The Red Book

2016–17

The Red Book

2016–17

Consultant Editors

Bill Dodwell LLB, LLM, CTA (Fellow), ACA

Kevin Prosser QC

Wolters Kluwer

Wolters Kluwer
145 London Road
Kingston upon Thames KT2 6SR
United Kingdom
Telephone: +44 (0) 844 561 8166
Fax: +44 (0) 208 547 2638
Email: cch@wolterskluwer.com
Website: www.cch.co.uk

Disclaimer

This publication is sold with the understanding that neither the publisher nor the authors, with regard to this publication, are engaged in rendering legal or professional services. The material contained in this publication neither purports, nor is intended to be, advice on any particular matter.

Although this publication incorporates a considerable degree of standardisation, subjective judgment by the user, based on individual circumstances, is indispensable. This publication is an "aid" and cannot be expected to replace such judgment.

Neither the publisher nor the authors can accept any responsibility or liability to any person, whether a purchaser of this publication or not, in respect of anything done or omitted to be done by any such person in reliance, whether sole or partial, upon the whole or any part of the contents of this publication.

Legislative and other material

While copyright in all statutory and other materials resides in the Crown or other relevant body, copyright in the remaining material in this publication is vested in the publisher.

The publisher advises that any statutory or other materials issued by the Crown or other relevant bodies and reproduced and quoted in this publication are not the authorised official versions of those statutory or other materials. In the preparation, however, the greatest care has been taken to ensure exact conformity with the law as enacted or other material as issued.

Crown copyright legislation is reproduced under the terms of Crown Copyright Policy Guidance issued by HMSO. Other Crown copyright material is reproduced with the permission of the controller of HMSO. European Communities Copyright material is reproduced with permission.

Telephone Helpline Disclaimer Notice

Where purchasers of this publication also have access to any Telephone Helpline Service operated by Wolters Kluwer (UK), then Wolters Kluwer's total liability to contract, tort (including negligence, or breach of statutory duty) misrepresentation, restitution or otherwise with respect to any claim arising out of its acts or alleged omissions in the provision of the Helpline Service shall be limited to the yearly subscription fee paid by the Claimant.

ISBN 978-1-78540-279-1

British Library Cataloguing-in-Publication Data.

A catalogue record for this book is available from the British Library.

Typeset by Innodata Inc., India

Printed and bound by Druckerei C.H. Beck, Nördlingen.

The Red Book

Senior Technical Editor

PAUL ROBBINS BA (Hons.), ACA, CTA

Technical Editors

SARAH ARNOLD ACA, CTA

Foreword

The *Finance Act* 2016 finally received Royal Assent on 15 September, its progress through Parliament having been delayed by the EU referendum. Many of the measures took effect from 1 or 6 April 2016, as is common in the modern era. The role of Parliament in enacting tax measures has effectively been reduced and there was a low level of debate in the House and in Committee for all but a handful of 'political' measures. This should be a matter of regret in a parliamentary democracy. Lawyers will note that the notion of a binding statement on the impact of the law by the relevant minister has all but disappeared. We should note the advantage of longer periods of public consultation, including on the drafting, which has helped improve some of what is eventually legislated. Yet the impact of adding over 600 pages to the statute book this year – and indeed every year since 2010 – cannot be underestimated. The resources demanded from everyone involved in the legislative process are substantial due to the wide range of different measures every year.

Simplification

This Act places the Office of Tax Simplification on a statutory basis in a strange juxtaposition to some of the more complicated income tax measures we've seen. The OTS was established in 2010 as a semi-independent part of HM Treasury. Its first Tax Policy Director, John Whiting, must take much of the credit for making over 200 recommendations which have been adopted by the Treasury and HMRC. The new statutory OTS '… must provide advice to the Chancellor of the Exchequer, on request or as the OTS considers appropriate, on the simplification of the tax system.' Allowing the OTS to take the initiative is an important safeguard to ensure that it doesn't look only at those projects requested by the Chancellor. Other safeguards include a requirement that the Chancellor publishes all OTS reports – and responds to them. The OTS must additionally publish an annual report and the Treasury must conduct a review of its activities every five years. For the first time, members of the OTS may be paid. However, it is up to the Treasury to determine the resources needed by the OTS, which puts a partial brake on expansionary ambitions. The Treasury Select Committee is also given the opportunity to interview a new chair before appointment and no doubt it will take evidence from the chair and tax director periodically. The OTS now seems to be entrusted to investigate wider areas of tax reform, such as the potential unification of income tax and National Insurance.

Savings and investments

This Act contains important changes to the income tax treatment of savings – and it is clear that interest income is favoured, whilst dividends and rental income do less well. With effect from 6 April 2016, there is a new personal savings allowance and also a new dividend allowance which is combined with higher taxation for dividends exceeding the allowance. The savings allowance is £1,000 for a basic rate taxpayer and £500 for a higher rate taxpayer – making them worth up to £200 p.a. for each category. However, this is an allowance and not an exemption – which means that the individual's income before the allowance is tested to determine the level. When combined with the £5,000 zero tax band on savings income, calculation of individual income taxation will be beyond most people.

The changes in the taxation of dividends, where the notional credit is abolished and replaced with a £5,000 allowance, is intended to levy more tax on those who provide services via their own companies. Cuts to the corporation rate had made it even more advantageous for a self-employed individual to incorporate. Imposing additional tax on dividends, combined with new anti-avoidance to limit opportunities to convert potential income into capital, is expected to raise about £2bn annually. It remains beneficial for individuals with profits below about £150,000 to incorporate, but those with higher incomes may look to disincorporate. The design of the measure means that many higher and additional rate taxpayers with dividends below £21,000 and £25,000 respectively, receive a tax cut, which is the inevitable outcome of the policy design. The Red Book figures showed that the Treasury expected a certain amount of acceleration of dividends, so as to mitigate the higher rates that now apply.

The long-standing transactions in securities rules are modified and a new targeted anti-avoidance rule introduced so as to limit the ability of individuals to retain profits in their companies and then claim capital gains tax rates on liquidation. The TAAR targets anyone who winds up one company and carries on a similar activity in a new company, with a main purpose of avoiding taxation. HMRC have confirmed that they will not give clearances in relation to the TAAR; instead individuals must rely upon guidance to ascertain their own position.

The previous Chancellor had put in train several new policies intended to make investment in buy-to-let or additional residential properties less attractive. From April 2020, finance costs will no longer be set-off in full against rental income, relief being given only at the basic rate. The latest change is the levy of an additional 3% stamp duty land tax charge on the purchase of an additional property. The intention seems to be that an individual's main residence should escape the 3% rate but there are too many cases where this isn't achieved in practice. One change introduced late to the Act allows a three-year period (increased from 18 months) to recover the 3% impost where a new main residence is purchased before the previous one is sold. It remains a poorly executed policy and it is understood that HMRC are receiving a significant number of queries from taxpayers uncertain whether and why the additional charge applies.

Finally, yet more changes to pensions come into effect. The lifetime allowance is cut to £1m, although nothing has been done to address the significant disparity in treatment between defined benefit schemes and defined contributions schemes. Effectively, a final salary scheme can produce a pension of £50,000 p.a. but a money purchase scheme produces a much lower pension (perhaps £30,000). For the well-off, a pension scheme has become an asset to be passed on to descendants, rather than simply a source of pension income that came to an end on the death of the pensioners.

International taxation

International corporate taxation has come under global scrutiny and the UK has played a leading role in the G20/OECD Base Erosion and Profit Shifting (BEPS) project. This Act introduces a number of changes which flow from the 15 Actions agreed in October 2015. The first change is to the UK's Patent Box, where the Forum on Harmful Tax Practices reached consensus that patent box regimes should be linked to undertaking the underlying research and development. The old regime is closed to new entrants but patents already in the scheme may continue to benefit until 2021. New patents will need to demonstrate the R&D link.

The UK becomes the first country to adopt Action 2 from the BEPS project – to counter hybrid mismatches. Hybrids are either instruments (loans or shares) or entities which are treated differently by two countries. The result can be that a group obtains a tax deduction in one country without recognising equivalent taxable income in another country – or that two deductions are given for the same economic cost. From 1 January 2017, the tax deduction will be denied where there is a hybrid involved. The UK is likely to be followed by Australia and New Zealand. There is also limited counteraction of hybrids in the EU's Anti-Tax Avoidance directive, which takes effect in 2019 – but which only counters hybrid mismatches between two EU states.

The UK has legislated to include the OECD's Transfer Pricing guidelines in UK law on transfer pricing. The Act now provides that changes made under BEPS Actions 8–10 are included in relation to accounting periods beginning on or after 1 April 2016 and for income tax purposes in 2016–17 and subsequently. Given that the Actions 8–10 report was mainly expressed as additional clarification of the 2010 guidelines, this change may just be to avoid any doubt as to the status of the 2015 report. The OECD continues to work on drafting changes as well as on developing additional guidance on the attribution of profits to permanent establishments and other areas.

There is currently consultation on the adoption of Action 4, which may limit interest deductions, where group interest expense exceeds £2m. The Government's original plan was to introduce interest limitations from 1 April 2017; no doubt the Chancellor will confirm in his Autumn Statement whether he plans to keep to this timetable.

Other BEPS Actions are likely to be implemented through changing the UK's double tax treaties, through the Multilateral Instrument. This is currently being negotiated by over 90 jurisdictions and is expected to be ratified by the UK and others in 2017. It is thus likely to take effect in 2018.

The UK has decided to bring its definition of royalties subject to withholding tax in line with the OECD Model Treaty definition. Additionally, it has legislated on the source of royalties by providing that where 'the payment is made in connection with a trade carried on by that person through a permanent establishment in the United Kingdom' withholding applies – even where the payments are made outside the UK and the payments are not necessarily deductible against branch profits. This clearly imposes a significant administration burden, not least because there is no royalty equivalent of the treaty passport system allowed for interest payments. There is also a treaty anti-abuse rule included, no doubt to limit the potential for so-called 'treaty shopping'.

This Government, and its predecessor, have imposed taxation in a number of areas where non-residents hold or realise gains from UK real property. This Act contains two important measures. First, the time when non-residents must pay capital gains tax on gains from UK residential property has been brought forward to 30 days after the disposal. This is a forerunner of a similar acceleration planned for UK residents disposing of property. Second, there is a new charge on non-resident individuals and companies realising gains from dealing in or the development of UK land. The original Budget announcement referred to companies and accompanied rapid changes to the double tax treaties with the Crown Dependencies.

At Committee Stage, significant amendments were made to add direct disposals by individuals, as well as indirect disposals of companies. There is also a treaty override, where the advantage sought 'is contrary to the object and purpose of the provisions of' the treaty.

Finally, the Government decided to accept an amendment proposed by an Opposition MP, supported by MPs from several parties. The amendment was put forward by Caroline Flint MP and enables HM Treasury to introduce regulations requiring that multinationals publish their 'country-by-country' template alongside their tax strategy. This template is introduced by the G20/OECD's Action 13 from the BEPS project and is required to be sent confidentially by multinationals with global turnover exceeding €750m (£586m) to tax authorities. Financial Secretary Jane Ellison told the House of Commons that the Government's policy remained that it thought public disclosure of tax information should be agreed internationally, otherwise UK-parented groups would be disadvantaged. The European Commission has proposed a Directive, which has not yet been debated by EU finance ministers.

In the courts

There have been a number of important cases before the Tribunals and higher courts over the last 12 months. The Supreme Court has continued to refine doctrines of statutory construction in the joined *UBS/Deutsche Bank* cases, which concerned employee remuneration planning from 2003. In each case the employer awarded shares in an SPV to its employees; the articles of association of the SPV provided that in certain circumstances the shares would be forfeited. The employers argued successfully in the Upper Tribunal and the Court of Appeal, that the shares thereby fell within ITEPA 2003, Pt. 7, Ch. 2 (restricted securities), with the result that the award was tax free. In particular, it did not matter that the forfeiture provisions in the articles had been inserted for tax purposes only. In that connection, the employers pointed out not only that Chapter 2 was highly prescriptive but contained no exception for tax avoidance, but also that one of the main purposes of Chapter 2 was to prevent a particular form of tax avoidance, namely the exploitation of the *Abbott v Philbin* principle, according to which an employee who acquires shares or other money's worth is taxable on their value at the time of acquisition, even if that value is low because they are subject to a risk of forfeiture or other restriction, and is not taxable on any higher value if and when that restriction subsequently falls away. Thus, the employers argued, it would defeat that statutory purpose to hold that Chapter 2 does not apply merely because the restriction is imposed for tax purposes. Indeed, this would mean that exploitation of the *Abbott v Philbin* principle was possible after all. However, the Supreme Court rejected these arguments. Lord Reed said 'Approaching the matter initially at a general level, the fact that Chapter 2 was introduced partly for the purpose of forestalling tax avoidance schemes self-evidently makes it difficult to attribute to Parliament an intention that it should apply to schemes which were carefully crafted to fall within its scope, purely for the purpose of tax avoidance.' Repeating the principle set out in *Scottish Provident*, his lordship added 'In summary, therefore, the reference in section 423(1) to "any contract, agreement, arrangement or condition which makes provision to which any of subsections (2) to (4) applies" is to be construed as being limited to provision having a business or commercial purpose, and not to commercially irrelevant conditions whose only purpose is the obtaining of the exemption.' The result was that the shares did not fit into the restricted securities exemption – but this did not mean that the employees were to be treated as receiving cash. Instead, the shares should be valued and tax levied accordingly.

Accelerated Payment Notices have been the subject of several applications for judicial review – but in all cases to date the application has been turned down. In *R (on the application of Vital Nut Co Ltd) v HMRC,* Charles J refused the application, despite criticising HMRC's approach. Financial Secretary Jane Ellison announced that over £3bn had been collected by HMRC under accelerated payment notices by early September 2016.

We congratulate the editors and publishers on speedily consolidating the provisions of the Finance Acts into these volumes.

Kevin Prosser QC
Bill Dodwell

September 2016

Publisher's Note

Volume 1A contains the text of the *Taxes Management Act* 1970, the *Income and Corporation Taxes Act* 1988, the *Taxation of Chargeable Gains Act* 1992 and the *Capital Allowances Act* 2001. It also contains all other significant Acts affecting the imposition and collection of income tax, corporation tax and capital gains tax, up to and including the *Transport Act* 2000. Enactments are presented in chronological order.

Volume 1B includes the key personal tax Acts: *Income Tax (Earnings and Pensions) Act* 2003, *Finance Act* 2004, the *Income Tax (Trading and Other Income) Act* 2005 and the *Income Tax Act* 2007. It also contains all other significant Acts relating to income tax, corporation tax and capital gains tax up to and including the *Income Tax Act* 2007, presented in chronological order.

Volume 1C includes the key corporation tax Acts: the *Corporation Tax Act* 2009, the *Corporation Tax Act* 2010 and the *Taxation (International and Other Provisions) Act* 2010. It also contains all other significant Acts relating to income tax, corporation tax and capital gains tax up to and including the *Taxation (International and Other Provisions) Act* 2010, presented in chronological order.

Volume 1D includes contains all significant Acts relating to income tax, corporation tax and capital gains tax from the *Finance Act* 2010 to *Finance Act* 2016, presented in chronological order. This volume also includes the legislation for the bank levy (*Finance Act* 2011), the annual tax on enveloped dwellings (*Finance Act* 2013), the diverted profits tax (*Finance Act* 2015) and the apprenticeship levy (*Finance Act* 2016).

Volume 1E includes UK statutory instruments and Scottish statutory instruments relevant to the taxes covered in Volumes 1A, 1B, 1C and 1D.

Volume 1F includes EC directives, HMRC directions, extra-statutory concessions, statements of practice, HMRC Briefs and extensive *Tax Bulletin* extracts relevant to the taxes covered in Volumes 1A, 1B, 1C and 1D.

Also in Volume 1F, a considerable number of other HMRC materials are reproduced as well as selected extracts from ICAEW technical releases and selected releases from the Chartered Institute of Taxation. Selected Accounting Standards are also included.

The Index volume covers material in Volumes 1A, 1B, 1C, 1D, 1E and 1F. It contains the comprehensive topic index, list of definitions and meanings and a consolidated destination table where pre-consolidation enactments can be traced in the *Income and Corporation Taxes Act* 1988, the *Taxation of Chargeable Gains Act* 1992, the *Capital Allowances Act* 2001, the *Income Tax (Earnings and Pensions) Act* 2003, the *Income Tax (Trading and Other Income) Act* 2005, the *Income Tax Act* 2007, the *Corporation Tax Act* 2009, the *Corporation Tax Act* 2010 and the *Taxation (International and Other Provisions) Act* 2010. The table also includes destinations for PAYE and sub-contractor regulations following the consolidations in the *Income Tax (Sub-contractors in the Construction Industry) Regulations* 1993 (SI 1993/743) and the *Income Tax (Employments) Regulations* 2003 (SI 2003/2682).

The Index volume also includes the "Stop Press" section which contains material that was issued too late to go in its normal location. In the main, the items normally included here are statutory instruments, some of which have been formally laid, but some of which may be the latest draft available at the time of going to press. These drafts have been included because, when laid, they will form an important part of the 2016–17 legislative picture. Readers should, however, be aware that they are potentially subject to amendment.

Volume 1G includes all relevant material on National Insurance contributions, tax credits, inheritance tax and petroleum revenue tax.

Volume 1H includes all relevant material on stamp taxes (including the land and buildings transaction tax in Scotland).

Volume 2 includes all relevant material on value added tax.

The legislation is reproduced so as to show those provisions which are in force in 2016–17. The Acts have been abridged by the omission of the full text of provisions which either amend earlier enactments (unless the amendment is prospective) or have been repealed. However, the *Finance Act* 2016 appears in full text in Volume 1D, in so far as it relates to income tax, corporation tax and capital gains tax, and in the relevant parts of Volume 1G and in Volumes 1H and 2 for the taxes dealt with in those volumes. The full text of *Finance (No. 2) Act* 2015 is also reproduced as this was not included in the 2015–16 edition.

Prospective changes for which no effective date in 2016–17 has been announced at the time of going to press, or where the effective date has been announced but is after 2016–17, are noted under the provisions to be amended or in the case of, for example, entirely new sections, at the place where they will appear when they enter into force, with reference made to the place where the text of the changes can be found. Prospective changes which enter into force during 2016–17 are made to the provisions amended, substituted, etc. with a "History" note setting out the "former" provisions in smaller type beneath. Where prospective legislation is amended before it takes effect it is shown in amended form at the place where it is introduced, but the "target" legislation to be amended carries only a brief description of the amendment.

Where, because of subsequent amendments, provisions do not appear as originally enacted, the former wording is reproduced only where it is either in force at some point in 2016–17 or likely to be of practical relevance to 2016–17 liabilities. Details of such amendments and, where appropriate, former wording in smaller type appear as "History" notes beneath the amended provisions. In some cases whole sections are involved and these appear in smaller type in their entirety.

Derivation notes under provisions of the *Income and Corporation Taxes Act* 1988, the *Taxation of Chargeable Gains Act* 1992, the *Capital Allowances Act* 2001, the *Income Tax (Earnings and Pensions) Act* 2003, the *Income Tax (Trading and Other Income) Act* 2005, the *Income Tax Act* 2007, the *Corporation Tax Act* 2009, the *Corporation Tax Act* 2010, and the *Taxation (International and Other Provisions) Act* 2010 indicate the former enactments.

Extensive cross references appear throughout, at the end of each section or paragraph, both to other provisions of the Taxes Acts and to extraneous legislation. Cross references under a section, paragraph, etc. mainly refer to provisions which explicitly mention that section, paragraph, etc. The order of cross references is first to list those involving the Act in point, then those involving the *Income and Corporation Taxes Act* 1988, then those involving other Taxes Acts in chronological order, and then those involving extraneous Acts, again in chronological order. Effective, or implicit, cross references are mentioned by way of editorial note (see below).

Relevant statutory instruments, extra-statutory concessions, statements of practice, *Tax Bulletin* decisions and interpretations (these are all reproduced) are noted. Other related materials (*Tax Bulletin* articles and special editions, HMRC press releases and booklets, releases from accountancy bodies and the Law Society, etc.) which affect particular provisions are also noted even if they are not reproduced. European material related to the provision in question is also noted, and editorial notes are inserted where additional comment is appropriate.

While Parliamentary materials or their equivalent had in other jurisdictions long been used as an aid to the interpretation of legislative acts, the decision of the House of Lords in *Pepper (HMIT) v Hart and related appeals* [1992] BTC 591 that ministerial statements may be so used in limited circumstances was an innovation in the UK. The cases in which such use can be made of Parliamentary material are at present limited to circumstances where: legislation is ambiguous, obscure or leads to an absurdity, the material relied upon consists of statements by a minister or other promoter of the Bill, and the statements relied upon are clear. A range of annotations covering Parliamentary material are grouped together under the generic heading of "Hansard Extracts" in the "Other materials" division. Editorial judgment has been used in selecting some of the more significant of such references, or those with the most widespread application; the coverage of Parliamentary material in the footnotes is by no means exhaustive.

As part of HMRC's response to the Government's code of practice on access to Government information, the HMRC guidance manuals have been made available to the public. The manuals provide HMRC staff with guidance on the interpretation of tax law and the operation of the tax system. References to useful material contained in the manuals appear under the heading "HMRC manuals". Editorial judgment has been used in selecting the references.

The publisher advises that the Acts, Regulations and other official material in this publication are not the authorised official versions. However, the greatest care has been taken to ensure exact conformity with the law as enacted and with the text of extra-statutory material. Some changes in printing style have been adopted for convenience and to improve readability. For example, marginal notes appearing in the official statutes have been reproduced in bold type in the first line of the section to which they relate. Many words and phrases have also been reproduced in bold where they are defined in the legislation so that the definitions can be located more easily.

Our role as publisher is not to guess which parts will be of greatest practical interest but rather to present all the legislation and related material accurately and to annotate it helpfully. We always welcome comments and suggestions from our readers and we thank those who have offered constructive thoughts over the past year.

ABBREVIATIONS

The following abbreviations are commonly used throughout this publication.

ACT	advance corporation tax
AEA 1925	Administration of Estates Act 1925
AIM	Alternative Investment Market
AIS	accrued income scheme
AL	aggregates levy
App.	appendix
APR	annual percentage rate
APRT	advance petroleum revenue tax
ARPA 2004	Age-Related Payments Act 2004
art.	article(s)
ATCSA 2001	Anti-Terrorism, Crime and Security Act 2001
ATED	Annual tax on enveloped dwellings
BB	Customs and Excise Business Briefs
BEN	business economic note
BES	business expansion scheme
BN	Budget Notes
BRNAA 2011	Budget Responsibility and National Audit Act 2011
BSA 1986	Building Societies Act 1986
B(S)A 1985	Bankruptcy (Scotland) Act 1985
BTC	British Tax Cases, 1982–current (CCH)
CA 1985	Companies Act 1985
CA 2006	Companies Act 2006
C & E Commrs	Commissioners of Customs and Excise
CAA 1968	Capital Allowances Act 1968
CAA 1990	Capital Allowances Act 1990
CAA 2001	Capital Allowances Act 2001
CCBSA 2014	Co-Operative and Community Benefit Societies Act 2014
CCH	CCH Information, a division of Wolters Kluwer (UK) Ltd
CCL	climate change levy
CED(GR)A 1979	Customs and Excise Duties (General Reliefs) Act 1979
CEMA 1979	Customs and Excise Management Act 1979
CFC	controlled foreign company
CGT	capital gains tax
CGTA 1979	Capital Gains Tax Act 1979
Ch.	Chapter(s) (of a statute/SI etc.)
CHA 2011	Charities Act 2011
CIC	close investment-holding company
CICA 2013	Crime (International Co-Operation) Act 2003
CIOT	Chartered Institute of Taxation
CJPA 2001	Criminal Justice and Police Act 2001
cl.	clause(s)
col.	column(s)
Commr; Commrs	commissioner; commissioners
Conv.	convention
CPA 1947	Crown Proceedings Act 1947
CPA 2014	Childcare Payments Act 2014
CRCA 2005	Commissioners for Revenue and Customs Act 2005
CRGA 2010	Constitutional Reform and Governance Act 2010
CRSA 2014	Courts Reform (Scotland) Act 2014
CRT	composite rate tax
CSPSSA 2000	Child Support, Pensions and Social Security Act 2000
CT	corporation tax
CTA 2009	Corporation Tax Act 2009
CTA 2010	Corporation Tax Act 2010
CTD	certificates of tax deposits

CTFA 2004	Child Trust Funds Act 2004
CT(NI)A 2015	Corporation Tax (Northern Ireland) Act 2015
CTT	capital transfer tax
CTTA 1984	Capital Transfer Tax Act 1984
DDA(S)A 2002	Debt Arrangement and Attachment (Scotland) Act 2002
Dir.	EC directives
DLT	development land tax
DLTA 1976	Development Land Tax Act 1976
DPA 1998	Data Protection Act 1998
DPT	Diverted Profits Tax
DSS	Department of Social Security
DTI	Department of Trade and Industry
EA 2002	Employment Act 2002
EA 2004	Energy Act 2004
EC	European Community/Communities
edn.	edition
EEC	European Economic Community
EEIG	European Economic Interest Grouping
e.g.	(exempli gratia) for example
EIS	enterprise investment scheme
ELPA 2010	Equitable Life (Payments) Act 2010
EMPA 2003	Electricity (Miscellaneous Provisions) Act 2003
ERA 1996	Employee Rights Act 1996
ESC	extra-statutory concession
ESOP	employee stock ownership plan
ESOT	employee share ownership trust
etc.	(et cetera) and so on
et seq.	(et sequens) and the following
EU	European Union
FA	Finance Act
FA 2016	Finance Act 2016
FI 1985	Films Act 1985
FIA 2000	Freedom of Information Act 2000
FII	franked investment income
F(No. 2)A	Finance (No. 2) Act
F(No. 2)A 2015	Finance (No. 2) Act 2015
F(No. 3)A	Finance (No. 3) Act
F(No. 3)A 2010	Finance (No. 3) Act 2010
FSMA 2000	Financial Services and Markets Act 2000
FYA	first-year allowance
GAAP	generally accepted accounting practice
Grp.	Group (VAT legislation)
HA 1988	Housing Act 1988
HM	Her Majesty
HMIT	Her Majesty's Inspector of Taxes
HMRC	HM Revenue & Customs
HMSO	Her Majesty's Stationery Office
HRA 1998	Human Rights Act 1998
IA	initial allowance
IA 1986	Insolvency Act 1986
ICAEW	Institute of Chartered Accountants in England and Wales
ICAS	Institute of Chartered Accountants of Scotland
ICTA 1970	Income and Corporation Taxes Act 1970
ICTA 1988	Income and Corporation Taxes Act 1988
i.e.	(id est) that is
IHT	inheritance tax
IHTA 1984	Inheritance Tax Act 1984
IHTPA 2014	Inheritance and Trustee's Power's Act 2014
INA 1978	Interpretation Act 1978

IoT	Institute of Taxation
IPT	insurance premium tax
IR Commrs	Commissioners of Inland Revenue
IRDec.	Inland Revenue decision
IRInt.	Inland Revenue interpretation
IRRA 1890	Inland Revenue Regulation Act 1890
IT	income tax
ITA 2007	Income Tax Act 2007
ITEPA 2003	Income Tax (Earnings and Pensions) Act 2003
ITTOIA 2005	Income Tax (Trading and Other Income) Act 2005
LA 2011	Localism Act 2011
LAUTRO	Life Assurance and Unit Trust Regulatory Organisation
LBTTSA 2013	Land and Buildings Transaction Tax (Scotland) Act 2013
LBTTSA 2016	Land and Buildings Transaction Tax (Amendment) (Scotland) Act 2016
LFT	landfill tax
LIFFE	London International Financial Futures and Options Exchange
LLPA 2000	Limited Liability Partnerships Act 2000
LPA 1907	Limited Partnerships Act 1907
LPA 1925	Law of Property Act 1925
LRRA 2006	Legislative and Regulatory Reform Act 2006
LSG	Law Society Gazette
MCT	mainstream corporation tax
MIRAS	mortgage interest relief at source
Misc.	miscellaneous items (denoted by number)
NB	(nota bene) note well
NHA 1980	National Heritage Act 1980
NI	Northern Ireland
NIC	National Insurance contributions
NICA 2002	National Insurance Contributions Act 2002
NICA 2004	National Insurance Contributions and Statutory Payments Act 2004
NICA 2006	National Insurance Contributions Act 2006
NICA 2008	National Insurance Contributions Act 2008
NICA 2014	National Insurance Contributions Act 2014
NICRCA 2015	National Insurance Contributions (Rate Ceilings) Act 2015
NICSPA 2004	National Insurance Contributions and Statutory Payments Act 2004
NR	Customs and Excise News Releases
O.	Order(s)
OJ	Official Journal of the European Communities
OJ "L" series	Official Journal of the European Communities, Legislation Series (cited by year, issue number and page, for example OJ 1989 L1/1 is the first page of the first issue of the legislation series of the Official Journal for 1989)
OPB	Occupational Pensions Board
Ors	others
OTA 1975	Oil Taxation Act 1975
OTA 1983	Oil Taxation Act 1983
p.; pp.	page; pages
PA 2004	Pensions Act 2004
PA 2007	Pensions Act 2007
PA 2011	Pensions Act 2011
PA 2014	Pensions Act 2014
PAA 2009	Perpetuities and Accumulations Act 2009
p.a.	per annum (each year)
PACE 1994	Police and Criminal Evidence Act 1994
para.	paragraph(s)
PAYE	pay as you earn
PCA 2002	Proceeds of Crime Act 2002
PCTA 1968	Provisional Collection of Taxes Act 1968
PEP	personal equity plan
PET	potentially exempt transfer

PLDA 1808	Probate and Legacy Duties Act 1808
PN	Customs and Excise Press Notices
PPS	personal pension scheme
PR	press release(s)
PRP	profit-related pay
PRT	petroleum revenue tax
PRTA 1980	Petroleum Revenue Tax Act 1980
PSA 1993	Pension Schemes Act 1993
PSA 2011	Postal Services Act 2011
PSA 2015	Pension Schemes Act 2015
PSO	Pensions Schemes Office
Pt.	Part(s)
QCB	qualifying corporate bond
r.	rule(s)
RA 1898	Revenue Act 1898 and similarly coded for appropriate subsequent years
RA 2005	Railways Act 2005
R & C Commrs	Revenue and Customs Commissioners
RDDA 1998	Regional Development Agencies Act 1998
reg.	regulations
Regulations	EC Regulations
RPI	retail prices index
RSC	Rules of the Supreme Court 1965
RSTPA 2014	Revenue Scotland and Tax Powers Act 2014
s.	section(s)
SA 1891	Stamp Act 1891
SAYE	save as you earn
SCA 1981	Supreme Court Act 1981
SCA 1998	Scotland Act 1998
SCA 2012	Scotland Act 2012
SCA 2016	Scotland Act 2016
SCDA 2012	Small Charitable Donations Act 2012
Sch.	Schedule(s)
SDLT	stamp duty land tax
SDLTCN	Stamp Duty Land Tax Customer Newsletter
SDMA 1891	Stamp Duty Management Act 1891
SDRT	stamp duty reserve tax
SD(TP)A 1992	Stamp Duty (Temporary Provisions) Act 1992
SERPS	state earnings-related pension scheme
SFO	Superannuation Funds Office
SI	statutory instrument
SMP	statutory maternity pay
SOCN	Stamp Office Customer Newsletter
SOCPA 2005	Serious Organised Crime and Police Act 2005
SP	Statement of practice
SPCA 2002	State Pension Credit Act 2002
SRO	self-regulating organisation
SR & O	statutory rules and orders
SSA 1975	Social Security Act 1975
SSA 1980	Social Security Act 1980
SSA 1986	Social Security Act 1986
SSA 1989	Social Security Act 1989
SSA 1998	Social Security Act 1998
SSAA 1992	Social Security Administration Act 1992
SSAP	Statement of Standard Accounting Practice
SSCBA 1992	Social Security Contributions and Benefits Act 1992
SS(CP)A 1992	Social Security (Consequential Provisions) Act 1992
SS(TF)A 1999	Social Security Contributions (Transfer of Functions, etc.) Act 1999
SSFA 2001	Social Security Fraud Act 2001
SSHBA 1982	Social Security Housing Benefits Act 1982

SS(MP)A 1977	Social Security (Miscellaneous Provisions) Act 1977
SSP	statutory sick pay
SSPA 1975	Social Security Pensions Act 1975
SSPA 1994	Statutory Sick Pay Act 1994
STA 1963	Stock Transfer Act 1963
STB	Stamp Taxes Bulletin
subcl.	subclause(s)
subpara.	subparagraph(s)
subs.	subsection(s)
TA 2000	Transport Act 2000
TAURUS	Transfer and Automated Registration of Uncertified Stock
TB	Tax Bulletin article
TBSE	Tax Bulletin special edition
TCA 2002	Tax Credits Act 2002
TCEA 2007	Tribunals, Courts and Enforcement Act 2007
TCGA 1992	Taxation of Chargeable Gains Act 1992
TCIA 2013	Trusts (Capital and Income) Act 2013
TCMWA 2016	Tax Collection and Management (Wales) Act 2016
TERA 2000	Terrorism Act 2000
TESSA	tax-exempt special savings account
TIOPA 2010	Taxation (International and Other Provisions) Act 2010
TMA 1970	Taxes Management Act 1970
TOPA 2014	Taxation of Pensions Act 2014
TR	technical release
TSA 2014	Tribunals (Scotland) Act 2014
TSBA 1985	Trustee Savings Bank Act 1985
TULR(C)A 1992	Trade Union and Labour Relations (Consolidation) Act 1992
TWDV	tax written-down value
UCITS	Undertakings for Collective Investment in Transferable Securities
UK	United Kingdom
USM	Unlisted Securities Market
VAT	value added tax
VATA 1983	Value Added Tax Act 1983
VATA 1994	Value Added Tax Act 1994
VCT	Venture Capital Trust
vol.	volume(s)
WA 2014	Wales Act 2014
WDA	writing down allowance
WDV	written-down value
WFT	windfall tax
WRA 2012	Welfare Reform Act 2012
WRPA 1999	Welfare Reform and Pensions Act 1999
¶	CCH paragraph

About the Publisher

Wolters Kluwer (UK) Limited is part of the international Wolters Kluwer Group. Wolters Kluwer is the leading publisher specialising in tax, business and law publishing throughout Europe, the US and the Asia Pacific region. The group produces a wide range of information services in different media for the accounting and legal professions and for business.

All Wolters Kluwer (UK) Limited publications are designed to be practical and authoritative reference works and guides and are written by our own highly qualified and experienced editorial team and specialist outside authors.

Wolters Kluwer (UK) Limited publishes information packages including electronic products, loose-leaf reporting services, newsletters and books on UK and European legal topics for distribution world-wide. The UK operation also acts as distributor of the publications of the overseas affiliates.

Wolters Kluwer
145 London Road
Kingston upon Thames KT2 6SR
United Kingdom
Telephone: 0844 561 8166
Facsimile: 0208 547 2638
Email: cch@wolterskluwer.com
Website: www.cch.co.uk

About the Consultant Editors

Bill Dodwell graduated from King's College, London, and Queens' College, Cambridge with LL.B and LL.M degrees in law. He became a partner in Deloitte in 2002, after 24 years with Arthur Andersen. He is a Fellow of the Chartered Institute of Taxation and a member of the ICAEW. Bill is President of the CIOT. Bill is Head of Tax Policy at Deloitte, responsible for consultation with the OECD, the European Commission the UK Treasury and tax authorities. He tweets as @ukbudget.

Kevin Prosser QC read law at University College, London and St Edmund Hall, Oxford. He was called to the Bar in 1982, and has been a QC since 1996. He specialises in all forms of tax advice and litigation. He was Chairman of the Revenue Bar Association from 2008 to 2014, and is now head of Pump Court Tax Chambers. He was a Recorder from 2000 to 2015 and a Deputy High Court Judge from 2008 to 2015.

Acknowledgement

CCH gratefully acknowledges the endorsement of this publication by the Chartered Institute of Taxation.

THE
CHARTERED
INSTITUTE OF
TAXATION

Table of Contents

INCOME, CORPORATION AND CAPITAL GAINS TAXES (pre-FA 2001)

Table of Contents

continued over

LIMITED PARTNERSHIPS ACT 1907

(1907 Chapter 24)

[*28th August 1907*]

ARRANGEMENT OF SECTIONS

1 Short title

1 This Act may be cited for all purposes as the Limited Partnerships Act 1907.

Prospective amendments – Repealed in relation to N. Ireland by CA 2006, s. 1286(2)(b) with effect from a date to be appointed.

2 Commencement of Act

2 [Repealed by Statute Law Revision Act 1927.]

3 Interpretation of terms

3 In the construction of this Act the following words and expressions shall have the meanings respectively assigned to them in this section, unless there be something in the subject or context repugnant to such construction:–

"Firm," "firm name," and **"business"** have the same meanings as in the Partnership Act 1890,

"General partner" shall mean any partner who is not a limited partner as defined by this Act.

Notes – S. 2 repealed in relation to N. Ireland by CA 2006, s. 1286(2)(b) with effect from 1 October 2009 (SI 2008/2860).

4 Definition and constitution of limited partnership

4(1) Limited partnerships may be formed in the manner and subject to the conditions by this Act provided.

4(2) A limited partnership must consist of one or more persons called general partners, who shall be liable for all debts and obligations of the firm, and one or more persons to be called limited partners, who shall at the time of entering into such partnership contribute thereto a sum or sums as capital or property valued at a stated amount, and who shall not be liable for the debts or obligations of the firm beyond the amount so contributed.

4(3) A limited partner shall not during the continuance of the partnership, either directly or indirectly, draw out or receive back any part of his contribution, and if he does so draw out or receive back any such part shall be liable for the debts and obligations of the firm up to the amount so drawn out or received back.

4(4) A body corporate may be a limited partner.

History – In s. 4(1) the words "From and after the commencement of this Act" omitted by the Statute Law Revision Act 1927.
In s. 4(2) the words "shall not consist … of more than twenty persons, and" omitted by SI 2002/3203, art. 3, with effect from 21 December 2002.
In s. 4(2) the words from "shall not consist … of more than twenty persons, and" omitted by SI 2002/3203, art. 3, with effect from 21 December 2002.
In s. 4(2) the words "in the case of a partnership" to "any other partnership" omitted by the Banking Act 1979, s. 51(2) and Sch. 7, with effect from 13 January 2004.

Cross references – SI 2013/1388, reg. 16(3): modification of s. 4 in its application to a partnership scheme in respect of which an authorisation order (under FSMA 2000, s. 261D(1)) is made.

Notes – S. 4 repealed in relation to N. Ireland by CA 2006, s. 1286(2)(b) with effect from 1 October 2009 (SI 2008/2860).

5 Registration of limited partnership required

5 Every limited partnership must be registered as such in accordance with the provisions of this Act, or in default thereof it shall be deemed to be a general partnership, and every limited partner shall be deemed to be a general partner.

Notes – S. 5 repealed in relation to N. Ireland by CA 2006, s. 1286(2)(b) with effect from 1 October 2009 (SI 2008/2860).

6 Modifications of general law in case of limited partnerships

6(1) A limited partner shall not take part in the management of the partnership business, and shall not have power to bind the firm:

Provided that a limited partner may by himself or his agent at any time inspect the books of the firm and examine into the state and prospects of the partnership business, and may advise with the partners thereon.

If a limited partner takes part in the management of the partnership business he shall be liable for all debts and obligations of the firm incurred while he so takes part in the management as though he were a general partner.

6(2) A limited partnership shall not be dissolved by the death or bankruptcy of a limited partner, and the lunacy of a limited partner shall not be a ground for dissolution of the partnership by the court unless the lunatic's share cannot be otherwise ascertained and realised.

6(3) In the event of the dissolution of a limited partnership its affairs shall be wound up by the general partners unless the court otherwise orders.

6(4) [Repealed by the Companies (Consolidation) Act 1908, s. 286 and Sch. 6 Pt. I.]

6(5) Subject to any agreement expressed or implied between the partners–

(a) Any difference arising as to ordinary matters connected with the partnership business may be decided by a majority of the general partners;

(b) A limited partner may, with the consent of the general partners, assign his share in the partnership, and upon such an assignment the assignee shall become a limited partner with all the rights of the assignor;

(c) The other partners shall not be entitled to dissolve the partnership by reason of any limited partner suffering his share to be charged for his separate debt;

(d) A person may be introduced as a partner without the consent of the existing limited partners;

(e) A limited partner shall not be entitled to dissolve the partnership by notice.

History – S. 6(4) repealed by the Companies (Consolidation) Act 1908, s. 286 and Sch. 6 Pt. I, with effect from 1 April 2009.

Cross references – SI 2013/1388, reg. 16(4): modification of s. 6 in its application to a partnership scheme in respect of which an authorisation order (under FSMA 2000, s. 261D(1)) is made.

Notes – S. 6 repealed in relation to N. Ireland by CA 2006, s. 1286(2)(b) with effect from 1 October 2009 (SI 2008/2860).

7 Law as to private partnerships to apply where not excluded by this Act

7 Subject to the provisions of this Act, the Partnership Act 1890, and the rules of equity and of common law applicable to partnerships, except so far as they are inconsistent with the express provisions of the last-mentioned Act, shall apply to limited partnerships.

Cross references – SI 2013/1388, reg. 16(5): modification of s. 7 in its application to a partnership scheme in respect of which an authorisation order (under FSMA 2000, s. 261D(1)) is made.

Notes – S. 7 repealed in relation to N. Ireland by CA 2006, s. 1286(2)(b) with effect from 1 October 2009 (SI 2008/2860).

8 Manner and particulars of registration

8 The registration of a limited partnership shall be effected by sending by post or delivering to the registrar at the register office in that part of the United Kingdom in which the principal place of business of the limited partnership is situated or proposed to be situated a statement signed by the partners containing the following particulars:–

(a) The firm name;

(b) The general nature of the business;

(c) The principal place of business;

(d) The full name of each of the partners;

(e) The term, if any, for which the partnership is entered into, and the date of its commencement;

(f) A statement that the partnership is limited, and the description of every limited partner as such;

(g) The sum contributed by each limited partner, and whether paid in cash or how otherwise.

Notes – S. 8 repealed in relation to N. Ireland by CA 2006, s. 1286(2)(b) with effect from 1 October 2009 (SI 2008/2860).

9 Registration of changes in partnerships

9(1) If during the continuance of a limited partnership any change is made or occurs in–

(a) the firm name,

(b) the general nature of the business,

(c) the principal place of business,

(d) the partners or the name of any partner,

(e) the term of character of the partnership,

(f) the sum contributed by any limited partner,

(g) the liability of any partner by reason of his becoming a limited instead of a general partner or a general instead of a limited partner.

a statement, signed by the firm, specifying the nature of the change, shall within seven days be sent by post or delivered to the registrar at the register office in that part of the United Kingdom in which the partnership is registered.

9(2) If default is made in compliance with the requirements of this section each of the general partners shall, on conviction under the Magistrates' Courts Act 1952, be liable to a fine not exceeding one pound for each day during which the default continues.

Cross references – SI 2013/1388, reg. 16(6): modification of s. 9 in its application to a partnership scheme in respect of which an authorisation order (under FSMA 2000, s. 261D(1)) is made.

Notes – S. 9 repealed in relation to N. Ireland by CA 2006, s. 1286(2)(b) with effect from 1 October 2009 (SI 2008/2860).

10 Advertisement in Gazette of statement of general partner becoming a limited partner and of assignment of share of limited partner

10(1) Notice of any arrangement or transaction under which any person will cease to be a general partner in any firm, and will become a limited partner in that firm, or under which the share of a limited partner in a firm will be assigned to any person, shall be forthwith advertised in the Gazette, and until notice of the arrangement or transaction is so advertised the arrangement or transaction shall, for the purposes of this Act, be deemed to be of no effect.

10(2) For the purposes of this section, the expression **"the Gazette"** means–

In the case of a limited partnership registered in England, the London Gazette;

In the case of a limited partnership registered in Scotland, the Edinburgh Gazette;

In the case of a limited partnership registered in Ireland, the Belfast Gazette.

Notes – S. 10 repealed in relation to N. Ireland by CA 2006, s. 1286(2)(b) with effect from 1 October 2009 (SI 2008/2860).

11 Ad valorem stamp duty on contributions by limited partners

11 [Repealed by FA 1973, s. 59(7) and Sch. 22, Pt. V.]

History – S. 11 repealed by FA 1973, s. 59(7) and Sch. 22, Pt. V, with effect from 25 July 1973.

12 Making false returns to be misdemeanor

12 [Repealed by Perjury Act 1911, s. 17 and Schedule]

History – S. 12 repealed by Perjury Act 1911, s. 17 and Schedule, itself subsequently repealed by Statute Law Revision Act 1927.

13 Registrar to file statement and issue certificate of registration

13 On receiving any statement made in pursuance of this Act the registrar shall cause the same to be filed, and he shall send by post to the firm from whom such statement shall have been received a certificate of the registration thereof.

Notes – S. 13 repealed in relation to N. Ireland by CA 2006, s. 1286(2)(b) with effect from 1 October 2009 (SI 2008/2860).

14 Register and index to be kept

14 At each of the register offices herein-after referred to the registrar shall keep, in proper books to be provided for the purpose, a register and an index of all the limited partnerships registered as aforesaid, and of all the statements registered in relation to such partnerships.

Notes – S. 14 repealed in relation to N. Ireland by CA 2006, s. 1286(2)(b) with effect from 1 October 2009 (SI 2008/2860).

15 Registrar of joint stock companies to be registrar under Act

15 The registrar of joint stock companies shall be the registrar of limited partnerships, and the several offices for the registration of joint stock companies in London, Edinburgh, and Belfast shall be the offices for the registration of limited partnerships carrying on business within those parts of the United Kingdom in which they are respectively situated.

Notes – S. 15 repealed in relation to N. Ireland by CA 2006, s. 1286(2)(b) with effect from 1 October 2009 (SI 2008/2860).

16 Inspection of statements registered

16(1) Any person may inspect the statements filed by the registrar in the register offices aforesaid; and any person may require a certificate of the registration of any limited partnership, or a copy of or extract from any registered statement, to be certified by the registrar.

16(2) A certificate of registration, or a copy of or extract from any statement registered under this Act, if duly certified to be a true copy under the hand of the registrar or one of the assistant registrars (whom it shall not be necessary to prove to be the registrar or assistant registrar) shall, in all legal proceedings, civil or criminal, and in all cases whatsoever be received in evidence.

History – In s. 16(1) the words ", and there shall be paid for such inspection such fees as may be appointed by the Board of Trade, not exceeding 5p for each inspection" repealed by CA 2006, s. 1063(7)(a)(i) and Sch. 16, and the words from "and there shall be paid for such certificate" to the end repealed by CA 2006, s. 1063(7)(a)(ii), s. 1295 and Sch. 16, with effect from 6 April 2007 by virtue of SI 2006/3428, art. 4(1)(a) and Sch. 4 (except for N. Ireland, art. 4(4)). Transitional provisions and savings apply, see art. 8 and Sch. 5, para. 6.

Previously, in s. 16(1) references to "5p", "10p", and "2p" substituted for references to shillings and pence by the Decimal Currency Act 1969, s. 10, made 16 May 1969.

Notes – S. 16 repealed in relation to N. Ireland by CA 2006, s. 1286(2)(b) with effect from 1 October 2009 (SI 2008/2860).

17 Power to Board of Trade to make rules

17 The Board of Trade may make rules concerning any of the following matters:–

(a) [Repealed by CA 2006, s. 1063(7)(b)(ii), s. 1295 and Sch. 16;]

(b) The duties or additional duties to be performed by the registrar for the purposes of this Act;

(c) The performance by assistant registrars and other officers of acts by this Act required to be done by the registrar;

(d) The forms to be used for the purposes of this Act;

(e) Generally the conduct and regulation of registration under this Act and any matters incidental thereto.

History – In s. 17 the words "(but as to fees with the concurrence of the Treasury)" repealed by CA 2006, s. 1063(7)(b)(i), s. 1295 and Sch. 16, with effect from 6 April 2007 by virtue of SI 2006/3428, art. 4(1)(a) and Sch. 4 (except for N. Ireland, art. 4(4)). Transitional provisions and savings apply, see art. 8 and Sch. 5, para. 6.

S. 17(a) repealed by CA 2006, s. 1063(7)(b)(ii), s. 1295 and Sch. 16, with effect from 6 April 2007 by virtue of SI 2006/3428, art. 4(1)(a) and Sch. 4 (except for N. Ireland, art. 4(4)). Transitional provisions and savings apply, see art. 8 and Sch. 5, para. 6.

Previously, in s. 17(a) reference to "25p" substituted for references to shillings and pence by the Decimal Currency Act 1969, s. 10, made 16 May 1969.

Notes – S. 17 repealed in relation to N. Ireland by CA 2006, s. 1286(2)(b) with effect from 1 October 2009 (SI 2008/2860).

LAW OF PROPERTY ACT 1925

(1925 Chapter 20)

[*9th April 1925*]

ARRANGEMENT OF SECTIONS

PART VII – PERPETUITIES AND ACCUMULATIONS

PERPETUITIES

ACCUMULATIONS

PART VII – PERPETUITIES AND ACCUMULATIONS

PERPETUITIES

161 Abolition of the double possibility rule

161(1) The rule of law prohibiting the limitation, after a life interest to an unborn person, of an interest in land to the unborn child or other issue of an unborn person is hereby abolished, but without prejudice to any other rule relating to perpetuities.

161(2) This section only applies to limitations or trusts created by an instrument coming into operation after the commencement of this Act.

162 Restrictions on the perpetuity rule

162(1) For removing doubts, it is hereby declared that the rule of law relating to perpetuities does not apply and shall be deemed never to have applied–

(a) [ceased to have effect by virtue of PAA 2009, s. 4 and repealed by TCEA 2007, s. 146 and Sch. 23, Pt. 4;]

(b) [ceased to have effect by virtue of PAA 2009, s. 4;]

(c) [ceased to have effect by virtue of PAA 2009, s. 4;]

(d) [ceased to have effect by virtue of PAA 2009, s. 4.]

162(2) [Ceased to have effect by virtue of PAA 2009, s. 4.]

History – S. 162(1)(a) repealed by TCEA 2007, s. 146 and Sch. 23, Pt. 4, with effect from 6 April 2014 (SI 2014/768, art. 2(b)).
S. 164 ceased to have effect by virtue of PAA 2009, s. 4, with effect in relation to an instrument taking effect on or after 6 April 2010, except in relation to a will executed before that day, and with effect in relation to an instrument made in the exercise of a special power of appointment only if the instrument creating the power takes effect on or after 6 April 2010. Former s. 162 read as follows:

"*Restrictions on the perpetuity rule*

162(1) For removing doubts, it is hereby declared that the rule of law relating to perpetuities does not apply and shall be deemed never to have applied–

(a) To any power to distrain on or to take possession of land or the income thereof given by way of indemnity against a rent, whether charged upon or payable in respect of any part of that land or not; or

(b) To any rentcharge created only as an indemnity against another rentcharge, although the indemnity rentcharge may only arise or become payable on breach of a condition or stipulation; or

(c) To any power, whether exercisable on breach of a condition or stipulation or not, to retain or withhold payment of any instalment of a rentcharge as an indemnity against another rentcharge; or

(d) To any grant, exception, or reservation of any right of entry on, or user of, the surface of land or of any easements, rights, or privileges over or under land for the purpose of–

(i) winning, working, inspecting, measuring, converting, manufacturing, carrying away, and disposing of mines and minerals;
(ii) inspecting, grubbing up, felling and carrying away timber and other trees, and the tops and lops thereof;
(iii) executing repairs, alterations, or additions to any adjoining land, or the buildings and erections thereon;
(iv) constructing, laying down, altering, repairing, renewing, cleansing, and maintaining sewers, watercourses, cesspools, gutters, drains, water-pipes, gas-pipes, electric wires or cables or other like works.

162(2) This section applies to instruments coming into operation before or after the commencement of this Act.".

163 Validation of certain gifts void for remoteness

163(1) Where in a will, settlement or other instrument the absolute vesting either of capital or income of property, or the ascertainment of a beneficiary or class of beneficiaries, is made to depend on the attainment by the beneficiary or members of the class of an age exceeding twenty-one years, and thereby the gift to that beneficiary or class or any member thereof, or any gift over, remainder, executory limitation, or trust arising on the total or partial failure of the original gift, is, or but for this section would be, rendered void for remoteness, the will, settlement, or other instrument shall take effect for the purposes of such gift, gift over, remainder, executory limitation, or trust as if the absolute vesting or ascertainment aforesaid had been made to depend on the beneficiary or member of the class attaining the age of twenty-one years, and that age shall be substituted for the age stated in the will, settlement, or other instrument.

163(2) This section applies to any instrument executed after the commencement of this Act and to any testamentary appointment (whether made in exercise of a general or special power), devise, or bequest contained in the will of a person dying after such commencement, whether the will is made before or after such commencement.

163(3) This section applies without prejudice to any provision whereby the absolute vesting or ascertainment is also made to depend on the marriage of any person, or any other event which may occur before the age stated in the will, settlement, or other instrument is attained.

ACCUMULATIONS

164 General restrictions on accumulation of income

164 [Ceased to have effect by virtue of PAA 2009, s. 13.]

History – S. 164 ceased to have effect by virtue of PAA 2009, s. 13, with effect in relation to an instrument taking effect on or after 6 April 2010, except in relation to a will executed before that day, and with effect in relation to an instrument made in the exercise of a special power of appointment only if the instrument creating the power takes effect on or after 6 April 2010. Former s. 164 read as follows:

"General restrictions on accumulation of income

164(1) No person may by any instrument or otherwise settle or dispose of any property in such manner that the income thereof shall save as hereinafter mentioned, be wholly or partially accumulated for any longer period than one of the following, namely:–

(a) the life of the grantor or settlor; or
(b) a term of twenty-one years from the death of the grantor, settlor or testator; or
(c) the duration of the minority – or respective minorities of any person or persons living or en ventre sa mere at the death of the grantor, settlor or testator; or
(c) the duration of the minority or respective minorities only of any person or persons who under the limitations of the instrument directing the accumulations would, for the time being, if of full age, be entitled to the income directed to be accumulated.

In every case where any accumulation is directed otherwise than as aforesaid, the direction shall (save as hereinafter mentioned) be void; and the income of the property directed to be accumulated shall, so long as the same is directed to be accumulated contrary to this section, go to and be received by the person or persons who would have been entitled thereto if such accumulation had not been directed.

164(2) This section does not extend to any provision–

(i) for payment of the debts of any grantor, settlor, testator or other person;
(ii) for raising portions for–
  (a) any child, children or remoter issue of any grantor, settlor or testator; or
  (b) any child, children or remoter issue of a person taking any interest under any settlement or other disposition directing the accumulations or to whom any interest is thereby limited;
(iii) respecting the accumulation of the produce of timber or wood;

and accordingly such provisions may be made as if no statutory restrictions on accumulation of income had been imposed.

164(3) The restrictions imposed by this section apply to instruments made on or after the twenty-eighth day of July, eighteen hundred, but in the case of wills only where the testator was living and of testamentary capacity after the end of one year from that date.".

165 Qualification of restrictions on accumulation

165 [Ceased to have effect by virtue of PAA 2009, s. 13.]

History – S. 165 ceased to have effect by virtue of PAA 2009, s. 13, with effect in relation to an instrument taking effect on or after 6 April 2010, except in relation to a will executed before that day, and with effect in relation to an instrument made in the exercise of a special power of appointment only if the instrument creating the power takes effect on or after 6 April 2010. Former s. 165 read as follows:

"Qualification of restrictions on accumulation

165 Where accumulations of surplus income are made during a minority under any statutory power or under the general law, the period for which such accumulations are made is not (whether the trust was created or the accumulations were made before or after the commencement of this Act) to be taken into account in determining the periods for which accumulations are permitted to be made by the last preceding section, and accordingly an express trust for accumulation for any other permitted period shall not be deemed to have been invalidated or become invalid, by reason of accumulations also having been made as aforesaid during such minority.".

166 Restriction on accumulation for the purchase of land

166 [Ceased to have effect by virtue of PAA 2009, s. 13.]

History – S. 166 ceased to have effect by virtue of PAA 2009, s. 13, with effect in relation to an instrument taking effect on or after 6 April 2010, except in relation to a will executed before that day, and with effect in relation to an instrument made in the exercise of a special power of appointment only if the instrument creating the power takes effect on or after 6 April 2010. Former s. 166 read as follows:

"Restriction on accumulation for the purchase of land

166(1) No person may settle or dispose of any property in such manner that the income thereof shall be wholly or partially accumulated for the purchase of land only, for any longer period than the duration of the minority or respective minorities of any person or persons who, under the limitations of the instrument directing the accumulation, would for the time being, if of full age, be entitled to the income so directed to be accumulated.

166(2) This section does not, nor do the enactments which it replaces, apply to accumulations to be held as capital money for the purposes of the Settled Land Act, 1925, or the enactments replaced by that Act, whether or not the accumulations are primarily liable to be laid out in the purchase of land.

166(3) This section applies to settlements and dispositions made after the twenty-seventh day of June eighteen hundred and ninety-two.".

FINANCE (NO. 2) ACT 1931

(21 & 22 Geo. 5, Chapter 49)

[*5th October 1931*]

22 Provisions in cases where Treasury has power to borrow money

22(1) Any securities issued by the Treasury under any Act may be issued with the condition that–

(a) so long as the securities are in the beneficial ownership of persons who are not resident in the United Kingdom, the interest thereon shall be exempt from income tax; and

(b) so long as the securities are in the beneficial ownership of persons who are neither domiciled nor resident in the United Kingdom, neither the capital thereof nor the interest thereon shall be liable to any taxation present or future.

History – In s. 22(1)(a) and (b), the word "ordinarily" omitted by FA 2013, s. 219 and Sch. 46, para. 114(1), with effect from 17 July 2013 (Royal Assent) (subject to the provisions of para. 114(2)–(6)).

Cross references – FA 1940, s. 60: extension of Treasury's power to issue securities carrying tax-free interest.
FA 1996, s. 154(1): FOTRA securities – extension of modifications rule in FA 1940, s. 60.

FINANCE ACT 1940

(3 & 4 Geo. 6, Chapter 29)

[*27th June 1940*]

60 Extension of power of Treasury to attach exemption from taxation to securities

60(1) The power of the Treasury under section twenty-two of the Finance (No. 2) Act, 1931, to issue securities with the condition as to exemption from taxation specified in that section shall extend to the issuing of securities with that condition so modified, whether as to the extent of the exemption or the cases in which the exemption is to operate, as the Treasury may specify in the terms of the issue.

Cross references – FA 1996, s. 154(1): FOTRA securities – modifications under s. 60.

FINANCE ACT 1942

(5 & 6 Geo, Chapter 21)

[*24th June 1942*]

PART V – MISCELLANEOUS AND GENERAL

47 Transfer and registration of Government Stock

47(1) The Treasury may by regulations provide–

(a) for the transfer in law by instrument in writing or otherwise of stock and registered bonds of the descriptions specified in Part I of the Eleventh Schedule to this Act;

(b) for the administration of such stock and bonds (including the registration of holders) by such one or more persons as the Treasury may appoint in accordance with the regulations and the closure of any register;

(bb) for the redemption of such stock and bonds;

(bc) for the exchange of any such stock and bonds (whenever issued) for strips thereof;

(bd) for exchanges by which such strips (whether deriving from the same security or from different securities) are consolidated into a single security of a description so specified;

(c) as to the issue, except in such cases as appear to the Treasury to be appropriate, of documents of title relating to such stock and bonds and as to evidence of title thereto;

(d) as to the transfer of such stock or bonds from England to Ireland and from Ireland to England;

(e) for any incidental, supplementary or transitional matters relating to such stock and bonds, and to transactions connected therewith, for which it appears to the Treasury to be necessary or expedient to provide.

47(1ZA) Regulations under subsection (1) of this section may make provision with respect to the purchase and sale of such stock and bonds by any person, or any description of person, through the Bank of England and, in relation to purchase and sale under the regulations, may–

(a) make provision with respect to the commission and fees payable, and

(b) make provision limiting the amount which any person, or any description of person, may purchase or sell on any day.

47(1A) Regulations under subsection (1) of this section may make provision authorising the Bank of England, in such circumstances and subject to such conditions as may be prescribed in the regulations, to transfer stock and bonds standing in their books in the name of a deceased person into the name of another person without requiring the production of probate, confirmation or letters of administration.

47(1B) In this section **"strip"**, in relation to any stock or bond, means a security issued under the National Loans Act 1968 which–

(a) is issued for the purpose of representing the right to, or of securing–

(i) a payment corresponding to a payment of interest or principal remaining to be made under the stock or bond, or

(ii) two or more payments each corresponding to a different payment remaining to be so made;

(b) is issued in conjunction with the issue of one or more other securities which, together with that security, represent the right to , or secure, payments corresponding to every payment remaining to be made under the stock or bond; and

(c) is not itself a security that represents the right to, or secures, payments corresponding to a part of every payment so remaining.

47(1C) For the purposes of subsection (1B) of this section, where the balance has been struck for a dividend on any stock or bond, any payment to be made in respect of that dividend shall, at times falling after that balance has been struck, be treated as not being a payment remaining to be made under the stock or bond.

47(1D) Without prejudice to the generality of the powers conferred by the preceding provisions of this section (but subject to subsection (1E) of this section), regulations made by virtue of paragraph (bc) or (bd) of subsection (1) of this section may–

(a) provide, for the purpose of authorising the making of exchanges, for any stock or bonds to be treated as issued on such terms as may be specified in the regulations;

(b) contain such provision as the Treasury think fit about the circumstances in which and the conditions subject to which exchanges may be effected; and

(c) contain any such provision as could be contained in rules made under section 14(3) of the National Loans Act 1968 (Treasury rules as to exchange of securities).

47(1E) Regulations made by virtue of subsection (1)(bc) or (bd) of this section shall not make provision for the exchange of any stock or bonds, or of any strips, in any cases other than those where the exchange is at the request of the holder or in accordance with an order made by a court.

47(1EA) Persons appointed in accordance with regulations under subsection (1)(b) shall be appointed on such terms (including terms as to the making of payments by the Treasury) as the Treasury consider appropriate, and the persons who may be so appointed include the Bank of England.

47(1F) Regulations under this section may make different provision for different cases and contain such exceptions and exclusions as the Treasury think fit; and the powers of the Treasury to make regulations under this section are without prejudice to any of their powers under the National Loans Act 1968.

47(2) As from the date on which the first regulations made under this section come into operation, all such stock and bonds as aforesaid shall be transferable in law in manner provided by regulations so made, and in no other manner, and accordingly the enactments and Order in Council set out in Part II of the Eleventh Schedule to this Act shall be amended to the extent specified in the third column of that Part, and the enactments and Order in Council set out in Part III of the said Schedule shall be repealed to the extent specified in the third column of that Part.

47(3) When the Treasury propose to make any regulations under this section, they shall lay a draft thereof before Parliament, and if either House of Parliament within the period of forty days beginning with the day on which the draft of the regulations is laid before it resolves that the regulations shall not be made, no further proceedings shall be taken thereon, but without prejudice to the laying of new draft regulations before Parliament.

In reckoning any such period of forty days as aforesaid no account shall be taken of any time during which Parliament is dissolved or prorogued or during which both Houses are adjourned for more than four days.

47(4) Nothing in this section shall affect–

(a) any stock in respect of which a stock certificate issued under Part V of the National Debt Act 1870, is for the time being outstanding, or any other bearer security;

(b) [repealed by FA 1964, s. 24 and Sch. 8, para. 2, s. 26(7) and Sch. 9;]

(c) the National Savings Stock Register or any stock or securities for the time being registered therein.

History – In s. 47(1)(a), words "or otherwise" inserted by Stock Transfer Act 1982, s. 3 and Sch. 2, para. 2.
S. 47(1)(b) substituted by FA 2002, s. 140, with effect from 11 March 2004, by virtue of SI 2004/689 (c. 23).
S. 47(1)(bb) inserted by FA 1989, s. 183(1).
S. 47(1)(bc),(bd) inserted by FA 1996, s. 202(1).
In s. 47(1)(c), words "except in such cases as appear to the Treasury to be appropriate" inserted by Stock Transfer Act 1982, s. 3 and Sch. 2, para. 2.
S. 47(1A) inserted by FA 1989, s. 183(1).
S. 47(1EA) inserted by FA 2002, s. 140, with effect from 11 March 2004, by virtue of SI 2004/689 (c. 23).
S. 47(1B)–(1F) inserted by FA 1996, s. 202(2).
S. 47(4)(b) repealed by FA 1964, s. 24 and Sch. 8, para. 2, s. 26(7) and Sch. 9, and words in s. 47(4)(c) repealed by National Debt Act 1958, s. 17(1) and Schedule. Words in s. 47(4)(c) "the National Savings Stock Register" substituted by Post Office Act 1969, s. 108(1)(d).
S. 47(1ZA) inserted by Bank of England Act 1998, s. 34, with effect from 1 June 1998 by virtue of SI 1998/1120 (C. 25).

Cross references – FA 2002, s. 139: Closure of UK gilts register kept in Ireland.

CROWN PROCEEDINGS ACT 1947

(10 & 11 Geo. 6, Chapter 44) [*31st July 1947*]

ARRANGEMENT OF SECTIONS

PART VI – EXTENT, COMMENCEMENT, SHORT TITLE, ETC.

PART I – SUBSTANTIVE LAW

1 Right to sue the Crown

1 Where any person has a claim against the Crown after the commencement of this Act, and, if this Act had not been passed, the claim might have been enforced, subject to the grant of Her Majesty's fiat, by petition of right, or might have been enforced by a proceeding provided by any statutory provision repealed by this Act, then, subject to the provisions of this Act, the claim may be enforced as of right, and without the fiat of Her Majesty, by proceedings taken against the Crown for that purpose in accordance with the provisions of this Act.

History – S. 1 amended by Statute Law Revision Act 1953 to refer to Her Majesty.

PART II – JURISDICTION AND PROCEDURE

THE HIGH COURT

13 Civil proceedings in the High Court

13 Subject to the provisions of this Act, all such civil proceedings by or against the Crown as are mentioned in the First Schedule to this Act are hereby abolished, and all civil proceedings by or against the Crown in the High Court shall be instituted and proceeded with in accordance with rules of court and not otherwise.

COUNTY COURTS

15 Civil proceedings in the county court

15(1) Subject to the provisions of this Act, and to any enactment limiting the jurisdiction of the county court (whether by reference to the subject matter of the proceedings to be brought or the amount sought to be recovered in the proceedings or otherwise) any civil proceedings against the Crown may be instituted in the county court.

15(2) Any proceedings by or against the Crown in the county court shall be instituted and proceeded with in accordance with rules of court and not otherwise.

History – In s. 15(1) and (2), the words "the county court" (in both places) substituted for the words "a county court" by Crime and Courts Act 2013, s. 17(5) and Sch. 9, para. 20(a), with effect from 22 April 2014 (SI 2014/954, art. 2).
In s. 15(2), the words "rules of court" substituted for the words "county court rules" by SI 2005/2712, art. 2 and Sch. 1, para. 1, with effect from 1 October 2005.

Cross references – County Courts Act 1984, s. 46; TMA 1970, s. 66: county court rules, replaced by Civil Procedure Rules 1998 (SI 1998/3132) as from 26 April 1999.

GENERAL

16 Interpleader

16 The Crown may obtain relief by way of interpleader proceedings, and may be made a party to such proceedings, in the same manner in which a subject may obtain relief by way of such proceedings or be made a party thereto, and may be made a party to such proceedings notwithstanding that the application for relief is made by a sheriff or other like officer; and all rules of court relating to interpleader proceedings shall, subject to the provisions of this Act, have effect accordingly.

History – In s. 16, the words "and county court rules" repealed by SI 2005/2712, art. 2 and Sch. 1, para. 2, with effect from 1 October 2005.

17 Parties to proceedings

17(1) The Minister for the Civil Service shall publish a list specifying the several Government departments which are authorised departments for the purposes of this Act, and the name and address for service of the person who is, or is acting for the purposes of this Act as, the solicitor for each such department, and may from time to time amend or vary the said list.

Any document purporting to be a copy of a list published under this section and purporting to be printed under the superintendence or the authority of Her Majesty's Stationery Office shall in any legal proceedings be received as evidence for the purpose of establishing what departments are authorised departments for the purposes of this Act, and what person is, or is acting for the purposes of this Act as, the solicitor for any such department.

17(2) Civil proceedings by the Crown may be instituted either by an authorised Government department in its own name, whether that department was or was not at the commencement of this Act authorised to sue, or by the Attorney-General.

17(3) Civil proceedings against the Crown shall be instituted against the appropriate authorised Government department, or, if none of the authorised Government departments is appropriate or the person instituting the proceedings has any reasonable doubt whether any and if so which of those departments is appropriate, against the Attorney-General.

17(4) Where any civil proceedings against the Crown are instituted against the Attorney-General, an application may at any stage of the proceedings be made to the court by or on behalf of the Attorney-General to have such of the authorised Government departments as may be specified in the application substituted for him as defendant to the proceedings; and where any such proceedings are brought against an authorised Government department, an application may at any stage of the proceedings be made to the court on behalf of that department to have the Attorney-General or such of the authorised Government departments as may be specified in the application substituted for the applicant as the defendant to the proceedings.

Upon any such application the court may if it thinks fit make an order granting the application on such terms as the court thinks just; and on such an order being made the proceedings shall continue as if they had been commenced against the department specified in that behalf in the order, or, as the case may require, against the Attorney-General.

17(5) No proceedings instituted in accordance with this Part of this Act by or against the Attorney-General or an authorised Government department shall abate or be affected by any change in the person holding the office of Attorney-General or in the person or body of persons constituting the department.

History – Reference to the "Minister for the Civil Service" substituted by SI 1968/1656.
S. 17 amended by Statute Law Revision Act 1953 to refer to Her Majesty.

18 Service of documents

18 All documents required to be served on the Crown for the purpose of or in connection with any civil proceedings by or against the Crown shall, if those proceedings are by or against an authorised Government department, be served on the solicitor, if any, for that department, or the person, if any, acting for the purposes of this Act as solicitor for that department, or if there is no such solicitor and no person so acting, or if the proceedings are brought by or against the Attorney-General, on the Solicitor for the affairs of Her Majesty's Treasury.

History – S. 18 amended by Statute Law Revision Act 1953 to refer to Her Majesty.

19 Venue and related matters

19 [Repealed by SI 2005/2712, art. 2 and Sch. 1, para. 3.]

History – S. 19 repealed by SI 2005/2712, art. 2 and Sch. 1, para. 3, with effect from 1 October 2005.

20 Removal and transfer of proceedings

20(1) [Repealed by SI 2005/2712, art. 2 and Sch. 1, para. 4(a).]

20(2) All rules of law and enactments relating to the removal or transfer of proceedings from the county court to the High Court, or the transfer of proceedings from the High Court to the county court, shall apply in relation to proceedings against the Crown.

History – S. 20(1) repealed by SI 2005/2712, art. 2 and Sch. 1, para. 4(a), with effect from 1 October 2005.
In s. 20(2), the words "the county court" (in both places) substituted for the words "a county court" by Crime and Courts Act 2013, s. 17(5) and Sch. 9, para. 20(a), with effect from 22 April 2014 (SI 2014/954, art. 2).
In s. 20(2), the words "Without prejudice to the rights of the Crown under the preceding provisions of this section,", which appeared before the words "All rules of law", repealed by SI 2005/2712, art. 2 and Sch. 1, para. 4(b), with effect from 1 October 2005.
Former proviso to s. 20(2) repealed by Senior Courts Act 1981, s. 152(4) and Sch. 7, with effect from 1 January 1982.

21 Nature of relief

21(1) In any civil proceedings by or against the Crown the court shall, subject to the provisions of this Act, have power to make all such orders as it has power to make in proceedings between subjects, and otherwise to give such appropriate relief as the case may require:

Provided that:–

(a) where in any proceedings against the Crown any such relief is sought as might in proceedings between subjects be granted by way of injunction or specific performance, the court shall not grant an injunction or make an order for specific performance, but may in lieu thereof make an order declaratory of the rights of the parties; and

(b) in any proceedings against the Crown for the recovery of land or other property the court shall not make an order for the recovery of the land or the delivery of the property, but may in lieu thereof make an order declaring that the plaintiff is entitled as against the Crown to the land or property or to the possession thereof.

21(2) The court shall not in any civil proceedings grant any injunction or make any order against an officer of the Crown if the effect of granting the injunction or making the order would be to give any relief against the Crown which could not have been obtained in proceedings against the Crown.

22 Appeals and stay of execution

22 Subject to the provisions of this Act, all enactments and rules of court relating to appeals and stay of execution shall, with any necessary modifications, apply to civil proceedings by or against the Crown as they apply to proceedings between subjects.

History – In s. 22, the words "and rules of court" substituted for the words ", rules of court and county court rules" by SI 2005/2712, art. 2 and Sch. 1, para. 5, with effect from 1 October 2005.

23 Scope of Part II

23(1) Subject to the provisions of this section, any reference in this Part of this Act to **"civil proceedings by the Crown"** shall be construed as a reference to the following proceedings only:–

(a) proceedings for the enforcement or vindication of any right or the obtaining of any relief which, if this Act had not been passed, might have been enforced or vindicated or obtained by any such proceedings as are mentioned in paragraph 1 of the First Schedule to this Act;

(b) proceedings for the enforcement or vindication of any right or the obtaining of any relief which, if this Act had not been passed, might have been enforced or vindicated or obtained by an action at the suit of any Government department or any officer of the Crown as such;

(c) all such proceedings as the Crown is entitled to bring by virtue of this Act;

and the expression **"civil proceedings by or against the Crown"** shall be construed accordingly.

23(2) Subject to the provisions of this section, any reference in this Part of this Act to **"civil proceedings against the Crown"** shall be construed as a reference to the following proceedings only:–

(a) proceedings for the enforcement or vindication of any right or the obtaining of any relief which, if this Act had not been passed, might have been enforced or vindicated or obtained by any such proceedings as are mentioned in paragraph 2 of the First Schedule to this Act;

(b) proceedings for the enforcement or vindication of any right or the obtaining of any relief which, if this Act had not been passed, might have been enforced or vindicated or obtained by an action against the Attorney-General, any Government department, or any officer of the Crown as such; and

(c) all such proceedings as any person is entitled to bring against the Crown by virtue of this Act;

and the expression **"civil proceedings by or against the Crown"** shall be construed accordingly.

23(3) [Not relevant to taxation; not reproduced here.]

23(4) Subject to the provisions of any order in council made under the provisions hereinafter contained, this part of this Act shall not affect proceedings initiated in any court other than the High Court or the county court.

History – In s. 23(4), the words "the county court" substituted for the words "a county court" by Crime and Courts Act 2013, s. 17(5) and Sch. 9, para. 20(a), with effect from 22 April 2014 (SI 2014/954, art. 2).

PART III – JUDGMENTS AND EXECUTION

24 Interest on debts, damages and costs

24(1) Section seventeen of the Judgments Act, 1838 (which provides that a judgment debt shall carry interest) and section 44A of the Administration of Justice Act 1970 (which enables the court to order an appropriate rate for a judgment debt expressed in a currency other than sterling) shall apply to judgment debts due from or to the Crown.

24(2) Where any costs are awarded to or against the Crown in the High Court, interest shall be payable upon those costs unless the court otherwise orders, and any interest so payable shall be at the same rate as that at which interest is payable upon judgment debts due from or to the Crown.

24(3) Section 35A of the Senior Courts Act 1981 and section 69 of the County Courts Act 1984 (which respectively empower the High Court and the county court to award interest on debts and damages) and section 3 of the Law Reform (Miscellaneous Provisions) Act 1934 (which empowers other courts of record to do so) shall apply to judgments given in proceedings by and against the Crown.

24(4) [Repealed by Statute Law (Repeals) Act 1993 s. 1(1), Sch. 1 Pt. 1.]

History – Respective powers to award interest on debts and damages substituted by County Courts Act 1984, s. 148(1) and Sch. 2, para. 21, with effect from 1 August 1984 and by the Administration of Justice Act 1982, Sch. 1, Pt. III, with effect from 1 January 1983. In s. 24(1), reference to the Administration of Justice Act 1970 inserted by the Private International Law (Miscellaneous Provisions) Act 1995 s. 4(1) with effect from 1 November 1996.
In s. 24(3), the words "the county court" substituted for the words "county courts" by Crime and Courts Act 2013, s. 17(5) and Sch. 9, para. 20(b), with effect from 22 April 2014 (SI 2014/954, art. 2).
In s. 24(3), the words "Senior Courts Act 1981" substituted for the words "Supreme Court Act 1981" by Constitutional Reform Act 2005, s. 59(5) and Sch. 11, para. 1(2), with effect from 1 October 2009 (SI 2009/1604, art. 2).
S. 24(4) repealed by Statute Law (Repeals) Act 1993 s. 1(1), Sch. 1, Pt. 1 with effect from 5 November 1993.

25 Satisfaction of orders against the Crown

25(1) Where in any civil proceedings by or against the Crown, or in any proceedings on the Crown side of the Queen's Bench Division, or in connection with any arbitration to which the Crown is a party, any order (including an order for costs) is made by any court in favour of any person against the Crown or against a Government department or against an officer of the Crown as such, the proper officer of the court shall, on an application in that behalf made by or on behalf of that person at any time after the expiration of twenty-one days from the date of the order or, in case the order provides for the payment of costs and the costs require to be taxed, at any time after the costs have been taxed, whichever is the later, issue to that person a certificate in the prescribed form containing particulars of the order:

Provided that, if the court so directs, a separate certificate shall be issued with respect to the costs (if any) ordered to be paid to the applicant.

25(2) A copy of any certificate issued under this section may be served by the person in whose favour the order is made upon the person for the time being named in the record as the solicitor, or as the person acting as solicitor, for the Crown or for the Government department or officer concerned.

25(3) If the order provides for the payment of any money by way of damages, of any costs, the certificate shall state the amount so payable, and the appropriate Government department shall, subject as hereinafter provided, pay to the person entitled or to his solicitor the amount appearing by the certificate to be due to him together with the interest, if any, lawfully due thereon:

Provided that the court by which any such order as aforesaid is made or any court to which an appeal against the order lies may direct that, pending an appeal or otherwise, payment of the whole of any amount so payable, or any part thereof, shall be suspended, and if the certificate has not been issued may order any such directions to be inserted therein.

25(4) Save as aforesaid no execution or attachment or process in the nature thereof shall be issued out of any court for enforcing payment by the Crown of any such money or costs as aforesaid, and no person shall be individually liable under any order for the payment by the Crown, or any Government department, or any officer of the Crown as such, of any such money or costs.

25(5) [Repealed by Statute Law (Repeals) Act 1993 s. 1(1), Sch. 1 Pt. 1.]

History – S. 25 amended by Statute Law Revision Act 1953 to refer to the Queen's Bench Division.
S. 25(5) repealed by Statute Law (Repeals) Act 1993 s. 1(1), Sch. 1, Pt. 1 with effect from 5 November 1993.

26 Execution by the Crown

26(1) Subject to the provisions of this Act, any order made in favour of the Crown against any person in any civil proceedings to which the Crown is a party may be enforced in the same manner as an order made in an action between subjects, and not otherwise.

26(2) Sections four and five of the Debtors Act, 1869 (which provide respectively for the abolition of imprisonment for debt, and for saving the power of committal in case of small debts), shall apply to sums of money payable and debts due to the Crown:

Provided that for the purpose of the application of the said section four to any sum of money payable or debt due to the Crown, the section shall have effect as if there were included among the exceptions therein mentioned default in payment of any sum payable in respect of death duties.

26(3) Nothing in this section shall affect any procedure which immediately before the commencement of this Act was available for enforcing an order made in favour of the Crown in proceedings brought by the Crown for the recovery of any fine or penalty.

History – S. 26(1) amended by Statute Law (Repeals) Act 1993 s. 1(1), Sch. 1, Pt. 1.
Default in payment of purchase tax removed from exceptions in s. 26(2) by FA 1972, Sch. 28, Pt. II, with effect from 1 March 1982 (see SI 1982/87).

Cross references – S. 49: application to Scotland.

27 Attachment of moneys payable by the Crown

27(1) Where any money is payable by the Crown to some person who, under any order of any court, is liable to pay any money to any other person, and that other person would, if the money so payable by the Crown were money payable by a subject, be entitled under rules of court to obtain an order for the attachment thereof as a debt due or accruing due, or an order for the appointment of a sequestrator or receiver to receive the money on his behalf, the High Court may, subject to the provisions of this Act and in accordance with rules of court, make an order restraining the first-mentioned person from receiving that money and directing payment thereof to that other person, or to the sequestrator or receiver:

Provided that no such order shall be made in respect of:–

(a) any wages or salary payable to any officer of the Crown as such;

(b) any money which is subject to the provisions of any enactment prohibiting or restricting assignment or charging or taking in execution.

27(2) The provisions of the preceding subsection shall, so far as they relate to forms of relief falling within the jurisdiction of the county court, have effect in relation to the county court as they have effect in relation to the High Court.

27(3) In their application to England and Wales the preceding provisions of this section shall have effect subject to any order for the time being in force under section 139(2) of the Senior Courts Act 1981.

History – Para. (c) of the proviso to s. 27(1) (precluding the making of an order under s. 27(1) in respect of money payable on account of a National Savings Bank deposit) was repealed and s. 27(3) inserted by Senior Courts Act 1981, s. 139(1), (4), 152(4) and Sch. 7, with effect from 1 January 1982 (see also cross reference).

In s. 27(2), the words "the county court" substituted for the words "a county court" and the words "the county court" substituted for the words "county courts" by Crime and Courts Act 2013, s. 17(5) and Sch. 9, para. 20, with effect from 22 April 2014 (SI 2014/954, art. 2).

In s. 27(2), the words ", but with the substitution of a reference to county court rules for any reference in the said subsection to rules of court", which appeared after the words "High Court", repealed by SI 2005/2712, art. 2 and Sch. 1, para. 6, with effect from 1 October 2005.

In s. 27(3), the words "Senior Courts Act 1981" substituted for the words "Supreme Court Act 1981" by Constitutional Reform Act 2005, s. 59(5) and Sch. 11, para. 1(2), with effect from 1 October 2009 (SI 2009/1604, art. 2).

Cross references – Senior Courts Act 1981, s. 139(2), (3): Lord Chancellor enabled to exclude deposits with the National Savings Bank.

PART IV – MISCELLANEOUS AND SUPPLEMENTAL

MISCELLANEOUS

28 Discovery

28(1) Subject to and in accordance with rules of court:–

(a) in any civil proceedings in the High Court or the county court to which the Crown is a party, the Crown may be required by the court to make discovery of documents and produce documents for inspection; and

(b) in any such proceedings as aforesaid, the Crown may be required by the court to answer interrogatories:

Provided that this section shall be without prejudice to any rule of law which authorises or requires the withholding of any document or the refusal to answer any question on the ground that the disclosure of the document or the answering of the question would be injurious to the public interest.

Any order of the court made under the powers conferred by paragraph (b) of this subsection shall direct by what officer of the Crown the interrogatories are to be answered.

28(2) Without prejudice to the proviso to the preceding subsection, any rules made for the purposes of this section shall be such as to secure that the existence of a document will not be disclosed if, in the opinion of a Minister of the Crown, it would be injurious to the public interest to disclose the existence thereof.

History – In s. 28(1)(a), the words "the county court" substituted for the words "a county court" by Crime and Courts Act 2013, s. 17(5) and Sch. 9, para. 20(a), with effect from 22 April 2014 (SI 2014/954, art. 2).

In s. 28(1), the words "and county court rules", which appeared after the words "rules of court", repealed by SI 2005/2712, art. 2 and Sch. 1, para. 7, with effect from 1 October 2005.

31 Application to the Crown of certain statutory provisions

31(1) This Act shall not prejudice the right of the Crown to take advantage of the provisions of an Act of Parliament although not named therein; and it is hereby declared that in any civil proceedings against the Crown the provisions of any Act of Parliament which could, if the proceedings were between subjects, be relied upon by the defendant as a defence to the proceedings, whether in whole or in part, or otherwise, may, subject to any express provision to the contrary, be so relied upon by the Crown.

31(2) Section six of the Debtors Act, 1869 (which empowers the court in certain circumstances to order the arrest of a defendant about to quit England) shall, with any necessary modifications, apply to civil proceedings in the High Court by the Crown.

32 No abatement on demise of Crown

32 No claim by or against the Crown, and no proceedings for the enforcement of any such claim, shall abate or be affected by the demise of the Crown.

SUPPLEMENTAL

35 Rules of court and county court rules

35(1) Any power to make rules of court shall include power to make rules for the purpose of giving effect to the provisions of this Act, and any such rules may contain provisions to have effect in relation to any proceedings by or against the Crown in substitution for or by way of addition to any of the provisions of the rules applying to proceedings between subjects.

35(2) Provision shall be made by rules of court with respect to the following matters:–

(a) for providing for service of process, or notice thereof, in the case of proceedings by the Crown against persons, whether British subjects or not, who are not resident in the United Kingdom;

(b) for securing that where any civil proceedings are brought against the Crown in accordance with the provisions of this Act the claimant shall provide the Crown with information as to the circumstances in which it is alleged that the liability of the Crown has risen and as to the departments and officers of the Crown concerned;

(c) [repealed by SI 2005/2712, art. 2 and Sch. 1, para. 8(c)(iii);]

(d) [repealed by SI 2005/2712, art. 2 and Sch. 1, para. 8(c)(iii);]

(e) [repealed by SI 2005/2712, art. 2 and Sch. 1, para. 8(c)(iii);]

(f) for enabling evidence to be taken on commission in proceedings by or against the Crown;

(g) for providing:–

(i) that a person shall not be entitled to avail himself of any set-off or counterclaim in any proceedings by the Crown for the recovery of taxes, duties or penalties, or to avail himself in proceedings of any other nature by the Crown of any set-off or counterclaim arising out of a right or claim to repayment in respect of any taxes, duties or penalties;

(ii) that a person shall not be entitled without the leave of the court to avail himself of any set-off or counterclaim in any proceedings by the Crown if either the subject-matter of the set-off or counterclaim does not relate to the Government department in the name of which the proceedings are brought or the proceedings are brought in the name of the Attorney-General;

(iii) that the Crown, when sued in the name of a Government department, shall not, without the leave of the court, be entitled to avail itself of any set-off or counterclaim if the subject-matter thereof does not relate to that department; and

(iv) that the Crown, when sued in the name of the Attorney-General, shall not be entitled to avail itself of any set-off or counterclaim without the leave of the court.

35(3) Provision may be made by rules of court for regulating any appeals to the High Court, whether by way of case stated or otherwise, under enactments relating to the revenue, and any rules made under this subsection may revoke any enactments or rules in force immediately before the commencement of this Act so far as they regulate any such appeals, and may make provision for any matters for which provision was made by any enactments or rules so in force.

History – In s. 35(1), the words " or county court rules", which appeared after the words "rules of court" repealed by SI 2005/2712, art. 2 and Sch. 1, para. 8(b), with effect from 1 October 2005.

In s. 35(2), the words "and county court rules ", which appeared after the words "rules of court", repealed by SI 2005/2712, art. 2 and Sch. 1, para. 8(c), with effect from 1 October 2005.

In s. 35(2)(b), the words "the claimant shall provide the Crown with information" substituted for the words "the plaintiff shall, before the Crown is required to take any step in the proceedings, provide the Crown with such information as the Crown may reasonably require" by SI 2005/2712, art. 2 and Sch. 1, para. 8(c), with effect from 1 October 2005.

S. 35(2)(c), (d) and (e) repealed by SI 2005/2712, art. 2 and Sch. 1, para. 8(c), with effect from 1 October 2005.

Cross references – S. 50: application to Scotland.

TMA 1970, s. 69: penalty, surcharge, or interest on overdue tax treated as tax for s. 35(2)(g)(i).

Notes – Senior Courts Act 1981, s. 84 and County Courts Act 1984: relevant power to make rules (those rules are RSC, O. 77 and CCR, O. 42, as replaced by Civil Procedure Rules 1998 (SI 1998/3132), r. 50.1(3), Sch. 1, r. 77 and Sch. 2, r. 42 as from 26 April 1999).

38 Interpretation

38(1) Any reference in this Act to the provisions of this Act shall, unless the context otherwise requires, include a reference to rules of court made for the purposes of this Act.

38(2) In this Act, except in so far as the context otherwise requires or it is otherwise expressly provided, the following expressions have the meanings hereby respectively assigned to them, that is to say:–

"Agent" when used in relation to the Crown, includes an independent contractor employed by the Crown;

"Civil proceedings" includes proceedings in the High Court or the county court for the recovery of fines or penalties, but does not include proceedings on the Crown side of the Queen's Bench Division;

"Officer", in relation to the Crown, includes any servant of Her Majesty, and accordingly (but without prejudice to the generality of the foregoing provision) includes a Minister of the Crown and a member of the Scottish Executive;

"Order" includes a judgment, decree, rule, award or declaration;

"Prescribed" means prescribed by rules of court;

"Proceedings against the Crown" includes a claim by way of set-off or counterclaim raised in proceedings by the Crown;

"Statutory duty" means any duty imposed by or under any Act of Parliament.

38(3) Any reference in this Act to **Her Majesty in Her private capacity** shall be construed as including a reference to Her Majesty in right of Her Duchy of Lancaster and to the Duke of Cornwall.

38(4) Any reference in Parts III or IV of this Act to **civil proceedings by or against the Crown**, or to **civil proceedings to which the Crown is a party**, shall be construed as including a reference to civil proceedings to which the Attorney-General, or any Government department, or any officer of the Crown as such is a party:

Provided that the Crown shall not for the purposes of Parts III and IV of this Act be deemed to be a party to any proceedings by reason only that they are brought by the Attorney-General upon the relation of some other person.

38(5) [Repealed by Armed Forces Act 1981, Sch. 5, Pt. I.]

38(6) References in this Act to any enactment shall be construed as references to that enactment as amended by or under any other enactment, including this Act.

History – S. 38 amended by Statute Law Revision Act 1953 to refer to Her Majesty and the Queen's Bench Division.
In s. 38(1), the words " or county court rules", which appeared after the words "rules of court", repealed by SI 2005/2712, art. 2 and Sch. 1, para. 9(a), with effect from 1 October 2005.
In s. 38(2), in definition of "officer", words "and a member of the Scottish Executive" inserted by Scotland Act 1998, s. 125 and Sch. 8, para. 7(2)(c).
In s. 38(2), the words "or county court rules, as the case may be", which appeared after the words "rules of court", repealed by SI 2005/2712, art. 2 and Sch. 1, para. 9(b), with effect from 1 October 2005.
The repeal of s. 38(5) has effect from 28 July 1981.

Cross references – S. 51(2): application to Scotland.

40 Savings

40(1) Nothing in this Act shall apply to proceedings by or against, or authorise proceedings in tort to be brought against Her Majesty in Her private capacity.

40(2) Except as therein otherwise expressly provided, nothing in this Act shall:–

(a) affect the law relating to prize salvage, or apply to proceedings in causes or matters within the jurisdiction of the High Court as a prize court or to any criminal proceedings; or

(b) authorise proceedings to be taken against the Crown under or in accordance with this Act in respect of any alleged liability of the Crown arising otherwise than in respect of Her Majesty's Government in the United Kingdom or the Scottish Administration, or affect proceedings against the Crown in respect of any such alleged liability as aforesaid; or

(c) affect any proceedings by the Crown otherwise than in right of Her Majesty's Government in the United Kingdom or the Scottish Administration; or

(d) subject the Crown to any greater liabilities in respect of the acts or omissions of any independent contractor employed by the Crown than those to which the Crown would be subject in respect of such acts or omissions if it were a private person; or

(e) [Repealed by the Highways (Miscellaneous Provisions) Act 1961, s. 1(6), (8) and 17(3).]

(f) affect any rules of evidence or any presumption relating to the extent to which the Crown is bound by any Act of Parliament; or

(g) affect any right of the Crown to demand a trial at bar or to control or otherwise intervene in proceedings affecting its rights, property or profits; or

(h) affect any liability imposed on the public trustee or on the Consolidated Fund of the United Kingdom or the Scottish Administration by the Public Trustee Act, 1906 and, without prejudice to the general effect of the foregoing provisions, Part III of this Act shall not apply to the Crown except in right of Her Majesty's Government in the United Kingdom or the Scottish Administration.

40(3) A certificate of a Secretary of State:–

(a) to the effect that any alleged liability of the Crown arises otherwise than in respect of Her Majesty's Government in the United Kingdom;

(b) to the effect that any proceedings by the Crown are proceedings otherwise than in right of Her Majesty's Government in the United Kingdom;

shall, for the purposes of this Act, be conclusive as to the matter so certified.

40(3A) A certificate of the Scottish Ministers to the effect that–

(a) any alleged liability of the Crown arises otherwise than in right of the Scottish Administration,

(b) any proceedings by the Crown are proceedings otherwise than in respect of the Scottish Administration,

shall, for the purposes of this Act, be conclusive as to that matter.

40(4) Where any property vests in the Crown by virtue of any rule of law which operates independently of the acts or the intentions of the Crown, the Crown shall not by virtue of this Act be subject to any liabilities in tort by reason only of the property being so vested; but the provisions of this subsection shall be without prejudice to the liabilities of the Crown under this Act in respect of any period after the Crown or any person acting for the Crown has in fact taken possession or control of any such property, or entered into occupation thereof.

40(5) This Act shall not operate to limit the discretion of the court to grant relief by way of mandamus in cases in which such relief might have been granted before the commencement of this Act, notwithstanding that by reason of the provisions of this Act some other and further remedy is available.

History – S. 40 amended by Statute Law Revision Act 1953 to refer to Her Majesty.
In s. 40(2), words "or the Scottish Administration" inserted in each place, and s. 40(3A) inserted, by Scotland Act 1998, s. 125 and Sch. 8, para. 7(3)(a), (b).

PART V – APPLICATION TO SCOTLAND

41 Application of Act to Scotland

41 The provisions of this Part of this Act shall have effect for the purpose of the application of this Act to Scotland.

42 Exclusion of certain provisions

42 Section one, Part II (except section thirteen so far as relating to proceedings mentioned in the First Schedule and section twenty-one), Part III (except section twenty-six) and section twenty-eight of this Act shall not apply to Scotland.

43 Interpretation for purposes of application to Scotland

43 In the application of this Act to Scotland:–

(a) for any reference to the High Court (except a reference to that Court as a prize court) there shall be substituted a reference to the Court of Session; for any reference to the county court there shall be substituted a reference to the sheriff court; the expression **"plaintiff"** means pursuer; the expression **"defendant"** means defender; the expression **"county court rules"** means Act of Sederunt applying to the sheriff court; and the expression **"injunction"** means interdict.

(b) [Repealed.]

44 Proceedings against the Crown in the sheriff court

44 Subject to the provisions of this Act and to any enactment limiting the jurisdiction of the sheriff court (whether by reference to the subject matter of the proceedings or otherwise) civil proceedings against the Crown may be instituted in the sheriff court in like manner as if the proceedings were against a subject:

Provided that where in any proceedings against the Crown in the sheriff court a certificate by the appropriate Law Officer is produced to the effect that the proceedings may involve an important question of law, or may be decisive of other cases, or are for other reasons more fit for trial in the Court of Session, the proceedings shall be remitted to the Court of Session, and where any proceedings have been so remitted to the Court of Session, and it appears to that Court that the remit has occasioned additional expense to the pursuer, the Court shall take account of the additional expense so occasioned in deciding any question as to expenses.

In this proviso, **"the appropriate Law Officer"** means–

(a) the Lord Advocate, where the proceedings are against any part of the Scottish Administration, and

(b) the Advocate General for Scotland, in any other case.

History – In the proviso, words "appropriate Law Officer" substituted for "Lord Advocate", and definition of "appropriate Law Officer" inserted, by Scotland Act 1998, s. 125 and Sch. 8, para. 7(4)(a), (b).

45 Satisfaction of orders granted against the Crown in Scotland

45(1) Where in any civil proceedings by or against the Crown or to which the Crown has been made a party, any order (including an award of expenses) is made by any court in favour of any person against the Crown or against a Government department or against an officer of the Crown as such, the clerk of court shall, on an application in that behalf made by or on behalf of that person at any time after the expiration of twenty-one days from the date of the order, or, in a case where there is an award of expenses and the expenses require to be taxed, at any time after taxation whichever is the later, issue to that person a certified copy of the order of the court.

45(2) A copy of any such order may be served by the person in whose favour the order is made upon the person for the time being named in the record as the solicitor, or the person acting as solicitor, for the Crown or for the Government department or officer concerned.

45(3) If the order decerns for the payment of any money or any expenses, the appropriate Government department shall, subject as hereinafter provided, pay to the person entitled or to his solicitor the amount appearing from the order to be due to him together with the interest, if any, lawfully due thereon:

Provided that the court by which any such order as aforesaid is made or any court to which an appeal against the order lies may direct that pending an appeal or otherwise payment of the whole of any amount so payable, or any part thereof, shall be suspended.

45(4) No such order as aforesaid shall warrant any diligence or execution against any person to enforce payment of any such money or expenses as aforesaid, and no person shall be individually liable under any order for the payment by the Crown, or any Government department or any officer of the Crown as such, of any such money or expenses.

46 Provisions as to arrestment

46 Arrestment in the hands of the Crown or of a Government department or of any officer of the Crown as such shall be competent in any case where arrestment in the hands of a subject would have been competent:

Provided that nothing in the foregoing provisions shall warrant the arrestment of:–

(a) [Repealed by Debtors (Scotland) Act 1987, Sch. 8.]

(b) any money which is subject to the provisions of any enactment prohibiting or restricting assignation or charging or taking in execution.

(c) [Repealed by Law Reform (Miscellaneous Provisions) (Scotland) Act 1985, s. 49(2) and Sch. 4.]

History – The repeal of para. (a) has effect from 30 November 1988 (SI 1988/1818 (C 66) (s. 170)).
The repeal of para. (c) has effect from 20 December 1985.

47 Recovery of documents in possession of Crown

47 Subject to and in accordance with Acts of Sederunt applying to the Court of Session and the sheriff court, commission and diligence for the recovery of documents in the possession of the Crown may be granted in any action whether or not the Crown is a party thereto, in like manner in all respects as if the documents were in the possession of a subject:

Provided that–

(i) this subsection shall be without prejudice to any rule of law which authorises or requires the withholding of any document on the ground that its disclosure would be injurious to the public interest; and

(ii) the existence of a document shall not be disclosed if, in the opinion of a Minister of the Crown, it would be injurious to the public interest to disclose the existence thereof.

49 Application to Scotland of section 26

49 Section twenty-six of this Act shall have effect as if for subsection (2) thereof there were substituted the following subsection:–

> "**26(2)** The exception in respect of taxes contained in section four of the Debtors (Scotland) Act, 1880, from the enactment therein contained abolishing imprisonment for debt shall apply only in respect of death duties."

History – Exception for purchase tax removed by FA 1972, s. 54(8) and Sch. 28, Pt. II, with effect from 1 March 1982 (SI 1982/87).

50 Application to Scotland of section 35

50 Section thirty-five of this Act shall have effect as if for subsection (2) thereof there were substituted the following subsection:–

> **"35(2)** The following provisions shall apply as regards proceedings in the Court of Session or the sheriff court:–
>
> (b) a person shall not be entitled to avail himself of any set-off or counterclaim in any proceedings by the Crown for the recovery of taxes, duties or penalties, or to avail himself in proceedings of any other nature by the Crown of any set-off or counterclaim arising out of a right or claim to repayment in respect of any taxes, duties or penalties;"

Cross references – TMA 1970, s. 69: penalties, surcharges and interest on overdue tax treated as tax for this purpose.

51 Application to Scotland of sections 36 and 38

51(1) [Repealed by Statute Law Repeals Act 1993, s. 1(1) and Sch. 1, Pt. 1.]

51(2) Section thirty-eight of this Act shall have effect as if in subsection (4) thereof:–

(i) there were included a reference to this Part of this Act;

(ii) for the reference to the Attorney-General there were substituted a reference to the Lord Advocate or the Advocate General for Scotland;

(iii) the proviso were omitted.

History – S. 51(1) repealed by Statute Law Repeals Act 1993, s. 1(1) and Sch. 1, Pt. 1.
In s. 51(2), reference to the Advocate General for Scotland inserted by Scotland Act 1998, s. 125 and Sch. 8, para. 7(6).

PART VI – EXTENT, COMMENCEMENT, SHORT TITLE, ETC.

52 Extent of Act

52 Subject to the provisions hereinafter contained with respect to Northern Ireland, this Act shall not affect the law enforced in courts elsewhere than in England and Scotland, or the procedure in any such courts.

53 Provisions as to Northern Ireland

53(1) Her Majesty may by Order in Council provide for extending this Act to Northern Ireland with such additions, exceptions and modifications as appear to Her Majesty to be expedient.

53(2) An Order in Council under this section may provide for amending the law both in its application to the Crown in right of Her Majesty's Government in the United Kingdom and in its application to the Crown in right of Her Majesty's Government in Northern Ireland.

53(3) An Order in Council under this section may provide for amending the law:–

(a) with respect to the right of the Crown to sue in a county court in Northern Ireland; and

(b) with respect to the award of costs to or against the Crown in Northern Ireland.

53(4) An Order in Council under this section may be varied or revoked by a further Order in Council made thereunder.

53(5) An Order in Council under this section may include such provisions as appear to Her Majesty to be incidental to or consequential on any provisions contained in such an Order by virtue of the preceding provisions of this section.

53(6) [Repealed by the Northern Ireland Constitution Act 1973, s. 41(1)(a) and Sch. 6, Pt. 1.]

53(7) An Order in Council under this section shall be laid before Parliament as soon as may be after it is made, and, if either House of Parliament, within the next twenty-eight days on which that House has sat after such an Order is laid before it, resolves that the Order be annulled, the Order shall thereupon cease to have effect except as respects things previously done or omitted to be done, without prejudice, however, to the making of a new Order.

History – S. 53(6) repealed by the Northern Ireland Constitution Act 1973, s. 41(1)(a) and Sch. 6, Pt. 1.
S. 53 amended by Statute Law Revision Act 1953 to refer to Her Majesty.

Statutory instruments – SR & O 1949/1836
Crown Proceedings (Northern Ireland) Order 1981 (SI 1981/233).

54 *Short title and commencement*

54(1) This Act may be cited as the Crown Proceedings Act, 1947.

54(2) [Repealed by Statute Law Revision Act 1950.]

PROVISIONAL COLLECTION OF TAXES ACT 1968

(1968 Chapter 2)

[*1st February 1968*]

ARRANGEMENT OF SECTIONS

1 Temporary statutory effect of House of Commons resolutions affecting income tax, purchase tax or customs or excise duties

1(1) This section applies only to income tax, capital gains tax, corporation tax, the bank levy, diverted profits tax, the apprenticeship levy, petroleum revenue tax, stamp duty reserve tax, stamp duty land tax, annual tax on enveloped dwellings, value added tax, climate change levy, insurance premium tax, landfill tax, aggregates levy, and duties of customs and excise.

1(1A) [Repealed by FA 1993, s. 205(3), s. 213 and Sch. 23, Pt. VI.]

1(2) Subject to that, and to the provisions of subsections (4) to (9) below, where the House of Commons passes a resolution which–

(a) provides for the renewal for a further period of any tax in force or imposed during the previous financial year (whether at the same or a different rate, and whether with or without modifications) or for the variation or abolition of any existing tax, and

(b) contains a declaration that it is expedient in the public interest that the resolution should have statutory effect under the provisions of this Act,

the resolution shall, for the period specified in the next following subsection, have statutory effect as if contained in an Act of Parliament and, where the resolution provides for the renewal of a tax, all enactments which were in force with reference to that tax as last imposed by Act of Parliament shall during that period have full force and effect with respect to the tax as renewed by the resolution.

In this section references to the renewal of a tax include references to its reimposition, and references to the abolition of a tax include references to its repeal.

1(3) The period is one expiring at the end of seven months after the date on which the resolution is expressed to take effect or, if no such date is expressed, after the date on which the resolution is passed.

1(4) A resolution shall cease to have statutory effect under this section unless within the next thirty days on which the House of Commons sits after the day on which the resolution is passed–

(a) a Bill renewing, varying or, as the case may be, abolishing the tax is read a second time by the House, or

(b) a Bill is amended by the House in Committee or on Report, or by any Public Bill Committee of the House so as to include provision for the renewal, variation or, as the case may be, abolition of the tax.

1(5) A resolution shall also cease to have statutory effect under this section if–

(a) the provisions giving effect to it are rejected during the passage of the Bill containing them through the House, or

(b) an Act comes into operation renewing, varying or, as the case may be, abolishing the tax, or

(c) Parliament is dissolved, or

(d) Parliament is prorogued.

1(5A) Subsection (5B) applies in relation to a resolution instead of subsection (5)(d) where Parliament is prorogued at the end of a session if–

(a) one of the following happens during the session–

  (i) a Bill renewing, varying or, as the case may be, abolishing the tax is read a first time by the House, or

  (ii) a Bill is amended by the House in Committee or on Report or by any Public Bill Committee of the House so as to include provision for the renewal, variation or, as the case may be, abolition of the tax,

(b) the Standing Orders or Sessional Orders of the House provide, or during the session the House orders, that proceedings on the Bill not completed before the end of the session shall be resumed in the next session, and

(c) proceedings on the Bill are not completed during the session.

1(5B) The resolution shall cease to have statutory effect under this section if, during the period of thirty sitting days beginning with the first sitting day of the next session, no Bill renewing, varying or, as the case may be, abolishing the tax is presented to the House.

1(5C) In subsection (5B) **"sitting day"** means a day on which the House sits.

1(5D) Where a Bill is amended as mentioned in subsection (5A)(a)(ii), it does not matter for the purposes of subsection (5A)(b) if the House orders as mentioned in subsection (5A)(b) before the amendment to the Bill is made.

1(6) Where, in the case of a resolution providing for the renewal or variation of a tax, the resolution ceases to have statutory effect by virtue of [subsection](4), (5) or (5B) above, or the period specified in subsection (3) above terminates, before an Act comes into operation renewing or varying the tax, any money paid in pursuance of the resolution shall be repaid or made good, and any deduction made in pursuance of the resolution shall be deemed to be an unauthorised deduction.

1(7) Where any tax as renewed or varied by a resolution is modified by the Act renewing or varying the tax, any money paid in pursuance of the resolution which would not have been payable under the new conditions affecting the tax shall be repaid or made good, and any deduction made in pursuance of the resolution shall, so far as it would not have been authorised under the new conditions affecting the tax, be deemed to be an unauthorised deduction.

1(8) When during any session a resolution has had statutory effect under this section, statutory effect shall not be again given under this section in the same session to the same resolution or to a resolution having the same effect.

1(9) Subsection (8) does not apply where the later resolution is passed in a different calendar year from that in which the earlier resolution is passed.

History – In s. 1(1), the words "the apprenticeship levy," inserted by FA 2016, s. 116, with effect from 15 September 2016 (Royal Assent).
In s. 1(1), the words "capital gains tax," inserted by FA 2016, s. 92, with effect from 15 September 2016 (Royal Assent).
In s. 1(1), the words "diverted profits tax," inserted by FA 2015, s. 115(5), with effect in relation to accounting periods beginning on or after 1 April 2015 (subject to the transitional provisions at FA 2015, s. 116(2)–(5)).
In s. 1(1), the words "annual tax on enveloped dwellings," inserted by FA 2013, s. 168 and Sch. 35, para. 1, with effect from 17 July 2013 (Royal Assent).
In s. 1(1), the words ", the bank levy" inserted by FA 2011, s. 73 and Sch. 19, para. 56, with effect from 19 July 2011.
In s. 1(1), the words "stamp duty land tax" inserted after "stamp duty reserve tax" by FA 2003, s. 123 and Sch. 18, para. 1 with effect from 10 July 2003 (date of Royal Assent to FA 2003) for transactions which are within the charge to stamp duty land tax from 1 December 2003 (the appointed day by virtue of SI 2003/2899 (C. 106)).
In s. 1(1), the words "aggregates levy," inserted by FA 2001, s. 49(1).
In s. 1(1), the words "climate change levy" inserted by FA 2000, Sch. 7, para. 1.
In s. 1(1), the words "(including advance corporation tax)" which followed "corporation tax" omitted by FA 1998, s. 31 and Sch. 3, para. 1(2), s. 165 and Sch. 27, Pt. III(2), in relation to distributions made after 5 April 1999.
In s. 1(1), the words "insurance premium tax," inserted by FA 1994, s. 64 and Sch. 7, para. 33, in relation to resolutions passed after 3 May 1994.
In s. 1(1), the words "corporation tax (including advance corporation tax)" inserted by FA 1993, s. 205 in relation to resolutions passed after 27 July 1993.
In s. 1(1), the words "car tax" repealed by FA 1993, s. 205(2) and s. 213 and Sch. 23, Pt. VI in relation to resolutions passed after 27 July 1993.
S. 1(1) amended by FA 1968, s. 51(2) but provisions including reference to purchase tax repealed by FA 1972, Sch. 28.
In s. 1(1), the words "landfill tax," inserted by FA 1998, s. 148(1).
S. 1(1A) repealed by FA 1993, s. 205(3) and s. 213 and Sch. 23, Pt. VI in relation to resolutions passed after 27 July 1993. S. 1(1A) was inserted by FA 1985, s. 97.
In s. 1(2), "(9)" substituted for "(8)" by FA 2011, s. 88(2), with effect from 30 December 2011 (SI 2011/2934).
S. 1(3) substituted by FA 2011, s. 88(3), with effect from 30 December 2011 (SI 2011/2934).
In former s. 1(3)(a), references to "November or December" and "5th May in the next calendar year" substituted and in s. 1(4), the word "thirty" substituted by FA 1993, s. 205(5) in relation to resolutions passedafter 27 July 1993.
S. 1(3)(aa) inserted by F(No. 2)A 1997, s. 50(1) in relation to resolutions passed after 31 July 1997.
S. 1(3A) omitted by FA 2014, s. 296 and Sch. 38, para. 13, with effect from 17 July 2014. S. 1(3A) had been prospectively inserted by SCA 2012, s. 26(7) (SCA 2012, s. 26 omitted by FA 2014, s. 296 and Sch. 38, para. 17, with effect from 17 July 2014).
In s. 1(4)(b), the words "Public Bill Committee" substituted for the words "Standing Committee" by FA 2007, s. 112(1), with effect from 19 July 2007.
In s. 1(4)(b), the words "in Committee … of the House" inserted by FA 1968, s. 60.
In s. 1(5)(c), the words "or prorogued" (which appeared after "dissolved"), omitted by FA 2011, s. 88(4)(a), with effect from 30 December 2011 (SI 2011/2934).
S. 1(5)(d) (and the word ", or" at the end of s. 1(5)(c)) inserted by FA 2011, s. 88(4)(b), with effect from 30 December 2011 (SI 2011/2934).
S. 1(5A), (5B), (5C) and (5D) inserted by FA 2011, s. 88(5), with effect from 30 December 2011 (SI 2011/2934).
In s. 1(6), "(4), (5) or (5B)" substituted for "(4) or (5)" by FA 2011, s. 88(6), with effect from 30 December 2011 (SI 2011/2934).
S. *1(9) inserted by FA 2011*, s. 88(7), with effect from 30 December 2011 (SI 2011/2934).
Application extended to petroleum revenue tax, stamp duty reserve tax, value added tax and car tax by OTA 1975, s. 11; FA 1986, s. 86(3); FA 1972, s. 1(5) and FA 1972, s. 52(11) and Sch. 7, para. 2(4) respectively.
References to provisions of ICTA 1988 substituted by Sch. 29, para. 32 of that Act.

Cross references – FA 1994, s. 64 and Sch. 7, para. 34(1): amount of insurance premium tax repayable by virtue of s. 1(6), (7) is the difference between the amount chargeable at the rate specified in the resolution and the amount that would have been chargeable at the lower rate.

2 Payments and deductions made on account, and before renewal, of any temporary tax within s. 1

2(1) Any payment or deduction made on account of a temporary tax to which section 1 above applies and within one month after the date of its expiry shall, if the payment or deduction would have been a legal payment or deduction if the tax had not expired, be deemed to be a legal payment or deduction, subject to the condition that–

(a) if a resolution for the renewal or reimposition of the tax is not passed by the House of Commons within that month, or such a resolution is passed within that month but ceases to have statutory effect under the said section 1, any money so paid or deducted shall be repaid or made good, and

(b) if the tax is ultimately renewed or reimposed at a different rate, or with modifications, any amount paid or deducted which could not properly have been paid or deducted under the new conditions affecting the tax shall be repaid or made good.

2(2) In this section **"temporary tax"** means a tax which has been imposed, or renewed or reimposed, for a limited period not exceeding eighteen months, and was in force or imposed during the previous financial year.

Cross references – ICTA 1988 s. 822: over-deductions of tax from interest payments made by companies as a result of the tax being reimposed at a lower rate.

5 House of Commons resolution giving provisional effect to motions affecting taxation

5(1) This section shall apply if the House of Commons resolves that provisional statutory effect shall be given to one or more motions to be moved by the Chancellor of the Exchequer, or some other Minister, and which, if agreed to by the House, would be resolutions–

(a) to which statutory effect could be given under section 1 of this Act, or

(b) to which section 3 of this Act could be applied,

(c) [Repealed by FA 1993, s. 205(6)(a), s. 213 and Sch. 23, Pt. VI.]

5(2) Subject to subsection (3) below, on the passing of the resolution under subsection (1) above, sections 1 to 3 of this Act and section 822 of the Income and Corporation Taxes Act 1988 (over-deductions from preference dividends before passing of annual Act) shall apply as if each motion to which the resolution applies had then been agreed to by a resolution of the House.

5(3) Subsection (2) above shall cease to apply to a motion if that motion, or a motion containing the same proposals with modifications, is not agreed to by a resolution of the House (in this section referred to as "a confirmatory resolution") within the next ten days on which the House sits after the resolution under subsection (1) above is passed, and, if it ceases to apply, all such adjustments, whether by way of discharge or repayment of tax, or discharge of security, or otherwise, shall be made as may be necessary to restore the position to what it would have been if subsection (2) above had never applied to that motion, and to make good any deductions which have become unauthorised deductions.

5(4) The enactments specified in subsection (2) above shall have effect as if–

(a) any confirmatory resolution passed within the said period of ten sitting days had been passed when the resolution under subsection (1) above was passed, and

(b) everything done in pursuance of the said subsection (2) by reference to the motion to which the confirmatory resolution relates had been done by reference to the confirmatory resolution,

but any necessary adjustments shall be made, whether by way of discharge or repayment of tax, or modification of the terms of any security, or further assessment, or otherwise, where the proposals in the confirmatory resolution are not the same as those in the original motion to which that resolution relates.

History – S. 5(1)(c) and word "or" immediately preceding it and in s. 5(2), reference to ICTA 1988, s. 822 substituted by FA 1993, s. 205(6), s. 213 and Sch. 23, Pt. VI, in relation to resolutions passed after 27 July 1993.
References to provisions of ICTA 1988 substituted by Sch. 29, para. 32 of that Act.

Cross references – S. 3: provisional collection of duties of customs and excise under resolutions not having statutory effect under s.1.
FA 1973, s. 50: corresponding provisions for stamp duty.
FA 1994, s. 64 and Sch. 7, para. 34(1): amount of insurance premium tax repayable by virtue of s. 5(3) is the difference between the amount specified in the resolution and the amount that would have been chargeable at the lower rate.

6 Short title, repeals and saving as respects Northern Ireland

6(1) This Act may be cited as the Provisional Collection of Taxes Act 1968.

6(2) [Amending provision, not reproduced here.]

6(3) [Repealed by Northern Ireland Constitution Act 1973, s. 41(1)(a) and Sch. 6, Pt. I, with effect from 18 July 1973.]

FINANCE ACT 1969

(1969 Chapter 32)

[*25th July 1969*]

PART VI – MISCELLANEOUS

58 Disclosure of information for statistical purposes by Board of Inland Revenue

58(1) For the purpose of any statistical survey conducted or to be conducted by the Department of Employment, the Department of Trade and Industry or the Central Statistical Office of the Chancellor of the Exchequer, the Board of Inland Revenue may disclose to an authorised officer of that Department or Office–

(a) the names and addresses of persons (in this section referred to as "employers") required under PAYE regulations to make deductions of tax from payments of, or on account of, earnings or amounts treated as earnings from an employment; and

(b) information concerning the number of persons (in this section referred to as "employees") in receipt of earnings or amounts treated as earnings paid by an employer.

58(1A) In subsection (1) **"earnings or amounts treated as earnings"** means earnings or amounts treated as earnings which constitute employment income (see section 7(2)(a) or (b) of the Income Tax (Earnings and Pensions) Act 2003).

58(2) For the purpose of any statistical survey relating to earnings conducted or to be conducted by the Central Statistical Office of the Chancellor of the Exchequer, the Board of Inland Revenue may disclose to an authorised officer of that Office the name and address of the employer of any person who is one of a number of employees selected (as a statistical sample) for the purpose of that survey.

58(3) Subsections (1) and (2) above shall have effect notwithstanding any obligation as to secrecy imposed on the Board or any officer of the Board under the Income Tax Management Act 1964 or otherwise.

58(4) Subject to subsection (5) below, no information obtained by virtue of this section by an officer of the Department of Employment, the Department of Trade and Industry or the Central Statistical Office of the Chancellor of the Exchequer may be disclosed except–

(a) to an officer of that Department or Office for the purpose of the statistical survey concerned, or

(b) to another department (including a department of the Government of Northern Ireland) for the purpose of a statistical survey conducted or to be conducted by that department, or

(c) to an authorised officer of any body specified in the first column of the following Table for the purposes of functions of that body under any enactment specified in relation to it in the second column of the Table.

TABLE

Body	*Enactment*
A local education authority in England and Wales.	Section 8 of the Employment and Training Act 1973.
An education authority in Scotland.	Section 126 of the Education (Scotland) Act 1980.
The Northern Ireland Training Authority.	The Industrial Training (Northern Ireland) Order 1984.
A local planning authority within the meaning of Part 2 or 6 of the Planning and Compulsory Purchase Act 2004 and any board which exercises for any area the functions of such an authority.	Part 2 or 6 of the Planning and Compulsory Purchase Act 2004
A planning authority as defined in section 172(3) of the Town and Country Planning (Scotland) Act 1997.	Part II of the Town and Country Planning (Scotland) Act 1997.
The Welsh Development Agency.	The Welsh Development Agency Act 1975.
Scottish Enterprise.	Part I of The Enterprise and New Towns (Scotland) Act 1990.

Body	*Enactment*
Highlands and Islands Enterprise.	Part I of the Enterprise and New Towns (Scotland) Act 1990.
A development corporation within the meaning of the New Towns Act 1981.	Section 4 of the New Towns Act 1981.
A development corporation within the meaning of the New Towns (Scotland) Act 1968.	Section 3 of the New Towns (Scotland) Act 1968.
A new town commission within the meaning of the New Towns Act (Northern Ireland) 1965.	Section 7 of the New Towns Act (Northern Ireland) 1965.

58(5) Subsection (4) above does not apply to the disclosure of any such information as is mentioned in subsection (1) or subsection (2) above–

(a) in the form of a summary so framed as not to enable particulars relating to an employer or employee to be ascertained from it, or

(b) in the case of such information as is mentioned in subsection (1) above, with the consent of the employer concerned and, in the case of such information as is mentioned in subsection (2) above, with the consent of the employee concerned.

58(6) If any person who has obtained any information by virtue of any provision of this section discloses that information otherwise than in accordance with paragraph (a) paragraph (b) or paragraph (c) of subsection (4) above or subsection (5) above, he shall be liable on summary conviction to a fine not exceeding £5,000, or on conviction on indictment to imprisonment for a term not exceeding two years or to fine or to both.

58(7) References in this section to the Department of Employment, the Department of Trade and Industry or the Central Statistical Office of the Chancellor of the Exchequer include references to any department of the Government of Northern Ireland carrying out similar functions.

History – References to provisions of ICTA 1988 substituted by Sch. 29, para. 32 to that Act.

In s. 58(1)(a), the words "PAYE regulations" substituted for the words "section 203 of the Taxes Act 1988 (pay as you earn)" by ITEPA 2003, Sch. 6, para. 122(2)(a) which has effect, for income tax purposes, for the tax year 2003–04 and subsequent tax years and, for corporation tax purposes, for accounting periods ending after 5 April 2003.

In s. 58(1)(a), the words "earnings or amounts treated as earnings from an employment" substituted for the words "emoluments to which that section applies" by ITEPA 2003, Sch. 6, para. 122(2)(b) which has effect, for income tax purposes, for the tax year 2003–04 and subsequent tax years and, for corporation tax purposes, for accounting periods ending after 5 April 2003.

In s. 58(1)(b), the words "earnings or amounts treated as earnings" substituted for the word "emoluments" by ITEPA 2003, Sch. 6, para. 122(3) which has effect, for income tax purposes, for the tax year 2003–04 and subsequent tax years and, for corporation tax purposes, for accounting periods ending after 5 April 2003.

S. 58(1A) inserted by ITEPA 2003, Sch. 6, para. 122(4) which has effect, for income tax purposes, for the tax year 2003–04 and subsequent tax years and, for corporation tax purposes, for accounting periods ending after 5 April 2003.

In s. 58(1), (4), (7) references to the Department of Trade and Industry and the Central Statistical Office of the Chancellor of the Exchequer substituted by SI 1989/992, with effect from 31 July 1989.

In s. 58(2), references to the Central Statistical Office of the Chancellor of the Exchequer substituted by SI 1995/2986, art. 11 and Schedule, with effect from 1 January 1996.

S. 58(4)(a) amended by Employment and Training Act 1973, s. 4(6), with effect from 1 January 1974.

In the entry in the Table in s. 58(4)(c) relating to local planning authorities, in column 1 the words "Part 2 or 6 of the Planning and Compulsory Purchase Act 2004" substituted for the words "the Town and Country Planning Act 1990" and in column 2 the words "Part 2 or 6 of the Planning and Compulsory Purchase Act 2004" substituted for the words "Part II of the Town and Country Planning Act 1990" by the Planning and Compulsory Purchase Act 2004, s. 118 and Sch. 7, para. 2, with effect from 28 September 2004 by virtue of SI 2004/2202, art. 2(i), subject to the transitional provisions and savings under SI 2004/2202, art. 4 and Sch. 2.

Entry in Table in s. 58(4)(c) relating to the Development Board for Rural Wales repealed by Government of Wales Act 1998, s. 152 and Sch. 18, Pt. IV, with effect from 1 July 1999 by virtue of SI 1998/3178.

References in Table in s. 58(4)(c) to Town and Country Planning Act 1990 substituted, with effect from 24 August 1990, for earlier references to the corresponding provisions of the Town and Country Planning Act 1971, by the Planning (Consequential Provisions) Act 1990, s. 4 and Sch. 23, para. 23 (England and Wales only).

Reference in first and second column of the Table in s. 58(4)(c) to the Town and Country Planning (Scotland) Act 1997 were substituted for reference to s. 172(3) of the Local Government (Scotland) Act 1973 and Pt. II of the Town and Country Planning (Scotland) Act 1972 respectively by s. 4 and Sch. 2, para. 18 of the Planning (Consequential Provisions) (Scotland) Act 1997, with effect from 27 May 1997.

References in Table in s. 58(4)(c) to Scottish Enterprise, Highlands and Islands Enterprise, and Pt. I of the Enterprise and New Towns (Scotland) Act 1990, substituted by s. 38(1) and Sch. 4, para. 2 of that Act, with effect from 1 April 1991 by virtue of SI 1990/1840 (C 48) (S 173), art. 4.

S. 58(4)(c) and Table inserted and reference in s. 58(6) consequently amended by F(No. 2)A 1987, s. 69(2), (3).

The fine in s. 58(6) was raised from £2,000 to £5,000 by SI 1992/333 for offences committed after 30 September 1992.

Notes – TMA 1970, s. 6(3), (4) and Sch. 4, para. 1 impose obligations as to secrecy on the Board and its officers.

In relation to Northern Ireland certain functions of Department of Employment etc. transferred to other bodies under SI 1970/1537.

For references to the Parliament of Northern Ireland, see also Northern Ireland Constitution Act 1973.

FA 1972, s. 127: disclosure of information between revenue departments.

FA 1989, s. 182: offence of unlawful disclosure.

FA 1997, s. 110: Revenue and Customs and Excise obtaining information from social security authorities.

61 Citation, interpretation, construction, extent and repeals

61(1) This Act may be cited as the Finance Act 1969.

61(2) In this Act, except where the context otherwise requires, **"the Board"** means the Commissioners of Inland Revenue.

61(4) Any reference in this Act to any other enactment shall, except so far as the context otherwise requires, be construed as a reference to that enactment as amended or applied by or under any other enactment, including this Act.

61(5) Except as otherwise expressly provided, such of the provisions of this Act as relate to matters in respect of which the Parliament of Northern Ireland has power to make laws shall not extend to Northern Ireland.

Notes – For reference to the Parliament of Northern Ireland, see also Northern Ireland Constitution Act 1973.

TAXES MANAGEMENT ACT 1970

(1970 Chapter 9) [*12th March 1970*]

ARRANGEMENT OF SECTIONS

PART 3A – REFERRAL OF QUESTIONS DURING ENQUIRY

PART IV – ASSESSMENT AND CLAIMS

91. Effect on interest of reliefs
91A. Reliefs etc.: effect on interest on development land tax
92. Remission in certain cases of interest on tax in arrear by reason of exchange restrictions

PART X – PENALTIES, ETC.

93. Failure to make return for income tax and capital gains tax
93A. Failure to make partnership return
94. Failure to make return for corporation tax
95. Incorrect return or accounts for income tax or capital gains tax
95A. Incorrect partnership return or accounts
96. Incorrect return or accounts for corporation tax
97. Incorrect return or accounts: supplemental
97AA. Failure to produce documents under section 19A
97A. Two or more tax-geared penalties in respect of same tax
98. Special returns, etc.
98A. Special penalties in the case of certain returns
98B. European Economic Interest Groupings
98C. Notification under Part 7 of Finance Act 2004
99. Assisting in preparation of incorrect return etc.
99A. Certificates of non-liability to income tax
99B. Declarations under Chapter 2 of Part 14 of ITA 2007
100. Determination of penalties by officer of Board
100A. Provisions supplementary to section 100
100B. Appeals against penalty determinations
100C. Penalty proceedings before First-tier Tribunal
100D. Penalty proceedings before court
101. Evidence for purposes of proceedings relating to penalties
102. Mitigation of penalties
103. Time limits for penalties
103ZA. Disapplication of sections 100 to 103 in the case of certain penalties
103A. Interest on penalties
104. Saving for criminal proceedings
105. Admissibility of evidence not affected by offer of settlement
106. Refusal to allow a deduction of income tax, and avoidance of agreements for payment without deduction

EVASION

106A. Offence of fraudulent evasion of income tax

OFFSHORE INCOME, ASSETS AND ACTIVITIES

106B. Offence of failing to give notice of being chargeable to tax
106C. Offence of failing to deliver return
106D. Offence of making inaccurate return
106E. Exclusions from offences under sections 106B to 106D
106F. Offences under sections 106B to 106D: supplementary provision
106G. Penalties for offences under sections 106B to 106D
106H. Regulations under sections 106E and 106F

SCOTLAND

107. Criminal liability for false statements made to obtain allowances

PART XI – MISCELLANEOUS AND SUPPLEMENTAL

SETTLEMENTS

107A. Relevant trustees

COMPANIES

108. Responsibility of company officers

PART I – ADMINISTRATION

1 Responsibility for certain taxes

1 The Commissioners for Her Majesty's Revenue and Customs shall be responsible for the collection and management of–

(a) income tax,

(b) corporation tax, and

(c) capital gains tax.

History – S. 1 substituted by CRCA 2005, s. 50 and Sch. 4, para. 12 with effect from 18 April 2005, by virtue of SI 2005/1126, reg. 2(2).

HMRC Manuals – IR, Business Income Manual, BIM75225: HMRC's view that the general/special commissioners do not have power to review the exercise of "care and management" powers. (See also *Steibelt v Paling* [1999] BTC 184).

2 General Commissioners

2 [Ceased to have effect by virtue of TCEA 2007, s. 48(1) and Sch. 8, para. 1(2) and repealed by TCEA 2007, s. 146 and Sch. 23, Pt. 1.]

History – S. 2 ceased to have effect by virtue of TCEA 2007, s. 48(1) and Sch. 8, para. 1(2) and repealed by TCEA 2007, s. 146 and Sch. 23, Pt. 1, with effect from 1 April 2009 (SI 2008/2696, art. 6(b)(i) and (c)(i)). However, former s. 2 shall continue to apply for the purpose of TMA 1970, s. 56 (statement of case for opinion of the High Court) arising from a decision of the General Commissioners made before 1 April 2009 (SI 2008/2696, art. 4). Former s. 2 read as follows:

"General Commissioners

2(1) For the purpose of exercising such powers relating to appeals and other matters as are conferred on them by the Taxes Acts or by Part II of the Social Security Contributions (Transfer of Functions, etc.) Act 1999 there shall be "Commissioners for the general purposes of the income tax" (in the Taxes Acts referred to as **"General Commissioners"**) who shall act for the same separate areas in Great Britain as heretofore or for the separate areas in Northern Ireland defined by an order made by the Lord Chancellor (in the Taxes Acts referred to as **"divisions"**).

2(2) General Commissioners for divisions in England and Wales or Northern Ireland shall be appointed by, and shall hold office during the pleasure of, the Lord Chancellor.

2(3) General Commissioners for divisions in Scotland shall be appointed by, and shall hold office during the pleasure of, the Secretary of State.

2(4) In Scotland a sheriff shall be ex officio a General Commissioner for any division wholly or partly within his sheriffdom, and a salaried sheriff-substitute shall be ex officio a General Commissioner for any division wholly or partly within his district.

2(5) The Lord Chancellor or, in Scotland, the Secretary of State shall pay General Commissioners by way of travelling allowance or subsistence allowance sums of such amounts and in such circumstances as he may, with the approval of the Treasury, determine.

2(6) The Lord Chancellor or, in Scotland, the Secretary of State may by order create a new division or abolish an existing division or alter in any other respect the divisions or their boundaries; and any such order may contain such consequential and transitional provisions as the Lord Chancellor or the Secretary of State, as the case may be, thinks fit and may be revoked or varied by a subsequent order under this subsection.

2(6A) The Lord Chancellor must consult the Lord Chief Justice of England and Wales or, in Northern Ireland, the Lord Chief Justice of Northern Ireland before exercising any function conferred on him by subsection (1) or (6).

2(6B) The Lord Chief Justice of England and Wales may nominate a judicial office holder (as defined in section 109(4) of the Constitutional Reform Act 2005) to exercise his functions under this section.

2(6C) The Lord Chief Justice of Northern Ireland may nominate one of the following to exercise his functions under this section–

(a) the holder of one of the offices listed in Schedule 1 to the Justice (Northern Ireland) Act 2002;

(b) a Lord Justice of Appeal (as defined in section 88 of that Act).

2(7) A General Commissioner shall not continue in office after he attains the age of seventy-five years.

2(8) The validity of any proceedings of General Commissioners shall not be affected by a defect in the appointment of any of them, or by a failure to observe the requirements of the last preceding subsection.

2(9) No action shall lie against a General Commissioner in respect of any act or omission of his–

(a) in the execution of his duty; and

(b) with respect to any matter within his jurisdiction.

2(10) No action shall lie against a General Commissioner in respect of any act or omission of his–

(a) in the purported execution of his duty; but

(b) with respect to any matter not within his jurisdiction,

unless it is proved that he acted in bad faith.

History – In s. 2(1), words "or by Part II of the Social Security (Transfer of Functions, etc.) Act 1999" inserted by Social Security Contributions (Transfer of Functions, etc.) Act 1999, s. 18 and Sch. 7, para. 1, with effect from 1 April 1999 by virtue of SI 1999/527, art. 2(b) and Sch. 2, but from 4 March 1999 for purposes connected with the making of regulations (SI 1999/527, art. 2(a) and Sch. 1). In s. 2(1), the words "or for the separate … Lord Chancellor", and in s. 2(2) the words "or Northern Ireland", were inserted by FA 1988, s. 134(1)(a), (b), (4), with effect from 3 April 1989 (SI 1989/473).

S. 2(3) amended by FA 1975, s. 57(1) and Sch. 13, Pt. II, with effect from 16 March 1975.

S. 2(5) substituted by F(No. 2)A 1992, s. 76 and Sch. 16, para. 2(1) with effect from 1 April 1994.

S. 2(6A) inserted by Constitutional Reform Act 2005, Sch. 4, para. 64, with effect from 3 April 2006 (by virtue of SI 2006/1014).

S. 2(6B) inserted by Constitutional Reform Act 2005, Sch. 4, para. 64, with effect from 3 April 2006 (by virtue of SI 2006/1014).

S. 2(6C) inserted by Constitutional Reform Act 2005, Sch. 4, para. 64, with effect from 3 April 2006 (by virtue of SI 2006/1014).

S. 2(7) only applies in respect of General Commissioners appointed on or before 31 December 1995. SI 1995/3192 (not reproduced) sets the retirement age at 70 for general commissioners appointed after that date.

S. 2(9), (10) inserted by Access to Justice Act 1999, s. 101, with effect from 1 April 2001 in so far as they extend to England and Wales and Northern Ireland only.

Cross references – TMA 1970, Pt.V: jurisdiction of and proceedings before the Commissioners.

F(No. 2)A 1992 s. 75: powers of the Lord Chancellor to make regulations to re-name the General and Special Commissioners.

FA 1972, s. 130: regulations may be made for the purpose of compensating clerks to general commissioners for loss of office etc., by virtue of the exercise of the powers conferred by s. 2(6).

FA 1973, s. 41: division boundaries are not affected by changes in local government areas.

TCEA 2007, s. 30, 35, 36 and Sch. 6: General Commissioners are a "scheduled tribunal" for purposes of that Act.

Statutory instruments – SI 1995/3192: Retirement Age of General Commissioners Order 1995 (not reproduced)."

2A General Commissioners: costs and expenses in legal proceedings

2A [Repealed by TCEA 2007, s. 146 and Sch. 23, Pt. 1.]

History – S. 2A repealed by TCEA 2007, s. 146 and Sch. 23, Pt. 1, with effect from 1 April 2009 (SI 2008/2696, art. 6(c)(i)). However, former s. 2A shall continue to apply for the purpose of TMA 1970, s. 56 (statement of case for opinion of the High Court) arising from a decision of the General Commissioners made before 1 April 2009 (SI 2008/2696, art. 4). Former s. 2A read as follows:

"General Commissioners: costs and expenses in legal proceedings

2A(1) A court may not order a General Commissioner to pay costs or (in Scotland) expenses in any proceedings in respect of any act or omission of his in the execution (or purported execution) of his duty as a General Commissioner.

2A(2) Subsection (1) above does not apply in relation to–

(a) any proceedings in which a General Commissioner is being tried for an offence or is appealing against a conviction; or

(b) any proceedings in which it is proved that a General Commissioner acted in bad faith in respect of the matters giving rise to the proceedings.

2A(3) Where a court is prevented by subsection (1) above from ordering a General Commissioner to pay costs or expenses in any proceedings, the court may instead order the making by the relevant Minister of a payment in respect of the costs or expenses of a person in the proceedings.

2A(4) The relevant Minister may by regulations made by statutory instrument make provision specifying–

(a) circumstances when a court shall or shall not exercise the power conferred on it by subsection (3) above; and

(b) how the amount of any payment ordered under that subsection is to be determined.

2A(5) No regulations may be made under subsection (4) above unless a draft of the statutory instrument containing them has been laid before, and approved by a resolution of, each House of Parliament.

2A(6) In this section **"relevant Minister"** means the Lord Chancellor or, in Scotland, the Secretary of State.

History – S. 2A inserted by Access to Justice Act 1999, s. 102 with effect from 1 April 2001 in respect of England and Wales and Northern Ireland (SI 2001/916) and with effect from 31 March 2003 in respect of Scotland (SI 2003/207).

Statutory instruments – SI 2001/1304: General Commissioners of Income Tax (Costs) Regulations 2001."

3 Clerk to General Commissioners

3 [Repealed by TCEA 2007, s. 146 and Sch. 23, Pt. 1.]

History – S. 3 repealed by TCEA 2007, s. 146 and Sch. 23, Pt. 1, with effect from 1 April 2009 (SI 2008/2696, art. 6(c)(i)). However, former s. 3 shall continue to apply for the purpose of TMA 1970, s. 56 (statement of case for opinion of the High Court) arising from a decision of the General Commissioners made before 1 April 2009 (SI 2008/2696, art. 4). Former s. 3 read as follows:

"Clerk to General Commissioners

3(1) The General Commissioners for every division shall appoint a clerk and, if they think it necessary, an assistant clerk, and persons appointed under this subsection shall hold office during the pleasure of the Commissioners and act under their direction.

3(2) The Lord Chancellor or, in Scotland, the Secretary of State shall pay a clerk such remuneration in respect of his services as the Lord Chancellor or Secretary of State may, with the approval of the Treasury, determine.

3(3) The Lord Chancellor or, in Scotland, the Secretary of State may, in such cases as he may in his discretion determine, pay to or in respect of any full-time clerk such pension allowance or gratuity, or make such provision for the payment of pension allowance or gratuity to or in respect of any full-time clerk, as he may, with the approval of the Treasury, determine.

In this subsection **"full-time clerk"** means a clerk as regards whom the Lord Chancellor or Secretary of State is satisfied that he is required to devote substantially the whole of his time to the duties of his office.

3(4) Without prejudice to the power of any General Commissioners to dismiss their clerk or assistant clerk, the Lord Chancellor or, in Scotland, the Secretary of State may, after consulting the General Commissioners for any division, dismiss their clerk or assistant clerk.

3(5) A clerk or assistant clerk shall not continue in office after he has attained the age of seventy years unless the General Commissioners for whom he acts think it desirable in the public interest and extend his term of office; and the term shall not be extended beyond the age of seventy-five years.

History – S. 3(2) substituted by F(No. 2)A 1992, s. 76 and Sch. 16, para. 2(3) with effect from 1 April 1994.

In s. 3(3), the words "The Lord Chancellor ... in his discretion determine", the words "he may, with the approval of the Treasury, determine" and the words "the Lord Chancellor ... is satisfied" substituted by F(No. 2)A 1992, s. 76 and Sch. 16, para. 2(4) with effect from 1 April 1994.

S. 3(3) amended by Superannuation Act 1972, s. 29 and Sch. 6, para. 77, with effect from 25 March 1972.

Cross references – FA 1972, s. 130: regulations may be made for the purpose of compensating clerks to general commissioners for loss of office etc."

3A General Commissioners and clerks: indemnity

3A [Repealed by TCEA 2007, s. 146 and Sch. 23, Pt. 1.]

History – S. 3A repealed by TCEA 2007, s. 146 and Sch. 23, Pt. 1, with effect from 1 April 2009 (SI 2008/2696, art. 6(c)(i)). However, former s. 3A shall continue to apply for the purpose of TMA 1970, s. 56 (statement of case for opinion of the High Court) arising from a decision of the General Commissioners made before 1 April 2009 (SI 2008/2696, art. 4). Former s. 3A read as follows:

"General Commissioners and clerks: indemnity

3A(1) A General Commissioner or a clerk may be indemnified by the relevant Minister in respect of–

(a) any costs or (in Scotland) expenses which the General Commissioner or clerk reasonably incurs in or in connection with proceedings in respect of anything done or omitted in the exercise (or purported exercise) of his duty as a General Commissioner or clerk;

(b) any costs or expenses which he reasonably incurs in taking steps to dispute any claim which might be made in such proceedings;

(c) any damages awarded against him or costs or expenses ordered to be paid by him in any such proceedings; and

(d) any sums payable by him in connection with a reasonable settlement of any such proceedings or claim,

unless it is proved, in respect of matters giving rise to the proceedings or claim in question, that he acted in bad faith.

3A(2) A General Commissioner or a clerk shall be indemnified by the relevant Minister in respect of any such costs or expenses, damages or sums as are mentioned in subsection (1)(a) to (d) above if, in respect of the matters giving rise to the proceedings or claim in question, he acted reasonably and in good faith.

3A(3) Any question whether, or to what extent, a person is to be indemnified under this section shall be determined by the relevant Minister.

3A(4) A determination under subsection (3) above with respect to any such costs or expenses or sums as are mentioned in subsection (1) (a), (b) or (d) above may, if the person claiming to be indemnified so requests, be made in advance before they are incurred or the settlement made.

3A(5) Any such determination in advance for indemnity in respect of costs or expenses to be incurred–

(a) shall be subject to such limitations, if any, as the relevant Minister thinks proper and to the subsequent determination of the amount of the costs or expenses reasonably incurred; and

(b) shall not affect any other determination which may fall to be made in connection with the proceedings or claim in question.

3A(6) In this section **"clerk"** means–

(a) any person appointed to be a clerk or assistant clerk to the General Commissioners for any division; or

(b) a person who assists any such person;

and **"relevant Minister"** means the Lord Chancellor or, in Scotland, the Secretary of State.

History – S. 3A inserted by Access to Justice Act 1999, s. 103 with effect from 1 April 2001 in relation to England and Wales and Northern Ireland (SI 2001/916) and with effect from 31 March 2003 in respect of Scotland (SI 2003/207)."

4 Special Commissioners

4 [Omitted by SI 2009/56, art. 3(1) and Sch. 1, para. 6.]

History – S. 4 omitted by SI 2009/56, art. 3(1) and Sch. 1, para. 6, operative from 1 April 2009, subject to transitional and saving provisions in SI 2009/56, Sch. 3.

4A Deputy Special Commissioners

4A [Omitted by SI 2009/56, art. 3(1) and Sch. 1, para. 6.]

History – S. 4A omitted by SI 2009/56, art. 3(1) and Sch. 1, para. 6, operative from 1 April 2009, subject to transitional and saving provisions in SI 2009/56, Sch. 3.

5 General and Special Commissioners

5 [Omitted by SI 2009/56, art. 3(1) and Sch. 1, para. 6.]

History – S. 5 omitted by SI 2009/56, art. 3(1) and Sch. 1, para. 6, operative from 1 April 2009, subject to transitional and saving provisions in SI 2009/56, Sch. 3.

6 Declarations on taking office

6(1) [Omitted by SI 2009/56, art. 3(1) and Sch. 1, para. 6 and repealed by TCEA 2007, s. 146 and Sch. 23, Pt. 1.]

6(2) [Repealed by TCEA 2007, s. 146 and Sch. 23, Pt. 1.]

6(3) [Repealed by CRCA 2005, s. 52 and Sch 5; see History note.]

6(4) [Repealed by CRCA 2005, s. 52 and Sch 5; see History note.]

6(5) [Omitted by SI 2009/56, art. 3(1) and Sch. 1, para. 6.]

History – S. 6(1) omitted by SI 2009/56, art. 3(1) and Sch. 1, para. 6, operative from 1 April 2009, subject to transitional and saving provisions in SI 2009/56, Sch. 3. S. 6(1) repealed by TCEA 2007, s. 146 and Sch. 23, Pt. 1, with effect from 1 April 2009 (SI 2008/2696, art. 6(c)(i) – subject to transitional provisions at art. 3).
Former s. 6(1)(b) repealed by FA 1982, Sch. 22, Pt. X .
In former s. 6(1)(c), the words "or section 704 of ITA 2007" inserted by ITA 2007, s. 1027 and Sch. 1, para. 243, with effect from 6 April 2007.
In former s. 6(1)(c), the reference to ICTA 1988, s. 707 substituted for the previous reference by ICTA 1988, Sch. 29, para. 32.
S. 6(2) repealed by TCEA 2007, s. 146 and Sch. 23, Pt. 1, with effect from 1 April 2009 (SI 2008/2696, art. 6(c)(i) – subject to transitional provisions at art. 3).
S. 6(3) and (4) ceased to have effect by virtue of CRCA 2005, s. 50, Sch. 4, para. 13 and repealed by CRCA 2005, s. 52 and Sch. 5, with effect from 18 April 2005 (SI 2005/1126, reg. 2(2)).
S. 6(5) omitted by SI 2009/56, art. 3(1) and Sch. 1, para. 6, operative from 1 April 2009, subject to transitional and saving provisions in SI 2009/56, Sch. 3.

Cross references – FA 1969, s. 58: disclosure for statistical purposes of information regarding employment.
FA 1972, s. 127: disclosure of information between revenue departments.
FA 1989, s. 182: offence of unlawful disclosure.
SSCTFA 1999, s. 3(5): in any declaration for the purposes of s. 6, reference to an offence relating to inland revenue is taken to include a reference to an offence relating to contributions, statutory sick pay or statutory maternity pay, or an offence under regulations made under Pension Schemes Act 1993, Pt. III, or pension schemes (Northern Ireland) Act 1993, Pt. III.
EA 2002, s. 5: reference in any declaration under s. 6 to an offence relating to Inland Revenue to be taken to include a reference to an offence relating to statutory paternity pay or statutory adoption pay.
TCA 2002, s. 2(6): in any declaration for the purposes of s. 6, reference to an offence relating to inland revenue is taken to include a reference to an offence relating to a tax credit.

PART II – RETURNS OF INCOME AND GAINS

INCOME TAX

7 Notice of liability to income tax and capital gains tax

7(1) Every person who–

(a) is chargeable to income tax or capital gains tax for any year of assessment, and

(b) falls within subsection (1A) or (1B),

shall, subject to subsection (3) below, within the notification period, give notice to an officer of the Board that he is so chargeable.

7(1A) A person falls within this subsection if the person has not received a notice under section 8 requiring a return for the year of assessment of the person's total income and chargeable gains.

7(1B) A person falls within this subsection if the person–

(a) has received a notice under section 8 requiring a return for the year of assessment of the person's total income and chargeable gains, and

(b) has received a notice under section 8B withdrawing the notice under section 8.

7(1C) In subsection (1) **"the notification period"** means–

(a) in the case of a person who falls within subsection (1A), the period of 6 months from the end of the year of assessment, or

(b) in the case of a person who falls within subsection (1B)–

(i) the period of 6 months from the end of the year of assessment, or

(ii) the period of 30 days beginning with the day after the day on which the notice under section 8 was withdrawn,

whichever ends later.

7(2) In the case of persons who are chargeable as mentioned in subsection (1) above as the relevant trustees of a settlement, that subsection and subsections (1A) to (1C) have effect as if references to a notice under section 8 were references to a notice under section 8A.

7(2A) A person who–

(a) falls within subsection (1A) or (1B), and

(b) is notified of a simple assessment for the year of assessment,

is not required to give notice under subsection (1) for that year unless the person is chargeable to income tax or capital gains tax for the year of assessment on any income or gain that is not included in the assessment.

7(3) A person shall not be required to give notice under subsection (1) above in respect of a year of assessment if for that year –

(a) the person's total income consists of income from sources falling within subsections (4) to (7) below,

(b) the person has no chargeable gains, and

(c) the person is not liable to a high income child benefit charge.

7(4) A source of income falls within this subsection in relation to a year of assessment if–

(a) all payments of, or on account of, income from it during that year, and

(b) all income from it for that year which does not consist of payments,

have or has been taken into account in the making of deductions or repayments of tax under PAYE regulations.

7(5) A source of income falls within this subsection in relation to any person and any year of assessment if all income from it for that year has been or will be taken into account–

(a) in determining that person's liability to tax, or

(b) in the making of deductions or repayments of tax under PAYE regulations.

7(6) A source of income falls within this subsection in relation to any person and any year of assessment if all income from it for that year is–

(a) income from which income tax has been deducted; or

(b) income from or on which income tax is treated as having been deducted or paid,

(c) [omitted by FA 2016, s. 5(9)(a)]

and that person is not for that year liable to tax at a rate other than the basic rate, the dividend nil rate, the Scottish basic rate, the dividend ordinary rate, the savings nil rate or the starting rate for savings.

7(6A) A source of income falls within this subsection in relation to any person and any year of assessment if for that year–

(a) all income from the source is dividend income (see section 19 of ITA 2007), and

(b) the person–

(i) is UK-resident,

(ii) is not liable to tax at the dividend ordinary rate,

(iii) is not liable to tax at the dividend upper rate,

(iv) is not liable to tax at the dividend additional rate, and

(v) is not charged to tax under section 832 of ITTOIA 2005 (relevant foreign income charged on remittance basis) on any dividend income.

7(7) A source of income falls within this subsection in relation to any person and any year of assessment if all income from it for that year is income on which he could not become liable to tax under a self-assessment made under section 9 of this Act in respect of that year.

7(8) [Omitted by FA 2008, s. 123 and Sch. 41, para. 25(a)(i).]

7(9) For the purposes of this Act the relevant trustees of a settlement are–

(a) in relation to income (other than gains treated as arising under Chapter 9 of Part 4 of ITTOIA 2005, the persons who are trustees when the income arises and any persons who subsequently become trustees; and

(aa) in relation to gains treated as arising under Chapter 9 of Part 4 of ITTOIA 2005, the persons who are trustees in the year of assessment in which the gains arise and any persons who subsequently become trustees; and

(b) in relation to chargeable gains, the persons who are trustees in the year of assessment in which the chargeable gains accrue and any persons who subsequently become trustees.

Prospective amendments – In s. 7(6), the words "the Welsh basic rate," inserted before the words "the dividend ordinary rate" by WA 2014, s. 9(12), with effect from a day to be appointed under s. 14.

History – S. 7(1)(b) substituted and in s. 7(1) the words "the notification period" substituted for the words "six months from the end of that year" by FA 2013, s. 233 and Sch. 51, para. 2(2), with effect in relation to a return under TMA 1970, s. 12AA for a partnership which includes one or more companies, in respect of a return for a relevant period (a period in respect of which a return is required) beginning on or after 6 April 2012 and in relation to a return under that section for any other partnership, or a return under TMA 1970, s. 8 or 8A, in respect of a return for a year of assessment beginning on or after 6 April 2012.
S. 7(1A), (1B) and (1C) inserted by FA 2013, s. 233 and Sch. 51, para. 2(3), with effect in relation to a return under TMA 1970, s. 12AA for a partnership which includes one or more companies, in respect of a return for a relevant period (a period in respect of which a return is required) beginning on or after 6 April 2012 and in relation to a return under that section for any other partnership, or a return under TMA 1970, s. 8 or 8A, in respect of a return for a year of assessment beginning on or after 6 April 2012.
In s. 7(2), the words "and subsections (1A) to (1C) have effect as if references to a notice under section 8 were references to a notice under section 8A." substituted for the words "shall have effect as if the reference to a notice under section 8 of this Act were a reference to a notice under section 8A of this Act" by FA 2013, s. 233 and Sch. 51, para. 2(4), with effect in relation to a return under TMA 1970, s. 12AA for a partnership which includes one or more companies, in respect of a return for a relevant period (a period in respect of which a return is required) beginning on or after 6 April 2012 and in relation to a return under that section for any other partnership, or a return under TMA 1970, s. 8 or 8A, in respect of a return for a year of assessment beginning on or after 6 April 2012.
In s. 7(2), the words "persons who are" and the words "the relevant trustees" substituted for the previous words by FA 1995, s. 103(1), 115(1), with effect as respects the year 1996–97 and subsequent years of assessment.
S. 7(2A) inserted by FA 2016, s. 167 and Sch. 23, para. 2, with effect in relation to the 2016–17 tax year and subsequent years.
S. 7(3) amended by FA 2012, s. 8 and Sch. 1, para. 2 with effect for the tax year 2012–13 and subsequent tax years.
In s. 7(4), the words "PAYE regulations" substituted by ITEPA 2003, Sch. 6, para. 124 for the tax year 2003–04 andsubsequent tax years.
In s. 7(5), the words "PAYE regulations" substituted by ITEPA 2003, Sch. 6, para. 124 for the tax year 2003–04 and subsequent tax years.
S. 7(6)(c) omitted, the word "or" at the end of para. (a) inserted, a comma substituted for the word" ; or" at the end of para. (b) and the words ", the dividend nil rate" inserted by FA 2016, s. 5(9)(a), with effect for the tax year 2016–17 and subsequent tax years. Former s. 7(6)(c) read as follows:
"(c) income chargeable under Chapter 3 of Part 4 of ITTOIA 2005 (dividends etc. from UK resident companies etc.),".
In s. 7(6) the words ", the savings nil rate" inserted by FA 2016, s. 4(15), with effect for the tax year 2016–17 and subsequent tax years.
In s. 7(6), the words "the Scottish basic rate," inserted after the words "the basic rate," by FA 2014, s. 296 and Sch. 38, para. 14(1), with effect in relation to the tax year 2016–17 and subsequent tax years (SI 2015/2000, art. 3).
In s. 7(6), the words "or the starting rate for savings" substituted by FA 2008, s. 5 and Sch. 1, para. 38, with effect for 2008–09 and subsequent tax years.
In s. 7(6), the words "savings rate" substituted by ITA 2007, s. 1027 and Sch. 1, para. 244, with effect from 6 April 2007.
In s. 7(6), the reference in sub-para (c) to Chapter 3 of Part 4 of ITTOIA 2005 substituted by ITTOIA 2005, s. 882(1) and Sch. 1, para. 358(2)(a); effective for 2005–06 onwards (ITTOIA 2005, s. 883(1)); the words ", the lower rate or the starting rate" substituted by FA 1999, s. 22(11)(a) for the year 1999–2000 and subsequent years of assessment; the words ", the Schedule F ordinary rate" inserted by F(No. 2)A 1997, s. 34 and Sch. 4, para. 1(1), with effect for the year 1999–2000 and subsequent years. The word "dividend" substituted for "Schedule F" in that phrase by ITTOIA 2005, s. 882(1) and Sch. 1, para. 358(2)(b); effective for 2005–06 onwards (ITTOIA 2005, s. 883(1)).
S. 7(6A) inserted by FA 2016, s. 5(9)(b), with effect for the tax year 2016–17 and subsequent tax years.
In s. 7(7) the words "income on which" substituted, and s. 7(9) inserted, by FA 1995, s. 103(2), with effect as respects the year 1996–97 and subsequent years of assessment.
S. 7(8) omitted by FA 2008, s. 123 and Sch. 41, para. 25(a)(i), with effect from 1 April 2010 (SI 2009/511, art. 2 and 3) subject to transitional provisions at SI 2009/511, art. 4).
In s. 7(9), the words "(other than gains treated as arising under Chapter II of Part XIII of the principal Act)" in para (a); and the whole of para. (aa) inserted by FA 1998, s. 86 and Sch. 14, para. 5, in relation to chargeable events happening on or after 6 April 1998. References to Chapter 9 of Part 4 of ITTOIA 2005 substituted for references to ICTA 1988, Pt. XIII, Ch. II by ITTOIA 2005, s. 882(1) and Sch. 1, para. 358(3); effective for income tax purposes for 2005–06 onwards and for corporation tax purposes for accounting periods ending after 5 April 2005 (ITTOIA 2005, s. 883(1)).
S. 7 substituted by FA 1994, s. 196 and Sch. 19, para. 1(1) with effect as respects the year 1995–96 and subsequent years of assessment.

Cross references – S. 59B(3): payment of income tax and capital gains tax under self-assessment.
S. 59C: surcharges on unpaid income tax and capital gains tax under self-assessment.
S. 100B: appeals against penalty determinations.
S. 102 Board's power to mitigate penalties.
FA 2004, s. 108(3) and s. 109(4): special withholding tax to be treated as income tax deducted at source for the purposes of this section.

HMRC Manuals – Enquiry Manual EM6052: Board's policy on abatement of tax-geared penalties.

7A Disregard of certain NRCGT gains for purposes of section 7

7A(1) This section applies where–

(a) a person ("P") is the taxable person in relation to an NRCGT return relating to a tax year ("year X") which is made and delivered to an officer of Revenue and Customs before the end of the notification period and contains an advance self-assessment,

(b) the return is in respect of a non-resident CGT disposal on which an NRCGT gain accrues, and

(c) P would (apart from this section) be required to give a notice under section 7 with respect to year X.

7A(2) For the purpose of determining whether or not P is required to give such a notice (and only for that purpose), P is regarded as not being chargeable to capital gains tax in respect of the NRCGT gain mentioned in subsection (1)(b).

7A(3) The reference in subsection (1) to the tax year to which an NRCGT return **"relates"** is to be interpreted in accordance with section 12ZB(7).

7A(4) In this section–

"advance self-assessment" has the meaning given by section 12ZE(1);

"the notification period" has the meaning given by section 7(1C);

the **"taxable person"**, in relation to a non-resident CGT disposal, means the person who would be chargeable to capital gains tax in respect of any chargeable NRCGT gain accruing on the disposal (were such a gain to accrue).

7A(5) See–

section 14B of the 1992 Act for the meaning of **"non-resident CGT disposal"**;

section 57B of, and Schedule 4ZZB to, the 1992 Act for the meaning of **"NRCGT gain"**.

History – S. 7A inserted by FA 2015, s. 37 and Sch. 7, para. 42, with effect in relation to disposals made on or after 6 April 2015.

8 Personal return

8(1) For the purpose of establishing the amounts in which a person is chargeable to income tax and capital gains tax for a year of assessment, and the amount payable by him by way of income tax for that year, he may be required by a notice given to him by an officer of the Board–

(a) to make and deliver to the officer, a return containing such information as may reasonably be required in pursuance of the notice, and

(b) to deliver with the return such accounts, statements and documents, relating to information contained in the return, as may reasonably be so required.

8(1A) [Omitted by FA 2007, s. 88(3) and repealed by s. 114 and Sch. 27, Pt. 5(3).]

8(1AA) For the purposes of subsection (1) above–

(a) the amounts in which a person is chargeable to income tax and capital gains tax are net amounts, that is to say, amounts which take into account any relief or allowance a claim for which is included in the return; and

(b) the amount payable by a person by way of income tax is the difference between the amount in which he is chargeable to income tax and the aggregate amount of any income tax deducted at source.

8(1B) In the case of a person who carries on a trade, profession, or business in partnership with one or more other persons, a return under this section shall include each amount which, in any relevant statement, is stated to be equal to his share of any income, loss, tax, credit or charge for the period in respect of which the statement is made.

8(1C) In subsection (1B) above **"relevant statement"** means a statement which, as respects the partnership, falls to be made under section 12AB of this Act for a period which includes, or includes any part of, the year of assessment or its basis period.

8(1D) A return under this section for a year of assessment (Year 1) must be delivered–

(a) in the case of a non-electronic return, on or before 31st October in Year 2, and

(b) in the case of an electronic return, on or before 31st January in Year 2.

8(1E) But subsection (1D) is subject to the following two exceptions.

8(1F) Exception 1 is that if a notice in respect of Year 1 is given after 31st July in Year 2 (but on or before 31st October), a return must be delivered–

(a) during the period of 3 months beginning with the date of the notice (for a non-electronic return), or

(b) on or before 31st January (for an electronic return).

8(1G) Exception 2 is that if a notice in respect of Year 1 is given after 31st October in Year 2, a return (whether electronic or not) must be delivered during the period of 3 months beginning with the date of the notice.

8(1H) The Commissioners–

(a) shall prescribe what constitutes an electronic return, and

(b) may make different provision for different cases or circumstances.

8(2) Every return under this section shall include a declaration by the person making the return to the effect that the return is to the best of his knowledge correct and complete.

8(3) A notice under this section may require different information, accounts and statements for different periods or in relation to different descriptions of source of income.

8(4) Notices under this section may require different information, accounts and statements in relation to different descriptions of person.

8(4A) Subsection (4B) applies if a notice under this section is given to a person within section 8ZA of this Act (certain persons employed etc by person not resident in United Kingdom who perform their duties for UK clients).

8(4B) The notice may require a return of the person's income to include particulars of any general earnings (see section 7(3) of ITEPA 2003) paid to the person.

8(5) In this section and sections 8A, 9 and 12AA of this Act, any reference to income tax deducted at source is a reference to income tax deducted or treated as deducted from any income or treated as paid on any income.

History – In s. 8(1)(a), former words ", on or before the day mentioned in subsection (1A) below" which followed "to make and deliver to the officer" omitted by FA 2007, s. 88(2) and repealed by FA 2007, s. 114 and Sch. 27, Pt. 5(3), with effect in respect of a return for a year of assessment beginning on or after 6 April 2007.
S. 8(1) (together with s. 8(1A), (1B), (1C)) substituted for s. 8(1) by FA 1994, s. 178(1).
S. 8(1A) omitted by FA 2007, s. 88(3) and repealed by FA 2007, s. 114 and Sch. 27, Pt. 5(3), with effect in respect of a return for a year of assessment beginning on or after 6 April 2007.
S. 8(1A) amended by FA 1995, s. 104(1)–(3) and further amended by FA 1996, s. 121(1)–(3), s. 205 and Sch. 41, Pt. V(6) as respects the year 1996–97 and subsequent years of assessment.
S. 8(1A) (together with s. 8(1), (1B), (1C)) substituted for s. 8(1) by FA 1994, s. 178(1).
In s. 8(1AA)(b) the words "and any tax credits to which section 397(1) or 397A(1) of ITTOIA 2005 applies" (which appeared after the word "source") omitted by FA 2016, s. 5 and Sch. 1 para. 51(2), with effect for the tax year 2016–17 and subsequent tax years.
In s. 8(1AA)(b), "397A(1)" substituted for "397A(2)" by FA 2009, s. 40 and Sch. 19, para. 9 (a), with effect for:

- qualifying distributions arising on or after 22 April 2009;
- cash dividends paid over to a person under ITEPA 2003, Sch. 2, para. 68(4) on or after 22 April 2009;
- dividends treated under ITTOIA 2005, s. 407 as paid to a person on or after 22 April 2009; and
- manufactured overseas dividends that are representative of any of the above distributions (FA 2009, Sch. 19, para. 14(1)).

In s. 8(1AA)(b), the reference to ITTOIA 2005, s. 397A(2) inserted by FA 2008, s. 34 and Sch. 12, para. 8, with effect for 2008–09 and subsequent tax years.
In s. 8(1AA)(b) the reference to s. 397(1) ITTOIA 2005 substituted by ITTOIA 2005, s. 882(1) and Sch. 1, para. 359; effective for 2005–06 onwards (ITTOIA 2005, s. 883(1)).
S. 8(1AA) inserted by FA 1996, s. 121(1)–(3), s. 205 and Sch. 41, Pt. V(6) as respects the year 1996–97 and subsequent years of assessment.
S. 8(1B) amended by FA 1995, s. 104(1)–(3) as respects the year 1996–97 and subsequent years of assessment.
S. 8(1B) (together with s. 8(1), (1A), (1C)) substituted for s. 8(1) by FA 1994, s. 178(1).
S. 8(1C) (together with s. 8(1), (1A), (1B)) substituted for s. 8(1) by FA 1994, s. 178(1).
S. 8(1D)–(1H) inserted by FA 2007, s. 88(4), with effect in respect of a return for a year of assessment beginning on or after 6 April 2007.
S. 8(4A) and (4B) inserted by TIOPA 2010, s. 371 and Sch. 7, para. 12, with effect for corporation tax purposes for accounting periods ending on or after 1 April 2010, for income tax and capital gains tax purposes for the tax year 2010–11 and subsequent tax years, and for petroleum revenue tax purposes for chargeable periods beginning on or after 1 July 2010.
S. 8(5) inserted by FA 1995, s. 104(1)–(3) by FA 1996, s. 121(1)–(3), s. 205 and Sch. 41, Pt. V(6) as respects the year 1996–97 and subsequent years of assessment.
S. 8 substituted by FA 1990, s. 90(1), (5), effective where a notice to deliver a return was, or fell to be, given after 5 April 1990.

Cross references – S. 9(1): a return must include a self-assessment.
S. 12(2): a return to include particulars in relation to capital gains tax.
S. 9ZA: amendment of personal or trustee return by taxpayer and s. 9ZB: amendment of personal or trustee return by Revenue.
S. 12ABA: amendment of partnership return by taxpayer.
S. 12ABB: correction of partnership return by Revenue.
S. 28A: "Filing date" for the purpose of s. 28A (amendment of self-assessment where enquiries made) is the date mentioned in s 8(1A) or 8A(1A) as the case may be.
S. 28B(4): where partnership return is amended under s. 28B, officer shall by notice to partners amend the partners' returns under s. 8 or s. 8A.
S. 28C: determination of tax under self-assessment where no return delivered.
S. 29: where self assessment found to be insufficient following submission of return under this section.
S. 30B: amendment of partnership return where loss of tax is discovered.
S. 33A: error or mistake in partnership return.
S. 50(9): where amounts in partnership statement are reduced or increased, officer shall by notice to partners amend the partners' self-assessments under s. 8 or s. 8A.
S. 59B: payment or repayment of income tax and capital gains tax following amendment or correction of return.
S. 93: penalties for failure to make return for income tax and capital gains tax.
S. 95: penalties for fraudulent or negligent delivery of incorrect returns under s. 8.
FA 1974, s. 24: particulars of income may be required from an overseas employer under s. 8.
ICTA 1988, s. 62A(3): time limit for giving notice of a change in basis period.
ICTA 1988, s. 379A(3): amendment to any prior s. 8 or s. 8A self-assessment may be required with a Sch. A loss claim.
TCGA 1992, s. 3A(1): in relation to the years 2003–04 and subsequent years, a statement to the effect that a person's chargeable gains do not exceed their annual exemption and the aggregate disposal consideration does not exceed four times that exemption is sufficient compliance with TMA 1970 s. 8 insofar as it relates to establishing that person's capital gains tax liability for the year.
FA 2002, s. 98: time limit for election to carry back gift aid donations.
TCA 2002, s. 19(4): enquiry window for Revenue enquiries into awards of working tax credit and child tax credit.
ITEPA 2003, s. 711(1): right to make a personal return.
FA 2004, s. 108(3) and s. 109(4): special withholding tax to be treated as income tax deducted at source for the purposes of this section.
FA 2009, Sch. 55: penalties for failure to make returns under s. 8(1)(a) or provide accounts, statements or documents under s. 8(1)(b) (subject to commencement order).
SI 2003/282: regulations governing electronic delivery of information to or by the Board under s. 8.

Statements of practice – A13: completion of return forms by attorneys.
SP 1/97: the electronic lodgment service.

Other material – HMRC helpsheet: Should I be in Self Assessment? is available at www.tax.org.uk/Resources/CIOT/Documents/2013/01/120118_3037_SA_Flyer_v6_PM.pdf.
IR press release, 4 April 1996: Under self-assessment, HMRC will, if requested, issue a tax return before the end of the tax year in which death occurred.
Tax Bulletin TB01/02-5: HMRC change of policy on use of provisional figures in returns: they will no longer send back a return that does not adequately explain why provisional figures are needed or does not give a date for the supply of final figures, but the omission of that information will be a factor to be taken into account in deciding whether to open an enquiry into the return.
Law Society's Gazette, 18 March 1992, p. 14 (not reproduced): HMRC accept there will be circumstances where taxpayer will not be able to sign return and are prepared in principle to accept the signature of an attorney in cases of physical incapacity to sign and mental incapacity.

8ZA Interpretation of section 8(4A)

8ZA(1) For the purposes of section 8(4A) of this Act, a person ("F") is within this section if each of conditions A to C is met.

8ZA(2) Condition A is that F performs in the United Kingdom, for a continuous period of 30 days or more, duties of an office or employment.

8ZA(3) Condition B is that the office or employment is under or with a person who–

(a) is not resident in the United Kingdom, but

(b) is resident outside the United Kingdom.

8ZA(4) Condition C is that the duties are performed for the benefit of a person who–

(a) is resident in the United Kingdom, or

(b) carries on a trade, profession or vocation in the United Kingdom.

History – S. 8ZA inserted by TIOPA 2010, s. 371 and Sch. 7, para. 13, with effect for corporation tax purposes for accounting periods ending on or after 1 April 2010, for income tax and capital gains tax purposes for the tax year 2010–11 and subsequent tax years, and for petroleum revenue tax purposes for chargeable periods beginning on or after 1 July 2010.

8A Trustee's return

8A(1) For the purpose of establishing the amounts in which the relevant trustees of a settlement, and the settlors and beneficiaries, are chargeable to income tax and capital gains tax for a year of assessment, and the amount payable by him by way of income tax for that year, an officer of the Board may by a notice given to any relevant trustee require the trustee–

(a) to make and deliver to the officer, a return containing such information as may reasonably be required in pursuance of the notice, and

(b) to deliver with the return such accounts, statements and documents, relating to information contained in the return, as may reasonably be so required;

and a notice may be given to any one trustee or separate notices may be given to each trustee or to such trustees as the officer thinks fit.

8A(1A) [Omitted by FA 2007, s. 89(3) and repealed by s. 114 and Sch. 27, Pt. 5(3).]

8A(1AA) For the purposes of subsection (1) above–

(a) the amounts in which a person is chargeable to income tax and capital gains tax are net amounts, that is to say, amounts which take into account any relief or allowance a claim for which is included in the return; and

(b) the amount payable by a person by way of income tax is the difference between the amount in which he is chargeable to income tax and the aggregate amount of any income tax deducted at source.

8A(1B) A return under this section for a year of assessment (Year 1) must be delivered–

(a) in the case of a non-electronic return, on or before 31st October in Year 2, and

(b) in the case of an electronic return, on or before 31st January in Year 2.

8A(1C) But subsection (1B) is subject to the following two exceptions.

8A(1D) Exception 1 is that if a notice in respect of Year 1 is given after 31st July in Year 2 (but on or before 31st October), a return must be delivered–

(a) during the period of 3 months beginning with the date of the notice (for a non-electronic return), or

(b) on or before 31st January (for an electronic return).

8A(1E) Exception 2 is that if a notice in respect of Year 1 is given after 31st October in Year 2, a return (whether electronic or not) must be delivered during the period of 3 months beginning with the date of the notice.

8A(1F) The Commissioners–

(a) shall prescribe what constitutes an electronic return, and

(b) may make different provision for different cases or circumstances.

8A(2) Every return under this section shall include a declaration by the person making the return to the effect that the return is to the best of his knowledge correct and complete.

8A(3) A notice under this section may require different information, accounts and statements for different periods or in relation to different descriptions of source of income.

8A(4) Notices under this section may require different information, accounts and statements in relation to different descriptions of settlement.

8A(5) The following references, namely–

(a) references in section 9 or 28C of this Act to a person to whom a notice has been given under this section being chargeable to tax; and

(b) references in section 29 of this Act to such a person being assessed to tax,

shall be construed as references to the relevant trustees of the settlement being so chargeable or, as the case may be, being so assessed.

History – In s. 8A(1)(a), former words ", on or before the day mentioned in subsection (1A) below" which followed "to make and deliver to the officer" omitted by FA 2007, s. 89(2) and repealed by FA 2007, s. 114 and Sch. 27, Pt. 5(3), with effect in respect of a return for a year of assessment beginning on or after 6 April 2007.
S. 8A(1A) omitted by FA 2007, s. 89(3) and repealed by FA 2007, s. 114 and Sch. 27, Pt. 5(3), with effect in respect of a return for a year of assessment beginning on or after 6 April 2007.
S. 8A(1), (1A) amended by FA 1995, s. 103(3), (4) and 104(1), and s. 8A(1) and (1A) amended, by FA 1996, s. 121(1)–(3), s. 205 and Sch. 41, Pt. V(6), as respects the year 1996–97 and subsequent years of assessment.
S. 8A(1) and (1A) substituted for s. 8A(1) by FA 1994, s. 178(2).
In s. 8A(1AA)(b) the words "and any tax credits to which section 397(1) or 397A(1) of ITTOIA 2005 applies" (which appeared after the word "source") omitted by FA 2016, s. 5 and Sch. 1 para. 51(3), with effect for the tax year 2016–17 and subsequent tax years.
In s. 8(1AA)(b), "397A(1)" substituted for "397A(2)" by FA 2009, s. 40 and Sch. 19, para. 9(a), with effect for:

- qualifying distributions arising on or after 22 April 2009;
- cash dividends paid over to a person under ITEPA 2003, Sch. 2, para. 68(4) on or after 22 April 2009;
- dividends treated under ITTOIA 2005, s. 407 as paid to a person on or after 22 April 2009; and
- manufactured overseas dividends that are representative of any of the above distributions (FA 2009, Sch. 19, para. 14(1)).

In s. 8A(1AA)(b), the reference to ITTOIA 2005, s. 397A(2) inserted by FA 2008, s. 34 and Sch. 12, para. 9, with effect for 2008–09 and subsequent tax years.
In s. 8A(1AA)(b) the reference to ITTOIA 2005 s. 397(1) substituted by ITTOIA 2005, s. 882(1) and Sch. 1, para. 360; effective for 2005–06 onwards (ITTOIA 2005, s. 883(1)).
S. 8A(1AA) inserted by FA 1995, s. 103(3), (4) by FA 1996, s. 121(1)–(3), s. 205 and Sch. 41, Pt. V(6), as respects the year 1996–97 and subsequent years of assessment.
S. 8A(1B)–(1F) inserted by FA 2007, s. 89(4), with effect in respect of a return for a year of assessment beginning on or after 6 April 2007.
S. 8A(5) inserted by FA 1995, s. 103(3), (4) by FA 1996, s. 121(1)–(3), s. 205 and Sch. 41, Pt. V(6), as respects the year 1996–97 and subsequent years of assessment.
S. 8A inserted by FA 1990, s. 90(1), (5), effective where a notice to deliver a return was, or falls to be, given after 5 April 1990.

Cross references – S. 9(1): a return must include a self-assessment.
S. 9ZA: amendment of personal or trustee return by taxpayer and s. 9ZB: amendment of personal or trustee return by Revenue.
S. 12(2): a return to include particulars in relation to capital gains tax.
S. 12ABA: amendment of partnership return by taxpayer.
S. 12ABB: correction of partnership return by Revenue.
S. 28A: "Filing date" for the purpose of s. 28A (amendment of self-assessment where enquiries made) is the date mentioned in s. 8(1A) or 8A(1A) as the case may be.
S. 28B(4): where partnership return is amended under s. 28B, officer shall by notice to partners amend the partners' returns under s. 8 or s. 8A.
S. 28C: determination of tax under self-assessment where no return delivered.
S. 29: where self assessment found to be insufficient following submission of return under this section.
S. 30B: amendment of partnership return where loss of tax is discovered.
S. 33A: error or mistake in partnership return.
S. 50(9): where amounts in partnership statement are reduced or increased, officer shall by notice to partners amend the partners' self-assessments under s. 8 or s. 8A.
S. 59B: payment or repayment of income tax and capital gains tax following amendment or correction of return.
S. 93: penalties for failure to make return for income tax and capital gains tax.
S. 95: penalties for fraudulent or negligent delivery of incorrect returns under s. 8A.
ICTA 1988, s. 379A(3): amendment to any prior s. 8 or s. 8A self-assessment may be required with a Sch. A loss claim.
TCGA 1992, Sch. 1, para. 1(5A) and 2(6A) (modification of annual exemption and reporting limits for trustees): references to TMA 1970, s. 8 in s. 3A(1) should be read as references to TMA 1970, s. 8A.
FA 2002, Sch. 22, para. 17(2): a return under s. 8A is a relevant return for the purposes of determining the extent to which change of basis period provisions of FA 2002, Sch. 22 apply to periods of account ending before 1 August 2002.
FA 2004, s. 108(3) and s. 109(4): special withholding tax to be treated as income tax deducted at source for the purposes of this section.
FA 2009, Sch. 55: penalties for failure to make returns under s. 8A(1)(a) or provide accounts, statements or documents under s. 8A(1)(b) (subject to commencement order).
SI 2003/282: regulations governing electronic delivery of information to or by the Board under this section.

Statements of practice – SP 1/97: the electronic lodgment service.

8B Withdrawal by HMRC of notice under section 8 or 8A

8B(1) This section applies to a person who is given a notice under section 8 or 8A.

8B(2) Before the end of the withdrawal period, HMRC may withdraw the notice (whether at the request of the person or otherwise).

8B(3) But the notice may not be withdrawn if–

(a) the person has made a return under section 8 or 8A in pursuance of the notice under that section, or

(b) the person has been served with notice of a determination under section 28C by virtue of the notice under section 8 or 8A having been given to the person.

8B(4) If HMRC decide to withdraw the notice under section 8 or 8A they must do so by giving the person a notice under this section.

8B(5) A notice under this section must specify the date on which the notice under section 8 or 8A is withdrawn.

8B(6) For the purposes of subsection (2) **"the withdrawal period"** means–

(a) the period of 2 years beginning with the end of the year of assessment to which the notice under section 8 or 8A relates, or

(b) in exceptional circumstances, such extended period as HMRC may determine.

8B(7) Withdrawal of a notice given to a person under section 8 or 8A in relation to a year of assessment does not prevent HMRC from giving the person a further notice under that section in relation to that year.

8B(8) See paragraph 17A of Schedule 55 to FA 2009 as to the cancellation of liability to a penalty under any paragraph of that Schedule by including provision in a notice under this section.

History – In s. 8B(2), the words "HMRC may withdraw the notice (whether at the request of the person or otherwise)" substituted for the words "the person may request HMRC to withdraw the notice" by FA 2016, s. 169(2), with effect in relation to any notice under TMA 1970, s. 8 or 8A given in relation to the 2014–15 tax year or any subsequent tax year (and it is immaterial whether the notice was given before or after 15 September 2016 (Royal Assent)).

In s. 8B(3), the words "the notice may not be withdrawn" substituted for the words "no request may be made" by FA 2016, s. 169(3), with effect in relation to any notice under TMA 1970, s. 8 or 8A given in relation to the 2014–15 tax year or any subsequent tax year (and it is immaterial whether the notice was given before or after 15 September 2016 (Royal Assent)).

In s. 8B(4), the words ", on receiving a request," (which appeared after the word "If") omitted by FA 2016, s. 169(4), with effect in relation to any notice under TMA 1970, s. 8 or 8A given in relation to the 2014–15 tax year or any subsequent tax year (and it is immaterial whether the notice was given before or after 15 September 2016 (Royal Assent)).

In s. 8B(6)(b) the word "determine" substituted for the words "agree with the person" by FA 2016, s. 169(5), with effect in relation to any notice under TMA 1970, s. 8 or 8A given in relation to the 2014–15 tax year or any subsequent tax year (and it is immaterial whether the notice was given before or after 15 September 2016 (Royal Assent)).

S. 8B inserted by FA 2013, s. 233 and Sch. 51, para. 3, with effect in relation to a return under TMA 1970, s. 12AA for a partnership which includes one or more companies, in respect of a return for a relevant period (a period in respect of which a return is required) beginning on or after 6 April 2012 and in relation to a return under that section for any other partnership, or a return under TMA 1970, s. 8 or 8A, in respect of a return for a year of assessment beginning on or after 6 April 2012.

9 Returns to include self-assessment

9(1) Subject to subsections (1A) and (2) below, every return under section 8 or 8A of this Act shall include a self-assessment, that is to say–

(a) an assessment of the amounts in which, on the basis of the information contained in the return and taking into account any relief or allowance a claim for which is included in the return, the person making the return is chargeable to income tax and capital gains tax for the year of assessment; and

(b) an assessment of the amount payable by him by way of income tax, that is to say, the difference between the amount in which he is assessed to income tax under paragraph (a) above and the aggregate amount of any income tax deducted at source

but nothing in this subsection shall enable a self-assessment to show as repayable any income tax treated as deducted or paid by virtue of section 246D(1) of the principal Act, section 626 of ITEPA 2003 or section 399(2) or 530(1) of ITTOIA 2005.

9(1A) The tax to be assessed on a person by a self-assessment shall not include any tax which–

(a) is chargeable on the scheme administrator of a registered pension scheme under Part 4 of the Finance Act 2004, or

(b) is chargeable on the person who is (or persons who are) the responsible person in relation to an employer-financed retirement benefits scheme under section 394(2) of ITEPA 2003.

9(2) A person shall not be required to comply with subsection (1) above if he makes and delivers his return for a year of assessment–

(a) on or before the 31st October next following the year, or

(b) where the notice under section 8 or 8A of this Act is given after the 31st August next following the year, within the period of two months beginning with the day on which the notice is given.

9(3) Where, in making and delivering a return, a person does not comply with subsection (1) above, an officer of the Board shall if subsection (2) above applies, and may in any other case–

(a) make the assessment on his behalf on the basis of the information contained in the return, and

(b) send him a copy of the assessment so made;

9(3A) An assessment under subsection (3) above is treated for the purposes of this Act as a self-assessment and as included in the return.

9(4) [Omitted by FA 2001, s. 88 and Sch. 29, para. 2.]

9(5) [Omitted by FA 2001, s. 88 and Sch. 29, para. 2.]

9(6) [Omitted by FA 2001, s. 88 and Sch. 29, para. 2.]

History – In s. 9(1)(b) the words "and any tax credits to which section 397(1) or 397A(1) of ITTOIA 2005 applies" (which appeared after the word "source") and the words", 400(2), 414(1), 421(1)" (which appeared after the words "section 399(2)") omitted by FA 2016, s. 5 and Sch. 1 para. 51(4), with effect for the tax year 2016–17 and subsequent tax years.
In s. 9(1)(b), "397A(1)" substituted for "397A(2)" by FA 2009, s. 40 and Sch. 19, para. 9(b), with effect for:

- qualifying distributions arising on or after 22 April 2009;
- cash dividends paid over to a person under ITEPA 2003, Sch. 2, para. 68(4) on or after 22 April 2009;
- dividends treated under ITTOIA 2005, s. 407 as paid to a person on or after 22 April 2009; and
- manufactured overseas dividends that are representative of any of the above distributions (FA 2009, Sch. 19, para. 14(_)(1)).

In s. 9(1)(b), the reference to ITTOIA 2005, s. 397A(2) inserted by FA 2008, s. 34 and Sch. 12, para. 10, with effect for 2008–09 and subsequent tax years.
In s. 9(1), the words "or 547(5) of the principal Act or section 626 of ITEPA 2003" substituted by ITEPA 2003, Sch. 6, para. 125(2) which has effect for the tax year 2003–04 and subsequent tax years. The reference in para. (b) to ITTOIA 2005, s. 397(1) substituted by ITTOIA 2005, s. 882(1) and Sch. 1, para. 361(a); effective for 2005–06 onwards (ITTOIA 2005, s. 883(1)). References to ICTA 1988, s. 233(1), 249(4), 421(1) and 547(5) omitted by ITTOIA 2005, s. 882(1) and Sch. 1, para. 361(b) and repealed by ITTOIA 2005, s 884, Sch. 3; effective for 2005–06 onwards (ITTOIA 2005, s. 883(1)). References to ITTOIA 2005, s. 399(2), 400(2), 414(1), 421(1) and 530(1) inserted by ITTOIA 2005, s. 882(1) and Sch. 1, para. 361; effective for 2005–06 onwards (ITTOIA 2005, s. 883(1)).
In s. 9(1A) the words after "any tax" substituted by FA 2004, s. 281 and Sch. 35, para. 1 with effect from 6 April 2006.
In s. 9(1A), the words "or under section 394(2) of ITEPA 2003" inserted by ITEPA 2003, Sch. 6, para. 125(3) which has effect for the tax year 2003–04 and subsequent tax years.
S. 9(1A) and reference to it in s. 9(1) inserted by FA 1998, s. 98(2) with effect for 1998–99 and subsequent years and with deemed effect for 1996–97 and 1997–98.
In s. 9(2), the words "31st October" substituted for "30th September" and the words "31st August" substituted for "31st July" by FA 2007, s. 91(1), with effect in respect of a return for a year of assessment beginning on or after 6 April 2007.
In s. 9(3) the words "and references in this Act to a person's self-assessment include references to an assessment made on a person's behalf under this subsection" omitted by FA 2001, s. 88 and Sch. 29, para. 1, with effect from 11 May 2001 in relation to returns–
(a) whether made before or after 11 May 2001, and
(b) whether relating to periods before or after 11 May 2001.
S. 9(3A) inserted by FA 2001, s. 88 and Sch. 29, para. 1, with effect from 11 May 2001 in relation to returns–
(a) whether made before or after 11 May 2001, and
(b) whether relating to periods before or after 11 May 2001.
S. 9(4)–(6) omitted by FA 2001, s. 88 and Sch. 29, para. 2, with effect from 11 May 2001 in relation to returns–
(a) whether made before or after 11 May 2001, and
(b) whether relating to periods before or after 11 May 2001.
S. 9 substituted by FA 1994, s. 179 and amended by FA 1995, s. 104(4), 115(2), 162 and Sch. 29, Pt. VIII(14), and by FA 1996, s. 121(4), 122(1) as respects the year 1996–97 and subsequent years of assessment. S. 9 previously substituted by FA 1990, s. 90(1), (5), effective where a notice to deliver a return was, or falls to be, given after 5 April 1990.

Cross references – TMA 1970, s. 28C(3): determination under s. 28C has effect as if it were a self-assessment until such time as it is superseded by a self-assessment under s. 9.
TMA 1970, s. 59A: payments on account of income tax.
TMA 1970, s. 65: recovery of tax due under s. 9 via the magistrates' court.
FA 1994, s. 197(1): references in the Tax Acts and Gains Tax Acts to a person being assessed include tax assessed or charged by self-assessment under s. 9.
SI 2003/282: regulations governing electronic delivery of information to or by the Board under this section.
FA 2004, s. 108(3) and s. 109(4): special withholding tax to be treated as income tax deducted at source for the purposes of this section.

9ZA Amendment of personal or trustee return by taxpayer

9ZA(1) A person may amend his return under section 8 or 8A of this Act by notice to an officer of the Board.

9ZA(2) An amendment may not be made more than twelve months after the filing date.

9ZA(3) In this section "the filing date", in respect of a return for a year of assessment (Year 1), means–

(a) 31st January of Year 2, or

(b) if the notice under section 8 or 8A is given after 31st October of Year 2, the last day of the period of three months beginning with the date of the notice.

History – S. 9ZA(3) substituted by FA 2007, s. 91(2), with effect in respect of a return for a year of assessment beginning on or after 6 April 2007.

Cross references – TCA 2002, s. 20(2)(a): revisions of decisions on working tax credit and child tax credit on an amendment under this section taking effect.
FA 2009, Sch. 53, para. 3: late payment interest in respect of amounts due following an assessment, amendment or determination.

HMRC interpretations – IRInt. 186: amending a self assessment return under what is now s. 9ZA does not preclude penalty action by Revenue if taxpayer has acted negligently or fraudulently in original submission of return.

9ZB *Correction of personal or trustee return by Revenue*

9ZB(1) An officer of the Board may amend a return under section 8 or 8A of this Act so as to correct–

(a) obvious errors or omissions in the return (whether errors of principle, arithmetical mistakes or otherwise), and

(b) anything else in the return that the officer has reason to believe is incorrect in the light of information available to the officer.

9ZB(2) A correction under this section is made by notice to the person whose return it is.

9ZB(3) No such correction may be made more than nine months after–

(a) the day on which the return was delivered, or

(b) if the correction is required in consequence of an amendment of the return under section 9ZA of this Act, the day on which that amendment was made.

9ZB(4) A correction under this section is of no effect if the person whose return it is gives notice rejecting the correction.

9ZB(5) Notice of rejection under subsection (4) above must be given–

(a) to the officer of the Board by whom the notice of correction was given,

(b) before the end of the period of 30 days beginning with the date of issue of the notice of correction.

History – S. 9ZB(1)(b) and the ", and" before it inserted (and s. 9ZB(1)(a) created from existing wording) by FA 2008, s. 119(1) with effect from 1 April 2010 (SI 2009/405).

S. 9ZB inserted by FA 2001, s. 88 and Sch. 29, para. 2 with effect from 11 May 2001 in relation to returns–

(a) whether made before or after 11 May 2001, and

(b) whether relating to periods before or after 11 May 2001.

Cross references – TCA 2002, s. 20(2)(b): revisions of decisions on working tax credit and child tax credit following issue of a notice of correction.

FA 2009, Sch. 53, para. 3: late payment interest in respect of amounts due following an assessment, amendment or determination.

9A Notice of enquiry

9A(1) An officer of the Board may enquire into a return under section 8 or 8A of this Act if he gives notice of his intention to do so (**"notice of enquiry"**)–

(a) to the person whose return it is (**"the taxpayer"**),

(b) within the time allowed.

9A(2) The time allowed is–

(a) if the return was delivered on or before the filing date, up to the end of the period of twelve months after the day on which the return was delivered;

(b) if the return was delivered after the filing date, up to and including the quarter day next following the first anniversary of the day on which the return was delivered;

(c) if the return is amended under section 9ZA of this Act, up to and including the quarter day next following the first anniversary of the day on which the amendment was made.

For this purpose the quarter days are 31st January, 30th April, 31st July and 31st October.

9A(3) A return which has been the subject of one notice of enquiry may not be the subject of another, except one given in consequence of an amendment (or another amendment) of the return under section 9ZA of this Act.

9A(4) An enquiry extends to–

(a) anything contained in the return, or required to be contained in the return, including any claim or election included in the return,

(b) consideration of whether to give the taxpayer a transfer pricing notice under section 168(1) of TIOPA 2010 (provision not at arm's length: medium-sized enterprise), but this is subject to the following limitation.

(c) consideration of whether to give the taxpayer a notice under section 81(2) of TIOPA 2010 (notice to counteract scheme or arrangement designed to increase double taxation relief).

9A(5) If the notice of enquiry is given as a result of an amendment of the return under section 9ZA of this Act–

(a) at a time when it is no longer possible to give notice of enquiry under subsection (2)(a) or (b) above, or

(b) after an enquiry into the return has been completed,

the enquiry into the return is limited to matters to which the amendment relates or which are affected by the amendment.

9A(6) In this section **"the filing date"** means, in relation to a return, the last day for delivering it in accordance with section 8 or 8A.

History – In s. 9A(2)(a), the words "after the day on which the return was delivered;" substituted for the words "after the filing date;" by FA 2007, s. 96(1) and applicable to returns which relate to the tax year 2007–08 or a later tax year.

In s. 9A(4)(b), the words "section 168(1) of TIOPA 2010" substituted for the words "paragraph 5C of Schedule 28AA to the principal Act" by TIOPA 2010, s. 374 and Sch. 8, para. 107, with effect for corporation tax purposes for accounting periods ending on or after 1 April 2010, for income tax and capital gains tax purposes for the tax year 2010–11 and subsequent tax years, and for petroleum revenue tax purposes for chargeable periods beginning on or after 1 July 2010.

In s. 9A(4)(c), the words "section 81(2) of TIOPA 2010 (notice to counteract scheme or arrangement designed to increase double taxation relief)" substituted for the words "section 804ZA of the principal Act (schemes and arrangements designed to increase relief)" by TIOPA 2010, s. 374 and Sch. 8, para. 2, with effect for corporation tax purposes for accounting periods ending on or after 1 April 2010, for income tax and capital gains tax purposes for the tax year 2010–11 and subsequent tax years, and for petroleum revenue tax purposes for chargeable periods beginning on or after 1 July 2010.

S. 9A(4)(c) inserted by FA 2005, s. 88(1) with effect from 10 February 2005 (where credit for foreign tax is affected by a scheme to which ICTA 1988, Sch. 28AB, para. 5 applies) or 16 March 2005 (where that credit is affected by any other scheme or arrangement prescribed by ICTA 1988, Sch. 28AB.)
S. 9A(4) substituted by FA 2004 s. 30 and Sch. 5, para. 1, with effect in relation to chargeable periods beginning on or after 1 April 2004.
In s. 9A(6), the words "means, in relation to a return, the last day for delivering it in accordance with section 8 or 8A" substituted for "means the day mentioned in section 8(1A) or, as the case may be, section 8A(1A) of this Act" by FA 2007, s. 91(3), with effect in respect of a return for a year of assessment beginning on or after 6 April 2007. See s. 8 or s. 8A History note as appropriate.
S. 9A substituted by FA 2001, s. 88 and Sch. 29, para. 4, with effect from 11 May 2001 in relation to returns–
(a) whether made before or after 11 May 2001, and
(b) whether relating to periods before or after 11 May 2001.
Former s. 9A inserted by FA 1994, s. 180, with effect for the year 1996–97 and subsequent years of assessment.

Cross references – TCA 2002, s. 19(7): effect of s. 9A enquiry on timescale for enquiries into awards of working tax credit and child tax credit.
SI 2003/282: regulations governing electronic delivery of information to or by the Board under this section.

Statements of practice – SP 1/99: where enquiries remain open after expiry of period within which notice of enquiry may be issued solely because of an unagreed capital gains tax valuation, HMRC will not normally raise further enquiries into matters unrelated to the valuation or the CGT computation unless the circumstances are such that, had the enquiry already been completed, the Revenue could have made a section 29 discovery.

HMRC Manuals – Enquiry Manual EM1551: Instructions on opening an enquiry.
Enquiry Manual EM1601: inspectors may give early confirmation that no enquiry is proposed into a return of a deceased taxpayer.

Other material – Code of Practice 11 (COP 11): 'enquiries into tax returns by local tax offices'
Taxline 2000/3 (not reproduced): time limits for enquiries (based on case law).

9B Amendment of return by taxpayer during enquiry

9B(1) This section applies if a return is amended under section 9ZA of this Act (amendment of personal or trustee return by taxpayer), or in accordance with Chapter 2 of Part 4 of the Finance Act 2014 (amendment of return after follower notice), at a time when an enquiry is in progress into the return.

9B(2) The amendment does not restrict the scope of the enquiry but may be taken into account (together with any matters arising) in the enquiry.

9B(3) So far as the amendment affects the amount stated in the self-assessment included in the return as the amount of tax payable, it does not take effect while the enquiry is in progress and–

(a) if the officer states in the closure notice that he has taken the amendment into account and that–

  (i) the amendment has been taken into account in formulating the amendments contained in the notice, or

  (ii) his conclusion is that the amendment is incorrect,

the amendment shall not take effect;

(b) otherwise, the amendment takes effect when the closure notice is issued.

9B(4) For the purposes of this section the period during which an enquiry is in progress is the whole of the period–

(a) beginning with the day on which notice of enquiry is given, and

(b) ending with the day on which the enquiry is completed.

History – In s. 9B(1), the words ", or in accordance with Chapter 2 of Part 4 of the Finance Act 2014 (amendment of return after follower notice)," inserted by FA 2014, s. 233 and Sch. 33, para. 1, with effect from 17 July 2014.
S. 9B substituted with s. 9A, 9C and 9D for former s. 9A by FA 2001, s. 88, Sch. 29, para. 4, with effect from 11 May 2001 in relation to returns–
(a) whether made before or after 11 May 2001, and
(b) whether relating to periods before or after 11 May 2001.

Cross references – FA 2009, Sch. 53, para. 3: late payment interest in respect of amounts due following an assessment, amendment or determination.

9C Amendment of self-assessment during enquiry to prevent loss of tax

9C(1) This section applies where an enquiry is in progress into a return as a result of notice of enquiry by an officer of the Board under section 9A(1) of this Act.

9C(2) If the officer forms the opinion–

(a) that the amount stated in the self-assessment contained in the return as the amount of tax payable is insufficient, and

(b) that unless the assessment is immediately amended there is likely to be a loss of tax to the Crown,

he may by notice to the taxpayer amend the assessment to make good the deficiency.

9C(3) In the case of an enquiry which under section 9A(5) of this Act is limited to matters arising from an amendment of the return, subsection (2) above only applies so far as the deficiency is attributable to the amendment.

9C(4) For the purposes of this section the period during which an enquiry is in progress is the whole of the period–

(a) beginning with the day on which notice of enquiry is given, and
(b) ending with the day on which the enquiry is completed.

History – S. 9C substituted with s. 9A, 9B and 9D for former s. 9A by FA 2001, s. 88, Sch. 29, para. 4, with effect from 11 May 2001 in relation to returns–
(a) whether made before or after 11 May 2001, and
(b) whether relating to periods before or after 11 May 2001.

Cross references – TMA 70, s. 31: right of appeal.
TCA 2002, s. 20(2)(c),(k): revisions of decisions on working tax credit and child tax credit following amendment of an assessment, or determination or settlement of an appeal.
FA 2009, Sch. 53, para. 3: late payment interest in respect of amounts due following an assessment, amendment or determination.

9D Choice between different Cases of Schedule D

9D [S. 9D omitted by ITTOIA 2005, s. 882(1) and Sch. 1, para. 362 and repealed by ITTOIA 2005, s. 884 and Sch. 3.]

History – S. 9D omitted by ITTOIA 2005, s. 882(1) and Sch. 1, para. 362 and repealed by ITTOIA 2005, s. 884 and Sch. 3; effective for 2005–06 onwards (ITTOIA 2005, s. 883(1)).

CORPORATION TAX

10 Notice of liability to corporation tax

10 [Repealed by FA 1998, s. 117(3) and Sch. 19, para. 1, s. 165 and Sch. 27, Pt. III(28).]

History – S. 10 repealed by FA 1998, s. 117(3) and Sch. 19, para. 1, s. 165 and Sch. 27 Pt. III(28) as respects accounting periods ending on or after 1 July 1999, the self-assessment appointed day by virtue of FA 1994, s. 199(2) and SI 1998/3173 (C. 78). The repealed provisions of s. 10 are superseded by FA 1998, Sch. 18, which has effect in relation to accounting periods ending on or after 1 July 1999 and which is construed and has effect as if it were contained in TMA 1970 (FA 1998, s. 117(2)).

11 Return of profits

11 [Repealed by FA 1998, s. 117(3) and Sch. 19, para. 1, s. 165 and Sch. 27, Pt. III(28).]

History – S. 11 repealed by FA 1998, s. 117(3) and Sch. 19, para. 1, s. 165 and Sch. 27 Pt. III(28) as respects accounting periods ending on or after 1 July 1999, the self-assessment appointed day by virtue of FA 1994, s. 199(2) and SI 1998/3173 (C. 78). The repealed provisions of s. 11 are superseded by FA 1998, Sch. 18, which has effect in relation to accounting periods ending on or after 1 July 1999 and which is construed and has effect as if it were contained in TMA 1970 (FA 1998, s. 117(2)).

11AA Return of profits to include self-assessment

11AA [Repealed by FA 1998, s. 117(3) and Sch. 19, para. 1, s. 165 and Sch. 27, Pt. III(28).]

History – S. 11AA repealed by FA 1998, s. 117(3) and Sch. 19, para. 1, s. 165 and Sch. 27 Pt. III(28) as respects accounting periods ending on or after 1 July 1999, the self-assessment appointed day by virtue of FA 1994, s. 199(2) and SI 1998/3173 (C. 78). The repealed provisions of s. 11AA are superseded by FA 1998, Sch. 18, which has effect in relation to accounting periods ending on or after 1 July 1999 and which is construed and has effect as if it were contained in TMA 1970 (FA 1998, s. 117(2)).

11AB Power to enquire into return of profits

11AB [Repealed by FA 1998, s. 117(3) and Sch. 19, para. 1, s. 165 and Sch. 27, Pt. III(28).]

History – S. 11AB repealed by FA 1998, s. 117(3) and Sch. 19, para. 1, s. 165 and Sch. 27 Pt. III(28) as respects accounting periods ending on or after 1 July 1999, the self-assessment appointed day by virtue of FA 1994, s. 199(2) and SI 1998/3173 (C. 78). The repealed provisions of s. 11AB are superseded by FA 1998, Sch. 18, which has effect in relation to accounting periods ending on or after 1 July 1999 and which is construed and has effect as if it were contained in TMA 1970 (FA 1998, s. 117(2)).

11AC Modifications of sections 11AA and 11AB in relation to non-annual accounting of general insurance business

11AC [Repealed by FA 1998, s. 117(3) and Sch. 19, para. 1, s. 165 and Sch. 27, Pt. III(28).]

History – S. 11AC repealed by FA 1998, s. 117(3) and Sch. 19, para. 1, s. 165 and Sch. 27 Pt. III(28) as respects accounting periods ending on or after 1 July 1999, the self-assessment appointed day by virtue of FA 1994, s. 199(2) and SI 1998/3173 (C. 78). The repealed provisions of s. 11AC are superseded by FA 1998, Sch. 18, which has effect in relation to accounting periods ending on or after 1 July 1999 and which is construed and has effect as if it were contained in TMA 1970 (FA 1998, s. 117(2)).

11AD Modifications of sections 11AA and 11AB for insurance companies with non-annual actuarial investigations

11AD [Repealed by FA 1998, s. 117(3) and Sch. 19 para. 1, s. 165 and Sch. 27 Pt. III(28).]

History – S. 11AD repealed by FA 1998, s. 117(3) and Sch. 19, para. 1, s. 165 and Sch. 27 Pt. III(28) as respects accounting periods ending on or after 1 July 1999, the self-assessment appointed day by virtue of FA 1994, s. 199(2) and SI 1998/3173 (C. 78). The repealed provisions of s. 11AD are superseded by FA 1998, Sch. 18, which has effect in relation to accounting periods ending on or after 1 July 1999 and which is construed and has effect as if it were contained in TMA 1970 (FA 1998, s. 117(2)).

11AE Modifications of sections 11AA and 11AB for friendly societies with non-annual actuarial investigations

11AE [Repealed by FA 1998, s. 117(3) and Sch. 19, para. 1, s. 165 and Sch. 27, Pt. III(28).]

History – S. 11AE repealed by FA 1998, s. 117(3) and Sch. 19, para. 1, s. 165 and Sch. 27 Pt. III(28) as respects accounting periods ending on or after 1 July 1999, the self-assessment appointed day by virtue of FA 1994, s. 199(2) and SI 1998/3173 (C. 78). The repealed provisions of s. 11AE are superseded by FA 1998, Sch. 18, which has effect in relation to accounting periods ending on or after 1 July 1999 and which is construed and has effect as if it were contained in TMA 1970 (FA 1998, s. 117(2)).

CAPITAL GAINS

11A Notice of liability to capital gains tax

11A [Repealed by FA 1995, s. 115(3), 162 and Sch. 29, Pt. VIII(14).]

History – S. 11A repealed by FA 1995, s. 115(3), 162 and Sch. 29, Pt. VIII(14) as respects the year 1996–97 and subsequent years of assessment.

12 Information about chargeable gains

12 [Omitted by SI 2009/2035, art. 2 and Schedule, para. 2.]

History – S. 12 omitted by SI 2009/2035, art. 2 and Schedule, para. 2, with effect from 13 August 2009.

NRCGT RETURNS

12ZA Interpretation of sections 12ZB to 12ZN

12ZA(1) In sections 12ZA to 12ZN–

"advance self-assessment" is to be interpreted in accordance with section 12ZE(1);

"amount notionally chargeable" is to be interpreted in accordance with section 12ZF(1);

"filing date", in relation to an NRCGT return, is to be interpreted in accordance with section 12ZB(8);

"interest in UK land" has the same meaning as in Schedule B1 to the 1992 Act (see paragraph 2 of that Schedule);

the **"taxable person"**, in relation to a non-resident CGT disposal, means the person who would be chargeable to capital gains tax in respect of any chargeable NRCGT gain (see section 57B of, and Schedule 4ZZB to, the 1992 Act) accruing on the disposal (were such a gain to accrue).

12ZA(2) In those sections, references to the tax year to which an NRCGT return **"relates"** are to be interpreted in accordance with section 12ZB(7).

12ZA(3) For the purposes of those sections the **"completion"** of a non-resident CGT disposal is taken to occur–

(a) at the time of the disposal, or

(b) if the disposal is under a contract which is completed by a conveyance, at the time when the asset is conveyed.

12ZA(4) For the meaning in those sections of **"non-resident CGT disposal"** see section 14B of the 1992 Act (and see also section 12ZJ).

12ZA(5) For the meaning of **"NRCGT group"** in those sections see section 288(1) of the 1992 Act.

12ZA(6) In this section **"conveyance"** includes any instrument (and "conveyed" is to be construed accordingly).

History – S. 12ZA inserted by FA 2015, s. 37 and Sch. 7, para. 43, with effect in relation to disposals made on or after 6 April 2015.

12ZB NRCGT return

12ZB(1) Where a non-resident CGT disposal is made, the appropriate person must make and deliver to an officer of Revenue and Customs, on or before the filing date, a return in respect of the disposal.

12ZB(2) In subsection (1) the **"appropriate person"** means–

(a) the taxable person in relation to the disposal, or

(b) if the disposal is made by a member of an NRCGT group, the relevant members of the group.

12ZB(3) A return under this section is called an **"NRCGT return"**.

12ZB(4) An NRCGT return must–

(a) contain the information prescribed by HMRC, and

(b) include a declaration by the person making it that the return is to the best of the person's knowledge correct and complete.

12ZB(5) Subsection (1) does not apply to a non-resident CGT disposal to which section 188C of the 1992 Act applies (transfers within NRCGT group).

12ZB(6) For the purposes of subsection (2)(b), the **"relevant members"** of the NRCGT group are–

(a) the companies which are members of that group when the disposal is made, and

(b) any other companies which are, at any time before the time of the disposal in the tax year to which the return relates, members of that group.

12ZB(7) An NRCGT return "relates to" the tax year in which any gains on the non-resident CGT disposal would accrue.

12ZB(8) The **"filing date"** for an NRCGT return is the 30th day following the day of the completion of the disposal to which the return relates. But see also section 12ZJ(5).

History – S. 12ZB inserted by FA 2015, s. 37 and Sch. 7, para. 43, with effect in relation to disposals made on or after 6 April 2015.

12ZBA Elective NRCGT return

12ZBA(1) A person is not required to make and deliver an NRCGT return under section 12ZB(1), but may do so, in circumstances to which this section applies.

12ZBA(2) The circumstances to which this section applies are where the disposal referred to in section 12ZB(1) is–

(a) a disposal on or after 6 April 2015 where, by virtue of any of the no gain/no loss provisions, neither a gain nor a loss accrues, or

(b) the grant of a lease on or after 6 April 2015 which is–

(i) for no premium,

(ii) to a person who is not connected with the grantor, and

(iii) under a bargain made at arm's length.

12ZBA(3) For the purposes of subsection (2)–

"connected" is to be construed in accordance with section 286 of 1992 Act;

"no gain/no loss provisions" has the meaning given by section 288(3A) of the 1992 Act;

"lease" and premium" have the meanings given by paragraph 10 of Schedule 8 to the 1992 Act.

12ZBA(4) The Treasury may by regulations made by statutory instrument add or remove circumstances to which this section applies.

12ZBA(5) Regulations under subsection (4) may–

(a) amend this section or any other enactment;

(b) make consequential provision.

12ZBA(6) A statutory instrument containing regulations under subsection (4) is subject to annulment in pursuance of a resolution of the House of Commons.

12ZBA(7) Paragraph 1 of Schedule 55 to the Finance Act 2009 (penalty for late returns) does not apply in relation to an NRCGT return which is made and delivered by virtue of this section.

History – S. 12ZBA inserted by FA 2016, s. 91, with effect from 15 September 2016 (Royal Assent).

12ZC Single return in respect of two or more non-resident CGT disposals

12ZC Where–

(a) a person is required to make and deliver an NRCGT return with respect to two or more non-resident CGT disposals,

(b) the date of the completion of each of the disposals is the same, and

(c) any gains accruing on the disposals would accrue in the same tax year,

the person is to make and deliver a single return with respect to all those disposals.

History – S. 12ZC inserted by FA 2015, s. 37 and Sch. 7, para. 43, with effect in relation to disposals made on or after 6 April 2015.

12ZD NRCGT returns: grant and exercise of options

12ZD(1) This section applies where–

(a) by virtue of section 144(2) of the 1992 Act, the grant of an option binding the grantor to sell an interest in UK land is, on the exercise of the option, treated as the same transaction as the sale, and

(b) both the grant of the option and the transaction entered into by the grantor in fulfilment of the grantor's obligations under the option ("the sale") would be non-resident CGT disposals (were they not treated as a single transaction).

12ZD(2) On completion of the sale–

(a) the grantor is to be subject to the same obligations under sections 12ZB, 12ZE and 59AA (duties relating to returns and payments on account) in relation to the grant of the option as the grantor would be subject to were the option never to be exercised, and

(b) the consideration for the option is to be disregarded (despite section 144(2) of the 1992 Act) in calculating under section 12ZF the amount of capital gains tax notionally chargeable at the completion date of the single transaction mentioned in subsection (1)(a).

12ZD(3) In this section **"sell"** is to be interpreted in accordance with section 144(6) of the 1992 Act.

History – S. 12ZD inserted by FA 2015, s. 37 and Sch. 7, para. 43, with effect in relation to disposals made on or after 6 April 2015.

12ZE NRCGT return to include advance self-assessment

12ZE(1) An NRCGT return ("the current return") relating to a tax year ("year Y") which a person ("P") is required to make in respect of one or more non-resident CGT disposals ("the current disposals") must include an assessment (an "advance self-assessment") of–

(a) the amount notionally chargeable at the filing date for the current return (see section 12ZF), and

(b) if P has made (or is to make) a prior NRCGT return, the amount of any increase in the amount notionally chargeable for year Y.

But see the exceptions in section 12ZG.

12ZE(2) In a case falling within subsection (1)(b)–

(a) there is an "increase in the amount notionally chargeable" for year Y if the amount notionally chargeable at the filing date for the current return exceeds the corresponding amount for the prior NRCGT return (or the prior NRCGT return which has the most recent filing date, if there is more than one), and

(b) the amount of that increase is the amount of the excess.

12ZE(3) **"Prior NRCGT return"** means an NRCGT return which–

(a) relates to year Y, and

(b) is in respect of a non-resident CGT disposal (or disposals) the completion date of which is earlier than that of the current disposals.

History – S. 12ZE inserted by FA 2015, s. 37 and Sch. 7, para. 43, with effect in relation to disposals made on or after 6 April 2015.

12ZF The "amount notionally chargeable"

12ZF(1) The **"amount notionally chargeable"** at the filing date for an NRCGT return ("the current return") is the amount of capital gains tax to which the person whose return it is ("P") would be chargeable under section 14D or 188D of the 1992 Act for the year to which the return relates ("year Y"), as determined–

(a) on the assumption in subsection (2),

(b) in accordance with subsection (3), and

(c) if P is an individual, on the basis of a reasonable estimate of the matters set out in subsection (4).

12ZF(2) The assumption mentioned in subsection (1)(a) is that in year Y no NRCGT gain or loss accrues to P on any disposal the completion of which occurs after the day of the completion of the disposals to which the return relates ("day X").

12ZF(3) In the determination of the amount notionally chargeable–

(a) all allowable losses accruing to P in year Y on disposals of assets the completion of which occurs on or before day X which are available to be deducted under paragraph (a) or (b) of section 14D(2) or (as the case may be) section 188D(2) of the 1992 Act are to be so deducted, and

(b) any other relief or allowance relating to capital gains tax which is required to be given in P's case is to be taken into account, so far as the relief would be available on the assumption in subsection (2).

12ZF(4) The matters mentioned in subsection (1)(c) are–

(a) whether or not income tax will be chargeable at the higher rate or the dividend upper rate in respect of P's income for year Y (see section 4(4) of the 1992 Act), and

(b) (if P estimates that income tax will not be chargeable as mentioned in paragraph (a)) what P's Step 3 income will be for year Y.

12ZF(5) An advance self-assessment must, in particular, give particulars of any estimate made for the purposes of subsection (1)(c).

12ZF(6) A reasonable estimate included in an NRCGT return in accordance with subsection (5) is not regarded as inaccurate for the purposes of Schedule 24 to the Finance Act 2007 (penalties for errors).

12ZF(7) Where P is the relevant body of an NRCGT group–

(a) the references to P in subsections (2) and (3)(a) are to be read as references to any member of the NRCGT group;

(b) the reference to P in subsection (3)(b) is to be read as including any member of the NRCGT group.

12ZF(8) For the purposes of this section–

an estimate is **"reasonable"** if it is made on a basis that is fair and reasonable, having regard to the circumstances in which it is made;

"Step 3 income", in relation to an individual, has the same meaning as in section 4 of the 1992 Act.

12ZF(9) In this section, references to the **"relevant body"** of an NRCGT group are to be interpreted in accordance with section 188D(4) of the 1992 Act.

12ZF(10) Section 989 of ITA 2007 (the definitions) applies for the purposes of this section as it applies for income tax purposes.

12ZF(11) For the meaning of **"NRCGT gain"** and **"NRCGT loss"** see section 57B of, and Schedule 4ZZB to, the 1992 Act.

History – S. 12ZF inserted by FA 2015, s. 37 and Sch. 7, para. 43, with effect in relation to disposals made on or after 6 April 2015.

12ZG Cases where advance self-assessment not required

12ZG(1) Where a person ("P") is required to make and deliver an NRCGT return relating to a tax year ("year Y"), section 12ZE(1) (requirement to include advance self-assessment in return) does not apply if condition A, B or C is met.

12ZG(2) Condition A is that P (or, if P is the trustees of a settlement, any trustee of the settlement) has been given, on or before the day on which the NRCGT return is required to be delivered, a notice under section 8 or 8A with respect to–

(a) year Y, or

(b) the previous tax year,

and that notice has not been withdrawn.

12ZG(3) Condition B is that P has been given, on or before the day on which the NRCGT return is required to be delivered, a notice under paragraph 3 of Schedule 18 to the Finance Act 1998 (notice requiring delivery of a company tax return) specifying a period which includes the whole or part of–

(a) year Y, or

(b) the previous tax year,

and that notice has not been withdrawn.

12ZG(4) Condition C is that an annual tax on enveloped dwellings return has been delivered by P (or a representative partner acting instead of P) for the preceding chargeable period.

12ZG(5) In subsection (4)–

"the preceding chargeable period" means the chargeable period (as defined in section 94(8) of the Finance Act 2013) which ends with the 31 March preceding year Y;

"representative partner" has the meaning given by section 167(6) of the Finance Act 2013.

12ZG(6) The Treasury may by regulations prescribe further circumstances in which section 12ZE(1) is not to apply.

12ZG(7) Regulations under subsection (6)–

(a) may make different provision for different purposes;

(b) may include incidental, consequential, supplementary or transitional provision.

History – S. 12ZG inserted by FA 2015, s. 37 and Sch. 7, para. 43, with effect in relation to disposals made on or after 6 April 2015.

12ZH NRCGT returns and annual self-assessment: section 8

12ZH(1) This section applies where a person ("P") (other than the relevant trustees of a settlement)–

(a) is not required to give a notice under section 7 with respect to a tax year ("year X"), and

(b) would be required to give such a notice in the absence of section 7A (which removes that duty in certain cases where the person has made an NRCGT return that includes an advance self-assessment).

12ZH(2) In this section, **"the relevant NRCGT return"** means–

(a) the NRCGT return by virtue of which P is not required to give a notice under section 7 with respect to year X, or

(b) if more than one NRCGT return falls within paragraph (a), the one relating to the disposal which has the latest completion date.

12ZH(3) P is treated for the purposes of the Taxes Acts as having been required to make and deliver to an officer of Revenue and Customs a return under section 8 for the purpose of establishing, with respect to year X, the matters mentioned in section 8(1).

12ZH(4) For the purposes of subsection (3), section 8 is to be read as if subsections (1E) to (1G) of that section were omitted.

12ZH(5) If P does not give a notice under subsection (6) before 31 January in the tax year after year X, the Taxes Acts have effect, from that date, as if the advance self-assessment contained in the relevant NRCGT return were a self-assessment included, for the purposes set out in section 9(1), in a return under section 8 made by P and delivered on that date.

12ZH(6) If P gives HMRC a notice under this subsection specifying an NRCGT return which–

(a) relates to year X, and

(b) contains an advance self-assessment,

the Taxes Acts are to have effect, from the effective date of the notice, as if that advance self-assessment were a self-assessment included, for the purposes set out in section 9(1), in a return under section 8 made by P and delivered on that date.

12ZH(7) References in the Taxes Acts to a return under section 8 (for example, references to amending, or enquiring into, a return under that section) are to be read in accordance with subsections (5) and (6).

12ZH(8) A notice under subsection (6)–

(a) must be given before 31 January in the tax year after year X;

(b) must state that P considers the advance self-assessment in question to be an accurate self-assessment in respect of year X for the purposes of section 9.

12ZH(9) The **"effective date"** of a notice under subsection (6) is–

(a) the day on which the NRCGT return specified in the notice is delivered, or

(b) if later, the day on which the notice is given.

12ZH(10) The self-assessment which subsection (5) or (6) treats as having been made by P is referred to in this section as the "section 9 self-assessment".

12ZH(11) If P–

(a) gives a notice under subsection (6), and

(b) makes and delivers a subsequent NRCGT return relating to year X which contains an advance self-assessment,

that advance self-assessment is to be treated as amending the section 9 self-assessment.

12ZH(12) For the purposes of subsection (11), an NRCGT return made and delivered by P ("return B") is "subsequent" to an NRCGT return to which P's notice under subsection (6) relates ("the notified return") if the day of the completion of the disposal to which return B relates is later than the day of the completion of the disposal to which the notified return relates.

History – S. 12ZH inserted by FA 2015, s. 37 and Sch. 7, para. 43, with effect in relation to disposals made on or after 6 April 2015.

12ZI NRCGT returns and annual self-assessment: section 8A

12ZI(1) This section applies where the relevant trustees of a settlement ("the trustees")–

(a) are not required to give a notice under section 7 with respect to a tax year ("year X"), and

(b) would be required to give such a notice in the absence of section 7A (which removes that duty in certain cases where the person has made an NRCGT return including an advance self-assessment).

12ZI(2) In this section, **"the relevant NRCGT return"** means–

(a) the NRCGT return by virtue of which P is not required to give a notice under section 7 with respect to year X, or

(b) if more than one NRCGT return falls within paragraph (a), the one relating to the disposal which has the latest completion date.

12ZI(3) The trustees are treated for the purposes of the Taxes Acts as having been required to make and deliver to an officer of Revenue and Customs a return under section 8A, for the purpose of establishing, with respect to year X, the matters mentioned in section 8A(1).

12ZI(4) For the purposes of subsection (3), section 8A is to be read as if–

(a) in subsection (1) of that section, ", and the settlors and beneficiaries," were omitted, and

(b) subsections (1C) to (1E) of that section were omitted.

12ZI(5) If the trustees do not give a notice under subsection (6) before 31 January in the tax year after year X, the Taxes Acts have effect, from that date, as if the advance self-assessment contained in the relevant NRCGT return were a self-assessment included, for the purposes set out in section 9(1), in a return under section 8A made by the trustees and delivered on that date.

12ZI(6) If the trustees give HMRC a notice under this subsection specifying an NRCGT return which–

(a) relates to year X, and

(b) contains an advance self-assessment,

the Taxes Acts are to have effect, from the effective date of the notice, as if that advance self-assessment were a self-assessment included, for the purposes set out in section 9(1), in a return under section 8A made by the trustees and delivered on that date.

12ZI(7) References in the Taxes Acts to a return under section 8A (for example, references to amending, or enquiring into, a return under that section) are to be read in accordance with subsections (5) and (6).

12ZI(8) A notice under subsection (6)–

(a) must be given before 31 January in the tax year after year X;

(b) must state that the trustees consider the advance self-assessment in question to be an accurate self-assessment in respect of year X for the purposes of section 9.

12ZI(9) The **"effective date"** of a notice under subsection (6) is–

(a) the day on which the NRCGT return specified in the notice is delivered, or

(b) if later, the day on which the notice is given.

12ZI(10) The self-assessment which subsection (5) or (6) treats as having been made by the trustees is referred to in this section as the **"section 9 self-assessment"**.

12ZI(11) If the trustees–

(a) give a notice under subsection (6), and

(b) make and deliver a subsequent NRCGT return relating to year X which contains an advance self-assessment,

that advance self-assessment is to be treated as amending the section 9 self-assessment.

12ZI(12) For the purposes of subsection (11), an NRCGT return made and delivered by the trustees ("return B") is "subsequent" to an NRCGT return to which the trustees' notice under subsection (6) relates ("the notified return") if the day of the completion of the disposal to which return B relates is later than the day of the completion of the disposal to which the notified return relates.

History – S. 12ZI inserted by FA 2015, s. 37 and Sch. 7, para. 43, with effect in relation to disposals made on or after 6 April 2015.

12ZJ Sections 12ZA to 12ZI: determination of residence status

12ZJ(1) For the purposes of sections 12ZA to 12ZI, the question whether or not a disposal of a UK residential property interest is a non-resident CGT disposal is to be determined in accordance with subsections (2) and (3).

12ZJ(2) A non-residence condition is to be taken to be met in relation to a disposal of a UK residential property interest if, at the time of the completion of the disposal–

(a) it is uncertain whether or not that condition will be met, but

(b) it is reasonable to expect that that condition will be met.

12ZJ(3) If (in a case within subsection (2)) it later becomes certain that neither of the non-residence conditions is met in relation to the disposal, the disposal is treated as not being, and as never having been, a non-resident CGT disposal (and any necessary repayments or adjustments are to be made accordingly).

12ZJ(4) Subsection (5) applies if–

(a) at the time of the completion of the disposal of a UK residential property interest it is uncertain whether or not the disposal is a non-resident CGT disposal because it is uncertain whether or not a non-residence condition will be met, but the case does not fall within subsection (2), and

(b) it later becomes certain that a non-residence condition is met in relation to the disposal.

12ZJ(5) For the purposes of this Act, the filing date for the NRCGT return is taken to be the 30th day following the day on which it becomes certain that a non-residence condition is met in relation to the disposal.

12ZJ(6) In this section **"a non-residence condition"** means condition A or B in section 14B of the 1992 Act.

History – S. 12ZJ inserted by FA 2015, s. 37 and Sch. 7, para. 43, with effect in relation to disposals made on or after 6 April 2015.

12ZK Amendment of NRCGT return by the taxpayer

12ZK(1) A person may, by notice to an officer of Revenue and Customs, amend the person's NRCGT return.

12ZK(2) An amendment may not be made more than 12 months after 31 January of the year following the relevant tax year.

12ZK(3) In subsection (2) **"the relevant tax year"** means the tax year in which any gains on the disposal to which the return relates would accrue.

History – S. 12ZK inserted by FA 2015, s. 37 and Sch. 7, para. 43, with effect in relation to disposals made on or after 6 April 2015.

12ZL Correction of NRCGT return by HMRC

12ZL(1) An officer of Revenue and Customs may amend an NRCGT return so as to correct–

(a) obvious errors or omissions in the return (whether errors of principle, arithmetical mistakes or otherwise), and

(b) anything else in the return that the officer has reason to believe is incorrect in the light of information available to the officer.

12ZL(2) A correction under this section is made by notice to the person whose return it is.

12ZL(3) No such correction may be made more than 9 months after–

(a) the day on which the return was delivered, or

(b) if the correction is required in consequence of an amendment of the return under section 12ZK (amendment by the taxpayer), the day on which that amendment was made.

12ZL(4) A correction under this section is of no effect if the person to whom the notice of correction was given gives notice rejecting the correction.

12ZL(5) Notice of rejection under subsection (4) must be given–

(a) to the officer of Revenue and Customs by whom the notice of correction was given,

(b) before the end of the period of 30 days beginning with the date of issue of the notice of correction.

History – S. 12ZL inserted by FA 2015, s. 37 and Sch. 7, para. 43, with effect in relation to disposals made on or after 6 April 2015.

12ZM Notice of enquiry

12ZM(1) An officer of Revenue and Customs may enquire into an NRCGT return if the officer gives notice of the intention to do so ("notice of enquiry")–

(a) to the person whose return it is,

(b) within the time allowed.

12ZM(2) The time allowed is–

(a) if the return was delivered on or before 31 January in the year following the relevant tax year (the "annual filing date"), up to the end of the period of 12 months after the day on which the return was delivered;

(b) if the return was delivered after the annual filing date, up to and including the quarter day next following the first anniversary of the day on which the return was delivered;

(c) if the return is amended under section 12ZL (correction by HMRC), up to and including the quarter day next following the first anniversary of the day on which the amendment was made.

For this purpose the quarter days are 31 January, 30 April, 31 July and 31 October.

12ZM(3) An enquiry extends to anything contained in the return, or required to be contained in the return, including any claim or election included in the return, subject to the following limitation.

12ZM(4) If the notice of enquiry is given as a result of an amendment of the return under section 12ZK (amendment by taxpayer)–

(a) at a time when it is no longer possible to give notice of enquiry under subsection (2)(a) or (b), or

(b) after an enquiry into the return has been completed,

the enquiry into the return is limited to matters to which the amendment relates or which are affected by the amendment.

12ZM(5) In subsection (2) **"the relevant tax year"** means the tax year in which any gain on the disposal to which the return relates would accrue.

History – S. 12ZM inserted by FA 2015, s. 37 and Sch. 7, para. 43, with effect in relation to disposals made on or after 6 April 2015.

12ZN Amendment of return by taxpayer during enquiry

12ZN(1) This section applies if an NRCGT return is amended under section 12ZK (amendment by taxpayer) at a time when an enquiry is in progress into the return.

12ZN(2) The amendment does not restrict the scope of the enquiry but may be taken into account (together with any matters arising) in the enquiry.

12ZN(3) So far as the amendment affects the amount notionally chargeable for the purposes of the return (see section 12ZF(1)), it does not take effect while the enquiry is in progress and–

(a) if the officer states in the closure notice that the officer has taken the amendment into account and that–

(i) the amendment has been taken into account in formulating the amendments contained in the notice, or

(ii) the officer's conclusion is that the amendment is incorrect,

the amendment is not to take effect;

(b) otherwise, the amendment takes effect when the closure notice is issued.

12ZN(4) For the purposes of this section the period during which an enquiry is in progress is the whole of the period–

(a) beginning with the day on which the notice of enquiry is given, and

(b) ending with the day on which the enquiry is completed.

History – S. 12ZN inserted by FA 2015, s. 37 and Sch. 7, para. 43, with effect in relation to disposals made on or after 6 April 2015.

PARTNERSHIPS

12AA Partnership return

12AA(1) Where a trade, profession or business is carried on by two or more persons in partnership, for the purpose of facilitating the establishment of the following amounts, namely–

(a) the amount in which each partner chargeable to income tax for any year of assessment is so chargeable and the amount payable by way of income tax by each such partner, and

(b) the amount in which each partner chargeable to corporation tax for any period is so chargeable,

an officer of the Board may act under subsection (2) or (3) below (or both).

12AA(1A) For the purposes of subsection (1) above–

(a) the amount in which a partner is chargeable to income tax or corporation tax is a net amount, that is to say, an amount which takes into account any relief or allowance for which a claim is made; and

(b) the amount payable by a partner by way of income tax is the difference between the amount in which he is chargeable to income tax and the aggregate amount of any income tax deducted at source.

12AA(2) An officer of the Board may by a notice given to the partners require such person as is identified in accordance with rules given with the notice or a successor of his–

(a) to make and deliver to the officer in respect of such period as may be specified in the notice, on or before such day as may be so specified, a return containing such information as may reasonably be required in pursuance of the notice, and

(b) to deliver with the return such accounts, statements and documents, relating to information contained in the return, as may reasonably be so required.

12AA(3) An officer of the Board may by notice given to any partner require the partner or a successor of his–

(a) to make and deliver to the officer in respect of such period as may be specified in the notice, on or before such day as may be so specified, a return containing such information as may reasonably be required in pursuance of the notice, and

(b) to deliver with the return such accounts and statements as may reasonably be so required;

and a notice may be given to any one partner or separate notices may be given to each partner or to such partners as the officer thinks fit.

12AA(4) In the case of a partnership which includes one or more individuals, a notice under subsection (2) or (3) above may specify different days depending on whether a return in respect of a year of assessment (Year 1) is electronic or non-electronic.

12AA(4A) The day specified for a non-electronic return must not be earlier than 31st October of Year 2.

12AA(4B) The day specified for an electronic return must not be earlier than 31st January of Year 2.

12AA(4C) But subsections (4A) and (4B) are subject to the following two exceptions.

12AA(4D) Exception 1 is that if the notice is given after 31st July in Year 2 (but on or before 31st October)–

(a) the day specified for a non-electronic return must be after the end of the period of three months beginning with the date of the notice, and

(b) the day specified for an electronic return must not be earlier than 31st January.

12AA(4E) Exception 2 is that if the notice is given after 31st October in Year 2, the day specified for a return (whether or not electronic) must be after the end of the period of three months beginning with the date of the notice.

12AA(5) In the case of a partnership which includes one or more companies, a notice may specify different dates depending on whether a notice in respect of a relevant period is electronic or non-electronic.

12AA(5A) The day specified for a non-electronic return must not be earlier than the end of the period of nine months beginning at the end of the relevant period.

12AA(5B) The day specified for an electronic return must not be earlier than the first anniversary of the end of the relevant period.

12AA(5C) But where the notice is given more than nine months after the end of the relevant period, the day specified for a return (whether or not electronic) must be after the end of the period of three months beginning with the date of the notice.

12AA(5D) For the purposes of this section **"relevant period"** means the period in respect of which the return is required.

12AA(5E) The Commissioners–

(a) shall prescribe what constitutes an electronic return for the purposes of this section, and

(b) may make different provision for different cases or circumstances.

12AA(6) Every return under this section shall include–

(a) a declaration of the name, residence and tax reference of each of the persons who have been partners–

(i) for the whole of the relevant period, or

(ii) for any part of that period,

and, in the case of a person falling within sub-paragraph (ii) above, of the part concerned; and

(b) a declaration by the person making the return to the effect that it is to the best of his knowledge correct and complete.

12AA(7) Every return under this section shall also include, if the notice under subsection (2) or (3) above so requires–

(a) with respect to any disposal of partnership property during a period to which the return relates, the like particulars as if the partnership were liable to tax on any chargeable gain accruing on the disposal, and

(b) [omitted by SI 2009/2035, art. 2 and Schedule, para. 3.]

12AA(8) A notice under this section may require different information, accounts and statements for different periods or in relation to different descriptions of source of income.

12AA(9) Notices under this section may require different information, accounts and statements in relation to different descriptions of partnership.

12AA(10) In this section **"residence"**, in relation to a company, means its registered office.

12AA(10A) In this Act a **"partnership return"** means a return in pursuance of a notice under subsection (2) or (3) above.

12AA(11) In this Act **"successor"**, in relation to a person who is required to make and deliver, or has made and delivered, a partnership return , but is no longer available, means–

(a) where a partner is for the time being nominated for the purposes of this subsection by a majority of the relevant partners, that partner; and

(b) where no partner is for the time being so nominated, such partner as–

(i) in the case of a notice under subsection (2) above, is identified in accordance with rules given with that notice; or

(ii) in the case of a notice under subsection (3) above, is nominated for the purposes of this subsection by an officer of the Board;

and **"predecessor"** and **"successor"**, in relation to a person so nominated or identified, shall be construed accordingly.

12AA(12) For the purposes of subsection (11) above a nomination under paragraph (a) of that subsection, and a revocation of such a nomination, shall not have effect in relation to any time before notice of the nomination or revocation is given to an officer of the Board.

12AA(13) In this section **"relevant partner"** means a person who was a partner at any time during the period for which the return was made or is required, or the personal representatives of such a person.

History – In s. 12AA(1A)(b), the words "and any tax credits to which section 397(1) or 397A(1) of ITTOIA 2005 applies" (which appeared after the word "source") omitted by FA 2016, s. 5 and Sch. 1 para. 51(5), with effect for the tax year 2016–17 and subsequent tax years.

In s. 12AA(1A)(b), "397A(1)" substituted for "397A(2)" by FA 2009, s. 40 and Sch. 19, para. 9(c), with effect for:

- qualifying distributions arising on or after 22 April 2009;
- cash dividends paid over to a person under ITEPA 2003, Sch. 2, para. 68(4) on or after 22 April 2009;
- dividends treated under ITTOIA 2005, s. 407 as paid to a person on or after 22 April 2009; and
- manufactured overseas dividends that are representative of any of the above distributions (FA 2009, Sch. 19, para. 14(1)).

In s. 12AA(1A)(b), the reference to ITTOIA 2005, s. 397A(2) inserted by FA 2008, s. 34 and Sch. 12, para. 11, with effect for 2008–09 and subsequent tax years.

In s. 12AA(1A)(b) the reference to ITTOIA 2005 substituted by ITTOIA 2005, s. 882(1) and Sch. 1, para. 363; effective for 2005–06 onwards (ITTOIA 2005, s. 883(1)).

S. 12AA(4)–(4E) substituted for s. 12AA(4) by FA 2007, s. 90(1), with effect in respect of a return for a year of assessment beginning on or after 6 April 2007.

S. 12AA(5)–(5E) substituted for s. 12AA(5) by FA 2007, s. 90(2), with effect in respect of a return for a period in respect of which a return is required (a "relevant period") beginning on or after 6 April 2007.

S. 12AA(7)(b) omitted by SI 2009/2035, art. 2 and Schedule, para. 3, with effect from 13 August 2009.

In former s. 12AA(7)(b), reference to FA 1998, Sch. 18, para. 13 inserted by FA 1998, s. 117(3) and Sch. 19 para. 3, with effect in relation to accounting periods ending on or after 1 July 1999, the self-assessment appointed day (see note above).

S. 12AA(10A) inserted by FA 2001, s. 88 and Sch. 29, para. 18, with effect from 11 May 2001 in relation to returns–

(a) whether made before or after 11 May 2001, and

(b) whether relating to periods before or after 11 May 2001.

S. 12AA(11) amended by FA 2001, s. 88 and Sch. 29, para. 18, substituting the words "a partnership return" for the previous words with effect from 11 May 2001 in relation to returns–

(a) whether made before or after 11 May 2001, and

(b) whether relating to periods before or after 11 May 2001.

S. 12AA inserted by FA 1994, s. 184 and amended by FA 1995, s. 104(6), 115(4), and by FA 1996, s. 121(6), (7) , 123 and 205 and Sch. 41, Pt. V(6), in so far as it relates to income tax and capital gains tax, as respects the year 1996–97 and subsequent years of assessment and, in so far as it relates to corporation tax, as respects accounting periods ending on or after 1 July 1999, the self-assessment appointed day by virtue of FA 1994, s. 199(2) and SI 1998/3173 (C. 78).

Cross references – S. 12AB: a return under s. 12 includes a partnership statement.

S. 93A: penalties for failure to deliver return.

S. 95: penalties for incorrect return.

ICTA 1988, s. 62A(3): time limit for giving notice of a change in basis period.

CAA 2001, s. 201: references to return in relation to elections under CAA 2001, s. 198 and s. 199 by persons in partnership mean a return under s. 12AA.

FA 2009, Sch. 55: penalties for failure to make returns under s. 12AA(2)(a) or (3A) or provide accounts, statements or documents under s. 12AA(2)(b) or (3)(b) (subject to commencement order).

SI 2003/282: regulations governing electronic delivery of information to or by the Board under this section .

Statements of practice – SP 1/97: the electronic lodgment service.

Other material – Taxline 1997/43 (not reproduced): HMRC confirmation that there is no formal procedure to follow in the appointment of a successor to a partner nominated to handle the partnership's tax affairs.

12AAA Withdrawal by HMRC of notice under section 12AA

12AAA(1) This section applies to a partner who is required by a notice under section 12AA to deliver a return.

12AAA(2) Before the end of the withdrawal period, the partner may request HMRC to withdraw the notice.

12AAA(3) But no request may be made if the partner has delivered a return under section 12AA in pursuance of the notice.

12AAA(4) If, on receiving a request, HMRC decide to withdraw the notice under section 12AA they must do so by giving the partner a notice under this section.

12AAA(5) A notice under this section must specify the date on which the notice under section 12AA is withdrawn.

12AAA(6) For the purposes of subsection (2) **"the withdrawal period"** means–

(a) in the case of a partnership which includes one or more companies, the period of 2 years beginning with the end of the period in respect of which the return under section 12AA was required by the notice under that section,

(b) in the case of any other partnership, the period of 2 years beginning with the end of the year of assessment to which the notice under section 12AA relates, or

(c) *in the case of any partnership,* such extended period as HMRC may agree with the partner in exceptional circumstances.

12AAA(7) Withdrawal of a notice under section 12AA in relation to the period in respect of which the return under that section was required or year of assessment (as the case may be) does not prevent HMRC from serving a further notice under section 12AA requiring a partner to deliver a return in relation to that period or year.

12AAA(8) References in subsections (2) to (6) to the partner include references to a successor of the partner (see section 12AA(11)).

12AAA(9) See paragraph 17B of Schedule 55 to FA 2009 as to the cancellation of liability to a penalty under any paragraph of that Schedule by including provision in a notice under this section.

History – S. 12AAA inserted by FA 2013, s. 233 and Sch. 51, para. 4, with effect in relation to a return under TMA 1970, s. 12AA for a partnership which includes one or more companies, in respect of a return for a relevant period (a period in respect of which a return is required) beginning on or after 6 April 2012 and in relation to a return under that section for any other partnership, or a return under TMA 1970, s. 8 or 8A, in respect of a return for a year of assessment beginning on or after 6 April 2012.

12AB Partnership return to include partnership statement

12AB(1) Every partnership return shall include a statement (a partnership statement) of the following amounts, namely–

(a) in the case of the period in respect of which the return is made and each period of account ending within that period–

(i) the amount of income or loss from each source which, on the basis of the information contained in the return and taking into account any relief or allowance a section 42(7) claim for which is included in the return, has accrued to or has been sustained by the partnership for the period in question,

(ia) the amount of the consideration which, on that basis, has accrued to the partnership in respect of each disposal of partnership property during that period, and

(ii) each amount of income tax which, on that basis, has been deducted or treated as deducted from any income of the partnership, or treated as paid on any such income, for that period,

(iii) [omitted by FA 2016, s. 5 and Sch. 1 para. 51(6)(a)]

(iv) [omitted by ITA 2007, s. 1027 and Sch. 1, para. 245(2)(b) and repealed by s. 1031 and Sch. 3, Pt. 1.]

(b) in the case of each such period as is mentioned in paragraph (a) above and each of the partners, the amount which, on that basis and (where applicable) taking into account any such relief or allowance, is equal to his share of that income, loss, consideration or tax.

12AB(2) [Omitted by FA 2001, s. 88 and Sch. 29, para. 3.]

12AB(3) [Omitted by FA 2001, s. 88 and Sch. 29, para. 3.]

12AB(4) [Omitted by FA 2001, s. 88 and Sch. 29, para. 3.]

12AB(5) In this section–

"section 42(7) claim" means a claim under any of the provisions mentioned in section 42(7) of this Act;

History – S. 12AB(1)(a)(iii) (and the word "and" preceding it) omitted and the word "and" at the end of sub-para. (ia) inserted by FA 2016, s. 5 and Sch. 1 para. 51(6)(a), with effect in relation to dividends paid or arising (or treated as paid), and other distributions made (or treated as made) in the tax year 2016–17 or at any later time. Former s. 12AB(1)(a)(iii) read as follows:

"(iii) the amount of each tax credit which, on that basis, has accrued to the partnership for that period,".

In s. 12AB(1)(b), the words "or tax" substituted for the words ", tax or credit" by FA 2016, s. 5 and Sch. 1 para. 51(6)(b), with effect in relation to dividends paid or arising (or treated as paid), and other distributions made (or treated as made) in the tax year 2016–17 or at any later time.

In s. 12AB(1) the words "partnership return" substituted by FA 2001, s. 88 and Sch. 29, para. 19 with effect from 11 May 2001.

In s. 12AB(1)(a) the word "and" inserted in sub-paragraph (ii) and deleted from sub-paragraph (iii) by ITA 2007, Sch. 1, para. 245(2)(a) and (b) and s. 12AB(1)(a)(iv) omitted by ITA 2007, s. 1027 and Sch. 1, para. 245(2)(b), and repealed by s. 1031 and Sch. 3, Pt. 1 and in s. 12AB(1)(b), the words "tax or credit" substituted for the words "tax, credit or charge" by ITA 2007, s. 1027 and Sch. 1, para. 245(3), all with effect from 6 April 2007.

S. 12AB(2)–(4) omitted by FA 2001, s. 88 and Sch. 29, para. 3 with effect from 11 May 2001.

In s. 12AB(5), the definition of "tax credit" omitted by FA 2016, s. 5 and Sch. 1 para. 51(6)(c), with effect in relation to dividends paid or arising (or treated as paid), and other distributions made (or treated as made) in the tax year 2016–17 or at any later time. The omitted definition read as follows:

""**tax credit**" means a tax credit to which section 1109 of CTA 2010 applies in the case of corporation tax and section 397(1) or 397A(1) of ITTOIA 2005.".

In s. 12AB(5), the words "section 1109 of CTA 2010" substituted for the words "section 231 of the principal Act" by CTA 2010, s. 1177 and Sch. 1, para. 153, with effect for corporation tax purposes for accounting periods ending on or after 1 April 2010, and for income tax and capital gains tax purposes for the tax year 2010–11 and subsequent tax years.

In s. 12AB(5), "397A(1)" substituted for "397A(2)" by FA 2009, s. 40 and Sch. 19, para. 9(c), with effect for:

- qualifying distributions arising on or after 22 April 2009;
- cash dividends paid over to a person under ITEPA 2003, Sch. 2, para. 68(4) on or after 22 April 2009;
- dividends treated under ITTOIA 2005, s. 407 as paid to a person on or after 22 April 2009; and
- manufactured overseas dividends that are representative of any of the above distributions (FA 2009, Sch. 19, para. 14(1)).

In s. 12AB(5), the reference to ITTOIA 2005, s. 397A(2) inserted by FA 2008, s. 34 and Sch. 12, para. 12 with effect for 2008–09 and subsequent tax years.

In s. 12AB(5), the words "in the case of corporation tax and section 397(1) of ITTOIA 2005 applies in the case of income tax" inserted by ITTOIA 2005, s. 882(1) and Sch. 1, para. 364; effective for income tax purposes for 2005–06 onwards and for corporation tax purposes for accounting periods ending after 5 April 2005 (ITTOIA 2005, s. 883(1)).

S. 12AB inserted by FA 1994 s. 185, and amended by FA 1995, s. 104(7), (8), and by FA 1996, s. 123(5), (6), in so far as it relates to income tax and capital gains tax, as respects the year 1996–97 and subsequent years of assessment and, in so far as it relates to corporation tax, as respects accounting periods ending on or after 1 July 1999, the appointed day (FA 1994, s. 199(2), (3)).

Cross references – FA 1998, Sch. 18 para. 12(2): a "relevant partnership statement" means a statement returned under s. 12AB.
SI 2003/282: regulations governing electronic delivery of information to or by the Board under this section.

12ABA Amendment of partnership return by taxpayer

12ABA(1) A partnership return may be amended by the partner who made and delivered the return, or his successor, by notice to an officer of the Board.

12ABA(2) An amendment may not be made more than twelve months after the filing date.

12ABA(3) Where a partnership return is amended under this section, the officer shall by notice to each of the partners amend–

(a) the partner's return under section 8 or 8A of this Act, or

(b) the partner's company tax return,

so as to give effect to the amendment of the partnership return.

12ABA(4) In this section **"the filing date"** means–

(a) in the case of a partnership which includes one or more individuals, in respect of a return for a year of assessment (Year 1)–

  (i) 31st January of Year 2, or

  (ii) if the notice under section 12AA is given after 31st October of Year 2, the last day of the period of three months beginning with the date of the notice, and

(b) in the case of a partnership which includes one or more companies, the end of the period specified in section 12AA(5B) or (5C).

History – S. 12ABA(4) substituted by FA 2007, s. 91(4), with effect in respect of a return for a year of assessment beginning on or after 6 April 2007 (for a partnership which includes one or more individuals) and in respect of a return for a period in respect of which a return is required (a "relevant period") beginning on or after 6 April 2007 (for a partnership which includes one or more companies).
S. 12ABA inserted by FA 2001, s. 88 and Sch. 29, para. 3 with effect from 11 May 2001.

Cross references – TCA 2002, s. 20(2)(d): revisions of decisions on working tax credit and child tax credit following amendment of a partnership return.

HMRC interpretations – IRInt. 186: amending a self assessment return under what is now s. 12ABA does not preclude penalty action by Revenue if taxpayer has acted negligently or fraudulently in original submission of return.

12ABB Correction of partnership return by Revenue

12ABB(1) An officer of the Board may amend a partnership return so as to correct–

(a) obvious errors or omissions in the return (whether errors of principle, arithmetical mistakes or otherwise), and

(b) anything else in the return that the officer has reason to believe is incorrect in the light of information available to the officer.

12ABB(2) A correction under this section is made by notice to the partner who made and delivered the return, or his successor.

12ABB(3) No such correction may be made more than nine months after–

(a) the day on which the return was delivered, or

(b) if the correction is required in consequence of an amendment of the return under section 12ABA of this Act, the day on which that amendment was made.

12ABB(4) A correction under this section is of no effect if the person to whom the notice of correction was given, or his successor, gives notice rejecting the correction.

12ABB(5) Notice of rejection under subsection (4) above must be given–

(a) to the officer of the Board by whom the notice of correction was given,

(b) before the end of the period of 30 days beginning with the date of issue of the notice of correction.

12ABB(6) Where a partnership return is corrected under this section, the officer shall by notice to each of the partners amend–

(a) the partner's return under section 8 or 8A of this Act, or

(b) the partner's company tax return,

so as to give effect to the correction of the partnership return.

Any such amendment shall cease to have effect if the correction is rejected.

History – S. 12ABB(1)(b) and the ", and" before it inserted (and s. 12ABB(1)(a) created from existing wording) by FA 2008, s. 119(2) with effect from 1 April 2010 (SI 2009/405).
S. 12ABB inserted by FA 2001, s. 88 and Sch. 29, para. 3 with effect from 11 May 2001.

Cross references – TCA 2002, s. 20(2)(e): revisions of decisions on working tax credit and child tax credit following amendment of a return under this section.

12AC Notice of enquiry

12AC(1) An officer of the Board may enquire into a partnership return if he gives notice of his intention to do so (**"notice of enquiry"**)–

(a) to the partner who made and delivered the return, or his successor,

(b) within the time allowed.

12AC(2) The time allowed is–

(a) if the return was delivered on or before the filing date, up to the end of the period of twelve months after the day on which the return was delivered;

(b) if the return was delivered after the filing date, up to and including the quarter day next following the first anniversary of the day on which the return was delivered;

(c) if the return is amended under section 12ABA of this Act, up to and including the quarter day next following the first anniversary of the day on which the amendment was made.

For this purpose the quarter days are 31st January, 30th April, 31st July and 31st October.

12AC(3) A return which has been the subject of one notice of enquiry may not be the subject of another, except one given in consequence of an amendment (or another amendment) of the return under section 12ABA of this Act.

12AC(4) An enquiry extends to anything contained in the return, or required to be contained in the return, including any claim or election included in the return, subject to the following limitation.

12AC(5) If the notice of enquiry is given as a result of an amendment of the return under section 12ABA of this Act–

(a) at a time when it is no longer possible to give notice of enquiry under subsection (2)(a) or (b) above, or

(b) after an enquiry into the return has been completed,

the enquiry into the return is limited to matters to which the amendment relates or which are affected by the amendment.

12AC(6) The giving of notice of enquiry under subsection (1) above at any time shall be deemed to include the giving of notice of enquiry–

(a) under section 9A(1) of this Act to each partner who at that time has made a return under section 8 or 8A of this Act or at any subsequent time makes such a return, or

(b) under paragraph 24 of Schedule 18 to the Finance Act 1998 to each partner who at that time has made a company tax return or at any subsequent time makes such a return.

12AC(7) In this section **"the filing date"** means the day specified in the notice under section 12AA(2) of this Act or, as the case may be, subsection (3) of that section.

History – In s. 12AC(2)(a), the words "after the day on which the return was delivered" substituted by FA 2007, s. 96(2) and applicable to returns which relate to the tax year 2007–08 or a later tax year.

Former s. 12AC(3) substituted by FA 1998, s. 117(3) and Sch. 19, para. 5 with effect in relation to accounting periods ending on or after 1 July 1999, the self-assessment appointed day by virtue of SI 1998/3173 (FA 1998, s. 117(4), (5) and FA 1994, s. 199(2)).

S. 12AC substituted (together with s. 12AD and 12AE) for former s. 12AC by FA 2001, s. 88 and Sch. 29, para. 5, with effect from 11 May 2001.

Cross references – SI 2003/282: regulations governing electronic delivery of information to or by the Board under this section.

Statements of practice – SP 1/99: where enquiries remain open after expiry of period within which notice of enquiry may be issued solely because of an unagreed capital gains tax valuation, Revenue will not normally raise further enquiries into matters unrelated to the valuation or the CGT computation unless the circumstances are such that, had the enquiry already been completed, the Revenue could have made a section 29 discovery.

HMRC Manuals – Enquiry Manual EM1551: instructions on opening enquiries.

12AD Amendment of partnership return by taxpayer during enquiry

12AD(1) This section applies if a partnership return is amended under section 12ABA of this Act (amendment of partnership return by taxpayer) at a time when an enquiry is in progress into the return.

12AD(2) The amendment does not restrict the scope of the enquiry but may be taken into account (together with any matters arising) in the enquiry.

12AD(3) So far as the amendment affects any amount stated in the partnership statement included in the return, it does not take effect while the enquiry is in progress and–

(a) if the officer states in the closure notice that he has taken the amendment into account and that–

(i) the amendment has been taken into account in formulating the amendments contained in the notice, or

(ii) his conclusion is that the amendment is incorrect,

the amendment shall not take effect;

(b) otherwise, the amendment takes effect when the closure notice is issued.

12AD(4) Where the effect of an amendment is deferred under subsection (3) above–

(a) no amendment to give effect to that amendment (**"the deferred amendment"**) shall be made under section 12ABA(3) of this Act (consequential amendment of partners' returns) while the enquiry is in progress;

(b) if the deferred amendment does not take effect but is taken into account as mentioned in subsection (3)(a)(i) above, section 28B(4) of this Act (amendment of partners' returns consequential on amendment of partnership return by closure notice) applies accordingly; and

(c) if the deferred amendment takes effect under subsection (3)(b) above, any necessary amendment under section 12ABA(3) of this Act may then be made.

12AD(5) For the purposes of this section the period during which an enquiry is in progress is the whole of the period–

(a) beginning with the day on which notice of enquiry is given, and

(b) ending with the day on which the enquiry is completed.

History – S. 12AD substituted (together with s. 12AC and s. 12AE) for former s. 12AC by FA 2001, s. 88 and Sch. 29, para. 5 with effect from 11 May 2001.

Cross references – SI 2003/282: regulations governing electronic delivery of information to or by the Board under this section.

12ADA AIFM firms

12ADA(1) An officer of Revenue and Customs may by notice require a partnership which has made an election under section 863H of ITTOIA 2005 (whether or not the election has been revoked) to provide the officer with such information as the officer may reasonably require for purposes connected with the operation of sections 863H to 863K of ITTOIA 2005.

12ADA(2) The information must be provided within such reasonable time as the officer may specify in the notice.

History – S. 12ADA inserted by FA 2014, s. 74 and Sch. 17, para. 16(2), with effect for the tax year 2014–15 and subsequent tax years.

12AE Choice between different Cases of Schedule D

12AE [Omitted by CTA 2009, s. 1322 and Sch. 1, para. 297 and repealed by CTA 2009, s. 1326 and Sch. 3, Pt. 1.]

History – S. 12AE omitted by CTA 2009, s. 1322 and Sch. 1, para. 297 and repealed by CTA 2009, s. 1326 and Sch. 3, Pt. 1, with effect for corporation tax purposes for accounting periods ending on or after 1 April 2009, and for income tax and capital gains tax purposes for the tax year 2009–10 and subsequent tax years.

12A European Economic Interest Groupings

12A(1) In this section **"grouping"** means a European Economic Interest Grouping formed in pursuance of Council Regulation (EEC) No. 2137/85 of 25th July 1985 (**"the Council Regulation"**), whether registered in Great Britain, in Northern Ireland, or elsewhere.

12A(2) For the purposes of securing that members of a grouping are assessed to income tax and capital gains tax or (as the case may be) corporation tax, an inspector may act under subsection (3) or (4) below.

12A(3) In the case of a grouping which is registered in Great Britain or Northern Ireland or has an establishment registered in Great Britain or Northern Ireland, an inspector may by a notice given to the grouping require the grouping–

(a) to make and deliver to the inspector within the time limited by the notice a return containing such information as may be required in pursuance of the notice, and

(b) to deliver with the return such accounts and statements as may be required in pursuance of the notice.

12A(4) In the case of any other grouping, an inspector may by a notice given to any member of the grouping resident in the United Kingdom, or if none is to any member of the grouping, require the member–

(a) to make and deliver to the inspector within the time limited by the notice a return containing such information as may be required in pursuance of the notice, and

(b) to deliver with the return such accounts and statements as may be required in pursuance of the notice,

and a notice may be given to any one of the members concerned or separate notices may be given to each of them or to such of them as the inspector thinks fit.

12A(5) Every return under this section shall include a declaration by the grouping or member making the return to the effect that the return is to the best of the maker's knowledge correct and complete.

12A(6) A notice under this section may require different information, accounts and statements for different periods, in relation to different descriptions of income or gains or in relation to different descriptions of member.

12A(7) Notices under this section may require different information, accounts and statements in relation to different descriptions of grouping.

12A(8) Subject to subsection (9) below, where a notice is given under subsection (3) above, everything required to be done shall be done by the grouping acting through its manager or, where there is more than one, any of them; but where the manager of a grouping (or each of them) is a person other than an individual, the grouping shall act through the individual, or any of the individuals, designated in accordance with the Council Regulation as the representative of the manager (or any of them).

12A(9) Where the contract for the formation of a grouping provides that the grouping shall be validly bound only by two or more managers acting jointly, any declaration required by subsection (5) above to be included in a return made by a grouping shall be given by the appropriate number of managers.

History – S. 12A(2) amended by FA 1994, s. 196 and Sch. 19, para. 2, substituting the words "securing that members ... (as the case may be) corporation tax", in so far as it relates to income tax and capital gains tax, as respects the year 1996–97 and subsequent years of assessment and, in so far as it relates to corporation tax, as respects accounting periods ending on or after 1 July 1999, the appointed day by virtue of FA 1994, s. 199(2), (3) and SI 1998/3173 (C. 78).
S. 12A inserted by FA 1990, s. 69 and Sch. 11, para. 2, 5, deemed to have effect from 1 July 1989.

Cross references – S. 98B(2): failure of European Economic Interest Grouping, or member of such a grouping, to comply with a notice under s. 12A.

European material – For Council Regulation 2137/85, see OJ 1985 L199/1.

HMRC Manuals – European Economic Interest Groupings EEIG191ff.: revenue procedures regarding returns under this section.

Other material – HMRC press release, 9 February 1994: from 1 January 1994 these provisions extended to all EEIGs established within the European Economic Area (currently all EU member states, Iceland, Norway and Liechtenstein).

RECORDS

12B Records to be kept for purposes of returns

12B(1) Any person who may be required by a notice under section 8, 8A or 12AA of this Act to make and deliver a return for a year of assessment or other period shall–

(a) keep all such records as may be requisite for the purpose of enabling him to make and deliver a correct and complete return for the year or period; and

(b) preserve those records until the end of the relevant day, that is to say, the day mentioned in subsection (2) below or, where a return is required by a notice given on or before that day, whichever of that day and the following is the latest, namely–

(i) where enquiries into the return are made by an officer of the Board, the day on which, by virtue of section 28A(1) or 28B(1) of this Act, those enquiries are completed; and

(ii) where no enquiries into the return are so made, the day on which such an officer no longer has power to make such enquiries.

12B(2) The day referred to in subsection (1) above is–

(a) in the case of a person carrying on a trade, profession or business alone or in partnership or a company, the fifth anniversary of the 31st January next following the year of assessment or (as the case may be) the sixth anniversary of the end of the period;

(b) otherwise, the first anniversary of the 31st January next following the year of assessment

or (in either case) such earlier day as may be specified in writing by the Commissioners for Her Majesty's Revenue and Customs (and different days may be specified for different cases).

12B(2A) Any person who–

(a) is required, by such a notice as is mentioned in subsection (1) above given at any time after the end of the day mentioned in subsection (2) above, to make and deliver a return for a year of assessment or other period; and

(b) has in his possession at that time any records which may be requisite for the purpose of enabling him to make and deliver a correct and complete return for the year or period,

shall preserve those records until the end of the relevant day, that is to say, the day which, if the notice had been given on or before the day mentioned in subsection (2) above, would have been the relevant day for the purposes of subsection (1) above.

12B(3) In the case of a person carrying on a trade, profession or business alone or in partnership–

(a) the records required to be kept and preserved under subsection (1) or (2A) above shall include records of the following, namely–

(i) all amounts received and expended in the course of the trade, profession or business and the matters in respect of which the receipts and expenditure take place, and

(ii) in the case of a trade involving dealing in goods, all sales and purchases of goods made in the course of the trade;

(b) [omitted by FA 2008, s. 115 and Sch. 37, para. 2(3).]

12B(3A) The Commissioners for Her Majesty's Revenue and Customs may by regulations–

(a) provide that the records required to be kept and preserved under this section include, or do not include, records specified in the regulations, and

(b) provide that those records include supporting documents so specified.

12B(4) The duty under subsection (1) or (2A) to preserve records may be discharged–

(a) by preserving them in any form and by any means, or

(b) by preserving the information contained in them in any form and by any means,

subject to subsection (4A) and any conditions or further exceptions specified in writing by the Commissioners for Her Majesty's Revenue and Customs.

12B(4A) Subsection (4)(b) does not apply in the case of the following kinds of records–

(a) any statement in writing such as is mentioned in–

(i) subsection (1) of section 1100 of CTA 2010 (amount of distribution, formerly amount of qualifying distribution and tax credit), or

(ii) section 495(1) or 975(2) or (4) of ITA 2007 (statements about deduction of income tax),

which is furnished by the company or person there mentioned, whether after the making of a request or otherwise;

(b) any record (however described) which is required by regulations under section 70(1)(c) of the Finance Act 2004 to be given to a sub-contractor (within the meaning of section 58 of that Act) on the making of a payment to which section 61 of that Act (deductions on account of tax) applies;

(c) any such record as may be requisite for making a correct and complete claim in respect of, or otherwise requisite for making a correct and complete return so far as relating to, an amount of tax–

(i) which has been paid under the laws of a territory outside the United Kingdom, or

(ii) which would have been payable under the law of a territory outside the United Kingdom ("territory F") but for a development relief.

12B(4B) In subsection (4A)(c) **"development relief"** means a relief–

(a) given under the law of territory F with a view to promoting industrial, commercial, scientific, educational or other development in a territory outside the United Kingdom, and

(b) about which provision is made in arrangements that have effect under section 2(1) of TIOPA 2010 (double taxation relief by agreement with territories outside the United Kingdom).

12B(5) Subject to subsections (5A) and (5B) below, any person who fails to comply with subsection (1) or (2A) above in relation to a year of assessment or accounting period shall be liable to a penalty not exceeding £3,000.

12B(5A) Subsection (5) above does not apply where the records which the person fails to keep or preserve are records which might have been requisite only for the purposes of claims, elections or notices which are not included in the return.

12B(5B) Subsection (5) above also does not apply where–

(a) the records which the person fails to keep or preserve are records falling within paragraph (a) of subsection (4A) above; and

(b) an officer of the Board is satisfied that any facts which he reasonably requires to be proved, and which would have been proved by the records, are proved by other documentary evidence furnished to him.

12B(5C) Regulations under this section may–

(a) make different provision for different cases, and

(b) make provision by reference to things specified in a notice published by the Commissioners for Her Majesty's Revenue and Customs in accordance with the regulations (and not withdrawn by a subsequent notice).

12B(6) *For the purposes of this section–*

(a) a person engaged in the letting of property shall be treated as carrying on a trade; and

(b) **"supporting documents"** includes accounts, books, deeds, contracts, vouchers and receipts.

History – In s. 12B(1), the words "(or under any of those sections as extended by section 12 of this Act)" omitted by SI 2009/2035, art. 2 and Schedule, para. 4, with effect from 13 August 2009.

In s. 12B(1)(b)(i) the words "or any amendment of the return" and "treated as" omitted and "28A(1) or 28B(1)" substituted by FA 2001, s. 88 and Sch. 29, para. 20 with effect from 11 May 2001.
In s. 12B(1)(b)(ii) the words "or any amendment of the return" omitted by FA 2001, s. 88 and Sch. 29, para. 20 with effect from 11 May 2001.
In s. 12B(1) reference to s. 11 omitted by FA 1998, s. 117(3), Sch. 19, para. 6, s. 165 and Sch. 27, Pt. III(28), with effect in relation to accounting periods ending on or after 1 July 1999, the self-assessment appointed day by virtue of FA 1994, s. 199(2) and SI 1998/3173 (C. 78).
In s. 12B(2) the word "otherwise" substituted for the words "in any other case" and the words "or (in either case) such earlier day as may be specified in writing by the Commissioners for Her Majesty's Revenue and Customs (and different days may be specified for different cases)." inserted by FA 2008, s. 115 and Sch. 37, para. 2(2) with effect from 1 April 2009 (SI 2009/402, art. 2).
S. 12B(3)(b), and the word "and" before it omitted by FA 2008, s. 115 and Sch. 37, para. 2(3) with effect from 1 April 2009 (SI 2009/402, art. 2).
S. 12B(3A) inserted by FA 2008, s. 115 and Sch. 37, para. 2(4) with effect from 1 April 2009 (SI 2009/402, art. 2).
S. 12B(4) substituted by FA 2008, s. 115 and Sch. 37, para. 2(5) with effect from 1 April 2009 (SI 2009/402, art. 2).
In s. 12B(4) the word "tribunal" substituted for the word "Commissioners" by SI 2009/56, art. 3(1) and Sch. 1, para. 7, operative from 1 April 2009, subject to transitional and saving provisions in SI 2009/56, Sch. 3.
In s. 12B(4A)(a)(i) the words "of distribution, formerly amount" inserted by FA 2016, s. 5 and Sch. 1 para. 51(7), with effect in relation to dividends paid or arising (or treated as paid), and other distributions made (or treated as made) in the tax year 2016–17 or at any later time.
In s. 12B(4A), the words "section 1100 of CTA 2010" substituted for the words "section 234 of the principal Act" by CTA 2010, s. 1177 and Sch. 1, para. 154, with effect for corporation tax purposes for accounting periods ending on or after 1 April 2010, and for income tax and capital gains tax purposes for the tax year 2010–11 and subsequent tax years.
In s. 12B(4A) the words "Subsection (4)(b) does not apply in the case of the following kinds of records" substituted for the words "The records that fall within this subsection are" by FA 2008, s. 115 and Sch. 37, para. 2(6) with effect from 1 April 2009 (SI 2009/402, art.2).
S. 12B(4A)(a)(ii) substituted by ITA 2007, s. 1027 and Sch. 1, para. 246, with effect from 6 April 2007.
S. 12B(4A)(b) substituted by FA 2004, s. 76 and Sch. 12, para. 1, from 6 April 2007 (FA 2004, s. 77).
In s. 12B(4A)(c)(ii) substituted by TIOPA 2010, s. 374 and Sch. 8, para. 3(2), with effect for corporation tax purposes for accounting periods ending on or after 1 April 2010, for income tax and capital gains tax purposes for the tax year 2010–11 and subsequent tax years, and for petroleum revenue tax purposes for chargeable periods beginning on or after 1 July 2010.
S. 12B(4B) inserted by TIOPA 2010, s. 374 and Sch. 8, para. 3(3), with effect for corporation tax purposes for accounting periods ending on or after 1 April 2010, for income tax and capital gains tax purposes for the tax year 2010–11 and subsequent tax years, and for petroleum revenue tax purposes for chargeable periods beginning on or after 1 July 2010.
S. 12B(5C) inserted by FA 2008, s. 115 and Sch. 37, para. 2(7), with effect from 1 April 2009 (SI 2009/402, art. 2).
S. 12B inserted by FA 1994, s. 196 and Sch. 19, para. 3 and amended by FA 1995, s. 105, 162 and Sch. 29, Pt. VIII(14), and by FA 1996, s. 124(2)–(5), in so far as it relates to income tax or capital gains tax, as respects the year 1996–97 and subsequent years of assessment.

Cross references – S. 102: Board's power to mitigate penalties.
S. 100B: appeals against penalty determinations.
FA 2004, s. 33(3): s. 12B(5) not to apply to records relating to an arm's length provision (for the purposes of ICTA 1988, Sch. 28AA) until 2006–07.
Sch. 1A, para. 2A(3), (5): preservation of records for the purposes of claims, etc. not included in returns.

HMRC Manuals – Enquiry Manual EM4650: Revenue's approach to penalties for failure to preserve records.

PART III – OTHER RETURNS AND INFORMATION

Cross references – S. 98: penalties for failure to make a return under this Part.

Notes – For returns by underwriting agents of syndicate profits or losses and apportioning between syndicate members the syndicate profits or losses as determined by an inspector, see FA 1993, s. 173 and Sch. 19, para. 2, 6.

13 Persons in receipt of taxable income belonging to others

13 [Omitted by FA 2011, s. 86 and Sch. 23, para. 51(2)(a).]

History – S. 13 omitted by FA 2011, s. 86 and Sch. 23, para. 51(2)(a), with effect from 1 April 2012, but in relation to a notice issued before that date, s. 13 continues to apply as if it had not been omitted (FA 2011, Sch. 23, para. 65). Former s. 13 read as follows

"Persons in receipt of taxable income belonging to others

13(1) Every person who, in whatever capacity, is in receipt of any money or value, or of any profits or gains from any of the sources mentioned in the Income Tax Acts, of or belonging to another person who is chargeable to income tax in respect thereof, or who would be so chargeable if he were resident in the United Kingdom and not an incapacitated person, shall, whenever required to do so by a notice given to him by an inspector, prepare and deliver, within the time mentioned in the notice, a return, signed by him, containing–

(a) a statement of all such money, value, profits or gains, and
(b) the name and address of every person to whom the same belong, and
(c) a declaration whether every such person is of full age, or is resident in the United Kingdom or is an incapacitated person.

13(2) If any person described above is acting jointly with any other person, he shall, in like manner, deliver a return of the names and addresses of all persons joined with him at the time of delivery of the return mentioned in subsection (1) above.

13(3) A notice under this section shall not require information as to any money, value, profits or gains received in a year of assessment ending more than three years before the date of the giving of the notice.".

Former s. 13(1) amended by FA 1970, Sch. 8, Pt. VII.
Former s. 13(1)(c) amended by FA 1988, s. 148 and Sch. 14, Pt. VIII by omitting the words, "or is a married woman,", with effect from 1990–91.
Former s. 13(3) inserted by FA 1988, s. 123(1), (5) with regard to notices given after 29 July 1988.

Cross references – S. 76: protection for certain returns of trustees, agents and receivers under s. 13.
S. 118(1): definition of "incapacitated person".
FA 1973, Sch. 15, para. 2: particulars which may be required from a licence-holder under Petroleum (Production) Act 1934.

Other material – Law Society's Gazette, 29 May 1991: Revenue should be discriminating in issuing s. 13 notices to solicitors, and should not normally send them to those who provide the necessary information satisfactorily in another manner. Following a nil return for two years, inspectors may use their discretion to dispense with returns altogether.

14 Return of lodgers and inmates

14 [Omitted by FA 2011, s. 86 and Sch. 23, para. 51(2)(b).]

History – S. 14 omitted by FA 2011, s. 86 and Sch. 23, para. 51(2)(b), with effect from 1 April 2012, but in relation to a notice issued before that date, s. 14 continues to apply as if it had not been omitted (FA 2011, Sch. 23, para. 65). Former s. 14 read as follows:

"Return of lodgers and inmates

14 Every person, when required to do so by a notice served on him by an inspector, shall, within the time limited by the notice, prepare and deliver to the inspector a return, in writing, containing to the best of his belief–

(a) the name of every lodger or inmate resident in his dwelling-house, and

(b) the name and ordinary place of residence of any such lodger or inmate who has any ordinary place of residence elsewhere at which he can be assessed and who desires to be assessed at such ordinary place of residence.".

15 Return of employees' earnings etc.

15 [Omitted by FA 2011, s. 86 and Sch. 23, para. 51(2)(c).]

History – S. 15 omitted by FA 2011, s. 86 and Sch. 23, para. 51(2)(c), with effect from 1 April 2012, but in relation to a notice issued before that date, s. 15 continues to apply as if it had not been omitted (FA 2011, Sch. 23, para. 65). Former s. 15 read as follows:

"Return of employees' earnings etc.

History – In the heading to s. 15, the words "Return of employees' earnings etc." substituted by ITEPA 2003, Sch. 6, para. 126(2) which has effect for the tax year 2003–04 and subsequent tax years.

15(1) Every employer, when required to do so by notice from an officer of the Board, shall, within the time limited by the notice, prepare and deliver to the officer a return relating to persons who are or have been employees of his, containing the information required under the following provisions of this section.

15(2) An employer shall not be required to include in his return information relating to any year of assessment if the notice is given more than five years after the 31st January next following that year.

15(3) A notice under subsection (1) above–

(a) shall specify the employees for whom a return is to be made and may, in particular, specify individuals (by name or otherwise) or all employees of an employer or all his employees who are or have been in employment which, for the purposes of the benefits code in ITEPA 2003, is a taxable employment under Part 2 of that Act (see section 66) but is not an excluded employment (see section 63 of that Act); and

(b) shall specify the years of assessment or other periods with respect to which the information is to be provided.

15(4) A notice under subsection (1) above may require the return to state the name and place of residence of an employee to whom it relates.

15(5) A notice under subsection (1) above may require the return to contain, in respect of an employee to whom it relates, the following particulars–

(a) in the case of relevant payments made by the employer, particulars of the payments;

(b) in the case of relevant payments not falling within paragraph (a) above the making of which by another person has been arranged by the employer–

(i) particulars of the payments; and

(ii) the name and business address of the other person; and

(c) in the case of relevant payments not falling within either of the preceding paragraphs, the name and business address of any person who has, to the employer's knowledge, made the payments.

15(6) Any payments made to an employee in respect of his employment are **relevant payments** for the purposes of this section, including–

(a) payments to him in respect of expenses (including sums put at his disposal and paid away by him);

(b) payments made on his behalf and not repaid; and

(c) payments to him for services rendered in connection with a trade or business, whether the services were rendered in the course of his employment or not.

15(7) Where, for the purposes of his return, an employer apportions expenses incurred partly in or in connection with a particular matter and partly in or in connection with other matters–

(a) the return shall contain a statement that the sum included in the return is the result of such an apportionment; and

(b) if required to do so by notice from an officer of the Board, the employer shall prepare and deliver to the officer, within the time limited by the notice, a return containing full particulars as to the amount apportioned and the manner in which, and the grounds on which, the apportionment has been made.

15(8) A notice under subsection (1) above may require the return–

(a) to state in respect of an employee to whom it relates whether any benefits are or have been provided for him (or for any other person) by reason of his employment, such as may give rise to charges to tax under the relevant provisions, that is to say, Chapters 4 to 10 of Part 3 and sections 222 and 223 of ITEPA 2003 (miscellaneous benefits in cash or in kind); and

(b) if such benefits are or have been provided, to contain such particulars of those benefits as may be specified in the notice.

15(9) Where such benefits are provided the notice may, without prejudice to subsection (8)(b) above, require the return to contain the following particulars–

(a) in the case of benefits which are or have been provided by the employer, particulars of the amounts which may be chargeable to tax by virtue of the relevant provisions;

(b) in the case of benefits not falling within paragraph (a) above the provision of which by another person is or has been arranged by the employer–

(i) particulars of the amounts which may be so chargeable; and

(ii) the name and business address of the other person; and

(c) in the case of benefits not falling within either of the preceding paragraphs, the name and business address of any person who has, to the employer's knowledge, provided the benefits.

15(10) Where it appears to an officer of the Board that a person has, in any year of assessment, been concerned in making relevant payments to, or providing benefits to or in respect of, employees of another, the officer may at any time up to five years after the 31st January next following that year by notice require that person–

(a) to deliver to the officer, within the time limited by the notice, such particulars of those payments or benefits, or of the amounts which may be chargeable to tax in respect of the benefits, as may be specified in the notice (so far as known to him); and

(b) to include with those particulars the names and addresses (so far as known to him) of the employees concerned.

15(11) In determining, in pursuance of a notice under subsection (1) or (10) above, amounts which may be chargeable to tax by virtue of the relevant provisions, a person–

(a) shall not make–

(i) any deduction or other adjustment which he is unable to show, by reference to information in his possession or otherwise available to him, is authorised or required by the relevant provisions; or

(ii) any deduction authorised by section 328(1), 362, 363, 364 or 365 of ITEPA 2003; but

(b) subject to that, shall make all such deductions and other adjustments as may be authorised or required by the relevant provisions.

15(12) Where the employer is a body of persons, the secretary of the body or other officer (by whatever name called) performing the duties of secretary shall be treated as the employer for the purposes of this section.

Where the employer is a body corporate, that body corporate, as well as the secretary or other officer, shall be liable to a penalty for failure to comply with this section.

15(13) In this section–

"arranged" includes guaranteed and in any way facilitated;

"employee" means an office holder or employee whose earnings are within the charge to tax under ITEPA 2003, and related expressions are to be construed accordingly;

"relevant payments" has the meaning given by subsection (6) above; and

"the relevant provisions" has the meaning given by section (8)(a) above.".

In the heading to former s. 15, the words "Return of employees' earnings etc." substituted by ITEPA 2003, Sch. 6, para 126(2) which has effect for the tax year 2003–04 and subsequent tax years.
In former s. 15(3)(a), the words "employment which … (see section 63 of that Act)" substituted by ITEPA 2003, Sch. 6, para. 126(3) which has effect for the tax year 2003–04 and subsequent tax years.
In former s. 15(8)(a), the words "the relevant provisions, that is to say, Chapters 4 to 10 of Part 3 and sections 222 and 223 of ITEPA 2003" substituted for the words "the relevant sections, that is to say, sections 141, 142, 143, 144A, 145, 146 and 154 to 165 of the principal Act" by ITEPA 2003, Sch. 6, para. 126(4) which has effect for the tax year 2003–04 and subsequent tax years.
In former s. 15(9)(a), the words "the relevant provisions" substituted by ITEPA 2003, Sch. 6, para. 126(5) which has effect for the tax year 2003–04 and subsequent tax years.
In former s. 15(11), the words "the relevant provisions" substituted in each place by ITEPA 2003, Sch. 6, para. 126(6)(a) which has effect for the tax year 2003–04 and subsequent tax years.
In former s. 15(11)(a)(ii), the words "section 328(1), 362, 363, 364 or 365 of ITEPA 2003" substituted by ITEPA 2003, Sch. 6, para. 126(6)(b) which has effect for the tax year 2003–04 and subsequent tax years.
In former s. 15(13), in the definition of "employee", the words "whose earnings are within the charge to tax under ITEPA 2003" substituted for the words "whose emoluments fall to be assessed under Schedule E" by ITEPA 2003, Sch. 6, para. 126(7)(a) which has effect for the tax year 2003–04 and subsequent tax years.
In former s. 15(13), the definition of "the relevant provisions" substituted for the definition of "the relevant sections" by ITEPA 2003, Sch. 6, para. 126(7)(b) which has effect for the tax year 2003–04 and subsequent tax years.
Former s. 15 substituted by FA 1995, s. 106, with effect for payments made or benefits provided on or after 6 April 1996.

Cross references – FA 1974, s. 24: s. 15 applies to returns of persons treated as employees of non-resident employers.
SI 2003/2682: PAYE regulations under which returns are required in respect of most employees.

15A Non-resident's staff are UK client's employees for section 15 purposes

15A [Omitted by FA 2011, s. 86 and Sch. 23, para. 51(2)(d).]

History – S. 15A omitted by FA 2011, s. 86 and Sch. 23, para. 51(2)(d), with effect from 1 April 2012, but in relation to a notice issued before that date, s. 15A continues to apply as if it had not been omitted (FA 2011, Sch. 23, para. 65). Former s. 15A read as follows:

"Non-resident's staff are UK client's employees for section 15 purposes

15A(1) Subsection (5) applies if each of conditions A to C is met.

15A(2) Condition A is that a person ("F") performs in the United Kingdom, for a continuous period of 30 days or more, duties of an office or employment.

15A(3) Condition B is that the office or employment is under or with a person who–

(a) is not resident in the United Kingdom, but
(b) is resident outside the United Kingdom.

15A(4) Condition C is that the duties are performed for the benefit of a person ("P") who–

(a) is resident in the United Kingdom, or
(b) carries on a trade, profession or vocation in the United Kingdom.

15A(5) Section 15 of this Act applies as if P were F's employer, but only so as to enable P to be required to make a return of F's name and place of residence.".

Former s. 15A inserted by TIOPA 2010, s. 371 and Sch. 7, para. 14, with effect for corporation tax purposes for accounting periods ending on or after 1 April 2010, for income tax and capital gains tax purposes for the tax year 2010–11 and subsequent tax years, and for petroleum revenue tax purposes for chargeable periods beginning on or after 1 July 2010.

16 Fees, commissions, etc.

16 [Omitted by FA 2011, s. 86 and Sch. 23, para. 51(2)(e).]

History – S. 16 omitted by FA 2011, s. 86 and Sch. 23, para. 51(2)(e), with effect from 1 April 2012, but in relation to a notice issued before that date, s. 16 continues to apply as if it had not been omitted (FA 2011, Sch. 23, para. 65). Former s. 16 read as follows:

"Fees, commissions, etc.

16(1) Every person carrying on a trade or business shall, if required to do so by notice from an inspector, make and deliver to the inspector a return of all payments of any kind specified in the notice made during a period so specified, being–

(a) payments made in the course of the trade or business, or of such part of the trade or business as may be specified in the notice, for services rendered by persons not employed in the trade or business, or
(b) payments for services rendered in connection with the formation, acquisition, development or disposal of the trade or business, or any part of it, by persons not employed in the trade or business, or
(c) periodical or lump sum payments made in respect of any copyright, public lending right, right in a registered design or design right.

16(2) Every body of persons carrying on any activity which does not constitute a trade or business shall, if required to do so by notice from an inspector, make and deliver to the inspector a return of all payments of a kind specified in the notice made during a period so specified, being–

(a) payments made in the course of carrying on the activity, or such part of the activity as may be specified in the notice, for services rendered by persons not employed by the said body of persons, or
(b) periodical or lump sum payments made in respect of any copyright, public lending right, right in a registered design or design right.

16(3) A return required under either of the preceding subsections shall, if the trade or business or other activity is carried on by an unincorporated body of persons (other than a company), be made and delivered by the person who is or performs the duties of secretary of the body, and the notice shall be framed accordingly.

16(4) A return under the preceding provisions of this section shall give the name of the person to whom each payment was made, the amount of the payment and such other particulars (including particulars as to the services or rights in respect of which the payment was made, the period over which any services were rendered and any business name and any business or home address of the person to whom payment was made) as may be specified in the notice.

16(5) No person shall be required under the preceding provisions of this section to include in a return–
(a) particulars of any payment from which income tax is deductible, or
(b) particulars of payments made to any one person where the total of the payments to that person which would otherwise fall to be included in the return does not exceed £15, or
(c) particulars of any payment made in a year of assessment ending more than three years before the service of the notice requiring him to make the return.
16(6) [Repealed by FA 1989, s. 163(6) and Sch. 17, Pt. VIII.]
16(7) In this section–
(a) references to payments for services include references to payments in the nature of commission of any kind and references to payments in respect of expenses incurred in connection with the rendering of services, and
(b) references to the making of payments include references to the giving of any valuable consideration,
and the requirement imposed by subsection (4) above to state the amount of a payment shall, in relation to any consideration given otherwise than in the form of money, be construed as a requirement to give particulars of the consideration.
16(8) In subsection (2) above references to a **body of persons** include references to any department of the Crown, any public or local authority and any other public body.".
In former s. 16(1)(c), (2)(b), the words ", public lending right … design right" were substituted by Copyright, Designs and Patents Act 1988, s. 303(1) and Sch. 7, para. 13, with effect from 1 August 1989 (SI 1989/816).
Former s. 16(6) repealed by FA 1989, s. 163(6) and Sch. 17, Pt. VIII, in relation to offences on or after 27 July 1989.
Former s. 16(8) added by FA 1988, s. 124, in respect of payments made in 1988–89 and subsequent years.

16A Agency workers

16A [Omitted by FA 2011, s. 86 and Sch. 23, para. 51(2)(f).]

History – S. 16A omitted by FA 2011, s. 86 and Sch. 23, para. 51(2)(f), with effect from 1 April 2012, but in relation to a notice issued before that date, s. 16A continues to apply as if it had not been omitted (FA 2011, Sch. 23, para. 65). Former s. 16A read as follows:

"Agency workers

16A(1) This section applies where–
(a) any services which an individual provides or is obliged to provide under an agency contract are treated under section 44(2) of ITEPA 2003 as the duties of an office or employment held by him with the agency, or
(b) any remuneration receivable under or in consequence of arrangements falling within section 45 of that Act is treated as earnings from an office or employment held by an individual with the agency.
16A(2) Where this section applies–
(a) section 15 above shall apply as if the individual were employed by the agency, and
(b) section 16 above shall not apply to any payments made to the individual under or in consequence of the agency contract or the arrangements.
16A(3) In this section **"agency contract"** and **"remuneration"** have the same meaning as in Chapter 7 of Part 2 of ITEPA 2003.".
Former s. 16A substituted by ITEPA 2003, Sch. 6, para. 127 which has effect for the tax year 2003–04 and subsequent tax years.

17 Interest paid or credited by banks, building societies etc. without deduction of income tax

17 [Omitted by FA 2011, s. 86 and Sch. 23, para. 51(2)(g).]

History – S. 17 omitted by FA 2011, s. 86 and Sch. 23, para. 51(2)(g), with effect from 1 April 2012, but in relation to a notice issued before that date, s. 17 continues to apply as if it had not been omitted (FA 2011, Sch. 23, para. 65). former s. 17 read as follows:

"Interest paid or credited by banks, building societies etc. without deduction of income tax

17(1) Every person carrying on a trade or business who, in the ordinary course of the operations thereof, receives or retains money in such circumstances that interest becomes payable thereon which is paid or credited without deduction of income tax or after deduction of income tax, and, in particular, every such person who is a bank or building society, shall, if required to do so by notice from an inspector, make and deliver to the inspector, within the time specified in the notice, a return of all interest paid or credited by him as aforesaid during a year of assessment specified in the notice in the course of his trade or business or any such part of his trade or business as may be so specified, giving the names and addresses of the persons to whom the interest was paid or credited and stating, in each case, the amount of the interest actually paid or credited and (where the interest was paid or credited after deduction of income tax) the amount of the interest from which the tax was deducted and the amount of the tax deducted:
Provided that–
(a) [omitted by FA 1990, s. 92(2)(c), 132 and Sch. 19, Pt. V]
(b) the years specified in a notice under this subsection shall not be a year ending more than three years before the date of the service of the notice.
17(1A) In this section **"bank"** has the meaning given by section 991 of ITA 2007.
17(2) Without prejudice to the generality of so much of subsection (1) above as enables different notices to be served thereunder in relation to different parts of a trade or business, separate notices may be served under that subsection as respects the transactions carried on at any branch or branches respectively specified in the notices, and any such separate notice shall, if served on the manager or other person in charge of the branch or branches in question, be deemed to have been duly served on the person carrying on the trade or business; and where such a separate notice is so served as respects the transactions carried on at any branch or branches, any notice subsequently served under the said subsection (1) on the person carrying on the trade or business shall not be deemed to extend to any transaction to which the said separate notice extends.
17(3) This section shall, with any necessary adaptations, apply in relation to the National Savings Bank as if it were a trade or business carried on by the Director of Savings.
17(4) This section shall apply only to money received or retained in the United Kingdom.
17(4A) If a person to whom any interest is paid or credited in respect of any money received or retained in the United Kingdom by notice in writing served on the person paying or crediting the interest–
(a) has declared that the person beneficially entitled to the interest is a company not resident in the United Kingdom, and
(b) has requested that the interest shall not be included in any return under this section,
the person paying or crediting the interest shall not be required to include the interest in any such return.
17(4B) [Repealed by FA 2000, s. 145(1) and Sch. 40, Pt. V.]
17(4C) [Repealed by FA 2000, s. 145(1) and Sch. 40, Pt. V.]
17(5) The Board may by regulations provide as mentioned in all or any of the following paragraphs–
(a) that a return under subsection (1) above shall contain such further information as is prescribed if the notice requiring the return specifies the information and requires it to be contained in the return;
(b) that a person required to make and deliver a return under subsection (1) above shall furnish with the return such further information as is prescribed if the notice requiring the return specifies the information and requires it to be so furnished;
(c) that if a person is required–

(i) to make and deliver a return under subsection (1) above;
(ii) to include information in such a return under any provision made under paragraph (a) above; or
(iii) to furnish information under any provision made under paragraph (b) above, and the notice under subsection (1) above specifies the form in which the return is to be made and delivered, or the information is to be included or furnished, the person shall make and deliver the return, or include or furnish the information, in that form;

(d) that a notice under subsection (1) above shall not require prescribed information;

and in this subsection **"prescribed"** means prescribed by the regulations.

The further information required as mentioned in paragraph (a) or (b) above may include, in prescribed cases, the name and address of the person beneficially entitled to the interest paid or credited.

17(6) Regulations under subsection (5) above–

(a) shall be made by statutory instrument subject to annulment in pursuance of a resolution of the House of Commons,
(aa) may make provision with respect to the furnishing of information by persons required–
(i) to make and deliver a return under subsection (1) above;
(ii) to include information in such a return under any provision made under subsection (5)(a) above; or
(iii) to furnish information under any provision made under subsection (5)(b) above,
including the inspection of books, documents and other records on behalf of the Board;
(b) may make different provision in relation to different cases or descriptions of case, and
(c) may include such supplementary, incidental, consequential or transitional provisions as appear to the Board to be necessary or expedient.

17(7) In the application of this section in relation to building societies, references to interest include references to dividends. For this purpose **"dividend"** includes any distribution (whether or not described as a dividend).

17(8) References in this section to interest include references to–

(a) alternative finance return within the meaning of Chapter 5 of Part 2 of the Finance Act 2005 (see section 57 of that Act), and
(b) alternative finance return within the meaning of Chapter 6 of Part 6 of CTA 2009 (see sections 511 to 513 of that Act).".

In the heading, the words ", building societies" inserted by ITA 2007, s. 1027 and Sch. 1, para. 247(5), with effect from 6 April 2007.
In former s. 17(1) the words "or building society" inserted by ITA 2007, s. 1027 and Sch. 1, para. 247(2), with effect from 6 April 2007.
In former s. 17(1), the words "such person who is a bank" substituted by FA 1996, s. 198 and Sch. 37, para. 11(3), with effect in relation to interest paid on or after 29 April 1996.
In former s. 17(1), the words "or after deduction of income tax" and "actually paid or credited … amount of the tax deducted" inserted and para. (a) of the proviso omitted by FA 1990, s. 92(1)–(3), 132 and Sch. 19, Pt. V, as regards a case where interest is paid or credited in the year 1991–92 or a subsequent year of assessment.
Former s. 17(1) amended by FA 1988, s. 123(2), (5) with respect to notices given after 29 July 1988 by inserting the words "of assessment".
In former s. 17(1A), the words "section 991 of ITA 2007" substituted for the words "section 840A of the principal Act" by ITA 2007, s. 1027 and Sch. 1, para. 247(3), with effect from 6 April 2007.
Former s. 17(1A) inserted by FA 1996, s. 198 and Sch. 37, para. 11(1), (2), with effect in relation to interest paid on or after 29 April 1996.
In former s. 17(4), words at the end of that subsection repealed by F(No. 2)A 1992, s. 29(1) and s. 82 and Sch. 18, Pt. VII (3) with effect in relation to interest paid or credited after 16 July 1992.
Former s. 17(4A)–(4C) substituted by F(No. 2)A 1992, s. 29(1), in relation to interest paid or credited after 16 July 1992.
Former s. 17(4B), (4C) repealed by FA 2000, s. 145(1) and Sch. 40, Pt. V, with effect in relation to amounts paid, credited or received on or after 6 April 2001.
Former s. 17(5), (6) inserted, by FA 1990, s. 92(1)–(3), 132 and Sch. 19, Pt. V, as regards a case where interest is paid or credited in the year 1991–92 or a subsequent year of assessment.
Former s. 17(5)(c), (5) respectively substituted, and amended by FA 2000, s. 145(2)(a), (b), with effect in relation to amounts paid, credited or received on or after 6 April 2001.
Former s. 17(6)(aa) inserted by FA 2000, s. 145(3), with effect in relation to amounts paid, credited or received on or after 6 April 2001.
Former s. 17(7) inserted by ITA 2007, Sch. 1, para. 247(4), with effect from 6 April 2007.
Former s. 17(8) inserted by CTA 2009, s. 1322 and Sch. 1, para. 298, with effectfor corporation tax purposes for accounting periods ending on or after 1 April 2009, and for income tax and capital gains tax purposes for the tax year 2009–10 and subsequent tax years.

Cross references – FA 2003, s. 199(4): regulations in respect of Community obligations for the taxation of savings income may provide for notices under those regulations to be combined with notices under TMA 1970 s. 17.
FA 2005, Sch. 2, para. 2: references in s. 17 to interest paid to include references to alternative finance return or profit share return.
National Savings Bank Act 1971, s. 12(3): provisions concerning secrecy in that Act have effect subject to s. 17(3).
SI 1990/2231, reg. 12: modifications of s. 17 in its application to a building society after 5 April 1991.
SI 2003/3297, reg. 15: combination of notice under s. 17 with that under the Savings Income regulations with effect from date to be specified by the Treasury (no earlier than 1 January 2005).

Statutory instruments – SI 1992/15 (as amended by SI 2001/405 and SI 2008/2688): made under s. 17(5) and (6).
SI 2011/22: made partly under s. 17(5) and (6).

18 Interest paid without deduction of income tax

18 [Omitted by FA 2011, s. 86 and Sch. 23, para. 51(2)(h).]

History – S. 18 omitted by FA 2011, s. 86 and Sch. 23, para. 51(2)(h), with effect from 1 April 2012, but in relation to a notice issued before that date, s. 18 continues to apply as if it had not been omitted (FA 2011, Sch. 23, para. 65). Former s. 18 read as follows:

"Interest paid without deduction of income tax

18(1) Any person by or through whom any interest is paid in the year 1969–70 or any subsequent year of assessment without deduction of income tax or after deduction of income tax shall, on being so required by a notice given to him by an inspector, furnish to the inspector, within the time limited by the notice–

(a) the name and address of the person to whom the interest has been paid or on whose behalf the interest has been received, and
(b) the amount of the interest actually paid or received and (where the interest has been paid or received after deduction of income tax) the amount of the interest from which the tax has been deducted and the amount of the tax deducted,

and any person by whom any such interest is received on behalf of another person shall on being so required furnish to the inspector the name and address of the person on whose behalf the interest has been received, and the amount actually received and (where the interest has been received after deduction of income tax) the amount of the interest from which the tax has been deducted and the amount of the tax deducted.

18(2) The persons to whom subsection (1) above applies include any officer in any public office or in any department of the Crown.

18(3) [Repealed by FA 2000, s. 145(5) and Sch. 40, Pt. V.]

18(3AA) [Repealed by FA 2000, s. 145(5) and Sch. 40, Pt. V.]

18(3A) A notice under this section shall not require information with respect to interest paid or received in a year of assessment ending more than three years before the date of the giving of the notice.

18(3B) The Board may by regulations provide as mentioned in all or any of the following paragraphs–
(a) that a person required to furnish information under subsection (1) above shall furnish at the same time such further information as is prescribed if the notice concerned specifies the information and requires it to be so furnished;
(b) that if a person is required to furnish information under subsection (1) above or under any provision made under paragraph (a) above, and the notice concerned specifies the form in which the information is to be furnished, the person shall furnish the information in that form;
(c) that a notice under subsection (1) above shall not require prescribed information;
and in this subsection **"prescribed"** means prescribed by the regulations.
The further information required as mentioned in paragraph (a) above may include, in prescribed cases, the name and address of the person beneficially entitled to the interest paid or received.
18(3C) Regulations under subsection (3B) above–
(a) shall be made by statutory instrument subject to annulment in pursuance of a resolution of the House of Commons,
(aa) may make provision with respect to the furnishing of information by persons required to furnish information under subsection (1) above, or under any provision made under subsection (3B)(a) above, including the inspection of books, documents and other records on behalf of the Board;
(b) may make different provision in relation to different cases or descriptions of case, and
(c) may include such supplementary, incidental, consequential or transitional provisions as appear to the Board to be necessary or expedient.
18(3D) For the purposes of this section interest shall be treated as received by any person if it is received by another person at his direction or with his consent.
18(3E) For the purposes of this section the following shall be treated as interest–
(a) any dividend in respect of a share in a building society;
(b) any amount to which a person holding a deeply discounted security is entitled on the redemption of that security; and
(c) any foreign dividend.
18(3F) In subsection (3E)(b) above **"deeply discounted security"** has the same meaning as in Chapter 8 of Part 4 of ITTOIA 2005 (profits from deeply discounted securities) (see section 430 of that Act).
18(3G) In subsection (3E)(c) above **"foreign dividend"** means any annual payment, interest or dividend payable out of, or in respect of the stocks, funds, shares or securities of–
(a) a body of persons that is not resident in the United Kingdom, or
(b) a government or public or local authority in a country outside the United Kingdom.
18(4) [Repealed by FA 1988, s. 148 and Sch. 14, Pt. IV.]
18(5) References in this section to interest include references to–
(a) alternative finance return within the meaning of Chapter 5 of Part 2 of the Finance Act 2005 (see section 57 of that Act), and
(b) alternative finance return within the meaning of Chapter 6 of Part 6 of CTA 2009 (see sections 511 to 513 of that Act).".
In former s. 18(1) the words "or after deduction of income tax" inserted, and the words "actually paid or received ... amount of the tax deducted" in para. (b) and "the amount actually received ... amount of the tax deducted" substituted, by FA 1990, s. 92(4), (5), as regards a case where interest is paid in 1991–92 or a subsequent year of assessment.
In former s. 18(1) the words "by or through whom" and "by whom any such interest is received" substituted by FA 2000, s. 145(4), with effect in relation to amounts paid, credited or received on or after 6 April 2001.
Former s. 18(2) amended by ICTA 1988, s. 844 and Sch. 29, para. 7(2) in relation to tax for 1988–89 and subsequent years of assessment, and for companies' accounting periods ending after 5 April 1988 by substituting the words "subsection (1) above" for "this section".
Former s. 18(3), (3AA) repealed by FA 2000, s. 145(5) and Sch. 40, Pt. V, with effect in relation to amounts paid, credited or received on or after 6 April 2001.
Former s. 18(3A) inserted by FA 1988, s. 123(3), (5) with respect to notices given after 29 July 1988.
In former s. 18(3A) the words "or received" inserted by FA 2000, s. 145(6) with effect in relation to amounts paid, credited or received on or after 6 April 2001.
Former s. 18(3B) inserted by FA 1990, s. 92(4), (6), as regards a case where interest is paid in 1991–92 or a subsequent year of assessment.
In former s. 18(3B) the final paragraph inserted by FA 2000, s. 145(7) with effect in relation to amounts paid, credited or received on or after 6 April 2001.
Former s. 18(3C) inserted by FA 1990, s. 92(4), (6), as regards a case where interest is paid in 1991–92 or a subsequent year of assessment.
Former s. 18(3C)(aa) inserted by FA 2000, s. 145(8), with effect in relation to amounts paid, credited or received on or after 6 April 2001.
Former s. 18(3D), (3E), (3F) and (3G) substituted for the previous (3D) by FA 2000, s. 145(9), with effect in relation to amounts paid, credited or received on or after 6 April 2001.
In former s. 18(3E)(b) "deeply" substituted for "relevant" by ITTOIA 2005, s. 882(1) and Sch. 1, para. 366(2); effective for for 2005–06 onwards (ITTOIA 2005, s. 883(1)).
Former s. 18(3F) substituted by ITTOIA 2005, s. 882(1) and Sch. 1, para. 366(3); effective for income tax purposes for 2005–06 onwards andfor corporation tax purposes for accounting periods ending after 5 April 2005 (ITTOIA 2005, s. 883(1A)). Previous version of the sub-section defined "relevant discounted security" by reference to FA 1996, Sch. 13, para. 3.
Former s. 18(4) repealed by FA 1988, s. 148 and Sch. 14, Pt. IV, with effect for 1988–89 and later years of assessment.
Former s. 18(5) inserted by CTA 2009, s. 1322 and Sch. 1, para. 299, with effect for corporation tax purposes for accounting periods ending on or after 1 April 2009, and for income tax and capital gains tax purposes for the tax year 2009–10 and subsequent tax years.
Cross references – FA 2005, Sch. 2, para. 2: references in s. 18 to interest paid to include references to alternative finance return or profit share return.
FA 2003, s. 199(4): regulations in respect of Community obligations for the taxation of savings income may provide for notices under those regulations to be combined with notices under TMA 1970, s. 18.
SI 2003/3297, reg. 15: combination of notice under s. 18 with that under the Savings Income regulations with effect from date to be specified by the Treasury (no earlier than 1 January 2005).
Statutory instruments – SI 1992/15 (as amended by SI 2001/405 and SI 2008/2688): made under s. 18(3B) and (3C).

18A Other payments and licences etc.

18A [Omitted by FA 2011, s. 86 and Sch. 23, para. 51(2)(i).]

History – *S. 18A omitted by FA 2011*, s. 86 and Sch. 23, para. 51(2)(i), with effect from 1 April 2012, but in relation to a notice issued before that date, s. 18A continues to apply as if it had not been omitted (FA 2011, Sch. 23, para. 65).
Former s. 18A inserted by FA 1988, s. 125.

18B Savings income: regulations about European and international aspects

18B(1) The Treasury may make regulations for implementing and for dealing with matters arising out of or related to–

(a) any EU obligation created with a view to ensuring the effective taxation of savings income under the law of the United Kingdom and the laws of the other member States, and

(b) any arrangements made with a territory other than a member State with a view to ensuring the effective taxation of savings income under the law of the United Kingdom and the law of the other territory.

18B(2) In this section **"savings income"** means–

(a) interest, apart from interest of a prescribed description, or

(b) other sums of a prescribed description.

18B(3) The power to make regulations under this section is exercisable by statutory instrument.

18B(4) A statutory instrument containing regulations under this section is subject to annulment in pursuance of a resolution of the House of Commons.

History – S. 18B inserted by TIOPA 2010, s. 371 and Sch. 7, para. 103, with effect for corporation tax purposes for accounting periods ending on or after 1 April 2010, for income tax and capital gains tax purposes for the tax year 2010–11 and subsequent tax years, and for petroleum revenue tax purposes for chargeable periods beginning on or after 1 July 2010.

18C Regulations under section 18B: provision about "paying agents"

18C(1) Regulations under section 18B may, in particular, require paying agents–

(a) to obtain and verify prescribed descriptions of information about the identity and residence of relevant payees to whom they make savings income payments, and

(b) to provide to the Commissioners for Her Majesty's Revenue and Customs, or an officer of Revenue and Customs, prescribed descriptions of information about relevant payees to whom they make savings income payments and about the savings income payments which they make to them.

18C(2) Regulations under section 18B may include provision for the inspection on behalf of the Commissioners of books, documents and other records of persons who are, or appear to an officer to be, paying agents.

18C(3) In this section **"paying agents"** means persons of a prescribed description who make savings income payments to other persons.

18C(4) In this section **"relevant payees"** means–

(a) persons of a prescribed description who are resident (within the meaning of regulations under section 18B) in a prescribed territory, and

(b) persons of any such other description as may be prescribed.

18C(5) For the purposes of this section, a person makes savings income payments to another person if the person–

(a) makes payments of savings income to the other person, or

(b) secures the payment of savings income for the other person.

18C(6) In this section **"savings income"** has the same meaning as in section 18B.

18C(7) The descriptions of persons who may be prescribed under subsection (3) include, in particular, public officers and government departments.

18C(8) The only territories which may be prescribed under subsection (4)(a) are–

(a) the other member States, and

(b) territories with which arrangements such as are mentioned in section 18B(1)(b) have been made.

History – S. 18C inserted by TIOPA 2010, s. 371 and Sch. 7, para. 103, with effect for corporation tax purposes for accounting periods ending on or after 1 April 2010, for income tax and capital gains tax purposes for the tax year 2010–11 and subsequent tax years, and for petroleum revenue tax purposes for chargeable periods beginning on or after 1 July 2010.

18D Content of regulations under section 18B: supplementary provision

18D(1) Regulations under section 18B may include provision for notices under such regulations to be combined with notices under paragraph 1 of Schedule 23 to the Finance Act 2011 (data-gathering powers).

18D(2) Regulations under section 18B may include provision about the time at or within which, and the manner in which, any requirement imposed by such regulations is to be complied with.

18D(3) Regulations under section 18B may include provision for penalties for failure to comply with requirements imposed by such regulations, including provision applying any provision of this Act about the determination of penalties or any other matter relating to penalties.

18D(4) Regulations under section 18B–

(a) may make different provision for different cases or descriptions of case, and

(b) may include incidental, supplemental, consequential and transitional provision and savings.

History – In s. 18D(1) "paragraph 1 of Schedule 23 to the Finance Act 2011 (data-gathering powers)" substituted for "sections 17 and 18" by FA 2012, s. 224(6), with effect from 1 April 2012.

S. 18D inserted by TIOPA 2010, s. 371 and Sch. 7, para. 103, with effect for corporation tax purposes for accounting periods ending on or after 1 April 2010, for income tax and capital gains tax purposes for the tax year 2010–11 and subsequent tax years, and for petroleum revenue tax purposes for chargeable periods beginning on or after 1 July 2010.

18E Interpretation of sections 18B to 18D: "prescribed" etc

18E(1) In sections 18B to 18D **"prescribed"** means prescribed by regulations under section 18B.

18E(2) The following provisions do not apply for the purposes of sections 18B to 18D–

(a) section 118 of this Act (interpretation), and

(b) section 18 of ITA 2007 (meaning of "savings income" in the Income Tax Acts).

History – S. 18E inserted by TIOPA 2010, s. 371 and Sch. 7, para. 103, with effect for corporation tax purposes for accounting periods ending on or after 1 April 2010, for income tax and capital gains tax purposes for the tax year 2010–11 and subsequent tax years, and for petroleum revenue tax purposes for chargeable periods beginning on or after 1 July 2010.

19 Information for purposes of charge on profits of UK property businesses or under Schedule A

19 [Omitted by FA 2011, s. 86 and Sch. 23, para. 51(2)(j).]

History – S. 19 omitted by FA 2011, s. 86 and Sch. 23, para. 51(2)(j), with effect from 1 April 2012, but in relation to a notice issued before that date, s. 19 continues to apply as if it had not been omitted (FA 2011, Sch. 23, para. 65). Former s. 19 read as follows:

"Information for purposes of charge on profits of UK property businesses or under Schedule A

19(1) For the purpose of obtaining particulars of profits or gains chargeable to tax under Chapter 3 of Part 3 of ITTOIA 2005, or under Chapter 3 of Part 4 of CTA 2009, as the profits of a UK property business (or, for chargeable periods ending before 6th April 1970, under Case VIII of Schedule D), the inspector may by notice in writing require–

(a) any lessee, occupier or former lessee or occupier of land (including any person having, or having had, the use of land) to give such information as may be prescribed by the Board as to the terms applying to the lease, occupation or use of the land, and where any of those terms are established by any written instrument, to produce the instrument to the inspector,

(b) any lessee or former lessee of land to give such information as may be so prescribed as to any consideration given for the grant or assignment to him of the tenancy,

(c) any person who as agent manages land or is in receipt of rent or other payments arising from land to furnish the inspector with such particulars relating to payments arising therefrom as may be specified in the notice.

19(2) [Omitted by CTA 2009, s. 1322 and Sch. 1, para. 300(3) and repealed by CTA 2009, s. 1326 and Sch. 3, Pt. 1.]

19(3) In this section–

(a) **"lease"** includes an agreement for a lease, and any tenancy, but does not include a mortgage or heritable security, and **"lessee"** shall be construed accordingly but shall include the successor in title of a lessee,

(b) in relation to Scotland **"assignment"** means an assignation.

19(4) A notice under this section shall not require information with respect to–

(a) the terms applying to the lease, occupation or use of the land, or

(b) consideration given, or

(c) payments arising,

in a year of assessment ending more than three years before the date of the giving of the notice.".

In heading to former s. 19 the words "charge on profits of UK property businesses or under" inserted by ITTOIA 2005, s. 882(1) and Sch. 1, para. 367(3); effective for income tax purposes for 2005–06 onwards and for corporation tax purposes for accounting periods ending after 5 April 2005 (ITTOIA 2005, s. 883(1)).

In former s. 19(1) the words ", or under Chapter 3 of Part 4 of CTA 2009, as the profits of a UK property business" substituted for the words "as the profits of a UK property business or under Schedule A" by CTA 2009, s. 1322 and Sch. 1, para. 300(2), with effect for corporation tax purposes for accounting periods ending on or after 1 April 2009, and for income tax and capital gains tax purposes for the tax year 2009–10 and subsequent tax years.

In former s. 19(1) the words "under Chapter 3 of Part 3 of ITTOIA 2005 as the profits of a UK property business or" inserted by ITTOIA 2005, s. 882(1) and Sch. 1, para. 367(2); effective for income tax purposes for 2005–06 onwards and for corporation tax purposes for accounting periods ending after 5 April 2005 (ITTOIA 2005, s. 883(1)).

Former s. 19(2) omitted by CTA 2009, s. 1322 and Sch. 1, para. 300(3) and repealed by CTA 2009, s. 1326 and Sch. 3, Pt. 1, with effect for corporation tax purposes for accounting periods ending on or after 1 April 2009, and for income tax and capital gains tax purposes for the tax year 2009–10 and subsequent tax years.

Former s.. 19(4) inserted by FA 1988, s. 123(4), (5) with respect to notices given after 29 July 1988.

Reference to provisions of the principal Act substituted by ICTA 1988, Sch. 29, para. 32, that Act becoming the principal Act (TMA 1970, s. 118(1)).

Cross references – ICTA 1988, s. 34–36: treatment of premiums etc. as rent or profits, charge on assignment of lease granted at an undervalue and charge on sale of land with right to reconveyance.

PRODUCTION OF ACCOUNTS, BOOKS AND OTHER INFORMATION

19A Power to call for documents for purposes of certain enquiries

19A [Omitted by FA 2008, s. 113 and Sch. 36, para. 66.]

History – S. 19A omitted by FA 2008, s. 113 and Sch. 36, para. 66, with effect from 1 April 2009 (SI 2009/404, art. 2, subject to savings at SI 2009/404, art. 3).

20 Power to call for documents of taxpayer and others

20 [Omitted by FA 2008, s. 113 and Sch. 36, para. 67.]

History – S. 20 omitted by FA 2008, s. 113 and Sch. 36, para. 67, with effect from 1 April 2009 (SI 2009/404, art. 2, subject to savings at SI 2009/404, art. 3).

Cross references – SI 2009/275, art. 3(a): any decision under s. 20(7), (8B) or (8G)(b) is an excluded decision for the purposes of TCEA 2007, s. 11(1) and 13(1).

20A Power to call for papers of tax accountant

20A [Omitted by FA 2012, s. 223 and Sch. 38, para. 45(a).]

History – S. 20A omitted by FA 2012, s. 223 and Sch. 38, para. 45(a), with effect from 1 April 2013 (SI 2013/279, art. 2) subject to savings provision at SI 2013/279, art. 3; where a notice is given under s. 20A on or before 31 March 2013, for the purposes of that notice the amendments made by FA 2012, Sch. 38, para. 44–47 shall be disregarded. Former s. 20A read as follows:

"Power to call for papers of tax accountant

20A(1) Where after the passing of the Finance Act 1976 a person–

(a) is convicted of an offence in relation to tax (whenever committed) by or before any court in the United Kingdom; or

(b) has a penalty imposed on him (whether before or after the passing of that Act) under section 99 of this Act,

and he has stood in relation to others as tax accountant, an inspector authorised by the Board for the purpose of this section may by notice in writing require the person to deliver to him such documents as are in his possession or power and as (in the inspector's reasonable opinion) contain information relevant to any tax liability to which any client of his is or has been, or may be or have been, subject, or to the amount of any such liability.

20A(1A) The reference to documents in subsection (1) above does not include–

(a) personal records (as defined in section 12 of the Police and Criminal Evidence Act 1984), or

(b) journalistic material (as defined in section 13 of that Act).

20A(1B) Subject to subsection (1A) above, the reference to documents in subsection (1) above is to those specified or described in the notice in question; and

(a) the notice shall require documents to be delivered within such time (which shall not be less than thirty days after the date of the notice) as may be specified in the notice; and

(b) the inspector may take copies of them or of extracts from them.

20A(2) Subsection (1) above does not have effect in relation to a person convicted or penalised as there mentioned for so long as an appeal is pending against the conviction or penalty; and–

(a) for this purpose an appeal is to be treated as pending (where one is competent but has not been brought) until the expiration of the time for bringing it or, in the case of a conviction in Scotland, until the expiration of 28 days from the date of conviction; and

(b) references here to appeal include further appeal but, in relation to the imposition of a penalty, do not include appeal against the amount of the penalty.

20A(3) A notice is not to be given to any person under this section unless with the consent of the appropriate judicial authority; and that authority is to give his consent only on being satisfied that in all the circumstances the inspector is justified in so proceeding.

20A(4) The power to give a notice under this section, by reference to a person's conviction or the imposition on him of a penalty, ceases at the expiration of the period of 12 months beginning with the date on which it was first exercisable in his case by virtue of that conviction or penalty.

20A(5) To the extent specified in section 20B below, the above provisions are subject to the restrictions of that section.".

Former s. 20A(1)(b), (2), (4) amended by FA 1989, s. 168(1), (2), by substituting "a penalty imposed on", "penalty" (as it first appears in s. 20A(2)), "imposition", "imposition on" and "penalty" (in s. 20A(4)), consequent to amendments to s. 100 permitting an inspector etc. to determine a penalty rather than take proceedings for the award of a penalty.

Former s. 20A(1A), (1B) substituted for final sentence of s. 20A(1) by FA 1989, s. 143, effective for notices given on or after 27 July 1989.

Former s. 20A inserted by FA 1976, Sch. 6, with effect from 1976–77.

Cross references – FA 1988, s. 127(2)–(4): ancillary rights of access to computer hardware.

Police and Criminal Evidence Act 1984, s. 12: "personal records" (see s. 20A(1A)(a)) defined as documentary and other records concerning an individual relating to his physical or mental health, spiritual counselling etc. given to him, or counselling etc. given to him for the purposes of his personal welfare by any voluntary organisation or certain individuals.

Police and Criminal Evidence Act 1984, s. 13: "journalistic material" (see s. 20A(1A)(b)) defined as material acquired or created for the purposes of journalism which is in the possession of the person who so acquired or created it.

HMRC Manuals – Capital Gains Manual CG 20224: although no statutory authority exists an inspector may request (where he believes such a list may have been made) a copy of a list of investments and assets held at a particular date. Note, such requests should not be routinely made nor the impression given that there is authority for such a request.

20B Restrictions on powers under section 20A

20B [Omitted by FA 2012, s. 223 and Sch. 38, para. 45(b).]

History – S. 20B omitted by FA 2012, s. 223 and Sch. 38, para. 45(b), with effect from 1 April 2013 (SI 2013/279, art. 2), subject to savings provision at SI 2013/279, art. 3; where a notice is given under s. 20A on or before 31 March 2013, for the purposes of that notice the amendments made by FA 2012, Sch. 38, para. 44–47 shall be disregarded. Former s. 20B read as follows:

"Restrictions on powers under section 20A

History – In s. 20B, in the heading the word "section" substituted for the words "ss. 20 and" by FA 2008, s. 113 and Sch. 36, para. 68(2), with effect from 1 April 2009 (SI 2009/404, art. 2, subject to savings at SI 2009/404, art. 3).

20B(1) Before a notice is given to a person by an inspector under section 20A, the person must have been given a reasonable opportunity to deliver the documents in question; and the inspector must not apply for consent under section 20A(3), until the person has been given that opportunity.

20B(1A) [Omitted by FA 2008, s. 113 and Sch. 36, para. 68(4).]

20B(1B) [Omitted by FA 2008, s. 113 and Sch. 36, para. 68(4).]

20B(2) A notice under section 20A does not oblige a person to deliver documents relating to the conduct of a pending appeal by the client.

"Appeal" means appeal relating to tax.

20B(3) An inspector cannot under section 20A(1), give notice to a relevant lawyer, but the notice must in any such case be given (if at all) by the Board; and accordingly in relation to a relevant lawyer for references in section 20A to the inspector, there are substituted references to the Board.

20B(4) To comply with a notice under section 20A(1), copies of documents may be delivered instead of the originals; but–

(a) the copies must be photographic or otherwise by way of facsimile; and

(b) if so required by the inspector (or, as the case may be, the Board) in the case of any documents specified in the requirement, the originals must be made available for inspection by a named officer of the Board (failure to comply with this requirement counting as failure to comply with the notice).

20B(5) [Omitted by FA 2008, s. 113 and Sch. 36, para. 68(8).]

20B(6) [Omitted by FA 2008, s. 113 and Sch. 36, para. 68(8).]

20B(7) [Omitted by FA 2008, s. 113 and Sch. 36, para. 68(8).]

20B(8) A notice under section 20A(1) does not oblige a relevant lawyer to deliver or make available, without his client's consent, any document with respect to which a claim to professional privilege could be maintained.

20B(9) [Omitted by FA 2008, s. 113 and Sch. 36, para. 68(10).]

20B(10) [Omitted by FA 2008, s. 113 and Sch. 36, para. 68(10).]

20B(11) [Omitted by FA 2008, s. 113 and Sch. 36, para. 68(10).]

20B(12) [Omitted by FA 2008, s. 113 and Sch. 36, para. 68(10).]

20B(13) [Omitted by FA 2008, s. 113 and Sch. 36, para. 68(10).]

20B(14) [Omitted by FA 2008, s. 113 and Sch. 36, para. 68(10).]

20B(15) In this section **"relevant lawyer"** means a barrister, advocate, solicitor or other legal representative communications with whom may be the subject of a claim to professional privilege."

In former s. 20B(1) the words"under section 20(1), (3) or (8A), or", "(or, in the case of section 20(3), to deliver or make available)", ", or to furnish the particulars in question" and "section 20(7) or (8A) or, as the case may be," omitted by FA 2008, s. 113 and Sch. 36, para. 68(3), with effect from 1 April 2009 (SI 2009/404, art. 2, subject to savings at SI 2009/404, art. 3).

In former s. 20B(1), the words "section 20(1), (3) or (8A)" and "section 20(7) or (8A)" substituted by FA 1988, s. 126(4)(a) in respect of notices given on or after 29 July 1988.

In former s. 20B(1), the words ", or to furnish the particulars in question" inserted by FA 1989, s. 144(2) in respect of notices given on or after 27 July 1989.

Former s. 20B(1A) omitted by FA 2008, s. 113 and Sch. 36, para. 68(4), with effect from 1 April 2009 (SI 2009/404, art. 2, subject to savings at SI 2009/404, art. 3).

Former s. 20B(1A) inserted by FA 1989, s. 144(3) in respect of notices given on or after 27 July 1989.

Former s. 20B(1B) omitted by FA 2008, s. 113 and Sch. 36, para. 68(4), with effect from 1 April 2009 (SI 2009/404, art. 2, subject to savings at SI 2009/404, art. 3).

In former s. 20B(1B) the words "the tribunal" substituted for the words "a General or Special Commissioner" and the words "tribunal is" substituted for the words"Commissioner is" by SI 2009/56, art. 3(1) and Sch. 1, para. 10(2), operative from 1 April 2009, subject to transitional and saving provisions in SI 2009/56, Sch. 3.

Former s. 20B(1B) inserted by FA 1989, s. 144(3) in respect of notices given on or after 27 July 1989.

In former s. 20B(2), the words "A notice under section 20(1) does not oblige a person to deliver documents or furnish particulars relating to the conduct of any pending appeal by him; a notice under section 20(3) or (8A) does not oblige a person to deliver or make available documents relating to the conduct of a pending appeal by the taxpayer; and" omitted by FA 2008, s. 113 and Sch. 36, para. 68(5), with effect from 1 April 2009 (SI 2009/404, art. 2, subject to savings at SI 2009/404, art. 3).

In former s. 20B(2), references to s. 20(8A) substituted by FA 1988, s. 126(4)(b) in respect of notices given on or after 20 July 1988.

In former s. 20B(2), the words "or furnish particulars" insertedby FA 1989, s. 144(4) in respect of notices given on or after 27 July 1989.

In former s. 20B(3), the words "relevant lawyer" substituted in both places for the words "barrister, advocate or solicitor", by the Legal Services Act 2007, s. 208 and Sch. 21, para. 25, with effect from 1 January 2010 (SI 2009/3250, art. 2(h)).

In former s. 20B(3), the words "under section 20(1) or (3) or" and "section 20(3) and (4) and" omitted by FA 2008, s. 113 and Sch. 36, para. 68(6), with effect from 1 April 2009 (SI 2009/404, art. 2, subject to savings at SI 2009/404, art. 3).

In former s. 20B(4) the words "section 20(1) or" and ", and as an alternative to delivering documents to comply with a notice under section 20(3) or (8A)" omitted by FA 2008, s. 113 and Sch. 36, para. 68(7), with effect from 1 April 2009 (SI 2009/404, art. 2, subject to savings at SI 2009/404, art. 3).

In former s. 20B(4), references to s. 20(8A) substituted by FA 1988, s. 126(4)(b) in respect of notices given on or after 20 July 1988.

Former s. 20B(5) omitted by FA 2008, s. 113 and Sch. 36, para. 68(8), with effect from 1 April 2009 (SI 2009/404, art. 2, subject to savings at SI 2009/404, art. 3).

In former s. 20B(5), the words "does not oblige a person" substituted by FA 1989, s. 144(5) in respect of notices given on or after 27 July 1989.

Former s. 20B(6) omitted by FA 2008, s. 113 and Sch. 36, para. 68(8), with effect from 1 April 2009 (SI 2009/404, art. 2, subject to savings at SI 2009/404, art. 3).

In former s. 20B(6)(a) the word "tribunal" substituted for the words "Commissioner giving consent" and in para. (b) the words "the tribunal" substituted for the words "a General or Special Commissioner" and in words following para. (b) the word "tribunal" substituted for the word "Commissioner" by SI 2009/56, art. 3(1) and Sch. 1, para. 10(2), operative from 1 April 2009, subject to transitional and saving provisions in SI 2009/56, Sch. 3.

Former s. 20B(7) omitted by FA 2008, s. 113 and Sch. 36, para. 68(8), with effect from 1 April 2009 (SI 2009/404, art. 2, subject to savings at SI 2009/404, art. 3).

In former s. 20B(7), words omitted by FA 1989, s. 144(6) in respect of notices given on or after 27 July 1989.

In former s. 20B(8), the words "relevant lawyer" substituted for the words "barrister, advocate or a solicitor", by the Legal Services Act 2007, s. 208 and Sch. 21, para. 25, with effect from 1 January 2010 (SI 2009/3250, art. 2(h)).

In former s. 20B(8) the words"section 20(3)or (8A) or" omitted by FA 2008, s. 113 and Sch. 36, para. 68(9), with effect from 1 April 2009 (SI 2009/404, art. 2, subject to savings at SI 2009/404, art. 3).

In former s. 20B(8), references to s. 20(8A) substituted by FA 1988, s. 126(4)(b) in respect of notices given on or after 20 July 1988.

Former s. 20B(9)–(14) omitted by FA 2008, s. 113 and Sch. 36, para. 68(10), with effect from 1 April 2009 (SI 2009/404, art. 2, subject to savings at SI 2009/404, art. 3).

Former s. 20B(9)–(14) substituted for the original s. 20B(9) by FA 1989, s. 144(7) in respect of notices given on or after 27 July 1989.

Former s. 20B(15) inserted by the Legal Services Act 2007, s. 208, Sch. 21, para. 25, with effect from 1 January 2010 (SI 2009/3250, art. 2(h)).

Former s. 20B inserted by FA 1976, Sch. 6, with effect from 1976–77.

Cross references – SI 2009/275, art. 3(a): any decision under s. 20B(1B) or (6) is an excluded decision for the purposes of TCEA 2007, s. 11(1) and 13(1).

FA 1988, s. 127(2)–(4): ancillary rights of access to computer hardware.

ICTA 1988, s. 767C(8): application of s. 20B(4) and (8)–(14) to the Board's powers to obtain information where company ownership changes.

FA 1990, s. 125(2)(b), (c): construction of s. 20B(2), (6) where, by virtue of s. 125(1), Revenue use powers under s. 20 to obtain information on behalf of the tax authorities of an EU member state.

FA 2000, s. 146(4)(b), (c): application of s. 20B(2), (6) to proceedings etc. or loss of tax under the law of any territory outside the UK.

FA 2006, s. 174(1): modification of s. 20B for international tax arrangements.

20BA Orders for the delivery of documents

20BA(1) The appropriate judicial authority may make an order under this section if satisfied on information on oath given by an authorised officer of the Board–

(a) that there is reasonable ground for suspecting that an offence involving serious fraud in connection with, or in relation to, tax is being, has been or is about to be committed, and

(b) that documents which may be required as evidence for the purposes of any proceedings in respect of such an offence are or may be in the power or possession of any person.

20BA(2) An order under this section is an order requiring the person who appears to the authority to have in his possession or power the documents specified or described in the order to deliver them to an officer of the Board within–

(a) ten working days after the day on which notice of the order is served on him, or

(b) such shorter or longer period as may be specified in the order.

For this purpose a **"working day"** means any day other than a Saturday, Sunday or public holiday.

20BA(3) Where in Scotland the information mentioned in subsection (1) above relates to persons residing or having places of business at addresses situated in different sheriffdoms–

(a) an application for an order may be made to the sheriff for the sheriffdom in which any of the addresses is situated, and

(b) where the sheriff makes an order in respect of a person residing or having a place of business in his own sheriffdom, he may also make orders in respect of all or any of the other persons to whom the information relates (whether or not they have an add[r]ess within the sheriffdom).

20BA(4) Schedule 1AA to this Act contains provisions supplementing this section.

History – S. 20BA inserted by FA 2000, s. 149(1).

Cross references – Criminal Justice and Police Act 2001, s. 59(7)(b)(iii): enhanced powers of seizure: applications to "appropriate judicial authority".
TCA 2002, s. 36(1): application of s. 20BA in relation to tax credits fraud.

20BB Falsification etc. of documents

20BB(1) Subject to subsections (2) and (3) below, a person shall be guilty of an offence if he intentionally falsifies, conceals, destroys or otherwise disposes of, or causes or permits the falsification, concealment, destruction or disposal of, a document which–

(a) he has been required by an order under section 20BA above,

(b) [omitted by FA 2012, s. 223 and Sch. 38, para. 46(2)(d),]

to deliver, or to deliver or make available for inspection.

20BB(2) A person does not commit an offence under subsection (1) above if he acts–

(a) with the written permission of the tribunal or an officer of the Board, or

(b) after the document has been delivered,

(c) [omitted by FA 2012, s. 223 and Sch. 38, para. 46(3)(d).]

20BB(3) A person does not commit an offence under subsection (1)(a) above if he acts after the end of the period of two years beginning with the date on which the order is made, unless before the end of that period an officer of Revenue and Customs has notified the person in writing that the order has not been complied with to the officer's satisfaction.

20BB(4) [Omitted by FA 2012, s. 223 and Sch. 38, para. 46(5).]

20BB(5) A person guilty of an offence under subsection (1) above shall be liable–

(a) on summary conviction, to a fine not exceeding the statutory maximum;

(b) on conviction on indictment, to imprisonment for a term not exceeding two years or to a fine or to both.

History – In s. 20BB(1), the words "subsections (2) and (3)" substituted for the words "subsections (2) to (4)" by FA 2012, s. 223 and Sch. 38, para. 46(2)(a), with effect from 1 April 2013 (SI 2013/279, art. 2), subject to savings provision at SI 2013/279, art. 3; where a notice is given under s. 20A on or before 31 March 2013, for the purposes of that notice the amendments made by FA 2013, Sch. 38, para. 44–47 shall be disregarded.
In s. 20BB(1)(a), the words "a notice under section 20A above or" omitted by FA 2012, s. 223 and Sch. 38, para. 46(2)(b), with effect from 1 April 2013 (SI 2013/279, art. 2), subject to savings provision at SI 2013/279, art. 3; where a notice is given under s. 20A on or before 31 March 2013, for the purposes of that notice the amendments made by FA 2012, Sch. 38, para. 44–47 shall be disregarded.
In s. 20BB(1)(a) the words "20 or" omitted by FA 2008, s, 113 and Sch. 36, para. 69(2), with effect from 1 April 2009 (SI 2009/404, art. 2, subject to savings at SI 2009/404, art. 3).
In s. 20BB(1)(a) words "or an order under section 20BA above" inserted by FA 2000, s. 149(3)(a).
S. 20BB(1)(b) (and the "or" before it) omitted by FA 2012, s. 223 and Sch. 38, para. 46(2), with effect from 1 April 2013 (SI 2013/279, art. 2), subject to savings provision at SI 2013/279, art. 3; where a notice is given under s. 20A on or before 31 March 2013, for the purposes of that notice the amendments made by FA 2012, Sch. 38, para. 44–47 shall be disregarded. Former s. 20BB(1)(b) read as follows:

"(b) he has been given an opportunity in accordance with section 20B(1) above,".

In s. 20BB(2)(a), the words ", the inspector" omitted by FA 2012, s. 223 and Sch. 38, para. 46(3)(a), with effect from 1 April 2013 (SI 2013/279, art. 2), subject to savings provision at SI 2013/279, art. 3; where a notice is given under s. 20A on or before 31 March 2013, for the purposes of that notice the amendments made by FA 2012, Sch. 38, para. 44–47 shall be disregarded.
In s. 20BB(2)(a), the words "the tribunal" substituted for the words "a General or Special Commissioner" by SI 2009/56, art. 3(1) and Sch. 1, para. 11, operative from 1 April 2009, subject to transitional and saving provisions in SI 2009/56, Sch. 3.
In s. 20BB(2)(b) the words "or, in a case within section 20(3) or (8A) above, inspected" omitted by FA 2008, s, 113 and Sch. 36, para. 69(3), with effect from 1 April 2009 (SI 2009/404, art. 2, subject to savings at SI 2009/404, art. 3).
S. 20BB(2)(c) (and the "or" before it) omitted (and the "or" in (a) inserted) by FA 2012, s. 223 and Sch. 38, para. 46(3), with effect from 1 April 2013 (SI 2013/279, art. 2), subject to savings provision at SI 2013/279, art. 3; where a notice is given under s. 20A on or before 31 March 2013, for the purposes of that notice the amendments made by FA 2012, Sch. 38, para. 44–47 shall be disregarded.
Former s. 20BB(2)(c) read as follows:
"(c) after a copy has been delivered in accordance with section 20B(4) or (14) above and the original has been inspected.".
In s. 20BB(3), the words "the order is made, unless before the end of that period an officer of Revenue and Customs has notified the person in writing that the order has not been complied with to the officer's satisfaction" substituted for the words "the notice is given or the order is made, unless before the end of that period the inspector or an officer of the Board has notified the person in writing that the notice or order has not been complied with to his satisfaction" by FA 2012, s. 223 and Sch. 38, para. 46(4), with effect from 1 April 2013 (SI 2013/279, art. 2), subject to savings provision at SI 2013/279, art. 3; where a notice is given under s. 20A on or before 31 March 2013, for the purposes of that notice the amendments made by FA 2012, Sch. 38, para. 44–47 shall be disregarded.
In s. 20BB(3) words "or the order is made" and "or order" inserted by FA 2000, s. 149(3)(b), (c) respectively.
S. 20BB(4) omitted by FA 2012, s. 223 and Sch. 38, para. 46(5), with effect from 1 April 2013 (SI 2013/279, art. 2), subject to savings provision at SI 2013/279, art. 3; where a notice is given under s. 20A on or before 31 March 2013, for the purposes of that notice the amendments made by FA 2012, Sch. 38, para. 44–47 shall be disregarded. Former s. 20BB(4) read as follows:
"20BB(4) A person does not commit an offence under subsection (1)(b) above if he acts–
(a) after the end of the period of six months beginning with the date on which an opportunity to deliver the document was given, or
(b) after an application for consent to a notice being given in relation to the document has been refused.".
S. 20BB inserted by FA 1989, s. 145 for any falsification, concealment, destruction or disposal on or after 27 July 1989.

Cross references – TCA 2002, s. 36(1): application of s. 20BB in relation to tax credits fraud.
FA 2006, s. 174(1): modification of s. 20BB for international tax arrangements.

20C Entry with warrant to obtain documents

20C [Omitted by FA 2007, s. 84(4) and Sch. 22, para. 4(a); repealed by FA 2007, s. 114 and Sch. 27, Pt. 5(1).]

History – S. 20C omitted by FA 2007, s. 84(4) and Sch. 22, para. 4(a) with effect from 1 December 2007 by virtue of SI 2007/3166, art. 3(a), and repealed by FA 2007, s. 114 and Sch. 27, Pt. 5(1) with effect from 8 November 2007 by virtue of SI 2007/3166, art. 2(c) in accordance with FA 2007, s. 84(5).
Previously, in s. 20C(1), the words "serious fraud" and "is being, has been or is about to be" substituted by FA 1989, s. 146(2) for warrants issued on or after 27 July 1989.
S. 20C(1AA) inserted by FA 2000, s. 150(2) with effect from 28 July 2000.
S. 20C(1A) and (1B) inserted by FA 1989, s. 146(3) in respect of warrants issued on or after 27 July 1989.
S. 20C(3) substituted by FA 1989, s. 146(4) in respect of warrants issued on or after 27 July 1989.
S. 20C(3A) inserted by FA 2000, s. 150(3) with effect from 28 July 2000.
In s. 20C(3A), the words "stored in any electronic form" substituted and "or from which it can readily be produced in a visible and legible form" inserted by the Criminal Justice and Police Act 2001, Sch. 2, para. 13(1) and (2)(d) with effect from 6 April 2003 (SI 2003/708, art. 2(k)).
S. 20C(4), (4A) and (4B) substituted by FA 2000, s. 150(4) with effect from 28 July 2000.
S. 20C(5)–(8) substituted by FA 1989, s. 146(4) in respect of warrants issued after 27 July 1989.
S. 20C(9) inserted by FA 2000, s. 150(5).
S. 20C inserted by FA 1976, Sch. 6, with effect from 1976–77.

Cross references – CRCA 2005, s. 13(3)(b); s. 14(2)(b): Board's power to approve an application for a search warrant is not able to be delegated.
Criminal Justice and Police Act 2001, s. 63(2)(e): power to obtain hard copies of information which is stored in electronic form to be treated as a power of seizure for the purposes of certain provisions of Pt. II of that Act.
Criminal Justice and Police Act 2001, Sch. 1, para. 13: power of seizure conferred by s. 20C is a power to which s. 50 of that Act applies.
TCA 2002, s. 36(2), (3): application of s. 20C in relation to tax credits fraud.

20CC Procedure where documents etc. are removed

20CC [Omitted by FA 2007, s. 84(4) and Sch. 22, para. 4(a); repealed by FA 2007, s. 114 and Sch. 27, Pt. 5(1).]

History – S. 20CC omitted by FA 2007, s. 84(4) and Sch. 22, para. 4(a) with effect from 1 December 2007 by virtue of SI 2007/3166, art. 3(a), and repealed by FA 2007, s. 114 and Sch. 27, Pt. 5(1) with effect from 8 November 2007 by virtue of SI 2007/3166, art. 2(c) in accordance with FA 2007, s. 84(5).
S. 20CC previously inserted by FA 1989, s. 147(1) for warrants issued on or after 27 July 1989.

Cross references – CJPA 2001, s. 57(1)(c): enhanced powers of seizure under s. 50, 51 of that Act.
TCA 2002, s. 36(2): application of s. 20CC in relation to tax credits fraud.

20D Interpretation of s. 20 to 20C

20D(1) For the purposes of section 20BA above, **"the appropriate judicial authority"** is–
(a) in England and Wales, a Circuit judge;
(b) in Scotland, a sheriff; and
(c) in Northern Ireland, a county court judge.

20D(2) [Omitted by FA 2012, s. 223 and Sch. 38, para. 47(b).]

20D(3) [Omitted by FA 2008, s. 113 and Sch. 36, para. 70(3).]

History – In s. 20D(1), the words "section 20BA" substituted for the words "sections 20A and 20BA" by FA 2012, s. 223 and Sch. 38, para. 47(a), with effect from 1 April 2013 (SI 2013/279, art. 2), subject to savings provision at SI 2013/279, art. 3; where a notice is given under s. 20A on or before 31 March 2013, for the purposes of that notice the amendments made by FA 2012, Sch. 38, para. 44–47 shall be disregarded.
In s. 20D(1), the words "sections 20A and 20BA" substituted by FA 2007, s. 84 and Sch. 22, para. 1 with effect from 1 December 2007, by virtue of SI 2007/3166, art. 3(a) in accordance with s. 84(4).
In s. 20D(1) reference to s. 20BA inserted by FA 2000, s. 149(4)with effect from 28 July 2000.
S. 20D(2) omitted by FA 2012, s. 223 and Sch. 38, para. 47(b), with effect from 1 April 2013 (SI 2013/279, art. 2), subject to savings provision at SI 2013/279, art. 3; where a notice is given under s. 20A on or before 31 March 2013, for the purposes of that notice the amendments made by FA 2012, Sch. 38, para. 44–47 shall be disregarded. Former s. 20D(2) read as follows:
"**20D(2)** For the purposes of section 20A, a person stands in relation to another as tax accountant at any time when he assists the other in the preparation or delivery of any information, return, accounts or other document which he knows will be, or is or are likely to be, used for any purpose of tax; and his clients are all those to whom he stands or has stood in that relationship.".
In s. 20D(2) the word "section" substituted for the words "sections 20 and" by FA 2008, s. 113 and Sch. 36, para. 70, with effect from 1 April 2009 (SI 2009/404, art. 2, subject to savings at SI 2009/404, art. 3).
S. 20(D)(2) amended by FA 1989, s. 148 by substituting the words "or delivery … likely to be, used" in respect of warrants issued on or after 27 July 1989.
S. 20D(3) omitted by FA 2008, s. 113 and Sch. 36, para. 70, with effect from 1 April 2009 (SI 2009/404, art. 2, subject to savings at SI 2009/404, art. 3).
Former s. 20D(3) substituted by Civil Evidence Act 1995, Sch. 1, para. 6, with effect from 31 January 1997 by virtue of SI 1996/3217 (C. 101).

Cross references – FA 1988, s. 127(1): construction of references in Taxes Acts to "document" and "copy of a document".
FA 1988, s. 127(2)–(4): ancillary rights of access to computer hardware.
FA 2006, s. 174(1): modification of s. 20D for international tax arrangements.

21 Transactions in securities etc.

21 [Omitted by FA 2011, s. 86 and Sch. 23, para. 51(2)(k).]

History – S. 21 omitted by FA 2011, s. 86 and Sch. 23, para. 51(2)(k), with effect from 1 April 2012, but in relation to a notice issued before that date, s. 21 continues to apply as if it had not been omitted (FA 2011, Sch. 23, para. 65). Former s. 21 read as follows:

"*Transactions in securities etc.*

21(1) The Board may exercise the powers conferred by this section as respects, and in connection with, any business consisting in or involving dealings in securities; and for the purposes of this section it shall be immaterial whether those dealings are or, as the case may be, were–
(a) on behalf of persons other than the person carrying on the business;
(b) by that person on his own behalf; or
(c) a mixture of the two.
21(2) With a view to obtaining information about securities transactions in the course of a business within subsection (1) above, the Board may serve on the person by whom the business is or has been carried on a notice requiring him to make available within a time specified in the notice, for inspection by an inspector or other officer of the Board, all such books, accounts and other documents in his possession or power as may be specified or described in the notice, being books, accounts or other documents which in the opinion of the Board contain or may contain information directly or indirectly relating to any such transactions.
21(3) The Board may serve on any broker a notice requiring him to make available within a time specified in the notice, for inspection by an inspector or other officer of the Board, all such books, accounts or other documents in his possession or power as may be specified or described in the notice, being books, accounts or other documents which in the opinion of the Board contain or may contain information relating directly or indirectly to securities transactions in the course of any business of a person other than the broker which is a business within subsection (1) above.
21(4) Where a person (**"the recipient"**) who is not a broker has directly or indirectly received from another person any payment which–
(a) is made by that other person in the course of a business within subsection (1) above, and
(b) is a payment treated by that other person as made in respect of interest on securities,
the Board may by notice in writing require the recipient to state, within a time specified in the notice, whether the amount received is in whole or in part received on behalf of, or for payment on to, a third person and (if it is) to furnish the name and address of that third person.
21(4A) Where a person (**"the payer"**) has directly or indirectly paid to another person any sum which–
(a) constitutes a receipt by that other person in the course of a business within subsection (1) above, and
(b) is a receipt treated by that other person as accruing in respect of interest on securities,
the Board may by notice in writing require the payer to state, within a time specified in the notice, whether the amount paid is in whole or in part received from, or paid on account of, a third person and (if it is) to furnish the name and address of that third person.
21(5) If, for the purpose of obtaining (from any persons at all) information directly or indirectly relating to any securities transactions in the course of a business within subsection (1) above, any person in whose name any securities are registered is so required by notice in writing by the Board, he shall state whether or not he is the beneficial owner of those securities, and, if not the beneficial owner of those securities or any of them, shall furnish the name and address of the person or persons on whose behalf the securities are registered in his name.
21(5A) Where it appears to the Board that a person may have incurred a liability to pay or account for tax under Chapter 2 of Part 11 or Chapter 9 of Part 15 of ITA 2007 (manufactured payments), the Board may by notice served on that person require him, within such period (not being less than 28 days) as may be specified in the notice, to provide the Board with information which–
(a) is available to that person; and
(b) is or may be relevant to whether that person has incurred such a liability, or to the extent of such liability.
21(6) The Board may not exercise their powers under the preceding provisions of this section for the purpose of obtaining information relating to transactions in any year of assessment ending more than six years before the service of the notice.
21(7) In this section–

"broker" means any person who is a member of a recognised investment exchange, within the meaning given by section 285(1)(a) of the Financial Services and Markets Act 2000;

"interest" includes dividends;

"securities" includes shares and stock; and

"securities transaction" means–
(a) any transaction in securities;
(b) any transaction under which a payment which is representative of any interest on a security has been, is to be or may be made; or
(c) the making or receipt of such a payment.".

Former section heading amended by CCH to reflect altered content (originally "Stock jobbers' transactions").
Former s. 21(1) substituted by FA 1997, s. 76 and Sch. 10, para. 14(1), (2), with effect, by virtue of SI 1997/991, from 1 July 1997.

In former s. 21(2), words "securities transactions" and "person" substituted by FA 1997, s. 76 and Sch. 10, para. 14(3) with effect, by virtue of SI 1997/991, from 1 July 1997.
In former s. 21(3) the words "securities transactions … broker which is" substituted by FA 1997, s. 76 and Sch. 10, para. 14(4), with effect, by virtue of SI 1997/991, from 1 July 1997.
Former s. 21(4), (4A) substituted for former s. 21(4) by FA 1997, s. 76 and Sch. 10, para. 14(5), with effect, by virtue of SI 1997/991, from 1 July 1997.
In former s. 21(5), words "at all" and "securities transactions" substituted by FA 1997, s. 76 and Sch. 10, para. 14(1), (6), (7), with effect by virtue of SI 1997/991, from 1 July 1977.
In former s. 21(5A), the words "Chapter 2 of Part 11 or Chapter 9 of Part 15 of ITA 2007" substituted for the words "Schedule 23A to the principal Act" by ITA 2007, s. 1027 and Sch. 1, para. 248, with effect from 6 April 2007.
Former s. 21(5A) inserted by FA 1997, s. 76 and Sch. 10, para. 14(1), (6), (7), with effect, by virtue of SI 1997/991, from 1 July 1997.
In former s. 21(7), in the definition of "broker", the words "given by section 285(1)(a) of the Financial Services and Markets Act 2000" substituted for "of the Financial Services Act 1986", by SI 2001/3629, art. 3 with effect from 1 December 2001.
Former s. 21(7) substituted by FA 1997, s. 76 and Sch. 10, para. 14(1), (8), with effect, by virtue of SI 1997/991, from 1 July 1997.

Cross references – CRCA 2005, s. 16 and Sch 2(2): power under this section may be exercised only in connection with functions relating to matters to which CRCA 2005, s. 7 applies.
Financial Services and Markets Act 2000, s. 285(1)(a) defines a "recognised investment exchange" as an investment exchange in relation to which a recognition order under s. 290 of that Act is in force.

SURTAX

22 Additional particulars for surtax

22 [Omitted by SI 2009/2035, art. 2 and Schedule, para. 5.]

History – S. 22 omitted by SI 2009/2035, art. 2 and Schedule, para. 5, with effect from 13 August 2009.

23 Power to obtain copies of registers of securities

23 [Omitted by FA 2011, s. 86 and Sch. 23, para. 51(2)(l).]

History – S. 23 omitted by FA 2011, s. 86 and Sch. 23, para. 51(2)(l), with effect from 1 April 2012, but in relation to a notice issued before that date, s. 23 continues to apply as if it had not been omitted (FA 2011, Sch. 23, para. 65). Former s. 23 read as follows:

"Power to obtain copies of registers of securities

23(1) The Board may cause to be served upon any body corporate a notice requiring them to deliver to the Board within a specified time, being not less than twenty-one days, a copy, certified by a duly authorised officer of such body, of the whole of, or any specified class of entries in, any register containing the names of the holders of any securities issued by them.
23(2) On delivery of the copy in accordance with the notice payment shall be made therefor at the rate of 25 pence in respect of each one hundred entries.
23(3) In this section, **"security"** includes shares, stock, debentures and debenture stock, and **"entry"** means, in relation to any register, so much thereof as relates to the securities held by any one person.".
Former s. 23(2) amended by Decimal Currency Act 1969, s. 10, 16(1), inserting the decimalised amount.

Cross references – CRCA 2005, s. 16 and Sch. 2(2): power under this section may be exercised only in connection with functions relating to matters to which CRCA 2005, s. 7 applies.

24 Power to obtain information as to income from securities

24 [Omitted by FA 2011, s. 86 and Sch. 23, para. 51(2)(m).]

History – S. 24 omitted by FA 2011, s. 86 and Sch. 23, para. 51(2)(m), with effect from 1 April 2012, but in relation to a notice issued before that date, s. 24 continues to apply as if it had not been omitted (FA 2011, Sch. 23, para. 65). Former s. 24 read as follows:

"Power to obtain information as to income from securities

24(1) The Board may by notice in writing require–
(a) any person, being a registered or inscribed holder of any United Kingdom securities, who, in any year of assessment, has received on behalf of any other person any income arising from any such securities, or
(b) any person by or through whom, in any year of assessment, any income in respect of United Kingdom securities has been paid in any case where–
  (i) the registered or inscribed holder of the securities is not the person to whom the income was paid or,
  (ii) the securities are bearer securities,

to furnish them, within such time as may be specified in the notice (not being less than twenty-eight days) with particulars of the amounts so received or, as the case may be, paid in that year (other than amounts received or paid in that year on behalf of or to any one person which did not exceed in the aggregate the sum of £15), the securities to which those amounts respectively relate, and the names and addresses of the persons on whose behalf or to whom those amounts were respectively received or paid.
24(2) The Board may similarly require any person who acts or has acted, directly or indirectly, as an intermediary or as one of a series of intermediaries between any such person as is specified in subsection (1)(a) or (b) above and the person or persons beneficially entitled to the income in question to furnish such information as the Board may require for the purpose of enabling them to ascertain the names and addresses of the person or persons beneficially entitled to the income and the respective amounts to which those persons were beneficially entitled.
24(3) Nothing in this section shall impose on any bank the obligation to disclose any particulars relating to income from securities in cases where the person beneficially entitled to the income is not resident in the United Kingdom.
24(3ZA) If–
(a) a person beneficially entitled to income from any securities is resident in a territory outside the United Kingdom, and
(b) there are double taxation arrangements with respect to income tax or corporation tax which relate to that territory,

subsection (3) does not exempt any bank from the duty of disclosing to the Board particulars relating to the income of that person.
24(3ZB) *In subsection (3ZA)* **"double taxation arrangements"** means arrangements which have effect under section 2(1) of TIOPA 2010 (double taxation relief by agreement with territories outside the United Kingdom).
24(3A) In this section **"bank"** has the meaning given by section 991 of ITA 2007.
24(4) In this section–

"securities" includes shares, stocks, bonds, debentures and debenture stock, and

"United Kingdom securities" means any securities issued by or on behalf of Her Majesty's Government in the United Kingdom or the Government of Northern Ireland and any securities of a body corporate incorporated in any part of the United Kingdom.".

Former s. 24(3ZA) and (3ZB) inserted by TIOPA 2010, s. 374 and Sch. 8, para. 4, with effect for corporation tax purposes for accounting periods ending on or after 1 April 2010, for income tax and capital gains tax purposes for the tax year 2010–11 and subsequent tax years, and for petroleum revenue tax purposes for chargeable periods beginning on or after 1 July 2010.

In former s. 24(3A), the words "section 991 of ITA 2007" substituted by ITA 2007, s. 1027 and Sch. 1, para. 249, with effect from 6 April 2007.

Former s. 24(3A) inserted by FA 1996, s. 198 and Sch. 37, para. 11(1), (2), (5), with effect in relation to requirements imposed on or after 29 April 1996.

Cross references – CRCA 2005, s. 16 and Sch. 2(2): power under this section may be exercised only in connection with functions relating to matters to which CRCA 2005, s. 7 applies.

ICTA 1988, s. 816(3): banks have an overriding duty to make disclosures in cases where double taxation treaties apply.

CHARGEABLE GAINS

25 Issuing houses, stockbrokers, auctioneers, etc.

25 [Omitted by FA 2011, s. 86 and Sch. 23, para. 51(2)(n).]

History – S. 25 omitted by FA 2011, s. 86 and Sch. 23, para. 51(2)(n), with effect from 1 April 2012, but in relation to a notice issued before that date, s. 25 continues to apply as if it had not been omitted (FA 2011, Sch. 23, para. 65). Former s. 25 read as follows:

"Issuing houses, stockbrokers, auctioneers, etc.

25(1) For the purpose of obtaining particulars of chargeable gains an inspector may by notice in writing require a return under any of the provisions of this section.

25(2) An issuing house or other person carrying on a business of effecting public issues of shares or securities in any company, or placings of shares or securities in any company, either on behalf of the company, or on behalf of holders of blocks of shares or securities which have not previously been the subject of a public issue or placing, may be required to make a return of all such public issues or placings effected by that person in the course of the business in the period specified in the notice requiring the return, giving particulars of the persons to or with whom the shares or securities are issued, allotted or placed, and the number or amount of the shares or securities so obtained by them respectively.

25(3) A person not carrying on such a business may be required to make a return as regards any such public issue or placing effected by that person and specified in the notice, giving particulars of the persons to or with whom the shares or securities are issued, allotted, or placed and the number or amount of the shares or securities so obtained by them respectively.

25(4) A member of a stock exchange in the United Kingdom, other than a market maker, may be required to make a return giving particulars of any transactions effected by him in the course of his business in the period specified in the notice requiring the return and giving particulars of–

(a) the parties to the transactions,
(b) the number or amount of the shares or securities dealt with in the respective transactions, and
(c) the amount or value of the consideration.

25(5) A person (other than a member of a stock exchange in the United Kingdom) who acts as an agent or broker in the United Kingdom in transactions in shares or securities may be required to make a return giving particulars of any such transactions effected by him after 5th April 1968 and in the period specified in the notice, and giving particulars of–

(a) the parties to the transactions,
(b) the number or amount of the shares or securities dealt with in the respective transactions, and
(c) the amount or value of the consideration.

25(6) The committee or other person or body of persons responsible for managing a clearing house for any terminal market in commodities may be required to make a return giving particulars of any transactions effected through the clearing house in the period specified in the notice requiring the return and giving particulars of–

(a) the parties to the transactions,
(b) the amounts dealt with in those transactions respectively, and
(c) the amount or value of the consideration.

25(7) An auctioneer, and any person carrying on a trade of dealing in any description of tangible movable property, or of acting as an agent or intermediary in dealings in any description of tangible movable property, may be required to make a return giving particulars of any transactions effected by or through him in which any asset which is tangible movable property is disposed of for a consideration the amount or value of which, in the hands of the recipient, exceeds £6,000.

25(8) No person shall be required under this section to include in a return particulars of any transaction effected more than three years before the service of the notice requiring him to make the return.

25(9) In this section **"company"** and **"shares"** shall be construed in accordance with sections 99, 103A and 288(1) of the 1992 Act.

25(10) In this section **"market maker"**, in relation to shares or securities, means a person who–

(a) holds himself out at all normal times in compliance with the rules of The Stock Exchange as willing to buy and sell shares or securities of the kind concerned at a price specified by him, and
(b) is recognised as doing so by the Council of The Stock Exchange.".

Former s. 25(4) amended by FA 1986, Sch. 18, para. 8(1) in relation to transactions after 26 October 1986, by substituting "market maker" for "jobber" and s. 25(10) accordingly inserted by para. 8(2).

Former s. 25(7) amended by FA 1989, s. 123(1)(c), (2) by substituting "£6,000" in relation to disposals after 5 April 1989.

References to provisions of the 1992 Act substituted by TCGA 1992, s. 290 and Sch. 10, para. 2(4).

In former s. 25(9), "103A" inserted by FA 2009, s. 44 and Sch. 22, para. 11(1)(a) with effect from 1 December 2009 (FA 2009, Sch. 22, para. 13(1)).

Cross references – FA 1986, Sch. 18, para. 8(4): the Board has power to make regulations concerning the interpretation of "The Stock Exchange" and "The Council of the Stock Exchange".

TCGA 1992, s. 99: application of tax on chargeable gains as if unit trust schemes were companies.

TCGA 1992, s. 288(1): "company" includes any body corporate or unincorporated association but not a partnership.

HMRC Manuals – Capital Gains CG10370: internal guidance refers to a limit under s. 25(7) of £20,000 per transaction.

26 Nominee shareholders

26 [Omitted by FA 2011, s. 86 and Sch. 23, para. 51(2)(o).]

History – S. 26 omitted by FA 2011, s. 86 and Sch. 23, para. 51(2)(o), with effect from 1 April 2012, but in relation to a notice issued before that date, s. 26 continues to apply as if it had not been omitted (FA 2011, Sch. 23, para. 65). Former s. 26 read as follows:

"Nominee shareholders

26(1) If, for the purpose of obtaining particulars of chargeable gains, any person in whose name any shares of a company are registered is so required by notice in writing by the Board or an inspector, he shall state whether or not he is the beneficial owner of those shares and, if not the beneficial owner of those shares or any of them, shall furnish the name and address of the person or persons on whose behalf the shares are registered in his name.
26(2) In this section references to shares include references to securities and loan capital.".

27 Settled property

27 [Omitted by FA 2011, s. 86 and Sch. 23, para. 51(2)(p).]

History – S. 27 omitted by FA 2011, s. 86 and Sch. 23, para. 51(2)(p), with effect from 1 April 2012, but in relation to a notice issued before that date, s. 27 continues to apply as if it had not been omitted (FA 2011, Sch. 23, para. 65). former s. 27 read as follows:

"Settled property

27(1) The Board may by notice in writing require any person, being a party to a settlement, to furnish them within such time as they may direct (not being less than twenty-eight days) with such particulars as they think necessary for the purposes of the 1992 Act.
27(2) In this section **"settlement"** has the meaning given by section 620 of ITTOIA 2005.".
In former s. 27(2) references to ICTA 1988, s. 660G(1), (2) substituted by FA 1995, s. 74 and Sch. 17, para. 21, with effect for the year 1995–96 and subsequent years of assessment and replaced with a reference to ITTOIA 2005, s. 620 by ITTOIA 2005, s. 882(1) and Sch. 1, para. 368; effective for income tax purposes for 2005–06 onwards and for corporation tax purposes for accounting periods ending after 5 April 2005 (ITTOIA 2005, s. 883(1)).
Reference to provisions of the principal Act substituted by ICTA 1988, Sch. 29, para. 32, that Act becoming the principal Act (TMA 1970, s. 118(1)).
References to the 1992 Act substituted by TCGA 1992, s. 290 and Sch. 10, para. 2(2).

Cross references – ICTA 1988, s. 660G(1): definition of settlement by inclusion of any disposition, trust, covenant, agreement or transfer of assets arrangement.
TCGA 1992, s. 98: special powers to obtain information for the purposes of the attribution of gains of non-resident or dual resident settlements etc. to beneficiaries.

28 Non-resident companies and trusts

28 [Omitted by SI 2009/2035, art. 2 and Schedule, para. 6.]

History – S. 28 omitted by SI 2009/2035, art. 2 and Schedule, para. 6, with effect from 13 August 2009.

PART 3A – REFERRAL OF QUESTIONS DURING ENQUIRY

History – Pt. 3A inserted by FA 2001, s. 88 and Sch. 29, para. 6. It applies:
(a) where the notice of enquiry is given after 11 May 2001, or
(b) where the enquiry is in progress immediately before 11 May 2001.
For the purposes of paragraph (b) an enquiry is in progress until the officer's enquiries fall to be treated as completed under s. 28A(5) or, as the case may be, s. 28B(5) of the Taxes Management Act 1970 (as those provisions had effect apart from the amendments made by FA 2001, Sch. 29).

28ZA Referral of questions during enquiry

28ZA(1) At any time when an enquiry is in progress under section 9A(1) or 12AC(1) of this Act, any question arising in connection with the subject-matter of the enquiry may be referred to the tribunal for its determination.

28ZA(2) Notice of referral must be given–

(a) jointly by the taxpayer and an officer of the Board,

(b) [Omitted by SI 2009/56, art. 3(1) and Sch. 1, para. 12(3).]

(c) to the tribunal.

28ZA(3) [Omitted by SI 2009/56, art. 3(1) and Sch. 1, para. 12(4).]

28ZA(4) More than one notice of referral may be given under this section in relation to an enquiry.

28ZA(5) For the purposes of this section the period during which an enquiry is in progress is the whole of the period–

(a) beginning with the day on which notice of enquiry is given, and

(b) ending with the day on which the enquiry is completed.

28ZA(6) In this section **"the taxpayer"** means–

(a) in relation to an enquiry under section 9A(1) of this Act, the person to whom the notice of enquiry was given;

(b) in relation to an enquiry under section 12AC(1) of this Act, the person to whom the notice of enquiry was given or his successor.

History – In s. 28ZA(1) the words "tribunal for its" substituted for the words "Special Commissioners for their" by SI 2009/56, art. 3(1) and Sch. 1, para. 12(2), operative from 1 April 2009, subject to transitional and saving provisions in SI 2009/56, Sch. 3.
In s. 28ZA(2)(b) omitted and in para. (c) the word "tribunal" substituted for the words "Special Commissioners" by SI 2009/56, art. 3(1) and Sch. 1, para. 12(3), operative from 1 April 2009, subject to transitional and saving provisions in SI 2009/56, Sch. 3.

In s. 28ZA(3) omitted by SI 2009/56, art. 3(1) and Sch. 1, para. 12(4), operative from 1 April 2009, subject to transitional and saving provisions in SI 2009/56, Sch. 3.
S. 28ZA inserted by FA 2001, s. 88 and Sch. 29, para. 6. It applies:
(a) where the notice of enquiry is given after 11 May 2001, or
(b) where the enquiry is in progress immediately before 11 May 2001.
For the purposes of para. (b) an enquiry is in progress until the officer's enquiries fall to be treated as completed under s. 28A(5) or, as the case may be, s. 28B(5) of the Taxes Management Act 1970 (as those provisions had effect apart from the amendments made by FA 2001, Sch. 29).

28ZB Withdrawal of notice of referral

28ZB(1) Either party may withdraw a notice of referral under section 28ZA of this Act.

28ZB(2) [Omitted by SI 2009/56, art. 3(1) and Sch. 1, para. 13(3).]

History – In s. 28ZB(1) the words "by notice in accordance with this section" omitted by SI 2009/56, art. 3(1) and Sch. 1, para. 13(2), operative from 1 April 2009, subject to transitional and saving provisions in SI 2009/56, Sch. 3.
In s. 28ZB(2) omitted by SI 2009/56, art. 3(1) and Sch. 1, para. 13(3), operative from 1 April 2009, subject to transitional and saving provisions in SI 2009/56, Sch. 3.
S. 28ZB inserted by FA 2001, s. 88 and Sch. 29, para. 6. It applies:
(a) where the notice of enquiry is given after 11 May 2001, or
(b) where the enquiry is in progress immediately before 11 May 2001.
For the purposes of paragraph (b) an enquiry is in progress until the officer's enquiries fall to be treated as completed under s. 28A(5) or, as the case may be, s. 28B(5) of the Taxes Management Act 1970 (as those provisions had effect apart from the amendments made by FA 2001, Sch. 29).

28ZC Regulations with respect to referrals

28ZC [Omitted by SI 2009/56, art. 3(1) and Sch. 1, para. 14.]

History – S. 28ZC omitted by SI 2009/56, art. 3(1) and Sch. 1, para. 14, operative from 1 April 2009, subject to transitional and saving provisions in SI 2009/56, Sch. 3.

28ZD Effect of referral on enquiry

28ZD(1) While proceedings on a referral under section 28ZA of this Act are in progress in relation to an enquiry–

(a) no closure notice shall be given in relation to the enquiry, and

(b) no application may be made for a direction to give such a notice.

28ZD(2) For the purposes of this section proceedings on a referral are in progress where–

(a) notice of referral has been given,

(b) the notice has not been withdrawn, and

(c) the questions referred have not been finally determined.

28ZD(3) For the purposes of subsection (2)(c) above a question referred is finally determined when–

(a) it has been determined by the tribunal, and

(b) there is no further possibility of that determination being varied or set aside (disregarding any power to give permission to appeal out of time).

History – In s. 28ZD(3)(a) the word "tribunal" substituted for the words "Special Commissioners" by SI 2009/56, art. 3(1) and Sch. 1, para. 15, operative from 1 April 2009, subject to transitional and saving provisions in SI 2009/56, Sch. 3.
S. 28ZD inserted by FA 2001, s. 88 and Sch. 29, para. 6. It applies:
(a) where the notice of enquiry is given after 11 May 2001, or
(b) where the enquiry is in progress immediately before 11 May 2001.
For the purposes of paragraph (b) an enquiry is in progress until the officer's enquiries fall to be treated as completed under s. 28A(5) or, as the case may be, s. 28B(5) of the Taxes Management Act 1970 (as those provisions had effect apart from the amendments made by FA 2001, Sch. 29).

28ZE Effect of determination

28ZE(1) The determination of a question referred to the tribunal under section 28ZA of this Act is binding on the parties to the referral in the same way, and to the same extent, as a decision on a preliminary issue in an appeal.

28ZE(2) The determination shall be taken into account by an officer of the Board–

(a) in reaching his conclusions on the enquiry, and

(b) in formulating any amendments of the return required to give effect to those conclusions.

28ZE(3) Any right of appeal under section 31(1)(a), (b) or (c) of this Act may not be exercised so as to reopen the question determined except to the extent (if any) that it could be reopened if it had been determined as a preliminary issue in that appeal.

History – In s. 28ZE(1) the word "tribunal" substituted for the words "Special Commissioners" by SI 2009/56, art. 3(1) and Sch. 1, para. 16, operative from 1 April 2009, subject to transitional and saving provisions in SI 2009/56, Sch. 3.
S. 28ZE inserted by FA 2001, s. 88 and Sch. 29, para. 6. It applies:
(a) where the notice of enquiry is given after 11 May 2001, or
(b) where the enquiry is in progress immediately before 11 May 2001.

For the purposes of paragraph (b) an enquiry is in progress until the officer's enquiries fall to be treated as completed under s. 28A(5) or, as the case may be, s. 28B(5) of the Taxes Management Act 1970 (as those provisions had effect apart from the amendments made by FA 2001, Sch. 29).

PART IV – ASSESSMENT AND CLAIMS

Cross references – SI 1993/743, reg. 14(2): application of Pt. IV to assessments under reg. 14(1).
SI 2002/2172, reg. 14(4): application of Pt. IV to determinations of working tax credit funding to be repaid by employers.

28A Completion of enquiry into personal or trustee return or NRCGT return

History – In the heading, the words "or NRCGT return" inserted by FA 2015, s. 37 and Sch. 7, para. 44(2), with effect in relation to disposals made on or after 6 April 2015.

28A(1) An enquiry under section 9A(1) or 12ZM of this Act is completed when an officer of the Board by notice (a **"closure notice"**) informs the taxpayer that he has completed his enquiries and states his conclusions.

In this section **"the taxpayer"** means the person to whom notice of enquiry was given.

28A(2) A closure notice must either–

(a) state that in the officer's opinion no amendment of the return is required, or

(b) make the amendments of the return required to give effect to his conclusions.

28A(3) A closure notice takes effect when it is issued.

28A(4) The taxpayer may apply to the tribunal for a direction requiring an officer of the Board to issue a closure notice within a specified period.

28A(5) Any such application is to be subject to the relevant provisions of Part 5 of this Act (see, in particular, section 48(2)(b)).

28A(6) The tribunal shall give the direction applied for unless satisfied that there are reasonable grounds for not issuing a closure notice within a specified period.

History – In s. 28A(1), the words "or 12ZM" inserted by FA 2015, s. 37 and Sch. 7, para. 44(2), with effect in relation to disposals made on or after 6 April 2015.
In s. 28A(4) the word "tribunal" substituted for the word "Commissioners" by SI 2009/56, art. 3(1) and Sch. 1, para. 17(2), operative from 1 April 2009, subject to transitional and saving provisions in SI 2009/56, Sch. 3.
S. 28A(5) substituted by SI 2009/56, art. 3(1) and Sch. 1, para. 17(3), operative from 1 April 2009, subject to transitional and saving provisions in SI 2009/56, Sch. 3.
In s. 28A(6) the word "tribunal" substituted for the words "Commissioners hearing the application" and the words "they are" omitted by SI 2009/56, art. 3(1) and Sch. 1, para. 17(2), operative from 1 April 2009, subject to transitional and saving provisions in SI 2009/56, Sch. 3.
s. 28A substituted by FA 2001, s. 88, Sch. 29, para. 8(1) with effect where the notice of enquiry is given after 11 May 2001, or where the enquiry is in progress immediately before that date (for these purposes, an "enquiry is in progress" until the officer's enquiries fall to be treated as completed under former s. 28A(5) prior to amendment).

Cross references – S. 12B(1): period for which records must be preserved.
Pt. 3A (referral of questions during enquiry): application if enquiry in progress, where completion under former s. 28A(5) (not made.
S. 31–31D (appeals): application to closure notices under s. 28A(1).
S. 43C: application of other provisions following amendment of tax return.
S. 46B–46D: questions to be determined by special commissioners; jurisdiction of special commissioners over certain claims included in returns; questions to be determined by Lands Tribunal.
S. 50(7A): procedure on appeals.
S. 59B(4A)(a): repayment postponed pending completion of enquiries.
Sch. 3ZA, para. 5: tax payable or repayable following amendment of a self assessment in personal or trustee return by closure notice following enquiry.
ICTA 1988, Sch. 13A, para. 14: standard provisions about enquiries into self-assessments.
ICTA 1988, Sch. 28AA, para. 6: "relevant notice" includes a notification given to a taxpayer of an enquiry's completion and conclusions under s. 28A(5).
FA 1998, s. 110(9): meaning of "closure notice" applies s. 28A(1).
FA 1998, s. 111(6): meaning of "relevant notice" applies s. 28A(1).
FA 2001, Sch. 29, para. 8(2): application of s. 28A, if enquiry in progress, where completion under former s. 28A(5) not made.
TCA 2002, s. 20(2): revisions of decisions on working tax credit and child tax credit following issue of a closure notice, or determination or settlement of an appeal.
FA 2009, Sch. 53, para. 3: late payment interest in respect of amounts due following an assessment, amendment or determination.

28AA Amendment of return of profits made for wrong period

28AA [Repealed by FA 1998, s. 117(3) and Sch. 19, para. 9, s. 165 and Sch. 27, Pt. III(28).]

History – S. 28AA repealed by FA 1998, s. 117(3) and Sch. 19, para. 9, s. 165 and Sch. 27, Pt. III(28) with effect in relation to accounting periods ending on or after 1 July 1999, the self-assessment appointed day by virtue of FA 1994, s. 199(2) and SI 1998/3173 (C. 78).
It was originally inserted by FA 1994, s. 138 and Sch. 24, para. 6, also in relation to accounting periods ending on or after the self-assessment appointed day.
These repealed provisions are superseded by FA 1998, Sch. 18 which has effect in relation to accounting periods ending on or after 1 July 1999 and is construed and has effect as if it were contained in TMA 1970 (FA 1998, s. 117(2)).

28AB Provisions supplementary to section 28AA

28AB [Repealed by FA 1998, s. 117(3) and Sch. 19, para. 9, s. 165 and Sch. 27, Pt. III(28).]

History – S. 28AB repealed by FA 1998, s. 117(3) and Sch. 19, para. 9, s. 165 and Sch. 27, Pt. III(28), with effect in relation to accounting periods ending on or after 1 July 1999, the self-assessment appointed day by virtue of FA 1994, s. 199(2) and SI 1998/3173 (C. 78).
Former s. 28AB inserted by FA 1994, s. 138 and Sch. 24, para. 6 , also in relation to accounting periods ending on or after the self-assessment appointed day.
These repealed provisions are superseded by FA 1998, Sch. 18 which has effect in relation to accounting periods ending on or after 1 July 1999 and is construed and has effect as if it were contained in TMA 1970 (FA 1998, s. 117(2)).

28B Completion of enquiry into partnership return

28B(1) An enquiry under section 12AC(1) of this Act is completed when an officer of the Board by notice (a **"closure notice"**) informs the taxpayer that he has completed his enquiries and states his conclusions.

In this section **"the taxpayer"** means the person to whom notice of enquiry was given or his successor.

28B(2) A closure notice must either–

(a) state that in the officer's opinion no amendment of the return is required, or

(b) make the amendments of the return required to give effect to his conclusions.

28B(3) A closure notice takes effect when it is issued.

28B(4) Where a partnership return is amended under subsection (2) above, the officer shall by notice to each of the partners amend–

(a) the partner's return under section 8 or 8A of this Act, or

(b) the partner's company tax return,

so as to give effect to the amendments of the partnership return.

28B(5) The taxpayer may apply to the tribunal for a direction requiring an officer of the Board to issue a closure notice within a specified period.

28B(6) Any such application is to be subject to the relevant provisions of Part 5 of this Act (see, in particular, section 48(2)(b)).

28B(7) The tribunal shall give the direction applied for unless satisfied that there are reasonable grounds for not issuing a closure notice within a specified period.

History – In s. 28B(5) the word "tribunal" substituted for the words "Commissioners" by SI 2009/56, art. 3(1) and Sch. 1, para. 18(2), operative from 1 April 2009, subject to transitional and saving provisions in SI 2009/56, Sch. 3.
S. 28B(6) substituted by SI 2009/56, art. 3(1) and Sch. 1, para. 17(4), operative from 1 April 2009, subject to transitional and saving provisions in SI 2009/56, Sch. 3.
In s. 28B(7) the word "tribunal" substituted for the words "Commissioners hearing the application" and the words "they are" omitted by SI 2009/56, art. 3(1) and Sch. 1, para. 18(2), operative from 1 April 2009, subject to transitional and saving provisions in SI 2009/56, Sch. 3.
S. 28B substituted by FA 2001, s. 88, Sch. 29, para. 9(1) with effect where the notice of enquiry is given after 11 May 2001, or where the enquiry is in progress immediately before that date (for these purposes, an "enquiry is in progress" until the officer's enquiries fall to be treated as completed under former s. 28B(5) prior to amendment).
Former s. 28B originally inserted by FA 1994, s. 189, and amended by FA 1996, s. 133 and Sch. 19, para. 2, 5, in so far as it relates to income tax and capital gains tax, as respects the year 1996–97 and, in its original form (i.e. including the corporation tax provisions in former s. 28B(4), (6B)), as respects corporation tax accounting periods ending on or after the self-assessment appointed day (FA 1994, s. 199(2), (3)).
Former s. 28B(4), (6B) substituted by FA 1998, Sch. 19 para. 10(2), (3) with effect in relation to accounting periods ending on or after 1 July 1999, the self-assessment appointed day by virtue of FA 1994, s. 199(2) and SI 1998/3173 (C.78). Those corporation tax provisions were superseded by provisions in FA 1998, Sch. 18 for accounting periods ending on or after 1 July 1999.

Cross references – S. 12B(1): period for which records must be preserved.
S. 12AB(5): source of the meaning of the term "period of account".
Pt. 3A (referral of questions during enquiry): application if enquiry in progress, where completion under former s. 28B(5) not made.
S. 31–31D (appeals): application to closure notices under s. 28B(1) .
S. 43C: application of other provisions following amendment of tax return.
S. 46B–46D: questions to be determined by special commissioners; jurisdiction of special commissioners over certain claims included in returns; questions to be determined by Lands Tribunal.
Sch. 3ZA, para. 8: tax payable or repayable following amendment of a self assessment in partnership return by closure notice following enquiry.
FA 1998, s. 110(9): meaning of "closure notice" applies s. 28B(1).
FA 1998, s. 111(6): meaning of "relevant notice" applies s. 28B(1).
FA 2001, Sch. 29, para. 9(2): application of s. 28B, if enquiry in progress, where completion under former s. 28B(5) not made.
TCA 2002, s. 20(2): revisions of decisions on working tax credit and child tax credit following amendment of return.

Notes – In former TMA 1970, s. 28B(2)(b) (as inserted) the word "was" appears to have been omitted after the word "return" in the Queen's Printer's version.

28C Determination of tax where no return delivered

28C(1) This section applies where–

(a) a notice has been given to any person under section 8 or 8A of this Act (the relevant section), and

(b) the required return is not delivered on or before the filing date.

28C(1A) An officer of the Board may make a determination of the following amounts, to the best of his information and belief, namely–

(a) the amounts in which the person who should have made the return is chargeable to income tax and capital gains tax for the year of assessment; and

(b) the amount which is payable by him by way of income tax for that year;

and subsection (1AA) of section 8 or, as the case may be, section 8A of this Act applies for the purposes of this subsection as it applies for the purposes of subsection (1) of that section.

28C(2) Notice of any determination under this section shall be served on the person in respect of whom it is made and shall state the date on which it is issued.

28C(3) Until such time (if any) as it is superseded by a self-assessment made under section 9 of this Act (whether by the taxpayer or an officer of the Board) on the basis of information contained in a return under the relevant section, a determination under this section shall have effect for the purposes of Parts VA, VI, IX and XI of this Act as if it were such a self-assessment.

28C(4) Where–

(a) proceedings have been commenced for the recovery of any tax charged by a determination under this section; and

(b) before those proceedings are concluded, the determination is superseded by such a self-assessment as is mentioned in subsection (3) above,

those proceedings may be continued as if they were proceedings for the recovery of so much of the tax charged by the self-assessment as is due and payable and has not been paid.

28C(4A) Where–

(a) action is being taken under Part 1 of Schedule 8 to the Finance (No. 2) Act 2015 (enforcement by deduction from accounts) for the recovery of an amount (**"the original amount"**) of tax charged by a determination under this section, and

(b) before that action is concluded, the determination is superseded by such a self-assessment as is mentioned in subsection (3),

that action may be continued as if it were action for the purposes of the recovery of so much of the tax charged by the self-assessment as is due and payable, has not been paid and does not exceed the original amount.

28C(5) No determination under this section, and no self-assessment superseding such a determination, shall be made otherwise than–

(a) before the end of the period of 3 years beginning with the filing date; or

(b) in the case of such a self-assessment, before the end of the period of twelve months beginning with the date of the determination.

28C(6) In this section **"the filing date"** in respect of a return for a year of assessment (Year 1) means either–

(a) 31st January of Year 2, or

(b) if the notice under section 8 or 8A was given after 31st October of Year 2, the last day of the period of three months beginning with the day on which the notice is given.

History – In s. 28C(4)(a) the words "proceedings have been commenced" substituted by FA 2001, s. 88, Sch. 29, para. 17(1) with effect in relation to proceedings begun after 11 May 2001.
S. 28C(4A) inserted by F(No. 2)A 2015, s. 51 and Sch. 8, para. 25, with effect from 18 November 2015 (Royal Assent).
In s. 28C(5)(a) "3 years" substituted for "five years" by FA 2008, s. 118 and Sch. 39, para. 2, with effect from 1 April 2010 (SI 2009/403, art. 2(2) subject to SI 2009/403, art. 3–10 – in particular art. 10).
S. 28C(6) substituted by FA 2007, s. 91(5), with effect in respect of a return for a year of assessment beginning on or after 6 April 2007. See s. 8 or s. 8A History note as appropriate.
S. 28C inserted by FA 1994 ss 190, 199 with effect for the tax year 1996–97 and subsequent tax years.

Cross references – S. 59B(5A): payment/repayment of tax where a determination under s. 28C which has effect as a person's self-assessment is superseded by his self-assessment under s. 9.
Sch. 1AB, para. 3A: determinations under s. 28C: special rules.
FA 2009, Sch. 53, para. 3: late payment interest in respect of amounts due following an assessment, amendment or determination.

Other material – Tax Bulletin TB08/95-7: equitable liability claims pre 1 April 2011.

28D Determination of corporation tax where no return delivered

28D [Repealed by FA 1998, s. 117(3) and Sch. 19, para. 11, s. 165 and Sch. 27, Pt. III(28).]

History – S. 28D repealed by FA 1998, s. 117(3) and Sch. 19, para. 11, s. 165 and Sch. 27, Pt. III(28) with effect in relation to accounting periods ending on or after 1 July 1999, the self-assessment appointed day by virtue of FA 1994, s. 199(2) and SI 1998/3173. Former s. 28D inserted by FA 1994, s. 138 and Sch. 24, para. 7, also in relation to accounting periods ending on or after the self-assessment appointed day.
These repealed provisions are superseded by FA 1998, Sch. 18 which has effect in relation to accounting periods ending on or after 1 July 1999 and is construed and has effect as if it were contained in TMA 1970 (FA 1998, s. 117(2)).

28E Determination of corporation tax where notice complied with in part

28E [Repealed by FA 1998, s. 117(3) and Sch. 19, para. 11, s. 165 and Sch. 27, Pt. III(28).]

History – S. 28E repealed by FA 1998, s. 117(3) and Sch. 19, para. 11, s. 165 and Sch. 27, Pt. III(28) as respects accounting periods ending on or after 1 July 1999, the self-assessment appointed day by virtue of FA 1994, s. 199(2) and SI 1998/3173.

Former s. 28E inserted by FA 1994, s. 138 and Sch. 24, para. 7, in relation to accounting periods ending on or after the self-assessment appointed day.
These repealed provisions are superseded by FA 1998, Sch. 18 which has effect in relation to accounting periods ending on or after 1 July 1999 and is construed and has effect as if it were contained in TMA 1970 (FA 1998, s. 117(2)).

28F Corporation tax determinations: supplementary

28F [Repealed by FA 1998, s. 117(3) and Sch. 19, para. 11, s. 165 and Sch. 27, Pt. III(28).]

History – S. 28F repealed by FA 1998, s. 117(3) and Sch. 19, para. 11, s. 165 and Sch. 27, Pt. III(28) with effect in relation to accounting periods ending on or after 1 July 1999, the self-assessment appointed day by virtue of FA 1994, s. 199(2) and SI 1998/3173.
Former s. 28F inserted by FA 1994, s. 138 and Sch. 24, para. 7, also in relation to accounting periods ending on or after the self-assessment appointed day.
These repealed provisions are superseded by FA 1998, Sch. 18 which has effect in relation to accounting periods ending on or after 1 July 1999 and is construed and has effect as if it were contained in TMA 1970 (FA 1998, s. 117(2)).

28G Determination of amount notionally chargeable where no NRCGT return delivered

28G(1) This section applies where it appears to an officer of Revenue and Customs that–

(a) a person is required to make and deliver in respect of a non-resident CGT disposal an NRCGT return containing an advance self-assessment, and

(b) the person has not delivered the required return by the filing date for the return.

28G(2) The officer may make a determination, to the best of the officer's information and belief, of the amount of capital gains tax which should have been assessed in the required return as the amount notionally chargeable.

28G(3) Notice of any determination under this section must be served on the person in respect of whom it is made and must state the date on which it is issued.

28G(4) Until such time (if any) as it is superseded by an advance self-assessment on the basis of information contained in an NRCGT return, a determination under this section is to have effect as if it were an advance self-assessment contained in an NRCGT return made by the person in respect of the disposal concerned.

28G(5) Where–

(a) proceedings have been commenced for the recovery of an amount payable by virtue of a determination under this section, and

(b) before those proceedings are concluded, the determination is superseded by an advance self-assessment made by the person in respect of the disposal,

those proceedings may be continued as if they were proceedings for the recovery of so much of the amount payable by virtue of the advance self-assessment as is due and payable and has not been paid.

28G(6) No determination under this section, and no advance self-assessment superseding such a determination may be made–

(a) after the end of the period of 3 years beginning with 31 January of the year following the tax year to which the determination relates, or

(b) in the case of such an advance self-assessment, after the end of the period of 12 months beginning with the date of the determination.

28G(7) In this section–

"advance self-assessment" is to be interpreted in accordance with section 12ZE(1);

"amount notionally chargeable" is to be interpreted in accordance with section 12ZF(1);

"filing date", in relation to an NRCGT return, is to be interpreted in accordance with section 12ZB(8).

28G(8) For the meaning in this section of **"non-resident CGT disposal"** see section 14B of the 1992 Act.

History – S. 28G inserted by FA 2015, s. 37 and Sch. 7, para. 45, with effect in relation to disposals made on or after 6 April 2015.

28H Simple assessments by HMRC: personal assessments

28H(1) HMRC may make a simple assessment for a year of assessment in respect of a person (other than a person to whom section 28I applies) if, when the assessment is made, the person is not excluded by subsection (2) in relation to that year.

28H(2) Subsection (1) does not apply to a person at any time in relation to that year of assessment if–

(a) the person has delivered a return under section 8 for that year, or

(b) the person is at that time subject to a requirement to make and deliver such a return by virtue of a notice under section 8.

but nothing in this subsection prevents HMRC from giving the person notice of a simple assessment at the same time as a notice withdrawing a notice under section 8.

28H(3) A simple assessment is–

(a) an assessment of the amounts in which the person is chargeable to income tax and capital gains tax for the year of assessment to which it relates, and

(b) an assessment of the amount payable by the person by way of income tax for that year, that is to say, the difference between the amount in which the person is assessed to income tax under paragraph (a) and the aggregate amount of any income tax deducted at source;

but nothing in this subsection enables an assessment to show as repayable any income tax which any provision of the Income Tax Acts provides is not repayable.

28H(4) The amounts in which a person is chargeable to income tax and capital gains are net amounts, taking into account any relief or allowance that is applicable.

28H(5) A simple assessment must be based on information relating to the person that is held by HMRC (whether or not supplied by the person to whom the assessment relates).

28H(6) The notice of a simple assessment required to be sent to the person by section 30A(3) must (among other things)–

(a) include particulars of the income and gains, and any relief or allowance, taken into account in the assessment, and

(b) state any amount payable by the person by virtue of section 59BA (with particulars of how it may be paid and the date by which it is payable).

28H(7) The tax to be assessed on a person by a simple assessment does not include any tax which–

(a) is chargeable on the scheme administrator of a registered pension scheme under Part 4 of Finance Act 2004,

(b) is chargeable on the sub-scheme administrator of a sub-scheme under Part 4 of the Finance Act 2004 as modified by the Registered Pension Schemes (Splitting of Schemes) Regulations 2006, or

(c) is chargeable on the person who is (or persons who are) the responsible person in relation to an employer-financed retirement benefits scheme under section 394(2) of ITEPA 2003.

28H(8) Nothing in this section prevents HMRC issuing more than one simple assessment to the same person in respect of the same year of assessment (whether or not any earlier simple assessment for that year is withdrawn).

28H(9) In this section references to a simple assessment are to an assessment under this section.

History – S. 28H inserted by FA 2016, s. 167 and Sch. 23, para. 3, with effect in relation to the 2016–17 tax year and subsequent years.

28I Simple assessments by HMRC: trustees

28I(1) HMRC may make a simple assessment for a year of assessment in respect of a settlement if, when the assessment is made, the relevant trustees of the settlement are not excluded by subsection (2) in relation to that year.

28I(2) Subsection (1) does not apply at any time in relation to that year of assessment if–

(a) a return under section 8A has been delivered for that year by the relevant trustees or any of them, or

(b) there is at that time a subsisting requirement to make and deliver such a return by virtue of a notice under section 8A;

but nothing in this subsection prevents HMRC from giving notice of a simple assessment at the same time as a notice withdrawing a notice under section 8A.

28I(3) A simple assessment is–

(a) an assessment of the amounts in which the relevant trustees are chargeable to income tax and capital gains tax for the year of assessment to which it relates, and

(b) an assessment of the amount payable by them by way of income tax for that year, that is to say, the difference between the amount in which they are assessed to income tax under paragraph (a) and the aggregate amount of any income tax deducted at source;

but nothing in this subsection enables an assessment to show as repayable any income tax which any provision of the Income Tax Acts provides is not repayable.

28I(4) *The amounts in which* the relevant trustees are chargeable to income tax and capital gains are net amounts, taking into account any relief or allowance that is applicable.

28I(5) A simple assessment must be based only on information relating to the settlement that is held by HMRC (whether or not supplied by the relevant trustees).

28I(6) The notice of a simple assessment required by section 30A(3) may be given to any one or more of the relevant trustees.

28I(7) That notice must (among other things)–

(a) include particulars of the income and gains, and any relief or allowance, taken into account in the assessment, and

(b) state any amount payable by the relevant trustees by virtue of section 59BA (with particulars of how it may be paid and the date by which it is payable).

28I(8) The tax to be assessed by a simple assessment does not include any tax which–

(a) is chargeable on the scheme administrator of a registered pension scheme under Part 4 of Finance Act 2004,

(b) is chargeable on the sub-scheme administrator of a sub-scheme under Part 4 of the Finance Act 2004 as modified by the Registered Pension Schemes (Splitting of Schemes) Regulations 2006, or

(c) is chargeable on the person who is (or persons who are) the responsible person in relation to an employer-financed retirement benefits scheme under section 394(2) of ITEPA 2003.

28I(9) Nothing in this section prevents HMRC issuing more than one simple assessment in respect of the same settlement and the same year of assessment (whether or not any earlier simple assessment for that year is withdrawn).

28I(10) In this section references to a **"simple assessment"** are to an assessment under this section.

28I(11) In this Act references to the person to whom a simple assessment relates are, in relation to one made under this section, to the relevant trustees of the settlement to which it relates.

History – S. 28I inserted by FA 2016, s. 167 and Sch. 23, para. 3, with effect in relation to the 2016–17 tax year and subsequent years.

28J Power to withdraw a simple assessment

28J(1) HMRC may withdraw a simple assessment by notice to the person to which it relates.

28J(2) An assessment that has been withdrawn ceases to have effect (and is to be taken as never having had any effect).

History – S. 28J inserted by FA 2016, s. 167 and Sch. 23, para. 3, with effect in relation to the 2016–17 tax year and subsequent years.

29 Assessment where loss of tax discovered

29(1) If an officer of the Board or the Board discover, as regards any person (the taxpayer) and a year of assessment–

(a) that any income which ought to have been assessed to income tax, or chargeable gains which ought to have been assessed to capital gains tax, have not been assessed, or

(b) that an assessment to tax is or has become insufficient, or

(c) that any relief which has been given is or has become excessive,

the officer or, as the case may be, the Board may, subject to subsections (2) and (3) below, make an assessment in the amount, or the further amount, which ought in his or their opinion to be charged in order to make good to the Crown the loss of tax.

29(2) Where–

(a) the taxpayer has made and delivered a return under section 8 or 8A of this Act in respect of the relevant year of assessment, and

(b) the situation mentioned in subsection (1) above is attributable to an error or mistake in the return as to the basis on which his liability ought to have been computed,

the taxpayer shall not be assessed under that subsection in respect of the year of assessment there mentioned if the return was in fact made on the basis or in accordance with the practice generally prevailing at the time when it was made.

29(3) Where the taxpayer has made and delivered a return under section 8 or 8A of this Act in respect of the relevant year of assessment, he shall not be assessed under subsection (1) above–

(a) in respect of the year of assessment mentioned in that subsection; and

(b) in the same capacity as that in which he made and delivered the return,

unless one of the two conditions mentioned below is fulfilled.

29(4) The first condition is that the situation mentioned in subsection (1) above was brought about carelessly or deliberately by the taxpayer or a person acting on his behalf.

29(5) The second condition is that at the time when an officer of the Board–

(a) ceased to be entitled to give notice of his intention to enquire into the taxpayer's return under section 8 or 8A of this Act in respect of the relevant year of assessment; or

(b) informed the taxpayer that he had completed his enquiries into that return,

the officer could not have been reasonably expected, on the basis of the information made available to him before that time, to be aware of the situation mentioned in subsection (1) above.

29(6) For the purposes of subsection (5) above, information is made available to an officer of the Board if–

(a) it is contained in the taxpayer's return under section 8 or 8A of this Act in respect of the relevant year of assessment (the return), or in any accounts, statements or documents accompanying the return;

(b) it is contained in any claim made as regards the relevant year of assessment by the taxpayer acting in the same capacity as that in which he made the return, or in any accounts, statements or documents accompanying any such claim;

(c) it is contained in any documents, accounts or particulars which, for the purposes of any enquiries into the return or any such claim by an officer of the Board, are produced or furnished by the taxpayer to the officer; or

(d) it is information the existence of which, and the relevance of which as regards the situation mentioned in subsection (1) above–

(i) could reasonably be expected to be inferred by an officer of the Board from information falling within paragraphs (a) to (c) above; or

(ii) are notified in writing by the taxpayer to an officer of the Board.

29(7) In subsection (6) above–

(a) any reference to the taxpayer's return under section 8 or 8A of this Act in respect of the relevant year of assessment includes–

(i) a reference to any return of his under that section for either of the two immediately preceding years of assessment;

(ia) a reference to any NRCGT return made and delivered by the taxpayer which contains an advance self-assessment relating to the relevant year of assessment or either of the two immediately preceding chargeable periods; and

(ii) where the return is under section 8 and the taxpayer carries on a trade, profession or business in partnership, a reference to any partnership return with respect to the partnership for the relevant year of assessment or either of those periods; and

(b) any reference in paragraphs (b) to (d) to the taxpayer includes a reference to a person acting on his behalf.

29(7A) The requirement to fulfil one of the two conditions mentioned above does not apply so far as regards any income or chargeable gains of the taxpayer in relation to which the taxpayer has been given, after any enquiries have been completed into the taxpayer's return, a notice under section 81(2) of TIOPA 2010 (notice to counteract scheme or arrangement designed to increase double taxation relief).

29(8) An objection to the making of an assessment under this section on the ground that neither of the two conditions mentioned above is fulfilled shall not be made otherwise than on an appeal against the assessment.

29(9) Any reference in this section to the relevant year of assessment is a reference to–

(a) in the case of the situation mentioned in paragraph (a) or (b) of subsection (1) above, the year of assessment mentioned in that subsection; and

(b) in the case of the situation mentioned in paragraph (c) of that subsection, the year of assessment in respect of which the claim was made.

29(10) [Repealed by FA 1998, s. 117(3) and Sch. 19, para. 12(6), s. 165 and Sch. 27, Pt. III(28).]

History – In s. 29(1), words "income which ought … capital gains tax" substituted by FA 1998, s. 117(3) and Sch. 19 para. 12(2) with effect from 1 July 1999 (see note above).

In s. 29(2), (3), (5)(a), (6)(a) and (7)(a), words "section 8 or 8A" substituted by FA 1998, Sch. 19, para. 12(4) with effect from 1 July 1999 (see note above).

In s. 29(3)(b), words "in the case of a return under section 8 or 8A" repealed by FA 1998, s. 117(3), Sch. 19, para. 12(5), s. 165 and Sch. 27, Pt. III(28), with effect from 1 July 1999 (see note above).

In s. 29(4) the words "was brought about carelessly or deliberately by" substituted for the words "is attributable to fraudulent or negligent conduct on the part of" by FA 2008, s. 118 and Sch. 39, para. 3, with effect from 1 April 2010 (SI 2009/403, art. 2(2) subject to SI 2009/403, art. 3–10 – in particular art. 10).

In s. 29(6)(c) the words omitted", whether in pursuance of a notice under section 19A of this Act or otherwise" by FA 2008, s. 113 and Sch. 36, para. 71, with effect from 1 April 2009 (SI 2009/404, art. 2, subject to savings at SI 2009/404, art. 3).

S. 29(7)(a)(ia) *inserted (and the "and" after (i) omitted)* by FA 2015, s. 37 and Sch. 7, para. 46, with effect in relation to disposals made on or after 6 April 2015.

In s. 29(7)(a)(ii), the words "any partnership return with respect to the partnership" substituted by FA 2001, s. 88, Sch. 29, para. 22 with effect from 11 May 2001 in relation to returns whether made before or after that date and whether relating to periods before or after then.

In s. 29(7A), the words "section 81(2) of TIOPA 2010 (notice to counteract scheme or arrangement designed to increase double taxation relief)" substituted for the words "section 804ZA of the principal Act" by TIOPA 2010, s. 374 and Sch. 8, para. 5, with effect

for corporation tax purposes for accounting periods ending on or after 1 April 2010, for income tax and capital gains tax purposes for the tax year 2010–11 and subsequent tax years, and for petroleum revenue tax purposes for chargeable periods beginning on or after 1 July 2010.
S. 29(7A) inserted by FA 2005, s. 88(2) with effect from 10 February 2005 where credit for foreign tax is affected by a scheme to which ICTA 1988, Sch. 28AB, para. 5 applies or 16 March 2005 where that credit is affected by any other scheme or arrangement prescribed by ICTA 1988, Sch. 28AB (FA 2005, s. 87(3), (5)).
S. 29(10) repealed by FA 1998, s. 117(3) and Sch. 19, para. 12(6), s. 165 and Sch. 27, Pt. III(28), with effect from 1 July 1999 (see note above).
In s. 29, "year of assessment" substituted for "chargeable period", wherever it occured, by FA 1998, s. 117(3) and Sch. 19 para. 12(3) with effect from 1 July 1999 (see note above).
S. 29 substituted by FA 1994, s. 191(1), (2) with effect for income tax and capital gains tax from 1996–97 in respect of partnerships trading before 6 April 1994 and from 1997–98 in all other cases. (It was also to have had effect for corporation tax purposes for accounting periods ending on or after 1 July 1999, but was superseded by FA 1998, Sch. 18, para. 41. Consequential amendments were made to s. 29 with effect in relation to accounting periods ending on or after 1 July 1999, the self-assessment appointed day by virtue of FA 1994, s. 199(2) and SI 1998/3173.)

Cross references – S. 7(8): penalty for failure to comply with s. 7(1) will not exceed tax assessed in respect of the year under this section or TMA 1970 s. 9.
S. 43A: time limits for certain discovery assessments.
S. 46(2): save as provided in this section, determination of commissioners final and conclusive.
S. 55(1): recovery of tax not postponed.
S. 59A(4B): payments on account of income tax.
S. 59B(6): income tax or capital gains tax due by virtue of assessment under s. 29 is payable 30 days from date of notice of assessment.
S. 113(1B): delegation of responsibility by officer of the Board for completing assessment procedure.
S. 114: want of form not to invalidate assessment.
S. 118(5)-(7): definition of carelessly and deliberately for purposes of s. 29(4).
ICTA 1988, s. 588(5): application of s. 29 to employers incurring training costs.
ICTA 1988, s. 804ZA: notices in respect of certain prescribed tax-avoidance schemes and arrangements designed to increase relief for foreign tax.
ICTA 1988, Sch. 3, para. 6E(1): disapplication of s. 29(1)–(4), (7), (8) in relation to assessments under ICTA 1988, Sch. 3, para. 6D (paying and collecting agents in respect of foreign dividends etc.).
ICTA 1988, Sch. 14, para. 7(3): s. 29 applicable to excess relief claim in relation to life assurance premiums.
ICTA 1988, Sch. 28AA, para. 6:"relevant notice" includes a notice of assessment under s. 29.
FA 1995, s. 73(4): power of Treasury to make regulations concerning tax credits on distributions from venture capital trusts, applying s. 29(1)(c) to repayments of income tax.
FA 1998, s. 110(9): Board approval required in transfer pricing cases for issue of a discovery assessment under s. 29 .
FA 1998, s. 111(6): a "relevant notice" includes assessments issued under s. 29.
FA 1998, Sch. 18, para. 44: time limit for making discovery assessments and determinations in respect of companies.
ITEPA 2003, s. 312(2): recovery of tax where exemption for retraining expenses withdrawn.
TCA 2002, s. 20(2): revisions of decisions on working tax credit and child tax credit following making of an assessment under s. 29(1), or determination or settlement of an appeal.
SI 1995/351, reg. 5, 6: assessment in respect of amount payable under stop-loss insurance to an individual or corporate member of Lloyd's is not out of time if made before end of underwriting year following the underwriting year in which amount received.
FA 2009, Sch. 53, para. 3: late payment interest in respect of amounts due following an assessment, amendment or determination.

Statements of practice – SP 8/91: principles applied by HMRC in determining whether "discovery" assessment should be made.

HMRC Manuals – Enquiry Manual EM3260: Revenue's view on when information is "made available."
Enquiry Manual EM3265: operational restriction on making discovery assessments.

Other material – Tax Bulletin TB06/96-1: discovery and disclosure under self assessment.
Tax Bulletin TB08/01-6: guidance on when HMRC will raise a "discovery" assessment without opening an enquiry.
Taxline 1996/124 (not reproduced): Revenue clarification that for self-assessment purposes the relevance of any accounts or computations submitted with a return does not need to be indicated, and it is to be assumed that the Revenue has received the information contained therein.

29A Non-resident CGT disposals: determination of amount which should have been assessed

29A(1) Subsection (2) applies if HMRC discover, as regards a non-resident CGT disposal made by a person ("P") (or two or more such disposals in a case falling within section 12ZC) and a tax year ("the relevant tax year") that–

(a) an amount that ought to have been assessed as the amount notionally chargeable in an advance self-assessment under section 12ZE(1) has not been so assessed by the filing date, or

(b) an assessment of the amount notionally chargeable for the purposes of section 12ZF(1) contained in an NRCGT return made and delivered by P has become insufficient.

29A(2) HMRC may determine that the amount or further amount which in its opinion ought to be assessed under section 12ZE to remedy the failure mentioned in subsection (1)(a) or the insufficiency mentioned in subsection (1)(b) is to be treated for the purposes of this Act as if it were so assessed in–

(a) an NRCGT return made by P in respect of the disposal, or

(b) (if P has made and delivered an NRCGT return in respect of the disposal) that return.

But see subsections (3) to (5).

29A(3) Where P has made and delivered in respect of the disposal an NRCGT return containing an advance self-assessment, HMRC may not make a determination under subsection (2) in respect of the disposal unless one of the two conditions mentioned below is met.

29A(4) The first condition is that the situation mentioned in subsection (1) was brought about carelessly or deliberately by P or a person acting on P's behalf.

29A(5) The second condition is that at the time when an officer of Revenue and Customs–

(a) ceased to be entitled to give notice of the officer's intention to enquire into the NRCGT return, or

(b) informed P of the completion of the officer's enquiries into the return,

the officer could not reasonably have been expected, on the basis of the information made available to the officer before that time, to be aware of the situation mentioned in subsection (1).

29A(6) For the purposes of subsection (5), information is made available to an officer of Revenue and Customs if–

(a) it is contained in an NRCGT return made and delivered by P which relates to the relevant tax year or either or the two immediately preceding tax years,

(b) it is contained in any return under section 8 or 8A made and delivered by P in respect of either of the two tax years immediately preceding the relevant tax year,

(c) it is contained in any claim made by P which relates to P's capital gains tax position with respect to the relevant tax year or either of the two immediately preceding tax years,

(d) it is contained in any accounts, statements or documents accompanying a return falling within paragraph (a) or (b) or a claim falling within paragraph (c),

(e) it is contained in any documents, accounts or particulars which, for the purposes of any enquiries by an officer of Revenue and Customs into a return falling within paragraph (a) or (b) or a claim falling within paragraph (c) are produced or provided by P to the officer, or

(f) it is information the existence of which, and the relevance of which as regards the situation mentioned in subsection (1)–

(i) could be reasonably expected to be inferred by an officer of Revenue and Customs from information falling within paragraphs (a) to (e), or

(ii) are notified in writing by the taxpayer to an officer of Revenue and Customs.

29A(7) In subsection (6)–

(a) any reference to a return made and delivered by P under section 8 in respect of a tax year includes, if P carries on a trade, profession or business in partnership, a reference to any partnership return with respect to the partnership for that tax year, and

(b) any reference to P includes a person acting on P's behalf.

29A(8) An objection to the making of a determination under subsection (2) on the ground that neither of the two conditions mentioned above is fulfilled may not be made otherwise than on an appeal against the assessment.

29A(9) In this section–

"advance self-assessment" has the meaning given by section 12ZE(1);

"amount notionally chargeable" is to be interpreted in accordance with section 12ZF(1);

"filing date", in relation to an NRCGT return, has the meaning given by section 12ZB(8).

29A(10) For the meaning in this section of **"non-resident CGT disposal"** see section 14B of the 1992 Act.

History – S. 29A inserted by FA 2015, s. 37 and Sch. 7, para. 47, with effect in relation to disposals made on or after 6 April 2015.

30 Recovery of overpayment of tax, etc.

30(1) Where an amount of income tax or capital gains tax has been repaid to any person which ought not to have been repaid to him, that amount of tax may be assessed and recovered as if it were unpaid tax.

30(1A) Subsection (1) above shall not apply where the amount of tax which has been repaid is assessable under section 29 of this Act.

30(1B) Subsections (2) to (8) of section 29 of this Act shall apply in relation to an assessment under subsection (1) above as they apply in relation to an assessment under subsection (1) of that section; and subsection (4) of that section as so applied shall have effect as if the reference to the loss of tax were a reference to the repayment of the amount of tax which ought not to have been repaid.

30(2) In any case where–

(a) a repayment of tax has been increased in accordance with section 824 of the principal Act or section 283 of the 1992 Act (supplements added to repayments of tax, etc.) or section 102 of the Finance Act 2009 (repayment interest); and

(b) the whole or any part of that repayment has been paid to any person but ought not to have been paid to him; and

(c) that repayment ought not to have been increased either at all or to any extent;

then the amount of the repayment assessed under subsection (1) above may include an amount equal to the amount by which the repayment ought not to have been increased.

30(2A) [Repealed by FA 1998, s. 117(3) and Sch. 19, para. 13(4), s. 165 and Sch. 27, Pt. III(28), as respects accounting periods ending on or after 1 July 1999, the appointed day.]

30(3) In any case where–

(a) a payment, other than a repayment of tax to which subsection (2) above applies, is increased in accordance with section 824 or 825 of the principal Act or section 283 of the 1992 Act; and

(b) that payment ought not to have been increased either at all or to any extent;

then an amount equal to the amount by which the payment ought not to have been increased may be assessed and recovered as if it were unpaid income tax.

30(3A) [Repealed by FA 1998, s. 117(3) and Sch. 19, para. 13(6), s. 165 and Sch. 27, Pt. III(28) as respects accounting periods ending on or after 1 July 1999, the appointed day.]

30(4) [Omitted by ITTOIA 2005, s. 882(1) and Sch. 1, para. 369 and repealed by ITTOIA 2005, s. 884 and Sch. 3.]

30(4A) [Repealed by FA 1998, s. 117(3) and Sch. 19, para. 13(8), s. 165 and Sch. 27, Pt. III(28) as respects accounting periods ending on or after 1 July 1999, the appointed day.]

30(5) An assessment under this section shall not be out of time under section 34 of this Act if it is made before the end of whichever of the following ends the later, namely–

(a) the year of assessment following that in which the amount assessed was repaid or paid as the case may be, or

(b) where a return delivered by the person concerned is enquired into by an officer of the Board, the period ending with the day on which, by virtue of section 28A(1) of this Act, the enquiry is completed.

30(6) Subsection (5) above is without prejudice to section 36 of this Act.

30(7) In this section any reference to an amount repaid or paid includes a reference to an amount allowed by way of set-off.

History – In s. 30(1), the words "income tax or capital gains tax" substituted for the word "tax" by FA 1998, s. 117(3) and Sch. 19, para. 13(2) with effect in relation to accounting periods ending on or after 1 July 1999, the self-assessment appointed day by virtue of FA 1994, s. 199(2) and SI 1998/3173 (C. 78).
The above amendment to s. 30(1), and the amendments by FA 1998 detailed in the notes below, effectively disapply s. 30 for the purposes of corporation tax for accounting periods ending on and after 1 July 1999, the appointed day. FA 1998, Sch. 18, which has effect in relation to accounting periods ending on or after 1 July 1999 and is construed and has effect as if it were contained in TMA 1970, contains equivalent provisions for corporation tax under self-assessment (FA 1998, s. 117(2)).
S. 30(1A) inserted by FA 1990, s. 105 in relation to amounts of tax repaid on or after 26 July 1990.
S. 30(1B) inserted by FA 1994, s. 196 and Sch. 19, para. 4, for income tax and capital gains tax, as respects the year 1996–97 and subsequent years of assessment, and originally also for corporation tax as respects accounting periods ending on or after 1 July 1999 (the appointed day: see above), but for corporation tax self-assessment see now FA 1998, Sch. 18.
In s. 30(2)(a), the words "or section 102 of the Finance Act 2009 (repayment interest)" inserted by SI 2014/992, art. 4(a), with effect from 6 May 2014 in relation to payments which are due and payable in respect of the tax year 2014–15 and subsequent tax years.
In s. 30(2)(a), reference to ICTA 1988, s. 825 omitted by FA 1998, s. 117(3) and Sch. 19, para. 13(3), s. 165 and Sch. 27, Pt. III(28) as respects accounting periods ending on or after 1 July 1999, the corporation tax self-assessment appointed day (see above).
In s. 30(2)(a) and (3)(a), references to "section 283 of the 1992 Act", substituted by TCGA 1992, s. 290 and Sch. 10, para. 2(6).
S. 30(2A) and (3A) repealed by FA 1998, s. 117(3) and Sch. 19, para. 13(4), (6) and (8), with effect in relation to accounting periods ending on or after 1 July 1999, the self-assessment appointed day (see above).
S. 30(4) omitted by ITTOIA 2005, s. 882(1) and Sch. 1, para. 369 and repealed by ITTOIA 2005, s. 884 and Sch. 3; effective for 2005–06 onwards.
S. 30(4A) repealed by FA 1998, s. 117(3) and Sch. 19, para. 13(4), (6) and (8), with effect in relation to accounting periods ending on or after 1 July 1999, the self-assessment appointed day (see above).
In s. 30(3), the words "or corporation tax" omitted by FA 1998, s. 117(3) and Sch. 19, para. 13(5), s. 165 and Sch. 27, Pt. III(27), with effectin relation to accounting periods ending on or after 1 July 1999, the corporation tax self-assessment appointed day (see above).
S. 30(4) substituted by FA 1998, s. 117(3) and Sch. 19, para. 13(5), with effect in relation to accounting periods ending on or after 1 July 1999, the corporation tax self-assessment appointed day (see above).
In s. 30(5)(a), the words "year of assessment" substituted for the words "chargeable period" by FA 1998, s. 117(3) and Sch. 19, para. 13(9), with effect in relation to accounting periods ending on or after 1 July 1999, the corporation tax self-assessment appointed day (see above).
In s. 30(5)(b), the words ", or an amendment of such a return," (which appeared after the words "the person concerned") omitted, "28A(1)" substituted for "28A(5)" and "the enquiry is" substituted for "the officer's enquiries are treated as", by FA 2001, s. 88, Sch. 29, para. 23, and the words omitted repealed by s. 110, Sch. 33, Pt. II(13), all with effect from 11 May 2001 in relation to returns whether made before or after that date and whether relating to periods before or after then.
S. 30(5), substituted by FA 1994, s. 196 and Sch. 19, para. 4(2), with effect for income tax purposes, for the year 1996–97 and subsequent years of assessment, and for corporation tax purposes, with effect for accounting periods ending on or after 1 July 1999 (SI 1998/3173, art. 2).
S. 30(6) amended by FA 1989, s. 149(3)(a) omitting reference to s. 37 and 39 consequent to the repeal (with saving) of those sections.
S. 30 substituted by FA 1982, s. 149(1) in relation to any amount repaid or paid from 6 April 1982.

Cross references – S. 107A: relevant trustees may be liable for payment under s. 30.
ICTA 1988, s. 252(2)–(4): recovery of overpaid interest on payments of tax credit.
ICTA 1988, s. 369(7): s. 30 applies to any overpayment to a MIRAS lender of tax deducted by a borrower and thus treated as paid by the lender as if it were income tax which ought not to have been repaid, or a relief which was not due.
ICTA 1988, s. 813(3): where tax credits have been incorrectly paid the amounts recoverable may be assessed and recovered as if they were unpaid tax, and s. 30 applies accordingly.
ICTA 1988, Sch. 14, para. 7(3): s. 30 applies to life assurance premium relief.

ICTA 1988, Sch. 19AB, para. 3(1): excess of provisional repayments of income tax borne by deduction or tax credit in respect of pension business of a life insurance company, over actual entitlement, treated as excessive repayment of corporation tax to the insurance company. See also para. 3(1ZA): modification of time limit where assessment made under s. 30 by virtue of para. 3(1) (pre-corporation tax self-assessment).
FA 1989, s. 57(3): s. 30 applies to excess relief for medical insurance payments.
FA 1991, s. 33(3)(b): application of s. 30 where the recipient of a payment in respect of a qualifying course of vocational training claims from the Board the amount of tax deducted by the payer, but is not entitled to do so.
FA 1995, s. 73(4): s. 30 may be applied where repayment of income tax made in respect of tax credits on distributions of venture capital trusts.
FA 2000, s. 46(2)(a): exemption under that section (small charitable trades) denied in respect of income which is chargeable to tax under s. 30.
SI 1987/1749, reg. 11(1): s. 30 applies in relation to certain payments by the Board under Occupational Pension Schemes (Additional Voluntary Contributions) Regulations 1987.
SI 1988/1012, reg. 6(1): similar provisions to those of s. 30 are applied to erroneous payments made by the Secretary of State by way of minimum contributions under SSA 1986.
SI 1988/1013, reg. 13(1): similar provisions to those of s. 30 are applied to certain excessive and erroneous payments made to a scheme administrator.
SI 1992/734, reg. 6: adaptation of s. 30 in relation to recovery of tax from training provider for purposes of vocational training relief.
SI 1994/1518, reg. 5: s. 30 modified as respects recovery of tax from payee of medical insurance premium.
SI 1995/351, reg. 5, 6: assessment in respect of amount payable under stop-loss insurance to an individual or corporate member of Lloyd's is not out of time if made before end of underwriting year following the underwriting year in which amount received.
SI 2001/56, reg. 3, 4, 5: application of s. 30 to incentive payments for electronic communication of individual and employer returns.
SI 2003/2495, reg. 4: recovery of overpaid incentives for PAYE filing.
FA 2009, Sch. 53, para. 5: late payment interest start date in respect of amounts recoverable under s. 30.

Extra-statutory concessions – B41: repayments of tax will be made outside the statutory six-year time limit where an overpayment of tax has arisen because of an error by the Revenue or another government department, and where there is no dispute or doubt as to the facts.

Statements of practice – SP 8/91: principles applied by Revenue in deciding whether "discovery" assessment should be made.

30A Assessing procedure

30A(1) Except as otherwise provided, all assessments to tax which are not self-assessments shall be made by an officer of the Board.

30A(2) All income tax which falls to be charged by an assessment which is not a self-assessment may, notwithstanding that it was chargeable under more than one Part or Chapter of ITEPA 2003 or ITTOIA 2005, be included in one assessment.

30A(3) Notice of any such assessment shall be served on the person assessed and shall state the date on which it is issued and the time within which any appeal against the assessment may be made.

30A(4) After the notice of any such assessment has been served on the person assessed, the assessment shall not be altered except in accordance with the express provisions of the Taxes Acts.

30A(5) Assessments to tax which under any provision in the Taxes Acts are to be made by the Board shall be made in accordance with this section.

History – In s. 30A(2) the words "Part or Chapter of ITEPA 2003 or ITTOIA 2005" substituted for the former word "Schedule" by ITTOIA 2005, s. 882(1) and Sch. 1, para. 370; effective for 2005–06 onwards (ITTOIA 2005, s. 883(1)).
S. 30A inserted by FA 1994, s. 196 and Sch. 19, para. 5(1) in respect of the year 1997–98 and subsequent years of assessment for partnerships whose trades, professions or businesses were set up or commenced before 6 April 1994 (FA 1994, Sch. 19, para. 5(2)) and otherwise in respect of the year 1996–97 and subsequent years of assessment (FA 1994, s. 199(2) and SI 1998/3173).

30AA Assessing income tax on trustees and personal representatives

30AA(1) Income tax charged on income arising to trustees of a settlement may be assessed and charged on, and in the name of, any one or more of the assessable trustees.

30AA(2) Income tax charged on income arising to the personal representatives of a deceased person may be assessed and charged on, and in the name of, any one or more of the assessable representatives.

30AA(3) In subsection (1) **"the assessable trustees"** means–

(a) the trustees of the settlement in the tax year in which the income arises, and

(b) any subsequent trustees of the settlement.

30AA(4) In subsection (2) **"the assessable representatives"** means–

(a) the persons who, in the tax year in which the income arises, are personal representatives of the deceased person, and

(b) any subsequent personal representatives of the deceased person.

History – S. 30AA inserted by TIOPA 2010, s. 371 and Sch. 7, para. 58, with effect for corporation tax purposes for accounting periods ending on or after 1 April 2010, for income tax and capital gains tax purposes for the tax year 2010–11 and subsequent tax years, and for petroleum revenue tax purposes for chargeable periods beginning on or after 1 July 2010.

30B Amendment of partnership statement where loss of tax discovered

30B(1) Where an officer of the Board or the Board discover, as regards a partnership statement made by any person (**the representative partner**) in respect of any period–

(a) that any profits which ought to have been included in the statement have not been so included, or

(b) that an amount of profits so included is or has become insufficient, or

(c) that any relief or allowance claimed by the representative partner is or has become excessive,

the officer or, as the case may be, the Board may, subject to subsections (3) and (4) below, by notice to that partner so amend the partnership return as to make good the omission or deficiency or eliminate the excess.

30B(2) Where a partnership return is amended under subsection (1) above, the officer shall by notice to each of the relevant partners amend–

(a) the partner's return under section 8 or 8A of this Act, or

(b) the partner's company tax return,

so as to give effect to the amendments of the partnership return.

30B(3) Where the situation mentioned in subsection (1) above is attributable to an error or mistake as to the basis on which the partnership statement ought to have been made, no amendment shall be made under that subsection if that statement was in fact made on the basis or in accordance with the practice generally prevailing at the time when it was made.

30B(4) No amendment shall be made under subsection (1) above unless one of the two conditions mentioned below is fulfilled.

30B(5) The first condition is that the situation mentioned in subsection (1) above was brought about carelessly or deliberately by–

(a) the representative partner or a person acting on his behalf, or

(b) a relevant partner or a person acting on behalf of such a partner.

30B(6) The second condition is that at the time when an officer of the Board–

(a) ceased to be entitled to give notice of his intention to enquire into the representative partner's partnership return; or

(b) informed that partner that he had completed his enquiries into that return,

the officer could not have been reasonably expected, on the basis of the information made available to him before that time, to be aware of the situation mentioned in subsection (1) above.

30B(7) Subsections (6) and (7) of section 29 of this Act apply for the purposes of subsection (6) above as they apply for the purposes of subsection (5) of that section; and those subsections as so applied shall have effect as if–

(a) any reference to the taxpayer were a reference to the representative partner;

(b) any reference to the taxpayer's return under section 8 or 8A were a reference to the representative partner's partnership return; and

(c) sub-paragraph (ii) of paragraph (a) of subsection (7) were omitted.

30B(8) An objection to the making of an amendment under subsection (1) above on the ground that neither of the two conditions mentioned above is fulfilled shall not be made otherwise than on an appeal against the amendment.

30B(9) In this section–

"profits"

(a) in relation to income tax, means income,

(b) in relation to capital gains tax, means chargeable gains, and

(c) in relation to corporation tax, means profits as computed for the purposes of that tax;

"relevant partner" means a person who was a partner at any time during the period in respect of which the partnership statement was made.

30B(10) Any reference in this section to the representative partner includes, unless the context otherwise requires, a reference to any successor of his.

History – In s. 30B(1), the words "amend the partnership return" substituted by FA 2001, s. 88, Sch. 29, para. 24(2) with effect from 11 May 2001 in relation to returns whether made before or after that date and whether relating to periods before or after then.

S. 30B(2) substituted by FA 2001, s. 88, Sch. 29, para. 24(3) with effect from 11 May 2001 in relation to returns whether made before or after that date and whether relating to periods before or after then. The effect of the amendment was to replace in para. (a) the reference to "the partner's self-assessment under section 9 of this Act" with the present wording and to replace the word "statement" with the word "return". S. 30B(2) had been substituted previously by FA 1998, s. 117(3) and Sch. 19, para. 14(2) as respects accounting periods ending on or after 1 July 1999, the corporation tax self-assessment appointed day by virtue of FA 1994, s. 199(2) and SI 1998/3173 (C. 78).

In s. 30B(5) the words "was brought about carelessly or deliberately by" substituted for the words "is attributable to fraudulent or negligent conduct on the part of" by FA 2008, s. 118 and Sch. 39, para. 4 with effect from 1 April 2010 (SI 2009/403, art. 2(2) subject to SI 2009/403, art. 3–10 – in particular art. 10).

In s. 30B(6)(a) and (7)(b) the words "partnership return" substituted for "return under section 12AA of this Act" by FA 2001, s. 88, Sch. 29, para. 24(4) with effect from 11 May 2001 in relation to returns whether made before or after that date and whether relating to periods before or after then.

In s. 30B(7)(b), reference to TMA 1970, s. 11 omitted by FA 1998, s. 117(3) and Sch. 19, para. 14(3) as respects accounting periods ending on or after 1 July 1999 – the corporation tax self-assessment appointed day (see above).

In s. 30B(9), the definition of "profits" substituted as respects accounting periods ending on or after 1 July 1999, the corporation tax self-assessment appointed day (see above).

S. 30B inserted by FA 1994, s. 196 and Sch. 19, para. 6, and amended by FA 1995, s. 115(5), for income tax and capital gains tax, as respects the year 1996–97 and subsequent years of assessment, and originally also for corporation tax as respects accounting periods ending on or after the self-assessment appointed day (FA 1994, s. 199(2), (3)), but now superseded by FA 1998, Sch. 18 for corporation tax self-assessment provisions.

Cross references – S. 31–31D (appeals) (as substituted by FA 2001, Sch. 29, para. 11): application to amendments of partnership returns under s. 30B(1) (as amended by FA 2001) where notice of the amendment is issued after 11 May 2001.
S. 46B–46D: questions to be determined by special commissioners; jurisdiction of special commissioners over certain claims included in returns; questions to be determined by Lands Tribunal.
Sch. 3ZA, para. 9: tax payable or repayable on consequential amendment under s. 30B(2)(a) of self-assessment in partner's return.

31 Appeals: right of appeal

31(1) An appeal may be brought against–

(a) any amendment of a self-assessment under section 9C of this Act (amendment by Revenue during enquiry to prevent loss of tax),

(b) any conclusion stated or amendment made by a closure notice under section 28A or 28B of this Act (amendment by Revenue on completion of enquiry into return),

(c) any amendment of a partnership return under section 30B(1) of this Act (amendment by Revenue where loss of tax discovered), or

(d) any assessment to tax which is not a self-assessment.

31(2) If an appeal under subsection (1)(a) above against an amendment of a self-assessment is made while an enquiry is in progress none of the steps mentioned in section 49A(2)(a) to (c) may be taken in relation to the appeal until the enquiry is completed.

31(3) [Omitted by CTA 2009, s. 1322 and Sch. 1, para. 301 and repealed by CTA 2009, s. 1326 and Sch. 3, Pt. 1.]

31(3A) In the case of a simple assessment, the right to appeal under subsection (1)(d) does not apply unless and until the person concerned has–

(a) raised a query about the assessment under section 31AA, and

(b) been given a final response to that query.

31(4) This section has effect subject to any express provision in the Taxes Acts, including in particular any provision making one kind of assessment conclusive in an appeal against another kind of assessment.

History – In s. 31(2) the word "If" and the word "is" (after "self-assessment") inserted and the words "none of the steps mentioned in section 49A(2)(a) to (c) may be taken in relation to the appeal" substituted for the words "shall not be heard and determined" by SI 2009/56, art. 3(1) and Sch. 1, para. 19, operative from 1 April 2009, subject to transitional and saving provisions in SI 2009/56, Sch. 3.
S. 31(3) omitted by CTA 2009, s. 1322 and Sch. 1, para. 301 and repealed by CTA 2009, s. 1326 and Sch. 3, Pt. 1, with effect for corporation tax purposes for accounting periods ending on or after 1 April 2009, and for income tax and capital gains tax purposes for the tax year 2009–10 and subsequent tax years.
In s. 31(3) the reference to TMA 1970, s. 9D omitted by ITTOIA 2005, s. 882(1) and Sch. 1, para. 371; effective 2005–06 onwards (ITTOIA 2005, s. 883(1)).
S. 31(3A) inserted by FA 2016, s. 167 and Sch. 23, para. 4, with effect in relation to the 2016–17 tax year and subsequent years.
S. 31–31D substituted for former s. 31 by FA 2001, Sch. 29, para. 11(1) with effect in relation to–
(a) amendments of a self assessment under s. 9C (as inserted by FA 2001, Sch. 29, para. 4, with effect from 11 May 2001);
(b) closure notices issued under s. 28A(1) or 28B(1) (as substituted by FA 2001, Sch. 29, para. 8 and 9, with effect from 11 May 2001);
(c) amendments of partnership returns under s. 30B(1) where notice of the amendment is issued after 11 May 2001, and
(d) assessments to tax which are not self assessments where the notice of the assessment is issued after 11 May 2001.

Cross references – ICTA 1988, s. 350, 445, 740, 743(1) and 747(4)(a): deduction of income tax at source; charge on investment income of overseas life insurance companies; liability of non-transferor on transfer of assets abroad; liability of transferor on transfer of assets abroad; and charge on profits of controlled foreign companies.
ICTA 1988, s. 830 (and FA 1973, s. 38): extended charge to tax in relation to the territorial sea of the UK and designated areas.
ICTA 1988, Sch. 27, para. 17: no appeal may be brought on the ground that an offshore fund should have been certified as a distributing fund.
FA 1988, s. 134(8): an election that certain proceedings in Northern Ireland instituted in front of special commissioners should not be transferred to general commissioners may be disregarded by virtue of former s. 31(5A)–(5E).
TCGA 1992, s. 276: extended charge to tax on chargeable gains in relation to the territorial sea of the UK and designated areas.
FA 1993, s. 173 and Sch. 19, para. 4(3): for 1992–93 and subsequent years of assessment former s. 31(5)–(5E) apply for the purposes of an election in respect of underwriters' agents' appeals against inspectors' determinations of Lloyd's syndicate profits and losses in the same way as for the purposes of s. 31(4).
FA 1993, s. 173 and Sch. 19, para. 7(2)(a): modified application of former s. 31 for 1992–93 and subsequent years of assessment where determination of a Lloyd's syndicate's profit or loss is varied or modified after issue of a notice of assessment on any syndicate member.
SSCTFA 1999, s. 12(5): former s. 31(5A)–(5E) have effect in relation to an election under SSCTFA 1999, s. 12(4) (election to bring appeal against a decision of an officer of the Board on certain contributions questions before the Special Commissioners) as they do in relation to an appeal under former s. 31(4).
SI 1993/2004, reg. 11(10): application of former s. 31 to an appeal against an assessment under reg. 11 (manufactured overseas dividends).
TCA 2002, s. 39(4): s. 31D(2)–(7) have effect for purposes of an election under TCA 2002, s. 39(3) (election to bring tax credits appeal before the Special Commissioners) but see also TCA 2002, s. 63 for transitional arrangements.

Notes – Express provisions requiring appeals against assessments to be made to the special commissioners:
- s. 47(3) (chargeable gains regarding the value of unquoted shares or securities in UK-resident companies);
- ICTA 1988, s. 75(5) (expenses of management);
- ICTA 1988, s. 584(9) (relief for unremittable overseas income).

For jurisdiction in appeals on claims see s. 42 and Sch. 2.

31A Appeals: notice of appeal

31A(1) Notice of an appeal under section 31 of this Act must be given–
(a) in writing,
(b) within 30 days after the specified date,
(c) to the relevant officer of the Board.

31A(2) In relation to an appeal under section 31(1)(a) or (c) of this Act–
(a) the specified date is the date on which the notice of amendment was issued, and
(b) the relevant officer of the Board is the officer by whom the notice of amendment was given.

31A(3) In relation to an appeal under section 31(1)(b) of this Act–
(a) the specified date is the date on which the closure notice was issued, and
(b) the relevant officer of the Board is the officer by whom the closure notice was given.

31A(4) In relation to an appeal under section 31(1)(d) of this Act (other than an appeal against a simple assessment)–
(a) the specified date is the date on which the notice of assessment was issued, and
(b) the relevant officer of the Board is the officer by whom the notice of assessment was given.

31A(4A) In relation to an appeal under section 31(1)(d) against a simple assessment–
(a) the specified date is the date on which the person concerned is given notice under section 31AA of the final response to the query the person is required by section 31(3A) to make, and
(b) the relevant officer of the Board is the officer by whom the notice of assessment was given.

31A(5) The notice of appeal must specify the grounds of appeal.

31A(6) [Omitted by SI 2009/56, art. 3(1) and Sch. 1, para. 20.]

History – In s. 31A(4) the words "(other than an appeal against a simple assessment)" inserted by FA 2016, s. 167 and Sch. 23, para. 5(2), with effect in relation to the 2016–17 tax year and subsequent years.
S. 31A(4A) inserted by FA 2016, s. 167 and Sch. 23, para. 5(3), with effect in relation to the 2016–17 tax year and subsequent years
S. 31A(6) omitted by SI 2009/56, art. 3(1) and Sch. 1, para. 20, operative from 1 April 2009, subject to transitional and saving provisions in SI 2009/56, Sch. 3.
S. 31–31D substituted for former s. 31 by FA 2001, Sch. 29, para. 11(1) with effect in relation to–
(a) amendments of a self assessment under s. 9C (as inserted by FA 2001, Sch. 29, para. 4);
(b) closure notices issued under s. 28A(1) or 28B(1) (as substituted by FA 2001, Sch. 29, para. 8 and 9);
(c) amendments of partnership returns under s. 30B(1) where notice of the amendment is issued after 11 May 2001; and
(d) assessments to tax which are not self assessments where the notice of the assessment is issued after that date.

Cross references – FA 1993, s. 173 and Sch. 19, para. 4(3): s. 31A(5) and (6) and 31D(2)–(7) apply for the purposes of an election in respect of underwriters' agents' appeals against inspectors' determinations of Lloyd's syndicate profits and losses in the same way as for the purposes of s. 31D(1).
FA 1993, s. 173 and Sch. 19, para. 7(2)(a): modified application of s. 31A where determination of a Lloyd's syndicate's profit or loss is varied or modified after issue of a notice of assessment on any syndicate member.

31AA Taxpayer's right to query simple assessment

31AA(1) This section applies where a person has been given notice of a simple assessment.

31AA(2) The person may query the simple assessment by notifying HMRC of–
(a) a belief that the assessment is or may be incorrect, and
(b) the reasons for that belief.

31AA(3) The person may exercise the power to query the simple assessment at any time within–
(a) the period of 60 days after the date on which the notice of assessment was issued, or
(b) such longer period as HMRC may allow.

31AA(4) If the simple assessment is queried, HMRC must–
(a) consider the query and the matters raised by it, and
(b) give a final response to the query.

31AA(5) The person may at any time withdraw a query (which terminates HMRC's duties under subsection (4)).

31AA(6) If it appears to HMRC that–
(a) they need time to consider the matters raised by the query, or
(b) further information (whether from the person or anyone else) is required,

HMRC may postpone the simple assessment in whole or part (according to how much of it is being queried by the person).

31AA(7) If the simple assessment is postponed in whole or part, HMRC must notify the person in writing–
(a) whether the assessment is postponed in whole or part, and

(b) if it is postponed in part, of the amount that remains payable under the assessment.

31AA(8) While the simple assessment is postponed the person is under no obligation to pay–

(a) the payable amount specified in the notice of assessment (if the whole assessment is postponed), or

(b) the postponed part of the payable amount so specified (if the assessment is postponed in part).

31AA(9) After considering the query the final response must be to–

(a) confirm the simple assessment,

(b) give the person an amended simple assessment (which supersedes the original assessment), or

(c) withdraw the simple assessment (without replacing it).

31AA(10) HMRC must notify the person in writing of their final response.

31AA(11) This section does not apply to an amended simple assessment given as a final response to the query.

31AA(12) Nothing in this section affects–

(a) a person's right to request an explanation from HMRC of a simple assessment or the information on which it is based, or

(b) HMRC's power to give a person such explanation or information as they consider appropriate, whether as part of the querying process under this section or otherwise.

31AA(13) In subsection (12) **"person"** means a person who has been given notice of a simple assessment[.]

History – S. 31AA inserted by FA 2016, s. 167 and Sch. 23, para. 6, with effect in relation to the 2016–17 tax year and subsequent years.

31B Appeals: appeals to General Commissioners

31B [Omitted by SI 2009/56, art. 3(1) and Sch. 1, para. 21.]

History – S. 31B omitted by SI 2009/56, art. 3(1) and Sch. 1, para. 21, operative from 1 April 2009, subject to transitional and saving provisions in SI 2009/56, Sch. 3.

31C Appeals: appeals to Special Commissioners

31C [Omitted by SI 2009/56, art. 3(1) and Sch. 1, para. 21.]

History – S. 31C omitted by SI 2009/56, art. 3(1) and Sch. 1, para. 21, operative from 1 April 2009, subject to transitional and saving provisions in SI 2009/56, Sch. 3.

31D Appeals: election to bring appeal before Special Commissioners

31D [Omitted by SI 2009/56, art. 3(1) and Sch. 1, para. 21.]

History – S. 31D omitted by SI 2009/56, art. 3(1) and Sch. 1, para. 21, operative from 1 April 2009, subject to transitional and saving provisions in SI 2009/56, Sch. 3.

OVERPAID TAX, EXCESSIVE ASSESSMENTS ETC

History – In the heading, the words "Overpaid tax, excessive assessments etc" substituted for "Relief for excessive assessments" by FA 2009, s. 100 and Sch. 52, para. 4 with effect in relation to claims made on or after 1 April 2010.

32 Double assessment

32(1) If on a claim made to the Board it appears to their satisfaction that a person has been assessed to tax more than once for the same cause and for the same chargeable period, they shall direct the whole, or such part of any assessment as appears to be an overcharge, to be vacated, and thereupon the same shall be vacated accordingly.

32(2) An appeal may be brought against the refusal of a claim under this section.

32(3) Notice of appeal under subsection (2) must be given–

(a) in writing;

(b) within 30 days after the day on which notice of the refusal is given;

(c) to the officer of Revenue and Customs by whom that notice was given.

History – S. 32(1) amended by FA 1985, Sch. 27, Pt. X, with effect from 19 March 1985 to remove references to development land tax. S. 32(2) and (3) substituted for former s. 32(2) by SI 2009/56, art. 3(1) and Sch. 1, para. 22, operative from 1 April 2009, subject to transitional and saving provisions in SI 2009/56, Sch. 3.

Cross references – FA 1995, Sch. 21, para. 3(2): modification of s. 32, as respects each partner for 1996–97, in case of partnership whose trade etc. was set up and commenced before 6 April 1994.

TCA 2002, s. 20(2): revisions of decisions on working tax credit and child tax credit following vacation of an assessment, or determination or settlement of appeal.

Extra-statutory concessions – B41: repayments of tax will be made outside the statutory six-year time limit where an overpayment of tax has arisen because of an error by the Revenue or another government department, and where there is no dispute or doubt as to the facts.

33 Recovery of overpaid tax etc

33 Schedule 1AB contains provision for and in connection with claims for the recovery of overpaid income tax and capital gains tax.

History – S. 33 substituted for former s. 33 and 33A by FA 2009, s. 100 and Sch. 52, para. 1 with effect in relation to claims made on or after 1 April 2010.
At the time of its substitution by FA 2009, s. 100 and Sch. 52, para. 1, former s. 33 was to have been amended prospectively: in former s. 33(1) the words "not more than 4 years after the end of" were to have been substituted for the words "not later than five years after the 31st January next following" by FA 2008, s. 118 and Sch. 39, para. 5, with effect from 1 April 2010 (SI 2009/403, art. 2(2) subject to SI 2009/403, art. 3–10 – in particular art. 10).

33A Error or mistake in partnership return

33A [Effectively repealed by FA 2009, s. 100 and Sch. 52, para. 1.]

History – S. 33A (together with former s. 33) substituted by new s. 33 by FA 2009, s. 100 and Sch. 52, para. 1 with effect in relation to claims made on or after 1 April 2010.
At the time of its substitution by FA 2009, s. 100 and Sch. 52, para. 1, former s. 33A was to have been amended prospectively: in former s. 33A(2) the words "not more than 4 years after the end of the year of assessment in question, or in which the relevant period ends," were to be substituted for the words "not later than 31st January of Year 6" by FA 2008, s. 118 and Sch. 39, para. 6, with effect from 1 April 2010 (SI 2009/403, art. 2(2) subject to SI 2009/403, art. 3–10 – in particular art. 10).

TIME LIMITS

34 Ordinary time limit of 4 years

History – In the heading to s. 34, "4 years" substituted for "six years" by FA 2008, s. 118 and Sch. 39, para. 7(3), with effect from 1 April 2010 (SI 2009/403, art. 2(2) subject to SI 2009/403, art. 3–10 – in particular art. 10).

34(1) Subject to the following provisions of this Act, and to any other provisions of the Taxes Acts allowing a longer period in any particular class of case, an assessment to income tax or capital gains tax may be made at any time not more than 4 years after the end of the year of assessment to which it relates.

34(1A) In subsection (1) the reference to an assessment to capital gains tax includes a determination under section 29A (non-resident CGT disposals: determination of amount which should have been assessed).

34(2) An objection to the making of any assessment on the ground that the time limit for making it has expired shall only be made on an appeal against the assessment.

34(3) In this section **"assessment"** does not include a self-assessment.

History – In s. 34(1) the words "not more than 4 years after the end of" substituted for the words "not later than five years after the 31st January next following" by FA 2008, s. 118 and Sch. 39, para. 7(2), with effect from 1 April 2010 (SI 2009/403, art. 2(2) subject to SI 2009/403, art. 3–10 – in particular art. 10).
In s. 34(1), the words from "an assessment to tax may be made" to the end of the subsection substituted by FA 1998, s. 117(3) and Sch. 19, para. 17(1), with effect in relation to accounting periods ending on or after 1 July 1999, the corporation tax self-assessment appointed day by virtue of FA 1994, s. 199(2) and SI 1998/3173 (C. 78).
The equivalent provisions under corporation tax self-assessment are to be found in FA 1998, Sch. 18, which has effect in relation to accounting periods ending on or after 1 July 1999 and is construed and has effect as if it were contained in TMA 1970 (FA 1998, 117(2)).
S. 34(1) formerly amended by FA 1994, s. 196 and Sch. 19, para. 10, in so far as it relates to income tax and capital gains tax, as respects the year 1996–97 and subsequent years of assessment, and originally also for corporation tax accounting periods ending on or after 1 July 1999, the appointed day (see notes above).
S. 34(1) formerly amended by FA 1985, Sch. 27, Pt. X, with effect from 19 March 1985, removing a reference to development land tax.
S. 34(1A) inserted by FA 2015, s. 37 and Sch. 7, para. 48, with effect in relation to disposals made on or after 6 April 2015.
S. 34(3) inserted by FA 2016, s. 168(2), with effect from 15 September 2016 (Royal Assent).

Cross references – OTA 1975, Sch. 2, para. 1(1): s. 34(2) applies for the purposes of oil taxation.
ICTA 1988, s. 246Q(10): disapplication of reference to s. 34 in ICTA 1988, s. 252(5) where it is applied by virtue of s. 246Q.
ICTA 1988, Sch. 3, para. 6E(2): for the purposes of s. 34, an assessment under ICTA 1988, Sch. 3, para. 6D (paying and collecting agents in respect of foreign dividends, etc.) is taken to relate to the year of assessment in which the quarter, to which the assessment relates, ends.
TCGA 1992, s. 248(2): assessment to withdraw roll-over on replacement of land compulsorily acquired where the dwelling-house in point becomes subject to principal private residence relief can be made at any time.
TCGA 1992, s. 256(2): gain crystallising where property ceasing to be subject to charitable trusts represents prior disposal consideration can ordinarily be assessed up to three years after the tax year in which it so ceases.
FA 1993, s. 178(3)(a): extension of ordinary six-year time limit where inspector not notified in time of an amount payable to a member of Lloyd's under a stop-loss insurance, or out of the High Level Stop Loss Fund, in respect of a loss in his underwriting business.
FA 1994, s. 225(1): allocation of stop-loss insurance recovery by corporate underwriter to later accounting period where inspector would otherwise be prevented from making an assessment by s. 34.
SI 1982/1236, reg. 19(6): assessments giving effect to a notice under ICTA 1988, s. 375(6) that interest is not "relevant loan interest".
SI 1995/352, reg. 6(2)(a): modifications applying to assessment of Lloyd's underwriters for 1992–93.
SI 1995/352, reg. 7(2)(a): modifications applying to assessment of Lloyd's underwriters for 1993–94 and 1994–95.

34A Ordinary time limit for self-assessments

34A(1) Subject to subsections (2) and (3), a self assessment contained in a return under section 8 or 8A may be made and delivered at any time not more than 4 years after the end of the year of assessment to which it relates.

34A(2) Nothing in subsection (1) prevents–

(a) a person who has received a notice under section 8 or 8A within that period of 4 years from delivering a return including a self-assessment within the period of 3 months beginning with the date of the notice,

(b) a person in respect of whom a determination under section 28C has been made from making a self-assessment in accordance with that section within the period allowed by subsection (5)(a) or (b) of that section.

34A(3) Subsection (1) has effect subject to the following provisions of this Act and to any other provisions of the Taxes Acts allowing a longer period in any particular class of case.

34A(4) This section has effect in relation to self-assessments for a year of assessment earlier than 2012–13 as if–

(a) in subsection (1) for the words from "not more" to the end there were substituted "on or before 5 April 2017", and

(b) in subsection (2)(a) for the words "within that period of 4 years" there were substituted "on or before 5 April 2017."

History – S. 34A inserted by FA 2016, s. 168(3), with effect from 15 September 2016 (Royal Assent).

35 Time limit: income received after year for which they are assessable

35(1) Where income to which this section applies is received in a year of assessment subsequent to that for which it is assessable, an assessment to income tax as respects that income may be made at any time not more than 4 years after the end of the year of assessment in which it was received.

35(2) This section applies to–

(a) employment income,

(b) pension income, and

(c) social security income.

History – In s. 35 the words "not more than 4 years after the end of" substituted for the words "within six years after" by FA 2008, s. 118 and Sch. 39, para. 8, with effect from 1 April 2010 (SI 2009/403, art. 2(2) subject to SI 2009/403, art. 3–10 – in particular art. 10).

S. 35 substituted by FA 2004, s. 92 and Sch. 17, para. 3(1) in relation to income assessable for 2004–05 and subsequent years of assessment. The previous version of the section had been repealed by FA 1998, s. 165 and Sch. 27, Pt. III(9) with effect from 6 April 1998.

36 Loss of tax brought about carelessly or deliberately etc

History – The heading to s. 36 substituted by FA 2008, s. 118 and Sch. 39, para. 9(6), with effect from 1 April 2010 (SI 2009/403, art. 2(2) subject to SI 2009/403, art. 3–10 – in particular art. 10). The former heading read: "Fraudulent or negligent conduct".

36(1) An assessment on a person in a case involving a loss of income tax or capital gains tax brought about carelessly by the person may be made at any time not more than 6 years after the end of the year of assessment to which it relates (subject to subsection (1A) and any other provision of the Taxes Acts allowing a longer period).

36(1A) An assessment on a person in a case involving a loss of income tax or capital gains tax–

(a) brought about deliberately by the person,

(b) attributable to a failure by the person to comply with an obligation under section 7,

(c) attributable to arrangements in respect of which the person has failed to comply with an obligation under section 309, 310 or 313 of the Finance Act 2004 (obligation of parties to tax avoidance schemes to provide information to Her Majesty's Revenue and Customs), or

(d) attributable to arrangements which were expected to give rise to a tax advantage in respect of which the person was under an obligation to notify the Commissioners for Her Majesty's Revenue and Customs under section 253 of the Finance Act 2014 (duty to notify Commissioners of promoter reference number) but failed to do so.

may be made at any time not more than 20 years after the end of the year of assessment to which it relates (subject to any provision of the Taxes Acts allowing a longer period).

36(1B) In subsections (1) and (1A), references to a loss brought about by the person who is the subject of the assessment include a loss brought about by another person acting on behalf of that person.

36(2) Where the person mentioned in subsection (1) or (1A) ("the person in default") carried on a trade, profession or business with one or more other persons at any time in the period for which the assessment is made, an assessment in respect of the profits or gains of the trade, profession or business in a case mentioned in subsection (1A) or (1B) may be made not only on the person in default but also on his partner or any of his partners.

36(3) If the person on whom the assessment is made so requires, in determining the amount of the tax to be charged for any chargeable period in any assessment made in a case mentioned in subsection (1) or

(1A) above, effect shall be given to any relief or allowance to which he would have been entitled for that chargeable period on a claim or application made within the time allowed by the Taxes Acts.

36(3A) In subsection (3) above, **"claim or application"** does not include an election under any of sections 47 to 49 of ITA 2007 (tax reductions for married couples and civil partners: elections to transfer relief).

36(4) Any act or omission such as is mentioned in section 98B below on the part of a grouping (as defined in that section) or member of a grouping shall be deemed for the purposes of subsections (1) and (1A) above to be the act or omission of each member of the grouping.

History – S. 36(1A)(d) inserted (and the "or" at the end of s. 36(1A)(b) omitted, and the ", or" at the end of s. 36(1A)(c) inserted), by FA 2104, s. 277(1), with effect from 17 July 2014. It is assumed that the full stop at the end of s. 36(1A)(d) is included due to a parliamentary drafting error.

S. 36(1), (1A) and (1B) substituted for former s. 36(1) by FA 2008, s. 118 and Sch. 39, para. 9(2), with effect from 1 April 2010 (SI 2009/403, art. 2(2) subject to SI 2009/403, art. 3–10 – in particular art. 10).

In former s. 36(1) the words "income tax or capital gains tax" substituted for "tax", and words from "not later than" to the end of the subsection substituted, by FA 1998, s. 117(3) and Sch. 19 para. 18(1), with effect in relation to accounting periods ending on or after 1 July 1999, the corporation tax self-assessment appointed day by virtue of FA 1994, s. 199(2) and SI 1998/3173 (C. 78).

The equivalent provisions under corporation tax self-assessment are to be found in FA 1998, Sch. 18, which has effect in relation to accounting periods ending on or after 1 July 1999 and is construed and has effect as if it were contained in TMA 1970 (FA 1998, s. 117(2)).

S. 36(1) formerly amended and s. 36(2) substituted, by FA 1994, s. 196 and Sch. 19, para. 11, in so far as it relates to income tax and capital gains tax, as respects the year 1996–97 and subsequent years of assessment, and originally also for corporation tax accounting periods ending on or after the self-assessment appointed day (see notes above).

In s. 36(2), the words "in a case" substituted for "for the purpose" by FA 2009, s. 99 and Sch. 51, para. 41 with effect from 1 April 2010 (SI 2010/867).

In s. 36(2), the words "Where the person mentioned in subsection (1) or (1A) ("the person in default")" substituted for the words "Where the person in default" and the words "subsection (1A) or (1B)" substituted for the words "subsection (1) above" by FA 2008, s. 118 and Sch. 39, para. 9(3), with effect from 1 April 2010 (SI 2009/403, art. 2(2) subject to SI 2009/403, art. 3–10 – in particular art. 10).

In s. 36(3), the words "in a case" substituted for "for the purpose" by FA 2009, s. 99 and Sch. 51, para. 41 with effect from 1 April 2010 (SI 2010/867).

In s. 36(3), "or (1A)" inserted by FA 2008, s. 118 and Sch. 39, para. 9(4), with effect from 1 April 2010 (SI 2009/403, art. 2(2) subject to SI 2009/403, art. 3–10 – in particular art. 10).

In s. 36(3A), the words "section 257BA of the principal Act or", which appeared after "election under", omitted by FA 2009, s. 5 and Sch. 1, para. 6(a)(i) with effect for the tax year 2010–11 and subsequent tax years.

In s. 36(3A), the words "or any of sections 47 to 49 of ITA 2007" inserted by ITA 2007, s. 1027 and Sch. 1, para. 251(a) and the words "(tax reductions for married couples and civil partners: elections to transfer relief)" substituted for the words "(elections as to transfer of married couple's allowance)" by ITA 2007, s. 1027 and Sch. 1, para. 251(b), with effect from 6 April 2007.

In s. 36(3A) the words "or under Schedule 13B to that Act (elections as to transfer of children's tax credit)" inserted by FA 1999, s. 30(4)(a) with effect for the year 2001–02 and subsequent years of assessment but then repealed by TCA 2002 s. 60 and Sch. 6 with effect from 6 April 2003 (SI 2003/962).

S. 36(3A) inserted, in relation to tax for 1993–94 and subsequent years of assessment, by F(No. 2)A 1992, s. 20 and Sch. 5, para. 9(1), (2).

In s. 36(4) the words "subsections (1) and (1A)" substituted for the words "subsection (1)" by FA 2008, s. 118 and Sch. 39, para. 9(5) with effect from 1 April 2010 (SI 2009/403, art. 2(2) subject to SI 2009/403, art. 3–10 – in particular art. 10).

S. 36(4) inserted by FA 1990, s. 69 and Sch. 11, para. 4(1), 5, deemed to have effect from 1 July 1989.

S. 36 substituted by FA 1989, s. 149(1), (7), with effect from 27 July 1989 but not affecting the making of assessments for any year before 1983–84 or for accounting periods which ended before 1 April 1983.

Cross references – S. 43C(1): application of s. 36(3) following amendment of tax return due to negligent or fraudulent conduct.

S. 98B: failure to deliver a return or document and fraudulent or negligent delivery of incorrect return etc. in respect of European Economic Interest Grouping.

S. 118(3): partnership assessment treated as made on individual partners.

OTA 1975, Sch. 2, para. 1(1): s. 36 applies with modifications for the purposes of oil taxation.

ICTA 1988, s. 307(5): assessments made for the purpose of withdrawing relief under the business expansion scheme (in relation to shares issued on or before 31 December 1993) or the enterprise investment scheme (in relation to shares issued on or after 1 January 1994) may, without prejudice to s. 36, be made within six years.

Former ICTA 1988, Sch. 3, para. 6E(2): for the purposes of s. 36(1), an assessment under ICTA 1988, Sch. 3, para. 6D (paying and collecting agents in respect of foreign dividends, etc.) is taken to relate to the year of assessment in which the quarter, to which the assessment relates, ends.

Former ICTA 1988, Sch. 3, para. 6E(3): modification of s. 36(2) in relation to an assessment under ICTA 1988, Sch. 3, para. 6D (paying and collecting agents in respect of foreign dividends, etc.).

ICTA 1988, Sch. 13, para. 10(1) and Sch. 16, para. 10(1): s. 36 applies to assessments to ACT and of income tax deductible at source on company payments which are not distributions.

FA 1993, s. 178(3)(b): modified application of s. 36 in relation to payments made to a member of Lloyd's under a stop-loss insurance or out of the High Level Stop Loss Fund in respect of an underwriting loss.

FA 1993, s. 173 and Sch. 19, para. 8: for 1992–93 and subsequent years, for the purposes of s. 36, acts or omissions of a Lloyd's underwriters' syndicate are attributable to each member of the syndicate (see ICTA 1988, s. 450 and Sch. 19A, para. 9 for prior years (from 1988–89)).

FA 1994, s. 225(3): allocation of stop-loss insurance recovery by corporate underwriter to later accounting period where inspector would otherwise be prevented from making an assessment by s. 36.

SI 1987/530, reg. 11(2)(b): application of s. 36 to non-resident entertainers and sportsmen.

SI 1995/352, reg. 6(2)(a): modifications applying to assessment of Lloyd's underwriters for 1992–93.

SI 1995/352, reg. 7(2)(a): modifications applying to assessment of Lloyd's underwriters for 1993–94 and 1994–95.

HMRC interpretations – IRInt. 148: confirmation that under self assessment s. 36(2) does not preserve composite assessment mechanism, merely allows HMRC to make individual assessments on each of the partners who have additional tax to pay on their revised share of partnership profit.

HMRC Manuals – Capital Allowances, CA2099b: HMRC guidance on consequences of claiming capital allowances which would have been due had a claim been made within the time limits where a further or discovery assessment is raised to recover tax which would have been lost through fraud or neglect.

37 Neglect: income tax and capital gains tax

37 [Repealed by FA 1989, s. 149(2) and Sch. 17, Pt. VIII.]

History – S. 37 repealed by FA 1989, s. 149(2) and Sch. 17, Pt. VIII from 27 July 1989 but not affecting the making of assessments for years before 1983–84 or for accounting periods which ended before 1 April 1983.

Cross references – F(No. 2)A 1987, s. 84(7): s. 37 does not apply to assessments made under s. 84 of that Act (amounts due by way of penalty).
ICTA 1988, s. 307(5): assessments made for the purpose of withdrawing relief under the business expansion scheme may, without prejudice to s. 37, be made within six years.
ICTA 1988, Sch. 16, para. 10(1): s. 37 applies to assessments in respect of income tax deductible at source on company payments which are not distributions.
ICTA 1988, Sch. 19A, para. 9; FA 1973, Sch. 16A, para. 9: for the purposes of s. 37, acts or omissions of a Lloyd's underwriting agent are attributable to each member of the syndicate.

37A Effect of assessment where allowances transferred

37A Where an assessment is made on any person in a case falling within section 36(1) or (1A), the fact that the person's liability to income tax or total income for any year of assessment is assessed as greater than it was previously taken to be shall not affect the validity of any deduction from net income or tax reduction made in the case of that person's spouse or civil partner by virtue of section 39, 51 or 52 of ITA 2007; and the entitlement in that case of the first-mentioned person for the year in question to any deduction from net income or tax reduction shall be treated as correspondingly reduced.

History – In s. 37A, the words "section 257BB or 265 of the principal Act or", which appeared after "by virtue of", omitted by FA 2009, s. 5 and Sch. 1, para. 6(a)(ii) with effect for the tax year 2010–11 and subsequent tax years.
In s. 37A the words "in a case falling within section 36(1) or (1A)" substituted for the words "for the purpose of making good a loss of tax wholly or partly attributable to fraudulent or negligent conduct" by FA 2008, s. 118 and Sch. 39, para. 10, with effect from 1 April 2010 (SI 2009/403, art. 2(2) subject to SI 2009/403, art. 3–10 – in particular art. 10).
In s. 37A the words "deduction from net income or tax reduction" were substituted in both places where the phrase occurred, by ITA 2007, s. 1027 and Sch. 1, para. 252(2), with effect from 6 April 2007; the words "or civil partner" inserted by ITA 2007, s. 1027 and Sch. 1, para. 252(3), with effect from 6 April 2007 and the words "or section 39, 51 or 52 of ITA 2007" inserted by ITA 2007, s. 1027 and Sch. 1, para. 252(4) with effect from 6 April 2007.
S. 37A amended by FA 1999, s. 30(4)(b) (inserting the words "or partner" and "or paragraph 4 of Schedule 13B to that Act") and by s. 139 and Sch. 20, Pt. III(3) (repealing a reference to 257D which appeared after "section 257BB"), all with effect for the year 2001–02 and subsequent years of assessment. The words "or partner" and "or paragraph 4 of Schedule 13B to that Act" being subsequently repealed by TCA 2002 s. 60 and Sch. 6 with effect from 6 April 2003 (SI 2003/962).
In s. 37A, the words "liability to income tax or" inserted; the words "any income tax reduction … that person's spouse" substituted for the words "any deduction made from the total income of the person's spouse" and the words "and the entitlement … treated as correspondingly reduced" substituted for the words "and where any such deduction has been made in such a case, the total amount which the first-mentioned person is entitled to deduct from total income for the year in question shall be correspondingly reduced" by FA 1994, s. 77 and Sch. 8, para. 13, with effect for 1994–95 and subsequent years of assessment (FA 1994, s. 77(7)).
"257BB" substituted for "257B", in relation to tax for 1993–94 and subsequent years of assessment, by F(No. 2)A 1992, s. 20 and Sch. 5, para. 9(1), (3).
S. 37A inserted by FA 1988, s. 35 and Sch. 3, para. 30, with effect from 1990–91; the amendment was made by FA 1989, s. 149(4)(a)(i), substituting "fraudulent or negligent conduct".

38 Modification of s. 37 in relation to partnerships

38 [Repealed by FA 1989, s. 149(2) and Sch. 17, Pt. VIII.]

History – S. 38 repealed by FA 1989, s. 149(2) and Sch. 17, Pt. VIII, with effect from 27 July 1989 but not affecting the making of assessments for years before 1983–84 or for accounting periods which ended before 1 April 1983.
S. 38(3A) dealt with development land tax.

39 Neglect: corporation tax

39 [Repealed by FA 1989, s. 149(2) and Sch. 17, Pt. VIII.]

History – S. 39 repealed by FA 1989, s. 149(2) and Sch. 17, Pt. VIII from 27 July 1989 but not affecting the making of assessments for years before 1983–84 or for accounting periods which ended before 1 April 1983.

Cross references – S. 118: definition of "neglect".

40 Assessment on personal representatives

40(1) For the purpose of the charge of tax on the executors or administrators of a deceased person in respect of the income, or chargeable gains, which arose or accrued to him before his death, the time allowed by section 34, 35 or 36 above shall in no case extend more than 4 years after the end of the year of assessment in which the deceased died.

40(2) In a case involving a loss of tax brought about carelessly or deliberately by a person who has died (or another person acting on that person's behalf before that person's death), an assessment on his personal representatives to tax for any year of assessment ending not earlier than six years before his death may be made at any time not more than 4 years after the end of the year of assessment in which he died.

40(3) In this section **"tax"** means income tax or capital gains tax.

40(4) Any act or omission such as is mentioned in section 98B below on the part of a grouping (as defined in that section) or member of a grouping shall be deemed for the purposes of subsection (2) above to be the act or omission of each member of the grouping.

History – In s. 40(1) the words "more than 4 years after the end of" substituted for the words "beyond the end of the period of three years beginning with the 31st January next following" by FA 2008, s. 118 and Sch. 39, para. 11(2), with effect from 1 April 2010 (SI 2009/403, art. 2(2) subject to SI 2009/403, art. 3–10 – in particular art. 10).
S. 40(1), (2) amended by FA 1994, s. 196 and Sch. 19, para. 12, by substituting the words "the period of three years beginning with the 31st January next following the year of assessment" for the previous words "the third year next following the year of assessment", as respects the year 1996–97 and subsequent years of assessment.
In s. 40(2) the words "In a case involving a loss of tax brought about carelessly or deliberately by a person who has died (or another person acting on that person's behalf before that person's death)" substituted for the words "For the purpose of making good to the Crown any loss of tax attributable to the fraudulent or negligent conduct of a person who has died" and the words "not more than 4 years after the end of" substituted for the words "before the end of the period of three years beginning with the 31st January next following" by FA 2008, s. 118 and Sch. 39, para. 11(3), with effect from 1 April 2010 (SI 2009/403, art. 2(2) subject to SI 2009/403, art. 3–10 – in particular art. 10).
S. 40(2) amended by FA 1989, Sch. 17, Pt. VIII omitting reference to s. 41 consequent on repeal of that section.
S. 40(2) amended by FA 1989, s. 149(4)(a)(ii) substituting "fraudulent or negligent conduct" for "fraud, wilful default or neglect" consequent to amendment of s. 36, with effect from 27 July 1989 but not affecting the making of assessments for years before 1983–84.
S. 40(4) inserted by FA 1990, s. 69 and Sch. 11, para. 4(2), 5, deemed to have effect from 1 July 1989.
Former s. 40(4), (5) dealt with development land tax and were repealed consequent on repeal of Development Land Tax Act 1976 by FA 1985, Sch. 27, Pt. X with effect from 19 March 1985.

Cross references – S. 74: deduction of tax paid out of the assets and effects of the deceased person.
S. 98B: failure to deliver a return or document and fraudulent or negligent delivery of incorrect return etc. in respect of European Economic Interest Grouping.
FA 1993, s. 173 and Sch. 19, para. 8: for 1992–93 and subsequent years, for the purposes of s. 40, acts or omissions of a Lloyd's underwriting agent are attributable to each member of the syndicate (see ICTA 1988, s. 450 and Sch. 19A, para. 9 for prior years (from 1988–89)).
FA 1993, s. 178(3)(b): modified application of s. 40(2) in relation to payments made to a member of Lloyd's under a stop-loss insurance or out of a High Level Stop Loss Fund in respect of an underwriting loss.
SI 1995/352, reg. 6(2)(b): modifications applying to assessment of Lloyd's underwriters for 1992–93.
SI 1995/352, reg. 7(2)(b): modifications applying to assessment of Lloyd's underwriters for 1993–94 and 1994–95.

41 Leave of General or Special Commissioners required for certain assessments

41 [Repealed by FA 1989, s. 149(2) and Sch. 17, Pt. VIII.]

History – S. 41 repealed by FA 1989, s. 149(2) and Sch. 17, Pt. VIII, with effect from 27 July 1989 but not affecting the making of assessments for years before 1983–84 or for accounting periods which ended before 1 April 1983.
S. 41(3) dealt with development land tax.

Cross references – ICTA 1988, Sch. 19A, para. 9; FA 1973, Sch. 16A, para. 9: for the purposes of s. 41, the acts or omissions of a Lloyd's underwriting agent are attributed to each member of the syndicate.

Notes – S. 41 does not apply to any assessment signed before 6 April 1965.

CORPORATION TAX DETERMINATIONS

41A Determination procedure

41A [Repealed by FA 1998, s. 117(3) and Sch. 19, para. 19, s. 165 and Sch. 27, Pt. III(28).]

History – S. 41A repealed by FA 1998, s. 117(3) and Sch. 19, para. 19, s. 165 and Sch. 27, Pt. III(28), with effect in relation to accounting periods ending on or after 1 July 1999, the self-assessment appointed day by virtue of FA 1994, s. 199(2) and SI 1998/3173 (C. 78). The repealed provisions of s. 41A are superseded by FA 1998, Sch. 18, which has effect in relation to accounting periods ending on or after 1 July 1999 and is construed and has effect as if it were contained in TMA 1970 (FA 1998, s. 117(2)).

41B Reduction of determination

41B [Repealed by FA 1998, s. 117(3) and Sch. 19, para. 19, s. 165 and Sch. 27, Pt. III(28).]

History – S. 41B repealed by FA 1998, s. 117(3) and Sch. 19, para. 19, s. 165 and Sch. 27, Pt. III(28), with effect in relation to accounting periods ending on or after 1 July 1999, the self-assessment appointed day by virtue of FA 1994, s. 199(2) and SI 1998/3173 (C. 78). The repealed provisions of s. 41B are superseded by FA 1998, Sch. 18, which has effect in relation to accounting periods ending on or after 1 July 1999 and is construed and has effect as if it were contained in TMA 1970 (FA 1998, s. 117(2)).

41C Time limits

41C [Repealed by FA 1998, s. 117(3) and Sch. 19, para. 19, s. 165 and Sch. 27, Pt. III(28).]

History – S. 41C repealed by FA 1998, s. 117(3) and Sch. 19 para. 19, s. 165 and Sch. 27 Pt. III(28), with effect in relation to accounting periods ending on or after 1 July 1999, the self-assessment appointed day by virtue of FA 1994, s. 199(2) and SI 1998/3173 (C. 78). The repealed provisions of s. 41C are superseded by FA 1998, Sch. 18, which has effect in relation to accounting periods ending on or after 1 July 1999 and is construed and has effect as if it were contained in TMA 1970 (FA 1998, s. 117(2)).

CLAIMS

42 Procedure for making claims etc.

42(1) Where any provision of the Taxes Acts provides for relief to be given, or any other thing to be done, on the making of a claim, this section shall, unless otherwise provided, have effect in relation to the claim.

42(1A) Subject to subsection (3) below, a claim for a relief, an allowance or a repayment of tax shall be for an amount which is quantified at the time when the claim is made.

42(2) Subject to subsections (3) to (3ZC) below, where notice has been given under section 8, 8A or 12AA of this Act, a claim shall not at any time be made otherwise than by being included in a return under that section if it could, at that or any subsequent time, be made by being so included.

42(3) Subsections (1A) and (2) above shall not apply in relation to any claim which falls to be taken into account in the making of deductions or repayments of tax under PAYE regulations.

42(3ZA) Subsection (2) above shall not apply in relation to any claim by the trustees of a charitable trust for an amount to be exempt from tax by virtue of–

(a) section 521(4) of ITA 2007 (gifts entitling donor to gift aid relief: charitable trusts),

(b) section 532 of that Act (exemption for savings and investment income),

(c) section 533 of that Act (exemption for public revenue dividends),

(d) section 536 of that Act (exemption for certain miscellaneous income), or

(e) section 537 of that Act (exemption for income from estates in administration).

42(3ZB) Subsection (2) also does not apply in relation to any claim for repayment of an amount of income tax which–

(a) is treated as having been paid by virtue of section 520(4) of ITA 2007 (gift aid relief: income tax treated as paid by trustees of charitable trust), or

(b) has been deducted at source from income to which any of the provisions mentioned in paragraphs (b) to (e) of subsection (3ZA) applies.

42(3ZC) Subsection (2) also does not apply in relation to any claim under section 210 of the Finance Act 2013 (claims for consequential relieving adjustments after counteraction of tax advantage under the general anti-abuse rule).

42(3A)–(3B) [Repealed by FA 1996, s. 128(1)(a), s. 205 and Sch. 41, Pt. V(6).]

42(4)–(4A) [Repealed by FA 1998, s. 117(3) and Sch. 19, para. 20(3), s. 165 and Sch. 27, Pt. III(28).]

42(5) The references in this section to a claim being included in a return include references to a claim being so included by virtue of an amendment of the return.

42(6) In the case of a trade, profession or business carried on by persons in partnership, a claim under any of the provisions mentioned in subsection (7) below shall be made–

(a) where subsection (2) above applies, by being included in a partnership return, and

(b) in any other case, by such one of those persons as may be nominated by them for the purpose.

42(7) The provisions are–

(a) sections 471, 472, 570, 571(4) and 732(4) of the principal Act;

(b) [Omitted by CTA 2009, s. 1322 and Sch. 1, para. 302 and repealed by CTA 2009, s. 1326 and Sch. 3, Pt. 1.]

(c) sections 3, 83, 89, 129, 131, 135, 177, 183, 266, 268, 290, 355, 381 and 569 of the Capital Allowances Act;

(d) sections 40B(5), sections 40D, sections 41 and 42 of the Finance (No. 2) Act 1992,

(e) sections 25A, 111(1), 126(2), 129(2), 143, 185, 194 and 326 of ITTOIA 2005,

(f) sections 668 and 669 of ITA 2007.

(g) sections 109(1), 124(2), 127(2), 178 and 268 of CTA 2009.

42(8) [Omitted by FA 2012, s. 222(1)(a).]

42(9) Where a claim has been made (whether by being included in a return under section 8, 8A or 12AA of this Act or otherwise) and the claimant subsequently discovers that an error or mistake has been made in the claim, the claimant may make a supplementary claim within the time allowed for making the original claim.

42(10) This section (except subsection (1A) above and subject to subsection (10A) below) shall apply in relation to any elections as it applies in relation to claims.

42(10A) Subsection (2) above does not apply in relation to an election under section 55C of ITA 2007 (election to transfer allowance to spouse or civil partner).

42(11) Schedule 1A to this Act shall apply as respects any claim or election which–

(a) is made otherwise than by being included in a return under section 8, 8A, 12ZB or 12AA of this Act.

(b) [repealed by FA 1995, s. 107(10).]

42(11A) Schedule 1B to this Act shall have effect as respects certain claims for relief involving two or more years of assessment.

42(12) [Repealed by FA 1996, s. 136 and Sch. 22, para. 6, s. 205 and Sch. 41, Pt. V(12).]

42(13) In this section **"profits"**–

(a) in relation to income tax, means income, and

(b) in relation to capital gains tax, means chargeable gains.

History – In s. 42(2), "(3ZC)" substituted for "(3ZB)" by FA 2013, s. 213(2), with effect in relation to any tax arrangements entered into on or after 17 July 2013 (subject to provisions of FA 2013, s. 215(2) and (3)).
In s. 42(2), "to (3ZB)" substituted for "and (3ZA)" by FA 2012, s. 51 and Sch. 15, para. 11(2), in relation to claims whenever made.
In s. 42(2), "(3ZA)" substituted for "(3A)" by FA 2010, s. 32 and Sch. 8, para. 4(2), in relation to claims whenever made.
In s. 42(2), (9) and (11) references to TMA 1970, s. 11 omitted by FA 1998, s. 117(3) and Sch. 19, para. 20(2), s. 165 and Sch. 27, Pt. III(28), with effect in relation to accounting periods ending on or after 1 July 1999, the self-assessment appointed day by virtue of FA 1994, s. 199(2) and SI 1998/3173 (C. 78).
In s. 42(3), the words "PAYE regulations" substituted by ITEPA 2003, Sch. 6, para. 128 which has effect for the tax year 2003–04 and subsequent tax years.
S. 42(3ZA) amended by FA 2012, s. 51 and Sch. 15, para. 11(3), in relation to claims whenever made.
S. 42(3ZA) inserted by FA 2010, s. 32 and Sch. 8, para. 4(3), in relation to claims whenever made.
S. 42(3ZB) inserted by FA 2012, s. 51 and Sch. 8, para. 11(4), in relation to claims whenever made.
S. 42(3ZC) inserted by FA 2013, s. 213(3), with effect in relation to any tax arrangements entered into on or after 17 July 2013 (subject to provisions of FA 2013, s. 215(2) and (3)).
S. 42(4), (4A) repealed by FA 1998, s. 117(3) and Sch. 19, para. 20(3), s. 165 and Sch. 27, Pt. III(28), with effect in relation to accounting periods ending on or after 1 July 1999, the corporation tax self-assessment appointed day (see notes above).
In s. 42(5), words at the end "and the reference in subsection (4) above to a claim for payment includes a reference to a claim resulting in payment" repealed by FA 1998, s. 117(3) and Sch. 19, para. 20(3), with effect in relation to accounting periods ending on or after 1 July 1999, the corporation tax self-assessment appointed day (see notes above).
(The repeals of s. 42(4), (4A), and the repeal in s. 42(5), noted above had already been made by F(No. 2)A 1997, s 34 and Sch. 4, para. 3(1), s. 52 and Sch. 8, Pt. II(9) with effect in relation to tax credits in respect of distributions made on or after 6 April 1999.)
In s. 42(6)(a) the words "partnership return" substituted for the words "return under section 12AA of this Act" by FA 2001, s. 88, Sch. 29, para. 26 with effect from 11 May 2001 in relation to returns whether made before or after that date and whether relating to periods beforeor after then.
In s. 42(7)(e), the words "25A," inserted by FA 2013, s. 17 and Sch. 4, para. 44, with effect for the tax year 2013–14 and subsequent tax years (subject to provisions of FA 2013, Sch. 4, para. 57).
In s. 42(7), ", 84, 91B, 101(2)," and "504, 531," omitted (and repealed by CTA 2009, s. 1326 and Sch. 3, Pt. 1) and the words "571(4) and 732(4) of the principal Act;" substituted for the words "571(4), 732(4), of, and paragraphs 2, 6 and 11 of Schedule 5 to, the principal Act"; para. (b) omitted (and repealed by CTA 2009, s. 1326 and Sch. 3, Pt. 1); the word "and" immediately after para. (e) omitted (and repealed by CTA 2009, s. 1326 and Sch. 3, Pt. 1) and para. (g) inserted by CTA 2009, s. 1322 and Sch. 1, para. 302, with effect for corporation tax purposes for accounting periods ending on or after 1 April 2009, and for income tax and capital gains tax purposes for the tax year 2009–10 and subsequent tax years.
In s. 42(7)(a) reference to ICTA 1988, s. 810 omitted by FA 2000, Sch. 40, Pt. II(13), with effect in relation to claims made on or after 1st April 2000.
In s. 42(7)(a):

- former reference to ICTA 1988, s. 579(4) repealed by FA 1998, s. 165 and Sch. 27, Pt. III(4), with effect for income tax purposes for the year 1998–99 and subsequent years of assessment, and for corporation tax purposes with effect from 1 April 1998;
- former reference to ICTA 1988, s. 120(2) repealed by FA 1997, s. 113 and Sch. 18, Pt. VI(2), with effect in relation to payments made on or after 6 April 1997;
- former references to s. 534, 535, 537A and 538 repealed by FA 1996, s. 128(1)(b), s. 205 and Sch. 41, Pt. V(6), with effect as respects claims made in relation to the year 1997–98 or later years of assessment;
- reference to s. 484 repealed by FA 1996, s. 205 and Sch. 41, Pt. V(3), in accordance with FA 1996, s. 105.
- reference to ICTA 1988, s. 723(3) omitted by ITA 2007, s. 1027 and Sch. 1, para. 253(a) and repealed by s. 1031 and Sch. 3, Pt. 1, with effect from 6 April 2007.

S. 42(7)(c), (d) substituted by CAA 2001, s. 578 and Sch. 2, para. 1 with effect as respects allowances and charges falling to be made for chargeable periods ending, for income tax purposes, on or after 6 April 2001.
In s. 42(7)(d) the word "and" at the end of the paragraph omitted by ITA 2007, s. 1027 and Sch. 1, para. 253(b) and repealed by s. 1031 and Sch. 3, Pt. 1, with effect from 6 April 2007.
S. 42(7)(e) inserted by ITTOIA 2005, s. 882(1) and Sch. 1, para. 372; effective for 2005–06 onwards (ITTOIA 2005, s. 883(1)).
S. 42(7)(f) inserted by ITA 2007, s. 1027 and Sch. 1, para. 253(c), with effect from 6 April 2007.
S. 42(8) omitted by FA 2012, s. 222(1)(a), with effect for the tax year 2012–13 and subsequent tax years.
In s. 42(10), the words "and subject to subsection (10A) below" inserted after the word "above" by FA 2014, s. 11(10)(a), with effect for the tax year 2015–16 and subsequent tax years.
S. 42(10A) inserted by FA 2014, s. 11(10)(b), with effect for the tax year 2015–16 and subsequent tax years.
In s. 42(11), "12ZB" inserted by FA 2015, s. 37 and Sch. 7, para. 49, with effect in relation to disposals made on or after 6 April 2015.
S. 42 substituted by FA 1994, s. 196 and Sch. 19, para. 13, and amended by FA 1995, s. 97(2), 107, 162 and Sch. 29, Pt. VIII(14), and by FA 1996, s. 128(1)(a), (c), 130(2)–(4), s. 136 and Sch. 22, para. 6 and s. 205 and Sch. 41, Pt. V(6), (7), and (12), in so far as it relates to income tax and capital gains tax, as respects the year 1996–97 and subsequent years of assessment, and originally also for corporation tax, as respects accounting periods ending on or after 1 July 1999, the day appointed by SI 1998/3173 for the purposes of FA 1994, s. 199(2), (3) (corporation tax self-assessment provisions now to be found in FA 1998, Sch. 18, Pt. VII: see notes above).

Cross references – Sch. 1B: claims for relief involving more than one year.
CAA 2001, s. 3(4): claims for certain specified allowances to be made under s. 42 (as not included in a return) and not under CAA 2001, s. 3(2).
CAA 2001, s. 3(6): claims to capital allowances under CAA 2001, s. 3 subject to s. 42(6), (7) (special provisions for partnerships).
CAA 2001, s. 201(5): s. 42 does not apply to an election under CAA 2001, s. 198 (election to apportion sale price on sale of qualifying interest) or 199 (election to apportion capital sum given by lessee on grant of lease).
CAA 2001, s. 227(5): s. 42 does not apply to an election under CAA 2001, s. 227 (special treatment for sale and leaseback cases).
TCGA 1992, s. 16(2A): s. 42 applied to claims for allowable capital losses.
FA 1993, s. 194(4): modifications of s. 42 in its application to a claim for double taxation relief in relation to petroleum revenue tax in respect of receipts attributable to UK use of foreign field assets.
FA 1996, s. 129(1): disapplication of s. 42 in relation to claims for medical insurance and vocational training relief.
SI 1982/1236, reg. 14(1): s. 42 is not applicable to claims made under this instrument (interest relief).
SI 1987/530, reg. 13: s. 42 applies to claims in respect of tax overpaid under this instrument (entertainers and sportsmen).
SI 1987/1749, reg. 9(1): s. 42 does not apply to a claim under Occupational Pension Schemes (Additional Voluntary Contributions) Regulations 1987.
SI 1988/1013, reg. 11(1): s. 42 does not apply to claims made under this instrument (personal pension schemes).
SI 1989/469, reg. 21(1): s. 42 does not apply to claims made under this instrument (personal equity plans).
SI 1993/743, reg. 20(3): application of s. 42 to an appeal of an inspector under reg. 20(1) (repayment of excess credits to subcontractor).

SI 1998/1870, reg. 27(1): disapplication of s. 42 to claims under the Individual Savings Account regulations.
SI 2004/1450, reg. 28(1): disapplication of s. 42 for the purposes of Child Trust Funds.

Statements of practice – SP A13: HMRC view that claims must normally be made personally, but relaxation where the taxpayer's health might suffer if he were required to provide a personal signature.
SP 8/91: HMRC practice on issue of "discovery" assessment following determination of appeal.

HMRC interpretations – IRInt. 211: HMRC's view on ability to make claims for an earlier year when, under self assessment, a carry back claim is treated as a claim for the year in which the event occurs, not that to which the carry back is made (and the earlier year is not, as a consequence, reopened).
IRInt. 254: *Mansworth v Jelley* implications.

HMRC Manuals – Capital Gains, vol. I, CG13861: if taxpayer does nothing within 30 days decision will stand; if claimant indicates he wishes to withdraw claim this is strictly a matter to be resolved by agreement (TMA 1970, s. 54) or by commissioners; however, unless a false claim is suspected, it is not appropriate to hold the taxpayer to a claim which he no longer wishes to pursue.
Capital Gains, vol. VI, CG 60606: prescribed form for claims to roll over relief.

Other material – Tax Bulletin TB08/95-8: requirement to submit vouchers in support of repayment claims.
Taxline 1993/57 (not reproduced): a statement in Lloyd's Market Bulletin (21 October 1992) that once loss relief was claimed under a particular section it could not be subsequently varied, is counter to established practice based on TMA 1970, s. 42. (This approach has now been modified (Lloyd's Market Bulletin (14 September 1993)).)
Committee on Enforcement Powers of the Revenue Departments (Keith Committee) (Cmnd. 8822), para. 3.5.13: Revenue practice to permit claims following assessments to "culpable tax" due to fraud or wilful default.
IR press release, 29 November 1994: form of roll-over relief claim determined by Board under s. 42(5).

Notes – S. 42(11) rewritten as ITA 2007, s. 1020(1).

43 Time limit for making claims

43(1) Subject to any provision of the Taxes Acts prescribing a longer or shorter period, no claim for relief in respect of income tax or capital gains tax may be made more than 4 years after the end of the year of assessment to which it relates.

43(2) A claim (including a supplementary claim) which could not have been allowed but for the making of an assessment to income tax or capital gains tax after the year of assessment to which the claim relates may be made at any time before the end of the year of assessment following that in which the assessment was made.

43(3) [Repealed by FA 1985, Sch. 27, Pt. X, with effect from 19 March 1985.]

History – In s. 43(1), the words "4 years after the end of" substituted for the words "five years after the 31st January next following" by FA 2008, s. 118 and Sch. 39, para. 12, with effect from 1 April 2010 (SI 2009/403, art. 2(2) subject to SI 2009/403, art. 3–10 – in particular art. 10).
S. 43(1) substituted by FA 1998, s. 117(3) and Sch. 19, para. 21, with effect in relation to accounting periods ending on or after 1 July 1999, the self-assessment appointed day by virtue of FA 1994, s. 199(2) and SI 1998/3173 (C. 78). Corporation tax self-assessment provisions formerly in s. 43(1) are superseded by FA 1998, Sch. 18, which has effect in relation to accounting periods ending on or after 1 July 1999 and is construed and has effect as if it were contained in TMA 1970 (FA 1998, s. 115(2)).
Former s. 43(1) amended and s. 43(3) repealed by FA 1985, Sch. 27, Pt. X, removing references to development land tax.

Cross references – S. 43C: application of s. 43(2) following amendment of tax return.
TCGA 1992, s. 16(2A): s. 43 applied to claims for allowable capital losses.
FA 1993, s. 194(4): modifications of s. 43 in its application to a claim for double taxation relief in relation to petroleum revenue tax in respect of receipts attributable to UK use of foreign field assets.
SI 1995/352, reg. 14, 15, Schedule: extended time limit under s. 43(1) for Lloyd's underwriters.

Extra-statutory concessions – B41: repayments of tax will be made outside the statutory six-year time limit where an overpayment of tax has arisen because of an error by HMRC or another government department, and where there is no dispute or doubt as to the facts.

Statements of practice – SP A13: HMRC view that claims must normally be made personally, but relaxation where the taxpayer's health might suffer if he were required to provide a personal signature.

Hansard – Commons Written Answer, 10 December 1985 (not reproduced): Financial Secretary explained that in the absence of statutory discretion, a presumption existed that time limits for claims and elections should be strictly applied; however, late claims may still be entertained following an error by the Revenue, where the taxpayer had given clear notice of intention to claim or where reason for delay is clearly beyond the taxpayer's control.

43A Further assessments: claims etc.

43A(1) This section applies where–

(a) by virtue of section 29 of this Act an assessment to income tax or capital gains tax is made on any person for a year of assessment, and

(b) the assessment is not made for the purpose of making good to the Crown any loss of tax brought about carelessly or deliberately by that person or by someone acting on behalf of that person.

43A(2) Without prejudice to section 43(2) above but subject to section 43B below, where this section applies–

(a) any relevant claim, election, application or notice which could have been made or given within the time allowed by the Taxes Acts may be made or given at any time within one year from the end of the year of assessment in which the assessment is made, and

(b) any relevant claim, election, application or notice previously made or given may at any such time be revoked or varied–

(i) in the same manner as it was made or given, and

(ii) by or with the consent of the same person or persons who made, gave or consented to it (or, in the case of any such person who has died, by or with the consent of his personal representatives),

except where by virtue of any enactment it is irrevocable.

43A(2A) In subsection (2) above, **"claim, election, application or notice"** does not include an election under–

(a) any of sections 47 to 49 of ITA 2007 (tax reductions for married couples and civil partners: elections to transfer relief),

(aa) section 55C of ITA 2007 (election to transfer allowance to spouse or civil partner),

(b) [Repealed by Statute Law (Repeals) Act 2013, s. 1 and Sch. 1, Pt. 10.]

(c) section 35(5) of the Taxation of Chargeable Gains Act 1992 (election for assets to be re-based to 1982).

43A(2B) For the purposes of this section and section 43B below, a claim under Schedule 1AB is relevant in relation to an assessment for a year of assessment if it relates to that year of assessment.

43A(3) For the purposes of this section and section 43B below, any other claim, election, application or notice is relevant in relation to an assessment for a year of assessment if–

(a) it relates to that year of assessment or is made or given by reference to an event occurring in that year of assessment, and

(b) it or, as the case may be, its revocation or variation has or could have the effect of reducing any of the liabilities mentioned in subsection (4) below.

43A(4) The liabilities referred to in subsection (3) above are–

(a) the increased liability to tax resulting from the assessment,

(b) any other liability to tax of the person concerned for–

(i) the year of assessment to which the assessment relates, or

(ii) any year of assessment which follows that year of assessment and ends not later than one year after the end of the year of assessment in which the assessment is made.

43A(5) Where a claim, election, application or notice is made, given, revoked or varied by virtue of subsection (2) above, all such adjustments shall be made, whether by way of discharge or repayment of tax or the making of assessments or otherwise, as are required to take account of the effect of the taking of that action on any person's liability to tax for any year of assessment.

43A(6) The provisions of this Act relating to appeals against decisions on claims shall apply with any necessary modifications to a decision on the revocation or variation of a claim by virtue of subsection (2) above.

History – S. 43A(1)(a) substituted by FA 1998, s. 117(3) and Sch. 19, para. 22(2), and FA 1999, s. 139 and Sch. 20, Pt. III(20), with effect in relation to accounting periods ending on or after 1 July 1999, the self-assessment appointed day by virtue of FA 1994, s. 199(2) and SI 1998/3173 (C. 78). The corporation tax element of the former text is re-enacted in FA 1998, Sch. 18 as respects accounting periods ending on or after 1 July 1999.

In s. 43A(1)(b) the words "brought about carelessly or deliberately by that person or by someone acting on behalf of that person." substituted for the words "attributable to his fraudulent or negligent conduct or the fraudulent or negligent conduct of a person acting on his behalf." by FA 2008, s. 118 and Sch. 39, para. 13, with effect from 1 April 2010 (SI 2009/403, art. 2(2) subject to SI 2009/403, art. 3–10 – in particular art. 10).

S. 43A(1) amended, by substituting reference to s. 29 for previous reference to s. 29(3), by FA 1994, s. 196 and Sch. 19, para. 15(1):

- in so far as it relates to partnerships whose trades, professions or businesses are set up and commenced before 6 April 1994, as respects the year 1997–98 and subsequent years of assessment (FA 1994, Sch. 19, para. 15(2)); and
- in so far as it relates to income tax and capital gains tax, other than in relation to partnerships whose trades were set up and commenced after 6 April 1994, as respects the year 1996–97 and subsequent years of assessment; and
- also originally as respects corporation tax accounting periods ending on or after the day appointed under FA 1994, s. 199(2), but see now FA 1998, Sch. 18.

References to "chargeable periods" replaced by the phrase "year of assessment" in subsections (2), (3), (4) and (5) by FA 1998, s. 117(3) and Sch. 19, para. 22(3), with effect in relation to accounting periods ending on or after 1 July 1999, the self-assessment appointed day (see above).

In s. 43A(2A)(a), the words "section 257BA of the principal Act or", which appeared at the beginning, omitted by FA 2009, s. 5 and Sch. 1, para. 6 (a)(iii) with effect for the tax year 2010–11 and subsequent tax years.

In s. 43A(2A)(a), the words "or any of sections 47 to 49 of ITA 2007" inserted by ITA 2007, s. 1027 and Sch. 1, para. 254(a) and the words "(tax reductions for married couples and civil partners: elections to transfer relief)" substituted for the words "(election as to transfer of married couple's allowance)" by ITA 2007, s. 1027 and Sch. 1, para. 254(b), with effect from 6 April 2007.

S. 43A(2A)(aa) inserted by FA 2014, s. 11(11), with effect for the tax year 2015–16 and subsequent tax years.

S. 43A(2A)(b) repealed by Statute Law (Repeals) Act 2013, s. 1 and Sch. 1, Pt. 10, with effect from 31 January 2013.

In former s. 43A(2A)(b), the words "the principal Act" substituted for the words "that Act" by ITA 2007, s. 1027 and Sch. 1, para. 254(c), with effect from 6 April 2007.

The reference in s. 43A(2A) to ICTA 1988 Sch. 13B was deleted by TCA 2002 s. 60 and Sch. 6 with effect from 5 April 2003 (SI 2003/962) but then amended by FA 2003, s. 207(2) with effect from 10 July 2003 to include elections under ICTA 1988 Sch. 13B and TCGA 1992 s. 35(5). Where the revised section applies to the amendment of a return, it only does so where that amendment is issued after 10 July 2003.

In s. 43A(2A), the words "or under Schedule 13B to that Act (elections as to transfer of children's tax credit)" inserted at the end by FA 1999, s. 30(4)(c) with effect for the year 2001–02 and subsequent years of assessment.

S. 43A(2A) inserted in relation to tax for 1993–94 and subsequent years of assessment, by F(No. 2)A 1992, s. 20 and Sch. 5, para. 9(1), (4).

S. 43A(2B) inserted by FA 2009, s. 100 and Sch. 52, para. 5(2) with effect in relation to claims made on or after 1 April 2010.
In s. 43A(3), the words "any other claim" to be substituted for the words "a claim" by FA 2009, s. 100 and Sch. 52, para. 5(3) with effect in relation to claims made on or after 1 April 2010.
S. 43A inserted by FA 1989, s. 150 for assessments notice of which is issued after 27 July 1989.

Cross references – S. 43C: application of s. 43A following amendment of tax return.
FA 1998, Sch. 18, para. 63(2): disapplication of s. 43A where altered liability accepted by third party following amendment to corporation tax assessment etc.

Extra-statutory concessions – B41: repayments of tax will be made outside the statutory six-year time limit where an overpayment of tax has arisen because of an error by HMRC or another government department, and where there is no dispute or doubt as to the facts.

Statements of practice – SP 6/94: s. 43A does not apply where assessment made to recover tax lost due to fraudulent or negligent conduct; s. 43A notice cannot reduce tax beyond amount due under late assessment, and only applies to the chargeable period for which late assessment is made.

43B Limits on application of section 43A

43B(1) If the effect of the exercise by any person of a power conferred by section 43A(2) above–

(a) to make or give a claim, election, application or notice, or

(b) to revoke or vary a claim, election, application or notice previously made or given,

would be to alter the liability to tax of another person, that power may not be exercised except with the consent in writing of that other person or, where he has died, his personal representatives.

43B(2) Where–

(a) a power conferred by subsection (2) of section 43A above is exercised in consequence of an assessment made on a person, and

(b) the exercise of the power increases the liability to tax of another person,

that section shall not apply by reason of any assessment made because of that increased liability.

43B(3) In any case where–

(a) one or more relevant claims, elections, applications or notices are made, given, revoked or varied by virtue of the application of section 43A above in the case of an assessment, and

(b) the total of the reductions in liability to tax which, apart from this subsection, would result from the action mentioned in paragraph (a) above would exceed the additional liability to tax resulting from the assessment,

the excess shall not be available to reduce any liability to tax.

43B(4) Where subsection (3) above has the effect of limiting either the reduction in a person's liability to tax for more than one period or the reduction in the liability to tax of more than one person, the limited amount shall be apportioned between the periods or persons concerned–

(a) except where paragraph (b) below applies, in such manner as may be specified by the inspector by notice in writing to the person or persons concerned, or

(b) where the person concerned gives (or the persons concerned jointly give) notice in writing to the inspector within the relevant period, in such manner as may be specified in the notice given by the person or persons concerned.

43B(5) For the purposes of paragraph (b) of subsection (4) above the relevant period is the period of 30 days beginning with the day on which notice under paragraph (a) of that subsection is given to the person concerned or, where more than one person is concerned, the latest date on which such notice is given to any of them.

History – S. 43B inserted by FA 1989, s. 150 for assessments notice of which is issued on or after 27 July 1989.

Cross references – S. 43C: application of s. 43B following amendment of tax return.

Extra-statutory concessions – B41: repayments of tax will be made outside the statutory six-year time limit where an overpayment of tax has arisen because of an error by HMRC or another government department, and where there is no dispute or doubt as to the facts.

43C Consequential claims etc.

43C(1) Where–

(a) a return is amended under section 28A(2)(b), 28B(2)(b) or 28B(4), and

(b) the amendment is made for the purpose of making good to the Crown any loss of tax brought about carelessly or deliberately by the taxpayer or a person acting on his behalf,

sections 36(3) and 43(2) apply in relation to the amendment as they apply in relation to any assessment under section 29.

43C(2) Where–

(a) a return is amended under section 28A(2)(b), 28B(2)(b) or 28B(4), and

(b) the amendment is not made for the purpose mentioned in subsection (1)(b) above, sections 43(2), 43A and 43B apply in relation to the amendment as they apply in relation to any assessment under section 29.

43C(3) References to an assessment in sections 36(3), 43(2), 43A and 43B, as they apply by virtue of subsection (1) or (2) above, shall accordingly be read as references to the amendment of the return.

43C(4) Where it is necessary to make any adjustment by way of an assessment on any person–

(a) in order to give effect to a consequential claim, or

(b) as a result of allowing a consequential claim,

the assessment is not out of time if it is made within one year of the final determination of the claim.

For this purpose a claim is not taken to be finally determined until it, or the amount to which it relates, can no longer be varied, on appeal or otherwise.

43C(5) In subsection (4) above **"consequential claim"** means any claim, supplementary claim, election, application or notice that may be made or given under section 36(3), 43(2) , 43A or 43D(6) (as it applies by virtue of subsection (1) or (2) above or otherwise).

History – In s. 43C(1)(b), the words "brought about carelessly or deliberately by" substituted for the words "attributable to fraudulent or negligent conduct on the part of" by FA 2008, s. 118 and Sch. 39, para. 14, with effect from 1 April 2010 (SI 2009/403, art. 2(2) subject to SI 2009/403, art. 3–10 – in particular art. 10).
In s. 43C(5), ", 43A or 43D(6)" substituted for "or 43A" by TIOPA 2010, s. 374 and Sch. 8, para. 6, with effect for corporation tax purposes for accounting periods ending on or after 1 April 2010, for income tax and capital gains tax purposes for the tax year 2010–11 and subsequent tax years, and for petroleum revenue tax purposes for chargeable periods beginning on or after 1 July 2010.
S. 43C inserted by FA 2003, s. 207(1) with effect from 10 July 2003. Where the section applies to an amendment to a return, it only does so where that amendment is issued after 10 July 2003.

43D Claims for double taxation relief in relation to petroleum revenue tax

43D(1) This section has effect in relation to a claim for relief under sections 2 to 6 of TIOPA 2010 in relation to petroleum revenue tax.

43D(2) The claim shall be for an amount which is quantified at the time when the claim is made.

43D(3) If, after the claim has been made, the claimant discovers that an error or mistake has been made in the claim, the claimant may make a supplementary claim within the time allowed for making the original claim.

43D(4) Schedule 1A to this Act applies as respects the claim, but as if the reference in paragraph 2A(4) to a year of assessment included a reference to a chargeable period.

43D(5) The claim may not be made more than 4 years after the end of the chargeable period to which it relates, but this is subject to any provision of the Taxes Acts prescribing a longer or shorter period.

43D(6) If the claim or a supplementary claim could not have been allowed but for the making of an assessment to petroleum revenue tax after the end of the chargeable period to which the claim relates, the claim or supplementary claim may be made at any time before the end of the chargeable period following that in which the assessment is made.

43D(7) In this section **"chargeable period"** has the same meaning as in the Oil Taxation Act 1975 (see section 1(3) and (4) of that Act, under which a period that is a chargeable period ends with 30 June or 31 December and, apart from the first chargeable period in relation to an oil field, is a period of 6 months).

History – S. 43D inserted by TIOPA 2010, s. 374 and Sch. 8, para. 7, with effect for corporation tax purposes for accounting periods ending on or after 1 April 2010, for income tax and capital gains tax purposes for the tax year 2010–11 and subsequent tax years, and for petroleum revenue tax purposes for chargeable periods beginning on or after 1 July 2010.

Transitional – TIOPA 2010, Sch. 9, para. 15: where SI 2009/403, art. 10 applies, s. 43D(5) has effect at times before 1 April 2012 as if for as if for "4 years after the end of" there were substituted "5 years after the 31 January next following".

43E Making of income tax claims by electronic communications etc

43E(1) The Commissioners for Her Majesty's Revenue and Customs may, by publishing them in a manner the Commissioners consider appropriate, give any claims directions that the Commissioners consider appropriate.

43E(2) In subsection (1) **"claims directions"** means general directions for the purposes of income tax relating to–

(a) the circumstances in which, and

(b) the conditions subject to which,

claims by individuals under the Tax Acts may be made by the use of an electronic communications service or otherwise without producing a claim in writing.

43E(3) Directions under subsection (1)–

(a) may not relate to the making of a claim by an individual in the individual's capacity as a trustee, partner or personal representative, but

(b) subject to that, may relate to claims made by an individual through another person acting on the individual's behalf.

43E(4) Directions under subsection (1) may not relate to–

(a) the making of a claim to which Schedule 1B to this Act applies, or

(b) the making of a claim under any provision of the Capital Allowances Act 2001.

43E(5) Directions under subsection (1)–

(a) cannot modify any requirement imposed by or under any enactment as to the period within which any claim is to be made or as to the contents of any claim, but

(b) may include provision as to how any requirement as to the contents of a claim is to be met when the claim is not produced in writing.

43E(6) Directions under subsection (1) may make different provision in relation to the making of claims of different descriptions.

43E(7) A direction under subsection (1) may revoke or vary any previous direction given under that subsection.

43E(8) In subsection (2) **"electronic communications service"** has the same meaning as in the Communications Act 2003 (see section 32 of that Act).

43E(9) In subsections (1) to (6), references to the making of a claim include references to any of the following–

(a) the making of an election,

(b) the giving of a notification or notice,

(c) the amendment of any return, claim, election, notification or notice, and

(d) the withdrawal of any claim, election, notification or notice,

and in those subsections **"claim"** is to be read accordingly.

43E(10) For the purposes of subsection (9)(c)–

(a) **"return"** includes any statement or declaration under the Income Tax Acts, and

(b) the definition of **"return"** given by section 118(1) of this Act does not apply.

History – S. 43E inserted by TIOPA 2010, s. 374 and Sch. 7, para. 86, with effect for corporation tax purposes for accounting periods ending on or after 1 April 2010, for income tax and capital gains tax purposes for the tax year 2010–11 and subsequent tax years, and for petroleum revenue tax purposes for chargeable periods beginning on or after 1 July 2010.

43F Effect of directions under section 43E

43F(1) If directions under section 43E(1) are in force in relation to the making of claims of any description to the Commissioners for Her Majesty's Revenue and Customs, claims of that description may be made to the Commissioners in accordance with the directions.

43F(2) If directions under section 43E(1) are in force in relation to the making of claims of any description to an officer of Revenue and Customs, claims of that description may be made to an officer in accordance with the directions.

43F(3) Subsections (1) and (2) apply despite any enactment or subordinate legislation which requires claims of the description concerned to be made in writing or by notice.

43F(4) If directions under section 43E(1) are in force in relation to the making of claims of any description, claims of that description that are made without producing the claim in writing must be made in accordance with the directions.

43F(5) In subsection (3) **"subordinate legislation"** has the same meaning as in the Interpretation Act 1978.

43F(6) Section 43E(9) read with section 43E(10) (interpretation of references to making a claim, and meaning of **"claim"**) applies for the purposes of subsections (1) to (4) (as well as for those of section 43E(1) to (6)).

History – S. 43F inserted by TIOPA 2010, s. 374 and Sch. 7, para. 86, with effect for corporation tax purposes for accounting periods ending on or after 1 April 2010, for income tax and capital gains tax purposes for the tax year 2010–11 and subsequent tax years, and for petroleum revenue tax purposes for chargeable periods beginning on or after 1 July 2010.

PART V – APPEALS AND OTHER PROCEEDINGS

JURISDICTION

Cross references – FA 2011, Sch. 23, para. 36: provisions of TMA 1970, Pt. V relating to appeals have effect in relation to appeals under FA 2011, Sch. 23, para. 36 as they have effect in relation to an appeal against an assessment to income tax (FA 2011, Sch. 23, para. 37(5)).

TCA 2002, s. 39(6): Pt. V applies in relation to tax credits appeals, subject to prescribed modifications (see SI 2003/1382; but see also TCA 2002, s. 63 for transitional arrangements).
CTFA 2004, s. 23: exercise of rights of appeal, TMA 1970, Pt. V, (appeals to Commissioners) applies in relation to appeals under CTFA 2004, s. 22 (as in relation to appeals under the Taxes Acts, within the meaning of that Act), but subject to such modifications as are prescribed by regulations.
FA 2004, s. 114(6): Part V applies in relation to appeals against withdrawal of, or the refusal to issue, certificates to avoid levy of special withholding tax.
SI 1987/1749, reg. 9(5): Pt. V applies to appeals on annual claims under the Occupational Pension Schemes (Additional Voluntary Contributions) Regulations 1987, and the special commissioners may vary the decision appealed against whether or not the variation is to the advantage of the appellant.
SI 1993/743, reg. 14(2), (4): application of Pt. V to an appeal against a formal determination against a contractor under reg. 14.
SI 1993/2004, reg. 11(10): application of Pt. V to an appeal against an assessment under reg. 11 (manufactured overseas dividends).
SI 2002/2172, reg. 14(4): application of Pt. V (except s. 55) to determinations of working tax credit funding to be repaid by employers.
SI 2004/1450, reg. 28(5): application of Pt. 5 for the purposes of Child Trust Funds appeals under SI 2004/1450, reg. 28(3).

44 General Commissioners

44 [Omitted by SI 2009/56, art. 3(1) and Sch. 1, para. 25.]

History – S. 44 omitted by SI 2009/56, art. 3(1) and Sch. 1, para. 25, operative from 1 April 2009, subject to transitional and saving provisions in SI 2009/56, Sch. 3.

45 Quorum of Special Commissioners

45 [Omitted by SI 2009/56, art. 3(1) and Sch. 1, para. 25.]

History – S. 45 omitted by SI 2009/56, art. 3(1) and Sch. 1, para. 25, operative from 1 April 2009, subject to transitional and saving provisions in SI 2009/56, Sch. 3.

46 General and Special Commissioners

46 [Omitted by SI 2009/56, art. 3(1) and Sch. 1, para. 25.]

History – S. 46 omitted by SI 2009/56, art. 3(1) and Sch. 1, para. 25, operative from 1 April 2009, subject to transitional and saving provisions in SI 2009/56, Sch. 3.

46A Regulations about jurisdiction

46A [Omitted by SI 2009/56, art. 3(1) and Sch. 1, para. 25.]

History – S. 46A omitted by SI 2009/56, art. 3(1) and Sch. 1, para. 25, operative from 1 April 2009, subject to transitional and saving provisions in SI 2009/56, Sch. 3.

46B Regulations about jurisdiction

46B [Omitted by SI 2009/56, art. 3(1) and Sch. 1, para. 25.]

History – S. 46B omitted by SI 2009/56, art. 3(1) and Sch. 1, para. 25, operative from 1 April 2009, subject to transitional and saving provisions in SI 2009/56, Sch. 3.

46C Jurisdiction of Special Commissioners over certain claims included in returns

46C [Omitted by SI 2009/56, art. 3(1) and Sch. 1, para. 25.]

History – S. 46C omitted by SI 2009/56, art. 3(1) and Sch. 1, para. 25, operative from 1 April 2009, subject to transitional and saving provisions in SI 2009/56, Sch. 3.

46D Questions to be determined by the relevant tribunal

History – In the heading to s. 46D, the words "the relevant tribunal" substituted for the words "Lands Tribunal" by SI 2009/1307, art. 5(1) and (2) and Sch. 1, para. 96(a), with effect from 1 June 2009 (subject to the transitional and savings provisions in SI 2009/1307, Sch. 5).

46D(1) In so far as the question in dispute on an appeal to which this section applies–

(a) is a question of the value of any land or of a lease of land, and

(b) arises in relation to the taxation of chargeable gains (whether under capital gains tax or corporation tax) or in relation to a claim under the 1992 Act,

the question shall be determined by the relevant tribunal.

46D(2) This section applies to–

(a) an appeal against an amendment of a self-assessment under section 9C of this Act or paragraph 30 of Schedule 18 to the Finance Act 1998;

(aa) an appeal against an amendment of a return under paragraph 34 of Schedule 18 to the Finance Act 1998;

(b) an appeal against a conclusion stated or amendment made by a closure notice under section 28A or 28B of this Act;

(c) an appeal against an amendment of a partnership return under section 30B(1) of this Act;

(d) an appeal against an assessment to tax which is not a self-assessment;

(e) an appeal against a conclusion stated or amendment made by a closure notice under paragraph 7(2) of Schedule 1A to this Act relating to a claim or election made otherwise than by being included in a return;

(f) an appeal against a decision contained in a closure notice under paragraph 7(3) of Schedule 1A to this Act disallowing in whole or in part a claim or election made otherwise than by being included in a return.

46D(3) In this section **"the relevant tribunal"** means–

(a) in relation to land in England and Wales, the Upper Tribunal;

(b) in relation to land in Scotland, the Lands Tribunal for Scotland;

(c) in relation to land in Northern Ireland, the Lands Tribunal for Northern Ireland.

History – In s. 46D(1), the words "relevant tribunal" substituted for the words "relevant Lands Tribunal" by SI 2009/1307, art. 5(1) and (2) and Sch. 1, para. 96(b), with effect from 1 June 2009 (subject to the transitional and savings provisions in SI 2009/1307, Sch. 5).
S. 46D(2)(a), (aa), (b) and (c) substituted for para. (a), (b) and (c) by FA 2001, s. 88, Sch. 29, para. 29(2) with effect from 11 May 2001 in relation to returns whether made before or after that date and whether relating to periods before or after then.
Former s. 46D(2)(a) substituted by FA 1998, s. 117(3) and Sch. 19, para. 24, with effect in relation to accounting periods ending on or after 1 July 1999, the appointed day for corporation tax self-assessment by virtue of FA 1994, s. 199(2), (3) and SI 1998/3173 (C. 78). S. 46D(2)(a) formerly referred only to TMA 1970, s. 28A(2), (4).
In s. 46D(2)(aa), "34" substituted for "34(2)" by FA 2008, s. 119(12)(a)(iii) with effect from 1 April 2010 (SI 2009/405).
In s. 46D(2)(e), the words "a conclusion stated or amendment made by a closure notice under paragraph 7(2) of Schedule 1A to this Act relating to" substituted and, in s. 46D(2)(f), the words "closure notice under paragraph 7(3)" substituted, by FA 2001, s. 88, Sch. 29, para. 29(3), (4) with effect from 11 May 2001 in relation to returns whether made before or after that date and whether relating to periods before or after then.
In s. 46D(3), the words "relevant tribunal" substituted for the words "relevant Lands Tribunal" and the words "Upper Tribunal" substituted for the words "Lands Tribunal" by SI 2009/1307, art. 5(1) and (2) and Sch. 1, para. 96(b) and (c), with effect from 1 June 2009 (subject to the transitional and savings provisions in SI 2009/1307, Sch. 5).
S. 46D, together with s. 46B and 46C, originally substituted for s. 47, by FA 1996, s. 136 and Sch. 22, para. 7, with effect in relation to any proceedings relating to the year 1996–97 or any subsequent year of assessment, and any proceedings relating to a company accounting period ending on or after 1 July 1999, the self-assessment appointed day (see above).

Cross references – SI 1994/1811, reg. 22(2): market value or apportionment of value may be proved in proceedings relating to tax on chargeable gains by certificate signed by clerk or registrar of appropriate tribunal.

47 Special jurisdiction relating to tax on chargeable gains

47 [Substituted by FA 1996, s. 136 and Sch. 22, para. 7.]

History – S. 46B–46D substituted for s. 47 by FA 1996, s. 136 and Sch. 22, para. 7, with effect in relation to any proceedings relating to the year 1996–97 or any subsequent year of assessment, and any proceedings relating to a corporation tax accounting period ending on or after 1 July 1999, the appointed day by virtue of FA 1994, s. 199(2), (3) and SI 1998/3173 (C. 78).

47A Special jurisdiction relating to development land tax

47A [Repealed by FA 1985, Sch. 27, Pt. X, with effect from 19 March 1985.]

History – S. 47A dealt with development land tax.

47B Special jurisdiction relating to business expansion scheme

47B If and so far as the question in dispute on any appeal against the refusal of relief under Chapter III of Part VII of the principal Act (relief for investment in corporate trades), or against an assessment withdrawing any such relief, is a question of the value of an interest in land (within the meaning of section 294(5) of that Act) it shall be determined–

(a) if the land is in England and Wales, on a reference to the Upper Tribunal;

(b) if the land is in Scotland, on a reference to the Lands Tribunal for Scotland; and

(c) if the land is in Northern Ireland, on a reference to the Lands Tribunal for Northern Ireland.

History – In s. 47B(a), the words "Upper Tribunal" substituted for the words "Lands Tribunal" by SI 2009/1307, art. 5(1) and (2) and Sch. 1, para. 97, with effect from 1 June 2009 (subject to the transitional and savings provisions in SI 2009/1307, Sch. 5).
Reference to provisions of the principal Act substituted by ICTA 1988, Sch. 29, para. 32, that Act becoming the principal Act (TMA 1970, s. 118(1)).
S. 47B inserted by FA 1986, Sch. 9, para. 22 in relation to shares issued after 18 March 1986.

APPEALS

History – The above heading substituted by SI 2009/56, art. 3(1) and Sch. 1, para. 26, operative from 1 April 2009, subject to transitional and saving provisions in SI 2009/56, Sch. 3. Former heading was "PROCEEDINGS BEFORE COMMISSIONERS".

47C Meaning of tribunal

47C In this Act **"tribunal"** means the First-tier Tribunal or, where determined by or under Tribunal Procedure Rules, the Upper Tribunal.

History – S. 47C inserted by SI 2009/56, art. 3(1) and Sch. 1, para. 27, operative from 1 April 2009, subject to transitional and saving provisions in SI 2009/56, Sch. 3.

48 Application to appeals and other proceedings

48(1) In the following provisions of this Part of this Act, unless the context otherwise requires–

(a) **"appeal"** means any appeal under the Taxes Acts;

(b) a reference to notice of appeal given, or to be given, to HMRC is a reference to notice of appeal given, or to be given, under any provision of the Taxes Acts.

48(2) In the case of–

(a) an appeal other than an appeal against an assessment, the following provisions of this Part of this Act shall, in their application to the appeal, have effect subject to any necessary modifications, including the omission of sections 54A to 54C and 56 below;

(b) any proceedings other than an appeal which, under the Taxes Acts, are to be subject to the relevant provisions of this Part of this Act, the relevant provisions–

(i) shall apply to the proceedings as they apply to appeals;

(ii) but shall, in that application, have effect subject to any necessary modifications, including (except in the case of applications under section 55 below) the omission of section 56 below.

48(3) In subsection (2), a reference to the relevant provisions of this Part of this Act is a reference to the following provisions of this Part, except sections 49A to 49I and 54A to 54C.

History – In s. 48(2)(a), the words "sections 54A to 54C and 56" substituted for the words "section 56" by TIOPA 2010, s. 371 and Sch. 7, para. 31(2), with effect for corporation tax purposes for accounting periods ending on or after 1 April 2010, for income tax and capital gains tax purposes for the tax year 2010–11 and subsequent tax years, and for petroleum revenue tax purposes for chargeable periods beginning on or after 1 July 2010.

In s. 48(3), the words "and 54A to 54C" inserted by TIOPA 2010, s. 371 and Sch. 7, para. 31(3), with effect for corporation tax purposes for accounting periods ending on or after 1 April 2010, for income tax and capital gains tax purposes for the tax year 2010–11 and subsequent tax years, and for petroleum revenue tax purposes for chargeable periods beginning on or after 1 July 2010.

S. 48 substituted by SI 2009/56, art. 3(1) and Sch. 1, para. 28, operative from 1 April 2009, subject to transitional and saving provisions in SI 2009/56, Sch. 3.

Former s. 48(2) amended by F(No. 2)A 1975, s. 45(4).

Cross references – OTA 1975, Sch. 2, para. 1(1): s. 48 applies with modifications for the purposes of oil taxation.

Social Security Contributions (Transfer of Functions, etc.) Act 1999, s. 13(2)(a)(ii): power of the Board, with the concurrence of the Lord Chancellor and the Lord Advocate, to make regulations making provision with respect to appeals on contributions matters, including any of the matters dealt with in s. 48.

SI 2003/1382: in its application to appeals under TCA 2002 s. 38, s. 48 was modified, with effect from 18 June 2003, by–

- the substitution, in subs. (1), of the words ""appeal" means an appeal against an employer penalty (as defined under section 63(11) of the Tax Credit Act 2002) to the General Commissioners or to the Special Commissioners" for the existing definition;
- the omission of subs. (2).

49 Late notice of appeal

49(1) This section applies in a case where–

(a) notice of appeal may be given to HMRC, but

(b) no notice is given before the relevant time limit.

49(2) Notice may be given after the relevant time limit if–

(a) HMRC agree, or

(b) where HMRC do not agree, the tribunal gives permission.

49(3) If the following conditions are met, HMRC shall agree to notice being given after the relevant time limit.

49(4) Condition A is that the appellant has made a request in writing to HMRC to agree to the notice being given.

49(5) Condition B is that HMRC are satisfied that there was reasonable excuse for not giving the notice before the relevant time limit.

49(6) Condition C is that HMRC are satisfied that request under subsection (4) was made without unreasonable delay after the reasonable excuse ceased.

49(7) If a request of the kind referred to in subsection (4) is made, HMRC must notify the appellant whether or not HMRC agree to the appellant giving notice of appeal after the relevant time limit.

49(8) In this section **"relevant time limit"**, in relation to notice of appeal, means the time before which the notice is to be given (but for this section).

History – S. 49 substituted by SI 2009/56, art. 3(1) and Sch. 1, para. 29, operative from 1 April 2009, subject to transitional and saving provisions in SI 2009/56, Sch. 3.

49A Appeal: HMRC review or determination by tribunal

49A(1) This section applies if notice of appeal has been given to HMRC.

49A(2) In such a case–

(a) the appellant may notify HMRC that the appellant requires HMRC to review the matter in question (see section 49B),

(b) HMRC may notify the appellant of an offer to review the matter in question (see section 49C), or

(c) the appellant may notify the appeal to the tribunal (see section 49D).

49A(3) See sections 49G and 49H for provision about notifying appeals to the tribunal after a review has been required by the appellant or offered by HMRC.

49A(4) This section does not prevent the matter in question from being dealt with in accordance with section 54 (settling appeals by agreement).

History – S. 49A inserted by SI 2009/56, art. 3(1) and Sch. 1, para. 30, operative from 1 April 2009, subject to transitional and saving provisions in SI 2009/56, Sch. 3.

49B Appellant requires review by HMRC

49B(1) Subsections (2) and (3) apply if the appellant notifies HMRC that the appellant requires HMRC to review the matter in question.

49B(2) HMRC must, within the relevant period, notify the appellant of HMRC's view of the matter in question.

49B(3) HMRC must review the matter in question in accordance with section 49E.

49B(4) The appellant may not notify HMRC that the appellant requires HMRC to review the matter in question and HMRC shall not be required to conduct a review if–

(a) the appellant has already given a notification under this section in relation to the matter in question,

(b) HMRC have given a notification under section 49C in relation to the matter in question, or

(c) the appellant has notified the appeal to the tribunal under section 49D.

49B(5) In this section **"relevant period"** means–

(a) the period of 30 days beginning with the day on which HMRC receive the notification from the appellant, or

(b) such longer period as is reasonable.

History – S. 49B inserted by SI 2009/56, art. 3(1) and Sch. 1, para. 30, operative from 1 April 2009, subject to transitional and saving provisions in SI 2009/56, Sch. 3.

49C HMRC offer review

49C(1) Subsections (2) to (6) apply if HMRC notify the appellant of an offer to review the matter in question.

49C(2) When HMRC notify the appellant of the offer, HMRC must also notify the appellant of HMRC's view of the matter in question.

49C(3) If, within the acceptance period, the appellant notifies HMRC of acceptance of the offer, HMRC must review the matter in question in accordance with section 49E.

49C(4) If the appellant does not give HMRC such a notification within the acceptance period, HMRC's view of the matter in question is to be treated as if it were contained in an agreement in writing under section 54(1) for the settlement of the matter.

49C(5) The appellant may not give notice under section 54(2) (desire to repudiate or resile from agreement) in a case where subsection (4) applies.

49C(6) Subsection (4) does not apply to the matter in question if, or to the extent that, the appellant notifies the appeal to the tribunal under section 49H.

49C(7) HMRC may not notify the appellant of an offer to review the matter in question (and, accordingly, HMRC shall not be required to conduct a review) if–

(a) HMRC have already given a notification under this section in relation to the matter in question,

(b) the appellant has given a notification under section 49B in relation to the matter in question, or

(c) the appellant has notified the appeal to the tribunal under section 49D.

49C(8) In this section **"acceptance period"** means the period of 30 days beginning with the date of the document by which HMRC notify the appellant of the offer to review the matter in question.

History – S. 49C inserted by SI 2009/56, art. 3(1) and Sch. 1, para. 30, operative from 1 April 2009, subject to transitional and saving provisions in SI 2009/56, Sch. 3.

49D *Notifying appeal to the tribunal*

49D(1) This section applies if notice of appeal has been given to HMRC.

49D(2) The appellant may notify the appeal to the tribunal.

49D(3) If the appellant notifies the appeal to the tribunal, the tribunal is to decide the matter in question.

49D(4) Subsections (2) and (3) do not apply in a case where–

(a) HMRC have given a notification of their view of the matter in question under section 49B, or

(b) HMRC have given a notification under section 49C in relation to the matter in question.

49D(5) In a case falling within subsection (4)(a) or (b), the appellant may notify the appeal to the tribunal, but only if permitted to do so by section 49G or 49H.

History – S. 49D inserted by SI 2009/56, art. 3(1) and Sch. 1, para. 30, operative from 1 April 2009, subject to transitional and saving provisions in SI 2009/56, Sch. 3.

49E Nature of review etc

49E(1) This section applies if HMRC are required by section 49B or 49C to review the matter in question.

49E(2) The nature and extent of the review are to be such as appear appropriate to HMRC in the circumstances.

49E(3) For the purpose of subsection (2), HMRC must, in particular, have regard to steps taken before the beginning of the review–

(a) by HMRC in deciding the matter in question, and

(b) by any person in seeking to resolve disagreement about the matter in question.

49E(4) The review must take account of any representations made by the appellant at a stage which gives HMRC a reasonable opportunity to consider them.

49E(5) The review may conclude that HMRC's view of the matter in question is to be–

(a) upheld,

(b) varied, or

(c) cancelled.

49E(6) HMRC must notify the appellant of the conclusions of the review and their reasoning within–

(a) the period of 45 days beginning with the relevant day, or

(b) such other period as may be agreed.

49E(7) In subsection (6) **"relevant day"** means–

(a) in a case where the appellant required the review, the day when HMRC notified the appellant of HMRC's view of the matter in question,

(b) in a case where HMRC offered the review, the day when HMRC received notification of the appellant's acceptance of the offer.

49E(8) Where HMRC are required to undertake a review but do not give notice of the conclusions within the time period specified in subsection (6), the review is to be treated as having concluded that HMRC's view of the matter in question (see sections 49B(2) and 49C(2)) is upheld.

49E(9) If subsection (8) applies, HMRC must notify the appellant of the conclusion which the review is treated as having reached.

History – S. 49E inserted by SI 2009/56, art. 3(1) and Sch. 1, para. 30, operative from 1 April 2009, subject to transitional and saving provisions in SI 2009/56, Sch. 3.

49F Effect of conclusions of review

49F(1) This section applies if HMRC give notice of the conclusions of a review (see section 49E(6) and (9)).

49F(2) The conclusions are to be treated as if they were an agreement in writing under section 54(1) for the settlement of the matter in question.

49F(3) The appellant may not give notice under section 54(2) (desire to repudiate or resile from agreement) in a case where subsection (2) applies.

49F(4) Subsection (2) does not apply to the matter in question if, or to the extent that, the appellant notifies the appeal to the tribunal under section 49G.

History – S. 49F inserted by SI 2009/56, art. 3(1) and Sch. 1, para. 30, operative from 1 April 2009, subject to transitional and saving provisions in SI 2009/56, Sch. 3.

49G Notifying appeal to tribunal after review concluded

49G(1) This section applies if–

(a) HMRC have given notice of the conclusions of a review in accordance with section 49E, or

(b) the period specified in section 49E(6) has ended and HMRC have not given notice of the conclusions of the review.

49G(2) The appellant may notify the appeal to the tribunal within the post-review period.

49G(3) If the post-review period has ended, the appellant may notify the appeal to the tribunal only if the tribunal gives permission.

49G(4) If the appellant notifies the appeal to the tribunal, the tribunal is to determine the matter in question.

49G(5) In this section **"post-review period"** means–

(a) in a case falling within subsection (1)(a), the period of 30 days beginning with the date of the document in which HMRC give notice of the conclusions of the review in accordance with section 49E(6), or

(b) in a case falling within subsection (1)(b), the period that–

(i) begins with the day following the last day of the period specified in section 49E(6), and

(ii) ends 30 days after the date of the document in which HMRC give notice of the conclusions of the review in accordance with section 49E(9).

History – S. 49G inserted by SI 2009/56, art. 3(1) and Sch. 1, para. 30, operative from 1 April 2009, subject to transitional and saving provisions in SI 2009/56, Sch. 3.

49H Notifying appeal to tribunal after review offered but not accepted

49H(1) This section applies if–

(a) HMRC have offered to review the matter in question (see section 49C), and

(b) the appellant has not accepted the offer.

49H(2) The appellant may notify the appeal to the tribunal within the acceptance period.

49H(3) But if the acceptance period has ended, the appellant may notify the appeal to the tribunal only if the tribunal gives permission.

49H(4) If the appellant notifies the appeal to the tribunal, the tribunal is to determine the matter in question.

49H(5) In this section **"acceptance period"** has the same meaning as in section 49C.

History – S. 49H inserted by SI 2009/56, art. 3(1) and Sch. 1, para. 30, operative from 1 April 2009, subject to transitional and saving provisions in SI 2009/56, Sch. 3.

49I Interpretation of sections 49A to 49H

49I(1) In sections 49A to 49H–

(a) **"matter in question"** means the matter to which an appeal relates;

(b) a reference to a notification is a reference to a notification in writing.

49I(2) In sections 49A to 49H, a reference to the appellant includes a person acting on behalf of the appellant except in relation to–

(a) notification of HMRC's view under section 49B(2);

(b) notification by HMRC of an offer of review (and of their view of the matter) under section 49C;

(c) notification of the conclusions of a review under section 49E(6); and

(d) notification of the conclusions of a review under section 49E(9).

49I(3) But if a notification falling within any of the paragraphs of subsection (2) is given to the appellant, a copy of the notification may also be given to a person acting on behalf of the appellant.

History – S. 49I inserted by SI 2009/56, art. 3(1) and Sch. 1, para. 30, operative from 1 April 2009, subject to transitional and saving provisions in SI 2009/56, Sch. 3.

50 Procedure

50(1)–(5) [Omitted by SI 1994/1813, Sch. 1, para. 6(a), with effect from 1 September 1994.]

50(6) If, on an appeal notified to the tribunal, the tribunal decides–

(a) that the appellant is overcharged by a self-assessment;

(b) that any amounts contained in a partnership statement are excessive; or

(c) that the appellant is overcharged by an assessment other than a self-assessment,

the assessment or amounts shall be reduced accordingly, but otherwise the assessment or statement shall stand good.

50(7) If, on an appeal notified to the tribunal, the tribunal decides–

(a) that the appellant is undercharged to tax by a self-assessment;

(b) that any amounts contained in a partnership statement are insufficient; or

(c) that the appellant is undercharged by an assessment other than a self-assessment, the assessment or amounts shall be increased accordingly.

50(7A) If, on an appeal notified to the tribunal, the tribunal decides that a claim or election which was the subject of a decision contained in a closure notice under section 28A of this Act should have been allowed or disallowed to an extent different from that specified in the notice, the claim or election shall be allowed or disallowed accordingly to the extent that the tribunal decides is appropriate, but otherwise the decision in the notice shall stand good.

50(8) Where, on an appeal notified to the tribunal against an assessment (other than a self-assessment) which–

(a) assesses an amount which is chargeable to tax, and

(b) charges tax on the amount assessed,

the tribunal decides as mentioned in subsection (6) or (7) above, the tribunal may, unless the circumstances of the case otherwise require, reduce or, as the case may be, increase only the amount assessed; and where any appeal notified to the tribunal is so determined the tax charged by the assessment shall be taken to have been reduced or increased accordingly.

50(9) Where any amounts contained in a partnership statement are reduced under subsection (6) above or increased under subsection (7) above, an officer of the Board shall by notice to each of the relevant partners amend–

(a) the partner's return under section 8 or 8A of this Act, or

(b) the partner's company tax return,

so as to give effect to the reductions or increases of those amounts.

50(10) Where an appeal is notified to the tribunal, the decision of the tribunal on the appeal is final and conclusive.

50(11) But subsection (10) is subject to–

(a) sections 9 to 14 of the TCEA 2007,

(b) Tribunal Procedure Rules, and

(c) the Taxes Acts.

History – S. 50(1)–(5) omitted by SI 1994/1813, Sch. 1, para. 6(a), Sch. 2, Pt. I, with effect from 1 September 1994.

In s. 50(6) the words "If, on an appeal notified to the tribunal, the tribunal decides–" substituted for the words "If, on an appeal, it appears to the majority of the Commissioners present at the hearing, by examination of the appellant on oath or affirmation, or by other evidence–" by SI 2009/56, art. 3(1) and Sch. 1, para. 31(2), operative from 1 April 2009, subject to transitional and saving provisions in SI 2009/56, Sch. 3.

In s. 50(6) the word "lawful" which appeared after the word "other" in the introductory paragraph omitted by SI 1994/1813, Sch. 1, para. 6(b), with effect from 1 September 1994.

In s. 50(6)–

- in para. (a), the words "by reason of an amendment under section 28A(2) or (4) of this Act or paragraph 30 or 34(2) of Schedule 18 to the Finance Act 1998", and
- in para. (b), the words "by reason of an amendment under section 28B(3) or 30B(1) of this Act,"

(both of which appeared after the word "that" in each para.) omitted and repealed by FA 2001, s. 88, Sch. 29, para. 30(2), (3) and s. 110, Sch. 33, Pt. 2(13) with effect from 11 May 2001 in relation to returns whether made before or after that date and whether relating to periods before or after then.

In s. 50(7) the words "If, on an appeal notified to the tribunal, the tribunal decides" substituted for the words "If, on an appeal, it appears to the Commissioners" by SI 2009/56, art. 3(1) and Sch. 1, para. 31(3), operative from 1 April 2009, subject to transitional and saving provisions in SI 2009/56, Sch. 3.

In s. 50(7)–

- in para. (a), the words "which has been amended under section 28A(2) or (4) of this Act or paragraph 30 or 34(2) of Schedule 18 to the Finance Act 1998", and
- in para. (b), the words "which has been amended under section 28B(3) or 30B(1) of this Act"

(which appeared after the words "self-assessment" and "partnership statement" respectively), omitted and repealed by FA 2001, s. 88, Sch. 29, para. 30(2), (3) and s. 110, Sch. 33, Pt. 2(13) with effect from 11 May 2001 in relation to returns whether made before or after that date and whether relating to periods before or after then.

Prior to the above repeal, in s. 50(6)(a) and (7)(a), the words "or paragraph 30 or 34(2) of Schedule 18 to the Finance Act 1998" had been inserted by FA 1998, s. 117(3) and Sch. 19, para. 27(4), with effect in relation to accounting periods ending on or after 1 July 1999, the corporation tax self-assessment appointed day by virtue of FA 1994, s. 199(2), (3) and SI 1998/3173 (C. 78).

Originally, s. 50(6), (7) had been substituted by FA 1994, s. 196 in so far as they relate to income tax and capital gains tax, as respects the year 1996–97 and subsequent years of assessment and, in so far as they relate to corporation tax, as respects accounting periods ending on or after 1 July 1999, the self-assessment appointed day (see above).

In s. 50(7A) the words "If, on an appeal notified to the tribunal, the tribunal decides" substituted for the words "If, on an appeal, it appears to the Commissioners" and the words "the tribunal decides is" substituted for the words "appears to them" by SI 2009/56, art. 3(1) and Sch. 1, para. 31(4), operative from 1 April 2009, subject to transitional and saving provisions in SI 2009/56, Sch. 3.

In s. 50(7A) the words "which was the subject of a decision contained in a closure notice under section 28A" substituted for the words "specified in a notice under section 28A(4A)" by FA 2001, s. 88, Sch. 29, para. 30(4) with effect from 11 May 2001 in relation to returns whether made before or after that date and whether relating to periods before or after then.

Originally, s. 50(7A) inserted by FA 1996, s. 133 and Sch. 19, para. 7, in so far as it relates to income tax and capital gains tax, as respects the year 1996–97 and subsequent years of assessment and, in so far as it relates to corporation tax, as respects accounting periods ending on or after 1 July 1999, the self-assessment appointed day (see above).

In s. 50(8) the words "notified to the tribunal" inserted twice; the words "the tribunal decides" substituted for the words "it appears to the Commissioners" and the words "the tribunal may" substituted for the words "they may" by SI 2009/56, art. 3(1) and Sch. 1, para. 31(5), operative from 1 April 2009, subjectto transitional and saving provisions in SI 2009/56, Sch. 3.

S. 50(8) amended, by the insertion of the words "(other than a self-assessment)" by FA 1994, s. 196 in so far as it relates to income tax and capital gains tax, as respects the year 1996–97 and subsequent years of assessment and, in so far as it relates to corporation tax, as respects accounting periods ending on or after 1 July 1999, the self-assessment appointed day (see above).

S. 50(8) originally inserted by F(No. 2)A 1975, s. 67(2).
S. 50(9)(a) substituted by FA 2001, s. 88, Sch. 29, para. 30(5) with effect from 11 May 2001 in relation to returns whether made before or after that date and whether relating to periods before or after then.
Former s. 50(9) substituted by FA 1998, s. 117(3) and Sch. 19, para. 27(4), with effect in relation to accounting periods ending on or after 1 July 1999, the self-assessment appointed day by virtue of FA 1994, s. 199(2), (3) and SI 1998/3173 (C. 78) (see above).
Former s. 50(9) originally inserted by FA 1994, s. 196 and Sch. 19, para. 17, in so far as it relates to income tax and capital gains tax, as respects the year 1996–97 and subsequent years of assessment and, in so far as it relates to corporation tax, as respects accounting periods ending on or after 1 July 1999, the self-assessment appointed day (see above).
S. 50(10) inserted by SI 2009/56, art. 3(1) and Sch. 1, para. 31(6), operative from 1 April 2009, subject to transitional and saving provisions in SI 2009/56, Sch. 3.
S. 50(11) inserted by SI 2009/56, art. 3(1) and Sch. 1, para. 31(6), operative from 1 April 2009, subject to transitional and saving provisions in SI 2009/56, Sch. 3.

Cross references – Sch. 3ZA, para. 11: tax payable or repayable on consequential amendment under s. 50(9)(a) of self assessment in partner's return following decision by commissioners on partnership.
S. 19A: disapplication of s. 50(6)–(8) on appeal under s. 19A(6).
S. 59C: disapplication of s. 50(6)–(8) on appeal under s. 59C(7) (appeal against imposition of a surcharge).
S. 88A(5): disapplication of s. 50(6)–(8) to an appeal against a determination under s. 88 (interest in cases of loss due to taxpayer's fault).
S. 93: disapplication of s. 50(6)–(8) on appeal against the determination under s. 100 of a penalty under s. 93(2), (4).
S. 93A: disapplication of s. 50(6)–(8) on appeal against the determination under s. 100 of a penalty under s. 93A(2), (4).
S. 100B(2): disapplication of s. 50(6)–(8) to an appeal against a determination under s. 100 (penalties).
ICTA 1988, s. 62A: disapplication of s. 50(6)–(8) on appeal under s. 62A(6).
FA 1995, Sch. 22, para. 12(6): disapplication of s. 50(6)–(8) with regard to appeals against notices issued under FA 1995, Sch. 22, para. 12(1) (transitional current-year basis anti-avoidance rules).
Social Security Contributions (Transfer of Functions, etc.) Act 1999, s. 13(2)(a)(ii): power of the Board, with the concurrence of the Lord Chancellor and the Lord Advocate, to make regulations making provision with respect to appeals on contributions matters, including any of the matters dealt with in s. 50.

Other material – Department of Constitutional Affairs booklets; *Appeals and other proceedings before the Special Commissioners* and *Tax Appeals: A guide to appealing against decisions of the Inland Revenue on tax and other matters.*

51 Power of Commissioners to obtain information from appellant

51 [Omitted by SI 1994/1813, Sch. 1, para. 7, Sch. 2, Pt. I.]

History – S. 51 omitted by SI 1994/1813, Sch. 1, para. 7, Sch. 2, Pt. I, with effect from 1 September 1994.

52 Evidence

52 [Omitted by SI 1994/1813, Sch. 1, para. 7.]

History – S. 52 omitted by SI 1994/1813, Sch. 1, para. 7, Sch. 2, Pt. I, with effect from 1 September 1994.

53 Appeals against summary determination of penalties

53 [Omitted by SI 2009/56, art. 3(1) and Sch. 1, para. 32.]

History – S. 53 omitted by SI 2009/56, art. 3(1) and Sch. 1, para. 32, operative from 1 April 2009, subject to transitional and saving provisions in SI 2009/56, Sch. 3.

54 Settling of appeals by agreement

54(1) Subject to the provisions of this section, where a person gives notice of appeal and, before the appeal is determined by the tribunal, the inspector or other proper officer of the Crown and the appellant come to an agreement, whether in writing or otherwise, that the assessment or decision under appeal should be treated as upheld without variation, or as varied in a particular manner or as discharged or cancelled, the like consequences shall ensue for all purposes as would have ensued if, at the time when the agreement was come to, the tribunal had determined the appeal and had upheld the assessment or decision without variation, had varied it in that manner or had discharged or cancelled it, as the case may be.

54(2) Subsection (1) of this section shall not apply where, within thirty days from the date when the agreement was come to, the appellant gives notice in writing to the inspector or other proper officer of the Crown that he desires to repudiate or resile from the agreement.

54(3) Where an agreement is not in writing–

(a) the preceding provisions of this section shall not apply unless the fact that an agreement was come to, and the terms agreed, are confirmed by notice in writing given by the inspector or other proper officer of the Crown to the appellant or by the appellant to the inspector or other proper officer; and

(b) the references in the said preceding provisions to the time when the agreement was come to shall be construed as references to the time of the giving of the said notice of confirmation.

54(4) Where–

(a) a person who has given a notice of appeal notifies the inspector or other proper officer of the Crown, whether orally or in writing, that he desires not to proceed with the appeal; and

(b) thirty days have elapsed since the giving of the notification without the inspector or other proper officer giving to the appellant notice in writing indicating that he is unwilling that the appeal should be treated as withdrawn, the preceding provisions of this section shall have effect as if, at the date of the appellant's notification, the appellant and the inspector or other proper officer had come to an agreement, orally or in writing, as the case may be, that the assessment or decision under appeal should be upheld without variation.

54(5) The references in this section to an agreement being come to with an appellant and the giving of notice or notification to or by an appellant include references to an agreement being come to with, and the giving of notice or notification to or by, a person acting on behalf of the appellant in relation to the appeal.

History – In s. 54(1) the word "tribunal" substituted for the word "Commissioners" twice by SI 2009/56, art. 3(1) and Sch. 1, para. 32, operative from 1 April 2009, subject to transitional and saving provisions in SI 2009/56, Sch. 3.

Cross references – FA 1982, s. 156 and Sch. 21, para. 4(1): s. 54 applies to the tribunal established under ICTA 1988, s. 706 in respect of the functions transferred to it by FA 1982, s. 156 (cancellation of tax advantage on certain transactions in securities).

Social Security Contributions (Transfer of Functions, etc.) Act 1999, s. 13(2)(a)(ii): power of the Board, with the concurrence of the Lord Chancellor and the Lord Advocate, to make regulations making provision with respect to appeals on contributions matters, including any of the matters dealt with in s. 54.

SI 2002/2926, reg. 3: application of s. 54, with modifications, to tax credits appeals.

SI 2003/1382: in its application to appeals under TCA 2002, s. 38, s. 54 is modified, with effect from 18 June 2003, by–

- the substitution, in subs. (1) of the words "set aside" in place of "discharged or cancelled" and the substitution of the words "had set it aside" for "had discharged or cancelled it";
- the substitution of the words "the officer of the Board" for "the inspector or other officer of the Crown" and "the inspector or other proper officer" in each place where they occur;
- the omission of the words "assessment or".

SI 2005/191, reg. 4: modification of s. 54 in its application to appeals against decisions of HMRC in respect of child trust funds.

Statements of practice – SP 8/91: if an assessment has been determined on appeal in accordance with s. 54, a discovery assessment should not be made in respect of any particular point which has been dealt with in the course of the determination of that appeal.

HMRC interpretations – IRInt. 64: where substantive point was squarely in issue in reaching agreement under s. 54, relief will not be available under s. 33.

Other material – Taxline 1999/146: where inspector has full information available to him to make his decision, the question whether he chooses to make enquiries or not is immaterial; if he comes to an agreement with the taxpayer following full disclosure of the facts, s. 54 applies.

CIOT technical release CIOT/TIR/7/97 (not reproduced): Revenue explanation of interaction of transfer pricing rules with s. 54:

- the UK Revenue may be willing to discuss the scope for entering into competent authority discussions before an assessment is settled;
- early notification to the UK Revenue of transfer pricing disputes with overseas revenues is welcome;
- the UK competent authority does not have the power to modify transfer pricing adjustments on settled years but will assist the group, of which the taxpayer is a member, in securing corresponding relief;
- a claim for a corresponding adjustment in respect of action by an overseas revenue must be made under TMA 1970, s. 43 within six years although in appropriate cases a protective claim may be accepted and a claim may be made within six years even if a section 54 agreement has been reached earlier;
- the means of ensuring relief from international double taxation in respect of transfer pricing adjustments is an evolving issue and the UK Revenue is open to receiving representations.

54A No questioning in appeal of amounts of certain social security income

54A(1) Subsection (2) applies if an amount is notified under section 54B(1) and–

(a) no objection is made to the notification within 60 days after its date of issue, or such further period as may be allowed under section 54B(4) and (5), or

(b) an objection is made but is withdrawn by the objector by notice.

54A(2) The amount is not to be questioned in any appeal against any assessment in respect of income including the amount.

54A(3) Subsection (4) applies if an amount is notified under section 54B(1) and–

(a) an objection is made to the notification within 60 days after its date of issue, or such further period as may be allowed under section 54B(4) and (5),

(b) the appropriate officer and the objector come to an agreement that the amount notified should be varied in a particular manner, and

(c) the officer confirms that agreement in writing.

54A(4) The amount, as varied, is not to be questioned in any appeal against any assessment in respect of income including that amount.

54A(5) Subsection (4) does not apply if, within 60 days from the date when the agreement was come to, the objector gives to the appropriate officer notice that the objector wishes to repudiate or resile from the agreement.

History – S. 54A inserted by TIOPA 2010, s. 371 and Sch. 7, para. 32, with effect for corporation tax purposes for accounting periods ending on or after 1 April 2010, for income tax and capital gains tax purposes for the tax year 2010–11 and subsequent tax years, and for petroleum revenue tax purposes for chargeable periods beginning on or after 1 July 2010.

54B Notifications of taxable amounts of certain social security income

54B(1) The appropriate officer may by notice notify a person who is liable to pay any income tax charged on any unemployment benefit, jobseeker's allowance or income support–

(a) of the amount on which the tax is charged, or

(b) of an alteration in an amount previously notified under paragraph (a) or this paragraph.

54B(2) A notification under subsection (1) must–

(a) state its date of issue, and

(b) state that the person notified may object to the notification by notice given within 60 days after that date.

54B(3) A notification under subsection (1)(b) cancels the previous notification concerned.

54B(4) An objection to a notification under subsection (1) may be made later than 60 days after its date of issue if, on an application for the purpose–

(a) the appropriate officer is satisfied–

(i) that there was a reasonable excuse for not objecting before the end of the 60 days, and

(ii) that the application was made without unreasonable delay after the end of the 60 days, and

(b) the officer gives consent in writing.

54B(5) If the officer is not so satisfied, the officer is to refer the application for determination by the tribunal.

History – S. 54B inserted by TIOPA 2010, s. 371 and Sch. 7, para. 32, with effect for corporation tax purposes for accounting periods ending on or after 1 April 2010, for income tax and capital gains tax purposes for the tax year 2010–11 and subsequent tax years, and for petroleum revenue tax purposes for chargeable periods beginning on or after 1 July 2010.

54C Interpretation of sections 54A and 54B: "appropriate officer" etc

54C(1) In sections 54A and 54B **"the appropriate officer"** means the appropriate officer–

(a) in Great Britain, of the Department for Work and Pensions, and

(b) in Northern Ireland, of the Department for Social Development.

54C(2) Section 48(1)(a) (meaning of "appeal" in the following provisions of Part 5) does not apply for the purposes of sections 54A and 54B.

History – S. 54C inserted by TIOPA 2010, s. 371 and Sch. 7, para. 32, with effect for corporation tax purposes for accounting periods ending on or after 1 April 2010, for income tax and capital gains tax purposes for the tax year 2010–11 and subsequent tax years, and for petroleum revenue tax purposes for chargeable periods beginning on or after 1 July 2010.

55 Recovery of tax not postponed

55(1) This section applies to an appeal to the tribunal against–

(a) an amendment of a self-assessment–

(i) under section 9C of this Act, or

(ii) under paragraph 30 or 34 of Schedule 18 to the Finance Act 1998,

(aa) a conclusion stated or amendment made by a closure notice under section 28A or 28B of this Act,

(b) an assessment to tax other than a self-assessment,

(c) [omitted by ITA 2007, s. 1027 and Sch. 1, para. 257(a), and repealed by s. 1031 and Sch. 3, Pt. 1,]

(d) [omitted by FA 2012, s. 180 and Sch. 20, para. 11.]

55(2) Except as otherwise provided by the following provisions of this section, the tax charged–

(a) by the amendment or assessment, or

(b) where the appeal is against a conclusion stated by a closure notice, as a result of that conclusion,

shall be due and payable as if there had been no appeal.

55(3) If the appellant has grounds for believing that the amendment or assessment overcharges the appellant to tax, or as a result of the conclusion stated in the closure notice the tax charged on the appellant is excessive, the appellant may–

(a) first apply by notice in writing to HMRC within 30 days of the specified date for a determination by them of the amount of tax the payment of which should be postponed pending the determination of the appeal;

(b) where such a determination is not agreed, refer the application for postponement to the tribunal within 30 days from the date of the document notifying HMRC's decision on the amount to be postponed.

An application under paragraph (a) must state the amount believed to be overcharged to tax and the grounds for that belief.

55(3A) An application under subsection (3) above may be made more than thirty days after the specified date if there is a change in the circumstances of the case as a result of which the appellant has grounds for believing that he is over-charged to tax by the amendment or assessment, or as a result of the conclusion stated in the closure notice, or where the notice of appeal has been given after the relevant time limit (see section 49).

55(4) If, after any determination of the amount of tax the payment of which should be so postponed–

(a) there is a change in the circumstances of the case as a result of which either party has grounds for believing that the amount so determined has become excessive or, as the case may be, insufficient, and

(b) the parties cannot agree on a revised determination,

the party mentioned in paragraph (a) may, at any time before the determination of the appeal, apply to the tribunal for a revised determination of that amount.

55(5) Any such application is to be subject to the relevant provisions of Part 5 of this Act (see, in particular, section 48(2)(b)).

55(6) The amount of tax the payment of which shall be postponed pending the determination of the appeal shall be the amount (if any) in which it appears that there are reasonable grounds for believing that the appellant is overcharged to tax; and–

(a) in the case of a determination made on an application under subsection (3) above, other than an application made by virtue of subsection (3A) above, the date on which any tax the payment of which is not so postponed is due and payable shall be determined as if the tax were charged by an amendment or assessment notice of which was issued on the date of that determination and against which there had been no appeal; and

(b) in the case of a determination made on an application under subsection (4) above–

(i) the date on which any tax the payment of which ceases to be so postponed is due and payable shall be determined as if the tax were charged by an amendment or assessment notice of which was issued on the date of that determination and against which there had been no appeal; and

(ii) any tax overpaid shall be repaid.

55(6A) Notwithstanding the provisions of sections 11 and 13 of the TCEA 2007, the decision of the tribunal shall be final and conclusive.

55(7) If the appellant and HMRC reach an agreement as to the amount of tax the payment of which should be postponed pending the determination of the appeal, the agreement shall not have effect unless–

(a) the agreement is in writing, or

(b) the fact that the agreement has been reached, and the terms of the agreement, are confirmed by notice in writing given–

(i) by the appellant to HMRC, or

(ii) by HMRC to the appellant.

55(8) [Omitted by SI 2009/56, art. 3(1) and Sch. 1, para. 34(10).]

55(8A) Where an agreement is made which has effect under subsection (7), references in subsection (6)(a) and (b) above to the date of the determination shall be construed as references to the date that the agreement is confirmed in writing.

55(8B) Subsections (8C) and (8D) apply where a person has been given an accelerated payment notice or partner payment notice under Chapter 3 of Part 4 of the Finance Act 2014 and that notice has not been withdrawn.

55(8C) Nothing in this section enables the postponement of the payment of (as the case may be)–

(a) the understated tax to which the payment specified in the notice under section 220(2)(b) of that Act relates,

(b) the disputed tax specified in the notice under section 221(2)(b) of that Act,

(c) the understated partner tax to which the payment specified in the notice under paragraph 4(1)(b) of Schedule 32 to that Act relates, or

(d) the amount of tax specified in an assessment under paragraph 76 of Schedule 18 to the Finance Act 1998 where–

(i) an asserted surrenderable amount is specified in the notice under section 220(2)(d) of the Finance Act 2014 or under paragraph 4(1)(d) of Schedule 32 to that Act, and

(ii) the claimant company has failed to act in accordance with paragraph 75(6) of Schedule 18 to the Finance Act 1998.

55(8D) Accordingly, if the payment of an amount of tax within subsection (8C)(b) is postponed by virtue of this section immediately before the accelerated payment notice is given, it ceases to be so postponed with effect from the time that notice is given, and the tax is due and payable–

(a) if no representations were made under section 222 of that Act in respect of the notice, on or before the last day of the period of 90 days beginning with the day the notice or partner payment notice is given, and

(b) if representations were so made, on or before whichever is later of–

(i) the last day of the 90 day period mentioned in paragraph (a), and

(ii) the last day of the period of 30 days beginning with the day on which HMRC's determination in respect of those representations is notified under section 222 of that Act.

55(9) On the determination of the appeal–

(a) the date on which any tax payable in accordance with that determination is due and payable shall, so far as it is tax the payment of which had been postponed, or which would not have been charged by the amendment or assessment, or as a result of the conclusion stated in the closure notice, if there had been no appeal, be determined as if the tax were charged by an amendment or assessment–

(i) notice of which was issued on the date on which HMRC issue to the appellant a notice of the total amount payable in accordance with the determination, and

(ii) against which there had been no appeal; and

(b) any tax overpaid shall be repaid.

55(10) [Omitted by SI 2009/56, art. 3(1) and Sch. 1, para. 34(13).]

55(10A) In this section **"the specified date"** means the date of–

(a) the issue of the notice of amendment or assessment, or

(b) in the case of an appeal against a conclusion stated or amendment made by a closure notice, the issue of the closure notice.

55(10B) References in this section to agreements between an appellant and HMRC, and to the giving of notices between the parties, include references to agreements, and the giving of notices, between a person acting on behalf of the appellant in relation to the appeal and HMRC.

55(11) [Omitted by SI 2009/56, art. 3(1) and Sch. 1, para. 34(13).]

History – In s. 55(1) the word "tribunal" substituted for the word "Commissioners" twice by SI 2009/56, art. 3(1) and Sch. 1, para. 34(2), operative from 1 April 2009, subject to transitional and saving provisions in SI 2009/56, Sch. 3.

In s. 55(1)(a)(ii), "34" substituted for "34(2)" by FA 2008, s. 119(12)(a)(iv) with effect from 1 April 2010 (SI 2009/405).

S. 55(1)(a) and (aa) substituted for the previous version of subs. (1)(a) by FA 2001, s. 88, Sch. 29, para. 31(2) with effect from 11 May 2001 in relation to returns whether made before or after that date and whether relating to periods before or after then.

S. 55(1)(a) and (b) (previously) substituted by FA 1998, s. 117(3) and Sch. 19, para. 28 with effect in relation to accounting periods ending on or after 1 July 1999, the corporation tax self-assessment appointed day by virtue of FA 1994, s. 199(2), (3) and SI 1998/3173 (C. 78).

S. 55(1)(d) omitted by FA 2012, s. 180 and Sch. 20, para. 11 in relation to accounting periods of controlled foreign companies beginning on or after 1 January 2013.

S. 55(1) previously substituted and s. 55(2)–(11) amended, by the substitution of the words "amendment or assessment" for "assessment" in each place where it occurred, by FA 1994, s. 196 and Sch. 19, para. 18, in so far as it relates to income tax and capital gains tax, as respects the year 1996–97 and subsequent years of assessment, and also originally as respects corporation tax accounting periods ending on or after 1 July 1999, the appointed day by virtue of SI 1998/3173 (but see now amendment made by FA 1998, s. 117(3) and Sch. 19, para. 28, above).

S. 55(1)(b) previously substituted by FA 1996, s. 132 and Sch. 18, para. 1:

- for the purposes of income tax and capital gains tax, as respects the year 1996–97 and subsequent years of assessment;
- for the purposes of corporation tax, as respects accounting periods ending on or after 1 July 1999, the appointed day by virtue of FA 1994, s. 199(2), (3) and SI 1998/3173 (C. 78); and
- so far as relating to partnerships whose trades, professions or businesses were set up and commenced before 6 April 1994, with effect as respects the year 1997–98 and subsequent years of assessment.

S. 55(1)(c) omitted by ITA 2007, s. 1027 and Sch. 1, para. 257(a), and repealed by s. 1031 and Sch. 3, Pt. 1 with effect from 6 April 2007.

In s. 55(1)(d), the words "the principal Act" substituted for "that Act" by ITA 2007, s. 1027 and Sch. 1, para. 257(b) with effect from 6 April 2007.

S. 55(1)(f) related to development land tax.

S. 55(1)(g) substituted by ICTA 1988, s. 844 and Sch. 29, para. 8(1) in relation to tax for 1988–89 and subsequent years of assessment, and for companies' accounting periods ending after 5 April 1988.

S. 55(2) amended, the amendment substituting subs. (2)(a), (b) for the words "by the amendment or assessment", by FA 2001, s. 88, Sch. 29, para. 31(3) with effect from 11 May 2001 in relation to returns whether made before or after that date and whether relating to periods before or after then.

S. 55(2), (6), (9) (previously in the case of (2)) amended by FA 1989, s. 156(2), (4) for tax charged by an assessment, notice of which is issued after 30 July 1982, to clarify wording consequent to previous amendments, see below.

S. 55(3) substituted by SI 2009/56, art. 3(1) and Sch. 1, para. 34(3), operative from 1 April 2009, subject to transitional and saving provisions in SI 2009/56, Sch. 3.

In former s. 55(3), the words "or as a result of the conclusion stated in the closure notice," inserted and the words "the specified date" substituted for the words "the date of the issue of the notice of amendment or assessment", by FA 2001, s. 88, Sch. 29, para. 31(4) with effect from 11 May 2001 in relation to returns whether made before or after that date and whether relating to periods before or after then.

In s. 55(3A) the words ", or where *the notice of appeal* has been given after the relevant time limit (see section 49)" inserted by *SI 2009/56, art. 3(1) and Sch. 1*, para. 34(4), operative from 1 April 2009, subject to transitional and saving provisions in SI 2009/56, *Sch. 3*.

In s. 55(3A), the words "the specified date" substituted for the words "the date of the issue of the notice of amendment or assessment" and the words "or as a result of the conclusion stated in the closure notice," inserted, by FA 2001, s. 88, Sch. 29, para. 31(5) with effect from 11 May 2001 in relation to returns whether made before or after that date and whether relating to periods before or after then.

S. 55(3A) originally inserted by FA 1982, s. 68(2) in relation to notices of assessment issued after 30 July 1982; s. 55(2), (6) amended accordingly by FA 1982, s. 68(1), (3).
S. 55(4) substituted by SI 2009/56, art. 3(1) and Sch. 1, para. 34(5), operative from 1 April 2009, subject to transitional and saving provisions in SI 2009/56, Sch. 3.
S. 55(5) substituted by SI 2009/56, art. 3(1) and Sch. 1, para. 34(6), operative from 1 April 2009, subject to transitional and saving provisions in SI 2009/56, Sch. 3.
In s. 55(6) the words "to the Commissioners, having regard to the representations made and any evidence adduced," omitted by SI 2009/56, art. 3(1) and Sch. 1, para. 34(7), operative from 1 April 2009, subject to transitional and saving provisions in SI 2009/56, Sch. 3.
In s. 55(6), the word "lawful" which appeared before the word "evidence" omitted by SI 1994/1813, Sch. 1, para. 9(a), Sch. 2, Pt. I, with effect from 1 September 1994.
S. 55(6A) substituted by SI 2009/56, art. 3(1) and Sch. 1, para. 34(8), operative from 1 April 2009, subject to transitional and saving provisions in SI 2009/56, Sch. 3.
Former s. 55(6A) inserted by ICTA 1988, s. 844 and Sch. 29, para. 8(2) in relation to tax for 1988–89 and subsequent years of assessment and for companies' accounting periods ending after 5 April 1988 – see previously FA 1984, s. 89(6).
S. 55(7) substituted by SI 2009/56, art. 3(1) and Sch. 1, para. 34(9), operative from 1 April 2009, subject to transitional and saving provisions in SI 2009/56, Sch. 3.
Former s. 55(7) amended by FA 1990, s. 104(2), (4), substituting "an inspector" for "the inspector", effective where notice of appeal is given on or after 26 July 1990.
S. 55(8) omitted by SI 2009/56, art. 3(1) and Sch. 1, para. 34(10), operative from 1 April 2009, subject to transitional and saving provisions in SI 2009/56, Sch. 3.
S. 55(8A) inserted by SI 2009/56, art. 3(1) and Sch. 1, para. 34(11), operative from 1 April 2009, subject to transitional and saving provisions in SI 2009/56, Sch. 3.
S. 55(8B), (8C) and (8D) inserted by FA 2014, s. 224(1), with effect from 17 July 2014.
S. 55(8C)(d) (and the ", or" before it) inserted (and the "or" after (b) omitted) by FA 2015, s. 118 and Sch. 18, para. 11, with effect from 26 March 2015.
In s. 55(9)(a)(i) the words "HMRC issue" substituted for the words "the inspector issues" by SI 2009/56, art. 3(1) and Sch. 1, para. 34(12), operative from 1 April 2009, subject to transitional and saving provisions in SI 2009/56, Sch. 3.
In s. 55(9)(a), the words "or as a result of the conclusion stated in the closure notice," inserted by FA 2001, s. 88, Sch. 29, para. 31(6) witheffect from 11 May 2001 in relation to returns whether made before or after that date and whether relating to periods before or after then.
S. 55(10) omitted by SI 2009/56, art. 3(1) and Sch. 1, para. 34(13), operative from 1 April 2009, subject to transitional and saving provisions in SI 2009/56, Sch. 3.
Former s. 55(10) substituted by FA 2001, s. 88, Sch. 29, para. 31(7) with effect from 11 May 2001 in relation to returns whether made before or after that date and whether relating to periods before or after then.
Former s. 55(10) previously amended by FA 1990, s. 104(2), (4), substituting "subsection (3) above" for "this section", effective where notice of appeal is given on or after 26 July 1990.
S. 55(10A) effectively inserted by FA 2001, s. 88, Sch. 29, para. 31(7) with effect from 11 May 2001 in relation to returns whether made before or after that date and whether relating to periods before or after then.
S. 55(10B) substituted by SI 2009/56, art. 3(1) and Sch. 1, para. 34(14), operative from 1 April 2009, subject to transitional and saving provisions in SI 2009/56, Sch. 3.
S. 55(10B) effectively inserted by FA 2001, s. 88, Sch. 29, para. 31(7) with effect from 11 May 2001 in relation to returns whether made before or after that date and whether relating to periods before or after then.
S. 55(11) omitted by SI 2009/56, art. 3(1) and Sch. 1, para. 34(15), operative from 1 April 2009, subject to transitional and saving provisions in SI 2009/56, Sch. 3.
In former s. 55(11), the words "or under regulations made pursuant to section 46A of this Act" inserted by SI 1994/1813, Sch. 1, para. 9(b), with effect from 1 September 1994.
Former s. 55(11) amended by FA 1984, Sch. 23, with effect, by virtue of SI 1984/1836, from 1 January 1985, removing a reference to s. 45(2) (repealed).
In s. 55 the word "tribunal" substituted for the word "Commissioners" twice by SI 2009/56, art. 3(1) and Sch. 1, para. 34(2), operative from 1 April 2009, subject to transitional and saving provisions in SI 2009/56, Sch. 3.
Reference to provisions of the principal Act substituted by ICTA 1988, Sch. 29, para. 32, that Act becoming the principal Act (TMA 1970, s. 118(1)).
S. 55 substituted by F(No. 2)A 1975, s. 45(1).

Cross references – S. 59B (as inserted by FA 1994, s. 193 as respects 1996–97 and subsequent years of assessment): payment of income tax and capital gains tax.
S. 59DA and SI 1998/3175, reg. 6(6): application to postpone payment of corporation tax under s. 55(3) or (4) may be combined with an application under s. 59DA(4) (determination of interim repayment) or an application under SI 1998/3175, reg. 6 (repayment of amounts in respect of a large company's total liability for an accounting period).
S. 86(1): income tax or capital gains tax due under s. 55 carries interest at the rate applicable under FA 1989, s. 178 from the "relevant date" until the date of payment.
Sch. 3ZA, para. 1(3): date by which payment to be made after amendment or correction of self assessment subject to postponement provisions of s. 55(6) and (9).
ICTA 1988, s. 306(8): claim for relief under the business expansion scheme (in relation to shares issued on or before 31 December 1993) or the enterprise investment scheme (in relation to shares issued on or after 1 January 1994) to precede an application under s. 55(3).
ICTA 1988, s. 374A(4)(a): assessment to recover certain amounts deducted under MIRAS to be treated as an assessment specified under s. 55(1).
ICTA 1988, s. 375(4): assessment of excess relief on payments relating to loan interest under MIRAS to be treated as an assessment specified under s. 55(1).
ICTA 1988, s. 747(4)(a): assessment as if corporation tax for liability in respect of a controlled foreign company.
ICTA 1988, s. 753(1), (3): notice or revised notice of direction regarding company with interest in a controlled foreign company.
ICTA 1988, Sch. 14, para. 6(2): TMA 1970 applies to any assessment to recover excess life assurance premium relief as though such an assessment were one specified in s. 55(1).
ICTA 1988, Sch. 16, para. 4(1), (9): due date for income tax under Sch. 16, 14 days from return period or from date of payment if outside an accounting period.
FA 1993, s. 173 and Sch. 19, para. 5; for 1992–93 and subsequent years, s. 55 applies, with modifications, to appeals by Lloyd's underwriting agents against inspectors' determinations of a syndicate's profits or losses and (para. 7(2)) effect of s. 55 in relation to an appeal by a Lloyd's syndicate member against a varied or modified determination of syndicate profits or losses (see ICTA 1988, s. 450 and Sch. 19A, para. 6 for prior years (from 1988–89)).
ICTA 1988, s. 754: special provisions as to assessment, recovery and postponement of tax in respect of a controlled foreign company.
FA 2000, Sch. 15, para. 40(7): application for postponement may not be made under s. 55(3) or s. 55(4) on the ground of eligibility for investment relief unless a claim has been made for the relief.

FA 2002, Sch. 16, para. 45: application for postponement may not be made under s. 55(3) or s. 55(4) on the ground of eligibility for community investment relief unless a claim has been made for the relief.
FA 2009, Sch. 53, para. 4: late payment interest in respect of amounts postponed under s. 55.
FA 2014, s. 227(9)(b): the period during which an accelerated payment notice is suspended under FA 2014, s. 227 does not count towards the periods mentioned in s. 55(8D).
SI 1987/352, reg. 6(6): TMA 1970 to apply to assessments made under those regulations (pension scheme surpluses) as if they were assessments as specified in s. 55(1).
SI 1987/530, reg. 14(2)(a): TMA 1970 to apply to assessments made under those regulations (entertainers and sportsmen) as if they were assessments as specified in s. 55(1).
SI 1989/469, reg. 28(3)(a): TMA 1970 to apply to assessments made under those regulations (personal equity plans) as if they were assessments as specified in s. 55(1).

HMRC Manuals – Company Taxation, vol. IV, CT10213: interaction of repayment claim under ICTA 1988, s. 10(4) and postponement application.

56 Payment of tax where there is a further appeal

56(1) This section applies if a party to an appeal against an assessment (the "initial appeal") makes a further appeal.

56(2) Tax is payable or repayable in accordance with the determination of the court or tribunal on the initial appeal, despite the further appeal having been made.

56(3) But in a case where the amount charged by the assessment is altered by the order or judgment of the Upper Tribunal or court–

(a) if too much tax has been paid, the amount overpaid shall be refunded with such interest, if any, as may be allowed by that order or judgment; and

(b) if too little tax has been charged, the amount undercharged shall be due and payable at the expiration of a period of thirty days beginning with the date on which HMRC issue to the other party a notice of the total amount payable in accordance with the order or judgment.

56(4) Subsection (5) applies where–

(a) an accelerated payment notice or partner payment notice has been given to a party to the appeal under Chapter 3 of Part 4 of the Finance Act 2014 (and not withdrawn), and

(b) the assessment has effect, or partly has effect, to counteract the whole or part of the asserted advantage (within the meaning of section 219(3) of that Act) by reason of which the notice was given.

56(5) If, on the application of HMRC, the relevant court or tribunal considers it necessary for the protection of the revenue, it may direct that subsection (2) does not apply so far as the tax relates to the counteraction of the whole or part of the asserted advantage, and–

(a) give permission to withhold all or part of any repayment, or

(b) require the provision of adequate security before repayment is made.

56(6) **"Relevant court or tribunal"** means the tribunal or court from which permission or leave to appeal is sought.

History – S. 56(4), (5) and (6) inserted by FA 2014, s. 225(1), with effect from 17 July 2014.
S. 56 substituted by SI 2009/56, art. 3(1) and Sch. 1, para. 35, operative from 1 April 2009, subject to transitional and saving provisions in SI 2009/56, Sch. 3. Former s. 56 read as follows:

"Statement of case for opinion of the High Court

56(1) [Omitted by SI 1994/1813, Sch. 1, para. 10(a).]
56(2) [Omitted by SI 1994/1813, Sch. 1, para. 10(a).]
56(3) Where a party to an appeal requires the Commissioners to state and sign a case under regulation 20(1) of the General Commissioners Regulations, he shall pay to the Commissioners a fee of £25 for and in respect of the same, before he is entitled to have the case stated.
56(4) [Omitted by SI 1994/1813, Sch. 1, para. 10(a).]
56(5) [Omitted by SI 1994/1813, Sch. 1, para. 10(a).]
56(6) The High Court shall hear and determine any question or questions of law arising on a case stated and transmitted to the High Court under regulation 22 of the General Commissioners Regulations and shall reverse, affirm or amend the determination in respect of which the case has been stated, or shall remit the matter to the Commissioners with the opinion of the Court thereon, or may make such other order in relation to the matter as to the Court may seem fit.
56(7) The High Court may cause the case to be sent back for amendment, and thereupon the case shall be amended accordingly, and judgment shall be delivered after it has been amended.
56(8) An appeal shall lie from the decision of the High Court to the Court of Appeal and thence to the House of Lords:
Provided that–

(a) no appeal shall lie to the House of Lords from the Court of Appeal unless leave has been given under and in accordance with section 1 of the Administration of Justice (Appeals) Act 1934, and

(b) this subsection has effect subject to Part II of the Administration of Justice Act 1969 (appeal from High Court to House of Lords).

56(9) Where a party to an appeal against an assessment has required a case to be stated under regulation 20(1) of the General Commissioners Regulations, then notwithstanding that the case has been required to be stated or is pending before the High Court, tax shall be paid in accordance with the determination of the Commissioners who have been required to state the case:
Provided that, if the amount charged by the assessment is altered by the order or judgment of the High Court, then–

(a) if too much tax has been paid the amount overpaid shall be refunded with such interest, if any, as the High Court may allow; or

(b) if too little tax has been charged, the amount undercharged shall be due and payable at the expiration of a period of thirty days beginning with the date on which the inspector issues to the other party a notice of the total amount payable in accordance with the order or judgment of that Court.

56(10) All matters within the jurisdiction of the High Court under this section shall be assigned in Scotland to the Court of Session sitting as the Court of Exchequer, and an appeal shall lie from the decision under this section of the Court of Session, as the Court of Exchequer in Scotland, to the House of Lords.

56(11) This section has effect in Northern Ireland subject to section 58 below.

History – S. 56(1), (2), (4), (5) omitted by SI 1994/1813, Sch. 1, para. 10(a), Sch. 2, Pt. I, with effect from 1 September 1994.
In s. 56(3) the words "the clerk to" repealed by TCEA 2007, s. 146 and Sch. 23, Pt. 1, with effect from 1 April 2009 (SI 2008/2696, art. 6(c)(i) – subject to transitional provisions at art. 3).
In s. 56(3) the words "Where a party to an appeal requires the Commissioners to state and sign a case under regulation 20(1) of the General Commissioners Regulations, he" substituted by SI 1994/1813, Sch. 1, para. 10(b), with effect from 1 September 1994.
S. 56(3) amended by FA 1984, s. 127 and Sch. 22, para. 6, substituting the sum of £25 with effect, by virtue of SI 1984/1836, from 1 January 1985.
In s. 56(6) the words "arising on a case stated and transmitted to the High Court under regulation 22 of the General Commissioners Regulations" substituted by SI 1994/1813, Sch. 1, para. 10(c), with effect from 1 September 1994.
S. 56(6) previously amended by FA 1985, Sch. 27, Pt. X, removing a reference to other officers of the Board, which related to development land tax.
In s. 56(9) the words "Where a party to an appeal against an assessment has required a case to be stated under regulation 20(1) of the General Commissioners Regulations, then notwithstanding that the case" substituted by SI 1994/1813, Sch. 1, para. 10(d), with effect from 1 September 1994.
S. 56(9) previously amended by FA 1989, s. 156(3), (4) for tax charged by an assessment, notice of which is issued after 30 July 1982 clarifying "the amount of" as being "the amount charged by" an assessment.

Cross references – S. 19A: case cannot be stated under s. 56 following determination of an appeal under s. 19A(6).
S. 33A: in relation to errors or mistakes in partnership statements, neither the representative partner nor the Board can require a case to be stated under s. 56 other than on a point of law arising in connection with the computation of profits.
ICTA 1988, s. 824(7), 825(6): no repayment supplement payable where the High Court allows such interest as in s. 55(9)(a).
SSCTFA 1999, s. 13(2)(a)(iii): power of the Board, with the concurrence of the Lord Chancellor and the Lord Advocate, to make regulations making provision with respect to appeals on contributions matters, including any of the matters dealt with in s. 56.
FA 2003, Sch. 17, para. 9(2)(c): corresponding provisions may be made for the purposes of Stamp Duty Land Tax.
SI 2003/1382: in the application of this Part of the Act to appeals under TCA 2002, s. 38 with effect from 18 June 2003, s. 56 is to be omitted.

Hansard – 22 March 1983, vol. 39, col. 394 (not reproduced): where a taxpayer has an appeal determined in his absence through failure to receive notice of the hearing, or through sickness, etc., if the commissioners are satisfied with the truth of the explanation for the failure to attend or submit documents, the inspector will not object to the commissioners recalling their determination and rehearing the appeal.

Other material – RSC, O. 91: procedure in the High Court on appeal from the general or special commissioners, as replaced by Civil Procedure Rules 1998 (SI 1998/3132), r. 50.1(3), Sch. 1, r. 91 as from 26 April 1999.

Notes – The following amendments to s. 56 never came into effect:

- In s. 56(8) the words "Supreme Court" substituted in the first place by Constitutional Reform Act 2005, s. 40 and Sch. 9, para. 21(2)(a), with effect from a day to be appointed.
- S. 56(8)(a) substituted by Constitutional Reform Act 2005, s. 40 and Sch. 9, para. 21(2)(b), with effect from a day to be appointed. New s. 56(8)(a) reads as follows:

  "(a) an appeal to the Supreme Court under this subsection lies only with the permission of the Court of Appeal or the Supreme Court, and"
- In s. 56(8)(b) the words "Supreme Court" substituted in each place by Constitutional Reform Act 2005, s. 40 and Sch. 9, para. 21(2)(c), with effect from a day to be appointed.
- In s. 56(10) the words "Supreme Court" substituted in each place by Constitutional Reform Act 2005, s. 40 and Sch. 9, para. 21(2)(c), with effect from a day to be appointed."

56A Appeals from the special commissioners

56A [Omitted by SI 2009/56, art. 3(1) and Sch. 1, para. 36.]

History – S. 56A omitted by SI 2009/56, art. 3(1) and Sch. 1, para. 36, operative from 1 April 2009, subject to transitional and saving provisions in SI 2009/56, Sch. 3.

56B Regulations about practice and procedure

56B [Omitted by SI 2009/56, art. 3(1) and Sch. 1, para. 36.]

History – S. 56B omitted by SI 2009/56, art. 3(1) and Sch. 1, para. 36, operative from 1 April 2009, subject to transitional and saving provisions in SI 2009/56, Sch. 3.

56C Power of Special Commissioners to order costs

56C [Omitted by SI 2009/56, art. 3(1) and Sch. 1, para. 36.]

History – S. 56C omitted by SI 2009/56, art. 3(1) and Sch. 1, para. 36, operative from 1 April 2009, subject to transitional and saving provisions in SI 2009/56, Sch. 3.

56D Power of Special Commissioners to publish reports of decisions

56D [Omitted by SI 2009/56, art. 3(1) and Sch. 1, para. 36.]

History – S. 56D omitted by SI 2009/56, art. 3(1) and Sch. 1, para. 36, operative from 1 April 2009, subject to transitional and saving provisions in SI 2009/56, Sch. 3.

CHARGEABLE GAINS

57 Regulations about appeals

57(1) The Commissioners for Her Majesty's Revenue and Customs may make regulations–

(a) as respects the conduct of appeals against assessments and decisions on claims under the 1992 Act,

(b) entitling persons, in addition to those who would be so entitled apart from the regulations, to be parties to such appeals,

(c) regulating the time within which such appeals or claims may be brought or made,

(d) where the market value of an asset on a particular date, or an apportionment or any other matter, may affect the liability to capital gains tax of two or more persons, enabling any such person to have the matter determined by the tribunal having jurisdiction to determine that matter if arising on an appeal against an assessment, and prescribing a procedure by which the matter is not determined differently on different occasions,

(e) authorising an officer of Revenue and Customs, notwithstanding the obligation as to secrecy imposed by virtue of this or any other Act, to disclose to a person entitled to appear on such an appeal the market value of an asset as determined by an assessment or decision on a claim, or to disclose to a person whose liability to tax may be affected by the determination of the market value of an asset on a particular date, or an apportionment or any other matter, any decision on the matter made by an officer of Revenue and Customs.

57(1A) Regulations under this section may not make provision for the practice and procedure to be followed in the First-tier Tribunal or Upper Tribunal.

57(2) [Repealed by FA 1971, Sch. 14, Pt. III.]

57(3) Regulations under this section may contain such supplemental and incidental provisions as appear to the Board to be expedient including in particular–

(a) [Omitted by SI 2009/56, art. 3(1) and Sch. 1, para. 37(4).]

(b) provisions corresponding to section 563 of the Capital Allowances Act (determination of apportionment affecting tax liability of two or more persons), and

(c) provisions authorising the giving of conditional decisions where, under section 46D of this Act or Tribunal Procedure Rules, questions on an appeal against an assessment or a decision on a claim may go partly to one tribunal and partly to another.

57(4) Regulations under this section–

(a) shall be made by statutory instrument subject to annulment in pursuance of a resolution of the House of Commons, and

(b) shall have effect notwithstanding anything in this Act.

History – In s. 57(1) the words "The Commissioners for Her Majesty's Revenue and Customs may make regulations" substituted for the words "The Board may make regulations"; in para. (b) the words "to be parties to" substituted for the words "to appear on" and in para. (e) the words "an officer of Revenue and Customs" substituted for the words "an inspector or other officer of the Board" twice by SI 2009/56, art. 3(1) and Sch. 1, para. 37(2), operative from 1 April 2009, subject to transitional and saving provisions in SI 2009/56, Sch. 3.

S. 57(1A) inserted by SI 2009/56, art. 3(1) and Sch. 1, para. 37(3), operative from 1 April 2009, subject to transitional and saving provisions in SI 2009/56, Sch. 3.

S. 57(2) repealed by FA 1971, Sch. 14, Pt. III.

S. 57(3)(a) omitted and in para. (c) the words "section 46D of this Act or Tribunal Procedure Rules" substituted for the words "section 46B, 46C or 46D of this Act" by SI 2009/56, art. 3(1) and Sch. 1, para. 37(4), operative from 1 April 2009, subject to transitional and saving provisions in SI 2009/56, Sch. 3.

S. 57(3)(b) substituted by CAA 2001, s. 578 and Sch. 2, para. 2 with effect as respects allowances and charges falling to be made for chargeable periods ending, for income tax purposes, on or after 6 April 2001, and for corporation tax purposes, on or after 1 April 2001. Under CAA 2001, Sch. 3, para. 8, where a person is affected by a change in the law brought into effect by CAA 2001, they may elect for the pre-consolidation law to apply for the chargeable period straddling the commencement of CAA 2001.

S. 57(3)(b) previously amended by CAA 1990, Sch. 1, para. 1(1), substituting reference to provisions of that Act on consolidation, for chargeable periods ending after 5 April 1990.

In s. 57(3)(c) reference to s. 46B–D substituted for previous reference to s. 47 by FA 1996, s. 136 and Sch. 22, para. 8, in relation to any proceedings relating to the year 1996–97 or any subsequent year of assessment, and any proceedings relating to an accounting period ending on or after 1 July 1999, the appointed day by virtue of FA 1994, s. 199(2), (3) and SI 1998/3173 (C. 78).

Reference to the 1992 Act in s. 57(1)(a) substituted by TCGA 1992, s. 290 and Sch. 10, para. 2(2).

Cross references – Sch. 3, para. 10: rules for assigning proceedings to general commissioners.

Statutory instruments – SI 1967/149 made under FA 1965, Sch. 10, para. 2, the predecessor of s. 57.

DEVELOPMENT LAND TAX

57A Regulations about appeals

57A(1)–(3) [Repealed by FA 1985, Sch. 27, Pt. X, with effect from 19 March 1985.]

PROCEDURAL RULES

57B *Commissioners: procedural rules*

57B [Repealed by F(No. 2)A 1992, s. 76 and Sch. 16, para. 5, s. 82 and Sch. 18, Pt. IX, with effect from 16 July 1992.]

NORTHERN IRELAND

History – This heading omitted by SI 2009/56, art. 3(1) and Sch. 1, para. 38, operative from 1 April 2009, subject to transitional and saving provisions in SI 2009/56, Sch. 3.

58 Proceedings in tax cases in Northern Ireland

58 [Omitted by SI 2009/56, art. 3(1) and Sch. 1, para. 38.]

History – S. 58 omitted by SI 2009/56, art. 3(1) and Sch. 1, para. 38, operative from 1 April 2009, subject to transitional and saving provisions in SI 2009/56, Sch. 3. Former s. 58 read as follows:

"Proceedings in tax cases in Northern Ireland

58(1) [Repealed by FA 1988, s. 134(2), (4), 148 and Sch. 14, Pt. IX.]

58(2) A case which is stated by the General Commissioners under regulation 22 of the General Commissioners Regulations in proceedings in Northern Ireland shall be a case for the opinion of the Court of Appeal in Northern Ireland, and the Taxes Acts shall have effect as if section 56 of this Act applied in relation to such proceedings–

(a) with the substitution for references to the High Court of references to the Court of Appeal in Northern Ireland, and

(b) with the omission of subsection (8) of that section,

and the procedure relating to the hearing and determination of the case by the Court of Appeal in Northern Ireland shall be that for the time being in force in Northern Ireland as respects cases stated by a county court in the exercise of its general jurisdiction.

58(2A) [Omitted by SI 1994/1813, Sch. 1, para. 12(b).]

58(2B) The Taxes Acts shall have effect as if section 56A of this Act applied in relation to any appeal to the Special Commissioners constituting proceedings in Northern Ireland–

(a) with the substitution for references to the High Court of references to the Court of Appeal in Northern Ireland, and

(b) with the omission of subsections (2) and (5) to (7).

58(2C) An appeal shall lie to the Supreme Court in accordance with section 42 of the Judicature (Northern Ireland) Act 1978 from a decision of the Court of Appeal in Northern Ireland on a case stated under regulation 22 of the General Commissioners Regulations or on an appeal under section 56A of this Act.

58(3) For the purposes of this section–

(a) **"proceedings in Northern Ireland"** means proceedings as respects which the place given by the rules in Schedule 3 to this Act is in Northern Ireland;

(b) proceedings under section 102, 113(5), 281(4), 343(10) or 783(9) of the principal Act (or the corresponding enactments repealed by that Act), section 186 of ITTOIA 2005, section 11 of or paragraph 22 of Schedule 7 to the Income and Corporation Taxes Act 1970 or section 563 of the Capital Allowances Act (determination of apportionment affecting tax liability of two or more persons) shall be proceedings in Northern Ireland if the place given by the rules in Schedule 3 to this Act in relation to each of the parties concerned in the proceedings is in Northern Ireland,

and sections 21 and 22 of the Interpretation Act (Northern Ireland) 1954 shall apply as if references in those provisions to any enactment included a reference to this section.

58(4) [Repealed by FA 1988, s. 148 and Sch. 14, Pt. IX.]

History – S. 58(1) repealed, and in s. 58(2) the former word "Special" before "Commissioners" omitted by FA 1988, s. 134(2), (4), 148 and Sch. 14, Pt. IX, with effect from 3 April 1989 (SI 1989/473).

S. 58(2) substituted by SI 1994/1813, Sch. 1, para. 12(a), with effect from 1 September 1994.

S. 58(2A) omitted and s. 58(2B), (2C) inserted by SI 1994/1813, Sch. 1, para. 12(b), with effect from 1 September 1994. Former s. 58(2A) was inserted, and s. 58(3) substituted, by FA 1988, s. 135(1), (2) and 324(4), with effect from 3 April 1989 (SI 1989/473).

In s. 58(2C) the words "Supreme Court" substituted for the words "House of Lords" by the Constitutional Reform Act 2005, s. 40 and Sch. 9, para. 21(4), with effect from 1 October 2009 (SI 2009/1604).

In s. 58(3)(b), the words "section 563 of the Capital Allowances Act (determination of apportionment affecting tax liability of two or more persons)" substituted for the words "section 151 of the Capital Allowances Act 1990 (proceedings to which more than one taxpayer is a party)" by CAA 2001, s. 578 and Sch. 2, para. 3 with effect as respects allowances and charges falling to be made for chargeable periods ending, for income tax purposes, on or after 6 April 2001, and for corporation tax purposes, on or after 1 April 2001. A reference to ITTOIA 2005, s. 186 inserted by ITTOIA 2005, s. 882(1) and Sch. 1, para. 375; effective for income tax purposes for 2005–06 onwards and for corporation tax purposes for accounting periods ending after 5 April 2005 (ITTOIA 2005, s. 883(1)).

In s. 58(3)(b), a reference to ICTA 1988 Sch. 13B was inserted by FA 1999 s. 30(4), (5) with effect from 2000–01 and repealed by TCA 2002 s. 60 and Sch. 6 with effect from 6 April 2003 (SI 2003/962). A reference to ICTA 1988, s. 260(3) repealed by FA 1999, s. 139 and Sch. 20, Pt. III(4) with effect for the year 2000–01 and subsequent years of assessment. S. 58(3)(b) was previously amended by CAA 1990, Sch. 1, para. 1(1), substituting reference to provisions of that Act on consolidation, for chargeable periods ending after 5 April 1990.

S. 58(4) repealed by FA 1988, s. 148 and Sch. 14, Pt. IX, with effect from 3 April 1989 (SI 1989/473).

Cross references – ICTA 1988, s. 102, 113(5) (for pre-6 April 1994 partnerships), 260(3), 281(4), 343(10) and 783(9): valuation of trading stock/work in progress; apportionment of profits on a continuation election; apportionment of additional personal allowance; determination of tax repayments to a wife; apportionment of receipts, expenses, assets or liabilities on company reconstructions without significant change of ownership; and apportionment of sums re certain leased assets.

OTA 1975, Sch. 2, para. 1(1): s. 58(2B), (2C), (3) apply with modifications for the purposes of oil taxation.

FA 1988, s. 134(6): s. 58(3) applies in respect of the transfer of certain proceedings from the special to the general commissioners after 3 April 1989.

FA 2003, Sch. 17, para. 9(2)(c) and (3)(c): provisions corresponding with s. 56 and s. 56A (as modified by s. 58) may be made for the purposes of stamp duty land tax.

SI 1994/1813, reg. 1(2): in s. 58(2) and (2C), the words "General Commissioners" shall be construed in accordance with TMA 1970, s. 2(1), with effect from 1 September 1994.

SI 1994/1813, reg. 1(2): in s. 58(2B), the words "Special Commissioners" are construed in accordance with TMA 1970, s. 4(1).

SI 2003/1382: in the application of this Part of the Act to appeals under TCA 2002, s. 38 with effect from 18 June 2003, s. 58 is to be omitted.

SI 2004/1363, reg. 25ff: modification of s. 58 for the purposes of SDLT.

Reg. 25(2): modification of s. 58(2B) inserting "as modified by regulation 25 of the Stamp Duty Land Tax (Appeals) Regulations 2004" after "section 56A of this Act", in relation to appeals from the general and special commissioners.

SI 2004/1363, reg. 25(2): modification of s. 58(3)(a) substituting "regulations 7 to 13 and 15 of the Stamp Duty Land Tax (Appeals) Regulations 2004" for "the rules in Schedule 3 to this Act", in relation to appeals from the general and special commissioners.

SI 2004/1363, reg. 26(8)–(10): modification of s. 58 in relation to referrals to the special commissioners under Sch. 10, para. 19 and Sch. 11, para. 12.

SI 2004/1363, reg. 26(12): modification of s. 58 omitting s. 58(2C) in relation to referrals to the special commissioners under Sch. 10, para. 19 and Sch. 11, para. 12."

59 Election for county court in Northern Ireland

59 [Repealed by FA 1988, s. 134(2), (4), 148 and Sch. 14, Pt. IX, with effect from 3 April 1989 (SI 1989/473 (C 17)).]

PART VA – PAYMENT OF TAX

History – Pt. VA inserted by FA 1994, s. 192–195, in so far as it relates to income tax and capital gains tax, as respects the year 1996–97 and subsequent years of assessment and, in so far as it relates to corporation tax, as respects accounting periods ending on or after 1 July 1999, the appointed day by virtue of FA 1994, s. 199(2), (3) and SI 1998/3173 (C. 78).

INCOME TAX AND CAPITAL GAINS TAX

History – Heading "INCOME TAX AND CAPITAL GAINS TAX" added by FA 1998, Sch. 19, para. 29(1) as respects accounting periods ending on or after 1 July 1999, the appointed day by virtue of FA 1994, s. 199(2), (3) and SI 1998/3173 (C. 78).

59A Payments on account of income tax

59A(1) Subject to subsection (9) below, this section applies to any person (the taxpayer) as regards a year of assessment if as regards the immediately preceding year–

(a) he is assessed to income tax under section 9 of this Act in any amount, and

(b) that amount (the assessed amount) exceeds the amount of any income tax which has been deducted at source, and

(c) the amount of the excess (the relevant amount) is not less than such amount as may be prescribed by regulations made by the Board, and

(d) the proportion which the relevant amount bears to the assessed amount is not less than such proportion as may be so prescribed.

59A(2) Subject to subsection (3) below, the taxpayer shall make two payments on account of his liability to income tax for the year of assessment–

(a) the first on or before the 31st January in that year, and

(b) the second on or before the next following 31st July;

and, subject to subsections (4) to (4B) below, each of those payments on account shall be of an amount equal to 50 per cent of the relevant amount.

59A(3) If, at any time before the 31st January next following the year of assessment, the taxpayer makes a claim under this subsection stating–

(a) his belief that he will not be assessed to income tax for that year, or that the amount in which he will be so assessed will not exceed the amount of income tax deducted at source, and

(b) his grounds for that belief,

each of the payments on account shall not be, and shall be deemed never to have been, required to be made.

59A(4) If, at any time before the 31st January next following the year of assessment, the taxpayer makes a claim under this subsection stating–

(a) his belief that the amount in which he will be assessed to income tax for that year will exceed the amount of income tax deducted at source by a stated amount which is less than the relevant amount, and

(b) his grounds for that belief,

the amount of each of the payments on account required to be made shall be, and shall be deemed always to have been, equal to 50 per cent of the stated amount.

59A(4A) If as regards the year immediately preceding the year of assessment–

(a) the taxpayer is assessed to income tax under section 9 of this Act after the date on or before which either payment on account is required to be made, or

(b) his assessment to income tax under that section is amended after that date

then, subject to subsections (3) and (4) above and subsection (4B) below and to any subsequent application of this subsection, the amount of the payment on account shall be, and shall be deemed always to have been, equal to 50 per cent of the relevant amount as determined on the basis of the assessment or, as the case may be, the assessment as amended.

59A(4B) *If as regards the year immediately preceding the year of assessment the taxpayer is assessed to* income tax under section 29 of this Act in any amount, then, subject to subsections (3) and (4) above and to any subsequent application of this subsection, the amount of each payment on account shall be, and shall be deemed always to have been, the total of–

(a) the amount which, immediately before the making of the assessment under section 29, is the amount of that payment, and

(b) an amount equal to 50 per cent of the amount in which he is assessed under that assessment;

and if that assessment is varied, the amount in which he is assessed under it shall be taken for the purposes of paragraph (b) above to be the amount of the assessment as varied.

59A(5) Where the taxpayer makes a claim under subsection (3) or (4) above or subsection (4A) or (4B) above applies there shall be made all such adjustments, whether by the repayment of amounts paid on account, by the making of payments or further payments on account or otherwise, as may be required to give effect to the provisions of that subsection.

59A(6) Where the taxpayer fraudulently or negligently makes any incorrect statement in connection with a claim under subsection (3) or (4) above, he shall be liable to a penalty not exceeding the difference between–

(a) the amount which would have been payable on account if he had made a correct statement, and

(b) the amount of the payment on account (if any) made by him.

59A(7) [Omitted by FA 2015, s. 37 and Sch. 7, para. 50.]

59A(8) In this section, in relation to a year of assessment, any reference to the amount of any income tax deducted at source is a reference to the amount by which the aggregate of the following, namely–

(a) any income tax deducted or treated as deducted from any income, or treated as paid on any income, in respect of the year, and

(b) any amounts which, in respect of the year, are to be deducted at source under PAYE regulations in subsequent years,

exceeds the aggregate of any amounts which, in the year, are deducted at source under the PAYE regulations in respect of previous years.

59A(9) If, at any time before the 31st January next following a year of assessment, an officer of the Board so directs–

(a) this section shall not apply, and shall be deemed never to have applied, as regards that year to any person specified in the direction; and

(b) there shall be made all such adjustments, whether by the repayment of amounts paid on account or otherwise, as may be required to give effect to the direction.

59A(10) PAYE regulations may provide that, for the purpose of determining the amount of any such excess as is mentioned in subsection (1) above, any necessary adjustments in respect of matters prescribed by the regulations shall be made to the amount of tax deducted at source under PAYE regulations.

History – S. 59A(4B), and references to that subsection in s. 59A(2), (4A) and (5), inserted by FA 1996, s. 132 and Sch. 18, para. 2, generally as respects 1996–97 and subsequent years of assessment, and, so far as relating to partnerships whose trades, professions or businesses were set up or commenced before 6 April 1994, with effect as respects the 1997–98 and subsequent years of assessment.
S. 59A(7) omitted by FA 2015, s. 37 and Sch. 7, para. 50, with effect in relation to disposals made on or after 6 April 2015.
In s. 59A(8)(b), the words "or are tax credits to which section 397(1) or 397A(1) of ITTOIA 2005 applies," omitted by FA 2016, s. 5 and Sch. 1 para. 51(8), with effect in relation to dividends paid or arising (or treated as paid), and other distributions made (or treated as made) in the tax year 2016–17 or at any later time.
In s. 59A(8)(b), "397A(1)" substituted for "397A(2)" by FA 2009, s. 40 and Sch. 19, para. 9(d), with effect for:

- qualifying distributions arising on or after 22 April 2009;
- cash dividends paid over to a person under ITEPA 2003, Sch. 2, para. 68(4) on or after 22 April 2009;
- dividends treated under ITTOIA 2005, s. 407 as paid to a person on or after 22 April 2009; and
- manufactured overseas dividends that are representative of any of the above distributions (FA 2009, Sch. 19, para. 14(1)).

In s. 59A(8)(b), the reference to ITTOIA 2005, s. 397A(2) inserted by FA 2008, s. 34 and Sch. 12, para. 13, with effect for 2008–09 and subsequent tax years.
In s. 59A(8)(b), the reference to ITTOIA 2005, s. 397(1) substituted by ITTOIA 2005, s. 882(1) and Sch. 1, para. 376; effective for 2005–06 onwards (ITTOIA 2005, s. 883(1)).
In s. 59A(8), the words "PAYE regulations" substituted by FA 2003, s. 145(7)(a) with effect from 10 July 2003.
In s. 59A(8)(b), the words "PAYE regulations" substituted by ITEPA 2003, Sch. 6, para. 130(a) which has effect for the tax year 2003–04 and subsequent tax years. In addition the words "the principal Act" substituted for "that Act" by FA 2004, s. 92 and Sch. 17, para 10(1) with effect from 22 July 2004.
S. 59A(10) inserted by FA 1996, s. 119(1), as respects the year 1996–97 and subsequent years of assessment.
In s. 59A(10), the words "PAYE regulations" substituted by ITEPA 2003, Sch. 6, para. 130(b) which has effect for the tax year 2003–04 and subsequent tax years.
In s. 59A(10) the words "PAYE regulations" substituted by FA 2003, s. 145(7)(b) with effect from 10 July 2003.
S. 59A inserted by FA 1994, s. 192 with respect to 1996–97 and subsequent years. Subs. (1), (2) and (5) amended by FA 1995, s. 108(1), (2), (4), subs. (4A) inserted by FA 1995 s. 108(3) and subs. (8) and (9) substituted in order to correct deficiencies in original legislation.

Cross references – TMA 1970, s. 86: interest on overdue tax.
TMA 1970, s. 107A(2): liability of trustees to make payments on account.
ICTA 1988, s. 42A(6): s. 59A may be modified by regulations regarding the taxation of the income of non-residents which is derived from property in the UK.
ICTA 1988, s. 824(3)(a): time from which entitlement to repayment supplement runs as respects the year 1996–97 and subsequent years of assessment.
ICTA 1988, s. 824(4): order of attribution of repayment of income tax to a person for a year of assessment.
FA 1995, Sch. 21, para. 2: payments on account of income tax for 1996–97.
FA 2004, s. 108(3): special withholding tax to be treated as income tax deducted at source for the purposes of this section.

SI 1996/781: as respects the year 1996–97 and subsequent years of assessment, for the purposes of repayment supplement, Lloyd's income (other than syndicate income) received under deduction of tax or tax credits received (other than in respect of syndicate income) are related to the year of assessment in which the underwriting year ends.
SI 1996/782: as respects the year 1995–96, for the purposes of repayment supplement, Lloyd's income (other than syndicate income) received under deduction of tax or tax credits received (other than in respect of syndicate income) are related to the year of assessment in which the underwriting year ends.
SI 1996/1654, reg. 1(2), 3: as respects the year 1996–97 and subsequent years of assessment, the prescribed amount for the purposes of s. 59A(1)(c) is £500.
SI 1996/1654, reg. 1(3), 4: as respects the year 1997–98 and subsequent years of assessment, the prescribed proportion for the purposes of s. 59A(1)(d) (i.e. the proportion which the relevant amount as mentioned in s. 59A(1)(c) bears to the assessed amount as mentioned in s. 59A(1)(b)) is the proportion of one to four.
SI 2001/56, reg. 3(2)(g) (incentive payments for electronic communication of individuals' returns): Board's direction may specify a condition that tax payable is paid in accordance with the provisions of s. 59A and s. 59B.
SI 2003/2682, reg. 185: adjustments in respect of tax that should have been deducted through PAYE.
FA 2009, s. 111(1)(a)(a): managed payment plans in respect of income tax payable under s. 59A(2).
FA 2009, Sch. 53, para. 1: late payment interest in respect of amounts claimed under s. 59A(3), (4).

Statutory instruments – SI 1996/1654 as amended by SI 1997/2491 (made under s. 59A(1)).
SI 2003/2682 PAYE regulations.
SI 2008/838: made under s. 59A(1).

Other material – Tax Bulletin TB04/98-4: personal insolvency under self assessment.
Tax Bulletin TB04/96-4: table of effective dates of payment when tax paid after 5 April 1996 by cheque, electronic funds transfer, bank giro, or girobank.
IR press release, 29 July 1996: self assessment: provision of information from taxpayer statements of account to authorised agents.

59AA Non-resident CGT disposals: payments on account of capital gains tax

59AA(1) Subsections (2) and (3) apply where a person ("P") is required to make, in relation to a tax year, an NRCGT return in respect of one or more non-resident CGT disposals containing an advance self-assessment and the amount in subsection (6)(a) is greater than the amount in subsection (6)(b).

59AA(2) With effect from the filing date for the return, the balancing amount is (or, where applicable, becomes) the amount payable by P on account of P's liability to capital gains tax for the tax year.

59AA(3) Where P is the relevant members of an NRCGT group, P is responsible for discharging the obligation of the taxable person to pay any balancing amounts and such amounts are payable on account of the taxable person's liability to capital gains tax for the tax year.

59AA(4) Subsection (5) applies where a person ("P") is required to make, in relation to a tax year, an NRCGT return containing an advance self-assessment and the amount in subsection (6)(a) is less than the amount in subsection (6)(b).

59AA(5) The balancing amount is repayable to P on the filing date for the return.

59AA(6) The amounts referred to in subsections (1) and (4) are–

(a) the amount notionally chargeable contained in the self-assessment, and

(b) the total of any amounts previously paid under this section on account of P's liability to capital gains tax for the tax year.

59AA(7) In subsections (2) and (5) **"the balancing amount"** means the difference between those amounts.

59AA(8) Where, in the case of a repayment, the NRCGT return is enquired into by an officer of Revenue and Customs–

(a) nothing in subsection (5) requires the repayment to be made before the day on which, by virtue of section 28A(1), the enquiry is completed, but

(b) the officer may at any time before that day make the repayment, on a provisional basis, to such extent as the officer thinks fit.

59AA(9) Subsection (10) applies to–

(a) any amount payable on account of capital gains tax as a result of the amendment or correction under section 12ZK, 12ZL or 28A of an advance self-assessment, and

(b) any amount paid on account of capital gains tax which is repayable as a result of such an amendment or correction.

59AA(10) The amount is payable or (as the case may be) repayable on or before the day specified by the relevant provision of Schedule 3ZA.

59AA(11) Subsection (12) applies where a determination under section 28G (determination of amount notionally chargeable where no NRCGT return delivered) which has effect as a person's advance self-assessment is superseded by an advance self-assessment in an NRCGT return made and delivered by the person under section 12ZB.

59AA(12) Any amount which is payable on account of capital gains tax, and any amount paid on account of capital gains tax which is repayable, by virtue of the supersession is to be payable or (as the case may be) repayable on or before the filing date for the return.

59AA(13) In this section–

"advance self-assessment" has the meaning given by section 12ZE(1);

"amount notionally chargeable" is to be interpreted in accordance with section 12ZF(1);

"filing date", in relation to an NRCGT return, has the meaning given by section 12ZB(8);

the **"taxable person"**, in relation to a non-resident CGT disposal, means the person who would be chargeable to capital gains tax in respect of any chargeable NRCGT gain accruing on the disposal (were such a gain to accrue).

59AA(14) For the meaning in this section of **"non-resident CGT disposal"** see section 14B of the 1992 Act.

59AA(15) For the meaning in this section of **"NRCGT group"** see section 288(1) of the 1992 Act.

History – S. 59AA inserted by FA 2015, s. 37 and Sch. 7, para. 51, with effect in relation to disposals made on or after 6 April 2015.

59AB Amounts payable on account: recovery

59AB The provisions of the Taxes Acts as to the recovery of tax shall apply to an amount falling to be paid on account of tax in the same manner as they apply to an amount of tax.

History – S. 59AB inserted by FA 2015, s. 37 and Sch. 7, para. 51, with effect in relation to disposals made on or after 6 April 2015.

59B Payments of income tax and capital gains tax: assessments other than simple assessments

History – In the heading the words ": assessments other than simple assessments" inserted by FA 2016, s. 167 and Sch. 23, para. 7(2), with effect in relation to the 2016–17 tax year and subsequent years.

59B(1) Subject to subsection (2) below, the difference between–

(a) the amount of income tax and capital gains tax contained in a person's self-assessment under section 9 of this Act for any year of assessment, and

(b) the aggregate of any payments on account made by him in respect of that year (whether under section 59A or 59AA of this Act or otherwise) and any income tax which in respect of that year has been deducted at source,

shall be payable by him or (as the case may be) repayable to him as mentioned in subsection (3) or (4) below but nothing in this subsection shall require the repayment of any income tax treated as deducted or paid by virtue of section 246D(1), of the principal Act, section 626 of ITEPA 2003 or section 399(2) or 530(1) of ITTOIA 2005.

59B(2) The following, namely–

(a) any amount which, in the year of assessment, is deducted at source under PAYE regulations in respect of a previous year, and

(b) any amount which, in respect of the year of assessment, is to be deducted at source under PAYE regulations in a subsequent year,

shall be respectively deducted from and added to the aggregate mentioned in subsection (1)(b) above.

59B(2A) The reference in subsection (1)(b) to payments on account under section 59AA does not include any amounts already repaid under section 59AA(5).

59B(3) In a case where the person–

(a) gave the notice required by section 7 of this Act within six months from the end of the year of assessment, but

(b) was not given notice under section 8 or 8A of this Act until after the 31st October next following that year,

the difference shall be payable or repayable at the end of the period of three months beginning with the day on which the notice under section 8 or 8A was given.

59B(4) In any other case, the difference shall be payable or repayable on or before the 31st January next following the year of assessment.

59B(4ZA) In a case in which the notice required by section 7 was given following the receipt of a notice under section 8B, subsections (3) and (4) apply as if–

(a) the reference to the notice required by section 7 were a reference to the original notice required by that section, and

(b) the references to notice under section 8 or 8A were references to the original notice under that section.

59B(4ZB) In subsection (4ZA) the references to original notices are to notices given before the notice under section 8B.

59B(4A) Where in the case of a repayment the return on the basis of which the person's self-assessment was made under section 9 of this Act is enquired into by an officer of the Board–

(a) nothing in subsection (3) or (4) above shall require the repayment to be made before the day on which, by virtue of section 28A(1) of this Act, the enquiry is completed; but

(b) the officer may at any time before that day make the repayment, on a provisional basis, to such extent as he thinks fit.

59B(5) An amount of tax which is payable or repayable as a result of the amendment or correction of a self-assessment under–

(a) section 9ZA, 9ZB, 9C or 28A of this Act (amendment or correction of return under section 8 or 8A of this Act), or

(b) section 12ABA(3)(a), 12ABB(6)(a), 28B(4)(a), 30B(2)(a), 33A(4)(a) or 50(9)(a) of this Act (amendment of partner's return to give effect to amendment or correction of partnership return),

is payable (or repayable) on or before the day specified by the relevant provision of Schedule 3ZA to this Act.

59B(5A) Where a determination under section 28C of this Act which has effect as a person's self-assessment is superseded by his self-assessment under section 9 of this Act, any amount of tax which is payable or repayable by virtue of the supersession shall be payable or (as the case may be) repayable on or before the day given by subsection (3) or (4) above.

59B(6) Any amount of income tax or capital gains tax which is payable by virtue of an assessment made otherwise than under section 9, 28H or 28I of this Act shall, unless otherwise provided, be payable on the day following the end of the period of 30 days beginning with the day on which the notice of assessment is given.

59B(7) In this section any reference to income tax deducted at source is a reference to income tax deducted or treated as deducted from any income or treated as paid on any income.

But such a reference does not include income tax repaid on a claim for repayment of income tax which–

(a) is treated as having been paid by virtue of section 520(4) of ITA 2007 (gift aid relief: income tax treated as paid by trustees of charitable trust), or

(b) has been deducted at source from income to which section 532, 533, 536 or 537 of that Act (certain sources of income exempt from income tax) applies.

59B(8) PAYE regulations may provide that, for the purpose of determining the amount of the difference mentioned in subsection (1) above, any necessary adjustments in respect of matters prescribed by the regulations shall be made to the amount of tax deducted at source under PAYE regulations.

History – In s. 59B(1), the words ", 400(2), 414(1), 421(1)" (which appeared after the words "section 399(2)") omitted by FA 2016, s. 5 and Sch. 1 para. 51(9)(a), with effect for the tax year 2016–17 and subsequent tax years.

In s. 59B(1), the final words beginning "but nothing in this subsection" inserted by FA 1996 s. 122(2) with respect to 1996–97 and subsequent years.

In s. 59B(1), the words "or 547(5) of the principal Act or section 626 of ITEPA 2003" substituted by ITEPA 2003, Sch. 6, para. 131(2) which has effect for the tax year 2003–04 and subsequent tax years.

In s. 59B(1) references to ICTA 1988, s. 233(1), 249(4), 421(1) and 547(5) omitted by ITTOIA 2005, s. 882(1) and Sch. 1, para. 377(2)(a) and repealed by ITTOIA 2005, s. 884 and Sch. 3; effective for 2005–06 onwards (ITTOIA 2005, s. 883(1)). References to ITTOIA 2005, s. 399(2), 400(2), 414(1), 421(1) and 530(1) substituted by ITTOIA 2005, s. 882(1) and Sch. 1, para. 377(2)(b); effective for 2005–06 onwards ((ITTOIA 2005, s. 883(1)).

In s. 59B(1)(b), the words "or 59AA" inserted by FA 2015, s. 37 and Sch. 7, para. 52(2), with effect in relation to disposals made on or after 6 April 2015.

In s. 59B(2)(b), the words "or is a tax credit to which section 397(1) or 397A(1) of ITTOIA 2005 applies," (which appeared after the word "year,") omitted by FA 2016, s. 5 and Sch. 1 para. 51(9)(b), with effect for the tax year 2016–17 and subsequent tax years.

In s. 59B(2)(b), "397A(1)" substituted for "397A(2)" by FA 2009, s. 40 and Sch. 19, para. 9(d), with effect for:

- qualifying distributions arising on or after 22 April 2009;
- cash dividends paid over to a person under ITEPA 2003, Sch. 2, para. 68(4) on or after 22 April 2009;
- dividends treated under ITTOIA 2005, s. 407 as paid to a person on or after 22 April 2009; and
- manufactured overseas dividends that are representative of any of the above distributions (FA 2009, Sch. 19, para. 14(1)).

In s. 59B(2)(a), the words "PAYE regulations" substituted by ITEPA 2003, Sch. 6, para. 131(3) which has effect for the tax year 2003–04 and subsequent tax years.

In s. 59B(2)(b), the reference to ITTOIA 2005, s. 397A(2) inserted by FA 2008, s. 34 and Sch. 12, para. 14, with effect for 2008–09 and subsequent tax years.

In s. 59B(2)(b), the words "PAYE regulations" substituted by FA 2003, s. 145(7)(b) with effect from 10 July 2003.

In s. 59B(2)(b), reference to ITTOIA 2005, s. 397(1) substituted by ITTOIA 2005, s. 882(1) and Sch. 1, para. 377(3); effective for 2005–06 onwards ((ITTOIA 2005, s. 883(1)).

S. 59B(2A) inserted by FA 2015, s. 37 and Sch. 7, para. 52(3), with effect in relation to disposals made on or after 6 April 2015.

S. 59B(4ZA) and (4ZB) inserted by FA 2013, s. 233 and Sch. 51, para. 5, with effect in relation to a return under TMA 1970, s. 12AA for a partnership which includes one or more companies, in respect of a return for a relevant period (a period in respect of which a return is required) beginning on or after 6 April 2012 and in relation to a return under that section for any other partnership, or a return under TMA 1970, s. 8 or 8A, in respect of a return for a year of assessment beginning on or after 6 April 2012.

In s. 59B(4A)(a), "28A(1)" substituted for "28A(5)" and "the enquiry is" substituted for "the officer's enquiries are treated as" and subs. (5) substituted, all by FA 2001, s. 88, Sch. 29, para. 14 with effect from 11 May 2001 in relation to returns whether made before or after that date and whether relating to periods before or after then.

S. 59B(4A) inserted by FA 1996, s. 127 with respect to 1996–97 and subsequent years.

S. 59B(5A) inserted by FA 1996, s. 125(4) with respect to 1996–97 and subsequent years.

In s. 59B(6) the words ", 28H or 28I" inserted by FA 2016, s. 167 and Sch. 23, para. 7(3), with effect in relation to the 2016–17 tax year and subsequent years.
In s. 59B(6) the words "otherwise than under section 9 of this Act shall, unless otherwise provided" substituted for "under section 29 of this Act shall" by FA 1995, s. 115(6) with respect to 1996–97 and subsequent years.
S. 59B(7) amended by FA 2012, s. 51 and Sch. 15, para. 9, with effect in relation to income tax repaid on gifts made or income received on or after 6 April 2006. Accordingly, any reference in that amendment to a provision of ITA 2007 is to be read as including a reference to any corresponding earlier enactment which was rewritten in that provision.
S. 59B(8) inserted by FA 1996, s. 126(2) with respect to 1996–97 and subsequent years.
In s. 59B(8), the words "PAYEregulations" substituted for the words "that section" by FA 2003, s. 145(7)(b) with effect from 10 July 2003.
In s. 59B(8), the words "PAYE regulations" substituted for the words "Regulations under section 203 of the principal Act (PAYE)" by ITEPA 2003, Sch. 6, para. 131(4) which has effect for the tax year 2003–04 and subsequent tax years.
S. 59B inserted by FA 1994, s. 193 with respect to 1996–97 and subsequent years, in order to correct deficiencies in original legislation.

Cross references – TMA 1970, s. 42(3A): claims in connection with prior years.
TMA 1970, s. 86: interest on overdue tax.
Sch. 3ZA, para. 1(2) (date for payment after amendment or correction of self assessment): priority of later date given by s. 59B(3), (4) over date given by Sch. 3ZA.
ICTA 1988, s. 824(3)(a): time from which entitlement to repayment supplement runs as respects the year 1996–97 and subsequent years.
ICTA 1988, ICTA 1988,s. 824(4): order of attribution of repayment of income tax to a person for a year of assessment
ICTA 1988, Sch. 4A, para. 7(3), 9(4): effect of creative artists averaging claim on aggregate amount of payments per s. 59B(1)(b).
FA 1995, Sch. 21, para. 3(1), (3): partnership taxation for 1996–97.
FA 2004, s. 108(3) and s. 109(4): special withholding tax to be treated as income tax deducted at source for the purposes of this section.
FA 2009, s. 111(1)(b): managed payment plans in respect of capital gains tax payable under s. 59B.
FA 2009, Sch. 56: penalties for failure to make payments under s. 59B(3), (4), (5A), (5), (6) on time (subject to commencement order)
SI 2001/56, reg. 3(2)(g) (incentive payments for electronic communication of individuals' returns): Board's direction may specify a condition that tax payable is paid in accordance with the provisions of s. 59A and s. 59B.
SI 2003/2682, reg. 185: adjustments in respect of tax that should have been deducted through PAYE.

Statutory instruments – SI 2003/2682 PAYE regulations.

Other material – Tax Bulletin TB04/96-4: table of effective dates of payment when tax paid after 5 April 1996 by cheque, electronic funds transfer, bank giro, or girobank.
IR press release, 31 May 2000: launch of voluntary tax savings scheme, at Barclay's Bank, for share fishermen.

59BA Payment of income tax and capital gains tax: simple assessments

59BA(1) This section applies where a person has been given a simple assessment in relation to a year of assessment.

59BA(2) Subject to subsection (3), the difference between–

(a) the amount of income tax and capital gains tax for that year contained in the simple assessment, and

(b) the aggregate of any payments on account made by the person in respect of that year (whether under section 59A or 59AA or otherwise) and any income tax which in respect of that year has been deducted at source,

is payable by that person as mentioned in subsection (4) or (5).

59BA(3) Nothing in subsection (2) is to be read as requiring the repayment of any income tax which any provision of the Income Tax Acts provides is not repayable.

59BA(4) In a case where the person is given notice of the simple assessment after the 31st October next after the year of assessment, the difference is payable at the end of the period of 3 months after the day on which that notice was given.

59BA(5) In any other case the difference is payable on or before the 31st January next after the end of the year of assessment.

59BA(6) Section 59B(7) (which explains references to income tax deducted at source) applies for the purposes of this section.

59BA(7) PAYE regulations may provide that, for the purpose of determining the amount of the difference mentioned in subsection (2), any necessary adjustments in respect of matters prescribed in the regulations shall be made to the amount of tax deducted at source under PAYE regulations.

History – S. 59BA inserted by FA 2016, s. 167 and Sch. 23, para. 8, with effect in relation to the 2016–17 tax year and subsequent years.

59C Surcharges on unpaid income tax and capital gains tax

59C [Omitted by SI 2011/702, art. 5.]

History – S. 59C omitted by SI 2011/702, art. 5, with effect from 1 April 2011, but subject to SI 2011/702, art. 23, which provides that the omission does not have effect in relation to a return or other document which is required to be made or delivered to HMRC, or an amount of tax which is payable, in relation to the tax year 2009–10 or any previous tax year.

CORPORATION TAX

History – Heading "CORPORATION TAX" added by FA 1998, Sch. 19, para. 29(2) as respects corporation tax accounting periods under self-assessment. See history note for further details.

59D General rule as to when corporation tax is due and payable

59D(1) Corporation tax for an accounting period is due and payable on the day following the expiry of nine months from the end of that period.

59D(2) If the tax payable is then exceeded by the total of any relevant amounts previously paid (as stated in the relevant company tax return), the excess shall be repaid.

59D(3) The tax payable means the amount computed in accordance with the first to fourth steps of paragraph 8 of Schedule 18 to the Finance Act 1998.

59D(4) Relevant amounts previously paid means any of the following, so far as relating to the accounting period in question–

(a) any amount of corporation tax paid by the company and not repaid;

(b) any corporation tax refund surrendered to the company by another group company;

(c) any amount by which the sums available for set off under Step 4 of the calculation in paragraph 8 of Schedule 18 to the Finance Act 1998 (amounts set off against overall tax liability) exceeds the amount against which they may be set off under that provision;

(d) any amount treated as corporation tax paid in respect of profits of the company by virtue of regulations under section 62 of the Finance Act 2004 (deductions from payments to sub-contractors).

59D(5) This section has effect subject to section 59E and section 357YQ of CTA 2010 (assessment of tax chargeable on restitution interest).

History – In s. 59D(3) the words "the first to fourth steps of" inserted by F(No. 2)A 2015, s. 38(4)(a), with effect in relation to interest (whether arising before or on or after 21 October 2015) which falls within F(No. 2)A 2015, s. 38(11).
In s. 59D(4)(d) the words "by virtue of regulations under section 62 of the Finance Act 2004" substituted by FA 2004 s. 76 and Sch. 12, para. 2 with effect from 6 April 2007 (FA 2004, s. 77).
In s. 59D(4)(d), words "under section 559" substituted by FA 2002, s. 40(3), with effect in relation to deductions made under s. 559 on or after 6 April 2002.
In s. 59D(5) the words "and section 357YQ of CTA 2010 (assessment of tax chargeable on restitution interest)" inserted by F(No. 2)A 2015, s. 38(4)(b), with effect in relation to interest (whether arising before or on or after 21 October 2015) which falls within F(No. 2)A 2015, s. 38(11).
S. 59D substituted (together with s. 59DA) by FA 1998, s. 117(3) and Sch. 19, para. 29(2), with effect in relation to corporation tax accounting periods ending on or after 1 July 1999, the self-assessment appointed day by virtue of FA 1994, s. 199(2), (3) and SI 1998/3173 (C. 78).
Former s. 59D inserted by FA 1994, s. 195 as respects accounting periods ending on or after the appointed day.

Cross references – F(No. 2)A 2015, Sch. 3, para. 16(10) (banking companies): in s. 59D(5), the reference to s. 59E is to be read as including a reference to F(No. 2)A 2015, Sch. 3, para. 16(5)–(9).
F(No. 2)A 2015, Sch. 3, para. 14(10) (banking companies): in s. 59D(5), the reference to s. 59E is to be read as including a reference to F(No. 2)A 2015, Sch. 3, para. 14(5)–(9).
F(No. 2)A 2015, Sch. 2, para. 1(9) (bank levy): in s. 59D(5), the reference to s. 59E is to be read as including a reference to F(No. 2)A 2015, Sch. 2, para. 1(4)–(8).
FA 2015, s. 76(11) (bank levy): in s. 59D(5), the reference to s. 59E is to be read as including a reference to FA 2015, s. 76(5)–(10).
FA 2013, s. 202(12) (bank levy): in s. 59D(5) the reference to s. 59E is to be read as including a reference to s. 202(6)–(11).
FA 2012, Sch. 34, para. 12: reference in s. 59D(5) to s. 59E to be read as including a reference to that paragraph.
ICTA 1988, s. 419: due date for tax on loans to participators etc. by close company.
FA 1998, Sch. 18, para. 38: determination of amount due may be accompanied by notice determining the due date.
SI 1998/3175: provisions for payment of corporation tax by instalments by large companies.
FA 2009, s. 111(1)(c): managed payment plans in respect of corporation tax payable under s. 59D.

59DA Claim for repayment in advance of liability being established

59DA(1) This section applies where a company has paid an amount of corporation tax for an accounting period and the circumstances of the company change, so that the company has grounds for believing that the amount paid exceeds its probable tax liability although that liability has not been finally established.

59DA(2) The company may, by notice given to an officer of the Board, claim repayment of the excess.

No such claim may be made before the date which under section 826 of the principal Act (interest on overpaid tax), subject to regulations under section 826A of that Act, is the material date in relation to that tax.

59DA(3) The notice must state–

(a) the amount which the company considers should be repaid, and

(b) its grounds for believing that the amount paid exceeds its probable tax liability.

59DA(4) If the company has appealed against an amendment of an assessment, or an assessment, relating to the tax liability in question, and the appeal has not been finally determined, it may apply to the tribunal for a determination of the amount which should be repaid to the company pending determination of the liability.

59DA(5) Any such application is to be subject to the relevant provisions of Part 5 of this Act (see, in particular, section 48(2)(b)).

59DA(6) If the company makes an application under section 55(3) or (4) (application to postpone payment pending determination of appeal), that application may be combined with an application under subsection (4) above.

59DA(7) If a company makes a claim or application under this section before it has delivered a company tax return for the period in question, any deductions under section 61 of the Finance Act 2004 (deductions from payments to certain subcontractors) shall be disregarded in considering whether the amount paid by the company exceeds its probable tax liability.

59DA(8) This section has effect subject to section 59E.

History – In s. 59DA(4) the word "tribunal" substituted for the words "Commissioners to whom the appeal stands referred" by SI 2009/56, art. 3(1) and Sch. 1, para. 40(2), operative from 1 April 2009, subject to transitional and saving provisions in SI 2009/56 Sch. 3.

S. 59DA(5) substituted by SI 2009/56, art. 3(1) and Sch. 1, para. 40(3), operative from 1 April 2009, subject to transitional and saving provisions in SI 2009/56, Sch. 3.

In s. 59DA(7), the words "section 61 of the Finance Act 2004" substituted by FA 2004, s. 76 and Sch. 12, para. 3 with effect from 6 April 2007 (FA 2004, s. 77).

S. 59DA (together with s. 59D) substituted for original s. 59D, superseding it in relation to corporation tax accounting periods ending on or after 1 July 1999, by FA 1998, s. 117(3) and Sch. 19, para. 29(2). 1 July 1999 is the appointed day for corporation tax self-assessment by virtue of FA 1994, s. 199(2), (3) and SI 1998/3173 (C. 78).

Cross references – ICTA 1988 s. 826A(4): power of Treasury to modify s. 59DA(2) in relation to companies of a prescribed description by varying the date before which a claim under s. 826(2) may not be made.

FA 1998, Sch. 18, para. 31(3): repayment claim under s. 56DA not affected by amendment to company return during an enquiry.

SI 1998/3175, reg. 6(8): s. 59A disapplied where reg. 6 (repayment of amounts in respect of a large company's total liability for an accounting period) applies.

SI 2003/282: regulations governing electronic delivery of information to or by the Board under this section revoking SI 2000/945 with effect from 5 March 2003.

Statutory instruments – SI 1998/3175: Corporation Tax (Instalment Payments) Regulations 1998.

59E Further provision as to when corporation tax is due and payable

59E(1) The Treasury may by regulations make provision, in relation to companies of such descriptions as may be prescribed for, or in connection with, treating amounts of corporation tax for an accounting period as becoming due and payable on dates which fall on or before the date on which corporation tax for that period would become due and payable apart from this section.

59E(2) Without prejudice to the generality of subsection (1) above, regulations under this section may make provision–

(a) for, or in connection with, the determination of amounts of corporation tax which are treated as becoming due and payable under the regulations;

(b) for, or in connection with, the determination of the dates on which amounts of corporation tax are treated as becoming due and payable under the regulations;

(c) for, or in connection with, the making of payments to the Board in respect of amounts of corporation tax which are treated as becoming due and payable under the regulations;

(d) for, or in connection with, the determination of the amount of any such payments as are mentioned in paragraph (c) above;

(e) for, or in connection with, the determination of the dates on which any such payments as are mentioned in paragraph (c) above become due and payable;

(f) for, or in connection with, any assumptions which are to be made for any purposes of the regulations;

(g) for, or in connection with, the payment to the Board of interest on amounts of corporation tax which are treated as becoming due and payable under the regulations;

(h) for, or in connection with, the repayment of amounts paid under the regulations;

(i) for, or in connection with, the payment of interest by the Board on amounts paid or repaid under the regulations;

(j) with respect to the furnishing of information to the Board;

(k) with respect to the keeping, production or inspection of any books, documents or other records;

(l) for, or in connection with, the imposition of such requirements as the Treasury think necessary or expedient for any purposes of the regulations;

(m) for, or in connection with, appeals in relation to questions arising under the regulations.

59E(3) Regulations under this section may make provision–

(a) for amounts of corporation tax for an accounting period to be treated as becoming due and payable on dates which fall within the accounting period;

(b) for payments in respect of any such amounts of corporation tax for an accounting period as are mentioned in paragraph (a) above to become due and payable on dates which fall within the accounting period.

59E(4) Where interest is charged by virtue of regulations under this section on any amounts of corporation tax for an accounting period which are treated as becoming due and payable under the regulations, the company shall, in such circumstances as may be prescribed, be liable to a penalty not exceeding twice the amount of that interest.

59E(5) Regulations under this section–

(a) may make such modifications of any provisions of the Taxes Acts, or

(b) may apply such provisions of the Taxes Acts,

as the Treasury think necessary or expedient for or in connection with giving effect to the provisions of this section.

59E(6) Regulations under this section which apply any provisions of the Taxes Acts may apply those provisions either without modifications or with such modifications as the Treasury think necessary or expedient for or in connection with giving effect to the provisions of this section.

59E(7) Regulations under this section–

(a) may make different provision for different purposes, cases or circumstances;

(b) may make different provision in relation to companies or accounting periods of different descriptions;

(c) may make such supplementary, incidental, consequential or transitional provision as appears to the Treasury to be necessary or expedient.

59E(8) Subject to subsection (9) below, regulations under this section may make provision in relation to accounting periods beginning before (as well as accounting periods beginning on or after) the date on which the regulations are made.

59E(9) Regulations under this section may not make provision in relation to accounting periods ending before the day appointed under section 199 of the Finance Act 1994 for the purposes of Chapter III of Part IV of that Act (corporation tax self-assessment).

59E(10) In this section–

"modifications" includes amendments, additions and omissions;

"prescribed" means prescribed by regulations made under this section.

59E(11) Any reference in this section to corporation tax includes a reference–

(a) to any amount due from a company under section 455 or 464A of CTA 2010 (charge to tax in case of loan or benefit to participator) as if it were an amount of corporation tax chargeable on the company;

(b) to any sum charged on a company at step 5 in section 371BC(1) of TIOPA 2010 (controlled foreign companies) as if it were an amount of corporation tax;

(ba) to any sum chargeable on a company under section 269DA of CTA 2010 (surcharge on banking companies) as if it were an amount of corporation tax chargeable on the company;

(c) to any sum chargeable on a company under section 330(1) of CTA 2010 (supplementary charge in respect of ring fence trades) as if it were an amount of corporation tax chargeable on the company.

(d) to the bank levy where treated as an amount of corporation tax chargeable on a company by paragraph 50 or 51 of Schedule 19 to the Finance Act 2011 (the bank levy).

59E(12) Without prejudice to the generality of any provision above–

(a) in relation to cases where the bank levy is treated as an amount of corporation tax chargeable on a company, regulations under this section may make provision–

(i) for amounts of the bank levy to be treated as becoming due and payable on dates which fall within the chargeable period (within the meaning of Schedule 19 to the Finance Act 2011);

(ii) for payments in respect of any such amounts of the bank levy as are mentioned in sub-paragraph (i) to become due and payable on dates which fall within that period;

(b) in relation to cases where a company on which the bank levy is treated as an amount of corporation tax chargeable for an accounting period has made payments in respect of corporation tax for that period, regulations under this section may make provision for or in connection with determining the extent to which those payments are to be treated as being payments of the bank levy;

(c) in relation to cases where a company ("the relevant company") has made payments in respect of corporation tax for an accounting period wholly or partly on the assumption that the bank levy will be treated as an amount of corporation tax chargeable on the relevant company for that period, regulations under this section may make provision for or in connection with treating those payments (wholly or partly) to have been made by another company if it turns out that the bank levy is not to be treated as an amount of corporation tax chargeable on the relevant company for that period;

(d) where regulations under this section impose a requirement within subsection (2)(j) above to furnish information for purposes related to the bank levy, the regulations may make provision for or in connection with applying Part 7 of Schedule 36 to the Finance Act 2008 in whole or in part (with or without modification) as if the requirement to furnish the information were contained in an information notice within the meaning of that Schedule.

History – In s. 59E(11)(a), the words "or 464A" and the words "or benefit" inserted by FA 2013, s. 79 and Sch. 30, para. 9, with effect from 20 March 2013.
In s. 59E(11)(a), the words "section 455 of CTA 2010 (charge to tax in case of loan to participator)" substituted for the words "section 419 of the principal Act (loans to participators etc)" by CTA 2010, s. 1177 and Sch. 1, para. 155(a), with effect for corporation tax purposes for accounting periods ending on or after 1 April 2010, and for income tax and capital gains tax purposes for the tax year 2010–11 and subsequent tax years.
S. 59E(11)(ba) inserted by F(No. 2)A 2015, s. 17 and Sch. 3, para. 2, with effect from 18 November 2015 (Royal Assent).
S. 59E(11)(b) substituted by FA 2012, s. 180 and Sch. 20, para. 12 in relation to accounting periods of controlled foreign companies beginning on or after 1 January 2013.
In s. 59E(11)(c), the words "section 330(1) of CTA 2010" substituted for the words "section 501A(1) of the principal Act" by CTA 2010, s. 1177 and Sch. 1, para. 155(b), with effect for corporation tax purposes for accounting periods ending on or after 1 April 2010, and for income tax and capital gains tax purposes for the tax year 2010–11 and subsequent tax years.
S. 59E(11)(c) inserted by FA 2002, s. 92(2) with effect from 24 July 2002.
S. 59E(11)(d) inserted by FA 2011, s. 73 and Sch. 19, para. 58(2), with effect from 19 July 2011, subject to the transitional provisions in FA 2011, Sch. 19, para. 65(9).
S. 59E(12) inserted by FA 2011, s. 73 and Sch. 19, para. 58(3), with effect from 19 July 2011, subject to the transitional provisions in FA 2011, Sch. 19, para. 65(9).
S. 59E inserted by FA 1998, s. 30(1).

Cross references – S. 87A(9): restriction on powers to make regulations under s. 59E.
S. 98: penalties etc. for failure to comply with regulations under s. 59E.
ICTA 1988, s. 826A(3): regulations made under s. 59E take priority over regulations made under s. 826A(3).
ICTA 1988, s. 826(7E): restriction on powers to make regulations under s. 59E.
FA 1998, s. 30(2): power of Treasury to make regulations to counter arrangements to avoid or mitigate the effects of regulations made under s. 59E.
FA 1998, Sch. 18, para. 38(2): determination of amount due may be accompanied by notice determining the due date.
FA 2009, Sch. 56: penalties for failure to make payments under regulations under s. 59E on time (subject to commencement order).
SI 1998/3175, reg. 13: circumstances prescribed for purposes of s. 59E(4).
SI 2003/282: regulations governing electronic delivery of information to or by the Board under this section revoking SI 2000/945 with effect from 5 March 2003.

Statutory instruments – SI 1998/3175 (as amended): Corporation Tax (Instalment Payments) Regulations 1998.
SI 2016/566: made under s. 59E.

Other material – IR press release 110/90 (8 June 1999) contains guidance notes on use of information and penalty powers in quarterly instalment payments cases.

Notes – The appointed day for corporation tax self-assessment (see s. 59E(9)) is 1 July 1999 by virtue of FA 1994, s. 199(2), (3) and SI 1998/3173 (C. 78).

59F Arrangements for paying tax on behalf of group members

59F(1) An officer of Revenue and Customs may enter into arrangements for the specified purpose with some or all of the members of a group.

59F(2) For the purposes of subsection (1), arrangements entered into with some or all of the members of a group are for "the specified purpose" if they are arrangements for one of those members to discharge any liability of each of those members to pay corporation tax for the accounting periods to which the arrangements relate.

59F(3) For the purposes of this section, a company and all its 51% subsidiaries form a group and, if any of those subsidiaries has 51% subsidiaries, the group includes them and their 51% subsidiaries, and so on.

59F(4) Arrangements entered into under subsection (1)–

(a) may make provision in relation to cases where companies become or cease to be members of a group,

(b) may make provision in relation to the discharge of liability to pay interest or penalties,

(c) may make provision in relation to the discharge of liability to pay any amount within subsection (6),

(d) may make provision for or in connection with the termination of the arrangements, and

(e) may make such supplementary, incidental, consequential or transitional provision as is necessary for the purposes of the arrangements.

59F(5) Arrangements entered into under subsection (1)–

(a) do not affect the liability to corporation tax, or to pay corporation tax, of any company to which the arrangements relate, and

(b) do not affect any other liability under the Tax Acts of any company to which the arrangements relate.

59F(6) The following amounts are within this subsection–

(a) an amount due from a company under section 455 or 464A of CTA 2010 (charge to tax in case of loan or benefit to participator in close company) as if it were an amount of corporation tax chargeable on the company, and

(b) a sum charged on a company at step 5 in section 371BC(1) of TIOPA 2010 (controlled foreign companies) as if it were an amount of corporation tax, and

(c) the bank levy where treated as an amount of corporation tax chargeable on a company by paragraph 50 or 51 of Schedule 19 to the Finance Act 2011 (the bank levy).

History – In s. 59F(6)(a), the words "or 464A" and the words "or benefit" inserted by FA 2013, s. 79 and Sch. 30, para. 10, with effect from 20 March 2013.
S. 59F(6)(b) and the word "and" after it substituted by FA 2012, s. 180 and Sch. 20, para. 12 in relation to accounting periods of controlled foreign companies beginning on or after 1 January 2013.
S. 59F(6)(c) inserted by FA 2011, s. 73 and Sch. 19, para. 59, with effect from 19 July 2011.
S. 59F inserted by TIOPA 2010, s. 371 and Sch. 7, para. 79, with effect for corporation tax purposes for accounting periods ending on or after 1 April 2010, for income tax and capital gains tax purposes for the tax year 2010–11 and subsequent tax years, and for petroleum revenue tax purposes for chargeable periods beginning on or after 1 July 2010.

59FA Exit charge payment plans

59FA(1) Schedule 3ZB contains provisions about exit charge payment plans in accordance with which companies may defer payment of certain corporation tax.

59FA(2) Parts 1 and 2 of the Schedule each make provision about the circumstances in which an exit charge payment plan may be entered into, and about determining the amount of corporation tax that may be deferred–

(a) see Part 1 in relation to a company which ceases to be resident in the United Kingdom, and

(b) see Part 2 in relation to a company which is not resident in the United Kingdom but which carries on, or has carried on, a trade in the United Kingdom through a permanent establishment there.

59FA(3) Part 3 of the Schedule contains provision about–

(a) entering into an exit charge payment plan,

(b) the effect of such a plan,

(c) the content of such a plan, and

(d) the methods in accordance with which tax deferred under such a plan may be paid.

History – S. 59FA inserted by FA 2013, s. 229 and Sch. 49, para. 2, with effect from 11 December 2012 in relation to an accounting period if the relevant day, in relation to that period, falls on or after 11 December 2012 (subject to provisions of FA 2013, Sch. 49, para. 8(2) and (3)).

MANAGED PAYMENT PLANS

History – Heading inserted by FA 2013, s. 229 and Sch. 49, para. 3, with effect from 11 December 2012 in relation to an accounting period if the relevant day, in relation to that period, falls on or after 11 December 2012 (subject to provisions of FA 2013, Sch. 49, para. 8(2) and (3)).

59G Managed payment plans

59G(1) This section applies if a person ("P") has entered into a managed payment plan in respect of–

(a) an amount on account of income tax which is to become payable in accordance with section 59A(2),

(b) an amount of income tax or capital gains tax which is to become payable in accordance with section 59B, or

(c) an amount of corporation tax which is to become payable in accordance with section 59D.

59G(2) P enters into a managed payment plan in respect of an amount if–

(a) P agrees to pay, and an officer of Revenue and Customs agrees to accept payment of, the amount by way of instalments,

(b) the instalments to be paid before the due date are balanced by the instalments to be paid after it (see section 59H), and

(c) the agreement meets such other requirements as may be specified in regulations made by the Commissioners for Her Majesty's Revenue and Customs.

59G(3) But this section does not apply, in the case of an amount of corporation tax, if an arrangement under section 59F has been made in relation to the amount.

59G(4) If P pays all of the instalments in accordance with the plan, P is to be treated as having paid, on the due date, the total of those instalments.

59G(5) If P–

(a) pays one or more instalments in accordance with the plan, but

(b) *fails* to pay one or more later instalments in accordance with it,

P is to be treated as having paid, on the due date, the total of the instalments paid before the failure (but this is subject to subsection (6)).

59G(6) If–

(a) subsection (5) applies in a case in which the first failure to pay an instalment occurs before the due date, and

(b) P would (in the absence of a managed payment plan) be entitled to be paid interest on any amount paid before that date,

then, despite that subsection, P is entitled to be paid that interest.

59G(7) If–

(a) subsection (5) applies,

(b) P makes one or more payments after the due date (whether or not in accordance with the plan), and

(c) an officer of Revenue and Customs gives P a notice specifying any or all of those payments,

P is not liable to a penalty or surcharge for failing to pay the amount of the specified payments on or before the due date.

59G(8) Regulations under this section may make different provision for different cases.

59G(9) In this section **"the due date"**, in relation to an amount mentioned in subsection (1), means the date on which it becomes payable.

History – S. 59G inserted by TIOPA 2010, s. 371 and Sch. 7, para. 80, with effect for corporation tax purposes for accounting periods ending on or after 1 April 2010, for income tax and capital gains tax purposes for the tax year 2010–11 and subsequent tax years, and for petroleum revenue tax purposes for chargeable periods beginning on or after 1 July 2010.

59H Balancing of instalments for the purposes of section 59G

59H(1) Subsection (2) applies for the purposes of section 59G(2)(b).

59H(2) The instalments to be paid before the due date are balanced by those to be paid after it if the time value of the instalments to be paid before that date is equal, or approximately equal, to the time value of the instalments to be paid after it.

59H(3) The time value of the instalments to be paid before the due date is the total of the time value of each of the instalments to be paid before that date (and the time value of the instalments to be paid after that date is to be read accordingly).

59H(4) The time value of an instalment is–

$$A \times T$$

where–

A is the amount of the instalment, and

T is the number of days before, or after, the due date that the instalment is to be paid.

59H(5) The Commissioners for Her Majesty's Revenue and Customs may by regulations make provision for the purpose of determining when an amount is approximately equal to another amount.

59H(6) Regulations under this section may make different provision for different cases.

History – S. 59H inserted by TIOPA 2010, s. 371 and Sch. 7, para. 80, with effect for corporation tax purposes for accounting periods ending on or after 1 April 2010, for income tax and capital gains tax purposes for the tax year 2010–11 and subsequent tax years, and for petroleum revenue tax purposes for chargeable periods beginning on or after 1 July 2010.

PART VI – COLLECTION AND RECOVERY

Cross references – TCA 1999, Sch. 2, para. 10(1); Sch. 4, para. 2(3), 4(3): application of Pt. VI in respect of working families tax credit and disabled person's tax credit.
TCA 2002, s. 29(3): overpayment of working tax credit to be treated as tax charged and due and repayable.
TCA 2002, Sch. 2, para. 7(1): a penalty payable under Pt. 1 of that Act is treated for the purposes of TMA 1970, Pt. VI as if it were tax charged in an assessment and due and payable.
CTFA 2004, s. 21(11): penalty to be treated for the purposes of TMA 1970, Pt. 6 (collection and recovery) as if it were tax charged in an assessment and due and payable.
SI 1993/743, reg. 14(2): application of Pt. VI to a formal determination against a contractor under reg. 14.
SI 2002/2172, reg. 14(4): application of Pt. VI to determinations of working tax credit funding to be repaid by employers.

HMRC Manuals – Insolvency Manual INS9307: set off of tax overpaid against amounts due to other Government Departments in an insolvency.

Other material – Tax Bulletin TB08/95-7: Revenue practice of "equitable liability", under which the Revenue may be prepared not to pursue its legal right to recovery of the full amount of tax due where to insist on doing so would be unconscionable (e.g. an estimated determination is excessive), provided that the liability assessed is greater than the amount which would have been charged had the returns, and necessary supporting documentation, been submitted at the proper time, and acceptable evidence is provided of what the liability should have been.
Taxline 1994/23 (not reproduced): because income tax is an annual tax, where an individual is made bankrupt after the Finance Act has received Royal Assent, his liability to income tax comes to an end and can only be recovered out of the assets held by the individual's trustee in bankruptcy. At the end of the year, that exemption is lost as a fresh liability is imposed by that year's Finance Act.

60 Issue of demand notes and receipts

60(1) Every collector shall, when the tax becomes due and payable, make demand of the respective sums given to him in charge to collect, from the persons charged therewith, or at the places of their last abode, or on the premises in respect of which the tax is charged, as the case may require.

60(2) On payment of the tax, the collector shall if so requested give a receipt.

Cross references – OTA 1975, Sch. 2, para. 1(1): s. 60 applies for the purposes of oil taxation.
ICTA 1988, s. 203: provisions as to PAYE.
ICTA 1988, s. 252: assessments to recover excessive tax credits treated as assessments to income or corporation tax.
ICTA 1988, s. 830; FA 1973, Sch. 15, para. 2, 4: collection of tax assessed on non-residents in connection with exploration or exploitation activities or rights.
FA 1993, s. 173 and Sch. 19, para. 2(3)–(5), 6(2), (3), 10(6)–(8); assessment and collection of tax on profits and gains of or penalties imposed on Lloyd's underwriters in relation to 1992–93 and subsequent years (see ICTA 1988, s. 450 and Sch. 19A, para. 3, 10 for prior years (from 1988–89)).
SI 1986/1711, Schedule, Pt. I, II: s. 60 applies for purposes of stamp duty reserve tax.
SI 1999/2537: modified application of s. 60 in relation to stamp duty penalties.

DISTRAINT AND POINDING

61 Distraint by collectors

61(1) If a person neglects or refuses to pay the sum charged, upon demand made by the collector, the collector may distrain upon the goods and chattels of the person charged (in this section referred to as **"the person in default"**).

61(1A) [Omitted by FA 2008, s. 129 and Sch. 43, para. 1(3).]

61(2) For the purpose of levying any such distress, a justice of the peace, on being satisfied by information on oath that there is reasonable ground for believing that a person is neglecting or refusing to pay a sum charged, may issue a warrant in writing authorising a collector to break open, in the daytime, any house or premises, calling to his assistance any constable.

Every such constable shall, when so required, aid and assist the collector in the execution of the warrant and in levying the distress in the house or premises.

61(3) A levy or warrant to break open shall be executed by, or under the direction of, and in the presence of, the collector.

61(4) A distress levied by the collector shall be kept for five days, at the costs and charges of the person in default.

61(5) If the person in default does not pay the sum due, together with the costs and charges, the distress shall be appraised by one or more independent persons appointed by the collector, and shall be sold by public auction by the collector for payment of the sum due and all costs and charges.

Any overplus coming by the distress, after the deduction of the costs and charges and of the sum due, shall be restored to the owner of the goods distrained.

61(6) The Treasury may by regulations make provision with respect to–

(a) the fees chargeable on or in connection with the levying of distress, and

(b) the costs and charges recoverable where distress has been levied;

and any such regulations shall be made by statutory instrument which shall be subject to annulment in pursuance of a resolution of the House of Commons.

61(7) This section extends only to Northern Ireland.

History – In s. 61(1), the words from "(a) in England and Wales, use the procedure in Schedule 12 to the Tribunals, Courts and Enforcement Act 2007 (taking control of goods) to recover that sum; (b) in Northern Ireland," omitted by FA 2008, s. 129 and Sch. 43, para. 1(2) with effect from 6 April 2014 (SI 2014/906, art. 2).
In s. 61(1), the words "– (a) in England and Wales, use the procedure in Schedule 12 to the Tribunals, Courts and Enforcement Act 2007 (taking control of goods) to recover that sum; (b) in Northern Ireland," inserted by TCEA 2007, s. 62(3) and Sch. 13, para. 33(2), with effect from 6 April 2014 (SI 2014/768, art. 2).
In s. 61(1), the words "the collector may … person in default)" substituted by FA 1989, s. 152 with effect from 1 February 1994 by virtue of SI 1994/87, the appointed day order for the purposes of FA 1989, s. 152(7).
S. 61(1A) omitted by FA 2008, s. 129 and Sch. 43, para. 1(3) with effect from 6 April 2014 (SI 2014/906, art. 2).
S. 61(1A) inserted by TCEA 2007, s. 62(3) and Sch. 13, para. 33(3), with effect from 6 April 2014 (SI 2014/768, art. 2).
In s. 61(2), the words "a justice of the peace … authorising a collector to" substituted by FA 1989, s. 152 with effect from 1 February 1994 by virtue of SI 1994/87, the appointed day order for the purposes of FA 1989, s. 152(7).
In s. 61(4), the words "in default" substituted by FA 1989, s. 152 with effect from 1 February 1994 by virtue of SI 1994/87, the appointed day order for the purposes of FA 1989, s. 152(7).
In s. 61(5), the words "in default" substituted; the words "within the said five days" which preceded the words ", the distress" omitted, the words "one or more independent … the collector" substituted and certain words which preceded "any overplus" omitted by FA 1989, s. 152 with effect from 1 February 1994 by virtue of SI 1994/87, the appointed day order for the purposes of FA 1989, s. 152(7).
S. 61(6) inserted by FA 1989, s. 152 with effect from 1 February 1994 by virtue of SI 1994/87, the appointed day order for the purposes of FA 1989, s. 152(7).
S. 61(7) inserted by FA 2008, s. 129 and Sch. 43, para. 1(4), with effect from 6 April 2014 (SI 2014/906, art. 2).

Cross references – OTA 1975, Sch. 2, para. 1(1): s. 61 applies, with modifications, for the purposes of oil taxation.
F(No. 2)A 1997, Sch. 2, para. 15(2): application, with modifications, to windfall tax.

SI 1986/1711, Schedule, Pt. I, II: s. 61 applies for purposes of stamp duty reserve tax.
SI 1999/2537: s. 61 applies in relation to stamp duty penalties.

Statutory instruments – SI 1994/236: fees and costs in connection with the levying of distress in default of a stamp duty penalty.

Other material – HMRC Codes of Practice 6 (Collection of tax) and 7 (Collection of amounts due from employers, and contractors in the construction industry).

62 Priority of claim for tax

62(1) If at any time at which any goods or chattels belonging to any person (in this section referred to as "**the person in default**") are liable to be taken by virtue of any execution or other process, warrant, or authority whatever, or by virtue of any assignment, on any account or pretence whatever, except at the suit of the landlord for rent, the person in default is in arrears in respect of any such sums as are referred to in subsection (1A) below, the goods or chattels may not be so taken unless on demand made by the collector the person at whose suit the execution or seizure is made, or to whom the assignment was made, pays or causes to be paid to the collector, before the sale or removal of the goods or chattels, all such sums as have fallen due at or before the date of seizure.

62(1A) The sums referred to in subsection (1) above are–

(a) sums due from the person in default on account of deductions of income tax from taxable earnings (as defined by section 10 of ITEPA 2003) paid during the period of twelve months next before the date of seizure, being deductions which the person in default was liable to make under PAYE regulations less the amount of the repayments of income tax which he was liable to make during that period; and

(b) sums due from the person in default in respect of deductions required to be made by him for that period under section 61 of the Finance Act 2004 (sub-contractors in the construction industry).

62(2) If the sums referred to in subsection (1) above are not paid within ten days of the date of the demand referred to in that subsection, the collector may distrain the goods and chattels notwithstanding the seizure or assignment, and may proceed to the sale thereof, as prescribed by this Act, for the purpose of obtaining payment of the whole of those sums, and the reasonable costs and charges attending such distress and sale, and every collector so doing shall be indemnified by virtue of this Act.

62(3) [Repealed by FA 1985, Sch. 27, Pt. X, with effect from 19 March 1985 and (so far as unrepealed) by FA 1989, Sch. 17, Pt. VIII.]

62(4) This section does not extend to England and Wales.

History – In s. 62(1), the words from the beginning to first "are", from "the person in default" to "the collector", and "such sums" to the end substituted by FA 1989, s. 153.
In s. 62(1A)(a), the words "taxable earnings (as defined by section 10 of ITEPA 2003)" substituted by ITEPA 2003, Sch. 6, para. 132(a) which has effect for the tax year 2003–04 and subsequent tax years.
In s. 62(1A)(a), the words "PAYE regulations" substituted by ITEPA 2003, Sch. 6, para. 132(b) which has effect for the tax year 2003–04 and subsequent tax years.
In s. 62(1A)(b), the words "section 61 of the Finance Act 2004" substituted by FA 2004, s. 76 and Sch. 12, para. 4 with effect from 6 April 2007 (FA 2004, s. 77)
S. 62(1A) inserted by FA 1989, s. 153.
In s. 62(2) the words from the beginning to "the collector may", and the words "may proceed" and "those sums" substituted by FA 1989, s. 153.
S. 62(3) dealt with development land tax.
S. 62(4) inserted by TCEA 2007, s. 62(3) and Sch. 13, para. 34, with effect from 6 April 2014 (SI 2014/768, art. 2).

Cross references – OTA 1975, Sch. 2, para. 1(1): s. 62 applies with modifications for the purposes of oil taxation.
SI 1987/530: tax due under assessments on non-resident entertainers and sportsmen to be treated as Sch. D tax (now tax on trading profits) for collection purposes.

63 Recovery of tax in Scotland

63 [Omitted by FA 2008, s. 129 and Sch. 43, para. 12(a).]

History – S. 63 omitted by FA 2008, s. 129 and Sch. 43, para. 12(a), with effect from 23 November 2009, by virtue of SI 2009/3024, art. 3, subject to transitional provisions in SI 2009/3024, art. 4.

63A Sheriff officer's fees and outlays

63A [Omitted by FA 2008, s. 129 and Sch. 43, para. 12(b).]

History – S. 63A omitted by FA 2008, s. 129 and Sch. 43, para. 12(b), with effect from 23 November 2009, by virtue of SI 2009/3024, art. 3, subject to transitional provisions in SI 2009/3024, art. 4.

64 Priority of claim for tax in Scotland

64(1) If at any time at which any moveable goods and effects belonging to any person (in this section referred to as "**the person in default**") are liable to be taken by virtue of any diligence whatever, or by any assignation, the person in default is in arrears in respect of any such sums as are referred to in subsection (1A) below, the goods and effects may not be so taken unless on demand made by the collector the person proceeding to take the said goods and effects pays such sums as have fallen due at or before the date of poinding or, as the case may be, other diligence or assignation.

64(1A) The sums referred to in subsection (1) above are–

(a) sums due from the person in default on account of deductions of income tax from taxable earnings (as defined by section 10 of ITEPA 2003) paid during the period of twelve months next before the date of poinding, being deductions which the person in default was liable to make under PAYE regulations less the amount of the repayments of income tax which he was liable to make during that period; and

(b) sums due from the person in default in respect of deductions required to be made by him for that period under section 61 of the Finance Act 2004 (sub-contractors in the construction industry).

64(2) If the sums referred to in subsection (1) above are not paid within ten days of the date of the demand referred to in that subsection, the sums shall, notwithstanding any proceedings for the purpose of taking the said moveable goods and effects, be recoverable by poinding and selling the said moveable goods and effects under warrant obtained in conformity with the provisions contained in section 63 above.

64(3) [Repealed by FA 1985, Sch. 27, Pt. X, with effect from 19 March 1985 and (so far as unrepealed) by FA 1989, Sch. 17, Pt. VIII.]

History – In s. 64(1) the words "poinding, sequestration for rent, or" omitted by Bankruptcy and Diligence etc. (Scotland) Act 2007, s. 226 and Sch. 6, Pt. 1, with effect from 22 April 2009 (SSI 2009/67, art. 3(3) and Sch. 2).
S. 64(1) amended by FA 1989, s. 155.
S. 64(1A) inserted by FA 1989, s. 155.
In s. 64(1A)(a), the words "taxable earnings (as defined by section 10 of ITEPA 2003)" substituted by ITEPA 2003, Sch. 6, para. 134(a) which has effect for the tax year 2003–04 and subsequent tax years.
In s. 64(1A)(a), the words "PAYE regulations" substituted by ITEPA 2003, Sch. 6, para. 134(b) which has effect for the tax year 2003–04 and subsequent tax years.
In s. 64(1A)(b), the words "section 61 of the Finance Act 2004" substituted by FA 2004, s. 76 and Sch. 12, para. 6, with effect from 6 April 2007 (FA 2004, s. 77).
S. 64(2) amended by FA 1989, s. 155.
S. 64(3) dealt with development land tax and was repealed subject to saving.

Cross references – OTA 1975, Sch. 2, para. 1(1): s. 64 applies with modifications for the purposes of oil taxation.

COURT PROCEEDINGS

65 Magistrates' courts

65(1) Any amount due and payable by way of income tax, capital gains tax or corporation tax which does not exceed £2,000 shall, without prejudice to any other remedy, be recoverable summarily as a civil debt by proceedings commenced in the name of a collector.

65(2) All or any of the sums due in respect of tax from any one person and payable to any one collector (being sums which are by law recoverable summarily) may, whether or not they are due under one assessment, be included in the same complaint, summons, order, warrant or other document required by law to be laid before justices or to be issued by justices, and every such document as aforesaid shall, as respects each such sum, be construed as a separate document and its invalidity as respects any one such sum shall not affect its validity as respects any other such sum.

65(3) Proceedings under this section may be brought in England and Wales at any time within one year from the time when the matter complained of arose.

65(4) It is hereby declared that in subsection (1) above the expression **"recoverable summarily as a civil debt"** in respect of proceedings in Northern Ireland means recoverable in proceedings under Article 62 of the Magistrates' Courts (Northern Ireland) Order 1981.

65(5) The Treasury may by order made by statutory instrument increase the sum specified in subsection (1) above and any statutory instrument shall be subject to annulment in pursuance of a resolution of the Commons House of Parliament.

History – S. 65(1) amended, by FA 1998, s. 117(3) and Sch. 19, para. 30(2), with effect in relation to accounting periods ending on or after 1 July 1999, the corporation tax self-assessment appointed day by virtue of FA 1994, s. 199(2), (3) and SI 1998/3173 (C. 78).
S. 65(1) amended, by the substitution of the words "the amount of … payment or tax", by FA 1994, s. 196 and Sch. 19, para. 19(1), in so far as it relates to income tax and capital gains tax, as respects the year 1996–97 and subsequent years of assessment, and also originally for corporation tax accounting periods ending on or after the appointed day (FA 1994, s. 199(2), (3)), but the corporation tax element of the former text is superseded by the amendment in FA 1998, Sch. 19, para. 30(2) (see the note above).
In s. 65(1), previous limit of £1,000 substituted from 1 September 1991 by SI 1991/1625; previously £500 from 11 September 1989 (SI 1989/1300).
In s. 65(3), words from "for the recovery of" to the end repealed by FA 1998, s. 117(3) and Sch. 19, para. 30(3), s. 165 and Sch. 27, Pt. III(28), with effect in relation to accounting periods ending on or after 1 July 1999, the corporation tax self-assessment appointed day by virtue of FA 1994, s. 199(2), (3) and SI 1998/3173 (C. 78).
Former s. 65(3) amended, by the substitution of para. (a) and (b) for the earlier words "any tax charged under Schedule E", by FA 1994, s. 196 and Sch. 19, para. 19(2), in so far as it relates to income tax and capital gains tax, as respects the year 1996–97 and subsequent years of assessment, and also originally for corporation tax accounting periods ending on or after the appointed day (FA 1994, s. 199(2), (3)), but the corporation tax element of the former text is superseded by the amendment in FA 1998, Sch. 19, para. 30(3) (see the note above).

S. 65(4) amended by FA 1984, s. 57(1) to insert the reference to the Magistrates' Courts (Northern Ireland) Order 1981 (SI 1981/1675 (NI 26)) in place of referencesto previous provisions.
S. 65(5) amended, by FA 1998, s. 117(3) and Sch. 19, para. 30(4), with effect in relation to accounting periods ending on or after 1 July 1999, the self-assessment appointed day by virtue of FA 1994, s. 199(2), (3) and SI 1998/3173 (C. 78) by the substitution of the word "sum" for the word "sums".
S. 65(5) inserted by FA 1984, s. 57(1).

Cross references – Administration of Justice Act 1970, s. 11–14 and Sch. 4: special enforcement proceedings.
Social Security Contributions (Transfer of Functions, etc.) Act 1999, Sch. 4, para. 2: recovery of NI contributions in magistrates' courts where income tax recovery provisions not applicable.
SI 1986/1711, Schedule, Pt. I, II: modified application of s. 65 for purposes of stamp duty reserve tax.
SI 1993/743, reg. 19(4): proceedings for recovery from contractors of total amounts of tax deductible in respect of payments to sub-contractors in the construction industry.
SI 1999/2537: modified application of provisions of s. 65 in relation to stamp duty penalties.

66 County courts

66(1) Tax due and payable may, in England and Wales, and in Northern Ireland where the amount does not exceed the limit specified in Article 10(1) of the County Courts (Northern Ireland) Order 1980, without prejudice to any other remedy, be sued for and recovered from the person charged therewith as a debt due to the Crown by proceedings in England and Wales in the county court or in Northern Ireland in a county court.

66(2) [Omitted by FA 2008, s. 137(2)(b).]

66(2A) [Omitted by SI 1991/724 (L 5).]

66(3) In this section as it applies in Northern Ireland the expression **"county court"** shall mean a county court held for a division under the County Courts (Northern Ireland) Order 1980.

66(4) Sections 21 and 42(2) of the Interpretation Act (Northern Ireland) 1954 shall apply as if any reference in those provisions to any enactment included a reference to this section, and Part III of the County Courts (Northern Ireland) Order 1980 (general civil jurisdiction) shall apply for the purposes of this section in Northern Ireland.

History – In s. 66(1), the words "in England and Wales in the county court or in Northern Ireland" inserted after "proceedings" by Crime and Courts Act 2013, s. 17 and Sch. 9, para. 132, with effect from 22 April 2014 (SI 2014/954, art. 2).
In s. 66(1), the words "commenced in the name of a collector" omitted by FA 2008, s. 137(2)(a), with effect from 21 July 2008.
In s. 66(1) the words "under any assessment" omitted and repealed by FA 2001, s. 89(1) and s. 110, Sch. 33, Pt. 2(14) in relation to proceedings begun after 11 May 2001.
In s. 66(1) words from the beginning to "(Northern Ireland) Order 1980," by SI 1991/724 (L 5), reg. 2(8) and Schedule, with effect from 1 July 1991.
S. 66(2) omitted by FA 2008, s. 137(2)(b) with effect from 21 July 2008.
S. 66(2A) omitted by SI 1991/724 (L 5), reg. 2(8) and Schedule, with effect from 1 July 1991.
S. 66(3) substituted by SI 1991/724 (L 5), reg. 2(8) and Schedule, with effect from 1 July 1991.

Cross references – OTA 1975, Sch. 2, para. 1(1): s. 66 applies for the purposes of oil taxation.
Administration of Justice Act 1970, s. 11–14 and Sch. 4: special enforcement provisions.
FA 1993, s. 173 and Sch. 19, para. 11(3): interest on payments due on account for tax on profits and gains of Lloyd's underwriters (1992–93 and subsequent years) treated for s. 66 as tax charged etc. (see ICTA 1988, s. 450 and Sch. 19A, para. 11(1) for prior years (from 1988–89)).
SI 1986/1711, Schedule, Pt. I, II: modified application of s. 66 for purposes of stamp duty reserve tax.
SI 1991/724 (L. 5), reg. 2(1)(f): a county court has jurisdiction under s. 66 whatever the amount involved in the proceedings and whatever the value of any fund or asset connected with the proceedings.
SI 1991/1877, reg. 2(1), (3): there is no right of appeal, in respect of proceedings in which the county court has jurisdiction under s. 66, without the leave of a judge either of the county court or of the Court of Appeal, where the value of the appeal does not exceed £5,000, or is unquantifiable.
SI 1993/743, reg. 19(4): proceedings for recovery from contractors of tax deductible in respect of payments to sub-contractors in the construction industry.
SI 1999/2537: modified application of provisions of s. 66 in relation to stamp duty penalties.

67 Inferior courts in Scotland

67(1) In Scotland, tax due and payable may, without prejudice to any other remedy, be sued for and recovered from the person charged therewith as a debt due to the Crown by proceedings commenced in the name of a collector in the sheriff court.

67(1A) An officer of the Board who is authorised by the Board to do so may address the court in any proceedings under this section.

67(2) Sections 65 and 66 above shall not apply in Scotland.

History – In s. 67(1) the words "under any assessment" omitted and repealed by FA 2001, s. 89(1) and s. 110, Sch. 33, Pt. 2(14) in relation to proceedings begun after 11 May 2001.
S. 67(1) amended by FA 1995, s. 156(2), (3), in relation to proceedings commenced after 1 May 1995.
S. 67(1) amended by FA 1976, s. 58 and Sch. 15, Pt. III, with effect from 1 September 1976.
S. 67(1A) inserted, by FA 1995, s. 156(2), (3), in relation to proceedings commenced after 1 May 1995.

Cross references – OTA 1975, Sch. 2, para. 1(1): s. 67 applies for the purposes of oil taxation.
SI 1986/1711, Schedule, Pt. I, II: modified application of s. 67 for purposes of stamp duty reserve tax.
SI 1993/743, reg. 19(4): proceedings for recovery from contractors of total amount of tax deductible in respect of payments to sub-contractors in the construction industry.
SI 1999/2537: modified application of provisions of s. 67 in relation to stamp duty penalties.

68 High Court, etc.

68(1) Any tax may be sued for and recovered from the person charged therewith in the High Court as a debt due to the Crown, or by any other means whereby any debt of record or otherwise due to the Crown can, or may at any time, be sued for and recovered, as well as by the other means specially provided by this Act for levying the tax.

68(2) All matters within the jurisdiction of the High Court under this section shall be assigned in Scotland to the Court of Session sitting as the Court of Exchequer.

Cross references – OTA 1975, Sch. 2, para. 1(1): s. 68 applies for the purposes of oil taxation.
SI 1986/1711, Schedule, Pt. I, II: s. 68 applies for purposes of stamp duty reserve tax.
SI 1999/2537: modified application of provisions of s. 68 in relation to stamp duty penalties.

SUPPLEMENTAL

69 Recovery of penalty or interest

69(1) This section applies to–

(a) penalties imposed under Part 2, 5A or 10 of this Act or Schedule 18 to the Finance Act 1998;

(b) penalties imposed under any paragraph of Schedule 56 to the Finance Act 2009 in respect of an amount falling within any of the following items of the Table in paragraph 1 of that Schedule–

 (i) item 1, 12, 18 or 19, or

 (ii) insofar as the tax falls within item 1, item 17, 23 or 24;

(c) interest charged under any provision of this Act (or recoverable as if it were interest so charged); and

(d) interest charged under section 101 of the Finance Act 2009.

69(2) An amount by way of penalty or interest to which this section applies shall be treated for the purposes of the following provisions as if it were an amount of tax.

69(3) Those provisions are–

(a) sections 61, 63 and 65 to 68 of this Act;

(b) section 35(2)(g)(i) of the Crown Proceedings Act 1947 (rules of court: restriction of set-off or counterclaim where proceedings, or set-off or counterclaim, relate to tax) and any rules of court imposing any such restriction;

(c) section 35(2)(b) of that Act as set out in section 50 of that Act (which imposes corresponding restrictions in Scotland).

History – In the heading to s. 69, the word ", surcharge", which appeared after the word "penalty", omitted by SI 2011/702, art. 6(c), with effect from 1 April 2011, but subject to SI 2011/702, art. 20, which provides that the omission does not have effect in relation to a return or other document which is required to be made or delivered to HMRC, or an amount of tax which is payable, in relation to the tax year 2009–10 or any previous tax year.
S. 69(1)(b) substituted by SI 2011/702, art. 6(a), with effect from 1 April 2011, but subject to SI 2011/702, art. 20, which provides that the substitution does not have effect in relation to a return or other document which is required to be made or delivered to HMRC, or an amount of tax which is payable, in relation to the tax year 2009–10 or any previous tax year.
S. 69(1)(d) (and the word "; and" at the end of s. 69(1)(c)) inserted by SI 2011/701, art. 7, with effect from 31 October 2011.
In s. 69(2), the word ", surcharge", which appeared after the word "penalty", omitted by SI 2011/702, art. 6(b), with effect from 1 April 2011, but subject to SI 2011/702, art. 20, which provides that the omission does not have effect in relation to a return or other document which is required to be made or delivered to HMRC, or an amount of tax which is payable, in relation to the tax year 2009–10 or any previous tax year.
S. 69 substituted by FA 2001, s. 89(2) for proceedings begun (or a counterclaim made) after 11 May 2001 and to a set-off first claimed after that date.
In former s. 69 the words "or under Schedule 18 to the Finance Act 1998" inserted by FA 1998, s. 117(3) and Sch. 19, para. 31 with effect in relation to accounting periods ending on or after 1 July 1999, the corporation tax self-assessment appointed day by virtue of FA 1994, s. 199(2), (3) and SI 1998/3173 (C. 78).
In former s. 69 before paragraph (a) the words "or recoverable under section 826(8A) of the principal Act as if it were interest so charged" inserted by FA 1998, s. 35 and Sch. 4, para. 3 with effect in relation to accounting periods ending on or after 1 July 1999, the corporation tax self-assessment appointed day (see note above). Former s. 69 after paragraph (c) the words "or if it is interest recoverable under section 826(8A) of the principal Act," inserted by FA 1998, s. 35 and Sch. 4, para. 3 with effect in relation to accounting periods ending on or after 1 July 1999, the self-assessment appointed day (see note above).
In former s. 69 the words "A penalty imposed under … Part IX of this Act" substituted for the former words "Interest charged under Part IX of this Act", and the words "if it is a penalty or surcharge …interest on, tax" substituted for the former words "if it is interest on tax" by FA 1994, s. 196 and Sch. 19, para. 20, in so far as it relates to income tax and capital gains tax, as respects the year 1996–97 and subsequent years of assessment.
Former s. 69 previously amended by F(No. 2)A 1987, s. 86(1), with respect to accounting periods ending after 30 September 1993 (under Pay and File) by virtue of SI 1992/3066, art. 3.

Cross references – OTA 1975, Sch. 2, para. 1(1): s. 69 applies with modifications for the purposes of supplementary petroleum duty.
SI 1986/1711, Schedule, Pt. I, II: *modified application* of s. 69 for purposes of stamp duty reserve tax.
SI 1999/2537: modified application of s. 69 in relation to stamp duty penalties.

Notes – For the purposes of SI 1986/1711, reg. 20 (which applies certain provisions of TMA 1970, in some cases subject to modifications, for the purposes of stamp duty reserve tax), the amendments made to the heading to s. 69 and to s. 69(1)(b) and (2) by SI 2011/702 have no effect (SI 2011/702, art. 22).

70 Evidence

70(1) [Omitted by FA 2008, s. 138 and Sch. 44, para. 1.]

70(2) [Omitted by FA 2008, s. 138 and Sch. 44, para. 1.]

70(3) [Ceases to have effect by virtue of FA 1994, s. 196 and Sch. 19, para. 21(2).]

70(4) A written statement as to the wages, salaries, fees, and other earnings or amounts treated as earnings paid for any period to the person against whom proceedings are brought under section 65, 66 or 67 of this Act, purporting to be signed by his employer for that period or by any responsible person in the employment of the employer, shall in such proceedings be prima facie evidence that the wages, salaries, fees and other earnings or amounts treated as earnings therein stated to have been paid to the person charged have in fact been so paid.

70(5) In subsection (4) **"earnings or amounts treated as earnings"** means earnings or amounts treated as earnings which constitute employment income (see section 7(2)(a) or (b) of ITEPA 2003).

History – S. 70(1) omitted by FA 2008, s. 138 and Sch. 44, para. 1 with effect from 21 July 2008.
S. 70(2) omitted by FA 2008, s. 138 and Sch. 44, para. 1 with effect from 21 July 2008.
In former s. 70(2)(a), the words ", the principal Act or ITEPA 2003" substituted for the words "or the principal Act" by ITEPA 2003, Sch. 6, para. 135(2) which has effect for the tax year 2003–04 and subsequent tax years.
In former s. 70(2)(a), the words "payable under any provision of this Act or the principal Act" substituted for the words "payable under Part IX of this Act" by FA 2001, s. 89(3) applicable to certificates tendered in evidence after 11 May 2001.
In s. 70(2)(a), the words "or under Schedule 18 to the Finance Act 1998" inserted by FA 1998, s. 117(3) and Sch. 19, para. 19(32) with effect in relation to accounting periods ending on or after 1 July 1999, the corporation tax self-assessment appointed day by virtue of FA 1994, s. 199(2), (3) and SI 1998/3173 (C. 78).
S. 70(2)(a) and (b) substituted for the former words "that interest is payable under section 86 or 87 of this Act and that payment of the interest has not been made to him, or, to the best of his knowledge and belief, to any other collector, or to any person acting on his behalf or on behalf of another collector" by FA 1994, s. 196 and Sch. 19, para. 21(1), and s. 70(3) repealed by virtue of FA 1994, s. 196 and Sch. 19, para. 21(2), in relation to income tax and capital gains tax, as respects the year 1996–97 and subsequent years of assessment and in relation to corporation tax, as respects accounting periods ending on or after the appointed day (1 July 1999 by virtue of FA 1994, s. 199(2), (3) and SI 1998/3173 (C. 78)).
S. 70(3) substituted by FA 1989, s. 160(3).
In s. 70(4), the words "earnings or amounts treated as earnings" substituted for the words "emoluments" by ITEPA 2003, Sch. 6, para. 135(3) which has effect for the tax year 2003–04 and subsequent tax years.
S. 70(5) inserted by ITEPA 2003, Sch. 6, para. 135(4) which has effect for the tax year 2003–04 and subsequent tax years.

Cross references – OTA 1975, Sch. 2, para. 1(1): s. 70(1)–(3) apply with modification to oil taxation.
SI 1999/2537: modified application of provisions of s. 70(2) in relation to stamp duty penalties.

Notes – Former s. 70(5) which was to have been inserted by F(No. 2)A 1987, s. 84(4), (9) was repealed by FA 1989, s. 187 and Sch. 17, Pt. VIII before it took effect.

70A Payments by cheque

70A(1) For the purposes of this Act and the provisions mentioned in subsection (2) below, where–

(a) any payment to an officer of the Board or the Board is made by cheque, and

(b) the cheque is paid on its first presentation to the banker on whom it is drawn,

the payment shall be treated as made on the day on which the cheque was received by the officer or the Board.

70A(2) The provisions are–

(a) sections 824 to 826 of the principal Act (repayment supplements and interest on tax overpaid);

(b) section 283 of the 1992 Act (repayment supplements); and

(c) section 102 of the Finance Act 2009 (repayment interest).

70A(3) This section is subject to regulations under section 95(1) of the Finance Act 2007 (payment by cheque).

History – S. 70A(2)(c) (and the "; and" before it) inserted (and the "and" after (a) omitted) by SI 2014/992, art. 4(b), with effect from 6 May 2014 in relation to payments which are due and payable in respect of the tax year 2014–15 and subsequent tax years
S. 70A(3) inserted by FA 2007, s. 95(7), with effect from Royal Assent 19 July 2007.
S. 70A inserted by FA 1994, s. 196 and Sch. 19, para. 22, as respects cheques received on or after 6 April 1996.

Cross references – SI 1993/743: effective date of cheque payments by subcontractors.

Other material – Tax Bulletin TB04/96-4: table of effective dates of payment when tax paid after 5 April 1996 by cheque, electronic funds transfer, bank giro, or girobank.

PART VII – PERSONS CHARGEABLE IN A REPRESENTATIVE CAPACITY, ETC.

INCOME TAX

71 Bodies of persons

71(1) Every body of persons shall be chargeable to income tax in like manner as any person is chargeable under the Income Tax Acts.

71(2) Subject to section 108 of this Act, the chamberlain or other officer acting as treasurer, auditor or receiver for the time being of any body of persons chargeable to income tax shall be answerable for doing all such acts as are required to be done under the Income Tax Acts for the purpose of the assessment of the body and for payment of the tax.

71(3) Every such officer as aforesaid may from time to time retain, out of any money coming into his hands on behalf of the body, so much thereof as is sufficient to pay the income tax charged upon the body, and shall be indemnified for all such payments made in pursuance of the Income Tax Acts.

History – In s. 71(1) the words "Subject to sections 6 to 12 and Parts VIII and XI of the principal Act (charge of corporation tax on companies)," omitted by CTA 2009, s. 1322 and Sch. 1, para. 304 and repealed by CTA 2009, s. 1326 and Sch. 3, Pt. 1, with effect for corporation tax purposes for accounting periods ending on or after 1 April 2009, and for income tax and capital gains tax purposes for the tax year 2009–10 and subsequent tax years.
Reference to provisions of the principal Act substituted by ICTA 1988, Sch. 29, para. 32, that Act becoming the principal Act (TMA 1970, s. 118(1)).

Cross references – SI 1986/1711, Schedule, Pt. I, II: modified application of s. 71 to stamp duty reserve tax.

72 Trustees, guardians, etc. of incapacitated persons

72 [Omitted by FA 2012, s. 222(1)(b).]

History – S. 72 omitted by FA 2012, s. 222(1)(b), with effect for the tax year 2012–13 and subsequent tax years.

Cross references – SSCBA 1992, Sch. 2, para. 5: Class 4 National Insurance contributions not payable by a trustee, guardian etc. in respect of the profits of a trade, profession or vocation.

Statements of practice – A13: HMRC view that returns must be signed by the taxpayer personally, with relaxation where the provision of a signature would be injurious to the taxpayer's health.

73 Further provision as to infants

73 [Omitted by FA 2012, s. 222(1)(c).]

History – S. 73 omitted by FA 2012, s. 222(1)(c), with effect for the tax year 2012–13 and subsequent tax years.
In former s. 73, the words "parent or guardian" substituted by Age of Legal Capacity (Scotland) Act 1991, s. 10 and Sch. 1, para. 33, with effect from 25 September 1991.

74 Personal representatives

74(1) If a person chargeable to income tax dies, the executor or administrator of the person deceased shall be liable for the tax chargeable on such deceased person, and may deduct any payments made under this section out of the assets and effects of the person deceased.

74(2) On neglect or refusal of payment, any person liable under this section may be proceeded against in like manner as any other defaulter.

Cross references – S. 40: assessment in respect of deceased's tax liability made on personal representative by reference to four-year time limit.
ICTA 1988, s. 113(6): liability of deceased partner's personal representatives for tax on share of partnership profits.
SI 1986/1711, Schedule, Pt. I and II: modified application of s. 74 to stamp duty reserve tax.

75 Receivers appointed by a court

75(1) A receiver appointed by any court in the United Kingdom which has the direction and control of any property in respect of which income tax is charged in accordance with the provisions of the Income Tax Acts shall be assessable and chargeable with the tax in like manner and to the like amount as would be assessed and charged if the property were not under the direction and control of the court.

75(2) Every such receiver shall be answerable for doing all matters and things required to be done under the Income Tax Acts for the purpose of assessment and payment of income tax.

Cross references – F(No. 2)A 1997, Sch. 2, para. 18(1), (2): modified application to windfall tax.

76 Protection for certain trustees, agents and receivers

76 [Omitted by FA 2011, s. 86 and Sch. 23, para. 51(2)(q).]

History – S. 76 omitted by FA 2011, s. 86 and Sch. 23, para. 51(2)(q), with effect from 1 April 2012, but in relation to a notice issued before that date, s. 76 continues to apply as if it had not been omitted (FA 2011, Sch. 23, para. 65). Former s. 76 read as follows:

"*Protection for certain trustees, agents and receivers*

76(1) A trustee who has authorised the receipt of profits arising from trust property by, or by the agent of, the person entitled thereto shall not, if–

(a) that person or agent actually received the profits under that authority, and

(b) the trustee makes a return, as required by section 13 of this Act, of the name, address and profits of that person,

be required to do any other act for the purpose of the assessment of that person to income tax.

76(2) An agent or receiver of any person resident in the United Kingdom, other than an incapacitated person, shall not, if he makes a return, as required by section 13 of this Act, of the name, address and profits of that person, be required to do any other act for the purpose of the assessment of that person to income tax.".

CAPITAL GAINS TAX

77 Application of Part VII to capital gains tax

77(1) This Part of this Act (except section 76 above) shall apply in relation to capital gains tax as it applies in relation to income tax, and subject to any necessary modifications.

77(2) This Part of this Act as applied by this section shall not affect the question of who is the person to whom chargeable gains accrue, or who is chargeable to capital gains tax, so far as that question is relevant for the purposes of any exemption, or of any provision determining the rate at which capital gains tax is chargeable.

History – S. 77(1) amended by FA 1971, s. 37 and Sch. 14, Pt. II, with effect from 6 April 1973.

DEVELOPMENT LAND TAX

77A Application of Part VII to development land tax

77A [Repealed by FA 1985, Sch. 27, Pt. X, with effect from 19 March 1985.]

PART 7A – HOLDERS OF LICENCES UNDER THE PETROLEUM ACT 1998

LICENCE-HOLDERS' LIABILITIES FOR TAX ASSESSED ON NON-UK RESIDENTS

History – Pt. 7A inserted by TIOPA 2010, s. 371 and Sch. 7, para. 2, with effect for corporation tax purposes for accounting periods ending on or after 1 April 2010, for income tax and capital gains tax purposes for the tax year 2010–11 and subsequent tax years, and for petroleum revenue tax purposes for chargeable periods beginning on or after 1 July 2010.

77B Pre-conditions for serving secondary-liability notice

77B(1) Conditions A to E are the pre-conditions for the purposes of section 77C.

77B(2) Condition A is that tax is assessed on a person not resident in the United Kingdom.

77B(3) Condition B is that the tax is assessed in reliance on–

(a) section 276 of the 1992 Act,

(b) section 874 of ITTOIA 2005, or

(c) section 1313 of CTA 2009.

77B(4) Condition C is that the tax assessed is not tax under ITEPA 2003.

77B(5) Condition D is that–

(a) there is a licence to which the tax assessed is related (see section 77J for the meaning of tax related to a licence),

(b) there is more than one licence to which the tax assessed is related, or

(c) there is a licence, or more than one licence, to which part of the tax assessed is related but in addition part of the tax assessed is not related to any licence.

77B(6) Condition E is that the tax is not paid in full within 30 days after it becomes due and payable.

77B(7) In this Part **"licence"** means a licence under Part 1 of the Petroleum Act 1998.

History – S. 77B inserted by TIOPA 2010, s. 371 and Sch. 7, para. 2, with effect for corporation tax purposes for accounting periods ending on or after 1 April 2010, for income tax and capital gains tax purposes for the tax year 2010–11 and subsequent tax years, and for petroleum revenue tax purposes for chargeable periods beginning on or after 1 July 2010.

77C Secondary-liability notices

77C(1) If each of the pre-conditions (see section 77B) is met, an officer of Revenue and Customs may serve on the holder of the licence concerned, or on the holder of any of the licences concerned, a notice–

(a) that states particulars of the assessment,

(b) that states the amount remaining unpaid and the date when it became payable,

(c) that requires the holder to pay, within 30 days of the service of the notice, the amount for which the holder is liable, and

(d) that, if the amount for which the holder is liable is given by subsection (3) or section 77G(7), gives particulars of how the amount was determined.

77C(2) For the purposes of subsection (1), the amount for which the holder is liable is the amount remaining unpaid, together with any interest on it under sections 86 and 87A, but this is subject to subsection (3) and section 77G(7).

77C(3) In a case within section 77B(5)(b) or (c), the amount for which the holder of the licence is liable is given by–

$$\frac{L}{T} \times (A + I)$$

77C(4) In subsection (3)–

A is the amount remaining unpaid,

I is any interest due on that amount under sections 86 and 87A,

T is the total amount of the profits or chargeable gains in respect of which the assessment is made, and

L is so much of that total amount as is profits or chargeable gains related to the licence.

77C(5) The power under subsection (1) is subject to section 77E (certain pre-1974 cases).

77C(6) In this Part **"secondary-liability notice"** means a notice under subsection (1).

History – S. 77C inserted by TIOPA 2010, s. 371 and Sch. 7, para. 2, with effect for corporation tax purposes for accounting periods ending on or after 1 April 2010, for income tax and capital gains tax purposes for the tax year 2010–11 and subsequent tax years, and for petroleum revenue tax purposes for chargeable periods beginning on or after 1 July 2010.

77D Payments under secondary-liability notices

77D(1) Any amount which a person is required to pay by a secondary-liability notice may be recovered from the person as if it were tax due and duly demanded from the person.

77D(2) If a person ("H") pays any amount which a secondary-liability notice requires H to pay, H may recover the amount from the person on whom the assessment concerned was made.

77D(3) A payment in pursuance of a secondary-liability notice is not allowed as a deduction in calculating any income, profits or losses for any tax purposes.

History – S. 77D inserted by TIOPA 2010, s. 371 and Sch. 7, para. 2, with effect for corporation tax purposes for accounting periods ending on or after 1 April 2010, for income tax and capital gains tax purposes for the tax year 2010–11 and subsequent tax years, and for petroleum revenue tax purposes for chargeable periods beginning on or after 1 July 2010.

77E Exception for certain pre-1974 cases

77E(1) Section 77C(1) does not give power to serve a secondary-liability notice on the holder of a licence if the profits arose, or the chargeable gains accrued, to the assessed person in consequence of a contract made by the holder before 23 March 1973.

77E(2) The exception under subsection (1) does not apply if–

(a) the assessed person is connected with the holder, or

(b) the contract was substantially varied on or after 23 March 1973.

77E(3) For the purposes of subsection (2), whether a person is connected with another is determined in accordance with section 1122 of CTA 2010.

History – S. 77E inserted by TIOPA 2010, s. 371 and Sch. 7, para. 2, with effect for corporation tax purposes for accounting periods ending on or after 1 April 2010, for income tax and capital gains tax purposes for the tax year 2010–11 and subsequent tax years, and for petroleum revenue tax purposes for chargeable periods beginning on or after 1 July 2010.

EXEMPTION CERTIFICATES

77F Issue, cancellation and effect of exemption certificates

77F(1) This section applies if there is a person ("T") who will or might become liable to tax which, if unpaid, could be recovered under this Part from a person ("H") who is the holder of a licence.

77F(2) If an officer of Revenue and Customs, on an application made by T, is satisfied that T will comply with any obligations imposed on T by the Taxes Acts, the officer may issue to H a certificate exempting H from section 77C with respect to any tax payable by T.

77F(3) If a certificate is issued to H under subsection (2), an officer of Revenue and Customs may, by notice in writing to H, cancel the certificate from the date specified in the notice.

77F(4) The date specified in a notice under subsection (3) may not be earlier than 30 days after the service of the notice.

77F(5) If a certificate is issued to H under subsection (2), section 77C does not apply to any tax payable by T which becomes due while the certificate is in force.

77F(6) If a certificate is issued to H under subsection (2) but is subsequently cancelled under subsection (3), section 77C also does not apply to any tax payable by T which–

(a) becomes due after the certificate is cancelled, but

(b) is in respect of profits arising, or chargeable gains accruing, while the certificate is in force.

History – S. 77F inserted by TIOPA 2010, s. 371 and Sch. 7, para. 3, with effect for corporation tax purposes for accounting periods ending on or after 1 April 2010, for income tax and capital gains tax purposes for the tax year 2010–11 and subsequent tax years, and for petroleum revenue tax purposes for chargeable periods beginning on or after 1 July 2010.

77G Liabilities for assessments made after exemption certificate cancelled

77G(1) Subsection (7) applies if–

(a) each of conditions A to C is met, and

(b) one of conditions D and E is met.

77G(2) Condition A is that, after the cancellation under section 77F(3) of a certificate issued under section 77F(2) to a person ("H") who is the holder of a licence, tax related to the licence is assessed on the applicant for the certificate.

77G(3) Condition B is that the tax is assessed in reliance on–

(a) section 276 of the 1992 Act,

(b) section 874 of ITTOIA 2005, or

(c) section 1313 of CTA 2009.

77G(4) Condition C is that the tax assessed is not tax under ITEPA 2003.

77G(5) Condition D is that–

(a) ignoring section 77F, H could be required by a secondary-liability notice to pay all of the tax remaining unpaid under the assessment, and

(b) the profits or chargeable gains in respect of which the assessment is made include (but are not limited to) profits arising, or chargeable gains accruing, while the certificate is in force.

77G(6) Condition E is that–

(a) as a result of section 77C(3), but ignoring section 77F, H could be required by a secondary-liability notice to pay some, but not all, of the tax remaining unpaid under the assessment, and

(b) the profits or chargeable gains that are–

(i) ones in respect of which the assessment is made, and

(ii) related to the licence,

include (but are not limited to) profits arising, or chargeable gains accruing, while the certificate is in force.

77G(7) If this subsection applies then, for the purposes of section 77C(1), the amount for which the holder of the licence is liable is the amount given by–

$$A \times \left(1 - \frac{CIF}{CIF + NIF}\right)$$

together with a corresponding proportion of any interest due under sections 86 and 87A on the amount remaining unpaid.

77G(8) In subsection (7)–

A is the amount that H could be required to pay as mentioned in paragraph (a) of whichever of conditions D and E is met ("the operative condition"),

CIF is the amount of the profits or chargeable gains mentioned in paragraph (b) of the operative condition that are ones arising, or accruing, while the certificate is in force, and

NIF is the amount of the profits or chargeable gains mentioned in paragraph (b) of the operative condition that are ones arising, or accruing, while the certificate is not in force.

History – S. 77G inserted by TIOPA 2010, s. 371 and Sch. 7, para. 3, with effect for corporation tax purposes for accounting periods ending on or after 1 April 2010, for income tax and capital gains tax purposes for the tax year 2010–11 and subsequent tax years, and for petroleum revenue tax purposes for chargeable periods beginning on or after 1 July 2010.

SUPPLEMENTARY

77H Calculations under sections 77C(3) and 77G(7)

77H(1) Subsection (2) applies for the purposes of calculating any of the following amounts of profits or chargeable gains–

(a) L in a calculation under section 77C(3),

(b) CIF in a calculation under section 77G(7), and

(c) CIF + NIF in a calculation under section 77G(7) when it is condition E in section 77G that is met.

77H(2) The amount is to be calculated as if for the purposes of making a separate assessment in respect of those profits or chargeable gains on the person on whom the assessment was made.

77H(3) An officer of Revenue and Customs applying subsection (2) is to make all such allocations and apportionments of receipts, expenses, allowances and deductions taken into account, or made, for the purposes of the actual assessment as appear to the officer to be just and reasonable in the circumstances.

History – S. 77H inserted by TIOPA 2010, s. 371 and Sch. 7, para. 4, with effect for corporation tax purposes for accounting periods ending on or after 1 April 2010, for income tax and capital gains tax purposes for the tax year 2010–11 and subsequent tax years, and for petroleum revenue tax purposes for chargeable periods beginning on or after 1 July 2010.

77I Information

77I [Omitted by FA 2011, s. 86 and Sch. 23, para. 51(2)(r).]

History – S. 77I omitted by FA 2011, s. 86 and Sch. 23, para. 51(2)(r), with effect from 1 April 2012, but in relation to a notice issued before that date, s. 77I continues to apply as if it had not been omitted (FA 2011, Sch. 23, para. 65). Former s. 77I read as follows:

"*Information*

77I(1) The holder of a licence must, if required to do so by a notice served on the holder by an officer of Revenue and Customs, give to the officer within the time specified by the notice (which is not to be less than 30 days) such particulars as may be required by the notice of–

(a) licence-related transactions (see subsection (2)),
(b) licence-related payments (see subsection (3)), or
(c) persons to whom licence-related payments have been paid or are payable.

77I(2) In subsection (1) **"licence-related transaction"** means a transaction in connection with activities authorised by the licence as a result of which any person is or might be liable to tax by virtue of–

(a) section 276 of the 1992 Act,
(b) section 874 of ITTOIA 2005, or
(c) section 1313 of CTA 2009.

77I(3) In subsection (1) **"licence-related payment"** means–

(a) earnings which constitute employment income (see section 7(2)(a) of ITEPA 2003),
(b) amounts which are treated as earnings and constitute employment income (see section 7(2)(b) of ITEPA 2003), or
(c) other payments,

paid or payable in respect of duties or services performed in an area in which activities authorised by the licence may be carried on under the licence.

77I(4) If a notice under subsection (1) is served on the holder of a licence, the holder must take reasonable steps to obtain the information necessary to enable the holder to comply with the notice.".

Former s. 77I inserted by TIOPA 2010, s. 371 and Sch. 7, para. 4, with effect for corporation tax purposes for accounting periods ending on or after 1 April 2010, for income tax and capital gains tax purposes for the tax year 2010–11 and subsequent tax years, and for petroleum revenue tax purposes for chargeable periods beginning on or after 1 July 2010.

77J Meaning of "related to a licence" as respects tax, or profits or gains

77J(1) Subsections (2) and (3) apply for the purposes of this Part.

77J(2) An amount of tax is related to a licence if the tax is in respect of profits or chargeable gains related to the licence.

77J(3) Profits or chargeable gains are related to a licence if they are–

(a) profits from activities authorised by the licence,
(b) profits from activities carried on in connection with activities authorised by the licence, or
(c) profits from, or chargeable gains accruing on the disposal of, exploration or exploitation rights connected with–
   (i) activities authorised by the licence, or
   (ii) activities carried on in connection with activities authorised by the licence.

77J(4) In this section–

(a) **"designated area"** means an area designated by Order in Council under section 1(7) of the Continental Shelf Act 1964,
(b) **"exploration or exploitation activities"** means activities carried on in connection with the exploration or exploitation of so much of the seabed and subsoil and their natural resources as is situated in the United Kingdom or a designated area,
(c) **"exploration or exploitation rights"** means rights to–
   (i) assets to be produced by exploration or exploitation activities,
   (ii) interests in such assets, or
   (iii) the benefit of such assets,
(d) any reference to the disposal of exploration or exploitation rights includes a reference to the disposal of unlisted shares deriving their value, or the greater part of their value, directly or indirectly from such rights,
(e) **"shares"** includes–
   (i) stock, and

(ii) securities not creating or evidencing a charge on assets,

(f) **"unlisted shares"** means shares that are not listed on a recognised stock exchange, and

(g) **"recognised stock exchange"** has the meaning given by section 1005(1) and (2) of ITA 2007.

History – S. 77J inserted by TIOPA 2010, s. 371 and Sch. 7, para. 4, with effect for corporation tax purposes for accounting periods ending on or after 1 April 2010, for income tax and capital gains tax purposes for the tax year 2010–11 and subsequent tax years, and for petroleum revenue tax purposes for chargeable periods beginning on or after 1 July 2010.

77K Other definitions in Part 7A

77K(1) This section applies for the purposes of this Part.

77K(2) **"Licence"** has the meaning given by section 77B(7).

77K(3) **"Secondary-liability notice"** has the meaning given by section 77C(6).

History – S. 77K inserted by TIOPA 2010, s. 371 and Sch. 7, para. 4, with effect for corporation tax purposes for accounting periods ending on or after 1 April 2010, for income tax and capital gains tax purposes for the tax year 2010–11 and subsequent tax years, and for petroleum revenue tax purposes for chargeable periods beginning on or after 1 July 2010.

PART VIII – CHARGES ON NON-RESIDENTS

INCOME TAX

78 Method of charging non-residents

78 [Repealed by FA 1995, s. 162 and Sch. 29, Pt. VIII(16) for the purposes of income tax and capital gains tax, in relation to the year 1996–97 and subsequent years of assessment, and for the purposes of corporation tax, in relation to accounting periods beginning after 31 March 1996.]

79 Profits from branch or agency

79 [Repealed by FA 1995, s. 162 and Sch. 29, Pt. VIII(16) for the purposes of income tax and capital gains tax, in relation to the year 1996–97 and subsequent years of assessment, and for the purposes of corporation tax, in relation to accounting periods beginning after 31 March 1996.]

80 Charge on percentage of turnover

80 [Repealed by FA 1995, s. 162 and Sch. 29, Pt. VIII(16) for the purposes of income tax and capital gains tax, in relation to the year 1996–97 and subsequent years of assessment, and for the purposes of corporation tax, in relation to accounting periods beginning after 31 March 1996.]

81 Taxation on basis of merchanting profit

81 [Repealed by FA 1995, s. 162 and Sch. 29, Pt. VIII(16) for the purposes of income tax and capital gains tax, in relation to the year 1996–97 and subsequent years of assessment, and for the purposes of corporation tax, in relation to accounting periods beginning after 31 March 1996.]

82 Savings

82 [Repealed by FA 1995, s. 162 and Sch. 29, Pt. VIII(16) for the purposes of income tax and capital gains tax, in relation to the year 1996–97 and subsequent years of assessment, and for the purposes of corporation tax, in relation to accounting periods beginning after 31 March 1996.]

83 Responsibilities and indemnification of persons in whose name a non-resident person is chargeable

83 [Repealed by FA 1995, s. 162 and Sch. 29, Pt. VIII(16) for the purposes of income tax and capital gains tax, in relation to the year 1996–97 and subsequent years of assessment, and for the purposes of corporation tax, in relation to accounting periods beginning after 31 March 1996.]

CAPITAL GAINS TAX

84 Gains from branch or agency

84 [Repealed by FA 1995, s. 162 and Sch. 29, Pt. VIII(16) for the purposes of income tax and capital gains tax, in relation to the year 1996–97 and subsequent years of assessment and for the purposes of corporation tax, in relation to accounting periods beginning after 31 March 1996.]

CORPORATION TAX

85 Application of Part VIII to corporation tax

85 [Repealed by FA 1995, s. 162 and Sch. 29, Pt. VIII(16) for the purposes of income tax and capital gains tax, in relation to the year 1996–97 and subsequent years of assessment and for the purposes of corporation tax, in relation to accounting periods beginning after 31 March 1996.]

DEVELOPMENT LAND TAX

85A Non-residents chargeable to development land tax

85A [Repealed by FA 1985, Sch. 27, Pt. X, with effect from 19 March 1985.]

PART IX – INTEREST ON OVERDUE TAX

Other material – ICAEW Technical Release TR 799 (not reproduced): interest under TMA 1970 will not accrue beyond the date of commencement of liquidation (compulsory/members' voluntary liquidation).

86 Interest on overdue income tax and capital gains tax

86(1) The following, namely–

(a) any amount on account of income tax which becomes due and payable in accordance with section 59A(2) of this Act, and

(b) any income tax or capital gains tax which becomes due and payable in accordance with section 55 or 59B of this Act,

shall carry interest at the rate applicable under section 178 of the Finance Act 1989 from the relevant date until payment.

86(2) For the purposes of subsection (1)(a) above the relevant date is whichever of the dates mentioned in section 59A(2) of this Act is applicable; and for the purposes of subsection (1)(b) above the relevant date is–

(a) in any such case as is mentioned in subsection (3) of section 59B of this Act, the last day of the period of three months mentioned in that subsection; and

(b) in any other case, the date mentioned in subsection (4) of that section.

86(3) Subsection (1) above applies even if the relevant date is a non-business day within the meaning of section 92 of the Bills of Exchange Act 1882.

86(4) Subsection (5) below applies where as regards a year of assessment–

(a) any person makes a claim under subsection (3) or (4) of section 59A of this Act in respect of the amounts (the section 59A amounts) payable by him in accordance with subsection (2) of that section, and

(b) an amount (the section 59B amount) becomes payable by him

(i) in accordance with section 59B(3), (4) or (5) of this Act, or

(ii) in accordance with section 59B(6) of this Act in respect of income tax assessed under section 29 of this Act.

86(5) Interest shall be payable under this section as if each of the section 59A amounts had been equal to–

(a) the aggregate of that amount and 50 per cent of the section 59B amount, or

(b) the amount which would have been payable in accordance with subsection (2) of section 59A of this Act if the claim under subsection (3) or (4) of that section had not been made,

whichever is the less.

86(6) In determining for the purposes of subsections (4) and (5) above what amount (if any) is payable by any person in accordance with section 59B(3), (4) or (5) of this Act or, in respect of income tax assessed under section 29 of this Act, in accordance with section 59B(6) of this Act–

(a) it shall be assumed that both of the section 59A amounts have been paid, and

(b) no account shall be taken of any amount which has been paid on account otherwise than under section 59A(2) of this Act or is payable by way of capital gains tax.

86(7) *Subsection (8) below* applies where as regards any person and a year of assessment–

(a) amounts (the section 59A amounts) become payable by him in accordance with section 59A(2) of this Act, and

(b) an amount (the section 59B amount) becomes repayable to him in accordance with section 59B(3), (4) or (5) of this Act.

86(8) So much of any interest payable under this section on either of the section 59A amounts as is not attributable to the amount by which that amount exceeds 50 per cent of the section 59B amount shall be remitted.

86(9) In determining for the purposes of subsections (7) and (8) above what amount (if any) is repayable to any person in accordance with section 59B(3), (4) or (5) of this Act, no account shall be taken of any amount which has been paid on account otherwise than under section 59A(2) of this Act or is payable by way of capital gains tax.

History – S. 86 amended by FA 1996, s.132 and Sch. 18, para. 3:

- in relation to partnerships whose trades, professions and businesses were set up and commenced before 6 April 1994, as respects the year 1997–98 and subsequent years of assessment (FA 1994, Sch. 19, para. 23(2));
- in so far as it relates to income tax and capital gains tax, other than in relation to partnerships whose trades, professions and businesses were set up and commenced before 6 April 1994, as respects the year 1996–97 and subsequent years of assessment (FA 1994, s. 199(2)).

In s. 86(2) reference to "section 92" substituted for previous reference to "section 93" by FA 1996, s. 131(2).
S. 86 substituted by FA 1994, s. 196 and Sch. 19, para. 23(1), as superseded by:

- FA 1995, s. 110(1) as respects the year 1996–97 and subsequent years generally;
- FA 1995, s. 110(2) in relation to any income tax or capital gains tax which is for the year 1995–96 or a previous year and is charged by an assessment made on or after 6 April 1998;
- FA 1995, s. 110(4) (as inserted by FA 1996, s. 131) so far as it relates to partnerships whose business commenced before 6 April 1994, as respects the year 1997–98 and subsequent years.

Cross references – S. 59D: general rule as to when corporation tax payable (nine months from the end of the accounting period).
S. 59E: further provision as to when corporation tax due and payable (regulatory powers).
S. 70(2): collector's certificate is sufficient evidence of non-payment.
S. 107A(2)(d): application of s. 86 to relevant trustees.
S. 109(2): s. 86(6) applies with modifications in relation to tax charged on close companies in connection with loans to participators under ICTA 1988, s. 419, 420.
FA 1984, Sch. 14, para. 6(4): no interest chargeable under s. 86 is charged where capital gains tax is postponed in respect of beneficiary's liability for tax of non-resident trustees for any period prior to the time when tax becomes payable.
F(No. 2)A 1987, s. 86(3), (7): reference to s. 86 in s. 92 shall include references to s. 87A (interest on overdue corporation tax etc.) in relation to accounting periods ending after 30 September 1993 (by virtue of SI 1992/3066, art. 2).
ICTA 1988, s. 203: PAYE.
ICTA 1988, s. 307(6): application of s. 86 to assessments made by virtue of s. 307.
ICTA 1988, s. 369(7), (8): application of s. 86 to MIRAS.
ICTA 1988, s. 375(4): assessments made in respect of excess relief under ICTA 1988, s. 375(3) to be treated as assessments as mentioned in s. 86(2).
ICTA 1988, s. 393A(1): set off of company trading losses against profits of the same or an earlier accounting period.
ICTA 1988, s. 767B(1): modification of s. 86, in so far as it applies in relation to accounting periods ending on or before 30 September 1993, where tax is assessed under ICTA 1988, s. 767A (change in company ownership: corporation tax).
ICTA 1988, Sch. 3, para. 9: 30 days from the date of issue of the notice of assessment.
ICTA 1988, Sch. 14, para. 7(3), (4): life assurance premium relief; payment of a sum claimed under ICTA 1988, s. 266(5)(b).
FA 1991, s. 33(3), (3A): vocational training relief; application of s. 86.
SSCBA 1992, Sch. 2, para. 6: application of s. 86 in relation to Class 4 National Insurance contributions.
TCGA 1992, s. 281(5): payment of capital gains tax on certain gifts by instalments is subject to interest under s. 88 in accordance with the revised due dates.
FA 1995, s. 73(4): application of s. 86 to certain sums payable in connection with venture capital trusts.
FA 2001, s. 107: relief for interest in certain circumstances (e.g. foot and mouth)
SI 1986/1711, Schedule, Pt. I, II: modified application of s. 86 to stamp duty reserve tax.
SI 1987/352, reg. 6(6)(b): s. 86(3), (4) does not apply to assessments under this instrument (pension surpluses) – also, reckonable dates for payment of tax under that instrument.
SI 1987/530, reg. 11(3)(b): application of s. 86–92 to withholding tax on entertainers and sportsmen.
SI 1989/469, reg. 28(3)(a); SI 1987/352, reg. 6(6)(a): assessments under these regulations (personal equity plan and pensions surpluses) are treated as assessments specified in s. 86.
SI 1989/1297, reg. 3: applicable rate of interest for the purposes of s. 86.
SI 1993/743, reg. 15(4): application of s. 86 rate to sub-contractors tax deduction scheme.
SI 1998/3175: corporation tax payment by instalments regulations.
SI 2011/701, art. 5: s. 86 does not apply to any self-assessment amount (as defined in SI 2011/701, art. 2) which becomes payable or repayable on or after 31 October 2011 (the date of the coming into force of FA 2009, s. 101–103).

Extra-statutory concessions – A17: where taxpayer dies before tax is due, the time for payment is extended until the personal representatives have obtained a grant of representation.

Hansard – 2 July 1975, col. 746 and confirmed in ICAEW Technical Release TR 798 (not reproduced): where a taxpayer simultaneously has tax due under one assessment and has overpaid on another and he draws this fact to the Revenue's attention and asks for a set-off, interest will not be charged on the tax due as of the date that the set-off request is made (to the extent that it can be met from the overpayment).
Written Answers, 17 November 1986, col. 81 (not reproduced): when tax is paid by bank giro, the Revenue treat the date stamped on the payslip by the bank cashier as the date of payment.

HMRC Manuals – Assessed Taxes, AT 12.502: how HMRC consider objections to an interest charge.

Other material – Taxline 1993/55 (not reproduced): HMRC regard SP 6/89 as not only protecting the taxpayer from interest charges under TMA 1970, s. 88, but as also protecting HMRC's entitlement to interest under s. 86. As a Sch. E assessment will only attract interest from the date it is agreed or determined, deductions and allowances must be reported as well as income.
Tax Bulletin TB04/96-4: table of effective dates of payment when tax paid after 5 April 1996 by cheque, electronic funds transfer, bank giro, or girobank.

86A Interest on development land tax unpaid on reckonable date

86A [Repealed by FA 1985, Sch. 27, Pt. X, with effect from 19 March 1985.]

87 Interest on overdue income tax deducted at source

87(1) Income tax which is assessable under Chapter 15 of Part 15 of ITA 2007 carries interest at the rate applicable under section 178 of the Finance Act 1989 from the date when it was due under section 951 of ITA 2007 until payment.

87(2) Subsection (1) applies–

(a) whether or not an assessment is made, and

(b) whether or not income tax which is assessed has been paid when the assessment is made.

87(3) Subsection (1) applies even if the date when the income tax should have been paid is a non-business day as defined by section 92 of the Bills of Exchange Act 1882.

87(4) Subsection (5) applies to any income tax which–

(a) was payable under Chapter 15 of Part 15 of ITA 2007 (collection: deposit-takers, building societies and certain companies) in respect of payments within section 946 of that Act made in a return period,

(b) was not paid on the date when it was due under section 951 of that Act, and

(c) has subsequently been discharged or repaid under section 953 of that Act because the person who made the payments received payments on which it suffered income tax by deduction in a later return period.

87(5) The income tax carries interest under subsection (1) from the date when it was due under section 951 of ITA 2007 until the earliest of–

(a) the date when the income tax was paid,

(b) the date when the person delivered a return for the later return period, and

(c) the expiry of 14 days after the end of that period,

but subsection (1) does not otherwise apply to the income tax.

87(6) In this section **"return period"** means a period for which a return is required to be made under Chapter 15 of Part 15 of ITA 2007.

History – S. 87 substituted by ITA 2007, s. 1027 and Sch. 1, para. 258, with effect from 6 April 2007.

87A Interest on overdue corporation tax etc.

87A(1) Corporation tax shall carry interest at the rate applicable under section 178 of the Finance Act 1989 from the date when the tax becomes due and payable (in accordance with section 59D of this Act) until payment.

87A(2) Subsection (1) above applies even if the date when the tax becomes due and payable (as mentioned in that subsection) is a non-business day within the meaning of section 92 of the Bills of Exchange Act 1882.

87A(3) In relation to corporation tax assessed or treated as assessed by virtue of section 346(2) or 347(1) of the principal Act, section 137(4), 139(7) or 190 of the 1992 Act paragraph 75A(2) of Schedule 18 to the Finance Act 1998, paragraph 69 of Schedule 29 to the Finance Act 2002 or Chapter 7 of Part 22 of CTA 2010 (which enable unpaid corporation tax assessed on a company to be assessed on other persons in certain circumstances), the reference in subsection (1) above to the date when the tax becomes due and payable is a reference to the date when it became due and payable by the company.

87A(4) [Repealed by FA 1998, s. 31 and Sch. 3, para. 4(2), s. 165 and Sch. 20, Pt. III(2).]

87A(4A) In a case where–

(a) there is for an accounting period of a company (**"the later period"**) a non-trading deficit on the company's loan relationships,

(b) as a result of a claim under section 389(1) or 459(1)(b) of CTA 2009 the whole or part of the deficit for the later period is set off against profits of an earlier accounting period (**"the earlier period"**), and

(c) if the claim had not been made, there would be an amount or, as the case may be, an additional amount of corporation tax for the earlier period which would carry interest in accordance with this section,

then, for the purposes of the determination at any time of whether any interest is payable under this section or of the amount of interest so payable, the amount mentioned in paragraph (c) above shall be taken to be an amount of unpaid corporation tax for the earlier period except so far as concerns interest for any time after the date on which any corporation tax for the later period became (or, as the case may be, would have become) due and payable as mentioned in subsection (8) below.

87A(4B) [Repealed by FA 1998, s. 31 and Sch. 3, para. 4(3), s. 165 and Sch. 20, Pt. III(2).]

87A(5) [Omitted by FA 2016, s. 5 and Sch. 1 para. 51(10).]

87A(6) In any case where–

(a) on a claim under section 37 of CTA 2010, the whole or any part of a loss incurred in an accounting period (**"the later period"**) has been relieved (whether under that section or section 42 of that Act) for the purposes of corporation tax against profits of a preceding accounting period (**"the earlier period"**);

(b) the earlier period does not fall wholly within the period of twelve months immediately preceding the later period; and

(c) if the claim had not been made, there would be an amount or, as the case may be, an additional amount of corporation tax for the earlier period which would carry interest in accordance with this section,

then, for the purposes of the determination at any time of whether any interest is payable under this section or of the amount of interest so payable, the amount mentioned in paragraph (c) above shall be taken to be an amount of unpaid corporation tax for the earlier period except so far as concerns interest for any time after the date on which any corporation tax for the later period became (or, as the case may be, would have become) due and payable as mentioned in subsection (8) below.

87A(7) [Repealed by FA 1998, s. 31 and Sch. 3, para. 4(3), s. 165 and Sch. 20, Pt. III(2).]

87A(8) In subsections (4), (4A) and (6) above, any reference to the date on which corporation tax for an accounting period became, or would have become, due and payable shall be construed on the basis that corporation tax for an accounting period becomes due and payable on the day following the expiry of nine months from the end of the accounting period.

87A(9) The power conferred by section 59E of this Act (alteration of date on which corporation tax becomes due and payable) does not include power to make provision in relation to subsection (4), (4A), (6) or (8) above the effect of which would be to change the meaning of references in subsection (4), (4A) or (6) above to the date on which corporation tax for an accounting period became, or would have become, due and payable (as mentioned in subsection (8) above).

History – S. 87A(1) amended by FA 1994, s. 196 and Sch. 19, para. 24, substituting the reference to TMA 1970, s. 59D for the former reference to ICTA 1988, s. 10, in relation to accounting periods ending on or after 1 July 1999, the appointed day by virtue of FA 1994, s. 199(2), (3) and SI 1998/3173 (C. 78).

In s. 87A(1), (5), the words "rate applicable under section 178 of the Finance Act 1989" substituted by FA 1989, s. 179(1)(b)(i) with effect from 1 October 1993 (the day from which FA 1989, s. 178 has effect for the purposes of s. 87A by virtue of SI 1993/2212).

In s. 87A(3), the words "Schedule 28 to the Finance Act 2000 or" omitted by CTA 2010, s. 1177 and Sch. 1, para 156(2)(a) and repealed by CTA 2010, s. 1181 and Sch. 3, Pt. 1, with effect for corporation tax purposes for accounting periods ending on or after 1 April 2010, and for income tax and capital gains tax purposes for the tax year 2010–11 and subsequent tax years.

In s. 87A(3), the words "or Chapter 7 of Part 22 of CTA 2010" inserted by CTA 2010, s. 1177 and Sch. 1, para. 156(2)(b), with effect for corporation tax purposes for accounting periods ending on or after 1 April 2010, and for income tax and capital gains tax purposes for the tax year 2010–11 and subsequent tax years.

In s. 87A(3), reference to FA 1998, Sch. 18, para. 75A(2) substituted for former reference to FA 1990, s. 96(8) by FA 1999, s. 92(5), with effect in relation to accounting periods ending on or after 1 July 1999.

In s. 87A(3), words "or treated as assessed" and words "or Schedule 28 of the Finance Act 2000" inserted by FA 2000, Sch. 28, para. 3 with effect in relation to unpaid corporation tax assessed on a non-resident company (the "taxpayer company"), for an accounting period beginning after 1st April 2000, and payable by a company other than the "taxpayer company" by virtue of FA 2000, Sch. 28.

In s. 87A(3), words "or treated as assessed" and "or 190" inserted by FA 2000, Sch. 29, para. 9(2) with effect for the purposes of TCGA 1992, s. 190 (tax recoverable from another group company or controlling director), in relation to gains accruing on or after 1st April 2000.

In s. 87A(3), word "or" preceding "paragraph 75A(2)" and the words "or 179(11)" repealed by FA 2000, Sch. 40, Pt. II(11) and (12) respectively.

In s. 87A(3), the words ", Schedule 28 to the Finance Act 2000 or paragraph 69 of Schedule29 to the Finance Act 2002" substituted by FA 2002, Sch. 29, para. 69(4) with effect from 1 April 2002.

S. 87A(4) repealed by FA 1998, s. 31 and Sch. 3, para. 4(2), s. 165 and Sch. 27, Pt. III(2), with effect where the "later period" referred to in that subsection begins on or after 6 April 1999.

Former s. 87A(4) amended by FA 1995, s. 130 and Sch. 24, para. 9(1), with deemed effect from 23 March 1995 (FA 1995, Sch. 24, para. 7, FA 1993, s. 165(7)(b) and SI 1994/3224 (C. 79)) (and by FA 1998: see note below).

In former s. 87A(4), s. 87A(4A) and (6), references to subsection (8) substituted for former references to subsection (1) by FA 1998, s. 35 and Sch. 4, para. 4(2), with effect where the accounting period whose due and payable date (as defined in FA 1998, Sch. 4, para. 4(6)) falls to be determined is an accounting period ending on or after 1 July 1999, the corporation tax self-assessment appointed day by virtue of FA 1994, s. 199(2), (3) and SI 1998/3173 (C. 78).

In s. 87A(4A)(b) the words "section 389(1) or 459(1)(b) of CTA 2009" substituted for the words "section 83(2)(c) of the Finance Act 1996 or paragraph 4(3) of Schedule 11 to that Act" by CTA 2009, s. 1322 and Sch. 1, para. 305, with effect for corporation tax purposes for accounting periods ending on or after 1 April 2009, and for income tax and capital gains tax purposes for the tax year 2009–10 and subsequent tax years.

In s. 87A(4A)(a), the words "a non-trading deficit on the company's loan relationships," substituted for the previous words "a relievable amount within the meaning of section 131 of the Finance Act 1993 (non-trading exchange gains and losses)," and in s. 87A(4A)(b) the words "section 83(2)(c) … set off against profits" substituted, by FA 1996, s. 104 and Sch. 14, para. 1(1), in relation to accounting periods ending after 31 March 1996.

S. 87A(4A) (as amended by FA 1995, s. 130 and Sch. 24, para. 8, with deemed effect from 23 March 1995) inserted by FA 1993, s. 170 and Sch. 18, para. 1, with effect where a company becomes entitled to qualifying assets or rights under a currency contract, or subject to qualifying liabilities or duties under a currency contract, on or after the first day of its first accounting period to begin after 22 March 1995 (FA 1993, s. 165 and SI 1994/3224 (C. 79)).

S. 87A(4B) repealedby FA 1998, s. 31 and Sch. 3, para. 4(3), s. 165 and Sch. 27, Pt. III(2), with effect where the "earlier period" referred to in that subsection begins on or after 6 April 1999.

Former s. 87A(4B) inserted by FA 1995, s. 130 and Sch. 24, para. 9 with deemed effect from 23 March 1995 (FA 1995, Sch. 24, para. 7, FA 1993, s. 165(7)(b) and SI 1994/3224 (C. 79)) and amended by FA 1996, s. 104 and Sch. 14, para. 1(2), in relation to accounting periods ending after 31 March 1996.
S. 87A(5) omitted by FA 2016, s. 5 and Sch. 1 para. 51(10), with effect in relation to dividends paid or arising (or treated as paid), and other distributions made (or treated as made) in the tax year 2016–17 or at any later time. Former s. 87A(5) read as follows:
"**(5)** A sum assessed on a company by such an assessment as is referred to in section 1111(2) of CTA 2010 (recovery of payment of tax credit or interest on such a payment) shall carry interest at the rate applicable under section 178 of the Finance Act 1989 from the date when the payment of tax credit or interest was made until the sum assessed is paid.".
In former s. 87A(5), the words "1111(2) of CTA 2010" substituted for the words "252(5) of the principal Act" by CTA 2010, s. 1177 and Sch. 1, para. 156(3), with effect for corporation tax purposes for accounting periods ending on or after 1 April 2010, and for income tax and capital gains tax purposes for the tax year 2010–11 and subsequent tax years.
In s. 87A(6)(a), the words "section 37 of CTA 2010" substituted for the words "section 393A(1) of the principal Act" by CTA 2010, s. 1177 and Sch. 1, para. 156(4)(a), with effect for corporation tax purposes for accounting periods ending on or after 1 April 2010, and for income tax and capital gains tax purposes for the tax year 2010–11 and subsequent tax years.
In s. 87A(6)(a), the words "relieved (whether under that section or section 42 of that Act)" substituted for the words "set off (whether under section 393A(1) or 393B(3))" by CTA 2010, s. 1177 and Sch. 1, para. 1596(4)(b), with effect for corporation tax purposes for accounting periods ending on or after 1 April 2010, and for income tax and capital gains tax purposes for the tax year 2010–11 and subsequent tax years.
In s. 87A(6)(a), the words "(whether under section 393A(1) or 393B(3))" inserted by FA 2008, s. 111 and Sch. 35, para. 1, with effect in relation to losses incurred in accounting periods beginning on or after 12 March 2008.
S. 87A(7) repealed by FA 1998, s. 31 and Sch. 3, para. 4(3), s. 165 and Sch. 27, Pt. III(2), with effect where the "earlier period" referred to in that subsection begins on or after 6 April 1999.
S. 87A(8) and (9) inserted by FA 1998, s. 35 and Sch. 4, para. 4(3) and (4), with effect where the accounting period whose due and payable date (as defined in FA 1998, Sch. 4, para. 4(6)) falls to be determined is an accounting period ending on or after 1 July 1999, the corporation tax self-assessment appointed day by virtue of FA 1994, s. 199(2), (3) and SI 1998/3173 (C. 78).
S. 87A inserted by F(No. 2)A 1987, s. 85; ICTA 1988, s. 844 and Sch. 29, para. 10(1), (4); FA 1990, s. 96(12) and FA 1993, s. 120 and Sch. 14, para. 4 (superseding FA 1991, s. 73 and Sch. 15, para. 2), with respect to accounting periods ending after 30 September 1993, the day appointed by virtueof SI 1992/3066 (under Pay and File).
Cross references – ICTA 1988, s. 393A(1): set off of company trading losses against profits of same or earlier accounting period.
ICTA 1988, s. 767B(1): modification of s. 87A where corporation tax assessed under ICTA 1988, s. 767A (change in company ownership: corporation tax).
ICTA 1988, Sch. 19AB, para. 5: transitional application of s. 87A to life insurance companies carrying on pension business which make provisional repayment claims. See also para. 3(3): disregard of words in s. 87A(1) "(in accordance with section 10 of the principal Act)" in application of s. 87A to interest payable by life insurance company on excessive provisional repayment in respect of pension business.
TCGA 1992, s. 137(5): restitution in respect of interest payable by a person charged with unpaid tax following nullification of the equation of original and new holdings by a finding that the exchange, reconstruction or amalgamation not effected for bona fide commercial reasons etc.
TCGA 1992, s. 139(8): restitution in respect of interest payable by a person charged with unpaid tax following nullification of the no gain, no loss provisions for transfers of business on a reconstruction or amalgamation by a finding that not effected for bona fide commercial reasons etc.
TCGA 1992, s. 179(11): restitution in respect of interest payable by a person charged with unpaid tax following crystallisation of gain when company leaves a group with asset transferred intra-group.
TCGA 1992, s. 189(4): restitution in respect of interest payable by a person charged with unpaid tax as the recipient of a capital distribution emanating from the asset in respect of which the gain arose.
TCGA 1992, s. 190(4): restitution in respect of interest payable by a person charged with unpaid tax as the principal company of the chargeable company's group or as a fellow group member previously owning the asset.
FA 1994, s. 250: modified application of s. 87A where tax due under FA 1994, s. 250(4) (disposal of assets by companies treated as non-resident).
FA 1998, Sch. 18, para. 52(6): interest charged on the recovery of excess repayments of corporation tax.
FA 2000, Sch. 15, para. 63(2): interest on corporation tax which becomes due following reduction or withdrawal of investment relief.
SI 1998/3175, reg. 7: modifications of s. 87A as it applies in relation to any unpaid amount in respect of the total liability of a large company for an accounting period.
SI 1989/1297, reg. 3A, 3ZA, 3ZB: applicable rate of interest on overdue corporation tax.
Other material – Tax Bulletin TB04/96-4: table of effective dates of payment when tax paid after 5 April 1996 by cheque, electronic funds transfer, bank giro, or girobank.
Notes – S. 87 rewritten as ITA 2007, Sch. 1 para. 258.

88 Interest on tax recovered to make good loss due to taxpayer's fault

88 [Repealed by FA 1996, s. 132 and Sch. 18, para. 4(1), s. 205 and Sch. 41, Pt. V(8).]

History – S. 88 repealed by FA 1996, s. 132 and Sch. 18, para. 4(1), s. 205 and Sch. 41, Pt. V(8). The repeal is effective generally for years after 1995–96. However, in the case of partnerships where the business was set up and commenced before 6 April 1994, the repeal is effective for years after 1996–97. The repeal also applies to income tax and capital gains tax charged by assessments made after 5 April 1998, but relating to 1995–96 and earlier years.

88A Determinations under section 88

88A [Repealed by FA 1996, s. 132 and Sch. 18, para. 4(2), s. 205 and Sch. 41, Pt. V(8).]

History – S. 88A repealed (in consequence of the repeal of s. 88), by FA 1996, s. 132 and Sch. 18, para. 4(2), s. 205 and Sch. 41, Pt. V(8). The repeal is effective generally for years after 1995–96. However, in the case of partnerships where the business was set up and commenced before 6 April 1994, the repeal is effective for years after 1996–97. The repeal also applies to income tax and capital gains tax charged by assessments made after 5 April 1998, but relating to 1995–96 and earlier years.
S. 88A inserted by FA 1989, s. 160(2) with effect from 27 July 1989.

89 The prescribed rate of interest

89 [Repealed by FA 1989, s. 187 and Sch. 17, Pt. X.]

History – The repeal of s. 89 has effect for periods beginning on or after 18 August 1989 by virtue of SI 1989/1298 (C. 44) for the enactments specified in para. 2(2) of that Order and from 1 October 1993 in relation to TMA 1970, s. 87A and ICTA 1988, s. 826 (the date from which FA 1989, s. 178 applies to TMA 1970, s. 87A and ICTA 1988, s. 826 by virtue of SI 1993/2212).

90 Interest on tax payable gross

History – The heading to s. 90 substituted for "Disallowance of relief for interest on tax" by CTA 2009, s. 1322 and Sch. 1, para. 306(4), with effect for corporation tax purposes for accounting periods ending on or after 1 April 2009, and for income tax and capital gains tax purposes for the tax year 2009–10 and subsequent tax years.

90(1) Interest payable under this Part of this Act–

(a) shall be paid without any deduction of income tax; and

(b) [Omitted by CTA 2009, s. 1322 and Sch. 1, para. 306(2) and repealed by CTA 2009, s. 1326 and Sch. 3, Pt. 1.]

90(2) [Omitted by CTA 2009, s. 1322 and Sch. 1, para. 306(3) and repealed by CTA 2009, s. 1326 and Sch. 3, Pt. 1.]

History – S. 90(1)(b), and the word "and" which followed it, omitted by CTA 2009, s. 1322 and Sch. 1, para. 306(2) and repealed by CTA 2009, s. 1326 and Sch. 3, Pt. 1, with effect for corporation tax purposes for accounting periods ending on or after 1 April 2009, and for income tax and capital gains tax purposes for the tax year 2009–10 and subsequent tax years, subject to the transitional provisions at CTA 2009, Sch. 2, para. 142.

In former s. 90(1)(b), the words "any corporation tax purpose (but see also sections 54 and 869 of ITTOIA 2005 for corresponding rule for income tax purposes)" substituted for the former wording by ITTOIA 2005, s. 882(1) and Sch. 1, para. 378; effective for income tax purposes for 2005–06 onwards and for corporation tax purposes for accounting periods ending after 5 April 2005 (ITTOIA 2005, s. 883(1)).

S. 90(2), and the word "and" which followed it, omitted by CTA 2009, s. 1322 and Sch. 1, para. 306(3) and repealed by CTA 2009, s. 1326 and Sch. 3, Pt. 1, with effect for corporation tax purposes for accounting periods ending on or after 1 April 2009, and for income tax and capital gains tax purposes for the tax year 2009–10 and subsequent tax years.

S. 90 amended by FA 1998, s. 33, with effect in relation to accounting periods ending on or after 1 July 1999, the corporation tax self-assessment appointed day by virtue of FA 1994, s. 199(2), (3) and SI 1998/3173, and in relation to interest on tax assessable in accordance with ICTA 1988, Sch. 13 or 16 for return periods in accounting periods ending on or after that day.

Cross references – FA 1993, s. 173 and Sch. 19, para. 11(5): for 1992–93 and subsequent years, s. 90 applies to interest on amounts payable by Lloyd's underwriting agents on account of the tax liabilities of syndicate members (see ICTA 1988, s. 450 and Sch. 19A, para. 3(4) for prior years (from 1988–89).

OTA 1975, Sch. 2, para. 1(1): s. 90 applies for the purposes of oil taxation.

SI 1986/1711, Schedule, Pt. I, II: s. 90 applies for purposes of stamp duty reserve tax.

91 Effect on interest of reliefs

91(1) Where any amount of interest is payable under section 86 of this Act in relation to an assessment, and relief from tax charged by the assessment is given to any person by a discharge of any of that tax, such adjustment shall be made of the said amount, and such repayment shall be made of any amounts previously paid under that section in relation to the assessment, as are necessary to secure that the total sum, if any, paid or payable under that section in relation to the assessment, is the same as it would have been if the tax discharged had never been charged.

91(1A) Where interest is payable under section 87A of this Act in respect of an amount of corporation tax for an accounting period, and relief from tax is given by a discharge of any of that corporation tax–

(a) such adjustment shall be made of the amount of interest payable under that section in respect of corporation tax for that accounting period, and

(b) such repayment shall be made of any amounts of interest previously paid under that section in respect of that corporation tax,

as are necessary to secure that the total sum (if any) paid or payable under that section in respect of corporation tax for that accounting period is the same as it would have been if the tax discharged had never been charged.

91(1B) Subsection (1A) above has effect subject to section 87A(4), (4A), (4B), (6) and (7) of this Act.

91(2) Subject to subsection (2A) below where relief from tax paid for any chargeable period is given to any person by repayment, he shall be entitled to require that the amount repaid shall be treated for the purposes of this section, so far as it will go, as if it were a discharge of the tax charged on him (whether alone or together with other persons) by or by virtue of any assessment for or relating to the same chargeable period, so, however, that it shall not be applied to any assessment made after the relief was given and that it shall not be applied to more than one assessment so as to reduce, without extinguishing, the amount of tax charged thereby.

91(2A) In any case where–

(a) relief from corporation tax is given to any person by repayment, and

(b) that tax was paid for an accounting period ending after the day which is the appointed day for the purposes of section 10 of the principal Act,

that person shall be entitled to require that the amount repaid shall be treated for the purposes of this section, so far as it will go, as if it were a discharge of the corporation tax charged on him for that period.

91(3) Notwithstanding anything in the preceding provisions of this section, no relief, whether given by way of discharge or repayment, shall be treated for the purposes of this section as–

(a) [Repealed by FA 1971, s. 37(1), 38(1), Sch. 6, para. 88(a) and Sch. 14, Pt. II.]

(b) affecting tax charged by any assessment to income tax made under Schedule A or Schedule D if either–

(i) [Repealed by FA 1971, s. 37(1), 38(1), Sch. 6, para. 88(a) and Sch. 14, Pt. II.]

(ii) it arises in connection with income taxable otherwise than under Schedule A or Schedule D, or

(iii) it relates to a source income from which is taxable otherwise than under Schedule A or Schedule D, or

(c) affecting tax charged at a rate other than the basic rate, the savings nil rate or the starting rate for savings on income from which tax has been deducted (otherwise than under PAYE regulations) or is treated as having been deducted, unless it is a relief from the tax so charged.

91(4) For the purposes of this section a relief from corporation tax or capital gains tax shall not be treated as affecting tax charged by any assessment unless the assessment is to the same tax.

History – In s. 91(1) reference to "section 88", which appeared after the reference to s. 86, repealed, and minor consequential amendments made, by FA 1996, s. 132 and Sch. 18, para. 4(2), s. 205 and Sch. 41, Pt. V(8). The repeal relating to s. 88 is effective generally for years after 1995–96. However, in the case of partnerships where the business was set up and commenced before 6 April 1994, the repeal is effective for years after 1996–97. The repeal also applies to income tax and capital gains tax charged by assessments made after 5 April 1988, but relating to 1995–96 and earlier years.

S. 91(1A) and s. 91(2A) (as amended by ICTA 1988, s. 844 and Sch. 29, para. 10(6)) inserted by F(No. 2)A 1987, s. 86(5)–(7): and s. 91(2) amended to make it subject to s. 91(2A), with respect to accounting periods ending after 30 September 1993 by virtue of SI 1992/3066, art. 2 (under Pay and File).

S. 91(1B) amended by FA 1995, s. 130 and Sch. 24, para. 10, with deemed effect from 23 March 1995 (FA 1995, Sch. 24, para. 7, FA 1993, s. 165 and SI 1994/3224) to include reference to s. 87A(4A) and (4B).

S. 91(1B) amended by FA 1993, s. 120 and Sch. 14, para. 5, inserting "(6) and (7)" after the words "section 84A(4)".

S. 91(2) amended by FA 1985, Sch. 27, Pt. X by removing a reference to development land tax.

S. 91(3)(a), (b)(i) repealed with effect from 1973–74.

In s. 91(3)(c) the words ", the savings nil rate" inserted by FA 2016, s. 4(16), with effect for the tax year 2016–17 and subsequent tax years.

In s. 91(3)(c), the words "or the starting rate for savings" substituted by FA 2008, s. 5 and Sch. 1, para. 39, with effect for 2008–09 and subsequent tax years.

In s. 91(3)(c), the words "savings rate" substituted by ITA 2007, s. 1027 and Sch. 1, para. 259, with effect from 6 April 2007.

In s. 91(3)(c), the words "PAYE regulations" substituted by ITEPA 2003, Sch. 6, para. 136 which has effect for the tax year 2003–04 and subsequent tax years.

S. 91(3)(c) inserted by FA 1971, Sch. 6, para. 88(b), with effect from 1973–74.

In s. 91(3)(c), words ", the lower rate or the starting rate" substituted by FA 1999, s. 22(11)(b) with effect for the year 1999–2000 and subsequent years of assessment. Former reference to the lower rate inserted by F(No. 2)A 1992, s. 19(2), for 1992–93 and subsequent years of assessment.

Reference to provisions of the principal Act substituted by ICTA 1988, Sch. 29, para. 32, that Act becoming the principal Act (TMA 1970, s. 118(1)).

Cross references – S. 107(4), (5): restricted application to tax re loans by close companies to participators.

ICTA 1988, s. 203: PAYE.

ICTA 1988, s. 306(9): restriction on application of s. 91 on discharge etc. in relation to business expansion scheme (in relation to shares issued on or before 31 December 1993) or enterprise investment scheme investment (in relation to shares issued on or after 1 January 1994).

ICTA 1988, s. 419(4): restriction on application of s. 91 on discharge or repayment of tax in respect of loans to participators in close companies; and for the purposes of s. 91 relief from tax under s. 419, 420 is only treated as affecting tax charged by an assessment where the assessment is under those sections.

91A Reliefs etc.: effect on interest on development land tax

91A [Repealed by FA 1985, Sch. 27, Pt. X, with effect from 19 March 1985.]

92 Remission in certain cases of interest on tax in arrear by reason of exchange restrictions

92(1) The provisions of this section shall have effect where the Board are satisfied as respects any tax carrying interest under section 86 of this Act–

(a) that the tax is in respect of income or chargeable gains arising in a country outside the United Kingdom, and

(b) that, as the result of action of the government of that country, it is impossible for the income or gains to be remitted to the United Kingdom, and

(c) that having regard to the matters aforesaid and to all the other circumstances of the case it is reasonable that the tax should for the time being remain uncollected,

and the Board allow the tax to remain uncollected accordingly.

92(2) Interest on the said tax shall, subject to subsection (3) below, cease to run under the said section 86 as from the date on which the Board were first in possession of the information necessary to enable them to be satisfied as aforesaid and, if the said date is not later than three months from the time when the tax became due and payable, the interest thereon under the said section 86 in respect of the period before the said date shall be remitted.

92(3) Where, under subsection (2) above, interest has ceased to run on any tax and thereafter demand is made by the collector or other proper officer for payment of all or any of that tax, interest under the said section 86 shall again begin to run from the date of the demand in respect of the amount demanded:

Provided that where all or any part of the amount demanded is paid not later than three months from the date of the demand, the interest under the said section 86 on the amount so paid running from the date of the demand shall be remitted.

Cross references – F(No. 2)A 1987, s. 86(3)(a), (7): the reference in s. 92 to s. 86 shall include, with respect to accounting periods ending after 30 September 1993 (by virtue of SI 1992/3066, art. 2), a reference to s. 87A.

PART X – PENALTIES, ETC.

93 Failure to make return for income tax and capital gains tax

93 [Omitted by SI 2011/702, art. 7(a).]

History – S. 93 omitted by SI 2011/702, art. 7(a) with effect from 1 April 2011, but subject to SI 2011/702, art. 20, which provides that the omission does not have effect in relation to a return or other document which is required to be made or delivered to HMRC, or an amount of tax which is payable, in relation to the tax year 2009–10 or any previous tax year.

Notes – For the purposes of SI 1986/1711, reg. 20 (which applies certain provisions of TMA 1970, in some cases subject to modifications, for the purposes of stamp duty reserve tax), the omission of s. 93 by SI 2011/702 has no effect (SI 2011/702, art. 22).

93A Failure to make partnership return

93A [Omitted by SI 2011/702, art. 7(b).]

History – S. 93A omitted by SI 2011/702, art. 7(b) with effect from 1 April 2011, but subject to SI 2011/702, art. 20, which provides that the omission does not have effect in relation to a return or other document which is required to be made or delivered to HMRC, or an amount of tax which is payable, in relation to the tax year 2009–10 or any previous tax year.

94 Failure to make return for corporation tax

94 [Repealed by FA 1998, s. 117(3) and Sch. 19, para. 33, s. 165 and Sch. 27, Pt. III(28).]

History – S. 94 repealed by FA 1998, s. 117(3) and Sch. 19, para. 33, with effect in relation to accounting periods ending on or after 1 July 1999, the corporation tax self-assessment appointed day by virtue of FA 1994, s. 199(2), (3) and SI 1998/3173 (C. 78).

95 Incorrect return or accounts for income tax or capital gains tax

95 [Omitted by FA 2007, s. 97 and Sch. 24, para. 29(a) and repealed by FA 2007, s. 114 and Sch. 27, Pt. 5(5).]

History – S. 95 omitted by FA 2007, s. 97 and Sch. 24, para. 29(a) and repealed by FA 2007, s. 114 and Sch. 27, Pt. 5(5), with effect as follows by virtue of SI 2008/568, art. 2:

- 1 April 2008 in relation to relevant documents relating to tax periods commencing on or after that date;
- 1 April 2008 in relation to assessments falling within paragraph 2 for tax periods commencing on or after that date;
- 1 July 2008 in relation to relevant documents relating to claims under the Thirteenth Council Directive (arrangements for the refund of value added tax to persons not established in Community territory) for years commencing on or after that date;
- 1 January 2009 in relation to relevant documents relating to claims under the Eighth Council Directive (arrangements for the refund of value added tax to taxable persons not established in the territory of the country) for years commencing on or after that date;
- 1 April 2009 in relation to documents relating to all other claims for repayments of relevant tax made on or after 1 April 2009 which are not related to a tax period; and
- in any other case, 1 April 2009 in relation to documents given where a person's liability to pay relevant tax arises on or after that date.

However, no person will be liable to a penalty under Sch. 24 in respect of any tax period for which a return is required to be made before 1 April 2009.

Previously, in s. 95(1)(a) reference to TMA 1970, s. 9 omitted, and in s. 95(3) the words at the end "; and the references in subsection (2) to the amount of income tax payable do not, in relation to anything done in connection with a partnership, include any income tax not chargeable in the partnership name" repealed by FA 1994, s. 196 and Sch. 19, para. 27(1), (2), s. 258 and Sch. 26, Pt. V(23), as respects the year 1996–97 and subsequent years of assessment.

In s. 95(1)(a) references to TMA 1970, s. 8A inserted and consequential amendment made by FA 1990, s. 90(4), (5), effective for notices given (or falling to be given) after 5 April 1990.

S. 95(1) amended by FA 1989, s. 163 reducing the maximum penalty from the "aggregate of (i) £50 and (ii) the amount, or, in the case of fraud, twice the amount of the difference specified in subsection (2) below" for returns, statements, declarations or accounts delivered, made or submitted on or after 27 July 1989.

S. 95(1)(a) amended by FA 1988, s. 148 and Sch. 14, Pt. VIII by removing the former reference to ICTA 1988, s. 284(4), with effect from 1990–91.

S. 95(3) amended by FA 1971, Sch. 6, para. 90, with effect from 1973–74.

Reference to provisions of the principal Act substituted by ICTA 1988, Sch. 29, para. 32, that Act becoming the principal Act (TMA 1970, s. 118(1)).

Cross references – FA 1993, Sch. 20A, para. 9(5) (introduced by FA 2004, s. 144 and Sch. 25 para. 3): this section is to apply where a Lloyd's member fraudulently or negligently fails to comply with the reporting requirements of Part 3 of that Schedule.

FA 2004, s. 33(5): delivery of an incorrect return not to be regarded as negligent if solely due to a failure to preserve records relating to an arm's length provision (until 2006–07 or for accounting periods ending on or before 31 March 2006).

FA 2004, s. 313(4)(a): a person is not liable to a penalty under s. 95 by reason of any failure to include in a return or account any number or other information required by FA 2004, s. 313(3)(a).

S. 8, 8A, 9 and 12: return of income, trustee's return, partnership return and capital gains.

S. 59C(6): where penalty incurred under s. 95, no part of the tax by reference to which the penalty was determined is regarded as unpaid for the purpose of surcharges on income tax and capital gains tax (s. 59C(2), (3)).

S. 107A: application of s. 95 to relevant trustees.

S. 118(3): partnership assessment treated as made on individual partners and tax charged treated accordingly.

ICTA 1988, s. 369(7): s. 95 applies to any overpayment to a MIRAS lender of tax deducted by a borrower and thus treated as paid by the lender as if it were income tax which ought not to have been repaid, or a relief which was not due.
ICTA 1988, Sch. 6A, para. 8(4): claim for alternative calculation to be applied in respect of private use by employee of a company van is, for the purposes of s. 95, to be taken as a claim for relief.
ICTA 1988, Sch. 14, para. 7(3)(d): s. 95 applies in relation to excess life assurance premium relief.
FA 1989, s. 57(3)(d): application to excessive relief for payments of medical insurance.
FA 1991, s. 33(3)(d): application of s. 95 where the recipient of a payment in respect of a qualifying course of vocational training claims from the Board, in excess of his entitlement, the amount of tax deducted from the payer.
FA 1993, s. 173 and Sch. 19, para. 2(3)–(5): (1992–93 and subsequent years) penalties for incorrect returns submitted by Lloyd's underwriting agents (see ICTA 1988, s. 450 and Sch. 19A, para. 2(4), (10) for prior years (from 1988–89)).
FA 1995, s. 73(4): regulations may apply s. 95 in cases where amounts equivalent to the tax credits on distributions are paid to any person by a venture capital trust.
ITEPA 2003, s. 164(4): claim for alternative calculation of value of shared availability of van.
SI 1986/1711, Schedule, Pt. I, II: modified application of s. 95 for purposes of stamp duty reserve tax.
SI 1989/469, reg. 9(6)(a) (false declaration on applying to subscribe to a personal equity plan): reg. 9(6)(b) (modifications to s. 95 in respect of applications to subscribe to personal equity plans) and reg. 18(4) (deductions where excessive relief given in respect of personal equity plans to be treated as deductions at source, and not repayable by virtue of s. 95(2)(a)).
SI 1998/1870, reg. 12(8): modified application of s. 95 in respect of applications to subscribe to an individual savings account – see also reg. 13(8) (applications by curator bonis).
SI 1998/1870, reg. 24(4): deduction to claw back excessive relief given in respect of an individual savings account is treated for the purposes of s. 95(2)(a) as an amount of income tax deducted at source and not repayable.

HMRC Manuals – Investigation Handbook, vol. III, IH5525ff: mitigation factors for tax geared penalties.

Other material – ICAEW Technical Release TAX 27/95 (not reproduced): professional conduct in relation to taxation.
IR press release, 18 October 1990: Board may accept a money settlement instead of instituting criminal proceedings in respect of fraud alleged to have been committed by a taxpayer, particularly where the taxpayer has made a full confession and co-operated in the investigation, but they can give no undertaking that they will do so.
Tax Bulletin TB12/98-1: HMRC guidance notes on penalties exigible where "a return is not submitted in accordance with the arm's length principle [for transfer pricing], it can be shown that the return was submitted fraudulently or negligently, and UK tax is lost as a result".

95A Incorrect partnership return or accounts

95A [Omitted by FA 2007, s. 97 and Sch. 24, para. 29(a) and repealed by FA 2007, s. 114 and Sch. 27, Pt. 5(5).]

History – S. 95A omitted by FA 2007, s. 97 and Sch. 24, para. 29(a) and repealed by FA 2007, s. 114 and Sch. 27, Pt. 5(5), with effect as follows by virtue of SI 2008/568, art. 2:

- 1 April 2008 in relation to relevant documents relating to tax periods commencing on or after that date;
- 1 April 2008 in relation to assessments falling within paragraph 2 for tax periods commencing on or after that date;
- 1 July 2008 in relation to relevant documents relating to claims under the Thirteenth Council Directive (arrangements for the refund of value added tax to persons not established in Community territory) for years commencing on or after that date;
- 1 January 2009 in relation to relevant documents relating to claims under the Eighth Council Directive (arrangements for the refund of value added tax to taxable persons not established in the territory of the country) for years commencing on or after that date;
- 1 April 2009 in relation to documents relating to all other claims for repayments of relevant tax made on or after 1 April 2009 which are not related to a tax period; and
- in any other case, 1 April 2009 in relation to documents given where a person's liability to pay relevant tax arises on or after that date.

However, no person will be liable to a penalty under Sch. 24 in respect of any tax period for which a return is required to be made before 1 April 2009.
In s. 95A(1)(a):

- in sub-para. (i), the words "incorrect partnership return" substituted for "incorrect return of a kind mentioned in section 12AA of this Act"; and
- in sub-para. (ii), "partnership return" substituted for "return of such a kind",

by FA 2001, s. 88, Sch. 29, para. 32 with effect from 11 May 2001 in relation to returns whether made before or after that date and whether relating to periods before or after then.
S. 95A inserted by FA 1994, s. 196 and Sch. 19, para. 28, and amended by FA 1996, s. 123(12), (13), in so far as it relates to income tax and capital gains tax, as respects the year 1996–97 and subsequent years of assessment and, in so far as it relates to corporation tax, as respects accounting periods ending on or after 1 July 1999, the appointed day by virtue of FA 1994, s. 199(2), (3) and SI 1998/3173 (C. 78).

Cross references – FA 2004, s. 33(6): delivery of an incorrect partnership return not to be regarded as negligent if solely due to a failure to preserve records relating to an arm's length provision (until 2006-07 or for accounting periods ending on or before 31 March 2006).

Other material – Tax Bulletin TB12/98-1: HMRC guidance on penalties exigible where "a return is not submitted in accordance with the arm's length principle [for transfer pricing], it can be shown that the return was submitted fraudulently or negligently, and UK tax is lost as a result".

96 Incorrect return or accounts for corporation tax

96 [Repealed by FA 1998, s. 117(3) and Sch. 19, para. 34, s. 165 and Sch. 27, Pt. III(28).]

History – S. 96 repealed by FA 1998, s. 117(3) and Sch. 19, para. 34, s. 165 and Sch. 27, Pt. III(28), with effect in relation to accounting periods ending on or after 1 July 1999, the corporation tax self-assessment appointed day by virtue of FA 1994, s. 199(2), (2) and SI 1998/3173 (C. 78).

97 Incorrect return or accounts: supplemental

97 [Omitted by FA 2007, s. 97 and Sch. 24, para. 29(a) and repealed by FA 2007, s. 114 and Sch. 27, *Pt. 5(5).]*

History – S. 97 omitted by FA 2007, s. 97 and Sch. 24, para. 29(a) and repealed by FA 2007, s. 114 and Sch. 27, Pt. 5(5), with effect as follows by virtue of SI 2008/568, art. 2:

- 1 April 2008 in relation to relevant documents relating to tax periods commencing on or after that date;
- 1 April 2008 in relation to assessments falling within paragraph 2 for tax periods commencing on or after that date;
- 1 July 2008 in relation to relevant documents relating to claims under the Thirteenth Council Directive (arrangements for the refund of value added tax to persons not established in Community territory) for years commencing on or after that date;

- 1 January 2009 in relation to relevant documents relating to claims under the Eighth Council Directive (arrangements for the refund of value added tax to taxable persons not established in the territory of the country) for years commencing on or after that date;
- 1 April 2009 in relation to documents relating to all other claims for repayments of relevant tax made on or after 1 April 2009 which are not related to a tax period; and
- in any other case, 1 April 2009 in relation to documents given where a person's liability to pay relevant tax arises on or after that date.

However, no person will be liable to a penalty under Sch. 24 in respect of any tax period for which a return is required to be made before 1 April 2009.

References to TMA 1970, s. 95 substituted for former references to s. 95 and 96 by FA 1998, s. 117(3) and Sch. 19, para. 35, with effect in relation to corporation tax accounting periods ending on or after 1 July 1999, the appointed day by virtue of FA 1994, s. 199(2), (3) and SI 1998/3173 (C. 78).

Cross references – SI 1989/469, reg. 28(4): s. 97(1) applies in the case of personal equity plans with modifications.
SI 1986/1711, Schedule, Pt. I, II: modified application of s. 97 for purposes of stamp duty reserve tax.

97AA Failure to produce documents under section 19A

97AA [Omitted by FA 2008, s. 113 and Sch. 36, para. 72.]

History – S. 97AA omitted by FA 2008, s. 113 and Sch. 36, para. 72, with effect from 1 April 2009 (SI 2009/404 art. 2, subject to savings at SI 2009/404, art. 3).

97A Two or more tax-geared penalties in respect of same tax

97A Where two or more penalties–

(a) are incurred by any person and fall to be determined by reference to any income tax or capital gains tax with which he is chargeable for a year of assessment,

(b) [Repealed by FA 1998, s. 117(3) and Sch. 19, para. 37, s. 165 and Sch. 27, Pt. III(28).]

each penalty after the first shall be so reduced that the aggregate amount of the penalties, so far as determined by reference to any particular part of the tax, does not exceed whichever is or, but for this section, would be the greater or greatest of them, so far as so determined.

History – S. 97A(b), and word "or" immediately preceding it, repealed by FA 1998, s. 117(3) and Sch. 19, para. 37, s. 165 and Sch. 27, Pt. III(28), with effect in relation to accounting periods ending on or after 1 July 1999, the appointed day by virtue of FA 1994, s. 199(2), (3) and SI 1998/3173 (C. 78).
S. 97A inserted by FA 1988, s. 129, with effect for 1988–89 and subsequent years of assessment, or for company accounting periods ending after 31 March 1989.

Cross references – FA 2016, Sch. 22, para. 21: in the application of section 97A, no account is to be taken of a penalty under FA 2016, Sch. 22 (asset-based penalty for offshore inaccuracies and failures).
FA 2014, s. 212(3): in the application of s. 97A, no account is to be taken of a penalty under FA 2014, s. 208 (penalty if corrective action not taken in response to a follower notice).

Other material – ICAEW Technical Release TR 739 (not reproduced): Revenue will decide on appropriate penalty taking account of all circumstances. A small penalty might be charged on a first offence being uncovered with a further penalty on a second offence being uncovered. The "first" penalty means the first to be charged.

98 Special returns, etc.

98(1) Subject to the provisions of this section and section 98A below, where any person–

(a) has been required, by a notice served under or for the purposes of any of the provisions specified in the first column of the Table below, to deliver any return or other document, to furnish any particulars, to produce any document, or to make anything available for inspection, and he fails to comply with the notice, or

(b) fails to furnish any information, give any certificate or produce any document or record in accordance with any of the provisions specified in the second column of the Table below,

he shall be liable, subject to subsections (3) and (4) below–

(i) to a penalty not exceeding £300, and

(ii) if the failure continues after a penalty is imposed under paragraph (i) above, to a further penalty or penalties not exceeding £60 for each day on which the failure continues after the day on which the penalty under paragraph (i) above was imposed (but excluding any day for which a penalty under this paragraph has already been imposed).

98(2) Subject to section 98A below, where a person fraudulently or negligently furnishes, gives, produces or makes any incorrect information, certificate, document, record or declaration of a kind mentioned in any of the provisions specified in either column of the Table below, he shall be liable to a penalty not exceeding £3,000.

98(3) No penalty shall be imposed under subsection (1) above in respect of a failure within paragraph (a) of that subsection at any time after the failure has been remedied.

98(4) No penalty shall be imposed under paragraph (ii) of subsection (1) above in respect of a failure within paragraph (b) of that subsection at any time after the failure has been remedied.

98(4A) If–

(a) a failure to comply with Chapter 15 or 16 of Part 15 of ITA 2007 arises from a person's failure to deliver an account, or show the amount, of a payment, and

(b) the payment is within subsection (4B), (4D), (4DA) or (4E) below,

subsection (1) above shall have effect as if for "£300" there were substituted "£3,000" and as if for "£60" there were substituted "£600".

98(4B) A payment is within this subsection if–

(a) the payment is made by a company, local authority or qualifying partnership (within the meaning of section 932 of ITA 2007) without an amount representing income tax on the payment being deducted from it,

(b) at the time the payment is made, the company, authority or partnership–

(i) does not believe that the payment is an excepted payment for the purposes of Chapter 11 of Part 15 of ITA 2007 (payments between companies etc: exception from duties to deduct), or

(ii) if it does so believe, cannot reasonably do so,

(c) the payment is one from which tax is deductible under Part 15 of ITA 2007 unless the company, authority or partnership reasonably believes that it is an excepted payment for the purposes of Chapter 11 of that Part, and

(d) the payment is not an excepted payment at the time the payment is made.

98(4C) [Omitted by ITA 2007, s. 1027 and Sch. 1, para. 260(4) and repealed by s. 1031 and Sch. 3, Pt. 1.]

98(4D) A payment is within this subsection if–

(a) it is a payment from which a sum representing income tax must be deducted under Chapter 6 (deduction from annual payments and patent royalties) or 7 (deduction from other payments connected with intellectual property) of Part 15 of ITA 2007,

(b) a company, purporting to rely on section 911 of that Act (double taxation arrangements: deduction at treaty rate), deducts less from the payment than required by those Chapters, and

(c) at the time the payment is made the payee (as defined in section 913 of that Act) is not entitled to relief under double taxation arrangements (as defined in section 1023 of that Act) and the company–

(i) does not believe that it is entitled to such relief, or

(ii) if it does so believe, cannot reasonably do so.

98(4DA) A payment is within this subsection if–

(a) it is a payment from which a sum representing income tax must be deducted under Chapter 6 (deduction from annual payments and patent royalties) or 7 (deduction from other payments connected with intellectual property) of Part 15 of ITA 2007,

(b) a company, purporting to rely on section 914 of ITA 2007 (EU companies: discretion to make payment gross), makes the payment without deducting a sum representing income tax, and

(c) at the time the payment is made the payment is not exempt from income tax as a result of section 758 of ITTOIA 2005 (exemption for certain interest and royalty payments) and the company–

(i) does not believe that the payment is so exempt, or

(ii) if it does so believe, cannot reasonably do so.

98(4E) A payment is within this subsection if–

(a) it is an interest distribution made to a unit holder by the trustees of an authorised unit trust,

(b) the trustees, in purported reliance on the reputable intermediary condition being fulfilled with respect to the unit holder, do not comply with the obligation under section 874 of ITA 2007 to make a deduction from the interest distribution,

(c) that obligation would apply if that condition were not so fulfilled, and

(d) the trustees did not believe that the unit holder was not ordinarily resident in the United Kingdom or could not reasonably have so believed (so that that condition was not so fulfilled).

Expressions used in this subsection have the same meaning as in regulations made under section 17(3) of the Finance (No. 2) Act 2005 (as at 1st April 2006, see the Authorised Investment Funds (Tax) Regulations 2006 (S.I. 2006/964)).

98(4F) If a person fails to furnish any information or produce any document or record in accordance with regulations under section 716B of ITEPA 2003, subsection (1) has effect as if–

(a) for "£300" there were substituted "£3,000", and

(b) for "£60" there were substituted "£600".

98(5) [Omitted by FA 2009, s. 37 and Sch. 17, para. 2(a).]

TABLE

1	2

Part III of this Act
Regulations under section 59E of this Act
In the principal Act–
section 310(4) and (5);
regulations under section 333;
	In the principal Act–
	section 310(1), (2), (2A) and (3);
	regulations under section 333;
	section 375(5);
	section 552;
	regulations under section 552ZA(6);
	regulations under section 552ZB;
	regulations under paragraph 7 of Schedule 14;
	Schedule 15, paragraph 14(4);
	Regulations under section 151 of the 1992 Act.
	Regulations 16 and 17 of the Income Tax (Interest Relief) Regulations 1982.
	Sections 45B(5) and (6), 45G(4) and (5), 45I(5) and (6), 118–120, 145(2) and (3) and 203 of the Capital Allowances Act.

Regulations under section 151 of the 1992 Act.	section 12ADA of this Act
Paragraph 2(9) of Schedule 1 to the 1992 Act.	Paragraph 12 of Schedule 4ZA to the 1992 Act
Section 98 of the 1992 Act	Paragraphs 2 to 6 of Schedule 5A to the 1992 Act.
Section 73 of the Finance Act 1989.	Regulation 11(2) of the Income Tax (Manufactured Overseas Dividends) Regulations 1993.
Paragraph 1(7) of Schedule 1 to the 1992 Act	
Paragraph 66 of Schedule 15 to the Finance Act 2000.	Regulations under section 73 of the Finance Act 1995.
Paragraph 10 of Schedule 34 to the Finance Act 2002.	Paragraph 64 or 65 of Schedule 15 to the Finance Act 2000.
Section 421J(4) of ITEPA 2003	Paragraph 93(2) of Schedule 22 to the Finance Act 2000.
Regulations under section 715 of ITEPA 2003	
Paragraph 93 of Schedule 2 to ITEPA 2003	Paragraph 129 of Schedule 22 to the Finance Act 2000.
Paragraph 45 of Schedule 3 to ITEPA 2003	Paragraph 6 of Schedule 34 to the Finance Act 2002.
Paragraph 33 of Schedule 4 to ITEPA 2003	
Paragraph 51 of Schedule 5 to ITEPA 2003	Regulations under section 589 of ITEPA 2003
Regulations under section 70(3) of the Finance Act 2004	Regulations under section 715 of ITEPA 2003
Section 401B of ITTOIA 2005	Regulations under section 716B of ITEPA 2003.
Section 421A of ITTOIA 2005	PAYE regulations
Regulations under Chapter 3 of Part 6 of ITTOIA 2005	Regulations under section 65(2), 69(1), 70(1)(a) or (c) or 71 of the Finance Act 2004
Section 40(1) of the Finance Act 2005	Regulations under section 251(1)(a) or (4) of the Finance Act 2004
Regulations under section 17(3) of the Finance (No. 2) Act 2005.	Section 75(4) of ITTOIA 2005
Sections 242 and 243(1) and (2) of ITA 2007	
Sections 257GG and 257GH(1) and (2) of ITA 2007	
Sections 257SG and 257SH(1) and (2) of ITA 2007	
Section 312A of ITA 2007	
Regulations under Chapter 5 of Part 6 of ITA 2007	

TABLE

1	2
Section 748(1) and (2) of ITA 2007	Regulations under Chapter 3 of Part 6 of ITTOIA 2005
Section 771 of ITA 2007	Section 37(3) of the Finance Act 2005
Regulations under section 871(1) of ITA 2007	Section 37(6) of the Finance Act 2005
Regulations under section 969(1) of ITA 2007	Section 106 of FA 2006 as modified by Schedule 17 of that Act
Regulations under section 971(1) of ITA 2007	Section 116 of FA 2006
Regulations 21 and 22 of the Income Tax (Purchased Life Annuities) Regulations 2008.	Regulations under section 116 of FA 2006
Section 31(3) and (4) of CTA 2010	Section 130 of FA 2006
Section 465(3) and (4) of CTA 2010	Sections 240 and 241 of ITA 2007
Section 832 of CTA 2010	Sections 257GE and 257GF of ITA 2007
Section 1052(4) and (5) of CTA 2010	Sections 257SE and 257SF of ITA 2007
Section 1101(5) and (6) of CTA 2010	Section 271(1) of ITA 2007
Section 1102(4) and (5) of CTA 2010	Regulations under Chapter 5 of Part 6 of ITA 2007
Regulations under section 283, 284, 285, 295 or 297 of TIOPA 2010	Section 373 of ITA 2007
Regulations under section 61(5) of the Finance Act 2012	Regulations under section 871(1) of ITA 2007
	Chapter 15 of Part 15 of ITA 2007
	Chapter 16 of Part 15 of ITA 2007
	Regulations under section 969(1) of ITA 2007
	Regulations under section 971(1) of ITA 2007
	Regulations under section 973(1) of ITA 2007
	Section 75(4) of CTA 2009 paragraph 4 of Schedule 17 to FA 2009.
	Section 260 of CTA 2010
	Regulations 7, 23 and 25 of the Income Tax (Purchased Life Annuities) Regulations 2008
	Section 1046(1) to (4) of CTA 2010
	Section 1095 of CTA 2010
	Section 1096 of CTA 2010
	Section 1052(1) to (3) of CTA 2010
	Section 1101(1), (2) and (4) of CTA 2010
	Section 228 of TIOPA 2010
	Regulations under paragraph 16 of Schedule 18 to the Finance Act 2011
	Regulations under section 61(5) of the Finance Act 2012
	Regulations under paragraph 3 of Schedule 22 to the Finance Act 2013
	Regulations under paragraph 8 of Schedule 6 to the Finance Act 2014
	paragraph 17 or 18 of Schedule 4 to FA 2016

The references in this Table to regulations under section 602 have effect only for the purpose of giving effect to any provision mentioned in paragraphs (a) and (b) of subsection (2) of that section.

References in this Table to sections 240, 241, 242 and 243(1) and (2) of ITA 2007 are to provisions that apply only in relation to shares issued after 5 April 2007.

Prospective amendments – In s. 98(4E)(d), the word "ordinarily" omitted by FA 2013, s. 219 and Sch. 46, para. 116(1), with effect from the coming into force of regulations under F(No. 2)A 2005, s. 17(3) by virtue of the amendment made by FA 2013, Sch. 46, para. 136.

History – S. 98(1), (2) amended, (3) substituted and (4) inserted by FA 1989, s. 164(1)–(4), (7) adding "Subject to section 98A below," and reference to subs. (4) and increasing the level of penalties for offences on or after 27 July 1989.

In s. 98(4A)(a), the words "Chapter 15 or 16 of Part 15 of ITA 2007" substituted for the words "section 350(1) of, or Schedule 16 to, the principal Act" by ITA 2007, Sch. 1, para. 260(2), with effect from 6 April 2007.

In s. 98(4A)(b), the reference to s. 98(4E) added by FA 2003, s. 203(11) in relation to interest distributions made on or after 16 October 2002: the reference to s. 98(4DA) inserted by FA 2004, s. 105(2) in relation to payments of interest or royalties on or after 1 January 2004.
S. 98(4A) inserted by FA 2001, s. 85(2) with application to payments made on or after 1 April 2001.
S. 98(4B)(a)–(d) substituted by ITA 2007, Sch. 1, para. 260(3), with effect from 6 April 2007.
In s. 98(4B), words:

- "local authority" inserted in para. (a);
- "authority" inserted in subpara. (b)(i) and para. (c);
- "either" substituted for "one" in subpara. (b)(i), (ii); and
- "neither" substituted for "none" in para. (d),

by FA 2002, s. 94(5), with effect in relation to payments made on or after 1 October 2002.
S. 98(4B) inserted by FA 2001, s. 85(2) with application to payments made on or after 1 April 2001.
S. 98(4C) omitted by ITA 2007, s. 1027 and Sch. 1, para. 260(4) and repealed by s. 1031 and Sch. 3, Pt. 1, with effect from 6 April 2007.
S. 98(4C) substituted by FA 2002, s. 94(6), with effect in relation to payments made on or after 1 October 2002.
S. 98(4C) inserted by FA 2001, s. 85(2) with application to payments made on or after 1 April 2001.
S. 98(4D) substituted by ITA 2007, Sch. 1, para. 260(5), with effect from 6 April 2007. The former s. 98(4D) and reference to it in s. 98(4A)(b) was inserted by FA 2002, s. 96(3), with effect in relation to payments made on or after 1 October 2002.
S. 98(4DA) substituted by ITA 2007, Sch. 1, para. 260(6), with effect from 6 April 2007. The former s. 98(4DA) was inserted by FA 2004, s. 105(3) in relation to payments of interest or royalties made on or after 1 January 2004.
In former s. 98(4DA) the reference to ITTOIA 2005, s. 758 substituted for a reference to FA 2004, s. 98 by ITTOA 2005, s. 882(1) and Sch. 2, para. 379(2); effective for income tax purposes for 2005–06 onwards (ITTOIA 2005, s. 883(1)).
In s. 98(4E)(b), the words "section 874 of ITA 2007" substituted by ITA 2007, Sch. 1, para. 260(7), with effect from 6 April 2007.
In s. 98(4E) the words "regulations made under section 17(3) of the Finance (No. 2) Act 2005 (as at 1st April 2006, see the Authorised Investment Funds (Tax) Regulations 2006 (S.I. 2006/964))" substituted by SI 2006/964, reg. 87(2)(a), with effect:

- for the purposes of income tax for the tax year 2006-07 and subsequent tax years, for distributions made on or after 6 April 2006;
- for the purposes of corporation tax on income, for accounting periods beginning on or after 1 April 2006 and on chargeable gains, in relation to disposals made on or after 1 April 2006, and for distributions made on or after 1 April 2006; and
- for the purposes of capital gains tax, in relation to disposals made on or after 6 April 2006.

S. 98(4E) inserted by FA 2003, s. 203(12) in relation to interest distributions made on or after 16 October 2002.
S. 98(4F) inserted by FA 2014, s. 18(3), with effect from 6 April 2015 (SI 2015/931, art. 2).
S. 98(5) omitted by FA 2009, s. 37 and Sch. 17, para. 2(a) with effect in relation to events taking place and transactions carried out on or after 1 July 2009.
Former s. 98(5) inserted by FA 1990, s. 68(3)(b) and s. 98(1) accordingly amended.
In former s. 98(5), in the table, in Col. 1, entry relating to FA 2002, Sch. 35, para. 11 omitted by FA 2012, Sch. 39, para. 5(2)(a)(i), with effect in relation to instruments executed on or after 6 April 2013.
In former s. 98(5), in the table, in Col. 2, entry relating to FA 2002, Sch. 35, para. 7 omitted by FA 2012, Sch. 39, para. 5(2)(a)(ii), with effect in relation to instruments executed on or after 6 April 2013.
Table and the immediately following paragraph substituted by ICTA 1988, s. 844 and Sch. 29, para. 9, in place of the former table which referred to relevant pre-consolidation provisions, with effect from 1988–89, and in respect of companies' accounting periods ending after 5 April 1988, various provisions inserting entries in the former table having been repealed by ICTA 1988, s. 844 and Sch. 31.
The final paragraph following the table inserted by ITA 2007, s. 1027 and Sch. 1, para. 260(10), with effect from 6 April 2007.
Col. 1 of Table amended as follows:

- Entry for FA 1973, Sch. 15, para. 2 omitted by FA 2011, s. 86 and Sch. 23, para. 51(3), with effect from 1 April 2012, but in relation to notice issued or request made before that date, this entry continues to apply as if it had not been omitted (FA 2011, Sch. 23, para. 65).
- Entry for ICTA 1988, s. 38(5) omitted by CTA 2009, s. 1322 and Sch. 1, para. 307(2)(a) and repealed by CTA 2009, s. 1326 and Sch. 3, Pt. 1, with effect for corporation tax purposes for accounting periods ending on or after 1 April 2009, and for income tax and capital gains tax purposes for the tax year 2009–10 and subsequent tax years. Former entry transposed from second col. by FA 1989, s. 164(5) and Sch. 17, Pt. VIII for offences on or after 27 July 1989;
- Entry (so far as it continued to have effect, see below) for ICTA 1988, s. 42 omitted by FA 2011, s. 86 and Sch. 23, para. 51(3), with effect from 1 April 2012, but in relation to notice issued or request made before that date, this entry continues to apply as if it had not been omitted (FA 2011, Sch. 23, para. 65).
- Entry for ICTA 1988, s. 42 omitted by TIOPA 2010, s. 371 and Sch. 7, para. 18(2) and repealed by TIOPA 2010, s. 378 and Sch. 10, Pt. 12, with effect for corporation tax purposes for accounting periods ending on or after 1 April 2010, for income tax and capital gains tax purposes for the tax year 2010–11 and subsequent tax years, and for petroleum revenue tax purposes for chargeable periods beginning on or after 1 July 2010. Former entry transposed from second col. by FA 1989, s. 164(5) and Sch. 17, Pt. VIII for offences on or after 27 July 1989;
- Entry for regulations under ICTA 1988, s. 42A omitted by ITA 2007, s. 1027 and Sch. 1, para. 260(8)(a), and repealed by s. 1031 and Sch. 3, Pt. 1, with effect from 6 April 2007. Former entry added by FA 1995, s. 40(2).
- Entry for regulations under TMA 1970, s. 59E added by FA 1999, s. 89(1);
- Entry for TMA 1970, s. 77I omitted by FA 2011, s. 86 and Sch. 23, para. 51(3), with effect from 1 April 2012, but in relation to notice issued or request made before that date, this entry continues to apply as if it had not been omitted (FA 2011, Sch. 23, para. 65).
- Entry for TMA 1970, s. 77I(1) inserted by TIOPA 2010, s. 371 and Sch. 7, para. 5(3), with effect for corporation tax purposes for accounting periods ending on or after 1 April 2010, for income tax and capital gains tax purposes for the tax year 2010–11 and subsequent tax years, and for petroleum revenue tax purposes for chargeable periods beginning on or after 1 July 2010.
- Entry for ICTA 1988, s. 76ZE(5) omitted by SI 2009/2035, art. 2 and Schedule, para. 8(3)(a), with effect from 13 August 2009. Former entry inserted by CTA 2009, s. 1322 and Sch. 1, para. 307(2)(b), with effect for corporation tax purposes for accounting periods ending on or after 1 April 2009, and for income tax and capital gains tax purposes for the tax year 2009–10 and subsequent tax years.
- Entry (so far as it continued to have effect, see below) for ICTA 1988, s. 217(4) omitted by FA 2011, s. 86 and Sch. 23, para. 51(3), with effect from 1 April 2012, but in relation to notice issued or request made before that date, this entry continues to apply as if it had not been omitted (FA 2011, Sch. 23, para. 65).
- Entry for ICTA 1988, s. 217(4) omitted by CTA 2010, s. 1177 and Sch. 1, para. 157(2)(a)(i) and repealed by CTA 2010, s. 1181 and Sch. 3, Pt. 1, with effect for corporation tax purposes for accounting periods ending on or after 1 April 2010, and for income tax and capital gains tax purposes for the tax year 2010–11 and subsequent tax years. Former entry substituted for ICTA 1988, s. 217 by SI 2009/2035, art. 2 and Schedule, para. 8(2)(a), with effect from 13 August 2009.
- Entry (so far as it continued to have effect, see below) for ICTA 1988, s. 226(4) omitted by FA 2011, s. 86 and Sch. 23, para. 51(3), with effect from 1 April 2012, but in relation to notice issued or request made before that date, this entry continues to apply as if it had not been omitted (FA 2011, Sch. 23, para. 65).
- Entry for ICTA 1988, s. 226(4) omitted by CTA 2010, s. 1177 and Sch. 1, para. 157(2)(a)(ii) and repealed by CTA 2010, s. 1181 and Sch. 3, Pt. 1, with effect for corporation tax purposes for accounting periods ending on or after 1 April 2010, and

for income tax and capital gains tax purposes for the tax year 2010–11 and subsequent tax years. Former entry substituted for ICTA 1988, s. 226(3) and (4) by SI 2009/2035, art. 2 and Schedule, para. 8(2)(b), with effect from 13 August 2009.

- Entry for ICTA 1988, s. 234(7)(b), (8) and (9) omitted by CTA 2010, s. 1177 and Sch. 1, para. 157(2)(a)(iii) and repealed by CTA 2010, s. 1181 and Sch. 3, Pt. 1, with effect for corporation tax purposes for accounting periods ending on or after 1 April 2010, and for income tax and capital gains tax purposes for the tax year 2010–11 and subsequent tax years.
- Entry for ICTA 1988, s. 246H omitted by SI 2009/2035, art. 2 and Schedule, para. 8(3)(a), with effect from 13 August 2009. Former entry added by FA 1994, s. 138 and Sch. 16, para. 10;
- Entry for ICTA 1988, s. 250(6) omitted by CTA 2010, s. 1177 and Sch. 1, para. 157(2)(a)(iv) and repealed by CTA 2010, s. 1181 and Sch. 3, Pt. 1, with effect for corporation tax purposes for accounting periods ending on or after 1 April 2010, and for income tax and capital gains tax purposes for the tax year 2010–11 and subsequent tax years. Former entry substituted for ICTA 1988, s. 250(6) and (7) by SI 2009/2035, art. 2 and Schedule, para. 8(2)(c), with effect from 13 August 2009.
- Entry for ICTA 1988, s. 272(7) omitted by SI 2009/2035, art. 2 and Schedule, para. 8(3)(a), with effect from 13 August 2009.
- Entry for regulations under ICTA 1988, s. 326C omitted by ITTOIA 2005, s. 882 and Sch. 1, para. 379(3)(a) and repealed by ITTOIA 2005, s. 884 and Sch. 3; effective for income tax purposes for 2005–06 onwards (ITTOIA 2005, s. 883(1)). Former entry added by FA 1990, s. 28(2);
- Entry for regulations under ICTA 1988, s. 333B omitted by FA 2007, s. 38 and Sch. 7, para. 1 and repealed by FA 2007, s. 114 and Sch. 27, Pt. 2(7), with effect for periods of account of insurance companies beginning on or after 1 January 2007, subject to the transitional provisions in FA 2007, Sch. 7, Pt. 2. Former entry added by FA 1998, s. 77(2);
- Entry for ICTA 1988, s. 431E(1) omitted by FA 2012, s. 146 and Sch. 16, para. 67(2)(a), with effect in relation to accounting periods beginning on or after 1 January 2013 (FA 2012, s. 148) but subject to transitional provisions in FA 2012, Sch. 17. Where an accounting period would otherwise straddle 1 January 2013, it is deemed to end on 31 December 2012 (FA 2012, s. 149). Former entry for regulations under ICTA 1988, s. 431E(1) added by FA 1995, s. 51 and Sch. 8, para. 50;
- Entry for regulations under ICTA 1988, s. 441A(3) omitted by FA 2007, s. 41 and Sch. 10, para. 16(2) and repealed by FA 2007, s. 114 and Sch. 27, Pt. 2(10), with effect from 19 July 2007. Former entry added by FA 1995, s. 51 and Sch. 8, para. 50.
- Entry for ICTA 1988, s. 468P(6) omitted by SI 2006/964, reg. 87(2)(b)(i), with effect:
  - for the purposes of income tax for the tax year 2006–07 and subsequent tax years, for distributions made on or after 6 April 2006;
  - for the purposes of corporation tax on income, for accounting periods beginning on or after 1 April 2006 and on chargeable gains, in relation to disposals made on or after 1 April 2006, and for distributions made on or after 1 April 2006; and
  - for the purposes of capital gains tax, in relation to disposals made on or after 6 April 2006.

  Former entry added by FA 2003, s. 203(13) in relation to interest distributions made on or after 16 October 2002.
- Entry for regulations under ICTA 1988, s. 468PB(3) omitted by SI 2006/964, reg. 87(2)(b)(ii), with effect:
  - for the purposes of income tax for the tax year 2006–07 and subsequent tax years, for distributions made on or after 6 April 2006;
  - for the purposes of corporation tax on income, for accounting periods beginning on or after 1 April 2006 and on chargeable gains, in relation to disposals made on or after 1 April 2006, and for distributions made on or after 1 April 2006; and
  - for the purposes of capital gains tax, in relation to disposals made on or after 6 April 2006.

  Former entry added by FA 2003, s. 203(13) in relation to interest distributions made on or after 16 October 2002.
- Entry for regulations under ICTA 1988, s. 476(1) omitted by ITA 2007, s. 1027 and Sch. 1, para. 260(8)(b), and repealed by s. 1031 and Sch. 3, Pt. 1 with effect from 6 April 2007.
- Entry for regulations under ICTA 1988, s. 477A(1) omitted by ITA 2007, s. 1027 and Sch. 1, para. 260(8)(c), and repealed by s. 1031 and Sch. 3, Pt. 1 with effect from 6 April 2007. Former entry added by FA 1990, s. 30 and Sch. 5, para. 15.
- Entry for ICTA 1988, s. 482(3) omitted by ITA 2007, s. 1027 and Sch. 1, para. 260(8)(d), and repealed by s. 1031 and Sch. 3, Pt. 1, with effect from 6 April 2007.
- Entry for regulations under ICTA 1988, s. 482(11) omitted by ITA 2007, s. 1027 and Sch. 1, para. 260(8)(e), and repealed by s. 1031 and Sch. 3, Pt. 1, with effect from 6 April 2007.
- Entry for ICTA 1988, s. 483 omitted by ITA 2007, s. 1027 and Sch. 1, para. 260(8)(f), and repealed by s. 1031 and Sch. 3, Pt. 1, with effect from 6 April 2007.
- Entry for regulations under ICTA 1988, s. 555(7) omitted by ITA 2007, s. 1027 and Sch. 1, para. 260(8)(g), and repealed by s. 1031 and Sch. 3, Pt. 1, with effect from 6 April 2007.
- Entry for ICTA 1988, s. 588(7) omitted by CTA 2009, s. 1322 and Sch. 1, para. 307(2)(c) and repealed by CTA 2009, s. 1326 and Sch. 3, Pt. 1, with effect for corporation tax purposes for accounting periods ending on or after 1 April 2009, and for income tax and capital gains tax purposes for the tax year 2009–10 and subsequent tax years, subject to the transitional provisions at CTA 2009, Sch. 2, para. 138.
- Entry for regulations under ICTA 1988, s. 602, 612 and 639 repealed by FA 2004, s. 326 and Sch. 42, Pt. 3 with effect from 6 April 2006.
- Entry for regulations under ICTA 1988, s. 605(1A)(b) repealed by FA 2004, s. 326 and Sch. 42, Pt. 3 with effect from 6 April 2006. Former entry added by FA 1994, s. 105(4)(a);
- Entry for regulations under ICTA 1988, s. 651A(1)(b)–(d) repealed by FA 2004, s. 326 and Sch. 42, Pt. 3 with effect from 6 April 2006. Former entry added by FA 1998, s. 96(3)(a);
- Entry for ICTA 1988, s. 660F omitted by ITTOIA 2005, s. 882 and Sch. 1, para. 379(3)(b) and repealed by ITTOIA 2005, s. 884 and Sch. 3; effective for income tax purposes for 2005–06 onwards (ITTOIA 2005, s. 883(1)). Former entry substituted for s. 669, 680 by FA 1995, s. 74 and Sch. 17, para. 23;
- Entry for ICTA 1988, s. 700(4) omitted by SI 2009/2035, art. 2 and Schedule, para. 8(3)(a), with effect from 13 August 2009.
- Entry for ICTA 1988, s. 708 omitted by SI 2009/2035, art. 2 and Schedule, para. 8(3)(a), with effect from 13 August 2009.
- Entry for ICTA 1988, s. 728 omitted by SI 2009/2035, art. 2 and Schedule, para. 8(3)(a), with effect from 13 August 2009.
- Entry for ICTA 1988, s. 729(11) repealed by FA 1996, Sch. 41, Pt. V(21), with effect from 6 November 2006.
- Entry for ICTA 1988, s. 730(8) omitted by FA 2009, s. 49 and Sch. 25, para. 9(3)(a) with effect in relation to transfers on or after 22 April 2009.
- Entry for ICTA 1988, s. 745(1) omitted by ITA 2007, s. 1027 and Sch. 1, para. 260(8)(h), and repealed by s. 1031 and Sch. 3, Pt. 1, with effect from 6 April 2007.
- Entry for ICTA 1988, s. 755 omitted by SI 2009/2035, art. 2 and Schedule, para. 8(3)(a), with effect from 13 August 2009.
- Entry for ICTA 1988, s. 765A(2)(b) omitted by FA 2009, s. 37 and Sch. 17, para. 2(b) with effect in relation to events taking place and transactions carried out on or after 1 July 2009. Former entry added by FA 1990, s. 68(3)(c).
- Entry for ICTA 1988, s. 767 omitted by FA 2008, s. 113 and Sch. 36, para. 73, with effect from 1 April 2009 (SI 2009/404, art. 2, subject to savings at SI 2009/404, art. 3). Former entry for ICTA 1988, s. 767C added by FA 1998, s. 115(2);
- Entry (so far as it continued to have effect, see below) for ICTA 1988, s. 768(9) omitted by FA 2011, s. 86 and Sch. 23, para. 51(3), with effect from 1 April 2012, but in relation to notice issued or request made before that date, this entry continues to apply as if it had not been omitted (FA 2011, Sch. 23, para. 65).

- Entry for ICTA 1988, s. 768(9) omitted by CTA 2010, s. 1177 and Sch. 1, para. 157(2)(a)(v) and repealed by CTA 2010, s. 1181 and Sch. 3, Pt. 1, with effect for corporation tax purposes for accounting periods ending on or after 1 April 2010, and for income tax and capital gains tax purposes for the tax year 2010–11 and subsequent tax years.
- Entry for ICTA 1988, s. 774(5) omitted by SI 2009/2035, art. 2 and Schedule, para. 8(3)(a), with effect from 13 August 2009.
- Entry for ICTA 1988, s. 778 omitted by CTA 2010, s. 1177 and Sch. 1, para. 157(2)(a)(vi) and repealed by CTA 2010, s. 1181 and Sch. 3, Pt. 1, with effect for corporation tax purposes for accounting periods ending on or after 1 April 2010, and for income tax and capital gains tax purposes for the tax year 2010–11 and subsequent tax years.
- Entry for ICTA 1988, s. 815 omitted by SI 2009/2035, art. 2 and Schedule, para. 8(3)(a), with effect from 13 August 2009.
- Entry for ICTA 1988, Sch. 5, para. 10 omitted by CTA 2009, s. 1322 and Sch. 1, para. 307(2)(d) and repealed by CTA 2009, s. 1326 and Sch. 3, Pt. 1, with effect for corporation tax purposes for accounting periods ending on or after 1 April 2009, and for income tax and capital gains tax purposes for the tax year 2009–10 and subsequent tax years.
- Entry for ICTA 1988, Sch. 6, para. 9 omitted by SI 2009/2035, art. 2 and Schedule, para. 8(3)(b), with effect from 13 August 2009.
- Entry for ICTA 1988, Sch. 15, para. 14(5) omitted by SI 2009/2035, art. 2 and Schedule, para. 8(3)(c), with effect from 13 August 2009.
- Entry for ICTA 1988, Sch. 15B, para. 5(2) omitted by ITA 2007, s. 1027 and Sch. 1, para. 260(8)(i), and repealed by s. 1031 and Sch. 3, Pt. 1, with effect from 6 April 2007. Former entry added by FA 1995, s. 71(3))
- Entry for ICTA 1988, Sch. 22, para. 4 omitted by SI 2009/2035, art. 2 and Schedule, para. 8(3)(d), with effect from 13 August 2009.
- Entry for regulations under ICTA 1988, Sch. 28B, para. 11B(5) omitted by ITA 2007, s. 1027 and Sch. 1, para. 260(8)(j), and repealed by s. 1031 and Sch. 3, Pt. 1, with effect from 6 April 2007. Former entry added by FA 2000, Sch. 18 para. 8(3) in relation to exchanges of shares or securities taking effect on or after 21 March 2000;
- Entry for FA 1973, Sch. 15, para. 2 omitted by TIOPA 2010, s. 371 and Sch. 7, para. 5(2) and repealed by TIOPA 2010, s. 378 and Sch. 10 , Pt. 12, with effect for corporation tax purposes for accounting periods ending on or after 1 April 2010, for income tax and capital gains tax purposes for the tax year 2010–11 and subsequent tax years, and for petroleum revenue tax purposes for chargeable periods beginning on or after 1 July 2010.
- Entry for FA 1973, s. 32 omitted by SI 2009/2035, art. 2 and Schedule, para. 8(3)(e), with effect from 13 August 2009.
- Entry for FA 1984, Sch. 14, para. 15(1) omitted by SI 2009/2035, art. 2 and Schedule, para. 8(3)(f), with effect from 13 August 2009.
- Entry for FA 1985, Sch. 22, para. 6(1) omitted by SI 2009/2035, art. 2 and Schedule, para. 8(3)(g), with effect from 13 August 2009.
- Entry for regulations under FA 1989, s. 57 omitted by SI 2009/2035, art. 2 and Schedule, para. 8(3)(h), with effect from 13 August 2009. Former entry added by FA 1989, s. 57(2);
- Entry for FA 1989, s. 73 added by FA 1989, s. 73(9);
- Entry (so far as it continued to have effect, see below) for FA 1989, Sch. 12, para. 3 omitted by FA 2011, s. 86 and Sch 23, para. 51(3), with effect from 1 April 2012, but in relation to notice issued or request made before that date, this entry continues to apply as if it had not been omitted (FA 2011, Sch. 23, para. 65).
- Entry for FA 1989, Sch. 12, para. 3 and 4 omitted by CTA 2010, s. 1177 and Sch. 1, para. 157(2)(a)(vii) and repealed by CTA 2010, s. 1181 and Sch. 3, Pt. 1, with effect for corporation tax purposes for accounting periods ending on or after 1 April 2010, and for income tax and capital gains tax purposes for the tax year 2010–11 and subsequent tax years. Former entry substituted for FA 1989, Sch. 12, para. 2 to 4 by SI 2009/2035, art. 2 and Schedule, para. 8(2)(d), with effect from 13 August 2009.
- Entry for regulations under FA 1991, s. 33 omitted by SI 2009/2035, art. 2 and Schedule, para. 8(3)(i), with effect from 13 August 2009. Former entry added by FA 1991, s. 33(2);
- Entry for references to the 1992 Act substituted on consolidation by TCGA 1992, s. 290 and Sch. 10, para. 2(10);
- Entry for TCGA 1992, s. 79(6) omitted by SI 2009/2035, art. 2 and Schedule, para. 8(3)(j), with effect from 13 August 2009.
- Entry for TCGA 1992 s. 169G(2) omitted by SI 2009/2035, art. 2 and Schedule, para. 8(3)(j), with effect from 13 August 2009. Former entry inserted by FA 2004, s. 116 and Sch. 21, para. 1, with effect for any notice given:
  - after 22 July 2004 (Royal Assent); and
  - in respect of 2003–04 or any subsequent year of assessment
- Entry for TCGA 1992, s. 235 omitted by SI 2009/2035, art. 2 and Schedule, para. 8(3)(j), with effect from 13 August 2009.
- Entry for TCGA 1992 Sch. 1 para. 1(7) inserted by FA 2003, s. 159 and Sch. 28, para. 6 in respect of the year 2002–03 and subsequent years provided the notice is given on or after 10 July 2003.
- Entry for TCGA 1992, Sch. 4ZA, para. 14 omitted by SI 2009/2035, art. 2 and Schedule, para. 8(3)(k), with effect from 13 August 2009. Former entry inserted by FA 2006, s. 88 and Sch. 12, para. 46(1), with effect from 6 April 2006.
- Entry for TCGA 1992, Sch. 5, para. 10 omitted by SI 2009/2035, art. 2 and Schedule, para. 8(3)(l), with effect from 13 August 2009.
- Entry for FA 1995, s. 86(12) added by FA 1995, s. 86(12) but omitted by ITA 2007, s. 1027 and Sch. 1, para. 260(8)(k), and repealed by s. 1031 and Sch. 3, Pt. 1, with effect from 6 April 2007.
- Entry for FA 2000, Sch. 15 para. 66 inserted by FA 2000, Sch. 16 para. 1(3);
- Entry for FA 2002, Sch. 34, para. 10 added by FA 2002, s. 111 and Sch. 34, para. 10, with effect from 24 April 2002;
- Entry for FA 2002, Sch. 35, para. 11 added by FA 2002, s. 113 and Sch. 35, para. 11, with effect from 24 April 2002;
- Entry for FA 2002, Sch. 33 added by FA 2002, s. 109 and Sch. 33, para. 15 with effect from 24 July 2002 but omitted by ITA 2007, s. 1027 and Sch. 1, para. 260(8)(l), and repealed by s. 1031 and Sch. 3, Pt. 1, with effect from 6 April 2007.
- Entry for Regulations under ITEPA 2003, s. 589 omitted by SI 2009/2035, art. 2 and Schedule, para. 8(3)(m), with effect from 13 August 2009. Former entry inserted by ITEPA 2003, Sch. 6, para. 137(3) which has effect, for income tax purposes, for the tax year 2003–04 and subsequent tax years, and, for corporation tax purposes, for accounting periods ending after 5 April 2003.
- Entries for Regulations under section 715 of ITEPA 2003, Paragraph 93 of Schedule 2 to ITEPA 2003, Paragraph 45 of Schedule 3 to ITEPA 2003, Paragraph 33 of Schedule 4 to ITEPA 2003, and Paragraph 51 of Schedule 5 to ITEPA 2003 inserted by ITEPA 2003, Sch. 6, para. 137(3) which has effect, for income tax purposes, for the tax year 2003–04 and subsequent tax years, and, for corporation tax purposes, for accounting periods ending after 5 April 2003.
- Entry for ITEPA 2003 s. 421J(4) added by FA 2003, s. 140 and Sch. 22, para. 47(1)(a) in accordance with the provisions made for the taking effect of the amendments to ITEPA 2003, Pt. 7 by FA 2003, Sch. 22, para. 3–10. Some amendments have effect on or after 16 April 2003; others have effect from the day appointed for the purposes of FA 2003, Sch. 22, para. 3(2).
- Entry for regulations under FA 2003, s. 199 omitted by TIOPA 2010, s. 371 and Sch. 7, para. 104(2) and repealed by TIOPA 2010, s. 378 and Sch. 10, Pt. 12, with effect for corporation tax purposes for accounting periods ending on or after 1 April 2010, for income tax and capital gains tax purposes for the tax year 2010–11 and subsequent tax years, and for petroleum revenue tax purposes for chargeable periods beginning on or after 1 July 2010. Former entry added by FA 2003, s. 199(5) with effect from 10 July 2003.
- Entry for regulations under section 70(3) of the Finance Act 2004 inserted by FA 2004, s. 76 and Sch. 12, para. 7, with effect from 6 April 2007.
- Entries for ITTOIA 2005, s. 75(5), 128 and 305 omitted by SI 2009/2035, art. 2 and Schedule, para. 8(3)(n), with effect from 13 August 2009. Former entries inserted by ITTOIA 2005, s. 882 and Sch. 1, para. 379(3)(c); effective for income tax

purposes for 2005–06 onwards and for corporation tax purposes for accounting periods ending after 5 April 2005 (ITTOIA 2005, s. 883(1)).

- Entry for ITTOIA 2005, s. 401B inserted by CTA 2010, s. 1177 and Sch. 1, para. 157(b), with effect for corporation tax purposes for accounting periods ending on or after 1 April 2010, and for income tax and capital gains tax purposes for the tax year 2010–11 and subsequent tax years.
- Entry for ITTOIA 2005, s. 421A inserted by CTA 2010, s. 1177 and Sch. 1, para. 157(b), with effect for corporation tax purposes for accounting periods ending on or after 1 April 2010, and for income tax and capital gains tax purposes for the tax year 2010–11 and subsequent tax years.
- Entry for ITTOIA 2005, s. 302B omitted by FA 2011, s. 86 and Sch. 23, para. 51(3), with effect from 1 April 2012, but in relation to notice issued or request made before that date, this entry continues to apply as if it had not been omitted (FA 2011, Sch. 23, para. 65).
- Entry for ITTOIA 2005, s. 302B inserted by TIOPA 2010, s. 371 and Sch. 7, para. 18(3), with effect for corporation tax purposes for accounting periods ending on or after 1 April 2010, for income tax and capital gains tax purposes for the tax year 2010–11 and subsequent tax years, and for petroleum revenue tax purposes for chargeable periods beginning on or after 1 July 2010.
- Entry for ITTOIA 2005, s. 647 omitted by FA 2011, s. 86 and Sch. 23, para. 51(3), with effect from 1 April 2012, but in relation to notice issued or request made before that date, this entry continues to apply as if it had not been omitted (FA 2011, Sch. 23, para. 65).
- Entries for ITTOIA 2005, s. 647 and Regulations under ITTOIA 2005, Pt. 6, Ch. 3 inserted by ITTOIA 2005, s. 882 and Sch. 1, para. 379(3)(c); effective for income tax purposes for 2005–06 onwards and for corporation tax purposes for accounting periods ending after 5 April 2005 (ITTOIA 2005, s. 883(1)).
- Entry for FA 2005, s. 40(1), inserted by FA 2005, s. 43(2) with effect from the tax year 2004–05 onwards.
- Entry for regulations under F(No. 2)A 2005, s. 17(3) inserted by SI 2006/964, reg. 87(2)(b)(iii), with effect:
  - for the purposes of income tax for the tax year 2006–07 and subsequent tax years, for distributions made on or after 6 April 2006;
  - for the purposes of corporation tax on income, for accounting periods beginning on or after 1 April 2006 and on chargeable gains, in relation to disposals made on or after 1 April 2006, and for distributions made on or after 1 April 2006; and
  - for the purposes of capital gains tax, in relation to disposals made on or after 6 April 2006.
- Entry for ITA 2007, s. 242 and 243(1) and (2), inserted by ITA 2007, s. 1027 and Sch. 1, para. 260(8)(m), with effect from 6 April 2007.
- Entry for ITA 2007, s. 257GG and s. 257GH(1) and (2), inserted by FA 2012, Sch. 6, para 23(a), in relation to shares issued on or after 6 April 2012.
- Entry for ITA 2007, s. 257SG and s. 257SH(1) and (2) inserted by FA 2014, s. 57 and Sch. 11, para. 2(2), with effect from 17 July 2014.
- Entry for ITA 2007, s. 271(2) omitted by SI 2009/2035, art. 2 and Schedule, para. 8(3)(o), with effect from 13 August 2009. Former entry inserted by ITA 2007, s. 1027 and Sch. 1, para. 260(8)(m), with effect from 6 April 2007.
- Entry for ITA 2007, s. 312A inserted by FA 2012, Sch. 8, para 17, with effect from 17 July 2012.
- Entry for regulations under ITA 2007, Ch. 5, Pt. 6, inserted by ITA 2007, s. 1027 and Sch. 1, para. 260(8)(m), with effect from 6 April 2007.
- Entry for regulations under ITA 2007, s. 330(5) omitted by SI 2009/2035, art. 2 and Schedule, para. 8(3)(p), with effect from 13 August 2009. Former entry inserted by ITA 2007, s. 1027 and Sch. 1, para. 260(8)(m), with effect from 6 April 2007.
- Entry for ITA 2007, s. 703 omitted by SI 2009/2035, art. 2 and Schedule, para. 8(3)(q), with effect from 13 August 2009. Former entry inserted by ITA 2007, s. 1027 and Sch. 1, para. 260(8)(m), with effect from 6 April 2007.
- Entry for ITA 2007, s. 748(1) and (2), inserted by ITA 2007, s. 1027 and Sch. 1, para. 260(8)(m), with effect from 6 April 2007.
- Entry for ITA 2007, s. 771, inserted by ITA 2007, s. 1027 and Sch. 1, para. 260(8)(m), with effect from 6 April 2007.
- Entry for ITA 2007, s. 788 omitted by SI 2009/2035, art. 2 and Schedule, para. 8(3)(q), with effect from 13 August 2009. Former entry inserted by ITA 2007, s. 1027 and Sch. 1, para. 260(8)(m), with effect from 6 April 2007.
- Entry for ITA 2007, s. 862 omitted by SI 2009/2035, art. 2 and Schedule, para. 8(3)(q), with effect from 13 August 2009. Former entry inserted by ITA 2007, s. 1027 and Sch. 1, para. 260(8)(m), with effect from 6 April 2007.
- Entry for regulations under ITA 2007, s. 871(1), inserted by ITA 2007, s. 1027 and Sch. 1, para. 260(8)(m), with effect from 6 April 2007.
- Entry for regulations under ITA 2007, s. 969(1), inserted by ITA 2007, s. 1027 and Sch. 1, para. 260(8)(m), with effect from 6 April 2007.
- Entry for regulations under ITA 2007, s. 971(1), inserted by ITA 2007, s. 1027 and Sch. 1, para. 260(8)(m), with effect from 6 April 2007.
- Entry for ITA 2007, Sch. 2, para. 155(5) omitted by SI 2009/2035, art. 2 and Schedule, para. 8(3)(r), with effect from 13 August 2009. Former entry inserted by ITA 2007, s. 1027 and Sch. 1, para. 260(8)(m), with effect from 6 April 2007.
- Entry for Regulations 21 and 22 of the *Income Tax (Purchased Life Annuities) Regulations* 2008 inserted by SI 2008/562, reg. 26, with effect in relation to an annuity under which the first payment to the annuitant is made on or after 6 April 2008, subject to the transitional provision in reg. 27 which reads as follows:

  "**27** In the case of an annuity–

  (a) the contract for which was made during the period beginning with 6th April 2007 and ending with (and including) 5th April 2008;

  (b) under which the payments by the insurer to the annuitant are made in arrears; and

  (c) under which the first payment to the annuitant is made on or after 6th April 2008,

  the mortality tables applicable shall be the ones which were in force when the annuity was made and not those prescribed by regulation 7(3).".
- Entry for CTA 2009, s. 75(5) omitted by SI 2009/2035, art. 2 and Schedule, para. 8(3)(s), with effect from 13 August 2009. Former entry inserted by CTA 2009, s. 1322 and Sch. 1, para. 307(2)(e), with effect for corporation tax purposes for accounting periods ending on or after 1 April 2009, and for income tax and capital gains tax purposes for the tax year 2009–10 and subsequent tax years.
- Entry for CTA 2009, s. 126 omitted by SI 2009/2035, art. 2 and Schedule, para. 8(3)(s), with effect from 13 August 2009. Former entry inserted by CTA 2009, s. 1322 and Sch. 1, para. 307(2)(e), with effect for corporation tax purposes for accounting periods ending on or after 1 April 2009, and for income tax and capital gains tax purposes for the tax year 2009–10 and subsequent tax years.
- *Entry for CTA 2009*, s. 241 omitted by FA 2011, s. 86 and Sch. 23, para. 51(3), with effect from 1 April 2012, but in relation to notice issued or request made before that date, this entry continues to apply as if it had not been omitted (FA 2011, Sch. 23, para. 65).
- Entry for CTA 2009, s. 241 inserted by CTA 2009, s. 1322 and Sch. 1, para. 307(2)(e), with effect for corporation tax purposes for accounting periods ending on or after 1 April 2009, and for income tax and capital gains tax purposes for the tax year 2009–10 and subsequent tax years.

- Entry for CTA 2009, s. 245 omitted by SI 2009/2035, art. 2 and Schedule, para. 8(3)(s), with effect from 13 August 2009. Former entry inserted by CTA 2009, s. 1322 and Sch. 1, para. 307(2)(e), with effect for corporation tax purposes for accounting periods ending on or after 1 April 2009, and for income tax and capital gains tax purposes for the tax year 2009–10 and subsequent tax years.
- Entry for CTA 2009, s. 966(1) omitted by SI 2009/2035, art. 2 and Schedule, para. 8(3)(s), with effect from 13 August 2009. Former entry inserted by CTA 2009, s. 1322 and Sch. 1, para. 307(2)(e), with effect for corporation tax purposes for accounting periods ending on or after 1 April 2009, and for income tax and capital gains tax purposes for the tax year 2009–10 and subsequent tax years.
- Entry for regulations under FA 2009, Sch. 15, para. 24, 25, 26, 36, 38 omitted by TIOPA 2010, s. 374 and Sch 8, para. 157(2) and repealed by TIOPA 2010, s. 378 and Sch. 10, Pt. 4, with effect for corporation tax purposes for accounting periods ending on or after 1 April 2010, for income tax and capital gains tax purposes for the tax year 2010–11 and subsequent tax years, and for petroleum revenue tax purposes for chargeable periods beginning on or after 1 July 2010. Former entry inserted by FA 2009, s. 35 and Sch. 15, para. 95 with effect in relation to periods of account of the worldwide group that begin on or after 1 January 2010 or to which FA 2009, Sch. 15, para. 98 applies.
- Entry for CTA 2010, s. 31(3) and (4) substituted for entry relating to CTA 2010, s. 31 by FA 2011, s. 86 and Sch. 23, para. 51(4)(a), with effect from 1 April 2012, but in relation to a notice issued or a request made before that date, the former entry continues to apply as if the substitution had not been made (FA 2011, Sch. 23, para. 65).
- Former entry for CTA 2010, s. 31 inserted by CTA 2010, s. 1177 and Sch. 1, para. 157(2)(c), with effect for corporation tax purposes for accounting periods ending on or after 1 April 2010, and for income tax and capital gains tax purposes for the tax year 2010–11 and subsequent tax years.
- Entry for CTA 2012, s. 465(3) and (4) substituted for the entry relating to CTA 2010, s. 465 by FA 2011, s. 86 and Sch. 23, para. 51(4)(b), with effect from 1 April 2012, but in relation to a notice issued or a request made before that date, the former entry continues to apply as if the substitution had not been made (FA 2011, Sch. 23, para. 65).
- Former entry for CTA 2010, s. 465 inserted by CTA 2010, s. 1177 and Sch. 1, para. 157(2)(c), with effect for corporation tax purposes for accounting periods ending on or after 1 April 2010, and for income tax and capital gains tax purposes for the tax year 2010–11 and subsequent tax years.
- Entry for CTA 2010, s. 728 omitted by FA 2011, s. 86 and Sch. 23, para. 51(3), with effect from 1 April 2012, but in relation to notice issued or request made before that date, this entry continues to apply as if it had not been omitted (FA 2011, Sch. 23, para. 65).
- Former entry for CTA 2010, s. 728 inserted by CTA 2010, s. 1177 and Sch. 1, para. 157(2)(c), with effect for corporation tax purposes for accounting periods ending on or after 1 April 2010, and for income tax and capital gains tax purposes for the tax year 2010–11 and subsequent tax years.
- Entry for CTA 2010, s. 832 inserted by CTA 2010, s. 1177 and Sch. 1, para. 157(2)(c), with effect for corporation tax purposes for accounting periods ending on or after 1 April 2010, and for income tax and capital gains tax purposes for the tax year 2010–11 and subsequent tax years.
- Entry for CTA 2010, s. 1046(5) to (7) omitted by FA 2011, s. 86 and Sch. 23, para. 51(3), with effect from 1 April 2012, but in relation to notice issued or request made before that date, this entry continues to apply as if it had not been omitted (FA 2011, Sch. 23, para. 65).
- Entry for former CTA 2010, s. 1046(5) to (7) inserted by CTA 2010, s. 1177 and Sch. 1, para. 157(2)(c), with effect for corporation tax purposes for accounting periods ending on or after 1 April 2010, and for income tax and capital gains tax purposes for the tax year 2010–11 and subsequent tax years.
- Entry for CTA 2010, s. 1052(4) and (5) inserted by CTA 2010, s. 1177 and Sch. 1, para. 157(2)(c), with effect for corporation tax purposes for accounting periods ending on or after 1 April 2010, and for income tax and capital gains tax purposes for the tax year 2010–11 and subsequent tax years.
- Entry for CTA 2010, s. 1097(1) and (2) omitted by FA 2011, s. 86 and Sch. 23, para. 51(3), with effect from 1 April 2012, but in relation to notice issued or request made before that date, this entry continues to apply as if it had not been omitted (FA 2011, Sch. 23, para. 65).
- Entry for CTA 2010, s. 1097(1) and (2) inserted by CTA 2010, s. 1177 and Sch. 1, para. 157(2)(c), with effect for corporation tax purposes for accounting periods ending on or after 1 April 2010, and for income tax and capital gains tax purposes for the tax year 2010–11 and subsequent tax years.
- Entry for CTA 2010, s. 1101(5) and (6) inserted by CTA 2010, s. 1177 and Sch. 1, para. 157(2)(c), with effect for corporation tax purposes for accounting periods ending on or after 1 April 2010, and for income tax and capital gains tax purposes for the tax year 2010–11 and subsequent tax years.
- Entry for CTA 2010, s. 1102(4) and (5) substituted for the entry relating to CTA 2010, s. 1102 by FA 2011, s. 86 and Sch. 23, para. 51(4)(c), with effect from 1 April 2012, but in relation to a notice issued or a request made before that date, the former entry continues to apply as if the substitution had not been made (FA 2011, Sch. 23, para. 65).
- Former entry for CTA 2010, s. 1102 inserted by CTA 2010, s. 1177 and Sch. 1, para. 157(2)(c), with effect for corporation tax purposes for accounting periods ending on or after 1 April 2010, and for income tax and capital gains tax purposes for the tax year 2010–11 and subsequent tax years.
- Entry for CTA 2010, s. 1109 omitted by FA 2016, s. 5 and Sch. 1, para. 51(11), with effect in relation to dividends paid or arising (or treated as paid), and other distributions made (or treated as made), in the tax year 2016–17 or at any later time.
- Former e for CTA 2010, s. 1109 inserted by CTA 2010, s. 1177 and Sch. 1, para. 157(2)(c), with effect for corporation tax purposes for accounting periods ending on or after 1 April 2010, and for income tax and capital gains tax purposes for the tax year 2010–11 and subsequent tax years.
- Entry for regulations under TIOPA 2010, s. 283, 284, 285, 295 or 297 inserted by TIOPA 2010, s. 374 and Sch. 8, para. 157(3), with effect for corporation tax purposes for accounting periods ending on or after 1 April 2010, for income tax and capital gains tax purposes for the tax year 2010–11 and subsequent tax years, and for petroleum revenue tax purposes for chargeable periods beginning on or after 1 July 2010.
- Entry for regulations under FA 2012, s. 61(5) inserted by FA 2012, s. 146 and Sch. 16, para. 67(2)(b), with effect in relation to accounting periods beginning on or after 1 January 2013 (FA 2012, s. 148) but subject to transitional provisions in FA 2012, Sch. 17. Where an accounting period would otherwise straddle 1 January 2013, it is deemed to end on 31 December 2012 (FA 2012, s. 149).

Col. 2 of Table amended as follows:

- Entry for TMA 1970, s. 12ADA inserted by FA 2014, s. 74 and Sch. 17, para. 16(3), with effect for the tax year 2014–15 and subsequent tax years.
- Entry for regulations under ICTA 1988, s. 42A omitted by ITA 2007, s. 1027 and Sch. 1, para. 260(9)(a), and repealed by s. 1031 and Sch. 3, Pt. 1, with effect from 6 April 2007. Former entry added by FA 1995, s. 40(2).
- Entry for ICTA 1988, s. 38(5) and 42 transposed to first col., s. 482(2) added by FA 1989, s. 164(5) for offences on or after 27 July 1989;
- Entry for regulations under ICTA 1988, s. 51B repealed by FA 1998, s. 165 and Sch. 27 Pt. 28, with effect in relation to payments of interest falling due after 31 March 1999. Former entry added by FA 1995, s. 78(2).
- Entry for ICTA 1988, s. 216 omitted by CTA 2010, s. 1177 and Sch. 1, para. 157(3)(a)(i) and repealed by CTA 2010, s. 1181 and Sch. 3, Pt. 1, with effect for corporation tax purposes for accounting periods ending on or after 1 April 2010, and for income tax and capital gains tax purposes for the tax year 2010–11 and subsequent tax years.

- Entry for ICTA 1988, s. 226(1) and (2) omitted by CTA 2010, s. 1177 and Sch. 1, para. 157(3)(a)(ii) and repealed by CTA 2010, s. 1181 and Sch. 3, Pt. 1, with effect for corporation tax purposes for accounting periods ending on or after 1 April 2010, and for income tax and capital gains tax purposes for the tax year 2010–11 and subsequent tax years.
- Entry for ICTA 1988, s. 234(5), (6) and (7)(a) omitted by CTA 2010, s. 1177 and Sch. 1, para. 157(3)(a)(iii) and repealed by CTA 2010, s. 1181 and Sch. 3, Pt. 1, with effect for corporation tax purposes for accounting periods ending on or after 1 April 2010, and for income tax and capital gains tax purposes for the tax year 2010–11 and subsequent tax years.
- Entry for ICTA 1988, s. 250(1) to (5) omitted by CTA 2010, s. 1177 and Sch. 1, para. 157(3)(a)(iv) and repealed by CTA 2010, s. 1181 and Sch. 3, Pt. 1, with effect for corporation tax purposes for accounting periods ending on or after 1 April 2010, and for income tax and capital gains tax purposes for the tax year 2010–11 and subsequent tax years.
- Entry for ICTA 1988, s. 76ZE(4) omitted by FA 2012, s. 146 and Sch. 16, para. 67(3)(a), with effect in relation to accounting periods beginning on or after 1 January 2013 (FA 2012, s. 148), subject to transitional provisions in FA 2012, Sch. 17. Where an accounting period would otherwise straddle 1 January 2013, it is deemed to end on 31 December 2012 (FA 2012, s. 149). Former entry for ICTA 1988, s. 76ZE(4) inserted by CTA 2009, s. 1322 and Sch. 1, para. 307(3)(a), with effect for corporation tax purposes for accounting periods ending on or after 1 April 2009, and for income tax and capital gains tax purposes for the tax year 2009–10 and subsequent tax years.
- In the entry for ICTA 1988, s. 310, (2A) inserted by FA 2001, s. 63 and Sch. 15, para. 39 in relation to shares issued on or after 6 April 2001, for claims for relief under ICTA 1988, Pt. 7, Ch. 3 made for the year 2000–01 or any later year of assessment;
- Entry for regulations under s. 326C omitted by ITTOIA 2005, s. 882 and Sch. 1, para. 379(4)(a) and repealed by ITTOIA 2005, s. 884 and Sch. 3; effective for income tax purposes for 2005–06 onwards (ITTOIA 2005, s. 883(1)). Former entry added by FA 1990, s. 28(2).
- Entry for regulations under ICTA 1988, s. 333B omitted by FA 2007, s. 38 and Sch. 7, para. 1 and repealed by FA 2007, s. 114 and Sch. 27, Pt. 2(7), with effect for periods of account of insurance companies beginning on or after 1 January 2007, subject to the transitional provisions in FA 2007, Sch. 7, Pt. 2. Former entry added by FA 1998, s. 77(2).
- Entry for ICTA 1988, s. 350(1) omitted by ITA 2007, s. 1027 and Sch. 1, para. 260(9)(b), and repealed by s. 1031 and Sch. 3, Pt. 1, with effect from 6 April 2007.
- Entry for ICTA 1988, s. 431E(1) omitted by FA 2012, s. 146 and Sch. 16, para. 67(3)(b), with effect in relation to accounting periods beginning on or after 1 January 2013 (FA 2012, s. 148), subject to transitional provisions in FA 2012, Sch. 17. Where an accounting period would otherwise straddle 1 January 2013, it is deemed to end on 31 December 2012 (FA 2012, s. 149). Former entry for regulations under ICTA 1988, s. 431E(1) added by FA 1995, s. 51 and Sch. 8, para. 50.
- Entry for regulations under ICTA 1988, s. 441A(3) omitted by FA 2007, s. 41 and Sch. 10, para. 16(2) and repealed by FA 2007, s. 114 and Sch. 27, Pt. 2(10), with effect from Royal Assent 19 July 2007. Former entry added by FA 1995, s. 51 and Sch. 8, para. 50.
- Entry for regulations under ICTA 1988, s. 444BB and 444BD omitted by FA 2012, s. 26(2), with effect in relation to accounting periods ending on or after 1 January 2016 (SI 2015/1999, art. 2);
- Entry for regulations under ICTA 1988, s. 444BB and 444BD added by FA 1996, s. 166 and Sch. 32, para. 2;
- Entry for regulations under ICTA 1988, s. 476(1) omitted by ITA 2007, s. 1027 and Sch. 1, para. 260(9)(c), and repealed by s. 1031 and Sch. 3, Pt. 1, with effect from 6 April 2007.
- Entry for regulations under ICTA 1988, s. 477A(1) omitted by ITA 2007, s. 1027 and Sch. 1, para. 260(9)(d), and repealed by s. 1031 and Sch. 3, Pt. 1, with effect from 6 April 2007. Former entry added by FA 1990, s. 30 and Sch. 5, para. 15.
- Entry for ICTA 1988, s. 482(2) omitted by ITA 2007, s. 1027 and Sch. 1, para. 260(9)(e), and repealed by s. 1031 and Sch. 3, Pt. 1, with effect from 6 April 2007. Former entry added by FA 1989, s. 164.
- Entry for regulations under ICTA 1988, s. 482(11) omitted by ITA 2007, s. 1027 and Sch. 1, para. 260(9)(f), and repealed by s. 1031 and Sch. 3, Pt. 1, with effect from 6 April 2007.
- Entry for ICTA 1988, s. 552 substituted for one to ICTA 1988, s. 552(1)–(4) and reference to regulations under ICTA 1988, s. 552ZA(6) substituted for one to regulations under ICTA 1988, s. 552(4A) by FA 2001, s. 83 and Sch. 28, para. 20, in relation to chargeable events happening on or after 6 April 2002;
- Entry for ICTA 1988, s. 552 added by FA 2001, s. 83 and Sch. 28, para. 20, with effect for chargeable events happening after 5 April 2002.
- Entry for regulations under ICTA 1988, s. 552ZA(6) added by FA 2001, s. 83 and Sch. 28, para. 20, with effect for chargeable events happening after 5 April 2002.
- Entry for regulations under ICTA 1988, s. 552ZB added by FA 2013, s. 25 and Sch. 9, para. 12, with effect from 17 July 2013.
- Entry for regulations under ICTA 1988, s. 555(7) omitted by ITA 2007, s. 1027 and Sch. 1, para. 260(9)(g), and repealed by s. 1031 and Sch. 3, Pt. 1, with effect from 6 April 2007.
- Entry for regulations under ICTA 1988, s. 566(1), (2) or (2A) added by FA 1996, s. 178(2);
- Entry for ICTA 1988, s. 577(4) omitted by CTA 2009, s. 1322 and Sch. 1, para. 307(3)(b) and repealed by CTA 2009, s. 1326 and Sch. 3, Pt. 1, with effect for corporation tax purposes for accounting periods ending on or after 1 April 2009, and for income tax and capital gains tax purposes for the tax year 2009–10 and subsequent tax years.
- Entry for ICTA 1988, s. 588(6) omitted by CTA 2009, s. 1322 and Sch. 1, para. 307(3)(c) and repealed by CTA 2009, s. 1326 and Sch. 3, Pt. 1, with effect for corporation tax purposes for accounting periods ending on or after 1 April 2009, and for income tax and capital gains tax purposes for the tax year 2009–10 and subsequent tax years, subject to the transitional provisions at CTA 2009, Sch. 2, para. 138.
- Entry for regulations under ICTA 1988, s. 602, 612 and 639 repealed by FA 2004, s. 326 and Sch. 42, Pt. 3 with effect from 6 April 2006.
- Entry for regulations under ICTA 1988, s. 605(1A) added by FA 1994, s. 105(4)(c) with effect from 3 May 1994 and subsequently repealed by FA 2004, s. 326 and Sch. 42, Pt. 3 with effect from 6 April 2006;
- Entry for regulations under ICTA 1988, s. 651A(1)(a) repealed by FA 2004, s. 326 and Sch. 42, Pt. 3 with effect from 6 April 2006. Former entry added by FA 1998, s. 96(3)(c).
- Entry for ICTA 1988, s. 765A(2)(a) omitted by FA 2009, s. 37 and Sch. 17, para. 2(c) with effect in relation to events taking place and transactions carried out on or after 1 July 2009.
- Entry for ICTA 1988, s. 765A(2)(a) added by FA 1990 s. 68(3)(d);
- Entry for regulations under ICTA 1988, Sch. 15B, para. 5(1) added by FA 1995, s. 71(3) and (4), with effect for the year 1995–96 and subsequent years of assessment but omitted by ITA 2007, s. 1027 and Sch. 1, para. 260(9)(h), and repealed by s. 1031 and Sch. 3, Pt. 1, with effect from 6 April 2007.
- Entry for ICTA 1988, Sch. 16, omitted by ITA 2007, s. 1027 and Sch. 1, para. 260(9)(i), and repealed by s. 1031 and Sch. 3, Pt. 1, with effect from 6 April 2007.
- Entry for ICTA 1988, Sch. 22, para. 2 omitted by SI 2009/2035, art. 2 and Schedule, para. 8(4)(a), with effect from 13 August 2009.
- Entry for FA 1984, Sch. 14, para. 15(3) omitted by SI 2009/2035, art. 2 and Schedule, para. 8(4)(b), with effect from 13 August 2009.
- Entry for regulations under FA 1989, s. 57 omitted by SI 2009/2035, art. 2 and Schedule, para. 8(4)(c), with effect from 13 August 2009. Former entry added by FA 1989, s. 57(2);

- Entry for regulations under FA 1991, s. 33 omitted by SI 2009/2035, art. 2 and Schedule, para. 8(4)(d), with effect from 13 August 2009. Former entry added by FA 1991, s. 33(2);
- Entry for F(No. 2)A 1992, s. 28(2) omitted by FA 2008, s. 113 and Sch. 36, para. 73 with effect from 1 April 2009 (SI 2009/404, art. 2, subject to savings at SI 2009/404, art. 3). Former entry for F(No. 2)A 1992, s. 28(2) added by F(No. 2) A 1992, s. 28(4);
- Entry for references to the 1992 Act substituted on consolidation by TCGA 1992, s. 290 and Sch. 10, para. 2(10);
- Entry for TCGA 1992, Sch. 5A, para. 2–6 added by FA 1994, s. 97(6);
- Entry for SSAA 1992, s. 110ZA omitted by NICSPA 2004, s. 12 and Sch. 2, with effect from 6 April 2005 (by virtue of SI 2004/1943, reg. 6). Former entry added by Social Security Contributions (Transfer of Functions, etc.) Act 1999, s. 5 and Sch. 5, para. 1.
- Entry for reg. 11(2) of the Income Tax (Manufactured Overseas Dividends) Regulations added by SI 1993/2004, reg. 11(13) with effect from 1 October 1993;
- Entry for regulations under FA 1995, s. 73 added by FA 1995, s. 73(5);
- Entry for FA 1999, s. 86(4) omitted by TIOPA 2010, s. 374 and Sch. 8, para. 108(2) and repealed by TIOPA 2010, s. 378 and Sch. 10, Pt. 2, with effect for corporation tax purposes for accounting periods ending on or after 1 April 2010, for income tax and capital gains tax purposes for the tax year 2010–11 and subsequent tax years, and for petroleum revenue tax purposes for chargeable periods beginning on or after 1 July 2010. Former entry added by FA 1999, s. 86(9);
- Entry for FA 2000, Sch. 15, para. 64 or 65 inserted by FA 2000, Sch. 16, para. 1(2);
- Entry for FA 2000, Sch. 22, para. 93(2) inserted by FA 2000, Sch. 22, para. 93(4);
- Entry for FA 2000, Sch. 22, para. 129 inserted by FA 2000, Sch. 22, para. 129(3);
- Entry for References to CAA 2001, s. 43(5), (6) omitted by FA 2008, s. 76(6)(a).
- Former entry for CAA 2001, s. 43(5) and (6) and references to CAA 2001, s. 118 to 120, 145(2) and (3) and 203 substituted for references to CAA 1990, s. 22B(4), 23(2), 33F(5), 48, 51(6A) and 53(1H) by CAA 2001, s. 578 and Sch. 2, para. 4(2).
- Entry for CAA 2001, s. 45B(5) and (6) inserted by FA 2001, s. 6 and Sch. 17, para. 5 with effect as respects allowances and charges falling to be made for chargeable periods ending, for income tax purposes, on or after 6 April 2001, and for corporation tax purposes, on or after 1 April 2001;
- Entry for CAA 2001, s. 45G(4) and (5) added by FA 2002, s. 63 and Sch. 21, para. 7(2), with effect in relation to expenditure incurred on or after 17 April 2002).
- Entry for CAA 2001, s. 45I(5) and (6) inserted by FA 2003, s. 167 and Sch. 30, para. 6 in relation to expenditure incurred on or after 1 April 2003.
- Entry for FA 2002, Sch. 16, para. 42 omitted by CTA 2010, s. 1177 and Sch. 1, para. 157(3)(a)(v) and repealed by CTA 2010, s. 1181 and Sch. 3, Pt. 1, with effect for corporation tax purposes for accounting periods ending on or after 1 April 2010, and for income tax and capital gains tax purposes for the tax year 2010–11 and subsequent tax years. Former entry inserted with effect from 23 January 2003 by The Finance Act 2002, Section 57(3) and (4)(a), (Appointed Day) Order 2003 (SI 2003/88) giving effect to FA 2002, Sch. 17, para. 1.
- Entry for regulations under FA 2002, Sch. 33 omitted by ITA 2007, s. 1027 and Sch. 1, para. 260(9)(j), and repealed by s. 1031 and Sch. 3, Pt. 1, with effect from 6 April 2007. Former entry added by FA 2002, s. 109 and Sch. 33, para. 15 with effect from 24 July 2002.
- Entry for FA 2002, Sch. 34, para. 6 added by FA 2002, s. 111 and Sch. 34, para. 6, with effect from 24 April 2002;
- Entry for FA 2002, Sch. 35, para. 7 added by FA 2002, s. 113 and Sch. 35, para. 7, with effect from 24 April 2002;
- Entry for ITEPA 2003, s. 421J(3) substituted for references to s. 432, 445, 465, 466, 486 of ITEPA 2003 by FA 2003, s. 140 and Sch. 22, para. 47(1)(b). Some amendments have effect on or after 16 April 2003; others have effect from the day appointed for the purposes of FA 2003, Sch. 22, para. 3(2). (The deleted references had in turn been inserted by ITEPA 2003, Sch. 6, para. 137(5), with effect, for income tax purposes, for the year 2003–04 and subsequent years, and for corporation tax purposes, for accounting periods ending after 5 April 2003.)
- Entry for ITEPA 2003, s. 421J(3) omitted by FA 2014, s. 51 and Sch. 8, para. 231, which is treated as having come into force on 6 April 2014.
- Entry for ITEPA 2003, Sch. 5, para. 52 omitted by FA 2014, s. 51 and Sch. 8, para. 221, which is treated as having come into force on 6 April 2014.
- Entry for regulations under s. 589 of ITEPA 2003, regulations under s. 715 of ITEPA 2003, PAYE regulations and para. 52 of Sch. 5 to ITEPA 2003 inserted by ITEPA 2003, Sch. 6, para. 137(5) which has effect, for income tax purposes, for the tax year 2003–04 and subsequent tax years, and, for corporation tax purposes, for accounting periods ending after 5 April 2003.
- Entry for Regulations under section 716B of ITEPA 2003. inserted by FA 2014, s. 18(4), with effect from 6 April 2015 (SI 2015/931, art. 2).
- Entry for FA 2004, s. 55 omitted by FA 2008, s. 123 and Sch. 41, para. 25(a)(ii) with effect from 1 April 2010 (SI 2009/511, art. 2 and 3 (subject to transitional provisions at SI 2009/511, art. 4). Former entry inserted by FA 2004, s. 55(6) with effect for accounting periods beginning on or after 22 July 2004.
- Entry for regulations under FA 2004, s. 251(1)(a) or (4) inserted by FA 2004, s. 258(1), with effect from 6 April 2006.
- Entry for regulations under section 65(2), 69(1), 70(1)(a) or (c) or 71 of the Finance Act 2004 inserted by FA 2004, s. 76 and Sch. 12, para. 7, with effect from 6 April 2007.
- Entry for ITTOIA 2005, s. 75(4) and regulations under ITTOIA 2005, Pt. 6, Ch. 3, inserted by ITTOIA 2005, s. 882(1) and Sch. 1, para. 379(4)(b); effective for income tax purposes for 2005–06 onwards (ITTOIA 2005, s. 883(1)).
- Entry for FA 2005, s. 37(3) and 37(6), inserted by FA 2005, s. 43(3) with effect from tax year 2004–05 onwards.
- Entry for FA 2006, s. 106 (as modified by Schedule 17 of that Act), s. 116 and FA 2006, s. 130 inserted by FA 2006, s. 140, in respect of notices required to be given for accounting periods beginning on or after 1 January 2007.
- Entry for regulations under FA 2006, s. 122 inserted by FA 2006, s. 140, in respect of notices required to be given for accounting periods beginning on or after 1 January 2007 but omitted by ITA 2007, s. 1027 and Sch. 1, para. 260(9)(k), and repealed by s. 1031 and Sch. 3, Pt. 1, with effect from 6 April 2007.
- Entry for TCGA 1992 , Sch. 4ZA, para. 12 inserted by FA 2006, s. 88 and Sch. 12, para. 46(2) with effect from 6 April 2006.
- Entry for ITA 2007, s. 240 and s. 241, inserted by ITA 2007, s. 1027 and Sch. 1, para. 260(9)(l) with effect from 6 April 2007.
- Entry for ITA 2007, s. 257GE and s. 257GF inserted by FA 2012, Sch. 6, para 23(b), in relation to shares issued on or after 6 April 2012.
- Entry for ITA 2007, s. 257SE and 257SF inserted by FA 2014, s. 57 and Sch. 11, para. 2(3), with effect from 17 July 2014.
- Entry for ITA 2007, s. 271(1), inserted by ITA 2007, s. 1027 and Sch. 1, para. 260(9)(l) with effect from 6 April 2007.
- Entry for regulations under ITA 2007, Pt. 6, Ch. 5, inserted by ITA 2007, s. 1027 and Sch. 1, para. 260(9)(l) with effect from 6 April 2007.
- Entry for ITA 2007, s. 373, inserted by ITA 2007, s. 1027 and Sch. 1, para. 260(9)(l) with effect from 6 April 2007.
- Entry for regulations under ITA 2007, s. 871(1), inserted by ITA 2007, s. 1027 and Sch. 1, para. 260(9)(l) with effect from 6 April 2007.
- Entry for ITA 2007, Pt. 15, Ch. 15, inserted by ITA 2007, s. 1027 and Sch. 1, para. 260(9)(l) with effect from 6 April 2007.
- Entry for ITA 2007, Pt. 15, Ch. 16, inserted by ITA 2007, s. 1027 and Sch. 1, para. 260(9)(l) with effect from 6 April 2007.
- Entry for regulations under ITA 2007, s. 969(1), inserted by ITA 2007, s. 1027 and Sch. 1, para. 260(9)(l) with effect from 6 April 2007.

- Entry for regulations under ITA 2007, s. 971(1), inserted by ITA 2007, s. 1027 and Sch. 1, para. 260(9)(l) with effect from 6 April 2007.
- Entry for regulations under ITA 2007, s. 973(1), inserted by ITA 2007, s. 1027 and Sch. 1, para. 260(9)(l) with effect from 6 April 2007.
- Entry for Regulations 7, 23 and 25 of the *Income Tax (Purchased Life Annuities) Regulations* 2008 inserted by SI 2008/562, reg. 26, with effect in relation to an annuity under which the first payment to the annuitant is made on or after 6 April 2008, subject to the transitional provision in reg. 27 which reads as follows:

  "**27** In the case of an annuity–

  (a) the contract for which was made during the period beginning with 6th April 2007 and ending with (and including) 5th April 2008;

  (b) under which the payments by the insurer to the annuitant are made in arrears; and

  (c) under which the first payment to the annuitant is made on or after 6th April 2008,

  the mortality tables applicable shall be the ones which were in force when the annuity was made and not those prescribed by regulation 7(3).".
- Entry for CTA 2009, s. 75(4) inserted by CTA 2009, s. 1322 and Sch. 1, para. 307(3)(d), with effect for corporation tax purposes for accounting periods ending on or after 1 April 2009, and for income tax and capital gains tax purposes for the tax year 2009–10 and subsequent tax years.
- Entry for FA 2009, Sch. 17, para. 4 inserted by FA 2009, s. 37 and Sch. 17, para. 10 with effect in relation to events taking place and transactions carried out on or after 1 July 2009.
- Entry for CTA 2010, s. 260 inserted by CTA 2010, s. 1177 and Sch. 1, para. 157(3)(b), with effect for corporation tax purposes for accounting periods ending on or after 1 April 2010, and for income tax and capital gains tax purposes for the tax year 2010–11 and subsequent tax years.
- Entry for CTA 2010, s. 1046(1) to (4) inserted by CTA 2010, s. 1177 and Sch. 1, para. 157(3)(b), with effect for corporation tax purposes for accounting periods ending on or after 1 April 2010, and for income tax and capital gains tax purposes for the tax year 2010–11 and subsequent tax years.
- Entry for CTA 2010, s. 1095 inserted by CTA 2010, s. 1177 and Sch. 1, para. 157(3)(b), with effect for corporation tax purposes for accounting periods ending on or after 1 April 2010, and for income tax and capital gains tax purposes for the tax year 2010–11 and subsequent tax years.
- Entry for CTA 2010, s. 1096 inserted by CTA 2010, s. 1177 and Sch. 1, para. 157(3)(b), with effect for corporation tax purposes for accounting periods ending on or after 1 April 2010, and for income tax and capital gains tax purposes for the tax year 2010–11 and subsequent tax years.
- Entry for CTA 2010, s. 1052(1) to (3) inserted by CTA 2010, s. 1177 and Sch. 1, para. 157(3)(b), with effect for corporation tax purposes for accounting periods ending on or after 1 April 2010, and for income tax and capital gains tax purposes for the tax year 2010–11 and subsequent tax years.
- Entry for CTA 2010, s. 1101(1), (2) and (4) inserted by CTA 2010, s. 1177 and Sch. 1, para. 157(3)(b), with effect for corporation tax purposes for accounting periods ending on or after 1 April 2010, and for income tax and capital gains tax purposes for the tax year 2010–11 and subsequent tax years.
- Entry for TIOPA 2010, s. 228 inserted by TIOPA 2010, s. 374 and Sch. 8, para. 108(3), with effect for corporation tax purposes for accounting periods ending on or after 1 April 2010, for income tax and capital gains tax purposes for the tax year 2010–11 and subsequent tax years, and for petroleum revenue tax purposes for chargeable periods beginning on or after 1 July 2010.
- Entry for regulations under FA 2011, Sch. 18, para. 16 inserted by FA 2014, s. 44 and Sch. 6, para. 11(2), with effect from 17 July 2014.
- Entry for FA 2012, s. 61(5) inserted by FA 2012, s. 146 and Sch. 16, para. 67(3)(c), with effect in relation to accounting periods beginning on or after 1 January 2013 (FA 2012, s. 148), subject to transitional provisions in FA 2012, Sch. 17. Where an accounting period would otherwise straddle 1 January 2013, it is deemed to end on 31 December 2012 (FA 2012, s. 149).
- Entry for regulations under FA 2013, Sch. 22, para. 3 inserted by FA 2014, s. 44 and Sch. 6, para. 11(3), with effect from 17 July 2014.
- Entry for regulations under FA 2014, Sch. 6, para. 8 inserted by FA 2014, s. 44 and Sch. 6, para. 11(3), with effect from 17 July 2014.
- Entry for FA 2016, Sch. 4, para. 17 or 18 inserted by FA 2016, s. 19(10) and Sch. 4, para. 20, with effect from 15 September 2016.

Cross references – ICTA 1988, s. 566(2E): exclusion of further penalty under s. 98 in relation to person already liable to penalty under s. 566(2C).

SSCBA 1992, Sch. 1, para. 6(7): s. 98 applies to regulations made under that paragraph as it applies to regulations under ICTA 1988, s. 203 (PAYE).

FA 1993, s. 187(8): s. 98 to have effect as if, in the first column of the Table there were included a reference to s. 178(2)–(6) of that Act (PRT).

FA 2005, s. 43(4): application of s. 98 where information, statements or declarations are made jointly by trustees and a "vulnerable person".

SI 1986/1711, Schedule, Pt. I, II: modified application of s. 98 to stamp duty reserve tax.

SI 1997/993, reg. 8(5), (6): modification of s. 98, Table, 2nd column, in relation to a return under reg. 8(2) (manufactured dividends: returns by persons other than UK-resident companies).

SI 2006/964, reg. 93A: modification of s. 98(4E).

SI 2008/562, reg. 26: modification of column 1 and 2 in Table in s. 98.

SI 2010/1187, reg. 11: Financial Assistance Scheme: modification of second column in Table in s. 98.

Other material – Misc. 03/2016: Chargeable Events – Penalties following Audits & Voluntary Disclosures

98A Special penalties in the case of certain returns

98A(1) PAYE regulations or regulations under section 70(1)(a) or 71 of the Finance Act 2004 (sub-contractors) may provide that this section shall apply in relation to any specified provision of the regulations.

98A(2) Where this section applies in relation to a provision of regulations, any person who fails to make a return in accordance with the provision shall be liable–

(a) to a penalty or penalties of the relevant monthly amount for each month (or part of a month) during which the failure continues, but excluding any month after the twelfth or for which a penalty under this paragraph has already been imposed, and

(b) if the failure continues beyond twelve months, without prejudice to any penalty under paragraph (a) above, to a penalty not exceeding

(i) in the case of a provision of PAYE regulations, so much of the amount payable by him in accordance with the regulations for the year of assessment to which the return relates as remained unpaid at the end of 19th April after the end of that year, or

(ii) in the case of a provision of regulations under section 70(1)(a) or 71 of the Finance Act 2004, £3,000

98A(3) For the purposes of subsection (2)(a) above, the relevant monthly amount in the case of a failure to make a return–

(a) where the number of persons in respect of whom particulars should be included in the return is fifty or less, is £100, and

(b) where that number is greater than fifty, is £100 for each fifty such persons and an additional £100 where that number is not a multiple of fifty.

98A(4) [Omitted by FA 2007, s. 97 and Sch. 24, para. 29(a) and repealed by FA 2007, s. 114 and Sch. 27, Pt. 5(5).]

History – In s. 98A(1), the words "section 70(1)(a) or 71 of the Finance Act 2004 (sub-contractors)" substituted for the words "section 566(1) (sub-contractors) of the principal Act" by FA 2004, s. 76 and Sch. 12, para. 8(2), with effect from 6 April 2007 (FA 2004, s. 77).

In s. 98A(1), the words "PAYE regulations or regulations under section" substituted for the words "Regulations under section 203(2) (PAYE) or" by ITEPA 2003, Sch. 6, para. 138 which has effect for the tax year 2003–04 and subsequent tax years.

In s. 98A(2)(b)(i) created from existing text and s. 98(2)(b)(ii) inserted by FA 2004 s. 76 and Sch. 12, para. 8(3), with effect from 6 April 2007 (FA 2004, s. 77).

S. 98A(4) omitted by FA 2007, s. 97 and Sch. 24, para. 29(a) and repealed by FA 2007, s. 114 and Sch. 27, Pt. 5(5), with effect as follows by virtue of SI 2008/568, art. 2:

- 1 April 2008 in relation to relevant documents relating to tax periods commencing on or after that date;
- 1 April 2008 in relation to assessments falling within paragraph 2 for tax periods commencing on or after that date;
- 1 July 2008 in relation to relevant documents relating to claims under the Thirteenth Council Directive (arrangements for the refund of value added tax to persons not established in Community territory) for years commencing on or after that date;
- 1 January 2009 in relation to relevant documents relating to claims under the Eighth Council Directive (arrangements for the refund of value added tax to taxable persons not established in the territory of the country) for years commencing on or after that date;
- 1 April 2009 in relation to documents relating to all other claims for repayments of relevant tax made on or after 1 April 2009 which are not related to a tax period; and
- in any other case, 1 April 2009 in relation to documents given where a person's liability to pay relevant tax arises on or after that date.

However, no person will be liable to a penalty under Sch. 24 in respect of any tax period for which a return is required to be made before 1 April 2009.

In s. 98A(4)(a) "(in the case of a provision of PAYE regulations) or a period (in the case of a provision of regulations under section 70(1)(a) or 71 of the Finance Act 2004)" inserted by FA 2004, s. 76 and Sch. 12, para. 8(4), with effect from 6 April 2007 (FA 2004, s. 77).

S. 98A inserted by FA 1989, s. 165 with effect from 27 July 1989, but with s. 98A(2)(a) modified as respects failures before 20 May 1995 (the day appointed by virtue of SI 1994/2503 (C. 50)).

Cross references – SSCBA 1992, Sch. 1, para. 7: application of s. 98A to returns of National Insurance contributions.

SI 2005/2045, reg. 4(12): application of s. 98A to monthly return by a contractor.

Statutory instruments – SI 2003/2682 (PAYE).

SI 2005/2045: Construction Industry Scheme Regulations.

Extra-statutory concessions – B46: 7-day period of grace for companies with statutory filing dates after 30 September 1995, and for employers' and contractors' returns for years following 1994–95.

Other material – IR press release, 14 June 1996: automatic penalties for employers' and contractors' returns filed late restricted to total amount of tax and NIC which should be shown on the return, or £100, whichever is the greater.

98B European Economic Interest Groupings

98B(1) In this section **"grouping"** means a European Economic Interest Grouping formed in pursuance of Council Regulation (EEC) No. 2137/85 of 25th July 1985, whether registered in Great Britain, in Northern Ireland, or elsewhere.

98B(2) Subsections (2A) to (4) below apply where a grouping or member of a grouping required by a notice given under section 12A of this Act to deliver a return or other document fails to comply with the notice.

98B(2A) The grouping or member shall be liable to a penalty not exceeding £300 multiplied by the number of members of the grouping at the time of the failure to comply.

98B(2B) If, on an application made to it by an officer of the Board, the tribunal so directs, the grouping or member shall be liable, for each day on which the failure continues after the day on which the grouping or member is notified of the direction (but excluding any day for which a penalty under this subsection has already been imposed), to a further penalty or penalties not exceeding £60 multiplied by the number of members of the grouping at the end of that day.

98B(3) No penalty shall be imposed under subsection (2A) or (2B) above in respect of a failure at any time after the failure has been remedied.

98B(4) If a grouping to which, or member to whom, a notice is given proves that there was no income or chargeable gain to be included in the return, the penalty under subsections (2A) and (2B) above shall not exceed £100.

98B(5) Where a grouping or member fraudulently or negligently delivers an incorrect return, accounts or statement, or makes an incorrect declaration in a return delivered, under section 12A above, the grouping or member shall be liable to a penalty not exceeding £3,000 multiplied by the number of members of the grouping at the time of delivery.

History – S. 98B(2) substituted by FA 1994, s. 196 and Sch. 19, para. 30, in so far as it applies to income tax and capital gains tax, as respects the year 1996–97 and subsequent years of assessment and, in so far as it applies to corporation tax, as respects accounting periods ending on or after 1 July 1999, the appointed day for corporation tax self-assessment by virtue of FA 1994, s. 199(2), (3) and SI 1998/3173 (C. 78).

S. 98B(2A) inserted by FA 1994, s. 196 and Sch. 19, para. 30, in so far as it applies to income tax and capital gains tax, as respects the year 1996–97 and subsequent years of assessment and, in so far as it applies to corporation tax, as respects accounting periods ending on or after 1 July 1999, the appointed day for corporation tax self-assessment by virtue of FA 1994, s. 199(2), (3) and SI 1998/3173 (C. 78).

In s. 98B(2B) the word "it" substituted for the word "them" and the words "[the] tribunal so directs" (if this substitution was carried out as provided then the word "the" would appear twice) substituted for the words "General or Special Commissioners so direct" by SI 2009/56, art. 3(1) and Sch. 1, para. 44, operative from 1 April 2009, subject to transitional and saving provisions in SI 2009/56, Sch. 3.

S. 98B(2B) inserted by FA 1994, s. 196 and Sch. 19, para. 30, in so far as it applies to income tax and capital gains tax, as respects the year 1996–97 and subsequent years of assessment and, in so far as it applies to corporation tax, as respects accounting periods ending on or after 1 July 1999, the appointed day for corporation tax self-assessment by virtue of FA 1994, s. 199(2), (3) and SI 1998/3173 (C. 78).

S. 98B(3), (4) amended by FA 1994, s. 196 and Sch. 19, para. 30, in so far as it applies to income tax and capital gains tax, as respects the year 1996–97 and subsequent years of assessment and, in so far as it applies to corporation tax, as respects accounting periods ending on or after 1 July 1999, the appointed day for corporation tax self-assessment by virtue of FA 1994, s. 199(2), (3) and SI 1998/3173 (C. 78).

S. 98B inserted by FA 1990, s. 69 and Sch. 11, para. 3, 5, deemed to have effect from 1 July 1989.

Cross references – S. 36(4): 20-year time limit for fraudulent or negligent conduct applies to each member of the grouping.

S. 40(3): time limit for assessment on personal representatives applies to each member of the grouping.

FA 1998, Sch. 18, para. 91: actions by one member of an EEIG deemed to be an act or omission of all members for certain purposes.

European material – For Council Regulation 2137/85, see OJ 1985 L199/1.

Other material – Inland Revenue press release, 9 February 1994: from 1 January 1994 these provisions extended to all EEIGs established within the European Economic Area (EU member states, Iceland, Norway and Liechtenstein).

98C Notification under Part 7 of Finance Act 2004

98C(1) A person who fails to comply with any of the provisions of Part 7 of the Finance Act 2004 (disclosure of tax avoidance schemes) mentioned in subsection (2) below shall be liable–

(a) to a penalty not exceeding

  (i) in the case of a provision mentioned in paragraph (a), (b), (c) or (ca) of that subsection, £600 for each day during the initial period (but see also subsections (2A), (2B) and (2ZC) below), and

  (ii) in any other case, £5,000, and

(b) if the failure continues after a penalty is imposed under paragraph (a) above, to a further penalty or penalties not exceeding £600 for each day on which the failure continues after the day on which the penalty under paragraph (a) was imposed (but excluding any day for which a penalty under this paragraph has already been imposed).

98C(2) Those provisions are–

(a) section 308(1) and (3) (duty of promoter in relation to notifiable proposals and notifiable arrangements),

(b) section 309(1) (duty of person dealing with promoter outside United Kingdom),

(c) section 310 (duty of parties to notifiable arrangements not involving promoter),

(ca) section 310A (duty to provide further information requested by HMRC),

(cb) section 310C (duty of promoters to provide updated information),

(d) section 312(2) (duty of promoter to notify client of reference number),

(da) section 312A(2) and (2A) (duty of client to notify parties of reference number),

(daa) section 312B (duty of client to provide information to promoter),

(db) section 313ZA (duty of promoter to provide details of clients),

(dc) section 313ZB (enquiry following disclosure of client details),

(dca) section 313ZC (duty of employer to provide details of employees etc),

(e) sections 313A and 313B (duty of promoter to respond to inquiry),

(f) section 313C (duty of introducer to give details of persons who have provided information or have been provided with information), and

(g) section 316A (duty to provide additional information).

98C(2ZA) In this section **"the initial period"** means the period–

(a) beginning with the relevant day, and

(b) ending with the earlier of the day on which the penalty under subsection (1)(a)(i) is determined and the last day before the failure ceases;

and for this purpose **"the relevant day"** is the day specified in relation to the failure in the following table.

TABLE

Failure	*Relevant day*
A failure to comply with subsection (1) or (3) of section 308 in so far as the subsection applies by virtue of an order under section 306A	The first day after the end of the period prescribed under section 306A(6)
A failure to comply with subsection (1) or (3) of section 308 in so far as the subsection applies by virtue of an order under section 308A(2)	The first day after the end of the period prescribed under subsections (5) and (6)(a) of section 308A (as it may have been extended by a direction under subsection (6)(b) of that section)
Any other failure to comply with subsection (1) of section 308	The first day after the end of the period prescribed under that subsection
Any other failure to comply with subsection (3) of section 308	The first day after the end of the period prescribed under that subsection
A failure to comply with subsection (1) of section 309	The first day after the end of the period prescribed under that subsection
A failure to comply with section 310	The first day after the latest time by which section 310 must be complied with in the case concerned
A failure to comply with section 310A	The first day after the end of the period within which the person must comply with section 310A.

98C(2ZB) The amount of a penalty under subsection (1)(a)(i) is to be arrived at after taking account of all relevant considerations, including the desirability of its being set at a level which appears appropriate for deterring the person, or other persons, from similar failures to comply on future occasions having regard (in particular)–

(a) in the case of a penalty for a promoter's failure to comply with section 308(1) or (3) or section 310A, to the amount of any fees received, or likely to have been received, by the promoter in connection with the notifiable proposal (or arrangements implementing the notifiable proposal), or with the notifiable arrangements, and

(b) in the case of a penalty for a relevant person's failure to comply with section 309(1), 310 or 310A, to the amount of any advantage gained, or sought to be gained, by the relevant person in relation to any tax prescribed under section 306(1)(b) in relation to the notifiable arrangements.

98C(2ZBA) In subsection (2ZB)–

(a) **"promoter"** has the same meaning as in Part 7 of the Finance Act 2004, and

(b) **"relevant person"** means a person who enters into any transaction forming part of notifiable arrangements within the meaning of that Part.

98C(2ZC) If the maximum penalty under subsection (1)(a)(i) above appears inappropriately low after taking account of those considerations, the penalty is to be of such amount not exceeding £1 million as appears appropriate having regard to those considerations.

98C(2ZD) Where it appears to an officer of Revenue and Customs that a penalty under subsection (1)(a)(i) above has been determined on the basis that the initial period begins with a day later than that which the officer considers to be the relevant day, an officer of Revenue and Customs may commence proceedings for a re-determination of the penalty.

98C(2ZE) The Treasury may by regulations vary–

(a) any of the sums for the time being specified in subsection (1) above, and

(b) the sum specified in subsection (2ZC) above.

98C(2A) Where a failure to comply with a provision mentioned in subsection (2) concerns a proposal or arrangements in respect of which an order has been made under section 306A of the Finance Act 2004 (doubt as to notifiability), the amounts specified in subsection (1)(a)(i) and (b) above shall be increased to the prescribed sum in relation to days falling after the prescribed period.

98C(2B) Where a failure to comply with a provision mentioned in subsection (2) concerns a proposal or arrangements in respect of which an order has been made under section 314A of the Finance Act 2004 (order to disclose), the amounts specified in subsection (1)(a)(i) and (b) above shall be increased to the prescribed sum in relation to days falling after the prescribed period.

98C(2C) In subsection (2A) and (2B)–

(a) **"the prescribed sum"** means a sum prescribed by the Treasury by regulations, and

(b) **"the prescribed period"** means a period beginning with the date of the order under section 306A or 314A and prescribed by the Commissioners by regulations.

98C(2D) The making of an order under section 306A or 314A of that Act does not of itself mean that, for the purposes of section 118(2) of this Act, a person either did or did not have a reasonable excuse for non-compliance before the order was made.

98C(2E) Where an order is made under section 306A or 314A of that Act then for the purposes of section 118(2) of this Act–

(a) the person identified in the order as the promoter of the proposal or arrangements cannot, in respect of any time after the end of the period mentioned in subsection (2B), rely on doubt as to notifiability as an excuse for failure to comply with section 308 of that Act, and

(b) any delay in compliance with that section after the end of that period is unreasonable unless attributable to something other than doubt as to notifiability.

98C(2EA) Where a person fails to comply with–

(a) section 309 of that Act and the promoter for the purposes of that section is a monitored promoter for the purposes of Part 5 of the Finance Act 2014, or

(b) section 310 of that Act and the arrangements for the purposes of that section are arrangements of such a monitored promoter,

then for the purposes of section 118(2) of this Act legal advice which the person took into account is to be disregarded in determining whether the person had a reasonable excuse, if the advice was given or procured by that monitored promoter.

98C(2EB) In determining for the purpose of section 118(2) of this Act whether or not a person who is a monitored promoter within the meaning of Part 5 of the Finance Act 2014 had a reasonable excuse for a failure to do anything required to be done under a provision mentioned in subsection (2), reliance on legal advice is to be taken automatically not to constitute a reasonable excuse if either–

(a) the advice was not based on a full and accurate description of the facts, or

(b) the conclusions in the advice that the person relied on were unreasonable.

98C(2F) Regulations under this section–

(a) may include incidental or transitional provision,

(b) shall be made by statutory instrument,

(c) in the case of regulations under subsection (2C)(a), shall not be made unless a draft has been laid before and approved by resolution of the House of Commons, and

(d) in the case of regulations under subsection (2ZE) or (2C)(b), shall be subject to annulment in pursuance of a resolution of the House of Commons.

98C(3) A person who fails to comply with subsection (1) of section 313 of the Finance Act 2004 (duties of parties to notifiable arrangements to notify Board of reference number, etc.) or regulations under subsection (3) of that section shall be liable to a penalty not exceeding the relevant sum.

98C(4) In subsection (3) above **"the relevant sum"** means–

(a) in relation to a person not falling within paragraph (b) or (c) below, £5,000 in respect of each scheme to which the failure relates,

(b) in relation to a person who has previously failed to comply with subsection (1) of section 313 or regulations under subsection (3) of that section on one (and only one) occasion during the period of 36 months ending with the date on which the current failure to comply with that provision began, £7,500 in respect of each scheme to which the current failure relates (whether or not the same as the scheme to which the previous failure relates), or

(c) in relation to a person who has previously failed to comply with subsection (1) of section 313 or regulations under subsection (3) of that section on two or more occasions during the period of 36 months ending with the date on which the current failure to comply with that provision began, £10,000 in respect of each scheme to which the current failure relates (whether or not the same as the schemes to which any of the previous failures relates).

98C(5) In subsection (4) above **"scheme"** means any notifiable arrangements within the meaning of Part 7 of the Finance Act 2004.

History – In s. 98C(1)(a)(i), ", (c) or (ca)" substituted for "or (c)" by FA 2014, s. 284(6), with effect from 17 July 2014.
S. 98C(1)(a)(i) and (ii) substituted for "£5,000" in s. 98C(1)(a) by FA 2010, s. 56 and Sch. 17, para. 10(2), with effect from 1 January 2011 (SI 2010/3019).
S. 98C(2)(ca) inserted by FA 2014, s. 284(7), with effect from 17 July 2014.
S. 98C(2)(cb) inserted by FA 2015, s. 117 and Sch. 17, para. 3 with effect from 26 March 2015.
S. 98C(2)(daa) inserted by FA 2013, s. 223(4), with effect from 17 July 2013.
In s 98C(2)(da) the words "and (2A)" inserted by FA 2015, s. 117 and Sch. 17, para. 8 with effect from 26 March 2015.
In s. 98C(2)(da), the word "and" omitted from the end by FA 2010, s. 56 and Sch. 17, para. 10(3)(a), with effect from 1 January 2011 (SI 2010/3019).
S. 98C(2)(db) inserted by FA 2010, s. 56 and Sch. 17, para. 10(3)(b), with effect from 1 January 2011 (SI 2010/3019).
S. 98C(2)(dc) inserted by FA 2013, s. 223(4), with effect from 17 July 2013.
S. 98C(2)(dca) inserted by FA 2015, s. 117 and Sch. 17, para. 11 with effect from 26 March 2015.
In s 98C(2)(f) the words "or have been provided with information" inserted by FA 2015, s. 117 and Sch. 17, para. 13 with effect from 26 March 2015.
S. 98C(2)(f), and the word "and" before it, inserted by FA 2010, s. 56 and Sch. 17, para. 10(3)(c), with effect from 1 January 2011 (SI 2010/3019).
S. 98C(2)(g), and the word "and" before it, inserted (and the word "and" preceding it omitted) by FA 2015, s. 117 and Sch. 17, para. 15 with effect from 26 March 2015.
In s. 98C(2), the word "312(2)" substituted for the word "312(1)" in paragraph (d) and, after that paragraph (but before the word "and"), para. (da) inserted by FA 2008, s. 116 and Sch. 38, para. 7(2), with effect from 1 November 2008 for purposes other than stamp duty land tax (SI 2008/1935), and with effect from 1 April 2010, for stamp duty land tax purposes (SI 2010/409).
In s. 98C(2), the word "or" at the end of paragraph (c) repealed by FA 2007, s. 114 and Sch. 27, Pt. 6(4) and paragraph (e) and the word ", and" preceding it inserted by FA 2007, s. 108(9)(a), with effect from 19 July 2007.
In s. 98C(2ZA), in the table, the entry relating to a failure to comply with FA 2004, s. 310A inserted by FA 2014, s. 284(8), with effect from 17 July 2014.
S. 98C(2ZA) inserted by FA 2010, s. 56 and Sch. 17, para. 10(4), with effect from 1 January 2011 (SI 2010/3019).
In s. 98C(2ZB)(a), the word "promoter's" substituted for the word "person's" by FA 2014, s. 284(9)(a)(i), with effect from 17 July 2014.
In s. 98C(2ZB)(a), the words "or section 310A" inserted by FA 2014, s. 284(9)(a)(ii), with effect from 17 July 2014.
In s. 98C(2ZB)(a), the word "promoter" substitutedfor the word "person" by FA 2014, s. 284(9)(a)(iii), with effect from 17 July 2014.
In s. 98C(2ZB)(b), the word "relevant" inserted before the word "person's" by FA 2014, s. 284(9)(b)(i), with effect from 17 July 2014.
In s. 98C(2ZB)(b), ", 310 or 310A" substituted for "or 310" by FA 2014, s. 284(9)(b)(ii), with effect from 17 July 2014.
In s. 98C(2ZB)(b), the word "relevant" inserted before the word "person" inserted by FA 2014, s. 284(9)(b)(iii) with effect from 17 July 2014.
S. 98C(2ZB) inserted by FA 2010, s. 56 and Sch. 17, para. 10(4), with effect from 1 January 2011 (SI 2010/3019).
S. 98C(2ZBA) inserted by FA 2014, s. 284(10), with effect from 17 July 2014.
S. 98C(2ZC) inserted by FA 2010, s. 56 and Sch. 17, para. 10(4), with effect from 1 January 2011 (SI 2010/3019).
S. 98C(2ZD) inserted by FA 2010, s. 56 and Sch. 17, para. 10(4), with effect from 1 January 2011 (SI 2010/3019).
S. 98C(2ZE) inserted by FA 2010, s. 56 and Sch. 17, para. 10(4), with effect from 1 January 2011 (SI 2010/3019).
In s. 98C(2A), the words "amounts specified in subsection (1)(a)(i) and (b) above shall be increased to the prescribed sum in relation to days falling after the prescribed period" substituted for the words "amount specified in subsection (1)(b) above shall be increased to the prescribed sum" by FA 2010, s. 56 and Sch. 17, para. 10(5), with effect from 1 January 2011 (SI 2010/3019).
In s. 98C(2B), the words "amounts specified in subsection (1)(a)(i) and (b)" substituted for the words "amount specified in subsection (1)(b)" by FA 2010, s. 56 and Sch. 17, para. 10(6), with effect from 1 January 2011 (SI 2010/3019).
In s. 98C(2C)(b), the words "306A or" inserted by FA 2010, s. 56 and Sch. 17, para. 10(7), with effect from 1 January 2011 (SI 2010/3019).
In s. 98C(2D), the words "306A or" inserted by FA 2010, s. 56 and Sch. 17, para. 10(8), with effect from 1 January 2011 (SI 2010/3019).
In s. 98C(2E), the words "306A or" inserted by FA 2010, s. 56 and Sch. 17, para. 10(9), with effect from 1 January 2011 (SI 2010/3019).
S. 98C(2EA) and (2EB) inserted by FA 2014, s. 275, with effect from 17 July 2014.
In s. 98C(2F), in the opening words, the words "this section" substituted for the words "subsection (2C)" by FA 2010, s. 56 and Sch. 17, para. 10(10)(a), with effect from 1 January 2011 (SI 2010/3019).
In s. 98C(2F)(c), the words "(2ZE) or" inserted by FA 2010, s. 56 and Sch. 17, para. 10(10)(b), with effect from 1 January 2011 (SI 2010/3019).
S. 98C(2A)–(2F) inserted by FA 2007, s. 108(9)(b), with effect from 19 July 2007.
In s. 98C(3), the words "penalty not exceeding the relevant sum" substituted for the words "penalty of the relevant sum" by FA 2015, s. 117 and Sch. 17, para. 18(a), with effect from 26 March 2015.
In s. 98C(3), the words "subsection(1) of section 313" substituted for the words "section 313(1)" and the words "or regulations under subsection (3) of that section" inserted by FA 2008, s. 116 and Sch. 38, para. 7(3), with effect from 1 November 2008 for purposes other than stamp duty land tax (SI 2008/1935), and with effect from 1 April 2010, for stamp duty land tax purposes (SI 2010/409).
In s. 98C(4)(a), the figure "£5,000" substituted for "£100"; in (b), the figure "£7,500" substituted for "£500"; and in (c), the figure "£10,000" substituted for "£1,000" by FA 2015, s. 117 and Sch. 17, para. 18(b), with effect from 26 March 2015.
In s. 98C(4), the words "subsection (1) of section 313 or regulations under subsection (3) of that section" substituted (in both places) for the words "313(1)" by FA 2008, s. 116 and Sch. 38, para. 7(4), with effect from 1 November 2008 for purposes other than stamp duty land tax (SI 2008/1935), and with effect from 1 April 2010, for stamp duty land tax purposes (SI 2010/409).
S. 98C inserted by FA 2004, s. 315(1) with effect from 1 August 2004.

Cross references – SI 2007/785, Pt. 3: provisions corresponding to s. 98C.
SI 2007/3104: where a penalty is imposed under s. 98C(1) following an order under FA 2004, s. 306A, or s. 314A the amount specified in s. 98C(1)(b) is increased to £5,000.

Statutory instruments – SI 2007/3103: made under s. 98C(2B) and (2C).
SI 2007/3104: made under s. 98C(2A)–(2C)(a).
SI 2012/1836: made partly under s. 98C(2A), (2B) and (2C)(b).

99 Assisting in preparation of incorrect return etc.

99 [Omitted by FA 2012, s. 223 and Sch. 38, para. 45(c).]

History – S. 99 omitted by FA 2012, s. 223 and Sch. 38, para. 45(c), with effect from 1 April 2013 (SI 2013/279, art. 2), subject to savings provision at SI 2013/279, art. 3; where a notice is given under s. 20A on or before 31 March 2013, for the purposes of that notice the amendments made by FA 2012, Sch. 38, para. 44–47 shall be disregarded.
S. 99 substituted by FA 1989, s. 166 in relation to assistance and inducements on or after 27 July 1989.

Cross references – S. 20A: imposition of penalty may result in notice to deliver papers as regards tax clients.
S. 100C(1A): appeals against penalties under s. 98C(1)(a) to be heard by the Special Commissioners.
OTA 1975, Sch. 2, para. 1(1): s. 99 applies for the purposes of oil taxation.
F(No. 2)A 1997, Sch. 2, para. 14(3): s. 99 applies for the purposes of windfall tax.

FA 2004, s. 33(7): a person is not to be taken to know that a return is incorrect solely due to a failure to preserve records relating to an arm's length provision (until 2006/07 or for accounting periods ending on or before 31 March 2006).
SI 1986/1711, Schedule, Pt. I and II: modified application of s. 99 for purposes of stamp duty reserve tax.

Statements of practice – A13: HMRC view that returns must be signed personally by taxpayers, with relaxation where the provision of a signature would damage the taxpayer's health.
SP1/97: applications for HMRC approval to transmit information via ELS will automatically be refused where a penalty has been imposed under s. 99 within three years of the application.

Other material – Taxline 2000/3 (not reproduced): advice to accountants worried about breaching the ICAEW ethical rule when requested to provide documents by HMRC.

99A Certificates of non-liability to income tax

99A If a person who gives a certificate of non-liability to income tax in pursuance of regulations under section 852 of ITA 2007–

(a) gives the certificate fraudulently or negligently, or

(b) fails to comply with any undertaking contained in the certificate in pursuance of the regulations,

he shall be liable to a penalty not exceeding £3,000.

History – In s. 99A, the words "section 852 of ITA 2007" substituted for the words "section 477A of the principal Act (building societies) or section 480B of that Act (deposit-takers)" by ITA 2007, Sch. 1, para. 261, with effect from 6 April 2007.
S. 99A inserted by FA 1991, s. 82, in relation to certificates given on or after 25 July 1991 so far as relating to the giving of a certificate, or, so far as relating to failure to comply with an undertaking contained in a certificate, in relation to certificates whenever given, but not so as to impose liability for a failure occurring before 25 July 1991.

Hansard – Standing Committee on the 1991 Finance Bill, 11 June 1991, col. 294 (not reproduced): the Financial Secretary, in discussing innocent failures within s. 99A(b), said that there would be cases where taxpayers registered by mistake but that, provided the taxpayer had acted in good faith, the question of a penalty would not arise.

Notes – Certificates of non-liability may be given under SI 1990/2231, reg. 5 (building societies) and SI 1990/2232, reg. 5 (deposit-takers).

99B Declarations under Chapter 2 of Part 14 of ITA 2007

99B Where a person fraudulently or negligently gives any incorrect information in a declaration under any of sections 858 to 861 of ITA 2007, the person shall be liable to a penalty not exceeding £3,000.

History – S. 99B inserted by ITA 2007, s. 1027 and Sch. 1, para. 262, with effect from 6 April 2007.

100 Determination of penalties by officer of Board

100(1) Subject to subsection (2) below and except where proceedings for a penalty have been instituted under section 100D below, an officer of the Board authorised by the Board for the purposes of this section may make a determination imposing a penalty under any provision of the Taxes Acts and setting it at such amount as, in his opinion, is correct or appropriate.

100(2) Subsection (1) above does not apply where the penalty is a penalty under–

(a) [omitted by SI 2011/702, art. 8(a),]

(b) section 94(1) above as it has effect before the substitution made by section 83 of the Finance (No.2) Act 1987,

(c) section 98(1) above as it has effect before the amendments made by section 164 of the Finance Act 1989 or section 98(1)(i) above as it has effect after those amendments, subject to subsection (2A), or

(d) paragraph (a)(i) of section 98A(2) above as it has effect by virtue of section 165(2) of the Finance Act 1989, or

(e) section 98B(2)(a) above, or

(f) section 98C(1)(a) above,

(g) [Omitted by FA 2009, s. 109 and Sch. 57, para. 13(2).]

100(2A) Subsection (2)(c) does not exclude the application of subsection (1) where the penalty relates to a failure to furnish any information or produce any document or record in accordance with regulations under section 716B of ITEPA 2003 (employment intermediaries to keep, preserve and provide information etc).

100(3) Notice of a determination of a penalty under this section shall be served on the person liable to the penalty and shall state the date on which it is issued and the time within which an appeal against the determination may be made.

100(4) After the notice of a determination under this section has been served the determination shall not be altered except in accordance with this section or on appeal.

100(5) If it is discovered by an officer of the Board authorised by the Board for the purposes of this section that the amount of a penalty determined under this section is or has become insufficient the officer may make a determination in a further amount so that the penalty is set at the amount which, in his opinion, is correct or appropriate.

100(6) In any case where–

(a) a determination under this section is of a penalty under paragraph 18(2) of Schedule 18 to the Finance Act 1998, and

(b) after the determination has been made it is discovered by an officer of the Board authorised by the Board for the purposes of this section that the amount which was taken into account as the relevant amount of tax is or has become excessive,

the determination shall be revised so that the penalty is set at the amount which is correct; and, where more than the correct amount has already been paid, the appropriate amount shall be repaid.

History – In s. 100(1), the words "or a penalty has been imposed by the Commissioners under section 53 of this Act" which appeared after the word "below" omitted by SI 1994/1813, Sch. 1, para. 14, with effect from 1 September 1994.
S. 100(2)(a) omitted by SI 2011/702, art. 8(a), with effect from 1 April 2011, but subject to SI 2011/702, art. 20, which provides that the omission does not have effect in relation to a return or other document which is required to be made or delivered to HMRC, or an amount of tax which is payable, in relation to the tax year 2009–10 or any previous tax year.
In s. 100(2)(c), the words ", subject to subsection (2A)" inserted by FA 2015, s. 18(2), with effect from 26 March 2015.
S. 100(2)(g) (and the word "or" preceding it) omitted by FA 2009, s. 109 and Sch. 57, para. 13(2) with effect from 21 July 2009.
S. 100(2)(g) inserted by FA 2008, s. 113 and Sch. 36, para. 74, with effect from 1 April 2009 (SI 2009/404, art. 2, subject to savings at SI 2009/404, art. 3).
S. 100(2)(e) inserted by FA 1990, Sch. 11 para. 3(2), (5), deemed to have effect from 1 July 1989.
S. 100(2)(f) inserted by FA 2004, s. 315(2) with effect from 1 August 2004.
S. 100(2A) inserted by FA 2015, s. 18(3), with effect from 26 March 2015.
In s. 100(6)(a), the words "section 93(2), (4) or (5) of this Act", which appeared after the words "of a penalty", omitted by SI 2011/702, art. 8(b)(i), with effect from 1 April 2011, but subject to SI 2011/702, art. 20, which provides that the omission does not have effect in relation to a return or other document which is required to be made or delivered to HMRC, or an amount of tax which is payable, in relation to the tax year 2009–10 or any previous tax year.
In s. 100(6)(a), the words "or section 260(1)(b) of the Finance Act 2004", which appeared before the word ", and" at the end, omitted by SI 2011/702, art. 8(b)(ii), with effect from 1 April 2011, but subject to SI 2011/702, art. 21, which provides that the omission does not have effect in respect of a return period ending on or before 31 December 2010.
In s. 100(6)(a) the words "or section 260(1)(b) of the Finance Act 2004" inserted by FA 2004, s. 260(5) with effect from 6 April 2006.
In s. 100(6)(a) the word "or" preceding the words "paragraph 18(2)" repealed by FA 2004, s. 326 and Sch. 42, Pt. 3 with effect from 6 April 2006, subject to the transitional provisions in Sch. 36.
In s. 100(6)(a) the words "section 93(2), (4) or (5) of this Act or" inserted by FA 2001, s. 91(1) in relation to penalties determined at any time whether before or after 11 May 2001.
In s. 100(6)(a), reference to FA 1998, Sch. 18, para. 18(2) substituted for reference to TMA 1970, s. 94(6) by FA 1998, s. 117(3) and Sch. 19, para. 38, with effect in relation to accounting periods ending on or after 1 July 1999, the corporation tax self-assessment appointed day by virtue of FA 1994, s. 199(2), (3) and SI 1998/3173 (C. 28).
S. 100 substituted by FA 1989, s. 167.

Cross references – S. 113(1D): delegation of responsibility by officer of the Board for completion of determination procedure.
S. 114: want of form not to invalidate determination.
FA 1988, s. 134(6), (8): proceedings instituted before the special commissioners in Northern Ireland before 3 April 1989 will not be transferred to the general commissioners until after that date.
SSCBA 1992, Sch. 1, para. 7: application of s. 100 to returns of National Insurance contributions.
ITEPA 2003, s. 421JE(7): s. 100 to 103 do not apply to a penalty under ITEPA 2003, s. 421JC or ITEPA 2003, s. 421JD.
ITEPA 2003, Sch. 2, para. 81J(8): s. 100 to 103 do not apply to a penalty under ITEPA 2003, Sch. 2, Pt. 10.
ITEPA 2003, Sch. 3, para. 40J(8): s. 100 to 103 do not apply to a penalty under ITEPA 2003, Sch. 3, Pt. 8.
ITEPA 2003, Sch. 4, para. 28J(8): s. 100 to 103 do not apply to a penalty under ITEPA 2003, Sch. 4, Pt. 7.
ITEPA 2003, Sch. 5, para. 57D(7): s. 100 to 103 do not apply to a penalty under ITEPA 2003, Sch. 5, Pt. 8.
SI 1986/1711, Schedule, Pt. I and II: modified application of s. 100 for purposes of stamp duty reserve tax.
SI 2001/1004, reg. 82: application with respect to National Insurance returns.
SI 2007/785, reg.15(2): modification of s. 100, substituting s. 100(2)(f).

Notes – For the purposes of SI 1986/1711, reg. 20 (which applies certain provisions of TMA 1970, in some cases subject to modifications, for the purposes of stamp duty reserve tax), the omission of s. 100(2)(a) by SI 2011/702 has no effect (SI 2011/702, art. 22).
In s. 100(2)(e), the reference to s. 98B(2)(a) refers to the pre-self-assessment version of s. 98B.

100A Provisions supplementary to section 100

100A(1) [Omitted by FA 2007, s. 97 and Sch. 24, para. 29(b) and repealed by FA 2007, s. 114 and Sch. 27, Pt. 5(5).]

100A(2) A penalty determined under section 100 above shall be due and payable at the end of the period of thirty days beginning with the date of the issue of the notice of determination.

100A(3) A penalty determined under section 100 above shall for all purposes be treated as if it were tax charged in an assessment and due and payable.

History – S. 100A(1) omitted by FA 2007, s. 97 and Sch. 24, para. 29(b) and repealed by FA 2007, s. 114 and Sch. 27, Pt. 5(5), with effect as follows by virtue of SI 2008/568, art. 2:

- 1 April 2008 in relation to relevant documents relating to tax periods commencing on or after that date;
- 1 April 2008 in relation to assessments falling within paragraph 2 for tax periods commencing on or after that date;
- 1 July 2008 in relation to relevant documents relating to claims under the Thirteenth Council Directive (arrangements for the refund of value added tax to persons not established in Community territory) for years commencing on or after that date;
- 1 January 2009 in relation to relevant documents relating to claims under the Eighth Council Directive (arrangements for the refund of value added tax to taxable persons not established in the territory of the country) for years commencing on or after that date;
- 1 April 2009 in relation to documents relating to all other claims for repayments of relevant tax made on or after 1 April 2009 which are not related to a tax period; and
- in any other case, 1 April 2009 in relation to documents given where a person's liability to pay relevant tax arises on or after that date.

However, no person will be liable to a penalty under Sch. 24 in respect of any tax period for which a return is required to be made before 1 April 2009.

S. 100A inserted by FA 1989, s. 167.

Cross references – SSCBA 1992, Sch. 1, para. 7: application of s. 100A to returns of National Insurance contributions.
ITEPA 2003, s. 421JE(7): s. 100 to 103 do not apply to a penalty under ITEPA 2003, s. 421JC or ITEPA 2003, s. 421JD.
ITEPA 2003, Sch. 2, para. 81J(8): s. 100 to 103 do not apply to a penalty under ITEPA 2003, Sch. 2, Pt. 10.
ITEPA 2003, Sch. 3, para. 40J(8): s. 100 to 103 do not apply to a penalty under ITEPA 2003, Sch. 3, Pt. 8.
ITEPA 2003, Sch. 4, para. 28J(8): s. 100 to 103 do not apply to a penalty under ITEPA 2003, Sch. 4, Pt. 7.
ITEPA 2003, Sch. 5, para. 57D(7): s. 100 to 103 do not apply to a penalty under ITEPA 2003, Sch. 5, Pt. 8.
SI 1986/1711, Schedule, Pt. I and II: modified application of s. 100A for purposes of stamp duty reserve tax.

100B Appeals against penalty determinations

100B(1) An appeal may be brought against the determination of a penalty under section 100 above and, subject to the following provisions of this section, the provisions of this Act relating to appeals shall have effect in relation to an appeal against such a determination as they have effect in relation to an appeal against an assessment to tax, except that references to the tribunal shall be taken to be references to the First-tier Tribunal.

100B(2) On an appeal against the determination of a penalty under section 100 above section 50(6) to (8) of this Act shall not apply but–

(a) in the case of a penalty which is required to be of a particular amount, the First-tier Tribunal may–

(i) if it appears that no penalty has been incurred, set the determination aside,

(ii) if the amount determined appears to be correct, confirm the determination, or

(iii) if the amount determined appears to be incorrect, increase or reduce it to the correct amount,

(b) in the case of any other penalty, the First-tier Tribunal may–

(i) if it appears that no penalty has been incurred, set the determination aside,

(ii) if the amount determined appears to be appropriate, confirm the determination,

(iii) if the amount determined appears to be excessive, reduce it to such other amount (including nil) as it considers appropriate, or

(iv) if the amount determined appears to be insufficient, increase it to such amount not exceeding the permitted maximum as it considers appropriate.

100B(3) In addition to any right of appeal on a point of law under section 11(2) of the TCEA 2007, the person liable to the penalty may appeal to the Upper Tribunal against the amount of the penalty which has been determined under subsection (2), but not against any decision which falls under section 11(5)(d) and (e) of the TCEA 2007 and was made in connection with the determination of the amount of the penalty.

100B(3A) Section 11(3) and (4) of the TCEA 2007 applies to the right of appeal under subsection (3) as it applies to the right of appeal under section 11(2) of the TCEA 2007.

100B(3B) On an appeal under this section the Upper Tribunal has the same powers as are conferred on the First-tier Tribunal by virtue of this section.

History – In s. 100B(1), the words "sections 93 and 93A of this Act and", which appeared after the words "subject to", omitted by SI 2011/702, art. 9(a), with effect from 1 April 2011, but subject to SI 2011/702, art. 20, which provides that the omission does not have effect in relation to a return or other document which is required to be made or delivered to HMRC, or an amount of tax which is payable, in relation to the tax year 2009–10 or any previous tax year.
In s. 100B(1) the words "sections 93 and 93A" substituted for the words "sections 93, 93A and 95A" by SI 2009/571, art. 8 and Sch. 1, para. 12, with effect from 1 April 2009.
In s. 100B(1) the words ", except that references to the tribunal shall be taken to be references to the First-tier Tribunal" inserted by SI 2009/56, art. 3(1) and Sch. 1, para. 45(2), operative from 1 April 2009, subject to transitional and saving provisions in SI 2009/56, Sch. 3.
In s. 100B(1), reference to TMA 1970, s. 93, 93A and 95A, and in s. 100B(2), reference to TMA 1970, s. 93(8) and 93A(7), inserted by FA 1994, s. 196 and Sch. 19, para. 31, FA 1995, s. 115(7), in so far as it relates to income tax and corporation tax, as respects the year 1996–97 and subsequent years of assessment and, in so far as it relates to corporation tax, as respects accounting periods ending on or after 1 July 1999, the appointed day for corporation tax self-assessment by virtue of FA 1994, s. 199(2), (3) and SI 1998/3173 (C. 78).
In s. 100B(2), the word "On" substituted for the words "Subject to sections 93(8) and 93A(7) of this Act on" by SI 2011/702, art. 9(b), with effect from 1 April 2011, but subject to SI 2011/702, art. 20, which provides that the substitution does not have effect in relation to a return or other document which is required to be made or delivered to HMRC, or an amount of tax which is payable, in relation to the tax year 2009–10 or any previous tax year.
In s. 100B(2) the words "First-tier Tribunal" substituted for the word "Commissioners" twice; the words "to them" omitted seven times and in para. (b)(iii) and (iv) the words"as it considers" substituted for the words "as they consider" by SI 2009/56, art. 3(1) and Sch. 1, para. 45(3), operative from 1 April 2009, subject to transitional and saving provisions in SI 2009/56, Sch. 3.
S. 100B(3), (3A) and (3B) substituted for former s. 100B(3) by SI 2009/56, art. 3(1) and Sch. 1, para. 45(4), operative from 1 April 2009, subject to transitional and saving provisions in SI 2009/56, Sch. 3.
In former s. 100B(3), thewords "any right to have a case stated under regulation 22 of the General Commissioners Regulations or any right of appeal under section 56A" substituted by SI 1994/1813, Sch. 1, para. 15, with effect from 1 September 1994.
S. 100B inserted by FA 1989, s. 167.

Cross references – S. 50(6)–(8): procedure for commissioners amending etc. assessments.
S. 56A: appeals from the special commissioners.
SSCBA 1992, Sch. 1, para. 7: application of s. 100B to returns of National Insurance contributions.
ITEPA 2003, s. 421JE(7): s. 100 to 103 do not apply to a penalty under ITEPA 2003, s. 421JC or ITEPA 2003, s. 421JD.
ITEPA 2003, Sch. 2, para. 81J(8): s. 100 to 103 do not apply to a penalty under ITEPA 2003, Sch. 2, Pt. 10.
ITEPA 2003, Sch. 3, para. 40J(8): s. 100 to 103 do not apply to a penalty under ITEPA 2003, Sch. 3, Pt. 8.
ITEPA 2003, Sch. 4, para. 28J(8): s. 100 to 103 do not apply to a penalty under ITEPA 2003, Sch. 4, Pt. 7.
ITEPA 2003, Sch. 5, para. 57D(7): s. 100 to 103 do not apply to a penalty under ITEPA 2003, Sch. 5, Pt. 8.
SI 1986/1711, Schedule, Pt. I and II: modified application of s. 100B for purposes of stamp duty reserve tax.

Notes – For the purposes of SI 1986/1711, reg. 20 (which applies certain provisions of TMA 1970, in some cases subject to modifications, for the purposes of stamp duty reserve tax), the amendments made to s. 100B(1) and (2) by SI 2011/702 have no effect (SI 2011/702, art. 22).

100C Penalty proceedings before First-tier Tribunal

History – In the heading to s. 100C the words "First-tier Tribunal" substituted for the word "Commissioners" by SI 2009/56, art. 3(1) and Sch. 1, para. 46(2), operative from 1 April 2009, subject to transitional and saving provisions in SI 2009/56, Sch. 3.

100C(1) An officer of the Board authorised by the Board for the purposes of this section may commence proceedings before the First-tier Tribunal for any penalty to which subsection (1) of section 100 above does not apply by virtue of subsection (2) of that section.

100C(1A) [Omitted by SI 2009/56, art. 3(1) and Sch. 1, para. 45(4).]

100C(2) The person liable to the penalty shall be a party to the proceedings.

100C(3) Any penalty determined by the First-tier Tribunal in proceedings under this section shall for all purposes be treated as if it were tax charged in an assessment and due and payable.

100C(4) In addition to any right of appeal on a point of law under section 11(2) of the TCEA 2007, the person liable to the penalty may appeal to the Upper Tribunal against the determination of a penalty in proceedings under subsection (1), but not against any decision which falls under section 11(5)(d) and (e) of the TCEA 2007 and was made in connection with the determination of the amount of the penalty.

100C(4A) Section 11(3) and (4) of the TCEA 2007 applies to the right of appeal under subsection (4) as it applies to the right of appeal under section 11(2) of the TCEA 2007.

100C(5) On any such appeal the Upper Tribunal may–

(a) if it appears that no penalty has been incurred, set the determination aside,

(b) if the amount determined appears to be appropriate, confirm the determination,

(c) if the amount determined appears to be excessive, reduce it to such other amount (including nil) as the Upper Tribunal considers appropriate, or

(d) if the amount determined appears to be insufficient, increase it to such amount not exceeding the permitted maximum as the Upper Tribunal considers appropriate.

History – In s. 100C(1) the words "First-tier Tribunal" substituted for the words "General or Special Commissioners" by SI 2009/56, art. 3(1) and Sch. 1, para. 46(3), operative from 1 April 2009, subject to transitional and saving provisions in SI 2009/56, Sch. 3.
S. 100C(1A) omitted by SI 2009/56, art. 3(1) and Sch. 1, para. 46(4), operative from 1 April 2009, subject to transitional and saving provisions in SI 2009/56, Sch. 3.
Former s. 100C(1A) inserted by FA 2004, s. 315(3) with effect from 1 August 2004.
S. 100C(2) substituted by SI 2009/56, art. 3(1) and Sch. 1, para. 46(5), operative from 1 April 2009, subject to transitional and saving provisions in SI 2009/56, Sch. 3.
In s. 100C(3) the words "First-tier Tribunal" substituted for the words "General or Special Commissioners" by SI 2009/56, art. 3(1) and Sch. 1, para. 46(6), operative from 1 April 2009, subject to transitional and saving provisions in SI 2009/56, Sch. 3.
S. 100C(4) and (4A) substituted for former s. 100C(4) by SI 2009/56, art. 3(1) and Sch. 1, para. 46(7), operative from 1 April 2009, subject to transitional and saving provisions in SI 2009/56, Sch. 3.
In s. 100C(5) the words "Upper Tribunal" substituted for the word "court" three times by SI 2009/56, art. 3(1) and Sch. 1, para. 46(8), operative from 1 April 2009, subject to transitional and saving provisions in SI 2009/56, Sch. 3.
S. 100C inserted by FA 1989, s. 167.

Cross references – SSCBA 1992, Sch. 1, para. 7: application of s. 100C to returns of National Insurance contributions.
ITEPA 2003, s. 421JE(7): s. 100 to 103 do not apply to a penalty under ITEPA 2003, s. 421JC or ITEPA 2003, s. 421JD.
ITEPA 2003, Sch. 2, para. 81J(8): s. 100 to 103 do not apply to a penalty under ITEPA 2003, Sch. 2, Pt. 10.
ITEPA 2003, Sch. 3, para. 40J(8): s. 100 to 103 do not apply to a penalty under ITEPA 2003, Sch. 3, Pt. 8.
ITEPA 2003, Sch. 4, para. 28J(8): s. 100 to 103 do not apply to a penalty under ITEPA 2003, Sch. 4, Pt. 7.
ITEPA 2003, Sch. 5, para. 57D(7): s. 100 to 103 do not apply to a penalty under ITEPA 2003, Sch. 5, Pt. 8.
SI 1986/1711, Schedule, Pt. I and II: modified application of s. 100C for purposes of stamp duty reserve tax.
SI 2007/785, reg.15(3): modification of s. 100C, substituting s. 100C(1A).
RSC, O. 91: procedure in the High Court on appeal from the general or special commissioners, as replaced by Civil Procedure Rules 1998 (SI 1998/3132), r. 50.1(3), Sch. 1, r. 91 as from 26 April 1999.

100D Penalty proceedings before court

100D(1) Where in the opinion of the Board the liability of any person for a penalty arises by reason of the fraud of that or any other person, proceedings for the penalty may be instituted before the High Court or, in Scotland, the Court of Session as the Court of Exchequer in Scotland.

100D(2) Proceedings under this section which are not instituted (in England, Wales or Northern Ireland) under the Crown Proceedings Act 1947 by and in the name of the Board as an authorised department for the purposes of that Act shall be instituted–

(a) in England and Wales, in the name of the Attorney General,

(b) in Scotland, in the name of the Lord Advocate, and

(c) in Northern Ireland, in the name of the Attorney General for Northern Ireland.

100D(3) Any proceedings under this section instituted in England and Wales shall be deemed to be civil proceedings by the Crown within the meaning of Part II of the Crown Proceedings Act 1947 and any such proceedings instituted in Northern Ireland shall be deemed to be civil proceedings within the meaning of that Part of that Act as for the time being in force in Northern Ireland.

100D(4) If in proceedings under this section the court does not find that fraud is proved but consider that the person concerned is nevertheless liable to a penalty, the court may determine a penalty notwithstanding that, but for the opinion of the Board as to fraud, the penalty would not have been a matter for the court.

History – S. 100D inserted by FA 1989, s. 167.

Cross references – SSCBA 1992, Sch. 1, para. 7: application of s. 100D to returns of National Insurance contributions.
ITEPA 2003, s. 421JE(7): s. 100 to 103 do not apply to a penalty under ITEPA 2003, s. 421JC or ITEPA 2003, s. 421JD.
ITEPA 2003, Sch. 2, para. 81J(8): s. 100 to 103 do not apply to a penalty under ITEPA 2003, Sch. 2, Pt. 10.
ITEPA 2003, Sch. 3, para. 40J(8): s. 100 to 103 do not apply to a penalty under ITEPA 2003, Sch. 3, Pt. 8.
ITEPA 2003, Sch. 4, para. 28J(8): s. 100 to 103 do not apply to a penalty under ITEPA 2003, Sch. 4, Pt. 7.
ITEPA 2003, Sch. 5, para. 57D(7): s. 100 to 103 do not apply to a penalty under ITEPA 2003, Sch. 5, Pt. 8.
SI 1986/1711, Schedule, Pt. I and II: s. 100D applies for purposes of stamp duty reserve tax.
SI 2001/1004, reg. 82: application with respect to National Insurance returns.

101 Evidence for purposes of proceedings relating to penalties

101 An assessment which can no longer be varied by the tribunal on an appeal notified to it or by order of any court is sufficient evidence, for the purposes of–

(a) the preceding provisions of this Part, and

(b) the provisions of Schedule 18 to the Finance Act 1998 relating to penalties,

that the amounts in respect of which tax is charged in the assessment arose or were received as stated in the assessment.

History – In s. 101 the words "the tribunal on an appeal notified to it" substituted for the words "any Commissioners on appeal" by SI 2009/56, art. 3(1) and Sch. 1, para. 47, operative from 1 April 2009, subject to transitional and saving provisions in SI 2009/56, Sch. 3.
S. 101 substituted by FA 1998, s. 117(3) and Sch. 19, para. 39, with effect in relation to accounting periods ending on or after 1 July 1999, the corporation tax self-assessment appointed day by virtue of FA 1994, s. 199(2), (3) and SI 1998/3173 (C. 78).
Former s. 101 amended by FA 1985, Sch. 27, Pt. X by removing a reference to development land tax, with effect from 19 March 1985.

Cross references – OTA 1975, Sch. 2, para. 1(1): s. 101 applies with modifications for the purposes of oil taxation.
ITEPA 2003, s. 421JE(7): s. 100 to 103 do not apply to a penalty under ITEPA 2003, s. 421JC or ITEPA 2003, s. 421JD.
ITEPA 2003, Sch. 2, para. 81J(8): s. 100 to 103 do not apply to a penalty under ITEPA 2003, Sch. 2, Pt. 10.
ITEPA 2003, Sch. 3, para. 40J(8): s. 100 to 103 do not apply to a penalty under ITEPA 2003, Sch. 3, Pt. 8.
ITEPA 2003, Sch. 4, para. 28J(8): s. 100 to 103 do not apply to a penalty under ITEPA 2003, Sch. 4, Pt. 7.
ITEPA 2003, Sch. 5, para. 57D(7): s. 100 to 103 do not apply to a penalty under ITEPA 2003, Sch. 5, Pt. 8.
SI 1986/1711, Schedule, Pt. I and II: modified application of s. 101 for purposes of stamp duty reserve tax.

102 Mitigation of penalties

102 The Board may in their discretion mitigate any penalty, or stay or compound any proceedings for a penalty, and may also, after judgment, further mitigate or entirely remit the penalty.

History – The words "a penalty" substituted for "recovery thereof" by FA 1989, s. 168(4), consequent to the substitution of s. 100 and the insertion of s. 100A–D.

Cross references – OTA 1975, Sch. 2, para. 1(1): s. 102 applies for the purposes of oil taxation.
SSCBA 1992, Sch. 1, para. 7: application of s. 102 to returns of National Insurance contributions.
ITEPA 2003, s. 421JE(7): s. 100 to 103 do not apply to a penalty under ITEPA 2003, s. 421JC or ITEPA 2003, s. 421JD.
ITEPA 2003, Sch. 2, para. 81J(8): s. 100 to 103 do not apply to a penalty under ITEPA 2003, Sch. 2, Pt. 10.
ITEPA 2003, Sch. 3, para. 40J(8): s. 100 to 103 do not apply to a penalty under ITEPA 2003, Sch. 3, Pt. 8.
ITEPA 2003, Sch. 4, para. 28J(8): s. 100 to 103 do not apply to a penalty under ITEPA 2003, Sch. 4, Pt. 7.
ITEPA 2003, Sch. 5, para. 57D(7): s. 100 to 103 do not apply to a penalty under ITEPA 2003, Sch. 5, Pt. 8.
SI 1986/1711, Schedule, Pt. I and II: s. 102 applies for purposes of stamp duty reserve tax.
SI 2001/1004, reg. 90K: application with respect to late payment of National Insurance Contributions due electronically.

HMRC Manuals – Enquiry Manual, EM5310: HMRC's policy on mitigation.

103 Time limits for penalties

103(1) Subject to subsection (2) below, where the amount of a penalty is to be ascertained by reference to tax payable by a person for any period, the penalty may be determined by an officer of the Board, or proceedings for the penalty may be commenced before the tribunal or a court–

(a) at any time within six years after the date on which the penalty was incurred, or

(b) at any later time within three years after the final determination of the amount of tax by reference to which the amount of the penalty is to be ascertained.

103(2) [Omitted by FA 2007, s. 97 and Sch. 24, para. 29(b) and repealed by FA 2007, s. 114 and Sch. 27, Pt. 5(5).]

103(3) [Omitted by FA 2012, s. 223 and Sch. 38, para. 48(a).]

103(4) A penalty to which subsection (1) does not apply may be so determined, or proceedings for such a penalty may be commenced before the tribunal or a court, at any time within six years after the date on which the penalty was incurred or began to be incurred.

History – *In s. 103(1)* the word "tribunal" substituted for the word "Commissioners" by SI 2009/56, art. 3(1) and Sch. 1, para. 48, operative from 1 April 2009, subject to transitional and saving provisions in SI 2009/56, Sch. 3.
S. 103(2) omitted by FA 2007, s. 97 and Sch. 24, para. 29(b) and repealed by FA 2007, s. 114 and Sch. 27, Pt. 5(5), with effect as follows by virtue of SI 2008/568, art. 2:

- 1 April 2008 in relation to relevant documents relating to tax periods commencing on or after that date;
- 1 April 2008 in relation to assessments falling within paragraph 2 for tax periods commencing on or after that date;

- 1 July 2008 in relation to relevant documents relating to claims under the Thirteenth Council Directive (arrangements for the refund of value added tax to persons not established in Community territory) for years commencing on or after that date;
- 1 January 2009 in relation to relevant documents relating to claims under the Eighth Council Directive (arrangements for the refund of value added tax to taxable persons not established in the territory of the country) for years commencing on or after that date;
- 1 April 2009 in relation to documents relating to all other claims for repayments of relevant tax made on or after 1 April 2009 which are not related to a tax period; and
- in any other case, 1 April 2009 in relation to documents given where a person's liability to pay relevant tax arises on or after that date.

However, no person will be liable to a penalty under Sch. 24 in respect of any tax period for which a return is required to be made before 1 April 2009.
In former s. 103(2), the words "the 31st January next following the chargeable period" substituted for the previous words "the end of the chargeable period" by FA 1994, s. 196 and Sch. 19, para. 32, in so far as it relates to income tax and capital gains tax, as respects the year 1996–97 and subsequent years of assessment and, in so far as it relates to corporation tax, as respects accounting periods ending on or after 1 July 1999, the appointed day for corporation tax self-assessment by virtue of FA 1994, s. 199(2), (3) and SI 1998/3173 (C. 78).
S. 103(3) omitted by FA 2012, s. 223 and Sch. 38, para. 48(a), with effect from 1 April 2013 (SI 2013/279, art. 2).
In s. 103(4), the words "subsection (1) does not apply" substituted for the words "neither subsection (1) nor subsection (3) above applies" by FA 2012, s. 223 and Sch. 38, para. 48(b), with effect from 1 April 2013 (SI 2013/279, art. 2).
In s. 103(4) the word "tribunal" substituted for the word "Commissioners" by SI 2009/56, art. 3(1) and Sch. 1, para. 48, operative from 1 April 2009, subject to transitional and saving provisions in SI 2009/56, Sch. 3.
S. 103 substituted by FA 1989, s. 169 with effect from 27 July 1989, but not affecting the application of the former s. 103(4) to proceedings under s. 100 before substitution by that Act.

Cross references – SSCBA 1992, Sch. 1, para. 7: application of s. 103 to returns of National Insurance contributions.
ITEPA 2003, s. 421JE(7): s. 100 to 103 do not apply to a penalty under ITEPA 2003, s. 421JC or ITEPA 2003, s. 421JD.
ITEPA 2003, Sch. 2, para. 81J(8): s. 100 to 103 do not apply to a penalty under ITEPA 2003, Sch. 2, Pt. 10.
ITEPA 2003, Sch. 3, para. 40J(8): s. 100 to 103 do not apply to a penalty under ITEPA 2003, Sch. 3, Pt. 8.
ITEPA 2003, Sch. 4, para. 28J(8): s. 100 to 103 do not apply to a penalty under ITEPA 2003, Sch. 4, Pt. 7.
ITEPA 2003, Sch. 5, para. 57D(7): s. 100 to 103 do not apply to a penalty under ITEPA 2003, Sch. 5, Pt. 8.
SI 1986/1711, Schedule, Pt. I and II: modified application of s. 103 for purposes of stamp duty reserve tax.
SI 2001/1004, reg. 90P: application with respect to non-delivery of National Insurance Contributions due electronically.

103ZA Disapplication of sections 100 to 103 in the case of certain penalties

103ZA Sections 100 to 103 do not apply to a penalty under –

(a) Schedule 24 to FA 2007 (penalties for errors),

(b) Schedule 36 to FA 2008 (information and inspection powers),

(c) Schedule 41 to that Act (penalties for failure to notify and certain other wrongdoing),

(d) Schedule 55 to FA 2009 (penalties for failure to make returns etc),

(e) Schedule 56 to that Act (penalties for failure to make payments on time),

(f) Schedule 23 to FA 2011 (data-gathering powers),

(g) Schedule 38 to FA 2012 (tax agents: dishonest conduct),

(ga) section 212A of the Finance Act 2013 (general anti-abuse rule),

(h) Part 4 of the Finance Act 2014 (follower notices and accelerated payments) or

(i) Part 5 of Schedule 18 to Finance Act 2016 (serial tax avoidance).

Prospective amendments – S. 103ZA(j) (and the word ", or" preceding it) inserted and the word "or" at the end of para. (h) omitted by FA 2016, s. 165 and Sch. 22, para. 20(1), with effect from a day to be appointed under s. 165(2).

History – In s. 103ZA(d), the word "or" at the end omitted by FA 2011, s. 86 and Sch. 23, para. 51(5)(a), with effect from 1 April 2012.
S. 103ZA(f) and the word "or" (at the end of s. 103ZA(e)) inserted by FA 2011, s. 86 and Sch. 23, para. 51(5)(b), with effect from 1 April 2012.
S. 103ZA(g) (and the ", or" before it) inserted (and the "or" in (e) omitted) by FA 2012, s. 223 and Sch. 38, para 49, with effect from 1 April 2013 (SI 2013/279, art. 2).
S. 103ZA(ga) (and the word "or" at the end) inserted and the word "or" at the end of para. (g) omitted by FA 2016, s. 158(10) with effect in relation to tax arrangements (FA 2013, Pt. 5) entered into on or after 15 September 2016 (Royal Assent).
S. 103ZA(h) inserted (and the "or" at the end of s. 103ZA(f) omitted, and the ", or" at the end of s. 103ZA(g) inserted), by FA 2014, s. 233 and Sch. 33, para. 2, with effect from 17 July 2014.
S. 103ZA(i) (and the word "or" preceding it) inserted and the word "or" at the end of para. (ga) omitted by FA 2016, s. 159 and Sch. 18, para. 59, with effect in relation to relevant defeats incurred after 15 September 2016 (Royal Assent) subject to Sch. 18, para. 64 and 65.
S. 103ZA inserted by FA 2009, s. 109 and Sch. 57, para. 13(3) with effect from 21 July 2009.

103A Interest on penalties

103A A penalty under any of the provisions of Part II, IV or VA or this Part of this Act, or Schedule 18 to the Finance Act 1998, shall carry interest at the rate applicable under section 178 of the Finance Act 1989 from the date on which it becomes due and payable until payment.

History – In s. 103A, the words ", or Schedule 18 to the Finance Act 1998," inserted by FA 1998, s. 117(3) and Sch. 19, para. 40, with effect in relation to accounting periods ending on or after 1 July 1999, the corporation tax self-assessment appointed day by virtue of FA 1994, s. 199(2), (3) and SI 1998/3173 (C. 78).
S. 103A inserted by FA 1994, s. 196 and Sch. 19, para. 33 and amended by FA 1995, s. 115(8), in so far as it relates to income tax and capital gains tax, as respects the year 1996–97 and subsequent years of assessment and, in so far as it relates to corporation tax, as respects accounting periods ending on or after 1 July 1999, the appointed day (see above).

Cross references – SI 1989/1297, reg. 3(1)(ab) (inserted by SI 1998/310) and SI 1998/311 (C. 7): applicable rate of interest under FA 1989, s. 178(1) as it applies to s. 103A for periods beginning on or after 9 March 1998.
SI 1999/2537: modified application of s. 103A in relation to stamp duty penalties.
SI 2001/1004, reg. 90P: application with respect to non-delivery of National Insurance Contributions due electronically.

104 Saving for criminal proceedings

104 The provisions of the Taxes Acts shall not, save so far as is otherwise provided, affect any criminal proceedings for any misdemeanour.

Cross references – OTA 1975, Sch. 2, para. 1(1): s. 104 applies for the purposes of oil taxation.
SSCBA 1992, Sch. 1, para. 7: application of s. 104 to returns of National Insurance contributions.
SI 1986/1711, Schedule, Pt. I and II: modified application of s. 104 for purposes of stamp duty reserve tax.
SI 2001/1004, reg. 82: application with respect to National Insurance returns.

Statements of practice – SP 2/88: civil tax penalties and criminal prosecution cases.

Notes – Felony–misdemeanour distinction abolished by Criminal Law Act 1967, s. 1(1).

105 Admissibility of evidence not affected by offer of settlement

History – Heading substituted for the words "Evidence in cases of fraud or wilful default" by FA 2003, s. 206(2).

105(1) Statements made or documents produced by or on behalf of a person shall not be inadmissible in any such proceedings as are mentioned in subsection (2) below by reason only that it has been drawn to his attention–

(a) that where serious tax fraud has been committed the Board may accept a money settlement and that the Board will accept such a settlement, and will not pursue a criminal prosecution, if he makes a full confession of all tax irregularities, or

(b) that the extent to which he is helpful and volunteers information is a factor that will be taken into account in determining the amount of any penalty,

105(2) The proceedings mentioned in subsection (1) above are–

(a) any criminal proceedings against the person in question for any form of fraudulent conduct in connection with or in relation to tax, and

(b) any proceedings against him for the recovery of any tax due from him, and

(c) any proceedings for a penalty or on appeal against the determination of a penalty.

History – In s. 105, the words "fraudulent conduct" substituted by FA 1989, s. 149(5) but not to affect the making of assessments for years of assessment before 1983–84 or for accounting periods ended before 1 April 1983.
In s. 105(1), para. (a) and (b) substituted by FA 2003, s. 206(1) in relation to statements made, or documents produced, on or after 10 July 2003. The previous paragraphs did not require a full confession to all tax irregularities for the acceptance of a money settlement in lieu of prosecution, it was merely a factor influencing the Board's decision.
S. 105(1)(a), the words "tax due from him, and" at the end of s. 105(2)(b) and s. 105(2)(c) substituted by FA 1989, s. 168(5).

Cross references – OTA 1975, Sch. 2, para. 1(1): s. 105 applies for the purposes of oil taxation.
SI 1986/1711, Schedule, Pt. I: s. 105 applies for purposes of stamp duty reserve tax.
SI 2001/1004, reg. 82: application with respect to National Insurance returns.

Statements of practice – SP 2/88: civil tax penalties and criminal prosecution cases.

106 Refusal to allow a deduction of income tax, and avoidance of agreements for payment without deduction

106(1) A person who refuses to allow a deduction of income tax authorised by the Taxes Acts to be made out of any payment shall incur a penalty of £50.

106(2) Every agreement for payment of interest, rent or other annual payment in full without allowing any such deduction shall be void.

EVASION

106A Offence of fraudulent evasion of income tax

106A(1) A person commits an offence if that person is knowingly concerned in the fraudulent evasion of income tax by that or any other person.

106A(2) A person guilty of an offence under this section is liable–

(a) on summary conviction, to imprisonment for a term not exceeding 12 months or a fine not exceeding the statutory maximum, or both, or

(b) on conviction on indictment, to imprisonment for a term not exceeding 7 years or a fine, or both.

106A(3) In the application of subsection (2)(a)–

(a) in England and Wales in relation to offences committed before the commencement of section 282(3) of the Criminal Justice Act 2003, and

(b) in Northern Ireland,

for "*12 months*" substitute "*6 months*".

106A(4) This section does not apply to things done or omitted before 1st January 2001.

History – S. 106A inserted by TIOPA 2010, s. 371 and Sch. 7, para. 95, with effect for corporation tax purposes for accounting periods ending on or after 1 April 2010, for income tax and capital gains tax purposes for the tax year 2010–11 and subsequent tax years, and for petroleum revenue tax purposes for chargeable periods beginning on or after 1 July 2010.

OFFSHORE INCOME, ASSETS AND ACTIVITIES

Prospective amendments – Heading inserted by FA 2016, s. 166(1), with effect form a day to be appointed under s. 166(2), subject to the transitional provisions in FA 2016, s. 166(4).

106B Offence of failing to give notice of being chargeable to tax

106B [Prospectively inserted by FA 2016, s. 166(1).]

Prospective amendments – S. 106B inserted by FA 2016, s. 166(1), with effect form a day to be appointed under s. 166(2), subject to the transitional provisions in FA 2016, s. 166(4).

106C Offence of failing to deliver return

106C [Prospectively inserted by FA 2016, s. 166(1).]

Prospective amendments – S. 106C inserted by FA 2016, s. 166(1), with effect form a day to be appointed under s. 166(2), subject to the transitional provisions in FA 2016, s. 166(4).

106D Offence of making inaccurate return

106D [Prospectively inserted by FA 2016, s. 166(1).]

Prospective amendments – S. 106D inserted by FA 2016, s. 166(1), with effect form a day to be appointed under s. 166(2), subject to the transitional provisions in FA 2016, s. 166(4).

106E Exclusions from offences under sections 106B to 106D

106E [Prospectively inserted by FA 2016, s. 166(1).]

Prospective amendments – S. 106E inserted by FA 2016, s. 166(1), with effect form a day to be appointed under s. 166(2), subject to the transitional provisions in FA 2016, s. 166(4).

106F Offences under sections 106B to 106D: supplementary provision

106F [Prospectively inserted by FA 2016, s. 166(1).]

Prospective amendments – S. 106F inserted by FA 2016, s. 166(1), with effect form a day to be appointed under s. 166(2), subject to the transitional provisions in FA 2016, s. 166(4).

106G Penalties for offences under sections 106B to 106D

106G [Prospectively inserted by FA 2016, s. 166(1).]

Prospective amendments – S. 106G inserted by FA 2016, s. 166(1), with effect form a day to be appointed under s. 166(2), subject to the transitional provisions in FA 2016, s. 166(4).

106H Regulations under sections 106E and 106F

106H [Prospectively inserted by FA 2016, s. 166(1).]

Prospective amendments – S. 106H inserted by FA 2016, s. 166(1), with effect form a day to be appointed under s. 166(2), subject to the transitional provisions in FA 2016, s. 166(4).

SCOTLAND

107 Criminal liability for false statements made to obtain allowances

107(1) This section applies only in Scotland.

107(2) If any person, for the purpose of obtaining any allowance, reduction, rebate or repayment in respect of tax, either for himself or for any other person, or, in any return made with reference to tax, knowingly makes any false statement or false representation, he shall be liable, on summary conviction, to imprisonment for a term not exceeding six months.

107(3) Notwithstanding anything in the Summary Jurisdiction (Scotland) Act 1954, proceedings for an offence under this section may be commenced at any time within three years from the time when the offence was committed.

107(4) The expression **"return"** in this section shall be construed without regard to the definition in section 118(1) of this Act.

Cross references – OTA 1975, Sch. 2, para. 1(1): s. 107(1)–(3) apply for the purposes of oil taxation.

Statements of practice – SP 2/88: civil tax penalties and criminal prosecution cases.

PART XI – MISCELLANEOUS AND SUPPLEMENTAL

SETTLEMENTS

107A Relevant trustees

107A(1) Subject to the following provisions of this section, anything which for the purposes of this Act is done at any time by or in relation to any one or more of the relevant trustees of a settlement shall be treated for those purposes as done at that time by or in relation to the other or others of those trustees.

107A(2) Subject to subsection (3) below, where the relevant trustees of a settlement are liable–

(a) to a penalty under section 12B or 95 of this Act or paragraph 2A of Schedule 1A to this Act or Schedule 24 to the Finance Act 2007 or Schedule 41 to the Finance Act 2008 or Schedule 55 to the Finance Act 2009, or to interest under section 101 of the Finance Act 2009 on such a penalty;

(b) to make a payment in accordance with an assessment under section 30 of this Act, or to make a payment under section 59A, 59AA or 59B of this Act;

(c) to a penalty under Schedule 56 to the Finance Act 2009, or to interest under section 101 of that Act on such a penalty; or

(d) to interest under section 86 of this Act or section 101 of the Finance Act 2009,

the penalty, interest or payment may be recovered (but only once) from any one or more of those trustees.

107A(3) No amount may be recovered by virtue of subsection (2)(a) or (c) above from a person who did not become a relevant trustee until after the relevant time, that is to say–

(a) in relation to–

(i) a penalty under paragraph 4 of Schedule 55 to the Finance Act 2009 in respect of a return or other document falling within item 1, 2 or 3 of the Table in paragraph 1 of that Schedule, or

(ii) interest under section 101 of that Act on a penalty within sub-paragraph (i),

the beginning of the penalty date as defined in paragraph 1(4) of that Schedule;

(b) in relation to a penalty under any provision of this Act mentioned in subsection (2)(a) above, or to interest under section 101 of the Finance Act 2009 on such a penalty, the time when the relevant act or omission occurred; and

(c) in relation to–

(i) a penalty under Schedule 56 to the Finance Act 2009 in respect of an amount falling within item 1, 12, 18 or 19 of the Table in paragraph 1 of that Schedule,

(ii) a penalty under that Schedule in respect of an amount falling within item 17, 23 or 24 of that Table so far as the tax falls within item 1, or

(iii) interest under section 101 of that Act on a penalty within sub-paragraph (i) or (ii),

the beginning of the penalty date as defined in paragraph 1(4) of that Schedule;

and in paragraph (b) above **"the relevant act or omission"** means the act or omission which caused the penalty to become payable.

107A(4) [Omitted by SI 2011/702, art. 10(4).]

Prospective amendments – In s. 107A(2) the words "or Schedule 22 to the Finance Act 2016" inserted after the words "Schedule 55 to the Finance Act 2009" by FA 2016, s. 165 and Sch. 22, para. 20(2)(a), with effect from a day to be appointed under s. 165(2).
In s. 107A(3)(aa) inserted and in the words after para. (c) the words "(aa) and" inserted after the word "paragraph" by FA 2016, s. 165 and Sch. 22, para. 20(2)(b) and (c), with effect from a day to be appointed under s. 165(2).

History – In s. 107A(2)(a), the words "section 101 of the Finance Act 2009" substituted for the words "section 103A of this Act" by SI 2011/702, art. 8(2)(a), with effect from 31 October 2011.
In s. 107A(2)(a), ", 93", which appeared after "section 12B", omitted by SI 2011/702, art. 10(2)(a)(i), with effect from 1 April 2011, but subject to SI 2011/702, art. 20, which provides that the omission does not have effect in relation to a return or other document which is required to be made or delivered to HMRC, or an amount of tax which is payable, in relation to the tax year 2009–10 or any previous tax year.
In s. 107A(2)(a), the words "or Schedule 55 to the Finance Act 2009" inserted by SI 2011/702, art. 10(2)(a)(ii), with effect from 1 April 2011, but subject to SI 2011/702, art. 20, which provides that the insertion does not have effect in relation to a return or other document which is required to be made or delivered to HMRC, or an amount of tax which is payable, in relation to the tax year 2009–10 or any previous tax year.
In s. 107A(2)(a), "7," omitted and the words "or Schedule 41 to the Finance Act 2008" inserted by SI 2010/530, art. 2 and Schedule, para. 3, with effect from 1 April 2010.
In s. 107A(2) ", 95" omitted (though this had already been effectively omitted by FA 2008 – see below) and the words "or Schedule 24 to the Finance Act 2007" inserted by SI 2009/571, art. 8 and Sch. 1, para. 13, with effect from 1 April 2009.
In s. 107A(2)(a) the words "or 95" substituted for the words ", 95 or 97AA" by FA 2008, s. 113 and Sch. 36, para. 75(2), with effect from 1 April 2009 (SI 2009/404, art. 2, subject to savings at SI 2009/404, art. 3).
In s. 107A(2)(b), ", 59AA" inserted by FA 2015, s. 37 and Sch. 7, para. 53, with effect in relation to disposals made on or after 6 April 2015.
In s. 107A(2)(c), the words ", or to interest under section 101 of that Act on such a penalty;" inserted by SI 2011/702, art. 8(2)(b), with effect from 31 October 2011.

S. 107A(2)(c) substituted by SI 2011/702, art. 10(2)(b), with effect from 1 April 2011, but subject to SI 2011/702, art. 20, which provides that the substitution does not have effect in relation to a return or other document which is required to be made or delivered to HMRC, or an amount of tax which is payable, in relation to the tax year 2009–10 or any previous tax year.
In s. 107A(2)(d), the words "or section 101 of the Finance Act 2009" inserted by SI 2011/702, art. 8(2)(c), with effect from 31 October 2011.
In s. 107A(2), in the closing words, the words "interest or payment" substituted for the words "interest, payment or surcharge" by SI 2011/702, art. 10(2)(c), with effect from 1 April 2011, but subject to SI 2011/702, art. 20, which provides that the substitutiondoes not have effect in relation to a return or other document which is required to be made or delivered to HMRC, or an amount of tax which is payable, in relation to the tax year 2009–10 or any previous tax year.
S. 107A(3)(a) substituted by SI 2011/701, art. 8(3)(a), with effect from 31 October 2011.
S. 107A(3)(a) substituted by SI 2011/702, art. 10(3)(a), with effect from 1 April 2011, but subject to SI 2011/702, art. 20, which provides that the substitution does not have effect in relation to a return or other document which is required to be made or delivered to HMRC, or an amount of tax which is payable, in relation to the tax year 2009–10 or any previous tax year.
In s. 107(3)(a) the words "or 97AA(1)(b)" omitted by FA 2008, s. 113 and Sch. 36, para. 75(3), with effect from 1 April 2009 (SI 2009/404, art. 2, subject to savings at SI 2009/404, art. 3).
In s. 107A(3)(b), the words "section 101 of the Finance Act 2009" substituted for the words "section 103A of this Act" by SI 2011/702, art. 8(3)(b), with effect from 31 October 2011.
In s. 107A(3)(b), the word "other", which appeared before the words "provision of this Act", omitted by SI 2011/702, art. 10(3)(b), with effect from 1 April 2011, but subject to SI 2011/702, art. 20, which provides that the omission does not have effect in relation to a return or other document which is required to be made or delivered to HMRC, or an amount of tax which is payable, in relation to the tax year 2009–10 or any previous tax year.
S. 107A(3)(c) substituted by SI 2011/702, art. 10(3)(c), with effect from 1 April 2011, but subject to SI 2011/702, art. 20, which provides that the substitution does not have effect in relation to a return or other document which is required to be made or delivered to HMRC, or an amount of tax which is payable, in relation to the tax year 2009–10 or any previous tax year.
S. 107A(3)(c)(iii) inserted (and the word "or" at the end of s. 107A(3)(c)(i) omitted, and the word "or" at the end of s. 107A(3)(c)(ii) inserted) by SI 2011/701, art. 8(3)(c), with effect from 31 October 2011.
S. 107A(4) omitted by SI 2011/702, art. 10(4), with effect from 1 April 2011, but subject to SI 2011/702, art. 20, which provides that the omission does not have effect in relation to a return or other document which is required to be made or delivered to HMRC, or an amount of tax which is payable, in relation to the tax year 2009–10 or any previous tax year.
S. 107A inserted by FA 1995, s. 103(5) as respects the year 1996–97 and subsequent years of assessment.
Cross references – SI 1999/2537: modified application of provisions of s. 107A in relation to stamp duty penalties.

COMPANIES

108 Responsibility of company officers

108(1) Everything to be done by a company under the Taxes Acts shall be done by the company acting through the proper officer of the company or, except where a liquidator has been appointed for the company, through such other person as may for the time being have the express, implied or apparent authority of the company to act on its behalf for the purpose, and service on a company of any document under or in pursuance of the Taxes Acts may be effected by serving it on the proper officer.

This subsection is without prejudice to Part VIII of this Act (charges on non-residents) as it applies to corporation tax.

108(2) Corporation tax or other tax chargeable under the Corporation Tax Acts on a company which is not a body corporate, or which is a body corporate not incorporated under any enactment forming part of the law of the United Kingdom, or by Charter, may, at any time after the tax becomes due, and without prejudice to any other method of recovery, be recovered from the proper officer of the company, and that officer may retain out of any money coming into his hands on behalf of the company sufficient sums to pay that tax, and, so far as he is not so reimbursed, shall be entitled to be indemnified by the company in respect of the liability so imposed on him.

108(3) For the purposes of this section–

(a) the proper officer of a company which is a body corporate shall be the secretary or person acting as secretary of the company, except that if a liquidator or administrator has been appointed for the company the liquidator or, as the case may be, administrator shall be the proper officer,

(b) the proper officer of a company which is not a body corporate or for which there is no proper officer within paragraph (a) above, shall be the treasurer or the person acting as treasurer, of the company.

108(4) For the purposes of subsection (3)(a), where two or more persons are appointed to act jointly or concurrently as the administrator of a company, the proper officer is–

(a) such one of them as is specified in a notice given to the Board by those persons for the purposes of this section, or

(b) where the Board is not so notified, such one or more of those persons as the Board may designate as the proper officer for those purposes.

History – In s. 108(1), words "or, except where … for the purpose" inserted by FA 1993, s. 120 and Sch. 14, para. 7.
In s. 108(2), the word "any" substituted for the words "the Companies Act 1985 or any other" by SI 2009/1890, art. 3(3)(c), with effect from 1 October 2009.
S. 108(2) amended by Companies Consolidation (Consequential Provisions) Act 1985, substituting a reference to the Companies Act 1985 for the previous reference to the Companies Act 1948.
In s. 108(3)(a), references to an administrator inserted by FA 2003, s. 196 and Sch. 41, para. 2(2) in relation to companies which enter administration on or after the commencement of Enterprise Act 2002, s. 248.

S. 108(4) inserted by FA 2003, s. 196 and Sch. 41, para. 2(3) in relation to companies which enter administration on or after the commencement of Enterprise Act 2002, s. 248.

Cross references – FA 2011, Sch. 23, para. 43: s. 108 applies for the purposes of that schedule as for the purposes of the Taxes Acts.
FA 2008, Sch. 36, para. 56: application of s. 108 for purposes of that schedule as for purposes of the Taxes Act.
OTA 1975, Sch. 2, para. 1(1): s. 108 applies for the purposes of oil taxation, with modifications to s. 108(2).
SI 1986/1711, Schedule, Pt. I and II: modified application of s. 108 for purposes of stamp duty reserve tax.
SI 1999/2537: modified application of provisions of s. 108 in relation to stamp duty penalties.
SI 2001/1817 reg. 4(3): application of s. 108(1) to notice under Social Security Contributions (Share Options) Act 2001, s. 1.
SI 2009/317, art. 3(2)(a), (3)(a): modification of meaning of "liquidator" and "administrator" in relation to liquidation or administration of banks.
FA 2012, Sch. 38, para.36: S. 108 to apply for the purposes of provisions relating to dishonest conduct by tax agents.

HMRC Manuals – Company Taxation, CT93170: HMRC will accept returns or amended returns showing an original signature if there is no reason to doubt the authority of the person signing. HMRC will also accept returns signed in the name of a firm of accountants.

Other material – ICAEW Technical Release TR 340: HMRC insist on the strict statutory position under s. 108 in respect of group income elections.

109 Corporation tax on close company in connection with loans or benefits to participators etc.

History – In the heading to s. 109 the words "or benefits" inserted by FA 2013, s. 79 and Sch. 30, para. 11(7), with effect from 20 March 2013.

109(1) The provisions of sections 455 to 459 and 464A and 464B of CTA 2010 (charge of tax in connection with loans or benefits to participators etc.) directing that tax be assessed and recoverable as if it were an amount of corporation tax shall be taken as applying, subject to the provisions of the Taxes Act, and to any necessary modifications, all enactments applying generally to corporation tax, including those relating to the assessing, collecting and receiving of corporation tax, those conferring or regulating a right of appeal and those concerning administration, penalties, interest on unpaid tax and priority of tax in cases of insolvency under the law of any part of the United Kingdom.

109(2) [Omitted by F(No. 2)A 1987, s. 91(1).]

109(3) For the purposes of section 87A of this Act as applied by subsection (1) above–

(a) the date when tax under section 455 of CTA 2010 became due and payable is that determined in accordance with subsection (3) of that section, and

(b) the date when tax under section 464A of CTA 2010 became due and payable is that determined in accordance with subsection (4) of that section.

109(3A) If

(a) there is such a repayment of the whole or any part of a loan or advance as is referred to in subsection (2) of section 458 of CTA 2010, or

(b) there is such a release or writing off of the whole or any part of the debt in respect of a loan or advance as is referred to in that subsection,

interest under section 87A of this Act on so much of the tax under section 455 of CTA 2010 as is referable to the amount repaid, released or written off shall not be payable in respect of any period after the date on which the repayment was made or the release or writing off occurred.

109(3B) If there is a payment which for the purposes of section 464B of CTA 2010 is a return payment in respect of a benefit conferred, interest under section 87A of this Act on so much of the tax under section 464A of CTA 2010 as is referable to the return payment is not payable in respect of any period after the date on which the return payment was made.

109(4) Section 91 of this Act shall not apply in consequence of any discharge or repayment of tax under section 458 or 464B of CTA 2010.

109(5) For the purposes of the said section 91, a relief from tax under sections 455 to 459 or 464A and 464B of CTA 2010 shall not be treated as affecting tax charged by any assessment unless the assessment is to tax under that section.

History – In s. 109(1), the words "and 464A and 464B" inserted and the words "or benefits" substituted for the words "by close companies" by FA 2013, s. 79 and Sch. 30, para. 11(2), with effect from 20 March 2013.
In s. 109(1), the words "sections 455 to 459 of CTA 2010" substituted for the words "sections 419 and 420 of the principal Act" by CTA 2010, s. 1177 and Sch. 1, para. 158(2), with effect for corporation tax purposes for accounting periods ending on or after 1 April 2010, and for income tax and capital gains tax purposes for the tax year 2010–11 and subsequent tax years.
S. 109(2) omitted and s. 109(3) amended by F(No. 2)A 1987, s. 91, with respect to loans or advances made (or treated as made) in any accounting period ending after 30 September 1993, (under Pay and File) by virtue of SI 1992/3066, art. 2.
S. 109(2) amended by F(No. 2)A 1975, s. 46(5) with effect from 1975–76.
S. 109(3) substituted by FA 2013, s. 79 and Sch. 30, para. 11(3), with effect from 20 March 2013.
In former s. 109(3), the words "section 455 of CTA 2010" substituted for the words "the said section 419" by CTA 2010, s. 1177 and Sch. 1, para. 158(3), with effect for corporation tax purposes for accounting periods ending on or after 1 April 2010, and for income tax and capital gains tax purposes for the tax year 2010–11 and subsequent tax years.
Former s. 109(3) amended by (F(No. 2)A 1975, s. 46(5) with effect from 1975–76.
In s. 109(3A), the words "subsection (2) of section 458 of CTA 2010" substituted for the words "subsection (4) of section 419 of the principal Act" by CTA 2010, s. 1177 and Sch. 1, para. 158(4)(a), with effect for corporation tax purposes for accounting periods ending on or after 1 April 2010, and for income tax and capital gains tax purposes for the tax year 2010–11 and subsequent tax years.

In s. 109(3A), the words "section 455 of CTA 2010" substituted for the words "the said section 419" by CTA 2010, s. 1177 and Sch. 1, para. 158(4)(b), with effect for corporation tax purposes for accounting periods ending on or after 1 April 2010, and for income tax and capital gains tax purposes for the tax year 2010–11 and subsequent tax years.
S. 109(3A) amended by FA 1998, s. 31 and Sch. 3, para. 6, by creating para. (a), inserting para. (b), and inserting the words ", released or written off" and "or the release or writing off occurred", with effect in relation to the release or writing off of the whole or part of a debt on or after 6 April 1999.
S. 109(3A) inserted, by F(No. 2)A 1987, s. 91, with respect to loans or advances made (or treated as made) in any accounting period ending after 30 September 1993, (under Pay and File) by virtue of SI 1992/3066, art. 2.
S. 109(3B) inserted by FA 2013, s. 79 and Sch. 30, para. 11(4), with effect from 20 March 2013.
In s. 109(4), the words "or 464B" inserted by FA 2013, s. 79 and Sch. 30, para. 11(5), with effect from 20 March 2013.
In s. 109(4), the words "section 458 of CTA 2010" substituted for the words "section 419(4) of the principal Act" by CTA 2010, s. 1177 and Sch. 1, para. 158(5), with effect for corporation tax purposes for accounting periods ending on or after 1 April 2010, and for income tax and capital gains tax purposes for the tax year 2010–11 and subsequent tax years.
In s. 109(5), the words "or 464A and 464B" inserted by FA 2013, s. 79 and Sch. 30, para. 11(6), with effect from 20 March 2013.
In s. 109(5), the words "sections 455 to 459 of CTA 2010" substituted for the words "the said sections 419 and 420" by CTA 2010, s. 1177 and Sch. 1, para. 158(6), with effect for corporation tax purposes for accounting periods ending on or after 1 April 2010, and for income tax and capital gains tax purposes for the tax year 2010–11 and subsequent tax years.
References to the principal Act substituted by ICTA 1988, Sch. 29, para. 32.
S. 109 substituted by FA 1972, Sch. 24, para. 13, with effect from 6 April 1973.

Cross references – SI 2009/317, art. 3(4)(a): modification of meaning of "insolvency legislation" and "the law of insolvency" in relation to liquidation or administration of banks. It is assumed that the modification was intended to cover the reference to "insolvency under the law of any part of the United Kingdom" in s. 109(1) but it is not clear whether or not that has been achieved.

Notes – ICTA 1988 failed to amend the words "that section" in s. 109(5) so as to be grammatically consistent with the substitution of "sections 419 and 420" for the previous "section 286".

109A Residence of companies

109A Chapter 3 of Part 2 of CTA 2009 (rules for determining residence of companies) applies for the purposes of this Act as it applies for the purposes of the Corporation Tax Acts.

History – S. 109A inserted by CTA 2009, s. 1322 and Sch. 1, para. 308, with effect for corporation tax purposes for accounting periods ending on or after 1 April 2009, and for income tax and capital gains tax purposes for the tax year 2009–10 and subsequent tax years.

COMPANIES CEASING TO BE UK RESIDENT

109B Provisions for securing payment by company of outstanding tax

109B(1) Each of conditions A to D must be met before a company ceases to be resident in the United Kingdom, subject to subsection (5A).

109B(2) Condition A is that the company gives to the Commissioners for Her Majesty's Revenue and Customs notice of its intention to cease to be resident in the United Kingdom.

109B(3) Condition B is that the notice specifies the time ("the migration time") when the company intends to cease to be resident in the United Kingdom.

109B(4) Condition C is that the company gives to the Commissioners–

(a) a statement of the amount which, in its opinion, is the amount of the tax which is or will be payable by it in respect of periods beginning before the migration time, and

(b) particulars of the arrangements which it proposes to make for securing the payment of that tax (which may include a proposal to enter into an exit charge payment plan in accordance with Schedule 3ZB).

109B(5) Condition D is that–

(a) arrangements are made by the company for securing the payment of the tax which is or will be payable by it in respect of periods beginning before the migration time, and

(b) those arrangements, as made by the company, are approved for the purposes of this subsection by the Commissioners.

109B(5A) Condition D does not apply to the extent that payment of the tax is to be secured by the company entering into an exit charge payment plan in accordance with Schedule 3ZB.

109B(6) If any question arises as to the amount which, for the purposes of subsection (5), should be regarded as the amount of tax which is or will be payable by the company in respect of periods beginning before the migration time, that question is to be referred to the tribunal.

109B(7) A decision of the tribunal under subsection (6) is final, despite sections 11 and 13 of the TCEA 2007 (appeals from tribunal decisions).

109B(8) If any information furnished by the company for the purpose of securing the Commissioners' approval under subsection (5) does not fully and accurately disclose all facts and considerations material for the Commissioners' decision under that subsection, any resulting approval is void.

History – In s. 109B(1), the words ", subject to subsection (5A)" inserted by FA 2013, s. 229 and Sch. 49, para. 4(2), with effect from 11 December 2012 in relation to an accounting period if the relevant day, in relation to that period, falls on or after 11 December 2012 (subject to provisions of FA 2013, Sch. 49, para. 8(2) and (3)).

In s. 109B(4)(b), the words "(which may include a proposal to enter into an exit charge payment plan in accordance with Schedule 3ZB)" inserted by FA 2013, s. 229 and Sch. 49, para. 4(3), with effect from 11 December 2012 in relation to an accounting period if the relevant day, in relation to that period, falls on or after 11 December 2012 (subject to provisions of FA 2013, Sch. 49, para. 8(2) and (3)).
S. 109B(5A) inserted by FA 2013, s. 229 and Sch. 49, para. 4(4), with effect from 11 December 2012 in relation to an accounting period if the relevant day, in relation to that period, falls on or after 11 December 2012 (subject to provisions of FA 2013, Sch. 49, para. 8(2) and (3)).
S. 109B inserted by TIOPA 2010, s. 371 and Sch. 7, para. 54, with effect for corporation tax purposes for accounting periods ending on or after 1 April 2010, for income tax and capital gains tax purposes for the tax year 2010–11 and subsequent tax years, and for petroleum revenue tax purposes for chargeable periods beginning on or after 1 July 2010.

109C Penalty for company's failure to comply with section 109B

109C If a company ceases to be resident in the United Kingdom at a time before each of conditions A to D in section 109B is met, the company is liable to a penalty not exceeding the amount of tax–

(a) which is or will be payable by it in respect of periods beginning before that time, and

(b) which has not been paid at that time.

History – S. 109C inserted by TIOPA 2010, s. 371 and Sch. 7, para. 54, with effect for corporation tax purposes for accounting periods ending on or after 1 April 2010, for income tax and capital gains tax purposes for the tax year 2010–11 and subsequent tax years, and for petroleum revenue tax purposes for chargeable periods beginning on or after 1 July 2010.

109D Penalty for other persons if company fails to comply with section 109B

109D(1) Subsection (5) applies if–

(a) condition E is met, and

(b) either of conditions F and G is met.

109D(2) Condition E is that in relation to a company ("the migrating company") any person ("P") does or is party to the doing of any act which to P's knowledge amounts to or results in, or forms part of a series of acts which together amount to or result in, or will amount to or result in, the migrating company ceasing to be resident in the United Kingdom at a time before each of conditions A to D in section 109B is met.

109D(3) Condition F is that P is–

(a) a director of the migrating company,

(b) a company which has control of the migrating company, or

(c) a director of a company which has control of the migrating company.

109D(4) Condition G is that the act mentioned in subsection (2) is a direction or instruction given–

(a) to persons within subsection (3), but

(b) otherwise than by way of advice given by a person acting in a professional capacity.

109D(5) If this subsection applies, P is liable to a penalty not exceeding the amount of tax–

(a) which is or will be payable by the migrating company in respect of periods beginning before the time mentioned in subsection (2), and

(b) which has not been paid at that time.

109D(6) Subsections (7) and (8) apply for the purposes of any proceedings against a person within subsection (3) for the recovery of a penalty under subsection (5).

109D(7) It is to be presumed that the person was party to every act of the migrating company unless the person proves that it was done without the person's consent or connivance.

109D(8) It is to be presumed, unless the contrary is proved, that any early-migration act was to the person's knowledge an early-migration act.

109D(9) In subsection (8) **"early-migration act"** means an act which in fact amounted to or resulted in, or formed part of a series of acts which together amounted to or resulted in, or would amount to or result in, the migrating company ceasing to be resident in the United Kingdom at a time before each of conditions A to D in section 109B is met.

History – S. 109D inserted by TIOPA 2010, s. 371 and Sch. 7, para. 54, with effect for corporation tax purposes for accounting periods ending on or after 1 April 2010, for income tax and capital gains tax purposes for the tax year 2010–11 and subsequent tax years, and for petroleum revenue tax purposes for chargeable periods beginning on or after 1 July 2010.

109E Liability of other persons for unpaid tax

109E(1) This section applies if–

(a) a company ("the migrating company") ceases to be resident in the United Kingdom at any time, and

(b) any tax which is payable by the company in respect of periods beginning before that time is not paid within 6 months from the time when it becomes payable.

109E(1A) The reference in subsection (1)(b) to the time when tax becomes payable is a reference to–

(a) in a case where an exit charge payment plan has been entered into in accordance with Schedule 3ZB in respect of the tax, the time when the tax becomes payable under the plan, and

(b) in any other case, the time when the tax becomes payable in accordance with section 59D or 59E.

109E(2) The Commissioners for Her Majesty's Revenue and Customs may, at any time before the end of the period of 3 years beginning with the relevant time, serve on any person within subsection (3) a notice–

(a) stating particulars of the tax payable, the amount remaining unpaid and the date when it became payable, and

(b) requiring that person to pay that amount within 30 days of the service of the notice.

109E(2A) In subsection (2) the **"relevant time"** means–

(a) in a case where an exit charge payment plan has been entered into in accordance with Schedule 3ZB in respect of the tax, the later of–

(i) the first day after the period of 12 months beginning immediately after the migration accounting period (as defined in Part 1 or 2 of Schedule 3ZB, as the case may be), and

(ii) the date on which the tax is payable under the plan, and

(b) in any other case, the time when the amount of the tax is finally determined.

109E(3) The persons within this subsection are–

(a) any company which is, or within the pre-migration year was, a member of the same group as the migrating company,

(b) any person who is, or within the pre-migration year was, a controlling director of the migrating company, and

(c) any person who is, or within the pre-migration year was, a controlling director of a company which has, or within the pre-migration year had, control over the migrating company.

109E(4) Any amount which a person is required to pay by a notice under this section may be recovered from the person as if it were tax due and duly demanded from the person.

109E(5) If a person ("P") pays any amount which a notice under this section requires P to pay, P may recover the amount from the migrating company.

109E(6) A payment in pursuance of a notice under this section is not allowed as a deduction in calculating any income, profits or losses for any tax purposes.

109E(7) In this section–

"controlling director", in relation to a company, means a director of the company who has control of the company,

"group" has the meaning which would be given by section 170 of the 1992 Act if in that section for references to 75 per cent subsidiaries there were substituted references to 51 per cent subsidiaries, and

"pre-migration year" means the period of 12 months ending with the time when the migrating company ceases to be resident in the United Kingdom.

History – S. 109E(1A) inserted by FA 2013, s. 229 and Sch. 49, para. 5(2), with effect from 11 December 2012 in relation to an accounting period if the relevant day, in relation to that period, falls on or after 11 December 2012 (subject to provisions of FA 2013, Sch. 49, para. 8(2) and (3)).

In s. 109(2) the words "the relevant time" substituted for the words "the time when the amount of the tax is finally determined" by FA 2013, s. 229 and Sch. 49, para. 5(3), with effect from 11 December 2012 in relation to an accounting period if the relevant day, in relation to that period, falls on or after 11 December 2012 (subject to provisions of FA 2013, Sch. 49, para. 8(2) and (3)).

S. 109E(2A) inserted by FA 2013, s. 229 and Sch. 49, para. 5(4), with effect from 11 December 2012 in relation to an accounting period if the relevant day, in relation to that period, falls on or after 11 December 2012 (subject to provisions of FA 2013, Sch. 49, para. 8(2) and (3)).

S. 109E inserted by TIOPA 2010, s. 371 and Sch. 7, para. 54, with effect for corporation tax purposes for accounting periods ending on or after 1 April 2010, for income tax and capital gains tax purposes for the tax year 2010–11 and subsequent tax years, and for petroleum revenue tax purposes for chargeable periods beginning on or after 1 July 2010.

109F Interpretation of sections 109B to 109E

109F(1) In sections 109B to 109E, any reference to the tax payable by a company includes a reference to–

(a) any amount which the company is liable to pay under section 77C (territorial extension of charge to tax),

(b) any amount of tax which the company is liable to pay under regulations made under section 684 of ITEPA 2003 (PAYE),

(c) any amount which the company is liable to pay under sections 61 and 62(1)(a) of the Finance Act 2004 (sub-contractors in the construction industry),

(d) any income tax which the company is liable to pay in respect of payments within section 946 of ITA 2007 (collection of tax: deposit-takers, building societies and certain companies), and

(e) any amount representing income tax which the company is liable to pay under section 966 of ITA 2007 (entertainers and sportsmen).

109F(2) In sections 109B to 109E read in accordance with subsection (1), any reference to the tax payable by a company in respect of periods beginning before any particular time includes a reference to any interest–

(a) on the tax so payable, or

(b) on tax paid by the company in respect of such periods,

which the company is liable to pay in respect of periods beginning before or after that time.

109F(3) In sections 109B to 109E **"director"**, in relation to a company, is to be read in accordance with the following provisions–

(a) section 67(1) and (2) of ITEPA 2003, and

(b) section 452 of CTA 2010.

109F(4) In sections 109B to 109E, any reference to a person having control of a company is to be read in accordance with sections 450 and 451 of CTA 2010.

History – S. 109F inserted by TIOPA 2010, s. 371 and Sch. 7, para. 54, with effect for corporation tax purposes for accounting periods ending on or after 1 April 2010, for income tax and capital gains tax purposes for the tax year 2010–11 and subsequent tax years, and for petroleum revenue tax purposes for chargeable periods beginning on or after 1 July 2010.

VALUATION

110 Valuation of land: power of entry

110 [Omitted by SI 2009/3054, art. 3 and Schedule, para. 1.]

History – S. 110 omitted by SI 2009/3054, art. 3 and Schedule, para. 1, with effect from 1 April 2010.

111 Valuation of assets: power to inspect

111 [Omitted by SI 2009/3054, art. 3 and Schedule, para. 1.]

History – S. 111 omitted by SI 2009/3054, art. 3 and Schedule, para. 1, with effect from 1 April 2010.

DOCUMENTS

112 Loss, destruction or damage to assessments, returns, etc.

112(1) Where any assessment to tax, or any duplicate of assessment to tax, or any return or other document relating to tax, has been lost or destroyed, or been so defaced or damaged as to be illegible or otherwise useless, HMRC may, notwithstanding anything in any enactment to the contrary, do all such acts and things as they might have done, and all acts and things done under or in pursuance of this section shall be as valid and effectual for all purposes as they would have been, if the assessment or duplicate of assessment had not been made, or the return or other document had not been made or furnished or required to be made or furnished.

Provided that, where any person who is charged with tax in consequence or by virtue of any act or thing done under or in pursuance of this section proves to the satisfaction of the tribunal that he has already paid any tax for the same chargeable period in respect of the subject matter and on the account in respect of and on which he is so charged, relief shall be given to the extent to which the liability of that person has been discharged by the payment so made either by abatement from the charge or by repayment, as the case may require.

112(1A) [Repealed by FA 1985, Sch. 27, Pt. X, with effect from 19 March 1985.]

112(2) [Omitted by SI 2009/56, art. 3(1) and Sch. 1, para. 49(3).]

112(3) The references in subsection (1) above to assessments to tax include references to determinations of penalties; and in its application to such determinations the proviso to that subsection shall have effect with the appropriate modifications.

History – In s. 112(1) the word "HMRC" substituted for the words "the Commissioners, inspectors, collectors and other officers having powers in relation to tax" and the word "tribunal" substituted for the words "Commissioners having jurisdiction in the case" by SI 2009/56, art. 3(1) and Sch. 1, para. 49(2), operative from 1 April 2009, subject to transitional and saving provisions in SI 2009/56, Sch. 3.

S. 112(1A) dealt with development land tax.

S. 112(2) omitted by SI 2009/56, art. 3(1) and Sch. 1, para. 49(3), operative from 1 April 2009, subject to transitional and saving provisions in SI 2009/56, Sch. 3.

S. 112(3) inserted by FA 1989, s. 168(6).

Cross references – OTA 1975, Sch. 2, para. 1(1): s. 112 applies for the purposes of oil taxation, with modifications to s. 112(1).

SI 1999/2537: modified application of provisions of s. 112 in relation to stamp duty penalties.

113 Form of returns and other documents

113(1) Any returns under the Taxes Acts shall be in such form as the Board prescribe, and in prescribing income tax forms under this subsection the Board shall have regard to the desirability of securing, so far as may be possible, that no person shall be required to make more than one return annually of the sources of his income and the amounts derived therefrom.

113(1A) Any notice or direction requiring any return to be made under the Taxes Acts to an inspector or other officer of the Board may be issued or given in the name of that officer, or as the case may be in the name of the Board, by any officer of the Board, and so as to require the return to be made to the first-mentioned officer.

113(1B) Where the Board or an inspector or other officer of the Board have in accordance with section 29 of this Act or paragraph 41 of Schedule 18 to the Finance Act 1998, or any other provision of the Taxes Acts, decided to make an assessment to tax, and have taken all other decisions needed for arriving at the amount of the assessment, they may entrust to some other officer of the Board responsibility for completing the assessing procedure, whether by means involving the use of a computer or otherwise, including responsibility for serving notice of the assessment on the person liable for tax.

113(1C) [Repealed by FA 1996, s. 132 and Sch. 18, para. 4(2)(c), s. 205 and Sch. 41, Pt. V(8).]

113(1D) Where an officer of the Board has decided to impose a penalty under section 100 of this Act and has taken all other decisions needed for arriving at the amount of the penalty, he may entrust to any other officer of the Board responsibility for completing the determination procedure, whether by means involving the use of a computer or otherwise, including responsibility for serving notice of the determination on the person liable to the penalty.

113(2) Any return or assessment or other document relating to chargeable gains or tax on capital gains may be combined with one relating to income or income tax.

113(3) Every assessment, determination of a penalty, duplicate, warrant, notice of assessment, of determination or of demand, or other document required to be used in assessing, charging, collecting and levying tax or determining a penalty shall be in accordance with the forms prescribed from time to time in that behalf by the Board, and a document in the form prescribed and supplied or approved by them shall be valid and effectual.

History – S. 113(1A) inserted by FA 1970, Sch. 4, para. 10.
S. 113(1B) amended by inserting the words "or paragraph 41 of Schedule 18 to the Finance Act 1998", by FA 1998, s. 117(3) and Sch. 19, para. 41, with effect in relation to accounting periods ending on or after 1 July 1999, the corporation tax self-assessment appointed day by virtue of FA 1994, s. 199(2), (3) and SI 1998/3173 (C. 78).
S. 113(1B) inserted by FA 1970, Sch. 4, para. 10.
S. 113(1C) repealed by FA 1996, s. 132 and Sch. 18, para. 4(2)(c), s. 205 and Sch. 41, Pt. V(8), with effect:

- as respects the year 1996–97 and subsequent years of assessment; and
- in relation to any income tax or capital gains tax which is charged by an assessment made on or after 6 April 1998 and is for the year 1995–96 or any earlier year of assessment.

So far as relating to partnerships whose trades, professions or businesses were set up and commenced before 6 April 1994, the repeal of s. 113(1C) has effect:

- as respects the year 1997–98 and subsequent years of assessment; and
- in relation to any income tax which is charged by an assessment made on or after 6 April 1998 and is for the year 1995–96 or any earlier year of assessment.

S. 113(1C) inserted by FA 1989, s. 159(4).
S. 113(1D) inserted by FA 1989, s. 168(7)(a).
Words "determination of a penalty,", ", of determination" and "or determining a penalty" inserted by FA 1989, s. 168(7)(b).

Cross references – CRCA 2005, s. 16 and Sch. 2(3): s. 113(3) has effect only in connection with functions relating to matters to which CRCA 2005, s. 7 applies.
OTA 1975, Sch. 2, para. 1(1): s. 113(1A) and, with modifications, s. 113(3) apply for the purposes of oil taxation.
SI 1995/351, reg. 8: s. 113(1B) applies to determinations and notices of determinations under FA 1993, Sch. 19 (Lloyd's underwriters).
SI 1999/2537: modified application of provisions of s. 113 in relation to stamp duty penalties.

Statutory instruments – SI 2003/2682 PAYE regulations.
SI 2005/2045: Construction Industry Scheme Regulations.
SI 2006/131: pension schemes.
SI 2007/2969: PAYE, partly made under s. 113(1).

Statements of practice – SP 5/87: Revenue approach towards acceptance of tax returns and other forms by way of facsimiles or photocopies, as substitutes for officially-produced printed forms.

114 Want of form or errors not to invalidate assessments, etc.

114(1) An assessment or determination, warrant or other proceeding which purports to be made in pursuance of any provision of the Taxes Acts shall not be quashed, or deemed to be void or voidable, for want of form, or be affected by reason of a mistake, defect or omission therein, if the same is in substance and effect in conformity with or according to the intent and meaning of the Taxes Acts, and if the person or property charged or intended to be charged or affected thereby is designated therein according to common intent and understanding.

114(2) An assessment or determination shall not be impeached or affected–

(a) by reason of a mistake therein as to–

(i) the name or surname of a person liable, or

(ii) the description of any profits or property, or

(iii) the amount of the tax charged, or

(b) by reason of any variance between the notice and the assessment or determination.

History – Words "or determination" inserted after the word "assessment" in each place where it occurs in s. 114 by FA 1989, s. 160(5).

Cross references – FA 2011, Sch. 23, para. 43: s. 114 applies for the purposes of that schedule as for the purposes of the Taxes Acts.
FA 2008, Sch. 36, para. 56: application of s. 114 for the purposes of that Schedule as for purposes of Taxes Acts.
OTA 1975, Sch. 2, para. 1(1): s. 114 applies with modifications for the purposes of oil taxation.
SI 1986/1711, Schedule, Pt. I and II: modified application of s.114 for purposes of stamp duty reserve tax.
SI 1999/2537: modified application of provisions of s. 114 in relation to stamp duty penalties.
FA 2012, Sch. 38, para.36: S. 114 to apply for the purposes of provisions relating to dishonest conduct by tax agents.

115 Delivery and service of documents

115(1) A notice or form which is to be served under the Taxes Acts on a person may be either delivered to him or left at his usual or last known place of residence.

115(2) Any notice or other document to be given, sent, served or delivered under the Taxes Acts may be served by post, and, if to be given, sent, served or delivered to or on any person by HMRC may be so served addressed to that person–

(a) at his usual or last known place of residence, or his place of business or employment, or

(b) in the case of a company, at any other prescribed place and, in the case of a liquidator of a company, at his address for the purposes of the liquidation or any other prescribed place.

115(3) In subsection (2) above **"prescribed"** means prescribed by regulations made by the Board, and the power of making regulations for the purposes of that subsection shall be exercisable by statutory instrument subject to annulment in pursuance of a resolution of the House of Commons.

115(4) [Omitted by SI 2009/56, art. 3(1) and Sch. 1, para. 50(3) and repealed by TCEA 2007, s. 146 and Sch. 23, Pt. 1.]

115(5) [Omitted by SI 2009/56, art. 3(1) and Sch. 1, para. 50(3).]

History – In s. 115(2) the words "by HMRC" substituted for the words "by the Board, by any officer of the Board, or by or on behalf of any body of Commissioners," by SI 2009/56, art. 3(1) and Sch. 1, para. 50(2), operative from 1 April 2009, subject to transitional and saving provisions in SI 2009/56, Sch. 3.
S. 115(4) omitted by SI 2009/56, art. 3(1) and Sch. 1, para. 50(3), operative from 1 April 2009, subject to transitional and saving provisions in SI 2009/56, Sch. 3 and repealed by TCEA 2007, s. 146 and Sch. 23, Pt. 1, with effect from 1 April 2009 (SI 2008/2696, art. 6(c)(i)).
S. 115(5) omitted by SI 2009/56, art. 3(1) and Sch. 1, para. 50(3), operative from 1 April 2009, subject to transitional and saving provisions in SI 2009/56, Sch. 3.
Former s. 115(5) inserted by SI 1994/1813, Sch. 1, para. 16, with effect from 1 September 1994.

Cross references – FA 2011, Sch. 23, para. 43: s. 115 applies for the purposes of that schedule as for the purposes of the Taxes Acts.
FA 2008, Sch. 36, para. 56: application of s. 115 for the purposes of that Schedule as for purposes of the Taxes Acts.
OTA 1975, Sch. 2, para. 1(1): s. 115(1)–(3) apply for the purposes of oil taxation.
INA 1978, s. 7: service by post is deemed to be effected by properly addressing, pre-paying and posting a letter containing the documents to be served.
SI 1999/2537: modified application of provisions of s. 115 in relation to stamp duty penalties.
SI 2009/317, art. 3(2)(a), (c): modification of meaning of "liquidator" and "liquidation" in relation to liquidation or administration of banks.
FA 2012, Sch. 38, para.36: S. 115 to apply for the purposes of provisions relating to dishonest conduct by tax agents.

115A Electronic lodgement of tax returns, etc.

115A Schedule 3A to this Act (which makes provision with respect to the electronic lodgement of tax returns and documents required in connection with tax returns) shall have effect.

Prospective amendments – S. 115A repealed by FA 1999, s. 139 and Sch. 20, Pt. VII with effect from a day to be appointed under FA 1999, s. 133(4).

History – S. 115A inserted by FA 1995, s. 153 and Sch. 28, para. 1.

116 Receipts, etc. exempt from stamp duty

116 [Repealed by FA 1970, Sch. 8, Pt. V, with effect from 1 February 1971.]

NORTHERN IRELAND

117 Action of ejectment in Northern Ireland

117 Unless other provision is made in that behalf by any enactment, an action of ejectment in Northern Ireland for non-payment of rent shall not be defeated on the ground that the person liable to pay the rent is entitled under the Income Tax Acts to a deduction which would reduce the amount due by him below a year's rent.

INTERPRETATION

118 Interpretation

118(1) In this Act, unless the context otherwise requires–

"Act" includes an Act of the Parliament of Northern Ireland and

"enactment" shall be construed accordingly,

"the Board" means the Commissioners of Inland Revenue,

"body of persons" means any body politic, corporate or collegiate, and any company, fraternity, fellowship and society of persons, whether corporate or not corporate,

"chargeable gain" has the same meaning as in the 1992 Act,

"chargeable period" means a year of assessment or a company's accounting period,

"collector" means any collector of taxes,

"company" has the meaning given by section 1121(1) of CTA 2010 (with section 617 of that Act),

"CTA 2009" means the Corporation Tax Act 2009,

"CTA 2010" means the Corporation Tax Act 2010,

"HMRC" means Her Majesty's Revenue and Customs;

"inspector" means any inspector of taxes,

"ITEPA 2003" means the Income Tax (Earnings and Pensions) Act 2003,

"ITTOIA 2005" means the Income Tax (Trading and Other Income) Act 2005,

"ITA 2007" means the Income Tax Act 2007,

"NRCGT return" has the meaning given by section 12ZB;

"partnership return" has the meaning given by section 12AA(10A) of this Act,

"the principal Act" means the Income and Corporation Taxes Act 1988,

"the relevant trustees", in relation to a settlement, shall be construed in accordance with section 7(9) of this Act.

"return" includes any statement or declaration under the Taxes Acts,

"successor", in relation to a person who is required to make and deliver, or has made and delivered, a partnership return, and

"predecessor" and **"successor,"** in relation to the successor of such a person, shall be construed in accordance with section 12AA(11) of this Act;

"tax", where neither income tax nor capital gains tax nor corporation tax nor development land tax is specified, means any of those taxes,

"the Taxes Acts" means this Act and–

(a) the Tax Acts, and

(b) the Taxation of Chargeable Gains Act 1992 and all other enactments relating to capital gains tax,

"the TCEA 2007" means the Tribunals, Courts and Enforcement Act 2007;

"the 1992 Act" means the Taxation of Chargeable Gains Act 1992,

"TIOPA 2010" means the Taxation (International and Other Provisions) Act 2010,

"trade" includes every trade, manufacture, adventure or concern in the nature of trade.

"the tribunal" is to be read in accordance with section 47C;

118(2) For the purposes of this Act, a person shall be deemed not to have failed to do anything required to be done within a limited time if he did it within such further time, if any, as the Board or the tribunal or officer concerned may have allowed; and where a person had a reasonable excuse for not doing anything required to be done he shall be deemed not to have failed to do it unless the excuse ceased and, after the excuse ceased, he shall be deemed not to have failed to do it if he did it without unreasonable delay after the excuse had ceased.

118(3) [Repealed by FA 1994, s. 196 and Sch. 19, para. 34(2) and s. 258 and Sch. 26, Pt. V(23).]

118(4) For the purposes of this Act, the amount of tax covered by any assessment shall not be deemed to be finally determined until that assessment can no longer be varied, whether by the tribunal on an appeal notified to it or by the order of any court.

118(5) For the purposes of this Act a loss of tax or a situation is brought about carelessly by a person if the person fails to take reasonable care to avoid bringing about that loss or situation.

118(6) Where–

(a) information is provided to Her Majesty's Revenue and Customs,

(b) the person who provided the information, or the person on whose behalf the information was provided, discovers some time later that the information was inaccurate, and

(c) that person fails to take reasonable steps to inform Her Majesty's Revenue and Customs,

any loss of tax or situation brought about by the inaccuracy shall be treated for the purposes of this Act as having been brought about carelessly by that person.

118(7) In this Act, references to a loss of tax or a situation brought about deliberately by a person include a loss of tax or a situation that arises as a result of a deliberate inaccuracy in a document given to Her Majesty's Revenue and Customs by or on behalf of that person.

History – In s. 118(1):

Definitions of "branch or agency" and "branch or agent" repealed by FA 2003, s. 216 and Sch. 43, Pt. 3(6) in relation to accounting periods beginning on or after 1 January 2003.

In the definition of "company", the words "section 1121(1) of CTA 2010 (with section 617 of that Act)" substituted for the words "section 992(1) of ITA 2007 (with section 468 of the principal Act)" by CTA 2010, s. 1177 and Sch. 1, para. 159(a), with effect for corporation tax purposes for accounting periods ending on or after 1 April 2010, and for income tax and capital gains tax purposes for the tax year 2010–11 and subsequent tax years.

In the definition of "company", the words "section 992(1) of ITA 2007 (with section 468 of the principal Act)" substituted for the words "section 832(1) of the principal Act (with section 468 of that Act)" by ITA 2007, s. 1027 and Sch. 1, para. 263(a), with effect from 6 April 2007.

Definition of "CTA 2009" inserted by CTA 2009, s. 1322 and Sch. 1, para. 309, with effect for corporation tax purposes for accounting periods ending on or after 1 April 2009, and for income tax and capital gains tax purposes for the tax year 2009–10 and subsequent tax years.

Definition of "CTA 2010" inserted by CTA 2010, s. 1177 and Sch. 1, para. 159(b), with effect for corporation tax purposes for accounting periods ending on or after 1 April 2010, and for income tax and capital gains tax purposes for the tax year 2010–11 and subsequent tax years.

Definition of "the General Commissioners Regulations" omitted by SI 2009/56, art. 3(1) and Sch. 1, para. 51(2), operative from 1 April 2009, subject to transitional and saving provisions in SI 2009/56, Sch. 3.

Definition of "HMRC" inserted by SI 2009/56, art. 3(1) and Sch. 1, para. 51(3), operative from 1 April 2009, subject to transitional and saving provisions in SI 2009/56, Sch. 3.

Definitions of "incapacitated person" and "infant" omitted by FA 2012, s. 222(4)(a), with effect for the tax year 2012–13 and subsequent tax years.

Definition of "infant" inserted by Age of Legal Capacity (Scotland) Act 1991, s. 10 and Sch. 1, para. 34, with effect from 25 September 1991.

Definition of "ITEPA 2003" inserted by ITEPA 2003, Sch. 6, para. 139 which has effect, for income tax purposes, for tax year 2003–04 and subsequent tax years and, for corporation tax purposes, for accounting periods ending after 5 April 2003.

Definition of "ITTOIA 2005" inserted by ITTOIA 2005, s. 882(1) and Sch. 1, para. 380; effective for income tax purposes for 2005–06 onwards and forcorporation tax purposes for accounting periods ending after 5 April 2005 (ITTOIA 2005, s. 883(1)).

Definition of "ITA 2007" inserted by ITA 2007, s. 1027 and Sch. 1, para. 263(b), with effect from 6 April 2007.

Definition of "neglect" (which previously appeared) repealed by FA 1989, s. 187 and Sch. 17, Pt. VIII, but not to affect the making of assessments for years of assessment before 1983–84 or for accounting periods which ended before 1 April 1983 (FA 1989, s. 149(7)).

Definition of "NRCGT return" inserted by FA 2015, s. 37 and Sch. 7, para. 54, with effect in relation to disposals made on or after 6 April 2015.

Definition of "partnership return" inserted by FA 2001, s. 88 and Sch. 29, para. 33(2) with effect from 11 May 2001 in relation to returns whether made before or after that date and whether relating to periods before or after then.

Definition of "the relevant trustees" inserted by FA 1995, s. 103(6), with effect, so far as it relates to income tax and capital gains tax, as respects the year 1996–97 and subsequent years of assessment, and so far as it relates to corporation tax, as respects accounting periods ending on or after 1 July 1999, the day appointed by virtue of FA 1994, s. 199(3) and SI 1998/3173 (C. 78)).

Definition of "successor" amended, substituting the words "a partnership return" for the words "a return under section 12AA of this Act", by FA 2001, s. 88, Sch. 29, para. 33(3) with effect from 11 May 2001 in relation to returns whether made before or after that date and whether relating to periods before or after then.

Definition of "successor" inserted by FA 1996, s. 123(14) (thereby substituted for the previous definition inserted by FA 1994, s. 196 and Sch. 19, para. 34) in so far as it relates to income tax and capital gains tax, as respects the year 1996–97 and subsequent years of assessment and, in so far as it relates to corporation tax, as respects accounting periods ending on or after 1 July 1999, the appointed day (FA 1994, s. 199(2),(3) and SI 1998/3173 (C. 78)).

Definition of "the Special Commissioners Regulations" omitted by SI 2009/56, art. 3(1) and Sch. 1, para. 51(2), operative from 1 April 2009, subject to transitional and saving provisions in SI 2009/56, Sch. 3.

In the definition of "tax", the words "except that in sections 20A, 20B and 20D it does not include development land tax," omitted by FA 2012, s. 223 and Sch. 38, para. 50, with effect from 1 April 2013 (SI 2013/279, art. 2).

In the definitionof "tax", "20," omitted by FA 2008, s. 113 and Sch. 36, para. 76, with effect from 1 April 2009 (SI 2009/404, art. 2, subject to savings at SI 2009/404, art. 3).

In the definition of "tax" the word ", 20C" omitted by FA 2007, s. 84(4) and Sch. 22, para. 4(b), with effect from 1 December 2007 by virtue of SI 2007/3166, art. 3(a), and repealed by FA 2007, s. 114 and Sch. 27, Pt. 5(1), with effect from 8 November 2007 by virtue of SI 2007/3166, art. 2(c) in accordance with FA 2007, s. 84(5).

In definition of "tax" the words "except that in sections 20, 20A, 20B, 20C and 20D it does not include development land tax," inserted by the FA 1976, s. 57(2).

In definition of "tax" the words "nor development land tax" inserted by the Development Land Tax Act 1976, s. 41 and Sch. 8, para. 32.

Definition of "Taxes Acts" further amended by ICTA 1988, s. 844 and Sch. 31 removing the reference to ICTA 1970, s. 526(2) (repealed), with effect for 1988–89 and subsequent years of assessment.

Definition of "the TCEA 2007" inserted by SI 2009/56, art. 3(1) and Sch. 1, para. 51(3), operative from 1 April 2009, subject to transitional and saving provisions in SI 2009/56, Sch. 3.

Definition of "TIOPA 2010" inserted by TIOPA 2010, s. 374 and Sch. 8, para. 314, with effect for corporation tax purposes for accounting periods ending on or after 1 April 2010, for income tax and capital gains tax purposes for the tax year 2010–11 and subsequent tax years, and for petroleum revenue tax purposes for chargeable periods beginning on or after 1 July 2010.

Definition of "the tribunal" inserted by SI 2009/56, art. 3(1) and Sch. 1, para. 51(3), operative from 1 April 2009, subject to transitional and saving provisions in SI 2009/56, Sch. 3.

In s. 118(2) the word "tribunal" substituted for the word "Commissioners" by SI 2009/56, art. 3(1) and Sch. 1, para. 51(4), operative from 1 April 2009, subject to transitional and saving provisions in SI 2009/56, Sch. 3.

S. 118(2) amended by FA 1970, s. 36 and Sch. 8 repealing the proviso; and further amended by F(No. 2)A 1987, s. 94 by inserting the words "not to have failed to do it unless the excuse ceased and, after the excuse ceased, he shall be deemed" after "deemed" in the second place where it occurs.
S. 118(3) repealed by FA 1994, s. 196 and Sch. 19, para. 34(2) and s. 258 and Sch. 26, Pt. V(23). The repeal has effect:

- in relation to partnerships whose trade, profession or business is set up and commenced before 6 April 1994, as respects the year 1997–98 and subsequent years of assessment; and
- in relation to other partnerships, as respects the year 1996–97 and subsequent years of assessment.

In s. 118(4) the words "the tribunal on an appeal notified to it" substituted for the words "any Commissioners on appeal" by SI 2009/56, art. 3(1) and Sch. 1, para. 51(5), operative from 1 April 2009, subject to transitional and saving provisions in SI 2009/56, Sch. 3.
S. 118(5), (6) and (7) inserted by FA 2008, s. 118 and Sch. 39, para. 15, with effect from 1 April 2010 (SI 2009/403, art. 2(2) subject to SI 2009/403, art. 3–10 – in particular art. 10).
References to the "1992 Act" and the "Taxation of Chargeable Gains Act 1992" substituted by TCGA 1992, s. 290 and Sch. 10, para. 2(11).
Words "section 36" in former s. 118(3) substituted by FA 1989, s. 149(3)(b), but not to affect the making of assessments for years of assessment before 1983–84 or for accounting periods which ended before 1 April 1983 (FA 1989, s. 149(7)).

Cross references – S. 88(7): s. 118(2) not to apply for the purposes of s. 88(1)(a) (assessment to recover loss of tax attributable to failure to give a notice etc.).
ICTA 1988, s. 705B(1)(b): modified application of s. 118 for purposes of proceedings in Northern Ireland.
FA 2003, Sch. 17, para. 1 (Stamp Duty Land Tax): Sch. 17 to be treated as part of "the Taxes Acts" for the purposes of TMA 1970, Pt. 1.
OTA 1975, Sch. 2, para. 1(1): s. 118(1), (2) apply for the purposes of oil taxation.
SI 1986/1711, Schedule, Pt. I and II: modified application of s. 118 for purposes of stamp duty reserve tax.
SI 1999/2537: modified application of s. 118(1) in relation to stamp duty penalties.

Statements of practice – A13: HMRC view that returns must be signed by the taxpayer personally, with relaxation where the provision of a signature would damage the taxpayer's health.

HMRC Manuals – Company Taxation, CT94140: HMRC's understanding of "reasonable excuse" and its application in relation to company tax returns.

Notes – CCH has taken the view that the definitions of "company", "tax" and "Taxes Acts" should exclude references to development land tax on the basis that FA 1985, Sch. 27, Pt. X repealed the whole of the Development Land Tax Act 1976 with effect from 19 March 1985 and therefore repealed those references by implication. The repeal of words relating to development land tax in the definition of "tax" by FA 2007, s. 84 and Sch. 22, para. 4 has not therefore been reflected.

PART XII – GENERAL

119 Commencement and construction

119(1) This Act shall come into force for all purposes on 6th April 1970 to the exclusion of the corresponding enactments repealed by the principal Act.

119(2) This Act, and the repeals made by the principal Act, have effect subject to Schedule 4 to this Act.

119(3) This Act, so far as it relates to income tax or corporation tax, shall be construed as one with the principal Act.

119(4) This Act, so far as it relates to chargeable gains, shall be construed as one with the 1992 Act and ITEPA 2003.

119(5) [Repealed by FA 1985, Sch. 27, Pt. X, with effect from 19 March 1985.]

History – In s. 119(4), the words "and ITEPA 2003" inserted by ITEPA 2003, Sch. 6, para. 140 which has effect, for income tax purposes, for tax year 2003–04 and subsequent tax years and, for corporation tax purposes, for accounting periods ending after 5 April 2003.
S. 119(5) dealt with development land tax.
References to the "1992 Act" in definitions of "chargeable gain" and "the Taxes Acts" substituted by TCGA 1992, s. 290 and Sch. 10, para. 2(2).

Notes – Sch. 4 dealt with savings and transitory provisions and is spent.

120 Short title

120 This Act may be cited as the Taxes Management Act 1970.

SCHEDULES

SCHEDULE 1 – FORMS OF DECLARATIONS

[Omitted by SI 2009/56, art. 3(1) and Sch. 1, para. 52.]

History – Sch. 1 omitted by SI 2009/56, art. 3(1) and Sch. 1, para. 52, operative from 1 April 2009, subject to transitional and saving provisions in SI 2009/56, Sch. 3.

SCHEDULE 1AA – ORDERS FOR PRODUCTION OF DOCUMENTS

Section 149(2)

History – Sch. 1AA inserted by FA 2000, s. 149(2) and Sch. 39.

Cross references – TCA 2002, s. 36(1): application of Sch. 1AA and regulations made thereunder in relation to tax credits fraud.

Statutory instruments – SI 2000/2875: regulations under various provisions of Sch. 1AA.

INTRODUCTION

1 The provisions of this Schedule supplement section 20BA.

AUTHORISED OFFICER OF THE BOARD

2(1) In section 20BA(1) an **"authorised officer of the Board"** means an officer of the Board authorised by the Board for the purposes of that section.

2(2) The Board may make provision by regulations as to–

(a) the procedures for approving in any particular case the decision to apply for an order under that section, and

(b) the descriptions of officer by whom such approval may be given.

Statutory instruments – SI 2000/2875, reg. 3: regulations under Sch. 1AA, para. 2(2).
SI 2007/881: made under para. 2(2).

NOTICE OF APPLICATION FOR ORDER

3(1) A person is entitled–

(a) to notice of the intention to apply for an order against him under section 20BA, and

(b) to appear and be heard at the hearing of the application,

unless the appropriate judicial authority is satisfied that this would seriously prejudice the investigation of the offence.

3(2) The Board may make provision by regulations as to the notice to be given, the contents of the notice and the manner of giving it.

Statutory instruments – SI 2000/2875, reg. 4: regulations under Sch. 1AA, para. 3(2).

OBLIGATIONS OF PERSON GIVEN NOTICE OF APPLICATION

4(1) A person who has been given notice of intention to apply for an order under section 20BA(4) shall not–

(a) conceal, destroy, alter or dispose of any document to which the application relates, or

(b) disclose to any other person information or any other matter likely to prejudice the investigation of the offence to which the application relates.

This is subject to the following qualifications.

4(2) Sub-paragraph (1)(a) does not prevent anything being done–

(a) with the leave of the appropriate judicial authority,

(b) with the written permission of an officer of the Board,

(c) after the application has been dismissed or abandoned, or

(d) after any order made on the application has been complied with.

4(3) Sub-paragraph (1)(b) does not prevent a professional legal adviser from disclosing any information or other matter–

(a) to, or to a representative of, a client of his in connection with the giving by the adviser of legal advice to the client; or

(b) to any person–

(i) in contemplation of, or in connection with, legal proceedings; and

(ii) for the purpose of those proceedings.

This sub-paragraph does not apply in relation to any information or other matter which is disclosed with a view to furthering a criminal purpose.

4(4) A person who fails to comply with the obligation in sub-paragraph (1)(a) or (b) above may be dealt with as if he had failed to comply with an order under section 20BA.

EXCEPTION OF ITEMS SUBJECT TO LEGAL PRIVILEGE

5(1) Section 20BA does not apply to items subject to legal privilege.

5(2) For this purpose **"items subject to legal privilege"** means–

(a) communications between a professional legal adviser and his client or any person representing his client made in connection with the giving of legal advice to the client;

(b) communications between a professional legal adviser and his client or any person representing his client or between such an adviser or his client or any such representative and any other person made in connection with or in contemplation of legal proceedings and for the purposes of such proceedings; and

(c) items enclosed with or referred to in such communications and made–

(i) in connection with the giving of legal advice; or

(ii) in connection with or in contemplation of legal proceedings and for the purposes of such proceedings,

when they are in the possession of a person who is entitled to possession of them.

5(3) Items held with the intention of furthering a criminal purpose are not subject to legal privilege.

RESOLUTION OF DISPUTES AS TO LEGAL PRIVILEGE

6(1) The Board may make provision by regulations for the resolution of disputes as to whether a document, or part of a document, is an item subject to legal privilege.

6(2) The regulations may, in particular, make provision as to–

(a) the custody of the document whilst its status is being decided;

(b) the appointment of an independent, legally qualified person to decide the matter;

(c) the procedures to be followed; and

(d) who is to meet the costs of the proceedings.

Statutory instruments – SI 2000/2875, reg. 7: regulations under Sch. 1AA, para. 6.

COMPLYING WITH AN ORDER

7(1) The Board may make provision by regulations as to how a person is to comply with an order under section 20BA.

7(2) The regulations may, in particular, make provision as to–

(a) the officer of the Board to whom the documents are to be produced,

(b) the address to which the documents are to be taken or sent, and

(c) the circumstances in which sending the documents by post complies with the order.

7(3) Where an order under section 20BA applies to a document in electronic or magnetic form, the order shall be taken to require the person to deliver the information recorded in the document in a form in which it is visible and legible.

Statutory instruments – SI 2000/2875, reg. 6: regulations under Sch. 1AA, para. 7(1), (2).

PROCEDURE WHERE DOCUMENTS ARE DELIVERED

8(1) The provisions of section 20CC(3) to (9) apply in relation to a document delivered to an officer of the Board in accordance with an order under section 20BA as they apply to a thing removed by an officer of the Board as mentioned in subsection (1) of section 20CC.

8(2) In section 20CC(9) as applied by sub-paragraph (1) above the reference to the warrant concerned shall be read as a reference to the order concerned.

SANCTION FOR FAILURE TO COMPLY WITH ORDER

9(1) If a person fails to comply with an order made under section 20BA, he may be dealt with as if he had committed a contempt of the court.

9(2) For this purpose **"the court"** means–

(a) in relation to an order made by a Circuit judge, the Crown Court;

(b) in relation to an order made by a sheriff, a sheriff court;

(c) in relation to an order made by a county court judge, a county court in Northern Ireland.

NOTICE OF ORDER ETC.

10 The Board may make provision by regulations as to the circumstances in which notice of an order under section 20BA, or of an application for such an order, is to be treated as having been given.

Statutory instruments – SI 2000/2875, reg. 5: regulations under Sch. 1AA, para. 10.

GENERAL PROVISIONS ABOUT REGULATIONS

11 Regulations under this Schedule–

(a) may contain such incidental, supplementary and transitional provision as appears to the Board to be appropriate, and

(b) shall be made by statutory instrument which shall be subject to annulment in pursuance of a resolution of either House of Parliament.

Statutory instruments – SI 2000/2875: regulations under Sch. 1AA, para. 11(a).

SCHEDULE 1AB – RECOVERY OF OVERPAID TAX ETC

Section 33

History – Sch. 1AB inserted by FA 2009, s. 100 and Sch. 52, para. 2 with effect in relation to claims made on or after 1 April 2010.
Cross references – FA 2009, Sch. 52, para. 10: modification of para. 3(1) in relation to certain claims made before 1 April 2012.

CLAIM FOR RELIEF FOR OVERPAID TAX ETC

1(1) This paragraph applies where–

(a) a person has paid an amount by way of income tax or capital gains tax but the person believes that the tax was not due, or

(b) a person has been assessed as liable to pay an amount by way of income tax or capital gains tax, or there has been a determination or direction to that effect, but the person believes that the tax is not due.

1(2) The person may make a claim to the Commissioners for repayment or discharge of the amount.

1(3) Paragraph 2 makes provision about cases in which the Commissioners are not liable to give effect to a claim under this Schedule.

1(4) Paragraphs 3 to 7 (and sections 42 to 43C and Schedule 1A) make further provision about making and giving effect to claims under this Schedule.

1(5) Paragraph 8 makes provision about the application of this Schedule to amounts paid under contract settlements.

1(6) The Commissioners are not liable to give relief in respect of a case described in sub-paragraph (1)(a) or (b) except as provided–

(a) by this Schedule and Schedule 1A (following a claim under this paragraph), or

(b) by or under another provision of the Income Tax Acts or an enactment relating to the taxation of capital gains.

1(7) For the purposes of this Schedule, an amount paid by one person on behalf of another is treated as paid by the other person.

CASES IN WHICH COMMISSIONERS NOT LIABLE TO GIVE EFFECT TO CLAIM

2(1) The Commissioners are not liable to give effect to a claim under this Schedule if or to the extent that the claim falls within a case described in this paragraph (see also paragraphs 3A and 4(5)).

2(2) Case A is where the amount paid, or liable to be paid, is excessive by reason of–

(a) a mistake in a claim, election or notice,

(b) a mistake consisting of making or giving, or failing to make or give, a claim, election or notice,

(c) a mistake in allocating expenditure to a pool for the purposes of the Capital Allowances Act or a mistake consisting of making, or failing to make, such an allocation, or

(d) a mistake in bringing a disposal value into account for the purposes of that Act or a mistake consisting of bringing, or failing to bring, such a value into account.

2(3) Case B is where the claimant is or will be able to seek relief by taking other steps under the Income Tax Acts or an enactment relating to the taxation of capital gains.

2(4) Case C is where the claimant–

(a) could have sought relief by taking such steps within a period that has now expired, and

(b) knew, or ought reasonably to have known, before the end of that period that such relief was available.

2(5) Case D is where the claim is made on grounds that–

(a) have been put to a court or tribunal in the course of an appeal by the claimant relating to the amount paid or liable to be paid, or

(b) have been put to Her Majesty's Revenue and Customs in the course of an appeal by the claimant relating to that amount that is treated as having been determined by a tribunal (by virtue of section 54 (settling of appeals by agreement)).

2(6) Case E is where the claimant knew, or ought reasonably to have known, of the grounds for the claim before the latest of the following–

(a) the date on which an appeal by the claimant relating to the amount paid, or liable to be paid, in the course of which the ground could have been put forward (a "relevant appeal") was determined by a court or tribunal (or is treated as having been so determined),

(b) the date on which the claimant withdrew a relevant appeal to a court or tribunal, and

(c) the end of the period in which the claimant was entitled to make a relevant appeal to a court or tribunal.

2(7) Case F is where the amount in question was paid or is liable to be paid–

(a) in consequence of proceedings enforcing the payment of that amount brought against the claimant by Her Majesty's Revenue and Customs, or

(b) in accordance with an agreement between the claimant and Her Majesty's Revenue and Customs settling such proceedings.

2(8) Case G is where–

(a) the amount paid, or liable to be paid, is excessive by reason of a mistake in calculating the claimant's liability to income tax or capital gains tax (other than a mistake in a PAYE assessment or PAYE calculation), and

(b) liability was calculated in accordance with the practice generally prevailing at the time.

2(9) Case H is where–

(a) the amount paid, or liable to be paid, is excessive by reason of a mistake in a PAYE assessment or PAYE calculation, and

(b) the assessment or calculation was made in accordance with the practice generally prevailing at the end of the period of 12 months following the tax year for which the assessment or calculation was made.

2(9A) Cases G and H do not apply where the amount paid, or liable to be paid, is tax which has been charged contrary to EU law.

2(9B) For the purposes of sub-paragraph (9A), an amount of tax is charged contrary to EU law if, in the circumstances in question, the charge to tax is contrary to–

(a) the provisions relating to the free movement of goods, persons, services and capital in Titles II and IV of Part 3 of the Treaty on the Functioning of the European Union, or

(b) the provisions of any subsequent treaty replacing the provisions mentioned in paragraph (a).

2(10) For the purposes of Cases G and H–

(a) **"PAYE assessment"** means an assessment on the claimant made in accordance with section 709 of ITEPA 2003 (assessment in connection with PAYE deductions), and

(b) **"PAYE calculation"** means a calculation of the amount of a deduction or repayment made or to be made under PAYE regulations in respect of tax estimated to be payable by the claimant.

History – In para. 2(1), "paragraphs 3A and 4(5)" substituted for "paragraph 4(5)" by SI 2011/1037, art. 2(2), with effect from 1 April 2001, and in relation to determinations (within the meaning of s. 28C) made before 1 April 2011 (as in relation to determinations made on or after that date). But the substitution does not apply in relation to a determination made before that date if a claim for relief in respect of it has already been refused before that date.

Para. 2(9A) inserted by FA 2013, s. 231(1), with effect in relation to any claim (in respect of overpaid tax, excessive assessments etc) made after the end of the six month period beginning on 17 July 2013.

Para. 2(9B) inserted by FA 2013, s. 231(1), with effect in relation to any claim (in respect of overpaid tax, excessive assessments etc) made after the end of the six month period beginning on 17 July 2013.

MAKING A CLAIM

3(1) A claim under this Schedule may not be made more than 4 years after the end of the relevant tax year.

3(2) In relation to a claim made in reliance on paragraph 1(1)(a), the relevant tax year is–

(a) where the amount paid, or liable to be paid, is excessive by reason of a mistake in a return or returns under section 8, 8A or 12AA of this Act, the tax year to which the return (or, if more than one, the first return) relates, and

(b) otherwise, the tax year in respect of which the payment was made.

3(3) In relation to a claim made in reliance on paragraph 1(1)(b), the relevant tax year is–

(a) where the amount liable to be paid is excessive by reason of a mistake in a return or returns under section 8, 8A or 12AA, the tax year to which the return (or, if more than one, the first return) relates, and

(b) otherwise, the tax year to which the assessment, determination or direction relates.

3(4) A claim under this Schedule may not be made by being included in a return under section 8, 8A or 12AA of this Act.

3(5) Sub-paragraph (1) is subject to paragraph 3A.

History – Para. 3(3)(a) and (b) (and the "–" before them) inserted by FA 2013, s. 232(1), with effect in relation to any claim (in respect of overpaid tax, excessive assessments etc.) made after the end of the six-month period beginning on 17 July 2013.
Para. 3(5) inserted by SI 2011/1037, art. 2(3), with effect from 1 April 2011, and in relation to determinations (within the meaning of s. 28C) made before 1 April 2011 (as in relation to determinations made on or after that date). But the insertion does not apply in relation to a determination made before that date if a claim for relief in respect of it has already been refused before that date.

Cross references – FA 2009, Sch. 52, para. 10: modification of para. 3(1) in relation to certain claims made before 1 April 2012.

DETERMINATIONS UNDER SECTION 28C: SPECIAL RULES

3A(1) This paragraph applies where–

(a) a determination has been made under section 28C of an amount that a person is liable to pay by way of income tax or capital gains tax, but the person believes the tax is not due or, if it has been paid, was not due,

(b) relief would be available under this Schedule but for the fact that–

(i) the claim falls within Case C (see paragraph 2(4)),

(ii) the claim falls within Case F(a) (see paragraph 2(7)(a)), or

(iii) more than 4 years have elapsed since the end of the relevant tax year (see paragraph 3(1)), and

(c) if the claim falls within Case F(a), the person was neither present nor legally represented during the enforcement proceedings in question.

3A(2) A claim under this Schedule for repayment or discharge of the amount may be made, and effect given to it, despite paragraph 2(4), paragraph 2(7)(a) or paragraph 3(1), as the case may be.

3A(3) But the Commissioners are not liable to give effect to a claim made in reliance on this paragraph unless conditions A, B and C are met.

3A(4) Condition A is that in the opinion of the Commissioners it would be unconscionable for the Commissioners to seek to recover the amount (or to withhold repayment of it, if it has already been paid).

3A(5) Condition B is that the person's affairs (as respects matters concerning the Commissioners) are otherwise up to date or arrangements have been put in place, to the satisfaction of the Commissioners, to bring them up to date so far as possible.

3A(6) Condition C is that either–

(a) the person has not relied on this paragraph on a previous occasion (whether in respect of the same or a different determination or tax), or

(b) the person has done so, but in the exceptional circumstances of the case should be allowed to do so again on the present occasion.

3A(7) For the purposes of sub-paragraph (6)–

(a) a person has relied on this paragraph on a previous occasion if the person has made a claim (or a composite set of claims involving one or more determinations, taxes and tax years) in reliance on this paragraph on a previous occasion, and

(b) it does not matter whether that claim (or set of claims) succeeded.

3A(8) A claim made in reliance on this paragraph must include (in addition to anything required by Schedule 1A) such information and documentation as is reasonably required for the purpose of determining whether conditions A, B and C are met.

History – Para. 3A inserted by SI 2011/1037, art. 2(4), with effect from 1 April 2011, and in relation to determinations (within the meaning of s. 28C) made before 1 April 2011 (as in relation to determinations made on or after that date). But the insertion does not apply in relation to a determination made before that date if a claim for relief in respect of it has already been refused before that date.

Notes – By virtue of SI 2011/1037, art. 4 (not reproduced), para. 3A(6) and (7) references to reliance "on this paragraph" include reliance before 1 April 2011 on the concession which para. 3A replaces (the "equitable liability" concession, described in TB 08/95-7).

THE CLAIMANT: ONE PERSON ACCOUNTABLE FOR AMOUNTS PAYABLE BY ANOTHER ETC

4(1) Sub-paragraph (2) applies where, under a relevant enactment, a person ("P") is accountable to the Commissioners for–

(a) an amount representing income tax or capital gains tax that is or is estimated to be payable by another person ("T"), or

(b) any other amount that, under a relevant enactment, has been or is to be set off against a liability of T.

4(2) A claim under this Schedule in respect of the amount may be made only by T.

4(3) Sub-paragraph (4) applies where–

(a) a person ("P") has paid an amount described in sub-paragraph (1)(a) or (b) in the belief that P was accountable to the Commissioners for the amount under a relevant enactment, but

(b) P was not so accountable.

4(4) A claim under this Schedule in respect of the amount may be made only by P.

4(5) The Commissioners are not liable to give effect to a claim under sub-paragraph (4) if or to the extent that the amount has been repaid to T or set against amounts payable to the Commissioners by T.

4(6) **"Relevant enactment"** means–

(a) PAYE regulations,

(b) Chapter 3 of Part 3 of the Finance Act 2004 or regulations under that Chapter (construction industry scheme), or

(c) any other provision of or made under the Taxes Acts.

THE CLAIMANT: PARTNERSHIPS

5(1) This paragraph applies where–

(a) a trade, profession or business is carried on by two or more persons in partnership,

(b) an amount is paid, or liable to be paid, by one or more of those persons in accordance with a self-assessment, and

(c) the amount is excessive by reason of a mistake in a partnership return.

5(2) A claim under this Schedule in respect of the amount–

(a) may be made by the relevant partner nominated to make the claim by all of the relevant partners, and

(b) may not be made by any other person.

5(3) In relation to such a claim, references in this Schedule to the claimant are to any of the relevant partners.

5(4) **"Relevant partner"** means–

(a) a person who was a partner in the partnership at any time during the period in respect of which the partnership return was made, or

(b) the personal representative of such a person.

ASSESSMENT OF CLAIMANT IN CONNECTION WITH CLAIM

6(1) This paragraph applies where–

(a) a claim is made under this Schedule,

(b) the grounds for giving effect to the claim also provide grounds for a discovery assessment or determination on the claimant in respect of any chargeable period, and

(c) such an assessment or determination could be made but for a relevant restriction.

6(2) **"Discovery assessment or determination"** means–

(a) an assessment under section 29(1), or

(b) a discovery assessment or discovery determination under Schedule 18 to the Finance Act 1998 (company tax return etc).

6(3) The following are relevant restrictions–

(a) the conditions in section 29(3) to (5),

(b) the restrictions in paragraphs 42 to 45 of Schedule 18 to the Finance Act 1998, and

(c) the expiry of a time limit for making a discovery assessment or determination.

6(4) Where this paragraph applies–

(a) the relevant restrictions are to be disregarded, and

(b) the discovery assessment or determination is not out of time if it is made before the final determination of the claim.

AMENDMENT OF PARTNERSHIP RETURN ETC IN CONNECTION WITH CLAIM

7(1) This paragraph applies where–

(a) a claim is made under this Schedule,

(b) the claimant is one of two or more persons carrying on a trade, profession or business in partnership,

(c) the grounds for giving effect to the claim also provide grounds for amending, under section 30B(1) (discovery of loss of tax from partnership), a return made by the partnership or any of the partners in respect of any period, and

(d) such an amendment could be made but for a relevant restriction.

7(2) The following are relevant restrictions–

(a) the conditions in section 30B(4) to (6), and

(b) the expiry of a time limit for making an assessment under that section.

7(3) Where this paragraph applies–

(a) the relevant conditions are to be disregarded, and

(b) the amendment is not out of time if it is made before the final determination of the claim.

CONTRACT SETTLEMENTS

8(1) In paragraph 1(1)(a), the reference to an amount paid by way of income tax or capital gains tax includes an amount paid under a contract settlement in connection with income tax or capital gains tax believed to be due from any person.

8(2) Sub-paragraphs (3) to (6) apply if the person who paid the amount under the contract settlement ("the payer") and the person from whom the tax was due ("the taxpayer") are not the same person.

8(3) In relation to a claim under this Schedule in respect of that amount–

(a) the references to the claimant in paragraph 2(5) to (7) (Cases D, E and F) have effect as if they included the taxpayer,

(b) the references to the claimant in paragraph 2(8) and (10) (Cases G and H) have effect as if they were references to the taxpayer,

(c) the references to the claimant in paragraphs 6(1)(b) and 7(1)(b) have effect as if they were references to the taxpayer, and

(d) references to tax in Schedule 1A (as it applies to a claim under this Schedule) include such an amount.

8(4) Sub-paragraph (5) applies where the grounds for giving effect to a claim by the payer in respect of the amount also provide grounds for a discovery assessment or determination on the taxpayer in respect of any chargeable period.

8(5) The Commissioners may set any amount repayable to the payer by virtue of the claim against any amount payable by the taxpayer by virtue of the assessment or determination.

8(6) The obligations of the Commissioners and the taxpayer are discharged to the extent of any set-off under sub-paragraph (5).

8(7) In this paragraph–

"contract settlement" means an agreement made in connection with any person's liability to make a payment to the Commissioners under or by virtue of an enactment;

"discovery assessment or determination" has the same meaning as in paragraph 6.

INTERPRETATION

9(1) In this Schedule **"the Commissioners"** means the Commissioners for Her Majesty's Revenue and Customs.

9(2) For the purposes of this Schedule, a claim is not finally determined until it, or the amount to which it relates, can no longer be varied (whether on appeal or otherwise).

SCHEDULE 1A – CLAIMS ETC. NOT INCLUDED IN RETURNS

Section 42

History – Sch. 1A inserted by FA 1994, s. 196 and Sch. 19, para. 35 and amended by FA 1995, s. 107(11) and Sch. 20 in so far as it relates to income tax and capital gains tax, as respects the year 1996–97 and subsequent years of assessment and, in so far as it relates to corporation tax, as respects accounting periods ending on or after 1 July 1999, the appointed day for the purposes of corporation tax self-assessment by virtue of FA 1994, s. 199(2), (3) and SI 1998/3173 (C. 78)).

Cross references – CTA 2010, s. 9A: Sch. 1A does not apply to an election under CTA 2010, s. 9A made before 19 July 2011 (FA 2011, s. 34 and Sch. 7, para. 8(4)).
FA 1998, Sch. 18, para. 9, 10: company tax return under self assessment – claims or elections that cannot be made without a return and other claims, etc. to be included in a return.
FA 1998, Sch. 18, para. 59: Sch. 1A applies to claims or elections not within FA 1998, Sch. 18, para. 57 (claims or elections affecting a single accounting period) or 58 (claims or elections involving more than one accounting period) whether or not included in a company tax return.
CAA 2001, s. 201(5): Sch. 1A does not apply to an election under CAA 2001, s. 198 (election to apportion sale price on sale of qualifying interest) or 199 (election to apportion capital sum given by lessee on grant of lease).
CAA 2001, s. 227(5): Sch. 1A does not apply to an election under CAA 2001, s. 227 (special treatment for sale and leaseback cases).
SI 2003/282: regulations governing electronic delivery of information to or by the Board under this Schedule revoking SI 2000/945 with effect from 5 March 2003.

Statements of practice – SP 5/01: HMRC's approach to extending time limits for making claims for loss relief, capital allowances and group relief.

PRELIMINARY

1 In this Schedule–

"claim" means a claim or election as respects which this Schedule applies;

"partnership claim" means a claim made in accordance with section 42(6)(b) of, or paragraph 5 of Schedule 1AB to, this Act or paragraph 51D of Schedule 18 to the Finance Act 1998 (claims for overpaid corporation tax);

"profits"–

(a) in relation to income tax, means income,

(b) in relation to capital gains tax, means chargeable gains, and

(c) in relation to corporation tax, means profits as computed for the purposes of that tax;

"relevant partner", in relation to a partnership claim, means any person who was a partner at any time during the period in respect of which the claim is made;

"successor", in relation to a person who–

(a) has made a partnership claim, but

(b) is no longer a partner or is otherwise no longer available,

means such other partner who may at any time be nominated for the purposes of this paragraph by the majority of the partners at that time, and

"predecessor" and **"successor"**, in relation to a person so nominated, shall be construed accordingly.

History – In para. 1, in the definition of "partnership claim", the words ", or paragraph 5 of Schedule 1AB to," inserted by FA 2009, s. 100 and Sch. 52, para. 6 with effect in relation to claims made on or after 1 April 2010.
In para. 1, in the definition of "partnership claim", the words "or paragraph 51D of Schedule 18 to the Finance Act 1998 (claims for overpaid corporation tax)" added by FA 2009, s. 100 and Sch. 52, para. 17 with effect in relation to claims made on or after 1 April 2010.
Definition of "profits" substituted by FA 1998, s. 117(3) and Sch. 19, para. 42(2) with effect in relation to company accounting periods ending on or after 1 July 1999, the corporation tax self-assessment appointed day (FA 1998, s. 117(4), (5) and FA 1994, s. 199(2), (3)).
Definition of "claim" amended by FA 1996, s. 130(5).

Notes – Para. 1 rewritten as ITA 2007, s. 1020(1).

MAKING OF CLAIMS

2(1) Subject to any provision in the Taxes Acts for a claim to be made to the Board, every claim shall be made to an officer of the Board.

2(2) No claim requiring the repayment of tax shall be made unless the claimant has documentary proof that the tax has been paid by deduction or otherwise.

2(3) A claim shall be made in such form as the Board may determine.

2(4) The form of claim shall provide for a declaration to the effect that all the particulars given in the form are correctly stated to the best of the information and belief of the person making the claim.

2(5) The form of claim may require–

(a) a statement of the amount of tax which will be required to be discharged or repaid in order to give effect to the claim;

(b) such information as is reasonably required for the purpose of determining whether and, if so, the extent to which the claim is correct; and

(bb) the delivery with the claim of such accounts, statements and documents, relating to information contained in the claim, as are reasonably required for the purpose mentioned in paragraph (b) above;

(c) [omitted by SI 2009/2035, art. 2 and Schedule, para. 9.]

2(6) In the case of a claim made by or on behalf of a person who is not resident, or who claims to be not resident or not domiciled, in the United Kingdom, an officer of the Board or the Board may require a statement or declaration in support of the claim to be made by affidavit.

History – In para. 2(5)(b) the word "and" at end inserted and para. (c) (and the word "and" which preceded it) omitted by SI 2009/2035, art. 2 and Schedule, para. 9, with effect from 13 August 2009.
Para. 2(5)(c) amended by inserting the words "or paragraph 13 of Schedule 18 to the Finance Act 1998", by FA 1998, s. 117(3) and Sch. 19, para. 42(3) as respects company accounting periods ending on or after 1 July 1999, the corporation tax self-assessment appointed day by virtue of FA 1994, s. 199(2), (3) and SI 1998/3173 (C. 78).
Para. 2(5)(b) and (bb) substituted for former para. 2(5)(b) by FA 1995, s. 107(11) and Sch. 20, para. 1, with effect from the year 1996–97 as respects income tax and capital gains tax and, as respects corporation tax, with effect in relation to accounting periods ending after 30 June 1999 (SI 1998/3173 art 2).
In para. 2(6), the words "or not ordinarily resident" omitted by FA 2013, s. 219 and Sch. 46, para. 117, with effect from 17 July 2013.
Notes – Para. 2(3), (4) and (5) rewritten as ITA 2007, s. 1020(1).

KEEPING AND PRESERVING OF RECORDS

2A(1) Any person who may wish to make a claim in relation to a year of assessment or other period shall–

(a) keep all such records as may be requisite for the purpose of enabling him to make a correct and complete claim; and

(b) shall preserve those records until the end of the relevant day.

2A(2) In relation to a claim, the relevant day for the purposes of sub-paragraph (1) above is whichever of the following is the latest, namely–

(a) where enquiries into the claim or any amendment of the claim are made by an officer of the Board, the day on which, by virtue of paragraph 7(1) below, those enquiries are completed; and

(b) where no enquiries into the claim or any amendment of the claim are so made, the day on which such an officer no longer has power to make such enquiries.

2A(2A) The Commissioners for Her Majesty's Revenue and Customs may by regulations–

(a) provide that the records required to be kept and preserved under sub-paragraph (1) include, or do not include, records specified in the regulations, and

(b) provide that those records include supporting documents so specified.

2A(3) The duty under sub-paragraph (1) to preserve records may be discharged–

(a) by preserving them in any form and by any means, or

(b) by preserving the information contained in them in any form and by any means,

subject to sub-paragraph (3A) and any conditions or further exceptions specified in writing by the Commissioners for Her Majesty's Revenue and Customs.

2A(3A) Sub-paragraph (3)(b) does not apply in the case of records of the kinds specified in section 12B(4A) or paragraph 22(3) of Schedule 18 to the Finance Act 1998.

2A(4) Subject to sub-paragraph (5) below, any person who fails to comply with sub-paragraph (1) above in relation to any claim which is made for a year of assessment or accounting period shall be liable to a penalty not exceeding £3,000.

2A(5) Sub-paragraph (4) above does not apply where–

(a) the records which the person fails to keep or preserve are records falling within paragraph (a) of section 12B(4A) of this Act or paragraph 22(3) of Schedule 18 to the Finance Act 1998; and

(b) an officer of the Board is satisfied that any facts which he reasonably requires to be proved, and which would have been proved by the records, are proved by other documentary evidence furnished to him.

2A(6) Regulations under this paragraph may–

(a) make different provision for different cases, and

(b) make provision by reference to things specified in a notice published by the Commissioners for Her Majesty's Revenue and Customs in accordance with the regulations (and not withdrawn by a subsequent notice).

2A(7) In this paragraph **"supporting documents"** includes accounts, books, deeds, contracts, vouchers and receipts.

History – In para. 2A(2)(a), "7(1)" substituted for "7(4)" and the words "treated as" (which appeared before the word "completed") omitted, by FA 2001, s. 88, Sch. 29, para. 34(2), and the words omitted repealed by s. 110, Sch. 33, Pt. 2(13), all with effect from 11 May 2001 in relation to returns whether made before or after that date and whether relating to periods before or after then.
Para. 2A(2A) inserted by FA 2008, s. 115 and Sch. 37, para. 3 with effect from 1 April 2009 (SI 2009/402, art. 2).
Para. 2A(3) and (3A) substituted for para. 2A(3) by FA 2008, s. 115 and Sch. 37, para. 3 with effect from 1 April 2009 (SI 2009/402, art. 2).
In former para. 2A(3) the word "tribunal" substituted for the word "Commissioners" by SI 2009/56, art. 3(1) and Sch. 1, para. 54, operative from 1 April 2009, subject to transitional and saving provisions in SI 2009/56, Sch. 3.
In former para. 2A(3) and (5)(a) the words "or paragraph 22(3) of Schedule 18 to the Finance Act 1998" inserted by FA 1998, s. 117(3) and Sch. 19, para. 42(4) with effect in relation to company accounting periods ending on or after 1 July 1999, the corporation tax self-assessment appointed day by virtue of FA 1994, s. 199(2), (3) and SI 1998/3173 (C. 78).
In para. 2A(3) the words "Except in the case … 12B(4A) of this Act," inserted by FA 1996, s. 124(6) and in para. 2A(4) the words "Subject to sub-paragraph (5) below," inserted by FA 1996, s. 124(7), for the purposes of income tax and capital gains tax, as respects the year 1996–97 and subsequent years of assessment, and for the purposes of corporation tax, as respects accounting periods ending on or after 1 July 1999, the appointed day (FA 1994, s. 199(2), (3)). These amendments do not have effect in relation to any time before 29 April 1996, or any records which a person fails to preserve before 29 April 1996.
Para. 2A(5) inserted by FA 1996, s. 124(8), for the purposes of income tax and capital gains tax, as respects the year 1996–97 and subsequent years of assessment, and for the purposes of corporation tax, as respects accounting periods ending on or after 1 July 1999, the appointed day (FA 1994, s. 199(2), (3)). This amendment does not have effect in relation to any time before 29 April 1996, or anyrecords which a person fails to preserve before 29 April 1996.
Para. 2A(6) inserted by FA 2008, s. 115 and Sch. 37, para. 3(4) with effect from 1 April 2009 (SI 2009/402, art. 2).
Para. 2A(7) inserted by FA 2008, s. 115 and Sch. 37, para. 3(4) with effect from 1 April 2009 (SI 2009/402, art. 2).

AMENDMENTS OF CLAIMS

3(1) Subject to sub-paragraph (2) below–

(a) at any time before the end of the period of nine months beginning with the day on which a claim is made, an officer of the Board may by notice to the claimant so amend the claim as to correct any obvious errors or mistakes in the claim (whether errors of principle, arithmetical mistakes or otherwise); and

(b) at any time before the end of the period of twelve months beginning with the day on which the claim is made, the claimant may amend his claim by notice to an officer of the Board.

3(2) No amendment of a claim may be made under sub-paragraph (1) above at any time during the period–

(a) beginning with the day on which an officer of the Board gives notice of his intention to enquire into the claim, and

(b) ending with the day on which the officer's enquiries into the claim are completed.

Cross references – FA 2013, Sch. 24, para. 6(6): para. 3(1)(b) does not apply in relation to an election under FA 2013, Sch. 24, para. 6(3).

GIVING EFFECT TO CLAIMS AND AMENDMENTS

4(1) Subject to sub-paragraphs (1A), (3) to (5) below, an officer of the Board or the Board shall, as soon as practicable after a claim other than a partnership claim is made, or such a claim is amended under paragraph 3 above, give effect to the claim or amendment by discharge or repayment of tax.

4(1A) In relation to a claim which would otherwise fall to be taken into account in the making of deductions or repayments of tax under PAYE regulations, sub-paragraph (1) above shall apply as if for the word "shall" there were substituted the word "may".

4(2) Subject to sub-paragraphs (3) to (5) below, an officer of the Board or the Board shall, as soon as practicable after a partnership claim is made, or such a claim is amended under paragraph 3 above, give effect to the claim or amendment, as respects each of the relevant partners, by discharge or repayment of tax.

4(3) Where any such claim or amendment as is mentioned in sub-paragraph (1) or (2) above is enquired into by an officer of the Board–

(a) that sub-paragraph shall not apply until the day on which, by virtue of paragraph 7(1) below, the enquiry is completed; but

(b) the officer may at any time before that day give effect to the claim or amendment, on a provisional basis, to such extent as he thinks fit.

4(4) Nothing in this paragraph applies in relation to a claim or an amendment of a claim if the claim is not one for discharge or repayment of tax.

4(5) This paragraph has effect subject to any provision in the Taxes Acts that–

(a) requires or allows effect to be given to a claim by other means, or

(b) provides that an amount is not to be discharged or repaid.

History – In para. 4(1), "to (5)" substituted for "and (4)" by FA 2009, s. 100 and Sch. 52, para. 7(2)(a) with effect in relation to claims made on or after 1 April 2010.

In para. 4(1), the words "and to any other provision in the Taxes Acts which otherwise provides", which appeared before ", and officer of the Board", omitted by FA 2009, s. 100 and Sch. 52, para. 7(2)(b) with effect in relation to claims made on or after 1 April 2010.
In para. 4(1A), the words "PAYE regulations" substituted for the words "section 203 of the principal Act" by ITEPA 2003, Sch. 6, para. 141 which has effect, for income tax purposes, for the tax year 2003–04 and subsequent tax years and, for corporation tax purposes, for accounting periods ending after 5 April 2003.
In para. 4(2), "to (5)" substituted for "and (4)" by FA 2009, s. 100 and Sch. 52, para. 7(3) with effect in relation to claims made on or after 1 April 2010.
In para. 4(3)(a), "7(1)" substituted for "7(4)" and the words "the enquiry is" substituted for "the officer's enquiries are treated as", by FA 2001, s. 88 and Sch. 29, para. 34(3) with effect from 11 May 2001 in relation to returns whether made before or after that date and whether relating to periods before or after then.
Para. 4(4) inserted, and references to it in para. 4(1) and (2) inserted, by FA 1996, s. 133 and Sch. 19, para. 8, for the purposes of income tax and capital gains tax, as respects the year 1996-97 and subsequent years of assessment, and for the purposes of corporation tax, as respects accounting periods ending on or after 1 July 1999, the day appointed for the purposes of self-assessment by virtue of FA 1994, s. 199 and SI 1998/3173 (C. 78).
Para. 4(5) inserted by FA 2009, s. 100 and Sch. 52, para. 7(4) with effect in relation to claims made on or after 1 April 2010.

POWER TO ENQUIRE INTO CLAIMS

5(1) An officer of the Board may enquire into–

(a) a claim made by any person, or

(b) any amendment made by any person of a claim made by him,

if, before the end of the period mentioned in sub-paragraph (2) below, he gives notice in writing of his intention to do so to that person or, in the case of a partnership claim, any successor of that person.

5(2) The period referred to in sub-paragraph (1) above is whichever of the following ends the latest, namely–

(a) the period ending with the quarter day next following the first anniversary of the day on which the claim or amendment was made;

(b) where the claim or amendment relates to a year of assessment, the period ending with the first anniversary of the 31st January next following that year; and

(c) where the claim or amendment relates to a period other than a year of assessment, the period ending with the first anniversary of the end of that period;

and the quarter days for the purposes of this sub-paragraph are 31st January, 30th April, 31st July and 31st October.

5(3) A claim or amendment which has been enquired into under sub-paragraph (1) above shall not be the subject of–

(a) a further notice under that sub-paragraph; or

(b) if it is subsequently included in a return, a notice under section 9A(1) or 12AC(1) of this Act or paragraph 24 of Schedule 18 to the Finance Act 1998.

History – In para. 5(3)(b) the words "under section 9A(1) or 12AC(1) of this Act or paragraph 24 of Schedule 18 to the Finance Act 1998" substituted by FA 1998, s. 117(3) and Sch. 19, para. 42(5) with effect in relation to company accounting periods ending on or after 1 July 1999, the corporation tax self-assessment appointed day by virtue of FA 1994, s. 199(2), (3) and SI 1998/3173 (C. 78).

Cross references – ICTA 1988, s. 488(11A)(b), (12): enquiry into a claim by a housing association.
ICTA 1988, s. 489(9A): enquiry into a claim by a self-build society.

POWER TO CALL FOR DOCUMENTS FOR PURPOSES OF ENQUIRIES

6 [Omitted by FA 2008, s. 113 and Sch. 36, para. 77.]

History – Para. 6 omitted by FA 2008, s. 113 and Sch. 36, para. 77, with effect from 1 April 2009 (SI 2009/404, art. 2, subject to savings at SI 2009/404, art. 3).

APPEAL AGAINST NOTICE TO PRODUCE DOCUMENTS, ETC.

6A [Omitted by FA 2008, s. 113 and Sch. 36, para. 77.]

History – Para. 6A omitted by FA 2008, s. 113 and Sch. 36, para. 77, with effect from 1 April 2009 (SI 2009/404, art. 2, subject to savings at SI 2009/404, art. 3).

COMPLETION OF ENQUIRY INTO CLAIM

7(1) An enquiry under paragraph 5 above is completed when an officer of the Board by notice (a **"closure notice"**) informs the claimant that he has completed his enquiries and states his conclusions.

7(2) In the case of a claim for discharge or repayment of tax, the closure notice must either–

(a) state that in the officer's opinion no amendment of the claim is required, or

(b) if in the officer's opinion the claim is insufficient or excessive, amend the claim so as to make good or eliminate the deficiency or excess.

In the case of an enquiry falling within paragraph 5(1)(b) above, paragraph (b) above only applies so far as the deficiency or excess is attributable to the claimant's amendment.

7(3) In the case of a claim that is not a claim for discharge or repayment of tax, the closure notice must either–

(a) allow the claim, or

(b) disallow the claim, wholly or to such extent as appears to the officer appropriate.

7(4) A closure notice takes effect when it is issued.

7(5) The claimant may apply to the tribunal for a direction requiring an officer of the Board to issue a closure notice within a specified period.

7(6) Any such application is to be subject to the relevant provisions of Part 5 of this Act (see, in particular, section 48(2)(b)).

7(7) The tribunal shall give the direction applied for unless satisfied that there are reasonable grounds for not issuing a closure notice within a specified period.

7(8) In relation to a partnership claim, references in this paragraph to the claimant are to the person who made the claim or his successor.

History – In para. 7(5) the word "tribunal" substituted for the word "Commissioners" by SI 2009/56, art. 3(1) and Sch. 1, para. 56(2), operative from 1 April 2009, subject to transitional and saving provisions in SI 2009/56, Sch. 3.
Para. 7(6) substituted by SI 2009/56, art. 3(1) and Sch. 1, para. 56(3), operative from 1 April 2009, subject to transitional and saving provisions in SI 2009/56, Sch. 3.
In para. 7(7) the word "tribunal" substituted for the word "Commissioners hearing the application" and the words they are omitted by SI 2009/56, art. 3(1) and Sch. 1, para. 56(4), operative from 1 April 2009, subject to transitional and saving provisions in SI 2009/56, Sch. 3.
Para. 7 and the heading which precedes it substituted by FA 2001, s. 88 and Sch. 29, para. 10(2) with effect where the notice of enquiry is given after 11 May 2001, or where the enquiry is in progress immediately before that date (for these purposes, an "enquiry is in progress" until the officer's enquiries fall to be treated as completed under former para. 7(4) prior to substitution).
Former para. 7(3A), (3B) inserted, and in former para. 7(4)(b) the words "whether the claim … what amount (if any)" substituted for "the amount which" by FA 1996, s. 133 and Sch. 19, para. 9, for the purposes of income tax and capital gains tax, as respects the year 1996–97 and subsequent years of assessment, and for the purposes of corporation tax, as respects accounting periods ending on or after 1 July 1999, the day appointed for the purposes of self-assessment by virtue of FA 1994, s. 199 and SI 1998/3173 (C. 78).

Cross references – Para. 9: appeals against amendments under para. 7.
FA 2001, Sch. 29, para. 12(8): application of para. 9 (as amended by FA 2001) to closure notices issued under the substituted version of para. 7.

GIVING EFFECT TO SUCH AMENDMENTS

8(1) An officer of the Board or the Board shall, within 30 days after the date of issue of a closure notice amending a claim other than a partnership claim under paragraph 7(2) above, give effect to the amendment by making such adjustment as may be necessary, whether–

(a) by way of assessment on the claimant, or

(b) by discharge of tax or, on proof to the satisfaction of the officer or the Board that any tax has been paid by the claimant by deduction or otherwise, by repayment of tax.

8(2) An officer of the Board or the Board shall, within 30 days after the date of issue of a closure notice amending a partnership claim under paragraph 7(2) above, give effect to the amendment, as respects each of the relevant partners, by making such adjustment as may be necessary, whether–

(a) by way of assessment on the partner, or

(b) by discharge of tax or, on proof to the satisfaction of the officer or the Board that any tax has been paid by the partner by deduction or otherwise, by repayment of tax.

8(3) An assessment made under sub-paragraph (1) or (2) above shall not be out of time if it is made within the time mentioned in that sub-paragraph.

History – In para. 8(1), the words "after the date of issue of a closure notice amending a claim other than a partnership claim under paragraph 7(2)" substituted for the words "of a claim other than a partnership claim being amended under paragraph 7(2) or (3)" and, in 8(2), the words "after the date of issue of a closure notice amending a partnership claim under paragraph 7(2)" substituted for "of a [partnership] claim being amended under paragraph 7(2) or (3)", by FA 2001, s. 88, Sch. 29, para. 34(4) and (5) respectively, with effect from 11 May 2001 in relation to returns whether made before or after that date and whether relating to periods before or after then. (The amending legislation omits the word "partnership" from the text of the original words in para. 8(2) which are to be substituted, although it is clear that it is to be replaced along with the rest of the wording.)

APPEALS AGAINST SUCH AMENDMENTS

9(1) An appeal may be brought against–

(a) any conclusion stated or amendment made by a closure notice under paragraph 7(2) above, or

(b) any decision contained in a closure notice under paragraph 7(3) above.

9(1A) Notice of the appeal must be given–

(a) in writing,

(b) within 30 days after the date on which the closure notice was issued,

(c) to the officer of the Board by whom the closure notice was given.

9(2) Where, in the case of such an appeal, the issues arising include–

(a) any question arising under section 278 of the principal Act or section 56 or 460 of ITA 2007 (residence etc of claimants);

(b) any question of residence, ordinary residence or domicile; or

(c) the question whether a fund is one to which section 615(3) of the principal Act applies (pension funds for service abroad),

the time for bringing the appeal shall be three months from the date mentioned in sub-paragraph (1A)(b) above.

9(3) In the case of an appeal against an amendment made by a closure notice under paragraph 7(2) above, if an appeal is notified to the tribunal under section 49D, 49G or 49H, the tribunal may vary the amendment appealed against whether or not the variation is to the advantage of the appellant.

9(4) Where any such amendment is varied, whether by HMRC or by the tribunal or by the order of any court, paragraph 8 above shall (with the necessary modifications) apply in relation to the variation as it applied in relation to the amendment.

9(5) If, on an appeal notified to the tribunal, the tribunal decides that a claim which was the subject of a decision contained in a closure notice under paragraph 7(3) above should have been allowed or disallowed to an extent different from that specified in the notice, the claim shall be allowed or disallowed accordingly to the extent that appears appropriate, but otherwise the decision in the notice shall stand good.

History – Para. 9(1) and (1A) substituted for former para. 9(1) by FA 2001, s. 88, Sch. 29, para. 12(2), with effect in relation to closure notices issued under para. 7 (as substituted by FA 2001, Sch. 29, para. 10).
Former para. 9(1) substituted by FA 1996, s. 133 and Sch. 19, para. 10, for the purposes of income tax and capital gains tax, as respects the year 1996–97 and subsequent years of assessment, and for the purposes of corporation tax, as respects accounting periods ending on or after 1 July 1999, the day appointed for the purposes of self-assessment by virtue of FA 1994, s. 199(2), (3) and SI 1998/3173.
In para. 9(2)(a), the words "or section 56 or 460 of ITA 2007 (residence etc of claimants)" substituted for the words "(personal reliefs for non-residents)" by ITA 2007, s. 1027 and Sch. 1, para. 264(a), with effect from 6 April 2007.
In para. 9(2)(c), the words "of the principal Act" substituted for the words "of that Act" by ITA 2007, s. 1027 and Sch. 1, para. 264(b), with effect from 6 April 2007.
In para. 9(2), "(1A)(b)" substituted for "(1)" by FA 2001, s. 88, Sch. 29, para. 12(3), with effect in relation to closure notices issued under para. 7 (as substituted by FA 2001, Sch. 29, para. 10).
Previously, in para. 9(2), the words "date mentioned in sub-paragraph (1) above" substituted for "making of the amendment under paragraph 7(3) above" by FA 1996, s. 133 and Sch. 19, para. 10, for the purposes of income tax and capital gains tax, as respects the year 1996–97 and subsequent years of assessment, and for the purposes of corporation tax, as respects accounting periods ending on or after 1 July 1999 (see note further above).
In para. 9(3) the words "In the case of" substituted for the word "On" and the words "if an appeal is notified to the tribunal under section 49D, 49G or 49H, the tribunal" substituted for the words "the Commissioners" by SI 2009/56, art. 3(1) and Sch. 1, para. 57(2), operative from 1 April 2009, subject to transitional and saving provisions in SI 2009/56, Sch. 3.
In para. 9(3) the words "amendment made by a closure notice under paragraph 7(2) above" substituted for the words "amendment under paragraph 7(3) above" by FA 2001, s. 88, Sch. 29, para. 12(4), with effect in relation to closure notices issued under para. 7 (as substituted by FA 2001, Sch. 29, para. 10).
Previously, in para. 9(3), the words "against an amendment under paragraph 7(3) above" substituted for "under this paragraph" by FA 1996, s. 133 andSch. 19, para. 10, for the purposes of income tax and capital gains tax, as respects the year 1996–97 and subsequent years of assessment, and for the purposes of corporation tax, as respects accounting periods ending on or after 1 July 1999 (see note further above).
In para. 9(4) the words "HMRC or by the tribunal" substituted for the word "the Commissioners" by SI 2009/56, art. 3(1) and Sch. 1, para. 57(3), operative from 1 April 2009, subject to transitional and saving provisions in SI 2009/56, Sch. 3.
In para. 9(4) the words "any such amendment" substituted for the words "an amendment made under paragraph 7(3) above" by FA 2001, s. 88, Sch. 29, para. 12(5), with effect in relation to closure notices issued under para. 7 (as substituted by FA 2001, Sch. 29, para. 10).
In para. 9(5) the words "an appeal notified to the tribunal, the tribunal decides" substituted for the word "appeal, it appears to the Commissioners" and the words "to them" omitted by SI 2009/56, art. 3(1) and Sch. 1, para. 57(3), operative from 1 April 2009, subject to transitional and saving provisions in SI 2009/56, Sch. 3.
In para. 9(5) the words "which was the subject of a decision contained in a closure notice under paragraph 7(3)" substituted for the words "specified in a notice under paragraph 7(3A)" by FA 2001, s. 88, Sch. 29, para. 12(6), with effect in relation to closure notices issued under para. 7 (as substituted by FA 2001, Sch. 29, para. 10).
Para. 9(5) originally inserted by FA 1996, s. 133 and Sch. 19, para. 10, for the purposes of income tax and capital gains tax, as respects the year 1996–97 and subsequent years of assessment, and for the purposes of corporation tax, as respects accounting periods ending on or after 1 July 1999 (see note further above).

10 [Omitted by SI 2009/56, art. 3(1) and Sch. 1, para. 58.]

History – Para. 10 omitted by SI 2009/56, art. 3(1) and Sch. 1, para. 58, operative from 1 April 2009, subject to transitional and saving provisions in SI 2009/56, Sch. 3.

11 [Omitted by SI 2009/56, art. 3(1) and Sch. 1, para. 58.]

History – Para. 11 omitted by SI 2009/56, art. 3(1) and Sch. 1, para. 58, operative from 1 April 2009, subject to transitional and saving provisions in SI 2009/56, Sch. 3.

SCHEDULE 1B – CLAIMS FOR RELIEF INVOLVING TWO OR MORE YEARS

Section 42

History – Sch. 1B inserted by FA 1996, s. 128 and Sch. 17, with effect as respects claims made (or deemed to be made) in relation to the year 1996–97 or later years of assessment.

Cross references – ICTA 1988, Sch. 4A (creative artists relief for fluctuating profits): two or more claims made by the same person are associated if each of them are a claim under TMA 1970, Sch. 1B or a claim under Sch. 4A. See para. 1 below.

HMRC interpretations – IRInt. 211: HMRC's view on ability to make claims for an earlier year when, under self-assessment, a carry back claim is treated as a claim for the year in which the event occurs, not that to which the carry back is made (under TMA 1970, Sch. 1B) and the earlier year is not, as a consequence, reopened.

PRELIMINARY

1(1) In this Schedule–

(a) any reference to a claim includes a reference to an election or notice; and

(b) any reference to the amount in which a person is chargeable to tax is a reference to the amount in which he is so chargeable after taking into account any relief or allowance for which a claim is made.

1(2) For the purposes of this Schedule, two or more claims made by the same person are associated with each other if each of them is a claim to which this Schedule applies and the same year of assessment is the earlier year in relation to each of those claims.

1(3) In sub-paragraph (2) above, any reference to claims includes a reference to amendments and revocations to which paragraph 4 below applies.

History – In para. 1(2), the words "is a claim to which this Schedule applies and the same" substituted for the former wording by ITTOIA 2005, s. 882(1) and Sch. 1, para. 382(1)(a); effective for income tax purposes for 2005–06 onwards (ITTOIA 2005, s. 883(1)).
In para. 1(3), the words "includes a reference to amendments and revocations to which paragraph 4 below applies." substituted for the former wording by ITTOIA 2005, s. 882(1) and Sch. 1, para. 382(1)(b); effective for income tax purposes for 2005–06 onwards (ITTOIA 2005, s. 883(1)).
Para. 1(2) and (3) substituted by FA 2001, s. 71, Sch. 24, para. 3(1) for the year 2000–01 and subsequent years of assessment.

LOSS RELIEF

2(1) This paragraph applies where a person makes a claim requiring relief for a loss incurred or treated as incurred, or a payment made, in one year of assessment (**"the later year"**) to be given in an earlier year of assessment (**"the earlier year"**).

2(2) Section 42(2) of this Act shall not apply in relation to the claim.

2(3) The claim shall relate to the later year.

2(4) Subject to sub-paragraph (5) below, the claim shall be for an amount equal to the difference between–

(a) the amount in which the person is chargeable to tax for the earlier year (**"amount A"**); and

(b) the amount in which he would be so chargeable on the assumption that effect could be, and were, given to the claim in relation to that year (**"amount B"**).

2(5) Where effect has been given to one or more associated claims, amounts A and B above shall each be determined on the assumption that effect could have been, and had been, given to the associated claim or claims in relation to the earlier year.

2(6) Effect shall be given to the claim in relation to the later year, whether by repayment or set-off, or by an increase in the aggregate amount given by section 59B(1)(b) of this Act, or otherwise.

2(7) For the purposes of this paragraph, any deduction made under section 62(2) of the 1992 Act (death: general provisions) in respect of an allowable loss shall be deemed to be made in pursuance of a claim requiring relief to be given in respect of that loss.

Cross references – ICTA 1988, s. 824(2C) (repayment supplement): application of ICTA 1988, s. 824(1) to repayment resulting from claim under para. 2.
FA 2009, Sch. 54, para. 7(a): repayment interest start date in respect of repaid following a claim under para. 2.

RELIEF FOR FLUCTUATING PROFITS OF FARMING ETC.

3(1) This paragraph applies where a person who is or has been carrying on a qualifying trade, profession or vocation (within the meaning of Chapter 16 of Part 2 of ITTOIA 2005) claims that Chapter 16 of Part 2 of ITTOIA 2005 shall have effect in relation to his profits from that trade, profession or vocation–

(a) in the case of a two-year claim, for two consecutive years of assessment, and

(b) in the case of a five-year claim, for five consecutive years of assessment.

3(2) The claim shall relate to the last of the two or five years.

3(3) Subject to sub-paragraph (4) below, in so far as the claim relates to the profits of an earlier year, the claim shall be for an amount equal to the difference between–

(a) the amount in which the person is chargeable to tax for the earlier year (**"amount A"**); and

(b) the amount in which he would be so chargeable on the assumption that effect could be, and were, given to the claim in relation to that year (**"amount B"**).

3(4) Where effect has been given to one or more associated claims, amounts A and B above shall each be determined on the assumption that effect could have been, and had been, given to the associated claim or claims in relation to the earlier year.

3(5) In so far as the claim relates to the profits of an earlier year, effect shall be given to the claim in relation to the last of the two or five years by an increase in the amount of tax payable or, as the case may require, in the aggregate amount given by section 59B(1)(b) of this Act.

3(6) Where this paragraph applies twice in relation to the same year of assessment, the increase or reduction in the amount of tax payable for that year which is required by sub-paragraph (5) above on the earlier application shall be disregarded in determining amounts A and B above for the purposes of the later application.

3(7) In this paragraph–

"two-year claim" means a claim under section 222 of ITTOIA 2005;

"five-year claim" means a claim under section 222A of ITTOIA 2005.

History – Para. 3(1)(a) and (b) substituted for the words" for two consecutive years of assessment (**"the earlier year"** and **"the later year"**)." by FA 2016, s. 25(10)(a), with effect for the tax year 2016–17 and subsequent tax years.
In para. 3(1), the words "a qualifying trade, profession or vocation (within the meaning of Chapter 16 of Part 2 of ITTOIA 2005) claims that Chapter 16 of Part 2 of ITTOIA 2005" substituted for the former words by ITTOIA 2005, s. 882(1) and Sch. 1, para. 382(3)(a); effective for income tax purposes for 2005–06 onwards (ITTOIA 2005, s. 883(1)); and the words "profession or vocation" inserted by ITTOIA 2005, s. 882(1) and Sch. 1, para. 382(3)(b); effective for income tax purposes for 2005–06 onwards (ITTOIA 2005, s. 883(1)).
In para. 3(2), the words "the last of the two or five years" substituted for the words "the later year" by FA 2016, s. 25(10)(b), with effect for the tax year 2016–17 and subsequent tax years.
In para. 3(3), the words "an earlier year" substituted for the words "the earlier year" by FA 2016, s. 25(10)(c), with effect for the tax year 2016–17 and subsequent tax years.
In para. 3(5), the words "an earlier year" substituted for the words "the earlier year" and the words "the last of the two or five years" substituted for the words "the later year" by FA 2016, s. 25(10)(d), with effect for the tax year 2016–17 and subsequent tax years.
Para. 3(7) inserted by FA 2016, s. 25(10)(e), with effect for the tax year 2016–17 and subsequent tax years.

Cross references – ICTA 1988, s. 824(2C) (repayment supplement): application of ICTA 1988, s. 824(1) to repayment resulting from claim under para. 3.

RELIEF CLAIMED BY VIRTUE OF SECTION 224(4) OF ITTOIA 2005

History – In the heading, the reference to ITTOIA 2005, s. 224(4) substituted for the former reference by ITTOIA 2005, s. 882(1) and Sch. 1, para. 382(5); effective for income tax purposes for 2005–06 onwards (ITTOIA 2005, s. 883(1)).

4(1) This paragraph applies where–

(a) a person who claims that Chapter 16 of Part 2 of ITTOIA 2005 shall have effect for two or five consecutive years of assessment makes or amends a claim for relief under any other provision of the Income Tax Acts for any of those years; and

(b) the making or amendment of the claim would be out of time but for section 224(4) of that Act.

4(2) The claim or amendment shall relate to the last of the two or five years.

4(3) Subject to sub-paragraph (4) below, in so far as the claim or amendment relates to income of an earlier year, the amount claimed, or (as the case may be) the increase or reduction in the amount claimed, shall be equal to the difference between–

(a) the amount in which the person is chargeable to tax for the earlier year (**"amount A"**); and

(b) the amount in which he would be so chargeable on the assumption that effect could be, and were, given to the claim or amendment in relation to that year (**"amount B"**).

4(4) Where effect has been given to one or more associated claims, amounts A and B above shall each be determined on the assumption that effect could have been, and had been, given to the associated claim or claims in relation to the earlier year.

4(5) In so far as the claim or amendment relates to income of an earlier year, effect shall be given to the claim or amendment in relation to the last of the two or five years by an increase in the amount of tax payable or, as the case may require, in the aggregate amount given by section 59B(1)(b) of this Act.

4(6) In this paragraph **"amend"** includes revoke and **"amendment"** shall be construed accordingly.

History – In para. 4(1), the words "or five" inserted, the words "("the earlier year" and "the later year")" (which appeared after the word "assessment") omitted and the word "any" substituted for the word "either" by FA 2016, s. 25(11)(a), with effect for the tax year 2016–17 and subsequent tax years.
In para. 4(1)(a), the words "claims that Chapter 16 of Part 2 of ITTOIA 2005" substituted for the former wording by ITTOIA 2005, s. 882(1) and Sch. 1, para. 382(4)(a); effective for income tax purposes for 2005–06 onwards (ITTOIA 2005, s. 883(1)).
In para. 4(1)(b), the words "section 224(4) of that Act" substituted for the former wording by ITTOIA 2005, s. 882(1) and Sch. 1, para. 382(4)(b); effective for income tax purposes for 2005–06 onwards (ITTOIA 2005, s. 883(1)).

In para. 4(2), the words "the last of the two or five years" substituted for the words "the later year" by FA 2016, s. 25(11)(b), with effect for the tax year 2016–17 and subsequent tax years.
In para. 4(3), the words "an earlier year" substituted for the words "the earlier year" by FA 2016, s. 25(11)(c), with effect for the tax year 2016–17 and subsequent tax years.
In para. 4(5), the words "an earlier year" substituted for the words "the earlier year" and the words "the last of the two or five years" substituted for the words "the later year" by FA 2016, s. 25(11)(d), with effect for the tax year 2016–17 and subsequent tax years.

CARRY-BACK OF POST-CESSATION ETC. RECEIPTS

5(1) This paragraph applies where a person who has received a sum to which section 257 of ITTOIA 2005 applies (election for carry-back) makes an election under that section requiring tax to he charged as if the sum were received on the date of cessation; and in this paragraph–

"the earlier year" means the year in which the sum is treated as received;

"the later year" means the year in which the sum is received.

5(2) The claim shall relate to the later year.

5(3) Subject to sub-paragraph (4) below, the claim shall be for an amount equal to the difference between–

(a) the amount in which the person is chargeable to tax for the earlier year (**"amount A"**); and

(b) the amount in which he would be so chargeable on the assumption that effect could be, and were, given to the claim in relation to that year (**"amount B"**).

5(4) Where effect has been given to one or more associated claims, amounts A and B above shall each be determined on the assumption that effect could have been, and had been, given to the associated claim or claims in relation to the earlier year.

5(5) In computing amount B for the purposes of this paragraph, no further deduction or relief shall be made or given in respect of any loss or allowance deducted in pursuance of section 254 of ITTOIA 2005.

5(6) Effect shall be given to the claim in relation to the later year by an increase in the amount of tax payable.

History – In para. 5(1), the reference to ITTOIA 2005, s. 254 substituted for the former reference to ICTA 1988, s. 108 and the words "the date of the cessation" substituted for the previous wording by ITTOIA 2005, s. 882(1) and Sch. 1, para. 382(6)(a); effective for income tax purposes for 2005–06 onwards (ITTOIA 2005, s. 883(1)).
In para. 5(5), the reference to ITTOIA 2005, s. 254 substituted for the former reference to ICTA 1988, s. 105 by ITTOIA 2005, s. 882(1) and Sch. 1, para. 382(6)(b); effective for income tax purposes for 2005–06 onwards (ITTOIA 2005, s. 883(1)).

BACKWARD SPREADING OF CERTAIN PAYMENTS

6 [Repealed by FA 2001, s. 110 and Sch. 33, Pt. 2(6).]

History – Para. 6 repealed by FA 2001, s. 110 and Sch. 33, Pt. 2(6) with effect in relation to payments actually receivable on or after 6 April 2001.

SCHEDULE 2 – JURISDICTION IN APPEALS ON CLAIMS

Section 42

[Repealed by FA 1996, s. 136 and Sch. 22, para. 6]

History – Sch. 2 repealed by FA 1996, s. 136 and Sch. 22, para. 6, s. 205 and Sch. 41, Pt. V(12), with effect in relation to any proceedings relating to the year 1996–97 or any subsequent year of assessment, and any proceedings relating to an accounting period ending on or after 1 July 1999, the appointed day for the purposes of corporation tax self-assessment by virtue of FA 1994, s. 199(2), (3) and SI 1998/3173 (C. 78).

SCHEDULE 3 – RULES FOR ASSIGNING PROCEEDINGS TO GENERAL COMMISSIONERS

Section 44

[Omitted by SI 2009/56, art. 3(1) and Sch. 1, para. 59.]

History – Sch. 3 omitted by SI 2009/56, art. 3(1) and Sch. 1, para. 59, operative from 1 April 2009, subject to transitional and saving provisions in SI 2009/56, Sch. 3.

SCHEDULE 3ZA – DATE BY WHICH PAYMENT TO BE MADE AFTER AMENDMENT OR CORRECTION OF SELF-ASSESSMENT

History – Sch. 3ZA inserted by FA 2001, s. 88, Sch. 29, para. 15 with application where the "relevant day" is, or is after, 11 May 2001 (the "relevant day" being the first day of the period of 30 days specified in the relevant provision of Sch. 3ZA – i.e. the period beginning with the day on which the appropriate notice was given).

Cross references – FA 2001, s. 88, Sch. 29, para. 16(2): definition of "relevant day" for commencement of application of Sch. 3ZA.

GENERAL

1(1) This Schedule specifies the day by which tax has to be paid (or repaid) following the amendment or correction of a self-assessment or an advance self-assessment (see section 12ZE(1)).

1(2) If in any case the general rules in section 59AA(2) or 59B(3) and (4) of this Act give a later day, those rules apply instead.

1(3) The provisions of this Schedule have effect subject to section 55(6) and (9) of this Act (provisions as to postponement of payment, etc. in case of appeal).

History – In para. 1(1), the words "or an advance self-assessment (see section 12ZE(1))" inserted by FA 2015, s. 37 and Sch. 7, para. 55(2)(a), with effect in relation to disposals made on or after 6 April 2015.
In para. 1(2), the words "59AA(2) or" inserted by FA 2015, s. 37 and Sch. 7, para. 55(2)(b), with effect in relation to disposals made on or after 6 April 2015.

AMENDMENT OF PERSONAL OR TRUSTEE RETURN BY THE TAXPAYER

2(1) This paragraph applies where an amount of tax is payable or repayable as a result of the amendment of a self-assessment under section 9ZA of this Act (amendment of personal or trustee return by taxpayer) or an amendment of an advance self-assessment under section 12ZK (amendment of NRCGT return by taxpayer).

2(2) Subject to sub-paragraph (3) below, the amount is payable (or repayable) on or before the day following the end of the period of 30 days beginning with the day on which the notice of amendment was given.

2(3) If section 9B(3) or 12ZN(3) of this Act applies (amendment of self-assessment or advance self-assessment by taxpayer during enquiry: deferral of effect), then–

(a) if the amendment is taken into account as mentioned in paragraph (a)(i) of that subsection, paragraph 5 below (amendment of personal or trustee return by closure notice) applies accordingly; and

(b) if the amendment takes effect under paragraph (b) of that subsection on the issue of the closure notice, the amount is payable (or repayable) on or before the day following the end of the period of 30 days beginning with the day on which the closure notice was given.

History – In para. 2(1), the words "or an amendment of an advance self-assessment under section 12ZK (amendment of NRCGT return by taxpayer)" inserted by FA 2015, s. 37 and Sch. 7, para. 55(3)(a), with effect in relation to disposals made on or after 6 April 2015.
In para. 2(3), the words "or 12ZN(3)" and the words "or advance self-assessment" inserted by FA 2015, s. 37 and Sch. 7, para. 55(3)(b), with effect in relation to disposals made on or after 6 April 2015.

CORRECTION OF PERSONAL OR TRUSTEE RETURN BY REVENUE

3(1) This paragraph applies where an amount of tax is payable or repayable as a result of the correction of a self-assessment under section 9ZB or 12ZL of this Act (correction of personal or trustee return or NRCGT return by the Revenue).

3(2) The amount is payable (or repayable) on or before the day following the end of the period of 30 days beginning with the day on which the notice of correction was given.

History – In para. 3(1), the words "or 12ZL" and the words "or NRCGT return" inserted by FA 2015, s. 37 and Sch. 7, para. 55(4), with effect in relation to disposals made on or after 6 April 2015.

AMENDMENT OF PERSONAL OR TRUSTEE RETURN TO PREVENT LOSS OF TAX

4(1) This paragraph applies where an amount of tax is payable or repayable as a result of the amendment of a self-assessment under section 9C of this Act (amendment of personal or trustee return by Revenue to prevent loss of tax).

4(2) The amount is payable (or repayable) on or before the day following the end of the period of 30 days beginning with the day on which the notice of amendment was given.

AMENDMENT OF PERSONAL OR TRUSTEE RETURN BY CLOSURE NOTICE

5(1) This paragraph applies where an amount of tax or an amount on account of capital gains tax is payable or repayable as a result of the amendment of a self-assessment or advance self-assessment under section 28A of this Act (amendment of return by closure notice following enquiry).

5(2) The amount is payable (or repayable) on or before the day following the end of the period of 30 days beginning with the day on which the closure notice was given.

History – In para. 5(1), the words "or an amount on account of capital gains tax" and the words "or advance self-assessment" inserted and the words "personal or trustee" (which appeared before the word "return") by FA 2015, s. 37 and Sch. 7, para. 55(5), with effect in relation to disposals made on or after 6 April 2015.

AMENDMENT CONSEQUENTIAL ON AMENDMENT OF PARTNERSHIP RETURN BY TAXPAYER

6(1) This paragraph applies where an amount of tax is payable or repayable as a result of the amendment of a self-assessment under section 12ABA(3)(a) of this Act (consequential amendment of partner's personal or trustee return where partnership return amended by taxpayer).

6(2) The amount is payable (or repayable) on or before the day following the end of the period of 30 days beginning with the day on which the notice under section 12ABA(3)(a) of this Act was given.

AMENDMENT CONSEQUENTIAL ON CORRECTION OF PARTNERSHIP RETURN BY REVENUE

7(1) This paragraph applies where an amount of tax is payable or repayable as a result of the amendment of a self-assessment under section 12ABB(6)(a) of this Act (consequential amendment of partner's personal or trustee return where partnership return corrected by Revenue).

7(2) The amount is payable (or repayable) on or before the day following the end of the period of 30 days beginning with the day on which the notice under section 12ABB(6)(a) of this Act was given.

AMENDMENT CONSEQUENTIAL ON AMENDMENT OF PARTNERSHIP RETURN BY CLOSURE NOTICE

8(1) This paragraph applies where an amount of tax is payable or repayable as a result of the amendment of a self-assessment under section 28B(4)(a) of this Act (consequential amendment of partner's personal or trustee return where partnership return amended by closure notice).

8(2) The amount is payable (or repayable) on or before the day following the end of the period of 30 days beginning with the day on which the notice under section 28B(4)(a) of this Act was given.

AMENDMENT CONSEQUENTIAL ON AMENDMENT OF PARTNERSHIP RETURN TO PREVENT LOSS OF TAX

9(1) This paragraph applies where an amount of tax is payable or repayable as a result of the amendment of a self-assessment under section 30B(2)(a) of this Act (consequential amendment of partner's personal or trustee return where partnership return amended by Revenue to prevent loss of tax).

9(2) The amount is payable (or repayable) on or before the day following the end of the period of 30 days beginning with the day on which the notice under section 30B(2)(a) of this Act was given.

AMENDMENT CONSEQUENTIAL ON AMENDMENT OF PARTNERSHIP RETURN BY WAY OF ERROR OR MISTAKE RELIEF

10 [Omitted by FA 2009, s. 100 and Sch. 52, para. 8.]

History – Para. 10 omitted by FA 2009, s. 100 and Sch. 52, para. 8 with effect in relation to claims made on or after 1 April 2010.

AMENDMENT CONSEQUENTIAL ON REDUCTION OR INCREASE ON APPEAL OF AMOUNTS STATED IN PARTNERSHIP STATEMENT

11(1) This paragraph applies where an amount of tax is payable or repayable as a result of the amendment of a self-assessment under section 50(9)(a) of this Act (consequential amendment of partner's personal or trustee return where partnership statement amended by Revenue following decision on appeal).

11(2) The amount is payable (or repayable) on or before the day following the end of the period of 30 days beginning with the day on which the notice under section 50(9)(a) of this Act was given.

SCHEDULE 3ZB – EXIT CHARGE PAYMENT PLANS

History – Sch. 3ZB inserted by FA 2013, s. 229 and Sch. 49, para. 6, with effect from 11 December 2012 in relation to an accounting period if the relevant day, in relation to that period, falls on or after 11 December 2012 (subject to provisions of FA 2013, Sch. 49, para. 8(2) and (3)).

Part 1 – Company Ceasing to Be Resident in UK

CIRCUMSTANCES IN WHICH EXIT CHARGE PAYMENT PLAN MAY BE ENTERED INTO

1(1) This Part of this Schedule and Part 3 of this Schedule apply where an eligible company–

(a) ceases to be resident in the United Kingdom,

(b) on ceasing to be so resident, becomes resident in another EEA state, and

(c) is liable to pay qualifying corporation tax in respect of the migration accounting period.

1(2) The company may defer payment of some or all of the qualifying corporation tax if it enters into an exit charge payment plan in respect of it in accordance with this Schedule.

1(3) The company may enter into an exit charge payment plan only if conditions A to C are met.

1(4) Condition A is that before the end of the period of 9 months beginning immediately after the migration accounting period–

(a) an application to enter into the exit charge payment plan is made to Her Majesty's Revenue and Customs, and

(b) the application contains details of all the matters which are required by Part 3 of this Schedule to be specified in the plan.

1(5) Condition B is that on ceasing to be resident in the United Kingdom, the company carries on a business in an EEA state.

1(6) Condition C is that, on becoming resident in the other EEA state, the company is not treated as resident in a territory outside the European Economic Area for the purposes of any double taxation arrangements.

1(7) In this paragraph–

"double taxation arrangements" means arrangements which are made by two or more territories with a view to affording relief from double taxation and which have effect at the time when the company ceases to be resident in the United Kingdom;

"eligible company" means a company that has a right to freedom of establishment protected by Article 49 of the Treaty on the functioning of the European Union or established by Article 31 of the Agreement on the European Economic Area.

1(8) In this Part of this Schedule–

(a) references to the migration accounting period are to–

  (i) in a case where an accounting period comes to an end on the company ceasing to be resident in the United Kingdom, that accounting period, and

  (ii) in a case not falling within sub-paragraph (i), the accounting period during which the company ceases to be resident in the United Kingdom,

(b) references to a Part 1 company are to a company in relation to which this Part of this Schedule applies, and

(c) references to Part 3 of this Schedule are to Part 3 of this Schedule as it applies to a Part 1 company.

QUALIFYING CORPORATION TAX

2(1) The company is liable to pay qualifying corporation tax in respect of the migration accounting period if CT1 is greater than CT2 where–

CT1 is the corporation tax which the company is liable to pay for the accounting period, and

CT2 is the corporation tax which the company would be liable to pay for the accounting period if any income, profits, gains, losses or debits arising only by virtue of the exit charge provisions were ignored,

(CT2 will be zero if the company would not be liable to pay any corporation tax for the period).

2(2) The amount of qualifying corporation tax which the company is liable to pay is the difference between CT1 and CT2.

2(3) **"Exit charge provisions"** means–

(a) section 185 of the 1992 Act,

(b) section 187(4) of that Act, where that subsection applies by virtue of section 187(4)(c),

(c) section 162 of CTA 2009, where that section applies by virtue of section 41(2)(b) of that Act,

(d) section 333 of that Act,

(e) section 609 of that Act,

(f) section 859 of that Act, where that section applies by virtue of section 859(2)(a), and

(g) section 862 of that Act, where that section applies by virtue of section 862(1)(c).

2(4) References in this Part of this Schedule and Part 3 of this Schedule to qualifying corporation tax are to be read in accordance with this paragraph.

INTERPRETATION: EXIT CHARGE ASSETS AND LIABILITIES

3(1) This paragraph applies for the purposes of this Part of this Schedule and Part 3 of this Schedule.

3(2) **"Exit charge assets"** and **"exit charge liabilities"** means assets or liabilities (as the case may be) in respect of which income, profits or gains arise in the migration accounting period by virtue of the exit charge provisions, and in particular–

(a) **"TCGA or trading stock exit charge assets"** means those exit charge assets, other than pre-FA 2002 intangible fixed assets, in respect of which income, profits or gains arise by virtue of the exit charge provision mentioned in paragraph 2(3)(a), (b) or (c),

(b) **"financial exit charge assets or liabilities"** means those exit charge assets or liabilities in respect of which income, profits or gains arise by virtue of the exit charge provision mentioned in paragraph 2(3)(d) or (e),

(c) **"intangible exit charge assets"** means–

   (i) those exit charge assets in respect of which income, profits or gains arise by virtue of the exit charge provision mentioned in paragraph 2(3)(f) or (g), and

   (ii) those exit charge assets which are pre-FA 2002 intangible fixed assets in respect of which income, profits or gains arise by virtue of the exit charge provision mentioned in paragraph 2(3)(a) or (b).

3(3) In sub-paragraph (2)–

(a) **"exit charge provisions"** has the meaning given in paragraph 2(3);

(b) **"pre-FA 2002 intangible fixed asset"** means an intangible fixed asset which is a pre-FA 2002 asset (as defined in section 881 of CTA 2009).

Part 2 – Non-UK Resident Companies with UK Permanent Establishments

CIRCUMSTANCES IN WHICH EXIT CHARGE PAYMENT PLAN MAY BE ENTERED INTO

4(1) This Part of this Schedule and Part 3 of this Schedule apply where–

(a) at any time during an accounting period ("the migration accounting period") an eligible company which is not resident in the United Kingdom carries on a trade in the United Kingdom through a permanent establishment there,

(b) one or more PE qualifying events occurs in respect of any assets or liabilities of the company as mentioned in sub-paragraph (4), and

(c) the company is liable to pay qualifying corporation tax in respect of the migration accounting period.

4(2) The company may defer payment of some or all of the qualifying corporation tax if it enters into an exit charge payment plan in respect of it in accordance with this Schedule.

4(3) The company may enter into an exit charge payment plan only if before the end of the period of 9 months beginning immediately after the migration accounting period–

(a) an application to enter into the exit charge payment plan is made to Her Majesty's Revenue and Customs, and

(b) the application contains details of all the matters which are required by Part 3 of this Schedule to be specified in the plan.

4(4) For the purposes of this Part of this Schedule, a "PE qualifying event" occurs in respect of an asset or liability of a company if–

(a) an event occurs which triggers–

   (i) a deemed disposal and reacquisition of the asset or liability under the exit charge provision mentioned in paragraph 5(3)(a), (c), (d) or (e), or

   (ii) a valuation of the asset under the exit charge provision mentioned in paragraph 5(3)(b),

(b) the event–
  (i) occurs during the migration accounting period, or
  (ii) causes the migration accounting period to come to an end, and
(c) at the time of the event, the company is not treated as resident in a territory outside the European Economic Area for the purposes of any double taxation arrangements.

4(5) In this Part of this Schedule, references to a PE qualifying asset or liability are to an asset or liability in respect of which a PE qualifying event occurs.

4(6) In this paragraph **"double taxation arrangements"** and **"eligible company"** have the meanings given in paragraph 1(7).

4(7) In this Part of this Schedule–
(a) references to the migration accounting period are to be read in accordance with this paragraph;
(b) references to a Part 2 company are to a company in relation to which this Part of this Schedule applies,
(c) references to Part 3 of this Schedule are to Part 3 of this Schedule as it applies to a Part 2 company, and
(d) **"permanent establishment"**, in relation to a company, is to be read in accordance with Chapter 2 of Part 24 of CTA 2010.

QUALIFYING CORPORATION TAX

5(1) The company is liable to pay qualifying corporation tax in respect of the migration accounting period if CT1 is greater than CT2 where–

CT1 is the corporation tax which the company is liable to pay for the accounting period, and

CT2 is the corporation tax which the company would be liable to pay for the accounting period if any income, profits, gains, losses or debits arising as a result of any PE qualifying events, and arising only by virtue of the exit charge provisions, were ignored,

(CT2 will be zero if the company would not be liable to pay any corporation tax for the period).

5(2) The amount of qualifying corporation tax which the company is liable to pay is the difference between CT1 and CT2.

5(3) Exit charge provisions means–
(a) section 25 of the 1992 Act,
(b) section 162 of CTA 2009, where that section applies by virtue of section 41(2)(b) of that Act,
(c) section 334 of that Act,
(d) section 610 of that Act, and
(e) section 859 of that Act, where that section applies by virtue of section 859(2)(b).

5(4) References in this Part of this Schedule and Part 3 of this Schedule to qualifying corporation tax are to be read in accordance with this paragraph.

INTERPRETATION: EXIT CHARGE ASSETS AND LIABILITIES

6(1) This paragraph applies for the purposes of this Part of this Schedule and Part 3 of this Schedule.

6(2) **"Exit charge assets"** and **"exit charge liabilities"** means any PE qualifying assets or liabilities (as the case may be) in respect of which income, profits or gains arise in the migration accounting period by virtue of the exit charge provisions, and in particular–
(a) **"TCGA or trading stock exit charge assets"** means those exit charge assets, other than pre-FA 2002 intangible fixed assets, in respect of which income, profits or gains arise by virtue of the exit charge provision mentioned in paragraph 5(3)(a) or (b);
(b) **"financial exit charge assets or liabilities"** means those exit charge assets or liabilities in respect of which income, profits or gains arise by virtue of the exit charge provision mentioned in paragraph 5(3)(c) or (d);
(c) **"intangible exit charge assets"** means–
  (i) those exit charge assets in respect of which income, profits or gains arise by virtue of the exit charge provision mentioned in paragraph 5(3)(e), and
  (ii) those exit charge assets which are pre-FA 2002 intangible fixed assets in respect of which income, profits or gains arise by virtue of the exit charge provision mentioned in paragraph 5(3)(a).

6(3) In sub-paragraph (2)–

(a) **"exit charge provisions"** has the meaning given in paragraph 5(3);

(b) **"pre-FA 2002 intangible fixed asset"** means an intangible fixed asset which is a pre-FA 2002 asset (as defined in section 881 of CTA 2009).

Part 3 – Entering into an Exit Charge Payment Plan

INTRODUCTION

7(1) As to when this Part of this Schedule applies, see–

(a) Part 1 of this Schedule (companies ceasing to be resident in the United Kingdom), and

(b) Part 2 of this Schedule (companies with permanent establishments in the United Kingdom).

7(2) In this Part of this Schedule, as it applies to a company in relation to which Part 1 of this Schedule applies, terms and expressions which are used in this Part and in that Part have the same meanings in this Part as in that Part.

7(3) In this Part of this Schedule, as it applies to a company in relation to which Part 2 of this Schedule applies, terms and expressions which are used in this Part and in that Part have the same meanings in this Part as in that Part.

ENTERING INTO AN EXIT CHARGE PAYMENT PLAN

8(1) A Part 1 company or a Part 2 company enters into an exit charge payment plan in respect of qualifying corporation tax in accordance with this Schedule if–

(a) the company agrees to pay, and an officer of Revenue and Customs agrees to accept payment of, the tax in accordance with the standard instalment method (see paragraph 13) or the realisation method (see paragraphs 14 to 17) or a combination of the two methods,

(b) the company agrees to pay interest on the tax in accordance with paragraph 9(3), and

(c) the plan meets the requirements set out in paragraphs 10 to 12 as to the matters that must be specified in it.

8(2) The exit charge payment plan may, in the circumstances mentioned in sub-paragraph (3), contain appropriate provision regarding security for Her Majesty's Revenue and Customs in respect of the deferred payment of the tax.

8(3) Those circumstances are where an officer of Her Majesty's Revenue and Customs considers that agreeing to accept payment of qualifying corporation tax in accordance with the plan would present a serious risk as to collection of the tax in the absence of provision regarding security in respect of that tax.

8(4) An exit charge payment plan is void if any information furnished by the company in connection with the plan does not fully and accurately disclose all facts and considerations material to the decision of the officer of Revenue and Customs to accept payment of qualifying corporation tax in accordance with the plan.

EFFECT OF EXIT CHARGE PAYMENT PLAN

9(1) This paragraph applies where an exit charge payment plan is entered into by a company in respect of qualifying corporation tax in accordance with this Schedule.

9(2) As regards when the tax is payable–

(a) the plan does not prevent the tax becoming due and payable under section 59D or 59E, but

(b) the Commissioners for Her Majesty's Revenue and Customs–

(i) may not seek payment of the tax otherwise than in accordance with the plan;

(ii) may make repayments in respect of any amount of the tax paid, or any amount paid on account of the tax, before the plan is entered into.

9(3) As regards interest–

(a) the tax carries interest in accordance with Part 9 as if the plan had not been entered into, and

(b) each time a payment is made under the plan, it is to be paid together with any interest payable on it.

9(4) As regards penalties, the company will be liable to penalties for late payment of the tax only if it fails to make payments in accordance with the plan (see item 6ZA of the Table at the end of paragraph 1 of Schedule 56 to the Finance Act 2009).

9(5) Qualifying corporation tax payable in accordance with an exit charge payment plan which is for the time being unpaid may be paid at any time before it becomes payable under the plan together with interest payable on it to the date of payment.

CONTENT OF EXIT CHARGE PAYMENT PLAN

10(1) An exit charge payment plan entered into by a Part 1 company must specify–

(a) the date on which the company ceased to be resident in the United Kingdom, and

(b) the EEA state in which the company has become resident.

10(2) An exit charge payment plan entered into by a Part 2 company must specify–

(a) the EEA state in which the company is resident, and

(b) if the company has ceased to carry on a trade in the United Kingdom through a permanent establishment there, the date on which it ceased to do so.

10(3) In either case an exit charge payment plan entered into by a company must also specify–

(a) the amount of qualifying corporation tax which, in the company's opinion, is payable by it in respect of the migration accounting period,

(b) the amount of that qualifying corporation tax which the company wishes to defer paying under the exit charge payment plan ("ECPP tax"), and

(c) whether the ECPP tax is to be paid in accordance with–

 (i) the standard instalment method (see paragraph 13),

 (ii) the realisation method (see paragraphs 14 to 17), or

 (iii) a combination of the two methods.

10(4) If the ECPP tax is to be paid in accordance with a combination of the two methods, the exit charge payment plan must also specify–

(a) in the case of each of the company's exit charge assets or liabilities (see paragraphs 3(2) or 6(2), as the case may be), the method in accordance with which the amount of ECPP tax attributable to the asset or liability (see sub-paragraph (6)) is to be paid, and

(b) the amount of the ECPP tax specified under sub-paragraph (3)(b) that is to be paid in accordance with each method.

10(5) But an exit charge payment plan may specify that any ECPP tax is to be paid in accordance with the standard instalment method only if–

(a) in the case of a plan entered into by a Part 1 company, the company's ceasing to be resident in the United Kingdom is not part of arrangements the main purpose of which, or one of the main purposes of which, is to defer the payment of any qualifying corporation tax payable by it;

(b) in the case of a plan entered into by a Part 2 company, none of the PE qualifying events occurring during the migration accounting period, or bringing that period to an end, is part of arrangements the main purpose of which, or one of the main purposes of which, is to defer the payment of any qualifying corporation tax payable by it.

10(6) The amount of ECPP tax attributable to each exit charge asset or liability is–

$$\frac{A}{B} \times T$$

where–

"A" is the income, profits or gains arising in respect of the asset or liability in the migration accounting period by virtue of the relevant exit charge provision only,

"B" is the total income, profits or gains arising in respect of all the exit charge assets and liabilities in the migration accounting period by virtue of the exit charge provisions only, and

"T" is the ECPP tax.

CONTENT: REALISATION METHOD

11(1) This paragraph applies if, under an exit charge payment plan, the amount of ECPP tax attributable to any exit charge asset or *liability* is to be paid in accordance with the realisation method.

11(2) The plan must specify–

(a) each such asset or liability (so far as not already specified under paragraph 10(4)(a)), and

(b) the amount of ECPP tax attributable to the asset or liability, calculated in accordance with paragraph 10(6).

11(3) The plan must also include requirements as to the ongoing provision of information by the company to Her Majesty's Revenue and Customs in relation to the asset or liability.

CONTENT: ADDITIONAL INFORMATION RELATING TO ASSETS AND LIABILITIES

12(1) This paragraph applies if, under an exit charge payment plan, the amount of ECPP tax attributable to an exit charge asset or liability is to be paid in accordance with the realisation method.

12(2) The plan must specify any additional information required by this paragraph in relation to the asset or liability.

12(3) Sub-paragraph (4) applies in the case of a financial exit charge asset or liability if, immediately after the migration accounting period, the remaining term of the loan relationship or derivative contract in question is less than 10 years.

12(4) The plan must specify, in relation to the asset or liability, how many years of the term of the loan relationship or derivative contract remain (rounded up to the nearest whole year).

12(5) Sub-paragraph (6) applies in the case of an intangible exit charge asset if, immediately after the migration accounting period, the remaining useful life of the asset for accountancy purposes is less than 10 years.

12(6) The plan must specify, in relation to the asset, how many years of the useful life of the asset remain (rounded up to the nearest whole year).

THE STANDARD INSTALMENT METHOD

13(1) This paragraph applies if, under an exit charge payment plan, some or all of the ECPP tax is to be paid in accordance with the standard instalment method.

13(2) The amount of the ECPP tax that is to be paid in accordance with the standard instalment method is payable in 6 instalments of equal amounts as follows–

(a) the first instalment is due on the first day after the period of 9 months beginning immediately after the migration accounting period, and

(b) the other 5 instalments are due one on each of the first 5 anniversaries of that day.

13(3) But if a relevant event occurs, the outstanding balance of the ECPP tax that is payable in accordance with the standard instalment method is payable on the date on which the next instalment of that tax would otherwise have been due under the plan.

13(4) A **"relevant event"** means–

(a) the company becoming insolvent or entering into administration,

(b) the appointment of a liquidator,

(c) any event under the law of an EEA state outside the United Kingdom corresponding to an event specified in paragraph (a) or (b), or

(d) the company ceasing to be resident in an EEA state and, on so ceasing, not becoming resident in any other EEA state.

THE REALISATION METHOD: TCGA OR TRADING STOCK EXIT CHARGE ASSETS

14(1) This paragraph applies if–

(a) under an exit charge payment plan, the amount of ECPP tax attributable to an exit charge asset is to be paid in accordance with the realisation method, and

(b) the asset is a TCGA or trading stock exit charge asset (see paragraph 3(2)(a) or 6(2)(a), as the case may be).

14(2) The amount of ECPP tax attributable to the asset under paragraph 10(6) is payable in relation to whichever is the first to occur of the following events–

(a) the disposal of that asset at any time after–

  (i) the company ceases to be resident in the United Kingdom (in the case of a Part 1 company), or

  (ii) the occurrence of the PE qualifying event in respect of the asset (in the case of a Part 2 company),

(b) the tenth anniversary of the end of the migration accounting period, or

(c) a relevant event (as defined in paragraph 13(4)).

14(3) The date on which the amount is payable is–

(a) in a case falling within sub-paragraph (2)(a) or (b), the date of the event referred to, and

(b) in a case falling within sub-paragraph (2)(c), the relevant date or, if that date has already passed, the next anniversary of that date.

14(4) In sub-paragraph (3)(b), **"relevant date"** means the first day after the period of 9 months beginning immediately after the migration accounting period.

14(5) Section 21(2) of the 1992 Act (part disposals of assets) applies for the purposes of sub-paragraph (2)(a) as it applies for the purposes of that Act.

14(6) Where part of an asset is disposed of at any time after the event mentioned in sub-paragraph (2)(a), the amount of ECPP tax attributable to the asset under paragraph 10(6) is to be apportioned on a just and reasonable basis for the purpose of applying this paragraph to the part of the asset disposed of and the part which remains undisposed of.

THE REALISATION METHOD: OTHER EXIT CHARGE ASSETS AND LIABILITIES

15(1) This paragraph applies if–

(a) under an exit charge payment plan, the ECPP tax attributable to an exit charge asset or liability is to be paid in accordance with the realisation method, and

(b) the asset or liability is–

  (i) a financial exit charge asset or liability, or

  (ii) an intangible exit charge asset,

(see paragraph 3(2)(b) and (c) or 6(2)(b) and (c), as the case may be).

15(2) The amount of ECPP tax attributable to any such asset or liability under paragraph 10(6) is payable in a number of annual instalments of equal amounts.

15(3) The number of annual instalments is–

(a) in a case where a number of years is specified in the plan in relation to the asset or liability by virtue of paragraph 12(4) or (6), that number, and

(b) otherwise, 10.

15(4) The instalments are due as follows–

(a) the first instalment is due on the first day after the period of 9 months beginning immediately after the migration accounting period, and

(b) the other instalments are due one on each of the subsequent anniversaries of that day (until they are all paid).

15(5) But see paragraphs 16 and 17 for circumstances in which all or part of the outstanding balance of the amount of ECPP tax attributable to the asset or liability under paragraph 10(6) ("the outstanding balance in respect of the asset or liability") becomes payable.

OUTSTANDING BALANCE BECOMING PAYABLE IN FULL

16(1) This paragraph applies where the amount of ECPP tax attributable to an asset or liability under paragraph 10(6) is payable in instalments in accordance with paragraph 15.

16(2) All of the outstanding balance in respect of the asset or liability (as defined in paragraph 15(5)) is payable in accordance with sub-paragraph (3) if–

(a) a trigger event occurs in relation to the asset or liability (see sub-paragraph (4)), or

(b) a relevant event occurs (as defined in paragraph 13(4)),

before the last instalment is payable in accordance with paragraph 15.

16(3) The outstanding balance is payable–

(a) in a case falling within sub-paragraph (2)(a), on the date of the trigger event, and

(b) in a case falling within sub-paragraph (2)(b), on the date on which the next instalment would otherwise have been due under the plan.

16(4) For the purposes of this paragraph, a trigger event occurs in relation to an asset or liability if–

(a) in the case of a financial exit charge asset or liability, the company ceases to be party to the loan relationship or derivative contract in question, or

(b) in the case of an intangible fixed asset, the asset is disposed of.

OUTSTANDING BALANCE BECOMING PAYABLE IN PART

17(1) This paragraph applies where–

(a) the amount of ECPP tax attributable to an asset or liability under paragraph 1C(6) is payable in instalments in accordance with paragraph 15, and

(b) a partial trigger event occurs in relation to the asset or liability (see sub-paragraph (4)) before the last instalment is payable.

17(2) On the occurrence of that event, part of the outstanding balance in respect of the asset or liability (as defined in paragraph 15(5)) is payable.

17(3) The part payable under sub-paragraph (2) is so much of the outstanding balance in respect of the asset or liability as is attributable to the transaction mentioned in sub-paragraph (4)(a) or (b).

17(4) For the purposes of sub-paragraph (2), a partial trigger event occurs in relation to an asset or liability if–

(a) in the case of a financial exit charge asset or liability–

(i) there is a disposal of rights or liabilities under the loan relationship or derivative contract in question which amounts to a related transaction (as defined in section 304 or 596 of CTA 2009 as the case may be), but

(ii) the transaction does not result in the company ceasing to be party to the relationship or contract, and

(b) in the case of an intangible exit charge asset, there is a transaction which–

(i) results in a reduction in the accounting value of the asset, but

(ii) does not result in the asset ceasing to be recognised in the company's balance sheet.

17(5) Where part of the outstanding balance in respect of an asset or liability is paid in accordance with sub-paragraphs (2) and (3), the remaining instalments due under paragraph 15 in respect of the asset or liability continue to be payable so far as they relate to the remaining asset or liability (subject to paragraph 16 and this paragraph).

17(6) In sub-paragraph (5), the **"remaining asset or liability"** means–

(a) in a case within sub-paragraph (4)(a), the loan relationship or derivative contract as it exists following the related transaction,

(b) in a case within sub-paragraph (4)(b), the asset as it continues to be recognised on the balance sheet following the transaction mentioned in that sub-paragraph.

17(7) For the purposes of sub-paragraphs (3) and (5)–

(a) the outstanding balance in respect of the asset or liability, and

(b) the remaining instalments due under paragraph 15 in respect of the asset or liability,

are to be apportioned on a just and reasonable basis between the transaction mentioned in sub-paragraph (4) (a) or (b) and the remaining asset or liability.

17(8) In relation to an intangible exit charge asset that has no balance sheet value (or no longer has a balance sheet value), sub-paragraph (4)(b) applies as if, immediately before the transaction, it did have a balance sheet value.

SCHEDULE 3A – ELECTRONIC LODGEMENT OF TAX RETURNS, ETC.

Section 115A

Prospective amendments – Sch. 3A repealed by FA 1999, s. 133(3), 139 and Sch. 20, Pt. VII, with effect from a date or dates to be appointed under FA 1999, s. 133(4).

History – Sch. 3A inserted by FA 1995, s. 153 and Sch. 28, para. 2.

Statements of practice – SP 1/97: the electronic lodgment service.

Other material – HMRC Press Release 26 September 2005; electronic lodgement service withdrawn from 31 March 2006.

Part I – Tax Returns: General

THE BASIC RULE

1(1) Sub-paragraph (2) below applies where a person is–

(a) required by a notice to which this Schedule applies, or

(b) subject to any other requirement to which this Schedule applies,

to deliver or make a return to an officer of the Board or to the Board.

1(2) The requirement to deliver or make the return shall be treated as fulfilled by the person subject to the requirement if–

(a) information is transmitted electronically in response to that requirement; and

(b) each of the conditions in Part III of this Schedule is met with respect to that transmission.

1(3) Sub-paragraphs (4) and (5) below apply where the requirement to deliver or make the return is fulfilled by virtue of sub-paragraph (2) above.

1(4) Any requirement–

(a) under any provision of Part II of this Act or Schedule 18 to the Finance Act 1998, that the return include a declaration by the person making the return to the effect that the return is to the best of his knowledge correct or complete, or–

(b) under or by virtue of any other provision of the Taxes Acts that the return be signed or include any description of declaration or certificate,

shall not apply.

1(5) The time at which the requirement to deliver or make the return is fulfilled is the end of the day during which the last of the conditions in Part III of this Schedule to be met with respect to the transmission is met.

1(6) In sub-paragraph (2)(a) above **"information"** includes any self-assessment, partnership statement, particulars or claim.

History – Para. 1(4)(a) amended by inserting the words "or Schedule 18 to the Finance Act 1998", by FA 1998, s. 117(3) and Sch. 19, para. 43(2) with effect in relation to company accounting periods ending on or after 1 July 1999, the corporation tax self-assessment appointed day by virtue of FA 1994, s. 199(2), (3) and SI 1998/3173 (C. 78).

RETURNS TO WHICH SCHEDULE APPLIES

2(1) This Schedule applies to a notice requiring a return to be delivered or made if–

(a) the notice is given under any provision of the Taxes Acts or of regulations made under the Taxes Acts;

(b) the provision is specified for the purposes of this Schedule by an order made by the Treasury; and

(c) the notice is given after the day appointed by the order in relation to notices under the provision so specified.

2(2) This Schedule applies to any other requirement to deliver or make a return if–

(a) the requirement is imposed by any provision of the Taxes Acts or of regulations made under the Taxes Acts;

(b) the provision is specified for the purposes of this Schedule by an order made by the Treasury; and

(c) the requirement is required to be fulfilled within a period beginning after the day appointed by the order in relation to the specified provision.

2(3) The power to make an order under this paragraph shall be exercisable by statutory instrument which shall be subject to annulment in pursuance of a resolution of the House of Commons.

2(4) For the purposes of this Schedule, any reference to a requirement to deliver a return includes, in relation to regulations made under the principal Act or under ITEPA 2003 or ITTOIA 2005, a reference to a requirement to render a return.

History – In para. 2(4), the reference to ITTOIA 2005 inserted by ITTOIA 2005, s. 882(1) and Sch. 1, para. 384; effective for income tax purposes for 2005–06 onwards (ITTOIA 2005, s. 883(1)).
In para. 2(4), the words "or under ITEPA 2003" inserted by ITEPA 2003, Sch. 6, para. 143 which has effect, for income tax purposes, for the tax year 2003–04 and subsequent tax years and, for corporation tax purposes, for accounting periods ending after 5 April 2003.

Statutory instruments – SI 1997/57: appoints 1 March 1997 pursuant to para. 2(1)(c) in relation to notices requiring returns to be delivered or made under TMA 1970, s. 8, 8A, 12AA.

Part II – Documents Supporting Certain Tax Returns

3(1) This paragraph applies where–

(a) a person is required by a notice to which this Schedule applies to deliver a return to an officer of the Board;

(b) the notice also requires any document other than the return (**"a supporting document"**) to be delivered;

(c) the provision under which the notice is given requires the supporting document to be delivered with the return;

(d) the notice states that the supporting document may be transmitted electronically; and

(e) the requirement to deliver the return is fulfilled by virtue of paragraph 1(2) of this Schedule.

3(2) The requirement to deliver the supporting document shall be treated as fulfilled by the person subject to the requirement if–

(a) information is transmitted electronically in response to that requirement; and

(b) each of the conditions in Part III of this Schedule is met with respect to that transmission.

3(3) If information is not transmitted electronically in response to the requirement to deliver the supporting document, that requirement shall have effect as a requirement to deliver the document on or before the day which is the last day for the delivery of the return.

3(4) For the purposes of sub-paragraph (1)(b) above the reference to a document includes in particular a reference to any accounts, statements or reports.

3(5) Where the requirement to deliver the supporting document is fulfilled by virtue of sub-paragraph (2) above, the time at which it is fulfilled is the end of the day during which the last of the conditions in Part III of this Schedule to be met with respect to the transmission is met.

Part III – The Conditions

APPROVED PERSONS

4(1) The first condition is that the transmission must be made by a person approved by the Board.

4(2) A person seeking approval under this paragraph shall be given notice of the grant or refusal of approval.

4(3) A person may be approved for the purpose of transmitting the information–

(a) on behalf of another person or other persons; or

(b) on his own behalf.

4(4) An approval under this paragraph may be withdrawn by notice with effect from such date as may be specified in the notice.

4(5) A notice refusing or withdrawing an approval shall state the grounds for the refusal or withdrawal.

4(6) A person who is refused approval or whose approval is withdrawn may appeal against the refusal or withdrawal.

4(7) The appeal shall be made by notice given to the Board before the end of the period of 30 days beginning with the day on which notice of the refusal or withdrawal was given to the appellant.

4(8) If an appeal is notified to the tribunal under section 49D, 49G or 49H, the tribunal shall not allow the appeal unless it appears that, having regard to all the circumstances, it is unreasonable for the approval to be refused or (as the case may be) withdrawn.

4(9) If the tribunal allows an appeal by a person who has been refused approval, it shall specify the date from which the approval is to have effect.

History – In para. 4(6) the words "to the Special Commissioners" omitted by SI 2009/56, art. 3(1) and Sch. 1, para. 61(2), operative from 1 April 2009, subject to transitional and saving provisions in SI 2009/56, Sch. 3.

In para. 4(8) the words "If an appeal is notified to the tribunal under section 49D, 49G or 49H, the tribunal" substituted for the words "The Special Commissioners" and the words "to them" omitted by SI 2009/56, art. 3(1) and Sch. 1, para. 61(3), operative from 1 April 2009, subject to transitional and saving provisions in SI 2009/56, Sch. 3.

In para. 4(9) the words "tribunal allows" substituted for the words "Special Commissioners allow" and the word "it" substituted for the word "they" by SI 2009/56, art. 3(1) and Sch. 1, para. 61(4), operative from 1 April 2009, subject to transitional and saving provisions in SI 2009/56, Sch. 3.

APPROVED MANNER OF TRANSMISSION

5(1) The second condition applies if the person who makes the transmission is notified by the Board of any requirements for the time being applicable to him as to the manner in which transmissions are to be made by him or as to the manner in which any description of transmission is to be made by him.

5(2) The second condition is that the transmission must comply with the requirements so notified.

5(3) The requirements referred to include in particular requirements as to–

(a) the hardware or type of hardware, or

(b) the software or type of software,

to be used to make transmissions or a description of transmissions.

CONTENT OF TRANSMISSION

6 The third condition is that the transmission must signify, in a manner approved by the Board, that before the transmission was made a hard copy of the information proposed to be transmitted was made and authenticated in accordance with Part IV of this Schedule.

PROCEDURE FOR ACCEPTING ELECTRONIC TRANSMISSIONS

7(1) The fourth condition is that the information transmitted must be accepted for electronic lodgement.

7(2) For the purposes of this Schedule, information is accepted for electronic lodgement if it is accepted under a procedure selected by the Board for the purposes of this Schedule.

7(3) The selected procedure may in particular consist of or include the use of specially designed software.

Part IV – Hard Copies of Information Transmitted

PROVISIONS ABOUT MAKING OF HARD COPIES

8(1) A hard copy is made in accordance with this Part of this Schedule if it is made under arrangements designed to ensure that the information contained in the hard copy is the information in fact transmitted.

8(2) A hard copy is authenticated in accordance with this Part of this Schedule if–

(a) where the transmission is made in response to a requirement imposed by a notice under Part II of this Act or Schedule 18 to the Finance Act 1998 to deliver a return, the hard copy is endorsed with a declaration by the relevant person that the hard copy is to the best of his knowledge correct and complete; and

(b) in any other case, if the hard copy is signed by the relevant person.

8(3) In sub-paragraph (2) above **"the relevant person"** means–

(a) where the transmission is made as mentioned in sub-paragraph (2)(a) above, the person who, but for paragraph 1(4)(a) of this Schedule, would have been required to make the declaration there mentioned;

(b) in any other case, the person subject to the requirement to deliver or make the return or, in the case of a document other than a return, deliver the document.

History – Paragraph 8(2)(a) amended by inserting the words "or Schedule 18 to the Finance Act 1998", by FA 1998, s. 117(3) and Sch. 19, para. 43(3) with effect in relation to company accounting periods ending on or after 1 July 1999, the corporation tax self-assessment appointed day by virtue of FA 1994, s. 199(2), (3) and SI 1998/3173 (C. 78).

MEANING OF "HARD COPY"

9 In this Part of this Schedule **"hard copy"**, in relation to information held electronically, means a printed out version of that information.

Part V – Status of Information

EXERCISE OF POWERS

10(1) Sub-paragraphs (2) to (5) below apply where information transmitted in response to a requirement to deliver or make a return is accepted for electronic lodgement.

10(2) An officer of the Board shall have all the powers that he would have had if the information accepted had been contained in a return delivered by post.

10(3) The Board shall have all the powers that they would have had if the information accepted had been contained in a return delivered by post.

10(4) Where the information is transmitted in response to a notice given under any provision of Part II of this Act, any power which, if the information had been contained in a return delivered by post, a person would have had under this Act to amend the return–

(a) by delivering a document, or

(b) by notifying amendments,

to an officer of the Board, shall have effect as if the power enabled that person to deliver a statement of amended information to the officer.

10(5) Any right that a person would have had, if the information transmitted had been contained in a return delivered by post, to claim that tax charged under an assessment was excessive by reason of some mistake or error in the return shall have effect as far as the claimant is concerned as if the information transmitted had been contained in a return delivered by post.

10(6) Where information transmitted in response to a requirement to deliver a document other than a return is accepted for electronic lodgement, an officer of the Board shall have all the powers that he would have had if the information had been contained in a document delivered by post.

10(7) This paragraph is subject to paragraph 11 of this Schedule.

PROCEEDINGS

11(1) Sub-paragraphs (2) to (4) below apply where–

(a) a person is required by a notice to which this Schedule applies, or subject to any other requirement to which this Schedule applies, to deliver or make a return; and

(b) that requirement is fulfilled by virtue of paragraph 1(2) of this Schedule.

11(2) A hard copy shown to have been made and authenticated in accordance with Part IV of this Schedule for the purposes of the transmission in question shall be treated for the purposes of any proceedings as if it were a return delivered or made in response to the requirement.

11(3) Sub-paragraph (4) below applies if no hard copy is shown to have been made and authenticated in accordance with Part IV of this Schedule for the purposes of the transmission in question.

11(4) A hard copy certified by an officer of the Board to be a true copy of the information transmitted shall be treated for the purposes of any proceedings in relation to which the certificate is given as if it–

(a) were a return delivered or made in response to the requirement in question, and

(b) contained any declaration or signature which would have appeared on a hard copy made and authenticated in accordance with Part IV of this Schedule for the purposes of the transmission.

11(5) Where–

(a) a person is required by a notice to which this Schedule applies to deliver any document other than a return, and

(b) that requirement is fulfilled by virtue of paragraph 3(2) of this Schedule,

sub-paragraphs (2) to (4) above shall apply as if any reference to a return delivered in response to the requirement were a reference to a document delivered in response to the requirement.

11(6) In this paragraph–

"hard copy" has the same meaning as in Part IV of this Schedule; and

"proceedings" includes proceedings before any tribunal having jurisdiction by virtue of any provision of the Taxes Acts.

History – In para. 11(6) the words "the General or Special Commissioners or" omitted by SI 2009/56, art. 3(1) and Sch. 1, para. 62, operative from 1 April 2009, subject to transitional and saving provisions in SI 2009/56, Sch. 3.

FINANCE ACT 1971

(1971 Chapter 68) [*5th August 1971*]

ARRANGEMENT OF SECTIONS

PART II – INCOME TAX AND CORPORATION TAX

CHAPTER I – GENERAL

PART V – MISCELLANEOUS

SCHEDULES

PART II – INCOME TAX AND CORPORATION TAX

Chapter I – General

21 Occupational pension schemes

21 [Omitted by ITA 2007, s. 1027 and Sch. 1, para. 265 and repealed by s. 1031 and Sch. 3, Pt. 1.]

History – S. 21 omitted by ITA 2007, s. 1027 and Sch. 1, para. 265, and repealed by s. 1031 and Sch. 3, Pt. 1, with effect from 6 April 2007.

PART V – MISCELLANEOUS

69 Citation, interpretation, construction, extent and repeals

69(1) This Act may be cited as the Finance Act 1971.

69(2) In this Act **"the Taxes Act"** means the Income and Corporation Taxes Act 1988.

69(3) In this Act–

Parts II and III, so far as they relate to income tax, shall be construed as one with the Income Tax Acts and, so far as they relate to corporation tax, shall be construed as one with the Corporation Tax Acts.

69(4) Except so far as the context otherwise requires, any reference in this Act to any enactment shall be construed as a reference to that enactment as amended, and as including a reference to that enactment as applied, by or under any other enactment, including this Act.

69(5) Except as otherwise expressly provided, such of the provisions of this Act as relate to matters in respect of which the Parliament of Northern Ireland has power to make laws do not extend to Northern Ireland.

69(6) If the Parliament of Northern Ireland passes provisions amending or replacing any enactment of that Parliament referred to in this Act the reference shall be construed as a reference to the enactment as so amended or, as the case may be, as a reference to those provisions.

History – Reference to ICTA 1988 substituted by Sch. 29, para. 32 of that Act.

SCHEDULE 3 – OCCUPATIONAL PENSION SCHEMES

Section 21

Part II – Taxation of Refunds of Contributions and Certain Other Payments

SCHEMES APPROVED UNDER OLD LAW TAXATION OF REFUNDS OF CONTRIBUTIONS AND COMMUTATION PAYMENTS

[Omitted by ITA 2007, s. 1027 and Sch. 1, para. 265 and repealed by s. 1031 and Sch. 3, Pt. 1.]

History – Sch. 3 omitted by ITA 2007, s. 1027 and Sch. 1, para. 265 and repealed by s. 1031 and Sch. 3, Pt. 1, with effect from 6 April 2007.

FINANCE ACT 1972

(1972 Chapter 41) *[27th July 1972]*

ARRANGEMENT OF SECTIONS

PART VII – MISCELLANEOUS

PART VII – MISCELLANEOUS

127 Disclosure of information between revenue departments

127 [Ceased to have effect by virtue of CRCA 2005, s. 50 and Sch. 4, para. 16 and repealed by s. 52 and Sch. 5.]

History – S. 127 ceased to have effect by virtue of CRCA 2005, s. 50 and Sch. 4, para. 16 and repealed by s. 52 and Sch. 5, with effect from 18 April 2005 (by virtue of SI 2005/1126, art. 2).

Notes – See note to FA 1989, s. 182 for occasions when the Revenue may disclose personal information to Government departments etc.
FA 1969, s. 58: disclosure for statistical purposes of information regarding employment.
FA 1997, s. 110: supply of information by social security authorities to Revenue and Customs.

129 Summary award of penalties

129 [Amends TMA 1970, s. 53(1).]

130 Compensation for loss of office etc. by clerks to General Commissioners

130 [Repealed by TCEA 2007, s. 146 and Sch. 23, Pt. 1.]

History – S. 130 repealed by TCEA 2007, s. 146 and Sch. 23, Pt. 1, with effect from 1 April 2009 (SI 2008/2696, art. 6(c)(iii)).

131 Post-war credits

131 [Spent]

134 Citation, interpretation, construction, extent and repeals

134(1) This Act may be cited as the Finance Act 1972.

134(2) In this Act **"the Taxes Act"** means the Income and Corporation Taxes Act 1988.

134(3) [Not reproduced.]

134(4) Except so far as the context otherwise requires, any reference in this Act to any enactment shall be construed as a reference to that enactment as amended, and as including a reference to that enactment as applied, by or under any other enactment, including this Act.

134(5) Except as otherwise expressly provided, such of the provisions of this Act as relate to matters in respect of which the Parliament of Northern Ireland has power to make laws do not extend to Northern Ireland.

134(6) If the Parliament of Northern Ireland passes provisions amending or replacing any enactment of that Parliament referred to in this Act the reference shall be construed as a reference to the enactment as so amended or, as the case may be, as a reference to those provisions.

History – Reference to ICTA 1988 substituted by Sch. 29, para. 32 of that Act.

FINANCE ACT 1973

(1973 Chapter 51)

[*25th July 1973*]

ARRANGEMENT OF SECTIONS

PART III – INCOME TAX, CORPORATION TAX AND CAPITAL GAINS TAX

32 Information as to arrangements for transferring relief, etc.

32 [Omitted by SI 2009/2035, art. 2 and Schedule, para. 10.]

History – S. 32 omitted by SI 2009/2035, art. 2 and Schedule, para. 10, with effect from 13 August 2009.

38 Territorial extension of charge to income tax, capital gains tax and corporation tax

38 [Omitted by TIOPA 2010, s. 371 and Sch. 7, para. 7 and repealed by TIOPA 2010, s. 378 and Sch. 10, Pt. 12.]

History – Omitted by TIOPA 2010, s. 371 and Sch. 7, para. 7 and repealed by TIOPA 2010, s. 378 and Sch. 10, Pt. 12, with effect for corporation tax purposes for accounting periods ending on or after 1 April 2010, for income tax and capital gains tax purposes for the tax year 2010–11 and subsequent tax years and for petroleum revenue tax purposes for chargeable periods beginning on or after 1 July 2010.

Notes – S. 38 rewritten as follows:
S. 38(2): TIOPA 2010, Sch. 7, para. 4.

41 General Commissioners' divisions

41 [Omitted by SI 2009/56, art. 3 and Sch. 1, para. 65.]

History – S. 41 omitted by SI 2009/56, art. 3 and Sch. 1, para. 65, with effect from 1 April 2009, subject to transitional and saving provisions in SI 2009/56, Sch. 3.

PART VI – MISCELLANEOUS AND GENERAL

59 Citation, interpretation, construction, extent and repeals

59(1) This Act may be cited as the Finance Act 1973.

59(2) In this Act–

(a) **"the Taxes Act 1970"** means the Income and Corporation Taxes Act 1970; and

(b) **"the Taxes Act 1988"** means the Income and Corporation Taxes Act 1988.

59(3) In this Act–

(c) Part III, so far as it relates to income tax, shall be construed as one with the Income Tax Acts, so far as it relates to corporation tax, shall be construed as one with the Corporation Tax Acts and, so far as it relates to capital gains tax, shall be construed as one with the Capital Gains Tax Act 1979; . . .

59(4) Except so far as the context otherwise requires, any reference in this Act to any enactment shall be construed as a reference to that enactment as amended, and as including a reference to that enactment as applied, by or under any other enactment, including this Act.

59(5) Except as otherwise expressly provided, such of the provisions of this Act as relate to matters in respect of which the Parliament of Northern Ireland has power to make laws do not extend to Northern Ireland.

59(6) If the Parliament of Northern Ireland passes provisions amending or replacing any enactment of that Parliament referred to in this Act the reference shall be construed as a reference to the enactment as so amended or, as the case may be, as a reference to those provisions.

History – S. 59(2) substituted by ICTA 1988, s. 844 and Sch. 29, para. 32 to reflect the consolidation effected by the Act.
Reference to interpretation of "the additional rate" omitted by FA 1984, Sch. 7, para. 3 consequent to the repeal of provisions relating to that rate for 1984–85 and subsequent years of assessment.
In relation to tax for 1992–93 and subsequent years of assessment, reference to CGTA 1979 to be construed as a reference to TCGA 1992 (by virtue of INA 1978, s. 17(2)).

SCHEDULE 15 – TERRITORIAL EXTENSION OF CHARGE TO TAX – SUPPLEMENTARY PROVISIONS

Section 38

[Omitted by TIOPA 2010, s. 371 and Sch. 7, para. 8 and repealed by TIOPA 2010, s. 378 and Sch. 10, Pt. 12.]

History – Omitted by TIOPA 2010, s. 371 and Sch. 7, para. 8 and repealed by TIOPA 2010, s. 378 and Sch. 10, Pt. 12, with effect for corporation tax purposes for accounting periods ending on or after 1 April 2010, for income tax and capital gains tax purposes for the tax year 2010–11 and subsequent tax years and for petroleum revenue tax purposes for chargeable periods beginning on or after 1 July 2010.

Notes – Sch. 15 rewritten as follows
Para. 2: TIOPA 2010, Sch. 7, para. 4.
Para. 4(1): TIOPA 2010, Sch. 7, para. 2, 3 and 4.
Para. 4(2): TIOPA 2010, Sch. 7, para. 2.
Para. 4(3): TIOPA 2010, Sch. 7, para. 2.
Para. 4A(1): TIOPA 2010, Sch. 7, para. 2.
Para. 4A(2): TIOPA 2010, Sch. 7, para. 2.
Para. 5: TIOPA 2010, Sch. 7, para. 2 and 3.
Para. 6: TIOPA 2010, Sch. 7, para. 2.
Para. 7: TIOPA 2010, Sch. 7, para. 3.
Para. 7A(1): TIOPA 2010, Sch. 7, para. 3.
Para. 7A(2): TIOPA 2010, Sch. 7, para. 3.
Para. 7A(3): TIOPA 2010, Sch. 7, para. 2 and 3.
Para. 7A(4): TIOPA 2010, Sch. 7, para. 3.
Para. 8: TIOPA 2010, Sch. 7, para. 3.
Para. 8A(1): TIOPA 2010, Sch. 7, para. 2 and 3.
Para. 8A(2): TIOPA 2010, Sch. 7, para. 4.
Para. 8A(3): TIOPA 2010, Sch. 7, para. 2.
Para. 8A(4): TIOPA 2010, Sch. 7, para. 2 and 3.

FINANCE ACT 1974

(1974 Chapter 30)

[*31st July 1974*]

PART II – INCOME TAX, CORPORATION TAX AND CAPITAL GAINS TAX (GENERAL)

24 Returns of persons treated as employees

24 [Omitted by TIOPA 2010, s. 371 and Sch. 7, para. 16 and repealed by TIOPA 2010, s. 378 and Sch. 10, Pt. 12.]

History – S. 24 omitted by TIOPA 2010, s. 371 and Sch. 7, para. 16 and repealed by TIOPA 2010, s 378 and Sch. 10, Pt. 12, with effect for corporation tax purposes for accounting periods ending on or after 1 April 2010, for income tax and capital gains tax purposes for the tax year 2010–11 and subsequent tax years, and for petroleum revenue tax purposes for chargeable periods beginning on or after 1 July 2010.

Notes – S. 24 rewritten at TIOPA 2010, Sch. 7, para. 12, 13 and 14.

INTERPRETATION ACT 1978

(1978 Chapter 30)

[*20th July 1978*]

ARRANGEMENT OF SECTIONS

GENERAL PROVISIONS AS TO ENACTMENT AND OPERATION

1 Words of enactment

1 Every section of an Act takes effect as a substantive enactment without introductory words.

3 Judicial notice

3 Every Act is a public Act to be judicially noticed as such, unless the contrary is expressly provided by the Act.

4 Time of commencement

4 An Act or provision of an Act comes into force–

(a) where provision is made for it to come into force on a particular day, at the beginning of that day;

(b) where no provision is made for its coming into force, at the beginning of the day on which the Act receives the Royal Assent.

INTERPRETATION AND CONSTRUCTION

5 Definitions

5 In any Act, unless the contrary intention appears, words and expressions listed in Schedule 1 to this Act are to be construed according to that Schedule.

6 Gender and number

6 In any Act, unless the contrary intention appears–

(a) words importing the masculine gender include the feminine;

(b) words importing the feminine gender include the masculine;

(c) words in the singular include the plural and words in the plural include the singular.

7 References to service by post

7 Where an Act authorises or requires any document to be served by post (whether the expression **"serve"** or the expression **"give"** or **"send"** or any other expression is used) then, unless the contrary intention appears, the service is deemed to be effected by properly addressing, pre-paying and posting a letter containing the document and, unless the contrary is proved, to have been effected at the time at which the letter would be delivered in the ordinary course of post.

Cross references – FA 2003, s. 84(3): for the purposes of stamp duty land tax, a notice or other document is properly addressed if addressed to an individual's usual or last known place of residence or business, or, in the case of a company, to its principal place of business, the address of its liquidator or any other place prescribed by regulations.

10 References to the Sovereign

10 In any Act a reference to the Sovereign reigning at the time of the passing of the Act is to be construed, unless the contrary intention appears, as a reference to the Sovereign for the time being.

11 Construction of subordinate legislation

11 Where an Act confers power to make subordinate legislation, expressions used in that legislation have, unless the contrary intention appears, the meaning which they bear in the Act.

STATUTORY POWERS AND DUTIES

12 Continuity of powers and duties

12(1) Where an Act confers a power or imposes a duty it is implied, unless the contrary intention appears, that the power may be exercised, or the duty is to be performed, from time to time as occasion requires.

12(2) Where an Act confers a power or imposes a duty on the holder of an office as such, it is implied, unless the contrary intention appears, that the power may be exercised, or the duty is to be performed, by the holder for the time being of the office.

13 Anticipatory exercise of powers

13 Where an Act which (or any provision of which) does not come into force immediately on its passing confers power to make subordinate legislation, or to make appointments, give notices, prescribe forms or do any other thing for the purposes of the Act, then, unless the contrary intention appears, the power may be exercised, and any instrument made thereunder may be made so as to come into force, at any time after the passing of the Act so far as may be necessary or expedient for the purpose–

(a) of bringing the Act or any provision of the Act into force; or

(b) of giving full effect to the Act or any such provision at or after the time when it comes into force.

14 Implied power to amend

14 Where an Act confers power to make–

(a) rules, regulations or byelaws; or

(b) Orders in Council, orders or other subordinate legislation to be made by statutory instrument,

it implies, unless the contrary intention appears, a power, exercisable in the same manner and subject to the same conditions or limitations, to revoke, amend or re-enact any instrument made under the power.

14A Power to include sunset and review provisions in subordinate legislation

14A(1) This section applies where an Act confers a power or a duty on a person to make subordinate legislation except to the extent that–

(a) the power or duty is exercisable by the Scottish Ministers, or

(b) the power or duty is exercisable by any other person within devolved competence (within the meaning of the Scotland Act 1998).

14A(2) The subordinate legislation may include–

(a) provision requiring the person to review the effectiveness of the legislation within a specified period or at the end of a specified period;

(b) provision for the legislation to cease to have effect at the end of a specified day or a specified period;

(c) if the power or duty is being exercised to amend other subordinate legislation, provision of the kind mentioned in paragraph (a) or (b) in relation to that other legislation.

14A(3) The provision that may be made by virtue of subsection (2)(a) includes provision requiring the person to consider whether the objectives which it was the purpose of the legislation to achieve remain appropriate and, if so, whether they could be achieved in another way.

14A(4) Subordinate legislation including provision of a kind mentioned in subsection (2) may make such provision generally or only in relation to specified provisions of the legislation or specified cases or circumstances.

14A(5) Subordinate legislation including provision of a kind mentioned in subsection (2) may make transitional, consequential, incidental or supplementary provision or savings in connection with such provision.

14A(6) In this section, **"specified"** means specified in the subordinate legislation.

History – S. 14A inserted by Enterprise and Regulatory Reform Act 2013, s. 59(2), with effect from 25 April 2013.

REPEALING ENACTMENTS

15 Repeal of repeals

15 Where an Act repeals a repealing enactment, the repeal does not revive any enactment previously repealed unless words are added reviving it.

16 General savings

16(1) Without prejudice to section 15, where an Act repeals an enactment, the repeal does not, unless the contrary intention appears–

(a) revive anything not in force or existing at the time at which the repeal takes effect;

(b) affect the previous operation of the enactment repealed or anything duly done or suffered under that enactment;

(c) affect any right, privilege, obligation or liability acquired, accrued or incurred under that enactment;

(d) affect any penalty, forfeiture or punishment incurred in respect of any offence committed against that enactment;

(e) affect any investigation, legal proceeding or remedy in respect of any such right, privilege, obligation, liability, penalty, forfeiture or punishment;

and any such investigation, legal proceeding or remedy may be instituted, continued or enforced, and any such penalty, forfeiture or punishment may be imposed, as if the repealing Act had not been passed.

16(2) This section applies to the expiry of a temporary enactment as if it were repealed by an Act.

17 Repeal and re-enactment

17(1) Where an Act repeals a previous enactment and substitutes provisions for the enactment repealed, the repealed enactment remains in force until the substituted provisions come into force.

17(2) Where an Act repeals and re-enacts, with or without modification, a previous enactment then, unless the contrary intention appears–

(a) any reference in any other enactment to the enactment so repealed shall be construed as a reference to the provision re-enacted;

(b) in so far as any subordinate legislation made or other thing done under the enactment so repealed, or having effect as if so made or done, could have been made or done under the provision re-enacted, it shall have effect as if made or done under that provision.

Cross references – ITEPA 2003, Sch. 7, para. 6: ITEPA 2003, Sch. 7, para. 1–5 have effect for the purposes of ITEPA 2003 instead of INA 1978, s. 17(2) but those paragraphs are without prejudice to any other provision of INA 1978; ITEPA 2003, Sch. 7, para. 6 has effect for the tax year 2003–04 and subsequent tax years.

FA 2012, Sch. 19, para. 2(8): FA 2012, Sch. 19, para. 2 has effect instead of INA 1978, s. 17(2) for the purposes of FA 2012, Part 3 (friendly societies carrying on long-term business); FA 2012, Sch. 19, para. 2(8) has effect in relation to accounting periods of companies beginning on or after 1 January 2013.

MISCELLANEOUS

18 Duplicated offences

18 Where an act or omission constitutes an offence under two or more Acts, or both under an Act and at common law, the offender shall, unless the contrary intention appears, be liable to be prosecuted and punished under either or any of those Acts or at common law, but shall not be liable to be punished more than once for the same offence.

19 Citation of other Acts

19(1) Where an Act cites another Act by year, statute, session or chapter, or a section or other portion of another Act by number or letter, the reference shall, unless the contrary intention appears, be read as referring–

(a) in the case of Acts included in any revised edition of the statutes printed by authority, to that edition;

(b) in the case of Acts not so included but included in the edition prepared under the direction of the Record Commission, to that edition;

(c) in any other case, to the Acts printed by the Queen's Printer, or under the superintendence or authority of Her Majesty's Stationery Office.

19(2) An Act may continue to be cited by the short title authorised by any enactment notwithstanding the repeal of that enactment.

20 References to other enactments

20(1) Where an Act describes or cites a portion of an enactment by referring to words, sections or other parts from or to which (or from and to which) the portion extends, the portion described or cited includes the words, sections or other parts referred to unless the contrary intention appears.

20(2) Where an Act refers to an enactment, the reference, unless the contrary intention appears, is a reference to that enactment as amended, and includes a reference thereto as extended or applied, by or under any other enactment, including any other provision of that Act.

Cross references – FA 1995, s. 39(3): construction of references to Sch. A provisions as applied or modified by FA 1995, s. 39 and Sch. 6.

20A References to EU instruments

20A Where an Act passed after the commencement of this section refers to a EU instrument that has been amended, extended or applied by another such instrument, the reference, unless the contrary intention appears, is a reference to that instrument as so amended, extended or applied.

History – In the heading to s. 20A, the words "EU instruments" substituted for the words "Community instruments" by the European Union (Amendment) Act 2008, s. 3 and Schedule, Pt. 2 with effect from 1 December 2009 (the date appointed by SI 2009/3143, art. 2).
In s. 20A, the words "EU instruments" substituted for the words "Community instruments" by the European Union (Amendment) Act 2008, s. 3 and Schedule, Pt. 2 with effect from 1 December 2009 (the date appointed by SI 2009/3143, art. 2).
S. 20A inserted by LRRA 2006, s. 25(1), with effect from 8 January 2007.

SUPPLEMENTARY

21 Interpretation etc.

21(1) In this Act **"Act"** includes a local and personal or private Act; and **"subordinate legislation"** means Orders in Council, orders, rules, regulations, schemes, warrants, byelaws and other instruments made or to be made under any Act.

21(2) This Act binds the Crown.

22 Application to Acts and Measures

22(1) This applies to itself, to any Act passed after the commencement of this Act (subject, in the case of section 20A, to the provision made in that section) and, to the extent specified in Part I of Schedule 2, to Acts passed before the commencement of this Act.

22(2) In any of the foregoing provisions of this Act a reference to an Act is a reference to an Act to which that provision applies; but this does not affect the generality of references to enactments or of the references in section 19(1) to other Acts.

History – In s. 22(1) the words "(subject, in the case of section 20A, to the provision made in that section)" inserted by LRRA 2006, s. 25(2), with effect from 8 January 2007.

23 Application to other instruments

23(1) The provisions of this Act, except sections 1 to 3 and 4(b), apply, so far as applicable and unless the contrary intention appears, to subordinate legislation made after the commencement of this Act and, to the extent specified in Part II of Schedule 2, to subordinate legislation made before the commencement of this Act, as they apply to Acts.

23(2) In the application of this Act to Acts passed or subordinate legislation made after the commencement of this Act, all references to an enactment include an enactment comprised in subordinate legislation whenever made, and references to the passing or repeal of an enactment are to be construed accordingly.

23(3) Sections 9 and 19(1) also apply to deeds and other instruments and documents as they apply to Acts and subordinate legislation; and in the application of section 17(2)(a) to Acts passed or subordinate legislation made after the commencement of this Act, the reference to any other enactment includes any deed or other instrument or document.

23(4) Subsections (1) and (2) of this section do not apply to Orders in Council made under section 5 of the Statutory Instruments Act 1946, section 1(3) of the Northern Ireland (Temporary Provisions) Act 1972 or Schedule 1 to the Northern Ireland Act 1974.

23A Acts of the Scottish Parliament etc.

23A(1) This Act applies in relation to an Act of the Scottish Parliament and an instrument made under such an Act only to the extent provided in this section.

23A(2) Except as provided in subsection (3) below, sections 15 to 18 apply to–

(a) an Act of the Scottish Parliament as they apply to an Act;

(b) an instrument made under an Act of the Scottish Parliament as they apply to subordinate legislation.

23A(3) In the application of those sections to an Act and to subordinate legislation–

(a) references to an enactment include an enactment comprised in, or in an instrument made under, an Act of the Scottish Parliament, and

(b) the reference in section 17(2)(b) to subordinate legislation includes an instrument made under an Act of the Scottish Parliament.

23A(4) In the application of section 20 to an Act and to subordinate legislation, references to an enactment include and enactment comprised in, or in an instrument made under, an Act of the Scottish Parliament.

History – S. 23A inserted by Scotland Act 1998, s. 125 and Sch. 8, para. 16(2), with effect from 1 July 1999 (SI 1998/3178).

23B Measures and Acts of the National Assembly for Wales etc.

23B(1) Subject as follows, the provisions of this Act–

(a) apply to a Measure or Act of the National Assembly for Wales as they apply to an Act, and

(a) apply to an instrument made under a Measure or Act of the National Assembly for Wales as they apply to other subordinate legislation.

23B(2) Sections 1 to 3 do not apply to a Measure or Act of the National Assembly for Wales.

23B(3) In this Act references to an enactment include an enactment comprised in, or in an instrument made under, a Measure or Act of the National Assembly for Wales.

23B(4) In the application of this Act to a Measure or Act of the National Assembly for Wales, references to the passing of an Act or an enactment are to be read as references to the enactment of the Measure or Act.

23B(5) Section 4(b) does not apply to a Measure of the National Assembly for Wales; but where such a Measure makes no provision for the coming into force of a provision contained in it, that provision comes into force at the beginning of the day on which the Measure is approved by Her Majesty in Council.

History – S. 23B inserted by the Government of Wales Act 2006, s. 160(1) and Sch. 10, para. 11, with effect from 3 May 2007 subject to s. 161(4)(5) which provides for certain provisions to come into force for specified purposes on 25 May 2007.

24 Application to Northern Ireland

24(1) This Act extends to Northern Ireland so far as it applies to Acts or subordinate legislation which so extend.

24(2) In the application of this Act to Acts passed or subordinate legislation made after the commencement of this Act, all references to an enactment include an enactment comprised in Northern Ireland legislation whenever passed or made; and in relation to such legislation references to the passing or repeal of an enactment include the making or revocation of an Order in Council.

24(3) In the application of section 14 to Acts passed after the commencement of this Act which extend to Northern Ireland, **"statutory instrument"** includes statutory rule for the purposes of the Statutory Rules (Northern Ireland) Order 1979.

24(3A) Section 20A applies to Northern Ireland legislation as it applies to Acts.

24(4) The following definitions contained in Schedule 1, namely those of–

The Communities and related expressions;

The Corporation Tax Acts;

EEA agreement and EEA state;

The Income Tax Acts;

The Tax Acts,

apply, unless the contrary intention appears, to Northern Ireland legislation as they apply to Acts.

24(5) In this section **"Northern Ireland legislation"** means–

(a) Acts of the Parliament of Ireland;

(b) Acts of the Parliament of Northern Ireland;

(c) Orders in Council under section 1(3) of the Northern Ireland (Temporary Provisions) Act 1972;

(d) Measures of the Northern Ireland Assembly established under section 1 of the Northern Ireland Assembly Act 1973;

(e) Orders in Council under Schedule 1 to the Northern Ireland Act 1974;

(f) Acts of the Northern Ireland Assembly; and

(g) Orders in Council under section 85 of the Northern Ireland Act 1998.

History – S. 24(3A) inserted by LRRA 2006, s. 25(3), with effect from 8 January 2007.
In s. 24(4), the words "EEA agreement and EEA state;" inserted by LRRA 2006, s. 26(2), with effect from 8 January 2007.
In s. 24(5) para. (d)–(g) substituted for previous para. (d) and (e) by *Northern Ireland Act* 1998, s. 99 and Sch. 13, para. 3, with effect from 2 December 1999, the date prescribed by the Northern Ireland Act 1998 (Commencement No 5) Order 1999, SI 1999/3209, reg. 2.

25 Repeals and savings

25(1) [Not reproduced.]

25(2) Without prejudice to section 17(2)(a), a reference to the Interpretation Act 1889, to any provision of that Act or to any other enactment repealed by this Act, whether occurring in another Act, in subordinate legislation, in Northern Ireland legislation or in any deed or other instrument or document, shall be construed as referring to this Act, or to the corresponding provision of this Act, as it applies to Acts passed at the time of the reference.

25(3) The provisions of this Act relating to Acts passed after any particular time to not affect the construction of Acts passed before that time, though continued or amended by Acts passed thereafter.

26 Commencement

26 This Act shall come into force on 1st January 1979.

27 Short title

27 This Act may be cited as the Interpretation Act 1978.

SCHEDULES

SCHEDULE 1 – WORDS AND EXPRESSIONS DEFINED

Section 5

Notes – The years or dates in square brackets following certain entries in this Schedule are relevant for the purposes of Sch. 2, para. 4 (application to existing enactments).

DEFINITIONS

"Associated state" means a territory maintaining a status of association with the United Kingdom in accordance with the West Indies Act 1967. [16th February 1967]

"Act" means an Act of Parliament.

"Bank of England" means, as the context requires, the Governor and Company of the Bank of England or the bank of the Governor and Company of the Bank of England.

"Bank of Ireland" means, as the context requires, the Governor and Company of the Bank of Ireland or the bank of the Governor and Company of the Bank of Ireland.

"British Islands" means the United Kingdom, the Channel Islands and the Isle of Man. [1889]

"British overseas territory" has the same meaning as in the British Nationality Act 1981.

"British possession" means any part of Her Majesty's dominions outside the United Kingdom; and where parts of such dominions are under both a central and a local legislature, all parts under the central legislature are deemed, for the purposes of this definition, to be one British possession. [1889]

"Building regulations", in relation to England and Wales, has the meaning given by section 122 of the Building Act 1984.

"Central funds", in an enactment providing in relation to England and Wales for the payment of costs out of central funds, means money provided by Parliament.

"Charity Commissioners" means the Charity Commission for England and Wales (see section 13 of the Charities Act 2011)

"Church Commissioners" means the Commissioners constituted by the Church Commissioners Measure 1947.

"Civil partnership" means a civil partnership which exists under or by virtue of the Civil Partnership Act 2004 (and any reference to a civil partner is to be read accordingly).

"Colonial legislature", and **"legislature"** in relation to a British possession, mean the authority, other than the Parliament of the United Kingdom or Her Majesty in Council, competent to make laws for the possession. [1889]

"Colony" means any part of Her Majesty's dominions outside the British Islands except–

(a) countries having fully responsible status within the Commonwealth;

(b) territories for whose external relations a country other than the United Kingdom is responsible;

(c) associated states;

and where parts of such dominions are under both a central and a local legislature, all parts under the central legislature are deemed for the purposes of this definition to be one colony. [1889]

"Commencement" in relation to an Act or enactment, means the time when the Act or enactment comes into force.

"Committed for trial" means–

(a) [revoked by the Constitutional Reform Act 2005, s. 59 and Sch. 11, para. 24.]

(b) in relation to Northern Ireland, committed in custody or on bail by a magistrates' court pursuant to Article 37 of the Magistrates' Courts (Northern Ireland) Order 1981, or by a court, judge, resident magistrate, or other authority having power to do so, with a view to trial on indictment. [1st January 1979]

"Comptroller and Auditor General" means the Comptroller-General of the receipt and issue of Her Majesty's Exchequer and Auditor-General of Public Accounts.

"Consular officer" *has the meaning* assigned by Article 1 of the Vienna Convention set out in Schedule 1 to the Consular Relations Act 1968.

"The Corporation Tax Acts" means the enactments relating to the taxation of the income and chargeable gains of companies and of company distributions (including provisions relating to income tax).

"County court" means–

(a) in relation to England and Wales, the county court established under section A1 of the County Courts Act 1984; [1846]

(b) in relation to Northern Ireland, a court held for a division under the County Courts (Northern Ireland) Order 1980. [1889]

"Court of Appeal" means–

(a) in relation to England and Wales, Her Majesty's Court of Appeal in England;

(b) in relation to Northern Ireland, Her Majesty's Court of Appeal in Northern Ireland.

"Court of Judicature" means the Court of Judicature of Northern Ireland.

"Court of summary jurisdiction", **"summary conviction"** and **"Summary Jurisdiction Acts"**, in relation to Northern Ireland, have the same meanings as in Measures of the Northern Ireland Assembly and Acts of the Parliament of Northern Ireland.

"Crown Court" means–

(a) in relation to England and Wales, the Crown Court constituted by section 4 of the Courts Act 1971;

(b) in relation to Northern Ireland, the Crown Court constituted by section 4 of the Judicature (Northern Ireland) Act 1978.

"Crown Estate Commissioners" means the Commissioners referred to in section 1 of the Crown Estate Act 1961.

"EEA agreement" means the agreement on the European Economic Area signed at Oporto on 2nd May 1992, together with the Protocol adjusting that Agreement signed at Brussels on 17th March 1993, as modified or supplemented from time to time. [The date of the coming into force of this paragraph.]

"EEA state", in relation to any time, means–

(a) a state which at that time is a member State; or

(b) any other state which at that time is a party to the EEA agreement. [The date of the coming into force of this paragraph.]

"Enactment" does not include an enactment comprised in, or in an instrument made under, an Act of the Scottish Parliament.

"England" means, subject to any alteration of boundaries under Part IV of the Local Government Act 1972, the area consisting of the counties established by section 1 of that Act, Greater London and the Isles of Scilly. [1st April 1974]

"The EU", or **"the EU Treaties"** and other expressions defined by section 1 of and Schedule 1 to the European Communities Act 1972 have the meanings prescribed by that Act.

"Financial year" means, in relation to matters relating to the Consolidated Fund, the National Loans Fund, or moneys provided by Parliament, or to the Exchequer or to central taxes or finance, the twelve months ending with 31st March. [1889]

"Governor-General" includes any person who for the time being has the powers of the Governor-General, and "Governor", in relation to any British possession, includes the officer for the time being administering the government of that possession. [1889]

"Her Majesty's Revenue and Customs" has the meaning given by section 4 of the Commissioners for Revenue and Customs Act 2005.

"High Court" means–

(a) in relation to England and Wales, Her Majesty's High Court of Justice in England;

(b) in relation to Northern Ireland, Her Majesty's High Court of Justice in Northern Ireland.

"The Immigration Acts" has the meaning given by section 61 of the UK Borders Act 2007.

"The Income Tax Acts" means all enactments relating to income tax, including any provisions of the Corporation Tax Acts which relate to income tax.

"Land" includes buildings and other structures, land covered with water, and any estate, interest, easement, servitude or right in or over land. [1st January 1979]

"Land Clauses Acts" means

(a) in relation to England and Wales, the Land Clauses Consolidation Act 1845 and the Lands Clauses Consolidation Acts Amendment Act 1860, and any Acts for the time being in force amending those Acts; [1889]

(b) in relation to Scotland, the Lands Clauses Consolidation (Scotland) Act 1845 and the Lands Clauses Consolidation Acts Amendment Act 1860, and any Acts for the time being in force amending those Acts; [1889]

(c) in relation to Northern Ireland, the enactments defined as such by section 46(1) of the Interpretation Act (Northern Ireland) 1954. [1889]

"Local land charges register", in relation to England and Wales, means the register kept pursuant to section 3 of the Local Land Charges Act 1975.

"London borough" means a borough described in Schedule 1 to the London Government Act 1963 "inner London borough" means one of the boroughs so described and numbered from 1 to 12 and "outer London borough" means one of the boroughs so described and numbered from 13 to 32, subject (in each case) to any alterations made under Part IV of the Local Government Act 1972 or Part II of the Local Government Act 1992.

"Lord Chancellor" means the Lord High Chancellor of Great Britain.

"Magistrates' court" has the meaning assigned to it–

(a) in relation to England and Wales, by section 148 of the Magistrates' Courts Act 1980;

(b) in relation to Northern Ireland, by Article 2(2) of the Magistrates' Courts (Northern Ireland) Order 1981.

"Month" means calendar month.

"National Debt Commissioners" means the Commissioners for the Reduction of the National Debt.

"Northern Ireland legislation" has the meaning assigned by section 24(5) of this Act. [1st January 1979]

"Oath" and **"affidavit"** include affirmation and declaration, and **"swear"** includes affirm and declare.

"Officer of Revenue and Customs" has the meaning given by section 2(1) of the Commissioners for Revenue and Customs Act 2005.

"Ordnance Map" means a map made under powers conferred by the Ordnance Survey Act 1841 or the Boundary Survey (Ireland) Act 1854.

"Parliamentary Election" means the election of a Member to serve in Parliament for a constituency. [1889]

"PAYE income" has the meaning given by section 683 of the Income Tax (Earnings and Pensions) Act 2003.

"PAYE regulations" means regulations under section 684 of that Act.

"Person" includes a body of persons corporate or unincorporate. [1889]

"Police area" and **"Police authority"** and other expressions relating to the police have the meaning or effect described–

(a) in relation to England and Wales, by section 101(1) of the Police Act 1996;

(b) in relation to Scotland, by sections 50 and 51(4) of the Police (Scotland) Act 1967.

"The Privy Council" means the Lords and others of Her Majesty's Most Honourable Privy Council.

"Rules of Court" in relation to any court means rules made by the authority having power to make rules or orders regulating the practice and procedure of that court, and in Scotland includes Acts of Adjournal and Acts of Sederunt; and the power of the authority to make rules of court (as above defined) includes power to make such rules for the purpose of any Act which directs or authorises anything to be done by rules of court. [1889]

"Secretary of State" means one of Her Majesty's Principal Secretaries of State.

"Senior Courts" means the Senior Courts of England and Wales.

"Sent for trial" means, in relation to England and Wales. sent by a magistrate's court to the Crown Court for trial pursuant to section 51 or 51A of the Crime and Disorder Act 1998.

"Sheriff" is to be construed in accordance with section 134(2) and (3) of the Courts Reform (Scotland) Act 2014.

"The standard scale", with reference to a fine or penalty for an offence triable only summarily,–

(a) in relation to England and Wales, has the meaning given by section 37 of the Criminal Justice Act 1982;

(b) in relation to Scotland, has the meaning given by section 225(1) of the Criminal Procedure (Scotland) Act 1995;

(c) in relation to Northern Ireland, has the meaning given by Article 5 of the Fines and Penalties (Northern Ireland) Order 1984.

"Statutory declaration" means a declaration made by virtue of the Statutory Declarations Act 1835.

"Statutory maximum", with reference to a fine or penalty on summary conviction for an offence,–

(a) in relation to England and Wales, means the prescribed sum within the meaning of section 32 of the Magistrates' Courts Act 1980;

(b) in relation to Scotland, means the prescribed sum within the meaning of section 225(8) of the Criminal Procedure (Scotland) Act 1995; and

(c) in relation to Northern Ireland, means the prescribed sum within the meaning of Article 4 of the Fines and Penalties (Northern Ireland) Order 1984.

"Supreme Court" means the Supreme Court of the United Kingdom.

"The Tax Acts" means the Income Tax Acts and the Corporation Tax Acts.

"Transfer for trial" means the transfer of proceedings against an accused to the Crown Court for trial under section 7 of the Magistrates' Courts Act 1980.

"The Treasury" means the Commissioners of Her Majesty's Treasury.

"Trust of land" and **"trustees of land"**, in relation to England and Wales, have the same meanings as in the Trusts of Land and Appointment of Trustees Act 1996.

"United Kingdom" means Great Britain and Northern Ireland. [12th April 1927]

"Wales" means the combined area of counties which were created by section 20 of the Local Government Act 1972, as originally enacted, but subject to any alteration made under section 73 of that Act (consequential alteration of boundary following alteration of watercourse).

"Writing" includes typing, printing, lithography, photography and other modes of representing or reproducing words in a visible form, and expressions referring to writing are construed accordingly.

CONSTRUCTION OF CERTAIN EXPRESSIONS RELATING TO OFFENCES

In relation to England and Wales–

(a) **"indictable offence"** means an offence which, if committed by an adult, is triable on indictment, whether it is exclusively so triable or triable either way;

(b) **"summary offence"** means an offence which, if committed by an adult, is triable only summarily;

(c) **"offence triable either way"** means an offence other than an offence triable on indictment only by virtue of Part V of the Criminal Justice Act 1988 which, if committed by an adult, is triable either on indictment or summarily;

and the terms **"indictable"**, **"summary"** and **"triable either way"**, in their application to offences, are to be construed accordingly.

In the above definitions references to the way or ways in which an offence is triable are to be construed without regard to the effect, if any, of section 22 of the Magistrates' Courts Act 1980 on the mode of trial in a particular case.

CONSTRUCTION OF CERTAIN REFERENCES TO RELATIONSHIPS

In relation to England and Wales–

(a) references (however expressed) to any relationship between two persons;

(b) references to a person whose father and mother were or were not married to each other at the time of his birth; and

(c) references cognate with references falling within paragraph (b) above,

shall be construed in accordance with section 1 of the Family Law Reform Act 1987. [4th April 1988]

Prospective amendments – In the definition of "county court", in para. (b), the words "for a division" omitted by Justice Act (Northern Ireland) 2015, s. 6 and Sch. 1, para. 75 and repealed by s. 105 and Sch. 9, Pt. 1, with effect from with effect from a date to be appointed under s. 106(2).

History – Definitions of "Act" and "Enactment" inserted by Scotland Act 1998, s. 125 and Sch. 8, para. 16(3), with effect from 1 July 1999 by virtue of SI 1998/3178.

The definition of "British overseas territory" inserted by the British Overseas Territories Act 2002, s. 1(3), with effect from 26 February 2002.

The definition of "Building regulations" amended by the Building Act 1984, Sch. 6, para. 19.

The definition of "Charity Commissioners" substituted by Charities Act 2011, s. 354 and Sch. 7, para. 35, with effect from the end of the period of 3 months beginning with 14 December 2011.

The definition of "Charity Commissioners" substituted by the Charities Act 1993, s. 98(1) and Sch. 6, para. 15.

The definition of "Civil partnership" inserted by the Civil Partnership Act 2004, Sch. 27, para. 59, with effect from 5 December 2005 (by virtue of SI 2005/3175, art. 2(2)).
In the definition of "Committed for trial", para. (a) repealed by Criminal Justice Act 2003, Sch. 37, Pt. 4, from 1 October 2009 (the date appointed by virtue of SI 2009/160, art. 2).
In the definition of "Committed for Trial", the words "justice of the peace" in para. (b) repealed by the Justice (Northern Ireland) Act 2002, s. 86 and Sch. 13, with effect from 1 April 2005 (SR 2005/109, art. 2 and Sch.).
The definition of "Committed for trial" substituted by the Magistrates' Courts Act 1980, Sch. 7, para. 169 and SI 1981/1675, Sch. 6, para. 56.
In the definition of "Comptroller and Auditor General", the words "appointed in pursuance of the Exchequer and Audit Departments Act 1866" (which appeared after "Public Accounts", omitted by the Budget Responsibility and National Audit Act 2011, s. 26 and Sch. 5, para. 12, with effect from 1 April 2012 (SI 2011/2576, art. 5).
The definition of "The Corporation Tax Acts" substituted by FA 1987, s. 71 and Sch. 15, para. 12.
In the definition of "County court", the words "the county court established under section A1 of" substituted for the words "a court held for a district under" by Crime and Courts Act 2013, s. 17(5) and Sch. 9, para. 68, with effect from 22 April 2014 (SI 2014/954, art. 2).
The definition of "County court" amended by the County Courts Act 1984, Sch. 2, para. 68 and SI 1980/397, Sch. 1, Pt. II.
The definition of "Court of Judicature" inserted by CRA 2005, s. 59(5) and Sch. 11, para. 24(b), with effect from 1 October 2009 (SI 2009/1604).
Definitions of "EEA agreement" and "EEA state" inserted by LRRA 2006, s. 26(1), with effect from 8 January 2007.
In the definitions, "The EU" or "the EU Treaties" substituted for "The Communities", "the Treaties" or "The community Treaties" in the appropriate places by the European Union (Amendment) Act 2008, s. 3 and Schedule, Pt. 2 with effect from 1 December 2009(by virtue of SI 2009/3143, art. 2).
The definition of "Her Majesty's Revenue and Customs" inserted by CRCA 2005, s. 4(3), with effect from 7 April 2005 (by virtue of SI 2005/1126, reg. 2(1)).
In the definition of "The Immigration Acts" the words "section 61 of the UK Borders Act 2007" substituted by UK Borders Act 2007, s. 61(4), with effect from 30 October 2007.
The definition of "The Immigration Acts" inserted by the Immigration, Asylum and Nationality Act 2006, s. 64(4), with effect from 30 March 2006.
In the definition of "Local land charges register", the words "the register" substitute for the words "a register" by Infrastructure Act 2015, s. 34 and Sch. 5, para. 34, with effect from 11 April 2015.
In the definition of "Local land charges register", the words "and the appropriate local land charges register has the meaning assigned by section 4 of that Act" (which appeared after the words "Local Land Charges Act 1975"), omitted by Infrastructure Act 2015, s. 34 and Sch. 5, para. 34, with effectfrom 11 April 2015.
The definition of "London borough" amended by the Local Government Act 1992, s. 27(1) and Sch. 3, para. 21.
The definition of "Officer of Revenue and Customs" inserted by CRCA 2005, s. 2(7), with effect from 7 April 2005 (by virtue of SI 2005/1126, reg. 2(1)).
Definitions of "PAYE income" and "PAYE regulations" inserted by ITEPA 2003, Sch. 6, para. 148 which has effect for the tax year 2003–04 and subsequent tax years.
Definitions of "police area" and "police authority" amended by Police Act 1996, s. 103 and Sch. 7, para. 32.
Definitions of "Police Service of Northern Ireland" and "Police Service of Northern Ireland Reserve" inserted by Police (Northern Ireland) Act 2000, s. 78 and Sch. 6, para. 5.
The definition of "Senior Courts" inserted by CRA 2005, s. 59(5) and Sch. 11, para. 24(b), with effect from 1 October 2009 (SI 2009/1604).
The definition of "Sent for trial" inserted by Criminal Justice Act 2003, s. 41 and Sch. 3, para. 49, with effect from 9 May 2005 (SI 2005/1267).
The definition of "Sheriff" substituted by SI 2015/700, art. 10 and Schedule, para. 10, with effect from 1 April 2015 (the same day as that on which CRSA 2014, s. 134(2) and (3) comes into force by virtue of SSI 2015/77).
Definitions of "the standard scale" and "statutory maximum" inserted and "offence triable either way" amended by Criminal Justice Act 1988, s. 170 and Sch. 15, para. 58, 59, with effect from 12 October 1988 (SI 1988/1676, reg. 4).
In definitions of "the standard scale" and "statutory maximum", references to the Criminal Procedure (Scotland) Act 1995 substituted by Criminal Procedure (Consequential Provisions) (Scotland) Act1995, Sch. 4, para. 17, with effect from 1 April 1996.
In definition of "statutory maximum", references to the Criminal Procedure (Scotland) Act 1995 substituted by Criminal Procedure (Consequential Provisions) (Scotland) Act 1995, Sch. 4, para. 17, with effect from 1 April 1996.
Definition of "statutory maximum" inserted by Criminal Justice Act 1988, s. 170 and Sch. 15, para. 58, 59, with effect from 12 October 1988 (SI 1988/1676, reg. 4).
In the definition of "Supreme Court" inserted by CRA 2005, s. 59(5) and Sch. 11, para. 24(a), with effect from 1 October 2009 (SI 2009/1604).
The definition of "The Tax Acts" substituted by FA 1987, s. 71 and Sch. 15, para. 12.
The definition of "Transfer for trial" inserted by the Criminal Justice and Public Order Act 1994, Sch. 4, para. 28(b).
Definitions of "trust of land" and "trustees of land" inserted by Trusts of Land and Appointment of Trustees Act 1996, Sch. 3, para. 16, with effect from 1 January 1997 (SI 1996/2974).
The definition of "Wales" substituted by the Local Government (Wales) Act 1994, Sch. 2, para. 9.
The definition of "offence triable either way" amended by the Magistrates' Court Act 1980, s. 154 and Sch. 7, para. 169 and the Criminal Justice Act 1988, s. 170(1) and Sch. 15, para. 59.
The words under the heading "Construction of certain references to relationships" amended by the Family Law Reform Act 1987, s. 33(1) and Sch. 2, para. 73.

SCHEDULE 2 – APPLICATION OF ACT TO EXISTING ENACTMENTS

Sections 22, 23

Part I – Acts

1 The following provisions of this Act apply to Acts whenever passed–

Section 6(a) and (c) so far as applicable to enactments relating to offences punishable on indictment or on summary conviction

Section 9

Section 10

Section 11 so far as it relates to subordinate legislation made after the year 1889
Section 14A
Section 18
Section 19(2).

History – In para. 1, entry relating to "Section 14A" inserted by Enterprise and Regulatory Reform Act 2013, s. 59(3), with effect from 25 April 2013.

2 The following apply to Acts passed after the year 1850–
Section 1
Section 3
Section 6(a) and (c) so far as not applicable to such Acts by virtue of paragraph 1
Section 15
Section 17(1)

3 The following apply to Acts passed after the year 1889–
Section 4
Section 7
Section 12
Section 13
Section 14 so far as it relates to rules, regulations or byelaws
Section 16(1)
Section 17(2)(a)
Section 19(1)
Section 20(1)

4(1) Subject to the following provisions of this paragraph–

(a) paragraphs of Schedule 1 at the end of which a year or date is specified or described apply, so far as applicable, to Acts passed on or after the date, or after the year, so specified or described; and

(b) paragraphs of the Schedule at the end of which no year or date is specified or described apply, so far as applicable, to Acts passed at any time.

4(2,3) [Not reproduced.]

4(4) The definition of **"Lord Chancellor"** does not apply to Acts passed before 1st October 1921 in which that expression was used in relation to Ireland only.

4(5) The definition of **"person"**, so far as it includes bodies corporate, applies to any provision of an Act whenever passed relating to an offence punishable on indictment or on summary conviction.

5 The following definitions shall be treated as included in Schedule 1 for the purposes specified in this paragraph–

(a) in any Act passed before 1st April 1974, a reference to England includes Berwick upon Tweed and Monmouthshire and, in the case of an Act passed before the Welsh Language Act 1967, Wales;

(b) in any Act passed before the commencement of this Act and after the year 1850, **"land"**, includes messuages, tenements and hereditaments, houses and buildings of any tenure;

(c) in any Act passed before the commencement of the Criminal Procedure (Scotland) Act 1975, **"the Summary Jurisdiction (Scotland) Acts"** means Part II of that Act.

Part II – Subordinate Legislation

6 Sections 4(a), 9 and 19(1), and so much of Schedule 1 as defines the following expressions, namely–
England;
Local land charges register and appropriate local land charges register;
Police area (and related expressions) in relation to Scotland;
United Kingdom;
Wales,

apply to subordinate legislation made at any time before the commencement of this Act as they apply to Acts passed at that time.

History – In para. 6 the words "British subject and Commonwealth citizen" repealed by British Nationality Act 1981, s. 52(8), Sch. 9.

7 The definition in Schedule 1 of **"county court"**, in relation to England and Wales, applies to Orders in Council made after the year 1846.

FINANCE ACT 1980

(1980 Chapter 48)

[*1st August 1980*]

ARRANGEMENT OF SECTIONS

PART III – INCOME TAX, CORPORATION TAX AND CAPITAL GAINS TAX

CHAPTER III – CAPITAL GAINS

PART III – INCOME TAX, CORPORATION TAX AND CAPITAL GAINS TAX

Chapter III – Capital Gains

79 General relief for gifts

79 [Repealed by FA 1989, s. 124(1), 187 and Sch. 17, Pt. VII, with effect in relation to disposals after 13 March 1989.]

History – S. 79 was repealed as mentioned above, but continues to be relevant in so far as various enactments operate in consequence of relief having been given thereby in respect of disposals made before 14 March 1989.

See now:

- TCGA 1992, s. 67 (outstanding claims under FA 1980, s. 79);
- TCGA 1992, s. 168 (clawback of relief when hold-over relief claimed under TCGA 1992, s. 165 (relief for gifts of business assets) and donee emigrates within six years of gift);
- TCGA 1992, Sch. 4, para. 2 (computation of held-over gain accruing before 31 March 1982 under FA 1980, s. 79).

The substance of s. 79(5), (6) is re-enacted in TCGA 1992, s. 67(2), (3). The elements of the claim were set out in s. 79(1)–(3), reproduced below for information:

"**79(1)** If after 5th April 1980 an individual (in this section referred to as **"the transferor"**) makes a disposal, otherwise than under a bargain at arm's length, to an individual resident or ordinarily resident in the United Kingdom (in this section referred to as **"the transferee"**) and the transferor and transferee make a claim for relief under this section–

(a) the amount of any chargeable gain which, apart from this section, would accrue to the transferor on the disposal; and

(b) the amount of the consideration for which, apart from this section, the transferee would be regarded for the purposes of capital gains tax as having acquired the asset in question,

shall each be reduced by an amount equal to the held-over gain on the disposal.

79(2) Subject to subsection (3) below, the reference in subsection (1) above to the held-over gain on a disposal is a reference to the chargeable gain which would have accrued on that disposal apart from this section.

79(3) In any case where–

(a) there is actual consideration (as opposed to the consideration equal to the market value which is deemed to be given by virtue of any provision of the Capital Gains Tax Act 1979) for a disposal in respect of which a claim for relief is made under this section; and

(b) that actual consideration exceeds the sums allowable as a deduction under section 32 of that Act,

the held-over gain on the disposal shall be reduced by the excess referred to in paragraph (b) above or, if part of the gain on the disposal is relieved under Schedule 20 to the Finance Act 1985 (retirement relief), by so much, if any, of that excess as exceeds the part so relieved."

FINANCE ACT 1982

(1982 Chapter 39)

[*30th July 1982*]

ARRANGEMENT OF SECTIONS

PART VII – MISCELLANEOUS AND SUPPLEMENTARY

PART VII – MISCELLANEOUS AND SUPPLEMENTARY

145 Certificates of tax deposit: extension of interest period

145 For the purposes of certificates of tax deposit issued by the Treasury under section 12 of the National Loans Act 1968 on terms published before 31st July 1980, the date which is the due date in relation to–

(a) income tax charged at a rate other than the basic rate, and

(b) capital gains tax,

is by virtue of this section postponed, with respect to the year 1980–81 and any subsequent year of assessment, from the date specified in the prospectuses concerned to 1st December following the end of the year of assessment for which the tax is payable.

147 Transfer of assets of British Gas Corporation

147(1) In this section–

"the Corporation" means the British Gas Corporation; and

"75 per cent subsidiary" has the meaning given by section 838 of the Taxes Act 1988.

147(2) If, in pursuance of a scheme made under section 10(2) of the Oil and Gas (Enterprise) Act 1982, any of the assets of the Corporation or of a 75 per cent subsidiary of the Corporation are transferred to another 75 per cent subsidiary of the Corporation, neither–

(a) section 278 of the Taxes Act 1970 (deemed disposals of assets for capital gains tax where member leaves group), nor

(b) section 21 of the Development Land Tax Act 1976 (deemed disposals of assets for development land tax where member leaves group),

shall have effect as respects any of the assets so transferred on that other subsidiary's ceasing to be a 75 per cent subsidiary of the Corporation.

147(3) If, for the purpose of enabling the Corporation to comply with a direction given under section 7(2) of the Gas Act 1972 requiring any asset to be disposed of, the asset to which the direction relates is transferred to a 75 per cent subsidiary of the Corporation, neither section 278 of the Taxes Act 1970 nor section 21 of the Development Land Tax Act 1976 shall have effect as respects any of the assets of that subsidiary on the subsidiary's ceasing to be a 75 per cent subsidiary of the Corporation.

History – References to provisions of the Taxes Act 1988 substituted by ICTA 1988, Sch. 29, para. 32, that Act being the Taxes Act 1988 (FA 1982, s. 157(2)(b)).

Notes – ICTA 1988, s. 838 defines 75 per cent subsidiary by reference to "ownership", "directly or indirectly" of not less than 75 per cent of "ordinary share capital".

FINANCE ACT 1984

(1984 Chapter 43)

[*26th July 1984*]

ARRANGEMENT OF SECTIONS

PART II – INCOME TAX, CORPORATION TAX AND CAPITAL GAINS TAX ETC.

CHAPTER III – CAPITAL GAINS

CHAPTER IV – INSURANCE

SCHEDULES

PART II – INCOME TAX, CORPORATION TAX AND CAPITAL GAINS TAX ETC.

Chapter III – Capital Gains

70 Postponement of tax due from beneficiaries on gains of non-resident trustees

70 [Repealed by TCGA 1992, s. 290 and Sch. 12, subject to saving in TCGA 1992, Sch. 11, para. 18(b) in relation to amounts of tax which are postponed under FA 1984, Sch. 14.]

History – S. 70 reproduced below for information in the light of the saving in TCGA 1992, Sch. 11, para. 18(b):

"**70(1)** The provisions of Schedule 14 to this Act have effect in any case where–

(a) before 6th April 1981, a chargeable gain accrued to the trustees of a settlement in such circumstances that section 17 of the Capital Gains Tax Act 1979 (non-resident trust) applies as respects that chargeable gain; and

(b) by virtue of that section a beneficiary under the settlement is treated for the purposes of that Act as if, in the year 1983–84 or any earlier year of assessment, an amount determined by reference to the chargeable gain which accrued to the trustees or, as the case may be, the whole or part of that gain had been a chargeable gain accruing to the beneficiary; and

(c) at 29th March 1983 some or all of the capital gains tax payable in respect of the chargeable gain accruing to the beneficiary had not been paid.

70(2) [Amends CGTA 1979, s. 17(3)(b).]

70(3) [Amends FA 1981, s. 80(8).]

70(4) [In this section and Schedule 14 to this Act **"settlement"**, **"settlor"** and **"settled property"** have the same meaning as in section 17 of the Capital Gains Tax Act 1979.]"

Chapter IV – Insurance

73 Insurance business of registered friendly societies

73(1)–(3) [Repealed by ICTA 1988, s. 844 and Sch. 31.]

73(4) In consequence of the preceding provisions of this section and subsection (5) below, in section 1 of the Friendly Societies Act (Northern Ireland) 1970 and section 7 of the Friendly Societies Act 1974 (societies which may be registered)–

(a) paragraph (a) of subsection (3), and

(b) subsection (3A),

shall not have effect with respect to benefits secured by contracts made after 13th March 1984.

73(5), (6) [Repealed by ICTA 1988, s. 844 and Sch. 31.]

73(7) If, after 13th March 1984, the committee of a registered society or branch whose rules make provision for it to carry on life or endowment business resolve to accept, in respect of any contract falling within subsection (8) below, premiums of amounts arrived at by deducting 15 per cent from the premiums provided for by the rules of the society or branch (that is to say by deducting the same amount as, apart from section 72 above, would have been deductible by way of relief under section 19 of the Taxes Act),–

(a) the resolution shall be deemed to be permitted by the principal Act and the rules of the society or branch; and

(b) nothing in the principal Act shall require the registration of the resolution; and

(c) together with the annual return of the society or branch for the year of account ending 31st December 1984, the society or branch shall send a copy of the resolution to the registrar.

73(8) Subsection (7) above applies to any contract entered into by a registered society or branch–

(a) which is for the assurance under life or endowment business of any gross sum; and

(b) which is entered into pursuant to a proposal received by the society or branch on or before 13th March 1984; and

(c) which is one which the society might lawfully have entered into on that date; and

(d) which is entered into after 13th March 1984 and before 1st May 1984.

73(9) In subsection (7) above **"the principal Act"** means, according to the enactment under which the society or branch is registered,–

(a) the Friendly Societies Act (Northern Ireland) 1970; or

(b) the Friendly Societies Act 1974;

and subsections (7) and (8) shall be construed as one with the principal Act.

History – S. 73(1)–(3), (5), (6) were repealed by ICTA 1988, s. 844 and Sch. 31. See now ICTA 1988, s. 460(2)(c)(ii), (4), (6) and 464(1).

SCHEDULE 14 – BENEFICIARY'S LIABILITY FOR TAX ON GAINS OF NON-RESIDENT TRUSTEES

Section 70

1–15 [Sch. 14 was repealed by TCGA 1992 (see History note).]

History – Sch. 14 was repealed by TCGA 1992, s. 290 and Sch. 12, subject to saving in TCGA 1992, Sch. 11, para. 18(b) in respect of amounts of tax postponed under Sch. 14. Sch. 14 is reproduced below for information:
In former para. 1, in the definition of "close relative", the words "or civil partner" inserted by SI 2005/3229, reg. 2, with effect from 5 December 2005.
Reference in former Sch. 14, para. 1, 7, 8, 12 and 15 to provisions of the Taxes Act 1988 substituted by ICTA 1988, Sch. 29, para. 32, that Act being the Taxes Act 1988 (FA 1984, s. 128(2)).

"INTERPRETATION

1(1) In this Schedule–

"attributed gain", in relation to the beneficiary, means the chargeable gain which, as mentioned in paragraph (b) of subsection (1) of the principal section, is treated as accruing to him;

"the beneficiary" means the beneficiary referred to in that paragraph and paragraph (c) of that subsection;

"claim" means a claim under paragraph 2(1) below;

"close relative", in relation to any person, means his spouse or civil partner or a child or remoter descendant of his;

"ineligible gain" shall be construed in accordance with paragraph 2(3) below;

"offshore income gain"has the same meaning as in Chapter V of Part XVII of the Taxes Act 1988;

"the principal Act" means the Capital Gains Tax Act 1979;

"the principal section" means section 70 of this Act;

"related settlement" shall be construed in accordance with paragraph 5(6) below;

"relevant benefit" shall be construed in accordance with paragraph 5 below; and

"the relevant year of assessment", in relation to an attributed gain, means the year of assessment in which the gain is treated as accruing to the beneficiary.

1(2) Subject to subsection (4) of the principal section, section 83 of the Finance Act 1981 (meaning of "capital payment" etc.) applies for the purposes of this Schedule as it applies for the purposes of sections 80 to 82 of that Act.

1(3) In any case where the beneficiary is a married woman, any reference in the following provisions of this Schedule to the payment of capital gains tax by the beneficiary shall be construed as including a reference to the payment by her husband of capital gains tax which, under subsection (1) of section 45 of the principal Act, is assessed and charged on him.

CLAIMS FOR POSTPONEMENT OF TAX

2(1) Subject to sub-paragraph (3) below, in a case falling within the principal section, the provisions of this Schedule have effect to determine whether, on a claim made to the Board, payment of any of the capital gains tax referable to an attributed gain may be postponed and, if so, to what extent and for how long.

2(2) A claim must be made before 1st July 1985 or, if it is later, the expiry of the period of thirty days beginning with the date of the issue of a notice of assessment requiring the payment of an amount of capital gains tax assessed, in whole or in part, by reason of an attributed gain to which the claim relates.

2(3) The provisions of this Schedule do not have effect to allow postponement of the payment of the capital gains tax referable to an attributed gain if the capital gains tax chargeable on the gain–

(a) has previously been postponed under section 17(4)(b) of the principal Act (pre-6th April 1965 settlements); or

(b) subject to sub-paragraph (4) below, carries interest, by virtue of section 88(1) of the Taxes Management Act 1970 (interest on tax recovered to make good tax lost due to fraud, wilful default or neglect), from the date on which the tax ought to have been paid until payment;

and an attributed gain falling within paragraph (a) or paragraph (b) above is in this Schedule referred to as an ineligible gain.

2(4) Sub-paragraph (3)(b) above does not apply where the tax carries interest by reason only of the neglect of any person and that neglect is remedied before 1st July 1985.

2(5) In relation to a claim, any reference in this Schedule to an attributed gain to which the claim relates is a reference to such a gain–
(a) which is specified in the claim, and
(b) which is not an ineligible gain, and
(c) in respect of which the claim is not out of time by virtue of sub-paragraph (2) above,
and any reference to the settlement to which the claim relates is a reference to the settlement under which the beneficiary is a beneficiary and to the trustees of which accrued the chargeable gain which gives rise to the attributed gain or gains to which the claim relates.
2(6) In a case where a claim relates to attributed gains accruing to the beneficiary by virtue of more than one settlement, the provisions of this Schedule shall have effect as if there were separate claims, each relating to the attributed gain or gains accruing by virtue of a single settlement.
2(7) Without prejudice to the application of sub-paragraph (2) above in a case where the personal representatives of the beneficiary receive a notice of assessment requiring the payment by them of an amount of capital gains tax assessed, in whole or in part, by reason of an attributed gain, if–
(a) before his death the beneficiary or, where paragraph 1(3) above applies, the beneficiary's husband received a notice of assessment requiring the payment by him of such an amount of capital gains tax, and
(b) at the time of his death the period within which he might make a claim in respect of any of the tax assessed by that notice had not expired,
a claim by his personal representatives relating to that tax may be made at any time before the expiry of the period of six months beginning on the date of the death of the beneficiary or, as the case may be, her husband (or, if it is later, before 1st July 1985).
2(8) In relation to any claim by the personal representatives of the beneficiary, references in this Schedule to the postponement of the payment of any tax shall be construed as references to the discharge of that tax and, accordingly, paragraphs 11 and 12 below do not apply where a claim is made by the personal representatives.

TAX REFERABLE TO ATTRIBUTED GAINS

3 Any reference in this Schedule to the tax referable to an attributed gain is a reference to the amount determined by multiplying the total capital gains tax on chargeable gains accruing to the beneficiary in the relevant year of assessment by a fraction–
(a) of which the numerator is the amount of the attributed gain; and
(b) the denominator is the total of the chargeable gains accruing to the beneficiary in the relevant year of assessment.

INITIAL CALCULATIONS RELEVANT TO TAX WHICH MAY BE POSTPONED

4(2) Subject to sub-paragraph (3) below, in this paragraph and paragraph 5 below **"the base year"** means the year of assessment which precedes the relevant year of assessment in relation to the attributed gain or, as the case may be, the earliest of the attributed gains to which the claim relates.
4(3) Where the relevant year of assessment referred to in sub-paragraph (2) above is the year 1965–66, the base year is also that year of assessment.
4(4) In relation to a claim **"the unpaid tax"** means the amount of tax–
(a) which is referable to the attributed gain (or attributed gains) to which the claim relates; and
(b) which remains unpaid at the date of the claim.
4(5) In relation to a claim, **"the tax already paid"** means the amount of tax–
(a) which has been paid at the date of the claim, excluding any tax which was so paid, or is or was otherwise borne, by the trustees of the settlement to which the claim relates; and
(b) which is referable to any attributed gains–
(i) which have accrued to the beneficiary by virtue of the settlement to which the claim relates; and
(ii) for which the relevant year of assessment is, or is later than, the base year; and
(iii) which are not ineligible gains.

RELEVANT BENEFITS

5(1) The provisions of this paragraph have effect to determine what are the relevant benefits to be taken into account (as mentioned in paragraph 4(1)(c) above) in relation to a claim; and in the following provisions of this paragraph **"the calculation period"** means the period beginning at the beginning of the base year and ending on 9th March 1981.
5(2) Subject to sub-paragraph (3) below, if, under or by reference to the settlement to which the claim relates or a related settlement, the beneficiary received a capital payment from the trustees of the settlement–
(a) at any time in the calculation period, or
(b) after the end of that period but before 6th April 1984, in so far as that payment represented a chargeable gain which, before 6th April 1981, accrued to the trustees of the settlement to which the claim relates,
the amount of that capital payment is a relevant benefit.
5(3) In any case where, apart from this sub-paragraph, sub-paragraph (2) above would bring into account, as a relevant benefit in relation to a claim, a capital payment received under or by reference to a related settlement, and either–
(a) on a claim relating to the related settlement, the payment falls to be taken into account under this paragraph as a relevant benefit, or
(b) it appears to the Board to be likely that the payment will fall to be so taken into account on a claim relating to the related settlement,
the payment shall not be taken into account as a relevant benefit in relation to the claim referred to in sub-paragraph (2) above except to the extent that it constitutes a surplus benefit by virtue of paragraph 6(5) below.
5(4) If, at any time in the period beginning at the beginning of the base year and ending at the beginning of the year of assessment in which the claim is made, the beneficiary disposed of his interest in the settlement to which the claim relates in circumstances such that, by virtue of section 58(1) of the principal Act, no chargeable gain could accrue on the disposal, then the amount or value of the consideration for the disposal is a relevant benefit.
5(5) Where the disposal referred to in sub-paragraph (4) above was made before 6th April 1984, the reference in that sub-paragraph to the consideration for the disposal shall be construed as a reference only to such consideration (if any) as was actually given for the disposal.
5(6) For the purposes of this Schedule, a settlement is a related settlement in relation to the settlement to which a claim relates if, by the exercise in the base year or later (whether before or after the making of the claim) of a power conferred by one of the settlements, or by the combination of such an exercise and any other transactions, property of any description forming part of the settled property of one of the settlements is at any time appointed to the other settlement or otherwise dealt with so as to increase the value of the settled property of the other settlement.

THE BASIC RULES AS TO POSTPONEMENT

6(1) Unless on a claim the aggregate of–
(a) the unpaid tax (as defined in paragraph 4(4) above), and
(b) the tax already paid (as defined in paragraph 4(5) above),
exceeds 30 per cent of the aggregate of the relevant benefits referred to in paragraph 4(1)(c) above, there is no postponement of the payment of any of the capital gains tax referable to the attributed gains to which the claim relates.
6(2) Subject to the following provisions of this Schedule, the amount of capital gains tax payment of which is, on a claim, postponed by virtue of this Schedule is whichever is the smaller of–
(a) the unpaid tax; and
(b) the amount of the excess referred to in sub-paragraph (1) above;

and, where the amount in paragraph (b) above is the smaller, payment of tax assessed for a later year shall be postponed in priority to payment of tax assessed for an earlier year.

6(3) Without prejudice to paragraph 2(8) above, if at any time after a claim is made the beneficiary dies, any tax the payment of which would, by virtue of this Schedule, still be postponed at the date of his death shall be discharged on that date.

6(4) Notwithstanding anything in Part IX of the Taxes Management Act 1970 (interest on overdue tax), where payment of an amount of capital gains tax is postponed by virtue of this Schedule none of that tax shall carry interest (or be taken to have carried interest) for any period before the time when the tax becomes payable in accordance with paragraph 11 below.

6(5) In any case where, by virtue of sub-paragraph (1) above, there is on a claim no postponement of the payment of capital gains tax, there shall be determined–

(a) whether there would still be no postponement if there were left out of account all relevant benefits (if any) referable to capital payments received under or by reference to a related settlement, and

(b) if so, what is the excess of all the other relevant benefits over 31/3 times the aggregate of the tax referred to in paragraphs (a) and (b) of sub-paragraph (1) above,

and so much of those other relevant benefits as are referable to capital payments falling within sub-paragraph (2) of paragraph 5 above and equal (or do not exceed) that excess shall be regarded as a surplus benefit for the purposes of sub-paragraph (3) of that paragraph.

EFFECT OF SUBSEQUENT CAPITAL PAYMENTS RECEIVED BY THE BENEFICIARY

7(1) The provisions of this paragraph apply if–

(a) on a claim there would, in accordance with paragraph 6(2) above, be an amount of capital gains tax payment of which is postponed by virtue of this Schedule; but

(b) before the beginning of the year of assessment in which the claim is made, the beneficiary has received from the trustees of the settlement to which the claim relates or a related settlement a capital payment which is not a relevant benefit and has not been brought into account under sub-sections (3) and (4) of section 80 of the Finance Act 1981 (new provisions as to gain of non-resident settlements) in determining whether chargeable gains or offshore income gains should be attributed to the beneficiary by reference to any trust gains for any previous year of assessment.

7(2) If the amount of capital gains tax referred to in paragraph (a) of sub-paragraph (1) above exceeds 30 per cent of the aggregate of the amount of the capital payments which fall within paragraph (b) of that sub-paragraph, then, subject to paragraph 9 below, the amount of capital gains tax payment of which is postponed by virtue of this Schedule is an amount equal to that excess.

7(3) If the amount of capital gains tax referred to in paragraph (a) of sub-paragraph (1) above is less than or equal to 30 per cent of the aggregate of the amount of the capital payments which fall within paragraph (b) of that sub-paragraph, then there is no postponement of the payment of any of that capital gains tax.

7(4) In any case where–

(a) the amount of capital gains tax referred to in sub-paragraph (1)(a) above equals or exceeds 30 per cent of the aggregate of those capital payments falling within sub-paragraph (1)(b) above which the beneficiary has received from the trustees of the settlement to which the claim relates, and

(b) apart from this paragraph, those capital payments would fall to be brought into account under subsections (3) and (4) of section 80 of the Finance Act 1981 (new provisions as to gains of non-resident settlements) in determining whether chargeable gains or offshore income gains should be attributed to the beneficiary by reference to any trust gains for the year of assessment in which the claim is made,

then, as respects that year of assessment and any subsequent year, those capital payments shall be left out of account for the purposes of the said subsections (3) and (4).

7(5) In any case where–

(a) the condition in sub-paragraph (4)(a) above is not fulfilled, but

(b) the condition in sub-paragraph (4)(b) above is fulfilled,

then, as respects the year of assessment in which the claim is made and any subsequent year, so much of the capital payments referred to in sub-paragraph (4) above as is equal to 31/3 times the amount of capital gains tax referred to in sub-paragraph (1)(a) above shall be left out of account for the purposes of subsections (3) and (4) of section 80 of the Finance Act 1981.

7(6) Where, by virtue of sub-paragraph (4) or sub-paragraph (5) above, the whole or any part of a capital payment falls to be left out of account as mentioned in that sub-paragraph–

(a) the payment shall to the same extent be left out of account for the purposes of the application on any other occasion of any provision of paragraphs 7 to 12 of this Schedule; and

(b) section 740 of the Taxes Act 1988 (transfer of assets abroad: liability of non-transferors) shall have effect in relation to a benefit received by the beneficiary which, in whole or in part, consists of that payment as if, in the year of assessment in which the claim is made, chargeable gains equal to so much of that payment as falls to be so left out of account were, by reason of that payment, treated under section 80 of that Act as accruing to the beneficiary.

7(7) Where any capital payments falling within sub-paragraph (1)(b) above which the beneficiary has received from the trustees of the settlement to which the claim relates are not such as are referred to in sub-paragraph (4)(b) above, sub-paragraph (6)(a) above shall apply to each of those payments in like manner as if it had been such a payment as is referred to in sub-paragraph (4)(b) above and the amount of it to be left out of account had been determined accordingly under sub-paragraph (4) or sub-paragraph (5) above.

8(1) The provisions of this paragraph apply if, in a case where paragraph 7 above applies, the amount of capital gains tax referred to in sub-paragraph (1)(a) of that paragraph exceeds 30 per cent of the aggregate of those capital payments falling within sub-paragraph (1)(b) of that paragraph which the beneficiary has received from the trustees of the settlement to which the claim relates.

8(2) In the following provisions of this paragraph–

(a) the capital payments falling within sub-paragraph (1)(b) of paragraph 7 above which the beneficiary has received otherwise than from the trustees of the settlement to which the claim relates are referred to as **"related payments"**; and

(b) any of those related payments which, apart from this paragraph, would fall to be brought into account as mentioned in sub-paragraph (4)(b) of paragraph 7 above is referred to as a **"related section 80 payment"**.

8(3) If sub-paragraph (2) of paragraph 7 above applies, then–

(a) as respects the year of assessment in which the claim is made and any subsequent year, any related section 80 payment shall be left out of account for the purposes of sub-paragraphs (3) and (4) of section 80 of the Finance Act 1981; and

(b) all the related payments shall be left out of account for the purposes of the application on any other occasion of any provision of paragraphs 7 to 12 of this Schedule.

8(4) If sub-paragraph (3) of paragraph 7 above applies, then–

(a) as respects the year of assessment in which the claim is made and any subsequent year, so much of any related section 80 payment as is equal to 31/3 times the amount of capital gains tax released by that payment shall be left out of account for the purposes of subsections (3) and (4) of section 80 of the Finance Act 1981; and

(b) so much of each of the related payments as is equal to 31/3 times the amount of capital gains tax released by the payment shall be left out of account for the purposes mentioned in sub-paragraph (3)(b) above.

8(5) For the purposes of sub-paragraph (4) above, the amount of capital gains tax released by a related payment shall be determined by the formula–

$$(A - B) \times \frac{C}{D}$$

where–

A is the capital gains tax referred to in sub-paragraph (1)(a) of paragraph 7 above;

B is an amount equal to 30 per cent of the aggregate of those capital payments falling within sub-paragraph (1)(b) of that paragraph which the beneficiary has received from the trustees of the settlement to which the claim relates;

C is the related payment in question; and

D is the aggregate of all the related payments.

8(6) Where, by virtue of sub-paragraph (3)(a) or sub-paragraph (4)(a) above, the whole or any part of a related section 80 payment falls to be left out of account as mentioned in that sub-paragraph, section 740 of the Taxes Act 1988 shall have effect in relation to the benefit received by the beneficiary which, in whole or in part, consists of that payment as if, in the year of assessment in which the claim is made, chargeable gains equal to so much of that payment as falls to be so left out of account were, by reason of that payment, treated under section 80 of that Act as accruing to the beneficiary.

EFFECT OF RELATED BENEFITS DERIVED FROM PAYMENTS RECEIVED BY CLOSE RELATIVES OF THE BENEFICIARY

9(1) The provisions of this paragraph apply if,–

(a) on a claim, payment of an amount of capital gains tax determined in accordance with paragraph 6(2) or paragraph 7(2) above would, apart from this paragraph, be postponed by virtue of this Schedule; and

(b) as a result of a capital payment received by a close relative of the beneficiary, there is, in accordance with paragraph 10 below, a related benefit which falls to be taken into account in relation to the claim.

9(2) If the amount of capital gains tax referred to in sub-paragraph (1)(a) above exceeds 30 per cent of the aggregate of the related benefits which fall to be taken into account in relation to the claim, then the amount of capital gains tax payment of which is postponed by virtue of this Schedule is an amount equal to that excess.

9(3) If the amount of capital gains tax referred to in sub-paragraph (1)(a) above is less than or equal to 30 per cent of the aggregate of the related benefits which fall to be taken into account in relation to the claim, then there is no postponement of the payment of any of that capital gains tax.

RELATED BENEFITS

10(1) The provisions of this paragraph have effect to determine what are, in relation to a claim, the related benefits which are to be taken into account under paragraph 9 above.

10(2) If, on or after 6th April 1984 and before the beginning of the year of assessment in which the claim is made, a close relative of the beneficiary has received from the trustees of the settlement to which the claim relates or a related settlement a capital payment which has not been brought into account under subsections (3) and (4) of section 80 of the Finance Act 1981 in determining whether chargeable gains or offshore income gains should be attributed to the close relative by reference to any trust gains for any previous year of assessment, then, subject to sub-paragraphs (3) and (4) below, that capital payment is a related benefit which falls to be taken into account in relation to the claim.

10(3) A capital payment falling within sub-paragraph (2) above is not a related benefit which falls to be taken into account as mentioned in that sub-paragraph to the extent that it has already been taken into account on any previous operation of sub-paragraph (4) or sub-paragraph (5) of paragraph 7 above on the occasion of a claim in respect of which the close relative himself or a close relative of his or a person whose close relative he was the beneficiary.

10(4) A capital payment falling within sub-paragraph (2) above is not a related benefit which falls to be taken into account as mentioned in that sub-paragraph if the Board so direct on the grounds that it appears likely that the payment will fall to be taken into account, either as giving rise to a relevant benefit or under paragraph 7 above, in relation to such a claim as is referred to in sub-paragraph (3) above.

10(5) Sub-paragraphs (3) to (6) of paragraph 8 above shall have effect for the purposes of this paragraph–

(a) as if any reference to a provision of paragraph 7 above were a reference to the corresponding provision of paragraph 9 above; and

(b) as if any reference to a related payment were a reference to a related benefit which falls to be taken into account as mentioned in sub-paragraph (2) above; and

(c) as if any reference to a related section 80 payment were a reference to a related benefit which falls to be taken into account as mentioned in sub-paragraph (2) above and which, apart from this paragraph, would fall to be taken into account under sub-paragraphs (3) and (4) of section 80 of the Finance Act 1981 in determining whether chargeable gains or offshore income gains should be attributed to the close relative concerned by reference to any trust gains for the year of assessement in which is made the claim referred to in sub-paragraph (2) above; and

(d) as if "B" in the formula in sub-paragraph (5) were nil; and

(e) as if any reference in sub-paragraph (6) to the beneficiary were a reference to the close relative concerned.

TIME WHEN POSTPONED TAX BECOMES PAYABLE

11(1) The provisions of this paragraph apply where, as a result of a claim, payment of an amount of capital gains tax, determined in accordance with paragraphs 6 to 9 above, is postponed by virtue of this Schedule; and, subject to sub-paragraph (6) below, any reference in the following provisions of this paragraph to postponed tax is a reference to tax the payment of which is so postponed.

11(2) Postponed tax shall become payable in accordance with sub-paragraph (5) below if, at any time in the year of assessment in which the claim is made or any later year, the beneficiary disposes of his interest in the settlement to which the claim relates in circumstances such that, by virtue of section 58(1) of the principal Act, no chargeable gain could accrue on the disposal; and in sub-paragraph (5) below **"the relevant consideration"** means the amount or value of the consideration for such a disposal.

11(3) Subject to paragraph 12 below, postponed tax shall become payable in accordance with sub-paragraph (5) below if, at any time in the year of assessment in which the claim is made or any later year, the beneficiary or a close relative of his receives a capital payment from the trustees of the settlement to which the claim relates or a related settlement.

11(4) In the following provisions of this paragraph and paragraph 12 below, any reference to a material year of assessment is a reference to one in which the beneficiary disposes of his interest as mentioned in sub-paragraph (2) above or in which sub-paragraph (3) above applies.

11(5) For any material year of assessment, so much of the postponed tax as does not exceed 30 per cent of the aggregate of–

(a) the relevant consideration in respect of any disposal in that year, and

(b) subject to paragraph 12 below, the capital payments received in that year as mentioned in sub-paragraph (3) above,

shall become payable as if it were capital gains tax assessed in respect of gains accruing in that year.

11(6) If, for any material year of assessment, the amount of the postponed tax exceeds 30 per cent of the aggregate referred to in sub-paragraph (5) above, only the excess shall continue after the end of that year to be postponed tax for the purposes of this paragraph, but without prejudice to the subsequent operation of this paragraph in relation to a later year of assessment which is a material year.

11(7) Where part, but not the whole, of any postponed tax becomes payable in accordance with sub-paragraph (5) above, tax assessed for an earlier year shall be regarded as becoming so payable before tax assessed for a later year.

BALANCE OF CAPITAL PAYMENTS

12(1) *If* any capital payments received in any year of assessment as mentioned in paragraph 11(3) above fall to be brought into account for that year for the purposes of subsections (3) and (4) of section 80 of the Finance Act 1981, those capital payments shall be disregarded for the purposes of sub-paragraph (5) or, as the case may be, sub-paragraph (6) of paragraph 11 above except to the extent that the aggregate of those payments exceeds the chargeable gains and offshore income gains which in that year are treated under the said section 80 as accruing to the beneficiary or, as the case may be, the close relative; and any such excess is in the following provisions of this paragraph referred to as the balance of section 80 payments for that year.

12(2) Subject to the following provisions of this paragraph, as respects any year of assessment subsequent to a material year of assessment for which there is a balance of section 80 payments there shall be left out of account for the purposes of subsections (3) and (4) of section 80 of the Finance Act 1981 so much of the capital payments as made up that balance.
12(3) If paragraph 11(6) above did not apply for any material year of assessment for which there is a balance of section 80 payments then, as respects years of assessment subsequent to that year, sub-paragraph (2) above shall apply only to so much of the capital payments mentioned therein as is equal to 31/8 times the amount of postponed tax released by that balance.
12(4) For any material year of assessment, the amount of postponed tax released by a balance of section 80 payments for that year shall be determined by the formula–

$$(E - F) \times \frac{G}{H}$$

where

E the postponed tax, within the meaning of paragraph 11 above;
F an amount equal to 30 per cent of any consideration for that year which falls within sub-paragraph (5)(a) of that paragraph;
G the balance of the section 80 payments for that year; and
H the aggregate of the capital payments (including that balance) taken into account under sub-paragraph (5)(b) of that paragraph for that year.

12(5) If, in a case where sub-paragraph (2) above applies in accordance with sub-paragraph (3) above, there were, for the material year of assessment concerned,–
(a) a balance of section 80 payments derived from payments received by the beneficiary, and
(b) another such balance derived from payments received by a close relative of his,
sub-paragraph (2) above shall apply (in accordance with sub-paragraph (3) above) to the capital payments which made up the balance derived from payments received by the beneficiary in priority to capital payments which made up the other balance.
12(6) Subject to sub-paragraph (5) above, where there is more than one capital payment to which sub-paragraph (2) above applies, the proportion of each of them which is left out of account as mentioned in that sub-paragraph shall be the same.
12(7) Where, by virtue of the preceding provisions of this paragraph, the whole or any part of a capital payment falls to be left out of account as mentioned in sub-paragraph (2) above, section 740 of the Taxes Act 1988 shall have effect in relation to a benefit which is received by the beneficiary or, as the case may be, a close relative of his and which, in whole or in part, consists of that payment as if, in the material year of assessment concerned, chargeable gains equal to so much of that payment as falls to be so left out of account were, by reason of that payment, treated under section 80 of that Act as accruing to the beneficiary or, as the case may be, the close relative.
13(1) Where, by virtue of sub-paragraph (2) of paragraph 12 above, the whole or any part of a capital payment falls to be left out of account as mentioned in that sub-paragraph, it shall to the same extent be left out of account for the purposes of the application on any other occasion of any provision of paragraphs 7 to 12 of this Schedule.
13(2) Where sub-paragraph (6) of paragraph 11 above applies for any material year of assessment, any capital payments which–
(a) fall to be taken into account under sub-paragraph (5)(b) of that paragraph for that year, and
(b) are not such as to fall within paragraph 12(1) above,
shall be left out of account for the purposes referred to in sub-paragraph (1) above.
13(3) Where sub-paragraph (6) of paragraph 11 above does not apply for any material year of assessment, so much of any capital payment falling within paragraphs (a) and (b) of sub-paragraph (2) above as is equal to 31/3 times the amount of postponed tax released by that payment shall be left out of account for the purposes referred to in sub-paragraph (1) above.
13(4) The amount of postponed tax released by a capital payment shall be determined for the purposes of sub-paragraph (3) above by the formula in paragraph 12(4) above, except that, in applying that formula for those purposes, "G" shall be the amount of the capital payment in question.
13(5) In this paragraph, **"material year of assessment"** shall be construed in accordance with paragraph 11(4) above.

SECOND AND LATER CLAIMS

14(1) This paragraph applies where–
(a) as a result of a claim (in this paragraph referred to as **"the earlier claim"**), payment of an amount of capital gains tax (in this paragraph referred to as **"the original tax"**), determined in accordance with paragraph 6 or paragraph 7 above, is or was postponed by virtue of this Schedule; and
(b) after the making of the earlier claim, another claim (in this paragraph referred to as **"the later claim"**) is made in relation to an attributed gain to which the earlier claim did not relate; and
(c) the settlement to which the earlier and the later claims relate is the same.
14(2) If the year of assessment which is the relevant year of assessment in relation to any attributed gain to which the later claim relates is earlier than the earliest year of assessment which is the relevant year of assessment in relation to any attributed gain to which the earlier claim related, then,–
(a) the earlier claim and the postponement resulting from it shall be set aside; and
(b) the provisions of this Schedule shall have effect as if (notwithstanding paragraph 2(2) above) the attributed gains to which the later claim relates included the attributed gains to which the earlier claim related.
14(3) Where sub-paragraph (2) above does not apply and, at the time the later claim is made, payment of any of the original tax remains postponed by virtue of this Schedule, then, subject to sub-paragraph (4) below,–
(a) paragraphs 4 to 10 above shall not apply in relation to the later claim; and
(b) payment of the tax referable to the attributed gain or gains to which the later claim relates shall be postponed by virtue of this Schedule; and
(c) paragraphs 11 and 12 above shall apply as if the payment of that tax had been postponed as a result of the earlier claim and, accordingly, that tax shall be added to the original tax.
14(4) If, in a case where sub-paragraph (3) above applies, the relevant year of assessment in relation to an attributed gain (in this sub-paragraph referred to as **"the later gain"**) to which the later claim relates is the same as the relevant year of assessment in relation to an attributed gain to which the earlier claim related,–
(a) paragraph 3 above shall not apply in relation to the later gain; and
(b) in relation to the later gain, the references in sub-paragraph (3) above to the tax referable to the gain shall be construed as references to the capital gains tax assessed by reason of the gain.
14(5) Where sub-paragraph (2) above does not apply and, at the time the later claim is made, there is no longer any postponement of the payment of any of the original tax, then, in the application of the provisions of this Schedule in relation to the later claim, paragraph 4(2) above shall not apply and **"the base year"** for the purposes of paragraphs 4 and 5 above shall be that year of assessment which was the base year in relation to the earlier claim.

INFORMATION

15(1) The Board may by notice in writing require any person to furnish them, within such time as they may direct, not being less than twenty-eight days, with such particulars as they think necessary for the purposes of section 70 of this Act and this Schedule.
15(2) Subsections (2) to (6) of section 745 of the Taxes Act 1988 shall have effect in relation to sub-paragraph (1) above as they have effect in relation to subsection (1) of that section; but, in the application of those subsections by virtue of this sub-paragraph, references to Chapter III of Part XVII of the Taxes Act shall be construed as references to section 70 of this Act and this Schedule.

15(3) In any case where–

(a) a claim has been made, and

(b) as a result of the claim, payment of an amount of capital gains tax was postponed by virtue of this Schedule, and

(c) at a time when any of that tax remains unpaid, there is a disposal to which paragraph 11(2) above applies or the beneficiary or a close relative of his receives such a capital payment as is referred to in paragraph 11(3)(a) above,

then, not later than three months after the end of the year of assessment in which the disposal occurs or the payment is received, the beneficiary shall inform the Board of the disposal or receipt, as the case may be.

15(4) [A Repealed by ICTA 1988, s. 844 and Sch. 31.]

Notes – The reference in former Sch. 14, para. 8 and 12 to "section 80 of that Act" is to FA 1981, s. 80."

COMPANIES ACT 1985

(1985 Chapter 6)

[*11th March 1985*]

ARRANGEMENT OF SECTIONS

PART X – ENFORCEMENT OF FAIR DEALING BY DIRECTORS

245D Disclosure of information held by Inland Revenue to persons authorised to apply to court

245D [Repealed by CA 2006, s. 1295 and Sch. 4, with effect from 6 April 2008 (SI 2007/3495, art. 8(a) and Sch. 2, Pt. 1).]

History – Former s. 245D inserted by the Companies (Audit, Investigations and Community Enterprise) Act 2004, s. 11, with effect from 6 April 2005.

Notes – S. 245D reflected in CA 2006 as follows:
S. 245D(1): CA 2006, s. 458(1).
S. 245D(2): CA 2006, s. 458(2).
S. 245D(3): CA 2006, s. 458(1)).

245E Restrictions on use and further disclosure of information disclosed under section 245D

245E [Repealed by CA 2006, s. 1295 and Sch. 4, with effect from 6 April 2008 (SI 2007/3495, art. 8(a) and Sch. 2, Pt. 1).]

History – Former s. 245E inserted by the Companies (Audit, Investigations and Community Enterprise) Act 2004, s. 11 with effect from 6 April 2005.

Notes – S. 245E reflected in the CA 2006 as follows:
S. 245D(1) and (2): CA 2006, s. 458(3).
S. 245D(3): CA 2006, s. 458(4) and (5).
S. 245D(4): CA 2006, s. 458(4).
S. 245D(5): CA 2006, s. 1126; 1130.

RESTRICTIONS ON DIRECTORS TAKING FINANCIAL ADVANTAGE

311 Prohibition on tax-free payments to directors

311 [Repealed by CA 2006, s. 1144(1) and Sch. 4.]

History – S. 311 repealed by CA 2006, s. 1295 and Sch. 4, with effect from 6 April 2007, by virtue of SI 2006/3428.

FILMS ACT 1985

(1985 Chapter 21)

[*23rd May 1985*]

ARRANGEMENT OF SECTIONS

SCHEDULES

6 Certification of British films

6 Schedule 1 to this Act has effect with respect to the certification by the Secretary of State of a film as a British film for the purposes of film tax relief.

History – S. 6 substituted by FA 2006, s. 42 and Sch. 5, para. 15, with effect from 1 January 2007 (FA 2006, s. 53(1)).

SCHEDULES

SCHEDULE 1 – CERTIFICATION OF BRITISH FILMS FOR PURPOSES OF FILM TAX RELIEF

Sections 3, 5 and 6

History – In the heading to Sch. 1, the words "Certification of British films for the purposes of film tax relief" substituted for "Certification for purposes of section 72 of Finance Act 1982 in case of British films" by FA 2006, s. 42 and Sch. 5, para. 16, with effect from 1 January 2007 (FA 2006, s. 53(1)).

PRELIMINARY

1(1) In this Schedule–

"film" includes any record, however made, of a sequence of visual images that is capable of being used as a means of showing that sequence as a moving picture;

"film production company" has the same meaning as in Part 15 of the Corporation Tax Act 2009 (see section 1182 of that Act).

1(2) For the purposes of this Schedule each part of a series of films is treated as a separate film, unless–

(a) the films form a series with not more than 26 parts,

(b) the combined playing time is not more than 26 hours, and

(c) the series constitutes a self-contained work or is a series of documentaries with a common theme,

in which case the films are treated as a single film.

1(3) References in this Schedule to a film include the film soundtrack.

1(4) For the purposes of this Schedule a film is completed when it is first in a form in which it can reasonably be regarded as ready for copies of it to be made and distributed for presentation to the general public.

History – In para. 1(1), in the definition of "film production company", the words "Part 15 of the Corporation Tax Act 2009 (see section 1182 of that Act)" substituted for the words "Chapter 3 of Part 3 of the Finance Act 2006 (see section 32 of that Act)" by CTA 2009, s. 1322 and Sch. 1, para. 319, with effect, for corporation tax purposes, for accounting periods ending on or after 1 April 2009 and, for income tax and capital gains tax purposes, for the tax year 2009–10 and subsequent years.

Para. 1 substituted by FA 2006, s. 42 and Sch. 5, para. 17, with effect from 1 January 2007 (FA 2006, s. 53(1)).

Cross references – SI 2006/643, art. 3: modifications (omission of definitions of "Commonwealth country" and "film production activity") in respect of films:

- where the first day of principal photography is after 1 April 2006, or
- where the first day of principal photography is before that date but production is not completed by 1 January 2007.

APPLICATIONS FOR CERTIFICATION

2(1) The film production company may apply to the Secretary of State for the certification of a film as a British film.

2(2) The application may be for an interim or final certificate.

2(3) An interim certificate is a certificate granted before the film is completed that the film, if completed in accordance with the proposals set out in the application, will be a British film.

2(4) A final certificate is a certificate granted after the film is completed that the film is a British film.

2(5) The applicant must–

(a) produce to the Secretary of State such books or other documents relating to the application, and

(b) provide the Secretary of State with such other information with respect to it,

as the Secretary of State may require for the purposes of determining the application.

2(6) The Secretary of State may require information provided for the purposes of the application to be accompanied by a statutory declaration, by the person providing it, as to the truth of the information.

History – Para. 2 substituted by FA 2006, s. 42 and Sch. 5, para. 18, with effect from 1 January 2007 (FA 2006, s. 53(1)).

Cross references – SI 2006/3430, art. 2: an application under para. 2 in relation to a film for which the first day of principal photography is on or after 1 January 2007 will be determined in accordance with Sch. 1 as modified by SI 2006/3430.

CERTIFICATION AND WITHDRAWAL OF CERTIFICATION

3(1) If the Secretary of State is satisfied that the requirements are met for interim or final certification of a film as a British film, he shall certify the film accordingly.

3(2) If the Secretary of State is not satisfied that those requirements are met, he shall refuse the application.

3(3) An interim certificate–

(a) may be given subject to conditions, and (unless the Secretary of State directs otherwise) is of no effect if the conditions are not met;

(b) may be expressed to expire after a specified period, and (unless the Secretary of State directs otherwise) ceases to have effect at the end of that period; and

(c) ceases to have effect when a final certificate is issued.

3(4) If it appears to the Secretary of State that a film certified by him under this Schedule ought not to have been certified, he shall revoke its certification.

Unless the Secretary of State directs otherwise, a certificate that is revoked is treated as never having had effect.

History – Para. 3 substituted by FA 2006, s. 42 and Sch. 5, para. 19, with effect from 1 January 2007 (FA 2006, s. 53(1)).

BRITISH FILMS FOR PURPOSES OF THE SCHEDULE

4(1) A film is a British film for the purposes of this Schedule if it passes the relevant cultural test (see paragraph 4A, 4B or 4C).

4(2) [Effectively repealed by FA 2006, s. 42 and Sch. 5, para. 20.]

4(3) [Effectively repealed by FA 2006, s. 42 and Sch. 5, para. 20.]

4(4) The third requirement is that not less than the requisite amount of labour costs (as determined under paragraph 7) represents payments paid or payable in respect of the labour or services of–

(a) Commonwealth citizens,

(b) citizens of a member State, or

(c) persons ordinarily resident in a Commonwealth country or a member State.

4(5) For the purpose of calculating the total expenditure incurred in the production of a film pursuant to sub-paragraph (3), the following shall be disregarded–

(a) any amount deducted under paragraph 7(2)(a) or, as the case may be, paragraph 7(2)(b) in calculating the amount which is the lesser amount for the purposes of paragraph 7(1);

(b) any expenditure incurred on the acquisition or licensing of copyright, trademarks or rights of a similar nature, other than copyright in works created for the purpose of their use in the film;

(c) any expenditure, including the payment of interest, incurred for the purposes of raising or servicing finance for making the film; and

(d) any business overheads attributable to the film.

4(6) A state shall be treated for the purposes of this paragraph as if it were a member State if–

(a) it is party to an *agreement* under Article 310 of the Treaty establishing the European Community; and

(b) the agreement requires a maker of a film who is ordinarily resident or registered in that state to be treated for the purposes of this Schedule in the same way as a maker of a film who is ordinarily resident or registered in a member State.

(7) Her Majesty may by Order in Council provide for films to be treated as British films for the purposes of this Schedule if they are made in accordance with the terms of any agreement between Her Majesty's Government in the United Kingdom and any other government, international organisation or authority.

History – Para. 4(1) substituted for para. 4(1), (2) and (3) by FA 2006, s. 42 and Sch. 5, para. 20, with effect from 1 January 2007 (FA 2006, s. 53(1)).

Cross references – SI 2015/86, art. 3–6: modifications (further amendments of para. 4A–4D) in relation to any film other than an excepted film (as defined in SI 2015/86, art. 2(2)).
SI 2006/3430, art. 3, 4: modifications (further substitution of para. 4A–4C and amendment of 4D) in respect of films where the first day of principal photography is on or after 1 January 2007.
SI 2006/643, art. 4: modifications (substitution of para. 4 and insertion of para 4A–4D) in respect of films:

- where the first day of principal photography is after 1 April 2006, or;
- where the first day of principal photography is before that date but production is not completed by 1 January 2007.

Statutory instruments – SI 1985/960: made under para. 4(5).
SI 2006/2656: made under para. 4(5)

EXCLUDED FILMS

5(1) A film must not be certified as a British film for the purposes of this Schedule if parts of the film whose playing time exceeds 10% of the total playing time of the film are derived from a previous film, unless–

(a) the two films have the same film production company or producer, and

(b) the previous film has not been certified under this Schedule.

5(2) The Secretary of State may direct that sub-paragraph (1) shall not apply in relation to a film if in his opinion–

(a) it is a documentary; and

(b) its subject matter makes it appropriate for sub-paragraph (1) not to be applied.

5(3) For the purposes of this paragraph–

(a) the film soundtrack shall be left out of account;

(b) **"producer"** means the person by whom the arrangements necessary for the making of the film are undertaken;

(c) in relation to certification before the commencement of Chapter 3 of part 3 of the Finance Act 2006, references to certification of a film shall be read as references to certification of the master negative, tape or disc of the film.

History – Para. 5(1) substituted by FA 2006, s. 42 and Sch. 5, para. 21(2) from 1 January 2007 (FA 2006, s. 53(1)).
Para. 5(3) inserted by FA 2006, s. 42 and Sch. 5, para. 21(3), with effect from 1 January 2007 (FA 2006, s. 53(1)).
Para. 5 substituted by SI 1999/2386, art. 7 with effect from 17 August 2002.

ASCERTAINMENT OF LABOUR COSTS AND PLAYING TIME

6(1) For the purposes of this Schedule the labour costs of a film shall be taken to be, subject to paragraph 8, the total amount of the payments paid or payable in respect of the labour or services of persons directly engaged in the making of the film, in so far as those payments are attributable to the making of that film, but shall not be taken to include payments in respect of copyright unless it is copyright in a work created for the purpose of its use in the film.

6(2) For the purposes of sub-paragraph (1)–

(a) the author of the scenario of a film shall be deemed to be a person directly engaged in the making of the film;

(b) a person shall not be taken to be directly engaged in the making of a film by reason only–

  (i) that he is financially interested in the making of the film or is engaged in a clerical capacity as a servant of an undertaking concerned with the making of the film; or

  (ii) that he supplies goods used in the making of the film or is in the employment of a person who supplies such goods;

(c) payments paid or payable to a person who is engaged in an administrative capacity as an officer or servant of an undertaking concerned with the making of a film shall not be taken to be attributable to the making of the film except in so far as they are payments in respect of services directly concerned with the making of that film.

6(3) [Omitted by SI 1999/2386, art. 8.]

History – S. 6(3) omitted by SI 1999/2386, art. 8, with effect from 27 August 2002.

Cross references – SI 2006/643, art. 5: modifications (omission of para. 6) in respect of films:

- where the first day of principal photography is after 1 April 2006, or;
- where the first day of principal photography is before that date but production is not completed by 1 January 2007.

DETERMINATION OF REQUISITE AMOUNT OF LABOUR COSTS

7(1) For the purposes of paragraph 4(4) the requisite amount of the labour costs of a film shall be taken to be whichever is the lesser of the two amounts specified in sub-paragraph (2) of this paragraph.

7(2) The amounts referred to in sub-paragraph (1) are–

(a) the amount arrived at by applying the fraction seven-tenths to the total labour costs of the film, after deducting from those costs, if the applicant on an application under paragraph 2 so desires, the amount of any payment which, as part of those costs, has been paid or is payable in respect of the labour or services of any one person who was not, while engaged in the making of the film–

(i) a Commonwealth citizen or a citizen of a member State, nor

(ii) a person ordinarily resident in a Commonwealth country or a member State; and

(b) the amount arrived at by applying the fraction three-quarters to the total labour costs of the film, after deducting from those costs the amount of any payments which, as part of those costs, have been paid or are payable in respect of the labour or services of any two persons neither of whom was, while engaged in the making of the film, such a citizen or person as is referred to in paragraph (a)(i) or (ii), and at least one of whom was so engaged in the capacity of an actor or actress and in no other capacity.

7(3) [Omitted by SI 1999/2386, art. 9.]

History – In para. 7(1), reference to para. 4(4) substituted and words "(subject to sub-paragraph (3) of this paragraph)" omitted by SI 1999/2386, art. 9, with effect from 27 August 1999.
In para. 7(2)(a), words "seven-tenths" substituted and in para. 7(2)(b) the words "three-quarters" substituted by SI 1999/2386, art. 9, with effect from 27 August 1999.
Para. 7(3), omitted by SI 1999/2386, art. 9, with effect from 27 August 1999.

Cross references – SI 2006/643, art. 5: modifications (omission of para. 7) in respect of films:
- where the first day of principal photography is after 1 April 2006, or
- where the first day of principal photography is before that date but production is not completed by 1 January 2007.

POWER OF SECRETARY OF STATE TO DIRECT ALTERATION OF LABOUR COSTS

8 Where it is material, in connection with an application under paragraph 2 in relation to a negative, tape or disc of a film, to ascertain the labour costs of the film or the proportion of those costs which represents payments in respect of the labour or services of persons of any particular class, then–

(a) if it appears to the Secretary of State that any sum which, as part of those costs, is paid or payable in respect of the labour or services of any particular person is so great as not to be a bona fide payment by way of remuneration for the said labour or services, the Secretary of State may direct that that sum, or part of that sum, shall be disregarded in ascertaining the said labour costs or the said proportion thereof, as the case may be; and

(b) if it appears to the Secretary of State that no sum or a sum so small as not bona fide to represent all the remuneration therefor is paid or payable as part of those costs in respect of the labour or services of any particular person, the Secretary of State may direct that such sum, or (as the case may be) such greater sum, as may be specified in the direction shall be treated as so paid or payable.

Cross references – SI 2006/643, art. 5: modifications (omission of para. 8) in respect of films:
- where the first day of principal photography is after 1 April 2006, or;
- where the first day of principal photography is before that date but production is not completed by 1 January 2007.

DETERMINATION OF DISPUTES

9(1) Any person who is aggrieved by any decision of the Secretary of State under paragraph 3 may, subject to rules of court, apply to the High Court, and the decision of that Court shall be final.

9(2) In relation to any person whose principal place of business is in Scotland, sub-paragraph (1) shall have effect as if for any reference to the High Court there were substituted a reference to the Court of Session.

History – In para. 9(1) the words "any decision of the Secretary of State under paragraph 3 may" substituted for the words "any decision of the Secretary of State to refuse an application under paragraph 2 or to revoke any certification under paragraph 3(1) may" by FA 2006, s. 42 and Sch. 5, para. 22, with effect from 1 January 2007 (FA 2006, s. 53(1)).

REGULATIONS AND ORDERS

10(1) The Secretary of State may make regulations–

(a) prescribing the form of applications under paragraph 2;

(b) prescribing the particulars and evidence necessary for satisfying the Secretary of State that a film is a British film for the purposes of this Schedule;

(c) providing that any statutory declaration which is required by paragraph 2(6) to be made by any person shall be deemed to be properly made if it is made on his behalf by any such person as may be specified in the regulations.

10(2) The Secretary of State with the approval of the Treasury may by order make such modifications of any of the provisions of paragraphs 1 and 4 to 5 as he considers appropriate; and any such order may contain such incidental, supplemental and transitional provisions as he considers appropriate in connection with the order.

10(3) In sub-paragraph (2) **"modifications"** includes additions, omissions and alterations.

10(4) Any regulations or order under this paragraph shall be made by statutory instrument.

10(5) Any regulations under this paragraph shall be laid before Parliament after being made; but no order shall be made under this paragraph unless it has been laid before Parliament and approved by a resolution of each House.

History – In para. 10(1)(c) a reference to paragraph "2(6)" substituted for the reference to paragraph "2(4)" by FA 2006, s. 42 and Sch. 5, para. 23(a), with effect from 1 January 2007 (FA 2006, s. 53(1)).
In para. 10(2) a reference to paragraphs "4 to 5" substituted for the reference to paragraphs "4 to 8" by FA 2006, s. 42 and Sch. 5, para. 23(b), with effect from 1 January 2007 (FA 2006, s. 53(1)).

Statutory instruments – SI 1985/994: made under para. 10(1).
SI 2006/643: made under para. 10(2).
SI 2006/3281: made under para. 10(1).
SI 2006/3430: made under para. 10(2).
SI 2015/86: made under para. 10(2).

BANKRUPTCY (SCOTLAND) ACT 1985

(1985 Chapter 66)

[*30th October 1985*]

ARRANGEMENT OF SECTIONS

SAFEGUARDING OF INTERESTS OF CREDITORS OF INSOLVENT PERSONS

34 Gratuitous alienations

34(1) Where this subsection applies, an alienation by a debtor shall be challengeable by–

(a) any creditor who is a creditor by virtue of a debt incurred on or before the date of sequestration, or before the granting of the trust deed or the debtor's death, as the case may be; or

(b) the permanent trustee, the trustee acting under the trust deed or the judicial factor, as the case may be.

34(2) Subsection (1) above applies where–

(a) by the alienation, whether before or after the coming into force of this section, any of the debtor's property has been transferred or any claim or right of the debtor has been discharged or renounced; and

(b) any of the following has occurred–

(i) his estate has been sequestrated (other than, in the case of a natural person, after his death); or

(ii) he has granted a trust deed which has become a protected trust deed; or

(iii) he has died and within 12 months after his death, his estate has been sequestrated; or

(iv) he has died and within the said 12 months, a judicial factor has been appointed under section 11A of the Judicial Fators (Scotland) Act 1889 to administer his estate and the estate was absolutely insolvent at the date of death; and

(c) the alienation took place on a relevant day.

34(3) For the purposes of paragraph (c) of subsection (2) above, the day on which an alienation took place shall be the day on which the alienation became completely effectual; and in that paragraph "relevant day" means, if the alienation has the effect of favouring–

(a) a person who is an associate of the debtor, a day not earlier than 5 years before the date of sequestration, the granting of the trust deed or the debtor's death, as the case may be; or

(b) any other person, a day not earlier than 2 years before the said date.

34(4) On a challenge being brought under subsection (1) above, the court shall grant decree of reduction or for such restoration of property to the debtor's estate or other redress as may be appropriate, but the court shall not grant such a decree if the person seeking to uphold the alienation establishes–

(a) that immediately, or at any other time, after the alienation the debtor's assets were greater than his liabilities; or

(b) that the alienation was made for adequate consideration; or

(c) that the alienation–

(i) was a birthday, Christmas or other conventional gift; or

(ii) was a gift made, for a charitable purpose, to a person who is not an associate of the debtor,

which having regard to all the circumstances, it was reasonable for the debtor to make:

Provided that this subsection shall be without prejudice to any right or interest acquired in good faith and for value from or through the transferee in the alienation.

34(5) In subsection (4) above, "charitable purpose" means any charitable, benevolent or philanthropic purpose whether or not it is charitable within the meaning of any rule of law.

34(6) For the purposes of the foregoing provisions of this section, an alienation in implementation of a prior obligation shall be deemed to be one for which there was no consideration or no adequate consideration to the extent that the prior obligation was undertaken for no consideration or no adequate consideration.

34(7) This section is without prejudice to the operation of section 2 of the Married Women's Policies of Assurance (Scotland) Act 1880 (policy of assurance may be effected in trust for spouse, future spouse and children) including the operation of that section as applied by section 132 of the Civil Partnership Act 2004.

34(8) A permanent trustee, the trustee acting under a protected trust deed and a judicial factor appointed under section 11A of the Judicial Factors (Scotland) Act 1889 shall have the same right as a creditor has under any rule of law to challenge an alienation of a debtor made for no consideration or for no adequate consideration.

34(9) The permanent trustee shall insert in the sederunt book a copy of any decree under this section affecting the sequestrated estate.

History – In s. 34(7), the words "including the operation of that section as applied by section 132 of the Civil Partnership Act 2004" inserted by CPA 2004, s. 261(2) and Sch. 28, para. 35, with effect from 5 December 2005 (SSI 2005/604, art. 2(a)).

DISTRIBUTION OF DEBTOR'S ESTATE

51 Order of priority in distribution

51(1) The funds of the debtor's estate shall be distributed by the trustee to meet the following debts in the order in which they are mentioned–

(a) the outlays and remuneration of the interim trustee in the administration of the debtor's estate;

(b) the outlays and remuneration of the trustee in the administration of the debtor's estate;

(c) where the debtor is a deceased debtor, deathbed and funeral expenses reasonably incurred and expenses reasonably incurred in administering the deceased's estate;

(d) the expenses reasonably incurred by a creditor who is a petitioner, or concurs in a debtor application, for sequestration;

(e) ordinary preferred debts (excluding any interest which has accrued thereon to the date of sequestration);

(ea) secondary preferred debts (excluding any interest which has accrued thereon to the date of sequestration);

(f) ordinary debts, that is to say a debt which is neither a secured debt nor a debt mentioned in any other paragraph of this subsection;

(g) interest at the rate specified in subsection (7) below on–

  (i) the ordinary preferred debts;

  (ia) the secondary preferred debts;

  (ii) the ordinary debts,

between the date of sequestration and the date of payment of the debt;

(h) any postponed debt.

51(2) In this Act—

(a) **"preferred debt"** means a debt listed in Part I of Schedule 3 to this Act,

(b) **"ordinary preferred debt"** means a debt within any of paragraphs 4 to 6B of Part I of Schedule 3 to this Act,

(c) **"secondary preferred debt"** means a debt within paragraph 6C or 6D of Part 1 of Schedule 3 to this Act, and

Part II of that Schedule shall have effect for the interpretation of Part I.

51(3) In this Act **"postponed debt"** means–

(a) a loan made to the debtor, in consideration of a share of the profits in his business, which is postponed under section 3 of the Partnership Act 1890 to the claims of other creditors;

(b) a loan made to the debtor by the debtor's spouse or civil partner;

(c) a creditor's right to anything vesting in the trustee by virtue of a successful challenge under section 34 of this Act or to the proceeds of sale of such a thing.

51(4) Any debt falling within any of paragraphs (c) to (h) of subsection (1) above shall have the same priority as any other debt falling within the same paragraph and, where the funds of the estate are inadequate to enable the debts mentioned in the paragraph to be paid in full, they shall abate in equal proportions.

51(5) Any surplus remaining, after all the debts mentioned in this section have been paid in full, shall be made over to the debtor or to his successors or assignees; and in this subsection **"surplus"** includes any kind of estate but does not include any unclaimed dividend.

51(5A) Subsection (5) above is subject to Article 35 of the EC Regulation (surplus in secondary proceedings to be transferred to main proceedings).

51(6) Nothing in this section shall affect–

(a) the right of a secured creditor which is preferable to the rights of the trustee; or

(b) any preference of the holder of a lien over a title deed or other document which has been delivered to the trustee in accordance with a requirement under section 38(4) of this Act.

51(7) The rate of interest referred to in paragraph (g) of subsection (1) above shall be whichever is the greater of–

(a) the prescribed rate at the date of sequestration; and

(b) the rate applicable to that debt apart from the sequestration.

History – In s. 51(1)(d), the words "a debtor application" substituted for the words "the petition" by Bankruptcy and Diligence etc. (Scotland) Act 2007, s. 36 and Sch. 1, para. 43, with effect from 1 April 2008 (SI 2008/115, art. 3).
S. 51(1)(e) and (ea) substituted for (e) by SI 2014/3486, art. 28(2)(a), with effect from 1 January 2015, subject to the transitional provision in SI 2014/3486, art. 3 (amendments have no effect in relation to any insolvency proceedings commenced before that date).
In s. 51(1)(g)(i), the word "ordinary" inserted by SI 2014/3486, art. 28(2)(a), with effect from 1 January 2015, subject to the transitional provision in SI 2014/3486, art. 3 (amendments have no effect in relation to any insolvency proceedings commenced before that date).
S. 51(1)(g)(ia) inserted by SI 2014/3486, art. 28(2)(a), with effect from 1 January 2015, subject to the transitional provision in SI 2014/3486, art. 3 (amendments have no effect in relation to any insolvency proceedings commenced before that date).
S. 51(2) substituted by SI 2014/3486, art. 28(2)(b), with effect from 1 January 2015, subject to the transitional provision in SI 2014/3486, art. 3 (amendments have no effect in relation to any insolvency proceedings commenced before that date).
In s. 51(3)(b) words "or civil partner" inserted at end by Civil Partnership Act 2004, Sch. 28, para. 39, with effect from 5 December 2005 (by virtue of Scottish SI 2005/604, art. 2(c)).
S. 51(5A) inserted by SI 2003/2109, reg. 14, with effect from 8 September 2003.
In s. 51 the word "permanent" which appeared before the word "trustee" in five places, omitted by the Bankruptcy and Diligence etc. (Scotland) Act 2007, s. 226(2) and Sch. 6, Pt. 1, with effect from 1 April 2008 (SSI 2008/115, art. 3 and Sch. 2, para. 8) subject to transitional provisions and savings at SSI 2008/115, art. 4–7, 10 and 15.

Notes – The commencement date for s. 51 is 29 December 1986 (s. 78(2), SI 1986/1913).

MISCELLANEOUS AND SUPPLEMENTARY

78 Short title, commencement and extent

78(1) This Act may be cited as the Bankruptcy (Scotland) Act 1985.

78(2) This Act, except this section, shall come into force on such day as the Secretary of State may by order made by statutory instrument appoint; and different days may be so appointed for different purposes and for different provisions.

78(3)–(4) [Transitional and saving provisions.]

78(5) This Act, except the provisions mentioned in subsection (6) below, extends to Scotland only.

78(6) [Not reproduced.]

Notes – The commencement date for s. 78 is 30 October 1985 (s. 78(2)).

SCHEDULE 3 – PREFERRED DEBTS

Section 51

Part I – List of Preferred Debts

DEBTS TO INLAND REVENUE

1 [Sch. 3, para. 1 repealed by the Enterprise Act 2002, s. 251(2)(a), s. 278(2), and Sch. 26.]

History – Sch. 3, para. 1 repealed by the Enterprise Act 2002, s. 251(2)(a), s. 278(2), and Sch. 26, with effect from 15 September 2003, by virtue of SI 2003/2093, art. 2 and Sch. 1. Art. 4 contains transitional provisions.
Previously, in Sch. 3, para. 1 the words "PAYE regulations" substituted for "section 203 of the Income and Corporation Taxes Act 1988 (pay as you earn)" by ITEPA 2003, s. 722 and Sch. 6, para. 153, with effect for income tax purposes, for the tax year 2003–2004 and subsequent tax years, and for corporation tax purposes, for accounting periods ending after 5 April 2003.
References to ICTA 1988 substituted by ICTA 1988, s. 844 and Sch. 29, para. 32.

Transitional – Enterprise Act 2002 (Commencement No. 4 and Transitional Provisions and Savings) Order 2003, SI 2003/2093, art. 4, contains transitional provisions so that the former rules remain in effect where insolvency arrangements are in place prior to 15 September 2003.

Notes – The commencement date for Sch. 3 is 29 December 1986 (s. 78(2), SI 1986/1913).

FINANCE ACT 1986

(1986 Chapter 41) *[25th July 1986]*

ARRANGEMENT OF SECTIONS

PART II – INCOME TAX, CORPORATION TAX AND CAPITAL GAINS TAX

CHAPTER I – GENERAL

EMPLOYEE SHAREHOLDING

CHAPTER IV – SECURITIES

SCHEDULES

PART II – INCOME TAX, CORPORATION TAX AND CAPITAL GAINS TAX

Chapter I – General

EMPLOYEE SHAREHOLDING

24 Approved profit sharing schemes: workers' co-operatives

24(4) [Repealed by Co-operative and Community Benefit Societies Act 2014, s. 151 and Sch. 7)]

24(5) [Repealed by Co-operative and Community Benefit Societies Act 2014, s. 151 and Sch. 7)]

History – S. 24(4) repealed (as relates to England, Wales and Scotland – see s. 153 of the Act) by Co-operative and Community Benefit Societies Act 2014, s. 151 and Sch. 7, with effect from 1 August 2014 (subject to the provisions of Sch. 5 and 6 of that Act). Former s. 24(4) as it continues to apply reads as follows:

"**24(4)** Where, for the purpose of securing (and maintaining) approval of its profit sharing scheme in accordance with Part I of Schedule 9 to the Taxes Act 1988, the rules of a society which is a workers' co-operative or which is seeking to be registered under the industrial and provident societies legislation as a workers' co-operative contain–

(a) provision for membership of the society by the trustees of the scheme,

(b) provision denying voting rights to those trustees, or

(c) other provisions which appear to the registrar to be reasonably necessary for that purpose,

those provisions shall be disregarded in determining whether the society should be or continue to be registered under the industrial and provident societies legislation as a bona fide co-operative society."

S. 24(5) repealed (as relates to England, Wales and Scotland – see s. 153 of the Act) by Co-operative and Community Benefit Societies Act 2014, s. 151 and Sch. 7, with effect from 1 August 2014 (subject to the provisions of Sch. 5 and 6 of that Act). Former s. 24(5) as it continues to apply reads as follows:

"**24(5)** In subsection (4) above **"the industrial and provident societies legislation"** means–

(a) [omitted by Co-operative and Community Benefit Societies Act 2014, s. 151 and Sch. 4, para. 37(a)]

(b) the Industrial and Provident Societies Act (Northern Ireland) 1969,

and **"registrar"** has the same meaning as in that Act and **"co-operative society"** has the same meaning as in section 1 of that Act."

Former s. 24(5)(a) omitted by Co-operative and Community Benefit Societies Act 2014, s. 151 and Sch. 4, para. 37(a), with effect from 1 August 2014 (subject to the provisions of Sch. 5 and 6 of that Act). Former s. 24(5)(a) read as follows:

"(a) the Industrial and Provident Societies Act 1965, or"

In former s. 24(5) the words "that Act" substituted for the words "each of those Acts" and the words "that Act" substituted for the words "those Acts" by Co-operative and Community Benefit Societies Act 2014, s. 151 and Sch. 4, para. 37(b) and (c), with effect from 1 August 2014 (subject to the provisions of Sch. 5 and 6 of that Act)

Reference to provisions of the Taxes Act 1988 in s. 24(4) substituted by ICTA 1988, Sch. 29, para. 32, that Act being the Taxes Act 1988 (FA 1986, s. 114(2)).

Notes – The term "registrar" is defined by reference to the chief registrar of friendly societies and any assistant registrar. The term "co-operative society" is defined by the exclusion of any society which carries on, or intends to carry on, business with the object of making profits mainly for the payment of interest, dividends or bonuses on money invested or deposited with, or lent to, the society or any other person.

Chapter IV – Securities

63 Other provisions

63 Schedule 18 to this Act (which contains other provisions about securities) shall have effect.

SCHEDULE 18 – SECURITIES: OTHER PROVISIONS

Section 63

INFORMATION

7 [Repealed by FA 1997, s. 76 and Sch. 10, para. 15, s. 113 and Sch. 18, Pt. VI(10).]

History – Para. 7 repealed by FA 1997, s. 76 and Sch. 10, para. 15, s. 113 and Sch. 18, Pt. VI(10), with effect in relation to any payment of a manufactured dividend or manufactured interest which is a payment made on or after 1 July 1997 (SI 1997/991 (C. 33)), but not affecting the exercise, on or after that date, of the powers conferred by TMA 1970, s. 21 or by any regulations modifying that section (FA 1997, Sch. 10, para. 16).

8(1) [Amends TMA 1970, s. 25(4).]

8(2) [Inserts TMA 1970, s. 25(10).]

8(3) Sub-paragraphs (1) and (2) above apply in relation to transactions on or after the day of The Stock Exchange reforms.

8(4) [Omitted by FA 2011, s. 86 and Sch. 23, para. 54.]

8(5) [Omitted by FA 2011, s. 86 and Sch. 23, para. 54.]

History – Para. 8(4) and (5) omitted by FA 2011, s. 86 and Sch. 23, para. 54, with effect from 1 April 2012, subject to transitional provisions in FA 2011, Sch. 23, para. 65

Notes – TMA 1970, s. 25(4), (5) and (10)(a) empower an inspector to require a return from certain members of a UK stock exchange or from certain UK agents or brokers of transactions in relation to chargeable gains.

MISCELLANEOUS

9 [Repealed by FA 1997, s. 76 and Sch. 10, para. 15, s. 113 and Sch. 18, Pt. VI(10).]

History – Para. 9 repealed by FA 1997, s. 76 and Sch. 10, para. 15, s. 113 and Sch. 18, Pt. VI(10), with effect in relation to any payment of a manufactured dividend or manufactured interest which is a payment made on or after 1 July 1997 (SI 1997/991 (C. 33)), but not affecting the exercise, on or after that date, of the powers conferred by TMA 1970, s. 21 or by any regulations modifying that section (FA 1997, Sch. 10, para. 16).

GENERAL

10(1) In this Schedule **"the day of The Stock Exchange reforms"** means the day on which the rule of The Stock Exchange that prohibits a person from carrying on business as both a broker and a jobber is abolished.

10(2) In this Schedule **"recognised investment exchange"** means a recognised investment exchange within the meaning given by section 285(1)(a) of the Financial Services and Markets Act 2001.

10(3) Any power to make regulations under this Schedule shall be exercisable by statutory instrument subject to annulment in pursuance of a resolution of the House of Commons.

History – In para. 10(2), the words "of the Financial Services Act 1986" were substituted by the words "given by section 285(1)(a) of the Financial Services and Markets Act 2000", by virtue of SI 2001/3629, art. 12 which came into force on 1 December 2001.

Notes – The day of The Stock Exchange reforms was 27 October 1986.
Section 285(1) of the Financial Services and Markets Act 2000 provides that:
"285(1) In this Act–
(a) **"recognised investment exchange"** means an investment exchange in relation to which a recognition order is in force; and
(b) **"recognised clearing house"** means a clearing house in relation to which a recognition order is in force."

INSOLVENCY ACT 1986

(1986 Chapter 45)

[*25th July 1986*]

ARRANGEMENT OF SECTIONS

PART IV – WINDING UP OF COMPANIES REGISTERED UNDER THE COMPANIES ACTS

CHAPTER I – PRELIMINARY

MODES OF WINDING UP

CHAPTER V – PROVISIONS APPLYING TO BOTH KINDS OF VOLUNTARY WINDING UP

CHAPTER VI – WINDING UP BY THE COURT

GROUNDS AND EFFECT OF WINDING-UP PETITION

COMMENCEMENT OF WINDING UP

CHAPTER VIII – PROVISIONS OF GENERAL APPLICATION IN WINDING UP

PREFERENTIAL DEBTS

EXECUTION, ATTACHMENT AND THE SCOTTISH EQUIVALENTS

PART IX – BANKRUPTCY

CHAPTER V – EFFECT OF BANKRUPTCY ON CERTAIN RIGHTS TRANSACTIONS, ETC.

ADJUSTMENT OF PRIOR TRANSACTIONS, ETC.

PART XII – PREFERENTIAL DEBTS IN COMPANY AND INDIVIDUAL INSOLVENCY

SCHEDULES

Notes – The Insolvency Act 1986 came into force on 29 December 1986. See also relevant parts of Bankruptcy (Scotland) Act 1985, reproduced above.

PART IV – WINDING UP OF COMPANIES REGISTERED UNDER THE COMPANIES ACTS

Chapter I – Preliminary

MODES OF WINDING UP

73 Scheme of this Part

73(1) This Part applies to the winding up of a company registered under the Companies Act 2006 in England and Wales or Scotland.

73(2) The winding up may be either–

(a) voluntary (see Chapters 2 to 5), or

(b) by the court (see Chapter 6).

73(3) This Chapter and Chapters 7 to 10 relate to winding up generally, except where otherwise stated.

History – S. 73 substituted by SI 2009/1941, art. 2 and Sch. 1, para. 75(2), with effect from 1 October 2009.

Chapter V – Provisions Applying to Both Kinds of Voluntary Winding Up

110 Acceptance of shares, etc., as consideration for sale of company property

110(1) This section applies, in the case of a company proposed to be, or being, wound up voluntarily, where the whole or part of the company's business or property is proposed to be transferred or sold

(a) to another company ("the transferee company"), whether or not the latter is a company registered under the Companies Act 2006, or

(b) to a limited liability partnership (the "transferee limited liability partnership").

110(2) With the requisite sanction, the liquidator of the company being, or proposed to be, wound up ("the transferor company") may receive, in compensation or part compensation for the transfer or sale–

(a) in the case of the transferee company, shares, policies or other like interests in the transferee company for distribution among the members of the transferor company, or

(b) in the case of the transferee limited liability partnership, membership in the transferee limited liability partnership for distribution among the members of the transferor company.

110(3) The sanction requisite under subsection (2) is–

(a) in the case of a members' voluntary winding up, that of a special resolution of the company, conferring either a general authority on the liquidator or an authority in respect of any particular arrangement, and

(b) in the case of a creditors' voluntary winding up, that of either the court or the liquidation committee.

110(4) Alternatively to subsection (2), the liquidator may (with that sanction) enter into any other arrangement whereby the members of the transferor company may–

(a) in the case of the transferee company, in lieu of receiving cash, shares, policies or other like interests (or in addition thereto) participate in the profits of, or receive any other benefit from, the transferee company, or

(b) in the case of the transferee limited liability partnership, in lieu of receiving cash or membership (or in addition thereto), participate in some other way in the profits of, or receive any other benefit from, the transferee limited liability partnership.

110(5) A sale or arrangement in pursuance of this section is binding on members of the transferor company.

110(6) A special resolution is not invalid for purposes of this section by reason that it is passed before or concurrently with a resolution for voluntary winding up or for appointing liquidators; but, if an order is made within a year for winding up the company by the court, the special resolution is not valid unless sanctioned by the court.

History – In s. 110(1)(a), the words "company registered under the Companies Act 2006" substituted for the words "company within the meaning of the Companies Act" by SI 2009/1941, art. 2 and Sch. 1, para. 75(11), with effect from 1 October 2009

In s. 110(1), para. (a) created from existing wording, and para. (b) and the ", or" before it inserted, by SI 2001/1090, reg. 9 and Sch. 5, para. 15(2), with effect from 6 April 2001.

In s. 110(2) the word "sale–" and para. (a) and (b) substituted for the words "sale, shares, policies or other like interests in the transferee company for distribution among the members of the transferor company." by SI 2001/1090, reg. 9 and Sch. 5, para. 15(3), with effect from 6 April 2001.
In s. 110(4) the words "company may–" and para. (a) and (b) substituted for the words "company may, in lieu of receiving cash, shares, policies or other like interests (or in addition thereto), participate in the profits of, or receive any other benefit from, the transferee company.." by SI 2001/1090, reg. 9 and Sch. 5, para. 15(4), with effect from 6 April 2001.

Chapter VI – Winding Up by the Court

GROUNDS AND EFFECT OF WINDING-UP PETITION

126 Power to stay or restrain proceedings against company.

126(1) At any time after the presentation of a winding-up petition, and before a winding-up order has been made, the company, or any creditor or contributory, may–

(a) where any action or proceeding against the company is pending in the High Court or Court of Appeal in England and Wales or Northern Ireland, apply to the court in which the action or proceeding is pending for a stay of proceedings therein, and

(b) where any other action or proceeding is pending against the company, apply to the court having jurisdiction to wind up the company to restrain further proceedings in the action or proceeding;

and the court to which the application is so made may (as the case may be) stay, sist or restrain the proceedings accordingly on such terms as it thinks fit.

126(2) In the case of a company registered but not formed under the Companies Act 2006, where the application to stay, sist or restrain is by a creditor, this section extends to actions and proceedings against any contributory of the company.

126(3) Subsection (1) applies in relation to any action being taken in respect of the company under Part 1 of Schedule 8 to the Finance (No. 2) Act 2015 (enforcement by deduction from accounts) as it applies in relation to any action or proceeding mentioned in paragraph (b) of that subsection.

History – In s. 126(2), the words "a company registered but not formed under the Companies Act 2006" substituted for the words "a company registered under section 680 of the Companies Act (pre-1862 companies; companies formed under legislation other than the Companies Acts) or the previous corresponding legislation" by SI 2009/1941, art. 2(1) and Sch. 1, para. 75(14), with effect from 1 October 2009, subject to the transitional provisions in SI 2009/1941, art. 8.
S. 126(3) inserted by F(No. 2)A 2015, s. 51 and Sch. 8, para. 27, with effect from 18 November 2015 (Royal Assent).

127 Avoidance of property dispositions, etc.

127(1) In a winding up by the court, any disposition of the company's property, and any transfer of shares, or alteration in the status of the company's members, made after the commencement of the winding up is, unless the court otherwise orders, void.

127(2) This section has no effect in respect of anything done by an administrator of a company while a winding-up petition is suspended under paragraph 40 of Schedule B1.

History – S. 127(1) created from existing text and s. 127(2) inserted by Enterprise Act 2002, s. 248(3) and Sch. 17, para. 15, with effect from 15 September 2003, subject to transitional provisions in SI 2003/2093, art. 3 (amendments have no effect where a petition for an administration order has been presented before that date) (SI 2003/2093, art. 2(1)).

128 Avoidance of attachments, etc.

128(1) Where a company registered in England and Wales is being wound up by the court, any attachment, sequestration, distress or execution put in force against the estate or effects of the company after the commencement of the winding up is void.

128(2) This section, so far as relates to any estate or effects of the company situated in England and Wales, applies in the case of a company registered in Scotland as it applies in the case of a company registered in England and Wales.

128(3) In subsection (1) **"attachment"** includes a hold notice or a deduction notice under Part 1 of Schedule 8 to the Finance (No. 2) Act 2015 (enforcement by deduction from accounts) and, if subsection (1) has effect in relation to a deduction notice, it also has effect in relation to the hold notice to which the deduction notice relates (whenever the hold notice was given).

History – S. 128(3) inserted by F(No. 2)A 2015, s. 51 and Sch. 8, para. 28, with effect from 18 November 2015 (Royal Assent).

COMMENCEMENT OF WINDING UP

129 Commencement of winding up by the court

129(1) If, before the presentation of a petition for the winding up of a company by the court, a resolution has been passed by the company for voluntary winding up, the winding up of the company is deemed to have commenced at the time of the passing of the resolution; and unless the court, on proof of fraud or mistake, directs otherwise, all proceedings taken in the voluntary winding up are deemed to have been validly taken.

129(1A) Where the court makes a winding-up order by virtue of paragraph 13(1)(e) of Schedule B1, the winding up is deemed to commence on the making of the order.

129(2) In any other case, the winding up of a company by the court is deemed to commence at the time of the presentation of the petition for winding up.

History – S. 129(1A) inserted by Enterprise Act 2002, s. 248(3) and Sch. 17, para. 16, with effect from 15 September 2003, subject to transitional provisions in SI 2003/2093, art. 3 (amendments have no effect where a petition for an administration order has been presented before that date) (SI 2003/2093, art. 2(1)).

130 Consequences of winding-up order

130(1) On the making of a winding-up order, a copy of the order must forthwith be forwarded by the company (or otherwise as may be prescribed) to the registrar of companies, who shall enter it in his records relating to the company.

130(2) When a winding-up order has been made or a provisional liquidator has been appointed, no action or proceeding shall be proceeded with or commenced against the company or its property, except by leave of the court and subject to such terms as the court may impose.

130(3) When an order has been made for winding up a company registered but not formed under the Companies Act 2006, no action or proceeding shall be commenced or proceeded with against the company or its property or any contributory of the company, in respect of any debt of the company, except by leave of the court, and subject to such terms as the court may impose.

130(3A) In subsections (2) and (3), the reference to an action or proceeding includes action in respect of the company under Part 1 of Schedule 8 to the Finance (No. 2) Act 2015 (enforcement by deduction from accounts).

130(4) An order for winding up a company operates in favour of all the creditors and of all contributories of the company as if made on the joint petition of a creditor and of a contributory.

History – In s. 130(3), the words "registered but not formed under the Companies Act 2006" substituted for the words "registered under section 680 of the Companies Act" by SI 2009/1941, art. 2(1) and Sch. 1, para. 75(15), with effect from 1 October 2009, subject to the transitional provisions in SI 2009/1941, art. 8.

S. 130(3A) inserted by F(No. 2)A 2015, s. 51 and Sch. 8, para. 29, with effect from 18 November 2015 (Royal Assent).

Chapter VIII – Provisions of General Application in Winding Up

PREFERENTIAL DEBTS

175 Preferential debts (general provision)

175(1) In a winding up the company's preferential debts shall be paid in priority to all other debts.

175(1A) Ordinary preferential debts rank equally among themselves after the expenses of the winding up and shall be paid in full, unless the assets are insufficient to meet them, in which case they abate in equal proportions.

175(1B) Secondary preferential debts rank equally among themselves after the ordinary preferential debts and shall be paid in full, unless the assets are insufficient to meet them, in which case they abate in equal proportions.

175(2) Preferential debts–

(a) [omitted by SI 2014/3486, art. 5(4);]

(b) so far as the assets of the company available for payment of general creditors are insufficient to meet them, have priority over the claims of holders of debentures secured by, or holders of, any floating charge created by the company, and shall be paid accordingly out of any property comprised in or subject to that charge.

175(3) In this section "preferential debts", "ordinary preferential debts" and "secondary preferential debts" each has the meaning given in section 386 in Part 12.

History – In s. 175(1), the words "(within the meaning given by section 386 in Part XII)" (which appeared after the words "preferential debts") omitted by SI 2014/3486, art. 5(2), with effect from 1 January 2015, subject to the transitional provision in SI 2014/3486, art. 3 (amendments have no effect in relation to any insolvency proceedings commenced before 1 January 2015).

S. 175(1A) and (1B) inserted by SI 2014/3486, art. 5(3), with effect from 1 January 2015, subject to the transitional provision in SI 2014/3486, art. 3 (amendments have no effect in relation to any insolvency proceedings commenced before 1 January 2015).

S. 175(2)(a) (and the "and" immediately following it) omitted by SI 2014/3486, art. 5(4), with effect from 1 January 2015, subject to the transitional provision in SI 2014/3486, art. 3 (amendments have no effect in relation to any insolvency proceedings commenced before 1 January 2015). Former s. 175(2) read as follows:

"(a) rank equally among themselves after the expenses of the winding up and shall be paid in full, unless the assets are insufficient to meet them, in which case they abate in equal proportions; and".

S. 175(3) inserted by SI 2014/3486, art. 5(5), with effect from 1 January 2015, subject to the transitional provision in SI 2014/3486, art. 3 (amendments have no effect in relation to any insolvency proceedings commenced before 1 January 2015).

176 Preferential charge on goods distrained, etc

176(1) This section applies where a company is being wound up by the court in England and Wales, and is without prejudice to section 128 (avoidance of attachments, etc.).

176(2) Subsection (2A) applies where–

(a) any person (whether or not a landlord or person entitled to rent) has distrained upon the goods or effects of the company, or

(b) Her Majesty's Revenue and Customs has been paid any amount from an account of the company under Part 1 of Schedule 8 to the Finance (No. 2) Act 2015 (enforcement by deduction from accounts),

in the period of 3 months ending with the date of the winding-up order.

176(2A) Where this subsection applies–

(a) in a case within subsection (2)(a), the goods or effects, or the proceeds of their sale, and

(b) in a case within subsection (2)(b), the amount in question,

is charged for the benefit of the company with the preferential debts of the company to the extent that the company's property is for the time being insufficient for meeting those debts.

176(3) Where by virtue of a charge under subsection (2A) any person surrenders any goods or effects to a company or makes a payment to a company, that person ranks, in respect of the amount of the proceeds of sale of those goods or effects by the liquidator or (as the case may be) the amount of the payment, as a preferential creditor of the company, except as against so much of the company's property as is available for the payment of preferential creditors by virtue of the surrender or payment.

History – In heading to s. 176, the words ", etc" inserted by F(No. 2)A 2015, s. 51 and Sch. 8, para. 30(4), with effect from 18 November 2015 (Royal Assent).

S. 176(2) and (2A) substituted for (2) by F(No. 2)A 2015, s. 51 and Sch. 8, para. 30(2), with effect from 18 November 2015 (Royal Assent). Former s. 176(2) read as follows:

"**176(2)** Where any person (whether or not a landlord or person entitled to rent) has distrained upon the goods or effects of the company in the period of 3 months ending with the date of the winding-up order, those goods or effects, or the proceeds of their sale, shall be charged for the benefit of the company with the preferential debts of the company to the extent that the company's property is for the time being insufficient for meeting them.".

In s. 176(3), "(2A)" substituted for "(2)" by F(No. 2)A 2015, s. 51 and Sch. 8, para. 30(3), with effect from 18 November 2015 (Royal Assent).

EXECUTION, ATTACHMENT AND THE SCOTTISH EQUIVALENTS

183 Effect of execution or attachment (England and Wales)

183(1) Where a creditor has issued execution against the goods or land of a company or has attached any debt due to it, and the company is subsequently wound up, he is not entitled to retain the benefit of the execution or attachment against the liquidator unless he has completed the execution or attachment before the commencement of the winding up.

183(2) However–

(a) if a creditor has had notice of a meeting having been called at which a resolution for voluntary winding up is to be proposed, the date on which he had notice is substituted, for the purpose of subsection (1), for the date of commencement of the winding up;

(b) a person who purchases in good faith under a sale by the enforcement officer or other officer charged with the execution of the writ any goods of a company on which execution has been levied in all cases acquires a good title to them against the liquidator; and

(c) the rights conferred by subsection (1) on the liquidator may be set aside by the court in favour of the creditor to such extent and subject to such terms as the court thinks fit.

183(3) For purposes of this Act–

(a) an execution against goods is completed by seizure and sale, or by making of a charging order under section 1 of the Charging Orders Act 1979;

(b) an attachment of a debt is completed by receipt of the debt; and

(c) *an execution against land is* completed by seizure, by the appointment of a receiver, or by the making of a charging order under section 1 of the Act above-mentioned.

183(4) In this section **"goods"** includes all chattels personal; and **"enforcement officer"** means an individual who is authorised to act as an enforcement officer under the Courts Act 2003.

183(4A) For the purposes of this section, Her Majesty's Revenue and Customs is to be regarded as having attached a debt due to a company if it has taken action under Part 1 of Schedule 8 to the Finance (No. 2) Act 2015 (enforcement by deduction for accounts) as a result of which an amount standing to the credit of an account held by the company is–

(a) subject to arrangements made under paragraph 6(3) of that Schedule, or

(b) the subject of a deduction notice under paragraph 13 of that Schedule.

183(5) This section does not apply in the case of a winding up in Scotland.

History – In s. 183(2)(b), the words "enforcement officer or other officer charged with the execution of the writ" substituted for the word "sheriff" by the Courts Act 2003, s. 109(1) and Sch. 8, para. 295(2), with effect from 15 March 2004, subject to the transitional provisions in SI 2004/401, art. 3 (SI 2004/401, art. 2(b)(vii)).
In s. 183(4), the words ""enforcement officer" means an individual who is authorised to act as an enforcement officer under the Courts Act 2003" substituted for the words ""the sheriff" includes any officer charged with the execution of a writ or other process." by the Courts Act 2003, s. 109(1) and Sch. 8, para. 295(3), with effect from 15 March 2004, subject to the transitional provisions in SI 2004/401, art. 3 (SI 2004/401, art. 2(b)(vii)).
S. 183(4A) inserted by F(No. 2)A 2015, s. 51 and Sch. 8, para. 31, with effect from 18 November 2015 (Royal Assent).

PART IX – BANKRUPTCY

Chapter V – Effect of Bankruptcy on Certain Rights Transactions, Etc.

ADJUSTMENT OF PRIOR TRANSACTIONS, ETC.

346 Enforcement procedures

346(1) Subject to section 285 in Chapter II (restriction on proceedings and remedies) and to the following provisions of this section, where the creditor of any person who is made bankrupt has, before the commencement of the bankruptcy–

(a) issued execution against the goods or land of that person, or

(b) attached a debt due to that person from another person,

that creditor is not entitled, as against the official reciever or trustee of the bankrupt's estate, to retain the benefit of the execution or attachment, or any sums paid to avoid it, unless the execution or attachment was completed, or the sums were paid, before the commencement of the bankruptcy.

346(1A) For the purposes of this section, Her Majesty's Revenue and Customs is to be regarded as having attached a debt due to a person if it has taken action under Part 1 of Schedule 8 to the Finance (No. 2) Act 2015 (enforcement by deduction from accounts) as a result of which an amount standing to the credit of an account held by that person is–

(a) subject to arrangements made under paragraph 6(3) of that Schedule, or

(b) the subject of a deduction notice under paragraph 13 of that Schedule.

346(2) Subject as follows, where any goods of a person have been taken in execution, then, if before the completion of the execution notice is given to the enforcement officer or other officer charged with the execution that that person has been made bankrupt–

(a) the enforcement officer or other officer shall on request deliver to the official receiver or trustee of the bankrupt's estate the goods and any money seized or recovered in part satisfaction of the execution, but

(b) the costs of the execution are a first charge on the goods or money so delivered and the official receiver or trustee may sell the goods or a sufficient part of them for the purpose of satisfying the charge.

346(3) Subject to subsection (6) below, where–

(a) under an execution in respect of a judgment for a sum exceeding such sum as may be prescribed for the purposes of this subsection, the goods of any person are sold or money is paid in order to avoid a sale, and

(b) before the end of the period of 14 days beginning with the day of the sale or payment the enforcement officer or other officer charged with the execution is given notice that a bankruptcy application has been made or a bankruptcy petition has been presented in relation to that person, and

(c) a bankruptcy order is or has been made as a result of that application or,

the balance of the proceeds of sale or money paid, after deducting the costs of execution, shall (in priority to the claim of the execution creditor) be comprised in the bankrupt's estate.

346(4) Accordingly, in the case of an execution in respect of a judgment for a sum exceeding the sum prescribed for the purposes of subsection (3), the enforcement officer or other officer charged with the execution–

(a) shall not dispose of the balance mentioned in subsection (3) at any time within the period of 14 days so mentioned or while proceedings on a bankruptcy application are ongoing or (as the case may be) there is pending a bankruptcy petition of which he has been given notice under that subsection, and

(b) shall pay that balance, where by virtue of that subsection it is comprised, in the bankrupt's estate, to the official receiver or (if there is one) to the trustee or that estate.

346(5) For the purposes of this section–

(a) an execution against goods is completed by seizure and sale or by the making of a charging order under section 1 of the Charging Orders Act 1979;

(b) an execution against land is completed by seizure, by the appointment of a receiver or by the making of a charging order under that section;

(c) an attachment of a debt is completed by the receipt of the debt.

346(6) The rights conferred by subsections (1) to (3) on the official receiver or the trustee may, to such extent and on such terms as it thinks fit, be set aside by the court in favour of the creditor who has issued the execution or attached the debt.

346(7) Nothing in this section entitles the trustee of a bankrupt's estate to claim goods from a person who has acquired them in good faith under a sale by an enforcement officer or other officer charged with an execution.

346(8) Neither subsection (2) nor subsection (3) applies in relation to any execution against property which has been acquired by or has devolved upon the bankrupt since the commencement of the bankruptcy, unless, at the time the execution is issued or before it is completed–

(a) the property has been or is claimed for the bankrupt's estate under section 307 (after-acquired property), and

(b) a copy of the notice given under that section has been or is served on the enforcement officer or other officer charged with the execution.

346(9) In this section **"enforcement officer"** means an individual who is authorised to act as an enforcement officer under the Courts Act 2003.

History – In s. 346(1) and (2), the word "made" substituted for the word "adjudged" by the Enterprise and Regulatory Reform Act 2013, s. 71(3) and Sch. 19, para. 56, with effect from 6 April 2016, but subject to savings that amendment has no effect in respect of a petition for a bankruptcy order presented to the court by a debtor before 6th April 2016 (SI 2016/191).
S. 346(1A) inserted by F(No. 2)A 2015, s. 51 and Sch. 8, para. 32, with effect from 18 November 2015 (Royal Assent).
In s. 346(2), (3)(b), (4) and (8)(b), the words "enforcement officer" substituted for the word "sheriff" (in each place) by the Courts Act 2003, s. 109(1) and Sch. 8, para. 297(2), with effect from 15 March 2004, subject to the transitional provisions in SI 2004/401, art. 3 (SI 2004/401, art. 2(b)(vii)).
In s. 346(3)(b), the words "bankruptcy application has been made or a" inserted by the Enterprise and Regulatory Reform Act 2013, s. 71(3) and Sch. 19, para. 39(3)(a), with effect from 6 April 2016, but subject to savings that amendment has no effect in respect of a petition for a bankruptcy order presented to the court by a debtor before 6th April 2016 (SI 2016/191).
In s. 346(3)(c), the words "as a result of that application or" inserted by the Enterprise and Regulatory Reform Act 2013, s. 71(3) and Sch. 19, para. 39(3)(b), with effect from 6 April 2016, but subject to savings that amendment has no effect in respect of a petition for a bankruptcy order presented to the court by a debtor before 6th April 2016 (SI 2016/191).
In s. 346(4)(a), the words "proceedings on a bankruptcy application are ongoing or (as the case may be)" inserted by the Enterprise and Regulatory Reform Act 2013, s. 71(3) and Sch. 19, para. 39(4), with effect from 6 April 2016, but subject to savings that amendment has no effect in respect of a petition for a bankruptcy order presented to the court by a debtor before 6th April 2016 (SI 2016/191).
In s. 346(7), the words "an enforcement officer" substituted for the words "a sheriff" by the Courts Act 2003, s. 109(1) and Sch. 8, para. 297(3), with effect from 15 March 2004, subject to the transitional provisions in SI 2004/401, art. 3 (SI 2004/401, art. 2(b)(vii)).
S. 346(9) inserted by the Courts Act 2003, s. 109(1) and Sch. 8, para. 297(4), with effect from 15 March 2004, subject to the transitional provisions in SI 2004/401, art. 3 (SI 2004/401, art. 2(b)(vii)).

347 Distress, etc.

347(1) The right of any landlord or other person to whom rent is payable to distrain upon the goods and effects of an undischarged bankrupt for rent due to him from the bankrupt is available (subject to sections 252(2)(b) and 254(1) above and subsection (5) below) against goods and effects comprised in the bankrupt's estate, but only for 6 months' rent accrued due before the commencement of the bankruptcy.

347(2) Where a landlord or other person to whom rent is payable has distrained for rent upon the goods and effects of an individual to whom a bankruptcy application or a bankruptcy petition relates and a bankruptcy order is subsequently made on that petition as a result of that application or, any amount recovered by way of that distress which–

(a) is in excess of the amount which by virtue of subsection (1) would have been recoverable after the commencement of the bankruptcy, or

(b) is in respect of rent for a period or part of a period after the distress was levied, shall be held for the bankrupt as apart of his estate.

347(3) Subsection (3A) applies where–

(a) any person (whether or not a landlord or person entitled to rent) has distrained upon the goods or effects of an individual who is made bankrupt before the end of the period of 3 months beginning with the distraint, or

(b) Her Majesty's Revenue and Customs has been paid any amount from an account of an individual under Part 1 of Schedule 8 to the Finance (No. 2) Act 2015 (enforcement by deduction from accounts) and the individual is adjudged bankrupt before the end of the period of 3 months beginning with the payment.

347(3A) Where this subsection applies–

(a) in a case within subsection (3)(a), the goods or effects, or the proceeds of their sale, and

(b) in a case within subsection (3)(b), the amount in question,

is charged for the benefit of the bankrupt's estate with the preferential debts of the bankrupt to the extent that the bankrupt's estate is for the time being insufficient for meeting them.

347(4) Where by virtue of any charge under subsection (3A) any person surrenders any goods or effects to the trustee of a bankrupt's estate or makes a payment to such a trustee, that person ranks, in respect of the amount of the proceeds of the sale of those goods or effects by the trustee or, as the case may be, the amount of the payment, as a preferential creditor of the bankrupt, except as against so much of the bankrupt's estate as is available for the payment of preferential creditors by virtue of the surrender or payment.

347(5) A landlord or other person to whom rent is payable is not at any time after the discharge of a bankrupt entitled to distrain upon any goods or effects comprised in the bankrupt's estate.

347(6) Where in the case of any execution–

(a) a landlord is (apart from this section) entitled under section 1 of the Landlord and Tenant Act 1709 or section 102 of the County Courts Act 1984 (claims for rent where goods seized in execution) to claim for an amount not exceeding one year's rent, and

(b) the person against whom the execution is levied is adjudged bankrupt before the notice of claim is served on the enforcement officer, or other officer charged with the execution,

the right of the landlord to claim under that section is restricted to a right to claim for an amount not exceeding 6 months' rent and does not extend to any rent payable in respect of a period after the notice of claim is so served.

347(7) Nothing in subsection (6) imposes any liability on an enforcement officer or other officer charged with an execution to account to the official receiver or the trustee of a bankrupt's estate for any sums paid by him to a landlord at any time before the enforcement officer or other officer was served with notice of the bankruptcy order in question.

But this subsection is without prejudice to the liability of the landlord.

347(8) Subject to sections 252(2)(b) and 254(1) above nothing in this Group of Parts affects any right to distrain otherwise than for rent; and any such right is at any time exerciseable without restriction against property comprised in a bankrupt's estate, even if that right is expressed by any enactment to be exerciseable in like manner as a right to distrain for rent.

347(9) Any right to distrain against property comprised in a bankrupt's estate is exerciseable notwithstanding that the property has vested in the trustee.

347(10) The provisions of this section are without prejudice to a landlord's right in a bankruptcy to prove for any bankruptcy debt in respect of rent.

347(11) In this section **"enforcement officer"** means an individual who is authorised to act as an enforcement officer under the Courts Act 2003.

History – In s. 347(1), the words "sections 252(2)(b) and 254(1) above and" inserted by the Insolvency Act 2003, s. 3 and Sch. 3, para. 14(a), with effect from 1 January 2003, subject to the transitional provisions in SI 2002/2711, art. 3–5 (SI 2002/2711, art. 2).

In s. 347(2), the words "a bankruptcy application or" and the words "as a result of that application or" inserted by the Enterprise and Regulatory Reform Act 2013, s. 71(3) and Sch. 19, para. 40(2), with effect from 6 April 2016, but subject to savings that amendment has no effect in respect of a petition for a bankruptcy order presented to the court by a debtor before 6th April 2016 (SI 2016/191).

In s. 347(3), the word "made" substituted for the word "adjudged" by the Enterprise and Regulatory Reform Act 2013, s. 71(3) and Sch. 19, para. 40(3), with effect from 6 April 2016, but subject to savings that amendment has no effect in respect of a petition for a bankruptcy order presented to the court by a debtor before 6th April 2016 (SI 2016/191).

S. 347(3) and (3A) substituted for (3) by F(No. 2)A 2015, s. 51 and Sch. 8, para. 33(1)(a), with effect from 18 November 2015 (Royal Assent). Former s. 347(3) read as follows:

"**347(3)** Where any person (whether or not a landlord or person entitled to rent) has distrained upon the goods or effects of an individual who is adjudged bankrupt before the end of the period of 3 months beginning with the distraint, so much of those goods or effects, or of the proceeds of their sale, as is not held for the bankrupt under subsection (2) shall be charged for the benefit of the bankrupt's estate with the preferential debts of the bankrupt to the extent that the bankrupt's estate is for the time being insufficient for meeting those debts.".

In s. 347(4), "(3A)" substituted for "(3)" by F(No. 2)A 2015, s. 51 and Sch. 8, para. 33(1)(b), with effect from 18 November 2015 (Royal Assent).
In s. 347(6), the words "enforcement officer," substituted for the word "sheriff" by the Courts Act 2003, s. 109(1) and Sch. 8, para. 298(2), with effect from 15 March 2004, subject to the transitional provisions in SI 2004/401, art. 3 (SI 2004/401, art. 2(b)(vii)).
In s. 347(7), the words "an enforcement officer" substituted for the words "a sheriff" and the words "the enforcement officer" substituted for the words "the sheriff" by the Courts Act 2003, s. 109(1) and Sch. 8, para. 298(3), with effect from 15 March 2004, subject to the transitional provisions in SI 2004/401, art. 3 (SI 2004/401, art. 2(b)(vii)).
In s. 347(8), the words "Subject to sections 252(2)(b) and 254(1) above." inserted by the Insolvency Act 2003, s. 3 and Sch. 3, para. 14(b), with effect from 1 January 2003, subject to the transitional provisions in SI 2002/2711, art. 3–5 (SI 2002/2711, art. 2).
S. 347(11) inserted by the Courts Act 2003, s. 109(1) and Sch. 8, para. 298(4), with effect from 15 March 2004, subject to the transitional provisions in SI 2004/401, art. 3 (SI 2004/401, art. 2(b)(vii)).

PART XII – PREFERENTIAL DEBTS IN COMPANY AND INDIVIDUAL INSOLVENCY

386 Categories of preferential debts

386(1) A reference in this Act to the **"preferential debts"** of a company or an individual is to the debts listed in Schedule 6 to this Act (contributions to occupational pension schemes; remuneration, &c. of employees; levies on coal and steel production; deposits covered by Financial Services Compensation Scheme; other deposits); and references to preferential creditors are to be read accordingly.

386(1A) A reference in this Act to the "ordinary preferential debts" of a company or an individual is to the preferential debts listed in any of paragraphs 8 to 15B of Schedule 6 to this Act.

386(1B) A reference in this Act to the "secondary preferential debts" of a company or an individual is to the preferential debts listed in paragraph 15BA or 15BB of Schedule 6 to this Act.

386(2) In Schedule 6 **"the debtor"** means the company or the individual concerned.

386(3) Schedule 6 is to be read with Schedule 4 to the Pensions Schemes Act 1993 (occupational pension scheme contributions).

History – In s. 386(1), the words "; other deposits" inserted by SI 2014/3486, art. 8(2), with effect from 1 January 2015, subject to the transitional provision in SI 2014/3486, art. 3 (amendments have no effect in relation to any insolvency proceedings commenced before 1 January 2015).
In s. 386(1), the words "; deposits covered by Financial Services Compensation Scheme" inserted (after the word "production") by Financial Services (Banking Reform) Act 2013, s. 13(2), with effect from 31 December 2014 (SI 2014/3160, art. 2).
In s. 386(1) the words "(contributions to occupational pension schemes; remuneration, &c. of employees; levies on coal and steel production)" substituted for the words "(money owed to the Inland Revenue for income tax deducted at source; VAT, insurance premium tax, landfill tax, climate change levy, aggregates levy, car tax, betting and gaming duties, beer duty, lottery duty, air passenger duty; social security and pension scheme contributions; remuneration etc. of employees; levies on coal and steel production)", by the Enterprise Act 2002, s. 251(3), with effect from 15 September 2003, by virtue of SI 2003/2093, art. 2 and Sch. 1. Art. 4 contains transitional provisions.
In s. 386(1), the words "aggregates levy" inserted by FA 2001, s. 27 and Sch. 5, para. 17.
In s. 386(1), the words "climate change levy" inserted by FA 2000, s. 30 and Sch. 7 para 3(1).
In s. 386(1), the words "landfill tax" inserted by FA 1996, s. 60 and Sch. 5, para. 12(1).
In s. 386(1), the words "air passenger duty" inserted by FA 1995, s. 17 with effect from 1 May 1995.
In s. 386(1), the words "lottery duty" inserted by FA 1993, s. 36 with effect from 1 December 1993.
In s. 386(1), the words "insurance premium tax," inserted by FA 1994, s. 64 and Sch. 7, para. 7(2), with effect from 3 May 1994.
In s. 386(1), the words "beer duty" inserted by FA 1991, s. 7 and Sch. 2, para. 21A as inserted by F(No. 2)A 1992, s. 9(1) with effect from 16 July 1992.
In s. 386(1), the words "; levies on coal and steel production" inserted by SI 1987/2093 with effect from 1 January 1988.
S. 386(1A) and (1B) inserted by SI 2014/3486, art. 8(3), with effect from 1 January 2015, subject to the transitional provision in SI 2014/3486, art. 3 (amendments have no effect in relation to any insolvency proceedings commenced before 1 January 2015).
In s. 386(2), the words "Schedule 6" substituted for the words "that Schedule" by SI 2014/3486, art. 8(4), with effect from 1 January 2015, subject to the transitional provision in SI 2014/3486, art. 3 (amendments have no effect in relation to any insolvency proceedings commenced before 1 January 2015).
In s. 386(3), the words "Schedule 4 to the Social Security Pensions Act 1975" substituted by the Pension Schemes Act 1993, Sch. 8, para. 18, with effect from 7 February 1994.

Cross references – SI 1986/1999, reg. 3, Sch. 1, Pt. II, para. 34: application to estates of deceased person dying before presentation of bankruptcy petition.

Transitional – Enterprise Act 2002 (Commencement No. 4 and Transitional Provisions and Savings) Order 2003, SI 2003/2093, art. 4, contains transitional provisions so that the former rules remain in effect where insolvency arrangements are in place prior to 15 September 2003.

SCHEDULE 6 – THE CATEGORIES OF PREFERENTIAL DEBTS

Section 386

CATEGORY 1: DEBTS DUE TO INLAND REVENUE

1 [Sch. 6, para. 1 repealed by the Enterprise Act 2002, s. 251(1)(a), s. 278(2), and Sch. 26.]

History – Sch. 6, para. 1 repealed by the Enterprise Act 2002, s. 251(1)(a), s. 278(2), and Sch. 26, with effect from 15 September 2003, by virtue of SI 2003/2093, art. 2 and Sch. 1. Art. 4 contains transitional provisions.

Sch. 6, para. 1 amended by ITEPA 2003, Sch. 6, para. 154, by substituting the words "taxable earnings (as defined by section 10 of the Income Tax (Earnings and Pensions) Act 2003)" for the word "emoluments", effective for the tax year 2003–04 and subsequent tax years.
Sch. 6, para. 1 amended by ITEPA 2003, Sch. 6, para. 154, by substituting the words "PAYE regulations" for the words "section 203 of the Income and Corporation Taxes Act 1988 (pay as you earn)", effective for the tax year 2003–04 and subsequent tax years.
Reference to provisions of ICTA 1988, s. 203 substituted by Sch. 29, para. 32 of that Act for companies' accounting periods ending after 5 April 1988.

Transitional – Enterprise Act 2002 (Commencement No. 4 and Transitional Provisions and Savings) Order 2003, SI 2003/2093, art. 4, contains transitional provisions so that the former rules remain in effect where insolvency arrangements are in place prior to 15 September 2003.

2 [Sch. 6, para. 2 repealed by the Enterprise Act 2002, s. 251(1)(a), s. 278(2), and Sch. 26.]

History – Sch. 6, para. 2 repealed by the Enterprise Act 2002, s. 251(1)(a), s. 278(2), and Sch. 26, with effect from 15 September 2003, by virtue of SI 2003/2093, art. 2 and Sch. 1. Art. 4 contains transitional provisions.
Reference to ICTA 1988, s. 559 substituted by Sch. 29, para. 32 of that Act for companies' accounting periods ending after 5 April 1988.

3–16 [Not reproduced.]

INCOME AND CORPORATION TAXES ACT 1988

(1988 Chapter 1)

[*9th February 1988*]

ARRANGEMENT OF SECTIONS

ICTA 1988

CHAPTER III – UNIT TRUST SCHEMES, DEALERS IN SECURITIES ETC.

CHAPTER IV – BUILDING SOCIETIES, BANKS, SAVINGS BANKS, INDUSTRIAL AND PROVIDENT SOCIETIES AND OTHERS

CHAPTER V – PETROLEUM EXTRACTION ACTIVITIES

CHAPTER 5A – SPECIAL RULES FOR LONG FUNDING LEASES OF PLANT OR MACHINERY: CORPORATION TAX

CHAPTER VI – MISCELLANEOUS BUSINESSES AND BODIES

PART XIII – MISCELLANEOUS SPECIAL PROVISIONS

CHAPTER I – INTELLECTUAL PROPERTY

CHAPTER II – LIFE POLICIES, LIFE ANNUITIES AND CAPITAL REDEMPTION POLICIES

CHAPTER III – ENTERTAINERS AND SPORTSMEN

CHAPTER IV – SUB-CONTRACTORS IN THE CONSTRUCTION INDUSTRY

CHAPTER V – SCHEMES FOR RATIONALISING INDUSTRY

CHAPTER VA – SHARE LOSS RELIEF

CHAPTER VI – OTHER PROVISIONS

PART XIV – PENSION SCHEMES, SOCIAL SECURITY BENEFITS, LIFE ANNUITIES ETC.

CHAPTER I – RETIREMENT BENEFIT SCHEMES

CHAPTER II – OTHER PENSION FUNDS AND SOCIAL SECURITY BENEFITS AND CONTRIBUTIONS

CHAPTER III – RETIREMENT ANNUITIES

CHAPTER IV – PERSONAL PENSION SCHEMES

CHAPTER V – PURCHASED LIFE ANNUITIES

CHAPTER VI – MISCELLANEOUS

PART XV – SETTLEMENTS

CHAPTER IA – LIABILITY OF SETTLOR

CHAPTER I – DISPOSITIONS FOR SHORT PERIODS

CHAPTER II – SETTLEMENTS ON CHILDREN

CHAPTER III – REVOCABLE SETTLEMENTS ETC.

CHAPTER IB – PROVISIONS AS TO CAPITAL SUMS PAID TO SETTLOR

PART I – THE CHARGE TO TAX

INCOME TAX

CORPORATION TAX

PART II – PROVISIONS RELATING TO THE SCHEDULE A CHARGE

ICTA 1988

PART V – PROVISIONS RELATING TO THE SCHEDULE E CHARGE

CHAPTER I – SUPPLEMENTARY CHARGING PROVISIONS OF GENERAL APPLICATION

MISCELLANEOUS PROVISIONS

SHAREHOLDINGS, LOANS ETC.

VOUCHERS ETC.

LIVING ACCOMMODATION

PAYMENTS ON RETIREMENT, SICK PAY ETC.

CHAPTER II – EMPLOYEES EARNING £8,500 OR MORE AND DIRECTORS

EXPENSES

BENEFITS IN KIND

PART VI – COMPANY DISTRIBUTIONS, TAX CREDITS ETC.

CHAPTER I – TAXATION OF COMPANY DISTRIBUTIONS

CHAPTER II – MATTERS WHICH ARE DISTRIBUTIONS FOR THE PURPOSES OF THE CORPORATION TAX ACTS

CHAPTER III – MATTERS WHICH ARE NOT DISTRIBUTIONS FOR THE PURPOSES OF THE CORPORATION TAX ACTS

PAYMENTS OF INTEREST

DEMERGERS

PURCHASE OF OWN SHARES

CHAPTER IV – SPECIAL PROVISIONS

CHAPTER V – RESIDENCE OF INDIVIDUALS

PART VIII – TAXATION OF INCOME AND CHARGEABLE GAINS OF COMPANIES

TAXATION OF INCOME

CHARGEABLE GAINS

PART IX – ANNUAL PAYMENTS AND INTEREST

ANNUAL PAYMENTS

PART XI – CLOSE COMPANIES

CHAPTER I – INTERPRETATIVE PROVISIONS

ADDITIONAL MATTERS TO BE TREATED AS DISTRIBUTIONS

CHAPTER II – CHARGES TO TAX IN CONNECTION WITH LOANS

CHAPTER III – APPORTIONMENT OF UNDISTRIBUTED INCOME ETC.

PART XII – SPECIAL CLASSES OF COMPANIES AND BUSINESSES

CHAPTER I – INSURANCE COMPANIES, UNDERWRITERS AND CAPITAL REDEMPTION BUSINESS

INSURANCE COMPANIES: GENERAL

CLASSES OF LIFE ASSURANCE BUSINESS

INTEREST DISTRIBUTIONS

DISTRIBUTIONS TO CORPORATE UNIT HOLDER

DEALERS IN SECURITIES, BANKS AND INSURANCE BUSINESSES

CHAPTER IV – BUILDING SOCIETIES, BANKS, SAVINGS BANKS, INDUSTRIAL AND PROVIDENT SOCIETIES AND OTHERS

CHAPTER V – PETROLEUM EXTRACTION ACTIVITIES

PART XIII – MISCELLANEOUS SPECIAL PROVISIONS

CHAPTER I – INTELLECTUAL PROPERTY

PATENTS AND KNOW-HOW

COPYRIGHT AND PUBLIC LENDING RIGHT

DESIGNS

ARTISTS' RECEIPTS

CHAPTER II – LIFE POLICIES, LIFE ANNUITIES AND CAPITAL REDEMPTION POLICIES

626. Modification of section 619 in relation to persons over 50
627. Lloyd's underwriters
628. Partnership retirement annuities
629. Annuity premiums of Ministers and other officers

CHAPTER IV – PERSONAL PENSION SCHEMES

PRELIMINARY

630. Interpretation
631. Approval of schemes
631A. Conversion of certain approved retirement benefits schemes

RESTRICTIONS ON APPROVAL

632. Establishment of schemes
632A. Eligibility to make contributions
632B. Eligibility to make contributions: concurrent membership
633. Scope of benefits
634. Annuity to member
634A. Income withdrawals by member
635. Lump sum to member
636. Annuity after death of member
636A. Income withdrawals after death of member
637. Death benefit
637A. Return of contributions on or after death of member
638. Other restrictions on approval
638ZA. Personal pension arrangements with more than one pension date etc
638A. Power to prescribe restrictions on approval

TAX RELIEFS

639. Member's contributions
640. Maximum amount of deductions
640A. Earnings cap
641. Carry-back of contributions
641A. Election for contributions to be treated as paid in previous year
642. Carry-forward of relief
643. Employer's contributions and personal pension income etc.
644. Meaning of "relevant earnings"
645. Earnings from pensionable employment
646. Meaning of "net relevant earnings"
646A. Earnings from associated employments
646B. Presumption of same level of relevant earnings etc. for 5 years
646C. Provisions supplementary to section 646B
646D. Higher level contributions after cessation of actual relevant earnings: modification of section 646B

CHARGE TO TAX

647. Unauthorised payments
648. Contributions under unapproved arrangements
648A. Annuities: charge under Schedule E
648B. Return of contributions after pension date

MISCELLANEOUS

649. Minimum contributions under Pension Schemes Act 1993
650. Withdrawal of approval
650A. Charge on withdrawal of approval from arrangements
651. Appeals
651A. Information powers
652. Information about payments
653. Information: penalties

CHAPTER IB – PROVISIONS AS TO CAPITAL SUMS PAID TO SETTLOR

CHAPTER IV – LIABILITY TO HIGHER RATE AND ADDITIONAL RATE TAX

LIABILITY OF SETTLORS

CHAPTER IC – LIABILITY OF TRUSTEES

CHAPTER ID – TRUST MANAGEMENT EXPENSES

CHAPTER V – MAINTENANCE FUNDS FOR HISTORIC BUILDINGS

PART XVI – ESTATES OF DECEASED PERSONS IN COURSE OF ADMINISTRATION

PART XVII – TAX AVOIDANCE

CHAPTER I – CANCELLATION OF CORPORATION TAX ADVANTAGES FROM CERTAIN TRANSACTIONS IN SECURITIES

CHAPTER II – TRANSFERS OF SECURITIES

TRANSFERS WITH OR WITHOUT ACCRUED INTEREST: INTRODUCTORY

TRANSFERS WITH OR WITHOUT ACCRUED INTEREST: CHARGE TO TAX AND RELIEFS

TRANSFERS WITH OR WITHOUT ACCRUED INTEREST: SUPPLEMENTAL

OTHER TRANSFERS OF SECURITIES

PURCHASE AND SALE OF SECURITIES

CHAPTER VI – MISCELLANEOUS

PART XVIII – DOUBLE TAXATION RELIEF

CHAPTER I – THE PRINCIPAL RELIEFS

CHAPTER II – RULES GOVERNING RELIEF BY WAY OF CREDIT

GENERAL

TAX UNDERLYING DIVIDENDS

MISCELLANEOUS RULES

FOREIGN DIVIDENDS: ONSHORE POOLING AND UTILISATION OF ELIGIBLE UNRELIEVED FOREIGN TAX

ICTA 1988

ICTA 1988

PART I – THE CHARGE TO TAX

INCOME TAX

1 The charge to income tax

1 [Omitted by ITA 2007, s. 1027 and Sch. 1, para. 2 and repealed by ITA 2007, s. 1031 and Sch. 3, Pt. 1 with effect for 2007–08 and subsequent tax years.]

Notes – S. 1 rewritten as follows:
S. 1(1): ITA 2007, s. 3(1), (2).
S. 1(2): ITA 2007, s. 4(1), 6(1), (2), 10(1), (2), (3), (4), 11(1), (2), 20(1), (2), 23.
S. 1(2A): ITA 2007, s. 4(1), 6(1), (2), 10(1), (2), (3), (4), 11(1), (2), 20(1), (2), 23.
S. 1(3): ITA 2007, s. 10(2), (3), 20(2).
S. 1(4): ITA 2007, s. 21(1), (2), (3).
S. 1(5A): ITA 2007, s. 21(4).
S. 1(6): ITA 2007, s. 21(5)
S. 1(6A): ITA 2007, s. 17(1), (2).

1A Application of lower rate to income from savings and distributions

1A [Omitted by ITA 2007, s. 1027 and Sch. 1, para. 2 and repealed by ITA 2007, s. 1031 and Sch. 3, Pt. 1 with effect for 2007–08 and subsequent tax years.]

Notes – S. 1A rewritten as follows:
S. 1A(1): ITA 2007, s. 12(1), (2), 13(1), 14(1), (2), 23.
S. 1A(1AA): ITA 2007, s. 13(1), 18(1), (2), 19(1), (2).
S. 1A(1A): ITA 2007, s. 12(1), 13(1), 14(1), 23.
S. 1A(1B): ITA 2007, s. 7, 23.
S. 1A(2): ITA 2007, s. 18(3), (4), 19(1), (2).
S. 1A(3): ITA 2007, s. 18(3), 19(1), (2).
S. 1A(2A): ITA 2007, s. 10(2), (3), 20(2).
S. 1A(4): ITA 2007, s. 13(1), 14(1), 16(7), 18(2).
S. 1A(5): ITA 2007, s. 16(1), (2), (3), (4), (5), (7).
S. 1A(6): ITA 2007, s. 1012(2), (3), (4), (5).
S. 1A(6A): ITA 2007, s. 17(1), (2).
S. 1A(8): ITA 2007, s. 19(3).

1B Rate of tax applicable to distribution income etc.

1B [Omitted by ITA 2007, s. 1027 and Sch. 1, para. 2 and repealed by ITA 2007, s. 1031 and Sch. 3, Pt. 1 with effect for 2007–08 and subsequent years.]

Notes – S. 1B rewritten as follows:
S. 1B(1): ITA 2007, s. 13(2), 19(1), (2), 23.
S. 1B(2): ITA 2007, s. 8(1), (2), 23.
S. 1B(3): ITA 2007, s. 19(3).

2 Fractions of a pound, and yearly assessments

2 [Omitted by ITA 2007, s. 1027 and Sch. 1, para. 2 and repealed by ITA 2007, s. 1031 and Sch. 3, Pt. 1 with effect for 2007–08 and subsequent years.]

Notes – S. 2 rewritten as follows:
S. 2(2): ITA 2007, s. 4(3), (5).

3 Certain income charged at basic rate

3 [Omitted by ITA 2007, s. 1027 and Sch. 1, para. 3 and repealed by ITA 2007, s. 1031 and Sch. 3, Pt. 1 with effect for 2007–08 and subsequent tax years.]

4 Construction of references in Income Tax Acts to deduction of tax

4 [Omitted by ITA 2007, s. 1027 and Sch. 1, para. 4 and repealed by ITA 2007, s. 1031 and Sch. 3, Pt. 1 with effect for 2007–08 and subsequent years.]

Notes – S. 4 rewritten as follows:
S. 4(1): ITA 2007, s. 851(2), 892(2), 900(2), 901(3), 902(2), 903(5), (6), (7), 906(5), 910(2), 928(2), 944(2).
S. 4(1A): ITA 2007, s. 851(2), 874(2), 889(4), 892(2), 902(3), (4), 919(1), (2).
S. 4(2): ITA 2007, s. 851(2), 874(2), 889(4), 892(2), 900(2), 901(3), 902(2), (3), 903(5), (6), (7), 906(5), 910(2), 919(1), (2), 928(2), 944(2).

5 Date for payment

5 [Repealed by FA 1994, s. 199(2) and s. 258 and Sch. 26, Pt. V(23) with effect for 1997–98 and subsequent tax years as respects partnerships whose trades, professions or businesses were set up and commenced before 6 April 1994 and with effect for 1996–97 and subsequent tax years in all other cases.]

CORPORATION TAX

6 The charge to corporation tax and exclusion of income tax and capital gains tax

6(1)–(3) [Omitted by CTA 2009, s. 1322 and Sch. 1, para. 2(2) and repealed by CTA 2009, s. 1326 and Sch. 3, Pt. 1.]

6(4) [Omitted by CTA 2010, s. 1177 and Sch. 1, para. 2 and repealed by CTA 2010, s. 1181 and Sch. 3, Pt. 1.]

6(4A) [Omitted by CTA 2009, s. 1322 and Sch. 1, para. 2(4) and repealed by CTA 2009, s. 1326 and Sch. 3, Pt. 1.]

6(5) [Omitted by TIOPA 2010, s. 371 and Sch. 7, para. 36 and repealed by TIOPA 2010, s. 378 and Sch. 10, Pt. 12.]

History – S. 6(1)–(3) omitted by CTA 2009, s. 1322 and Sch. 1, para. 2(2) and repealed by CTA 2009, s. 1326 and Sch. 3, Pt. 1, with effect for corporation tax purposes for accounting periods ending on or after 1 April 2009, and for income tax and capital gains tax purposes for the tax year 2009–10 and subsequent tax years.
S. 6(4) omitted by CTA 2010, s. 1177 and Sch. 1, para. 2 and repealed by CTA 2010, s. 1181 and Sch. 3, Pt. 1, with effect for corporation tax purposes for accounting periods ending on or after 1 April 2010, and for income and capital gains tax purposes for the tax year 2010–11 and subsequent tax years.
S. 6(4A) omitted by CTA 2009, s. 1322 and Sch. 1, para. 2(4) and repealed by CTA 2009, s. 1326 and Sch. 3, Pt. 1, with effect for corporation tax purposes for accounting periods ending on or after 1 April 2009, and for income tax and capital gains tax purposes for the tax year 2009–10 and subsequent tax years.
Former s. 6(4A) inserted by ITTOIA 2005, s. 882(1) and Sch. 1, para. 6; effective for income tax purposes for 2005–06 onwards and for corporation tax purposes for accounting periods ending after 5 April 2005 (ITTOIA 2005, s. 883(1)).
S. 6(5) omitted by TIOPA 2010, s. 371 and Sch. 7, para. 36 and repealed by TIOPA 2010, s. 378 and Sch. 10, Pt. 12, with effect for corporation tax purposes for accounting periods ending on or after 1 April 2010, for income tax and capital gains tax purposes for the tax year 2010–11 and subsequent tax years, and for petroleum revenue tax purposes for chargeable periods beginning on or after 1 July 2010.

Derivations – S. 6(1)–(4) (as originally enacted): ICTA 1970, s. 238(1)–(4), as amended (s. 238(2)) by FA 1971, s. 37(2), 38(1) and Sch. 14, Pt. II.

Notes – S. 6(2) rewritten for income tax purposes as ITA 2007, s. 5(1).
S. 6 rewritten for corporation tax purposes as follows:
S. 6(1): CTA 2009, s. 2(1).
S. 6(2): CTA 2009, s. 3(1), (2).
S. 6(3): CTA 2009, s. 4.
S. 6(4): CTA 2009, s. 2(2), 33, 1219(3), 1305(3), Sch. 1, para. 273(3), CTA 2010, s. 36(4), 37(3), 62(3), 188(1), (2), 190(2), 626(5), 673(5), 939(5), 957(2), 1070(6), 1071(3), (4), (6).

7 Treatment of certain payments and repayment of income tax

7 [Omitted by CTA 2010, s. 1177 and Sch. 1, para. 3 and repealed by CTA 2010, s. 1181 and Sch. 3, Pt. 1.]

History – S. 7 omitted by CTA 2010, s. 1177 and Sch. 1, para. 3 and repealed by CTA 2010, s. 1181 and Sch. 3, Pt. 1, with effect for corporation tax purposes for accounting periods ending on or after 1 April 2010, and for income and capital gains tax purposes for the tax year 2010–11 and subsequent tax years.

Notes – S. 7 rewritten for income tax purposes as follows:
S. 7(1): ITA 2007, s. 899(4), 977(1).
S. 7(4): ITA 2007, s. 977(2).
S. 7 rewritten for corporation tax purposes as follows:
S. 7(2): CTA 2010, s. 967(1), (2), (3).
S. 7(3): CTA 2010: Sch. 1, para. 33.
S. 7(4): CTA 2010: s. 967(4).

8 General scheme of corporation tax

8 [Omitted by CTA 2009, s. 1322 and Sch. 1, para. 3 and repealed by CTA 2009, s. 1326 and Sch. 3, Pt. 1.]

History – S. 8 omitted by CTA 2009, s. 1322 and Sch. 1, para. 3 and repealed by CTA 2009, s. 1326 and Sch. 3, Pt. 1, with effect for corporation tax purposes for accounting periods ending on or after 1 April 2009, and for income tax and capital gains tax purposes for the tax year 2009–10 and subsequent tax years.

Notes – S. 8 rewritten as follows:
S. 8(1): CTA 2009, s. 5(1), (4).
S. 8(2): CTA 2009, s. 6(1), (2), 7.
S. 8(3): CTA 2009, s. 8(1), (2), (5).

8A Resolutions to reduce corporation tax

8A [Repealed by FA 1996, s. 138 and Sch. 24, para. 10 and s. 205 and Sch. 41, Pt. V(13) with effect from 29 April 1996.]

9 Computation of income: application of income tax principles

9(1)–(4) [Omitted by CTA 2009, s. 1322 and Sch. 1, para. 4(2) and repealed by CTA 2009, s. 1326 and Sch. 3, Pt. 1.]

9(5) Where any enactment applies both to income tax and to corporation tax–

(a) it shall not be affected in its operation by the fact that they are distinct taxes but, so far as is consistent with the Corporation Tax Acts, shall apply in relation to income tax and corporation tax as if they were one tax, so that, in particular, a matter which in a case involving two individuals is relevant for both of them in relation to income tax shall in a like case involving an individual and a company be relevant for him in relation to that tax and for it in relation to corporation tax; and

(b) for that purpose references in any such enactment to a relief from or charge to income tax, or to a specified provision of the Income Tax Acts shall, in the absence of or subject to any express adaptation, be construed as being or including a reference to any corresponding relief from or charge to corporation tax, or to any corresponding provision of the Corporation Tax Acts.

9(6) [Omitted by CTA 2009, s. 1322 and Sch. 1, para. 4(4) and repealed by CTA 2009, s. 1326 and Sch. 3, Pt. 1.]

History – S. 9(1) and (2) omitted by CTA 2009, s. 1322 and Sch. 1, para. 4(2) and repealed by CTA 2009, s. 1326 and Sch. 3, Pt. 1, with effect for corporation tax purposes for accounting periods ending on or after 1 April 2009, and for income tax and capital gains tax purposes for the tax year 2009–10 and subsequent tax years.
In former s. 9(2), "(a)" inserted after the words "except that it does not include", and para. (b) inserted by ITA 2007, s. 1027 and Sch. 1, para. 6(2) with effect in relation to accounting periods ending after 5 April 2007.
Former s. 9(2A)–(2C) inserted by ITTOIA 2005, s. 882(1) and Sch. 1, para. 7(2); effective for income tax purposes for 2005–06 onwards and for corporation tax purposes for accounting periods ending after 5 April 2005 (ITTOIA 2005, s. 883(1)).
S. 9(3) omitted by CTA 2009, s. 1322 and Sch. 1, para. 4(2) and repealed by CTA 2009, s. 1326 and Sch. 3, Pt. 1, with effect for corporation tax purposes for accounting periods ending on or after 1 April 2009, and for income tax and capital gains tax purposes for the tax year 2009–10 and subsequent tax years.
In former s. 9(3)(a) the words "and D" and "Schedule D" substituted by ITTOIA 2005, s. 882(1) and Sch. 1, para. 7(3); effective for income tax purposes for 2005–06 onwards and for corporation tax purposes for accounting periods ending after 5 April 2005 (ITTOIA 2005, s. 883(1)).
In former s. 9(3)(a) the words ", as they apply for income tax" which appeared at the end of s. 9(3)(a) omitted by ITTOIA 2005, s. 882(1) and Sch. 1, para. 7(3) and repealed by s. 884 and Sch. 3; effective for income tax purposes for 2005–06 onwards and for corporation tax purposes for accounting periods ending after 5 April 2005 (ITTOIA 2005, s. 883(1)).
In former s. 9(3), the words "the like Schedules and Cases as apply for purposes of income tax" replaced by para. (a) and (b) by ITEPA 2003, Sch. 6, para. 4(a) which has effect, for corporation tax purposes, for accounting periods ending after 5 April 2003.
In former s. 9(3), the words "and those Parts" inserted by ITEPA 2003, Sch. 6, para. 4(b) which has effect, for corporation tax purposes, for accounting periods ending after 5 April 2003.
S. 9(4) omitted by CTA 2009, s. 1322 and Sch. 1, para. 4(2) and repealed by CTA 2009, s. 1326 and Sch. 3, Pt. 1, with effect for corporation tax purposes for accounting periods ending on or after 1 April 2009, and for income tax and capital gains tax purposes for the tax year 2009–10 and subsequent tax years.
In former s. 9(4), the words "and ITA 2007" inserted by ITA 2007, s. 1027 and Sch. 1, para. 6(3) with effect in relationto accounting periods ending after 5 April 2007.
In former s. 9(4) the words "(other than ITTOIA 2005)" inserted by ITTOIA 2005, s. 882(1) and Sch. 1, para. 7(4); effective for income tax purposes for 2005–06 onwards and for corporation tax purposes for accounting periods ending after 5 April 2005 (ITTOIA 2005, s. 883(1)).
In s. 9(5), the words ", by virtue of this section or otherwise," omitted by CTA 2009, s. 1322 and Sch. 1, para. 4(3) and repealed by CTA 2009, s. 1326 and Sch. 3, Pt. 1, with effect for corporation tax purposes for accounting periods ending on or after 1 April 2009, and for income tax and capital gains tax purposes for the tax year 2009–10 and subsequent tax years.
S. 9(6) omitted by CTA 2009, s. 1322 and Sch. 1, para. 4(4) and repealed by CTA 2009, s. 1326 and Sch. 3, Pt. 1, with effect for corporation tax purposes for accounting periods ending on or after 1 April 2009, and for income tax and capital gains tax purposes for the tax year 2009–10 and subsequent tax years.
In former s. 9(6), the words "The provisions of the Income Tax Acts applied by this section do not include sections 1 to 5, Part VII or sections 348 to 350 of this Act; and" that formerly appeared at the start of that subsection omitted by ITA 2007, s. 1027 and Sch. 1, para. 6(4) and repealed by ITA 2007, s. 1031 and Sch. 3, Pt. 1 with effect for accounting periods ending after 5 April 2007.
In former s. 9(6) the words "60 to 69" omitted by ITTOIA 2005, s. 882(1) and Sch. 1, para. 7(5) and repealed by s. 884 and Sch. 3; effective for income tax purposes for 2005–06 onwards and for corporation tax purposes for accounting periods ending after 5 April 2005 (ITTOIA 2005, s. 883(1)).

Derivations – S. 9(1): ICTA 1970, s. 250(1).
S. 9(2): ICTA 1970, s. 250(2), as amended by FA 1971, s. 37(2), 38(1) and Sch. 14, Pt. II.
S. 9(3)–(5): ICTA 1970, s. 250(3)–(5).
S. 9(6): ICTA 1970, s. 250(6), as amended by FA 1971, s. 56(3) and Sch. 14, Pt. IV.

Cross references – S. 30(4): company chargeable in respect of deductions for expenditure on sea walls, apportionment of deductions in year of assessment between accounting periods comprising that year.
S. 831(1), (2) and the Interpretation Act 1978, Sch. 1: meaning of the terms "the Income Tax Acts", "the Corporation Tax Acts" and "the Tax Acts".
ITEPA 2003, Sch. 7, para. 90(4): reference to the meaning of "income tax law"as provided in section 9(2).
ITTOIA 2005, Sch. 2, para. 8: general savings provision in respect of s. 9(5).

Notes – S. 9 rewritten as follows:
S. 9(1): CTA 2009, s. 2(4), 35, 209, 299(1), 752, 933(1), 969(1), (2), (3), 972(1), 974(1), 977(1), 979(1).
S. 9(2): CTA 2009, s. 35, 209, 299(1), 752, 933(1), 969(1), (5), 972(1), 974(1), 977(1), 979(1).
S. 9(2B): CTA 2009, s. 35, 209, 299(1), 752, 933(1), 972(1), 974(1), 977(1), 979(1).
S. 9(2C): CTA 2009, s. 35, 209, 299(1), 752, 933(1), 972(1), 974(1), 977(1), 979(1).
S. 9(3): CTA 2009, s. 35, 209, 299(1), 752, 933(1), 969(4), 972(1), 974(1), 977(1), 979(1), Sch. 1, para. 276.
S. 9(4): CTA 2009, s. 2(4), 969(4), 979(2).

10 Time for payment of tax

10 [Repealed by FA 1994, s. 258 and Sch. 26, Pt. V(23), as respects accounting periods ending on or after 1 July 1999 (FA 1994, s. 199(2), (3) and SI 1998/3173 (C. 78)).]

11 Companies not resident in United Kingdom

11(1)–(2A) [Omitted by CTA 2009, s. 1322 and Sch. 1, para. 5 and repealed by CTA 2009, s. 1326 and Sch. 3, Pt. 1.]

11(3) [Omitted by CTA 2010, s. 1177 and Sch. 1, para. 4 and repealed by CTA 2010, s. 1181 and Sch. 3, Pt. 1.]

11(4) [Omitted by CTA 2010, s. 1177 and Sch. 1, para. 4 and repealed by CTA 2010, s. 1181 and Sch. 3, Pt. 1.]

History – S. 11(1)–(2A) omitted by CTA 2009, s. 1322 and Sch. 1, para. 5 and repealed by CTA 2009, s. 1326 and Sch. 3, Pt. 1, with effect for corporation tax purposes for accounting periods ending on or after 1 April 2009, and for income tax and capital gains tax purposes for the tax year 2009–10 and subsequent tax years.
Former s. 11(1), (2) and (2A) substituted for previous s. 11(1) and (2) by FA 2003, s. 149(1) in relation to accounting periods beginning on or after 1 January 2003.
S. 11(3) omitted by CTA 2010, s. 1177 and Sch. 1, para. 4 and repealed by CTA 2010, s. 1181 and Sch. 3, Pt. 1, with effect for corporation tax purposes for accounting periods ending on or after 1 April 2010, and for income and capital gains tax purposes for the tax year 2010–11 and subsequent tax years.
S. 11(4) omitted by CTA 2010, s. 1177 and Sch. 1, para. 4 and repealed by CTA 2010, s. 1181 and Sch. 3, Pt. 1, with effect for corporation tax purposes for accounting periods ending on or after 1 April 2010, and for income and capital gains tax purposes for the tax year 2010–11 and subsequent tax years.

Derivations – S. 11(1) (as originally enacted): ICTA 1970, s. 246(1).
S. 11(2): ICTA 1970, s. 246(2), as amended by CGTA 1979, s. 157(2) and Sch. 7, para. 9.
S. 11(3): ICTA 1970, s. 246(3).
S. 11(4): FA 1982, s. 26(7).

Statements of practice – SP 4/92: capital gains tax rebasing elections; gives guidance on the treatment of persons becoming UK-resident after 6 April 1988.

Other material – ICAEW Technical Release TR 500 (not reproduced): an overseas company may qualify for the small companies' rate of tax in respect of its UK branch or agency profits if it can benefit from a non-discrimination clause in a double tax treaty.
Taxline 1993/17 (not reproduced): Revenue advised that a backlog of work on the presentation and submission of accounts and computations for earlier periods will not be regarded as a reasonable excuse for late delivery of a company's first return under Pay and File.

Notes – S. 11(1) rewritten for income tax purposes as ITA 2007, s. 5(1).
S. 11 rewritten for corporation tax purposes as follows:
S. 11(1): CTA 2009, s. 5(2), 19(1).
S. 11(2): CTA 2009, s. 5(3), (4), 19(2), (3).
S. 11(2A): CTA 2009, s. 19(2), (3).
S. 11(3): CTA 2010, s. 968(1), (2).
S. 11(4): CTA 2010, Sch. 1, para. 33.

ICTA 1988

11AA Determination of profits attributable to permanent establishment

11AA [Omitted by CTA 2009, s. 1322 and Sch. 1, para. 6 and repealed by CTA 2009, s. 1326 and Sch. 3, Pt. 1.]

History – S. 11AA omitted by CTA 2009, s. 1322 and Sch. 1, para. 6 and repealed by CTA 2009, s. 1326 and Sch. 3, Pt. 1, with effect for corporation tax purposes for accounting periods ending on or after 1 April 2009, and for income tax and capital gains tax purposes for the tax year 2009–10 and subsequent tax years.

Notes – S. 11AA rewritten as follows:
S. 11AA(1): CTA 2009, s. 19(2), 20(1).
S. 11AA(2): CTA 2009, s. 21(1).
S. 11AA(3): CTA 2009, s. 21(2), 30.
S. 11AA(4): CTA 2009, s. 29(1), (2), (5).
S. 11AA(5): CTA 2009, s. 24(1), (2), (3).

11A Overseas life insurance companies: interpretation of sections 11B and 11C

11A [ICTA 1988 is treated as being modified, in relation to overseas life insurance companies, by the insertion of s. 11A.]

Notes – S. 11A is treated as inserted as a modification in relation to overseas life insurance companies for accounting periods beginning after 31 December 1992 – see Sch. 19AC, para. 4 for the text of the modifying section.

11B Overseas life insurance companies: attribution of assets

11B [ICTA 1988 is treated as being modified, in relation to overseas life insurance companies, by the insertion of s. 11B.]

Notes – S. 11B is treated as inserted as a modification in relation to overseas life insurance companies for accounting periods beginning after 31 December 1992 – see Sch. 19AC, para. 4 for the text of the modifying section.

11C Overseas life insurance companies: additional income and gains

11C [ICTA 1988 is treated as being modified, in relation to overseas life insurance companies, by the insertion of s. 11C.]

Notes – S. 11C is treated as inserted as a modification in relation to overseas life insurance companies for accounting periods beginning after 31 December 1992 – see Sch. 19AC, para. 4 for the text of the modifying section.

12 Basis of, and periods for, assessment

12(1)–(7ZA) [Omitted by CTA 2009, s. 1322 and Sch. 1, para. 7 and repealed by CTA 2009, s. 1326 and Sch. 3, Pt. 1.]

12(7A) [Omitted by SI 2008/381, art. 3.]

12(7B) [Omitted by FA 2007, s. 40 and Sch. 9, para. 1(2)(a) and s. 41 and Sch. 10, para. 14(2)(a) and repealed by FA 2007, s. 114 and Sch. 27, Pt. 2(9) and (10).]

12(7C) [Omitted by SI 2008/381, art. 3.]

12(8) Where it appears to the inspector that the beginning or end of any accounting period of a company is uncertain, he may make an assessment on the company for such period, not exceeding 12 months, as appears to him appropriate, and that period shall be treated for all purposes as an accounting period of the company unless either–

(a) the inspector on further facts coming to his knowledge sees fit to revise it; or

(b) on an appeal against the assessment in respect of some other matter the company shows the true accounting periods;

and if on an appeal against an assessment made by virtue of this subsection the company shows the true accounting periods, the assessment appealed against shall, as regards the period to which it relates, have effect as an assessment or assessments for the true accounting periods, and there may be made such other assessments for any such periods or any of them as might have been made at the time when the assessment appealed against was made.

12(9) [Omitted by CTA 2009, s. 1322 and Sch. 1, para. 7 and repealed by CTA 2009, s. 1326 and Sch. 3, Pt. 1.]

History – S. 12(1)–(7ZA) omitted by CTA 2009, s. 1322 and Sch. 1, para. 7 and repealed by CTA 2009, s. 1326 and Sch. 3, Pt. 1, with effect for corporation tax purposes for accounting periods ending on or after 1 April 2009, and for income tax and capital gains tax purposes for the tax year 2009–10 and subsequent tax years.
Former s. 12(3)(da) inserted by FA 2003, s. 196 and Sch. 41, para. 1(2) in relation to companies which enter administration on or after 15 September 2003 (SI 2003/2093, art. 2 and Sch. 1, transitional rules in art. 3) commencement of section 248 of the Enterprise Act 2002.
In former s. 12(5), words "Subject to subsection (5A) below" inserted by and words "as the company may determine" substituted by FA 1996, s. 138 and Sch. 24, para. 11 where each of the different dates referred to in s. 12(5) occurs on or after 1 July 1999, the appointed day for self-assessment to corporation tax by virtue of FA 1994, s. 199 and SI 1998/3173 (C. 78).
Former s. 12(5A) inserted by FA 1996, s. 138 and Sch. 24, para. 11 where each of the different dates referred to in s. 12(5) occurs on or after 1 July 1999, the appointed day for self-assessment to corporation tax (see above).
Former s. 12(5B) inserted by FA 2003, s. 196 and Sch. 41, para. 1(3) in relation to companies which enter administration on or after 15 September 2003 (SI 2003/2093, art. 2 and Sch. 1, transitional rules in art. 3) commencement of section 248 of the Enterprise Act 2002.
In former s. 12(7), the reference to s. 12(7ZA) inserted by FA 2003, s. 196 and Sch. 41, para. 1(4) in relation to companies which enter administration on or after commencement of section 248 of the Enterprise Act 2002.
Former s. 12(7ZA) inserted by FA 2003, s. 196 and Sch. 41, para. 1(5) in relation to companies which enter administration on or after 15 September 2003 (SI 2003/2093, art. 2 and Sch. 1, transitional rules in art. 3) commencement of section 248 of the Enterprise Act 2002.
Former s. 12(7A) omitted by SI 2008/381, art. 3, with effect from 19 February 2008 in relation to transfers of business taking place on or after that date.
In former s. 12(7A), the reference to s. 12(7ZA) inserted by FA 2003, s. 196 and Sch. 41, para. 1(6) in relation to companies which enter administration on or after 15 September 2003 (SI 2003/2093, art. 2 and Sch. 1, transitional rules in art. 3) commencement of section 248 of the Enterprise Act 2002.
In former s. 12(7A) words from "an insurance business" to "long-term insurance" substituted by SI 2001/3629, art. 14(2), with effect in relation to any transfer under a scheme falling within Financial Services and Markets Act 2000, s. 105, including an excluded scheme falling within Case 2, 3 or 4 of s. 105(3).
Former s. 12(7A) inserted by FA 1990, s. 48 and Sch. 9, para. 3, in relation to transfers of business taking place on or after 1 January 1990. The words "Part I of Schedule 2C to the Insurance Companies Act 1982" in that section substituted by FA 1995, s. 53 and Sch. 9, para. 1, for transfers sanctioned or authorised after 30 June 1994.
S. 12(7B), to the extent not omitted by FA 2007, s. 40 and Sch. 9, para. 1(2)(a), is omitted by FA 2007, s. 41 and Sch. 10, para. 14(2)(a) and repealed by FA 2007, s. 114 and Sch. 27, Pt. 2(10), with effect in relation to periods of account beginning on or after 1 January 2007.
In s. 12(7B), definition of "insurance business transfer scheme" omitted by FA 2007, s. 40 and Sch. 9, para. 1(2)(a) and repealed by FA 2007, s. 114 and Sch. 27, Pt. 2(9), with effect for periods of account of insurance companies beginning on or after 1 January 2007.
S. 12(7B) inserted by SI 2001/3629, art. 14(3), with effect in relation to any transfer under a scheme falling within Financial Services and Markets Act 2000, s. 105, including an excluded scheme falling within Case 2, 3 or 4 of s. 105(3).
S. 12(7C) omitted by SI 2008/381, art. 3, with effect from 19 February 2008 in relation to transfers of business taking place on or after that date.
Former s. 12(7C) substituted by FA 2007, s. 40 and Sch. 9, para. 3(2), with effect for periods of account of insurance companies beginning on or after 1 January 2007.
In former s. 12(7C), the words "and subject to subsection (7C) below" inserted by F(No. 2)A 2005, s. 42 and Sch. 9, para. 20(2), with effect in relation to insurance business transfer schemes taking place on or after 16 March 2005.
Former s. 12(7C) inserted by F(No. 2)A 2005, s. 42 and Sch. 9, para. 20(3), with effect in relation to insurance business transfer schemes taking place on or after 16 March 2005.
S. 12(9) omitted by CTA 2009, s. 1322 and Sch. 1, para. 7 and repealed by CTA 2009, s. 1326 and Sch. 3, Pt. 1, with effect for corporation tax purposes for accounting periods ending on or after 1 April 2009, and for income tax and capital gains tax purposes for the tax year 2009–10 and subsequent tax years.
Former s. 12(9) inserted by FA 2006, s. 82 and Sch. 10, para. 43(2); with effect, in relation to any qualifying change of a company's ownership and any qualifying change in a company's interest in a business occurring, on or after 5 December 2005 (Sch. 10, para. 2).

Derivations – S. 12(1), (2): ICTA 1970, s. 247(1), (2).
S. 12(3): ICTA 1970, s. 247(3), as amended by FA 1972, s. 107(1), (4).
S. 12(4)–(6) (as originally enacted): ICTA 1970, s. 247(4)–(6).

S. 12(7): ICTA 1970, s. 247(7), as amended by Insolvency Act 1986, Sch. 14.
S. 12(8): ICTA 1970, s. 247(8).

Cross references – S. 342(3A) (as inserted by FA 1998, Sch. 4, para. 6(3)): in new subsection (3A) (no corporation tax on final accounting period in a company liquidation where interest income is less than a stipulated maximum), "the company's final accounting period" means "the accounting period of the company which, in accordance with section 12(7), ends by reason of the completion of the winding up.".
S. 342A(7) and (8): tax assessments on companies in administration – assumption as to date of relevant event.
S. 751(3): modification of s. 12(3), (5), (7) in its application to controlled foreign companies.
S. 831(1), (2) and the Interpretation Act 1978, Sch. 1: meaning of the terms "the Income Tax Acts", "the Corporation Tax Acts" and "the Tax Acts".
Sch. 19AC, para. 4A: in relation to overseas life insurance companies, the reference in s. 12(7A) to a transfer of the whole or part of a company's long-term business is treated as including a reference to a qualifying overseas transfer.
TCGA 1992, s. 280: tax on chargeable gain where consideration due in instalments may be payable in instalments in cases of hardship.
FA 1998, Sch. 18, para. 26(1): in the case of a company tax return which appears to the Inland Revenue has become a return for the wrong period as a result of a direction under s. 12(5A), the power to enquire into the return includes power to enquire into the period for which the return ought to have been made.
FA 2006, Sch. 15, para. 11: on a change of the accounting approach used to calculate business profits following the implementation of "Application Note G" to FRS 5 and "UITF Abstract 40" if a positive adjustment required is subject to spreading: any short accounting period that results from a change of accounting date or s. 12(7ZA), (7A) or (7B) are to be taken into account when determining the one third amount of the original adjustment that determines the limits of the permitted spreading.
FA 2006, Sch. 15, para. 12: following the implementation of "Application Note G" to FRS 5 and "UITF Abstract 40" if a claim to spread any charge is made and before the whole adjustment is taxed an accounting period ends by virtue of the commencement of winding-up proceedings then the rule in Sch. 15, para. 10(4) (any untaxed balance to be taxed in one accounting period) is to be applied to that accounting period.
SI 2006/3271, reg. 4: modification of s. 12 with effect from 31 December 2006 in relation to accounting periods ending on or after that date.
SI 2006/3389, reg. 2: modification of s. 12 with effect from 8 January 2007 with effect for periods of account beginning on or after 1 April 2006.

Extra-statutory concessions – C12: co-operative societies having half-yearly or quarterly accounting periods normally allowed annual corporation tax accounting periods.

Statements of practice – SP 1/91: procedure for making a valid claim.

Other material – ICAEW Technical Release TR 500 (not reproduced): subject to certain conditions, a company may vary its annual accounting period slightly, e.g. to make up accounts to the first Saturday of a calendar year; treatment of writing-down allowances on the transfer of a trade part way through an accounting period.

Notes – S. 12 rewritten as follows:
S. 12(1): CTA 2009, s. 8(3), (4), 942(1).
S. 12(2): CTA 2009, s. 9(1).
S. 12(3): CTA 2009, s. 10(1).
S. 12(4): CTA 2009, s. 9(2).
S. 12(5): CTA 2009, s. 11(1), (2).
S. 12(5A): CTA 2009, s. 11(3).
S. 12(5B): CTA 2009, s. 10(4).
S. 12(6): CTA 2009, s. 9(3).
S. 12(7): CTA 2009, s. 9(4), 10(5), 12(1), (2), (3), (4), (6), (7).
S. 12(7ZA): CTA 2009, s. 10(1), (2), (3).
S. 12(9): CTA 2009, s. 9(5), 10(6), 12(6).

SMALL COMPANIES' RATE

13 Small companies' relief

13 [Omitted by CTA 2010, s. 1177 and Sch. 1, para. 5 and repealed by CTA 2010, s. 1181 and Sch. 3, Pt. 1.]

History – S. 13 omitted by CTA 2010, s. 1177 and Sch. 1, para. 5 and repealed by CTA 2010, s. 1181 and Sch. 3, Pt. 1, with effect for corporation tax purposes for accounting periods ending on or after 1 April 2010, and for income and capital gains tax purposes for the tax year 2010–11 and subsequent tax years.

Notes – S. 13 rewritten for corporation tax purposes as follows:
S. 13(1): CTA 2010, s. 3(2), (3), 18.
S. 13(2): CTA 2010, s. 19(1), (2), (3), 20(1),(2).
S. 13(3): CTA 2010, s. 24(2), (3).
S. 13(4): CTA 2010, s. 25(3), (4), (5), 27(1), (2).
S. 13(4A): CTA 2010, s. 27(3), 27(5).
S. 13(4B): CTA 2010, s. 27(3).
S. 13(4C): CTA 2010, s. 27(4), (6).
S. 13(5): CTA 2010, s. 25(1), (2).
S. 13(6): CTA 2010, s. 24(4).
S. 13(7): CTA 2010, s. 32(1), (2), (3).
S. 13(7A): CTA 2010, s. 32(3).
S. 13(8): CTA 2010, s. 18, 19(2), 20(2).
S. 13(8AA): Not rewritten (unnecessary).
S. 13(8AB): CTA 2010, s. 1126(3), (4).

13ZA Interpretation of section 13(7)

13ZA [Omitted by CTA 2010, s. 1177 and Sch. 1, para. 5 and repealed by CTA 2010, s. 1181 and Sch. 3, Pt. 1.]

History – S. 13ZA omitted by CTA 2010, s. 1177 and Sch. 1, para. 5 and repealed by CTA 2010, s. 1181 and Sch. 3, Pt. 1, with effect for corporation tax purposes for accounting periods ending on or after 1 April 2010, and for income and capital gains tax purposes for the tax year 2010–11 and subsequent tax years.

Notes – S. 13ZA rewritten for corporation tax purposes as follows:
S. 13ZA(1): CTA 2010, s. 33(3).
S. 13ZA(2): CTA 2010, s. 33(1), (2).
S. 13ZA(3): CTA 2010, s. 33(4), (5), (6).
S. 13ZA(4): CTA 2010, s. 33(7).

13AA Corporation tax starting rate

13AA [Omitted by CTA 2010, s. 1177 and Sch. 1, para. 5 and repealed by CTA 2010, s. 1181 and Sch. 3, Pt. 1.]

History – S. 13AA omitted by CTA 2010, s. 1177 and Sch. 1, para. 5 and repealed by CTA 2010, s. 1181 and Sch. 3, Pt. 1, with effect for corporation tax purposes for accounting periods ending on or after 1 April 2010, and for income and capital gains tax purposes for the tax year 2010–11 and subsequent tax years.

13AB The non-corporate distribution rate

13AB [Omitted by CTA 2010, s. 1177 and Sch. 1, para. 5 and repealed by CTA 2010, s. 1181 and Sch. 3, Pt. 1.]

History – S. 13AB omitted by CTA 2010, s. 1177 and Sch. 1, para. 5 and repealed by CTA 2010, s. 1181 and Sch. 3, Pt. 1, with effect for corporation tax purposes for accounting periods ending on or after 1 April 2010, and for income and capital gains tax purposes for the tax year 2010–11 and subsequent tax years

13A Close investment-holding companies

13A [Omitted by CTA 2010, s. 1177 and Sch. 1, para. 5 and repealed by CTA 2010, s. 1181 and Sch. 3, Pt. 1.]

History – S. 13A omitted by CTA 2010, s. 1177 and Sch. 1, para. 5 and repealed by CTA 2010, s. 1181 and Sch. 3, Pt. 1, with effect for corporation tax purposes for accounting periods ending on or after 1 April 2010, and for income and capital gains tax purposes for the tax year 2010–11 and subsequent tax years.

Notes – S. 13A rewritten as follows:
S. 13A(1): CTA 2010, s. 34(1).
S. 13A(2): CTA 2010, s. 34(1), (2), (3), (4).
S. 13A(3): CTA 2010, s. 34(6).
S. 13A(4): CTA 2010, s. 34(5).
S. 13A(5): CTA 2010, s. 34(7).
S. 13A(6): CTA 2009, s. 1316(1), CTA 2010, s. 1176(1).

ADVANCE CORPORATION TAX

14 Advance corporation tax and qualifying distributions

14 [Omitted by CTA 2010, s. 1177 and Sch. 1, para. 6 and repealed by CTA 2010, s. 1181 and Sch. 3, Pt. 1.]

History – S. 14 omitted by CTA 2010, s. 1177 and Sch. 1, para. 6 and repealed by CTA 2010, s. 1181 and Sch. 3, Pt. 1, with effect for corporation tax purposes for accounting periods ending on or after 1 April 2010, and for income and capital gains tax purposes for the tax year 2010–11 and subsequent tax years.

Notes – S. 14 rewritten for corporation tax purposes as follows:
S. 14(2): CTA 2010, s. 1136(1), (2).

THE SIX SCHEDULES

15 Schedule A

15 [Omitted by CTA 2009, s. 1322 and Sch. 1, para. 8 and repealed by CTA 2009, s. 1326 and Sch. 3, Pt. 1.]

History – S. 15 omitted by CTA 2009, s. 1322 and Sch. 1, para. 8 and repealed by CTA 2009, s. 1326 and Sch. 3, Pt. 1, with effect for corporation tax purposes for accounting periods ending on or after 1 April 2009, and for income tax and capital gains tax purposes for the tax year 2009–10 and subsequent tax years.

Notes – The rewritten income tax provisions are located as follows:
S. 15(1) (Sch. A, para. 1(1)): ITTOIA 2005, s. 264, 266(1), 268 and 269(1).
S. 15(1) (Sch. A, para. 1(2)): ITTOIA 2005, s. 264.
S. 15(1) (Sch. A, para. 1(3)): ITTOIA 2005, s. 264 and 859(2).
S. 15(1) (Sch. A, para. 1(4)): ITTOIA 2005, s. 266(3).
S. 15(1) (Sch. A, para. 2(1)): ITTOIA 2005, s. 267.
S. 15(1) (Sch. A, para. 2(2)): ITTOIA 2005, s. 262(1) and (2), 267 and 273(1).
S. 15(1) (Sch. A, para. 3(1)): ITTOIA 2005, s. 266(4).
S. 15(1) (Sch. A, para. 3(2)): ITTOIA 2005, s. 875(1) and 878(1).
S. 15(1) (Sch. A, para. 4(1)): ITTOIA 2005, s. 308(1).
S. 15(1) (Sch. A, para. 4(2)): ITTOIA 2005, s. 308(3).
S. 15(1) (Sch. A, para. 4(3)): ITTOIA 2005, s. 308(2).
S. 15(1) (Sch. A, para. 4(4)): ITTOIA 2005, s. 308(4).
S. 15 rewritten for corporation tax purposes as follows:
S. 15(1) (Sch. A, para. 1(1)): CTA 2009, s. 205, 207(1), 209.
S. 15(1) (Sch. A, para. 1(2)): CTA 2009, s. 205.
S. 15(1) (Sch. A, para. 1(3)): CTA 2009, s. 205, 1270(2).
S. 15(1) (Sch. A, para. 1(4)): CTA 2009, s. 207(3).
S. 15(1) (Sch. A, para. 2(1)):CTA 2009, s. 208.
S. 15(1) (Sch. A, para. 2(2)): CTA 2009, s. 208, 213(1), 288(1), (2).
S. 15(1) (Sch. A, para. 2(3)): CTA 2009, s. 211(1), (2).

S. 15(1) (Sch. A, para. 3(1)): CTA 2009, s. 207(4).
S. 15(1) (Sch. A, para. 3(2)): CTA 2009, s. 1314(1), (4).
S. 15(1) (Sch. A, para. 4(1)): CTA 2009, s. 248(1).
S. 15(1) (Sch. A, para. 4(2)): CTA 2009, s. 248(3).
S. 15(1) (Sch. A, para. 4(3)): CTA 2009, s. 248(2).
S. 15(1) (Sch. A, para. 4(4)): CTA 2009, s. 248(4), 1314(1), (2).

16 Schedule B

16 [S. 16 repealed by FA 1988, s. 148 and Sch. 14, Pt. V, with effect from 6 April 1988.]

17 Schedule C

17 [S. 17 repealed, as part of the abolition of Sch. C, by FA 1996, s. 79 and Sch. 7, para. 3 and s. 205 and Sch. 41, Pt. V(2) for 1996–97 (income tax) and accounting periods ending after 31 March 1996 (corporation tax), subject to FA 1996, Sch. 7, para. 33–35.]

18 Schedule D

18 [Omitted by CTA 2009, s. 1322 and Sch. 1, para. 9 and repealed by CTA 2009, s. 1326 and Sch. 3, Pt. 1.]

History – S. 18 omitted by CTA 2009, s. 1322 and Sch. 1, para. 9 and repealed by CTA 2009, s. 1326 and Sch. 3, Pt. 1, with effect for corporation tax purposes for accounting periods ending on or after 1 April 2009, and for income tax and capital gains tax purposes for the tax year 2009–10 and subsequent tax years.

Notes – The rewritten income tax provisions are now located as follows (see table of destinations for full details):

(a) Cases I and II: ITTOIA 2005, Pt. 2, Ch. 2.

(b) Case III: ITTOIA 2005, Pt. 4, Ch. 2 (interest), Ch. 7 (purchased life annuity payments), Ch. 8 (deeply discounted securities), Ch. 10 (distributions from unauthorised unit trusts); and Pt. 5, Ch. 2 (receipts from intellectual property) – but royalties only, Ch. 4 (certain telecommunication rights: non-trading income) and Ch. 7 (annual payments not otherwise charged).

(c) Cases IV and V: except for foreign dividends, foreign income charged under these Cases has been integrated with the charge on equivalent types of UK income in ITTOIA 2005. Foreign dividends charged under Case V is rewritten in ITTOIA 2005, Pt. 4, Ch. 4.

(d) Case VI: ITTOIA 2005, Pt. 2, Ch. 17 (adjustment income: trades, professions and vocations) and Ch. 18 (post-cessation receipts: trades, professions and vocations); Pt. 3, Ch. 7 (adjustment income: UK property businesses), Ch. 8 (rent receivable in connection with a UK section 12 concern), Ch. 9 (rent receivable for UK electric-line wayleaves) and Ch. 10 (post-cessation receipts); Pt 4, Ch. 9 (gains from contracts for life insurance etc.), Ch. 11 (transactions in deposits) and Ch. 12 (disposals of futures and options involving guaranteed returns); and s. 579 (royalties and other income from intellectual property), s. 583 (income from disposals of know-how), s. 587 (income from sales of patent rights), Pt. 5, Ch. 3 (films and sound recordings: non-trade businesses), Ch. 4 (certain telecommunication rights: non-trading income), Ch. 5 (settlements amounts treated as income of settlor), s. 682(3) (assessments, adjustments and claims after the administration period) and Pt. 5, Ch. 8 (income not otherwise charged).

However, ITTOIA 2005 does not rewrite the words in ICTA 1988, s. 18(3), Case III(a) "whether such payment is payable within or out of the United Kingdom" as the place of payment is only one of the factors that determine the source of interest. (See ITTOIA 2005, Explanatory Notes, Annex 1, Table 1 (Change 158).)
Also, ITTOIA 2005, s. 369 does not rewrite the words in ICTA 1988, s. 18(3), Case III(a) "of money, whether yearly or otherwise": the words "of money" were held to refer to the debt rather than the interest (*Riches v Westminster Bank Ltd* (1947) 51 TC 293 HL) and therefore add nothing; the words "yearly or otherwise" in this context ceased to be relevant in 1918 when the charging provisions for yearly and short interest were merged. (See ITTOIA 2005, Explanatory Notes, Annex 1, Table 1 (Change 158).)
Also, ITTOIA 2005 does not (unlike ICTA 1988, s. 18(3), Case III(a)) give a list of examples of annual payments so as to avoid the risk of misleading readers in believing that omitted examples do not constitute annual payments and vice versa. (See ITTOIA 2005, Explanatory Notes, Annex 1, Table 1 (Change 158).)
Also, ITTOIA 2005 omits the words "any annuity or other" in ICTA 1988, s. 18(3), Case III(a) as most annuities are in fact charged under Pt. 4 and therefore a reference to them here could be misleading. (See ITTOIA 2005, Explanatory Notes, Annex 1, Table 1 (Change 158).)
Also, ITTOIA 2005 does not rewrite the separate provision in ICTA 1988, s. 18(3), Case III(c) charging "income from securities which is payable out of the public revenue of the United Kingdom or Northern Ireland" as any income that would fall into this category can be charged to tax elsewhere under ITTOIA 2005. (See ITTOIA 2005, Explanatory Notes, Annex 1, Table 1 (Change 158).)
Also, ITTOIA 2005 does not rewrite ICTA 1988, s. 18(6) (inserted by FA 2004, s. 105(4)) as it is unnecessary. (See ITTOIA 2005, Explanatory Notes, Annex 1, Table 1 (Change 158).)
The main receipts falling within specific charges under Sch. D, Case VI are as follows:

Receipts from land		
S. 15	Rent from furnished lettings (for income tax, only up to and including 1994–95, and for corporation tax, before 1 April 1998)	
S. 34(6)	Lease premiums paid to person other than landlord	(for income tax, only up to and including 1997–98, and for corporation tax, before 1 April 1998)
S. 35	Assignment of lease granted at undervalue	
S. 36	Sale of land with right to reconveyance	
S. 776	Transactions in land	
S. 780	Surrender and lease back	
Income from settlements		
S. 660C	Income deemed by s. 660A and 660B to be settlor's	
S. 677	Capital payments deemed to be income	
S. 740	Transfer of assets abroad: liability of non-transferors	
S. 743	Transfer of assets abroad: income chargeable under s. 739	

Transactions in bonds and securities etc.	
S. 56	Transactions in deposits
S. 582	Funding bonds issued in respect of interest on debts
S. 703	Cancellation of tax advantage
S. 714(2)	Accrued interest on securities transferred
S. 716(3)	Securities transferred with unrealised interest
S. 723(4)	Accrued interest on securities: delayed remittances
S. 729	"Bond washing": sale and repurchase of securities
S. 730	Sale of income arising from securities
S. 761	Offshore income gains
S. 786	Transactions associated with loans or credit
Sch. 5AA, para. 1	Guaranteed returns on transactions in futures and options
Annuities and pensions	
S. 547(1)(b), (6)	Gains on life annuity contracts
S. 599(3)	Commutation of pension: charge on administrator
S. 596A(3)	Certain benefits under non-approved schemes
S. 599A	Payments out of surplus funds
S. 601(5)	Repayments to employer
S. 602(1)	Pension fund surpluses
S. 607	Pilots' benefit funds: unauthorised payments
S. 650A	Personal pension funds: charge on withdrawal of approval
SI 1956/1230, reg. 14, 15	Underpayment of tax
SI 1987/352, reg. 6	Assessment on employer and administrator
Intellectual property	
S. 524	Sale of patent rights
S. 531	Sale of know-how
S. 775	Sale of income derived from personal activities
Withdrawal of capital allowances	
S. 384	Withdrawal of allowances: leasing by individuals
S. 528(4)	Balancing charges: patent rights
Withdrawal of other reliefs	
S. 79, 79A	Withdrawal of relief for contributions to local enterprise agencies, etc.
S. 307	Withdrawal of relief under business expansion/enterprise investment scheme
S. 399	Withdrawal of loss relief: sales of commodity futures
S. 700	Excess relief given during administration of estate
S. 788, 790, 804	Excess double taxation relief
Sch. 4, para. 11(5)	Excess relief on early redemption of deep discount security.
TMA 1970, s. 30	Tax repayment made in error
FA 1994, Sch. 20, para. 11(3)	Self-assessment: excessive double tax relief for years before 1996–97
FA 1998, Sch. 18, para. 52	Recovery of excessive repayments under self-assessment for corporation tax
Miscellaneous receipts	
S. 103, 104	Post-cessation receipts
S. 127(2)	Enterprise allowance
S. 135(7)	Certain unapproved share option scheme gains
S. 491	Receipts of assets distributed by mutual company
S. 571	Repayments under rationalisation and redundancy schemes
S. 781	Lease of assets other than land
S. 821	Under-deduction of tax before Act passed
S. 214(1)	Demergers: chargeable payments within five years
S. 553(6)	Gains on offshore life assurance policies
FA 1989, s. 68, 71	Employee share ownership trusts

SI 1989/469, reg. 22	Assessment for recovering tax
F(No. 2)A 1992, Sch. 12, para. 3	Untaxed income of banks in compulsory liquidation
FA 1993, s. 130	Non-trading foreign exchange gains
FA 1998, s. 47	Gifts in kind for relief in poor countries: benefits received by donor
FA 2002, Sch. 16, para. 27(2), (4)	Community investment tax relief withdrawn or reduced
FA 2002, Sch. 22, para. 4(2)(b)	Positive adjustment on change of accounting basis
FA 2002, Sch. 29, para. 34(4)	Non-trading gains on intangible fixed assets

S. 18 rewritten for corporation tax purposes as follows:
S. 18(1): CTA 2009, s. 35, 201(1), (2), 209, 287, 299(1), 752, 933(1), 972(1), 974(1), 977(1), 979(1), (2), 982(2).
S. 18(2): CTA 2009, s. 35, 201(1), (2), 209, 287, 299(1), 752, 933(1), 974(1), 977(1), 982(2).
S. 18(3): 201(2).
S. 18(3) ("Case I"): CTA 2009, s. 35, 201(1), 287.
S. 18(3) ("Case II"): Not rewritten, see CTA 2009 Explanatory Notes, Annex 1, Change 2.
S. 18(3) ("Case III"): CTA 2009, s. 299(1), 972(1), 977(1), (3), 982(2).
S. 18(3) ("Case V"): CTA 2009, s. 35, 209, 287, 933(1), (2), 974(1), 977(1), 979(1).
S. 18(3) ("Case VI"): CTA 2009, s. 287, 299(1), 752, 979(1), 982(2).
S. 18(3A): CTA 2009, s. 299, 972(1), 977(1), (3).
S. 18(3B): CTA 2009, s. 974(1), (3), (4), (5), 975(2).
S. 18(3C): CTA 2009, s. 975(1).
S. 18(3D): CTA 2009, s. 975(2).
S. 18(3E): CTA 2009, s. 974(6), 975(3).

19 Schedule E

19 [Omitted by ITEPA 2003, Sch. 6, para. 6 and repealed by ITEPA 2003, Sch. 8, Pt. 1.]

History – S. 19 omitted by ITEPA 2003, Sch. 6, para. 6 and repealed by ITEPA 2003, Sch. 8, Pt. 1, which have effect, for income tax purposes, for the tax year 2003–04 and subsequent tax years and, for corporation tax purposes, for accounting periods ending after 5 April 2003.

Notes – The rewritten income tax provisions are now located as follows:
In s. 19(1), the opening words in para. 1 of Schedule E of "Tax under this Schedule shall be charged in respect of any office or employment on emoluments therefrom which fall under one or more than one of the following Cases": ITEPA 2003, s. 6(1), s. 7(2), (3) and s. 10(2).
In s. 19(1), Case I of para. 1 of Schedule E: ITEPA 2003, s. 10(2), s. 15(1), s. 21(1) and s. 22(1).
In s. 19(1), Case II of para. 1 of Schedule E: ITEPA 2003, s. 10(2), s. 25(1) and s. 27(1).
In s. 19(1), Case III of para. 1 of Schedule E: ITEPA 2003, s. 10(2), s. 22(1), (2) and s. 26(1).
In s. 19(1), the concluding words in para. 1 of Schedule E of "and tax shall not be chargeable in respect of emoluments of an office or employment under any other paragraph of this Schedule" are unnecessary and so they have not been rewritten into the provisions of ITEPA 2003.
In s. 19(1), para. 2 of Schedule E: ITEPA 2003, s. 569(1), s. 577(1) and (2).
In s. 19(1), para. 3 of Schedule E: ITEPA 2003, s. 569(1).
In s. 19(1), para. 4 of Schedule E: ITEPA 2003, s. 615(1)–(6).
In s. 19(1), para. 5 of Schedule E: ITEPA 2003, s. 6(1) and s. 7(6).
S. 19(2) and (3)are unnecessary and so have not been rewritten into the provisions of ITEPA 2003.

20 Schedule F

20(1) [Omitted by ITTOIA 2005, s. 882(1) and Sch. 1, para. 10 and repealed by s. 884 and Sch. 3.]

History – S. 20 omitted by ITTOIA 2005, s. 882(1) and Sch. 1, para. 10 and repealed by s. 884 and Sch. 3; effective for income tax purposes for 2005–06 onwards and for corporation tax purposes for accounting periods ending after 5 April 2005 (ITTOIA 2005, s. 883(1)).

Notes – S. 20 is rewritten as follows:
S. 20(1): ITTOIA 2005, s. 383(1), (2), (3), 384(1), 385(1) and 398(1) and (2).
S. 20(2): ITTOIA 2005, s. 366(1), (2), (3), 367(2) and (3) and 687(1).

PART II – PROVISIONS RELATING TO THE SCHEDULE A CHARGE

GENERAL

21 Persons chargeable and basis of assessment

21 [Omitted by ITTOIA 2005, s. 882 and Sch. 1, para. 11 and repealed by s. 884 and Sch. 3.]

History – S. 21 omitted by ITTOIA 2005, s. 882(1) and Sch. 1, para. 2 and repealed by s. 884 and Sch. 3; effective for income tax purposes for 2005–06 onwards and for corporation tax purposes for accounting periods ending after 5 April 2005 (ITTOIA 2005, s. 883(1)).

Notes – S. 21 has been rewritten as follows:
S. 21(1): ITTOIA 2005, s. 271.
S. 21(2): ITTOIA 2005, s. 270(1).

21A Computation of amount chargeable

21A [Omitted by CTA 2009, s. 1322 and Sch. 1, para. 10 and repealed by CTA 2009, s. 1326 and Sch. 3, Pt. 1.]

History – S. 21A omitted by CTA 2009, s. 1322 and Sch. 1, para. 10 and repealed by CTA 2009, s. 1326 and Sch. 3, Pt. 1, with effect for corporation tax purposes for accounting periods ending on or after 1 April 2009, and for income tax and capital gains tax purposes for the tax year 2009–10 and subsequent tax years.

Notes – The rewritten income tax provisions are now located as follows:
S. 21A(1): ITTOIA 2005, s. 272(1) and 274(1)–(3).
S. 21A(2): ITTOIA 2005, s. 272(2) and 275(2) and (3).
S. 21A(4): ITTOIA 2005, s. 272(2).
S. 21A rewritten for corporation tax purposes as follows:
S. 21A(1): CTA 2009, s. 210(1), 214(1), (2), (3).
S. 21A(2): CTA 2009, s. 210(2), 985(2), (3), 986(2), (3), 999(3), (4), 1000(2), (3).
S. 21A(4): CTA 2009, s. 210(2).
S. 21A(5): CTA 2009, s. 210(1), 1147(2), (6), (7).

21B Application of other rules applicable to Case I of Schedule D

21B [Omitted by CTA 2009, s. 1322 and Sch. 1, para. 11 and repealed by CTA 2009, s. 1326 and Sch. 3, Pt. 1.]

History – S. 21B omitted by CTA 2009, s. 1322 and Sch. 1, para. 11 and repealed by CTA 2009, s. 1326 and Sch. 3, Pt. 1, with effect for corporation tax purposes for accounting periods ending on or after 1 April 2009, and for income tax and capital gains tax purposes for the tax year 2009–10 and subsequent tax years.

Notes – S. 21B has been rewritten as ITTOIA 2005, s. 310(1)–(3), 329(1)–(3), 330(1)–(4), 333(1)–(3), 334(1) and (2), 349, 350(1), 351(2), 353(1)–(3), 354(2), 355(1)–(4) and 361(1) and (2).
S. 21B rewritten for corporation tax purposes as CTA 2009, s. 210(1), (2), 249(1), (2), (3), 261(1), (2), (3), 262(1), (2), (3), (4), (5), (6), 280, 281(1), 282(1), (2), 283(2), 284(1), (2), (3), (4), 285, 1267(1), (4), 1269.

21C The Schedule A charge and mutual business

21C [Omitted by CTA 2009, s. 1322 and Sch. 1, para. 12 and repealed by CTA 2009, s. 1326 and Sch. 3, Pt. 1.]

History – S. 21C omitted by CTA 2009, s. 1322 and Sch. 1, para. 12 and repealed by CTA 2009, s. 1326 and Sch. 3, Pt. 1, with effect for corporation tax purposes for accounting periods ending on or after 1 April 2009, and for income tax and capital gains tax purposes for the tax year 2009–10 and subsequent tax years.

Notes – The rewritten income tax provisions are now located as follows:
S. 21C(1): ITTOIA 2005, s. 321(1).
S. 21C(2): ITTOIA 2005, s. 321(1).
S. 21C(3): ITTOIA 2005, s. 321(2).
S. 21C(4): ITTOIA 2005, s. 321(2).
S. 21C rewritten for corporation tax purposes as follows:
S. 21C(1): CTA 2009, s. 260(1).
S. 21C(2): CTA 2009, s. 260(1).
S. 21C(3): CTA 2009, s. 260(2).
S. 21C(4): CTA 2009, s. 260(2).
S. 21C(5): CTA 2009, s. 260(3).

22 Assessments

22 [Repealed by FA 1995, s. 39 and Sch. 6, para. 3, s. 162 and Sch. 29, Pt. VIII(1) with effect for 1995–96 and subsequent years of assessment (subject to FA 1995, s. 39(5)) and for corporation tax in relation to accounting periods ending on or after 31 March 1995.]

23 Collections from lessees and agents

23 [Repealed by FA 1995, s. 39(4) and Sch. 6, para. 3, s. 162 and Sch. 29, Pt. VIII(1) with effect for 1995–96 and subsequent years of assessment (subject to FA 1995, s. 39(5)) and for corporation tax in relation to accounting periods ending on or after 31 March 1995.]

24 Construction of Part II

24 [Omitted by CTA 2010, s. 1177 and Sch. 1, para. 7(1) and repealed by CTA 2010, s. 1181 and Sch. 3, Pt. 2; also omitted by TIOPA 2010, s. 374 and Sch. 8, para. 241 and repealed by TIOPA 2010, s. 378 and Sch. 10, Pt. 9.]

History – S. 24 omitted by CTA 2010, s. 1177 and Sch. 1, para. 7(1) and repealed by CTA 2010, s. 1181 and Sch. 3, Pt. 2, with effect for corporation tax purposes for accounting periods ending on or after 1 April 2010. S. 24 also omitted by TIOPA 2010, s. 374 and Sch. 8, para. 241 and repealed by TIOPA 2010, s. 378 and Sch. 10, Pt. 9, with effect for corporation tax purposes for accounting periods ending on or after 1 April 2010, for income tax and capital gains tax purposes for the tax year 2010–11 and subsequent tax years, and for petroleum revenue tax purposes for chargeable periods beginning on or after 1 July 2010.

Notes – The rewritten income tax provisions are now located as follows:
S. 24(1): ITTOIA 2005, s. 307(1) and 878(5).
S. 24(2): ITTOIA 2005, s. 306(1)–(3).
S. 24(3): ITTOIA 2005, s. 306(5).
S. 24(5): ITTOIA 2005, s. 307(3).

ITTOIA 2005 does not rewrite the definition of "lease" in ICTA 1988, s. 24(6)(a) on the basis that it is now redundant. (See ITTOIA 2005, Explanatory Notes, Annex 1, Table 1 (Change 158).)
S. 24 rewritten as follows:
S. 24(1): CTA 2009, s. 247(1), 291(1), (2), 1316(1), 1320(1), CTA 2010, s. 862(2), (3), (4), (5), 1166(1).
S. 24(2): CTA 2009, s. 246(1), (2), (3).
S. 24(3): CTA 2009, s. 246(5).
S. 24(4): CTA 2009, s. 246(4), 247(2).
S. 24(5): CTA 2009, s. 247(3), 1320(1), CTA 2010, s. 1166(1).
S. 24(6): CTA 2009, s. 207(2), CTA 2010, s. 862(5).
S. 24 rewritten in TIOPA 2010 as follows:
S. 24(1), (6): TIOPA 2010, Sch. 4, para. 3.

DEDUCTIONS AND OTHER ALLOWANCES

25 Deductions from rent: general rules

25 [Repealed by FA 1998, s. 38 and Sch. 5, para. 6, s. 165 and Sch. 27, Pt. III(4).]

History – By virtue of FA 1995, s. 39 and Sch. 6, para. 4, s. 25 ceased to apply for income tax purposes for 1995–96 and subsequent years of assessment except in so far as it continued to apply in certain circumstances for 1995–96 only by virtue of FA 1995, s. 39(5).
S. 25 repealed by FA 1998, s. 38 and Sch. 5, para. 6, s. 165 and Sch. 27, Pt. III(4) with effect for corporation tax from 1 April 1998 (subject to transitional provisions in FA 1998, Sch. 5, Pt. IV).

26 Deductions from rent: land managed as one estate

26 [Repealed by FA 1998, s. 39, s. 165 and Sch. 27, Pt. III(5).]

History – S. 26 repealed by FA 1998, s. 39, s. 165 and Sch. 27, Pt. III(5), with effect for income tax purposes on or after 6 April 2001 and, for corporation tax purposes, for accounting periods beginning on or after 1 April 2001.

27 Deductions from rent: maintenance funds for historic buildings

27 [Repealed by FA 1998, s. 39, s. 165 and Sch. 27, Pt. III(5).]

History – S. 27 repealed by FA 1998, s. 39, s. 165 and Sch. 27, Pt. III(5), with effect for income tax purposes on or after 6 April 2001 and, for corporation tax purposes, for accounting periods beginning on or after 1 April 2001.

28 Deductions from receipts other than rent

28 [Repealed by FA 1998, Sch. 5, para. 9, s. 165 and Sch. 27, Pt. III(4).]

History – S. 28 repealed by FA 1998, Sch. 5, para. 9, s. 165 and Sch. 27, Pt. III(4) for the purposes of corporation tax with effect from 1 April 1998 (subject to transitional provisions in FA 1998, Sch. 5, Pt. IV).
S. 28 ceases to have effect for income tax purposes by virtue of FA 1995, s. 39 and Sch. 6, para. 4, for (subject to FA 1995, s. 39(5)) 1995–96 and subsequent years of assessment.

29 Sporting rights

29 [Repealed by FA 1998, Sch. 5, para. 10, s. 165 and Sch. 27, Pt. III(4).]

History – S. 29 repealed by FA 1998, Sch. 5, para. 10, s. 165 and Sch. 27, Pt. III(4), for the purposes of corporation tax, with effect from 1 April 1998 (subject to transitional provisions in FA 1998, Sch. 5, Pt. IV).
S. 29 ceased to have effect for income tax purposes by virtue of FA 1995, s. 39 and Sch. 6, para. 4, for (subject to FA 1995, s. 39(5)) 1995–96 and subsequent years of assessment.

30 Expenditure on making sea walls

30 [Omitted by CTA 2009, s. 1322 and Sch. 1, para. 14 and repealed by CTA 2009, s. 1326 and Sch. 3, Pt. 1.]

History – S. 30 omitted by CTA 2009, s. 1322 and Sch. 1, para. 14 and repealed by CTA 2009, s. 1326 and Sch. 3, Pt. 1, with effect for corporation tax purposes for accounting periods ending on or after 1 April 2009, and for income tax and capital gains tax purposes for the tax year 2009–10 and subsequent tax years.

Notes – The rewritten income tax provisions are now located as follows:
S. 30(1): ITTOIA 2005, s. 315(1)–(4).
S. 30(2): ITTOIA 2005, s. 316(1), (2) and (4) and 318(1)–(3).
S. 30(3): ITTOIA 2005, s. 316(6) and 317(1)–(3).
S. 30(5): ITTOIA 2005, s. 315(5).
S. 30 rewritten for corporation tax purposes as follows:
S. 30(1): CTA 2009, s. 254(1), (2), (3), (4).
S. 30(2): CTA 2009, s. 255(1), (2), (4), (5).
S. 30(2A): CTA 2009, s. 257(1), (2), (3), (4).
S. 30(3): CTA 2009, s. 255(6), 256(1), (2), (3).
S. 30(4): CTA 2009, s. 254(5).
S. 30(5): CTA 2009, s. 254(7).

31 Provisions supplementary to sections 25 to 30

31 [Repealed by FA 1998, Sch. 5, para. 12, s. 165 and Sch. 27, Pt. III(4); see History note below.]

History – By virtue of FA 1995, s. 39 and Sch. 6, para. 4, s. 31 ceased to have effect for income tax purposes for (subject to FA 1995, s. 39(5)) 1995–96 and subsequent years of assessment.

S. 31 repealed by FA 1998, Sch. 5, para. 12, s. 165 and Sch. 27, Pt. III(4), for the purposes of corporation tax, with effect from 1 April 1998 (subject to transitional provisions in FA 1998, Sch. 5, Pt. IV).

31ZA Deduction for expenditure on energy-saving items

31ZA [Omitted by CTA 2009, s. 1322 and Sch. 1, para. 15 and repealed by CTA 2009, s. 1326 and Sch. 3, Pt. 1.]

History – Omitted by CTA 2009, s. 1322 and Sch. 1, para. 15 and repealed by CTA 2009, s. 1326 and Sch. 3, Pt. 1, with effect for corporation tax purposes for accounting periods ending on or after 1 April 2009, and for income tax and capital gains tax purposes for the tax year 2009–10 and subsequent tax years.

Notes – S. 31ZA rewritten as follows:
S. 31ZA(1): CTA 2009, s. 251(1).
S. 31ZA(2): CTA 2009, s. 251(2).
S. 31ZA(3): CTA 2009, s. 251(3).
S. 31ZA(4): CTA 2009, s. 251(4).
S. 31ZA(5): CTA 2009, s. 251(5).
S. 31ZA(6): CTA 2009, s. 251(6).
S. 31ZA(7): CTA 2009, s. 251(7).
S. 31ZA(8): CTA 2009, s. 251(8).

31ZB Restrictions on relief

31ZB [Omitted by CTA 2009, s. 1322 and Sch. 1, para. 15 and repealed by CTA 2009, s. 1326 and Sch. 3, Pt. 1.]

History – S. 31ZB omitted by CTA 2009, s. 1322 and Sch. 1, para. 15 and repealed by CTA 2009, s. 1326 and Sch. 3, Pt. 1, with effect for corporation tax purposes for accounting periods ending on or after 1 April 2009, and for income tax and capital gains tax purposes for the tax year 2009–10 and subsequent tax years.

Notes – S. 31ZB rewritten as follows:
S. 31ZB(1): CTA 2009, s. 252(1).
S. 31ZB(2): CTA 2009, s. 252(2).
S. 31ZB(3): CTA 2009, s. 252(3).
S. 31ZB(4): CTA 2009, s. 252(4).
S. 31ZB(5): CTA 2009, s. 252(5).

31ZC Regulations

31ZC [Omitted by CTA 2009, s. 1322 and Sch. 1, para. 15 and repealed by CTA 2009, s. 1326 and Sch. 3, Pt. 1.]

History – S. 31ZC omitted by CTA 2009, s. 1322 and Sch. 1, para. 15 and repealed by CTA 2009, s. 1326 and Sch. 3, Pt. 1, with effect for corporation tax purposes for accounting periods ending on or after 1 April 2009, and for income tax and capital gains tax purposes for the tax year 2009–10 and subsequent tax years.

Notes – S. 31ZC rewritten as follows:
S. 31ZC(1): CTA 2009, s. 253(1).
S. 31ZC(2): CTA 2009, s. 253(2).
S. 31ZC(3): CTA 2009, s. 253(3).

31A Deductions for expenditure by landlords on energy-saving items

Other material – Taxline 2004/11 (not reproduced): energy saving expenditure by landlords. Maximum claim £1,500. This is per building and not per claimant or per year.

31A [Omitted by ITTOIA 2005, s. 882 and Sch. 1, para. 16 and repealed by s. 884 and Sch. 3.]

History – S. 31A omitted by ITTOIA 2005, s. 882(1) and Sch. 1, para. 16 and repealed by s. 884 and Sch. 3; effective for income tax purposes for 2005–06 onwards and for corporation tax purposes for accounting periods ending after 5 April 2005 (ITTOIA 2005, s. 883(1)).

Notes – S. 31A has been rewritten as follows:
S. 31A(2): ITTOIA 2005, s. 312(2) and (3).
S. 31A(3): ITTOIA 2005, s. 312(1) and (3).
S. 31A(4): ITTOIA 2005, s. 312(1).
S. 31A(5): ITTOIA 2005, s. 312(1).
S. 31A(6): ITTOIA 2005, s. 312(1).
S. 31A(7): ITTOIA 2005, s. 312(1).
S. 31A(8): ITTOIA 2005, s. 312(1).
S. 31A(9): ITTOIA 2005, s. 312(1).
S. 31A(10): ITTOIA 2005, s. 313(2).
S. 31A(11): ITTOIA 2005, s. 313(3).
S. 31A(12): ITTOIA 2005, s. 313(4).
S. 31A(13): ITTOIA 2005, s. 314(1) and (2).
S. 31A(14): ITTOIA 2005, s. 313(1).

31B Provisions supplementary to section 31A

31B [Omitted by ITTOIA 2005, s. 882 and Sch. 1, para. 16 and repealed by s. 884 and Sch. 3.]

History – S. 31B omitted by ITTOIA 2005, s. 882(1) and Sch. 1, para. 16 and repealed by s. 884 and Sch. 3; effective for income tax purposes for 2005–06 onwards and for corporation tax purposes for accounting periods ending after 5 April 2005 (ITTOIA 2005, s. 883(1)).

Notes – S. 31B has been rewritten as follows:
S. 31B(1): ITTOIA 2005, s. 312(1), (3)–(7) and 313(1) and (5).

S. 31B(1): ITTOIA 2005, s. 313(1).
S. 31B(2): ITTOIA 2005, s. 312(1).
S. 31B(4): ITTOIA 2005, s. 312(3) and (4).
S. 31B(5): ITTOIA 2005, s. 313(5).
S. 31B(6): ITTOIA 2005, s. 312(5).
S. 31B(7): ITTOIA 2005, s. 312(5).
S. 31B(8): ITTOIA 2005, s. 312(7).
S. 31B(9): ITTOIA 2005, s. 312(6).
S. 31B(11): ITTOIA 2005, s. 312(1).

32 Capital allowances for machinery and plant used in estate management

32 [Repealed by FA 1997 s. 85 and Sch. 15, para. 1 and s. 113 and Sch. 18, Pt. VI(11), with effect for income tax purposes for 1997–98 and subsequent years of assessment and for corporation tax purposes in relation to accounting periods ending on or after 1 April 1997.]

33 Agricultural land: allowance for excess expenditure on maintenance

33 [Repealed by FA 1998, Sch. 5, para. 13, s. 165 and Sch. 27, Pt. III(4); see History note below.]

History – S. 33 repealed by FA 1998, Sch. 5, para. 13, s. 165 and Sch. 27, Pt. III(4), for the purposes of corporation tax, with effect from 1 April 1998 (subject to transitional provisions in FA 1998, Sch. 5, Pt. IV).
S. 33 ceased to apply for income tax purposes by virtue of FA 1995, s. 39 and Sch. 6, para. 4, for (subject to FA 1995, s. 39(5)) 1995–96 and subsequent years of assessment.

CONNECTED PERSONS

33A Rents or receipts payable by a connected person

33A [Repealed by FA 1998, Sch. 5, para. 14, s. 165 and Sch. 27, Pt. III(4); see History note.]

History – S. 33A repealed by FA 1998, Sch. 5, para. 14, s. 165 and Sch. 27, Pt. III(4), for the purposes of corporation tax, with effect from 1 April 1998 (subject to transitional provisions in FA 1998, Sch. 5, Pt. IV).
S. 33A ceased to apply for income tax purposes (subject to FA 1995, s. 39(5)) for 1995–96 and subsequent years of assessment by virtue of FA 1995, s. 39 and Sch. 6, para. 4.

33B Rents or receipts relating to land in respect of which a connected person makes payments to a third party

33B [Repealed by FA 1998, Sch. 5, para. 14, s. 165 and Sch. 27, Pt. III(4); see History note below.]

History – S. 33B repealed by FA 1998, Sch. 5, para. 14, s. 165 and Sch. 27, Pt. III(4), with effect, for the purposes of corporation tax, from 1 April 1998 (subject to transitional provisions in FA 1998, Sch. 5, Pt. IV).
S. 33B ceased to apply for income tax purposes (subject to FA 1995, s. 39(5)) for 1995–96 and subsequent years of assessment by virtue of FA 1995, s. 39 and Sch. 6, para. 4.

PREMIUMS, LEASES AT UNDERVALUE ETC.

34 Treatment of premiums etc. as rent

34 [Omitted by CTA 2009, s. 1322 and Sch. 1, para. 16 and repealed by CTA 2009, s. 1326 and Sch. 3, Pt. 1.]

History – S. 34 omitted by CTA 2009, s. 1322 and Sch. 1, para. 16 and repealed by CTA 2009, s. 1326 and Sch. 3, Pt. 1, with effect for corporation tax purposes for accounting periods ending on or after 1 April 2009, and for income tax and capital gains tax purposes for the tax year 2009–10 and subsequent tax years.

Notes – The rewritten income tax provisions are now located as follows:
S. 34(1): ITTOIA 2005, s. 277(1)–(4), 279(1)–(4), 280(1)–(4) and 281(1)–(4), (6).
S. 34(2): ITTOIA 2005, s. 278(1)–(3).
S. 34(3): ITTOIA 2005, s. 278(4) and (5).
S. 34(4): ITTOIA 2005, s. 279(1)–(4) and (6) and 280(1)–(4).
S. 34(5): ITTOIA 2005, s. 281(1)–(4), (6).
S. 34(6): ITTOIA 2005, s. 277(2)–(4), 279(2)–(4) and 281(2)–(4).
S. 34(7): ITTOIA 2005, s. 281(1) and 878(5).
S. 34(7A): ITTOIA 2005, s. 277(3), 279(3), 280(3) and 281(3).
S. 34(8): ITTOIA 2005, s. 299(1)–(3).
S. 34 rewritten for corporation tax purposes as follows:
S. 34(1): CTA 2009, s. 217(1), (2), (3), (4), 219(1), (2), (3), (4), 220(1), (2), (3), (4), 221(1), (2), (3), (4).
S. 34(2): CTA 2009, s. 218(1), (2), (3).
S. 34(3): CTA 2009, s. 218(4), (5).
S. 34(4): CTA 2009, s. 219(1), (2), (3), (4), (6), 220(1), (2), (3), (4).
S. 34(5): CTA 2009, s. 221(1), (2), (3), (4), (6).
S. 34(6): CTA 2009, s. 217(2), (3), (4), 219(2), (3), (4), 220(2), (3), (4), 221(2), (3), (4).
S. 34(7): CTA 2009, s. 221(1), 1316(1).
S. 34(7A): CTA 2009, s. 217(3), 219(3), 220(3), 221(3).
S. 34(8): CTA 2009, s. 236(1), (2), (3).

35 Charge on assignment of lease granted at an undervalue

35 [Omitted by CTA 2009, s. 1322 and Sch. 1, para. 16 and repealed by CTA 2009, s. 1326 and Sch. 3, Pt. 1.]

History – S. 35 omitted by CTA 2009, s. 1322 and Sch. 1, para. 16 and repealed by CTA 2009, s. 1326 and Sch. 3, Pt. 1, with effect for corporation tax purposes for accounting periods ending on or after 1 April 2009, and for income tax and capital gains tax purposes for the tax year 2009–10 and subsequent tax years.

Notes – The rewritten income tax provisions are now located as follows:
S. 35(1): ITTOIA 2005, s. 282(1) and 283(2)–(4).
S. 35(2): ITTOIA 2005, s. 282(1)–(3) and 283(5).
S. 35(2A): ITTOIA 2005, s. 282(3).
S. 35(1): ITTOIA 2005, s. 300(1)–(3).
S. 35 rewritten for corporation tax purposes as follows:
S. 35(1): CTA 2009, s. 222(1), 223(2), (3), (4).
S. 35(2): CTA 2009, s. 222(1), (2), (3), (4), 223(5).
S. 35(2A): CTA 2009, s. 222(3).
S. 35(3): CTA 2009, s. 237(1), (2), (3).

36 Charge on sale of land with right to reconveyance

36 [Omitted by CTA 2009, s. 1322 and Sch. 1, para. 16 and repealed by CTA 2009, s. 1326 and Sch. 3, Pt. 1.]

History – S. 36 omitted by CTA 2009, s. 1322 and Sch. 1, para. 16 and repealed by CTA 2009, s. 1326 and Sch. 3, Pt. 1, with effect for corporation tax purposes for accounting periods ending on or after 1 April 2009, and for income tax and capital gains tax purposes for the tax year 2009–10 and subsequent tax years.

Notes – The rewritten income tax provisions are now located as follows:
S. 36(1): ITTOIA 2005, s. 284(1)–(4) and 285(1)–(5).
S. 36(2): ITTOIA 2005, s. 286(2)–(5), 301(1)–(3) and 302(1)–(3).
S. 36(3): ITTOIA 2005,s. 285(1) and (3)–(5), 286(4) and (5) and 302(1)–(3).
S. 36(4): ITTOIA 2005, s. 285(2).
S. 36(4A): ITTOIA 2005, s. 284(3) and 285(4).
S. 36(4B): ITTOIA 2005, s. 286(6).
S. 36(5): ITTOIA 2005, s. 878(5).
S. 36 rewritten for corporation tax purposes as follows:
S. 36(1): CTA 2009, s. 224(1), (2), (3), (4), 225(1), (3), (4), (5).
S. 36(2): CTA 2009, s. 226(2), (3), (4), (5), 238(1), (2), (3), 239(1), (2), (3).
S. 36(3): CTA 2009, s. 225(1), (3), (4), (5), 226(4), (5), 239(1), (2), (3).
S. 36(4): CTA 2009, s. 225(2).
S. 36(4A): CTA 2009, s. 224(3), 225(4).
S. 36(4B): CTA 2009, s. 226(6).
S. 36(5): CTA 2009, s. 1316(1).

37 Premiums paid etc.: deductions from premiums and rent received

37 [Omitted by CTA 2009, s. 1322 and Sch. 1, para. 16 and repealed by CTA 2009, s. 1326 and Sch. 3, Pt. 1.]

History – S. 37 omitted by CTA 2009, s. 1322 and Sch. 1, para. 16 and repealed by CTA 2009, s. 1326 and Sch. 3, Pt. 1, with effect for corporation tax purposes for accounting periods ending on or after 1 April 2009, and for income tax and capital gains tax purposes for the tax year 2009–10 and subsequent tax years.

Notes – The rewritten income tax provisions are now located as follows:
S. 37(1): ITTOIA 2005, s. 287(4) and 290(2).
S. 37(2): ITTOIA 2005, s. 277(5), 279(5), 280(5), 282(5), 287(1)–(3), 288(2)–(4) and 289(4) and (5).
S. 37(3): ITTOIA 2005, s. 287(1)–(3), 288(2) and (3) and 289(2)–(5).
S. 37(4): ITTOIA 2005, s. 291(1)–(3) and 292(1), (3) and (4).
S. 37(5): ITTOIA 2005, s. 293(1)–(4).
S. 37(6): ITTOIA 2005, s. 294(1)–(6).
S. 37(7): ITTOIA 2005, s. 288(4) and (6).
S. 37(8): ITTOIA 2005, s. 290(3) and (4).
S. 37(9): ITTOIA 2005, s. 287(5), 288(3), 289(4), 290(1), (5) and (6), 291(4) and 295(1) and (2).
S. 37 rewritten for corporation tax purposes as follows:
S. 37(1): CTA 2009, s. 227(4), 230(2).
S. 37(2): CTA 2009, s. 217(5), 219(5), 220(5), 222(5), 227(1), (2), (3), 228(2), (3), (4), 229(4), (5).
S. 37(3): CTA 2009, s. 227(1), (3), 228(2), (3), 229(2), (3), (4), (5).
S. 37(4): CTA 2009, s. 231(1), (2), (3), 232(1), (3), (4).
S. 37(5): CTA 2009, s. 233(1), (2), (3), (4).
S. 37(6): CTA 2009, s. 234(1), (2), (3), (4), (5), (6), (7).
S. 37(7): CTA 2009, s. 228(4), (6), 233(6).
S. 37(8): CTA 2009, s. 230(3), (4).
S. 37(9): CTA 2009, s. 227(5), 228(3), 229(4), 230(1), (5), (6), 231(4), 235(1), (2), (3).
S. 37(10): CTA 2009, s. 247(4).

37A Section 37(4) and reductions in receipts under ITTOIA 2005

37A [Omitted by CTA 2009, s. 1322 and Sch. 1, para. 16 and repealed by CTA 2009, s. 1326 and Sch. 3, Pt. 1.]

History – S. 37A omitted by CTA 2009, s. 1322 and Sch. 1, para. 16 and repealed by CTA 2009, s. 1326 and Sch. 3, Pt. 1, with effect for corporation tax purposes for accounting periods ending on or after 1 April 2009, and for income tax and capital gains tax purposes for the tax year 2009–10 and subsequent tax years.

Notes – S. 37A rewritten as follows:
S. 37A(1): CTA 2009, s. 233(1).
S. 37A(2): CTA 2009, s. 233(2), (3).
S. 37A(3): CTA 2009, s. 233(4).
S. 37A(4): CTA 2009, s. 234(1), (2).
S. 37A(5): CTA 2009, s. 234(3), (4), (5), (6), (7).
S. 37A(6): CTA 2009, s. 233(6).
S. 37A(7): CTA 2009, s. 233(6).
S. 37A(8): CTA 2009, s. 233(1), 234(1).
S. 37A(9): CTA 2009, s. 247(4).

38 Rules for ascertaining duration of leases

38 [Omitted by CTA 2009, s. 1322 and Sch. 1, para. 16 and repealed by CTA 2009, s. 1326 and Sch. 3, Pt. 1.]

History – S. 38 omitted by CTA 2009, s. 1322 and Sch. 1, para. 16 and repealed by CTA 2009, s. 1326 and Sch. 3, Pt. 1, with effect for corporation tax purposes for accounting periods ending on or after 1 April 2009, and for income tax and capital gains tax purposes for the tax year 2009–10 and subsequent tax years.

Notes – The rewritten income tax provisions are now located as follows:
S. 38(1): ITTOIA 2005, s. 303(1) and (3) and 878(5).
S. 38(2): ITTOIA 2005, s. 304(1).
S. 38(3): ITTOIA 2005, s. 304(2).
S. 38(4): ITTOIA 2005, s. 304(3)–(6).
S. 38(5):ITTOIA 2005, s. 305(1)–(4).
S. 38(5): ITTOIA 2005, s. 303(3).
S. 38 rewritten for corporation tax purposes as follows:
S. 38(1): CTA 2009, s. 243(1), 1316(1).
S. 38(2): CTA 2009, s. 244(1).
S. 38(3): CTA 2009, s. 244(2).
S. 38(4): CTA 2009, s. 244(3), (4), (5), (6).
S. 38(5): CTA 2009, s. 245(1), (2), (3), (4).
S. 38(6): CTA 2009, s. 243(4).

39 Saving for pre-1963 leases, and special relief for individuals

39 [Omitted by CTA 2009, s. 1322 and Sch. 1, para. 16 and repealed by CTA 2009, s. 1326 and Sch. 3, Pt. 1.]

History – Omitted by CTA 2009, s. 1322 and Sch. 1, para. 16 and repealed by CTA 2009, s. 1326 and Sch. 3, Pt. 1, with effect for corporation tax purposes for accounting periods ending on or after 1 April 2009, and for income tax and capital gains tax purposes for the tax year 2009–10 and subsequent tax years.

Notes – S. 39(1) has been rewritten for income tax purposes into the provisions of ITTOIA 2005, Sch. 2, para. 63–66.
S. 39 rewritten for corporation tax purposes as follows: CTA 2009, Sch. 2, para. 35, 36, 37, 38.

SUPPLEMENTARY PROVISIONS

40 Tax treatment of receipts and outgoings on sale of land

40 [Omitted by CTA 2009, s. 1322 and Sch. 1, para. 17 and repealed by CTA 2009, s. 1326 and Sch. 3, Pt. 1.]

History – S. 40 omitted by CTA 2009, s. 1322 and Sch. 1, para. 17 and repealed by CTA 2009, s. 1326 and Sch. 3, Pt. 1, with effect for corporation tax purposes for accounting periods ending on or after 1 April 2009, and for income tax and capital gains tax purposes for the tax year 2009–10 and subsequent tax years.

Notes – S. 40(3) is rewritten as ITTOIA 2005, s. 320(1) and (2).
ITTOIA 2005 does not rewrite certain provisions of ICTA 1988, s. 40 as they are redundant following the merger of the property income rules with those for trading income. (See ITTOIA 2005, Explanatory Notes, Annex 1, Table 1 (Change 158).)
S. 40 rewritten for corporation tax purposes as follows:
S. 40(3): CTA 2009, s. 259(1), (2).

41 Relief for rent etc. not paid

41 [Repealed by FA 1998, Sch. 5, para. 21, s. 165 and Sch. 27, Pt. III(4).]

History – S. 41 repealed for income tax purposes for 1995–96 and subsequent years of assessment (subject to s. 39(5)) by virtue of FA 1995, s. 39 and Sch. 6, para. 4. Subsequently, s. 41 repealed for the purposes of corporation tax by FA 1998, Sch. 5, para. 21, s. 165 and Sch. 29, Pt. III(4) with effect from 1 April 1998 (subject to transitional provisions in FA 1998, Sch. 5, Pt. IV).

42 Appeals against determinations under Chapter 4 of Part 3 of ITTOIA 2005

42 [Omitted by TIOPA 2010, s. 371 and Sch. 7, para. 20 and repealed by TIOPA 2010, s. 378 and Sch. 10, Pt. 12.]

History – S. 42(7), so far as it continued to have effect (see TIOPA 2010, s. 381), omitted by FA 2011, s. 86 and Sch. 23, para. 55(a), with effect from 1 April 2012, subject to transitional provisions in FA 2011, Sch. 23, para. 65.
S. 42 omitted by TIOPA 2010, s. 371 and Sch. 7, para. 20 and repealed by TIOPA 2010, s. 378 and Sch. 10, Pt. 12, with effect for corporation tax purposes for accounting periods ending on or after 1 April 2010, for income tax and capital gains tax purposes for the tax year 2010–11 and subsequent tax years, and for petroleum revenue tax purposes for chargeable periods beginning on or after 1 July 2010.

Notes – Former s. 42 rewritten in CTA 2009 as follows:
Former s. 42(1): CTA 2009, s. 240(1), (2).
Former s. 42 rewritten in TIOPA 2010, Sch. 7, para. 22.

42A Non-residents and their representatives

42A [Omitted by ITA 2007, s. 1027 and Sch. 1, para. 7 and repealed by ITA 2007, s. 1031 and Sch. 3, Pt. 1 with effect for income tax purposes for 2007–08 and subsequent tax years and for corporation tax purposes in relation to accounting periods ending after 5 April 2007.]

Notes – S. 42A rewritten as follows:
S. 42A(1): ITA 2007, s. 971(1), (2).
S. 42A(2): ITA 2007, s. 971(3).
S. 42A(3): ITA 2007, s. 971(4), (5).
S. 42A(4): ITA 2007, s. 972(1).
S. 42A(5): ITA 2007, s. 972(2).
S. 42A(6): ITA 2007, s. 972(3), (4).
S. 42A(7): ITA 2007, s. 972(5).

43 Non-residents

43 [S. 43 repealed by FA 1995, s. 40(3), s. 162 and Sch. 29, Pt. VIII(16), in relation to any payment made on or after 6 April 1996.]

43A Finance agreement: interpretation

43A [S. 43A ceases to have effect by virtue of FA 2006, s. 76 and Sch. 6, para. 1(1); and is repealed by FA 2006, s. 178(1) and Sch. 26, Pt. 3(12).]

History – S. 43A ceases to have effect by virtue of FA 2006, s. 76 and Sch. 6, para. 1(1); and is repealed by FA 2006, s. 178(1) and Sch. 26, Pt. 3(12) with effect in relation to transactions entered into on or after 6 June 2006 (Sch. 6, para. 1(2)).
S. 43A(2) repealed by FA 2002, s. 141 and Sch. 40, Pt. 3(16).

Notes – The rules in s. 43A–43G ("rent factoring") are effectively subsumed into the new ICTA 1988, s. 774A–774G ("structured finance arrangements").

43B Transfer of rent

43B [S. 43B ceases to have effect by virtue of FA 2006, s. 76 and Sch. 6, para. 1(1); and is repealed by FA 2006, s. 178(1) and Sch. 26, Pt. 3(12).]

History – S. 43B ceases to have effect by virtue of FA 2006, s. 76 and Sch. 6, para. 1(1); and is repealed by FA 2006, s. 178(1) and Sch. 26, Pt. 3(12) with effect in relation to transactions entered into on or after 6 June 2006 (Sch. 6, para. 1(2)).

Cross references – CTA 2010, s. 1180 and Sch. 2, para. 87: Transitional provisions in respect of arrangements made before 6 June 2006.

Notes – The rules in s. 43A–43G ("rent factoring") are effectively subsumed into the new ICTA 1988, s. 774A–774G ("structured finance arrangements").

43C Transfer of rent: exceptions, &c.

43C [S. 43C ceases to have effect by virtue of FA 2006, s. 76 and Sch. 6, para. 1(1); and is repealed by FA 2006, s. 178(1) and Sch. 26, Pt. 3(12).]

History – S. 43C ceases to have effect by virtue of FA 2006, s. 76 and Sch. 6, para. 1(1); and is repealed by FA 2006, s. 178(1) and Sch. 26, Pt. 3(12) with effect in relation to transactions entered into on or after 6 June 2006 (Sch. 6, para. 1(2)).

Notes – The rules in s. 43A–43G ("rent factoring") are effectively subsumed into the new ICTA 1988, s. 774A–774G ("structured finance arrangements").

43D Interposed lease

43D [S. 43D ceases to have effect by virtue of FA 2006, s. 76 and Sch. 6, para. 1(1); and is repealed by FA 2006, s. 178(1) and Sch. 26, Pt. 3(12).]

History – S. 43D ceases to have effect by virtue of FA 2006, s. 76 and Sch. 6, para. 1(1); and is repealed by FA 2006, s. 178(1) and Sch. 26, Pt. 3(12), with effect in relation to transactions entered into on or after 6 June 2006 (Sch. 6, para. 1(2)).

Notes – The rules in s. 43A–43G ("rent factoring") are effectively subsumed into the new ICTA 1988, s. 774A–774G ("structured finance arrangements").

43E Interposed lease: exceptions, &c.

43E [S. 43E ceases to have effect by virtue of FA 2006, s. 76 and Sch. 6, para. 1(1); and is repealed by FA 2006, s. 178(1) and Sch. 26, Pt. 3(12).]

History – S. 43E ceases to have effect by virtue of FA 2006, s. 76 and Sch. 6, para. 1(1); and is repealed by FA 2006, s. 178(1) and Sch. 26, Pt. 3(12) with effect in relation to transactions entered into on or after 6 June 2006 (Sch. 6, para. 1(2)).

Notes – The rules in s. 43A–43G ("rent factoring") are effectively subsumed into the new ICTA 1988, s. 774A–774G ("structured finance arrangements").

43F Insurance business

43F [S. 43F ceases to have effect by virtue of FA 2006, s. 76 and Sch. 6, para. 1(1); and is repealed by FA 2006, s. 178(1) and Sch. 26, Pt. 3(12).]

History – S. 43F ceases to have effect by virtue of FA 2006, s. 76 and Sch. 6, para 1(1); and is repealed by FA 2006, s. 178(1) and Sch. 26, Pt. 3(12) with effect in relation to transactions entered into on or after 6 June 2006 (Sch. 6, para. 1(2)).

Notes – The rules in s. 43A–43G ("rent factoring") are effectively subsumed into the new ICTA 1988, s. 774A–774G ("structured finance arrangements").

43G Interpretation

43G [S. 43G ceases to have effect by virtue of FA 2006, s. 76 and Sch. 6, para. 1(1); and is repealed by FA 2006, s. 178(1) and Sch. 26, Pt. 3(12).]

History – S. 43G ceases to have effect by virtue of FA 2006, s. 76 and Sch. 6, para 1(1); and is repealed by FA 2006, s. 178(1) and Sch. 26, Pt. 3(12) with effect in relation to transactions entered into on or after 6 June 2006 (Sch. 6, para. 1(2)).

Notes – The rules in s. 43A–43G ("rent factoring") are effectively subsumed into the new ICTA 1988, s. 774A–774G ("structured finance arrangements").

PART III – GOVERNMENT SECURITIES

GENERAL

44 Income tax: mode of charge

44 [Repealed by FA 1996, s. 79 and Sch. 7, para. 7 and s. 205 and Sch. 41, Pt. V(2).]

45 Interpretation of Part III

45 [Repealed by FA 1996, s. 79 and Sch. 7, para. 8 and s. 205 and Sch. 41, Pt. V(2).]

GOVERNMENT SECURITIES: EXEMPTIONS FROM TAX

46 Savings certificates and tax reserve certificates

46 [Omitted by CTA 2009, s. 1322 and Sch. 1, para. 19 and repealed by CTA 2009, s. 1326 and Sch. 3, Pt. 1.]

History – S. 46 omitted by CTA 2009, s. 1322 and Sch. 1, para. 19 and repealed by CTA 2009, s. 1326 and Sch. 3, Pt. 1, with effect for corporation tax purposes for accounting periods ending on or after 1 April 2009, and for income tax and capital gains tax purposes for the tax year 2009–10 and subsequent tax years.

Notes – The rewritten income tax provisions are now located as follows:
S. 46(1): ITTOIA 2005, s. 692(1) and 693(1).
S. 46(2): ITTOIA 2005, s. 750.
S. 46(3): ITTOIA 2005, s. 692(1) and (2), 693(5) and Sch. 2, para. 138.
S. 46(4): ITTOIA 2005, s. 692(4) and 693(1)–(3).
S. 46(5): ITTOIA 2005, s. 693(6).
S. 46(6): ITTOIA 2005, s. 692(3).
S. 46 rewritten for corporation tax purposes as follows:
S. 46(1): CTA 2009, s. 1281(1), 1282(1).
S. 46(2): CTA 2009, s. 1283.
S. 46(3): CTA 2009, s. 1281(1), (2), 1282(4), Sch. 2, para. 136.
S. 46(4): CTA 2009, s. 1281(4), 1282(1), (2), (3).
S. 46(5): CTA 2009, s. 1282(5).
S. 46(6): CTA 2009, s. 1281(3).
S. 46(7): CTA 2009, s. 1282(6).

47 United Kingdom government securities held by non-residents

47 [Repealed by FA 1996, s. 154 and Sch. 28, para. 1 and s. 205 and Sch. 41, Pt. V(18) for 1996–97 and later years of assessment.]

48 Securities of foreign states

48 [Repealed by FA 1996, s. 79 and Sch. 7, para. 9 and s. 205 and Sch. 41, Pt. V(2).]

49 Stock and dividends in name of Treasury etc.

49(1) No tax shall be chargeable in respect of the stock or dividends–

(a) transferred, in pursuance of any Act of Parliament, to accounts in the books of the Bank of England in the name of the Treasury or the National Debt Commissioners, or

(b) transferred, in pursuance of any Act of Parliament, to the Treasury or the National Debt Commissioners and in respect of which the Treasury or those Commissioners are entered as holder in the registers kept by the Registrar of Government Stock,

but the Bank of England and the Registrar of Government Stock shall each transmit to the Board an account of the total amount thereof in those books or registers as the case may be.

49(2) No tax shall be chargeable in respect of the stock or dividends belonging to the Crown, in whatever name they may stand in the books of the Bank of England or in the registers kept by the Registrar of Government Stock.

49(3) In this section **"dividends"** means any interest, public annuities, dividends or shares of annuities.

49(4) In this section **"Registrar of Government Stock"** means the person or persons appointed in accordance with regulations under section 47(1)(b) of the Finance Act 1942 (see regulation 3 of the Government Stock Regulations 2004).

History – S. 49(1) substituted by SI 2004/2744, Schedule, para. 2(2)(a), with effect from 15 November 2004 subject to the transitional provision contained in SI 2004/2744, reg. 3, which reads as follows:

"**3(1)** Anything done, or treated as done, by or in relation to the Bank of England, or any officer of the Bank of England, under any transferred function before the commencement day shall continue to have effect on and after that day, but as if it had been done by or in relation to the Registrar of Government Stock.

3(2) Paragraph (1) is without prejudice to the application of the Interpretation Act 1978 and is subject to paragraph (3).

3(3) Nothing in this article shall have the effect of transferring any liability from the Bank of England, or an officer of the Bank of England, to the Registrar of Government Stock.

3(4) In this article–

"commencement day" means the day on which this Order comes into force;

"Registrar of Government Stock" means the person or persons appointed in accordance with regulations under section 47(1)(b) of the Finance Act 1942 (see regulation 3 of the Government Stock Regulations 2004);

"transferred function" means any function which–

(a) before the commencement day was a function of the Bank of England or of an officer of the Bank of England, but

(b) on that day becomes a function of the Registrar of Government Stock by virtue of any amendment made by the Schedule.

3(5) Where the effect of any amendment made by the Schedule is to replace, with modifications, a function of the Bank of England, or of an officer of the Bank of England, with a function of the Registrar of Government Stock, the functions shall be regarded for the purposes of this article as one and the same function and that function shall accordingly be regarded for these purposes as a transferred function."

In s. 49(2) the words "or in the registers kept by the Registrar of Government Stock" inserted by SI 2004/2744, Schedule, para. 2(2)(b), with effect from 15 November 2004 subject to the transitional provision contained in SI 2004/2744, reg. 3 (reproduced above).

S. 49(3) inserted by FA 1996, s. 79 and Sch. 7, para. 10 for 1996–97 and later years of assessment (income tax) and for accounting periods ending after 31 March 1996 (corporation tax), subject to FA 1996, Sch. 7, para. 33–35.

S. 49(4) inserted by SI 2004/2744, Schedule, para. 2(2)(c), with effect from 15 November 2004 subject to the transitional provision contained in SI 2004/2744, reg. 3 (reproduced above).

Derivations – ICTA 1970, s. 106(1)–(2).

GOVERNMENT SECURITIES: INTEREST PAYABLE WITHOUT DEDUCTION OF TAX

50 United Kingdom securities: Treasury directions for payment without deduction of tax

50 [Omitted by ITA 2007, s. 1027 and Sch. 1, para. 8 and repealed by ITA 2007, s. 1031 and Sch. 3, Pt. 1 with effect for income tax purposes for 2007–08 and subsequent tax years and for corporation tax purposes in relation to accounting periods ending after 5 April 2007.]

Notes – S. 50 rewritten as follows:
S. 50(A1): ITA 2007, s. 892(1), 893(1), (2).
S. 50(1): ITA 2007, s. 892(1), 893(1), (2), 894(1), (2).
S. 50(2): ITA 2007, s. 895(1), (2).
S. 50(3): ITA 2007, s. 892(1), 893(1), 895(3).
S. 50(4): ITA 2007, s. 895(2), (3).
S. 50(5): ITA 2007, s. 896(1), (2), (3).
S. 50(6): ITA 2007, s. 895(4), (5).
S. 50(7): ITA 2007, s. 1024
S. 50(7) ("registered"): ITA 2007, s. 895(6)
S. 50(7) ("the Registrar"): ITA 2007, s. 895(6)
S. 50(7) ("gilt-edged securities"): ITTOIA 2005, s. 153(1).

51 Treasury directions as respects Northern Ireland securities

51 [Omitted by ITA 2007, s. 1027 and Sch. 1, para. 8 and repealed by ITA 2007, s. 1031 and Sch. 3, Pt. 1 with effect for income tax purposes for 2007–08 and subsequent tax years and for corporation tax purposes in relation to accounting periods ending after 5 April 2007.]

Notes – S. 51 rewritten as follows:
S. 51(1): ITA 2007, s. 893(2), 894(3), (4).
S. 51(2): ITA 2007, s. 894(3).

51AA Commencement of direction under section 50 or 51

51AA [Omitted by ITA 2007, s. 1027 and Sch. 1, para. 8 and repealed by ITA 2007, s. 1031 and Sch. 3, Pt. 1 with effect for income tax purposes for 2007–08 and subsequent tax years and for corporation tax purposes in relation to accounting periods ending after 5 April 2007.]

Notes – S. 51AA rewritten as ITA 2007, s. 894(5).

51A Gilt-edged securities held under authorised arrangements

51A [Repealed by F(No. 2)A 1997, s. 37(5) and s. 52 and Sch. 8, Pt. II(13).]

History – S. 51A repealed by F(No. 2)A 1997, s. 37(5) and s. 52 and Sch. 8, Pt. II(13) with effect in relation to payments of interest falling due on or after 6 April 1998.

51B Periodic accounting for tax on interest on gilt-edged securities

51B [Repealed by FA 1998, s. 37, s. 165 and Sch. 27, Pt. III(3).]

History – S. 51B repealed by FA 1998, s. 37, s. 165 and Sch. 27, Pt. III(3) with effect in relation to payments of interest falling due on or after 1 April 1999 by virtue of SI 1999/619 (C 16).

52 Taxation of interest on converted government securities and interest which becomes subject to deduction

52 [Repealed by FA 1996, s. 79 and Sch. 7, para. 12 and s. 205 and Sch. 41, Pt. V(2).]

PART IV – PROVISIONS RELATING TO THE SCHEDULE D CHARGE

Chapter I – Supplementary Charging Provisions

53 Farming and other commercial occupation of land (except woodlands)

53 [Omitted by CTA 2009, s. 1322 and Sch. 1, para. 20 and repealed by CTA 2009, s. 1326 and Sch. 3, Pt. 1.]

History – S. 53 omitted by CTA 2009, s. 1322 and Sch. 1, para. 20 and repealed by CTA 2009, s. 1326 and Sch. 3, Pt. 1, with effect for corporation tax purposes for accounting periods ending on or after 1 April 2009, and for income tax and capital gains tax purposes for the tax year 2009–10 and subsequent tax years.

Notes – Rewritten income tax provisions are now located as follows:
S. 53(1): ITTOIA 2005, s. 9(1).
S. 53(2): ITTOIA 2005, s. 9(2) and 859(1). The references in ICTA 1988, s. 53(2) to "body of persons" are not rewritten by ITTOIA 2005 as it is generally understood that a body of persons acting in a representative or fiduciary capacity is treated as a separate entity from those persons acting on their own behalf. (See ITTOIA 2005, Explanatory Notes, Annex 1, Table 1 (Change 158).)
S. 53(3): ITTOIA 2005, s. 10(1)–(3) and 11(2).
S. 53(4): ITTOIA 2005, s. 10(3) and 11(1).
S. 53 rewritten for corporation tax purposes as follows:
S. 53(1): CTA 2009, s. 36(1).
S. 53(2): CTA 2009, s. 36(2), 1270(1).
S. 53(3): CTA 2009, s. 37(2), 38(1), (2), (3).
S. 53(4): CTA 2009, s. 37(1), 38(3).
S. 53(5): CTA 2009, s. 36(3), 38(3).

54 Woodlands managed on a commercial basis

54 [Repealed by FA 1988, s. 65 and Sch. 6, para. 3(1) and by s. 148 and Sch. 14, Pt. V, with effect from 15 March 1988.]

55 Mines, quarries and other concerns

55 [Omitted by CTA 2009, s. 1322 and Sch. 1, para. 21 and repealed by CTA 2009, s. 1326 and Sch. 3, Pt. 1.]

History – S. 55 omitted by CTA 2009, s. 1322 and Sch. 1, para. 21 and repealed by CTA 2009, s. 1326 and Sch. 3, Pt. 1, with effect for corporation tax purposes for accounting periods ending on or after 1 April 2009, and for income tax and capital gains tax purposes for the tax year 2009–10 and subsequent tax years.

Notes – The rewritten income tax provisions are now located as follows:
S. 55(1): ITTOIA 2005, s. 12(1)–(3).
S. 55(2): ITTOIA 2005, s. 12(4).
S. 55 rewritten for corporation tax purposes as follows:
S. 55(1): CTA 2009, s. 39(1), (2), (3).
S. 55(2): CTA 2009, s. 39(4).
S. 55(3): CTA 2009, s. 39(5).

56 Transactions in deposits with and without certificates or in debts

56(1) Subsection (2) below applies to the following rights–

(a) the right to receive the amount, with or without interest, stated in a certificate of deposit;

(b) the right to receive an amount payable with interest–

(i) in a transaction in which no certificate of deposit or security is issued, and

(ii) which is payable by a bank or similar institution or a person regularly engaging in similar transactions;

and the right to receive that interest.

56(2) Profits or gains arising to a company from the disposal of a right to which this subsection applies or, except so far as it is a right to receive interest, from the exercise of any such right (whether by the person to whom the certificate was issued or by some other person, or, as the case may be, by the person who acquired the right in the transaction referred to in subsection (1) above or by some person acquiring it directly or indirectly from that person), shall, if not falling to be taken into account as a trading receipt, be treated as an amount to which the charge to corporation tax on income applies

56(3) Subsection (2) above and section 551 of ITTOIA 2005 (charge to income tax on profits from disposal of deposit rights) do not apply in the case of the disposal or exercise of a right to receive an amount stated in a certificate of deposit or interest on such an amount–

(a) if the company disposing of the right acquired it before 7th March 1973;

(b) to any profits or gains arising to a fund or scheme in the case of which provision is made by section 613(4) or 614(2) or (3) or section 186 of the Finance Act 2004 for exempting the whole or part of its income from income tax;

(c) [omitted by CTA 2010, s. 1177 and Sch. 1, para. 8 and repealed by CTA 2010, s. 1181 and Sch. 3, Pt. 1.]

56(3A) [Repealed by FA 2002, s. 141 and Sch. 40.]

56(4) [Omitted by FA 2008, s. 43 and Sch. 17, para. 24(1).]

56(4A) This section and section 56A shall not apply for the purposes of corporation tax except in relation to rights in existence before 1st April 1996.

56(4B) For the purposes of corporation tax, where any profits or gains arising from the disposal or exercise of a right in existence before 1st April 1996 are, or (if there were any) would be, chargeable under this section, nothing in Part 5 of CTA 2009 (loan relationships) shall require any amount relating to that disposal, or to the exercise of that right, to be brought into account for the purposes of that Part.

56(5) In this section–

"certificate of deposit" means a document relating to money, in any currency, which has been deposited with the issuer or some other person, being a document which recognises an obligation to pay a stated amount to bearer or to order, with or without interest, and being a document by the delivery of which, with or without endorsement, the right to receive that stated amount, with or without interest, is transferable; and

"security" has the same meaning as in section 132 of the 1992 Act.

History – In s. 56(2) "an amount to which the charge to corporation tax on income applies" substituted for the words "annual profits or gains chargeable to corporation tax under Case VI of Schedule D" by CTA 2009, s. 1322 and Sch. 1, para. 22(2), with effect for corporation tax purposes for accounting periods ending on or after 1 April 2009, and for income tax and capital gains tax purposes for the tax year 2009–10 and subsequent tax years.

In s. 56(2) the words "company" and "corporation tax" substituted by ITTOIA 2005, s. 882(1) and Sch. 1, para. 34(2); effective for income tax purposes for 2005–06 onwards and for corporation tax purposes for accounting periods ending after 5 April 2005 (ITTOIA 2005, s. 883(1)).

In s. 56(3) the words "and section 551 of ITTOIA 2005 (charge to income tax on profits from disposal of deposit rights) do" and "company" substituted by ITTOIA 2005, s. 882(1) and Sch. 1, para. 34(3); effective for income tax purposes for 2005–06 onwards and for corporation tax purposes for accounting periods ending after 5 April 2005 (ITTOIA 2005, s. 883(1)).

In s. 56(3)(b), the words "613(4) or 614(2) or (3) or section 186 of the Finance Act 2004" substituted for the words "592(2), 613, 614(1) to (3) or 620(6)" by FA 2004, s. 281(1) and Sch. 35, para. 4 with effect from 6 April 2006 (FA 2004, s. 284(1)).

S. 56(3)(c) omitted by CTA 2010, s. 1177 and Sch. 1, para. 8 and repealed by CTA 2010, s. 1181 and Sch. 3, Pt. 1, with effect for corporation tax purposes for accounting periods ending on or after 1 April 2010, and for income and capital gains tax purposes for the tax year 2010–11 and subsequent tax years, subject to transitional provisions in CTA 2010, s. 1180 and Sch. 2, para. 70.

In former s. 56(3)(c), the words "charitable company" substituted by ITA 2007, s. 1027 and Sch. 1, para. 9 with effect for income tax purposes for 2007–08 and subsequent tax years and for corporation tax purposes for accounting periods ending after 5 April 2007.

S. 56(3A)–(3D) repealed by FA 2002, s. 141 and Sch. 40, Pt. 3(10), with effect in relation to accounting periods beginning on or after 1 October 2002.

S. 56(3A)–(3D) inserted by FA 1993, s. 170 and Sch. 18, para. 2, with effect where a company becomes entitled to a qualifying asset or to rights and duties under a currency contract, or subjectto a qualifying liability on or after 23 March 1995 (the commencement day for the purposes of FA 1993, s. 165(7) by virtue of SI 1994/3224 (C. 79)).

S. 56(4) omitted by FA 2008, s. 43 and Sch. 17, para. 24(1), with effect from 21 July 2008.

In s. 56(4), words "for the purposes of" substituted by FA 1996, s. 164(4) for accounting periods beginning on or after 1 January 1996, subject to FA 1996, s. 164(6).

S. 56(4A), 56(4B) inserted by FA 1996, s. 104 and Sch. 14 para. 6 for accounting periods ending after 31 March 1996, subject to FA 1996, Sch. 15.

In s. 56(4B), the words "Part 5 of CTA 2009" and "that Part" substituted for "Chapter II of Part IV of the Finance Act 1995" and "that Chapter" respectively by CTA 2009, s. 1322 and Sch. 1, para. 22(3), with effect for corporation tax purposes for accounting periods ending on or after 1 April 2009, and for income tax and capital gains tax purposes for the tax year 2009–10 and subsequent tax years.
In s. 56(5), references to the "1992 Act" substituted by TCGA 1992, s. 290 and Sch. 10, para. 14(3).

Derivations – S. 56(1)(a): FA 1973, s. 26(1).
S. 56(1)(b): FA 1974, s. 30(1).
S. 56(2): FA 1973, s. 26(1) and FA 1974, s. 30(1).
S. 56(3): FA 1973, s. 26(1), as amended by F(No. 2)A 1975, s. 50(1).
S. 56(4) (as originally enacted): FA 1973, s. 26(3), as further applied by FA 1974, s. 30(2).
S. 56(5) (as originally enacted): FA 1973, s. 26(4), FA 1968, s. 55, as further applied by FA 1974, s. 30(2); and from FA 1974, s. 30(1), as amended by CGTA 1979, s. 157(2) and Sch. 7, para. 9.

Cross references – S. 608(2)(c): exemption for superannuation funds approved immediately before 6 April 1980 for profits which would be chargeable to tax by virtue of s. 56.
Sch. 22, para. 7(3)(c): pension scheme surpluses – restriction of exemptions under s. 56 to specified percentage of profits or gains.
TCGA 1992, s. 132: definition of security by reference to the inclusion of any loan stock or similar security of a government, public or local authority or company whether secured or unsecured.
FA 1995, s. 128(3): income chargeable to tax under Sch. D, Case VI by virtue of s. 56 falls within the provisions on the limit on income chargeable on non-residents.
FA 1996, Pt. IV, Ch. II: loan relationships.
FA 2003, s. 151(2)(b): extent of charge to income tax in respect of non-resident companies.
SI 2002/2006, reg. 14: any amount treated as income under s. 56 is also treated as notional income of the claimant for the purposes of a claim to tax credit.
SI 2003/1633, the Uncertificated Securities (Amendment) (Eligible Debt Securities) Regulations 2003, reg. 15 and Sch. 2, para. 6: references in s. 56(1), (3) and (5):

- to a certificate of deposit include references to corresponding uncertificated units of an eligible debt security;
- to amounts stated in a certificate of deposit include references to a principal amount stated in, or determined in accordance with, the current terms of issue of such an eligible debt security.

Transitional – CTA 2009, Sch. 2, para. 55: certain references to CTA 2009, Pt. 5 to include references to FA 1996, Sch. 15 (loan relationships; savings and transitional provisions).

Other material – ICAEW Technical Release TR 117: (not reproduced) certificates of deposit do not include bearer bonds.
Bank of England notice, 29 April 1986 (not reproduced): Revenue confirmation that the arrangements for taxation of the return earned by holders of sterling commercial paper are those applying to certificates of deposit.

Notes – S. 56 rewritten as follows:
S. 56(1):ITTOIA 2005, s. 552(1).
S. 56(2):ITTOIA 2005, s. 366(1) and 551(1) and (2).
S. 56(3): ITA 2007, s. 534(1), (2), (3), (4), 538(2).
S. 56(5) ("certificate of deposit"): ITA 2007, s. 1019.
S. 56(5): ITTOIA 2005, s. 552(2).
ITTOIA 2005, Pt. 4, Ch. 11 does not rewrite the provision in ICTA 1988, s. 56(3)(a) which applies only to certificates of deposit issued before 7 March 1973. As such certificates are in practice issued for a maximum of five years, this provision is obsolescent or obsolete. Its effect is preserved in ITTOIA 2005, Sch. 2, para. 92. (See ITTOIA 2005, Explanatory Notes, Annex 1, Table 1 (Change 158).)
ITTOIA 2005 does not rewrite parts of ICTA 1988, s. 56 and 56A where their effect is more simply achieved byICTA 1988, s. 59. (See ITTOIA 2005, Explanatory Notes, Annex 1, Table 1 (Change 158).)

56A Disposal or exercise of rights in pursuance of deposits

56A(1) This section applies where there is an arrangement under which–

(a) there is a right to receive an amount (with or without interest) in pursuance of a deposit of money,

(b) when the right comes into existence there is no certificate of deposit in respect of the right, and

(c) the person for the time being entitled to the right is entitled to call for the issue of a certificate of deposit in respect of the right.

56A(2) In such a case–

(a) the right shall be treated as not falling within section 56(1)(b), and

(b) if there is a disposal or exercise of the right before such time (if any) as a certificate of deposit is issued in respect of it, section 56(2) shall apply to it by virtue of this paragraph.

56A(3) In the application of section 56 by virtue of this section–

(a) subsection (2) shall have effect as if the words from "(whether" to "person)" read "(whether by the person originally entitled to the right or by some other person)", and

(b) subsection (3) shall have effect as if the words "stated in a certificate of deposit" read "under an arrangement".

56A(4) In this section **"certificate of deposit"** has the meaning given by section 56(5).

History – S. 56A inserted by F(No. 2)A 1992, s. 34 and Sch. 8, para. 1 in relation to arrangements made after 16 July 1992.

Cross references – S. 56: disapplication of s. 56A. This section shall not apply for corporation tax purposes, except in relation to rights in existence before 1 April 1996.
SI 2003/1633, the Uncertificated Securities (Amendment) (Eligible Debt Securities) Regulations 2003, reg. 15 and Sch. 2, para. 6: references in s. 56A(1) and (2):

- to a certificate of deposit include references to corresponding uncertificated units of an eligible debt security;
- to amounts stated in a certificate of deposit include references to a principal amount stated in, or determined in accordance with, the current terms of issue of such an eligible debt security.

Notes – S. 56A rewritten as follows:
S. 56A(1): ITTOIA 2005, s. 552(1) and (2) and ITA 2007, s. 534(5).
S. 56A(2): ITTOIA 2005, s. 551(1) and (2) and s. 552(1).
S. 56A(3): ITA 2007, s. 534(1), (3), (4).
S. 56A(4): ITTOIA 2005, s. 552(2) and ITTA 2007, s. 534(5).

However, ITTOIA 2005 does not rewrite parts of ICTA 1988, s. 56 and 56A where their effect is more simply achieved by ICTA 1988, s. 59. (See ITTOIA 2005, Explanatory Notes, Annex 1, Table 1 (Change 158).)

57 Deep discount securities

57 [Repealed by FA 1996, s. 205 and Sch. 41, Pt. V(3) for accounting periods ending after 31 March 1996 (corporation tax) and for 1996–97 and subsequent years of assessment (income tax), subject to FA 1996, Sch. 15.]

58 Foreign pensions

58 [Omitted by ITEPA 2003, Sch. 6, para. 8 and repealed by ITEPA 2003, Sch. 8, Pt. 1.]

History – S. 58 omitted by ITEPA 2003, Sch. 6, para. 8 and repealed by ITEPA 2003, Sch. 8, Pt. 1 which have effect for the tax year 2003–04 and subsequent tax years.

Notes – S. 58 rewritten as follows:
S. 58(1): ITEPA 2003, s. 573(1).
S. 58(2): ITEPA 2003, s. 574 and s. 633.

59 Persons chargeable

59(1) [Omitted by ITTOIA 2005, s. 882 and Sch. 1, para. 35(2) and repealed by s. 884 and Sch. 3.]

59(2) [Omitted by ITTOIA 2005, s. 882 and Sch. 1, para. 35(2) and repealed by s. 884 and Sch. 3.]

59(3) [Omitted by TIOPA 2010, s. 374 and Sch. 8, para. 292 and repealed by TIOPA 2010, s. 378 and Sch. 10, Pt. 13.]

59(4) [Omitted by TIOPA 2010, s. 374 and Sch. 8, para. 292 and repealed by TIOPA 2010, s. 378 and Sch. 10, Pt. 13.]

History – S. 59(1) and (2) omitted by ITTOIA 2005, s. 882(1) and Sch. 1, para. 35(2) and repealed by s. 884 and Sch. 3; effective for income tax purposes for 2005–06 onwards and for corporation tax purposes for accounting periods ending after 5 April 2005 (ITTOIA 2005, s. 883(1)).
S. 59(3) and (4) omitted by TIOPA 2010, s. 374 and Sch. 8, para. 292 and repealed by TIOPA 2010, s. 378 and Sch. 10, Pt. 13, with effect for corporation tax purposes for accounting periods ending on or after 1 April 2010, for income tax and capital gains tax purposes for the tax year 2010–11 and subsequent tax years, and for petroleum revenue tax purposes for chargeable periods beginning on or after 1 July 2010.

Derivations – ICTA 1970, s. 114.

Notes – S. 59(1) has been rewritten as ITTOIA 2005, s. 8, 230, 245, 271, 332, 338, 348, 352, 360, 371, 404(1), 425, 549, 554, 573, 581, 611, 616, 685 and 689.
The references in ICTA 1988, s. 59(2) to persons carrying on a s. 55 concern and the agents or other officers who have the direction or management of the concern or who receive the profits is not rewritten by ITTOIA 2005. In the main these would be people who would receive or be entitled to the profits and it was thought that profits from such concerns should not be taxed more widely than profits from a trade. (See ITTOIA 2005, Explanatory Notes, Annex 1, Table 1 (Change 158).)
S. 59(3) and (4) not rewritten in TIOPA 2010, as unnecessary (see change 15 in Annex 1 to the Explanatory Notes to TIOPA 2010).

Chapter II – Income Tax: Basis of Assessment etc.

CASES I AND II

60 Assessment on current year basis

60 [Omitted by ITTOIA 2005, s. 882 and Sch. 1, para. 36 and repealed by s. 884 and Sch. 3.]

History – S. 60 omitted by ITTOIA 2005, s. 882(1) and Sch. 1, para. 36 and repealed by s. 884 and Sch. 3; effective for income tax purposes for 2005–06 onwards and for corporation tax purposes for accounting periods ending after 5 April 2005 (ITTOIA 2005, s. 883(1)).

Notes – S. 60 has been rewrittenas follows:
S. 60(1): ITTOIA 2005, s. 7(1) and 200(4).
S. 60(2): ITTOIA 2005, s. 7(2).
S. 60(3): ITTOIA 2005, s. 198(1) and (2), 200(3) and 201(1).
S. 60(5): ITTOIA 2005, s. 197(1).
ICTA 1988, s. 60(4) is not rewritten by ITTOIA 2005 as there will no longer be adjustments for previous years following a trader's death. (See ITTOIA 2005, Explanatory Notes, Annex 1, Table 1 (Change 158).)

61 Basis of assessment at commencement

61 [Omitted by ITTOIA 2005, s. 882 and Sch. 1, para. 36 and repealed by s. 884 and Sch. 3.]

History – S. 61 omitted by ITTOIA 2005, s. 882(1) and Sch. 1, para. 36 and repealed by s. 884 and Sch. 3; effective for income tax purposes for 2005–06 onwards and for corporation tax purposes for accounting periods ending after 5 April 2005 (ITTOIA 2005, s. 883(1)).

Notes – S. 61 has been rewritten as follows:
S. 61(1: ITTOIA 2005, s. 199(1) and 202(2).
S. 61(2): ITTOIA 2005, s. 200(2).

62 Change of basis period

62 [Omitted by ITTOIA 2005, s. 882 and Sch. 1, para. 36 and repealed by s. 884 and Sch. 3.]

History – S. 62 omitted by ITTOIA 2005, s. 882(1) and Sch. 1, para. 36 and repealed by s. 884 and Sch. 3; effective for income tax purposes for 2005–06 onwards and for corporation tax purposes for accounting periods ending after 5 April 2005 (ITTOIA 2005, s. 883(1)).

Notes – S. 62 has been rewritten as follows:
S. 62(1): ITTOIA 2005, s. 214(1), 215(1) and 216(1).
S. 62(2): ITTOIA 2005, s. 197(2), 200(3), 214(2) and (3), 215(1) and (2) and 216(2) and (3).
S. 62(3): ITTOIA 2005, s. 216(4) and s. 219(1).
S. 62(4): ITTOIA 2005, s. 219(2) and (3).
S. 62(5): ITTOIA 2005, s. 214(1).

62A Conditions for such a change

62A [Omitted by ITTOIA 2005, s. 882 and Sch. 1, para. 36 and repealed by s. 884 and Sch. 3.]

History – S. 62A omitted by ITTOIA 2005, s. 882(1) and Sch. 1, para. 36 and repealed by s. 884 and Sch. 3; effective for income tax purposes for 2005–06 onwards and for corporation tax purposes for accounting periods ending after 5 April 2005 (ITTOIA 2005, s. 883(1)).

Notes – S. 62A has been rewritten as follows:
S. 62A(1): ITTOIA 2005, s. 217(3), (4) and (6).
S. 62A(2): ITTOIA 2005, s. 217(3).
S. 62A(3): ITTOIA 2005, s. 217(2).
S. 62A(4): ITTOIA 2005, s. 217(4) and (5).
S. 62A(5): ITTOIA 2005, s. 217(6) and 218(1)–(3).
S. 62A(6): ITTOIA 2005, s. 218(4).
S. 62A(7): ITTOIA 2005, s. 218(7).
S. 62A(8): ITTOIA 2005, s. 218(5) and (7).
S. 62A(9): ITTOIA 2005, s. 218(6).

63 Basis of assessment on discontinuance

63 [Omitted by ITTOIA 2005, s. 882 and Sch. 1, para. 36 and repealed by s. 884 and Sch. 3.]

History – S. 63 omitted by ITTOIA 2005, s. 882(1) and Sch. 1, para. 36 and repealed by s. 884 and Sch. 3; effective for income tax purposes for 2005–06 onwards and for corporation tax purposes for accounting periods ending after 5 April 2005 (ITTOIA 2005, s. 883(1)).

Notes – S. 63 has been rewritten into the provisions of ITTOIA 2005, s. 200(5), 202(1), 215(1) and 216(1).

63A Overlap profits and overlap losses

63A [Omitted by ITTOIA 2005, s. 882 and Sch. 1, para. 36 and repealed by s. 884 and Sch. 3.]

History – S. 63A omitted by ITTOIA 2005, s. 882(1) and Sch. 1, para. 36 and repealed by s. 884 and Sch. 3; effective for income tax purposes for 2005–06 onwards and for corporation tax purposes for accounting periods ending after 5 April 2005 (ITTOIA 2005, s. 883(1)).

Notes – S. 63A has been rewritten as follows:
S. 63A(1): ITTOIA 2005, s. 220(1) and (2).
S. 63A(2): ITTOIA 2005, s. 220(3).
S. 63A(3): ITTOIA 2005, s. 205(1) and (2).
S. 63A(4): ITTOIA 2005, s. 206.
S. 63A(5): ITTOIA 2005, s. 204.

CASES III, IV AND V

64 Case III assessments

64 [Omitted by ITTOIA 2005, s. 882 and Sch. 1, para. 37 and repealed by s. 884 and Sch. 3.]

History – S. 64 omitted by ITTOIA 2005, s. 882(1) and Sch. 1, para. 37 and repealed by s. 884 and Sch. 3; effective for income tax purposes for 2005–06 onwards and for corporation tax purposes for accounting periods ending after 5 April 2005 (ITTOIA 2005, s. 883(1)).

Notes – S. 64 has been rewritten into the provisions of ITTOIA 2005, s. 370(1), 424(1), 428(1), 580(1), 615(1) and 684(1).
ITTOIA 2005 does not rewrite the words in ICTA 1988, s. 64 "without any deduction" as one of the defining features of an annual payment is that the recipient may make no deductions for expenses. (See ITTOIA 2005, Explanatory Notes, Annex 1, Table 1 (Change 158).)

65 Cases IV and V assessments: general

65 [Omitted by ITTOIA 2005, s. 882 and Sch. 1, para. 38 and repealed by s. 884 and Sch. 3.]

History – S. 65 omitted by ITTOIA 2005, s. 882(1) and Sch. 1, para. 38 and repealed by s. 884 and Sch. 3; effective for income tax purposes for 2005–06 onwards and for corporation tax purposes for accounting periods ending after 5 April 2005 (ITTOIA 2005, s. 883(1)).

Notes – S. 65 has been rewritten as follows:
S. 65(1): ITTOIA 2005, s. 7(4), 270(1), 370(1), 403(1),424(1), 428(1), 572(1)–(2), 580(1), 582(2)–(5), 610(1), 612(2)–(5),615(1), 617(3)–(6), 657(1), 684(1), 688(1), 838(1) and 839(1)–(5).
S. 65(2): ITTOIA 2005, Sch. 1, para. 605, 606 and 608.
S. 65(3): ITTOIA 2005, s. 7(1), (2) and (4), 19(1)–(3) and 227(1).
S. 65(4): ITTOIA 2005, s. 7(4), 227(1), 229(2), 269(3),358, 580(2), 582(2)–(5), 610(3), 612(2)–(5), 615(3), 617(3)-(6), 831(1)–(4), 838(2), 839(5) and Sch. 1, para. 605, 606 and 608.
S. 65(5): ITTOIA 2005, s. 359 and 832(1)–(4).
S. 65(6): ITTOIA 2005, s. 833(1), (3), (7) and (9).
S. 65(7): ITTOIA 2005, s. 834(1)–(3).

S. 65(8): ITTOIA 2005, s. 833(3), (6) and (9) and 834(4).
S. 65(9): ITTOIA 2005, s. 833(1), (3), (7) and (9).

65A Case V income from land outside UK: income tax

65A [Omitted by ITTOIA 2005, s. 882 and Sch. 1, para. 39 and repealed by s. 884 and Sch. 3.]

History – S. 65A omitted by ITTOIA 2005, s. 882(1) and Sch. 1, para. 39 and repealed by s. 884 and Sch. 3; effective for income tax purposes for 2005–06 onwards and for corporation tax purposes for accounting periods ending after 5 April 2005 (ITTOIA 2005, s. 883(1)).

Notes – S. 65A has been rewritten as follows:
S. 65A(1): ITTOIA 2005, s. 261 265, 266(1), (3) and (4) and 269(2).
S. 65A(2): ITTOIA 2005, s. 265, 266(1)–(4), 267, 273(1), 875(1) and (2) and 878(1).
S. 65A(3): ITTOIA 2005, s. 265.
S. 65A(4): ITTOIA 2005, s. 265 and 859(3).
S. 65A(5): ITTOIA 2005, s. 265, 266(2), 272(1) and (2), 274(1)–(3), 275(2) and (3), 277(1)–(5), 278(1)–(5), 279(1)–(6), 280(1)–(5), 281(1)–(4) and (6), 282(1)–(5), 283(2)–(5), 284(1)–(4), 285(1) and (3)–(5), 286(2)–(6), 287(1)–(5), 288(2)–(4) and (6), 289(2)–(5), 290(1)–(6), 291(1)–(4), 292(1), (3) and (4), 284(1)–(4), 293(1)–(4), 294(1)–(6), 295(1) and (2), 308(1)–(4), 311(1), (2) and (4)–(6), 312(1)–(7), 313(1)–(5), 314(1) and (2), 315(1)–(5), 316(1), (2) and (4)–(6), 317(1)–(3), 318(1)–(3), 320(1) and (2), 321(1) and (2), 361(1) and (2) and 364(1) and (2).
S. 65A(6): ITTOIA 2005, s. 272(2).
S. 65A(8): ITTOIA 2005, s. 363(1) and (2).

66 Special rules for fresh income

66 [Repealed by FA 1994, s. 207(4) and s. 258 and Sch. 26, Pt. V(24) for 1994–95.]

67 Special rules where source of income disposed of or yield ceases

67 [Repealed by FA 1994, s. 207(4), and s. 258 and Sch. 26, Pt. V(24).]

68 Special rules where property etc. situated in Republic of Ireland

68 [Omitted by ITTOIA 2005, s. 882 and Sch. 1, para. 40 and repealed by s. 884 and Sch. 3.]

History – S. 68 omitted by ITTOIA 2005, s. 882(1) and Sch. 1, para. 40 and repealed by s. 884 and Sch. 3; effective for income tax purposes for 2005–06 onwards and for corporation tax purposes for accounting periods ending after 5 April 2005 (ITTOIA 2005, s. 883(1)).

Notes – S. 68 has been rewritten as follows:
S. 68(1): ITTOIA 2005, s. 269(3), 270(1), 358, 370(1), 403(1), 424(1), 428(1), 572(1) and (2), 580(1), 582(2)–(5), 610(1), 612(2)–(5), 615(1), 617(3)–(6), 657(1), 684(1), 688(1), 831(5), 838(1) and (2) and 839(1)–(5).
S. 68(2): ITTOIA 2005, Sch. 1, para. 605, 606 and 608.
S. 68(3): ITTOIA 2005, s. 7(1), s. 19(1)–(3), s. 227(1), s. 831(5), s. 839(1)–(5) and Sch. 1, para. 605, 606 and 608.
S. 68(4): ITTOIA 2005, Sch. 1, para. 166.
S. 68(5): ITTOIA 2005, Sch. 1, para. 605, 606 and 608.

68A Share incentive plans: application of section 68B

68A [Omitted by ITTOIA 2005, s. 882 and Sch. 1, para. 41 and repealed by s. 884 and Sch. 3.]

History – S. 68A omitted by ITTOIA 2005, s. 882(1) and Sch. 1, para. 41 and repealed by s. 884 and Sch. 3; effective for income tax purposes for 2005–06 onwards and for corporation tax purposes for accounting periods ending after 5 April 2005 (ITTOIA 2005, s. 883(1)).

Notes – S. 68A has been rewritten as follows:
S. 68A(1): ITTOIA 2005, s. 405(1).
S. 68A(2): ITTOIA 2005, s. 405(2).
S. 68A(3): ITTOIA 2005, s. 405(2).

68B Share incentive plans: cash dividends and dividend shares

68B [Omitted by ITTOIA 2005, s. 882 and Sch. 1, para. 41 and repealed by s. 884 and Sch. 3.]

History – S. 68B omitted by ITTOIA 2005, s. 882(1) and Sch. 1, para. 41 and repealed by s. 884 and Sch. 3; effective for income tax purposes for 2005–06 onwards and for corporation tax purposes for accounting periods ending after 5 April 2005 (ITTOIA 2005, s. 883(1)).

Notes – S. 68B has been rewritten as follows:
S. 68B(1): ITTOIA 2005, s. 403(2), 404(2) and 406(1)–(5).
S. 68B(2): ITTOIA 2005, s. 403(2), 404(2) and 407(1)–(4).
S. 68B(3): ITTOIA 2005, s. 408(1).
S. 68B(4): ITTOIA 2005, s. 402(3).

68C Share incentive plans: interpretation

68C [Omitted by ITTOIA 2005, s. 882 and Sch. 1, para. 41 and repealed by s. 884 and Sch. 3.]

History – S. 68C omitted by ITTOIA 2005, s. 882(1) and Sch. 1, para. 41 and repealed by s. 884 and Sch. 3; effective for income tax purposes for 2005–06 onwards and for corporation tax purposes for accounting periods ending after 5 April 2005 (ITTOIA 2005, s. 883(1)).

Notes – S. 68C has been rewritten as follows:
S. 68C(1): ITTOIA 2005, s. 405(3).
S. 68C(2): ITTOIA 2005, s. 405(4).
S. 68C(3): ITTOIA 2005, s. 406(5) and 407(3).

CASE VI

69 Case VI assessments

69 [Omitted by ITTOIA 2005, s. 882 and Sch. 1, para. 42 and repealed by s. 884 and Sch. 3.]

History – S. 69 omitted by ITTOIA 2005, s. 882(1) and Sch. 1, para. 42 and repealed by s. 884 and Sch. 3; effective for income tax purposes for 2005–06 onwards and for corporation tax purposes for accounting periods ending after 5 April 2005 (ITTOIA 2005, s. 883(1)).

Notes – S. 69 has been rewritten into the provisions of ITTOIA 2005, s. 229(1), 244(1), 331, 337(1), 347, 351(1), 553, 556(1), 580(1), 582(2)–(5), 585(1), 591(1), 592(1), 610(1), 612(2)-(5), 615(1), 617(3)–(6), 621 and 688(1).

Chapter III – Corporation Tax: Basis of Assessment etc.

70 Basis of assessment etc.

70 [Omitted by CTA 2009, s. 1322 and Sch. 1, para. 23 and repealed by CTA 2009, s. 1326 and Sch. 3, Pt. 1.]

History – S. 70 omitted by CTA 2009, s. 1322 and Sch. 1, para. 23 and repealed by CTA 2009, s. 1326 and Sch. 3, Pt. 1, with effect for corporation tax purposes for accounting periods ending on or after 1 April 2009, and for income tax and capital gains tax purposes for the tax year 2009–10 and subsequent tax years.

Notes – S. 70 rewritten as follows:
S. 70(2): CTA 2009, s. 180(1).
S. 70(3): CTA 2009, s. 933(1).

70A Case V income from land outside UK: corporation tax

70A [Omitted by CTA 2009, s. 1322 and Sch. 1, para. 24 and repealed by CTA 2009, s. 1326 and Sch. 3, Pt. 1.]

History – S. 70A omitted by CTA 2009, s. 1322 and Sch. 1, para. 24 and repealed by CTA 2009, s. 1326 and Sch. 3, Pt. 1, with effect for corporation tax purposes for accounting periods ending on or after 1 April 2009, and for income tax and capital gains tax purposes for the tax year 2009–10 and subsequent tax years.

Notes – S. 70A rewritten as follows:
S. 70A(1): CTA 2009, s. 206, 207(1), (3), (4), 287.
S. 70A(2): CTA 2009, s. 206, 207(1), (2), (3), (4), 208, 213(1), 1314(1), (2).
S. 70A(3): CTA 2009, s. 206.
S. 70A(4): CTA 2009, s. 206, 1270(3).
S. 70A(5): CTA 2009, s. 206, 207(2), 210(1), (2), 211(1), 214(1), (2), (3), 217(1), (2), (3), (4), (5), 218(1), (2), (3), (4), (5), 219(1), (2), (3), (4), (5), (6), 220(1), (2), (3), (4), (5), 221(1), (2), (3), (4), (6), 222(1), (2), (3), (4), (5), 223(2), (3), (4), (5), 224(1), (2), (3), (4), 225(1), (3), (4), (5), 226(2), (3), (4), (5), (6), 227(1), (2), (3), (4), (5), 228(2), (3), (4), (6), 229(2), (3), (4), (5), 230(1), (2), (3), (4), (5), (6), 231(1), (2), (3), (4), 232(1), (3), (4), 233(1), (2), (3), (4), 234(1), (2), (3), (4), (5), (6), (7), 235(1), (2), (3), 248(1), (2), (3), (4), 250(1), (2), (4), (5), (6), 254(1), (2), (3), (4), (5), (7), 255(1), (2), (4), (5), (6), 256(1), (2), (3), 257(1), (2), (3), (4), 259(1), (2), 260(1), (2), (3), 291(1), (2).
S. 70A(6): CTA 2009, s. 210(2).
S. 70A(7): CTA 2009, s. 290(1), (2).

Chapter IV – Provisions Supplementary to Chapters II and III

71 Computation of income tax where no profits in year of assessment

71 [Omitted by ITTOIA 2005, s. 882 and Sch. 1, para. 43 and repealed by s. 884 and Sch. 3.]

History – S. 71 omitted by ITTOIA 2005, s. 882(1) and Sch. 1, para. 43 and repealed by s. 884 and Sch. 3; effective for income tax purposes for 2005–06 onwards and for corporation tax purposes for accounting periods ending after 5 April 2005 (ITTOIA 2005, s. 883(1)).

Notes – S. 71 is not rewritten by ITTOIA 2005 as it became redundant on the abolition of the preceding year basis of assessment. (See ITTOIA 2005, Explanatory Notes, Annex 1, Table 1 (Change 158).)

72 Apportionments etc. for purposes of Cases I, II and VI

72 [Omitted by CTA 2009, s. 1322 and Sch. 1, para. 25 and repealed by CTA 2009, s. 1326 and Sch. 3, Pt. 1.]

History – S. 72 omitted by CTA 2009, s. 1322 and Sch. 1, para. 25 and repealed by CTA 2009, s. 1326 and Sch. 3, Pt. 1, with effect for corporation tax purposes for accounting periods ending on or after 1 April 2009, and for income tax and capital gains tax purposes for the tax year 2009–10 and subsequent tax years.

Notes – Rewritten income tax provisions are now located as follows:
S. 72(1): ITTOIA 2005, s. 203(2), 275(2) and 871(1) and (3).
S. 72(2): ITTOIA 2005, s. 203(3), 275(3) and 871(4).
S. 72 rewritten for corporation tax purposes as follows:
S. 72(1): CTA 2009, s. 52(1), (2), 1307(1), (3).
S. 72(2): CTA 2009, s. 52(3), 1307(4).

73 Single assessments for purposes of Cases III, IV and V

73 [Repealed by FA 1995, s. 115(9), s. 162 and Sch. 29, Pt. VIII(14).]

History – S. 73 repealed for income tax purposes with effect for the year 1996–97 and subsequent years of assessment and, for corporation tax purposes, with effect for accounting periods ending on or after 1 July 1999 (the appointed day for self-assessment to corporation tax by virtue of FA 1994, s. 199(2), (3) and SI 1998/3173 (C. 78)), by FA 1995, s. 115(9) and s. 162 and Sch. 29, Pt. VIII(14).

Chapter V – Computational Provisions

Cross references – S. 21A(2): application of Pt. IV, Ch. V in computing profits of a Sch. A business.

DEDUCTIONS

74 General rules as to deductions not allowable

74 [Omitted by CTA 2009, s. 1322 and Sch. 1, para. 26 and repealed by CTA 2009, s. 1326 and Sch. 3, Pt. 1.]

History – S. 74 omitted by CTA 2009, s. 1322 and Sch. 1, para. 26 and repealed by CTA 2009, s. 1326 and Sch. 3, Pt. 1, with effect for corporation tax purposes for accounting periods ending on or after 1 April 2009, and for income tax and capital gains tax purposes for the tax year 2009–10 and subsequent tax years.

Notes – Rewritten income tax provisions are now located as follows:
S. 74(1): ITTOIA 2005, s. 29, 33, 34(1) and (2), 35(1) and (2), 51, 68(1)–(3), 106(1) and (2) and 291(2).
However, ICTA 1988, s. 74(1)(b) is not rewritten by ITTOIA 2005 as it is covered by ITTOIA 2005, s. 34. (See ITTOIA 2005, Explanatory Notes, Annex 1, Table 1 (Change 158).)
ITTOIA 2005 does not rewrite the rule in ICTA 1988, s. 74(1)(c) that prohibits the deduction for the domestic element of rents paid as this is covered by ICTA 1988, s. 74(1)(a). (See ITTOIA 2005, Explanatory Notes, Annex 1, Table 1 (Change 158).)
ITTOIA 2005 does not rewrite ICTA 1988, s. 74(1)(g) as it is covered by the general prohibition against the deduction for items of a capital nature. (See ITTOIA 2005, Explanatory Notes, Annex 1, Table 1 (Change 158).)
ICTA 1988, s. 74(1)(h) is not rewritten by ITTOIA 2005 as accounts prepared under generally accepted accounting practice would not contain a deduction for notional interest. (See ITTOIA 2005, Explanatory Notes, Annex 1, Table 1 (Change 158).)
ICTA 1988, s. 74(1)(k) by ITTOIA 2005 is not rewritten as it is not necessary in respect of accounts prepared under generally accepted accounting practice. (See ITTOIA 2005, Explanatory Notes, Annex 1, Table 1 (Change 158).)
ICTA 1988, s. 74(1)(m) is not rewritten by ITTOIA 2005 as it deals with amounts "payable out of the profits" and is therefore irrelevant when calculating the profits themselves. (See ITTOIA 2005, Explanatory Notes, Annex 1, Table 1 (Change 158).)
ICTA 1988, s. 74(1)(o) is not rewritten by ITTOIA 2005 as it is thought unlikely that any interest could satisfy its conditions and be deductible when calculating trade profits. (See ITTOIA 2005, Explanatory Notes, Annex 1, Table 1 (Change 158).)
S. 74(2): ITTOIA 2005, s. 35(1) and 259.
S. 74 rewritten for corporation tax purposes as follows:
S. 74(1): CTA 2009, s. 53(1), (2), 54(1), (2), 59, 68(1), (2), (3), 103(1), (2), 231(2).

75 Expenses of management: companies with investment business

75 [Omitted by CTA 2009, s. 1322 and Sch. 1, para. 27 and repealed by CTA 2009, s. 1326 and Sch. 3, Pt. 1.]

History – S. 75 omitted by CTA 2009, s. 1322 and Sch. 1, para. 27 and repealed by CTA 2009, s. 1326 and Sch. 3, Pt. 1, with effect for corporation tax purposes for accounting periods ending on or after 1 April 2009, and for income tax and capital gains tax purposes for the tax year 2009–10 and subsequent tax years.

Notes – S. 75 rewritten as follows:
S. 75(1): CTA 2009, s. 1219(1).
S. 75(2): CTA 2009, s. 985(3), 999(4), 1000(3), 1219(3), 1232.
S. 75(2A): CTA 2009, s. 1248(1), (2).
S. 75(2B): CTA 2009, s. 1248(3), (5).
S. 75(2C): CTA 2009, s. 1248(4).
S. 75(3): CTA 2009, s. 1219(3), 1221(1).
S. 75(4): CTA 2009, s. 1218(3), 1219(2).
S. 75(5): CTA 2009, s. 1220(1).
S. 75(5A): CTA 2009, s. 1220(2), (3).
S. 75(6): CTA 2009, s. 1222(1), (2), (3).
S. 75(7): CTA 2009, s. 1221(2), (3), 1233(1), (2).
S. 75(8): CTA 2009, s. 1223(1), (2).
S. 75(9): CTA 2009, s. 1223(2), (3).
S. 75(10): CTA 2009, s. 1219(4), 1220(4).
S. 75(11): CTA 2009, s. 1220(5), 1248(5).

75A Accounting period to which expenses of management are referable

75A [Omitted by CTA 2009, s. 1322 and Sch. 1, para. 28 and repealed by CTA 2009, s. 1326 and Sch. 3, Pt. 1.]

History – S. 75A omitted by CTA 2009, s. 1322 and Sch. 1, para. 28 and repealed by CTA 2009, s. 1326 and Sch. 3, Pt. 1, with effect for corporation tax purposes for accounting periods ending on or after 1 April 2009, and for income tax and capital gains tax purposes for the tax year 2009–10 and subsequent tax years.

Notes – S. 75A rewritten as follows:
S. 75A(1): CTA 2009, s. 1224(1).
S. 75A(2): CTA 2009, s. 1225(1).
S. 75A(3): CTA 2009, s. 1225(2).
S. 75A(4): CTA 2009, s. 1225(2).
S. 75A(5): CTA 2009, s. 1225(3).

S. 75A(6): CTA 2009, s. 1226(1), (2).
S. 75A(7): CTA 2009, s. 1227(1), (2).
S. 75A(8): CTA 2009, s. 1227(1), (2).
S. 75A(9): CTA 2009, s. 1224(2).
S. 75A(10): CTA 2009, s. 1255(1), (3).

75B Amounts reversing expenses of management deducted: charge to tax

75B [Omitted by CTA 2009, s. 1322 and Sch. 1, para. 29 and repealed by CTA 2009, s. 1326 and Sch. 3, Pt. 1.]

History – S. 75B omitted by CTA 2009, s. 1322 and Sch. 1, para. 29 and repealed by CTA 2009, s. 1326 and Sch. 3, Pt. 1, with effect for corporation tax purposes for accounting periods ending on or after 1 April 2009, and for income tax and capital gains tax purposes for the tax year 2009–10 and subsequent tax years.

Notes – S. 75B rewritten as follows:
S. 75B(1): CTA 2009, s. 1229(1), 1231(3).
S. 75B(2): CTA 2009, s. 1229(2).
S. 75B(3): CTA 2009, s. 1230(2), (3), 1231(3).
S. 75B(4): CTA 2009, s. 1229(3).
S. 75B(5): CTA 2009, s. 1229(5).
S. 75B(6): CTA 2009, s. 1229(6).
S. 75B(7): CTA 2009, s. 1229(3), (4).
S. 75B(8): CTA 2009, s. 1255(2).
S. 75B(9): CTA 2009, s. 1231(1), (2).
S. 75B(10): CTA 2009, s. 1231(2), 1255(2).
S. 75B(11): CTA 2009, s. 1228.
S. 75B(12): CTA 2009, s. 1255(3).

76 Expenses of insurance companies

76 [Omitted by FA 2012, s. 146 and Sch. 16, para. 2.]

History – S. 76 omitted by FA 2012, s. 146 and Sch. 16, para. 2 with effect in relation to accounting periods of companies beginning on or after 1 January 2013, subject to transitional provisions contained in FA 2012, Sch. 17. For accounting periods straddling 1 January 2013, FA 2012, s. 149 provides for a deemed cessation on 31 December 2012.

Derivations – S. 76(1) (as originally enacted): ICTA 1970, s. 305(1).
S. 76(2) (as originally enacted): ICTA 1970, s. 305(2), as amended by FA 1972, Sch. 18, para. 1(1) and Sch. 28, Pt. VI; and from FA 1972, Sch. 18, para. 1(2).
S. 76(3), (4) (as originally enacted): FA 1972, Sch. 18, para. 1(1), (3).
S. 76(5) (as originally enacted): ICTA 1970, s. 305(2).
S. 76(5A): FA 1996, Sch. 33, para. 1(1).
S. 76(6): ICTA 1970, s. 317, but see also s. 323(2).
S. 76(7) (as originally enacted): FA 1976, s. 47.
S. 76(8) (former provision): ICTA 1970, s. 305(3), but see also s. 323(2).

Payments for restrictive undertakings

76ZA Payments for restrictive undertakings

76ZA [Omitted by FA 2012, s. 146 and Sch. 16, para. 3.]

History – S. 76ZA omitted by FA 2012, s. 146 and Sch. 16, para. 3 with effect in relation to accounting periods of companies beginning on or after 1 January 2013, subject to transitional provisions contained in FA 2012, Sch. 17. For accounting periods straddling 1 January 2013, FA 2012, s. 149 provides for a deemed cessation on 31 December 2012.

Seconded employees

76ZB Employees seconded to charities and educational establishments

76ZB [Omitted by FA 2012, s. 146 and Sch. 16, para. 4.]

History – S. 76ZB omitted by FA 2012, s. 146 and Sch. 16, para. 4 with effect in relation to accounting periods of companies beginning on or after 1 January 2013, subject to transitional provisions contained in FA 2012, Sch. 17. For accounting periods straddling 1 January 2013, FA 2012, s. 149 provides for a deemed cessation on 31 December 2012.

Counselling and retraining expenses

76ZC Counselling and other outplacement services

76ZC [Omitted by FA 2012, s. 146 and Sch. 16, para. 5.]

History – S. 76ZC omitted by FA 2012, s. 146 and Sch. 16, para. 5 with effect in relation to accounting periods of companies beginning on or after 1 January 2013, subject to transitional provisions contained in FA 2012, Sch. 17. For accounting periods straddling 1 January 2013, FA 2012, s. 149 provides for a deemed cessation on 31 December 2012.

76ZD Retraining courses

76ZD [Omitted by FA 2012, s. 146 and Sch. 16, para. 5.]

History – S. 76ZD omitted by FA 2012, s. 146 and Sch. 16, para. 5 with effect in relation to accounting periods of companies beginning on or after 1 January 2013, subject to transitional provisions contained in FA 2012, Sch. 17. For accounting periods straddling 1 January 2013, FA 2012, s. 149 provides for a deemed cessation on 31 December 2012.

76ZE Retraining courses: recovery of tax

76ZE [Omitted by FA 2012, s. 146 and Sch. 16, para. 5.]

History – S. 76ZE omitted by FA 2012, s. 146 and Sch. 16, para. 5 with effect in relation to accounting periods of companies beginning on or after 1 January 2013, subject to transitional provisions contained in FA 2012, Sch. 17. For accounting periods straddling 1 January 2013, FA 2012, s. 149 provides for a deemed cessation on 31 December 2012.
Former s. 76ZE(5) omitted by SI 2009/2035, art. 2 and Schedule, para. 12, with effect from 13 August 2009.
Former s. 76ZE(6) omitted by SI 2009/2035, art. 2 and Schedule, para. 12, with effect from 13 August 2009.

Redundancy payments etc

76ZF Redundancy payments and approved contractual payments

76ZF [Omitted by FA 2012, s. 146 and Sch. 16, para. 6.]

History – S. 76ZF omitted by FA 2012, s. 146 and Sch. 16, para. 6 with effect in relation to accounting periods of companies beginning on or after 1 January 2013, subject to transitional provisions contained in FA 2012, Sch. 17. For accounting periods straddling 1 January 2013, FA 2012, s. 149 provides for a deemed cessation on 31 December 2012.

76ZG Payments in respect of employment wholly in employer's business

76ZG [Omitted by FA 2012, s. 146 and Sch. 16, para. 6.]

History – S. 76ZG omitted by FA 2012, s. 146 and Sch. 16, para. 6 with effect in relation to accounting periods of companies beginning on or after 1 January 2013, subject to transitional provisions contained in FA 2012, Sch. 17. For accounting periods straddling 1 January 2013, FA 2012, s. 149 provides for a deemed cessation on 31 December 2012.

76ZH Payments in respect of employment in more than one capacity

76ZH [Omitted by FA 2012, s. 146 and Sch. 16, para. 6.]

History – S. 76ZH omitted by FA 2012, s. 146 and Sch. 16, para. 6 with effect in relation to accounting periods of companies beginning on or after 1 January 2013, subject to transitional provisions contained in FA 2012, Sch. 17. For accounting periods straddling 1 January 2013, FA 2012, s. 149 provides for a deemed cessation on 31 December 2012.

76ZI Additional payments

76ZI [Omitted by FA 2012, s. 146 and Sch. 16, para. 6.]

History – S. 76ZI omitted by FA 2012, s. 146 and Sch. 16, para. 6 with effect in relation to accounting periods of companies beginning on or after 1 January 2013, subject to transitional provisions contained in FA 2012, Sch. 17. For accounting periods straddling 1 January 2013, FA 2012, s. 149 provides for a deemed cessation on 31 December 2012.

76ZJ Payments by the Government

76ZJ [Omitted by FA 2012, s. 146 and Sch. 16, para. 6.]

History – S. 76ZJ omitted by FA 2012, s. 146 and Sch. 16, para. 6 with effect in relation to accounting periods of companies beginning on or after 1 January 2013, subject to transitional provisions contained in FA 2012, Sch. 17. For accounting periods straddling 1 January 2013, FA 2012, s. 149 provides for a deemed cessation on 31 December 2012.

Contributions to local enterprise organisations or urban regeneration companies

76ZK Contributions to local enterprise organisations or urban regeneration companies

76ZK [Omitted by FA 2012, s. 146 and Sch. 16, para. 7.]

History – S. 76ZK omitted by FA 2012, s. 146 and Sch. 16, para. 7 with effect in relation to accounting periods of companies beginning on or after 1 January 2013, subject to transitional provisions contained in FA 2012, Sch. 17. For accounting periods straddling 1 January 2013, FA 2012, s. 149 provides for a deemed cessation on 31 December 2012.

Unpaid remuneration

76ZL Unpaid remuneration

76ZL [Omitted by FA 2012, s. 146 and Sch. 16, para. 8.]

History – S. 76ZL omitted by FA 2012, s. 146 and Sch. 16, para. 8 with effect in relation to accounting periods of companies beginning on or after 1 January 2013, subject to transitional provisions contained in FA 2012, Sch. 17. For accounting periods straddling 1 January 2013, FA 2012, s. 149 provides for a deemed cessation on 31 December 2012.

76ZM Unpaid remuneration: supplementary

76ZM [Omitted by FA 2012, s. 146 and Sch. 16, para. 8.]

History – S. 76ZM omitted by FA 2012, s. 146 and Sch. 16, para. 8 with effect in relation to accounting periods of companies beginning on or after 1 January 2013, subject to transitional provisions contained in FA 2012, Sch. 17. For accounting periods straddling 1 January 2013, FA 2012, s. 149 provides for a deemed cessation on 31 December 2012.

Car or motor cycle hire

76ZN Car or motor cycle hire

76ZN [Omitted by FA 2012, s. 146 and Sch. 16, para. 9.]

History – S. 76ZN omitted by FA 2012, s. 146 and Sch. 16, para. 9 with effect in relation to accounting periods of companies beginning on or after 1 January 2013, subject to transitional provisions contained in FA 2012, Sch. 17. For accounting periods straddling 1 January 2013, FA 2012, s. 149 provides for a deemed cessation on 31 December 2012.

76ZO Hiring cars (but not motor cycles) with low CO_2 emissions before 1 April 2013

76ZO [Omitted by FA 2009, s. 30 and Sch. 11, para. 61.]

History – S. 76ZO omitted by FA 2009, s. 30 and Sch. 11, para. 61, with effect in relation to expenses incurred on the hiring of a car or motorcycle under an agreement under which the hire period begins or after 1 April 2009 (for corporation tax purposes) or 6 April 2009 (for income tax purposes), subject to an election for transitional rules in FA 2009, Sch. 11, para. 67.

76A Levies and repayments under the Financial Services and Markets Act 2000

76A [Omitted by CTA 2009, s. 1322 and Sch. 1, para. 46 and repealed by CTA 2009, s. 1326 and Sch. 3, Pt. 1.]

History – S. 76A omitted by CTA 2009, s. 1322 and Sch. 1, para. 46 and repealed by CTA 2009, s. 1326 and Sch. 3, Pt. 1, with effect for corporation tax purposes for accounting periods ending on or after 1 April 2009, and for income tax and capital gains tax purposes for the tax year 2009–10 and subsequent tax years.

Notes – S. 76A rewritten as follows:
S. 76A(1): CTA 2009, s. 92(1), 104(1), (2).
S. 76A(2): CTA 2009, s. 92(3).
S. 76A(3): CTA 2009, s. 104(3).
S. 76A(4): not rewritten (see CTA 2009 Explanatory Notes, Annex 1, Change 22).
S. 76A(5): CTA 2009, s. 92(3), 104(4), 1254(3).
S. 76A(6): CTA 2009, s. 92(3).

76B Levies and repayments under the Financial Services and Markets Act 2000: investment companies

76B [Omitted by CTA 2009, s. 1322 and Sch. 1, para. 47 and repealed by CTA 2009, s. 1326 and Sch. 3, Pt. 1.]

History – S. 76B omitted by CTA 2009, s. 1322 and Sch. 1, para. 47 and repealed by CTA 2009, s. 1326 and Sch. 3, Pt. 1, with effect for corporation tax purposes for accounting periods ending on or after 1 April 2009, and for income tax and capital gains tax purposes for the tax year 2009–10 and subsequent tax years.

Notes – S. 76B rewritten as follows:
S. 76B(1): CTA 2009, s. 1232, 1246(1).
S. 76B(2): CTA 2009, s. 1254(1).
S. 76B(3): CTA 2009, s. 1246(3).
S. 76B(4): CTA 2009, s. 1246(2).
S. 76B(5): CTA 2009, s. 1254(2).

77 Incidental costs of obtaining loan finance

77 [Omitted by ITTOIA 2005, s. 882 and Sch. 1, para. 47 and repealed by s. 884 and Sch. 3.]

History – S. 77 omitted by ITTOIA 2005, s. 882(1) and Sch. 1, para. 47 and repealed by s. 884 and Sch. 3; effective for income tax purposes for 2005–06 onwards and for corporation tax purposes for accounting periods ending after 5 April 2005 (ITTOIA 2005, s. 883(1)).

Notes – S. 77 has been rewritten as follows:
S. 77(1): ITTOIA 2005, s. 58(1).
S. 77(2): ITTOIA 2005, s. 58(1).
S. 77(3): ITTOIA 2005, s. 59(1) and (2).
S. 77(4): ITTOIA 2005, s. 59(3).
S. 77(5): ITTOIA 2005, s. 59(4)–(6).
S. 77(6): ITTOIA 2005, s. 58(2)–(4).
S. 77(7): ITTOIA 2005, s. 58(4).

78 Discounted bills of exchange

78 [Repealed by FA 1996, s. 104 and Sch. 14, para. 10 and s. 205 and Sch. 41, Pt. V(3) except in relation to bills drawn before 1 April 1996.]

79 Contributions to local enterprise agencies

79 [Omitted by CTA 2009, s. 1322 and Sch. 1, para. 48 and repealed by CTA 2009, s. 1326 and Sch. 3, Pt. 1.]

History – S. 79 omitted by CTA 2009, s. 1322 and Sch. 1, para. 48 and repealed by CTA 2009, s. 1326 and Sch. 3, Pt. 1, with effect for corporation tax purposes for accounting periods ending on or after 1 April 2009, and for income tax and capital gains tax purposes for the tax year 2009–10 and subsequent tax years.

Notes – Rewritten income tax provisions are now located as follows:
S. 79(1): ITTOIA 2005, s. 31(1)–(3), 82(1) and (2) and 83(1).
S. 79(3): ITTOIA 2005, s. 82(3) and (4).
S. 79(4): ITTOIA 2005, s. 83(2), 84(1), (3) and (4) and 85(3).
S. 79(5): ITTOIA 2005, s. 84(2).
S. 79(6): ITTOIA 2005, s. 84(5).
S. 79(7): ITTOIA 2005, s. 84(6).
S. 79(8): ITTOIA 2005, s. 85(2), (4) and (5).
S. 79(9): ITTOIA 2005, s. 82(5) and (6).

S. 79(10): ITTOIA 2005, s. 878(5).
S. 79 rewritten for corporation tax purposes as follows:
S. 79(1): CTA 2009, s. 51(1), (2), 82(1), (2), 83(1).
S. 79(2): CTA 2009, s. 1232, 1244(1), (2).
S. 79(2A): CTA 2009, s. Sch. 1, para. 41.
S. 79(3): CTA 2009, s. 82(3), (4), 1244(3), (4), Sch. 1, para. 41.
S. 79(4): CTA 2009, s. 83(2), 84(1), (3), (4), 85(3).
S. 79(5): CTA 2009, s. 84(2).
S. 79(6): CTA 2009, s. 84(5).
S. 79(5): CTA 2009, s. 84(2).
S. 79(6): CTA 2009, s. 84(5).
S. 79(7): CTA 2009, s. 84(6).
S. 79(8): CTA 2009, s. 85(2), (4), (5).
S. 79(9): CTA 2009, s. 82(5), (6), 283(2), 1253(1), (2), Sch. 1, para. 41.
S. 79(10): CTA 2009, s. 1316(1).

79A Contributions to training and enterprise councils and local enterprise companies

79A [Omitted by CTA 2009, s. 1322 and Sch. 1, para. 49 and repealed by CTA 2009, s. 1326 and Sch. 3, Pt. 1.]

History – S. 79A omitted by CTA 2009, s. 1322 and Sch. 1, para. 49 and repealed by CTA 2009, s. 1326 and Sch. 3, Pt. 1, with effect for corporation tax purposes for accounting periods ending on or after 1 April 2009, and for income tax and capital gains tax purposes for the tax year 2009–10 and subsequent tax years.

Notes – Rewritten income tax provisions are now located as follows:
S. 79A(1): ITTOIA 2005, s. 82(1) and (2) and 83(1).
S. 79A(3): ITTOIA 2005, s. 82(3) and (4).
S. 79A(4): ITTOIA 2005, s. 82(5) and (6).
S. 79A(5): ITTOIA 2005, s. 83(3)–(5).
S. 79A(6): ITTOIA 2005, s. 878(5).
S. 79A rewritten for corporation tax purposes as follows:
S. 79A(1): CTA 2009, s. 51(1), (2), 82(1), (2), 83(1).
S. 79A(2): CTA 2009, s. 1232, 1244(1), (2).
S. 79A(2A): CTA 2009, s. Sch. 1, para. 41.
S. 79A(3): CTA 2009, s. 82(3), (4), 1244(3), (4), Sch. 1, para. 41.
S. 79A(4): CTA 2009, s. 82(5), (6), 1253(1), (2), Sch. 1, para. 41.
S. 79A(5): CTA 2009, s. 83(3), (4), (5).
S. 79A(6): CTA 2009, s. 1316(1).

79B Contributions to urban regeneration companies

79B [Omitted by CTA 2009, s. 1322 and Sch. 1, para. 50 and repealed by CTA 2009, s. 1326 and Sch. 3, Pt. 1.]

History – S. 79B omitted by CTA 2009, s. 1322 and Sch. 1, para. 50 and repealed by CTA 2009, s. 1326 and Sch. 3, Pt. 1, with effect for corporation tax purposes for accounting periods ending on or after 1 April 2009, and for income tax and capital gains tax purposes for the tax year 2009–10 and subsequent tax years.

Notes – Rewritten income tax provisions are now located as follows:
S. 79B(1): ITTOIA 2005, s. 82(1) and (2).
S. 79B(3): ITTOIA 2005, s. 82(3) and (4).
S. 79B(4): ITTOIA 2005, s. 82(5) and (6).
S. 79B(5): ITTOIA 2005, s. 86(1).
S. 79B(6): ITTOIA 2005, s. 86(2).
S. 79B(7): ITTOIA 2005, s. 86(2).
S. 79B(8): ITTOIA 2005, s. 86(3).
S. 79B rewritten for corporation tax purposes as follows:
S. 79B(1): CTA 2009, s. 51(1), (2), 82(1), (2).
S. 79B(2): CTA 2009, s. 1232, 1244(1), (2).
S. 79B(2A): CTA 2009, Sch. 1, para. 41.
S. 79B(3): CTA 2009, s. 82(3), (4), 1244(3), (4), Sch. 1, para. 41.
S. 79B(4): CTA 2009, s. 82(5), (6), 1253(1), (2), Sch. 1, para. 41.
S. 79B(5): CTA 2009, s. 86(1).
S. 79B(6): CTA 2009, s. 86(2).
S. 79B(7): CTA 2009, s. 86(2).
S. 79B(8): CTA 2009, s. 86(3).
S. 79B(9): CTA 2009, s. 1316(1).

80 Expenses connected with foreign trades etc.

80 [Omitted by ITTOIA 2005, s. 882 and Sch. 1, para. 51 and repealed by s. 884 and Sch. 3.]

History – S. 80 omitted by ITTOIA 2005, s. 882(1) and Sch. 1, para. 51 and repealed by s. 884 and Sch. 3; effective for income tax purposes for 2005–06 onwards and for corporation tax purposes for accounting periods ending after 5 April 2005 (ITTOIA 2005, s. 883(1)).

Notes – S. 80 has been rewritten into the provisions of ITTOIA 2005 as follows:
S. 80(1): ITTOIA 2005, s. 92(1) and (4).
S. 80(2): ITTOIA 2005, s. 92(2) and (3) and s. 93(1).
S. 80(3): ITTOIA 2005, s. 92(1).
S. 80(4): ITTOIA 2005, s. 93(1) and (2).
S. 80(5): ITTOIA 2005, s. 92(1), (3) and (4).
S. 80(6): ITTOIA 2005, s. 94(1) and (2).

S. 80(7): ITTOIA 2005, s. 92(2).
S. 80(8): ITTOIA 2005, s. 94(3).
S. 80(9): ITTOIA 2005, s. 93(3).

81 Travel between trades etc.

81 [Omitted by ITTOIA 2005, s. 882 and Sch. 1, para. 52 and repealed by s. 884 and Sch. 3.]

History – S. 81 omitted by ITTOIA 2005, s. 882(1) and Sch. 1, para. 52 and repealed by s. 884 and Sch. 3; effective for income tax purposes for 2005–06 onwards and for corporation tax purposes for accounting periods ending after 5 April 2005 (ITTOIA 2005, s. 883(1)).

Notes – S. 81 has been rewritten into the provisions of ITTOIA 2005 as follows:
S. 81(1): ITTOIA 2005, s. 92(1)–(4) and 93(4).
S. 81(2): ITTOIA 2005, s. 93(4).
S. 80(4): ITTOIA 2005, s. 92(1).
S. 80(5): ITTOIA 2005, s. 93(5).

82 Interest paid to non-residents

82 [Omitted by ITTOIA 2005, s. 882 and Sch. 1, para. 53 and repealed by s. 884 and Sch. 3.]

History – S. 82 omitted by ITTOIA 2005, s. 882(1) and Sch. 1, para. 53 and repealed by s. 884 and Sch. 3; effective for income tax purposes for 2005–06 onwards and for corporation tax purposes for accounting periods ending after 5 April 2005 (ITTOIA 2005, s. 883(1)).

Notes – ICTA 1988, s. 82 is not rewritten by ITTOIA 2005 as it no longer achieves its original purpose and is, in part, out of step with modern tax principles. (See ITTOIA 2005, Explanatory Notes, Annex 1, Table 1 (Change 158).)

82A Expenditure on research and development

82A [Omitted by CTA 2009, s. 1322 and Sch. 1, para. 51 and repealed by CTA 2009, s. 1326 and Sch. 3, Pt. 1.]

History – S. 82A omitted by CTA 2009, s. 1322 and Sch. 1, para. 51 and repealed by CTA 2009, s. 1326 and Sch. 3, Pt. 1, with effect for corporation tax purposes for accounting periods ending on or after 1 April 2009, and for income tax and capital gains tax purposes for the tax year 2009–10 and subsequent tax years.

Notes – Rewritten income tax provisions are now located as follows:
S. 82A(1): ITTOIA 2005, s. 31(1)–(3) and 87(1).
S. 82A(2): ITTOIA 2005, s. 87(2).
S. 82A(3): ITTOIA 2005, s. 87(3).
S. 82A(4): ITTOIA 2005, s. 87(4).
S. 82A(5): ITTOIA 2005, s. 87(5).
S. 82A rewritten for corporation tax purposes as follows:
S. 82A(1): CTA 2009, s. 51(1), (2), 87(1).
S. 82A(2): CTA 2009, s. 87(2).
S. 82A(3): CTA 2009, s. 87(3).
S. 82A(4): CTA 2009, s. 87(4).
S. 82A(5): CTA 2009, s. 87(5).

82B Payments to research associations, universities etc.

82B [Omitted by CTA 2009, s. 1322 and Sch. 1, para. 52 and repealed by CTA 2009, s. 1326 and Sch. 3, Pt. 1.]

History – S. 82B omitted by CTA 2009, s. 1322 and Sch. 1, para. 52 and repealed by CTA 2009, s. 1326 and Sch. 3, Pt. 1, with effect for corporation tax purposes for accounting periods ending on or after 1 April 2009, and for income tax and capital gains tax purposes for the tax year 2009–10 and subsequent tax years.

Notes – Rewritten income tax provisions are now located as follows:
S. 82B(1): ITTOIA 2005, s. 31(1)–(3) and 88(1), (2) and (4).
S. 82B(2): ITTOIA 2005, s. 88(3).
S. 82B(3): ITTOIA 2005, s. 88(5).
S. 82B(4): ITTOIA 2005, s. 88(6).
S. 82B(5): ITTOIA 2005, s. 88(7).
S. 82B rewritten for corporation tax purposes as follows:
S. 82B(1): CTA 2009, s. 51(1), (2), 88(1), (2), (4).
S. 82B(2): CTA 2009, s. 88(3).
S. 82B(3): CTA 2009, s. 88(5).
S. 82B(4): CTA 2009, s. 88(6).
S. 82B(5): CTA 2009, s. 88(7).

83 Patent fees etc. and expenses

83 [Omitted by CTA 2009, s. 1322 and Sch. 1, para. 53 and repealed by CTA 2009, s. 1326 and Sch. 3, Pt. 1.]

History – S. 83 omitted by CTA 2009, s. 1322 and Sch. 1, para. 53 and repealed by CTA 2009, s. 1326 and Sch. 3, Pt. 1, with effect for corporation tax purposes for accounting periods ending on or after 1 April 2009, and for income tax and capital gains tax purposes for the tax year 2009–10 and subsequent tax years.

Notes – S. 83 rewritten for income tax purposes as ITTOIA 2005, s. 31(1)–(3), 89(1) and 90(1).
S. 83 rewritten for corporation tax purposes as CTA 2009, s. 51(1), (2), 89, 90.

83A Gifts in kind to charities etc.

83A [Omitted by CTA 2009, s. 1322 and Sch. 1, para. 54 and repealed by CTA 2009, s. 1326 and Sch. 3, Pt. 1.]

History – S. 83A omitted by CTA 2009, s. 1322 and Sch. 1, para. 54 and repealed by CTA 2009, s. 1326 and Sch. 3, Pt. 1, with effect for corporation tax purposes for accounting periods ending on or after 1 April 2009, and for income tax and capital gains tax purposes for the tax year 2009–10 and subsequent tax years.

Notes – Rewritten income tax provisions are now located as follows:
S. 83A(1): ITTOIA 2005, s. 107 and 108(1) and (4).
S. 83A(2): ITTOIA 2005, s. 108(1).
S. 83A(3): ITTOIA 2005, s. 108(2).
S. 83A(4): ITTOIA 2005, s. 109(1) and (2).
S. 83A(5): ITTOIA 2005, s. 878(5).
S. 83A rewritten for corporation tax purposes as follows:
S. 83A(1): CTA 2009, s. 105(1), (4).
S. 83A(2): CTA 2009, s. 105(1).
S. 83A(3): CTA 2009, s. 105(2).
S. 83A(4): CTA 2009, s. 108(1), (3).
S. 83A(5): CTA 2009, s. 1316(1).

84 Gifts to educational establishments

84 [Omitted by CTA 2009, s. 1322 and Sch. 1, para. 55 and repealed by CTA 2009, s. 1326 and Sch. 3, Pt. 1.]

History – S. 84 omitted by CTA 2009, s. 1322 and Sch. 1, para. 55 and repealed by CTA 2009, s. 1326 and Sch. 3, Pt. 1, with effect for corporation tax purposes for accounting periods ending on or after 1 April 2009, and for income tax and capital gains tax purposes for the tax year 2009–10 and subsequent tax years.

Notes – Rewritten income tax provisions are now located as follows:
S. 84(1): ITTOIA 2005, s. 107 and 108(1).
S. 84(3): ITTOIA 2005, s. 108(2).
S. 84(4): ITTOIA 2005, s. 109(1).
S. 84(5): ITTOIA 2005, s. 108(3) and 110(1) and (2).
S. 84(6): ITTOIA 2005, s. 110(3).
S. 84(7): ITTOIA 2005, s. 110(4) and (5).
S. 84(8): ITTOIA 2005, s. 110(6).
S. 84(9): ITTOIA 2005, s. 878(5).
S. 84 rewritten for corporation tax purposes as follows:
S. 84(1): CTA 2009, s. 105(1).
S. 84(2): not rewritten (see CTA 2009 Explanatory Notes, Annex 1, Change 26).
S. 84(3): CTA 2009, s. 105(2).
S. 84(3A): not rewritten (see CTA 2009 Explanatory Notes, Annex 1, Change 28).
S. 84(4): CTA 2009, s. 108(1), (3).
S. 84(5): CTA 2009, s. 105(3), 106(1), (2).
S. 84(6): CTA 2009, s. 106(3).
S. 84(7): CTA 2009, s. 106(4), (5), (6).
S. 84(8): CTA 2009, s. 106(7).
S. 84(9): CTA 2009, s. 1316(1).

84A Costs of establishing share option or profit sharing schemes: relief

84A [Omitted by TIOPA 2010, s. 371 and Sch. 7, para. 26 and repealed by TIOPA 2010, s. 378 and Sch. 10, Pt. 12.]

History – S. 84A omitted by TIOPA 2010, s. 371 and Sch. 7, para. 26 and repealed by TIOPA 2010, s. 378 and Sch. 10, Part 12, with effect for corporation tax purposes for accounting periods ending on or after 1 April 2010, for income tax and capital gains tax purposes for the tax year 2010–11 and subsequent tax years, and for petroleum revenue tax purposes for chargeable periods beginning on or after 1 July 2010.

Notes – S. 84A rewritten for corporation tax purposes as follows:
S. 84A(2): CTA 2009, s. 1221(2), (3).
S. 84A rewritten in TIOPA 2010, Sch. 7, para. 28.

85 Payments to trustees of approved profit sharing schemes

85 [Omitted by CTA 2009, s. 1322 and Sch. 1, para. 57 and repealed by CTA 2009, s. 1326 and Sch. 3, Pt. 1.]

History – S. 85 omitted by CTA 2009, s. 1322 and Sch. 1, para. 57 and repealed by CTA 2009, s. 1326 and Sch. 3, Pt. 1, with effect for corporation tax purposes for accounting periods ending on or after 1 April 2009, and for income tax and capital gains tax purposes for the tax year 2009–10 and subsequent tax years.

85A Costs of establishing employee share ownership trusts: relief

85A [Omitted by CTA 2009, s. 1322 and Sch. 1, para. 58 and repealed by CTA 2009, s. 1326 and Sch. 3, Pt. 1.]

History – S. 85A omitted by CTA 2009, s. 1322 and Sch. 1, para. 58 and repealed by CTA 2009, s. 1326 and Sch. 3, Pt. 1, with effect for corporation tax purposes for accounting periods ending on or after 1 April 2009, and for income tax and capital gains tax purposes for the tax year 2009–10 and subsequent tax years.

Notes – S. 85A rewritten as follows:
S. 85A(1): CTA 2009, s. 1000(1).
S. 85A(2): CTA 2009, s. 1000(2), (3), (4), 1221(2), (3).

S. 85A(3): CTA 2009, s. 1000(5).
S. 85A(3A): CTA 2009, s. 1000(5).
S. 85A(4): CTA 2009, s. 1000(1).
S. 85A(5): CTA 2009, s. 1000(6).

85B Approved share incentive plans

85B [Omitted by CTA 2009, s. 1322 and Sch. 1, para. 59 and repealed by CTA 2009, s. 1326 and Sch. 3, Pt. 1.]

History – Omitted by CTA 2009, s. 1322 and Sch. 1, para. 59 and repealed by CTA 2009, s. 1326 and Sch. 3, Pt. 1, with effect for corporation tax purposes for accounting periods ending on or after 1 April 2009, and for income tax and capital gains tax purposes for the tax year 2009–10 and subsequent tax years.

86 Employees seconded to charities and educational establishments

86 [Omitted by CTA 2009, s. 1322 and Sch. 1, para. 60 and repealed by CTA 2009, s. 1326 and Sch. 3, Pt. 1.]

History – S. 86 omitted by CTA 2009, s. 1322 and Sch. 1, para. 60 and repealed by CTA 2009, s. 1326 and Sch. 3, Pt. 1, with effect for corporation tax purposes for accounting periods ending on or after 1 April 2009, and for income tax and capital gains tax purposes for the tax year 2009–10 and subsequent tax years.

Notes – Rewritten income tax provisions are now located as follows:
S. 86(1): ITTOIA 2005, s. 31(1)–(3) and 70(1)–(3).
S. 86(2): ITTOIA 2005, s. 70(2) and 878(1).
S. 86(3): ITTOIA 2005, s. 70(1) and (3).
S. 86(4): ITTOIA 2005, s. 71(1).
S. 86(5): ITTOIA 2005, s. 71(2). However, ICTA 1988, s. 86(5)(d) is not rewritten by ITTOIA 2005 as schools covered by it were abolished on 1 April 2003. (See ITTOIA 2005, Explanatory Notes, Annex 1, Table 1 (Change 158).)
S. 86(6): ITTOIA 2005, s. 71(3).
S. 86 rewritten for corporation tax purposes as follows:
S. 86(1): CTA 2009, s. 51(1), (2), 70(1), (2), (3), 1232, 1235(1), (2), (3), Sch. 1, para. 32.
S. 86(2): CTA 2009, s. 70(2), 1221(2), (3), 1235(2), Sch. 1, para. 32.
S. 86(3): CTA 2009, s. 70(1), (3), 71(1), (2), (3), 1235(1), (3), Sch. 1, para. 32.
S. 86(4): CTA 2009, s. 71(1).
S. 86(5): CTA 2009, s. 71(2).
S. 86(6): CTA 2009, s. 71(3).

86A Charitable donations: contributions to agent's expenses

86A [Omitted by CTA 2009, s. 1322 and Sch. 1, para. 61 and repealed by CTA 2009, Sch. 3, Pt. 1.]

History – S. 86A omitted by CTA 2009, s. 1322 and Sch. 1, para. 61 and repealed by CTA 2009, Sch. 3, Pt. 1, with effect for corporation tax purposes for accounting periods ending on or after 1 April 2009, and for income tax and capital gains tax purposes for the tax year 2009–10 and subsequent tax years.

Notes – S. 86A is rewritten as follows:
S. 86A(1): ITTOIA 2005, s. 72(1).
S. 86A(1A): ITTOIA 2005, s. 72(3).
S. 86A(2): ITTOIA 2005, s. 72(2).
S. 86A(3): ITTOIA 2005, s. 72(2).
S. 86A rewritten as follows:
S. 86A(1): CTA 2009, s. 72(1), 1236(1).
S. 86A(1A): CTA 2009, s. 72(3), 1236(4).
S. 86A(2): CTA 2009, s. 72(2), 1221(2), (3), 1232, 1236(1), (2).
S. 86A(3): CTA 2009, s. 72(2), 1236(3).

87 Taxable premiums etc.

87 [Omitted by CTA 2009, s. 1322 and Sch. 1, para. 62 and repealed by CTA 2009, Sch. 3, Pt. 1.]

History – Omitted by CTA 2009, s. 1322 and Sch. 1, para. 62 and repealed by CTA 2009, Sch. 3, Pt. 1, with effect for corporation tax purposes for accounting periods ending on or after 1 April 2009, and for income tax and capital gains tax purposes for the tax year 2009–10 and subsequent tax years.

Notes – Rewritten income tax provisions are now located as follows:
S. 87(1): ITTOIA 2005, s. 60(1).
S. 87(2): ITTOIA 2005, s. 60(2) and (3) and 61(1) and (3)–(5).
S. 87(3): ITTOIA 2005, s. 61(3) and (5).
S. 87(4): ITTOIA 2005, s. 63(1) and (2).
S. 87(5): ITTOIA 2005, s. 64(1)–(4) and 65(1)–(6).
S. 87(6): ITTOIA 2005, s. 63(3).
S. 87(7): ITTOIA 2005, s. 62(1)–(3).
S. 87(8): ITTOIA 2005, s. 60(5).
S. 87(9): ITTOIA 2005, s. 61(4) and (5).
S. 87 rewritten as follows:
S. 87(1): CTA 2009, s. 62(1).
S. 87(2): CTA 2009, s. 62(2), (3), 63(1), (3), (4), (5).
S. 87(3): CTA 2009, s. 63(3), (5).
S. 87(4): CTA 2009, s. 65(1), (2).
S. 87(5): CTA 2009, s. 66(1), (2), (3), (4), (5), 67(1), (2), (3), (4), (5), (6).
S. 87(6): CTA 2009, s. 65(3).
S. 87(7): CTA 2009, s. 64(1), (2), (3).
S. 87(8): CTA 2009, s. 62(5).
S. 87(9): CTA 2009, s. 63(4), (5).
S. 87(9A): CTA 2009, s. 62(6).

87A Section 87(2) and (3) and reductions in receipts under ITTOIA 2005

87A [Omitted by CTA 2009, s. 1322 and Sch. 1, para. 62 and repealed by CTA 2009, Sch. 3, Pt. 1.]

History – S. 87A omitted by CTA 2009, s. 1322 and Sch. 1, para. 62 and repealed by CTA 2009, Sch. 3, Pt. 1, with effect for corporation tax purposes for accounting periods ending on or after 1 April 2009, and for income tax and capital gains tax purposes for the tax year 2009–10 and subsequent tax years.

Notes – S. 87A rewritten as follows:
S. 87A(1): CTA 2009, s. 66(1), 67(1).
S. 87A(2): CTA 2009, s. 66(2), (3), (4), (5), 67(2), (3), (4), (5), (6).
S. 87A(3): CTA 2009, s. 66(1).

88 Payments to Export Credit Guarantee Department

88 [Omitted by CTA 2009, s. 1322 and Sch. 1, para. 63 and repealed by CTA 2009, Sch. 3, Pt. 1.]

History – S. 88 omitted by CTA 2009, s. 1322 and Sch. 1, para. 63 and repealed by CTA 2009, Sch. 3, Pt. 1, with effect for corporation tax purposes for accounting periods ending on or after 1 April 2009, and for income tax and capital gains tax purposes for the tax year 2009–10 and subsequent tax years.

Notes – S. 88 rewritten as ITTOIA 2005, s. 91.
S. 88 rewritten for corporation tax purposes as CTA 2009, s. 91, 1221(2), (3), 1232, 1245(1), (2).

88A Debts of overseas governments etc.

88A [Repealed by FA 1996, s. 205 and Sch. 41, Pt. V(3) for accounting periods ending after 31 March 1996 (corporation tax) and for 1996–97 (income tax), subject to FA 1996, Sch. 15.]

88B Section 88A debts: restriction on deductions under section 74(j)

88B [Repealed by FA 1996, s. 205 and Sch. 41, Pt. V(3) for accounting periods ending after 31 March 1996 (corporation tax) and for 1996–97 (income tax), subject to FA 1996, Sch. 15.]

88C Section 88A debts: restriction on other deductions

88C [Repealed by FA 1996, s. 205 and Sch. 41, Pt. V(3) for accounting periods ending after 31 March 1996 (corporation tax) and for 1996–97 (income tax), subject to FA 1996, Sch. 15.]

88D Restriction of deductions in respect of certain debts

88D [Omitted by CTA 2009, s. 1322 and Sch. 1, para. 64 and repealed by CTA 2009, Sch. 3, Pt. 1.]

History – S. 88D omitted by CTA 2009, s. 1322 and Sch. 1, para. 64 and repealed by CTA 2009, Sch. 3, Pt. 1, with effect for corporation tax purposes for accounting periods ending on or after 1 April 2009, and for income tax and capital gains tax purposes for the tax year 2009–10 and subsequent tax years.

Notes – S. 88D rewritten as follows:
S. 88D(1): CTA 2009, s. 55(1), 970(1).
S. 88D(2): CTA 2009, s. 55(2), 970(2).
S. 88D(3): CTA 2009, s. 970(3).
S. 88D(4): CTA 2009, s. 970(2).

89 Debts proving to be irrecoverable after discontinuance etc

89 [Omitted by CTA 2009, s. 1322 and Sch. 1, para. 65 and repealed by CTA 2009, Sch. 3, Pt. 1.]

History – S. 89 omitted by CTA 2009, s. 1322 and Sch. 1, para. 65 and repealed by CTA 2009, Sch. 3, Pt. 1, with effect for corporation tax purposes for accounting periods ending on or after 1 April 2009, and for income tax and capital gains tax purposes for the tax year 2009–10 and subsequent tax years.

Notes – S. 89 rewritten as CTA 2009, s. 55(2).

90 Additional payments to redundant employees

90 [Omitted by CTA 2009, s. 1322 and Sch. 1, para. 66 and repealed by CTA 2009, Sch. 3, Pt. 1.]

History – S. 90 omitted by CTA 2009, s. 1322 and Sch. 1, para. 66 and repealed by CTA 2009, Sch. 3, Pt. 1, with effect for corporation tax purposes for accounting periods ending on or after 1 April 2009, and for income tax and capital gains tax purposes for the tax year 2009–10 and subsequent tax years.

Notes – Rewritten income tax provisions are now located as follows:
S. 90(1): ITTOIA 2005, s. 31(1)–(3) and 79(1), (3), (5) and (6).
S. 90(2): ITTOIA 2005, s. 79(4).
S. 90(3): ITTOIA 2005, s. 79(2).
S. 90(3): ITTOIA 2005, s. 79(1) and (4).
S. 90 rewritten for corporation tax purposes as follows:
S. 90(1): CTA 2009, s. 51(1), (2), 79(1), (2), (4), (5), 1221(2), (3), 1232, 1242(1), (2), (4), Sch. 1, para. 39.
S. 90(1A): CTA 2009, s. Sch. 1, para. 39.
S. 90(2): CTA 2009, s. 79(3), 1242(3), Sch. 1, para. 39.
S. 90(3): CTA 2009, s. 80(1), (2).
S. 90(4): CTA 2009, s. 79(1), (3), 1242(1), (3), Sch. 1, para. 39.

91 Cemeteries

91 [Omitted by CTA 2009, s. 1322 and Sch. 1, para. 67 and repealed by CTA 2009, Sch. 3, Pt. 1.]

History – S. 91 omitted by CTA 2009, s. 1322 and Sch. 1, para. 67 and repealed by CTA 2009, Sch. 3, Pt. 1, with effect for corporation tax purposes for accounting periods ending on or after 1 April 2009, and for income tax and capital gains tax purposes for the tax year 2009–10 and subsequent tax years.

Notes – Rewritten income tax provisions are now located as follows:
S. 91(1): ITTOIA 2005, s. 169(1), 170(1) and (2) and 171(1) and (4).
S. 91(2): ITTOIA 2005, s. 169(4).
S. 91(3): ITTOIA 2005, s. 171(2)–(4).
S. 91(4): ITTOIA 2005, s. 170(5) and 171(1), (2) and (4).
S. 91(5): ITTOIA 2005, s. 169(4) and (5), 170(1), (2) and (4) and 171(4).
S. 91(6): ITTOIA 2005, s. 170(3) and 171(2).
S. 91(7): ITTOIA 2005, s. 169(1), 170(1) and (2) and 171(1) and (4).
S. 91(8): ITTOIA 2005, s. 169(2), (3) and (6) and 171(3) and (4).
S. 91(9): ITTOIA 2005, s. 170(5) and 171(1), (3)–(5).
Reference in s. 91(8)(c) to FA 1954 substituted by CCH for erroneous reference in HMSO text to FA 1952.
S. 91 rewritten for corporation tax purposes as follows:
S. 91(1): CTA 2009, s. 146(1), 147(1), (2), 148(1), (4).
S. 91(2): CTA 2009, s. 146(4).
S. 91(3): CTA 2009, s. 148(2, (3), (4)).
S. 91(4): CTA 2009, s. 147(5), 148(1), (2), (4).
S. 91(5): CTA 2009, s. 146(4), (5), 147(1), (2), (4), 148(4).
S. 91(6): CTA 2009, s. 147(3), 148(2).
S. 91(7): CTA 2009, s. 146(1), (4), 147(1), (2), 148(1), (4).
S. 91(8): CTA 2009, s. 146(2), (3), (6), 148(3), (4).
S. 91(9): CTA 2009, s. 147(5), 149(1), (3), (4), (5).

91A Waste disposal: restoration payments

91A [Omitted by CTA 2009, s. 1322 and Sch. 1, para. 68 and repealed by CTA 2009, Sch. 3, Pt. 1.]

History – S. 91A omitted by CTA 2009, s. 1322 and Sch. 1, para. 68 and repealed by CTA 2009, Sch. 3, Pt. 1, with effect for corporation tax purposes for accounting periods ending on or after 1 April 2009, and for income tax and capital gains tax purposes for the tax year 2009–10 and subsequent tax years.

Notes – Rewritten income tax provisions are now located as follows:
S. 91A(1): ITTOIA 2005, s. 168(1) and (2).
S. 91A(2): ITTOIA 2005, s. 168(2) and (3).
S. 91A(3): ITTOIA 2005, s. 168(4).
S. 91A(4): ITTOIA 2005, s. 168(5).
S. 91A(5): ITTOIA 2005, s. 168(5).
S. 91A(6): ITTOIA 2005, s. 167(1) and 168(5).
S. 91A(7): ITTOIA 2005, s. 168(6).
S. 91A rewritten for corporation tax purposes as follows:
S. 91A(1): CTA 2009, s. 145(1), (2).
S. 91A(2): CTA 2009, s. 145(2), (3).
S. 91A(3): CTA 2009, s. 145(4).
S. 91A(4): CTA 2009, s. 145(5).
S. 91A(5): CTA 2009, s. 145(5).
S. 91A(6): CTA 2009, s. 144(1), 145(5).
S. 91A(7): CTA 2009, s. 145(6).

91B Waste disposal: preparation expenditure

91B [Omitted by CTA 2009, s. 1322 and Sch. 1, para. 69 and repealed by CTA 2009, Sch. 3, Pt. 1.]

History – S. 91B omitted by CTA 2009, s. 1322 and Sch. 1, para. 69 and repealed by CTA 2009, Sch. 3, Pt. 1, with effect for corporation tax purposes for accounting periods ending on or after 1 April 2009, and for income tax and capital gains tax purposes for the tax year 2009–10 and subsequent tax years.

Notes – Rewritten income tax provisions are now located as follows:
S. 91B(1): ITTOIA 2005, s. 165(1).
S. 91B(2): ITTOIA 2005, s. 165(1) and (2) and 166(1).
S. 91B(3): ITTOIA 2005, s. 165(2) and 166(1).
S. 91B(4): ITTOIA 2005, s. 166(2) and 167(1).
S. 91B(5): ITTOIA 2005, s. 166(2).
S. 91B(6): ITTOIA 2005, s. 166(2).
S. 91B(7): ITTOIA 2005, s. 165(1).
S. 91B(8): ITTOIA 2005, s. 166(1).
S. 91B(9): ITTOIA 2005, s. 166(2) and (3).
S. 91B(10): ITTOIA 2005, s. 166(2), (3) and (4).
S. 91B(10A): ITTOIA 2005, s. 167(2).
S. 91B(11): ITTOIA 2005, s. 166(1) and (3) and 167(1).
S. 91B rewritten for corporation tax purposes as follows:
S. 91B(1): CTA 2009, s. 142(1).
S. 91B(2): CTA 2009, s. 142(1), (2), 143(1).
S. 91B(3): CTA 2009, s. 142(2), 143(1).
S. 91B(4): CTA 2009, s. 143(2), 144(2).
S. 91B(5): CTA 2009, s. 143(2).
S. 91B(6): CTA 2009, s. 143(2).
S. 91B(7): CTA 2009, s. 142(1), 143(1).
S. 91B(8): CTA 2009, s. 143(1).

S. 91B(9): CTA 2009, s. 143(2), (3).
S. 91B(10): CTA 2009, s. 143(2) (3), (4),.
S. 91B(10A): CTA 2009, s. 144(3).
S. 91B(11): CTA 2009, s. 143(1), (3), 144(2).

91BA Waste disposal: entitlement of successor to allowances

91BA [Omitted by CTA 2009, s. 1322 and Sch. 1, para. 69 and repealed by CTA 2009, Sch. 3, Pt. 1.]

History – S. 91BA omitted by CTA 2009, s. 1322 and Sch. 1, para. 69 and repealed by CTA 2009, Sch. 3, Pt. 1, with effect for corporation tax purposes for accounting periods ending on or after 1 April 2009, and for income tax and capital gains tax purposes for the tax year 2009–10 and subsequent tax years.

Notes – Rewritten income tax provisions are now located as follows:
S. 91BA(1): ITTOIA 2005, s. 165(1) and (3), s. 167(1) and Sch. 2, para. 44.
S. 91BA(2): ITTOIA 2005, s. 165(4).
S. 91BA(3): ITTOIA 2005, s. 165(3).
S. 91BA(4): ITTOIA 2005, s. 165(1).
S. 91BA rewritten for corporation tax purposes as follows:
S. 91BA(1): CTA 2009, s. 142(1), (3), 144(2), Sch. 2, para. 30.
S. 91BA(2): CTA 2009, s. 142(4).
S. 91BA(3): CTA 2009, s. 142(3).
S. 91BA(4): CTA 2009, s. 142(1).
S. 91BA(5): CTA 2009, s. 142(1).

91C Mineral exploration and access

91C [Omitted by CTA 2009, s. 1322 and Sch. 1, para. 70 and repealed by CTA 2009, Sch. 3, Pt. 1.]

History – S. 91C omitted by CTA 2009, s. 1322 and Sch. 1, para. 70 and repealed by CTA 2009, Sch. 3, Pt. 1, with effect for corporation tax purposes for accounting periods ending on or after 1 April 2009, and for income tax and capital gains tax purposes for the tax year 2009–10 and subsequent tax years.

Notes – Rewritten income tax provisions are now located at ITTOIA 2005, s. 161(1)–(3).
S. 91C rewritten for corporation tax purposes as CTA 2009, s. 137(1), (2), (3).

TREATMENT OF REGIONAL DEVELOPMENT AND OTHER GRANTS AND DEBTS RELEASED ETC.

92 Regional development grants

92 [Omitted by CTA 2009, s. 1322 and Sch. 1, para. 71 and repealed by CTA 2009, Sch. 3, Pt. 1.]

History – S. 92 omitted by CTA 2009, s. 1322 and Sch. 1, para. 71 and repealed by CTA 2009, Sch. 3, Pt. 1, with effect for corporation tax purposes for accounting periods ending on or after 1 April 2009, and for income tax and capital gains tax purposes for the tax year 2009–10 and subsequent tax years.

Notes – S. 92 is not rewritten by ITTOIA 2005 as there are no payments outstanding in respect of grants under the Industrial Development Act 1982 (see ITTOIA 2005, Explanatory Notes, Annex 1, Table 1 (Change 158)).

93 Other grants under Industrial Development Act 1982 etc.

93 [Omitted by CTA 2009, s. 1322 and Sch. 1, para. 72 and repealed by CTA 2009, Sch. 3, Pt. 1.]

History – S. 93 omitted by CTA 2009, s. 1322 and Sch. 1, para. 72 and repealed by CTA 2009, Sch. 3, Pt. 1, with effect for corporation tax purposes for accounting periods ending on or after 1 April 2009, and for income tax and capital gains tax purposes for the tax year 2009–10 and subsequent tax years.

Notes – Rewritten income tax provisions are now located as follows:
S. 93(1): ITTOIA 2005, s. 105(1) and (2).
S. 93(2): ITTOIA 2005, s. 105(1) and (2). However, ITTOIA 2005 does not rewrite the references in ICTA 1988, s. 93(2) to the Industry Act 1972 and its Northern Ireland equivalents. These statutes were repealed in 1982 and there are no outstanding instalments under them. (See ITTOIA 2005, Explanatory Notes, Annex 1, Table 1 (Change 158).)
S. 93(3): ITTOIA 2005, s. 105(2). However, ITTOIA 2005 excludes all grants in respect of corporation tax liabilities under ICTA 1988, s. 93(3). (See ITTOIA 2005, Explanatory Notes, Annex 1, Table 1 (Change 158).)
S. 93 rewritten for corporation tax purposes as follows:
S. 93(1): CTA 2009, s. 102(1), (2), 1252(1), (2), (3).
S. 93(2): CTA 2009, s. 102(1), (2), 1252(1), (2), (3).
S. 93(3): CTA 2009, s. 102(2), 1252(2).

94 Debts deducted and subsequently released

94 [Omitted by CTA 2009, s. 1322 and Sch. 1, para. 73 and repealed by CTA 2009, Sch. 3, Pt. 1.]

History – S. 94 omitted by CTA 2009, s. 1322 and Sch. 1, para. 73 and repealed by CTA 2009, Sch. 3, Pt. 1, with effect for corporation tax purposes for accounting periods ending on or after 1 April 2009, and for income tax and capital gains tax purposes for the tax year 2009–10 and subsequent tax years.

Notes – Rewritten income tax provisions are now located as follows:
S. 94(1): ITTOIA 2005, s. 97(1) and (2).
S. 94(2): ITTOIA 2005, s. 97(2).
S. 94 rewritten for corporation tax purposes as follows:
S. 94(1): CTA 2009, s. 94(1), (2).

95 Taxation of dealers in respect of distributions etc.

95 [Omitted by CTA 2009, s. 1322 and Sch. 1, para. 74 and repealed by CTA 2009, Sch. 3, Pt. 1.]

History – S. 95 omitted by CTA 2009, s. 1322 and Sch. 1, para. 74 and repealed by CTA 2009, Sch. 3, Pt. 1, with effect for corporation tax purposes for accounting periods ending on or after 1 April 2009, and for income tax and capital gains tax purposes for the tax year 2009–10 and subsequent tax years.

Notes – Rewritten income tax provisions are now located as follows:
S. 95(1): ITTOIA 2005, s. 366(1).
S. 95(1A): ITTOIA 2005, s. 398(2).
S. 95 rewritten for corporation tax purposes as follows:
S. 95(1): CTA 2009, s. 130(1), (3), (4).
S. 95(1A): CTA 2009, s. 130(2).
S. 95(2): CTA 2009, s. 130(1), (3), (4).
S. 95(2A): CTA 2009, s. 130(5).

95ZA Taxation of UK distributions received by insurance companies

95ZA(1) If the total amount of relevant distributions received by a company in an accounting period exceeds £50,000, those distributions are to be taken into account in calculating for corporation tax purposes the profits of the company in that period (and accordingly section 130(2) of CTA 2009 does not apply in relation to those distributions).

95ZA(2) A company ("company A") receives a "relevant distribution" if–

(a) it receives a distribution made by a company ("company B"),

(b) the value of the shares or stock in respect of which the distribution is made ("the holding") is materially reduced by reason of the distribution,

(c) a profit on the sale of the holding (to anyone other than company B) would be taken into account in calculating company A's profits in respect of relevant insurance business, and

(d) either–

  (i) the holding amounts to, or is an ingredient in a holding amounting to, 10% of all holdings of the same class in company B, or

  (ii) the period between the acquisition by company A of the holding and that company first taking steps to dispose of the holding does not exceed 30 days.

95ZA(3) In this section **"relevant insurance business"** means any kind of insurance business other than business in relation to which section 111 of the Finance Act 2012 applies.

95ZA(4) Section 177(7) of TCGA 1992 (provision supplementing provision corresponding to subsection (2)(d)(i) above) applies for the purposes of subsection (2)(d)(i).

95ZA(5) Section 731(4) below (interpretation of "taking steps to dispose of securities") applies for the purposes of subsection (2)(d)(ii) as if the reference to the securities were to the holding.

History – In s. 95ZA(1), "section 130(2)" substituted for "section 1285" by FA 2009, s. 34 and Sch. 14, para. 5(2), with effect in relation to distributions paid on or after 1 July 2009.
In s. 95ZA(1), the words "section 1285 of CTA 2009" substituted for the words "section 208" by CTA 2009, s. 1322 and Sch. 1, para. 75, with effect for corporation tax purposes for accounting periods ending on or after 1 April 2009, and for income tax and capital gains tax purposes for the tax year 2009–10 and subsequent tax years.
In s. 95ZA(2)(a), the words "resident in the United Kingdom", which appeared after "company", omitted by FA 2009, s. 34 and Sch. 14, para. 5(3), with effect in relation to distributions paid on or after 1 July 2009.
In s. 95ZA(3), the words "business in relation to which section 111 of the Finance Act 2012 applies" substituted for "life assurance business" by FA 2012, s. 146 and Sch. 16, para. 10 with effect in relation to accounting periods of companies beginning on or after 1 January 2013, subject to transitional provisions contained in FA 2012, Sch. 17. For accounting periods straddling 1 January 2013, FA 2012, s. 149 provides for a deemed cessation.
S. 95ZA inserted by FA 2008, s. 43 and Sch. 17, para. 16(1), with effect in relation to distributions made on or after 1 April 2008.

SPECIAL PROVISIONS

95A Creative artists: relief for fluctuating profits

95A [Omitted by ITTOIA 2005, s. 882 and Sch. 1, para. 75 and repealed by s. 884 and Sch. 3.]

History – S. 95A omitted by ITTOIA 2005, s. 882(1) and Sch. 1, para. 75 and repealed by s. 884 and Sch. 3; effective for income tax purposes for 2005–06 onwards and for corporation tax purposes for accounting periods ending after 5 April 2005 (ITTOIA 2005, s. 883(1)).

96 Farming and market gardening: relief for fluctuating profits

96 [Omitted by ITTOIA 2005, s. 882 and Sch. 1, para. 76 and repealed by s. 884 and Sch. 3.]

History – S. 96 omitted by ITTOIA 2005, s. 882(1) and Sch. 1, para. 76 and repealed by s. 884 and Sch. 3; effective for income tax purposes for 2005–06 onwards and for corporation tax purposes for accounting periods ending after 5 April 2005 (ITTOIA 2005, s. 883(1)).

Cross references – ITTOIA 2005, Sch. 2, para. 55: averaging profits of farmers and creative artists.

Notes – S. 96 has been rewritten as follows:
S. 96(1): ITTOIA 2005, s. 221(1) and (2) and 222(1) and (2).
S. 96(2): ITTOIA 2005, s. 222(1) and 223(1) and (3).

S. 96(3): ITTOIA 2005, s. 222(1) and 223(1) and (4).
S. 96(4): ITTOIA 2005, s. 222(2)–(4).
S. 96(5): ITTOIA 2005, s. 224(1) and (3) and 225(1)–(3).
S. 96(6): ITTOIA 2005, s. 221(1).
S. 96(7): ITTOIA 2005, s. 221(4). However, ITTOIA 2005 does not rewrite the reference in ICTA 1988, s. 96(7)(c) to stock relief as it is now spent. (See ITTOIA 2005, Explanatory Notes, Annex 1, Table 1 (Change 158).)
S. 96(8): ITTOIA 2005, s. 222(5) and (6) and 225(4).
S. 96(9): ITTOIA 2005, s. 224(4) and (5).

97 Treatment of farm animals etc.

97 [Omitted by CTA 2009, s. 1322 and Sch. 1, para. 76 and repealed by CTA 2009, Sch. 3, Pt. 1.]

History – S. 97 omitted by CTA 2009, s. 1322 and Sch. 1, para. 76 and repealed by CTA 2009, Sch. 3, Pt. 1, with effect for corporation tax purposes for accounting periods ending on or after 1 April 2009, and for income tax and capital gains tax purposes for the tax year 2009–10 and subsequent tax years.

98 Tied premises: receipts and expenses treated as those of trade

98 [Omitted by CTA 2009, s. 1322 and Sch. 1, para. 77 and repealed by CTA 2009, Sch. 3, Pt. 1.]

History – S. 98 omitted by CTA 2009, s. 1322 and Sch. 1, para. 77 and repealed by CTA 2009, Sch. 3, Pt. 1, with effect for corporation tax purposes for accounting periods ending on or after 1 April 2009, and for income tax and capital gains tax purposes for the tax year 2009–10 and subsequent tax years.

Notes – Rewritten income tax provisions are now located as follows:
S. 98(1): ITTOIA 2005, s. 19(1) and (2).
S. 98(2): ITTOIA 2005, s. 19(1).
S. 98(3): ITTOIA 2005, s. 19(3).
S. 98(1): ITTOIA 2005, s. 19(1).
S. 98 rewritten for corporation tax purposes as follows:
S. 98(1): CTA 2009, s. 42(1).
S. 98(2): CTA 2009, s. 42(1), (2).
S. 98(3): CTA 2009, s. 42(3).
S. 98(4): CTA 2009, s. 42(1).

99 Dealers in land

99 [Omitted by CTA 2009, s. 1322 and Sch. 1, para. 78 and repealed by CTA 2009, Sch. 3, Pt. 1.]

History – S. 99 omitted by CTA 2009, s. 1322 and Sch. 1, para. 78 and repealed by CTA 2009, Sch. 3, Pt. 1, with effect for corporation tax purposes for accounting periods ending on or after 1 April 2009, and for income tax and capital gains tax purposes for the tax year 2009–10 and subsequent tax years.

Notes – Rewritten income tax provisions are now located as follows:
S. 99(1): ITTOIA 2005, s. 156(1)–(3).
S. 99(2): ITTOIA 2005, s. 158(1)–(3).
S. 99(3): ITTOIA 2005, s. 158(4) and (5).
S. 99(4): ITTOIA 2005, Sch. 2, para. 42.
S. 99 rewritten for corporation tax purposes as follows:
S. 99(1): CTA 2009, s. 134(1), (2), (3).
S. 99(2): CTA 2009, s. 136(1), (2), (3).
S. 99(3): CTA 2009, s. 136(4), (5).
S. 99(4): CTA 2009, s. Sch. 2, para. 29.

Chapter VI – Discontinuance

History – Former words "and Change of Basis of Computation" in Chapter VI heading repealed by FA 1998, s. 165 and Sch. 27, Pt. III(6), applying to a change of accounting basis taking effect on or after 6 April 1999.

VALUATION OF TRADING STOCK ETC.

100 Valuation of trading stock at discontinuance of trade

100 [Omitted by CTA 2009, s. 1322 and Sch. 1, para. 79 and repealed by CTA 2009, Sch. 3, Pt. 1.]

History – S. 100 omitted by CTA 2009, s. 1322 and Sch. 1, para. 79 and repealed by CTA 2009, Sch. 3, Pt. 1, with effect for corporation tax purposes for accounting periods ending on or after 1 April 2009, and for income tax and capital gains tax purposes for the tax year 2009–10 and subsequent tax years.

Notes – Rewritten income tax provisions are now located as follows:
S. 100(1): ITTOIA 2005, s. 173(1), 175(1), (2) and (4) and s. 181(1).
S. 100(1ZA): ITTOIA 2005, s. 173(2).
S. 100(1A): ITTOIA 2005, s. 176(1) and (2), 177 and 181(2).
S. 100(1B): ITTOIA 2005, s. 175(3).
S. 100(1C): ITTOIA 2005, s. 178(1)–(4).
S. 100(1D): ITTOIA 2005, s. 178(5).
S. 100(1E): ITTOIA 2005, s. 180(1) and (2).
S. 100(1F): ITTOIA 2005, s. 179 and 878(6).
S. 100(1G): ITTOIA 2005, s. 181(2).
S. 100(2): ITTOIA 2005, s. 174(1)–(3).
S. 100(3): ITTOIA 2005, s. 176(3), 178(6) and 181(2).
S. 100 rewritten for corporation tax purposes as follows:
S. 100(1): CTA 2009, s. 162(1), 164(1), (2), (4), 170(1).
S. 100(1ZA): CTA 2009, s. 162(2).

S. 100(1A): CTA 2009, s. 165(1), (2), 166(1), (2), 170(2).
S. 100(1B): CTA 2009, s. 164(3).
S. 100(1C): CTA 2009, s. 167(1), (2), (3), (4).
S. 100(1D): CTA 2009, s. 167(5).
S. 100(1E): CTA 2009, s. 169(1), (2).
S. 100(1F): CTA 2009, s. 168, 1316(2).
S. 100(1G): CTA 2009, s. 170(2).
S. 100(2): CTA 2009, s. 163(1), (2), (3).
S. 100(3): CTA 2009, s. 165(3), 167(6), 170(2).

101 Valuation of work in progress at discontinuance of profession or vocation

101 [Omitted by CTA 2009, s. 1322 and Sch. 1, para. 80 and repealed by CTA 2009, Sch. 3, Pt. 1.]

History – S. 101 omitted by CTA 2009, s. 1322 and Sch. 1, para. 80 and repealed by CTA 2009, Sch. 3, Pt. 1, with effect for corporation tax purposes for accounting periods ending on or after 1 April 2009, and for income tax and capital gains tax purposes for the tax year 2009–10 and subsequent tax years.

Notes – Rewritten income tax provisions are now located as follows:
S. 101(1): ITTOIA 2005, s. 182(1) and 184(1) and (2).
S. 101(2): ITTOIA 2005, s. 185(1) and (2).
S. 101(2A): ITTOIA 2005, s. 185(2).
S. 101(3): ITTOIA 2005, s. 174(2) and (3) and 183(1) and (2).
S. 101 rewritten for corporation tax purposes as follows:
S. 101(1)–(2A): not rewritten for corporation tax purposes (see CTA 2009 Explanatory Notes, Annex 1, Change 39).
S. 101(3): CTA 2009, s. 163(3).

102 Provisions supplementary to sections 100 and 101

102 [Omitted by CTA 2009, s. 1322 and Sch. 1, para. 82 and repealed by CTA 2009, s. 1326 and Sch. 3, Pt. 1.]

History – S. 102 omitted by CTA 2009, s. 1322 and Sch. 1, para. 82 and repealed by CTA 2009, s. 1326 and Sch. 3, Pt. 1, with effect for corporation tax purposes for accounting periods ending on or after 1 April 2009, and for income tax and capital gains tax purposes for the tax year 2009–10 and subsequent tax years.

Notes – Rewritten income tax provisions are now located as follows:
S. 102(1): ITTOIA 2005, s. 186(1)–(4).
S. 102(2): ITTOIA 2005, s. 173(3) and (4) and 182(2) and (3).
S. 102 rewritten for corporation tax purposes as follows:
S. 102(1): CTA 2009, s. 171.
S. 102(2): CTA 2009, s. 162(3), (4).

CASE VI CHARGES ON RECEIPTS

103 Receipts after discontinuance: earnings basis charge and related charge affecting conventional basis

103 [Omitted by CTA 2009, s. 1322 and Sch. 1, para. 82 and repealed by CTA 2009, s. 1326 and Sch. 3, Pt. 1.]

History – S. 103 omitted by CTA 2009, s. 1322 and Sch. 1, para. 82 and repealed by CTA 2009, s. 1326 and Sch. 3, Pt. 1, with effect for corporation tax purposes for accounting periods ending on or after 1 April 2009, and for income tax and capital gains tax purposes for the tax year 2009–10 and subsequent tax years.

Notes – Rewritten income tax provisions are now located as follows:
S. 103(1): ITTOIA 2005, s. 243(1), (4) and (5), 246(1), 350(1) and 353(1).
S. 103(2): ITTOIA 2005, s. 243(1), 246(1), 350(1) and 353(1).
S. 103(3): ITTOIA 2005, s. 243(3), 252(1) and 253(1)–(3).
S. 103(4): ITTOIA 2005, s. 249(1) and (2) and 354(2).
S. 103(4A): ITTOIA 2005, s. 354(2).
S. 103(5): ITTOIA 2005, s. 248(1), (2) and (4) and 354(2).
S. 103 rewritten for corporation tax purposes as follows:
S. 103(1): CTA 2009, s. 188, 189(1), (4), 190(1), 280, 281(1), 282(1).
S. 103(2): CTA 2009, s. 189(1), 190(1), 281(1), 282(1).
S. 103(3): CTA 2009, s. 189(3), 195(1).
S. 103(4): CTA 2009, s. 193(1), (2), 283(2).
S. 103(5): CTA 2009, s. 192(1), (2), 283(2).

104 Conventional basis: general charge on receipts after discontinuance

104 [Omitted by CTA 2009, s. 1322 and Sch. 1, para. 82 and repealed by CTA 2009, s. 1326 and Sch. 3, Pt. 1.]

History – S. 104 omitted by CTA 2009, s. 1322 and Sch. 1, para. 82 and repealed by CTA 2009, s. 1326 and Sch. 3, Pt. 1, with effect for corporation tax purposes for accounting periods ending on or after 1 April 2009, and for income tax and capital gains tax purposes for the tax year 2009–10 and subsequent tax years.

Notes – Rewritten income tax provisions are now located as follows:
S. 104(1): ITTOIA 2005, s. 243(1) and (4), 246(1), 350(1) and 353(1).
S. 104(2): ITTOIA 2005, s. 243(1), 246(1), 350(1) and 353(1).
S. 104(6): ITTOIA 2005, s. 252(1).

S. 104 rewritten for corporation tax purposes as follows:
S. 104(1): CTA 2009, s. 188, 189(1), (4), 190(1), 280, 281(1), 282(1).
S. 104(2): CTA 2009, s. 189(1), 190(1), 281(1), 282(1).
S. 104(6): CTA 2009, s. 195(1).

105 Allowable deductions

105 [Omitted by CTA 2009, s. 1322 and Sch. 1, para. 82 and repealed by CTA 2009, s. 1326 and Sch. 3, Pt. 1.]

History – S. 105 omitted by CTA 2009, s. 1322 and Sch. 1, para. 82 and repealed by CTA 2009, s. 1326 and Sch. 3, Pt. 1, with effect for corporation tax purposes for accounting periods ending on or after 1 April 2009, and for income tax and capital gains tax purposes for the tax year 2009–10 and subsequent tax years.

Notes – Rewritten income tax provisions are now located as follows:
S. 105(1): ITTOIA 2005, s. 254(1) and (2) and 351(2).
S. 105(2): ITTOIA 2005, s. 254(3) and 351(2).
S. 105(3): ITTOIA 2005, s. 255(1)–(3) and 351(2).
ITTOIA 2005 does not rewrite the references to capital allowances in ICTA 1988, s. 105(1) and (3) as they are no longer needed now that capital allowances are given as trading expenses. (See ITTOIA 2005, Explanatory Notes, Annex 1, Table 1 (Change 158).)
S. 105 rewritten for corporation tax purposes as follows:
S. 105(1): CTA 2009, s. 196(1), (2), 285.
S. 105(2): CTA 2009, s. 196(3), 285.
S. 105(3): CTA 2009, s. 197(1), (2), (3) , 285.

106 Application of charges where rights to payments transferred

106 [Omitted by CTA 2009, s. 1322 and Sch. 1, para. 82 and repealed by CTA 2009, s. 1326 and Sch. 3, Pt. 1.]

History – S. 106 omitted by CTA 2009, s. 1322 and Sch. 1, para. 82 and repealed by CTA 2009, s. 1326 and Sch. 3, Pt. 1, with effect for corporation tax purposes for accounting periods ending on or after 1 April 2009, and for income tax and capital gains tax purposes for the tax year 2009–10 and subsequent tax years.

Notes – Rewritten income tax provisions are now located as follows:
S. 106(1): ITTOIA 2005, s. 98(3), 251(1)–(4), 310(3) and 355(1)–(4).
S. 106(2): ITTOIA 2005, s. 98(1)–(3), 251(4), 310(1)–(3) and 355(4).
S. 106 rewritten for corporation tax purposes as follows:
S. 106(1): CTA 2009, s. 95(3), 194(1), (2), (3), (4), 249(3), 284(1), (2), (3), (4).
S. 106(2): CTA 2009, s. 95(1), (2), (3), 194(4), 249(1), (2), (3), 284(4).

RELIEFS

107 Treatment of receipts as earned income

107 [Omitted by ITTOIA 2005, s. 882 and Sch. 1, para. 86 and repealed by s. 884 and Sch. 3.]

History – S. 107 omitted by ITTOIA 2005, s. 882(1) and Sch. 1, para. 86 and repealed by s. 884 and Sch. 3; effective for income tax purposes for 2005–06 onwards and for corporation tax purposes for accounting periods ending after 5 April 2005 (ITTOIA 2005, s. 883(1)).

108 Election for carry-back

108 [Omitted by ITTOIA 2005, s. 882 and Sch. 1, para. 87 and repealed by s. 884 and Sch. 3.]

History – S. 108 omitted by ITTOIA 2005, s. 882(1) and Sch. 1, para. 87 and repealed by s. 884 and Sch. 3; effective for income tax purposes for 2005–06 onwards and for corporation tax purposes for accounting periods ending after 5 April 2005 (ITTOIA 2005, s. 883(1)).

109 Charge under section 104: relief for individuals born before 6th April 1917

109 [Omitted by ITTOIA 2005, s. 882 and Sch. 1, para. 88 and repealed by s. 884 and Sch. 3.]

History – S. 109 omitted by ITTOIA 2005, s. 882(1) and Sch. 1, para. 88; effective for income tax purposes for 2005–06 onwards and for corporation tax purposes for accounting periods ending after 5 April 2005 (ITTOIA 2005, s. 883(1)).

109A Relief for post-cessation expenditure

109A [Omitted by ITA 2007, s. 1027 and Sch. 1, para. 11 and repealed by ITA 2007, s. 1031 and Sch. 3, Pt. 1 with effect for income tax purposes for 2007–08 and subsequent tax years and for corporation tax purposes in relation to accounting periods ending after 5 April 2007.]

Notes – Rewritten income tax provisions are now located as follows:
S. 109A(1): ITA 2007, s. 23, 24(1), 96(1), (2), (3), (4), 125(1), (2), (3), (4).
S. 109A(2): ITA 2007, s. 97(1), (2), (3), (4), (5).
S. 109A(3): ITTOIA 2005, s. 250(1)–(4), 255(4), 351(2) and 354(2).
S. 109A(4): ITA 2007, s. 98(2), (3).
S. 109A(4): ITTOIA 2005, s. 248(3) and (4), 255(4), 351(2) and 354(2).
S. 109A(4A): ITA 2007, s. 98(5), (6), (7), (8).
S. 109A(4A): ITTOIA 2005, s. 248(3) and (4), 255(4), 351(2) and 354(2).
S. 109A(5): ITA 2007, s. 99(1), (2), (3), (4), (5).
S. 109A(6): ITA 2007, s. 100(1), (2).
S. 109A(6A): ITA 2007, s. 23, 24(1), 125(1), (2), (3), (4).

SUPPLEMENTAL

110 Interpretation etc.

110 [Omitted by CTA 2009, s. 1322 and Sch. 1, para. 83 and repealed by CTA 2009, s. 1326 and Sch. 3, Pt. 1.]

History – S. 110 omitted by CTA 2009, s. 1322 and Sch. 1, para. 83 and repealed by CTA 2009, s. 1326 and Sch. 3, Pt. 1, with effect for corporation tax purposes for accounting periods ending on or after 1 April 2009, and for income tax and capital gains tax purposes for the tax year 2009–10 and subsequent tax years.

Notes – Rewritten income tax provisions are now located as follows:
S. 110(1A): ITA 2007, s. 62(3), 96(1), 125(1).
S. 110(1B): ITA 2007, s. 96(5).
S. 110(1D): ITA 2007, s. 125(5).
S. 110(2): ITTOIA 2005, s. 246(2)–(4), 249(3), 353(2) and (3) and 362(1) and (2).
S. 110(6): ITTOIA 2005, s. 252(3).
S. 110 rewritten for corporation tax purposes as follows:
S. 110(1A): CTA 2009, s. 190(2).
S. 110(1B): CTA 2009, s. 190(2), 289(1), (2).
S. 110(1C): CTA 2009, s. 282(2).
S. 110(1D): CTA 2009, s. 282(2).
S. 110(6): CTA 2009, s. 195(2).

CHANGE OF RESIDENCE

History – Cross-heading repealed by ITTOIA 2005, s. 884 and Sch. 3; effective for income tax purposes for 2005–06 onwards and for corporation tax purposes for accounting periods ending after 5 April 2005 (ITTOIA 2005, s. 883(1)).

110A Change of residence

110A [Omitted by ITTOIA 2005, s. 882 and Sch. 1, para. 91 and repealed by s. 884 and Sch. 3.]

History – S. 110A omitted by ITTOIA 2005, s. 882(1) and Sch. 1, para. 91 and repealed by s. 884 and Sch. 3; effective for income tax purposes for 2005–06 onwards and for corporation tax purposes for accounting periods ending after 5 April 2005 (ITTOIA 2005, s. 883(1)).

Notes – S. 110A has been rewritten into the provisions of ITTOIA 2005 as follows:
S. 110A(1): ITTOIA 2005, s. 17(1)–(4).
S. 110A(2): ITTOIA 2005, s. 17(1).

ICTA 1988

Chapter VII – Partnerships and Successions

Cross references – FA 2007, Sch. 4, para. 3 (restriction on trade losses: application of rules introduced into ITA 2007 for 2006–07 losses where basis period ends on or after 2 March 2007.

GENERAL

111 Treatment of partnerships

111(1) [Omitted by CTA 2009, s. 1322 and Sch. 1, para. 84 and repealed by CTA 2009, s. 1326 and Sch. 3, Pt. 1.]

111(2)-(13) [Omitted by ITTOIA 2005, s. 882 and Sch. 1, para. 92(3) and repealed by s. 884 and Sch. 3.]

History – S. 111(1) omitted by CTA 2009, s. 1322 and Sch. 1, para. 84 and repealed by CTA 2009, s. 1326 and Sch. 3, Pt. 1, with effect for corporation tax purposes for accounting periods ending on or after 1 April 2009, and for income tax and capital gains tax purposes for the tax year 2009–10 and subsequent tax years.
S. 111(2)–(13) omitted by ITTOIA 2005, s. 882 and Sch. 1, para. 92(3) and repealed by ITTOIA 2005, s. 884 and Sch. 3, effective for income tax purposes for 2005–06 onwards and for corporation tax purposes for accounting periods ending after 5 April 2005.

Notes – Rewritten income tax provisions are now located as follows:
S. 111(1): ITTOIA 2005, s. 848.
S. 111(2): ITTOIA 2005, s. 849(2);.
S. 111(3): ITTOIA 2005, s. 850(1);.
S. 111(4): ITTOIA 2005, s. 246(3) and (4), 353(2) and (3), 852(1)–(5) and 853(1) and (2);.
S. 111(5): ITTOIA 2005, s. 853(2);.
S. 111(6): ITTOIA 2005, s. 853(3);.
S. 111(7): ITTOIA 2005, s. 851(1) and (2);
S. 111(8): ITTOIA 2005, s. 854(1)–(4) and 855(1)–(3);.
S. 111(10): ITTOIA 2005, s. 847(2);.
S. 111(11): ITTOIA 2005, s. 847(3);.
S. 111(12): ITTOIA 2005, s. 854(6).
S. 111 rewritten for corporation tax purposes as follows:
S. 111(1): CTA 2009, s. 1258.

112 Partnerships controlled abroad

112 [Omitted by ITTOIA 2005, s. 882 and Sch. 1, para. 93 and repealed by s. 884 and Sch. 3.]

History – S. 112 omitted by ITTOIA 2005, s. 882(1) and Sch. 1, para. 93 and repealed by s. 884 and Sch. 3; effective for income tax purposes for 2005–06 onwards and for corporation tax purposes for accounting periods ending after 5 April 2005 (ITTOIA 2005, s. 883(1)).

Notes – S. 112 has been rewritten as follows:
S. 112(1): ITTOIA 2005, s. 849(3).
S. 112(1A): ITTOIA 2005, s. 243(5), 830(1) and 857(1)–(3).
S. 112(1B): ITTOIA 2005, s. 852(6) and (7) and 854(5).
S. 112(4): ITTOIA 2005, s. 858(1) and (2).
S. 112(5): ITTOIA 2005, s. 858(3).

113 Effect, for income tax, of change in ownership of trade, profession or vocation

113 [Omitted by ITTOIA 2005, s. 882 and Sch. 1, para. 94 and repealed by s. 884 and Sch. 3.]

History – S. 113 omitted by ITTOIA 2005, s. 882(1) and Sch. 1, para. 94 and repealed by s. 884 and Sch. 3; effective for income tax purposes for 2005–06 onwards and for corporation tax purposes for accounting periods ending after 5 April 2005 (ITTOIA 2005, s. 883(1)).

Notes – S. 113 has been rewritten as follows:
S. 113(1): ITTOIA 2005, s. 246(3) and (4) and 353(2) and (3).
S. 113(2): ITTOIA 2005, s. 77(5), 79(2), 173(3), 182(2), 246(3) and (4), 353(2) and (3) and 860(1) and (2).
S. 113(7): ITTOIA 2005, s. 258(1) and (2) and 361(1) and (2).
S. 113(6) is not rewritten by ITTOIA 2005 as it is covered by the general rule in TMA 1970, s. 74. (See ITTOIA 2005, Explanatory Notes, Annex 1, Table 1 (Change 158).)

PARTNERSHIPS INVOLVING COMPANIES

114 Special rules for computing profits and losses

114 [Omitted by CTA 2009, s. 1322 and Sch. 1, para. 85 and repealed by CTA 2009, s. 1326 and Sch. 3, Pt. 1.]

History – S. 114 omitted by CTA 2009, s. 1322 and Sch. 1, para. 85 and repealed by CTA 2009, s. 1326 and Sch. 3, Pt. 1, with effect for corporation tax purposes for accounting periods ending on or after 1 April 2009, and for income tax and capital gains tax purposes for the tax year 2009–10 and subsequent tax years.

Notes – S. 114 rewritten as follows:
S. 114(1): CTA 2009, s. 77(5), (6), 80(1), (2), 162(3), (4), 1259(3), (4), (5), 1260(1), (2), 1261(1), (2), (3), (4), (5), (6), 1267(3), (4), 1268(1), Sch. 1, para. 484, 485, 486, 487, 488, 489, 520(3).
S. 114(2): CTA 2009, s. 1262(1), (2), (4), 1265(1), (2).

115 Provisions supplementary to section 114

115 [Omitted by CTA 2009, s. 1322 and Sch. 1, para. 85 and repealed by CTA 2009, s. 1326 and Sch. 3, Pt. 1.]

History – S. 115 omitted by CTA 2009, s. 1322 and Sch. 1, para. 85 and repealed by CTA 2009, s. 1326 and Sch. 3, Pt. 1, with effect for corporation tax purposes for accounting periods ending on or after 1 April 2009, and for income tax and capital gains tax purposes for the tax year 2009–10 and subsequent tax years.

Notes – S. 115 rewritten as follows:
S. 115(4): CTA 2009, s. 1259(4), 1261(6).
S. 115(5): CTA 2009, s. 1266(1), Sch. 1, para. 365(3).
S. 115(5A): CTA 2009, s. 1266(2), Sch. 1, para. 365(3).
S. 115(5B): CTA 2009, s. 1266(3).
S. 115(5C): CTA 2009, s. 1266(4).

116 Arrangements for transferring relief

116 [Omitted by CTA 2010, s. 1177 and Sch. 1, para. 11 and repealed by CTA 2010, s. 1181 and Sch. 3, Pt. 1.]

History – S. 116 omitted by CTA 2010, s. 1177 and Sch. 1, para. 11 and repealed by CTA 2010, s. 1181 and Sch. 3, Pt. 1, with effect for corporation tax purposes for accounting periods ending on or after 1 April 2010, and for income and capital gains tax purposes for the tax year 2010–11 and subsequent tax years.

Notes – S. 116 rewritten for corporation tax purposes as follows:
S. 116(1): CTA 2010, s. 958, 959(1), (2), (3), (4), (5).
S. 116(2): CTA 2010, s. 960(1), (2), (3).
S. 116(3): CTA 2010, s. 960(4).
S. 116(4): CTA 2010, s. 961(1), (2), (3).
S. 116(6): CTA 2010, s. 962(1).
S. 116(7): CTA 2010, s. 1176(1).

LIMITED PARTNERS

117 Restriction on relief: individuals

117 [Omitted by ITA 2007, s. 1027 and Sch. 1, para. 13 and repealed by ITA 2007, s. 1031 and Sch. 3, Pt. 1 with effect for 2007–08 and later tax years.]

Notes – S. 117 rewritten as follows:
S. 117(1): ITA 2007, s. 104(1), (2), (3), (4), 107(1), (3), (4), (5).
S. 117(2): ITA 2007, s. 104(1), (4), (5), (6), 106(1), (2), (3), 107(1), (5), (6), (7).
S. 117(3): ITA 2007, s. 105(2), (4), (5), (6), (7).
S. 117(5): ITA 2007, s. 105(11).

118 Restriction on relief: companies

118 [Omitted by CTA 2010, s. 1177 and Sch. 1, para. 12 and repealed by CTA 2010, s. 1181 and Sch. 3, Pt. 1.]

History – S. 118 omitted by CTA 2010, s. 1177 and Sch. 1, para. 12 and repealed by CTA 2010, s. 1181 and Sch. 3, Pt. 1, with effect for corporation tax purposes for accounting periods ending on or after 1 April 2010, and for income and capital gains tax purposes for the tax year 2010–11 and subsequent tax years.

Notes – S. 118 rewritten for corporation tax purposes as follows:
S. 118(1): CTA 2010, s. 56(1), (2), (3), 59(1), (2), (3).
S. 118(2): CTA 2010, s. 56(1), (3), (4), (5),58(1), (2), (3), 59(1), (3), (4), (5), Sch. 2, paras 23, 24(1).
S. 118(3): CTA 2010, s. 57 (2), 57 (4), (5), (6), (7).

LIMITED LIABILITY PARTNERSHIPS

118ZA Treatment of limited liability partnerships

118ZA [Omitted by CTA 2010, s. 1177 and Sch. 1, para. 12 and repealed by CTA 2010, s. 1181 and Sch. 3, Pt. 1.]

History – S. 118ZA omitted by CTA 2010, s. 1177 and Sch. 1, para. 12 and repealed by CTA 2010, s. 1181 and Sch. 3, Pt. 1, with effect for corporation tax purposes for accounting periods ending on or after 1 April 2010, and for income and capital gains tax purposes for the tax year 2010–11 and subsequent tax years.
Former s. 118ZA omitted by CTA 2009, s. 1322 and Sch. 1, para. 87 and repealed by CTA 2009, s. 1326 and Sch. 3, Pt. 1, with effect for corporation tax purposes for accounting periods ending on or after 1 April 2009, and for income tax and capital gains tax purposes for the tax year 2009–10 and subsequent tax years.

Notes – Rewritten income tax provisions are now located as follows:
S. 118ZA(1): ITTOIA 2005, s. 863(1).
S. 118ZA(2): ITTOIA 2005, s. 863(2).
S. 118ZA(3): ITTOIA 2005, s. 863(3).
S. 118ZA(4): ITTOIA 2005, s. 863(4).
S. 118ZA rewritten for corporation tax purposes as follows:
S. 118ZA(1): CTA 2009, s. 1273(1).
S. 118ZA(2): CTA 2009, s. 1273(2).
S. 118ZA(3): CTA 2009, s. 1273(3).
S. 118ZA(4): CTA 2009, s. 1273(4).

118ZB Restriction on relief: companies

118ZB [Omitted by CTA 2010, s. 1177 and Sch. 1, para. 12 and repealed by CTA 2010, s. 1181 and Sch. 3, Pt. 1.]

History – S. 118ZB omitted by CTA 2010, s. 1177 and Sch. 1, para. 12 and repealed by CTA 2010, s. 1181 and Sch. 3, Pt. 1, with effect for corporation tax purposes for accounting periods ending on or after 1 April 2010, and for income and capital gains tax purposes for the tax year 2010–11 and subsequent tax years.

Notes – S. 118ZB is rewritten for income tax purposes as follows:
S. 118ZB(1): ITA 2007, s. 107(1), (3), (4), (5), (6), (7), 108(2), (7).
S. 118ZB(2): ITA 2007, s. 107(2).
S. 118ZB rewritten for corporation tax as follows:
S. 118ZB: CTA 2010, s. 59(1),(3), (5), 60(2), (7)

118ZC Member's contribution to trade

118ZC [Omitted by CTA 2010, s. 1177 and Sch. 1, para. 12 and repealed by CTA 2010, s. 1181 and Sch. 3, Pt. 1.]

History – S. 118ZC omitted by CTA 2010, s. 1177 and Sch. 1, para. 12 and repealed by CTA 2010, s. 1181 and Sch. 3, Pt. 1, with effect for corporation tax purposes for accounting periods ending on or after 1 April 2010, and for income and capital gains tax purposes for the tax year 2010–11 and subsequent tax years.

Notes – S. 118ZC is rewritten for income tax purposes as follows:
S. 118ZC(1): ITA 2007, s. 108(2), (7).
S. 118ZC(2): ITA 2007, s. 108(2), (7).
S. 118ZC(3): ITA 2007, s. 108(2), (5), (6).
S. 118ZC(4): ITA 2007, s. 108(8).
S. 118ZC(5): ITA 2007, s. 108(9).
S. 118ZC is rewritten for corporation tax purposes as follows:
S. 118ZC(1): CTA 2010, s. 60(2), (7).
S. 118ZC(2): CTA 2010, s. 60(2), (7).
S. 118ZC(3): CTA 2010, s. 60(2), (5), (6)
S. 118ZC(4): CTA 2010, s. 60(8).

118ZD Carry forward of unrelieved losses

118ZD [Omitted by CTA 2010, s. 1177 and Sch. 1, para. 12 and repealed by CTA 2010, s. 1181 and Sch. 3, Pt. 1.]

History – S. 118ZD omitted by CTA 2010, s. 1177 and Sch. 1, para. 12 and repealed by CTA 2010, s. 1181 and Sch. 3 Pt. 1, with effect for corporation tax purposes for accounting periods ending on or after 1 April 2010, and for income and capital gains tax purposes for the tax year 2010–11 and subsequent tax years.

Notes – S. 118ZD is rewritten for income tax purposes as follows:
S. 118ZD(1): ITA 2007, s. 109(1), (2).
S. 118ZD(2): ITA 2007, s. 109(1), (2).

S. 118ZD(3): ITA 2007, s. 109(3).
S. 118ZD is rewritten for corporation tax purposes as follows:
S. 118ZD(1): CTA 2010, s. 61(1), (2), Sch. 2, para. 24(2).
S. 118ZD(2): CTA 2010, s. 61(1), (2), Sch. 2, para. 24(2).
S. 118ZD(3): CTA 2010, s. 61(3), (4), Sch. 2, para. 24(2).

NON-ACTIVE GENERAL PARTNERS AND NON-ACTIVE MEMBERS OF LIMITED LIABILITY PARTNERSHIPS

118ZE Restriction on relief for non-active partners

118ZE [Omitted by ITA 2007, s. 1027 and Sch. 1, para. 18 and repealed by ITA 2007, s. 1031 and Sch. 3, Pt. 1 with effect for income tax purposes for 2007–08 and subsequent tax years and for corporation tax purposes in relation to accounting periods ending after 5 April 2007.]

Notes – S. 118ZE is rewritten as follows:
S. 118ZE(1): ITA 2007, s. 110(1).
S. 118ZE(2): ITA 2007, s. 110(2), (3), (4).
S. 118ZE(3): ITA 2007, s. 112(1), (6), Sch. 2 para. 32.
S. 118ZE(4): ITA 2007, s. 112(1), (6).
S. 118ZE(5): ITA 2007, s. 62(3).
S. 118ZE(6): ITA 2007, s. 62(3).
S. 118ZE(7): ITA 2007, s. 110(8).

118ZF Meaning of "the aggregate amount"

118ZF [Omitted by ITA 2007, s. 1027 and Sch. 1, para. 18 and repealed by ITA 2007, s. 1031 and Sch. 3, Pt. 1 with effect for income tax purposes for 2007–08 and subsequent tax years and for corporation tax purposes in relation to accounting periods ending after 5 April 2007.]

Notes – S. 118ZF is rewritten as follows:
S. 118ZF(1): ITA 2007, s. 110(4), (5), Sch. 2 para. 33(2).
S. 118ZF(1A): ITA 2007, s. 110(6).
S. 118ZF(2): ITA 2007, s. 110(5), Sch. 2 para. 33(2).

118ZG "The individual's contribution to the trade"

118ZG [Omitted by ITA 2007, s. 1027 and Sch. 1, para. 18 and repealed by ITA 2007, s. 1031 and Sch. 3, Pt. 1 with effect for income tax purposes for 2007–08 and subsequent tax years and for corporation tax purposes in relation to accounting periods ending after 5 April 2007.]

Notes – S. 118ZG is rewritten as ITA 2007, s. 110(4), 111(1), (2), (2), (2), (4), (5), (5), (6), (7), (11), (12), Sch. 2 para. 33(10), (11).

118ZH "A significant amount of time"

118ZH [Omitted by ITA 2007, s. 1027 and Sch. 1, para. 18 and repealed by ITA 2007, s. 1031 and Sch. 3, Pt. 1 with effect for income tax purposes for 2007–08 and subsequent tax years and for corporation tax purposes in relation to accounting periods ending after 5 April 2007.]

Notes – S. 118ZH is rewritten as ITA 2007, s. 112(2), (3), (4), (5).

118ZI Carry forward of unrelieved losses of non-active partners

118ZI [Omitted by ITA 2007, s. 1027 and Sch. 1, para. 18 and repealed by ITA 2007, s. 1031 and Sch. 3, Pt. 1 with effect for income tax purposes for 2007–08 and subsequent tax years and for corporation tax purposes in relation to accounting periods ending after 5 April 2007.]

Notes – S. 118ZI is rewritten as follows:
S. 118ZI(1): ITA 2007, s. 113(1), (2), (3).
S. 118ZI(2): ITA 2007, s. 113(8).
S. 118ZI(3): ITA 2007, s. 113(3).
S. 118ZI(4): ITA 2007, s. 113(4).
S. 118ZI(5): ITA 2007, s. 113(5).
S. 118ZI(6): ITA 2007, s. 113(6).
S. 118ZI(7): ITA 2007, s. 113(7).
S. 118ZI(8): ITA 2007, s. 113(5).

118ZJ Commencement: the first restricted year

118ZJ [Omitted by ITA 2007, s. 1027 and Sch. 1, para. 18 and repealed by ITA 2007, s. 1031 and Sch. 3, Pt. 1 with effect for income tax purposes for 2007–08 and subsequent tax years and for corporation tax purposes in relation to accounting periods ending after 5 April 2007.]

Notes – S. 118ZJ is rewritten as ITA 2007, Sch. 2 para. 33(3), (9).

118ZK Transitional provision for years after the first restricted year

118ZK [Omitted by ITA 2007, s. 1027 and Sch. 1, para. 18 and repealed by ITA 2007, s. 1031 and Sch. 3, Pt. 1 with effect for income tax purposes for 2007–08 and subsequent tax years and for corporation tax purposes in relation to accounting periods ending after 5 April 2007.]

Notes – S. 118ZK is rewritten as follows:
S. 118ZK(1): ITA 2007, Sch. 2 para. 33(3).
S. 118ZK(2): ITA 2007, Sch. 2 para. 33(5).
S. 118ZK(3): ITA 2007, Sch. 2 para. 33(4).
S. 118ZK(4): ITA 2007, Sch. 2 para. 33(7).
S. 118ZK(5): ITA 2007, Sch. 2 para. 33(6).
S. 118ZK(6): ITA 2007, Sch. 2 para. 33(8), (9).

118ZL Partnerships exploiting films

118ZL [Omitted by ITA 2007, s. 1027 and Sch. 1, para. 19 and repealed by ITA 2007, s. 1031 and Sch. 3, Pt. 1 with effect for income tax purposes for 2007–08 and subsequent tax years and for corporation tax purposes in relation to accounting periods ending after 5 April 2007.]

Notes – S. 118ZL is rewritten as follows:
S. 118ZL(1): ITA 2007, s. 115(1), (2), (3).
S. 118ZL(2): ITA 2007, s. 115(1).
S. 118ZL(3): ITA 2007, s. 115(5), (6), (8), (9).
S. 118ZL(4): ITA 2007, s. 116(1).
S. 118ZL(5): ITA 2007, s. 116(1).
S. 118ZL(6): ITA 2007, s. 116(2), (5).

118ZM Partnerships exploiting films: supplementary

118ZM [Omitted by ITA 2007, s. 1027 and Sch. 1, para. 19 and repealed by ITA 2007, s. 1031 and Sch. 3, Pt. 1 with effect for income tax purposes for 2007–08 and subsequent tax years and for corporation tax purposes in relation to accounting periods ending after 5 April 2007.]

Notes – S. 118ZM is rewritten as follows:
S. 118ZM(1): ITA 2007, s. 115(1), (10), 116(5).
S. 118ZM(2): ITA 2007, s. 112(2), (3), (5), 115(1).
S. 118ZM(3): ITA 2007, s. 115(7).
S. 118ZM(4): ITA 2007, s. 116(5).
S. 118ZM(5): ITA 2007, s. 116(3).
S. 118ZM(6): ITA 2007, s. 116(4).
S. 118ZM(7): ITA 2007, s. 116(4).
S. 118ZM(8): ITA 2007, s. 109(1), (2), 113(3).

PARTNERS: MEANING OF "CONTRIBUTION TO THE TRADE"

118ZN Partners: meaning of "contribution to the trade"

118ZN [Omitted by ITA 2007, s. 1027 and Sch. 1, para. 20 and repealed by ITA 2007, s. 1031 and Sch. 3, Pt. 1 with effect for income tax purposes for 2007–08 and subsequent tax years and for corporation tax purposes in relation to accounting periods ending after 5 April 2007.]

Notes – S. 118ZN is rewritten as follows:
S. 118ZN(1): ITA 2007, s. 114(1), Sch. 2 para. 34(1).
S. 118ZN(2): ITA 2007, s. 114(1), (2).
S. 118ZN(3): ITA 2007, s. 114(3).
S. 118ZN(4): ITA 2007, s. 114(4).
S. 118ZN(5): ITA 2007, s. 114(5).

118ZO Meaning of "relevant loss" in section 118ZN

118ZO [Omitted by ITA 2007, s. 1027 and Sch. 1, para. 20 and repealed by ITA 2007, s. 1031 and Sch. 3, Pt. 1 with effect for income tax purposes for 2007–08 and subsequent tax years and for corporation tax purposes in relation to accounting periods ending after 5 April 2007.]

Notes – S. 118ZO is rewritten as ITA 2007, Sch. 2 para. 34(1).

Chapter VIIA – Paying and Collecting Agents

History – Ch. VIIA repealed by FA 2000, s. 111(1), 156 and Sch. 40, Pt. II(17), for relevant payments or receipts in relation to which the chargeable date for the purposes of Ch. VIIA is on or after 1 April 2001.
Ch. VIIA inserted by FA 1996, s. 156 and Sch. 29, para. 1 with effect from 29 April 1996.

118A-118K [Repealed by FA 2000, s. 111(1), 156 and Sch. 40, Pt. II(17).]

History – Pt. IV, Ch. VIIA repealed by FA 2000, s. 111(1), 156 and Sch. 40, Pt. II(17), for relevant payments or receipts in relation to which the chargeable date for the purposes of Ch. VIIA is on or after 1 April 2001.

Chapter VIII – Miscellaneous and Supplemental

119 Rent etc. payable in connection with mines, quarries and similar concerns

119 [Omitted by CTA 2009, s. 1322 and Sch. 1, para. 88 and repealed by CTA 2009, s. 1326 and Sch. 3, Pt. 1.]

History – S. 119 omitted by CTA 2009, s. 1322 and Sch. 1, para. 88 and repealed by CTA 2009, s. 1326 and Sch. 3, Pt. 1, with effect for corporation tax purposes for accounting periods ending on or after 1 April 2009, and for income tax and capital gains tax purposes for the tax year 2009–10 and subsequent tax years.

Notes – Rewritten income tax provisions are now located as follows:
S. 119(1): ITTOIA 2005, s. 262(1), 335, 336(1) and (2) and 337(2).
S. 119(2): ITTOIA 2005, s. 336(1)–(3).
However, ITTOIA 2005 does not rewrite the provisions in s. 119 that treated rent as "rent in kind". The original purpose was to ensure that rent was paid without the deduction of tax. However, as rent ceased to be subject to such deductions, the deeming provision ceased to be needed. (See ITTOIA 2005, Explanatory Notes, Annex 1, Table 1 (Change 158).)
S. 119 rewritten for corporation tax purposes as follows:
S. 119(1): CTA 2009, s. 270, 271(1), (2), 288(1).
S. 119(2): not rewritten (see CTA 2009 Explanatory Notes, Annex 1, Change 53).
S. 119(3): CTA 2009, s. 271(1), (2), (3).

120 Rent etc. payable in respect of electric line wayleaves

120 [Omitted by CTA 2009, s. 1322 and Sch. 1, para. 89 and repealed by CTA 2009, s. 1326 and Sch. 3, Pt. 1.]

History – S. 120 omitted by CTA 2009, s. 1322 and Sch. 1, para. 89 and repealed by CTA 2009, s. 1326 and Sch. 3, Pt. 1, with effect for corporation tax purposes for accounting periods ending on or after 1 April 2009, and for income tax and capital gains tax purposes for the tax year 2009–10 and subsequent tax years.

Notes – Rewritten income tax provisions are now located as follows:
S. 120(1): ITTOIA 2005, s. 262(2), 344 and 345(1).
S. 120(1A): ITTOIA 2005, s. 346(1) and (2).
S. 120(5): ITTOIA 2005, s. 22(4) and (6) and 345(1)–(3).
S. 120 rewritten for corporation tax purposes as follows:
S. 120(1): CTA 2009, s. 45(1), (2), (5), 277, 278(1), 288(2).
S. 120(1A): CTA 2009, s. 45(1), 279(1), (2).
S. 120(5): CTA 2009, s. 45(4), (6), 278(1), (2), (3).

121 Management expenses of owner of mineral rights

121 [Omitted by CTA 2009, s. 1322 and Sch. 1, para. 90 and repealed by CTA 2009, s. 1326 and Sch. 3, Pt. 1.]

History – S. 121 omitted by CTA 2009, s. 1322 and Sch. 1, para. 90 and repealed by CTA 2009, s. 1326 and Sch. 3, Pt. 1, with effect for corporation tax purposes for accounting periods ending on or after 1 April 2009, and for income tax and capital gains tax purposes for the tax year 2009–10 and subsequent tax years.

Notes – S. 121(1) has been rewritten as ITTOIA 2005, s. 339(1) and (2).
S. 121 rewritten for corporation tax purposes as follows:
S. 121(3): CTA 2009, s. 272(1), (2).

122 Relief in respect of mineral royalties

122 [Omitted by CTA 2009, s. 1322 and Sch. 1, para. 91 and repealed by CTA 2009, s. 1326 and Sch. 3, Pt. 1.]

History – S. 122 omitted by CTA 2009, s. 1322 and Sch. 1, para. 91 and repealed by CTA 2009, s. 1326 and Sch. 3, Pt. 1, with effect for corporation tax purposes for accounting periods ending on or after 1 April 2009, and for income tax and capital gains tax purposes for the tax year 2009–10 and subsequent tax years.

Notes – Rewritten income tax provisions are now located as follows:
S. 122(1): ITTOIA 2005, s. 157(1) and (2), 319(1) and (2) and 340(1) and (2).
S. 122(2): ITTOIA 2005, s. 319(2) and 340(2).
S. 122(5): ITTOIA 2005, s. 157(3), 319(3), 341(2) and 343.
S. 122(6): ITTOIA 2005, s. 157(3), 319(3) and 341(1) and (3).
S. 122(7): ITTOIA 2005, s. 157(3), 319(3) and 342(1)–(3).
S. 122(4) is not rewritten by ITTOIA 2005 as it became redundant when the requirement to deduct income tax from the payment of rent within ICTA 1988, s. 119 was removed by FA 1995. (See ITTOIA 2005, Explanatory Notes, Annex 1, Table 1 (Change 158).)
S. 122 rewritten for corporation tax purposes as follows:
S. 122(1): CTA 2009, s. 135(1), (2), 258(1), (2), 273(1), (2).
S. 122(2): CTA 2009, s. 258(2), 273(2).
S. 122(5): CTA 2009, s. 135(3), 258(3), 274(2), 276.
S. 122(6): CTA 2009, s. 135(3), 258(3), 274(1), (3).
S. 122(7): CTA 2009, s. 135(3), 258(3), 275(1), (2), (3).

123 Foreign dividends

123 [Repealed, as part of the abolition of Sch. C, by FA 1996, s. 79 and Sch. 7, para. 13 and s. 205 and Sch. 41, Pt. V(2)]

124 Interest on quoted Eurobonds

124 [Repealed by FA 2000, s. 111(2)(b), 156 and Sch. 40, Pt. II(17), in relation to payments of interest made on or after 1 April 2001.]

125 Annual payments for dividends or non-taxable consideration

125 [Omitted by CTA 2009, s. 1322 and Sch. 1, para. 92 and repealed by CTA 2009, s. 1326 and Sch. 3, Pt. 1.]

History – S. 125 omitted by CTA 2009, s. 1322 and Sch. 1, para. 92 and repealed by CTA 2009, s. 1326 and Sch. 3, Pt. 1, with effect for corporation tax purposes for accounting periods ending on or after 1 April 2009, and for income tax and capital gains tax purposes for the tax year 2009–10 and subsequent tax years.

Notes – Rewritten income tax provisions are now located as follows:
S. 125(1): ITA 2007, s. 843, 899(5), 903(2), 904(1), (2), (3), (4), (5), (6), (7).
S. 125(2): ITA 2007, s. 904(1), (2), (3).
S. 125(2): ITTOIA 2005, s. 729(2).
S. 125(3): ITA 2007, s. 904(1), (4), (5), (6), (7).
S. 125(3): ITTOIA 2005, s. 729(3)–(5) and Sch. 2, para. 147.
S. 125(4): ITA 2007, s. 904(8).
S. 125 rewritten for corporation tax purposes as follows:
S. 125(1): CTA 2009, s. 1301(1), (2), (3), (4), (5), (6).
S. 125(2): CTA 2009, s. 1301(2), (3).
S. 125(3): CTA 2009, s. 1301(4), (5), (6).
S. 125(4): CTA 2009, s. 1301(8).

126 Treasury securities issued at a discount

126 [Repealed by FA 1996, s. 205 and Sch. 41, Pt. V(3).]

126A Charge to tax on appropriation of securities and bonds

126A [Repealed by FA 1996, s. 205 and Sch. 41, Pt. V(3).]

127 Enterprise allowance

Notes – S. 127 has been rewritten into the provisions of ITTOIA 2005 as follows:
S. 127(1): ITTOIA 2005, s. 207(1) and (3).

127 [Omitted by ITTOIA 2005, s. 882 and Sch. 1, para. 108 and repealed by s. 884 and Sch. 3.]

History – S. 127 omitted by ITTOIA 2005, s. 882(1) and Sch. 1, para. 108 and repealed by s. 884 and Sch. 3; effective for income tax purposes for 2005–06 onwards and for corporation tax purposes for accounting periods ending after 5 April 2005 (ITTOIA 2005, s. 883(1)).

127A Futures and options: transactions with guaranteed returns

127A [Omitted by ITTOIA 2005, s. 882 and Sch. 1, para. 109 and repealed by s. 884 and Sch. 3.]

History – S. 127A omitted by ITTOIA 2005, s. 882(1) and Sch. 1, para. 109 and repealed by s. 884 and Sch. 3; effective for income tax purposes for 2005–06 onwards and for corporation tax purposes for accounting periods ending after 5 April 2005 (ITTOIA 2005, s. 883(1)).

128 Commodity and financial futures etc.: losses and gains

128(1) [Omitted by ITTOIA 2005, s. 882 and Sch. 1, para. 110 and repealed by s. 884 and Sch. 3.]

128(2)–(3) [Omitted by CTA 2009, s. 1322 and Sch. 1, para. 93 and repealed by CTA 2009, s. 1326 and Sch. 3, Pt. 1.]

History – S. 128(1) omitted by ITTOIA 2005, s. 882 and Sch. 1, para. 110 and repealed by s. 884 and Sch. 3, effective for income tax purposes for 2005–06 onwards and for corporation tax purposes for accounting periods ending after 5 April 2005.
S. 128(2) and (3) omitted by CTA 2009, s. 1322 and Sch. 1, para. 93 and repealed by CTA 2009, s. 1326 and Sch. 3, Pt. 1, with effect for corporation tax purposes for accounting periods ending on or after 1 April 2009, and for income tax and capital gains tax purposes for the tax year 2009–10 and subsequent tax years.

Notes – Rewritten income tax provisions are now located as follows:
S. 128(1): ITTOIA 2005, s. 779(1).
S. 128(3): ITTOIA 2005, s. 779(2) and (3).
S. 128 rewritten for corporation tax purposes as follows:
S. 128(2): CTA 2009, s. 981(1).
S. 128(3): CTA 2009, s. 981(2), (3).

129 Stock lending

129 [Repealed by FA 1997, s. 76 and Sch. 10, para. 1(1) and s. 113 and Sch. 18, Pt. VI(10).]

History – S. 129 repealed by FA 1997, s. 76 and Sch. 10, para. 1(1) and s. 113 and Sch. 18, Pt. VI(10), with effect in relation to, and to transfers under, any arrangement made on or after 1 July 1997 (SI 1997/991 (c. 33)).

129A Stock lending: interest on cash collateral

129A [Repealed by FA 1997, s. 76 and Sch. 10, para. 1(2) and s. 113 and Sch. 18, Pt. VI(10).]

History – S. 129A repealed by FA 1997, s. 76 and Sch. 10, para. 1(2) and s. 113 and Sch. 18, Pt. VI(10), with effect in relation to, and to transfers under, any arrangement made on or after 1 July 1997 by SI 1997/991 (c. 33).

129B Stock lending fees

129B(1) The income which, as income deriving from investments of a description specified in any of the relevant provisions, is eligible for relief from tax by virtue of that provision shall be taken to include any relevant stock lending fee.

129B(2) For the purposes of this section the relevant provisions are sections 613(4) and 614(3) and section 186 of the Finance Act 2004.

129B(3) In this section **"relevant stock lending fee"**, in relation to investments of any description, means any amount, in the nature of a fee, which is payable in connection with any stock lending arrangement relating to investments which, but for any transfer under the arrangement, would be investments of that description.

129B(4) In this section **"stock lending arrangement"** has the same meaning as in section 263B of the 1992 Act.

History – In s. 129B(2), the words "sections 613(4) and 614(3) and section 186 of the Finance Act 2004" substituted for the words "sections 592(2), 608(2)(a), 613(4), 614(3), 620(6) and 643(2)" by FA 2004, s. 281 and Sch. 35, para. 6 with effect from 6 April 2006 (FA 2004, s. 284(1)).
In s. 129B(3), the word "any" is substituted for the words "an approved" by FA 1997, s. 76 and Sch. 10, para. 2(1), with effect in relation to, and to transfers under, any arrangement made on or after 1 July 1997, for the purposes of FA 1997, Sch. 10, para. 7(1) by virtue of SI 1997/991.
S. 129B(4) is substituted by FA 1997, s. 76 and Sch. 10, para. 2(2), with effect in relation to, and to transfers under, any arrangement made on or after 1 July 1997, for the purposes of FA 1997, Sch. 10, para. 12(4).
S. 129B inserted by FA 1996, s. 157 in relation to any arrangements entered into on or after 2 January 1996

Cross references – S. 592(2): exemption for certain income from investments or deposits of exempt approved retirement benefit schemes.
S. 608(2)(a): exemption from income tax for income from investments and deposits of an approved superannuation fund.
S. 613(4): exemption from income tax for income from Parliamentary pension funds.
S. 614(3): exemption for income derived from investments or deposits of certain overseas pension funds.
S. 620(6): exemption from income tax for income from funds maintained to provide retirement annuities for individuals in or connected with particular occupations.
S. 643(2): exemption from income tax for income from investments and deposits held by a person for the purposes of an approved personal pension scheme.
S. 659D: treatment of income from property investment LLPs.

130 Meaning of "investment company" in Part 4.

130 In this Part of this Act–

"investment company", means any company whose business consists wholly or mainly in the making of investments and the principal part of whose income is derived therefrom, but includes any savings bank or other bank for savings except any which, for the purposes of the Trustee Savings Bank Act 1985, is a successor or a further successor to a trustee savings bank.

History – Definition of "company with investment business" omitted by CTA 2009, s. 1322 and Sch. 1, para. 94(2–3) and repealed by Sch. 3, Pt. 1 and section heading accordingly changed with effect for corporation tax purposes for accounting periods ending on or after 1 April 2009, and for income tax and capital gains tax purposes for the tax year 2009–10 and subsequent tax years.
Former definition of "company with investment business" inserted and section heading accordingly changed by FA 2004, s. 38(3) and (4) with effect for accounting periods beginning on or after 1 April 2004, subject to the transitional provisions in FA 2004, s. 43 and 44 and Sch. 6 (FA 2004, s. 42).

Derivations – ICTA 1970, s. 304(5), as amended by FA 1980, s. 59(2) and Sch. 11, para. 1, and by TSBA 1981, Sch. 6, para. 1 (and see also TSBA 1985, Sch. 2, para. 6(6)).

Cross references – S. 75: expenses of companies with investment business.
S. 468(4): s. 75 to apply whether or not an authorised unit trust is an investment company.
S. 487(4): a credit union is not to be regarded as an investment company for the purposes of s. 75.
S. 768B: deductions on change in ownership of an investment company.
S. 768C(7): deductions where assets transferred to an investment company within a group.
SI 1997/1154: application of s. 75 to open-ended investment companies (insertion of s. 468(4A)).

HMRC Manuals – Company Taxation, vol. IV, vol. I, CT 817: a company left with income yielding assets after cessation does not automatically become an investment company.

Other material – British Venture Capital Association/Inland Revenue Statement, 26 May 1987 (not reproduced): where the general partner in a venture capital investment fund run through a limited partnership is a company, it will normally be an investment company. Tax Bulletin TB08/04-5: guidance on changes introduced by FA 2004.

Notes – S. 130 rewritten for corporation tax purposes as CTA 2009, s. 1218(1).

PART V – PROVISIONS RELATING TO THE SCHEDULE E CHARGE

Chapter I – Supplementary Charging Provisions of General Application

MISCELLANEOUS PROVISIONS

131 Chargeable emoluments

131 [Omitted by ITEPA 2003, Sch. 6, para. 14 and repealed by ITEPA 2003, Sch. 8, Pt. 1.]

History – S. 131 omitted by ITEPA 2003, Sch. 6, para. 14 and repealed by ITEPA 2003, Sch. 8, Pt. 1 which have effect for the tax year 2003–04 and subsequent tax years.

Notes – S. 131(1) has been rewritten into the provisions of ITEPA 2003, s. 10(2), s. 62(2) and s. 327.
S. 131(2) is unnecessary and so has not been rewritten into the provisions of ITEPA 2003.

132 Place of performance, and meaning of emoluments received in the UK

132 [Omitted by ITEPA 2003, Sch. 6, para. 14 and repealed by ITEPA 2003, Sch. 8, Pt. 1.]

History – S. 132 omitted by ITEPA 2003, Sch. 6, para. 14 and repealed by ITEPA 2003, Sch. 8, Pt. 1 which have effect for the tax year 2003–04 and subsequent tax years.

Notes – S. 132 rewritten as follows:
S. 132(1): ITEPA 2003, s. 38.
S. 132(2): ITEPA 2003, s. 39(1) and (2).
S. 132(3): ITEPA 2003, s. 39(3) and s. 383(4).
S. 132(4): ITEPA 2003, s. 25(1), s. 27(1), s. 28(1), (2), (3) and s. 40.
S. 132(5): ITEPA 2003, s. 33(1)–(6) and s. 34(2)–(7).

133 Voluntary pensions

133 [Omitted by ITEPA 2003, Sch. 6, para. 14 and repealed by ITEPA 2003, Sch. 8, Pt. 1.]

History – S. 133 omitted by ITEPA 2003, Sch. 6, para. 14 and repealed by ITEPA 2003, Sch. 8, Pt. 1 which have effect for the tax year 2003–04 and subsequent tax years.

Notes – S. 133 rewritten as follows:
S. 133(1): ITEPA 2003, s. 570 and s. 633.
S. 133(2): ITEPA 2003, s. 570 and s. 615(7).

134 Workers supplied by agencies

134 [Omitted by ITEPA 2003, Sch. 6, para. 14 and repealed by ITEPA 2003, Sch. 8, Pt. 1.]

History – S. 134 omitted by ITEPA 2003, Sch. 6, para. 14 and repealed by ITEPA 2003, Sch. 8, Pt. 1 which have effect for the tax year 2003–04 and subsequent tax years.

Notes – S. 134 rewritten as follows:
S. 134(1): ITEPA 2003, s. 7(5), s. 44(1), (2) and s. 47(1).
S. 134(2): ITEPA 2003, s. 46(1).
S. 134(3): ITEPA 2003, s. 46(1) and (2).
S. 134(4): ITEPA 2003, s. 44(2).
S. 134(5): ITEPA 2003, s. 44(1) and s. 47(2).
S. 134(6): ITEPA 2003, s. 45.
S. 134(7): ITEPA 2003, s. 47(3).

SHAREHOLDINGS, LOANS ETC.

135 Gains by directors and employees from share options

135 [Omitted by ITEPA 2003, Sch. 6, para. 15 and repealed by ITEPA 2003, Sch. 8, Pt. 1.]

History – S. 135 omitted by ITEPA 2003, Sch. 6, para. 15 and repealed by ITEPA 2003, Sch. 8, Pt. 1 which have effect for the tax year 2003–04 and subsequent tax years.

Cross references – ITEPA 2003, Sch. 7, para. 67(1) (Sch. 7: transitionals and savings): share options (includes a reference to s. 135); para. 67 applies where certain transactions occurred in the tax year 2002–03.
ITEPA 2003, Sch. 7, para. 82(3) (Sch. 7: transitionals and savings): enterprise management incentives (includes a reference to s. 135); para. 82 relates to the operation of ITEPA 2003, s. 541(2) (effects on tax charges where shares cease to be conditional only or are converted) in relation to a FA 2000 option which was exercised before 6 April 2003.

Notes – S. 135(1): ITEPA 2003, s. 7(6), s. 10(3), s. 471(1), (2), s. 476(1), (2), (4) and s. 478(1).
S. 135(2) has been rewritten into the provision of ITEPA 2003, s. 474.
S. 135(3): ITEPA 2003, s. 479(1), (2), s. 480(1), (2) and s. 484(2).
S. 135(4): ITEPA 2003, s. 479(3), s. 480(3) and s. 484(3).
S. 135(5): ITEPA 2003, s. 475(1), (2) and s. 478(2).
S. 135(6): ITEPA 2003, s. 471(1), s. 477(1), (2), s. 478(1), s. 479(2) and s. 480(2).
S. 135(7): ITEPA 2003, s. 477(5) and (6).
S. 135(8): ITEPA 2003, s. 483(1).
S. 135(9) is unnecessary and so has not been rewritten into the provisions of ITEPA 2003.

136 Provisions supplementary to section 135

136 [Omitted by ITEPA 2003, Sch. 6, para. 15 and repealed by ITEPA 2003, Sch. 8, Pt. 1.]

History – S. 136 omitted by ITEPA 2003, Sch. 6, para. 15 and repealed by ITEPA 2003, Sch. 8, Pt. 1 which have effect for the tax year 2003–04 and subsequent tax years.

Notes – S. 136 rewritten as follows:
S. 136(1): ITEPA 2003, s. 485(1)–(4).
S. 136(2): ITEPA 2003, s. 485(5).
S. 136(3): ITEPA 2003, s. 485(6).
S. 136(4) is spent and so has not been rewritten into the provisions of ITEPA 2003.
S. 136(5): ITEPA 2003, s. 483(2) and s. 487(1).
S. 136(6): ITEPA 2003, s. 486(1)–(3).
S. 136(7): ITEPA 2003, s. 486(5).
S. 136(8): ITEPA 2003, s. 486(4).

137 Payment of tax under section 135 by instalments

137 [Omitted by ITEPA 2003, Sch. 6, para. 15 and repealed by ITEPA 2003, Sch. 8, Pt. 1.]

History – S. 137 omitted by ITEPA 2003, Sch. 6, para. 15 and repealed by ITEPA 2003, Sch. 8, Pt. 1 which have effect for the tax year 2003–04 and subsequent tax years.

Notes – S. 137 is spent and so has not been rewritten into the provisions of ITEPA 2003.

138 Share acquisitions by directors and employees

138 [Omitted by FA 2008, s. 50(1). Previously repealed by FA 1988, s. 148 and Sch. 14, Pt. VI, in relation to acquisitions on or after 26 October 1987.]

History – S. 138 omitted by FA 2008, s. 50(1), with effect for the tax year 2008–09 and subsequent tax years.
S. 138 repealed by FA 1988, s. 148 in relation to acquisitions of shares or interests in shares on or after 26 October 1987. Until its omission by FA 2008, s. 138 continued to apply in relation to shares or interests in shares acquired before 26 October 1987, as confirmed in ITEPA 2003, s. 418(4) and ITEPA 2003, Sch. 7, para. 57 which have effect for the tax year 2003–04 and subsequent tax years.

139 Provisions supplementary to section 138

139 [Omitted by FA 2008, s. 50(1). Previously repealed by FA 1988, s. 148 and Sch. 14, Pt. VI, in relation to acquisitions on or after 26 October 1987.]

History – S. 139 omitted by FA 2008, s. 50(1), with effect for the tax year 2008–09 and subsequent tax years.
S. 139 repealed by FA 1988, s. 148 in relation to shares or interests in shares acquired on or after 26 October 1987. Until its omission by FA 2008, s. 139 continued to apply in relation to shares or interests in shares acquired before 26 October 1987, as confirmed in ITEPA 2003, s. 418(4) and ITEPA 2003, Sch. 7, para. 57 which have effect for the tax year 2003–04 and subsequent tax years.

Notes – ITEPA 2003, Sch. 7, para. 57(a) provides that ICTA 1988, s. 139 continues to apply in relation to shares or interests in shares acquired before 26 October 1987.

140 Further interpretation of sections 135 to 139

140 [Omitted by ITEPA 2003, Sch. 6, para. 17 and repealed by ITEPA 2003, Sch. 8, Pt. 1, except, as applicable to ICTA 1988, s. 138 and s. 139, in relation to acquisitions before 26 October 1987.]

History – S. 140 omitted by ITEPA 2003, Sch. 6, para. 17 and repealed by ITEPA 2003, Sch. 8, Pt. 1 which have effect for the tax year 2003–04 and subsequent tax years. However, s. 140, as it applies to ICTA 1988, s. 138 and s. 139, continues to apply in relation to shares or interests in shares acquired before 26 October 1987, by virtue of ITEPA 2003, s. 418(4) and ITEPA 2003, Sch. 7, para. 57 which have effect for the tax year 2003–04 and subsequent tax years.

140A Conditional acquisition of shares

140A [Omitted by ITEPA 2003, Sch. 6, para. 18 and repealed by ITEPA 2003, Sch. 8, Pt. 1.]

History – S. 140A omitted by ITEPA 2003, Sch. 6, para. 18 and repealed by ITEPA 2003, Sch. 8, Pt. 1 which have effect for the tax year 2003–04 and subsequent tax years.
S. 140A(2) repealed by FA 1999, s. 42(2), s. 139 and Sch. 20, Pt. III(8), with effect in relation to shares acquired on or after 27 July 1999.
S. 140A inserted by FA 1998, s. 50(1), in relation to interests acquired on or after 17 March 1998.

140B Consideration for shares conditionally acquired

140B [Omitted by ITEPA 2003, Sch. 6, para. 18 and repealed by ITEPA 2003, Sch. 8, Pt. 1.]

History – S. 140B omitted by ITEPA 2003, Sch. 6, para. 18 and repealed by ITEPA 2003, Sch. 8, Pt. 1 which have effect for the tax year 2003–04 and subsequent tax years.

Notes – S. 140B rewritten as follows:
S. 140B(1): ITEPA 2003, s. 429(1).
S. 140B(2): ITEPA 2003, s. 429(2).
S. 140B(3): ITEPA 2003, s. 429(3).
S. 140B(4): ITEPA 2003, s. 429(4).
S. 140B(5): ITEPA 2003, s. 429(5).
S. 140B(6): ITEPA 2003, s. 429(6).
S. 140B(7): ITEPA 2003, s. 430(1)–(5).

140C Cases where interest to be treated as only conditional

140C [Omitted by ITEPA 2003, Sch. 6, para. 18 and repealed by ITEPA 2003, Sch. 8, Pt. 1.]

History – S. 140C omitted by ITEPA 2003, Sch. 6, para. 18 and repealed by ITEPA 2003, Sch. 8, Pt. 1 which have effect for the tax year 2003–04 and subsequent tax years.

Notes – S. 140C rewritten as follows:
S. 140C(1): ITEPA 2003, s. 424(1), (4) and s. 434(1) ("market value").
S. 140C(1A): ITEPA 2003, s. 424(2).
S. 140C(2): ITEPA 2003, s. 424(2).
S. 140C(3): ITEPA 2003, s. 424(2) and (6).
S. 140C(3A): ITEPA 2003, s. 424(2) and (6).
S. 140C(4): ITEPA 2003, s. 424(2).
S. 140C(5): ITEPA 2003, s. 424(3).
S. 140C(6): ITEPA 2003, s. 424(7).

140D Convertible shares

140D [Omitted by ITEPA 2003, Sch. 6, para. 18 and repealed by ITEPA 2003, Sch. 8, Pt. 1.]

History – S. 140D omitted by ITEPA 2003, Sch. 6, para. 18 and repealed by ITEPA 2003, Sch. 8, Pt. 1 which have effect for the tax year 2003–04 and subsequent tax years.

Notes – S. 140D rewritten as follows:
S. 140D(1): ITEPA 2003, s. 435(1).
S. 140D(2): ITEPA 2003, s. 435(2).
S. 140D(3): ITEPA 2003, s. 7(6), s. 10(3), s. 438(1) and (2).
S. 140D(4): ITEPA 2003, s. 7(6), s. 10(3), s. 438(2) and (3).
S. 140D(5): ITEPA 2003, s. 439(1).
S. 140D(6): ITEPA 2003, s. 439(2) and (3).
S. 140D(7): ITEPA 2003, s. 439(6).
S. 140D(8): ITEPA 2003, s. 440(1).
S. 140D(9): ITEPA 2003, s. 440(2) and (3).
S. 140D(10): ITEPA 2003, s. 441.

140E Consideration for convertible shares

140E [Omitted by ITEPA 2003, Sch. 6, para. 18 and repealed by ITEPA 2003, Sch. 8, Pt. 1.]

History – S. 140E omitted by ITEPA 2003, Sch. 6, para. 18 and repealed by ITEPA 2003, Sch. 8, Pt. 1 which have effect for the tax year 2003–04 and subsequent tax years.

Notes – S. 140E rewritten as follows:
S. 140E(1): ITEPA 2003, s. 442(1).
S. 140E(2): ITEPA 2003, s. 442(2).
S. 140E(3): ITEPA 2003, s. 442(3).
S. 140E(4): ITEPA 2003, s. 442(4).
S. 140E(5): ITEPA 2003, s. 442(5).
S. 140E(6): ITEPA 2003, s. 442(6).
S. 140E(7): ITEPA 2003, 443(1)–(5).

140F Supplemental provision with respect to convertible shares

140F [Omitted by ITEPA 2003, Sch. 6, para. 18 and repealed by ITEPA 2003, Sch. 8, Pt. 1.]

History – S. 140F omitted by ITEPA 2003, Sch. 6, para. 18 and repealed by ITEPA 2003, Sch. 8, Pt. 1 which have effect for the tax year 2003–04 and subsequent tax years.

Notes – S. 140F rewritten as follows:
S. 140F(1): ITEPA 2003, s. 444.
S. 140F(2): ITEPA 2003, s. 435(3).
S. 140F(3): ITEPA 2003, s. 439(5).
S. 140F(4): ITEPA 2003, s. 440(5).
S. 140F(5): ITEPA 2003, s. 440(4).
S. 140F(6): ITEPA 2003, s. 435(1), s. 439(2), s. 442(1) and (2).
S. 140F(7): ITEPA 2003, s. 719.

140G Information for the purposes of sections 140A to 140F

140G [Omitted by ITEPA 2003, Sch. 6, para. 18 and repealed by ITEPA 2003, Sch. 8, Pt. 1.]

History – S. 140G omitted by ITEPA 2003, Sch. 6, para. 18 and repealed by ITEPA 2003, Sch. 8, Pt. 1 which have effect for the tax year 2003–04 and subsequent tax years.

Cross references – ITEPA 2003, Sch. 7, para. 47 (Sch. 7: transitionals and savings): conditional interests in shares – operation of ITEPA 2003, s. 432 (duty to notify provision of conditional interests in shares) where, in the tax year 2002–03, a person provided an individual with a conditional interest in shares in certain circumstances.
ITEPA 2003, Sch. 7, para. 48 (Sch. 7: transitionals and savings): conditional interests in shares – operation of ITEPA 2003, s. 433 (duty to notify events resulting in charges under s. 427) where, in the tax year 2002–03, the conditions, pertaining to the interest in shares, cease in certain circumstances.
ITEPA 2003, Sch. 7, para. 53 (Sch. 7: transitionals and savings): convertible shares – operation of ITEPA 2003, s. 445 (duty to notify conversions of shares) where shares, provided to an individual, are converted in the tax year 2002–03 in certain circumstances.
ITEPA 2003, Sch. 7, para. 60 (Sch. 7: transitionals and savings): post-acquisition benefits from shares – operation of ITEPA 2003, s. 465 (general duty to notify acquisitions of shares or interests in shares) where any acquisition of shares or an interest in shares within s. 465(1) ibid. was made in the tax year 2002–03.

Notes – S. 140G rewritten as follows:
S. 140G(1): ITEPA 2003, s. 432(1) and (2).
S. 140G(2): ITEPA 2003, s. 433(1) and (2).

ICTA 1988

S. 140G(3): ITEPA 2003, s. 445(1) and (2).
S. 140G(4): ITEPA 2003, s. 432(2), s. 433(2) and s. 445(2).
S. 140G(5): ITEPA 2003, s. 432(3), s. 433(3) and s. 445(3).
S. 140G(6): ITEPA 2003, s. 434(1) ("shares"), s. 435(2), s. 445(1) and (2).

140H Construction of sections 140A to 140G

140H [Omitted by ITEPA 2003, Sch. 6, para. 18 and repealed by ITEPA 2003, Sch. 8, Pt. 1.]

History – S. 140H omitted by ITEPA 2003, Sch. 6, para. 18 and repealed by ITEPA 2003, Sch. 8, Pt. 1 which have effect for the tax year 2003–04 and subsequent tax years.

Notes – S. 140H rewritten as follows:
S. 140H(1): ITEPA 2003, s. 423(1), s. 434(1) ("shares") and s. 436(1).
S. 140H(2): ITEPA 2003, s. 423(2) and s. 436(2).
S. 140H(3): ITEPA 2003, s. 425 and s. 437.
S. 140H(4): ITEPA 2003, s. 423(3), (4), (5), s. 434(1) ("shares"), s. 436(3), (4) and (5).
S. 140H(5): ITEPA 2003, s. 424(1) and s. 435(2).
S. 140H(6): ITEPA 2003, s. 434(1) ("terms") and s. 446(1) ("terms").
S. 140H(7): ITEPA 2003, s. 423(1), (2), (3), s. 436(1), (2), (3) and s. 437(1).
S. 140H(8): ITEPA 2003, s. 430(6), s. 434(1) ("director", "employee", "shares"), s. 443(6) and s. 446(1) ("director", "employee", "shares").
S. 140H(9): ITEPA 2003, s. 718.

VOUCHERS ETC.

141 Non-cash vouchers

141 [Omitted by ITEPA 2003, Sch. 6, para. 19 and repealed by ITEPA 2003, Sch. 8, Pt. 1.]

History – S. 141 omitted by ITEPA 2003, Sch. 6, para. 19 and repealed by ITEPA 2003, Sch. 8, Pt. 1 which have effect for the tax year 2003–04 and subsequent tax years.

Notes – S. 141 rewritten as follows:
S. 141(1): ITEPA 2003, s. 7(5), s. 82(1), s. 87(1), (2), (3), s. 88 and s. 95(1), (2) and (3).
S. 141(2): ITEPA 2003, s. 88.
S. 141(3): ITEPA 2003, s. 328(1), s. 329(1), (5), s. 353(4) and s. 362.
S. 141(4): ITEPA 2003, s. 87(2).
S. 141(5): ITEPA 2003, s. 82(3).
S. 141(6): ITEPA 2003, s. 86(1) and (2).
S. 141(6A): ITEPA 2003, s. 266(1).
S. 141(6B): ITEPA 2003, s. 266(1).
S. 141(6C): ITEPA 2003, s. 268(1)–(5).
S. 141(7): ITEPA 2003, s. 84(1), (2), (3), (4), s. 86(3), s. 87(4), s. 95(4) and s. 721(1).

142 Credit-tokens

142 [Omitted by ITEPA 2003, Sch. 6, para. 19 and repealed by ITEPA 2003, Sch. 8, Pt. 1.]

History – S. 142 omitted by ITEPA 2003, Sch. 6, para. 19 and repealed by ITEPA 2003, Sch. 8, Pt. 1 which have effect for the tax year 2003–04 and subsequent tax years.

Notes – S. 142 rewritten as follows:
S. 142(1): ITEPA 2003, s. 7(5), s. 90(1), s. 94(1)–(3) and s. 95(1)–(3).
S. 142(2): ITEPA 2003, s. 328(1), s. 329(1) and s. 363.
S. 142(3): ITEPA 2003, s. 94(1)–(3), s. 329(5) and s. 353(4).
S. 142(3A) and (3B): ITEPA 2003, s. 267.
S. 142(3C): ITEPA 2003, s. 268(1)–(5).
S. 142(3D): ITEPA 2003, s. 268(2), (3) and (6).
S. 142(4): ITEPA 2003, s. 92(1), (2), (4) and s. 721(1) ("credit token").
S. 142(5): ITEPA 2003, s. 92(3).

143 Cash vouchers taxable under P.A.Y.E.

143 [Omitted by ITEPA 2003, Sch. 6, para. 19 and repealed by ITEPA 2003, Sch. 8, Pt. 1.]

History – S. 143 omitted by ITEPA 2003, Sch. 6, para. 19 and repealed by ITEPA 2003, Sch. 8, Pt. 1 which have effect for the tax year 2003–04 and subsequent tax years.

Notes – S. 143 rewritten as follows:
S. 143(1): ITEPA 2003, s. 7(5), s. 73(1), s. 81, s. 95(1) and (2).
S. 143(2): ITEPA 2003, s. 73(3).
S. 143(3): ITEPA 2003, s. 75 and s. 80.
S. 143(4): ITEPA 2003, s. 76.
S. 143(5): ITEPA 2003, s. 79.

144 Supplementary provisions

144 [Omitted by ITEPA 2003, Sch. 6, para. 19 and repealed by ITEPA 2003, Sch. 8, Pt. 1.]

History – S. 144 omitted by ITEPA 2003, Sch. 6, para. 19 and repealed by ITEPA 2003, Sch. 8, Pt. 1 which have effect for the tax year 2003–04 and subsequent tax years.

Notes – S. 144 rewritten as follows:
S. 144(1): ITEPA 2003, s. 96(1)–(4).
S. 144(2): ITEPA 2003, s. 96(5)–(8).
S. 144(3): ITEPA 2003, s. 77, s. 87(6) and s. 94(4).

S. 144(4): ITEPA 2003, s. 73(2), s. 74, s. 82(2), s. 83, s. 90(2) and s. 91.
S. 144(4A): ITEPA 2003, s. 91 and s. 95.
S. 144(5): ITEPA 2003, s. 66, s. 75, s. 84, s. 92(1) and s. 721(4).

144A Payments etc. received free of tax

144A [Omitted by ITEPA 2003, Sch. 6, para. 20 and repealed by ITEPA 2003, Sch. 8, Pt. 1.]

History – S. 144A omitted by ITEPA 2003, Sch. 6, para. 20 and repealed by ITEPA 2003, Sch. 8, Pt. 1 which have effect for the tax year 2003–04 and subsequent tax years.

Notes – S. 144A rewritten as follows:
S. 144A(1): ITEPA 2003, s. 7(5), s. 222(1) and (2).
S. 144A(2): ITEPA 2003, s. 222(3).

LIVING ACCOMMODATION

145 Living accommodation provided for employee

145 [Omitted by ITEPA 2003, Sch. 6, para. 21 and repealed by ITEPA 2003, Sch. 8, Pt. 1.]

History – S. 145 omitted by ITEPA 2003, Sch. 6, para. 21 and repealed by ITEPA 2003, Sch. 8, Pt. 1 which have effect for the tax year 2003–04 and subsequent tax years.

Notes – S. 145 rewritten as follows:
S. 145(1): ITEPA 2003, s. 7(5), s. 97(1), s. 102(1) and s. 105(2).
S. 145(2): ITEPA 2003, s. 105(3) and (4).
S. 145(3): ITEPA 2003, s. 328(1), s. 329(1), (5), s. 353(4) and s. 364.
S. 145(4): ITEPA 2003, s. 99(1), (2), s. 100 and s. 314.
S. 145(5): ITEPA 2003, s. 99(3) and (4).
S. 145(6): ITEPA 2003, s. 97(1).
S. 145(7): ITEPA 2003, s. 97(2) and s. 98.
S. 145(8): ITEPA 2003, s. 66, s. 67, s. 68, s. 69, s. 99(5) and s. 721(5).

146 Additional charge in respect of certain living accommodation

146 [Omitted by ITEPA 2003, Sch. 6, para. 21 and repealed by ITEPA 2003, Sch. 8, Pt. 1.]

History – S. 146 omitted by ITEPA 2003, Sch. 6, para. 21 and repealed by ITEPA 2003, Sch. 8, Pt. 1 which have effect for the tax year 2003–04 and subsequent tax years.

Other material – Taxline 2000/8 (not reproduced): the inclusion of shadow directors within the charge.

Notes – S. 146 rewritten as follows:
S. 146(1): ITEPA 2003, s. 97(1), s. 98, s. 99(1), (2), s. 100, s. 102(1), s. 105(1) and s. 106(1).
S. 146(2): ITEPA 2003, s. 7(5), s. 106(2) and (3).
S. 146(3): ITEPA 2003, s. 106(2).
S. 146(4): ITEPA 2003, s. 104, s. 106(2) and s. 107(3).
S. 146(5): ITEPA 2003, s. 104, s. 106(2) and s. 107(3).
S. 146(6): ITEPA 2003, s. 107(2) and (3).
S. 146(7): ITEPA 2003, s. 112.
S. 146(8): ITEPA 2003, Sch. 7, para. 21.
S. 146(9): ITEPA 2003, s. 328(1), s. 329(1) and s. 364.
S. 146(10): ITEPA 2003, s. 66 and s. 97.
S. 146(11): ITEPA 2003, s. 104, s. 106(2), s. 107(3), (4), s. 113 and s. 718.

146A Priority of rules applying to living accommodation

146A [Omitted by ITEPA 2003, Sch. 6, para. 21 and repealed by ITEPA 2003, Sch. 8, Pt. 1.]

History – S. 146A omitted by ITEPA 2003, Sch. 6, para. 21 and repealed by ITEPA 2003, Sch. 8, Pt. 1 which have effect for the tax year 2003–04 and subsequent tax years.

Notes – S. 146A rewritten as ITEPA 2003, s. 64(1), (2) and s. 109.

147 Occupation of Chevening House

147 [Omitted by ITEPA 2003, Sch. 6, para. 21 and repealed by ITEPA 2003, Sch. 8, Pt. 1.]

History – S. 147 omitted by ITEPA 2003, Sch. 6, para. 21 and repealed by ITEPA 2003, Sch. 8, Pt. 1 which have effect for the tax year 2003–04 and subsequent tax years.

Notes – S. 147 rewritten as ITEPA 2003, s. 101.

PAYMENTS ON RETIREMENT, SICK PAY ETC.

148 Payments and other benefits in connection with termination of employment, etc.

148 [Omitted by ITEPA 2003, Sch. 6, para. 22 and repealed by ITEPA 2003, Sch. 8, Pt. 1.]

History – S. 148 omitted by ITEPA 2003, Sch. 6, para. 22 and repealed by ITEPA 2003, Sch. 8, Pt. 1 which have effect for the tax year 2003–04 and subsequent tax years.

Notes – S. 148 rewritten as follows:
S. 148(1): ITEPA 2003, s. 401(1), (3), s. 403(1), (4) and s. 404.
S. 148(2): ITEPA 2003, s. 402(1).

S. 148(2A): ITEPA 2003, s. 239(1), (2), s. 310(1), s. 402(2), (3) and s. 405.
S. 148(3): ITEPA 2003, s. 7(6), s. 10(3), s. 402(4), s. 403(1) and (2).
S. 148(4): ITEPA 2003, s. 403(3).
S. 148(5) has not been rewritten into the provisions of ITEPA 2003 as it is unnecessary.
S. 148(6): ITEPA 2003, s. 401(1), (4), s. 403(5), s. 404, s. 406, s. 407, s. 411, s. 412, s. 413(1), (3)–(6), s. 414(1)–(5), s. 415 and s. 416.
S. 148(7): ITEPA 2003, s. 5(1) and (2).

149 Sick pay

149 [Omitted by ITEPA 2003, Sch. 6, para. 22 and repealed by ITEPA 2003, Sch. 8, Pt. 1.]

History – S. 149 omitted by ITEPA 2003, Sch. 6, para. 22 and repealed by ITEPA 2003, Sch. 8, Pt. 1 which have effect for the tax year 2003–04 and subsequent tax years.

Notes – S. 149 rewritten as follows:
S. 149(1): ITEPA 2003, s. 7(5), s. 221(1)–(3) and (5)–(7).
S. 149(2): ITEPA 2003, s. 221(4).
S. 149(3): ITEPA 2003, s. 221(5)–(7) and s. 721(4).

150 Job release scheme allowances, maternity pay and statutory sick pay

150 [Omitted by ITEPA 2003, Sch. 6, para. 22 and repealed by ITEPA 2003, Sch. 8, Pt. 1.]

History – S. 150 omitted by ITEPA 2003, Sch. 6, para. 22 and repealed by ITEPA 2003, Sch. 8, Pt. 1 which have effect for the tax year 2003–04 and subsequent tax years.

Notes – S. 150(a) and (b) are spent and so have not been rewritten into the provisions of ITEPA 2003.
S. 150(c)–(e)rewritten as ITEPA 2003, s. 660.

151 Income support etc.

151 [Omitted by ITEPA 2003, Sch. 6, para. 22 and repealed by ITEPA 2003, Sch. 8, Pt. 1.]

History – S. 151 omitted by ITEPA 2003, Sch. 6, para. 22 and repealed by ITEPA 2003, Sch. 8, Pt. 1 which have effect for the tax year 2003–04 and subsequent tax years.

Notes – S. 151 rewritten as follows:
S. 151(1): ITEPA 2003, s. 660 and s. 665(1).
S. 151(2): ITEPA 2003, s. 665(2) and s. 669(1).
S. 151(3): ITEPA 2003, s. 667.
S. 151(4) is spent and so has not been rewritten into the provisions of ITEPA 2003.
S. 151(5): ITEPA 2003, s. 668.
S. 151(6) is spent and so has not been rewritten into the provisions of ITEPA 2003.
S. 151(7): ITEPA 2003, s. 668 and s. 669(1).
S. 151(8) is spent and so has not been rewritten into the provisions of ITEPA 2003.
S. 151(9): ITEPA 2003, s. 669(2).

151A Jobseeker's allowance

151A [Omitted by ITEPA 2003, Sch. 6, para. 22 and repealed by ITEPA 2003, Sch. 8, Pt. 1.]

History – S. 151A omitted by ITEPA 2003, Sch. 6, para. 22 and repealed by ITEPA 2003, Sch. 8, Pt. 1 which have effect for the tax year 2003–04 and subsequent tax years.

Notes – S. 151A rewritten as follows:
S. 151A(1): ITEPA 2003, s. 660.
S. 151A(2): ITEPA 2003, s. 671.
S. 151A(3): ITEPA 2003, s. 672.
S. 151A(4): ITEPA 2003, s. 673(3).
S. 151A(5): ITEPA 2003, s. 674(3).
S. 151A(6): ITEPA 2003, s. 673(2).
S. 151A(7): ITEPA 2003, s. 674(2).
S. 151A(8): ITEPA 2003, s. 673(4).
S. 151A(9): ITEPA 2003, s. 675(1) and (2).

152 Notification of taxable amount of certain benefits

152 [Omitted by TIOPA 2010, s. 371 and Sch. 7, para. 34 and repealed by TIOPA 2010, s. 378 and Sch. 10, Pt. 12.]

History – S. 152 omitted by TIOPA 2010, s. 371 and Sch. 7, para. 34 and repealed by TIOPA 2010, s. 378 and Sch. 10, Pt. 12, with effect for corporation tax purposes for accounting periods ending on or after 1 April 2010, for income tax and capital gains tax purposes for the tax year 2010–11 and subsequent tax years, and for petroleum revenue tax purposes for chargeable periods beginning on or after 1 July 2010.

Notes – S. 152 rewritten in TIOPA 2010, Sch. 7, para. 32.

Chapter II – Employees Earning £8,500 or More and Directors

History – Heading to Pt. V, Ch. II substituted by FA 1989, s. 53(2)(a).

EXPENSES

153 Payments in respect of expenses

153 [Omitted by ITEPA 2003, Sch. 6, para. 24 and repealed by ITEPA 2003, Sch. 8, Pt. 1.]

History – S. 153 omitted by ITEPA 2003, Sch. 6, para. 24 and repealed by ITEPA 2003, Sch. 8, Pt. 1 which have effect for the tax year 2003–04 and subsequent tax years.

Notes – S. 153 rewritten as follows:
S. 153(1): ITEPA 2003, s. 7(5), s. 70(1), (3)–(5) and s. 72(1).
S. 153(2): ITEPA 2003, s. 72(2) and (3).
S. 153(3): ITEPA 2003, s. 70(2).

BENEFITS IN KIND

154 General charging provision

154 [Omitted by ITEPA 2003, Sch. 6, para. 24 and repealed by ITEPA 2003, Sch. 8, Pt. 1.]

History – S. 154 omitted by ITEPA 2003, Sch. 6, para. 24 and repealed by ITEPA 2003, Sch. 8, Pt. 1 which have effect for the tax year 2003–04 and subsequent tax years.

Notes – S. 154 rewritten as follows:
S. 154(1): ITEPA 2003, s. 7(5), s. 201(1), (2), (4) and s. 203(1).
S. 154(2): ITEPA 2003, s. 201(2) and s. 202.
S. 154(3): ITEPA 2003, s. 209.

155 Exceptions from the general charge

155 [Omitted by ITEPA 2003, Sch. 6, para. 24 and repealed by ITEPA 2003, Sch. 8, Pt. 1.]

History – S. 155 omitted by ITEPA 2003, Sch. 6, para. 24 and repealed by ITEPA 2003, Sch. 8, Pt. 1 which have effect for the tax year 2003–04 and subsequent tax years.

Notes – S. 155 rewritten as follows:
S. 155(1): ITEPA 2003, s. 239(4), (5) and s. 240(3).
S. 155(1A): ITEPA 2003, s. 237(1) and (3).
S. 155(1B): ITEPA 2003, s. 240(2), (4) and s. 241(1).
S. 155(1C): ITEPA 2003, s. 240(4) and s. 241.
S. 155(2) was repealed by FA 2000, s. 156 and Sch. 40, Pt. II(2) and so has not been rewritten into the provisions of ITEPA.
S. 155(3): ITEPA 2003, s. 313.
S. 155(4): ITEPA 2003, s. 307(1) and (2).
S. 155(5): ITEPA 2003, s. 317(1).
S. 155(6): ITEPA 2003, s. 325.
S. 155(7): ITEPA 2003, s. 265 and s. 718.

155ZA Accommodation, supplies or services used in performing duties of employment

155ZA [Omitted by ITEPA 2003, Sch. 6, para. 24 and repealed by ITEPA 2003, Sch. 8, Pt. 1.]

History – S. 155ZA omitted by ITEPA 2003, Sch. 6, para. 24 and repealed by ITEPA 2003, Sch. 8, Pt. 1 which have effect for the tax year 2003–04 and subsequent tax years.

Notes – S. 155ZA rewritten as follows:
S. 155ZA(1): ITEPA 2003, s. 316(1).
S. 155ZA(2): ITEPA 2003, s. 316(2).
S. 155ZA(3): ITEPA 2003, s. 316(4).
S. 155ZA(4): ITEPA 2003, s. 316(6) and (7).
S. 155ZA(5): ITEPA 2003, s. 316(5).
S. 155ZA(6): ITEPA 2003, s. 316(3).

155ZB Power to provide for exemption of minor benefits

155ZB [Omitted by ITEPA 2003, Sch. 6, para. 24 and repealed by ITEPA 2003, Sch. 8, Pt. 1.]

History – S. 155ZB omitted by ITEPA 2003, Sch. 6, para. 24 and repealed by ITEPA 2003, Sch. 8, Pt. 1 which have effect for the tax year 2003–04 and subsequent tax years.

Notes – S. 155ZB rewritten as follows:
S. 155ZB(1): ITEPA 2003, s. 210(1).
S. 155ZB(2): ITEPA 2003, s. 210(2).
S. 155ZB(3): ITEPA 2003, s. 266(4) and (5).

155AA Mobile telephones

155AA [Omitted by ITEPA 2003, Sch. 6, para. 24 and repealed by ITEPA 2003, Sch. 8, Pt. 1.]

History – S. 155AA omitted by ITEPA 2003, Sch. 6, para. 24 and repealed by ITEPA 2003, Sch. 8, Pt. 1 which have effect for the tax year 2003–04 and subsequent tax years.

Notes – S. 155AA rewritten as follows:
S. 155AA(1): ITEPA 2003, s. 319(1).
S. 155AA(2): ITEPA 2003, s. 319(2) and (3).
S. 155AA(3) is unnecessary and so has not been rewritten into the provisions of ITEPA 2003.
S. 155AA(4) and (5) have been rewritten into the provision of ITEPA 2003, s. 319(3).
S. 155AA(6) is unnecessary and so has not been rewritten into the provisions of ITEPA 2003.

155A Care for children

155A [Omitted by ITEPA 2003, Sch. 6, para. 24 and repealed by ITEPA 2003, Sch. 8, Pt. 1.]

History – S. 155A omitted by ITEPA 2003, Sch. 6, para. 24 and repealed by ITEPA 2003, Sch. 8, Pt. 1 which have effect for the tax year 2003–04 and subsequent tax years.

Notes – S. 155A rewritten as follows:
S. 155A(1): ITEPA 2003, s. 318(1) and (2).
S. 155A(2): ITEPA 2003, s. 318(3) — (6).
S. 155A(3): ITEPA 2003, s. 318(3).
S. 155A(4): ITEPA 2003, s. 318(6).
S. 155A(5): ITEPA 2003, s. 318(7).
S. 155A(6): ITEPA 2003, s. 318(4) and (5).
S. 155A(7): ITEPA 2003, s. 318(3).
S. 155A(8): ITEPA 2003, s. 318(3), (4) and (8).

156 Cash equivalents of benefits charged under section 154

156 [Omitted by ITEPA 2003, Sch. 6, para. 24 and repealed by ITEPA 2003, Sch. 8, Pt. 1.]

History – S. 156 omitted by ITEPA 2003, Sch. 6, para. 24 and repealed by ITEPA 2003, Sch. 8, Pt. 1 which have effect for the tax year 2003–04 and subsequent tax years.

Notes – S. 156 rewritten as follows:
S. 156(1): ITEPA 2003, s. 203(2).
S. 156(2): ITEPA 2003, s. 203(3) and s. 204.
S. 156(3): ITEPA 2003, s. 203(3) and s. 206.
S. 156(4): ITEPA 2003, s. 203(3) and s. 206.
S. 156(5): ITEPA 2003, s. 203(3) and s. 205.
S. 156(6): ITEPA 2003, s. 203(3), s. 205 and s. 207(1).
S. 156(7): ITEPA 2003, s. 203(3) and s. 205.
S. 156(8): ITEPA 2003, s. 328(1), s. 329(1), (5), s. 353(4), s. 365(1) and (2).
S. 156(9): ITEPA 2003, s. 205 and s. 206.

156A Limited exemption for computer equipment

156A [Omitted by ITEPA 2003, Sch. 6, para. 24 and repealed by ITEPA 2003, Sch. 8, Pt. 1.]

History – S. 156A omitted by ITEPA 2003, Sch. 6, para. 24 and repealed by ITEPA 2003, Sch. 8, Pt. 1 which have effect for the tax year 2003–04 and subsequent tax years.

Notes – S. 156A rewritten as follows:
S. 156A(1): ITEPA 2003, s. 320(1), (4) and (5).
S. 156A(2): ITEPA 2003, s. 320(4)–(6).
S. 156A(3): ITEPA 2003, s. 320(1)–(5).
S. 156A(4) and (5) have been rewritten into the provision of ITEPA 2003, s. 320(7).

157 Cars available for private use

157 [Omitted by ITEPA 2003, Sch. 6, para. 24 and repealed by ITEPA 2003, Sch. 8, Pt. 1.]

History – S. 157 omitted by ITEPA 2003, Sch. 6, para. 24 and repealed by ITEPA 2003, Sch. 8, Pt. 1 which have effect for the tax year 2003–04 and subsequent tax years.

Notes – S. 157 rewritten as follows:
S. 157(1): ITEPA 2003, s. 7(5), s. 114(1), (3) and s. 120.
S. 157(2): ITEPA 2003, s. 121(1).
S. 157(3): ITEPA 2003, s. 239(1), (2), s. 269(1) and s. 721(4).
S. 157(4) and (5) were repealed by FA 1993, Sch. 3, para. 2(2) and so have not been rewritten into the provisions of ITEPA 2003.

157A Cars available for private use: cash alternative, etc.

157A [Omitted by ITEPA 2003, Sch. 6, para. 24 and repealed by ITEPA 2003, Sch. 8, Pt. 1.]

History – S. 157A omitted by ITEPA 2003, Sch. 6, para. 24 and repealed by ITEPA 2003, Sch. 8, Pt. 1 which have effect for the tax year 2003–04 and subsequent tax years.

Notes – S. 157A rewritten as ITEPA 2003, s. 119.

158 Car fuel

158 [Omitted by ITEPA 2003, Sch. 6, para. 24 and repealed by ITEPA 2003, Sch. 8, Pt. 1.]

History – S. 158 omitted by ITEPA 2003, Sch. 6, para. 24 and repealed by ITEPA 2003, Sch. 8, Pt. 1 which have effect for the tax year 2003–04 and subsequent tax years.

Notes – S. 158 rewritten as follows:
S. 158(1): ITEPA 2003, s. 7(5) and s. 149(1).
S. 158(2): ITEPA 2003, s. 150(1) and (2).
S. 158(3): ITEPA 2003, s. 149(3) and s. 721(1) ("credit-token", "non-cash voucher").
S. 158(4): ITEPA 2003, s. 170(5) and (6).
S. 158(5): ITEPA 2003, s. 152(1).
S. 158(6): ITEPA 2003, s. 151.
S. 158(6A): ITEPA 2003, s. 152(2).
S. 158(7) was repealed by FA 1998, Sch. 27, Pt. 3(10) and so has not been rewritten into the provisions of ITEPA 2003.
S. 158(8): ITEPA 2003, s. 152(4).
S. 158(9): ITEPA 2003, s. 149(4).

159 Pooled cars

159 [Omitted by ITEPA 2003, Sch. 6, para. 24 and repealed by ITEPA 2003, Sch. 8, Pt. 1.]

History – S. 159 omitted by ITEPA 2003, Sch. 6, para. 24 and repealed by ITEPA 2003, Sch. 8, Pt. 1 which have effect for the tax year 2003–04 and subsequent tax years.

Notes – S. 159 rewritten as follows:
S. 159(1): ITEPA 2003, s. 167(1).
S. 159(2): ITEPA 2003, s. 167(3).
S. 159(3): ITEPA 2003, s. 167(2).
S. 159(4), (5) and (6) were repealed by FA 1996, Sch. 20, para. 8 and so have not been rewritten into the provisions of ITEPA 2003.

159AA Vans available for private use

159AA [Omitted by ITEPA 2003, Sch. 6, para. 24 and repealed by ITEPA 2003, Sch. 8, Pt. 1.]

History – S. 159AA omitted by ITEPA 2003, Sch. 6, para. 24 and repealed by ITEPA 2003, Sch. 8, Pt. 1 which have effect for the tax year 2003–04 and subsequent tax years.

Notes – S. 159AA rewritten as follows:
S. 159AA(1): ITEPA 2003, s. 7(5), s. 114(1), (3) and s. 154.
S. 159AA(2) is unnecessary and so has not been rewritten into the provisions of ITEPA 2003.
S. 159AA(3): ITEPA 2003, s. 239(1), (2), s. 269(1) and s. 721(4).

159AB Pooled vans

159AB [Omitted by ITEPA 2003, Sch. 6, para. 24 and repealed by ITEPA 2003, Sch. 8, Pt. 1.]

History – S. 159AB omitted by ITEPA 2003, Sch. 6, para. 24 and repealed by ITEPA 2003, Sch. 8, Pt. 1 which have effect for the tax year 2003–04 and subsequent tax years.

Notes – S. 159AB: ITEPA 2003, s. 168.

159AC Heavier commercial vehicles available for private use

159AC [Omitted by ITEPA 2003, Sch. 6, para. 24 and repealed by ITEPA 2003, Sch. 8, Pt. 1.]

History – S. 159AC omitted by ITEPA 2003, Sch. 6, para. 24 and repealed by ITEPA 2003, Sch. 8, Pt. 1 which have effect for the tax year 2003–04 and subsequent tax years.

Notes – S. 159AC rewritten as follows:
S. 159AC(1): ITEPA 2003, s. 238(1)–3).
S. 159AC(2): ITEPA 2003, s. 238(1), s. 239(4) and (5).
S. 159AC(3): ITEPA 2003, s. 239(1), (2), s. 269(1) and s. 721(4).
S. 159AC(4): ITEPA 2003, s. 238(4) ("heavy goods vehicle").
S. 159AC(5): ITEPA 2003, s. 238(4) ("private use").

159A Mobile telephones

159A [Repealed by FA 1999, s. 44(2), 139 and Sch. 20, Pt. III(9), with effect for the year 1999–2000 and subsequent years of assessment.]

160 Beneficial loan arrangements

160 [Omitted by ITEPA 2003, Sch. 6, para. 24 and repealed by ITEPA 2003, Sch. 8, Pt. 1.]

History – S. 160 omitted by ITEPA 2003, Sch. 6, para. 24 and repealed by ITEPA 2003, Sch. 8, Pt. 1 which have effect for the tax year 2003–04 and subsequent tax years.

Notes – S. 160 rewritten as follows:
S. 160(1): ITEPA 2003, s. 7(5), s. 174(1), s. 175(1), (2), s. 184(1), (2) and (3).
S. 160(1A): ITEPA 2003, s. 184(2)–(5).
S. 160(1B): ITEPA 2003, s. 187(1), (2), (3) and (5).
S. 160(1BA): ITEPA 2003, s. 187(1) and (4).
S. 160(1C) was repealed by FA 2000, Sch. 10, para. 4(2) and so has not been rewritten into the provisions of ITEPA 2003.
S. 160(2): ITEPA 2003, s. 7(5), s. 174(1) and s. 188(1).
S. 160(3): ITEPA 2003, s. 188(2).
S. 160(3A): ITEPA 2003, s. 188(3).
S. 160(4): ITEPA 2003, s. 174(1), s. 175(3) and (4).
S. 160(4A): ITEPA 2003, s. 191(1), (2) and (5).
S. 160(5): ITEPA 2003, s. 173(2) and s. 181.
S. 160(6): ITEPA 2003, s. 174(6).
S. 160(7): ITEPA 2003, Sch. 7, para. 25.

161 Exceptions from section 160

161 [Omitted by ITEPA 2003, Sch. 6, para. 24 and repealed by ITEPA 2003, Sch. 8, Pt. 1.]

History – S. 161 omitted by ITEPA 2003, Sch. 6, para. 24 and repealed by ITEPA 2003, Sch. 8, Pt. 1 which have effect for the tax year 2003–04 and subsequent tax years.

Notes – S. 161 rewritten as follows:
S. 161(1): ITEPA 2003, s. 180(1)–(3).
S. 161(1A) and (1B) were repealed by FA 2000, Sch. 10, para. 5(4) and so have not been rewritten into the provisions of ITEPA 2003.
S. 161(2): ITEPA 2003, s. 177(1), (2) and (5).
S. 161(3): ITEPA 2003, s. 177(3), (4), (5) and s. 718.
S. 161(4): ITEPA 2003, s. 174(5).
S. 161(5): ITEPA 2003, s. 189.
S. 161(6): ITEPA 2003, s. 190.
S. 161(7): ITEPA 2003, Sch. 7, para. 25.

161A Treatment of qualifying loans

161A [Omitted by ITEPA 2003, Sch. 6, para. 24 and repealed by ITEPA 2003, Sch. 8, Pt. 1.]

History – S. 161A omitted by ITEPA 2003, Sch. 6, para. 24 and repealed by ITEPA 2003, Sch. 8, Pt. 1 which have effect for the tax year 2003–04 and subsequent tax years.

Notes – S. 161A rewritten as follows:
S. 161A(1): ITEPA 2003, s. 180(5).
S. 161A(2): ITEPA 2003, s. 178.

161B Beneficial loans: loans on ordinary commercial terms

161B [Omitted by ITEPA 2003, Sch. 6, para. 24 and repealed by ITEPA 2003, Sch. 8, Pt. 1.]

History – S. 161B omitted by ITEPA 2003, Sch. 6, para. 24 and repealed by ITEPA 2003, Sch. 8, Pt. 1 which have effect for the tax year 2003–04 and subsequent tax years.

Notes – S. 161B rewritten as follows:
S. 161B(1): ITEPA 2003, s. 176(1).
S. 161B(2): ITEPA 2003, s. 176(2).

162 Employee shareholdings

162 [Omitted by ITEPA 2003, Sch. 6, para. 24 and repealed by ITEPA 2003, Sch. 8, Pt. 1.]

History – S. 162 omitted by ITEPA 2003, Sch. 6, para. 24 and repealed by ITEPA 2003, Sch. 8, Pt. 1 which have effect for the tax year 2003–04 and subsequent tax years.

Notes – S. 162 rewritten as follows:
S. 162(1): ITEPA 2003, s. 7(5), s. 192(1), (2), s. 193(1)–(4), s. 197(1) ("employee"), s. 198(3), s. 200(1) ("employee") and Sch. 7, para. 28.
S. 162(2): ITEPA 2003, s. 193(1), (2), (5), s. 194(1) and (2).
S. 162(3): ITEPA 2003, s. 194(1)–(3) and s. 195(1).
S. 162(4): ITEPA 2003, s. 195(1).
S. 162(5): ITEPA 2003, s. 195(2) and (3).
S. 162(6): ITEPA 2003, s. 198(1), (3), s. 199(1), (3) and Sch. 7, para. 30.
S. 162(7): ITEPA 2003, s. 199(4).
S. 162(8): ITEPA 2003, s. 199(2).
S. 162(9): ITEPA 2003, s. 192(1), (2), s. 193(1), (2), s. 194(1), s. 197(1) ("interest in shares"), s. 198(1), s. 199(5) and s. 200(1) ("interest in shares").
S. 162(10): ITEPA 2003, s. 197(1) ("market value", "shares"), (2), (3), s. 200(1) ("market value", "shares"), (2) and s. 718.
S. 162(11): ITEPA 2003, s. 64(1), (2), s. 194(2) and s. 196.

163 Expenses connected with living accommodation

163 [Omitted by ITEPA 2003, Sch. 6, para. 24 and repealed by ITEPA 2003, Sch. 8, Pt. 1.]

History – S. 163 omitted by ITEPA 2003, Sch. 6, para. 24 and repealed by ITEPA 2003, Sch. 8, Pt. 1 which have effect for the tax year 2003–04 and subsequent tax years.

Notes – S. 163 rewritten as follows:
S. 163(1): ITEPA 2003, s. 315(1) and (2).
S. 163(2): ITEPA 2003, s. 315(1) and (3).
S. 163(3): ITEPA 2003, s. 315(3).
S. 163(4): ITEPA 2003, s. 315(4) and (5).
S. 163(5): ITEPA 2003, s. 315(4) and (5).

164 Director's tax paid by employer

164 [Omitted by ITEPA 2003, Sch. 6, para. 24 and repealed by ITEPA 2003, Sch. 8, Pt. 1.]

History – S. 164 omitted by ITEPA 2003, Sch. 6, para. 24 and repealed by ITEPA 2003, Sch. 8, Pt. 1 which have effect for the tax year 2003–04 and subsequent tax years.

Notes – S. 164 rewritten as follows:
S. 164(1): ITEPA 2003, s. 7(5), s. 223(1) — (4) and (6).
S. 164(2): ITEPA 2003, s. 223(7).
S. 164(3): ITEPA 2003, s. 223(5) and (6).

165 Scholarships

165 [Omitted by ITEPA 2003, Sch. 6, para. 24 and repealed by ITEPA 2003, Sch. 8, Pt. 1.]

History – S. 165 omitted by ITEPA 2003, Sch. 6, para. 24 and repealed by ITEPA 2003, Sch. 8, Pt. 1 which have effect for the tax year 2003–04 and subsequent tax years.

Notes – S. 165 rewritten as follows:
S. 165(1): ITEPA 2003, s. 215.
S. 165(2): ITEPA 2003, s. 212.
S. 165(3): ITEPA 2003, s. 213.
S. 165(4) and (5) have been rewritten into the provision of ITEPA 2003, Sch. 7, para. 32.
S. 165(6): ITEPA 2003, s. 212, s. 213 and s. 718.

GENERAL SUPPLEMENTARY PROVISIONS

166 Notice of nil liability under this Chapter

166 [Omitted by ITEPA 2003, Sch. 6, para. 24 and repealed by ITEPA 2003, Sch. 8, Pt. 1.]

History – S. 166 omitted by ITEPA 2003, Sch. 6, para. 24 and repealed by ITEPA 2003, Sch. 8, Pt. 1 which have effect for the tax year 2003–04 and subsequent tax years.

Notes – S. 166 rewritten as follows:
S. 166(1): ITEPA 2003, s. 65(1), (2), (3) and (5).
S. 166(2): ITEPA 2003, s. 65(6) – (9).
S. 166(3) and (4): ITEPA 2003, Sch. 7, para. 15.

167 Employment to which this Chapter applies

167 [Omitted by ITEPA 2003, Sch. 6, para. 24 and repealed by ITEPA 2003, Sch. 8, Pt. 1.]

History – S. 167 omitted by ITEPA 2003, Sch. 6, para. 24 and repealed by ITEPA 2003, Sch. 8, Pt. 1 which have effect for the tax year 2003–04 and subsequent tax years.

Notes – S. 167 rewritten as follows:
S. 167(1): ITEPA 2003, s. 216(1)–(4), s. 217(1) and s. 218(1).
S. 167(2): ITEPA 2003, s. 218(1), (3), (4), s. 219(5) and (6).
S. 167(2A) was repealed by FA 1994, Sch. 26, Pt. V(5) and so has not been rewritten into the provisions of ITEPA 2003.
S. 167(2B): ITEPA 2003, s. 218(1) and s. 219(1)–(4).
S. 167(2C): ITEPA 2003, s. 219(2), (3) and (4).
S. 167(2D): ITEPA 2003, s. 218(1).
S. 167(3): ITEPA 2003, s. 220.
S. 167(4): ITEPA 2003, s. 220(3).
S. 167(5): ITEPA 2003, s. 216(3).

168 Other interpretative provisions

168 [Omitted by ITEPA 2003, Sch. 6, para. 24 and repealed by ITEPA 2003, Sch. 8, Pt. 1.]

History – S. 168 omitted by ITEPA 2003, Sch. 6, para. 24 and repealed by ITEPA 2003, Sch. 8, Pt. 1 which have effect for the tax year 2003–04 and subsequent tax years.

Notes – S. 168 rewritten as follows:
S. 168(1) is unnecessary and so has not been rewritten into the provisions of ITEPA 2003.
S. 168(2): ITEPA 2003, s. 66.
S. 168(3): ITEPA 2003, s. 71, s. 192(3), s. 198(4) and s. 201(3).
S. 168(4): ITEPA 2003, s. 721(5).
S. 168(5): ITEPA 2003, s. 115(1) ("car"), (2) ("goods vehicle", "invalid carriage", "motor cycle"), s. 118(2), s. 171(1) ("business travel"), (2), (3), s. 329(5) and s. 353(4).
S. 168(5A): ITEPA 2003, s. 115(1) ("van"), (2) ("design weight", "goods vehicle", "motor cycle"), s. 118(2), s. 171(1) ("business travel"), (2) and(3).
S. 168(6): ITEPA 2003, s. 117 and s. 118(1).
S. 168(7): ITEPA 2003, s. 208.
S. 168(8): ITEPA 2003, s. 67(1) and s. 223(8).
S. 168(9): ITEPA 2003, s. 67(2) and s. 223(8).
S. 168(10): ITEPA 2003, s. 67(3).
S. 168(11): ITEPA 2003, s. 68 and s. 223(8).
S. 168(12): ITEPA 2003, s. 69.
S. 168(13): ITEPA 2003, s. 721(1) ("tax year").

168A Price of a car as regards a year

168A [Omitted by ITEPA 2003, Sch. 6, para. 24 and repealed by ITEPA 2003, Sch. 8, Pt. 1.]

History – S. 168A omitted by ITEPA 2003, Sch. 6, para. 24 and repealed by ITEPA 2003, Sch. 8, Pt. 1 which have effect for the tax year 2003–04 and subsequent tax years.

Notes – S. 168A rewritten as follows:
S. 168A(1): ITEPA 2003, s. 122 and s. 126(5).
S. 168A(2): ITEPA 2003, s. 123.
S. 168A(3) is unnecessary and so has not been rewritten into the provisions of ITEPA 2003.
S. 168A(4): ITEPA 2003, s. 126(1), (2), s. 127(1) and s. 128(1).
S. 168A(5): ITEPA 2003, s. 126(1), (4) and s. 127(1).
S. 168A(6): ITEPA 2003, s. 126(1), (2), (4) and s. 127(1).
S. 168A(7): ITEPA 2003, s. 126(2) and s. 127(1).
S. 168A(8): ITEPA 2003, s. 124.
S. 168A(9): ITEPA 2003, s. 123, s. 124, s. 125(4), s. 128 and s. 171(1) ("relevant taxes").

S. 168A(10): ITEPA 2003, s. 125(1).
S. 168A(11): ITEPA 2003, s. 125(2).
S. 168A(12): ITEPA 2003, s. 116(2).

168AA Equipment to enable disabled person to use car

168AA [Omitted by ITEPA 2003, Sch. 6, para. 24 and repealed by ITEPA 2003, Sch. 8, Pt. 1.]

History – S. 168AA omitted by ITEPA 2003, Sch. 6, para. 24 and repealed by ITEPA 2003, Sch. 8, Pt. 1 which have effect for the tax year 2003–04 and subsequent tax years.

Notes – S. 168AA rewritten as follows:
S. 168AA(1): ITEPA 2003, s. 172(1).
S. 168AA(2): ITEPA 2003, s. 172(1) and (2).
S. 168AA(3): ITEPA 2003, s. 171(4).
S. 168AA(4): ITEPA 2003, s. 116(2).

168AB Equipment etc. to enable car to run on road fuel gas

168AB [Omitted by ITEPA 2003, Sch. 6, para. 24 and repealed by ITEPA 2003, Sch. 8, Pt. 1.]

History – S. 168AB omitted by ITEPA 2003, Sch. 6, para. 24 and repealed by ITEPA 2003, Sch. 8, Pt. 1 which have effect for the tax year 2003–04 and subsequent tax years.

Notes – S. 168AB rewritten as follows:
S. 168AB(1): ITEPA 2003, s. 125(2).
S. 168AB(2): ITEPA 2003, s. 146(1) and (2).
S. 168AB(3): ITEPA 2003, s. 171(1).
S. 168AB(4): ITEPA 2003, s. 125(3) and s. 146(1).

168B Price of a car: accessories not included in list price

168B [Omitted by ITEPA 2003, Sch. 6, para. 24 and repealed by ITEPA 2003, Sch. 8, Pt. 1.]

History – S. 168B omitted by ITEPA 2003, Sch. 6, para. 24 and repealed by ITEPA 2003, Sch. 8, Pt. 1 which have effect for the tax year 2003–04 and subsequent tax years.

Notes – S. 168B rewritten as follows:
S. 168B(1): ITEPA 2003, s. 126(1) and (2).
S. 168B(2): ITEPA 2003, s. 126(1) and s. 127(1).
S. 168B(3): ITEPA 2003, s. 126(4).
S. 168B(4): ITEPA 2003, s. 129(1).
S. 168B(5): ITEPA 2003, s. 130(1).
S. 168B(6): ITEPA 2003, s. 129(2) and s. 130(2).
S. 168B(7): ITEPA 2003, s. 129(2) and s. 130(2).
S. 168B(8): ITEPA 2003, s. 116(2) s. 125(1) and (2).

168C Price of a car: accessories available after car first made available

168C [Omitted by ITEPA 2003, Sch. 6, para. 24 and repealed by ITEPA 2003, Sch. 8, Pt. 1.]

History – S. 168C omitted by ITEPA 2003, Sch. 6, para. 24 and repealed by ITEPA 2003, Sch. 8, Pt. 1 which have effect for the tax year 2003–04 and subsequent tax years.

Notes – S. 168C rewritten as follows:
S. 168C(1): ITEPA 2003, s. 126(3).
S. 168C(2): ITEPA 2003, s. 126(1) and s. 127(2).
S. 168C(3): ITEPA 2003, s. 116(2), s. 125(1) and (2).
S. 168C(4): ITEPA 2003, s. 126(4), s. 129 and s. 130.
S. 168C(5): ITEPA 2003, s. 170(1) and (2).

168D Price of a car: capital contributions

168D [Omitted by ITEPA 2003, Sch. 6, para. 24 and repealed by ITEPA 2003, Sch. 8, Pt. 1.]

History – S. 168D omitted by ITEPA 2003, Sch. 6, para. 24 and repealed by ITEPA 2003, Sch. 8, Pt. 1 which have effect for the tax year 2003–04 and subsequent tax years.

Notes – S. 168D rewritten as follows:
S. 168D(1): ITEPA 2003, s. 132(1).
S. 168D(2): ITEPA 2003, s. 132(2).
S. 168D(3) and (4) have been rewritten into the provision of ITEPA 2003, s. 132(3).
S. 168D(5): ITEPA 2003, s. 125(1) and (2).
S. 168D(6): ITEPA 2003, s. 170(1) and (2).

168E Price of a car: replacement accessories

168E [Omitted by ITEPA 2003, Sch. 6, para. 24 and repealed by ITEPA 2003, Sch. 8, Pt. 1.]

History – S. 168E omitted by ITEPA 2003, Sch. 6, para. 24 and repealed by ITEPA 2003, Sch. 8, Pt. 1 which have effect for the tax year 2003–04 and subsequent tax years.

Notes – S. 168E is unnecessary and so has not been rewritten into the provisions of ITEPA 2003.

168F Price of a car: classic cars

168F [Omitted by ITEPA 2003, Sch. 6, para. 24 and repealed by ITEPA 2003, Sch. 8, Pt. 1.]

History – S. 168F omitted by ITEPA 2003, Sch. 6, para. 24 and repealed by ITEPA 2003, Sch. 8, Pt. 1 which have effect for the tax year 2003–04 and subsequent tax years.

Notes – S. 168F rewritten as follows:
S. 168F(1): ITEPA 2003, s. 147(1).
S. 168F(2): ITEPA 2003, s. 147(2).
S. 168F(3): ITEPA 2003, s. 147(3) and (4).
S. 168F(4): ITEPA 2003, s. 147(3).
S. 168F(5): ITEPA 2003, s. 147(2), (5) and (6).
S. 168F(6): ITEPA 2003, s. 147(6).
S. 168F(7) and (8) have been rewritten into the provision of ITEPA 2003, s. 147(7).
S. 168F(9): ITEPA 2003, s. 125(1) and (2).
S. 168F(10): ITEPA 2003, s. 116(2).
S. 168F(11): ITEPA 2003, s. 170(1) and (2).

168G Price of a car: cap for expensive car

168G [Omitted by ITEPA 2003, Sch. 6, para. 24 and repealed by ITEPA 2003, Sch. 8, Pt. 1.]

History – S. 168G omitted by ITEPA 2003, Sch. 6, para. 24 and repealed by ITEPA 2003, Sch. 8, Pt. 1 which have effect for the tax year 2003–04 and subsequent tax years.

Notes – S. 168G rewritten as follows:
S. 168G(1): ITEPA 2003, s. 121(1).
S. 168G(2): ITEPA 2003, s. 170(1) and (2).

Chapter III – Profit-Related Pay

History – Ch. III repealed by FA 1997, s. 61(2) and s. 113 and Sch. 18, Pt. VI(3) in relation to payments made by reference to profit periods beginning on or after 1 January 2000.

Cross references – FA 1997, s. 61(3): schemes cannot be registered under Pt. V, Ch. III if the only payments for which it provides are by reference to profit periods beginning on or after 1 January 2000, and registration under that chapter will end on 31 December 2000. FA 1998, Sch. 11: transitional provisions for profit related pay.

PRELIMINARY

169 Interpretation

169 [Repealed by FA 1997, s. 61(2) and s. 113 and Sch. 18, Pt, VI(3), with effect in relation to payments made by reference to profit periods beginning on or after 1 January 2000.]

170 Taxation of profit-related pay

170 [Repealed by FA 1989, s. 42(4), 187 and Sch. 17, Pt. IV, with effect for 1989–90 and subsequent years of assessment.]

THE RELIEF

171–184 [Repealed by FA 1997, s. 61(2) and s. 113 and Sch. 18, Pt, VI(3), with effect in relation to payments made by reference to profit periods beginning on or after 1 January 2000.]

Chapter IV – Other Exemptions and Reliefs

SHARE OPTION AND PROFIT SHARING SCHEMES

185 Approved share option schemes

185 [Omitted by ITEPA 2003, Sch. 6, para. 25 and repealed by ITEPA 2003, Sch. 8, Pt. 1.]

History – S. 185 omitted by ITEPA 2003, Sch. 6, para. 25 and repealed by ITEPA 2003, Sch. 8, Pt. 1 which have effect for the tax year 2003–04 and subsequent tax years.

Notes – S. 185 rewritten as follows:
S. 185(1): ITEPA 2003, s. 517 and s. 522.
S. 185(2): ITEPA 2003, s. 518 and s. 523.
S. 185(3): ITEPA 2003, s. 519(1), s. 520(1), (2), s. 524(1) and s. 525.
S. 185(4): ITEPA 2003, s. 519(2), (3) and s. 520(1).
S. 185(5): ITEPA 2003, s. 524(1)–(3) and s. 525(1).
S. 185(6): ITEPA 2003, s. 7(6), s. 10(3) and s. 526(1)–(3).
S. 185(7) is unnecessary and so has not been rewritten into the provisions of ITEPA 2003.
S. 185(8): ITEPA 2003, s. 194(2), s. 479(2) and s. 480(2).
S. 185(9) is spent and so has not been rewritten into the provisions of ITEPA 2003.
S. 185(10) is unnecessary and so has not been rewritten into the provisions of ITEPA 2003.

186 Approved profit sharing schemes

186(1) The provisions of this section apply where, after 5th April 1979 and before 1st January 2003, the trustees of an approved profit sharing scheme appropriate shares–

(a) which have previously been acquired by the trustees, and

(b) as to which the conditions in Part II of Schedule 9 are fulfilled,

to an individual who participates in the scheme (**"the participant"**).

186(2) Notwithstanding that, by virtue of such an appropriation of shares as is mentioned in subsection (1) above, the beneficial interest in the shares passes to the participant to whom they are appropriated–

(a) the value of the shares at the time of the appropriation shall be treated as not being income of his chargeable to tax under Schedule E; and

(b) he shall not be chargeable to income tax under that Schedule by virtue of section 78 or 79 of the Finance Act 1988 in respect of the shares or by virtue of section 162 in any case where the shares are appropriated to him at an under-value within the meaning of that section.

186(3) Subject to the provisions of this section and paragraph 4 of Schedule 10, if, in respect of or by reference to any of a participant's shares, the trustees become or the participant becomes entitled, before the release date, to receive any money or money's worth (**"a capital receipt"**), the appropriate percentage (determined as at the time the trustees become or the participant becomes so entitled) of so much of the amount or value of the receipt as exceeds the appropriate allowance for that year, as determined under subsection (12) below, counts as employment income of the participant for the year of assessment in which the entitlement arises.

186(4) If the trustees dispose of any of a participant's shares at any time before the release date or, if it is earlier, the date of the participant's death, then, subject to subsections (6) and (7) below, the appropriate percentage of the locked-in value of the shares at the time of the disposal counts as employment income of the participant for the year of assessment in which the disposal takes place.

186(5) Subject to paragraphs 5 and 6(6) of Schedule 10, the locked-in value of a participant's shares at any time is–

(a) if prior to that time he has become entitled to a capital receipt (within the meaning of subsection (3) above) which is referable to those shares and–,

  (i) an amount calculated by reference to that capital receipt counts as his employment income by virtue of subsection (3) above, or

  (ii) if the entitlement to the capital receipt arose before 6th April 2003, he was chargeable to income tax by virtue of that subsection (as it had effect before that date) in respect of that capital receipt,

  the amount by which their initial market value exceeds the amount or value of that capital receipt or, if there has been more than one such receipt, the aggregate of them; and

(b) in any other case, their initial market value.

186(6) Subject to subsection (7) below, if, on a disposal of shares falling within subsection (4) above, the proceeds of the disposal are less than the locked-in value of the shares at the time of the disposal, subsection (4) above shall have effect as if that locked-in value were reduced to an amount equal to the proceeds of the disposal.

186(7) If, at any time prior to the disposal of any of a participant's shares, a payment was made to the trustees to enable them to exercise rights arising under a rights issue, then, subject to subsection (8) below, subsections (4) and (6) above shall have effect as if the proceeds of the disposal were reduced by an amount equal to that proportion of that payment or, if there was more than one, of the aggregate of those payments which, immediately before the disposal, the market value of the shares disposed of bore to the market value of all the participant's shares held by the trustees at that time.

186(8) For the purposes of subsection (7) above–

(a) no account shall be taken of any payment to the trustees if or to the extent that it consists of the proceeds of a disposal of rights arising under a rights issue; and

(b) in relation to a particular disposal the amount of the payment or, as the case may be, of the aggregate of the payments referred to in that subsection shall be taken to be reduced by an amount equal to the total of the reduction (if any) previously made under that subsection in relation to earlier disposals;

and any reference in subsection (7) or paragraph (a) above to the rights arising under a rights issue is a reference to rights conferred in respect of a participant's shares, being rights to be allotted, on payment, other shares or securities or rights of any description in the same company.

186(9) If at any time the participant's beneficial interest in any of his shares is disposed of, the shares in question shall be treated for the purposes of the relevant provisions as having been disposed of at that time by the trustees for (subject to subsection (10) below) the like consideration as was obtained for the disposal of the beneficial interest; and for the purposes of this subsection there is no disposal of the participant's beneficial interest if and at the time when–

(a) in England and Wales or Northern Ireland, that interest becomes vested in any person on the insolvency of the participant or otherwise by operation of law, or

(b) in Scotland, that interest becomes vested in a judicial factor, in a trustee on the participant's sequestrated estate or in a trustee for the benefit of the participant's creditors.

186(10) If–

(a) a disposal of shares falling within subsection (4) above is a transfer to which paragraph 2(2)(c) of Schedule 9 applies, or

(b) any other disposal falling within that subsection is not at arm's length,

(c) a disposal of shares falling within that subsection is one which is treated as taking place by virtue of subsection (9) above and takes place within the period of retention,

then for the purposes of the relevant provisions the proceeds of the disposal shall be taken to be equal to the market value of the shares at the time of the disposal.

186(11) Where the trustees of an approved scheme acquire any shares as to which the requirements of Part II of Schedule 9 are fulfilled and, within the period of 18 months beginning with the date of their acquisition, those shares are appropriated in accordance with the scheme, section 686 shall not apply to income consisting of dividends on those shares received by the trustees; and, for the purpose of determining whether any shares are appropriated within that period, shares which were acquired at an earlier time shall be taken to be appropriated before shares of the same class which were acquired at a later time.

186(12) For the purposes of subsection (3) above, **"the appropriate allowance"**, in relation to any year of assessment, means a sum which, subject to a maximum of £60, is the product of multiplying £20 by 1 plus the number of years which fall within the period of three years immediately preceding the year in question and in which shares were appropriated to the participant under the scheme; and if in any year (and before the release date) the trustees become or the participant becomes entitled, in respect of or by reference to any of his shares, to more than one capital receipt, the receipts shall be set against the appropriate allowance for that year in the order in which they are received.

186(13) Schedule 10 shall have effect with respect to profit sharing schemes.

History – In s. 186(1), words "and before 1st January 2003" inserted by FA 2000, s. 49(3).

In s. 186(2)(b), the words "section 78 or 79 of the Finance Act 1988 in respect of the shares" substituted by FA 1988, s. 89(a) in relation to acquisitions of shares or interests in shares on or after 26 October 1987.

In s. 186(3), the words "the participant shall be chargeable to income tax under Schedule E for the year of assessment in which the entitlement arises on" omitted by ITEPA 2003, Sch. 6, para. 26(2)(a) and repealed by ITEPA 2003, Sch. 8, Pt. 1 which have effect for the tax year 2003–04 and subsequent tax years.

In s. 186(3), the words "counts as employment income of the participant for the year of assessment in which the entitlement arises" added by ITEPA 2003, Sch. 6, para. 26(2)(b) which has effect for the tax year 2003–04 and subsequent tax years.

In s. 186(4), the words "the participant shall be chargeable to income tax under Schedule E for the year of assessment in which the disposal takes place on" omitted by ITEPA 2003, Sch. 6, para. 26(3)(a) and repealed by ITEPA 2003, Sch. 8, Pt. 1 which have effect for the tax year 2003–04 and subsequent tax years.

In s. 186(4), the words "counts as employment income of the participant for the year of assessment in which the disposal takes place" added by ITEPA 2003, Sch. 6, para. 26(3)(b) which has effect for the tax year 2003–04 and subsequent tax years.

In s. 186(5)(a), the words "entitled to a capital receipt (within the meaning of subsection (3) above) which is referable to those shares and– (i) an amount calculated by reference to that capital receipt counts as his employment income by virtue of subsection (3) above, or (ii) if the entitlement to the capital receipt arose before 6th April 2003, he was chargeable to income tax by virtue of that subsection (as it had effect before that date) in respect of that capital receipt," substituted for the words "chargeable to income tax by virtue of subsection (3) above on a percentage of the amount or value of any capital receipt which is referable to those shares," by ITEPA 2003, Sch. 6, para. 26(4) which has effect for the tax year 2003–04 and subsequent tax years.

In s. 186(10), sub-para. (b) substituted for former sub-para. (b) and in sub-para. (c) words "that subsection" substituted for "that sub-paragraph" by s. 134 and Sch. 20, para. 11 for 1996–97 and later years of assessment.

In s. 186(12), "£60" and "three years" substituted respectively for "£100" and "five years" by FA 1996, s. 118 with effect for 1997–98 and subsequent years of assessment.

Derivations – S. 186(1): FA 1978, s. 53(1).

S. 186(2) (as originally enacted): FA 1978, s. 53(3).

S. 186(3): FA 1978, s. 56(1), as amended by FA 1982, s. 42(1).

S. 186(4)–(7): FA 1978, s. 55(1)–(4).

S. 186(8): FA 1978, s. 55(5), (9).

S. 186(9), (10): FA 1978, s. 55(7), (8).

S. 186(11): FA 1978, s. 53(6).

S. 186(12) (as originally enacted): FA 1978, s. 56(6), as originally inserted by FA 1980, s. 46(6), substituted by FA 1982, s. 42(2) and amended by FA 1985, s. 45(4).

Cross references – ICTA 1988, s. 187: interpretations.

S. 686: liability to tax at the rate applicable to trusts in respect of certain income of discretionary trusts.

Sch. 10, para. 4: certain receipts not to be "capital receipts" within s. 186(3).

Sch. 10, para. 5: provisions relating to company reconstructions.

Sch. 10, para. 6(6): locked-in value equated with market value of excess or unauthorised shares.

Sch. 10, para. 7: requirement for trustees to deduct tax at source.

Sch. 10, para. 7(2): where s. 186(9) applies, consideration paid by the trustees is deemed to have been received by them as disposal proceeds of shares.

TCGA 1992, s. 238: capital gains tax treatment of approved profit-sharing schemes.

FA 2000, s. 49: phasing out of approved profit sharing (APS) schemes.

FA 2000, s. 49(1), (2): Board may not approve a profit sharing scheme under Sch. 9 unless the application for approval is received before 6 April 2001.

ITEPA 2003, s. 418(3): other provisions about share-related income and exemptions.

ITEPA 2003, Sch. 7, para. 76 (Sch. 7: transitionals and savings): approved company share option plan (CSOP) schemes.

SI 1979/591 reg. 19(1)(1): payment by way of or derived from shares appropriated under a profit sharing scheme to be disregarded for purposes of earnings-related contributions.

Other material – IR booklet IR 95(not reproduced): *Approved Profit-Sharing Schemes. An outline for employees.*

Notes – In view of FA 2000, s. 49 which provides for the phasing out of approved profit sharing (APS) schemes, s. 186 has not been rewritten into the provisions of ITEPA 2003.

187 Interpretation of sections 185 and 186 and Schedules 9 and 10

187(1) [Except so far as relating to profit sharing schemes, this subsection omitted by ITEPA 2003, Sch. 6, para. 27 and repealed by ITEPA 2003, Sch. 8, Pt. 1.]

187(2) [Except so far as relating to profit sharing schemes, this subsection omitted by ITEPA 2003, Sch. 6, para. 27 and repealed by ITEPA 2003, Sch. 8, Pt. 1.]

187(3) [Except so far as relating to profit sharing schemes, this subsection omitted by ITEPA 2003, Sch. 6, para. 27 and repealed by ITEPA 2003, Sch. 8, Pt. 1.]

187(4) [Except so far as relating to profit sharing schemes, this subsection omitted by ITEPA 2003, Sch. 6, para. 27 and repealed by ITEPA 2003, Sch. 8, Pt. 1.]

187(5) For the purposes of subsection (2) above, a participant's salary for a year of assessment means such of the emoluments of the office or employment by virtue of which he is entitled to participate in a profit sharing scheme as are liable to be paid in that year under deduction of tax pursuant to section 203 after deducting therefrom amounts included by virtue of Chapter II of this Part.

187(6) [Except so far as relating to profit sharing schemes, this subsection omitted by ITEPA 2003, Sch. 6, para. 27 and repealed by ITEPA 2003, Sch. 8, Pt. 1.]

187(7) [Except so far as relating to profit sharing schemes, this subsection omitted by ITEPA 2003, Sch. 6, para. 27 and repealed by ITEPA 2003, Sch. 8, Pt. 1.]

187(8) Where the disposal referred to in section 186(4) is made from a holding of shares which were appropriated to the participant at different times, then, in determining for the purposes of the relevant provisions–

(a) the initial market value and the locked-in value of each of those shares,

(b) [Repealed by FA 1996, s. 117(2) and s. 205 and Sch. 41, Pt. V(5)]

the disposal shall be treated as being of shares which were appropriated earlier before those which were appropriated later.

187(9) Any of the relevant provisions with respect to–

(a) the order in which any of a participant's shares are to be treated as disposed of for the purposes of those provisions, or

(b) the shares in relation to which an event is to be treated as occurring for any such purpose,

shall have effect in relation to a profit sharing scheme notwithstanding any direction given to the trustees with respect to shares of a particular description or to shares appropriated to the participant at a particular time.

187(10) In the relevant provisions **"workers' cooperative"** means a registered society, as defined in section 1119 of CTA 2010 which is a cooperative society and the rules of which include provisions which secure–

(a) that the only persons who may be members of it are those who are employed by, or by a subsidiary of, the society and those who are the trustees of its profit sharing scheme; and

(b) that, subject to any provision about qualifications for membership which is from time to time made by the members of the society by reference to age, length of service or other factors of any description, all such persons may be members of the society;

and in this subsection **"cooperative society"** has the same meaning as in section 2 of the Co-operative and Community Benefit Societies Act 2014 or, as the case may be, section 1 of the Industrial and Provident Societies (Northern Ireland) Act 1969.

History – In s. 187(10), the words "registered society" substituted for the words "registered industrial and provident society", the words "section 2 of the Co-operative and Community Benefit Societies Act 2014" substituted for the words "section 1 of the Industrial and Provident Societies Act 1965" and the words "section 1 of" inserted by Co-operative and Community Benefit Societies Act 2014, s. 151 and Sch. 4, para. 40, with effect from 1 August 2014.

In s. 187(10), the words "section 1119 of CTA 2010" substituted for the words "section 834(1)" by CTA 2010, s. 1177 and Sch. 1, para. 13, with effect for corporation tax purposes for accounting periods ending on or after 1 April 2010, and for income and capital gains tax purposes for the tax year 2010–11 and subsequent tax years.

In s. 187(10), the words ", as defined in section 834(1)" substituted for ", within the meaning of section 486," by CTA 2009, s. 1322 and Sch. 1, para. 95, with effect for corporation tax purposes for accounting periods ending on or after 1 April 2009, and for income tax and capital gains tax purposes for the tax year 2009–10 and subsequent tax years.

Except so far as relating to profit sharing schemes, s. 187(1)–(4), (6) and (7) omitted by ITEPA 2003, Sch. 6, para. 27 and repealed by ITEPA 2003, Sch. 8, Pt. 1 which have effect, for income tax purposes, for the tax year 2003–04 and subsequent tax years and, for corporation tax purposes, for accounting periods ending after 5 April 2003.

For the purposes of profit sharing schemes, s. 187(1)–(4), (6) and (7) read as follows:

"**187(1)** In sections 185 and 186, this section and Schedules 9 and 10 **"the relevant provisions"** means those sections (including this section) and Schedules.

187(2) For the purposes of the relevant provisions, except where the context otherwise requires–

"appropriate percentage" shall be construed in accordance with paragraph 3 of Schedule 10;

"approved", in relation to a scheme, means approved under Schedule 9;

"associated company" has the same meaning as in section 416, except that, for the purposes of paragraph 23 of Schedule 9, subsection (1) of that section shall have effect with the omission of the words "or at any time within one year previously";

"bonus date" has the meaning given by paragraph 17 of Schedule 9;

"capital receipt" means money or money's worth to which the trustees of or a participant in a profit sharing scheme become or becomes entitled as mentioned in section 186(3), but subject to paragraph 4 of Schedule 10;

"certified contractual savings scheme" has the meaning given by section 326;

"control" has the same meaning as in section 840;

"grantor", in relation to any scheme, means the company which has established the scheme;

"group scheme" and, in relation to such a scheme, **"participating company"** have the meanings given by paragraph 1(3) and (4) of Schedule 9;

"initial market value", in relation to shares in a profit sharing scheme, has the meaning given by paragraph 30(4) of Schedule 9;

"locked-in value", in relation to any shares, shall be construed in accordance with section 186(5);

"market value" has the same meaning as in Part VIII of the 1992 Act;

"new holding" has the meaning given by section 126(1)(b) of the 1992 Act;

"participant", in relation to a profit sharing scheme, means an individual to whom the trustees of the scheme have appropriated shares;

"participant's shares", in relation to a participant in a profit sharing scheme, means, subject to paragraph 5(4) of Schedule 10, shares which have been appropriated to the participant by the trustees;

"period of retention" has the meaning given by paragraph 2 of Schedule 10;

"release date", in relation to any of the shares of a participant in a profit sharing scheme, means the third anniversary of the date on which they were appropriated to him;

"relevant amount", in relation to a participant in a profit sharing scheme, means an amount which is not less than £3,000 and not more than £8,000 but which, subject to that, is 10 per cent of his salary (determined under subsection (5) below) for the year of assessment in question or the preceding year of assessment, whichever is the greater;

"relevant requirements" has the meaning given by paragraph 1 of Schedule 9;

"savings-related share option scheme" has the meaning given by paragraph 1 of Schedule 9;

"scheme" means a savings-related share option scheme, a share option scheme which is not a savings-related share option scheme or a profit sharing scheme, as the context may require;

"shares" includes stock;

"specified age", in relation to a scheme, means the age specified in pursuance of paragraph 8A of Schedule 9 as the specified age for the purposes of the scheme;

"the trustees", in relation to an approved profit sharing scheme or the shares of a participant in such a scheme, means the body of persons for the establishment of which the scheme must provide as mentioned in paragraph 30 of Schedule 9; and

"the trust instrument", in relation to an approved profit sharing scheme, means the instrument referred to in paragraph 30(1)(c) of Schedule 9.

187(3) For the purposes of the application of the relevant provisions in relation to any share option scheme or profit sharing scheme, a person has a material interest in a company if he, either on his own or with one or more associates, or if any associate of his with or without such other associates,–

(a) is the beneficial owner of, or able, directly or through the medium of other companies, or by any other indirect means to control, more than 25 per cent or, in the case of a share option scheme which is not a savings-related share option scheme, more than 10 per cent, of the ordinary share capital of the company, or

(b) where the company is a close company, possesses, or is entitled to acquire, such rights as would, in the event of the winding-up of the company or in any other circumstances, give an entitlement to receive more than 25 per cent, or in the case of a share option scheme which is not a savings-related share option scheme more than 10 per cent, of the assets which would then be available for distribution among the participators.

In this subsection **"associate"** has the meaning given by section 417(3) and (4) and **"participator"** has the meaning given by section 417(1).

187(4) Subsection (3) above shall have effect subject to the provisions of Part VI of Schedule 9.

187(6) Section 839 shall apply for the purposes of the relevant provisions.

187(7) For the purposes of the relevant provisions a company is a member of a consortium owning another company if it is one of a number of companies which between them beneficially own not less than three-quarters of the other company's ordinary share capital and each of which beneficially owns not less than one-twentieth of that capital."

S. 187(2): definition of "pensionable age" repealed by Pensions Act 1995 s. 126 and Sch. 4, para. 12(a) with effect from 19 July 1995.

In s. 187(2): in definition of "release date", "third" substituted for "fifth" by FA 1996, s. 116 where the third anniversary of the appropriation of the shares to the participant occurs on or after 29 April 1996.

In s. 187(2), in the definition of "relevant amount", the words "not less than £3,000 and not more than £8,000" substituted by FA 1991, s. 41 for 1991–92 and subsequent years of assessment. Definition of "specified age" inserted by FA 1991, s. 33(4), with effect in relation to a scheme not approved before 25 July 1991.

In s. 187(3), the words "in a company" to the end of para.(b) were substituted, and the words "and "participator" has" to the end were inserted, by FA 1989, s. 107 and Sch. 12, para. 9, in relation to accounting periods beginning after 31 March 1989.

References to provisions of the 1992 Act in s. 187(2) (definitions of "market value" and "new holding") substituted by TCGA 1992, s. 290 and Sch. 10, para. 14(13).

S. 187(8)(b) repealed by FA 1996, s. 117(2) and s. 205 and Sch. 41, Pt. V(5) in relation to events on or after 29 April 1996 giving rise to anincome tax charge under s. 186, 187 or Sch. 9, 10.

Derivations – In s. 187(2):
definition of "appropriate percentage": FA 1978, s. 61(1);
definition of "approved": FA 1978, s. 53(2); see also FA 1978, s. 61(1) ("approved scheme"), FA 1980, Sch. 10, para 1(1) and FA 1984, Sch. 10, para. 1(1);
definition of "associated company": FA 1980, Sch. 10, para. 26(1) (as amended by FA 1982, s. 40(8)); FA 1984, Sch. 10, para. 15(1);
definition of "bonus date": FA 1980, Sch. 10, para. 26(1);
definition of "capital receipt": FA 1978, s. 56(1);
the reference to "certified contractual savings scheme": FA 1980, Sch. 10, para. 5(b);

definition of "control": FA 1978, Sch. 9, para. 16; FA 1980, Sch. 10, para. 26(1) and FA 1984, Sch. 10, para. 15(1);
definition of "grantor": FA 1984, Sch. 10, para. 1(1), 15(1); see also FA 1978, Sch. 9, para. 1(1); FA 1980, Sch. 10, para. 1(1) (references to "the company concerned") (now Sch. 9, para. 1(1));
definitions of "group scheme", and "participating company": FA 1978, s. 61(1); FA 1980, Sch. 10, para. 26(1); FA 1984, Sch. 10, para. 15(1); see also FA 1978, Sch. 9, para. 1(2); FA 1980, Sch. 10, para. 1(3); FA 1984, Sch. 10, para. 1(3), (4) (now Sch. 9, para. 1(3), (4));
definition of "initial market value": FA 1978, s. 61(1);
references to "locked-in value": FA 1978, s. 61(1);
definition of "market value": FA 1978, s. 61(1) (as amended by CGTA 1979, s. 157(2) and Sch. 7, para. 9); FA 1980, Sch. 10, para. 26(1) and FA 1984, Sch. 10, para. 15(1);
definition of "new holding": FA 1978, s. 54(2)(a) (as amended by CGTA 1979, s. 157(2) and Sch. 7, para. 9), 57(1);
definition of "participant": FA 1978, s. 53(2)(a); and see FA 1978, s. 61(1);
definition of "participant's shares": FA 1978, s. 53(2)(b); see also FA 1978, s. 57(4) (now Sch. 10, para. 5(4));
reference to "pensionable age" (as originally enacted): FA 1978, s. 54(4)(b); FA 1980, Sch. 10, para. 8;
for "period of retention" see FA 1978, s. 54(4), as amended by FA 1980, s. 46(3) (now Sch. 10, para. 2), 61(1));
definition of "release date" (as originally enacted): FA 1978, s. 54(6) (as amended by FA 1980, s. 46(4) and FA 1985, s. 45(2)), 61(1);
definition of "relevant amount" (as originally enacted): FA 1978, s. 61(1), inserted therein by FA 1983, s. 25(1);
for definition of "savings-related share option scheme", see FA 1980, Sch. 10, para. 1(1)(a) (see now Sch. 9, para. 1(1));
definition of "shares": FA 1978, s. 61(1); FA 1980, Sch. 10, para. 26(1) and FA 1984, Sch. 10, para. 15(1);
definition of "the trustees": FA 1978, s. 61(1);
definition of "the trust instrument": FA 1978, s. 61(1).
S. 187(3) (as originally enacted): ICTA 1970, s. 285(6) (as amended by FA 1971, s. 37 and Sch. 6, para. 30; FA 1980, s. 122 and Sch. 20, Pt. VIII); FA 1978, Sch. 9, para. 11(3)(b); FA 1980, Sch. 10, para. 26(2) and FA 1984, Sch. 10, para. 4(4).
S. 187(4): FA 1987, s. 33(2).
S. 187(5): FA 1978, s. 61(4), as inserted by FA 1983, s. 25(2).
S. 187(6): FA 1980, Sch. 10, para. 26(4) and FA1984, Sch. 10, para. 15(3).
S. 187(7): FA 1978, Sch. 9, para. 17; FA 1980, Sch. 10, para. 26(5) (both provisions as amended by FA 1986, s. 23(5)) and FA 1984, Sch. 10, para. 15(4).
S. 187(8): FA 1978, s. 55(6).
S. 187(9): FA 1978, s. 61(2).
S. 187(10): FA 1978, Sch. 9, para. 18, as inserted by FA 1986, s. 24(1).

Cross references – S. 203: deduction of tax at source from Sch. E payments.
S. 326: schemes within regulations made under FA 1969, s. 52 or National Loans Act 1968, s. 12 providing for the payment of periodical contributions and repayment with bonuses or interest and certified by the Treasury.
Pt. V, Ch. II: Sch. E charge on benefits of directors and employees earning £8,500 or more.
S. 486(12): registered industrial and provident society to be registered under the Industrial and Provident Societies Act 1965 or the Industrial and Provident Societies Act (Northern Ireland) 1969.
Pt. XI: provisions for apportionment to participators of non-trading income of close companies.
S. 839: circumstances in which persons are connected.
Sch. 9, para. 30: scheme must provide for UK resident trustees to perform specified functions.
Sch. 9, para. 30(1)(c): instrument must comply with provisions of Sch. 9, para. 31–34 (requirements of trustees concerning notification of appropriation, prohibition of certain disposals, accounting for moneys received, dealing with participants, rights, maintaining records and giving information to participants).
Sch. 10, para. 4: certain receipts not to be "capital receipts".
Sch. 10, para. 5(4): saving provisions for changes in participant's shares on company reconstructions.
Sch. 10, para. 6(4): chargeable events deemed first to relate to scheme shares and not to excess or unauthorised shares, subject to s. 187(8).
TCGA 1992, 126(1)(b): in relation to a reorganisation, "new holding" by reference to the shares and securities which thereafter represent the original shares, including any original shares and securities which remain.
TCGA 1992, s. 238: capital gains tax treatment of approved profit sharing schemes and share option schemes.
SSCBA 1992, s. 122(1): pensionable age is 65 for men, 60 for women.
Industrial and Provident Societies Act 1965, s. 1(3); Industrial and Provident Societies Act (Northern Ireland) 1969, s. 1(3): "cooperative society" does not include a society carrying on business with the object of making profits for the payment of interest etc. on money invested with the society.
FA 2000, s. 49: phasing out of approved profit sharing (APS) schemes.
ITEPA 2003, s. 418(3): other provisions about share-related income and exemptions.
ITEPA 2003, Sch. 7, para. 76: approved company share option plan (CSOP) schemes.

HMRC Manuals – Employee Share Scheme Unit Manual, ESS 30065ff: Revenue practice on determining the initial market value.

Other material – ICAEW Technical Release TR 511 (not reproduced): "salary" in s. 187(5) means salary net of pension contributions.

Notes – S. 187 rewritten as follows:
S. 187(1) has not been rewritten into the provisions of ITEPA 2003, because:
(a) for the purposes of profit sharing schemes, s. 187(1) has not been omitted by ITEPA 2003, Sch. 6, para. 27 and not been repealed by ITEPA 2003, Sch. 8, Pt. 1; and
(b) for other purposes, although s. 187(1) has been omitted by ITEPA 2003, Sch. 6, para. 27 and repealed by ITEPA 2003, Sch. 8, Pt. 1, it is unnecessary.

For the purposes of profit sharing schemes, s. 187(2) has not been rewritten into the provisions of ITEPA 2003 because, for these purposes, s. 187(2) has not been omitted by ITEPA 2003, Sch. 6, para. 27 and not been repealed by ITEPA 2003, Sch. 8, Pt. 1. For other purposes, s. 187(2) has been rewritten as ITEPA 2003, s. 516(4), s. 521(4), s. 719, Sch. 3, para. 35, para. 47, para. 48, Sch. 4, para. 35 and para. 36.
For the purposes of profit sharing schemes, s. 187(3) has not been rewritten into the provisions of ITEPA 2003 because, for these purposes, s. 187(3) has not been omitted by ITEPA 2003, Sch. 6, para. 27 and not been repealed by ITEPA 2003, Sch. 8, Pt. 1. For other purposes, s. 187(3) has been rewritten as ITEPA 2003, Sch. 3, para. 11, para. 12, para. 14, Sch. 4, para. 9, para. 10 and para. 12.
For the purposes of profit sharing schemes, s. 187(4) has not been rewritten into the provisions of ITEPA 2003 because, for these purposes, s. 187(4) has not been omitted by ITEPA 2003, Sch. 6, para. 27 and not been repealed by ITEPA 2003, Sch. 8, Pt. 1. For other purposes, s. 187(4) has been rewritten as:ITEPA 2003, Sch. 3, para. 11 and Sch. 4, para. 9.
For the purposes of profit sharing schemes, s. 187(6) has not been rewritten into the provisions of ITEPA 2003 because, for these purposes, s. 187(6)has not been omitted by ITEPA 2003, Sch. 6, para. 27 and not been repealed by ITEPA 2003, Sch. 8, Pt. 1. For other purposes, s. 187(6) has been rewritten as: ITEPA 2003, s. 718.
For the purposes of profit sharing schemes, s. 187(7) has not been rewritten into the provisions of ITEPA 2003 because, for these purposes, s. 187(7) has not been omitted by ITEPA 2003, Sch. 6, para. 27 and not been repealed by ITEPA 2003, Sch. 8, Pt. 1. For other purposes, s. 187(7) has been rewritten as:ITEPA 2003, Sch. 3, para. 48 and Sch. 4, para. 36.

CONTRIBUTIONS IN RESPECT OF SHARE OPTION GAINS

187A Relief for contributions in respect of share option gains

187A [Omitted by ITEPA 2003, Sch. 6, para. 28 and repealed by ITEPA 2003, Sch. 8, Pt. 1.]

History – S. 187A omitted by ITEPA 2003, Sch. 6, para. 28 and repealed by ITEPA 2003, Sch. 8, Pt. 1 which have effect for the tax year 2003–04 and subsequent tax years.

Notes – S. 187A rewritten as follows:
S. 187A(1): ITEPA 2003, s. 481(1).
S. 187A(2): ITEPA 2003, s. 481(2).
S. 187A(3): ITEPA 2003, s. 481(3).
S. 187A(4): ITEPA 2003, s. 478(1), (2) and s. 481(1).
S. 187A(5) is unnecessary and so has not been rewritten into the provisions of ITEPA 2003.
S. 187A(6): ITEPA 2003, s. 481(1) and (5).
S. 187A(7): ITEPA 2003, s. 481(5) and s. 487(1) ("secondary Class 1 contributions", "the Contributions and Benefits Act").

RETIREMENT BENEFITS ETC.

188 Exemptions from section 148

188 [Repealed by FA 1998, s. 165 and Sch. 27, Part III(9).]

History – S. 188 repealed by FA 1998, s. 165 and Sch. 27, Part III(9) with application to payments or other benefits received (within the meaning of s. 148 as substituted by FA 1998, s. 58(1)) on or after 6 April 1998, except where the payment or other benefit or the right to receive it has been brought into charge to tax before that date (FA 1998, 58(4)).

189 Lump sum benefits on retirement

189 [Omitted by ITEPA 2003, Sch. 6, para. 28 and repealed by ITEPA 2003, Sch. 8, Pt. 1.]

History – S. 189 omitted by ITEPA 2003, Sch. 6, para. 28 and repealed by ITEPA 2003, Sch. 8, Pt. 1 which have effect for the tax year 2003–04 and subsequent tax years.

Notes – S. 189 rewritten as ITEPA 2003, s. 637.

190 Payments to MPs and others

190 [Omitted by ITEPA 2003, Sch. 6, para. 28 and repealed by ITEPA 2003, Sch. 8, Pt. 1.]

History – S. 190 omitted by ITEPA 2003, Sch. 6, para. 28 and repealed by ITEPA 2003, Sch. 8, Pt. 1 which have effect for the tax year 2003–04 and subsequent tax years.

Notes – S. 190 rewritten as follows:
S. 190(1): ITEPA 2003, s. 291(1).
S. 190(2) and (3): ITEPA 2003, s. 291(2).
S. 190(4): ITEPA 2003, s. 291(3).

191 Job release scheme allowances not to be treated as income

191 [Omitted by ITEPA 2003, Sch. 6, para. 28 and repealed by ITEPA 2003, Sch. 8, Pt. 1.]

History – S. 191 omitted by ITEPA 2003, Sch. 6, para. 28 and repealed by ITEPA 2003, Sch. 8, Pt. 1 which have effect for the tax year 2003–04 and subsequent tax years.

Notes – S. 191 is spent and so has not been rewritten into the provisions of ITEPA 2003.

REMOVAL EXPENSES AND BENEFITS

191A Removal expenses and benefits

191A [Omitted by ITEPA 2003, Sch. 6, para. 28 and repealed by ITEPA 2003, Sch. 8, Pt. 1.]

History – S. 191A omitted by ITEPA 2003, Sch. 6, para. 28 and repealed by ITEPA 2003, Sch. 8, Pt. 1 which have effect for the tax year 2003–04 and subsequent tax years.

Notes – S. 191A introduces the repealed ICTA 1988, Schedule 11A and so has not been rewritten into the provisions of ITEPA 2003; ICTA 1988, Schedule 11A repealed by ITEPA 2003, Sch. 8, Pt. 1.

191B Removal benefits: beneficial loan arrangements

191B [Omitted by ITEPA 2003, Sch. 6, para. 28 and repealed by ITEPA 2003, Sch. 8, Pt. 1.]

History – S. 191B omitted by ITEPA 2003, Sch. 6, para. 28 and repealed by ITEPA 2003, Sch. 8, Pt. 1 which have effect for the tax year 2003–04 and subsequent tax years.

Notes – S. 191B rewritten as follows:
S. 191B(1): ITEPA 2003, s. 288(1) and (2).
S. 191B(2): ITEPA 2003, s. 288(1) and (2).
S. 191B(3) and (4) have been rewritten into the provision of ITEPA 2003, s. 288(5).
S. 191B(5)–(7) have been rewritten into the provisions of ITEPA 2003, s. 288(1) and (3).
S. 191B(8): ITEPA 2003, s. 288(1) and s. 289(1)–(3).
S. 191B(9): ITEPA 2003, s. 288(1).
S. 191B(10), (11) and (12) have been rewritten into the provision of ITEPA 2003, s. 288(4).

S. 191B(13): ITEPA 2003, s. 191(4), (5), s. 288(6) and s. 289(4).
S. 191B(14) was repealed by FA 1994, Sch. 26, Pt. V(5) and so has not been rewritten into the provisions of ITEPA 2003.
S. 191B(15): ITEPA 2003, s. 274(1) and (2).
S. 191B(16): ITEPA 2003, s. 5, s. 276 and s. 721(5).

FOREIGN EMOLUMENTS AND EARNINGS, PENSIONS AND CERTAIN TRAVEL FACILITIES

192 Relief from tax for foreign emoluments

192 [Omitted by ITEPA 2003, Sch. 6, para. 28 and repealed by ITEPA 2003, Sch. 8, Pt. 1.]

History – S. 192 omitted by ITEPA 2003, Sch. 6, para. 28 and repealed by ITEPA 2003, Sch. 8, Pt. 1 which have effect for the tax year 2003–04 and subsequent tax years.

Notes – S. 192 rewritten as follows:
S. 192(1): ITEPA 2003, s. 22(1), s. 23(2), s. 355(2), (3), s. 390 and s. 721(1) ("foreign employer").
S. 192(2): ITEPA 2003, s. 22(1) and s. 23(2).
S. 192(3): ITEPA 2003, s. 328(1), s. 329(1), s. 334(1), s. 355(1) and (4)–(6).
S. 192(4) is spent and so has not been rewritten into the provisions of ITEPA 2003.
S. 192(5): ITEPA 2003, s. 23(3), s. 24(1), (2), (3), (5), (6), s. 329(1) and s. 331(2).

192A Foreign earnings deduction for seafarers

192A [Omitted by ITEPA 2003, Sch. 6, para. 28 and repealed by ITEPA 2003, Sch. 8, Pt. 1.]

History – S. 192A omitted by ITEPA 2003, Sch. 6, para. 28 and repealed by ITEPA 2003, Sch. 8, Pt. 1 which have effect for the tax year 2003–04 and subsequent tax years.

Notes – S. 192A rewritten as follows:
S. 192A(1) has been rewritten into the provisions ITEPA 2003, s. 328(4), (5), s. 329(1), s. 378(1), (2) and s. 379(1).
S. 192A(2) has been rewritten into the provisions ITEPA 2003, s. 40(3)–(6) and s. 384.
S. 192A(3) has been rewritten into the provisions ITEPA 2003, s. 40(3)–(6) and s. 385.
S. 192A(4) has been rewritten into the provisions ITEPA 2003, s. 329(1), s. 330(1), s. 331(2), s. 380, s. 381, s. 382 and s. 383(1)–(3).

193 Foreign earnings and travel expenses

193 [Omitted by ITEPA 2003, Sch. 6, para. 28 and repealed by ITEPA 2003, Sch. 8, Pt. 1.]

History – S. 193 omitted by ITEPA 2003, Sch. 6, para. 28 and repealed by ITEPA 2003, Sch. 8, Pt. 1 which have effect for the tax year 2003–04 and subsequent tax years.

Notes – S. 193 rewritten as follows:
S. 193(1) was repealed by FA 1998, s. 63(1) and so has not been rewritten into the provisions of ITEPA 2003.
S. 193(2): ITEPA 2003, s. 341(1)–(4), s. 376(1) and s. 721(1) ("foreign employer").
S. 193(3): ITEPA 2003, s. 341(1)–(6).
S. 193(4): ITEPA 2003, s. 328(1), s. 329(1), s. 369(1) and s. 376(1)–(3).
S. 193(5): ITEPA 2003, s. 342(1)–(7) and s. 721(1) ("foreign employer").
S. 193(6): ITEPA 2003, s. 342(1)–(8).
S. 193(7): ITEPA 2003, but separate identification is not possible because the provisions are very numerous.

194 Other foreign travel expenses

194 [Omitted by ITEPA 2003, Sch. 6, para. 28 and repealed by ITEPA 2003, Sch. 8, Pt. 1.]

History – S. 194 omitted by ITEPA 2003, Sch. 6, para. 28 and repealed by ITEPA 2003, Sch. 8, Pt. 1 which have effect for the tax year 2003–04 and subsequent tax years.

Notes – S. 194 rewritten as follows:
S. 194(1): ITEPA 2003, s. 328(4), (5), s. 329(1), s. 369(1), s. 370(1), (2), s. 371(1) and (2).
S. 194(2): ITEPA 2003, s. 371(3)–(7).
S. 194(3): ITEPA 2003, s. 370(4).
S. 194(4): ITEPA 2003, s. 370(4) and (5).
S. 194(5) and (6) have been rewritten into the provision of ITEPA 2003, s. 370(3).
S. 194(7): ITEPA 2003, s. 372.
S. 194(8): ITEPA 2003, s. 370(5).
S. 194(9): ITEPA 2003, s. 330(1).
S. 194(10) has been rewritten into provisions of ITEPA 2003, but separate identification is not possible because the provisions are very numerous.

195 Travel expenses of employees not domiciled in the United Kingdom

195 [Omitted by ITEPA 2003, Sch. 6, para. 28 and repealed by ITEPA 2003, Sch. 8, Pt. 1.]

History – S. 195 omitted by ITEPA 2003, Sch. 6, para. 28 and repealed by ITEPA 2003, Sch. 8, Pt. 1 which have effect for the tax year 2003–04 and subsequent tax years.

Notes – S. 195 rewritten as follows:
S. 195(1): ITEPA 2003, s. 373(1) and s. 374(1).
S. 195(2): ITEPA 2003, s. 373(2), (3), s. 374(2), (3) and s. 375(1).
S. 195(3): ITEPA 2003, s. 375(2), (3) and (4).
S. 195(4): ITEPA 2003, s. 375(3) and (4).
S. 195(5): ITEPA 2003, s. 373(1) and (4).
S. 195(6): ITEPA 2003, s. 374(1), (3)–(5) and (8).
S. 195(7): ITEPA 2003, s. 328(4), (5), s. 329(1), s. 369(1), s. 373(1), (2), (5), s. 374(1), (2), (6) and (9).
S. 195(8): ITEPA 2003, s. 373(6) and s. 374(7).

S. 195(9): ITEPA 2003, s. 373(4) and s. 374(3).
S. 195(10): ITEPA 2003, s. 374(9).
S. 195(11): ITEPA 2003, but separate identification is not possible because the provisions are very numerous.
S. 195(12): ITEPA 2003, s. 330(1).
S. 195(13) is spent and so has not been rewritten into the provisions of ITEPA 2003.

196 Foreign pensions

196 [Omitted by ITEPA 2003, Sch. 6, para. 28 and repealed by ITEPA 2003, Sch. 8, Pt. 1.]

History – S. 196 omitted by ITEPA 2003, Sch. 6, para. 28 and repealed by ITEPA 2003, Sch. 8, Pt. 1 which have effect for the tax year 2003–04 and subsequent tax years.

Notes – S. 196: ITEPA 2003, s. 617.

197 Leave travel facilities for the armed forces

197 [Omitted by ITEPA 2003, Sch. 6, para. 28 and repealed by ITEPA 2003, Sch. 8, Pt. 1.]

History – S. 197 omitted by ITEPA 2003, Sch. 6, para. 28 and repealed by ITEPA 2003, Sch. 8, Pt. 1 which have effect for the tax year 2003–04 and subsequent tax years.

Notes – S. 197 rewritten as follows:
S. 197(1): ITEPA 2003, s. 228(1) and s. 296(1).
S. 197(2): ITEPA 2003, s. 266(3) and s. 296.

197A Car parking facilities

197A [Omitted by ITEPA 2003, Sch. 6, para. 28 and repealed by ITEPA 2003, Sch. 8, Pt. 1.]

History – S. 197A omitted by ITEPA 2003, Sch. 6, para. 28 and repealed by ITEPA 2003, Sch. 8, Pt. 1 which have effect for the tax year 2003–04 and subsequent tax years.

Notes – S. 197A rewritten as ITEPA 2003, s. 237(2), (3) and s. 266(1).

197AA Works bus services

197AA [Omitted by ITEPA 2003, Sch. 6, para. 28 and repealed by ITEPA 2003, Sch. 8, Pt. 1.]

History – S. 197AA omitted by ITEPA 2003, Sch. 6, para. 28 and repealed by ITEPA 2003, Sch. 8, Pt. 1 which have effect for the tax year 2003–04 and subsequent tax years.

Notes – S. 197AA rewritten as follows:
S. 197AA(1): ITEPA 2003, s. 242(1).
S. 197AA(2): ITEPA 2003, s. 242(2) ("works transport service").
S. 197AA(3): ITEPA 2003, s. 242(3) ("bus") and s. 249 ("qualifying journey").
S. 197AA(4): ITEPA 2003, s. 242(1).
S. 197AA(5): ITEPA 2003, s. 242(1) and (2) ("children").
S. 197AA(6): ITEPA 2003, s. 266(2) and (5).
S. 197AA(7): ITEPA 2003, s. 249 ("workplace").
S. 197AA(8): ITEPA 2003, s. 242(5).
S. 197AA(9): ITEPA 2003, s. 242(4) and (6).

197AB Support for public transport bus services

197AB [Omitted by ITEPA 2003, Sch. 6, para. 28 and repealed by ITEPA 2003, Sch. 8, Pt. 1.]

History – S. 197AB omitted by ITEPA 2003, Sch. 6, para. 28 and repealed by ITEPA 2003, Sch. 8, Pt. 1 which have effect for the tax year 2003–04 and subsequent tax years.

Notes – S. 197AB rewritten as follows:
S. 197AB(1): ITEPA 2003, s. 243(1) and (2).
S. 197AB(2): ITEPA 2003, s. 243(5) and s. 249 ("qualifying journey").
S. 197AB(3): ITEPA 2003, s. 243(1).
S. 197AB(3A): ITEPA 2003, s. 243(3).
S. 197AB(4): ITEPA 2003, s. 5, s. 243(4), (5) and s. 249 ("workplace").
S. 197AB(5): ITEPA 2003, s. 266(2) and (5).

197AC Provision of cycle or cyclist's safety equipment

197AC [Omitted by ITEPA 2003, Sch. 6, para. 28 and repealed by ITEPA 2003, Sch. 8, Pt. 1.]

History – S. 197AC omitted by ITEPA 2003, Sch. 6, para. 28 and repealed by ITEPA 2003, Sch. 8, Pt. 1 which have effect for the tax year 2003–04 and subsequent tax years.

Notes – S. 197AC rewritten as follows:
S. 197AC(1): ITEPA 2003, s. 244(1) and (2).
S. 197AC(2): ITEPA 2003, s. 244(5).
S. 197AC(3): ITEPA 2003, s. 244(4).
S. 197AC(4): ITEPA 2003, s. 244(3) and s. 249 ("qualifying journey").
S. 197AC(5): ITEPA 2003, s. 266(2) and (5).
S. 197AC(6): ITEPA 2003, s. 5 and s. 249 ("workplace").

MILEAGE ALLOWANCES

197AD Mileage allowance payments

197AD [Omitted by ITEPA 2003, Sch. 6, para. 28 and repealed by ITEPA 2003, Sch. 8, Pt. 1.]

History – S. 197AD omitted by ITEPA 2003, Sch. 6, para. 28 and repealed by ITEPA 2003, Sch. 8, Pt. 1 which have effect for the tax year 2003–04 and subsequent tax years.

Notes – S. 197AD rewritten as follows:
S. 197AD(1): ITEPA 2003, s. 229(1).
S. 197AD(2): ITEPA 2003, s. 229(2).
S. 197AD(3): ITEPA 2003, s. 229(3).
S. 197AD(4): ITEPA 2003, s. 229(4).

197AE Passenger payments

197AE [Omitted by ITEPA 2003, Sch. 6, para. 28 and repealed by ITEPA 2003, Sch. 8, Pt. 1.]

History – S. 197AE omitted by ITEPA 2003, Sch. 6, para. 28 and repealed by ITEPA 2003, Sch. 8, Pt. 1 which have effect for the tax year 2003–04 and subsequent tax years.

Notes – S. 197AE rewritten as follows:
S. 197AE(1): ITEPA 2003, s. 233(1) and (2).
S. 197AE(2): ITEPA 2003, s. 233(3).
S. 197AE(3): ITEPA 2003, s. 233(4).
S. 197AE(4): ITEPA 2003, s. 233(5).

197AF Mileage allowance relief

197AF [Omitted by ITEPA 2003, Sch. 6, para. 28 and repealed by ITEPA 2003, Sch. 8, Pt. 1.]

History – S. 197AF omitted by ITEPA 2003, Sch. 6, para. 28 and repealed by ITEPA 2003, Sch. 8, Pt. 1 which have effect for the tax year 2003–04 and subsequent tax years.

Notes – S. 197AF rewritten as follows:
S. 197AF(1): ITEPA 2003, s. 231(1).
S. 197AF(2): ITEPA 2003, s. 231(3).
S. 197AF(3): ITEPA 2003, s. 231(2).
S. 197AF(4) is unnecessary and so has not been rewritten into the provisions of ITEPA 2003.

197AG Giving effect to mileage allowance relief

197AG [Omitted by ITEPA 2003, Sch. 6, para. 28 and repealed by ITEPA 2003, Sch. 8, Pt. 1.]

History – S. 197AG omitted by ITEPA 2003, Sch. 6, para. 28 and repealed by ITEPA 2003, Sch. 8, Pt. 1 which have effect for the tax year 2003–04 and subsequent tax years.

Notes – S. 197AG rewritten as follows:
S. 197AG(1): ITEPA 2003, s. 232(1).
S. 197AG(2): ITEPA 2003, s. 232(2).
S. 197AG(3): ITEPA 2003, s. 232(3) and (4).
S. 197AG(4): ITEPA 2003, s. 232(5).
S. 197AG(5): ITEPA 2003, s. 232(6).

197AH Interpretation of sections 197AD to 197AG

197AH [Omitted by ITEPA 2003, Sch. 6, para. 28 and repealed by ITEPA 2003, Sch. 8, Pt. 1.]

History – S. 197AH omitted by ITEPA 2003, Sch. 6, para. 28 and repealed by ITEPA 2003, Sch. 8, Pt. 1 which have effect for the tax year 2003–04 and subsequent tax years.

Notes – S. 197AH is unnecessary and so has not been rewritten into the provisions of ITEPA 2003.

197B Limit on chargeable mileage profit

197B [Repealed by FA 2001, s. 107 and Sch. 33, Pt. 2(1)]

History – S. 197B repealed by FA 2001, s. 107 and Sch. 33, Pt. 2(1) with effect for the year 2002–03 and subsequent years of assessment.

197C Definition of mileage profit

197C [Repealed by FA 2001, s. 107 and Sch. 33, Pt. 2(1).]

History – S. 197C repealed by FA 2001, s. 107 and Sch. 33, Pt. 2(1) with effect for the year 2002–03 and subsequent years of assessment.

197D Definition of taxed mileage profit

197D [Repealed by FA 2001, s. 107 and Sch. 33, Pt. 2(1).]

History – S. 197D repealed by FA 2001, s. 107 and Sch. 33, Pt. 2(1) with effect for the year 2002–03 and subsequent years of assessment.

197E Exception from section 197B

197E [Repealed by FA 2001, s. 107 and Sch. 33, Pt. 2(1).]

History – S. 197E repealed by FA 2001, s. 107 and Sch. 33, Pt. 2(1) with effect for the year 2002–03 and subsequent years of assessment.

197F Other interpretative provisions

197F [Repealed by FA 2001, s. 107 and Sch. 33, Pt. 2(1).]

History – S. 197F repealed by FA 2001, s. 107 and Sch. 33, Pt. 2(1) with effect for the year 2002–03 and subsequent years of assessment.

SPORTING AND RECREATIONAL FACILITIES

197G Sporting and recreational facilities

197G [Omitted by ITEPA 2003, Sch. 6, para. 28 and repealed by ITEPA 2003, Sch. 8, Pt. 1.]

History – S. 197G omitted by ITEPA 2003, Sch. 6, para. 28 and repealed by ITEPA 2003, Sch. 8, Pt. 1 which have effect for the tax year 2003–04 and subsequent tax years.

Notes – S. 197G rewritten as follows:
S. 197G(1): ITEPA 2003, s. 261(1) and s. 266(3).
S. 197G(2): ITEPA 2003, s. 261(2) and (3).
S. 197G(3): ITEPA 2003, s. 261(2), (4), (5), s. 262(1) and s. 263.
S. 197G(4): ITEPA 2003, s. 261(6).
S. 197G(5): s. 263.
S. 197G(6): ITEPA 2003, s. 262(2), s. 263, s. 721(1) and (5).

OTHER EXPENSES, SUBSCRIPTIONS ETC.

198 Relief for necessary expenses

198 [Omitted by ITEPA 2003, Sch. 6, para. 28 and repealed by ITEPA 2003, Sch. 8, Pt. 1.]

History – S. 198 omitted by ITEPA 2003, Sch. 6, para. 28 and repealed by ITEPA 2003, Sch. 8, Pt. 1 which have effect for the tax year 2003–04 and subsequent tax years.

Notes – S. 198 rewritten as follows:
S. 198(1): ITEPA 2003, s. 328(1), s. 329(1), s. 330(1), s. 333(1), (2), s. 334(1), s. 336(1), (3), s. 337(1) and s. 338(1).
S. 198(1A): ITEPA 2003, s. 337(1), s. 338(1)–(5) and s. 339.
S. 198(1B): ITEPA 2003, s. 340(1)–(7).
S. 198(2): ITEPA 2003, s. 328(4), (5), s. 335(2), (3), s. 354(1) and (2).
S. 198(3): ITEPA 2003, s. 328(1), (4), (5), s. 329(1), s. 330(1), s. 335(3), s. 353(1)–(3) and s. 354(2).
S. 198(4): ITEPA 2003, s. 360.
S. 198(5): ITEPA 2003, s. 359.

198A Interpretation of section 198

198A [Repealed by FA 1998, s. 165 and Sch. 27, Part III(10).]

History – S. 198Arepealed by FA 1998, s. 165 and Sch. 27, Part III(10).

199 Expenses necessarily incurred and defrayed from official emoluments

199 [Omitted by ITEPA 2003, Sch. 6, para. 28 and repealed by ITEPA 2003, Sch. 8, Pt. 1.]

History – S. 199 omitted by ITEPA 2003, Sch. 6, para. 28 and repealed by ITEPA 2003, Sch. 8, Pt. 1 which have effect for the tax year 2003–04 and subsequent tax years.

Notes – S. 199 rewritten as follows:
S. 199(1): ITEPA 2003, s. 328(3), s. 329(1), s. 368(1) and (2).
S. 199(2): ITEPA 2003, s. 330(2) and s. 368(3).

200 Expenses of Members of Parliament

200 [Omitted by ITEPA 2003, Sch. 6, para. 28 and repealed by ITEPA 2003, Sch. 8, Pt. 1.]

History – S. 200 omitted by ITEPA 2003, Sch. 6, para. 28 and repealed by ITEPA 2003, Sch. 8, Pt. 1 which have effect for the tax year 2003–04 and subsequent tax years.

Notes – S. 200 rewritten as follows:
S. 200(1): ITEPA 2003, s. 292.
S. 200(2): ITEPA 2003, s. 228(2) and s. 294(1).
S. 200(3): ITEPA 2003, s. 294(2).
S. 200(4): ITEPA 2003, s. 294(3).
S. 200(5): ITEPA 2003, s. 294(4).

200ZA Expenses of members of Scottish Parliament, National Assembly for Wales or Northern Ireland Assembly

200ZA [Omitted by ITEPA 2003, Sch. 6, para. 28 and repealed by ITEPA 2003, Sch. 8, Pt. 1.]

History – S. 200ZA omitted by ITEPA 2003, Sch. 6, para. 28 and repealed by ITEPA 2003, Sch. 8, Pt. 1 which have effect for the tax year 2003–04 and subsequent tax years.

Notes – S. 200ZA rewritten as follows:
S. 200ZA(1): ITEPA 2003, s. 293(2) and s. 294(1).
S. 200ZA(2): ITEPA 2003, s. 228(2), s. 293(1) and s. 294(1).
S. 200ZA(3): ITEPA 2003, s. 293(3) and s. 294(2).
S. 200ZA(4): ITEPA 2003, s. 294(3).
S. 200ZA(5): ITEPA 2003, s. 294(4).

200AA Incidental benefits for holders of certain offices etc.

200AA [Omitted by ITEPA 2003, Sch. 6, para. 28 and repealed by ITEPA 2003, Sch. 8, Pt. 1.]

History – S. 200AA omitted by ITEPA 2003, Sch. 6, para. 28 and repealed by ITEPA 2003, Sch. 8, Pt. 1 which have effect for the tax year 2003–04 and subsequent tax years.

Notes – S. 200AA rewritten as follows:
S. 200AA(1): ITEPA 2003, s. 228(2) s. 295(1) and (2).
S. 200AA(2): ITEPA 2003, s. 295(3) and (4).
S. 200AA(3) was repealed by FA 1999, s. 44(5) and so has not been rewritten into the provisions of ITEPA 2003.
S. 200AA(4): ITEPA 2003, s. 721(5).
S. 200AA(5): ITEPA 2003, s. 295(5).
S. 200AA(6): ITEPA 2003, s. 295(6).

200A Incidental overnight expenses

200A [Omitted by ITEPA 2003, Sch. 6, para. 28 and repealed by ITEPA 2003, Sch. 8, Pt. 1.]

History – S. 200A omitted by ITEPA 2003, Sch. 6, para. 28 and repealed by ITEPA 2003, Sch. 8, Pt. 1 which have effect for the tax year 2003–04 and subsequent tax years.
For the purposes of ITEPA 2003, Sch. 7, para. 34, s. 200A(5) is modified as follows: the words "the aggregate of the exemption provisions total in respect of the period (as defined in section 241 of ITEPA 2003) and" inserted immediately after the words "exceeded by", by virtue of ITEPA 2003, Sch. 7, para. 34. Accordingly, for the purposes of ITEPA 2003, Sch. 7, para. 34, s. 200A is treated as having read as follows:

"Incidental overnight expenses

200A(1) Subject to subsection (2) below, sums paid to or on behalf of any person holding an office or employment, to the extent that they are paid wholly and exclusively for the purpose of defraying, or of being used for defraying, any expenses which–
(a) are incidental to that person's being away from his usual place of abode during a qualifying absence from home, but
(b) would not be deductible under sections 193, 194,195 or 332 or (in the absence of sections 197AD to 197AF) 198 if incurred out of that person's emoluments,

shall not be regarded as emoluments of the office or employment for any purpose of Schedule E.

200A(2) Subsection (1) above shall not apply in the case of any qualifying absence in relation to which the authorised maximum is exceeded.

200A(3) For the purposes of this section a qualifying absence from home, in relation to a person holding an office or employment, is any continuous period throughout which that person is obliged to stay away from his usual place of abode and during which he–
(a) has at least one overnight stay away from that place; but
(b) does not on any occasion stay overnight at a place other than a place the expenses of travelling to which are–
(i) expenses incurred out of his emoluments and deductible, otherwise than by virtue of section 193(4), 194(2) or 195(6), under any of the provisions mentioned in subsection (1)(b) above, or
(ii) expenses which would be so deductible if so incurred, or
(iii) expenses the amount of which, having been paid or reimbursed by the person under whom he holds that office or employment, is excluded from his emoluments in pursuance of section 200B, or
(iv) expenses the amount of which would be so excluded if it were so paid or reimbursed, or
(v) expenses the amount of which, having been paid or reimbursed by the person under whom he holds that office or employment, is excluded from his emoluments in pursuance of section 200E, or
(vi) expenses the amount of which would be so excluded if it were so paid or reimbursed.

200A(4) In this section **"the authorised maximum"**, in relation to each qualifying absence from home by any person, means the aggregate amount equal to the sum of the following amounts–
(a) £5 for every night (if any) during that absence which is a night the whole of which is spent by that person in the United Kingdom; and
(b) £10 for every night (if any) during that absence which is a night the whole or any part of which is spent by that person outside the United Kingdom.

200A(5) For the purposes of this section the authorised maximum is exceeded in relation to a qualifying absence from home by any person if that maximum is exceeded by the aggregate of the exemption provisions total in respect of the period (as defined in section 241 of ITEPA 2003) and the amount which, in the absence of subsection (2) above and of the other requirements of this Act that that maximum is not exceeded, would fall by virtue of this section and sections 141(6C), 142(3C) and 155(1B) to be disregarded, in relation to that qualifying absence, in determining the amount of that person's emoluments.

200A(6) The Treasury may by order increase either or both of the sums for the time being specified in subsection (4)(a) and (b) above; and such an order shall have effect for determining what emoluments are received by any person on or after the date when the order comes into force."

Cross references – ITEPA 2003, s. 241: incidental overnight expenses and benefits – overall exemption limit.
ITEPA 2003, Sch. 7, para. 34 (Sch. 7: transitionals and savings): incidental overnight expenses and benefits.
S. 141(6C) and (6D): exemption for incidental overnight expenses met by means of non-cash voucher.
S. 142(3C) and (3D): exemption for incidental overnight expenses met by means of credit-token.
S. 155(1B) and (1C): charge on benefits in kind for persons in director's or higher-paid employment does not apply in respect of incidental overnight expenses up to authorised maximum.
S. 332: expenses allowable in assessing income tax chargeable upon a clergyman or minister of any religious denomination.

Notes – S. 200A rewritten as follows:
S. 200A(1): ITEPA 2003, s. 240(1), s. 329(5) and s. 353(4).
S. 200A(2): ITEPA 2003, s. 240(3) and s. 241(1).
S. 200A(3): ITEPA 2003, s. 240(4)–(7), s. 329(5) and s. 353(4).
S. 200A(4): ITEPA 2003, s. 241(3).
S. 200A(5): ITEPA 2003, s. 241(1) and (2).
S. 200A(6): ITEPA 2003, s. 716(1)–(3).

200B Work-related training provided by employers

200B [Omitted by ITEPA 2003, Sch. 6, para. 28 and repealed by ITEPA 2003, Sch. 8, Pt. 1.]

History – S. 200B omitted by ITEPA 2003, Sch. 6, para. 28 and repealed by ITEPA 2003, Sch. 8, Pt. 1 which have effect for the tax year 2003–04 and subsequent tax years.

Notes – S. 200B rewritten as follows:
S. 200B(1), (2) and (3): ITEPA 2003, s. 250(1).
S. 200B(4): ITEPA 2003, s. 250(2).
S. 200B(5): ITEPA 2003, s. 251(1).
S. 200B(6): ITEPA 2003, s. 251.
S. 200B(7): ITEPA 2003, s. 718.

200C Expenditure excluded from section 200B

200C [Omitted by ITEPA 2003, Sch. 6, para. 28 and repealed by ITEPA 2003, Sch. 8, Pt. 1.]

History – S. 200C omitted by ITEPA 2003, Sch. 6, para. 28 and repealed by ITEPA 2003, Sch. 8, Pt. 1 which have effect for the tax year 2003–04 and subsequent tax years.

Notes – S. 200C rewritten as follows:
S. 200C(1): ITEPA 2003, s. 253(1), (2) and (4).
S. 200C(2): ITEPA 2003, s. 252(1), (2) and (3).
S. 200C(2A): ITEPA 2003, s. 252(4), s. 329(5) and s. 353(4).
S. 200C(3): ITEPA 2003, s. 254(1) and (2).
S. 200C(4) and (5) are unnecessary and so have not been rewritten into the provisions of ITEPA 2003.
S. 200C(6): ITEPA 2003, s. 253(3).
S. 200C(7): ITEPA 2003, s. 252(5), s. 253(2) and s. 254(3).
S. 200C(8): ITEPA 2003, s. 718.

200D Other work-related training

200D [Omitted by ITEPA 2003, Sch. 6, para. 28 and repealed by ITEPA 2003, Sch. 8, Pt. 1.]

History – S. 200D omitted by ITEPA 2003, Sch. 6, para. 28 and repealed by ITEPA 2003, Sch. 8, Pt. 1 which have effect for the tax year 2003–04 and subsequent tax years.

Notes – S. 200D rewritten as ITEPA 2003, s. 250(1).

200E Education and training funded by employers

200E [Omitted by ITEPA 2003, Sch. 6, para. 28 and repealed by ITEPA 2003, Sch. 8, Pt. 1.]

History – S. 200E omitted by ITEPA 2003, Sch. 6, para. 28 and repealed by ITEPA 2003, Sch. 8, Pt. 1 which have effect for the tax year 2003–04 and subsequent tax years.

Notes – S. 200E rewritten as follows:
S. 200E(1) and (2): ITEPA 2003, s. 255(1).
S. 200E(3): ITEPA 2003, s. 255(3).
S. 255(4): ITEPA 2003, s. 256.
S. 200E(5) and (6): ITEPA 2003, s. 255(2).

200F Section 200E: exclusion of expenditure not directly related to training

200F [Omitted by ITEPA 2003, Sch. 6, para. 28 and repealed by ITEPA 2003, Sch. 8, Pt. 1.]

History – S. 200F omitted by ITEPA 2003, Sch. 6, para. 28 and repealed by ITEPA 2003, Sch. 8, Pt. 1 which have effect for the tax year 2003–04 and subsequent tax years.

Notes – S. 200F rewritten as follows:
S. 200F(1): ITEPA 2003, s. 258(1) and (2).
S. 200F(2): ITEPA 2003, s. 257(1), (2) and (3).
S. 200F(2A): ITEPA 2003, s. 257(4), s. 329(5) and s. 353(4).
S. 200F(3): ITEPA 2003, s. 259(1) and (2).
S. 200F(4): ITEPA 2003, s. 258(3).
S. 200F(5): ITEPA 2003, s. 257(5) and s. 259(3).

200G Section 200E: exclusion of expenditure if contributions not generally available to staff

200G [Omitted by ITEPA 2003, Sch. 6, para. 28 and repealed by ITEPA 2003, Sch. 8, Pt. 1.]

History – S. 200G omitted by ITEPA 2003, Sch. 6, para. 28 and repealed by ITEPA 2003, Sch. 8, Pt. 1 which have effect for the tax year 2003–04 and subsequent tax years.

Notes – S. 200G rewritten as follows:
S. 200G(1): ITEPA 2003, s. 260(1) and (2).
S. 200G(2): ITEPA 2003, s. 260(1).
S. 200G(3): ITEPA 2003, s. 260(3), (4) and (5).

200H Section 200E: exclusion of expenditure otherwise relieved

200H [Omitted by ITEPA 2003, Sch. 6, para. 28 and repealed by ITEPA 2003, Sch. 8, Pt. 1.]

History – S. 200H omitted by ITEPA 2003, Sch. 6, para. 28 and repealed by ITEPA 2003, Sch. 8, Pt. 1 which have effect for the tax year 2003–04 and subsequent tax years.

Notes – S. 200H is unnecessary and so has not been rewritten into the provisions of ITEPA 2003.

200J Education or training funded by third parties

200J [Omitted by ITEPA 2003, Sch. 6, para. 28 and repealed by ITEPA 2003, Sch. 8, Pt. 1.]

History – S. 200J omitted by ITEPA 2003, Sch. 6, para. 28 and repealed by ITEPA 2003, Sch. 8, Pt. 1 which have effect for the tax year 2003–04 and subsequent tax years.

Notes – S. 200J rewritten asITEPA 2003, s. 255(1) and s. 260(1).

201 Fees and subscriptions to professional bodies, learned societies etc.

201 [Omitted by ITEPA 2003, Sch. 6, para. 28 and repealed by ITEPA 2003, Sch. 8, Pt. 1.]

History – S. 201 omitted by ITEPA 2003, Sch. 6, para. 28 and repealed by ITEPA 2003, Sch. 8, Pt. 1 which have effect for the tax year 2003–04 and subsequent tax years.

Other material – Taxline 2000/4 (not reproduced): payment for a practicing certificate does not fall within the list of approved subs unless it is required for employment (this goes for the premium for professional indemnity as well).

Notes – S. 201 rewritten as follows:
S. 201(1): ITEPA 2003, s. 328(1), s. 329(1), s. 333(1), (2), s. 334(1), s. 343(1) and s. 344(1).
S. 201(2): ITEPA 2003, s. 343(2).
S. 201(3): ITEPA 2003, s. 344(2) and (3).
S. 201(4): ITEPA 2003, s. 344(5) and (6).
S. 201(5): ITEPA 2003, s. 343(1) and s. 344(1).
S. 201(6): ITEPA 2003, s. 344(7) and s. 345(1).
S. 201(7): ITEPA 2003, s. 345(2) and (3).

201AA Employee liabilities and indemnity insurance

201AA [Omitted by ITEPA 2003, Sch. 6, para. 28 and repealed by ITEPA 2003, Sch. 8, Pt. 1.]

History – S. 201AA omitted by ITEPA 2003, Sch. 6, para. 28 and repealed by ITEPA 2003, Sch. 8, Pt. 1 which have effect for the tax year 2003–04 and subsequent tax years.

Notes – S. 201AA rewritten as follows:
S. 201AA(1): ITEPA 2003, s. 328(1), s. 329(1), s. 333(1), (2), s. 334(1), s. 346(1), s. 347(1)and s. 558(1).
S. 201AA(2): ITEPA 2003, s. 348 and s. 559.
S. 201AA(3): ITEPA 2003, s. 349(2)–(5) and s. 560(2)–(5).
S. 201AA(4): ITEPA 2003, s. 349(2).
S. 201AA(5): ITEPA 2003, s. 350(1)–(3) and s. 561(1)–(3).
S. 201AA(6): ITEPA 2003, s. 350(4)–(6) and s. 561(4)–(6).
S. 201AA(7): ITEPA 2003, s. 346(3) and s. 558(3).
S. 201AA(8): ITEPA 2003, s. 346(2) and s. 558(2).
S. 201AA(9): ITEPA 2003, s. 346(3) and s. 558(3).

201A Expenses of entertainers

201A [Omitted by ITEPA 2003, Sch. 6, para. 28 and repealed by ITEPA 2003, Sch. 8, Pt. 1.]

History – S. 201A omitted by ITEPA 2003, Sch. 6, para. 28 and repealed by ITEPA 2003, Sch. 8, Pt. 1 which have effect for the tax year 2003–04 and subsequent tax years.

Notes – S. 201A rewritten as follows:
S. 201A(1): ITEPA 2003, s. 328(1) and s. 352(1).
S. 201A(2) and (2A): ITEPA 2003, s. 329(1), s. 333(1), (2), s. 334(1), s. 352(1) and (5).
S. 201A(3) and (3A): ITEPA 2003, s. 352(6).
S. 201A(4): ITEPA 2003, s. 352(2).
S. 201A(4A): ITEPA 2003, s. 352(1).
S. 201A(5): ITEPA 2003, s. 352(4).
S. 201A(6) is unnecessary and so has not been rewritten into the provisions of ITEPA 2003.

202 Donations to charity: payroll deduction scheme

202 [Omitted by ITEPA 2003, Sch. 6, para. 28 and repealed by ITEPA 2003, Sch. 8, Pt. 1.]

History – S. 202 omitted by ITEPA 2003, Sch. 6, para. 28 and repealed by ITEPA 2003, Sch. 8, Pt. 1 which have effect for the tax year 2003–04 and subsequent tax years.

Notes – S. 202 rewritten as follows:
S. 202(1): ITEPA 2003, s. 713(1) and (2).
S. 202(2): ITEPA 2003, s. 713(3)(4) and (5).
S. 202(3): ITEPA 2003, s. 714(1) and (2).
S. 202(4): ITEPA 2003, s. 714(2) and (3).
S. 202(5): ITEPA 2003, s. 713(1) and s. 714(1).
S. 202(6): ITEPA 2003, s. 714(1).
S. 202(7) was repealed by FA 200, s. 38(5) and (7) and so has not been rewritten into the provisions of ITEPA 2003.
S. 202(8): ITEPA 2003, s. 715(1) and (2).
S. 202(9) and (10): ITEPA 2003, s. 715(3).
S. 202(11): ITEPA 2003, s. 714(2).

Chapter V – Assessment, Collection, Recovery and Appeals

202A Assessment on receipts basis

202A [Omitted by ITEPA 2003, Sch. 6, para. 29 and repealed by ITEPA 2003, Sch. 8, Pt. 1.]

History – S. 202A omitted by ITEPA 2003, Sch. 6, para. 29 and repealed by ITEPA 2003, Sch. 8, Pt. 1 which have effect for the tax year 2003–04 and subsequent tax years.

Notes – S. 202A rewritten as follows:
S. 202A(1): ITEPA 2003, s. 10(2), s. 15(2), s. 21(2), s. 22(2), s. 25(2), s. 26(2) and s. 27(2).
S. 202A(2): ITEPA 2003, s. 15(3), s. 21(3), s. 22(3), s. 25(3), s. 26(3) and s. 27(3).
S. 202A(3): ITEPA 2003, s. 13(4) and (5).
S. 202A(4) is unnecessary and so has not been rewritten into the provisions of ITEPA 2003.

202B Receipts basis: meaning of receipt

202B [Omitted by ITEPA 2003, Sch. 6, para. 29 and repealed by ITEPA 2003, Sch. 8, Pt. 1.]

History – S. 202B omitted by ITEPA 2003, Sch. 6, para. 29 and repealed by ITEPA 2003, Sch. 8, Pt. 1 which have effect for the tax year 2003–04 and subsequent tax years.

Notes – S. 202B(1) and (2) have been rewritten into the provisions of ITEPA 2003, s. 18(1) and s. 31(1).
S. 202B(3): ITEPA 2003, s. 18(2) and s. 31(2).
S. 202B(4): ITEPA 2003, s. 18(1) and s. 31(1).
S. 202B(5): ITEPA 2003, s. 18(3), (4), s. 31(3), (4) and s. 686(3).
S. 202B(6): ITEPA 2003, s. 18(3), (4), s. 31(3), (4) and s. 686(4).
S. 202B(7): ITEPA 2003, s. 19(1) and s. 32(1).
S. 202B(8): ITEPA 2003, s. 19(2), (3) and s. 32(1)–(3).
S. 202B(9) and (10) have been rewritten into the provisions of ITEPA 2003, s. 19(2), s. 32(1) and (2).
S. 202B(11): ITEPA 2003, s. 19(4), s. 32(1) and (4).

203 Pay as you earn

203 [Omitted by ITEPA 2003, Sch. 6, para. 30 and repealed by ITEPA 2003, Sch. 8, Pt. 1.]

History – S. 203 omitted by ITEPA 2003, Sch. 6, para. 30 and repealed by ITEPA 2003, Sch. 8, Pt. 1 which have effect for the tax year 2003–04 and subsequent tax years.

Notes – S. 203 rewritten as follows:
S. 203(1): ITEPA 2003, s. 684(6).
S. 203(2): ITEPA 2003, s. 684(1), (2) and (7).
S. 203(3): ITEPA 2003, s. 684(3).
S. 203(3A) is spent and so has not been rewritten into the provisions of ITEPA 2003.
S. 203(4) was repealed by FA 1989, s. 45(3) and so has not been rewritten into the provisions of ITEPA 2003.
S. 203(5): ITEPA 2003, s. 684(5).
S. 203(6): ITEPA 2003, s. 685(1).
S. 203(7): ITEPA 2003, s. 685(2).
S. 203(8): ITEPA 2003, s. 685(3).
S. 203(9): ITEPA 2003, s. 684(4).
S. 203(10): ITEPA 2003, s. 684(2).

203A PAYE: meaning of payment

203A [Omitted by ITEPA 2003, Sch. 6, para. 30 and repealed by ITEPA 2003, Sch. 8, Pt. 1.]

History – S. 203A omitted by ITEPA 2003, Sch. 6, para. 30 and repealed by ITEPA 2003, Sch. 8, Pt. 1 which have effect for the tax year 2003–04 and subsequent tax years.

Notes – S. 203A rewritten as follows:
S. 203A(1) and (2): ITEPA 2003, s. 686(1).
S. 203A(3): ITEPA 2003, s. 686(2).
S. 203A(4): ITEPA 2003, s. 686(1).
S. 203A(5): ITEPA 2003, s. 686(3) and (4).

203B PAYE: payment by intermediary

203B [Omitted by ITEPA 2003, Sch. 6, para. 30 and repealed by ITEPA 2003, Sch. 8, Pt. 1.]

History – S. 203B omitted by ITEPA 2003, Sch. 6, para. 30 and repealed by ITEPA 2003, Sch. 8, Pt. 1 which have effect for the tax year 2003–04 and subsequent tax years.

Notes – S. 203B rewritten as follows:
S. 203B(1): ITEPA 2003, s. 687(1).
S. 203B(2): ITEPA 2003, s. 687(2).
S. 203B(3): ITEPA 2003, s. 687(3).
S. 203B(4): ITEPA 2003, s. 687(4).
S. 203B(5): ITEPA 2003, s. 718.

203C PAYE: employee of non-UK employer

203C [Omitted by ITEPA 2003, Sch. 6, para. 30 and repealed by ITEPA 2003, Sch. 8, Pt. 1.]

History – S. 203C omitted by ITEPA 2003, Sch. 6, para. 30 and repealed by ITEPA 2003, Sch. 8, Pt. 1 which have effect for the tax year 2003–04 and subsequent tax years.

Notes – S. 203C rewritten as follows:
S. 203C(1): ITEPA 2003, s. 689(1).
S. 203C(2): ITEPA 2003, s. 689(2).
S. 203C(3): ITEPA 2003, s. 689(3).

S. 203C(3A): ITEPA 2003, s. 689(4).
S. 203C(3B): ITEPA 2003, s. 689(5).
S. 203C(4): ITEPA 2003, s. 689(6).
S. 203C(5): ITEPA 2003, s. 689(5) and s. 718.

203D PAYE: employee non-resident, etc.

203D [Omitted by ITEPA 2003, Sch. 6, para. 30 and repealed by ITEPA 2003, Sch. 8, Pt. 1.]

History – S. 203D omitted by ITEPA 2003, Sch. 6, para. 30 and repealed by ITEPA 2003, Sch. 8, Pt. 1 which have effect for the tax year 2003–04 and subsequent tax years.

Notes – S. 203D rewritten as follows:
S. 203D(1): ITEPA 2003, s. 690(1).
S. 203D(2): ITEPA 2003, s. 690(2).
S. 203D(3): ITEPA 2003, s. 690(3).
S. 203D(4): ITEPA 2003, s. 690(4).
S. 203D(5): ITEPA 2003, s. 690(5).
S. 203D(6): ITEPA 2003, s. 690(6).
S. 203D(7): ITEPA 2003, s. 690(7).
S. 203D(8): ITEPA 2003, s. 690(8).
S. 203D(9): ITEPA 2003, s. 690(9).

203E PAYE: mobile UK workforce

203E [Omitted by ITEPA 2003, Sch. 6, para. 30 and repealed by ITEPA 2003, Sch. 8, Pt. 1.]

History – S. 203E omitted by ITEPA 2003, Sch. 6, para. 30 and repealed by ITEPA 2003, Sch. 8, Pt. 1 which have effect for the tax year 2003–04 and subsequent tax years.

Notes – S. 203E rewritten as follows:
S. 203E(1): ITEPA 2003, s. 691(1).
S. 203E(2): ITEPA 2003, s. 691(2).
S. 203E(3): ITEPA 2003, s. 691(3).
S. 203E(4): ITEPA 2003, s. 691(4).
S. 203E(5): ITEPA 2003, s. 691(5).

203F PAYE: [readily convertible] assets

203F [Omitted by ITEPA 2003, Sch. 6, para. 30 and repealed by ITEPA 2003, Sch. 8, Pt. 1.]

History – S. 203F omitted by ITEPA 2003, Sch. 6, para. 30 and repealed by ITEPA 2003, Sch. 8, Pt. 1 which have effect for the tax year 2003–04 and subsequent tax years.

Notes – S. 203F rewritten as follows:
S. 203F(1): ITEPA 2003, s. 696(1).
S. 203F(2): ITEPA 2003, s. 702(1).
S. 203F(3): ITEPA 2003, s. 696(2).
S. 203F(3A): ITEPA 2003, s. 702(2).
S. 203F(3B): ITEPA 2003, s. 702(4).
S. 203F(3C): ITEPA 2003, s. 702(5).
S. 203F(4): ITEPA 2003, s. 701(2) and s. 721(1) ("cash voucher", "credit-token", "non-cash voucher").
S. 203F(5): ITEPA 2003, s. 701(1).
S. 203F(6): ITEPA 2003, s. 702(6) and s. 721(5).

203FA PAYE: enhancing the value of an asset

203FA [Omitted by ITEPA 2003, Sch. 6, para. 30 and repealed by ITEPA 2003, Sch. 8, Pt. 1.]

History – S. 203FA omitted by ITEPA 2003, Sch. 6, para. 30 and repealed by ITEPA 2003, Sch. 8, Pt. 1 which have effect for the tax year 2003–04 and subsequent tax years.

Notes – S. 203FA rewritten as follows:
S. 203FA(1): ITEPA 2003, s. 697(1) and (2).
S. 203FA(2): ITEPA 2003, s. 697(2).
S. 203FA(3): ITEPA 2003, s. 697(3).
S. 203FA(4): ITEPA 2003, s. 697(5).
S. 203FA(5) is unnecessary and so has not been rewritten into the provisions of ITEPA 2003.

203FB PAYE: gains from share options etc.

203FB [Omitted by ITEPA 2003, Sch. 6, para. 30 and repealed by ITEPA 2003, Sch. 8, Pt. 1.]

History – S. 203FB omitted by ITEPA 2003, Sch. 6, para. 30 and repealed by ITEPA 2003, Sch. 8, Pt. 1 which have effect for the tax year 2003–04 and subsequent tax years.

Notes – S. 203FB rewritten as follows:
S. 203FB(1): ITEPA 2003, s. 698(1), s. 699(1) and s. 700(1).
S. 203FB(2): ITEPA 2003, s. 700(2).
S. 203FB(3): ITEPA 2003, s. 700(3).
S. 203FB(4): ITEPA 2003, s. 698(3).
S. 203FB(5): ITEPA 2003, s. 699(3).
S. 203FB(6): ITEPA 2003, s. 699(4).
S. 203FB(6A): ITEPA 2003, s. 700(4).
S. 203FB(7): ITEPA 2003, s. 698(4) and s. 699(5).
S. 203FB(8): ITEPA 2003, s. 700(5).
S. 203FB(9): ITEPA 2003, s. 700(6) and s. 721(1) ("cash voucher", "credit-token", "non-cash voucher").
S. 203FB(10): ITEPA 2003, s. 698(2), (5), s. 699(2), (6), s. 700(7) and (8).

203G PAYE: non-cash vouchers

203G [Omitted by ITEPA 2003, Sch. 6, para. 30 and repealed by ITEPA 2003, Sch. 8, Pt. 1.]

History – S. 203G omitted by ITEPA 2003, Sch. 6, para. 30 and repealed by ITEPA 2003, Sch. 8, Pt. 1 which have effect for the tax year 2003–04 and subsequent tax years.

Notes – S. 203G rewritten as follows:
S. 203G(1): ITEPA 2003, s. 694(1).
S. 203G(2): ITEPA 2003, s. 694(2) and s. 721(1) ("non-cash voucher").
S. 203G(3): ITEPA 2003, s. 694(3).
S. 203G(4): ITEPA 2003, s. 694(4).
S. 203G(5): ITEPA 2003, s. 694(7).

203H PAYE: credit-tokens

203H [Omitted by ITEPA 2003, Sch. 6, para. 30 and repealed by ITEPA 2003, Sch. 8, Pt. 1.]

History – S. 203H omitted by ITEPA 2003, Sch. 6, para. 30 and repealed by ITEPA 2003, Sch. 8, Pt. 1 which have effect for the tax year 2003–04 and subsequent tax years.

Notes – S. 203H rewritten as follows:
S. 203H(1): ITEPA 2003, s. 695(1).
S. 203H(2) was repealed by FA 1998, s. 68(2) and so has not been rewritten into the provisions of ITEPA 2003.
S. 203H(3): ITEPA 2003, s. 695(3).
S. 203H(4): ITEPA 2003, s. 721(1) ("credit-token").

203I PAYE: cash vouchers

203I [Omitted by ITEPA 2003, Sch. 6, para. 30 and repealed by ITEPA 2003, Sch. 8, Pt. 1.]

History – S. 203I omitted by ITEPA 2003, Sch. 6, para. 30 and repealed by ITEPA 2003, Sch. 8, Pt. 1 which have effect for the tax year 2003–04 and subsequent tax years.

Notes – S. 203I rewritten as follows:
S. 203I(1): ITEPA 2003, s. 693(1).
S. 203I(2): ITEPA 2003, s. 693(4).
S. 203I(3): ITEPA 2003, s. 693(5).

ICTA 1988

203J S. 203B to s. 203I: accounting for tax

203J [Omitted by ITEPA 2003, Sch. 6, para. 30 and repealed by ITEPA 2003, Sch. 8, Pt. 1.]

History – S. 203J omitted by ITEPA 2003, Sch. 6, para. 30 and repealed by ITEPA 2003, Sch. 8, Pt. 1 which have effect for the tax year 2003–04 and subsequent tax years.

Notes – S. 203J rewritten as follows:
S. 203J(1): ITEPA 2003, s. 710(1).
S. 203J(2): ITEPA 2003, s. 710(2).
S. 203J(3): ITEPA 2003, s. 710(3) and (4).
S. 203J(4): ITEPA 2003, s. 710(5).
S. 203J(5): ITEPA 2003, s. 710(6).

203K "Trading arrangements"

203K [Omitted by ITEPA 2003, Sch. 6, para. 30 and repealed by ITEPA 2003, Sch. 8, Pt. 1.]

History – S. 203K omitted by ITEPA 2003, Sch. 6, para. 30 and repealed by ITEPA 2003, Sch. 8, Pt. 1 which have effect for the tax year 2003–04 and subsequent tax years.

Notes – S. 203K(1)–(3) were repealed by FA 1998, Sch. 27, Pt. 3(12) and so have not been rewritten into the provisions of ITEPA 2003. S. 203K(4) rewritten as ITEPA 2003, s. 702(3).

203L S. 203B to s. 203K: interpretation, etc.

203L [Omitted by ITEPA 2003, Sch. 6, para. 30 and repealed by ITEPA 2003, Sch. 8, Pt. 1.]

History – S. 203L omitted by ITEPA 2003, Sch. 6, para. 30 and repealed by ITEPA 2003, Sch. 8, Pt. 1 which have effect for the tax year 2003–04 and subsequent tax years.

Notes – S. 203L rewritten as follows:
S. 203L(1): ITEPA 2003, s. 712(1).
S. 203L(1A): ITEPA 2003, s. 688(1).
S. 203L(1B): ITEPA 2003, s. 688(2).
S. 203L(1C): ITEPA 2003, s. 688(3) and s. 718.
S. 203L(2) is unnecessary and so has not been rewritten into the provisions of ITEPA 2003.
S. 203L(3): ITEPA 2003, s. 684(8).
S. 203L(4): ITEPA 2003, s. 684(2).

204 PAYE repayments

204 [Omitted by ITEPA 2003, Sch. 6, para. 30 and repealed by ITEPA 2003, Sch. 8, Pt. 1.]

History – S. 204 omitted by ITEPA 2003, Sch. 6, para. 30 and repealed by ITEPA 2003, Sch. 8, Pt. 1 which have effect for the tax year 2003–04 and subsequent tax years.

Notes – S. 204 rewritten as ITEPA 2003, s. 708(1) and (2).

205 Assessments unnecessary in certain circumstances

205 [Omitted by ITEPA 2003, Sch. 6, para. 31 and repealed by ITEPA 2003, Sch. 8, Pt. 1.]

History – S. 205 omitted by ITEPA 2003, Sch. 6, para. 31 and repealed by ITEPA 2003, Sch. 8, Pt. 1 which have effect for the tax year 2003–04 and subsequent tax years.

Notes – S. 205 rewritten as follows:
S. 205(1) to (3) are unnecessary and so have not been rewritten into the provisions of ITEPA 2003.
S. 205(4): ITEPA 2003, s. 711.
S. 205(5) is unnecessary and so has not been rewritten into the provisions of ITEPA 2003.

206 Additional provision for certain assessments

206 [Omitted by ITEPA 2003, Sch. 6, para. 31 and repealed by ITEPA 2003, Sch. 8, Pt. 1.]

History – S. 206 omitted by ITEPA 2003, Sch. 6, para. 31 and repealed by ITEPA 2003, Sch. 8, Pt. 1 which have effect for the tax year 2003–04 and subsequent tax years.

Notes – S. 206 rewritten as ITEPA 2003, s. 709.

206A PAYE settlement agreements

206A [Omitted by ITEPA 2003, Sch. 6, para. 32 and repealed by ITEPA 2003, Sch. 8, Pt. 1.]

History – S. 206A omitted by ITEPA 2003, Sch. 6, para. 32 and repealed by ITEPA 2003, Sch. 8, Pt. 1 which have effect for the tax year 2003–04 and subsequent tax years.

Notes – S. 206A rewritten as follows:
S. 206A(1): ITEPA 2003, s. 703.
S. 206A(2): ITEPA 2003, s. 704(1).
S. 206A(3): ITEPA 2003, s. 705.
S. 206A(4): ITEPA 2003, s. 706.
S. 206A(5) is unnecessary and so has not been rewritten into the provisions of ITEPA 2003.
S. 206A(6): ITEPA 2003, s. 684(2).
S. 206A(7) is unnecessary and so has not been rewritten into the provisions of ITEPA 2003.
S. 206A(8): ITEPA 2003, s. 704(2).
S. 206A(9): ITEPA 2003, s. 707.

207 Disputes as to domicile or ordinary residence

207 [Omitted by ITEPA 2003, Sch. 6, para. 33 and repealed by ITEPA 2003, Sch. 8, Pt. 1.]

History – S. 207 omitted by ITEPA 2003, Sch. 6, para. 33 and repealed by ITEPA 2003, Sch. 8, Pt. 1 which have effect for the tax year 2003–04 and subsequent tax years.

Notes – S. 207 rewritten as ITEPA 2003, s. 42 and s. 43.

PART VI – COMPANY DISTRIBUTIONS, TAX CREDITS ETC

Chapter I – Taxation of Company Distributions

207A Application of lower rate to company distributions

207A [Repealed by FA 1996, s. 205 and Sch. 41, Pt. V(1) for 1996–97 and later years of assessment.]

208 UK company distributions not generally chargeable to corporation tax

208 [Omitted by CTA 2009, s. 1322 and Sch. 1, para. 96 and repealed by CTA 2009, s. 1326 and Sch. 3, Pt. 1.]

History – S. 208 omitted by CTA 2009, s. 1322 and Sch. 1, para. 96 and repealed by CTA 2009, s. 1326 and Sch. 3, Pt. 1, with effect for corporation tax purposes for accounting periods ending on or after 1 April 2009, and for income tax and capital gains tax purposes for the tax year 2009–10 and subsequent tax years.

Notes – S. 208 rewritten as CTA 2009, s. 1285(1), (2), (3), (4).

Chapter II – Matters which are Distributions for the Purposes of the Corporation Tax Acts

209 Meaning of "distribution"

History – Chapter II of Part VI omitted by CTA 2010, s. 1177 and Sch. 1, para. 14 and repealed by CTA 2010, s. 1181 and Sch. 3, Pt. 1.

209 [Omitted by CTA 2010, s. 1177 and Sch. 1, para. 14 and repealed by CTA 2010, s. 1181 and Sch. 3, Pt. 1.]

History – Chapter II of Part VI (of which s. 209 formed a part) omitted by CTA 2010, s. 1177 and Sch. 1, para. 14 and repealed by CTA 2010, s. 1181 and Sch. 3, Pt. 1, with effect for corporation tax purposes for accounting periods ending on or after 1 April 2010, and for income and capital gains tax purposes for the tax year 2010–11 and subsequent tax years.

Notes – S. 209 rewritten for corporation tax purposes as follows:
S. 209(1): CTA 2010, s. 999(1), 1030.
S. 209(1A): CTA 2010, s. 1031.
S. 209(2): CTA 2010, s. 1000(1), 1003(1), (2), 1004(1), (2), 1005, 1015(1), (2), (3), (4), (5), (6); 1017(2), Sch. 2, para. 103(1), (2).

S. 209(3): CTA 2010, s. 1006, 1018(1), Sch. 2, para. 102, 104.
S. 209(3A): CTA 2010, s. 1007(1), (2), (3), 1018(2), (3).
S. 209(3AA): CTA 2010, s. 1008(1), (2), (3), (4).
S. 209(3B): CTA 2010, s. 1017(1).
S. 209(4): CTA 2010, s. 1020(1), (2), (3).
S. 209(5): CTA 2010, s. 1002(2), (3), 1021(1).
S. 209(6): CTA 2010, s. 1002(1), (4), 1021(4), (5).
S. 209(6A): CTA 2010, s. 1019(1), (2), (3).
S. 209(7): CTA 2010, s. 1021(1), (2), (3).
S. 209(8): CTA 2010, s. 1003(3), 1004(3).
S. 209(9): CTA 2010, s. 1016(1), (2), (3).
S. 209(10): CTA 2010, s. 1017(4).
S. 209(11): CTA 2010, s. 1017(3).

209A Section 209(3AA): link to shares of company or associated company

History – Chapter II of Part VI omitted by CTA 2010, s. 1177 and Sch. 1, para. 14 and repealed by CTA 2010, s. 1181 and Sch. 3, Pt. 1.

209A [Omitted by CTA 2010, s. 1177 and Sch. 1, para. 14 and repealed by CTA 2010, s. 1181 and Sch. 3, Pt. 1.]

History – Chapter II of Part VI (of which s. 209A formed a part) omitted by CTA 2010, s. 1177 and Sch. 1, para. 14 and repealed by CTA 2010, s. 1181 and Sch. 3, Pt. 1, with effect for corporation tax purposes for accounting periods ending on or after 1 April 2010, and for income and capital gains tax purposes for the tax year 2010–11 and subsequent tax years.

Notes – S. 209A rewritten for corporation tax purposes as follows:
S. 209A(1): CTA 2010, s. 1009(1).
S. 209A(2): CTA 2010, s. 1009(2).
S. 209A(3): CTA 2010, s. 1010(1), (2), (3).
S. 209A(4): CTA 2010, s. 1009(3).
S. 209A(5): CTA 2010, s. 1011(1).
S. 209A(6): CTA 2010, s. 1011(2).
S. 209A(7): CTA 2010, s. 1011(3).

209B Section 209(3AA): hedging arrangements

History – Chapter II of Part VI omitted by CTA 2010, s. 1177 and Sch. 1, para. 14 and repealed by CTA 2010, s. 1181 and Sch. 3, Pt. 1.

209B [Omitted by CTA 2010, s. 1177 and Sch. 1, para. 14 and repealed by CTA 2010, s. 1181 and Sch. 3, Pt. 1.]

History – Chapter II of Part VI (of which s. 209B formed a part) omitted by CTA 2010, s. 1177 and Sch. 1, para. 14 and repealed by CTA 2010, s. 1181 and Sch. 3, Pt. 1, with effect for corporation tax purposes for accounting periods ending on or after 1 April 2010, and for income and capital gains tax purposes for the tax year 2010–11 and subsequent tax years.

Notes – S. 209B rewritten for corporation tax purposes as follows:
S. 209B(1): CTA 2010, s. 1012(1).
S. 209B(2): CTA 2010, s. 1013(1).
S. 209B(3): CTA 2010, s. 1012(2).
S. 209B(4): CTA 2010, s. 1013(2), (3).
S. 209B(5): CTA 2010, s. 1013(4), (5).
S. 209B(6): CTA 2010, s. 1013(6).
S. 209B(7): CTA 2010, s. 1013(7).
S. 209B(8): CTA 2010, s. 1014(1), (2), (3), (4), (5), (6).
S. 209B(9): CTA 2010, s. 1013(8).

210 Bonus issue following repayment of share capital

History – Chapter II of Part VI omitted by CTA 2010, s. 1177 and Sch. 1, para. 14 and repealed by CTA 2010, s. 1181 and Sch. 3, Pt. 1.

210 [Omitted by CTA 2010, s. 1177 and Sch. 1, Part 1, para. 14 and repealed by CTA 2010, s. 1181 and Sch. 3, Pt. 1.]

History – Chapter II of Part VI (of which s. 210 formed a part) omitted by CTA 2010, s. 1177 and Sch. 1, para. 14 and repealed by CTA 2010, s. 1181 and Sch. 3, Pt. 1, with effect for corporation tax purposes for accounting periods ending on or after 1 April 2010, and for income and capital gains tax purposes for the tax year 2010–11 and subsequent tax years.

Notes – S. 210 rewritten for corporation tax purposes as follows:
S. 210(1): CTA 2010, s. 1022(1), (2), (3), (4), Sch. 2, para. 105(1).
S. 210(2): CTA 2010, s. 1023(3), Sch. 2, para. 105(2), (3).
S. 210(3): CTA 2010, s. 1023(1), (2), Sch. 2, para. 105(4).
S. 210(4): CTA 2010, s. 1023(4), (5).

211 Matters to be treated or not to be treated as repayments of share capital

History – Chapter II of Part VI omitted by CTA 2010, s. 1177 and Sch. 1, para. 14 and repealed by CTA 2010, s. 1181 and Sch. 3, Pt. 1.

211 [Omitted by CTA 2010, s. 1177 and Sch. 1, para. 14 and repealed by CTA 2010, s. 1181 and Sch. 3, Pt. 1.]

History – Chapter II of Part VI (of which s. 211 formed a part) omitted by CTA 2010, s. 1177 and Sch. 1, para. 14 and repealed by CTA 2010, s. 1181 and Sch. 3, Pt. 1, with effect for corporation tax purposes for accounting periods ending on or after 1 April 2010, and for income and capital gains tax purposes for the tax year 2010–11 and subsequent tax years.

Notes – S. 211 rewritten for corporation tax purposes as follows:
S. 211(1): CTA 2010, s. 1026(1), (2), 1027(1), (2), (4), Sch. 2, para. 106(1), (2), (3).

S. 211(2): CTA 2010, s. 1026(3).
S. 211(3): CTA 2010, s. 1027(3).
S. 211(4): CTA 2010, s. 1026(4).
S. 211(5): CTA 2010, s. 1025(1), (2).
S. 211(6): CTA 2010, s. 1025(3).
S. 211(7): CTA 2010, s. 1024.

Chapter III – Matters which are not Distributions for the Purposes of the Corporation Tax Acts

History – Chapter III of Part VI omitted by CTA 2010, s. 1177 and Sch. 1, para. 15 and repealed by CTA 2010, s. 1181 and Sch. 3, Pt. 1.

PAYMENTS OF INTEREST

212 Interest etc. paid in respect of certain securities

History – Chapter III of Part VI omitted by CTA 2010, s. 1177 and Sch. 1, para. 15 and repealed by CTA 2010, s. 1181 and Sch. 3, Pt. 1.

212 [Omitted by CTA 2010, s. 1177 and Sch. 1, para. 15 and repealed by CTA 2010, s. 1181 and Sch. 3, Pt. 1.]

History – Chapter III of Part VI (of which s. 212 formed a part) omitted by CTA 2010, s. 1177 and Sch. 1, para. 15 and repealed by CTA 2010, s. 1181 and Sch. 3, Pt. 1, with effect for corporation tax purposes for accounting periods ending on or after 1 April 2010, and for income and capital gains tax purposes for the tax year 2010–11 and subsequent tax years.

Notes – S. 212 rewritten for corporation tax purposes as follows:
S. 212(1): CTA 2010, s. 1032(1).
S. 212(2): CTA 2010, Sch. 2, para. 107(1), (2).
S. 212(3): CTA 2010, s. 1032(2).

DEMERGERS

History – Chapter III of Part VI omitted by CTA 2010, s. 1177 and Sch. 1, para. 15 and repealed by CTA 2010, s. 1181 and Sch. 3, Pt. 1.

213 Exempt distributions

213 [Omitted by CTA 2010, s. 1177 and Sch. 1, para. 15 and repealed by CTA 2010, s. 1181 and Sch. 3, Pt. 1.]

History – Chapter III of Part VI (of which s. 213 formed a part) omitted by CTA 2010, s. 1177 and Sch. 1, para. 15 and repealed by CTA 2010, s. 1181 and Sch. 3, Pt. 1, with effect for corporation tax purposes for accounting periods ending on or after 1 April 2010, and for income and capital gains tax purposes for the tax year 2010–11 and subsequent tax years.

Notes – S. 213 rewritten for corporation tax purposes as follows:
S. 213(1): CTA 2010, s. 1074(1), (2).
S. 213(2): CTA 2010, s. 1075(1), 1076, 1077(2).
S. 213(3): CTA 2010, s. 1075(2), 1076, 1077(1), 1079, 1080(2), (3).
S. 213(4): CTA 2010, s. 1081(1), (2).
S. 213(5): CTA 2010, s. 1081(2).
S. 213(6): CTA 2010, s. 1082(1), (2).
S. 213(7): CTA 2010, s. 1082(4).
S. 213(8): CTA 2010, s. 1083(1), (2), (3), (4), (5).
S. 213(9): CTA 2010, s. 1084(2).
S. 213(10): CTA 2010, s. 1081(3).
S. 213(11): CTA 2010, s. 1081(4), (5), (6), (7).
S. 213(12): CTA 2010, s. 1082(3), 1084(1), 1085(1), (2), (3).

213A Exempt distributions: division of business

History – Chapter III of Part VI omitted by CTA 2010, s. 1177 and Sch. 1, para. 15 and repealed by CTA 2010, s. 1181 and Sch. 3, Pt. 1.

213A [Omitted by CTA 2010, s. 1177 and Sch. 1, para. 15 and repealed by CTA 2010, s. 1181 and Sch. 3, Pt. 1.]

History – Chapter III of Part VI (of which s. 213A formed a part) omitted by CTA 2010, s. 1177 and Sch. 1, para. 15 and repealed by CTA 2010, s. 1181 and Sch. 3, Pt. 1, with effect for corporation tax purposes for accounting periods ending on or after 1 April 2010, and for income and capital gains tax purposes for the tax year 2010–11 and subsequent tax years.

Notes – S. 213A rewritten for corporation tax purposes as follows:
S. 213A(1): CTA 2010, s. 1075(1), 1078(1), (2).
S. 213A(2): CTA 2010, s. 1075(2)
S. 213A(3): CTA 2010, s. 1079, 1080(4).

214 Chargeable payments connected with exempt distributions

History – Chapter III of Part VI omitted by CTA 2010, s. 1177 and Sch. 1, para. 15 and repealed by CTA 2010, s. 1181 and Sch. 3, Pt. 1.

214 [Omitted by CTA 2010, s. 1177 and Sch. 1, para. 15 and repealed by CTA 2010, s. 1181 and Sch. 3, Pt. 1.]

History – Chapter III of Part VI (of which s. 214 formed a part) omitted by CTA 2010, s. 1177 and Sch. 1, para. 15 and repealed by CTA 2010, s. 1181 and Sch. 3, Pt. 1, with effect for corporation tax purposes for accounting periods ending on or after 1 April 2010, and for income and capital gains tax purposes for the tax year 2010–11 and subsequent tax years.

Notes – S. 214(1) rewritten as ITA 2007, s. 928(1), (2), (5).
S. 214 rewritten for corporation tax purposes as follows:
S. 214(1): CTA 2010, s. 1028(1), 1086(1), (2), (3), 1087.
S. 214(1A): CTA 2010, s.1086(4), (5).
S. 214(1B): CTA 2010, s.1086(2).
S. 214(2): CTA 2010, s.1028(3), 1088(1), (2), (3), (4), (5), (6), 1089(3), (4), (5).
S. 214(3): CTA 2010, s.1028(3), 1088(1), 1089(1), (2), (3), (4), (5), (6).
S. 214(4): CTA 2010, s.1090(1), (2).
S. 214(5): CTA 2010, s.1090(3).
S. 214(6): CTA 2010, s.1086(6).

215 Advance clearance by Board of distributions and payments

History – Chapter III of Part VI omitted by CTA 2010, s. 1177 and Sch. 1, para. 15 and repealed by CTA 2010, s. 1181 and Sch. 3, Pt. 1.

215 [Omitted by CTA 2010, s. 1177 and Sch. 1, para. 15 and repealed by CTA 2010, s. 1181 and Sch. 3, Pt. 1.]

History – Chapter III of Part VI (of which s. 215 formed a part) omitted by CTA 2010, s. 1177 and Sch. 1, para. 15 and repealed by CTA 2010, s. 1181 and Sch. 3, Pt. 1, with effect for corporation tax purposes for accounting periods ending on or after 1 April 2010, and for income and capital gains tax purposes for the tax year 2010–11 and subsequent tax years.

Notes – S. 215 rewritten for corporation tax purposes as follows:
S. 215(1): CTA 2010, s. 1091(1), (2).
S. 215(2): CTA 2010, s.1092(1), (2), (3).
S. 215(3): CTA 2010, s.1092(4), (5).
S. 215(4): CTA 2010, s.1086(6).
S. 215(5): CTA 2010, s.1093(1), (2), (3), (4).
S. 215(6): CTA 2010, s.1094(1).
S. 215(7): CTA 2010, s.1094(2), (3), (4), (5).
S. 215(8): CTA 2010, s.1094(6), (7).

216 Returns

History – Chapter III of Part VI omitted by CTA 2010, s. 1177 and Sch. 1, para. 15 and repealed by CTA 2010, s. 1181 and Sch. 3, Pt. 1.

216 [Omitted by CTA 2010, s. 1177 and Sch. 1, para. 15 and repealed by CTA 2010, s. 1181 and Sch. 3, Pt. 1.]

History – Chapter III of Part VI (of which s. 216 formed a part) omitted by CTA 2010, s. 1177 and Sch. 1, para. 15 and repealed by CTA 2010, s. 1181 and Sch. 3, Pt. 1, with effect for corporation tax purposes for accounting periods ending on or after 1 April 2010, and for income and capital gains tax purposes for the tax year 2010–11 and subsequent tax years.

Notes – S. 216 rewritten for corporation tax purposes as follows:
S. 216(1): CTA 2010, s. 10951(1), (2), (3).
S. 216(2): CTA 2010, s.1096(1), (2), (8).
S. 216(3): CTA 2010, s.1096(3), (4), (6), (7), (8).
S. 216(4): CTA 2010, s.1096(5).

217 Information

History – Chapter III of Part VI omitted by CTA 2010, s. 1177 and Sch. 1, para. 15 and repealed by CTA 2010, s. 1181 and Sch. 3, Pt. 1.

217 [Omitted by CTA 2010, s. 1177 and Sch. 1, para. 15 and repealed by CTA 2010, s. 1181 and Sch. 3, Pt. 1.]

History – S. 217(4), so far as it continued to have effect (see CTA 2010, s. 1184), omitted by FA 2011, s. 86 and Sch. 23, para. 55(b), with effect from 1 April 2012, subject to transitional provisions in FA 2011, Sch. 23, para. 65.
Chapter III of Part VI (of which s. 217 formed a part) omitted by CTA 2010, s. 1177 and Sch. 1, para. 15 and repealed by CTA 2010, s. 1181 and Sch. 3, Pt. 1, with effect for corporation tax purposes for accounting periods ending on or after 1 April 2010, and for income and capital gains tax purposes for the tax year 2010–11 and subsequent tax years.

Notes – Former s. 217 rewritten for corporation tax purposes as follows:
Former s. 217(4): CTA 2010, s. 1097(1), (2).

218 Interpretation of sections 213 to 217

History – Chapter 3 of Part 6 omitted by CTA 2010, s. 1177 and Sch. 1, para. 15 and repealed by CTA 2010, s. 1181 and Sch. 3, Pt. 1.

218 [Omitted by CTA 2010, s. 1177 and Sch. 1, para. 15 and repealed by CTA 2010, s. 1181 and Sch. 3, Pt. 1.]

History – Chapter III of Part VI (of which s. 218 formed a part) omitted by CTA 2010, s. 1177 and Sch. 1, para. 15 and repealed by CTA 2010, s. 1181 and Sch. 3, Pt. 1, with effect for corporation tax purposes for accounting periods ending on or after 1 April 2010, and for income and capital gains tax purposes for the tax year 2010–11 and subsequent tax years.

Notes – S. 218 rewritten for corporation tax purposes as follows:
S. 218(1): CTA 2010, s. 1028(3), 1075(2), 1098(1), (2), (3), 1099(1), 1117(1).
S. 218(2): CTA 2010, s. 1099(2).
S. 218(3): CTA 2010, s. 1099(3), (4).
S. 218(4): CTA 2010, s. 1176(1).

PURCHASE OF OWN SHARES

History – Chapter III of Part VI omitted by CTA 2010, s. 1177 and Sch. 1, para. 15 and repealed by CTA 2010, s. 1181 and Sch. 3, Pt. 1.

219 Purchase by unquoted trading company of own shares

History – Chapter III of Part VI omitted by CTA 2010, s. 1177 and Sch. 1, para. 15 and repealed by CTA 2010, s. 1181 and Sch. 3, Pt. 1.

219 [Omitted by CTA 2010, s. 1177 and Sch. 1, para. 15 and repealed by CTA 2010, s. 1181 and Sch. 3, Pt. 1.]

History – Chapter III of Part VI (of which s. 219 formed a part) omitted by CTA 2010, s. 1177 and Sch. 1, para. 15 and repealed by CTA 2010, s. 1181 and Sch. 3, Pt. 1, with effect for corporation tax purposes for accounting periods ending on or after 1 April 2010, and for income and capital gains tax purposes for the tax year 2010–11 and subsequent tax years.

Notes – S. 219 rewritten for corporation tax purposes as follows:
S. 219(1): CTA 2010, s. 1033(1), (2), (3), (5).
S. 219(2): CTA 2010, s. 1033(4).

220 Conditions as to residence and period of ownership

History – Chapter III of Part VI omitted by CTA 2010, s. 1177 and Sch. 1, para. 15 and repealed by CTA 2010, s. 1181 and Sch. 3, Pt. 1.

220 [Omitted by CTA 2010, s. 1177 and Sch. 1, para. 15 and repealed by CTA 2010, s. 1181 and Sch. 3, Pt. 1.]

History – Chapter III of Part VI (of which s. 220 formed a part) omitted by CTA 2010, s. 1177 and Sch. 1, para. 15 and repealed by CTA 2010, s. 1181 and Sch. 3, Pt. 1, with effect for corporation tax purposes for accounting periods ending on or after 1 April 2010, and for income and capital gains tax purposes for the tax year 2010–11 and subsequent tax years.

Notes – S. 220 rewritten for corporation tax purposes as follows:
S. 220(1): CTA 2010, s. 1034(1), (2).
S. 220(3): CTA 2010, s. 1034(3).
S. 220(4): CTA 2010, s. 1034(4).
S. 220(5): CTA 2010, s. 1035(1).
S. 220(6): CTA 2010, s. 1036(1), (2).
S. 220(7): CTA 2010, s. 1036(3).
S. 220(8): CTA 2010, s. 1035(2).
S. 220(9): CTA 2010, s. 1035(3).

221 Reduction of vendor's interest as shareholder

History – Chapter III of Part VI omitted by CTA 2010, s. 1177 and Sch. 1, para. 15 and repealed by CTA 2010, s. 1181 and Sch. 3, Pt. 1.

221 [Omitted by CTA 2010, s. 1177 and Sch. 1, para. 15 and repealed by CTA 2010, s. 1181 and Sch. 3, Pt. 1.]

History – Chapter III of Part VI (of which s. 221 formed a part) omitted by CTA 2010, s. 1177 and Sch. 1, para. 15 and repealed by CTA 2010, s. 1181 and Sch. 3, Pt. 1, with effect for corporation tax purposes for accounting periods ending on or after 1 April 2010, and for income and capital gains tax purposes for the tax year 2010–11 and subsequent tax years.

Notes – S. 221 rewritten for corporation tax purposes as follows:
S. 221(1): CTA 2010, s. 1037(1).
S. 221(2): CTA 2010, s. 1037(2).
S. 221(3): CTA 2010, s. 1037(6).
S. 221(4): CTA 2010, s. 1037(3), (4), (5).
S. 221(5): CTA 2010, s. 1038(1).
S. 221(6): CTA 2010, s. 1038(2).
S. 221(7): CTA 2010, s. 1038(3), (4), (5).
S. 221(8): CTA 2010, s. 1038(6).

222 Conditions applicable where purchasing company is member of group

History – Chapter III of Part VI omitted by CTA 2010, s. 1177 and Sch. 1, para. 15 and repealed by CTA 2010, s. 1181 and Sch. 3, Pt. 1.

222 [Omitted by CTA 2010, s. 1177 and Sch. 1, para. 15 and repealed by CTA 2010, s. 1181 and Sch. 3, Pt. 1.]

History – Chapter III of Part VI (of which s. 222 formed a part) omitted by CTA 2010, s. 1177 and Sch. 1, para. 15 and repealed by CTA 2010, s. 1181 and Sch. 3, Pt. 1, with effect for corporation tax purposes for accounting periods ending on or after 1 April 2010, and for income and capital gains tax purposes for the tax year 2010–11 and subsequent tax years.

Notes – S. 222 rewritten for corporation tax purposes as follows:
S. 222(1): CTA 2010, s. 1039(1), (3), (5).
S. 222(2): CTA 2010, s. 1040(3).
S. 222(3): CTA 2010, s. 1039(1), (4), (5).
S. 222(4): CTA 2010, s. 1040(4).
S. 222(5): CTA 2010, s. 1040(2).
S. 222(6): CTA 2010, s. 1040(1).
S. 222(7): CTA 2010, s. 1041(1), (2).
S. 222(8): CTA 2010, s. 1041(3).
S. 222(9): CTA 2010, s. 1047(1).

S. 222(10): CTA 2010, s. 1047(2).
S. 222(11): CTA 2010, s. 1047(3).
S. 222(12): CTA 2010, s. 1047(4).

223 Other conditions

History – Chapter III of Part VI omitted by CTA 2010, s. 1177 and Sch. 1, para. 15 and repealed by CTA 2010, s. 1181 and Sch. 3, Pt. 1.

223 [Omitted by CTA 2010, s. 1177 and Sch. 1, para. 15 and repealed by CTA 2010, s. 1181 and Sch. 3, Pt. 1.]

History – Chapter III of Part VI (of which s. 223 formed a part) omitted by CTA 2010, s. 1177 and Sch. 1, para. 15 and repealed by CTA 2010, s. 1181 and Sch. 3, Pt. 1, with effect for corporation tax purposes for accounting periods ending on or after 1 April 2010, and for income and capital gains tax purposes for the tax year 2010–11 and subsequent tax years.

Notes – S. 223 rewritten for corporation tax purposes as follows:
S. 223(1): CTA 2010, s. 1042(1), (5), (5).
S. 223(2): CTA 2010, s. 1042(2), (3), (5).
S. 223(3): CTA 2010, s. 1042(4).

224 Relaxation of conditions in certain cases

History – Chapter III of Part VI omitted by CTA 2010, s. 1177 and Sch. 1, para. 15 and repealed by CTA 2010, s. 1181 and Sch. 3, Pt. 1.

224 [Omitted by CTA 2010, s. 1177 and Sch. 1, para. 15 and repealed by CTA 2010, s. 1181 and Sch. 3, Pt. 1.]

History – Chapter III of Part VI (of which s. 224 formed a part) omitted by CTA 2010, s. 1177 and Sch. 1, para. 15 and repealed by CTA 2010, s. 1181 and Sch. 3, Pt. 1, with effect for corporation tax purposes for accounting periods ending on or after 1 April 2010, and for income and capital gains tax purposes for the tax year 2010–11 and subsequent tax years.

Notes – S. 224 rewritten for corporation tax purposes as follows:
S. 224: CTA 2010, s. 1043(1), (2).

225 Advance clearance of payments by Board

History – Chapter III of Part VI omitted by CTA 2010, s. 1177 and Sch. 1, para. 15 and repealed by CTA 2010, s. 1181 and Sch. 3, Pt. 1.

225 [Omitted by CTA 2010, s. 1177 and Sch. 1, para. 15 and repealed by CTA 2010, s. 1181 and Sch. 3, Pt. 1.]

History – Chapter III of Part VI (of which s. 225 formed a part) omitted by CTA 2010, s. 1177 and Sch. 1, para. 15 and repealed by CTA 2010, s. 1181 and Sch. 3, Pt. 1, with effect for corporation tax purposes for accounting periods ending on or after 1 April 2010, and for income and capital gains tax purposes for the tax year 2010–11 and subsequent tax years.

Notes – S. 225 rewritten for corporation tax purposes as follows:
S. 225(1): CTA 2010, s. 1044(1), (2), (3).
S. 225(2): CTA 2010, s. 1045(1), (2), (3).
S. 225(3): CTA 2010, s. 1045(4).
S. 225(4): CTA 2010, s. 1045(5).
S. 225(5): CTA 2010, s. 1045(6).

226 Returns and information

History – S. 226(4), so far as it continued to have effect (see CTA 2010, s. 1184), omitted by FA 2011, s. 86 and Sch. 23, para. 55(c), with effect from 1 April 2012, subject to transitional provisions in FA 2011, Sch. 23, para. 65.
Chapter III of Part VI omitted by CTA 2010, s. 1177 and Sch. 1, para. 15 and repealed by CTA 2010, s. 1181 and Sch. 3, Pt. 1.

226 [Omitted by CTA 2010, s. 1177 and Sch. 1, para. 15 and repealed by CTA 2010, s. 1181 and Sch. 3, Pt. 1.]

History – Chapter III of Part VI (of which s. 226 formed a part) omitted by CTA 2010, s. 1177 and Sch. 1, para. 15 and repealed by CTA 2010, s. 1181 and Sch. 3, Pt. 1, with effect for corporation tax purposes for accounting periods ending on or after 1 April 2010, and for income and capital gains tax purposes for the tax year 2010–11 and subsequent tax years.

Notes – Former s. 226 rewritten for corporation tax purposes as follows:
Former s. 226(1): CTA 2010, s. 1046(1), (2).
Former s. 226(2): CTA 2010, s. 1046(3), (4).
Former s. 226(4): CTA 2010, s. 1046(5), (6), (7).

227 Associated persons

History – Chapter III of Part VI omitted by CTA 2010, s. 1177 and Sch. 1, para. 15 and repealed by CTA 2010, s. 1181 and Sch. 3, Pt. 1.

227 [Omitted by CTA 2010, s. 1177 and Sch. 1, para. 15 and repealed by CTA 2010, s. 1181 and Sch. 3, Pt. 1.]

History – Chapter III of Part VI (of which s. 227 formed a part) omitted by CTA 2010, s. 1177 and Sch. 1, para. 15 and repealed by CTA 2010, s. 1181 and Sch. 3, Pt. 1, with effect for corporation tax purposes for accounting periods ending on or after 1 April 2010, and for income and capital gains tax purposes for the tax year 2010–11 and subsequent tax years.

Notes – S. 227 rewritten for corporation tax purposes as follows:
S. 227(1): CTA 2010, s. 1059(1).
S. 227(2): CTA 2010, s. 1059(2), (3).
S. 227(3): CTA 2010, s. 1059(4).
S. 227(4): CTA 2010, s. 1059(5).

S. 227(5): CTA 2010, s. 1060(1).
S. 227(6): CTA 2010, s. 1061(1).
S. 227(7): CTA 2010, s. 1059(6).
S. 227(8): CTA 2010, s. 1060(2), (3), (5).
S. 227(9): CTA 2010, s. 1060(4), 1061(2).

228 Connected persons

History – Chapter III of Part VI omitted by CTA 2010, s. 1177 and Sch. 1, para. 15 and repealed by CTA 2010, s. 1181 and Sch. 3, Pt. 1.

228 [Omitted by CTA 2010, s. 1177 and Sch. 1, para. 15 and repealed by CTA 2010, s. 1181 and Sch. 3, Pt. 1.]

History – Chapter III of Part VI (of which s. 228 formed a part) omitted by CTA 2010, s. 1177 and Sch. 1, para. 15 and repealed by CTA 2010, s. 1181 and Sch. 3, Pt. 1, with effect for corporation tax purposes for accounting periods ending on or after 1 April 2010, and for income and capital gains tax purposes for the tax year 2010–11 and subsequent tax years.

Notes – S. 228 rewritten for corporation tax purposes as follows:
S. 228(1): CTA 2010, s. 1062(1).
S. 228(2): CTA 2010, s. 1062(2).
S. 228(3): CTA 2010, s. 1062(3).
S. 228(4): CTA 2010, s. 1062(4), (5), (6).
S. 228(5): CTA 2010, s. 1062(7).
S. 228(6): CTA 2010, s. 1063(1), (2).
S. 228(7): CTA 2010, s. 1063(3).
S. 228(8): CTA 2010, s. 1063(4)

229 Other interpretative provisions

History – Chapter III of Part VI omitted by CTA 2010, s. 1177 and Sch. 1, para. 15 and repealed by CTA 2010, s. 1181 and Sch. 3, Pt. 1.

229 [Omitted by CTA 2010, s. 1177 and Sch. 1, para. 15 and repealed by CTA 2010, s. 1181 and Sch. 3, Pt. 1.]

History – Chapter III of Part VI (of which s. 229 formed a part) omitted by CTA 2010, s. 1177 and Sch. 1, para. 15 and repealed by CTA 2010, s. 1181 and Sch. 3, Pt. 1, with effect for corporation tax purposes for accounting periods ending on or after 1 April 2010, and for income and capital gains tax purposes for the tax year 2010–11 and subsequent tax years.

Notes – S. 229 rewritten for corporation tax purposes as follows:
S. 229(1): CTA 2010, s. 1048(1), (2), 1119, 1176(2).
S. 229(2): CTA 2010, s. 1048(3).
S. 229(3): CTA 2010, s. 1033(6).

STOCK DIVIDENDS

History – Chapter III of Part VI omitted by CTA 2010, s. 1177 and Sch. 1, para. 15 and repealed by CTA 2010, s. 1181 and Sch. 3, Pt. 1.

230 Stock dividends: distributions

History – Chapter III of Part VI omitted by CTA 2010, s. 1177 and Sch. 1, para. 15 and repealed by CTA 2010, s. 1181 and Sch. 3, Pt. 1.

230 [Omitted by CTA 2010, s. 1177 and Sch. 1, para. 15 and repealed by CTA 2010, s. 1181 and Sch. 3, Pt. 1.]

History – Chapter III of Part VI (of which s. 230 formed a part) omitted by CTA 2010, s. 1177 and Sch. 1, para. 15 and repealed by CTA 2010, s. 1181 and Sch. 3, Pt. 1, with effect for corporation tax purposes for accounting periods ending on or after 1 April 2010, and for income and capital gains tax purposes for the tax year 2010–11 and subsequent tax years.

Notes – S. 230 rewritten for corporation tax purposes as follows:
S. 230: CTA 2010, s. 1049(1), (3).

INDUSTRIAL AND PROVIDENT SOCIETY DIVIDENDS ETC

History – Chapter III of Part VI omitted by CTA 2010, s. 1177 and Sch. 1, para. 15 and repealed by CTA 2010, s. 1181 and Sch. 3, Pt. 1.

230A Dividend or bonus granted by industrial and provident society

History – Chapter III of Part VI omitted by CTA 2010, s. 1177 and Sch. 1, para. 15 and repealed by CTA 2010, s. 1181 and Sch. 3, Pt. 1.

230A [Omitted by CTA 2010, s. 1177 and Sch. 1, para. 15 and repealed by CTA 2010, s. 1181 and Sch. 3, Pt. 1.]

History – Chapter 3 of Part 6 (of which s. 230A formed a part) omitted by CTA 2010, s. 1177 and Sch. 1, Part 1, para. 15 and repealed by CTA 2010, s. 1181 and Sch. 3, Pt. 1, with effect for corporation tax purposes for accounting periods ending on or after 1 April 2010, and for income and capital gains tax purposes for the tax year 2010–11 and subsequent tax years.

Notes – S. 230A rewritten for corporation tax purposes as follows:
S. 230A(1): CTA 2010, s. 1056(1).
S. 230A(2): CTA 2010, s. 1056(2).

Chapter IV – Tax Credits

231 Tax credits for certain recipients of qualifying distributions

231 [Omitted by CTA 2010, s. 1177 and Sch. 1, para. 16 and repealed by CTA 2010, s. 1181 and Sch. 3, Pt. 1.]

History – S. 231 omitted by CTA 2010, s. 1177 and Sch. 1, para. 16 and repealed by CTA 2010, s. 1181 and Sch. 3, Pt. 1, with effect for corporation tax purposes for accounting periods ending on or after 1 April 2010, and for income and capital gains tax purposes for the tax year 2010–11 and subsequent tax years.

Notes – S. 231 rewritten for income tax purposes as follows:
S. 231(1): ITTOIA 2005, s. 385(1) and 397(1) and (6).
S. 231(1A): ITTOIA 2005, s. 397(1).
S. 231(3): ITTOIA 2005, s. 397(2).
S. 231(3AA): ITTOIA 2005, s. 397(2) and (3).
S. 231(4): ITTOIA 2005, s. 385(1) and 397(5).
Partnership statement under TMA 1970, s. 12AB must also take account of partnership tax credits.
S. 231 rewritten for corporation tax purposes as follows:
S. 231(1): CTA 2010, s. 1109(1), (2), (5), Sch. 2, para. 111
S. 231(1A): CTA 2010, s. 1109(2).
S. 231(1B): CTA 2010, s. 1109(1).
S. 231(4): CTA 2010, s. 1109(3).

231A Restrictions on the use of tax credits by pension funds

231A [Repealed by F(No. 2)A 1997, s. 30(8), s. 52 and Sch. 8, Pt. II(9).]

History – S. 231A repealed by F(No. 2)A 1997, s. 30(8), s. 52 and Sch. 8, Pt. II(9), in relation to distributions made on or after 6 April 1999.

ICTA 1988

231AA No tax credit for borrower under stock lending arrangement or interim holder under repurchase agreement

231AA [Omitted by CTA 2010, s. 1177 and Sch. 1, para. 17 and repealed by CTA 2010, s. 1181 and Sch. 3, Pt. 1.]

History – S. 231AA omitted by CTA 2010,s. 1177 and Sch. 1, para. 17 and repealed by CTA 2010, s. 1181 and Sch. 3, Pt. 1, with effect for corporation tax purposes for accounting periods ending on or after 1 April 2010, and for income and capital gains tax purposes for the tax year 2010–11 and subsequent tax years.

Notes – S. 231AA rewritten for income tax purposes as follows:
S. 231AA(1): ITA 2007, s. 592(1), (2), 593(1), (2)
S. 231AA(1A): ITA 2007, s. 592(3), 593(3).
S. 231AA(2): ITA 2007, s. 568(1), (2), (3), (4), (5), (6).
S. 231AA(3): ITA 2007, s. 569(1), (2), (3), (4), 593(1)
S. 231AA(4): ITA 2007, s. 592(1), 593(1), 595, 596(2), 601(1), (2), (3), 602(1), (2), 606(1), (8).
S. 231AA rewritten for corporation tax purposes as follows:
S. 231AA(1): CTA 2010, s. 808(1), (2), 809(1), (2)
S. 231AA(2): CTA 2010, s. 805(1), (2), (3), (4), (5), (6), 806(1), (2).
S. 231AA(3): CTA 2010, s. 807.
S. 231AA(4): CTA 2010, s. 781(1), 808(1), 809(1), 812(2), 812(6).
S. 231AA(5): CTA 2010, s. 809(3).

231AB No tax credit for original owner under repurchase agreement in respect of certain manufactured dividends

231AB [Omitted by CTA 2010, s. 1177 and Sch. 1, para. 18 and repealed by CTA 2010, s. 1181 and Sch. 3, Pt. 1.]

History – S. 231AB omitted by CTA 2010, s. 1177 and Sch. 1, para. 18 and repealed by CTA 2010, s. 1181 and Sch. 3, Pt. 1, with effect for corporation tax purposes for accounting periods ending on or after 1 April 2010, and for income and capital gains tax purposes for the tax year 2010–11 and subsequent tax years.

Notes – S. 231AB rewritten for income tax purposes as follows:
S. 231AB(1): ITA 2007, s. 594(1), (2).
S. 231AB(1A): ITA 2007, s. 594(3).
S. 231AB(2): ITA 2007, s. 569(1), (2), (3), (4), 594(1).
S. 231AB(3): ITA 2007, s. 594(1), 595, 601(1), (2), (3), 602(1), (2), 606(1), (8)
S. 231AB rewritten for corporation tax purposes as follows:
S. 231AB(1): CTA 2010, s. 810(1), (2).
S. 231AB(2): CTA 2010, s. 807.
S. 231AB(3): CTA 2010, s. 781(1), 812(6).

231B Consequences of certain arrangements to pass on the value of a tax credit

231B [Omitted by FA 2016, s. 5 and Sch. 1, para. 52(2).]

History – S. 231B omitted by FA 2016, s. 5 and Sch. 1, para. 52(2), with effect in relation to dividends paid or arising (or treated as paid), and other distributions made (or treated as made), in the tax year 2016–17 or at any later time. Former s. 231B read as follows:

"Consequences of certain arrangements to pass on the value of a tax credit

231B(1) This section applies in any case where–
(a) a person ("A") is entitled to a tax credit in respect of a qualifying distribution;
(b) arrangements subsist such that another person ("B") obtains, whether directly or indirectly, a payment representing any of the value of the tax credit;
(c) the arrangements (whether or not made directly between A and B) were entered into for an unallowable purpose; and
(d) the condition in subsection (2) below is satisfied.

231B(2) The condition is that if B had been the person entitled to the tax credit and the qualifying distribution to which it relates, and had received the distribution when it was made, then–
(a) B would not have been entitled to obtain any payment under section 231(2) or (3) in respect of the tax credit; and
(b) if B is a company, B could not have used the income consisting of the distribution to frank a distribution actually made in the accounting period in which it would have received the distribution to which the tax credit relates.

231B(3) This section does not apply if and to the extent that any other provision of the Tax Acts has the effect of cancelling or reducing the tax advantage which would otherwise be obtained by virtue of the arrangements.

231B(4) Where this section applies–
(a) no claim shall be made under section 231(2) for payment of the amount of the tax credit;
(b) no claim shall be made under section 397(2) of ITTOIA 2005 in respect of the tax credit; and
(c) the income consisting of the distribution in respect of which A is entitled to the tax credit shall not be regarded for the purposes of section 241 as franked investment income;
(d) [omitted by FA 2011, s. 91 and Sch. 26, para. 2(a).]

231B(5) For the purposes of this section, the question whether any arrangements were entered into for an "unallowable purpose" shall be determined in accordance with subsections (6) and (7) below.

231B(6) Arrangements are entered into for an unallowable purpose if the purposes for which at least one person is a party to the arrangements include a purpose which is not amongst the business or other commercial purposes of that person.

231B(7) Where one of the purposes for which a person enters into any arrangements is the purpose of securing that that person or another obtains a tax advantage, that purpose shall be regarded as a business or other commercial purpose of the person only if it is neither the main purpose, nor one of the main purposes, for which the person enters into the arrangements.

231B(8) Any reference in this section to a person obtaining a tax advantage includes a reference to a person obtaining a payment representing any of the value of a tax credit in circumstances where, had the person obtaining the payment been entitled to the tax credit and the qualifying distribution to which it relates, that person–
(a) would not have been entitled to obtain any payment under section 231(2) or (3) in respect of the tax credit; and
(b) if that person is a company, could not have used the income consisting of the distribution to frank a distribution actually made in the accounting period in which it would have received the distribution to which the tax credit relates.

231B(9) If an amount representing any of the value of a tax credit to which a person is entitled is applied at the direction of, or otherwise in favour of, some other person (whether by way of set off or otherwise), the case shall be treated for the purposes of this section as one where that other person obtains a payment representing any of the value of the tax credit.

231B(10) In determining for the purposes of subsections (2)(b) and (8)(b) above whether a company could have used the income consisting of the distribution in question to frank a distribution of the company, the company shall be taken to use its actual franked investment income to frank distributions before using the income consisting of the distribution in question.

231B(11) References in this section to using franked investment income to frank a distribution of a company have the same meaning as in Chapter V of Part VI.

231B(12) In this section–

"arrangements" means arrangements of any kind, whether in writing or not (and includes a series of arrangements, whether or not between the same parties);

"business or other commercial purposes" includes the efficient management of investments;

"franked investment income" has the same meaning as in Chapter V of Part VI and references to income consisting of a distribution shall be construed accordingly;

"tax advantage" has the meaning given by section 1139 of CTA 2010.

History – S. 231B(4)(d) and the "and" before it omitted (and the "and" at the end of s. 231B(4)(b) inserted) by FA 2011, s. 91 and Sch. 26, para. 2(a), with effect from 19 July 2011.
In s. 231B(4)(b) the words "section 397(2) of ITTOIA 2005" substituted by ITTOIA 2005, s. 882(1) and Sch. 1, para. 116; effective for income tax purposes for 2005–06 onwards and for corporation tax purposes for accounting periods ending after 5 April 2005 (ITTOIA 2005, s. 883(1)).
Reference in s. 231B(4)(b) to s. 441A(7) repealed by F(No. 2)A 1997, s. 34 and Sch. 4, para. 26, s. 52 and Sch. 8, Pt. II(10), with effect in relation to distributions made on or after 6 April 1999.
In s. 231B(12), "section 1139 of CTA 2010" substituted for "section 840ZA" by CTA 2010, s. 1177 and Sch. 1, para. 19, with effect for corporation tax purposes for accounting periods ending on or after 1 April 2010, and for income and capital gains tax purposes for the tax year 2010–11 and subsequent tax years.
In s. 231B(12), definition of "tax advantage" substituted by ITA 2007, s. 1027 and Sch. 1, para. 26 with effect for income tax purposes for 2007–08 and subsequent tax years and for corporation tax purposes in relation to accounting periods ending after 5 April 2007.
S. 231B inserted by F(No. 2)A 1997, s. 28, with effect in relation to distributions made on or after 2 July 1997."

232 Tax credits for non-UK residents

232 [Omitted by ITTOIA 2005, s. 882 and Sch. 1, para. 117 and repealed by s. 884 and Sch. 3.]

History – S. 232 omitted by ITTOIA 2005, s. 882(1) and Sch. 1, para. 117 and repealed by s. 884 and Sch. 3; effective for income tax purposes for 2005–06 onwards and for corporation tax purposes for accounting periods ending after 5 April 2005 (ITTOIA 2005, s. 883(1)).

Notes – S. 232 rewritten as follows:
S. 232(1): ITTOIA 2005, s. 397(1) and (4). However, ITTOIA 2005 does not rewrite the words in ICTA 1988, s. 232(1) "having made a claim in that behalf" as they are unnecessary as a claim for personal allowances would have to be made in any event. (See ITTOIA 2005, Explanatory Notes, Annex 1, Table 1 (Change 158).)

233 Taxation of certain recipients of distributions and in respect of non-qualifying distributions

233 [Omitted by ITTOIA 2005, s. 882 and Sch. 1, para. 118 and repealed by s. 884 and Sch. 3.]

History – S. 233 omitted by ITTOIA 2005, s. 882(1) and Sch. 1, para. 118 and repealed by s. 884 and Sch. 3; effective for income tax purposes for 2005–06 onwards and for corporation tax purposes for accounting periods ending after 5 April 2005 (ITTOIA 2005, s. 883(1)).

Notes – S. 233 rewritten as follows:
S. 233(1): ITTOIA 2005, s. 399(1)–(3) and (7), 400(1)–(3) and Sch. 1, para. 146.
S. 233(1A): ITTOIA 2005, s. 399(1) and (3)–(6).
S. 233(1B): ITTOIA 2005, s. 400(4) and (5).
S. 233(2): ITTOIA 2005, 400(6) and 401(1)–(6).

234 Information relating to distributions

234 [Omitted by CTA 2010, s. 1177 and Sch. 1, para. 20 and repealed by CTA 2010, s. 1181 and Sch. 3, Pt. 1.]

History – S. 234 omitted by CTA 2010, s. 1177 and Sch. 1, para. 20 and repealed by CTA 2010, s. 1181 and Sch. 3, Pt. 1, with effect for corporation tax purposes for accounting periods ending on or after 1 April 2010, and for income and capital gains tax purposes for the tax year 2010–11 and subsequent tax years.

Notes – S. 234 rewritten for corporation tax purposes as follows:
S. 234(1): CTA 2010, s. 1100(1), (2), (3), (4), (5), (6).
S. 234(2): CTA 2010, s. 1100(4).
S. 234(5): CTA 2010, s. 1101(1), 1101(3).
S. 234(6): CTA 2010, s. 1101(2).
S. 234(7): CTA 2010, s. 1101(4), (5), (7).
S. 234(8): CTA 2010, s. 1101(6), (7).
S. 234(9): CTA 2010, s. 1102(1), (2), (3), (4), (5), (6).

234A Information relating to distributions: further provisions

234A [Omitted by CTA 2010, s. 1177 and Sch. 1, para. 21 and repealed by CTA 2010, s. 1181 and Sch. 3, Pt. 1.]

History – S. 234A omitted by CTA 2010, s. 1177 and Sch. 1, para. 21 and repealed by CTA 2010, s. 1181 and Sch. 3, Pt. 1, with effect for corporation tax purposes for accounting periods ending on or after 1 April 2010, and for income and capital gains tax purposes for the tax year 2010–11 and subsequent tax years.

Notes – S. 234A rewritten for corporation tax purposes as follows:
S. 234A(1): CTA 2010, s. 1104(1).
S. 234A(2): CTA 2010, s. 1104(3).
S. 234A(3): CTA 2010, s. 1104(2).
S. 234A(4): CTA 2010, s. 1105(1), (3).
S. 234A(5): CTA 2010, s. 1105(2).
S. 234A(6): See CTA 2010, Explanatory Notes, Annex 1, Change 58.
S. 234A(7): CTA 2010, s. 1106(4), (5), (6).
S. 234A(8): CTA 2010, s. 1106(3).
S. 234A(8A): CTA 2010, s. 1106(2).
S. 234A(9): CTA 2010, s. 1107(1), (2).
S. 234A(10): CTA 2010, s. 1108(1).
S. 234A(11): CTA 2010, s. 1108(2).

235 Distributions of exempt funds etc.

235 [Repealed by F(No. 2)A 1997, s. 34 and Sch. 4, para. 7, s. 52 and Sch. 8, Pt. II(9).]

History – S. 235 repealed by F(No. 2)A 1997, s. 34 and Sch. 4, para. 7, s. 52 and Sch. 8, Pt. II(9), with effect in relation to distributions made on or after 6 April 1999.

236 Provisions supplementary to section 235

236 [Repealed by F(No. 2)A 1997, s. 34 and Sch. 4, para. 7, s. 52 and Sch. 8, Pt. II(9).]

History – S. 236 repealed by F(No. 2)A 1997, s. 34 and Sch. 4, para. 7, s. 52 and Sch. 8, Pt. II(9), with effect in relation to distributions made on or after 6 April 1999.

237 Disallowance of reliefs in respect of bonus issues

237 [Repealed by F(No. 2)A 1997, s. 34 and Sch. 4, para. 7, s. 52 and Sch. 8, Pt. II(9).]

History – S. 237 repealed by F(No. 2)A 1997, s. 34 and Sch. 4, para. 7, s. 52 and Sch. 8, Pt. II(9), with effect in relation to distributions made on or after 6 April 1999.

Chapter V – Advance Corporation Tax and Franked Investment Income

238 Interpretation of terms and collection of ACT

238 [Repealed by FA 1998, Sch. 3, para 11(1), s. 165 and Sch. 27, Pt. III(2).]

History – S. 238 repealed by FA 1998, Sch. 3, para 11(1), s. 165 and Sch. 27, Pt. III(2), with effect in relation to accounting periods beginning on or after 6 April 1999.

239 Set-off of ACT against liability to corporation tax

239 [Repealed by FA 1998, Sch. 3, para 12(1), s. 165 and Sch. 27, Pt. III(2).]

History – S. 239 repealed by FA 1998, Sch. 3, para 12(1), s. 165 and Sch. 27, Pt. III(2), with effect in relation to accounting periods beginning on or after 6 April 1999.

240 Set-off of company's surplus ACT against subsidiary's liability to corporation tax

240 [Repealed by FA 1998, Sch. 3, para 13(1), s. 165 and Sch. 27, Pt. III(2).]

History – S. 240 repealed by FA 1998, Sch. 3, para 13(1), s. 165 and Sch. 27, Pt. III(2), with effect in relation to accounting periods of the surrendering company beginning on or after 6 April 1999.

241 Calculation of ACT where company receives franked investment income

241 [Repealed by FA 1998, Sch. 3, para. 14(1), s. 165 and Sch. 27, Pt. III(2).]

History – S. 241 repealed by FA 1998, Sch. 3, para. 14(1), s. 165 and Sch. 27, Pt. III(2) with effect in relation to accounting periods beginning on or after 6 April 1999.

242 Set-off of losses etc. against surplus of franked investment income

242 [Repealed by F(No. 2)A 1997, s. 20(5), 52 and Sch. 8, Pt. II(4).]

History – Repealed by F(No. 2)A 1997, s. 20(5), 52 and Sch. 8, Pt. II(4) with effect in relation to accounting periods beginning on or after 2 July 1997.

243 Set-off of loss brought forward, or terminal loss

243 [Repealed by F(No. 2)A 1997, s. 20(5), 52 and Sch. 8, Pt. II(4).]

History – Repealed by F(No. 2)A 1997, s. 20(5), 52 and Sch. 8, Pt. II(4) with effect in relation to accounting periods beginning on or after 2 July 1997.

244 Further provisions relating to claims under section 242 or 243

244 [Repealed by F(No. 2)A 1997, s. 20(5), 52 and Sch. 8, Pt. II(4).]

History – S. 244 repealed by F(No. 2)A 1997, s. 20(5), 52 and Sch. 8, Pt. II(4) with effect in relation to accounting periods beginning on or after 2 July 1997.

245 Calculation etc. of ACT on change of ownership of company

245 [Repealed by FA 1998, Sch. 3, para 15(1), s. 165 and Sch. 27, Pt. III(2).]

History – S. 245 repealed by FA 1998, Sch. 3, para 15(1), s. 165 and Sch. 27, Pt. III(2), with effect in relation to distributions made on or after 6 April 1999.

245A Restriction on application of section 240 in certain circumstances

245A [Repealed by FA 1998, Sch. 3, para. 16(1), s. 165 and Sch. 27, Pt. III(2).]

History – S. 245A repealed by FA 1998, Sch. 3, para. 16(1), s. 165 and Sch. 27, Pt. III(2), with effect in relation to distributions made on or after 6 April 1999.

245B Restriction on set-off where asset transferred after change in ownership of company

245B [Repealed by FA 1998, Sch. 3, para. 17(1), s. 165 and Sch. 27, Pt. III(2).]

History – S. 245B repealed by FA 1998, Sch. 3, para. 17(1), s. 165 and Sch. 27, Pt. III(2), with effect in relation to distributions made on or after 6 April 1999.

246 Charge of ACT at previous rate until new rate fixed, and changes of rate

246 [Repealed by FA 1998, Sch. 3, para. 18(1), s. 165 and Sch. 27, Pt. III(2).]

History – S. 246 repealed by FA 1998, Sch. 3, para. 18(1), s. 165 and Sch. 27, Pt. III(2), with effect in relation to distributions made on or after 6 April 1999.

Chapter VA – Foreign Income Dividends

ELECTION BY COMPANY PAYING DIVIDEND

246A Election by company paying dividend

246A [Repealed by F(No. 2A) 1997, s. 36 and Sch. 6, para. 3(1), s. 52 and Sch. 8, Pt. II(11).]

History – S. 246A repealed by F(No. 2A) 1997, s. 36 and Sch. 6, para. 3(1), s. 52 and Sch. 8, Pt. II(11), with effect in relation to distributions made on or after 6 April 1999.

246B Procedure for making election

246B [Repealed by F(No. 2A) 1997, s. 36 and Sch. 6, para. 3(1), s. 52 and Sch. 8, Pt. II(11).]

History – S. 246B repealed by F(No. 2A) 1997, s. 36 and Sch. 6, para. 3(1), s. 52 and Sch. 8, Pt. II(11), with effect in relation to distributions made on or after 6 April 1999.

RECIPIENT OF FOREIGN INCOME DIVIDEND

246C No tax credit for recipient

246C [Repealed by F(No. 2A) 1997, s. 36 and Sch. 6, para. 3(1), s. 52 and Sch. 8, Pt. II(11).]

History – S. 246C repealed by F(No. 2A) 1997, s. 36 and Sch. 6, para. 3(1), s. 52 and Sch. 8, Pt. II(11), with effect in relation to distributions made on or after 6 April 1999.

246D Individuals etc.

246D [Repealed by F(No. 2A) 1997, s. 36 and Sch. 6, para. 3(1), s. 52 and Sch. 8, Pt. II(11).]

History – S. 246D repealed by F(No. 2A) 1997, s. 36 and Sch. 6, para. 3(1), s. 52 and Sch. 8, Pt. II(11), with effect in relation to distributions made on or after 6 April 1999.

COMPANIES: PAYMENTS AND RECEIPTS

246E Foreign income dividend not franked payment

246E [Repealed by F(No. 2A) 1997, s. 36 and Sch. 6, para. 3(1), s. 52 and Sch. 8, Pt. II(11).]

History – S. 246E repealed by F(No. 2A) 1997, s. 36 and Sch. 6, para. 3(1), s. 52 and Sch. 8, Pt. II(11), with effect in relation to distributions made on or after 6 April 1999.

246F Calculation of ACT where company receives foreign income dividend

246F [Repealed by F(No. 2A) 1997, s. 36 and Sch. 6, para. 3(1), s. 52 and Sch. 8, Pt. II(11).]

History – S. 246F repealed by F(No. 2A) 1997, s. 36 and Sch. 6, para. 3(1), s. 52 and Sch. 8, Pt. II(11), with effect for accounting periods beginning on or after 6 April 1999.

246G Information relating to foreign income dividends

246G [Repealed by F(No. 2A) 1997, s. 36 and Sch. 6, para. 3(1), s. 52 and Sch. 8, Pt. II(11).]

History – S. 246G repealed by F(No. 2A) 1997, s. 36 and Sch. 6, para. 3(1), s. 52 and Sch. 8, Pt. II(11), with effect in relation to distributions made on or after 6 April 1999.

246H Power of inspector to require information

246H [Repealed by F(No. 2A) 1997, s. 36 and Sch. 6, para. 3(1), s. 52 and Sch. 8, Pt. II(11).]

History – S. 246H repealed by F(No. 2A) 1997, s. 36 and Sch. 6, para. 3(1), s. 52 and Sch. 8, Pt. II(11), with effect for accounting periods beginning on or after 6 April 1999.

FOREIGN SOURCE PROFIT AND DISTRIBUTABLE FOREIGN PROFIT

246I Foreign source profit and distributable foreign profit

246I [Repealed by F(No. 2A) 1997, s. 36 and Sch. 6, para. 3(1), s. 52 and Sch. 8, Pt. II(11).]

History – S. 246I repealed by F(No. 2A) 1997, s. 36 and Sch. 6, para. 3(1), s. 52 and Sch. 8, Pt. II(11), with effect for accounting periods beginning on or after 6 April 1999.

MATCHING OF DIVIDEND WITH DISTRIBUTABLE FOREIGN PROFIT

246J Matching of dividend with distributable foreign profit

246J [Repealed by F(No. 2A) 1997, s. 36 and Sch. 6, para. 3(1), s. 52 and Sch. 8, Pt. II(11).]

History – S. 246J repealed by F(No. 2A) 1997, s. 36 and Sch. 6, para. 3(1), s. 52 and Sch. 8, Pt. II(11), with effect for accounting periods beginning on or after 6 April 1999.

246K Matching: subsidiaries

246K [Repealed by F(No. 2A) 1997, s. 36 and Sch. 6, para. 3(1), s. 52 and Sch. 8, Pt. II(11).]

History – S. 246K repealed by F(No. 2A) 1997, s. 36 and Sch. 6, para. 3(1), s. 52 and Sch. 8, Pt. II(11), with effect for accounting periods of the parent beginning on or after 6 April 1999.

246L Requirement as to subsidiaries

246L [Repealed by F(No. 2A) 1997, s. 36 and Sch. 6, para. 3(1), s. 52 and Sch. 8, Pt. II(11).]

History – S. 246L repealed by F(No. 2A) 1997, s. 36 and Sch. 6, para. 3(1), s. 52 and Sch. 8, Pt. II(11), with effect for accounting periods of the parent beginning on or after 6 April 1999.

246M Matching: further provisions

246M [Repealed by F(No. 2A) 1997, s. 36 and Sch. 6, para. 3(1), s. 52 and Sch. 8, Pt. II(11).]

History – S. 246M repealed by F(No. 2A) 1997, s. 36 and Sch. 6, para. 3(1), s. 52 and Sch. 8, Pt. II(11), with effect for accounting periods of the parent beginning on or after 6 April 1999.

REPAYMENT OR SET-OFF OF ADVANCE CORPORATION TAX

246N ACT to be repaid or set off against corporation tax liability

246N [Repealed by F(No. 2A) 1997, s. 36 and Sch. 6, para. 3(1), s. 52 and Sch. 8, Pt. II(11).]

History – S. 246N repealed by F(No. 2A) 1997, s. 36 and Sch. 6, para. 3(1), s. 52 and Sch. 8, Pt. II(11), with effect for accounting periods beginning on or after 6 April 1999.

246P Notional foreign source advance corporation tax

246P [Repealed by F(No. 2A) 1997, s. 36 and Sch. 6, para. 3(1), s. 52 and Sch. 8, Pt. II(11).]

History – S. 246P repealed by F(No. 2A) 1997, s. 36 and Sch. 6, para. 3(1), s. 52 and Sch. 8, Pt. II(11), with effect for accounting periods beginning on or after 6 April 1999.

246Q Repayment or set-off: supplementary

246Q [Repealed by F(No. 2A) 1997, s. 36 and Sch. 6, para. 3(1), s. 52 and Sch. 8, Pt. II(11).]

History – S. 246Q repealed by F(No. 2A) 1997, s. 36 and Sch. 6, para. 3(1), s. 52 and Sch. 8, Pt. II(11), with effect for accounting periods beginning on or after 6 April 1999.

246R Supplementary claims

246R [Repealed by F(No. 2A) 1997, s. 36 and Sch. 6, para. 3(1), s. 52 and Sch. 8, Pt. II(11).]

History – S. 246R repealed by F(No. 2A) 1997, s. 36 and Sch. 6, para. 3(1), s. 52 and Sch. 8, Pt. II(11), with effect for accounting periods beginning on or after 6 April 1999.

INTERNATIONAL HEADQUARTERS COMPANIES

246S International headquarters companies

246S [Repealed by F(No. 2A) 1997, s. 36 and Sch. 6, para. 3(1), s. 52 and Sch. 8, Pt. II(11).]

History – S. 246S repealed by F(No. 2A) 1997, s. 36 and Sch. 6, para. 3(1), s. 52 and Sch. 8, Pt. II(11), with effect for accounting periods beginning on or after 6 April 1999.

246T Liability to pay ACT displaced

246T [Repealed by F(No. 2A) 1997, s. 36 and Sch. 6, para. 3(1), s. 52 and Sch. 8, Pt. II(11).]

History – S. 246T repealed by F(No. 2A) 1997, s. 36 and Sch. 6, para. 3(1), s. 52 and Sch. 8, Pt. II(11), with effect for accounting periods beginning on or after 6 April 1999.

246U Settlement of liability by IHC as to ACT

246U [Repealed by F(No. 2A) 1997, s. 36 and Sch. 6, para. 3(1), s. 52 and Sch. 8, Pt. II(11).]

History – S. 246U repealed by F(No. 2A) 1997, s. 36 and Sch. 6, para. 3(1), s. 52 and Sch. 8, Pt. II(11), with effect for accounting periods beginning on or after 6 April 1999.

246V Settlement of liability by non-IHC as to ACT

246V [Repealed by F(No. 2A) 1997, s. 36 and Sch. 6, para. 3(1), s. 52 and Sch. 8, Pt. II(11).]

History – S. 246V repealed by F(No. 2A) 1997, s. 36 and Sch. 6, para. 3(1), s. 52 and Sch. 8, Pt. II(11), with effect for accounting periods beginning on or after 6 April 1999.

246W Payments and repayments where further matching takes place

246W [Repealed by F(No. 2A) 1997, s. 36 and Sch. 6, para. 3(1), s. 52 and Sch. 8, Pt. II(11).]

History – S. 246W repealed by F(No. 2A) 1997, s. 36 and Sch. 6, para. 3(1), s. 52 and Sch. 8, Pt. II(11), with effect for accounting periods beginning on or after 6 April 1999.

ADJUSTMENTS

246X Adjustments where profits or foreign tax altered

246X [Repealed by F(No. 2A) 1997, s. 36 and Sch. 6, para. 3(1), s. 52 and Sch. 8, Pt. II(11).]

History – S. 246X repealed by F(No. 2A) 1997, s. 36 and Sch. 6, para. 3(1), s. 52 and Sch. 8, Pt. II(11), with effect for accounting periods beginning on or after 6 April 1999.

APPLICATION OF THIS CHAPTER

246Y Application of this Chapter

246Y [Repealed by F(No. 2A) 1997, s. 36 and Sch. 6, para. 3(1), s. 52 and Sch. 8, Pt. II(11).]

History – S. 246Y repealed by F(No. 2A) 1997, s. 36 and Sch. 6, para. 3(1), s. 52 and Sch. 8, Pt. II(11), with effect for accounting periods beginning on or after 6 April 1999.

Chapter VI – Miscellaneous and Supplemental

GROUP INCOME

History – Chapter VI of Part VI omitted by CTA 2010, s. 1177 and Sch. 1, para. 22 and repealed by CTA 2010, s. 1181 and Sch. 3, Pt. 1.

247 Dividends etc. paid by one member of a group to another

History – Chapter VI of Part VI omitted by CTA 2010, s. 1177 and Sch. 1, para. 22 and repealed by CTA 2010, s. 1181 and Sch. 3, Pt. 1.

247 [Omitted by CTA 2010, s. 1177 and Sch. 1, para. 22 and repealed by CTA 2010, s. 1181 and Sch. 3, Pt. 1.]

History – Chapter VI of Part VI (of which s. 247 formed a part) omitted by CTA 2010, s. 1177 and Sch. 1, para 22 and repealed by CTA 2010, s. 1181 and Sch. 3, Pt. 1, with effect for corporation tax purposes for accounting periods ending on or after 1 April 2010, and for income and capital gains tax purposes for the tax year 2010–11 and subsequent tax years. Former s. 247 repealed by FA 2001, s. 85(5), Sch. 33, Pt. 2(10), in relation to payments made after 11 May 2001.

248 Provisions supplementary to section 247

History – Chapter VI of Part VI omitted by CTA 2010, s. 1177 and Sch. 1, para. 22 and repealed by CTA 2010, s. 1181 and Sch. 3, Pt. 1.

248 [Omitted by CTA 2010, s. 1177 and Sch. 1, para. 22 and repealed by CTA 2010, s. 1181 and Sch. 3, Pt. 1.]

History – Chapter VI of Part VI (of which s. 248 formed a part) omitted by CTA 2010, s. 1177 and Sch. 1, para. 22 and repealed by CTA 2010, s. 1181 and Sch. 3, Pt. 1, with effect for corporation tax purposes for accounting periods ending on or after 1 April 2010, and for income and capital gains tax purposes for the tax year 2010–11 and subsequent tax years. Former s. 248 repealed by FA 2001, s. 85(5), Sch. 33, Pt. 2(10), in relation to payments made after 11 May 2001.

STOCK DIVIDENDS

249 Stock dividends treated as income

History – Chapter VI of Part VI omitted by CTA 2010, s. 1177 and Sch. 1, para. 22 and repealed by CTA 2010, s. 1181 and Sch. 3, Pt. 1.

249 [Omitted by CTA 2010, s. 1177 and Sch. 1, para. 22 and repealed by CTA 2010, s. 1181 and Sch. 3, Pt. 1.]

History – Chapter VI of Part VI (of which s. 249 formed a part) omitted by CTA 2010, s. 1177 and Sch. 1, para. 22 and repealed by CTA 2010, s. 1181 and Sch. 3, Pt. 1, with effect for corporation tax purposes for accounting periods ending on or after 1 April 2010, and for income and capital gains tax purposes for the tax year 2010–11 and subsequent tax years.

Notes – S. 249 rewritten as follows:
S. 249(1): ITTOIA 2005, s. 410(1).
S. 249(3): ITTOIA 2005, s. 413(5) and (6).
S. 249(4): ITTOIA 2005, s. 409(1), 410(1), (2) and (6),411(1) and (2), 412(1)–(3),413(2), 414(1)–(5) and Sch. 1, para. 46.
S. 249(5): ITTOIA 2005, s. 410(1), (4) and (5), 413(4) and 664(1) and (2).
S. 249(6): ITTOIA 2005, s. 409(1), 410(1), (3) and (6), 411(1) and (2), 413(3), 414(1) and (2) and Sch. 1, para. 46.
S. 249 rewritten for corporation tax purposes as follows:
S. 249(1): CTA 2010, s. 1049(1), 1051(2).
S. 249(2): CTA 2010, s. 1049(2).
S. 249(8): CTA 2010, Sch. 1, para. 464(3), Sch. 2, para. 108.
S. 249(9): CTA 2010, s. 1050(1), (2), (3), (4), (5), Sch. 1, para. 452.

250 Returns

History – Chapter VI of Part VI omitted by CTA 2010, s. 1177 and Sch. 1, para. 22 and repealed by CTA 2010, s. 1181 and Sch. 3, Pt. 1.

250 [Omitted by CTA 2010, s. 1177 and Sch. 1, para. 22 and repealed by CTA 2010, s. 1181 and Sch. 3, Pt. 1.]

History – Chapter VI of Part VI (of which s. 250 formed a part) omitted by CTA 2010, s. 1177 and Sch. 1, para. 22 and repealed by CTA 2010, s. 1181 and Sch. 3, Pt. 1, with effect for corporation tax purposes for accounting periods ending on or after 1 April 2010, and for income and capital gains tax purposes for the tax year 2010–11 and subsequent tax years.

Notes – S. 250 rewritten for corporation tax purposes as follows:
S. 250(1): CTA 2010, s. 1052(1), (2).
S. 250(2): CTA 2010, s. 1053(1), (2).
S. 250(3): CTA 2010, s. 1052(2).

S. 250(4): CTA 2010, s. 1052(1).
S. 250(5): CTA 2010, s. 1052(3).
S. 250(6): CTA 2010, s. 1052(4), (5), (6), (7).

251 Interpretation of sections 249 and 250

History – Chapter VI of Part VI omitted by CTA 2010, s. 1177 and Sch. 1, Part 1, para. 22 and repealed by CTA 2010, s. 1181 and Sch. 3, Pt. 1.

251 [Omitted by CTA 2010, s. 1177 and Sch. 1, para. 22 and repealed by CTA 2010, s. 1181 and Sch. 3, Pt. 1.]

History – Chapter VI of Part VI (of which s. 251 formed a part) omitted by CTA 2010, s. 1177 and Sch. 1, para. 22 and repealed by CTA 2010, s. 1181 and Sch. 3, Pt. 1, with effect for corporation tax purposes for accounting periods ending on or after 1 April 2010, and for income and capital gains tax purposes for the tax year 2010–11 and subsequent tax years.

Notes – S. 251 rewritten as follows:
S. 251(1): ITTOIA 2005, s. 410(6), 411(2) and 413(6).
S. 251(2): ITTOIA 2005, s. 412(1)–(4).
S. 251(3): ITTOIA 2005, s. 412(4) and (5).
S. 251(5): ITTOIA 2005, s. 412(5).
S. 251(6): ITTOIA 2005, s. 412(5).
S. 251 rewritten for corporation tax purposes as follows:
S. 251(1): CTA 2010, s. 1051(1), (3), (4), Sch. 1, para. 454.

APPROVED SHARE INCENTIVE PLANS

History – Chapter VI of Part VI omitted by CTA 2010, s. 1177 and Sch. 1, para. 22 and repealed by CTA 2010, s. 1181 and Sch. 3, Pt. 1.

251A Application of sections 251B and 251C

History – Chapter VI of Part VI omitted by CTA 2010, s. 1177 and Sch. 1, para. 22 and repealed by CTA 2010, s. 1181 and Sch. 3, Pt. 1.

251A [Omitted by CTA 2010, s. 1177 and Sch. 1, para. 22 and repealed by CTA 2010, s. 1181 and Sch. 3, Pt. 1.]

History – Chapter VI of Part VI (of which s. 251A formed a part) omitted by CTA 2010, s. 1177 and Sch. 1, para. 22 and repealed by CTA 2010, s. 1181 and Sch. 3, Pt. 1, with effect for corporation tax purposes for accounting periods ending on or after 1 April 2010, and for income and capital gains tax purposes for the tax year 2010–11 and subsequent tax years. Former s. 251A omitted by ITTOIA 2005, s. 882(1) and Sch. 1, para. 122 and repealed by s. 884 and Sch. 3; effective for income tax purposes for 2005–06 onwards and for corporation tax purposes for accounting periods ending after 5 April 2005 (ITTOIA 2005, s. 883(1)).

Notes – S. 251A rewritten as follows:
S. 251A(1): ITTOIA 2005, s. 392(1).
S. 251A(2): ITTOIA 2005, s. 392(2), (3), (5) and (6).
S. 251A(3): ITTOIA 2005, s. 392(4).

251B Treatment of cash dividend retained and then later paid out

History – Chapter VI of Part VI omitted by CTA 2010, s. 1177 and Sch. 1, para. 22 and repealed by CTA 2010, s. 1181 and Sch. 3, Pt. 1.

251B [Omitted by CTA 2010, s. 1177 and Sch. 1, para. 22 and repealed by CTA 2010, s. 1181 and Sch. 3, Pt. 1.]

History – Chapter VI of Part VI (of which s. 251B formed a part) omitted by CTA 2010, s. 1177 and Sch. 1, para. 22 and repealed by CTA 2010, s. 1181 and Sch. 3, Pt. 1, with effect for corporation tax purposes for accounting periods ending on or after 1 April 2010, and for income and capital gains tax purposes for the tax year 2010–11 and subsequent tax years. Former s. 251B omitted by ITTOIA 2005, s. 882(1) and Sch. 1, para. 122 and repealed by s. 884 and Sch. 3; effective for income tax purposes for 2005–06 onwards and for corporation tax purposes for accounting periods ending after 5 April 2005 (ITTOIA 2005, s. 883(1)).

Notes – S. 251B rewritten as follows:
S. 251B(1): ITTOIA 2005, s. 384(1) and (2), 385(2) and 393(1)–(4).
S. 251B(2): ITTOIA 2005, s. 393(3). However, ITTOIA 2005 does not rewrite the words in ICTA 1988, s. 251B(2) "except to the extent that it represents a foreign cash dividend" as they are no longer necessary. (See ITTOIA 2005, Explanatory Notes, Annex 1, Table 1 (Change 158).)
S. 251B(3): ITTOIA 2005, s. 393(5).

251C Charge on dividend shares ceasing to be subject to plan

History – Chapter VI of Part VI omitted by CTA 2010, s. 1177 and Sch. 1, para. 22 and repealed by CTA 2010, s. 1181 and Sch. 3, Pt. 1.

251C [Omitted by CTA 2010, s. 1177 and Sch. 1, para. 22 and repealed by CTA 2010, s. 1181 and Sch. 3, Pt. 1.]

History – Chapter VI of Part VI (of which s. 251C formed a part) omitted by CTA 2010, s. 1177 and Sch. 1, para. 22 and repealed by CTA 2010, s. 1181 and Sch. 3, Pt. 1, with effect for corporation tax purposes for accounting periods ending on or after 1 April 2010, and for income and capital gains tax purposes for the tax year 2010–11 and subsequent tax years. Former s. 251C omitted by ITTOIA 2005, s. 882(1) and Sch. 1, para. 122 and repealed by s. 884 and Sch. 3; effective for income tax purposes for 2005–06 onwards and for corporation tax purposes for accounting periods ending after 5 April 2005 (ITTOIA 2005, s. 883(1)).

Notes – S. 251C rewritten as follows:
S. 251C(1): ITTOIA 2005, s. 384(1) and (2), 385(2) and 394(1)–(4).
S. 251C(2): ITTOIA 2005, s. 394(3).
S. 251C(3): ITTOIA 2005, s. 394(5).

S. 251C(4): ITTOIA 2005, s. 395(1) and (2).
S. 251C(5): ITTOIA 2005, s. 395(3).
S. 251C(6): ITTOIA 2005, s. 382(3).

251D Interpretation of sections 251A to 251C

History – Chapter VI of Part VI omitted by CTA 2010, s. 1177 and Sch. 1, para. 22 and repealed by CTA 2010, s. 1181 and Sch. 3, Pt. 1.

251D [Omitted by CTA 2010, s. 1177 and Sch. 1, para. 22 and repealed by CTA 2010, s. 1181 and Sch. 3, Pt. 1.]

History – Chapter VI of Part VI (of which s. 251C formed a part) omitted by CTA 2010, s. 1177 and Sch. 1, para. 22 and repealed by CTA 2010, s. 1181 and Sch. 3, Pt. 1, with effect for corporation tax purposes for accounting periods ending on or after 1 April 2010, and for income and capital gains tax purposes for the tax year 2010–11 and subsequent tax years. Former s. 251D omitted by ITTOIA 2005, s. 882(1) and Sch. 1, para. 122 and repealed by s. 884 and Sch. 3; effective for income tax purposes for 2005–06 onwards and for corporation tax purposes for accounting periods ending after 5 April 2005 (ITTOIA 2005, s. 883(1)).

Notes – S. 251D rewritten as follows:
S. 251D(1): ITTOIA 2005, s. 396(1).
S. 251D(2): ITTOIA 2005, s. 396(2).
S. 251D(3): ITTOIA 2005, s. 396(3) and (4).

SUPPLEMENTAL

252 Rectification of excessive set-off etc. of [ACT or] tax credit

History – Chapter VI of Part VI omitted by CTA 2010, s. 1177 and Sch. 1, para. 22 and repealed by CTA 2010, s. 1181 and Sch. 3, Pt. 1.

252 [Omitted by CTA 2010, s. 1177 and Sch. 1, para. 22 and repealed by CTA 2010, s. 1181 and Sch. 3, Pt. 1.]

History – Chapter VI of Part VI (of which s. 252 formed a part) omitted by CTA 2010, s. 1177 and Sch. 1, para. 22 and repealed by CTA 2010, s. 1181 and Sch. 3, Pt. 1, with effect for corporation tax purposes for accounting periods ending on or after 1 April 2010, and for income and capital gains tax purposes for the tax year 2010–11 and subsequent tax years.

Notes – S. 252 rewritten for corporation tax purposes as follows:
S. 252(1): CTA 2010, s. 1110(1), (2), (3), (4), Sch. 1, para. 449.
S. 252(2): CTA 2010, s. 1110(5), (6).
S. 252(3): CTA 2010, s. 1111(1).
S. 252(4): CTA 2010, Sch. 2, para. 112.
S. 252(5): CTA 2010, s. 1111(2), (3), (4), Sch. 1, para. 449.

253 Power to modify or replace section 234(5) to (9) and Schedule 13

History – Chapter VI of Part VI omitted by CTA 2010, s. 1177 and Sch. 1, Part 1, para. 22 and repealed by CTA 2010, s. 1181 and Sch. 3, Pt. 1.

253 [Omitted by CTA 2010, s. 1177 and Sch. 1, para. 22 and repealed by CTA 2010, s. 1181 and Sch. 3, Pt. 1.]

History – Chapter VI of Part VI (of which s. 253 formed a part) omitted by CTA 2010, s. 1177 and Sch. 1, para. 22 and repealed by CTA 2010, s. 1181 and Sch. 3, Pt. 1, with effect for corporation tax purposes for accounting periods ending on or after 1 April 2010, and for income and capital gains tax purposes for the tax year 2010–11 and subsequent tax years.

Notes – S. 253 rewritten for corporation tax purposes as follows:
S. 253(1): CTA 2010, s. 1103(1), (2), (3).
S. 253(3): CTA 2010, s. 1103(4), (5), (6).
S. 253(4): CTA 2010, s. 1103(7).

254 Interpretation of Part VI

History – Chapter VI of Part VI omitted by CTA 2010, s. 1177 and Sch. 1, para. 22 and repealed by CTA 2010, s. 1181 and Sch. 3, Pt. 1.

254 [Omitted by CTA 2010, s. 1177 and Sch. 1, para. 22 and repealed by CTA 2010, s. 1181 and Sch. 3, Pt. 1.]

History – Chapter VI of Part VI (of which s. 254 formed a part) omitted by CTA 2010, s. 1177 and Sch. 1, para. 22 and repealed by CTA 2010, s. 1181 and Sch. 3, Pt. 1, with effect for corporation tax purposes for accounting periods ending on or after 1 April 2010, and for income and capital gains tax purposes for the tax year 2010–11 and subsequent tax years.

Notes – S. 254 rewritten for corporation tax purposes as follows:
S. 254(1): CTA 2010, s. 1072(4), 1113(6), 1114(3), (6), 1115(1), 1117(1), Sch. 1, para. 454.
S. 254(2): CTA 2010, s. 1113(1),1114(1), Sch. 1, para. 454.
S. 254(3): CTA 2010, s. 1072(1), (2).
S. 254(4): CTA 2010, s. 1072(3), 1113(2), 1114(2).
S. 254(5): CTA 2010, s. 1115(2), (3), Sch. 1, para. 454.
S. 254(6): CTA 2010, s. 1115(4), (5), Sch. 1, para. 454.
S. 254(7): CTA 2010, s. 1115(6), Sch. 1, para. 454.
S. 254(8): CTA 2010, s. 811(1), (2), 1112(1), (2), (3), Sch. 1, para. 454.
S. 254(9): CTA 2010, s. 1117(3), (4).
S. 254(10): CTA 2010, s. 1117(5).
S. 254(11): CTA 2010, s. 1117(6).
S. 254(12): CTA 2010, s. 1113(3), (4), 1114(4), (5), 1117(7), (8), Sch. 1, para. 454.

255 "Gross rate" and "gross amount" of distributions to include ACT

History – Chapter VI of Part VI omitted by CTA 2010, s. 1177 and Sch. 1, para. 22 and repealed by CTA 2010, s. 1181 and Sch. 3, Pt. 1.

255 [Omitted by CTA 2010, s. 1177 and Sch. 1, para. 22 and repealed by CTA 2010, s. 1181 and Sch. 3, Pt. 1.]

History – Chapter VI of Part VI (of which s. 255 formed a part) omitted by CTA 2010, s. 1177 and Sch. 1, para. 22 and repealed by CTA 2010, s. 1181 and Sch. 3, Pt. 1, with effect for corporation tax purposes for accounting periods ending on or after 1 April 2010, and for income and capital gains tax purposes for the tax year 2010–11 and subsequent tax years. Former s. 255 repealed by FA 1998, Sch. 3, para. 23, s. 165 and Sch. 27, Pt. III(2), with effect in relation to distributions made on or after 6 April 1999.

PART VII – GENERAL PROVISIONS RELATING TO TAXATION OF INCOME OF INDIVIDUALS

Cross references – S. 9(6): disapplication of Pt. VII to computation of income for purposes of corporation tax.

Chapter I – Personal Reliefs

Cross references – Sch. 15B, para. 1(6): computation of income tax relief on investment in venture capital trusts.
TMA 1970, Sch. 2, para. 2(2): appeal from an inspector's decision lies exclusively to the general commissioners.
FA 1995, s. 128(1): calculation of maximum amount of income tax chargeable on non-residents.
SSCBA 1992, Sch. 2, para. 3(2)(a) (formerly SSA 1975, Sch. 2, para. 3(2)(a)): personal reliefs not applicable to calculation of Class 4 contributions.

THE RELIEFS

256 General

256 [Omitted by FA 2009, s. 5 and Sch. 1, para. 2(a).]

History – S. 256 omitted by FA 2009, s. 5 and Sch. 1, para. 2(a), with effect for the tax year 2010–11 and subsequent tax years.
Notes – S. 256 rewritten for income tax purposes as follows:
S. 256(1): ITA 2007, s. 23, 35, 36(1), 37(1), 38(1), 39(2), 45(1), 46(1), 51(4), 52(3).
S. 256(2): ITA 2007, s. 23, 29(2), 45(1), 46(1), 47(1), 48(1), 49(1), 53(1), (2).
S. 256(3): ITA 2007, s. 27(4), (5), 53(1), (2).

256A Meaning of "adjusted net income"

256A [Omitted by FA 2009, s. 5 and Sch. 1, para. 2(b).]

History – S. 256A omitted by FA 2009, s. 5 and Sch. 1, para. 2(b), with effect for the tax year 2010–11 and subsequent tax years.

256B Meaning of "the minimum amount"

256B [Omitted by FA 2009, s. 5 and Sch. 1, para. 2(c).]

History – S. 256B omitted by FA 2009, s. 5 and Sch. 1, para. 2(c), with effect for the tax year 2010–11 and subsequent tax years.

257 Personal allowance

257 [Omitted by FA 2009, s. 5 and Sch. 1, para. 2(d).]

History – S. 257 omitted by FA 2009, s. 5 and Sch. 1, para. 2(d), with effect for the tax year 2010–11 and subsequent tax years.
Notes – S. 257 rewritten for income tax purposes as follows:
S. 257(1): ITA 2007, s. 23, 35.
S. 257(2): ITA 2007, s. 23, 35, 36(1).
S. 257(3): ITA 2007, s. 23, 36(1), 37(1).
S. 257(4): ITA 2007, s. 41(2), (3).
S. 257(5): ITA 2007, s. 36(2), 37(2).

257AA Children's tax credit

257AA [Repealed by TCA 2002, s. 60 and Sch. 6.]

History – S. 257AA repealed by TCA 2002, s. 60 and Sch. 6, with effect from 6 April 2003 (SI 2003/962).
S. 257AA inserted by FA 1999, s. 30(1), FA 2000, s. 34 and FA 2001, s. 52, with effect for 2001–02 and subsequent years.

257A Married couple's allowance (pre-5th December 2005 marriages)

257A [Omitted by FA 2009, s. 5 and Sch. 1, para. 2(e).]

History – S. 257A omitted by FA 2009, s. 5 and Sch. 1, para. 2(e), with effect for the tax year 2010–11 and subsequent tax years.
Notes – S. 257A rewritten for income tax purposes as follows:
S. 257A(2): ITA 2007, s. 23, 26(1), 27(4), (5), 45(1), (2), (3).
S. 257A(3): ITA 2007, s. 23, 26(1), 27(4), (5), 45(1), (2), (3).
S. 257A(3A): ITA 2007, s. 44(1), 45(2).
S. 257A(4): ITA 2007, s. 55(2).
S. 257A(5): ITA 2007, s. 45(4).

S. 257A(5A): ITA 2007, s. 43, 45(5), Sch. 1 para. 28.
S. 257A(6): ITA 2007, s. 54(1), (2), (4), (6), 55(1).

257AB Married couple's allowance (post-5th December 2005 marriages and civil partnerships etc.)

257AB [Omitted by FA 2009, s. 5 and Sch. 1, para. 2(e).]

History – S. 257AB omitted by FA 2009, s. 5 and Sch. 1, para. 2(e), with effect for the tax year 2010–11 and subsequent tax years.

Notes – S. 257AB rewritten for income tax purposes as follows:
S. 257AB(1): ITA 2007, s. 44(1), 46(1), (2).
S. 257AB(2): ITA 2007, s. 46(1), (3).
S. 257AB(3): ITA 2007, s. 55(2).
S. 257AB(4): ITA 2007, s. 46(4).
S. 257AB(5): ITA 2007, s. 43, 46(5), Sch. 1 para. 28.
S. 257AB(6): ITA 2007, s. 55(1).
S. 257AB(7): ITA 2007, s. 54(1), (2), (4), (6).
S. 257AB(8): ITA 2007, s. 44(3).
S. 257AB(9): ITA 2007, s. 46(6).

257BA Elections as to transfer of relief under section 257A or 257AB

257BA [Omitted by FA 2009, s. 5 and Sch. 1, para. 2(e).]

History – S. 257BA omitted by FA 2009, s. 5 and Sch. 1, para. 2(e), with effect for the tax year 2010–11 and subsequent tax years.

Notes – S. 257BA rewritten for income tax purposes as follows:
S. 257BA(1): ITA 2007, s. 47(1), (2), (3), (4).
S. 257BA(2): ITA 2007, s. 48(1), (2), (3), (4).
S. 257BA(3): ITA 2007, s. 49(1), (2).
S. 257BA(4): ITA 2007, s. 50(2), (5).
S. 257BA(5): ITA 2007, s. 50(3).
S. 257BA(6): ITA 2007, s. 54(5).
S. 257BA(7): ITA 2007, s. 50(3), (4).
S. 257BA(8): ITA 2007, s. 50(5), (6), (7).
S. 257BA(9): ITA 2007, s. 55(1).

257BB Transfer of relief under section 257A or 257AB where relief exceeds income

257BB [Omitted by FA 2009, s. 5 and Sch. 1, para. 2(e).]

History – S. 257BB omitted by FA 2009, s. 5 and Sch. 1, para. 2(e), with effect for the tax year 2010–11 and subsequent tax years.

Notes – S. 257BB rewritten for income tax purposes as follows:
S. 257BB(1): ITA 2007, s. 51(1), (2), (3), (5), 53(3).
S. 257BB(2): ITA 2007, s. 51(4).
S. 257BB(3): ITA 2007, s. 52(1), (2), (4), 53(3).
S. 257BB(3A): ITA 2007, s. 51(3), 52(2).
S. 257BB(4): ITA 2007, s. 52(3).
S. 257BB(5): ITA 2007, s. 53(4).

257C Indexation of amounts in sections 256B, 257, 257A and 257AB

257C [Omitted by FA 2009, s. 5 and Sch. 1, para. 2(f).]

History – S. 257C omitted by FA 2009, s. 5 and Sch. 1, para. 2(f), with effect for the tax year 2010–11 and subsequent tax years.

Notes – S. 257C rewritten for income tax purposes as follows:
S. 257C(1): ITA 2007, s. 57(1), (2), (3), (4).
S. 257C(2A): ITA 2007, s. 57(5).
S. 257C(3): ITA 2007, s. 57(6).

257D Transitional relief: husband with excess allowances

257D [Repealed by FA 1999, s. 32(2), 139 and Sch. 20, Pt. III(3).]

History – S. 257D repealed by FA 1999, s. 32(2), 139 and Sch. 20, Pt. III(3), with effect for the year 2000–01 and subsequent years of assessment.

257E Transitional relief: the elderly

257E [Repealed by FA 1999, s. 32(2), 139 and Sch. 20, Pt. III(3).]

History – S. 257E repealed by FA 1999, s. 32(2), 139 and Sch. 20, Pt. III(3), with effect for the year 2000–01 and subsequent years of assessment.

257F Transitional relief: separated couples

257F [Repealed by FA 1999, s. 32(2), 139 and Sch. 20, Pt. III(3).]

History – S. 257F repealed by FA 1999, s. 32(2), 139 and Sch. 20, Pt. III(3), with effect for the year 2000–01 and subsequent years of assessment.

258 Widower's or widow's housekeeper

258 [Repealed by FA 1988, s. 25(3) and Sch. 14, Pt. IV.]

History – S. 258 repealed by FA 1988, s. 25(3) and Sch. 14, Pt. IV, effective for tax year 1988–89 and later years.

259 Additional relief in respect of children

259 [Repealed by FA 1999, s. 33, 139 and Sch. 20, Pt. III(4).]

History – S. 259 repealed by FA 1999, s. 33, 139 and Sch. 20, Pt. III(4), with effect for the year 2000–01 and subsequent years of assessment.

260 Apportionment of relief under section 259

260 [Repealed by FA 1999, s. 33, 139 and Sch. 20, Pt. III(4).]

History – S. 260 repealed by FA 1999, s. 33, 139 and Sch. 20, Pt. III(4), with effect for the year 2000–01 and subsequent years of assessment.

261 Claims under section 259 for year of marriage

261 [Repealed by FA 1999, s. 33, 139 and Sch. 20, Pt. III(4).]

History – S. 261 repealed by FA 1999, s. 33, 139 and Sch. 20, Pt. III(4), with effect for the year 2000–01 and subsequent years of assessment.

261A Additional relief in respect of children for year of separation

261A [Repealed by FA 1999, s. 33, 139 and Sch. 20, Pt. III(4).]

History – S. 261A repealed by FA 1999, s. 33, 139 and Sch. 20, Pt. III(4), with effect for the year 2000–01 and subsequent years of assessment.

262 Widows' bereavement allowance

262 [Repealed by FA 1999, s. 34, 139 and Sch. 20, Pt. III(5).]

History – S. 262 repealed by FA 1999, s. 34, 139 and Sch. 20, Pt. III(5), with effect in relation to deaths occurring on or after 6 April 2000.

263 Dependent relatives

263 [Repealed by FA 1988, s. 25(3) and Sch. 14, Pt. IV.]

History – S. 263 repealed by FA 1988, s. 25(3) and Sch. 14, Pt. IV, effective for 1988–89 and later years.

264 Claimant depending on services of a son or daughter

264 [Repealed by FA 1988, s. 25(3) and Sch. 14, Pt. IV.]

History – S. 264 repealed by FA 1988, s. 25(3) and Sch. 14, Pt. IV, effective for 1988–89 and later years.

265 Blind person's allowance

265 [Omitted by FA 2009, s. 5 and Sch. 1, para. 2(g).]

History – S. 265 omitted by FA 2009, s. 5 and Sch. 1, para. 2(g), with effect for the tax year 2010–11 and subsequent tax years.

Notes – S. 265 rewritten for income tax purposes as follows:
S. 265(1): ITA 2007, s. 23, 38(1), (2), (3).
S. 265(1A): ITA 2007, s. 57(1).
S. 265(2): ITA 2007, s. 23, 39(1), (2), (3).
S. 265(5): ITA 2007, s. 39(2), 40(1).
S. 265(6): ITA 2007, s. 40(2).
S. 265(7): ITA 2007, s. 38(2), (3).

266 Life assurance premiums

266(1) Subject to the provisions of this section, section 274 and Schedules 14 and 15 and sections 192 to 194 of the Finance Act 2004, an eligible individual who pays any such premium as is specified in subsection (2) below shall (without making any claim) be entitled to relief under this section.

266(1A) For the purposes of subsection (1) above an individual is an eligible individual if the individual–

(a) is resident in the United Kingdom, or

(b) meets the conditions in section 56(3) of ITA 2007.

266(2) The premiums referred to in subsection (1) above are any premiums paid by an individual under a policy of insurance or contract for a deferred annuity, where–

(a) the payments are made to –

(i) a person who has permission under Part 4A of the Financial Services and Markets Act 2000 or under paragraph 15 of Schedule 3 to that Act (as a result of qualifying for authorisation under paragraph 12(1) of that Schedule) to effect or carry out contracts of long-term insurance; or

(ii) a member of the Society who effects or carries out contracts of long-term insurance in accordance with Part 19 of the Financial Services and Markets Act 2000;

(iii) a friendly society; or

(iv) in the case of a deferred annuity, the National Debt Commissioners; and

(b) the insurance or, as the case may be, the deferred annuity is on the life of the individual or on the life of his spouse or civil partner; and

(c) the insurance or contract was made by him or his spouse or civil partner.

266(3) Subject to subsections (10) and (11) below, no relief under this section shall be given–

(a) except in respect of premiums payable under policies for securing a capital sum on death, whether in conjunction with any other benefit or not;

(b) in respect of premiums payable under any policy issued in respect of an insurance made after 19th March 1968 unless the policy is a qualifying policy;

(c) in respect of premiums payable under any policy issued in respect of an insurance made after 13th March 1984;

(d) in respect of premiums payable during the period of deferment in respect of a policy of deferred assurance.

266(4) Subject to subsection (8) below, relief under this section in respect of any premiums paid by an individual in a year of assessment shall be given by making good to the person to whom they are paid any deficiency arising from the deductions authorised under subsection (5) below; and this section and Schedule 14 shall have effect in relation to any premium or part of a premium which is paid otherwise than in the year of assessment in which it becomes due and payable as if it were paid in that year.

266(5) Subject to the provisions of Schedule 14–

(a) an individual resident in the United Kingdom who is entitled to relief under this section in respect of any premium may deduct from any payment in respect of the premium and retain an amount equal to 12.5 per cent of the payment; and

(b) the person to whom the payment is made shall accept the amount paid after the deduction in discharge of the individual's liability to the same extent as if the deduction had not been made and may recover the deficiency from the Board.

266(6) [Omitted by ITA 2007, s. 1027 and Sch. 1, para. 36(4) and repealed by ITA 2007, s. 1031 and Sch. 3, Pt. 1.]

266(6A) [Omitted by ITA 2007, s. 1027 and Sch. 1, para. 46(4) and repealed by ITA 2007, s. 1031 and Sch. 3, Pt. 1, with effect for 2007–08 and subsequent tax years.]

266(7) [Omitted by FA 2009, s. 5 and Sch. 1, para. 3(6).]

266(8) Where the individual is not resident in the United Kingdom (but is entitled to relief by virtue of subsection (1A)(b)), subsection (4) above shall not apply but the like relief shall be given to him under paragraph 6 of Schedule 14.

266(9) Subsections (5) and (8) above shall apply in relation to an individual who is not resident in the United Kingdom but is a member of the armed forces of the Crown or the spouse or civil partner of such a member as if the individual were so resident.

266(10) Subsection (3)(b) above shall not apply–

(a) to any policy of life insurance having as its sole object the provision on an individual's death or disability of a sum substantially the same as any amount then outstanding under a mortgage of his residence, or of any premises occupied by him for the purposes of a business, being a mortgage the principal amount secured by which is repayable by instalments payable annually or at shorter regular intervals; or

(b) to any policy of life insurance issued in connection with an approved scheme as defined in Chapter I of Part XIV.

In the application of this subsection to Scotland, for any reference to a mortgage there shall be substituted a reference to a heritable security within the meaning of the Conveyancing (Scotland) Act 1924 (but including a security constituted by ex facie absolute disposition or assignation).

266(11) Subsection (3)(a) and (d) above shall not affect premiums payable–

(a) under policies or contracts made in connection with any superannuation or bona fide pension scheme for the benefit of the employees of any employer, or of persons engaged in any particular trade, profession, vocation or business, or for the benefit of the spouse, civil partner, widow, widower, surviving civil partner or children or other dependants of any such employee or person, or

(b) under policies taken out by teachers in the schools known in the year 1918 as secondary schools, pending the establishment of a superannuation or pension scheme for those teachers.

266(12) Schedule 14 shall have effect for the purpose of modifying, for certain cases, and supplementing the provisions of this section.

266(13) In Schedule 14, **"friendly society"** means the same as in the Friendly Societies Act 1992 (and includes any society that by virtue of section 96(2) of that Act is to be treated as a registered friendly society within the meaning of that Act).

266(14) In subsection (2)(a)

"contracts of long-term insurance" means contracts which fall within Part II of Schedule 1 to the Financial Services and Markets Act 2000 (Regulated Activities) Order 2001; and

"member of the Society" has the same meaning as in Lloyd's Act 1982.

Prospective amendments – S. 266 repealed by FA 2012, Sch. 39, para. 28(1) with effect on a date to be appointed.

History – In s. 266(1), the words "eligible individual" substituted for "individual" by FA 2009, s. 5 and Sch. 1, para. 3(2)(a), with effect for the tax year 2010–11 and subsequent tax years.

In s. 266(1), the words "or makes a payment falling within subsection (7) below", which appeared after the words "subsection (2) below" omitted by FA 2009, s. 5 and Sch. 1, para. 3(2)(b), with effect for the tax year 2010–11 and subsequent tax years.

In s. 266(1) the words "section 274 and Schedules 14 and 15 and sections 192 to 194 of the Finance Act 2004," substituted for the words "sections 274 and 619(6) and Schedules 14 and 15," by FA 2004, s. 281 and Sch. 35, para. 9 with effect from 6 April 2006, subject to FA 2004, Sch. 36.

S. 266(1A) inserted by FA 2009, s. 5 and Sch. 1, para. 3(3), with effect for the tax year 2010–11 and subsequent tax years.

In s. 266(2)(a)(i), the words "Part 4A" substituted for the words "Part 4" by Financial Services Act 2012, s. 114(1) and Sch. 18, para. 58(2), with effect from 1 April 2013 (SI 2013/423).

In s. 266(2)(b) and (c) the words "or civil partner" inserted by SI 2005/3229, reg. 57(2), with effect from 5 December 2005.

S. 266(2)(a)(i), (ii) substituted for former para. (a)(i)–(iii) by SI 2001/3629, art. 18(2), with effect from 1 December 2001.

In s. 266(3), "(7),", which appeared after "Subject to subsections", omitted by FA 2009, s. 5 and Sch. 1, para. 3(4), with effect for the tax year 2010–11 and subsequent tax years.

In s. 266(3)(c), the words ", except where the relief relates to part only of any such payment as falls within subsection (6) below" omitted by ITA 2007, s. 1027 and Sch. 1, para. 36(2) and repealed by ITA 2007, s. 1031 and Sch. 3, Pt. 1 with effect for 2007–08 and subsequent tax years.

In s. 266(4), "subsection" substituted for "subsections (7) and" by FA 2009, s. 5 and Sch. 1, para. 3(5), with effect for the tax year 2010–11 and subsequent tax years.

In s. 266(4), the words "subsections 7 and 8" substituted by ITA 2007, s. 1027 and Sch. 1, para. 36(3) with effect for 2007–08 and later tax years.

S. 266(5) amended by FA 1988, s. 29 substituting 12.5 per cent, effective on or after 6 April 1989.

S. 266(6) and (6A) omitted by ITA 2007, s. 1027 and Sch. 1, para. 36(4) and repealed by ITA 2007, s. 1031 and Sch. 3, Pt. 1 with effect for 2007–08 and subsequent tax years.

Former s. 266(6)(c) and (6A): insertions made by FA 1996, s. 171(3), (4).

In former s. 266(6)(a) reference to "friendly society" substituted by F(No. 2)A 1992, s. 56 and Sch. 9, para. 2(2) with effect from19 February 1993 (SI 1993/236).

S. 266(7) omitted by FA 2009, s. 5 and Sch. 1, para. 3(6), with effect for the tax year 2010–11 and subsequent tax years.

In former s. 266(7)(b), the words "in calculating his net income there shall be deducted" substituted by ITA 2007, s. 1027 and Sch. 1, para. 36(5) with effect for 2007–08 and subsequent tax years.

In s. 266(8), the words "(but is entitled to relief by virtue of subsection (1A)(b))" substituted for the words "and is entitled to relief by virtue of section 278(2) or (2ZA)" by FA 2009, s. 5 and Sch. 1, para. 3(7), with effect for the tax year 2010–11 and subsequent tax years.

In s. 266(8), the words "and is entitled" substituted and the reference "or (2ZA)" inserted by ITA 2007, s. 1027 and Sch. 1, para. 36(6) with effect for 2007–08 and subsequent tax years.

In s. 266(8), the words "(subject to section 278(3))" omitted by ITA 2007, s. 1027 and Sch. 1, para. 36(6)(c) and repealed by ITA 2007, s. 1031 and Sch. 3, Pt. 1 with effect for 2007–08 and subsequent tax years.

In s. 266(9) the words "or civil partner" inserted by SI 2005/3229, reg. 57(3), with effect from 5 December 2005.

In s. 266(9), the word "spouse" substituted by FA 1988, s. 35 and Sch. 3, para. 9, for 1990–91 and subsequent years of assessment.

In s. 266(11)(a) the words "civil partner" and ", surviving civil partner" inserted by SI 2005/3229, reg. 57(4), with effect from 5 December 2005.

In s. 266(11)(a), the words "spouse", to "or person", substituted by FA 1988, s. 35 and Sch. 3, para. 9, for 1990–91 and subsequent years of assessment.

In s. 266(13), the words "this section and" omitted by ITA 2007, s. 1027 and Sch. 1, para. 36(7) and ITA 2007, s. 1031 and Sch. 3, Pt. 1 with effect for 2007–08 and later tax years.

S. 266(13) inserted by F(No. 2)A 1992, s. 56 and Sch. 9, para. 2(3) with effect from 19 February 1993 (SI 1993/236).

S. 266(14) added by SI 2001/3629, art. 18(3), with effect from 1 December 2001.

Derivations – S. 266(1): ICTA 1970, s. 19(1), as amended by FA 1976, s. 34 and Sch. 4, para. 1, 3(1).

S. 266(2) (as originally enacted): ICTA 1970, s. 19(2), as amended by FA 1976, s. 34, 36(5) and Sch. 4, para. 3(2); Insurance Companies Act 1981, Sch. 5, Pt. I and Insurance Companies Act 1982, s. 99(2) and Sch. 5, para. 10.

S. 266(3): ICTA 1970, s. 19(3), (4) and FA 1984, s. 72(1).

S. 266(4): FA 1976, s. 34 and Sch. 4, para. 4(1) and FA 1978, s. 25 and Sch. 3, para. 2.

S. 266(5) (as originally enacted): FA 1976, Sch. 4, para. 5, amended by FA 1980, s. 29.

S. 266(6) (as originally enacted), (7): FA 1978, Sch. 3, para. 11(1), 12, as amended by FA 1981, s. 33.

S. 266(8), (9) (as originallyenacted): FA 1976, Sch. 4, para. 4(2), 5A, as inserted by FA 1978, Sch. 3, para. 5. See also Armed Forces Act 1981, Sch. 3, para. 1.

S. 266(10): ICTA 1970, s. 19(4)(a), (c). Para. (c) was inserted by FA 1971, Sch. 3, para. 11.

S. 266(11) (as originally enacted): ICTA 1970, s. 19(3)(i), (ii).

Cross references – S. 431(2): life assurance business includes annuity business.
S. 466(2): life and endowment business exempt from tax (subject to certain exceptions).
Pt. XIV, Ch. I: rules as to approved retirement benefit schemes.
S. 619(6): relief excluded where relief also available on premiums in respect of a retirement annuity contract.
Sch. 14: modifying and supplementary provisions and power to make regulations governing s. 266.
Sch. 15: rules as to qualifying policies.
FA 2012, Sch. 39, para. 23: s. 266 applies only if premium (or part of premium) becomes due and payable before 6 April 2015 and is actually paid before 6 July 2015.
Extra-statutory concessions – A32: relief continues to be available in respect of certain pre-1980–81 non-qualifying policies.
Statements of practice – SP 4/79: policies on the lives of children under 12 not in general to qualify.
SP 11/79: exceptional qualification for policies on the lives of children under 12 in respect of certain Friendly Society policies (and transitional (1979) provisions).
SP 4/97: where the taxpayer receives commission from the life office only the premium net of commission is relieved.
Other material – IR press release, 4 February 1981 (not reproduced): relief for premiums paid to UK branch of overseas life office.
ICAEW Technical Release TR 224 (not reproduced): generally, commission received by a policyholder, or an agent on his own insurance, is not taxed.
Notes – S. 266 rewritten for income tax purposes as follows:
S. 266(1): ITA 2007, s. 457(1), 458(1).
S. 266(7): ITA 2007, s. 23, 24(1), 457(1), (2), (4), (5), 458(1), (2), (4), (5).

266A Life assurance premiums paid by employer

266A(1) This section applies if–

(a) pursuant to an employer-financed retirement benefits scheme, the employer in any year of assessment pays a sum with a view to the provision of any relevant benefits for or in respect of any employee of that employer, and

(b) the payment is made under such an insurance or contract as is mentioned in section 266.

This section applies whether or not the accrual of the relevant benefits is dependent on any contingency.

266A(2) Relief, if not otherwise allowable, shall be given to that employee under section 266 in respect of the payment to the extent, if any, to which such relief would have been allowable to him if–

(a) the payment had been made by him, and

(b) the insurance or contract under which the payment is made had been made with him.

266A(3) For the purposes of subsection (1)(a) benefits are provided in respect of an employee if they are provided for the employee's spouse or civil partner, widow or widower or surviving civil partner, children, dependants or personal representatives.

266A(4) If a sum within subsection (1) is paid with a view to the provision of benefits for or in respect of more than one employee of the employer, part of it is to be treated as paid for or in respect of each of them.

266A(5) The amount treated as paid for or in respect of each employee is–

$$A \times \frac{B}{C}$$

where–

A is the sum paid,

B is the amount which would have had to be paid to secure the benefits to be provided for or in respect of the employee in question, and

C is the total amount which would have had to be paid to secure the benefits to be provided for or in respect of all the employees if separate payments had been made in the case of each of them.

266A(6) This section does not apply if–

(a) in the year of assessment in which the sum is paid the earnings from the employee's employment are (or, if there are none, would be if there were any) earnings charged on remittance, or

(b) the employee is not domiciled in the United Kingdom in the tax year in which the sum is paid and the conditions in subsection (7) are met.

266A(7) Those conditions are–

(a) that the employment is with a foreign employer, and

(b) that, on a claim made by the employee, the Board are satisfied that the pension scheme corresponds to a registered pension scheme.

266A(8) In subsection (6)(a) **"earnings charged on remittance"** means earnings which are taxable earnings under–

(a) section 22 of ITEPA 2003 (chargeable overseas earnings for year when remittance basis applies and employee outside section 26), or

(b) section 26 of that Act (foreign earnings for year when remittance basis applies and employee meets section 26A requirement).

ICTA 1988

266A(9) In this section–

"employer-financed retirement benefits scheme", and

"relevant benefits",

have the same meaning as in Chapter 2 of Part 6 of ITEPA 2003 (see sections 393A and 393B of that Act).

Prospective amendments – S. 266A repealed by FA 2012, Sch. 39, para. 28(1) with effect on a date to be appointed.

History – In s. 266A(1) the words "an employer-financed" substituted for the words "a non-approved" by FA 2004, s. 281 and Sch. 35, para. 10(2) with effect from 6 April 2006, subject to FA 2004, Sch. 36.

S. 266A(3)–(9) substituted for s. 266A(3)–(6) by FA 2004, s. 281 and Sch. 35, para. 10(3) with effect, subject to FA 2004, Sch. 36, from 6 April 2006.

In former s. 266A(3)(b) the words "or civil partner" and "or surviving civil partner" inserted by SI 2005/3229, reg. 58, with effect from 5 December 2005.

In s. 266A(8)(a) the words "remittance basis applies and employee outside section 26" substituted for the words "employee resident and ordinarily resident, but not domiciled, in UK" and in para. (b) the words "remittance basis applies and employee meets section 26A requirement" substituted for the words "employee resident, but not ordinarily resident, in UK" by FA 2013, s. 219 and Sch. 46, para. 16, with effect in relation to an individual's foreign income and gains for the tax year 2013–14 or any subsequent tax year (subject to the savings at FA 2013, Sch. 46, para. 26).

S. 266A inserted by ITEPA 2003, Sch. 6, para. 36 which has effect for the tax year 2003–04 and subsequent tax years.

267 Qualifying policies

267 Schedule 15, Part I of which contains the basic rules for determining whether or not a policy is a qualifying policy, Part II of which makes provision for the certification etc. of policies as qualifying policies and Part III of which modifies Parts I and II in their application to certain policies issued by non-resident companies, shall have effect for the purpose of determining whether or not a policy is a qualifying policy; and, accordingly, any reference in this Act to a qualifying policy shall be construed in accordance with that Schedule.

268 Early conversion or surrender of life policies

268 [Omitted by FA 2012, Sch. 39, para. 31(1).]

History – S. 268 omitted by FA 2012, Sch. 39, para. 31(1) with effect in relation to events occurring on or after 6 April 2015. Former s. 268 read as follows:

"Early conversion or surrender of life policies

268(1) Where a policy of life insurance to which this section applies has been issued and, within four years from the making of the insurance in respect of which it was issued, any of the following events happens, that is to say–

(a) the surrender of the whole or part of the rights conferred by the policy;

(b) the falling due (otherwise than on death) of a sum payable in pursuance of a right conferred by the policy to participate in profits; and

(c) the conversion of the policy into a paid-up or partly paid-up policy;

the body by whom the policy was issued shall pay to the Board, out of the sums payable by reason of the surrender or, as the case may be, out of the sum falling due or out of the fund available to pay the sums which will be due on death or on the maturity of the policy, a sum determined in accordance with the following provisions of this section, unless the body is wound up and the event is a surrender or conversion effected in connection with the winding-up.

268(2) The sum payable under subsection (1) above shall, subject to the following provisions of this section, be equal to the lower of the following, that is to say–

(a) the appropriate percentage of the premiums payable under the policy up to the happening of the event; and

(b) the surrender value of the policy at the time of the happening of the event less the complementary percentage of the premiums mentioned in paragraph (a) above.

268(3) If the event is one of those mentioned below, the sum payable to the Board shall not exceed the following limit, that is to say–

(a) if it is the surrender of part of the rights conferred by the policy, the value of the rights surrendered at the time of the surrender;

(b) if it is the conversion of the policy into a partly paid-up policy, the surrender value at the time of the conversion, of so much of the policy as is paid up; and

(c) if it is the falling due of a sum, that sum.

268(4) If the event was preceded by the happening of such an event as is mentioned in subsection (1) above, subsection (2) above shall apply–

(a) as if the lower of the amounts mentioned therein were reduced by the sum paid under this section in respect of the earlier event; and

(b) if the earlier event was such an event as is mentioned in paragraph (a) or (c) of subsection (3) above, as if the surrender value of the policy were increased by the amount which, under that paragraph, limited or might have limited the sum payable under this section in respect of the earlier event.

268(5) For the purposes of this section the appropriate percentage, in relation to any event, is the percentage equal to the following fraction of the percentage found by doubling that mentioned in section 266(5)(a) as in force for the year of assessment in which the event happened, that is to say–

(a) if the event happens in the first two of the four years mentioned in subsection (1) above, three-sixths;

(b) if it happens in the third of those years, two-sixths; and

(c) if it happens in the last of those years, one-sixth;

and the complementary percentage, in relation to any event, is 100 per cent less the appropriate percentage.

268(6) Where the annual amount of the premiums payable under a policy of life insurance is at any time increased (whether under the policy or by any contract made after its issue) so as to exceed by more than 25 per cent–

(a) if the insurance was made on or before 26th March 1974, the annual amount as at that date, or

(b) in the case of any other insurance, the first annual amount so payable,

the additional rights attributable to the excess shall be treated for the purposes of this section as conferred by a new policy issued in respect of an insurance made at that time, and the excess shall be treated as premiums payable under the new policy.

268(7) This section applies to any policy of life insurance which is a qualifying policy unless–
(a) it is a policy in respect of the premiums on which relief under section 266 is not available by virtue of subsection (3)(c) of that section; or
(b) it is a policy of life insurance issued in connection with a registered pension scheme;
and in relation to a policy of life insurance issued in respect of an insurance made before 27th March 1974 applies only in accordance with subsection (6) above.

History – In s. 268(7)(b) the words "a registered pension scheme;" substituted for the words "an approved scheme, as defined in Chapter 1 of Part 14;", by FA 2004, s. 281 and Sch. 35, para. 11 with effect from 6 April 2006.

Derivations – S. 268(1)–(5): FA 1975, s. 7(1)–(5), as amended by FA 1976, Sch. 4, para. 19(1).
S. 268(6), (7): FA 1975, s. 7(6)–(8), as amended by FA 1984, s. 72(5).

Cross references – Pt. XIV, Ch. I: rules as to approved retirement benefit schemes.

Extra-statutory concessions – A41: relaxation of statutory condition re back-dating of policies, reduction in first year premiums, certain trivial infringements and back-dating of certification."

269 Surrender etc. of policies after four years

269 [Omitted by FA 2012, Sch. 39, para. 31(1).]

History – S. 269 omitted by FA 2012, Sch. 39, para. 31(1) in relation to events occurring on or after 6 April 2015. Former s. 269 read as follows:

"Surrender etc. of policies after four years

269(1) Where a policy of life insurance to which this section applies has been issued and, in the fifth or any later year from the making of the insurance in respect of which it was issued, either of the following events happens, that is to say–
(a) the surrender of the whole or part of the rights conferred by the policy; and
(b) the falling due (otherwise than on death or maturity) of a sum payable in pursuance of a right conferred by the policy to participate in profits;
then, if either of those events has happened before, the body by whom the policy was issued shall pay to the Board, out of the sums payable by reason of the surrender, or, as the case may be, out of the sum falling due, a sum determined in accordance with the following provisions of this section.
269(2) The sum payable under subsection (1) above shall, subject to the following provisions of this section, be equal to the applicable percentage of the lower of the following–
(a) the total of the premiums which are payable in that year under the policy; and
(b) the sums payable by reason of the surrender or, as the case may be, the sum falling due;
and the percentage to be applied for this purpose shall be a percentage equal to that mentioned in section 266(5)(a) as in force for the year of assessment in which the event happens.
269(3) Where, after a sum has become payable under subsection (1) above, and within the same year from the making of the insurance, another such event happens as is mentioned therein, the sums payable under that subsection in respect of both or all of the events shall not exceed the applicable percentage of the total mentioned in subsection (2)(a) above.
269(4) Where, on the happening of an event in the fifth or any later year from the making of the insurance, any sum is payable under subsection (1) of section 268 as applied by subsection (6) of that section as well as under subsection (1) above, subsection (2) above shall apply as if the sums or sum mentioned in paragraph (b) thereof were reduced by the sum payable under that section.
269(5) This section applies to any policy of life insurance which is a qualifying policy unless–
(a) it is a policy in respect of the premiums on which relief under section 266 is not available by virtue of subsection (3)(c) of that section; or
(b) it is a policy issued in the course of an industrial insurance business; or
(c) it was issued in respect of an insurance made before 27th March 1974.

Derivations – FA 1975, s. 8(1), (2), as amended by FA 1976, s. 34 and Sch. 4, para. 19(2).
S. 269(3)–(5): FA 1975, s. 8(3)–(5), as amended by FA 1984, s. 72(5)."

270 Provisions supplementary to sections 268 and 269

270 [Omitted by FA 2012, Sch. 39, para. 31(1).]

History – S. 270 omitted by FA 2012, Sch. 39, para. 31(1) with effect in relation to events occurring on or after 6 April 2015. Former s. 270 read as follows:

"Provisions supplementary to sections 268 and 269

270(1) Where on the happening of an event in relation to a policy of life insurance a sum is payable under section 268 or 269, relief under section 266 in respect of the relevant premiums paid under the policy shall be reduced by the sum so payable or, as the case may be, by so much of the sum as does not exceed the amount of that relief (or as does not exceed so much of that amount as remains after any previous reduction under this section).
270(2) For the purposes of this section the relevant premiums are–
(a) in relation to a sum payable under section 268, the premiums payable under the policy up to the happening of the event by reason of which the sum is payable; and
(b) in relation to a sum payable under section 269, the premiums payable in the year (from the making of the insurance) in which the event happens by reason of which the sum is payable.
270(3) Where the relevant premiums are payable in more than one year of assessment the reduction in relief under this section shall, so far as possible, reduce relief for an earlier year of assessment before reducing relief for a later one.
270(4) Any sum paid under section 268 or 269 by reason of any event shall be treated–
(a) as between the parties, as received by the person by whom the premiums under the policy were paid; and
(b) for the purposes of section 266, as a sum paid by that person in satisfaction of his liability resulting from the reduction of relief under this section;
and where that sum exceeds that liability he shall be entitled, on a claim made by him not later than 4 years after the end of the year of assessment in which the event happens, to repayment of the excess.

History – In s. 270(4), the words "4 years" substituted for the words "six years" by FA 2008, s. 118 and Sch. 39, para. 21, with effect from 1 April 2010 (SI 2009/403, art. 2(2), but subject to SI 2009/403, art. 3–10, in particular art. 10).

Derivations – S. 270(1)–(4): FA 1975, s. 9(1)–(4), as amended by FA 1976, s. 34 and Sch. 4, para. 19(3).

Extra-statutory concessions – A51: excessive clawback qualifies for repayment supplement."

271 Deemed surrender in cases of certain loans

271 [Omitted by FA 2012, Sch. 39, para. 31(1).]

History – S. 271 omitted by FA 2012, Sch. 39, para. 31(1) with effect in relation to events occurring on or after 6 April 2015. Former s. 271 read as follows:

"Deemed surrender in cases of certain loans

271(1) Where–

(a) by virtue of section 465 of ITTOIA 2005 a gain arising in connection with a policy would be treated as forming part of an individual's total income; and

(b) the policy was issued in respect of an insurance made after 26th March 1974; and

(c) any sum is at any time after the making of the insurance lent to or at the direction of that individual by or by arrangement with the body issuing the policy;

then, subject to subsection (2) below, the same results shall follow under sections 268 to 270 as if at the time the sum was lent there had been a surrender of part of the rights conferred by the policy and the sum had been paid as consideration for the surrender (and if the policy is a qualifying policy, whether or not the premiums under it are eligible for relief under section 266, those results shall follow under section 269, whether or not a gain would be treated as arising on the surrender).

271(2) Subsection (1) above does not apply–

(a) in relation to a policy if–

(i) it is a qualifying policy; and

(ii) either interest at a commercial rate is payable on the sum lent or the sum is lent to a full-time employee of the body issuing the policy for the purpose of assisting him in the purchase or improvement of a dwelling used or to be used as his only or main residence; or

(b) [Repealed by FA 1994, s. 146 and Sch. 17, para. 2 and s. 258 and Sch. 26, Pt. V(22).]

History – In s. 271(1)(a) the words "by virtue of section 465 of ITTOIA 2005" substituted by ITTOIA 2005, s. 882(1) and Sch. 1, para. 123; effective for income tax purposes for 2005–06 onwards and for corporation tax purposes for accounting periods ending after 5 April 2005 (ITTOIA 2005, s. 883(1)).

In s. 271, words mistakenly included in consolidation of the Tax Acts in 1988 repealed and deemed never to have had effect by FA 1994, s. 146 and Sch. 17, para. 2, and s. 258 and Sch. 26, Pt. V(22).

Derivations – S. 271(1): FA 1975, Sch. 2, para. 16(1), as amended by FA 1976, s. 35.
S. 271(2): FA 1975, Sch. 2, para. 16(3).

Cross references – S. 353: general relief for interest paid.
S. 365: interest relief available in respect of interest on a loan to purchase a life annuity.
S. 547: method of charging gain arising under a policy on a chargeable event.
S. 548: parallel provisions crystallising a charge to higher rate tax ("a chargeable event")."

272 Collection of sums payable under sections 268 and 269

272 [Omitted by FA 2012, Sch. 39, para. 31(1).]

History – S. 272 omitted by FA 2012, Sch. 39, para. 31(1) with effect in relation to events occurring on or after 6 April 2015. Former s. 272 read as follows:

"Collection of sums payable under sections 268 and 269

272(1) Any body by whom a policy to which section 268 or 269 applies has been issued shall, within 30 days of the end of each period of 12 months ending with 31st March in every year, make a return to the collector of the sums which, in that period, have become payable by it under either of those sections.

272(2) Any sum which is to be included in a return made under subsection (1) above shall be due at the time by which the return is to be made and shall be paid without being demanded.

272(3) Where any sum which was or ought to have been included in such a return is not paid by the end of the period for which the return was to be made, it may be recovered by an assessment as if it were income tax for the year of assessment in which that period ends; and where it appears to the inspector that a sum which ought to have been so included had not been included or that a return is not correct he may make such an assessment to the best of his judgment.

272(4) All the provisions of the Income Tax Acts relating to the assessment and collection of tax, interest on unpaid tax, appeals and penalties shall, with the necessary modifications, apply in relation to sums due under this section; and for the purposes of those provisions so far as they relate to interest on unpaid tax, a sum assessed in pursuance of this section shall be treated as having been payable when it would have been payable had it been included in a return under subsection (1) above.

272(5) Where, on an appeal against an assessment made in pursuance of this section, it is determined that a greater sum has been assessed than was payable, the excess, if paid, shall be repaid.

272(6) Where a body has paid a sum which is payable under section 268 or 269 it shall give within 30 days to the person by whom the sum is, under section 270(4), treated as received a statement specifying that sum and showing how it has been arrived at.

272(7) [Omitted by SI 2009/2035, art. 2 and Sch., para. 17.]

History – S. 272(7) omitted by SI 2009/2035, art. 2 and Sch., para. 17, with effect from 13 August 2009.

Derivations – FA 1975, Sch. 1, para. 1–4(1).

Cross references – TMA 1970, s. 98: penalties for failure to comply with notice under s. 272(7).

Notes – In s. 272(7)(b) reference to documents to be construed in accordance with Civil Evidence Act 1968, Pt. I: see FA 1988, s. 127(1) (Civil Evidence Act 1968, s. 10 is reproduced in a note to said s. 127(1)). This has the effect of giving the Revenue access under s. 272(7)(b) to computer records. See FA 1988, s. 127(2)–(4) for ancillary rights of access to computer hardware. For application to Scotland and Northern Ireland, see FA 1988, s. 127(5)."

273 Payments securing annuities

273 [Omitted by FA 2009, s. 5 and Sch. 1, para. 2(h).]

History – S. 273 omitted by FA 2009, s. 5 and Sch. 1, para. 2(h), with effect for the tax year 2010–11 and subsequent tax years.

Notes – S. 273 rewritten for income tax purposes as follows:
S. 273(1): ITA 2007, s. 23, 26(1), 27(4), (5), 459(1), (2), (6).
S. 273(2): ITA 2007, s. 459(5).

274 Limits on relief under section 266

History – In the heading to s. 274, "section 266" substituted for "sections 266 and 273" by FA 2009, s. 5 and Sch. 1, para 4(6), with effect for the tax year 2010–11 and subsequent tax years.

274(1) The aggregate of the premiums in respect of which relief is given to any person under section 266 shall not exceed £1,500 in any year of assessment or one-sixth of that person's total income, whichever is the greater.

274(2) The aggregate of the relief given under section 266 in respect of premiums payable for securing any benefits other than capital sums on death shall not exceed the amount of the income tax calculated at 12.5% on £100.

274(3) [Omitted by FA 2009, s. 5 and Sch. 1, para. 4(4).]

274(4) War insurance premiums shall not be taken into account in calculating the limits of one-sixth of total income or of £100 mentioned in this section.

In this subsection **"war insurance premiums"** means any additional premium paid in order to extend an existing life insurance policy to risks arising from war or war service abroad, and any part of any premium paid in respect of a life insurance policy covering those risks, or either of them, which is attributable to those risks, or either of them.

Prospective amendments – S. 274 repealed by FA 2012, Sch. 39, para. 28(1) with effect on a date to be appointed.

History – In s. 274(1), the words "or other sums", which appeared after "premiums", omitted by FA 2009, s. 5 and Sch. 1, para 4(2), with effect for the tax year 2010–11 and subsequent tax years.
In s. 274(2), "section 266" substituted for "sections 266 and 273" by FA 2009, s. 5 and Sch. 1, para. 4(3)(a), with effect for the tax year 2010–11 and subsequent tax years.
In s. 274(2), the words "or sums", which appeared after "premiums", omitted by FA 2009, s. 5 and Sch. 1, para. 4(3)(b), with effect for the tax year 2010–11 and subsequent tax years.
In s. 274(2), "12.5%" substituted for "the appropriate rate" by FA 2009, s. 5 and Sch. 1, para. 4(3)(c), with effect for the tax year 2010–11 and subsequent tax years.
S. 274(3) omitted by FA 2009, s. 5 and Sch. 1, para. 4(4), with effect for the tax year 2010–11 and subsequent tax years.
S. 274(3) amended by FA 1988, s. 29 substituting "12.5 per cent" for "15 per cent", effective on or after 6 April 1989.
In s. 274(4), the words "or other sum" omitted in both places (where they appeared after "premium") by FA 2009, s. 5 and Sch. 1, para. 4(5), with effect for the tax year 2010–11 and subsequent tax years.
In s. 274(4) the word "is" substituted by FA 1996, s. 134 and Sch. 20, para. 20 for 1996–97 and later years of assessment.

Derivations – S. 274(1): ICTA 1970, s. 21(1), as amended by FA 1976, s. 34 and Sch. 4, para. 21(2).
S. 274(2): ICTA 1970, s. 21(3), as amended by FA 1975, s. 10 and Sch. 2, para. 6 and FA 1976, s. 34 and Sch. 4, para. 21(4).
S. 274(3) (as originally enacted): ICTA 1970, s. 21(4), as amended by FA 1975, s. 10 and Sch. 2, para. 6; FA 1976, s. 34 and Sch. 4, para. 21(5); FA 1980, s. 29; and by FA 1987, s. 71 and Sch. 15, para. 2(5).
S. 274(4): ICTA 1970, s. 21(5), as amended by FA 1975, s. 10 and Sch. 2, para. 6(1)(d).

Notes – S. 274(2) rewritten for income tax purposes as ITA 2007, s. 457(3), 458(3), 459(3).

SUPPLEMENTAL

275 Meaning of "relative"

275 [Repealed by FA 1988, s. 25 and Sch. 14, Pt. IV.]

History – Repealed by FA 1988, s. 25 and Sch. 14, Pt. IV, effective for 1988–89 and later years.

276 Effect on relief of charges on income

276 [Omitted by ITA 2007, s. 1027 and Sch. 1, para. 38 and repealed by ITA 2007, s. 1031 and Sch. 3, Pt. 1 with effect for 2007–08 and subsequent tax years.]

277 Partners

277 [Omitted by ITA 2007, s. 1027 and Sch. 1, para. 39 and repealed by ITA 2007, s. 1031 and Sch. 3, Pt. 1 with effect for 2007–08 and subsequent tax years.]

278 Non-residents

278 [Omitted by FA 2009, s. 5 and Sch. 1, para. 2(i).]

History – S. 278 omitted by FA 2009, s. 5 and Sch. 1, para. 2(i), with effect for the tax year 2010–11 and subsequent tax years.

Notes – S. 278 rewritten for income tax purposes as follows:
S. 278(1): ITA 2007, s. 35, 36(1), 37(1), 38(1), 39(1), 45(2), 46(2), 47(2), 48(2), 51(4), 56(2), 457(1), 458(1), 459(1), 460(2).
S. 278(2): ITA 2007, s. 35, 36(1), 37(1), 38(1), 39(1), 45(2), 46(2), 47(2), 48(2), 51(4), 56(2), (3), 460(2), (3).

Chapter II – Taxation of Income of Spouses and Civil Partners

History – In the heading to Ch. II the words "and Civil Partners" inserted by SI 2005/3229, reg. 61, with effect from 5 December 2005.

GENERAL RULES

279 Aggregation of wife's income with husband's

279 [Repealed by FA 1988, s. 32, 148 and Sch. 14, Pt. VIII.]

History – Repealed by FA 1988, s. 32, 148 and Sch. 14, Pt. VIII for 1990–91 and subsequent years of assessment.

280 Transfer of reliefs

280 [Repealed by FA 1988, s. 148 and Sch. 14, Pt. VIII.]

History – S. 280 repealed by FA 1988, s. 148 and Sch. 14, Pt. VIII for 1990–91 and subsequent years of assessment.

281 Tax repayments to wives

281 [Repealed by FA 1988, s. 148 and Sch. 14, Pt. VIII.]

History – S. 281 repealed by FA 1988, s. 148 and Sch. 14, Pt. VIII, for 1990–91 and subsequent years of assessment.

282 Construction of references to spouses or civil partners living together

History – In the heading to s. 282 the words "spouses or civil partners" substituted for the words "husband and wife" by SI 2005/3229, reg. 62(b), with effect from 5 December 2005.

282 [Omitted by ITA 2007, s. 1027 and Sch. 1, para. 41 and repealed by ITA 2007, s. 1031 and Sch. 3, Pt. 1 with effect for 2007–08 and subsequent tax years.]

Notes – S. 282 rewritten for income tax purposes as ITA 2007, s. 1011.

282A Jointly held property

282A [Omitted by ITA 2007, s. 1027 and Sch. 1, para. 42 and repealed by ITA 2007, s. 1031 and Sch. 3, Pt. 1 with effect for 2007–08 and subsequent tax years.]

Notes – S. 282A rewritten for income tax purposes as follows:
S. 282A(1): ITA 2007, s. 836(1), (2), (3).
S. 282A(2): ITA 2007, s. 836(3).
S. 282A(3): ITA 2007, s. 836(3), 837(1).
S. 282A(4): ITA 2007, s. 836(3).
S. 282A(4A): ITA 2007, s. 836(3).
S. 282A(5): ITA 2007, s. 836(3).
S. 282A(6): ITA 2007, s. 836(1).

282B Jointly held property: declarations

282B [Omitted by ITA 2007, s. 1027 and Sch. 1, para. 42 and repealed by ITA 2007, s. 1031 and Sch. 3, Pt. 1 with effect for 2007–08 and later tax years.]

Notes – S. 282B rewritten for income tax purposes as follows:
S. 282B(1): ITA 2007, s. 837(1), (2).
S. 282B(2): ITA 2007, s. 837(4).
S. 282B(3): ITA 2007, s. 837(3).
S. 282B(4): ITA 2007, s. 837(1).
S. 282B(5): ITA 2007, s. 837(5).

SEPARATE ASSESSMENTS

283 Option for separate assessment

283 [Repealed by FA 1988, s. 148 and Sch. 14, Pt. VIII.]

History – S. 283 repealed by FA 1988, s. 148 and Sch. 14, Pt. VIII for 1990–91 and subsequent years of assessment.

284 Effect of separate assessment on personal reliefs

284 [Repealed by FA 1988, s. 148 and Sch. 14, Pt. VIII.]

History – S. 284 repealed by FA 1988, s. 148 and Sch. 14, Pt. VIII for 1990–91 and subsequent years of assessment.

285 Collection from wife of tax assessed on husband but attributable to her income

285 [Repealed by FA 1988, s. 148 and Sch. 14, Pt. VIII.]

History – S. 285 repealed by FA 1988, s. 148 and Sch. 14, Pt. VIII for 1990–91 and subsequent years of assessment.

286 Right of husband to disclaim liability for tax on deceased wife's income

286 [Repealed by FA 1988, s. 148 and Sch. 14, Pt. VIII.]

History – S. 286 repealed by FA 1988, s. 148 and Sch. 14, Pt. VIII, for 1990–91 and subsequent years of assessment.

SEPARATE TAXATION

287 Separate taxation of wife's earnings

287 [Repealed by FA 1988, s. 148 and Sch. 14, Pt. VIII.]

History – S. 287 repealed by FA 1988, s. 148 and Sch. 14, Pt. VIII for 1990–91 and subsequent years of assessment.

288 Elections under section 287

288 [Repealed by FA 1988, s. 148 and Sch. 14, Pt. VIII.]

History – S. 288 repealed by FA 1988, s. 148 and Sch. 14, Pt. VIII, for 1990–91 and subsequent years of assessment.

Chapter III – Enterprise Investment Scheme

History – Pt. VII, Ch. III omitted by ITA 2007, s. 1027 and Sch. 1, para. 627 and repealed by ITA 2007, Sch. 3, Pt. 2, with the effect in relation to shares issued after 5 April 2007, with the exception of s. 305A, which is omitted by ITA 2007, s. 1027 and Sch. 1, para. 43 and repealed by ITA 2007, s. 1031 and Sch. 3, Pt. 1 with effect for 2007–08 and subsequent tax years. The provisions, as they apply in relation to shares issued before 6 April 2007, are reproduced below.
Heading to Pt. VII, Ch. III substituted by FA 1994, s. 137 and Sch. 15, para. 1, 2. The former heading read: "Relief for Investment in New Corporate Trades: The Business Expansion Scheme".

Cross references – TCGA 1992, s. 150: capital gains tax interaction with former BES relief – identification rules in s. 107 of that Act do not apply to shares in respect of which relief under Ch. III has been given and not withdrawn.
TCGA 1992, s. 150A: capital gains tax interaction with enterprise investment scheme relief.
TCGA 1992, s. 231: interaction of former BES relief and roll-over relief on disposal of shares to a qualifying employee share ownership trust by virtue of which the replacement shares are treated as being non-chargeable assets, thereby preventing roll-over relief.
TCGA 1992, Sch. 5B: enterprise investment scheme – reinvestment.
FA 2000, Sch. 15, para. 55(4)(a)(ii): corporate venturing scheme: where "replacement value" received under para. 54 so that investment relief is not reduced or withdrawn, person who subscribes for shares is not eligible for any relief under Pt. VII, Ch. III.

Other material – IR press release, 21 December 1990: guidelines regarding approval of BES investment funds.
IR leaflet IR137 (not reproduced): a guide to the enterprise investment scheme.

289 Eligibility for relief

289 [Omitted by ITA 2007, s. 1027 and Sch. 1, para. 627 and repealed by ITA 2007, s. 1031 and Sch. 3, Pt. 2 with effect in relation to shares issued after 5 April 2007.]

History – S. 289 omitted by ITA 2007, s. 1027 and Sch. 1, para. 627 and repealed by ITA 2007, s. 1031 and Sch. 3, Pt. 2 with effect in relation to shares issued after 5 April 2007. In so far as it continues to apply to shares issued before 6 April 2007, the text of s. 289 is as follows:

"Eligibility for relief

289(1) For the purposes of this Chapter, an individual is eligible for relief, subject to the following provisions of this Chapter, if–
(a) eligible shares in a qualifying company for which he has subscribed are issued to him and, under section 291, he qualifies for relief in respect of those shares,
(aza) he subscribed for the shares (other than any of them which are bonus shares) wholly in cash,
(aa) at the time when they are issued the shares (other than any of them which are bonus shares) are fully paid up,
(b) the shares (other than any of them which are bonus shares) are issued in order to raise money for the purpose of a qualifying business activity,
(ba) the requirements of subsection (1A) below are satisfied in relation to the company,
(c) at least 80 per cent of the money raised by the issue of–
(i) the shares, and
(ii) all other eligible shares (if any) in the company of the same class which are issued on the same day,
is employed wholly for the purpose of the activity mentioned in paragraph (b) above not later than the time mentioned in subsection (3) below, and
(d) all of the money so raised is employed wholly for that purpose not later than 12 months after that time.

289(1A) The requirements of this subsection are satisfied in relation to the qualifying company if at no time in the relevant period is any of the following, namely–
(a) the relevant qualifying trade,
(b) relevant preparation work (if any), and
(c) relevant research and development (if any),
being carried on by a person other than the qualifying company or a qualifying 90% subsidiary of that company.

289(1B) In a case where relevant preparation work is carried on by the qualifying company or a qualifying 90% subsidiary of that company, there is to be disregarded, for the purpose of determining whether the requirements of subsection (1A) above are satisfied in relation to the qualifying company, the carrying on of the relevant qualifying trade by a company other than–
(a) the qualifying company, or
(b) a subsidiary of that company,
at any time in the relevant period before the qualifying company or any qualifying 90% subsidiary of that company carries on that trade.

289(1C) The requirements of subsection (1A) above are not to be regarded as failing to be satisfied in relation to the qualifying company if–
(a) by reason only of anything done as a consequence of the qualifying company or any other company being in administration or receivership, or
(b) by reason only of the qualifying company or any other company being wound up or dissolved without winding up,

the relevant qualifying trade ceases to be carried on in the relevant period by the qualifying company or any qualifying 90% subsidiary of that company and is subsequently carried on in that period by a person who is not at any time in the period of restriction connected with the qualifying company.

289(1D) Subsection (1C) above applies only if (as the case may be)–

(a) the entry into administration or receivership and everything done as a consequence of the company concerned being in administration or receivership, or

(b) the winding up or dissolution,

is for bona fide commercial reasons and is not part of a scheme or arrangement the main purpose of which or one of the main purposes of which is the avoidance of tax.

289(1E) In this section–

"relevant preparation work" means preparations falling within subsection (2)(a)(ii) below which are the subject of the qualifying business activity mentioned in subsection (1) above,

"the relevant qualifying trade" means the qualifying trade which is the subject of that qualifying business activity,

"relevant research and development" means–

(a) research and development falling within subsection (2)(b) below which is the subject of that qualifying business activity, and

(b) any other preparations for the carrying on of the qualifying trade which is the subject of that activity.

289(2) In this Chapter **"qualifying business activity"**, in relation to a company, means–

(a) the company or any qualifying 90% subsidiary of that company–

(i) carrying on a qualifying trade which, on the date the shares are issued, the company or any such subsidiary is carrying on, or

(ii) preparing to carry on, or carrying on, a qualifying trade which, on that date, is intended to be carried on wholly or mainly in the United Kingdom by the company or any such subsidiary and which is begun to be carried on by the company or any such subsidiary within two years after that date,

but only if, at any time in the relevant period when the qualifying trade is so carried on, it is carried on wholly or mainly in the United Kingdom, or

(b) the company or any qualifying 90% subsidiary of that company carrying on research and development–

(i) which, on the date the shares are issued, the company or any such subsidiary is carrying on or which the company or any such subsidiary begins to carry on immediately afterwards, and

(ii) from which it is intended that a qualifying trade which the company or any such subsidiary will carry on wholly or mainly in the United Kingdom will be derived,

but only if, at any time in the relevant period when the research and development or the qualifying trade derived from it is carried on, it is carried on wholly or mainly in the United Kingdom.

(c) [Omitted by FA 2001, Sch. 15, para. 2(b) and Sch. 33, Pt. 2(3).]

289(3) The time referred to in subsection (1)(c) above is–

(a) the end of the period of twelve months beginning with the issue of the eligible shares, or

(b) in the case of money raised only for the purpose referred to in subsection (2)(a) above, the end of that period or, if later, the end of the period of twelve months beginning when the company or a qualifying 90% subsidiary of that company begins to carry on the qualifying trade,

and for the purposes of this Chapter, the conditions in subsection (1)(c) and (d) above do not fail to be satisfied by reason only of the fact that an amount of money which is not significant is employed for another purpose.

289(3A) In determining–

(a) for the purposes of subsection (2)(a)(ii) or (3)(b) above when a qualifying trade is begun to be carried on by a qualifying 90% subsidiary of a company, or

(b) for the purposes of subsection (2)(b)(i) above when research and development is begun to be carried on by such a subsidiary of a company,

there shall be disregarded any carrying on of the trade or, as the case may be, the research and development by it before it became such a subsidiary of the company.

289(4)–(5) [Repealed by FA 2001, Sch. 15, para. 2(c) and Sch. 33, Pt. 2(3).]

289(6) An individual is not eligible for relief in respect of any shares unless the shares are subscribed for, and issued, for bona fide commercial purposes and not as part of a scheme or arrangement the main purpose or one of the main purposes of which is the avoidance of tax.

289(7) In this Chapter **"eligible shares"** means new ordinary shares which, throughout the period–

(a) beginning with the issue of the shares, and

(b) ending immediately before the termination date relating to those shares,

carry no present or future preferential right to dividends or to a company's assets on its winding up and no present or future right to be redeemed.

289(8) Section 312(1A)(b) applies to determine the relevant period for the purposes of this section.

289(8A) Shares are not fully paid up for the purposes of subsection (1)(aa) above if there is any undertaking to pay cash to any person at a future date in respect of the acquisition of the shares.

289(9) Section 190 of ITA 2007 (meaning of **"qualifying 90% subsidiary"**) applies for the purposes of this Chapter.

History – In s. 289(1)(a) the words "wholly in cash" repealed following "subscribed" by FA 2004, s. 93, Sch. 18, para. 1(2)(a), and s. 326, Sch. 42, Pt. 2(13), with effect in relation to shares issued on or after 17 March 2004.

In s. 289(1)(a), words "wholly in cash" inserted, s. 289(1)(aa) inserted, in s. 289(1)(b) words "and all other shares comprised in the same issue" inserted, and in s. 289(1)(c) words "the activity mentioned in paragraph (b) above" substituted for "that activity", by FA 1998, s. 74(1) and Sch. 13, para. 1(1), with effect in relation to shares issued on or after 6 April 1998.

S. 289(1)(aza) inserted by FA 2004, s. 93 and Sch. 18, para. 1(2)(b), with effect in relation to shares issued on or after 17 March 2004.

In s. 289(1)(aa) the words "(other than any of them which are bonus shares) are fully paid up" substituted for the words "are fully paid up (disregarding for this purpose any undertaking to pay cash to the company at a future date)" by FA 2004, s. 93 and Sch. 18, para. 1(2)(c), with effect in relation to shares issued on or after 17 March 2004.

In s. 289(1)(b) the words "(other than any of them which are bonus shares)"substituted for the words "and all other shares comprised in the same issue" by FA 2004, s. 93 and Sch. 18, para. 1(2)(d), with effect in relation to shares issued on or after 17 March 2004.

S. 289(1)(ba) inserted before the word "and" formerly at the end of para. (b) by FA 1997, s. 74 and Sch. 8, para. 2(1), with effect in relation to shares issued after 26 November 1996, and with effect after 26 November 1996 in relation to shares which were issued on or after 1 January 1994 but before 27 November 1996, and immediately before 27 November 1996 were held by an individual and at that time were shares to which relief (within the meaning of Pt. VII, Ch. III) was attributable.

S. 289(1)(c) substitutedby FA 2004, s. 93 and Sch. 18, para. 1(2)(e), with effect in relation to shares issued on or after 17 March 2004. Former s. 289(1)(c) read as follows:

"(c) at least 80% of the money raised by the issue mentioned in paragraph (b) above is employed wholly for the purpose of the activity mentioned in that paragraph not later than the time mentioned in subsection (3) below, and".

S. 289(1)(c), (d) substituted for former s. 289(1)(c), and s. 289(1)(ba) and 289(3) consequentially amended, by FA 2001, Sch. 15, para. 6 and Sch. 33, Pt. 2(3) in relation to shares issued on or after 7 March 2001; and in respect of the application of ICTA 1988, Pt. VII, Ch. III and TCGA 1992, Sch. 5B, on or after 7 March 2001 in relation to shares:

- that were issued after 31 December 1993 but before 7 March 2001, and
- to which income tax relief or deferral relief was attributable immediately before 7 March 2001.

S. 289(1A)–(1E) substituted for (1A)–(1D) by FA 2004, s. 93 and Sch. 18, para. 1(3), with effect in relation to shares issued on or after 17 March 2004. Former s. 289(1A)–(1D) read as follows:
"**289(1A)** The requirements of this subsection are satisfied in relation to a qualifying company if throughout the relevant period the active company–
(a) is a company which–
(i) is such a company as is mentioned in section 293(2)(a), and
(ii) if it is a subsidiary of the qualifying company, is a 90 per cent subsidiary of that company, or
(b) would be a company falling within paragraph (a) above if its purposes were disregarded to the extent that they consist in the carrying on of activities such as are mentioned in section 293(3D)(a) and (b) and (3E)(a), or
(c) is a 90 per cent subsidiary of the qualifying company and falls within subsection (1B) below.
289(1B) A subsidiary of the qualifying company falls within this subsection if–
(a) apart from purposes capable of having no significant effect (other than in relation to incidental matters) on the extent of its activities, it exists wholly for the purpose of carrying on activities such as are mentioned in section 293(3D)(b); or
(b) it has no profits for the purposes of corporation tax and no part of its business consists in the making of investments.
289(1C) In subsection (1A) above **"the active company"** means the qualifying company or, where the qualifying business activity mentioned in subsection (1) above consists in a subsidiary of that company carrying on or preparing to carry on a qualifying trade orresearch and development, that subsidiary.
289(1D) Subsections (4A) and (6) of section 293 shall apply in relation to the requirements of subsection (1A) above as they apply in relation to subsection (2) of that section.".
Former s. 289(1A)(a) substituted, and in para. (b) words "a company falling within paragraph (a) above" substituted for "such a company" by FA 1999, s. 71(1), with effect in relation to shares issued on or after 6 April 1999. As it has effect in relation to shares issued before that date, para. (a) provides as follows:
"(a) is such a company as is mentioned in section 293(2)(a), or"
In former s. 289(1A)(c), words "90 per cent subsidiary" substituted for by FA 1998, s. 74(1) and Sch. 13, para. 1(2), with effect in relation to shares issued on or after 6 April 1998.
S. 289(1A), (1B), (1C), (1D) inserted by FA 1997, s. 74 and Sch. 8, para. 2(2), with effect in relation to shares issued after 26 November 1996, and with effect after 26 November 1996 in relation to shares which were issued on or after 1 January 1994 but before 27 November 1996, and immediately before 27 November 1996 were held by an individual and at that time were shares to which relief (within the meaning of Pt. VII, Ch. III) was attributable.
In former s. 289(1C), reference to oil exploration omitted by FA 2001, Sch. 15, para. 2(a) in relation to shares issued on or after 7 March 2001; and in respect of the application of ICTA 1988, Pt. VII, Ch. III and TCGA 1992, Sch. 5B, on or after 7 March 2001 in relation to shares:

- that were issued after 31 December 1993 but before 7 March 2001, and
- to which income tax relief or deferral relief was attributable immediately before 7 March 2001.

In former s. 289(1D), words "Subsections (4A) and (6)" substituted for "Subsection (6)", and "they apply" for "it applies", by FA 2000, s. 64 and Sch. 17, para. 9(2), with effect in relation to shares issued on or after 21 March 2000, and in respect of the application of s. 293 on or after that date in relation to shares that were issued after 31 December 1993 but before 21 March 2000, and to which enterprise investment scheme or CGT deferral relief was attributable immediately before 21 March 2000.
In s. 289(2)(a) the words "qualifying 90% subsidiary of that company" substituted for "subsidiary" by FA 2004, s. 93 and Sch. 18, para. 1(4)(a), with effect in relation to shares issued on or after 17 March 2004.
In s. 289(2)(a)(i) the words "the company or any such subsidiary" substituted for "it" by FA 2004, s. 93 and Sch. 18, para. 1(4)(b), with effect in relation to shares issued on or after 17 March 2004.
In s. 289(2)(a)(ii) the words "preparing to carry on, or carrying on," substituted for "preparing to carry on", "is intended to be carried" substituted for "it intends to carry" and "by the company or any such subsidiary and which is begun to be carried on by the company or any such subsidiary" substituted for "and which it begins to carry on" by FA 2004, s. 93 and Sch. 18, para. 1(4)(c), with effect in relation to shares issued on or after 17 March 2004.
In s. 289(2)(a), in the words at the end, "trade is so" substituted for "trade is" by FA 2004, s. 93 and Sch. 18, para. 1(4)(d), with effect in relation to shares issued on or after 17 March 2004.
In s. 289(2)(b), in the words at the beginning, "qualifying 90% subsidiary of that company"substituted for "subsidiary" by FA 2004, s. 93 and Sch. 18, para. 1(4)(e), with effect from 21 July 2004.
In s. 289(2)(b)(i) the words "the companyor any such subsidiary is carrying on or which the company or any such subsidiary" substituted for "it is carrying on or which it" by FA 2004, s. 93 and Sch. 18, para. 1(4)(e), with effect in relation to shares issued on or after 17 March 2004.
In s. 289(2)(b)(ii) the words "such subsidiary" substituted for "subsidiary" by FA 2004, s. 93 and Sch. 18, para. 1(4)(e), with effect in relation to shares issued on or after 17 March 2004.
S. 289(2)(c), (4) and (5) omitted, and s. 289(2)(a) and (b) consequentially amended, by FA 2001, Sch. 15, para. 2(b) and (c) and Sch. 33, Pt. 2(3) in relation to shares issued on or after 7 March 2001; and in respect of the application of ICTA 1988, Pt. VII, Ch. III and TCGA 1992, Sch. 5B, on or after 7 March 2001 in relation to shares:

- that were issued after 31 December 1993 but before 7 March 2001, and
- to which income tax relief or deferral relief was attributable immediately before 7 March 2001.

In s. 289(3)(b) the words "a qualifying 90% subsidiary of that company" substituted for "subsidiary concerned" by FA 2004, s. 93 and Sch. 18, para. 1(5), with effect in relation to shares issued on or after 17 March 2004.
S. 289(3A) inserted by FA 2004, s. 93 and Sch. 18, para. 1(6), with effect in relation to shares issued on or after 17 March 2004.
In s. 289(6), word "for" inserted after "subscribed" by FA 1998, s. 74(1) and Sch. 13, para. 1(3), with effect in relation to shares issued on or after 6 April 1998.
In s. 289(7), words "throughout the period–", and para. (a) and (b), substituted for "throughout the period of five years beginning with the date on which they are issued," by FA 2000, s. 64 and Sch. 17, para. 1, with effect in relation to shares issued on or after 6 April 2000.
In s. 289(7), word "preferential", in the second place where it occurred between "future" and "right", omitted by FA 1998, s. 74(1) and Sch. 13, para. 1(4), s. 165 and Sch. 27, Pt. III(14), with effect in relation to shares issued on or after 6 April 1998.
S. 289(8A) inserted by FA 2004, s. 93 and Sch. 18, para. 1(7), with effect in relation to shares issued on or after 17 March 2004.
S. 289(9) substituted for former s. 289(9)-(13) by FA 2007, s. 51 and Sch. 16, para. 16(1)(a), with effect from 6 April 2007. Former s. 289(9)(d) amended by SI 2007/1820, art 2(2), with effect, for income tax purposes, for 2007–08 and subsequent tax years and, for corporation tax purposes, for accounting periods ending after 5 April 2007.
S. 289(9)–(13) substituted for s. 289(9) by FA 2004, s. 93 and Sch. 18, para. 1(8), with effect in relation to shares issued on or after 17 March 2004. Former s. 289(9) read as follows:
"**289(9)** In this section **"90 per cent subsidiary"**, in relation to the qualifying company, means a subsidiary of a kind which the company might hold by virtue of section 308 if–
(a) the references in subsection (2) of that section to 75 per cent were references to 90 per cent; and
(b) subsection (4) of that section were omitted.".
S. 289(9) inserted by FA 1998, s. 74(1) and Sch. 13, para. 1(5), with effect in relation to shares issued on or after 6 April 1998.

S. 289 (and s. 289A and 289B) substituted for former s. 289 by FA 1994, s. 137, Sch. 15, para. 2, in relation to shares issued on or after 1 January 1994 with effect for 1993–94 and subsequent years of assessment. For the wording of s. 289 as it applies to shares issued prior to that date, see History note to s. 289B.

Cross references – TCGA 1992, Sch. 5B: capital gains tax deferral on reinvestment in EIS qualifying shares.

HMRC interpretations – IRInt. 141: practical consequences (e.g. completion of form EIS 1, etc.) where there is more than one qualifying business activity, for example two trades carried on by different subsidiaries, or a trade carried on by one subsidiary and research and development carried on by another.

Other material – HMRC press release, 25 September 2000: establishment of Small Company Enterprise Centre to deal with claims regarding eligibility."

Notes – S. 289 rewritten for income tax purposes as follows:
S. 289(1): ITA 2007, s. 157(1), 173(1), (3), 174, 175(1), 180.
S. 289(1A): ITA 2007, s. 183(1).
S. 289(1B): ITA 2007, s. 183(2), (3).
S. 289(1C): ITA 2007, s. 183(4), (5).
S. 289(1D): ITA 2007, s. 183(6).
S. 289(1E): ITA 2007, s. 183(7).
S. 289(2): ITA 2007, s. 179(1), (2), (3), (4), (5).
S. 289(3): ITA 2007, s. 175(2), (3).
S. 289(3A): ITA 2007, s. 175(4), 179(6).
S. 289(6): ITA 2007, s. 165, 178.
S. 289(7): ITA 2007, s. 173(2).
S. 289(8): ITA 2007, s. 173(2), 179(3), (5), 183(3).
S. 289(8A): ITA 2007, s. 173(4).
S. 289(9): ITA 2007, s. 190(1), 1021(2).
S. 289(10): ITA 2007, s. 190(2).
S. 289(11): ITA 2007, s. 190(2).
S. 289(12): ITA 2007, s. 190(3).
S. 289(13): ITA 2007, s. 190(4).

289A Form of relief

289A [Omitted by ITA 2007, s. 1027 and Sch. 1, para. 627 and repealed by ITA 2007, Sch. 3, Pt. 2 with effect in relation to shares issued after 5 April 2007.]

History – S. 289A omitted by ITA 2007, s. 1027 and Sch. 1, para. 627 and repealed by ITA 2007, s. 1031 and Sch. 3, Pt. 2 with effect in relation to shares issued after 5 April 2007. In so far as it continues to apply to shares issued before 6 April 2007, the text of s. 289A is as follows:

"**289A(1)** Where an individual eligible for relief in respect of any amount subscribed for eligible shares makes a claim, then, subject to the following provisions of this Chapter, the amount of his liability for the year of assessment in which the shares were issued (**"the current year"**) to income tax on his total income shall be the following amount.

289A(2) That amount is the amount to which he would be so liable apart from this section less whichever is the smaller of–
(a) an amount equal to tax at the lower rate for the current year on the amount or, as the case may be, the aggregate of the amounts subscribed for eligible shares issued in that year in respect of which he is eligible for relief, and
(b) the amount which reduces his liability to nil.

289A(3) Subject to subsection (4) below, if in the case of any issue of relevant shares, that is, shares–
(a) which are issued before 6th October in the current year, and
(b) in respect of the amount subscribed for which the individual is eligible for relief,

the individual so requests in his claim, subsection (1) above shall apply as if, in respect of such part of that issue as may be specified in his claim, the shares had been issued in the preceding year of assessment; and his liability to income tax for both years of assessment shall be determined accordingly.

289A(4) Not more than half of the relevant shares comprised in any issue may be treated by virtue of subsection (3) above as issued in the previous year; and the number of relevant shares (comprised in any issues) so treated as issued in a particular year shall not be such that the total amount subscribed for them exceeds £50,000.

289A(5) In determining for the purposes of subsection (2) above the amount of income tax to which a person would be liable apart from this section, no account shall be taken of–
(a) any income tax reduction under Chapter I of Part VII of this Act or under section 347B,
(b) any income tax reduction under section 353(1A),
(c) any income tax reduction under section 54(3A) of the Finance Act 1989,
(ca) any income tax reduction under paragraph 19(2) of Schedule 16 to the Finance Act 2002 (community investment tax relief),
(d) any relief by way of a reduction of liability to tax which is given in accordance with any arrangements having effect by virtue of section 788 or by way of a credit under section 790(1), or
(e) any tax at the basic rate on so much of that person's income as is income the income tax on which he is entitled to charge against any other person or to deduct, retain or satisfy out of any payment.

289A(6) A claim for relief in respect of eligible shares issued by a company shall not be allowed unless subsection (7) below is complied with in relation to the issue of shares in question but, where it is complied with, the relief may be given at any time when it appears that the conditions for the relief may be satisfied.

289A(7) This subsection is complied with if–
(a) in a case where the money raised by an issue of eligible shares is raised wholly for the purpose of a qualifying business activity falling within paragraph (a) of section 289(2), the trade concerned has been carried on for four months by no person other than the qualifying company or a qualifying 90% subsidiary of that company, and
(b) in a case where the money raised by an issue of eligible shares is raised wholly or partly for the purpose of a qualifying business activity falling within paragraph (b) of that subsection the research and development concerned has been carried on for four months by no person other than the qualifying company or a qualifying 90% subsidiary of that company,
(c) [omitted by FA 2001, Sch. 15, para. 3 and Sch. 33, Pt. 2(3).]

289A(8) Where–
(a) by reason only of the qualifying company or any other company being wound up or dissolved without winding up–
 (i) *the trade concerned* is carried on as mentioned in subsection (7)(a) above, or
 (ii) the research and development concerned is carried on as mentioned in subsection (7)(b) above,
 for a period shorter than four months, and
(b) the winding up or dissolution is for bona fide commercial reasons and is not part of a scheme or arrangement the main purpose or one of the main purposes of which is the avoidance of tax,

subsection (7)(a) or, as the case may be, (7)(b) above shall have effect as if it referred to that shorter period.

289A(8A) Where, by reason only of anything done as a consequence of the qualifying company or any other company being in administration or receivership–

(a) the trade concerned is carried on as mentioned in subsection (7)(a) above for a period shorter than four months, or

(b) the research and development concerned is carried on as mentioned in subsection (7)(b) above for a period shorter than four months,

subsection (7)(a) or, as the case may be, (7)(b) above shall have effect as if it referred to that shorter period.

This applies only if–

(a) the entry into administration or receivership, and

(b) everything done as a consequence of the company concerned being in administration or receivership,

is for bona fide commercial reasons and is not part of a scheme or arrangement the main purpose or one of the main purposes of which is the avoidance of tax.

289A(9) [Omitted by FA 2001, Sch. 15, para. 9 and Sch. 33, Pt. 2(3).]"

In s. 289A(4) "£50,000" substituted for "£25,000" by FA 2006, s. 91 and Sch. 14, para. 5(1), with effect in relation to shares issued on or after 6 April 2006.

In s. 289A(4) the upper limit on carry-back of relief raised to £25,000 (from £15,000) by FA 1998, s. 74(1) and Sch. 13, para. 2, with effect in relation to shares issued on or after 6 April 1998.

S. 289A(5)(ca) inserted by FA 2002, s. 57 and Sch. 17, para. 2, with effect years of assessment ending on or after 17 April 2002, the day appointed by virtue of SI 2003/88 (C. 5).

In s. 289A(6) the words "A claim for relief in respect of eligible shares issued by a company shall not be allowed unless subsection (7) below is complied with in relation to the issue of shares in question" substituted for "A claim for relief shall not be allowed unless subsection (7) below is complied with" by FA 2004, s. 93 and Sch. 18, para. 2(2), with effect in relation to shares issued on or after 17 March 2004.

In s. 289A(7)(a) the words "a case where the money raised by an issue of eligible shares is raised wholly" substituted for "the case of shares issued" and the words "trade concerned has been carried on for four months by no person other than the qualifying company or a qualifying 90% subsidiary of that company" substituted for "company or subsidiary concerned has carried on the trade for four months" by FA 2004, s. 93 and Sch. 18, para. 2(3(a), with effect in relation to shares issued on or after 17 March 2004.

In s. 289A(7)(b) the words "acase where the money raised by an issue of eligible shares is raised wholly or partly" substituted for "the case of shares issued" and "the research and development concerned has been carried on for four months by no person other than the qualifying company or a qualifying 90% subsidiary of that company" substituted for "or within both paragraph (a) and paragraph (b) of that subsection, the company or subsidiary concerned has carried on the research and development for four months" by FA 2004, s. 93 and Sch. 18, para. 2(3), with effect in relation to shares issued on or after 17 March 2004.

S. 289A(7)(c) omitted and s. 289A(7)(a) and (b) consequentially amended, by FA 2001, Sch. 15, para. 3 and Sch. 33, Pt. 2(3) in relation to repayments of tax on or after 7 March 2001.

S. 289A(8)(a) substituted by FA 2004, s. 93 and Sch. 18, para. 2(4)(a), with effect in relation to shares issued on or after 17 March 2004. Former s. 289A(8)(a) read as follows:

"(a) the company or subsidiary concerned, by reason of its being wound up, or dissolved without winding up, carries on a trade for a period shorter than four months, and".

In s. 289A(8)(b), the words "it is shown that" repealed by FA 2004, s. 93 and Sch. 18, para. 2(4)(b), and s. 326, Sch. 42, Pt. 2(13) in relation to shares issued on or after 17 March 2004.

In s. 289A(8)(b) words "is for" substituted for "was for", "is not" substituted for "not as" and "which is" substituted for "which was" by FA 2004, s. 93 and Sch. 18, para. 2(4)(b), with effect in relation to shares issued on or after 17 March 2004.

In s. 289A(8)(b), in the words at the end, "or, as the case may be, (7)(b)" inserted by FA 2004, s. 93 and Sch. 18, para. 2(4)(c), with effect in relation to shares issued on or after 17 March 2004.

In s. 289A(8A), the words from the start to the end of the first s. 289(8A)(b) substituted for "Where the company or subsidiary concerned, by reason of anything done as a consequence of its being in administration or receivership, carries on a trade for a period shorter than four months, subsection (7)(a) above shall have effect as if it referred to that shorter period." by FA 2004, s. 93 and Sch. 18, para. 2(5)(a), with effect in relation to shares issued on or after 17 March 2004.

In s. 289A(8A)(b), the word "concerned" inserted by FA 2004, s. 93 and Sch. 18, para. 2(5)(b), with effect in relation to shares issued on or after 17 March 2004.

In s. 289A(8A) the words "the entry into administration or receivership" substituted for "the making of the order in question" bySI 2003/2096, art. 4 and Sch., para. 16 with effect from 15 September 2003. Transitional provisions are contained in art. 6.

S. 289A(8A) originally inserted by FA 2000, s. 64 and Sch. 17, para. 9(3), with effect in relation to shares issued on or after 21 March 2000, and in respect of the application of s. 293 on or after that date in relation to shares that were issued after 31 December 1993 but before March 2000, and to which EIS relief or CGT deferral relief was attributable immediately before 21 March 2000.

S. 289A(9) repealed by FA 2001, Sch. 15, para. 9 and Sch. 33, Pt. 2(3) in relation to repayments of tax on or after 7 March 2001.

S. 289A (and s. 289 and 289B) substituted for former s. 289 by FA 1994, s. 137 and Sch. 15, para. 2 in relation to shares issued on or after 1 January 1994 with effect for 1993–94 and subsequent years of assessment. For the wording of s. 289 as it applies to shares issued prior to that date, see History note to s. 289B.

Cross references – Pt. VII, Ch. I: personal reliefs.
S. 347B: qualifying maintenance payments.
S. 353(1A): relief for interest payments.
S. 788: double taxation agreements.
S. 790: unilateral double taxation relief.
S. 824: repayment supplement normally payable from 12 months after the end of the tax year for which tax was overpaid.
Sch. 15B(6): interaction with relief for investment in venture capital trusts.
FA 1989, s. 54(3A): relief on premiums for medical insurance where surviving spouse not aged 60 or over.
TCGA 1992, s. 150A: capital gains tax interaction with enterprise investment scheme relief.
TCGA 1992, Sch. 5B: capital gains tax deferral on reinvestment in EIS qualifying shares.
FA 1990, s. 25(7)(a): s. 289A(5)(e) to apply to the donor of a charitable gift as if any reference to income tax which he is entitled to charge against any person included a reference to tax treated as deducted from the gift under FA 1990, s. 25.

HMRC interpretations – IRInt. 141: practical consequences for purposes of s. 289A(6), (7) where there is more than one qualifying business activity, for example two trades carried on by different subsidiaries, or a trade carried on by one subsidiary and research and development carried on by another.

Notes – S. 289A rewritten for income tax purposes as follows:
S. 289A(1): ITA 2007, s. 23, 26(1), 158(1).
S. 289A(2): ITA 2007, s. 23, 26(1), 29(2), 158(2).
S. 289A(3): ITA 2007, s. 158(4).
S. 289A(4): ITA 2007, s. 158(5).
S. 289A(5): ITA 2007, s. 23, 27(4), (5).
S. 289A(6): ITA 2007, s. 176(1).
S. 289A(7): ITA 2007, s. 176(1), (2), (3).
S. 289A(8): ITA 2007, s. 176(4).
S. 289A(8A): ITA 2007, s. 176(5).

289B Attribution of relief to shares

289B [Omitted by ITA 2007, s. 1027 and Sch. 1, para. 627 and repealed by ITA 2007, s. 1031 and Sch. 3, Pt. 2 with effect in relation to shares issued after 5 April 2007.]

History – S. 289B omitted by ITA 2007, s. 1027 and Sch. 1, para. 627 and repealed by ITA 2007, s. 1031 and Sch. 3, Pt. 2 with effect in relation to shares issued after 5 April 2007. In so far as it continues to apply in relation to shares issued before 6 April 2007, the text of s. 289B is as follows:

"**289B(1)** References in this Chapter, in relation to any individual, to the relief attributable to any shares or issue of shares shall be read, subject to the provisions of this Chapter providing for the reduction or withdrawal of relief, as references to any reduction made in the individual's liability to income tax which is attributed to those shares or that issue in accordance with this section.

289B(2) Where an individual's liability to income tax is reduced in any year of assessment (**"the current year"**) under section 289A, then–

(a) where the reduction is given by reason of an issue of shares made (or treated as made) in the current year, the amount of the reduction shall be attributed to that issue, and

(b) where the reduction is given by reason of two or more issues of shares made (or treated as made) in the current year, the reduction–

(i) shall be apportioned between those issues in the same proportions as the amounts subscribed by the individual for each issue, and

(ii) shall be attributed to those issues accordingly.

289B(3) Where under this section an amount of any reduction of income tax is attributed to an issue of shares (**"the original issue"**) in a company to an individual–

(a) a proportionate part of that amount shall be attributed to each share comprised in the original issue, and

(b) if any corresponding bonus shares in that company are issued to him at any subsequent time–

(i) a proportionate part of the total amount attributed immediately before that time to shares comprised in the original issue shall be attributed to each of the shares in the holding comprising those shares and the bonus shares, and

(ii) this Chapter shall apply as if the original holding had comprised all those shares.

289B(3A) In subsection (3) above **"corresponding bonus shares"**means bonus shares which–

(a) are issued in respect of the shares comprised in the original issue; and

(b) are of the same class, and carry the same rights, as those shares.

289B(4) Subject to subsection (5) below, in this Chapter references (however expressed) to an issue of eligible shares in any company to an individual are references to any eligible shares in the company that are of the same class and are issued to him on the same day, but this subsection does not apply in relation to section 289A(6) and (7).

289B(5) Where section 289A(1) applies in the case of any issue of shares as if part of the issue had been issued in a previous year, this section and sections 299(4) and 306(1) shall have effect as if that part and the remainder were separate issues of shares (and that part had been issued on a day in the previous year).

289B(6) Where, at a time when any relief is attributable to, or to any part of, any issue of shares, the relief falls to be withdrawn or reduced under this Chapter–

(a) where it falls to be withdrawn, the relief attributable to each of the shares in question shall be reduced to nil, and

(b) where it falls to be reduced by any amount, the relief attributable to each of the shares in question shall be reduced by a proportionate part of that amount."

In s. 289B(3)(b), words "corresponding bonus shares in that company" substituted for "bonus shares in that company which are eligible shares", and s. 289(3A) inserted, by FA 1998, s. 74(1) and Sch. 13, para. 3(1), (2), with effect in relation to bonus shares issued on or after 6 April 1998.

In s. 289B(4), the words "same day, but this subsection does not apply in relation to section 289A(6) and (7)" substituted for "same day" by FA 2004, s. 93 and Sch. 18, para. 3, with effect in relation to shares issued on or after 17 March 2004.

S. 289B(4) substituted by FA 1998, s. 74(1) and Sch. 13, para. 3(3), with effect in relation to shares issued on or after 6 April 1998. The wording of the subsection as it applied prior to this substitution was:

"**289B(4)** Subject to subsection (5) below, in this Chapter references to an issue of shares in any company to an individual are to any shares in the company issued to him on the same day."

In S. 289(5), words "sections 299(4) and 306(1)" substituted for "the following provisions of this Chapter (except section 290(1))" by FA 1998, s. 74(1) and Sch. 13, para. 3(4), with effect in relation to shares issued on or after 6 April 1998.

S. 289, 289A and 289B substituted for former s. 289 by FA 1994, s. 137 and Sch. 15, para. 2, in relation to shares issued on or after 1 January 1994 with effect for 1993–94 and subsequent years of assessment. The wording of s. 289 as it applies to shares issued prior to that date is:

"*The relief*

289(1) This Chapter has effect for affording relief from income tax where an individual who qualifies for the relief subscribes for eligible shares in a qualifying company, and either–

(a) those shares are issued to him after 5th April 1983 and before the end of 1993 for the purpose of raising money for a qualifying trade which is being carried on by the company or which it intends to carry on; or

(b) those shares are issued to him after 18th March 1986 and before the end of 1993 for the purpose of raising money–

(i) for research and development which is being carried on by the company or by any subsidiary of the company on the date on which the shares are issued, or begins so to be carried on immediately thereafter, and from which it is intended that a qualifying trade (to be so carried on) will be derived; or

(ii) both for any such research and development and the resulting trade; or

(c) those shares are issued to him after 5th April 1985 and before 19th March 1986 for the purpose of raising money–

(i) for research and development which is being carried on at the time when the shares are issued, or begins immediately thereafter, and from which the company intends to derive a qualifying trade which will be carried on by it; or

(ii) both for any such research and development and the resulting trade; or

(d) those shares are issued to him after the passing of the Finance Act 1986 (25th July 1986) and before the end of 1993 for the purpose of raising money for oil exploration which–

(i) is being carried on by the company, or by any subsidiary of the company, on the date on which the shares are issued; or

(ii) begins so to be carried on immediately thereafter;

and from which it is intended that a qualifying trade (to be so carried on) will be derived.

289(2) Subsection (1)(d) above shall not apply unless–

(a) throughout the period of three years beginning with the date on which the shares were issued the company, or any subsidiary of the company, holds an exploration licence which was granted to it, or to another such subsidiary;

(b) the exploration is carried out solely within the area to which the licence applies; and

(c) on the date on which the shares are issued, neither the company nor any subsidiary of the company holds an appraisal licence or a development licence relating to that area or any part of that area.

289(3) Where, at any time after the issue of the shares but before the end of the period mentioned in subsection (2)(a) above, the company, or any subsidiary of the company, comes to hold an appraisal licence or development licence which relates to the area, or any part of the area, to which the exploration licence relates, the exploration licence and that other licence shall be treated for the purposes of subsection (2)(a) above as a single exploration licence.

289(4) In this Chapter **"eligible shares"** means new ordinary shares which, throughout the period of five years beginning with the date on which they are issued, carry no present or future preferential right to dividends or to a company's assets on its winding up and no present or future preferential right to be redeemed.
289(5) Subject to subsection (6) below, the relief in respect of the amount subscribed by an individual for any eligible shares shall be given as a deduction of that amount from his total income for the year of assessment in which the shares are issued, and references in this Chapter to the amount of the relief are references to the amount of that deduction.
289(6) If–
(a) the shares are issued before 6th October in a year of assessment; and
(b) the claimant so requests in his claim for relief;
the relief shall be given partly by way of deduction from the claimant's total income for the year of assessment in which the shares are issued and partly by way of deduction from his total income for the preceding year of assessment.
289(7) A deduction from the claimant's total income for the year of assessment preceding that in which the shares are issued shall be of such amount as may be specified in the claim; but
(a) that amount shall not exceed one half of the total relief in respect of the shares; and
(b) the aggregate of that amount and the amounts of any other deductions made by virtue of subsection (6) above from the claimant's total income for the year of assessment preceding that in which the shares are issued shall not exceed £5,000.
289(8) The relief shall be given on a claim and shall not be allowed–
(a) in a case falling within subsection (1)(a)–
(i) unless and until the company has carried on the trade for four months; and
(ii) if the company is not carrying on that trade at the time when the shares are issued, unless the company begins to carry it on within two years after that time;
(b) in a case falling within subsection (1)(b) or (c) unless and until the company or (as the case may be) the subsidiary has carried on the research and development for four months;
(c) in a case falling within subsection (1)(d) unless and until the company has carried on the exploration for four months.
289(9) A claim for relief may be allowed–
(a) under subsection (1)(a), (c) or (d) at any time after the trade, the research and development or the exploration (as the case may be) has been carried on by the company for four months;
(b) under subsection (1)(b) at any time after the research and development has been carried on for four months;
if the conditions for the relief are then satisfied.
289(10) In the case of a claim allowed before the end of the relevant period, the relief shall be withdrawn if by reason of any subsequent event it appears that the claimant was not entitled to the relief allowed.
289(11) An individual is not entitled to relief in respect of any shares unless the shares are subscribed for and issued for bona fide commercial purposes and not as part of a scheme or arrangement the main purpose, or one of the main purposes of which, is the avoidance of tax.
289(12) In this Chapter **"the relevant period"**, in relation to relief in respect of any eligible shares issued by a company, means–
(a) as respects sections 291, 299, 299A, 300, 302 and 303, the period beginning with the incorporation of the company (or, if the company was incorporated more than two years before the date on which the shares were issued, beginning two years before that date) and ending five years after the issue of the shares; and
(b) as respects sections 290A, 293, 294, 297, 308 and 309, the period beginning with the date on which the shares were issued and ending either–
(i) three years after that date; or
(ii) in a case falling within subsection (1)(a), where the company was not at that date carrying on a qualifying trade, three years after the date on which it subsequently began to carry on such a trade.
289(12A) In arriving at the relevant period for the purposes of sections 294 to 296 any time falling on or after 29th November 1994 shall be ignored; and subsection (12) above shall have effect subject to the preceding provisions of this subsection.
289(13) Where by reason of its being wound up, or dissolved without winding up, the company carries on the qualifying trade for a period shorter than four months, subsection (8)(a) above shall have effect as if it referred to that shorter period but only if it is shown that the winding up or dissolution was for bona fide commercial reasons and not as part of a scheme or arrangement the main purpose or one of the main purposes of which was the avoidance of tax.
289(14) The relief shall be treated for the purposes of section 835(5) as a deduction to be made under Chapter I of this Part after all other deductions under that Chapter and shall be disregarded for the purposes of calculating relief under section 550(2), and paragraphs 4 and 16 of Schedule 11 where an election has effect under paragraph 12 of that Schedule.
289(15) Where effect is given to a claim for relief by repayment of tax, section 824 shall have effect in relation to the repayment as if the time from which the 12 months mentioned in subsections (1)(b) and (3)(a) of that section are to be calculated were the end of the year of assessment in which the shares are issued or, if the period mentioned in subsection (8)(a) above ends in a later year, the end of that later year."
In former s. 289(1)(a), (b) and (d) the words "and before the end of 1993" were inserted by F(No. 2)A 1992, s. 38.
In former s. 289(12)(a), reference to s. 299A inserted by FA 1993, s. 111(2).
Former s. 289(12A) inserted by FA 1995, s. 68(2) in relation to shares issued before 1 January 1994.

Derivations – Former s. 289(1) (as originally enacted) was derived as follows:
- Opening words from FA 1983, Sch. 5, para. 2(1).
- Para. (a) from FA 1983, s. 26(1) (as amended by FA 1986, s. 40(2)) and Sch. 5, para. 2(1).
- Para. (b) from FA 1983, Sch. 5, para. 2A(1), (2), as inserted by FA 1985, s. 44(2), and as amended by FA 1986, s. 40 and Sch. 9, para. 3.
- Para. (c) from FA 1983, Sch. 5, para. 2A(2) as it read prior to its amendment by FA 1986.
- Para. (d) from FA 1983, Sch. 5, para. 2B(2) (modifying para. 2(1)(b)) as inserted by FA 1986, s. 40 and Sch. 9, para. 4(1).

Former s. 289(2): FA 1983, Sch. 5, para. 2B(2) (modifying para. 2(1)(c)–(e)), as inserted by FA 1986, s. 40 and Sch. 9, para. 4(1).
Former s. 289(3): FA 1983, Sch. 5, para. 2B(3) (inserting para. 2(1A) by way of modification), as inserted by FA 1986, s. 40 and Sch. 9, para. 4(1).
Former s. 289(4), (5): FA 1983, Sch. 5, para. 2(2), (3), as amended by FA 1987, s. 42(1).
Former s. 289(6), (7): FA 1983, Sch. 5, para. 2(4A), (4B), as inserted by FA 1987, s. 42(1).
Former s. 289(8): FA 1983, Sch. 5, para. 2(4); para. (b) is derived from Sch. 5, para. 2A(3) (inserted by FA 1985, s. 44(2) and amended by FA 1986, s. 40 and Sch. 9, para. 3); and para. (c) is derived from Sch. 5, para. 2B(4) (inserted by FA 1986, s. 40 and Sch. 9, para. 4(1)).
Former s. 289(9): FA 1983, Sch. 5, para. 2(5); from para. 2B(5) (inserted by FA 1986, s. 40 and Sch. 9, para. 4(1)); and from para. 2A(4) (inserted by FA 1985, s. 44(2) and amended by FA 1986, s. 40 and Sch. 9, para. 3).
Former s. 289(10), (11): FA 1983, Sch. 5, para. 2(b), 11.
Former s. 289(12): FA 1983, Sch. 5, para. 2(7), as amended by FA 1986, s. 40 and Sch. 9, para. 2; and from para. 2A(5) (inserted by FA 1985, s. 44(2)) and para. 2B(6) (inserted by FA 1986, s. 40 and Sch. 9, para. 4(1)).
Former s. 289(13): FA 1983, Sch. 5, para. 2(8).
Former s. 289(14): FA 1981, s. 52(7), as modified by FA 1983, Sch. 5, para. 2(9) (substituted by FA 1987, s. 42(2)).
Former s. 289(15): FA 1983, Sch. 5, para. 2(10), as substituted by FA 1987, s. 42(2); see also FA 1981, s. 52(8).

Cross references – S. 550(2): computation of top-slicing relief in cases where a chargeable event occurs in respect of a life or capital redemption policy or life annuity contract.

S. 835(5): personal reliefs to be deducted after all other deductions from total income.
Sch. 11, para. 4, 12 and 16: election for modified top-slicing relief for payments on retirement or removal from office or employment under obligations pre-10 March 1981.
FA 1988, s. 50 and Sch. 4, para. 2: modifications of former s. 289 where eligible shares are issued for the purpose of raising finance for private rented housing.

Notes – S. 289B rewritten for income tax purposes as follows:
S. 289B(1): ITA 2007, s. 201(1).
S. 289B(2): ITA 2007, s. 201(2).
S. 289B(3): ITA 2007, s. 201(3), (4).
S. 289B(3A): ITA 2007, s. 201(5).
S. 289B(4): ITA 2007, s. 255(1), (2).
S. 289B(5): ITA 2007, s. 201(6), 202(2), 210(2), 219(1), (2), 228(1), (2).
S. 289B(6): ITA 2007, s. 201(7).

290 Minimum and maximum subscriptions

290 [Omitted by ITA 2007, s. 1027 and Sch. 1, para. 627 and repealed by ITA 2007, s. 1031 and Sch. 3, Pt. 2 with effect in relation to shares issued after 5 April 2007.]

History – S. 290 omitted by ITA 2007, s. 1027 and Sch. 1, para. 627 and repealed by ITA 2007, s. 1031 and Sch. 3, Pt. 2 with effect in relation to shares issued on or after 5 April 2007. In so far as it continues to apply in relation to shares issued before 6 April 2007, the text of s. 290 is as follows:
"**290(1)** Subject to section 311(3), the relief shall not be given in respect of any amount subscribed by an individual for eligible shares issued to him by any company in any year of assessment unless the amount or total amount subscribed by him for the eligible shares issued to him by the company in that year is £500 or more.
290(2) An individual shall not be eligible for relief in any year of assessment in respect of any amount subscribed for eligible shares exceeding £400,000 (whether the shares are issued in that or a subsequent year)."
In s. 290(2) the amount of £400,000 (the maximum amount eligible for relief in any year) substituted for the former amount (£200,000) by FA 2006, s. 91(1) and Sch. 14, para. 6(1), with effect for 2006–07 and subsequent years of assessment.
In s. 290(2), the figure "£200,000" substituted for "£150,000" by FA 2004, s. 93 and Sch. 18, para. 4(1), with effect for the year 2004–05 and subsequent years of assessment.
Previously in s. 290(2) the maximum annual subscription limit raised to £150,000 (from £100,000) by FA 1998, s. 74(1) and Sch. 13, para. 4 in relation to shares issued on or after 6 April 1998.
S. 290(2) substituted by FA 1994, s. 137 and Sch. 15, para. 3(1), with effect for 1994–95 and subsequent years of assessment.

Derivations – FA 1983, Sch. 5, para. 3(1), (2) substituted by FA 1987, s. 42(3).

Cross references – FA 1994, Sch. 15, para. 3(3): in 1993–94 a limit of £40,000 on the amounts qualifying for relief applied to the aggregate of investments under the business expansion and enterprise investment schemes.

Notes – S. 290 rewritten for income tax purposes as follows:
S. 290(1): ITA 2007, s. 157(2), (3).
S. 290(2): ITA 2007, s. 158(2).

290A Restriction of relief where amounts raised exceed permitted maximum

290A [Repealed by FA 1998, s. 74(1) and Sch. 13, para. 5, s. 165 and Sch. 27, Pt. III(14).]

History – S. 290A repealed by FA 1998, s. 74(1) and Sch. 13, para. 5, s. 165 and Sch. 27, Pt. III(14) with effect in relation to shares issued on or after 6 April 1998.

291 Individuals qualifying for relief

291 [Omitted by ITA 2007, s. 1027 and Sch. 1, para. 627 and repealed by ITA 2007, s. 1031 and Sch. 3, Pt. 2 with effect in relation to shares issued after 5 April 2007.]

History – S. 291 omitted by ITA 2007, s. 1027 and Sch. 1, para. 627 and repealed by ITA 2007, s. 1031 and Sch. 3, Pt. 2 with effect in relation to shares issued after 5 April 2007. In so far as it continues to apply in relation to shares issued before 6 April 2007, s. 291 is as follows:
"**291(1)** An individual qualifies for relief in respect of eligible shares in a company (referred to in this section and sections 291A and 291B as the **"issuing company"**) if–
(a) he subscribes for the shares on his own behalf, and
(b) subject to section 291A(4), he is not at any time in the period–
 (i) beginning two years before the issue of the shares, and
 (ii) ending immediately before the termination date relating to those shares,
 connected with the company (whether before or after its incorporation).
291(2) For the purposes of this section, an individual is **connected with the issuing company** if he, or an associate of his, is–
(a) an employee of, or of a partner of, the issuing company or any subsidiary,
(b) a partner of the issuing company or any subsidiary, or
(c) subject to section 291A, a director of, or of a company which is a partner of, the issuing company or any subsidiary,
or if he, or an associate of his, is so connected by virtue of section 291B.
291(3) In subsection (2) above "subsidiary", in relation to the issuing company, means a company which at any time in the relevant period is a 51 per cent subsidiary of the issuing company, whether or not it is such a subsidiary while the individual concerned or his associate is such an employee, partner or director as is mentioned in that subsection.
291(4) For the purposes of subsections (2) and (3) above and section 291A, in the case of a person who is both a director and an employee of a company–
(a) references (however expressed) to him in his capacity as a director of the company include him in his capacity as an employee of the company, but
(b) *(apart from that) he is not to be treated as an employee of the company.*
291(5) Section 312(1A)(a) applies to determine the relevant period for the purposes of this section and sections 291A and 291B.
291(6) [Repealed by FA 2001, Sch. 33, Pt. 2(3).]"
S. 291(1)(b) substituted by FA 2001, Sch. 15, para. 10 in relation to shares issued on or after 7 March 2001; and in respect of the application of ICTA 1988, Pt. VII, Ch. III and TCGA 1992, Sch. 5B, on or after 7 March 2001 in relation to shares:
- that were issued after 31 December 1993 but before 7 March 2001, and
- to which income tax relief or deferral relief was attributable immediately before 7 March 2001.

In former s. 291(1)(b), the word "designated" was substituted for "seven year" by FA 2000, s. 64 and Sch. 17, para. 2(a), with effect in relation to shares issued on or after 6 April 2000. The words "the seven year period … after its incorporation" were substituted by FA 1998, s. 74(1) and Sch. 13, para. 6(1), with effect in relation to shares issued on or after 6 April 1998.
In s. 291(2), words "and sections 291A and 291B" repealed by FA 1998, s. 74(1) and Sch. 13, para. 6(2), s. 165 and Sch. 27, Pt. III(14), with effect in relation to shares issued on or after 6 April 1998.
S. 291(3) substituted by FA 1998, s. 74(1) and Sch. 13, para. 6(3), with effect in relation to shares issued on or after 6 April 1998. The text of s. 291(3) as it applies to shares issued prior to that date was as follows:
"**291(3)** In subsection (2) above **"subsidiary"**, in relation to the issuing company, means a 51 per cent subsidiary of the issuing company–
(a) whether it becomes such a subsidiary before, during or after the year of assessment in respect of which the individual concerned claims relief, and
(b) whether or not it is such a subsidiary while he or his associate is such an employee, partner or director."
S. 291(6) repealed by FA 2001, Sch. 33, Pt. 2(3) in relation to shares issued on or after 7 March 2001; and in respect of the application of ICTA 1988, Pt. VII, Ch. III and TCGA 1992, Sch. 5B, on or after 7 March 2001 in relation to shares:
- that were issued after 31 December 1993 but before 7 March 2001, and
- to which income tax relief or deferral relief was attributable immediately before 7 March 2001.

Former s. 291(6) substituted by FA 2000, s. 64 and Sch. 17, para. 2(b), with effect in relation to shares issued on or after 6 April 2000. The wording of s. 291(6) as it applies to shares issued prior to that date was as follows:
"**291(6)** In this Chapter "the seven year period", in relation to relief in respect of any eligible shares issued by a company, means the period beginning two years before, and ending five years after, the issue of the shares."
Former s. 291(6) inserted by FA 1998, s. 74(1) and Sch. 13, para. 6(4), with effect in relation to shares issued on or after 6 April 1998.
S. 291 (and s. 291A and 291B) substituted for former s. 291 by FA 1994, s. 137 and Sch. 15, para. 5. For text of former s. 291, see History note to s. 291B.

HMRC Manuals – Inspector's Manual, IM6935 ff.: scope of "connection with the company".

Notes – S. 291 rewritten for income tax purposes as follows:
S. 291(1): ITA 2007, s. 157(1), 163(1), (2).
S. 291(2): ITA 2007, s. 166(1), 167(1).
S. 291(3): ITA 2007, s. 167(2).
S. 291(4): ITA 2007, s. 167(3).
S. 291(5): ITA 2007, s. 167(2), 168(5), 169(1), 170(7).

291A Connected persons: directors

291A [Omitted by ITA 2007, s. 1027 and Sch. 1, para. 627 and repealed by ITA 2007, s. 1031 and Sch. 3, Pt. 2 with effect in relation to shares issued after 5 April 2007.]

History – S. 291A omitted by ITA 2007, s. 1027 and Sch. 1, para. 627 and repealed by ITA 2007, s. 1031 and Sch. 3, Pt. 2 with effect in relation to shares issued after 5 April 2007. In so far as it continues to apply in relation to shares issued before 5 April 2007, s. 291A is as follows:
"**291A(1)** An individual is not connected with the issuing company by reason only that he, or an associate of his, is a director of that or another company unless he or his associate (or a partnership of which he or his associate is a member)–
(a) receives a payment from the issuing company or a related person during the period mentioned in section 291(1)(b), or
(b) is entitled to receive such a payment in respect of that period or any part of it.
291A(2) In this section–
(a) **"related person"**, in relation to the issuing company, means–
(i) any company of which the individual or his associate is a director and which is a subsidiary or a partner of the issuing company or of a subsidiary, and
(ii) any person connected with the issuing company or with a company falling within sub-paragraph (i) above, and
(b) any reference to a payment to an individual includes a payment made to him indirectly or to his order or for his benefit.
291A(3) For the purposes of subsection (1) above there shall be disregarded–
(a) any payment or reimbursement of travelling or other expenses wholly, exclusively and necessarily incurred by him or his associate in the performance of his duties as a director,
(b) any interest which represents no more than a reasonable commercial return on money lent to the issuing company or a related person,
(c) any dividend or other distribution which does not exceed a normal return on the investment,
(d) any payment for the supply of goods which does not exceed their market value,
(e) any payment of rent for any property occupied by the issuing company or a related person which does not exceed a reasonable and commercial rent for the property, and
(f) any reasonable and necessary remuneration which–
(i) is paid for services rendered to the issuing company or related person in the course of a trade or profession carried on wholly or partly in the United Kingdom (not being secretarial or managerial services or services of a kind provided by the person to whom they are rendered), and
(ii) is taken into account in calculating for tax purposes the profits of that trade or profession.
291A(4) An individual (**"the subscriber"**) who subscribes for eligible shares (**"the relevant shares"**) may qualify for the relief notwithstanding his connection with the company at any time in the relevant period if–
(a) he is so connected by reason only of his, or his associate's, being a director of, or of a company which is a partner of, the issuing company or a subsidiary in receipt of, or entitled to receive, remuneration as such, and
(b) the following conditions are satisfied;
and in this subsection and subsection (5) below **"remuneration"** includes any benefit or facility.
291A(5) The conditions are that–
(a) in relation to the director (whether he is the subscriber or his associate), his remuneration, or the remuneration to which he is entitled, (leaving out of account any reasonable and necessary remuneration falling within subsection (3)(f) above) consists only of remuneration which is reasonable remuneration for services rendered to the company of which he is a director in his capacity as such,
(b) the subscriber was issued with eligible shares (whether the relevant shares or a previous issue of eligible shares) at a time when he had never been–
(i) connected with the issuing company, or
(ii) involved in carrying on (whether on his own account or as a partner, director or employee) the whole or any part of the trade carried on by the issuing company or a subsidiary, and
(c) where the issue of the relevant shares did not satisfy paragraph (b) above, they were not issued after the end of the period–
(i) beginning with the date of the latest issue of eligible shares which satisfied that paragraph, and
(ii) ending immediately before the termination date in relation to those eligible shares,
and in paragraph (b) above **"trade"** includes any business, profession or vocation.
291A(6) In this section **"subsidiary,"** in relation to the issuing company, means a 51 per cent subsidiary of the issuing company."

S. 291A(1)(a) amended by FA 2001, Sch. 15, para. 11 in relation to shares issued on or after 7 March 2001; and in respect of the application of ICTA 1988, Pt. VII, Ch. III and TCGA 1992, Sch. 5B, on or after 7 March 2001 in relation to shares:

- that were issued after 31 December 1993 but before 7 March 2001, and
- to which income tax relief or deferral relief was attributable immediately before 7 March 2001.

In s. 291A(1)(a), word "designated" substituted for "seven year" by FA 2000, s. 64 and Sch. 17, para. 3(2), with effect in relation to shares issued on or after 6 April 2000. The words "seven year period" were substituted by FA 1998, s. 74(1) and Sch. 13, para. 7(1), with effect in relation to shares issued on or after 6 April 1998.
In s. 291A(3)(f) the words "carried on wholly or partly in the United Kingdom" inserted and the words "in calculating for tax purposes the profits of that trade or profession" substituted by ITTOIA 2005, s. 882(1) and Sch. 1, para. 126; effective for income tax purposes for 2005–06 onwards and for corporation tax purposes for accounting periods ending after 5 April 2005 (ITTOIA 2005, s. 883(1)).
In s. 291A(3)(f)(ii), "profits" substituted for "profits or gains" by FA 1998, s. 46(3) and Sch. 7, para. 1.
S. 291A(5)(b)(ii) substituted by FA 1998, s. 74(1) and Sch. 13, para. 7(2)(a), with effect in relation to shares issued on or after 6 April 1998.
In s. 291A(5)(c), para. (i) created, and para. (ii) inserted, by FA 2000, s. 64 and Sch. 17, para. 3(3), with effect in relation to shares issued on or after 6 April 2000.
In s. 291A(5), words at the end "and the reference to a trade previously carried on includes part of such a trade" repealed by FA 1998, s. 74(1) and Sch. 13, para. 7(2)(b), s. 165 and Sch. 27, Pt. III(14) , in relationto shares issued on or after 6 April 1998.
S. 291A (and s. 291 and 291B) substituted for former s. 291 by FA 1994, s. 137 and Sch. 15, para. 5. For the text of former s. 291, see History note to s. 291B.

HMRC Manuals – Inspector's Manual, IM6959: definition of "associate".
Notes – S. 291A rewritten for income tax purposes as follows:
S. 291A(1): ITA 2007, s. 168(1).
S. 291A(2): ITA 2007, s. 168(4), 167(1).
S. 291A(3): ITA 2007, s. 168(2), (3).
S. 291A(4): ITA 2007, s. 169(1), (6).
S. 291A(5): ITA 2007, s. 169(2), (3), (4), (5).
S. 291A(6): ITA 2007, s. 168(5).

291B Connected persons: persons interested in capital etc. of company

291B [Omitted by ITA 2007, s. 1027 and Sch. 1, para. 627 and repealed by ITA 2007, s. 1031 and Sch. 3, Pt. 2 with effect in relation to shares issued after 5 April 2007.]

History – S. 291B omitted by ITA 2007, s. 1027 and Sch. 1, para. 627 and repealed by ITA 2007, s. 1031 and Sch. 3, Pt. 2 with effect in relation to shares issued after 5 April 2007. In so far as it continues to apply in relation to shares issued before 6 April 2007, s. 291B is as follows:
"**291B(1)** An individual is **connected with the issuing company** if he directly or indirectly possesses or is entitled to acquire more than 30 per cent of–
(a) the issued ordinary share capital of the company or any subsidiary,
(b) the loan capital and issued share capital of the company or any subsidiary, or
(c) the voting power in the company or any subsidiary.
291B(2) An individual is **connected with the issuing company** if he directly or indirectly possesses or is entitled to acquire such rights as would, in the event of the winding up of the company or any subsidiary or in any other circumstances, entitle him to receive more than 30 per cent of the assets of the company or subsidiary (the **"company in question"**) which would then be available for distribution to equity holders of the company in question.
291B(3) For the purposes of subsection (2) above–
(a) the persons who are equity holders of the company in question, and
(b) the percentage of the assets of the company in question to which the individual would be entitled,
shall be determined in accordance with paragraphs 1 and 3 of Schedule 18, taking references in paragraph 3 to the first company as references to an equity holder and references to a winding up as including references to any other circumstances in which assets of the company in question are available for distribution to its equity holders.
291B(4) An individual is **connected with a company** if he has control of it or of any subsidiary.
291B(5) Where an individual subscribes for shares in a company with which (apart from this subsection) he is not connected, he shall nevertheless be treated as connected with it if he subscribes for the shares as part of any arrangement which provides for another person to subscribe for shares in another company with which (assuming it to be an issuing company) that or any other individual who is a party to the arrangement is connected.
291B(5A) An individual is not connected with a company by reason only of the fact that one or more shares in the company are held by him, or by an associate of his, at a time when the company–
(a) has not issued any shares other than subscriber shares; and
(b) has not begun to carry on, or to make preparations for carrying on, any trade or business.
291B(6) In this section **"subsidiary"**, in relation to the issuing company, means a company which at any time in the relevant period is a 51 per cent subsidiary of the issuing company, whether or not it is such a subsidiary while the individual concerned has, or is entitled to acquire, such capital, voting power, rights or control as are mentioned in this section.
291B(7) For the purposes of this section the loan capital of a company shall be treated as including any debt incurred by the company–
(a) for any money borrowed or capital assets acquired by the company,
(b) for any right to receive income created in favour of the company, or
(c) for consideration the value of which to the company was (at the time when the debt was incurred) substantially less than the amount of the debt (including any premium on it).
291B(8) For the purposes of this section an individual shall be treated as entitled to acquire anything which he is entitled to acquire at a future date or will at a future date be entitled to acquire, and there shall be attributed to any person any rights or powers of any other person who is an associate of his.
291B(9) In determining for the purposes of this section whether an individual is connected with a company, no debt incurred by the company or any subsidiary by overdrawing an account with a person carrying on a business of banking shall be treated as loan capital of the company or subsidiary if the debt arose in the ordinary course of that business.
291B(10) Section 995 of ITA 2007 applies for the purposes of this section."
S. 291B(5A) inserted by FA 1998, s. 74(1) and Sch. 13, para. 8(1), with effect in relation to shares issued on or after 6 April 1998.
S. 291B(6) substituted by FA 1998, s. 74(1) and Sch. 13, para. 8(2), with effect in relation to shares issued on or after 6 April 1998. The former text of subsection (6) was as follows:
"**291B(6)** In this section **"subsidiary"**, in relation to the issuing company, means a 51 per cent subsidiary of the issuing company–
(a) whether it becomes such a subsidiary before, during or after the year of assessment in respect of which the individual concerned claims relief, and
(b) whether or not it is such a subsidiary while he has, or is entitled to acquire, such capital, voting power, rights or control as are mentioned in this section."

In s. 291B(10) the words "995 of ITA 2007" substituted for "840" by SI 2007/1820, art. 2(2), with effect, for income tax purposes, for 2007–08 and subsequent tax years, and, for corporation tax purposes, for accounting periods ending after 5 April 2007.
S. 291, 291A and 291B substituted for s. 291 by FA 1994, s. 137 and Sch. 15, para. 5, in relation to shares issued on or after 1 January 1994 with effect for 1993–94 and subsequent years of assessment. The wording of s. 291 as it applies to shares issued prior to that date was as follows:
"**291(1)** Subject to section 292, an individual qualifies for the relief if he–
(a) subscribes for the eligible shares on his own behalf,
(b) is resident and ordinarily resident in the United Kingdom at the time when they are issued, and
(c) is not at any time in the relevant period connected with the company;
and, in relation to shares issued after 5th April 1986, an individual who is at any time performing duties which are treated by virtue of section 132(4)(a) as performed in the United Kingdom shall be treated for the purposes of this section as resident and ordinarily resident in the United Kingdom at that time.
291(2) An individual is connected with the company if he, or an associate of his, is–
(a) an employee of the company or of a partner of the company;
(b) a partner of the company; or
(c) subject to subsection (3) below, a director of the company or of another company which is a partner of that company.
291(3) An individual is not connected with a company by reason only that he, or an associate of his, is a director unless he or his associate (or a partnership of which he or his associate is a member) receives a payment from the company during the period of five years beginning with the date on which the shares are issued or is entitled to receive such a payment in respect of that period or any part of it; but for that purpose there shall be disregarded–
(a) any payment or reimbursement of travelling or other expenses wholly, exclusively and necessarily incurred by him or his associate in the performance of his duties as a director of the company;
(b) any interest which represents no more than a reasonable commercial return on money lent to the company;
(c) any dividend or other distribution which does not exceed a normal return on the investment;
(d) any payment for the supply of goods which does not exceed their market value; and
(e) any reasonable and necessary remuneration which–
(i) is paid for services rendered to the company in the course of a trade or profession (not being secretarial or managerial services or services of a kind provided by the company itself); and
(ii) is taken into account in computing the profits or gains of the trade or profession under Case I or II of Schedule D or would be so taken into account if it fell in a period on the basis of which those profits or gains are assessed under that Schedule.
291(4) An individual is **connected** with the company if he directly or indirectly possesses or is entitled to acquire more than 30 per cent of–
(a) the issued ordinary share capital of the company; or
(b) the loan capital and issued share capital of the company; or
(c) the voting power in the company.
291(5) For the purposes of subsection (4)(b) above the loan capital of a company shall be treated as including any debt incurred by the company–
(a) for any money borrowed or capital assets acquired by the company; or
(b) for any right to receive income created in favour of the company; or
(c) for consideration the value of which to the company was (at the time when the debt was incurred) substantially less than the amount of the debt (including any premium thereon).
291(6) An individual is connected with the company if he directly or indirectly possesses or is entitled to acquire such rights as would, in the event of the winding up of the company or in any other circumstances, entitle him to receive more than 30 per cent of the assets of the company which would then be available for distribution to equity holders of the company, and for the purposes of this subsection–
(a) the persons who are equity holders of the company, and
(b) the percentage of the assets of the company to which the individual would be entitled,
shall be determined in accordance with paragraphs 1 and 3 of Schedule 18, taking references in paragraph 3 to the first company as references to an equity holder and references to a winding up as including references to any other circumstances in which assets of the company are available for distribution to its equity holders.
291(7) An individual is connected with a company if he has control of it within the meaning of section 840.
291(8) For the purposes of this section an individual shall be treated as entitled to acquire anything which he is entitled to acquire at a future date or will at a future date be entitled to acquire, and there shall be attributed to any person any rights or powers of any other person who is an associate of his.
291(9) In determining for the purposes of this section whether an individual is connected with a company, no debt incurred by the company by overdrawing an account with a person carrying on a business of banking shall be treated as loan capital of the company if the debt arose in the ordinary course of that business.
291(10) Where an individual subscribes for shares in a company with which he is not connected (either within the meaning of this section or by virtue of section 309(6)(b)) he shall nevertheless be treated as connected with it if he subscribes for the shares as part of any arrangement which provides for another person to subscribe for shares in another company with which that or any other individual who is a party to the arrangement is connected (within the meaning of this section or by virtue of section 309(6)(b))."

Derivations – Former s. 291(1): FA 1983, Sch. 5, para. 4(1) (as amended by F(No. 2)A 1983, s. 5 and Sch. 1) and para. 4(5), as inserted by FA 1986, s. 40 and Sch. 9, para. 5(1).
Former s. 291(2)–(8): FA 1981, s. 54(2)–(8), and FA 1983, Sch. 5, para. 4(2).
Former s. 291(9), (10): FA 1983, Sch. 5, para. 4(3), (4).

Cross references – S. 132(4)(a): duties of Crown servants performed abroad treated as performed in the UK.
S. 840: control is defined by reference to the power of a person to secure that the affairs of a body corporate are conducted in accordance with his wishes.
Sch. 18: definition of assets available for distribution to equity holders.
FA 1988, s. 50(1), (2) and Sch. 4, para. 4: individual deemed connected with a company in certain circumstances; provisions inserted as s. 291(1A) only where eligible shares are issued for the purpose of raising finance for private rented housing.

Other material – Taxline 2004/9 (not reproduced): meaning of "entitled to acquire" – look only at the issued share capital at the time and ignore shares that might be issued in the future.

Notes – S. 291B rewritten for income tax purposes as follows:
S. 291B(1): ITA 2007, s. 170(1).
S. 291B(2): ITA 2007, s. 170(2).
S. 291B(3): ITA 2007, s. 170(3), (4).
S. 291B(4): ITA 2007, s. 170(6).
S. 291B(5): ITA 2007, s. 171(1), (2).
S. 291B(5A): ITA 2007, s. 170(5).
S. 291B(6): ITA 2007, s. 170(7).
S. 291B(7): ITA 2007, s. 170(8).
S. 291B(8): ITA 2007, s. 170(9).
S. 291B(9): ITA 2007, s. 170(10).
S. 291B(10): ITA 2007, s. 1021(2).

292 Parallel trades

292 [Omitted by ITA 2007, s. 1027 and Sch. 1, para. 627 and repealed by ITA 2007, s. 1031 and Sch. 3, Pt. 2 with effect in relation to shares issued after 5 April 2007.]

History – S. 292 omitted by ITA 2007, s. 1027 and Sch. 1, para. 627 and repealed by ITA 2007, s. 1031 and Sch. 3, Pt. 2 with effect in relation to shares issued after 5 April 2007. In so far as it continues to apply in relation to shares issued before 6 April 2007, s. 292 is as follows:

"**292(1)** An individual is not eligible for relief in respect of any shares in a company if, at the date mentioned in subsection (2) below–
(a) he is one of a group of persons–
(i) who control the company; or
(ii) to whom belongs an interest amounting in the aggregate to more than a half share in the trade carried on by the company;
(b) he is also an individual, or one of a group of persons–
(i) controlling another company; or
(ii) to whom belongs an interest amounting in the aggregate to more than a half share in another trade; and
(c) the trade carried on by the company, or a substantial part of it–
(i) is concerned with the same or similar types of property or parts thereof or provides the same or similar services or facilities; and
(ii) serves substantially the same or similar outlets or markets;
as the other trade or (as the case may be) the trade carried on by the other company.

292(2) The date mentioned in subsection (1) above is–
(a) the date on which the shares are issued; or
(b) if later, the date on which the company begins to carry on the trade.

292(3) For the purposes of subsection (1) above–
(a) the persons to whom a trade belongs, and (where a trade belongs to two or more persons) their respective shares in that trade, shall be determined in accordance with section 344(1)(a) and (b), (2) and (3); and
(b) any interest, rights or powers of a person who is an associate of another person shall be treated as those of that other person.

292(4) For the purposes of this section–
(a) references to a **"company's trade"** include references to the trade of any company which is a 51 per cent subsidiary of that company on the date referred to in subsection (2) above; and
(b) **"trade"** in the expressions "another trade", "other trade" and "trade carried on by the other company" includes any business, profession or vocation.

292(5) This section shall not apply where the shares mentioned in subsection (1) above are issued on or after 29th November 1994."

In s. 292(1), the words "An individual … (2) below" substituted for former words "An individual is not entitled to relief in respect of any shares in a company which are issued after 18th March 1986 where at the date mentioned in subsection (2) below" by FA 1994, s. 137 and Sch. 15, para. 6(a), in relation to shares issued on or after 1 January 1994 with effect for 1993–94 and subsequent years of assessment.

In s. 292(4)(a), the words "any company … subsection (2) above" substituted for former words "of any of its subsidiaries" by FA 1994, s. 137 and Sch. 15, para. 6(b), in relation to shares issued on or after 1 January 1994 with effect for 1993–94 and subsequent years of assessment.

S. 292(5) inserted by FA 1995, s. 66(2) in relation to shares issued on or after 1 January 1994 (enterprise investment scheme).

Derivations – S. 292(1) (as originally enacted): FA 1983, Sch. 5, para. 10A(1) (as inserted by FA 1986, s. 40 and Sch. 9, para. 12) and FA 1986, Sch. 9, para. 1(2).
S. 292(2)–(4) (as originally enacted): FA 1983, Sch. 5, para. 10A(2)–(4), as inserted by FA 1986, s. 40 and Sch. 9, para. 12.

Cross references – S. 344(1)(a): trade belongs to persons carrying it on in the shares in which they are entitled to the profits.
S. 344(1)(b): trade belonging to non-charitable trustees treated as belonging to the persons entitled to the trust income.
S. 344(2), (3): trade belonging to a company deemed normally to belong to its ordinary shareholders in proportion to their holdings, subject to special rules for subsidiaries.
FA 1988, Sch. 4, para. 5: s. 292 does not apply where eligible shares issued for the purpose of raising finance for private rented housing under BES.

293 Qualifying companies

293 [Omitted by ITA 2007, s. 1027 and Sch. 1, para. 627 and repealed by ITA 2007, s. 1031 and Sch. 3, Pt. 2 with effect in relation to shares issued after 5 April 2007.]

History – S. 293 omitted by ITA 2007, s. 1027 and Sch. 1, para. 627 and repealed by ITA 2007, s. 1031 and Sch. 3, Pt. 2 with effect in relation to shares issued after 5 April 2007. In so far as it continues to apply in relation to shares issued before 6 April 2007, s. 293 is as follows:

"**293(1)** Subject to section 294, a company is a qualifying company (whether it is resident in the United Kingdom or elsewhere) if it complies with the requirements of this section.

293(1A) At the beginning of the relevant period, the company must be–
(a) an unquoted company, and
(b) a company to which subsection (1B) below does not apply.

293(1B) This subsection applies to a company–
(a) if arrangements are in existence for it to cease to be an unquoted company; or
(b) if–
(i) arrangements are in existence for it to become a subsidiary of another company (**"the new company"**) by virtue of an exchange of shares, or shares and securities, in relation to which section 304A (certain exchanges resulting in acquisition of share capital by new company) applies, and
(ii) arrangements have been made with a view to the new company ceasing to be an unquoted company.

293(2) The company must, throughout the relevant period, be–
(a) a company which exists wholly for the purpose of carrying on one or more qualifying trades or which so exists apart from purposes capable of having no significant effect (other than in relation to incidental matters) on the extent of the company's activities, or
(aa) the parent company of a trading group.

293(3) In this section **"qualifying subsidiary"**, in relation to a company, means a subsidiary of a kind which that company may hold *by virtue of section 308.*

293(3A) For the purposes of this section a company is the parent company of a trading group if–
(a) it has one or more subsidiaries;
(b) each of its subsidiaries is a qualifying subsidiary of the company; and
(c) the requirements of subsection (3B) below are fulfilled by what would be the business of the company and its subsidiaries if all the activities, taken together, of the company and its subsidiaries were regarded as one business.

293(3B) A business fulfils the requirements of this subsection if neither the business nor a substantial part of it consists in, or in either of, the following, that is to say–
(a) activities falling within section 297(2)(a) to (g) but not within subsection (3C) below; and
(b) activities (other than research and development) carried on otherwise than in the course of a trade.
293(3C) The activities falling within this subsection are–
(a) the receiving of royalties or licence fees in circumstances where the requirement mentioned in section 297(4) is satisfied in relation to the company receiving them;
(b) the letting of ships, other than offshore installations or pleasure craft, on charter in circumstances where the requirements mentioned in paragraphs (a) to (d) of section 297(6) are satisfied in relation to the company so letting them.
293(3D) Activities of a company or of any of its subsidiaries shall be disregarded for the purposes of subsections (3A) to (3C) above to the extent that they consist in–
(a) the holding of shares in or securities of, or the making of loans to, one or more of the company's subsidiaries; or
(b) the holding and managing of property used by the company or any of its subsidiaries for the purposes of–
(i) research and development from which it is intended that a qualifying trade to be carried on by the company or any of its subsidiaries will be derived; or
(ii) one or more qualifying trades so carried on.
293(3E) Activities of a subsidiary of a company shall also be disregarded for the purposes of subsections (3A) to (3C) above to the extent that they consist in–
(a) the making of loans to the company; or
(b) in the case of a mainly trading subsidiary, activities carried on otherwise than in pursuance of its main purpose.
293(3F) For the purposes of subsection (3E) above–
(a) **"mainly trading subsidiary"** means a subsidiary which, apart from purposes capable of having no significant effect (other than in relation to incidental matters) on the extent of its activities, exists wholly for the purpose of carrying on one or more qualifying trades; and
(b) that purpose shall be taken to be its main purpose.
293(4) [Repealed by FA 1994, s. 137 and Sch. 15, para. 7(b) and s. 258 and Sch. 26, Pt. V(17).]
293(4A) A company shall not be regarded as ceasing to comply with subsection (2) above by reason only of anything done as a consequence of the company, or any of its subsidiaries, being in administration or receivership.
This subsection has effect subject to subsection (4B) and subsection (5) below.
293(4B) Subsection (4A) applies only if–
(a) the entry into administration or receivership, and
(b) everything done as a consequence of the company concerned being in administration or receivership,
is for bona fide commercial reasons and is not part of a scheme or arrangement the main purpose or one of the main purposes of which is the avoidance of tax.
293(5) Without prejudice to the generality of subsection (2) above, but subject to subsection (6) below, a company ceases to comply with that subsection if before the end of the relevant period a resolution is passed, or an order is made, for the winding up of the company or any of its subsidiaries (or, in the case of a winding up otherwise than under the Insolvency Act 1986 or the Insolvency (Northern Ireland) Order 1989, any other act is done for the like purpose) or the company or any of its subsidiaries is dissolved without winding up.
293(6) A company shall not be regarded as ceasing to comply with subsection (2) above if it does so by reason only of the company or any of its subsidiaries being wound up or dissolved without winding up and–
(a) the winding up or dissolution is for bona fide commercial reasons and is not part of a scheme or arrangement the main purpose or one of the main purposes of which is the avoidance of tax;
(b) [repealed by FA 2000, s. 64 and Sch. 17, para. 10, s. 156 and Sch. 40, Pt. II(5).]
293(6ZA) The company must not at any time in the relevant period have a property managing subsidiary which is not a qualifying 90% subsidiary of the company.
293(6ZB) **"Property managing subsidiary"** means a subsidiary of the company whose business consists wholly or mainly in the holding or managing of land or any property deriving its value from land.
293(6ZC) In subsection (6ZB) above, **"land"** and **"property deriving its value from land"** have the same meaning as in section 776.
293(6A) The value of the relevant assets
(a) must not exceed £7 million immediately before the issue of the eligible shares; and
(b) must not exceed £8 million immediately afterwards.
293(6B) Subject to subsection (6C) below, the reference in subsection (6A) above to the value of the relevant assets is a reference–
(a) in relation to a time when the company did not have any qualifying subsidiaries, to the value of the gross assets of the company at that time; and
(b) in relation to any other time, to the aggregate value at that time of the gross assets of all the companies in the company's group.
293(6C) For the purposes of subsection (6B) above assets of any member of the company's group that consist in rights against, or in shares in or securities of, another member of the group shall be disregarded.
293(6D) In subsections (6B) and (6C) above references, in relation to any time, to the company's group are references to the company and its qualifying subsidiaries at that time.
293(7) [Repealed by FA 1998, s. 74(1) and Sch. 13, para. 9(4), s. 165 and Sch. 27, Pt. III(14).]
293(8) Subject to section 304A, the company must not at any time in the relevant period–
(a) control (whether on its own or together with any person connected with it) any company which is not a qualifying subsidiary, or
(b) be–
(i) a 51% subsidiary of another company, or
(ii) under the control of another company (or of another company and any other person connected with that other company), without being a 51% subsidiary of that other company,
and no arrangements must be in existence at any time in that period by virtue of which the company could fall within paragraph (a) or (b) above (whether during that period or otherwise).
293(8AA) In subsection (8)(b) above **"control"** has the meaning given by section 995 of ITA 2007.
293(8A) Section 312(1A)(b) applies to determine the relevant period for the purposes of this section and sections 294, 295 and 296.
293(8B) In arriving at the relevant period for the purposes of sections 294 to 296 any time falling on or after 29th November 1994 shall be ignored; and subsection (8A) above shall have effect subject to the preceding provisions of this subsection.
293(9)–(11) [Repealed by FA 1994, s. 137 and Sch. 15, para. 7(e) and s. 258 and Sch. 26, Pt. V(17).]"
S. 293(1)–(3) substituted, and s. 293(4) repealed, by FA 1994, s. 137 and Sch. 15, para. 7(a), (b), and s. 258 and Sch. 26, Pt. V(17), in relation to shares issued on or after 1 January 1994 with effect for 1993–94 and subsequent years of assessment.
S. 293(1A) and (1B) inserted, and s. 293(2) consequentially amended by FA 2001, Sch. 15, para. 12 in relation to shares issued on or after 7 March 2001; and in respect of the application of ICTA 1988, Pt. VII, Ch. III and TCGA 1992, Sch. 5B, on or after 7 March 2001 in relation to shares:
- that were issued after 31 December 1993 but before 7 March 2001, and
- to which income tax relief or deferral relief was attributable immediately before 7 March 2001.

S. 293(2)(aa) substituted for former para. (b) by FA 1997, s. 74 and Sch. 8, para. 4(1) with effect in relation to shares issued after 26 November 1996, and with effect after 26 November 1996 in relation to shares which were issued on or after 1 January 1994 but before 27 November 1996, and immediately before 27 November 1996 were held by an individual and at that time were shares to which relief (within the meaning of Pt. VII, Ch. III) was attributable. In so far as it continues to apply to other shares, former para. (b) reads as follows:

"(b) a company whose business consists wholly of–
(i) the holding of shares or securities of, or the making of loans to, one or more qualifying subsidiaries of the company, or
(ii) both the holding of such shares or securities, or the making of such loans, and the carrying on of one or more qualifying trades."

S. 293(3A), (3B), (3C), (3D), (3E) and (3F) inserted by FA 1997, s. 74 and Sch. 8, para. 4(2) with effect in relation to shares issued after 26 November 1996, and with effect after 26 November 1996 in relation to shares which were issued on or after 1 January 1994 but before 27 November 1996, and immediately before 27 November 1996 were held by an individual and at that time were shares to which relief (within the meaning of Pt. VII, Ch. III) was attributable.

In s. 293(3B)(b) reference to oil exploration omitted by FA 2001, Sch. 15, para. 4 in relation to shares issued on or after 7 March 2001; and in respect of the application of ICTA 1988, Pt. VII, Ch. III and TCGA 1992, Sch. 5B, on or after 7 March 2001 in relation to shares:

- that were issued after 31 December 1993 but before 7 March 2001, and
- to which income tax relief or deferral relief was attributable immediately before 7 March 2001.

In s. 293(3B)(b) the words "(other than research and development and oil exploration)" inserted by FA 1998, s. 74(1) and Sch. 13, para. 9(3), with effect in relation to shares issued on or after 6 April 1998.

In s. 293(3C)(b) the words "offshore installations" substituted for "oil rigs" inserted by FA 2004, s. 146 and Sch. 27, para. 4(2), with effect, subject to the provisions at FA 2004, Sch. 27, para. 4(6), in relation to shares issued on or after 6 April 2004.

In s. 293(3C) reference to s. 297(5) deemed, by FA 2001, Sch. 15, para. 14, never to have been made.

In s. 293(4B) the words "the entry into administration or receivership" substituted for "the making of the order in question" by SI 2003/2096, art. 4 and Sch., para. 17 with effect from 15 September 2003. Transitional provisions are contained in art. 6.

In s. 293(4A), the words "which is in administration or receivership" following "a company" omitted by FA 2004, s. 93 and Sch. 18, para. 5(2)(a), and repealed by s. 326, Sch. 42, Pt. 2(13) with effect in relation to shares issued on or after 17 March 2004.

In s. 293(4A), the word "only" inserted following "by reason" by FA 2004, s. 93 and Sch. 18, para. 5(2)(b), with effect in relation to shares issued on or after 17 March 2004.

In s. 293(4A), the words "the company, or any of its subsidiaries," substituted for "its" by FA 2004, s. 93 and Sch. 18, para. 5(2)(c), with effect in relation to shares issued on or after 17 March 2004.

S. 293(4A) and (4B) inserted by FA 2000, s. 64 and Sch. 17, para. 9(1), with effect in relation to shares issued on or after 21 March 2000, and in respect of the application of s. 293 on or after that date in relation to shares that were issued after 31 December 1993 but before 21 March 2000, and to which EIS relief or CGT deferral relief was attributable immediately before 21 March 2000.

In s. 293(4B)(b), the word "concerned" inserted by FA 2004, s. 93 and Sch. 18, para. 5(3), with effect in relation to shares issued on or after 17 March 2004.

In s. 293(5), the words "or any of its subsidiaries," inserted in two places by FA 2004, s. 93 and Sch. 18, para. 5(4), with effect in relation to shares issued on or after 17 March 2004.

In s. 293(5) the words "Insolvency (Northern Ireland) Order 1989" substituted by SI 1989/2405 (NI 19), Sch. 9, para. 59, operative from 1 October 1991 (SI 1991/411 (C 20)).

In s. 293(6), the words "by reason only of the company or any of its subsidiaries" substituted for "by reason of" by FA 2004, s. 93 and Sch. 18, para. 5(5)(a), with effect in relation to shares issued on or after 17 March 2004.

In s. 293(6)(a), the words "and is not" substituted for "and not" by FA 2004, s. 93 and Sch. 18, para. 5(5), with effect in relation to shares issued on or after 17 March 2004.

At the start of s. 293(6)(a) the words "it is shown that" repealed by FA 1998, s. 74(1) and Sch. 13, para. 9(2), s. 165 and Sch. 27, Pt. III(14), in relation to events occurring on or after 6 April 1998.

S. 293(6)(b), and the word "and" immediately before it, were repealed by FA 2000, s. 64 and Sch. 17, para. 10, s. 156 and Sch. 40, Pt. II(5), with effect in relation to shares issued on or after 21 March 2000, and in respect of the application of s. 293 on or after that date in relation to shares that were issued after 31 December 1993 but before 21 March 2000, and to which EIS relief or CGT deferral relief was attributable immediately before 21 March 2000. The former text of s. 291(6)(b) read as follows:

"(b) the company's net assets, if any, are distributed to its members or dealt with as bona vacantia before the end of the relevant period or, in the case of a winding up, the end (if later) of three years from the commencement of the winding up."

S. 293(6ZA) inserted by FA 2004, s. 93 and Sch. 18, para. 5(6), with effect in relation to shares issued on or after 17 March 2004.
S. 293(6ZB) inserted by FA 2004, s. 93 and Sch. 18, para. 5(6), with effect in relation to shares issued on or after 17 March 2004.
S. 293(6ZC) inserted by FA 2004, s. 93 and Sch. 18, para. 5(6), with effect in relation to shares issued on or after 17 March 2004.

In s. 293(6A)(a) the words "£7 million" substituted for the words "£15 million" by FA 2006, s. 91 and Sch. 14, para. 1(1)(a), with effect in relation to shares issued on or after 6 April 2006 except for any shares issued on or after that date (Sch. 14, para. 1(2)–(4)):

- that were subscribed for before 22 March 2006; or
- that were issued to the managers of an investment fund approved under ICTA 1988, s. 311; where the fund was approved before 22 March 2006 and the investment was accepted before 6 April 2006 and the shares were issued to the mangers as nominee for the investor.

In s. 293(6A)(b) the words "£8 million" substituted for the words "£16 million" by FA 2006, s. 91 and Sch. 14, para. 1(1)(b), with effect in relation to shares issued on or after 6 April 2006 except for any shares issued on or after that date (Sch. 14, para. 1(2)–(4)):

- that were subscribed for before 22 March 2006; or
- that were issued to the managers of an investment fund approved under ICTA 1988, s. 311; where the fund was approved before 22 March 2006 and the investment was accepted before 6 April 2006 and the shares were issued to the mangers as nominee for the investor.

S. 293(6A)–(6D) inserted by FA 1998, s. 74(1) and Sch. 13, para. 9(3), with effect in relation to shares issued on or after 6 April 1998.

S. 293(7) repealed by FA 1998, s. 74(1) and Sch. 13, para. 9(4), s. 165 and Sch. 27, Pt. III(14), with effect in relation to shares issued on or after 6 April 1998. S. 293(7) formerly read as follows:

"**293(7)** The company's share capital must not, at any time in the relevant period, include any issued shares that are not fully paid up or would not be fully paid up if any undertaking to pay cash to the company at a future date were disregarded."

In former s. 293(7), the words "or would … disregarded" inserted by FA 1994, s. 137 and Sch. 15, para. 7(c), in relation to shares issued on or after 1 January 1994 with effect for 1993–94 and subsequent years of assessment.

In s. 293(8AA) the words "995 of ITA 2007" substituted for "840" by SI 2007/1820, art. 2(2), with effect, for income tax purposes, for 2007–08 and subsequent tax years, and, for corporation tax purposes, for accounting periods ending after 5 April 2007.

S. 293(8) and (8AA) substituted for former s. 293(8) by FA 2000, s. 63 and Sch. 17, para. 11, with effect in relation to shares issued on or after 21 March 2000, and in respect of the application of s. 293 on or after that date in relation to shares that were issued after 31 December 1993 but before 21 March 2000, and to which EIS relief or CGT deferral relief was attributable immediately before 21 March 2000. The former text of s. 293(8) read as follows:

"**293(8)** Subject to sections 304A and 308, the company must not–
(a) at any time in the relevant period control (or together with any person connected with it control) another company or be under the control of another company (or another company and any other person connected with that other company), or
(b) at any such time be a 51 per cent subsidiary of another company or itself have a 51 per cent subsidiary,

and no arrangements must be in existence at any time in that period by virtue of which the company could fall within paragraph (a) or (b) above."

In former s. 293(8) for EIS shares, words "Subject to sections 304A and 308" substituted for "Subject to section 308" by FA 1998, s. 74(1) and Sch. 13, para. 9(5), with effect in relation to shares issued on or after 6 April 1998.

Former s. 293(8), and s. 293(8A), substituted for the earlier s. 293(8), and s. 293(9)–(11) repealed, by FA 1994, s. 137 and Sch. 15, para. 7(d), (e), and s. 258 and Sch. 26, Pt. V(17), in relation to shares issued on or after 1 January 1994 with effect for 1993–94 and subsequent years of assessment. S. 293(8)–(11) formerly provided as follows:

"**293(8)** Subject to sections 304A, 308 and 309, the company must not at any time in the relevant period–

(a) control (or together with any person connected with it control) another company or be under the control of another company (or another company and any other person connected with that other company); or

(b) be a 51 per cent subsidiary of another company or itself have a 51 per cent subsidiary;

and no arrangements must be in existence at any time in that period by virtue of which the company could fall within paragraph (a) or (b) above.

293(9) A company is not a qualifying company in relation to shares issued before 19th March 1986 if–

(a) an individual has acquired a controlling interest in the company's trade after 5th April 1983; and

(b) at any time in the period mentioned in subsection (10) below he has, or has had, a controlling interest in another trade; and

(c) the trade carried on by the company or a substantial part of it–

(i) is concerned with the same or similar types of property or parts thereof or provides the same or similar services or facilities as the other trade, or

(ii) serves substantially the same or similar outlets or markets as the other trade.

Section 298(1) and (2) shall apply for the purposes of this subsection.

293(10) The period referred to in subsection (9) above is the period beginning two years before and ending three years after–

(a) the date on which the shares were issued; or

(b) if later, the date on which the company began to carry on the trade.

293(11) In subsections (9) and (10) above references to a **company's trade** include references to the trade of any of its subsidiaries."

In former s. 293(8) (immediately above) for BES shares, words "Subject to sections 304A, 308 and 309" substituted for "Subject to sections 308 and 309" by FA 1998, s. 74(1) and Sch. 13, para. 38(1), with effect in relation to new shares (within the meaning of s. 304A) issued on or after 6 April 1998.

S. 293(8B) inserted by FA 1995, s. 66(3), in relation to shares issued on or after 1 January 1994 (enterprise investment scheme).

Derivations – S. 293(1) (as originally enacted): FA 1983, Sch. 5, para. 5(1), as amended by FA 1986, s. 40 and Sch. 9, para. 6(2).
S. 293(2) (as originally enacted): FA 1983, Sch. 5, para. 5(2), as amended by F(No. 2)A 1983, s. 5 and Sch. 1, para. 3(a).
S. 293(3) (as originally enacted): FA 1983, Sch. 5, para. 5(3).
Former s. 293(4): FA 1983, Sch. 5, para. 5(3A) (as inserted by FA 1986, s. 40 and Sch. 9, para. 6(3)), and FA 1985, Sch. 9, para. 1(2).
S. 293(5) (as originally enacted): FA 1983, Sch. 5, para. 5(4), as amended by Insolvency Act 1986, Sch. 14, and SI 1986/1032 (NI 6).
S. 293(6)–(8) (as originally enacted): FA 1983, Sch. 5, para. 5(5)–(7).
Former s. 293(9), (10): FA 1983, Sch. 5, para. 5(8)–(10), which was repealed by FA 1986, s. 40 and Sch. 9, para. 6(4), in relation to shares issued at any time after 18 March 1986.
Former s. 293(11): FA 1983, Sch. 5, para. 5(11) (inserted by F(No. 2)A 1983, s. 5 and Sch. 1, para. 3(b)) which was repealed by FA 1986, s. 40 and Sch. 9, para. 6(4), in relation to shares issued at any time after 18 March 1986.

Cross references – S. 576(4)–(4B): modified application of s. 293 in defining "qualifying trading company" for relief for losses on shares in unlisted trading companies.
FA 1988, Sch. 4, para. 6: modifications of s. 293 where eligible shares issued for the purpose of raising finance for private rented housing under BES.
TCGA 1992, Sch. 5B: capital gains tax relief for reinvestment in enterprise investment scheme shares.

Statements of practice – SP 2/00: application of gross asset rules in s. 293(6A).

Other material – ICAEW Technical Release TR 798 (not reproduced): Revenue confirm that a company falling within former s. 293(2)(a) for a part of the relevant period and then former s. 293(2)(b) for the remainder of that period would be regarded as a qualifying company throughout the relevant period.
Law Society's Gazette, 15 June 1994 (not reproduced): meeting between Revenue and revenue law committee of Law Society – Revenue said that expression in s. 293(2)(a) "capable of having no significant effect … on the extent of the company's activities" indicated that *de minimis* non-qualifying activities could be ignored.

Notes – S. 293 rewritten for income tax purposes as follows:
S. 293(1): ITA 2007, s. 180.
S. 293(1A): ITA 2007, s. 143(1), 184(1), Sch. 1 para. 128.
S. 293(1B): ITA 2007, s. 143(1), 184(1), Sch. 1 para. 128.
S. 293(2): ITA 2007, s. 137(1), (7), 181(1), (2), (8), Sch. 1 para. 122.
S. 293(3A): ITA 2007, s. 137(3), 140(1), 181(4), 187, 257(1), Sch. 1 para. 122, 125.
S. 293(3B): ITA 2007, s. 137(1), (7), 181(2), (8), Sch. 1 para. 122.
S. 293(3C): ITA 2007, s. 137(7), 181(8), Sch. 1 para. 122.
S. 293(3D): ITA 2007, s. 137(5), 181(6), Sch. 1 para. 122.
S. 293(3E): ITA 2007, s. 137(4), (5), 181(5), (6), Sch. 1 para. 122.
S. 293(3F): ITA 2007, s. 137(7), 181(8), Sch. 1 para. 122.
S. 293(4A): ITA 2007, s. 138(1), 182(1), Sch. 1 para. 123.
S. 293(4B): ITA 2007, s. 138(2), 182(2), Sch. 1 para. 123.
S. 293(5): ITA 2007, s. 138(3), 182(3), Sch. 1 para. 123.
S. 293(6): ITA 2007, s. 138(4), 182(4), Sch. 1 para. 123.
S. 293(6A): ITA 2007, s. 142(1), (2), 186(1), (2), (3), Sch. 1 para. 127.
S. 293(6B): ITA 2007, s. 142(1), (2), (3), 186(1), (2), (3), Sch. 1 para. 127.
S. 293(6C): ITA 2007, s. 142(3), 186(3), Sch. 1 para. 127.
S. 293(6ZA): ITA 2007, s. 141(1), 188(1), Sch. 1 para. 126.
S. 293(6ZB): ITA 2007, s. 141(2), 188(2), Sch. 1 para. 126.
S. 293(6ZC): ITA 2007, s. 188(3).
S. 293(8): ITA 2007, s. 139(1), (2), (3), 185(1), (2), (3), Sch. 1 para. 124.
S. 293(8AA): ITA 2007, s. 1021(2).
S. 293(8A): ITA 2007, s. 181(1), 182(3), 184(1), (6), 185(1), (2), 188(1).

294 Companies with interests in land

294 [Omitted by ITA 2007, s. 1027 and Sch. 1, para. 627 and repealed by ITA 2007, s. 1031 and Sch. 3, Pt. 2 with effect in relation to shares issued on or after 5 April 2007.]

ICTA 1988

History – S. 294 omitted by ITA 2007, s. 1027 and Sch. 1, para. 627 and repealed by ITA 2007, s. 1031 and Sch. 3, Pt. 2 with effect in relation to shares issued after 5 April 2007. In so far as it continues to apply in relation to shares issued before 6 April 2007, s. 294 is as follows:

"**294(1)** Subject to section 296, a company is not a qualifying company in relation to any shares if at any time during the relevant period–

(a) the value of the interests in land held by the company at that time; or

(b) where lower, the value of the interests in land which were held by the company immediately after the issue of the shares (adjusted in accordance with section 295);

is greater than half the value of the company's assets as a whole.

294(2) For the purposes of this section, the value of the interests in land held by a company on any date shall be arrived at by first aggregating the market value on that date of each of those interests and then deducting–

(a) the amount of any debts of the company which are secured on any of those interests (including any debt secured by a floating charge on property which comprises any of those interests);

(b) the amount of any unsecured debts of the company which do not fall due for payment before the expiry of the period of 12 months beginning with that date; and

(c) the amount paid up in respect of those shares of the company (if any) which carry a present or future preferential right to the company's assets on its winding up.

294(3) For the purposes of this section, the value of a company's assets as a whole shall be arrived at by first aggregating the market value of each of those assets and then deducting the amount of the debts and liabilities of the company.

294(4) For the purposes of subsection (3) above, the amount paid up in respect of those shares of a company (if any) which carry a present or future preferential right to the company's assets on its winding up shall be treated as a debt of the company, but otherwise a company's share capital, share premium account and reserves shall not be treated for those purposes as debts or liabilities of the company.

294(5) In this section **"interest in land"** means any estate or interest in land, any right in or over land or affecting the use or disposition of land, and any right to obtain such an estate, interest or right from another which is conditional on that other's ability to grant the estate, interest or right in question, except that it does not include–

(a) the interest of a creditor (other than a creditor in respect of a rentcharge) whose debt is secured by way of a mortgage, an agreement for a mortgage or a charge of any kind over land; or

(b) in Scotland, the interest of a creditor in a charge or security of any kind over land.

294(5A) For the purposes of this section, the value of an interest in any building or other land shall be adjusted by deducting the market value of any machinery or plant which is so installed or otherwise fixed in or to the building or other land as to become, in law, part of it.

294(6) In arriving at the value of any interest in land for the purposes of this section–

(a) it shall be assumed that there is no source of mineral deposits in the land of a kind which it would be practicable to exploit by extracting them from underground otherwise than by means of opencast mining or quarrying; and

(b) any borehole on the land shall be disregarded if it was made in the course of oil exploration.

294(7) Where a company is a member of a partnership which holds any interest in land–

(a) that interest shall, for the purposes of this section and sections 295 and 296, be treated as an interest in land held by the company; but

(b) its value at any time shall, for those purposes, be taken to be such fraction of its value (apart from this subsection) as is equal to the fraction of the assets of the partnership to which the company would be entitled if the partnership were dissolved at that time.

294(8) Where a qualifying company has one or more subsidiaries, the company and its subsidiaries (**"the group"**) shall be treated as a single company for the purposes of this section and sections 295 and 296; but any debt owed by, or liability of, one member of the group to another shall be disregarded for those purposes.

294(9) The Treasury may by order amend subsection (1) above by substituting a different fraction for the fraction for the time being specified there."

In s. 294(1), the words "Subject to … relevant period" substituted for former words "subject to section 296, a company is not a qualifying company in relation to shares issued after 18th March 1986 if at any time during the relevant period" by FA 1994, s. 137 and Sch. 15, para. 8, in relation to shares issued on or after 1 January 1994 with effect for 1993–94 and subsequent years of assessment.

S. 294(5A) was inserted by FA 1988, s. 52(1), with effect in respect of valuations falling to be made after 29 July 1988.

Derivations – (as originally enacted) – S. 294(1): FA 1983, Sch. 5, para. 5A(1) (as inserted by FA 1986, s. 40 and Sch. 9, para. 7) and FA 1986, Sch. 9, para. 1(2).

S. 294(2)–(5): FA 1983, Sch. 5, para. 5A(2)–(5), as inserted by FA 1986, s. 40 and Sch. 9, para. 7.

S. 294(6)–(9): FA 1983, Sch. 5, para. 5A(6)–(9), as inserted by FA 1986, s. 40 and Sch. 9, para. 7.

Cross references – FA 1988, Sch. 4, para. 7: s. 294 does not apply where eligible shares issued for the purpose of raising finance for private rented housing under BES.

TMA 1970, s. 47B: appeal against refusal of relief, or against assessment withdrawing relief, including a question of an interest in land, lies to the appropriate Lands Tribunal.

Other material – Taxline 1991/19 (not reproduced): Revenue confirmation that, where unsecured loan stock issued with a redemption date outside the period in s. 294(2)(b) but with a right of conversion into ordinary shares at an earlier time, conversion constitutes payment within s. 294; and, since "payment" can occur at any time, the requirements of s. 294(2)(b) are not fulfilled.

295 Valuation of interests in land for purposes of section 294(1)(b)

295 [Omitted by ITA 2007, s. 1027 and Sch. 1, para. 627 and repealed by ITA 2007, s. 1031 and Ch. 3, Pt. 2 with effect in relation to shares issued after 5 April 2007.]

History – S. 295 omitted by ITA 2007, s. 1027 and Sch. 1, para. 627 and repealed by ITA 2007, s. 1031 and Sch. 3, Pt. 2 with effect in relation to shares issued after 5 April 2007. In so far as it continues to apply in relation to shares issued before 6 April 2007, s. 295 is as follows:

"**295(1)** For the purposes of section 294(1)(b), the value of the interests in land held by a company immediately after the issue of the shares in question (**"the original interests"**) shall be adjusted by–

(a) adding–

(i) the cost of any interests in land subsequently acquired by the company (**"the later interests"**); and

(ii) any expenditure (whenever payable) incurred by the company wholly and exclusively in enhancing the value of any of the original or later interests;

(b) deducting any consideration received by the company on the disposal of any of the original or later interests or on the grant by the company of any interest in land out of any of those interests;

(c) deducting any consideration otherwise derived by the company from its ownership of any of the original or later interests.

295(2) Any sum which is received by a company by way of rent, or which is attributable to the use of any premises by the company, shall be disregarded for the purposes of subsection (1)(c) above.

295(3) For the purposes of this section–
(a) the cost of an interest in land acquired by a company shall be taken to be the amount or value of the consideration given by the company, or on its behalf, wholly and exclusively for the acquisition of the interest;
(b) consideration shall be brought into account without any discount for the postponement of the right to receive any part of it; and
(c) the grant of an interest in land out of any of the original interests shall be treated as a disposal of the original interest in question.
295(4) Where–
(a) the interest of a company as lessee under a lease (**"the lease"**) falls to be valued at any time for the purposes of section 294 or the cost of acquiring that interest falls to be calculated for the purposes of this section; and
(b) the aggregate amount of the rent payable by the lessee under the lease before the end of the relevant period exceeds that which would be so payable under a lease of the premises at a full market rent (but otherwise on the same terms and conditions as the lease);
the value of the company's interest at that time shall be calculated on the assumption that the aggregate amount payable as mentioned in paragraph (b) above is a nominal amount and, where the interest was acquired after the issue of the shares in question, it shall be assumed that the company paid the appropriate premium when acquiring the interest.
295(5) In determining, for the purposes of this section, the consideration for the disposal or acquisition of an interest in land, no account shall be taken in the first instance of any contingent liability assumed by the company or by any other person.
295(6) If it is subsequently shown to the satisfaction of the Board that a contingent liability which was not taken into account in determining the consideration for a disposal or acquisition has become enforceable and is being or had been enforced, such adjustment, whether by way of a further assessment or the discharge or repayment of tax or otherwise, shall be made as is required in consequence.
295(7) Where the relief obtainable under subsection (6) above requires a discharge or repayment of tax, it shall be given on a claim to the Board and such a claim may be made at any time."

Derivations – FA 1983, Sch. 5, para. 5B(1)–(7), as inserted by FA 1986, s. 40 and Sch. 9, para. 7.

Cross references – FA 1988, Sch. 4, para. 7: s. 295 does not apply where eligible shares issued for the purpose of raising finance for private rented housing under BES.

296 Section 294 disapplied where amounts raised total £50,000 or less

296 [Omitted by ITA 2007, s. 1027 and Sch. 1, para. 627 and repealed by ITA 2007, s. 1031 and Sch. 3, Pt. 2 with effect in relation to shares issued after 5 April 2007.]

History – S. 296 omitted by ITA 2007, s. 1027 and Sch. 1, para. 627 and repealed by ITA 2007, s. 1031 and Sch. 3, Pt. 2 with effect in relation to shares issued after 5 April 2007. In so far as it continues to apply in relation to shares issued before 6 April 2007, s. 296 is as follows:
"296(1) Where a company raises any amount through the issue of eligible shares, section 294–
(a) shall not have effect to deny relief in relation to those shares if the aggregate of that amount and of all other amounts (if any) so raised within the period of 12 months ending with the date of that issue does not exceed £50,000; and
(b) where that aggregate exceeds £50,000, shall have effect to deny relief only in relation to the excess.
296(2) Where–
(a) at any time within the relevant period, the company in question or any of its subsidiaries carries on any trade or part of a trade in partnership, or as a party to a joint venture, with one or more other persons; and
(b) that other person, or at least one of those other persons, is a company;
each reference to £50,000 in subsection (1)(a) and (b) above shall have effect as if it were a reference to–

$$\frac{£50,000}{1 + A}$$

where A is the total number of companies (apart from the company in question or any of its subsidiaries) which are members of any such partnership or parties to any such joint venture during the relevant period.
296(3) Where section 294, as read with this section, requires a restriction to be placed on the relief given on claims in respect of shares issued to two or more individuals, the available relief shall be divided between them in proportion to the amounts which have been respectively subscribed by them for the shares to which their claims relate and which would, apart from the restrictions, be eligible for the relief.
296(4) A claimant who is dissatisfied with the manner in which the available relief is divided under this section between him and any other claimant or claimants may apply to the appropriate Commissioners who shall, after giving the other claimant or claimants an opportunity to appear and be heard or to make representations in writing, determine the question for all the claimants in the same way as an appeal.
296(5) In this section **"the appropriate Commissioners"** means–
(a) in a case where the same body of General Commissioners has jurisdiction with respect to all the claimants, those Commissioners, unless all the claimants agree that the question should be determined by the Special Commissioners;
(b) in a case where different bodies of General Commissioners have jurisdiction with respect to the claimants, such of those bodies as the Board may direct, unless all the claimants agree that the question should be determined by the Special Commissioners;
(c) in any other case, the Special Commissioners.
296(6) [Repealed by FA 1994, s. 137 and Sch. 15, para. 9, and s. 258 and Sch. 26, Pt. V(17).]"
S. 296(6) repealed by FA 1994, s. 137 and Sch. 15, para. 9, and s. 258 and Sch. 26, Pt. V(17), in relation to shares issued on or after 1 January 1994 with effect for 1993–94 and subsequent years of assessment. Former s. 296(6) provided as follows:
"296(6) In calculating the aggregate mentioned in subsection (1)(a) above in respect of any period of 12 months which begins on or before 18th March 1986, any amount raised by the issue of eligible shares on or before that date shall be disregarded.".

Derivations – (as originally enacted) – FA 1983, Sch. 5, para. 5C(1)–(6) (as inserted by FA 1986, s. 40(1) and Sch. 9, para. 7).

Cross references – S. 293(8B): any time on or after 29 November 1994 to be ignored in arriving at the relevant period for the purposes of s. 294–296.
FA 1988, Sch. 4, para. 7: s. 296 does not apply where eligible shares issued for the purpose of raising finance for private rented housing under BES.

297 Qualifying trades

297 [Omitted by ITA 2007, s. 1027 and Sch. 1, para. 627 and repealed by ITA 2007, Sch. 3, Pt. 2 with effect in relation to shares issued after 5 April 2007.]

History – S. 297 omitted by ITA 2007, s. 1027 and Sch. 1, para. 627 and repealed by ITA 2007, s. 1031 and Sch. 3, Pt. 2 with effect in relation to shares issued after 5 April 2007. In so far as it continues to apply in relation to shares issued before 6 April 2007, s. 297 is as follows:

"**297(1)** A trade is a qualifying trade if it complies with the requirements of this section.

297(2) Subject to subsection (9) below, the trade must not at any time in the relevant period consist of one or more of the following activities if that activity amounts, or those activities when taken together amount, to a substantial part of the trade–

(a) dealing in land, in commodities or futures or in shares, securities or other financial instruments;

(b) dealing in goods otherwise than in the course of an ordinary trade of wholesale or retail distribution;

(c) banking, insurance, money-lending, debt-factoring, hire-purchase financing or other financial activities;

(d) [Omitted by FA 2001, Sch. 15, para. 5 and Sch. 33, Pt. 2(3).]

(e) leasing (including letting ships on charter or other assets on hire) or receiving royalties or licence fees;

(f) providing legal or accountancy services;

(fa) property development;

(fb) farming or market gardening;

(fc) holding, managing or occupying woodlands, any other forestry activities or timber production;

(fd) operating or managing hotels or comparable establishments or managing property used as an hotel or comparable establishment;

(fe) operating or managing nursing homes or residential care homes, or managing property used as a nursing home or residential care home;

(g) providing services or facilities for any trade carried on by another person (other than a company of which the company providing the services or facilities is the subsidiary) which consists to any substantial extent of activities within any of paragraphs (a) to (fe) above and in which a controlling interest is held by a person who also has a controlling interest in the trade carried on by the company;

(h-j) [Repealed by FA 1994, s. 137 and Sch. 15, para. 10, and s. 258 and Sch. 26, Pt. V(17).]

297(3) For the purposes of subsection (2)(b) above–

(a) a trade of wholesale distribution is one in which the goods are offered for sale and sold to persons for resale by them, or for processing and resale by them, to members of the general public for their use or consumption;

(b) a trade of retail distribution is one in which the goods are offered for sale and sold to members of the general public for their use or consumption;

(c) a trade is not an ordinary trade of wholesale or retail distribution if–

(i) it consists to a substantial extent of dealing in goods of a kind which are collected or held as an investment or of that activity and any other activity of a kind falling within subsection (2)(a) to (g) above, taken together; and

(ii) a substantial proportion of those goods are held by the company for a period which is significantly longer than the period for which a vendor would reasonably be expected to hold them while endeavouring to dispose of them at their market value; and

(d) in determining whether a trade is an ordinary trade of wholesale or retail distribution regard shall be had to the extent to which it has the following features, that is to say–

(i) the goods are bought by the trader in quantities larger than those in which he sells them;

(ii) the goods are bought and sold by the trader in different markets;

(iii) the trader employs staff and incurs expenses in the trade in addition to the cost of the goods and, in the case of a trade carried on by a company, in addition to any remuneration paid to any person connected with it;

(iv) there are purchases or sales from or to persons who are connected with the trader;

(v) purchases are matched with forward sales or vice versa;

(vi) the goods are held by the trader for longer than is normal for goods of the kind in question;

(vii) the trade is carried on otherwise than at a place or places commonly used for wholesale or retail trade;

(viii) the trader does not take physical possession of the goods;

those features in sub-paragraphs (i) to (iii) being regarded as indications that the trade is such an ordinary trade and those in sub-paragraphs (iv) to (viii) being regarded as indications of the contrary.

297(3A) For the purposes of this Chapter the activities of a person shall not be taken to fall within paragraph (fd) or (fe) of subsection (2) above except where that person has an estate or interest in, or is in occupation of, the hotels or comparable establishments or, as the case may be, the nursing homes or residential care homes.

297(4) A trade shall not be treated as failing to comply with this section by reason only that at some time in the relevant period it consists to a substantial extent in the receiving of royalties or licence fees if the royalties and licence fees (or all but for a part that is not a substantial part in terms of value) are attributable to the exploitation of relevant intangible assets.

297(5) For this purpose an intangible asset is a **"relevant intangible asset"** if the whole or greater part (in terms of value) of it has been created–

(a) by the company mentioned in section 293(1), or

(b) by a company which was a subsidiary of that company throughout a period during which it created the whole or greater part (in terms of value) of the intangible asset.

297(5A) For the purposes of subsection (5) above–

(a) in the case of an intangible asset that is intellectual property, references to the creation of the asset by a company are to its creation in circumstances in which the right to exploit it vests in the company (whether alone or jointly with others);

(b) [omitted by FA 2007, s. 51 and Sch. 16, para. 11(1)(b) and repealed by s. 114 and Sch. 27, Pt. 2(16);]

(c) [omitted by FA 2007, s. 51 and Sch. 16, para. 11(1)(b) and repealed by s. 114 and Sch. 27, Pt. 2(16).]

297(5B) For the purposes of subsections (4) to (5A) above **"intangible asset"** means any asset which falls to be treated as an intangible asset in accordance with generally accepted accounting practice.

297(5C) In subsection (5A)(a) above **"intellectual property"** means–

(a) any patent, trade mark, registered design, copyright, design right, performer's right or plant breeder's right; and

(b) any rights under the law of a country or territory outside the United Kingdom which correspond or are similar to those falling within paragraph (a) above.

297(5D) If–

(a) the company mentioned in section 293(1) ("the issuing company") acquired all the shares ("old shares") in another company ("the old company") at a time when the only shares issued in the issuing company were subscriber shares, and

(b) the consideration for the old shares consisted wholly of the issue of shares in the issuing company,

references in subsection (5) above to the company mentioned in section 293(1) include the old company.

297(6) A trade shall not be treated as failing to comply with this section by reason only of its consisting of letting ships, other than offshore installations or pleasure craft, on charter if–

(a) every ship let on charter by the company carrying on the trade is beneficially owned by the company;

(b) every ship beneficially owned by the company is registered in the United Kingdom; and

(c) throughout the relevant period the company is solely responsible for arranging the marketing of the services of its ships; and

(d) the conditions mentioned in subsection (7) below are satisfied in relation to every letting on charter by the company;

but where any of the requirements mentioned in paragraphs (a) to (d) above are not satisfied in relation to any lettings of such ships, the trade shall not thereby be treated as failing to comply with this section if those lettings and any other activity of a kind falling within subsection (2)(a) to (g) above do not, when taken together, amount to a substantial part of the trade.

297(7) The conditions are that–

(a) the letting is for a period not exceeding 12 months and no provision is made at any time (whether in the lease or otherwise) for extending it beyond that period otherwise than at the option of the lessee;

(b) during the period of the letting there is no provision in force (whether made in the lease or otherwise) for the grant of a new letting to end, otherwise than at the option of the lessee, more than 12 months after that provision is made;

(c) the letting is by way of a bargain made at arms length between the company and a person who is not connected with it;
(d) under the terms of the charter the company is responsible as principal–
(i) for taking, throughout the period of the charter, management decisions in relation to the ship, other than those of a kind generally regarded by persons engaged in trade of the kind in question as matters of husbandry; and
(ii) for defraying all expenses in connection with the ship throughout that period, or substantially all such expenses, other than those directly incidental to a particular voyage or to the employment of the ship during that period; and
(e) no arrangements exist by virtue of which a person other than the company may be appointed to be responsible for the matters mentioned in paragraph (d) above on behalf of the company;

but this subsection shall have effect, in relation to any letting between the company in question and its subsidiary, or between it and another company of which it is a subsidiary or between it and a company which is a subsidiary of the same company of which it is a subsidiary, as if paragraph (c) were omitted.

297(8) The trade must, during the relevant period, be conducted on a commercial basis and with a view to the realisation of profits.

297(9) [Omitted by FA 2001, Sch. 15, para. 5 and Sch. 33, Pt. 2(3).]"

In s. 297(1), the words "Subject to section 298(7) below," which appeared at the start of the subsection repealed by FA 1998, s 74(1) and Sch. 13, para. 10, s. 165 and Sch. 27, Pt. III(14), with effect in relation to shares issued on or after 6 April 1998.

In s. 297(1), the words "(6) and" which appeared before "(7)" repealed by FA 1994, s. 137 and Sch. 15, para. 10(a), and s. 258 and Sch. 26, Pt. V(17), in relation to shares issued on or after 1 January 1994 with effect for 1993–94 and subsequent years of assessment.

In s. 297(2)(a), the words "land … instruments" substituted for former words "commodities, shares, securities, land or futures" and in s. 297(2)(g) the words in parentheses inserted by FA 1994, s. 137 and Sch. 15, para. 10(b), in relation to shares issued on or after 1 January 1994 with effect for 1993–94 and subsequent years of assessment.

S. 297(2)(d) omitted by FA 2001, Sch. 15, para. 5 and Sch. 33, Pt. II(3) in relation to shares issued on or after 7 March 2001; and in respect of the application of ICTA 1988, Pt. VII, Ch. III and TCGA 1992, Sch. 5B, on or after 7 March 2001 in relation to shares:

- that were issued after 31 December 1993 but before 7 March 2001, and
- to which income tax relief or deferral relief was attributable immediately before 7 March 2001.

S. 297(2)(fa)–(fe) inserted by FA 1998, s. 70(1) and Sch. 12, para. 1(1) and reference to "(fe)" substituted for "(f)" in s. 297(2)(g) by Sch. 12, para. 1(2), with effect in relation to shares issued on or after 17 March 1998.

S. 297(2)(h) and (j) repealed by FA 1994, s. 137 and Sch. 15, para. 10(b), and s. 258 and Sch. 26, Pt. V(17), in relation to shares issued on or after 1 January 1994 with effect for 1993–94 and subsequent years of assessment.

In s. 297(3)(c)(i), "(2)(a) to (g)" substituted for "(2)" by FA 1997, s. 74 and Sch. 8, para. 5 with effect in relation to shares issued after 26 November 1996, and with effect after 26 November 1996 in relation to shares which were issued on or after 1 January 1994 but before 27 November 1996, and immediately before 27 November 1996 were held by an individual and at that time were shares to which relief (within the meaning of Pt. VII, Ch. III) was attributable.

S. 297(3A) inserted by FA 1998, s. 70(1) and Sch. 12, para. 1(3), with effect in relation to shares issued on or after 17 March 1998.

S. 297(5)(a) and (b) substituted by FA 2007, s. 51 and Sch. 16, para. 11(1)(a), with effect from 6 April 2007 (subject to the transitional provisions at FA 2007, Sch. 16, para. 14). Former s. 297(5)(a) and (b) read as follows:

"(a) by the company carrying on the trade, or
(b) by a company which at all times during which it created the intangible asset was–
(i) the parent company of the company carrying on the trade, or
(ii) a qualifying subsidiary of that parent company.".

S. 297(5A)(b) and (c) and the words "For the purposes of paragraph (c) above, section 308 shall have effect as if the references in that section to the qualifying company were to that parent company." which followed para. (c) omitted by FA 2007, s. 51 and Sch. 16, para. 11(1)(b) and repealed by s. 114 and Sch. 27, Pt. 2(16), with effect from 6 April 2007 (subject to the transitional provisions at FA 2007, Sch. 16, para. 14). Former s. 297(5A)(b) and (c) read as follows:

"(b) **"parent company"** means a company that–
(i) has one or more 51% subsidiaries, but
(ii) is not itself a 51% subsidiary of another company; and
(c) a subsidiary of the parent company referred to in subsection (5)(b) above is a **"qualifying subsidiary"** of that company if it is a subsidiary of a kind which the parent company may hold by virtue of section 308."

In former s. 297(5), the words "A trade … if" substituted for former words "A trade shall not be treated as failing to comply with this section by reason only of its consisting to a substantial extent of receiving royalties or licence fees if" by FA 1994, s. 137 and Sch 15, para. 10(c), in relation to shares issued on or after 1 January 1994 with effect for 1993–94 and subsequent years of assessment.

In s. 297(5B), words "generally accepted accounting practice" substituted for "normal accounting practice" by FA 2002, s. 103(4)(a), and second sentence (which defined "normal accounting practice" as normal accounting practice in relation to the accounts of companies incorporated in any part of the UK) repealed by FA 2002, s. 141 and Sch. 40, Pt. 3(16).

S. 297(5D) inserted by FA 2007, s. 51 and Sch. 16, para. 11(1)(c), with effect from 6 April 2007 (subject to the transitional provisions at FA 2007, Sch. 16, para. 14).

S. 297(4)–(5C) substituted for former s. 297(4), (5) by FA 2000, s. 64 and Sch. 17, para. 13(1), with effect in relation to shares issued on or after 6 April 2000. S. 297(4), (5) previously read as follows:

"**297(4)** A trade shall not be treated as failing to comply with this section by reason only of its consisting to a substantial extent of receiving royalties or licence fees if–
(a) the company carrying on the trade is engaged throughout the relevant period in–
(i) the production of films; or
(ii) the production of films and the distribution of films produced by it in the relevant period; and
(b) all royalties and licence fees received by it in that period are in respect of films produced by it in that period or sound recordings in relation to such films or other products arising from such films.

297(5) A trade shall not be treated as failing to comply with this section by reason only that it consists to a substantial extent of receiving royalties or licence fees if–
(a) the company carrying on the trade is engaged in research and development throughout the relevant period; and
(b) all royalties and licence fees received by it in that period are attributable to research and development which it has carried out.".

In s. 297(6) the words "offshore installations" substituted for "oil rigs" by FA 2004, s. 146 and Sch. 27, para. 4(3), with effect, subject to the provisions at FA 2004, Sch. 27, para. 4(6), in relation to shares issued on or after 6 April 2004.

In s. 297(6), in the words after para. (d), "(2)(a) to (g)" substituted for "(2)" by FA 1997, s. 74 and Sch. 8, para. 5 with effect in relation to shares issued after 26 November 1996, and with effect after 26 November 1996 in relation to shares which were issued on or after 1 January 1994 but before 27 November 1996, and immediately before 27 November 1996 were held by an individual and at that time were shares to which relief (within the meaning of Pt. VII, Ch. III) was attributable.

S. 297(9) omitted by FA 2001, Sch. 15, para. 5 and Sch. 33, Pt. 2(3) in relation to shares issued on or after 7 March 2001; and in respect of the application of ICTA 1988, Pt. VII, Ch. III and TCGA 1992, Sch. 5B, on or after 7 March 2001 in relation to shares:

- that were issued after 31 December 1993 but before 7 March 2001, and
- to which income tax relief or deferral relief was attributable immediately before 7 March 2001.

Derivations – S. 297(1) (as originally enacted): FA 1983, Sch. 5, para. 6(1).

S. 297(2)(a)–(g) (as originally enacted): FA 1983, Sch. 5, para. 6(2), as substituted by FA 1986, s. 40(1) and Sch. 9, para. 8(2). See also s. 298(7).

Former s. 297(2)(h): FA 1985, s. 44(3), amending FA 1983, Sch. 5, para. 6(2) prior to substitution by FA 1986, Sch. 9, para. 8(2). See also s. 298(6)(b).
Former s. 297(2)(j): FA 1984, s. 37(1), amending FA 1983, Sch. 5, para. 6(2) prior to substitution by FA 1986, Sch. 9, para. 8(2). See also s. 298(6)(c).
S. 297(3)(a)–(c): FA 1983, Sch. 5, para. 6(2A), as substituted by FA 1986, s. 40(1) and Sch. 9, para. 8(4).
S. 297(3)(d): FA 1983, Sch. 5, para. 6(4), as substituted by FA 1986, s. 40(1), Sch. 9, para. 8(4), and FA 1981, s. 56(3).
S. 297(3)(d)(i)–(viii): FA 1983, Sch. 11, para. 1–8.
S. 297(4): FA 1983, Sch. 5, para. 6(2A), as inserted by FA 1984, s. 37(2), and amended by FA 1987, s. 43(1) by substituting new subpara. (a) and (b).
S. 297(5) (as originally enacted): FA 1983, Sch. 5, para. 6(2AA), as inserted by FA 1985, s. 44(4).
S. 297(6): FA 1983, Sch. 5, para. 8(2B), as substituted by FA 1986, s. 40(1) and Sch. 9, para. 8(3).
S. 297(7): FA 1983, Sch. 5, para. 6(2C), as substituted by FA 1986, s. 40(1) and Sch. 9, para. 8(3).
S. 297(8): FA 1983, Sch. 5, para. 6(3).
S. 297(9) (as originally enacted): FA 1983, Sch. 5, para. 2B(7), as inserted by FA 1986, s. 40(1) and Sch. 9, para. 4(1).

Cross references – S. 576(4A)(d): modified application of s. 297 in defining "qualifying trading company" for relief for losses on shares in unlisted trading companies.
S. 836A: meaning of generally accepted accounting practice (s. 297(5B)).
FA 1988, Sch. 4, para. 8: disapplication where eligible shares issued for the purpose of raising finance for private rented housing under BES.

HMRC interpretations – IRInt. 227: qualifying trade – leasing, receiving royalties and receiving licence fees.

Hansard – HC Standing Committee on Finance Bill 1986, 17 July 1986, col. 1268 (not reproduced): "substantial", in relation to non-qualifying activities, means, as a rule of thumb, about 20 per cent of the trade (confirmed Hansard 9 May 1988, col. 42).

HMRC Manuals – Inspector's Manual, IM6998: excluded activities.
Inspector's Manual, vol. III, IM 7003: definition of controlling interest.

Other material – ICAEW Technical Release TR 676 (not reproduced): Revenue confirm that, for s. 297(4)(a)(ii), it is not necessary for film production to be carried on throughout the qualifying period.

Notes – S. 297 rewritten for income tax purposes as follows:
S. 297(2): ITA 2007, s. 189(1), 192(1), 199(1).
S. 297(3): ITA 2007, s. 193(3), (4), (5), (6), (7).
S. 297(3A): ITA 2007, s. 197(3), 198(4).
S. 297(4): ITA 2007, s. 195(2), (3).
S. 297(5): ITA 2007, s. 195(4).
S. 297(5A): ITA 2007, s. 195(5), (6), 257(1).
S. 297(5B): ITA 2007, s. 195(6).
S. 297(5C): ITA 2007, s. 195(6).
S. 297(6): ITA 2007, s. 194(1), (3), (4), (7).
S. 297(7): ITA 2007, s. 194(5), (6).
S. 297(8): ITA 2007, s. 189(1).

Accounting Standard – Explanations of "generally accepted accounting practice" in specified circumstances.

298 Provisions supplementary to sections 293 and 297

298 [Omitted by ITA 2007, s. 1027 and Sch. 1, para. 627 and repealed by ITA 2007, s. 1031 and Sch. 3, Pt. 2 with effect in relation to shares issued after 5 April 2007.]

History – S. 298 omitted by ITA 2007, s. 1027 and Sch. 1, para. 627 and repealed by ITA 2007, s. 1031 and Sch. 3, Pt. 2 with effect in relation to shares issued on or after 5 April 2007. In so far as it continues to apply in relation to shares issued before 6 April 2007, s. 298 is as follows:

"298(1) For the purposes of section 297 a person has a controlling interest in a trade–
(a) in the case of a trade carried on by a company, if–
(i) he controls the company;
(ii) the company is a close company and he or an associate of his is a director of the company and the beneficial owner of, or able directly or through the medium of other companies or by any other indirect means to control, more than 30 per cent of the ordinary share capital of the company; or
(iii) not less than half of the trade could in accordance with section 344(2) be regarded as belonging to him;
(b) in any other case, if he is entitled to not less than half of the assets used for, or the income arising from, the trade.

298(2) For the purposes of subsection (1) above, there shall be attributed to any person any rights or powers of any other person who is an associate of his.

298(3) References in this section and section 297 to a trade shall be construed without regard to section 989 of ITA 2007 (which defines "trade" as including any venture in the nature of trade); but the foregoing provisions do not affect the construction of references in section 297(2)(g) or subsection (1) above to a trade carried on by a person other than the company and those references shall be construed as including a reference to any business, profession or vocation.

298(4) The Treasury may by order amend sections 293 and 297 and this section in such manner as they consider expedient.

298(5) In section 297–

"film" means an original master negative of a film, an original master film disc or an original master film tape;

"nursing home" means any establishment which exists wholly or mainly for the provision of nursing care for persons suffering from sickness, injury or infirmity or for women who are pregnant or have given birth to children;

"pleasure craft" means any ship of a kind primarily used for sport or recreation;

"property development" means the development of land–
(a) by a company which has, or at any time has had, an interest in the land, and
(b) with the sole or main object of realising a gain from the disposal of an interest in the land when it is developed;

"residential care home" means any establishment which exists wholly or mainly for the provision of residential accommodation, together with board and personal care, for persons in need of personal care by reason of old age, mental or physical disabilities, past or present dependence on alcohol or drugs or any past illnesses or past or present mental disorders; and

"sound recording" means, in relation to a film, its sound track, original master audio disc or, as the case may be, original master audio tape;

and section 312(1A)(b) shall apply to determine the relevant period for the purposes of that section.

298(5A) References in this section, in relation to an hotel, to a comparable establishment are references to a guest house, hostel or other establishment the main purpose of maintaining which is the provision of facilities for overnight accommodation (whether with or without catering services).

298(5B) Subject to subsection (5C) below, the reference in subsection (5) above to an interest in land is a reference to–

(a) any estate, interest or right in or over land, including any right affecting the use or disposition of land; or
(b) any right to obtain such an estate, interest or right from another which is conditional on the other's ability to grant the estate, interest or right.

298(5C) References in this section to an interest in land do not include references to–
(a) the interest of a creditor (other than a creditor in respect of a rentcharge) whose debt is secured by way of mortgage, an agreement for a mortgage or a charge of any kind over land; or
(b) in the case of land in Scotland, the interest of a creditor in a charge or security of any kind over land

298(6)–(8) [Repealed by FA 1994, s. 137 and Sch. 15, para. 11, and s. 258 and Sch. 26, Pt. V(17).]"

In s. 298(1) words "section 297" substituted for "sections 293(9) and 297" by FA 1998, s. 74(1) and Sch. 13, para. 11, with effect in relation to shares issued on or after 6 April 1998.

In s. 298(3) the words "section 989 of ITA 2007 (which defines "trade" as including any venture in the nature of trade)" substituted for the words "so much of the definition of "trade" in section 832(1) as relates to adventures or concerns in the nature of trade" by SI 2007/1820, art 2(3), with effect, for income tax purposes, for 2007–08 and subsequent tax years and, for corporation tax purposes, for accounting periods ending after 5 April 2007.

In s. 298(4) words "sections 293 and 297" substituted for "section 297" by FA 1998, s. 70(2) as respects Treasury orders in relation to shares issued on or after 13 March 1998.

S. 298(4) substituted by FA 1994, s. 137 and Sch. 15, para. 11(a), in relation to shares issued on or after 1 January 1994 with effect for 1993–94 and subsequent years of assessment. S. 298(4) formerly read as follows:

"**298(4)** The Treasury may by order amend section 297 and this section except in relation to shares issued before 19th March 1986, in such manner as they think expedient.".

In s. 298(5) the definition of "oil rig" repealed by FA 2004, s. 146 and Sch. 27, para. 4(4), and s. 326, Sch. 42, Pt. 2(19) with effect, subject to the provisions at FA 2004, Sch. 27, para. 4(6), in relation to shares issued on or after 6 April 2004. The former definition provided as follows:

""**oil rig**" means any ship which is an offshore installation for the purposes of the Mineral Workings (Offshore Installations) Act 1971;"

S. 298(5) the definitions of "nursing home", "property development" and "residential care home" inserted by FA 1998, s. 70(1) and Sch. 12, para. 2, with effect in relation to shares issued on or after 17 March 1998.

In s. 298(4), the definition of "property development" repealed by FA 1994, s. 137 and Sch. 15, para. 11(b), and s. 258 and Sch. 26, Pt. V(17), and the words "and section … that section" inserted by FA 1994, s. 137 and Sch. 15, para. 11(c), in relation to shares issued on or after 1 January 1994 with effect for 1993–94 and subsequent years of assessment. The former definition provided as follows:

""**property development**" means the development of land, by a company which has, or at any time has had, an interest in the land (within the meaning of section 294(5)), with the sole or main object of realising a gain from disposing of the land when developed;".

S. 298(5A), (5B) and (5C) inserted by FA 1998, s. 70(1) and Sch. 12, para. 2(3), with effect in relation to shares issued on or after 17 March 1998.

S. 298(6)–(8) repealed by FA 1994, s. 137 and Sch. 15, para. 11(d), and s. 258 and Sch. 26, Pt. V(17), in relation to shares issued on or after 1 January 1994 with effect for 1993–94 and subsequent years of assessment. Former s. 298(6)–(8) provided as follows:

"**298(6)** Section 297 shall have effect in relation to shares issued before 19th March 1986 subject to the following modifications–
(a) in subsection (2) the words "or those activities when taken together amount" shall be omitted;
(b) subsection (2)(h) shall not apply unless the shares were issued after 19th March 1985;
(c) subsection (2)(j) shall not apply unless the shares were issued after 13th March 1984;
(d) in subsection (3) the words in paragraph (a) "to members of the general public for their use or consumption" and paragraph (c) shall be omitted; and
(e) subsections (6) and (7) shall be omitted;

and in relation to shares issued after 18th March 1986 section 297(2) shall have effect with the omission of paragraphs (h) and (j)

298(7) Section 297(2) shall have effect so far as it relates to oil extraction only in relation to shares issued after 25th July 1986.

298(8) Section 297(4) shall have effect in relation to shares issued before 17th March 1987 with the omission of paragraph (a) (ii) together with the word "or" immediately before it, (but not the word "and" at the end of it) and the words in paragraph (b) "in that period" in the second place where they appear.".

Derivations – (as originally enacted) – In relation to shares issued before 19 March 1986, s. 298(1) derived from FA 1981, s. 56(8) as applied by FA 1983, Sch. 5, para. 5(9).

In relation to shares issued after 18 March 1986, s. 298(1) derived from FA 1983, Sch. 5, para. 6(5) as substituted for former para. 6(4) by FA 1986, s. 40(1) and Sch. 9, para. 1(2), 8(4).

In relation to shares issued before 19 March 1986, s. 298(2) derived from FA 1981, s. 56(9) as applied by FA 1983, Sch. 5, para. 5(9).

In relation to shares issued after 18 March 1986, s. 298(2) derived from FA 1983, Sch. 5, para. 6(6) as substituted for former para. 6(4) by FA 1986, s. 40(1) and Sch. 9, para. 1(2), 8(4).

In relation to shares issued before 19 March 1986, s. 298(3) derived from FA 1981, s. 56(10) as applied by FA 1983, Sch. 5, former para. 6(4).

In relation to shares issued after 18 March 1986, s. 298(3) derived from FA 1983, Sch. 5, para. 6(7) as substituted for former para. 6(4) by FA 1986, s. 40(1) and Sch. 9, para. 1(2), 8(4).

S. 298(4): FA 1983, Sch. 5, para. 6(8) (as substituted for former para. 6(4) by FA 1986, s. 40(1) and Sch. 9, para. 8(4); FA 1986, s. 40(1) and Sch. 9, para. 1(2).

S. 298(5): FA 1983, Sch. 5, para. 6(10) (as substituted for former para. 6(4) by FA 1986, s. 40(1) and Sch. 9, para. 8(4)), and, in relation to shares issued before 19 March 1986, from FA 1983, Sch. 5, former para. 6(2B) (as inserted by FA 1984, s. 37(2) and amended by FA 1985, s. 44(5)).

S. 298(7): FA 1986, Sch. 9. para. 8(5).

Cross references – S. 344(2), (3): trade belonging to a company deemed normally to belong to its ordinary shareholders in proportion to their holdings, subject to detailed provisions as to deemed shareholdings and subsidiaries.

S. 576(4B)(c): modified application of s. 298(5) in defining "qualifying trading company" for relief for losses on shares in unlisted trading companies.

FA 1988, Sch. 4, para. 8: s. 298 does not apply where eligible shares issued for the purpose of raising finance for private rented housing under BES.

Mineral Workings (Offshore Installations) Act 1971, s. 1(3) (not reproduced): an offshore installation is any installation maintained or intended to be established for underwater exploration or exploitation of mineral resources.

Notes – S. 298 rewritten for income tax purposes as follows:
S. 298(1): ITA 2007, s. 199(3), (4).
S. 298(2): ITA 2007, s. 199(5).
S. 298(3): ITA 2007, s. 189(2), 199(5).
S. 298(4): ITA 2007, s. 144, 200, Sch. 1 para. 129.
S. 298(5): ITA 2007, s. 189(1), 194(4), (8), 196(2), 198(2), (3).
S. 298(5A): ITA 2007, s. 197(2).
S. 298(5B): ITA 2007, s. 196(3).
S. 298(5C): ITA 2007, s. 196(4).

299 Disposal of shares

299 [Omitted by ITA 2007, s. 1027 and Sch. 1, para. 627 and repealed by ITA 2007, s. 1031 and Sch. 3, Pt. 2 with effect in relation to shares issued after 5 April 2007.]

History – S. 299 omitted by ITA 2007, s. 1027 and Sch. 1, para. 627 and repealed by ITA 2007, s. 1031 and Sch. 3, Pt. 3 with effect in relation to shares issued on or after 5 April 2007. In so far as it continues to apply in relation to shares issued before 6 April 2007, s. 299 is as follows:

"**299(1)** Subject to section 304(1), where an individual makes, before the end of the relevant period, any disposal of eligible shares to which relief is attributable, then–

(a) if the disposal is made otherwise than by way of a bargain made at arm's length, the relief attributable to those shares shall be withdrawn, and

(b) in the case of any disposal made by way of a bargain made at arm's length–

(i) if, apart from this subsection, the relief attributable to those shares is greater than the amount mentioned in subsection (2) below, it shall be reduced by that amount, and

(ii) if sub-paragraph (i) above does not apply, the relief attributable to those shares shall be withdrawn.

299(2) The amount referred to in subsection (1) above is an amount equal to tax at the lower rate for the year of assessment for which the relief was given on the amount or value of the consideration which the individual receives for the shares.

299(3) Where, in relation to any issue of eligible shares held by any individual, the disposal referred to in subsection (1) above is a disposal of part of the issue, that subsection shall apply to the relief that was attributable to that part.

299(4) Where an individual's liability to income tax has been reduced in any year of assessment under section 289A in respect of any issue of eligible shares issued in that year (or treated by section 289B(5) as so issued) and the amount of the reduction ("A") is less than the amount ("B") which is equal to tax at the lower rate for that year on the amount subscribed for the issue, subsection (2) above shall have effect as if the amount or value referred to in that subsection were reduced by multiplying it by the fraction–

$$\frac{A}{B}$$

299(5) Where an option, the exercise of which would bind the grantor to purchase any shares, is granted to an individual during the relevant period, any relief attributable to the shares to which the option relates shall be withdrawn.

299(5A) The shares to which such an option relates shall be taken to be those which, if–

(a) the option were exercised immediately after the grant; and

(b) any shares in the company acquired by the individual after the grant were disposed of immediately after being acquired,

would be treated for the purposes of this section as disposed of in pursuance of the option.

299(6) Where shares of any class in a company have been acquired by an individual on different days, any disposal by him of shares of that class shall be treated for the purposes of this section as relating to those acquired on an earlier day rather than to those acquired on a later day.

299(6A) Where shares of any class in a company have been acquired by an individual on the same day, any of those shares disposed of by him shall be treated for the purposes of this section as disposed of in the following order, namely–

(a) first any to which neither relief under this Chapter nor deferral relief is attributable;

(b) next any to which deferral relief, but not relief under this Chapter, is attributable;

(c) next any to which relief under this Chapter, but not deferral relief, is attributable; and

(d) finally any to which both relief under this Chapter and deferral relief are attributable;

and in this subsection and subsection (6C) below "deferral relief" has the same meaning as in Schedule 5B to the 1992 Act.

299(6B) Any shares falling within paragraph (c) or (d) of subsection (6A) above which are treated by section 289B(5) as issued on an earlier day shall be treated as disposed of before any other shares falling within that paragraph.

299(6C) The following, namely–

(a) any shares to which relief under this Chapter is attributable and which were transferred to an individual as mentioned in section 304; and

(b) any shares to which deferral relief, but not relief under this Chapter, is attributable and which were acquired by an individual on a disposal to which section 58 of the 1992 Act applies,

shall be treated for the purposes of subsections (6) and (6A) above as acquired by him on the day on which they were issued.

299(6D) In a case to which section 127 of the 1992 Act applies (including a case where that section applies by virtue of any enactment relating to chargeable gains), shares comprised in the new holding shall be treated for the purposes of subsections (6) and (6A) above as acquired when the original shares were acquired.

In this subsection "new holding" and "original shares" have the same meaning as in section 127 of the 1992 Act (or, as the case may be, that section as applied by virtue of the enactment concerned).

299(7) [Repealed by FA 1998, s. 74(1) and Sch. 13, para. 12(6), s. 165 and Sch. 27, Pt. III(14) in relation to disposals made on or after 6 April 1998.]

299(8) For the purposes of this section–

(a) [repealed by FA 1998, s. 74(1) and Sch. 13, para. 12(7), s. 165 and Sch. 27, Pt. III(14) as respects shares issued on or after 6 April 1998.]

(b) references to a disposal of shares include references to the grant of an option the exercise of which would bind the grantor to sell the shares, and

(c) section 312(1A)(a) applies to determine the relevant period."

In s. 299(1) the words from the beginning to "relief is attributable" substituted for "Where an individual makes any disposal of eligible shares before the end of the relevant period", and references to "the relief" substituted for "any relief", by FA 1998, s. 74(1) and Sch. 13, para. 12(1), in relation to disposals made on or after 6 April 1998.

In s. 299(3) the words "any issue of eligible shares held by any individual" substituted for "any issue of shares held by any person", and "the issue" substituted for "the shares", by FA 1998, s. 74(1) and Sch. 13, para. 12(2) in relation to shares issued on or after 6 April 1998.

In s. 299(4) the words "eligible" inserted by FA 1998, s. 74(1) and Sch. 13, para. 12(3)(a) in relation to shares issued on or after 6 April 1998, and words "issued in that year (or treated by section 289B(5) as so issued)" inserted by FA 1998, s. 74(1) and Sch. 13, para. 12(3)(b) in relation to disposals made on or after 6 April 1998.

S. 299(5A) inserted by FA 1998, s. 74(1) and Sch. 13, para. 12(4) in relation to options granted on or after 6 April 1998.

In s. 299(6D), the words "including a case where that section applies by virtue of any enactment relating to chargeable gains" substituted for the words "whether or not by virtue of section 135(3) of that Act" and the words "have the same meaning as in section 127 of the 1992 Act (or, as the case may be, that section as applied by virtue of the enactment concerned" substituted for the words "shall be construed in accordance with sections 126, 127, 135 and 136 of the 1992 Act" by FA 2002, Sch. 9, para. 4(2)(a),with effect for disposal after 16 April 2002.

S. 299(6)–(6D) substituted for former s. 299(6) by FA 1998, s. 74(1) and Sch. 13, para. 12(5) in relation to disposals made on or after 6 April 1998.

S. 299(7) repealed by FA1998, s. 74(1) and Sch. 13, para. 12(6), s. 165 and Sch. 27, Pt. III(14), in relation to disposals made on or after 6 April 1998.

S. 299(8)(a) repealed by FA 1998, s. 74(1) and Sch. 13, para. 12(7), s. 165 and Sch. 27, Pt. III(14), in relation to shares issued on or after 6 April 1998. The repealed subsection (8)(a) read: "shares in a company shall not be treated as being of the same class unless they would be so treated if dealt with on the Stock Exchange"
S. 299 substituted by FA 1994, s. 137 and Sch. 15, para. 12, in relation to shares issued on or after 1 January 1994 with effect for 1993–94 and subsequent years of assessment. Former s. 299 provided as follows:
"299(1) Subject to section 304(5), where an individual disposes of any eligible shares before the end of the relevant period, then–
(a) if the disposal is otherwise than by way of a bargain made at arm's length, he shall not be entitled to any relief in respect of those shares; and
(b) in any other case, the amount of relief to which he is entitled in respect of those shares shall be reduced by the amount or value of the consideration which he receives for them.
299(2) Where after 18th March 1986 an option, the exercise of which would bind the grantor to purchase any shares, is granted to an individual during the relevant period, the individual shall not be entitled to any relief in respect of the shares to which the option relates.
299(3) Where an individual holds ordinary shares of any class in a company and the relief has been given (and not withdrawn) in respect of some shares of that class but not others, any disposal by him of ordinary shares of that class in the company, and any option of the kind mentioned in subsection (2) above, shall be treated for the purposes of this section as relating–
(a) first, to those (if any) in respect of which relief has been given (and not withdrawn) under Chapter II of Part IV of the Finance Act 1981 rather than to others; and
(b) then, to those in respect of which relief has been given (and not withdrawn) under this Chapter (or Schedule 5 to the Finance Act 1983).
299(4) Where shares of any class in a company have been acquired by an individual on different days, any disposal by him of shares of that class shall, subject to subsection (3) above, be treated for the purposes of this section as relating to those acquired on an earlier day rather than to those acquired on a later day.
299(4A) Where shares of any class in a company have been acquired by an individual on the same day, any disposal by him of shares of that class shall, subject to subsection (3) above, be treated for the purposes of this section as relating to those in respect of which relief has not been given, or has been withdrawn, rather than to those in respect of which relief has been given and has not been withdrawn.
299(4B) Any shares in respect of which relief has been given and has not been withdrawn and which were transferred to an individual as mentioned in section 304 shall be treated for the purposes of subsections (4) and (4A) above as acquired by him on the day on which they were issued.
299(4C) In a case to which section 127 of the 1992 Act applies (whether or not by virtue of section 135(3) of that Act), shares comprised in the new holding shall be treated for the purposes of subsections (4) and (4A) above as acquired when the original shares were acquired.
In this subsection "new holding" and "original shares" shall be construed in accordance with section 126, 127, 135 and 136 of the 1992 Act.
299(5) Where shares in respect of which the relief was given have by virtue of any such allotment as is mentioned in section 126(2)(a) of the 1992 Act (not being an allotment for payment) fallen to be treated under section 127 of that Act as the same asset as a new holding–
(a) a disposal of the whole or part of the new holding shall be treated for the purposes of this section as a disposal of the whole or a corresponding part of those shares; and
(b) the new holding shall be treated for the purposes of subsection (3) above as shares in respect of which the relief has been given.
299(6) For the purposes of this section–
(a) shares in a company shall not be treated as being of the same class unless they would be so treated if dealt with on the Stock Exchange; and
(b) references to a disposal of shares include references to the grant of an option (after 18th March 1986) the exercise of which would bind the grantor to sell the shares."
At the beginning of s. 299(1) the words "subject to section. 304(5)" inserted by FA 1998, s. 74(1) and Sch. 13, para. 39(1), with effect in relation to disposals made on or after 6 April 1998.
S. 299(4) to (4C) substituted for former s. 299(4) by FA 1998, s. 74(1) and Sch. 13, para. 39(2), with effect in relation to disposals made on or after 6 April 1998 of shares issued prior to 1 January 1994.

Cross references – TCGA 1992, s. 105A: election for alternative order of disposal for purposes of s. 299(6A) and (6B) of approved-scheme EIS shares acquired on the same day.
TCGA 1992, s. 126(2)(a): reorganisation of share capital where persons allotted securities in proportion to their holdings in the company.
TCGA 1992, s. 127: on reorganisation of share capital new holding equated with original shares.
TCGA 1992, s. 150: identification of BES shares for capital gains tax purposes.
TCGA 1992, s. 150A(4): identification of enterprise investment scheme shares for capital gains tax purposes determined as for s. 299 purposes.
TCGA 1992, Sch. 5B: capital gains tax deferral on reinvestment in EIS qualifying shares.

Notes – S. 299 rewritten for income tax purposes as follows:
S. 299(1): ITA 2007, s. 209(1), (2), (3), (4).
S. 299(2): ITA 2007, s. 209(3).
S. 299(4): ITA 2007, s. 210(1), (2), 219(1), (2), 220(1), 228(1), (2), 229(1), (2).
S. 299(5): ITA 2007, s. 189(1), 194(4), (8), 196(2), 198(2), (3).
S. 299(5A): ITA 2007, s. 212(3).
S. 299(6): ITA 2007, s. 246(2).
S. 299(6A): ITA 2007, s. 246(3), (7).
S. 299(6B): ITA 2007, s. 246(4).
S. 299(6C): ITA 2007, s. 246(5).
S. 299(6D): ITA 2007, s. 246(6), (7).
S. 299(8): ITA 2007, s. 209(1), 211(1), (2), 212(1).

299A Loan linked investments

299A [Omitted by ITA 2007, s. 1027 and Sch. 1, para. 627 and repealed by ITA 2007, s. 1031 and Sch. 3, Pt. 2 with effect in relation to shares issued after 5 April 2007.]

History – S. 299A omitted by ITA 2007, s. 1027 and Sch. 1, para. 627 and repealed by ITA 2007, s. 1031 and Sch. 3, Pt. 2 with effect in relation to shares issued after 5 April 2007. In so far as it continues to apply in relation to shares issued before 6 April 2007, s. 299A is as follows:
"299A(1) An individual is not eligible for relief in respect of any shares in a company if–
(a) there is a loan made by any person, at any time in the relevant period, to that individual or any associate of his; and
(b) the loan is one which would not have been made, or would not have been made on the same terms, if that individual had not subscribed for those shares or had not been proposing to do so.

ICTA 1988

299A(2) References in this section to the making by any person of a loan to any individual or an associate of his include references–
(a) to the giving by that person of any credit to that individual or any associate of his; and
(b) to the assignment or assignation to that person of any debt due from that individual or any associate of his;
and the references in section 307(6)(ca) to the making of a loan shall be construed accordingly.
299A(3) Section 312(1A)(a) applies to determine the relevant period for the purposes of this section."
S. 299A(1), (2) inserted by FA 1993, s. 111(1), in relation to any case in which the claim for relief is made on or after 16 March 1993. In s. 299A(1), the words "An individual … if" substituted for former words "An individual shall not be entitled to relief in respect of any shares issued on or after 16th March 1993 if", and s. 299A(3) inserted, by FA 1994, s. 137 and Sch. 15, para. 13, in relation to shares issued on or after 1 January 1994 with effect for 1993–94 and subsequent years of assessment.

Statements of practice – SP 6/98: Revenue understanding of way in which loan linked investments rules operate.

Notes – S. 299A rewritten for income tax purposes as follows:
S. 299A(1): ITA 2007, s. 164(1), (2).
S. 299A(2): ITA 2007, s. 164(3), 239(2).
S. 299A(3): ITA 2007, s. 164(1).

299B Pre-arranged exits

299B [Omitted by ITA 2007, s. 1027 and Sch. 1, para. 627 and repealed by ITA 2007, s. 1031 and Sch. 3, Pt. 2, with effect in relation to shares issued after 5 April 2007.]

History – S. 299B omitted by ITA 2007, s. 1027 and Sch. 1, para. 627 and repealed by ITA 2007, s. 1031 and Sch. 3, Pt. 3 with effect in relation to shares issued after 5 April 2007. In so far as it continues to apply in relation to shares issued before 6 April 2007, s. 299B is as follows:
"**299B(1)** An individual is not eligible for relief in respect of any shares in a company if the relevant arrangements include–
(a) arrangements with a view to the subsequent repurchase, exchange or other disposal of those shares or of other shares in or securities of the same company;
(b) arrangements for or with a view to the cessation of any trade which is being or is to be or may be carried on by the company or a person connected with the company;
(c) arrangements for the disposal of, or of a substantial amount of, the assets of the company or of a person connected with the company;
(d) arrangements the main purpose of which, or one of the main purposes of which, is (by means of any insurance, indemnity or guarantee or otherwise) to provide partial or complete protection for persons investing in shares in that company against what would otherwise be the risks attached to making the investment.
299B(2) The arrangements referred to in subsection (1)(a) above do not include any arrangements with a view to such an exchange of shares, or shares and securities, as is mentioned in section 304A(1).
299B(3) The arrangements referred to in subsection (1)(b) and (c) above do not include any arrangements applicable only on the winding up of a company except in a case where–
(a) the relevant arrangements include arrangements for the company to be wound up; or
(b) the company is wound up otherwise than for bona fide commercial reasons.
299B(4) The arrangements referred to in subsection (1)(d) above do not include any arrangements which are confined to the provision–
(a) for the company itself, or
(b) in the case of a company which is a parent company of a trading group, for the company itself, for the company itself and one or more of its subsidiaries or for one or more of its subsidiaries,
of any such protection against the risks arising in the course of carrying on its business as it might reasonably be expected so to provide in normal commercial circumstances.
299B(5) The reference in subsection (4) above to the parent company of a trading group shall be construed in accordance with the provision contained for the purposes of section 293 in that section.
299B(6) In this section **"the relevant arrangements"** means–
(a) the arrangements under which the shares are issued to the individual; and
(b) any arrangements made before the issue of the shares to him in relation to or in connection with that issue.
299B(7) [Repealed by FA 2000, s. 156 and Sch. 40, Pt. II(5).]"
S. 299B(7) repealed by FA 2000, s. 156 and Sch. 40, Pt. II(5), in accordance with FA 2000, Sch. 17, para. 14. Former s. 299B(7) read as follows:
"**299B(7)** In this section "arrangements" includes any scheme, agreement or understanding, whether or not legally enforceable."
S. 299B inserted by FA 1998, s. 71(1), with effect in relation to shares issued on or after 2 July 1998.

Notes – S. 299B rewritten for income tax purposes as follows:
S. 299B(1): ITA 2007, s. 177(1).
S. 299B(2): ITA 2007, s. 177(2).
S. 299B(3): ITA 2007, s. 177(3).
S. 299B(4): ITA 2007, s. 177(4).
S. 299B(5): ITA 2007, s. 177(4).
S. 299B(6): ITA 2007, s. 177(5).

300 Value received from company

300 [Omitted by ITA 2007, s. 1027 and Sch. 1, para. 627 and repealed by ITA 2007, s. 1031 and Sch. 3, Pt. 2 with effect in relation to shares issued after 5 April 2007.]

History – S. 300 omitted by ITA 2007, s. 1027 and Sch. 1, para. 627 and repealed by ITA 2007, s. 1031 and Sch. 3, Pt. 2 with effect in relation to shares issued after 5 April 2007. In so far as it continues to apply in relation to shares issued before 6 April 2007, s. 300 is as follows:
"**300(1)** Subsection (1A) below applies where an individual who subscribes for eligible shares in a company receives any value (other than insignificant value) from the company at any time in the period of restriction.
300(1A) Where any relief is attributable to those shares, then (unless the amount of the relief has already been reduced on account of the value received) –
(a) if it is greater than the amount mentioned in subsection (1B) below, it shall be reduced by that amount, and
(b) if paragraph (a) above does not apply, the relief shall be withdrawn.
300(1AA) This section is subject to section 300A.
300(1B) The amount referred to in subsection (1A) above is an amount equal to tax at the lower rate for the year of assessment for which the relief was given on the amount of the value received; and section 299(4) above applies for the purposes of this subsection as it applies for the purposes of subsection (2) of that section.
300(1BA) Where–
(a) an individual subscribes for two or more issues of eligible shares in a company, being issues comprising shares in respect of which the individual obtains relief, and

(b) the individual receives any value from the company at any time in the periods of restriction relating to the shares comprised in two or more of those issues,

this section has effect in relation to the shares comprised in each of the issues referred to in paragraph (b) above as if the amount of the value received were reduced by multiplying it by the fraction specified in subsection (1BB) below.

300(1BB) The fraction is–

$$\frac{A}{B}$$

where–

A is the amount subscribed by the individual for the eligible shares comprised in the issue in question, and

B is the aggregate of that amount and the corresponding amount or amounts for eligible shares comprised in the other issue or issues.

300(1BC) Where–

(a) an individual who subscribes for eligible shares in a company receives value (**"the relevant receipt"**) from the company during the period of restriction,

(b) the individual has received from the company one or more receipts of insignificant value at a time or times–

(i) during that period, but

(ii) not later than the time of the relevant receipt, and

(c) the aggregate amount of the value of the receipts within paragraphs (a) and (b) above is not an amount of insignificant value,

the individual shall be treated for the purposes of this Chapter as if the relevant receipt had been a receipt of an amount of value equal to the aggregate amount.

For this purpose a receipt does not fall within paragraph (b) above if it has previously been aggregated under this subsection.

300(1C) Any reference in subsection (1), (1BA) or (1BC) above to the receipt of value (however expressed) from a company includes a reference to the receipt of value from a person who at any time in the relevant period is connected with the company, whether or not he is so connected at the time when the individual concerned receives the value from him; and other references to the company in this section and section 301 shall be read accordingly.

300(1D) Notwithstanding anything in subsection (2) below, for the purposes of this section an individual is not to be treated as recovering value from a company by reason only of the payment to him, or any associate of his, of any remuneration for services rendered to the company as a director if the remuneration is reasonable remuneration.

300(1E) Section 291(4) applies for the purposes of subsection (1D) above as it applies for the purposes of section 291A, and the reference in subsection (1D) above to the payment of remuneration includes the provision of any benefit or facility.

300(2) For the purposes of this section an individual receives value from the company if the company–

(a) repays, redeems or repurchases any of its share capital or securities which belong to the individual or makes any payment to him for giving up his right to any of the company's share capital or any security on its cancellation or extinguishment;

(b) repays, in pursuance of any arrangements for or in connection with the acquisition of the shares in respect of which the relief is claimed, any debt owed to the individual other than a debt which was incurred by the company–

(a) on or after the date of issue of those shares; and

(b) otherwise than in consideration of the extinguishment of a debt incurred before that date;

(c) makes to the individual any payment for giving up his right to any debt (other than a debt in respect of a payment of the kind mentioned in section 291A(3)(a) or (f) or an ordinary trade debt) on its extinguishment;

(d) releases or waives any liability of the individual to the company or discharges, or undertakes to discharge, any liability of his to a third person;

(e) makes a loan or advance to the individual which has not been repaid in full before the issue of the shares in respect of which relief is claimed;

(f) provides a benefit or facility for the individual;

(g) transfers an asset to the individual for no consideration or for consideration less than its market value or acquires an asset from him for consideration exceeding its market value; or

(h) makes to him any other payment except a payment of the kind mentioned in any of the paragraphs of section 291A(3) or a payment in discharge of an ordinary trade debt.

300(3) For the purposes of this section an individual also receives value from the company if he receives in respect of ordinary shares held by him any payment or asset in a winding up or in connection with a dissolution of the company, being a winding up or dissolution falling within section 293(6).

300(4) The value received by an individual is–

(a) in a case within paragraph (a), (b) or (c) of subsection (2) above, the amount received by the individual or, if greater, the market value of the shares, securities or debt in question;

(b) in a case within paragraph (d) of that subsection, the amount of the liability;

(c) in a case within paragraph (e) of that subsection, the amount of the loan or advance reduced by the amount of any repayment made before the issue of the shares in respect of which relief is claimed;

(d) in a case within paragraph (f) of that subsection, the cost to the company of providing the benefit or facility less any consideration given for it by the individual;

(e) in a case within paragraph (g) of that subsection, the difference between the market value of the asset and the consideration (if any) given for it;

(f) in a case within paragraph (h) of that subsection, the amount of the payment; and

(g) in a case within subsection (3) above, the amount of the payment or, as the case may be, the market value of the asset.

300(5) For the purposes of this section an individual also receives value from the company if any person who would, for the purposes of section 291, be treated as connected with the company–

(a) purchases any of its share capital or securities which belong to the individual; or

(b) makes any payment to him for giving up any right in relation to any of the company's share capital or securities;

and the value received by the individual is the amount received by the individual or, if greater, the market value of the shares or securities in question.

300(6) Where by reason of an individual's disposal of shares in a company any relief attributable to those shares is withdrawn or reduced under section 299, the individual shall not be treated for the purposes of this section as receiving value from the company in respect of the disposal."

S. 300(1) amended by FA 2001, Sch. 15, para. 15(1) and (2) with effect:

(1) in relation to shares issued on or after 7 March 2001, and

(2) in relation to shares issued before that date, in respect of the application of ICTA 1988, Pt. VII, Ch. III and TCGA 1992, Sch. 5B, in relation to:

(a) value received (within the meaning of ICTA 1988, s. 300 or TCGA 1992, Sch. 5B, para. 13), and

(b) repayments made (see s. 300(1) or TCGA 1992, Sch. 5B, para. 14(1)),

on or after that date.

In s. 300(1), "designated" substituted for "seven year" by FA 2000, s. 64 and Sch. 17, para. 4, with effect in relation to shares issued on or after 6 April 2000.

S. 300(1) substituted by FA 1998, s. 74(1) and Sch. 13, para. 13(1), in relation to shares issued on or after 6 April 1998. The wording of former s. 300(1) was as follows:

"**300(1)** Subsection (1A) below applies where an individual who subscribes for eligible shares in a company–

(a) has, before the issue of the shares but within the relevant period, received any value from the company, or

(b) after their issue but before the end of the relevant period, receives any such value."

S. 300(1AA) and (1BA)–(1BC) inserted, and s. 300(1C) amended, by FA 2001, Sch. 15, para. 15(3)–(5), with effect from the time mentioned in the first amendment noted above.

S. 300(1C) substituted by FA 1998, s. 74(1) and Sch. 13, para. 13(2), in relation to shares issued on or after 6 April 1998. The wording of former s. 300(1C) was as follows:

"**300(1C)** References in subsection (1) above to the receipt of value from a company include references to the receipt of value from a 51 per cent subsidiary of that company, whether it becomes such a subsidiary before or after the individual concerned receives any value from it; and other references to the company in this section and section 301 shall be read accordingly."

Former s. 300(1)–(1E) substituted for former s. 300(1) by FA 1994, s. 137 and Sch. 15, para. 14(a), in relation to shares issued on or after 1 January 1994 with effect for 1993–94 and subsequent years of assessment. Former s. 300(1) provided as follows:

"**300(1)** Subject to section 299, where an individual who subscribes for eligible shares in a company–

(a) has, before the issue of the shares but within the relevant period, received any value from the company; or

(b) after their issue but before the end of the relevant period, receives any such value;

the amount of the relief to which he is entitled in respect of the shares shall be reduced by the value received; but the value received shall be disregarded to the extent to which relief under Schedule 5 to the Finance Act 1983 or under this Chapter has been reduced on its account.".

S. 300(2)(b) substituted by FA 2004, s. 93 and Sch. 18, para. 6, with effect in relation to shares issued on or after 17 March 2004, but not in relation to the repayment of a debt incurred before 17 March 2004 if the shares were subscribed for before that date, and the debt was incurred on or after the date on which the shares were subscribed for. Former s. 300(2)(b) read as follows:

"(b) repays any debt owed to the individual other than a debt which was incurred by the company–

(i) on or after the date on which he subscribed for the shares in respect of which the relief is claimed; and

(ii) otherwise than in consideration of the extinguishment of a debt incurred before that date;".

In s. 300(2)(c), "291A(3)(a) or (f)" substituted for former "291(3)(a) or (e)", and in s. 300(2)(h), the words "any of the paragraphs of section 291A(3)" substituted for former words "section 291(3)(a), (b), (c), (d) or (e)" by FA 1994, s. 137 and Sch. 15, para. 14(b), in relation to shares issued on or after 1 January 1994 with effect for 1993–94 and subsequent years of assessment.

In s. 300(4)(a) and (5), "received" substituted for "receivable" by FA 2001, Sch. 15, para. 6, with effect from the time mentioned in the first amendment noted above.

S. 300(6) inserted by FA 1998, s. 74(1) and Sch. 13, para. 13(1), in relation to disposals made on or after 6 April 1998.

Derivations – Former s. 300(1): FA 1983, Sch. 5, para. 8(1), as amended by FA 1986, Sch. 9, para. 10(2).

S. 300(2)–(4) (as originally enacted): FA 1981, s. 58(2)–(4), as applied and modified by FA 1983, Sch. 3, para. 8(2) (as substituted by FA 1986, s. 40(1) and Sch. 9, para. 10(3)).

S. 300(5): FA 1983, Sch. 5, para. 8(3), as amended by F(No. 2)A 1983, s. 5 and Sch. 1, para. 5.

Cross references – TCGA 1992, s. 150B(1)(a): reduction of CGT relief where s. 300(1A)(a) applies.

TCGA 1992, Sch. 5B: capital gains tax deferral on reinvestment in EIS qualifying shares.

HMRC Manuals – Inspector's Manual, IM7027 ff.: circumstances in which individuals receive value.

Notes – S. 300 rewritten for income tax purposes as follows:

S. 300(1): ITA 2007, s. 213(1), (3), 214(1).
S. 300(1A): ITA 2007, s. 213(2), (4).
S. 300(1AA): ITA 2007, s. 213(3).
S. 300(1B): ITA 2007, s. 213(2), 219(1), (2), 220(1).
S. 300(1BA): ITA 2007, s. 218(1), (2), (3).
S. 300(1BB): ITA 2007, s. 218(2).
S. 300(1BC): ITA 2007, s. 214(2), (3).
S. 300(1C): ITA 2007, s. 221.
S. 300(1D): ITA 2007, s. 216(8).
S. 300(1E): ITA 2007, s. 216(9).
S. 300(2): ITA 2007, s. 216(2).
S. 300B(3): ITA 2007, s. 216(5).
S. 300(4): ITA 2007, s. 217.
S. 300(5): ITA 2007, s. 216(6), 217.
S. 300(6): ITA 2007, s. 216(7).

300A Receipt of replacement value

300A [Omitted by ITA 2007, s. 1027 and Sch. 1, para. 627 and repealed by ITA 2007, s. 1031 and Sch. 3, Pt. 2 with effect in relation to shares issued after 5 April 2007.]

History – S. 300A omitted by ITA 2007, s. 1027 and Sch. 1, para. 627 and repealed by ITA 2007, s. 1031 and Sch. 3, Pt. 2 with effect in relation to shares issued after 5 April 2007. In so far as it continues to apply in relation to shares issued before 6 April 2007, s. 300A is as follows:

"**300A(1)** Where–

(a) any relief attributable to any eligible shares comprised in an issue of shares subscribed for by an individual (**"the individual"**) would, in the absence of this section, be reduced or withdrawn under section 300 by reason of a receipt of value within subsection (2) or (5) of that section (**"the original value"**),

(b) the original supplier receives value (**"the replacement value"**) from the original recipient by virtue of a qualifying receipt, and

(c) the amount of the replacement value is not less than the amount of the original value,

the receipt of the original value shall be disregarded for the purposes of section 300.

This is subject to subsections (7) and (8) below.

300A(2) For the purposes of this section–

"the original recipient" means the person who receives the original value, and

"the original supplier" means the person from whom that value was received.

300A(3) Where the amount of the original value is, by virtue of subsection (1BA) of section 300, treated as reduced for the purposes of that section as it applies in relation to the eligible shares in question, the reference in subsection (1)(c) above to the amount of the original value shall be read as a reference to the amount of that value disregarding the reduction.

300A(4) A receipt of the replacement value is a qualifying receipt for the purposes of subsection (1) above if it arises–

(a) by reason of the original recipient doing one or more of the following–

(i) making a payment to the original supplier, other than a payment which falls within paragraph (c) below or to which subsection (5) below applies;

(ii) acquiring any asset from the original supplier for a consideration the amount or value of which is more than the market value of the asset;
(iii) disposing of any asset to the original supplier for no consideration or for a consideration the amount or value of which is less than the market value of the asset;
(b) where the receipt of the original value was within section 300(2)(d), by reason of an event the effect of which is to reverse the event which constituted the receipt of the original value; or
(c) where the receipt of the original value was within section 300(5), by reason of the original recipient repurchasing the share capital or securities in question, or (as the case may be) reacquiring the right in question, for a consideration the amount or value of which is not less than the amount of the original value.

300A(5) This subsection applies to–
(a) any payment for any goods, services or facilities, provided (whether in the course of a trade or otherwise) by–
(i) the original supplier, or
(ii) any other person who, at any time in the period of restriction, is an associate of, or connected with, that supplier (whether or not he is such an associate, or so connected, at the material time),
which is reasonable in relation to the market value of those goods, services or facilities;
(b) any payment of any interest which represents no more than a reasonable commercial return on money lent to–
(i) the original recipient, or
(ii) any person who, at any time in the period of restriction, is an associate of his (whether or not he is such an associate at the material time);
(c) any payment for the acquisition of an asset which does not exceed its market value;
(d) any payment, as rent for any property occupied by–
(i) the original recipient, or
(ii) any person who, at any time in the period of restriction, is an associate of his (whether or not he is such an associate at the material time),
of an amount not exceeding a reasonable and commercial rent for the property;
(e) any payment in discharge of an ordinary trade debt; and
(f) any payment for shares in or securities of any company in circumstances that do not fall within subsection (4)(a)(ii) above.

300A(6) For the purposes of this section, the amount of the replacement value is–
(a) in a case within paragraph (a) of subsection (4) above, the aggregate of–
(i) the amount of any payment within sub-paragraph (i) of that paragraph, and
(ii) the difference between the market value of any asset to which sub-paragraph (ii) or (iii) of that paragraph applies and the amount or value of the consideration (if any) received for it,
(b) in a case within subsection (4)(b) above, the same as the amount of the original value, and
(c) in a case within subsection (4)(c) above, the amount or value of the consideration received by the original supplier,
and section 300(4) and (5) shall apply for the purposes of determining the amount of the original value.

300A(7) The receipt of the replacement value by the original supplier shall be disregarded for the purposes of this section, as it applies in relation to the eligible shares, to the extent to which that receipt has previously been set (under this section) against any receipts of value which are, in consequence, disregarded for the purposes of section 300 as that section applies in relation to those shares or any other shares subscribed for by the individual.

300A(8) The receipt of the replacement value by the original supplier (**"the event"**) shall be disregarded for the purposes of this section if–
(a) the event occurs before the start of the period of restriction, or
(b) in a case where the event occurs after the time the original recipient receives the original value, it does not occur as soon after that time as is reasonably practicable in the circumstances, or
(c) where an appeal has been brought by the individual against an assessment to withdraw or reduce any relief attributable to the eligible shares by reason of the receipt of the original value, the event occurs more than 60 days after the amount of relief which falls to be withdrawn has been finally determined.
But nothing in this section requires the replacement value to be received after the original value.

300A(9) Subsection (10) below applies where–
(a) the receipt of the replacement value by the original supplier is a qualifying receipt (for the purposes of subsection (1) above) in consequence of which any receipts of value are disregarded for the purposes of section 300 as that section applies in relation to the shares in question or any other shares subscribed for by the individual in question, and
(b) the event which gives rise to the receipt is (or includes) a subscription for shares by–
(i) the individual, or
(ii) any person who, at any time in the period of restriction, is an associate of his, whether or not he is such an associate at the material time.

300A(10) Where this subsection applies, the person who subscribes for the shares as mentioned in subsection (9)(b) above shall not–
(a) be eligible for any relief under this Chapter in relation to those shares or any other shares in the same issue, or
(b) by virtue of his subscription for those shares or any other shares in the same issue, be treated as making a qualifying investment for the purposes of Schedule 5B to the 1992 Act (enterprise investment scheme: reinvestment).

300A(11) In this section–
(a) any reference to a payment to a person (however expressed) includes a reference to a payment made to him indirectly or to his order or for his benefit, and
(b) references to **"the period of restriction"** are to the period of restriction relating to the shares mentioned in subsection (1) (a) above."

S. 300A inserted by FA 2001, Sch. 15, para. 16, with effect:
(1) in relation to shares issued on or after 7 March 2001, and
(2) in relation to shares issued before that date, in respect of the application of ICTA 1988, Pt. VII, Ch. III and TCGA 1992, Sch. 5B, in relation to:
(a) value received (within the meaning of ICTA 1988, s. 300 or TCGA 1992, Sch. 5B, para. 13), and
(b) repayments made (see s. 303(1) or TCGA 1992, Sch. 5B, para. 14(1))
on or after that date.

Notes – S. 300A rewritten for income tax purposes as follows:
S. 300A(1): ITA 2007, s. 222(1), 223(5).
S. 300A(2): ITA 2007, s. 222(2), 223(5).
S. 300A(3): ITA 2007, s. 222(3).
S. 300A(4): ITA 2007, s. 222(4).
S. 300A(5): ITA 2007, s. 222(5).
S. 300A(6): ITA 2007, s. 222(6).
S. 300A(7): ITA 2007, s. 223(1).
S. 300A(8): ITA 2007, s. 223(2).
S. 300A(9): ITA 2007, s. 223(3).
S. 300A(10): ITA 2007, s. 223(4).
S. 300A(11): ITA 2007, s. 222(5), (7), 223(2), (3).

301 Provisions supplementary to section 300

301 [Omitted by ITA 2007, s. 1027 and Sch. 1, para. 627 and repealed by ITA 2007, s. 1031 and Sch. 3, Pt. 2 with effect in relation to shares issued after 5 April 2007.]

History – S. 301 omitted by ITA 2007, s. 1027 and Sch. 1, para. 627 and repealed by ITA 2007, s. 1031 and Sch. 3, Pt. 2 with effect in relation to shares issued after 5 April 2007. In so far as it continues to apply in relation to shares issued before 6 April 2007, s. 301 is as follows:

"**301(1), (2)** [Repealed by FA 1994, s. 137 and Sch. 15, para. 15(a), and s. 258 and Sch. 26, Pt. V(17).]

301(3) For the purposes of section 300(2)(d) a company shall be treated as having released or waived a liability if the liability is not discharged within 12 months of the time when it ought to have been discharged.

301(4) For the purposes of section 300(2)(e) there shall be treated as if it were a loan made by the company to the individual–

(a) the amount of any debt (other than an ordinary trade debt) incurred by the individual to the company; and

(b) the amount of any debt due from the individual to a third person which has been assigned to the company.

301(4A) For the purposes of this section and sections 300 and 300A, an individual who acquires any eligible shares on such a transfer as is mentioned in section 304 shall be treated as if he subscribed for those shares.

301(5) In this section and sections 300 and 300A, **"an ordinary trade debt"** means any debt for goods or services supplied in the ordinary course of a trade or business where any credit given does not exceed six months and is not longer than that normally given to the customers of the person carrying on the trade or business.

301(6) In this section and section 300 –

(a) any reference to a payment or transfer to an individual includes a reference to a payment or transfer made to him indirectly or to his order or for his benefit; and

(b) any reference to an individual includes a reference to an associate of his and any reference to the company includes a reference to any person connected with the company.

301(6A) Section 312(1A)(a) applies to determine the relevant period for the purposes of section 300.

301(7) [Repealed by FA 1994, s. 137 and Sch. 15, para. 15(c), and s. 258 and Sch. 26, Pt. V(17).]"

S. 301(1), (2) repealed by FA 1994, s. 137 and Sch. 15, para. 15(a), and s. 258 and Sch. 26, Pt. V(17), in relation to shares issued on or after 1 January 1994 with effect for 1993–94 and subsequent years of assessment. Former s. 301(1), (2) provided as follows:

"**301(1)** Where by virtue of section 300 any relief is withheld or withdrawn in the case of an individual to whom ordinary shares in a company have been issued at different times before 19th March 1986 the relief shall be withheld or withdrawn in respect of shares issued earlier rather than in respect of shares issued later.

301(2) Where relief to which an individual is entitled in respect of eligible shares issued after 18th March 1986 is reduced by virtue of section 300, effect shall be given to the reduction by apportioning it, as between any such eligible shares held by him, in such a way as appears to the inspector, or on an appeal to the Commissioners concerned, to be just and reasonable."

In s. 301(4A) and (5), reference to s. 300A inserted by FA 2001, Sch. 15, para. 17, with effect:

(1) in relation to shares issued on or after 7 March 2001, and

(2) in relation to shares issued before that date, in respect of the application of ICTA 1988, Pt. VII, Ch. III and TCGA 1992, Sch. 5B, in relation to:

 (a) value received (within the meaning of ICTA 1988, s. 300 or TCGA 1992, Sch. 5B, para. 13), and

 (b) repayments made (see s. 300(1) or TCGA 1992, Sch. 5B, para. 14(1)),

on or after that date.

S. 301(4A) inserted by FA 1998, s. 74(1) and Sch. 13, para. 14(1), in relation to value received (within the meaning of s. 300) on or after 6 April 1998.

S. 301(5) the words "any credit" substituted for the words "the credit" by FA 1998, s. 74(1) and Sch. 13, para. 14(2), in relation to shares issued on or after 6 April 1998.

S. 301(6A) inserted by FA 1994, s. 137 and Sch. 15, para. 15(b), in relation to shares issued on or after 1 January 1994 with effect for 1993–94 and subsequent years of assessment.

S. 301(7) repealed by FA 1994, s. 137 and Sch. 15, para. 15(c), and s. 258 and Sch. 26, Pt. V(17), in relation to shares issued on or after 1 January 1994 with effect for 1993–94 and subsequent years of assessment. Former s. 301(7) provided as follows:

"**301(7)** Section 300 shall apply in relation to shares issued before 19th March 1986 with the omission–

(a) in subsection (2)(e) of the words "which has not been repaid in full before the issue of the shares in respect of which relief is claimed"; and

(b) in subsection (4)(c) of the words "reduced by the amount of any repayment made before the issue of the shares in respect of which relief is claimed".".

Derivations – Former s. 301(1): FA 1981, s. 58(5) as applied by FA 1983, Sch. 5, former para. 8(2) (before being substituted by FA 1986, Sch. 9, para. 10(3)).

Former s. 301(2): FA 1983, Sch. 5, para. 8(4) as inserted by FA 1986, s. 40(1) and Sch. 9, para. 1(2), 10(4).

S. 301(3), (4): FA 1981, s. 58(6), (7), as applied by FA 1983, Sch. 5, para. 8(2) (as amended by FA 1986, s. 40(1) and Sch. 9, para. 10(3)).

S. 301(5): FA 1981, s. 58(8) (as amended by FA 1987, Sch. 15, para. 14(2)) as applied by FA 1983, Sch. 5, para. 8(2) (as amended by FA 1986, s. 40(1) and Sch. 9, para. 10(3)).

S. 301(6): FA 1981, s. 58(9) as applied by FA 1983, Sch. 5, para. 8(2) (as amended by FA 1986, s. 40(1) and Sch. 9, para. 10(3)).

Former s. 301(7): FA 1986, Sch. 9, para. 1(2), 10(3).

Notes – S. 301 rewritten for income tax purposes as follows:

S. 301(3): ITA 2007, s. 216(3).

S. 301(4): ITA 2007, s. 216(4).

S. 301(4A): ITA 2007, s. 213(5).

S. 301(5): ITA 2007, s. 216(10), 222(7).

S. 301(6): ITA 2007, s. 221.

S. 301(6A): ITA 2007, s. 221.

Former s. 301(7)(a) modified s. 300(2)(e) so as to reflect FA 1981, s. 58(2)(e) as applied by FA 1983, Sch. 5, para. 8(2) before its amendment by FA 1986, s. 40(1) and Sch. 9, para. 1(2), 10(3).

Former s. 301(7)(b) modified s. 300(4)(c) so as to reflect FA 1981, s. 58(4)(c) as applied by FA 1983, Sch. 5, para. 8(2) before its amendment by FA 1986, s. 40(1) and Sch. 9, para. 1(2), 10(3).

301A Receipts of insignificant value: supplementary provision

301A [Omitted by ITA 2007, s. 1027 and Sch. 1, para. 627 and repealed by ITA 2007, s. 1031 and Sch. 3, Pt. 2 with effect in relation to shares issued after 5 April 2007.]

History – S. 301A omitted by ITA 2007, s. 1027 and Sch. 1, para. 627 and repealed by ITA 2007, s. 1031, Sch. 3, Pt. 2 with effect in relation to shares issued after 5 April 2007. In so far as it continues to apply in relation to shares issued before 6 April 2007, s. 301A is as follows:

"**301A(1)** In this section and section 300 references to a receipt of insignificant value (however expressed) are references to a receipt of an amount of insignificant value.
This is subject to subsection (3) below.
301A(2) For the purposes of this section and section 300 **"an amount of insignificant value"** means an amount of value which–
(a) does not exceed £1,000, or
(b) if it exceeds that amount, is insignificant in relation to the amount subscribed by the individual in question for the eligible shares in question.
301A(3) For the purposes of section 300, if, at any time in the period–
(a) beginning one year before the eligible shares in question are issued, and
(b) expiring at the end of the issue date,
arrangements are in existence which provide for the individual in question to receive or to be entitled to receive, at any time in the period of restriction relating to those shares, any value from the company that issued those shares, no amount of value received by the individual shall be treated as a receipt of insignificant value.
301A(4) For the purposes of this section–
(a) references to the individual include references to any person who, at any time in the period of restriction relating to the shares in question, is an associate of his (whether or not he is such an associate at the material time), and
(b) the reference in subsection (3) above to the company includes a reference to any person who, at any time in the period of restriction relating to the shares in question, is connected with the company (whether or not that person is so connected at the material time).
301A(5) For the purposes of this section, an individual who acquires any eligible shares on such a transfer as is mentioned in section 304 shall be treated as if he subscribed for those shares."
S. 301A inserted by FA 2001, Sch. 15, para. 18, with effect:
(1) in relation to shares issued on or after 7 March 2001, and
(2) in relation to shares issued before that date, in respect of the application of ICTA 1988, Pt. VII, Ch. III and TCGA 1992, Sch. 5B, in relation to:
(a) value received (within the meaning of ICTA 1988, s. 300 or TCGA 1992, Sch. 5B, para. 13), and
(b) repayments made (see s. 300(1) or TCGA 1992, Sch. 5B, para. 14(1)),
on or after that date.

Notes – S. 301A rewritten for income tax purposes as follows:
S. 301A(1): ITA 2007, s. 215(2).
S. 301A(2): ITA 2007, s. 215(2).
S. 301A(3): ITA 2007, s. 215(3), (4).
S. 301A(4): ITA 2007, s. 215(5).
S. 301A(5): ITA 2007, s. 213(5).

ICTA 1988

302 Replacement capital

302 [Omitted by ITA 2007, s. 1027 and Sch. 1, para. 627 and repealed by ITA 2007, s. 1031 and Sch. 3, Pt. 2 with effect in relation to shares issued after 5 April 2007.]

History – S. 302 omitted by ITA 2007, s. 1027 and Sch. 1, para. 627 and repealed by ITA 2007, s. 1031 and Sch. 3, Pt. 2 with effect in relation to shares issued after 5 April 2007. In so far as it continues to apply in relation to shares issued before 6 April 2007, s 302 is as follows:
"**302(1)** Any relief attributable to any shares in a company held by an individual shall be withdrawn if–
(a) at any time in the relevant period, the company or any subsidiary–
(i) begins to carry on as its trade or as part of its trade a trade which was previously carried on at any time in that period otherwise than by the company or any subsidiary, or
(ii) acquires the whole, or a greater part, of the assets used for the purposes of a trade previously so carried on, and
(b) subsection (2) below applies in relation to that individual.
302(2) This subsection applies in relation to an individual where–
(a) any person or group of persons to whom an interest amounting in the aggregate to more than a half share in the trade (as previously carried on) belonged, at any time in the relevant period, is or are a person or group of persons to whom such an interest in the trade carried on by the company belongs or has, at any such time, belonged; or
(b) any person or group of persons who control or, at any such time, have controlled the company is or are a person or group of persons who, at any such time, controlled another company which previously carried on the trade;
and the individual is that person or one of those persons.
302(3) Any relief attributable to any shares in a company held by an individual shall be withdrawn if–
(a) the company comes to acquire all of the issued share capital of another company, at any time in the relevant period; and
(b) any person or group of persons who control or have, at any such time, controlled the company is or are a person or group of persons who, at any such time, controlled that other company;
and that individual is that person or one of those persons.
302(4) For the purposes of subsection (2) above–
(a) the persons to whom a trade belongs and, where a trade belongs to two or more persons, their respective shares in that trade shall be determined in accordance with section 344(1)(a) and (b), (2) and (3); and
(b) any interest, rights or powers of a person who is an associate of another person shall be treated as those of that other person.
302(4A) In determining whether any relief attributable to any shares in a company (the **"issuing company"**) held by a person who–
(a) is a director of, or of a company which is a partner of, the issuing company or any subsidiary, and
(b) is in receipt of, or entitled to receive, remuneration as such a director falling within section 291A(5)(a),
is to be withdrawn, the second reference in paragraph (b) of each of subsections (2) and (3) above and, so far as relating to those paragraphs, in subsection (1)(a)(i) above to any time in the relevant period shall be read as a reference to any time before the end of the relevant period.
302(4B) Section 291(4) applies for the purposes of subsection (4A) above as it applies for the purposes of section 291A, and in subsection (4A) above **"remuneration"** includes any benefit or facility.
302(5) In this section–

"subsidiary" means a company which would be a subsidiary if the relevant period for the purposes of section 308 were the period referred to in section 312(1A)(a); and

"trade" includes any business, profession or vocation, and references to a trade previously carried on include references to part of such a trade;
and section 312(1A)(a) applies to determine the relevant period for the purposes of this section."
S. 302(1) substituted by FA 1994, s. 137 and Sch. 15, para. 16(a), in relation to shares issued on or after 1 January 1994 with effect for 1993–94 and subsequent years of assessment. Former s. 302(1) provided as follows:

"**302(1)** An individual is not entitled to relief in respect of any shares in a company where–
(a) at any time in the relevant period, the company or any of its subsidiaries–
(i) begins to carry on as its trade or as part of its trade a trade which was previously carried on at any time in that period otherwise than by the company or any of its subsidiaries; or
(ii) acquires the whole, or greater part, of the assets used for the purposes of a trade previously so carried on; and
(b) subsection (2) below applies in relation to that individual.".

In s. 302(3), the words "Any relief … withdrawn if" substituted for former words "An individual is not entitled to relief in respect of any shares in a company where" by FA 1994, s. 137 and Sch. 15, para. 16(b), in relation to shares issued on or after 1 January 1994 with effect for 1993–94 and subsequent years of assessment.

S. 302(4A), (4B) inserted by FA 1994, s. 137 and Sch. 15, para. 16(c), in relation to shares issued on or after 1 January 1994 with effect in 1993–94 and subsequent years of assessment.

In s. 302(5), definition of "subsidiary" substituted, and the words at the end "and section … this section" inserted, by FA 1994, s. 137 and Sch. 15, para. 16(d), in relation to shares issued on or after 1 January 1994 with effect for 1993–94 and subsequent years of assessment. The former definition provided: ""subsidiary" means a subsidiary of a kind which a qualifying company may have by virtue of sections 308 and 309".

Derivations – (as originally enacted) – FA 1983, Sch. 5, para. 9(1)–(5), as amended by F(No. 2)A 1983, s. 5 and Sch. 1, para. 6.

Cross references – FA 1988, Sch. 4, para. 9(1)–(4): modification of s. 302(1), (2), (4) and (5) where eligible shares issued for the purpose of raising finance for private rented housing under BES.

Notes – S. 302 rewritten for income tax purposes as follows:
S. 302(1): ITA 2007, s. 232(1).
S. 302(2): ITA 2007, s. 232(1), (2), (3).
S. 302(3): ITA 2007, s. 233(1), (2).
S. 302(4): ITA 2007, s. 232(4).
S. 302(4A): ITA 2007, s. 232(5), 233(3).
S. 302(4B): ITA 2007, s. 232(6), 233(4).
S. 302(5): ITA 2007, s. 232(1), (2), (3), (7), 233(1), (2), (3).

303 Value received by persons other than claimants

303 [Omitted by ITA 2007, s. 1027 and Sch. 1, para. 627 and repealed by ITA 2007, s. 1031 and Sch. 3, Pt. 2 with effect in relation to shares issued after 5 April 2007.]

History – S. 303 omitted by ITA 2007, s. 1027 and Sch. 1, para. 627 and repealed by ITA 2007, s. 1031 and Sch. 3, Pt. 2 with effect in relation to shares issued after 5 April 2007. In so far as it continues to apply in relation to shares issued before 6 April 2007, s. 303 is as follows:

"**303(1)** Where, in the case of an issue of eligible shares in a company, any relief is attributable to any shares comprised in the issue which are held by an individual, subsection (1A) below shall apply if at any time in the period of restriction the company or any subsidiary–
(a) repays, redeems or repurchases any of its share capital which belongs to any member other than that individual or a person who falls within subsection (1B) below, or
(b) makes any payment to any such member for giving up his right to any of the share capital of the company or subsidiary on its cancellation or extinguishment.

303(1A) The relief–
(a) if it is greater than the amount mentioned in subsection (1C) below, shall be reduced by that amount, and
(b) if paragraph (a) above does not apply, shall be withdrawn.

303(1AA) This section is subject to sections 303AA and 303A.

303(1B) A person falls within this sub-paragraph if the repayment, redemption, repurchase or payment in question–
(a) causes any relief attributable to his shares in the company to be withdrawn or reduced by virtue of section 299 or 300(2)(a), or
(b) gives rise to a qualifying chargeable event (within the meaning of paragraph 14(4) of Schedule 5B to the 1992 Act) in respect of him, or
(c) causes any investment relief attributable to shares held by that person (within the meaning of Schedule 15 to the Finance Act 2000) to be withdrawn or reduced by virtue of paragraph 46 (disposal of shares) or 49(1)(a) (repayment etc. of share capital or securities) of that Schedule,

or it would have the effect mentioned in paragraph (a), (b) or (c) above were it not a receipt of insignificant value for the purposes of section 300 above, paragraph 13 of Schedule 5B to the 1992 Act or paragraph 47 of the Finance Act 2000, as the case may be.

303(1C) The amount referred to in subsection (1A) above is an amount equal to tax at the lower rate for the year of assessment for which the relief was given–
(a) where subsection (1) above does not apply in the case of any other individual, on the amount received by the member;
(b) where that subsection also applies in the case of one or more other individuals, on the appropriate fraction of that amount;

and subsection (4) of section 299 applies for the purposes of this subsection as it applies for the purposes of subsection (2) of that section.

303(1D) In subsection (1C) above "the appropriate fraction" is–

$$\frac{A}{B}$$

where–

A = the amount subscribed by the individual for eligible shares which are comprised in the issue and to which relief is or, but for subsection (1A)(b) above, would be attributable;

B = the aggregate of that amount and the amount or amounts subscribed by the other individual or individuals for such shares.

303(2) Where the repayment, redemption, repurchase or payment mentioned in subsection (1) above falls within the applicable periods for two or more issues of eligible shares in the company, subsection (1A) above shall have effect in relation to each of those issues as if the amount receivable by the member were reduced by multiplying it by the fraction–

$$\frac{C}{D}$$

where–

C = the amount subscribed by individuals for eligible shares which are comprised in the issue and to which relief is or, but for subsection (1A)(b) above, would be attributable;

D = the aggregate of that amount and the corresponding amount or amounts for the other issue or issues.

303(2A) For the purposes of subsection (2) above "the applicable period" for an issue of eligible shares is–
(a) if the shares were issued before 6th April 2000, the period beginning two years before the issue of the shares and ending immediately before the fifth anniversary of the issue date,
(b) if the shares were issued on or after 6th April 2000 but before 7th March 2001, the period beginning two years before the issue of the shares and ending immediately before the termination date relating to those shares,
(c) in any other case, the period of restriction for the issue.
303(3)–(7) [Repealed by FA 2001, Sch. 15, para. 19(6) and Sch. 33, Pt. 2(3).]
303(8) [Repealed by FA 1994, s. 137 and Sch. 15, para. 17(d), and s. 258 and Sch. 26, Pt. V(17).]
303(9) Where–
(a) a company issues share capital (**"the original shares"**) of nominal value equal to the authorised minimum (within the meaning of the Companies Act 1985) for the purposes of complying with the requirements of section 117 of that Act (public company not to do business unless requirements as to share capital complied with); and
(b) after the registrar of companies has issued the company with a certificate under section 117, it issues eligible shares;
subsection (1) above shall not apply in relation to any redemption of any of the original shares within 12 months of the date on which those shares were issued.
In relation to companies incorporated under the law of Northern Ireland references in this subsection to the Companies Act 1985 and to section 117 of that Act shall have effect as references to the Companies (Northern Ireland) Order 1986 and to Article 127 of that Order.
303(9A) References in this section and sections 303AA and 303A to a subsidiary of a company are references to a company which at any time in the relevant period is a 51 per cent subsidiary of the first mentioned company, whether or not it is such a subsidiary at the time of the repayment, redemption, repurchase or payment in question.
303(9B) Section 312(1A)(a) applies to determine the relevant period for the purposes of this section.
303(10), (11) [Repealed by FA 1994, s. 137 and Sch. 15, para. 17(f), and s. 258 and Sch. 26, Pt. V(17).]"
In s. 303(1), "period of restriction" substituted for "designated period" by FA 2001, Sch. 15, para. 19(1), with effect:
(1) in relation to shares issued on or after 7 March 2001, and
(2) in relation to shares issued before that date, in respect of the application of ICTA 1988, Pt. VII, Ch. III and TCGA 1992, Sch. 5B, in relation to:
(a) value received (within the meaning of ICTA 1988, s. 300 or TCGA 1992, Sch. 5B, para. 13), and
(b) repayments made (see s. 300(1) or TCGA 1992, Sch. 5B, para. 14(1)),
on or after that date.
In s. 303(1), "designated" substituted for "seven year" by FA 2000, s. 64 and Sch. 17, para. 5(2), with effect in relation to shares issued on or after 6 April 2000.
S. 303(1) to (2) substituted by FA 1998, s. 74(1) and Sch. 13, para. 15(1), in relation to shares issued on or after 6 April 1998. The wording of s. 303(1)–(2) was as follows:
"303(1) Where any relief is attributable to any shares in a company held by an individual, subsection (1A) below shall apply if at any time in the relevant period the company or any subsidiary repays, redeems or repurchases any of its share capital which belongs to any member other than–
(a) that individual, or
(b) another individual the relief attributable to whose shares in the company is thereby withdrawn or reduced by virtue of section 299 or 300(2)(a),
or makes any payment to any such member for giving up his right to any of the share capital of the company or subsidiary on its cancellation or extinguishment.
303(1A) The relief–
(a) if it is greater than the amount mentioned in subsection (1B) below, shall be reduced by that amount, and
(b) if paragraph (a) above does not apply, shall be withdrawn.
303(1B) The amount referred to in subsection (1A) above is an amount equal to tax at the lower rate for the year of assessment for which the relief was given on the amount receivable by the member or, if greater, the nominal value of the share capital in question; and section 299(4) above applies for the purposes of this subsection as it applies for the purposes of subsection (2) of that section.
303(2) Where subsection (1) above applies, the amount of relief to which an individual is entitled shall be reduced by the amount receivable by the member or, if greater, the nominal value of the share capital in question; and where, apart from this subsection, two or more individuals would be entitled to relief the reduction shall be made in proportion to the amounts of relief to which they would, apart from this subsection, have been entitled."
Former s. 303(1), (1A), (1B) substituted for the earlier s. 303(1) by FA 1994, s. 137 and Sch. 15, para. 17(a), in relation to shares issued on or after 1 January 1994 with effect for 1993–94 and subsequent years of assessment. The earlier version of s. 303(1) provided as follows:
"303(1) The relief to which an individual is entitled in respect of any shares in a company shall be reduced in accordance with subsection (2) below if at any time in the relevant period the company repays, redeems or repurchases any of its share capital which belongs to any member other than–
(a) that individual; or
(b) another individual whose relief is thereby withdrawn or reduced by virtue of section 299 or reduced by virtue of section 300(2)(a);
or makes any payment to any such member for giving up his right to any of the company's share capital on its cancellation or extinguishment."
In s. 303(1AA) reference to s. 303AA inserted by FA 2001, Sch. 15, para. 19(2), with effect from the time mentioned in the first amendment noted above.
S. 303(1AA) inserted by FA 2000, s. 63(2) and Sch. 16, para. 2(2), in relation to shares issued on or after 1 April 2000 but before 1 April 2010.
S. 303(1B) amended by FA 2001, Sch. 15, para. 19(3), with effect from the time mentioned in the first amendment noted above.
S. 303(1B)(c) inserted by FA 2000, s. 63(2) and Sch. 16, para. 2(2), in relation to shares issued on or after 1 April 2000 but before 1 April 2010.
In s. 303(1C), "received" substituted for "receivable" by FA 2001, Sch. 15, para. 19(4), with effect from the time mentioned in the first amendment noted above.
S. 303(2A)(b) and (c) substituted for former para. (b) by FA 2001, Sch. 15, para. 19(5), with effect from the time mentioned in the first amendment noted above.
In s. 303(2), "the applicable periods" substituted for "the seven year periods" by FA 2000, s. 64 and Sch. 17, para. 5(3), with effect in relation to shares issued on or after 6 April 2000.
S. 303(2A) inserted by FA 2000, s. 64 and Sch. 17, para. 5(4), with effect in relation to shares issued on or after 6 April 2000.
S. 303(3)–(7) repealed by FA 2001, Sch. 15, para. 19(6) and Sch. 33, Pt. 2(3), with effect from the time mentioned in the first amendment noted above.
In s. 303(3), "designated" substituted for "seven year" by FA 2000, s. 64 and Sch. 17, para. 5(5), with effect in relation to shares issued on or after 6 April 2000. The words "the seven year period" were substituted by FA 1998, s. 74(1) and Sch. 13, para. 15(2) in place of the words "the relevant period" in relation to shares issued on or after 6 April 1998.
In s. 303(3), "291B(1)" and "291B" substituted for former "291(4)" and "291" respectively, by FA 1994, s. 137 and Sch. 15, para. 17(b) in relation to shares issued on or after 1 January 1994 with effect for 1993–94 and subsequent years of assessment.

S. 303(6A) inserted by FA 1994, s. 137 and Sch. 15, para. 17(c), in relation to shares issued on or after 1 January 1994 with effect for 1993–94 and subsequent years of assessment.
S. 303(8) repealed, by FA 1994, s. 137 and Sch. 15, para. 17(d), and s. 258 and Sch. 26, Pt. V(17), in relation to shares issuedon or after 1 January 1994 with effect for 1993–94 and subsequent years of assessment. S. 303(8) formerly provided as follows:
"**303(8)** Subsection (1) above does not apply in relation to the redemption of any share capital for which the redemption date was fixed before 15th March 1983.".
In s. 303(9A) "sections 303AA and 303A" substituted for "section 303AA" by FA 2004, s. 93 and Sch. 18, para. 7, with effect in relation to any repayment (within the meaning of ICTA 1988, section 303A) made on or after 17 March 2004.
In s. 303(9A), reference to s. 303AA inserted by FA 2001, Sch. 15, para. 19(7), and concluding words "or, as the case may be, the receipt of value in question" omitted by FA 2001, Sch. 33, Pt. 2(3), both with effect from the time mentioned in the first amendment noted above.
S. 303(9A) substituted by FA 1998, s. 74(1) and Sch. 13, para. 15(2), in relation to shares issued on or after 6 April 1998. The wording of former s. 303(9A) was as follows:
"**303(9A)** References in this section to a subsidiary of a company are references to a 51 per cent subsidiary of the company, whether it becomes such a subsidiary before or after the redemption, repayment, repurchase or payment in question or, as the case may be, the receipt of value in question."
Former s. 303(9A) and s. 303(9B) inserted by FA 1994, s. 137 and Sch. 15, para. 17(e); and s. 303(10), (11) repealed by FA 1994, s. 137 and Sch. 15, para. 17(f), and s. 258 and Sch. 26, Pt. V(17), in relation to shares issued on or after 1 January 1994 with effect for 1993–94 and subsequent years of assessment. The wording of former s. 303(10) and (11) was as follows:
"**303(10)** Where relief to which an individual is entitled in respect of eligible shares issued after 18th March 1986 is reduced by virtue of this section, effect shall be given to the reduction by apportioning it as between any such eligible shares held by him in such a way as appears to the inspector, or on appeal to the Commissioners concerned, to be just and reasonable.
303(11) In relation to shares issued before 19th March 1986, subsection (1)(b) above shall have effect with the omission of the words "withdrawn or reduced by virtue of section 299 or".".

Derivations – Former s. 303(1): FA 1983, Sch. 5, para. 10(1), as amended by FA 1986, Sch. 9, para. 11(2).
S. 303(2)–(7) (as originally enacted): FA 1981, s. 59(3)–(8), as amended and applied by FA 1983, Sch. 5, para. 10(2).
S. 303(8), (9) (as originally enacted): FA 1983, Sch. 5, para. 10(3), (4), as amended by the Companies Consolidation (Consequential Provisions) Act 1985, Sch. 2, and FA 1987, Sch. 15, para. 15(1).
Former s. 303(10): FA 1983, Sch. 5, para. 10(5A), inserted by F(No. 2)A 1983, s. 5 and Sch. 1 and substituted by FA 1986, Sch. 9, para. 11(3).
Former s. 303(11): FA 1983, Sch. 5, para. 10(1) and FA 1986, Sch. 9, para. 1(2).

Cross references – TCGA 1992, s. 150B(1)(b): reduction of CGT relief where s. 303(1A)(a) applies.
TCGA 1992, Sch. 5B: capital gains tax deferral on reinvestment in EIS qualifying shares.

Notes – S. 303 rewritten for income tax purposes as follows:
S. 303(1): ITA 2007, s. 224(1).
S. 303(1A): ITA 2007, s. 224(2).
S. 303(1AA): ITA 2007, s. 224(3).
S. 303(1B): ITA 2007, s. 224(4), (5).
S. 303(1C): ITA 2007, s. 224(2), 227(1), 228(1), (2), 229(1), (2).
S. 303(1D): ITA 2007, s. 227(2).
S. 303(2): ITA 2007, s. 226(1), (2).
S. 303(2A): ITA 2007, s. 226(1).
S. 302(9): ITA 2007, s. 230(1), (2), (3).
S. 302(9A): ITA 2007, s. 224(7).
S. 302(9B): ITA 2007, s. 224(7).

303AA Insignificant repayments disregarded for purposes of section 303(1)

303AA [Omitted by ITA 2007, s. 1027 and Sch. 1, para. 627 and repealed by ITA 2007, s. 1031 and Sch. 3, Pt. 2 with effect in relation to shares issued after 5 April 2007.]

History – S. 303AA omitted by ITA 2007, s. 1027 and Sch. 1, para. 627 and repealed by ITA 2007, s. 1031 and Sch. 3, Pt. 2 with effect in relation to shares issued after 5 April 2007. In so far as it continues to apply in relation to shares issued before 6 April 2007, s. 303AA is as follows:
"**303AA(1)** Any repayment shall be disregarded for the purposes of section 303(1) (repayments etc. which cause withdrawal or reduction of relief) if whichever is the greater of–
(a) the market value of the shares to which it relates (**"the target shares"**) immediately before the event occurs, and
(b) the amount received by the member in question,
is insignificant in relation to the market value of the remaining issued share capital of the company in question (or, as the case may be, subsidiary in question) immediately after the event occurs.
This is subject to subsection (4) below.
303AA(2) For the purposes of this section **"repayment"** means a repayment, redemption, repurchase or payment mentioned in section 303(1) (repayments etc. which cause withdrawal or reduction of relief).
303AA(3) For the purposes of subsection (1) above it shall be assumed that the target shares are cancelled at the time the repayment is made.
303AA(4) Where an individual subscribes for eligible shares in a company, subsection (1) above does not apply to prevent section 303(1) having effect in relation to those shares if, at a relevant time, arrangements are in existence that provide–
(a) for a repayment by the company or any subsidiary of the company (whether or not it is such a subsidiary at the time the arrangements are made), or
(b) for anyone to be entitled to such a repayment,
at any time in the period of restriction relating to those shares.
303AA(5) For the purposes of subsection (4) above **"a relevant time"** means any time in the period–
(a) beginning one year before the eligible shares were issued, and
(b) expiring at the end of the issue date."
S. 303AA inserted by FA 2001, Sch. 15, para. 20, with effect:
(1) in relation to shares issued on or after 7 March 2001, and
(2) in relation to shares issued before that date, in respect of the application of ICTA 1988, Pt. VII, Ch. III and TCGA 1992, Sch. 5B, in relation to:
(a) value received (within the meaning of ICTA 1988, s. 300 or TCGA 1992, Sch. 5B, para. 13), and
(b) repayments made (see s. 300(1) or TCGA 1992, Sch. 5B, para. 14(1)),
on or after that date.

Notes – S. 303AA rewritten for income tax purposes as follows:
S. 303AA(1): ITA 2007, s. 225(1).
S. 303AA(2): ITA 2007, s. 224(7).
S. 303AA(3): ITA 2007, s. 225(2).
S. 303AA(4): ITA 2007, s. 225(3), (4).
S. 303AA(5): ITA 2007, s. 225(3).

303A Restriction on withdrawal of relief under section 303

303A [Omitted by ITA 2007, s. 1027 and Sch. 1, para. 627 and repealed by ITA 2007, s. 1031 and Sch. 3, Pt. 2 with effect in relation to shares issued after 5 April 2007.]

History – S. 303A omitted by ITA 2007, s. 1027 and Sch. 1, para. 627 and repealed by ITA 2007, s. 1031 and Sch. 3, Pt. 2 with effect in relation to shares issued after 5 April 2007. In so far as it continues to apply in relation to shares issued before 6 April 2007, s. 303A is as follows:
"303A(1) Subsections (4) and (7) below apply where, by reason of a repayment, any investment relief which is attributable under Schedule 15 to the Finance Act 2000 to any shares is withdrawn under paragraph 56(2) of that Schedule.
303A(2) For the purposes of this section **"repayment"** has the meaning given in section 303AA(2) above.
303A(3) For the purposes of this section **"the relevant amount"**is the amount determined by the formula–

$$X - 5Y$$

Where–

X is the amount of the repayment, and
Y is the aggregate amount of investment relief withdrawn by reason of the repayment.

303A(4) Where the relevant amount does not exceed £1,000 the repayment shall be disregarded for the purposes of section 303(1), unless repayment arrangements are in existence at any time in the period–
(a) beginning one year before the shares mentioned in subsection (1) above are issued, and
(b) expiring at the end of the issue date of those shares.
303A(5) For this purpose **"repayment arrangements"** means arrangements which provide–
(a) for a repayment by the company that issued the shares ("the issuing company") or any subsidiary of that company, or
(b) for anyone to be entitled to such a repayment,
at any time.
303A(6) Subsection (5)(a) above applies in relation to a subsidiary of the issuing company whether or not it is such a subsidiary–
(a) [omitted by FA 2004, s. 93 and Sch. 18, para. 8 and repealed by s. 326 and Sch. 42, Pt. 2(13).]
(b) when the arrangements were made.
303A(7) Where the repayment is not disregarded by virtue of subsection (4) above, the amount receivable by reason of the repayment shall be treated for the purposes of section 303(1C)(a) as an amount equal to the relevant amount.
303A(8) [Repealed by FA 2001, Sch. 15, para. 21(b) and Sch. 33, Pt. 2(3).]
303A(9) In this section–
(a) **"investment relief"** has the same meaning as in Schedule 15 to the Finance Act 2000 (corporate venturing scheme), and
(b) references to the withdrawal of investment relief include its reduction."

S. 303A(2) substituted, s. 303A(8) repealed, and s. 303A(9) amended by FA 2001, Sch. 15, para. 21(a) and Sch. 33, Pt 2(3), with effect:
(1) in relation to shares issued on or after 7 March 2001, and
(2) in relation to shares issued before that date, in respect of the application of ICTA 1988, Pt. VII, Ch. III and TCGA 1992, Sch. 5B, in relation to:
  (a) value received (within the meaning of ICTA 1988, s. 300 or TCGA 1992, Sch. 5B, para. 13), and
  (b) repayments made (see s. 300(1) or TCGA 1992, Sch. 5B, para. 14(1)),

on or after that date.
S. 303A(6)(a) omitted by FA 2004, s. 93 and Sch. 18, para. 8 and repealed by s. 326 and Sch. 42, Pt. 2(13) in relation to any repayment (within the meaning of ICTA 1988, s. 303A) made on or after 17 March 2004.
S. 303A inserted by FA 2000, s. 63(2) and Sch. 16, para. 2(3), in relation to shares issued on or after 1 April 2000 but before 1 April 2010.

Notes – S. 303A rewritten for income tax purposes as follows:
S. 303A(1): ITA 2007, s. 231(1).
S. 303A(2): ITA 2007, s. 224(7).
S. 303A(3): ITA 2007, s. 231(2).
S. 303A(4): ITA 2007, s. 231(3).
S. 303A(5): ITA 2007, s. 231(4).
S. 303A(6): ITA 2007, s. 231(5).
S. 303A(7): ITA 2007, s. 231(6).
S. 303A(9): ITA 2007, s. 231(7).

304 Spouses and civil partners

History – In the heading to s. 304 the words "Spouses and civil partners" substituted for the words "Husband and wife" by SI 2005/3229, reg. 65(c), with effect from 5 December 2005.

304 [Omitted by ITA 2007, s. 1027 and Sch. 1, para. 627 and repealed by ITA 2007, s. 1031 and Sch. 3, Pt. 2 with effect in relation to shares issued after 5 April 2007.]

History – S. 304 omitted by ITA 2007, s. 1027 and Sch. 1, para. 627 and repealed by ITA 2007, s. 1031 with effect in relation to shares issued after 5 April 2007. In so far as it continues to apply in relation to shares issued before 6 April 2007, s. 304 is as follows:
"304(1) Section 299(1) shall not apply to a disposal of shares to which an amount of relief is attributable made by an individual to his spouse or civil partner at a time when they are living together.
304(2) Where such shares issued to one of them (**"the transferor"**) are transferred to the other (**"the transferee"**) by a transaction inter vivos to which that section does not apply, this Chapter shall have effect, in relation to any subsequent disposal or other event, as if–
(a) the transferee were the person who had subscribed for the shares,
(b) the transferee's liability to income tax had been reduced under section 289A in respect of those shares for the same year of assessment as that for which the transferor's liability was so reduced and, accordingly, that amount of relief had continued to be attributable to the shares notwithstanding the transfer.
304(3) Any assessment for reducing or withdrawing the relief by reason of any such disposal or other event shall be made on the transferee.
304(4) Subsections (6) to (6D) of section 299 shall apply for the purposes of this section as they apply for the purposes of that section."

ICTA 1988

In s. 304(1) the words "an individual to his spouse or civil partner" substituted for the words "a married man to his wife or a married woman to her husband" by SI 2005/3229, reg. 65(b) with effect from 5 December 2005.
S. 304(4) inserted by FA 1998, s. 74(1) and Sch. 13, para. 16(1), with effect in relation to disposals made on or after 6 April 1998.
S. 304 substituted by FA 1994, s. 137 and Sch. 15, para. 18, in relation to shares issued on or after 1 January 1994 with effect for 1993–94 and subsequent years of assessment. As it has effect in relation to shares issued before 1 January 1994, s. 304 (as amended by FA 1988, s. 35 and Sch. 3, para. 12(1)(b) including the repeal of s. 304(1)–(4)) provides as follows:
"**304(5)** Subsection (1) of section 299 shall not apply to a disposal made by an individual to his spouse or civil partner at a time when they are living together; but where shares issued to one of them have been transferred to the other by a transaction inter vivos that subsection shall apply on the disposal of the shares by the transferee to a third person and any assessment for withdrawing relief in respect of the shares shall be made on the transferee.
304(6) If any relief given for the year 1989–90 or any earlier year of assessment in respect of shares for which a married man or married woman has subscribed and which were issued while they were living together falls to be withdrawn in the year 1990–91 or any subsequent year of assessment by virtue of a disposal of those shares by the person who subscribed for them, any assessment for withdrawing that relief shall be made on the person making the disposal and shall be made by reference to the reduction of tax flowing from the amount of the relief regardless of any allocation of that relief under section 280 or of any allocation of the reduction under section 284 for the year of assessment for which the relief was given.
304(7) Subsections (3) to (4C) of section 299 shall apply for the purposes of this section as they apply for the purposes of that section."
In former s. 304(5) the words "an individual to his spouse or civil partner" substituted for the words "a married man to his wife or a married woman to her husband" by SI 2005/3229, reg. 65(a) with effect from 5 December 2005.
Former s. 304(7) inserted by FA 1998, s. 74(1) and Sch. 13, para. 40(1), with effect in relation to disposals made on or after 6 April 1998 of shares issued prior to 1 January 1994.

Cross references – S. 301A: receipts of insignificant value: supplementary provision.
TCGA 1992, s. 150A(3): limitation of CGT exemption on disposal of enterprise investment scheme shares.
TCGA 1992, Sch. 5B, para. 4: chargeable events in relation to EIS shares.

Notes – S. 304 rewritten for income tax purposes as follows:
S. 304(1): ITA 2007, s. 209(4).
S. 304(2): ITA 2007, s. 245(1), (2), (3).
S. 304(3): ITA 2007, s. 245(4).
S. 304(4): ITA 2007, s. 246(2), (3), (4), (5), (6), (7).

304A Acquisition of share capital by new company

304A [Omitted by ITA 2007, s. 1027 and Sch. 1, para. 627 and repealed by ITA 2007, s. 1031 and Sch. 3, Pt. 2 with effect in relation to shares issued after 5 April 2007.]

History – S. 304A omitted by ITA 2007, s. 1027 and Sch. 1, para. 627 and repealed by ITA 2007, s. 1031 and Sch. 3, Pt. 2 with effect in relation to shares issued after 5 April 2007. In so far as it continues to apply in relation to shares issued before 6 April 2007, s. 304A is as follows:
"**304A(1)** This section applies where–
(a) a company ("the new company") in which the only issued shares are subscriber shares acquires all the shares ("old shares") in another company ("the old company");
(b) the consideration for the old shares consists wholly of the issue of shares ("new shares") in the new company;
(c) the consideration for new shares of each description consists wholly of old shares of the corresponding description;
(d) new shares of each description are issued to the holders of old shares of the corresponding description in respect of and in proportion to their holdings;
(e) at some time before the issue of the new shares–
(i) the old company issued eligible shares; and
(ii) a certificate in relation to those eligible shares was issued by that company for the purposes of subsection (2) of section 306 and in accordance with that section; and
(f) before the issue of the new shares, the Board have, on the application of the new company or the old company, notified that company that the Board are satisfied that the exchange of shares–
(i) will be effected for bona fide commercial reasons; and
(ii) will not form part of any such scheme or arrangements as are mentioned in section 137(1) of the 1992 Act.
304A(2) For the purposes of this Chapter–
(a) the exchange of shares shall not be regarded as involving any disposal of the old shares or any acquisition of the new shares; and
(b) any relief under this Chapter which is attributable to any old shares shall be attributable instead to the new shares for which they are exchanged.
304A(3) Where, in the case of any new shares held by an individual to which relief becomes so attributable, the old shares for which they are exchanged were subscribed for by and issued to the individual, this Chapter (except section 297(5D)) shall have effect as if–
(a) the new shares had been subscribed for by him at the time when, and for the amount for which, the old shares were subscribed for by him;
(b) the new shares had been issued to him by the new company at the time when the old shares were issued to him by the old company;
(c) the claim for relief made in respect of the old shares had been made in respect of the new shares; and
(d) his liability to income tax had been reduced under section 289A in respect of the new shares for the same year of assessment as that for which his liability was so reduced in respect of the old shares.
304A(4) Where, in the case of any new shares held by an individual to which relief becomes so attributable, the old shares for which they are exchanged were transferred to the individual as mentioned in section 304, this Chapter (except section 297(5D)) shall have effect in relation to any subsequent disposal or other event as if–
(a) the new shares had been subscribed for by him at the time when, and for the amount for which, the old shares were subscribed for;
(b) the new shares had been issued by the new company at the time when the old shares were issued by the old company;
(c) the claim for relief made in respect of the old shares had been made in respect of the new shares; and
(d) his liability to income tax had been reduced under section 289A in respect of the new shares for the same year of assessment as that for which the liability of the individual who subscribed for the old shares was so reduced in respect of those shares.
304A(5) Where relief becomes so attributable to any new shares–
(a) this Chapter shall have effect as if anything which, under section 306(2), 307(1A) or 310, has been done, or is required to be done, by or in relation to the old company had been done, or were required to be done, by or in relation to the new company; and
(b) any appeal brought by the old company against a notice under section 307(1A)(b) may be prosecuted by the new company as if it had been brought by that company.

304A(6) For the purposes of this section old shares and new shares are of a corresponding description if, on the assumption that they were shares in the same company, they would be of the same class and carry the same rights; and in subsection (1) above references to shares, except in the expressions "eligible shares" and "subscriber shares", include references to securities.
304A(7) Nothing in section 293(8) shall apply in relation to such an exchange of shares, or shares and securities, as is mentioned in subsection (1) above or arrangements with a view to such an exchange.
304A(8) Subsection (2) of section 138 of the 1992 Act shall apply for the purposes of subsection (1)(f) above as it applies for the purposes of subsection (1) of that section."
In s. 304A(3) the words "(except section 297(5D))" inserted by FA 2007, s. 51 and Sch. 16, para. 11(2), with effect from 6 April 2007 (subject to the transitional provisions at FA 2007, Sch. 16, para. 14).
In s. 304A(4) the words "(except section 297(5D))" inserted by FA 2007, s. 51 and Sch. 16, para. 11(2), with effect from 6 April 2007 (subject to the transitional provisions at FA 2007, Sch. 16, para. 14).
S. 304A inserted by FA 1998, s. 74 and Sch. 13, para. 17 with effect in relation to new shares (within the meaning of ICTA 1988, s. 304A) issued on or after 6 April 1998.
S. 304A also inserted into Pt. VII, Ch. III, as it has effect in relation to shares issued before 1 January 1994, by FA 1998, s. 74(1) and Sch. 13, para. 41, with effect in relation to new shares (within the meaning of ICTA 1988, s. 304A) issued on or after 6 April 1998.

Cross references – ICTA 1988, s. 293(1B)(b)(i) : unquoted company requirement.
ICTA 1988. s. 576(4)–(4B): relief for losses on unlisted shares in trading companies.
TCGA 1992, s. 150A(8D): disapplication of restriction of relief where shares issued on or after 6 April 1998 and subsequently transferred under s. 304A.

Notes – S. 304A rewritten for income tax purposes as follows:
S. 304A(1): ITA 2007, s. 145(1), 247(1), Sch. 1 para. 130.
S. 304A(2): ITA 2007, s. 145(2), 247(3), Sch. 1 para. 130.
S. 304A(3): ITA 2007, s. 146(1), (2), 249(1), (2), Sch. 1 para. 131.
S. 304A(4): ITA 2007, s. 146(1), (2), 249(3), (4).
S. 304A(5): ITA 2007, s. 248(1), (2), (3).
S. 304A(6): ITA 2007, s. 145(1), (4), 247(1), (5), Sch. 1 para. 130.
S. 304A(7): ITA 2007, s. 145(3), 247(4), Sch. 1 para. 130.
S. 304A(8): ITA 2007, s. 247(2).

305 Reorganisation of share capital

305 [Omitted by ITA 2007, s. 1027 and Sch. 1, para. 627 and repealed by ITA 2007, s. 1031 and Sch. 3, Pt. 2 with effect in relation to shares issued after 5 April 2007.]

History – S. 305 omitted by ITA 2007, s. 1027 and Sch. 1, para. 627 and repealed by s. 1031 and Sch. 3, Pt. 2 with effect in relation to shares issued after 5 April 2007. In so far as it continues to apply in relation to shares issued before 6 April 2007, s. 305 is as follows:
"**305(1)** Subsection (2) below applies where–
(a) there is by virtue of any allotment in the relevant period, being such an allotment for payment as is mentioned in section 126(2)(a) of the 1992 Act, a reorganisation affecting ordinary shares,
(b) immediately before the reorganisation an amount of relief ("X") is attributable to the shares, and
(c) both–
(i) the amount subscribed for the shares ("Z"), and
(ii) the market value of the shares immediately before the reorganisation,
exceed the market value of the shares immediately after the reorganisation.
305(2) Where this subsection applies, the relief attributable to the shares shall be reduced by the following amount–

$$\frac{X \times Y}{Z}$$

where "Y" is whichever is the smaller of the amounts by which Z, and the market value of the shares immediately before the reorganisation, exceed the market value of the shares immediately after the reorganisation.
305(3) Subsection (2) above also applies where–
(a) an individual, who at any time in the relevant period has received, or become entitled to receive, in respect of any ordinary shares in a company, a provisional allotment of shares in or debentures of the company, disposes of his rights, and
(b) that subsection would have applied if he had not disposed of the rights but the allotment had been made to him by virtue of those rights.
305(4) Section 312(1A)(a) applies to determine the relevant period for the purposes of this section.
305(5) Subsection (2) above shall not apply where the reorganisation occurs on or after 29th November 1994.
305(6) Subsection (2) above shall not apply by virtue of subsection (3) above where the rights are disposed of on or after 29th November 1994."
S. 305(5), (6) inserted by FA 1995, s. 66(4) in relation to shares issued on or after 1 January 1994.
S. 305 substituted by FA 1994, s. 137 and Sch. 15, para. 19, in relation to shares issued on or after 1 January 1994 with effect for 1993–94 and subsequent years of assessment. Former s. 305 provided as follows:
"**305(1)** Where shares in respect of which relief has been given and not withdrawn have by virtue of any such allotment, otherwise than for payment, as is mentioned in section 126(2)(a) of the 1992 Act fallen to be treated under section 127 of that Act as the same asset as a new holding–
(a) a disposal of the whole or part of the new holding shall be treated for the purposes of this Part as a disposal of the whole or a corresponding part of those shares; and
(b) the new holding shall be treated for the purposes of section 299(3) as shares in respect of which relief has been given and not withdrawn.
305(2) Where–
(a) there is, by virtue of any such allotment for payment as is mentioned in section 126(2)(a) of the 1992 Act, a reorganisation affecting ordinary shares in respect of which relief has been given; and
(b) immediately before the reorganisation the relief had not been withdrawn; and
(c) the amount of relief (or, where the relief has been reduced, the amount remaining) and the market value of the shares immediately before the reorganisation, exceeds their market value immediately after the reorganisation
the relief shall be reduced by an amount equal to whichever is the smaller of those excesses.
305(3) Subsection (2) above shall also apply where–
(a) an individual who has received, or become entitled to receive, in respect of any ordinary shares in a company, a provisional allotment of shares in or debentures of the company disposes of his rights; and
(b) subsection (2) above would have applied (apart from this subsection) had those rights not been disposed of but an allotment of shares or debentures made to him.
305(4) This section has effect in relation to reorganisations occurring after 18th March 1986.
305(5) Subsection (2) above shall not apply where the reorganisation occurs on or after 29th November 1994.

305(6) Subsection (2) above shall not apply by virtue of subsection (3) above where the rights are disposed of on or after 29th November 1994."
References to provisions of the 1992 Act substituted by TCGA 1992, Sch. 10, para. 14(17).

Derivations – Former s. 305(1)–(3) (as originally enacted): FA 1983, Sch. 5, para. 16A(1), (2), (4), inserted by FA 1986, Sch. 9, para. 17(1).
Former s. 305(4): FA 1986, Sch. 9, para. 17(2).

Cross references – TCGA 1992, s. 126(2)(a): reorganisation of share capital where securities allotted to members in proportion to their existing holdings.
TCGA 1992, s. 127: equation of original shares and new holding on reorganisation.
TCGA 1992, s. 150(10): effect of reduction of BES relief for capital gains tax purposes.
TCGA 1992, s. 150A(9): effect of reduction of enterprise investment scheme relief for capital gains tax purposes.

Other material – Taxline 1991/19 (not reproduced): Revenue confirmation that a clawback of relief under former s. 305(2) triggered only where the shares under the rights issue are issued below the original price.

Notes – S. 305 rewritten for income tax purposes as follows:
S. 305(1): ITA 2007, s. 145(1), 247(1), Sch. 1 para. 130.
S. 305(2): ITA 2007, s. 145(2), 247(3), Sch. 1 para. 130.
S. 305(3): ITA 2007, s. 146(1), (2), 249(1), (2), Sch. 1 para. 131.
S. 305(4): ITA 2007, s. 146(1), (2), 249(3), (4).
S. 305(5): ITA 2007, s. 248(1), (2), (3).
S. 305(6): ITA 2007, s. 145(1), (4), 247(1), (5), Sch. 1 para. 130.

305A Relief for loss on disposal of shares

305A [Omitted by ITA 2007. s. 1027 and Sch. 1, para. 43 and repealed by ITA 2007, s. 1031 and Sch. 3, Pt. 1 with effect for 2007–08 and subsequent tax years.]

Notes – S. 305A rewritten for income tax purposes as follows:
S. 305A(1): ITA 2007, s. 131(1), (2).
S. 305A(2): ITA 2007, s. 136(1).

306 Claims

306 [Omitted by ITA 2007, s. 1027 and Sch. 1, para. 627 and repealed by ITA 2007, s. 1031 and Sch. 3, Pt. 2 with effect in relation to shares issued after 5 April 2007.]

History – S. 306 omitted by ITA 2007, s. 1027 and Sch. 1, para. 627 and repealed by ITA 2007, s. 1031 and Sch. 3, Pt. 2 with effect in relation to shares issued after 5 April 2007. In so far as it continues to apply in relation to shares issued before 6 April 2007, s. 306 is as follows:

"**306(1)** A claim for relief in respect of eligible shares issued by a company in any year of assessment (or treated by section 289B(5) as so issued) shall be made–
(a) not earlier than the requirement in section 289A(6) is first satisfied; and
(b) not later than the fifth anniversary of the 31st January next following that year of assessment.

306(2) No claim for relief in respect of eligible shares in a company may be made unless the person making the claim has received from the company a certificate issued by the company in such form as the Board may direct and certifying that, except so far as they fall to be satisfied by that person, the conditions for the relief are satisfied in relation to those shares.

306(3) Before issuing a certificate for the purposes of subsection (2) above a company shall furnish the inspector with a statement to the effect that, except so far as they fall to be satisfied by the persons to whom eligible shares comprised in the share issue have been issued, the conditions for the relief–
(a) are satisfied in relation to that issue; and
(b) have been so satisfied at all times since the beginning of the relevant period.

306(3A) A company may not furnish an inspector with a statement in respect of any shares issued in any year of assessment–
(a) later than two years after the end of that year of assessment, or
(b) if the period of four months referred to in subsection (1)(a) above ended after the end of that year, later than two years after the end of that period.

306(4) No certificate shall be issued for the purposes of subsection (2) above without the authority of the inspector; but where the company, or a person connected with the company, has given notice to the inspector under section 310(2) or paragraph 16(2) or (4) of Schedule 5B to the 1992 Act, the authority must be given or renewed after the receipt of the notice.

306(5) Any statement under subsection (3) above shall be in such form as the Board may direct and shall contain–
(a) such additional information as the Board may reasonably require, including in particular information relating to the persons who have requested the issue of certificates under subsection (2) above;
(b) a declaration that the statement is correct to the best of the company's knowledge and belief; and
(c) such other declarations as the Board may reasonably require.

306(6) Where a company has issued a certificate for the purposes of subsection (2) above, or furnished a statement under subsection (3) above and–
(a) the certificate or statement is made fraudulently or negligently; or
(b) the certificate was issued in contravention of subsection (4) above;
the company shall be liable to a penalty not exceeding £3,000.

306(7) For the purposes of PAYE regulations no regard shall be had to the relief unless a claim for it has been duly made and admitted.

306(8) No application shall be made under section 55(3) or (4) of the Management Act (application for postponement of payment of tax pending appeal) on the ground that the applicant is eligible for the relief unless a claim for the relief has been duly made by him.

306(9) For the purposes of section 86 of the Management Act (interest on overdue tax), tax charged by an assessment–
(a) shall be regarded as due and payable notwithstanding that relief from the tax (whether by discharge or repayment) is subsequently given on a claim for the relief; but
(b) shall, unless paid earlier or due and payable later, be regarded as paid on the date of the making of the claim on which the relief is given;
and section 91 of that Act (effect on interest of reliefs) shall not apply in consequence of any discharge or repayment for giving effect to the relief.

306(10) For the purposes of the provisions of the Management Act relating to appeals against decisions on claims, the refusal of the inspector to authorise the issue of a certificate under subsection (2) above shall be taken to be a decision refusing a claim made by the company.

306(11) Section 312(1A)(b) applies to determine the relevant period for the purposes of this section."
In s. 306(1), the words "(or so treated … as so issued)" inserted by FA 1998, s. 74(1) and Sch. 13, para. 19(1), with effect in relation to shares issued on or after 6 April 1998.

S. 306(1)(a)substituted by FA 2001, Sch. 15, para. 22, with effect in relation to shares issued on or after 6 April 2001.
In s. 306(1) as it has effect in relation to shares issued on or after 1 January 1994, para. (b) substituted by FA 1996, s. 135 and Sch. 21, para. 7 for 1996–97 and later years of assessment. As it previously had effect, para. (b) read as follows:
"(b) not later than twelve months after an inspector authorises the issue of a certificate for the purpose of subsection (2) below".
In s. 306(1), "289A(7)(a), (b) or (c)" substituted for former "s. 289(8)(a), (b) or (c)", and former para. (b) substituted, by FA 1994, s. 137 and Sch. 15, para. 21(a), in relation to shares issued on or after 1 January 1994 with effect for 1993–94 and subsequent years of assessment. Former para. (b) provided as follows:
"(b) not later than two years after the end of that year of assessment or, if that period of four months ended after the end of that year, not later than two years after the end of that period.".
In s. 306(2), the words ", except so far … conditions for the relief" substituted for the words "the conditions for the relief, so far as applying to the company and the trade" by FA 1998, s. 74(1) and Sch. 13, para. 19(2), with effect in relation to shares issued on or after 6 April 1998.
In s. 306(2) words "No claim for relief in respect of eligible shares in a company may be made unless the person making the claim has received from the company" substituted for "A claim for relief in respect of eligible shares in a company shall not be allowed unless it is accompanied by" by FA 1996, s. 134 and Sch. 20, para. 22 for shares issued on or after 6 April 1996.
S. 306(3) substituted by FA 1998, s. 74(1) and Sch. 13, para. 19(3), with effect in relation to shares issued on or after 6 April 1998. As it has effect in relation to shares issued before that date, para. 19(3) provides as follows:
"**19(3)** Before issuing a certificate for the purposes of subsection (2) above a company shall furnish the inspector with a statement to the effect that it satisfies the conditions for the relief, so far as they apply in relation to the company and the trade, and has done so at all times since the beginning of the relevant period."
In s. 306(3A), the words following para. (b), "but section 289B(5) shall not apply for the purposes of this subsection" repealed by FA 1998, s. 74(1) and Sch. 13, para. 19(4), s. 165 and Sch. 27, Pt. III(14), with effect in relation to shares issued on or after 6 April 1998.
S. 306(3A) inserted by FA 1994, s. 137 and Sch. 15, para. 21(b), in relation to shares issued on or after 1 January 1994 with effect for 1993–94 and subsequent years of assessment.
S. 306(4) and (5) substituted by FA 1998, s. 74(1) and Sch. 13, para. 19(5), with effect in relation to shares issued on or after 6 April 1998. As they had effect in relation to shares issued before that date, s. 306(4), (5) provided as follows:
"**306(4)** No such certificate shall be issued without the authority of the inspector or where the company, or a person connected with the company, has given notice to the inspector under section 310(2).
306(5) Any statement under subsection (3) above shall contain such information as the Board may reasonably require, shall be in such form as the Board may direct and shall contain a declaration that it is correct to the best of the company's knowledge and belief."
In s. 306(7), the words "PAYE regulations" substituted for the words "regulations made under section 203" by ITEPA 2003, Sch. 6, para. 37 which has effect for the tax year 2003–04 and subsequent tax years.
In s. 306(8), the words "eligible for" substituted for former words "entitled to" by FA 1994, s. 137 and Sch. 15, para. 21(c), in relation to shares issued on or after 1 January 1994 with effect for 1993–94 and subsequent years of assessment.
In s. 306(10), the concluding sentence "This subsection shall not apply in relation to shares issued before 19th March 1986." repealed by FA 1994, s. 137 and Sch. 15, para. 21(d) and s. 258 and Sch. 26, Pt. V(17), and s. 306(11) inserted by FA 1994, s. 137 and Sch. 15, para. 21(e) in relation to shares issued on or after 1 January 1994 with effect for 1993–94 and subsequent years of assessment.

Derivations – S. 306(1)–(7) (as originally enacted): FA 1983, Sch. 5, para. 13(1)–(7).
S. 306(8): FA 1981, s. 61(6), applied by FA 1983, Sch. 5, para. 13(8).
S. 306(9), (10): FA 1983, Sch. 5, para. 13(9), (10), inserted by FA 1986, Sch. 1, para. 13.

Cross references – TMA 1970, s. 42: procedure for making claims, etc. (see s. 306(10)).
FA 1988, Sch. 4, para. 10: modification of s. 306(2), (3) where eligible shares issued for the purpose of raising finance for private rented housing under BES.
TCGA 1992, s. 150: capital gains tax relief on disposal of business expansion scheme shares.
TCGA 1992, s. 150A: capital gains tax relief on disposal of enterprise investment scheme shares.
TCGA 1992, Sch. 5B, para. 6: claims for relief in respect of relevant EIS shares.
SI 1995/352, reg. 14, 15, Sch.: extended time limits under s. 306(1)(b) for Lloyd's underwriters.

HMRC interpretations – IRInt. 141: practical consequences (e.g. completion of form EIS 1, etc.) where there is more than one qualifying business activity, for example two trades carried on by different subsidiaries, or a trade carried on by one subsidiary and research and development carried on by another.

Notes – S. 306 rewritten for income tax purposes as follows:
S. 306(1): ITA 2007, s. 202(1).
S. 306(2): ITA 2007, s. 203(1), 204(1).
S. 306(3): ITA 2007, s. 204(2), 205(1), (2).
S. 306(3A): ITA 2007, s. 205(4).
S. 306(4): ITA 2007, s. 204(3), (4).
S. 306(5): ITA 2007, s. 205(3).
S. 306(6): ITA 2007, s. 207.
S. 306(7): ITA 2007, s. 203(2).
S. 306(8): ITA 2007, s. 203(3).
S. 306(10): ITA 2007, s. 206.
S. 306(11): ITA 2007, s. 205(1).

307 Withdrawal of relief

307 [Omitted by ITA 2007, s. 1027 and Sch. 1, para. 627 and repealed by ITA 2007, s. 1031 and Sch. 3, Pt. 3 with effect in relation to shares issued after 5 April 2007.]

History – S. 307 omitted by ITA 2007, s. 1027 and Sch. 1, para. 627 and repealed by ITA 2007, s. 1031 and Sch. 3, Pt. 2 with effect in relation to shares issued after 5 April 2007. In so far as it continues to apply in relation to shares issued before 6 April 2007, s. 307 is as follows:
"**307(1)** Where any relief has been given which is subsequently found not to have been due, it shall be withdrawn by the making of an assessment to income tax for the year of assessment for which the relief was given.
307(1A) Relief may not be withdrawn, in relation to shares issued by a company on any date, on the ground that the company is not a qualifying company or that the requirements of section 289(1)(b), (ba), (c) or (d) are not met unless–
(a) the company has given notice under section 310 or paragraph 16(2) or (4) of Schedule 5B to the 1992 Act, or
(b) an inspector has given notice to the company stating that, by reason of that ground, the whole or any part of the relief given to individuals to whom the shares were issued on that date was not, in his opinion, due.
307(1B) The giving of notice by an inspector under subsection (1A) above shall be taken, for the purposes of the provisions of the Management Act relating to appeals against decisions on claims, to be a decision refusing a claim made by the company.
307(1C) Where any issue has been determined on an appeal brought by virtue of paragraph 1A(6) of Schedule 5B to the 1992 Act (appeal against notice that shares never have been, or have ceased to be, eligible shares), the determination shall be conclusive for the purposes of any appeal brought by virtue of subsection (1B) above on which that issue arises.

307(2) Subject to subsections (3) to (7) below, no assessment for withdrawing relief may be made, and no notice may be given under subsection (1A) above, more than six years after the end of the year of assessment–

(a) in which the time mentioned in section 289(3) falls, or

(b) in which the event by reason of which the claimant ceases to be eligible for relief occurs,

whichever is the later.

307(3) No assessment for withdrawing relief in respect of shares issued to any person shall be made by reason of any event occurring after his death.

307(4) Where a person has, by a disposal or disposals to which section 299(1)(b) applies, disposed of all the eligible shares issued to him by a company, no assessment for withdrawing relief in respect of any of those shares shall be made by reason of any subsequent event unless it occurs at a time when he is connected with the company within the meaning of section 291.

307(5) Subsection (2) above is without prejudice to section 36 of the Management Act (fraudulent or negligent conduct).

307(6) In its application to an assessment made by virtue of this section, section 86 of the Management Act (interest on overdue tax) shall have effect as if the relevant date were–

(a) in the case of relief withdrawn by virtue of section 289(6) or 299B(1) –

(i) so far as effect has been given to the relief in accordance with PAYE regulations, 5th April in the year of assessment in which effect was so given;

(ii) so far as effect has not been so given, the date on which the relief was granted.

(aa) in the case of relief withdrawn by virtue of section 289(1)(c) or (d), the date on which the relief was granted;

(b) in the case of relief withdrawn by virtue of section 289(1)(ba), 291, 293, 297, 302, 303(1) or 305 in consequence of any event after the grant of the relief, the date of that event;

(c) in the case of relief withdrawn by virtue of section 299(1) in consequence of a disposal after the grant of the relief, the date of the disposal;

(cca) in the case of relief withdrawn by virtue of section 299(5), the date on which the option was granted;

(ca) in the case of relief withdrawn by virtue of section 299A in consequence of the making of any loan after the grant of the relief, the date of the making of the loan;

(d) in the case of relief withdrawn by virtue of section 300 in consequence of a receipt of value after the grant of the relief, the date of the receipt.

307(7) For the purposes of subsection (6) above the date on which the relief is granted is the date on which a repayment of tax for giving effect to the relief was made or, if there was no such repayment, the date on which the inspector issued a notice to the claimant showing the amount of tax payable after giving effect to the relief.

307(8) Where a company has ceased to be a qualifying company in consequence of the operation of section 294, subsection (6) above shall apply as if the relief was withdrawn in consequence of an event which occurred at the time when the company so ceased to be a qualifying company.

307(8A) References in this section to the withdrawal of relief include its reduction.

307(9) [Repealed by FA 1994, s. 137 and Sch. 15, para. 22(e) and s. 258 and Sch. 26, Pt. V(17).]"

In s. 307(1) the words "to income tax" substituted by ITTOIA 2005, s. 882(1) and Sch. 1, para. 127; effective for income tax purposes for 2005–06 onwards and for corporation tax purposes for accounting periods ending after 5 April 2005 (ITTOIA 2005, s. 883(1)).

In s. 307(1), the following concluding words omitted by FA 1994, s. 137 and Sch. 15, para. 22(a), and s. 258 and Sch. 26, Pt. V(17), in relation to shares issued on or after 1 January 1994 with effect for 1993–94 and subsequent years of assessment:

"; but where by virtue of section 289(6) relief has been given for each of two consecutive years of assessment, any withdrawal of relief shall be made for the first of those years before being made for the second.".

In s. 307(1A) reference to s. 289(1)(d) inserted by FA 2001, Sch. 15, para. 7(a) in relation to shares issued on or after 7 March 2001; and in respect of the application of ICTA 1988, Pt. VII, Ch. III and TCGA 1992, Sch. 5B, on or after 7 March 2001 in relation to shares:

- that were issued after 31 December 1993 but before 7 March 2001, and
- to which income tax relief or deferral relief was attributable immediately before 7 March 2001.

In s. 307(1A), reference to ICTA 1988, s. 289(1)(b) and to TCGA 1995, Sch. 5B, para. 16(2) and (4) inserted by FA 1998, s. 74(1) and Sch. 13, para. 20(1), with effect in relation to shares issued on or after 6 April 1998.

S. 307(1A), (1B) and (2) substituted for former s. 307(2) by FA 1994, s. 137 and Sch. 15, para. 22(b), in relation to shares issued on or after 1 January 1994 with effect for 1993–94 and subsequent years of assessment. Former s. 307(2) provided as follows:

"**307(2)** Subject to subsections (3) to (7) below, any assessment for withdrawing relief which is made by reason of an event occurring after the date of the claim may be made within six years after the end of the year of assessment in which that event occurs.".

S. 307(1C) inserted by FA 1998, s. 74(1) and Sch. 13, para. 20(2), with effect in relation to shares issued on or after 6 April 1998.

In s. 307(4), the words "eligible shares" substituted for the words "ordinary shares" by FA 1998, s. 74(1) and Sch. 13, para. 20(3), with effect in relation to shares issued on or after 6 April 1998.

S. 307(5) amended by FA 1989, s. 149(4)(b), (7) substituting reference to TMA 1970, s. 36 with effect from 27 July 1989, but not affecting the making of assessments for years before 1983–84 or for accounting periods which ended before 1 April 1983.

S. 307(6): "relevant date" substituted for "reckonable date" by FA 1996, s. 132 and Sch. 18, para. 5, 17(3) for 1996–97 and later years of assessments and for income or capital gains tax relating to any earlier year of assessment and charged in an assessment made on or after 6 April 1998.

In s. 307(6)(a)(i), the words "PAYE regulations" substituted for the words "regulations under section 203" by ITEPA 2003, Sch. 6, para. 38 which has effect for the tax year 2003–04 and subsequent tax years.

In s. 307(6)(a), reference to ICTA 1988, s. 299B(1) inserted by FA 1998, s. 71(2), with effect in relation to shares issued on or after 6 April 1998.

In s. 307(6)(a), "289(6)" substituted for "289(11)", and s. 307(6)(aa) and (cca) inserted, by FA 1994, s. 137 and Sch. 15, para. 22(c), in relation to shares issued on or after 1 January 1994 with effect for 1993–94 and subsequent years of assessment.

In s. 307(6)(aa) reference to s. 289(1)(d) inserted by FA 2001, Sch. 15, para. 7(b) in relation to shares issued on or after 7 March 2001; and in respect of the application of ICTA 1988, Pt. VII, Ch. III and TCGA 1992, Sch. 5B, on or after 7 March 2001 in relation to shares:

- that were issued after 31 December 1993 but before 7 March 2001, and
- to which income tax relief or deferral relief was attributable immediately before 7 March 2001.

In s. 307(6)(b), reference to ICTA 1988, s. 289(1)(ba) inserted by FA 1998, s. 74(1) and Sch. 13, para. 20(4), with effect in relation to shares issued on or after 6 April 1998.

S. 307(6)(ca) inserted by FA 1993, s. 111(3), in relation to any case in which the claim for relief is made on or after 16 March 1993.

S. 307(8A) inserted by FA 1994, s. 137 and Sch. 15, para. 22(d), and s. 307(9) repealed, by FA 1994, s. 137 and Sch. 15, para. 22(e), and s. 258 and Sch. 26, Pt. V(17), in relation to shares issued on or after 1 January 1994 with effect for 1993–94 and subsequent years of assessment. Former s. 307(9) provided as follows:

"**307(9)** Subsections (1) to (7) above apply in relation to relief under Chapter II of Part IV of the Finance Act 1981 as they apply in relation to relief under this Chapter (or Schedule 5 to the Finance Act 1983) but–

(a) with the substitution for references to sections 299 (in both places), 291, 289(11), 293, 297, 302, 303(1), 305 and 300 of this Act of references respectively to sections 57, 54, 59(1), 53(7), 54, 55, 56, 59(2) and 58 of the Finance Act 1981; and

(b) with the omission of subsection (6)(a)(i).".

Derivations – S. 307(1) (as originally enacted): FA 1983, Sch. 5, para. 14(1) and (1A), inserted by FA 1987, s. 42(5).

S. 307(2)–(7) (as originally enacted): FA 1981, s. 62(2)–(7), as amended and applied by FA 1983, Sch. 5, para. 14(2), (as amended by F(No. 2)A 1983, s. 5 and Sch. 1, para. 8; FA 1986, Sch. 9, para. 14).

S. 307(8): FA 1983, Sch. 5, para. 5A(10), inserted by FA 1986. Sch. 9, para. 7.

Former s. 307(9): FA 1981, s. 62(6) and FA 1983, Sch. 5, para. 14(2).
Cross references – S. 203 and regulations made thereunder: PAYE.
TCGA 1992, Sch. 5B, para. 1A(6): decisions under s. 307(1B) shall be final and conclusive in relation to any subsequent appeal on which that issue arises.
Notes – S. 307 rewritten for income tax purposes as follows:
S. 307(1): ITA 2007, s. 234(1), 235.
S. 307(1A): ITA 2007, s. 234(2), (3).
S. 307(1B): ITA 2007, s. 236(1).
S. 307(1C): ITA 2007, s. 236(2).
S. 307(2): ITA 2007, s. 237(1), (2).
S. 307(3): ITA 2007, s. 238(1).
S. 307(4): ITA 2007, s. 238(2), (3).
S. 307(5): ITA 2007, s. 237(3).
S. 307(6): ITA 2007, s. 239(1).
S. 307(8A): ITA 2007, s. 235, 237(1), (2), 238(1), (2), (3), 239(1).

308 Application to subsidiaries

308 [Omitted by ITA 2007, s. 1027 and Sch. 1, para. 627 and repealed by ITA 2007, s. 1031 and Sch. 3, Pt. 3 with effect in relation to shares issued after 5 April 2007.]

308(6) [Repealed by FA 1994, s. 137 and Sch. 15, para. 23(b), and s. 258 and Sch. 26, Pt. V(17).]

History – S. 308 omitted by ITA 2007, s. 1027 and Sch. 1, para. 627 and repealed by ITA 2007, s. 1031 and Sch. 3, Pt. 2 with effect in relation to shares issued after 5 April 2007. In so far as it continues to apply in relation to shares issued before 6 April 2007, s. 308 is as follows:
"**308(1)** A qualifying company may, in the relevant period, have one or more subsidiaries if–
(a) the conditions mentioned in subsection (2) below are satisfied in respect of the subsidiary or, as the case may be, each subsidiary;
(b) [repealed by FA 1996, s. 74 and Sch. 8, para. 6(a) and s. 113 and Sch. 18, Pt. VI(8).]
308(2) The conditions referred to are–
(a) [omitted by FA 2004, s. 93 and Sch. 18, para. 9(b) and repealed by s. 326 and Sch. 42, Pt. 2(13).]
(b) [omitted by FA 2004, s. 93 and Sch. 18, para. 9(b) and repealed by s. 326 and Sch. 42, Pt. 2(13).]
(c) [omitted by FA 2004, s. 93 and Sch. 18, para. 9(b) and repealed by s. 326 and Sch. 42, Pt. 2(13).]
(ca) that more than 50 per cent. of the ordinary share capital of the subsidiary is owned directly or indirectly by the qualifying company;
(d) that no person other than the qualifying company or another of its subsidiaries has control of the subsidiary within the meaning of section 995 of ITA 2007; and
(e) that no arrangements are in existence by virtue of which either of the conditions in paragraphs (ca) and (d) above would cease to be satisfied.
308(3) The conditions shall not be regarded as ceasing to be satisfied by reason only of the subsidiary or any other company being wound up, or dissolved without winding up, if–
(a) the winding up or dissolution is for bona fide commercial reasons and is not part of a scheme or arrangement the main purpose or one of the main purposes of which is the avoidance of tax;
(b) [omitted by FA 2004, s. 93 and Sch. 18, para. 9(e).]
308(3A) The conditions shall not be regarded as ceasing to be satisfied by reason only of anything done as a consequence of the subsidiary or any other company being in administration or receivership if–
(a) the entry into administration or receivership, and
(b) everything done as a consequence of the company concerned being in administration or receivership,
is for bona fide commercial reasons and is not part of a scheme or arrangement the main purpose of which or one of the main purposes of which is the avoidance of tax.
308(4) The conditions shall not be regarded as ceasing to be satisfied by reason only of arrangements being in existence for the disposal by the qualifying company or (as the case may be) by another subsidiary of all its interest in the subsidiary if the disposal is to be for bona fide commercial reasons and is not to be part of a scheme or arrangement the main purpose or one of the main purposes of which is the avoidance of tax.
308(5) [Omitted by FA 2004, s. 93 and Sch. 18, para. 9(h).]
308(5A) Section 312(1A)(b) applies to determine the relevant period for the purposes of this section.
308(5B) Subsections (2) to (10) of section 838 apply for the purposes of subsection (2)(ca) above as they apply for the purposes of subsection (1) of that section."
In s. 308(1), the word "and" at the end of para. (a) and all of para. (b) repealed by FA 1997, s. 74 and Sch. 8, para. 6(a) and s. 113 and Sch. 18, Pt. VI(8), with effect in relation to shares issued after 26 November 1996, and with effect after 26 November 1996 in relation to shares which were issued on or after 1 January 1994 but before 27 November 1996, and immediately before 27 November 1996 were held by an individual and at that time were shares to which relief (within the meaning of Pt. VII, Ch. III) was attributable. In so far as it continues to apply to other shares, former para. (b) reads as follows:
"(b) the subsidiary or, as the case may be, each subsidiary exists wholly, or substantially wholly, for the purpose of carrying on one or more qualifying trades or is a property managing, or dormant, subsidiary."
In s. 308(1)(a) words "and, except as provided by subsection (3) below, continue to be so satisfied until the end of the relevant period" omitted by FA 2004, s. 93 and Sch. 18, para. 9(a), and repealed by s. 326, Sch. 42, Pt. 2(13), with effect, in relation to shares issued on or after 17 March 2004.
S. 308(2)(a)–(c) omitted by FA 2004, s. 93 and Sch. 18, para. 9(b), and repealed by s. 326 and Sch. 42, Pt. 2(13), with effect in relation to shares issued on or after 17 March 2004. The wording of former s. 308(2)(a)–(c) was as follows:
"(a) that the qualifying company, or another of its subsidiaries, possesses not less than 75 per cent of the issued share capital of, and not less than 75 per cent of the voting power in, the subsidiary;
(b) that the qualifying company, or another of its subsidiaries, would in the event of a winding up of the subsidiary or in any other circumstances be beneficially entitled to receive not less than 75 per cent of the assets of the subsidiary which would then be available for distribution to the equity holders of the subsidiary;
(c) that the qualifying company or another of its subsidiaries is beneficially entitled to not less than 75 per cent of any profits of the subsidiary which are available for distribution to the equity holders of the subsidiary;".
In s. 308(2), references to "75 per cent" substituted for "90 per cent" in each place by FA 1998, s. 74 and Sch. 13, para. 21 with effect in relation to shares issued on or after 6 April 1998.
S. 308(2)(ca) inserted by FA 2004, s. 93 and Sch. 18, para. 9(b), with effect in relation to shares issued on or after 17 March 2004.
In s. 308(2)(d) the words "995 of ITA 2007" substituted for "840" by SI 2007/1820, art. 2(2), with effect, for income tax purposes, for 2007–08 and subsequent tax years, and, for corporation tax purposes, for accounting periods ending after 5 April 2007.

In s. 308(2)(e) words "either of the conditions in paragraphs (ca) and" substituted for "the conditions in paragraphs (a) to" and "would" substituted for "could" by FA 2004, s. 93 and Sch. 18, para. 9(b), with effect in relation to shares issued on or after 17 March 2004.
S. 308(3) the words "any other company" substitued for "the qualifying company" by FA 2004, s. 93 and Sch. 18, para. 9(c), with effect in relation to shares issued on or after 17 March 2004.
S. 308(3)(a) the words "it is shown that" at the beginning omitted by FA 2004, s. 93 and Sch. 18, para.9, and repealed by s. 326, Sch. 42, Pt. 2(13), with effect in relation to shares issued on or after 17 March 2004.
S. 308(3)(a) the words "and is not" substitued for "and not" by FA 2004, s. 93 and Sch. 18, para. 9(d), with effect in relation to shares issued on or after 17 March 2004.
S. 308(3)(b) and the word "and" preceding it, omitted by FA 2004, s. 93 and Sch. 18, para. 9(e) and repealed by s. 326, Sch. 42, Pt. 2(13), with effect in relation to shares issued on or after 17 March 2004. The wording of former s. 308(3)(b) was as follows:
"(b) the net assets, if any, of the subsidiary or, as the case may be, the qualifying company are distributed to its members or dealt with as bona vacantia before the end of the relevant period, or in the case of a winding up, the end (if later) of three years from the commencement of the winding up.".
S. 308(3A) inserted by FA 2004, s. 93 and Sch. 18, para. 9(f), with effect in relation to shares issued on or after 17 March 2004.
Ins. 308(4) the words "arrangements being in existence for" inserted by FA 2004, s. 93 and Sch. 18, para. 9(g), with effect in relation to shares issued on or after 17 March 2004.
In s. 308(4) the words "within the relevant period" which followed "another subsidiary" omitted by FA 2004, s. 93 and Sch. 18, para. 9(g), and repealed by s. 326 and Sch. 42, Pt. 2(13), with effect in relation to shares issued on or after 17 March 2004.
In s. 308(4) the words "it is shown that" which followed "subsidiary if" omitted by FA 2004, s. 93 and Sch. 18, para. 9(g), and repealed by s. 326 and Sch. 42, Pt. 2(13), with effect in relation to shares issued on or after 17 March 2004.
In s. 308(4) the words "to be" inserted following "disposal is" by FA 2004, s. 93 and Sch. 18, para. 9(g), with effect in relation to shares issued on or after 17 March 2004.
In s. 308(4) the words "and is not to be" substituted for "and not" by FA 2004, s. 93 and Sch. 18, para. 9(g), with effect in relation to shares issued on or after 17 March 2004.
S. 308(5) omitted by FA 2004, s. 93 and Sch. 18, para. 9(h), and repealed by s. 326 and Sch. 42, Pt. 2(13), with effect in relation to shares issued on or after 17 March 2004. Former s. 308(5) read as follows:
"**308(5)** For the purposes of this section–
(a) [Repealed by FA 1997, s. 74 and Sch. 8, para. 6(b) and s. 113 and Sch. 18, Pt. VI(8).]
(b) [Repealed by FA 1997, s. 74 and Sch. 8, para. 6 and s. 113 and Sch. 18, Pt. VI(8).]
(c) the persons who are equity holders of a subsidiary and the percentage of the assets of a subsidiary to which an equity holder would be entitled shall be determined in accordance with paragraphs 1 and 3 of Schedule 18, taking references in paragraph 3 to the first company as references to an equity holder and references to a winding up as including references to any other circumstances in which assets of the subsidiary are available for distribution to its equity holders.".
In former s. 308(5), para. (a) and (b) repealed FA 1997, s. 74 and Sch. 8, para. 6(b) and s. 113 and Sch. 18, Pt. VI(8) with effect in relation to shares issued after 26 November 1996, and with effect after 26 November 1996 in relation to shares which were issued on or after 1 January 1994 but before 27 November 1996, and immediately before 27 November 1996 were held by an individual and at that time were shares to which relief (within the meaning of Pt. VII, Ch. III) was attributable. In so far as they continue to apply to other shares, former para. (a) and (b) read as follows:
"(a) a subsidiary of a qualifying company is a **"property managing subsidiary"** if it exists wholly, or substantially wholly, for the purpose of holding and managing property used by the qualifying company, or by any of its subsidiaries, for the purposes of–
(i) research and development from which it is intended that a qualifying trade to be carried on by the company or any of its subsidiaries will be derived; or
(ii) one or more qualifying trades so carried on;
(b) a subsidiary is a **"dormant subsidiary"** if it has no profits for the purposes of corporation tax and no part of its business consists in the making of investments; and"
S. 308(5A) inserted by FA 1994, s. 137 and Sch. 15, para. 23(a), and s. 308(6) repealed by FA 1994, s. 137 and Sch. 15, para. 23(b), and s. 258 and Sch. 26, Pt. V(17), in relation to shares issued on or after 1 January 1994 with effect for 1993–94 and subsequent years of assessment. Former s. 308(6) provided as follows:
"**308(6)** In relation to shares issued before 19th March 1986 this section shall have effect subject to the following modifications–
(a) the following paragraph shall be substituted for subsection (1)(b)–
"(b) the subsidiary or each subsidiary was incorporated in the United Kingdom and is a company falling within section 293(2)(a).";
(b) the following subsection shall be substituted for subsection (2)–
"**308(2)** The conditions referred to in subsection (1)(a) above are–
(a) that the qualifying company possesses all the issued share capital of, and all the voting power in, the subsidiary; and
(b) that no other person has control of the subsidiary within the meaning of section 840; and
(c) that no arrangements are in existence by virtue of which the conditions in paragraphs (a) and (b) above could cease to be satisfied."; and
(c) subsections (4) and (5) shall be omitted."
S. 308(5B) inserted by FA 2004, s. 93 and Sch. 18, para. 9, with effect in relation to shares issued on or after 17 March 2004.

Derivations – S. 308(1): FA 1983, Sch. 5, para. 17(1) substituted by FA 1986, Sch. 9, para. 18.
S. 308(2)–(5): FA 1983, Sch. 5, para. 17(1A)–(1D), inserted by FA 1986, Sch. 9, para. 18, and amended by FA 1987, Sch. 15, para. 15(2).
Former s. 308(6)(a) and (c): FA 1983, Sch. 5, para. 17(1) as enacted prior to amendment by FA 1986, Sch. 9, para. 18.
Former s. 308(6)(b): FA 1981, s. 65(2).

Cross references – ICTA 1988, s. 576: relief for losses on unlisted shares in trading companies.
TCGA 1992, Sch. 5B, para. 16(7): persons from whom information can be required in connection with a claim.
FA 1988, Sch. 4, para. 11: modification of s. 308(1) where eligible shares issued for the purposes of raising finance for private rented housing under BES.

Notes – S. 308 rewritten for income tax purposes as follows:
S. 308(1): ITA 2007, s. 140(1), 187, Sch. 1 para. 125.
S. 308(2): ITA 2007, s. 191(2), 1021(2).
S. 308(3): ITA 2007, s. 191(3).
S. 308(3A): ITA 2007, s. 191(4).
S. 308(4): ITA 2007, s. 191(5).
S. 308(5): ITA 2007, s. 237(3).
S. 308(5A): ITA 2007, s. 187.
S. 308(5B): ITA 2007, s. 191(2).

309 Further provisions as to subsidiaries

309 [Repealed by FA 1994, s. 137 and Sch. 15, para. 24, and s. 258 and Sch. 26, Pt. V(17), in relation to shares issued on or after 1 January 1994 with effect for 1993–94 and subsequent years of assessment.]

History – Former s. 309 provided as follows:
"**309(1)** Where a qualifying company has one or more subsidiaries in the relevant period, this Chapter shall have effect subject to subsections (2) to (8) below.
309(2) The shares issued by the qualifying company may, instead of or as well as being issued for the purpose mentioned in subsection (1)(a) of section 289, be issued for the purpose of raising money for a qualifying trade which is being carried on by a subsidiary or which a subsidiary intends to carry on; and, where shares are so issued, subsections (8), (9), (12)(b)(ii) and (13) of that section shall have effect as if references to the company were or, as the case may be, included references to the subsidiary.
309(3) In relation to a qualifying trade carried on by a subsidiary the reference in section 297(2)(g) to another person shall not include a reference to the company of which it is a subsidiary.
309(4) In section 303(1) references to the company (except the first) shall include references to a company which during the relevant period is a subsidiary of the company whether it becomes a subsidiary before or after the redemption, repayment, repurchase or payment referred to in that subsection.
309(5) In subsections (2), (4) and (6) of section 291, references to the company (except, in each subsection, the first such reference) include references to a company which is during the relevant period a subsidiary of that company–
(a) whether it becomes a subsidiary before, during or after the year of assessment in respect of which the individual concerned claims relief; or
(b) whether or not it is such a subsidiary while he is such an employee, partner or director as is mentioned in subsection (2) or while he has or is entitled to acquire such capital or voting power or rights as are mentioned in subsections (4) and (6).
309(6) Without prejudice to the provisions of section 291 (as it has effect in accordance with subsection (5) above), an individual shall be treated as connected with a company if–
(a) he has at any time in the relevant period had control (within the meaning of section 840) of another company which has since that time and before the end of the relevant period become a subsidiary of the company; or
(b) he directly or indirectly possesses or is entitled to acquire any loan capital of a subsidiary of that company.
309(7) Section 291(5) and (8) shall apply for the purposes of this section.
309(8) In sections 300(1) and 303(3) references to the receipt of value from the company shall include references to the receipt of value from any company which during the relevant period is a subsidiary of that company, whether it becomes a subsidiary before or after the individual concerned receives any value from it, and other references to the company in sections 300 and 301 and in section 303(6) shall be construed accordingly.".

Derivations – S. 309(1): FA 1983, Sch. 5, para. 17(2).
S. 309(2)–(4): FA 1983, Sch. 5, para. 18(1)–(3).
S. 309(5), (6): FA 1981, Sch. 12, para. 2(1), (1B), substituted by FA 1982, s. 52(2).
S. 309(7): FA 1983, Sch. 5, para. 18(5).
S. 309(8): FA 1981, Sch. 12, para. 4, as amended by FA 1982, s. 52(3).

Cross references – S. 840: control is defined by reference to the power of a person to secure that the affairs of a body corporate are conducted in accordance with his wishes.
FA 1988, Sch. 4, para. 12: modifications of s. 309(2) where eligible shares issued for the purpose of raising finance for private rented housing under BES.

310 Information

310 [Omitted by ITA 2007, s. 1027 and Sch. 1, para. 627 and repealed by ITA 2007, s. 1031 and Sch. 3, Pt. 2 with effect in relation to shares issued after 5 April 2007.]

History – S. 310 omitted by ITA 2007, s. 1027 and Sch. 1, para. 627 and repealed by ITA 2007, s. 1031 and Sch. 3, Pt. 2 with effect in relation to shares issued after 5 April 2007. In so far as it continues to apply in relation to shares issued before 6 April 2007, s. 310 is as follows:
"**310(1)** Where an event occurs by reason of which any relief given to an individual falls to be withdrawn by virtue of sections 291, 299, 299A or 300, or would fall to be withdrawn under section 300 were it not for the application of section 300A, the individual shall within 60 days of his coming to know of the event give a notice to the inspector containing particulars of the event.
310(2) Where an event occurs by reason of which any relief in respect of any shares in a company falls to be withdrawn by virtue of section 289(1)(ba), (c) or (d), 293, 300, 302 or 303, or would fall to be withdrawn under section 300 were it not for the application of section 300A,–
(a) the company; and
(b) any person connected with the company who has knowledge of that matter;
shall within 60 days of the event or, in the case of a person within paragraph (b) above, of his coming to know of it, give a notice to the inspector containing particulars of the event.
310(2A) Where–
(a) a person is required to give notice under subsection (1) or (2) above of an event by reason of which any relief in respect of any shares in a company–
(i) falls to be withdrawn under section 300, or
(ii) would fall to be so withdrawn were it not for the application of section 300A, and
(b) that person has knowledge of the replacement value received (or expected to be received) from the original recipient by the original supplier by reason of a qualifying receipt,
the notice shall include particulars of that receipt of the replacement value (or expected receipt).
In this subsection **"the replacement value"**, **"the original recipient"**, **"the original supplier"** and **"qualifying receipt"** shall be construed in accordance with section 300A.
310(3) Where–
(a) a company has issued a certificate under section 306(2) in respect of any eligible shares in the company; and
(b) it appears to the company, or to any person connected with the company who has knowledge of the matter, that section 294 may have effect to deny relief in respect of those shares;
the company or (as the case may be) that person or (where it so appears to each of them) both the company and that person shall give notice to the inspector setting out the particulars of the case.
310(4) If the inspector has reason to believe
(a) that a person has not given a notice which he is required to give under subsection (1) or (2) above in respect of any event, or under subsection (3) above in respect of any particular case, or
(b) that a person has given or received value (within the meaning of section 300(2) or (5)) which, but for the fact that the amount given or received was an amount of insignificant value (within the meaning of section 301A(2)), would have triggered a requirement to give a notice under subsection (1) or (2) above, or
(c) that a person has made or received any repayment (within the meaning of section 303AA(2)) which, but for the fact that it falls to be disregarded for the purposes of section 303(1) by virtue of section 303AA(1), would have triggered a requirement to give a notice under subsection (2) above,
the inspector may by notice require that person to furnish him within such time (not being less than 60 days) as may be specified in the notice with such information relating to the event or case as the inspector may reasonably require for the purposes of this Chapter.

ICTA 1988

310(5) Where relief is claimed in respect of shares in a company and the inspector has reason to believe that it may not be due by reason of any such arrangement or scheme as is mentioned in 289(1D), (6) or (9)(e), 289A(8)(b) or (8A), 291B(5), 293(4B), (6) or (8),s. 299B(1) or 308(2)(e), (3), (3A) or (4), he may by notice require any person concerned to furnish him within such time (not being less than 60 days) as may be specified in the notice with–

(a) a declaration in writing stating whether or not, according to the information which that person has or can reasonably obtain, any such arrangement or scheme exists or has existed;

(b) such other information as the inspector may reasonably require for the purposes of the provision in question and as that person has or can reasonably obtain.

310(6) For the purposes of subsection (5) above the persons who are persons concerned are–

(a) in relation to section 289(6) or 293(4B) or (6), the claimant, the company and any person controlling the company;

(aa) in relation to section 289(1D), 289A(8)(b) or (8A) or 308(3), (3A) or (4), the claimant, the company, any other company in question and any person controlling the company or any other company in question;

(b) in relation to section 291B(5), the claimant;

(c) in relation to section 289(9)(e) , 293(8) or 308(2)(e), the company and any person controlling the company; and

(d) in relation to section 299B(1), the claimant, the company and any person connected with the company;

and for those purposes references in this subsection to the claimant include references to any person to whom the claimant appears to have made a transfer such as is mentioned in section 304(1) of any of the shares in question.

310(6A) The references in subsections (5) and (6) above to subsections (3), (3A) and (4) of section 308 are to be read as including those provisions as applied by section 289(10) and (11).

310(7) Where relief has been given in respect of shares in a company–

(a) any person who receives from the company any payment or asset which may constitute value received (by him or another) for the purposes of sections 300 and 303(3); and

(b) any person on whose behalf such a payment or asset is received,

shall, if so required by the inspector, state whether the payment or asset received by him or on his behalf is received on behalf of any person other than himself and, if so, the name and address of that person.

310(8) Where relief has been claimed in respect of shares in a company, any person who holds or has held shares in the company and any person on whose behalf any such shares are or were held shall, if so required by the inspector, state whether the shares which are or were held by him or on his behalf are or were held on behalf of any person other than himself and, if so, the name and address of that person.

310(9) No obligation as to secrecy imposed by statute or otherwise shall preclude the inspector from disclosing to a company that relief has been given or claimed in respect of a particular number or proportion of its shares.

310(9A) References in this section to withdrawal of relief include its reduction.

310(10), (11) [Repealed by FA 1994, s. 137, Sch. 15, para. 25(e) and s. 258 and Sch. 26, Pt. V(17).]"

In s. 310(1), (2) the words "or would fall to be withdrawn under section 300 were it not for the application of section 300A" inserted by FA 2001, Sch. 15, para. 23 in relation to events occurring on or after 7 March 2001.

In s. 310(1), reference to s. 304 omitted by FA 1998, s. 74(1) and Sch. 13, para. 22(1), with effect in relation to events occurring on or after 6 April 1998.

In s. 310(1) and former (10)(a), references to s. 299A inserted by FA 1993, s. 111(2), in relation to any case in which the claim for relief is made on or after 16 March 1993.

In s. 310(1), former reference to s. 304 substituted for earlier reference to s. 304(2) to (6), in s. 310(2), "289(1)(c) or (6)" substituted for former "289(11)", in s. 310(5), the numbers "289(6), 291B(5)" substituted for former "289(11), 291(10)", in s. 310(6), the number "289(6)" substituted for former "291(11)" in both places, and "291B(5)" substituted for "291(10)", by FA 1994, s. 137 and Sch. 15, para. 25(a)–(d), in relation to shares issued on or after 1 January 1994 with effect for 1993–94 and subsequent years of assessment.

In s. 310(2) a reference to s. 289(1)(d) inserted by FA 2001, Sch. 15, para. 8 in relation to shares issued on or after 7 March 2001; and in respect of the application of ICTA 1988, Pt. VII, Ch. III and TCGA 1992, Sch. 5B, on or after 7 March 2001 in relation to shares:

- that were issued after 31 December 1993 but before 7 March 2001, and
- to which income tax relief or deferral relief was attributable immediately before 7 March 2001.

In s. 310(1) and (2), the words "or would … 300A," inserted by FA 2001, Sch. 15, para. 23(1) and (2) in relation to events occurring on or after 7 March 2001.

In s. 310(2), references to s. 289(6) and s. 297 omitted and reference to s. 289(1)(ba) inserted by FA 1998, s. 74(1) and Sch. 13, para. 22(2), and the words "or payment" at the end "or payment" repealed by FA 1998, s. 74(1) and Sch. 13, para. 22(2), s. 165 and Sch. 27, Pt. III(14), with effect in relation to events occurring on or after 6 April 1998.

S. 310(2A), and s. 310(4)(b) and (c), inserted by FA 2001, Sch. 15, para. 23(3) and (4) in relation to events occurring on or after 7 March 2001.

In s. 310(5) words "289(1D), (6) or (9)(e), 289A(8)(b) or (8A)" substituted for "289(6)," by FA 2004, s. 93 and Sch. 18, para. 10(1)(a), with effect in relation to any notice given after 22 July 2004 in respect of shares issued on or after 17 March 2004.

In s. 310(5) words "293(4B), (6) or (8)," substituted for "293(8)," by FA 2004, s. 93 and Sch. 18, para. 10(1)(a), with effect in relation to any notice given after 22 July 2004 in respect of shares issued on or after 17 March 2004.

In s. 310(5) words "or 308(2)(e), (3), (3A) or (4)" substituted for "or 308(2)(e)" by FA 2004, s. 93 and Sch. 18, para. 10(1)(a), with effect in relation to any notice given after 22 July 2004 in respect of shares issued on or after 17 March 2004.

In s. 310(5), reference to s. 299B(1) inserted by FA 1998, s. 71(3), witheffect in relation to shares issued on or after 2 July 1997.

In s. 310(6)(a) words "or 293(4B) or (6)" inserted by FA 2004, s. 93 and Sch. 18, para. 10(1)b), with effect in relation to any notice given after 22 July 2004 in respect of shares issued on or after 17 March 2004.

S. 310(6)(aa) inserted by FA 2004, s. 93 and Sch. 18, para. 10(1)(b), with effect in relation to any notice given after 22 July 2004 in respect of shares issued on or after 17 March 2004.

S. 310(6) substituted by FA 1998, s. 71(4), with effect in relation to shares issued on or after 2 July 1997. As it has effect in relation to shares issued before that date, s. 310(6) provides as follows:

"**310(6)** References in subsection (5) above to the person concerned are references, in relation to sections 289(6), 291B(5) and 308(2)(e), to the claimant and, in relation to sections 289(6), 293(8) and 308(2)(e), to the company and any person controlling the company."

In s. 310(6)(c) words "289(9)(e)," inserted by FA 2004, s. 93 and Sch. 18, para. 10(1)(b), with effect in relation to any notice given after 22 July 2004 in respect of shares issued on or after 17 March 2004.

S. 310(6A) inserted by FA 2004, s. 93 and Sch. 18, para. 10(1)(c), with effect in relation to any notice given after 22 July 2004 in respect of shares issued on or after 17 March 2004.

In s. 310(7), reference to s. 301 omitted by FA 1998, s. 74(1) and Sch. 13, para. 22(3), with effect in relation to events occurring on or after 6 April 1998.

S. 310(9A) inserted by FA 1998, s. 74 and Sch. 13, para. 22(4), with effect in relation to events occurring on or after 6 April 1998.

S. 310(10), (11) omitted by FA 1994, s. 137 and Sch. 15, para. 25(e) and s. 258 and Sch. 26, Pt. V(17) in relation to shares issued on or after 1 January 1994 with effect for 1993–94 and subsequent years of assessment.

Former s. 310(10) and (11) provided as follows:

"**310(10)** This section shall have effect in relation to relief under Chapter II of Part IV of the Finance Act 1981 as it has effect in relation to relief under this Chapter but with the substitution–

(a) in subsection (1) for "291, 299, 299A, 300 or 304(2) to (6)" of "54, 57, 58 and 60(6) of the Finance Act 1981";

(b) for subsection (3) of the following subsection–

"**310(3)** Where the company is notified by the inspector that relief has been given in respect of any shares issued by the company on a specified date, then, if any shares in the company (whether or not shares in respect of which relief has been given) are transferred at any time in the period of five years beginning with that date, the company shall within 60 days of–
(a) coming to know of the transfer; or
(b) receiving the notification from the inspector,
whichever is the later, give a notice to the inspector containing particulars of the transfer.";
(c) in subsection (5) for references to sections 289(11), 291(10), 293(8) and 308(2)(e) of references to sections 54(9), 55(8) and 59(1) of the 1981 Act;
(d) in subsection (6) for "289(11), 293(10) and 308(2)(e)" and "289(11), 293(8) and 308(2)(e)" of "54(9) and 59(1) of the Finance Act 1981" and "55(8) and 59(1) of that Act", respectively;
(e) in subsection (7) for "300, 301 or 303(3)" of "58 or 59(4) of the Finance Act 1981".
310(11) In any case where this section has effect in accordance with subsection (10) above and the qualifying company has one or more subsidiaries–
(a) subsection (3) above shall, where the inspector has notified the subsidiary that relief has been given in respect of shares in the company of which it is a subsidiary, apply to the subsidiary as respects any transfer of its shares as it applies to the company as respects any transfer of shares in the company; and
(b) subsections (5) and (6) above shall have effect in relation to any such arrangements as are mentioned in paragraph (c) of subsection (2) of section 308 (as that subsection has effect by virtue of subsection (6) of that section) as they have effect in relation to any such arrangement as is mentioned in section 289(11).".

Derivations – S. 310(1), (2) as originally enacted: FA 1983, Sch. 5, para. 15(1), (2).
S. 310(3): FA 1983, Sch. 5, para. 15A(1), inserted by FA 1986, Sch. 9, para. 15.
S. 310(4): FA 1983, Sch. 5, para. 15(3) and 15A(2), inserted by FA 1986, Sch. 9, para. 15.
S. 310(5) as originally enacted: FA 1983, Sch. 5, para. 15(4) and 18(4), as amended by FA 1986, Sch. 9, para. 19(2).
S. 310(6) as originally enacted: FA 1983, Sch. 5, para. 15(5).
S. 310(7): FA 1981, s. 63(7) and FA 1983, Sch. 5, para. 15(6).
S. 310(8), (9): FA 1981, s. 63(8), (9).
Former s. 310(10): FA 1981, s. 63(3) and FA 1983, s. 26(2).
Former s. 310(11): FA 1981, Sch. 12, para. 6 and 7.

Cross references – TMA 1970, s. 98: penalties for failure to furnish information or comply with notice under s. 310(1)–(5).
FA 1981, Pt. IV, Ch. II: the business expansion scheme was originally introduced as the business start-up scheme under which only investment in a company beginning a new trade was eligible for relief.
TCGA 1992, Sch. 5B, para. 1A(5)(a): provisions do not apply unless a company has given notice *inter alia* under s. 310(2).

Notes – S. 310 rewritten for income tax purposes as follows:
S. 310(1): ITA 2007, s. 240(1), (2).
S. 310(2): ITA 2007, s. 241(1), (2), (3), (4), (5).
S. 310(2A): ITA 2007, s. 240(3), (4), 241(6), (7).
S. 310(4): ITA 2007, s. 242(1), (2), (3), (4).
S. 310(5): ITA 2007, s. 243(1), (2), (3).
S. 310(6): ITA 2007, s. 243(4).
S. 310(6A): ITA 2007, s. 243(1).
S. 310(7): ITA 2007, s. 243(5).
S. 310(8): ITA 2007, s. 243(6).
S. 310(9): ITA 2007, s. 244.
S. 310(9A): ITA 2007, s. 240(1), 241(1).

311 Nominees, bare trustees and approved investment funds

311 [Omitted by ITA 2007, s. 1027 and Sch. 1, para. 627 and repealed by ITA 2007, s. 1031 and Sch. 3, Pt. 2 with effect in relation to shares issued after 5 April 2007.]

History – S. 311 omitted by ITA 2007, s. 1027 and Sch. 1, para. 627 and repealed by ITA 2007, s. 1031, Sch. 3, Pt. 2 with effect in relation to shares issued on or after 5 April 2007. In so far as it continues to apply in relation to shares issued before 6 April 2007, s. 311 is as follows:
"**311(1)** Shares subscribed for, issued to, held by or disposed of for an individual by a nominee shall be treated for the purposes of this Chapter as subscribed for, issued to, held by or disposed of by that individual.
311(2) Where eligible shares are held on a bare trust for two or more beneficiaries, this Chapter shall have effect (with the necessary modifications) as if–
(a) each beneficiary had subscribed as an individual for all of those shares; and
(b) the amount subscribed by each beneficiary was equal to the total amount subscribed on the issue of those shares divided by the number of beneficiaries.
311(2A) Subsection (2B) below applies where an individual claims relief in respect of eligible shares in a company and–
(a) the shares have been issued to the managers of an approved fund as nominee for the individual;
(b) the fund has closed, that is to say, no further investments in the fund are to be accepted; and
(c) the amounts which the managers have, as nominee for the individual, subscribed for eligible shares issued within six months after the closing of the fund represent not less than 90 per cent of his investment in the fund;
and in this section **"the managers of an approved fund"** means the person or persons having the management of an investment fund approved for the purposes of this section by the Board.
311(2B) In any case where this subsection applies, sections 289A and 289B shall have effect as if–
(a) any reference to the year of assessment or other period in which the shares are issued were a reference to the year of assessment or other period in which the fund closes; and
(b) any reference to the time of the issue of the shares, or the time of the subscription for the shares, were a reference to the time of the closing of the fund.
311(3) Section 290(1) shall not apply where the amount is subscribed as nominee for an individual by the managers of an approved fund.
311(4) Where an individual claims relief in respect of eligible shares in a company which have been issued to the managers of an approved fund as nominee for that individual, section 306(2) shall apply–
(a) as if it required the certificate referred to in that section to be issued by the company to the managers; and
(b) as if it provided that no claim for relief may be made unless the person making the claim has received from the managers a certificate issued by the managers, in such form as the Board may authorise, certifying that the managers hold certificates issued to them by the companies concerned, for the purposes of sections 306(2), in respect of the holdings of eligible shares shown on the managers' certificate.
311(5) The managers of an approved fund may be required by a notice given to them by an inspector or other officer of the Board to deliver to the officer, within the time limited by the notice, a return of the holdings of eligible shares shown on certificates issued by them in accordance with subsection (4) above in the year of assessment to which the return relates.

311(6) Section 306(6) shall not apply in relation to any certificate issued by the managers of an approved fund for the purposes of subsection (4) above."

In s. 311(2), the words "Where eligible shares … beneficiaries" substituted for the former words "Where eligible shares issued after 18th March 1986 are held on a bare trust for two or more beneficiaries", by FA 1994, s. 137 and Sch. 15, para. 26(a) in relation to shares issued on or after 1 January 1994 with effect for 1993–94 and subsequent years of assessment.

In s. 311(2B), the words "In any case … as if" substituted for former words "In any case where this subsection applies, subsections (5) to (7) of section 289 and subsections (1) to (3) and (6) of section 304 shall have effect as if" by FA 1994, s. 137 and Sch. 15, para. 26(b), in relation to shares issued on or after 1 January 1994 with effect for 1993–94 and subsequent years of assessment.

S. 311(2A)–(3) substituted for former s. 311(3) by FA 1988, s. 53(1), in relation to approved funds closing after 15 March 1988.

In s. 311(4) words "as if it required … the managers" substituted for "as if it required–(a) the certificate referred to in that section to be issued by the company to the managers; (b) the claim for relief to be accompanied by" by FA 1996, s. 134 and Sch. 20, para. 23 for shares issued on or after 6 April 1996.

Derivations – S. 311(1): FA 1983, Sch. 5, para. 19(1).
S. 311(2): FA 1983, Sch. 5, para. 19A, inserted by FA 1986, Sch. 9, para. 20.
S. 311 (3) as originally enacted, (4)–(6): FA 1983, Sch. 5, para. 19(2)–(5).

Other material – HMRC guidelines on approval of investment funds (s. 311(2A)) and applications for approval, 1 August 1994 (obtainable from Company Tax Division, Room M22, West Wing, Somerset House, London WC2R 1LB).

In the Queen's Printer's version of the Act, the reference to "sections 306(2)" should apparently be "section 306(2)", i.e. in the singular.

Notes – S. 311 rewritten for income tax purposes as follows:
S. 311(1): ITA 2007, s. 250(1).
S. 311(2): ITA 2007, s. 250(2), (3).
S. 311(2A): ITA 2007, s. 250(3), 251(1).
S. 311(2B): ITA 2007, s. 251(2).
S. 311(3): ITA 2007, s. 251(3).
S. 311(4): ITA 2007, s. 250(3), 251(4), (5).
S. 311(5): ITA 2007, s. 250(3), 251(6).
S. 311(6): ITA 2007, s. 251(7).

312 Interpretation of Chapter III

312 [Omitted by ITA 2007, s. 1027 and Sch. 1, para. 627 and repealed by ITA 2007, s. 1031 and Sch. 3, Pt. 2 with effect in relation to shares issued after 5 April 2007.]

History – S. 312 omitted by ITA 2007, s. 1027 and Sch. 1, para. 627 and repealed by ITA 2007, s. 1031 and Sch. 3, Pt. 2 with effect in relation to shares issued after 5 April 2007. In so far as it continues to apply in relation to shares issued before 6 April 2007, s. 312 is as follows:

"Interpretation of Chapter III

312(1) In this Chapter–

"arrangements" includes any scheme, agreement or understanding, whether or not legally enforceable;

"associate" has the meaning given in subsections (3) and (4) of section 417 except that in those subsections "relative" shall not include a brother or sister;

"bonus shares" means shares which are issued otherwise than for payment (whether in cash or otherwise);

"control", except in sections 289(9), 291B(4), 293(8)(b)) and 308(2), shall be construed in accordance with section 416(2) to (6);

"debenture" has the meaning given by section 744 of the Companies Act 1985;

"director" shall be construed in accordance with section 417(5);

"eligible for relief" has the meaning given by section 289(1);

"eligible shares" has the meaning given by section 289(7);

"ordinary shares" means shares forming part of a company's ordinary share capital;

"the period of restriction", in relation to any eligible shares issued by a company, means the period–
(a) beginning one year before the shares are issued, and
(b) ending immediately before the termination date relating to the shares;

"relief" means relief under this Chapter,

"research and development" has the meaning given by section 1006 of ITA 2007;

"qualifying 90% subsidiary", in relation to any company, is to be construed in accordance with section 289(9);

"subsidiary", in relation to any company (except in the expression "51 per cent subsidiary" or where otherwise defined), means a subsidiary of that company of a kind which that company may hold under section 308,

"51 per cent subsidiary", in relation to any company, means (except in the case of references to a company which is a 51 per cent subsidiary on a particular date or at a particular time) a company which is a 51 per cent subsidiary of that company at any time in the relevant period (applying subsection (1A)(a) below),

"termination date" in relation to any eligible shares issued by a company, means the third anniversary of the issue date or if–
(a) the money raised by the issue was raised wholly or mainly for the purpose of a qualifying business activity falling within section 289(2)(a) (company meeting trading activities requirement by reason of the company or a qualifying 90% subsidiary of the company carrying on or preparing to carry on a qualifying trade), and
(b) neither the company nor any of its qualifying 90% subsidiaries had begun to carry on the trade in question on the issue date, the third anniversary of the date on which the company or any qualifying 90% subsidiary of the company begins to carry on that trade; and

"unquoted company" means a company none of whose shares, stocks, debentures or other securities are marketed to the general public.

312(1A) In any provision of this Chapter **"relevant period"**, in relation to any eligible shares issued by a company, means whichever of the following periods is applied for the purposes of that provision–
(a) the period beginning either–
  (i) with the incorporation of the company, or
  (ii) if the company was incorporated more than two years before the date on which the shares were issued, two years before that date,

  and ending immediately before the termination date relating to the shares, and
(b) the period beginning with the issue of the shares and ending immediately before the termination date relating to them.

312(1ZA) In determining, for the purposes of the definition of **"termination date"** in subsection (1) above, when a qualifying trade is begun to be carried on by a qualifying 90% subsidiary of a company there shall be disregarded any carrying on of the trade by it before it became such a subsidiary of the company.
312(1B) For the purposes of the definition of "unquoted company" in subsection (1) above, shares, stocks, debentures or other securities are marketed to the general public if they are–
(a) listed on a recognised stock exchange,
(b) listed on a designated exchange in a country outside the United Kingdom, or
(c) dealt in outside the United Kingdom by such means as may be designated.
312(1C) In subsection (1B) above **"designated"** means designated by an order made by the Board for the purposes of that subsection; and an order made for the purposes of paragraph (b) of that subsection may designate an exchange by name, or by reference to any class or description of exchanges, including a class or description framed by reference to any authority or approval given in a country outside the United Kingdom.
312(1D) Section 828(1) does not apply to an order made for the purposes of subsection (1B) above.
312(1E) Where a company is an unquoted company at the time when any shares are issued ("the relevant time"), it shall not be treated for the purposes of this Chapter as ceasing to be an unquoted company in relation to those shares at any subsequent time by reason only that any shares, stocks, debentures or other securities of the company are at that time–
(a) listed on a stock exchange that is a recognised stock exchange by virtue of an order made under section 1005(1)(b) of ITA 2007, or
(b) listed on an exchange, or dealt in by any means, designated by an order made for the purposes of subsection (1B) above,
if the order was made after the relevant time.
312(2) Section 993 of ITA 2007 applies for the purposes of this Chapter other than section 291, section 291A(1), (4) and (5) and section 291B.
312(2A) References in this Chapter to a company being in administration or receivership shall be construed as follows–
(a) references to a company being "in administration" are to–
(i) it being in administration within the meaning of Schedule B1 to the Insolvency Act 1986 (c. 45) or Schedule B1 to the Insolvency (Northern Ireland) Order 1989 (S.I. 1989/2405 (N.I. 19)), or
(ii) there being in force in relation to it, under the law of a country or territory outside the United Kingdom, any appointment corresponding to an appointment of an administrator under either of those Schedules;
(b) references to a company being "in receivership" are to there being in force in relation to it–
(i) an order for the appointment of an administrative receiver, a receiver and manager or a receiver under Chapter I or II of Part III of the Insolvency Act 1986 or Part IV of the Insolvency (Northern Ireland) Order 1989, or
(ii) any corresponding order under the law of a country or territory outside the United Kingdom.
312(3) References in this Chapter to a disposal of shares include references to a disposal of an interest or right in or over the shares and an individual shall be treated for the purposes of this Chapter as disposing of any shares which he is treated by virtue of section 136 of the 1992 Act as exchanging for other shares.
312(4) In this Chapter–
(a) references in any provision to the reduction of any relief attributable to any shares include a reference–
(i) to the reduction of the relief to nil, and
(ii) where no relief has yet been given, to the reduction of the amount which apart from that provision would be the relief, and
(b) references to the withdrawal of any relief, in respect of any shares, are to the withdrawal of the relief attributable to those shares or, in a case where no relief has yet been given, to ceasing to be eligible for relief in respect of those shares.
312(4A) In this Chapter references (however expressed) to an issue of eligible shares in any company are to any eligible shares in the company that are of the same class and are issued on the same day.
312(4B) For the purposes of this Chapter shares in a company shall not be treated as being of the same class unless they would be so treated if dealt with on the Stock Exchange.
312(5) For the purposes of this Chapter, the market value at any time of any asset shall be taken to be the price which it might reasonably be expected to fetch on a sale at that time in the open market free from any interest or right which exists by way of security in or over it.
312(6) References in this Chapter to relief given to an individual in respect of eligible shares, and to the withdrawal of such relief, include respectively references to relief given to him in respect of those shares at any time after he has disposed of them and references to the withdrawal of such relief at any such time.
312(7)–(8) [Repealed by FA 2001, Sch. 33, Pt. 2(3).]

History – In s. 312(1):
- definition of "appraisal licence" omitted by FA 2001, in relation to shares issued on or after 7 March 2001; and in respect of the application of ICTA 1988, Pt. VII, Ch. III and TCGA 1992, Sch. 5B, on or after 7 March 2001 in relation to shares:
  - that were issued after 31 December 1993 but before 7 March 2001, and
  - to which income tax relief or deferral relief was attributable immediately before 7 March 2001.
- definition of "arrangements" inserted by FA 2000, s. 64 and Sch. 17, para. 14(1), with effect in relation to shares issued on or after 6 April 2000, and in respect of the application of s. 312 on or after that date in relation to shares that were issued after 31 December 1993 but before March 2000, and to which EIS relief or CGT deferral relief was attributable immediately before 21 March 2000.
- definition of "bonus shares" inserted by FA 2004, s. 93 and Sch. 18, para. 11(2)(a), with effect in relation to shares issued on or after 17 March 2004.
- in definition of "control", reference to s. 293(8)(b) inserted by FA 2000, s. 64 and Sch. 17, para. 14(1), with effect in relation to shares issued on or after 6 April 2000, and in respect of the application of s. 312 on or after that date in relation to shares that were issued after 31 December 1993 but before March 2000, and to which EIS relief or CGT deferral relief was attributable immediately before 21 March 2000.
- in definition of "control", "289(9)," inserted by FA 2004, s. 93 and Sch. 18, para. 11(2)(b), with effect in relation to shares issued on or after 17 March 2004.
- in definition of "control", the words "291B(4) and 308(2)" substituted for former words "291(7), 308(2) and 309(6)(a)" by FA 1994, s. 137 and Sch. 15, para. 27(a)(i), (ii), (v), (vi) in relation to shares issued on or after 1 January 1994 with effect for 1993–94 and subsequent years of assessment.
- definition of "the designated period" (inserted by FA 2000, s. 64 and Sch. 17, para. 6(2), with effect in relation to shares issued on or after 6 April 2000) omitted by FA 2001, Sch. 33, Pt. 2(3), with effect from the time mentioned in the first History note, above.
- definition of "development licence" omitted by FA 2001, Sch. 33, Pt. 2(3), with effect from the time mentioned in the first 2001 History note, above.
- definition of "eligible for relief" inserted; and definitions of "relief", "subsidiary", "51 per cent subsidiary" and "unquoted company" substituted, by FA 1994, s. 137 and Sch. 15, para. 27(a)(i), (ii), (v), (vi) in relation to shares issued on or after 1 January 1994 with effect for 1993–94 and subsequent years of assessment.
- definition of "eligible shares" inserted; and definitions of "relief", "subsidiary", "51 per cent subsidiary" and "unquoted company" substituted, by FA 1994, s. 137 and Sch. 15, para. 27(a)(i), (ii), (v), (vi) in relation to shares issued on or after 1 January 1994 with effect for 1993–94 and subsequent years of assessment.

- definition of "exploration licence" omitted by FA 2001, Sch. 33, Pt. 2(3), with effect from the time mentioned in the first 2001 History note, above.
- definition of "fixed-rate preference share capital" omitted by FA 1994, s. 137 and Sch. 15, para. 27(a)(iii), and (iv) and s. 258 and Sch. 26, Pt. V(17) in relation to shares issued on or after 1 January 1994 with effect for 1993–94 and subsequent years of assessment. The former definition was as follows:

  "**"fixed-rate preference share capital"** means share capital consisting of shares which–
  (a) are issued for consideration which is or includes new consideration; and
  (b) do not carry any right either to conversion into shares or securities of any other description or to the acquisition of any additional shares or securities; and
  (c) do not carry any right to dividends other than dividends which–
   (i) are of a fixed amount or at a fixed rate per cent of the nominal value of the shares, and
   (ii) represent no more than a reasonable commercial return on the new consideration received by the company in respect of the issue of the shares; and
  (d) on repayment do not carry any rights to an amount exceeding that new consideration except in so far as those rights are reasonably comparable with those general for fixed dividend shares listed in the Official List of the Stock Exchange;".
- definition of "modified appraisal licence", omitted by FA 2001, Sch. 33, Pt. 2(3), with effect from the time mentioned in the first 2001 History note, above.
- definition of "modified development licence" omitted by FA 2001, Sch. 33, Pt. 2(3), with effect from the time mentioned in the first 2001 History note, above.
- definition of "modified exploration licence" omitted by FA 2001, Sch. 33, Pt. 2(3), with effect from the time mentioned in the first 2001 History note, above.
- definition of "new consideration" repealed by FA 1998, s. 74(1) and Sch. 13, para. 23(1)(a), s. 165 and Sch. 27, Pt. III(14), with effect in relation to shares issued on or after 6 April 1998. As it has effect in relation to shares issued before that date, the definition provides as follows:

  "**"new consideration"** has the same meaning as in Part VI;".
- definition of "Northern Ireland licence" (and, in relation to such a licence "the initial term", "the 30 year renewal term" and "the five year renewal term") omitted by FA 2001, Sch. 33, Pt. 2(3), with effect from the time mentioned in the first 2001 History note, above.
- definition of "the 30 year renewal term" omitted by FA 2001, Sch. 33, Pt. 2(3), with effect from the time mentioned in the first 2001 History note, above.
- definition of "the five year renewal term") omitted by FA 2001, Sch. 33, Pt. 2(3), with effect from the time mentioned in the first 2001 History note, above.
- definition of "oil" omitted by FA 2001, Sch. 33, Pt. 2(3), with effect from the time mentioned in the first 2001 History note, above.
- definition of "oil extraction activities" omitted by FA 2001, Sch. 33, Pt. 2(3), with effect from the time mentioned in the first 2001 History note, above.
- definition of "oil exploration" omitted by FA 2001, Sch. 33, Pt. 2(3), with effect from the time mentioned in the first 2001 History note, above.
- definition of "the period of restriction" inserted by FA 2001, Sch. 15, para. 24, with effect from the time mentioned in the the first History note, above.
- in the definition of "qualifying 90% subsidiary", "to (13)" omitted by FA 2007, s. 51 and Sch. 16, para. 16(1)(b) and repealed by s. 114 and Sch. 27, Pt. 2(16), with effect from 6 April 2007.
- definition of "qualifying 90% subsidiary" inserted by FA 2004, s. 93 and Sch. 18, para. 11(2)(c), with effect in relation to shares issued on or after 17 March 2004.
- definition of "the relevant period" omitted by FA 1994, s. 137 and Sch. 15, para. 27(a)(iii), and (iv) and s. 258 and Sch. 26, Pt. V(17) in relation to shares issued on or after 1 January 1994 with effect for 1993–94 and subsequent years of assessment. The former definition was as follows:

  "**"the relevant period"** has the meaning given in section 289(12);".
- definition of "relief" was substituted in identical terms by FA 1998, s. 74(1) and Sch. 13, para. 23(1)(b), with effect in relation to shares issued on or after 6 April 1998.
- definition of "relief" substituted by FA 1994, s. 137 and Sch. 15, para. 27(a)(i), (ii), (v), (vi) in relation to shares issued on or after 1 January 1994 with effect for 1993–94 and subsequent years of assessment. Former definition was as follows:

  "**"the relief"** and

  "relief", except where the reference is to relief under Chapter II of Part IV of the Finance Act 1981, means relief under section 289 (and includes relief under Schedule 5 to the Finance Act 1983), and references to the amount of the relief shall be construed in accordance with section 289(5);".
- in the definition of "research and development", the words "1006 of ITA 2007" substituted for the words "837A" by SI 2007/1820, art 2(4), with effect, for income tax purposes, for 2007–08 and subsequent tax years and, for corporation tax purposes, for accounting periods ending after 5 April 2007.
- definition of "research and development" substituted by FA 2000, s. 64 and Sch. 17, para. 15(1), with effect in relation to shares issued on or after 6 April 2000, but not affecting the operation of any provision of Ch. III in relation to shares issued before 6 April 2000. The former definition (substituted by FA 1998, s. 74(1) and Sch. 13, para. 23(1)(b), with effect in relation to shares issued on or after 6 April 1998) was identical to that which it replaced and was as follows:

  "**"research and development"** means any activity which is intended to result in a patentable invention (within the meaning of the Patents Act 1977) or in a computer program;".
- definition of "the seven year period" repealed by FA 2000, s. 156 and Sch. 40, Pt. II(5), with effect in relation to shares issued on or after 6 April 2000. The former text of the definition is as follows:

  "**"the seven year period"** has the meaning given by section 291(6);".
- definition of of "the seven year period" inserted by FA 1998, s. 74(1) and Sch. 13, para. 23(1)(b), with effect in relation to shares issued on or after 6 April 1998.
- definition of "subsidiary" substituted by FA 1994, s. 137 and Sch. 15, para. 27(a)(i), (ii), (v), (vi) in relation to shares issued on or after 1 January 1994 with effect for 1993–94 and subsequent years of assessment.
- definition of "51 per cent subsidiary" substituted by FA 1994, s. 137 and Sch. 15, para. 27(a)(i), (ii), (v), (vi) in relation to shares issued on or after 1 January 1994 with effect for 1993–94 and subsequent years of assessment.
- definition of "termination date", the words "the money raised by the issue was raised wholly or mainly" substituted for "the shares were issued wholly or mainly in order to raise money", "qualifying 90% subsidiary of the company" substituted for "subsidiary", "neither the company nor any of its qualifying 90% subsidiaries had" substituted for "the company or subsidiary concerned had not", and "the company or any qualifying 90% subsidiary of the company" substituted for "it" in the words at the end, by FA 2004, s. 93 and Sch. 18, para. 11(2)(d), with effect in relation to shares issued on or after 17 March 2004.
- definition of "termination date" inserted by FA 2000, s. 64 and Sch. 17, para. 6(3), with effect in relation to shares issued on or after 6 April 2000.
- definition of "unquoted company" substituted, by FA 1994, s. 137 and Sch. 15, para. 27(a)(i), (ii), (v), (vi) in relation to shares issued on or after 1 January 1994 with effect for 1993–94 and subsequent years of assessment. Former definition was as follows:

"**"unquoted company"** means a company none of whose shares, stocks or debentures are listed in the Official List of the Stock Exchange or dealt in on the Unlisted Securities Market. ".

- definition of "the 1984 Regulations", and the word "and" immediately preceding that definition, omitted by FA 2001, Sch. 33, Pt. 2(3), with effect from the time mentioned in the first 2001 History note, above.

S. 312(1A) substituted by FA 2000, s. 64 and Sch. 17 with effect in relation to shares issued on or after 6 April 2000. In relation to shares issued before that date, the text of s. 312(1A) is as follows:

"**312(1A)** In any provision of this Chapter **"relevant period"**, in relation to relief in respect of any eligible shares issued by a company, means whichever of the following periods is applied for the purposes of that provision–

(a) the period beginning with the incorporation of the company (or, if the company was incorporated more than two years before the date on which the shares were issued, beginning two years before that date) and ending five years after the issue of the shares, and

(b) the period beginning with the date on which the shares were issued and ending either–

(i) three years after that date, or

(ii) in a case falling within section 289(2)(a) where the company or subsidiary concerned had not begun to carry on the trade in question on that date, three years after the date on which it begins to carry on that trade."

S. 312(1ZA) inserted by FA 2004, s. 93 and Sch. 18, para. 11(3), with effect in relation to shares issued on or after 17 March 2004.

In former s. 312(1A), the words "(disregarding section 289B(5))" which appeared at the end of the opening words, and the words "dealt in on the Unlisted Securities Market or" at the beginning of s. 312(1B)(c) repealed by FA 1998, s. 74(1) and Sch. 13, para. 23(2) and (3), s. 165 and Sch. 27, Pt. III(14), with effect in relation to shares issued on or after 6 April 1998.

In s. 312(1E)(a), the words "section 1005(1)(b) of ITA 2007" substituted for the words "section 841" by FA 2007, s. 109 and Sch. 26, para. 7(3), with effect from 19 July 2007.

S. 312(1E) amended by FA 2001, Sch. 15, para. 13, with effect from the time mentioned in the first History note, above.

S. 312(1A)–(1E) inserted, and in s. 312(2) "sections 291 to 291B" substituted for former "section 291", by FA 1994, s. 137 and Sch. 15, para. 27(b), (c), in relation to shares issued on or after 1 January 1994 with effect for 1993–94 and subsequent years of assessment.

In s. 312(2), the words "993 of ITA 2007" substituted for the words "839" by SI 2007/1820, art 2(5), with effect, for income tax purposes, for 2007–08 and subsequent tax years and, for corporation tax purposes, for accounting periods ending after 5 April 2007.

In s. 312(2), para. (a) substituted by ITA 2007, s. 1027 and Sch. 1, para. 42 with effect for 2007–08 and subsequent tax years, as it applies in relation to shares issued before 6 April 2007.

In s. 312(2), reference to section 291A(1), (4) and (5) inserted by FA 1998, s. 74(1) and Sch. 13, para. 23(4), with effect in relation to shares issued on or after 6 April 1998.

S. 312(2A)(a) substituted by SI 2003/2096, art. 4 and Sch., para. 18 with effect from 15 September 2003. Transitional provisions are contained in art. 6. S. 321(2A)(a) previously read follows:

"(a) references to a company being "in administration" are to there being in force in relation to it–

(i) an administration order under Part II of the Insolvency Act 1986 or Part III of the Insolvency (Northern Ireland) Order 1989, or

(ii) any corresponding order under the law of a country or territory outside the United Kingdom;".

S. 312(2A) inserted by FA 2000, s. 64 and Sch. 17, para. 9(4), with effect in relation to shares issued on or after 21 March 2000, and in respect of the application of s. 293 on or after that date in relation to shares that were issued after 31 December 1993 but before March 2000, and to which EIS relief or CGT deferral relief was attributable immediately before 21 March 2000.

In s. 312(3), "136" substituted for "136(1)" by FA 2002, s. 45 and Sch. 9, para. 4(3), with effect in relation to disposals of shares or debentures (or any interests falling to be treated as shares or debentures for the purposes of TCGA 1992, s. 135 or 136 issued on or after 17 April 2002.

In s. 312(3), reference to the 1992 Act substituted by TCGA 1992, s. 290 and Sch. 10, para. 14(18).

S. 312(4) and (5) substituted by FA 1994, s. 137 and Sch. 15, para. 27(d), (e), in relation to shares issued on or after 1 January 1994 with effect for 1993–94 and subsequent years of assessment. Former s. 312(4), (5) provided as follows:

"**312(4)** References in this Chapter to the reduction of any amount include references to its reduction to nil.

312(5) For the purposes of this Chapter–

(a) in relation to shares issued after 18th March 1986, the **market value** at any time of any asset shall be taken to be the price which it might reasonably be expected to fetch on a sale at that time in the open market free from any interest or right which exists by way of security in or over it;

(b) in relation to shares issued before 19th March 1986, **"market value"** shall be construed in accordance with section 272 of the 1992 Act.".

S. 312(4A) and (4B) inserted by FA 1998, s. 74(1) and Sch. 13, para. 23(5), with effect in relation to shares issued on or after 6 April 1998.

S. 312(7) and (8) repealed by FA 2001, Sch. 33, Pt. 2(3), with effect from the time mentioned in the first History note, above.

In former s. 312(7), the words "subsection (2)(c) of section 289" substituted for former words "section 289(2)(c)" by FA 1998, s. 74 and Sch. 13, para. 23(6), with effect in relation to shares issued on or after 6 April 1998.

In former s. 312(7) reference to "289(2)(c)" substituted for former "289(1)(d)" by FA 1994, s. 137 and Sch. 15, para. 27(d), (e), in relation to shares issued on or after 1 January 1994 with effect for 1993–94 and subsequent years of assessment.

Derivations – S. 312(1) (as originally enacted): FA 1981, s. 67(1) and FA 1983, Sch. 5, para. 20(2), as amended by FA 1985, s. 44(6), by FA 1986, Sch. 9, para. 21(1) and (2), and by the Companies Consolidation (Consequential Provisions) Act 1985, Sch. 2.

S. 312(2)–(4) (as originally enacted): FA 1981, s. 67(2)–(4).

S. 312(5)–(8) (as originally enacted): FA 1983, Sch. 5, para. 20(3)–(6), inserted by FA 1986, Sch. 9, para. 21(3).

Cross references – S. 254(1): new consideration is consideration provided otherwise than out of the company's assets.

S. 416(2)–(6): control normally defined by reference to possession of or entitlement to acquire the majority of a company's share capital or voting power, the majority of income on a distribution or the majority of the assets on a winding up (subject to deeming provisions and extensions).

S. 416(3): definition of "associate" in relation to a person by reference to a relative, partner or trustee of a settlement made by that person or a relative of his, the trustees of a settlement comprising shares in which that person is interested and where that person is a company, any other company interested in those shares.

S. 417(4): relative means ancestor, sibling, spouse or descendant.

S. 417(5): extended definition of director to include shadow directors and managers with the ability to control more than 20 per cent of a company's assets.

S. 502(1): oil is any substance capable of being won under a licence granted under the Petroleum (Production) Act 1934 or Petroleum (Production) Act (Northern Ireland) 1964, other than methane won in the course of mine safety operations; oil extraction activities includes searching for, extracting, transporting to dry land and initial treatment or storage of oil.

S. 576: relief for losses on unlisted shares in trading companies.

S. 828: requirement for orders or regulations under the Tax Acts to be made by statutory instrument.

S. 839: circumstances in which persons are connected.

TCGA 1992, s. 136(1): shares issued by a company to shareholders of another company in proportion to their holdings in connection with amalgamation or reconstruction.

Patents Act 1977, s. 1(1) (not reproduced): inventions which are new, involve inventive steps and which are capable of industrial application, subject to exclusions.

Companies Act 1985, s. 744: debenture includes any debenture stock, bonds and any other securities whether constituting a charge on the company's assets or not. Provisions in the Companies Act 1985 to be substituted by the Companies Act 2006 on dates to be appointed (expected to be between 2007 and 2008).
ITEPA 2003, Sch. 5, para. 11(10): application of s. 312(2A) to enterprise management incentives.

HMRC interpretations – IRInt. 141: where there are two different dates under s. 312(1A)(b), HMRC view that relevant period lasts until second date is reached."

Notes – S. 312 rewritten for income tax purposes as follows:
S. 312(1): ITA 2007, s. 139(4), 143(3), 156(1), 159(4), 168(5), 184(2), 213(1), 214(2), 215(4), (5), 218(3), 222(5), 223(2), (3), 224(1), 225(4), 253(1), (2), 256(1), 257(1), (3), 1022(1), Sch. 1 para. 124, 128.
S. 312(1A): ITA 2007, s. 159(2), (3).
S. 312(1ZA): ITA 2007, s. 256(2).
S. 312(1B): ITA 2007, s. 184(3).
S. 312(1C): ITA 2007, s. 184(4), (5).
S. 312(1D): ITA 2007, s. 1014(2).
S. 312(1E): ITA 2007, s. 143(2), 184(6), Sch. 1 para. 128.
S. 312(2): ITA 2007, s. 257(2).
S. 312(2A): ITA 2007, s. 252(2), (3).
S. 312(3): ITA 2007, s. 254(1), (2).
S. 312(4): ITA 2007, s. 257(4).
S. 312(4A): ITA 2007, s. 255(1).
S. 312(4B): ITA 2007, s. 257(5).
S. 312(5): ITA 2007, s. 257(6).
S. 312(6): ITA 2007, s. 257(7).

Chapter IV – Special Provisions

313 Taxation of consideration for certain restrictive undertakings

313 [Omitted by ITEPA 2003, Sch. 6, para. 39 and repealed by ITEPA 2003, Sch. 8, Pt. 1.]

History – S. 313 omitted by ITEPA 2003, Sch. 6, para. 39 and repealed by ITEPA 2003, Sch. 8, Pt. 1 which have effect for the tax year 2003–04 and subsequent tax years.

Notes – S. 313 rewritten as follows:
S. 313(1): ITEPA 2003, s. 7(5), s. 225(1), (3) and (8).
S. 313(2): ITEPA 2003, s. 225(1), (2) and (4).
S. 313(3): ITEPA 2003, s. 225(5).
S. 313(4): ITEPA 2003, s. 226(1).
S. 313(5) was repealed by FA 1988, s. 73(1) and so has not been rewritten into the provisions of ITEPA 2003.
S. 313(6): ITEPA 2003, s. 225(6), (7) and s. 226(2).

314 Divers and diving supervisors

314 [Omitted by ITTOIA 2005, s. 882 and Sch. 1, para. 128 and repealed by s. 884 and Sch. 3.]

History – S. 314 omitted by ITTOIA 2005, s. 882(1) and Sch. 1, para. 128 and repealed by s. 884 and Sch. 3; effective for income tax purposes for 2005–06 onwards and for corporation tax purposes for accounting periods ending after 5 April 2005 (ITTOIA 2005, s. 883(1)).

Notes – S. 314 rewritten as follows:
S. 314(1): ITTOIA 2005, s. 15(1)–(3).
S. 314(2): ITTOIA 2005, s. 15(1).

315 Wounds and disability pensions

315 [Omitted by ITEPA 2003, Sch. 6, para. 41 and repealed by ITEPA 2003, Sch. 8, Pt. 1.]

History – S. 315 omitted by ITEPA 2003, Sch. 6, para. 41 and repealed by ITEPA 2003, Sch. 8, Pt. 1 which have effect for the tax year 2003–04 and subsequent tax years.

Notes – S. 315 rewritten as follows:
S. 315(1) and (2): ITEPA 2003, s. 641(1).
S. 315(3): ITEPA 2003, s. 641(2).

316 Allowances, bounties and gratuities

316 [Omitted by ITEPA 2003, Sch. 6, para. 41 and repealed by ITEPA 2003, Sch. 8, Pt. 1.]

History – S. 316 omitted by ITEPA 2003, Sch. 6, para. 41 and repealed by ITEPA 2003, Sch. 8, Pt. 1 which have effect for the tax year 2003–04 and subsequent tax years.

Notes – S. 316 rewritten as follows:
S. 316(1) and (2) are spent and so have not been rewritten into the provisions of ITEPA 2003.
S. 316(3): ITEPA s. 228(2) and s. 297.
S. 316(4): ITEPA s. 228(2) and s. 298.
S. 316(5) is spent and so has not been rewritten into the provisions of ITEPA 2003.

317 Victoria Cross and other awards

317 [Omitted by ITEPA 2003, Sch. 6, para. 41 and repealed by ITEPA 2003, Sch. 8, Pt. 1.]

History – S. 317 omitted by ITEPA 2003, Sch. 6, para. 41 and repealed by ITEPA 2003, Sch. 8, Pt. 1 which have effect for the tax year 2003–04 and subsequent tax years.

Notes – S. 317 rewritten as ITEPA 2003, s. 638.

318 Other pensions in respect of death due to war service etc.

318 [Omitted by ITEPA 2003, Sch. 6, para. 41 and repealed by ITEPA 2003, Sch. 8, Pt. 1.]

History – S. 318 omitted by ITEPA 2003, Sch. 6, para. 41 and repealed by ITEPA 2003, Sch. 8, Pt. 1 which have effect for the tax year 2003–04 and subsequent tax years.

Notes – S. 318 rewritten as follows:
S. 318(1) and (2): ITEPA 2003, s. 639.
S. 318(3): ITEPA 2003, s. 640.

319 Crown servants: foreign service allowance

319 [Omitted by ITEPA 2003, Sch. 6, para. 42 and repealed by ITEPA 2003, Sch. 8, Pt. 1.]

History – S. 319 omitted by ITEPA 2003, Sch. 6, para. 42 and repealed by ITEPA 2003, Sch. 8, Pt. 1 which have effect for the tax year 2003–04 and subsequent tax years.

Notes – S. 319 rewritten as follows:
S. 319(1): ITEPA 2003, s. 228(2) and s. 299(1).
S. 319(2): ITEPA 2003, s. 299(2).

320 Commonwealth Agents-General and official agents etc.

320 [Omitted by ITA 2007, s. 1027 and Sch. 1, para. 45 and repealed by ITA 2007, s. 1031 and Sch. 3, Pt. 1 with effect for 2007–08 and subsequent tax years.]

Notes – S. 320 rewritten for income tax purposes as follows:
S. 320(2): ITA 2007, s. 841(2), (6).
S. 320(3): ITA 2007, s. 841(1), (3), (4).
S. 320(4): ITA 2007, s. 841(5), (7).

321 Consuls and other official agents

321 [Omitted by ITEPA 2003, Sch. 6, para. 43 and repealed by ITEPA 2003, Sch. 8, Pt. 1.]

History – S. 321 omitted by ITEPA 2003, Sch. 6, para. 43 and repealed by ITEPA 2003, Sch. 8, Pt. 1 which have effect for the tax year 2003–04 and subsequent tax years.

Notes – S. 321 rewritten as follows:
S. 321(1): ITEPA 2003, s. 228(2), s. 300(1), (2), s. 301(1), (2) and (4).
S. 321(2): ITEPA 2003, s. 300(1), (2), s. 301(1), (2) and (3).
S. 321(3): ITEPA 2003, s. 300(3), s. 301(5) and (6).

322 Consular officers and employees

322 [Omitted by ITTOIA 2005, s. 882 and Sch. 1, para. 129 and repealed by s. 884 and Sch. 3.]

History – S. 322 omitted by ITTOIA 2005, s. 882(1) and Sch. 1, para. 129 and repealed by s. 884 and Sch. 3; effective for income tax purposes for 2005–06 onwards and for corporation tax purposes for accounting periods ending after 5 April 2005 (ITTOIA 2005, s. 883(1)).

Notes – S. 322 rewritten as follows:
S. 322(1): ITTOIA 2005, s. 771(1)–(4) and Sch. 1, para. 610 and 613.
S. 322(1A): ITTOIA 2005, s. 771(1) and Sch. 1, para. 610 and 613.
S. 322(3): ITTOIA 2005, s. 771(5) and Sch. 1, para. 610 and 613.
S. 322(4): ITTOIA 2005, s. 771(1) and Sch. 1, para. 610 and 613.
S. 322(5): ITTOIA 2005, s. 772(1)–(4).

323 Visiting forces

323 [Omitted by ITA 2007, s. 1027 and Sch. 1, para. 46 and repealed by ITA 2007, s. 1031 and Sch. 3, Pt. 1 with effect for 2007–08 and subsequent tax years.]

Notes – S. 323 rewritten for income tax purposes as follows:
S. 323(2): ITA 2007, s. 833(1), (3), (4).
S. 323(3): ITA 2007, s. 833(5).
S. 323(4): ITA 2007, s. 833(1), (6).
S. 323(5): ITA 2007, s. 833(2).
S. 323(6): ITA 2007, s. 833(3).
S. 323(8): ITA 2007, s. 833(7).

324 Designated international organisations

324 [Omitted by ITTOIA 2005, s. 882 and Sch. 1, para. 130 and repealed by s. 884 and Sch. 3.]

History – S. 324 omitted by ITTOIA 2005, s. 882(1) and Sch. 1, para. 130 and repealed by s. 884 and Sch. 3 effective for income tax purposes for 2005–06 onwards and for corporation tax purposes for accounting periods ending after 5 April 2005 (ITTOIA 2005, s. 883(1)).

Notes – S. 324 rewritten as follows:
S. 324(1): ITTOIA 2005, s. 774(5)–(7).
S. 324(2): ITTOIA 2005, s. 774(1)–(4).

325 Interest on deposits with National Savings Bank

325 [Omitted by ITTOIA 2005, s. 882 and Sch. 1, para. 131 and repealed by s. 884 and Sch. 3.]

History – S. 325 omitted by ITTOIA 2005, s. 882(1) and Sch. 1, para. 131 and repealed by s. 884 and Sch. 3; effective for income tax purposes for 2005–06 onwards and for corporation tax purposes for accounting periods ending after 5 April 2005 (ITTOIA 2005, s. 883(1)).

Notes – S. 325 rewritten as ITTOIA 2005, s. 691(1) and (2) and 783(2).

326 Interest etc. under contractual savings schemes

326 [Omitted by ITTOIA 2005, s. 882 and Sch. 1, para. 132 and repealed by s. 884 and Sch. 3.]

History – S. 326 omitted by ITTOIA 2005, s. 882(1) and Sch. 1, para. 132 and repealed by s. 884 and Sch. 3; effective for income tax purposes for 2005–06 onwards and for corporation tax purposes for accounting periods ending after 5 April 2005 (ITTOIA 2005, s. 883(1)).

Notes – S. 326 rewritten as follows:
S. 326(1): ITTOIA 2005, s. 702(1), (3) and (4) and 704(2) and (4)–(6). However, ITTOIA 2005 does not rewrite the words in ICTA 1988, s. 326(1) "other sum" as they add nothing to the provision (except possible confusion). (See ITTOIA 2005, Explanatory Notes, Annex 1, Table 1 (Change 158).)
S. 326(2): ITTOIA 2005, s. 703(2), 704(2) and 705(1).
S. 326(3): ITTOIA 2005, s. 703(2), 704(5) and 705(1).
S. 326(4): ITTOIA 2005, s. 703(2), 704(5) and 705(1).
S. 326(5): ITTOIA 2005, s. 703(2), 704(6) and 705(1).
S. 326(6): ITTOIA 2005, s. 702(1) and 707(1).
S. 326(7): ITTOIA 2005, s. 707(1).
S. 326(8): ITTOIA 2005, s. 707(2).

326A Tax-exempt special savings accounts

326A [Omitted by ITTOIA 2005, s. 882 and Sch. 1, para. 133 and repealed by s. 884 and Sch. 3.]

History – S. 326A omitted by ITTOIA 2005, s. 882(1) and Sch. 1, para. 133 and repealed by s. 884 and Sch. 3; effective for income tax purposes for 2005–06 onwards and for corporation tax purposes for accounting periods ending after 5 April 2005 (ITTOIA 2005, s. 883(1)).

326B Loss of exemption for special savings accounts

326B [Omitted by ITTOIA 2005, s. 882 and Sch. 1, para. 133 and repealed by s. 884 and Sch. 3.]

History – S. 326B omitted by ITTOIA 2005, s. 882(1) and Sch. 1, para. 133 and repealed by s. 884 and Sch. 3; effective for income tax purposes for 2005–06 onwards and for corporation tax purposes for accounting periods ending after 5 April 2005 (ITTOIA 2005, s. 883(1)).

326BB Follow-up TESSAs

326BB [Omitted by ITTOIA 2005, s. 882 and Sch. 1, para. 133 and repealed by s. 884 and Sch. 3.]

History – S. 326BB omitted by ITTOIA 2005, s. 882(1) and Sch. 1, para. 133 and repealed by s. 884 and Sch. 3; effective for income tax purposes for 2005–06 onwards and for corporation tax purposes for accounting periods ending after 5 April 2005 (ITTOIA 2005, s. 883(1)).

326C Tax-exempt special savings accounts: supplementary

326C [Omitted by ITTOIA 2005, s. 882 and Sch. 1, para. 133 and repealed by s. 884 and Sch. 3.]

History – S. 326C omitted by ITTOIA 2005, s. 882(1) and Sch. 1, para. 133 and repealed by s. 884 and Sch. 3; effective for income tax purposes for 2005–06 onwards and for corporation tax purposes for accounting periods ending after 5 April 2005 (ITTOIA 2005, s. 883(1)).

326D Tax-exempt special savings accounts: tax representatives

326D [Omitted by ITTOIA 2005, s. 882 and Sch. 1, para. 133 and repealed by s. 884 and Sch. 3.]

History – S. 326D omitted by ITTOIA 2005, s. 882(1) and Sch. 1, para. 133 and repealed by s. 884 and Sch. 3; effective for income tax purposes for 2005–06 onwards and for corporation tax purposes for accounting periods ending after 5 April 2005 (ITTOIA 2005, s. 883(1)).

327 Disabled persons' vehicle maintenance grant

Notes – S. 327 rewritten as ITTOIA 2005, s. 780(1) and (2).

327 [Omitted by ITTOIA 2005, s. 882 and Sch. 1, para. 134 and repealed by s. 884 and Sch. 3.]

History – S. 327 omitted by ITTOIA 2005, s. 882(1) and Sch. 1, para. 134 and repealed by s. 884 and Sch. 3; effective for income tax purposes for 2005–06 onwards and for corporation tax purposes for accounting periods ending after 5 April 2005 (ITTOIA 2005, s. 883(1)).

327A Payments to adopters

Notes – S. 327A rewritten as follows:
S. 327A(1): ITTOIA 2005, s. 744, 745 and 746.
S. 327A(2): ITTOIA 2005, s. 747.

327A [Omitted by ITTOIA 2005, s. 882 and Sch. 1, para. 135 and repealed by s. 884 and Sch. 3.]

History – S. 327A omitted by ITTOIA 2005, s. 882(1) and Sch. 1, para. 135 and repealed by s. 884 and Sch. 3; effective for income tax purposes for 2005–06 onwards and for corporation tax purposes for accounting periods ending after 5 April 2005 (ITTOIA 2005, s. 883(1)).

328 Funds in court

328 [Repealed by FA 1999, s. 68(2), s. 139 and Sch. 20, Pt. III(17).]

History – S. 328 repealed by FA 1999, s. 68(2), s. 139 and Sch. 20, Pt. III(17), with effect in relation to any income arising to a common investment fund on or after 6 April 1999, and any distribution made by such a fund for a distribution period beginning on or after that date.

329 Interest on damages for personal injuries

329 [Omitted by ITTOIA 2005, s. 882 and Sch. 1, para. 136 and repealed by s. 884 and Sch. 3.]

History – S. 329 omitted by ITTOIA 2005, s. 882(1) and Sch. 1, para. 136 and repealed by s. 884 and Sch. 3; effective for income tax purposes for 2005–06 onwards and for corporation tax purposes for accounting periods ending after 5 April 2005 (ITTOIA 2005, s. 883(1)).

Notes – S. 329 rewritten as follows:
S. 329(1): ITTOIA 2005, s. 751(1) and (3).
S. 329(2): ITTOIA 2005, s. 751(1).
S. 329(3): ITTOIA 2005, s. 751(2).
S. 329(4): ITTOIA 2005, s. 751(3).

329AA Personal injury damages in the form of periodical payments

329AA [Omitted by ITTOIA 2005, s. 882 and Sch. 1, para. 136 and repealed by s. 884 and Sch. 3.]

History – S. 329AA omitted by ITTOIA 2005, s. 882(1) and Sch. 1, para. 136 and repealed by s. 884 and Sch. 3; effective for income tax purposes for 2005–06 onwards and for corporation tax purposes for accounting periods ending after 5 April 2005 (ITTOIA 2005, s. 883(1)).

Notes – S. 329AA rewritten as follows:
S. 329AA(1): ITTOIA 2005, s. 731(1) and 733.
S. 329AA(2): ITTOIA 2005, s. 733 and 734(1)–(3).
S. 329AA(3): ITTOIA 2005, s. 731(1) and (3) and 733.
S. 329AA(4): ITTOIA 2005, s. 734(1)–(3).
S. 329AA(5): ITTOIA 2005, s. 731(5) and 732(3).
S. 329AA(6): ITTOIA 2005, s. 731(4).
S. 329AA(7): ITTOIA 2005, s. 731(1), (2) and (6) and 733.

329AB Compensation for personal injury under statutory or other schemes

329AB [Omitted by ITTOIA 2005, s. 882 and Sch. 1, para. 136 and repealed by s. 884 and Sch. 3.]

History – S. 329AB omitted by ITTOIA 2005, s. 882(1) and Sch. 1, para. 136 and repealed by s. 884 and Sch. 3; effective for income tax purposes for 2005–06 onwards and for corporation tax purposes for accounting periods ending after 5 April 2005 (ITTOIA 2005, s. 883(1)).

Notes – S. 329AB rewritten as follows:
S. 329AB(1): ITTOIA 2005, s. 732(1) and 733.
S. 329AB(2): ITTOIA 2005, s. 732(3).
S. 329AB(3): ITTOIA 2005, s. 732(3).

329A Annuities purchased for certain persons

329A [Not reproduced]

Notes – S. 329A is superseded by s. 329AA for payments received after 29 April 1996 irrespective of when the agreement or order referred to in s. 329AA was made or took effect (FA 1996, s. 150, Sch. 26 and s. 205, Sch. 41, Pt. V(16)).

329B Annuities assigned in favour of certain persons

329B [Not reproduced]

Notes – S. 329B is superseded by s. 329AA (inserted by FA 1996, s. 143(1) and Sch. 25 for payments received after 29 April 1996 irrespective of when the agreement or order referred to in s. 329AA was made or took effect. (FA 1996, s. 150, Sch. 26 and s. 205, Sch. 41, Pt. V(16)).

329C Annuities: criminal injuries

329C [Not reproduced]

History – S. 329C never took effect, being superseded by s. 329AB with effect in relation to payments received after the passing of the Criminal Injuries Compensation Act 1995, s. 8, which inserted s. 329C.

330 Compensation for National-Socialist persecution

330 [Omitted by ITEPA 2003, Sch. 6, para. 46 and repealed by ITEPA 2003, Sch. 8, Pt. 1.]

History – S. 330 omitted by ITEPA 2003, Sch. 6, para. 46 and repealed by ITEPA 2003, Sch. 8, Pt. 1 which have effect for the tax year 2003–04 and subsequent tax years.

Notes – S. 330 rewritten as ITEPA 2003, s. 642.

331 Scholarship income

331 [Omitted by ITTOIA 2005, s. 882 and Sch. 1, para. 137 and repealed by s. 884 and Sch. 3.]

History – S. 331 omitted by ITTOIA 2005, s. 882(1) and Sch. 1, para. 137 and repealed by s. 884 and Sch. 3; effective for income tax purposes for 2005–06 onwards and for corporation tax purposes for accounting periods ending after 5 April 2005 (ITTOIA 2005, s. 883(1)).

Notes – S. 331 rewritten as follows:
S. 331(1): ITTOIA 2005, s. 776(3).
S. 331(2): ITTOIA 2005, s. 776(1).

331A Student loans: certain interest to be disregarded

331A [Omitted by ITTOIA 2005, s. 882 and Sch. 1, para. 138 and repealed by s. 884 and Sch. 3.]

History – S. 331A omitted by ITTOIA 2005, s. 882(1) and Sch. 1, para. 138 and repealed by s. 884 and Sch. 3; effective for income tax purposes for 2005–06 onwards and for corporation tax purposes for accounting periods ending after 5 April 2005 (ITTOIA 2005, s. 883(1)).

Notes – S. 331A rewritten as follows:
S. 331A(1): ITTOIA 2005, s. 753(1).
S. 331A(2): ITTOIA 2005, s. 753(2).

332 Expenditure and houses of ministers of religion

332(1) [Omitted by ITEPA 2003, Sch. 6, para. 47(2) and repealed by ITEPA 2003, Sch. 8, Pt. 1.]

332(2) [Omitted by ITEPA 2003, Sch. 6, para. 47(2) and repealed by ITEPA 2003, Sch. 8, Pt. 1.]

332(3) [Omitted by ITTOIA 2005, s. 882 and Sch. 1, para. 139 and repealed by s. 884 and Sch. 3.]

332(3A) [Omitted by ITEPA 2003, Sch. 6, para. 47(4) and repealed by ITEPA 2003, Sch. 8, Pt. 1.]

332(3B) [Omitted by ITEPA 2003, Sch. 6, para. 47(4) and repealed by ITEPA 2003, Sch. 8, Pt. 1.]

332(4) [Omitted by ITEPA 2003, Sch. 6, para. 47(4) and repealed by ITEPA 2003, Sch. 8, Pt. 1.]

History – S. 332(1) and (2) omitted by ITEPA 2003, Sch. 6, para. 47(2) and repealed by ITEPA 2003, Sch. 8, Pt. 1 which have effect for the tax year 2003–04 and subsequent tax years.
S. 332(3) omitted by ITTOIA 2005, s. 882(1) and Sch. 1, para. 139 and repealed by s. 884 and Sch. 3; effective for income tax purposes for 2005–06 onwards and for corporation tax purposes for accounting periods ending after 5 April 2005 (ITTOIA 2005, s. 883(1)).
S. 332(3A), (3B) and (4) were omitted by ITEPA 2003, Sch. 6, para. 47(4) and repealed by ITEPA 2003, Sch. 8, Pt. 1 which have effect for the tax year 2003–04 and subsequent tax years.
S. 332(3A) and (3B) inserted by FA 2001, s. 57(3) and (4) and Sch. 12, para. 10 with effect from the year 2002–03.

Derivations – Former s. 332(3): ICTA 1970, s. 194(3), (4).

Notes – S. 332(3) rewritten as ITTOIA 2005, s. 159(1)–(4).

332A Venture capital trusts: relief

332A [Omitted by ITA 2007, s. 1027 and Sch. 1, para. 47 and repealed by ITA 2007, s. 1031 and Sch. 3, Pt. 1 with effect for 2007–08 and subsequent tax years.]

Notes – S. 332A rewritten for income tax purposes as ITA 2007, s. 258.

333 Investment plan regulations

333 Regulations under Chapter 3 of Part 6 of ITTOIA 2005 (income from individual investment plans) may include provision generally for the purpose of the administration of corporation tax in relation to plans.

History – S. 333 substituted by ITTOIA 2005, s. 882(1) and Sch. 1, para. 141; effective for income tax purposes for 2005–06 onwards and for corporation tax purposes for accounting periods ending after 5 April 2005 (ITTOIA 2005, s. 883(1)).

Statutory instruments – SI 1989/469: Personal Equity Plan Regulations.
SI 1998/1870: Individual Savings Account Regulations.

Notes – S. 333 rewritten as follows:
S. 333(1): ITTOIA 2005, s. 694(1).
S. 333(1A): ITTOIA 2005, s. 695(2) and 696(2)
S. 333(2): ITTOIA 2005, s. 694(1), (3) and (5).
S. 333(3): ITTOIA 2005, s. 694(3) and (4), 695(1), (3) and (4), 696(1)–(3) and 701(3).
S. 333(4): ITTOIA 2005, s. 699(1)–(8), 700(1)–6) and 701(1) and (2).

333A Personal equity plans: tax representatives

333A [Omitted by ITTOIA 2005, s. 882 and Sch. 1, para. 142 and repealed by s. 884 and Sch. 3.]

History – S. 333A omitted by ITTOIA 2005, s. 882(1) and Sch. 1, para. 142 and repealed by s. 884 and Sch. 3; effective for income tax purposes for 2005–06 onwards and for corporation tax purposes for accounting periods ending after 5 April 2005 (ITTOIA 2005, s. 883(1)).

Notes – S. 333A rewritten as follows:
S. 333A(1): ITTOIA 2005, s. 697(1).
S. 333A(2): ITTOIA 2005, s. 697(1) and 698(2).
S. 333A(3): ITTOIA 2005, s. 697(1) and 698(3).
S. 333A(4): ITTOIA 2005, s. 697(1) and 698(4).
S. *333A(5): ITTOIA 2005, s. 698(2).*
S. 333A(6): ITTOIA 2005, s. 697(3).
S. 333A(7): ITTOIA 2005, s. 698(5).
S. 333A(8): ITTOIA 2005, s. 698(5).
S. 333A(9): ITTOIA 2005, s. 698(6).
S. 333A(10): ITTOIA 2005, s. 698(6).
S. 333A(11): ITTOIA 2005, s. 697(1) and (2).
S. 333A(12): ITTOIA 2005, s. 697(2).

333B Involvement of insurance companies with plans and accounts

333B [Omitted by FA 2007, s. 38 and Sch. 7, para. 4 and repealed by s. 114 and Sch. 27, Pt. 2(7).]

History – S. 333B omitted by FA 2007, s. 38 and Sch. 7, para. 4 and repealed by s. 114 and Sch. 27, Pt. 2(7), with effect for the purposes of corporation tax, for periods of account of insurance companies beginning on or after 1 January 2007, and for the purposes of income tax, for the tax year 2007–08 and subsequent tax years (but see transitional provisions at FA 2007, Sch. 7, para. 80–84).

Notes – S. 333B rewritten as follows:
S. 333B(4): ITTOIA 2005, s. 697(2).
S. 333B(9): ITTOIA 2005, s. 697(4).
FA 2001, s. 87(5): Sch. 19AB, as modified, does not apply to tax credits in respect of distributions made after 5 April 2004.

Chapter V – Residence of Individuals

334 Commonwealth citizens and others temporarily abroad

334 [Omitted by ITA 2007, s. 1027 and Sch. 1, para. 48 and repealed by ITA 2007, s. 1031 and Sch. 3, Pt. 1 with effect for 2007–08 and subsequent tax years.]

Notes – S. 334 rewritten for income tax purposes as ITA 2007, s. 829(1), (2).

335 Residence of persons working abroad

335 [Omitted by ITA 2007, s. 1027 and Sch. 1, para. 49 and repealed by ITA 2007, s. 1031 and Sch. 3, Pt. 1 with effect for 2007–08 and subsequent tax years.]

Notes – S. 335 rewritten for income tax purposes as follows:
S. 335(1): ITA 2007, s. 830(1), (2), (3), (4), (6).
S. 335(2): ITA 2007, s. 830(5).

336 Temporary residents in the United Kingdom

336 [Omitted by ITA 2007, s. 1027 and Sch. 1, para. 50 and repealed by ITA 2007, s. 1031 and Sch. 3, Pt. 1 with effect for 2007–08 and subsequent tax years.]

Notes – S. 336 rewritten for income tax purposes as follows:
S. 336(1): ITA 2007, s. 831(1), (2), (4), (5).
S. 336(1A): ITA 2007, s. 831(2), (5).
S. 336(2): ITA 2007, s. 832(1), (2), (3), (4).
S. 336(3): ITA 2007, s. 831(1), 832(1).

PART VIII – TAXATION OF INCOME AND CHARGEABLE GAINS OF COMPANIES

TAXATION OF INCOME

History – S. 337–338B, as inserted by FA 2002, s. 84(2) and Sch. 30, para. 1, replaced former s. 337, 337A and 338, and are consequential upon the introduction, by FA 2002, s. 84(1) and Sch. 29, of a code for the tax treatment of intangible fixed assets created or acquired on or after 1 April 2002. The text of former s. 337, 337A and 338 is set out in the History notes to the FA 2002 versions.

337 Companies beginning or ceasing to carry on trade

337 [Omitted by CTA 2009, s. 1322 and Sch. 1, para. 103 and repealed by CTA 2009, s. 1326 and Sch. 3, Pt. 1.]

History – S. 337 omitted by CTA 2009, s. 1322 and Sch. 1, para. 103 and repealed by CTA 2009, s. 1326 and Sch. 3, Pt. 1, with effect for corporation tax purposes for accounting periods ending on or after 1 April 2009, and for income tax and capital gains tax purposes for the tax year 2009–10 and subsequent tax years.

Notes – Rewritten income tax provisions are now located as follows:
S. 337(1): ITTOIA 2005, s. 18(2).
S. 337(2): ITTOIA 2005, s. 362(1) and (2).
S. 337 rewritten as for corporation tax purposes as follows:
S. 337(1): CTA 2009, s. 41(2), Sch. 1, para. 520(3).
S. 337(2): CTA 2009, s. 289(1), (2).

337A Computation of company's profits or income: exclusion of general deductions

337A(1) [Omitted by CTA 2010, s. 1177 and Sch. 1, para. 23 and repealed by CTA 2010, s. 1181 and Sch. 3, Pt. 1.]

337A(2) [Omitted by TIOPA 2010, s. 371 and Sch. 7, para. 37 and repealed by TIOPA 2010, s. 378 and Sch. 10, Pt. 12.]

History – S. 337A(1) omitted by CTA 2010, s. 1177 and Sch. 1, para. 23 and repealed by CTA 2010, s. 1181 and Sch. 3, Pt. 1, with effect for corporation tax purposes for accounting periods ending on or after 1 April 2010, and for income and capital gains tax purposes for the tax year 2010–11 and subsequent tax years.
S. 337A(2) omitted by TIOPA 2010, s. 371 and Sch. 7, para. 37 and repealed by TIOPA 2010, s. 378 and Sch. 10, Pt. 12, with effect for corporation tax purposes for accounting periods ending on or after 1 April 2010, for income tax and capital gains tax purposes for

the tax year 2010–11 and subsequent tax years, and for petroleum revenue tax purposes for chargeable periods beginning on or after 1 July 2010.

Transitional – CTA 2009, Sch. 2, para. 55: certain references to CTA 2009, Pt. 5 to include references to FA 1996, Sch. 15 (loan relationships; savings and transitional provisions).

Notes – S. 337A rewritten as for corporation tax purposes as follows:
S. 337A(1): CTA 2009, s. 1305(1), (2), CTA 2010, Sch. 1, para. 680.
S. 337A(2) rewritten in TIOPA 2010, Sch. 7, para. 39.

338 Charges on income deducted from total profits

338 [Omitted by CTA 2010, s. 1177 and Sch. 1, para. 24 and repealed by CTA 2010, s. 1181 and Sch. 3, Pt. 1.]

History – S. 338 omitted by CTA 2010, s. 1177 and Sch. 1, para. 24 and repealed by CTA 2010, s. 1181 and Sch. 3, Pt. 1, with effect for corporation tax purposes for accounting periods ending on or after 1 April 2010, and for income and capital gains tax purposes for the tax year 2010–11 and subsequent tax years.

Notes – S. 338 rewritten as for corporation tax purposes as follows:
S. 338(1): CTA 2010, s. 189(1).
S. 338(2): CTA 2010, s. 189(2).
S. 338(3): CTA 2010, s. 189(3).
S. 338(4): CTA 2010, s. 189(4).
S. 338(5): CTA 2010, s. 189(5).

338A Meaning of "charges on income"

338A [Omitted by CTA 2010, s. 1177 and Sch. 1, para. 25 and repealed by CTA 2010, s. 1181 and Sch. 3, Pt. 1.]

History – S. 338A omitted by CTA 2010, s. 1177 and Sch. 1, para. 25 and repealed by CTA 2010, s. 1181 and Sch. 3, Pt. 1, with effect for corporation tax purposes for accounting periods ending on or after 1 April 2010, and for income and capital gains tax purposes for the tax year 2010–11 and subsequent tax years.

Notes – S. 338A rewritten as for corporation tax purposes as follows:
S. 338A(1): CTA 2010, s. 190(1), (2).
S. 338A(2): CTA 2010, s. 190(1).
S. 338A(3): CTA 2010, s. 190(2).

338B Charges on income: annuities or other annual payments

338B [Repealed by F(No. 2)A 2005, s. 70(1) and Sch. 11, Pt. 2(7).]

History – S. 338B repealed by F(No. 2)A 2005, s. 70(1) and Sch. 11, Pt. 2(7) with effect in relation to payments made on or after 16 March 2005 in respect of annuities or other annual payments (F(No. 2)A 2005, s. 38(7) and (13)).

339 Charges on income: donations to charity

339 [Omitted by CTA 2010, s. 1177 and Sch. 1, para. 26 and repealed by CTA 2010, s. 1181 and Sch. 3, Pt. 1.]

History – S. 339 omitted by CTA 2010, s. 1177 and Sch. 1, para. 26 and repealed by CTA 2010, s. 1181 and Sch. 3, Pt. 1, with effect for corporation tax purposes for accounting periods ending on or after 1 April 2010, and for income and capital gains tax purposes for the tax year 2010–11 and subsequent tax years.

Notes – S. 339(4) rewritten for income tax purposes as ITA 2007, s. 522(1), (3), (4), (5), (6).
S. 339 rewritten for corporation tax purposes as follows:
S. 339(1): CTA 2010, s. 190(2), 191(1), (2), (6), 194(1).
S. 339(1A): CTA 2010, s. 194(2).
S. 339(1B): CTA 2010, s. 194(3).
S. 339(3B): CTA 2010, s. 191(3), (7), 195(1), (2), 196, 197(1), (2), (3).
S. 339(3BA): CTA 2010, s. 192(1), (2), (3), (4), (5).
S. 339(3BB): CTA 2010, s. 192(6).
S. 339(3C): CTA 2010, s. 197(2), (3).
S. 339(3D): CTA 2010, s. 197(3), (4).
S. 339(3DA): CTA 2010, s. 197(2).
S. 339(3DB): CTA 2010, s. 198(1), (2), (3), (4), (6).
S. 339(3DC): CTA 2010, s. 198(1), (5), (7).
S. 339(3DD): CTA 2010, s. 198(1), (6), (7), (8).
S. 339(3E): CTA 2010, s. 191(5), 193(1), (2).
S. 339(3G): CTA 2010, s. 191(4).
S. 339(4): CTA 2010, s. 473(1), (2), 476(1), 477(1).
S. 339(7AA): CTA 2010, s. 199(1), (2), (3).
S. 339(7AB): CTA 2010, s. 200(1), (2), (3), (5).
S. 339(7AC): CTA 2010, s. 200(4).
S. 339(7A): CTA 2010, s. 201, 1176(1).
S. 339(9): CTA 2010, s. 202.

339A Maximum qualifying donations

339A [Repealed by FA 1991, s. 71(1), 123 and Sch. 19, Pt. V with effect in relation to accounting periods beginning on or after 19 March 1991 (FA 1991, s. 71(3)).]

History – The repeal of s. 339A has effect in relation to accounting periods beginning on or after 19 March 1991 (FA 1991, s. 71(3)).

340 Charges on income: interest payable to non-residents

340 [Repealed by FA 1996, s. 104 and Sch. 14 para. 17 and s. 205 and Sch. 41, Pt. V(3) for accounting periods ending after 31 March 1996 (corporation tax), subject to FA 1996, Sch. 15.]

341 Payments of interest etc. between related companies

341 [Repealed by FA 1996, s. 104 and Sch. 14 para. 17 and s. 205 and Sch. 41, Pt. V(3) for accounting periods ending after 31 March 1996 (corporation tax), subject to FA 1996, Sch. 15.]

342 Tax on company in liquidation

342 [Omitted by CTA 2010, s. 1177 and Sch. 1, para. 27 and repealed by CTA 2010, s. 1181 and Sch. 3, Pt. 1.]

History – S. 342 omitted by CTA 2010, s. 1177 and Sch. 1, para. 27 and repealed by CTA 2010, s. 1181 and Sch. 3, Pt. 1, with effect for corporation tax purposes for accounting periods ending on or after 1 April 2010, and for income and capital gains tax purposes for the tax year 2010–11 and subsequent tax years.

Notes – S. 342 rewritten for corporation tax purposes as follows:
S. 342(1): CTA 2010, s. 626(2).
S. 342(2): CTA 2010, s. 627(1), (2), 628(2), (3), (4), (5).
S. 342(3): CTA 2010, s. 627(1), (2), 628(2), (3), (4.
S. 342(3A): CTA 2010, s. 633(1), (2), (3), (4).
S. 342(4): CTA 2010, s. 629(1), (2).
S. 342(5): CTA 2010, s. 629(1), (3).
S. 342(6): CTA 2010, s. 629(4), (5), (6).
S. 342(7): CTA 2010, s. 632(2), (3), (4), (5).
S. 342(8): CTA 2010, s. 628(6), (7).

342A Tax on companies in administration

342A [Omitted by CTA 2010, s. 1177 and Sch. 1, para. 28 and repealed by CTA 2010, s. 1181 and Sch. 3, Pt. 1.]

History – S. 342A omitted by CTA 2010, s. 1177 and Sch. 1, para. 28 and repealed by CTA 2010, s. 1181 and Sch. 3, Pt. 1, with effect for corporation tax purposes for accounting periods ending on or after 1 April 2010, and for income and capital gains tax purposes for the tax year 2010–11 and subsequent tax years.

Notes – S. 342A rewritten for corporation tax purposes as follows:
S. 342A(1): CTA 2010, s. 626(3), (4).
S. 342A(2): CTA 2010, s. 627(1), (2), 630(2), (3), (4), (5).
S. 342A(3): CTA 2010, s. 627(1), (2), 630(2), (3), (4.
S. 342A(4): CTA 2010, s. 633(1), (2), (3).
S. 342A(5): CTA 2010, s. 633(4).
S. 342A(6): CTA 2010, s. 631(1), (2).
S. 342A(7): CTA 2010, s. 631(1), (3).
S. 342A(8): CTA 2010, s. 631(4), (5), (6), (3).
S. 342A(9): CTA 2010, s. 632(2), (3), (4), (5).
S. 342A(10): CTA 2010, s. 630(6), (7).

343 Company reconstructions without a change of ownership

343 [Omitted by CTA 2010, s. 1177 and Sch. 1, para. 29 and repealed by CTA 2010, s. 1181 and Sch. 3, Pt. 1.]

History – S. 343 omitted by CTA 2010, s. 1177 and Sch. 1, para. 29 and repealed by CTA 2010, s. 1181 and Sch. 3, Pt. 1, with effect for corporation tax purposes for accounting periods ending on or after 1 April 2010, and for income and capital gains tax purposes for the tax year 2010–11 and subsequent tax years.

Notes – S. 343 rewritten for corporation tax purposes as follows:
S. 343(1): CTA 2010, s. 939(2), 940, 941(1), (2), (3), (4), 943(1), (2), (3), 944(1), 948(1), 951(2), (4), Sch. 1, para. 354.
S. 343(2): CTA 2010, s. 948(1), (2), (3), (4), (5), 949(1), (2), (3), (4), (5), (6), (7), Sch. 1, para. 354, Sch. 2, para. 100.
S. 343(3): CTA 2010, s. 944(3), (4).
S. 343(4): CTA 2010, s. 945(1), (4), (5), Sch. 2, para. 99.
S. 343(4A): CTA 2010, s. 944(2).
S. 343(7): CTA 2010, s. 953(1), (2), (3), (4), (5), (6), (7).
S. 343(8): CTA 2010, s. 951(1), (2), (3), (4).
S. 343(9): CTA 2010, s. 952(1).
S. 343(10): CTA 2010, s. 952(2), (3).

343ZA Transfers of trade to obtain balancing allowances

343ZA [Omitted by CTA 2010, s. 1177 and Sch. 1, para. 30 and repealed by CTA 2010, s. 1181 and Sch. 3, Pt. 1.]

History – S. 343ZA omitted by CTA 2010, s. 1177 and Sch. 1, para. 30 and repealed by CTA 2010, s. 1181 and Sch. 3, Pt. 1, with effect for corporation tax purposes for accounting periods ending on or after 1 April 2010, and for income and capital gains tax purposes for the tax year 2010–11 and subsequent tax years.

Notes – S. 343ZA rewritten for corporation tax purposes as follows:
S. 343ZA(1): CTA 2010, s. 954(1).
S. 343ZA(2): CTA 2010, s. 955(1).
S. 343ZA(3): CTA 2010, s. 957(1).

S. 343ZA(4): CTA 2010, s. 954(1), (2), (3), (4), (5), (7), 955(1), (2), (4), (5), (6), (8).
S. 343ZA(5): CTA 2010, s. 954(6).
S. 343ZA(6): CTA 2010, s. 955(3), (7).
S. 343ZA(7): CTA 2010, s. 956(1).
S. 343ZA(8): CTA 2010, s. 956(2), (3).

343A Company reconstructions involving business of leasing plant or machinery

343A [Omitted by CTA 2010, s. 1177 and Sch. 1, para. 31 and repealed by CTA 2010, s. 1181 and Sch. 3, Pt. 1.]

History – S. 343A omitted by CTA 2010, s. 1177 and Sch. 1, para. 31 and repealed by CTA 2010, s. 1181 and Sch. 3, Pt. 1, with effect for corporation tax purposes for accounting periods ending on or after 1 April 2010, and for income and capital gains tax purposes for the tax year 2010–11 and subsequent tax years.

Notes – S. 343A rewritten for corporation tax purposes as follows:
S. 343A(1): CTA 2010, s. 950(1).
S. 343A(2): CTA 2010, s. 950(2), (3).
S. 343A(3): CTA 2010, s. 950(4).
S. 343A(4): CTA 2010, s. 950(5).
S. 343A(5): CTA 2010, s. 950(2), (6).

344 Company reconstructions: supplemental

344 [Omitted by CTA 2010, s. 1177 and Sch. 1, para. 32 and repealed by CTA 2010, s. 1181 and Sch. 3, Pt. 1.]

History – S. 344 omitted by CTA 2010, s. 1177 and Sch. 1, para. 32 and repealed by CTA 2010, s. 1181 and Sch. 3, Pt. 1, with effect for corporation tax purposes for accounting periods ending on or after 1 April 2010, and for income and capital gains tax purposes for the tax year 2010–11 and subsequent tax years.

Notes – S. 344 rewritten for corporation tax purposes as follows:
S. 344(1): CTA 2010, s. 941(5), (6).
S. 344(2): CTA 2010, s. 941(6), 942(1), (4), (5).
S. 344(3): CTA 2010, s. 942(2), (3), (6), (7), (8).
S. 344(4): CTA 2010, s. 941(7), (8).
S. 344(5): CTA 2010, s. 945(3), 947(2), (6).
S. 344(6): CTA 2010, s. 945(2), 946(2), (5), (7).
S. 344(7): CTA 2010, s. 945(2), 947(3).
S. 344(8): CTA 2010, s. 946(3), (4).
S. 344(9): CTA 2010, s. 946(5), (6), (7).
S. 344(10): CTA 2010, s. 947(4).
S. 344(11): CTA 2010, s. 946(8).
S. 344(12): CTA 2010, s. 946(9).

CHARGEABLE GAINS

345 Computation of chargeable gains

345 [Repealed by TCGA 1992, s. 290 and Sch. 12 in relation to tax for 1992–93 and subsequent years of assessment.]

Notes – See now TCGA 1992, s. 8.

346 Capital distribution of chargeable gains: recovery of tax from shareholder

346 [Repealed by TCGA 1992, s. 290 and Sch. 12 in relation to tax for 1992–93 and subsequent years of assessment.]

Notes – See now TCGA 1992, s. 189.

347 Tax on one member of group recoverable from another member

347 [Repealed by TCGA 1992, s. 290 and Sch. 12 in relation to tax for 1992–93 and subsequent years of assessment.]

Notes – See now TCGA 1992, s. 190.

PART IX – ANNUAL PAYMENTS AND INTEREST

ANNUAL PAYMENTS

347A General rule

347A [Omitted by FA 2007, s. 30 and Sch. 5, para. 1(4) and repealed by s. 114 and Sch. 27, Pt. 2(3).]

History – S. 347A omitted by FA 2007, s. 30 and Sch. 5, para. 1(4) and repealed by s. 114 and Sch. 27, Pt. 2(3), with effect in relation to payments made on or after 6 April 2007.

Notes – Rewritten income tax provisions are now located as follows:
S. 347A(1): ITA 2007, s. 900(1).
S. 347A(1): ITTOIA 2005, s. 727(1).
S. 347A(2): ITA 2007, s. 900(1), 901(2).
S. 347A(2): ITTOIA 2005, s. 727(1) and 2, 728, 729(1)–(5) and Sch. 2, para. 147.
S. 347A(3): ITA 2007, s. 901(2).
S. 347A(3): ITTOIA 2005, s. 727(3) and 730(6).
S. 347A(4): ITTOIA 2005, s. 730(1) and (2).
S. 347A(5): ITTOIA 2005, s. 839(1) and (3). The reference to ITEPA 2003, s. 355 in ICTA 1988, s. 347A(5) is not rewritten by ITTOIA 2005 as its effect is already given under ITEPA 2003, s. 355. (See ITTOIA 2005, Explanatory Notes, Annex 1, Table 1 (Change 158).)
S. 347A(6): ITA 2007, s. 905.
S. 347A(6): ITTOIA 2005, s. 727(4).

347B Qualifying maintenance payments

347B [Omitted by ITA 2007, s. 1027 and Sch. 1, para. 53 and repealed by ITA 2007, s. 1031 and Sch. 3, Pt. 1 with effect for 2007–08 and subsequent tax years.]

Notes – S. 347B rewritten for income tax purposes as follows:
S. 347B(1): ITA 2007, s. 454(1), (2), (4), (5), (6).
S. 347B(1A): ITA 2007, s. 454(3).
S. 347B(2): ITA 2007, s. 23, 26(1), 453(1), (2).
S. 347B(3): ITA 2007, s. 453(2).
S. 347B(5A): ITA 2007, s. 29(2), 453(2).
S. 347B(5B): ITA 2007, s. 27(4), (5).
S. 347B(7): ITA 2007, s. 454(9).
S. 347B(8): ITA 2007, s. 454(7).
S. 347B(9): ITA 2007, s. 455(1).
S. 347B(10): ITA 2007, s. 455(2).
S. 347B(11): ITA 2007, s. 454(8), 455(3).
S. 347B(12): ITA 2007, s. 456(1), (2).
S. 347B(13): ITA 2007, s. 456(3).

348 Payments out of profits or gains brought into charge to income tax: deduction of tax

348 [Omitted by ITA 2007, s. 1027 and Sch. 1, para. 54 and repealed by ITA 2007, s. 1031 and Sch. 3, Pt. 1.]

History – S. 348 omitted by ITA 2007, s. 1027 and Sch. 1, para. 54 and repealed by ITA 2007, s. 1031 and Sch. 3, Pt. 1 with effect in relation to accounting periods ending after 5 April 2007.

Notes – Rewritten income tax provisions are now located as follows:
S. 348(1): ITA 2007, s. 24(2), 448(1), (2), (4), 449(1), (2), (5), 505(1), (2), 848(1), 900(1), (2), 901(1), (3), (4), 942(1), (2), (3), 964(1), (3), (4), 1025(1), (2), (4).
S. 348(1): ITTOIA 2005, s. 426, 550, 602, 618 and 686(1).
S. 348(1A): ITA 2007, s. 899(2), (3), (4), (5), 941(3), (5).
S. 348(2): ITA 2007, s. 448(1), (2), 449(1), (2), 903(1),(3), (5), (6), 964(1), (3), (4), 1025(1), (2), (4).
S. 348(2): ITTOIA 2005, s. 602 and 618.
S. 348(3): ITA 2007, s. 899(5).
S. 348(4): ITA 2007, s. 1026.

349 Payments not out of profits or gains brought into charge to income tax, and annual interest

349 [Omitted by ITA 2007, s. 1027 and Sch. 1, para. 55 and repealed by ITA 2007, s. 1031 and Sch. 3, Pt. 1.]

History – S. 349 omitted by ITA 2007, s. 1027 and Sch. 1, para. 55 and repealed by ITA 2007, s. 1031 and Sch. 3, Pt. 1 with effect in relation to accounting periods ending after 5 April 2007.

Notes – Rewritten income tax provisions are now located as follows:
S. 349(1): ITA 2007, s. 848(1), 900(1), (2), 901(1), (3), (4), 903(1), (3), (5), (6), (7), 906(5), 910(2), 928(2), 942(1), (2), (3), 944(2), 1025(1), (2), (4).
S. 349(1): ITTOIA 2005, s. 426, 602, 618 and 686(1).
S. 349(1A): ITA 2007, s. 899(2), (3), (4), (5), 941(3), (5).
S. 349(1B): ITA 2007, s. 899(5).
S. 349(2): ITA 2007, s. 874(1), (2), (6), 875.
S. 349(3): ITA 2007, s. 876(1), (2), 878(1), 879(1), 881, 882, 883, 884(1), 885(1), 886(1), (2).
S. 349(3AA): ITA 2007, s. 878(2), 879(2).
S. 349(3AB): ITA 2007, s. 879(4).
S. 349(3A): ITA 2007, s. 889(1), (2), (3), (4).
S. 349(3B): ITA 2007, s. 889(3).
S. 349(3C): ITA 2007, s. 892(1), (2).
S. 349(4): ITA 2007, s. 889(7), 987.
S. 349(4) ("certificate of deposit"): ITA 2007, s. 1019.
S. 349(4) ("qualifying certificate of deposit"): ITA 2007, s. 985(1), (2), 986(1), (2).
S. 349(4) ("UK public revenue dividend"): ITA 2007, s. 891.
S. 349(4) ("uncertificated eligible debt security units"): ITA 2007, s. 986(3).
S. 349(5): ITA 2007, s. 984(1).
S. 349(6): ITA 2007, s. 886(3), 984(2).
ITTOIA 2005 does not rewrite the provisions in ICTA 1988, s. 349(7) as it is covered by the general disregard provision in ITTOIA 2005, Pt. 6, Ch. 10. (See ITTOIA 2005, Explanatory Notes, Annex 1, Table 1 (Change 158).)

349ZA Extension of section 349: proceeds of sale of UK patent rights

349ZA [Omitted by ITA 2007, s. 1027 and Sch. 1, para. 56 and repealed by ITA 2007, s. 1031 and Sch. 3, Pt. 1 with effect for income tax purposes for 2007–08 and subsequent tax years and for corporation tax purposes in relation to accounting periods ending after 5 April 2007.]

Notes – S. 349ZA rewritten for income tax purposes as follows:
S. 349ZA(1): ITA 2007, s. 910(1).
S. 349ZA(2): ITA 2007, s. 910(2), (3).
S. 349ZA(3): ITA 2007, s. 910(3).
S. 349ZA(4): ITA 2007, s. 910(4).
S. 349ZA(5): ITA 2007, s. 910(5).

349A Exceptions to section 349 for payments between companies etc.

349A [Omitted by ITA 2007, s. 1027 and Sch. 1, para. 57 and repealed by ITA 2007, s. 1031 and Sch. 3, Pt. 1 with effect for income tax purposes for 2007–08 and subsequent tax years and for corporation tax purposes in relation to accounting periods ending after 5 April 2007.]

Notes – S. 349A rewritten for income tax purposes as follows:
S. 349A(1): ITA 2007, s. 930(1).
S. 349A(2): ITA 2007, s. 930(3).
S. 349A(3): ITA 2007, s. 930(2).
S. 349A(4): ITA 2007, s. 930(2).
S. 349A(5): ITA 2007, s. 930(4).
S. 349A(6): ITA 2007, s. 930(1), 932.

349B The conditions mentioned in section 349A(1)

349B [Omitted by ITA 2007, s. 1027 and Sch. 1, para. 57 and repealed by ITA 2007, s. 1031 and Sch. 3, Pt. 1 with effect for income tax purposes for 2007–08 and subsequent tax years and for corporation tax purposes in relation to accounting periods ending after 5 April 2007.]

Notes – S. 349B rewritten for income tax purposes as follows:
S. 349B(1): ITA 2007, s. 933.
S. 349B(2): ITA 2007, s. 934(1), (2), (3), (4).
S. 349B(3): ITA 2007, s. 936(1), (2).
S. 349B(4): ITA 2007, s. 935(1), (2), (3).
S. 349B(6): ITA 2007, s. 937(1), (2), (3).
S. 349B(7): ITA 2007, s. 937(4), (5), (6).
S. 349B(8): ITA 2007, s. 936(3), 937(7).

349C Directions disapplying section 349A(1)

349C [Omitted by ITA 2007, s. 1027 and Sch. 1, para. 57 and repealed by ITA 2007, s. 1031 and Sch. 3, Pt. 1 with effect for income tax purposes for 2007–08 and subsequent tax years and for corporation tax purposes in relation to accounting periods ending after 5 April 2007.]

Notes – S. 349C rewritten for income tax purposes as follows:
S. 349C(1): ITA 2007, s. 931(1).
S. 349C(2): ITA 2007, s. 931(2).
S. 349C(3): ITA 2007, s. 931(3).
S. 349C(4): ITA 2007, s. 931(1), 932.

349D Section 349A(1): consequences of reasonable but incorrect belief

349D [Omitted by ITA 2007, s. 1027 and Sch. 1, para. 57 and repealed by ITA 2007, s. 1031 and Sch. 3, Pt. 1 with effect for income tax purposes for 2007–08 and subsequent tax years and for corporation tax purposes in relation to accounting periods ending after 5 April 2007.]

Notes – S. 349D rewritten for income tax purposes as follows:
S. 349D(1): ITA 2007, s. 938(1), (2).
S. 349D(2): ITA 2007, s. 932, 938(1).

349E Deductions under section 349(1): payment of royalties overseas

349E [Omitted by ITA 2007, s. 1027 and Sch. 1, para. 58 and repealed by ITA 2007, s. 1031 and Sch. 3, Pt. 1 with effect for income tax purposes for 2007–08 and subsequent tax years and for corporation tax purposes in relation to accounting periods ending after 5 April 2007.]

Notes – S. 349E rewritten for income tax purposes as follows:
S. 349E(1): ITA 2007, s. 911(1), (2), (4), 913(2), 1023.
S. 349E(2): ITA 2007, s. 911(3).
S. 349E(3): ITA 2007, s. 912(1), (2).
S. 349E(4): ITA 2007, s. 912(3).
S. 349E(5): ITA 2007, s. 911(4), 913(1), (2).
S. 349E(6): ITA 2007, Sch. 1 para. 385(2).
S. 349E(7): ITA 2007, Sch. 1 para. 385(3).

350 Charge to tax where payments made under section 349

350 [Omitted by ITA 2007, s. 1027 and Sch. 1, para. 59 and repealed by ITA 2007, s. 1031 and Sch. 3, Pt. 1 with effect for income tax purposes for 2007–08 and for corporation tax purposes in relation to accounting periods ending after 5 April 2007.]

Notes – S. 350 rewritten for income tax purposes as follows:
S. 350(1): ITA 2007, s. 946, 963(1), (2), (3), 964(1), (3), (4).
S. 350(3): ITA 2007, s. 963(4).
S. 350(4): ITA 2007, s. 946, 962(1), (6).
S. 350(5): ITA 2007, s. 962(2).
S. 350(6): ITA 2007, s. 962(3), (4).
S. 350(7): ITA 2007, s. 962(5).

350A UK public revenue dividends: deduction of tax

350A [Omitted by ITA 2007, s. 1027 and Sch. 1, para. 60 and repealed by ITA 2007, s. 1031 and Sch. 3, Pt. 1 with effect for income tax prposes for 2007–08 and for corporation tax purposes in relation to accounting periods ending after 5 April 2007.]

Notes – S. 350A rewritten for income tax purposes as follows:
S. 350A(1): ITA 2007, s. 897(1).
S. 350A(2): ITA 2007, s. 897(2).
S. 350A(3): ITA 2007, s. 897(3).

351 Small maintenance payments

351 [Repealed by FA 1988, s. 148 and Sch. 14, Pt. IV, (1)–(7) in relation to payments made after 5 April 1989, and (8) in relation to orders and variations made after that date.]

352 Certificates of deduction of tax

352 [Omitted by ITA 2007, s. 1027 and Sch. 1, para. 61 and repealed by ITA 2007, s. 1031 and Sch. 3, Pt. 1 with effect for 2007–08 and subsequent tax years.]

Notes – S. 352 rewritten for income tax purposes as follows:
S. 352(1): ITA 2007, s. 495(1), (2), 975(1), (2), (3), (4), (5).
S. 352(2): ITA 2007, s. 495(3), 975(6).

RELIEF FOR PAYMENTS OF INTEREST (EXCLUDING MIRAS)

353 General provision

353(1) Where a person pays interest in any year of assessment, that person, if he makes a claim to the relief, shall for that year of assessment be entitled (subject to section 52 of ITTOIA 2005) to relief in accordance with this section in respect of so much (if any) of the amount of that interest as is eligible for relief under this section by virtue of section 365.

353(1A) Where a person is entitled for a year of assessment to relief under this section in respect of an amount of interest which is eligible for relief by virtue of section 365, the relief is given as a tax reduction for that tax year.

353(1AA) The amount of the tax reduction is 23% of the amount of the interest.

353(1AB) The tax reduction is given effect at Step 6 of the calculation in section 23 of ITA 2007.

353(1B) [Omitted by ITA 2007, s. 1027 and Sch. 1, para. 62(4) and repealed by ITA 2007, s. 1031 and Sch. 3, Pt. 1.]

353(1C)–(1D) [Repealed by FA 1995, s. 162 and Sch. 29, Pt. VIII(2); see History note.]

353(1E) Where any person is entitled for any year of assessment to relief in respect of any amount of interest which is eligible for that relief partly as mentioned in subsection (1A) above and partly as mentioned in section 383 of ITA 2007 (relief for interest payments), that amount of interest shall be apportioned between the cases to which each of those provisions applies without regard to what parts of the total amount borrowed remain outstanding but according to–

(a) the proportions of the total amount borrowed which were applied for different purposes;

(b) [repealed by FA 1995, s. 162 and Sch. 29, Pt. VIII(2); see History note];

and subsection (1A) above or section 383 of ITA 2007 shall apply accordingly to the case in which that subsection or section applies.

353(1F) [Omitted by ITA 2007, s. 1027 and Sch. 1, para. 62(6) and repealed by ITA 2007, s. 1031 and Sch. 3, Pt. 1.]

353(1G) [Omitted by ITA 2007, s. 1027 and Sch. 1, para. 62(6) and repealed by ITA 2007, s. 1031 and Sch. 3, Pt. 1.]

353(1H) [Omitted by ITA 2007, s. 1027 and Sch. 1, para. 62(6) and repealed by ITA 2007, s. 1031 and Sch. 3, Pt. 1.]

353(2) This section does not apply to a payment of relevant loan interest to which section 369 applies.

353(3) Relief under this section shall not be given in respect of–

(a) interest on a debt incurred by overdrawing an account or by debiting the account of any person as the holder of a credit card or under similar arrangements; or

(b) where interest is paid at a rate in excess of a reasonable commercial rate, so much of the interest as represents the excess.

353(4,5) [Repealed by FA 1994, s. 81 and Sch. 9, para. 3, and s. 258 and Sch. 26, Pt. V(2).]

History – In s. 353(1), the words "sections 359 to 368 of this Act and" omitted by ITA 2007, s. 1027 and Sch. 1, para. 62(2)(a) and repealed by ITA 2007, s. 1031 and Sch. 3, Pt. 1 with effect for income tax purposes for 2007–08 and subsequent tax years and for corporation tax purposes in relation to accounting periods ending after 5 April 2007.

In s. 353(1), the words "section 365" substituted by ITA 2007, s. 1027 and Sch. 1, para. 62(2)(b) with effect for income tax purposes for 2007–08 and subsequent tax years and for corporation tax purposes in relation to accounting periods ending after 5 April 2007.

In s. 353(1) the words "of this Act and section 52 of ITTOIA 2005" inserted by ITTOIA 2005, s. 882(1) and Sch. 1, para. 152; effective for income tax purposes for 2005–06 onwards and for corporation tax purposes for accounting periods ending after 5 April 2005 (ITTOIA 2005, s. 883(1)).

S. 353(1A), (1AA) and (1AB) substituted for former s. 353(1A) by ITA 2007, s. 1027 and Sch. 1, para. 62(3) with effect for income tax purposes for 2007–08 and subsequent tax years and for corporation tax purposes in relation to accounting periods ending after 5 April 2007.

S. 353(1B) omitted by ITA 2007, s. 1027 and Sch. 1, para. 62(4) and repealed by ITA 2007, s. 1031 and Sch. 3, Pt. 1 with effect for income tax purposes for 2007–08 and subsequent tax years and for corporation tax purposes in relation to accounting periods ending after 5 April 2007.

S. 353(1), former (1A), former (1B) amended, so as to remove references to s. 354-358, and s. 353(1G) substituted, by FA 1999, s. 38, Sch. 4, para. 1, s. 139 and Sch. 20, Pt. III(7), with effect in relation to a payment of interest made on or after 6 April 2000 (whenever falling due), or a payment of interest made before that date but not before 9 March 1999 which was:

- not due until on or after 6 April 2000, or
- was made in accordance with any scheme made for a tax avoidance purpose (see FA 1999, s. 38(5)) on or after 9 March 1999 (whether or not before the making of the payment).

In s. 353(1G), words "23 per cent" substituted by FA 2000, s. 83(2), with effect in relation to payments of interest made on or after 6 April 2000.

The following repeals in s. 353 made by FA 1995, s. 162 and Sch. 29, Pt. VIII(2), with effect in relation to any payment of interest made on or after 6 April 1995, subject to the provisions of FA 1995, s. 42(4)–(6):

- in s. 353(1A), para. (b) and the word "and" immediately preceding it;
- in s. 353(1B), para. (b) and the word "or" immediately preceding it;
- s. 353(1C), (1D); and
- in s. 353(1E), the words "the following factors, that is to say" which appeared after "but according to"; and para. (b) and the word "and" immediately preceding it.

S. 353(1) substituted, and s. 353(1A)–(1H) inserted, by FA 1994, s. 81(1), (2), in relation to interest payments made on or after 6 April 1994 (whenever falling due).

In former s. 353(1B), words "(subject to section 237(5)(b))" substituted by FA 1995, s. 42(2)(a), with effect in relation to any payment of interest made on or after 6 April 1995, subject to the provisions of FA 1995, s. 42(4)–(6).

In s. 353(1E), the words "under this section" omitted by ITA 2007, s. 1027, Sch. 1, para. 62(5)(a) and repealed by ITA 2007, s. 1031 and Sch. 3, Pt. 1; and the words "section 383 of ITA 2007 (relief for interest payments", "those provisions" and "and subsection (1A) above or section 383 of ITA 2007 shall apply accordingly to the case in which that subsection or section applies" substituted by ITA 2007, s. 1027 and Sch. 1, para. 62(5) with effect for income tax purposes for 2007–08 and later tax years and for corporation tax purposes in relation to accounting periods ending after 5 April 2007.

S. 353 (1F), (1G) and (1H) omitted by ITA 2007, s. 1027 and Sch. 1, para. 62(6) and repealed by ITA 2007, s. 1031 and Sch. 3, Pt. 1 with effect for income tax purposes for 2007–08 and subsequent tax years and for corporation tax purposes in relation to accounting periods ending after 5 April 2007.

S. 353(4), (5) repealed by FA 1994, s. 81 and Sch. 9, para. 3, and s. 258 and Sch. 26, Pt. V(2), in relation to interest payments made on or after 6 April 1994 (whenever falling due).

Former s. 353(4), (5) added by FA 1991, s. 27(1), in relation to payments of interest made on or after 6 April 1991 (whenever falling due), subject to the provisions of s. 27 (3), (5) in relation to certain bridging loans. S. 353(5) previously amended by FA 1993, s. 79 and Sch. 6, para. 1, by substituting the words "by virtue of … the lower rate," in relation to 1993–94 and subsequent years of assessment.

Derivations – S. 353(1) (as originally enacted): FA 1972, s. 75(1) (as amended by FA 1974, s. 19(1)); FA 1972, s. 75(6) (as substituted by FA 1976, s. 49(5)); FA 1973, s. 23(5)(b).

S. 353(2): FA 1982, s. 26(1).

S. 353(3)(a): FA 1972, s. 75(1A), inserted by FA 1974, s. 19(1).

S. 353(3)(b): FA 1972, s. 75(2).

Cross references – S. 117: restrictions on relief under this section for individual members of limited partnerships.

S. 118ZE (inserted by FA 2004, s. 124(1)): non-active general partners and non-active members of limited liability partnerships – restriction on relief for non-active partners.

Pt. VI, Ch. I (s. 256–278): personal allowances.

S. 271(2): relief under this section for interest on loan annuity contracts by elderly.

S. 280(2): relief under this section may be claimed by other spouse to extent income of the entitled spouse is insufficient.

S. 289A(5)(b): form of enterprise investment scheme relief.

S. 787: restriction on relief under this section where transaction designed for sole or main purpose of tax reduction.

S. 788: double taxation relief agreements.

S. 790: unilateral double taxation relief.

Sch. 15B, para. 1(6)(c): any income tax reduction under s. 353(1A) not taken into account in computing total income for purposes of granting relief under Sch. 15B, Pt. I (venture capital trusts: relief on investment).

FA 1988, Sch. 6, para. 3(3), (4): certain interest payments are not eligible for relief under s. 353 if paid on or after 15 March 1988 in respect of a business consisting of the occupation of commercial woodlands.

FA 1989, s. 54(3C)(b): calculation of medical insurance relief.

SSCBA 1992, Sch. 2, para. 3: application of s. 353 as regards the computation of profits or gains on which Class 4 NICs are chargeable.

TCGA 1992, s. 6: rate of capital gains tax determined by reference to rate of income tax effectively as if gain were added as top slice of income.

FA 1995, Sch. 22, para. 2, 5: restriction of relief under s. 353 where transitional self-assessment rules exploited by partnership with a view to artificially increasing profits or gains of transitional period, or overlap period.
FA 1999, s. 38(1): ineligibility for relief under s. 353 by virtue of s. 354 of any payment of interest falling within FA 1999, s. 38(3), (4) (broadly, mortgage interest payments made on or after 6 April 2000, or on or after 9 March 1999 and before 6 April 2000 but not falling due until on or after 6 April 2000, or made between those dates in pursuance of a tax avoidance scheme made on or after 9 March 1999).
ITEPA 2003, s. 178: exception for loans where interest qualifies for tax relief.
ITEPA 2003, s. 180(5): threshold for benefit of loan to be treated as earnings.
FA 2006, s. 75(1): the amount of loan interest eligible for relief in respect of a film partnership is restricted to, under specified conditions, 40 per cent of the interest that would otherwise be eligible for relief.

Extra-statutory concessions – ESC A89: circumstances in which relief for interest on a loan to buy property used for both residential and business purposes may be allowed in part under s. 353 and in part as a deduction in computing profits or losses.

Statements of practice – SP 2/03 and SP 1/05: directions by HMRC under FA 1998, s. 118: circumstances in which an amendment to a return to make a claim to relief under s. 353, or an amendment to a claim made in the return, may be made by telephone.

HMRC interpretations – IRInt. 57: Revenue view on what factors are relevant in determining whether income has a UK source, and is thus within the charge to tax under Sch. D, Case III.

HMRC Manuals – Inspector's Manual, IM784: relief for mortgage interest where there is business use of home.

Other material – Taxline 1992/43 (not reproduced): Revenue confirmation that where overdraft used solely for qualifying purpose and replaced by a loan within 12 months, relief (given for the loan interest only provided all other relief conditions met) is extended to other qualifying purposes (partnership loans, etc.).
HMRC press release, 10 February 1995 (not reproduced): relief of interest under transitional Sch. A rules.

Notes – S. 353 rewritten for income tax purposes as follows:
S. 353(1): ITA 2007, s. 23, 24(1), 383(1), (2).
S. 353(1A): ITA 2007, s. 23, 26(1).
S. 353(1B): ITA 2007, s. 23, 383(3), (4).
S. 353(1F): ITA 2007, s. 29(2).
S. 353(1H): ITA 2007, s. 27(4), (5).
S. 353(3): ITA 2007, s. 384(1), (2).

354 Loans to buy land, etc.

354 [Repealed by FA 1999, s. 38 and Sch. 4, para. 2, s. 139 and Sch. 20, Pt. III(7).]

History – S. 354 repealed by FA 1999, s. 38 and Sch. 4, para. 2, s. 139 and Sch. 20, Pt. III(7), with effect (FA 1999, s. 38(3), (4)) in relation to a payment of interest made on or after 6 April 2000 (whenever falling due), or a payment of interest made before that date but not before 9 March 1999 which was:

- not due until on or after 6 April 2000, or
- was made in accordance with any scheme made for a tax avoidance purpose (see FA 1999, s. 38(5)) on or after 9 March 1999 (whether or not before the making of the payment).

355 Matters excluded from section 354

355 [Repealed by FA 1999, s. 38 and Sch. 4, para. 2, s. 139 and Sch. 20, Pt. III(7).]

History – S. 355 repealed by FA 1999, s. 38 and Sch. 4, para. 2, s. 139 and Sch. 20, Pt. III(7), with effect (FA 1999, s. 38(3), (4)) in relation to a payment of interest made on or after 6 April 2000 (whenever falling due), or a payment of interest made before that date but not before 9 March 1999 which was:

- not due until on or after 6 April 2000, or
- was made in accordance with any scheme made for a tax avoidance purpose (see FA 1999, s. 38(5)) on or after 9 March 1999 (whether or not before the making of the payment).

356 Job-related accommodation

356 [Repealed by FA 1999, s. 38 and Sch. 4, para. 2, s. 139 and Sch. 20, Pt. III(7).]

History – S. 356 repealed by FA 1999, s. 38 and Sch. 4, para. 2, s. 139 and Sch. 20, Pt. III(7), with effect (FA 1999, s. 38(3), (4)) in relation to a payment of interest made on or after 6 April 2000 (whenever falling due), or a payment of interest made before that date but not before 9 March 1999 which was:

- not due until on or after 6 April 2000, or
- was made in accordance with any scheme made for a tax avoidance purpose (see FA 1999, s. 38(5)) on or after 9 March 1999 (whether or not before the making of the payment).

356A Limit on relief for home loans: residence basis

356A [Repealed by FA 1999, s. 38 and Sch. 4, para. 2, s. 139 and Sch. 20, Pt. III(7).]

History – S. 356A repealed by FA 1999, s. 38 and Sch. 4, para. 2, s. 139 and Sch. 20, Pt. III(7), with effect (FA 1999, s. 38(3), (4)) in relation to a payment of interest made on or after 6 April 2000 (whenever falling due), or a payment of interest made before that date but not before 9 March 1999 which was:

- not due until on or after 6 April 2000, or
- was made in accordance with any scheme made for a tax avoidance purpose (see FA 1999, s. 38(5)) on or after 9 March 1999 (whether or not before the making of the payment).

356B Residence basis: married couples

356B [Repealed by FA 1999, s. 38 and Sch. 4, para. 2, s. 139 and Sch. 20, Pt. III(7).]

History – S. 356B repealed by FA 1999, s. 38 and Sch. 4, para. 2, s. 139 and Sch. 20, Pt. III(7), with effect (FA 1999, s. 38(3), (4)) in relation to a payment of interest made on or after 6 April 2000 (whenever falling due), or a payment of interest made before that date but not before 9 March 1999 which was:

- not due until on or after 6 April 2000, or
- was made in accordance with any scheme made for a tax avoidance purpose (see FA 1999, s. 38(5)) on or after 9 March 1999 (whether or not before the making of the payment).

356C Payments to which sections 356A and 356B apply

356C [Repealed by FA 1999, s. 38 and Sch. 4, para. 2, s. 139 and Sch. 20, Pt. III(7).]

History – S. 356C repealed by FA 1999, s. 38 and Sch. 4, para. 2, s. 139 and Sch. 20, Pt. III(7), with effect (FA 1999, s. 38(3), (4)) in relation to a payment of interest made on or after 6 April 2000 (whenever falling due), or a payment of interest made before that date but not before 9 March 1999 which was:
- not due until on or after 6 April 2000, or
- was made in accordance with any scheme made for a tax avoidance purpose (see FA 1999, s. 38(5)) on or after 9 March 1999 (whether or not before the making of the payment).

356D Provisions supplementary to sections 356A to 356C

356D [FA 1999, s. 38 and Sch. 4, para. 2, s. 139 and Sch. 20, Pt. III(7).]

History – S. 356D repealed by FA 1999, s. 38 and Sch. 4, para. 2, s. 139 and Sch. 20, Pt. III(7), with effect (FA 1999, s. 38(3), (4)) in relation to a payment of interest made on or after 6 April 2000 (whenever falling due), or a payment of interest made before that date but not before 9 March 1999 which was:
- not due until on or after 6 April 2000, or
- was made in accordance with any scheme made for a tax avoidance purpose (see FA 1999, s. 38(5)) on or after 9 March 1999 (whether or not before the making of the payment).

357 Limit on amount of loan eligible for relief by virtue of section 354

357 [Repealed by FA 1999, s. 38 and Sch. 4, para. 2, s. 139 and Sch. 20, Pt. III(7).]

History – S. 357 repealed by FA 1999, s. 38 and Sch. 4, para. 2, s. 139 and Sch. 20, Pt. III(7), with effect (FA 1999, s. 38(3), (4)) in relation to a payment of interest made on or after 6 April 2000 (whenever falling due), or a payment of interest made before that date but not before 9 March 1999 which was:
- not due until on or after 6 April 2000, or
- was made in accordance with any scheme made for a tax avoidance purpose (see FA 1999, s. 38(5)) on or after 9 March 1999 (whether or not before the making of the payment).

357A Substitution of security

357A [Repealed by FA 1999, s. 38 and Sch. 4, para. 2, s. 139 and Sch. 20, Pt. III(7).]

History – S. 357A repealed by FA 1999, s. 38 and Sch. 4, para. 2, s. 139 and Sch. 20, Pt. III(7), with effect (FA 1999, s. 38(3), (4)) in relation to a payment of interest made on or after 6 April 2000 (whenever falling due), or a payment of interest made before that date but not before 9 March 1999 which was:
- not due until on or after 6 April 2000, or
- was made in accordance with any scheme made for a tax avoidance purpose (see FA 1999, s. 38(5)) on or after 9 March 1999 (whether or not before the making of the payment).

357B Treatment of loans following security substitution

357B [Repealed by FA 1999, s. 38 and Sch. 4, para. 2, s. 139 and Sch. 20, Pt. III(7).]

History – S. 357B repealed by FA 1999, s. 38 and Sch. 4, para. 2, s. 139 and Sch. 20, Pt. III(7), with effect (FA 1999, s. 38(3), (4)) in relation to a payment of interest made on or after 6 April 2000 (whenever falling due), or a payment of interest made before that date but not before 9 March 1999 which was:
- not due until on or after 6 April 2000, or
- was made in accordance with any scheme made for a tax avoidance purpose (see FA 1999, s. 38(5)) on or after 9 March 1999 (whether or not before the making of the payment).

357C Substitution of security: supplemental

357C [Repealed FA 1999, s. 38 and Sch. 4, para. 2, s. 139 and Sch. 20, Pt. III(7).]

History – S. 357C repealed by FA 1999, s. 38 and Sch. 4, para. 2, s. 139 and Sch. 20, Pt. III(7), with effect (FA 1999, s. 38(3), (4)) in relation to a payment of interest made on or after 6 April 2000 (whenever falling due), or a payment of interest made before that date but not before 9 March 1999 which was:
- not due until on or after 6 April 2000, or
- was made in accordance with any scheme made for a tax avoidance purpose (see FA 1999, s. 38(5)) on or after 9 March 1999 (whether or not before the making of the payment).

358 Relief where borrower deceased

358 [Repealed by FA 1999, s. 38 and Sch. 4, para. 2, s. 139 and Sch. 20, Pt. III(7).]

History – S. 358 repealed by FA 1999, s. 38 and Sch. 4, para. 2, s. 139 and Sch. 20, Pt. III(7), with effect (FA 1999, s. 38(3), (4)) in relation to a payment of interest made on or after 6 April 2000 (whenever falling due), or a payment of interest made before that date but not before 9 March 1999 which was:
- not due until on or after 6 April 2000, or
- was made in accordance with any scheme made for a tax avoidance purpose (see FA 1999, s. 38(5)) on or after 9 March 1999 (whether or not before the making of the payment).

359 *Loan to buy machinery or plant*

359 [Omitted by ITA 2007, s. 1027 and Sch. 1, para. 63 and repealed by ITA 2007, s. 1031 and Sch. 3, Pt. 1 with effect for 2007–08 and subsequent tax years.]

Notes – S. 359 rewritten for income tax purposes as follows:
S. 359(1): ITA 2007, s. 383(2), 385(1), 388(1), (2), 389(2), (3).
S. 359(2): ITA 2007, s. 389(4), (5).
S. 359(3): ITA 2007, s. 383(2), 385(1), 390(1), (2), (4), 391(2), (3).
S. 359(4): ITA 2007, s. 391(4), (5).

360 Loan to buy interest in close company

360 [Omitted by ITA 2007, s. 1027 and Sch. 1, para. 64 and repealed by ITA 2007, s. 1031 and Sch. 3, Pt. 1 with effect for 2007–08 and subsequent tax years.]

Notes – S. 360 rewritten for income tax purposes as follows:
S. 360(1): ITA 2007, s. 383(2), 385(1), 392(1), (2), (4), 393(1).
S. 360(2): ITA 2007, s. 393(1), (2), (4).
S. 360(3): ITA 2007, s. 385(1), 393(1), (2), (3).
S. 360(3A): ITA 2007, s. 392(3), Sch. 2 para. 91, 92.
S. 360(4): ITA 2007, s. 392(4), 394(5), 395(6).

360A Meaning of "material interest" in section 360

360A [Omitted by ITA 2007, s. 1027 and Sch. 1, para. 66 and repealed by ITA 2007, s. 1031 and Sch. 3, Pt. 1 with effect for 2007–08 and subsequent tax years.]

Notes – S. 360A rewritten for income tax purposes as follows:
S. 360A(1): ITA 2007, s. 394(1), (2), (3), (4).
S. 360A(2): ITA 2007, s. 395(1), (6).
S. 360A(4): ITA 2007, s. 395(2), Sch. 2 para. 94.
S. 360A(5): ITA 2007, s. 395(6), Sch. 2 para. 94.
S. 360A(6): ITA 2007, s. 395(3).
S. 360A(7): ITA 2007, s. 395(4), (5).
S. 360A(8): ITA 2007, Sch. 2 para. 93(1).
S. 360A(9): ITA 2007, Sch. 2 para. 93(2), (3), (4), (5).
S. 360A(10): ITA 2007, s. 394(5), 395(6).

361 Loan to buy interest in co-operative or employee-controlled company

361 [Omitted by ITA 2007, s. 1027 and Sch. 1, para. 66 and repealed by ITA 2007, s. 1031 and Sch. 3, Pt. 1 with effect for 2007–08 and subsequent tax years.]

Notes – S. 361 rewritten for income tax purposes as follows:
S. 361(1): ITA 2007, s. 383(2), 385(1), 401(1), (2), (3), 402(1).
S. 361(2): ITA 2007, s. 402(2), (3), (4), Sch. 2 para. 97.
S. 361(3): ITA 2007, s. 396(1), (2), 397(1).
S. 361(4): ITA 2007, s. 396(2), 397(2), (3), (4), (5).
S. 361(5): ITA 2007, s. 396(3).
S. 361(6): ITA 2007, s. 396(4).
S. 361(8): ITA 2007, s. 396(5), 397(6).

362 Loan to buy into partnership

362 [Omitted by ITA 2007, s. 1027 and Sch. 1, para. 68 and repealed by ITA 2007, s. 1031 and Sch. 3, Pt. 1 with effect for 2007–08 and subsequent tax years.]

Notes – S. 362 rewritten for income tax purposes as follows:
S. 362(1): ITA 2007, s. 383(2), 385(1), 398(1), (2), 399(1).
S. 362(2): ITA 2007, s. 399(2), (3).

363 Provisions supplementary to sections 360 to 362

363 [Omitted by ITA 2007, s. 1027 and Sch. 1, para. 68 and repealed by ITA 2007, s. 1031 and Sch. 3, Pt. 1 with effect for 2007–08 and subsequent tax years.]

Notes – S. 363 rewritten for income tax purposes as follows:
S. 363(1): ITA 2007, s. 406(1), (2), (3), (4), (5).
S. 363(2): ITA 2007, s. 407(1), (2), (3), (4).
S. 363(3): ITA 2007, s. 1008(1).
S. 363(4): ITA 2007, s. 408(2), (3), (4), (5).
S. 363(5): ITA 2007, s. 401(3).

364 Loan to pay inheritance tax

364 [Omitted by ITA 2007, s. 1027 and Sch. 1, para. 69 and repealed by ITA 2007, s. 1031 and Sch. 3, Pt. 1 with effect for 2007–08 and subsequent tax years.]

Notes – S. 364 rewritten for income tax purposes as follows:
S. 364(1): ITA 2007, s. 383(2), 385(1), 403(1), (2), 404.
S. 364(2): ITA 2007, s. 405(1), (2), (3).
S. 364(3): ITA 2007, s. 403(3).
S. 364(4): ITA 2007, s. 403(4), 404.

365 Loan to buy life annuity

365(1) Subject to the following provisions of this section, interest is eligible for relief under section 353 if it is interest on a loan in respect of which the following conditions are satisfied–

(aa) that the loan was made before 9th March 1999;

(a) that the loan was made as part of a scheme under which not less than nine-tenths of the proceeds of the loan were applied to the purchase by the person to whom it was made of an annuity ending with his life or with the life of the survivor of two or more persons (**"the annuitants"**) who include the person to whom the loan was made;

(b) that at the time the loan was made the person to whom it was made or each of the annuitants had attained the age of 65 years;

(c) that the loan was secured on land in the United Kingdom or the Republic of Ireland and the person to whom it was made or one of the annuitants owns an estate or interest in that land; and

(d) that, if the loan was made after 26th March 1974, the person to whom it was made or each of the annuitants used the land on which it was secured as his only or main residence immediately before 9th March 1999.

365(1AA) Where–

(a) a loan made on or after 9th March 1999 was made in pursuance of an offer made by the lender before that date, and

(b) the offer was either in writing or evidenced by a note or memorandum made by the lender before that date,

the loan shall be deemed for the purposes of subsection (1)(aa) above to have been made before that date.

365(1AB) Subject to subsection (1AC) below, the conditions in paragraphs (aa) and (a) of subsection (1) above shall be treated as satisfied in relation to a loan ("the new loan") if–

(a) the new loan was made on or after the day on which the Finance Act 1999 was passed;

(b) the new loan was made as part of a scheme ("the scheme") under which the whole or any part of the proceeds of the loan was used to defray money applied in paying off another loan ("the old loan"); and

(c) the conditions in subsection (1) above were, or were treated by virtue of this subsection as, satisfied with respect to the old loan.

365(1AC) If only part of the proceeds of the new loan was used to defray money applied in paying off the old loan, subsection (lAB) above applies only if, under the scheme, not less than nine-tenths of the remaining part of the proceeds of the new loan was applied to the purchase by the person to whom it was made of an annuity ending with his life or with the life of the survivor of two or more persons who include him.

365(1AD) In subsection (1AC) above **"the remaining part"** means the part of the proceeds of the new loan that was not used to defray money applied in paying off the old loan.

365(1A) The condition in subsection (1)(d) above shall be treated as satisfied in relation to a loan if–

(a) the person to whom the loan was made, or any of the annuitants, ceased to use the land as his only or main residence at a time falling within the period of twelve months ending with 8th March 1999, and

(b) the intention at that time of the person to whom the loan was made, or each of the annuitants owning an estate or interest in the land, was to take steps, before the end of the period of twelve months after the day on which the land ceased to be so used, with a view to the disposal of his estate or interest.

365(1B) If it appears to the Board reasonable to do so, having regard to all circumstances of a particular case, they may direct that in relation to that case subsection (1A) above shall have effect as if for the reference to 12 months there were substituted a reference to such longer period as meets the circumstances of that case.

365(2) Interest is not eligible for relief by virtue of this section unless it is payable by the person to whom the loan was made or by one of the annuitants.

365(3) If the loan was made after 26th March 1974 interest on it is eligible for relief by virtue of this section only to the extent that the amount on which it is payable does not exceed the sum of £30,000; and if the interest is payable by two or more persons the interest payable by each of them is so eligible only to the extent that the amount on which it is payable does not exceed such amount as bears to that sum the same proportion as the interest payable by him bears to the interest payable by both or all of them.

History – S. 365(1)(aa) and (1AA) inserted by FA 1999, s. 39, with effect for the year 1998–99 and subsequent years of assessment.

In s. 365(1)(d), words "used the land" to the end substituted for "uses the land on which it was secured as his only or main residence at the time the interest is paid" by FA 1999, s. 40(2), with effect in relation to any payment of interest (whenever falling due) made on or after 27 July 1999.
S. 365(1AB)–(1AD) inserted by FA 1999, s. 40(3), and s. 365(1A) substituted by FA 1999, s. 40(4)), with effect in relation to any payment of interest (whenever falling due) made on or after 27 July 1999.
Former s. 365(1A), and s. 365(1B) inserted by FA 1993, s. 57(3), in relation to payments of interest made on or after 16 March 1993 (whenever falling due).
In s. 365(3), words "the sum of £30,000" and "that sum" substituted by FA 2000, s. 83(1), with effect in relation to payments of interest made on or after 6 April 2000.

Derivations – FA 1974, Sch. 1, para. 24, as amended by FA 1984, s. 22(3).

366 Information

366(1) A person who claims relief under section 353 in respect of any payment of interest shall furnish to the inspector a statement in writing by the person to whom the payment is made, showing–

(a) the date when the debt was incurred;

(b) the amount of the debt when incurred;

(c) the interest paid in the year of assessment for which the claim is made; and

(d) the name and address of the debtor.

366(2) Where any such interest as is mentioned in section 353 is paid, the person to whom it is paid shall, if the person who pays it so requests in writing, furnish him with such statement as regards that interest as is mentioned in subsection (1) above; and the duty imposed by this subsection shall be enforceable at the suit or instance of the person making the request.

366(3) Subsections (1) and (2) above do not apply to interest paid to a building society, or to a local authority.

History – In s. 366(1)(c), the words "(or, in the case of relief by virtue of section 364(2), the year of assessment for which the claim would be made but for an insufficiency of income)" omitted by ITA 2007, s. 1027 and Sch. 1, para. 70 and repealed by ITA 2007, s. 1031 and Sch. 3, Pt. 1 with effect for income tax purposes for 2007–08 and subsequent tax years and for corporation tax purposes in relation to accounting periods ending after 5 April 2007.
In s. 366(1)(c), former reference to s. 355(4) (which appeared before reference to s. 364(2)) repealed by FA 1995, s. 162 and Sch. 29, Pt. VIII(2), with effect in relation to any payment of interest made on or after 6 April 1995, subject to the provisions of FA 1995, s. 42(4)–(8).

Derivations – S. 366(1) (as originally enacted): FA 1972, Sch. 10, para. 7, as amended by FA 1974, Sch. 1, para. 25(1).
S. 366(2), (3): FA 1972, Sch. 10, para. 8, 9.

HMRC interpretations – IRInt. 106: forms in use under s. 366(2) by types of lender and for types of loan.

Notes – S. 366 rewritten for income tax purposes as follows:
S. 366(1): ITA 2007, s. 412(1), (3).
S. 366(2): ITA 2007, s. 412(1), (2), (4).
S. 366(3): ITA 2007, s. 412(5).

367 Provisions supplementary to sections 354 to 366

367(1) [Repealed by FA 1999, s. 38 and Sch. 4, para. 3, s. 139 and Sch. 20, Pt. III(7).]

367(2) [Omitted by ITA 2007, s. 1027 and Sch. 1, para. 71 and repealed by ITA 2007, s. 1031 and Sch. 3, Pt. 1.]

367(3) [Omitted by ITA 2007, s. 1027 and Sch. 1, para. 71 and repealed by ITA 2007, s. 1031 and Sch. 3, Pt. 1.]

367(4) [Omitted by ITA 2007, s. 1027 and Sch. 1, para. 71 and repealed by ITA 2007, s. 1031 and Sch. 3, Pt. 1.]

367(5) In section 365(3) references to the qualifying maximum for the year of assessment are references to such sum as Parliament may determine for the purpose for that year.

History – S. 367(1) and reference to s. 354(1) in s. 367(2) repealed by FA 1999, s. 38 and Sch. 4, para. 3(1), s. 139 and Sch. 20, Pt. III(7), and s. 367(3), (4) and (5) amended to remove references to s. 354 and s. 356A to 357 by FA 1999, s. 38 and Sch. 4, para. 3(2)–(4), with effect (FA 1999, s. 38(3), (4)) in relation to a payment of interest made on or after 6 April 2000 (whenever falling due), or a payment of interest made before that date but not before 9 March 1999 which was:

- not due until on or after 6 April 2000, or
- was made in accordance with any scheme made for a tax avoidance purpose (see FA 1999, s. 38(5)) on or after 9 March 1999 (whether or not before the making of the payment).

S. 367(2), (3) and (4) omitted by ITA 2007, s. 1027 and Sch. 1, para. 71 and repealed by ITA 2007, s. 1031 and Sch. 3, Pt. 1 with effect for 2007–08 and subsequent tax years.

Derivations – S. 367(1) (as originally enacted): FA 1972, Sch. 9, para. 9 and 5A, inserted by FA 1974, Sch. 1, para. 3; FA 1974, Sch. 1, para. 4(4).
S. 367(2)–(4): FA 1972, Sch. 9, para. 2, 14, 15 and FA 1974, Sch. 1, para. 23.
S. 367(5) (as originally enacted): FA 1974, Sch. 1, para. 5(1A), inserted by FA 1984, s. 22(1)(c).

Notes – S. 367 rewritten for income tax purposes as follows:
S. 367(2): ITA 2007, s. 385(2), (3).
S. 367(3): ITA 2007, s. 385(4).
S. 367(4): ITA 2007, s. 386(1), (2).

367A Alternative finance arrangements

367A(1) Sections 353 and 365 have effect as if–

(a) purchase and resale arrangements involved the making of a loan, and

(b) alternative finance return were interest.

367A(2) Section 366 has effect accordingly.

367A(3) In this section–

"alternative finance return" has the meaning given in sections 564I to 564L of ITA 2007, and

"purchase and resale arrangements" means arrangements to which section 564C of ITA 2007 applies.

History – S. 367A inserted by TIOPA 2010, s. 365 and Sch. 2, para. 47, with effect for corporation tax purposes for accounting periods ending on or after 1 April 2010, for income tax and capital gains tax purposes for the tax year 2010–11 and subsequent tax years, and for petroleum revenue tax purposes for chargeable periods beginning on or after 1 July 2010.

Cross references – TIOPA 2010, Sch. 9, para. 37: application of alternative finance provisions to arrangements entered into before certain dates.

368 Exclusion of double relief etc.

368 [Omitted by ITA 2007, and Sch. 1, para. 72 and repealed by ITA 2007, Sch. 3, Pt. 1.]

History – S. 368 omitted by ITA 2007, and Sch. 1, para. 72 and repealed by ITA 2007, Sch. 3, Pt. 1 with effect in relation to accounting periods ending after 5 April 2007.

Notes – Rewritten income tax provisions are now located as follows:
S. 368(1): ITA 2007, s. 387(1).
S. 368(3): ITA 2007, s. 387(2), (3), (4).
S. 368(4): ITTOIA 2005, s. 52(1) and (2).
S. 368(5): ITA 2007, s. 387(5), (6).
S. 368(5): ITTOIA 2005, s. 52(3) and (4).
S. 368(6): ITA 2007, s. 387(7).
S. 368(6): ITTOIA 2005, s. 52(5).

MORTGAGE INTEREST RELIEF AT SOURCE

369 Mortgage interest payable under deduction of tax

369(1) If a person who is a qualifying borrower makes a payment of relevant loan interest to which this section applies, he shall be entitled, on making the payment, to deduct and retain out of it a sum equal to the applicable percentage thereof.

369(1A) In subsection (1) above **"the applicable percentage"** means 23 per cent.

369(2) Where a sum is deducted under subsection (1) above from a payment of relevant loan interest–

(a) the person to whom the payment is made shall allow the deduction on receipt of the residue;

(b) the borrower shall be acquitted and discharged of so much money as is represented by the deduction as if the sum had been actually paid; and

(c) the sum deducted shall be treated as income tax paid by the person to whom the payment is made.

369(3) The following payments, that is to say–

(a) payments of relevant loan interest to which this section applies, and

(b) payments which would be such payments but for section 373(5),

shall not be allowable as deductions for any purpose of the Income Tax Acts except in so far as they fall to be treated as such payments by virtue only of section 375(2) and would be allowable apart from this subsection.

369(3A)–(5B) [See History note.]

369(6) Sections 967(2) and 968(2) of CTA 2010 do not apply to a payment of relevant loan interest to which this section applies, but any person by whom such a payment is received shall be entitled to recover from the Board, in accordance with regulations, an amount which by virtue of subsection (2)(c) above is treated as income tax paid by him; and any amount so recovered shall be treated for the purposes of the Tax Acts in like manner as the payment of relevant loan interest to which it relates.

369(7) The following provisions of the Management Act, namely–

(a) section 29(1)(c) (excessive relief) as it has effect apart from section 29(2) to (10) of that Act;

(b) section 30 (tax repaid in error etc.) apart from subsection (1B),

(c) section 86 (interest), and

(d) section 95 (incorrect return or accounts),

shall apply in relation to an amount which is paid to any person by the Board as an amount recoverable in accordance with regulations made by virtue of subsection (6) above but to which that person is not entitled as if it were income tax which ought not to have been repaid and, where that amount was claimed by that person, as if it had been repaid as respects a chargeable period as a relief which was not due.

369(8) In the application of section 86 of the Management Act by virtue of subsection (7) above in relation to sums due and payable by virtue of an assessment made for the whole or part of a year of assessment (**"the relevant year of assessment"**) under section 29(1)(c) or 30 of that Act, as applied by that subsection, the relevant date–

(a) is 1st January in the relevant year of assessment in a case where the person falling within subsection (6) above has made a relevant interim claim; and

(b) in any other case, is the later of the following dates, that is to say–

(i) 1st January in the relevant year of assessment; or

(ii) the date of the making of the payment by the Board which gives rise to the assessment.

369(9) In this section–

"financial year", in relation to any person, means a financial year of that person for the purposes of the relevant regulations;

"interim claim" means an interim claim within the meaning of the relevant regulations;

"relevant interim claim" means, in relation to an assessment made for a period coterminous with, or falling wholly within, a person's financial year, an interim claim made for a period falling wholly or partly within that financial year; and

"the relevant regulations" means regulations made under section 378(3) for the purposes of subsection (6) above.

History – In s. 369(1), the words "the applicable percentage thereof" substituted by FA 1994, s. 81(3), in relation to interest payments made on or after 6 April 1994 and to interest payments becoming due on or after, which have been made at any time before, that date but on or after 30 November 1993.

In s. 369(1A), words "23 per cent" substituted by FA 2000, s. 83(3) with effect in relation to payments of interest made on or after 6 April 2000.

S. 369(1A) substituted by FA 1999, s. 38 and Sch. 4, para. 4, with effect (FA 1999, s. 38(3), (4)) in relation to a payment of interest made on or after 6 April 2000 (whenever falling due), or a payment of interest made before that date but not before 9 March 1999 which was:

- not due until on or after 6 April 2000, or
- was made in accordance with any scheme made for a tax avoidance purpose (see FA 1999, s. 38(5)) on or after 9 March 1999 (whether or not before the making of the payment).

S. 369(3) substituted for former s. 369(3)–(5B), by FA 1994, s. 81(4), in relation to interest payments made on or after 6 April 1994 and to interest payments becoming due on or after, which have been made at any time before, that date but on or after 30 November 1993.

In s. 369(6), the words "Sections 967(2) and 968(2) of CTA 2010 do not apply to a payment of relevant loan interest to which this section applies, but any person by whom such a payment" substituted for the words "Any person by whom a payment of relevant loan interest to which this section applies" by CTA 2010, s. 1177 and Sch. 1, para. 33, with effect for corporation tax purposes for accounting periods ending on or after 1 April 2010, and for income and capital gains tax purposes for the tax year 2010–11 and subsequent tax years.

In s. 369(7), para. (a) substituted; in para. (b) words "apart from subsection (1B)" inserted ; in para (c) reference to section 86 substituted for reference to section 88 and in words following para. (d) words "as respects a chargeable period" inserted by FA 1996, s. 132 and Sch. 18, para. 6(1) with effect as provided by para. 17.

S. 369(7) inserted by FA 1993, s. 58 but not in relation to any payment if the payment, or the claim on which it is made, was made before 27 July 1993.

S. 369(8), (9) inserted by FA 1996, s. 132 and Sch. 18, para. 6(2) with effect as provided by FA 1996, Sch. 18, para. 17.

Derivations – S. 369(1), (2) (as originally enacted): FA 1982, s. 26(1), (2).

S. 369(3)–(6) (as originally enacted): FA 1982, s. 26(4)–(7).

Cross references – S. 7(3), 11(4): s. 7(2) (income tax borne to be set off against corporation tax) and 11(3) (set-off of tax deducted at source) do not apply to a payment of interest to which s. 369 applies.

S. 74(1)(o): interest to which s. 369 applies is not an allowable deduction under Sch. D, Case I or II unless s. 375(2) (interest ceasing to be relevant loan interest or borrower ceasing to qualify: payment subsequently made under deduction of tax) applies to it.

S. 262(4)(a): any deduction made on account of loan interest payments due to which s. 369 applies is disregarded in computing total income of a widow's late husband for the purpose of determining widow's entitlement to married couple's allowance.

S. 266(5): life assurance premium relief – deduction of 12.5 per cent by UK residents.

S. 273: relief for payments securing widow's and children's annuities.

S. 276: income, the tax on which a person is entitled to charge against another person, is not available for personal reliefs at the basic rate.

S. 477A(8): exclusion from general provisions applicable to deduction of basic rate income tax at source for interest on building society advances does not apply to interest within s. 369.

S. 824(2B): eligibility for repayment supplement of amount paid to the borrower under s. 375(8) (repayment to borrower of under-deduction of relevant loan interest).

Sch. 14, para. 6: claim available where full relief is not given by deduction.

TCGA 1992, s. 6: rate of capital gains tax determined by reference to rate of income tax effectively as if gain were added as top slice of income.

FA 1994, s. 81(7): references in mortgage agreements to the basic rate of tax are treated as references to "the applicable percentage".

FA 1999, s. 38(2): disapplication of s. 369(1) to mortgage interest payments made (broadly) on or after 6 April 2000, or between 9 March 1999 and 6 April 2000 but not falling due until on or after 6 April 2000, or made between those dates in pursuance of a tax avoidance scheme made on or after 9 March 1999.

ITEPA 2003, s. 178: exception for loans where interest qualifies for tax relief.

ITEPA 2003, s. 180(5): threshold for benefit of loan to be treated as earnings.

ITEPA 2003, s. 184(5): interest treated as paid.

ITEPA 2003, s. 399(4): employment-related loans – interest treated as paid.

ITEPA 2003, s. 416(4): notional interest treated as paid if amount charged for beneficial loan.

Extra-statutory concessions – ESC A89: circumstances in which relief for interest on a loan to buy property used for both residential and business purposes may be allowed in part under s. 353 and in part as a deduction in computing profits or losses.

Other material – TAXline 1997/8 and 1998/12 (not reproduced): FICO practice that if lenders fail to act on information from borrowers giving details of changes in circumstances, any excessive relief given is recovered from the lender and not the borrower. See also Revenue Manual, Relief, Re 547.

TAXline 1998/31: confirmation from FICO that court costs in mortgage possession proceedings, where added to the loan, are to be treated as 'qualifying expenditure' and their addition to the loan capital should never lead to disqualification from MIRAS.

370 Relevant loan interest

370(1) Subject to this section and sections 373 to 376, in this Part **"relevant loan interest"** means interest which is paid and payable in the United Kingdom to a qualifying lender and to which subsection (2) below applies.

370(2) Subject to subsection (4) below, this subsection applies to interest if, disregarding section 353(2) and any other provision applying to interest falling to be treated as relevant loan interest–

(a) it is interest falling within section 365; and

(b) apart (where applicable) from section 365(3), the whole of the interest would be eligible for relief under section 353;

(c) [repealed by FA 1999, s. 39 and Sch. 4, para. 5(3), s. 139 and Sch. 20, Pt. III(7).]

370(3) [Repealed by FA 1999, s. 38 and Sch. 4, para. 5(4), s. 139 and Sch. 20, Pt. III(7).]

370(4) [Repealed by FA 1999, s. 38 and Sch. 4, para. 5(4), s. 139 and Sch. 20, Pt. III(7).]

370(5) In determining whether subsection (2) above applies to any interest, section 365 shall have effect as if the words "or the Republic of Ireland" were omitted.

370(6) [Repealed by FA 1999, s. 38 and Sch. 4, para. 5(4), s. 139 and Sch. 20, Pt. III(7).]

370(6A) [Repealed by FA 1995, s. 162 and Sch. 29, Pt. VIII(2); see History note.]

370(7) [Repealed by FA 1999, s. 38 and Sch. 4, para. 5(4), s. 139 and Sch. 20, Pt. III(7).]

History – S. 370(1) amended, removing references to s. 372 and to subsection (3), by FA 1999, s. 38 and Sch. 4, para. 5(1), s. 139 and Sch. 20, Pt. III(7), with effect (FA 1999, s. 38(3), (4)) in relation to a payment of interest made on or after 6 April 2000 (whenever falling due), or a payment of interest made before that date but not before 9 March 1999 which was:

- not due until on or after 6 April 2000, or
- was made in accordance with any scheme made for a tax avoidance purpose (see FA 1999, s. 38(5)) on or after 9 March 1999 (whether or not before the making of the payment).

In s. 370(1), reference to s. 372 substituted by FA 1993, s. 57(4)(c), in relation to payments made on or after 16 March 1993 (whenever falling due).

In s. 370(2)(b) the words "would be eligible for relief under section 353" substituted by ITTOIA 2005, s. 882(1) and Sch. 1, para. 155; effective for income tax purposes for 2005–06 onwards and for corporation tax purposes for accounting periods ending after 5 April 2005 (ITTOIA 2005, s. 883(1)).

In s. 370(2), references to s. 354(1), 356A and 357, and para. (c) and word "and" immediately preceding it, repealed by FA 1999, s. 38 and Sch. 4, para. 5(3), s. 139 and Sch. 20, Pt. III(7), with effect (FA 1999, s. 38(3), (4)) in relation to a payment of interest made on or after 6 April 2000 (whenever falling due), or a payment of interest made before that date but not before 9 March 1999 which was:

- not due until on or after 6 April 2000, or
- was made in accordance with any scheme made for a tax avoidance purpose (see FA 1999, s. 38(5)) on or after 9 March 1999 (whether or not before the making of the payment).

In s. 370(2), the words "and any other … relevant loan interest" inserted, and in s. 370(2)(b) the words "(where applicable) from" substituted by FA 1994, s. 81 and Sch. 9, para. 10(1) in relation to interest payments made on or after 6 April 1994 (whenever falling due), and to interest payments becoming due on or after that date, but which were made before that date and on or after 30 November 1993.

S. 370(3), (4), (6) and (7) repealed by FA 1999, s. 38 and Sch. 4, para. 5(4), s. 139 and Sch. 20, Pt. III(7), with effect (FA 1999, s. 38(3), (4)) in relation to a payment of interest made on or after 6 April 2000 (whenever falling due), or a payment of interest made before that date but not before 9 March 1999 which was:

- not due until on or after 6 April 2000, or
- was made in accordance with any scheme made for a tax avoidance purpose (see FA 1999, s. 38(5)) on or after 9 March 1999 (whether or not before the making of the payment).

S. 370(5) amended, effectively removing reference to s. 354(1), by FA 1999, s. 38 and Sch. 4, para. 5(5), s. 139 and Sch. 20, Pt. III(7), with effect (FA 1999, s. 38(3), (4)) in relation to a payment of interest made on or after 6 April 2000 (whenever falling due), or a payment of interest made before that date but not before 9 March 1999 which was:

- not due until on or after 6 April 2000, or
- was made in accordance with any scheme made for a tax avoidance purpose (see FA 1999, s. 38(5)) on or after 9 March 1999 (whether or not before the making of the payment).

Derivations – S. 370(1)–(4) (as originally enacted): FA 1982, 370(5)–Sch. 7, para. 2(3)–(3), (7). S. 370(5)–(7), as originally enacted: FA 1982, Sch. 7, para. 3(1)–(3).

Cross references – FA 1988, s. 43(3): exclusion of interest paid by a housing association on a house improvement loan after 5 April 1988.

SI 1982/1236, reg. 7B: modification of s. 370(3) where interest is paid by certain trustees in respect of option mortgages continuing after 31 March 1983.

371 Second loans

371 [Repealed by FA 1993, s. 57(4)(b), s. 213 and Sch. 23, Pt. III(1) in relation to payments of interest made on or after 16 March 1993 (whenever falling due).]

372 Home improvement loans

372 [Repealed by FA 1999, s. 38 and Sch. 4, para. 6, s. 139 and Sch. 20, Pt. III(7).]

History – S. 372 repealed by FA 1999, s. 38 and Sch. 4, para. 6, s. 139 and Sch. 20, Pt. III(7), with effect (FA 1999, s. 38(3), (4)) in relation to a payment of interest made on or after 6 April 2000 (whenever falling due), or a payment of interest made before that date but not before 9 March 1999 which was:

- not due until on or after 6 April 2000, or
- was made in accordance with any scheme made for a tax avoidance purpose (see FA 1999, s. 38(5)) on or after 9 March 1999 (whether or not before the making of the payment).

373 Loans in excess of the qualifying maximum, and joint borrowers

373(1) The provisions of this section have effect in relation to a loan where, by virtue of section 365(3), only part of the interest on the loan would (apart from section 353(2)) be eligible for relief under section 353; and in this section any such loan is referred to as a **"limited loan"**.

373(2) None of the interest on a limited loan is relevant loan interest unless–

(a) the loan is made on or after 6th April 1987; or

(b) the qualifying lender to whom the interest is payable has given notice to the Board in accordance with regulations that he is prepared to have limited loans of a description which includes that limited loan brought within the tax deduction scheme.

373(3) [Repealed by FA 1999, s. 38 and Sch. 4, para. 7, s. 139 and Sch. 20, Pt. III(7).]

373(4) [Repealed by FA 1999, s. 38 and Sch. 4, para. 7(2)(b), s. 139 and Sch. 20, Pt. III(7).]

373(5) Where the condition in paragraph (a) or (b) of subsection (2) above is fulfilled only so much of the interest as (apart from section 353(2)) would be eligible for relief under section 353 is relevant loan interest.

373(6) Where a loan on which interest is payable by the borrower was made jointly to the borrower and another person who is not the borrower's husband or wife, the interest on the loan is not relevant loan interest unless–

(a) each of the persons to whom the loan was made is a qualifying borrower; and

(b) in relation to each of them considered separately, the whole of that interest is relevant loan interest, in accordance with section 370 and this section.

373(7) In subsection (6) above references to the borrower's husband or wife do not include references to a separated husband or wife.

History – S. 373(1), (5), (6) and (7) amended, effectively removing references to s. 356A, 357(1), 367(1), 372 and subsections (3) and (4), and subsections (3) and (4) repealed, by FA 1999, s. 38 and Sch. 4, para. 7, s. 139 and Sch. 20, Pt. III(7), with effect (FA 1999, s. 38(3), (4)) in relation to a payment of interest made on or after 6 April 2000 (whenever falling due), or a payment of interest made before that date but not before 9 March 1999 which was:

- not due until on or after 6 April 2000, or
- was made in accordance with any scheme made for a tax avoidance purpose (see FA 1999, s. 38(5)) on or after 9 March 1999 (whether or not before the making of the payment).

Derivations – S. 373(1), as originally enacted: FA 1982, Sch. 7, para. 5(1).
S. 373(2): FA 1982, Sch. 7, para. 5(2), as amended by FA 1985, s. 37(2).
S. 373(3), as originally enacted: FA 1982, Sch. 7, para. 5(3).
S. 373(4): FA 1982, Sch. 7, para. 5(3A), inserted by FA 1983, s. 17(2).
S. 373(5): FA 1982, Sch. 7, para. 5(4), as amended by FA 1983, s. 17(2) and FA 1985, s. 37(3).
S. 373(6), (7): FA 1982, Sch. 7, para. 6(1), (2).

Cross references – S. 74(1)(o): deduction of relevant loan interest in computing profits and gains.

374 Conditions for application of section 369

374(1) Section 369 does not apply to any relevant loan interest unless–

(a) in the case of a loan of a description specified by regulations for the purposes of this paragraph, the borrower or, in the case of joint borrowers, each of them has given notice to the lender in the prescribed form certifying–

(i) that he is a qualifying borrower; and

(ii) that the interest is relevant loan interest; and

(iii) such other matters as may be prescribed; or

(b) the Board have given notice to the lender and the borrower that the interest may be paid under deduction of tax; or

(c) [Repealed by FA 1999, s. 38 and Sch. 4, para. 8, s. 139 and Sch. 20, Pt. III(7).]

(d) the loan to which the interest relates is of a description specified by regulations for the purposes of this paragraph and was made–

ICTA 1988

(i) if sub-paragraph (2) of paragraph 2 of Schedule 7 to the Finance Act 1982 applied to interest on the loan which became due on or after a date earlier than 6th April 1983, being a date specified by the Board in pursuance of sub-paragraph (5) of that paragraph, before that earlier date; or

(ii) if the qualifying lender is a building society or a local authority, before 1st April 1983; or

(iii) if sub-paragraphs (i) and (ii) above do not apply and the interest falls within section 370(2), before 6th April 1983.

374(2) Where notice has been given as mentioned in paragraph (a) or (b) of subsection (1) above, section 369 applies to any relevant loan interest to which the notice relates and which becomes due on or after the relevant date, as defined by subsection (3) below; and in a case falling within paragraph (d) of subsection (1) above, section 369 applies to the relevant loan interest referred to in that paragraph.

374(3) In subsection (2) above **"the relevant date"** means–

(a) in the case of a notice under subsection (1)(a) above, the date the notice is given, and

(b) in the case of a notice under subsection (1)(b) above, a date specified in the notice as being the relevant date (which may be earlier than the date so specified as the date from which the interest may be paid under deduction of tax).

History – S. 374(1)(c), and reference to it in s. 374(2), repealed by FA 1999, s. 38 and Sch. 4, para. 8, s. 139 and Sch. 20, Pt. III(7), with effect (FA 1999, s. 38(3), (4)) in relation to a payment of interest made on or after 6 April 2000 (whenever falling due), or a payment of interest made before that date but not before 9 March 1999 which was:

- not due until on or after 6 April 2000, or
- was made in accordance with any scheme made for a tax avoidance purpose (see FA 1999, s. 38(5)) on or after 9 March 1999 (whether or not before the making of the payment).

Derivations – FA 1982, Sch. 7, para. 7(1)–(5).

374A Interest which never has been relevant loan interest etc.

374A(1) This section applies where, in the case of any loan, interest on the loan never has been relevant loan interest or the borrower never has been a qualifying borrower.

374A(2) Without prejudice to subsection (3) below, in relation to a payment of interest–

(a) as respects which either of the conditions mentioned in paragraphs (a) and (b) of section 374(1) is fulfilled, and

(b) from which a deduction was made as mentioned in section 369(1),

section 369 shall have effect as if the payment of interest were a payment of relevant loan interest made by a qualifying borrower.

374A(3) Nothing in subsection (2) above shall be taken as regards the borrower as entitling him to make any deduction or to retain any amount deducted and, accordingly, where any amount has been deducted, he shall be liable to make good that amount and an officer of the Board may make such assessments as may in his judgment be required for recovering that amount.

374A(4) The Management Act shall apply to an assessment under subsection (3) above as if it were an assessment to income tax for the year of assessment in which the deduction was made.

374A(5) If the borrower fraudulently or negligently makes any false statement or representation in connection with the making of any deduction, he shall be liable to a penalty not exceeding the amount deducted.

History – S. 374A(4): words at end deleted by FA 1996, s. 132 and Sch. 18, para. 7 and s. 205 and Sch. 41, Pt. V(8) with effect for 1996–97 and subsequent years of assessment and in relation to assessments made on or after 6 April 1998 in respect of capital gains tax or income tax which is for 1995–96 or an earlier year of assessment.

S. 374A inserted by FA 1995, s. 112(1), in relation to deductions made by borrowers, and payments made by the Board, after 1 May 1995.

375 Interest ceasing to be relevant loan interest etc.

375(1) If at any time–

(a) the interest on a loan ceases to be relevant loan interest; or

(b) a person making payments of relevant loan interest ceases to be a qualifying borrower;

the borrower shall give notice of the fact to the lender.

375(2) Without prejudice to subsection (3) below, in relation to a payment of interest–

(a) which is due after the time referred to in subsection (1) above and before the date on which notice is given under that subsection, and

(aa) as respects which any of the conditions mentioned in section 374(1) is fulfilled, and

(b) from which a deduction was made as mentioned in section 369(1),

section 369 shall have effect as if the payment were a payment of relevant loan interest made by a qualifying borrower.

375(3) Nothing in subsection (2) above shall be taken as regards the borrower as entitling him to any deduction or to retain any amount deducted and, accordingly, where any amount that has been deducted exceeds the amount which ought to have been deducted, he shall be liable to make good the excess and an inspector may make such assessments as may in his judgment be required for recovering the excess.

375(4) The Management Act shall apply to an assessment under subsection (3) above as if it were an assessment to income tax for the year of assessment in which the deduction was made.

375(4A) If there is any unreasonable delay in the giving of a notice under subsection (1) above, the borrower shall be liable to a penalty not exceeding so much of the aggregate amount that he is liable to make good under subsection (3) above as is attributable to that delay.

375(5) If, as a result of receiving a notice under subsection (1) above or otherwise, a qualifying lender has reason to believe that any interest is no longer relevant loan interest or that a borrower is no longer a qualifying borrower, the lender shall furnish the Board with such information as is in his possession with respect to those matters.

375(6) Where it appears to the Board that any of the provisions of sections 370 to 373 is not or may not be fulfilled with respect to any interest, or that a qualifying borrower has or may have ceased to be a qualifying borrower, they shall give notice of that fact to the lender and the borrower specifying the description of relevant loan interest concerned or, as the case may be, that the borrower has or may have ceased to be a qualifying borrower.

375(7) Section 369 shall not apply to any payment of relevant loan interest of a description to which a notice under subsection (6) above relates and which becomes due or is made after such date as may be specified in the notice and before such date as may be specified in a further notice given by the Board to the lender and the borrower.

375(8) In any case where–

(a) section 369 applies to any relevant loan interest by virtue of a notice under section 374(1)(b), and

(b) the relevant date specified in the notice is earlier than the date from which the interest begins to be paid under deduction of tax, and

(c) a payment of that interest was made on or after the relevant date but not under deduction of tax,

regulations may provide for a sum to be paid by the Board of an amount equal to that which the borrower would have been able to deduct from that payment by virtue of section 369 if it had been made after the relevant date.

375(8A) In any case where an amount to which a person is not entitled is paid to him by the Board in pursuance of regulations made by virtue of subsection (8) above, regulations may–

(a) provide for an officer of the Board to make such assessments as may in his judgment be required for recovering that amount from that person; and

(b) make provision corresponding to that made by subsection (4A) above and subsections (4) and (5) of section 374A.

375(8B) Subsections (1), (5) and (6) above shall not apply where interest ceases to be relevant loan interest by virtue of section 38 of the Finance Act 1999.

375(9) [Repealed by FA 1999, s. 38 and Sch. 4, para. 9(2), s. 139 and Sch. 20, Pt. III(7).]

375(10) [Repealed by FA 1999, FA 1999, s. 38 and Sch. 4, para. 9(2), s. 139 and Sch. 20, Pt. III(7).]

History – S. 375(2)(aa), (8A) inserted, and s. 375(4), (4A) substituted for former s. 375(4), by FA 1995, s. 112(2)–(4), in relation to deductions made by borrowers, and payments made by the Board, after 1 May 1995.
In s. 375(3), the words "shall be … been deducted" substituted by FA 1994, s. 81 and Sch. 9, para. 11, in relation to interest payments made on or after 6 April 1994 and to interest payments becoming due on or after, which have been made at any time before, that date but on or after 30 November 1993.
S. 375(4): words "as if it were an assessment to income tax for the year of assessment in which the deduction was made" substituted by FA 1996, s. 132 and Sch. 18, para. 8 with effect as provided by para. 17.
S. 375(8B) inserted by FA 1999, s. 38 and Sch. 4, para. 9(1), and s. 375(9), (10) repealed by FA 1999, s. 38 and Sch. 4, para. 9(2), s. 139 and Sch. 20, Pt. III(7), with effect (FA 1999, s. 38(3), (4)) in relation to a payment of interest made on or after 6 April 2000 (whenever falling due), or a payment of interest made before that date but not before 9 March 1999 which:

- was not due until on or after 6 April 2000, or
- was made in accordance with any scheme made for a tax avoidance purpose (see FA 1999, s. 38(5)) on or after 9 March 1999 (whether or not before the making of the payment).

Derivations – FA 1982, Sch. 7, para. 8–9(1), 10–12.

Cross references – S. 74(1)(o): interest to which s. 375(2) applies may be an allowable deduction for Sch. D, Case I or II purposes notwithstanding the general disallowance of relevant loan interest within s. 369.
S. 824(2B): eligibility for repayment supplement of amount paid to the borrower under s. 375(8) (repayment to borrower of under-deduction of relevant loan interest).
TMA 1970, s. 98: penalties for failure to furnish information etc. under s. 375(5).
FA 2009, Sch. 54, para. 8: sets repayment interest start date for payments under regulations under s. 375(8), for the purposes of FA 2009, s. 102.

Other material – Taxline 1997/8 and 1998/12 (not reproduced): FICO practice that if lenders fail to act on information from borrowers giving details of changes in circumstances, any excessive relief given is recovered from the lender and not the borrower. See also Revenue Manual, Relief, Re 547.

375A Option to deduct interest for the purposes of Schedule A

375A [Repealed by FA 1999, s. 38 and Sch. 4, para. 10, s. 139 and Sch. 20, Pt. III(7).]

History – S. 375A repealed by FA 1999, s. 38 and Sch. 4, para. 10, s. 139 and Sch. 20, Pt. III(7), with effect (FA 1999, s. 38(3), (4)) in relation to a payment of interest made on or after 6 April 2000 (whenever falling due), or a payment of interest made before that date but not before 9 March 1999 which:

- was not due until on or after 6 April 2000, or
- was made in accordance with any scheme made for a tax avoidance purpose (see FA 1999, s. 38(5)) on or after 9 March 1999 (whether or not before the making of the payment).

376 Qualifying borrowers and qualifying lenders

376(1) Subject to subsection (2) below, an individual is a qualifying borrower with respect to the interest on any loan.

376(2) In relation to interest paid at a time when the borrower or the borrower's husband or wife holds an office or employment which would, but for some special exemption or immunity from tax, be a taxable employment under Part 2 of ITEPA 2003 (as defined by section 66(3) of that Act), the borrower is not a qualifying borrower.

376(3) In subsection (2) above references to the borrower's husband or wife do not include references to a separated husband or wife.

376(4) The following bodies are qualifying lenders:

(a) a building society;

(b) a local authority;

(c) the Bank of England;

(d) the Post Office;

(e) a person who has permission under Part 4A of the Financial Services and Markets Act 2000 to effect or carry out contracts of long-term insurance;

(f) any company to which property and rights belonging to a trustee savings bank were transferred by section 3 of the Trustee Savings Bank Act 1985;

(g) [omitted by SI 2001/3629, art. 23(2)(b)];

(h) a development corporation within the meaning of the New Towns Act 1981 or the New Towns (Scotland) Act 1968;

(j) the Homes and Communities Agency;

(ja) the Greater London Authority so far as exercising its housing or regeneration functions or its new towns and urban development functions;

(k) the regulator of Social Housing;

(ka) the Secretary of State if the loan is made by him under section 79 of the Housing Associations Act 1985;

(l) the Northern Ireland Housing Executive;

(m) the Scottish Special Housing Association;

(n) [repealed by Government of Wales Act 1998, s. 152 and Sch. 18, Pt. IV];

(o) the Church of England Pensions Board;

(p) any body which is for the time being registered under section 376.

376(4A) [Omitted by SI 2001/3629, art. 23(3).]

376(5) [Repealed by FA 1994, s. 142(1)(b), and s. 258 and Sch. 26, Pt. V(19).]

376(6) [Repealed by FA 1999, s. 38 and Sch. 4, para. 11, s. 139 and Sch. 20, Pt. III(7)(b).]

History – In s. 376(2), the words "an office or employment which would, but for some special exemption or immunity from tax, be a taxable employment under Part 2 of ITEPA 2003 (as defined by section 66(3) of that Act)" substituted for the words "an office or employment in respect of the emoluments of which he or she would but for some special exemption or immunity from tax be chargeable to tax under Case I, II or III of Schedule E" by ITEPA 2003, Sch. 6, para. 52 which has effect for the tax year 2003–04 and subsequent tax years.

In s. 376(3), reference to definition of "separated" in s. 376(1), repealed by FA 1999, s. 38 and Sch. 4, para. 11(a), s. 139 and Sch. 20, Pt. III(7), with effect (FA 1999, s. 38(3), (4)) in relation to a payment of interest made on or after 6 April 2000 (whenever falling due), or a payment of interest made before that date but not before 9 March 1999 which:

- was not due until on or after 6 April 2000, or
- was made in accordance with any scheme made for a tax avoidance purpose (see FA 1999, s. 38(5)) on or after 9 March 1999 (whether or not before the making of the payment).

In s. 376(4)(e), the words "Part 4A" substituted for the words "Part 4" by Financial Services Act 2012, s. 114(1) and Sch. 18, para. 58(3), with effect from 1 April 2013 (SI 2013/423).

S. 376(4)(e) substituted by SI 2001/3629, art. 23(2)(a), with effect from 1 December 2001.

S. 376(4)(g) omitted by SI 2001/3629, art. 23(2)(b), with effect from 1 December 2001.

S. 376(4)(ja) inserted by the Localism Act 2011, s. 195 and Sch. 19, para. 24, with effect from 1 April 2012 (SI 2012/628).

S. 376(4)(k) substituted by the Housing and Regeneration Act 2008, s. 277 and Sch. 9, para. 12, with effect from 1 April 2010 (SI 2010/862).

S. 376(4)(j) substituted by the Housing and Regeneration Act 2008, s. 56 and Sch. 8, para. 42, with effect from 1 December 2008 (SI 2008/3068).
S. 376(4)(ka) substituted by Government of Wales Act 1998, s. 140 and Sch. 16, para. 55, with effect from 1 November 1998 by virtue of SI 1998/2244.
S. 376(4)(n) repealed by Government of Wales Act 1998, s. 152 and Sch. 18, Pt. IV, with effect from 1 October 1998 by virtue of SI 1998/2244.
S. 376(4)(p) substituted by SI 2001/3629, art. 23(2)(c), with effect from 1 December 2001.
In s. 376(4)(p), the words "for the … 376A below" and "Board" substituted by FA 1994, s. 142(1)(a), with effect from 3 May 1994.
S. 376(4A) omitted by SI 2001/3629, art. 23(3), with effect from 1 December 2001.
S. 376(5) repealed by FA 1994, s. 142(1)(b), and s. 258 and Sch. 26, Pt. V(19), with effect from 3 May 1994.
S. 376(6) repealed by FA 1999, s. 38 and Sch. 4, para. 11(b), s. 139 and Sch. 20, Pt. III(7), with effect (FA 1999, s. 38(3), (4)) in relation to a payment of interest made on or after 6 April 2000 (whenever falling due), or a payment of interest made before that date but not before 9 March 1999 which:

- was not due until on or after 6 April 2000, or
- was made in accordance with any scheme made for a tax avoidance purpose (see FA 1999, s. 38(5)) on or after 9 March 1999 (whether or not before the making of the payment).

Derivations – S. 376(1)–(3): FA 1982, Sch. 7, para. 13.
S. 376(4) (as originally enacted): FA 1982, Sch. 7, para. 14(1) (as amended by Building Societies Act 1986, Sch. 18, para. 15(3), by the Insurance Companies Act 1982, s. 99(2) and Sch. 5, para. 28(b), by TSBA 1985, Sch. 2, para. 7(1), and by FA 1983, s. 17(3)); Banking Act 1987, Sch. 6, para. 13.
Former s. 376(5): FA 1982, Sch. 7, para. 14(2), as amended by FA 1983, s. 17(4) and FA 1985, s. 37(4).
S. 376(6): FA 1982, Sch. 7, para. 15.

Cross references – FA 1994, s. 142(3): entitlement of a body previously prescribed for the purposes of s. 376 to be entered in the register maintained under s. 376A upon the coming into force of FA 1994.

376A The register of qualifying lenders

376A(1) The Board shall maintain, and publish in such manner as they consider appropriate, a register for the purposes of section 376(4).

376A(1A) The following are entitled to be registered–

(a) a person who has permission under Part 4A of the Financial Services and Markets Act 2000–
  (i) to accept deposits; or
  (ii) to effect or carry out contracts of general insurance;

(b) a 90 per cent subsidiary of a person mentioned in–
  (i) section 376(4)(e); or
  (ii) paragraph (a) above;

(c) any other body whose activities and objects appear to the Board to qualify it for registration.

376A(2) If the Board are satisfied that an applicant for registration is entitled to be registered, they may register the applicant generally or in relation to any description of loan specified in the register, with effect from such date as may be so specified; and a body which is so registered shall become a qualifying lender in accordance with the terms of its registration.

376A(3) The registration of any body may be varied by the Board–

(a) where it is general, by providing for it to be in relation to a specified description of loan, or

(b) where it is in relation to a specified description of loan, by removing or varying the reference to that description of loan,

and where they do so, they shall give the body written notice of the variation and of the date from which it is to have effect.

376A(4) If it appears to the Board at any time that a body which is registered under this section would not be entitled to be registered if it applied for registration at that time, the Board may by written notice given to the body cancel its registration with effect from such date as may be specified in the notice.

376A(5) The date specified in a notice under subsection (3) or (4) above shall not be earlier than the end of the period of 30 days beginning with the date on which the notice is served.

376A(6) Any body which is aggrieved by the failure of the Board to register it under this section, or by the variation or cancellation of its registration, may appeal, by notice given to the Board before the end of the period of 30 days beginning with the date on which the body is notified of the Board's decision.

History – In s. 376A(1A)(a), the words "Part 4A" substituted for the words "Part 4" by Financial Services Act 2012, s. 114(1) and Sch. 18, para. 58(4), with effect from 1 April 2013 (SI 2013/423).
S. 376A(1A) inserted by SI 2001/3629, art. 24, with effect from 1 December 2001.
S. 376A inserted by FA 1994, s. 142(2), with effect from 3 May 1994.
In s. 376A(6), the words "appeal" inserted by SI 2009/56, art. 3(1) and Sch. 1, para. 138(a), operative from 1 April 2009, subject to transitional and saving provisions in SI 2009/56, Sch. 3.
In s. 376A(6), the words ", require the matter to be determined by the Special Commissioners; and the Special Commissioners shall thereupon hear and determine the matter in like manner as an appeal.", which appeared after "Board's decision", omitted by SI 2009/56, art. 3(1) and Sch. 1, para. 138(b), operative from 1 April 2009, subject to transitional and saving provisions in SI 2009/56, Sch. 3.

Cross references – FA 1994, s. 142(3): entitlement of existing prescribed qualifying lenders to be entered on s. 376A register, etc.

Other material – HMRC press release, 4 July 1994, 17 October 1994 and 19 January 1995 (not reproduced): details of publication and updating of s. 376A register.

377 Variation of terms of repayment of certain loans

377 [Repealed by FA 1999, s. 38 and Sch. 4, para. 12, s. 139 and Sch. 20, Pt. III(7).]

History – S. 377 repealed by FA 1999, s. 38 and Sch. 4, para. 12, s. 139 and Sch. 20, Pt. III(7), with effect (FA 1999, s. 38(3), (4)) in relation to a payment of interest made on or after 6 April 2000 (whenever falling due), or a payment of interest made before that date but not before 9 March 1999 which:
- was not due until on or after 6 April 2000, or
- was made in accordance with any scheme made for a tax avoidance purpose (see FA 1999, s. 38(5)) on or after 9 March 1999 (whether or not before the making of the payment).

378 Supplementary regulations

378(1) [Repealed by FA 1999, s. 38 and Sch. 4, para. 13(a), s. 139 and Sch. 20, Pt. III(7)(b).]

378(2) [Repealed by FA 1999, s. 38 and Sch. 4, para. 13(a), s. 139 and Sch. 20, Pt. III(7)(b).]

378(3) The Board may by regulations make provision–

(a) for the purposes of any provision of sections 369 to 376A which relates to any matter or thing to be specified by or done in accordance with regulations;

(b) for the application of those sections in relation to loan interest paid by personal representatives and trustees;

(c) with respect to the furnishing of information by borrowers or lenders, including, in the case of lenders, the inspection of books, documents and other records on behalf of the Board;

(d) for, and with respect to, appeals to the tribunal against the refusal of the Board to issue a notice under section 374(1)(b) or the issue of a notice under section 375(6) or (7); and

(e) generally for giving effect to sections 369 to 376A.

378(4) [Repealed by FA 1999, s. 38 and Sch. 4, para. 13(a), s. 139 and Sch. 20, Pt. III(7)(b).]

History – S. 378(1), (2) and (4) repealed, and s. 378(3) amended by substituting references to s. 376A for those to s. 377, by FA 1999, s. 38 and Sch. 4, para. 13, s. 139 and Sch. 20, Pt. III(7), with effect (FA 1999, s. 38(3), (4)) in relation to a payment of interest made on or after 6 April 2000 (whenever falling due), or a payment of interest made before that date but not before 9 March 1999 which:
- was not due until on or after 6 April 2000, or
- was made in accordance with any scheme made for a tax avoidance purpose (see FA 1999, s. 38(5)) on or after 9 March 1999 (whether or not before the making of the payment).

In s. 378(3), the words "the tribunal." substituted for "the General Commissioners or the Special Commissioners" by SI 2009/56, art. 3(1) and Sch. 1, para. 139, operative from 1 April 2009, subject to transitional and saving provisions in SI 2009/56, Sch. 3.

Derivations – S. 378(1), (4)(a): FA 1982, s. 29(1), as amended by FA 1984, s. 56(2) and Housing (Consequential Provisions) Act 1985, Sch. 2, para. 54(2).
S. 378(2), (3): FA 1982, s. 29(2), (3).
S. 378(4)(b): FA 1982, s. 29(4).

Cross references – S. 488: co-operative housing associations approved by the Secretary of State or the Head of the Department of the Environment for Northern Ireland.
S. 489: self-build societies approved by the Secretary of State or the Head of the Department of the Environment for Northern Ireland.

Statutory instruments – SI 1982/1236: made under s. 378 or its predecessor.

379 Interpretation of sections 369 to 378

379 In sections 369 to 378–

"contracts of general insurance" means contracts which fall within Part I of Schedule 1 to the Financial Services and Markets Act 2000 (Regulated Activities) Order 2001 and **"contracts of long-term insurance"** means contracts which fall within Part II of that Schedule;

"prescribed" means prescribed by the Board;

"qualifying borrower" has the meaning given by section 376(1) to (3);

"qualifying lender" has the meaning given by section 376(4);

"regulations" means regulations made by the Board under section 378;

"relevant loan interest" has the meaning given by section 370(1);

"separated" means separated under an order of a court of competent jurisdiction or by deed of separation or in such circumstances that the separation is likely to be permanent.

History – In s. 379, definition of "contracts of general insurance" inserted by SI 2001/3629, art. 25, with effect from 1 December 2001.
In s. 379, definitions of "qualifying lender" and "regulations" amended by effectively removing references to s. 376(6) and 378(1), (2), and definition of "separated" inserted, by FA 1999, s. 38 and Sch. 4, para. 14, s. 139 and Sch. 20, Pt. III(7), with effect (FA 1999, s. 38(3), (4)) in relation to a payment of interest made on or after 6 April 2000 (whenever falling due), or a payment of interest made before that date but not before 9 March 1999 which:
- was not due until on or after 6 April 2000, or
- was made in accordance with any scheme made for a tax avoidance purpose (see FA 1999, s. 38(5)) on or after 9 March 1999 (whether or not before the making of the payment).

Words in definition of "prescribed" repealed by FA 1994, s. 258 and Sch. 26, Pt. V(19), with effect from 3 May 1994.

Derivations – FA 1982, s. 26(3), 28(5), (7) and Sch. 7, para. 1, 4(1)(a), 13(1), (2), 14(1).

PART X – LOSS RELIEF AND GROUP RELIEF
Chapter I – Loss Relief: Income Tax

LOSSES FROM UK PROPERTY BUSINESS OR OVERSEAS PROPERTY BUSINESS

History – Pt. X, Ch. 1 omitted by ITA 2007, s. 1027 and Sch. 1, para. 73 and repealed by ITA 2007, s. 1031 and Sch. 3, Pt. 1 with effect for 2007–08 and subsequent tax years.
In the cross-heading the words "UK property business" substituted by ITTOIA 2005, s. 882(1) and Sch. 1, para. 156(8); effective for income tax purposes for 2005–06 onwards (ITTOIA 2005, s. 883(1)).

379A Losses from UK property business

History – The heading to s. 379A substituted by ITTOIA 2005, s. 882(1) and Sch. 1, para. 156(7); effective for income tax purposes for 2005–06 onwards (ITTOIA 2005, s. 883(1)).

379A [Omitted by ITA 2007, s. 1027 and Sch. 1, para. 73 and repealed by ITA 2007, s. 1031 and Sch. 1, Pt. 1 with effect for 2007–08 and later tax years.]

Notes – S. 379A rewritten for income tax purposes as follows:
S. 379A(1): ITA 2007, s. 23, 24(1), 25(4), 118(1), (2), (3), (4), 119.
S. 379A(2): ITA 2007, s. 120(1), 123(2), (3).
S. 379A(3): ITA 2007, s. 23, 24(1), 118(5), 120(2), 121(1), 124(1), (2).
S. 379A(4): ITA 2007, s. 118(4), 121(1), 122(2), (3), (4), (5).
S. 379A(5): ITA 2007, s. 120(4), 121(1).
S. 379A(6): ITA 2007, s. 118(4), 121(2), (3).
S. 379A(8): ITA 2007, s. 123(5).
S. 379A(9): ITA 2007, s. 123(6), (7).
S. 379A(10): ITA 2007, s. 123(4).

ICTA 1988

379B Losses from overseas property business

379B [Omitted by ITA 2007, s. 1027 and Sch. 1, para. 73 and repealed by ITA 2007, s. 1031 and Sch. 3, Pt. 1 with effect for 2007–08 and subsequent tax years.]

Notes – S. 379B rewritten for income tax purposes as ITA 2007, s. f118(1), (2), (3), (4), (5), 119, 120(1), (2), (4), 121(1), (2), (3), 122(2), (3), (4), (5), 123(2), (3), (4), (5), (6), (7), 124(1), (2).

TRADE ETC. LOSSES

380 Set-off against general income

380 [Omitted by ITA 2007 and Sch. 1, para. 73 and repealed by ITA 2007, s. 1031 and Sch. 3, Pt. 1 with effect for 2007–08 and subsequent tax years.]

Notes – S. 380 rewritten for income tax purposes as follows:
S. 380(1): ITA 2007, s. 23, 24(1), 25(4), 63, 64(1), (2), (5), 65(1), 72(3), 128(1), (2), (5), 129(1).
S. 380(2): ITA 2007, s. 65(2), (3), 129(2), (3).

381 Further relief for individuals for losses in early years of trade

381 [Omitted by ITA 2007, s. 1027 and Sch. 1, para. 73 and repealed by ITA 2007, s. 1031 and Sch. 3, Pt. 1 with effect for 2007–08 and subsequent tax years.]

Notes – S. 381 rewritten for income tax purposes as follows:
S. 381(1): ITA 2007, s. 23, 24(1), 72(1).
S. 381(2): ITA 2007, s. 25(4), 72(2), 73.
S. 381(3): ITA 2007, s. 63.
S. 381(4): ITA 2007, s. 74(1), (2), (3).
S. 381(5): ITA 2007, s. 74(4), (5).
S. 381(7): ITA 2007, s. 72(4), 74(6).

382 Provisions supplementary to sections 380 and 381

382 [Omitted by ITA 2007, s. 1027 and Sch. 1, para. 73 and repealed by ITA 2007, s. 1031 and Sch. 3, Pt. 1 with effect for 2007–08 and subsequent tax years.]

Notes – S. 382 rewritten for income tax purposes as follows:
S. 382(3): ITA 2007, s. 61(2), 62(2).

383 Extension of right of set-off to capital allowances

383 [Repealed by FA 1994, s. 214(1)(b), and s. 258 and Sch. 26, Pt. V(24), with effect for 1994–95 and subsequent years of assessment in relation to trades etc. commenced after 5 April 1994 and for 1997–98 and subsequent years in relation to other trades etc.]

384 Restrictions on right of set-off

384 [Omitted by ITA 2007, s. 1027 and Sch. 1, para. 73 and repealed by ITA 2007, s. 1031 and Sch. 3, Pt. 1 with effect for 2007–08 and later tax years.]

Notes – S. 384 rewritten for income tax purposes as follows:
S. 384(1): ITA 2007, s. 66(1), (2), (4).
S. 384(2): ITA 2007, s. 66(6).
S. 384(3): ITA 2007, s. 66(5).
S. 384(4): ITA 2007, s. 60(3).
S. 384(6): ITA 2007, s. 75(1), (2), (5), (6).
S. 384(7): ITA 2007, s. 75(1), (2), (3).
S. 384(8): ITA 2007, s. 79(1).
S. 384(9): ITA 2007, s. 66(3).
S. 384(10): ITA 2007, s. 66(7).
S. 384(11): ITA 2007, s. 79(2).

384A Restriction of set-off of allowances against general income

384A [Omitted by ITA 2007, s. 1027 and Sch. 1, para. 73 and repealed by ITA 2007, s. 1031 and Sch. 3, Pt. 1 with effect for 2007–08 and subsequent tax years.]

Notes – S. 384A rewritten for income tax purposes as follows:
S. 384A(1): ITA 2007, s. 76.
S. 384A(2): ITA 2007, s. 77(1), (2), (3).
S. 384A(3): ITA 2007, s. 77(3).
S. 384A(4): ITA 2007, s. 78(1), (2), (3).
S. 384A(4): ITA 2007, s. 60(3).
S. 384A(5): ITA 2007, s. 78(4), (5), (6).
S. 384A(6): ITA 2007, s. 79(1).
S. 384A(7): ITA 2007, s. 1021(1).
S. 384A(8): ITA 2007, s. 79(2).

385 Carry-forward against subsequent profits

385 [Omitted by ITA 2007, s. 1027 and Sch. 1, para. 73 and repealed by ITA 2007, s. 1031 and Sch. 3, Pt. 1 with effect for 2007–08 and subsequent tax years.]

Notes – S. 385 rewritten for income tax purposes as follows:
S. 385(1): ITA 2007, s. 23, 24(1), 25(4), 61(2), 62(2), 83(1), (2), (3), (4), (5), 84.
S. 385(4): ITA 2007, s. 78(1), (2), (3).
S. 385(4): ITA 2007, s. 25(4), 85(1), (2), (3).
S. 385(7): ITA 2007, s. 63.

386 Carry-forward where business transferred to a company

386 [Omitted by ITA 2007, s. 1027 and Sch. 1, para. 73 and repealed by ITA 2007, s. 1031 and Sch. 3, Pt. 1 with effect for 2007–08 and later tax years.]

Notes – S. 386 rewritten for income tax purposes as follows:
S. 386(1): ITA 2007, s. 86(1), (2), (4), (5), (6).
S. 386(3): ITA 2007, s. 86(3).

387 Carry-forward as losses of amounts taxed under section 350

387 [Omitted by ITA 2007, s. 1027 and Sch. 1, para. 73 and repealed by ITA 2007, s. 1031 and Sch.3, Pt. 1 with effect for 2007–08 and subsequent tax years.]

388 Carry-back of terminal losses

388 [Omitted by ITA 2007, s. 1027 and Sch. 1, para. 73 and repealed by ITA 2007, s. 1031 and Sch. 3, Pt. 1 with effect for 2007–08 and subsequent tax years.]

Notes – S. 388 rewritten for income tax purposes as follows:
S. 388(1): ITA 2007, s. 23, 24(1), 25(4), 89(1), (2), (3).
S. 388(2): ITA 2007, s. 63.
S. 388(3): ITA 2007, s. 91.
S. 388(4): ITA 2007, s. 25(4), 92(1), (2), (3).
S. 388(6): ITA 2007, s. 90(1).
S. 388(7): ITA 2007, s. 90(2).

389 Supplementary provisions relating to carry-back of terminal losses

389 [Omitted by ITA 2007, s. 1027 and Sch. 1, para. 73 and repealed by ITA 2007, s. 1031 and Sch. 3, Pt. 1 with effect for 2007–08 and subsequent tax years.]

Notes – S. 389 rewritten for income tax purposes as follows:
S. 389(2): ITA 2007, s. 93(1), (2), (3), (4).
S. 389(4): ITA 2007, s. 62(3), 89(1).

390 Treatment of interest as a loss for purposes of carry-forward and carry-back

390 [Omitted by ITA 2007, s. 1027 and Sch. 1, para. 73 and repealed by ITA 2007, s. 1031 and Sch. 3, Pt. 1 with effect for 2007–08 and subsequent tax years.]

Notes – S. 390 rewritten for income tax purposes as ITA 2007, s. 88(1), (2), 94(1), (2).

391 Losses from trade etc. carried on abroad

391 [Omitted by ITA 2007, s. 1027 and Sch. 1, para. 73 and repealed by ITA 2007, s. 1031 and Sch. 3, Pt. 1 with effect for 2007–08 and later tax years.]

Notes – S. 391 rewritten for income tax purposes as ITA 2007, s. 95(1), (2), (3), (4), (5), (6).

CASE VI LOSSES

392 Losses from miscellaneous transactions

392 [Omitted by ITA 2007, s. 1027 and Sch. 1, para. 73 and repealed by ITA 2007, s. 1031 and Sch. 3, Pt. 1 with effect for 2007–08 and subsequent tax years.]

Notes – S. 392 rewritten for income tax purposes as follows:
S. 392(1): ITA 2007, s. 23, 24(1), 152(1), (2), (8).
S. 392(2): ITA 2007, s. 23, 24(1), 25(4), 152(5), (7), (8), 153.
S. 392(3): ITA 2007, s. 152(6).
S. 392(4): ITA 2007, s. 152(6), (8).
S. 392(5): ITA 2007, s. 153.
S. 392(6): ITA 2007, s. 155(1).
S. 392(7): ITA 2007, s. 155(2).
S. 392(8): ITA 2007, Sch. 2 para. 37(1), (2).

ICTA 1988

Chapter II – Loss Relief: Corporation Tax

LOSSES FROM UK PROPERTY BUSINESS OR OVERSEAS PROPERTY BUSINESS

History – Chapter II of Part X omitted by CTA 2010, s. 1177 and Sch. 1, para. 34 and repealed by CTA 2010, s. 1181 and Sch. 3, Pt. 1.

392A UK property business losses

392A [Omitted by CTA 2010, s. 1177 and Sch. 1, para. 34 and repealed by CTA 2010, s. 1181 and Sch. 3, Pt. 1.]

History – Chapter II of Part X (of which s. 392A formed a part) omitted by CTA 2010, s. 1177 and Sch. 1, para. 34 and repealed by CTA 2010, s. 1181 and Sch. 3, Pt. 1, with effect for corporation tax purposes for accounting periods ending on or after 1 April 2010, and for income and capital gains tax purposes for the tax year 2010–11 and subsequent tax years, subject to transitional provisions in CTA 2010, s. 1180 and Sch. 2, para. 17.

Notes – S. 392A rewritten for corporation tax purposes as follows:
S. 392A(1): CTA 2010, s. 62(1), (2), (3).
S. 392A(2): CTA 2010, s. 62(4), (5).
S. 392A(3): CTA 2010, s. 63(1), (2), (3).
S. 392A(4): CTA 2010, s. 62(1).
S. 392A(5): CTA 2010, s. 64(1), 67(1).
S. 392A(6): CTA 2010, s. 64(2), (3), 67(2), (3).
S. 392A(7): CTA 2010, s. 64(1), 67(1).

392B Losses from overseas property business

392B [Omitted by CTA 2010, s. 1177 and Sch. 1, para. 34 and repealed by CTA 2010, s. 1181 and Sch. 3, Pt. 1.]

History – Chapter II of Part X (of which s. 392B formed a part) omitted by CTA 2010, s. 1177 and Sch. 1, para. 34 and repealed by CTA 2010, s. 1181 and Sch. 3, Pt. 1, with effect for corporation tax purposes for accounting periods ending on or after 1 April 2010, and for income and capital gains tax purposes for the tax year 2010–11 and subsequent tax years, subject to transitional provisions in CTA 2010, s. 1180 and Sch. 2, para. 17. Former s. 392B read as follows:

"*Losses from overseas property business*

392B(1) Where in any accounting period a company incurs a loss in an overseas property business (whether carried on by it solely or in partnership) –

(a) the loss shall be carried forward to the succeeding accounting period and set against any profits of the business for that period,

(b) if there are no profits of the business for that period, or if the profits for that period are exceeded by the amount of the loss, the loss or the remainder of it shall be carried forward again and set against any profits of the business for the next succeeding accounting period,

and so on.

392B(2) Subsections (5) to (7) of section 392A apply in relation to relief under subsection (1) above and an overseas property business as they apply in relation to relief under section 392A(1) to (3) and a UK property business.".

Notes – S. 392B rewritten for corporation tax purposes as follows:
S. 392B(1): CTA 2010, s. 66(1), (2), (3).
S. 392B(2): CTA 2010, s. 67(1), (2), (3).

TRADE ETC. LOSSES

393 Losses other than terminal losses

393 [Omitted by CTA 2010, s. 1177 and Sch. 1, para. 34 and repealed by CTA 2010, s. 1181 and Sch. 3, Pt. 1.]

History – Chapter II of Part X (of which s. 393 formed a part) omitted by CTA 2010, s. 1177 and Sch. 1, para. 34 and repealed by CTA 2010, s. 1181 and Sch. 3, Pt. 1, with effect for corporation tax purposes for accounting periods ending on or after 1 April 2010, and for income and capital gains tax purposes for the tax year 2010–11 and subsequent tax years, subject to transitional provisions in CTA 2010, s. 1180 and Sch. 2, para. 17. Former s. 393 read as follows:

"Losses other than terminal losses

393(1) Where in any accounting period a company carrying on a trade incurs a loss in the trade, the loss shall be set off for the purposes of corporation tax against any trading income from the trade in succeeding accounting periods; and (so long as the company continues to carry on the trade) its trading income from the trade in any succeeding accounting period shall then be treated as reduced by the amount of the loss, or by so much of that amount as cannot be relieved under this subsection, or (if a claim is made under section 393A(1)) under section 393A(1) or 393B(3), against income or profits of an earlier accounting period.
393(2)–(6) [Repealed by FA 1991, s. 73(2), 123 and Sch. 19, Pt. V.]
393(7) The amount of a loss incurred in a trade in an accounting period shall be computed for the purposes of this section in the same way as trading income from the trade in that period would have been computed.
393(8) For the purposes of this section **"trading income"** means, in relation to any trade, the income which falls or would fall to be included in respect of the trade in the total profits of the company; but where–

(a) in an accounting period a company incurs a loss in a trade in respect of which it is within the charge to corporation tax under Chapter 2 of Part 3 of CTA 2009 and
(b) in any later accounting period to which the loss or any part of it is carried forward under subsection (1) above relief in respect thereof cannot be given, or cannot wholly be given, because the amount of the trading income of the trade is insufficient,

any interest or dividends on investments which would fall to be taken into account as trading receipts in computing that trading income but for the fact that they have been subjected to tax under other provisions shall be treated for the purposes of subsection (1) above as if they were trading income of the trade.
393(9) Where in an accounting period the charges on income paid by a company–

(a) exceed the amount of the profits against which they are deductible, and
(b) include payments made wholly and exclusively for the purposes of a trade carried on by the company,

then, up to the amount of that excess or of those payments, whichever is the less, the charges on income so paid shall in computing a loss for the purposes of subsection (1) above be deductible as if they were trading expenses of the trade.
393(10) In this section references to a company carrying on a trade refer to the company carrying it on so as to be within the charge to corporation tax in respect of it.
393(11) [Repealed by FA 1990, s. 99(2), s. 132 and Sch. 19, Pt. V, and FA 1991, s. 73(2) and Sch. 15, para. 8, s. 123 and Sch. 19, Pt. V.]".

Notes – S. 393 rewritten for corporation tax purposes as follows:
S. 393(1): CTA 2010, s. 45(1), (2), (3), (4).
S. 393(7): CTA 2010, s. 35(3).
S. 393(8): CTA 2010, s. 45(4), (5), 46(1), (2), (3).
S. 393(10): CTA 2010, s. 36(3).

393A Losses: set off against profits of the same, or an earlier, accounting period

393A [Omitted by CTA 2010, s. 1177 and Sch. 1, para. 34 and repealed by CTA 2010, s. 1181 and Sch. 3, Pt. 1.]

History – Chapter II of Part X (of which s. 393A formed a part) omitted by CTA 2010, s. 1177 and Sch. 1, para. 34 and repealed by CTA 2010, s. 1181 and Sch. 3, Pt. 1, with effect for corporation tax purposes for accounting periods ending on or after 1 April 2010, and for income and capital gains tax purposes for the tax year 2010–11 and subsequent tax years, subject to transitional provisions in CTA 2010, s. 1180 and Sch. 2, para. 18.

Notes – S. 393A rewritten for corporation tax purposes as follows:
S. 393A(1): CTA 2010, s. 37(1), (2), (3), (4), (6), (8).
S. 393A(2): CTA 2010, s. 37(3), 38(1), (2), (3).
S. 393A(2A): CTA 2010, s. 39(2), 40(2).
S. 393A(2B): CTA 2010, s. 39(1), (3), (4), (5).
S. 393A(2C): CTA 2010, s. 40(1), 40 (3).
S. 393A(2E): CTA 2010, s. 41.
S. 393A(3): CTA 2010, s. 37(5), (6), 44(1), (2), (4).
S. 393A(4): CTA 2010, s. 44(1), (3).
S. 393A(9): CTA 2010, s. 35(3), 36(3).
S. 393A(10): CTA 2010, s. 37(7).
S. 393A(11): CTA 2010, s. 43(1).
S. 393A(11A): CTA 2010, s. 43(2), (3).
S. 393A(12): CTA 2010, s. 40(1), 43(1).

393B Losses of ring fence trade: set off against profits of an earlier accounting period

393B [Omitted by CTA 2010, s. 1177 and Sch. 1, para. 34 and repealed by CTA 2010, s. 1181 and Sch. 3, Pt. 1.]

History – Chapter II of Part X (of which s. 393B formed a part) omitted by CTA 2010, s. 1177 and Sch. 1, para. 34 and repealed by CTA 2010, s. 1181 and Sch. 3, Pt. 1, with effect for corporation tax purposes for accounting periods ending on or after 1 April 2010, and for income and capital gains tax purposes for the tax year 2010–11 and subsequent tax years.

Notes – S. 393B rewritten for corporation tax purposes as follows:
S. 393B(1): CTA 2010, s. 42(1).
S. 393B(2): CTA 2010, s. 42(2), (3).

S. 393B(3): CTA 2010, s. 42(3), (4), (7).
S. 393B(4): CTA 2010, s. 42(5).
S. 393B(5): CTA 2010, s. 42(5).
S. 393B(6): CTA 2010, s. 42(6).
S. 393B(7): CTA 2010, s. 42(6).
S. 393B(8): CTA 2010, s. 42(8).

394 Terminal losses

394(1)–(6) [Omitted by CTA 2010, s. 1177 and Sch. 1, para. 34 and repealed by CTA 2010, s. 1181 and Sch. 3, Pt. 1.]

History – Chapter 2 of Part 10 (of which s. 394 formed a part) omitted by CTA 2010, s. 1177 and Sch. 1, para. 34 and repealed by CTA 2010, s. 1181 and Sch. 3, Pt. 1, with effect for corporation tax purposes for accounting periods ending on or after 1 April 2010, and for income and capital gains tax purposes for the tax year 2010–11 and subsequent tax years. Former s. 394 repealed by FA 1991, s. 73(2), s. 123 and Sch. 19, Pt. V, with effect in relation to losses incurred in accounting periods ending on or after 1 April 1991.

395 Leasing contracts and company reconstructions

395 [Omitted by CTA 2010, s. 1177 and Sch. 1, para. 34 and repealed by CTA 2010, s. 1181 and Sch. 3, Pt. 1.]

History – Chapter II of Part X (of which s. 395 formed a part) omitted by CTA 2010, s. 1177 and Sch. 1, para. 34 and repealed by CTA 2010, s. 1181 and Sch. 3, Pt. 1, with effect for corporation tax purposes for accounting periods ending on or after 1 April 2010, and for income and capital gains tax purposes for the tax year 2010–11 and subsequent tax years.

Notes – S. 395 rewritten for corporation tax purposes as follows:
S. 395(1): CTA 2010, s. 53(1), (2), (3), Sch. 2, para. 22.
S. 395(2): CTA 2010, s. 53(4), 1176(1).
S. 395(3): CTA 2010, s. 53(6).
S. 395(4): CTA 2010, s. 53(7).
S. 395(5): CTA 2010, s. 53(5).

CASE VI LOSSES

396 Losses from miscellaneous transactions

396 [Omitted by CTA 2010, s. 1177 and Sch. 1, para. 34 and repealed by CTA 2010, s. 1181 and Sch. 3, Pt. 1.]

History – Chapter II of Part X (of which s. 396 formed a part) omitted by CTA 2010, s. 1177 and Sch. 1, para. 34 and repealed by CTA 2010, s. 1181 and Sch. 3, Pt. 1, with effect for corporation tax purposes for accounting periods ending on or after 1 April 2010, and for income and capital gains tax purposes for the tax year 2010–11 and subsequent tax years, subject to transitional provisions in CTA 2010, s. 1180 and Sch. 2, para. 17.

Notes – S. 396 rewritten for corporation tax purposes as follows:
S. 396(1): CTA 2010, s. 91(1), (2), (3), (4), (5), (6), (7).
S. 396(2): CTA 2010, s. 91(7).
S. 396(2A): CTA 2010, Sch. 2, para. 25.
S. 396(2B): CTA 2010, Sch. 2, para. 25.

Chapter III – Loss Relief: Miscellaneous Provisions

397 Restriction of relief in case of farming and market gardening

397 [Omitted by CTA 2010, s. 1177 and Sch. 1, para. 35 and repealed by CTA 2010, s. 1181 and Sch. 3, Pt. 1.]

History – S. 397 omitted by CTA 2010, s. 1177 and Sch. 1, para. 35 and repealed by CTA 2010, s. 1181 and Sch. 3, Pt. 1, with effect for corporation tax purposes for accounting periods ending on or after 1 April 2010, and for income and capital gains tax purposes for the tax year 2010–11 and subsequent tax years.

Notes – S. 397 rewritten for income tax purposes as follows:
S. 397(1): ITA 2007, s. 67(2).
S. 397(3): ITA 2007, s. 67(3), 68(3), (4).
S. 397(4): ITA 2007, s. 67(3).
S. 397(5): ITA 2007, s. 67(2), 68(5), 996(1).
S. 397(7): ITA 2007, s. 70(6).
S. 397(8): ITA 2007, s. 67(3), 69(2).
S. 397(10): ITA 2007, s. 69(3), (4), (5), (6), (7), 70(2), (3).
S. 397 rewritten for corporation tax purposes as follows:
S. 397(2): CTA 2010, s. 48(2).
S. 397(3): CTA 2010, s. 48(3), 49(3), (4).
S. 397(4): CTA 2010, s. 48(3).
S. 397(5): CTA 2010, s. 48(2), 49(5), (6).
S. 397(7): CTA 2010, s. 48(4).
S. 397(8): CTA 2010, s. 48(3), 50(1).
S. 397(9): CTA 2010, s. 50(3).
S. 397(10): CTA 2010, s. 50(4), (5), 51(1), (2), (3).

398 Transactions in deposits with and without certificates or in debts

398 Where a company sustains a loss on the exercise or disposal of a right to receive any amount, being a right to which section 56(2) applies, in a case where–

(a) if a profit had arisen from that exercise or disposal, that profit would have been chargeable to corporation tax by virtue of section 56(2), and

(b) the company is chargeable to corporation tax under Part 5 of CTA 2009 (loan relationships) in respect of interest payable on that amount,

then the amount of its loss may be set off under section 91 of CTA 2010.

History – In s. 398, the words "section 91 of CTA 2010" substituted for the words "section 396" by CTA 2010, s. 1177 and Sch. 1, para. 36, with effect for corporation tax purposes for accounting periods ending on or after 1 April 2010, and for income and capital gains tax purposes for the tax year 2010–11 and subsequent tax years.
In s. 398, the words "a company", the words "the company is chargeable to corporation tax under Schedule D" and the words "the amount of its loss may be set off under section 396" substituted and the word "corporation" inserted by ITA 2007, s. 1027 and Sch. 1, para. 75 with effect for income tax purposes for 2007–08 and later tax years and for corporation tax purposes in relation to accounting periods ending after 5 April 2007.
In s. 398, the words "above or Chapter 11 of Part 4 of ITTOIA 2005 (transactions in deposits)" and the words "above or that Chapter" in para. (a) omitted by ITA 2007, s. 1027 and Sch. 1, para. 75(3) and repealed by ITA 2007, s. 1031 and Sch. 3, Pt. 1 with effect for income tax purposes for 2007–08 and later tax years and for corporation tax purposes in relation to accounting periods ending after 5 April 2007.
In s. 398 the former words "above or Chapter 11 of Part 4 of ITTOIA 2005 (transactions in deposits)" and "above or that Chapter" inserted and the words "corporation tax under Schedule D or income tax under that Act" substituted by ITTOIA 2005, s. 882(1) and Sch. 1, para. 170; effective for income tax purposes for 2005–06 onwards and for corporation tax purposes for accounting periods ending after 5 April 2005 (ITTOIA 2005, s. 883(1)).
Reference in s. 398 to Sch. C repealed by FA 1996, s. 79 and Sch. 7, para. 16 and s. 205 and Sch. 41, Pt. V(2) for 1996–97 and later years of assessment (income tax) and accounting periods ending after 31 March 1996 (corporation tax), subject to FA 1996, Sch. 7, para. 33–35.
S. 398 amended by FA 1993, s. 120 and Sch. 14, para. 8(4), by substituting the words "the amountof his loss" to the end in relation to any case where under Pay and File losses may be set off under s. 396(1) without the making of a claim (Pay and File applies in respect of accounting periods ending after 30 September 1993 by virtue of SI 1992/3066).
In s. 398(b), the words "Part 5 of CTA 2009 (loan relationships)" substituted for "Schedule D" by CTA 2009, s. 1322 and Sch. 1, para. 114, with effect for corporation tax purposes for accounting periods ending on or after 1 April 2009, and for income tax and capital gains tax purposes for the tax year 2009–10 and subsequent tax years.

Derivations – (as originally enacted) – FA 1973, s. 26(2), as amended by FA 1974, s. 30(2).

Cross references – S. 56(2): Sch. D, Case VI charge on disposals of rights under certificates of deposit, deposits or debts.

Transitional – CTA 2009, Sch. 2, para. 55: certain references to CTA 2009, Pt. 5 to include references to FA 1996, Sch. 15 (loan relationships; savings and transitional provisions).

Notes – S. 398 rewritten for income tax purposes as ITA 2007, s. 154(1), (2), (3).

399 Dealings in commodity futures etc.: withdrawal of loss relief

399 [Omitted by CTA 2010, s. 1177 and Sch. 1, para. 37 and repealed by CTA 2010, s. 1181 and Sch. 3, Pt. 1.]

History – S. 399 omitted by CTA 2010, s. 1177 and Sch. 1, para. 37 and repealed by CTA 2010, s. 1181 and Sch. 3, Pt. 1, with effect for corporation tax purposes for accounting periods ending on or after 1 April 2010, and for income and capital gains tax purposes for the tax year 2010–11 and subsequent tax years.

Notes – S. 399 rewritten for income tax purposes as follows:
S. 399(2): ITA 2007, s. 81(1), (2), (3), (4), (5).
S. 399(3): ITA 2007, s. 81(6).
S. 399(4): ITA 2007, Sch. 2 para. 24.
S. 399(5): ITA 2007, s. 81(7).
S. 399 rewritten for corporation tax purposes as follows:
S. 399(2): CTA 2010, s. 52(1), (2), (3).
S. 399(2): CTA 2010, s. 52(1), (2), (3).
S. 399(3): CTA 2010, s. 52(4).
S. 399(4): CTA 2010, Sch. 2, para. 21.
S. 399(5): CTA 2010, s. 52(5).

400 Write-off of government investment

400 [Omitted by CTA 2010, s. 1177 and Sch. 1, para. 38 and repealed by CTA 2010, s. 1181 and Sch. 3, Pt. 1.]

History – S. 400 omitted by CTA 2010, s. 1177 and Sch. 1, para. 38 and repealed by CTA 2010, s. 1181 and Sch. 3, Pt. 1, with effect for corporation tax purposes for accounting periods ending on or after 1 April 2010, and for income and capital gains tax purposes for the tax year 2010–11 and subsequent tax years.

Notes – S. 400 rewritten for corporation tax as follows:
S. 400(1): CTA 2010, s. 92(1), (2), (3); Sch. 2, para. 26.
S. 400(2): CTA 2010, s. 95(1).
S. 400(3): CTA 2010, s. 95(4).
S. 400(4): CTA 2010, s. 95(2), (3).
S. 400(5): CTA 2010, s. 93(1), (2), (3).
S. 400(6): CTA 2010, s. 96(1), (2), (3).
S. 400(7): CTA 2010, s. 94(1), (5).
S. 400(8): CTA 2010, s. 94(3), (4), (5).
S. 400(9): CTA 2010, s. 94(2), (5).
S. 400(9A): CTA 2010, s. 96(4).
S. 400(10): CTA 2010, s. 92(4), 93(4), 94(5).

401 Relief for pre-trading expenditure

401 [Omitted by CTA 2009, s. 1322 and Sch. 1, para. 117 and repealed by CTA 2009, s. 1326 and Sch. 3, Pt. 1.]

History – S. 401 omitted by CTA 2009, s. 1322 and Sch. 1, para. 117 and repealed by CTA 2009, s. 1326 and Sch. 3 Pt. 1, with effect for corporation tax purposes for accounting periods ending on or after 1 April 2009, and for income tax and capital gains tax purposes for the tax year 2009–10 and subsequent tax years.

Notes – Rewritten income tax provisions are now located as follows:
S. 401(1): ITTOIA 2005, s. 57(2).
S. 401 rewritten for corporation tax purposes as follows:
S. 401(1): CTA 2009, s. 61(1), (2).
S. 401(1AA): CTA 2009, s. 61(3).
S. 401(1AB): CTA 2009, s. 330(1), (2), (3).
S. 401(1AC): CTA 2009, s. 330(3), (4), (5).

Chapter IV – Group Relief

History – Chapter IV of Part X omitted by CTA 2010, s. 1177 and Sch. 1, para. 39 and repealed by CTA 2010, s. 1181 and Sch. 3, Pt. 1.

402 Surrender of relief between members of groups and consortia

History – Chapter IV of Part X omitted by CTA 2010, s. 1177 and Sch. 1, para. 39 and repealed by CTA 2010, s. 1181 and Sch. 3, Pt. 1.

402 [Omitted by CTA 2010, s. 1177 and Sch. 1, para. 39 and repealed by CTA 2010, s. 1181 and Sch. 3, Pt. 1.]

History – Chapter IV of Part X (of which s. 402 formed a part) omitted by CTA 2010, s. 1177 and Sch. 1,para. 39 and repealed by CTA 2010, s. 1181 and Sch. 3, Pt. 1, with effect for corporation tax purposes for accounting periods ending on or after 1 April 2010, and for income and capital gains tax purposes for the tax year 2010–11 and subsequent tax years.

Notes – S. 402 rewritten for corporation tax as follows:
S. 402(1): CTA 2010, s. 97(2), 99(2), 113(2), 130(2), 135(2).
S. 402(2): CTA 2010, s. 99(1), 131(1), 134, 135(2).
S. 402(2A): CTA 2010, s. 112, 136(2), (3).
S. 402(2B): CTA 2010, s. 112,.
S. 402(3): CTA 2010, s. 132(2), (3), 133(1), (2), 153(1), (3).
S. 402(3A): CTA 2010, s. 99(1), 130(2), 132(2), (3), 133(1), (2).
S. 402(3B): CTA 2010, s. 99(1), 130(2), 132(2), (3), 133(1), (2).
S. 402(4): CTA 2010, s. 132(4), (5), 133(3), (4).
S. 402(5): CTA 2010, s. 130(3), 135(3).
S. 402(6): CTA 2010, s. 183 (1), (2).

403 Amounts which may be surrendered by way of group relief

History – Chapter IV of Part X omitted by CTA 2010, s. 1177 and Sch. 1, para. 39 and repealed by CTA 2010, s. 1181 and Sch. 3, Pt. 1.

403 [Omitted by CTA 2010, s. 1177 and Sch. 1, para. 39 and repealed by CTA 2010, s. 1181 and Sch. 3, Pt. 1.]

History – Chapter IV of Part X (of which s. 403 formed a part) omitted by CTA 2010, s. 1177 and Sch. 1, para. 39 and repealed by CTA 2010, s. 1181 and Sch. 3, Pt. 1, with effect for corporation tax purposes for accounting periods ending on or after 1 April 2010, and for income and capital gains tax purposes for the tax year 2010–11 and subsequent tax years.

Notes – S. 403 rewritten for corporation tax as follows:
S. 403(1): CTA 2010, s. 99(1), 103(1), 104(1), 137(1), (2).
S. 403(2): CTA 2010, s. 99(3).
S. 403(3): CTA 2010, s. 99(4), 105(1), (2), (3), (4).
S. 403(4): CTA 2010, s. 99(5), 105(5), 137(3).

403ZA Amounts eligible for group relief: trading losses

History – Chapter IV of Part X omitted by CTA 2010, s. 1177 and Sch. 1, para. 39 and repealed by CTA 2010, s. 1181 and Sch 3, Pt. 1.

403ZA [Omitted by CTA 2010, s. 1177 and Sch. 1, para. 39 and repealed by CTA 2010, s. 1181 and Sch. 3, Pt. 1.]

History – Chapter IV of Part X (of which s. 403ZA formed a part) omitted by CTA 2010, s. 1177 and Sch. 1, para. 39 and repealed by CTA 2010, s. 1181 and Sch. 3, Pt. 1, with effect for corporation tax purposes for accounting periods ending on or after 1 April 2010, and for income and capital gains tax purposes for the tax year 2010–11 and subsequent tax years.

Notes – S. 403ZA rewritten for corporation tax as follows:
S. 403ZA(1): CTA 2010, s. 100(1).
S. 403ZA(2): CTA 2010, s. 100(2).
S. 403ZA(3): CTA 2010, s. 147(1), (2), (3).
S. 403ZA(4): CTA 2010, s. 147(4).

403ZB Amounts eligible for group relief: excess capital allowances

History – Chapter IV of Part X omitted by CTA 2010, s. 1177 and Sch. 1, para. 39 and repealed by CTA 2010, s. 1181 and Sch. 3, Pt. 1.

403ZB [Omitted by CTA 2010, s. 1177 and Sch. 1, para. 39 and repealed by CTA 2010, s. 1181 and Sch. 3, Pt. 1.]

History – Chapter IV of Part X (of which s. 403ZB formed a part) omitted by CTA 2010, s. 1177 and Sch. 1, para. 39 and repealed by CTA 2010, s. 1181 and Sch. 3, Pt. 1, with effect for corporation tax purposes for accounting periods ending on or after 1 April 2010, and for income and capital gains tax purposes for the tax year 2010–11 and subsequent tax years.

Notes – S. 403ZB rewritten for corporation tax as follows:
S. 403ZB(1): CTA 2010, s. 101(1).
S. 403ZB(2): CTA 2010, s. 101(1), (3).
S. 403ZB(3): CTA 2010, s. 101(4).

403ZC Amounts eligible for group relief: non-trading deficit on loan relationships

History – Chapter IV of Part X omitted by CTA 2010, s. 1177 and Sch. 1, ara. 39 and repealed by CTA 2010, s. 1181 and Sch. 3, Pt. 1.

403ZC [Omitted by CTA 2010, s. 1177 and Sch. 1, para. 39 and repealed by CTA 2010, s. 1181 and Sch. 3, Pt. 1.]

History – Chapter IV of Part X (of which s. 403ZC formed a part) omitted by CTA 2010, s. 1177 and Sch. 1, para. 39 and repealed by CTA 2010, s. 1181 and Sch. 3, Pt. 1, with effect for corporation tax purposes for accounting periods ending on or after 1 April 2010, and for income and capital gains tax purposes for the tax year 2010–11 and subsequent tax years.

Notes – S. 403ZC rewritten for corporation tax as follows:
S. 403ZC(1): CTA 2010, s. 99(1).

403ZD Other amounts available by way of group relief

History – Chapter IV of Part X omitted by CTA 2010, s. 1177 and Sch. 1, para. 39 and repealed by CTA 2010, s. 1181 and Sch. 3, Pt. 1.

403ZD [Omitted by CTA 2010, s. 1177 and Sch. 1, para. 39 and repealed by CTA 2010, s. 1181 and Sch. 3, Pt. 1.]

History – Chapter IV of Part X (of which s. 403ZD formed a part) omitted by CTA 2010, s. 1177 and Sch. 1, para. 39 and repealed by CTA 2010, s. 1181 and Sch. 3, Pt. 1, with effect for corporation tax purposes for accounting periods ending on or after 1 April 2010, and for income and capital gains tax purposes for the tax year 2010–11 and subsequent tax years.

Notes – S. 403ZD rewritten for corporation tax as follows:
S. 403ZD(1): CTA 2010, s. 99(1).
S. 403ZD(2): CTA 2010, s. 99(1).
S. 403ZD(3): CTA 2010, s. 102(1), (2).
S. 403ZD(4): CTA 2010, s. 103(1), (2).
S. 403ZD(6): CTA 2010, s. 104(1), (2).

403ZE Computation of gross profits

History – Chapter IV of Part X omitted by CTA 2010, s. 1177 and Sch. 1, para. 39 and repealed by CTA 2010, s. 1181 and Sch. 3, Pt. 1.

403ZE [Omitted by CTA 2010, s. 1177 and Sch. 1, para. 39 and repealed by CTA 2010, s. 1181 and Sch. 3, Pt. 1.]

History – Chapter IV of Part X (of which s. 403ZE formed a part) omitted by CTA 2010, s. 1177 and Sch. 1, para. 39 and repealed by CTA 2010, s. 1181 and Sch. 3, Pt. 1, with effect for corporation tax purposes for accounting periods ending on or after 1 April 2010, and for income and capital gains tax purposes for the tax year 2010–11 and subsequent tax years.

403A Limits on group relief

History – Chapter IV of Part X omitted by CTA 2010, s. 1177 and Sch. 1, para. 39 and repealed by CTA 2010, s. 1181 and Sch. 3, Pt. 1.

403A [Omitted by CTA 2010, s. 1177 and Sch. 1, para. 39 and repealed by CTA 2010, s. 1181 and Sch. 3, Pt. 1.]

History – Chapter IV of Part X (of which s. 403A formed a part) omitted by CTA 2010, s. 1177 and Sch. 1, para. 39 and repealed by CTA 2010, s. 1181 and Sch. 3, Pt. 1, with effect for corporation tax purposes for accounting periods ending on or after 1 April 2010, and for income and capital gains tax purposes for the tax year 2010–11 and subsequent tax years.

Notes – S. 403A rewritten for corporation tax as follows:
S. 403A(1): CTA 2010, s. 138, 139(1).
S. 403A(2): CTA 2010, s. 139(1), 140(1).
S. 403A(3): CTA 2010, s. 139(2), 140(2).
S. 403A(4): CTA 2010, s. 139(3), (4), (5), (6), 140(6).
S. 403A(5): CTA 2010, s.140(3), (4), (5).
S. 403A(7): CTA 2010, s.141(1).
S. 403A(8): CTA 2010, s.142(1).
S. 403A(9): CTA 2010, s.142(2).
S. 403A(10): CTA 2010, s.142(3).
S. 403A(11): CTA 2010, s.142(3).

403B Apportionments under section 403A

History – Chapter IV of Part X omitted by CTA 2010, s. 1177 and Sch. 1, para. 39 and repealed by CTA 2010, s. 1181 and Sch. 3, Pt. 1.

403B [Omitted by CTA 2010, s. 1177 and Sch. 1, para. 39 and repealed by CTA 2010, s. 1181 and Sch. 3, Pt. 1.]

History – Chapter IV of Part X (of which s. 403B formed a part) omitted by CTA 2010, s. 1177 and Sch. 1, para. 39 and repealed by CTA 2010, s. 1181 and Sch. 3, Pt. 1, with effect for corporation tax purposes for accounting periods ending on or after 1 April 2010, and for income and capital gains tax purposes for the tax year 2010–11 and subsequent tax years.

Notes – S. 403B rewritten for corporation tax as follows:
S. 403B(1): CTA 2010, s. 139(2), (5), (6),140(2), (6).
S. 403B(2): CTA 2010, s. 141(3).

403C Amount of relief in consortium cases

History – Chapter IV of Part X omitted by CTA 2010, s. 1177 and Sch. 1, para. 39 and repealed by CTA 2010, s. 1181 and Sch. 3, Pt. 1.

403C [Omitted by CTA 2010, s. 1177 and Sch. 1, para. 39 and repealed by CTA 2010, s. 1181 and Sch. 3, Pt. 1.]

History – Chapter IV of Part X (of which s. 403C formed a part) omitted by CTA 2010, s. 1177 and Sch. 1, para. 39 and repealed by CTA 2010, s. 1181 and Sch. 3, Pt. 1, with effect for corporation tax purposes for accounting periods ending on or after 1 April 2010, and for income and capital gains tax purposes for the tax year 2010–11 and subsequent tax years.

Notes – S. 403C rewritten for corporation tax as follows:
S. 403C(1): CTA 2010, s. 143(1), 144(1).
S. 403C(2): CTA 2010, s. 143(1), (2), (3), (4), 144(1).
S. 403C(3): CTA 2010, s. 144(2), (3), (4).
S. 403C(4): CTA 2010, s. 143(5), 144(5).
S. 403C(5): CTA 2010, s. 143(6), 144(6).

403D Relief for or in respect of UK losses of non-resident companies

History – Chapter IV of Part X omitted by CTA 2010, s. 1177 and Sch. 1, para. 39 and repealed by CTA 2010, s. 1181 and Sch. 3, Pt. 1.

403D [Omitted by CTA 2010, s. 1177 and Sch. 1, para. 39 and repealed by CTA 2010, s. 1181 and Sch. 3, Pt. 1.]

History – Chapter IV of Part X (of which s. 403D formed a part) omitted by CTA 2010, s. 1177 and Sch. 1, para. 39 and repealed by CTA 2010, s. 1181 and Sch. 3, Pt. 1, with effect for corporation tax purposes for accounting periods ending on or after 1 April 2010, and for income and capital gains tax purposes for the tax year 2010–11 and subsequent tax years.

Notes – S. 403D rewritten for corporation tax as follows:
S. 403D(1): CTA 2010, s. 107(1), (2), (3), (4), (5), (6).
S. 403D(2): CTA 2010, s. 108(3), 140(8).
S. 403D(3): CTA 2010, s. 108(1), (2).
S. 403D(4): CTA 2010, s. 108(3).
S. 403D(5): CTA 2010, s. 107(7).
S. 403D(6): CTA 2010, s. 107(8), (9).
S. 403D(7): CTA 2010, s. 186(1).
S. 403D(8): CTA 2010, s. 186(3).
S. 403D(9): CTA 2010, s. 187(1), (2).
S. 403D(10): CTA 2010, s. 186(2).

403E Relief for overseas losses of UK resident companies

History – Chapter IV of Part X omitted by CTA 2010, s. 1177 and Sch. 1, para. 39 and repealed by CTA 2010, s. 1181 and Sch. 3, Pt. 1.

403E [Omitted by CTA 2010, s. 1177 and Sch. 1, para. 39 and repealed by CTA 2010, s. 1181 and Sch. 3, Pt. 1.]

History – Chapter IV of Part X (of which s. 403E formed a part) omitted by CTA 2010, s. 1177 and Sch. 1, para. 39 and repealed by CTA 2010, s. 1181 and Sch. 3, Pt. 1, with effect for corporation tax purposes for accounting periods ending on or after 1 April 2010, and for income and capital gains tax purposes for the tax year 2010–11 and subsequent tax years.

Notes – S. 403E rewritten for corporation tax as follows:
S. 403E(1): CTA 2010, s. 106(1), (2).
S. 403E(2): CTA 2010, s. 106(5).
S. 403E(4): CTA 2010, s. 106(3), (4).
S. 403E(5): CTA 2010, s. 106(4).
S. 403E(6): CTA 2010, s. 106(2).
S. 403E(7): CTA 2010, s. 108(1), (2), (3), 187(1), (2).
S. 403E(8): CTA 2010, s. 106(6), (7).

403F Relief in respect of overseas losses of non-resident companies

History – Chapter IV of Part X omitted by CTA 2010, s. 1177 and Sch. 1, para. 39 and repealed by CTA 2010, s. 1181 and Sch. 3, Pt. 1.

403F [Omitted by CTA 2010, s. 1177 and Sch. 1, para. 39 and repealed by CTA 2010, s. 1181 and Sch. 3, Pt. 1.]

History – Chapter IV of Part X (of which s. 403F formed a part) omitted by CTA 2010, s. 1177 and Sch. 1, para. 39 and repealed by CTA 2010, s. 1181 and Sch. 3, Pt. 1, with effect for corporation tax purposes for accounting periods ending on or after 1 April 2010, and for income and capital gains tax purposes for the tax year 2010–11 and subsequent tax years.

Notes – S. 403F rewritten for corporation tax as follows:
S. 403F(1): CTA 2010, s. 112, 113(1).
S. 403F(2): CTA 2010, s. 113(2).
S. 403F(5): CTA 2010, s. 113(2).

403G Unallowable overseas losses of non-resident companies

History – Chapter IV of Part X omitted by CTA 2010, s. 1177 and Sch. 1, para. 39 and repealed by CTA 2010, s. 1181 and Sch. 3, Pt. 1.

403G [Omitted by CTA 2010, s. 1177 and Sch. 1, para. 39 and repealed by CTA 2010, s. 1181 and Sch. 3, Pt. 1.]

History – Chapter IV of Part X (of which s. 403G formed a part) omitted by CTA 2010, s. 1177 and Sch. 1, para. 39 and repealed by CTA 2010, s. 1181 and Sch. 3, Pt. 1, with effect for corporation tax purposes for accounting periods ending on or after 1 April 2010, and for income and capital gains tax purposes for the tax year 2010–11 and subsequent tax years.

Notes – S. 403G rewritten for corporation tax as follows:
S. 403G(1): CTA 2010, s. 127(1).
S. 403G(2): CTA 2010, s. 127(1).
S. 403G(3): CTA 2010, s. 127(2).
S. 403G(4): CTA 2010, s. 127(3).
S. 403G(5): CTA 2010, Sch. 2, para. 52.
S. 403G(6): CTA 2010, s. 127(1), (4).

404 Limitation of group relief in relation to certain dual resident companies

History – Chapter IV of Part X omitted by CTA 2010, s. 1177 and Sch. 1, para. 39 and repealed by CTA 2010, s. 1181 and Sch. 3, Pt. 1.

404 [Omitted by CTA 2010, s. 1177 and Sch. 1, para. 39 and repealed by CTA 2010, s. 1181 and Sch. 3, Pt. 1.]

History – Chapter IV of Part X (of which s. 404 formed a part) omitted by CTA 2010, s. 1177 and Sch. 1, para. 39 and repealed by CTA 2010, s. 1181 and Sch. 3, Pt. 1, with effect for corporation tax purposes for accounting periods ending on or after 1 April 2010, and for income and capital gains tax purposes for the tax year 2010–11 and subsequent tax years.

Notes – S. 404 rewritten for corporation tax as follows:
S. 404(1): CTA 2010, s. 109(1), (2).
S. 404(2): CTA 2010, s. 109(1).
S. 404(4): CTA 2010, s. 109(1).
S. 404(5): CTA 2010, s. 109(3).
S. 404(6): CTA 2010, s. 109(4), (5).

405 Claims relating to losses etc. of members of both group and consortium

History – Chapter IV of Part X omitted by CTA 2010, s. 1177 and Sch. 1, para. 39 and repealed by CTA 2010, s. 1181 and Sch. 3, Pt. 1.

405 [Omitted by CTA 2010, s. 1177 and Sch. 1, para. 39 and repealed by CTA 2010, s. 1181 and Sch. 3, Pt. 1.]

History – Chapter IV of Part X (of which s. 405 formed a part) omitted by CTA 2010, s. 1177 and Sch. 1, para. 39 and repealed by CTA 2010, s. 1181 and Sch. 3, Pt. 1, with effect for corporation tax purposes for accounting periods ending on or after 1 April 2010, and for income and capital gains tax purposes for the tax year 2010–11 and subsequent tax years.

Notes – S. 405 rewritten for corporation tax as follows:
S. 405(1): CTA 2010, s. 148(1), (2), (3), (4).
S. 405(2): CTA 2010, s. 148(5).
S. 405(3): CTA 2010, s. 148(6).
S. 405(4): CTA 2010, s. 149(1), (2), (3), (4).
S. 405(5): CTA 2010, s. 149(5).
S. 405(6): CTA 2010, s. 149(6).

406 Claims relating to losses etc. of consortium company or group member

History – Chapter IV of Part X omitted by CTA 2010, s. 1177 and Sch. 1, para. 39 and repealed by CTA 2010, s. 1181 and Sch. 3, Pt. 1.

406 [Omitted by CTA 2010, s. 1177 and Sch. 1, para. 39 and repealed by CTA 2010, s. 1181 and Sch. 3, Pt. 1.]

History – Chapter IV of Part X (of which s. 406 formed a part) omitted by CTA 2010, s. 1177 and Sch. 1, para. 39 and repealed by CTA 2010, s. 1181 and Sch. 3, Pt. 1, with effect for corporation tax purposes for accounting periods ending on or after 1 April 2010, and for income and capital gains tax purposes for the tax year 2010–11 and subsequent tax years.

Notes – S. 406 rewritten for corporation tax as follows:
S. 406(1): CTA 2010, s. 133(1), (2).
S. 406(2): CTA 2010, s. 133(1), (3), (4), 145(2), 147(2), 148(2), 149(2).
S. 406(3): CTA 2010, s. 142(2), (3).
S. 406(4): CTA 2010, s. 146(2), (3), (8).
S. 406(5): CTA 2010, s. 133(2), (3), (4).
S. 406(6): CTA 2010, s. 145(3).
S. 406(7): CTA 2010, s. 142(2), (3).
S. 406(8): CTA 2010, s. 146(5), (6), (7), (8).

407 Relationship between group relief and other relief

History – Chapter IV of Part X omitted by CTA 2010, s. 1177 and Sch. 1, para. 39 and repealed by CTA 2010, s. 1181 and Sch. 3, Pt. 1.

407 [Omitted by CTA 2010, s. 1177 and Sch. 1, para. 39 and repealed by CTA 2010, s. 1181 and Sch. 3, Pt. 1.]

History – Chapter IV of Part X (of which s. 407 formed a part)omitted by CTA 2010, s. 1177 and Sch. 1, para. 39 and repealed by CTA 2010, s. 1181 and Sch. 3, Pt. 1, with effect for corporation tax purposes for accounting periods ending on or after 1 April 2010, and for income and capital gains tax purposes for the tax year 2010–11 and subsequent tax years.

Notes – S. 407 rewritten for corporation tax as follows:
S. 407(1): CTA 2010, s. 137(4), (6).
S. 407(2): CTA 2010, s. 137(5).
S. 407(13: CTA 2010, s. 137(4), (5).

408 Corresponding accounting periods

History – Chapter IV of Part X omitted by CTA 2010, s. 1177 and Sch. 1, para. 39 and repealed by CTA 2010, s. 1181 and Sch. 3, Pt. 1.

408 [Omitted by CTA 2010, s. 1177 and Sch. 1, para. 39 and repealed by CTA 2010, s. 1181 and Sch. 3, Pt. 1.]

History – Chapter IV of Part X (of which s. 408 formed a part) omitted by CTA 2010, s. 1177 and Sch. 1, para. 39 and repealed by CTA 2010, s. 1181 and Sch. 3, Pt. 1, with effect for corporation tax purposes for accounting periods ending on or after 1 April 2010, and for income and capital gains tax purposes for the tax year 2010–11 and subsequent tax years.

409 Companies joining or leaving group or consortium

History – Chapter IV of Part X omitted by CTA 2010, s. 1177 and Sch. 1, para. 39 and repealed by CTA 2010, s. 1181 and Sch. 3, Pt. 1.

409 [Omitted by CTA 2010, s. 1177 and Sch. 1, para. 39 and repealed by CTA 2010, s. 1181 and Sch. 3, Pt. 1.]

History – Chapter IV of Part X (of which s. 409 formed a part) omitted by CTA 2010, s. 1177 and Sch. 1, para. 39 and repealed by CTA 2010, s. 1181 and Sch. 3, Pt. 1, with effect for corporation tax purposes for accounting periods ending on or after 1 April 2010, and for income and capital gains tax purposes for the tax year 2010–11 and subsequent tax years.

410 Arrangements for transfer of company to another group or consortium

History – Chapter IV of Part X omitted by CTA 2010, s. 1177 and Sch. 1, para. 39 and repealed by CTA 2010, s. 1181 and Sch. 3, Pt. 1.

410 [Omitted by CTA 2010, s. 1177 and Sch. 1, para. 39 and repealed by CTA 2010, s. 1181 and Sch. 3, Pt. 1.]

History – Chapter IV of Part X (of which s. 410 formed a part) omitted by CTA 2010, s. 1177 and Sch. 1, para. 39 and repealed by CTA 2010, s. 1181 and Sch. 3, Pt. 1, with effect for corporation tax purposes for accounting periods ending on or after 1 April 2010, and for income and capital gains tax purposes for the tax year 2010–11 and subsequent tax years.

Notes – S. 410 rewritten for corporation tax as follows:
S. 410(1): CTA 2010, s. 154(1), (2), (3).
S. 410(2): CTA 2010, s. 155(1), (2), (3), (5).
S. 410(3): CTA 2010, s. 155(5).
S. 410(4): CTA 2010, s. 154(4), 155(4).
S. 410(5): CTA 2010, s. 155(3), 156(2), 1176(2).
S. 410(6): CTA 2010, s. 156(3).
S. 410(7): CTA 2010, s. 156(2).

411 Exclusion of double allowances

History – Chapter IV of Part X omitted by CTA 2010, s. 1177 and Sch. 1, para. 39 and repealed by CTA 2010, s. 1181 and Sch. 3, Pt. 1.

411 [Omitted by CTA 2010, s. 1177 and Sch. 1, para. 39 and repealed by CTA 2010, s. 1181 and Sch. 3, Pt. 1.]

History – Chapter IV of Part X (of which s. 411 formed a part) repealed by CTA 2010, s. 1181 and Sch. 3, Pt. 1, with effect for corporation tax purposes for accounting periods ending on or after 1 April 2010, and for income and capital gains tax purposes for the tax year 2010–11 and subsequent tax years.

Notes – S. 411 rewritten for corporation tax as follows:
S. 411(1): CTA 2010, s. 137(7).
S. 411(10): CTA 2010, s. 184.

411ZA No relief where deduction of relevant return under alternative finance arrangements disallowed

History – Chapter IV of Part X omitted by CTA 2010, s. 1177 and Sch. 1, para. 39 and repealed by CTA 2010, s. 1181 and Sch. 3, Pt. 1.

411ZA [Omitted by CTA 2010, s. 1177 and Sch. 1, para. 39 and repealed by CTA 2010, s. 1181 and Sch. 3, Pt. 1.]

History – Chapter IV of Part X (of which s. 411ZA formed a part) omitted by CTA 2010, s. 1177 and Sch. 1, para. 39 and repealed by CTA 2010, s. 1181 and Sch. 3, Pt. 1, with effect for corporation tax purposes for accounting periods ending on or after 1 April 2010, and for income and capital gains tax purposes for the tax year 2010–11 and subsequent tax years.

Notes – S. 411ZA rewritten for corporation tax as follows:
S. 411ZA(1): CTA 2010, s. 110(1).
S. 411ZA(2): CTA 2010, s. 110(2).

411A Group relief by way of substitution for loss relief

History – Chapter IV of Part X omitted by CTA 2010, s. 1177 and Sch. 1, para. 39 and repealed by CTA 2010, s. 1181 and Sch. 3, Pt. 1.

411A [Omitted by CTA 2010, s. 1177 and Sch. 1, para. 39 and repealed by CTA 2010, s. 1181 and Sch. 3, Pt. 1.]

History – Chapter IV of Part X (of which s. 411A formed a part) omitted by CTA 2010, s. 1177 and Sch. 1, para. 39 and repealed by CTA 2010, s. 1181 and Sch. 3, Pt. 1, with effect for corporation tax purposes for accounting periods ending on or after 1 April 2010, and for income and capital gains tax purposes for the tax year 2010–11 and subsequent tax years.

412 Claims and adjustments

History – Chapter IV of Part X omitted by CTA 2010, s. 1177 and Sch. 1, para. 39 and repealed by CTA 2010, s. 1181 and Sch. 3, Pt. 1.

412 [Omitted by CTA 2010, s. 1177 and Sch. 1, para. 39 and repealed by CTA 2010, s. 1181 and Sch. 3, Pt. 1.]

History – Chapter IV of Part X (of which s. 412A formed a part) omitted by CTA 2010, s. 1177 and Sch. 1 para. 39 and repealed by CTA 2010, s. 1181 and Sch. 3, Pt. 1, with effect for corporation tax purposes for accounting periods ending on or after 1 April 2010, and for income and capital gains tax purposes for the tax year 2010–11 and subsequent tax years.

Notes – S. 412 rewritten for corporation tax as follows:
S. 412(1): CTA 2010, s. 97(9).
S. 412(2): CTA 2010, s. 97(9).

413 Interpretation of Chapter IV

History – Chapter IV of Part X omitted by CTA 2010, s. 1177 and Sch. 1, para. 39 and repealed by CTA 2010, s. 1181 and Sch. 3, Pt. 1.

413 [Omitted by CTA 2010, s. 1177 and Sch. 1, para. 39 and repealed by CTA 2010, s. 1181 and Sch. 3, Pt. 1.]

History – Chapter IV of Part X (of which s. 413 formed a part) omitted by CTA 2010, s. 1177 and Sch. 1, para. 39 and repealed by CTA 2010, s. 1181 and Sch. 3, Pt. 1, with effect for corporation tax purposes for accounting periods ending on or after 1 April 2010, and for income and capital gains tax purposes for the tax year 2010–11 and subsequent tax years.

Notes – S. 413 rewritten for corporation tax as follows:
S. 413(1): CTA 2010, s. 188(1).
S. 413(2): CTA 2010, s. 188(1).
S. 413(2A): CTA 2010, s. 130(2), 135(2).
S. 413(3): CTA 2010, s. 152, 185(1), (2), 188(1).
S. 413(4): CTA 2010, s. 151(1), (2).
S. 413(5): CTA 2010, s. 151(3).
S. 413(6): CTA 2010, s. 153(1), (2), (3).
S. 413(7): CTA 2010, s. 151(4).

PART XI – CLOSE COMPANIES

Chapter I – Interpretative Provisions

History – Chapter I of Part XI omitted by CTA 2010, s. 1177 and Sch. 1, para. 40 and repealed by CTA 2010, s. 1181 and Sch. 3, Pt. 1.

414 Close companies

History – Chapter I of Part XI omitted by CTA 2010, s. 1177 and Sch. 1, para. 40 and repealed by CTA 2010, s. 1181 and Sch. 3, Pt. 1.

414 [Omitted by CTA 2010, s. 1177 and Sch. 1, para. 40 and repealed by CTA 2010, s. 1181 and Sch. 3, Pt. 1.]

History – Chapter I of Part XI (of which s. 414 formed a part) omitted by CTA 2010, s. 1177 and Sch. 1, para. 40 and repealed by CTA 2010, s. 1181 and Sch. 3, Pt. 1, with effect for corporation tax purposes for accounting periods ending on or after 1 April 2010, and for income and capital gains tax purposes for the tax year 2010–11 and subsequent tax years.

Notes – S. 414 rewritten as follows:
S. 414(1): CTA 2009, Sch. 1, para. 272(2), CTA 2010, s. 439(1), (2), 442, 443(1).
S. 414(2): CTA 2010, s. 439(1), (3), 442.
S. 414(2A): CTA 2010, s. 440(2).
S. 414(2B): CTA 2010, s. 440(3).
S. 414(2C): CTA 2010, s. 441(1), (2), (3), (4).
S. 414(2D): CTA 2010, s. 439(5).
S. 414(4): CTA 2010, s. 443(2), (3).
S. 414(5): CTA 2010, s. 444(1), (2), (3).
S. 414(6): CTA 2010, s. 444(4).
S. 414(7): CTA 2010, s. 445(1), (2), (3).

415 Certain quoted companies not to be close companies

History – Chapter I of Part XI omitted by CTA 2010, s. 1177 and Sch. 1, para. 40 and repealed by CTA 2010, s. 1181 and Sch. 3, Pt. 1.

415 [Omitted by CTA 2010, s. 1177 and Sch. 1, para. 40 and repealed by CTA 2010, s. 1181 and Sch. 3, Pt. 1.]

History – Chapter I of Part XI (of which s. 415 formed a part)omitted by CTA 2010, s. 1177 and Sch. 1, para. 40 and repealed by CTA 2010, s. 1181 and Sch. 3, Pt. 1, with effect for corporation tax purposes for accounting periods ending on or after 1 April 2010, and for income and capital gains tax purposes for the tax year 2010–11 and subsequent tax years.

Notes – S. 415 rewritten as follows:
S. 415(1): CTA 2010, s. 446(1), (6).
S. 415(2): CTA 2010, s. 446(2).
S. 415(3): CTA 2010, s. 447(1), (2), (4).
S. 415(4): CTA 2010, s. 447(1).
S. 415(5): CTA 2010, s. 447(2), (3), (6).
S. 415(6): CTA 2010, s. 446(3), (4), 447(5), (7).
S. 415(7): CTA 2010, s. 446(5), 447(7).
S. 415(8): CTA 2010, s. 446(6), 447(8).

416 Meaning of "associated company" and "control"

History – Chapter I of Part XI omitted by CTA 2010, s. 1177 and Sch. 1, para. 40 and repealed by CTA 2010, s. 1181 and Sch. 3, Pt. 1.

416 [Omitted by CTA 2010, s. 1177 and Sch. 1, para. 40 and repealed by CTA 2010, s. 1181 and Sch. 3, Pt. 1.]

History – Chapter I of Part XI (of which s. 416 formed a part) omitted by CTA 2010, s. 1177 and Sch. 1, para. 40 and repealed by CTA 2010, s. 1181 and Sch. 3, Pt. 1, with effect for corporation tax purposes for accounting periods ending on or after 1 April 2010, and for income and capital gains tax purposes for the tax year 2010–11 and subsequent tax years.

Notes – S. 416 rewritten as follows:
S. 416(1): CTA 2010, s. 449.
S. 416(2): CTA 2010, s. 450(1), (2), (3), (4), 1069(3).
S. 416(3): CTA 2010, s. 450(5), 1069(3).
S. 416(4): CTA 2010, s. 451(1), (2), 1069(3).
S. 416(5): CTA 2010, s. 451(1), (3),1069(3).
S. 416(6): CTA 2010, s. 451(1), (4), (5), (6),1069(3).

417 Meaning of "participator", "associate", "director" and "loan creditor"

History – Chapter I of Part XI omitted by CTA 2010, s. 1177 and Sch. 1, para. 40 and repealed by CTA 2010, s. 1181 and Sch. 3, Pt. 1.

417 [Omitted by CTA 2010, s. 1177 and Sch. 1, para. 40 and repealed by CTA 2010, s. 1181 and Sch. 3, Pt. 1.]

History – Chapter I of Part XI (of which s. 417 formed a part) omitted by CTA 2010, s. 1177 and Sch. 1, para. 40 and repealed by CTA 2010, s. 1181 and Sch. 3, Pt. 1, with effect for corporation tax purposes for accounting periods ending on or after 1 April 2010, and for income and capital gains tax purposes for the tax year 2010–11 and subsequent tax years.

Notes – S. 417 rewritten for income tax purposes as follows:
S. 417(3): ITA 2007, s. 253(1).
S. 417(4): ITA 2007, s. 253(2).
S. 417 rewritten for corporation tax purposes as follows:
S. 417(1): CTA 2010, s. 454(1), (2), (3), (4), 1068(1), 1069(3).
S. 417(2): CTA 2010, s. 454(6), 1068(2).
S. 417(3): CTA 2010, s. 448(1), 1069(3).
S. 417(4): CTA 2010, s. 448(2).
S. 417(5): CTA 2010, s. 452(1), (2).
S. 417(6): CTA 2010, s. 452(3).
S. 417(7): CTA 2010, s. 453(1), (2).
S. 417(8): CTA 2010, s. 453(3).
S. 417(9): CTA 2010, s. 453(4).

ADDITIONAL MATTERS TO BE TREATED AS DISTRIBUTIONS

History – Chapter I of Part XI omitted by CTA 2010, s. 1177 and Sch. 1, para. 40 and repealed by CTA 2010, s. 1181 and Sch. 3, Pt. 1.

418 "Distribution" to include certain expenses of close companies

History – Chapter I of Part XI omitted by CTA 2010, s. 1177 and Sch. 1, para. 40 and repealed by CTA 2010, s. 1181 and Sch. 3, Pt. 1.

418 [Omitted by CTA 2010, s. 1177 and Sch. 1, para. 40 and repealed by CTA 2010, s. 1181 and Sch. 3, Pt. 1.]

History – Chapter I of Part XI (of which s. 418 formed a part) omitted by CTA 2010, s. 1177 and Sch. 1, para. 40 and repealed by CTA 2010, s. 1181 and Sch. 3, Pt. 1, with effect for corporation tax purposes for accounting periods ending on or after 1 April 2010, and for income and capital gains tax purposes for the tax year 2010–11 and subsequent tax years.

Notes – For income tax purposes, s. 418(2) rewritten as ITTOIA 2005, s. 385(1).
S. 418 rewritten for corporation tax as follows;
S. 418(1): CTA 2010, s. 1000(2), 1064(2), (4).
S. 418(2): CTA 2010, s. 1064(1), (2), (4).
S. 418(3): CTA 2010, s. 1065.
S. 418(4): CTA 2010, s. 1064(3).
S. 418(5): CTA 2010, s. 1066(1).
S. 418(6): CTA 2010, s. 1066(2), (3).
S. 418(7): CTA 2010, s. 1067(1), (2), (3).
S. 418(8): CTA 2010, s. 1069(1), (2).

Chapter II – Charges to Tax in Connection with Loans

History – Chapter II of Part XI omitted by CTA 2010, s. 1177 and Sch. 1, para. 41 and repealed by CTA 2010, s. 1181 and Sch. 3, Pt. 1.

419 Loans to participators etc.

History – Chapter II of Part XI omitted by CTA 2010, s. 1177 and Sch. 1, para. 41 and repealed by CTA 2010, s. 1181 and Sch. 3, Pt. 1.

419 [Omitted by CTA 2010, s. 1177 and Sch. 1, para. 41 and repealed by CTA 2010, s. 1181 and Sch. 3, Pt. 1.]

History – Chapter II of Part XI (of which s. 419 formed a part) repealed by CTA 2010, s. 1181 and Sch. 3, Pt. 1, with effect for corporation tax purposes for accounting periods ending on or after 1 April 2010, and for income and capital gains tax purposes for the tax year 2010–11 and subsequent tax years.

Notes – S. 419 rewritten for corporation tax as follows;
S. 419(1): CTA 2010, s. 455(1), 2), 456(1).
S. 419(2): CTA 2010, s. 455(4).
S. 419(3): CTA 2010, s. 455(3).
S. 419(4): CTA 2010, s. 458(1), (2), (3).
S. 419(4A): CTA 2010, s. 458(4), (5).
S. 419(4B): CTA 2010, s. 458(6).
S. 419(5): CTA 2010, s. 459(1), (2), (3).
S. 419(6): CTA 2010, s. 455(6).
S. 419(7): CTA 2010, s. 455(5), 459(4).

420 Exceptions from section 419

History – Chapter II of Part XI omitted by CTA 2010, s. 1177 and Sch. 1, para. 41 and repealed by CTA 2010, s. 1181 and Sch. 3, Pt. 1.

420 [Omitted by CTA 2010, s. 1177 and Sch. 1, para. 41 and repealed by CTA 2010, s. 1181 and Sch. 3, Pt. 1.]

History – Chapter II of Part XI (of which s. 420 formed a part) omitted by CTA 2010, s. 1177 and Sch. 1, para. 41 and repealed by CTA 2010, s. 1181 and Sch. 3, Pt. 1, with effect for corporation tax purposes for accounting periods ending on or after 1 April 2010, and for income and capital gains tax purposes for the tax year 2010–11 and subsequent tax years.

Notes – S. 420 rewritten for corporation tax as follows;
S. 420(1): CTA 2010, s. 456(2).
S. 420(2): CTA 2010, s. 456(3), (4), (5), (6), (7), 457(1), Sch. 2, para. 69(1), (2), (3).

421 Taxation of borrower when loan under section 419 released etc.

History – Chapter II of Part XI omitted by CTA 2010, s. 1177 and Sch. 1, para. 41 and repealed by CTA 2010, s. 1181 and Sch. 3, Pt. 1.

421 [Omitted by CTA 2010, s. 1177 and Sch. 1, para. 41 and repealed by CTA 2010, s. 1181 and Sch. 3, Pt. 1.]

History – Chapter II of Part XI (of which s. 421 formed a part) omitted by CTA 2010, s. 1177 and Sch. 1, para. 41 and repealed by CTA 2010, s. 1181 and Sch. 3, Pt. 1, with effect for corporation tax purposes for accounting periods ending on or after 1 April 2010, and for income and capital gains tax purposes for the tax year 2010–11 and subsequent tax years.

Notes – Rewritten income tax provisions are now located as follows:
S. 421(1): ITTOIA 2005, s. 415(1), 416(1)–(3), 417(1) and (2), 421(1)–(5) and Sch. 1, para. 146.
S. 421(2): ITTOIA 2005, s. 416(3), 417(2), 419(1)–(3), 420(1) and (2), 664(1) and (2) and Sch. 1, para. 146.
S. 421(3): ITTOIA 2005, s. 418(1)–(6).
S. 421(4): ITTOIA 2005, s. 415(5).
S. 421 rewritten for corporation tax as follows;
S. 421(1): CTA 2010, s. 463(1), (2), (3), (4), (5), (6), (7).

422 Extension of section 419 to loans by companies controlled by close companies

History – Chapter II of Part XI omitted by CTA 2010, s. 1177 and Sch. 1, para. 41 and repealed by CTA 2010, s. 1181 and Sch. 3, Pt. 1.

422 [Omitted by CTA 2010, s. 1177 and Sch. 1, para. 41 and repealed by CTA 2010, s. 1181 and Sch. 3, Pt. 1.]

History – Chapter II of Part XI (of which s. 422 formed a part) omitted by CTA 2010, s. 1177 and Sch. 1, para. 41 and repealed by CTA 2010, s. 1181 and Sch. 3, Pt. 1, with effect for corporation tax purposes for accounting periods ending on or after 1 April 2010, and for income and capital gains tax purposes for the tax year 2010–11 and subsequent tax years.

Notes – For income tax purposes, s. 422(5) rewritten as ITTOIA 2005, s. 415(3) and (4) and s. 422(6) as ITTOIA 2005,s. 415(3)–(5).
S. 422 rewritten for corporation tax as follows;
S. 422(1): CTA 2010, s. 460(1), (2), (5).
S. 422(2): CTA 2010, s. 460(1), (3),(5).
S. 422(3): CTA 2010, s. 460(4).
S. 422(4): CTA 2010, s. 461(1), (2).
S. 422(5): CTA 2010, s. 462(1), (2), 464(1), (2).
S. 422(6): CTA 2010, s. 460(1), (2), (3), (4), (7), 461(1), (2), 462(1), (2).

Chapter III – Apportionment of Undistributed Income etc.

Cross references – FA 1989, Sch. 12, Pt. I: administrative provisions in connection with close companies.

Notes – For accounting periods beginning after 31 March 1989, s. 423–430 have, following their repeal by FA 1989, s. 103, 187 and Sch. 17, Pt. V, been replaced by FA 1989, s. 104 and 105 (close investment-holding companies).

423 Apportionment of certain income, deductions and interest

423 [Repealed by FA 1989, s. 103, 187 and Sch. 17, Pt. V in relation to accounting periods beginning after 31 March 1989.]

424 Exclusions from section 423

424 [Repealed by FA 1989, s. 103, 187 and Sch. 17, Pt. V in relation to accounting periods beginning after 31 March 1989.]

425 Manner of apportionment

425 [Repealed by FA 1989, s. 103, 187 and Sch. 17, Pt. V in relation to accounting periods beginning after 31 March 1989.]

426 Charge to income tax where apportionment is to an individual

426 [Repealed by FA 1989, s. 103, 187 and Sch. 17, Pt. V in relation to accounting periods beginning after 31 March 1989.]

427 Reduction of charge under section 426 in certain cases

427 [Repealed by FA 1989, s. 103, 187 and Sch. 17, Pt. V in relation to accounting periods beginning after 31 March 1989.]

428 Increase of apportioned sum etc. by reference to ACT

428 [Repealed by FA 1989, s. 103, 187 and Sch. 17, Pt. V in relation to accounting periods beginning after 31 March 1989.]

429 Payment and collection of income tax

429 [Repealed by FA 1989, s. 103, 187 and Sch. 17, Pt. V in relation to accounting periods beginning after 31 March 1989.]

430 Consequences of apportionment: ACT

430 [Repealed by FA 1989, s. 103, 187 and Sch. 17, Pt. V in relation to accounting periods beginning after 31 March 1989.]

PART XII – SPECIAL CLASSES OF COMPANIES AND BUSINESSES

Chapter I – Insurance Companies, Underwriters and Capital Redemption Business

INSURANCE COMPANIES: GENERAL

Cross references – FA 1989, s. 90A: meaning of expressions used in ICTA 1988, Pt. XII, Ch. I applied to FA 1989, s. 82 to s. 90 and FA 1989, Sch. 8A.
TCGA 1992, s. 214BA: meaning of expressions used in ICTA 1988, Pt. XII, Ch. I applied to TCGA 1992, Pt. VI, Ch. III.

Notes – See also FA 1989, s. 82ff.

431 Interpretative provisions relating to insurance companies

431 [Omitted by FA 2012, s. 146 and Sch. 16, para. 11.]

History – S. 431 omitted by FA 2012, s. 146 and Sch. 16, para. 11 with effect in relation to accounting periods of companies beginning on or after 1 January 2013, subject to transitional provisions contained in FA 2012, Sch. 17. For accounting periods straddling 1 January 2013, FA 2012, s. 149 provides for a deemed cessation on 31 December 2012.

431ZA Election that assets not be foreign business assets

431ZA [Omitted by FA 2012, s. 146 and Sch. 16, para. 12.]

History – S. 431ZA omitted by FA 2012, s. 146 and Sch. 16, para. 12 with effect in relation to accounting periods of companies beginning on or after 1 January 2013, subject to transitional provisions contained in FA 2012, Sch. 17. For accounting periods straddling 1 January 2013, FA 2012, s. 149 provides for a deemed cessation on 31 December 2012.

431AA Relevant benefits for purposes of section 431(4)(d) and (e)

431AA(1) [Repealed by FA 1995, s. 162 and Sch. 29, Pt. VIII(5), with effect in relation to accounting periods beginning on or after 1 January 1995.]

431AB Friendly societies: Meaning of "long-term" insurance fund

431AB [Modification: SI 1997/473, reg. 7A (as inserted by SI 2004/822) inserts s. 431AB. in the case of a Friendly Society not required to keep a separate fund for long-term business.]

431A Amendment of Chapter etc

431A [Omitted by FA 2012, s. 146 and Sch. 16, para. 13.]

History – S. 431A omitted by FA 2012, s. 146 and Sch. 16, para. 13 with effect in relation to accounting periods of companies beginning on or after 1 January 2013, subject to transitional provisions contained in FA 2012, Sch. 17. For accounting periods straddling 1 January 2013, FA 2012, s. 149 provides for a deemed cessation on 31 December 2012.

CLASSES OF LIFE ASSURANCE BUSINESS

431B Meaning of "pension business"

431B [Omitted by FA 2012, s. 146 and Sch. 16, para. 14.]

History – S. 431B omitted by FA 2012, s. 146 and Sch. 16, para. 14 with effect in relation to accounting periods of companies beginning on or after 1 January 2013, subject to transitional provisions contained in FA 2012, Sch. 17. For accounting periods straddling 1 January 2013, FA 2012, s. 149 provides for a deemed cessation on 31 December 2012.

431BA Meaning of "child trust fund business"

431BA [Omitted by FA 2012, s. 146 and Sch. 16, para. 15.]

History – S. 431BA omitted by FA 2012, s. 146 and Sch. 16, para. 15 with effect in relation to accounting periods of companies beginning on or after 1 January 2013, subject to transitional provisions contained in FA 2012, Sch. 17. For accounting periods straddling 1 January 2013, FA 2012, s. 149 provides for a deemed cessation on 31 December 2012.

431BB Meaning of "individual savings account business"

431BB [Omitted by FA 2012, s. 146 and Sch. 16, para. 16.]

History – S. 431BB omitted by FA 2012, s. 146 and Sch. 16, para. 16 with effect in relation to accounting periods of companies beginning on or after 1 January 2013, subject to transitional provisions contained in FA 2012, Sch. 17. For accounting periods straddling 1 January 2013, FA 2012, s. 149 provides for a deemed cessation on 31 December 2012.

431C Meaning of "life reinsurance business"

431C [Omitted by FA 2012, s. 146 and Sch. 16, para. 17.]

History – S. 431C omitted by FA 2012, s. 146 and Sch. 16, para. 17 with effect in relation to accounting periods of companies beginning on or after 1 January 2013, subject to transitional provisions contained in FA 2012, Sch. 17. For accounting periods straddling 1 January 2013, FA 2012, s. 149 provides for a deemed cessation on 31 December 2012.

431D Meaning of "overseas life assurance business"

431D [Omitted by FA 2012, s. 146 and Sch. 16, para. 18.]

History – S. 431D omitted by FA 2012, s. 146 and Sch. 16, para. 18 with effect in relation to accounting periods of companies beginning on or after 1 January 2013, subject to transitional provisions contained in FA 2012, Sch. 17. For accounting periods straddling 1 January 2013, FA 2012, s. 149 provides for a deemed cessation on 31 December 2012.

431E Overseas life assurance business: regulations

431E [Omitted by FA 2012, s. 146 and Sch. 16, para. 18.]

History – S. 431E omitted by FA 2012, s. 146 and Sch. 16, para. 18 with effect in relation to accounting periods of companies beginning on or after 1 January 2013, subject to transitional provisions contained in FA 2012, Sch. 17. For accounting periods straddling 1 January 2013, FA 2012, s. 149 provides for a deemed cessation on 31 December 2012.

431EA Meaning of "gross roll-up business"

431EA [Omitted by FA 2012, s. 146 and Sch. 16, para. 19.]

History – S. 431EA omitted by FA 2012, s. 146 and Sch. 16, para. 19 with effect in relation to accounting periods of companies beginning on or after 1 January 2013, subject to transitional provisions contained in FA 2012, Sch. 17. For accounting periods straddling 1 January 2013, FA 2012, s. 149 provides for a deemed cessation on 31 December 2012.

431F Meaning of "basic life assurance and general annuity business"

431F [Omitted by FA 2012, s. 146 and Sch. 16, para. 20.]

History – S. 431F omitted by FA 2012, s. 146 and Sch. 16, para. 20 with effect in relation to accounting periods of companies beginning on or after 1 January 2013, subject to transitional provisions contained in FA 2012, Sch. 17. For accounting periods straddling 1 January 2013, FA 2012, s. 149 provides for a deemed cessation on 31 December 2012.

431FA Meaning of "tax exempt life assurance business"

431FA [See note below.]

Cross references – SI 2007/2145, reg. 5 introduced s. 431FA as modification for business which is exempt from corporation tax by virtue of ICTA 1988, s. 460(11) or (12), s. 461(4) or (4A) or s. 461B(5) or (6A).

BASIS OF TAXATION ETC

History – Cross heading substituted for the cross heading before s. 432 which read "SEPARATION OF DIFFERENT CATEGORIES OF BUSINESS" by FA 2007, s. 39 and Sch. 8, para. 4, with effect for periods of account of insurance companies beginning on or after 1 January 2007. Former heading inserted by FA 1995, s. 51 and Sch. 8, para. 51(2) in relation to accounting periods beginning on or after 1 January 1995.

431G Company carrying on life assurance business

431G [Omitted by FA 2012, s. 146 and Sch. 16, para. 21.]

History – S. 431G omitted by FA 2012, s. 146 and Sch. 16, para. 21 with effect in relation to accounting periods of companies beginning on or after 1 January 2013, subject to transitional provisions contained in FA 2012, Sch. 17. For accounting periods straddling 1 January 2013, FA 2012, s. 149 provides for a deemed cessation on 31 December 2012.

431H Company carrying on life assurance business and other insurance business

431H [Omitted by FA 2012, s. 146 and Sch. 16, para. 22.]

History – S. 431H omitted by FA 2012, s. 146 and Sch. 16, para. 22 with effect in relation to accounting periods of companies beginning on or after 1 January 2013, subject to transitional provisions contained in FA 2012, Sch. 17. For accounting periods straddling 1 January 2013, FA 2012, s. 149 provides for a deemed cessation on 31 December 2012.

432 Separation of different categories of business

432 [Substituted with s. 431G and 431H by FA 2007, s. 39 and Sch. 8, para. 4.]

History – S. 432 substituted with s. 431G and 431H by FA 2007, s. 39 and Sch. 8, para. 4, with effect for periods of account of insurance companies beginning on or after 1 January 2007.

Derivations – (as originally enacted) – ICTA 1970, s. 307.

432YA PHI business – adjustment consequent on change in Insurance Prudential Sourcebook

432YA [Omitted by FA 2012, s. 146 and Sch. 16, para. 23.]

History – S. 432YA omitted by FA 2012, s. 146 and Sch. 16, para. 23 with effect in relation to accounting periods of companies beginning on or after 1 January 2013, subject to transitional provisions contained in FA 2012, Sch. 17. For accounting periods straddling 1 January 2013, FA 2012, s. 149 provides for a deemed cessation on 31 December 2012.

432ZA Linked assets

432ZA [Omitted by FA 2012, s. 146 and Sch. 16, para. 24.]

History – S. 432ZA omitted by FA 2012, s. 146 and Sch. 16, para. 24 with effect in relation to accounting periods of companies beginning on or after 1 January 2013, subject to transitional provisions contained in FA 2012, Sch. 17. For accounting periods straddling 1 January 2013, FA 2012, s. 149 provides for a deemed cessation on 31 December 2012.

432A Apportionment of income and gains

432A [Omitted by FA 2012, s. 146 and Sch. 16, para. 25.]

History – S. 432A omitted by FA 2012, s. 146 and Sch. 16, para. 25 with effect in relation to accounting periods of companies beginning on or after 1 January 2013, subject to transitional provisions contained in FA 2012, Sch. 17. For accounting periods straddling 1 January 2013, FA 2012, s. 149 provides for a deemed cessation on 31 December 2012.

432AA UK property business or overseas property business

432AA [Omitted by FA 2012, s. 146 and Sch. 16, para. 26.]

History – S. 432AA omitted by FA 2012, s. 146 and Sch. 16, para. 26 with effect in relation to accounting periods of companies beginning on or after 1 January 2013, subject to transitional provisions contained in FA 2012, Sch. 17. For accounting periods straddling 1 January 2013, FA 2012, s. 149 provides for a deemed cessation on 31 December 2012.

432AB Losses from UK property business or overseas property business

432AB [Omitted by FA 2012, s. 146 and Sch. 16, para. 27.]

History – S. 432AB omitted by FA 2012, s. 146 and Sch. 16, para. 27 with effect in relation to accounting periods of companies beginning on or after 1 January 2013, subject to transitional provisions contained in FA 2012, Sch. 17. For accounting periods straddling 1 January 2013, FA 2012, s. 149 provides for a deemed cessation on 31 December 2012.

432B Apportionment of receipts brought into account

432B [Omitted by FA 2012, s. 146 and Sch. 16, para. 28.]

History – S. 432B omitted by FA 2012, s. 146 and Sch. 16, para. 28 with effect in relation to accounting periods of companies beginning on or after 1 January 2013, subject to transitional provisions contained in FA 2012, Sch. 17. For accounting periods straddling 1 January 2013, FA 2012, s. 149 provides for a deemed cessation on 31 December 2012.

432C Section 432B apportionment: non-participating funds

432C [Omitted by FA 2012, s. 146 and Sch. 16, para. 28.]

History – S. 432C omitted by FA 2012, s. 146 and Sch. 16, para. 28 with effect in relation to accounting periods of companies beginning on or after 1 January 2013, subject to transitional provisions contained in FA 2012, Sch. 17. For accounting periods straddling 1 January 2013, FA 2012, s. 149 provides for a deemed cessation on 31 December 2012.

432CA Apportionment of asset value increase where line 51 amount decreases

432CA [Omitted by FA 2012, s. 146 and Sch. 16, para. 28.]

History – S. 432CA omitted by FA 2012, s. 146 and Sch. 16, para. 28 with effect in relation to accounting periods of companies beginning on or after 1 January 2013, subject to transitional provisions contained in FA 2012, Sch. 17. For accounting periods straddling 1 January 2013, FA 2012, s. 149 provides for a deemed cessation on 31 December 2012.

432CB Transfers of business involving excess assets

432CB [Omitted by FA 2012, s. 146 and Sch. 16, para. 28.]

History – S. 432CB omitted by FA 2012, s. 146 and Sch. 16, para. 28 with effect in relation to accounting periods of companies beginning on or after 1 January 2013, subject to transitional provisions contained in FA 2012, Sch. 17. For accounting periods straddling 1 January 2013, FA 2012, s. 149 provides for a deemed cessation on 31 December 2012.

432D Section 432B apportionment: value of non-participating funds

432D [Omitted by FA 2007, s. 38 and Sch. 7, para. 18 and repealed by FA 2007, s. 114 and Sch. 27, Pt. 2(7).]

History – S. 432D omitted by FA 2007, s. 38 and Sch. 7, para. 18 and repealed by s. 114 and Sch. 27, Pt. 2(7), with effect for the purposes of corporation tax, for periods of account of insurance companies beginning on or after 1 January 2007, and for the purposes of income tax, for the tax year 2007–08 and subsequent tax years (but see transitional provisions at FA 2007, Sch. 7, para. 80–84).

432E Section 432B apportionment: participating funds

432E [Omitted by FA 2012, s. 146 and Sch. 16, para. 28.]

History – S. 432E omitted by FA 2012, s. 146 and Sch. 16, para. 28 with effect in relation to accounting periods of companies beginning on or after 1 January 2013, subject to transitional provisions contained in FA 2012, Sch. 17. For accounting periods straddling 1 January 2013, FA 2012, s. 149 provides for a deemed cessation on 31 December 2012.

432F Section 432B apportionment: supplementary provisions

432F [Omitted by FA 2012, s. 146 and Sch. 16, para. 28.]

History – S. 432F omitted by FA 2012, s. 146 and Sch. 16, para. 28 with effect in relation to accounting periods of companies beginning on or after 1 January 2013, subject to transitional provisions contained in FA 2012, Sch. 17. For accounting periods straddling 1 January 2013, FA 2012, s. 149 provides for a deemed cessation on 31 December 2012.

432G Section 432B apportionment: business transfers-in

432G [Omitted by FA 2012, s. 146 and Sch. 16, para. 28.]

History – S. 432G omitted by FA 2012, s. 146 and Sch. 16, para. 28 with effect in relation to accounting periods of companies beginning on or after 1 January 2013, subject to transitional provisions contained in FA 2012, Sch. 17. For accounting periods straddling 1 January 2013, FA 2012, s. 149 provides for a deemed cessation on 31 December 2012.

433 Profits reserved for policy holders and annuitants

433 [Repealed by FA 1989, s. 84 and Sch. 8, para. 2, s. 187 and Sch. 17, Pt. IV, with effect from 14 March 1989; but relevant for the purposes of FA 1989, s. 82B(4), as inserted by FA 2003, Sch. 33, para. 1(1).]

MISCELLANEOUS PROVISIONS RELATING TO LIFE ASSURANCE BUSINESS

History – Heading inserted by FA 1995, s. 51 and Sch. 8, para. 51(4) in relation to accounting periods beginning on or after 1 January 1995.

434 Franked investment income etc.

434 [Omitted by FA 2012, s. 146 and Sch. 16, para. 29.]

History – S. 434 omitted by FA 2012, s. 146 and Sch. 16, para. 29 with effect in relation to accounting periods of companies beginning on or after 1 January 2013, subject to transitional provisions contained in FA 2012, Sch. 17. For accounting periods straddling 1 January 2013, FA 2012, s. 149 provides for a deemed cessation on 31 December 2012.

434A Computation of losses and limitation on relief

434A [Omitted by FA 2012, s. 146 and Sch. 16, para. 30.]

History – S. 434A omitted by FA 2012, s. 146 and Sch. 16, para. 30 with effect in relation to accounting periods of companies beginning on or after 1 January 2013, subject to transitional provisions contained in FA 2012, Sch. 17. For accounting periods straddling 1 January 2013, FA 2012, s. 149 provides for a deemed cessation on 31 December 2012.

434AZA Reduced loss relief for additions to non-profit funds

434AZA [Omitted by FA 2012, s. 146 and Sch. 16, para. 31.]

History – S. 434AZA omitted by FA 2012, s. 146 and Sch. 16, para. 31 with effect in relation to accounting periods of companies beginning on or after 1 January 2013, subject to transitional provisions contained in FA 2012, Sch. 17. For accounting periods straddling 1 January 2013, FA 2012, s. 149 provides for a deemed cessation on 31 December 2012.

434AZB Additions to non-profit funds: amount of loss reduction

434AZB [Omitted by FA 2012, s. 146 and Sch. 16, para. 31.]

History – S. 434AZB omitted by FA 2012, s. 146 and Sch. 16, para. 31 with effect in relation to accounting periods of companies beginning on or after 1 January 2013, subject to transitional provisions contained in FA 2012, Sch. 17. For accounting periods straddling 1 January 2013, FA 2012, s. 149 provides for a deemed cessation on 31 December 2012.

434AZC Sections 434AZA and 434AZB: supplementary

434AZC [Omitted by FA 2012, s. 146 and Sch. 16, para. 31.]

History – S. 434AZC omitted by FA 2012, s. 146 and Sch. 16, para. 31 with effect in relation to accounting periods of companies beginning on or after 1 January 2013, subject to transitional provisions contained in FA 2012, Sch. 17. For accounting periods straddling 1 January 2013, FA 2012, s. 149 provides for a deemed cessation on 31 December 2012.

434AA Treatment of annuities

434AA [S. 434AA is treated as inserted in relation to overseas life insurance companies with effect from 31 December 2006 for accounting periods ending on or after that date. See SI 2006/3271, reg. 10.]

Notes – S. 434AA is treated as inserted by SI 2006/3271, reg. 10 in relation to overseas life insurance companies with effect from 31 December 2006 for accounting periods ending on or after that date.

434AB Treatment of annuities

434AB [S. 434AB is treated as inserted in relation to overseas life insurance companies for accounting periods beginning on or after 1 January 1995. See Sch. 19AC, para. 9B for wording.]

Notes – S. 434AB is treated as inserted in relation to overseas life insurance companies for accounting periods beginning on or after 1 January 1995. See Sch. 19AC, para. 9B for wording.

434B Treatment of interest and annuities

434B(1) [Repealed by FA 1996, s. 165(3) and s. 205 and Sch. 41, Pt. V(25).]

434B(2) [Repealed by FA 1997, s. 113 and Sch. 18, Pt. VI(6).]

History – S. 434B(1) repealed by FA 1996, s. 165(3) and s. 205 and Sch. 41, Pt. V(25) for accounting periods beginning on or after 1 January 1996, subject to FA 1996, s. 165(5).
S. 434B(2) repealed by FA 1997, s. 113 and Sch. 18, Pt. VI(6) in relation to accounting periods beginning after 5 March 1997.

434C Interest on repayment of advance corporation tax

434C [Repealed by FA 1998, s. 31 and Sch. 3, para. 26; s. 165 and Sch. 27, Pt. III(2).]

History – S. 434C repealed by FA 1998, s. 31 and Sch. 3, para. 26; s. 165 and Sch. 27, Pt. III(2) with effect in relation to distributions made on or after 6 April 1999.

434D Capital allowances: management assets

434D [Repealed by CAA 2001, s. 578 and Sch. 2, para. 39, s. 580 and Sch. 4.]

History – S. 434D repealed by CAA 2001, s. 578 and Sch. 2, para. 39, s. 580 and Sch. 4, with effect as respects allowances and charges falling to be made for chargeable periods ending, for income tax purposes, on or after 6 April 2001, and, for corporation tax purposes, on or after 1 April 2001.

Notes – S. 434D and 434E are rewritten as CAA 2001, s. 255 to 257, 544 and 545.

434E Capital allowances: investment assets

434E [Repealed by CAA 2001, s. 578 and Sch. 2, para. 39, s. 580 and Sch. 4.]

History – S. 434E repealed by CAA 2001, s. 578 and Sch. 2, para. 39, s. 580 and Sch. 4, with effect as respects allowances and charges falling to be made for chargeable periods ending, for income tax purposes, on or after 6 April 2001, and, for corporation tax purposes, on or after 1 April 2001.

Notes – S. 434D and 434E are rewritten as CAA 2001, s. 255 to 257, 544 and 545.

435 Taxation of gains reserved for policy holders and annuitants

435 [Repealed by FA 1989, s. 84 and Sch. 8, para. 5, s. 187 and Sch. 17, Pt. IV, with respect to accounting periods beginning on or after 1 January 1990 (including the 1990 component period within FA 1989, s. 84(3)).]

436 Pension business: separate charge on profits

History – In the heading for s. 436 the words "Pension business" substituted by FA 1995, s. 51 and Sch. 8, para. 51(5), with effect in relation to accounting periods beginning on or after 1 January 1995.

436 [Omitted by FA 2007, s. 38 and Sch. 7, para. 24 and repealed by s. 114 and Sch. 27, Pt. 2(7).]

History – S. 436 omitted by FA 2007, s. 38 and Sch. 7, para. 24 and repealed by s. 114 and Sch. 27, Pt. 2(7), with effect for the purposes of corporation tax, for periods of account of insurance companies beginning on or after 1 January 2007, and for the purposes of income tax, for the tax year 2007–08 and subsequent tax years (but see transitional provisions at FA 2007, Sch. 7 para. 80–84). Former s. 436 read as follows:

"Pension business: separate charge on profits

History – In the heading for s. 436 the words "Pension business" substituted by FA 1995, s. 51 and Sch. 8, para. 51(5), with effect in relation to accounting periods beginning on or after 1 January 1995.

436(1) Subject to the provisions of this section, profits arising to an insurance company from pension business shall be treated as income within Schedule D, and be chargeable under Case VI of that Schedule, and for that purpose–

(a) that business shall be treated separately, and

(b) subject to paragraph (a) above, and to subsection (3) below, the profits therefrom shall be computed in accordance with the provisions of this Act applicable to Case I of Schedule D.

436(2) Subsection (1) above shall not apply to an insurance company charged to corporation tax in accordance with the provisions applicable to Case I of Schedule D in respect of the profits of its ordinary life assurance business.

436(3) In making the computation referred to in subsection (1) above–

(a) sections 82 and 82B to 83AB of the Finance Act 1989 shall apply with the necessary modifications

(aa) [Repealed by FA 1996, s. 163, Sch. 31, para. 7 and s. 205, Sch. 41, Pt. V(23).]

(b) [Repealed by FA 1989, s. 87(4), (5), 187 and Sch. 17, Pt. IV;]

ICTA 1988

(c) there may be set off against the profits any loss, to be computed on the same basis as the profits, which has arisen from pension business in any previous accounting period or year of assessment;

(d)–(e) [Repealed by F(No. 2)A 1997, s. 23 and Sch. 3, para. 5(1), s. 52 and Sch. 8, Pt. II(6).]

436(4) Section 396 shall not be taken to apply to a loss incurred by a company on its pension business.

436(5) Nothing in section 128 or 399(1) shall affect the operation of this section.

History – In s. 436(1), words "general annuity business or" which appeared before words "pension business" repealed by FA 1991, s. 48 and Sch. 7, para. 4(1)(a), s. 123 and Sch. 19, Pt. V, and words "that business" substituted by FA 1991, s. 48 and Sch. 7, para. 4(1)(b), effective with respect to accounting periods beginning on or after 1 January 1992.

In s. 436(3)(a), the reference to "82B to 83AB" inserted in place of "83" by FA 2003, s. 170 and Sch. 33, para. 1(3) with effect for accounting periods beginning on or after 1 January 2003.

In s. 436(3)(a), the words which followed the word "modifications", i.e. "and in particular with the omission of all references to policy holders (other than holders of policies referable to pension business) and of the words "and any amounts of tax which are expended on behalf of" in section 82(1)(a)"; omitted by FA 2003, s. 170 and Sch. 33, para. 1(3); FA 2003, s. 216 and Sch. 43, Pt. 3(12) with effect for accounting periods beginning on or after 1 January 2003.

In s. 436(3)(a), the words "and any amounts of tax which are expended on behalf of" substituted for "tax or" by FA 2000, s. 103 and Sch. 30, para. 18(3) with effect in relation to periods of account beginning on or after 1 April 2000. (S. 436(3)(a) formerly provided for the omission of the words "tax or" in FA 1989, s. 82(1)(a) for certain purposes but this amendment was necessaryas a consequence of other amendments to s. 82(1)(a) itself by FA 2000.)

In s. 436(3)(a), words from "and of ..." to the end inserted by FA 1990, s. 43(2), with respect to accounting periods beginning on or after 1 January 1990 (including the 1990 component period within FA 1989, s. 84(3)).

In s. 436(3)(a), words "sections 82 and 83 of the Finance Act 1989" previously substituted by FA 1989, s. 84 and Sch. 8, para. 6, with effect from 14 March 1989.

S. 436(3)(aa) inserted by FA 1995, s. 51 and Sch. 8, para. 16(4), with effect in relation to accounting periods ending on or after 1 January 1995, but repealed by FA 1996, s. 163, Sch. 31, para. 7 and s. 205, Sch. 41, Pt. V(23) for periods of account beginning on or after 1 January 1996, subject to FA 1996, Sch. 31, para. 9.

The repeal of s. 436(3)(b) has effect with respect to accounting periods beginning on or after 1 January 1990, in accordance with FA 1989, s. 83(5).

In s. 436(3)(c), words "or general annuity business" which appeared after words "pension business", in s. 436(3)(e) words "general annuity business or" which appeared before words "pension business", and in s. 436(4) the "general annuity business or" which appeared before words "pension business", repealed by FA 1991, s. 48 and Sch. 7, para. 4(2), (3), s. 123 and Sch. 19, Pt. V, effective with respect to accounting periods beginning on or after 1 January 1992.

S. 436(3)(d) repealed by F(No. 2)A 1997, s. 23 and Sch. 3, para. 5(1), s. 52 and Sch. 8, Pt. II(6), with effect in relation to distributions made on or after 2 July 1997.

S. 436(3)(d)(i) substituted by FA 1990, s. 41 and Sch. 6, para. 5, with deemed effect from 1 January 1990, but subject to the provisions of FA 1990, Sch. 6, para. 11, 12.

In s. 436(3)(d), words from "and" immediately preceding subpara. (ii) to the end of the paragraph repealed by FA 1995, s. 162 and Sch. 29, Pt. VIII(5), with effect in relation to accounting periods beginning on or after 1 January 1995.

S. 436(3)(e) repealed by F(No. 2)A 1997, s. 23 and Sch. 3, para. 5(1), s. 52 and Sch. 8, Pt. II(6), with effect in relation to distributions made on or after 2 July 1997.

Derivations – S. 436(1) (as originally enacted): ICTA 1970, s. 312(1), as amended by FA 1970, s. 26(3) and Sch. 5, Pt. III, para. 11(3).

S. 436(2): proviso to ICTA 1970, s. 312(1).

S. 436(3)(a)–(c) (as originally enacted): ICTA 1970, s. 312(2), as amended by FA 1970, s. 26(3) and Sch. 5, Pt. III, para. 11(6)(a), (b); FA 1987, Sch. 16, Pt. VII.

S. 436(3)(d) (as originally enacted): ICTA 1970, s. 314(5), as amended by FA 1970, s. 26(3) and Sch. 5, Pt. III, para. 11(3).

S. 436(3)(e) (as originally enacted): FA 1972, Sch. 18, para. 5(1)(a).

S. 436(4) (as originally enacted): ICTA 1970, s. 312(3), as amended by FA 1970, s. 26(3) and Sch. 5, Pt. III, para. 11(3).

S. 436(5): FA 1985, s. 72(7).

Cross references – S. 76(2B): inclusion of Sch. D Case VI profits chargeable under ICTA 1988, s. 436; s. 439B; and s. 441 in the computation of "relevant income".

S. 128: non-trading profits from transactions in commodity and financial futures and qualifying options not taxable under Sch. D.

S. 337(2)(b): annuities paid not deductible.

S. 396: set-off and carry-forward of Sch. D, Case VI losses.

S. 399(1): non-trading losses arising from transactions in commodity and financial futures and qualifying options not available for loss relief.

S. 724: transfer of securities taken into account for s. 436 not to fall under s. 713(2)(a), (3)(a) (transfers with/without accrued interest).

S. 761 and Sch. 28, para. 3(4): where profit attributable to material disposal in offshore fund is taken into account in computation under s. 436 (subject to s. 437(2)) any unindexed gain computed as if TCGA 1992, s. 37(1) (exclusion of amounts charged as income) did not apply.

S. 808: interest or dividends tax-exempt under double taxation arrangements received by non-resident carrying on insurance business in UK not to be excluded from profits so as to create a loss to be set off under s. 436(3)(c).

Sch. 28, para. 3(4)(a): in relation to offshore income gains, unindexed gain where profit within s. 436 (without reference to s. 437(2)) ignores TCGA 1992, s. 37(1) (exclusion of certain sums).

FA 1989, s. 43(13): in s. 436(1)(b) reference to "this Act" is deemed to include a reference to FA 1989, s. 43 (Sch. D computation following change to receipts basis of assessment for Sch. E).

FA 1989, s. 88(3A): inclusion of Sch. D Case VI profits chargeable under ICTA 1988, s. 436; s. 439B; and s. 441 in the computation of "relevant profits".

FA 1989, s. 89(1A): treatment of Sch. D Case VI profits chargeable under ICTA 1988, s. 436; s. 439B; and s. 441 in the computation of "the policy holders' share of the relevant profits".

CAA 2001, s. 256(3)(a): giving effect to allowances and charges where a company is charged to tax under s. 436.

CAA 2001, s. 545(5)(a): if a company is charged to tax under s. 436, no allowance on any investment asset may be taken into account in calculating its profits from life assurance business.

SI 2005/2014, reg. 13: modification of s. 436 to make it applicable to friendly societies carrying on life assurance business (which is not entirely exempt).

Statements of practice – SP 4/95: computation of profit of long term insurance business."

436A Gross roll-up business: separate charge on profits

436A *[Omitted by FA 2012, s. 146 and Sch. 16, para. 32.]*

History – S. 436A omitted by FA 2012, s. 146 and Sch. 16, para. 32 with effect in relation to accounting periods of companies beginning on or after 1 January 2013, subject to transitional provisions contained in FA 2012, Sch. 17. For accounting periods straddling 1 January 2013, FA 2012, s. 149 provides for a deemed cessation on 31 December 2012.

436B Gains referable to gross roll-up business not to be chargeable gains

436B [Omitted by FA 2012, s. 146 and Sch. 16, para. 33.]

History – S. 436B omitted by FA 2012, s. 146 and Sch. 16, para. 33 with effect in relation to accounting periods of companies beginning on or after 1 January 2013, subject to transitional provisions contained in FA 2012, Sch. 17. For accounting periods straddling 1 January 2013, FA 2012, s. 149 provides for a deemed cessation on 31 December 2012.

437 General annuity business

437 [Omitted by FA 2012, s. 146 and Sch. 16, para. 34.]

History – S. 437 omitted by FA 2012, s. 146 and Sch. 16, para. 34 with effect in relation to accounting periods of companies beginning on or after 1 January 2013, subject to transitional provisions contained in FA 2012, Sch. 17. For accounting periods straddling 1 January 2013, FA 2012, s. 149 provides for a deemed cessation on 31 December 2012.

437A Meaning of "steep-reduction annuity" etc.

437A [Omitted by FA 2012, s. 146 and Sch. 16, para. 34.]

History – S. 437A omitted by FA 2012, s. 146 and Sch. 16, para. 34 with effect in relation to accounting periods of companies beginning on or after 1 January 2013, subject to transitional provisions contained in FA 2012, Sch. 17. For accounting periods straddling 1 January 2013, FA 2012, s. 149 provides for a deemed cessation on 31 December 2012.

438 Pension business: exemption from tax

438 [Omitted by FA 2012, s. 146 and Sch. 16, para. 35.]

History – S. 438 omitted by FA 2012, s. 146 and Sch. 16, para. 35 with effect in relation to accounting periods of companies beginning on or after 1 January 2013, subject to transitional provisions contained in FA 2012, Sch. 17. For accounting periods straddling 1 January 2013, FA 2012, s. 149 provides for a deemed cessation on 31 December 2012.

438A Pension business: payments on account of tax credits and deducted tax

438A [Repealed by FA 2001, s. 87, 110 and Sch. 33, Pt. 2(12).]

History – Repealed by FA 2001, s. 87, 110 and Sch. 33, Pt. 2(12) with effect in relation to income tax deducted from payments received after 30 September 2001 and with effect in relation to tax credits in accordance with the deferred repeal of Sch. 19AB (see History note at the start of that schedule).

438B Income or gains arising from property investment LLP

438B [Omitted by FA 2007, s. 38 and Sch. 7, para. 27 and repealed by s. 114 and Sch. 27, Pt. 2(7).]

History – S. 438B omitted by FA 2007, s. 38 and Sch. 7, para. 27 and repealed by s. 114 and Sch. 27, Pt. 2(7), with effect for the purposes of corporation tax, for periods of account of insurance companies beginning on or after 1 January 2007, and for the purposes of income tax, for the tax year 2007-08 and subsequent tax years (but see transitional provisions at FA 2007, Sch. 7, para. 80–84).

438C Determination of policy holders' share for purposes of s. 438B

438C [Omitted by FA 2007, s. 38 and Sch. 7, para. 28 and repealed by s. 114 and Sch. 27, Pt. 2(7).]

History – S. 438C omitted by FA 2007, s. 38 and Sch. 7, para. 28 and repealed by FA 2007, s. 114 and Sch. 27, Pt. 2(7), with effect for the purposes of corporation tax, for periods of account of insurance companies beginning on or after 1 January 2007, and for the purposes of income tax, for the tax year 2007–08 and subsequent tax years (but see transitional provisions at FA 2007, Sch. 7, para. 80–84).

439 Restricted government securities

439 [Omitted by FA 2007, s. 38 and Sch. 7, para. 29 and repealed by s. 114 and Sch. 27, Pt. 2(7).]

History – S. 439 omitted by FA 2007, s. 38 and Sch. 7, para. 29 and repealed by s. 114 and Sch. 27, Pt. 2(7), with effect for the purposes of corporation tax, for periods of account of insurance companies beginning on or after 1 January 2007, and for the purposes of income tax, for the tax year 2007–08 and subsequent tax years (but see transitional provisions at FA 2007, Sch. 7, para. 80–84).

439A Taxation of pure reinsurance business

439A [Omitted by FA 2007, s. 39 and Sch. 8, para. 7 and repealed by FA 2007, s. 114 and Sch. 27, Pt. 2(8).]

History – S. 439A omitted by FA 2007, s. 39 and Sch. 8, para. 7 and repealed by s. 114 and Sch. 27, Pt. 2(8), with effect for periods of account of insurance companies beginning on or after 1 January 2007.

440 Transfers of assets etc.

440 [Omitted by FA 2012, s. 146 and Sch. 16, para. 36.]

History – S. 440 omitted by FA 2012, s. 146 and Sch. 16, para. 36 with effect in relation to accounting periods of companies beginning on or after 1 January 2013, subject to transitional provisions contained in FA 2012, Sch. 17. For accounting periods straddling 1 January 2013, FA 2012, s. 149 provides for a deemed cessation on 31 December 2012.

440A Securities

440A [Omitted by FA 2012, s. 146 and Sch. 16, para. 37.]

History – S. 440A omitted by FA 2012, s. 146 and Sch. 16, para. 37 with effect in relation to accounting periods of companies beginning on or after 1 January 2013, subject to transitional provisions contained in FA 2012, Sch. 17. For accounting periods straddling 1 January 2013, FA 2012, s. 149 provides for a deemed cessation on 31 December 2012.

440B Modifications where tax charged under section 35 of CTA 2009

440B [Omitted by FA 2012, s. 146 and Sch. 16, para. 38.]

History – S. 440B omitted by FA 2012, s. 146 and Sch. 16, para. 38 with effect in relation to accounting periods of companies beginning on or after 1 January 2013, subject to transitional provisions contained in FA 2012, Sch. 17. For accounting periods straddling 1 January 2013, FA 2012, s. 149 provides for a deemed cessation on 31 December 2012.

440C Modifications for change of tax basis

440C [Omitted by FA 2012, s. 146 and Sch. 16, para. 39.]

History – S. 440C omitted by FA 2012, s. 146 and Sch. 16, para. 39 with effect in relation to accounting periods of companies beginning on or after 1 January 2013, subject to transitional provisions contained in FA 2012, Sch. 17. For accounting periods straddling 1 January 2013, FA 2012, s. 149 provides for a deemed cessation on 31 December 2012.

440D Modifications in relation to BLAGAB group reinsurers

440D [Omitted by FA 2012, s. 146 and Sch. 16, para. 40.]

History – S. 440D omitted by FA 2012, s. 146 and Sch. 16, para. 40 with effect in relation to accounting periods of companies beginning on or after 1 January 2013, subject to transitional provisions contained in FA 2012, Sch. 17. For accounting periods straddling 1 January 2013, FA 2012, s. 149 provides for a deemed cessation on 31 December 2012.

441 Overseas life assurance business

441 [Omitted by FA 2007, s. 38 and Sch. 7, para. 34 and repealed by s. 114 and Sch. 27, Pt. 2(7).]

History – S. 441 omitted by FA 2007, s. 38 and Sch. 7, para. 34 and repealed by s. 114 and Sch. 27, Pt. 2(7), with effect for the purposes of corporation tax, for periods of account of insurance companies beginning on or after 1 January 2007, and for the purposes of income tax, for the tax year 2007–08 and subsequent tax years (but see transitional provisions at FA 2007, Sch. 7, para. 80–84).

441A Section 441: distributions

441A(1) [Repealed by F(No. 2)A 1997, s. 23 and Sch. 3, para. 9(2), s. 52 and Sch. 8, Pt. II(6).]

441A(2)–(8) [Repealed by F(No. 2)A 1997, s. 34 and Sch. 4, para. 28(1), s. 52 and Sch. 8, Pt. II(10).]

History – S. 441A(1) repealed by F(No. 2)A 1997, s. 23 and Sch. 3, para. 9(2), s. 52 and Sch. 8, Pt. II(6) in relation to distributions made on or after 2 July 1996.
S. 441A(2)–(8) repealed by F(No. 2)A 1997, s. 34 and Sch. 4, para. 28(1), s. 52 and Sch. 8, Pt. II(10), with effect in relation to distributions made on or after 6 April 1999.

441B Treatment of UK land

441B [Repealed by SI 2007/2086, reg. 6(2)(a).]

History – S. 441B repealed by SI 2007/2086, reg. 6(2)(a), with effect for accounting periods beginning on or after 13 August 2007.

442 Overseas business of UK companies

442 [Omitted by FA 2012, s. 146 and Sch. 16, para. 41.]

History – S. 442 omitted by FA 2012, s. 146 and Sch. 16, para. 41 with effect in relation to accounting periods of companies beginning on or after 1 January 2013, subject to transitional provisions contained in FA 2012, Sch. 17. For accounting periods straddling 1 January 2013, FA 2012, s. 149 provides for a deemed cessation on 31 December 2012.

442A Taxation of investment return where risk reinsured

442A [Omitted by FA 2012, s. 146 and Sch. 16, para. 42.]

History – S. 442A omitted by FA 2012, s. 146 and Sch. 16, para. 42 with effect in relation to accounting periods of companies beginning on or after 1 January 2013, subject to transitional provisions contained in FA 2012, Sch. 17. For accounting periods straddling 1 January 2013, FA 2012, s. 149 provides for a deemed cessation on 31 December 2012.

443 Life policies carrying rights not in money

443 [Omitted by FA 2007, s. 41 and Sch. 10, para. 16(3)(d) and repealed by s. 114 and Sch. 27, Pt. 2(10).]

History – S. 443 omitted by FA 2007, *s. 41 and Sch. 10*, para. 16(3)(d) and repealed by s. 114 and Sch. 27, Pt. 2(10), with effect from 19 *July 2007*.

Notes – ICTA 1988, s. 443 is not rewritten by ITTOIA 2005 as it is no longer necessary. (See ITTOIA 2005, Explanatory Notes, Annex 1, Table 1 (Change 158).)

444 Life policies issued before 5th August 1965

444 [Omitted by FA 2007, s. 41 and Sch. 10, para. 16(3)(e) and repealed by s. 114 and Sch. 27, Pt. 2(10).]

History – S. 444 omitted by FA 2007, s. 41 and Sch. 10, para. 16(3)(e) and repealed by s. 114 and Sch. 27, Pt. 2(10), with effect from 19 July 2007.

444A Transfers of business

444A [Omitted by FA 2012, s. 146 and Sch. 16, para. 43.]

History – S. 444A omitted by FA 2012, s. 146 and Sch. 16, para. 43 with effect in relation to accounting periods of companies beginning on or after 1 January 2013, subject to transitional provisions contained in FA 2012, Sch. 17. For accounting periods straddling 1 January 2013, FA 2012, s. 149 provides for a deemed cessation on 31 December 2012.

444AZA Transfers of life assurance business: gross roll-up business losses of the transferor

444AZA [Omitted by FA 2012, s. 146 and Sch. 16, para. 43.]

History – S. 444AZA omitted by FA 2012, s. 146 and Sch. 16, para. 43 with effect in relation to accounting periods of companies beginning on or after 1 January 2013, subject to transitional provisions contained in FA 2012, Sch. 17. For accounting periods straddling 1 January 2013, FA 2012, s. 149 provides for a deemed cessation on 31 December 2012.

444AZB Transfers of life assurance business: trade losses of the transferor

444AZB [Omitted by FA 2012, s. 146 and Sch. 16, para. 43.]

History – S. 444AZB omitted by FA 2012, s. 146 and Sch. 16, para. 43 with effect in relation to accounting periods of companies beginning on or after 1 January 2013, subject to transitional provisions contained in FA 2012, Sch. 17. For accounting periods straddling 1 January 2013, FA 2012, s. 149 provides for a deemed cessation on 31 December 2012.

444AA Transfers of business: deemed periodical returns

444AA [Omitted by FA 2012, s. 146 and Sch. 16, para. 43.]

History – S. 444AA omitted by FA 2012, s. 146 and Sch. 16, para. 43 with effect in relation to accounting periods of companies beginning on or after 1 January 2013, subject to transitional provisions contained in FA 2012, Sch. 17. For accounting periods straddling 1 January 2013, FA 2012, s. 149 provides for a deemed cessation on 31 December 2012.

444AB Transfer schemes: transferor

444AB [Omitted by FA 2012, s. 146 and Sch. 16, para. 43.]

History – S. 444AB omitted by FA 2012, s. 146 and Sch. 16, para. 43 with effect in relation to accounting periods of companies beginning on or after 1 January 2013, subject to transitional provisions contained in FA 2012, Sch. 17. For accounting periods straddling 1 January 2013, FA 2012, s. 149 provides for a deemed cessation on 31 December 2012.

444ABA Non long-term fund transferred assets

444ABA [Omitted by FA 2012, s. 146 and Sch. 16, para. 43.]

History – S. 444ABA omitted by FA 2012, s. 146 and Sch. 16, para. 43 with effect in relation to accounting periods of companies beginning on or after 1 January 2013, subject to transitional provisions contained in FA 2012, Sch. 17. For accounting periods straddling 1 January 2013, FA 2012, s. 149 provides for a deemed cessation on 31 December 2012.

444ABAA Non-profit fund transferred assets

444ABAA [Omitted by FA 2012, s. 146 and Sch. 16, para. 43.]

History – S. 444ABAA omitted by FA 2012, s. 146 and Sch. 16, para. 43 with effect in relation to accounting periods of companies beginning on or after 1 January 2013, subject to transitional provisions contained in FA 2012, Sch. 17. For accounting periods straddling 1 January 2013, FA 2012, s. 149 provides for a deemed cessation on 31 December 2012.

444ABB Retained assets

444ABB [Omitted by FA 2012, s. 146 and Sch. 16, para. 43.]

History – S. 444ABB omitted by FA 2012, s. 146 and Sch. 16, para. 43 with effect in relation to accounting periods of companies beginning on or after 1 January 2013, subject to transitional provisions contained in FA 2012, Sch. 17. For accounting periods straddling 1 January 2013, FA 2012, s. 149 provides for a deemed cessation on 31 December 2012.

444ABBA Transfers of business: election for transferee to pay tax of transferor

444ABBA [Omitted by FA 2012, s. 146 and Sch. 16, para. 43.]

History – S. 444ABBA omitted by FA 2012, s. 146 and Sch. 16, para. 43 with effect in relation to accounting periods of companies beginning on or after 1 January 2013, subject to transitional provisions contained in FA 2012, Sch. 17. For accounting periods straddling 1 January 2013, FA 2012, s. 149 provides for a deemed cessation on 31 December 2012.

444ABC Transfer scheme transferring part of business: transferor

444ABC [Omitted by SI 2008/381, art. 15.]

History – S. 444ABC omitted by SI 2008/381, art. 15, with effect in relation to transfers of business taking place on or after 1 July 2008.

444ABD Transferor's period of account including transfer

444ABD [Omitted by FA 2012, s. 146 and Sch. 16, para. 43.]

History – S. 444ABD omitted by FA 2012, s. 146 and Sch. 16, para. 43 with effect in relation to accounting periods of companies beginning on or after 1 January 2013, subject to transitional provisions contained in FA 2012, Sch. 17. For accounting periods straddling 1 January 2013, FA 2012, s. 149 provides for a deemed cessation on 31 December 2012.

444AC Transfer schemes: reduction of income of transferee

444AC [Omitted by FA 2012, s. 146 and Sch. 16, para. 43.]

History – S. 444AC omitted by FA 2012, s. 146 and Sch. 16, para. 43 with effect in relation to accounting periods of companies beginning on or after 1 January 2013, subject to transitional provisions contained in FA 2012, Sch. 17. For accounting periods straddling 1 January 2013, FA 2012, s. 149 provides for a deemed cessation on 31 December 2012.

444ACZA Transfer schemes transferring part of business: reduction in income of transferee

444ACZA [Omitted by SI 2008/381, art. 18.]

History – S. 444ACZA omitted by SI 2008/381, art. 18, with effect in relation to transfers of business taking place on or after 1 July 2008.
Former s. 444AC substituted by s. 444AC and 444ACZA by FA 2007, s. 40 and Sch. 9, para. 6(1), with effect from 11 March 2008, in relation to transfers of business taking place on or after 1 July 2008, and subject to any provision made by an order under Sch. 9, para. 16 on or after 11 March 2008, by virtue of SI 2008/379.

444ACA Transfers of business: transferor shares are assets of transferee's long-term insurance fund etc

444ACA [Omitted by FA 2007, s. 41 and Sch. 10, para. 2(2) and repealed by s. 114 and Sch. 27, Pt. 2(10).]

History – S. 444ACA omitted by FA 2007, s. 41 and Sch. 10, para. 2(2) and repealed by s. 114 and Sch. 27, Pt. 2(10), with effect in relation to periods of account beginning on or after 1 January 2007.

444AD Transfers of business: modification of s. 83(2B) FA 1989

444AD [Omitted by FA 2007, s. 40 and Sch. 9, para. 7(1) and repealed by s. 114 and Sch. 27, Pt. 2(9).]

History – S. 444AD omitted by FA 2007, s. 40 and Sch. 9, para. 7(1) and repealed by s. 114 and Sch. 27, Pt. 2(9), with effect from 11 March 2008, in relation to transfers of business taking place on or after 1 July 2008, and subject to any provision made by an order under Sch. 9, para. 16 on or after 11 March 2008, by virtue of SI 2008/379.

444AE Transfers of business: FAFTS

444AE [Omitted by FA 2012, s. 146 and Sch. 16, para. 43.]

History – S. 444AE omitted by FA 2012, s. 146 and Sch. 16, para. 43 with effect in relation to accounting periods of companies beginning on or after 1 January 2013, subject to transitional provisions contained in FA 2012, Sch. 17. For accounting periods straddling 1 January 2013, FA 2012, s. 149 provides for a deemed cessation on 31 December 2012.

444AEA Transfer schemes: anti-avoidance rule

444AEA [Omitted by FA 2012, s. 146 and Sch. 16, para. 43.]

History – S. 444AEA omitted by FA 2012, s. 146 and Sch. 16, para. 43 with effect in relation to accounting periods of companies beginning on or after 1 January 2013, subject to transitional provisions contained in FA 2012, Sch. 17. For accounting periods straddling 1 January 2013, FA 2012, s. 149 provides for a deemed cessation on 31 December 2012.

444AEB Life assurance trade profits advantage: transferor

444AEB [Omitted by FA 2012, s. 146 and Sch. 16, para. 43.]

History – S. 444AEB omitted by FA 2012, s. 146 and Sch. 16, para. 43 with effect in relation to accounting periods of companies beginning on or after 1 January 2013, subject to transitional provisions contained in FA 2012, Sch. 17. For accounting periods straddling 1 January 2013, FA 2012, s. 149 provides for a deemed cessation on 31 December 2012.

444AEC Life assurance trade profits advantage: transferee

444AEC [Omitted by FA 2012, s. 146 and Sch. 16, para. 43.]

History – S. 444AEC omitted by FA 2012, s. 146 and Sch. 16, para. 43 with effect in relation to accounting periods of companies beginning on or after 1 January 2013, subject to transitional provisions contained in FA 2012, Sch. 17. For accounting periods straddling 1 January 2013, FA 2012, s. 149 provides for a deemed cessation on 31 December 2012.

444AECA Parts of transfer scheme arrangements: anti-avoidance rule

444AECA [Omitted by FA 2012, s. 146 and Sch. 16, para. 43.]

History – S. 444AECA omitted by FA 2012, s. 146 and Sch. 16, para. 43 with effect in relation to accounting periods of companies beginning on or after 1 January 2013, subject to transitional provisions contained in FA 2012, Sch. 17. For accounting periods straddling 1 January 2013, FA 2012, s. 149 provides for a deemed cessation on 31 December 2012.

444AECB Parts of transfer scheme arrangements: life assurance trade profits advantage transferor

444AECB [Omitted by FA 2012, s. 146 and Sch. 16, para. 43.]

History – S. 444AECB omitted by FA 2012, s. 146 and Sch. 16, para. 43 with effect in relation to accounting periods of companies beginning on or after 1 January 2013, subject to transitional provisions contained in FA 2012, Sch. 17. For accounting periods straddling 1 January 2013, FA 2012, s. 149 provides for a deemed cessation on 31 December 2012.

444AECC Parts of transfer scheme arrangements: life assurance trade profits advantage transferee

444AECC [Omitted by FA 2012, s. 146 and Sch. 16, para. 43.]

History – S. 444AECC omitted by FA 2012, s. 146 and Sch. 16, para. 43 with effect in relation to accounting periods of companies beginning on or after 1 January 2013, subject to transitional provisions contained in FA 2012, Sch. 17. For accounting periods straddling 1 January 2013, FA 2012, s. 149 provides for a deemed cessation on 31 December 2012.

444AED Clearance: no avoidance or group advantage

444AED [Omitted by FA 2012, s. 146 and Sch. 16, para. 43.]

History – S. 444AED omitted by FA 2012, s. 146 and Sch. 16, para. 43 with effect in relation to accounting periods of companies beginning on or after 1 January 2013, subject to transitional provisions contained in FA 2012, Sch. 17. For accounting periods straddling 1 January 2013, FA 2012, s. 149 provides for a deemed cessation on 31 December 2012.

SURPLUSES OF MUTUAL AND FORMER MUTUAL BUSINESSES

History – heading inserted by FA 2006, s. 86 and Sch. 11, para. 5(1) in relation to periods of account ending on or after 29 September 2005.

444AF Demutualisation surplus: life assurance business

444AF [Omitted by FA 2012, s. 146 and Sch. 16, para. 44.]

History – S. 444AF omitted by FA 2012, s. 146 and Sch. 16, para. 44 with effect in relation to accounting periods of companies beginning on or after 1 January 2013, subject to transitional provisions contained in FA 2012, Sch. 17. For accounting periods straddling 1 January 2013, FA 2012, s. 149 provides for a deemed cessation on 31 December 2012.

444AG Section 444AF: "demutualisation transfer surplus"

444AG [Omitted by FA 2012, s. 146 and Sch. 16, para. 44.]

History – S. 444AG omitted by FA 2012, s. 146 and Sch. 16, para. 44 with effect in relation to accounting periods of companies beginning on or after 1 January 2013, subject to transitional provisions contained in FA 2012, Sch. 17. For accounting periods straddling 1 January 2013, FA 2012, s. 149 provides for a deemed cessation on 31 December 2012.

444AH Modification of section 444AG etc for gross roll-up businesses

444AH [Omitted by FA 2012, s. 146 and Sch. 16, para. 44.]

History – S. 444AH omitted by FA 2012, s. 146 and Sch. 16, para. 44 with effect in relation to accounting periods of companies beginning on or after 1 January 2013, subject to transitional provisions contained in FA 2012, Sch. 17. For accounting periods straddling 1 January 2013, FA 2012, s. 149 provides for a deemed cessation on 31 December 2012.

444AI Section 444AF: "reduction in company's unappropriated surplus"

444AI [Omitted by FA 2012, s. 146 and Sch. 16, para. 44.]

History – S. 444AI omitted by FA 2012, s. 146 and Sch. 16, para. 44 with effect in relation to accounting periods of companies beginning on or after 1 January 2013, subject to transitional provisions contained in FA 2012, Sch. 17. For accounting periods straddling 1 January 2013, FA 2012, s. 149 provides for a deemed cessation on 31 December 2012.

444AJ Sections 444AF and 444AK: "relevant receipts reduction"

444AJ [Omitted by FA 2012, s. 146 and Sch. 16, para. 44.]

History – S. 444AJ omitted by FA 2012, s. 146 and Sch. 16, para. 44 with effect in relation to accounting periods of companies beginning on or after 1 January 2013, subject to transitional provisions contained in FA 2012, Sch. 17. For accounting periods straddling 1 January 2013, FA 2012, s. 149 provides for a deemed cessation on 31 December 2012.

444AK Mutual surplus: gross roll-up business

444AK [Omitted by FA 2012, s. 146 and Sch. 16, para. 44.]

History – S. 444AK omitted by FA 2012, s. 146 and Sch. 16, para. 44 with effect in relation to accounting periods of companies beginning on or after 1 January 2013, subject to transitional provisions contained in FA 2012, Sch. 17. For accounting periods straddling 1 January 2013, FA 2012, s. 149 provides for a deemed cessation on 31 December 2012.

444AL Interpretation of sections 444AF to 444AK

444AL [Omitted by FA 2012, s. 146 and Sch. 16, para. 44.]

History – S. 444AL omitted by FA 2012, s. 146 and Sch. 16, para. 44 with effect in relation to accounting periods of companies beginning on or after 1 January 2013, subject to transitional provisions contained in FA 2012, Sch. 17. For accounting periods straddling 1 January 2013, FA 2012, s. 149 provides for a deemed cessation on 31 December 2012.

PROVISIONS APPLYING IN RELATION TO OVERSEAS LIFE INSURANCE COMPANIES

444B Modification of Act in relation to overseas life insurance companies

444B [Repealed by SI 2006/3271, reg. 43 and Schedule, Pt. 1.]

History – S. 444B repealed by SI 2006/3271, reg. 43 and Schedule, Pt. 1 with effect from 31 December 2006 in relation to accounting periods ending on or after that date. S. 444B previously gave effect to Sch. 19AC.
S. 444B inserted by FA 1993, s. 97(1).

444BA Equalisation reserves for general business

444BA [Repealed by FA 2012, s. 26(1).]

History – S. 444BA repealed by FA 2012, s. 26(1) with effect in relation to accounting periods ending on or after 1 January 2016 (SI 2015/1999, art. 2), subject to transitional provisions in FA 2012, s. 26(4) to (9). Former s. 444BA read as follows:

"Equalisation reserves for general business

444BA(1) Subject to the following provisions of this section and to sections 444BB to 444BD, the rules in subsection (2) below shall apply in making any computation, for the purposes of section 35 of CTA 2009 (charge on trade profits), of the profits or losses for any accounting period of an insurance company whose business has at any time been or included business in respect of which it was required, by virtue of equalisation reserves rules, to maintain an equalisation reserve.

444BA(2) Those rules are–

(a) that amounts which, in accordance with equalisation reserves rules, are transferred into the equalisation reserve in respect of the company's business for the accounting period in question are to be deductible;

(b) that amounts which, in accordance with any such regulations, are transferred out of the reserve in respect of the company's business for that period are to be treated as receipts of that business; and

(c) that it must be assumed that all such transfers as are required by equalisation reserves rules to be made into or out of the reserve in respect of the company's business for any period are made as required.

444BA(3) Where an insurance company having any business in respect of which it is required, by virtue of equalisation reserves rules, to maintain an equalisation reserve ceases to trade–

(a) any balance which exists in the reserve at that time for the purposes of the Tax Acts shall be deemed to have been transferred out of the reserve immediately before the company ceases to trade; and

(b) that transfer out shall be deemed to be a transfer in respect of the company's business for the accounting period in which the company so ceases and to have been required by equalisation reserves rules.

444BA(4) Where–

(a) an amount is transferred into an equalisation reserve in respect of the business of an insurance company for any accounting period,

(b) the rule in subsection (2)(a) above would apply to the transfer of that amount but for this subsection,

(c) that company by notice in writing to an officer of the Board makes an election in relation to that amount for the purposes of this subsection, and

(d) the notice of the election is given not more than two years after the end of that period,

the rule mentioned in subsection (2)(a) above shall not apply to that transfer of that amount and, instead, the amount transferred (the "unrelieved transfer" shall be carried forward for the purposes of subsection (5) below to the next accounting period and (subject to subsection (6) below) from accounting period to accounting period.

444BA(5) Where–

(a) in accordance with equalisation reserves rules, a transfer is made out of an equalisation reserve in respect of an insurance company's business for any accounting period,

(b) the rule in subsection (2)(b) above would apply to the transfer but for this subsection, and

(c) the accounting period is one to which any amount representing one or more unrelieved transfers has been carried forward under subsection (4) above,

that rule mentioned in subsection (2)(b) above shall not apply to that transfer except to the extent (if any) that the amount of the transfer exceeds the aggregate of the amounts representing unrelieved transfers carried forward to that period.

444BA(6) Where in the case of any company–

(a) any amount representing one or more unrelieved transfers is carried forward to an accounting period in accordance with subsection (4) above, and

(b) by virtue of subsection (5) above the rule in subsection (2)(b) above does not apply to an amount representing the whole or any part of any transfer out of an equalisation reserve in respect of the company's business for that period,

the amount mentioned in paragraph (a) above shall not be carried forward under subsection (4) above to the next accounting period except to the extent (if any) that it exceeds the amount mentioned in paragraph (b) above.

444BA(7) To the extent that any actual or assumed transfer in accordance with equalisation reserves rules of any amount into an equalisation reserve is attributable to arrangements entered into wholly or mainly for tax purposes–

(a) the rule in subsection (2)(a) above shall not apply to that transfer; and

(b) the making of that transfer shall be disregarded in determining, for the purposes of the Tax Acts, whether and to what extent there is subsequently any requirement to make a transfer into or out of the reserve in accordance with equalisation reserves rules;

and this subsection applies irrespective of whether the insurance company in question is a party to the arrangements.

444BA(8) For the purposes of this section the transfer of an amount into an equalisation reserve is attributable to arrangements entered into wholly or mainly for tax purposes to the extent that the arrangements to which it is attributable are arrangements–

(a) the sole or main purpose of which is, or
(b) the sole or main benefit accruing from which might (but for subsection (7) above) be expected to be,

the reduction by virtue of this section of any liability to tax.

444BA(9) Where–

(a) any transfer made into or out of an equalisation reserve maintained by an insurance company is made in accordance with equalisation reserves rules in respect of business carried on by that company over a period ("the equalisation period"), and
(b) parts of the equalisation period are in different accounting periods,

the amount transferred shall be apportioned for the purposes of this section between the different accounting periods in the proportions that correspond to the number of days in the equalisation period that are included in each of those accounting periods.

444BA(10) The Treasury may by regulations provide in relation to any accounting periods ending on or after 1st April 1996 for specified transitional provisions contained in equalisation reserves rules to be disregarded for the purposes of the Tax Acts in determining how much is required, on any occasion, to be transferred into or out of any equalisation reserve in accordance with the rules.

444BA(11) In this section, and in sections 444BB to 444BD, **"equalisation reserves rules"** means the rules in chapter 1.4 of the Insurance Prudential Sourcebook.".

In former s. 444BA(1), the words "section 35 of CTA 2009 (charge on trade profits)" substituted for "Case I or V of Schedule D" by CTA 2009, s. 1322 and Sch. 1, para. 155, with effect for corporation tax purposes for accounting periods ending on or after 1 April 2009, and for income tax and capital gains tax purposes for the tax year 2009–10 and subsequent tax years.

In former s. 444BA(11), "chapter 1.4 of the Insurance Prudential Sourcebook" substituted for "chapter 7.5 of the Integrated Prudential Sourcebook" by SI 2008/2673, reg. 2, with effect in relation to periods of account ending on or after 29 October 2008.

In former s. 444BA(11) the words "chapter 7.5 of the Integrated Prudential Sourcebook" substituted by F(No. 2)A 2005, s. 42 and Sch. 9, para. 9(2) effective in relation to periods of account ending on or after 31 December 2004 (Sch. 9, para. 9(3)).

In former s. 444BA: the words "equalisation reserves rules" substituted wherever that expression occurred; in s. 444BA(10), the words "the rules" substituted for "the regulations"; and s. 444BA(11) substituted, by SI 2001/3629, reg. 13 and 30(1)–(4) in relation to periods of account ending on or after 1 December 2001.

Former s. 444BA inserted by FA 1996, s. 166 and Sch. 32, para. 1.

Cross references – SI 2009/2039: modification of s. 444BA in relation to reserves maintained by a corporate member or a partnership member that are equivalent to equalisation reserves.

444BB Modification of s. 444BA for mutual or overseas business and for non-resident companies

444BB [Repealed by FA 2012, s. 26(1).]

History – S. 444BB repealed by FA 2012, s. 26(1) with effect in relation to accounting periods ending on or after 1 January 2016 (SI 2015/1999, art. 2), subject to transitional provisions in FA 2012, s. 26(4) to (9). Former s. 444BB read as follows:

"Modification of s. 444BA for mutual or overseas business and for non-resident companies

444BB(1) The Treasury may by regulations make provision modifying section 444BA so as, in cases mentioned in subsection (2) below–

(a) to require–
  (i) sums by reference to which the amount of any transfer into or out of an equalisation reserve falls to be computed, or
  (ii) the amount of any such transfer,

  to be apportioned between different parts of the business carried on for any period by an insurance company; and
(b) to provide for the purposes of corporation tax for the amounts taken to be transferred into or out of an equalisation reserve to be computed disregarding any such sum or, as the case may be, any such part of a transfer as is attributed, in accordance with the regulations, to a part of the business described for the purpose in the regulations.

444BB(2) Those cases are cases where an insurance company which, in accordance with equalisation reserves rules, is required to make transfers into or out of an equalisation reserve in respect of any business carried on by that company for any period is carrying on, for the whole or any part of that period–

(a) any business the income and gains of which fall to be disregarded in making a computation of the company's profits in accordance with the rules applicable for the purposes of section 35 of CTA 2009 (charge on trade profits), or
(b) any business by reference to which double taxation relief is afforded in respect of any income or gains.

444BB(3) Section 444BA shall have effect (subject to any regulations under subsection (1) above) in the case of an equalisation reserve maintained by an insurance company which–

(a) is not resident in the United Kingdom, and
(b) carries on business in the United Kingdom through a permanent establishment,

only if such conditions as may be prescribed by regulations made by the Treasury are satisfied in relation to that company and in relation to transfers into or out of that reserve.

444BB(4) Regulations under this section prescribing conditions subject to which section 444BA is to apply in the case of any equalisation reserve maintained by an insurance company may–

(a) contain conditions imposing requirements on the company to furnish the Board with information with respect to any matters to which the regulations relate, or to produce to the Board documents or records relating to any such matters; and
(b) provide that, where any prescribed condition is not, or ceases to be, satisfied in relation to the company or in relation to transfers into or out of that reserve, there is to be deemed for the purposes of the Tax Acts to have been a transfer out of that reserve of an amount determined under the regulations.

444BB(5) Regulations under this section may–

(a) provide for apportionments under the regulations to be made in such manner, and by reference to such factors, as may be specified or described in the regulations;
(b) make different provision for different cases;
(c) contain such supplementary, incidental, consequential and transitional provision as the Treasury may think fit;
(d) make provision having retrospective effect in relation to accounting periods beginning not more than one year before the time when the regulations are made;

and the powers conferred by this section in relation to transfers into or out of any reserve shall be exercisable in relation to both actual and assumed transfers.

444BB(6) In this section **"double taxation relief"** means–

(a) relief under double taxation arrangements which takes the form of a credit allowed against corporation tax, or
(b) relief under section 18(1)(b) and (2) of TIOPA 2010 which takes that form;

and **"double taxation arrangements"** here means arrangements which have effect under section 2(1) of that Act (double taxation relief by agreement with territories outside the United Kingdom)."

In former s. 444BB(2), the words "for the purposes of section 35 of CTA 2009 (charge on trade profits)" substituted for "to Case I of Schedule D" by CTA 2009, s. 1322 and Sch. 1, para. 156, with effect for corporation tax purposes for accounting periods ending on or after 1 April 2009, and for income tax and capital gains tax purposes for the tax year 2009–10 and subsequent tax years.

In former s. 444BB(2), the words "equalisation reserves rules" substituted by SI 2001/3629, reg. 13 and 30(1) in relation to periods of account ending on or after 1 December 2001.

In former s. 444BB(3)(b), the words "permanent establishment" substituted by FA 2003, 153(1)(a), with effect for accounting periods beginning on or after 1 January 2003.
In former s. 444B(6)(b), the words "relief under section 18(1)(b) and (2) of TIOPA 2010" substituted for the words "unilateral relief under section 790(1)" by TIOPA 2010, s. 374 and Sch. 8, para. 9 with effect for corporation tax purposes for accounting periods ending on or after 1 April 2010, for income tax and capital gains tax purposes for the tax year 2010–11 and subsequent tax years, and for petroleum revenue tax purposes for chargeable periods beginning on or after 1 July 2010.
In former s. 444B(6)(b), the words "which have effect under section 2(1) of that Act (double taxation relief by agreement with territories outside the United Kingdom)" substituted for the words "having effect by virtue of section 788" by TIOPA 2010, s. 374 and Sch. 8, para 9 with effect for corporation tax purposes for accounting periods ending on or after 1 April 2010, for income tax and capital gains tax purposes for the tax year 2010–11 and subsequent tax years, and for petroleum revenue tax purposes for chargeable periods beginning on or after 1 July 2010.
Former s. 444BB inserted by FA 1996, s. 166 and Sch. 32, para. 1.

Cross references – S. 788: double taxation relief by agreement with other countries.
S. 790(1): unilateral double taxation relief by way of credit.

Statutory instruments – SI 1999/1408: Non-resident Companies (General Insurance Business) (Regulations) 1999.
SI 2008/2679: Insurance Companies (Reserves) (Tax) (Amendment) Regulations 2008, made partly under s. 444BB(1), (3), (4) and (5).

444BC Modification of s. 444BA for non-annual accounting etc.

444BC [Repealed by FA 2012, s. 26(1).]

History – S. 444BC repealed by FA 2012, s. 26(1) with effect in relation to accounting periods ending on or after 1 January 2016 (SI 2015/1999, art. 2), subject to transitional provisions in FA 2012, s. 26(4) to (9). Former s. 444BC read as follows:

"Modification of s. 444BA for non-annual accounting etc.

444BC(1) The Treasury may by regulations make provision modifying the operation of section 444BA in relation to cases where an insurance company has, for the purpose of preparing the documents it is required to prepare for the purposes of section 9.3 of the Prudential Sourcebook (Insurers), applied for any period an accounting method described in paragraphs 57 to 59 in Section E of Part 2 of Schedule 3 to the Large and Medium-sized Companies and Groups (Accounts and Reports) Regulations 2008 (accounting on a non-annual basis).

444BC(2) Subsection (5) of section 444BB applies for the purposes of this section as it applies for the purposes of that section.".

In former s. 444BC(1), the words "paragraphs 57 to 59 in Section E of Part 2 of Schedule 3 to the Large and Medium-sized Companies and Groups (Accounts and Reports) Regulations 2008" substituted for the words "paragraph 52 or 53 of Schedule 9A to the Companies Act 1985" by SI 2009/1890, art. 5(1), with effect from 1 October 2009.
In former s. 444BC, the words "9.3 of the Prudential Sourcebook (Insurers)" substituted by SI 2001/3629, reg. 13 and 30(5) in relation to periods of account ending on or after 1 December 2001.
Former s. 444BC inserted by FA 1996, s. 166 and Sch. 32, para. 1.

Cross references – SI 2008/410: Large and Medium-sized Companies and Groups (Accounts and Reports) Regulations 2008.

Statutory instruments – SI 2008/2679: Insurance Companies (Reserves) (Tax) (Amendment) Regulations 2008, made partly under s. 444BC.

444BD Application of s. 444BA rules to other equalisation reserves

444BD [Repealed by FA 2012, s. 26(1).]

History – S. 444BD repealed by FA 2012, s. 26(1) with effect in relation to accounting periods ending on or after 1 January 2016 (SI 2015/1999, art. 2), subject to transitional provisions in FA 2012, s. 26(4) to (9). Former s. 444BD read as follows:

"Application of s. 444BA rules to other equalisation reserves

444BD(1) The Treasury may by regulations provide for section 444BA to have effect, in such cases and subject to such modifications as may be specified in the regulations, in relation to any equivalent reserves as it has effect in relation to equalisation reserves maintained by virtue of equalisation reserves rules.

444BD(2) For the purposes of this section a reserve is an equivalent reserve if–

(a) it is maintained, otherwise than by virtue of equalisation reserves rules, either–
  (i) by an EEA firm of the kind mentioned in paragraph 5(d) of Schedule 3 to the Financial Services and Markets Act 2000 which has permission under paragraph 15 of that Schedule (as a result of qualifying for authorisation under paragraph 12(1) of that Schedule) to effect or carry out contracts of insurance in the United Kingdom, or
  (ii) by a firm which has permission under paragraph 4 of Schedule 4 to that Act (as a result of qualifying for authorisation under paragraph 2 of that Schedule) to effect or carry out contracts of insurance in the United Kingdom, or;
  (iii) in respect of any business which consists of the effecting or carrying out of contracts of insurance and which is carried on outside the United Kingdom by a company resident in the United Kingdom;

and

(b) the purpose for which, or the manner in which, it is maintained is such as to make it equivalent to an equalisation reserve maintained by virtue of equalisation reserves rules.

444BD(3) For the purposes of this section a reserve is also an equivalent reserve if it is maintained in respect of any credit insurance business in accordance with requirements imposed either–

(a) by or under any enactment, or
(b) under so much of the law of any territory as secures compliance with the requirements of Article 1 of the credit insurance directive (equalisation reserves for credit insurance).

444BD(4) Without prejudice to the generality of subsection (1) above, the modifications made by virtue of that subsection may–

(a) provide for section 444BA to apply in the case of an equivalent reserve only where such conditions as may be specified in the regulations are satisfied in relation to the company maintaining the reserve or in relation to transfers made into or out of it; and
(b) contain any other provision corresponding to any provision which, in the case of a reserve maintained by virtue of equalisation reserves rules, may be made under sections 444BA to 444BC.

444BD(5) Subsections (4) and (5) of section 444BB shall apply for the purposes of this section as they apply for the purposes of that section.

444BD(6) Without prejudice to the generality of section 444BB(5), the transitional provision which by virtue of subsection (5) above may be contained in regulations under this section shall include–

(a) provision for treating the amount of any transfers made into or out of an equivalent reserve in respect of business carried on for any specified period as increased by the amount by which they would have been increased if no transfers into the reserve had been made in respect of business carried on for an earlier period; and

(b) provision for excluding from the rule in section 444BA(2)(b) so much of any amount transferred out of an equivalent reserve as represents, in pursuance of an apportionment made under the regulations, the transfer out of that reserve of amounts in respect of which there has been no entitlement to relief by virtue of section 444BA(2)(a).

444BD(7) In this section–

"credit insurance business" means business which consists of the effecting or carrying out of contracts of insurance against risks of loss to the persons insured arising from–

(a) the insolvency of debtors of theirs, or

(b) from the failure (otherwise than through insolvency) of debtors of theirs to pay their debts when due;

"the credit insurance directive" means Council Directive 87/343/EEC of 22nd June 1987 amending, as regards credit insurance and suretyship insurance, First Directive 73/239 on the coordination of laws, regulations and administrative provisions relating to the taking-up and pursuit of the business of direct insurance other than life assurance.".

In former s. 444BD:

- the words "equalisation reserves rules" substituted wherever that expression occurs
- in subs. (2)(a), subpara. (i), (ii) and (ii) substituted; and
- in subs. (7), the definition of "credit insurance business" substituted and the definition of "EC company" and the word 'and" that appeared immediately before it omitted,

all by SI 2001/3629, reg. 13 and 30(1) and (6)–(8) in relation to periods of account ending on or after 1 December 2001.
Former s. 444BD inserted by FA 1996, s. 166 and Sch. 32, para. 1.

Statutory instruments – SI 1999/1408: Non-resident Companies (General Insurance Business) (Regulations) 1999.
SI 2008/2679: Insurance Companies (Reserves) (Tax) (Amendment) Regulations 2008, made partly under s. 444BD(1), (4) and (5).

444C Modification of section 440

444C [Repealed by FA 1995, s. 162 and Sch. 29, Pt. VIII(5), with effect in relation to accounting periods beginning on or after 1 January 1995, except for s. 444C(2)(a) which is repealed with effect in relation to accounting periods beginning on or after 1 November 1994.]

444D Qualifying distributions, tax credits, etc.

444D [Repealed by FA 1995, s. 162 and Sch. 29, Pt. VIII(5), with effect in relation to accounting periods beginning on or after 1 January 1995.]

444E Income from investments attributable to BLAGAB, etc.

444E [Repealed by FA 1995, s. 162 and Sch. 29, Pt. VIII(5), with effect in relation to accounting periods beginning on or after 1 January 1995.]

PROVISIONS APPLYING ONLY TO OVERSEAS LIFE INSURANCE COMPANIES

445 Charge to tax on investment income

445 [Repealed by FA 1993, s. 103(2)(a), s. 213 and Sch. 23, Pt. III(9) in relation to accounting periods beginning after 31 December 1992.]

446 Annuity business

446(1) [Repealed by FA 1993, s. 103(2)(b), s. 213 and Sch. 23, Pt. III(9) in relation to accounting periods beginning after 31 December 1992.]

446(2), (3) [Repealed by FA 1991, s. 48 and Sch. 7, para. 7(1), s. 123 and Sch. 19, Pt. V.]

446(4) [Repealed by FA 1990, s. 132 and Sch. 19, Pt. IV.]

447 Set-off of income tax and tax credits against corporation tax

447(1), (2) [Repealed by FA 1993, s. 103(2)(c), s. 213 and Sch. 23, Pt. III(9) in relation to accounting periods beginning after 31 December 1992.]

447(3) [Repealed by FA 1991, s. 48 and Sch. 7, para. 7(3), s. 123 and Sch. 19, Pt. V.]

447(4) [Repealed by FA 1993, s. 103(2)(c), s. 213 and Sch. 23, Pt. III(9) in relation to accounting periods beginning after 31 December 1992.]

448 Qualifying distributions and tax credits

448 [Repealed by FA 1993, s. 103(2)(d), s. 213 and Sch. 23, Pt. III(9) in relation to accounting periods beginning after 31 December 1992.]

449 Double taxation agreements

449 [Repealed by FA 1993, s. 103(2)(d), s. 213 and Sch. 23, Pt. III(9) in relation to accounting periods beginning after 31 December 1992.]

UNDERWRITERS

450 Assessment, set-off of losses and reinsurance

450 [Repealed by FA 1993, s. 213 and Sch. 23, Pt. III(12) with effect for 1992–93 and subsequent years of assessment, except for s. 450(6) where the repeal has effect in relation to acquisitions made, or treated as made, after 31 December 1993.]

451 Regulations

451 [Repealed by FA 1993, s. 213 and Sch. 23, Pt. III(12) with effect for 1992–93 and subsequent years of assessment.]

452 Special reserve funds

452 [Repealed by FA 1993, s. 213 and Sch. 23, Pt. III(12), with effect for 1992–93 and subsequent years of assessment.]

453 Payments into premiums trust fund on account of losses

453 [Repealed by FA 1993, s. 213 and Sch. 23, Pt. III(12), with effect for 1992–93 and subsequent years of assessment.]

454 Income tax consequences on payments into and out of special reserve fund

454 [Repealed by FA 1993, s. 213 and Sch. 23, Pt. III(12), with effect for 1992–93 and subsequent years of assessment.]

455 Income tax consequences on death of underwriter

455 [Repealed by FA 1993 s. 213 and Sch. 23, Pt. III(12), with effect for 1992–93 and subsequent years of assessment.]

456 Unearned income, variation of arrangements and cancellation of approval etc.

456 [Repealed by FA 1993, s. 213 and Sch. 23, Pt. III(12), with effect for 1992–93 and subsequent years of assessment.]

457 Interpretation of sections 450 to 456

457 [Repealed by FA 1993, s. 213 and Sch. 23, Pt. III(12), with effect for 1992–93 and subsequent years of assessment.]

CAPITAL REDEMPTION BUSINESS

458 Capital redemption business

458 [Omitted by FA 2007, s. 38 and Sch. 7, para. 39 and repealed by s. 114 and Sch. 27, Pt. 2(7).]

History – S. 458 omitted by FA 2007, s. 38 and Sch. 7, para. 39 and repealed by s. 114 and Sch. 27, Pt. 2(7), with effect for the purposes of corporation tax, for periods of account of insurance companies beginning on or after 1 January 2007, and for the purposes of income tax, for the tax year 2007–08 and subsequent tax years (but see transitional provisions at FA 2007, Sch. 7, para. 80–84).

458A Capital redemption business: power to apply life assurance provisions

458A [Omitted by FA 2007, s. 38 and Sch. 7, para. 39 and repealed by s. 114 and Sch. 27, Pt. 2(7).]

History – S. 458A omitted by FA 2007, s. 38 and Sch. 7, para. 39 and repealed by s. 114 and Sch. 27, Pt. 2(7), with effect for the purposes of corporation tax, for periods of account of insurance companies beginning on or after 1 January 2007, and for the purposes of income tax, for the tax year 2007–08 and subsequent tax years (but see transitional provisions at FA 2007, Sch. 7, para. 80–84).

Chapter II – Friendly Societies, Trade Unions and Employers' Associations

UNREGISTERED FRIENDLY SOCIETIES

459 Exemption from tax

459 [Omitted by FA 2012, s. 176 and Sch. 18, para. 2.]

History – S. 459 omitted by FA 2012, s. 176 and Sch. 18, para. 2 with effect in relation to accounting periods of companies beginning on or after 1 January 2013, subject to transitional provisions in FA 2012, Sch. 19. For accounting periods straddling 1 January 2013, FA 2012, s. 179 provides for a deemed cessation on 31 December 2012.

REGISTERED FRIENDLY SOCIETIES

460 Exemption from tax in respect of life or endowment business

460 [Omitted by FA 2012, s. 176 and Sch. 18, para. 3.]

History – S. 460 omitted by FA 2012, s. 176 and Sch. 18, para. 3 with effect in relation to accounting periods of companies beginning on or after 1 January 2013, subject to transitional provisions in FA 2012, Sch. 19. For accounting periods straddling 1 January 2013, FA 2012, s. 179 provides for a deemed cessation on 31 December 2012.

461 Taxation in respect of other business

461 [Omitted by FA 2012, s. 176 and Sch. 18, para. 4.]

History – S. 461 omitted by FA 2012, s. 176 and Sch. 18, para. 4 with effect in relation to accounting periods of companies beginning on or after 1 January 2013, subject to transitional provisions in FA 2012, Sch. 19. For accounting periods straddling 1 January 2013, FA 2012, s. 179 provides for a deemed cessation on 31 December 2012.

Cross references – FA 2012, Sch. 19, para.1: anything which, as a result of s. 461(11), is treated as having been done by HMRC under a provision of ICTA repealed by FA 2012 is to continue to be treated as having been done by HMRC on that date under the provision of FA 2012, Pt. 3 corresponding to the repealed provision.

461A Taxation in respect of other business: incorporated friendly societies qualifying for exemption

461A [Omitted by FA 2012, s. 176 and Sch. 18, para. 5.]

History – S. 461A omitted by FA 2012, s. 176 and Sch. 18, para. 5 with effect in relation to accounting periods of companies beginning on or after 1 January 2013, subject to transitional provisions in FA 2012, Sch. 19. For accounting periods straddling 1 January 2013, FA 2012, s. 179 provides for a deemed cessation on 31 December 2012.

Cross references – FA 2012, Sch. 19, para.1: anything which, as a result of s. 461A(4), is treated as having been done by HMRC under a provision of ICTA repealed by FA 2012 is to continue to be treated as having been done by HMRC on that date under the provision of FA 2012, Pt. 3 corresponding to the repealed provision.

461B Taxation in respect of other business: incorporated friendly societies etc.

461B [Omitted by FA 2012, s. 176 and Sch. 18, para. 5.]

History – S. 461B omitted by FA 2012, s. 176 and Sch. 18, para. 5 with effect in relation to accounting periods of companies beginning on or after 1 January 2013, subject to transitional provisions in FA 2012, Sch. 19. For accounting periods straddling 1 January 2013, FA 2012, s. 179 provides for a deemed cessation on 31 December 2012.

461C Taxation in respect of other business: withdrawal of "qualifying" status from incorporated friendly society

461C [Omitted by FA 2012, s. 176 and Sch. 18, para. 5.]

History – S. 461C omitted by FA 2012, s. 176 and Sch. 18, para. 5 with effect in relation to accounting periods of companies beginning on or after 1 January 2013, subject to transitional provisions in FA 2012, Sch. 19. For accounting periods straddling 1 January 2013, FA 2012, s. 179 provides for a deemed cessation on 31 December 2012.

461D Transfers of other business

461D [Omitted by FA 2012, s. 176 and Sch. 18, para. 6.]

History – S. 461D omitted by FA 2012, s. 176 and Sch. 18, para. 6 with effect in relation to accounting periods of companies beginning on or after 1 January 2013, subject to transitional provisions in FA 2012, Sch. 19. For accounting periods straddling 1 January 2013, FA 2012, s. 179 provides for a deemed cessation on 31 December 2012.

461E Apportionments following transfer of other business

461E [See cross-reference note below.]

Cross references – SI 2008/1942, reg. 7: insertion of s. 461E as modification in relation to certain transfers of engagements and amalgamations of friendly societies taking place on or after 21 July 2008.

461F Apportionment of income and gains

461F [See cross-reference note below.]

Cross references – SI 2008/1942, reg. 7: insertion of s. 461F as modification in relation to certain transfers of engagements and amalgamations of friendly societies taking place on or after 21 July 2008.

461G Apportionment of expenses

461G [See cross-reference note below.]

Cross references – SI 2008/1942, reg. 7: insertion of s. 461G as modification in relation to certain transfers of engagements and amalgamations of friendly societies taking place on or after 21 July 2008.

462 Conditions for tax exempt business

462 [Omitted by FA 2012, s. 176 and Sch. 18, para. 7.]

History – S. 462 omitted by FA 2012, s. 176 and Sch. 18, para. 7 with effect in relation to accounting periods of companies beginning on or after 1 January 2013, subject to transitional provisions in FA 2012, Sch. 19. For accounting periods straddling 1 January 2013, FA 2012, s. 179 provides for a deemed cessation on 31 December 2012.

462A Election as to tax exempt business

462A [Omitted by FA 2008, s. 44 and Sch. 18, para. 5(1).]

History – S. 462A omitted by FA 2008, s. 44 and Sch. 18, para. 5(1), with effect from 21 July 2008.

463 Long-term business: application of the Corporation Tax Acts

463 [Omitted by FA 2012, s. 176 and Sch. 18, para. 8.]

History – S. 463 omitted by FA 2012, s. 176 and Sch. 18, para. 8 with effect in relation to accounting periods of companies beginning on or after 1 January 2013, subject to transitional provisions in FA 2012, Sch. 19. For accounting periods straddling 1 January 2013, FA 2012, s. 179 provides for a deemed cessation on 31 December 2012.

464 Maximum benefits payable to members

464 [Omitted by FA 2012, s. 176 and Sch. 18, para. 9.]

History – S. 464 omitted by FA 2012, s. 176 and Sch. 18, para. 9 with effect in relation to accounting periods of companies beginning on or after 1 January 2013, subject to transitional provisions in FA 2012, Sch. 19. For accounting periods straddling 1 January 2013, FA 2012, s. 179 provides for a deemed cessation on 31 December 2012.

465 Old societies

465 [Omitted by FA 2012, s. 176 and Sch. 18, para. 10.]

History – S. 465 omitted by FA 2012, s. 176 and Sch. 18, para. 10 with effect in relation to accounting periods of companies beginning on or after 1 January 2013, subject to transitional provisions in FA 2012, Sch. 19. For accounting periods straddling 1 January 2013, FA 2012, s. 179 provides for a deemed cessation on 31 December 2012.

465A Assets of branch of registered friendly society to be treated as assets of society after incorporation

465A [Omitted by FA 2012, s. 176 and Sch. 18, para. 11.]

History – S. 465A omitted by FA 2012, s. 176 and Sch. 18, para. 11 with effect in relation to accounting periods of companies beginning on or after 1 January 2013, subject to transitional provisions in FA 2012, Sch. 19. For accounting periods straddling 1 January 2013, FA 2012, s. 179 provides for a deemed cessation on 31 December 2012.

466 Interpretation of Chapter II

466 [Omitted by FA 2012, s. 176 and Sch. 18, para. 12.]

History – S. 466 omitted by FA 2012, s. 176 and Sch. 18, para. 12 with effect in relation to accounting periods of companies beginning on or after 1 January 2013, subject to transitional provisions in FA 2012, Sch. 19. For accounting periods straddling 1 January 2013, FA 2012, s. 179 provides for a deemed cessation on 31 December 2012.

TRADE UNIONS AND EMPLOYERS' ASSOCIATIONS

467 Exemption for trade unions and employers' associations

467 [Omitted by CTA 2010, s. 1177 and Sch. 1, para. 52 and repealed by CTA 2010, s. 1181 and Sch. 3, Pt. 1.]

History – S. 467 omitted by CTA 2010, s. 1177 and Sch. 1, para. 52 and repealed by CTA 2010, s. 1181 and Sch. 3, Pt. 1, with effect for corporation tax purposes for accounting periods ending on or after 1 April 2010, and for income and capital gains tax purposes for the tax year 2010–11 and subsequent tax years.

Notes – S. 467 rewritten for corporation tax purposes as follows:
S. 467(1): CTA 2010, s. 981(1), (2), (3), 982(1).
S. 467(2): CTA 2010, s. 982(2).
S. 467(3): CTA 2010, s. 981(4).
S. 467(3A): CTA 2010, s. 981(5).
S. 467(4): CTA 2010, s. 983(1), (2), (3), (4).

Chapter III – Unit Trust Schemes, Dealers in Securities etc.

UNIT TRUST SCHEMES

468 Authorised unit trusts

468 [Omitted by CTA 2010, s. 1177 and Sch. 1, para. 53 and repealed by CTA 2010, s. 1181 and Sch. 3, Pt. 1.]

History – S. 468 omitted by CTA 2010, s. 1177 and Sch. 1, para. 53 and repealed by CTA 2010, s. 1181 and Sch. 3, Pt. 1, with effect for corporation tax purposes for accounting periods ending on or after 1 April 2010, and for income and capital gains tax purposes for the tax year 2010–11 and subsequent tax years.

Notes – S. 468 rewritten for corporation tax purposes as follows:
S. 468(1): CTA 2010, s. 617(1), (3), (4).
S. 468(1A): CTA 2010, s. 618.
S. 468(3): CTA 2010, s. 617(2).
S. 468(6): CTA 2010, s. 616(1), (2), (3).
S. 468(7): CTA 2010, s. 619(3).
S. 468(8): CTA 2010, s. 619(1), (2).
S. 468(9): CTA 2010, s. 619(4), (5).

468A Open-ended investment companies

468A [Omitted by CTA 2010, s. 1177 and Sch. 1, para. 54 and repealed by CTA 2010, s. 1181 and Sch. 3, Pt. 1.]

History – S. 468A omitted by CTA 2010, s. 1177 and Sch. 1, para. 54 and repealed by CTA 2010, s. 1181 and Sch. 3, Pt. 1, with effect for corporation tax purposes for accounting periods ending on or after 1 April 2010, and for income and capital gains tax purposes for the tax year 2010–11 and subsequent tax years.

Notes – S. 468A rewritten for corporation tax purposes as follows:
S. 468A(1): CTA 2010, s. 614.
S. 468A(2): CTA 2010, s. 613.
S. 468A(3): CTA 2010, s. 615(3), (4).
S. 468A(4): CTA 2010, s. 615(1), (2).

468AA Authorised unit trusts: futures and options

468AA [Repealed by FA 2002, s. 83(1)(b), Sch. 27, para. 6 and s. 141, Sch. 40, Pt. 3(13) in relation to accounting periods beginning on or after 1 October 2002. For the text of this section as it applies for earlier periods, see History note below.]

History – S. 468AA omitted by FA 2002, s. 83(1)(b), Sch. 27, para. 6 and repealed by s. 141, Sch. 40, Pt. 3(13) in relation to accounting periods beginning on or after 1 October 2002.
Former s. 468AA inserted by FA 1990, s. 81(1), (5) in relation to income derived after 26 July 1990.

468A Certified unit trusts

468A [Repealed by FA 1990, s. 132 and Sch. 19, Pt. IV, effective for distribution periods ending after 31 December 1990.]

Notes – A different version of s. 468A ("Open-ended investment companies") was inserted immediately after s. 468 by F(No. 2)A 2005, s. 16 with effect from 20 July 2005. Purely for the purposes of distinguishing electronically the two versions of s. 468A (both now repealed), CCH have added a hyphen to the numbering of the version that appears second in the order of sections.

468B Certified unit trusts: corporation tax

468B [Repealed by FA 1990, s. 52(5), 132 and Sch. 19, Pt. IV, as regards an accounting period ending after 31 December 1990.]

468C Certified unit trusts: distributions

468C [Repealed by FA 1990, s. 52(6), 132 and Sch. 19, Pt. IV, as regards a distribution period ending after 31 December 1990.]

468D Funds of funds: distributions

468D [Repealed by FA 1990, s. 52(7), 132 and Sch. 19, Pt. IV, as regards a distribution period ending after 31 December 1990.]

468E Authorised unit trusts: corporation tax

468E [Repealed by FA 1996, s. 73 and Sch. 6, para. 10(3) and FA 1996, s. 205 and Sch. 41, Pt. V(1), for any accounting period ending after 31 March 1996 except in so far as it relates to the financial year 1995.]

468EE Corporation tax: cases where lower rate applies

468EE [Repealed by FA 1996, s. 73 and Sch. 6, para. 10(3) and FA 1996, s. 205 and Sch. 41, Pt. V(1), for any accounting period ending after 31 March 1996 except in so far as it relates to the financial year 1995.]

468F Authorised unit trusts: distributions

468F [Repealed by FA 1994, s. 112 and Sch. 14, para. 4, and s. 258 and Sch. 26, Pt. V(13), in relation to distribution periods beginning on or after 1 April 1994.]

History – S. 468F repealed by FA 1994, s. 112 and Sch. 14, para. 4, and s. 258 and Sch. 26, Pt. V(13), in relation to distribution periods beginning on or after 1 April 1994.

468G Dividends paid to investment trusts

468G [Repealed by FA 1994, s. 112 and Sch. 14, para. 4, and s. 258 and Sch. 26, Pt. V(13), in relation to distribution periods beginning on or after 1 April 1994.]

History – S. 468G repealed by FA 1994, s. 112 and Sch. 14, para. 4, and s. 258 and Sch. 26, Pt. V(13), in relation to distribution periods beginning on or after 1 April 1994.

DISTRIBUTIONS OF AUTHORISED UNIT TRUSTS: GENERAL

468H Interpretation

468H [Ceased to have effect by virtue of F(No. 2)A 2005, s. 17(1)(a) and repealed by F(No. 2)A 2005, s. 70 and Sch. 11, Pt. 2(3).]

History – S. 468H ceased to have effect by virtue of F(No. 2)A 2005, s. 17(1)(a) and repealed by F(No. 2)A 2005, s. 70 and Sch. 11, Pt. 2(3) with effect from the following dates (by virtue of SI 2006/982):

- for the purposes of income tax for the year 2006–07 and subsequent years of assessment, and for distributions made on or after 6 April 2006;
- for the purposes of corporation tax on income, for accounting periods beginning on or after 1 April 2006, on chargeable gains, in relation to disposals made on or after 1 April 2006, and for distributions made on or after 1 April 2006.

Notes – S. 468H has been rewritten for income tax purposes as follows:
S. 468H(2): ITTOIA 2005, s. 375(1), 378, 388(1) and 391.
S. 468H(3): ITTOIA 2005, s. 375(1), 378, 388(1) and 391.
S. 468H(4): ITTOIA 2005, s. 374(2)–(4), 377(2)–(4), 387(2)–(4) and 390(2)–(4).
S. 468H(6): ITTOIA 2005, s. 373(5), 375(1), 376(7), 378, 386(5), 388(1), 389(6) and 391.

468I Distribution accounts

468I [Ceased to have effect by virtue of F(No. 2)A 2005, s. 17(1)(a) and repealed by F(No. 2)A 2005, s. 70 and Sch. 11, Pt. 2(3).]

History – S. 468I ceased to have effect by virtue of F(No. 2)A 2005, s. 17(1)(a) and repealed by F(No. 2)A 2005, s. 70 and Sch. 11, Pt. 2(3) with effect from the following dates (by virtue of SI 2006/982):

- for the purposes of income tax for the year 2006–07 and subsequent years of assessment, and for distributions made on or after 6 April 2006;
- for the purposes of corporation tax on income, for accounting periods beginning on or after 1 April 2006, on chargeable gains, in relation to disposals made on or after 1 April 2006, and for distributions made on or after 1 April 2006.

DIVIDEND AND FOREIGN INCOME DISTRIBUTIONS

468J Dividend distributions

468J [Ceased to have effect by virtue of F(No. 2)A 2005, s. 17(1)(a) and repealed by F(No. 2)A 2005, s. 70 and Sch. 11, Pt. 2(3).]

History – S. 468J ceased to have effect by virtue of F(No. 2)A 2005, s. 17(1)(a) and repealed by F(No. 2)A 2005, s. 70 and Sch. 11, Pt. 2(3) with effect from the following dates (by virtue of SI 2006/982):

- for the purposes of income tax for the year 2006–07 and subsequent years of assessment, and for distributions made on or after 6 April 2006;
- for the purposes of corporation tax on income, for accounting periods beginning on or after 1 April 2006, on chargeable gains, in relation to disposals made on or after 1 April 2006, and for distributions made on or after 1 April 2006.

Notes – Rewritten income tax provisions are now located as follows:
S. 468J(1): ITTOIA 2005, s. 386(1) and (3) and 389(1) and (3).
S. 468J(2): ITTOIA 2005, s. 386(1), (3) and (4), 387(2)–(4), 389(1), (3), (4) and (5) and 390(2)–(4).

468K Foreign income distributions

468K [Repealed by F(No. 2)A 1997, s. 36 and Sch. 6, para. 8(4), s. 52 and Sch. 8, Pt. II(11).]

History – S. 468K (which was inserted by *FA 1994, s. 112 and Sch. 14, para. 2* in relation to distribution periods beginning on or after 1 April 1994) *repealed by F(No. 2)A 1997, s. 36 and Sch. 6, para. 8(4), s. 52 and Sch. 8, Pt. II(11)*, with effect for distribution periods the distribution date for which falls on or after 6 April 1999.

INTEREST DISTRIBUTIONS

468L Interest distributions

468L [Ceased to have effect by virtue of F(No. 2)A 2005, s. 17(1)(a) and repealed by F(No. 2)A 2005, s. 70 and Sch. 11, Pt. 2(3).]

History – S. 468L ceased to have effect by virtue of F(No. 2)A 2005, s. 17(1)(a) and repealed by F(No. 2)A 2005, s. 70 and Sch. 11, Pt. 2(3) with effect from the following dates (by virtue of SI 2006/982):

- for the purposes of income tax for the year 2006–07 and subsequent years of assessment, and for distributions made on or after 6 April 2006;
- for the purposes of corporation tax on income, for accounting periods beginning on or after 1 April 2006, on chargeable gains, in relation to disposals made on or after 1 April 2006, and for distributions made on or after 1 April 2006.

Notes – Rewritten income tax provisions are now located as follows:
S. 468L(1): ITTOIA 2005, s. 373(1) and (3) and 376(6).
S. 468L(1A): ITTOIA 2005, s. 373(6) and 376(1), (3) and (5).
S. 468L(2): ITTOIA 2005, s. 373(1) and (3)–(5), 374(2)–(4), 376(1) and (3)–(5) and 377(2)–(4).

468M Cases where no obligation to deduct tax

468M [Ceased to have effect by virtue of F(No. 2)A 2005, s. 17(1)(a) and repealed by F(No. 2)A 2005, s. 70 and Sch. 11, Pt. 2(3).]

History – S. 468M ceased to have effect by virtue of F(No. 2)A 2005, s. 17(1)(a) and repealed by F(No. 2)A 2005, s. 70 and Sch. 11, Pt. 2(3) with effect from the following dates (by virtue of SI 2006/982):

- for the purposes of income tax for the year 2006–07 and subsequent years of assessment, and for distributions made on or after 6 April 2006;
- for the purposes of corporation tax on income, for accounting periods beginning on or after 1 April 2006, on chargeable gains, in relation to disposals made on or after 1 April 2006, and for distributions made on or after 1 April 2006.

468N Deduction of tax (mixed funds)

468N [Effectively repealed by FA 2003, s. 203(3) (together with the substitution of an entirely new s. 468M) with effect for interest distributions made on or after 16 October 2002.]

468O Residence condition and reputable intermediary condition

468O [Ceased to have effect by virtue of F(No. 2)A 2005, s. 17(1)(a) and repealed by F(No. 2)A 2005, s. 70 and Sch. 11, Pt. 2(3).]

History – S. 468O ceased to have effect by virtue of F(No. 2)A 2005, s. 17(1)(a) and repealed by F(No. 2)A 2005, s. 70 and Sch. 11, Pt. 2(3) with effect from the following dates (by virtue of SI 2006/982):

- for the purposes of income tax for the year 2006–07 and subsequent years of assessment, and for distributions made on or after 6 April 2006;
- for the purposes of corporation tax on income, for accounting periods beginning on or after 1 April 2006, on chargeable gains, in relation to disposals made on or after 1 April 2006, and for distributions made on or after 1 April 2006.

468P Residence declarations

468P [Ceased to have effect by virtue of F(No. 2)A 2005, s. 17(1)(a) and repealed by F(No. 2)A 2005, s. 70 and Sch. 11, Pt. 2(3).]

History – S. 468P ceased to have effect by virtue of F(No. 2)A 2005, s. 17(1)(a) and repealed by F(No. 2)A 2005, s. 70 and Sch. 11, Pt. 2(3) with effect from the following dates (by virtue of SI 2006/982):

- for the purposes of income tax for the year 2006–07 and subsequent years of assessment, and for distributions made on or after 6 April 2006;
- for the purposes of corporation tax on income, for accounting periods beginning on or after 1 April 2006, on chargeable gains, in relation to disposals made on or after 1 April 2006, and for distributions made on or after 1 April 2006.

468PA Section 468O(1A): consequences of reasonable but incorrect belief

468PA [Ceased to have effect by virtue of F(No. 2)A 2005, s. 17(1)(a) and repealed by F(No. 2)A 2005, s. 70 and Sch. 11, Pt. 2(3).]

History – S. 468PA ceased to have effect by virtue of F(No. 2)A 2005, s. 17(1)(a) and repealed by F(No. 2)A 2005, s. 70 and Sch. 11, Pt. 2(3) with effect from the following dates (by virtue of SI 2006/982):

- for the purposes of income tax for the year 2006–07 and subsequent years of assessment, and for distributions made on or after 6 April 2006;
- for the purposes of corporation tax on income, for accounting periods beginning on or after 1 April 2006, on chargeable gains, in relation to disposals made on or after 1 April 2006, and for distributions made on or after 1 April 2006.

468PB Regulations supplementing sections 468M to 468PA

468PB [Ceased to have effect by virtue of F(No. 2)A 2005, s. 17(1)(a) and repealed by F(No. 2)A 2005, s. 70 and Sch. 11, Pt. 2(3).]

History – S. 468PB ceased to have effect by virtue of F(No. 2)A 2005, s. 17(1)(a) and repealed by F(No. 2)A 2005, s. 70 and Sch. 11, Pt. 2(3) with effect from the following dates (by virtue of SI 2006/982):

- for the purposes of income tax for the year 2006–07 and subsequent years of assessment, and for distributions made on or after 6 April 2006;
- for the purposes of corporation tax on income, for accounting periods beginning on or after 1 April 2006, on chargeable gains, in relation to disposals made on or after 1 April 2006, and for distributions made on or after April 2006.

DISTRIBUTIONS TO CORPORATE UNIT HOLDER

468Q Dividend distribution to corporate unit holder

468Q [Ceased to have effect by virtue of F(No. 2)A 2005, s. 17(1)(a) and repealed by F(No. 2)A 2005, s. 70 and Sch. 11, Pt. 2(3).]

History – S. 468Q ceased to have effect by virtue of F(No. 2)A 2005, s. 17(1)(a) and repealed by F(No. 2)A 2005, s. 70 and Sch. 11, Pt. 2(3) with effect from the following dates (by virtue of SI 2006/982):

- for the purposes of income tax for the year 2006–07 and subsequent years of assessment, and for distributions made on or after 6 April 2006;
- for the purposes of corporation tax on income, for accounting periods beginning on or after 1 April 2006, on chargeable gains, in relation to disposals made on or after 1 April 2006, and for distributions made on or after 1 April 2006.

468R Foreign income distribution to corporate unit holder

468R [Repealed by F(No. 2)A 1997, s. 36 and Sch. 6, para. 8(7), s. 52 and Sch. 8, Pt. II(11).]

History – S. 468R repealed by F(No. 2)A 1997, s. 36 and Sch. 6, para. 8(7), s. 52 and Sch. 8, Pt. II(11) with effect for distribution periods the distribution date for which falls on or after 6 April 1999.

469 Other unit trusts

469 [Omitted by CTA 2010, s. 1177 and Sch. 1, para. 55 and repealed by CTA 2010, s. 1181 and Sch. 3, Pt. 1.]

History – S. 469 omitted by CTA 2010, s. 1177 and Sch. 1, para. 55 and repealed by CTA 2010, s. 1181 and Sch. 3, Pt. 1, with effect for corporation tax purposes for accounting periods ending on or after 1 April 2010, and for income and capital gains tax purposes for the tax year 2010–11 and subsequent tax years.

Notes – Rewritten income tax provisions are now located as follows:
S. 469(1): ITA 2007, s. 504(1).
S. 469(2): ITA 2007, s. 504(2), (3).
S. 469(2A): ITA 2007, s. 504(4).
S. 469(2B): ITA 2007, s. 504(4).
S. 469(3): ITA 2007, s. 941(2), (3), (5).
S. 469(3): ITTOIA 2005, s. 547(1) and (2), 548(1) and (2), 549 and 550.
S. 469(4): ITA 2007, s. 941(2), (3), (5), 964(2).
S. 469(4): ITTOIA 2005, s. 547(2) and 548(1) and (2).
S. 469(5): ITA 2007, s. 941(2), (3), (5), 964(2).
S. 469(5): ITTOIA 2005, s. 548(3) and (4).
S. 469(5A): ITA 2007, s. 942(4).
S. 469(5B): ITA 2007, s. 942(5).
S. 469(5C): ITA 2007, s. 943(1), (2), (3).
S. 469(6): ITA 2007, s. 941(2), (3), (5).
S. 469(6): ITTOIA 2005, s. 548(5)–(7).
S. 469(6A): ITA 2007, s. 989.
S. 469(7): ITA 2007, s. 1007(1), (2).
S. 469(8): ITA 2007, s. 1007(3).
S. 469(9): ITA 2007, s. 504(4), (5).
S. 469 rewritten for corporation tax purposes as follows:
S. 469(1): CTA 2010, s. 621(1), 622(1), 1119.
S. 469(2): CTA 2010, s. 621(2), 622(2).
S. 469(4A): CTA 2009, s. 972(1), (2).
S. 469(4B): CTA 2009, s. 973(1).
S. 469(4C): CTA 2009, s. 973(2).
S. 469(5): CTA 2009, s. 973(3), (4).
S. 469(6): CTA 2009, s. 973(5), (6), (7).

469A Court common investment funds

469A [Omitted by CTA 2010, s. 1177 and Sch. 1, para. 56 and repealed by CTA 2010, s. 1181 and Sch. 3, Pt. 1.]

History – S. 469A omitted by CTA 2010, s. 1177 and Sch. 1, para. 56 and repealed by CTA 2010, s. 1181 and Sch. 3, Pt. 1, with effect for corporation tax purposes for accounting periods ending on or after 1 April 2010, and for income and capital gains tax purposes for the tax year 2010–11 and subsequent tax years.

Notes – S. 469A rewritten for corporation tax purposes as follows:
S. 469A(1): CTA 2010, s. 620(1), (2).
S. 469A(1A): CTA 2010, s. 620(3).
S. 469A(2): CTA 2010, s. 620(4).

470 Transitional provisions relating to unit trusts

470 [S. 470(1), (3) repealed by FA 1998, s. 165 and Sch. 27, Pt. III(23); s. 470(2) ceased to have effect on 29 April 1988 (SI 1988/745).]

DEALERS IN SECURITIES, BANKS AND INSURANCE BUSINESSES

471 Exchange of securities in connection with conversion operations, nationalisation etc.

471 [S. 471 repealed by FA 1998, s. 101(1), s. 165 and Sch. 27, Pt. III(23).]

History – S. 471 repealed by FA 1998, s. 101(6), s. 165 and Sch. 27, Pt. III(23) with effect in relation to exchanges made after 31 July 1998 (FA 1998, s. 101(3)).

472 Distribution of securities issued in connection with nationalisation etc.

472 [S. 472 repealed by FA 1998, s. 101(2), s. 165 and Sch. 27, Pt. III(23).]

History – S. 472 repealed by FA 1998, s. 101(2); s. 165 and Sch. 27, Pt. III(23), with effect in relation to issues of securities occurring after 31 July 1998 (FA 1998, s. 101(4)).

472A Trading profits etc. from securities: taxation of amounts taken to reserves

472A [Omitted by CTA 2009, s. 1322 and Sch. 1, para. 158 and repealed by CTA 2009, s. 1326 and Sch. 3, Pt. 1, with effect for corporation tax purposes for accounting periods ending on or after 1 April 2009, and for income tax and capital gains tax purposes for the tax year 2009–10 and subsequent tax years.]

Notes – Rewritten income tax provisions are now located as follows:
S. 472A(1): ITTOIA 2005, s. 149(1).
S. 472A(2): ITTOIA 2005, s. 149(2).
S. 472A(3): ITTOIA 2005, s. 149(3).
S. 472A(4): ITTOIA 2005, s. 149(4).
S. 472A rewritten for corporation tax purposes as follows:
S. 472A(1): CTA 2009, s. 128(1).
S. 472A(2): CTA 2009, s. 128(2).
S. 472A(3): CTA 2009, s. 128(3).
S. 472A(4): CTA 2009, s. 128(4).

473 Conversion etc. of securities held as circulating capital

473 [Omitted by CTA 2009, s. 1322 and Sch. 1, para. 159 and repealed by CTA 2009, s. 1326 and Sch. 3, Pt. 1.]

History – S. 473 omitted by CTA 2009, s. 1322 and Sch. 1, para. 159 and repealed by CTA 2009, s. 1326 and Sch. 3, Pt. 1, with effect for corporation tax purposes for accounting periods ending on or after 1 April 2009, and for income tax and capital gains tax purposes for the tax year 2009–10 and subsequent tax years.

Notes – Rewritten income tax provisions are now located as follows:
S. 473(1): ITTOIA 2005, s. 150(1).
S. 473(2): ITTOIA 2005, s. 150(2).
S. 473(2A): ITTOIA 2005, s. 150(3).
S. 473(3): ITTOIA 2005, s. 150(4).
S. 473(4): ITTOIA 2005, s. 150(5) and (6).
S. 473(6): ITTOIA 2005, s. 150(8).
S. 473(7): ITTOIA 2005, s. 150(7).
S. 473 rewritten for corporation tax purposes as follows:
S. 473(1): CTA 2009, s. 129(1).
S. 473(2): CTA 2009, s. 129(2).
S. 473(2A): CTA 2009, s. 129(3).
S. 473(3): CTA 2009, s. 129(1), (4).
S. 473(4): CTA 2009, s. 129(5), (6).
S. 473(6): CTA 2009, s. 129(8).
S. 473(7): CTA 2009, s. 129(7).

474 Treatment of tax-free income

474 [Repealed by FA 1996, s. 154 and Sch. 28, para. 2, and s. 79 and Sch. 7, para. 18 and s. 205 and Sch. 41, Pt. V(2), (18) for 1996–97 and later years of assessment (income tax) and accounting periods ending after 31 March 1996 (corporation tax).]

475 Tax-free Treasury securities: exclusion of interest on borrowed money

475 [Omitted by TIOPA 2010, s. 371 and Sch. 7, para. 41 and repealed by TIOPA 2010, s. 378 and Sch. 10, Pt. 12.]

History – S. 475 omitted by TIOPA 2010, s. 371 and Sch. 7, para. 41 and repealed by TIOPA 2010, s. 378 and Sch. 10, Pt. 12, with effect for corporation tax purposes for accounting periods ending on or after 1 April 2010, for income tax and capital gains tax purposes for the tax year 2010–11 and subsequent tax years, and for petroleum revenue tax purposes for chargeable periods beginning on or after 1 July 2010.

Notes – S. 475 rewritten in CTA 2009 as follows:
S. 475(2)(B): CTA 2009, s. 405(2).
S. 475 rewritten in TIOPA 2010, Sch. 7, para. 43.

Chapter IV – Building Societies, Banks, Savings Banks, Industrial and Provident Societies and Others

476 Building societies: regulations for payment of tax

476 [Repealed by FA 1990, s. 30 and Sch. 5, para. 2, s. 132 and Sch. 19, Pt. IV, with effect for 1991–92 and subsequent years of assessment.]

477 Investments becoming or ceasing to be relevant building society investments

477 [Repealed by FA 1990, s. 30 and Sch. 5, para. 3, s. 132 and Sch. 19, Pt. IV, with effect as regards any time falling on or after 6 April 1991.]

477A Building societies: regulations for loan relationships

477A [Omitted by CTA 2010, s. 1177 and Sch. 1, para. 57 and repealed by CTA 2010, s. 1181 and Sch. 3, Pt. 1.]

History – S. 477A omitted by CTA 2010, s. 1177 and Sch. 1, para. 57 and repealed by CTA 2010, s. 1181 and Sch. 3, Pt. 1, with effect for corporation tax purposes for accounting periods ending on or after 1 April 2010, and for income and capital gains tax purposes for the tax year 2010–11 and subsequent tax years.

Notes – S. 477A rewritten as follows:
S. 477A(1): ITA 2007, s. 852(1), (2), (3), 871(1), (2), (3), 872(1), (4), 946, 962(1), Sch. 1 para. 247.
S. 477A(1A): ITA 2007, s. 870(2), 872(5).
S. 477A(2): ITA 2007, s. 852(1), (2), (3), 871(1), (2), (3), 872(3), 962(1), Sch. 1 para. 247.
S. 477A(2A): ITA 2007, s. 871(1), (2), (3).
S. 477A(5): ITTOIA 2005, s. 367(3) and 372(1).
S. 477A(6): ITTOIA 2005, s. 367(3) and 372(1).
S. 477A(7): ITA 2007, s. 880.
S. 477A(9): ITTOIA 2005, s. 367(3) and 372(1) and (2).
S. 477A(10): ITA 2007, s. 870(2).
S. 477A rewritten for corporation tax purposes as follows:
S. 477A(3): CTA 2009, s. 498(1), (2), (3), (5); CTA 2010, s. 1054(1), (2).
S. 477A(4): CTA 2009, s. 498(4).
S. 477A(9): CTA 2010, s. 1054(1), (2).
S. 477A(10): CTA 2009, s. 498(5).

477B Building societies: incidental costs of issuing qualifying shares

477B [Omitted by CTA 2009, s. 1322 and Sch. 1, para. 162 and repealed by CTA 2009, s. 1326 and Sch. 3, Pt. 1.]

History – S. 477B omitted by CTA 2009, s. 1322 and Sch. 1, para. 162 and repealed by CTA 2009, s. 1326 and Sch. 3, Pt. 1, with effect for corporation tax purposes for accounting periods ending on or after 1 April 2009, and for income tax and capital gains tax purposes for the tax year 2009–10 and subsequent tax years.

Notes – S. 477B rewritten as follows:
S. 477B(1): CTA 2009, s. 131(1).
S. 477B(1A): CTA 2009, s. 131(3).
S. 477B(2): CTA 2009, s. 131(2).
S. 477B(3): CTA 2009, s. 131(4), (5), (6).
S. 477B(4): CTA 2009, s. 131(6).
S. 477B(5): CTA 2009, s. 131(1), (2).

478 Building societies: time for payment of tax

478 [Repealed by FA 1994, s. 258 and Sch. 26, Pt. V(23) with effect for accounting periods ending on or after 1 July 1999, the self-assessment appointed day.]

479 Interest paid on deposits with banks etc.

479 [Repealed by FA 1990, s. 30 and Sch. 5, para. 5, s. 132 and Sch. 19, Pt. IV, with effect as regards interest paid or credited on or after 6 April 1991.]

480 Deposits becoming or ceasing to be composite rate deposits

480 [Repealed by FA 1990, s. 30 and Sch. 5, para. 6, s. 132 and Sch. 19, Pt. IV, with effect as regards any time falling on or after 6 April 1991.]

480A Relevant deposits: deduction of tax from interest payments

480A [Omitted by ITA 2007, s. 1027 and Sch. 1, para. 89 and repealed by ITA 2007, s. 1031 and Sch. 3, Pt. 1 with effect for 2007–08 and subsequent tax years]

Notes – S. 480A rewritten for income tax purposes as follows:
S. 480A(1): ITA 2007, s. 851(1), (2), 855(1).
S. 480A(2): ITA 2007, s. 946.
S. 480A(3): ITA 2007, s. 946, 953(6), (7).
S. 480A(4): ITA 2007, s. 948(1), 953(7).
S. 480A(5): ITA 2007, s. 850(6).

480B Relevant deposits: exception from section 480A

480B [Omitted by ITA 2007, s. 1027 and Sch. 1, para. 89 and repealed by ITA 2007, s. 1031 and Sch. 3, Pt. 1 with effect for 2007–08 and subsequent tax years.]

Notes – S. 480B rewritten for income tax purposes as follows:
S. 480B(1): ITA 2007, s. 852(1), (4).
S. 480B(2): ITA 2007, s. 852(2), (4).
S. 480B(3): ITA 2007, s. 852(3).
S. 480B(4): ITA 2007, s. 850(6).

480C Relevant deposits: computation of tax on interest

480C [Omitted by ITTOIA 2005, s. 882 and Sch. 1, para. 185 and repealed by s. 884 and Sch. 3.]

History – S. 480C omitted by ITTOIA 2005, s. 882(1) and Sch. 1, para. 185 and repealed by s. 884 and Sch. 3; effective for income tax purposes for 2005–06 onwards and for corporation tax purposes for accounting periods ending after 5 April 2005 (ITTOIA 2005, s. 883(1)).

ICTA 1988

481 "Deposit-taker", 'deposit' and 'relevant deposit'

481 [Omitted by ITA 2007, s. 1027 and Sch. 1, para. 89 and repealed by ITA 2007, s. 1031 and Sch. 3, Pt. 1 with effect for 2007–08 and subsequent tax years.]

Notes – S. 481 rewritten for income tax purposes as follows:
S. 481(2): ITA 2007, s. 853(1), (2), (3), (4), (5), (6), 854(1).
S. 481(3): ITA 2007, s. 855(2), 983.
S. 481(4): ITA 2007, s. 856(1), (2), (3), (4), (5), (6).
S. 481(4A): ITA 2007, s. 873(1), (2).
S. 481(5): ITA 2007, s. 858(2), (3), 859(2), (3), 860(2), (3), 861(2), (3), 863(1), 864, 865, 866(1), 867(1), (2), 868(1), (2), 870(1), (2), 1022(1).
S. 481(5B): ITA 2007, Sch. 2 para. 154(1), (2), (3).
S. 481(6): ITA 2007, s. 872(1), (2), (4).

482 Supplementary provisions

482 [Omitted by ITA 2007, s. 1027 and Sch. 1, para. 89 and repealed by ITA 2007, s. 1031 and Sch. 3, Pt. 1 with effect for 2007–08 and subsequent tax years.]

Notes – S. 482 rewritten for income tax purposes as follows:
S. 482(1): ITA 2007, s. 850(6).
S. 482(2): ITA 2007, s. 858(2), (4), 859(2), (4), 860(2), 861(2), (4).
S. 482(2A): ITA 2007, s. 858(2), 859(2).
S. 482(3): ITA 2007, s. 862(1), (2).
S. 482(4): ITA 2007, s. 862(2), (3).
S. 482(5): ITA 2007, s. 857(1), (2), (3).
S. 482(5A): ITA 2007, s. 873(3), (4), (5), (6).
S. 482(6) ("appropriate person"): ITA 2007, s. 858(5), 859(5), 860(4), 861(5).
S. 482(6) ("certificate of deposit"): ITA 2007, s. 1019.
S. 482(6) ("general client account deposit"): ITA 2007, s. 863(2), (3).
S. 482(6) ("qualifying certificate of deposit"): ITA 2007, s. 985(1), (2), 986(1), (2).
S. 482(6) ("qualifying time deposit"): ITA 2007, s. 866(2), (3).
S. 482(6) ("uncertificated eligible debt security units"): ITA 2007, s. 986(3).
S. 482(7): ITA 2007, s. 868(4).
S. 482(8): ITA 2007, Sch. 2 para. 157(1), (2).
S. 482(9): ITA 2007, Sch. 2 para. 158(1), (2), (3).
S. 482(10): ITA 2007, s. 854(2), (3).
S. 482(11): ITA 2007, s. 871(1).
S. 482(11A): ITA 2007, s. 871(3).
S. 482(12): ITA 2007, s. 871(2), 872(3).

482A Audit powers in relation to non-residents

482A [Repealed by FA 2000, s. 145(10), 156 and Sch. 40, Pt. V.]

History – S. 482A repealed by FA 2000, s. 145(10), 156 and Sch. 40, Pt. V, with effect in relation to amounts paid, credited or received on or after 6 April 2001.

483 Determination of reduced rate for building societies and composite rate for banks etc.

483(1)–(3) [Repealed by FA 1990, s. 30, Sch. 5, para. 12, s. 132 and Sch. 19, Pt. IV.]

483(4) [Spent.]

483(5) [Repealed by FA 1990, s. 30, Sch. 5, para. 12, s. 132 and Sch. 19, Pt. IV.]

484 Savings banks: exemption from tax

484 [Repealed by FA 1996, s. 104 and Sch. 14, para. 29 and s. 205 and Sch. 41, Pt. V(3).]

History – S. 484 repealed by FA 1996, s. 104 and Sch. 14 para. 29 and s. 205 and Sch. 41, Pt. V(3) for accounting periods ending after 31 March 1996 (corporation tax), subject to FA 1996, Sch. 15.

485 Savings banks: supplemental

485 [Repealed by FA 1996, s. 104 and Sch. 14, para. 29 and s. 205 and Sch. 41, Pt. V(3).]

History – S. 485 repealed by FA 1996, s. 104 and Sch. 14 para. 29 and s. 205 and Sch. 41, Pt. V(3) for accounting periods ending after 31 March 1996 (corporation tax), subject to FA 1996, Sch. 15.

486 Industrial and provident societies and co-operative associations

486 [Omitted by CTA 2010, s. 1177 and Sch. 1, para. 58 and repealed by CTA 2010, s. 1181 and Sch. 3, Pt. 1.]

History – S. 486 omitted by CTA 2010, s. 1177 and Sch. 1, para. 58 and repealed by CTA 2010, s. 1181 and Sch. 3, Pt. 1, with effect for corporation tax purposes for accounting periods ending on or after 1 April 2010, and for income and capital gains tax purposes for the tax year 2010–11 and subsequent tax years.

Notes – Rewritten income tax provisions are now located as follows:
S. 486(1): ITTOIA 2005, s. 367(3) and 379(1).
S. 486(2): ITA 2007, s. 887(1).
S. 486(3): ITA 2007, s. 874(5), 887(1).
S. 486(4): ITTOIA 2005, s. 367(3), 379(1), and 830(1) and (2).
S. 486(6): ITA 2007, s. 887(2), (3).
S. 486(9): ITTOIA 2005, s. 379(1) and (2).
S. 486(12): ITA 2007, s. 151(1), 887(5), (6), Sch. 1 para. 132.
S. 486(12): ITTOIA 2005, s. 379(1)–(5).
S. 486 rewritten for corporation tax purposes as follows:
S. 486(1): CTA 2009, s. 499(1), 500(2); CTA 2010, s. 1055(1), (2), (3), 1057(1), (2), (3).
S. 486(4): CTA 2009, s. 499(2).
S. 486(7): CTA 2009, s. 500(1), (2).
S. 486(8): CTA 2010, Sch. 1, para. 248.
S. 486(9): CTA 2010, s. 1057(1), (2), Sch. 1, para. 248
S. 486(10): CTA 2009, s. 132(1), (2), (3), (4).
S. 486(11): CTA 2009, s. Sch. 1, para. 100.
S. 486(12): CTA 2009, s. 499(1), (4), (5), (6), 500(2), Sch. 1, para. 272(2); CTA 2010, s. 1055(1), (2), (4); 1057(1), (2), (4); (4); 1058(2), (3), (4), Sch. 1, para. 248.

487 Credit unions

487 [Omitted by CTA 2009, s. 1322 and Sch. 1, para. 164 and repealed by CTA 2009, s. 1326 and Sch. 3, Pt. 1.]

History – S. 487 omitted by CTA 2009, s. 1322 and Sch. 1, para. 164 and repealed by CTA 2009, s. 1326 and Sch. 3, Pt. 1, with effect for corporation tax purposes for accounting periods ending on or after 1 April 2009, and for income tax and capital gains tax purposes for the tax year 2009–10 and subsequent tax years.

Notes – S. 487 rewritten as follows:
S. 487(1): CTA 2009, s. 40(1), 397(1).
S. 487(2): CTA 2009, s. 397(2).
S. 487(3): CTA 2009, s. 133.
S. 487(3A): CTA 2009, s. 397(3).
S. 487(4): CTA 2009, s. 1218(2).
S. 487(5): CTA 2009, s. 40(2)

488 Co-operative housing associations

488 [Omitted by CTA 2010, s. 1177 and Sch. 1, para. 59 and repealed by CTA 2010, s. 1181 and Sch. 3, Pt. 1.]

History – S. 488 omitted by CTA 2010, s. 1177 and Sch. 1, para. 59 and repealed by CTA 2010, s. 1181 and Sch. 3, Pt. 1, with effect for corporation tax purposes for accounting periods ending on or after 1 April 2010, and for income and capital gains tax purposes for the tax year 2010–11 and subsequent tax years, subject to transitional provisions in CTA 2010, s. 1180 and Sch. 2, para. 80.

Notes – S. 488 rewritten as follows:
S. 488(1): CTA 2010, s. 642(1), (2), (3).
S. 488(2): CTA 2010, s. 642(4).
S. 488(4): CTA 2010, s. 648(1).
S. 488(5): CTA 2010, s. 643(1), (2).
S. 488(6): CTA 2010, s. 644(1), (2), 645(1), (2), (3), (4), (5), (6), 1166(1).
S. 488(7): CTA 2010, s. 644(3).
S. 488(7A): CTA *2010*, s. *646*(1), (2).
S. 488(8): CTA 2010, s. 649(1), (2), (3), (4), (5), (6).
S. 488(9): CTA 2010, s. 647(1).
S. 488(10): CTA 2010, s. 647(2), (3), (4).
S. 488(11): CTA 2010, s. 647(2).
S. 488(11A): CTA 2010, s. 648(2), (3), (4).

489 Self-build societies

489 [Omitted by CTA 2010, s. 1177 and Sch. 1, para. 60 and repealed by CTA 2010, s. 1181 and Sch. 3, Pt. 1.]

History – S. 489 omitted by CTA 2010, s. 1177 and Sch. 1, para. 60 and repealed by CTA 2010, s. 1181 and Sch. 3, Pt. 1, with effect for corporation tax purposes for accounting periods ending on or after 1 April 2010, and for income and capital gains tax purposes for the tax year 2010–11 and subsequent tax years, subject to transitional provisions in CTA 2010, s. 1180 and Sch. 2, para. 81.

Notes – S. 489 rewritten as follows:
S. 489(1): CTA 2010, s. 651(1).
S. 489(2): CTA 2010, s. 656(1).
S. 489(3): CTA 2010, s. 652(1), (2).
S. 489(4): CTA 2010, s. 653(1), (2), (3).
S. 489(5): CTA 2010, s. 653(4).
S. 489(5A): CTA 2010, s. 654(1), (2).
S. 489(6): CTA 2010, s. 657(1), (2), (3), (4).
S. 489(7): CTA 2010, s. 655(1).
S. 489(8): CTA 2010, s. 655(2), (3), (4).
S. 489(9): CTA 2010, s. 655(2).
S. 489(9A): CTA 2010, s. 656(2), (3), (4).
S. 489(10): CTA 2010, s. 655(5).
S. 489(11): CTA 2010, s. 650(1), (2), (3), 651(2), (3).
S. 489(12): CTA 2010, s. 653(1), (2), (3), (4), 657(5), (6), (7).

490 Companies carrying on a mutual business or not carrying on a business

490 [Omitted by CTA 2010, s. 1177 and Sch. 1, para. 61 and repealed by CTA 2010, s. 1181 and Sch. 3, Pt. 1.]

History – S. 490 omitted by CTA 2010, s. 1177 and Sch. 1, para. 61 and repealed by CTA 2010, s. 1181 and Sch. 3, Pt. 1, with effect for corporation tax purposes for accounting periods ending on or after 1 April 2010, and for income and capital gains tax purposes for the tax year 2010–11 and subsequent tax years.

Notes – S. 490 rewritten as follows:
S. 490(1): CTA 2010, s. 1070(1), (2), (3).
S. 490(2): CTA 2010, s. 1070(4).
S. 490(3): CTA 2010, s. 1070(5).
S. 490(4): CTA 2010, s. 1071(1), (2), (3),(4), (5).

491 Distribution of assets of body corporate carrying on mutual business

491 [Omitted by CTA 2009, s. 1322 and Sch. 1, para. 165 and repealed by CTA 2009, s. 1326 and Sch. 3, Pt. 1.]

History – S. 491 omitted by CTA 2009, s. 1322 and Sch. 1, para. 165 and repealed by CTA 2009, s. 1326 and Sch. 3, Pt. 1, with effect for corporation tax purposes for accounting periods ending on or after 1 April 2009, and for income tax and capital gains tax purposes for the tax year 2009–10 and subsequent tax years.

Notes – Rewritten income tax provisions are now located as follows:
S. 491(1): ITTOIA 2005, s. 104(1), (4) and (6).
S. 491(2): ITTOIA 2005, s. 104(5).
S. 491(3): ITTOIA 2005, s. 104(1)–(3).
S. 491(4): ITTOIA 2005, s. 104(1) and (2).
S. 491(6): ITTOIA 2005, s. 104(3).
S. 491(8): ITTOIA 2005, s. 104(1).
S. 491(10): ITTOIA 2005, s. 104(1)–(3).
S. 491(11): ITTOIA 2005, s. 104(7).
ITTOIA 2005 does not rewrite the references in ICTA 1988, s. 491(9) and (11) to mutual insurance and industrial and provident societies as they are thought no longer helpful. (See ITTOIA 2005, Explanatory Notes, Annex 1, Table 1 (Change 158).)
S. 491 rewritten for corporation tax purposes as follows:
S. 491(1): CTA 2009, s. 101(1), (4), (6).
S. 491(2): CTA 2009, s. 101(5).
S. 491(3): CTA 2009, s. 101(1), (2), (3), 283(2).
S. 491(4): CTA 2009, s. 101(1), (2).
S. 491(6): CTA 2009, s. 101(3), 283(2).
S. 491(7): CTA 2009, s. 197(1).
S. 491(8): CTA 2009, s. 101(1).
S. 491(10): not rewritten (see CTA 2009 Explanatory Notes, Annex 1, Change 2).
S. 491(11): CTA 2009, s. 101(7).

Chapter V – Petroleum Extraction Activities

492 Treatment of oil extraction activities etc. for tax purposes

492 [Omitted by CTA 2010, s. 1177 and Sch. 1, para. 62 and repealed by CTA 2010, s. 1181 and Sch. 3, Pt. 1.]

History – S. 492 omitted by CTA 2010, s. 1177 and Sch. 1, para. 62 and repealed by CTA 2010, s. 1181 and Sch. 3, Pt. 1, with effect for corporation tax purposes for accounting periods ending on or after 1 April 2010, and for income and capital gains tax purposes for the tax year 2010–11 and subsequent tax years.

Notes – Rewritten income tax provisions are now located at:
S. 492(1): ITTOIA 2005, s. 16(1) and (2)
S. 492(2): ITA 2007, s. 80(1), (2).

S. 492(4): ITA 2007, s. 87(1), (2).
S. 492 rewritten for corporation tax purposes as follows:
S. 492(1): CTA 2010, s. 274, 279.
S. 492(3): CTA 2010, s. 304(1).
S. 492(3A): CTA 2010, s. 303.
S. 492(4): CTA 2010, s. 304(2), (3), (4), (5), (6).
S. 492(6): CTA 2010, s. 306(1).
S. 492(7): CTA 2010, s. 306(2), (3).
S. 492(8): CTA 2010, s. 305(1).

493 Valuation of oil disposed of or appropriated in certain circumstances

493(A1) [Omitted by CTA 2010, s. 1177 and Sch. 1, para. 63 and repealed by CTA 2010, s. 1181 and Sch. 3, Pt. 1.]

493(A2) [Omitted by CTA 2010, s. 1177 and Sch. 1, para. 63 and repealed by CTA 2010, s. 1181 and Sch. 3, Pt. 1.]

493(A3) [Omitted by CTA 2010, s. 1177 and Sch. 1, para. 63 and repealed by CTA 2010, s. 1181 and Sch. 3, Pt. 1.]

493(1) [Omitted by CTA 2010, s. 1177 and Sch. 1, para. 63 and repealed by CTA 2010, s. 1181 and Sch. 3, Pt. 2; also omitted by TIOPA 2010, s. 374 and Sch. 8, para. 181 and repealed by TIOPA 2010, s. 378 and Sch. 10, Pt. 6.]

493(1A) [Omitted by CTA 2010, s. 1177 and Sch. 1, para. 63 and repealed by CTA 2010, s. 1181 and Sch. 3, Pt. 2; also omitted by TIOPA 2010, s. 374 and Sch. 8, para. 181 and repealed by TIOPA 2010, s. 378 and Sch. 10, Pt. 6.]

493(2) [Omitted by CTA 2010, s. 1177 and Sch. 1, para. 63 and repealed by CTA 2010, s. 1181 and Sch. 3, Pt. 2; also omitted by TIOPA 2010, s. 374 and Sch. 8, para. 181 and repealed by TIOPA 2010, s. 378 and Sch. 10, Pt. 6.]

493(3) [Omitted by CTA 2010, s. 1177 and Sch. 1, para. 63 and repealed by CTA 2010, s. 1181 and Sch. 3, Pt. 2; also omitted by TIOPA 2010, s. 374 and Sch. 8, para. 181 and repealed by TIOPA 2010, s. 378 and Sch. 10, Pt. 6.]

493(4) [Omitted by CTA 2010, s. 1177 and Sch. 1, para. 63 and repealed by CTA 2010, s. 1181 and Sch. 3, Pt. 2; also omitted by TIOPA 2010, s. 374 and Sch. 8, para. 181 and repealed by TIOPA 2010, s. 378 and Sch. 10, Pt. 6.]

493(5) [Omitted by CTA 2010, s. 1177 and Sch. 1, para. 63 and repealed by CTA 2010, s. 1181 and Sch. 3, Pt. 2; also omitted by TIOPA 2010, s. 374 and Sch. 8, para. 181 and repealed by TIOPA 2010, s. 378 and Sch. 10, Pt. 6.]

493(6) [Omitted by CTA 2010, s. 1177 and Sch. 1, para. 63 and repealed by CTA 2010, s. 1181 and Sch. 3, Pt. 2; also omitted by TIOPA 2010, s. 374 and Sch. 8, para. 181 and repealed by TIOPA 2010, s. 378 and Sch. 10, Pt. 6.]

History – S. 493(A1)–(A3) repealed by CTA 2010, s. 1181 and Sch. 3, Pt. 1, with effect for corporation tax purposes for accounting periods ending on or after 1 April 2010, and for income and capital gains tax purposes for the tax year 2010–11 and subsequent tax years.
S. 493(1)–(6) omitted by CTA 2010, s. 1177 and Sch. 1, para. 63 and repealed by CTA 2010, s. 1181 and Sch. 3, Pt. 2 with effect for corporation tax purposes for accounting periods ending on or after 1 April 2010. S. 493(1)–(6) also omitted by TIOPA 2010, s. 374 and Sch. 8, para. 181 and repealed by TIOPA 2010, s. 378 and Sch. 10, Pt. 6, with effect for corporation tax purposes for accounting periods ending on or after 1 April 2010, for income tax and capital gains tax purposes for the tax year 2010–11 and subsequent tax years, and for petroleum revenue tax purposes for chargeable periods beginning on or after 1 July 2010.

Notes – S. 493 rewritten in CTA 2010 as follows:
S. 493(A1): CTA 2010, s. 280(1), (3), (9).
S. 493(A2): CTA 2010, s. 280(2), (4), (5), (6), (7), (8).
S. 493(A3): CTA 2010, s. 280(10).
S. 493(1): CTA 2010, s. 281(1), (2).
S. 493(1A): CTA 2010, s. 278, 283(1), (2), (3).
S. 493(2): CTA 2010, s. 284(1), (2), (3), (4), (5), (6).
S. 493(3): CTA 2010, s. 282(1), (2), (3), (4), (5).
S. 493(4): CTA 2010, s. 285(1), (2), (3), (4), (5).
S. 493(5): CTA 2010, s. 282(6), (7), 285(6), (7).
S. 493(6): CTA 2010, s. 282(6), 285(6).
S. 493 rewritten in TIOPA 2010 as follows:
S. 493(1), (1A), (2), (3), (4), (5), (6): TIOPA 2010, Sch. 1, para. 2.

494 Loan relationships etc.

494 [Omitted by CTA 2010, s. 1177 and Sch. 1, para. 64 and repealed by CTA 2010, s. 1181 and Sch. 3, Pt. 1.]

History – S. 494 omitted by CTA 2010, s. 1177 and Sch. 1, para. 64 and repealed by CTA 2010, s. 1181 and Sch. 3, Pt. 1, with effect for corporation tax purposes for accounting periods ending on or after 1 April 2010, and for income and capital gains tax purposes for the tax year 2010–11 and subsequent tax years.

Notes – S. 494 rewritten as follows:
S. 494(2): CTA 2010, s. 286(1), (2), (3), (4) , (6), 287(2), (3), (4), (6), 1176(1).

S. 494(2ZA): CTA 2010, s. 287(1), (2), (3), (4), (6).
S. 494(2A): CTA 2010, s. 286(5), 287(5).

494AA Sale and lease-back

494AA [Omitted by CTA 2010, s. 1177 and Sch. 1, para. 64 and repealed by CTA 2010, s. 1181 and Sch. 3, Pt. 1.]

History – S. 494AA omitted by CTA 2010, s. 1177 and Sch. 1, para. 64 and repealed by CTA 2010, s. 1181 and Sch. 3, Pt. 1, with effect for corporation tax purposes for accounting periods ending on or after 1 April 2010, and for income and capital gains tax purposes for the tax year 2010–11 and subsequent tax years.

Notes – S. 494AA rewritten as follows:
S. 494AA(1): CTA 2010, s. 288(1), (2), (3), (4).
S. 494AA(2): CTA 2010, s. 288(5).
S. 494AA(3): CTA 2010, s. 288(6).
S. 494AA(4): CTA 2010, s. 288(7).
S. 494AA(5): CTA 2010, s. 288(8).
S. 494AA(6): CTA 2010, s. 288(9).

494A Computation of amount available for surrender by way of group relief

494A [Omitted by CTA 2010, s. 1177 and Sch. 1, para. 64 and repealed by CTA 2010, s. 1181 and Sch. 3, Pt. 1.]

History – S. 494A omitted by CTA 2010, s. 1177 and Sch. 1, para. 64 and repealed by CTA 2010, s. 1181 and Sch. 3, Pt. 1, with effect for corporation tax purposes for accounting periods ending on or after 1 April 2010, and for income and capital gains tax purposes for the tax year 2010–11 and subsequent tax years.

Notes – S. 494A rewritten as follows:
S. 494A(1): CTA 2010, s. 305(2).
S. 494A(2): CTA 2010, s. 305(3).
S. 494A(3): CTA 2010, s. 305(3).

ICTA 1988

495 Regional development grants

495 [Omitted by CTA 2010, s. 1177 and Sch. 1, para. 65 and repealed for corporation tax purposes only by CTA 2010, s. 1181 and Sch. 3, Pt. 2; also omitted by TIOPA 2010, s. 374 and Sch. 8, para. 182 and repealed by TIOPA 2010, s. 378 and Sch. 10, Pt. 6.]

History – S. 495 omitted by CTA 2010, s. 1177 and Sch. 1, para. 65 and repealed by CTA 2010, s. 1181 and Sch. 3, Pt. 2, with effect for corporation tax purposes for accounting periods ending on or after 1 April 2010. S. 495 also omitted by TIOPA 2010, s. 374 and Sch. 8, para. 182 and repealed by TIOPA 2010, s. 378 and Sch. 10, Pt. 6, with effect for corporation tax purposes for accounting periods ending on or after 1 April 2010, for income tax and capital gains tax purposes for the tax year 2010-11 and subsequent tax years, and for petroleum revenue tax purposes for chargeable periods beginning on or after 1 July 2010.
At the time of its repeal by CTA 2010, s. 1181 and Sch. 3, Pt. 2, in former s. 495(1)(b), the words ", 3" and ", industrial buildings" and in s. 495(3)(b), the word ", 3" were to be omitted by FA 2008, s. 84 and Sch. 27, para. 21, with effect in relation to chargeable periods beginning on or after 1 April 2011 (corporation tax) and 6 April 2011 (income tax).

Notes – S. 495 rewritten for corporation tax as follows:
S. 495(1): CTA 2010, s. 289(1), (2), (3).
S. 495(2): CTA 2010, s. 289(4), (5).
S. 495(3): CTA 2010, s. 290(1), (2), (3, (4).
S. 495(4): CTA 2010, s. 290(5), (6).
S. 495(5): CTA 2010, s. 290(7).
S. 495(6): CTA 2010, s. 290(8).
S. 495(7): CTA 2010, s. 289(6), 290(2), (4), (9).
S. 495 rewritten in TIOPA 2010 as follows:
S. 495(1), (2), (3), (4), (5), (6), (7): TIOPA 2010, Sch. 1, para. 2.

496 Tariff receipts and tax-exempt tariffing receipts

496 [Omitted by CTA 2010, s. 1177 and Sch. 1, para. 66 and repealed for corporation tax purposes only by CTA 2010, s. 1181 and Sch. 3, Pt. 2; also omitted by TIOPA 2010, s. 374 and Sch. 8, para. 183 and repealed by TIOPA 2010, s. 378 and Sch. 10, Pt. 6.]

History – S. 496 omitted by CTA 2010, s. 1177 and Sch. 1, Part 1, para. 66 and repealed by CTA 2010, s. 1181 and Sch. 3, Pt. 2, with effect for corporation tax purposes for accounting periods ending on or after 1 April 2010. S. 496 also omitted by TIOPA 2010, s. 374 and Sch. 8, para. 183 and repealed by TIOPA 2010, s. 378 and Sch. 10, Pt. 6, with effect for corporation tax purposes for accounting periods ending on or after 1 April 2010, for income tax and capital gains tax purposes for the tax year 2010–11 and subsequent tax years, and for petroleum revenue tax purposes for chargeable periods beginning on or after 1 July 2010.

Notes – S. 496 rewritten for corporation tax as follows:
S. 496(1): CTA 2010, s. 291(1), (2), (3), (4), (5).
S. 496(2): CTA 2010, s. 291(6).
S. 496(3): CTA 2010, s. 291(7).
S. 496(4): CTA 2010, s. 291(8).
S. 496 rewritten in TIOPA 2010 as follows:
S. 496(1), (2), (3), (4): TIOPA 2010, Sch. 1, para. 2.

496A Exploration expenditure supplement

496A Schedule 19B to this Act (exploration expenditure supplement) shall have effect.

History – S. 496A inserted by FA 2004, s. 286(2), with effect from 22 July 2004. Sch. 19B applies to companies carrying on a ring-fence trade making a claim, to supplement, in respect of accounting periods ending on or after 1 January 2004.

496B Ring fence expenditure supplement

496B [Omitted by CTA 2010, s. 1177 and Sch. 1, para. 67 and repealed by CTA 2010, s. 1181 and Sch. 3, Pt. 1.]

History – S. 496B omitted by CTA 2010, s. 1177 and Sch. 1, para. 67 and repealed by CTA 2010, s. 1181 and Sch. 3, Pt. 1, with effect for corporation tax purposes for accounting periods ending on or after 1 April 2010, and for income and capital gains tax purposes for the tax year 2010–11 and subsequent tax years.

497 Restriction on setting ACT against income from oil extraction activities etc.

497 [Repealed by FA 1998, s. 31 and Sch. 3, para. 29, s. 165 and Sch. 27, Pt. III(2).]

History – S. 497 repealed by FA 1998, s. 31 and Sch. 3, para. 29, s. 165 and Sch. 27, Pt. III(2), with effect in relation to accounting periods beginning on or after 6 April 1999.

498 Limited right to carry back surrendered ACT

498 [Repealed by FA 1998, s. 31 and Sch. 3, para. 30(1), s. 165 and Sch. 27, Pt. III(2).]

History – S. 498 repealed by FA 1998, s. 31 and Sch. 3, para. 30(1), s. 165 and Sch. 27, Pt. III(2), with effect in relation to accounting periods of the surrendering company beginning on or after 6 April 1999.

499 Surrender of ACT where oil extraction company etc. owned by a consortium

499 [Repealed by FA 1998, s. 31 and Sch. 3, para. 31, s. 165 and Sch. 27, Pt. III(2).]

History – S. 499 repealed by FA 1998, s. 31 and Sch. 3, para. 31, s. 165 and Sch. 27, Pt. III(2), with effect in relation to distributions made on or after 6 April 1999.

500 Deduction of PRT in computing income for corporation tax purposes

500 [Omitted by CTA 2010, s. 1177 and Sch. 1, para. 68 and repealed by CTA 2010, s. 1181 and Sch. 3, Pt. 1.]

History – S. 500 omitted by CTA 2010, s. 1177 and Sch. 1, para. 68 and repealed by CTA 2010, s. 1181 and Sch. 3, Pt. 1, with effect for corporation tax purposes for accounting periods ending on or after 1 April 2010, and for income and capital gains tax purposes for the tax year 2010–11 and subsequent tax years.

Notes – S. 500 rewritten as follows:
S. 500(1): CTA 2010, s. 299(1), (2).
S. 500(2): CTA 2010, s. 299(3).
S. 500(3): CTA 2010, s. 299(4).
S. 500(4): CTA 2010, s. 300(1), (2), (3), (4).
S. 500(5): CTA 2010, s. 301(1), (2),.
S. 500(6): CTA 2010, s. 301(7).
S. 500(7): CTA 2010, s. 301(3), (4).
S. 500(8): CTA 2010, s. 301(4), (5).
S. 500(9): CTA 2010, s. 301(6).
S. 500(10): CTA 2010, s. 278, 301(7).

501 Interest on repayment of PRT

501 [Omitted by CTA 2010, s. 1177 and Sch. 1, para. 68 and repealed by CTA 2010, s. 1181 and Sch. 3, Pt. 1.]

History – S. 501 omitted by CTA 2010, s. 1177 and Sch. 1, para. 68 and repealed by CTA 2010, s. 1181 and Sch. 3, Pt. 1, with effect for corporation tax purposes for accounting periods ending on or after 1 April 2010, and for income and capital gains tax purposes for the tax year 2010–11 and subsequent tax years.

Notes – S. 501 rewritten as follows:
S. 501: CTA 2010, s. 302(1), (3).

501A Supplementary charge in respect of ring fence trades

501A [Omitted by CTA 2010, s. 1177 and Sch. 1, para. 68 and repealed by CTA 2010, s. 1181 and Sch. 3, Pt. 1.]

History – S. 501A omitted by CTA 2010, s. 1177 and Sch. 1, para. 68 and repealed by CTA 2010, s. 1181 and Sch. 3, Pt. 1, with effect for corporation tax purposes for accounting periods ending on or after 1 April 2010, and for income and capital gains tax purposes for the tax year 2010–11 and subsequent tax years.

Notes – *S. 501A rewritten as follows:*
S. 501A(1): CTA 2010, s. 330(1).
S. 501A(2): CTA 2010, s. 330(2).
S. 501A(3): CTA 2010, s. 330(3).
S. 501A(4): CTA 2010, s. 331(2).
S. 501A(5): CTA 2010, s. 331(3), (9).
S. 501A(6): CTA 2010, s. 331(4).
S. 501A(7): CTA 2010, s. 331(5).

S. 501A(8): CTA 2010, s. 331(6), (8).
S. 501A(9): CTA 2010, s. 331(7), (8).
S. 501A(10): CTA 2010, s. 331(9).
S. 501A(11): CTA 2010, s. 331(9).
S. 501A(12): CTA 2010, s. 330(5).

501B Assessment, recovery and postponement of supplementary charge

501B [Omitted by CTA 2010, s. 1177 and Sch. 1, para. 68 and repealed by CTA 2010, s. 1181 and Sch. 3, Pt. 1.]

History – S. 501B omitted by CTA 2010, s. 1177 and Sch. 1, para. 68 and repealed by CTA 2010, s. 1181 and Sch. 3, Pt. 1, with effect for corporation tax purposes for accounting periods ending on or after 1 April 2010, and for income and capital gains tax purposes for the tax year 2010–11 and subsequent tax years.

Notes – S. 501B rewritten as follows:
S. 501B(1): CTA 2010, s. 332(1), (2), (3).
S. 501B(2): CTA 2010, s. 332(4).
S. 501B(3): CTA 2010, s. 332(5).
S. 501B(4): CTA 2010, s. 332(6).

502 Interpretation of Chapter V

502(1) [Omitted by CTA 2010, s. 1177 and Sch. 1, para. 69 and repealed for corporation tax purposes only by CTA 2010, s. 1181 and Sch. 3, Pt. 2; also omitted by TIOPA 2010, s. 374 and Sch. 8, para. 184 and repealed by TIOPA 2010, s. 378 and Sch. 10, Pt. 6.]

502(1A) [Omitted by CTA 2010, s. 1177 and Sch. 1, para. 69 and repealed by CTA 2010, s. 1181 and Sch. 3, Pt. 1.]

502(2) [Omitted by CTA 2010, s. 1177 and Sch. 1, para. 69 and repealed for corporation tax purposes only by CTA 2010, s. 1181 and Sch. 3, Pt. 2; also omitted by TIOPA 2010, s. 374 and Sch. 8, para. 184 and repealed by TIOPA 2010, s. 378 and Sch. 10, Pt. 6.]

502(3) [Omitted by CTA 2010, s. 1177 and Sch. 1, para. 69 and repealed by CTA 2010, s. 1181 and Sch. 3, Pt. 1.]

502(3A) [Omitted by CTA 2010, s. 1177 and Sch. 1, para. 69 and repealed by CTA 2010, s. 1181 and Sch. 3, Pt. 1.]

502(4) [Omitted by CTA 2010, s. 1177 and Sch. 1, para. 69 and repealed by CTA 2010, s. 1181 and Sch. 3, Pt. 1.]

History – S. 502(1) omitted by CTA 2010, s. 1177 and Sch. 1, para. 69 and repealed by CTA 2010, s. 1181 and Sch. 3, Pt. 2, with effect for corporation tax purposes for accounting periods ending on or after 1 April 2010. S. 502(1) also omitted by TIOPA 2010, s. 374 and Sch. 8, para. 184 and repealed by TIOPA 2010, s. 378 and Sch. 10, Pt. 6, with effect for corporation tax purposes for accounting periods ending on or after 1 April 2010, for income tax and capital gains tax purposes for the tax year 2010–11 and subsequent tax years, and for petroleum revenue tax purposes for chargeable periods beginning on or after 1 July 2010.
S. 502(1A) omitted by CTA 2010, s. 1177 and Sch. 1, para. 69 and repealed by CTA 2010, s. 1181 and Sch. 3, Pt. 1, with effect for corporation tax purposes for accounting periods ending on or after 1 April 2010, and for income and capital gains tax purposes for the tax year 2010–11 and subsequent tax years.
S. 502(2) omitted by CTA 2010, s. 1177 and Sch. 1, Part 1, para. 69 and repealed by CTA 2010, s. 1181 and Sch. 3, Pt. 2, with effect for corporation tax purposes for accounting periods ending on or after 1 April 2010. S. 502(2) also omitted by TIOPA 2010, s. 374 and Sch. 8, para. 184 and repealed by TIOPA 2010, s. 378 and Sch. 10, Pt. 6 with effect for corporation tax purposes for accounting periods ending on or after 1 April 2010, for income tax and capital gains tax purposes for the tax year 2010–11 and subsequent tax years, and for petroleum revenue tax purposes for chargeable periods beginning on or after 1 July 2010.
S. 502(3) omitted by CTA 2010, s. 1177 and Sch. 1, para. 69 and repealed by CTA 2010, s. 1181 and Sch. 3, Pt. 1, with effect for corporation tax purposes for accounting periods ending on or after 1 April 2010, and for income and capital gains tax purposes for the tax year 2010–11 and subsequent tax years.
S. 502(3A) omitted by CTA 2010, s. 1177 and Sch. 1, para. 69 and repealed by CTA 2010, s. 1181 and Sch. 3, Pt. 1, with effect for corporation tax purposes for accounting periods ending on or after 1 April 2010, and for income and capital gains tax purposes for the tax year 2010–11 and subsequent tax years.
S. 502(4) omitted by CTA 2010, s. 1177 and Sch. 1, para. 69 and repealed by CTA 2010, s. 1181 and Sch. 3, Pt. 1, with effect for corporation tax purposes for accounting periods ending on or after 1 April 2010, and for income and capital gains tax purposes for the tax year 2010–11 and subsequent tax years.

Notes – S. 502 rewritten for income tax purposes as follows:
S. 502(1): ITA 2007, s. 80(3); TIOPA 2010, Sch. 1, para. 2.
S. 502(1) ("oil extraction activities" and "oil rights"): ITTOIA 2005, s. 16(3).
S. 502(2): TIOPA 2010, Sch. 1, para. 2.
S. 502 rewritten for corporation tax purposes as follows:
S. 502(1): CTA 2010, s. 272(1), (2), (3), (4), (5), (6), (7), 273, 275,276, 277, 278.
S. 502(1A): CTA 2010, s. 276.
S. 502(2): CTA 2010, s. 272(8), (9), (10), 278.
S. 502(3): CTA 2010, s. 271(1).
S. 502(3A): CTA 2010, s. 271(2).
S. 502(4): CTA 2010, s. 271(1), (3).

CHAPTER 5A – SPECIAL RULES FOR LONG FUNDING LEASES OF PLANT OR MACHINERY: CORPORATION TAX

History – Chapter 5A of Part XII omitted by CTA 2010, s. 1177 and Sch. 1, para. 70 and repealed by CTA 2010, s. 1181 and Sch. 3, Pt. 1.

INTRODUCTORY

History – Chapter 5A of Part XII omitted by CTA 2010, s. 1177 and Sch. 1, para. 70 and repealed by CTA 2010, s. 1181 and Sch. 3, Pt. 1.

502A Scope of Chapter 5A

History – Chapter 5A of Part XII omitted by CTA 2010, s. 1177 and Sch. 1, para. 70 and repealed by CTA 2010, s. 1181 and Sch. 3, Pt. 1.

502A [Omitted by CTA 2010, s. 1177 and Sch. 1, para. 70 and repealed by CTA 2010, s. 1181 and Sch. 3, Pt. 1.]

History – Chapter 5A of Part XII (of which s. 502A formed a part) omitted by CTA 2010, s. 1177 and Sch. 1, para. 70 and repealed by CTA 2010, s. 1181 and Sch. 3, Pt. 1, with effect for corporation tax purposes for accounting periods ending on or after 1 April 2010, and for income and capital gains tax purposes for the tax year 2010–11 and subsequent tax years.

LESSORS UNDER LONG FUNDING FINANCE LEASES

502B Lessor under long funding finance lease: rental earnings

History – Chapter 5A of Part XII omitted by CTA 2010, s. 1177 and Sch. 1, para. 70 and repealed by CTA 2010, s. 1181 and Sch. 3, Pt. 1.

502B [Omitted by CTA 2010, s. 1177 and Sch. 1, para. 70 and repealed by CTA 2010, s. 1181 and Sch. 3, Pt. 1.]

History – Chapter 5A of Part XII (of which s. 502B formed a part) omitted by CTA 2010, s. 1177 and Sch. 1, para. 70 and repealed by CTA 2010, s. 1181 and Sch. 3, Pt. 1, with effect for corporation tax purposes for accounting periods ending on or after 1 April 2010, and for income and capital gains tax purposes for the tax year 2010–11 and subsequent tax years.

Notes – S. 502B rewritten for corporation tax as follows:
S. 502B(1): CTA 2010, s. 360(1).
S. 502B(2): CTA 2010, s. 360(2).
S. 502B(3): CTA 2010, s. 360(3).
S. 502B(4): CTA 2010, s. 360(4).

502C Lessor under long funding finance lease: exceptional items

History – Chapter 5A of Part XII omitted by CTA 2010, s. 1177 and Sch. 1, para. 70 and repealed by CTA 2010, s. 1181 and Sch. 3, Pt. 1.

502C [Omitted by CTA 2010, s. 1177 and Sch. 1, para. 70 and repealed by CTA 2010, s. 1181 and Sch. 3, Pt. 1.]

History – Chapter 5A of Part XII (of which s. 502C formed a part) omitted by CTA 2010, s. 1177 and Sch. 1, para. 70 and repealed by CTA 2010, s. 1181 and Sch. 3, Pt. 1, with effect for corporation tax purposes for accounting periods ending on or after 1 April 2010, and for income and capital gains tax purposes for the tax year 2010–11 and subsequent tax years.

Notes – S. 502C rewritten for corporation tax as follows:
S. 502C(1): CTA 2010, s. 361(1).
S. 502C(2): CTA 2010, s. 361(1), (2), (5).
S. 502C(3): CTA 2010, s. 361(3), (4).
S. 502C(4): CTA 2010, s. 361(6).

502D Lessor under long funding finance lease making termination payment

History – Chapter 5A of Part XII omitted by CTA 2010, s. 1177 and Sch. 1, para. 70 and repealed by CTA 2010, s. 1181 and Sch. 3, Pt. 1.

502D [Omitted by CTA 2010, s. 1177 and Sch. 1, para. 70 and repealed by CTA 2010, s. 1181 and Sch. 3, Pt. 1.]

History – Chapter 5A of Part XII (of which s. 502D formed a part) omitted by CTA 2010, s. 1177 and Sch. 1, para. 70 and repealed by CTA 2010, s. 1181 and Sch. 3, Pt. 1, with effect for corporation tax purposes for accounting periods ending on or after 1 April 2010, and for income and capital gains tax purposes for the tax year 2010–11 and subsequent tax years.

Notes – S. 502D rewritten for corporation tax as follows:
S. 502D(1): CTA 2010, s. 362(1).
S. 502D(2): CTA 2010, s. 362(1), (2).
S. 502D(3): CTA 2010, s. 362(3).

LESSORS UNDER LONG FUNDING OPERATING LEASES

502E Lessor under long funding operating lease: periodic deduction

History – Chapter 5A of Part XII omitted by CTA 2010, s. 1177 and Sch. 1, para. 70 and repealed by CTA 2010, s. 1181 and Sch. 3, Pt. 1.

502E [Omitted by CTA 2010, s. 1177 and Sch. 1, para. 70 and repealed by CTA 2010, s. 1181 and Sch. 3, Pt. 1.]

History – Chapter 5A of Part XII (of which s. 502E formed a part) omitted by CTA 2010, s. 1177 and Sch. 1, para. 70 and repealed by CTA 2010, s. 1181 and Sch. 3, Pt. 1, with effect for corporation tax purposes for accounting periods ending on or after 1 April 2010, and for income and capital gains tax purposes for the tax year 2010–11 and subsequent tax years.
S. 502E inserted by FA 2006, s. 81 and Sch. 8, para. 11. For commencement, see History note under Chapter 5A heading.

Notes – S. 502E rewritten for corporation tax as follows:
S. 502E(1): CTA 2010, s. 363(1).
S. 502E(2): CTA 2010, s. 363(2).
S. 502E(3): CTA 2010, s. 363(3).
S. 502E(4): CTA 2010, s. 364(3), (4), (5), (6), (7), 365(2).
S. 502E(5): CTA 2010, s. 364(3), (4), (5), (6), 365(4), (5).
S. 502E(6): CTA 2010, s. 363(4).
S. 502E(7): CTA 2010, s. 363(3), (5).
S. 502E(8): CTA 2010, s. 363(5).
S. 502E(9): CTA 2010, s. 363(3).

502F Long funding operating lease: lessor's additional expenditure

History – Chapter 5A of Part XII omitted by CTA 2010, s. 1177 and Sch. 1, para. 70 and repealed by CTA 2010, s. 1181 and Sch. 3, Pt. 1.

502F [Omitted by CTA 2010, s. 1177 and Sch. 1, para. 70 and repealed by CTA 2010, s. 1181 and Sch. 3, Pt. 1.]

History – Chapter 5A of Part XII (of which s. 502F formed a part) omitted by CTA 2010, s. 1177 and Sch. 1, para. 70 and repealed by CTA 2010, s. 1181 and Sch. 3, Pt. 1, with effect for corporation tax purposes for accounting periods ending on or after 1 April 2010, and for income and capital gains tax purposes for the tax year 2010–11 and subsequent tax years.

Notes – S. 502F rewritten for corporation tax as follows:
S. 502F(1): CTA 2010, s. 366(1), (7).
S. 502F(2): CTA 2010, s. 366(7).
S. 502F(3): CTA 2010, s. 366(2).
S. 502F(4): CTA 2010, s. 366(3).
S. 502F(5): CTA 2010, s. 367(1), (2), 368(1), (2), (3).
S. 502F(6): CTA 2010, s. 367(1), (2), (3), (4), 368(1), (2), (3), (4), (5).
S. 502F(7): CTA 2010, s. 366(4).
S. 502F(8): CTA 2010, s. 366(3), (6).
S. 502F(9): CTA 2010, s. 366(6).
S. 502F(10): CTA 2010, s. 366(3).
S. 502F(11): CTA 2010, s. 366(2).

502G Lessor under long funding operating lease: termination of lease

History – Chapter 5A of Part XII omitted by CTA 2010, s. 1177 and Sch. 1, para. 70 and repealed by CTA 2010, s. 1181 and Sch. 3, Pt. 1.

502G [Omitted by CTA 2010, s. 1177 and Sch. 1, para. 70 and repealed by CTA 2010, s. 1181 and Sch. 3, Pt. 1.]

History – Chapter 5A of Part XII (of which s. 502G formed a part) omitted by CTA 2010, s. 1177 and Sch. 1, para 70 and repealed by CTA 2010, s. 1181 and Sch. 3, Pt. 1, with effect for corporation tax purposes for accounting periods ending on or after 1 April 2010, and for income and capital gains tax purposes for the tax year 2010–11 and subsequent tax years.

Notes – S. 502G rewritten for corporation tax as follows:
S. 502G(1): CTA 2010, s. 369(1).
S. 502G(2): CTA 2010, s. 369(2), (3), (4).
S. 502G(3): CTA 2010, s. 369(6).
S. 502G(4): CTA 2010, s. 369(7).
S. 502G(5): CTA 2010, s. 369(2), (4).
S. 502G(6): CTA 2010, s. 369(2), (3), (4).
S. 502G(7): CTA 2010, s. 369(3), (4).
S. 502G(8): CTA 2010, s. 369(2), (3), (4).
S. 502G(9): CTA 2010, s. 369(5).

LESSORS UNDER LONG FUNDING FINANCE OR OPERATING LEASES: AVOIDANCE ETC

History – Chapter 5A of Part XII omitted by CTA 2010, s. 1177 and Sch. 1, para. 70 and repealed by CTA 2010. s. 1181 and Sch. 3, Pt. 1.

502GA Cases where s. 502B to 502G do not apply: plant or machinery held as trading stock

History – Chapter 5A of Part XII omitted by CTA 2010, s. 1177 and Sch. 1, para. 70 and repealed by CTA 2010 s. 1181 and Sch. 3, Pt. 1.

502GA [Omitted by CTA 2010, s. 1177 and Sch. 1, para. 70 and repealed by CTA 2010, s. 1181 and Sch. 3, Pt. 1.]

History – Chapter 5A of Part XII (of which s. 502GA formed a part) omitted by CTA 2010, s. 1177 and Sch. 1, para. 70 and repealed by CTA 2010, s. 1181 and Sch. 3, Pt. 1, with effect for corporation tax purposes for accounting periods ending on or after 1 April 2010, and for income and capital gains tax purposes for the tax year 2010–11 and subsequent tax years.

Notes – S. 502GA rewritten for corporation tax as follows:
S. 502GA(1): CTA 2010, s. 370(1).
S. 502GA(2): CTA 2010, s. 370(2).
S. 502GA(3): CTA 2010, s. 370(3).
S. 502GA(4): CTA 2010, s. 371(1), (2).
S. 502GA(5): CTA 2010, s. 371(3).

502GB Cases where s. 502B to 502G do not apply: lessor also lessee under non-long funding lease

History – Chapter 5A of Part XII omitted by CTA 2010, s. 1177 and Sch. 1, para. 70 and repealed by CTA 2010, s. 1181 and Sch. 3, Pt. 1.

502GB [Omitted by CTA 2010, s. 1177 and Sch. 1, para. 70 and repealed by CTA 2010, s. 1181 and Sch. 3, Pt. 1.]

History – Chapter 5A of Part XII (of which s. 502GB formed a part) omitted by CTA 2010, s. 1177 and Sch. 1, para. 70 and repealed by CTA 2010, s. 1181 and Sch. 3, Pt. 1, with effect for corporation tax purposes for accounting periods ending on or after 1 April 2010, and for income and capital gains tax purposes for the tax year 2010–11 and subsequent tax years.

Notes – S. 502GB rewritten for corporation tax as follows:
S. 502GB(1): CTA 2010, s. 372(1).
S. 502GB(2): CTA 2010, s. 372(2).
S. 502GB(3): CTA 2010, s. 372(3).

502GC Cases where s. 502B to 502G do not apply: other avoidance

History – Chapter 5A of Part XII omitted by CTA 2010, s. 1177 and Sch. 1, para. 70 and repealed by CTA 2010, s. 1181 and Sch. 3, Pt. 1.

502GC [Omitted by CTA 2010, s. 1177 and Sch. 1, para. 70 and repealed by CTA 2010, s. 1181 and Sch. 3, Pt. 1.]

History – Chapter 5A of Part XII (of which s. 502GC formed a part) omitted by CTA 2010, s. 1177 and Sch. 1, para. 70 and repealed by CTA 2010, s. 1181 and Sch. 3, Pt. 1, with effect for corporation tax purposes for accounting periods ending on or after 1 April 2010, and for income and capital gains tax purposes for the tax year 2010–11 and subsequent tax years.

Notes – S. 502GC rewritten for corporation tax as follows:
S. 502GC(1): CTA 2010, s. 373(1).
S. 502GC(2): CTA 2010, s. 373(2), 374(1).
S. 502GC(3): CTA 2010, s. 373(3), (4), (5).
S. 502GC(4): CTA 2010, s. 374(4).
S. 502GC(5): CTA 2010, s. 373(6).
S. 502GC(6): CTA 2010, s. 374(5).
S. 502GC(7): CTA 2010, s. 374(2).
S. 502GC(8): CTA 2010, s. 374(3).
S. 502GC(9): CTA 2010, s. 375(1), (2).
S. 502GC(10): CTA 2010, s. 375(3).

502GD Cases where ss 502B to 502G do not apply: films

History – Chapter 5A of Part XII omitted by CTA 2010, s. 1177 and Sch. 1, para. 70 and repealed by CTA 2010, s. 1181 and Sch. 3, Pt. 1.

502GD [Omitted by CTA 2010, s. 1177 and Sch. 1, para. 70 and repealed by CTA 2010, s. 1181 and Sch. 3, Pt. 1.]

History – Chapter 5A of Part XII (of which s. 502GD formed a part) omitted by CTA 2010, s. 1177 and Sch. 1, para. 70 and repealed by CTA 2010, s. 1181 and Sch. 3, Pt. 1, with effect for corporation tax purposes for accounting periods ending on or after 1 April 2010, and for income and capital gains tax purposes for the tax year 2010–11 and subsequent tax years.

Notes – S. 502GD rewritten for corporation tax as follows:
S. 502GD(1): CTA 2010, s. 376(1).
S. 502GD(2): CTA 2010, s. 376(2).

INSURANCE COMPANY AS LESSOR

History – Chapter 5A of Part XII omitted by CTA 2010, s. 1177 and Sch. 1, para. 70 and repealed by CTA 2010, s. 1181 and Sch. 3, Pt. 1.

502H Insurance company as lessor

History – Chapter 5A of Part XII omitted by CTA 2010, s. 1177 and Sch. 1, para. 70 and repealed by CTA 2010, s. 1181 and Sch. 3, *Pt. 1.*

502H [Omitted by CTA 2010, s. 1177 and Sch. 1, para. 70 and repealed by CTA 2010, s. 1181 and Sch. 3, Pt. 1.]

History – Chapter 5A of Part XII (of which s. 502H formed a part) omitted by CTA 2010, s. 1177 and Sch. 1, para. 70 and repealed by CTA 2010, s. 1181 and Sch. 3, Pt. 1, with effect for corporation tax purposes for accounting periods ending on or after 1 April 2010, and for income and capital gains tax purposes for the tax year 2010–11 and subsequent tax years.

LESSEES UNDER LONG FUNDING FINANCE LEASES

History – Chapter 5A of Part XII omitted by CTA 2010, s. 1177 and Sch. 1, para. 70 and repealed by CTA 2010, s. 1181 and Sch. 3, Pt. 1.

502I Lessee under long funding finance lease: limit on deductions

History – Chapter 5A of Part XII omitted by CTA 2010, s. 1177 and Sch. 1, para. 70 and repealed by CTA 2010, s. 1181 and Sch. 3, Pt. 1.

502I [Omitted by CTA 2010, s. 1177 and Sch. 1, para. 70 and repealed by CTA 2010, s. 1181 and Sch. 3, Pt. 1.]

History – Chapter 5A of Part XII (of which s. 502I formed a part) omitted by CTA 2010, s. 1177 and Sch. 1, para. 70 and repealed by CTA 2010, s. 1181 and Sch. 3, Pt. 1, with effect for corporation tax purposes for accounting periods ending on or after 1 April 2010, and for income and capital gains tax purposes for the tax year 2010–11 and subsequent tax years.

Notes – S. 502I rewritten for corporation tax as follows:
S. 502I(1): CTA 2010, s. 377(1), (2).
S. 502I(2): CTA 2010, s. 377(2), (3).
S. 502I(3): CTA 2010, s. 377(4).

502J Lessee under long funding finance lease: termination

History – Chapter 5A of Part XII omitted by CTA 2010, s. 1177 and Sch. 1, para. 70 and repealed by CTA 2010, s. 1181 and Sch. 3, Pt. 1.

502J [Omitted by CTA 2010, s. 1177 and Sch. 1, para. 70 and repealed by CTA 2010, s. 1181 and Sch. 3, Pt. 1.]

History – Chapter 5A of Part XII (of which s. 502J formed a part) omitted by CTA 2010, s. 1177 and Sch. 1, para. 70 and repealed by CTA 2010, s. 1181 and Sch. 3, Pt. 1, with effect for corporation tax purposes for accounting periods ending on or after 1 April 2010, and for income and capital gains tax purposes for the tax year 2010–11 and subsequent tax years.

Notes – S. 502J rewritten for corporation tax as follows:
S. 502J(1): CTA 2010, s. 378(1).
S. 502J(2): CTA 2010, s. 378(2).
S. 502J(3): CTA 2010, s. 378(3).

LESSEES UNDER LONG FUNDING OPERATING LEASES

History – Chapter 5A of Part XII omitted by CTA 2010, s. 1177 and Sch. 1, para. 70 and repealed by CTA 2010, s. 1181 and Sch. 3, Pt. 1.

502K Lessee under long funding operating lease

History – Chapter 5A of Part XII omitted by CTA 2010, s. 1177 and Sch. 1, para. 70 and repealed by CTA 2010, s. 1181 and Sch. 3, Pt. 1.

502K [Omitted by CTA 2010, s. 1177 and Sch. 1, para. 70 and repealed by CTA 2010, s. 1181 and Sch. 3, Pt. 1.]

History – Chapter 5A of Part XII (of which s. 502K formed a part) omitted by CTA 2010, s. 1177 and Sch. 1, para. 70 and repealed by CTA 2010, s. 1181 and Sch. 3, Pt. 1, with effect for corporation tax purposes for accounting periods ending on or after 1 April 2010, and for income and capital gains tax purposes for the tax year 2010–11 and subsequent tax years.

Notes – S. 502K rewritten for corporation tax as follows:
S. 502K(1): CTA 2010, s. 379(1).
S. 502K(2): CTA 2010, s. 379(2).
S. 502K(3): CTA 2010, s. 379(3).
S. 502K(4): CTA 2010, s. 380(2), (3), (4).
S. 502K(5): CTA 2010, s. 380(5), (6), (7).
S. 502K(6): CTA 2010, s. 379(4), (6).
S. 502K(7): CTA 2010, s. 379(7).
S. 502K(8): CTA 2010, s. 379(7).
S. 502K(9): CTA 2010, s. 379(7).

INTERPRETATION OF CHAPTER

History – Chapter 5A of Part XII omitted by CTA 2010, s. 1177 and Sch. 1, para. 70 and repealed by CTA 2010, s. 1181 and Sch. 3, Pt. 1.

502L Interpretation of this Chapter

History – Chapter 5A of Part XII omitted by CTA 2010, s. 1177 and Sch. 1, para. 70 and repealed by CTA 2010, s. 1181 and Sch. 3, Pt. 1.

502L [Omitted by CTA 2010, s. 1177 and Sch. 1, para. 70 and repealed by CTA 2010, s. 1181 and Sch. 3, Pt. 1.]

History – Chapter 5A of Part XII (of which s. 502L formed a part) omitted by CTA 2010, s. 1177 and Sch. 1, para. 70 and repealed by CTA 2010, s. 1181 and Sch. 3, Pt. 1, with effect for corporation tax purposes for accounting periods ending on or after 1 April 2010, and for income and capital gains tax purposes for the tax year 2010–11 and subsequent tax years.

Notes – S. 502L rewritten for corporation tax as follows:
S. 502L(1): CTA 2010, s. 381(4).
S. 502L(2): CTA 2010, s. 381(5).
S. 502L(3): CTA 2010, s. 381(2).
S. 502L(4): CTA 2010, s. 381(1).

Chapter VI – Miscellaneous Businesses and Bodies

503 Letting of furnished holiday accommodation treated as a trade for certain corporation tax purposes

503 [Omitted by CTA 2010, s. 1177 and Sch. 1, para. 71 and repealed by CTA 2010, s. 1181 and Sch. 3, Pt. 1.]

History – S. 503 omitted by CTA 2010, s. 1177 and Sch. 1, para. 71 and repealed by CTA 2010, s. 1181 and Sch. 3, Pt. 1, with effect for corporation tax purposes for accounting periods ending on or after 1 April 2010, and for income and capital gains tax purposes for the tax year 2010–11 and subsequent tax years.

Notes – S. 503 rewritten for corporation tax as follows:
S. 503(1): CTA 2010, s. 65(1), (2), (3),(4).
S. 503(4): CTA 2010, s. 65(5).
S. 503(5): CTA 2010, s. 65(4).

504 Supplementary provisions

504 [Omitted by CTA 2009, s. 1322 and Sch. 1, para. 173 and repealed by CTA 2009, s. 1326 and Sch. 3, Pt. 1.]

History – S. 504 omitted by CTA 2009, s. 1322 and Sch. 1, para. 173 and repealed by CTA 2009, s. 1326 and Sch. 3, Pt. 1, with effect for corporation tax purposes for accounting periods ending on or after 1 April 2009, and for income tax and capital gains tax purposes for the tax year 2009–10 and subsequent tax years.

Notes – Rewritten income tax provisions are now located as follows:
S. 504(2): ITTOIA 2005, s. 323(2) and (3).
S. 504(3): ITTOIA 2005, s. 323(3) and 325(1)–(6).
S. 504(4): ITTOIA 2005, s. 324(2)–(4) and 325(2), (3) and (5).
S. 504(6): ITTOIA 2005, s. 326(1) and (2).
S. 504(6A): ITTOIA 2005, s. 326(6).
S. 504(7): ITTOIA 2005, s. 326(3) and (4).
S. 504(8): ITTOIA 2005, s. 326(5).
S. 504(9): ITTOIA 2005, s. 323(1).
S. 504 rewritten for corporation tax purposes as follows:
S. 504(2): CTA 2009, s. 265(2), (3).
S. 504(3): CTA 2009, s. 265(3), 267(1), (2), (3), (4), (5), (6).
S. 504(5): CTA 2009, s. 266(2), (3), (4), 267(2), (3), (5).
S. 504(6): CTA 2009, s. 268(1), (2).
S. 504(6A): CTA 2009, s. 268(6).
S. 504(7): CTA 2009, s. 268(3), (4).
S. 504(8): CTA 2009, s. 268(5).
S. 504(9): CTA 2009, s. 265(1).

504A Letting of furnished holiday accommodation treated as trade for certain income tax purposes

504A [Omitted by ITA 2007, s. 1027 and Sch. 1, para. 93 and repealed by ITA 2007, s. 1031 and Sch. 3, Pt. 1 with effect for 2007–08 and subsequent tax years.]

Notes – S. 504A rewritten as follows:
S. 504A(1): ITA 2007, s. 127(1), (2), (3), 836(3).
S. 504A(2): ITA 2007, s. 127(3), 836(3), Sch. 1 para. 473(2), (4).
S. 504A(3): ITA 2007, s. 127(4), (5), (6).
S. 504A(4): ITA 2007, s. 127(7), Sch. 1 para. 473(4).
S. 504A(5): ITA 2007, s. 63.

505 Charitable companies: general

505 [Omitted by CTA 2010, s. 1177 and Sch. 1, para. 72 and repealed by CTA 2010, s. 1181 and Sch. 3, Pt. 1.]

History – S. 505 omitted by CTA 2010, s. 1177 and Sch. 1, para. 72 and repealed by CTA 2010, s. 1181 and Sch. 3, Pt. 1, with effect for corporation tax purposes for accounting periods ending on or after 1 April 2010, and for income and capital gains tax purposes for the tax year 2010–11 and subsequent tax years, subject to transitional provisions in CTA 2010, s. 1180 and Sch. 2, para. 77.

Notes – S. 505 rewritten as follows:
S. 505(1): ITA 2007, s. 521(4), 522(5), 523(5), 524(1), (2), (3), (4), 525(1), 530(1), (2), (3), 531(1), (2), (3), 532(1), (2), (3), (4), (5), 533(1), 536(1), (2), (3), 538(1).
S. 505(1AA): ITA 2007, s. 536(4).
S. 505(1A): ITA 2007, s. 533(2).
S. 505(1B): ITA 2007, s. 525(2), (3), (4).
S. 505(2): ITA 2007, s. 523(1), (2), (3), (4), (5), (6), (7).
S. 505(3): ITA 2007, s. 540(3), 562(4), (5).
S. 505(4): ITA 2007, s. 539(2), 540(1), (2), 541(2), (3), (4), Sch. 1 para. 326, 327.
S. 505(5): ITA 2007, s. 562(1), (2), (3), 563(2), (3), (4), (5), 564.
S. 505(6): ITA 2007, s. 563(2), (3), (5).
S. 505(7): ITA 2007, s. 541(2), 542(2), (3), (4), (5), (6), Sch. 1 para. 327.
S. 505 rewritten for corporation tax as follows:
S. 505(1): CTA 2010, s. 472(2), (4), 473(2), (3), 474(3), (5), 475(5), 476(1), 477(1), 478(1), (2), (3), (5), 479(1), 484(1), (2), (3), (4), 485(1), (2), (3), (4), (5), 486(1), (2), (3), (4), (5), (6), 487(1), (3), 488(1), (2), (3), (4), Sch. 2, para. 71
S. 505(1A): CTA 2010, s. 487(2).
S. 505(1B): CTA 2010, s. 479(2), (3), (4).

S. 505(2): CTA 2010, s. 474(1), (2), (3), (4).
S. 505(3): CTA 2010, s. 492(2), (3), 493(3), 515(4), (5), (6), (7).
S. 505(4): CTA 2010, s. 492(2), (3), 493(1), (2), 494(2), (3), (4).
S. 505(5): CTA 2010, s. 515(1), (2), (3), 516(2), (3), (4), (5), 517.
S. 505(6): CTA 2010, s. 516(2), (3), (5).
S. 505(7):CTA 2010, s. 495(2), (3), (4), (5), (6).

506 Charitable and non-charitable expenditure

506 [Omitted by CTA 2010, s. 1177 and Sch. 1, para. 73 and repealed by CTA 2010, s. 1181 and Sch. 3, Pt. 1.]

History – S. 506 omitted by CTA 2010, s. 1177 and Sch. 1, para. 73 and repealed by CTA 2010, s. 1181 and Sch. 3, Pt. 1, with effect for corporation tax purposes for accounting periods ending on or after 1 April 2010, and for income and capital gains tax purposes for the tax year 2010–11 and subsequent tax years, subject to transitional provisions in CTA 2010, s. 1180 and Sch. 2, para. 77.

Notes – S. 506 is rewritten for income tax purposes as follows:
S. 506(1): ITA 2007, s. 519, 543(1).
S. 506(1) ("charity"): ITTOIA 2005, s. 878(1).
S. 506(2): ITA 2007, s. 546(1), (2), (3), (4).
S. 506(3): ITA 2007, s. 547.
S. 506(4): ITA 2007, s. 543(1), 1019.
S. 506(5): ITA 2007, s. 548(1), (2).
Where the substituted s. 505 (above) and s. 506 cause any amount to be treated as non-charitable expenditure of an earlier chargeable period, the relief or exemption to be disallowed in that earlier period is not to exceed that which would have been disallowed prior to the substitution (FA 2006, s. 55(5)).
Institutions registered with charity commissioners conclusively presumed to be charities.
S. 506 rewritten for corporation tax as follows:
S. 506(1): CTA 2010, s. 467, 496(1), 1119.
S. 506(2): CTA 2010, s. 499(1), (2), (3), (4).
S. 506(3): CTA 2010, s. 500.
S. 506(4): CTA 2010, s. 496(1).
S. 506(5): CTA 2010, s. 501(1), (2).

506A Transactions with substantial donors

506A [Omitted by CTA 2010, s. 1177 and Sch. 1, para. 74 and repealed by CTA 2010, s. 1181 and Sch. 3, Pt. 1.]

History – S. 506A omitted by CTA 2010, s. 1177 and Sch. 1, para. 74 and repealed by CTA 2010, s. 1181 and Sch. 3, Pt. 1, with effect for corporation tax purposes for accounting periods ending on or after 1 April 2010, and for income and capital gains tax purposes for the tax year 2010–11 and subsequent tax years.

Notes – S. 506A is rewritten for income tax purposes as follows:
S. 506A(1): ITA 2007, s. 549(1).
S. 506A(2): ITA 2007, s. 549(2), (3).
S. 506A(3): ITA 2007, s. 543(1), 551(1).
S. 506A(4): ITA 2007, s. 543(1), 551(2), (3).
S. 506A(5): ITA 2007, s. 543(1), 551(5).
S. 506A rewritten for corporation tax as follows:
S. 506A(1): CTA 2010, s. 502(1).
S. 506A(2): CTA 2010, s. 502(2), (3), Sch. 2, para. 75.
S. 506A(3): CTA 2010, s. 496(1), 504(1).
S. 506A(4): CTA 2010, s. 496(1), 504(2), (3).
S. 506A(5): CTA 2010, s. 496(1), 504(5).

506B Section 506A: exceptions

506B [Omitted by CTA 2010, s. 1177 and Sch. 1, para. 75 and repealed by CTA 2010, s. 1181 and Sch. 3, Pt. 1.]

History – S. 506B omitted by CTA 2010, s. 1177 and Sch. 1, para. 75 and repealed by CTA 2010, s. 1181 and Sch. 3, Pt. 1, with effect for corporation tax purposes for accounting periods ending on or after 1 April 2010, and for income and capital gains tax purposes for the tax year 2010–11 and subsequent tax years.

Notes – S. 506B is rewritten for income tax purposes as follows:
S. 506B(1): ITA 2007, s. 554(1).
S. 506B(2): ITA 2007, s. 554(2).
S. 506B(3): ITA 2007, s. 554(3).
S. 506B(4): ITA 2007, s. 554(4).
S. 506B(5): ITA 2007, s. 554(5).
S. 506B(6): ITA 2007, s. 554(5).
S. 506B(7): ITA 2007, s. 553(1), (2), (3).
S. 506B(8): ITA 2007, s. 555(1).
S. 506B(9): ITA 2007, s. 555(2), (3), (4).
S. 506B rewritten for corporation tax as follows:
S. 506B(1): CTA 2010, s. 507(1).
S. 506B(2): CTA 2010, s. 507(2).
S. 506B(3): CTA 2010, s. 507(3).
S. 506B(4): CTA 2010, s. 507(4).
S. 506B(5): CTA 2010, s. 507(5).
S. 506B(6): CTA 2010, s. 507(5).
S. 506B(7): CTA 2010, s. 506(1), (2), (3).
S. 506B(8): CTA 2010, s. 508(1).
S. 506B(9): CTA 2010, s. 508(2), (3), (4).

506C Sections 506A and 506B: supplemental

506C [Omitted by CTA 2010, s. 1177 and Sch. 1, para. 76 and repealed by CTA 2010, s. 1181 and Sch. 3, Pt. 1.]

History – S. 506C omitted by CTA 2010, s. 1177 and Sch. 1, para. 76 and repealed by CTA 2010, s. 1181 and Sch. 3, Pt. 1, with effect for corporation tax purposes for accounting periods ending on or after 1 April 2010, and for income and capital gains tax purposes for the tax year 2010–11 and subsequent tax years.

Notes – S. 506C is rewritten for income tax purposes as follows:
S. 506C(1): ITA 2007, s. 550.
S. 506C(2): ITA 2007, s. 551(4).
S. 506C(3): ITA 2007, s. 549(4).
S. 506C(4): ITA 2007, s. 552(1), (2), (3).
S. 506C(5): ITA 2007, s. 556(1), (2).
S. 506C(6): ITA 2007, s. 551(6).
S. 506C(7): ITA 2007, s. 557(1).
S. 506C(8): ITA 2007, s. 557(2).
S. 506C(9): ITA 2007, s. 557(3).
S. 506C rewritten for corporation tax as follows:
S. 506C(1): CTA 2010, s. 503.
S. 506C(2): CTA 2010, s. 504(4).
S. 506C(3): CTA 2010, s. 502(4).
S. 506C(4): CTA 2010, s. 505(1), (2), (3).
S. 506C(5): CTA 2010, s. 509(1), (2).
S. 506C(6): CTA 2010, s. 504(6).
S. 506C(7): CTA 2010, s. 510(1), 1176(1).
S. 506C(8): CTA 2010, s. 510(2).
S. 506C(9): CTA 2010, s. 510(3).

507 The National Heritage Memorial Fund, the Historic Buildings and Monuments Commission for England and the British Museum

507 [Omitted by CTA 2010, s. 1177 and Sch. 1, para. 77 and repealed by CTA 2010, s. 1181 and Sch. 3, Pt. 1.]

History – S. 507 omitted by CTA 2010, s. 1177 and Sch. 1, para. 77 and repealed by CTA 2010, s. 1181 and Sch. 3, Pt. 1, with effect for corporation tax purposes for accounting periods ending on or after 1 April 2010, and for income and capital gains tax purposes for the tax year 2010–11 and subsequent tax years.

Notes – S. 507(1) is rewritten for income tax purposes as ITA 2007, s. 430(1).
S. 507 rewritten for corporation tax as follows:
S. 507(1): CTA 2010, s. 468, 475(5), (6), (8), 476(1), (2), (3), 490(1), (2), (3).

508 Scientific research organisations

508 [Omitted by CTA 2010, s. 1177 and Sch. 1, para. 78 and repealed by CTA 2010, s. 1181 and Sch. 3, Pt. 1.]

History – S. 508 omitted by CTA 2010, s. 1177 and Sch. 1, para. 78 and repealed by CTA 2010, s. 1181 and Sch. 3, Pt. 1, with effect for corporation tax purposes for accounting periods ending on or after 1 April 2010, and for income and capital gains tax purposes for the tax year 2010–11 and subsequent tax years.

Notes – S. 508 rewritten for corporation tax as follows:
S. 508(1): CTA 2010, s. 469(1), (2), (3), 477(1), (2), (3), (4), 491(3), (4).
S. 508(1A): CTA 2010, s. 469(5).
S. 508(1B): CTA 2010, s. 469(6).
S. 508(2): CTA 2010, s. 469(4).
S. 508(3): CTA 2010, s. 469(2), 470(1).
S. 508(4): CTA 2010, s. 470(2).

508A Investment trusts investing in housing

508A [Ceased to have effect by virtue of FA 2006, s. 143(a) and repealed by FA 2006, s. 178 and Sch. 26, Pt. 4.]

History – S. 508A ceased to have effect by virtue of FA 2006, s. 143(a) and repealed by FA 2006, s. 178, Sch. 26, Pt. 4 in relation to accounting periods beginning on or after 19 July 2006 (FA 2006, s. 145(2)).

508A- Contemplative religious communities: profits exempt from corporation tax

Notes – In what is assumed to have been a drafting error, a second version of s. 508A was inserted into ICTA 1988 several years after the repeal of the original version of s. 508A. Purely for the purposes of distinguishing electronically the two versions of s. 508A, CCH have added a hyphen to the numbering of this later version.

508A-(1) Subsection (2) applies in a case where members of a qualifying contemplative religious community transfer all their income and assets, or covenant all their income, to the community ("the *independent community*") (and for this purpose it is irrelevant whether or not the community is part of an order or religious institution).

508A-(2) As respects each chargeable period of the independent community, and each person who is a qualifying member of the independent community at any time in that period, the independent community shall be treated for the purposes of corporation tax as if an amount of its profits for the chargeable period equal to the relevant amount (see subsections (5) to (7)) were income of the qualifying member.

508A-(3) Subsection (4) applies in a case where–

(a) one or more qualifying contemplative religious communities ("constituent communities") are part of an order or religious institution ("the parent body"), and

(b) members of the constituent communities transfer all their income and assets, or covenant all their income, to the parent body.

508A-(4) As respects each chargeable period of the parent body, and each person who is a qualifying member of a constituent community at any time in that period, the parent body shall be treated for the purposes of corporation tax as if an amount of its profits for the chargeable period equal to the relevant amount (see subsections (5) to (7)) were income of the qualifying member.

508A-(5) For the purposes of subsections (2) and (4), the relevant amount, in relation to a chargeable period, is the amount of the annual personal allowance for persons born after 5 April 1948 (see section 35 of ITA 2007) for–

(a) the tax year which begins in the chargeable period, or

(b) if no tax year begins in the chargeable period, the tax year which is current when the chargeable period begins.

508A-(6) But, if the chargeable period is less than 12 months, the relevant amount is–

$$\frac{P}{365} \times A$$

where–

P is the number of days in the chargeable period;

A is the amount determined under subsection (5) in relation to the chargeable period.

508A-(7) If, during the chargeable period, an individual ceases to be a qualifying member of the independent community or a constituent community (otherwise than on death), the relevant amount, in relation to the chargeable period and that qualifying member, is–

$$\frac{Q}{P} \times B$$

where–

Q is the number of days in the chargeable period for which the individual is a qualifying member of the independent community or constituent community;

P is the number of days in the chargeable period;

B is the amount determined under subsection (5), or subsections (5) and (6), in relation to the chargeable period.

508A-(8) So far as the exemption from corporation tax conferred by this section calls for repayment of tax, no repayment shall be made except on a claim made by the independent community or parent body.

508A-(9) In a case where a member of an independent community or constituent community–

(a) has transferred or covenanted income to the community (in the case of an independent community) or the parent body (in the case of a constituent community), and

(b) has income for a tax year which does not exceed 20% of the annual personal allowance for persons born after 5 April 1948 (see section 35 of ITA 2007) for that tax year,

the member is, for the purposes of this section, to be taken to have transferred or covenanted all his or her income for that tax year to the community or parent body.

508A-(10) For the purposes of this section a contemplative religious community is a **"qualifying"** contemplative religious community if–

(a) the community is established in the United Kingdom,

(b) the members of the community live and practise their religion in a communal establishment, and

(c) the community is not a charity, but the religion that is professed by the members of the community does not prevent the community from being a charity.

508A-(11) In this section–

"member", in relation to a religious community, means an individual who–

(a) is living in the community, and

(b) has taken vows or made equivalent commitments (whether probationary or not);

"qualifying member", in relation to a religious community, means a member of the community who–

(a) has been a member of the community for a period of at least six months, and

(b) has transferred all his or her income and assets, or covenanted all his or her income, to the community (in the case of an independent community) or the parent body (in the case of a constituent community).

History – In s. 508A(5), "born after 5 April 1948" to be substituted for "under 65" by FA 2012, s. 4(7) with effect for the tax year 2013–14 and subsequent tax years.

In s. 508A(9)(b), "born after 5 April 1948" to be substituted for "under 65" by FA 2012, s. 4(7) with effect for the tax year 2013–14 and subsequent tax years.

S. 508A inserted by SI 2010/157, art. 6(1), with effect in relation to chargeable periods beginning on or after 1 April 2010.

508B Interpretation of section 508A

508B [Ceased to have effect by virtue of FA 2006, s. 143(a) and repealed by FA 2006, s. 178 and Sch. 26, Pt. 4.]

History – S. 508B ceased to have effect by virtue of FA 2006, s. 143(a) and repealed by FA 2006, Sch. 26, Pt. 4 in respect of accounting periods beginning on or after 19 July 2006 (FA 2006, s. 145(2)).

508B- Contemplative religious communities: gains exempt from corporation tax

Notes – In what is assumed to have been a drafting error, a second version of s. 508B was inserted into ICTA 1988 several years after the repeal of the original version of s. 508B. Purely for the purposes of distinguishing electronically the two versions of s. 508B, CCH have added a hyphen to the numbering of this later version.

508B-(1) Subsection (2) applies if, as respects a chargeable period–

(a) section 508A(2) applies in relation to an independent community,

(b) the profits of the independent community in the chargeable period are less than the total of the amounts that fall to be treated as income of the qualifying members of the community in accordance with section 508A(2), and

(c) the independent community has chargeable gains in the chargeable period.

508B-(2) As respects the chargeable period and each qualifying member of the independent community, the community shall be treated for the purposes of corporation tax as if the relevant amount of its chargeable gains for that period were income of the qualifying member.

508B-(3) Subsection (4) applies if, as respects a chargeable period–

(a) section 508A(4) applies in relation to a parent body,

(b) the profits of the parent body in the chargeable period are less than the total of the amounts that fall to be treated as income of the qualifying members of the constituent communities in accordance with section 508A(4), and

(c) the parent body has chargeable gains in the chargeable period.

508B-(4) As respects the chargeable period and each qualifying member of a constituent community, the parent body shall be treated for the purposes of corporation tax as if the relevant amount of its chargeable gains for that period were income of the qualifying member.

508B-(5) For the purposes of subsections (2) and (4), the relevant amount, in relation to a qualifying member of the independent community or a constituent community, is the smaller of–

(a) the shortfall in profits, and

(b) the average gain.

508B-(6) The shortfall in profits is the difference between–

(a) the relevant amount determined under section 508A(5) to (7) in relation to the qualifying member, and

(b) the amount that has actually been treated as the income of the qualifying member.

508B-(7) The average gain is–

$$\frac{G}{N}$$

where–

G is the amount of the chargeable gains which the independent community or parent body has in the chargeable period;

N is the number calculated by adding together the relevant value for each qualifying member of the independent community or constituent communities who, under section 508A(2) or (4), falls to be treated as having income.

508B-(8) For the purposes of calculating "N" in subsection (7)–

(a) the relevant value for a qualifying member is 1;

(b) but, if section 508A(7) applies in relation to the qualifying member, the relevant value for that member is–

$$I \times \frac{Q}{P}$$

where Q and P have the same meanings as in section 508A(7).

508B-(9) So far as the exemption from corporation tax conferred by this section calls for repayment of tax, no repayment shall be made except on a claim made by the independent community or parent body.

History – S. 508B inserted by SI 2010/157, art. 6(1), with effect in relation to chargeable periods beginning of or after 1 April 2010.

509 Reserves of marketing boards and certain other statutory bodies

509 [Omitted by CTA 2009, s. 1322 and Sch. 1, para. 176 and repealed by CTA 2009, s. 1326 and Sch. 3, Pt. 1.]

History – S. 509 omitted by CTA 2009, s. 1322 and Sch. 1, para. 176 and repealed by CTA 2009, s. 1326 and Sch. 3, Pt. 1, with effect for corporation tax purposes for accounting periods ending on or after 1 April 2009, and for income tax and capital gains tax purposes for the tax year 2009–10 and subsequent tax years.

Notes – S. 509 rewritten as follows:
S. 509(1): CTA 2009, s. 153(1), (2), (3), (4), (5), 155(1), (2).
S. 509(2): CTA 2009, s. 154(2), (3), (4), (5), 155(1), (2).
S. 509(3): CTA 2009, s. 153(5), 155(1), (2).

510 Agricultural societies

510 [Omitted by CTA 2010, s. 1177 and Sch. 1, para. 79 and repealed by CTA 2010, s 1181 and Sch. 3, Pt. 1.]

History – S. 510 omitted by CTA 2010, s. 1177 and Sch. 1, para. 79 and repealed by CTA 2010, s. 1181 and Sch. 3, Pt. 1, with effect for corporation tax purposes for accounting periods ending on or after 1 April 2010, and for income and capital gains tax purposes for the tax year 2010–11 and subsequent tax years.

Notes – S. 510 rewritten for corporation tax as follows:
S. 510(1): CTA 2010, s. 989(1).
S. 510(2): CTA 2010, s. 989(2).

510A European Economic Interest Groupings

510A [Omitted by CTA 2010, s. 1177 and Sch. 1, para. 80 and repealed by CTA 2010, s. 1181 and Sch. 3, Pt. 1.]

History – S. 510A omitted by CTA 2010, s. 1177 and Sch. 1, para. 80 and repealed by CTA 2010, s. 1181 and Sch. 3, Pt. 1, with effect for corporation tax purposes for accounting periods ending on or after 1 April 2010, and for income and capital gains tax purposes for the tax year 2010–11 and subsequent tax years.

Notes – S. 510A is rewritten for income tax purposes as follows:
S. 510A(1): ITA 2007, s. 842(5), Sch. 1 para. 341.
S. 510A(2): ITA 2007, s. 842(1), Sch. 1 para. 341.
S. 510A(3): ITA 2007, s. 842(1), Sch. 1 para. 341.
S. 510A(4): ITA 2007, s. 842(2), Sch. 1 para. 341.
S. 510A(5): ITA 2007, s. 842(3), (4), Sch. 1 para. 341.
S. 510A(6): ITA 2007, s. 842(1), Sch. 1 para. 341.
S. 510A rewritten for corporation tax as follows:
S. 510A(1): CTA 2010, s. 990(7).
S. 510A(2): CTA 2010, s. 990(1).
S. 510A(3): CTA 2010, s. 990(1).
S. 510A(4): CTA 2010, s. 990(2).
S. 510A(5): CTA 2010, s. 990(3), (4).
S. 510A(6): CTA 2010, s. 990(1).
S. 510A(6A): CTA 2010, s. 990(5), (6).

511 The Electricity Council and Boards, the Northern Ireland Electricity Service and the Gas Council

511(1) [Repealed by Electricity Act 1989, s. 112(4) and Sch. 18.]

511(2) [Repealed by Electricity Act 1989, s. 112(4) and Sch. 18.]

511(3) [Repealed by Electricity Act 1989, s. 112(4) and Sch. 18.]

511(4) [Repealed by Electricity (Northern Ireland) Order 1992.]

511(5) [Repealed by Electricity (Northern Ireland) Order 1992.]

511(6) [Repealed by Electricity Act 1989, s. 112(4) and Sch. 18.]

511(7) [Omitted by CTA 2010, s. 1177 and Sch. 1, para. 81 and repealed by CTA 2010, s. 1181 and Sch. 3, Pt. 1.]

History – S. 511(1)–(3), (6) repealed by Electricity Act 1989, s. 112(4) and Sch. 18, with effect from 9 November 2001 (the day appointed by The Electricity Act 1989 (Commencement No. 3) Order 2002 (SI 2001/3419)).
S. 511(4), (5) repealed by Electricity (Northern Ireland) Order 1992, with effect from 1 February 1999 by virtue of SI 1998/441 (C. 20).
S. 511(7) omitted by CTA 2010, s. 1177 and Sch. 1, para. 81 and repealed by CTA 2010, s. 1181 and Sch. 3, Pt. 1, with effect for corporation tax purposes for accounting periods ending on or after 1 April 2010, and for income and capital gains tax purposes for the tax year 2010–11 and subsequent tax years.

Derivations – S. 511(1)–(3): ICTA 1970, s. 349(1)–(3).
S. 511(4), (5): FA 1981, s. 50(3), (4).
S. 511(6): ICTA 1970, s. 349(4).
S. 511(7): ICTA 1970, s. 350(3).

Cross references – Gas Act 1986, s. 60: British Gas plc treated as same person as the British Gas Corporation for corporation tax purposes.

512 Atomic Energy Authority and National Radiological Protection Board

512(1) [Omitted by F(No.2)A 2005, s. 46(2)(c) and repealed by F(No.2)A 2005, s. 70 and Sch. 11, Part 2(12).]

512(2) [Omitted by F(No.2)A 2005, s. 46(2)(d) and repealed by F(No.2)A 2005, s. 70 and Sch. 11, Part 2(12).]

512(3) [Omitted by F(No.2)A 2005, s. 46(2)(c) and repealed by F(No.2)A 2005, s. 70 and Sch. 11, Part 2(12).]

History – S. 512(1) ceased to have effect by virtue of F(No. 2)A 2005, s. 46(2)(c); and repealed by F(No. 2)A 2005, s. 70 and Sch. 11, Pt. 2(12) so far as relating to the UKAEA, effective on and after 1 April 2005; and so far as relating to the NRPB, effective after 1 April 2005 (F(No. 2)A 2005, s. 46(4)(c), (d)).
S. 512(2) ceased to have effect by virtue of F(No. 2)A 2005, s. 46(2)(d); and repealed by F(No. 2)A 2005, s. 70 and Sch. 11, Pt. 2(12), effective in relation to income arising on or after 1 April 2005 (F(No. 2)A 2005, s. 46(4)(e)). S. 512(2) was formerly prospectively repealed by FA 2004, s. 326 and Sch. 42, Pt. 3, with effect from 6 April 2006.
S. 512(3) ceased to have effect by virtue of F(No. 2)A 2005, s. 46(2)(c) and repealed by F(No. 2)A 2005, s. 70 and Sch. 11, Pt. 2(12) so far as relating to the UKAEA, effective on and after 1 April 2005; and so far as relating to the NRPB, effective after 1 April 2005 (F(No. 2)A 2005, s. 46(4)(c), (d)).

Derivations – S. 512(1) (as originally enacted), (2): ICTA 1970, s. 351(1), (2).

513 British Airways Board and National Freight Corporation

513 [Omitted by CTA 2010, s. 1177 and Sch. 1, para. 82 and repealed by CTA 2010, s. 1181 and Sch. 3, Pt. 1.]

History – S. 513 omitted by CTA 2010, s. 1177 and Sch. 1, para. 82 and repealed by CTA 2010, s. 1181 and Sch. 3, Pt. 1, with effect for corporation tax purposes for accounting periods ending on or after 1 April 2010, and for income and capital gains tax purposes for the tax year 2010–11 and subsequent tax years.

514 Funds for reducing the National Debt

514 [Omitted by ITTOIA 2005, s. 882 and Sch. 1, para. 200 and repealed by s. 884 and Sch. 3.]

History – S. 514 omitted by ITTOIA 2005, s. 882(1) and Sch. 1, para. 200 and repealed by s. 884 and Sch. 3; effective for income tax purposes for 2005–06 onwards and for corporation tax purposes for accounting periods ending after 5 April 2005 (ITTOIA 2005, s. 883(1)).

Notes – S. 514 rewritten as ITTOIA 2005, s. 775.

515 Signatories to Operating Agreement for INMARSAT

515 [Omitted by ITA 2007, s. 1027 and Sch. 1, para. 103 and repealed by ITA 2007, s. 1031 and Sch. 3, Pt. 1 with effect for income tax purposes for 2007–08 and subsequent tax years and for corporation tax purposes in relation to accounting periods ending after 5 April 2007.]

516 Government securities held by non-resident central banks

516 [Omitted by ITA 2007, s. 1027 and Sch. 1, para. 104 and repealed by ITA 2007, Sch. 3, Pt. 1 with effect for income tax purposes for 2007–08 and subsequent tax years and for corporation tax purposes in relation to accounting periods ending after 5 April 2007.]

Notes – S. 516 is rewritten for income tax purposes as follows:
S. 516(1): ITA 2007, s. 840(1).
S. 516(2): ITA 2007, s. 840(2).
S. 516(3): ITA 2007, Sch. 1 para. 340(3).
S. 516(4): ITA 2007, s. 840(3), Sch. 1 para. 340(3).
S. 516(5): ITA 2007, s. 840(4), Sch. 1 para. 340(3).

517 Issue departments of the Reserve Bank of India and the State Bank of Pakistan

517 [Omitted by CTA 2010, s. 1177 and Sch. 1,para. 83 and repealed by CTA 2010, s. 1181 and Sch. 3, Pt. 1.]

History – S. 517 omitted by CTA 2010, s. 1177 and Sch. 1, para. 83 and repealed by CTA 2010, s. 1181 and Sch. 3, Pt. 1, with effect for corporation tax purposes for accounting periods ending on or after 1 April 2010, and for income and capital gains tax purposes for the tax year 2010–11 and subsequent tax years.

Notes – S. 517 is rewritten for income tax purposes as ITA 2007, s. 839.

518 Harbour reorganisation schemes

518 [Omitted by CTA 2010, s. 1177 and Sch. 1, para. 84 and repealed by CTA 2010, s. 1181 and Sch. 3, Pt. 1.]

History – S. 518 omitted by CTA 2010, s. 1177 and Sch. 1, para. 84 and repealed by CTA 2010, s. 1181 and Sch. 3, Pt. 1, with effect for corporation tax purposes for accounting periods ending on or after 1 April 2010, and for income and capital gains tax purposes for the tax year 2010–11 and subsequent tax years.

Notes – S. 518 rewritten for corporation tax as follows:
S. 518(1): CTA 2010, s. 991(1), 994(1).
S. 518(2): CTA 2010, s. 991(2).
S. 518(3): CTA 2010, s. 991(3), (4), (5).
S. 518(4): CTA 2010, s. 992(1), (2), (3).
S. 518(5): CTA 2010, s. 992(4).
S. 518(7): CTA 2010, s. 993(1), (2).
S. 518(8): CTA 2010, s. 994(1), (2), (3).
S. 518(9): CTA 2010, s. 994(4), (5).
S. 518(10): CTA 2010, s. 995(2), (3), (4), (5), (6).

518A Asbestos compensation settlements

518A [F(No. 3)A 2010, Sch. 14, para. 3(5) provides that ICTA 1988 is to be treated for the tax year 2006–07 as including, after s. 518, an amendment corresponding to the insertion of ITA 2007, s. 838A by Sch. 14, para. 3(3). For ease of reference CCH has given this provision the number 518A although that is not actually specified in F(No. 3)A 2010.]

519 Local authorities

519 [Omitted by CTA 2010, s. 1177 and Sch. 1, para. 85 and repealed by CTA 2010, s. 1181 and Sch. 3, Pt. 1.]

History – S. 519 omitted by CTA 2010, s. 1177 and Sch. 1, para. 85 and repealed by CTA 2010, s. 1181 and Sch. 3, Pt. 1, with effect for corporation tax purposes for accounting periods ending on or after 1 April 2010, and for income and capital gains tax purposes for the tax year 2010–11 and subsequent tax years.

Notes – S. 519 is rewritten for income tax purposes as follows:
S. 519(1): ITA 2007, s. 838(1), (3).
S. 519(2): ITA 2007, s. 838(2), (3).
S. 519(3): ITA 2007, s. 1000(1), (2), (3), (4), (5).
S. 519 rewritten for corporation tax as follows:
S. 519(1): CTA 2010, s. 984(1).
S. 519(2): CTA 2010, s. 984(2).
S. 519(3): CTA 2010, s. 113(1), (2), (3), (4).

519A Health service bodies

519A [Omitted by CTA 2010, s. 1177 and Sch. 1, para. 86 and repealed by CTA 2010, s. 1181 and Sch. 3, Pt. 1.]

History – S. 519A omitted by CTA 2010, s. 1177 and Sch. 1, para. 86 and repealed by CTA 2010, s. 1181 and Sch. 3, Pt. 1, with effect for corporation tax purposes for accounting periods ending on or after 1 April 2010, and for income and capital gains tax purposes for the tax year 2010–11 and subsequent tax years.

Notes – S. 519A rewritten for corporation tax as follows:
S. 519A(1): CTA 2010, s. 985(1).
S. 519A(2): CTA 2010, s. 986.
S. 519A(3): CTA 2010, s. 987(1).
S. 519A(4): CTA 2010, s. 987(5).
S. 519A(5): CTA 2010, s. 987(6), (7).
S. 519A(6): CTA 2010, s. 987(8).
S. 519A(7): CTA 2010, s. 987(2), (3), (9).
S. 519A(8): CTA 2010, s. 987(4).

PART XIII – MISCELLANEOUS SPECIAL PROVISIONS

Chapter I – Intellectual Property

PATENTS AND KNOW-HOW

520 Allowances for expenditure on purchase of patent rights: post-31st March 1986 expenditure

520 [Repealed by CAA 2001, s. 578, Sch. 2, para. 44, s. 580 and Sch. 4.]

History – S. 520 repealed by CAA 2001, s. 578, Sch. 2, para. 44, s. 580 and Sch. 4, with effect for income tax purposes, as respects allowances and charges falling to be made for chargeable periods ending on or after 6 April 2001, and for corporation tax purposes, as respects allowances and charges falling to be made for chargeable periods ending on or after 1 April 2001, subject to transitional provisions contained in CAA 2001, Sch. 3, para. 8.

Notes – S. 520–523 are rewritten as CAA 2001, Pt. 8.

521 Provisions supplementary to section 520

521 [Repealed by CAA 2001, s. 578, Sch. 2, para. 44, s. 580 and Sch. 4.]

History – S. 521 repealed by CAA 2001, s. 578, Sch. 2, para. 44, s. 580 and Sch. 4, with effect for income tax purposes, as respects allowances and charges falling to be made for chargeable periods ending on or after 6 April 2001, and for corporation tax purposes, as respects allowances and charges falling to be made for chargeable periods ending on or after 1 April 2001, subject to transitional provisions contained in CAA 2001, Sch. 3, para. 8.

Notes – S. 520–523 are rewritten as CAA 2001, Pt. 8.

522 Allowances for expenditure on purchase of patent rights: pre-1st April 1986 expenditure

522 [Repealed by CAA 2001, s. 578, Sch. 2, para. 44, s. 580 and Sch. 4.]

History – S. 522 repealed by CAA 2001, s. 578, Sch. 2, para. 44, s. 580 and Sch. 4, with effect for income tax purposes, as respects allowances and charges falling to be made for chargeable periods ending on or after 6 April 2001, and for corporation tax purposes, as respects allowances and charges falling to be made for chargeable periods ending on or after 1 April 2001, subject to transitional provisions contained in CAA 2001, Sch. 3, para. 8.

Notes – S. 520–523 are rewritten as CAA 2001, Pt. 8.

523 Lapses of patent rights, sales etc.

523 [Repealed by CAA 2001, s. 578, Sch. 2, para. 44, s. 580 and Sch. 4.]

History – S. 523 repealed by CAA 2001, s. 578, Sch. 2, para. 44, s. 580 and Sch. 4, with effect for income tax purposes, as respects allowances and charges falling to be made for chargeable periods ending on or after 6 April 2001, and for corporation tax purposes, as respects allowances and charges falling to be made for chargeable periods ending on or after 1 April 2001, subject to transitional provisions contained in CAA 2001, Sch. 3, para. 8.

Notes – S. 520–523 are rewritten as CAA 2001, Pt. 8.

524 Taxation of receipts from sale of patent rights

524 [Omitted by CTA 2009, s. 1322 and Sch. 1, para. 179 and repealed by CTA 2009, s. 1326 and Sch. 3, Pt. 1.]

History – S. 524 omitted by CTA 2009, s. 1322 and Sch. 1, para. 179 and repealed by CTA 2009, s. 1326 and Sch. 3, Pt. 1, with effect for corporation tax purposes for accounting periods ending on or after 1 April 2009, and for income tax and capital gains tax purposes for the tax year 2009–10 and subsequent tax years.

Notes – Rewritten income tax provisions are now located as follows:
S. 524(1): ITTOIA 2005, s. 587(1) and (2), 588(1) and (2), 589 and 590(2) and (4).
S. 524(2): ITTOIA 2005, s. 590(3), (5) and (6).
S. 524(2A): ITTOIA 2005, s. 590(6).
S. 524(3): ITA 2007, s. 910(1), (2), (3).
S. 524(3): ITTOIA 2005, s. 587(1) and (2), 588(1) and (2), 589, 591(1), 592(1), 595(1) and Sch. 1, para. 148.
S. 524(4): ITTOIA 2005, s. 591(2)–(4), 592(2)–(4), 595(3) and 596(1)–(3).
S. 524(5): ITTOIA 2005, s. 587(3).
S. 524(7): ITTOIA 2005, s. 588(3).
S. 524(8): ITTOIA 2005, s. 588(1), (2) and (4).
S. 524(9): ITTOIA 2005, s. 595(2) and s. 596(1). ITTOIA 2005 does not rewrite ICTA 1988, s. 524(10) on the basis that it is superfluous. (See ITTOIA 2005, Explanatory Notes, Annex 1, Table 1 (Change 158).)
S. 524 rewritten for corporation tax purposes as follows:
S. 524(1): CTA 2009, s. 912(1), 913(1), (2), 914(2), (3), 915(2), (3).
S. 524(2): CTA 2009, s. 914(4), (5), 915(4), (5).
S. 524(2A): CTA 2009, s. 914(5), 915(5).
S. 524(3): CTA 2009, s. 912(1), (2), 913(1), (2), 916(2), 917(2), 919(1).
S. 524(6): CTA 2009, s. 916(3), (4), (5), (6), 917(3), (4), (5), (6).
S. 524(7): CTA 2009, s. 913(1), (2), (4).
S. 524(8): CTA 2009, s. 913(3).
S. 524(9): CTA 2009, s. 919(2), (3).
S. 524(9A): CTA 2009, s. 920.

525 Capital sums: winding up or partnership change

525 [Omitted by CTA 2009, s. 1322 and Sch. 1, para. 180 and repealed by CTA 2009, s. 1326 and Sch. 3, Pt. 1.]

History – S. 525 omitted by CTA 2009, s. 1322 and Sch. 1, para. 180 and repealed by CTA 2009, s. 1326 and Sch. 3, Pt. 1, with effect for corporation tax purposes for accounting periods ending on or after 1 April 2009, and for income tax and capital gains tax purposes for the tax year 2009–10 and subsequent tax years.

Notes – Rewritten income tax provisions are now located as follows:
S. 525(1): ITTOIA 2005, s. 593(1), 594(1) and (2) and 862(2).
S. 525(2): ITTOIA 2005, s. 593(2)–(4) and 862(5) and (6).
S. 525(3): ITTOIA 2005, s. 862(1) and (2).
S. 525(4): ITTOIA 2005, s. 862(3) and (4).

S. 525 rewritten for corporation tax purposes as follows:
S. 525(1): CTA 2009, s. 918(1), (2).
S. 525(3): CTA 2009, s. 1272(1), (2).
S. 525(4): CTA 2009, s. 1272(2).

526 Relief for expenses

526 [Omitted by CTA 2009, s. 1322 and Sch. 1, para. 181 and repealed by CTA 2009, s. 1326 and Sch. 3, Pt. 1.]

History – S. 526 omitted by CTA 2009, s. 1322 and Sch. 1, para. 181 and repealed by CTA 2009, s. 1326 and Sch. 3, Pt. 1, with effect for corporation tax purposes for accounting periods ending on or after 1 April 2009, and for income tax and capital gains tax purposes for the tax year 2009–10 and subsequent tax years.

Notes – Rewritten income tax provisions are now located as follows:
S. 526(1): ITTOIA 2005, s. 600(1), (3) and (4) and 601(2).
S. 526(2): ITTOIA 2005, s. 600(1), (2) and (5) and 601(2).
S. 526 rewritten for corporation tax purposes as follows:
S. 526(1): CTA 2009, s. 924(1), (2), (3), 925(2).

527 Spreading of royalties over several years

527(1) Where–

(a) a royalty or other sum is paid to a company in respect of the user of a patent,

(b) the user extended over a period of six complete years or more, and

(c) the payment is one from which a sum representing income tax must be deducted under section 903 of ITA 2007,

the company may on the making of a claim require that the corporation tax payable by it by reason of the receipt of that sum shall be reduced so as not to exceed the total amount of corporation tax which would have been payable by it if that royalty or sum had been paid in six equal instalments at yearly intervals, the last of which was paid on the date on which the payment was in fact made.

527(2) Subsection (1) above shall apply in relation to a royalty or other sum where the period of the user is two complete years or more but less than six complete years as it applies to the royalties and sums mentioned in that subsection, but with the substitution for the reference to six equal instalments of a reference to so many equal instalments as there are complete years comprised in that period.

527(3) [Repealed by FA 1988, s. 148 and Sch. 14, Pt. VIII.]

527(4) [Omitted by ITA 2007, s. 1027 and Sch. 1, para. 108(3) and repealed by ITA 2007, s. 1031 and Sch. 3, Pt. 1.]

History – S. 527(1) substituted by ITA 2007, s. 1027 and Sch. 1, para. 108(2) with effect for income tax purposes for 2007–08 and subsequent tax years and for corporation tax purposes in relation to accounting periods ending after 5 April 2007.
S. 527(3) repealed by FA 1988, s. 148 and Sch. 14, Pt. VIII with effect in relation to tax payable for 1990–91 and subsequent years of assessment.
S. 527(4) omitted by ITA 2007, s. 1027 and Sch. 1, para. 108(3) and repealed by ITA 2007, s. 1031 and Sch. 3, Pt. 1 with effect for income tax purposes for 2007–08 and subsequent tax years and for corporation tax purposes in relation to accounting periods ending after 5 April 2007.

Derivations – S. 527(1): ICTA 1970, s. 384(1), as amended by FA 1971, s. 37 and Sch. 14, Pt. II.
S. 527(2): ICTA 1970, s. 384(2).
S. 527(4): ICTA 1970, s. 384(4).

Notes – S. 527 is rewritten for income tax purposes as follows:
S. 527(1): ITA 2007, s. 461(1), (2), (3).
S. 527(2): ITA 2007, s. 461(1), (3).
S. 527(3): ITA 2007, s. 461(1).
S. 527(4): ITA 2007, s. 461(1).

528 Manner of making allowances and charges

528 [Omitted by CTA 2009, s. 1322 and Sch. 1, para. 182 and repealed by CTA 2009, s. 1326 and Sch. 3, Pt. 1.]

History – S. 528 omitted by CTA 2009, s. 1322 and Sch. 1, para. 182 and repealed by CTA 2009, s. 1326 and Sch. 3, Pt. 1, with effect for corporation tax purposes for accounting periods ending on or after 1 April 2009, and for income tax and capital gains tax purposes for the tax year 2009–10 and subsequent tax years.

Notes – Rewritten income tax provisions are now located as follows:
S. 528(2): ITTOIA 2005, s. 600(1) and 601(1)–(3).
S. 528(3): ITTOIA 2005, s. 600(1) and 601(5).
S. 528 rewritten for corporation tax purposes as follows:
S. 528(2): CTA 2009, s. 924(1).
S. 528(3): CTA 2009, s. 924(1), 925(1), (2), (3).
S. 528(3A): CTA 2009, s. 925(5).

529 Patent income to be earned income in certain cases

529 [Omitted by ITTOIA 2005, s. 882 and Sch. 1, para. 206 and repealed by s. 884 and Sch. 3.]

History – S. 529 omitted by ITTOIA 2005, s. 882(1) and Sch. 1, para. 529 and repealed by s. 884 and Sch. 3; effective for income tax purposes for 2005–06 onwards and for corporation tax purposes for accounting periods ending after 5 April 2005 (ITTOIA 2005, s. 883(1)).

530 Disposal of know-how

530 [Repealed by CAA 2001, s. 578, Sch. 2, para. 47, s. 580 and Sch. 4.]

History – S. 530 repealed by CAA 2001, s. 578, Sch. 2, para. 47, s. 580 and Sch. 4, with effect for income tax purposes, as respects allowances and charges falling to be made for chargeable periods ending on or after 6 April 2001, and for corporation tax purposes, as respects allowances and charges falling to be made for chargeable periods ending on or after 1 April 2001, subject to transitional provisions contained in CAA 2001, Sch. 3, para. 8.

Notes – S. 530 is rewritten as CAA 2001, Pt. 7.

531 Provisions supplementary to section 530

531 [Omitted by CTA 2009, s. 1322 and Sch. 1, para. 183 and repealed by CTA 2009, s. 1326 and Sch. 3, Pt. 1.]

History – S. 531 omitted by CTA 2009, s. 1322 and Sch. 1, para. 183 and repealed by CTA 2009, s. 1326 and Sch. 3, Pt. 1, with effect for corporation tax purposes for accounting periods ending on or after 1 April 2009, and for income tax and capital gains tax purposes for the tax year 2009–10 and subsequent tax years.

Notes – Rewritten income tax provisions are now located as follows:
S. 531(1): ITTOIA 2005, s. 193(1) and (2).
S. 531(2): ITTOIA 2005, s. 194(1)–(3) and Sch. 1, para. 443(1) and (2).
S. 531(3): ITTOIA 2005, s. 194(4)–(6) and Sch. 1, para. 443(2).
S. 531(4): ITTOIA 2005, s. 585(2) and (3).
S. 531(5): ITTOIA 2005, s. 583(1), 584(2) and (3) and 586.
S. 531(6): ITTOIA 2005, Sch. 1, para. 337(5).
S. 531(7): ITTOIA 2005, s. 195(1)–(3), 584(4) and (5) and 878(6).
S. 531(8): ITTOIA 2005, s. 192(3) and (4), 583(1) and (2) and 878(6). But ITTOIA 2005 does not rewrite the words in ICTA 1988, s. 531(8) "whether absolute or qualified" as they are superfluous. (See ITTOIA 2005, Explanatory Notes, Annex 1, Table 1 (Change 158).)
S. 531 rewritten for corporation tax purposes as follows:
S. 531(1): CTA 2009, s. 177(1), (2).
S. 531(2): CTA 2009, s. 178(1), (2), (3).
S. 531(3): CTA 2009, s. 178(4), (5), (6).
S. 531(3A): CTA 2009, s. 178(7).
S. 531(4): CTA 2009, s. 908(1), 909(2), (3), (4).
S. 531(5): CTA 2009, s. 910(1), (2).
S. 531(7): CTA 2009, s. 179(1), (2), (3), 909(5), (6), 1316(2).
S. 531(8): CTA 2009, s. 176(3), (4), 908(1), (2).

532 Application of Capital Allowances Act

532 [Omitted by CTA 2009, s. 1322 and Sch. 1, para. 184 and repealed by CTA 2009, s. 1326 and Sch. 3, Pt. 1.]

History – S. 532 omitted by CTA 2009, s. 1322 and Sch. 1, para. 184 and repealed by CTA 2009, s. 1326 and Sch. 3, Pt. 1, with effect for corporation tax purposes for accounting periods ending on or after 1 April 2009, and for income tax and capital gains tax purposes for the tax year 2009–10 and subsequent tax years.

Notes – Rewritten income tax provisions are now located as follows:
S. 532: ITA 2007, s. 910(5).
S. 532(1): ITTOIA 2005, s. 192(2), (5) and (6), 193(3)–(6), 603(1) and (2), 604(1)–(4), 605(1)–(5), 606(1)–(4), 607(1) and (2), 608, 861(1)–(6), 878(6) and Sch. 1, para. 148.
S. 532 rewritten as CTA 2009, s. 908(5), 926(1), (2), 927(1), (2), (3), (4), 928(1), (2), (3), (4), (5), 929(1), (2), (3), (4), 930(1), (2), 931, 1316(2).

533 Interpretation of sections 520 to 532

533 [Omitted by CTA 2009, s. 1322 and Sch. 1, para. 185 and repealed by CTA 2009, s. 1326 and Sch. 3, Pt. 1.]

History – S. 533 omitted by CTA 2009, s. 1322 and Sch. 1, para. 185 and repealed by CTA 2009, s. 1326 and Sch. 3, Pt. 1, with effect for corporation tax purposes for accounting periods ending on or after 1 April 2009, and for income tax and capital gains tax purposes for the tax year 2009–10 and subsequent tax years.

Notes – Rewritten income tax provisions are now located as follows:
S. 533(1): ITTOIA 2005, s. 601(4) and 587(2) and (4).
S. 533(2): ITA 2007, s. 910(4).
S. 533(2): ITTOIA 2005, s. 597(1) and (2) and Sch. 1, para. 148.
S. 533(3): ITA 2007, s. 910(4).
S. 533(3): ITTOIA 2005, s. 597(3) and (4) and Sch. 1, para. 148.
S. 533(4): ITA 2007, s. 910(4).
S. 533(4): ITTOIA 2005, s. 599(1)–(3). But ITTOIA 2005 does not rewrite the references in ICTA 1988, s. 533(4) to sections of the Patents Act 1949 as patents under those sections will have ceased to have effect. (See ITTOIA 2005, Explanatory Notes, Annex 1, Table 1 (Change 158).)
S. 533(5): ITA 2007, s. 910(4).
S. 533(5): ITTOIA 2005, s. 598(1)–(3) and Sch. 1, para. 148.
S. 533(6): ITA 2007, s. 910(4).
S. 533(6): ITTOIA 2005, s. 598(1) and Sch. 1, para. 148.
S. 533(7): ITTOIA 2005, s. 192(1) and 583(4) and (5).

S. 533 rewritten for corporation tax purposes as follows:
S. 533(1): CTA 2009, s. 912(2), (3), 925(4).
S. 533(2): CTA 2009, s. 921(1), (2).
S. 533(3): CTA 2009, s. 921(3), (4).
S. 533(4): CTA 2009, s. 923(1), (2),(3).
S. 533(5): CTA 2009, s. 922(1), (2), (3).
S. 533(6): CTA 2009, s. 922(1).
S. 533(7): CTA 2009, s. 908(4).

COPYRIGHT AND PUBLIC LENDING RIGHT

534 Relief for copyright payments etc.

534 [Repealed by FA 2001, s. 71(3), s. 110 and Sch. 33, Pt. 2(6).]

History – S. 534 repealed by FA 2001, s. 71(3), s. 110 and Sch. 33, Pt. 2(6), with effect in relation to payments actually receivable on or after 6 April 2001.

535 Relief where copyright sold after ten years or more

535 [Repealed by FA 2001, s. 71(3), s. 110 and Sch. 33, Pt. 2(6).]

History – S. 535 repealed by FA 2001, s. 71(3), s. 110 and Sch. 33, Pt. 2(6), with effect in relation to payments actually receivable on or after 6 April 2001.

536 Taxation of royalties where owner abroad

536 [Omitted by ITA 2007, s. 1027 and Sch. 1, para. 110 and repealed by ITA 2007, s. 1031 and Sch. 3, Pt. 1 with effect for 2007–08 and subsequent tax years.]

Notes – S. 536 is rewritten for income tax purposes as follows:
S. 536(1): ITA 2007, s. 906(1), (2), (3), (5), 907(1), 909(3).
S. 536(2): ITA 2007, s. 906(3), (4), 907(2).
S. 536(3): ITA 2007, s. 908(1).
S. 536(4): ITA 2007, s. 908(2).
S. 536(5): ITA 2007, s. 909(1).
S. 536(6): ITA 2007, s. 909(2).

537 Public lending right

537 [Omitted by ITA 2007, s. 1027 and Sch. 1, para. 110 and repealed by ITA 2007, s. 1031 and Sch. 3, Pt. 1 with effect for 2007–08 and subsequent tax years.]

Notes – S. 537 is rewritten for income tax purposes as ITA 2007, s. 906(1), (5), 907(1).

DESIGNS

537A Relief for payments in respect of designs

537A [Repealed by FA 2001, s. 71(3), s. 110 and Sch. 33, Pt. 2(6).]

History – S. 537A repealed by FA 2001, s. 71(3), s. 110 and Sch. 33, Pt. 2(6), with effect in relation to payments actually receivable on or after 6 April 2001.

537B Taxation of design royalties where owner abroad

537B [Omitted by ITA 2007, s. 1027 and Sch. 1, para. 110 and repealed by ITA 2007, s. 1031 and Sch. 3, Pt. 1 with effect for 2007–08 and subsequent tax years.]

Notes – S. 537B is rewritten for income tax purposes as follows:
S. 537B(1): ITA 2007, s. 906(1), (2), (3), (5), 907(1), 909(3).
S. 537B(2): ITA 2007, s. 906(3), (4), 907(2).
S. 537B(3): ITA 2007, s. 908(1).
S. 537B(4): ITA 2007, s. 908(2).
S. 537B(5): ITA 2007, s. 909(1).
S. 537B(6): ITA 2007, s. 909(2).

ARTISTS' RECEIPTS

538 Relief for painters, sculptors and other artists

538 [Repealed by FA 2001, s. 71(3), s. 110 and Sch. 33, Pt. 2(6).]

History – S. 538 repealed by FA 2001, s. 71(3), s. 110 and Sch. 33, Pt. 2(6), with effect in relation to payments actually receivable on or after 6 April 2001.

Chapter II – Life Policies, Life Annuities and Capital Redemption Policies

Cross references – FA 2003, Sch. 34, para. 3: any event happening before 9th April 2003 in relation to a policy of life insurance which, at the time of the event, was a pure protection group life policy (i.e. a group life policy whose terms do not provide for any sums or other benefits to be paid or conferred except on death or disability) shall be deemed not to have been a chargeable event.
Sch. 34, para. 4: time permitted for compliance with requirements of section 539A.

539 Introductory

539 [Omitted by FA 2008, s. 36 and Sch. 14, para. 3.]

History – S. 539 omitted by FA 2008, s. 36 and Sch. 14, para. 3, with effect:
- so far as relating to corporation tax, for accounting periods beginning on or after 1 April 2008;
- so far as relating to income tax, for the tax year 2008–09 and subsequent tax years.

Notes – Rewritten income tax provisions are now located as follows:
S. 539(1): ITTOIA 2005, s. 473(1).
S. 539(2): ITTOIA 2005, s. 478(1)–(3), 479, 480(1) and (3), 483(1) and (2), 879(1) and Sch. 2, para. 86.
S. 539(3): ITTOIA 2005, s. 473(2), 480(2) and (3),483(3), 545(1) and 879(1).
S. 539(3A): ITTOIA 2005, s. 505(2).
S. 539(4): ITTOIA 2005, s. 484(1) and 500.
S. 539(5): ITTOIA 2005, Sch. 2, para. 96(1).
S. 539(6): ITTOIA 2005, Sch. 2, para. 96(2).
S. 539(7): ITTOIA 2005, Sch. 2, para. 96(3).
S. 539(9): ITTOIA 2005, s. 501(7) and Sch. 2, para. 107(2) and (3) and 108(2) and (3).

539ZA Application of this Chapter etc. to policies and contracts in which persons other than companies are interested

539ZA [Omitted by FA 2008, s. 36 and Sch. 14, para. 3.]

History – S. 539ZA omitted by FA 2008, s. 36 and Sch. 14, para. 3, with effect:
- so far as relating to corporation tax, for accounting periods beginning on or after 1 April 2008;
- so far as relating to income tax, for the tax year 2008–09 and subsequent tax years.

539A The conditions for being an excepted group life policy

539A [Omitted by FA 2008, s. 36 and Sch. 14, para. 3.]

History – S. 539A omitted by FA 2008, s. 36 and Sch. 14, para. 3, with effect:
- so far as relating to corporation tax, for accounting periods beginning on or after 1 April 2008;
- so far as relating to income tax, for the tax year 2008–09 and subsequent tax years.

Notes – ITTOIA 2005 amends s. 539A(see History note below for details) leaving it effective for corporation tax purposes only, for accounting periods ending after 5 April 2005 (ITTOIA 2005, s. 883(1)). Rewritten income tax provisions are now located as follows:
S. 539A(1): ITTOIA 2005, s. 481(2)–(4) and (6) and 482(2), (3) and (5).
S. 539A(2): ITTOIA 2005, s. 481(2).
S. 539A(3): ITTOIA 2005, s. 481(3).
S. 539A(4): ITTOIA 2005, s. 481(4) and (5).
S. 539A(5): ITTOIA 2005, s. 481(6).
S. 539A(6): ITTOIA 2005, s. 482(2) and 878(1).
S. 539A(7): ITTOIA 2005, s. 482(3) and (4) and 878(5).
S. 539A(8): ITTOIA 2005, s. 482(4)–(6) and 878(5).

540 Life policies: chargeable events

540 [Omitted by FA 2008, s. 36 and Sch. 14, para. 3.]

History – S. 540 omitted by FA 2008, s. 36 and Sch. 14, para. 3, with effect:
- so far as relating to corporation tax, for accounting periods beginning on or after 1 April 2008;
- so far as relating to income tax, for the tax year 2008–09 and subsequent tax years.

Notes – Rewritten income tax provisions are now located as follows:
S. 540(1): ITTOIA 2005, s. 462(1), 484(1), 485(2), (3) and (5), 498(1), 507(2)–(5) and 509(1) and (5). But ITTOIA 2005 does not rewrite the words in ICTA 1988, s. 540(1)(b) "whether or not the premiums thereunder are eligible for relief under section 266" as they add nothing. (See ITTOIA 2005, Explanatory Notes, Annex 1, Table 1 (Change 158).)
S. 540(3): ITTOIA 2005, Sch. 2, para. 102(1) and (2).
S. 540(4): ITTOIA 2005, s. 487.
S. 540(5): ITTOIA 2005, s. 485(6).
S. 540(5A): ITTOIA 2005, s. 485(2)–(4) and Sch. 2, para. 107(1).
S. 540(6): ITTOIA 2005, s. 542(1).

541 Life policies: computation of gain

541 [Omitted by FA 2008, s. 36 and Sch. 14, para. 3.]

History – S. 541 omitted by FA 2008, s. 36 and Sch. 14, para. 3, with effect:
- so far as relating to corporation tax, for accounting periods beginning on or after 1 April 2008;
- so far as relating to income tax, for the tax year 2008–09 and subsequent tax years.

Notes – Rewritten income tax provisions are now located as follows:
S. 541(1): ITTOIA 2005, s. 461(1), 491(2) and (3), 492(1), 493(1), (2), (5) and (7), 494(1) and 507(2)–(5).
S. 541(2): ITTOIA 2005, s. 493(1) and (2).
S. 541(3): ITTOIA 2005, s. 493(6) and 878(5).
S. 541(3A): ITTOIA 2005, s. 495(4).
S. 541(4A): ITTOIA 2005, s. 496(1) and (2).

S. 541(4B): ITTOIA 2005, s. 496(4), (5) and (7).
S. 541(4C): ITTOIA 2005, s. 496(3) and (7).
S. 541(4D): ITTOIA 2005, s. 496(6) and (7).
S. 541(5): ITTOIA 2005, s. 491(2), (3), (5) and (6), 492(1) and (2), 493(1), (2), (5) and (7), 494(1) and (3) and 495(3) and (5).
S. 541(6): ITTOIA 2005, Sch. 2, para. 105.

542 Life annuity contracts: chargeable events

542 [Omitted by FA 2008, s. 36 and Sch. 14, para. 3.]

History – S. 542 omitted by FA 2008, s. 36 and Sch. 14, para. 3, with effect:
- so far as relating to corporation tax, for accounting periods beginning on or after 1 April 2008;
- so far as relating to income tax, for the tax year 2008–09 and subsequent tax years.

Notes – Rewritten income tax provisions are now located as follows:
S. 542(1): ITTOIA 2005, s. 462(1), 484(1), 498(1), 507(2)–(5) and 509(1) and (5).
S. 542(2): ITTOIA 2005, s. 484(1), 493(1) and (2), 499(3), 500 and Sch. 2, para. 99.
S. 542(3): ITTOIA 2005, Sch. 2, para. 102(1) and (2).
S. 542(4): ITTOIA 2005, s. 487.

543 Life annuity contracts: computation of gain

543 [Omitted by FA 2008, s. 36 and Sch. 14, para. 3.]

History – S. 543 omitted by FA 2008, s. 36 and Sch. 14, para. 3, with effect:
- so far as relating to corporation tax, for accounting periods beginning on or after 1 April 2008;
- so far as relating to income tax, for the tax year 2008–09 and subsequent tax years.

Notes – Rewritten income tax provisions are now located as follows:
S. 543(1): ITTOIA 2005, s. 461(1), 491(2) and (3), 492(1), 493(1), (2) and (5), 494(1), 507(2)–(5) and 545(2) and (3).
S. 543(2): ITTOIA 2005, s. 493(5) and (6) and 878(5).
S. 543(2A): ITTOIA 2005, s. 495(4).
S. 543(3): ITTOIA 2005, s. 491(2) and (3), 492(1) and 494(1).

544 Second and subsequent assignment of life policies and contracts

544 [Omitted by FA 2008, s. 36 and Sch. 14, para. 3.]

History – S. 544 omitted by FA 2008, s. 36 and Sch. 14, para. 3, with effect:
- so far as relating to corporation tax, for accounting periods beginning on or after 1 April 2008;
- so far as relating to income tax, for the tax year 2008–09 and subsequent tax years.

Notes – Rewritten income tax provisions are now located as follows:
S. 544(1): ITTOIA 2005, Sch. 2, para. 102(2).
S. 544(2): ITTOIA 2005, s. 545(2) and (3) and Sch. 2, para. 102(2).
S. 544(3): ITTOIA 2005, and Sch. 2, para. 102(1) and (3)–(5).
S. 544(4): ITTOIA 2005, s. 487.
S. 544(5): ITTOIA 2005, Sch. 2, para. 102(5) and (8).
S. 544(6): ITTOIA 2005, Sch. 2, para. 102(6).
S. 544(7): ITTOIA 2005, Sch. 2, para. 102(7).
S. 544(8): ITTOIA 2005, Sch. 2, para. 102(9).

545 Capital redemption policies

545 [Omitted by FA 2008, s. 36 and Sch. 14, para. 3.]

History – S. 545 omitted by FA 2008, s. 36 and Sch. 14, para. 3, with effect:
- so far as relating to corporation tax, for accounting periods beginning on or after 1 April 2008;
- so far as relating to income tax, for the tax year 2008–09 and subsequent tax years.

Notes – Rewritten income tax provisions are now located as follows:
S. 545(1): ITTOIA 2005, s. 462(1), 484(1), 486, 498(1), 507(2)–(5) and 509(1) and (5).
S. 545(2): ITTOIA 2005, s. 487.
S. 545(3): ITTOIA 2005, s. 461(1), 491(2), (3) and (6), 492(1) and (2), 493(1), (2) and (5), 494(1) and (3), 495(3)–(5) and 507(2)–(5).
S. 545(4): ITTOIA 2005, s. 491(2) and (3), 492(1) and 494(1) and (2).

546 Calculation of certain amounts for purposes of sections 540, 542 and 545

546 [Omitted by FA 2008, s. 36 and Sch. 14, para. 3.]

History – S. 546 omitted by FA 2008, s. 36 and Sch. 14, para. 3, with effect:
- so far as relating to corporation tax, for accounting periods beginning on or after 1 April 2008;
- so far as relating to income tax, for the tax year 2008–09 and subsequent tax years.

Notes – Rewritten income tax provisions are now located as follows:
S. 546(1): ITTOIA 2005, s. 498(1) and (2), 507(2)–(6), 508(1), 509(1), 510(3), 545(2) and (3) and Sch. 2, para. 100(1)–(6).
S. 546(2): ITTOIA 2005, s. 507(2)–(5).
S. 546(3): ITTOIA 2005, s. 507(2)–(5).
S. 546(4): ITTOIA 2005, s. 499(1) and (3)–(5).
S. 546(5): ITTOIA 2005, Sch. 2, para. 105.
S. 546(6): ITTOIA 2005, s. 508(4).

546A Treatment of certain assignments etc involving co-ownership

546A [Omitted by FA 2008, s. 36 and Sch. 14, para. 3.]

History – S. 546A omitted by FA 2008, s. 36 and Sch. 14, para. 3, with effect:
- so far as relating to corporation tax, for accounting periods beginning on or after 1 April 2008;
- so far as relating to income tax, for the tax year 2008–09 and subsequent tax years.

ICTA 1988

Notes – Rewritten income tax provisions are now located as follows:
S. 546A(1): ITTOIA 2005, s. 505(1) and (3)–(8).
S. 546A(2): ITTOIA 2005, s. 505(1).
S. 546A(3): ITTOIA 2005, s. 505(6)–(8) and 506(2)–(6).
S. 546A(4): ITTOIA 2005, s. 505(6)–(8) and 506(2)–(4).

546B Special provision in respect of certain section 546 excesses

546B [Omitted by FA 2008, s. 36 and Sch. 14, para. 3.]

History – S. 546B omitted by FA 2008, s. 36 and Sch. 14, para. 3, with effect:
- so far as relating to corporation tax, for accounting periods beginning on or after 1 April 2008;
- so far as relating to income tax, for the tax year 2008–09 and subsequent tax years.

Notes – Rewritten income tax provisions are now located as follows:
S. 546B(1): ITTOIA 2005, s. 509(1) and 514(1).
S. 546B(A1): ITTOIA 2005, s. 485(3) and (5).
S. 546B(2): ITTOIA 2005, s. 509(1), (3) and (4) and 514(1).
S. 546B(3): ITTOIA 2005, s. 509(1).
S. 546B(4): ITTOIA 2005, s. 499(1).

546C Charging the section 546 excess to tax where section 546B applies

546C [Omitted by FA 2008, s. 36 and Sch. 14, para. 3.]

History – S. 546C omitted by FA 2008, s. 36 and Sch. 14, para. 3, with effect:
- so far as relating to corporation tax, for accounting periods beginning on or after 1 April 2008;
- so far as relating to income tax, for the tax year 2008–09 and subsequent tax years.

Notes – Rewritten income tax provisions are now located as follows:
S. 546C(1): ITTOIA 2005, s. 510(1) and (2).
S. 546C(2): ITTOIA 2005, s. 508(4), 510(1) and (2), 511(2)–(4) and 512(1), (3) and (4).
S. 546C(3): ITTOIA 2005, s. 508(4), 510(3), 511(2)–(4) and 512(1), (3) and (4).
S. 546C(4): ITTOIA 2005, s. 510(4).
S. 546C(5): ITTOIA 2005, s. 510(1) and (2) and 512(3).
S. 546C(6): ITTOIA 2005, s. 508(4), 511(2)–(4) and 512(1), (2) and (3).
S. 546C(7): ITTOIA 2005, s. 462(1), 484(1), 512(2) and 514(1).
S. 546C(8): ITTOIA 2005, s. 463(2) and 514(3) and (4).
S. 546C(9): ITTOIA 2005, s. 510(5) and 514(5).
S. 546C(10): ITTOIA 2005, s. 499(1) and (3)–(5).

546D Modifications of s. 546C for final year ending with terminal chargeable event

546D [Omitted by FA 2008, s. 36 and Sch. 14, para. 3.]

History – S. 546D omitted by FA 2008, s. 36 and Sch. 14, para. 3, with effect:
- so far as relating to corporation tax, for accounting periods beginning on or after 1 April 2008;
- so far as relating to income tax, for the tax year 2008–09 and subsequent tax years.

Notes – Rewritten income tax provisions are now located as follows:
S. 546D(1): ITTOIA 2005, s. 513(1) and (4).
S. 546D(2): ITTOIA 2005, s. 513(3).
S. 546D(3): ITTOIA 2005, s. 513(1), (2) and (4).
S. 546D(4): ITTOIA 2005, s. 513(4).
S. 546D(5): ITTOIA 2005, s. 513(4) and (5).
S. 546D(6): ITTOIA 2005, s. 513(1), (2) and (4).

547 Method of charging gain to tax

547 [Omitted by FA 2008, s. 36 and Sch. 14, para. 3.]

History – S. 547 omitted by FA 2008, s. 36 and Sch. 14, para. 3, with effect:
- so far as relating to corporation tax, for accounting periods beginning on or after 1 April 2008;
- so far as relating to income tax, for the tax year 2008–09 and subsequent tax years.

Notes – Rewritten income tax provisions are now located as follows:
S. 547(1): ITTOIA 2005, s. 461(1), 463(1), 465(1)–(5), 467(1)–(6), 468(1) and 664(1) and (2).
S. 547(2): ITTOIA 2005, s. 507(2)–(5) and 527(1) and (2).
S. 547(4): ITTOIA 2005, s. 464(3) and 468(6).
S. 547(4A): ITTOIA 2005, Sch. 2, para. 112(1) and 114(1).
S. 547(5): ITTOIA 2005, s. 530(1)–(7) and Sch. 1, para. 146.
S. 547(5AA): ITTOIA 2005, s. 530(1) and (2).
S. 547(5A): ITTOIA 2005, s. 531(1) and (3), Sch. 1, para. 146 and Sch. 2, para. 98 and 109(1) and (3).
S. 547(6): ITTOIA 2005, s. 461(1), 531(1) and (3) and Sch. 2, para. 109(2).
S. 547(6A): ITTOIA 2005, s. 532(1)–(5), 533(2)–(7) and 534(2).
S. 547(7): ITTOIA 2005, s. 531(1) and (3) and 545(1).
S.547(7A): ITTOIA 2005, s. 466(1) and (2).
S. 547(9): ITTOIA 2005, s. 467(1)–(3) and (5)–(7).
S. 547(9A): ITTOIA 2005, s. 467(7).
S. 547(10): ITTOIA 2005, s. 468(1)–(3).
S. 547(11): ITTOIA 2005, s. 468(1), (2) and (4).
S. 547(12): ITTOIA 2005, s. 468(1).
S. 547(13): ITTOIA 2005, s. 465(6), 468(5) and 532(5).

547A Method of charging gain to tax: multiple interests

547A [Omitted by FA 2008, s. 36 and Sch. 14, para. 3.]

History – S. 547A omitted by FA 2008, s. 36 and Sch. 14, para. 3, with effect:
- so far as relating to corporation tax, for accounting periods beginning on or after 1 April 2008;
- so far as relating to income tax, for the tax year 2008–09 and subsequent tax years.

Notes – Rewritten income tax provisions are now located as follows:
S. 547A(1): ITTOIA 2005, s. 464(5) and 469(1) and (3)–(5).
S. 547A(2): ITTOIA 2005, s. 469(7).
S. 547A(3): ITTOIA 2005, s. 470(2)–(7).
S. 547A(4): ITTOIA 2005, s. 464(5) and 469(3)–(5).
S. 547A(5): ITTOIA 2005, s. 471(2)–(5).
S. 547A(6): ITTOIA 2005, s. 472(1) and (2).
S. 547A(7): ITTOIA 2005, s. 472(4) and (5).
S. 547A(8): ITTOIA 2005, s. 472(6) and (7).
S. 547A(9): ITTOIA 2005, s. 472(5).
S. 547A(10): ITTOIA 2005, s. 472(3).
S. 547A(11): ITTOIA 2005, s. 471(1).
S. 547A(12): ITTOIA 2005, s. 471(7).
S. 547A(13): ITTOIA 2005, s. 471(7).
S. 547A(14): ITTOIA 2005, s. 469(6).
S. 547A(15): ITTOIA 2005, s. 468(5) and 878(1).
S. 547A(16): ITTOIA 2005, s. 470(7) and 471(6).

548 Deemed surrender of certain loans

548 [Omitted by FA 2008, s. 36 and Sch. 14, para. 3.]

History – S. 548 omitted by FA 2008, s. 36 and Sch. 14, para. 3, with effect:
- so far as relating to corporation tax, for accounting periods beginning on or after 1 April 2008;
- so far as relating to income tax, for the tax year 2008–09 and subsequent tax years.

Notes – Rewritten income tax provisions are now located as follows:
S. 548(1): ITTOIA 2005, s. 492(1), 494(1), 500, 501(1)–(6), 507(2)–(5), 508(2) and Sch. 2, para. 97.
S. 548(2): ITTOIA 2005, s. 494(1) and 545(2) and (3).
S. 548(3): ITTOIA 2005, s. 501(7), 502(1)–(3) and 503(1)–(3).
S. 548(3A): ITTOIA 2005, Sch. 2, para. 108(1).
S. 548(4): ITTOIA 2005, s. 499(3)–(5).

548A Effect of rebated or reinvested commission in certain cases

548A [Omitted by FA 2008, s. 36 and Sch. 14, para. 3.]

History – S. 548A omitted by FA 2008, s. 36 and Sch. 14, para. 3, with effect:
- so far as relating to corporation tax, for accounting periods beginning on or after 1 April 2008;
- so far as relating to income tax, for the tax year 2008–09 and subsequent tax years.

548B Section 548A: further definitions

548B [Omitted by FA 2008, s. 36 and Sch. 14, para. 3.]

History – S. 548B omitted by FA 2008, s. 36 and Sch. 14, para. 3, with effect:
- so far as relating to corporation tax, for accounting periods beginning on or after 1 April 2008;
- so far as relating to income tax, for the tax year 2008–09 and subsequent tax years.

549 Certain deficiencies allowable as deductions

549 [Omitted by ITTOIA 2005, s. 882 and Sch. 1, para. 219 and repealed by s. 884 and Sch. 3.]

History – S. 549 omitted by ITTOIA 2005, s. 882(1) and Sch. 1, para. 219 and repealed by s. 884 and Sch. 3; effective for income tax purposes for 2005–06 onwards and for corporation tax purposes for accounting periods ending after 5 April 2005 (ITTOIA 2005, s. 883(1)).

Notes – S. 549 rewritten as follows:
S. 549(1): ITTOIA 2005,s. 507(2)–(5), 539(1), 540(1)–(4), 541(2)–(4) and Sch. 2, para. 117(1).
S. 549(1A): ITTOIA 2005,s. 541(4).
S. 549(2): ITTOIA 2005,s. 539(3)–(6) and Sch. 2, para. 109(4).
S. 549(3): ITTOIA 2005,s. 499(3)–(5).

550 Relief where gain charged at a higher rate

550 [Omitted by ITTOIA 2005, s. 882 and Sch. 1, para. 220 and repealed by s. 884 and Sch. 3.]

History – S. 550 omitted by ITTOIA 2005, s. 882(1) and Sch. 1, para. 220 and repealed by s. 884 and Sch. 3; effective for income tax purposes for 2005–06 onwards and for corporation tax purposes for accounting periods ending after 5 April 2005 (ITTOIA 2005, s. 883(1)).

Notes – S. 550: ITTOIA 2005 as follows:
S. 550(1): ITTOIA 2005,s. 535(1), (3) and (4).
S. 550(2): ITTOIA 2005,s. 535(1)–(4), 536(1) and 537.
S. 550(3): ITTOIA 2005, s. 536(1) and 537.
S. 550(4): ITTOIA 2005, s. 528(5) and (6) and 536(4) and (5).
S. 550(5): ITTOIA 2005, s. 536(2) and (4).
S. 550(5A): ITTOIA 2005, s. 536(3).
S. 550(6): ITTOIA 2005, s. 537.
S. 550(7): ITTOIA 2005, s. 535(3)–(5).

551 Right of individual to recover tax from trustees

551 [Omitted by ITTOIA 2005, s. 882 and Sch. 1, para. 221 and repealed by s. 884 and Sch. 3.]

History – S. 551 omitted by ITTOIA 2005, s. 882(1) and Sch. 1, para. 221 and repealed by s. 884 and Sch. 3; effective for income tax purposes for 2005–06 onwards and for corporation tax purposes for accounting periods ending after 5 April 2005 (ITTOIA 2005, s. 883(1)).

Notes – S. 551: ITTOIA 2005 as follows:
S. 551(1): ITTOIA 2005, s. 538(1)–(3).
S. 551(2): ITTOIA 2005, s. 538(4).
S. 551(3): ITTOIA 2005, s. 538(5) and (6).

551A Right of company to recover tax from trustees

551A [Omitted by FA 2008, s. 36 and Sch. 14, para. 3.]

History – S. 551A omitted by FA 2008, s. 36 and Sch. 14, para. 3, with effect:
- so far as relating to corporation tax, for accounting periods beginning on or after 1 April 2008;
- so far as relating to income tax, for the tax year 2008–09 and subsequent tax years.

552 Information: duty of insurers

552(1) Where a chargeable event has happened in relation to any policy or contract, the body by or with whom the policy or contract was issued, entered into or effected shall–

(a) unless satisfied that no gain is to be treated as arising by reason of the event, deliver to the appropriate policy holder before the end of the relevant three month period a certificate specifying the information described in subsection (5) below; and

(b) if the condition in paragraph (a) or (b) of subsection (2) below is satisfied, deliver to the inspector before the end of the relevant three month period a certificate specifying the information described in subsection (5) below together with the name and address of the appropriate policy holder.

552(2) For the purposes of this section–

(a) the condition in this paragraph is that the event is an assignment for money or money's worth of the whole of the rights conferred by the policy or contract; or

(b) the condition in this paragraph is that the amount of the gain, or the aggregate amount of the gain and any gains connected with it, exceeds one half of the basic rate limit for the relevant year of assessment.

552(3) If, in the case of every certificate which a body delivers under subsection (1)(a) above which relates to a gain attributable to a year of assessment, the body also delivers to the inspector–

(a) before the end of the relevant three month period for the purposes of subsection (1)(b) above,

(b) by a means prescribed by the Board for the purposes of this subsection under section 552ZA(5), and

(c) in a form so prescribed in the case of that means,

a certificate specifying the same information as the certificate under subsection (1)(a) together with the name and address of the appropriate policy holder, the body shall be taken to have complied with the requirements of subsection (1)(b) above in relation to that year of assessment so far as relating to the chargeable events to which the certificates relate.

552(4) Where a certificate is not required to be delivered under subsection (1)(b) above in the case of any chargeable event–

(a) the inspector may by notice require the body to deliver to him a copy of any certificate that the body was required to deliver under subsection (1)(a) above which relates to the chargeable event; and

(b) it shall be the duty of the body to deliver such a copy within 30 days of receipt of the notice.

552(5) The information to be given to the appropriate policy holder pursuant to subsection (1)(a) above or the inspector pursuant to subsection (1)(b) above is–

(a) any unique identifying designation given to the policy or contract;

(b) the nature of the chargeable event and–

(i) the date on which it happened; and

(ii) if it is a chargeable event by virtue of section 514(1) of ITTOIA 2005 (chargeable events where transaction-related calculations show gains), the date on which the insurance year ends;

(c) if the event is the assignment of all the rights conferred by the policy or contract, such of the following as may be required for computing the amount of the gain to be treated as arising by virtue of Chapter 9 of Part 4 of ITTOIA 2005–

(i) the amount or value of any capital sums of a kind referred to in section 492(1)(b) to (e) of ITTOIA 2005;

(ii) the amounts previously paid under the policy or contract by way of premiums or otherwise by way of consideration for an annuity;

(iii) the amount of so much of any payment previously made on account of an annuity as is exempt under section 717 of ITTOIA 2005;

(iv) the value of any previously assigned parts of or shares in the rights conferred by the policy or contract;

(v) the total of the amounts of gains treated as arising on previous chargeable events within section 509(1) or 514(1) of ITTOIA 2005;

(d) except where paragraph (c) above applies, the amount of the gain treated as arising by reason of the event;

(e) the number of years relevant for computing the annual equivalent of the amount of the gain for the purposes of subsection (1) of section 536 of ITTOIA 2005 (top slicing relieved liability: one chargeable event), apart from subsections (6) and (8) of that section;

(f) on the assumption that section 465 of ITTOIA 2005 (person liable: individuals) has effect in relation to the gain–

(i) whether an individual would fall to be treated as having paid income tax at the basic rate on the amount of the gain in accordance with section 530 of that Act; and

(ii) if so, except in a case where paragraph (c) above applies, the amount of such tax that would fall to be so treated as paid.

552(6) For the purposes of subsection (1)(a) above, the relevant three month period is whichever of the following periods ends the latest–

(a) the period of three months following the happening of the chargeable event;

(b) if the event is a surrender or assignment which is a chargeable event by virtue of section 514(1) of ITTOIA 2005, the period of three months following the end of the insurance year in which the event happens;

(c) if the event is a death or an assignment of the whole of the rights or a surrender or assignment which is a chargeable event by virtue of section 514(1) of ITTOIA 2005, the period of three months beginning with receipt of written notification of the event.

552(7) For the purposes of subsection (1)(b) above, the relevant three month period is whichever of the following periods ends the latest–

(a) the period of three months following the end of the year of assessment in which the event happened;

(b) if the event is a surrender or assignment which is a chargeable event by virtue of section 514(1) of ITTOIA 2005, the period of three months following the end of the insurance year in which the event happens;

(c) if the event is a death or an assignment, the period of three months beginning with receipt of written notification of the event;

(d) if a certificate under subsection (1)(b) above would not be required in respect of the event apart from the happening of another event, and that other event is one of those mentioned in paragraph (c) above, the period of three months beginning with receipt of written notification of that other event.

552(8) For the purposes of this section the cases where a gain is connected with another gain are those cases where–

(a) both gains arise in connection with policies or contracts containing obligations which, immediately before the chargeable event, were obligations of the same body;

(b) the policy holder of those policies or contracts is the same;

(c) both gains are attributable to the same year of assessment;

(d) the terms of the policies or contracts are the same, apart from any difference in their maturity dates; and

(e) the policies or contracts were issued in respect of insurances made, or were entered into or effected, on the same date.

552(9) For the purposes of this section, the year of assessment to which a gain is attributable is–

(a) in the case of a gain treated as arising by virtue of subsection (1) of section 514 of ITTOIA 2005, the year of assessment which includes the end of the insurance year mentioned in subsection (3) and (4) of that section; or

(b) in any other case, the year of assessment in which happens the chargeable event by reason of which the gain is treated as arising.

552(10) In this section–

"amount", in relation to any gain, means the amount of the gain apart from section 528 of ITTOIA 2005;

"appropriate policy holder" means–

(a) in relation to an assignment of part of or a share in the rights conferred by a policy or contract, any person who is both–

(i) the policy holder, or one of the policy holders, immediately before the assignment; and

(ii) the assignor or one of the assignors; and

(b) in relation to any other chargeable event, the person who is the policy holder immediately before the happening of the event;

"chargeable event" means an event which is a chargeable event within the meaning of Chapter 9 of Part 4 of ITTOIA 2005;

"insurance year" has the same meaning as in Chapter 9 of Part 4 of ITTOIA 2005 (see section 499 of that Act);

"the relevant year of assessment", in the case of any gain, means–

(a) the year of assessment to which the gain is attributable,

(b) [omitted by FA 2008, s. 36 and Sch. 14, para. 4(8),]

552(11) [Omitted by FA 2008, s. 36 and Sch. 14, para. 4(9).]

552(12) This section is supplemented by section 552ZA.

552(13) For the purposes of this section–

(a) section 491(2) of ITTOIA 2005 is taken to have effect as if, in the definition of "PG", the words from "but" to the end were omitted, and

(b) no account is to be taken of the effect of section 465B or 541A of that Act.

552(14) For the purposes of this section no account is to be taken of the effect of sections 528 and 528A of ITTOIA 2005.

History – In s. 552(1) the words "within the meaning of this Chapter" omitted by ITTOIA 2005, s. 882(1) and Sch. 1, para. 222(2) and repealed by s. 884 and Sch. 3; effective for income tax purposes for 2005–06 onwards and for corporation tax purposes for accounting periods ending after 5 April 2005 (ITTOIA 2005, s. 883(1)).

In s. 552(3), the words "(or, where the appropriate policy holder is a company, the corresponding financial year)" and ", and the corresponding financial year,", which appeared after the words "year of assessment", omitted by FA 2008, s. 36 and Sch. 14, para. 4(2), with effect:

- so far as relating to corporation tax, for accounting periods beginning on or after 1 April 2008;
- so far as relating to income tax, for the tax year 2008–09 and subsequent tax years.

In s. 552(5)(b)(ii) the words "of this Act and section 514(1) of ITTOIA 2005 (chargeable events where transaction-related calculations show gains), the date on which the year and the insurance year end;" substituted; in para. (c) the words "and Chapter 9 of Part 5 of ITTOIA 2005", "and the amount or value of any capital sums of a kind referred to in section 492(1)(b) to (e) of ITTOIA 2005", "determined in accordance with section 656 and the amount of so much of any payment previously made on account of an annuity as is exempt under section 717 of ITTOIA 2005" and "and the total of the amounts of gains treated as arising on previous chargeable events within section 509(1) or 514(1) of ITTOIA 2005" inserted; and para. (e) and (f) substituted by ITTOIA 2005, s. 882(1) and Sch. 1, para. 222(3); effective for income tax purposes for 2005–06 onwards and for corporation tax purposes for accounting periods ending after 5 April 2005 (ITTOIA 2005, s. 883(1)).

In s. 552(5)(b), the words "section 546C(7)(a) of this Act and", which appeared before "section 514(1) of ITTOIA 2005", omitted and the words "the insurance year ends" substituted for the words "the year and the insurance year end" by FA 2008, s. 36 and Sch. 14, para. 4(3)(a), with effect:

- so far as relating to corporation tax, for accounting periods beginning on or after 1 April 2008;
- so far as relating to income tax, for the tax year 2008–09 and subsequent tax years.

In s. 552(5)(c), the words "this Chapter and", in sub-para. (i) the words "the amount or value of any relevant capital payments and", in sub-para. (iii) the words "the capital element in any payment previously made on account of an annuity determined in accordance with section 656 and " and in sub-para. (v) the words " the total of the amounts of gains treated as arising on previous chargeable events by reason, or in consequence, of the occurrence of a section 546 excess at the end of a year and " (which appeared at the start of each sub-para.) omitted by FA 2008, s. 36 and Sch. 14, para. 4(3)(b), with effect:

- so far as relating to corporation tax, for accounting periods beginning on or after 1 April 2008;
- so far as relating to income tax, for the tax year 2008–09 and subsequent tax years.

In s. 552(5)(f)(i), the words "basic rate" substituted for the words "savings rate" by FA 2008, s. 5 and Sch. 1, para. 43, with effect for the tax year 2008–09 and subsequent tax years.

In s. 552(5)(f)(i), the words "savings rate" substituted by ITA 2007, s. 1027 and Sch. 1, para. 112 with effect for income tax purposes for 2007–08 and subsequent tax years and for corporation tax purposes in relation to accounting periods ending after 5 April 2007.

In s. 552(6)(b), the words "section 546C(7)(a) of this Act (and", which appeared before "section 514(1) of ITTOIA 2005", and the closing bracket after "2005" omitted and the words "the insurance year" substituted for the words "the year (and the insurance year)" by FA 2008, s. 36 and Sch. 14, para. 4(4)(a), with effect:

- so far as relating to corporation tax, for accounting periods beginning on or after 1 April 2008;
- so far as relating to income tax, for the tax year 2008–09 and subsequent tax years.

In s. 552(6)(b) the words "of this Act (and section 514(1) of ITTOIA 2005)" and "(and the insurance year)" inserted; and in para. (c) the words "of this Act (and section 514(1) of ITTOIA 2005)" inserted by ITTOIA 2005, s. 882(1) and Sch. 1, para. 222(4); effective for income tax purposes for 2005–06 onwards and for corporation tax purposes for accounting periods ending after 5 April 2005 (ITTOIA 2005, s. 883(1)).

In s. 552(6)(c), the words "section 546C(7)(a) of this Act (and", which appeared before "section 514(1) of ITTOIA 2005", and the closing bracket after "2005" omitted by FA 2008, s. 36 and Sch. 14, para. 4(4)(b), with effect:

- so far as relating to corporation tax, for accounting periods beginning on or after 1 April 2008;
- so far as relating to income tax, for the tax year 2008–09 and subsequent tax years.

In s. 552(7)(a), the words ", or, where the policy holder is a company, the financial year,", which appeared after "year of assessment" omitted and in para. (b) the words "section 514(1) of ITTOIA 2005, the period of three months following the end of the insurance year" substituted for the words "section 546C(7)(a) of this Act (and section 514(1) of ITTOIA 2005), the period of three months following the end of the year (and the insurance year) " by FA 2008, s. 36 and Sch. 14, para. 4(5), with effect:

- so far as relating to corporation tax, for accounting periods beginning on or after 1 April 2008;
- so far as relating to income tax, for the tax year 2008–09 and subsequent tax years.

In s. 552(7)(b) the words "of this Act (and section 514(1) of ITTOIA 2005)" and "(and the insurance year)" inserted by ITTOIA 2005, s. 882(1) and Sch. 1, para. 222(5); effective for income tax purposes for 2005–06 onwards and for corporation tax purposes for accounting periods ending after 5 April 2005 (ITTOIA 2005, s. 883(1)).
In s. 552(8)(c), the words " or, where the policy holder is a company, to the same financial year", which appeared at the end, omitted by FA 2008, s. 36 and Sch. 14, para. 4(6), with effect:

- so far as relating to corporation tax, for accounting periods beginning on or after 1 April 2008;
- so far as relating to income tax, for the tax year 2008–09 and subsequent tax years.

In s. 552(9), in the words before para. (a) and in para. (b), the words "or financial year", which appeared after the words "year of assessment", omitted and in para. (a) the words "subsection (1) of section 514 of ITTOIA 2005, the year of assessment which includes the end of the insurance year mentioned in subsection (3) and (4) of that section;" substituted for the words "section 546C(7)(b) of this Act (and section 514(1) of ITTOIA 2005), the year of assessment or financial year which includes the end of the year as at which the section 546 excess in question occurs (and the end of the insurance year mentioned in section 514(3) and (4) of ITTOIA 2005);" by FA 2008, s. 36 and Sch. 14, para. 4(7), with effect:

- so far as relating to corporation tax, for accounting periods beginning on or after 1 April 2008;
- so far as relating to income tax, for the tax year 2008–09 and subsequent tax years.

In s. 552(9)(a) the words "of this Act (and section 514(1) of ITTOIA 2005)" and "(and the end of the insurance year mentioned in section 514(3) and (4) of ITTOIA 2005)" inserted by ITTOIA 2005, s. 882(1) and Sch. 1, para. 222(6); effective for income tax purposes for 2005–06 onwards and for corporation tax purposes for accounting periods ending after 5 April 2005 (ITTOIA 2005, s. 883(1)).
In s. 552(10), in the definition of "amount", the words "section 553(3) of this Act and", which appeared before "section 528 of ITTOIA 2005" omitted, in the definition of "chargeable event", the words "this Chapter and", which appeared before "Chapter 9 of Part 4 of ITTOIA 2005" omitted, the definitions of "financial year", "section 546 excess" and "year" omitted, the definition of "insurance year" inserted, and, in the definition of "the relevant year of assessment", para. (b) and the word "or" before it omitted by FA 2008, s. 36 and Sch. 14, para. 4(8), with effect:

- so far as relating to corporation tax, for accounting periods beginning on or after 1 April 2008;
- so far as relating to income tax, for the tax year 2008–09 and subsequent tax years.

In s. 552(10) in the definition of "amount" the words "of this Act and section 528 of ITTOIA 2005" and the definition of "chargeable event" inserted by ITTOIA 2005, s. 882(1) and Sch. 1, para. 222(6); effective for income tax purposes for 2005–06 onwards and for corporation tax purposes for accounting periods ending after 5 April 2005 (ITTOIA 2005, s. 883(1)).
S. 552(11) omitted by FA 2008, s. 36 and Sch. 14, para. 4(9), with effect:

- so far as relating to corporation tax, for accounting periods beginning on or after 1 April 2008;
- so far as relating to income tax, for the tax year 2008–09 and subsequent tax years.

In s. 552(13) the words "section 465B or 541A" substituted for the words "section 541A" by FA 2013, s. 218 and Sch. 45, para 144, with effect if the year of departure (as defined at FA 2013, Sch. 45, Pt. 4) is the tax year 2013–14 or a subsequent tax year (subject to the transitional provisions at FA 2013, Sch. 45, para. 154–159).
S. 552(13) substituted by FA 2012, s. 11(3) with effect in relation to:

- any policy issued in respect of an insurance made on or after 21 March 2012 or any contract made on or after that date; and to any insurance or contract made before 21 March 2012 if on or after that date either the policy or contract is varied resulting in an increase in the benefits secured, there is an assignment of rights or a share of the rights conferred by the policy or contract or some of those rights become held as security for a debt.

In former s. 552(13) the words "section 548A above or", which appeared before "section 541A of ITTOIA 2005" omitted by FA 2008, s. 36 and Sch. 14, para. 4(10), with effect:

- so far as relating to corporation tax, for accounting periods beginning on or after 1 April 2008;
- so far as relating to income tax, for the tax year 2008–09 and subsequent tax years.

Former s. 552(13) inserted by FA 2007, s. 29(2), with effect in relation to a policy or contract if it is made on or after 21 March 2007, or on or after that date, any of its terms are varied, or a right under it is exercised, so as to increase the benefits under it.
S. 552(14) inserted by FA 2013, s. 24 and Sch. 8, para. 6, with effect in relation to any policy of life assurance issued in respect of an insurance made on or after 6 April 2013 or any contract constituting a capital redemption policy made on or after that date (subject to FA 2013, Sch. 8, para. 7(2)–(4)).
S. 552 substituted by FA 2001, s. 83 and Sch. 28, para. 18, with effect in relation to chargeable events happening on or after 6 April 2002.

Derivations – (as originally enacted prior to substitution by FA 2001) – S. 552(1): ICTA 1970, s. 402(1) and FA 1975, Sch. 2, para. 20(1).
S. 522(2): ICTA 1970, s. 402(2).
S. 522(3)–(5): FA 1975, Sch. 2, para. 20(2)–(4).

Cross references – TMA 1970, s. 98: penalties for failure to furnish information etc. under s. 552.
SI 1998/1870, reg. 36 (as amended by SI 1998/3194): application of s. 552 to gains on policies held under ISAs.
SI 1999/881: Overseas Insurers (Tax Representatives) Regulations 1999.
SI 1999/1029, reg. 6: modifications in relation to certain gains arising in connection with a personal portfolio bond.
SI 2004/1450 (Child Trust Funds Regulations 2004), reg. 38(7): modification of s. 552.

Statutory instruments – SI 1997/265 (Life Assurance and Other Policies (Keeping of Information and Duties of Insurers) Regulations 1997) as amended by SI 2002/444.

Extra-statutory concessions – ESC B53: non-residents and gains on life insurance policies - amended.

552ZA Information: supplementary provisions

552ZA(1) This section supplements section 552 and shall be construed as one with it.

552ZA(2) Where the obligations under any policy or contract of the body that issued, entered into or effected it ("the original") are at any time the obligations of another body ("the transferee") to whom there has been a transfer of the whole or any part of a business previously carried on by the original insurer, section 552 shall have effect in relation to that time, except where the chargeable event–

(a) happened before the transfer, and

(b) in the case of a death or an assignment, is an event of which the notification mentioned in subsection (6) or (7) of that section was given before the transfer,

as if the policy or contract had been issued, entered into or effected by the transferee.

ICTA 1988

552ZA(3) Where, in consequence of section 514(1) of ITTOIA 2005, paragraph (a) or (b) of section 552(1) requires certificates to be delivered in respect of two or more surrenders, happening in the same year, of part of or a share in the rights conferred by the policy or contract, a single certificate may be delivered under the paragraph in question in respect of all those surrenders (and may treat them as if they together constituted a single surrender) unless between the happening of the first and the happening of the last of them there has been–

(a) an assignment of part of or a share in the rights conferred by the policy or contract; or

(b) an assignment, otherwise than for money or money's worth, of the whole of the rights conferred by the policy or contract.

552ZA(4) Where the appropriate policy holder is two or more persons–

(a) section 552(1)(a) requires a certificate to be delivered to each of them; but

(b) nothing in section 552 or this section requires a body to deliver a certificate under subsection (1)(a) of that section to any person whose address has not been provided to the body (or to another body, at a time when the obligations under the policy or contract were obligations of that other body).

552ZA(5) A certificate under section 552(1)(b) or (3)–

(a) shall be in a form prescribed for the purpose by the Board; and

(b) shall be delivered by any means prescribed for the purpose by the Board;

and different forms, or different means of delivery, may be prescribed for different cases or different purposes.

552ZA(6) The Board may by regulations make such provision as they think fit for securing that they are able–

(a) to ascertain whether there has been or is likely to be any contravention of the requirements of section 552 or this section; and

(b) to verify any certificate under that section.

552ZA(7) Regulations under subsection (6) above may include, in particular, provisions requiring persons to whom premiums under any policy are or have at any time been payable–

(a) to supply information to the Board; and

(b) to make available books, documents and other records for inspection on behalf of the Board.

552ZA(8) Regulations under subsection (6) above may–

(a) make different provision for different cases; and

(b) contain such supplementary, incidental, consequential or transitional provision as appears to the Board to be appropriate.

History – In s. 552ZA(3), the words "section 546C(7)(a) of this Act and" which appeared before the words "section 514(1) of ITTOIA 2005" omitted by FA 2008, s. 36 and Sch. 14, para. 5, with effect:

- so far as relating to corporation tax, for accounting periods beginning on or after 1 April 2008;
- so far as relating to income tax, for the tax year 2008–09 and subsequent tax years.

In s. 552ZA(3) the words "of this Act (and section 514(1) of ITTOIA 2005" inserted by ITTOIA 2005, s. 882(1) and Sch. 1, para. 223; effective for income tax purposes for 2005–06 onwards and for corporation tax purposes for accounting periods ending after 5 April 2005 (ITTOIA 2005, s. 883(1)).

S. 552ZA inserted by FA 2001, s. 83 and Sch. 28, para. 18, with effect in relation to chargeable events happening on or after 6 April 2002.

Cross references – TMA 1970, s. 98: penalties for failure to furnish information etc. under regulations made under s. 552ZA(6).
SI 1998/1870, reg. 36(6A): modification of s. 552ZA for purposes of individual savings accounts.
SI 1999/1029, reg. 6(7A): modification of s. 552ZA for purposes of personal portfolio bonds.
SI 2004/1450 (Child Trust Funds Regulations 2004), reg. 38(8): modification of s. 552ZA.

Statutory instruments – SI 2002/444: amends SI 1997/265 (Life Assurance and Other Policies (Keeping of Information and Duties of Insurers) Regulations 1997 to include s. 552ZA within the scope of the principal regulations (which, prior to SI 2002/444, only covered s. 552).
SI 2008/2628, made under s. 552ZA(6)–(8): amends SI 1997/265.

Extra-statutory concessions – ESC B53: non-residents and gains on life insurance policies - amended.

552ZB Regulations in relation to qualifying policies

552ZB(1) The Commissioners for Her Majesty's Revenue and Customs may make regulations–

(a) requiring relevant persons–

  (i) to provide prescribed information to persons who apply for the issue of qualifying policies or who are, or may be, required to make statements under paragraph B3(2) of Schedule 15;

  (ii) to provide to an officer of Revenue and Customs prescribed information about qualifying policies which have been issued by them or in relation to which they are or have been a relevant transferee;

(b) making such provision (not falling within paragraph (a)) as the Commissioners think fit for securing that an officer of Revenue and Customs is able–

(i) to ascertain whether there has been or is likely to be any contravention of the requirements of the regulations or of paragraph B3(2) of Schedule 15;

(ii) to verify any information provided to an officer of Revenue and Customs as required by the regulations.

552ZB(2) The provision that may be made by virtue of subsection (1)(b) includes, in particular, provision requiring relevant persons to make available books, documents and other records for inspection by or on behalf of an officer of Revenue and Customs.

552ZB(3) The regulations may–

(a) make different provision for different cases or circumstances, and

(b) contain incidental, supplementary, consequential, transitional, transitory or saving provision.

552ZB(4) In this section–

"prescribed" means prescribed by the regulations,

"qualifying policy" includes a policy which would be a qualifying policy apart from–

(a) paragraph A1(2), B1(2), B2(2) or B3(3) of Schedule 15, or

(b) paragraph 17(2)(za) of that Schedule (including as applied by paragraph 18), and

"relevant person" means a person–

(a) who issues, or has issued, qualifying policies, or

(b) who is, or has been, a relevant transferee in relation to qualifying policies.

552ZB(5) For the purposes of this section a person ("X") is at any time a **"relevant transferee"** in relation to a qualifying policy if the obligations under the policy of its issuer are at that time the obligations of X as a result of there having been a transfer to X of the whole or any part of a business previously carried on by the issuer.

History – S. 552ZB inserted by FA 2013, s. 25 and Sch. 9, para. 10, with effect from 17 July 2013 (Royal Assent).

Statutory instruments – SI 2013/1820: partly made under s. 552ZB(1).

552A Tax representatives

552A(1) This section has effect for the purpose of securing that, where it applies to an overseas insurer, another person is the overseas insurer's tax representative.

552A(2) In this section **"overseas insurer"** means a person not resident in the United Kingdom who carries on, or has at any time carried on, a business which consists of, or includes, the provision in the United Kingdom of services under–

(a) policies of life insurance,

(b) contracts for life annuities, or

(c) capital redemption policies,

otherwise than through a branch or agency of his in the United Kingdom.

552A(3) This section applies to an overseas insurer–

(a) if the condition in subsection (4) below is satisfied on the designated day; or

(b) where that condition is not satisfied on that day, if it has subsequently become satisfied.

552A(4) The condition mentioned in subsection (3) above is that–

(a) there are in force relevant insurances the obligations under which are obligations of the overseas insurer in question or of an overseas insurer connected with him; and

(b) the total amount or value of the gross premiums paid under those relevant insurances is £1 million or more.

552A(5) In this section **"relevant insurance"** means any policy of life insurance, contract for a life annuity or capital redemption policy in the case of which–

(a) the holder is resident in the United Kingdom;

(b) the obligations of the insurer are obligations of a person not resident in the United Kingdom; and

(c) those obligations are not attributable to a branch or agency of that person's in the United Kingdom.

552A(6) Before the expiration of the period of three months following the day on which this section first applies to an overseas insurer, the overseas insurer must nominate to the Board a person to be his tax representative.

552A(7) A person shall not be a tax representative unless–

(a) if he is an individual, he is resident in the United Kingdom and has a fixed place of residence there, or

(b) if he is not an individual, he has a business establishment in the United Kingdom,

ICTA 1988

and, in either case, he satisfies such other requirements (if any) as are prescribed in regulations made for the purpose by the Board.

552A(8) A person shall not be an overseas insurer's tax representative unless–

(a) his nomination by the overseas insurer has been approved by the Board; or

(b) he has been appointed by the Board.

552A(9) The Board may by regulations make provision supplementing this section; and the provision that may be made by any such regulations includes provision with respect to–

(a) the making of a nomination by an overseas insurer of a person to be his tax representative;

(b) the information which is to be provided in connection with such a nomination;

(c) the form in which such a nomination is to be made;

(d) the powers and duties of the Board in relation to such a nomination;

(e) the procedure for approving, or refusing to approve, such a nomination, and any time limits applicable to doing so;

(f) the termination, by the overseas insurer or the Board, of a person's appointment as a tax representative;

(g) the appointment by the Board of a person as the tax representative of an overseas insurer (including the circumstances in which such an appointment may be made);

(h) the nomination by the overseas insurer, or the appointment by the Board, of a person to be the tax representative of an overseas insurer in place of a person ceasing to be his tax representative;

(j) circumstances in which an overseas insurer to whom this section applies may, with the Board's agreement, be released (subject to any conditions imposed by the Board) from the requirement that there must be a tax representative;

(k) appeals to the tribunal against decisions of the Board under this section or regulations under it.

552A(10) The provision that may be made by regulations under subsection (9) above also includes provision for or in connection with the making of other arrangements between the Board and an overseas insurer for the purpose of securing the discharge by or on behalf of the overseas insurer of the relevant duties, within the meaning of section 552B.

552A(11) Section 1122 of CTA 2010 (connected persons) applies for the purposes of this section.

552A(12) In this section–

"capital redemption policy" means a capital redemption policy in relation to which Chapter 9 of Part 4 of ITTOIA 2005 has effect;

"contract for a life annuity" means a contract for a life annuity in relation to which Chapter 9 of Part 4 of ITTOIA 2005 has effect;

"the designated day" means such day as the Board may specify for the purpose in regulations;

"policy of life insurance" means a policy of life insurance in relation to which Chapter 9 of Part 4 of ITTOIA 2005 has effect;

"tax representative" means a tax representative under this section.

History – In s. 552A(5) the words "in relation to which this Chapter has effect and" omitted by ITTOIA 2005, s. 882(1) and Sch. 1, para. 224(2) and repealed by s. 884 and Sch. 3; effective for income tax purposes for 2005–06 onwards and for corporation tax purposes for accounting periods ending after 5 April 2005 (ITTOIA 2005, s. 883(1)).

In s. 552A(9)(k), the word "tribunal" substituted for "Special Commissioners" by SI 2009/56, art. 3(1) and Sch. 1, para. 148, operative from 1 April 2009, subject to transitional and saving provisions in SI 2009/56, Sch. 3.

In s. 552A(11), the words "Section 1122 of CTA 2010" substituted for the words "Section 839" by CTA 2010, s. 1177 and Sch. 1, para. 87, with effect for corporation tax purposes for accounting periods ending on or after 1 April 2010, and for income and capital gains tax purposes for the tax year 2010–11 and subsequent tax years.

In s. 552A(12), the words "this Chapter and" which appeared before the words "Chapter 9 of Part 4 of ITTOIA 2005" omitted three times and the word "has" substituted for the word "have" three times by FA 2008, s. 36 and Sch. 14, para. 6, with effect:

- so far as relating to corporation tax, for accounting periods beginning on or after 1 April 2008;
- so far as relating to income tax, for the tax year 2008–09 and subsequent tax years.

In s. 552A(12) the definitions of "capital redemption policy", "contract for life annuity" and "policy of life insurance" inserted by ITTOIA 2005, s. 882(1) and Sch. 1, para. 224(3); effective for income tax purposes for 2005–06 onwards and for corporation tax purposes for accounting periods ending after 5 April 2005 (ITTOIA 2005, s. 883(1)).

S. 552A inserted by FA 1998, s. 87 and effective from 6 April 1999, by virtue of SI 1999/881.

Statutory instruments – SI 1999/881 as amended by SI 2002/443: Overseas Insurers (Tax Representatives) Regulations 1999, as amended by SI 2001/2726.

552B Duties of overseas insurers' tax representatives

552B(1) It shall be the duty of an overseas insurer's tax representative to secure (where appropriate by acting on the overseas insurer's behalf) that the relevant duties are discharged by or on behalf of the overseas insurer.

552B(2) For the purposes of this section **"the relevant duties"** are–

(a) the duties imposed by section 552,

(b) the duties imposed by section 552ZA(2), (4) or (5),

(c) any duties imposed by regulations made under subsection (6) of section 552ZA by virtue of subsection (7) of that section, and

(d) any duties imposed by regulations under section 552ZB,

so far as relating to relevant insurances under which the overseas insurer in question has any obligations.

552B(3) An overseas insurer's tax representative shall be personally liable–

(a) in respect of any failure to secure the discharge of the relevant duties, and

(b) in respect of anything done for purposes connected with acting on the overseas insurer's behalf,

as if the relevant duties were imposed jointly and severally on the tax representative and the overseas insurer.

552B(4) In the application of this section in relation to any particular tax representative, it is immaterial whether any particular relevant duty arose before or after his appointment.

552B(5) This section has effect in relation to relevant duties relating to chargeable events happening on or after the day by which section 552A(6) requires the nomination of the overseas insurer's first tax representative to be made.

552B(5A) In subsection (5) **"chargeable event"** has the same meaning as in section 552 (see subsection (10) of that section).

552B(6) Expressions used in this section and in section 552A have the same meaning in this section as they have in that section.

History – S. 552B(2)(d) (and the word "and" before it) inserted (and the word "and" at the end of para. (b) omitted) by FA 2013, s. 25 and Sch. 9, para. 11, with effect from 17 July 2013 (Royal Assent).

S. 552B(2) substituted by FA 2001, s. 83 and Sch. 28, para. 19, with effect in relation to chargeable events happening on or after 6 April 2002.

S. 552B(5A) inserted by ITTOIA 2005, s. 882(1) and Sch. 1, para. 225; effective for income tax purposes for 2005–06 onwards and for corporation tax purposes for accounting periods ending after 5 April 2005 (ITTOIA 2005, s. 883(1)).

S. 552B inserted by FA 1998, s. 87 and effective from 6 April 1999, by virtue of SI 1999/881.

Cross references – SI 1999/881: Overseas Insurers (Tax Representatives) Regulations 1999.

553 Non-resident policies and off-shore capital redemption policies

553 [Omitted by FA 2008, s. 36 and Sch. 14, para. 7.]

History – S. 553 omitted by FA 2008, s. 36 and Sch. 14, para. 7, with effect:

- so far as relating to corporation tax, for accounting periods beginning on or after 1 April 2008;
- so far as relating to income tax, for the tax year 2008–09 and subsequent tax years.

Notes – Rewritten income tax provisions are now located as follows:

S. 553(1): ITTOIA 2005, s. 485(7) and 543(1) and (2).
S. 553(2): ITTOIA 2005, s. 474(4).
S. 553(3): ITTOIA 2005, s. 528(1)–(4).
S. 553(4): ITTOIA 2005, s. 528(5) and (6).
S. 553(5): ITTOIA 2005, s. 529(1) and Sch. 2, para. 106(1)–(3).
S. 553(5A): ITTOIA 2005, s. 529(1) and Sch. 2, para. 110(1) and (2).
S. 553(6): ITTOIA 2005, s. 461(1), 466(1) and 531(1) and (3).
S. 553(6A): ITTOIA 2005, s. 532(1)–(5), 533(2)–(7) and 534(2).
S. 553(7): ITTOIA 2005, s. 531(5) and (6).
S. 553(7A): ITTOIA 2005, s. 466(1) and (2).
S. 553(8): ITTOIA 2005, s. 536(7) and (8).
S. 553(9): ITTOIA 2005, s. 536(6).
S. 553(10): ITTOIA 2005, s. 476(3) and Sch. 2, para. 104 and 113.

553A Overseas life assurance business

553A [Omitted by FA 2008, s. 36 and Sch. 14, para. 7.]

History – S. 553A omitted by FA 2008, s. 36 and Sch. 14, para. 7, with effect:

- so far as relating to corporation tax, for accounting periods beginning on or after 1 April 2008;
- so far as relating to income tax, for the tax year 2008–09 and subsequent tax years.

Notes – Rewritten income tax provisions are now located as follows:

S. 553A(1): ITTOIA 2005, s. 476(3) and Sch. 2, para. 111(1).
S. 553A(2): ITTOIA 2005, s. 474(5).
S. 553A(3): ITTOIA 2005, s. 531(5) and (6).
S. 553A(4): ITTOIA 2005, s. 476(3) and Sch. 2, para. 111(1).
S. 553A(5): ITTOIA 2005, s. 531(5) and (6).
S. 553A(6): ITTOIA 2005, Sch. 2, para. 111(2) and (3).

553B Overseas life assurance business: capital redemption policies

553B [Omitted by FA 2008, s. 36 and Sch. 14, para. 7.]

History – S. 553B omitted by FA 2008, s. 36 and Sch. 14, para. 7, with effect:

- so far as relating to corporation tax, for accounting periods beginning on or after 1 April 2008;
- so far as relating to income tax, for the tax year 2008–09 and subsequent tax years.

Notes – Rewritten income tax provisions are now located as follows:
S. 553B(1): ITTOIA 2005, s. 476(3) and Sch. 2, para. 113.
S. 553B(2): ITTOIA 2005, s. 476(3) and Sch. 2, para. 113.
S. 553B(3): ITTOIA 2005, s. 476(3) and Sch. 2, para. 113.

553C Personal portfolio bonds

553C [Omitted by FA 2008, s. 36 and Sch. 14, para. 7.]

History – S. 553C omitted by FA 2008, s. 36 and Sch. 14, para. 7, with effect:
- so far as relating to corporation tax, for accounting periods beginning on or after 1 April 2008;
- so far as relating to income tax, for the tax year 2008–09 and subsequent tax years.

Notes – Rewritten income tax provisions are located as follows:
S. 553C(1): ITTOIA 2005, s. 526(1).
S. 553C(3): ITTOIA 2005, s. 526(1).
S. 553C(6): ITTOIA 2005, s. 526(2).
S. 553C(7): ITTOIA 2005, s. 526(1).
S. 553C(9): ITTOIA 2005, s. 526(3).
S. 553C(10): ITTOIA 2005, s. 516(5), 519(5) and 521(5).
S. 553C(11): ITTOIA 2005, s. 878(5).
Date of Royal Assent to FA 1998 was 31 July 1998.

554 Borrowings on life policies to be treated as income in certain cases

554 [Omitted by ITTOIA 2005, s. 882 and Sch. 1, para. 229 and repealed by s. 884 and Sch. 3.]

History – S. 554 omitted by ITTOIA 2005, s. 882(1) and Sch. 1, para. 229 and repealed by s. 884 and Sch. 3; effective for income tax purposes for 2005–06 onwards and for corporation tax purposes for accounting periods ending after 5 April 2005 (ITTOIA 2005, s. 883(1)).

Notes – S. 554 is not rewritten by ITTOIA 2005 as it is spent. (See ITTOIA 2005, Explanatory Notes, Annex 1, Table 1 (Change 158).)

Chapter III – Entertainers and Sportsmen

555 Payment of tax

555 [Omitted by ITA 2007, s. 1027 and Sch. 1, para. 113 and repealed by ITA 2007, s. 1031 and Sch. 3, Pt. 1.]

History – S. 555 omitted by ITA 2007, s. 1027 and Sch. 1, para. 113 and repealed by ITA 2007, s. 1031 and Sch. 3, Pt. 1 with effect for 2007–08 and subsequent tax years.

Notes – S. 555 rewritten as follows:
S. 555(1): ITA 2007, s. 966(1), (7).
S. 555(1): ITTOIA 2005, s. 13(1) and (8).
S. 555(2): ITA 2007, s. 966(1), (2), (3), (7).
S. 555(3): ITA 2007, s. 966(1), (2), (4), (7).
S. 555(4): ITA 2007, s. 967(1), (2).
S. 555(5): ITA 2007, s. 970(4), Sch. 1 para. 495.
S. 555(6): ITA 2007, s. 966(6), Sch. 1 para. 114, 495.
S. 555(7): ITA 2007, s. 969(1).
S. 555(8): ITA 2007, s. 968(1), (2), (3).
S. 555(9): ITA 2007, s. 968(4).
S. 555(10): ITA 2007, s. 968(5), (6).
S. 555(11): ITA 2007, s. 968(7).

556 Activity treated as trade etc. and attribution of income

556 [Omitted by CTA 2009, s. 1322 and Sch. 1, para. 186.]

History – S. 556 omitted by CTA 2009, s. 1322 and Sch. 1, para. 186, with effect for corporation tax purposes for accounting periods ending on or after 1 April 2009, and for income tax and capital gains tax purposes for the tax year 2009–10 and subsequent tax years.

Notes – Rewritten income tax provisions are now located as follows:
S. 556(1): ITTOIA 2005, s. 13(2)–(4) and (8).
S. 556(2): ITTOIA 2005, s. 13(5).
S. 556(3): ITTOIA 2005, s. 14(1).
S. 556(4): ITTOIA 2005, s. 13(2)–(5) and 14(1).
S. 556(5): ITA 2007, Sch. 1 para. 114.
S. 556(5): ITTOIA 2005, s. 13(6) and (8).
S. 556 rewritten for corporation tax purposes as follows:
S. 556(2): CTA 2009, s. 1309(1), (2).
S. 556(3): CTA 2009, s. 1309(4).
S. 556(4): CTA 2009, s. 1309(1), (2), (4).
S. 556(4A): CTA 2009, s. 1309(5).
S. 556(5): CTA 2009, s. 1309(3).

557 Charge on profits

557 [Omitted by ITTOIA 2005, s. 882 and Sch. 1, para. 231 and repealed by s. 884 and Sch. 3.]

History – S. 557 omitted by ITTOIA 2005, s. 882(1) and Sch. 1, para. 231 and repealed by s. 884 and Sch. 3; effective for income tax purposes for 2005–06 onwards and for corporation tax purposes for accounting periods ending after 5 April 2005 (ITTOIA 2005, s. 883(1)).

Notes – Rewritten income tax provisions are now located as follows:
S. 557(1): ITTOIA 2005, s. 13(7) and (8).
S. 557(2): ITTOIA 2005, s. 14(2).

S. 557(3): ITTOIA 2005, s. 14(3).
S. 557(4): ITTOIA 2005, s. 13(7) and 14(2).

558 Supplementary provisions

558(1) [Omitted by ITA 2007, s. 1027 and Sch. 1, para. 115 and repealed by ITA 2007, s. 1031 and Sch. 3, Pt. 1.]

558(2) [Omitted by ITA 2007, s. 1027 and Sch. 1, para. 115 and repealed by ITA 2007, s. 1031 and Sch. 3, Pt. 1.]

558(3) [Omitted by ITA 2007, s. 1027 and Sch. 1, para. 115 and repealed by ITA 2007 s. 1031 and Sch. 3, Pt. 1.]

558(4) [Omitted by ITA 2007, s. 1027 and Sch. 1, para. 115 and repealed by ITA 2007, s. 1031 and Sch. 3, Pt. 1.]

558(5)–(6) [Omitted by CTA 2009, s. 1322 and Sch. 1, para. 187 and repealed by CTA 2009, s. 1326 and Sch. 3, Pt. 1]

History – S. 558(5) and (6) omitted by CTA 2009, s. 1322 and Sch. 1, para. 187 and repealed by CTA 2009, s. 1326 and Sch. 3, Pt. 1, with effect for corporation tax purposes for accounting periods ending on or after 1 April 2009, and for income tax and capital gains tax purposes for the tax year 2009–10 and subsequent tax years.

Notes – Rewritten income tax provisions are now located as follows:
S. 558(1): ITA 2007, s. 970(1).
S. 558(2): ITA 2007, s. 967(3).
S. 558(3): ITA 2007, s. 967(4).
S. 558(4): ITA 2007, s. 970(2), (3).
S. 558(5): ITA 2007, s. 969(2).
S. 558(6): ITA 2007, s. 970(5).
S. 558 rewritten for corporation tax purposes as follows:
S. 558(5): CTA 2009, s. 1309(4).
S. 558(6): CTA 2009, s. 1309(5).

Chapter IV – Sub-Contractors in the Construction Industry

History – Ch. IV omitted and repealed by FA 2004, s. 76 and Sch. 12, para. 9(2) and FA 2004, s. 326 and Sch. 42, Pt. 2(7), with effect in relation to payments made on or after 6 April 2007 under contracts relating to construction operations (FA 2004, s. 77).

"Chapter IV – Sub-Contractors in the Construction Industry

Deductions on account of tax etc. from payments to certain sub-contractors

559 [Omitted and repealed by FA 2004, s. 76 and Sch. 12, para. 9(2) and FA 2004, s. 326 and Sch. 42, Pt. 2(7), with effect in relation to payments made on or after 6 April 2007 under contracts relating to construction operations (FA 2004, s. 77).]

Treatment of sums deducted under s. 559

559A [Omitted and repealed by FA 2004, s. 76 and Sch. 12, para. 9(2) and FA 2004, s. 326 and Sch. 42, Pt. 2(7), with effect in relation to payments made on or after 6 April 2007 under contracts relating to construction operations (FA 2004, s. 77).]

Persons who are sub-contractors or contractors for purposes of Chapter IV

560 [Omitted and repealed by FA 2004, s. 76 and Sch. 12, para. 9(2) and FA 2004, s. 326 and Sch. 42, Pt. 2(7), with effect in relation to payments made on or after 6 April 2007 under contracts relating to construction operations (FA 2004, s. 77).]

Exceptions from section 559

561 [Omitted and repealed by FA 2004, s. 76 and Sch. 12, para. 9(2) and FA 2004, s. 326 and Sch. 42, Pt. 2(7), with effect in relation to payments made on or after 6 April 2007 under contracts relating to construction operations (FA 2004, s. 77).]

Conditions to be satisfied by individuals

562 [Omitted and repealed by FA 2004, s. 76 and Sch. 12, para. 9(2) and FA 2004, s. 326 and Sch. 42, Pt. 2(7), with effect in relation to payments made on or after 6 April 2007 under contracts relating to construction operations (FA 2004, s. 77).]

Conditions to be satisfied by partners who are individuals

563 [Repealed by FA 1995, s. 139 and Sch. 27, para. 5, s. 162 and Sch. 29, Pt. VIII(21).]

History – S. 563 repealed by FA 1995, s. 139 and Sch. 27, para. 5, s. 162 and Sch. 29, Pt. VIII(21) with effect in relation to any application for the issue or renewal of a certificate which is made with respect to any period beginning on or after 1 August 1999 (the appointed day by virtue of FA 1995, Sch. 27, para. 8(1) and SI 1998/2620 (C. 62), art. 3).

Conditions to be satisfied by firms

564 [Omitted and repealed by FA 2004, s. 76 and Sch. 12, para. 9(2) and FA 2004, s. 326 and Sch. 42, Pt. 2(7), with effect in relation to payments made on or after 6 April 2007 under contracts relating to construction operations (FA 2004, s. 77).]

Conditions to be satisfied by companies

565 [Omitted and repealed by FA 2004, s. 76 and Sch. 12, para. 9(2) and FA 2004, s. 326 and Sch. 42, Pt. 2(7), with effect in relation to payments made on or after 6 April 2007 under contracts relating to construction operations (FA 2004, s. 77).]

General powers to make regulations under Chapter IV

566 [Omitted and repealed by FA 2004, s. 76 and Sch. 12, para. 9(2) and FA 2004, s. 326 and Sch. 42, Pt. 2(7), with effect in relation to payments made on or after 6 April 2007 under contracts relating to construction operations (FA 2004, s. 77).]

Meaning of "construction operations"

567 [Omitted and repealed by FA 2004, s. 76 and Sch. 12, para. 9(2) and FA 2004, s. 326 and Sch. 42, Pt. 2(7), with effect in relation to payments made on or after 6 April 2007 under contracts relating to construction operations (FA 2004, s. 77).]"

Chapter V – Schemes for Rationalising Industry

568 Deductions from profits of contributions paid under certified schemes

568(1) Notwithstanding anything contained in section 33 of ITTOIA 2005 or section 53 of CTA 2009 (no deduction for capital expenditure) but subject to the following provisions of this Chapter, where a person pays, wholly and exclusively for the purposes of a trade in respect of which he is chargeable under Part 2 of ITTOIA 2005 or Part 3 of CTA 2009, a contribution in furtherance of a scheme which is for the time being certified by the Secretary of State under this section, the contribution shall, in so far as it is paid in furtherance of the primary object of the scheme, be allowed to be deducted as an expense in computing the profits of that trade.

568(2) The Secretary of State shall certify a scheme under this section if he is satisfied–

(a) that the primary object of the scheme is the elimination of redundant works or machinery or plant from use in an industry in the United Kingdom; and

(b) that the scheme is in the national interest and in the interests of that industry as a whole; and

(c) that such number of persons engaged in that industry as are substantially representative of the industry are liable to pay contributions in furtherance of the primary object of the scheme by agreement between them and the body of persons carrying out the scheme.

References in this subsection to an industry in the United Kingdom shall include references to the business carried on by owners of ships or of a particular class of ships, wherever that business is carried on, and, in relation to that business, references in this subsection to works or machinery or plant shall include references to ships.

568(3) The Secretary of State shall cancel any certificate granted under this section if he ceases to be satisfied as to any of the matters referred to in subsection (2) above.

568(4) The Secretary of State may at any time require the body of persons carrying out a scheme certified under this section to produce any books or documents of whatever nature relating to the scheme and, if the requirement is not complied with, he may cancel the certificate.

568(5) In this section and in section 569 **"contribution"**, in relation to a scheme, does not include a sum paid by a person by way of loan or subscription of share capital, or in consideration of the transfer of assets to him, or by way of a penalty for contravening or failing to comply with the scheme.

History – In s. 568(1), the words "section 74 of this Act or", which appeared after "anything contained in", omitted by CTA 2009, s. 1322 and Sch. 1, para. 188(a) and repealed by CTA 2009, s. 1326 and Sch. 3, Pt. 1, with effect for corporation tax purposes for accounting periods ending on or after 1 April 2009, and for income tax and capital gains tax purposes for the tax year 2009–10 and subsequent tax years.

In s. 568(1), the words "or section 53 of CTA 2009 (no deduction for capital expenditure)" inserted by CTA 2009, s. 1322 and Sch. 1, para. 188(b), with effect for corporation tax purposes for accounting periods ending on or after 1 April 2009, and for income tax and capital gains tax purposes for the tax year 2009–10 and subsequent tax years.

In s. 568(1), the words "under Part 2 of ITTOIA 2005 or Part 3 of CTA 2009," substituted for "under Case I of Schedule D or under Part 2 of ITTOIA 2005," by CTA 2009, s. 1322 and Sch. 1, para. 188(c), with effect for corporation tax purposes for accounting periods ending on or after 1 April 2009, and for income tax and capital gains tax purposes for the tax year 2009–10 and subsequent tax years.

In s. 568(1) the words "of this Act or section 33 of ITTOIA 2005" and "or under Part 2 of ITTOIA 2005," inserted by ITTOIA 2005, s. 882(1) and Sch. 1, para. 232; effective for income tax purposes for 2005–06 onwards and for corporation tax purposes for accounting periods ending after 5 April 2005 (ITTOIA 2005, s. 883(1)).

In s. 568(1), "profits" substituted for "profits or gains" by FA 1998, s. 46(3) and Sch. 7, para. 1.

Derivations – ICTA 1970, s. 406 and SI 1970/1537.

Cross references – S. 74: general rules as to deductions not allowable in computing trading profits.

569 Repayment of contributions

569(1) In the event of the repayment, whether directly or by way of distribution of assets on a winding up or otherwise, of a contribution or any part of a contribution which has been allowed to be deducted under section 568, the deduction of the contribution, or so much of it as has been repaid, shall be deemed to be an unauthorised deduction in respect of which an assessment shall be made, and, notwithstanding the provisions of the Tax Acts requiring assessments to be made within six years after the end of the chargeable period to which they relate, any such assessment and any consequential assessment may be made at any time within three years after the end of the chargeable period in which the repayment was made.

569(2) For the purposes of this section, a sum received by any person by way of repayment of contributions shall be deemed to be by way of repayment of the last contribution paid by him, and, if the sum exceeds the amount of that contribution, by way of repayment of the penultimate contribution so paid, and so on.

Derivations – ICTA 1970, s. 407, as amended by FA 1971, Sch. 12, para. 45.

570 Payments under certified schemes which are not repayments of contributions

570(1) Subject to the provisions of this section, where, under any scheme which is for the time being certified or has at any time been certified by the Secretary of State under section 568, any payment (not being a payment made by way of repayment of contributions) is made to a person carrying on a trade to which the scheme relates, that payment shall be treated for the purposes of the Tax Acts as a trading receipt of the trade, and shall accordingly be taken into account in computing the profits of the trade for those purposes.

570(2) Where the payments which have been made under such a scheme in respect of a trade (not being payments made by way of repayment of contributions) have been made wholly or partly in respect of damage in respect of which no relief may be given under the Tax Acts and a claim is made to that effect, then, subject to and in accordance with the provisions of Schedule 21–

(a) relief shall be given in respect of those payments by reducing the amounts which are to be treated as trading receipts of the trade under subsection (1) above; but

(b) where such relief is given, section 568 shall, in relation to contributions subsequently paid under the scheme in respect of the trade, have effect subject to the modifications specified in Part III of that Schedule;

and paragraph 6 of that Schedule applies for the purposes of this subsection as it applies for the purposes of that Schedule.

570(3) The provisions of this section and Schedule 21 shall apply in relation to any payment made to a person who has ceased to carry on a trade to which any such scheme as is mentioned in subsection (1) above relates as they apply in relation to payments made to a person carrying on such a trade, subject to the modification that so much of that payment as falls to be treated as a trading receipt by virtue of those provisions shall be deemed for the purposes of those provisions to have been made to him on the last day on which he was engaged in carrying on the trade.

570(4) In determining for the purposes of this section and of Schedule 21–

(a) whether any trade has ceased to be carried on; or

(b) whether any contribution is paid in respect of a trade in respect of which a payment has been made; or

(c) whether any payment is made in respect of a trade in respect of which a contribution has been paid,

no regard shall be had to any event which, by virtue of section 18 of ITTOIA 2005 or section 41 of CTA 2009 (company starting or ceasing to be within charge to corporation tax) is to be treated as effecting a cessation of trading.

History – In s. 570(1), "profits" substituted for "profits or gains" by FA 1998, s. 46(3) and Sch. 7, para. 1.

S. 570(2) partially repealed; the words "and a claim is made to that effect," inserted; reference to "Schedule 21" substituted; and endpiece added by FA 1996, s. 134 and Sch. 20, para. 31 for 1996–97 and later years of assessment (income tax) and accounting periods ending on or after the appointed day for self-assessment to corporation tax (1 July 1999 by virtue of FA 1994, s. 199 and SI 1998/3173 (C. 78)).

In s. 570(4), after para. (c), the words "section 18 of ITTOIA 2005 or section 41 of CTA 2009 (company starting or ceasing to be within charge to corporation tax) is to be treated as effecting a cessation of trading." substituted for the words "section 337(1) above or section 18 of ITTOIA 2005 (companies beginning or ceasing to carry on trade), is to be treated as effecting a discontinuance of a trade" by CTA 2009, s. 1322 and Sch. 1, para. 189, with effect for corporation tax purposes for accounting periods ending on or after 1 April 2009, and for income tax and capital gains tax purposes for the tax year 2009–10 and subsequent tax years.

In s. 570(4) the words "section 337(1) above or section 18 of ITTOIA 2005 (companies beginning or ceasing to carry on trade)" substituted by ITTOIA 2005, s. 882(1) and Sch. 1, para. 233; effective for income tax purposes for 2005–06 onwards and for corporation tax purposes for accounting periods ending after 5 April 2005 (ITTOIA 2005, s. 883(1)).

Derivations – ICTA 1970, s. 408.

Cross references – S. 113: deemed cessation and recommencement of a trade on change in persons carrying it on.

S. 337(1): deemed cessation and recommencement of a trade where a company begins or ceases to carry it on or to be within the corporation tax charge.

Sch. 21, Pt. II, III: computational provisions as to relief in respect of damage, and exclusion of further relief where such relief has been given.

TMA 1970, s. 42(6), (7): procedure for claims by partnerships under self-assessment.

571 Cancellation of certificates

571(1) Where any certificate granted with respect to a scheme under section 568 is cancelled by the Secretary of State, and any deductible contributions paid in furtherance of the scheme have not been repaid at the expiration of one year from the cancellation, the body of persons carrying out the scheme shall, for the chargeable period in which that year expires, be charged to tax upon the aggregate amount of the deductible contributions which have not been repaid at that time.

571(1A) An amount charged to income tax under subsection (1) above is treated for income tax purposes as an amount of income.

571(1B) So far as relating to corporation tax, the charge to tax under subsection (1) has effect as an application of the charge to corporation tax on income.

571(2) The charge to tax under subsection (1) above shall not be made if the total amount of any contributions, other than deductible contributions, which have been paid under the scheme and have not been repaid before that time is greater than the available resources of the scheme, and shall not in any case be made upon an amount greater than the excess, if any, of those resources over that total amount.

571(3) In subsection (2) above **"the available resources"**, in relation to any scheme, means a sum representing the total funds held for the purposes of the scheme at the expiration of one year from the cancellation of the certificate plus a sum representing any funds held for the purposes of the scheme which, during that year, have been applied otherwise than in accordance with the provisions of the scheme as in force when the certificate was granted.

571(4) Where the body of persons carrying out a scheme are charged to tax by virtue of subsection (1) above, and, after the expiration of one year from the cancellation of the certificate, any deductible contribution paid in furtherance of the scheme is repaid, the amount upon which the charge is made shall on the making of a claim be reduced by the amount repaid, and all such repayments of tax shall be made as are necessary to give effect to the provisions of this subsection.

571(5) In this section **"contribution"** includes a part of a contribution, and **"deductible contribution"** means a contribution allowed to be deducted under section 568, any reduction under Part III of Schedule 21 being left out of account.

571(6) For the purposes of this section, a sum received by any person by way of repayment of contributions shall be deemed to be by way of repayment of the last contribution paid by him, and, if the sum exceeds the amount of that contribution, by way of repayment of the penultimate contribution so paid, and so on.

History – In s. 571(1), the words from "(in the case of corporation tax, under Case VI of Schedule D)", which appeared after "charged to tax", omitted by CTA 2009, s. 1322 and Sch. 1, para. 190(2) and repealed by CTA 2009, s. 1326 and Sch. 3, Pt. 1, with effect for corporation tax purposes for accounting periods ending on or after 1 April 2009, and for income tax and capital gains tax purposes for the tax year 2009–10 and subsequent tax years.

In s. 571(1) the words "(in the case of corporation tax, under Case VI of Schedule D)" substituted by ITTOIA 2005, s. 882(1) and Sch. 1, para. 234; effective for income tax purposes for 2005–06 onwards and for corporation tax purposes for accounting periods ending after 5 April 2005 (ITTOIA 2005, s. 883(1)).

S. 571(1A) inserted by ITA 2007, s. 1027 and Sch. 1, para. 116 with effect for income tax purposes for 2007–08 and later tax years and for corporation tax purposes in relation to accounting periods ending after 5 April 2007.

S. 571(1B) inserted by CTA 2009, s. 1322 and Sch. 1, para. 190(3), with effect for corporation tax purposes for accounting periods ending on or after 1 April 2009, and for income tax and capital gains tax purposes for the tax year 2009–10 and subsequent tax years.

Derivations – ICTA 1970, s. 409.

Cross references – TMA 1970, s. 42(6), (7): procedure for claims by partnerships, under s. 571(4), under self-assessment.

572 Application to statutory redundancy schemes

572(1) Sections 569 to 571 and Schedule 21 shall, subject to the adaptations specified in subsection (2) below, apply in relation to a statutory redundancy scheme as they apply in relation to a scheme certified under section 568.

572(2) The adaptations referred to above are as follows, that is to say–

(a) for any reference to a contribution allowed to be deducted under section 568 there shall be substituted a reference to a contribution allowed to be deducted under any provision of the Tax Acts other than that section;

(b) any provision that section 568 shall, in relation to contributions, have effect subject to modifications, shall be construed as a provision that so much of any provision of the Tax Acts other than that section as authorises the deduction of contributions shall, in relation to the contributions in question, have effect subject to the modifications in question;

(c) for any reference to the cancellations of a certificate with respect to a scheme there shall be substituted a reference to the scheme ceasing to have effect; and

(d) for any reference to the provisions of the scheme as in force when the certificate was granted there shall be substituted a reference to the provisions of the scheme as in force when the contributions were first paid thereunder.

572(3) In this section **"statutory redundancy scheme"** means a scheme for the elimination or reduction of redundant works, machinery or plant, or for other similar purposes, to which effect is given by or under any Act, whether passed before or after this Act.

Derivations – ICTA 1970, s. 410.

Chapter VA – Share Loss Relief

History – Chapter VA of Part XIII omitted by CTA 2010, s. 1177 and Sch. 1, para. 88 and repealed by CTA 2010, s. 1181 and Sch. 3, Pt. 1.

573 Relief for companies

573 [Omitted by CTA 2010, s. 1177 and Sch. 1, para. 88 and repealed by CTA 2010, s. 1181 and Sch. 3, Pt. 1.]

History – Chapter VA of Part XIII (of which s. 573 formed a part) omitted by CTA 2010, s. 1177 and Sch. 1, para. 88 and repealed by CTA 2010, s. 1181 and Sch. 3, Pt. 1, with effect for corporation tax purposes for accounting periods ending on or after 1 April 2010, and for income and capital gains tax purposes for the tax year 2010–11 and subsequent tax years.

Notes – S. 573(4) rewritten for income tax purposes as ITA 2007, Sch. 1 para. 309.
S. 573 rewritten for corporation tax purposes as follows:
S. 573(1): CTA 2010, s. 68(1), 69(2), (3), (4).
S. 573(2): CTA 2010, s. 70(2), (3), (4), 71(1), (2), (4).
S. 573(3): CTA 2010, s. 70(2), 71(1), 72(2), (3).
S. 573(4A): CTA 2010, s. 71(5).
S. 573(5): CTA 2010, s. 69(5), (6).
S. 573(6): CTA 2010, s. 73(1), (2).

RELIEF FOR LOSSES ON UNQUOTED SHARES IN TRADING COMPANIES

History – Chapter VA of Part XIII omitted by CTA 2010, s. 1177 and Sch. 1, para. 88 and repealed by CTA 2010, s. 1181 and Sch. 3, Pt. 1.

574 Relief for individuals

574 [Omitted by CTA 2010, s. 1177 and Sch. 1, para. 88 and repealed by CTA 2010, s. 1181 and Sch. 3, Pt. 1.]

History – Chapter VA of Part XIII (of which s. 574 formed a part) omitted by CTA 2010, s. 1177 and Sch. 1, para. 88 and repealed by CTA 2010, s. 1181 and Sch. 3, Pt. 1, with effect for corporation tax purposes for accounting periods ending on or after 1 April 2010, and for income and capital gains tax purposes for the tax year 2010–11 and subsequent tax years. Former s. 574 omitted by ITA 2007, s. 1027 and Sch. 1, para. 118 and repealed by ITA 2007, s. 1031 and Sch. 3, Pt. 1 with effect for 2007–08 and later tax years.

Notes – S. 574 rewritten for income tax purposes as follows:
S. 574(1): ITA 2007, s. 23, 24(1), 25(4), 131(1) and (2), 132(1), (3) and (4), 133(1) and Sch. 1, para. 309.
S. 574(2): ITA 2007, s. 133(3) and (4).
S. 574(3): ITA 2007, s. 135(2), 135(3) and s. 150(2).

575 Exclusion of relief under section 573 in certain cases

575 [Omitted by CTA 2010, s. 1177 and Sch. 1, para. 88 and repealed by CTA 2010, s. 1181 and Sch. 3, Pt. 1.]

History – Chapter VA of Part XIII (of which s. 575 formed a part) omitted by CTA 2010, s. 1177 and Sch. 1, para. 88 and repealed by CTA 2010, s. 1181 and Sch. 3, Pt. 1, with effect for corporation tax purposes for accounting periods ending on or after 1 April 2010, and for income and capital gains tax purposes for the tax year 2010–11 and subsequent tax years.

Notes – S. 575 rewritten for income tax purposes as follows:
S. 575(1): ITA 2007, s. 131(3).
S. 575(2): ITA 2007, s. 136(2), (3), (4), (5).
S. 575(3): ITA 2007, s. 131(4).
S. 575 rewritten for corporation tax purposes as follows:
S. 575(1): CTA 2010, s. 68(2).
S. 575(2): CTA 2010, s. 74(1), (2), (3), (4), (3).
S. 575(3): CTA 2010, s. 68(3).
S. 575(4): CTA 2010, s. 74(4).

576 Provisions supplementary to sections 573 and 575

576 [Omitted by CTA 2010, s. 1177 and Sch. 1, para. 88 and repealed by CTA 2010, s. 1181 and Sch. 3, Pt. 1.]

History – Chapter VA of Part XIII (of which s. 576 formed a part) omitted by CTA 2010, s. 1177 and Sch. 1, para. 88 and repealed by CTA 2010, s. 1181 and Sch. 3, Pt. 1, with effect for corporation tax purposes for accounting periods ending on or after 1 April 2010, and for income and capital gains tax purposes for the tax year 2010–11 and subsequent tax years.

Notes – S. 576 rewritten as follows:
S. 576(1): ITA 2007, s. 147(1), (2), (3), (4), (5), (6), 148(1), (2), (3), (4), (5).
S. 576(1A): ITA 2007, s. 148(3).
S. 576(1B): ITA 2007, s. 148(6).
S. 576(2): ITA 2007, Sch. 1 para. 309.
S. 576(3): ITA 2007, Sch. 1 para. 309.
S. 576(4): ITA 2007, s. 134(1), (2), (3), (4), (5), Sch. 1 para. 121.
S. 576(4A): ITA 2007, s. 137(1), (3), (4), (5), (7), (8), 138(1), (2), (3), (4), 139(1), (2), (3), (4), 140(1), 141(1), (2), 142(1), (2), (3), 143(1), (2), (3), 144, 145(1), (2), (3), (4), 146(1), (2), Sch. 1 para. 122, 123, 124, 125, 126, 127, 128, 129, 130, 131
S. 576(5): ITA 2007, s. 134(5), 136(4), 148(8), 151(1), (3), (4), (6), (7), Sch. 1 para. 121, 132.
"The 1992 Act" is TCGA 1992 (s. 831(3)).
S. 576 rewritten for corporation tax purposes as follows:
S. 576(1): CTA 2010, s. 75(1), (2), (3), (4), (5), (6), 76(1), (2), (3), (4), (5).
S. 576(1C): CTA 2010, s. 76(2), (3), (6).
S. 576(1D): CTA 2010, s. 76(8).

576A Qualifying trading companies

576A [Omitted by CTA 2010, s. 1177 and Sch. 1, para. 88 and repealed by CTA 2010, s. 1181 and Sch. 3, Pt. 1.]

History – Chapter VA of Part XIII (of which s. 576A formed a part) omitted by CTA 2010, s. 1177 and Sch. 1, para. 88 and repealed by CTA 2010, s. 1181 and Sch. 3, Pt. 1, with effect for corporation tax purposes for accounting periods ending on or after 1 April 2010, and for income and capital gains tax purposes for the tax year 2010–11 and subsequent tax years.

Notes – S. 576A rewritten for corporation tax purposes as follows:
S. 576A(1): CTA 2010, s. 78(1).
S. 576A(2): CTA 2010, s. 78(2).
S. 576A(3): CTA 2010, s. 78(3).
S. 576A(4): CTA 2010, s. 78(4).
S. 576A(5): CTA 2010, s. 78(5).

QUALIFYING TRADING COMPANIES: THE REQUIREMENTS

History – Chapter VA of Part XIII omitted by CTA 2010, s. 1177 and Sch. 1, para. 88 and repealed by CTA 2010, s. 1181 and Sch. 3, Pt. 1.

576B The trading requirement

576B [Omitted by CTA 2010, s. 1177 and Sch. 1, para. 88 and repealed by CTA 2010, s. 1181 and Sch. 3, Pt. 1.]

History – Chapter VA of Part XIII (of which s. 576B formed a part) omitted by CTA 2010, s. 1177 and Sch. 1, para. 88 and repealed by CTA 2010, s. 1181 and Sch. 3, Pt. 1, with effect for corporation tax purposes for accounting periods ending on or after 1 April 2010, and for income and capital gains tax purposes for the tax year 2010–11 and subsequent tax years.

Notes – S. 576B rewritten for corporation tax purposes as follows:
S. 576B(1): CTA 2010, s. 79(1).
S. 576B(2): CTA 2010, s. 79(2).
S. 576B(3): CTA 2010, s. 79(3).
S. 576B(4): CTA 2010, s. 79(4).
S. 576B(5): CTA 2010, s. 79(5).
S. 576B(6): CTA 2010, s. 79(6).
S. 576B(7): CTA 2010, s. 79(7).
S. 576B(8): CTA 2010, s. 79(8).
S. 576B(9): CTA 2010, s. 79(9).

576C Ceasing to meet the trading requirement because of administration or receivership

576C [Omitted by CTA 2010, s. 1177 and Sch. 1, para. 88 and repealed by CTA 2010, s. 1181 and Sch. 3, Pt. 1.]

History – Chapter VA of Part XIII (of which s. 576C formed a part) omitted by CTA 2010, s. 1177 and Sch. 1, para. 88 and repealed by CTA 2010, s. 1181 and Sch. 3, Pt. 1, with effect for corporation tax purposes for accounting periods ending on or after 1 April 2010, and for income and capital gains tax purposes for the tax year 2010–11 and subsequent tax years.

Notes – S. 576C rewritten for corporation tax purposes as follows:
S. 576C(1): CTA 2010, s. 80(1).
S. 576C(2): CTA 2010, s. 80(2).
S. 576C(3): CTA 2010, s. 80(3).
S. 576C(4): CTA 2010, s. 80(4).
S. 576C(5): CTA 2010, s. 80(5).

576D The control and independence requirement

576D [Omitted by CTA 2010, s. 1177 and Sch. 1, para. 88 and repealed by CTA 2010, s. 1181 and Sch. 3, Pt. 1.]

History – Chapter VA of Part XIII (of which s. 576D formed a part) omitted by CTA 2010, s. 1177 and Sch. 1, para. 88 and repealed by CTA 2010, s. 1181 and Sch. 3, Pt. 1, with effect for corporation tax purposes for accounting periods ending on or after 1 April 2010, and for income and capital gains tax purposes for the tax year 2010–11 and subsequent tax years.

Notes – S. 576D rewritten for corporation tax purposes as follows:
S. 576D(1): CTA 2010, s. 81(1).
S. 576D(2): CTA 2010, s. 81(2).
S. 576D(3): CTA 2010, s. 81(3).
S. 576D(3A): CTA 2010, s. 1176(1).
S. 576D(4): CTA 2010, s. 81(4), 1176(2).

576E The qualifying subsidiaries requirement

576E [Omitted by CTA 2010, s. 1177 and Sch. 1, para. 88 and repealed by CTA 2010, s. 1181 and Sch. 3, Pt. 1.]

History – Chapter VA of Part XIII (of which s. 576E formed a part) omitted by CTA 2010, s. 1177 and Sch. 1, para. 88 and repealed by CTA 2010, s. 1181 and Sch. 3, Pt. 1, with effect for corporation tax purposes for accounting periods ending on or after 1 April 2010, and for income and capital gains tax purposes for the tax year 2010–11 and subsequent tax years.

Notes – S. 576E rewritten for corporation tax purposes as follows:
S. 576E(1): CTA 2010, s. 82(1).
S. 576E(2): CTA 2010, s. 82(2).

576F The property managing subsidiaries requirement

576F [Omitted by CTA 2010, s. 1177 and Sch. 1, para. 88 and repealed by CTA 2010, s. 1181 and Sch. 3, Pt. 1.]

History – Chapter VA of Part XIII (of which s. 576F formed a part) omitted by CTA 2010, s. 1177 and Sch. 1, para. 88 and repealed by CTA 2010, s. 1181 and Sch. 3, Pt. 1, with effect for corporation tax purposes for accounting periods ending on or after 1 April 2010, and for income and capital gains tax purposes for the tax year 2010–11 and subsequent tax years.

Notes – S. 576F rewritten for corporation tax purposes as follows:
S. 576F(1): CTA 2010, s. 83(1).
S. 576F(2): CTA 2010, s. 83(2).

576G The gross assets requirement

576G [Omitted by CTA 2010, s. 1177 and Sch. 1, para. 88 and repealed by CTA 2010, s. 1181 and Sch. 3, Pt. 1.]

History – Chapter VA of Part XIII (of which s. 576G formed a part) omitted by CTA 2010, s. 1177 and Sch. 1, para. 88 and repealed by CTA 2010, s. 1181 and Sch. 3, Pt. 1, with effect for corporation tax purposes for accounting periods ending on or after 1 April 2010, and for income and capital gains tax purposes for the tax year 2010–11 and subsequent tax years.

Notes – S. 576G rewritten for corporation tax purposes as follows:
S. 576G(1): CTA 2010, s. 84(1).
S. 576G(2): CTA 2010, s. 84(2).
S. 576G(3): CTA 2010, s. 84(3).
S. 576G(4): CTA 2010, s. 84(4).

576H The unquoted status requirement

576H [Omitted by CTA 2010, s. 1177 and Sch. 1, para. 88 and repealed by CTA 2010, s. 1181 and Sch. 3, Pt. 1.]

History – Chapter VA of Part XIII (of which s. 576H formed a part) omitted by CTA 2010, s. 1177 and Sch. 1, para. 88 and repealed by CTA 2010, s. 1181 and Sch. 3, Pt. 1, with effect for corporation tax purposes for accounting periods ending on or after 1 April 2010, and for income and capital gains tax purposes for the tax year 2010–11 and subsequent tax years.

Notes – S. 576H rewritten for corporation tax purposes as follows:
S. 576H(1): CTA 2010, s. 85(1).
S. 576H(2): CTA 2010, s. 85(2).
S. 576H(3): CTA 2010, s. 85(3).

576I Power to amend requirements by Treasury order

576I [Omitted by CTA 2010, s. 1177 and Sch. 1, para. 88 and repealed by CTA 2010, s 1181 and Sch. 3, Pt. 1.]

History – Chapter VA of Part XIII (of which s. 576I formed a part) omitted by CTA 2010, s. 1177 and Sch. 1 para. 88 and repealed by CTA 2010, s. 1181 and Sch. 3, Pt. 1, with effect for corporation tax purposes for accounting periods ending on or after 1 April 2010, and for income and capital gains tax purposes for the tax year 2010–11 and subsequent tax years.

Notes – S. 576I rewritten for corporation tax purposes as follows:
S. 576I: CTA 2010, s. 86.

QUALIFYING TRADING COMPANIES: SUPPLEMENTARY PROVISIONS

History – Chapter VA of Part XIII omitted by CTA 2010, s. 1177 and Sch. 1, para. 88 and repealed by CTA 2010, s. 1181 and Sch. 3, Pt. 1.

576J Relief after an exchange of shares for shares in another company

576J [Omitted by CTA 2010, s. 1177 and Sch. 1, para. 88 and repealed by CTA 2010, s. 1181 and Sch. 3, Pt. 1.]

History – Chapter VA of Part XIII (of which s. 576J formed a part) omitted by CTA 2010, s. 1177 and Sch. 1, para. 88 and repealed by CTA 2010, s. 1181 and Sch. 3, Pt. 1, with effect for corporation tax purposes for accounting periods ending on or after 1 April 2010, and for income and capital gains tax purposes for the tax year 2010–11 and subsequent tax years.

Notes – S. 576J rewritten for corporation tax purposes as follows:
S. 576J(1): CTA 2010, s. 87(1).
S. 576J(2): CTA 2010, s. 87(2).
S. 576J(3): CTA 2010, s. 87(3).
S. 576J(4): CTA 2010, s. 87(4).
S. 576J(5): CTA 2010, s. 87(5).

576K Substitution of new shares for old shares

576K [Omitted by CTA 2010, s. 1177 and Sch. 1, para. 88 and repealed by CTA 2010, s. 1181 and Sch. 3, Pt. 1.]

History – Chapter VA of Part XIII (of which s. 576K formed a part) omitted by CTA 2010, s. 1177 and Sch. 1, para. 88 and repealed by CTA 2010, s. 1181 and Sch. 3, Pt. 1, with effect for corporation tax purposes for accounting periods ending on or after 1 April 2010, and for income and capital gains tax purposes for the tax year 2010–11 and subsequent tax years.

Notes – S. 576K rewritten for corporation tax purposes as follows:
S. 576K(1): CTA 2010, s. 88(1).
S. 576K(2): CTA 2010, s. 88(2).
S. 576K(3): CTA 2010, s. 73(1).
S. 576K(4): CTA 2010, s. 88(3).

SUPPLEMENTAL

History – Chapter VA of Part XIII omitted by CTA 2010, s. 1177 and Sch. 1, para. 88 and repealed by CTA 2010, s. 1181 and Sch. 3, Pt. 1.

576L Interpretation of Chapter

576L [Omitted by CTA 2010, s. 1177 and Sch. 1, para. 88 and repealed by CTA 2010, s. 1181 and Sch. 3, Pt. 1.]

History – Chapter VA of Part XIII (of which s. 576L formed a part) omitted by CTA 2010, s. 1177 and Sch. 1, para. 88 and repealed by CTA 2010, s. 1181 and Sch. 3, Pt. 1, with effect for corporation tax purposes for accounting periods ending on or after 1 April 2010, and for income and capital gains tax purposes for the tax year 2010–11 and subsequent tax years.

Notes – S. 576L rewritten for corporation tax purposes as follows:
S. 576L(1): CTA 2010, s. 90(1).
S. 576L(2): CTA 2010, s. 90(3).
S. 576L(3): CTA 2010, s. 90(4).
S. 576L(4): CTA 2010, s. 90(5).
S. 576L(5): CTA 2010, s. 90(6).

Chapter VI – Other Provisions

MISCELLANEOUS

577 Business entertaining expenses

577 [Omitted by CTA 2009, s. 1322 and Sch. 1, para. 191 and repealed by CTA 2009, s. 1326 and Sch. 3, Pt. 1.]

History – S. 577 omitted by CTA 2009, s. 1322 and Sch. 1, para. 191 and repealed by CTA 2009, s. 1326 and Sch. 3, Pt. 1, with effect for corporation tax purposes for accounting periods ending on or after 1 April 2009, and for income tax and capital gains tax purposes for the tax year 2009–10 and subsequent tax years.

Notes – Rewritten income tax provisions are now located as follows:
S. 577(1): ITTOIA 2005, s. 45(2), 46(1) and (3), 47(1) and (4) and 867(6).
S. 577(1)(b): ITEPA 2003, s. 356(1).
S. 577(3): ITTOIA 2005, s. 45(4) and 867(3).
In s. 577(3), the former words of para. (a) and (b): ITEPA 2003, s. 357.
S. 577(5): ITTOIA 2005, s. 45(1) and 867(3).
S. 577(7): ITTOIA 2005, s. 45(1) and (4), 47(1) and (3) and 867(3) and (6).
S. 577(8): ITTOIA 2005, s. 45(1) and (4), 47(1) and (3) and 867(3) and (6).
S. 577(9): ITTOIA 2005, s. 47(1) and (5).
S. 577(10): ITTOIA 2005, s. 46(1) and (2) and 47(1) and (2).
S. 577 rewritten for corporation tax purposes as follows:
S. 577(1): CTA 2009, s. 1298(1), (2).
S. 577(3): CTA 2009, s. 1298(3), 1299(1), 1300(1).
S. 577(5): CTA 2009, s. 1298(1), (5), 1299(1), (3), 1300(1), (4).
S. 577(7): CTA 2009, s. 1298(1), (5).
S. 577(8): CTA 2009, s. 1298(1), (5), 1300(1), (3).
S. 577(9): CTA 2009, s. 1300(1), (5).
S. 577(10): CTA 2009, s. 1299(1), (2), 1300(1), (2).

577A Expenditure involving crime

577A [Omitted by CTA 2009, s. 1322 and Sch. 1, para. 192 and repealed by CTA 2009, s. 1326 and Sch. 3, Pt. 1.]

History – S. 577A omitted by CTA 2009, s. 1322 and Sch. 1, para. 192 and repealed by CTA 2009, s. 1326 and Sch. 3, Pt. 1, with effect for corporation tax purposes for accounting periods ending on or after 1 April 2009, and for income tax and capital gains tax purposes for the tax year 2009–10 and subsequent tax years.

Notes – Rewritten income tax provisions are now located as follows:
S. 577A(1): ITTOIA 2005, s. 55(1) and 870(2).
S. 577A(1A): ITTOIA 2005, s. 55(2) and 870(3).
S. 577A rewritten for corporation tax purposes as follows:
S. 577A(1): CTA 2009, s. 1304(1), (4).
S. 577A(1A): CTA 2009, s. 1304(1), (5).
S. 577A(2): CTA 2009, s. 1304(2), (3).

578 Housing grants

578 [Omitted by CTA 2009, s. 1322 and Sch. 1, para. 193 and repealed by CTA 2009, s. 1326 and Sch. 3, Pt. 1.]

History – S. 578 omitted by CTA 2009, s. 1322 and Sch. 1, para. 193 and repealed by CTA 2009, s. 1326 and Sch. 3, Pt. 1, with effect for corporation tax purposes for accounting periods ending on or after 1 April 2009, and for income tax and capital gains tax purposes for the tax year 2009–10 and subsequent tax years.

Notes – S. 578 rewritten as follows:
S. 578(1): CTA 2009, s. 1284(1), (2).
S. 578(2): CTA 2009, s. 1284(3).

578A Expenditure on car hire

578A [Omitted by CTA 2009, s. 1322 and Sch. 1, para. 194 and repealed by CTA 2009, s. 1326 and Sch. 3, Pt. 1.]

History – S. 578A omitted by CTA 2009, s. 1322 and Sch. 1, para. 194 and repealed by CTA 2009, s. 1326 and Sch. 3, Pt. 1, with effect for corporation tax purposes for accounting periods ending on or after 1 April 2009, and for income tax and capital gains tax purposes for the tax year 2009–10 and subsequent tax years.

Notes – Rewritten income tax provisions are now located as follows:
S. 578A(1): ITTOIA 2005, s. 48(1).
S. 578A(2): ITTOIA 2005, s. 48(1).
S. 578A(2A): ITTOIA 2005, s. 50(1).
S. 578A(2B): ITTOIA 2005, s. 50(2).
S. 578A(3): ITTOIA 2005, s. 48(2).
S. 578A(4): ITTOIA 2005, s. 48(3) and (4).
S. 578A rewritten for corporation tax purposes as follows:
S. 578A(1): CTA 2009, s. 56(1), 1251(1), Sch. 1, para. 44.
S. 578A(2): CTA 2009, s. 56(1), 1251(1), Sch. 1, para. 44.
S. 578A(2A): CTA 2009, s. 58(1), 1251(7), Sch. 1, para. 45.
S. 578A(2B): CTA 2009, s. 58(2), 1251(7), Sch. 1, para. 45.
S. 578A(3): CTA 2009, s. 56(2), 1251(2), Sch. 1, para. 44.
S. 578A(4): CTA 2009, s. 56(3), (4), (5), 1231(3), 1251(3), (4), (5), Sch. 1, para. 44.

578B Expenditure on car hire: supplementary

578B [Omitted by CTA 2009, s. 1322 and Sch. 1, para. 194 and repealed by CTA 2009, s. 1326 and Sch. 3, Pt. 1.]

History – S. 578B omitted by CTA 2009, s. 1322 and Sch. 1, para. 194 and repealed by CTA 2009, s. 1326 and Sch. 3, Pt. 1, with effect for corporation tax purposes for accounting periods ending on or after 1 April 2009, and for income tax and capital gains tax purposes for the tax year 2009–10 and subsequent tax years.

Notes – Rewritten income tax provisions are now located as follows:
S. 578B(1): ITTOIA 2005, s. 49(1).
S. 578B(2): ITTOIA 2005, s. 49(2)–(5).
S. 578B(3): ITTOIA 2005, s. 49(6).
S. 578B(4): ITTOIA 2005, s. 48(5).
S. 578B rewritten for corporation tax purposes as follows:
S. 578B(1): CTA 2009, s. 57(1), 1251(7), Sch. 1, para. 44.
S. 578B(2): CTA 2009, s. 57(2), (3), (4), (5), 1251(7), Sch. 1, para. 44.
S. 578B(3): CTA 2009, s. 57(6), 1251(7), Sch. 1, para. 44.
S. 578B(4): CTA 2009, s. 56(6), 1251(6), Sch. 1, para. 44.

579 Statutory redundancy payments

579 [Omitted by CTA 2009, s. 1322 and Sch. 1, para. 195 and repealed by CTA 2009, s. 1326 and Sch. 3, Pt. 1.]

History – S. 579 omitted by CTA 2009, s. 1322 and Sch. 1, para. 195 and repealed by CTA 2009, s. 1326 and Sch. 3, Pt. 1, with effect for corporation tax purposes for accounting periods ending on or after 1 April 2009, and for income tax and capital gains tax purposes for the tax year 2009–10 and subsequent tax years.

Notes – Rewritten income tax provisions are now located as follows:
S. 579(1): ITEPA 2003, s. 309(1), (3) and (4).
S. 579(2): ITTOIA 2005, s. 31(1)–(3), 76(1) and 77(1)–(6).
S. 579(5): ITTOIA 2005, s. 76(1), 77(6) and 78(1)–(3).
S. 579(6): ITTOIA 2005, s. 80(1) and (2).
S. 579 rewritten for corporation tax purposes as follows:
S. 579(2): CTA 2009, s. 51(1), (2), 76(1), 77(1) (2), (3), (4), (5), (6), (7),.
S. 579(3): CTA 2009, s. 1221(2), (3), 1232, 1239(1), 1240(1), (2), (3), 1243(1), Sch. 1, para. 36, 37, 40.
S. 579(3A): CTA 2009, s. 1240(4), Sch. 1, para. 37.
S. 579(5): CTA 2009, s. 76(1), 77(7), 78(1), (2), (3), 1239(1), 1241(1), (2), (3), Sch. 1, para. 36, 38.
S. 579(6): CTA 2009, s. 81(1), (2), 1243(1), (2), (3), Sch. 1, para. 40.

580 Provisions supplementary to section 579

580 [Omitted by CTA 2009, s. 1322 and Sch. 1, para. 195 and repealed by CTA 2009, s. 1326 and Sch. 3, Pt. 1.]

History – S. 580 omitted by CTA 2009, s. 1322 and Sch. 1, para. 195 and repealed by CTA 2009, s. 1326 and Sch. 3, Pt. 1, with effect for corporation tax purposes for accounting periods ending on or after 1 April 2009, and for income tax and capital gains tax purposes for the tax year 2009–10 and subsequent tax years.

Notes – Rewritten income tax provisions are now located as follows:
S. 580(1): ITTOIA 2005, s. 76(2) and (3), 77(3), 78(2), 79(1) and (4) and 80(1).
S. 580(3): ITEPA 2003, s. 309(2) and.(3).
S. 580 rewritten for corporation tax purposes as follows:
S. 580(1): CTA 2009, s. 76(2), (3), 77(3), 78(2), 79(1), (3), 81(1), 1239(2), (3), 1240(3), 1241(2), 1242(1), (3), 1243(1), Sch. 1, para. 36, 37, 38, 39, 40.

580A Relief from tax on annual payments under certain insurance policies

580A [Omitted by ITTOIA 2005, s. 882 and Sch. 1, para. 240 and repealed by s. 884 and Sch. 3.]

History – S. 580A omitted by ITTOIA 2005, s. 882(1) and Sch. 1, para. 240 and repealed by s. 884 and Sch. 3; effective for income tax purposes for 2005–06 onwards and for corporation tax purposes for accounting periods ending after 5 April 2005 (ITTOIA 2005, s. 883(1)).

Notes – S. 580A rewritten as follows:
S. 580A(1): ITTOIA 2005, s. 735(1).
S. 580A(2): ITTOIA 2005, s. 735(1), 737(1), 739(1) and 740(1).
S. 580A(3): ITTOIA 2005, s. 736(1) and (2).
S. 580A(4): ITTOIA 2005, s. 737(2)–(4).
S. 580A(5): ITTOIA 2005, s. 738(1)–(3).
S. 580A(6): ITTOIA 2005, s. 735(1).
S. 580A(7): ITTOIA 2005, s. 743(1)–(3) and Sch. 1, para. 591 and 609.
S. 580A(8): ITTOIA 2005, s. 741(1)–(3).
S. 580A(9): ITTOIA 2005, s. 742.
S. 580A(10): ITTOIA 2005, s. 736(3).

580B Meaning of "self-contained" for the purposes of s. 580A

580B [Omitted by ITTOIA 2005, s. 882 and Sch. 1, para. 240 and repealed by s. 884 and Sch. 3.]

History – S. 580B omitted by ITTOIA 2005, s. 882(1) and Sch. 1, para. 240 and repealed by s. 884 and Sch. 3; effective for income tax purposes for 2005–06 onwards and for corporation tax purposes for accounting periods ending after 5 April 2005 (ITTOIA 2005, s. 883(1)).

Notes – S. 580B rewritten as follows:
S. 580B(1): ITTOIA 2005, s. 739(4) and 740(4).
S. 580B(2): ITTOIA 2005, s. 739(1)–(3).
S. 580B(3): ITTOIA 2005, s. 740(1)–(3).
ITTOIA 2005 does not rewrite ICTA 1988, s. 580B(4) as it seems unnecessary to state that the terms of a policy include fixing the premium or otherwise in respect of insurance against risk. (See ITTOIA 2005, Explanatory Notes, Annex 1, Table 1 (Change 158).)

580C Relief from tax on annual payments under immediate needs annuities

580C [Omitted by ITTOIA 2005, s. 882 and Sch. 1, para. 240 and repealed by s. 884 and Sch. 3.]

History – S. 580C omitted by ITTOIA 2005, s. 882(1) and Sch. 1, para. 240 and repealed by s. 884 and Sch. 3; effective for income tax purposes for 2005–06 onwards and for corporation tax purposes for accounting periods ending after 5 April 2005 (ITTOIA 2005, s. 883(1)).

Notes – S. 580C rewritten as follows:
S. 580C(1): ITTOIA 2005, s. 725(1).
S. 580C(2): ITTOIA 2005, s. 725(1).
S. 580C(3): ITTOIA 2005, s. 725(2) and (3).
S. 580C(4): ITTOIA 2005, s. 725(5) and 726(1)–(5).
S. 580C(5): ITTOIA 2005, s. 726(2)–(5).
S. 580C(6): ITTOIA 2005, s. 725(4).
S. 580C(7): ITTOIA 2005, s. 725(5).
S. 580C(8): ITTOIA 2005, s. 725(6) and 726(6).

581 Borrowing in foreign currency by local authorities and statutory corporations

581 [Omitted by ITTOIA 2005, s. 882 and Sch. 1, para. 241 and repealed by s. 884 and Sch. 3.]

History – S. 581 omitted by ITTOIA 2005, s. 882(1) and Sch. 1, para. 241 and repealed by s. 884 and Sch. 3; effective for income tax purposes for 2005–06 onwards and for corporation tax purposes for accounting periods ending after 5 April 2005 (ITTOIA 2005, s. 883(1)).

Notes – S. 581 rewritten as follows:
S. 581(1): ITTOIA 2005, s. 755(1) and (2), 756(1) and Sch. 1, para. 241.
S. 581(2): ITTOIA 2005, s. 756(2), (5) and (6).
S. 581(3): ITTOIA 2005, s. 755(3).
S. 581(4): ITTOIA 2005, s. 755(1)–(3) and 756(2), (4) and (6).
S. 581(5): ITTOIA 2005, s. 755(4).
S. 581(6): ITTOIA 2005, s. 756(2)–(6).

581A Interest on foreign currency securities etc.

581A [Omitted by ITA 2007, s. 1027 and Sch. 1, para. 133 and repealed by ITA 2007, s. 1031 and Sch. 3, Pt. 1 with effect for income tax purposes for 2007–08 and later tax years and for corporation tax purposes in relation to accounting periods ending after 5 April 2007.]

Notes – S. 581A rewritten as ITA 2007, s. 981.

582 Funding bonds issued in respect of interest on certain debts

582 [Omitted by CTA 2009, s. 1322 and Sch. 1, para. 196 and repealed by CTA 2009, s. 1326 and *Sch. 3, Pt. 1.]*

History – S. 582 omitted by CTA 2009, s. 1322 and Sch. 1, para. 196 and repealed by CTA 2009, s. 1326 and Sch. 3, Pt. 1, with effect for corporation tax purposes for accounting periods ending on or after 1 April 2009, and for income tax and capital gains tax purposes for the tax year 2009–10 and subsequent tax years.

Notes – Rewritten income tax provisions are now located as follows:
S. 582(1): ITTOIA 2005, s. 380(1) and (2) and 754(1).

S. 582(2): ITA 2007, s. 939(1), (2), (3), (4), 940(1), (2), (3).
S. 582(2): ITTOIA 2005, s. 371.
S. 582(2A): ITA 2007, s. 939(2).
S. 582(3): ITTOIA 2005, s. 380(1).
S. 582(4): ITA 2007, s. 939(6).
S. 582(4): ITTOIA 2005, s. 380(3) and 754(2).
S. 582 rewritten for corporation tax purposes as follows:
S. 582(1): CTA 2009, s. 413(1), (2), 414(1).
S. 582(2): CTA 2009, s. 299(1).
S. 582(2A): CTA 2009, s. 299(1).
S. 582(3): CTA 2009, s. 413(1).
S. 582(3A): CTA 2009, s. 413(2).
S. 582(4): CTA 2009, s. 413(3), 414(2).

582A Designated international organisations: miscellaneous exemptions

582A [Omitted by ITA 2007, s. 1027 and Sch. 1, para. 135 and repealed by ITA 2007, s. 1031 and Sch. 3, Pt. 1 with effect for income tax purposes for 2007–08 and later tax years and for corporation tax purposes in relation to accounting periods ending after 5 April 2007.]

Notes – S. 582A rewritten as follows:
S. 582A(1): ITA 2007, s. 979(1), Sch. 1 para. 459, 461.
S. 582A(4): ITA 2007, s. 979(3), (4).
S. 582A(5): ITA 2007, s. 979(2).
S. 582A(6): ITA 2007, Sch. 1 para. 459, 461.

583 Inter-American Development Bank

Notes – S. 583 rewritten as ITTOIA 2005, s. 773(1)–(4).

583 [Omitted by ITTOIA 2005, s. 882 and Sch. 1, para. 244 and repealed by s. 884 and Sch. 3.]

History – S. 583 omitted by ITTOIA 2005, s. 882(1) and Sch. 1, para. 244 and repealed by s. 884 and Sch. 3; effective for income tax purposes for 2005–06 onwards and for corporation tax purposes for accounting periods ending after 5 April 2005 (ITTOIA 2005, s. 883(1)).

ICTA 1988

584 Relief for unremittable overseas income

584 [Omitted by CTA 2009, s. 1322 and Sch. 1, para. 197 and repealed by CTA 2009, s. 1326 and Sch. 3, Pt. 1.]

History – S. 584 omitted by CTA 2009, s. 1322 and Sch. 1, para. 197 and repealed by CTA 2009, s. 1326 and Sch. 3, Pt. 1, with effect for corporation tax purposes for accounting periods ending on or after 1 April 2009, and for income tax and capital gains tax purposes for the tax year 2009–10 and subsequent tax years.
Notes – Rewritten income tax provisions are now located as follows:
S. 584(1): ITTOIA 2005, s. 841(1), (3) and (4) and 842(1).
S. 584(2): ITTOIA 2005, s. 842(1).
S. 584(2A): ITTOIA 2005, s. 843(1) and (3)–(5).
S. 584(4): ITTOIA 2005, s. 830(3) and 844(1)–(4).
S. 584(5): ITTOIA 2005, s. 842(3) and (4) and 843(1), (2), (4) and (5).
S. 584(6): ITTOIA 2005, s. 842(5).
S. 584(7): ITTOIA 2005, s. 843(7).
S. 584(8): ITTOIA 2005, s. 845(1)–(3).
S. 584 rewritten for corporation tax purposes as follows:
S. 584(1): CTA 2009, s. 1274(1), (3), (4), 1275(1).
S. 584(2): CTA 2009, s. 1275(1). Full rewrite not necessary (see CTA 2009 Explanatory Notes, Annex 1, Change 90).
S. 584(2A): CTA 2009, s. 1276(1), (3), (4), (5).
S. 584(4): CTA 2009, s. 1277(1), (2), (3), (4).
S. 584(5): CTA 2009, s. 1275(3), (4), 1276(1), (2), (4), (5).
S. 584(6): CTA 2009, s. 1275(5).
S. 584(8): CTA 2009, s. 1278(1), (2), (3).
S. 584(10): CTA 2009, s. Sch. 2, para. 135.

585 Relief from tax on delayed remittances

585 [Omitted by ITTOIA 2005, s. 882 and Sch. 1, para. 246 and repealed by s. 884 and Sch. 3.]

History – S. 585 omitted by ITTOIA 2005, s. 882(1) and Sch. 1, para. 246 and repealed by s. 884 and Sch. 3; effective for income tax purposes for 2005–06 onwards and for corporation tax purposes for accounting periods ending after 5 April 2005 (ITTOIA 2005, s. 883(1)).

Notes – S. 585 rewritten as follows:
S. 585(1): ITTOIA 2005, s. 835(1)–(3).
S. 585(2): ITTOIA 2005, s. 836(1)–(3).
S. 585(3): ITTOIA 2005, s. 835(4) and (5).
S. 585(4): ITTOIA 2005, Sch. 2, para. 151(2), (3) and (5).
S. 585(6): ITTOIA 2005, s. 837(1).
S. 585(7): ITTOIA 2005, s. 837(2) and (3).
S. 585(8): ITTOIA 2005, s. 837(4)-(6).
S. 585(9): ITTOIA 2005, Sch. 2, para. 151(4).
ITTOIA 2005 does not rewrite the rules in ICTA 1988, s. 585(3)–(5) which relate to periods before Self Assessment. (See ITTOIA 2005, Explanatory Notes, Annex 1, Table 1 (Change 158).)

586 Disallowance of deductions for war risk premiums

586 [Omitted by CTA 2009, s. 1322 and Sch. 1, para. 198 and repealed by CTA 2009, s. 1326 and Sch. 3, Pt. 1.]

History – S. 586 omitted by CTA 2009, s. 1322 and Sch. 1, para. 198 and repealed by CTA 2009, s. 1326 and Sch. 3, Pt. 1, with effect for corporation tax purposes for accounting periods ending on or after 1 April 2009, and for income tax and capital gains tax purposes for the tax year 2009–10 and subsequent tax years.

Notes – ICTA 1988, s. 586 is not rewritten by ITTOIA 2005 as it is obsolete. (See ITTOIA 2005, Explanatory Notes, Annex 1, Table 1 (Change 158).)
S. 586 not rewritten by CTA 2009 (see CTA 2009 Explanatory Notes, Annex 1, Change 99).

587 Disallowance of certain payments in respect of war injuries to employees

587 [Omitted by CTA 2009, s. 1322 and Sch. 1, para. 198 and repealed by CTA 2009, s. 1326 and Sch. 3, Pt. 1.]

History – S. 587 omitted by CTA 2009, s. 1322 and Sch. 1, para. 198 and repealed by CTA 2009, s. 1326 and Sch. 3, Pt. 1, with effect for corporation tax purposes for accounting periods ending on or after 1 April 2009, and for income tax and capital gains tax purposes for the tax year 2009–10 and subsequent tax years.

Notes – ICTA 1988, s. 587 is not rewritten by ITTOIA 2005 as it is obsolete. (See ITTOIA 2005, Explanatory Notes, Annex 1, Table 1 (Change 158).)
S. 587: Not rewritten by CTA 2009 (see CTA 2009 Explanatory Notes, Annex 1, Change 99).

587A New issues of securities: extra return

587A [Omitted by ITA 2007, s. 1027 and Sch. 1, para. 136 and repealed by ITA 2007, s. 1031 and Sch. 3, Pt. 1 with effect for income tax purposes for 2007–08 and later tax years and for corporation tax purposes in relation to accounting periods ending after 5 April 2007.]

Notes – S. 587A rewritten as follows:
S. 587A(1): ITA 2007, s. 845(1), (2).
S. 587A(2): ITA 2007, s. 845(3).
S. 587A(3): ITA 2007, s. 845(4), 846(6).
S. 587A(4): ITA 2007, s. 846(2).
S. 587A(5): ITA 2007, s. 846(3), (4).
S. 587A(6): ITA 2007, s. 846(4), (5).

587B Gifts of shares, securities and real property to charities etc

587B [Omitted by CTA 2010, s. 1177 and Sch. 1, para. 89 and repealed by CTA 2010, s. 1181 and Sch. 3, Pt. 1.]

History – S. 587B omitted by CTA 2010, s. 1177 and Sch. 1, para. 89 and repealed by CTA 2010, s. 1181 and Sch. 3, Pt. 1, with effect for corporation tax purposes for accounting periods ending on or after 1 April 2010, and for income and capital gains tax purposes for the tax year 2010–11 and subsequent tax years.

Notes – S. 587B rewritten as follows:
S. 587B(1): ITA 2007, s. 431(1).
S. 587B(2): ITA 2007, s. 23, 24(1), 431(1), (2), 445(1), Sch. 1 para. 536.
S. 587B(3): ITA 2007, Sch. 1 para. 328.
S. 587B(4): ITA 2007, s. 434(1), (2).
S. 587B(5): ITA 2007, s. 434(1), (2), 1021(1).
S. 587B(6): ITA 2007, s. 434(1).
S. 587B(7): ITA 2007, s. 434(2), (4), 436(1), (2), (3).
S. 587B(8A): ITA 2007, s. 437(1).
S. 587B(8B): ITA 2007, s. 437(1), 439(1), (2).
S. 587B(8C): ITA 2007, s. 439(3), (4), (5).
S. 587B(8D): ITA 2007, s. 439(6).
S. 587B(8E): ITA 2007, s. 440(1).
S. 587B(8F): ITA 2007, s. 440(2).
S. 587B(8G): ITA 2007, s. 440(2).
S. 587B(9): ITA 2007, s. 432(1), (2), 435, 439(7), 446.
S. 587B(9A): ITA 2007, s. 433(1).
S. 587B(9B): ITA 2007, s. 433(2), (3).
S. 587B(9C): ITA 2007, s. 433(4), (6).
S. 587B(9D): ITA 2007, s. 433(5).
S. 587B(9E): ITA 2007, s. 433(6).
S. 587B(10): ITA 2007, s. 438(1).
S. 587B(10A): ITA 2007, s. 1021(1).
S. 587B(11): ITA 2007, s. 438(2).
S. 587B rewritten for corporation tax purposes as follows:
S. 587B(1): CTA 2010, s. 203(1).
S. 587B(2): CTA 2010, s. 203(1), (2), (3).
S. 587B(4): CTA 2010, s. 206(1), (2).
S. 587B(5): CTA 2010, s. 206(1), (2), 1176(1).
S. 587B(6): CTA 2010, s. 206(1).
S. 587B(7): CTA 2010, s. 206(4), 208.
S. 587B(8A): CTA 2010, s. 209(1).
S. 587B(8B): CTA 2010, s. 209(1), 211(1), (2).
S. 587B(8C): CTA 2010, s. 211(3), (4), (5).
S. 587B(8D): CTA 2010, s. 211(6).

S. 587B(8E): CTA 2010, s. 212(1).
S. 587B(8F): CTA 2010, s. 212(2).
S. 587B(8G): CTA 2010, s. 212(2).
S. 587B(9): CTA 2010, s. 204(1), (2), 207, 209(1),210(3), 211(7), 212(1),217.
S. 587B(9ZA): CTA 2010, s. 204(3).
S. 587B(9ZB): CTA 2010, s. 204(4).
S. 587B(9A): CTA 2010, s. 205(1).
S. 587B(9B): CTA 2010, s. 205(2), (3).
S. 587B(9C): CTA 2010, s. 205(4), (6).
S. 587B(9D): CTA 2010, s. 205(5).
S. 587B(9E): CTA 2010, s. 205(6).
S. 587B(10): CTA 2010, s. 210(1).
S. 587B(10A): CTA 2010, s. 1176(1).
S. 587B(11): CTA 2010, s. 210(2).

587BA Qualifying interests in land held jointly

587BA [Omitted by CTA 2010, s. 1177 and Sch. 1, para. 90 and repealed by CTA 2010, s. 1181 and Sch. 3, Pt. 1.]

History – S. 587BA omitted by CTA 2010, s. 1177 and Sch. 1, para. 90 and repealed by CTA 2010, s. 1181 and Sch. 3, Pt. 1, with effect for corporation tax purposes for accounting periods ending on or after 1 April 2010, and for income and capital gains tax purposes for the tax year 2010–11 and subsequent tax years.

Notes – S. 587BA rewritten for corporation tax purposes as follows:
S. 587BA(1): CTA 2010, s. 214(1).
S. 587BA(2): CTA 2010, s. 214(2), (3).
S. 587BA(3): CTA 2010, s. 214(6).
S. 587BA(4): CTA 2010, s. 214(7).
S. 587BA(5): CTA 2010, s. 214(4).
S. 587BA(6): CTA 2010, s. 215(2), (3), (4).
S. 587BA(7): CTA 2010, s. 215(5).
S. 587BA(8): CTA 2010, s. 215(9).
S. 587BA(9): CTA 2010, s. 215(6).
S. 587BA(10): CTA 2010, s. 215(7).
S. 587BA(11): CTA 2010, s. 215(8).
S. 587BA(13): CTA 2010, s. 214(5).

587C Supplementary provision for gifts of real property

587C [Omitted by CTA 2010, s. 1177 and Sch. 1, para. 91 and repealed by CTA 2010, s. 1181 and Sch. 3, Pt. 1.]

History – S. 587C omitted by CTA 2010, s. 1177 and Sch. 1, para. 91 and repealed by CTA 2010, s. 1181 and Sch. 3, Pt. 1, with effect for corporation tax purposes for accounting periods ending on or after 1 April 2010, and for income and capital gains tax purposes for the tax year 2010–11 and subsequent tax years.

Notes – S. 587C rewritten as follows:
S. 587C(1): ITA 2007, s. 441(1), 442(1), 444(1).
S. 587C(2): ITA 2007, s. 442(2), (3).
S. 587C(3): ITA 2007, s. 442(3), (4), (5), (6), (7).
S. 587C(4): ITA 2007, s. 441(2).
S. 587C(5): ITA 2007, s. 441(3).
S. 587C(6): ITA 2007, s. 444(2).
S. 587C(7): ITA 2007, s. 444(3).
S. 587C(8): ITA 2007, s. 444(4), (5).
S. 587C(9): ITA 2007, s. 444(6).
S. 587C(10): ITA 2007, s. 444(7).
S. 587C rewritten for corporation tax as follows:
S. 587C(1): CTA 2010, s. 213(1), 216(1).
S. 587C(4): CTA 2010, s. 213(2).
S. 587C(5): CTA 2010, s. 213(3).
S. 587C(6): CTA 2010, s. 216(2).
S. 587C(7): CTA 2010, s. 216(3).
S. 587C(8): CTA 2010, s. 216(4).
S. 587C(8A): CTA 2010, s. 216(5).
S. 587C(9): CTA 2010, s. 216(6).
S. 587C(10): CTA 2010, s. 216(7).
S. 587C(11): CTA 2010, s. 1176(1).

588 Training courses for employees

588 [Omitted by CTA 2009, s. 1322 and Sch. 1, para. 200 and repealed by CTA 2009, s. 1326 and Sch. 3, Pt. 1.]

History – S. 588 omitted by CTA 2009, s. 1322 and Sch. 1, para. 200 and repealed by CTA 2009, s. 1326 and Sch. 3, Pt. 1. with effect for corporation tax purposes for accounting periods ending on or after 1 April 2009, and for income tax and capital gains tax purposes for the tax year 2009–10 and subsequent tax years.

Notes – Rewritten income tax provisions are now located as follows:
S. 588(1): ITTOIA 2005, s. 74(1) and (2).
S. 588(3): ITTOIA 2005, s. 31(1)–(3) and 74(1) and (2).
S. 588(5): ITTOIA 2005, s. 75(1)–(3).
S. 588(5)(a): ITEPA 2003, s. 312(1).
S. 588(6): ITTOIA 2005, s. 75(4).
S. 588(7): ITTOIA 2005, s. 75(5) and (6).

S. 588 rewritten for corporation tax purposes as follows:
S. 588(4): CTA 2009, s. 1221(2), (3), 1232, 1238(1), (2), Sch. 1, para. 34.
S. 588(5): CTA 2009, s. 75(1), (2), (3), 1238(4), Sch. 1, para. 35.
S. 588(5A): CTA 2009, s. Sch. 1, para. 35.
S. 588(6): CTA 2009, s. 75(4), 1238(4), Sch. 1, para. 35.
S. 588(7): CTA 2009, s. 75(5), (6), 1238(4), Sch. 1, para. 35.
In the circumstances set out in ITEPA 2003, Sch. 7, para. 37(1), the repeal of s. 588(5)(a), s. 589(3) and (4) by ITEPA 2003, Sch. 8, Pt. 1 does not affect the operations of s. 588(5), (6) and (7).
In the circumstances set out in ITEPA 2003,Sch. 7, para. 37(2), s. 588(6) and (7) apply as if s. 588(6) referred to a failure to comply with any provision of s. 589(3) or (4) instead of a failure to meet such a condition as is mentioned in ITEPA 2003, s. 312(1)(b)(i) or (ii).

589 Qualifying courses of training etc.

Notes – In the circumstances set out in ITEPA 2003, Sch. 7, para. 37(1), the repeal of s. 588(5)(a), s. 589(3) and (4) by ITEPA 2003, Sch. 8, Pt. 1 does not affect the operations of s. 588(5), (6) and (7).

589 [Omitted by ITEPA 2003, Sch. 6, para. 68 and repealed by ITEPA 2003, Sch. 8, Pt. 1 which have effect for the tax year 2003–04 and subsequent tax years.]

History – S. 589 omitted by ITEPA 2003, Sch. 6, para. 68 and repealed by ITEPA 2003, Sch. 8, Pt. 1 which have effect for the tax year 2003–04 and subsequent tax years. However, in the circumstances set out in ITEPA 2003, Sch. 7, para. 37(1), the repeal of s. 589(3) and (4) by ITEPA 2003, Sch. 8, Pt. 1 does not affect the operations of s. 588(5), (6) and (7).
Notes – S. 589 rewritten as follows:
S. 589(1): ITEPA 2003, s. 311(3).
S. 589(2): ITEPA 2003, s. 311(3) and (4).
S. 589(3) and (4): ITEPA 2003, s. 311(4).
S. 589(5): ITEPA 2003, s. 311(2).
S. 589(6): ITEPA 2003, s. 311(5), s. 329(5) and s. 353(4).
S. 589(6A): ITEPA 2003, s. 311(6).
S. 589(7): ITEPA 2003, s. 5.

589A Counselling services for employees

589A [Omitted by CTA 2009, s. 1322 and Sch. 1, para. 201 and repealed by CTA 2009, s. 1326 and Sch. 3, Pt. 1.]

History – S. 589A omitted by CTA 2009, s. 1322 and Sch. 1, para. 201 and repealed by CTA 2009, s. 1326 and Sch. 3, Pt. 1, with effect for corporation tax purposes for accounting periods ending on or after 1 April 2009, and for income tax and capital gains tax purposes for the tax year 2009–10 and subsequent tax years.

Notes – Rewritten income tax provisions are now located as follows:
S. 589A(1): ITTOIA 2005, s. 73(1) and (2).
S. 589A(1A): ITTOIA 2005, s. 73(3).
S. 589A(2), (3), and (5) are spent and so have not been rewritten.
S. 589A(4) and (6): ITEPA 2003, s. 310(1).
S. 589A(7): ITTOIA 2005, s. 73(1).
S. 589A(8): ITTOIA 2005, s. 31(1)–(3) and 73(1).
S. 589A(10) is spent and so has not been rewritten.
S. 589A rewritten for corporation tax purposes as follows:
S. 589A(1): CTA 2009, s. 73(1), (2), 1237(1), (3), Sch. 1, para. 33.
S. 589A(1A): CTA 2009, s. 73(3), 1237(4), Sch. 1, para. 33.
S. 589A(7): CTA 2009, s. 73(1), 1237(1), Sch. 1, para. 33.
S. 589A(8): CTA 2009, s. 51(1), (2), 73(1), 1232, 1237(1), (2), Sch. 1, para. 33.
S. 589A(9): CTA 2009, s. 1221(2), (3), 1232, 1237(1), (2), Sch. 1, para. 33.

589B Qualifying counselling services etc.

589B(1)–(4A) [Omitted by ITEPA 2003, Sch. 6, para. 70(2) and repealed by ITEPA 2003, Sch. 8, Pt. 1]

589B(5) [Omitted by CTA 2009, s. 1322 and Sch. 1, para. 202 and repealed by CTA 2009, s. 1326 and Sch. 3, Pt. 1.]

History – S. 589B(1)–(4A) omitted by ITEPA 2003, Sch. 6, para. 70(2) and repealed by ITEPA 2003, Sch. 8, Pt. 1 which have effect, for income tax purposes, for the tax year 2003–04 and subsequent tax years, and, for corporation tax purposes, for accounting periods ending after 5 April 2003.
S. 589B(5) omitted by CTA 2009, s. 1322 and Sch. 1, para. 202 and repealed by CTA 2009, s. 1326 and Sch. 3, Pt. 1, with effect for corporation tax purposes for accounting periods ending on or after 1 April 2009, and for income tax and capital gains tax purposes for the tax year 2009–10 and subsequent tax years.

Notes – S. 589B(1) is spent and so has not been rewritten into the provisions of ITEPA 2003.
S. 589B(2): ITEPA 2003, s. 310(2) to (5).
S. 589B(3) is unnecessary and so has not been rewritten into the provisions of ITEPA 2003.
S. 589B(4): ITEPA 2003, s. 310(6), s. 329(5) and s. 353(4).
S. 589B(4A): ITEPA 2003, s. 310(7).
S. 589B(5): ITTOIA 2005, s. 73(1).
In s. 589B(5), the former words "this section or", which preceded the words "section 589A", are incorporated into the rewrite-provision of ITEPA 2003, s. 5.
S. 589B rewritten for corporation tax purposes as follows:
S. 589B(5): CTA 2009, s. 73(1).

PART XIV – PENSION SCHEMES, SOCIAL SECURITY BENEFITS, LIFE ANNUITIES ETC.

Chapter I – Retirement Benefit Schemes

Cross references – FA 2004, s. 283 and Sch. 36, para. 1(a): any pension scheme which, immediately before 6 April 2006, is a retirement benefits scheme approved for the purposes of Chapter 1 of Pt. 14 is to be treated as becoming a registered pension scheme on that date.
FA 2004, s. 283 and Sch. 36, para. 4: (continuity of administration) the person or persons who administer; or who are responsible for; a pension scheme immediately before 6 April 2006, are treated as becoming the scheme administrators on that date.
FA 2004, s. 283 and Sch. 36, para. 6: (continuity of obligation) any liabilities or obligations of the administrator of a Chapter 1 of Pt. 14 approved retirement benefits scheme, incurred in relation to the scheme before 6 April 2006, are to be treated as liabilities and obligations of the administrator of the registered pension scheme from that date.
FA 2003, Sch. 24, para. 8(b): disapplication of rules in Sch. 24 that restrict the deduction allowable for contributions towards employee benefits where the contribution is made to a retirement benefits scheme under ICTA 1988, Pt. 14, Ch. 1.
FA 2000, Sch. 8, para. 83(2)(a): partnership share money deducted from an employee's salary in accordance with a partnership share agreement under an employee share ownership plan is disregarded for the purposes of ascertaining the employee's remuneration for the purposes of Pt. XIV, Ch. I.
Electricity Act 1989, Sch. 15: power of Secretary of State to make regulations amending the Scottish Pension Schemes to secure that they continue to be approved for the purposes of (inter alia) Pt. XIV, Ch. I, notwithstanding privatisation.
SI 1989/469: application of ICTA 1988, Pt. XIV, Ch. I to PEP feeder funds.
SI 1996/1584: application of ICTA 1988, Pt. XIV, Ch. I to pension funds pooling schemes.

Extra-statutory concessions – A95: where members of certain small lump sum retirement benefits schemes are also contributing to a personal pension or retirement annuity scheme, they may be able to retain their pensions provided they give up their entitlement to lump sum benefits under the retirement benefits scheme.

APPROVAL OF SCHEMES

590 Conditions for approval of retirement benefit schemes

590 [Repealed by FA 2004, s. 326 and Sch. 42, Pt. 3.]

History – S. 590 repealed by FA 2004, s. 326 and Sch. 42, Pt. 3, with effect from 6 April 2006 (subject to FA 2004, Sch. 36).

Derivations – Former s. 590(1): FA 1970, s. 19(1), as substituted by FA 1971, s. 21(2).
Former s. 590(2), as originally enacted: FA 1970, s. 19(2)(a)–(e), (g).
Former s. 590(3), as originally enacted: FA 1970, s. 19(2A), (2B), as inserted by FA 1971, s. 21, and as amended by F(No. 2)A 1987, s. 58 and Sch. 3, para. 1.
Former s. 590(4): FA 1970, s. 19(2A), as inserted by FA 1971, s. 21(3).
Former s. 590(7): FA 1970, s. 19(5).

590A Section 590: supplementary provisions

590A [Repealed by FA 2004, s. 326 and Sch. 42, Pt. 3.]

History – S. 590A repealed by FA 2004, s. 326 and Sch. 42, Pt. 3, with effect from 6 April 2006 (subject to FA 2004, Sch. 36).

590B Section 590: further supplementary provisions

590B [Repealed by FA 2004, s. 326 and Sch. 42, Pt. 3.]

History – S. 590B repealed by FA 2004, s. 326 and Sch. 42, Pt. 3, with effect from 6 April 2006 (subject to FA 2004, Sch. 36).

590C Earnings cap

590C [Repealed by FA 2004, s. 326 and Sch. 42, Pt. 3.]

History – S. 590C repealed by FA 2004, s. 326 and Sch. 42, Pt. 3, with effect from 6 April 2006 (subject to FA 2004, Sch. 36).

591 Discretionary approval

591 [Repealed by FA 2004, s. 326 and Sch. 42, Pt. 3.]

History – S. 591 repealed by FA 2004, s. 326 and Sch. 42, Pt. 3, with effect from 6 April 2006 (subject to FA 2004, Sch. 36).

Derivations – Former s. 591(1): FA 1970, s. 20(1), as amended by F(No. 2)A 1987, s. 58 and Sch. 3, para. 3(2).
Former s. 591(2): FA 1970, s. 20(2), as substituted by FA 1971, s. 21(4), para. (g) substituted and para. (h) inserted by F(No. 2)A 1987, s. 58 and Sch. 3, para. 3(3), (4).
Former s. 591(3): FA 1970, s. 20(2A), as inserted by FA 1981, s. 32(2), as amended by Insurance Companies Act 1982, s. 99(1), Sch. 4, para. 22.
Former s. 591(4): FA 1970, s. 20(3), as amended by FA 1987, s. 71 and Sch. 15, para. 3.
Former s. 591(5), (6): FA 1970, s. 20(4)–(6), as inserted by F(No. 2)A 1987, s. 58 and Sch. 3, para. 3(5).

591A Effect on approved schemes of regulations under section 591

591A [Repealed by FA 2004, s. 326 and Sch. 42, Pt. 3.]

History – S. 591A repealed by FA 2004, s. 326 and Sch. 42, Pt. 3, with effect from 6 April 2006 (subject to FA 2004, Sch. 36).

591B Cessation of approval: general provisions

591B [Repealed by FA 2004, s. 326 and Sch. 42, Pt. 3.]

History – S. 591B repealed by FA 2004, s. 326 and Sch. 42, Pt. 3, with effect from 6 April 2006 (subject to FA 2004, Sch. 36).

591C Cessation of approval: tax on certain schemes

591C [Repealed by FA 2004, s. 326 and Sch. 42, Pt. 3.]

History – S. 591C repealed by FA 2004, s. 326 and Sch. 42, Pt. 3, with effect from 6 April 2006 (subject to FA 2004, Sch. 36).

591D Section 591C: supplementary

591D [Repealed by FA 2004, s. 326 and Sch. 42, Pt. 3.]

History – S. 591D repealed by FA 2004, s. 326 and Sch. 42, Pt. 3, with effect from 6 April 2006 (subject to FA 2004, Sch. 36).
Notes – Former s. 591D(6) rewritten as ITEPA 2003, s. 397(9).

TAX RELIEFS

592 Exempt approved schemes

592 [Repealed by FA 2004, s. 326 and Sch. 42, Pt. 3.]

History – S. 592 repealed by FA 2004, s. 326 and Sch. 42, Pt. 3, with effect from 6 April 2006 (subject to FA 2004, Sch. 36).
Derivations – Former s. 592(1)–(6): FA 1970, s. 21(1)–(3), as inserted (s. 21(2A)) by FA 1971, s. 21(5).
Former s. 592(7): FA 1970, s. 21(4), as amended by F(No. 2)A 1987, s. 58; Sch. 3, para. 4(1) and Sch. 9, Pt. I.
Former s. 592(8) (as originally enacted), (9): FA 1970, s. 21(4A), (5), as inserted (s. 21(4A)) by F(No. 2)A 1987, s. 58 and Sch. 3, para. 4(1).
Former s. 592(10)–(12): FA 1970, s. 21(7A)–(9), as inserted (s. 21(7A)) by F.(No. 2) A. 1987, s. 58 and Sch. 3, para. 5.

593 Relief by way of deductions from contributions

593 [Repealed by FA 2004, s. 326 and Sch. 42, Pt. 3.]

History – S. 593 repealed by FA 2004, s. 326 and Sch. 42, Pt. 3, with effect from 6 April 2006 (subject to FA 2004, Sch. 36).
Derivations – FA 1970, Sch. 5, Pt. II, para. 6A, as inserted by F(No. 2)A 1987, s. 58 and Sch. 3, para. 12.

594 Exempt statutory schemes

594 [Repealed by FA 2004, s. 326 and Sch. 42, Pt. 3.]

History – S. 594 repealed by FA 2004, s. 326 and Sch. 42, Pt. 3, with effect from 6 April 2006 (subject to FA 2004, Sch. 36).
Derivations – Former s. 594(1): FA 1970, s. 22(2), as amended by FA 1972, s. 74(3) and by F(No. 2)A 1987, s. 58 and Sch. 3, para. 6(1).
Former s. 594(2): FA 1970, s. 22(2A), as inserted by F(No. 2)A 1987, s. 58 and Sch. 3, para. 6(1).

CHARGE TO TAX IN CERTAIN CASES

595 Charge to tax in respect of certain sums paid by employer etc.

595 [Omitted by ITEPA 2003, Sch. 6, para. 74 and repealed by ITEPA 2003, Sch. 8, Pt. 1.]

History – S. 595 omitted by ITEPA 2003, Sch. 6, para. 74 and repealed by ITEPA 2003, Sch. 8, Pt. 1 which have effect for the tax year 2003–04 and subsequent tax years.
Cross references – ITEPA 2003, s. 394A: pre-December 1993 schemes – chargeability of certain lump sums.
ITEPA 2003, s. 395: application of sections 396 and 397 – general rules.
ITEPA 2003, Sch. 7, para. 41 (Sch. 7: transitionals and savings): benefits from non-approved pension schemes.
Notes – S. 595 rewritten as follows:
S. 595(1): ITEPA 2003, s. 7(6), s. 10(3) and s. 386(1) to (4). For the purposes of the references made in ITEPA 2003, s. 394A and s. 395, the former s. 595(1) is reproduced in the History Note above; ITEPA 2003, s. 394A is inserted, as a modification, by ITEPA 2003, Sch. 7, para. 41.
S. 595(2) and (3) were repealed by FA 1989, Sch. 6, para. 7 and so have not been rewritten.
S. 595(4): ITEPA 2003, s. 388.
S. 595(5): ITEPA 2003, s. 386(6).

596 Exceptions from section 595

596 [Omitted by ITEPA 2003, Sch. 6, para. 74 and repealed by ITEPA 2003, Sch. 8, Pt. 1.]

History – S. 596 omitted by ITEPA 2003, Sch. 6, para. 74 and repealed by ITEPA 2003, Sch. 8, Pt. 1 which have effect for the tax year 2003–04 and subsequent tax years.
Notes – S. 596 rewritten as follows:
S. 596(1): ITEPA 2003, s. 386(1) and s. 387(2).
S. 596(2): ITEPA 2003, s. 389, s. 390 and s. 721(1) ("foreign employer").
S. 596(3): ITEPA 2003, s. 392(1) to (5).
S. 596(4): ITEPA 2003, s. 392(6) and (7).

596A Charge to tax: benefits under non-approved schemes

596A [Omitted by ITEPA 2003, Sch. 6, para. 75 and repealed by ITEPA 2003, Sch. 8, Pt. 1.]

History – S. 596A omitted by ITEPA 2003, Sch. 6, para. 75 and repealed by ITEPA 2003, Sch. 8, Pt. 1 which has effect for the tax year 2003–04 and subsequent tax years.
Notes – S. 596A rewritten as follows:
S. 596A(1): ITEPA 2003, s. 393(1), s. 394(1), (2), (3) and s. 400(1).
S. 596A(2): ITEPA 2003, s. 7(6), s. 10(3), s. 393(1), s. 394(1) and (3).

S. 596A(3): ITEPA 2003, s. 394(2) and (3).
S. 596A(4): ITEPA 2003, s. 398.
S. 596A(5): ITEPA 2003, s. 394(3) and (4).
S. 596A(6): ITEPA 2003, s. 393(2).
S. 596A(7) is unnecessary and so has not been rewritten into the provisions of ITEPA 2003.
S. 596A(8): ITEPA 2003, s. 395(2), (3), (4), s. 396(1), s. 397(2) to (5) and s. 400(1).
S. 596A(9): ITEPA 2003, s. 395(3), (4) and s. 397(1).
S. 596A(10): ITEPA 2003, s. 397(2), (3) and (4).
S. 596A(11): ITEPA 2003, s. 397(5) and s. 400(1).
S. 596A(12) and (13): ITEPA 2003, s. 397(6).
S. 596A(14): ITEPA 2003, s. 397(7).
S. 596A(15): ITEPA 2003, s. 395(5), s. 396(2) and s. 397(8).
S. 596A(16): ITEPA 2003, s. 718.
S. 596A(17): ITEPA 2003, s. 397(10).

596B Section 596A: supplementary provisions

596B [Omitted by ITEPA 2003, Sch. 6, para. 75 and repealed by ITEPA 2003, Sch. 8, Pt. 1.]

History – S. 596B omitted by ITEPA 2003, Sch. 6, para. 75 and repealed by ITEPA 2003, Sch. 8, Pt. 1 which have effect for the tax year 2003–04 and subsequent tax years.

Notes – S. 596B rewritten as ITEPA 2003, s. 398, s. 415(3) to (7) and s. 718.

596C Notional interest treated as paid if amount charged in respect of beneficial loan

596C [Omitted by ITEPA 2003, Sch. 6, para. 75 and repealed by ITEPA 2003, Sch. 8, Pt. 1.]

History – S. 596C omitted by ITEPA 2003, Sch. 6, para. 75 and repealed by ITEPA 2003, Sch. 8, Pt. 1 which have effect for the tax year 2003–04 and subsequent tax years.

Notes – S. 596C rewritten as ITEPA 2003, s. 399.

ICTA 1988

597 Charge to tax: pensions

597 [Omitted by ITEPA 2003, Sch. 6, para. 76 and repealed by ITEPA 2003, Sch. 8, Pt. 1.]

History – S. 597 omitted by ITEPA 2003, Sch. 6, para. 76 and repealed by ITEPA 2003, Sch. 8, Pt. 1 which have effect for the tax year 2003–04 and subsequent tax years.

Notes – S. 597 rewritten as follows:
S. 597(1): ITEPA 2003, s. 580(a).
S. 597(2) is unnecessary and so has not been rewritten.
S. 597(3): ITEPA 2003, s. 580(b).

598 Charge to tax: repayment of employee's contributions

598 [Repealed by FA 2004, s. 326 and Sch. 42, Pt. 3.]

History – S. 598 repealed by FA 2004, s. 326 and Sch. 42, Pt. 3, with effect from 6 April 2006 (subject to FA 2004, Sch. 36).

Derivations – FA 1970, Sch. 5, Pt. II, para. 2(1)–(4), (5)(a), (6), (7), as substituted by FA 1971, s. 21 and Sch. 3, para. 7.

599 Charge to tax: commutation of entire pension in special circumstances

599 [Repealed by FA 2004, s. 326 and Sch. 42, Pt. 3.]

History – S. 599 repealed by FA 2004, s. 326 and Sch. 42, Pt. 3, with effect from 6 April 2006 (subject to FA 2004, Sch. 36).

Derivations – Former s. 599(1)–(6): FA 1970, Sch. 5, Pt. II, para. 3(1)–(5), as substituted by FA 1971, s. 21 and Sch. 3, para. 7, as amended (s. 599(1)) by F(No. 2)A 1987, s. 58 and Sch. 3, para. 9(1).
Former s. 599(7), (8): FA 1970, Sch. 5, Pt. II, para. 3(7), (8), as inserted by F(No. 2)A 1987, s. 58 and Sch. 3, para. 10.
Former s. 599(9): FA 1970, Sch. 5, Pt. II, para. 3(1)(i).

599A Charge to tax: payments out of surplus funds

599A [Repealed by FA 2004, s. 326 and Sch. 42, Pt. 3.]

History – S. 599A repealed by FA 2004, s. 326 and Sch. 42, Pt. 3, with effect from 6 April 2006 (subject to FA 2004, Sch. 36).

Notes – S. 599A rewritten as follows:
S. 599A(5): ITEPA 2003, s. 624, s. 625 and s. 626(1).
S. 599A(6): ITEPA 2003, s. 626(2).
S. 599A(8): ITEPA 2003, s. 625.

600 Charge to tax: unauthorised payments to or for employees

600 [Omitted by ITEPA 2003, Sch. 6, para. 78 and repealed by ITEPA 2003, Sch. 8, Pt. 1.]

History – S. 600 omitted by ITEPA 2003, Sch. 6, para. 78 and repealed by ITEPA 2003, Sch. 8, Pt. 1 which have effect for the tax year 2003–04 and subsequent tax years.

Notes – S. 600 rewritten as follows:
S. 600(1): ITEPA 2003, s. 583(3), (4), (5), s. 586(1) and s. 593(1).
S. 600(2): ITEPA 2003, s. 583(3), s. 584, s. 585 and s. 593(1).
S. 600(3): ITEPA 2003, s. 583(6).
S. 600(4): ITEPA 2003, s. 583(7), s. 584 and s. 593(3).

601 Charge to tax: payments to employers

601 [Repealed by FA 2004, s. 326 and Sch. 42, Pt. 3.]

History – S. 601 repealed by FA 2004, s. 326 and Sch. 42, Pt. 3, with effect from 6 April 2006 (subject to FA 2004, Sch. 36).

Derivations – Former s. 601(1)–(4): FA 1986, Sch. 12, para. 1(1)–(3), (5)–(8), (11)–(13).
Former s. 601(5): FA 1986, Sch. 12, para. 1(4) and FA 1970, Sch. 5, para. 4(1), as amended by FA 1971, Sch. 3, para. 12(5)(a), para. 4(2).
Former s. 601(6): FA 1986, Sch. 12, para. 1(9), 3 and FA 1970, Sch. 5, para. 4(3), as inserted by FA 1971, Sch. 3, para. 12(5)(b).

PENSION FUND SURPLUSES

602 Regulations relating to surpluses

602 [Repealed by FA 2004, s. 326 and Sch. 42, Pt. 3.]

History – S. 602 repealed by FA 2004, s. 326 and Sch. 42, Pt. 3, with effect from 6 April 2006 (subject to FA 2004, Sch. 36).

Derivations – FA 1986, Sch. 12, para. 2(1), (2), (4)–(6), and (s. 602(1)), 3(2).

603 Reduction of surpluses

603 [Repealed by FA 2004, s. 326 and Sch. 42, Pt. 3.]

History – S. 603 repealed by FA 2004, s. 326 and Sch. 42, Pt. 3, with effect from 6 April 2006 (subject to FA 2004, Sch. 36).

SUPPLEMENTARY PROVISIONS

604 Application for approval of a scheme

604 [Repealed by FA 2004, s. 326 and Sch. 42, Pt. 3.]

History – S. 604 repealed by FA 2004, s. 326 and Sch. 42, Pt. 3, with effect from 6 April 2006 (subject to FA 2004, Sch. 36).

Derivations – FA 1970, Sch. 5, para. 6, as amended by F(No. 2)A 1987, s. 58 and Sch. 3, para. 11.

605 Information

605 [Repealed by FA 2004, s. 326 and Sch. 42, Pt. 3.]

History – S. 605 repealed by FA 2004, s. 326 and Sch. 42, Pt. 3, with effect from 6 April 2006 (subject to FA 2004, Sch. 36).

Derivations – Former s. 605(1), (2): FA 1970, Sch. 5, para. 7 (para. 7(2) inserted by F(No. 2)A 1987, s. 58 and Sch. 3, para. 13).
Former s. 605(3), (4), as originally enacted: FA 1970, Sch. 5, para. 8(1)–(3), as amended (para. 8(2)) by F(No. 2)A 1987, s. 58 and Sch. 3, para. 14.

605A False statements etc.

605A [Repealed by FA 2004, s. 326 and Sch. 42, Pt. 3.]

History – S. 605A repealed by FA 2004, s. 326 and Sch. 42, Pt. 3, with effect from 6 April 2006 (subject to FA 2004, Sch. 36).

606 Default of administrator etc.

606 [Repealed by FA 2004, s. 326 and Sch. 42, Pt. 3.]

History – S. 606 repealed by FA 2004, s. 326 and Sch. 42, Pt. 3, with effect from 6 April 2006 (subject to FA 2004, Sch. 36).

Derivations – Former s. 606(1)–(3): FA 1970, Sch. 5, para. 9, as inserted (para. 9(1)) by F(No. 2)A 1987, s. 58 and Sch. 3, para. 15.

606A Recourse to scheme members

606A [Repealed by FA 2004, s. 326 and Sch. 42, Pt. 3.]

History – S. 606A repealed by FA 2004, s. 326 and Sch. 42, Pt. 3, with effect from 6 April 2006 (subject to FA 2004, Sch. 36).

607 Pilots' benefit fund

607 [Repealed by FA 2004, s. 326 and Sch. 42, Pt. 3.]

History – S. 607 repealed by FA 2004, s. 326 and Sch. 42, Pt. 3, with effect from 6 April 2006 (subject to FA 2004, Sch. 36).

Derivations – Former s. 607(1)–(3): FA 1980, s. 35(1)–(3), and (s. 607(3)) Pilotage Act 1987, Sch. 2, para. 4.
Former s. 607(4): FA 1980, s. 35(4), as amended by Pilotage Act 1983, Sch. 3.

Notes – S. 607(3)(b)(iv) is unnecessary and so has not been rewritten into the provisions of ITEPA 2003.

608 Superannuation funds approved before 6th April 1980

608 [Repealed by FA 2004, s. 326 and Sch. 42, Pt. 3.]

History – S. 608 repealed by FA 2004, s. 326 and Sch. 42, Pt. 3, with effect from 6 April 2006 (subject to FA 2004, Sch. 36).

Derivations – FA 1980, s. 36(1), (2), (4), (6), as amended (s. 36(1)) by FA 1987, Sch. 16, Pt. VII.

Notes – S. 608(4) rewritten as ITEPA 2003, s. 590 and s. 591.

609 Schemes approved before 23rd July 1987

609 [Repealed by FA 2004, s. 326 and Sch. 42, Pt. 3.]

History – S. 609 repealed by FA 2004, s. 326 and Sch. 42, Pt. 3, with effect from 6 April 2006 (subject to FA 2004, Sch. 36).

610 Amendments of schemes

610 [Repealed by FA 2004, s. 326 and Sch. 42, Pt. 3.]

History – S. 610 repealed by FA 2004, s. 326 and Sch. 42, Pt. 3 with effect from 6 April 2006 (subject to FA 2004, Sch. 36).
Derivations – FA 1971, s. 22(1)–(3).

611 Definition of "retirement benefits scheme"

611 [Repealed by FA 2004, s. 326 and Sch. 42, Pt. 3.]

History – S. 611 repealed by FA 2004, s. 326 and Sch. 42, Pt. 3, with effect from 6 April 2006 (subject to FA 2004, Sch. 36).
Derivations – Former s. 611(1)–(4): FA 1970, s. 25.
Former s. 611(5): FA 1971, Sch. 3, para. 5(2).

611AA Definition of the administrator

611AA [Repealed by FA 2004, s. 326 and Sch. 42, Pt. 3.]

History – S. 611AA repealed by FA 2004, s. 326 and Sch. 42, Pt. 3, with effect from 6 April 2006 (subject to FA 2004, Sch. 36).

611A Definition of relevant statutory scheme

611A [Repealed by FA 2004, s. 326 and Sch. 42, Pt. 3.]

History – S. 611A repealed by FA 2004, s. 326 and Sch. 42, Pt. 3, with effect from 6 April 2006 (subject to FA 2004, Sch. 36).

612 Other interpretative provisions, and regulations for purposes of this Chapter

612 [Repealed by FA 2004, s. 326 and Sch. 42, Pt. 3.]

History – S. 612 repealed by FA 2004, s. 326 and Sch. 42, Pt. 3, with effect from 6 April 2006 (subject to FA 2004, Sch. 36)
Derivations – Former s. 612(1): FA 1970, s. 26(1), as amended by F(No. 2)A 1987, s. 58 and Sch. 3, para. 7(2), (3); FA 1973, Sch. 22, Pt. II; FA 1971, Sch. 3, para. 12(4); FA 1986, Sch. 12, para. 1(10) and Northern Ireland Constitution Act 1973, Sch. 5, para. 8.
Former s. 612(2): FA 1970, s. 26(2), as amended by F(No. 2)A 1987, Sch. 3, para. 8.
Former s. 612(3): FA 1970, Sch. 5, Pt. II, para. 10 and FA 1971, Sch. 3, para. 13(3).

Chapter II – Other Pension Funds and Social Security Benefits and Contributions

613 Parliamentary pension funds

613(1) The salary of a Member of the House of Commons shall, for all the purposes of the Income Tax Acts, be treated as reduced by the amounts deducted in pursuance of section 4 of the House of Commons Members' Fund Act 2016; but a Member shall not by reason of any such deduction be entitled to relief under any other provision of the Income Tax Acts.

613(2) In subsection (1) above the reference to salary shall be construed as mentioned in subsection (3) of section 1 of the House of Commons Members' Fund Act 1939, the reference to amounts deducted includes a reference to amounts required to be set aside under that subsection, and "deduction" shall be construed accordingly.

613(3) [Omitted by ITEPA 2003, Sch. 6, para. 83 and repealed by ITEPA 2003, Sch. 8, Pt. 1.]

613(4) The trustees of–

(a) the House of Commons Members' Fund specified in section 1 of the 2016 Act;

(b) [omitted by FA 2004, s. 281 and Sch. 35, para. 26(a); and repealed by FA 2004, s. 326 and Sch. 42, Pt. 3;]

(bb) [omitted by FA 2004, s. 281 and Sch. 35, para. 26(a); and repealed by FA 2004, s. 326 and Sch. 42, Pt. 3;]

(c) [omitted by FA 2004, s. 281 and Sch. 35, para. 26(a); and repealed by FA 2004, s. 326 and Sch. 42, Pt. 3;]

(d) [omitted by FA 2004, s. 281 and Sch. 35, para. 26(a); and repealed by FA 2004, s. 326 and Sch. 42, Pt. 3;]

shall be entitled to exemption from income tax in respect of all income derived from that Fund or any investment of that Fund.

A claim under this subsection shall be made to the Board.

History – In s. 613(1), the words "amounts deducted in pursuance of section 4 of the House of Commons Members' Fund Act 2016" substituted for the words "amounts deducted in pursuance of section 1 of the House of Commons Members' Fund Act 1939" by the House of Commons Members' Fund Act 2016, s. 8(2)(a), with effect at the end of the period of three months beginning with 12 May 2016 (Royal Assent).

S. 613(1) and (2) treated as not having been repealed by ITEPA 2003 (see Note below) by FA 2005, s. 101 and Sch. 10, para. 63, with effect from 7 April 2005 (Royal Assent)

S. 613(2) omitted by the House of Commons Members' Fund Act 2016, s. 8(2)(b), with effect at the end of the period of three months beginning with 12 May 2016 (Royal Assent). Former s. 613(2) read as follows:

"**613(2)** In subsection (1) above the reference to salary shall be construed as mentioned in subsection (3) of section 1 of the House of Commons Members' Fund Act 1939, the reference to amounts deducted includes a reference to amounts required to be set aside under that subsection, and "deduction" shall be construed accordingly.".

S. 613(1)–(3) omitted by ITEPA 2003, Sch. 6, para. 83 and repealed by ITEPA 2003, Sch. 8, Pt. 1 which have effect for the tax year 2003–04 and subsequent tax years.

In s. 613(4)(a), the words "specified in section 1 of the 2016 Act" substituted for the words "established under section 1 of that Act of 1939" by the House of Commons Members' Fund Act 2016, s. 8(2)(c), with effect at the end of the period of three months beginning with 12 May 2016 (Royal Assent).

In s. 613(4), the word "respective" preceding "trustees" and para. (b), (bb), (c) and (d) omitted by FA 2004, s. 281 and Sch. 35, para. 26(a); and repealed by FA 2004, s. 326 and Sch. 42, Pt. 3, with effect from 6 April 2006 (subject to FA 2004, Sch. 36).

In s. 613(4), in both places, the words "that Fund" substituted for the words "those funds" by FA 2004, s. 281 and Sch. 35, para. 26(b), with effect from 6 April 2006 (subject to FA 2004, Sch. 36).

Former s. 613(4)(bb) inserted, and in the closing words of s. 613(4) "funds" substituted for "Funds", by FA 1999, s. 52 and Sch. 5, para. 4, with effect for the year 1999–2000 and subsequent years of assessment.

Derivations – ICTA 1970, s. 211(1), (2), (4), as amended (s. 211(2)) by FA 1981, s. 50(1); Parliamentary and other Pensions Act 1972, s. 1, 36(1)(a) and Sch. 3; Parliamentary and other Pensions Act 1987, s. 6(1) and Sch. 3, para. 2(1).

Cross references – FA 2004, s. 283 and Sch. 36, para. 1: any pension scheme which, immediately before 6 April 2006, is a scheme or fund mentioned in s. 613(4)(b) to (d) is to be treated as becoming a registered pension scheme on that date.

FA 2004, s. 283 and Sch. 36, para. 4: (continuity of administration) the person or persons who administer; or who are responsible for; a pension scheme immediately before 6 April 2006, are treated as becoming the scheme administrators on that date.

FA 2004, s. 283 and Sch. 36, para. 6: (continuity of obligation) any liabilities or obligations of the administrator of the scheme or fund as in s. 613(4)(b) to (d), incurred in relation to the scheme before 6 April 2006, are to be treated as liabilities and obligations of the administrator of the registered pension scheme from that date.

S. 56(3)(b): exemption from Sch. D, Case VI charge on profits or gains arising from the disposal of rights connected with certificates of deposit.

S. 118G: payments exempt under s. 613(4) are not chargeable payments/receipts under the rules for paying and collecting agents.

S. 129B: exempt income under s. 613(4) includes stocklending fees.

S. 349B(3)(j): payment under s. 349A to trustees of an exempt Parliamentary pension fund within s. 613(4) may be made without deduction of tax.

S. 659A(1): "investment" in s. 613(4) includes futures contracts and options contracts, and income derived from transactions relating to such contracts regarded as income derived from (or income from) such contracts.

S. 659D(2): exemption under s. 613(4) does not apply to property investment LLPs.

S. 730A(7), 737D(1): power of Treasury to determine extent to which relief under s. 613(4) applies to price differential on sale and repurchase of securities treated as income under s. 730A(2), and to manufactured payments.

TMA 1970, s. 42: procedure for making claims.

TCGA 1992, s. 271(1)(b): exemption from capital gains tax for fund mentioned in s. 613(4).

FA 1996, Sch. 13, para. 7: treatment of losses on relevant discounted securities where income is exempt.

Extra-statutory concessions – C19: exemption where manufactured payments received by approved pension fund under terms of a stock lending arrangement approved within s. 129, to extent that dividends on interest arising would have been exempt under s. 613(4).

Notes – S. 613 rewritten as follows:

S. 613(1) and (2) are unnecessary and so have not been rewritten.

S. 613(3): ITEPA 2003, s. 619 and s. 621.

S. 235, 237: disallowance of relief in s. 613(4) in case of dividend stripping etc.

614 Exemptions and reliefs in respect of income from investments etc. of certain pension schemes

614(1) [Repealed by FA 1994, s. 258 and Sch. 26, Pt. V(22).]

614(2) Any interest or dividends received by the person in whom is vested any of the Family Pension Funds mentioned in section 273 of the Government of India Act 1935, and having effect as a scheme made under section 2 of the Overseas Pensions Act 1973, on sums forming part of that fund shall be exempt from income tax.

614(2A) The reference in subsection (2) above to interest on sums forming part of a fund include references to any amount which is treated as income by virtue of Chapter 8 of Part 4 of ITTOIA 2005 (profits from deeply discounted securities) and derives from any investment forming part of that fund.

614(3) Income derived from investments or deposits of any fund referred to in section 648, 649, 650 or 651 of ITEPA 2003 shall not be charged to income tax, and any income tax deducted from any such income shall be repaid by the Board to the persons entitled to receive the income.

614(4) In respect of income derived from investments or deposits of the Overseas Service Pensions Fund established pursuant to section 7(1) of the Overseas Aid Act 1966, the Board shall give by way of repayment such relief from income tax as is necessary to secure that the income is exempt to the like extent (if any) as if it were income of a person not domiciled and not resident in the United Kingdom.

614(5) In respect of dividends and other income derived from investments, deposits or other property of a superannuation fund to which section 615(3) applies the Board shall give by way of repayment such relief from income tax as is necessary to secure that the income is exempt to the like extent (if any) as if it were income of a person not domiciled and not resident in the United Kingdom.

614(6) A claim under this section shall be made to the Board.

History – S. 614(1) repealed by FA 1994, s. 258 and Sch. 26, Pt. V(22), with effect from 3 May 1994.
In s. 614(2A) the words "Chapter 8 of Part 4 of ITTOIA 2005 profits from deeply" substituted by ITTOIA 2005, s. 882(1) and Sch. 1, para. 261; effective for income tax purposes for 2005–06 onwards and for corporation tax purposes for accounting periods ending after 5 April 2005 (ITTOIA 2005, s. 883(1)).
S. 614(2A) inserted by FA 1996, s. 104 and Sch. 14 para. 34 for 1996–97 and later years of assessment, subject to FA 1996, Sch. 15.
In s. 614(3), the words "section 648, 649, 650 or 651 of ITEPA 2003" substituted for the words "paragraph (b), (c), (d) or (f) of subsection (2) of section 615" by ITEPA 2003, Sch. 6, para. 84 which has effect for the tax year 2003–04 and subsequent tax years.
In s. 614(4) the words "not domiciled and not resident" substituted for the words "not domiciled, ordinarily resident or resident" by FA 2013, s. 219 and Sch. 46, para. 28(a), with effect for the purposes of a person's liability to income tax for the tax year 2013–14 or any subsequent tax year but without prejudice to any provision of FA 2013, Sch. 46, Pt. 2 about the application of a particular amendment (and subject to the savings at FA 2013, Sch. 46, para. 73).
In s. 614(5) the words "not domiciled and not resident" substituted for the words "not domiciled, ordinarily resident or resident" by FA 2013, s. 219 and Sch. 46, para. 28, with effect for the purposes of a person's liability to income tax for the tax year 2013–14 or any subsequent tax year but without prejudice to any provision of FA 2013, Sch. 46, Pt. 2 about the application of a particular amendment (and subject to the savings at FA 2013, Sch. 46, para. 73).

Derivations – S. 614(1): ICTA 1970, s. 212(1), as amended by SS(CP)A 1975, s. 3 and Sch. 2, para. 38.
S. 614(2): ICTA 1970, s. 213(1) and Overseas Pensions Act 1973, s. 2.
S. 614(3): ICTA 1970, s. 214(2), 216(2), as amended by FA 1973, s. 53(1).
S. 614(4): ICTA 1970, s. 217(2), (4).
S. 614(5): ICTA 1970, s. 218(1).
S. 614(6): ICTA 1970, s. 212(3), 213(1), 214(3), 216(2), 217(2), 218(1), as amended by FA 1987, Sch. 15, para. 2(13).

Cross references – S. 56(3)(b): exemption from Sch. D, Case VI charge on profits or gains arising from the disposal of rights connected with certificates of deposit for schemes or funds under s. 614(1)–(3). S. 614(1) formerly exempted income receivable from any source for the purposes of any supplementary scheme under SSA 1975, s. 158 or Social Security (Northern Ireland) Act 1975, s. 149, by the body charged with the administration of the scheme.
S. 118G: payments exempt under s. 614(2)-(4) are not chargeable payments/receipts under the rules for paying and collecting agents.
S. 129B: exempt income under s. 614(3) includes stocklending fees.
S. 235, 237: disallowance of relief in case of dividend stripping etc.
S. 349B(3)(k): payment under s. 349A to persons entitled to receive the income of an exempt scheme within s. 614(3) may be made without deduction of tax.
S. 659A(1): "investments" in s. 614(3), (4) includes futures contracts and options contracts, and income derived from transactions relating to such contracts regarded as income derived from (or income from) such contracts.
S. 659D(2): exemption under s. 614(3), (4), (5) does not apply to property investment LLPs.
S. 730A(7), 737D(1): power of Treasury to determine extent to which relief under s. 614(2), (3), (4) applies to price differential on sale and repurchase of securities treated as income under s. 730A(2) and to manufactured payments.
TMA 1970, s. 42: procedure for making claims etc.
TCGA 1992, s. 271(1)(b), (c): exemption from capital gains tax for schemes or funds under s. 614(1), (2).
FA 1996, Sch. 13, para. 7: treatment of losses on relevant discounted securities where income is exempt.
Government of India Act 1935, s. 273(1): the Indian Military Widows and Orphans Fund, Superior Services (India) Family Pension Fund, Indian Military Family Pension Fund, Indian Civil Service Family Pension Fund.
Overseas Pensions Act 1973, s. 2 and Sch. 1: schemes established by the Secretary of State providing pensions for persons including those entitled under Government of India Act 1935, s. 273.
SSA 1975, s. 158 and Sch. 19; SSA (NI) 1975, s. 149 and Sch. 16: schemes supplementing the right of employed earners suffering industrial injuries, diseases, disablement or death. (Now repealed.)

Extra-statutory concessions – C19: exemption where manufactured payments received by approved pension fund under terms of a stock lending arrangement approved within s. 129, to extent that dividends or interest arising would have been exempt under s. 614(2), (3) or (4).

Notes – S. 614 formerly exempted income recoverable from any source for the purposes of any supplementary scheme under SSA 1975, s. 158 or Social Security (Northern Ireland) Act 1975, s. 149, by the body charged with the administration of the scheme.

615 Exemption from tax in respect of certain pensions

615(1) [Omitted by ITEPA 2003, Sch. 6, para. 85 and repealed by ITEPA 2003, Sch. 8, Pt. 1.]

615(2) [Omitted by ITEPA 2003, Sch. 6, para. 85 and repealed by ITEPA 2003, Sch. 8, Pt. 1.]

615(3) Where an annuity is paid from a superannuation fund to which this subsection applies to a person who is not resident in the United Kingdom, income tax shall not be deducted from any payment of the annuity or accounted for under Chapter 6 of Part 15 of ITA 2007 (deduction from annual payments and patent royalties) by the trustees or other persons having the control of the fund.

615(4) [Omitted by ITEPA 2003, Sch. 6, para. 85 and repealed by ITEPA 2003, Sch. 8, Pt. 1.]

615(5) [Omitted by ITEPA 2003, Sch. 6, para. 85 and repealed by ITEPA 2003, Sch. 8, Pt. 1.]

615(6) Subsection (3) above applies to any superannuation fund which–

(a) is bona fide established under irrevocable trusts in connection with some trade or undertaking carried on wholly or partly outside the United Kingdom;

(b) has for its sole purpose (subject to any enactment or Northern Ireland legislation requiring or allowing provision for the value of any rights to be transferred between schemes or between members of the same scheme) the provision of superannuation benefits in respect of persons' employment in the trade or undertaking wholly outside the United Kingdom; and

(c) is recognised by the employer and employed persons in the trade or undertaking;

and for the purposes of this subsection duties performed in the United Kingdom the performance of which is merely incidental to the performance of other duties outside the United Kingdom shall be treated as performed outside the United Kingdom.

615(7) In this section–

"pension" includes a gratuity or any sum payable on or in respect of death or, in the case of a pension falling within subsection (2)(g) above, ill-health, and a return of contributions with or without interest thereon or any other addition thereto;

"overseas territory" means any territory or country outside the United Kingdom;

"the Pensions (Increase) Acts" means the Pensions (Increase) Act 1971 and any Act passed after that Act for purposes corresponding to the purposes of that Act;

"United Kingdom trust territory" means a territory administered by the government of the United Kingdom under the trusteeship system of the United Nations.

615(8) [Omitted by ITEPA 2003, Sch. 6, para. 85 and repealed by ITEPA 2003, Sch. 8, Pt. 1.]

615(9) For the purposes of this section, a person shall be taken to be employed in the public service of an overseas territory at any time when–

(a) he is employed in any capacity under the government of that territory, or under any municipal or other local authority in it,

(b) he is employed, in circumstances not falling within paragraph (a) above, by a body corporate established for any public purpose in that territory by an enactment of a legislature empowered to make laws for that territory, or

(c) he is the holder of a public office in that territory in circumstances not falling within either paragraph (a) or (b).

615(10) For the purposes of subsection (9), references to the government of an overseas territory include references to a government constituted for two or more overseas territories, and to any authority established for the purpose of providing or administering services which are common to, or relate to matters of common interest to, two or more such territories.

History – S. 615(1) and (2) omitted by ITEPA 2003, Sch. 6, para. 85 and repealed by ITEPA 2003, Sch. 8, Pt. 1 which have effect for the tax year 2003–04 and subsequent tax years.
In s. 615(3), the words "Chapter 6 of Part 15 of ITA 2007 (deduction from annual payments and patent royalties)" substituted by ITA 2007, s. 1027 and Sch. 1, para. 140 with effect for 2007–08 and subsequent tax years.
S. 615(4) and (5) omitted by ITEPA 2003, Sch. 6, para. 85 and repealed by ITEPA 2003, Sch. 8, Pt. 1 which have effect for the tax year 2003–04 and subsequent tax years.
In s. 615(6)(b), words in parentheses inserted by FA 1999, s. 79 and Sch. 10, para. 11.
S. 615(8) omitted by ITEPA 2003, Sch. 6, para. 85 and repealed by ITEPA 2003, Sch. 8, Pt. 1 which have effect for the tax year 2003–04 and subsequent tax years.
S. 615(9) and (10) inserted, by International Development Act 2002, Sch. 3, para. 9 with effect from 17 June 2002.

Derivations – S. 615(3): ICTA 1970, s. 218(3).
S. 615(6): ICTA 1970, s. 218(4).
S. 615(7): ICTA 1970, s. 214(5), 215(3), 216(4) and Pensions (Increase) Act 1971.

Cross references – TMA 1970, Sch. 1A, para. 9(2): time for appealing inspector's amendment of claim regarding whether a fund is one to which s. 615(3) applies.
TMA 1970, s. 42: procedure for making claims.
IHTA 1984, s. 151, 152: treatment of overseas superannuation funds for inheritance tax.
TCGA 1992, Sch. 1, para. 2(7), (8): settlement comprising funds to which s. 615(3) applies is not grouped with others made by the same settlor in spreading the capital gains tax annual exemption.
FA 1989, s. 76(6B): deduction for expenses related to a superannuation fund which satisfies the requirements of s. 615(6).
Overseas Service Act 1958, s. 2, 4; Overseas Pensions Act 1973, s. 2: schemes established by the Secretary of State providing pensions for persons formerly engaged in overseas civilian or police service.
Overseas Aid Act 1966, s. 7(1): pensions payable to persons by reason of service in an overseas territory under an authority or body corporate approved in the Overseas Service Pensions Scheme.
Overseas Pensions Act 1973, s. 1: pensions payable in the UK by the UK Government under agreements with overseas governments.
Overseas Development and Co-operation Act 1980 s. 10(2): persons employed in public service if employed under the government or a local or municipal authority, by a body corporate established for public purpose or is otherwise the holder of a public office.
Pensions (India, Pakistan and Burma) Act 1985; Overseas Pensions Act 1973, s. 2: schemes established by the Secretary of State providing pensions for persons including those entitled under pensions arrangements in respect of sub-continental naval, military and civilian service taken over from the government of India by the UK.
FA 2004, Sch. 36, para. 56: inheritance tax where s. 615(3) does not apply to fund or scheme.
SI 1996/1584: pension funds pooling schemes

Statutory instruments – Federation of Rhodesia and Nyasaland (Dissolution) Order 1963 (SI 1963/2085), art. 24: pensions payable to persons by reason of former employment in public service of the Federation of Rhodesia and Nyasaland.

Extra-statutory concessions – A10: income tax not charged on lump sum relevant benefits receivable by an employee (or personal representative or dependent of his) from any superannuation fund accepted as being within s. 615(6).
B39: where payments or provisions are made in respect of a superannuation fund to which s. 615(3) applies, deduction may be allowed even if requirements of FA 1989, s. 76 not fulfilled.

HMRC Manuals – Schedule E Manual, vol. I, SE 2716: application of ESC A10 to superannuation funds within s. 615(6).

Notes – S. 615 rewritten as follows
S. 615(1): ITEPA 2003, s. 647(1), (2), s. 648(1), s. 649(1), s. 650(1), s. 651(1), s. 652(1), s. 653(1) and s. 654(1).
S. 615(2): ITEPA 2003, s. 648, s. 649(1), (2), (3), s. 650, s. 651(1), s. 652(1), (2), (4), (5), s. 653(1), (2), s. 654(1) and (2).
S. *615(4): ITEPA 2003, s. 651*(2), (4) and s. 654(3).
The terms in s. 615(7), which subsection still exists, have also been rewritten into the provisions of ITEPA 2003, s. 647(3), s. 649(5), s. 651(3), s. 651(4), s. 653(3) and s. 654(4).
S. 615(8): ITEPA 2003, s. 649(4), s. 650(2), s. 652(4)-(7) and s. 654(2).

616 Other overseas pensions

616 [Omitted by ITEPA 2003, Sch. 6, para. 86 and repealed by ITEPA 2003, Sch. 8, Pt. 1.]

History – S. 616 omitted by ITEPA 2003, Sch. 6, para. 86 and repealed by ITEPA 2003, Sch. 8, Pt. 1 which have effect for the tax year 2003–04 and subsequent tax years.

Notes – S. 616 rewritten as follows:
S. 616(1) and (2): ITEPA 2003, s. 643.
S. 616(3): ITEPA 2003, s. 629(1), s. 629(2) and s. 630(2).
S. 616(4): ITEPA 2003, s. 630(1) and s. 643.

617 Social security benefits and contributions

617 [Omitted by CTA 2009, s. 1322 and Sch. 1, para. 203 and repealed by CTA 2009, s. 1326 and Sch. 3, Pt. 1.]

History – S. 617 omitted by CTA 2009, s. 1322 and Sch. 1, para. 203 and repealed by CTA 2009, s. 1326 and Sch. 3, Pt. 1, with effect for corporation tax purposes for accounting periods ending on or after 1 April 2009, and for income tax and capital gains tax purposes for the tax year 2009–10 and subsequent tax years.

Notes – Rewritten income tax provisions are now located as follows:
S. 617(1): ITEPA 2003, s. 577(1), (2), s. 645, s. 660, s. 664(1), s. 676 and s. 677(1) Table B.
S. 617(2): ITEPA 2003, s. 666, s. 670 and s. 677(1) Table B.
S. 617(3): ITTOIA 2005, s. 53(1), 868(3)–(5) and Sch. 1, para. 593(2) and (3).
S. 617(4): ITTOIA 2005, s. 53(1)–(3), 868(3)–(5) and Sch. 1, para. 593(2) and (3).
S. 617 rewritten for corporation tax purposes as follows:
S. 617(3): CTA 2009, s. 1302(1), (2), 1306(1).
S. 617(4): CTA 2009, s. 1302(1), (2), (3).
S. 617(5): CTA 2009, s. 1302(4).

617A Tax Credits under Part I of Tax Credits Act 2002

617A [Omitted by ITEPA 2003, Sch. 6, para. 88 and repealed by ITEPA 2003, Sch. 8, Pt. 1.]

History – S. 617A omitted by ITEPA 2003, Sch. 6, para. 88 and repealed by ITEPA 2003, Sch. 8, Pt. 1 which have effect for the tax year 2003–04 and subsequent tax years.

Notes – S. 617A rewritten as ITEPA 2003, s. 677(1) Table B.

Chapter III – Retirement Annuities

Cross references – FA 2000, Sch. 8, para. 83(2)(b): partnership share money deducted from an employee's salary in accordance with a partnership share agreement under an employee share ownership plan is disregarded for the purposes of ascertaining the employee's relevant earnings for the purposes of Pt. XIV, Ch. III.
SI 1988/1436: disapplication of ICTA 1988, Sch. 23 in cases of bad investment advice.
SI 1990/586: disapplication of the earnings cap in cases of bad investment advice.
SI 1990/2101: disapplication of certain provisions of FA 1989, Sch. VI, Pt. II in cases of bad investment advice.

618 Termination of relief under this Chapter, and transitional provisions

618 [Repealed by FA 2004, s. 326 and Sch. 42, Pt. 3.]

History – S. 618 repealed by FA 2004, s. 326 and Sch. 42, Pt. 3, with effect from 6 April 2006 (subject to FA 2004, Sch. 36).

Derivations – F(No. 2)A 1987, s. 54(1), (3)–(6).

619 Exemption from tax in respect of qualifying premiums

619 [Repealed by FA 2004, s. 326 and Sch. 42, Pt. 3.]

History – S. 619 repealed by FA 2004, s. 326 and Sch. 42, Pt. 3, with effect from 6 April 2006 (subject to FA 2004, Sch. 36).

Derivations – Former s. 619(1): ICTA 1970, s. 226(1), (4), 227(1).
Former s. 619(2): ICTA 1970, s. 227(1A), as inserted by FA 1971, s. 20(2), and amended by FA 1980, s. 31(1).
Former s. 619(3): ICTA 1970, s. 227(1B), as inserted by FA 1971, s. 20(2), and amended by FA 1980, s. 31(2).
Former s. 619(4): ICTA 1970, s. 227(1BB), as inserted by FA 1980, s. 33(2).
Former s. 619(5)–(7): ICTA 1970, s. 227(10), (11), (13).

620 Qualifying premiums

620 [Repealed by FA 2004, s. 326 and Sch. 42, Pt. 3.]

History – S. 620 repealed by FA 2004, s. 326 and Sch. 42, Pt. 3, with effect from 6 April 2006 (subject to FA 2004, Sch. 36).

Derivations – Former s. 620(1): ICTA 1970, s. 226(1)(b), as amended by FA 1971, s. 20(1).
Former s. 620(2): ICTA 1970, s. 226(2), as amended by FA 1976, s. 30(2); FA 1980, s. 33(1).
Former s. 620(3): ICTA 1970, s. 226(2), as inserted by FA 1971, s. 20(3); see also s. 226A(5), as inserted by FA 1971, Sch. 2, para. 1.
Former s. 620(4): ICTA 1970, s. 226(3) (as amended by FA 1983, s. 19(1)), s. 226A(5) (as inserted by FA 1971, Sch. 2, para. 1).
Former s. 620(5)–(8): ICTA 1970, s. 226(5)–(7), (12).
Former s. 620(9): ICTA 1970, s. 226(13), as amended by F(No. 2)A 1987, s. 57 and Sch. 2, para. 1.

621 Other approved contracts

621 [Repealed by FA 2004, s. 326 and Sch. 42, Pt. 3.]

History – S. 621 repealed by FA 2004, s. 326 and Sch. 42, Pt. 3, with effect from 6 April 2006 (subject to FA 2004, Sch. 36).

Derivations – Former s. 621(1): ICTA 1970, s. 226A(1), as inserted by FA 1971, s. 20 and Sch. 2, para. 1, and amended by FA 1980, s. 33(1), 122 and Sch. 20.
Former s. 621(2): ICTA 1970, s. 226A(2), as inserted by FA 1971, s. 20 and Sch. 2, para. 1.

Former s. 621(3): ICTA 1970, s. 226A(3), as inserted by FA 1971, s. 20 and Sch. 2, para. 1, and amended by FA 1980, s. 33(1); FA 1976, s. 30(2).
Former s. 621(4)–(6): ICTA 1970, s. 226A(4), (6), (7), as inserted by FA 1971, s. 20 and Sch. 2, para. 1.

622 Substituted retirement annuity contracts

622 [Repealed by FA 2004, s. 326 and Sch. 42, Pt. 3.]

History – S. 622 repealed by FA 2004, s. 326 and Sch. 42, Pt. 3, with effect from 6 April 2006 (subject to FA 2004, Sch. 36).

Derivations – FA 1978, s. 26(1)–(3), as amended (s. 26(1)) by F(No. 2)A 1987, Sch. 2, para. 4.

623 Relevant earnings

623 [Repealed by FA 2004, s. 326 and Sch. 42, Pt. 3.]

History – S. 623 repealed by FA 2004, s. 326 and Sch. 42, Pt. 3, with effect from 6 April 2006 (subject to FA 2004, Sch. 36).

Derivations – Former s. 623(2) (as originally enacted): ICTA 1970, s. 226(9), as amended by FA 1972, s. 111 and Sch. 24, para. 17 and by FA 1987, s. 72 and Sch. 16, Pt. VII.
Former s. 623(3), (4): ICTA 1970, s. 226(10), as amended (s. 623(3)) by FA 1976, s. 30(2).
Former s. 623(5): ICTA 1970, s. 227(4); FA 1986, s. 56(7) and Sch. 13, para. 2(5); FA 1971, Sch. 8, para. 16(5).
Former s. 623(6) (as originally enacted): ICTA 1970, s. 227(5), as amended by FA 1980, s. 33(3), 122 and Sch. 20 and by FA 1981, s. 35(4)(a).
Former s. 623(7), (8) (as originally enacted): ICTA 1970, s. 227(6), (8).
Former s. 623(9): ICTA 1970, s. 227(9), as amended by FA 1987, Sch. 16, Pt. VII; FA 1981, s. 35(4)(a); FA 1980, s. 33(4).

624 Sponsored superannuation schemes and controlling directors

624 [Repealed by FA 2004, s. 326 and Sch. 42, Pt. 3.]

History – S. 624 repealed by FA 2004, s. 326 and Sch. 42, Pt. 3, with effect from 6 April 2006 (subject to FA 2004, Sch. 36).

Derivations – Former s. 624(1), (2): ICTA 1970, s. 226(11).
Former s. 624(3): ICTA 1970, s. 226(9), 224(1) (which was not repealed for the purpose of s. 226(9)).

625 Carry-forward of unused relief under section 619

625 [Repealed by FA 2004, s. 326 and Sch. 42, Pt. 3.]

History – S. 625 repealed by FA 2004, s. 326 and Sch. 42, Pt. 3, with effect from 6 April 2006 (subject to FA 2004, Sch. 36).

Derivations – ICTA 1970, s. 227A, as inserted by FA 1980, s. 32(1).

626 Modification of section 619 in relation to persons over 50

626 [Repealed by FA 2004, s. 326 and Sch. 42, Pt. 3.]

History – S. 626 repealed by FA 2004, s. 326 and Sch. 42, Pt. 3, with effect from 6 April 2006 (subject to FA 2004, Sch. 36).

Derivations – ICTA 1970, s. 228, as substituted by F(No. 2)A 1987, s. 54(2).

627 Lloyd's underwriters

627 [Repealed by FA 1994, s. 228(2)(a), and s. 258 and Sch. 26, Pt. V(25) with effect for 1997–98 and subsequent years of assessment.]

628 Partnership retirement annuities

628 [Repealed by FA 2004, s. 326 and Sch. 42, Pt. 3.]

History – S. 628 repealed by FA 2004, s. 326 and Sch. 42, Pt. 3, with effect from 6 April 2006 (subject to FA 2004, Sch. 36).

Derivations – Former s. 628(1) (as originally enacted): FA 1974, s. 16(1), as amended by FA 1984, Sch. 7, para. 3 and by FA 1980, s. 34(2).
Former s. 628(2): FA 1974, s. 16(2).
Former s. 628(3): FA 1974, s. 16(2A), as inserted by FA 1982, s. 39(1).
Former s. 628(4), (5): FA 1974, s. 16(3), (4), as inserted by FA 1980, s. 34(3).

629 Annuity premiums of Ministers and other officers

629(1) For the purposes of this Chapter so much of any salary which–

(a) is payable to the holder of a qualifying office who is also a Member of the House of Commons, and

(b) is payable for a period in respect of which the holder is not a participant in relation to that office in arrangements contained in the Parliamentary pension scheme but is a participant in relation to his membership of the House of Commons in any such arrangements, or for any part of such a period,

as is equal to the difference between a Member's pensionable salary and the salary which (in accordance with any such resolution as is mentioned in subsection (3)(a) below) is payable to him as a Member holding that qualifying office shall be treated as remuneration from the office of Member and not from the qualifying office.

629(2) In this section–

"Member's pensionable salary" means a Member's ordinary salary under any resolution of the House of Commons which, being framed otherwise than as an expression of opinion, is for the time being in force relating to the remuneration of Members or, if the resolution provides for a

Member's ordinary salary thereunder to be treated for pension purposes as being at a higher rate, a notional yearly salary at that higher rate;

"qualifying office" means an office mentioned in section 2(2)(b), (c) or (d) of the Parliamentary and other Pensions Act 1987;

"the Parliamentary pension scheme" has the same meaning as in that Act;

and without prejudice to the power conferred by virtue of paragraph 13 of Schedule 1 to that Act, regulations under section 2 of that Act may make provision specifying the circumstances in which a person is to be regarded for the purposes of this section as being or not being a participant in relation to his Membership of the House of Commons, or in relation to any office, in arrangements contained in the Parliamentary pension scheme.

629(3) In subsection (2) above **"a Member's ordinary salary"**, in relation to any resolution of the House of Commons, means–

(a) if the resolution provides for salary to be paid to Members at different rates according to whether or not they are holders of particular offices, or are in receipt of salaries or pensions as the holders or former holders of particular offices, a Member's yearly salary at the higher or highest rate; and

(b) in any other case, a Member's yearly salary at the rate specified in or determined under the resolution.

Derivations – S. 629(1): ICTA 1970, s. 229(1), as amended by Parliamentary and other Pensions Act 1972, s. 32(1); Parliamentary and Other Pensions and Salaries Act 1976, s. 1(3), (4); Parliamentary and other Pensions Act 1987, Sch. 3, para. 2(2).
S. 629(2), (3): ICTA 1970, s. 229(1A), (1B), as inserted by Parliamentary and other Pensions Act 1987, Sch. 3, para. 2(c).

Cross references – FA 1999, Sch. 5, para. 6(2): application of s. 629 to the salary of a member of the Scottish Executive who is also a member of the Scottish Parliament (MSP), where provision is made under the Scotland Act 1998 for the salary paid to an MSP who is also a member of the Scottish Executive to be lower than that of other MSPs.
Parliamentary and other Pensions Act 1987, s. 2(2): qualifying offices are those of ministers, whips, opposition leaders and certain committee chairmen.
Parliamentary and other Pensions Act 1987, Sch. 1, para. 13: regulations may be made modifying the Act.

ICTA 1988

Chapter IV – Personal Pension Schemes

Cross references – FA 2004, s. 283 and Sch. 36, para. 1: any pension scheme which, immediately before 6 April 2006, is a personal pension scheme approved under Chapter 4 of Pt. 14 is treated as becoming a registered pension scheme on that date.
FA 2004, s. 283 and Sch. 36, para. 4: (continuity of administration) the person or persons who administer; or who are responsible for; a pension scheme immediately before 6 April 2006, are treated as becoming the scheme administrators on that date.
FA 2004, s. 283 and Sch. 36, para. 6: (continuity of obligation) any liabilities or obligations of the administrator of a Chapter 4 of Pt. 14 personal pension scheme, incurred in relation to the scheme before 6 April 2006, are treated as liabilities and obligations of the administrator of the registered pension scheme from that date.
FA 2000, Sch. 8, para. 83(2)(b): partnership share money deducted from an employee's salary in accordance with a partnership share agreement under an employee share ownership plan is disregarded for the purposes of ascertaining the employee's relevant earnings for the purposes of Pt. XIV, Ch. IV.
FA 2003, Sch. 24, para. 8(c): disapplication of rules in Sch. 24 that restrict the deduction allowable for contributions towards employee benefits where the contribution is made to a personal pension scheme under ICTA 1988, Pt. 14, Ch. 4.
SI 1988/137 (Personal Pension Schemes (Appropriate Schemes) Regulations 1988), reg. 2 (not reproduced): forms of schemes which may be appropriate schemes.

Extra-statutory concessions – A95: where members of certain small lump sum retirement benefit schemes are also contributing to a personal pension or retirement annuity scheme, they may be able to retain their pensions provided they give up their entitlement to lump sum benefits under the retirement benefit scheme.
A102: personal pension contributions from 6 April 2001 may be used to reduce an individual's total income for the purposes only of determining the level of age related allowances available under ICTA 1988, s. 257(5) and 257A(5).

PRELIMINARY

630 Interpretation

630 [Repealed by FA 2004, s. 326 and Sch. 42, Pt. 3.]

History – S. 630 repealed by FA 2004, s. 326 and Sch. 42, Pt. 3, with effect from 6 April 2006 (subject to FA 2004, Sch. 36).
Derivations – F(No. 2)A 1987, s. 18.

631 Approval of schemes

631 [Repealed by FA 2004, s. 326 and Sch. 42, Pt. 3.]

History – S. 631 repealed by FA 2004, s. 326 and Sch. 42, Pt. 3, with effect from 6 April 2006 (subject to FA 2004, Sch. 36).
Derivations – F(No. 2)A 1987, s. 19.

631A Conversion of certain approved retirement benefits schemes

631A [Repealed by FA 2004, s. 326 and Sch. 42, Pt. 3.]

History – S. 631A repealed by FA 2004, s. 326 and Sch. 42, Pt. 3, with effect from 6 April 2006 (subject to FA 2004, Sch. 36)
Former s. 631A inserted by FA 2000, s. 61 and Sch. 13, para. 7.

RESTRICTIONS ON APPROVAL

632 Establishment of schemes

632 [Repealed by FA 2004, s. 326 and Sch. 42, Pt. 3.]

History – S. 632 repealed by FA 2004, s. 326 and Sch. 42, Pt. 3, with effect from 6 April 2006 (subject to FA 2004, Sch. 36).

Derivations – (as originally enacted) – F(No. 2)A 1987, s. 20(1)–(4).

632A Eligibility to make contributions

632A [Repealed by FA 2004, s. 326 and Sch. 42, Pt. 3.]

History – S. 632A repealed by FA 2004, s. 326 and Sch. 42, Pt. 3, with effect from 6 April 2006 (subject to FA 2004, Sch. 36).

632B Eligibility to make contributions: concurrent membership

632B [Repealed by FA 2004, s. 326 and Sch. 42, Pt. 3.]

History – S. 632B repealed by FA 2004, s. 326 and Sch. 42, Pt. 3, with effect from 6 April 2006 (subject to FA 2004, Sch. 36).

633 Scope of benefits

633 [Repealed by FA 2004, s. 326 and Sch. 42, Pt. 3.]

History – S. 633 repealed, by FA 2004, s. 326 and Sch. 42, Pt. 3, with effect from 6 April 2006 (subject to FA 2004, Sch. 36).

Derivations – F(No. 2)A 1987, s. 21.

634 Annuity to member

634 [Repealed by FA 2004, s. 326 and Sch. 42, Pt. 3.]

History – S. 634 repealed by FA 2004, s. 326 and Sch. 42, Pt. 3, with effect from 6 April 2006 (subject to FA 2004, Sch. 36).

Derivations – F(No. 2)A 1987, s. 22.

634A Income withdrawals by member

634A [Repealed by FA 2004, s. 326 and Sch. 42, Pt. 3.]

History – S. 634A repealed by FA 2004, s. 326 and Sch. 42, Pt. 3, with effect from 6 April 2006 (subject to FA 2004, Sch. 36).

635 Lump sum to member

635 [Repealed by FA 2004, s. 326 and Sch. 42, Pt. 3.]

History – S. 635 repealed by FA 2004, s. 326 and Sch. 42, Pt. 3, with effect from 6 April 2006 (subject to FA 2004, Sch. 36).

Derivations – F(No. 2)A 1987, s. 23.

636 Annuity after death of member

636 [Repealed by FA 2004, s. 326 and Sch. 42, Pt. 3.]

History – S. 636 repealed by FA 2004, s. 326 and Sch. 42, Pt. 3, with effect from 6 April 2006 (subject to FA 2004, Sch. 36).

Derivations – F(No. 2)A 1987, s. 24.

636A Income withdrawals after death of member

636A [Repealed by FA 2004, s. 326 and Sch. 42, Pt. 3.]

History – S. 636A repealed by FA 2004, s. 326 and Sch. 42, Pt. 3, with effect from 6 April 2006 (subject to FA 2004, Sch. 36).

637 Death benefit

637 [Repealed by FA 2004, s. 326 and Sch. 42, Pt. 3.]

History – S. 637 repealed by FA 2004, s. 326 and Sch. 42, Pt. 3, with effect from 6 April 2006 (subject to FA 2004, Sch. 36).

Derivations – F(No. 2)A 1987, s. 25, 26.

637A Return of contributions on or after death of member

637A [Repealed by FA 2004, s. 326 and Sch. 42, Pt. 3.]

History – S. 637A repealed, by FA 2004, s. 326 and Sch. 42, Pt. 3, with effect from 6 April 2006 (subject to FA 2004, Sch. 36).

638 Other restrictions on approval

638 [Repealed by FA 2004, s. 326 and Sch. 42, Pt. 3.]

History – S. 638 repealed by FA 2004, s. 326 and Sch. 42, Pt. 3, with effect from 6 April 2006 (subject to FA 2004, Sch. 36).

Derivations – Former s. 638(1)–(6): F(No. 2)A 1987, s. 27, 28(1), 29, 30(1).

Notes – In former s. 638(13), the definition of "employee share ownership plan", which is omitted by ITEPA 2003, Sch. 6, para. 90(5)(a) and repealed by ITEPA 2003, Sch. 8, Pt. 1, is unnecessary and so has not been rewritten into the provisions of ITEPA 2003.

638ZA Personal pension arrangements with more than one pension date etc

638ZA [Repealed by FA 2004, s. 326 and Sch. 42, Pt. 3.]

History – S. 638ZA repealed by FA 2004, s. 326 and Sch. 42, Pt. 3, with effect from 6 April 2006 (subject to FA 2004, Sch. 36)

638A Power to prescribe restrictions on approval

638A [Repealed by FA 2004, s. 326 and Sch. 42, Pt. 3.]

History – S. 638A repealed by FA 2004, s. 326 and Sch. 42, Pt. 3, with effect from 6 April 2006 (subject to FA 2004, Sch. 36).

TAX RELIEFS

639 Member's contributions

639 [Repealed by FA 2004, s. 326 and Sch. 42, Pt. 3.]

History – S. 639 repealed by FA 2004, s. 326 and Sch. 42, Pt. 3, with effect from 6 April 2006 (subject to FA 2004, Sch. 36)

Derivations – Former s. 639(1): F(No. 2)A 1987, s. 31, 46.
Former s. 639(2)–(5): F(No. 2)A 1987, s. 45(1)–(4).
Former s. 639(6)–(8): F(No. 2)A 1987, s. 48, 49.

640 Maximum amount of deductions

640 [Repealed by FA 2004, s. 326 and Sch. 42, Pt. 3.]

History – S. 640 repealed by FA 2004, s. 326 and Sch. 42, Pt. 3, with effect from 6 April 2006 (subject to FA 2004, Sch. 36).
Derivations – F(No. 2)A 1987, s. 32.

640A Earnings cap

640A [Repealed by FA 2004, s. 326 and Sch. 42, Pt. 3.]

History – S. 640A repealed by FA 2004, s. 326 and Sch. 42, Pt. 3, with effect from 6 April 2006 (subject to FA 2004, Sch. 36).

641 Carry-back of contributions

641 [Repealed by FA 2000, s. 156 and Sch. 40, Pt. II(4).]

History – S. 641 repealed by FA 2000, s. 156 and Sch. 40, Pt. II(4), with effect in relation to contributions paid on or after 6 April 2001.

641A Election for contributions to be treated as paid in previous year

641A [Repealed by FA 2004, s. 326 and Sch. 42, Pt. 3.]

History – S. 641A repealed by FA 2004, s. 326 and Sch. 42, Pt. 3, with effect from 6 April 2006 (subject to FA 2004, Sch. 36).

642 Carry-forward of relief

642 [Repealed by FA 2000, s. 156 and Sch. 40, Pt. II(4).]

History – S. 642 repealed by FA 2000, s. 156 and Sch. 40, Pt. II(4), with effect for the year 2001–02 and subsequent years of assessment.

643 Employer's contributions and personal pension income etc.

643 [Repealed by FA 2004, s. 326 and Sch. 42, Pt. 3.]

History – S. 643 repealed by FA 2004, s. 326 and Sch. 42, Pt. 3, with effect from 6 April 2006 (subject to FA 2004, Sch. 36).
Derivations – F(No. 2)A 1987, s. 38, 39(1), 41(1), (2).

Notes – Former s. 643(1): ITEPA 2003, s. 308(1).
The words "shall be assessable to tax under Schedule E (and section 203 shall apply accordingly) and", in former s. 643(5), have been rewritten into the provisions of ITEPA 2003, s. 598 and s. 599.

644 Meaning of "relevant earnings"

644 [Repealed by FA 2004, s. 326 and Sch. 42, Pt. 3.]

History – S. 644 repealed by FA 2004, s. 326 and Sch. 42, Pt. 3, with effect from 6 April 2006 (subject to FA 2004, Sch. 36).
Derivations – F(No. 2)A 1987, s. 35(2)–(6).

645 Earnings from pensionable employment

645 [Repealed by FA 2004, s. 326 and Sch. 42, Pt. 3.]

History – S. 645 repealed by FA 2004, s. 326 and Sch. 42, Pt. 3, with effect from 6 April 2006 (subject to FA 2004, Sch. 36).
Derivations – F(No. 2)A 1987, s. 36.

646 Meaning of "net relevant earnings"

646 [Repealed by FA 2004, s. 326 and Sch. 42, Pt. 3.]

History – S. 646 repealed by FA 2004, s. 326 and Sch. 42, Pt. 3, with effect from 6 April 2006 (subject to FA 2004, Sch. 36).

Derivations – F(No. 2)A 1987, s. 37.

646A Earnings from associated employments

646A [Repealed by FA 2004, s. 326 and Sch. 42, Pt. 3.]

History – S. 646A repealed by FA 2004, s. 326 and Sch. 42, Pt. 3, with effect from 6 April 2006 (subject to FA 2004, Sch. 36).

646B Presumption of same level of relevant earnings etc. for 5 years

646B [Repealed by FA 2004, s. 326 and Sch. 42, Pt. 3.]

History – S. 646B repealed by FA 2004, s. 326 and Sch. 42, Pt. 3, with effect from 6 April 2006 (subject to FA 2004, Sch. 36).

646C Provisions supplementary to section 646B

646C [Repealed by FA 2004, s. 326 and Sch. 42, Pt. 3.]

History – S. 646C repealed by FA 2004, s. 326 and Sch. 42, Pt. 3, with effect from 6 April 2006 (subject to FA 2004, Sch. 36).

646D Higher level contributions after cessation of actual relevant earnings: modification of section 646B

646D [Repealed by FA 2004, s. 326 and Sch. 42, Pt. 3.]

History – S. 646D repealed by FA 2004, s. 326 and Sch. 42, Pt. 3, with effect from 6 April 2006 (subject to FA 2004, Sch. 36).

CHARGE TO TAX

647 Unauthorised payments

647 [Omitted by ITEPA 2003, Sch. 6, para. 96 and repealed by ITEPA 2003, Sch. 8, Pt. 1.]

History – S. 647 omitted by ITEPA 2003, Sch. 6, para. 96 and repealed by ITEPA 2003, Sch. 8, Pt. 1 which have effect for the tax year 2003–04 and subsequent tax years.

Notes – S. 647 rewritten as follows:
S. 647(1): ITEPA 2003, s. 601(2).
S. 647(2): ITEPA 2003, s. 601(4), (5) and (6).
S. 647(3): ITEPA 2003, s. 602 and s. 603.
S. 647(4): ITEPA 2003, s. 601(7).

648 Contributions under unapproved arrangements

648 [Omitted by ITEPA 2003, Sch. 6, para. 96 and repealed by ITEPA 2003, Sch. 8, Pt. 1.]

History – S. 648 omitted by ITEPA 2003, Sch. 6, para. 96 and repealed by ITEPA 2003, Sch. 8, Pt. 1 which have effect for the tax year 2003–04 and subsequent tax years.

Notes – S. 648 rewritten as ITEPA 2003, s. 7(5), s. 224(1) and (2).

648A Annuities: charge under Schedule E

History – The heading "Annuities: charge to tax" which preceded s. 648A omitted by FA 1995, s. 58 and Sch. 11, para. 12 in relation to approvals of schemes or amendments under ICTA 1988, Pt. XIV, Ch. IV after 1 May 1995.

648A [Omitted by ITEPA 2003, Sch. 6, para. 96 and repealed by ITEPA 2003, Sch. 8, Pt. 1.]

History – S. 648A omitted by ITEPA 2003, Sch. 6, para. 96 and repealed by ITEPA 2003, Sch. 8, Pt. 1 which have effect for the tax year 2003–04 and subsequent tax years.

Notes – S. 648A rewritten as follows:
S. 648A(1): ITEPA 2003, s. 595.
S. 648A(2) is unnecessary and so has not been rewritten into the provisions of ITEPA 2003.

648B Return of contributions after pension date

648B [Repealed by FA 2004, s. 326 and Sch. 42, Pt. 3.]

History – S. 648B repealed by FA 2004, s. 326 and Sch. 42, Pt. 3, with effect from 6 April 2006 (subject to FA 2004, Sch. 36).

MISCELLANEOUS

649 Minimum contributions under Pension Schemes Act 1993

649 [Repealed by FA 2004, s. 326 and Sch. 42, Pt. 3.]

History – S. 649 repealed by FA 2004, s. 326 and Sch. 42, Pt. 3, with effect from 6 April 2006 (subject to FA 2004, Sch. 36).

Derivations – F(No. 2)A 1987, s. 42(1)–(5), (7).

650 Withdrawal of approval

650 [Repealed by FA 2004, s. 326 and Sch. 42, Pt. 3.]

History – S. 650 repealed by FA 2004, s. 326 and Sch. 42, Pt. 3, with effect from 6 April 2006 (subject to FA 2004, Sch. 36).
Derivations – F(No. 2)A 1987, s. 43.

650A Charge on withdrawal of approval from arrangements

650A [Repealed by FA 2004, s. 326 and Sch. 42, Pt. 3.]

History – S. 650A repealed by FA 2004, s. 326 and Sch. 42, Pt. 3, with effect from 6 April 2006 (subject to FA 2004, Sch. 36)

651 Appeals

651 [Repealed by FA 2004, s. 326 and Sch. 42, Pt. 3.]

History – S. 651 repealed by FA 2004, s. 326 and Sch. 42, Pt. 3, with effect from 6 April 2006 (subject to FA 2004, Sch. 36).
Derivations – TMA 1970, s. 115: service of notices.
F(No. 2)A 1987, s. 47.

651A Information powers

651A [Repealed by FA 2004, s. 326 and Sch. 42, Pt. 3.]

History – S. 651A repealed by FA 2004, s. 326 and Sch. 42, Pt. 3, with effect from 6 April 2006 (subject to FA 2004, Sch. 36).

652 Information about payments

652 [Repealed by FA 1998, s. 96(2); s. 165 and Sch. 27, Pt. III(21).]

History – S. 652 repealed by FA 1998, s. 96(2); s. 165 and Sch. 27, Pt. III(21) with effect from 1 October 2000 (SI 2000/2319 (C. 62)).

653 Information: penalties

653 [Repealed by FA 2004, s. 326 and Sch. 42, Pt. 3.]

History – S. 653 repealed by FA 2004, s. 326 and Sch. 42, Pt. 3, with effect from 6 April 2006 (subject to FA 2004, Sch. 36).
Derivations – F(No. 2)A 1987, s. 51(1).

653A Notices to be given to scheme administrator

653A [Repealed by FA 2004, s. 326 and Sch. 42, Pt. 3.]

History – S. 653A repealed by FA 2004, s. 326 and Sch. 42, Pt. 3, with effect from 6 April 2006 (subject to FA 2004, Sch. 36).

654 Remuneration of Ministers and other officers

654 [Repealed by FA 2004, s. 326 and Sch. 42, Pt. 3.]

History – S. 654 repealed by FA 2004, s. 326 and Sch. 42, Pt. 3, with effect from 6 April 2006 (subject to FA 2004, Sch. 36).
Derivations – F(No. 2)A 1987, s. 52.

655 Transitional provisions

655 [Repealed by FA 2004, s. 326 and Sch. 42, Pt. 3.]

History – S. 655 repealed by FA 2004, s. 326 and Sch. 42, Pt. 3, with effect from 6 April 2006 (subject to FA 2004, Sch. 36).
Derivations – F(No. 2)A 1987, s. 55, 56(1), (2).

Chapter V – Purchased Life Annuities

656 Purchased life annuities other than retirement annuities

656 [Omitted by FA 2008, s. 36 and Sch. 14, para. 8.]

History – S. 656 omitted by FA 2008, s. 36 and Sch. 14, para. 8, with effect:
- so far as relating to corporation tax, for accounting periods beginning on or after 1 April 2008;
- so far as relating to income tax, for the tax year 2008–09 and subsequent tax years.

Notes – Rewritten income tax provisions are now located as follows:
S. 656(1): ITTOIA 2005, s. 717(1).
S. 656(2): ITTOIA 2005, s. 719(4) and (5), 721(1)–(4), 722(1) and 724(1). But ITTOIA 2005 does not rewrite ICTA 1988, s. 656(2)(a) as it is otiose. (See ITTOIA 2005, Explanatory Notes, Annex 1, Table 1 (Change 158).)
S. 656(3): ITTOIA 2005, s. 719(3), (4), (5) and (8), 720(1) and (2) and 722(1).
S. 656(4): ITTOIA 2005, s. 720(3) and (4), 722(1)–(4) and 724(1).
S. 656(5): ITTOIA 2005, s. 723(3) and 724(2).
S. 656(6): ITTOIA 2005, s. 723(5) and (6) and 724(2).
S. 656(7): ITTOIA 2005, s. 720(4) and 721(3) and (4).
S. 656(8): ITTOIA 2005, s. 721(5).
S. 656(9): ITTOIA 2005, s. 720(5).

657 Purchased life annuities to which section 656 applies

657 [Omitted by FA 2008, s. 36 and Sch. 14, para. 8.]

History – S. 657 omitted by FA 2008, s. 36 and Sch. 14, para. 8, with effect:
- so far as relating to corporation tax, for accounting periods beginning on or after 1 April 2008;
- so far as relating to income tax, for the tax year 2008–09 and subsequent tax years.

Notes – Rewritten income tax provisions are now located as follows:
S. 657(1): ITTOIA 2005, s. 423(1) and (2).
S. 657(2): ITTOIA 2005, s. 718(1)–(3).

658 Supplementary

658 [Omitted by FA 2008, s. 36 and Sch. 14, para. 8.]

History – S. 658 omitted by FA 2008, s. 36 and Sch. 14, para. 8, with effect:
- so far as relating to corporation tax, for accounting periods beginning on or after 1 April 2008;
- so far as relating to income tax, for the tax year 2008–09 and subsequent tax years.

Notes – Rewritten income tax provisions are now located as follows:
S. 658(1): ITTOIA 2005, s. 723(1) and (2) and 724(2).
S. 658(2): ITTOIA 2005, s. 724(1).
S. 658(3): ITTOIA 2005, s. 724(1).
S. 658(4): ITTOIA 2005, s. 724(2) and (3).
S. 658(5): ITTOIA 2005, s. 723(7).

Chapter VI – Miscellaneous

658A Charges and assessments on administrators

658A [Repealed by FA 2004, s. 326 and Sch. 42, Pt. 3.]

History – S. 658A repealed by FA 2004, s. 326 and Sch. 42, Pt. 3, with effect from 6 April 2006 (subject to FA 2004, Sch. 36).

659 Financial futures and traded options

659 [Repealed by FA 1990, s. 81(4), s. 132 and Sch. 19, Pt. IV, with effect in relation to income derived and disposals made after 26 July 1990.]

659A Futures and options

659A(1) For the purposes of sections 613(4), 614(3) and (4)–

(a) **"investments"** (or **"investment"**) includes futures contracts and options contracts, and

(b) income derived from transactions relating to such contracts shall be regarded as income derived from (or income from) such contracts.

659A(2) For the purposes of subsection (1) above a contract is not prevented from being a futures contract or an options contract by the fact that any party is or may be entitled to receive or liable to make, or entitled to receive and liable to make, only a payment of a sum (as opposed to a transfer of assets other than money) in full settlement of all obligations.

History – In s. 659A(1) the words: "592(2), 608(2)(a),"; the words", 620(6) and 643(2)"; and the words "and paragraph 7(3)(a) of Schedule 22 to this Act shall be construed accordingly." repealed by FA 2004, s. 326 and Sch. 42, Pt. 3, with effect from 6 April 2006 (subject to FA 2004, Sch. 36).
S. 659A inserted by FA 1990, s. 81(2) in relation to income derived after 26 July 1990.

Cross references – S. 592(2): retirement benefit schemes.
S. 608(2)(a): superannuation funds approved before 6 April 1980.
S. 613(4): certain Parliamentary pension funds.
S. 614(3), (4): certain overseas service pension funds.
S. 620(6): retirement annuity funds.
S. 643(2): personal pension schemes.
Sch. 22, para. 7(3)(a), (d): reduction of pension fund surpluses – relief from income tax and CGT to be given only to extent of percentage of liabilities over assets where administrator fails to reduce surplus etc.
TCGA 1992, s. 271(1)(g), (h), (2): exemption from CGT on disposal of investments of an exempt approved scheme, approved personal pension scheme, and pre-6 April 1980 approved superannuation fund.

Statements of practice – 4/88: transactions in financial futures and options.

659B Definition of insurance company

659B [Repealed by FA 2004, s. 326 and Sch. 42, Pt. 3.]

History – S. 659B repealed by FA 2004, s. 326 and Sch. 42, Pt. 3, with effect from 6 April 2006 (subject to FA 2004, Sch. 36).

659C Effect of appointment or arrangements under section 659B

659C [Repealed by FA 2004, s. 326 and Sch. 42, Pt. 3.]

History – S. 659C repealed by FA 2004, s. 326 and Sch. 42, Pt. 3, with effect from 6 April 2006 (subject to FA 2004, Sch. 36).

659D Interpretation of provisions about pension sharing

659D [Repealed by FA 2004, s. 326 and Sch. 42, Pt. 3.]

History – S. 659D repealed by FA 2004, s. 326 and Sch. 42, Pt. 3, with effect from 6 April 2006 (subject to FA 2004, Sch. 36).

659E Treatment of income from property investment LLPs

Notes – S. 659E inserted by FA 2001, s. 76 and Sch. 25, para. 2. The section is initially referred to (in Sch. 25, para. 2) as s. 659D, which already exists (see above); this was clearly an error. From references in later enactments it is clear that the section is, in fact, intended to be s. 659E.

659E(1) The exemptions specified below do not apply to income derived from investments, deposits or other property held as a member of a property investment LLP (see section 1004 of ITA 2007).

659E(2) The exemptions are those provided by–

section 613(4) (Parliamentary pension funds),

section 614(3) (certain colonial, &c. pension funds),

section 614(4) (the Overseas Service Pension Fund),

section 614(5) (other pension funds for overseas employees).

659E(3) The income to which subsection (1) above applies includes relevant stock lending fees, in relation to any investments, to which any of the provisions listed in subsection (2) above would apply by virtue of section 129B.

659E(4) Section 659A (treatment of futures and options) applies for the purposes of subsection (1) above.

History – In s. 659E(1) the words "(see section 1004 of ITA 2007)" inserted by ITA 2007, s. 1027 and Sch. 1, para. 143 with effect for income tax purposes for 2007–08 and subsequent tax years and for corporation tax purposes in relation to accounting periods ending after 5 April 2007.
In s. 659E(2), the references to ICTA 1988, s. 592(2), 608(2)(a), 620(6) and 643(2) repealed by FA 2004, s. 326 and Sch. 42, Pt 3, with effect from 6 April 2006 (subject to FA 2004, Sch. 36).
S. 659E (as s. 659D) inserted by FA 2001, s. 76 and Sch. 25, para. 2, with effect from 6 April 2001.

PART XV – SETTLEMENTS

Chapter IA – Liability of Settlor

History – Ch. 1A substituted for former s. 660–676 and s. 683–685 by FA 1995, s. 74 and Sch. 17, para. 1 with effect for 1995–96 and subsequent years of assessment in relation to every settlement wherever and whenever it was made or entered into.

Cross references – FA 2000, s. 44(1): Ch. IA does not apply to any qualifying income which arises under a UK trust if it is given by the trustees to a charity in the tax year in which it arises, or it is income to which a charity is entitled under the terms of the trust.
FA 2000, s. 45(1): in Ch. IA, "settlement" does not include any arrangement so far as it consists of a loan of money made by an individual to a charity either for no consideration, or for a consideration which consists only of interest, where income arises on or after 6 April 2000 whether on loans made before or after that date.

MAIN PROVISIONS

660A Income arising under settlement where settlor retains an interest

660A [Omitted by ITTOIA 2005, s. 882 and Sch. 1, para. 271 and repealed by s. 884 and Sch. 3.]

History – S. 660A omitted by ITTOIA 2005, s. 882(1) and Sch. 1, para. 271 and repealed by s. 884 and Sch. 3; effective for income tax purposes for 2005–06 onwards and for corporation tax purposes for accounting periods ending after 5 April 2005 (ITTOIA 2005, s. 883(1)).

Notes – S. 660A rewritten as follows:
S. 660A(1): ITTOIA 2005, s. 622 and 624(1).
S. 660A(2): ITTOIA 2005, s. 625(1).
S. 660A(3): ITTOIA 2005, s. 625(4).
S. 660A(4): ITTOIA 2005, s. 625(2).
S. 660A(5): ITTOIA 2005, s. 625(3).
S. 660A(6): ITTOIA 2005, s. 626(1)–(4).
S. 660A(8): ITTOIA 2005, s. 627(1).
S. 660A(9): ITTOIA 2005, s. 627(2) and Sch. 2, para. 132(1) and (2).
S. 660A(10): ITTOIA 2005, s. 625(5) and 626(5).
S. 660A(11): ITTOIA 2005, s. 627(3) and Sch. 2, para. 132(1) and (3).
S. 660A(12): ITTOIA 2005, Sch. 2, para. 132(1) and (3).

660B Payments to unmarried minor children of settlor

660B [Omitted by ITTOIA 2005, s. 882 and Sch. 1, para. 271 and repealed by s. 884 and Sch. 3.]

History – S. 660B omitted by ITTOIA 2005, s. 882(1) and Sch. 1, para. 271 and repealed by s. 884 and Sch. 3; effective for income tax purposes for 2005–06 onwards and for corporation tax purposes for accounting periods ending after 5 April 2005 (ITTOIA 2005, s. 883(1)).

Notes – S. 660B rewritten as follows:
S. 660B(1): ITTOIA 2005, s. 629(1) and (2).
S. 660B(2): ITTOIA 2005, s. 631(1)–(3).
S. 660B(3): ITTOIA 2005, s. 631(4) and (5).
S. 660B(3A): ITTOIA 2005, s. 631(6) and (7).

S. 660B(4): ITTOIA 2005, s. 632(1)–(3).
S. 660B(5): ITTOIA 2005, s. 629(3) and (4).
S. 660B(6): ITTOIA 2005, s. 629(7).

660C Nature of charge on settlor

660C(1) [Omitted by ITTOIA 2005, s. 882 and Sch. 1, para. 272(2) and repealed by s. 884 and Sch. 3.]

660C(1A) [Omitted by ITTOIA 2005, s. 882 and Sch. 1, para. 272(2) and repealed by s. 884 and Sch. 3.]

660C(2) [Omitted by ITTOIA 2005, s. 882 and Sch. 1, para. 272(2) and repealed by s. 884 and Sch. 3.]

660C(3) [Omitted by ITA 2007, s. 1027 and Sch. 1, para. 144 and repealed by ITA 2007, s. 1031 and Sch. 3, Pt. 1.]

660C(4) [Omitted by FA 2007, s. 30 and Sch. 5, para. 2(1) and repealed by s. 114 and Sch. 27, Pt. 2(3).]

History – S. 660C(1) omitted by ITTOIA 2005, s. 882(1) and Sch. 1, para. 272(2) and repealed by s. 884 and Sch. 3; effective for income tax purposes for 2005–06 onwards and for corporation tax purposes for accounting periods ending after 5 April 2005 (ITTOIA 2005, s. 883(1)).
S. 660C(1A) omitted by ITTOIA 2005, s. 882(1) and Sch. 1, para. 272(2) and repealed by s. 884 and Sch. 3; effective for income tax purposes for 2005–06 onwards and for corporation tax purposes for accounting periods ending after 5 April 2005 (ITTOIA 2005, s. 883(1)).
S. 660C(2) omitted by ITTOIA 2005, s. 882(1) and Sch. 1, para. 272(2) and repealed by s. 884 and Sch. 3; effective for income tax purposes for 2005–06 onwards and for corporation tax purposes for accounting periods ending after 5 April 2005 (ITTOIA 2005, s. 883(1)).
S. 660C(3) omitted by ITA 2007, s. 1027 and Sch. 1, para. 144 and repealed by ITA 2007, s. 1031 and Sch. 3, Pt. 1 with effect for income tax purposes for 2007–08 and subsequent tax years and for corporation tax purposes in relation to accounting periods ending after 5 April 2007.
S. 660C(4) omitted by FA 2007, s. 30 and Sch. 5, para. 2(1) and repealed by s. 114 and Sch. 27, Pt. 2(3), with effect in relation to accounting periods ending on or after 6 March 2007 (but income which arises in an accounting period beginning before that date is to be chargeable to corporation tax as a result of that amendment only if it arises on or after that date).

Notes – S. 660C rewritten as follows:
S. 660C(1): ITTOIA 2005, s. 619(1) and (2) and 621.
S. 660C(1A): ITTOIA 2005, s. 619(3) and (4) and 621. But ITTOIA 2005 does not rewrite ICTA 1988, s. 660C(1A)(c)–(e) as they are unnecessary. (See ITTOIA 2005, Explanatory Notes, Annex 1, Table 1 (Change 158).)
S. 660C(2): ITTOIA 2005, s. 623(1) and (2).
S. 660C(3): ITA 2007, Sch. 1 para. 551.

660D Adjustments between settlor and trustees, etc.

660D [Omitted by ITTOIA 2005, s. 882 and Sch. 1, para. 273 and repealed by s. 884 and Sch. 3.]

History – S. 660D omitted by ITTOIA 2005, s. 882(1) and Sch. 1, para. 273 and repealed by s. 884 and Sch. 3; effective for income tax purposes for 2005–06 onwards and for corporation tax purposes for accounting periods ending after 5 April 2005 (ITTOIA 2005, s. 883(1)).

Notes – S. 660D rewritten as follows:
S. 660D(1): ITTOIA 2005, s. 646(1)–(3).
S. 660D(2): ITTOIA 2005, s. 646(4)–(7).
S. 660D(3): ITTOIA 2005, s. 646(8).

SUPPLEMENTARY PROVISIONS

660E Application to settlements by two or more settlors

660E [Omitted by ITTOIA 2005, s. 882 and Sch. 1, para. 273 and repealed by s. 884 and Sch. 3.]

History – S. 660E omitted by ITTOIA 2005, s. 882(1) and Sch. 1, para. 273 and repealed by s. 884 and Sch. 3; effective for income tax purposes for 2005–06 onwards and for corporation tax purposes for accounting periods ending after 5 April 2005 (ITTOIA 2005, s. 883(1)).

Notes – S. 660E rewritten as follows:
S. 660E(1): ITTOIA 2005, s. 644(1) and (2).
S. 660E(2): ITTOIA 2005, s. 644(3).
S. 660E(3): ITTOIA 2005, s. 644(4).
S. 660E(4): ITTOIA 2005, s. 644(5).
S. 660E(5): ITTOIA 2005, s. 645(1).
S. 660E(6): ITTOIA 2005, s. 645(2).
S. 660E(7): ITTOIA 2005, s. 645(3) and (4).

660F Power to obtain information

660F [Omitted by ITTOIA 2005, s. 882 and Sch. 1, para. 273 and repealed by s. 884 and Sch. 3.]

History – S. 660F omitted by ITTOIA 2005, s. 882(1) and Sch. 1, para. 273 and repealed by s. 884 and Sch. 3; effective for income tax purposes for 2005–06 onwards and for corporation tax purposes for accounting periods ending after 5 April 2005 (ITTOIA 2005, s. 883(1)).

Notes – S. 660F rewritten as ITTOIA 2005, s. 647(1) and (2).

660G Meaning of "settlement" and related expressions

660G [Omitted by ITTOIA 2005, s. 882 and Sch. 1, para. 273 and repealed by s. 884 and Sch. 3.]

History – S. 660G omitted by ITTOIA 2005, s. 882(1) and Sch. 1, para. 273 and repealed by s. 884 and Sch. 3; effective for income tax purposes for 2005–06 onwards and for corporation tax purposes for accounting periods ending after 5 April 2005 (ITTOIA 2005, s. 883(1)).

Notes – S. 660G rewritten as follows:
S. 660G(1): ITTOIA 2005, s. 620(1).
S. 660G(2): ITTOIA 2005, s. 620(2) and (3).
S. 660G(3): ITTOIA 2005, s. 648(1).
S. 660G(4): ITTOIA 2005, s. 648(2)–(5).

Chapter I – Dispositions for Short Periods

Notes – S. 660–676 and s. 683–685 replaced by Ch. IA by virtue of FA 1995, s. 74 and Sch. 17, para. 1 with effect for 1995–96 and subsequent years of assessment in relation to every settlement, wherever and whenever it was made or entered into.

660 Dispositions for period which cannot exceed six years

660 [Repealed by FA 1995, s. 162 and Sch. 29, Pt. VIII(8) with effect for 1995–96 and subsequent years of assessment.]

661 Adjustments between disponor and trustees

661 [Repealed by FA 1995, s. 162 and Sch. 29, Pt. VIII(8) with effect for 1995–96 and subsequent years of assessment.]

662 Application of Chapter I to dispositions by two or more disponors

662 [Repealed by FA 1995, s. 162 and Sch. 29, Pt. VIII(8) with effect for 1995–96 and subsequent years of assessment.]

ICTA 1988

Chapter II – Settlements on Children

Notes – S. 660–676 and s. 683–685 replaced by Ch. IA by virtue of s. 74 and Sch. 17, para. 1 in relation to every settlement, wherever and whenever it was made or entered into.

663 The general rule

663 [Repealed by FA 1995, s. 162 and Sch. 29, Pt. VIII(8) with effect for 1995–96 and subsequent years of assessment.]

664 Accumulation settlements

664 [Repealed by FA 1995, s. 162 and Sch. 29, Pt. VIII(8) with effect for 1995–96 and subsequent years of assessment.]

665 Meaning of "irrevocable"

665 [Repealed by FA 1995, s. 162 and Sch. 29, Pt. VIII(8) with effect for 1995–96 and subsequent years of assessment.]

666 Interest paid by trustees

666 [Repealed by FA 1995, s. 162 and Sch. 29, Pt. VIII(8) with effect for 1995–96 and subsequent years of assessment.]

667 Adjustments between disponor and trustees

667 [Repealed by FA 1995, s. 162 and Sch. 29, Pt. VIII(8) with effect for 1995–96 and subsequent years of assessment.]

668 Application of Chapter II to settlements by two or more settlors

668 [Repealed by FA 1995, s. 162 and Sch. 29, Pt. VIII(8) with effect for 1995–96 and subsequent years of assessment.]

669 Power to obtain information under Chapter II

669 [Repealed by FA 1995, s. 162 and Sch. 29, Pt. VIII(8) with effect for 1995–96 and subsequent years of assessment.]

670 Interpretation of Chapter II

670 [Repealed by FA 1995, s. 162 and Sch. 29, Pt. VIII(8) with effect for 1995–96 and subsequent years of assessment.]

Chapter III – Revocable Settlements etc.

Cross references – S. 720: Pt. XV, Ch. III applies to charges and reliefs under the accrued income scheme as for ordinary income.

Notes – S. 660–676 and s. 683–685 were replaced by Ch. IA by virtue of FA 1995, s. 74 and Sch. 17, para. 1 with effect for 1995–96 and subsequent years of assessment in relation to every settlement, wherever and whenever it was made or entered into.

671 Revocable settlements allowing release of obligation

671 [Repealed by FA 1995, s. 162 and Sch. 29, Pt. VIII(8) with effect for 1995–96 and subsequent years of assessment.]

672 Revocable settlements allowing reversion of property

672 [Repealed by FA 1995, s. 162 and Sch. 29, Pt. VIII(8) with effect for 1995–96 and subsequent years of assessment.]

673 Settlements where settlor retains an interest

673 [Repealed by FA 1995, s. 162 and Sch. 29, Pt. VIII(8) with effect for 1995–96 and subsequent years of assessment.]

674 Settlements: discretionary power for benefit of settlor etc.

674 [Repealed by FA 1995, s. 162 and Sch. 29, Pt. VIII(8) with effect for 1995–96 and subsequent years of assessment.]

674A Other settlements where settlor retains interest in settled property

674A [Repealed by FA 1995, s. 162 and Sch. 29, Pt. VIII(8) with effect for 1995–96 and subsequent years of assessment.]

675 Provisions supplementary to sections 671 to 674

675 [Repealed by FA 1995, s. 162 and Sch. 29, Pt. VIII(8) with effect for 1995–96 and subsequent years of assessment.]

676 Disallowance of deduction from total income of certain sums paid by settlor

676 [Repealed by FA 1995, s. 162 and Sch. 29, Pt. VIII(8) with effect for 1995–96 and subsequent years of assessment.]

Chapter IB – Provisions as to Capital Sums Paid to Settlor

History – Heading inserted by FA 1995, s. 74 and Sch. 17 para. 8 with effect for 1995–96 and subsequent years of assessment in relation to every settlement, wherever and whenever it was made or entered into.

677 Sums paid to settlor otherwise than as income

677 [Omitted by ITTOIA 2005, s. 882 and Sch. 1, para. 274 and repealed by s. 884 and Sch. 3.]

History – S. 677 omitted by ITTOIA 2005, s. 882(1) and Sch. 1, para. 274 and repealed by s. 884 and Sch. 3; effective for income tax purposes for 2005–06 onwards and for corporation tax purposes for accounting periods ending after 5 April 2005 (ITTOIA 2005, s. 883(1)).

Notes – S. 677 rewritten as follows:
S. 677(1): ITTOIA 2005, s. 633(1)–(5).
S. 677(2): ITTOIA 2005, s. 635(1)–(3) and Sch. 2, para. 134(2) and (3).
S. 677(3): ITTOIA 2005, s. 418(1)–(3) and 639(1) and (2).
S. 677(4): ITTOIA 2005, s. 638(1)–(3).
S. 677(5): ITTOIA 2005, s. 638(4) and (5).
S. 677(6): ITTOIA 2005, s. 640(1).
S. 677(7): ITTOIA 2005, s. 619(1), 621 and 640(2) and (3).
S. 677(7A): ITTOIA 2005, s. 640(4).
S. 677(7B): ITTOIA 2005, s. 640(5).
S. 677(7C): ITTOIA 2005, s. 640(6) and (7).
S. 677(8): ITTOIA 2005, s. 623(1) and (2).
S. 677(9): ITTOIA 2005, s. 620(4), 634(1)–(4) and (7) and Sch. 2, para. 134(4).
S. 677(10): ITTOIA 2005, s. 634(4) and (5) and Sch. 2, para. 134(5).

678 Capital sums paid by body connected with settlement

678 [*Omitted* by ITTOIA 2005, s. 882 and Sch. 1, para. 275 and repealed by s. 884 and Sch. 3.]

History – S. 678 omitted by ITTOIA 2005, s. 882(1) and Sch. 1, para. 275 and repealed by s. 884 and Sch. 3; effective for income tax purposes for 2005–06 onwards and for corporation tax purposes for accounting periods ending after 5 April 2005 (ITTOIA 2005, s. 883(1)).

Notes – S. 678 rewritten as follows:
S. 678(1): ITTOIA 2005, s. 641(1).
S. 678(2): ITTOIA 2005, s. 641(3)–(6).
S. 678(3): ITTOIA 2005, s. 643(3).
S. 678(4): ITTOIA 2005, s. 643(4).
S. 678(5): ITTOIA 2005, s. 634(1) and s. 643(1).
S. 678(6): ITTOIA 2005, s. 642(1)–(4).
S. 678(7): ITTOIA 2005, Sch. 2, para. 135.

679 Application of Chapter III to settlements by two or more settlors

679 [Repealed by FA 1995, s. 162 and Sch. 29, Pt. VIII(8) with effect for 1995–96 and subsequent years of assessment.]

680 Power to obtain information for purposes of Chapter III

680 [Repealed by FA 1995, s. 162 and Sch. 29, Pt. VIII(8) with effect for 1995–96 and subsequent years of assessment.]

681 Interpretation of Chapter III

681 [Repealed by FA 1995, s. 162 and Sch. 29, Pt. VIII(8) with effect for 1995–96 and subsequent years of assessment.]

682 Ascertainment of undistributed income

682 [Omitted by ITTOIA2005, s. 882 and Sch. 1, para. 276 and repealed by s. 884 and Sch. 3.]

History – S. 682 omitted by ITTOIA 2005, s. 882(1) and Sch. 1, para. 276 and repealed by s. 884 and Sch. 3; effective for income tax purposes for 2005–06 onwards and for corporation tax purposes for accounting periods ending after 5 April 2005 (ITTOIA 2005, s. 883(1)).

Notes – S. 682 rewritten as follows:
S. 682(1): ITTOIA 2005, s. 636(1)–(6) and 637(1).
S. 682(2): ITTOIA 2005, s. 637(2).
S. 682(3): ITTOIA 2005, s. 637(3).
S. 682(4): ITTOIA 2005, s. 637(4) and (5).
S. 682(5): ITTOIA 2005, s. 637(6).
S. 682(6): ITTOIA 2005, s. 637(7).

682A Supplementary provisions

682A [Omitted by ITTOIA 2005, s. 882 and Sch. 1, para. 276 and repealed by s. 884 and Sch. 3.]

History – S. 682A omitted by ITTOIA 2005, s. 882(1) and Sch. 1, para. 276 and repealed by s. 884 and Sch. 3; effective for income tax purposes for 2005–06 onwards and for corporation tax purposes for accounting periods ending after 5 April 2005 (ITTOIA 2005, s. 883(1)).

Notes – S. 682A rewritten as follows:
S. 682A(1): ITTOIA 2005, s. 620(1)–(3), 644(1) and (2), 645(1)–(4), 647(1) and (2) and 648(1)–(5).
S. 682A(2): ITTOIA 2005, s. 637(8) and 878(6).

Chapter IV – Liability to Higher Rate and Additional Rate Tax

Cross references – S. 720: Pt. XV, Ch. IV applies to charges and reliefs under the accrued income scheme as for ordinary income.

Notes – Former references in this Chapter to tax at a rate equal to the sum of the basic and additional rates of tax largely substituted, by virtue of FA 1993, by reference to tax at the rate applicable to trusts.

LIABILITY OF SETTLORS

683 Settlements made after 6th April 1965

683 [Repealed by FA 1995, s. 162 and Sch. 29, Pt. VIII(8) with effect for 1995–96 and subsequent years of assessment.]

684 Settlements made before 7th April 1965 but after 9th April 1946

684 [Repealed by FA 1995, s. 162 and Sch. 29, Pt. VIII(8) with effect for 1995–96 and subsequent years of assessment.]

685 Provisions supplementary to sections 683 and 684

685 [Repealed by FA 1995, s. 162 and Sch. 29, Pt. VIII(8), with effect for 1995–96 and subsequent years of assessment.]

Chapter IC – Liability of Trustees

History – Heading substituted by FA 1995, s. 74 and Sch. 17, para. 12, with effect for 1995–96 in relation to every settlement, wherever and whenever it was made or entered into.

685A Meaning of "settled property"

685A [Omitted by ITA 2007, s. 1027 and Sch. 1, para. 145 and repealed by ITA 2007, s. 1031 and Sch. 3, Pt. 1 with effect for 2007–08 and subsequent tax years.]

Notes – S. 685A rewritten as follows:
S. 685A(1): ITA 2007, s. 466(1), (2), (3), (4).
S. 685A(2): ITA 2007, s. 466(1), (5), (6).

685B Meaning of "settlor"

685B [Omitted by ITA 2007, s. 1027 and Sch. 1, para. 145 and repealed by ITA 2007, s. 1031 and Sch. 3, Pt. 1 with effect for 2007–08 and subsequent tax years.]

Notes – S. 685B rewritten as follows:
S. 685B(1): ITA 2007, s. 467(1), (2).
S. 685B(2): ITA 2007, s. 467(3), (4).
S. 685B(3): ITA 2007, s. 467(5).
S. 685B(4): ITA 2007, s. 467(6).
S. 685B(5): ITA 2007, s. 467(4), 468(1), (2), (3), (4), (5).
S. 685B(6): ITA 2007, s. 469(1), (2).
S. 685B(7): ITA 2007, s. 465(7).
S. 685B(8): ITA 2007, s. 465(8).

685C Transfer between settlements: identification of settlor

685C [Omitted by ITA 2007, s. 1027 and Sch. 1, para. 145 and repealed by ITA 2007, s. 1031 and Sch. 3, Pt. 1 with effect for 2007–08 and subsequent tax years.]

Notes – S. 685C rewritten as follows:
S. 685C(1): ITA 2007, s. 470(1).
S. 685C(2): ITA 2007, s. 470(3).
S. 685C(3): ITA 2007, s. 471(1), (2), (3).
S. 685C(4): ITA 2007, s. 471(1), (4).
S. 685C(5): ITA 2007, s. 471(5).
S. 685C(6): ITA 2007, s. 470(2).
S. 685C(7): ITA 2007, s. 470(4).

685D Variation of will or intestacy, etc: identification of settlor

685D [Omitted by ITA 2007, s. 1027 and Sch. 1, para. 145 and repealed by ITA 2007, s. 1031 and Sch. 3, Pt. 1 with effect for 2007–08 and later tax years.]

Notes – S. 685D rewritten as follows:
S. 685D(1): ITA 2007, s. 472(1), 473(1).
S. 685D(2): ITA 2007, s. 472(2).
S. 685D(3): ITA 2007, s. 472(3).
S. 685D(4): ITA 2007, s. 472(4), (5).
S. 685D(5): ITA 2007, s. 473(2), (3).
S. 685D(6): ITA 2007, s. 473(4).
S. 685D(7): ITA 2007, s. 473(5).
S. 685D(8): ITA 2007, s. 473(6).

685E Trustees of settlements

685E [Omitted by ITA 2007, s. 1027 and Sch. 1, para. 145 and repealed by ITA 2007, s. 1031 and Sch. 3, Pt. 1 with effect for 2007–08 and subsequent tax years.]

Notes – S. 685E rewritten as follows:
S. 685E(1): ITA 2007, s. 474(1).
S. 685E(2): ITA 2007, s. 475(1), (2).
S. 685E(3): ITA 2007, s. 475(4).
S. 685E(4): ITA 2007, s. 475(5), 476(2), (3).
S. 685E(5): ITA 2007, s. 476(2), (3), (4), (5).
S. 685E(6): ITA 2007, s. 475(6).
S. 685E(7): ITA 2007, s. 475(3).
S. 685E(8): ITA 2007, s. 474(2), (3).

685F Application of section 739 and 740

685F [Omitted by ITA 2007, s. 1027 and Sch. 1, para. 145 and repealed by ITA 2007, s. 1031 and Sch. 3, Pt. 1 with effect for 2007–08 and subsequent tax years.]

Notes – *S. 685F rewritten as follows:*
S. 685F(1): ITA 2007, Sch. 2 para. 134(1), (2), (3), (4).
S. 685F(2): ITA 2007, s. Sch. 2 para. 135(1), (2), (3), (4), (5).

685G Sub-funds

685G [Omitted by ITA 2007, s. 1027 and Sch. 1, para. 145 and repealed by ITA 2007, s. 1031 and Sch. 3, Pt. 1 with effect for 2007–08 and subsequent tax years.]

Notes – S. 685G rewritten as follows:
S. 685G(1): ITA 2007, s. 477(1), (2), (3), (4), (5), (6).
S. 685G(2): ITA 2007, s. 477(2), (4), (6), (7).
S. 685G(3): ITA 2007, s. 477(7).

686 Accumulation and discretionary trusts: special rates of tax

History – Sidenote substituted by F(No. 2)A 1997, s. 32(8), with effect in relation to distributions made on or after 6 April 1999.

686 [Omitted by ITA 2007, s. 1027 and Sch. 1, para. 145 and repealed by ITA 2007, s. 1031 and Sch. 3, Pt. 1 with effect for 2007–08 and later tax years.]

Notes – S. 686 rewritten as follows:
S. 686(1): ITA 2007, s. 479(1), (2), 481(2).
S. 686(1AA): ITA 2007, s. 479(3), (4), 481(3), (4).
S. 686(1A): ITA 2007, s. 9(1), (2).
S. 686(2): ITA 2007, s. 479(1), 480(1), (2), (3), (4).
S. 686(2): ITTOIA 2005, s. 568 and Sch. 2, para. 95.
S. 686(2AA): ITA 2007, s. 484(1), (2), (4), (5), 486(1), Sch. 2 para. 102.
S. 686(2A): ITA 2007, s. 487(1), (2), (3), (4), 1023.
S. 686(2B): ITA 2007, s. 487(5), (6).
S. 686(5A): ITA 2007, s. 479(3), 481(3).
S. 686(5B): ITA 2007, s. 19(3).
S. 686(6): ITA 2007, s. 463(1), 483(1), (2), (3).
S. 686(6A): ITA 2007, s. 480(4).
S. 686(6ZA): ITA 2007, s. 480(3), (5).
S. 686(6ZB): ITA 2007, s. 480(6).

686A Receipts to be treated as income to which section 686 applies

686A [Omitted by ITA 2007, s. 1027 and Sch. 1, para. 145 and repealed by ITA 2007, s 1031 and Sch. 3, Pt. 1 with effect for 2007–08 and subsequent tax years.]

Notes – In former s. 686A(2)(a), the words "by way of qualifying distribution" inserted by FA 2007, s. 55(1), with effect in respect of payments made to the trustees of a settlement on or after 6 April 2006. This amendment was therefore in force for the tax year 2006–07 only.
S. 686A rewritten as follows:
S. 686A(1): ITA 2007, s. 481(1), (2), (3), (4).
S. 686A(2): ITA 2007, s. 482.

686B Share incentive plans: distributions in respect of unappropriated shares

686B [Omitted by ITA 2007, s. 1027 and Sch. 1, para. 145 and repealed by ITA 2007. s. 1031 and Sch. 3, Pt. 1 with effect for 2007–08 and subsequent tax years.]

Notes – S. 686B rewritten as follows:
S. 686B(1): ITA 2007, s. 488(1).
S. 686B(2): ITA 2007, s. 488(2), (3), (4).
S. 686B(3): ITA 2007, s. 489(2), (3), (5), (7).
S. 686B(4): ITA 2007, s. 489(2), (4), (5), (7).
S. 686B(5): ITA 2007, s. 489(6), (7).
S. 686B(6): ITA 2007, s. 488(5).
S. 686B(7): ITA 2007, s. 490(3).
S. 686B(8): ITA 2007, s. Sch. 2 para. 103(1), (3), (4), (5), (6).

686C Interpretation of section 686B

686C [Omitted by ITA 2007, s. 1027 and Sch. 1, para. 145 and repealed by ITA 2007, s. 1031 and Sch. 3, Pt. 1 with effect for 2007–08 and subsequent tax years.]

Notes – S. 686C rewritten as follows:
S. 686C(1): ITA 2007, s. 490(1).
S. 686C(2): ITA 2007, s. 490(2).
S. 686C(3): ITA 2007, s. 488(6).
S. 686C(4): ITA 2007, s. 489(7).
S. 686C(5): ITA 2007, s. 489(8).

686D Special trust rates not to apply to first slice of trust income

686D [Omitted by ITA 2007, s. 1027 and Sch. 1, para. 145 and repealed by ITA 2007, s. 1031 and Sch. 3, Pt. 1 with effect for 2007–08 and subsequent tax years.]

Notes – S. 686D rewritten as follows:
S. 686D(1): ITA 2007, s. 491(1), (2).
S. 686D(2): ITA 2007, s. 491(1), (2).
S. 686D(3): ITA 2007, s. 491(1), (2).
S. 686D(4): ITA 2007, s. 491(3), (4).
S. 686D(5): ITA 2007, s. 491(3).
S. 686D(6): ITA 2007, s. 491(3).

S. 686D(7): ITA 2007, s. 491(3).
S. 686D(8): ITA 2007, s. 491(3), (5).

686E Application of section 686D where settlor has made more than one settlement

686E [Omitted by ITA 2007, s. 1027 and Sch. 1, para. 145 and repealed by ITA 2007, s. 1031 and Sch. 3, Pt. 1 with effect for 2007–08 and subsequent tax years.]

Notes – S. 686E rewritten as follows:
S. 686E(1): ITA 2007, s. 492(1).
S. 686E(2): ITA 2007, s. 492(2), (3).
S. 686E(3): ITA 2007, s. 492(1), (4).
S. 686E(4): ITA 2007, s. 492(5).

687 Payments under discretionary trusts

687 [Omitted by ITA 2007, s. 1027 and Sch. 1, para. 1027 and Sch. 3, Pt. 1 with effect for 2007–08 and subsequent tax years.]

Notes – S. 687 rewritten as follows:
S. 687(1): ITA 2007, s. 493(1), (2), (3), 899(5).
S. 687(2): ITA 2007, s. 23, 30(2), 494(1), (2), (3), (4), 496(1), (2), (3), (4), (5).
S. 687(3): ITA 2007, s. 497(1), (2), (3), 498(1), (2).
S. 687(3A): ITA 2007, s. 498(1).
S. 687(4): ITA 2007, s. 463(1).
S. 687(5): ITA 2007, s. 493(5).

687A Discretionary payments by trustees to companies

687A [Omitted by CTA 2010, s. 1177 and Sch. 1, para. 92 and repealed by CTA 2010, s. 1181 and Sch. 3, Pt. 1.]

History – S. 687A omitted by CTA 2010, s. 1177 and Sch. 1, para. 92 and repealed by CTA 2010, s. 1181 and Sch. 3, Pt. 1, with effect for corporation tax purposes for accounting periods ending on or after 1 April 2010, and for income and capital gains tax purposes for the tax year 2010–11 and subsequent tax years.

Notes – S. 687A rewritten for corporation tax purposes as follows:
S. 687A(1): CTA 2010, s. 610(1).
S. 687A(2): CTA 2010, s. 610(2).
S. 687A(3): CTA 2010, s. 610(3).
S. 687A(4): CTA 2010, s. 610(4).

688 Schemes for employees and directors to acquire shares

688 [Omitted by ITTOIA 2005, s. 882 and Sch.1, para. 279 and repealed by s. 884 and Sch. 3.]

History – S. 688 omitted by ITTOIA 2005, s. 882(1) and Sch. 1, para. 279 and repealed by s. 884 and Sch. 3; effective for income tax purposes for 2005–06 onwards and for corporation tax purposes for accounting periods ending after 5 April 2005 (ITTOIA 2005, s. 883(1)).
Notes – S. 688 rewritten as ITTOIA 2005, s. 752(1) and (2).

689 Recovery from trustees of discretionary trusts of higher rate tax due from beneficiaries

689 [Repealed by FA 1995, s. 74 and Sch. 17, para. 15 and s. 162 and Sch. 29, Pt. VIII(8) with effect for 1995–96 and subsequent years of assessment.]

Chapter ID – Trust Management Expenses

689A Disregard of expenses where beneficiary non-resident

689A [Omitted by ITA 2007, s. 1027 and Sch. 1, para. 147 and repealed by ITA 2007, s. 1031 and Sch. 3, Pt. 1 with effect for 2007–08 and subsequent tax years.]

Notes – S. 689A rewritten as follows:
S. 689A(1): ITA 2007, s. 499(1), 501(1), 502(1), 1023.
S. 689A(2): ITA 2007, s. 501(2), (3).
S. 689A(3): ITA 2007, s. 501(4).
S. 689A(4): ITA 2007, s. 501(5).
S. 689A(5): ITA 2007, s. 502(2), (3).

689B Order in which expenses to be set against income

689B [Omitted by CTA 2010, s. 1177 and Sch. 1, para. 93 and repealed by CTA 2010, s. 1181 and Sch. 3, Pt. 1.]

History – S. 689B omitted by CTA 2010, s. 1177 and Sch. 1, para. 93 and repealed by CTA 2010, s. 1181 and Sch. 3, Pt. 1, with effect for corporation tax purposes for accounting periods ending on or after 1 April 2010, and for income and capital gains tax purposes for the tax year 2010–11 and subsequent tax years.

Notes – S. 689B rewritten as follows:
S. 689B(1): ITA 2007, s. 484(2), 486(1), 503(2).
S. 689B(2): ITA 2007, s. 486(1), (2), 503(2), (3).

S. 689B(2A): ITA 2007, s. 486(1), 503(2).
S. 689B(3): ITA 2007, s. 486(1), 503(2).
S. 689B rewritten for corporation tax purposes as follows:
S. 689B: CTA 2010, s. 611(1), (2).

Chapter V – Maintenance Funds for Historic Buildings

690 Schedule 4 directions

690 [Omitted by ITA 2007, s. 1027 and Sch. 1, para. 149 and repealed by ITA 2007, s. 1031 and Sch. 3, Pt. 1 with effect for 2007–08 and subsequent tax years.]

Notes – S. 690 rewritten as ITA 2007, s. 507(2).

691 Certain income not to be income of settlor etc.

691 [Omitted by ITA 2007, s. 1027 and Sch. 1, para. 149 and repealed by ITA 2007, s. 1031 and Sch. 3, Pt. 1 with effect for 2007–08 and subsequent tax years.]

Notes – S. 691 rewritten as follows:
S. 691(1): ITA 2007, s. 507(2), 508(1).
S. 691(2): ITA 2007, s. 508(1), (2), (3), (4).
S. 691(3): ITA 2007, s. 510(1), (2).
S. 691(4): ITA 2007, s. 508(5).
S. 691(5): ITA 2007, s. 509(1), (3), (4).

692 Reimbursement of settlor

692 [Omitted by ITA 2007, s. 1027 and Sch. 1, para. 149 and repealed by ITA 2007, s. 1031 and Sch. 3, Pt. 1 with effect for 2007–08 and subsequent tax years.]

Notes – S. 692 rewritten as follows:
S. 692(1): ITA 2007, s. 507(2), 511(1).
S. 692(2): ITA 2007, s. 511(2).

693 Severance of settled property for certain purposes

693 [Omitted by ITA 2007, s. 1027 and Sch. 1, para. 149 and repealed by ITA 2007, s. 1031 and Sch. 3, Pt. 1 with effect for 2007–08 and subsequent tax years.]

Notes – S. 693 rewritten as ITA 2007, s. 507(2), (3).

694 Trustees chargeable to income tax in certain cases at higher rate reduced by rate applicable to trusts

History – The section sidenote (heading) amended by FA 2004, s. 29 and Sch. 4, para. 2. It formerly read "Trustees chargeable to income tax at 30 per cent in certain cases".

694 [Omitted by ITA 2007, s. 1027 and Sch. 1, para. 149 and repealed by ITA 2007, s. 1031 and Sch. 3, Pt. 1 with effect for 2007–08 and subsequent tax years.]

Notes – S. 694 rewritten as follows:
S. 694(1): ITA 2007, s. 507(2), 512(1), (2), (3), (4).
S. 694(2): ITA 2007, s. 513(1), (2).
S. 694(2A): ITA 2007, s. 515.
S. 694(3): ITA 2007, s. 517(1), (2).
S. 694(4): ITA 2007, s. 513(3), (4), 514.
S. 694(5): ITA 2007, s. 512(1), (5), (6).
S. 694(6): ITA 2007, s. 516(1), (2), (3).
S. 694(7): ITA 2007, s. 516(4).

PART XVI – ESTATES OF DECEASED PERSONS IN COURSE OF ADMINISTRATION

695 Limited interests in residue

695 [Omitted by CTA 2009, s. 1322 and Sch. 1, para. 204 and repealed by CTA 2009, s. 1326 and Sch. 3, Pt. 1.]

History – S. 695 omitted by CTA 2009, s. 1322 and Sch. 1, para. 204 and repealed by CTA 2009, s. 1326 and Sch. 3, Pt. 1, with effect for corporation tax purposes for accounting periods ending on or after 1 April 2009, and for income tax and capital gains tax purposes for the tax year 2009–10 and subsequent tax years.

Notes – Rewritten income tax provisions are now located as follows:
S. 695(1): ITTOIA 2005, s. 653(1) and 659(1).
S. 695(2): ITTOIA 2005, s. 649(1) and (3), 654(2) and (4), 656(1) and (2), 659(1), 661(1), 674(4) and (5) and 675.
S. 695(3): ITTOIA 2005, s. 649(1) and (3), 654(3) and (4), 656(1) and (2), 659(1), 661(1), 674(4) and (5) and 675.
S. 695(4): ITTOIA 2005, s. 649(1) and (3), 656(1)–(3), 657(2), (3) and (5), 658(2), 661(1), 662, 675 and 830(1) and (2).
S. 695(5): ITTOIA 2005, s. 678(1) and (2).
S. 695 rewritten for corporation tax purposes as follows:
S. 695(1): CTA 2009, s. 938(1).

S. 695(2): CTA 2009, s. 934(1), 939(2), (4), 941(1), (2), 944(1), 957(3), (5), 958.
S. 695(3): CTA 2009, s. 934(1), 939(3), (4), 941(1), (2), 944(1), 957(4), (5), 958.
S. 695(4): CTA 2009, s. 934(1), 941(1), (2), (3) , 942(1), (2), (3), (5), 944(1), 945, 958.
S. 695(5): CTA 2009, s. 961(1), (2).
S. 695(6): not rewritten (see CTA 2009 Explanatory Notes, Annex 1, Change 74, and commentary on clause 961).
S. 695(7): CTA 2009, s. 946(5).

696 Absolute interests in residue

696 [Omitted by CTA 2009, s. 1322 and Sch. 1, para. 205 and repealed by CTA 2009, s. 1326 and Sch. 3, Pt. 1.]

History – S. 696 omitted by CTA 2009, s. 1322 and Sch. 1, para. 205 and repealed by CTA 2009, s. 1326 and Sch. 3, Pt. 1, with effect for corporation tax purposes for accounting periods ending on or after 1 April 2009, and for income tax and capital gains tax purposes for the tax year 2009–10 and subsequent tax years.

Notes – Rewritten income tax provisions are now located as follows:
S. 696(1): ITTOIA 2005, s. 659(1).
S. 696(2): ITTOIA 2005, s. 667(1) and (2).
S. 696(3): ITTOIA 2005, s. 649(1) and (3), 652(1) and (2), 656(1) and (2), 659(1) and 660(1) and (2).
S. 696(3A): ITTOIA 2005, s. 660(1) and (2) and 665(1)–(3).
S. 696(3B): ITTOIA 2005, s. 665(1)–(3).
S. 696(4): ITTOIA 2005, s. 656(1)–(3) and 660(1).
S. 696(5): ITTOIA 2005, s. 652(3),660(2) and 665(1)-(3).
S. 696(6): ITTOIA 2005, s. 649(1),657(2), (3) and (5), 658(2) and 830(1) and (2).
S. 696(7): ITTOIA 2005, s. 677(1) and (2).
S. 696 rewritten for corporation tax purposes as follows:
S. 696(2): CTA 2009, s. 950(1), (2), (3).
S. 696(3): CTA 2009, s. 934(1), 937(1), (2), 941(1), (2), 943(1), (2).
S. 696(3A): CTA 2009, s. 943(1), (2), 948(1), (2), (3).
S. 696(3B): CTA 2009, s. 948(1), (2), (3).
S. 696(4): CTA 2009, s. 941(1), (2), (3), 943(1).
S. 696(5): CTA 2009, s. 937(3), 943(2), 948(1), (2), (3).
S. 696(6): CTA 2009, s. 934(1), 942(1), (2), (3), (5).
S. 696(7): CTA 2009, s. 960(1), (2).
S. 696(8): CTA 2009, s. 950(3).
S. 696(9): CTA 2009, s. 946(5).

697 Supplementary provisions as to absolute interests in residue

697 [Omitted by CTA 2009, s. 1322 and Sch. 1, para. 206 and repealed by CTA 2009, s. 1326 and Sch. 3, Pt. 1.]

History – S. 697 omitted by CTA 2009, s. 1322 and Sch. 1, para. 206 and repealed by CTA 2009, s. 1326 and Sch. 3, Pt. 1, with effect for corporation tax purposes for accounting periods ending on or after 1 April 2009, and for income tax and capital gains tax purposes for the tax year 2009–10 and subsequent tax years.

Notes – Rewritten income tax provisions are now located as follows:
S. 697(1): ITTOIA 2005, s. 666(1)–(3) and (5).
S. 697(1A): ITTOIA 2005, s. 666(2) and (6).
S. 697(2): ITTOIA 2005, s. 668(1)–(3).
S. 697(3): ITTOIA 2005, s. 668(1) and (5).
S. 697(4): ITTOIA 2005, s. 671(5) and (6).
S. 697 rewritten for corporation tax purposes as follows:
S. 697(1): CTA 2009, s. 949(1), (2), (3), (5).
S. 697(1A): CTA 2009, s. 949(2), (6).
S. 697(2): CTA 2009, s. 951(1), (2), (3).
S. 697(3): CTA 2009, s. 951(1), (5).
S. 697(4): CTA 2009, s. 954(5), (6), (7).
S. 697(5): CTA 2009, s. 954(6), (7).

698 Special provisions as to certain interests in residue

698 [Omitted by CTA 2009, s. 1322 and Sch. 1, para. 207 and repealed by CTA 2009, s. 1326 and Sch. 3, Pt. 1.]

History – S. 698 omitted by CTA 2009, s. 1322 and Sch. 1, para. 207 and repealed by CTA 2009, s. 1326 and Sch. 3, Pt. 1, with effect for corporation tax purposes for accounting periods ending on or after 1 April 2009, and for income tax and capital gains tax purposes for the tax year 2009–10 and subsequent tax years.

Notes – Rewritten income tax provisions are now located as follows:
S. 698(1): ITTOIA 2005, s. 650(5). But ITTOIA 2005 does not rewrite the provisions in ICTA 1988, s. 698(1) that deem income from an interest in another deceased person's estate to be part of the aggregate income of the estate as that result would arise in any event. (See ITTOIA 2005, Explanatory Notes, Annex 1, Table 1 (Change 158).)
S. 698(1A): ITTOIA 2005, s. 672(1), 673(1), 674(1) and (2) and 675.
S. 698(1B): ITTOIA 2005, s. 659(2)–(4), 672(1)–(4), 673(1)–(4) and (6), 674(3)–(5) and 675.
S. 698(2): ITTOIA 2005, s. 659(3) and 671(1) and (2).
S. 698(3): ITTOIA 2005, s. 649(1) and (3), 650(3), (4) and (6), 655(1), 656(1)–(3), 657(2), (3) and (5), 658(2), 659(2), 662 and 678(1) and (2).
S. 698 rewritten for corporation tax purposes as follows:
S. 698(1): CTA 2009, s. 935(5).
S. 698(1A): CTA 2009, s. 955(1), 956(1), 957(1), (2), 958.
S.698(1B): CTA 2009, s. 955(1), (2), (3), (4), 956(1), (2), (3), (4), (6), 957(3), (4), (5), 958.
S. 698(2): CTA 2009, s. 954(1), (2).
S. 698(3): CTA 2009, s. 934(1), 935(3), (4), (6), 940(1), 941(1), (2), (3), 942(1), (2), (3), (5), 945, 961(1), (2).
S. 698(4): CTA 2009, s. 953(1).
S. 698(5): CTA 2009, s. 953(3).
S. 698(6): CTA 2009, s. 953(3).

698A Taxation of income of beneficiaries at lower rate or at rates applicable to distribution income

History – In the heading to s. 698A the word "distribution" substituted by ITTOIA 2005, s. 882(1) and Sch. 1, para. 288(5); effective for income tax purposes for 2005–06 onwards and for corporation tax purposes for accounting periods ending after 5 April 2005 (ITTOIA 2005, s. 883(1)).

698A [Omitted by ITA 2007, s. 1027 and Sch. 1, para. 150 and repealed by ITA 2007, s. 1031 and Sch.3, Pt. 1 with effect for 2007–08 and subsequent tax years.]

Notes – S. 698A rewritten as follows:
S. 698A(1): ITA 2007, Sch. 1 para. 566.
S. 698A(2): ITA 2007, Sch. 1 para. 566.
S. 698A(3): ITA 2007, Sch. 1 para. 566.

699 Relief from higher rate tax for inheritance tax on accrued income

699 [Omitted by ITTOIA 2005, s. 882 and Sch. 1, para. 289 and repealed by s. 884 and Sch. 3.]

History – S. 699 omitted by ITTOIA 2005, s. 882(1) and Sch. 1, para. 289 and repealed by s. 884 and Sch. 3; effective for income tax purposes for 2005–06 onwards and for corporation tax purposes for accounting periods ending after 5 April 2005 (ITTOIA 2005, s. 883(1)).

Notes – S. 699: ITTOIA 2005 as follows:
S. 699(1): ITTOIA 2005, s. 669(1) and (2).
S. 699(2): ITTOIA 2005, s. 669(3).
S. 699(3): ITTOIA 2005, s. 669(4).
S. 699(4): ITTOIA 2005, s. 669(5) and (6).
S. 699(5): ITTOIA 2005, s. 669(7) and (8).
S. 699(6): ITTOIA 2005, s. 669(4). But ITTOIA 2005 does not rewrite ICTA 1988, s. 699(6)(b) as it is spent. (See ITTOIA 2005, Explanatory Notes, Annex 1, Table 1 (Change 158).)

699A Untaxed sums comprised in the income of the estate

699A [Omitted by CTA 2009, s. 1322 and Sch. 1, para. 208 and repealed by CTA 2009, s. 1326 and Sch. 3, Pt. 1.]

History – S. 699A omitted by CTA 2009, s. 1322 and Sch. 1, para. 208 and repealed by CTA 2009, s. 1326 and Sch. 3, Pt. 1, with effect for corporation tax purposes for accounting periods ending on or after 1 April 2009, and for income tax and capital gains tax purposes for the tax year 2009–10 and subsequent tax years.

Notes – Rewritten income tax provisions are now located as follows:
S. 699A(1): ITTOIA 2005, s. 680(1)–(4). But ITTOIA 2005 does not rewrite ICTA 1988, s. 699A(1)(b) as it serves no useful purpose on the basis that the income to which ICTA 1988, s. 699A(1)(a) applies is not directly assessable in any event. (See ITTOIA 2005, Explanatory Notes, Annex 1, Table 1 (Change 158).)
S. 699A(1A): ITTOIA 2005, s. 680(1)–(3).
S. 699A(1B): ITTOIA 2005, s. 651(4) and (5).
S. 699A(2): ITTOIA 2005, s. 663(2) and 659(2)–(6).
S. 699A(3): ITTOIA 2005, s. 657(3) and (4).
S. 699A(4): ITTOIA 2005, s. 663(2) and 680(1)–(4).
S. 699A(5): ITTOIA 2005, s. 680(5).
S. 699A(6): ITTOIA 2005, Sch. 1, para. 146.
S. 699A rewritten for corporation tax purposes as follows:
S. 699A(1): CTA 2009, s. 963(1), (2), (3), (4).
S. 699A(1A): CTA 2009, s. 963(1), (2), (3).
S. 699A(1B): CTA 2009, s. 936(4), (5).
S. 699A(2): CTA 2009, s. 946(2), 962(2), (3), (4), (5), (6).
S. 699A(3): CTA 2009, s. 942(3), (4).
S. 699A(4): CTA 2009, s. 946(2), 963(1), (2), (3), (4).
S. 699A(5): CTA 2009, s. 963(5).

700 Adjustments and information

700 [Omitted by TIOPA 2010, s. 371 and Sch. 7, para. 45 and repealed by TIOPA 2010, s. 378 and Sch. 10, Pt. 12.]

History – S. 700 omitted by TIOPA 2010, s. 371 and Sch. 7, para. 45 and repealed by TIOPA 2010, s. 378 and Sch. 10, Pt. 12, with effect for corporation tax purposes for accounting periods ending on or after 1 April 2010, for income tax and capital gains tax purposes for the tax year 2010–11 and subsequent tax years, and for petroleum revenue tax purposes for chargeable periods beginning on or after 1 July 2010.

Notes – S. 700 rewritten in ITTOIA 2005 as follows:
S. 700(1): ITTOIA 2005, s. 682(1) and (2).
S. 700(2): ITTOIA 2005, s. 682(3) and (4).
S. 700 rewritten by TIOPA 2010 as follows:
S. 700(5), (6): TIOPA 2010, Sch. 7, para. 47 (but words after s. 700(6)(b) not rewritten, as unnecessary).
S. 700(7): not rewritten, as unnecessary.
S. 700 rewritten for corporation tax purposes as follows:
S. 700(1): CTA 2009, s. 965(1), (2).
S. 700(2): CTA 2009, s. 965(3), (4).
S. 700(3): CTA 2009, s. 965(5).
S. 700(4): CTA 2009, s. 966(1), (2), (3), (4).
S. 700(5): CTA 2009, s. 967(1), (2), (3).
S. 700(6): CTA 2009, s. 967(4).

701 Interpretation

701 [Omitted by CTA 2009, s. 1322 and Sch. 1, para. 210 and repealed by CTA 2009, s. 1326 and Sch. 3, Pt. 1.]

History – S. 701 omitted by CTA 2009, s. 1322 and Sch. 1, para. 210 and repealed by CTA 2009, s. 1326 and Sch. 3, Pt. 1, with effect for corporation tax purposes for accounting periods ending on or after 1 April 2009, and for income tax and capital gains tax purposes for the tax year 2009–10 and subsequent tax years.

Notes – Rewritten income tax provisions are now located as follows:
S. 701(2): ITTOIA 2005, s. 650(1), (4) and (6).
S. 701(3): ITTOIA 2005, s. 650(2), (4) and (6).
S. 701(3A): ITTOIA 2005, s. 663(1)–(4), 670(1)–(5) and 679(2) and (3).
S. 701(4): ITTOIA 2005, s. 663(1)–(4), 670(1)–(5) and 679(2) and (3).
S. 701(5): ITTOIA 2005, s. 664(6).
S. 701(8): ITTOIA 2005, s. 664(1)–(5).
S. 701(9): ITTOIA 2005, s. 651(1)–(3).
S. 701(10): ITTOIA 2005, s. 651(1).
S. 701(10A): ITTOIA 2005, s. 651(1), (4) and (5).
S. 701(11): ITTOIA 2005, s. 649(4).
S. 701(12): ITTOIA 2005, s. 681(1)–(4).
S. 701(13): ITTOIA 2005, s. 653(1).
ITTOIA 2005 does not rewrite some of the provisions in ICTA 1988, s. 701(6) as the restricted meaning of annual payments makes these provisions otiose. Consequently, ICTA 1988, s. 701(7) need not be rewritten. (See ITTOIA 2005, Explanatory Notes, Annex 1, Table 1 (Change 158).)
S. 701 rewritten for corporation tax purposes as follows:
S. 701(2): CTA 2009, s. 935(1), (4), (6).
S. 701(3): CTA 2009, s. 935(2), (4), (6).
S. 701(3A): CTA 2009, s. 946(1), (2), (3), (4), 952(1), (2), (3), (4), (5), 962(2), (3).
S. 701(4): CTA 2009, s. 968.
S. 701(5): CTA 2009, s. 947(6).
S. 701(6): not rewritten (see CTA 2009 Explanatory Notes, Annex 1, Change 70).
S. 701(7): not rewritten (see CTA 2009 Explanatory Notes, Annex 1, Change 70).
S. 701(8): CTA 2009, s. 947(1), (2), (3), (4), (5).
S. 701(9): CTA 2009, s. 936(1), (2), (3).
S. 701(10): CTA 2009, s. 936(1).
S. 701(10A): CTA 2009, s. 936(1), (4), (5).
S. 701(11): CTA 2009, s. 934(3).
S. 701(12): CTA 2009, s. 964(1), (2), (3), (4).
S. 701(13): CTA 2009, s. 938(1).

702 Application to Scotland

702 [Omitted by CTA 2009, s. 1322 and Sch. 1, para. 211 and repealed by CTA 2009, s. 1326 and Sch. 3, Pt. 1.]

History – S. 702 omitted by CTA 2009, s. 1322 and Sch. 1, para. 211 and repealed by CTA 2009, s. 1326 and Sch. 3, Pt. 1, with effect for corporation tax purposes for accounting periods ending on or after 1 April 2009, and for income tax and capital gains tax purposes for the tax year 2009–10 and subsequent tax years.

Notes – Rewritten income tax provisions are now located at ITTOIA 2005, s. 653(2) and 664(6).
S. 702 rewritten for corporation tax purposes as CTA 2009, s. 938(2), 947(6).

PART XVII – TAX AVOIDANCE

Hansard – HC Debates, 10 April 1984, col. 254 (not reproduced): "…The House of Lords made it clear that [Ramsay/Furniss] is an evolving area of law, but the emerging principles do not in any way call in question the tax treatment of covenants, leasing transactions and other straightforward commercial transactions. Nor is there any question of HMRC challenging for example the tax treatment of straightforward transfers of assets between members of the same group of companies…"

Chapter I – Cancellation of Corporation Tax Advantages from Certain Transactions in Securities

History – Chapter I of Part XVII omitted by CTA 2010, s. 1177 and Sch. 1, para. 94 and repealed by CTA 2010, s. 1181 and Sch. 3, Pt. 1.

703 Cancellation of corporation tax advantage

History – Chapter I of Part XVII omitted by CTA 2010, s. 1177 and Sch. 1, para. 94 and repealed by CTA 2010, s. 1181 and Sch. 3, Pt. 1.

703 [Omitted by CTA 2010, s. 1177 and Sch. 1, para. 94 and repealed by CTA 2010, s. 1181 and Sch. 3, Pt. 1.]

History – Chapter I of Part XVII (of which s. 703 formed a part) omitted by CTA 2010, s. 1177 and Sch. 1, para. 94 and repealed by CTA 2010, s. 1181 and Sch. 3, Pt. 1, with effect for corporation tax purposes for accounting periods ending on or after 1 April 2010, and for income and capital gains tax purposes for the tax year 2010–11 and subsequent tax years, subject to transitional provisions in CTA 2010, s. 1180 and Sch. 2, para. 84.

Notes – S. 703 rewritten for income tax purposes as follows:
S. 703(1): ITA 2007, s. 682(1), 684(1), (2), 685(1), (2), (3).
S. 703(2): ITA 2007, s. 684(3).
S. 703(3): ITA 2007, s. 695(1), 698(1), (2), (4).
S. 703(3A): ITA 2007, s. 699(1), (2), (3).

S. 703(9): ITA 2007, s. 695(1), (2), 696(1), (2), (3), 698(1).
S. 703(10): ITA 2007, s. 696(1), (2), (3), 697(1), (2), (3), (4), (5), (6), 698(1).
S. 703(11): ITA 2007, s. 712(1), (2), (3).
S. 703(12): ITA 2007, s. 698(5), (7).
S. 703 rewritten for corporation tax as follows:
S. 703(1): CTA 2010, s. 731(1), 733(1), (2),734(1), (2), (3).
S. 703(2): CTA 2010, s. 733(3).
S. 703(3): CTA 2010, s. 743(1), 746(1), (2), (4).
S. 703(9): CTA 2010, s. 743(1), (2), 744(1), (2), (3), 746(1).
S. 703(10): CTA 2010, s. 744(1), (2), (3), 745(1), (2), (3), (4), (5), (6), 746(1).
S. 703(12): CTA 2010, s. 746(5), (7).

704 The prescribed circumstances

History – Chapter I of Part XVII omitted by CTA 2010, s. 1177 and Sch. 1, para. 94 and repealed by CTA 2010, s. 1181 and Sch. 3, Pt. 1.

704 [Omitted by CTA 2010, s. 1177 and Sch. 1, para. 94 and repealed by CTA 2010, s. 1181 and Sch. 3, Pt. 1.]

History – Chapter I of Part XVII (of which s. 704 formed a part) omitted by CTA 2010, s. 1177 and Sch. 1, para. 94 and repealed by CTA 2010, s. 1181 and Sch. 3, Pt. 1, with effect for corporation tax purposes for accounting periods ending on or after 1 April 2010, and for income and capital gains tax purposes for the tax year 2010–11 and subsequent tax years.

Notes – S. 704 rewritten for income tax purposes as follows:
S. 704, para. A: ITA 2007, s. 686(2), (3), (4).
S. 704, para. B(1): ITA 2007, s. 687(2), (3), (4), (5), 688(4), (5), (9).
S. 704, para. C(1): ITA 2007, s. 688(2), (3), (4), (5), (6), (9), 689(3), (4).
S. 704, para. C(2): ITA 2007, s. 688(7), 689(5).
S. 704, para. D(1): ITA 2007, s. 689(2), (3), (4), (5).
S. 704, para. D(2): ITA 2007, s. 691(1), (2), (3).
S. 704, para. D(3): ITA 2007, s. 691(4).
S. 704, para. E(1): ITA 2007, s. 690(2), (3), (4), (7), (8).
S. 704, para. E(2): ITA 2007, s. 690(5), 700(1), (2).
S. 704, para. E(3): ITA 2007, s. 690(3), (6), (7), (8), 700(3), (4).
S. 704 rewritten for corporation tax as follows:
S. 704(A): CTA 2010, s. 735(2), (3), (4).
S. 704(C1): CTA 2010, s. 736(2), (3), (4), 737(3), (4).
S. 704(C2): CTA 2010, s. 736(5), 737(5).
S. 704(D1): CTA 2010, s. 737(2), (3), (4), (5).
S. 704(D2): CTA 2010, s. 739(1), (2), (3), 737(3), (4).
S. 704(D3): CTA 2010, s. 739(4).
S. 704(E1): CTA 2010, s. 738(2), (3), (4), (7), (8).
S. 704(E2): CTA 2010, s. 738(5), 747(1), (2).
S. 704(E3): CTA 2010, s. 738(3), (6), (7), (8),747(3), (4).

705 Appeals against Board's notices under section 703

History – Chapter I of Part XVII omitted by CTA 2010, s. 1177 and Sch. 1, para. 94 and repealed by CTA 2010, s. 1181 and Sch. 3, Pt. 1.

705 [Omitted by CTA 2010, s. 1177 and Sch. 1, para. 94 and repealed by CTA 2010, s. 1181 and Sch. 3, Pt. 1.]

History – Chapter I of Part XVII (of which s. 705 formed a part) omitted by CTA 2010, s. 1177 and Sch. 1, para. 94 and repealed by CTA 2010, s. 1181 and Sch. 3, Pt. 1, with effect for corporation tax purposes for accounting periods ending on or after 1 April 2010, and for income and capital gains tax purposes for the tax year 2010–11 and subsequent tax years.

Notes – S. 705 rewritten for income tax purposes as follows:
S. 705(1): ITA 2007, s. 705(1), (2).
S. 705(2): ITA 2007, s. 706(1), (2), (3).
S. 705(3): ITA 2007, s. 706(3), (4), (6).
S. 705(5): ITA 2007, s. 705(3), (4), 706(5), 707(6).
S. 705 rewritten for corporation tax as follows:
s. 705(1): CTA 2010, s. 750(1), (2).
s. 705(5): CTA 2010, s. 750(3), (4).

705A Statement of case by tribunal for opinion of High Court

History – Chapter I of Part XVII omitted by CTA 2010, s. 1177 and Sch. 1, para. 94 and repealed by CTA 2010, s. 1181 and Sch. 3, Pt. 1.

705A [Omitted by CTA 2010, s. 1177 and Sch. 1, para. 94 and repealed by CTA 2010, s. 1181 and Sch. 3, Pt. 1.]

History – Chapter I of Part XVII (of which s. 705A formed a part) omitted by CTA 2010, s. 1177 and Sch. 1, para. 94 and repealed by CTA 2010, s. 1181 and Sch. 3, Pt. 1, with effect for corporation tax purposes for accounting periods ending on or after 1 April 2010, and for income and capital gains tax purposes for the tax year 2010–11 and subsequent tax years. Former s. 705A omitted by SI 2009/56, art. 3(1) and Sch. 1, para. 152, operative from 1 April 2009, subject to transitional and saving provisions in SI 2009/56, Sch. 3.
Note that when former s. 705A was repealed, there were prospective amendments pending as follows:

> "In s. 705A(8), the words "Supreme Court" substituted for the words "House of Lords" by Constitutional Reform Act 2005, s. 40 and Sch. 9, para. 47(2)(a), operative from a day to be appointed.
> In s. 705A(9), the words "Supreme Court" substituted for the words "House of Lords" for the words from "unless leave has been given" to the end of the subsection substitute "except with the leave of the Court of Appeal or of the Supreme Court." by Constitutional Reform Act 2005, s. 40 and Sch. 9, para. 47(2)(b), operative from a day to be appointed.
> In s. 705A(12), the words "Supreme Court" substituted for the words "House of Lords" by Constitutional Reform Act 2005, s. 40 and Sch. 9, para. 47(2)(c), operative from a day to be appointed.".

Notes – S. 705A rewritten for income tax purposes as follows:
S. 705A(1): ITA 2007, s. 707(1).
S. 705A(2): ITA 2007, s. 707(2).
S. 705A(3): ITA 2007, s. 707(3).
S. 705A(4): ITA 2007, s. 707(4), (5).
S. 705A(5): ITA 2007, s. 707(5).
S. 705A(6): ITA 2007, s. 708(1), (2).
S. 705A(7): ITA 2007, s. 708(3), (4).
S. 705A(8): ITA 2007, s. 710(1), (2).
S. 705A(9): ITA 2007, s. 710(3).
S. 705A(10): ITA 2007, s. 709(1), (2).
S. 705A(11): ITA 2007, s. 709(3), (4), (5).
S. 705A(12): ITA 2007, s. 707(2), (5), (7), 708(1), (2), 709(1), (3), (4), (5), 710(4).

705B Proceedings in Northern Ireland

History – Chapter I of Part XVII omitted by CTA 2010, s. 1177 and Sch. 1, para. 94 and repealed by CTA 2010, s. 1181 and Sch. 3, Pt. 1.

705B [Omitted by CTA 2010, s. 1177 and Sch. 1, para. 94 and repealed by CTA 2010, s. 1181 and Sch. 3, Pt. 1.]

History – Chapter I of Part XVII (of which s. 705B formed a part) omitted by CTA 2010, s. 1177 and Sch. 1, para. 94 and repealed by CTA 2010, s. 1181 and Sch. 3, Pt. 1, with effect for corporation tax purposes for accounting periods ending on or after 1 April 2010, and for income and capital gains tax purposes for the tax year 2010–11 and subsequent tax years. Former s. 705B omitted by SI 2009/56, art. 3(1) and Sch. 1, para. 152, operative from 1 April 2009, subject to transitional and saving provisions in SI 2009/56, Sch. 3.
Note that when s. 705B was repealed, there was a prospective amendment pending as follows:

> "In s. 705B(2), the words "Supreme Court" substituted for the words "House of Lords" by Constitutional Reform Act 2005, s. 40 and Sch. 9, para. 47(3), operative from a day to be appointed.".

Notes – S. 705B rewritten for income tax purposes as follows:
S. 705B(1): ITA 2007, s. 711(1), (2).
S. 705B(2): ITA 2007, s. 711(3), (4).
S. 705B(3): ITA 2007, s. 711(5).
S. 705B(4): ITA 2007, s. 711(6).

706 The tribunal

History – Chapter I of Part XVII omitted by CTA 2010, s. 1177 and Sch. 1, para. 94 and repealed by CTA 2010, s. 1181 and Sch. 3, Pt. 1.

706 [Omitted by CTA 2010, s. 1177 and Sch. 1, para. 94 and repealed by CTA 2010, s. 1181 and Sch. 3, Pt. 1.]

History – Chapter I of Part XVII (of which s. 706 formed a part) omitted by CTA 2010, s. 1177 and Sch. 1, para. 94 and repealed by CTA 2010, s. 1181 and Sch. 3, Pt. 1, with effect for corporation tax purposes for accounting periods ending on or after 1 April 2010, and for income and capital gains tax purposes for the tax year 2010–11 and subsequent tax years. Former s. 706 omitted by SI 2009/56, art. 3(1) and Sch. 1, para. 152, operative from 1 April 2009, subject to transitional and saving provisions in SI 2009/56, Sch. 3.

Notes – S. 706 rewritten for income tax purposes as follows:
S. 706(1): ITA 2007, s. 704(1), (3).
S. 706(2): ITA 2007, s. 704(2).

707 Procedure for clearance in advance

History – Chapter I of Part XVII omitted by CTA 2010, s. 1177 and Sch. 1, para. 94 and repealed by CTA 2010, s. 1181 and Sch. 3, Pt. 1.

707 [Omitted by CTA 2010, s. 1177 and Sch. 1, para. 94 and repealed by CTA 2010, s. 1181 and Sch. 3, Pt. 1.]

History – Chapter I of Part XVII (of which s. 707 formed a part) omitted by CTA 2010, s. 1177 and Sch. 1, para. 94 and repealed by CTA 2010, s. 1181 and Sch. 3, Pt. 1, with effect for corporation tax purposes for accounting periods ending on or after 1 April 2010, and for income and capital gains tax purposes for the tax year 2010–11 and subsequent tax years.

Notes – S. 707 rewritten for income tax purposes as follows:
S. 707(1): ITA 2007, s. 701(1), (2), (3), (4), (5), 702(1), (2).
S. 707(2): ITA 2007, s. 702(4).
S. 707(3): ITA 2007, s. 702(3).
S. 707 rewritten for corporation tax as follows:
S. 707(1): CTA 2010, s. 748(1), (2), (3), (4), (5), 749(1), (2).
S. 707(2): CTA 2010, s. 749(4).
S. 707(3): CTA 2010, s. 749(3).

708 Power to obtain information

History – Chapter I of Part XVII omitted by CTA 2010, s. 1177 and Sch. 1, para. 94 and repealed by CTA 2010, s. 1181 and Sch. 3, Pt. 1.

708 [Omitted by CTA 2010, s. 1177 and Sch. 1, para. 94 and repealed by CTA 2010, s. 1181 and Sch. 3, Pt. 1.]

History – Chapter I of Part XVII (of which s. 708 formed a part) omitted by CTA 2010, s. 1177 and Sch. 1, para. 94 and repealed by CTA 2010, s. 1181 and Sch. 3, Pt. 1, with effect for corporation tax purposes for accounting periods ending on or after 1 April 2010, and for income and capital gains tax purposes for the tax year 2010–11 and subsequent tax years. Former s. 708 omitted by SI 2009/2035, art. 2 and Sch., para. 19, with effect from 13 August 2009.

Notes – Former. 708 rewritten for income tax purposes as ITA 2007, s. 703(1), (2), (3), (4), (5), (6).

709 Meaning of "corporation tax advantage" and other expressions

History – Chapter I of Part XVII omitted by CTA 2010, s. 1177 and Sch. 1, para. 94 and repealed by CTA 2010, s. 1181 and Sch 3, Pt. 1.

709 [Omitted by CTA 2010, s. 1177 and Sch. 1, para. 94 and repealed by CTA 2010, s. 1181 and Sch. 3, Pt. 1.]

History – Chapter I of Part XVII (of which s. 709 formed a part) omitted by CTA 2010, s. 1177 and Sch. 1, para. 94 and repealed by CTA 2010, s. 1181 and Sch. 3, Pt. 1, with effect for corporation tax purposes for accounting periods ending on or after 1 April 2010, and for income and capital gains tax purposes for the tax year 2010–11 and subsequent tax years.

Notes – S. 709 rewritten for income tax purposes as follows:
S. 709(1): ITA 2007, s. 683(1), (2), Sch. 1 para. 225.
S. 709(2): ITA 2007, s. 713.
S. 709(2A): ITA 2007, s. 683(3), Sch. 1 para. 225.
S. 709(3): ITA 2007, s. 686(3), 687(3), (4), 688(3), (4), (8), 689(2), (6), 690(8).
S. 709(4): ITA 2007, s. 692(1), (2), 693(1), (2), 694(1), (2).
S. 709(5): ITA 2007, s. 694(3), (4), (5).
S. 709(6): ITA 2007, s. 693(3), (4).
S. 709 rewritten for corporation tax as follows:
S. 709(1): CTA 2010, s. 732(1), (2).
S. 709(2): CTA 2010, s. 751.
S. 709(3): CTA 2010, s. 735(3), 736(3),(6), 737(2), (6), 738(8).
S. 709(4): CTA 2010, s. 740(1), (2), 741(1), (2),742(1), (2).
S. 709(5): CTA 2010, s. 742(3), (4), (5).
S. 709(6): CTA 2010, s. 741(3), (4).

Chapter II – Transfers of Securities

TRANSFERS WITH OR WITHOUT ACCRUED INTEREST: INTRODUCTORY

710 Meaning of "securities", "transfer" etc. for purposes of sections 711 to 728

710 [Omitted by ITA 2007 and Sch. 1, para. 162 and repealed by ITA 2007, s. 1031 and Sch. 3, Pt. 1 with effect for 2007–08 and subsequent tax years.]

Notes – S. 710 rewritten as follows:
S. 710(2): ITA 2007, s. 619(1), (2).
S. 710(2A): ITA 2007, s. 619(1).
S. 710(3): ITA 2007, s. 619(3), (5).
S. 710(3A): ITA 2007, s. 619(4).
S. 710(4): ITA 2007, s. 619(6).
S. 710(5): ITA 2007, s. 620(1), (2), 648(7).
S. 710(6): ITA 2007, s. 620(3).
S. 710(7): ITA 2007, s. 675(1).
S. 710(8): ITA 2007, s. 675(2).
S. 710(9): ITA 2007, s. 639(5).
S. 710(10): ITA 2007, s. 675(3).
S. 710(11): ITA 2007, s. 676(1), (2).
S. 710(12): ITA 2007, s. 677(1), (2).
S. 710(13): ITA 2007, s. 620(1), (4), (7), 621(2), 673(4), (5).
S. 710(13A): ITA 2007, s. 673(4), (5).

711 Meaning of "interest", "transfers with or without accrued interest" etc.

711 [Omitted by ITA 2007, s. 1027 and Sch. 1, para. 162 and repealed by ITA 2007, s. 1031 and Sch. 3, Pt. 1 with effect for 2007–08 and subsequent tax years.]

Notes – S. 711 rewritten as follows:
S. 711(2): ITA 2007, s. 672(1), (2).
S. 711(3): ITA 2007, s. 673(1).
S. 711(4): ITA 2007, s. 673(1).
S. 711(5): ITA 2007, s. 623(1), 624(1).
S. 711(6): ITA 2007, s. 623(2), (3), (4), 624(2), (3), (4).
S. 711(6A): ITA 2007, s. 648(5), (6).
S. 711(7): ITA 2007, s. 632(4), (5), (6), 633(4), (5), (6).
S. 711(8): ITA 2007, s. 632(4), (5), (6), 633(4), (5), (6).
S. 711(9): ITA 2007, s. 671(1), (2).

712 Meaning of "settlement day" for purposes of sections 711 to 728

712 [Omitted by ITA 2007, s. 1027 and Sch. 1, para. 162 and repealed by ITA 2007, s. 131 and Sch. 3, Pt. 1 with effect for 2007–08 and subsequent tax years.]

Notes – S. 712 rewritten as follows:
S. 712(2): ITA 2007, s. 674(1).
S. 712(3): ITA 2007, s. 674(3).
S. 712(4): ITA 2007, s. 674(4), (5).
S. 712(5): ITA 2007, s. 674(6), (7).

TRANSFERS WITH OR WITHOUT ACCRUED INTEREST: CHARGE TO TAX AND RELIEFS

713 Deemed sums and reliefs

713 [Omitted by ITA 2007, s. 1027 and Sch. 1, para. 162 and repealed by ITA 2007, s. 1031 and Sch. 3, Pt. 1 with effect for 2007–08 and subsequent tax years.]

Notes – S. 713 rewritten as follows:
S. 713(1): ITA 2007, s. 632(1).
S. 713(2): ITA 2007, s. 632(1).
S. 713(3): ITA 2007, s. 633(1).
S. 713(4): ITA 2007, s. 632(2), (3), (4), (5), (6).
S. 713(5): ITA 2007, s. 633(2), (3), (4), (5), (6).
S. 713(6): ITA 2007, s. 632(5), (6), 633(4), (5), (6).
S. 713(7): ITA 2007, s. 664(1), (2), (3), (4), (5), 665(2).
S. 713(8): ITA 2007, s. 664(1), (2), (3), (4), (5), 665(2).
S. 713(9): ITA 2007, s. 664(6), 665(5).

714 Treatment of deemed sums and reliefs

714 [Omitted by ITA 2007, s. 1027 and Sch. 1, para. 162 and repealed by ITA 2007, s. 1031 and Sch. 3, Pt. 1 with effect for 2007–08 and subsequent tax years.]

Notes – S. 714 rewritten as follows:
S. 714(1): ITA 2007, s. 628(3), (4), (5), 629(1).
S. 714(2): ITA 2007, s. 615(2), 616, 617(2), (3), 628(3), (4), (5), 629(1).
S. 714(2A): ITA 2007, s. 617(1).
S. 714(2B): ITA 2007, s. 618(1).
S. 714(3): ITA 2007, s. 615(4), 628(6), 629(2), 679(1).
S. 714(4): ITA 2007, s. 615(4), 628(6), 629(2), 637(1), (2), 679(1).
S. 714(5): ITA 2007, s. 637(1), (2), 679(1), (2).

715 Exceptions from sections 713 and 714

715 [Omitted by ITA 2007, s. 1027 and Sch. 1, para. 162 and repealed by ITA 2007, s. 1031 and Sch. 3, Pt. 1 with effect for 2007–08 and subsequent tax years.]

Notes – S. 715 rewritten as follows:
S. 715(1): ITA 2007, s. 638(2), (3), 639(1), (2), (3), (4), 640(1), (2), (3), (4), 641(1), (2), (3), (4), 642(1), 643(1), (3), (4), 644(1), (2), 645(1), (2), (3), 646.
S. 715(2): ITA 2007, s. 638(2), (3), 639(1), (2), 640(1), (2), 641(1), (2), 642(2), 643(1), 644(1), (3), 645(1), (3), 646.
S. 715(3): ITA 2007, s. 652(1), (2), (3).
S. 715(4): ITA 2007, s. 643(1).
S. 715(5): ITA 2007, s. 643(2), (3), (4).
S. 715(6): ITA 2007, s. 638(2), (3), 647(2), (3), (4), (6), 663(1), (2), (3).
S. 715(7): ITA 2007, s. 663(4).
S. 715(8): ITA 2007, s. 641(4), 643(5), (6).

716 Transfer of unrealised interest

716 [Omitted by ITA 2007, s. 1027 and Sch. 1, para. 162 and repealed by ITA 2007, s. 1031 and Sch. 3, Pt. 1 with effect for 2007–08 and subsequent tax years.]

Notes – S. 716 rewritten as follows:
S. 716(1): ITA 2007, s. 625(1), (2).
S. 716(2): ITA 2007, s. 615(2), (4), 616, 617(2), 622(3), 628(3), (4), (5), (6), 629(1), (2), 634(1), (2).
S. 716(3): ITA 2007, s. 615(2), 616, 617(3), 630(1), (2), 631(1).
S. 716(3A): ITA 2007, s. 617(1).
S. 716(3B): ITA 2007, s. 618(1).
S. 716(4): ITA 2007, s. 681(1), (2), (3), (4), (5), (6).
S. 716(5): ITA 2007, s. 638(2), (3), 639(2), 640(2), 641(2), 642(1), (2), 643(1), (2), (3), (4), 644(1), 645(1), 646, 681(1), (2), (3), (4), (5), (6), Sch. 2 para. 128.
S. 716(6): ITA 2007, s. 664(1), (2), (3), (4), (5), (6), 665(2), (5).

717 Variable interest rate

717 [Omitted by ITA 2007, s. 1027 and Sch. 1, para. 162 and repealed by ITA 2007, s. 1031 and Sch. 3, Pt. 1 with effect for 2007–08 and subsequent tax years.]

Notes – S. 717 rewritten as follows:
S. 717(1): ITA 2007, s. 627(1).
S. 717(2): ITA 2007, s. 627(1), (2).
S. 717(3): ITA 2007, s. 627(3).
S. 717(6): ITA 2007, s. 630(1), (2), 635(1), 639(3), 640(3), 641(3).
S. 717(7): ITA 2007, s. 630(1), (2), 635(1), 638(2), (3), 639(3), (4), 640(3), (4), 641(3), (4).
S. 717(8): ITA 2007, s. 620(1), (5), 621(3), 630(1), (2), 638(2), (3), 639(3), (4), 640(3), (4), 641(3), (4).
S. 717(9): ITA 2007, s. 631(3), 635(2), (3), (4), 638(2), (3).
S. 717(10): ITA 2007, s. 617(3), 630(1), (2), 639(3), (4), 640(3), (4), 641(3), (4), 667(5).
S. 717(11): ITA 2007, s. 617(3), 630(1), (2), 639(3), (4), 640(3), (4), 641(3), (4), 667(5).

718 Interest in default

718 [Omitted by ITA 2007, s. 1027 and Sch. 1, para. 162 and repealed by ITA 2007, s. 1031 and Sch. 3, Pt. 1 with effect for 2007–08 and subsequent tax years.]

Notes – S. 718 rewritten as follows:
S. 718(1): ITA 2007, s. 659(1).
S. 718(2): ITA 2007, s. 659(2).

719 Unrealised interest in default

719 [Omitted by ITA 2007, s. 1027 and Sch. 1, para. 162 and repealed by ITA 2007, s. 1031 and Sch. 3, Pt. 1 with effect for 2007–08 and subsequent tax years.]

Notes – S. 719 rewritten as follows:
S. 719(1): ITA 2007, s. 660(1).
S. 719(2): ITA 2007, s. 660(2), (3).
S. 719(3): ITA 2007, s. 681(1), (2), (3), (4), (5), (6).
S. 719(4): ITA 2007, s. 660(2), (3), (5), 661(1), (3), (4), (5), (6), 665(3), (4), (5), 681(1), (2), (3), (4), (5), (6), (7), Sch. 2, para. 127.

TRANSFERS WITH OR WITHOUT ACCRUED INTEREST: SUPPLEMENTAL

720 Nominees, trustees etc.

720 [Omitted by ITA 2007, s. 1027 and Sch. 1, para. 162 and repealed by ITA 2007, s. 1031 and Sch. 3, Pt. 1 with effect for 2007–08 and subsequent tax years.]

Notes – S. 720 rewritten as follows:
S. 720(1): ITA 2007, s. 666(1), (2), (6), (7), (8).
S. 720(2): ITA 2007, s. 666(3), (4), (5).
S. 720(4): ITA 2007, s. 651(1), (2), (3).
S. 720(5): ITA 2007, s. 482.
S. 720(6): ITA 2007, s. 667(1), (2), (3), (4), (5).
S. 720(7): ITA 2007, s. 680(1), (2).
S. 720(8): ITA 2007, s. 667(4).

721 Death

721 [Omitted by ITA 2007, s. 1027 and Sch. 1, para. 162 and repealed by ITA 2007, s. 1031 and Sch. 3, Pt. 1 with effect for 2007–08 and subsequent tax years.]

Notes – S. 721 rewritten as follows:
S. 721(2): ITA 2007, s. 636(1), (2), (3).
S. 721(3): ITA 2007, s. 636(4), (5).

722 Trading stock

722 [Omitted by ITA 2007, s. 1027 and Sch. 1, para. 162 and repealed by ITA 2007, s. 1031 and Sch. 3, Pt. 1 with effect for 2007–08 and subsequent tax years.]

Notes – S. 722 rewritten as follows:
S. 722(1): ITA 2007, s. 650(1), (2).
S. 722(2): ITA 2007, s. 650(3), (4), (5), (6).

722A Gilt strips: deemed transfer

722A [Omitted by ITA 2007, s. 1027 and Sch. 1, para. 162 and repealed by ITA 2007, s. 1031 and Sch. 3, Pt. 1 with effect for 2007–08 and subsequent tax years.]

Notes – S. 722A rewritten as follows:
S. 722A(1): ITA 2007, s. 648(1), (2).
S. 722A(2): ITA 2007, s. 648(1), (2).
S. 722A(3): ITA 2007, s. 648(3), (4).
S. 722A(4): ITA 2007, s. 648(3), (4).
S. 722A(5): ITA 2007, s. 648(8), (9), 673(6), 1024.

723 Foreign securities: delayed remittances

723 [Omitted by ITA 2007, s. 1027 and Sch. 1, para. 162 and repealed by ITA 2007, s. 1031 and Sch. 3, Pt. 1 with effect for 2007–08 and subsequent tax years.]

Notes – S. 723 rewritten as follows:
S. 723(1): ITA 2007, s. 668(1), (4), 669(1).
S. 723(2): ITA 2007, s. 668(2), 669(2).
S. 723(3): ITA 2007, s. 668(2), 669(2).
S. 723(4): ITA 2007, s. 615(2), 616, 617(1), (4), 618(1), 670(1), (2), (3).
S. 723(5): ITA 2007, s. 668(1), (5), 669(1).
S. 723(6): ITA 2007, s. 668(7), 669(4).
S. 723(7): ITA 2007, s. 668(8), 669(5).
S. 723(8): ITA 2007, s. 668(6).

724 Insurance companies

724 [Repealed by FA 1996, s. 205 and Sch. 41, Pt. V(3) for accounting periods ending after 31 March 1996, subject to transitional provisions in FA 1996, Sch. 15.]

725 Lloyd's underwriters

725 [Repealed by FA 1993, s. 213 and Sch. 23, Pt. III(12), with effect for the underwriting year 1994 (syndicate profits of which were assessed in 1997–98) and subsequent underwriting years.]

726 Building societies

726 [Repealed by FA 1991, s. 123 and Sch. 19, Pt. V, for the year 1991–92 and subsequent years of assessment.]

726A New issues of securities

726A [Omitted by ITA 2007, s. 1027 and Sch. 1, para. 162 and repealed by ITA 2007, s. 1031 and Sch. 3, Pt. 1 with effect for 2007–08 and subsequent tax years.]

Notes – S. 726A rewritten as follows:
S. 726A(1): ITA 2007, s. 649(1), (2).
S. 726A(2): ITA 2007, s. 627(4), 649(4), (5), (6), 673(1).
S. 726A(3): ITA 2007, s. 662(1), (2).
S. 726A(4): ITA 2007, s. 662(3), (2), (3).
S. 726A(5): ITA 2007, s. 664(1), (2), (3), (4), (5), (6), 665(2), (5).
S. 726A(6): ITA 2007, s. 662(4).
S. 726A(7): ITA 2007, s. 627(4), 649(3).
S. 726A(8): ITA 2007, s. 627(5), 649(8).
S. 726A(9): ITA 2007, s. 649(8).

727 Stock lending

727 [Omitted by ITA 2007, s. 1027 and Sch. 1, para. 162 and repealed by ITA 2007, s. 1031 and Sch. 3, Pt. 1 with effect for 2007–08 and subsequent tax years.]

Notes – S. 727(2) rewritten as ITA 2007, s. 653.

727A Exception for sale and repurchase of securities

727A [Omitted by ITA 2007, s. 1027 and Sch. 1, para. 162 and repealed by ITA 2007, s. 1031 and Sch. 3, Pt. 1 with effect for 2007–08 and subsequent tax years.]

Notes – S. 727A rewritten as follows:
S. 727A(1): ITA 2007, s. 654(2), 655(1), (2).
S. 727A(2): ITA 2007, s. 654(3).
S. 727A(3): ITA 2007, s. 1021(1).
S. 727A(4): ITA 2007, s. 654(4), (7), (8).
S. 727A(5): ITA 2007, s. 654(4), (5).

728 Information

728 [Omitted by SI 2009/2035, art. 2 and Sch., para. 20.]

History – S. 728 omitted by SI 2009/2035, art. 2 and Sch., para. 20, with effect from 13 August 2009.
Derivations – Former s. 728(1)–(5) (as originally enacted): FA 1985, Sch. 23, para. 44(1)–(5).
S. 728(6): FA 1985, Sch. 23, para. 44(5A), as inserted by FA 1986, Sch. 17, para. 6(2).
S. 728(7), (8): FA 1986, Sch. 17, para. 6(4)–(6).

OTHER TRANSFERS OF SECURITIES

729 Sale and repurchase of securities

729 [Repealed by FA 1996, s. 159(1), s. 205 and Sch. 41, Pt. V(21).]

History – S. 729 repealed by FA 1996, s. 159(1), s. 205 and Sch. 41, Pt. V(21) where the initial agreement to sell or transfer the securities or other property was made on or after 6 November 1996 (SI 1996/2646).

730 Transfers of rights to receive distributions in respect of shares

730 [Omitted by FA 2009, s. 49 and Sch. 25, para. 9(1)(a).]

History – S. 730 omitted by *FA 2009*, s. 49 and Sch. 25, para. 9(1)(a), with effect in relation to transfers on or after 22 April 2009.

730A Treatment of price differential on sale and repurchase of securities

730A [Omitted by FA 2007, s. 47 and Sch. 14, para. 4; repealed by s. 114 and Sch. 27, Pt. 2(14).]

History – S. 730A omitted by FA 2007, s. 47 and Sch. 14, para. 4 and repealed by s. 114 and Sch. 27, Pt. 2(14), with effect in relation to arrangements coming into force on or after 1 October 2007, by virtue of SI 2007/2483, art. 3.

Notes – S. 730A rewritten for income tax as follows:
S. 730A(1): ITA 2007, s. 569(1), (2), (3), (4), 607(1), (2).
S. 730A(2): ITA 2007, s. 607(2), (3), (4).
S. 730A(3): ITA 2007, s. 607(5).
S. 730A(4): ITA 2007, s. 609(1), (2), (3), (4), (7), Sch. 1 para. 331.
S. 730A(4A): ITA 2007, s. 609(4).
S. 730A(7): ITA 2007, s. 609(5), (6).
S. 730A(8): ITA 2007, s. 608(1), (2), (3), (4).
S. 730A(8A): ITA 2007, s. 607(6), (7).
S. 730A(9): ITA 2007, s. 610(1), (2).

730B Interpretation of section 730A

730B [Omitted by FA 2007, s. 47 and Sch. 14, para. 4 and repealed by s. 114 and Sch. 27, Pt. 2(14).]

History – S. 730B omitted by FA 2007, s. 47 and Sch. 14, para. 4 and repealed by s. 114 and Sch. 27, Pt. 2(14), with effect in relation to arrangements coming into force on or after 1 October 2007, by virtue of SI 2007/2483, art. 3.

Notes – S. 730B rewritten as follows:
S. 730B(1): ITA 2007, s. 571, 654(3).
S. 730B(2): ITA 2007, s. 570(1), (2), (3), (4), 654(4), (5), (6).
S. 730B(3): ITA 2007, s. 569(1), (3), 607(1).
S. 730B(4): ITA 2007, s. 570(1), (5), (6), 654(7), (8).
S. 730B(5): ITA 2007, s. 1021(1).

730BB Exchange gains and losses on sale and repurchase of securities

730BB [Omitted by FA 2007, s. 47 and Sch. 14, para. 4 and repealed by s. 114 and Sch. 27, Pt. 2(14).]

History – S. 730BB omitted by FA 2007, s. 47 and Sch. 14, para. 4 and repealed by s. 114 and Sch. 27, Pt. 2(14), with effect in relation to arrangements coming into force on or after 1 October 2007, by virtue of SI 2007/2483, art. 3.

730C Exchanges of gilts: traders etc.

730C [Omitted by ITTOIA 2005, s. 882 and Sch. 1, para. 301 and repealed by s. 884 and Sch. 3.]

History – S. 730C omitted by ITTOIA 2005, s. 882(1) and Sch. 1, para. 301 and repealed by s. 884 and Sch. 3; effective for income tax purposes for 2005–06 onwards and for corporation tax purposes for accounting periods ending after 5 April 2005 (ITTOIA 2005, s. 883(1)).

Notes – S. 730C: ITTOIA 2005 as follows:
S. 730C(1): ITTOIA 2005, s. 151(1) and 152(1).
S. 730C(2): ITTOIA 2005, s. 151(1)–(4).
S. 730C(3): ITTOIA 2005, s. 152(1)–(3).
S. 730C(4): ITTOIA 2005, s. 151(5) and 152(4).
S. 730C(5): ITTOIA 2005, s. 150(2).
S. 730C(6): ITTOIA 2005, s. 154(1) and (3).
S. 730C(7): ITTOIA 2005, s. 154(2).
S. 730C(9): ITTOIA 2005, s. 153(1)–(5).

PURCHASE AND SALE OF SECURITIES

731 Application and interpretation of sections 732 to 734

731 [Omitted by FA 2008, s. 66(1)(c).]

History – S. 731 omitted by FA 2008, s. 66(1)(c) with effect in relation to cases where the purchase by the first buyer (within the meaning of s. 731(2)) is made on or after 1 April 2008.

732 Dealers in securities

732 [Omitted by FA 2008, s. 66(1)(c).]

History – S. 732 omitted by FA 2008, s. 66(1)(c) with effect in relation to cases where the purchase by the first buyer (within the meaning of s. 731(2)) is made on or after 1 April 2008.

733 Persons entitled to exemptions

733 [Omitted by FA 2008, s. 66(1)(c).]

History – S. 733 omitted by FA 2008, s. 66(1)(c) with effect in relation to cases where the purchase by the first buyer (within the meaning of s. 731(2)) is made on or after 1 April 2008.

734 Persons other than dealers in securities

734 [Omitted by FA 2008, s. 66(1)(c).]

History – S. 734 omitted by FA 2008, s. 66(1)(c) with effect in relation to cases where the purchase by the first buyer (within the meaning of s. 731(2)) is made on or after 1 April 2008.

735 Meaning of "appropriate amount in respect of" interest

735 [Omitted by FA 2008, s. 66(1)(c).]

History – S. 735 omitted by FA 2008, s. 66(1)(c) with effect in relation to cases where the purchase by the first buyer (within the meaning of s. 731(2)) is made on or after 1 April 2008.

MISCELLANEOUS PROVISIONS RELATING TO SECURITIES

736 Company dealing in securities: distribution materially reducing value of holding

736 [Omitted by FA 2008, s. 66(1)(d).]

History – S. 736 omitted by FA 2008, s. 66(1)(d), with effect in relation to distributions made on or after 1 April 2008.
Derivations – ICTA 1970, s. 476.
Cross references – S. 839: circumstances in which persons are connected.
TCGA 1992, s. 29 ff. and Sch. 11, para. 10: provisions relating to value-shifting for capital gains tax purposes.

736A Manufactured dividends and interest

736A [Omitted by CTA 2010, s. 1177 and Sch. 1, para. 95 and repealed by CTA 2010, s. 1181 and Sch. 3, Pt. 1.]

History – S. 736A omitted by CTA 2010, s. 1177 and Sch. 1, para. 95 and repealed by CTA 2010, s. 1181 and Sch. 3, Pt. 1, with effect for corporation tax purposes for accounting periods ending on or after 1 April 2010, and for income and capital gains tax purposes for the tax year 2010–11 and subsequent tax years.

736B Deemed manufactured payments in the case of stock lending arrangements

736B [Omitted by CTA 2010, s. 1177 and Sch. 1, para. 96 and repealed by CTA 2010, s. 1181 and Sch. 3, Pt. 1.]

History – S. 736B omitted by CTA 2010, s. 1177 and Sch. 1, para. 96 and repealed by CTA 2010, s. 1181 and Sch. 3, Pt. 1, with effect for corporation tax purposes for accounting periods ending on or after 1 April 2010, and for income and capital gains tax purposes for the tax year 2010–11 and subsequent tax years. :

Notes – S. 736B rewritten as follows:
S. 736B(1): ITA 2007, s. 596(1).
S. 736B(2): ITA 2007, s. 596(2), (3), (4).
S. 736B(2A): ITA 2007, s. 596(3), (4).
S. 736B(3): ITA 2007, s. 568(1), (2), (3), (4), (5), (6).
S. 736A rewritten for corporation tax purposes as follows:
S. 736B(1): CTA 2010, s. 812(1).
S. 736B(2): CTA 2010, s. 812(2), (3), (6).
S. 736B(2A): CTA 2010, s. 812(3).
S. 736B(2B): CTA 2010, s. 812(4), (5).
S. 736B(3): CTA 2010, s. 805(1), (2), (3), (4), (5), (6), 806(1), (2), 812(1), 814(1).

736C Deemed interest: cash collateral under stock lending arrangements

736C [Omitted by FA 2009, s. 48 and Sch. 24, para. 8(a)(i).]

History – S. 736C omitted by FA 2009, s. 48 and Sch. 24, para. 8(a)(i), with effect from 22 April 2009, subject to transitional provisions in FA 2009, Sch. 24, para. 13].
Transitional – CTA 2009, Sch. 2, para. 55: certain references to CTA 2009, Pt. 5 to include references to FA 1996, Sch. 15 (loan relationships; savings and transitional provisions).

Notes – S. 736C rewritten as follows:
S. 736C(1): ITA 2007, s. 597(1).
S. 736C(2): ITA 2007, s. 597(2).
S. 736C(3): ITA 2007, s. 597(3).
S. 736C(4): ITA 2007, s. 597(4).
S. 736C(5): ITA 2007, s. 597(5).
S. 736C(6): ITA 2007, s. 597(6).
S. 736C(7): ITA 2007, s. 597(7).
S. 736C(8): ITA 2007, s. 598(2).
S. 736C(10): ITA 2007, s. 598(3).
S. 736C(11): ITA 2007, s. 568(1), 597(1).
S. 736C(12): ITA 2007, s. 568(2), (3), (4), (5), (6), 598(4).
S. 736C(13): ITA 2007, s. 598(5).
S. 736C(14): ITA 2007, s. 598(6).

736D Quasi-stock lending arrangements and quasi-cash collateral

736D [Omitted by FA 2009, s. 48 and Sch. 24, para. 8(a)(ii).]

History – S. 736D omitted by FA 2009, s. 48 and Sch. 24, para. 8(a)(ii), with effect from 22 April 2009, subject to transitional provisions in FA 2009, Sch. 24, para. 13.

Notes – S. 736D rewritten as follows:
S. 736D(1): ITA 2007, s. 600(1), (2), (3).
S. 736D(2): ITA 2007, s. 600(4).
S. 736D(3): ITA 2007, s. 600(5).
S. 736D(4): ITA 2007, s. 596(5), 599(1).
S. 736D(5): ITA 2007, s. 599(2).
S. 736D(6): ITA 2007, s. 600(6).
S. 736D(7): ITA 2007, s. 599(3).
S. 736D(8): ITA 2007, s. 599(4).
S. 736D(9): ITA 2007, s. 1021(1).
S. 736D(10): ITA 2007, s. 599(5), 600(7).

737 Manufactured dividends: treatment of tax deducted

737 [Repealed by FA 1997, s. 76, Sch. 10, para. 8, s. 113 and Sch. 18, Pt. VI(10).]

History – S. 737 repealed by FA 1997, s. 76, Sch. 10, para. 8, s. 113 and Sch. 18, Pt. VI(10), with effect in relation to any payment of a manufactured dividend or manufactured interest which is a payment made on or after 1 July 1997. The repeal of s. 737(8) has effect subject to FA 1997, Sch. 10, para. 16(3).

Derivations – S. 737(8): ICTA 1970, s. 477(7).

737A Sale and repurchase of securities: deemed manufactured payments

737A [Omitted by FA 2007, s. 47 and Sch. 14, para. 7; repealed by s. 114 and Sch. 27, Pt. 2(14).]

History – S. 737A omitted by FA 2007, s. 47 and Sch. 14, para. 7 and repealed by s. 114 and Sch. 27, Pt. 2(14), with effect in relation to arrangements coming into force on or after 1 October 2007, by virtue of SI 2007/2483, art. 3.

Notes – S. 737A rewritten as follows:
S. 737A(1): ITA 2007, s. 601(1).
S. 737A(2): ITA 2007, s. 601(1), (2), 606(1), (3).
S. 737A(2A): ITA 2007, s. 601(3), 606(1), (3).
S. 737A(3): ITA 2007, s. 601(2), (3).
S. 737A(4): ITA 2007, s. 602(1).
S. 737A(5): ITA 2007, s. 602(1), 606(1), (3), (8).
S. 737A(5A): ITA 2007, s. 602(3), (4).
S. 737A(6): ITA 2007, s. 602(1), 606(1), (8).
The day appointed under s. 737B(9) for the purposes of s. 737A in relation to agreements to sell United Kingdom equities and United Kingdom securities is 1 May 1995 by virtue of SI 1995/1007 (C. 25). The appointed day in relation to agreements to sell overseas securities is 6 November 1996 by virtue of SI 1996/2645 (C. 74).

737B Interpretation of section 737A

737B [Omitted by FA 2007, s. 47 and Sch. 14, para. 7; repealed by s. 114 and Sch. 27, Pt. 2(14).]

History – S. 737B omitted by FA 2007, s. 47 and Sch. 14, para. 7 and repealed by s. 114 and Sch. 27, Pt. 2(14) with effect in relation to arrangements coming into force on or after 1 October 2007, by virtue of SI 2007/2483, art. 3.

Notes – S. 737B rewritten as follows:
S. 737B(1): ITA 2007, s. 569(1), (3), 601(1), 606(1), (3), 607(1), 613(2), Sch. 1 para. 336, 337.
S. 737B(2): ITA 2007, s. 566(1), (2), (3), (4), 567(1), (2), (3), 569(3), 601(1), 607(1).
S. 737B(3): ITA 2007, s. 571.
S. 737B(4): ITA 2007, s. 606(1), (7).
S. 737B(5): ITA 2007, s. 570(1), (2).
S. 737B(6): ITA 2007, s. 570(1), (5), (6).
S. 737B(7): ITA 2007, s. 570(1), (2), (3).
S. 737B(8): ITA 2007, s. 1021(1).
The day appointed under s. 737B(9) forthe purposes of s. 737A is 1 May 1995 in relation to agreements to sell United Kingdom equities and United Kingdom securities (SI 1995/1007).
The day appointed under s. 737B(9) for the purposes of s. 737A is 6 November 1996 in relation to agreements to sell overseas securities (SI 1996/2645).

737C Deemed manufactured payments: further provisions

737C [Omitted by FA 2007, s. 47 and Sch. 14, para. 7; repealed by s. 114 and Sch. 27, Pt. 2(14).]

History – S. 737C omitted by FA 2007, s. 47 and Sch. 14, para. 7 and repealed by s. 114 and Sch. 27, Pt. 2(14), with effect in relation to arrangements coming into force on or after 1 October 2007, by virtue of SI 2007/2483, art. 3.

Notes – S. 737C rewritten as follows:
S. 737C(1): ITA 2007, s. 603(1), 604(1), (2), (3), (4), (5).
S. 737C(2): ITA 2007, s. 602(2), 604(1), (2).
S. 737C(3): ITA 2007, s. 602(2), 604(2).
S. 737C(3A): ITA 2007, s. 602(2), 603(1), (2), 604(1), (3), 606(10).
S. 737C(7): ITA 2007, s. 602(2), 603(1), 604(1), (4).
S. 737C(8): ITA 2007, s. 602(2), 603(3), 604(4), 606(1), (9).
S. 737C(9): ITA 2007, s. 604(4).
S. 737C(10): ITA 2007, s. 602(2), 603(1), 604(1), (5).
S. 737C(11): ITA 2007, s. 602(2), 603(4), 604(5), 606(1), (9).
S. 737C(11A): ITA 2007, s. 605(1), (2), (3), (4), Sch. 1 para. 330.
S. 737C(12): ITA 2007, s. 566(1), (2), (3), (4), 567(1), (2), (3), 606(1), (7).

SUPPLEMENTAL

737D Power to provide for manufactured payments to be eligible for relief

737D [Omitted by FA 2008, s. 43 and Sch. 17, para. 35(1).]

History – S. 737D omitted by FA 2008, s. 43 and Sch. 17, para. 35(1), with effect from 21 July 2008.

Notes – S. 737D rewritten as follows:
S. 737D(1): ITA 2007, s. 587(1), (2).
S. 737D(2): ITA 2007, s. 587(1).

737E Power to modify sections 730A, 730BB and 737A to 737C

737E [Omitted by FA 2007, s. 47 and Sch. 14, para. 8; repealed by s. 114 and Sch. 27, Pt. 2(14).]

History – S. 737E omitted by FA 2007, s. 47 and Sch. 14, para. 8 and repealed by s. 114 and Sch. 27, Pt. 2(14), with effect in relation to arrangements coming into force on or after 1 October 2007, by virtue of SI 2007/2483, art. 3.

Notes – S. 737E rewritten as follows:
S. 737E(1): ITA 2007, s. 612(1), (2), (3), (4), (5), (6), (7), (8), (9), 656(1), (2), (3), (4), (5), (6), (7), (8), (9), Sch. 1 para. 336.
S. 737E(2): ITA 2007, s. 613(1), (2), 657(1), (2), Sch. 1 para. 337.
S. 737E(3): ITA 2007, s. 611(1), Sch. 1 para. 332.
S. 737E(4): ITA 2007, s. Sch. 1 para. 336, 337, 338.
S. 737E(5): ITA 2007, s. 611(2), (3), 614(1), (2), 658(1), (2), Sch. 1 para. 332, 338.
S. 737E(6): ITA 2007, s. 611(4), 614(3), Sch. 1 para. 332, 338.
S. 737E(7): ITA 2007, s. 611(5), (6), 614(4), (5), 658(3), (4), Sch. 1 para. 332, 338.
S. 737E(8): ITA 2007, s. 569(1), (2), (4), 612(2), 613(1), (2), 654(2), 656(2), Sch. 1 para. 336, 337.
S. 737E(9): ITA 2007, s. 569(1), (3), 570(1), (2), (3), (4), (5), (6), 571, 612(2), (3), (4), (5), (6), (7), (8), (9), 613(2), 654(3), (4), (5), (6), (7), (8), 656(2), (4), (5), (9), 657(2), 658(5), 1021(1), Sch. 1 para. 336, 337.

738 Power to amend sections 732, 735 and 737

738 [Omitted by FA 2008, s. 66(4)(a).]

History – S. 738 omitted by FA 2008, s. 66(4)(a) with effect in relation to cases where the purchase by the first buyer (within the meaning of s. 731(2)) is made on or after 1 April 2008.

Chapter III – Transfer of Assets Abroad

739 Prevention of avoidance of income tax

739 [Omitted by ITA 2007, s. 1027 and Sch. 1, para. 177 and repealed by ITA 2007, s. 1031 and Sch. 3, Pt. 1 with effect for 2007–08 and subsequent tax years.]

Notes – S. 739 rewritten as follows:
S. 739(1): ITA 2007, s. 716(1), 718(1), 720(1), 721(1), 727(1), 728(1).
S. 739(1A): ITA 2007, s. 721(5), 728(3).
S. 739(2): ITA 2007, s. 718(1), 720(2), (3), (5), 721(1), (2), (3), (4), (5).
S. 739(3): ITA 2007, s. 718(1), 727(2), (3), (4), 728(1), (3), 729(1).
S. 739(4): ITA 2007, s. 729(3).
S. 739(5): ITA 2007, s. 729(3).
S. 739(6): ITA 2007, s. 729(2).

740 Liability of non-transferors

740 [Omitted by ITA 2007, s. 1027 and Sch. 1, para. 177 and repealed by ITA 2007, s. 1031 and Sch. 3, Pt. 1 with effect for 2007–08 and subsequent tax years.]

Notes – S. 740 rewritten as follows:
S. 740(1): ITA 2007, s. 716(1), 718(1), 732(1).
S. 740(2): ITA 2007, s. 731(1), (2), (3), 732(1), (2), 733(1).
S. 740(3): ITA 2007, s. 718(1), 733(1).
S. 740(4): Not rewritten, as obsolete.
S. 740(5): ITA 2007, s. 735(1), (2), (3), (4), (5), (6).
S. 740(6): ITA 2007, s. 734(1), (2), (3), (4).
S. 740(7): ITA 2007, Sch. 2, para. 133(1), (2).

741 Exemption from sections 739 and 740 (transactions before 5th December 2005)

History – In heading, the words "(transactions before 5th December 2005)" added by FA 2006, s. 79 and Sch. 7, para. 2(4) and taken to have come into force on 5 December 2005.

Notes – S. 741 rewritten as ITA 2007, s. 739(2), (3), (4), 751.

741 [Omitted by ITA 2007, s. 1027 and Sch. 1, para. 177 and repealed by ITA 2007, s. 1031 and Sch. 3, Pt. 1 with effect for 2007–08 and subsequent tax years.]

741A Exemption from sections 739 and 740 (transactions on or after 5th December 2005)

741A [Omitted by ITA 2007, s. 1027 and Sch. 1, para. 177 and repealed by ITA 2007, s. 1031 and Sch. 3, Pt. 1 with effect for 2007–08 and subsequent tax years.]

Notes – S. 741A rewritten as follows:
S. 741A(1): ITA 2007, s. 737(2).
S. 741A(2): ITA 2007, s. 737(3).
S. 741A(3): ITA 2007, s. 737(4).
S. 741A(4: ITA 2007, s. 737(5), (6).
S. 741A(5): ITA 2007, s. 738(1), (2).
S. 741A(6): ITA 2007, s. 738(4), 1021(1).
S. 741A(7): ITA 2007, s. 737(7).
S. 741A(7) ("commercial transaction"): ITA 2007, s. 738(1), (2), (3).
S. 741A(7) ("independent persons"): ITA 2007, s. 738(3), (4).
S. 741A(8): ITA 2007, s. 737(8).
S. 741A(9): ITA 2007, s. 751.

741B Application of sections 741 and 741A

741B [Omitted by ITA 2007, s. 1027 and Sch. 1, para. 177 and repealed by ITA 2007, s. 1031 and Sch. 3, Pt. 1 with effect for 2007–08 and subsequent tax years.]

Notes – S. 741B rewritten as follows:
S. 741B(2) ("new transaction"): ITA 2007, s. 736(3).
S. 741B(2) ("old transaction"): ITA 2007, s. 736(3).
S. 741B(2) ("relevant transactions"): ITA 2007, s. 715(1).
S. 741B(2) ("the relevant date"): ITA 2007, s. 736(3).
S. 741B(3): ITA 2007, s. 736(2), 739(1).
S. 741B(4): ITA 2007, s. 736(2), 737(1).
S. 741B(5): ITA 2007, s. 736(2), 740(1).

741C Cases where there are both old transactions and new transactions

741C [Omitted by ITA 2007, s. 1027 and Sch. 1, para. 177 and repealed by ITA 2007, s 1031 and Sch. 3, Pt. 1 with effect for 2007–08 and subsequent tax years.]

Notes – S. 741C rewritten as follows:
S. 741C(1) ("new transaction"): ITA 2007, s. 740(1).
S. 741C(2) ("old transaction"): ITA 2007, s. 740(2).
S. 741C(3) ("relevant transactions"): ITA 2007, s. 740(2).
S. 741C(4) ("the relevant date"): ITA 2007, s. 740(3).
S. 741C(5): ITA 2007, s. 740(3).
S. 741C(6): ITA 2007, s. 740(4).
S. 741C(7): ITA 2007, s. 733(1), 740(5).
S. 741C(8): ITA 2007, s. 740(6), (7).

741D Section 739: just and reasonable apportionment in certain cases

741D [Omitted by ITA 2007, s. 1027 and Sch. 1, para. 177 and repealed by ITA 2007, s. 1031 and Sch. 3, Pt. 1 with effect for 2007–08 and subsequent tax years.]

Notes – S. 741D rewritten as follows:
S. 741D(1): ITA 2007, s. 741(1).
S. 741D(2): ITA 2007, s. 741(2), (5).
S. 741D(3): ITA 2007, s. 741(1).
S. 741D(4): ITA 2007, s. 741(3).
S. 741D(5): ITA 2007, s. 741(4), (5).
S. 741D(6): ITA 2007, s. 742(1), (2).
S. 741D(7): ITA 2007, s. 742(3).
S. 741D(8): ITA 2007, s. 751.
S. 741D(9): ITA 2007, s. 741(2), (3).

742 Interpretation of this Chapter

History – In heading, the words "this Chapter" substituted for the words "sections 739 to 741" by FA 2006, s. 79 and Sch. 7, para. 6(5) and taken to have come into force on 5 December 2005.

742 [Omitted by ITA 2007, s. 1027 and Sch. 1, para. 177 and repealed by ITA 2007, s. 1031 and Sch. 3, Pt. 1 with effect for 2007–08 and subsequent tax years.]

Notes – S. 742 rewritten as follows:
S. 742(1): ITA 2007, s. 719(1), (2).
S. 742(1A): ITA 2007, s. 716(1), 728(1), 732(1).
S. 742(1B): ITA 2007, s. 721(1), (2).
S. 742(2): ITA 2007, s. 718(1), 722(1), 723(1), (2), (3), (4), (5), (6), (7), 747(7).
S. 742(3): ITA 2007, s. 722(3), (4).
S. 742(4): ITA 2007, s. 718(1), 747(1).
S. 742(5): ITA 2007, s. 747(2), (3).
S. 742(6): ITA 2007, s. 747(4), (5).
S. 742(7): ITA 2007, s. 747(6).
S. 742(8): ITA 2007, s. 718(2), Sch. 2 para. 138.
S. 742(9): ITA 2007, s. 714(4), 716(2), 717.
S. 742(9A): ITA 2007, s. 718(2).

743 Supplemental provisions

743 [Omitted by ITA 2007, s. 1027 and Sch. 1, para. 177 and repealed by ITA 2007, s. 1031 and Sch. 3, Pt. 1 with effect for 2007–08 and subsequent tax years.]

Notes – S. 743 rewritten as follows:
S. 743(1): ITA 2007, s. 720(2), 727(2), 745(1), (3), (4).
S. 743(1ZA): ITA 2007, s. 745(3), (4).
S. 743(1A): ITA 2007, s. 745(3), (4).
S. 743(1B): ITA 2007, s. 745(3), (4).
S. 743(2): ITA 2007, s. 746(1), (2).
S. 743(3): ITA 2007, s. 726(1), (2), (3), 730(1), (2), (3).
S. 743(4): ITA 2007, s. 743(4).
S. 743(5): ITA 2007, s. 724(1), (2), (3), 745(2).

744 No duplication of charge

744 [Omitted by ITA 2007, s. 1027 and Sch. 1, para. 177 and repealed by ITA 2007, s. 1031 and Sch. 3, Pt. 1 with effect for 2007–08 and subsequent tax years.]

Notes – S. 744 rewritten as follows:
S. 744(1): ITA 2007, s. 743(1), (2), 751.
S. 744(2): ITA 2007, s. 744(2), (3), (4).

745 Power to obtain information

745 [Omitted by ITA 2007, s. 1027 and Sch. 1, para. 177 and repealed by ITA 2007, s. 1031 and Sch.3, Pt. 1 with effect for 2007–08 and subsequent tax years.]

Notes – S. 745 rewritten as follows:
S. 745(1): ITA 2007, s. 748(1), (2).
S. 745(2): ITA 2007, s. 748(3).
S. 745(3): ITA 2007, s. 718(1), 748(4), 749(1), (2), (3), (4), (5).
S. 745(4): ITA 2007, s. 749(6), Sch. 2 para. 139(1), (2).
S. 745(5): ITA 2007, s. 750(1), (2), (3).
S. 745(5A): ITA 2007, s. 750(4).
S. 745(6): ITA 2007, s. 749(7), 750(4).

746 Persons resident in the Republic of Ireland

746 [Omitted by ITA 2007, s. 1027 and Sch. 1, para. 177 and repealed by ITA 2007 and Sch. 3, Pt. 1 with effect for 2007–08 and subsequent tax years.]

Chapter IV – Controlled Foreign Companies

History – Ch. 4 omitted by FA 2012, s. 180 and Sch. 20, para. 14. The repeal has no effect for accounting periods beginning before 1 January 2013, subject to transitional rules in FA 2012, Sch. 20, para. 50 for companies with accounting periods straddling that date. Former Ch. 4 read as follows:

"Chapter IV – Controlled Foreign Companies

Cross references – Sch. 28AA, para. 6B(1)(b): compensating adjustment where advantaged person is a controlled foreign company. FA 1993, s. 94AA(6), 94AB(3) (for accounting periods beginning before 1 October 2002 – FA 1993, s. 94(9)): Ch. IV unaffected by operation of FA 1993, s. 94AA, 94AB (previously FA 1993, s. 94) (computation of corporation tax in currencies other than sterling: rules for ascertaining currency equivalents).

HMRC Manuals – IR, Assessed Taxes Manual, AT6.605: collection procedure in respect of controlled foreign companies.

Other material – IR press release, 9 November 1994: clearance procedure for non-trading controlled foreign companies.

Imputation of chargeable profits and creditable tax of controlled foreign companies

747(1) If in any accounting period a company–
(a) is resident outside the United Kingdom, and
(b) is controlled by persons resident in the United Kingdom, and
(c) is subject to a lower level of taxation in the territory in which it is resident,
the provisions of this Chapter shall apply in relation to that accounting period.

747(1A) A company which would not, apart from this subsection, fall to be regarded as controlled by persons resident in the United Kingdom shall be taken for the purposes of this Chapter to be so controlled if–
(a) there are two persons who, taken together, control the company;
(b) one of those persons is resident in the United Kingdom and is a person in whose case the 40 per cent test in section 755D(3) is satisfied; and
(c) the other is a person in whose case the 40 per cent test in section 755D(4) is satisfied.

747(1B) In determining, for the purposes of any provision of this Chapter except subsection (1)(a) above, whether a company is a person resident in the United Kingdom, section 18 of CTA 2009 (under which a company is treated as non-resident if it is so treated for double taxation relief purposes) shall be disregarded.

747(2) A company which falls within paragraphs (a) to (c) of subsection (1) above is in this Chapter referred to as a **"controlled foreign company"**.

747(3) *Subject to section 748,* where the provisions of this Chapter apply in relation to an accounting period of a controlled foreign company, the chargeable profits of that company for that period and its creditable tax (if any) for that period shall each be apportioned in accordance with section 752 among the persons (whether resident in the United Kingdom or not) who had an interest in that company at any time during that accounting period.

747(3A) In the case of an apportionment to a company resident in the United Kingdom which has made an application under section 751A, 751AA, 751AB or 751AC which has been granted, subsection (3) above has effect subject to that section.

747(4) Where, on such an apportionment of a controlled foreign company's chargeable profits for an accounting period as is referred to in subsection (3) above, an amount of those profits is apportioned to a company resident in the United Kingdom then, subject to subsection (5) below–

(a) a sum equal to corporation tax at the appropriate rate on that apportioned amount of profits, less the portion of the controlled foreign company's creditable tax for that period (if any) which is apportioned to the resident company, shall be chargeable on the resident company as if it were an amount of corporation tax chargeable on that company;

(b) [Omitted by ITA 2007, s. 1027 and Sch. 1, para. 178 and repealed by ITA 2007, s. 1031 and Sch. 3, Pt. 1.]

and for the purposes of paragraph (a) above **"the appropriate rate"** means the rate of corporation tax applicable to profits of that accounting period of the resident company in which ends the accounting period of the controlled foreign company which is mentioned in subsection (1) above or, if there is more than one such rate, the average rate over the whole of that accounting period of the resident company.

747(4A) [Repealed by FA 2005, s. 104 and Sch. 11, Pt. 2(6).]

747(4B) [Repealed by FA 2005, s. 104 and Sch. 11, Pt. 2(6).]

747(5) Tax shall not, by virtue of subsection (4) above, be chargeable on a company resident in the United Kingdom unless, on the apportionment in question, the aggregate of–

(a) the amount of the controlled foreign company's chargeable profits for the accounting period in question which is apportioned to the resident company, and

(b) any amounts of those chargeable profits which are apportioned to persons who are connected or associated with the resident company,

is at least 25 per cent of the total of those chargeable profits.

747(5A) Where the resident company has made an application under section 751A, 751AA, 751AB or 751AC which has been granted, it shall be assumed for the purposes of subsection (5) above that–

(a) each of the persons who are connected or associated with the resident company has made an application under that section to the same effect, and

(b) all the applications have been granted.

747(6) In relation to a company resident outside the United Kingdom–

(a) any reference in this Chapter to its **"chargeable profits"** for an accounting period is a reference to the amount which, on the assumptions in Schedule 24, would be the amount of the total profits of the company for that period on which, after allowing for any deductions available against those profits, corporation tax would be chargeable;

(aa) any reference in this Chapter to its chargeable profits for an accounting period includes (subject to subsections (7) to (9)) income which accrues during that accounting period to the trustees of a settlement in relation to which the company is a settlor or a beneficiary; and

(b) any reference in this Chapter to **"profits"** does not include a reference to chargeable gains but otherwise (except as provided by paragraph (a) above) has the same meaning as it has for the purposes of corporation tax.

747(7) Where there is more than one settlor or beneficiary in relation to the settlement mentioned in subsection (6)(aa), the income is to be apportioned between the company and the other settlors or beneficiaries on a just and reasonable basis.

747(8) Where income within subsection (6)(aa) is included in the chargeable profits of a company, any dividend or other distribution received by the company which derives from that income is not included in the chargeable profits of the company to the extent that it is so derived.

747(9) Any income within subsection (6)(aa) which would (apart from this subsection)–

(a) be included in the chargeable profits of a company which is a beneficiary in relation to a settlement and apportioned under subsection (3), and

(b) be included in the chargeable profits of a company which is a settlor in relation to the settlement and apportioned under that subsection,

is not to be included in the chargeable profits of the company which is a settlor.

History – In s. 747(1), words "the Board have reason to believe that" after "If" and "and the Board so direct" at the start of the closing words repealed by FA 1998, s. 113 and Sch. 17, para. 1(2); s. 165 and Sch. 27, Pt. III(27), with effect in relation to accounting periods of UK resident companies ending on or after 1 July 1999, the self-assessment appointed day by virtue of FA 1994, s. 199(2) and SI 1998/3173 (C. 78), subject to transitional provisions in FA 1998, Sch. 17, para. 37(2), (3), (4).

S. 747(1A) inserted by FA 2000, s. 104 and Sch. 31, para. 2, with effect on and after 21 March 2000.

In s. 747(1B), the words "section 18 of CTA 2009" substituted for "section 249 of the Finance Act 1994" by CTA 2009, s. 1322 and Sch. 1, para. 217, with effect for corporation tax purposes for accounting periods ending on or after 1 April 2009, and for income tax and capital gains tax purposes for the tax year 2009–10 and subsequent tax years.

S. 747(1B) inserted by FA 2002, s. 90(1), the insertion–

(a) being deemed to have come into force on 1 April 2002, and

(b) does not apply to a company that–

(i) by virtue of FA 1994, s. 249 was treated as resident outside the UK, and not resident in the UK, immediately before that date, and

(ii) has not subsequently ceased to be so treated.

In s. 747(3), words "Subject to s. 748, where" substituted for "Where, by virtue of a direction under subsection (1) above," by FA 1998, s. 113 and Sch. 17, para. 1(3) with effect in relation to accounting periods of UK resident companies ending on or after 1 July 1999, the self-assessment appointed day (see note above).

In s. 747(3A), ", 751AA, 751AB or 751AC" substituted for "or 751AA" by FA 2011, s. 47 and Sch. 12, para. 10(a), with effect in relation to accounting periods of controlled foreign companies beginning on or after 1 January 2011.

In s. 747(3A), "or 751AA" inserted by FA 2009, s. 36 and Sch. 16, para. 22(a), with effect in relation to accounting periods of controlled foreign companies ending on or after 1 January 2010.

S. 747(3A) inserted by FA 2007, s. 48 and Sch. 15, para. 1(2), with effect in relation to accounting periods of controlled foreign companies beginning on or after 6 December 2006 (subject to the transitional provisions at FA 2007, Sch. 15, para. 10(2)–(4)).

In s. 747(4)(a), words "chargeable on" substituted for "assessed on and recoverable from"; and in words following s. 747(4)(b) words "which is mentioned in subsection (1) above" substituted for "to which the direction under subsection (1) above relates", by FA 1998, s. 113 and Sch. 17, para. 1(4) with effect in relation to accounting periods of UK resident companies ending on or after 1 July 1999, the self-assessment appointed day (see note above).

In s. 747(4), para. (b) and the word "and" immediately preceding it omitted by ITA 2007, s. 1027 and Sch. 1, para. 178 and repealed by ITA 2007, s. 1031 and Sch. 3, Pt. 1 with effect in relation to accounting periods ending after 5 April 2007.

S. 747(4A) and (4B) repealed by FA 2005, s. 104 and Sch. 11, Pt. 2(6), with effect in relation to periods of account beginning on or after 16 March 2005.

S. 747(4A) and (4B) inserted by FA 1995, s. 133 and Sch. 25, para. 3, with effect from 1 May 1995.

In s. 747(5), words "chargeable on" substituted for "assessed on and recoverable from"; and "25 per cent" substituted for "10 per cent", by FA 1998, s. 113 and Sch. 17, para. 1(5) with effect in relation to accounting periods of UK resident companies ending on or after 1 July 1999, the self-assessment appointed day (see note above).

In s. 747(5A), ", 751AA, 751AB or 751AC" substituted for "or 751AA" by FA 2011, s. 47 and Sch. 12, para. 10(a), with effect in relation to accounting periods of controlled foreign companies beginning on or after 1 January 2011.

In s. 747(5A), "or 751AA" inserted by FA 2009, s. 36 and Sch. 16, para. 22(a), with effect in relation to accounting periods of controlled foreign companies ending on or after 1 January 2010.

S. 747(5A) inserted by FA 2007, s. 48 and Sch. 15,para. 1(3), with effect in relation to accounting periods of controlled foreign companies beginning on or after 6 December 2006 (subject to the transitional provisions at FA 2007, Sch. 15, para. 10(2)–(4)).
S. 747(6)(aa) inserted by FA 2008, s. 64(2)(a), with effect in relation to income accruing on or after 12 March 2008.
S. 747(7) inserted by FA 2008, s. 64(2)(b), with effect in relation to income accruing on or after 12 March 2008.
S. 747(8) inserted by FA 2008, s. 64(2)(b), with effect in relation to income accruing on or after 12 March 2008.
S. 747(9) inserted by FA 2008, s. 64(2)(b), with effect in relation to income accruing on or after 12 March 2008.

Derivations – FA 1984, s. 82 (as originally enacted).

Cross references – S. 739: provisions charging income arising to non-UK residents or domiciliaries to tax as the income of UK individuals where there is a transfer of assets abroad.
S. 801C: relief for underlying tax – provisions for separate streaming of dividend so far as representing dividend of a controlled foreign company paid in order to avoid an apportionment under 747(3) by pursuing an acceptable distribution policy (s. 748(1)(a)).
Sch. 24: provisions for computing profits etc. of controlled foreign companies.
Sch. 25, Pt. I: acceptable distribution policy as regards controlled foreign companies.
Sch. 28AA, para. 6B: compensating adjustment where advantaged person is a controlled foreign company.
TMA 1970, s. 46B(4): appeal lies to the special commissioners in respect of a question as to the application of s. 747(4)(a).
TMA 1970, s. 55(1): application of TMA 1970, s. 55 (recovery of tax not postponed) to appeals against notices under s. 753(1) or (3) where the appellant is assessed under s. 747(4)(a).
TMA 1970, s. 59E: further provision as to when corporation tax is due and payable under self-assessment.
TCGA 1992, Sch. 7AC, para. 5 (exemption of gains on substantial shareholdings): circumstances in which exemption will not apply – profits will not be treated as "untaxed" if an amount equal to those profits has been apportioned under s. 747 to a UK resident company prior to the disposal of shares (and, therefore, exemption is still due).
FA 2000, Sch. 22, para. 54(1): no s. 747 liability for a tonnage tax company in any accounting period in respect of profits of a controlled foreign company (CFC) if in that period distributions made by the CFC to the tonnage tax company would be relevant shipping income of the latter.
FA 2000, Sch. 22, para. 57(1)(b): any relief or set-off against a company's tax liability for an accounting period does not apply in relation to so much of that tax liability as is attributable to tonnage profits of a controlled foreign company apportioned to the company under s. 747(3).
FA 2002, Sch. 29, para. 116: assumptions to be made in computing profits of controlled foreign companies for purposes of gains and losses from intangible fixed assets.
F(No. 2)A 2005, Sch. 3, para. 3(2): the imputation of chargeable profits under s. 747(3) does not (of itself) satisfy the requirements of F(No. 2)A 2005, Sch. 3, para. 3(1)(b) regarding the conditions for a "hybrid entity" to exist for the tax arbitrage avoidance rules to apply.
Commonwealth Development Corporation Act 1999, Sch. 3, para. 2: exemption from corporation tax, and from any liability on profits arising under s. 747(4)(a), during the exempt period of the Corporation.
SI 1994/3226, reg. 1(5): transitional rules relating to exchange gains and losses where a direction under s. 747 has been given for the company's accounting period which includes 22 March 1995.
SI 1998/3081: disapplication of s. 747(3) in cases where the controlled foreign company is resident in a territory specified in the regulations, and certain conditions are satisfied. Applies in relation to any accounting period of a UK-resident company ending on or after 1 July 1999 (the corporation tax self-assessment appointed day).
SI 1999/358 (as amended by SI 2003/1861), reg. 20: set-off of unrelieved surplus ACT (as at 6 April 1999) against liability to corporation tax on profits of a controlled foreign company apportioned to a company resident in the UK.

Other material – IR press release, 5 October 1993: "excluded countries list" for periods prior to corporation tax self-assessment.

Notes – S. 747(4) rewritten as ITA 2007, s. 725(1), (2), 728(2).

Special rule for computing chargeable profits

747A [Ceased to have effect by virtue of FA 2005, s. 80(1) and Sch. 4, para. 24 and repealed by FA 2005. s. 104 and Sch. 11, Pt. 2(6).]

History – S. 747A ceased to have effect by virtue of FA 2005, s. 80(1) and Sch. 4, para. 24(1) and repealed by FA 2005, s. 104 and Sch. 11, Pt. 2(6), with effect in relation to periods of account beginning on or after 16 March 2005.

Cases where section 747(3) does not apply

History – Sidenote (heading) to s. 748 substituted by FA 1998, s. 113 and Sch. 17, para. 3(5) with effect in relation to accounting periods of UK resident companies ending on or after 1 July 1999, the self-assessment appointed day by virtue of FA 1994, s. 199(2) and SI 1998/3173 (C. 78)), subject to transitional provisions in FA 1998, Sch. 17, para. 37(2), (3), (4). Former wording was "Limitations on direction-making power".

748(1) No apportionment under section 747(3) falls to be made as regards an accounting period of a controlled foreign company if–
(a) [Omitted by FA 2009, s. 36 and Sch. 16, para. 1(2).]
(b) throughout that period the company is, within the meaning of Part II of Schedule 25, engaged in exempt activities;
(ba) the company is exempt for that period by virtue of Part 2A of that Schedule (exemption for trading companies with limited UK connection); or
(bb) the company is exempt for that period by virtue of Part 2B of that Schedule (exemption for companies exploiting intellectual property with limited UK connection); or
(c) [Omitted by FA 2007, s. 48 and Sch. 15, para. 8(1) and repealed by s. 114 and Sch. 27, Pt. 2(15).]
(d) the chargeable profits of the accounting period do not exceed £50,000 or, if the accounting period is less than 12 months, a proportionately reduced amount; or
(da) the relevant profits for the accounting period, after any adjustment required by subsection (3C), do not exceed–
(i) £200,000, or
(ii) if the accounting period is less than 12 months, a proportionately reduced amount; or
(e) as respects the accounting period, the company is, within the meaning of regulations made by the Board for the purposes of this paragraph, resident in a territory specified in the regulations and satisfies–
(i) such conditions with respect to its income or gains as may be so specified; and
(ii) such other conditions (if any) as may be so specified; or
(f) the accounting period ends during an exempt period in relation to the company (see Part 3A of Schedule 25).

748(1A) Regulations under paragraph (e) of subsection (1) above may–
(a) make different provision for different cases or with respect to different territories;
(b) make provision having effect in relation to accounting periods of controlled foreign companies ending not more than one year before the date on which the regulations are made; and
(c) contain such supplementary, incidental, consequential and transitional provision as the Board may think fit.

748(2) [Repealed by FA 1998, s. 113 and Sch. 17, para. 3(6); s. 165 and Sch. 27, Pt. III(27) – see History note.]

748(3) Notwithstanding that none of paragraphs (a) to (f) of subsection (1) above applies to an accounting period of a controlled foreign company, no apportionment under section 747(3) falls to be made as regards that accounting period if it is the case that–

(a) in so far as any of the transactions the results of which are reflected in the profits arising in that accounting period, or any two or more transactions taken together, the results of at least one of which are so reflected, achieved a reduction in United Kingdom tax, either the reduction so achieved was minimal or it was not the main purpose or one of the main purposes of that transaction or, as the case may be, of those transactions taken together to achieve that reduction, and

(b) it was not the main reason or, as the case may be, one of the main reasons for the company's existence in that accounting period to achieve a reduction in United Kingdom tax by a diversion of profits from the United Kingdom,

and Part IV of Schedule 25 shall have effect with respect to the preceding provisions of this subsection.

748(3A) The reference in subsection (1)(da) to the relevant profits for an accounting period are to the sum of–

(a) the profits of the company for that period calculated in accordance with generally accepted accounting practice (disregarding any exempt distributions and any capital gains or losses), before any adjustment required or authorised by law in calculating chargeable profits,

(b) any amount which accrues during that period to the trustees of a settlement in relation to which the company is a settlor or a beneficiary, and

(c) the company's share of any income which accrues during that period to a partnership of which the company is a partner.

748(3B) For the purposes of subsection (3A)–

(a) **"exempt distribution"** means a distribution (within the meaning of Part 23 of CTA 2010) which would be excluded from the company's chargeable profits by reason of it being exempt for the purposes of Part 9A of CTA 2009 (company distributions),

(b) where there is more than one settlor or beneficiary in relation to the settlement mentioned in subsection (3A)(b), the income is to be apportioned between the company and the other settlors or beneficiaries on a just and reasonable basis, and

(c) the company's share of any income which accrues to a partnership as mentioned in subsection (3A)(c) is to be determined by apportioning that income between the company and the other partners on a just and reasonable basis;

and in subsection (3A) and this subsection **"partnership"** includes an entity established under the law of a country or territory outside the United Kingdom of a similar character to a partnership; and **"partner"** is to be read accordingly.

748(3C) For the purposes of subsection (1)(da), Part 4 of TIOPA 2010 (transfer pricing) applies in relation to the calculation of the relevant profits for the accounting period as it applies in relation to the calculation of the chargeable profits for that period.

748(3D) But where the difference made in the amount of the relevant profits for the period as a result of the application of subsection (3C) would (disregarding this subsection) not exceed £50,000, no adjustment under that subsection is to be made.

748(4) [Repealed by FA 2005, s. 104 and Sch. 11, Pt. 2(6).]

748(5) [Repealed by FA 2005, s. 104 and Sch. 11, Pt. 2(6).]

748(6) This section is subject to sections 748ZA and 748A.

History – In s. 748(1)(b), the words "Schedule 25" substituted for the words "that Schedule" by FA 2011, s. 47 and Sch. 12, para. 1(2), with effect in relation to accounting periods of controlled foreign companies beginning on or after 1 January 2011.

S. 748(1)(ba) and (bb) inserted by FA 2011, s. 47 and Sch. 12, para. 1(3), with effect in relation to accounting periods of controlled foreign companies beginning on or after 1 January 2011.

S. 748(1)(da) inserted by FA 2011, s. 47 and Sch. 12, para. 4(2), with effect in relation to accounting periods of controlled foreign companies beginning on or after 1 January 2011.

S. 748(1)(f) (and the "; or" at the end of s. 748(1)(e)) inserted by FA 2011, s. 47 and Sch. 12, para. 6(2), with effect in relation to accounting periods of controlled foreign companies beginning on or after 1 January 2011.

S. 748(1)(a) including the word "or" at the end of it omitted by FA 2009, s. 36 and Sch. 16, para. 1(2) with effect in relation to accounting periods of controlled foreign companies beginning on or after 1 July 2009, subject to rules for accounting periods straddling 1 July 2009 in FA 2009, Sch. 16, para. 7 and transitional provisions in FA 2009, Sch. 16, para. 8. The wording of former s. 748(1)(a) was "in respect of that period the company pursues, within the meaning of Part I of Schedule 25, an acceptable distribution policy;".

S. 748(1)(c) and word "or" at end of it omitted by FA 2007, s. 48 and Sch. 15, para. 8(1) and repealed by s. 114 and Sch. 27, Pt. 2(15), with effect in relation to accounting periods of controlled foreign companies beginning on or after 6 December 2006 (subject to the transitional provisions at FA 2007, Sch. 15, para. 10(2)–(4)).

In s. 748(1), words "No apportionment under section 747(3) falls to be made as regards an accounting period of a controlled foreign company if–" substituted for "No direction may be given under section 747(1) with respect to an accounting period of a controlled foreign company if–" by FA 1998, s. 113 and Sch. 17, para. 3(2). In s. 748(1)(d), "£50,000" substituted for "£20 000" by FA 1998, s. 113 and Sch. 17, para. 3(3). S. 748(1)(e) inserted by FA 1998, s. 113 and Sch. 17, para. 3(4). All changes have effect in relation to accounting periods of UK resident companies endingon or after 1 July 1999, the self-assessment appointed day (see note above), subject to transitional provisions in FA 1998, Sch. 17, para. 37(2), (3), (4).

S. 748(1A) inserted by FA 1998, s. 113 and Sch. 17, para. 3(5) with effect in relation to accounting periods of UK resident companies ending on or after 1 July 1999, the self-assessment appointed day (see note above), subject to transitional provisions in FA 1998, Sch. 17, para. 37(2), (3), (4).

S. 748(2) repealed by FA 1998, s. 113 and Sch. 17, para. 3(6); s. 165 and Sch. 27, Pt. III(27) with effect in relation to accounting periods of UK resident companies ending on or after 1 July 1999, the self-assessment appointed day (see note above), subject to transitional provisions in FA 1998, Sch. 17, para. 37(2), (3), (4).

In s. 748(3), "(f)" substituted for"(e)" by FA 2011, s. 47 and Sch. 12, para. 6(3), with effect in relation to accounting periods of controlled foreign companies beginning on or after 1 January 2011.

In s. 748(3), "(a) to (e)" substituted for "(a) to (d)" by FA 1998, s. 113 and Sch. 17, para. 3(7), and the words "no apportionment under section 747(3) falls to be made as regards that accounting period if it is the case that" substituted for "no direction may be given under section 747(1) with respect to that accounting period if it appears to the Board that", both changes having effect in relation to accounting periods of UK resident companies ending on or after 1 July 1999, the self-assessment appointed day (see note above), subject to transitional provisions in FA 1998, Sch. 17, para. 37(2), (3), (4).

In s. 748(3)(a) the words "or any two…so reflected" substituted by FA 1996, s. 182 and Sch. 36, para. 2 in relation to accountingperiods of a controlled foreign company beginning on or after 28 November 1995.

S. 748(3A), (3B), (3C) and (3D) inserted by FA 2011, s. 47 and Sch. 12, para. 4(3), with effect in relation to accounting periods of controlled foreign companies beginning on or after 1 January 2011.

S. 748(4) repealed by FA 2005, s. 104 and Sch. 11, Pt. 2(6), with effect in relation to periods of account beginning on or after 16 March 2005.

Former s. 748(4) and (5) inserted by FA 1995, s. 133 and Sch. 25, para. 4, with effect from 1 May 1995.

S. 748(5) repealed by FA 2005, s. 104 and Sch. 11, Pt. 2(6), with effect in relation to periods of account beginning on or after 16 March 2005.

In s. 748(6), the words "sections 748ZA and" substituted for "section" by FA 2011, s. 47 and Sch. 12, para. 4(4), with effect in relation to accounting periods of controlled foreign companies beginning on or after 1 January 2011.

S. 748(6) inserted by FA 2002, s. 89(1) in relation to accounting periods of controlled foreign companies beginning on or after 24 July 2002.

Derivations – FA 1984, s. 83 (as originally enacted).

Cross references – S. 801: relief for UK and third country taxes for dividends paid between related companies.

S. 801C: relief for underlying tax – provisions for separate streaming of dividend so far as representing dividend of a controlled foreign company paid in order to satisfy s. 748(1)(a) (acceptable distribution policy).

Sch. 25: extended definitions relating to these provisions.

Statutory instruments – SI 1998/3081 (as amended): disapplication of s. 747(3) in cases where the controlled foreign company is resident in a territory specified in the regulations, and certain conditions are satisfied. Applies in relation to any accounting period of a UK-resident company ending on or after 1 July 1999 (the corporation tax self-assessment appointed day).

Other material – IR press release, 5 October 1993 (not reproduced): "excluded countries list" for periods prior to corporation tax self-assessment.
IR press release, 9 November 1994: clearance procedure for non-trading controlled foreign companies.

Exclusion of small profits exemptions

748ZA(1) Nothing in section 748(1)(da) prevents an apportionment falling to be made as regards an accounting period ("the relevant accounting period") of a controlled foreign company ("X") if condition A, B or C is met.
748ZA(2) Condition A is that at any time before the end of the relevant accounting period a scheme is entered into and–
(a) in the absence of this subsection, in consequence of the scheme, section 748(1)(da) would apply to prevent an apportionment falling to be made as regards the relevant accounting period of X, and
(b) the main purpose, or one of the main purposes, of any party to the scheme in entering into the scheme is to secure that section 748(1)(da) prevents an apportionment falling to be made as regards that period, or that period and one or more other accounting periods of X.
748ZA(3) Condition B is that at any time before the end of the relevant accounting period a scheme is entered into and–
(a) in consequence of the scheme profits are shifted to X from another company ("Y"),
(b) the main purpose or one of the main purposes of any party to the scheme in entering into the scheme is to ensure that section 748(1)(da) prevents an apportionment falling to be made as regards the chargeable profits of one or more controlled foreign companies for one or more accounting periods, and
(c) the relevant accounting period of X falls wholly or partly within that accounting period or those accounting periods.
748ZA(4) For the purposes of subsection (3), profits are shifted to X from Y if it is reasonable to suppose that in the absence of the scheme, and any similar scheme, the whole or a part of the income which is reflected in X's profits would have been reflected in Y's profits.
748ZA(5) Condition C is that, in determining X's chargeable profits for the relevant accounting period–
(a) [omitted by FA 2011, s. 30 and Sch. 5, para. 7(2)(a).]
(b) Part 21B of CTA 2010 (group mismatch schemes) has effect so as to exclude an amount from being brought into account as a debit or credit for the purposes of Part 5 of CTA 2009 (loan relationships) or Part 7 of that Act (derivative contracts).
748ZA(6) For the purposes of this section–
"apportionment" means an apportionment under section 747(3);
"scheme" means any scheme, arrangements or understanding of any kind whatever, whether or not legally enforceable, involving one or more transactions.

History – S. 748ZA(5)(a) omitted by FA 2011, s. 30 and Sch. 5, para. 7(2)(a), with effect in relation to loan relationships to which a company is a party (or to which it is treated as a party under CTA 2009, s. 418(6A)) on or after 19 July 2011, subject to transitional provisions in FA 2011, Sch. 5, para. 7(4).
S. 748ZA inserted by FA 2011, s. 47 and Sch. 12, para. 5, with effect in relation to accounting periods of controlled foreign companies beginning on or after 1 January 2011.

Territorial exclusions from exemption under section 748

748A(1) Nothing in section 748 prevents an apportionment under section 747(3) falling to be made as regards an accounting period of a controlled foreign company if the company–
(a) is a company incorporated in a territory to which this section applies as respects that accounting period; or
(b) is at any time in that accounting period liable to tax in such a territory by reason of domicile, residence or place of management; or
(c) at any time in that accounting period carries on business through a permanent establishment in such a territory.
748A(2) The condition in subsection (1)(c) above is not satisfied as regards an accounting period of a controlled foreign company if the business carried on by the company in that period through permanent establishments in territories to which this section applies, taken as a whole, is only a minimal part of the whole of the business carried on by the company in that period.
748A(3) The territories to which this section applies as respects an accounting period of a controlled foreign company are those specified as such in regulations made by the Treasury.
748A(4) Regulations under subsection (3) above–
(a) may make different provision for different cases or with respect to different territories; and
(b) may contain such incidental, supplemental, consequential or transitional provision as the Treasury may think fit.
748A(5) A statutory instrument containing regulations under subsection (3) above shall not be made unless a draft of the instrument has been laid before, and approved by a resolution of, the House of Commons.

History – In s. 748A(1)(c) the words "permanent establishment" substituted for the words "branch or agency"and in s. 748A(2) the words "permanent establishments" substituted for the words "branches or agencies" by FA 2003, s. 153(1)(a), in relation to accounting periods beginning on or after 1 January 2003.
S. 748A inserted by FA 2002, s. 89(2) in relation to accounting periods of controlled foreign companies beginning on or after 24 July 2002.

Residence

749(1) Subject to subsections (2) to (4) and (6) below, in any accounting period in which a company is resident outside the United Kingdom, it shall be regarded for the purposes of this Chapter as resident in that territory in which, throughout that period, it is liable to tax by reason of domicile, residence or place of management.
749(2) If, in the case of any company,–
(a) there are in any accounting period two or more territories falling within subsection (1) above, and
(b) no election or designation made under paragraph (d) or (e) of subsection (3) below in relation to an earlier accounting period of the company has effect by virtue of section 749A(1) in relation to that accounting period,

subsection (3) below shall apply with respect to that company and that accounting period.
749(3) Where this subsection applies, the company shall in that accounting period be regarded for the purposes of this Chapter as resident in only one of those territories, namely–
(a) if, throughout the accounting period, the company's place of effective management is situated in one of those territories only, in that territory;
(b) if, throughout the accounting period, the company's place of effective management is situated in two or more of those territories, in that one of them in which, at the end of the accounting period, the greater amount of the company's assets is situated;
(c) if neither paragraph (a) nor paragraph (b) above applies, in that one of the territories falling within subsection (1) above in which, at the end of the accounting period, the greater amount of the company's assets is situated;

(d) if–
(i) paragraph (a) above does not apply, and
(ii) neither paragraph (b) nor paragraph (c) above produces one, and only one, of those territories,
in that one of them (if any) which is specified in an election made in relation to that accounting period by any one or more persons who together have a majority assessable interest in the company in that accounting period; and
(e) if, in a case falling within paragraph (d) above, the time by which any election under that paragraph in relation to that accounting period must be made in accordance with section 749A(3)(b) expires without such an election having been made, in that one of those territories which the Board justly and reasonably designates in relation to that accounting period.

749(4) If, in the case of any company,–
(a) there are in any accounting period two or more territories falling within subsection (1) above, and
(b) an election or designation made under paragraph (d) or (e) of subsection (3) above in relation to an earlier accounting period of the company has effect by virtue of section 749A(1) in relation to the accounting period mentioned in paragraph (a) above,
the company shall in that accounting period be regarded for the purposes of this Chapter as resident in that one of those territories which is the subject of the election or designation.

749(5) If, in the case of any company, there is in any accounting period no territory falling within subsection (1) above, then, for the purposes of this Chapter, it shall be conclusively presumed that the company is in that accounting period resident in a territory in which it is subject to a lower level of taxation.

749(6) In any case where it becomes necessary for the purposes of subsection (3) above to determine in which of two or more territories the greater amount of a company's assets is situated at the end of an accounting period–
(a) account shall be taken only of those assets which, immediately before the end of that period, are situated in those territories; and
(b) the amount of them shall be determined by reference to their market value at that time.

749(7) This section is without prejudice to the provision that may be made in regulations under section 748(1)(e).

749(8) For the purposes of this section, one or more persons together have a "majority assessable interest" in a controlled foreign company in an accounting period of the company if–
(a) each of them has an assessable interest in the company in that accounting period; and
(b) it is likely that, were an apportionment of the chargeable profits of the company for that accounting period made under section 747(3), the aggregate of the amounts which would be apportioned to them is greater than 50 per cent of the aggregate of the amounts which would be apportioned to all the persons who have an assessable interest in the company in that accounting period.

749(9) For the purposes of subsection (8) above, a person has an "assessable interest" in a controlled foreign company in an accounting period of the company if he is one of the persons who it is likely would be chargeable to tax under section 747(4)(a) on an apportionment of the chargeable profits and creditable tax (if any) of the company for that accounting period under section 747(3).

749(10) For the purposes of subsection (8) and (9) above, the effect of any application under section 751A, 751AA, 751AB or 751AC shall be disregarded.

History – S. 749 substituted by FA 1998, s. 113 and Sch. 17, para. 4 with effect in relation to accounting periods of UK resident companies ending on or after 1 July 1999, the self-assessment appointed day by virtue of FA 1994, s. 199(2) and SI 1998/3173 (C. 78), subject to transitional provisions in FA 1998, Sch. 17, para. 37(2), (3), (4).
Former s. 749(4A) (inserted by FA 1990, s. 67(1), with effect on and after 20 March 1990) repealed by FA 1994, s. 251(4), and s. 258 and Sch. 26, Pt. VIII(1), with effect from 30 November 1993.
In s. 749(10), ", 751AA, 751AB or 751AC" substituted for "or 751AA" by FA 2011, s. 47 and Sch. 12, para. 10(b), with effect in relation to accounting periods of controlled foreign companies beginning on or after 1 January 2011.
In s. 749(10), "or 751AA" inserted by FA 2009, s. 36 and Sch. 16, para. 22(b), with effect in relation to accounting periods of controlled foreign companies ending on or after 1 January 2010.
S. 749(10) inserted by FA 2007, s. 48 and Sch. 15, para. 2, with effect in relation to accounting periods of controlled foreign companies beginning on or after 6 December 2006 (subject to the transitional provisions at FA 2007, Sch. 15, para. 10(2)–(4)).

Derivations – FA 1984, s. 84 (as originally enacted).

Cross references – S. 788: double taxation treaty relief.
Sch. 25, para. 5: cases where section 747(3) does not apply.
FA 1994, s. 249: with effect from 30 November 1993, dual resident companies treated as non-UK resident for all tax purposes, even if they are incorporated in the UK.

Elections and designations under section 749: supplementary provisions

749A(1) An election under paragraph (d) or a designation under paragraph (e) of section 749(3) shall have effect in relation to–
(a) the accounting period in relation to which it is made ("the original accounting period"), and
(b) each successive accounting period of the controlled foreign company in question which precedes the next one in which the eligible territories are different,
and shall so have effect notwithstanding any change in the persons who have interests in the company or any change in the interests which those persons have in the company.

749A(2) For the purposes of subsection (1)(b) above, an accounting period of the controlled foreign company is one in which the eligible territories are different if in the case of that accounting period–
(a) at least one of the two or more territories which fell within subsection (1) of section 749 in the original accounting period does not fall within that subsection; or
(b) some other territory also falls within that subsection.

749A(3) Any election under section 749(3)(d)–
(a) must be made by notice given to an officer of the Board;
(b) must be made no later than twelve months after the end of the controlled foreign company's accounting period in relation to which it is made;
(c) must state, as respects each of the persons making it, the percentage of the chargeable profits and creditable tax (if any) of the controlled foreign company for that accounting period which it is likely would be apportioned to him on an apportionment under section 747(3) if one were made;
(d) must be signed by the persons making it; and
(e) is irrevocable.

749A(4) Nothing in–
(a) paragraph 10 of Schedule 18 to the Finance Act 1998 (claims or elections in company tax returns), or
(b) Schedule 1A to the Management Act (claims or elections not included in returns),
shall apply, whether by virtue of section 754 or otherwise, to an election under section 749(3)(d).

749A(5) A designation under section 749(3)(e) is irrevocable.

749A(6) Where the Board make a designation under section 749(3)(e), notice of the making of the designation shall be given to every company resident in the United Kingdom which appears to the Board to have had an assessable interest in the controlled foreign company at any time during the accounting period of the controlled foreign company in relation to which the designation is made.

749A(7) A notice under subsection (6) above shall specify–
(a) the date on which the designation was made;
(b) the controlled foreign company to which the designation relates;
(c) the accounting period of the controlled foreign company in relation to which the designation is made; and
(d) the territory designated.

749A(8) subsection (9) of section 749 has effect for the purposes of subsection (6) above as it has effect for the purposes of subsection (8) of that section.

749A(9) For the purposes of this section the effect of any application under section 751A, 751AA, 751AB or 751AC shall be disregarded.

History – In s. 749A(9), ", 751AA, 751AB or 751AC" substituted for "or 751AA" by FA 2011, s. 47 and Sch. 12, para. 10(c), with effect in relation to accounting periods of controlled foreign companies beginning on or after 1 January 2011.
In s. 749A(9), "or 751AA" inserted by FA 2009, s. 36 and Sch. 16, para. 22(c), with effect in relation to accounting periods of controlled foreign companies ending on or after 1 January 2010.
S. 749A(9) inserted by FA 2007, s. 48 and Sch. 15, para. 3, with effect in relation to accounting periods of controlled foreign companies beginning on or after 6 December 2006 (subject to the transitional provisions at FA 2007, Sch. 15, para. 10(2)–(4)).
S. 749A inserted by FA 1998, s. 113 and Sch. 17, para. 4 with effect in relation to accounting periods of UK resident companies ending on or after 1 July 1999, the self-assessment appointed day by virtue of FA 1994, s. 199(2) and SI 1998/3173 (C. 78), subject to transitional provisions in FA 1998, Sch. 17, para. 37(2), (3), (4).

Interests in companies

749B(1) For the purposes of this Chapter, the following persons have an interest in a company–
(a) any person who possesses, or is entitled to acquire, share capital or voting rights in the company;
(b) any person who possesses, or is entitled to acquire, a right to receive or participate in distributions of the company;
(c) any person who is entitled to secure that income or assets (whether present or future) of the company will be applied directly or indirectly for his benefit; and
(d) any other person who, either alone or together with other persons, has control of the company.

749B(2) Rights which a person has as a loan creditor of a company do not constitute an interest in the company for the purposes of this Chapter.

749B(3) For the purposes of subsection (1)(b) above, the definition of **"distribution"** in Part 23 of CTA 2010 shall be construed without any limitation to companies resident in the United Kingdom.

749B(4) References in subsection (1) above to being entitled to do anything apply where a person–
(a) is presently entitled to do it at a future date, or
(b) will at a future date be entitled to do it;
but a person whose entitlement to secure that any income or assets of the company will be applied as mentioned in paragraph (c) of that subsection is contingent upon a default of the company or any other person under any agreement shall not be treated as falling within that paragraph unless the default has occurred.

749B(5) Where a company has an interest in another company and a third person has, or two or more persons together have, an interest in the first company (as in a case where one company has a shareholding in a controlled foreign company and the first company is controlled by a third company or by two or more persons together) subsections (6) and (7) below apply.

749B(6) Where this subsection applies, the person who has, or each of the persons who together have, the interest in the first company shall be regarded for the purposes of this Chapter as thereby having an interest in the second company.

749B(7) In any case where this subsection applies, in construing references in this Chapter to one person having the same interest as another, the person or as the case may be, each of the persons who together have, the interest in the first company shall be treated as having, to the extent of that person's interest in that company, the same interest as the first company has in the second company.

749B(8) Where two or more persons jointly have an interest in a company otherwise than in a fiduciary or representative capacity, they shall be treated for the purposes of this Chapter as having the interest in equal shares.

History – In s. 749B(3), the words "Part 23 of CTA 2010" substituted for the words "Part VI" by CTA 2010, s. 1177 and Sch. 1, para. 97, with effect for corporation tax purposes for accounting periods ending on or after 1 April 2010, and for income and capital gains tax purposes for the tax year 2010–11 and subsequent tax years.
S. 749B inserted by FA 1998, s. 113 and Sch. 17, para. 4, with effect in relation to accounting periods of UK resident companies ending on or after 1 July 1999, the self-assessment appointed day by virtue of FA 1994, s. 199(2) and SI 1998/3173 (C. 78), subject to transitional provisions in FA 1998, Sch. 17, para. 37(2), (3), (4).

Territories with a lower level of taxation

750(1) Without prejudice to subsection (5) of section 749, a company which, by virtue of any of subsections (1) to (4) of that section, is to be regarded as resident in a particular territory outside the United Kingdom shall be considered to be subject to a lower level of taxation in that territory if, after giving effect to subsections (1A) and (1B) below, the amount of tax (**"the local tax"**) which is paid under the law of that territory in respect of the profits of the company which arise in any accounting period is less than three-quarters of the corresponding United Kingdom tax on those profits.

750(1A) If in the case of that accounting period there is any income, or any income and any expenditure, of the company–
(a) which is brought into account in determining the profits of the company in respect of which tax is paid under the law of that territory, but
(b) which does not also fall to be brought into account in determining the chargeable profits of the company,
the local tax shall be treated for the purposes of this Chapter as reduced to what it would have been had that income and any such expenditure not been so brought into account.

750(1B) If–
(a) under the law of that territory any tax ("the company's tax") falls to be paid by the company in respect of profits of the company arising in that accounting period,
(b) under that law, any repayment of tax, or any payment in respect of a credit for tax, is made to a person other than the company, and
(c) that payment or repayment is directly or indirectly in respect of the company's tax,
the local tax shall be treated for the purposes of this Chapter as reduced (or further reduced) by the amount of that payment or repayment.

750(2) For the purposes of this Chapter, the amount of the corresponding United Kingdom tax on the profits arising in an accounting period of a company resident outside the United Kingdom is the amount of corporation tax which, on the assumptions set out in Schedule 24 and subject to subsection (3) below, would be chargeable in respect of the chargeable profits of the company for that accounting period.

750(3) In determining the amount of corporation tax which, in accordance with subsection (2) above, would be chargeable in respect of the chargeable profits of an accounting period of a company resident outside the United Kingdom–
(a) it shall be assumed for the purposes of Schedule 24 that an apportionment under section 747(3) falls to be made as regards that period; and
(ab) there shall be disregarded the effect of any application under section 751A, 751AA, 751AB or 751AC; and
(b) there shall be disregarded so much of any relief from corporation tax in respect of income as would be attributable to the local tax and would fall to be given by virtue of any provision of Part 2 of TIOPA 2010 (double taxation relief); and

(c) there shall be deducted from what would otherwise be the amount of that corporation tax–
  (i) any amount which (on the assumptions set out in Schedule 24) would fall to be set off against corporation tax by virtue of section 967 of CTA 2010; and
  (ii) any amount of income tax or corporation tax actually charged in respect of any of those chargeable profits.

750(4) The references in subsection (3)(c) above to an amount falling to be set off or an amount actually charged do not include so much of any such amount as has been or falls to be repaid to the company whether on the making of a claim or otherwise.
750(5) [Repealed by FA 2005, s. 104 and Sch. 11, Pt. 2(6).]
750(6) [Repealed by FA 2005, s. 104 and Sch. 11, Pt. 2(6).]
750(7) [Repealed by FA 2005, s. 104 and Sch. 11, Pt. 2(6).]
750(8) [Repealed by FA 2005, s. 104 and Sch. 11, Pt. 2(6).]

History – In s. 750(1) the words ", after giving effect to subsections (1A) and (1B) below," inserted by F(No. 2)A 2005, s. 44(2) with effect in relation to accounting periods of companies resident outside the United Kingdom beginning on or after 2 December 2004 (F(No. 2)A 2005, s. 44(4)).
In s. 750(1), "subsection (5)" substituted for "subsection (3)"; and "any of subsections (1) to (4)" substituted for "subsection (1) or subsection (2)" by FA 1998, s. 113 and Sch. 17, para. 5(2), with effect in relation to accounting periods of UK resident companies ending on or after 1 July 1999, the self-assessment appointed day by virtue of FA 1994, s. 199(2) and SI 1998/3173 (C. 78), subject to transitional provisions in FA 1998, Sch. 17, para. 37(2), (3), (4).
In s. 750(1), "three-quarters" substituted by FA 1993, s. 119(1), in relation to accounting periods beginning on or after 16 March 1993.
S. 750(1A) inserted by F(No. 2)A 2005, s. 44(3) with effect in relation to accounting periods of companies resident outside the United Kingdom beginning on or after 2 December 2004 (F(No. 2)A 2005, s. 44(4)).
S. 750(1B) inserted by F(No. 2)A 2005, s. 44(3) with effect in relation to accounting periods of companies resident outside the United Kingdom beginning on or after 2 December 2004 (F(No. 2)A 2005, s. 44(4)).
In s. 750(3)(ab), ", 751AA, 751AB or 751AC" substituted for "or 751AA" by FA 2011, s. 47 and Sch. 12, para. 10(d), with effect in relation to accounting periods of controlled foreign companies beginning on or after 1 January 2011.
In s. 750(3)(ab), "or 751AA" inserted by FA 2009, s. 36 and Sch. 16, para. 22(d), with effect in relation to accounting periods of controlled foreign companies ending on or after 1 January 2010.
S. 750(3)(ab) inserted by FA 2007, s. 48 and Sch. 15, para. 4, with effect in relation to accounting periods of controlled foreign companies beginning on or after 6 December 2006 (subject to the transitional provisions at FA 2007, Sch. 15, para. 10(2)–(4)).
S. 750(3)(a) substituted by FA 1998, s. 113 and Sch. 17, para. 5(3), with effect in relation to accounting periods of UK resident companies ending on or after 1 July 1999, the self-assessment appointed day (see note above), subject to transitional provisions in FA 1998, Sch. 17, para. 37(2), (3), (4).
In s. 750(3)(b), words at end "other than section 810" repealed by FA 2000, s. 156 and Sch. 40, with effect in relation to claims made on or after 1 April 2000.
In s. 750(3)(b), the words "Part 2 of TIOPA 2010 (double taxation relief)" substituted for the words "Part XVIII" by TIOPA 2010, s. 374 and Sch. 8, para 10 with effect for corporation tax purposes for accounting periods ending on or after 1 April 2010, for income tax and capital gains tax purposes for the tax year 2010–11 and subsequent tax years, and for petroleum revenue tax purposes for chargeable periods beginning on or after 1 July 2010.
In s. 750(3)(c)(i), the words "section 967 of CTA 2010" substituted for the words "section 7(2)" by CTA 2010, s. 1177 and Sch. 1, para. 98, with effect for corporation tax purposes for accounting periods ending on or after 1 April 2010, and for income and capital gains tax purposes for the tax year 2010–11 and subsequent tax years.
S. 750(5)–(8) repealed by FA 2005, s. 104 and Sch. 11, Pt. 2(6), with effect in relation to periods of account beginning on or after 16 March 2005.
Former s. 750(5)–(8) inserted by FA 1995, s. 133 and Sch. 25, para. 5, with effect from 1 May 1995.

Derivations – FA 1984, s. 85 (as originally enacted).

Cross references – S. 751: definition of "accounting period".
Pt. XVIII: provisions for double taxation relief.
Sch. 24: provisions for computing corresponding UK tax etc.
F(No. 2)A 2005, s. 44(5): special rules for determining the accounting period of a non-UK resident company for the purposes of ICTA 1988, Part 17, Chap. 4 where there has been an amendment to the actual accounting period (which would otherwise fall on or after 2 December 2004) and the amended accounting period would otherwise end prior to 2 December 2004.
SI 1998/3081: disapplication of s. 747(3) in cases where the controlled foreign company is resident in a territory specified in the regulations, and certain conditions are satisfied. Applies in relation to any accounting period of a UK-resident company ending on or after 1 July 1999 (the corporation tax self-assessment appointed day).

Statutory instruments – SI 2000/3158 Controlled Foreign Companies (Designer Rate Tax Provisions) Regulations 2000 (made under s. 750A(2) to (4)).

Other material – IR press release, 8 March 1991, as updated by press releases of 26 April 1993 and 5 October 1993 (not reproduced): list of excluded countries for the purposes of the controlled foreign companies provisions (applies in relation to periods prior to corporation tax self-assessment – superseded by SI 1998/3173 (see above)).

Deemed lower level of taxation: designer rate tax provisions

750A(1) Where–
(a) in any accounting period a company is to be regarded by virtue of any of subsections (1) to (4) of section 749 as resident in a particular territory outside the United Kingdom, and
(b) within the meaning of section 750(1), the local tax in respect of the profits arising to the company in that accounting period is equal to or greater than three-quarters of the corresponding United Kingdom tax on those profits, but
(c) that local tax is determined under designer rate tax provisions,

the company shall be taken for the purposes of this Chapter to be subject to a lower level of taxation in that territory in that accounting period.
750A(2) In subsection (1) above **"designer rate tax provisions"** means provisions–
  (a) which appear to the Board to be designed to enable companies to exercise significant control over the amount of tax which they pay; and
  (b) which are specified in regulations made by the Board.

750A(3) Regulations under subsection (2) above–
(a) may make different provision for different cases or with respect to different territories; and
(b) may contain such supplementary, incidental, consequential or transitional provision as the Board may think fit.

750A(4) The first regulations under subsection (2) above may make provision having effect in relation to accounting periods beginning not more than fifteen months before the date on which the regulations are made.

History – S. 750A inserted by FA 2000, s. 104 and Sch. 31, para. 3, with effect in relation to any accounting period of a company resident outside the UK which begins on or after 6 October 1999.

Accounting periods and creditable tax

751(1) For the purposes of this Chapter, an accounting period of a company resident outside the United Kingdom shall begin–

(a) whenever the company comes under the control of persons resident in the United Kingdom;

(b) whenever the company commences to carry on business unless an accounting period of the company has previously begun as respects which an apportionment under section 747(3) falls or has fallen to be made; and

(c) whenever an accounting period of the company ends without the company then ceasing either to carry on business or to have any source of income whatsoever.

751(2) For the purposes of this Chapter, an accounting period of a company resident outside the United Kingdom shall end if and at the time when–

(a) the company ceases to be under the control of persons resident in the United Kingdom; or

(b) the company becomes, or ceases to be, liable to tax in a territory; or

(bb) [Repealed by FA 1994, s. 251(4), and s. 258 and Sch. 26, Pt. VIII(1).]

(c) the company ceases to have any source of income whatsoever;

and for the purposes of paragraph (b) above **"liable to tax"** means liable to tax by reason of domicile, residence or place of management.

751(3) Without prejudice to subsections (1) and (2) above, sections 10(1) and (5), 11(1) and (2) and 12 of CTA 2009 shall apply for the purposes of this Chapter as they apply for the purposes of corporation tax, but with the omission of so much of those provisions as relates to a company coming or ceasing to be within the charge to corporation tax.

751(4) Where it appears to the Board that the beginning or end of any accounting period of a company resident outside the United Kingdom is uncertain, the Board may by notice specify as an accounting period of the company such period, not exceeding 12 months, as appears to the Board to be appropriate, and that period shall be treated for the purposes of this Chapter as an accounting period of the company unless the notice is subsequently amended under subsection (5) below.

751(5) If, on further facts coming to the knowledge of the Board after the giving of a notice under subsection (4) above, it appears to the Board that any accounting period specified in the notice is not the true accounting period, the Board shall amend the notice so as to specify the true period.

751(5A) Any notice under subsection (4) above, and notice of any amendment of such a notice under subsection (5) above, shall be given to every person who has an assessable interest, (as defined in section 749(9)) in the company in the accounting period in question.

751(6) In this Chapter, in relation to an accounting period of a controlled foreign company as regards which an apportionment under section 747(3) falls to be made, the **"creditable tax"** means the aggregate of–

(a) the amount of any relief from corporation tax in respect of income which (on the assumptions set out in Schedule 24 and assuming the company to be liable for corporation tax on the chargeable profits of that accounting period) would fall to be given to the company by virtue of any provision of Part 2 of TIOPA 2010 (double taxation relief) in respect of foreign tax attributable to any income which is brought into account in determining those chargeable profits; and

(b) any amount which (on those assumptions) would fall to be set off against corporation tax on those chargeable profits by virtue of section 967 of CTA 2010; and

(c) the amount of any income tax or corporation tax actually charged in respect of the chargeable profits of that accounting period, less any of that tax which has been or falls to be repaid to the company, whether on the making of a claim or otherwise.

History – In s. 751(1)(a), the word "persons" was substituted retrospectively by FA 1990, s. 89 and Sch. 14, para. 9.

In s. 751(1)(b), words "not being the subject of an earlier direction under section 747(1)" which came after "company" repealed, and words "unless an accounting period of the company has previously begun as respects which an apportionment under section 747(3) falls or has fallen to be made" inserted by FA 1998, s. 113 and Sch. 17, para. 6(2); s. 165 and Sch. 27, Pt. III(27), with effect in relation to accounting periods of UK resident companies ending on or after 1 July 1999, the self-assessment appointed day by virtue of FA 1994, s. 199(2) and SI 1998/3173 (C. 78), subject to transitional provisions in FA 1998, Sch. 17, para. 37(2), (3), (4).

S. 751(2)(bb) (inserted by FA 1990, s. 67(2), with effect on and after 20 March 1990) repealed by FA 1994, s. 251(4), and s. 258 and Sch. 26, Pt. VIII(1), with effect from 30 November 1993.

In s. 751(3), the words "sections 10(1) and (5), 11(1) and (2) and 12 of CTA 2009" substituted for "subsections (3), (5) and (7) of section 12" by CTA 2009, s. 1322 and Sch. 1, para. 218 , with effect for corporation tax purposes for accounting periods ending on or after 1 April 2009, and for income tax and capital gains tax purposes for the tax year 2009–10 and subsequent tax years.

In s. 751(4), words "the Board may by notice" substituted for "a direction under section 747(1) may", and reference to "the notice" substituted for reference to "the direction", by FA 1998, s. 113 and Sch. 17, para. 6(3), with effect in relation to accounting periods of UK resident companies ending on or after 1 July 1999, the self-assessment appointed day (see note above), subject to transitional provisions in FA 1998, Sch. 17, para. 37(2), (3), (4).

In s. 751(5), words "giving of a notice under subsection (4) above" substituted for "making of a direction (including facts emerging on an appeal against notice of the making of the direction)", and references to "notice" substituted for references to "direction", by FA 1998, s. 113 and Sch. 17, para. 6(4), with effect in relation to accounting periods of UK resident companies ending on or after 1 July 1999, the self-assessment appointed day (see note above), subject to transitional provisions in FA 1998, Sch. 17, para. 37(2), (3), (4).

S. 751(5A) inserted by FA 1998, s. 113 and Sch. 17, para. 6(5), with effect in relation to accounting periods of UK resident companies ending on or after 1 July 1999, the self-assessment appointed day (see note above), subject to transitional provisions in FA 1998, Sch. 17, para. 37(2), (3), (4).

In s. 751(6)(a), the words "Part 2 of TIOPA 2010 (double taxation relief)" substituted for the words "Part XVIII" by TIOPA 2010, s. 374 and Sch. 8, para. 11 with effect for corporation tax purposes for accounting periods ending on or after 1 April 2010, for income tax and capital gains tax purposes for the tax year 2010–11 and subsequent tax years, and for petroleum revenue tax purposes for chargeableperiods beginning on or after 1 July 2010.

In s. 751(6)(b), the words "section 967 of CTA 2010" substituted for the words "section 7(2)" by CTA 2010, s. 1177 and Sch. 1, para. 99, with effect for corporation tax purposes for accounting periods ending on or after 1 April 2010, and for income and capital gains tax purposes for the tax year 2010–11 and subsequent tax years.

In s. 751(6), words "as regards which an apportionment under section 747(3) falls to be made" substituted for "in respect of which a direction is given under section 747(1)" by FA 1998, s. 113 and Sch. 17, para. 6(6), with effect in relation to accounting periods of UK resident companies ending on or after 1 July 1999, the self-assessment appointed day (see note above), subject to transitional provisions in FA 1998, Sch. 17, para. 37(2), (3), (4).

Derivations – FA 1984, s. 86 (as originally enacted).

Cross references – S. 12(3), (5) and (7): general provisions for ascertaining corporation tax accounting periods.

Sch. 24: provisions for computing the profits etc. of controlled foreign companies.

Sch. 25, para. 3(4A): "unrestricted creditable tax" is the amount which would be a company's creditable tax for an accounting period if the reference in s. 751(6)(a) to Pt. XVIII did not include s. 797.

FA 1993, s. 168A: application of FA 1993, Pt. II, Ch. II (exchange gains and losses) to certain companies becoming resident in the UK.

FA 1994, s. 249: with effect from 30 November 1993, dual resident companies treated as non-UK resident for all tax purposes, even if they are incorporated in the UK.

Reduction in chargeable profits for certain activities of EEA business establishments

751A(1) This section applies if–
(a) an apportionment under section 747(3) falls to be made as regards an accounting period ("the relevant accounting period") of a controlled foreign company,
(b) throughout that period the controlled foreign company has a business establishment in an EEA territory,
(c) throughout that period there are individuals who work for the controlled foreign company in that territory and
(d) a company resident in the United Kingdom ("the UK resident company") has a relevant interest in the controlled foreign company in that period.

751A(2) The UK resident company may make an application to the Commissioners for Her Majesty's Revenue and Customs for the chargeable profits of the controlled foreign company for the relevant accounting period to be reduced by an amount ("the specified amount") specified in the application (including to nil).

751A(3) If the Commissioners grant the application–
(a) those chargeable profits are treated as reduced by the specified amount, and
(b) the controlled foreign company's creditable tax (if any) for that period is treated as reduced by so much of that tax as, on a just and reasonable basis, relates to the reduction in those chargeable profits,

for the purpose of applying section 747(3) to (5) for determining the sum (if any) chargeable on the UK resident company under section 747(4)(a) (but for no other purpose).

751A(4) The Commissioners may grant the application only if–
(a) they are satisfied that the specified amount does not exceed the amount (if any) equal to so much of those chargeable profits as can reasonably be regarded as representing the net economic value which–
(i) arises to the appropriate body of persons (taken as a whole), and
(ii) is created directly by qualifying work, and
(b) they have not previously granted an application made by the UK resident company in respect of the relevant accounting period under section 751AB or 751AC.

751A(5) For the purposes of subsection (4) "net economic value" does not include any value which derives directly or indirectly from the reduction or elimination of any liability of any person to any tax or duty imposed under the law of any territory.

751A(6) For the purposes of subsection (4) **"the appropriate body of persons"** means–
(a) if the controlled foreign company is not a member of a group of companies, the controlled foreign company and the persons who have an interest in it at any time in the relevant accounting period, and
(b) if the controlled foreign company is a member of a group of companies, all the persons falling within paragraph (a) and any other person who is a member of that group of companies,

and for the purposes of this subsection **"group of companies"** means a company and any other companies of which it has control.

751A(7) For the purposes of subsection (4) **"qualifying work"** means work which–
(a) is done in any EEA territory in which the controlled foreign company has a business establishment throughout the relevant accounting period, and
(b) is done in that territory by individuals working for the-controlled foreign company there.

751A(8) Any reference in this section to a business establishment of a controlled foreign company in an EEA territory is to be construed in accordance with paragraph 7 of Schedule 25 (but as if the reference in that paragraph to the territory in which the company is resident were to the EEA territory).

751A(9) For the purposes of this section individuals are not to be regarded as working for a company in any territory unless–
(a) they are employed by the company in the territory, or
(b) they are otherwise directed by the company to perform duties on its behalf in the territory.

History – S. 751(4) substituted by FA 2011, s. 47 and Sch. 12, para. 11, with effect in relation to accounting periods of controlled foreign companies beginning on or after 1 January 2011.
S. 751A inserted by FA 2007, s. 48 and Sch. 15, para. 5, with effect in relation to accounting periods of controlled foreign companies beginning on or after 6 December 2006 (subject to the transitional provisions at FA 2007, Sch. 15, para. 10(2)–(4)).

Reduction in chargeable profits for certain financing income

751AA(1) This section applies if–
(a) an apportionment under section 747(3) falls to be made as regards an accounting period ("the relevant accounting period") of a controlled foreign company,
(b) the chargeable profits of the controlled foreign company for the relevant accounting period would, apart from this section, include an amount of income in respect of a payment made by another company ("the payer"),
(c) the amount that the payer brings into account for the purposes of corporation tax in respect of the payment is reduced (in part or in full) by virtue of Part 3 of Schedule 15 to FA 2009 (tax treatment of financing costs and income), and
(d) a company resident in the United Kingdom ("the UK resident company") has a relevant interest in the controlled foreign company in the relevant accounting period.

751AA(2) The UK resident company may make an application to the Commissioners for Her Majesty's Revenue and Customs for the chargeable profits of the controlled foreign company for the relevant accounting period ("the chargeable profits") to be reduced by an amount ("the specified amount") specified in the application (including to nil).

751AA(3) If the Commissioners grant the application–
(a) the chargeable profits are treated as reduced by the specified amount, and
(b) the controlled foreign company's creditable tax (if any) for that period is treated as reduced by so much of that tax as, on a just and reasonable basis, relates to the reduction in the chargeable profits,

for the purpose of applying section 747(3) to (5) for determining the sum (if any) chargeable on the UK resident company under section 747(4)(a) (but for no other purpose).

751AA(4) The Commissioners may grant the application only if they are satisfied that the specified amount does not exceed the relevant amount.

751AA(5) In subsection (4) **"the relevant amount"** means the amount (if any) by which it is just and reasonable that the chargeable profits should be treated as reduced, having regard to the effect of Parts 3 and 4 of Schedule 15 to FA 2009 on amounts brought into account for the purposes of corporation tax by the payer, or any other company.

History – S. 751AA inserted by FA 2009, s. 36 and Sch. 16, para. 23, with effect in relation to accounting periods of controlled foreign companies ending on or after 1 January 2010.

Reduction in chargeable profits: failure to qualify for exemptions

751AB(1) This section applies if–
(a) an apportionment under section 747(3) would fall to be made as regards an accounting period ("the relevant accounting period") of a controlled foreign company,
(b) but for a relevant failure, section 748(1)(ba) or (bb) would have prevented such an apportionment, and
(c) a company resident in the United Kingdom ("the UK resident company") has a relevant interest in the controlled foreign company in that period.

751AB(2) **"Relevant failure"** means–
(a) in the case of section 748(1)(ba), one or both of the following–
(i) a failure to satisfy the requirement of paragraph 12E of Schedule 25 (requirement as to company's UK connection) in circumstances where the requirement would be satisfied if the reference in sub-paragraph (3)(a) of that paragraph to 10% were a reference to 50%, and
(ii) a failure to satisfy the requirement of paragraph 12F of that Schedule (finance income and relevant IP income) in circumstances where the relevant IP income of the controlled foreign company for the accounting period does not exceed 5% of the company's gross income for that period, and
(b) in the case of section 748(1)(bb), a failure to satisfy the requirement of paragraph 12M of that Schedule (finance income).
751AB(3) The UK resident company may make an application to the Commissioners for Her Majesty's Revenue and Customs for the chargeable profits of the controlled foreign company for the relevant accounting period ("the chargeable profits") to be reduced to an amount specified in the application ("the specified amount"). The specified amount may be nil.
751AB(4) If the Commissioners grant the application–
(a) the chargeable profits are treated as reduced to the specified amount, and
(b) the controlled foreign company's creditable tax (if any) for that period is treated as reduced by so much of that tax as, on a just and reasonable basis, relates to the reduction in the chargeable profits,
for the purpose of applying section 747(3) to (5) for determining the sum (if any) chargeable on the UK resident company under section 747(4)(a) (but for no other purpose).
751AB(5) The Commissioners may grant the application only if–
(a) they are satisfied that the specified amount is not less than the relevant amount, and
(b) they have not previously granted an application made by the UK resident company in respect of the relevant accounting period under section 751A or 751AC.
751AB(6) **"The relevant amount"** means–
(a) if the relevant failure is within subsection (2)(a), the sum of–
(i) the excess finance and IP income (if any) for the relevant accounting period, and
(ii) in a case where there is a failure specified in subsection (2)(a)(i), so much (if any) of the net chargeable profits for that period as are not excluded by subsection (8), and
(b) if the relevant failure is within subsection (2)(b)–
(i) the amount (if any) by which the controlled foreign company's finance income for the relevant accounting period exceeds 5% of its gross income for that period, or
(ii) if that amount is a negligible amount, nil.
751AB(7) **"The excess finance and IP income"** for the relevant accounting period means–
(a) the amount (if any) by which the total of the controlled foreign company's finance income and relevant IP income for that period exceeds 5% of its gross income for that period, or
(b) if that amount is a negligible amount, nil.
751AB(8) Net chargeable profits are excluded by this subsection if, and to the extent that, they can reasonably be regarded–
(a) as representing the net economic value which–
(i) arises to the appropriate body of persons (taken as a whole), and
(ii) is created directly by qualifying work, or
(b) as not being wholly or partly attributable, directly or indirectly, to transactions with persons within the charge to United Kingdom tax.
751AB(9) In subsection (8)(a) **"qualifying work"** means work which–
(a) is done in the territory in which the controlled foreign company is resident, and
(b) is done in that territory by individuals working for the controlled foreign company there.
751AB(10) A transaction with a company which is within the charge to United Kingdom tax only because it carries on a trade in the United Kingdom through a permanent establishment there is within subsection (8)(b) only if the transaction is attributable to activities carried on through that establishment.
751AB(11) For the purposes of subsections (8) and (9)–
(a) section 751A(5), (6) and (9) applies as it applies for the purposes of the equivalent provisions of section 751A, and
(b) paragraph 5(2) to (5) of Schedule 25 (residence of controlled foreign company) applies as it applies in relation to Part 2 of that Schedule.
751AB(12) In this section–
"finance income" has the meaning given by paragraph 12F(3) of Schedule 25 (with references to C read as references to the controlled foreign company);
"relevant IP income" has the meaning given by paragraph 12F(4) of that Schedule;
"net chargeable profits" means chargeable profits excluding so much of those profits as is directly attributable to the finance income or relevant IP income of the controlled foreign company;
"UK-connected gross income" has the same meaning as in paragraph 12E of Schedule 25;
"United Kingdom tax" means corporation tax or income tax;
and paragraph 12G of that Schedule (gross income) applies for the purposes of this section as it applies for the purposes of Part 2A of that Schedule (with references to C read as references to the controlled foreign company).

History – S. 751AB inserted by FA 2011, s. 47 and Sch. 12, para. 2, with effect in relation to accounting periods of controlled foreign companies beginning on or after 1 January 2011.

Reduction in chargeable profits following an exempt period

751AC(1) This section applies if–
(a) an exempt period in relation to a controlled foreign company ends in accordance with paragraph 15F(2) of Schedule 25 (time exempt period ends if there is an early termination event), other than by reason of an early termination event within paragraph 15F(3)(b),
(b) an accounting period ("the relevant accounting period") of the company ends after that exempt period but before the time the exempt period would have ended had paragraph 15F(2) of that Schedule not applied,
(c) an apportionment under section 747(3) would fall to be made as regards the relevant accounting period, and
(d) a company resident in the United Kingdom ("the UK resident company") has a relevant interest in the controlled foreign company in that period.
751AC(2) The UK resident company may make an application to the Commissioners for Her Majesty's Revenue and Customs for the chargeable profits of the controlled foreign company for that accounting period ("the chargeable profits") to be reduced to an amount ("the specified amount") specified in the application (which may be nil).
751AC(3) If the Commissioners grant the application–
(a) the chargeable profits are treated as reduced to the specified amount, and
(b) the controlled foreign company's creditable tax (if any) for that period is treated as reduced by so much of that tax as, on a just and reasonable basis, relates to the reduction in the chargeable profits,
for the purpose of applying section 747(3) to (5) for determining the sum (if any) chargeable on the UK resident company under section 747(4)(a) (but for no other purpose).

751AC(4) The Commissioners may grant the application only if–
(a) they are satisfied that the specified amount is not less than the relevant amount, and
(b) they have not previously granted an application made by the UK resident company in respect of the relevant accounting period under section 751A or 751AB.
751AC(5) **"The relevant amount"** means the amount (if any) equal to so much of the chargeable profits as it is just and reasonable to regard as referable to–
(a) the relevant transaction which triggered the end of the exempt period, or
(b) any later relevant transaction occurring before the time the exempt period would have ended had paragraph 15F(2) of Schedule 25 not applied.
751AC(6) **"Relevant transaction"** has the meaning given by paragraph 15E of Schedule 25 (and it does not matter if the transaction occurs pursuant to an agreement entered into by the controlled foreign company before the relevant time (within the meaning of paragraph 15G of that Schedule)).

History – S. 751AC inserted by FA 2011, s. 47 and Sch. 12, para. 7, with effect in relation to accounting periods of controlled foreign companies beginning on or after 1 January 2011.

Sections 751A to 751AC: supplementary

751B(1) An application by a company under section 751A, 751AA, 751AB or 751AC–
(a) must be made in such form as the HMRC Commissioners may determine,
(b) must be accompanied by such documents (or copies of documents) in the company's possession or power as those Commissioners may reasonably require for the purpose of determining whether to grant the application, and
(c) must contain such information as those Commissioners may reasonably require for that purpose.
751B(2) An application by a company under section 751A, 751AA, 751AB or 751AC–
(a) may be made at any time before the end of the application period, and
(b) may be amended or withdrawn at any time before the application is determined by those Commissioners.
751B(3) If an application by a company under section 751A, 751AA, 751AB or 751AC is granted after the company has delivered its relevant company tax return, it has 30 days beginning with the day on which the application is granted in which to amend that return to give effect to section 751A, 751AA, 751AB or 751AC.
751B(4) The time limits otherwise applicable to an amendment of a company tax return do not prevent an amendment being made under subsection (3).
751B(5) If the HMRC Commissioners refuse an application by a company under section 751A, 751AA, 751AB or 751AC, the company may appeal against the refusal.
751B(6) Notice of an appeal must be given in writing to the HMRC Commissioners within 30 days after the application is refused.
751B(7) On an appeal–
(a) if the tribunal is satisfied that the relevant amount is a different amount from the amount specified in the application, it must direct the HMRC Commissioners to grant the application as if the amount specified in it were that different amount,
(b) if the tribunal is satisfied that the relevant amount is the amount specified in the application, it must direct the HMRC Commissioners to grant the application, and
(c) in any other case, the tribunal must confirm the refusal.
751B(8) For the purposes of subsection (7) **"the relevant amount"**–
(a) in the case of an appeal in respect of the refusal of an application under section 751A, means the amount (if any) equal to so much of the chargeable profits mentioned in subsection (4) of section 751A as can reasonably be regarded as representing the value mentioned in that subsection,
(b) in the case of an appeal in respect of the refusal of an application under section 751AA, has the meaning given by subsection (5) of that section,
(c) in the case of an appeal in respect of the refusal of an application under section 751AB, has the meaning given by subsection (6) of that section, and
(d) in the case of an appeal in respect of the refusal of an application under section 751AC, has the meaning given by subsection (5) of that section.
751B(9) Part 5 of the Management Act (appeals), apart from section 50, applies in relation to an appeal under this section as it applies in relation to an appeal against an assessment to tax.
751B(10) In this section–

"the application period" means–
(a) the period within which an amendment to the relevant company tax return may be made by virtue of paragraph 15(4) of Schedule 18 to the Finance Act 1998 (disregarding any extension of that period provided by subsections (3) and (4) of this section or any other enactment), or
(b) if the relevant company tax return is amended under paragraph 34(2)(b) or (2A) of that Schedule as a consequence of the application of this Chapter–
  (i) the period of 30 days beginning when the amendment was notified to the company, or
  (ii) if an appeal is brought against such an amendment, the period of 30 days beginning when that appeal is finally determined;

"relevant company tax return", in relation to a company, means the return for the accounting period for which–
(a) any sum is chargeable on the company under section 747(4)(a), or
(b) any sum would be so chargeable but for section 751A, 751AA, 751AB or 751AC,

in respect of the chargeable profits of the company for the accounting period mentioned in section 751A, 751AA, 751AB or 751AC.
751B(11) In this section **"the HMRC Commissioners"** means the Commissioners for Her Majesty's Revenue and Customs.

History – In the heading to s. 751B, "to 751AC" substituted for "and 751AA" by FA 2011, s. 47 and Sch. 12, para. 12(6), with effect in relation to accounting periods of controlled foreign companies beginning on or after 1 January 2011.
In the heading to s. 751B, "Sections 751A and 751AA" substituted for "Section 751A" by FA 2009, s. 36 and Sch. 16, para. 24(2), with effect in relation to accounting periods of controlled foreign companies ending on or after 1 January 2010.
In s. 751B(1), ", 751AA, 751AB or 751AC" substituted for "or 751AA" by FA 2011, s. 47 and Sch. 12, para. 12(2), with effect in relation to accounting periods of controlled foreign companies beginning on or after 1 January 2011.
In s. 751B(1), "or 751AA" inserted by FA 2009, s. 36 and Sch. 16, para. 24(3), with effect in relation to accounting periods of controlled foreign companies ending on or after 1 January 2010.
In s. 751B(2), ", 751AA, 751AB or 751AC" substituted for "or 751AA" by FA 2011, s. 47 and Sch. 12, para. 12(2), with effect in relation to accounting periods of controlled foreign companies beginning on or after 1 January 2011.
S. 751B(2)(a) substituted by FA 2011, s. 47 and Sch. 12, para. 12(3), with effect in relation to accounting periods of controlled foreign companies beginning on or after 1 January 2011.
In s. 751B(2), "or 751AA" inserted by FA 2009, s. 36 and Sch. 16, para. 24(3), with effect in relation to accounting periods of controlled foreign companies ending on or after 1 January 2010.
In s. 751B(3), ", 751AA, 751AB or 751AC" substituted for "or 751AA" in each place by FA 2011, s. 47 and Sch. 12, para. 12(2), with effect in relation to accounting periods of controlled foreign companies beginning on or after 1 January 2011.
In s. 751B(3), "or 751AA" inserted in each place by FA 2009, s. 36 and Sch. 16, para. 24(3), with effect in relation to accounting periods of controlled foreign companies ending on or after 1 January 2010.

In s. 751B(5), ", 751AA, 751AB or 751AC" substituted for "or 751AA" by FA 2011, s. 47 and Sch. 12, para. 12(2), with effect in relation to accounting periods of controlled foreign companies beginning on or after 1 January 2011.
In s. 751B(5), "or 751AA" inserted by FA 2009, s. 36 and Sch. 16, para. 24(3), with effect in relation to accounting periods of controlled foreign companies ending on or after 1 January 2010.
In s. 751B(5), the words "to the Special Commissioners", which appeared after "may appeal", omitted by SI 2009/56, art. 3(1) and Sch. 1, para. 154(2), operative from 1 April 2009, subject to transitional and saving provisions in SI 2009/56, Sch. 3.
In s. 751B(7)(a), the words "the tribunal is" and "it" substituted for "the Special Commissioners are" and "they" respectively by SI2009/56, art. 3(1) and Sch. 1, para. 154(3)(a), operative from 1 April 2009, subject to transitional and saving provisions in SI 2009/56, Sch. 3.
In s. 751B(7)(b), the words "the tribunal is" and "it" substituted for "the Special Commissioners are" and "they" respectively by SI 2009/56, art. 3(1) and Sch. 1, para. 154(3)(a), operative from 1 April 2009, subject to transitional and saving provisions in SI 2009/56, Sch. 3.
In s. 751B(7)(c), the word "tribunal" substituted for "Special Commissioners" by SI 2009/56, art. 3(1) and Sch. 1, para. 154(3)(b), operative from 1 April 2009, subject to transitional and saving provisions in SI 2009/56, Sch. 3.
S. 751B(8)(c) and (d) inserted (and the "and" before s. 751B(8)(b) omitted) by FA 2011, s. 47 and Sch. 12, para. 12(4), with effect in relation to accounting periods of controlled foreign companies beginning on or after 1 January 2011.
S. 751B(8), para. (a) created (and the "—" before para. (a) inserted), and the words "in the case of an appeal in respect of the refusal of an application under section 751A," inserted, by FA 2009, s. 36 and Sch. 16, para. 24(4)(a), with effect in relation to accounting periods of controlled foreign companies ending on or after 1 January 2010.
S. 751B(8)(b) (and the "and" before it) inserted by FA 2009, s. 36 and Sch. 16, para. 24(4)(b), with effect in relation to accounting periods of controlled foreign companies ending on or after 1 January 2010.
In s. 751B(9), "(appeals)" substituted for "(appeals against assessments to tax)" by SI 2009/56, art. 3(1) and Sch. 1, para. 154(4), operative from 1 April 2009, subject to transitional and saving provisions in SI 2009/56, Sch. 3.
S. 751B(10) substituted by FA 2011, s. 47 and Sch. 12, para. 12(5), with effect in relation to accounting periods of controlled foreign companies beginning on or after 1 January 2011.
In former s. 751B(10), "or 751AA" and "or 751AA(1)" inserted by FA 2009, s. 36 and Sch. 16, para. 24(5), with effect in relation to accounting periods of controlled foreign companies ending on or after 1 January 2010.
S. 751B inserted by FA 2007, s. 48 and Sch. 15, para. 5, with effect in relation to accounting periods of controlled foreign companies beginning on or after 6 December 2006 (subject to the transitional provisions at FA 2007, Sch. 15, para. 10(2)–(4)).

Apportionment of chargeable profits and creditable tax

752(1) This section applies in any case where an apportionment under section 747(3) falls to be made as regards an accounting period of a controlled foreign company.
752(2) Where–
(a) the persons who have relevant interests in the controlled foreign company at any time in the relevant accounting period have those interests by virtue only of directly or indirectly holding ordinary shares of the company,
(b) each of those persons satisfies the condition that he is either–
(i) resident in the United Kingdom throughout that accounting period, or
(ii) resident in the United Kingdom at no time in that accounting period, and
(c) no company which has an intermediate interest in the controlled foreign company at any time in the relevant accounting period has that interest otherwise than by virtue of directly or indirectly holding ordinary shares of the controlled foreign company,

subsection (3) below shall apply.
752(3) Where this subsection applies, the apportionment of the controlled foreign company's chargeable profits and creditable tax (if any) for the relevant accounting period shall be made among the persons who have relevant interests in the company at any time in that period in direct proportion to the percentage of the issued ordinary shares of the controlled foreign company which, in accordance with section 752B, each of those relevant interests represents.
752(4) Where subsection (3) above does not apply, the apportionment of the controlled foreign company's chargeable profits and creditable tax (if any) for the relevant accounting period shall be made on a just and reasonable basis among the persons who have relevant interests in the company at any time in that period.

History – S. 752 substituted by FA 1998, s. 113 and Sch. 17, para. 7, with effect in relation to accounting periods of UK resident companies ending on or after 1 July 1999, the self-assessment appointed day by virtue of FA 1994, s. 199(2) and SI 1998/3173 (C. 78), subject to transitional provisions in FA 1998, Sch. 17, para. 37(2), (3), (4).
Derivations – FA 1984, s. 87 (as originally enacted).

Relevant interests

752A(1) This section has effect for the purpose of determining for the purposes of this Chapter who has a relevant interest in a controlled foreign company at any time; and references in this Chapter to relevant interests shall be construed accordingly.
752A(2) A UK resident company which has a direct or indirect interest in a controlled foreign company has a relevant interest in the company by virtue of that interest unless subsection (3) below otherwise provides.
752A(3) A UK resident company which has an indirect interest in a controlled foreign company does not have a relevant interest in the company by virtue of that interest if it has the interest by virtue of having a direct or indirect interest in another UK resident company.
752A(4) A related person who has a direct or indirect interest in a controlled foreign company has a relevant interest in the company by virtue of that interest unless subsection (5) or (6) below otherwise provides.
752A(5) A related person who has an indirect interest in a controlled foreign company does not have a relevant interest in the company by virtue of that interest if he has the interest by virtue of having a direct or indirect interest in–
(a) a UK resident company; or
(b) another related person.
752A(6) A related person who has a direct or indirect interest in a controlled foreign company does not have a relevant interest in the company by virtue of that interest to the extent that a UK resident company–
(a) has the whole or any part of the same interest indirectly, by virtue of having a direct or indirect interest in the related person, and
(b) by virtue of that indirect interest in the controlled foreign company, has a relevant interest in the company by virtue of subsection (2) above.
752A(7) A person who–
(a) has a direct interest in a controlled foreign company, but
(b) does not by virtue of subsections (2) to (6) above have a relevant interest in the company by virtue of that interest,

has a relevant interest in the company by virtue of that interest unless subsection (8) below otherwise provides.
752A(8) A person does not by virtue of subsection (7) above have a relevant interest in a controlled foreign company by virtue of having a direct interest in the company to the extent that another person–
(a) has the whole or any part of the same interest indirectly, and
(b) by virtue of that indirect interest, has a relevant interest in the company by virtue of subsections (2) to (6) above.

752A(9) No person has a relevant interest in a controlled foreign company otherwise than as provided by subsections (2) to (8) above.
752A(10) In this section–

"related person" means a person who–
(a) is not a UK resident company, but
(b) is connected or associated with a UK resident company which has by virtue of subsection (2) above a relevant interest in the controlled foreign company in question;

"UK resident company" means a company resident in the United Kingdom.

History – S. 752A inserted by FA 1998, s. 113 and Sch. 17, para. 7, with effect in relation to accounting periods of UK resident companies ending on or after 1 July 1999, the self-assessment appointed day by virtue of FA 1994, s. 199(2) and SI 1998/3173 (C. 78), subject to transitional provisions in FA 1998, Sch. 17, para. 37(2), (3), (4).

Section 752(3): the percentage of shares which a relevant interest represents

752B(1) For the purposes of section 752(3) above, where a person has a relevant interest in a controlled foreign company by virtue of indirectly holding issued ordinary shares of the company, the percentage of the issued ordinary shares of the company which the relevant interest represents is equal to–

$$P \times S$$

where–
P is the product of the appropriate fractions of that person and each of the share-linked companies through which he indirectly holds the shares in question, other than the lowest share-linked company; and
S is the percentage of issued ordinary shares of the controlled foreign company which is held directly by the lowest share-linked company.

752B(2) In subsection (1) above and this subsection–

"the appropriate fraction", in the case of a person who directly holds ordinary shares of a share-linked company, means that fraction of the issued ordinary shares of that company which his holding represents;

"the lowest share-linked company", in relation to a person who indirectly holds ordinary shares of a controlled foreign company, means the share-linked company which directly holds the shares in question;

"share-linked company" means a company which is share-linked to the controlled foreign company in question.

752B(3) Where a person has different indirect holdings of shares of the controlled foreign company (as in a case where different shares are held through different companies which are share-linked to the controlled foreign company) –
(a) subsection (1) above shall apply separately in relation to the different holdings with any necessary modifications; and
(b) for the purposes of section 752(3) above the percentage of the issued ordinary shares of the company which the relevant interest represents is the aggregate of the percentages resulting from those separate applications.

752B(4) Where, for the purposes of subsection (3) of section 752, the percentage of the issued ordinary shares of the controlled foreign company which a person directly or indirectly holds varies during the relevant accounting period, he shall be treated for the purposes of that subsection as holding throughout that period that percentage of the issued ordinary shares of the company which is equal to the sum of the relevant percentages for each holding period in the relevant accounting period.

752B(5) For the purposes of subsection (4) above–

"holding period", in the case of any person, means a part of the relevant accounting period during which the percentage of the issued ordinary shares of the controlled foreign company which the person holds (whether directly or indirectly) remains the same;

"the relevant percentage", in the case of a holding period, means the percentage equal to–

$$\frac{P \times H}{A}$$

where–
P is the percentage of the issued ordinary shares of the controlled foreign company which the person in question directly or indirectly holds in the holding period, as calculated in accordance with subsections (1) to (3) above so far as applicable;
H is the number of days in the holding period; and
A is the number of days in the relevant accounting period.

History – S. 752B inserted by FA 1998, s. 113 and Sch. 17, para. 7, with effect in relation to accounting periods of UK resident companies ending on or after 1 July 1999, the self-assessment appointed day by virtue of FA 1994, s. 199(2) and SI 1998/3173 (C. 78), subject to transitional provisions in FA 1998, Sch. 17, para. 37(2), (3), (4).

Interpretation of apportionment provisions

752C(1) In this section **"the relevant provisions"** means sections 752 to 752B and this section.
752C(2) For the purposes of the relevant provisions–
(a) a person has a direct interest in a company if (and only if) he has an interest in the company otherwise than by virtue of having an interest in another company;
(b) a person has an indirect interest in a company if (and only if) he has an interest in the company by virtue of having an interest in another company;
(c) a person indirectly holds shares of a controlled foreign company if (and only if) he directly holds ordinary shares of a company which is share-linked to the controlled foreign company.

752C(3) For the purposes of the relevant provisions, a company is "share-linked" to a controlled foreign company if it has an interest in the controlled foreign company only by virtue of directly holding ordinary shares–
(a) of the controlled foreign company, or
(b) of the controlled foreign company or of one or more companies which are share-linked to the controlled foreign company by virtue of paragraph (a) above, or
(c) of the controlled foreign company or of one or more companies which are share-linked to the controlled foreign company by virtue of paragraph (a) or (b) above

and so on.

752C(4) For the purposes of the relevant provisions, a company ("company A") has an intermediate interest in a controlled foreign company if (and only if)–
(a) it has a direct or indirect interest in the controlled foreign company; and
(b) one or more other persons have relevant interests in the controlled foreign company by virtue of having a direct or indirect interest in company A.

752C(5) Any interest or shares held by a nominee or bare trustee shall be treated for the purposes of the relevant provisions as held by the person or persons for whom the nominee or bare trustee holds the interest or shares.

752C(6) Where–
(a) an interest in a controlled foreign company is held in a fiduciary or representative capacity, and
(b) subsection (5) above does not apply, but
(c) there are one or more identifiable beneficiaries,
the interest shall be treated for the purposes of the relevant provisions as held by that beneficiary or, as the case may be, as apportioned on a just and reasonable basis among those beneficiaries.

752C(7) In the relevant provisions–

"bare trustee" means a person acting as trustee–
(a) for a person absolutely entitled as against the trustee; or
(b) for any person who would be so entitled but for being a minor or otherwise under a disability; or
(c) for two or more persons who are or would, but for all or any of them being a minor or otherwise under a disability, be jointly so entitled;

"ordinary shares", in the case of any company, means shares of a single class, however described, which is the only class of shares issued by the company;

"the relevant accounting period" means the accounting period mentioned in section 752(1);

"share" includes a reference to a fraction of a share.

History – S. 752C inserted by FA 1998, s. 113 and Sch. 17, para. 7, with effect in relation to accounting periods of UK resident companies ending on or after 1 July 1999, the self-assessment appointed day by virtue of FA 1994, s. 199(2) and SI 1998/3173 (C. 78), subject to transitional provisions in FA 1998, Sch. 17, para. 37(2), (3), (4).

Notices and Appeals

753 [Repealed by FA 1998, s. 113 and Sch. 17, para. 8; s. 165 and Sch. 27, Pt. III(27).]

History – S. 753 repealed by FA 1998, s. 113 and Sch. 17, para. 8; s. 165 and Sch. 27, Pt. III(27), with effect in relation to accounting periods of UK resident companies ending on or after 1 July 1999, the self-assessment appointed day by virtue of FA 1994, s. 199(2) and SI 1998/3173 (C. 78), subject to transitional provisions in FA 1998, Sch. 17, para. 37(2), (3), (4).

Assessment, recovery and postponement of tax

754(1) Subject to the following provisions of this section, the provisions of section 747(4)(a) relating to the charging of a sum as if it were an amount of corporation tax shall be taken as applying, subject to the provisions of the Taxes Acts, and to any necessary modifications, all enactments applying generally to corporation tax, including those relating to company tax returns, those relating to the assessing, collecting and receiving of corporation tax, those conferring or regulating a right of appeal and those concerning administration, penalties, interest on unpaid tax and priority of tax in cases of insolvency under the law of any part of the United Kingdom.

754(1A) Accordingly (but without prejudice to subsection (1) above) the Management Act shall have effect as if–
(a) any reference to corporation tax included a reference to a sum chargeable under section 747(4)(a) as if it were an amount of corporation tax; and
(b) any reference to profits of a company included a reference to an amount of chargeable profits of a controlled foreign company which falls to be apportioned to a company under section 747(3).

754(2) For the purposes of the Taxes Acts, any sum chargeable on a company under section 747(4)(a) is chargeable for the accounting period of the company in which ends that one of the controlled foreign company's accounting periods the chargeable profits of which give rise to that sum.

754(2A) Where–
(a) an apportionment under section 747(3) falls to be made as regards an accounting period of a controlled foreign company, and
(b) the apportionment falls to be made in accordance with section 752(4) on a just and reasonable basis, and
(c) a company tax return is made or amended using for the apportionment a particular basis adopted by the company making the return,
the Board may determine that another basis is to be used for the apportionment.

754(2B) [Omitted by SI 2009/2035, art. 2 and Schedule, para. 21.]

754(2C) [Omitted by SI 2009/2035, art. 2 and Schedule, para. 21.]

754(2D) Once the Board have determined under subsection (2A) above the basis to be used for the apportionment, matters shall proceed as if that were the only basis allowed by the Tax Acts.

754(2E) A determination under subsection (2A) above may be questioned on an appeal against an amendment, made under paragraph 30 or 34 of Schedule 18 to the Finance Act 1998, of the company's company tax return, but only on the ground that the basis of apportionment determined by the Board is not just and reasonable.

754(3) Subsection (3B) shall apply where any appeal–
(a) under paragraph 34(3) of Schedule 18 to the Finance Act 1998 against an amendment of a company tax return, or
(b) under paragraph 48 of that Schedule against a discovery assessment or discovery determination under paragraph 41 of that Schedule (including an assessment by virtue of paragraph 52 of that Schedule),
involves any question concerning the application of this Chapter in relation to any particular person, and the question is one whose resolution is likely to affect the liability of more than one person under this Chapter in respect of the controlled foreign company concerned.

754(3A) [Omitted by SI 2009/56, art. 3(1) and Sch. 1, para. 155(3).]

754(3B) Where this subsection applies–
(a) each of the persons whose liability under this Chapter in respect of the controlled foreign company concerned is likely to be affected by the resolution of the question shall be entitled to be a party to any proceedings;
(b) the tribunal shall determine that question separately from any other questions in those proceedings; and
(c) the tribunal's determination on that question shall have effect as if made in an appeal to which each of those persons was a party.

754(4) [Repealed by FA 1998, s. 113 and Sch. 17, para. 9(7).]

754(5) Schedule 26 shall have effect with respect to the reliefs which may be claimed by a company resident in the United Kingdom which has a liability for tax in respect of an amount of chargeable profits; and no reliefs other than those provided for by that Schedule shall be allowed against any such liability.

754(6) In any case where–
(a) the whole or any part of the tax chargeable on a company (**"the chargeable company"**) by virtue of section 747(4)(a) is not paid before the date on which it is due and payable in accordance with this Act or, as the case may be, the Management Act; and
(b) the Board serve a notice of liability to tax under this subsection on another company (**"the responsible company"**) which is resident in the United Kingdom and holds or has held (whether directly or indirectly) the whole or any part of the same interest in the controlled foreign company as is or was held by the chargeable company,
the whole or, as the case may be, the corresponding part of the tax chargeable on the chargeable company or, as the case may be, so much of it as remains unpaid shall be payable by the responsible company upon service of the notice.

754(7) Where a notice of liability is served under subsection (6) above–

(a) the whole, or (as the case may be) the corresponding part, of any interest due on the tax chargeable on the chargeable company and not paid; and

(b) any interest accruing due on that tax after the date of service (so far as referable to tax payable by the responsible company by virtue of the notice),

shall be payable by the responsible company.

754(8) In any case where–

(a) a notice of liability is served on the responsible company under subsection (6) above, and

(b) the relevant tax and any interest payable by the responsible company under subsection (7) above is not paid by that company before the expiry of the period of three months beginning on the date of service of the notice,

that tax and interest may, without prejudice to the right of recovery from the responsible company, be recovered from the chargeable company.

754(9) In this section **"the Taxes Acts"** has the same meaning as in the Management Act.

History – In s. 754(1), words "the charging" substituted for "assessment and recovery", and words "those relating to company tax returns" inserted, by FA 1998, s. 113 and Sch. 17, para. 9(2), with effect in relation to accounting periods of UK resident companies ending on or after 1 July 1999, the self-assessment appointed day by virtue of FA 1994, s. 199(2) and SI 1998/3173 (C. 78), subject to transitional provisions in FA 1998, Sch. 17, para. 37(2), (3), (4).

S. 754(1A) inserted by FA 1998, s. 113 and Sch. 17, para. 9(3), with effect in relation to accounting periods of UK resident companies ending on or after 1 July 1999, the self-assessment appointed day (see note above), subject to transitional provisions in FA 1998, Sch. 17, para. 37(2), (3), (4).

S. 754(2) substituted, and s. 754(2A), (2B), (2C), (2D), (2E) inserted by FA 1998, s. 113 and Sch. 17, para. 9(4) and (5), with effect in relation to accounting periods of UK resident companies ending on or after 1 July 1999, the self-assessment appointed day (see note above), subject to transitional provisions in FA 1998, Sch. 17, para. 37(2), (3), (4).

S. 754(2B) and (2C) omitted by SI 2009/2035, art. 2 and Schedule, para. 21, with effect from 13 August 2009.

In s. 754(2E), "34" substituted for "34(2)" by FA 2008, s. 119(12)(b), with effect from 1 April 2010 (SI 2009/405).

In s. 754(3), the words "Subsection (3B) shall apply where" substituted for "Where" by SI 2009/56, art. 3(1) and Sch. 1, para. 155(2)(a), operative from 1 April 2009, subject to transitional and saving provisions in SI 2009/56, Sch. 3.

In s. 754(3), the words "and the question is one whose resolution is likely to affect the liability of more than one person under this Chapter in respect of the controlled foreign company concerned" substituted for "that appeal shall be to the Special Commissioners" by SI 2009/56, art. 3(1) and Sch. 1, para. 155(2)(b), operative from 1 April 2009,subject to transitional and saving provisions in SI 2009/56, Sch. 3.

S. 754(3A) omitted by SI 2009/56, art. 3(1) and Sch. 1, para. 155(3), operative from 1 April 2009, subject to transitional and saving provisions in SI 2009/56, Sch. 3.

S. 754(3) substituted, and s. 754(3A), (3B) inserted by FA 1998, s. 113 and Sch. 17, para. 9(6), with effect in relation to accounting periods of UK resident companies ending on or after 1 July 1999, the self-assessment appointed day (see note above), subject to transitional provisions in FA 1998, Sch. 17, para. 37(2), (3), (4).

In s. 754(3B)(a), the words "to be a party to any proceedings" substituted for "to appear and be heard by the Special Commissioners, or to make representations to them in writing" by SI 2009/56, art. 3(1) and Sch. 1, para. 155(4)(a), operative from 1 April 2009, subject to transitional and saving provisions in SI 2009/56, Sch. 3.

In s. 754(3B)(b), the words "tribunal" substituted for "Special Commissioners" by SI 2009/56, art. 3(1) and Sch. 1, para. 155(4)(b), operative from 1 April 2009, subject to transitional and saving provisions in SI 2009/56, Sch. 3.

In s. 754(3B)(c), the words "the tribunal's" substituted for "their" by SI 2009/56, art. 3(1) and Sch. 1, para. 155(4)(c), operative from 1 April 2009, subject to transitional and saving provisions in SI 2009/56, Sch. 3.

S. 754(4) repealed by FA 1998, s. 113 and Sch. 17, para. 9(7), with effect in relation to accounting periods of UK resident companies ending on or after 1 July 1999, the self-assessment appointed day (see note above), subject to transitional provisions in FA 1998, Sch. 17, para. 37(2), (3), (4).

In s. 754(6):

- "chargeable" substituted for references to "assessed" or "assessable";
- in para. (a), "747(4)(a)". substituted for "752(6)";
- in para. (b), words "the whole or any part of" inserted; and
- words "the whole or, as the case may be, the corresponding part of" inserted.

Above changes made by FA 1998, s. 113 and Sch. 17, para. 9(8), with effect in relation to accounting periods of UK resident companies ending on or after 1 July 1999, the self-assessment appointed day (see note above), subject to transitional provisions in FA 1998, Sch. 17, para. 37(2), (3), (4).

In s. 754(7):

- in para. (a), words "the whole or, as the case may be, the corresponding part of" inserted, and "chargeable" substituted for references to "assessed" or "assessable";
- in para. (b), words "(so far as referable to tax payable by the responsible company by virtue of the notice)" inserted.

Above changes made by FA 1998, s. 113 and Sch. 17, para. 9(9), with effect in relation to accounting periods of UK resident companies ending on or after 1 July 1999, the self-assessment appointed day (see note above), subject to transitional provisions in FA 1998, Sch. 17, para. 37(2), (3), (4).

In s. 754(8), "chargeable" substituted for "assessable" by FA 1998, s. 113 and Sch. 17, para. 9(10), with effect in relation to accounting periods of UK resident companies ending on or after 1 July 1999, the self-assessment appointed day (see note above), subject to transitional provisions in FA 1998, Sch. 17, para. 37(2), (3), (4).

Derivations – FA 1984, s. 89(1)–(4), (7)–(11) (as originally enacted).

Returns where it is not established whether acceptable distribution policy applies

754A [Omitted by FA 2009, s. 36 and Sch. 16, para. 2(2).]

History – S. 754A omitted by FA 2009, s. 36 and Sch. 16, para. 2(2), with effect in relation to accounting periods of controlled foreign companies beginning on or after 1 July 2009, subject to rules for accounting periods straddling 1 July 2009 in FA 2009, Sch. 16, para. 7 and transitional provisions in FA 2009, Sch. 16, para. 8.

Former s. 754A inserted by FA 1998, s. 113 and Sch. 17, para. 10, with effect in relation to accounting periods of UK resident companies ending on or after 1 July 1999, the self-assessment appointed day by virtue of FA 1994, s. 199(2) and SI 1998/3173 (C. 78), subject to transitional provisions in FA 1998, Sch. 17, para. 37(2), (3), (4).

Determinations requiring the sanction of the Board

754B(1) This section has effect where a determination requiring the Board's sanction is made for any of the following purposes, that is to say–

(a) the giving of a closure notice; or

(b) the making of a discovery assessment.

754B(2) If the closure notice or, as the case may be, notice of the discovery assessment is given to any person without–
(a) the determination, so far as it is taken into account in the closure notice or the discovery assessment, having been approved by the Board, or
(b) notification of the Board's approval having been served on that person at or before the time of the giving of the notice,
the closure notice or, as the case may be, the discovery assessment shall be deemed to have been given or made (and in the case of an assessment notified) in the terms (if any) in which it would have been given or made had that determination not been taken into account.
754B(3) A notification under subsection (2)(b) above–
(a) must be in writing;
(b) must state that the Board have given their approval on the basis that–
(i) an amount of chargeable profits, and
(ii) an amount of creditable tax (which may be nil),
for the accounting period of the controlled foreign company in question fall to be apportioned under section 747(3) to the person in question;
(c) must state the amounts mentioned in sub-paragraphs (i) and (ii) of paragraph (b) above; and
(d) subject to paragraphs (a) to (c) above, may be in such form as the Board may determine.
754B(4) For the purposes of this section, the Board's approval of a determination requiring their sanction–
(a) must be given specifically in relation to the case in question and must apply to the amount determined; but
(b) subject to that, may be given by the Board (either before or after the making of the determination) in any such form or manner as they may determine.
754B(5) In this section references to a determination requiring the Board's sanction are references (subject to subsection (6) below) to any determination of the amount of chargeable profits or creditable tax for an accounting period of a controlled foreign company which falls to be apportioned to a particular person under section 747(3).
754B(6) For the purposes of this section, a determination shall be taken, in relation to a closure notice or a discovery assessment, not to be a determination requiring the Board's sanction if–
(a) an agreement about the relevant amounts has been made between an officer of the Board and the person in whose case it is made;
(b) that agreement is in force at the time of the giving of the closure notice or, as the case may be, notice of the assessment; and
(c) the matters to which the agreement relates include the amount determined.
754B(7) In paragraph (a) of subsection (6) above, **"the relevant amounts"** means
(a) the amount of chargeable profits, and
(b) the amount of creditable tax (which may be nil),
for the accounting period of the controlled foreign company in question which fall to be apportioned under section 747(3) to the person mentioned in that paragraph.
754B(8) For the purposes of subsection (6) above an agreement made between an officer of the Board and any person ("the taxpayer") in relation to any matter shall be taken to be in force at any time if, and only if–
(a) the agreement is one which has been made or confirmed in writing;
(b) that time is after the end of the period of thirty days beginning–
(i) in the case of an agreement made in writing, with the day of the making of the agreement, and
(ii) in any other case, with the day of the agreement's confirmation in writing; and
(c) the taxpayer has not, before the end of that period of thirty days, served a notice on an officer of the Board stating that he is repudiating or resiling from the agreement.
754B(9) The references in subsection (8) above to the confirmation in writing of an agreement are references to the service on the taxpayer by an officer of the Board of a notice–
(a) stating that the agreement has been made; and
(b) setting out the terms of the agreement.
754B(10) The matters that may be questioned on so much of any appeal by virtue of any provision of the Management Act or Schedule 18 to the Finance Act 1998 (company tax returns, assessments and related matters) as relates to a determination the making of which has been approved by the Board for the purposes of this section shall not include the Board's approval, except to the extent that the grounds for questioning the approval are the same as the grounds for questioning the determination itself.
754B(11) In this section–

"closure notice" means a notice under paragraph 32 of Schedule 18 to the Finance Act 1998 (completion of enquiry and statement of conclusions);

"discovery assessment" means a discovery assessment or discovery determination under paragraph 41 of that Schedule (including an assessment by virtue of paragraph 52 of that Schedule).

History – S. 754B inserted by FA 1998, s. 113 and Sch. 17, para. 9(11), with effect in relation to accounting periods of UK resident companies ending on or after 1 July 1999, the self-assessment appointed day by virtue of FA 1994, s. 199(2) and SI 1998/3173 (C. 78), subject to transitional provisions in FA 1998, Sch. 17, para. 37(2), (3), (4).

Cross references – SI 1999/1408, reg. 5: modifications of s. 755B in any case where a non-resident company–
(a) carries on general insurance business, and
(b) draws up accounts relating to that business using a method falling within s. 755B(2).

Information relating to controlled foreign companies

755 [Repealed by FA 1998, s. 113 and Sch. 17, para. 12; s. 165 and Sch. 27, Pt. III(27).]

History – S. 755 repealed by FA 1998, s. 113 and Sch. 17, para. 12; s. 165 and Sch. 27, Pt. III(27), with effect in relation to accounting periods of UK resident companies ending on or after 1 July 1999, the self-assessment appointed day by virtue of FA 1994, s. 199(2) and SI 1998/3173 (C. 78,) subject to transitional provisions in FA 1998, Sch. 17, para. 37(2), (3), (4).

Treatment of chargeable profits and creditable tax apportioned to company carrying on life assurance business

755A(1) This section applies in any case where–
(a) an amount ("the apportioned profit") of a controlled foreign company's chargeable profits for an accounting period falls to be apportioned under section 747(3) to a company resident in the United Kingdom ("the UK company");
(b) the UK company carries on life assurance business in that one of its accounting periods ("the relevant accounting period") in which ends the accounting period of the controlled foreign company; and
(c) the property or rights which represent the UK company's relevant interest in the controlled foreign company constitute to any extent assets of the UK company's long-term insurance fund.
755A(2) subsections (3) and (4) below apply if, in the case of the relevant accounting period, the UK company is charged to tax under the I minus E basis in respect of life assurance business.
755A(3) Where this subsection applies, the "appropriate rate" for the purposes of section 747(4)(a) and paragraph 1 of Schedule 26 in relation to the policy holders' part of any BLAGAB apportioned profit shall be–
(a) if a single rate of tax under section 88(1) of the Finance Act 1989 (lower corporation tax rate on certain insurance company profits) is applicable in relation to the relevant accounting period, that rate; or

(b) if more than one such rate of tax is applicable in relation to the relevant accounting period, the average of those rates over the whole of that period.

755A(4) Where this subsection applies, the "appropriate rate" for the purposes of section 747(4)(a) and paragraph 1 of Schedule 26 shall be nil in relation to so much of the apportioned profit as is referable to gross roll-up business carried on by the UK company.

755A(4A) In any case where–

(a) paragraph 4 of Schedule 26 to this Act applies to a dividend received by the UK company, and

(b) but for this subsection, subsection (5) of section 97 of TIOPA 2010 would apply to that dividend,

the amount of credit for foreign tax in respect of that dividend shall be treated, for the purposes of that section, as wholly attributable to basic life assurance and general annuity business.

755A(5) If, in the case of the relevant accounting period, the UK company is charged to tax under section 35 of CTA 2009 (charge on trade profits) in respect of its profits from life assurance business, the "appropriate rate" for the purposes of–

(a) section 747(4)(a), and

(b) paragraph 1 of Schedule 26,

shall be nil in relation to so much of the apportioned profit as is referable to the UK company's relevant interest so far as represented by assets of its long-term insurance fund.

755A(6) If, in the case of the relevant accounting period,–

(a) the UK company is charged to tax under the I minus E basis in respect of life assurance business,

(b) any creditable tax of the controlled foreign company falls to be apportioned to the UK company, and

(c) the apportioned profit is to any extent referable to gross roll-up business,

so much of the creditable tax so apportioned as is attributable to the apportioned profit so far as so referable shall be left out of account for the purposes of this Chapter, other than section 747(3) and this section, and shall be treated as extinguished.

755A(7) If, in the case of the relevant accounting period,–

(a) the UK company is charged to tax under section 35 of CTA 2009 in respect of its profits from life assurance business, and

(b) any creditable tax of the controlled foreign company falls to be apportioned to the UK company,

so much of the creditable tax so apportioned as is attributable to so much of the apportioned profit as is referable to the UK company's relevant interest so far as represented by assets of the UK company's long-term insurance fund shall be left out of account for the purposes of this Chapter, other than section 747(3) and this section, and shall be treated as extinguished.

755A(8) Any set off under paragraph 1 or 2 of Schedule 26 against the UK company's liability to tax under section 747(4)(a) in respect of the apportioned profit shall be made against only so much of that liability as is attributable to the eligible part of the apportioned profit.

755A(9) [Omitted by SI 2006/3270, reg. 8(c).]

755A(10) For the purposes of this section, the "eligible part" of the apportioned profit is any BLAGAB apportioned profit, other than the policy holders' part.

755A(11) For the purposes of this section the policy holders' part of any BLAGAB apportioned profit is–

(a) where subsection (11A) below applies, the whole of that profit, and

(b) in any other case, the relevant fraction (within the meaning of subsection (11B) below) of that profit.

755A(11A) This subsection applies if–

(a) the UK company's life assurance business is mutual business,

(b) the policy holders' share of the UK company's relevant profits for the relevant accounting period is equal to all those profits, or

(c) the policy holders' share of the UK company's relevant profits for the relevant accounting period is more than its BLAGAB profits for that period.

755A(11B) The relevant fraction for the purposes of subsection (11)(b) above is the fraction arrived at by dividing–

(a) the policy holders' share of the UK company's relevant profits for the relevant accounting period, by

(b) the UK company's BLAGAB profits for that period.

755A(11BA) But where the BLAGAB profits for the relevant accounting period are nil, the relevant fraction–

(a) if there are section 35 profits of the accounting period in respect of its life assurance business, is nil, and

(b) otherwise, is such fraction as is just and reasonable;

and for this purpose there are section 35 profits if there are profits computed in accordance with the life assurance trade profits provisions after making adjustments in respect of losses in accordance with section 85A(4) of the Finance Act 1989.

755A(11C) In subsections (11A) and (11B) above–

(a) references to the policy holders' share of the UK company's share of the relevant profits are to be construed in accordance with sections 88(3) and 89 of the Finance Act 1989,

(b) [omitted by FA 2008, s. 43 and Sch. 17, para. 18(2).]

755A(12) In this section–

"BLAGAB apportioned profit" means so much of the apportioned profit as is referable to basic life assurance and general annuity business carried on by the UK company;

755A(13) For the purposes of this section, the part of the apportioned profit which is referable to–

(a) basic life assurance and general annuity business, or

(ba) gross roll-up business,

carried on by the UK company is the part which would have been so referable under section 432A had the apportioned profit been a dividend paid to the UK company at the end of the accounting period mentioned in subsection (1)(a) above in respect of the property or rights which represent the UK company's relevant interest in the controlled foreign company.

755A(14) For the purposes of this section, any attribution of creditable tax to a particular part of the apportioned profit shall be made in the proportion which that part of the apportioned profit bears to the whole of the apportioned profit.

History – In s. 755A(1)(c), (5), (7) and (12) (in the definition of "long-term insurance fund"), words "long-term insurance fund" substituted for "long term business fund" by SI 2001/3629, art. 52(1)(j), with effect from 1 December 2001.

In s. 755A(2), the words "charged to tax under the I minus E basis in respect of" substituted for the words "not charged to tax under Case I of Schedule D in respect of its profits from" by FA 2007, s. 39 and Sch. 8, para. 10, with effect for periods of account of insurance companies beginning on or after 1 January 2007.

In s. 755A(3) "88(1)" substituted for "88A(1)" by FA 2003, s. 170 and Sch. 33, para. 13(8), with effect for the financial year 2003 and subsequent financial years.

In s. 755A(4), the words "gross roll-up business carried on by the UK company" substituted for the words reproduced below by FA 2007, s. 38 and Sch. 7, para. 47(2), with effect for the purposes of corporation tax, for periods of account of insurance companies beginning on or after 1 January 2007, and for the purposes of income tax, for the tax year 2007-08 and subsequent tax years (but see transitional provisions at FA 2007, Sch. 7, para. 80–84).

In s. 755A(4A)(b), the words "subsection (5) of section 97 of TIOPA 2010" substituted for the words "subsection (4) of section 804B of this Act" by TIOPA 2010, s. 374 and Sch. 8, para. 12 with effect for corporation tax purposes for accounting periods ending on or after 1 April 2010, for income tax and capital gains tax purposes for the tax year 2010–11 and subsequent tax years, and for petroleum revenue tax purposes for chargeable periods beginning on or after 1 July 2010.

S. 755A(4A) inserted by SI 2006/3270, reg. 8(a) with effect from 31 December 2006 in relation to accounting periods ending on or after that date.

In s. 755A(5), the words "section 35 of CTA 2009 (charge on trade profits)" substituted for "Case I of Schedule D" by CTA 2009, s. 1322 and Sch. 1, para. 219(2), with effect for corporation tax purposes for accounting periods ending on or after 1 April 2009, and for income tax and capital gains tax purposes for the tax year 2009–10 and subsequent tax years.

In s. 755A(6)(a), the words "charged to tax under the I minus E basis in respect of" substituted for the words "not charged to tax under Case I of Schedule D in respect of its profits from" by FA 2007, s. 39 and Sch. 8, para. 10, with effect for periods of account of insurance companies beginning on or after 1 January 2007.
In s. 755A(6)(c), the words "gross roll-up business" substituted for the words "a category of business specified in paragraphs (a) to (c) of subsection (4) above" by FA 2007, s. 38 and Sch. 7, para. 47(3),with effect for the purposes of corporation tax, for periods of account of insurance companies beginning on or after 1 January 2007, and for the purposes of income tax, for the tax year 2007-08 and subsequent tax years (but see transitional provisions at FA 2007, Sch. 7, para. 80–84). The former words read as follows:
In s. 755A(7), the words "section 35 of CTA 2009 (charge on trade profits)" substituted for "Case I of Schedule D" by CTA 2009, s. 1322 and Sch. 1, para. 219(3), with effect for corporation tax purposes for accounting periods ending on or after 1 April 2009, and for income tax and capital gains tax purposes for the tax year 2009–10 and subsequent tax years.
In s. 755A(8) words "or 2" omitted by SI 2006/3270, reg. 8(b) with effect from 31 December 2006 in relation to accounting periods ending on or after that date.
S. 755A(9) omitted by SI 2006/3270, reg. 8(c) with effect from 31 December 2006 in relation to accounting periods ending on or after that date.
S. 755A(11A) substituted (with s. 755A(11B) and (11C)) for former s. 755A(11) by FA 2003, s. 170 and Sch. 33, para. 13(9), with effect for the financial year 2003 and subsequent financial years.
S. 755A(11B) substituted (with s. 755A(11A) and (11C)) for former s. 755A(11) by FA 2003, s. 170 and Sch. 33, para. 13(9), with effect for the financial year 2003 and subsequent financial years.
In s. 755A(11BA), the words "section 35 profits" substituted for "Case I profits" in both places by CTA 2009, s. 1322 and Sch. 1, para. 219(4)(a), with effect for corporation tax purposes for accounting periods ending on or after 1 April 2009, and for income tax and capital gains tax purposes for the tax year 2009–10 and subsequent tax years.
In s. 755A(11BA), the words "life assurance trade profits provisions" substituted for "provisions applicable to Case I of Schedule D" by CTA 2009, s. 1322 and Sch. 1, para. 219(4)(b), with effect for corporation tax purposes for accounting periods ending on or after 1 April 2009, and for income tax and capital gains tax purposes for the tax year 2009–10 and subsequent tax years.
S. 755A(11BA) inserted by FA 2008, s. 43 and Sch. 17, para. 14, with effect in relation to accounting periods beginning on or after 1 January 2008 and ending on or after 12 March 2008.
S. 755A(11C)(b) and the word "and" before it omitted by FA 2008, s. 43 and Sch. 17, para. 18(2), with effect in relation to accounting periods beginning on or after 1 January 2008.
S. 755A(11C) substituted (with s. 755A(11A) and (11B)) for former s. 755A(11) by FA 2003, s. 170 and Sch. 33, para. 13(9), with effect for the financial year 2003 and subsequent financial years.
In s. 755A(12), definition of "long-term insurance fund" omitted by FA 2007, s. 41 and Sch. 10, para. 14(2)(d) and repealedby s. 114 and Sch. 27, Pt. 2(10), with effect in relation to periods of account beginning on or after 1 January 2007.
S. 755A(13)(a) and (ba) substituted for s. 755A(13)(a)–(d) by FA 2007, s. 38 and Sch. 7, para. 47(4), with effect for the purposes of corporation tax, for periods of account of insurance companies beginning on or after 1 January 2007, and for the purposes of income tax, for the tax year 2007-08 and subsequent tax years (but see transitional provisions at FA 2007, Sch. 7, para. 80–84).
S. 755A inserted by FA 1998, s. 113 and Sch. 17, para. 13, with effect in relation to accounting periods of UK resident companies ending on or after 1 July 1999, the self-assessment appointed day by virtue of FA 1994, s. 199(2) and SI 1998/3173 (C. 78), subject to transitional provisions in FA 1998, Sch. 17, para. 37(2), (3), (4).

Cross references – SI 2005/2014, reg. 22: modification of s. 755A to make it applicable to friendly societies carrying on life assurance business (which is not entirely exempt).
SI 2007/2145, reg. 12 modification of s. 755A for business which is exempt from corporation tax by virtue of ICTA 1988, s. 460(11) or (12), s. 461(4) or (4A) or s. 461B(5) or (6A).

Amendment of return where general insurance business of foreign company accounted for on non-annual basis

755B(1) This section applies where–
(a) a controlled foreign company carries on general insurance business in an accounting period;
(b) an amount of the company's chargeable profits, and an amount of its creditable tax (if any), for that accounting period falls to be apportioned under section 747(3) to a company resident in the United Kingdom ("the UK company");
(c) the UK company delivers a company tax return for that one of its accounting periods in which the controlled foreign company's accounting period ends; and
(d) in making or amending the return, the UK company has regard to accounts of the controlled foreign company drawn up using a method falling within subsection (2) below.

755B(2) The methods which fall within this subsection are–
(a) the method described in paragraph 58 in Section E of Part 2 of Schedule 3 to the Large and Medium-sized Companies and Groups (Accounts and Reports) Regulations 2008 (which provides for a technical provision to be made in the accounts which is later replaced by a provision for estimated claims outstanding); and
(b) any method which would have fallen within paragraph (a) above, had final replacement of the technical provision, as described in sub-paragraph (4) of paragraph 58 of that Schedule, taken place, and been required to take place, no later than the end of the year referred to in that sub-paragraph as the third year following the underwriting year.

755B(3) Where this section applies–
(a) the UK company may make any amendments of its company tax return arising from the replacement of the technical provision in the controlled foreign company's accounts at any time within twelve months from the date on which the provision was replaced; and
(b) notice of intention to enquire into the return under paragraph 24 of Schedule 18 to the Finance Act 1998 may be given at any time up to two years from that date (or at any later time in accordance with the general rule in sub-paragraph (3) of that paragraph).

755B(4) If, in a case where this section applies, the accounts of the controlled foreign company are drawn up using a method falling within paragraph (b) of subsection (2) above–
(a) the controlled foreign company, and
(b) any person with an interest in the controlled foreign company,

shall be treated for the purposes of this section as if final replacement of the technical provision, as described in sub-paragraph (4) of paragraph 58 of Schedule 3 to those Regulations, had taken place at, and been required to take place no later than, the end of the year referred to in that sub-paragraph as the third year following the underwriting year.

755B(5) Regulations under section 755C may make provision with respect to the determination of the amount of the provision by which the technical provision is to be treated as replaced in cases falling within subsection (4) above.

755B(6) In this section **"general insurance business"** means business which consists of the effecting or carrying out of contracts which fall within Part I of *Schedule 1 to the Financial* Services and Markets Act 2000 (Regulated Activities) Order 2001.

History – In s. 755B(2)(a), the words "paragraph 58 in Section E of Part 2 of Schedule 3 to the Large and Medium-sized Companies and Groups (Accounts and Reports) Regulations 2008" substituted for the words "paragraph 52 of Schedule 9A to the Companies Act 1985" by SI 2009/1890, art. 5(2)(a), with effect from 1 October 2009.
In s. 755B(2)(b), "58" substituted for "52" by SI 2009/1890, art. 5(3), with effect from 1 October 2009.
In s. 755B(4), the words "58 of Schedule 3 to those Regulations" substituted for the words "52 of Schedule 9A to the Companies Act 1985" by SI 2009/1890, art. 5(4), with effect from 1 October 2009.

S. 755B(6) substituted, by SI 2001/3629, reg. 13 and 44 which came into force on 1 December 2001.
S. 755B inserted by FA 1998, s. 113 and Sch. 17, para. 14, with effect in relation to accounting periods of UK resident companies ending on or after 1 July 1999, the self-assessment appointed day by virtue of FA 1994, s. 199(2) and SI 1998/3173 (C. 78), subject to transitional provisions in FA 1998, Sch. 17, para. 37(2), (3), (4).

Cross references – SI 2008/410: Large and Medium-sized Companies and Groups (Accounts and Reports) Regulations 2008.

Statutory instruments – SI 1999/1408: Non-resident Companies (General Insurance Business) Regulations 1999: made partly under s. 755B(5).

Application of Chapter where general insurance business of foreign company accounted for on non-annual basis

755C(1) The Treasury may by regulations provide for the provisions of this Chapter to have effect with prescribed modifications in any case where a non-resident company–
(a) carries on general insurance business; and
(b) draws up accounts relating to that business using a method falling within subsection (2) of section 755B.

755C(2) Regulations under subsection (1) above may–
(a) make different provision for different cases;
(b) make provision having effect in relation to accounting periods of non-resident companies ending not more than one year before the date on which the regulations are made; and
(c) contain such supplementary, incidental, consequential and transitional provision as the Treasury may think fit.

755C(3) In this section–

"general insurance business" has the same meaning as in section 755B;

"non-resident company" means a company resident outside the United Kingdom;

"prescribed" means prescribed in regulations under this section.

History – S. 755C inserted by FA 1998, s. 113 and Sch. 17, para. 15, with effect in relation to accounting periods of UK resident companies ending on or after 1 July 1999, the self-assessment appointed day by virtue of FA 1994, s. 199(2) and SI 1998/3173 (C. 78), subject to transitional provisions in FA 1998, Sch. 17, para. 37(2), (3), (4).

Statutory instruments – SI 1999/1408 Non-resident Companies (General Insurance Business) Regulations 1999: made partly under s. 755C.
SI 2008/2643, made under s. 755C: amends SI 1999/1408.

'Control' and the two '40 per cent tests'

755D(1) For the purposes of this Chapter **"control"**, in relation to a company, means the power of a person to secure–
(a) by means of the holding of shares or the possession of voting power in or in relation to the company or any other company, or
(b) by virtue of any powers conferred by the articles of association or other document regulating the company or any other company,

that the affairs of the company are conducted in accordance with his wishes.

755D(1A) For the purposes of this Chapter a person also controls a company if the person possesses, or is entitled to acquire, such rights as would–
(a) if the whole of the income of the company were distributed, entitle the person to receive the greater part of the amount so distributed,
(b) if the whole of the company's share capital were disposed of, entitle the person to receive the greater part of the proceeds of the disposal, or
(c) in the event of the winding-up of the company or in any other circumstances, entitle the person to receive the greater part of the assets of the company which would then be available for distribution.

755D(2) Where two or more persons, taken together, have the power mentioned in subsection (1) above or satisfy subsection (1A) above, they shall be taken for the purposes of this Chapter to control the company.

755D(3) The 40 per cent test in this subsection is satisfied in the case of one of two persons who, taken together, control a company if that one of them has interests, rights and powers representing at least 40 per cent of the holdings, rights and powers in respect of which the pair of them fall to be taken as controlling the company.

755D(4) The 40 per cent test in this subsection is satisfied in the case of one of two persons who, taken together, control a company if that one of them has interests, rights and powers representing–
(a) at least 40 per cent, but
(b) not more than 55 per cent,

of the holdings, rights and powers in respect of which the pair of them fall to be taken as controlling the company.

755D(5) For the purposes of this Chapter any question–
(a) whether a company is controlled by a person, or by two or more persons taken together, or
(b) whether, in the case of any company, the applicable 40 per cent test is satisfied in the case of each of two persons who, taken together, control the company,

shall be determined after attributing to each of the persons all the rights and powers mentioned in subsection (6) below that are not already attributed to that person for the purposes of subsections (1) to (4) above.

755D(6) The rights and powers referred to in subsection (5) above are–
(a) rights and powers which the person is entitled to acquire at a future date or which he will, at a future date, become entitled to acquire;
(b) rights and powers of other persons, to the extent that they are rights or powers falling within subsection (7) below;
(c) if the person is resident in the United Kingdom, rights and powers of any person who is resident in the United Kingdom and connected with the person; and
(d) if the person is resident in the United Kingdom, rights and powers which for the purposes of subsection (5) above would be attributed to a person who is resident in the United Kingdom and connected with the person (a "UK connected person") if the UK connected person were himself the person.

755D(7) Rights and powers fall within this subsection to the extent that they–
(a) are required, or may be required, to be exercised in any one or more of the following ways, that is to say–
  (i) on behalf of the person;
  (ii) under the direction of the person; or
  (iii) for the benefit of the person; and
(b) are not confined, in a case where a loan has been made by one person to another, to rights and powers conferred in relation to property of the borrower by the terms of any security relating to the loan.

755D(8) In subsections (6)(b) to (d) and (7) above, the references to a person's rights and powers include references to any rights or powers which he either–
(a) is entitled to acquire at a future date, or
(b) will, at a future date, become entitled to acquire.

755D(9) In paragraph (d) of subsection (6) above, the reference to rights and powers which would be attributed to a UK connected person if he were the person includes a reference to rights and powers which, by applying that paragraph wherever one person resident in the United Kingdom is connected with another person, would be so attributed to him through a number of persons each of whom is resident in the United Kingdom and connected with at least one of the others.

755D(10) In determining for the purposes of this section whether one person is connected with another in relation to a company, section 1122(4) of CTA 2010 shall be disregarded.

755D(11) References in this section–

(a) to rights and powers of a person, or

(b) to rights and powers which a person is or will become entitled to acquire,

include references to rights or powers which are exercisable by that person, or (when acquired by that person) will be exercisable, only jointly with one or more other persons.

History – S. 755D(1A) inserted by FA 2008, s. 64(3)(a), with effect for determining whether, at any time on or after 12 March 2008, a company is controlled by persons resident in the United Kingdom for the purposes of ICTA 1988, Pt. 17, Ch. 4.

In s. 755D(2), the words "or satisfy subsection (1A) above" inserted by FA 2008, s. 64(3)(b), with effect for determining whether, at any time on or after 12 March 2008, a company is controlled by persons resident in the United Kingdom for the purposes of ICTA 1988, Pt. 17, Ch. 4.

In s. 755D(10), the words "section 1122(4) of CTA 2010" substituted for the words "subsection (7) of section 839" by CTA 2010, s. 1177 and Sch. 1, para. 100, with effect for corporation tax purposes for accounting periods ending on or after 1 April 2010, and for income and capital gains tax purposes for the tax year 2010–11 and subsequent tax years.

S. 755D inserted by FA 2000, s. 104 and Sch. 31, para. 4(1), with effect–

(a) for the purposes of determining whether at any time on or after 21 March 2000 a company resident outside the UK is to be regarded for the purposes of Pt. XVII, Ch. IV as controlled by persons resident in the UK; and

(b) for any accounting period of a company resident outside the UK which begins on or after 21 March 2000.

Interpretation and construction of Chapter IV

756(1) In this Chapter **"company tax return"** means a return required to be made under Schedule 18 to the Finance Act 1998; **"trading company"** means a company whose business consists wholly or mainly of the carrying on of a trade or trades.

756(1A) In this Chapter **"EEA territory"**, in relation to any time, means a territory which is an EEA state at that time other than the United Kingdom.

756(1B) But a territory is not to be regarded for the purposes of subsection (1A) above as an EEA state at any time if–

(a) it is not a member State at that time, and

(b) there are no arrangements made in relation to the territory having effect by virtue of section 173 of the Finance Act 2006 (international tax enforcement arrangements) at that time.

756(2) For the purposes of this Chapter–

(a) section 1122 of CTA 2010 applies; and

(b) subsections (2) to (7) of section 882 of CTA 2010 (meaning of associates) apply.

756(3) In this Chapter **"loan creditor"** has the meaning given by section 453 of CTA 2010.

History – In s. 756(1), definition of "company tax return" inserted by FA 1998, s. 113 and Sch. 17, para. 16, with effect in relation to accounting periods of UK resident companies ending on or after 1 July 1999, the self-assessment appointed day by virtue of FA 1994, s. 199(2) and (SI 1998/3173 (C. 78), subject to transitional provisions in FA 1998, Sch. 17, para. 37(2), (3), (4).

S. 756(1A) inserted by FA 2007, s. 48 and Sch. 15, para. 6, with effect in relation to accounting periods of controlled foreign companies beginning on or after 6 December 2006 (subject to the transitional provisions at FA 2007, Sch. 15, para. 10(2)–(4)).

S. 756(1B) inserted by FA 2007, s. 48 and Sch. 15, para. 6, with effect in relation to accounting periods of controlled foreign companies beginning on or after 6 December 2006 (subject to the transitional provisions at FA 2007, Sch. 15, para. 10(2)–(4)).

In s. 756(2)(a), the words "section 1122 of CTA 2010" substituted for the words "section 839" by CTA 2010, s. 1177 and Sch. 1, para. 101(2)(a), with effect for corporation tax purposes for accounting periods ending on or after 1 April 2010, and for income and capital gains tax purposes for the tax year 2010–11 and subsequent tax years.

S. 756(2)(b), substituted by CTA 2010, s. 1177 and Sch. 1, para. 101(2)(b), with effect for corporation tax purposes for accounting periods ending on or after 1 April 2010, and for income and capital gains tax purposes for the tax year 2010–11 and subsequent tax years.

S. 756(3) substituted by CTA 2010, s. 1177 and Sch. 1, para. 101(3), with effect for corporation tax purposes for accounting periods ending on or after 1 April 2010, and for income and capital gains tax purposes for the tax year 2010–11 and subsequent tax years.

In s. 756(3), para. (a) and words following para. (b) repealed by FA 2000, s. 104 and Sch. 31, para. 4(2), s. 156 and Sch. 40, Pt. II(14), with effect–

(a) for the purposes of determining whether at any time on or after 21 March 2000 a company resident outside the UK is to be regarded for the purposes of Pt. XVII, Ch. IV as controlled by persons resident in the UK; and

(b) for any accounting period of a company resident outside the UK which begins on or after 21 March 2000.

Derivations – FA 1984, s. 91(1)–(3) (as originally enacted).

Cross references – S. 416: circumstances in which companies are associated, and in which a person controls a company.

S. 417(7)–(9): circumstances in which persons are "loan creditors".

S. 783(10): circumstances in which persons are associated.

S. 839: circumstances in which persons are connected.".

Chapter V – Offshore Funds

History – Ch. V repealed by SI 2009/3001, reg. 13(2) and Sch. 2, with effect from 1 December 2009 for various purposes (in accordance with the provisions of SI 2009/3001, reg. 1), subject to transitional and savings provisions in SI 2009/3001, Sch. 1.

MEANING OF OFFSHORE FUND

756A General definition of offshore fund

756A [Repealed by SI 2009/3001, reg. 13(2) and Sch. 2.]

History – S. 756A repealed by SI 2009/3001, reg. 13(2) and Sch. 2, with effect from 1 December 2009 for various purposes (in accordance with the provisions of SI 2009/3001, reg. 1), subject to transitional and savings provisions in SI 2009/3001, Sch. 1.

At the time of the repeal of s. 756A by SI 2009/3001, former s. 756A(4) was to have been omitted prospectively by FA 2008, s. 41(6)(a), with effect from a day which was to have been appointed (FA 2008, s. 41(8).

756B Treatment of umbrella funds

756B [Repealed by SI 2009/3001, reg. 13(2) and Sch. 2.]

History – S. 756B repealed by SI 2009/3001, reg. 13(2) and Sch. 2, with effect from 1 December 2009 for various purposes (in accordance with the provisions of SI 2009/3001, reg. 1), subject to transitional and savings provisions in SI 2009/3001, Sch. 1.
At the time of the repeal of s. 756B by SI 2009/3001, the words following former s. 756B(1)(b), and s. 756B(3), were to have been omitted prospectively by FA 2008, s. 41(6)(b), with effect from a day which was to have been appointed (FA 2008, s. 41(8)).

756C Treatment of funds comprising more than one class of interest

756C [Repealed by SI 2009/3001, reg. 13(2) and Sch. 2.]

History – S. 756C repealed by SI 2009/3001, reg. 13(2) and Sch. 2, with effect from 1 December 2009 for various purposes (in accordance with the provisions of SI 2009/3001, reg. 1), subject to transitional and savings provisions in SI 2009/3001, Sch. 1.
At the time of the repeal of s. 756C by SI 2009/3001, former s. 756C(2)(b) (and the word "or" before it) and former s. 756C(3) were to have been omitted prospectively by FA 2008, s. 41(6)(c), with effect from a day which was to have been appointed (FA 2008, s. 41(8)).

MATERIAL INTERESTS IN NON-QUALIFYING OFFSHORE FUNDS

Cross references – TCGA 1992, Sch. 7AD, para. 7(1) (gains of insurance company from venture capital investment partnership): nothing in TCGA 1992, Sch. 7AD affects Pt. 17, Ch. 5.

757 Disposal of material interests in non-qualifying offshore funds

757 [Repealed by SI 2009/3001, reg. 13(2) and Sch. 2.]

History – S. 757 repealed by SI 2009/3001, reg. 13(2) and Sch. 2, with effect from 1 December 2009 for various purposes (in accordance with the provisions of SI 2009/3001, reg. 1), subject to transitional and savings provisions in SI 2009/3001, Sch. 1
At the time of its repeal by SI 2009/3001, s. 757 was to have been omitted prospectively by FA 2008, s. 41(6)(d), with effect from a day which was to have been appointed (FA 2008, s. 41(8)).

Derivations – Former S. 757(1) (as originally enacted): FA 1984, s. 92(1), (7) and FA 1987, Sch. 16, Pt. VI.
Former S. 757(2)–(6) (as originally enacted): FA 1984, s. 92(2)–(6).
Former S. 757(7) (as originally enacted): FA 1984, s. 92(8).

758 Offshore funds operating equalisation arrangements

758 [Repealed by SI 2009/3001, reg. 13(2) and Sch. 2.]

History – S. 758 repealed by SI 2009/3001, reg. 13(2) and Sch. 2, with effect from 1 December 2009 for various purposes (in accordance with the provisions of SI 2009/3001, reg. 1), subject to transitional and savings provisions in SI 2009/3001, Sch. 1.
At the time of its repeal by SI 2009/3001, s. 758 was to have been omitted prospectively by FA 2008, s. 41(6)(d), with effect from a day which was to have been appointed (FA 2008, s. 41(8)).

Derivations – (as originally enacted) – FA 1984, s. 93.

759 Material interests in offshore funds

759 [Repealed by SI 2009/3001, reg. 13(2) and Sch. 2.]

History – S. 759 repealed by SI 2009/3001, reg. 13(2) and Sch. 2, with effect from 1 December 2009 for various purposes (in accordance with the provisions of SI 2009/3001, reg. 1), subject to transitional and savings provisions in SI 2009/3001, Sch. 1.
At the time of its repeal by SI 2009/3001, s. 759 was to have been omitted prospectively by FA 2008, s. 41(6)(d), with effect from a day which was to have been appointed (FA 2008, s. 41(8)).

Derivations – Former s. 759(1) (as originally enacted): FA 1984, s. 94(1); FA 1987, Sch. 16, Pt. VI.
Former s. 759(2)–(9) (as originally enacted): FA 1984, s. 94(2)–(9).

760 Non-qualifying offshore funds

760 [Repealed by SI 2009/3001, reg. 13(2) and Sch. 2.]

History – S. 760 repealed by SI 2009/3001, reg. 13(2) and Sch. 2, with effect from 1 December 2009 for various purposes (in accordance with the provisions of SI 2009/3001, reg. 1), subject to transitional and savings provisions in SI 2009/3001, Sch. 1.
At the time of its repeal by SI 2009/3001, s. 760 was to have been omitted prospectively by FA 2008, s. 41(6)(d), with effect from a day which was to have been appointed (FA 2008, s. 41(8)).

Derivations – FA 1984, s. 95 (as originally enacted).

CHARGE TO TAX OF OFFSHORE INCOME GAINS

761 Charge to income tax or corporation tax of offshore income gain

761 [Repealed by SI 2009/3001, reg. 13(2) and Sch. 2.]

History – S. 761 repealed by SI 2009/3001, reg. 13(2) and Sch. 2, with effect from 1 December 2009 for various purposes (in accordance with the provisions of SI 2009/3001, reg. 1), subject to transitional and savings provisions in SI 2009/3001, Sch. 1.
At the time of its repeal by SI 2009/3001, s. 761 was to have been omitted prospectively by FA 2008, s. 41(6)(d), with effect from a day which was to have been appointed (FA 2008, s. 41(8)).

Derivations – FA 1984, s. 96(1)–(7), as substituted (s. 96(6)) by FA 1987, Sch. 15, para. 16(1) (as originally enacted).

Notes – S. 761(6) rewritten as ITA 2007, s. 535(1), (2), 538(2).

762 Offshore income gains accruing to persons resident or domiciled abroad

762 [Repealed by SI 2009/3001, reg. 13(2) and Sch. 2.]

History – S. 762 repealed by SI 2009/3001, reg. 13(2) and Sch. 2, with effect from 1 December 2009 for various purposes (in accordance with the provisions of SI 2009/3001, reg. 1), subject to transitional and savings provisions in SI 2009/3001, Sch. 1.
At the time of its repeal by SI 2009/3001, s. 762 was to have been omitted prospectively by FA 2008, s. 41(6)(d), with effect from a day which was to have been appointed (FA 2008, s. 41(8)).

Derivations – (as originally enacted) – FA 1984, s. 97.

Other material – Tax Bulletin TB10/04-2: background to FA 2004 changes.

762ZA Offshore income gains: application of transfer of assets abroad provisions

762ZA [Repealed by SI 2009/3001, reg. 13(2) and Sch. 2.]

History – S. 762ZA repealed by SI 2009/3001, reg. 13(2) and Sch. 2, with effect from 1 December 2009 for various purposes (in accordance with the provisions of SI 2009/3001, reg. 1), subject to transitional and savings provisions in SI 2009/3001, Sch. 1.

762ZB Income treated as arising under section 761(1): remittance basis

762ZB [Repealed by SI 2009/3001, reg. 13(2) and Sch. 2.]

History – S. 762ZB repealed by SI 2009/3001, reg. 13(2) and Sch. 2, with effect from 1 December 2009 for various purposes (in accordance with the provisions of SI 2009/3001, reg. 1), subject to transitional and savings provisions in SI 2009/3001, Sch. 1.

762A Exchange of interests of different classes

762A [Repealed by SI 2009/3001, reg. 13(2) and Sch. 2.]

History – S. 762A repealed by SI 2009/3001, reg. 13(2) and Sch. 2, with effect from 1 December 2009 for various purposes (in accordance with the provisions of SI 2009/3001, reg. 1), subject to transitional and savings provisions in SI 2009/3001, Sch. 1.
At the time of its repeal by SI 2009/3001, s. 762A was to have been omitted prospectively by FA 2008, s. 41(6)(d), with effect from a day which was to have been appointed (FA 2008, s. 41(8)).

763 Deduction of offshore income gain in determining capital gain

763 [Repealed by SI 2009/3001, reg. 13(2) and Sch. 2.]

History – S. 763 repealed by SI 2009/3001, reg. 13(2) and Sch. 2, with effect from 1 December 2009 for various purposes (in accordance with the provisions of SI 2009/3001, reg. 1), subject to transitional and savings provisions in SI 2009/3001, Sch. 1.
At the time of its repeal by SI 2009/3001, s. 763 was to have been omitted prospectively by FA 2008, s. 41(6)(d), with effect from a day which was to have been appointed (FA 2008, s. 41(8)).

Derivations – FA 1984, s. 98 (as originally enacted).

764 Offshore income gains of trustees

764 [Omitted by FA 2006, s. 89 and Sch. 13, para. 23 and repealed by FA 2006, s. 178 and Sch. 26, Pt. 3(15)]

History – S. 764 omitted by FA 2006, s. 89 and Sch. 13, para. 23 and repealed by FA 2006, s. 178 and Sch. 26, Pt. 3(15) with effect from 6 April 2006 in relation to settlements whenever created.

Derivations – (as originally enacted) – FA 1984, s. 100(1).

Chapter VI – Miscellaneous

MIGRATION ETC. OF COMPANY

765 Migration etc. of companies

765 [Omitted by FA 2009, s. 37 and Sch. 17, para. 1(a).]

History – S. 765 omitted by FA 2009, s. 37 and Sch. 17, para. 1(a), with effect in relation to events taking place and transactions carried out on or after 1 July 2009 (but see cross reference note below).

765A Movements of capital between residents of member States

765A [Omitted by FA 2009, s. 37 and Sch. 17, para. 1(b).]

History – S. 765A omitted by FA 2009, s. 37 and Sch. 17, para. 1(b), with effect in relation to events taking place and transactions carried out on or after 1 July 2009.

766 Offences under section 765

766 [Omitted by FA 2009, s. 37 and Sch. 17, para. 1(c).]

History – S. 766 omitted by FA 2009, s. 37 and Sch. 17, para. 1(c), with effect in relation to events taking place and transactions carried out on or after 1 July 2009.

767 Interpretation and commencement of sections 765 and 766

767 [Omitted by FA 2009, s. 37 and Sch. 17, para. 1(d).]

History – S. 767 omitted by FA 2009, s. 37 and Sch. 17, para. 1(d), with effect in relation to events taking place and transactions carried out on or after 1 July 2009.
The repeal of s. 767(1)–(4) and of words in s. 767(5) by FA 1988, s. 148 and Sch. 14, Pt. IV have effect from 15 March 1988. The changes were made in consequence of new rules as to company migration, and the inability of UK-registered companies to change their residence for tax purposes.

Derivations – S. 767(5): ICTA 1970, s. 482(10) and Companies Consolidation (Consequential Provisions) Act 1985, Sch. 2.
S. 767(6): ICTA 1970, s. 482(12).

CHANGE IN OWNERSHIP OF COMPANY

767A Change in company ownership: corporation tax

767A [Omitted by CTA 2010, s. 1177 and Sch. 1, para. 102 and repealed by CTA 2010, s. 1181 and Sch. 3, Pt. 1.]

History – S. 767A omitted by CTA 2010, s. 1177 and Sch. 1, para. 102 and repealed by CTA 2010, s. 1181 and Sch. 3, Pt 1, with effect for corporation tax purposes for accounting periods ending on or after 1 April 2010, and for income and capital gains tax purposes for the tax year 2010–11 and subsequent tax years.

Notes – S. 767A rewritten for corporation tax purposes as follows:
S. 767A(1): CTA 2010, s. 710(1), (2), (3).
S. 767A(2): CTA 2010, s. 706(1), (2), (3).
S. 767A(3): CTA 2010, s. 709(2), (3).
S. 767A(4): CTA 2010, s. 711(2).
S. 767A(5): CTA 2010, s. 711(3).
S. 767A(6): CTA 2010, s. 711(4), (5).
S. 767A(7): CTA 2010, s. 711(5).
S. 767A(8): CTA 2010, s. 710(2).
S. 767A(9): CTA 2010, s. 710(1).
S. 767A(10): CTA 2010, s. 710(4).

767AA Change in company ownership: postponed corporation tax

767AA [Omitted by CTA 2010, s. 1177 and Sch. 1, para. 102 and repealed by CTA 2010, s. 1181 and Sch. 3, Pt. 1.]

History – S. 767AA omitted by CTA 2010, s. 1177 and Sch. 1, para. 102 and repealed by CTA 2010, s. 1181 and Sch. 3, Pt. 1, with effect for corporation tax purposes for accounting periods ending on or after 1 April 2010, and for income and capital gains tax purposes for the tax year 2010–11 and subsequent tax years.

Notes – S. 767AA rewritten for corporation tax purposes as follows:
S. 767AA(1): CTA 2010, s. 713(1), (2).
S. 767AA(2): CTA 2010, s. 714(1), (2), (3).
S. 767AA(3): CTA 2010, s. 714(4), (5).
S. 767AA(4): CTA 2010, s. 706(1), (2), (3).
S. 767AA(5): CTA 2010, s. 709(2), (3).
S. 767AA(6): CTA 2010, s. 715(2).
S. 767AA(7): CTA 2010, s. 715(3), (4), (5), (6).
S. 767AA(8): CTA 2010, s. 718(2).
S. 767AA(9): CTA 2010, s. 713(3).
S. 767AA(10): CTA 2010, s. 713(4).

767B Change of company ownership: supplementary

767B [Omitted by CTA 2010, s. 1177 and Sch. 1, para. 102 and repealed by CTA 2010, s. 1181 and Sch. 3, Pt. 1.]

History – S. 767B omitted by CTA 2010, s. 1177 and Sch. 1, para. 102 and repealed by CTA 2010, s. 1181 and Sch. 3, Pt. 1, with effect for corporation tax purposes for accounting periods ending on or after 1 April 2010, and for income and capital gains tax purposes for the tax year 2010–11 and subsequent tax years.

Notes – S. 767B rewritten for corporation tax purposes as follows:
S. 767B(1): CTA 2010, s. 716(1), (2).
S. 767B(1A): CTA 2010, s. 716(1), (2).
S. 767B(2): CTA 2010, s. 717(1), (2).
S. 767B(3): CTA 2010, s. 717(1).
S. 767B(4): CTA 2010, s. 707(2), (3), (4), (5), 708(2), (3), (4), (5), (6).
S. 767B(5): CTA 2010, s. 707(3).
S. 767B(6): CTA 2010, s. 707(5).
S. 767B(7): CTA 2010, s. 712(2), (3), (4), (5), (6).
S. 767B(8): CTA 2010, s. 711(5).
S. 767B(9): CTA 2010, s. 1176(1).
S. 767B(10): CTA 2010, s. 728(1), (2).

767C Change in company ownership: information

767C [Omitted by CTA 2010, s. 1177 and Sch. 1, para. 102 and repealed by CTA 2010, s. 1181 and Sch. 3, Pt. 1.]

History – S. 767C omitted by CTA 2010, s. 1177 and Sch. 1, para. 102 and repealed by CTA 2010, s. 1181 and Sch. 3, Pt. 1, with effect for corporation tax purposes for accounting periods ending on or after 1 April 2010, and for income and capital gains tax purposes for the tax year 2010–11 and subsequent tax years. Former s. 767C omitted by FA 2008, s. 113 and Sch. 36, para. 81, with effect from 1 April 2009 (SI 2009/404, art. 2, but subject to provisions of SI 2009/404, art. 3–12).

768 Change in ownership of company: disallowance of trading losses

768 [Omitted by CTA 2010, s. 1177 and Sch. 1, para. 102 and repealed by CTA 2010, s. 1181 and Sch. 3, Pt. 1]

History – S. 768(9), so far as it continued to have effect (see CTA 2010, s. 1184), omitted by FA 2011, s. 86 and Sch. 23, para. 55(d), with effect from 1 April 2012, subject to transitional provisions in FA 2011, Sch. 23, para. 65.
S. 768 omitted by CTA 2010, s. 1177 and Sch. 1, para. 102 and repealed by CTA 2010, s. 1181 and Sch. 3, Pt. 1, with effect for corporation tax purposes for accounting periods ending on or after 1 April 2010, and for income and capital gains tax purposes for the tax year 2010–11 and subsequent tax years.

Notes – Former s. 768 rewritten for corporation tax purposes as follows:
Former s. 768(1): CTA 2010, s. 673(1), (2), (3), 674(2), (6).
Former s. 768(2): CTA 2010, s. 674(3).
Former s. 768(3): CTA 2010, s. 674(4), (5).
Former s. 768(4): CTA 2010, s. 673(4).
Former s. 768(5): CTA 2010, s. 676.
Former s. 768(6): CTA 2010, s. 675(1), (2), (3), 687(4), (5).
Former s. 768(7): CTA 2010, s. 675(4), 687(6).
Former s. 768(8): CTA 2010, s. 727.
Former s. 768(9): CTA 2010, s. 728(1), (2).

768A Change in ownership: disallowance of carry back of trading losses

768A [Omitted by CTA 2010, s. 1177 and Sch. 1, para. 102 and repealed by CTA 2010, s. 1181 and Sch. 3, Pt. 1.]

History – S. 768A omitted by CTA 2010, s. 1177 and Sch. 1, para. 102 and repealed by CTA 2010, s. 1181 and Sch. 3, Pt. 1, with effect for corporation tax purposes for accounting periods ending on or after 1 April 2010, and for income and capital gains tax purposes for the tax year 2010–11 and subsequent tax years.

Notes – S. 768A rewritten for corporation tax purposes as follows:
S. 768A(1): CTA 2010, s. 673(1), (2), (3), 674(1).
S. 768A(2): CTA 2010, s. 673(4), 674(3), (4), (5), 727, 728(1), (2).

768B Change in ownership of company with investment business: deductions generally

768B [Omitted by CTA 2010, s. 1177 and Sch. 1, para. 102 and repealed by CTA 2010, s. 1181 and Sch. 3, Pt. 1.]

History – S. 768B omitted by CTA 2010, s. 1177 and Sch. 1, para. 102 and repealed by CTA 2010, s. 1181 and Sch. 3, Pt. 1, with effect for corporation tax purposes for accounting periods ending on or after 1 April 2010, and for income and capital gains tax purposes for the tax year 2010–11 and subsequent tax years.

Notes – S. 768B rewritten for corporation tax purposes as follows:
S. 768B(1): CTA 2010, s. 677(1), (2), (3), (4).
S. 768B(2): CTA 2010, s. 677(2).
S. 768B(3): CTA 2010, s. 677(5).
S. 768B(4): CTA 2010, s. 678(2), (3).
S. 768B(5): CTA 2010, s. 678(3).
S. 768B(6): CTA 2010, s. 682(2).
S. 768B(8): CTA 2010, s. 682(3).
S. 768B(9): CTA 2010, s. 682(4).
S. 768B(10): CTA 2010, s. 679(1), 680(1).
S. 768B(12): CTA 2010, s. 687(1), (2), (3), (4), (5), (6), 727, 728(1), (2).
S. 768B(13): CTA 2010, s. 687(1), (2), (3).
S. 768B(14): CTA 2010, s. 729.

768C Deductions: asset transferred within group

768C [Omitted by CTA 2010, s. 1177 and Sch. 1, para. 102 and repealed by CTA 2010, s. 1181 and Sch. 3, Pt. 1.]

History – S. 768C omitted by CTA 2010, s. 1177 and Sch. 1, Part 1, para. 102 and repealed by CTA 2010, s. 1181 and Sch. 3, Pt. 1, with effect for corporation tax purposes for accounting periods ending on or after 1 April 2010, and for income and capital gains tax purposes for the tax year 2010–11 and subsequent tax years.

Notes – S. 768C rewritten for corporation tax purposes as follows:
S. 768C(1): CTA 2010, s. 692(1), (2), (3), (4), (7).
S. 768C(2): CTA 2010, s. 692(5), (6).
S. 768C(3): CTA 2010, s. 695(2), (3).
S. 768C(4): CTA 2010, s. 695(3).
S. 768C(5): CTA 2010, s. 699(2), (3).
S. 768C(6): CTA 2010, s. 696(2), 697(2), 699(4).
S. 768C(7): CTA 2010, s. 699(5).
S. 768C(8): CTA 2010, s. 693(1), (2), (3).
S. 768C(9): CTA 2010, s. 696(1), 697(1).
S. 768C(11): CTA 2010, s. 727, 728(1), (2).

S. 768C(12): CTA 2010, s. 694, 729.
S. 768C(13): CTA 2010, s. 692(3), (4), (7),693(1), 694, 699(4), 702(2).

768D Change in ownership of company carrying on property business

768D [Omitted by CTA 2010, s. 1177 and Sch. 1, para. 102 and repealed by CTA 2010, s. 1181 and Sch. 3, Pt. 1.]

History – S. 768D omitted by CTA 2010, s. 1177 and Sch. 1, Part 1, para. 102 and repealed by CTA 2010, s. 1181 and Sch. 3, Pt. 1, with effect for corporation tax purposes for accounting periods ending on or after 1 April 2010, and for income and capital gains tax purposes for the tax year 2010–11 and subsequent tax years.

Notes – S. 768D rewritten for corporation tax purposes as follows:
S. 768D(1): CTA 2010, s. 677(1), 692(1), 704(1), (2), (3), (10), 705(1), (2), (3), (9).
S. 768D(2): CTA 2010, s. 683(1), 684(1), 700(1), 701(1), 704(4), 705(4).
S. 768D(3): CTA 2010, s. 678(2), 695(2), 704(5),705(5).
S. 768D(4): CTA 2010, s. 678(3), 695(3), 704(6), (7),705(6), (7).
S. 768D(5): CTA 2010, s. 683(2), 700(3), 704(8).

768E Change in ownership of company with unused non-trading loss on intangible fixed assets

768E [Omitted by CTA 2010, s. 1177 and Sch. 1, para. 102 and repealed by CTA 2010, s. 1181 and Sch. 3, Pt. 1.]

History – S. 768E omitted by CTA 2010, s. 1177 and Sch. 1, para. 102 and repealed by CTA 2010, s. 1181 and Sch. 3, Pt. 1, with effect for corporation tax purposes for accounting periods ending on or after 1 April 2010, and for income and capital gains tax purposes for the tax year 2010–11 and subsequent tax years.

Notes – S. 768E rewritten for corporation tax purposes as follows:
S. 768E(1): CTA 2010, s. 677(1), 681(1), 692(1), 698(1).
S. 768E(2): CTA 2010, s. 678(2), 695(2).
S. 768E(3): CTA 2010, s. 678(3), 685(3),695(3), 702(3).
S. 768E(4): CTA 2010, s. 681(2), 698(3).
S. 768E(5): CTA 2010, s. 681(3), 698(2), (4), (5).
S. 768E(6): CTA 2010, s. 727, 728(1), (2).
S. 768E(7): CTA 2010, s. 729.

769 Rules for ascertaining change in ownership of company

769 [Omitted by CTA 2010, s. 1177 and Sch. 1, para. 102 and repealed by CTA 2010, s. 1181 and Sch. 3, Pt. 1.]

History – S. 769 omitted by CTA 2010, s. 1177 and Sch. 1, para. 102 and repealed by CTA 2010, s. 1181 and Sch. 3, Pt. 1, with effect for corporation tax purposes for accounting periods ending on or after 1 April 2010, and for income and capital gains tax purposes for the tax year 2010–11 and subsequent tax years.

Notes – S. 769 rewritten for corporation tax purposes as follows:
S. 769(1): CTA 2010, s. 719(1), (2), (3), (4).
S. 769(2): CTA 2010, s. 720(1), (2), (3), (4), (5), (6), 1176(1).
S. 769(2A): CTA 2010, s. 722(1), (2), (3), (4).
S. 769(3): CTA 2010, s. 721(1), (2), (3), (4).
S. 769(3A): CTA 2010, s. 721(1), (2), (3), (4).
S. 769(4): CTA 2010, s. 725(1), (2).
S. 769(5): CTA 2010, s. 724(1), (2), (3).
S. 769(6): CTA 2010, s. 723(1), (2), (3), (4), (5).
S. 769(6A): CTA 2010, s. 723(6).
S. 769(6B): CTA 2010, s. 724(1), (2), (4), (5).
S. 769(6C): CTA 2010, s. 724(6).
S. 769(7): CTA 2010, s. 726.
S. 769(8): CTA 2010, s. 725(1), (3), (4), (5), (6).
S. 769(9): CTA 2010, s. 725(1).

TRANSACTIONS BETWEEN ASSOCIATED PERSONS

770 Sales etc. at an undervalue or overvalue

770 [Superseded by ICTA 1988, s. 770A – see History note.]

History – S. 770A substituted for s. 770–773 by FA 1998, s. 108(1), with effect for accounting periods and years of assessment ending on or after 1 July 1999, the day appointed for the commencement of company self-assessment by virtue of FA 1994, s. 199 and SI 1998/3173 (C. 78).

770A Provision not at arm's length

770A [Omitted by TIOPA 2010, s. 374 and Sch. 8, para. 110 and repealed by TIOPA 2010, s. 378 and Sch. 10, Pt. 2.]

History – S. 770A omitted by TIOPA 2010, s. 374 and Sch. 8, para. 110 and repealed by TIOPA 2010, s. 378 and Sch. 10, Pt. 2, with effect for corporation tax purposes for accounting periods ending on or after 1 April 2010, for income tax and capital gains tax purposes for the tax year 2010–11 and subsequent tax years, and for petroleum revenue tax purposes for chargeable periods beginning on or after 1 July 2010.

771 Transactions by petroleum companies

771 [Superseded by ICTA 1988, s. 770A – see History note.]

History – S. 770A substituted for s. 770–773 by FA 1998, s. 108(1), with effect for accounting periods and years of assessment ending on or after 1 July 1999, the day appointed for the commencement of corporation tax self-assessment (FA 1994, s. 199 and SI 1998/3173 (C. 78)).

772 Information for purposes of section 770 and appeals

772 [Superseded by ICTA 1988, s. 770A – see History note.]

History – S. 770A substituted for s. 770–773 by FA 1998, s. 108(1) with effect for accounting periods and years of assessment ending on or after 1 July 1999, the day appointed for the commencement of corporation tax self-assessment (FA 1994, s. 199 and SI 1998/3173 (C. 78)).

773 Interpretations of sections 770 and 771

773 [Superseded by ICTA 1988, s. 770A – see History note.]

History – S. 770A substituted for s. 770–773 by FA 1998, s. 108(1) with effect for accounting periods and years of assessment ending on or after 1 July 1999, the day appointed for the commencement of corporation tax self-assessment (FA 1994, s. 199 and SI 1998/3173 (C. 78)).

774 Transactions between dealing company and associated company

774 [Repealed by Statute Law (Repeals) Act 2013, s. 1 and Sch. 1, Pt. 10.]

History – S. 774 repealed by Statute Law (Repeals) Act 2013, s. 1 and Sch. 1, Pt. 10, with effect from 31 January 2013.

Derivations – ICTA 1970, s. 486.

FACTORING OF INCOME RECEIPTS ETC

774A Meaning of "structured finance arrangement" for purposes of s. 774B

774A [Omitted by CTA 2010, s. 1177 and Sch. 1, para. 104 and repealed by CTA 2010, s. 1181 and Sch. 3, Pt. 2; also omitted by TIOPA 2010, s. 374 and Sch. 8, para. 265 and repealed by TIOPA 2010, s. 378 and Sch. 10, Pt. 10.]

History – S. 774A omitted by CTA 2010, s. 1177 and Sch. 1, para. 104 and repealed by CTA 2010, s. 1181 and Sch. 3, Pt. 2, with effect for corporation tax purposes for accounting periods ending on or after 1 April 2010. S. 774A also omitted by TIOPA 2010, s. 374 and Sch. 8, para. 265 and repealed by TIOPA 2010, s. 378 and Sch. 10, Pt. 10, with effect for corporation tax purposes for accounting periods ending on or after 1 April 2010, for income tax and capital gains tax purposes for the tax year 2010–11 and subsequent tax years, and for petroleum revenue tax purposes for chargeable periods beginning on or after 1 July 2010.

Notes – S. 774A rewritten for corporation tax as follows:
S. 774A(1): CTA 2010, s. 758(1).
S. 774A(2): CTA 2010, s. 758(2), (3).
S. 774A(3): CTA 2010, s. 758(4).
S. 774A(4): CTA 2010, s. 758(5), 759(5), 760(4).
S. 774A rewritten for income tax by TIOPA 2010, Sch. 5, para. 2.

774B Disregard of intended effects of arrangement involving disposals of assets

774B [Omitted by CTA 2010, s. 1177 and Sch. 1, para. 104 and repealed by CTA 2010, s. 1181 and Sch. 3, Pt. 2; also omitted by TIOPA 2010, s. 374 and Sch. 8, para. 265 and repealed by TIOPA 2010, s. 378 and Sch. 10, Pt. 10.]

History – S. 774B omitted by CTA 2010, s. 1177 and Sch. 1, para. 104 and repealed by CTA 2010, s. 1181 and Sch. 3, Pt. 2, with effect for corporation tax purposes for accounting periods ending on or after 1 April 2010. S. 774B also omitted by TIOPA 2010, s. 374 and Sch. 8, para. 265 and repealed by TIOPA 2010, s. 378 and Sch. 10, Pt. 10, with effect for corporation tax purposes for accounting periods ending on or after 1 April 2010, for income tax and capital gains tax purposes for the tax year 2010–11 and subsequent tax years, and for petroleum revenue tax purposes for chargeable periods beginning on or after 1 July 2010.

Notes – S. 774B rewritten for corporation tax as follows:
S. 774B(1): CTA 2010, s. 759(1), 760(1).
S. 774B(1A): CTA 2010, s. 759(1), (2).
S. 774B(1B): CTA 2010, s. 760(1), (2), (3), (5).
S. 774B(2): CTA 2010, s. 759(3), 760(4).
S. 774B(3): CTA 2010, s. 759(4), 760(4).
S. 774B(5): CTA 2010, s. 761(1), (2), (3), 762(1), (2), (3).
S. 774B(6): CTA 2010, s. 762(3).
S. 774B(7): CTA 2010, s. 761(4), 762(4).
S. 774B(8): CTA 2010, s. 761(4), 762(3), (4).
S. 774B rewritten for income tax by TIOPA 2010, Sch. 5, para. 2.

774C Meaning of "structured finance arrangement" for purposes of s. 774D

774C [Omitted by CTA 2010, s. 1177 and Sch. 1, para. 104 and repealed by CTA 2010, s. 1181 and Sch. 3, Pt. 2; also omitted by TIOPA 2010, s. 374 and Sch. 8, para. 265 and repealed by TIOPA 2010, s. 378 and Sch. 10, Pt. 10.]

History – S. 774C omitted by CTA 2010, s. 1177 and Sch. 1, para. 104 and repealed by CTA 2010, s. 1181 and Sch. 3, Pt. 2, with effect for corporation tax purposes for accounting periods ending on or after 1 April 2010. S. 774C also omitted by TIOPA 2010, s. 374 and Sch. 8, para. 265 and repealed by TIOPA 2010, s. 378 and Sch. 10, Pt. 10, with effect for corporation tax purposes for accounting periods ending on or after 1 April 2010, for income tax and capital gains tax purposes for the tax year 2010–11 and subsequent tax years, and for petroleum revenue tax purposes for chargeable periods beginning on or after 1 July 2010.

Notes – S. 774C rewritten for corporation tax as follows:
S. 774C(1): CTA 2010, s. 763(1), 767(1).
S. 774C(2): CTA 2010, s. 763(2), (3), 764(5).
S. 774C(3): CTA 2010, s. 763(4).
S. 774C(4): CTA 2010, s. 764(5), 767(2), (3).
S. 774C(5): CTA 2010, s. 767(4).
S. 774C(6): CTA 2010, s. 764(1), (2), (3), (4), (5).
S. 774C(7): CTA 2010, s. 764(3), (4), (5).
S. 774C rewritten for income tax as follows:
S. 774C(1): TIOPA 2010, Sch. 5, para. 3, 4.
S. 774C(2), (3): TIOPA 2010, Sch. 5, para. 3.
S. 774C(4): TIOPA 2010, Sch. 5, para. 3, 4.
S. 774C(5): TIOPA 2010, Sch. 5, para. 4.
S. 774C(6), (7): TIOPA 2010, Sch. 5, para. 3.

774D Disregard of intended effects of arrangement involving change in relation to a partnership

774D [Omitted by CTA 2010, s. 1177 and Sch. 1, para. 104 and repealed by CTA 2010, s. 1181 and Sch. 3, Pt. 2; also omitted by TIOPA 2010, s. 374 and Sch. 8, para. 265 and repealed by TIOPA 2010, s. 378 and Sch. 10, Pt. 10.]

History – S. 774D omitted by CTA 2010, s. 1177 and Sch. 1, para. 104 and repealed by CTA 2010, s. 1181 and Sch. 3, Pt. 2, with effect for corporation tax purposes for accounting periods ending on or after 1 April 2010. S. 774D also omitted by TIOPA 2010, s. 374 and Sch. 8, para. 265 and repealed by TIOPA 2010, s. 378 and Sch. 10, Pt. 10, with effect for corporation tax purposes for accounting periods ending on or after 1 April 2010, for income tax and capital gains tax purposes for the tax year 2010–11 and subsequent tax years, and for petroleum revenue tax purposes for chargeable periods beginning on or after 1 July 2010.

Notes – S. 774D rewritten for corporation tax as follows:
S. 774D(1): CTA 2010, s. 765(1), 768(1).
S. 774D(2): CTA 2010, s. 765(3), 768(2).
S. 774D(2A): CTA 2010, s. 765(4), 768(5).
S. 774D(3): CTA 2010, s. 765(2), (3), 768(3), (4), 769(6).
S. 774D(4): CTA 2010, s. 765(2), 768(4).
S. 774D(7): CTA 2010, s. 766(1), (2), (3).
S. 774D(8): CTA 2010, s. 766(4).
S. 774D(10): CTA 2010, s. 769(1), (2), (3).
S. 774D(11): CTA 2010, s. 769(4).
S. 774D(12): CTA 2010, s. 766(5), 769(5).
S. 774D(13): CTA 2010, s. 766(5), 769(5).
S. 774D rewritten for income tax as follows:
S. 774D(1), (2), (2A), (3), (4): TIOPA 2010, Sch. 5, para. 3, 4.
S. 774D(5): not rewritten, as unnecessary.
S. 774D(6): TIOPA 2010, Sch. 5, para. 3.
S. 774D(7): not rewritten, as not applicable to income tax.
S. 774D(8): TIOPA 2010, Sch. 5, para. 3.
S. 774D(9): TIOPA 2010, Sch. 5, para. 4.
S. 774D(10): not rewritten, as not applicable to income tax.
S. 774D(11): TIOPA 2010, Sch. 5, para. 4.
S. 774D(12), (13): TIOPA 2010, Sch. 5, para. 3, 4.
S. 774D(14): not rewritten, as unnecessary.

774E Sections 774B and 774D: exceptions

774E [Omitted by CTA 2010, s. 1177 and Sch. 1, para. 104 and repealed by CTA 2010, s. 1181 and Sch. 3, Pt. 2; also omitted by TIOPA 2010, s. 374 and Sch. 8, para. 265 and repealed by TIOPA 2010, s. 378 and Sch. 10, Pt. 10.]

History – S. 774E omitted by CTA 2010, s. 1177 and Sch. 1, para. 104 and repealed by CTA 2010, s. 1181 and Sch. 3, Pt. 2, with effect for corporation tax purposes for accounting periods ending on or after 1 April 2010. S. 774E also omitted by TIOPA 2010, s. 374 and Sch. 8, para. 265 and repealed by TIOPA 2010, s. 378 and Sch. 10, Pt. 10, with effect for corporation tax purposes for accounting periods ending on or after 1 April 2010, for income tax and capital gains tax purposes for the tax year 2010–11 and subsequent tax years, and for petroleum revenue tax purposes for chargeable periods beginning on or after 1 July 2010.

Notes – S. 774E rewritten for corporation tax as follows:
S. 774E(1): CTA 2010, s. 771(1).
S. 774E(2): CTA 2010, s. 771(2).
S. 774E(3): CTA 2010, s. 771(3), (4).
S. 774E(4): CTA 2010, s. 771(5), (6).

S. 774E(5): CTA 2010, s. 771(7), (9).
S. 774E(6): CTA 2010, s. 771(8).
S. 774E(7): CTA 2010, s. 772(2), (3), (4).
S. 774E rewritten for income tax byTIOPA 2010, Sch. 5, para. 5.

774F Sections 774B and 774D: power to provide further exceptions

774F [Omitted by CTA 2010, s. 1177 and Sch. 1, para. 104 and repealed by CTA 2010, s. 1181 and Sch. 3, Pt. 2; also omitted by TIOPA 2010, s. 374 and Sch. 8, para. 265 and repealed by TIOPA 2010, s. 378 and Sch. 10, Pt. 10.]

History – S. 774F omitted by CTA 2010, s. 1177 and Sch. 1, para. 104 and repealed by CTA 2010, s. 1181 and Sch. 3, Pt. 2, with effect for corporation tax purposes for accounting periods ending on or after 1 April 2010. S. 774F also omitted TIOPA 2010, s. 374 and Sch. 8, para. 265 and repealed by TIOPA 2010, s. 378 and Sch. 10, Pt. 10, with effect for corporation tax purposes for accounting periods ending on or after 1 April 2010, for income tax and capital gains tax purposes for the tax year 2010–11 and subsequent tax years, and for petroleum revenue tax purposes for chargeable periods beginning on or after 1 July 2010.

Notes – S. 774F rewritten for corporation tax as follows:
S. 774F(1): CTA 2010, s. 773(1).
S. 774F(2): CTA 2010, s. 773(2).
S. 774F(3): CTA 2010, s. 773(3).
S. 774F rewritten for income tax by TIOPA 2010, Sch. 5, para. 5.

774G Sections 774A to 774D: minor definitions etc

774G [Omitted by CTA 2010, s. 1177 and Sch. 1, para. 104 and repealed by CTA 2010, s. 1181 and Sch. 3, Pt. 2; also omitted by TIOPA 2010, s. 374 and Sch. 8, para. 265 and repealed by TIOPA 2010, s. 378 and Sch. 10, Pt. 10.]

History – S. 774G omitted by CTA 2010, s. 1177 and Sch. 1, para. 104 and repealed by CTA 2010, s. 1181 and Sch. 3, Pt. 2, with effect for corporation tax purposes for accounting periods ending on or after 1 April 2010. S. 774G also omitted by TIOPA 2010, s. 374 and Sch. 8, para. 265 and repealed by TIOPA 2010, s. 378 and Sch. 10, Pt. 10, with effect for corporation tax purposes for accounting periods ending on or after 1 April 2010, for income tax and capital gains tax purposes for the tax year 2010–11 and subsequent tax years, and for petroleum revenue tax purposes for chargeable periods beginning on or after 1 July 2010.

Notes – S. 774G rewritten for corporation tax as follows:
S. 774G(1): CTA 2010, s. 775.
S. 774G(2): CTA 2010, s. 759(6), 760(4), 765(5), 768(6).
S. 774G(3): CTA 2010, s. 776(2), (3), (4).
S. 774G(4): CTA 2010, s. 1176(1).
S. 774G(5): CTA 2010, s. 774(2).
S. 774G(5A): CTA 2010, s. 774(3).
S. 774G(6): CTA 2010, s. 774(4).
S. 774G(7): CTA 2010, Sch. 1, para. 588.
S. 774G rewritten for income tax as follows:
S. 774G(1): TIOPA 2010, Sch. 5, para. 6.
S. 774G(2): TIOPA 2010, Sch. 5, para. 2, 3, 4.
S. 774G(3): TIOPA 2010, Sch. 5, para. 6.
S. 774G(4): rewrite unnecessary, as ITA 2007, s. 993 will apply (see ITA 2007, s. 1021(1)).
S. 774G(5), (5A), (6): TIOPA 2010, Sch. 5, para. 6.
S. 774G(7): TIOPA 2010, Sch. 8, para. 268.

OTHER PROVISIONS

775 Sale by individual of income derived from his personal activities

775 [Omitted by ITA 2007, s. 1027 and Sch. 1, para. 182 and repealed by ITA 2007, s. 1031 and Sch. 3, Pt. 1 with effect for 2007–08 and subsequent tax years.]

Notes – S. 775 rewritten as follows:
S. 775(1): ITA 2007, s. 773(2), 777(1), (3), (5), 778(1).
S. 775(2): ITA 2007, s. 778(2), (3), 779(3).
S. 775(2A): ITA 2007, s. 776(1), (2), (3).
S. 775(3): ITA 2007, s. 774, 777(4), 785(4).
S. 775(4): ITA 2007, s. 784(1), (2), (4), (5).
S. 775(5): ITA 2007, s. 785(1), (2), (3).
S. 775(6): ITA 2007, s. 784(6).
S. 775(7): ITA 2007, s. 776(2), 777(1), 778(1), 779(1), (2), (3), (4).
S. 775(8): ITA 2007, s. 777(6).
S. 775(9): ITA 2007, s. 777(1), (2).

775A Transfers of rights to receive annual payments

775A [Omitted by FA 2009, s. 49 and Sch. 25, para. 9(1)(b).]

History – S. 775A omitted by FA 2009, s. 49 and Sch. 25, para. 9(1)(b), with effect in relation to transfers on or after 22 April 2009.

776 Transactions in land: taxation of capital gains

776 [Omitted by CTA 2010, s. 1177 and Sch. 1, para. 105 and repealed by CTA 2010, s. 1181 and Sch. 3, Pt. 1.]

History – S. 776 omitted by CTA 2010, s. 1177 and Sch. 1, para. 105 and repealed by CTA 2010, s. 1181 and Sch. 3, Pt. 1, with effect for corporation tax purposes for accounting periods ending on or after 1 April 2010, and for income and capital gains tax purposes for the tax year 2010–11 and subsequent tax years.

Notes – S. 776 rewritten as follows:
S. 776(1): ITA 2007, s. 752(1).
S. 776(2): ITA 2007, s. 752(2), 756(1), (3), (4), 757(1), (2).
S. 776(3): ITA 2007, s. 756(1), (2), 759(2).
S. 776(3A): ITA 2007, s. 755(1).
S. 776(3B): ITA 2007, s. 758(1), 759(1), (3).
S. 776(4): ITA 2007, s. 753(1), (2), 757(1).
S. 776(5): ITA 2007, s. 756(5), 757(3).
S. 776(6): ITA 2007, s. 760(1), (2), (3), (4), (5), (6), (7).
S. 776(7): ITA 2007, s. 765(1), (2), (3).
S. 776(8): ITA 2007, s. 759(4), (5), (6).
S. 776(9): ITA 2007, s. 767.
S. 776(10): ITA 2007, s. 766(1), (2), (3), (4).
S. 776(11): ITA 2007, s. 770(1), (2), (3), (4), (5).
S. 776(12): ITA 2007, s. 770(6).
S. 776(13): ITA 2007, s. 188(3), 299(3), 756(1), (3), 772(2), 1021(1).
S. 776(14): ITA 2007, s. 756(1), 759(8).
S. 776 rewritten for corporation tax purposes as follows:
S. 776(1): CTA 2010, s. 815(1).
S. 776(2): CTA 2010, s. 815(2), 819(1), (2), (3), 820(1), (2).
S. 776(3): CTA 2010, s. 818(1), (2), 819(1), 821(1), (2).
S. 776(3A): CTA 2010, s. 818(1).
S. 776(4): CTA 2010, s. 816(1), (2), 820(1).
S. 776(5): CTA 2010, s. 819(4), 820(3).
S. 776(6): CTA 2010, s. 822(1), (2), (3), (4), (5), (6), (7).
S. 776(7): CTA 2010, s. 827(1), (2), (3).
S. 776(8): CTA 2010, s. 821(3), (4), (5).
S. 776(10): CTA 2010, s. 828(1), (2), (3), (4).
S. 776(11): CTA 2010, s. 831(1), (2), (3), (4), (5).
S. 776(12): CTA 2010, s. 831(6).
S. 776(13): CTA 2010, s. 819(1), (2), 833(2), 1176(1).
S. 776(14): CTA 2010, s. 819(1).

777 Provisions supplementary to section 776

777 [Omitted by CTA 2010, s. 1177 and Sch. 1, para. 105 and repealed by CTA 2010, s. 1181 and Sch. 3, Pt. 1.]

History – S. 777 omitted by CTA 2010, s. 1177 and Sch. 1, para. 105 and repealed by CTA 2010, s. 1181 and Sch. 3, Pt. 1, with effect for corporation tax purposes for accounting periods ending on or after 1 April 2010, and for income and capital gains tax purposes for the tax year 2010–11 and subsequent tax years.

Notes – S. 777 rewritten as follows:
S. 777(2): ITA 2007, s. 761(1), (2), 780(1), (2).
S. 777(3): ITA 2007, s. 761(3), 780(3).
S. 777(5): ITA 2007, s. 762(1), (2), (3), 781(1), (2), (3).
S. 777(6): ITA 2007, s. 764(1), (2), 783(1), (2).
S. 777(7): ITA 2007, s. 763(1), (2), (3), (4), 782(1), (2), (3), (4).
S. 777(8): ITA 2007, s. 768(1), (3), (4), (5), (6), 769(1), (2), 786(1), (3), (4), (5), (6), 787(1), (2).
S. 777(9): ITA 2007, s. 944(1), (2), (3).
S. 777(10): ITA 2007, s. 754, 775.
S. 777(11): ITA 2007, Sch. 1 para. 321.
S. 777(12): ITA 2007, Sch. 1 para. 299, 300.
S. 777(13): ITA 2007, s. 768(2), 772(1), (3), 777(7), 778(4), 786(2), 789.
S. 777 rewritten for corporation tax purposes as follows:
S. 777(2): CTA 2010, s. 823(1), (2).
S. 777(3): CTA 2010, s. 823(3).
S. 777(5): CTA 2010, s. 824(1), (2), (3).
S. 777(6): CTA 2010, s. 826(1), (2).
S. 777(7): CTA 2010, s. 825(1), (2), (3), (4).
S. 777(8): CTA 2010, s. 829(1), (3), (4), (5), 830(1), (2).
S. 777(10): CTA 2010, s. 817.
S. 777(11): CTA 2010, Sch. 1, para. 238.
S. 777(12): CTA 2010,Sch. 1, para. 226, 227.
S. 777(13): CTA 2010, s. 829(2), 833(1), (3).

778 Power to obtain information

778 [Omitted by CTA 2010, s. 1177 and Sch. 1, para. 105 and repealed by CTA 2010, s 1181 and Sch. 3, Pt. 1.]

History – S. 778 omitted by CTA 2010, s. 1177 and Sch. 1, para. 105 and repealed by CTA 2010, s. 1181 and Sch. 3, Pt 1, with effect for corporation tax purposes for accounting periods ending on or after 1 April 2010, and for income and capital gains tax purposes for the tax year 2010–11 and subsequent tax years.
At the time of its repeal by CTA 2010, s. 1181 and Sch. 3, Pt. 1, in s. 778(3), the words "relevant lawyer" were to be substituted for the word "solicitor" by the Legal Services Act 2007, s. 208 and Sch. 21, para. 74, with effect from a day to be appointed by order of the Lord Chancellor.
At the time of its repeal by CTA 2010, s. 1181 and Sch. 3, Pt. 1, new s. 778(4) was to be inserted by the Legal Services Act 2007, s. 208 and Sch. 21, para. 74, with effect from a day to be appointed by order of the Lord Chancellor.

Notes – S. 778 rewritten as follows:
S. 778(1): ITA 2007, s. 771(1), (2), 788(1), (2).
S. 778(2): ITA 2007, s. 771(3), 788(3).
S. 778(3): ITA 2007, s. 771(4), (5), (6), 788(4), (5), (6).
S. 778 rewritten for corporation tax purposes as follows:
S. 778(1): CTA 2010, s. 832(1), (2).
S. 778(2): CTA 2010, s. 832(3).
S. 778(3): CTA 2010, s. 832(4), (5), (6).

779 Sale and lease-back: limitation on tax reliefs

779 [Omitted by CTA 2010, s. 1177 and Sch. 1, para. 106 and repealed by CTA 2010, s. 1181 and Sch. 3, Pt. 2; also omitted by TIOPA 2010, s. 374 and Sch. 8, para. 242 and repealed by TIOPA 2010, s. 378 and Sch. 10, Pt. 9.]

History – S. 779 omitted by CTA 2010, s. 1177 and Sch. 1, para. 106 and repealed by CTA 2010, s. 1181 and Sch. 3, Pt. 2, with effect for corporation tax purposes for accounting periods ending on or after 1 April 2010. S. 779 also omitted by TIOPA 2010, s. 374 and Sch. 8, para. 242 and repealed by TIOPA 2010, s. 378 and Sch. 10, Pt. 9 with effect for corporation tax purposes for accounting periods ending on or after 1 April 2010, for income tax and capital gains tax purposes for the tax year 2010–11 and subsequent tax years, and for petroleum revenue tax purposes for chargeable periods beginning on or after 1 July 2010.

Notes – S. 779 rewritten for corporation tax purposes as follows:
S. 779(1): CTA 2010, s. 835(1), (2), (5), (6), 838(1), 839(1).
S. 779(2): CTA 2010, s. 836(1), (2), (5), (6), 838(1), 839(1).
S. 779(3): CTA 2010, s. 835(3), (4), 836(3), (4).
S. 779(4): CTA 2010, s. 838(3), 839(3).
S. 779(5): CTA 2010, s. 838(3), 840(2), (3), (4).
S. 779(6): CTA 2010, s. 838(1), (3),839(1), 840(5),841(1), (2), (3), (4), 843(1), (2), (4).
S. 779(7): CTA 2010, s. 838(3), 842(1), (2), (3), (4).
S. 779(8): CTA 2010, s. 844(1), (3), (4).
S. 779(9): CTA 2010, s. 845(1), (2), (4).
S. 779(10): CTA 2010, s. 846(1), (4), (5).
S. 779(11): CTA 2010, s. 847(1),(2), (3), (4), (5).
S. 779(12): CTA 2010, s. 843(5), 845(3), 846(1), (2), (3), 848.
S. 779(13): CTA 2010, s. 835(2), 836(2), 837, 860.
S. 779(14): CTA 2010, s. 835(7), 836(7).
S. 779 rewritten for income tax purposes as follows:
S. 779(1)–(12): TIOPA 2010, Sch. 4, para. 2.
S. 779(13): TIOPA 2010, Sch. 4, para. 2, 3 (but s. 779(13)(f), reference to woodlands not rewritten as obsolete).
S. 779(14): TIOPA 2010, Sch. 4, para. 2.

780 Sale and lease-back: taxation of consideration received

780 [Omitted by CTA 2010, s. 1177 and Sch. 1, para. 106 and repealed by CTA 2010, s. 1181 and Sch. 3, Pt. 2; also omitted by TIOPA 2010, s. 374 and Sch. 8, para. 242 and repealed by TIOPA 2010, s. 378 and Sch. 10, Pt. 9.]

History – S. 780 omitted by CTA 2010, s. 1177 and Sch. 1, para. 106 and repealed by CTA 2010, s. 1181 and Sch. 3, Pt. 2, with effect for corporation tax purposes for accounting periods ending on or after 1 April 2010. S. 780 also omitted by TIOPA 2010, s. 374 and Sch. 8, para. 242 and repealed by TIOPA 2010, s. 378 and Sch. 10, Pt. 9 with effect for corporation tax purposes for accounting periods ending on or after 1 April 2010, for income tax and capital gains tax purposes for the tax year 2010–11 and subsequent tax years, and for petroleum revenue tax purposes for chargeable periods beginning on or after 1 July 2010.

Notes – S. 780 rewritten for corporation tax purposes as follows:
S. 780(1): CTA 2010, s. 850(1), (2), (3), (4), (5), 851(1), (2), 853(1), (2), (3), 860.
S. 780(2): CTA 2010, s. 854(2), 855(1), (2), 856(1), (2), 857(1), (2),858(1), (2).
S. 780(3): CTA 2010, s. 851(1), (2), (3), (4), (5), (6), (7), (8).
S. 780(3A): CTA 2010, s. 851(8).
S. 780(4): CTA 2010, s. 852(1), (2), (3), (4).
S. 780(6): CTA 2010, s. 859(1), (2), (3), (4), (5), (6).
S. 780(7): CTA 2010, s. 850(4), 851(6), 856(1), (2), 857(1), (2), 858(1), 861(1), (2).
S. 780(8): CTA 2010, s. 851(1), 855(2), (3), 862(1), (2), (3), (4), (5), 1166(1), Sch. 2, para. 95(4).
S. 780(9): CTA 2010, s. 850(6), Sch. 2, para. 95(1), (2), (3).
S. 780 rewritten for income tax as follows:
S. 780(1)–(7): TIOPA 2010, Sch. 4, para. 2.
S. 780(8): TIOPA 2010, Sch. 4, para. 2, Sch. 9, para. 41(4).
S. 780(9): TIOPA 2010, Sch. 4, para. 2, Sch. 9, para. 41(1), (2), (3).

781 Assets leased to traders and others

781 [Omitted by CTA 2010, s. 1177 and Sch. 1, para. 106 and repealed by CTA 2010, s. 1181 and Sch. 3, Pt. 2; also omitted by TIOPA 2010, s. 374 and Sch. 8, para. 242 and repealed by TIOPA 2010, s. 378 and Sch. 10, Pt. 9.]

History – S. 781 omitted by CTA 2010, s. 1177 and Sch. 1, para. 106 and repealed by CTA 2010, s. 1181 and Sch. 3, Pt. 2, with effect for corporation tax purposes for accounting periods ending on or after 1 April 2010. S. 781 also omitted by TIOPA 2010, s. 374 and Sch. 8, para. 242 and repealed by TIOPA 2010, s. 378 and Sch. 10, Pt. 9 with effect for corporation tax purposes for accounting periods ending on or after 1 April 2010, for income tax and capital gains tax purposes for the tax year 2010–11 and subsequent tax years, and for petroleum revenue tax purposes for chargeable periods beginning on or after 1 July 2010.

Notes – S. 781 rewritten for corporation tax purposes as follows:
S. 781(1): CTA 2010, s. 871, 872(1), 873(1), (2), (3), (4), (5), 874(1), (2), 879(1).
S. 781(1B): CTA 2010, s. 874(1).
S. 781(2): CTA 2010, s. 874(4).

S. 781(3): CTA 2010, s. 872(4).
S. 781(4): CTA 2010, s. 886.
S. 781(6): CTA 2010, s. 874(5), (6), (7).
S. 781(7): CTA 2010, s. 876(1), (2).
S. 781(8): CTA 2010, s. 876(3), (4).
S. 781(8A): CTA 2010, s. 876(3).
S. 781(9): CTA 2010, s. 873(6), (7).
S. 781 rewritten for income tax purposes as follows:
S. 781(1), (1A): TIOPA 2010, Sch. 4, para. 5.
S. 781(1B): not rewritten, as applicable to corporation tax only.
S. 781(2), (3), (4): TIOPA 2010, Sch. 4, para. 5 (but reference to woodlands in s. 781(4)(e) not rewritten, as obsolete).
S. 781(5): not rewritten, as spent.
S. 781(6)–(9): TIOPA 2010, Sch. 4, para. 5.

782 Leased assets: special cases

782 [Omitted by CTA 2010, s. 1177 and Sch. 1, para. 106 and repealed by CTA 2010, s. 1181 and Sch. 3, Pt. 2; also omitted by TIOPA 2010, s. 374 and Sch. 8, para. 242 and repealed by TIOPA 2010, s. 378 and Sch. 10, Pt. 9.]

History – S. 782 omitted by CTA 2010, s. 1177 and Sch. 1, para. 106 and repealed by CTA 2010, s. 1181 and Sch. 3, Pt. 2, with effect for corporation tax purposes for accounting periods ending on or after 1 April 2010. S. 782 also omitted by TIOPA 2010, s. 374 and Sch. 8, para. 242 and repealed by TIOPA 2010, s. 378 and Sch. 10, Pt. 9 with effect for corporation tax purposes for accounting periods ending on or after 1 April 2010, for income tax and capital gains tax purposes for the tax year 2010–11 and subsequent tax years, and for petroleum revenue tax purposes for chargeable periods beginning on or after 1 July 2010.

Notes – S. 782 rewritten for corporation tax purposes as follows:
S. 782(1): CTA 2010, s. 864(1), (2), (3), (4), 865(1), 872(2), (3).
S. 782(1A): CTA 2010, s. 865(1), 866(1), (2).
S. 782(2): CTA 2010, s. 865(3).
S. 782(3): CTA 2010, s. 865(3).
S. 782(4): CTA 2010, s. 865(3).
S. 782(6): CTA 2010, s. 867(1), (3), (4), (5), (6).
S. 782(7): CTA 2010, s. 867(7).
S. 782(8): CTA 2010, s. 864(5).
S. 782(9): CTA 2010, s. 864(6).
S. 782(10): CTA 2010, s. 864(4).
S. 782 rewritten for income tax purposes as follows:
S. 782(1), (1A), (2), (3): TIOPA 2010, Sch. 4, para. 4.
S. 782(4): TIOPA 2010, Sch. 4, para. 4. Para. (a)–(c) not rewritten: unnecessary for income tax purposes as a result of change 11 in Annex 1 to the Explanatory Notes to TIOPA 2010.
S. 782(5): Not rewritten. Unnecessary for income tax purposes as a result of change 11 in Annex 1 to the Explanatory Notes to TIOPA 2010.
S. 782(6), (7), (8), (9), (10): TIOPA 2010, Sch. 4, para. 4.

783 Leased assets: supplemental

783 [Omitted by CTA 2010, s. 1177 and Sch. 1, para. 106 and repealed by CTA 2010, s. 1181 and Sch. 3, Pt. 2; also omitted by TIOPA 2010, s. 374 and Sch. 8, para. 242 and repealed by TIOPA 2010, s. 378 and Sch. 10, Pt. 9.]

History – S. 783 omitted by CTA 2010, s. 1177 and Sch. 1, para. 106 and repealed by CTA 2010, s. 1181 and Sch. 3, Pt. 2, with effect for corporation tax purposes for accounting periods ending on or after 1 April 2010. S. 783 also omitted by TIOPA 2010, s. 374 and Sch. 8, para. 242 and repealed by TIOPA 2010, s. 378 and Sch. 10, Pt. 9 with effect for corporation tax purposes for accounting periods ending on or after 1 April 2010, for income tax and capital gains tax purposes for the tax year 2010–11 and subsequent tax years, and for petroleum revenue tax purposes for chargeable periods beginning on or after 1 July 2010.

Notes – S. 783 rewritten for corporation tax purposes as follows:
S. 783(1): CTA 2010, s. 877, 878(1), (2).
S. 783(2): CTA 2010, s. 877, 878(3), (4).
S. 783(3): CTA 2010, s. 873(2), (4).
S. 783(4): CTA 2010, s. 879(1), (2).
S. 783(5): CTA 2010, s. 879(3).
S. 783(6): CTA 2010, s. 880(4), (5).
S. 783(7): CTA 2010, s. 880(6), (7), (8).
S. 783(8): CTA 2010, s. 880(2), (3).
S. 783(9): CTA 2010, s. 881(1), (2), (3).
S. 783(10): CTA 2010, s. 882(2), (3), (4), (5), (6), (7).
S. 783(11): CTA 2010, s. 882(7), 1176(2).
S. 783 rewritten for income tax purposes as follows:
S. 783(1), (2), (3), (4), (5), (6), (7), (8), (9), (10), (11): TIOPA 2010, Sch. 4, para. 5.

784 Leased assets subject to hire-purchase agreements

784 [Omitted by CTA 2010, s. 1177 and Sch. 1, para. 106 and repealed by CTA 2010, s. 1181 and Sch. 3, Pt. 2; also omitted by TIOPA 2010, s. 374 and Sch. 8, para. 242 and repealed by TIOPA 2010, s. 378 and Sch. 10, Pt. 9.]

History – S. 784 omitted by CTA 2010, s. 1177 and Sch. 1, para. 106 and repealed by CTA 2010, s. 1181 and Sch. 3, Pt. 2, with effect for corporation tax purposes for accounting periods ending on or after 1 April 2010. S. 784 also omitted by TIOPA 2010, s. 374 and Sch. 8, para. 242 and repealed by TIOPA 2010, s. 378 and Sch. 10, Pt. 9 with effect for corporation tax purposes for accounting periods ending on or after 1 April 2010, for income tax and capital gains tax purposes for the tax year 2010–11 and subsequent tax years, and for petroleum revenue tax purposes for chargeable periods beginning on or after 1 July 2010.

Notes – S. 784 rewritten for corporation tax purposes as follows:
S. 784(1): CTA 2010, s. 875(1), (4).
S. 784(2): CTA 2010, s. 875(2).
S. 784(3): CTA 2010, s. 875(3).
S. 784(4): CTA 2010, s. 875(5).
S. 784(5): CTA 2010, s. 875(6), (7), (8).
S. 784(6): CTA 2010, s. 1129(1), (2), (3), (4), (5), (6).
S. 784 rewritten for income tax purposes as follows:
S. 784(1), (2), (3), (4), (5): TIOPA 2010, Sch. 4, para. 5.
S. 784(6): TIOPA 2010, Sch. 8, para. 257.

785 Meaning of "asset", "capital sum" and "lease" for purposes of sections 781 to 784

785 [Omitted by CTA 2010, s. 1177 and Sch. 1, para. 106 and repealed by CTA 2010, s. 1181 and Sch. 3, Pt. 2; also omitted by TIOPA 2010, s. 374 and Sch. 8, para. 242 and repealed by TIOPA 2010, s. 378 and Sch. 10, Pt. 9.]

History – S. 785 omitted by CTA 2010, s. 1177 and Sch. 1, para. 106 and repealed by CTA 2010, s. 1181 and Sch. 3, Pt. 2, with effect for corporation tax purposes for accounting periods ending on or after 1 April 2010. S. 784 also omitted by TIOPA 2010, s. 374 and Sch. 8, para. 242 and repealed by TIOPA 2010, s. 378 and Sch. 10, Pt. 9, with effect for corporation tax purposes for accounting periods ending on or after 1 April 2010, for income tax and capital gains tax purposes for the tax year 2010–11 and subsequent tax years, and for petroleum revenue tax purposes for chargeable periods beginning on or after 1 July 2010.

Notes – S. 785 rewritten for corporation tax purposes as follows:
S. 785: CTA 2010, s. 868(2), (3), 869, 883, 884(2), (3), 885.
S. 785 rewritten for income tax purposes as follows:
S. 785: TIOPA 2010, Sch. 4, para. 4, 5. Reference to woodland not rewritten as obsolete.

785ZA Restrictions on use of losses: leasing partnerships

785ZA [Omitted by CTA 2010, s. 1177 and Sch. 1, para. 107 and repealed by CTA 2010, s. 1181 and Sch. 3, Pt. 1.]

History – S. 785ZA omitted by CTA 2010, s. 1177 and Sch. 1, para. 107 and repealed by CTA 2010, s. 1181 and Sch. 3, Pt. 1, with effect for corporation tax purposes for accounting periods ending on or after 1 April 2010, and for income and capital gains tax purposes for the tax year 2010–11 and subsequent tax years.

Notes – S. 785ZA rewritten for corporation tax purposes as follows:
S. 785ZA(1): CTA 2010, s. 887(1).
S. 785ZA(2): CTA 2010, s. 887(2).
S. 785ZA(3): CTA 2010, s. 887(3).
S. 785ZA(4): CTA 2010, s. 887(4).
S. 785ZA(5): CTA 2010, s. 888(1).
S. 785ZA(6): CTA 2010, s. 888(2).
S. 785ZA(7): CTA 2010, s. 888(3).
S. 785ZA(8): CTA 2010, s. 888(4).
S. 785ZA(9): CTA 2010, s. 888(5).

785ZB Section 785ZA: definitions

785ZB [Omitted by CTA 2010, s. 1177 and Sch. 1, para. 108 and repealed by CTA 2010, s. 1181 and Sch. 3, Pt. 1.]

History – S. 785ZB omitted by CTA 2010, s. 1177 and Sch. 1, para. 108 and repealed by CTA 2010, s. 1181 and Sch. 3, Pt. 1, with effect for corporation tax purposes for accounting periods ending on or after 1 April 2010, and for income and capital gains tax purposes for the tax year 2010–11 and subsequent tax years.

Notes – S. 785ZB rewritten for corporation tax purposes as follows:
S. 785ZB(1): CTA 2010, s. 887(5), 888(6), 889(1).
S. 785ZB(2): CTA 2010, s. 887(5).
S. 785ZB(3): CTA 2010, s. 889(1).
S. 785ZB(4): CTA 2010, s. 889(1).
S. 785ZB(5): CTA 2010, s. 889(1).
S. 785ZB(6): CTA 2010, s. 889(1).
S. 785ZB(7): CTA 2010, s. 888(6).
S. 785ZB(8): CTA 2010, s. 888(6).

785A Rent factoring of leases of plant or machinery

785A [Omitted by FA 2009, s. 49 and Sch. 25, para. 9(1)(c).]

History – S. 785A omitted by FA 2009, s. 49 and Sch. 25, para. 9(1)(c), with effect in relation to transfers on or after 22 April 2009.

785B Plant and machinery leases: capital receipts to be treated as income

785B [Omitted by CTA 2010, s. 1177 and Sch. 1, para. 109 and repealed by CTA 2010, s. 1181 and Sch. 3, Pt. 1.]

History – S. 785B omitted by CTA 2010, s. 1177 and Sch. 1, para. 109 and repealed by CTA 2010, s. 1181 and Sch. 3, Pt. 1, with effect for corporation tax purposes for accounting periods ending on or after 1 April 2010, and for income and capital gains tax purposes for the tax year 2010–11 and subsequent tax years.

Notes – S. 785B rewritten for corporation tax purposes as follows:
S. 785B(1): CTA 2010, s. 890(1).
S. 785B(2): CTA 2010, s. 890(2).
S. 785B(3): CTA 2010, s. 890(3), (4).

785C Section 785B: interpretation

785C [Omitted by CTA 2010, s. 1177 and Sch. 1, para. 110 and repealed by CTA 2010, s. 1181 and Sch. 3, Pt. 1.]

History – S. 785C omitted by CTA 2010, s. 1177 and Sch. 1, para. 110 and repealed by CTA 2010, s. 1181 and Sch. 3, Pt. 1, with effect for corporation tax purposes for accounting periods ending on or after 1 April 2010, and for income and capital gains tax purposes for the tax year 2010–11 and subsequent tax years.

Notes – S. 785C rewritten for corporation tax purposes as follows:
S. 785C(1): CTA 2010, s. 894(1).
S. 785C(2): CTA 2010, s. 893(2).
S. 785C(3): CTA 2010, s. 894(2).
S. 785C(4): CTA 2010, s. 894(3), (4), (5).
S. 785C(5): CTA 2010, s. 894(6), (7).
S. 785C(6): CTA 2010, s. 893(3).
S. 785C(7): CTA 2010, s. 893(4).
S. 785C(8): CTA 2010, s. 893(5).
S. 785C(9): CTA 2010, s. 893(6).
S. 785C(9A): CTA 2010, s. 893(7).
S. 785C(9B): CTA 2010, s. 893(7).
S. 785C(10): CTA 2010, s. 893(8), (9).

785D Section 785B: lease of plant and machinery and other property

785D [Omitted by CTA 2010, s. 1177 and Sch. 1, para. 111 and repealed by CTA 2010, s. 1181 and Sch. 3, Pt. 1.]

History – S. 785D omitted by CTA 2010, s. 1177 and Sch. 1, para. 111 and repealed by CTA 2010, s. 1181 and Sch. 3, Pt. 1, with effect for corporation tax purposes for accounting periods ending on or after 1 April 2010, and for income and capital gains tax purposes for the tax year 2010–11 and subsequent tax years.

Notes – S. 785D rewritten for corporation tax purposes as follows:
S. 785D(1): CTA 2010, s. 891(1).
S. 785D(2): CTA 2010, s. 891(2).
S. 785D(3): CTA 2010, s. 891(3).
S. 785D(4): CTA 2010, s. 891(4).

785E Section 785B: expectation that relevant capital payment will not be paid

785E [Omitted by CTA 2010, s. 1177 and Sch. 1, para. 112 and repealed by CTA 2010, s. 1181 and Sch. 3, Pt. 1.]

History – S. 785E omitted by CTA 2010, s. 1177 and Sch. 1, para. 112 and repealed by CTA 2010, s. 1181 and Sch. 3, Pt. 1, with effect for corporation tax purposes for accounting periods ending on or after 1 April 2010, and for income and capital gains tax purposes for the tax year 2010–11 and subsequent tax years.

Notes – S. 785E rewritten for corporation tax purposes as follows:
S. 785E(1): CTA 2010, s. 892(1).
S. 785E(2): CTA 2010, s. 892(2).
S. 785E(3): CTA 2010, s. 892(3).
S. 785E(4): CTA 2010, s. 892(4).

786 Transactions associated with loans or credit

786 [Omitted by CTA 2010, s. 1177 and Sch. 1, para. 113 and repealed by CTA 2010, s. 1181 and Sch. 3, Pt. 2; also omitted by TIOPA 2010, s. 374 and Sch. 8, para. 266 and repealed by TIOPA 2010, s. 378 and Sch. 10, Pt. 10.]

History – S. 786 omitted by CTA 2010, s. 1177 and Sch. 1, para. 113 and repealed by CTA 2010, s. 1181 and Sch. 3, Pt. 2, with effect for corporation tax purposes for accounting periods ending on or after 1 April 2010. S. 786 also omitted by TIOPA 2010, s. 374 and Sch. 8, para. 266 and repealed by TIOPA 2010, s. 378 and Sch. 10, Pt. 10, with effect for corporation tax purposes for accounting periods ending on or after 1 April 2010, for income tax and capital gains tax purposes for the tax year 2010–11 and subsequent tax years, and for petroleum revenue tax purposes for chargeable periods beginning on or after 1 July 2010.

Notes – S. 786 rewritten for corporation tax as follows:
S. 786(1): CTA 2010, s. 777(2), (3).
S. 786(2): CTA 2010, s. 777(4), (5).
S. 786(3): CTA 2010, s. 778(1), (2).
S. 786(3A): CTA 2010, s. 778(1).
S. 786(5): CTA 2010, s. 779(1), (2), (3), (4).
S. 786(5ZA): CTA 2010, s. 779(1), (4).
S. 786(6): CTA 2010, s. 779(5), (6).
S. 786(7): CTA 2010, s. 779(7).
S. 786(8): CTA 2010, s. 1176(1).
S. 786 rewritten for income tax purposes as follows:
S. 786(1), (2), (3), (3A), (5), (5ZA), (5A), (6), (7), (8): TIOPA 2010, Sch. 5, para. 7.

787 Restriction of relief for payments of interest

787 [Omitted by TIOPA 2010, s. 371 and Sch. 7, para. 49 and repealed by TIOPA 2010, s. 378 and Sch. 10, Pt. 12.]

History – S. 787 omitted by TIOPA 2010, s. 371 and Sch. 7, para. 49 and repealed by TIOPA 2010, s. 378 and Sch. 10, Part 12, with effect for corporation tax purposes for accounting periods ending on or after 1 April 2010, for income tax and capital gains tax purposes for the tax year 2010-11 and subsequent tax years, and for petroleum revenue tax purposes for chargeable periods beginning on or after 1 July 2010.

Notes – S. 787 rewritten as follows:
S. 787(1A): CTA 2009, s. 443(1), (2), (3), (4).
S. 787(3): CTA 2009, s. 443(5), (6).
S. 787 rewritten for income tax purposes as follows:
S. 787(1), (2): TIOPA 2010, Sch. 7, para. 52.

PART XVIII – DOUBLE TAXATION RELIEF

Cross references – FA 1996, s. 91F(2): where the Treasury add, remove or vary a "Condition" for purposes of FA 1996, s. 91B(6)(b), the Treasury may amend also ICTA 1988, Part XVIII by way of regulations.
FA 2009, s. 56: Pt. XVIII applies in relation to MEPs' pay, allowances and pensions under European Parliament Statute as if the pay etc. were payable under the law of a territory outside the UK.

sChapter I – The Principal Reliefs

Cross references – FA 2004, Pt. 3, Ch. 7: double taxation relief in respect of "special withholding tax" (as defined at FA 2004, s. 107(3)). Double taxation relief under this Chapter is not available in respect of such withholding tax and credit under this Chapter against income tax or capital gains tax is given in priority to credit for special withholding tax.

788 Relief by agreement with other territories

788 [Omitted by TIOPA 2010, s. 374 and Sch. 8, para. 13 and repealed by TIOPA 2010, s. 378 and Sch. 10, Pt. 1.]

History – S. 788 omitted by TIOPA 2010, s. 374 and Sch. 8, para. 13 and repealed by TIOPA 2010, s. 378 and Sch. 10, Pt. 1, with effect for corporation tax purposes for accounting periods ending on or after 1 April 2010, for income tax and capital gains tax purposes for the tax year 2010–11 and subsequent tax years, and for petroleum revenue tax purposes for chargeable periods beginning on or after 1 July 2010, subject to saving provisions in TIOPA 2010, Sch. 9, para. 26.

Notes – S. 788 rewritten for income tax purposes as follows:
S. 788(1): TIOPA 2010, s. 2(1), (2), (3).
S. 788(3): TIOPA 2010, s. 6(1), (2), (3), (4).
S. 788(4): TIOPA 2010, s. 18(1), (3).
S. 788(5): TIOPA 2010, s. 4(1), (2), (3), 20(1), (2), (3), (4), (5), (6), (7).
S. 788(6): TIOPA 2010, s. 6(6).
S. 788(7): TIOPA 2010, s. 134(1), (3), (4), (5), (6).
S. 788(8): TIOPA 2010, s. 3(1), (2).
S. 788(9): TIOPA 2010, s. 5(1).
S. 788(10): TIOPA 2010, s. 5(2).

789 Arrangements made under old law

789 [Omitted by TIOPA 2010, s. 374 and Sch. 8, para. 14 and repealed by TIOPA 2010, s. 378 and Sch. 10, Pt. 1.]

History – S. 789 omitted by TIOPA 2010, s. 374 and Sch. 8, para. 14 and repealed by TIOPA 2010, s. 378 and Sch. 10, Pt. 1, with effect for corporation tax purposes for accounting periods ending on or after 1 April 2010, for income tax and capital gains tax purposes for the tax year 2010–11 and subsequent tax years, and for petroleum revenue tax purposes for chargeable periods beginning on or after 1 July 2010.

Notes – S. 789 rewritten for income tax purposes as follows:
S. 789(1): TIOPA 2010, Sch. 9, para. 11(1), (2), (3), (4).
S. 789(3): Not rewritten as unnecessary.

790 Unilateral relief

790 [Omitted by TIOPA 2010, s. 374 and Sch. 8, para. 15 and repealed by TIOPA 2010, s. 378 and Sch. 10, Pt. 1.]

History – S. 790 omitted by TIOPA 2010, s. 374 and Sch. 8, para. 15 and repealed by TIOPA 2010, s. 378 and Sch. 10, Pt. 1, with effect for corporation tax purposes for accounting periods ending on or after 1 April 2010, for income tax and capital gains tax purposes for the tax year 2010–11 and subsequent tax years, and for petroleum revenue tax purposes for chargeable periods beginning on or after 1 July 2010, subject to saving provisions in TIOPA 2010, Sch. 9, para. 26.

Notes – S. 790 rewritten for income tax purposes as follows:
S. 790(1): TIOPA 2010, s. 18(1), (3).
S. 790(2): Not rewritten as unnecessary.
S. 790(3): TIOPA 2010, s. 8(1), 18(1), (3), 41(5).
S. 790(4): TIOPA 2010, s. 9(1), (2), (3).
S. 790(5): TIOPA 2010, s. 9(7), (8), 10(4), 11(1), 12(1), 13(1), (2), 14(1), (2), 15(1), (2), 16(1), (2).
S. 790(6): TIOPA 2010, s. 12(2), 14(2), (3), (4), (5), 15(2), (3), (4), (5), (6), (10), 16(2), (3), (4), (5), (6), (10), Sch. 9, para. 14(1), (2), 16(1), (2).
S. 790(6A): TIOPA 2010, s. 14(3), 15(3), 16(3).
S. 790(7): TIOPA 2010, s. 15(6), 16(6).
S. 790(8): TIOPA 2010, s. 15(6), (7), (8), (10), 16(6), (7), (8), (10).

S. 790(9): TIOPA 2010, s. 15(9), 16(9).
S. 790(10): TIOPA 2010, s. 12(3), (4).
S. 790(10A): TIOPA 2010, s. 17(1).
S. 790(10B): TIOPA 2010, s. 17(2), (3).
S. 790(10C): TIOPA 2010, s. 17(4), (5).
S. 790(11): TIOPA 2010, s. 134(2), (3), (4), (5), (6).
S. 790(12): TIOPA 2010, s. 8(2), (3), 9(1), (2), (4), (5), (6), 29(2), (4), 30(3), (4), 129(3), (4).

791 Power to make regulations for carrying out section 788

791 [Omitted by TIOPA 2010, s. 374 and Sch. 8, para. 16 and repealed by TIOPA 2010, s. 378 and Sch. 10, Pt. 1.]

History – S. 791 omitted by TIOPA 2010, s. 374 and Sch. 8, para. 16 and repealed by TIOPA 2010, s. 378 and Sch. 10, Pt. 1, with effect for corporation tax purposes for accounting periods ending on or after 1 April 2010, for income tax and capital gains tax purposes for the tax year 2010–11 and subsequent tax years, and for petroleum revenue tax purposes for chargeable periods beginning on or after 1 July 2010.

Notes – S. 791 rewritten for income tax purposes as follows:
S. 791: TIOPA 2010, s. 7(1), (2), (3), (4), (5).

Chapter II – Rules Governing Relief by Way of Credit

GENERAL

792 Interpretation of credit code

792 [Omitted by TIOPA 2010, s. 374 and Sch. 8, para. 17 and repealed by TIOPA 2010, s. 378 and Sch. 10, Pt. 1.]

History – S. 792 omitted by TIOPA 2010, s. 374 and Sch. 8, para. 17 and repealed by TIOPA 2010, s. 378 and Sch. 10, Pt. 1, with effect for corporation tax purposes for accounting periods ending on or after 1 April 2010, for income tax and capital gains tax purposes for the tax year 2010–11 and subsequent tax years, and for petroleum revenue tax purposes for chargeable periods beginning on or after 1 July 2010, subject to saving provisions in TIOPA 2010, Sch. 9, para. 26.

Notes – S. 792 rewritten for income tax purposes as follows:
S. 792(1): TIOPA 2010, s. 18(1), 21(1), (2), 26(1), 27, 28(5), 30(6).
S. 792(2): TIOPA 2010, s. 63(6), 64(7), 68(8), 70(4), 71(5).
S. 792(3): TIOPA 2010, s. 18(3), 21(1).

793 Reduction of United Kingdom taxes by amount of credit due

793 [Omitted by TIOPA 2010, s. 374 and Sch. 8, para. 17 and repealed by TIOPA 2010, s. 378 and Sch. 10, Pt. 1.]

History – S. 793 omitted by TIOPA 2010, s. 374 and Sch. 8, para. 17 and repealed by TIOPA 2010, s. 378 and Sch. 10, Pt. 1, with effect for corporation tax purposes for accounting periods ending on or after 1 April 2010, for income tax and capital gains tax purposes for the tax year 2010–11 and subsequent tax years, and for petroleum revenue tax purposes for chargeable periods beginning on or after 1 July 2010.

Notes – S. 793 rewritten for income tax purposes as follows:
S. 793(1): TIOPA 2010, s. 18(1), (2), (4).
S. 793(2): TIOPA 2010, s. 18(5).
S. 793(3): TIOPA 2010, s. 18(6).

793A No double relief etc.

793A [Omitted by TIOPA 2010, s. 374 and Sch. 8, para. 17 and repealed by TIOPA 2010, s. 378 and Sch. 10, Pt. 1.]

History – S. 793A omitted by TIOPA 2010, s. 374 and Sch. 8, para. 17 and repealed by TIOPA 2010, s. 378 and Sch. 10, Pt. 1, with effect for corporation tax purposes for accounting periods ending on or after 1 April 2010, for income tax and capital gains tax purposes for the tax year 2010–11 and subsequent tax years, and for petroleum revenue tax purposes for chargeable periods beginning on or after 1 July 2010.

Notes – S. 793A rewritten for income tax purposes as follows:
S. 793A(1): TIOPA 2010, s. 25(1), (2).
S. 793A(2): TIOPA 2010, s. 9(8), 10(4), 11(2).
S. 793A(3): TIOPA 2010, s. 9(8), 10(4), 11(3).

794 Requirement as to residence

794 [Omitted by TIOPA 2010, s. 374 and Sch. 8, para. 17 and repealed by TIOPA 2010, s. 378 and Sch. 10, Pt. 1.]

History – S. 794 omitted by TIOPA 2010, s. 374 and Sch. 8, para. 17 and repealed by TIOPA 2010, s. 378 and Sch. 10, Pt. 1, with effect for corporation tax purposes for accounting periods ending on or after 1 April 2010, for income tax and capital gains tax purposes for the tax year 2010–11 and subsequent tax years, and for petroleum revenue tax purposes for chargeable periods beginning on or after 1 July 2010.

Notes – S. 794 rewritten for income tax purposes as follows:
S. 794(1): TIOPA 2010, s. 26(1), (2).
S. 794(2): TIOPA 2010, s. 28(1), (2), (3), (4), 29(1), (2), (3), (4), 30(1), (2), (3), (4), (5).

795 Computation of income subject to foreign tax

795 [Omitted by TIOPA 2010, s. 374 and Sch. 8, para. 17 and repealed by TIOPA 2010, s. 378 and Sch. 10, Pt. 1.]

History – S. 795 omitted by TIOPA 2010, s. 374 and Sch. 8, para. 17 and repealed by TIOPA 2010, s. 378 and Sch. 10, Pt. 1, with effect for corporation tax purposes for accounting periods ending on or after 1 April 2010, for income tax and capital gains tax purposes for the tax year 2010–11 and subsequent tax years, and for petroleum revenue tax purposes for chargeable periods beginning on or after 1 July 2010.

Notes – S. 795 rewritten for income tax purposes as follows:
S. 795(1): TIOPA 2010, s. 32(1), (2).
S. 795(2): TIOPA 2010, s. 31(1), (2), (3).
S. 795(3): TIOPA 2010, 31(4), 32(5).
S. 795(3A): TIOPA 2010, Sch. 9, para. 16.
S. 795(4): TIOPA 2010, 31(5).
S. 795(5): TIOPA 2010, 31(6), 32(6).

795A Limits on credit: minimisation of the foreign tax

795A [Omitted by TIOPA 2010, s. 374 and Sch. 8, para. 17 and repealed by TIOPA 2010, s. 378 and Sch. 10, Pt. 1.]

History – S. 795A omitted by TIOPA 2010, s. 374 and Sch. 8, para. 17 and repealed by TIOPA 2010, s. 378 and Sch. 10, Pt. 1, with effect for corporation tax purposes for accounting periods ending on or after 1 April 2010, for income tax and capital gains tax purposes for the tax year 2010–11 and subsequent tax years, and for petroleum revenue tax purposes for chargeable periods beginning on or after 1 July 2010.

Notes – S. 795A rewritten for income tax purposes as follows:
S. 795A(1): TIOPA 2010, s. 33(1).
S. 795A(2): TIOPA 2010, s. 33(2).
S. 795A(3): TIOPA 2010, s. 33(3).

796 Limits on credit: income tax

796 [Omitted by TIOPA 2010, s. 374 and Sch. 8, para. 17 and repealed by TIOPA 2010, s. 378 and Sch. 10, Pt. 1.]

History – S. 796 omitted by TIOPA 2010, s. 374 and Sch. 8, para. 17 and repealed by TIOPA 2010, s. 378 and Sch. 10, Pt. 1, with effect for corporation tax purposes for accounting periods ending on or after 1 April 2010, for income tax and capital gains tax purposes for the tax year 2010–11 and subsequent tax years, and for petroleum revenue tax purposes for chargeable periods beginning on or after 1 July 2010.

Notes – S. 796 rewritten for income tax purposes as follows:
S. 796(1): TIOPA 2010, s. 36(1), (2), 36(4), (5), 40(1), (2), (4), (5).
S. 796(2): TIOPA 2010, s. 36(2), (3), (4), 40(2), (3), (4).
S. 796(2A): TIOPA 2010, s. 36(6).
S. 796(3): TIOPA 2010, s. 41(1), (2), (4), (5).

797 Limits on credit: corporation tax

797 [Omitted by TIOPA 2010, s. 374 and Sch. 8, para. 17 and repealed by TIOPA 2010, s. 378 and Sch. 10, Pt. 1.]

History – S. 797 omitted by TIOPA 2010, s. 374 and Sch. 8, para. 17 and repealed by TIOPA 2010, s. 378 and Sch. 10, Pt. 1, with effect for corporation tax purposes for accounting periods ending on or after 1 April 2010, for income tax and capital gains tax purposes for the tax year 2010–11 and subsequent tax years, and for petroleum revenue tax purposes for chargeable periods beginning on or after 1 July 2010.

Notes – S. 797 rewritten for income tax purposes as follows:
S. 797(1): TIOPA 2010, s. 42(1), (2).
S. 797(2): TIOPA 2010, s. 42(2), (3), (4).
S. 797(2A): TIOPA 2010, s. 43(1), (2).
S. 797(3): TIOPA 2010, s. 42(3), 52(1), (2), 54(2), 56(2).
S. 797(3A): TIOPA 2010, s. 42(3), 55(1), (2), (3), (4), (5).
S. 797(3B): TIOPA 2010, s. 42(3), 53(1), (2).
S. 797(6): TIOPA 2010, s. 53(3).

797A Foreign tax on items giving rise to a non-trading credit: loan relationships

797A [Omitted by TIOPA 2010, s. 374 and Sch. 8, para. 17 and repealed by TIOPA 2010, s. 378 and Sch. 10, Pt. 1.]

History – S. 797A omitted by TIOPA 2010, s. 374 and Sch. 8, para. 17 and repealed by TIOPA 2010, s. 378 and Sch. 10, Pt. 1, with effect for corporation tax purposes for accounting periods ending on or after 1 April 2010, for income tax and capital gains tax purposes for the tax year 2010–11 and subsequent tax years, and for petroleum revenue tax purposes for chargeable periods beginning on or after 1 July 2010.

Notes – S. 797A rewritten for income tax purposes as follows:
S. 797A(1): TIOPA 2010, s. 50(1), (3), (4), 54(1), (3), (6), (7), 55(2), (3), (6).
S. 797A(2): TIOPA 2010, s. 50(2), (4).
S. 797A(3): TIOPA 2010, s. 42(3), 54(2).
S. 797A(4): TIOPA 2010, s. 54(2), (7).
S. 797A(5): TIOPA 2010, s. 54(2), (5), (7).

S. 797A(6): TIOPA 2010, s. 42(3), 53(1), (2).
S. 797A(7): TIOPA 2010, s. 42(3), 54(3), (4), (5).
S. 797A(8): TIOPA 2010, s. 53(3).

797B Foreign tax on items giving rise to a non-trading credit: intangible fixed assets

797B [Omitted by TIOPA 2010, s. 374 and Sch. 8, para. 17 and repealed by TIOPA 2010, s. 378 and Sch. 10, Pt. 1.]

History – S. 797B omitted by TIOPA 2010, s. 374 and Sch. 8, para. 17 and repealed by TIOPA 2010, s. 378 and Sch. 10, Pt. 1, with effect for corporation tax purposes for accounting periods ending on or after 1 April 2010, for income tax and capital gains tax purposes for the tax year 2010–11 and subsequent tax years, and for petroleum revenue tax purposes for chargeable periods beginning on or after 1 July 2010.

Notes – S. 797B rewritten for income tax purposes as follows:
S. 797B(1): TIOPA 2010, s. 51(1), (3), (4), 56(4), (5).
S. 797B(2): TIOPA 2010, s. 51(2).
S. 797B(3): TIOPA 2010, s. 42(3), 56(1), (2).
S. 797B(4): TIOPA 2010, s. 56(3), (5).

798 Section 796: trade income

798 [Omitted by TIOPA 2010, s. 374 and Sch. 8, para. 17 and repealed by TIOPA 2010, s. 378 and Sch. 10, Pt. 1.]

History – S. 798 omitted by TIOPA 2010, s. 374 and Sch. 8, para. 17 and repealed by TIOPA 2010, s. 378 and Sch. 10, Pt. 1, with effect for corporation tax purposes for accounting periods ending on or after 1 April 2010, for income tax and capital gains tax purposes for the tax year 2010–11 and subsequent tax years, and for petroleum revenue tax purposes for chargeable periods beginning on or after 1 July 2010.

Notes – S. 798 rewritten for income tax purposes as follows:
S. 798(1): TIOPA 2010, s. 37(1).
S. 798(1A): TIOPA 2010, s. 37(2), (3), (4), (5), (6).
S. 798(2): TIOPA 2010, s. 37(4).
S. 798(3): TIOPA 2010, s. 37(6).
S. 798(4): TIOPA 2010, s. 38(1), (2), (3).
S. 798(5): TIOPA 2010, s. 37(7). S. 798(5)(c) not rewritten: spent.

798A Section 797: trade income

798A [Omitted by TIOPA 2010, s. 374 and Sch. 8, para. 17 and repealed by TIOPA 2010, s. 378 and Sch. 10, Pt. 1.]

History – S. 798A omitted by TIOPA 2010, s. 374 and Sch. 8, para. 17 and repealed by TIOPA 2010, s. 378 and Sch. 10, Pt. 1, with effect for corporation tax purposes for accounting periods ending on or after 1 April 2010, for income tax and capital gains tax purposes for the tax year 2010–11 and subsequent tax years, and for petroleum revenue tax purposes for chargeable periods beginning on or after 1 July 2010.

Notes – S. 798A rewritten for income tax purposes as follows:
S. 798A(1): TIOPA 2010, s. 44(1).
S. 798A(2): TIOPA 2010, s. 44(2). References to gains in s. 798A(2) and (3) not rewritten as unnecessary (they refer to chargeable gains which are not trade income).
S. 798A(3): TIOPA 2010, s. 44(3), (4), (5).
S. 798A(3A): TIOPA 2010, s. 44(3), 49(1).
S. 798A(3B): TIOPA 2010, s. 49(2).
S. 798A(3C): TIOPA 2010, s. 49(3), (4).
S. 798A(4): TIOPA 2010, s. 44(6).
S. 798A(5): TIOPA 2010, s. 44(7).

798B Section 798A: special cases

798B [Omitted by TIOPA 2010, s. 374 and Sch. 8, para. 17 and repealed by TIOPA 2010, s. 378 and Sch. 10, Pt. 1.]

History – S. 798B omitted by TIOPA 2010, s. 374 and Sch. 8, para. 17 and repealed by TIOPA 2010, s. 378 and Sch. 10, Pt. 1, with effect for corporation tax purposes for accounting periods ending on or after 1 April 2010, for income tax and capital gains tax purposes for the tax year 2010–11 and subsequent tax years, and for petroleum revenue tax purposes for chargeable periods beginning on or after 1 July 2010.

Notes – S. 798B rewritten for income tax purposes as follows:
S. 798B(1): TIOPA 2010, s. 46(1), (2).
S. 798B(2): TIOPA 2010, s. 46(3), (4).
S. 798B(3): TIOPA 2010, s. 47(1), (2), (3).
S. 798B(4): TIOPA 2010, s. 45(1).
S. 798B(4A): TIOPA 2010, s. 45(2).
S. 798B(4B): TIOPA 2010, s. 45(3).
S. 798B(4C): TIOPA 2010, s. 45(4), (5), (6).
S. 798B(5): TIOPA 2010, s. 48(1), (2), (3), (4), (5).

798C Disallowed credit: use as a deduction

798C [Omitted by TIOPA 2010, s. 374 and Sch. 8, para. 17 and repealed by TIOPA 2010, s. 378 and Sch. 10, Pt. 1.]

History – S. 798C omitted by TIOPA 2010, s. 374 and Sch. 8, para. 17 and repealed by TIOPA 2010, s. 378 and Sch. 10, Pt. 1, with effect for corporation tax purposes for accounting periods ending on or after 1 April 2010, for income tax and capital gains tax purposes for the tax year 2010–11 and subsequent tax years, and for petroleum revenue tax purposes for chargeable periods beginning on or after 1 July 2010.

Notes – S. 798C rewritten for income tax purposes as follows:
S. 798C(1): TIOPA 2010, s. 35(1), (3).
S. 798C(2): TIOPA 2010, s. 35(2), (4).
S. 798C(3): TIOPA 2010, s. 35(5).
S. 798C(4): TIOPA 2010, s. 35(6).

TAX UNDERLYING DIVIDENDS

799 Computation of underlying tax

799 [Omitted by TIOPA 2010, s. 374 and Sch. 8, para. 18 and repealed by TIOPA 2010, s. 378 and Sch. 10, Pt. 1.]

History – S. 799 omitted by TIOPA 2010, s. 374 and Sch. 8, para. 18 and repealed by TIOPA 2010, s. 378 and Sch. 10, Pt. 1, with effect for corporation tax purposes for accounting periods ending on or after 1 April 2010, for income tax and capital gains tax purposes for the tax year 2010–11 and subsequent tax years, and for petroleum revenue tax purposes for chargeable periods beginning on or after 1 July 2010.

Notes – S. 799 rewritten for income tax purposes as follows:
S. 799(1): TIOPA 2010, s. 57(1), (2), 58(1), 61.
S. 799(1A): TIOPA 2010, s. 57(2), 58(1).
S. 799(1B): TIOPA 2010, s. 60(1), (2), (3).
S. 799(2): TIOPA 2010, s. 57(2), 58(1), 61.
S. 799(2A): TIOPA 2010, s. 57(3).
S. 799(3): TIOPA 2010, s. 59(1), (2), (3), (4), (5), 62(1), (2), (3), (4).
S. 799(3A): TIOPA 2010, s. 59(2), (3).
S. 799(4): TIOPA 2010, s. 59(4), (5), (6), (7), 62(2), (4), (5), (6), (7).
S. 799(5): TIOPA 2010, s. 59(4), (5).
S. 799(6): TIOPA 2010, s. 59(8).
S. 799(7): TIOPA 2010, s. 59(8).

800 Dividends paid between related companies but not covered by arrangements

800 [Repealed by FA 2000, s. 103 and Sch. 30, para. 10, s. 156 and Sch. 40, Pt. II(13), with effect in relation to dividends paid on or after 1 April 2000.]

801 Dividends paid between related companies: relief for UK and third country taxes

801 [Omitted by TIOPA 2010, s. 374 and Sch. 8, para. 18 and repealed by TIOPA 2010, s. 378 and Sch. 10, Pt. 1.]

History – S. 801 omitted by TIOPA 2010, s. 374 and Sch. 8, para. 18 and repealed by TIOPA 2010, s. 378 and Sch. 10, Pt. 1, with effect for corporation tax purposes for accounting periods ending on or after 1 April 2010, for income tax and capital gains tax purposes for the tax year 2010–11 and subsequent tax years, and for petroleum revenue tax purposes for chargeable periods beginning on or after 1 July 2010.

Notes – S. 801 rewritten for income tax purposes as follows:
S. 801(1): TIOPA 2010, s. 63(1), (5), 64(1), (2), 65(2).
S. 801(1A): TIOPA 2010, s. 63(3), (4).
S. 801(2): TIOPA 2010, s. 64(1), (3), (4), (5), 65(1), (2), (3), (4).
S. 801(2A): TIOPA 2010, s. 65(6), (7).
S. 801(3): TIOPA 2010, s. 64(1), (4), (5), (4), (5), 65(1), (2), (3), (4), (6), (7).
S. 801(4): TIOPA 2010, s. 65(4), 66(1), (2), (3).
S. 801(5): TIOPA 2010, s. 63(2), 64(6).
S. 801(5A): TIOPA 2010, s. 64(6), 65(5).

801A Restriction of relief for underlying tax

801A [Omitted by TIOPA 2010, s. 374 and Sch. 8, para. 18 and repealed by TIOPA 2010, s. 378 and Sch. 10, Pt. 1.]

History – S. 801A omitted by TIOPA 2010, s. 374 and Sch. 8, para. 18 and repealed by TIOPA 2010, s. 378 and Sch. 10, Part 1, with effect for corporation tax purposes for accounting periods ending on or after 1 April 2010, for income tax and capital gains tax purposes for the tax year 2010-11 and subsequent tax years, and for petroleum revenue tax purposes for chargeable periods beginning on or after 1 July 2010.

Notes – S. 801A rewritten for income tax purposes as follows:
S. 801A(1): TIOPA 2010, s. 67(1), (2), (3), (4), (5).
S. 801A(2): TIOPA 2010, s. 67(6).
S. 801A(3): TIOPA 2010, s. 67(7).
S. 801A(4): TIOPA 2010, s. 67(7).
S. 801A(5): TIOPA 2010, s. 67(8).
S. 801A(6): TIOPA 2010, s. 68(1), (2).
S. 801A(7): TIOPA 2010, s. 68(1), (3), (4).
S. 801A(8): TIOPA 2010, s. 68(9).
S. 801A(9): TIOPA 2010, s. 68(6).

S. 801A(10): TIOPA 2010, s. 68(5).
S. 801A(11): TIOPA 2010, s. 68(7).

801B Dividends paid out of transferred profits

801B [Omitted by TIOPA 2010, s. 374 and Sch. 8, para. 18 and repealed by TIOPA 2010, s. 378 and Sch. 10, Pt. 1.]

History – S. 801B omitted by TIOPA 2010, s. 374 and Sch. 8, para. 18 and repealed by TIOPA 2010, s. 378 and Sch. 10, Pt. 1, with effect for corporation tax purposes for accounting periods ending on or after 1 April 2010, for income tax and capital gains tax purposes for the tax year 2010–11 and subsequent tax years, and for petroleum revenue tax purposes for chargeable periods beginning on or after 1 July 2010.

Notes – S. 801B rewritten for income tax purposes as follows:
S. 801B(1): TIOPA 2010, s. 69(1).
S. 801B(2): TIOPA 2010, s. 69(2).
S. 801B(3): TIOPA 2010, s. 69(3).

801C Separate streaming of dividend so far as representing an ADP dividend of a CFC

801C [Omitted by FA 2009, s. 36 and Sch. 16, para. 2(4).]

History – S. 801C omitted by FA 2009, s. 36 and Sch. 16, para. 2(4), with effect in relation to accounting periods of controlled foreign companies beginning on or after 1 July 2009, subject to rules for accounting periods straddling 1 July 2009 in FA 2009, Sch. 16, para. 7 and transitional provisions in FA 2009, Sch. 16, para. 8.
Former s. 801C inserted by FA 2000, s. 103 and Sch. 30, para. 13(1), with effect in relation to any claim for an allowance by way of credit made on or after 31 March 2001 in respect of a dividend paid by a company resident outside the United Kingdom to a company resident in the United Kingdom, unless the dividend was paid before that date.

ICTA 1988

802 UK insurance companies trading overseas

802 [Repealed by FA 2000, s. 103 and Sch. 30, para. 14, s. 156 and Sch. 40, Pt. II(13).]

History – S. 802 repealed by FA 2000, s. 103 and Sch. 30, para. 14, s. 156 and Sch. 40, Pt. II(13), with effect in relation to accounting periods beginning on or after 1 April 2000.

803 Underlying tax reflecting interest on loans

803 [Omitted by TIOPA 2010, s. 374 and Sch. 8, para. 19 and repealed by TIOPA 2010, s. 378 and Sch. 10, Pt. 1.]

History – S. 803 omitted by TIOPA 2010, s. 374 and Sch. 8, para. 19 and repealed by TIOPA 2010, s. 378 and Sch. 10, Pt 1, with effect for corporation tax purposes for accounting periods ending on or after 1 April 2010, for income tax and capital gains tax purposes for the tax year 2010–11 and subsequent tax years, and for petroleum revenue tax purposes for chargeable periods beginning on or after 1 July 2010.

Notes – S. 803 rewritten for income tax purposes as follows:
S. 803(1): TIOPA 2010, s. 70(1).
S. 803(2): TIOPA 2010, s. 70(2).
S. 803(3): TIOPA 2010, s. 70(2).
S. 803(10): TIOPA 2010, s. 70(3).

803A Foreign taxation of group as a single entity

803A [Omitted by TIOPA 2010, s. 374 and Sch. 8, para. 19 and repealed by TIOPA 2010, s. 378 and Sch. 10, Pt. 1.]

History – S. 803A omitted by TIOPA 2010, s. 374 and Sch. 8, para. 19 and repealed by TIOPA 2010, s. 378 and Sch. 10, Pt. 1, with effect for corporation tax purposes for accounting periods ending on or after 1 April 2010, for income tax and capital gains tax purposes for the tax year 2010–11 and subsequent tax years, and for petroleum revenue tax purposes for chargeable periods beginning on or after 1 July 2010.

Notes – S. 803A rewritten for income tax purposes as follows:
S. 803A(1): TIOPA 2010, s. 71(1).
S. 803A(2): TIOPA 2010, s. 71(2), (3).
S. 803A(3): TIOPA 2010, s. 71(4).

MISCELLANEOUS RULES

804 Relief against income tax in respect of income arising in years of commencement

804 [Omitted by TIOPA 2010, s. 374 and Sch. 8, para. 19 and repealed by TIOPA 2010, s. 378 and Sch. 10, Pt. 1.]

History – S. 804 omitted by TIOPA 2010, s. 374 and Sch. 8, para. 19 and repealed by TIOPA 2010, s. 378 and Sch. 10, Pt. 1, with effect for corporation tax purposes for accounting periods ending on or after 1 April 2010, for income tax and capital gains tax purposes for the tax year 2010–11 and subsequent tax years, and for petroleum revenue tax purposes for chargeable periods beginning on or after 1 July 2010.

Notes – S. 804 rewritten for income tax purposes as follows:
S. 804(1): TIOPA 2010, s. 22(1), (2).
S. 804(2): TIOPA 2010, s. 22(3).

S. 804(3): TIOPA 2010, s. 22(4), (5), (6).
S. 804(4): TIOPA 2010, s. 22(7).
S. 804(5): TIOPA 2010, s. 24(1).
S. 804(5A): TIOPA 2010, s. 24(2), (3).
S. 804(5B): TIOPA 2010, s. 24(4), (5), (6).
S. 804(5C): TIOPA 2010, s. 24(7).
S. 804(7): TIOPA 2010, s. 23(1), (2), (3).
S. 804(8): TIOPA 2010, s. 22(8), 24(8).

804ZA Schemes and arrangements designed to increase relief

804ZA [Omitted by TIOPA 2010, s. 374 and Sch. 8, para. 19 and repealed by TIOPA 2010, s. 378 and Sch. 10, Pt. 1.]

History – S. 804ZA omitted by TIOPA 2010, s. 374 and Sch. 8, para. 19 and repealed by TIOPA 2010, s. 378 and Sch. 10, Pt. 1, with effect for corporation tax purposes for accounting periods ending on or after 1 April 2010, for income tax and capital gains tax purposes for the tax year 2010–11 and subsequent tax years, and for petroleum revenue tax purposes for chargeable periods beginning on or after 1 July 2010.

Notes – S. 804ZA rewritten for income tax purposes as follows:
S. 804ZA(1): TIOPA 2010, s. 81(1), (2), 82(2).
S. 804ZA(2): TIOPA 2010, s. 82(2).
S. 804ZA(3): TIOPA 2010, s. 82(3).
S. 804ZA(4): TIOPA 2010, s. 82(4).
S. 804ZA(5): TIOPA 2010, s. 82(5).
S. 804ZA(6): TIOPA 2010, s. 82(5), (6), 95(4).
S. 804ZA(7): TIOPA 2010, s. 82(6).
S. 804ZA(8): TIOPA 2010, s. 81(2).
S. 804ZA(9): TIOPA 2010, s. 89(1), (2).
S. 804ZA(10): TIOPA 2010, s. 89(1), (3).
S. 804ZA(11): TIOPA 2010, s. 83(1).
S. 804ZA(11A): TIOPA 2010, s. 81(4), 82(7), 89(4).
S. 804ZA(12): TIOPA 2010, s. 95(4), (8).

804ZB Effect of notice under section 804ZA

804ZB [Omitted by TIOPA 2010, s. 374 and Sch. 8, para. 19 and repealed by TIOPA 2010, s. 378 and Sch. 10, Pt. 1.]

History – S. 804ZB omitted by TIOPA 2010, s. 374 and Sch. 8, para. 19 and repealed by TIOPA 2010, s. 378 and Sch. 10, Pt. 1, with effect for corporation tax purposes for accounting periods ending on or after 1 April 2010, for income tax and capital gains tax purposes for the tax year 2010–11 and subsequent tax years, and for petroleum revenue tax purposes for chargeable periods beginning on or after 1 July 2010.

Notes – S. 804ZB rewritten for income tax purposes as follows:
S. 804ZB(1): TIOPA 2010, s. 90(1).
S. 804ZB(2): TIOPA 2010, s. 90(1), (2).

804ZC Notices under section 804ZA: further provision

804ZC [Omitted by TIOPA 2010, s. 374 and Sch. 8, para. 19 and repealed by TIOPA 2010, s. 378 and Sch. 10, Pt. 1.]

History – S. 804ZC omitted by TIOPA 2010, s. 374 and Sch. 8, para. 19 and repealed by TIOPA 2010, s. 378 and Sch. 10, Pt. 1, with effect for corporation tax purposes for accounting periods ending on or after 1 April 2010, for income tax and capital gains tax purposes for the tax year 2010–11 and subsequent tax years, and for petroleum revenue tax purposes for chargeable periods beginning on or after 1 July 2010.

Notes – S. 804ZC rewritten for income tax purposes as follows:
S. 804ZC(1): TIOPA 2010, s. 91(1).
S. 804ZC(2): TIOPA 2010, s. 91(1), (2).
S. 804ZC(3): TIOPA 2010, s. 92(1), (2).
S. 804ZC(4): TIOPA 2010, s. 92(3).
S. 804ZC(5): TIOPA 2010, s. 92(4).
S. 804ZC(6): TIOPA 2010, s. 92(6), 94(1), (2), (3), (4), (5), (6), (7).
S. 804ZC(7): TIOPA 2010, s. 92(5).
S. 804ZC(8): TIOPA 2010, s. 93(1), (2).
S. 804ZC(9): TIOPA 2010, s. 93(3), (5).
S. 804ZC(10): TIOPA 2010, s. 93(4), (5).
S. 804ZC(11): TIOPA 2010, s. 91(3), 93(6).
S. 804ZC(12): TIOPA 2010, s. 95(3), (6), (7).

804A Life assurance companies with overseas branches etc: restriction of credit.

804A [Omitted by TIOPA 2010, s. 374 and Sch. 8, para. 19 and repealed by TIOPA 2010, s. 378 and Sch. 10, Pt. 1.]

History – S. 804A *omitted by TIOPA 2010*, s. 374 and Sch. 8, para. 19 and repealed by TIOPA 2010, s. 378 and Sch. 10, Pt. 1, with effect for corporation tax purposes for accounting periods ending on or after 1 April 2010, for income tax and capital gains tax purposes for the tax year 2010–11 and subsequent tax years, and for petroleum revenue tax purposes for chargeable periods beginning on or after 1 July 2010.

Notes – S. 804A rewritten for income tax purposes as follows:
S. 804A(1): TIOPA 2010, s. 96(1).
S. 804A(1A): TIOPA 2010, s. 96(2).

S. 804A(1B): TIOPA 2010, s. 96(3).
S. 804A(2): TIOPA 2010, s. 96(4).
S. 804A(3): TIOPA 2010, s. 96(5).
S. 804A(4): TIOPA 2010, s. 96(6).
S. 804A(5): TIOPA 2010, s. 96(7).

804B Insurance companies carrying on more than one category of business: restriction of credit

804B [Omitted by TIOPA 2010, s. 374 and Sch. 8, para. 19 and repealed by TIOPA 2010, s. 378 and Sch. 10, Pt. 1.]

History – S. 804B omitted by TIOPA 2010, s. 374 and Sch. 8, para. 19 and repealed by TIOPA 2010, s. 378 and Sch. 10, Pt. 1, with effect for corporation tax purposes for accounting periods ending on or after 1 April 2010, for income tax and capital gains tax purposes for the tax year 2010–11 and subsequent tax years, and for petroleum revenue tax purposes for chargeable periods beginning on or after 1 July 2010.

Notes – S. 804B rewritten for income tax purposes as follows:
S. 804B(1): TIOPA 2010, s. 97(1).
S. 804B(2): TIOPA 2010, s. 97(2).
S. 804B(3): TIOPA 2010, s. 97(3).
S. 804B(3A): TIOPA 2010, s. 97(4).
S. 804B(4): TIOPA 2010, s. 97(5).
S. 804B(5): TIOPA 2010, s. 97(6).
S. 804B(6): TIOPA 2010, s. 98(2).
S. 804B(7): TIOPA 2010, s. 98(3).
S. 804B(7A): TIOPA 2010, s. 98(4).
S. 804B(8): TIOPA 2010, s. 97(7).
S. 804B(9): TIOPA 2010, s. 97(8).

804C Insurance companies: allocation of expenses etc in computations under section 35 of CTA 2009

804C [Omitted by TIOPA 2010, s. 374 and Sch. 8, para. 19 and repealed by TIOPA 2010, s. 378 and Sch. 10, Pt. 1.]

History – S. 804C omitted by TIOPA 2010, s. 374 and Sch. 8, para. 19 and repealed by TIOPA 2010, s. 378 and Sch. 10, Pt. 1, with effect for corporation tax purposes for accounting periods ending on or after 1 April 2010, for income tax and capital gains tax purposes for the tax year 2010–11 and subsequent tax years, and for petroleum revenue tax purposes for chargeable periods beginning on or after 1 July 2010.

Notes – S. 804C rewritten for income tax purposes as follows:
S. 804C(1): TIOPA 2010, s. 99(1).
S. 804C(2): TIOPA 2010, s. 99(2).
S. 804C(3): TIOPA 2010, s. 100(1).
S. 804C(4): TIOPA 2010, s. 101(1), (3).
S. 804C(5): TIOPA 2010, s. 99(3).
S. 804C(6): TIOPA 2010, s. 100(2).
S. 804C(7): TIOPA 2010, s. 100(3).
S. 804C(8): TIOPA 2010, s. 100(4).
S. 804C(9): TIOPA 2010, s. 101(2).
S. 804C(10): TIOPA 2010, s. 99(4).
S. 804C(11): TIOPA 2010, s. 99(5).
S. 804C(12): TIOPA 2010, s. 99(6).
S. 804C(13): TIOPA 2010, s. 99(7), 104(1), (2), (3).
S. 804C(14): TIOPA 2010, s. 102(1), 103(1).

804D Interpretation of section 804C in relation to life assurance business etc

804D [Omitted by TIOPA 2010, s. 374 and Sch. 8, para. 19 and repealed by TIOPA 2010, s. 378 and Sch. 10, Pt. 1.]

History – S. 804D omitted by TIOPA 2010, s. 374 and Sch. 8, para. 19 and repealed by TIOPA 2010, s. 378 and Sch. 10, Pt. 1, with effect for corporation tax purposes for accounting periods ending on or after 1 April 2010, for income tax and capital gains tax purposes for the tax year 2010–11 and subsequent tax years, and for petroleum revenue tax purposes for chargeable periods beginning on or after 1 July 2010.

Notes – S. 804D rewritten for income tax purposes as follows:
S. 804D(1): TIOPA 2010, s. 102(1).
S. 804D(2): TIOPA 2010, s. 102(2).
S. 804D(3): TIOPA 2010, s. 102(3).
S. 804D(4): TIOPA 2010, s. 102(4).
S. 804D(5): TIOPA 2010, s. 102(5).

804E Interpretation of section 804C in relation to other insurance business

804E [Omitted by TIOPA 2010, s. 374 and Sch. 8, para. 19 and repealed by TIOPA 2010, s. 378 and Sch. 10, Pt. 1.]

History – S. 804E omitted by TIOPA 2010, s. 374 and Sch. 8, para. 19 and repealed by TIOPA 2010, s. 378 and Sch. 10, Pt. 1, with effect for corporation tax purposes for accounting periods ending on or after 1 April 2010, for income tax and capital gains tax purposes for the tax year 2010–11 and subsequent tax years, and for petroleum revenue tax purposes for chargeable periods beginning on or after 1 July 2010.

Notes – S. 804E rewritten for income tax purposes as follows:
S. 804E(1): TIOPA 2010, s. 103(1).
S. 804E(2): TIOPA 2010, s. 103(2).
S. 804E(3): TIOPA 2010, s. 103(3).
S. 804E(4): TIOPA 2010, s. 103(4).
S. 804E(5): TIOPA 2010, s. 103(5).
S. 804E(6): TIOPA 2010, s. 103(6).
S. 804E(7): TIOPA 2010, s. 103(7).

804F Interpretation of sections 804A to 804E

804F [Omitted by FA 2007, s. 41 and Sch. 10, para. 14(2)(e) and repealed by s. 114 and Sch. 27, Pt. 2(10).]

History – S. 804F omitted by FA 2007, s. 41 and Sch. 10, para. 14(2)(e) and repealed by s. 114 and Sch. 27, Pt. 2(10), with effect in relation to periods of account beginning on or after 1 January 2007.

804G Reduction in credit: payment by reference to foreign tax

804G [Omitted by TIOPA 2010, s. 374 and Sch. 8, para. 19 and repealed by TIOPA 2010, s. 378 and Sch. 10, Pt. 1.]

History – S. 804G omitted by TIOPA 2010, s. 374 and Sch. 8, para. 19 and repealed by TIOPA 2010, s. 378 and Sch. 10, Pt. 1, with effect for corporation tax purposes for accounting periods ending on or after 1 April 2010, for income tax and capital gains tax purposes for the tax year 2010–11 and subsequent tax years, and for petroleum revenue tax purposes for chargeable periods beginning on or after 1 July 2010.

Notes – S. 804G rewritten for income tax purposes as follows:
S. 804G(1): TIOPA 2010, s. 34(1).
S. 804G(2): TIOPA 2010, s. 34(2).
S. 804G(3): TIOPA 2010, s. 34(3).

805 Elections against credit

805 [Omitted by TIOPA 2010, s. 374 and Sch. 8, para. 19 and repealed by TIOPA 2010, s. 378 and Sch. 10, Pt. 1.]

History – S. 805 omitted by TIOPA 2010, s. 381 and Sch. 8, para. 19 and repealed by TIOPA 2010, s. 378 and Sch. 10, Pt. 1, with effect for corporation tax purposes for accounting periods ending on or after 1 April 2010, for income tax and capital gains tax purposes for the tax year 2010–11 and subsequent tax years, and for petroleum revenue tax purposes for chargeable periods beginning on or after 1 July 2010.

Notes – S. 805 rewritten for income tax purposes as follows:
S. 805: TIOPA 2010, s. 27.

806 Time limit for claims etc.

806 [Omitted by TIOPA 2010, s. 374 and Sch. 8, para. 19 and repealed by TIOPA 2010, s. 378 and Sch. 10, Pt. 1.]

History – S. 806 omitted by TIOPA 2010, s. 374 and Sch. 8, para. 19 and repealed by TIOPA 2010, s. 378 and Sch. 10, Pt. 1, with effect for corporation tax purposes for accounting periods ending on or after 1 April 2010, for income tax and capital gains tax purposes for the tax year 2010–11 and subsequent tax years, and for petroleum revenue tax purposes for chargeable periods beginning on or after 1 July 2010.

Notes – S. 806 rewritten for income tax purposes as follows:
S. 806(1): TIOPA 2010, s. 19(1), (2), (3).
S. 806(2): TIOPA 2010, s. 79(1), (2), (3).
S. 806(3): TIOPA 2010, s. 80(1), (2), (3).
S. 806(4): TIOPA 2010, s. 80(3).
S. 806(5): TIOPA 2010, s. 80(1), (5).
S. 806(6): TIOPA 2010, s. 80(4).

FOREIGN DIVIDENDS: ONSHORE POOLING AND UTILISATION OF ELIGIBLE UNRELIEVED FOREIGN TAX

806A Eligible unrelieved foreign tax on dividends: introductory

806A [Omitted by FA 2009, s. 34 and Sch. 14, para. 9.]

History – Following the omission of s. 806A by FA 2009, s. 34 and Sch. 14, para. 9, s. 806A amended by TIOPA 2010, s. 374 and Sch. 8, para. 20 as follows, with effect for corporation tax purposes for accounting periods ending on or after 1 April 2010, for income tax and capital gains tax purposes for the tax year 2010–11 and subsequent tax years, and for petroleum revenue tax purposes for chargeable periods beginning on or after 1 July 2010, subject to transitional provisions in TIOPA 2010, Sch. 9, para. 25:

- in s. 806A(2)(c) the words "section 67(6) of TIOPA 2010" substituted for the words "section 801A", and the words "section 67(3) of that Act" substituted for the words "subsection (1)(b) of that section";
- in s. 806A(2)(d) the words "section 70(2) of TIOPA 2010" substituted for the words "section 803", and the words "section 70(1)(d) of that Act" substituted for the words "subsection (1)(b) of that section";
- in s. 806A(2)(e) the words "section 112 of TIOPA 2010" substituted for the words "section 811";
- in s. 806A(4)(a) the words "section 42(2) of TIOPA 2010" substituted for the words "section 797"; and

- in s. 806A(5) the words "section 57(1) of TIOPA 2010" substituted for the words "section 799(1)", the words "section 65(4) of TIOPA 2010" substituted for the words "section 801(2) or (3)", and the words "section 65(4) of TIOPA 2010" substituted for the words "subsection (2) or (3) of section 801".

Following the omission of s. 806A by FA 2009, s. 34 and Sch. 14, para, 9, s. 806A(2) amended by CTA 2010, s. 1177 and Sch. 1, para. 114 as follows, with effect for corporation tax purposes for accounting periods ending on or after 1 April 2010, and for income and capital gains tax purposes for the tax year 2010–11 and subsequent tax years:

- in s. 806A(2)(a), the words"a profit of the trade for the purposes of section 45 of CTA 2010" substituted for the words "trading income fro the purposes of section 393"; and
- in s. 806A(2)(b), the words "subsection (1)(a) and (b) of section 46 of CTA 2010, would by virtue of that section fail to be treated as a profit of the trade for the purposes of section 45 of that Act" substituted for the words "paragraphs (a) and (b) of subsection (8) of section 393, would by virtue of that subsection fall to be treated as trading income for the purposes of subsection (1) of that section".

S. 806A omitted by FA 2009, s. 34 and Sch. 14, para. 9, with effect in relation to distributions paid on or after 1 July 2009.

In former s. 806A(2), the words "which are chargeable under Chapter 2 of Part 10 of CTA 2009 (dividends of non-UK resident companies), or which would be so chargeable but for section 982 of that Act (priority rules)" substituted for "chargeable under Case V of Schedule D" by CTA 2009, s. 1322 and Sch. 1, para. 252, with effect for corporation tax purposes for accounting periods ending on or after 1 April 2009, and for income tax and capital gains tax purposes for the tax year 2009–10 and subsequent tax years.

In former s. 806A(5) the words from "But if that is so in any case by reason only" to the end inserted by FA 2001, s. 81 and Sch. 27, para. 4(2) with effect in relation to:

(a) dividends arising on or after 31 March 2001 to companies resident in the UK from companies resident outside the UK; and
(b) foreign tax in respect of such dividends,

(whenever the dividend mentioned was paid).

Former s. 806A inserted by FA 2000, s. 103 and Sch. 30, para. 21(1) with effect in relation to:

(a) dividends arising on or after 31 March 2001 to companies resident in the UK from companies resident outside the UK; and
(b) foreign tax in respect of such dividends,

(whenever the dividend mentioned was paid).

Cross references – TIOPA 2010, Sch. 9, para. 26 and 27: application of "the saved rules" in relation to distributions paid before 1 July 2009 but in accounting periods ending on or after 1 April 2010.

806B The amounts that are eligible unrelieved foreign tax

806B [Omitted by FA 2009, s. 34 and Sch. 14, para. 9.]

History – Following the omission of s. 806B by FA 2009, s. 34 and Sch. 14, para. 9, s. 806B amended by TIOPA 2010, s. 374 and Sch. 8, para. 21 as follows, with effect for corporation tax purposes for accounting periods ending on or after 1 April 2010, for income tax and capital gains tax purposes for the tax year 2010–11 and subsequent tax years, and for petroleum revenue tax purposes for chargeable periods beginning on or after 1 July 2010, subject to transitional provisions in TIOPA 2010, Sch. 9, para. 25:

- in s. 806B(2)(b), the words "section 42 of TIOPA 2010" substituted for the words "section 797";
- in s. 806B(3)(b), the words "section 57(1) of TIOPA 2010" substituted for the words "section 799(1)";
- in s. 806B(4)(a), the words "section 57(1) of TIOPA 2010" substituted for the words "section 799(1)";
- in s. 806B(4)(b), the words "Step 3 in section 58(1) of TIOPA 2010" substituted for the words "section 799(1A)";
- in s. 806B(4)(b), "M" substituted for "M%";
- in s. 806B(4)(b)(ii), "PA" substituted for "U";
- in s. 806B(5), the words "section 65(4) of TIOPA 2010" substituted for the words "subsection (2) or (3) of section 801";
- in each of the paragraphs 806B(5)(a), (b)(ii) and (c)(ii), the words "section 65(4) of TIOPA 2010" substituted for the words "subsection (2) or (3), as the case may be, of section 801";
- in s. 806B(5), the words "Step 3 in section 58(1) of TIOPA 2010" substituted for the words "section 799(1A)";
- in s. 806B(5), "M" substituted for "M%";
- in s. 806B(5), "PA" substituted for "U";
- in s. 806B(7)(b), the words "section 59 of TIOPA 2010" substituted for the words "section 799(1)";
- in s. 806B(10), in the definition of "lower level dividend" the words "section 65(4) of TIOPA 2010" substituted for the words "section 801(2) or (3)";
- in s. 806B(10), in paragraph (a) of the definition of "the relevant tax" the words "section 57(1) of TIOPA 2010" substituted for the words "section 799(1)", and in paragraph (b) of that definition, the words "section 65(4) of TIOPA 2010" substituted for the words "section 801(2) or (3)".

S. 806B omitted by FA 2009, s. 34 and Sch. 14, para. 9, with effect in relation to distributions paid on or after 1 July 2009.

In former s. 806B(3), (4) and (5), the words "dividend falling within section 806A(2)" substituted for Case V dividend by CTA 2009, s. 1322 and Sch. 1, para. 253(2), with effect for corporation tax purposes for accounting periods ending on or after 1 April 2009, and for income tax and capital gains tax purposes for the tax year 2009–10 and subsequent tax years.

Former s. 806B(3)-(6) and the words "4(b) or 5(c)"in former s. 806B(9) substituted by FA 2001, s. 81 and Sch 27, para. 5(2) with effect in relation to:

(a) dividends arising on or after 31 March 2001 to companies resident in the UK from companies resident outside the UK; and
(b) foreign tax in respect of such dividends,

(whenever any such dividend as is mentioned in s. 801(2) or (3) was paid).

In former s. 806B(10), the definition of "the Case V dividend" omitted by CTA 2009, s. 1322 and Sch. 1, para. 253(3)(a) and repealed by CTA 2009, s. 1326 and Sch. 3, Pt. 1, with effect for corporation tax purposes for accounting periods ending on or after 1 April 2009, and for income tax and capital gains tax purposes for the tax year 2009–10 and subsequent tax years.

In former s. 806B(10), in the definition of "higher level dividend", para. (b) substituted by CTA 2009, s. 1322 and Sch. 1, para. 253(3)(b), with effect for corporation tax purposes for accounting periods ending on or after 1 April 2009, and for income tax and capital gains tax purposes for the tax year 2009–10 and subsequent tax years.

In former s. 806B(10) in paragraph (a) of the definition of "the relevant tax", the words "dividend falling within section 806A(2)" substituted for "Case V dividend" by CTA 2009, s. 1322 and Sch. 1, para. 253(3)(c), with effect for corporation tax purposes for accounting periods ending on or after 1 April 2009, and for income tax and capital gains tax purposes for the tax year 2009–10 and subsequent tax years.

Former s. 806B inserted by FA 2000, s. 103 and Sch. 30, para. 21(1) with effect in relation to:

(a) dividends arising on or after 31 March 2001 to companies resident in the UK from companies resident outside the UK; and
(b) foreign tax in respect of such dividends,

(whenever any such dividend as is mentioned in s. 801(2) or (3) was paid).

Cross references – TIOPA 2010, Sch. 9, para. 26 and 27: application of "the saved rules" in relation to distributions paid before 1 July 2009 but in accounting periods ending on or after 1 April 2010.

806C Onshore pooling

806C [Omitted by FA 2009, s. 34 and Sch. 14, para. 9.]

History – Following the omission of s. 806C by FA 2009, s. 34 and Sch. 14, para. 9, s. 806C amended by TIOPA 2010, s. 374 and Sch. 8, para. 22 as follows, with effect for corporation tax purposes for accounting periods ending on or after 1 April 2010, for income tax and capital gains tax purposes for the tax year 2010–11 and subsequent tax years, and for petroleum revenue tax purposes for chargeable periods beginning on or after 1 July 2010, subject to transitional provisions in TIOPA 2010, Sch. 9, para. 25:

- in s. 806C(3) and (4), the words "Part 2 of TOIPA 2010" substituted for the words "this Part".

S. 806C omitted by FA 2009, s. 34 and Sch. 14, para. 9, with effect in relation to distributions paid on or after 1 July 2009.
Former s. 806C inserted by FA 2000, s. 103 and Sch. 30, para. 21(1), with effect in relation to:
(a) dividends arising on or after 31 March 2001; and
(b) foreign tax in respect of such dividends,
and accordingly the "single related dividend" or "single unrelated dividend" which by virtue of former s. 806C fell to be treated as arising in any chargeable period did not include any dividend arising on or before 30 March 2001.

Cross references – TIOPA 2010, Sch. 9, para. 26 and 27: application of "the saved rules" in relation to distributions paid before 1 July 2009 but in accounting periods ending on or after 1 April 2010.

806D Utilisation of eligible unrelieved foreign tax

806D [Omitted by FA 2009, s. 34 and Sch. 14, para. 9.]

History – Following the omission of s. 806D by FA 2009, s. 34 and Sch. 14, para. 9, s. 806D amended by TIOPA 2010, s. 374 and Sch. 8, para. 23 as follows, with effect for corporation tax purposes for accounting periods ending on or after 1 April 2010, for income tax and capital gains tax purposes for the tax year 2010–11 and subsequent tax years, and for petroleum revenue tax purposes for chargeable periods beginning on or after 1 July 2010, subject to transitional provisions in TIOPA 2010, Sch. 9, para. 25:

- in s. 806D(3), (4) and (5), the words "Part 2 of TOIPA 2010" substituted for the words "this Part".

S. 806D omitted by FA 2009, s. 34 and Sch. 14, para. 9, with effect in relation to distributions paid on or after 1 July 2009.
Former s. 806D inserted by FA 2000, s. 103 and Sch. 30, para. 21(1), with effect in relation to:
(a) dividends arising on or after 31 March 2001; and
(b) foreign tax in respect of such dividends,
and accordingly the "single related dividend" or "single unrelated dividend" which by virtue of former s. 806C fell to be treated as arising in any chargeable period did not include any dividend arising on or before 30 March 2001.

Cross references – TIOPA 2010, Sch. 9, para. 26 and 27: application of "the saved rules" in relation to distributions paid before 1 July 2009 but in accounting periods ending on or after 1 April 2010.

806E Rules for carry back of relievable tax under section 806D

806E [Omitted by FA 2009, s. 34 and Sch. 14, para. 9.]

History – S. 806E omitted by FA 2009, s. 34 and Sch. 14, para. 9, with effect in relation to distributions paid on or after 1 July 2009.
Former s. 806E inserted by FA 2000, s. 103 and Sch. 30, para. 21(1), with effect in relation to:
(a) dividends arising on or after 31 March 2001; and
(b) foreign tax in respect of such dividends,
and accordingly the "single related dividend" or "single unrelated dividend" which by virtue of former s. 806C fell to be treated as arising in any chargeable period did not include any dividend arising on or before 30 March 2001.

Cross references – TIOPA 2010, Sch. 9, para 26 and 27: application of "the saved rules" in relation to distributions paid before 1 July 2009 but in accounting periods ending on or after 1 April 2010.

806F Credit to be given for underlying tax before other foreign tax etc.

806F [Omitted by FA 2009, s. 34 and Sch. 14, para. 9.]

History – Following the omission of s. 806F by FA 2009, s. 34 and Sch. 14, para. 9, s. 806F amended by TIOPA 2010, s. 374 and Sch. 8, para. 24 as follows, with effect for corporation tax purposes for accounting periods ending on or after 1 April 2010, for income tax and capital gains tax purposes for the tax year 2010–11 and subsequent tax years, and for petroleum revenue tax purposes for chargeable periods beginning on or after 1 July 2010, subject to transitional provisions in TIOPA 2010, Sch. 9, para. 25:

- in s. 806F(1) and (2), the words "Part 2 of TOIPA 2010" substituted for the words "this Part".

S. 806F omitted by FA 2009, s. 34 and Sch. 14, para. 9, with effect in relation to distributions paid on or after 1 July 2009.
Former s. 806F inserted by FA 2000, s. 103 and Sch. 30, para. 21(1), with effect in relation to:
(a) dividends arising on or after 31 March 2001; and
(b) foreign tax in respect of such dividends.

Cross references – TIOPA 2010, Sch. 9, para. 26 and 27: application of "the saved rules" in relation to distributions paid before 1 July 2009 but in accounting periods ending on or after 1 April 2010.

806G Claims for the purposes of section 806D(4) or (5)

806G [Omitted by FA 2009, s. 34 and Sch. 14, para. 9.]

History – S. 806G omitted by FA 2009, s. 34 and Sch. 14, para. 9, with effect in relation to distributions paid on or after 1 July 2009.
Former s. 806G inserted by FA 2000, s. 103 and Sch. 30, para. 21(1), with effect in relation to:
(a) dividends arising on or after 31 March 2001; and
(b) foreign tax in respect of such dividends,
and accordingly the "single related dividend" or "single unrelated dividend" which by virtue of former s. 806C fell to be treated as arising in any chargeable period did not include any dividend arising on or before 30 March 2001.

Cross references – TIOPA 2010, Sch. 9, para. 26 and 27: application of "the saved rules" in relation to distributions paid before 1 July 2009 but in accounting periods ending on or after 1 April 2010.

806H Surrender of relievable tax by one company in a group to another

806H [Omitted by FA 2009, s. 34 and Sch. 14, para. 9.]

History – S. 806H omitted by FA 2009, s. 34 and Sch. 14, para. 9, with effect in relation to distributions paid on or after 1 July 2009.

Former s. 806H inserted by FA 2000, s. 103 and Sch. 30, para. 21(1), with effect in relation to:
(a) dividends arising on or after 31 March 2001; and
(b) foreign tax in respect of such dividends.

Cross references – TIOPA 2010, Sch. 9, para. 26 and 27: application of "the saved rules" in relation to distributions paid before 1 July 2009 but in accounting periods ending on or after 1 April 2010.

Statutory instruments – SI 2001/1163 The Double Taxation Relief (Surrender of Relievable Tax Within a Group) Regulations 2001 (as amended by SI 2001/3873, SI 2003/1829 and 2008/2681).

806J Interpretation of foreign dividend provisions of this Chapter

806J [Omitted by FA 2009, s. 34 and Sch. 14, para. 9.]

History – Following the omission of s. 806J by FA 2009, s. 34 and Sch. 14, para. 9, s. 806J amended by TIOPA 2010, s. 374 and Sch 8, para. 25 as follows, with effect for corporation tax purposes for accounting periods ending on or after 1 April 2010, for income tax and capital gains tax purposes for the tax year 2010–11 and subsequent tax years, and for petroleum revenue tax purposes for chargeable periods beginning on or after 1 July 2010, subject to transitional provisions in TIOPA 2010, Sch. 9, para. 25:

- in s. 806J(5)(b), the words "section 15 or 16 of TIOPA 2010" substituted for the words "subsection (6)(b) of section 790";
- in s. 806J(5), the words "section 12(3) of TIOPA 2010" substituted for the words "subsection (10) of that section";
- s. 806J(6) substituted as follows:

"**806J(6)** For the purposes of the foreign dividend provisions of this Chapter a company is related to another company if that other company–
(a) controls directly or indirectly, or
(b) is a subsidiary of a company which controls directly or indirectly,
at least 10% of the voting power in the first-mentioned company.";

- in s. 806J(7), in the definition of "the mixer cap", the words "Step 6 in section 58(1) of TIOPA 2010" substituted for the words "section 799(1)".

S. 806J omitted by FA 2009, s. 34 and Sch. 14, para. 9, with effect in relation to distributions paid on or after 1 July 2009.
Former s. 806J inserted by FA 2000, s. 103 and Sch. 30, para. 21(1), with effect in relation to:
(a) dividends arising on or after 31 March 2001; and
(b) foreign tax in respect of such dividends,
and accordingly the "single related dividend" or "single unrelated dividend" which by virtue of former s. 806C fell to be treated as arising in any chargeable period did not include any dividend arising on or before 30 March 2001.

Cross references – TIOPA 2010, Sch. 9, para. 26 and 27: application of "the saved rules" in relation to distributions paid before 1 July 2009 but in accounting periods ending on or after 1 April 2010.

APPLICATION OF FOREIGN DIVIDEND PROVISIONS TO BRANCHES OR AGENCIES IN THE UK OF PERSONS RESIDENT ELSEWHERE

806K Application of foreign dividend provisions to branches or agencies in the UK of persons resident elsewhere

806K [Omitted by FA 2009, s. 34 and Sch. 14, para. 9.]

History – S. 806K omitted by FA 2009, s. 34 and Sch. 14, para. 9, with effect in relation to distributions paid on or after 1 July 2009.
Former s. 806K inserted by FA 2000, s. 103 and Sch. 30, para. 22(1), with effect in relation to:
(a) dividends arising on or after 31 March 2001; and
(b) foreign tax in respect of such dividends,
and accordingly the "single related dividend" or "single unrelated dividend", which, by virtue of former s. 806C as modified by former s. 806K, fell to be treated as arising in any chargeable period, did not include any dividend arising on or before 30 March 2001.

UNRELIEVED FOREIGN TAX: PROFITS OF OVERSEAS BRANCH OR AGENCY

806L Carry forward or carry back of unrelieved foreign tax

806L [Omitted by TIOPA 2010, s. 374 and Sch. 8, para. 26 and repealed by TIOPA 2010, s. 378 and Sch. 10, Pt. 1.]

History – S. 806L omitted by TIOPA 2010, s. 374 and Sch. 8, para. 26 and repealed by TIOPA 2010, s. 378 and Sch. 10, Pt. 1, with effect for corporation tax purposes for accounting periods ending on or after 1 April 2010, for income tax and capital gains tax purposes for the tax year 2010–11 and subsequent tax years, and for petroleum revenue tax purposes for chargeable periods beginning on or after 1 July 2010.

Notes – S. 806L rewritten for income tax purposes as follows:
S. 806L(1): TIOPA 2010, s. 72(1).
S. 806L(2): TIOPA 2010, s. 73(1), (4), 74(4).
S. 806L(3): TIOPA 2010, s. 74(1), (2), (3).
S. 806L(4): TIOPA 2010, s. 72(1), 74(2), (3).
S. 806L(5): TIOPA 2010, s. 72(2).
S. 806L(6): TIOPA 2010, s. 73(3).
S. 806L(7): TIOPA 2010, s. 78(1), (2).

806M Provisions supplemental to section 806L

806M [Omitted by TIOPA 2010, s. 374 and Sch. 8, para. 26 and repealed by TIOPA 2010, s. 378 and Sch. 10, Pt. 1.]

History – S. 806M omitted by TIOPA 2010, s. 374 and Sch. 8, para. 26 and repealed by TIOPA 2010, s. 378 and Sch. 10, Pt. 1, with effect for corporation tax purposes for accounting periods ending on or after 1 April 2010, for income tax and capital gains tax purposes for the tax year 2010–11 and subsequent tax years, and for petroleum revenue tax purposes for chargeable periods beginning on or after 1 July 2010.

Notes – S. 806M rewritten for income tax purposes as follows:
S. 806M(1): TIOPA 2010, s. 73(2), 75(1), (2), 76(1), (2), 77(1), (2), (3), 78(1), (2).
S. 806M(2): TIOPA 2010, s. 73(2).
S. 806M(3): TIOPA 2010, s. 76(1).
S. 806M(4): TIOPA 2010, s. 75(1), (2), (3).
S. 806M(5): TIOPA 2010, s. 77(1).
S. 806M(6): TIOPA 2010, s. 77(2).
S. 806M(7): TIOPA 2010, s. 77(3).

Chapter III – Miscellaneous Provisions

807 Sale of securities with or without accrued interest

807 [Omitted by TIOPA 2010, s. 374 and Sch. 8, para. 27 and repealed by TIOPA 2010, s. 378 and Sch. 10, Pt. 1.]

History – S. 807 omitted by TIOPA 2010, s. 374 and Sch. 8, para. 27 and repealed by TIOPA 2010, s. 378 and Sch. 10, Pt. 1, with effect for corporation tax purposes for accounting periods ending on or after 1 April 2010, for income tax and capital gains tax purposes for the tax year 2010–11 and subsequent tax years, and for petroleum revenue tax purposes for chargeable periods beginning on or after 1 July 2010.

Notes – S. 807 rewritten for income tax purposes as follows:
S. 807(1): TIOPA 2010, s. 10(1), (2), (3), (5).
S. 807(2): TIOPA 2010, s. 39(1), (2), (3), (4), (5).
S. 807(3): Not rewritten: unnecessary.
S. 807(4): TIOPA 2010, s. 112(1), (2).
S. 807(5): TIOPA 2010, s. 10(6), 39(6).

807A Disposals and acquisitions of company loan relationships with or without interest

807A [Omitted by TIOPA 2010, s. 374 and Sch. 8, para. 27 and repealed by TIOPA 2010, s. 378 and Sch. 10, Pt. 1.]

History – S. 807A omitted by TIOPA 2010, s. 374 and Sch. 8, para. 27 and repealed by TIOPA 2010, s. 378 and Sch. 10, Pt. 1, with effect for corporation tax purposes for accounting periods ending on or after 1 April 2010, for income tax and capital gains tax purposes for the tax year 2010–11 and subsequent tax years, and for petroleum revenue tax purposes for chargeable periods beginning on or after 1 July 2010.

Notes – S. 807A rewritten for income tax purposes as follows:
S. 807A(1): TIOPA 2010, s. 107(1), 108(1).
S. 807A(2): TIOPA 2010, s. 107(2), 108(2).
S. 807A(2A): TIOPA 2010, s. 108(3), 109(1), 110(1), Sch. 9, para. 22(4), (5).
S. 807A(6A): TIOPA 2010, s. 109(2), 110(2), Sch. 9, para. 22(5).
S. 807A(6B): TIOPA 2010, s. 109(2), (3).
S. 807A(6C): TIOPA 2010, s. 110(2), (3).
S. 807A(7): TIOPA 2010, s. 107(3).

EUROPEAN CROSS-BORDER TRANSFERS OF BUSINESS

807B Introduction to section 807C

807B [Omitted by TIOPA 2010, s. 374 and Sch. 8, para. 28 and repealed by TIOPA 2010, s. 378 and Sch. 10, Pt. 1.]

History – S. 807B omitted by TIOPA 2010, s. 374 and Sch. 8, para. 28 and repealed by TIOPA 2010, s. 378 and Sch. 10, Pt. 1, with effect for corporation tax purposes for accounting periods ending on or after 1 April 2010, for income tax and capital gains tax purposes for the tax year 2010–11 and subsequent tax years, and for petroleum revenue tax purposes for chargeable periods beginning on or after 1 July 2010.

Notes – S. 807B rewritten for income tax purposes as follows:
S. 807B(1): TIOPA 2010, s. 116(1).
S. 807B(2): TIOPA 2010, s. 116(2).
S. 807B(3): TIOPA 2010, s. 116(3).
S. 807B(4): TIOPA 2010, s. 116(4).
S. 807B(5): TIOPA 2010, s. 116(5).
S. 807B(6): TIOPA 2010, s. 116(6).
S. 807B(7): TIOPA 2010, s. 116(7).
S. 807B(8): TIOPA 2010, s. 116(8).
S. 807B(9): TIOPA 2010, s. 123.

807C Tax treated as chargeable in respect of transfer of loan relationship, derivative contract or intangible fixed assets

807C [Omitted by TIOPA 2010, s. 374 and Sch. 8, para. 28 and repealed by TIOPA 2010, s. 378 and Sch. 10, Pt. 1.]

History – S. 807C omitted by TIOPA 2010, s. 374 and Sch. 8, para. 28 and repealed by TIOPA 2010, s. 378 and Sch. 10, Pt. 1, with effect for corporation tax purposes for accounting periods ending on or after 1 April 2010, for income tax and capital gains tax purposes for the tax year 2010–11 and subsequent tax years, and for petroleum revenue tax purposes for chargeable periods beginning on or after 1 July 2010.

Notes – S. 807C rewritten for income tax purposes as follows:
S. 807C(1): TIOPA 2010, s. 117(1).
S. 807C(2): TIOPA 2010, s. 117(2).
S. 807C(3): TIOPA 2010, s. 117(3).
S. 807C(4): TIOPA 2010, s. 117(4).
S. 807C(5): TIOPA 2010, s. 117(5).
S. 807C(6): TIOPA 2010, s. 117(6).

EUROPEAN CROSS-BORDER MERGERS

807D Introduction to section 807E

807D [Omitted by TIOPA 2010, s. 374 and Sch. 8, para. 28 and repealed by TIOPA 2010, s. 378 and Sch. 10, Pt. 1.]

History – S. 807D omitted by TIOPA 2010, s. 374 and Sch. 8, para. 28 and repealed by TIOPA 2010, s. 378 and Sch. 10, Pt. 1, with effect for corporation tax purposes for accounting periods ending on or after 1 April 2010, for income tax and capital gains tax purposes for the tax year 2010–11 and subsequent tax years, and for petroleum revenue tax purposes for chargeable periods beginning on or after 1 July 2010.

Notes – S. 807D rewritten for income tax purposes as follows:
S. 807D(1): TIOPA 2010, s. 118(1).
S. 807D(2): TIOPA 2010, s. 118(2).
S. 807D(3): TIOPA 2010, s. 118(3).
S. 807D(4): TIOPA 2010, s. 118(4).
S. 807D(5): TIOPA 2010, s. 118(5).
S. 807D(6): TIOPA 2010, s. 118(6).
S. 807D(7): TIOPA 2010, s. 118(7).
S. 807D(8): TIOPA 2010, s. 118(8).
S. 807D(9): TIOPA 2010, s. 118(9).
S. 807D(10): TIOPA 2010, s. 118(10).
S. 807D(11): TIOPA 2010, s. 118(11), 123.
S. 807D(12): TIOPA 2010, s. 119(6).

807E Tax treated as chargeable in respect of transfer of loan relationship, derivative contract or intangible fixed assets

807E [Omitted by TIOPA 2010, s. 374 and Sch. 8, para. 28 and repealed by TIOPA 2010, s. 378 and Sch. 10, Pt. 1.]

History – S. 807E omitted by TIOPA 2010, s. 374 and Sch. 8, para. 28 and repealed by TIOPA 2010, s. 378 and Sch. 10, Pt. 1, with effect for corporation tax purposes for accounting periods ending on or after 1 April 2010, for income tax and capital gains tax purposes for the tax year 2010–11 and subsequent tax years, and for petroleum revenue tax purposes for chargeable periods beginning on or after 1 July 2010.

Notes – S. 807E rewritten for income tax purposes as follows:
S. 807E(1): TIOPA 2010, s. 119(1).
S. 807E(2): TIOPA 2010, s. 119(2).
S. 807E(3): TIOPA 2010, s. 119(3).
S. 807E(4): TIOPA 2010, s. 119(4).
S. 807E(5): TIOPA 2010, s. 119(5).

TRANSPARENT ENTITIES INVOLVED IN CROSS-BORDER TRANSFERS AND MERGERS

807F Introduction to section 807G

807F [Omitted by TIOPA 2010, s. 374 and Sch. 8, para. 28 and repealed by TIOPA 2010, s. 378 and Sch. 10, Pt. 1.]

History – S. 807F omitted by TIOPA 2010, s. 374 and Sch. 8, para. 28 and repealed by TIOPA 2010, s. 378 and Sch. 10, Pt. 1, with effect for corporation tax purposes for accounting periods ending on or after 1 April 2010, for income tax and capital gains tax purposes for the tax year 2010–11 and subsequent tax years, and for petroleum revenue tax purposes for chargeable periods beginning on or after 1 July 2010.

Notes – S. 807F rewritten for income tax purposes as follows:
S. 807F(1): TIOPA 2010, s. 120(1).
S. 807F(2): TIOPA 2010, s. 120(2).
S. 807F(3): TIOPA 2010, s. 120(3).
S. 807F(4): TIOPA 2010, s. 120(4).
S. 807F(5): TIOPA 2010, s. 120(5).
S. 807F(6): TIOPA 2010, s. 120(6), 123.

807G Tax treated as chargeable in respect of relevant transactions

807G [Omitted by TIOPA 2010, s. 374 and Sch. 8, para. 28 and repealed by TIOPA 2010, s. 378 and Sch. 10, Pt. 1.]

History – S. 807G omitted by TIOPA 2010, s. 374 and Sch. 8, para. 28 and repealed by TIOPA 2010, s. 378 and Sch. 10, Pt. 1, with effect for corporation tax purposes for accounting periods ending on or after 1 April 2010, for income tax and capital gains tax purposes for the tax year 2010–11 and subsequent tax years, and for petroleum revenue tax purposes for chargeable periods beginning on or after 1 July 2010.

Notes – S. 807G rewritten for income tax purposes as follows:
S. 807G(1): TIOPA 2010, s. 121(1).
S. 807G(2): TIOPA 2010, s. 121(2).
S. 807G(3): TIOPA 2010, s. 121(3).

808 Restriction on deduction of interest or dividends from trading income

808 [Omitted by CTA 2010, s. 1177 and Sch. 1, para. 115 and repealed by CTA 2010, s. 1181 and Sch. 3, Pt. 1.]

History – S. 808 omitted by CTA 2010, s. 1177 and Sch. 1, para. 115 and repealed by CTA 2010, s. 1181 and Sch. 3, Pt. 1, with effect for corporation tax purposes for accounting periods ending on or after 1 April 2010, and for income and capital gains tax purposes for the tax year 2010–11 and subsequent tax years.

Notes – S. 808 rewritten for corporation tax purposes as follows:
S. 808: CTA 2010, s. 54(1), (2), (3).

808A Interest: special relationship

808A [Omitted by TIOPA 2010, s. 374 and Sch. 8, para. 29 and repealed by TIOPA 2010, s. 378 and Sch. 10, Pt. 1.]

History – S. 808A omitted by TIOPA 2010, s. 374 and Sch. 8, para. 29 and repealed by TIOPA 2010, s. 378 and Sch. 10, Pt. 1, with effect for corporation tax purposes for accounting periods ending on or after 1 April 2010, for income tax and capital gains tax purposes for the tax year 2010–11 and subsequent tax years, and for petroleum revenue tax purposes for chargeable periods beginning on or after 1 July 2010.

Notes – S. 808A rewritten for income tax purposes as follows:
S. 808A(1): TIOPA 2010, s. 131(1), (2).
S. 808A(2): TIOPA 2010, s. 131(3).
S. 808A(3): TIOPA 2010, s. 131(6).
S. 808A(4): TIOPA 2010, s. 131(5).
S. 808A(5): TIOPA 2010, s. 131(4).

808B Royalties: special relationship

808B [Omitted by TIOPA 2010, s. 374 and Sch. 8, para. 29 and repealed by TIOPA 2010, s. 378 and Sch. 10, Pt. 1.]

History – S. 808B omitted by TIOPA 2010, s. 374 and Sch. 8, para. 29 and repealed by TIOPA 2010, s. 378 and Sch. 10, Pt. 1, with effect for corporation tax purposes for accounting periods ending on or after 1 April 2010, for income tax and capital gains tax purposes for the tax year 2010–11 and subsequent tax years, and for petroleum revenue tax purposes for chargeable periods beginning on or after 1 July 2010.

Notes – S. 808B rewritten for income tax purposes as follows:
S. 808B(1): TIOPA 2010, s. 132(1), (2).
S. 808B(2): TIOPA 2010, s. 132(3).
S. 808B(3): TIOPA 2010, s. 132(4).
S. 808B(4): TIOPA 2010, s. 132(5).
S. 808B(5): TIOPA 2010, s. 133(1).
S. 808B(6): TIOPA 2010, s. 133(2), (3), (4).
S. 808B(7): TIOPA 2010, s. 133(2), (4).
S. 808B(8): TIOPA 2010, s. 132(6).
S. 808B(9): TIOPA 2010, s. 132(7), (8), 157(1), 158(4), 159(1), 160(1).

809 Relief in respect of discretionary trusts

809 [Omitted by TIOPA 2010, s. 374 and Sch. 8, para. 29 and repealed by TIOPA 2010, s. 378 and Sch. 10, Pt. 1.]

History – S. 809 omitted by TIOPA 2010, s. 374 and Sch. 8, para. 29 and repealed by TIOPA 2010, s. 378 and Sch. 10, Pt. 1, with effect for corporation tax purposes for accounting periods ending on or after 1 April 2010, for income tax and capital gains tax purposes for the tax year 2010–11 and subsequent tax years, and for petroleum revenue tax purposes for chargeable periods beginning on or after 1 July 2010.

Notes – S. 809 rewritten for income tax purposes as follows:
S. 809(1): TIOPA 2010, s. 111(1), (2), (3), (4), (5), (6).
S. 809(2): TIOPA 2010, s. 111(7).

810 Postponement of capital allowances to secure double taxation relief

810 [Repealed by FA 2000, s. 103 and Sch. 30, para. 26(1), s. 156 and Sch. 40, Pt. II(13), with effect in relation to claims made on or after 1 April 2000.]

811 Deduction for foreign tax where no credit allowable

811 [Omitted by TIOPA 2010, s. 374 and Sch. 8, para. 29 and repealed by TIOPA 2010, s. 378 and Sch. 10, Pt. 1.]

History – S. 811 omitted by TIOPA 2010, s. 374 and Sch. 8, para. 29 and repealed by TIOPA 2010, s. 378 and Sch. 10, Pt. 1, with effect for corporation tax purposes for accounting periods ending on or after 1 April 2010, for income tax and capital gains tax purposes for the tax year 2010–11 and subsequent tax years, and for petroleum revenue tax purposes for chargeable periods beginning on or after 1 July 2010.

Notes – S. 811 rewritten for income tax purposes as follows:
S. 811(1): TIOPA 2010, s. 112(1), (6).
S. 811(2): TIOPA 2010, s. 112(4).
S. 811(3): TIOPA 2010, s. 112(5).
S. 811(3A): TIOPA 2010, s. 112(3).
S. 811(3B): TIOPA 2010, s. 112(7).
S. 811(4): TIOPA 2010, s. 114(1), (2), (3), (4).
S. 811(5): TIOPA 2010, s. 115(1), (3), (4).
S. 811(6): TIOPA 2010, s. 115(4).
S. 811(7): TIOPA 2010, s. 115(1), (7).
S. 811(8): TIOPA 2010, s. 115(5).
S. 811(9): TIOPA 2010, s. 115(5).
S. 811(10): TIOPA 2010, s. 115(6).

812 Withdrawal of right to tax credit of certain non-resident companies connected with unitary states

812 [Repealed by Statute Law (Repeals) Act 2013, s. 1 and Sch. 1, Pt. 10.]

History – S. 812 repealed by Statute Law (Repeals) Act 2013, s. 1 and Sch. 1, Pt. 10, with effect from 31 January 2013.

Derivations – S. 812(1): FA 1985, s. 54(1), (3).
S. 812(2): FA 1985, Sch. 13, para. 5(1).
S. 812(3), (4) (as originally enacted): FA 1985, s. 54(4), (5).
S. 812(5)(b)–(d): FA 1985, Sch. 13, para. 5(1), (2).
S. 812(5)(e): FA 1985, s. 54(6).
S. 812(6): FA 1985, s. 54(7)(b) and Sch. 13, para. 5(1).
S. 812(7) (as originally enacted): FA 1985, s. 54(7)(c).
S. 812(8): FA 1985, s. 54(2), (7)(a).
S. 812(9): FA 1985, s. 54(8).

813 Recovery of tax credits incorrectly paid

813 [Repealed by Statute Law (Repeals) Act 2013, s. 1 and Sch. 1, Pt. 10.]

History – S. 813 repealed by Statute Law (Repeals) Act 2013, s. 1 and Sch. 1, Pt. 10, with effect from 31 January 2013.

Derivations – FA 1985, Sch. 13, para. 1.

814 Arrangements to avoid section 812

814 [Repealed by Statute Law (Repeals) Act 2013, s. 1 and Sch. 1, Pt. 10.]

History – S. 814 repealed by Statute Law (Repeals) Act 2013, s. 1 and Sch. 1, Pt. 10, with effect from 31 January 2013.

Derivations – FA 1985, Sch. 13, para. 3.

815 Power to inspect documents

815 [Omitted by SI 2009/2035, art. 2 and Schedule, para. 23.]

History – S. 815 omitted by SI 2009/2035, art. 2 and Schedule, para. 23, with effect from 13 August 2009.

Derivations – FA 1985, Sch. 13, para. 4(1). "Notice": see s. 832(1).

815A Transfer of a non-UK trade

815A [Omitted by TIOPA 2010, s. 374 and Sch. 8, para. 32 and repealed by TIOPA 2010, s. 378 and Sch. 10, Pt. 1.]

History – S. 815A omitted by TIOPA 2010, s. 374 and Sch. 8, para. 32 and repealed by TIOPA 2010, s. 378 and Sch. 10, Pt. 1, with effect for corporation tax purposes for accounting periods ending on or after 1 April 2010, for income tax and capital gains tax purposes for the tax year 2010–11 and subsequent tax years, and for petroleum revenue tax purposes for chargeable periods beginning on or after 1 July 2010.

Notes – S. 815A rewritten for income tax purposes as follows:
S. 815A(1): TIOPA 2010, s. 122(1), (2).
S. 815A(2): TIOPA 2010, s. 122(1), (3), (4).
S. 815A(5): TIOPA 2010, s. 122(5).
S. 815A(6): TIOPA 2010, s. 122(2), 123.

815AZA UK residents and foreign enterprises

815AZA [Omitted by TIOPA 2010, s. 374 and Sch. 8, para. 32 and repealed by TIOPA 2010, s. 378 and Sch. 10, Pt. 1.]

History – S. 815AZA omitted by TIOPA 2010, s. 374 and Sch. 8, para. 32 and repealed by TIOPA 2010, s. 378 and Sch. 10, Pt. 1, with effect for corporation tax purposes for accounting periods ending on or after 1 April 2010, for income tax and capital gains tax purposes for the tax year 2010–11 and subsequent tax years, and for petroleum revenue tax purposes for chargeable periods beginning on or after 1 July 2010.

Notes – S. 815AZA rewritten for income tax purposes as follows:
S. 815AZA(1): TIOPA 2010, s. 130(1), (4).
S. 815AZA(2): TIOPA 2010, s. 130(2), (3).
S. 815AZA(3): TIOPA 2010, s. 130(6).
S. 815AZA(4): TIOPA 2010, s. 130(5).

815AA Mutual agreement procedure and presentation of cases under arrangements

815AA [Omitted by TIOPA 2010, s. 374 and Sch. 8, para. 32 and repealed by TIOPA 2010, s. 378 and Sch. 10, Pt. 1.]

History – S. 815AA omitted by TIOPA 2010, s. 374 and Sch. 8, para. 32 and repealed by TIOPA 2010, s. 378 and Sch. 10, Pt. 1, with effect for corporation tax purposes for accounting periods ending on or after 1 April 2010, for income tax and capital gains tax purposes for the tax year 2010–11 and subsequent tax years, and for petroleum revenue tax purposes for chargeable periods beginning on or after 1 July 2010.

Notes – S. 815AA rewritten for income tax purposes as follows:
S. 815AA(1): TIOPA 2010, s. 124(1).
S. 815AA(2): TIOPA 2010, s. 124(2), (3).
S. 815AA(3): TIOPA 2010, s. 124(4).
S. 815AA(4): TIOPA 2010, s. 125(1).
S. 815AA(5): TIOPA 2010, s. 125(2).
S. 815AA(6): TIOPA 2010, s. 125(3).

815B The Arbitration Convention

815B [Omitted by TIOPA 2010, s. 374 and Sch. 8, para. 32 and repealed by TIOPA 2010, s. 378 and Sch. 10, Pt. 1.]

History – S. 815B omitted by TIOPA 2010, s. 374 and Sch. 8, para. 32 and repealed by TIOPA 2010, s. 378 and Sch. 10, Pt. 1, with effect for corporation tax purposes for accounting periods ending on or after 1 April 2010, for income tax and capital gains tax purposes for the tax year 2010–11 and subsequent tax years, and for petroleum revenue tax purposes for chargeable periods beginning on or after 1 July 2010.

Notes – S. 815B rewritten for income tax purposes as follows:
S. 815B(1): TIOPA 2010, s. 127(1), (2).
S. 815B(2): TIOPA 2010, s. 127(3), (4).
S. 815B(3): TIOPA 2010, s. 127(5).
S. 815B(4): TIOPA 2010, s. 126.

815C Exchange of information with other territories

815C [Repealed by FA 2006, s. 178 and Sch. 26, Pt. 8(2).]

History – S. 815C repealed by FA 2006, s. 178 and Sch. 26, Pt. 8(2) with effect from 19 July 2006.

816 Disclosure of information

816 [Omitted by TIOPA 2010, s. 374 and Sch. 8, para. 32 and repealed by TIOPA 2010, s. 378 and Sch. 10, Pt. 1.]

History – S. 816(3), so far as it continued to have effect (see TIOPA 2010, s. 381), omitted by FA 2011, s. 86 and Sch. 23, para. 55(e), with effect from 1 April 2012, subject to transitional provisions in FA 2011, Sch. 23, para. 65.
S. 816 omitted by TIOPA 2010, s. 374 and Sch. 8, para. 32 and repealed by TIOPA 2010, s. 378 and Sch. 10, Pt. 1, with effect for corporation tax purposes for accounting periods ending on or after 1 April 2010, for income tax and capital gains tax purposes for the tax year 2010–11 and subsequent tax years, and for petroleum revenue tax purposes for chargeable periods beginning on or after 1 July 2010.

Notes – Former s. 816 rewritten for income tax purposes as follows:
Former s. 816(1): TIOPA 2010, s. 129(1), (2), (3), (4).
Former s. 816(2A): TIOPA 2010, s. 126, 128(1).
Former s. 816(3): TIOPA 2010, Sch. 8, para. 4.
Former s. 816(4): Not rewritten.
Former s. 816(5): TIOPA 2010, s. 128(2), 129(5).

PART XIX – SUPPLEMENTAL

MISCELLANEOUS

817 Deductions not to be allowed in computing profits or gains

817 [Omitted by CTA 2009, s. 1322 and Sch. 1, para. 265 and repealed by CTA 2009, s. 1326 and Sch. 3, Pt. 1.]

History – S. 817 omitted by CTA 2009, s. 1322 and Sch. 1, para. 265 and repealed by CTA 2009, s. 1326 and Sch. 3, Pt. 1, with effect for corporation tax purposes for accounting periods ending on or after 1 April 2009, and for income tax and capital gains tax purposes for the tax year 2009–10 and subsequent tax years.

Notes – ICTA 1988, s. 817 is not rewritten by ITTOIA 2005 as it is no longer necessary to provide that deductions are available only where "expressly enumerated in the Tax Acts". (See ITTOIA 2005, Explanatory Notes, Annex 1, Table 1 (Change 158).)
S. 817: not rewritten (see CTA 2009, Explanatory Notes, Annex 1, Change 101).

818 Arrangements for payments of interest less tax or of fixed net amount

818 [Omitted by ITA 2007, s. 1027 and Sch. 1, para. 203 and repealed by ITA 2007, s. 1031 and Sch. 3, Pt. 1 with effect for income tax purposes for 2007–08 and subsequent tax years and for corporation tax purposes in relation to accounting periods ending after 5 April 2007.]

Notes – S. 818 rewritten as follows:
S. 818(1): ITA 2007, s. 976(1), (2), (3).
S. 818(2): ITA 2007, s. 976(1), (2), (4), (5).
S. 818(3): ITA 2007, s. 976(6).

819 Old references to standard rate tax

819 [Omitted by ITA 2007, s. 1027 and Sch. 1, para. 204 and repealed by ITA 2007, s. 1031 and Sch. 3, Pt. 1 with effect for 2007–08 and subsequent tax years.]

820 Application of Income Tax Acts from year to year

820 In order to ensure the collection in due time of income tax which may be granted for any year commencing on 6th April, all such provisions contained in the Income Tax Acts as were in force on the preceding day shall have full force and effect with respect to tax which may be so granted, in the same manner as if that tax had been actually granted by Act of Parliament and those provisions had been applied thereto by the Act.

Derivations – ICTA 1970, s. 520.

Cross references – ITTOIA 2005, Sch. 2, para. 160: application of s. 820 to ITTOIA 2005.

821 Under-deductions from payments made before passing of annual Act

821(1) Where, in any year of assessment or accounting period, any half-yearly or quarterly payments (or half-periodic or quarterly payments) have been made on account of any interest, dividends or other annual profits or gains, previously to the passing of the Act imposing income or corporation tax for that year or period, and tax has not been charged thereon or deducted therefrom or has not been charged thereon or deducted therefrom at the rate ultimately imposed for that year or period–

(a) the amount not so charged or deducted shall be charged in respect of those payments to income tax under Chapter 2 of Part 4 of ITTOIA 2005 (interest) or shall be charged to corporation tax; and

(b) the agents entrusted with the payment of the interest, dividends or other annual profits or gains shall furnish to the Board a list containing the names and addresses of the persons to whom payments have been made and the amount of those payments, upon a requisition made by the Board in that behalf.

821(2) Any person liable to pay any rent, interest or annuity, or to make any other annual payment–

(a) shall be authorised–

(i) to make any deduction on account of income tax for any year of assessment which he has failed to make previously to the passing of the Act imposing the tax for that year, or

(ii) to make up any deficiency in any such deduction which has been so made, on the occasion of the next payment of the rent, interest or annuity or making of the other annual payment after the passing of the Act so imposing the tax, in addition to any other deduction which he may be by law authorised to make; and

(b) shall also be entitled, if there is no future payment from which the deduction may be made, to recover the sum which might have been deducted as if it were a debt due from the person as against whom the deduction could originally have been made if the Act imposing the tax for the year had been in force.

821(3) Subsection (2) above shall apply with respect to–

(a) any payment to which section 906 of ITA 2007 applies (certain royalties etc where usual place of abode of owner is abroad), and

(aa) [Omitted by ITA 2007, s. 1027 and Sch. 1, para. 205(b) and repealed by ITA 2007, s. 1031 and Sch. 3, Pt. 1.]

(b) any royalty or other sum paid in respect of the user of a patent;

as it applies with respect to any rent, interest, annuity or other annual payment.

821(4) In this section **"interest"** and **"dividends"** do not include any interest or dividend which is a distribution.

History – In s. 821(1)(a), the words "under Case III of Schedule D", which appeared after "corporation tax", omitted by CTA 2009, s. 1322 and Sch. 1, para. 266 and repealed by CTA 2009, s. 1326 and Sch. 3, Pt. 1, with effect for corporation tax purposes for accounting periods ending on or after 1 April 2009, and for income tax and capital gains tax purposes for the tax year 2009–10 and subsequent tax years.

In s. 821(1) the words "or accounting period", "(or half-periodic or quarterly payments)", "or corporation", "or period" and "in respect of those payments to income tax under Chapter 2 of Part 4 of ITTOIA 2005 (interest) or shall be charged to corporation tax [under]" (the word in square brackets not necessary) inserted and the words "in respect of those payments" omitted (and repealed by s. 884 and Sch. 3) by ITTOIA 2005, s. 882(1) and Sch. 1, para. 330; effective for income tax purposes for 2005–06 onwards and for corporation tax purposes for accounting periods ending after 5 April 2005 (ITTOIA 2005, s. 883(1)).

In s. 821(1)(a), words "under Case III … those payments; and" substituted by FA 1996, s. 73 and Sch. 6, para. 22 for 1996–97 and later years of assessment.

In s. 821(3), para. (a) substituted by ITA 2007, s. 1027 and Sch. 1, para. 205(a) and para. (aa) and the word "and" immediately after it omitted by ITA 2007, s. 1027 and Sch. 1, para. 205(b) and repealed by ITA 2007, s. 1031 and Sch. 3, Pt. 1 with effect for income tax purposes for 2007–08 and subsequent tax years and for corporation tax purposes in relation to accounting periods ending after 5 April 2007.
Former s. 821(3)(aa) inserted by Copyright, Designs and Patents Act 1988, s. 303(1) and Sch. 7, para. 36(7), with effect from 1 August 1989 (SI 1989/816).
S. 821(3)(c) and the word "and" immediately preceding it repealed by FA 1997, s. 113 and Sch. 18, Pt. VI(2) with effect in relation to payments made on or after 6 April 1997.

Derivations – S. 821(1), (2) (as originally enacted): ICTA 1970, s. 521(1), (2).
S. 821(3) (as originally enacted): ICTA 1970, s. 521(3)(b)–(d); FA 1983, s. 27(b).
S. 821(4): ICTA 1970, s. 521(4), as inserted by FA 1972, s. 111 and Sch. 24, para. 29.

Cross references – S. 120: electricity line wayleave rents subject to deduction of tax in the same way as patent royalties.
S. 348: discretion to deduct tax from payments made out of income charged to income tax.
S. 349: requirement to deduct tax from payments made otherwise than out of income charged to income tax.
S. 536: requirement to deduct tax from copyright royalties paid to non-resident.
S. 537B: taxation of design royalties where owner abroad.

822 Over-deductions from interest on loan capital etc. made before passing of annual Act

822(1) If in any year of assessment (**"the year"**) a resolution having statutory effect under the Provisional Collection of Taxes Act 1968 provides for the charging of income tax at a lower rate less than that charged for the previous year, the following provisions of this section shall have effect with respect to deductions in respect of income tax by any body corporate, from payments of interest (not being a distribution) on any of its securities.

822(2) Any deduction which was made before the expiration of one month from the passing of the resolution and which would, if the tax had been renewed at the rate imposed for the previous year, have been a legal deduction, shall be deemed to be a deduction rendered legal by section 2 of the Provisional Collection of Taxes Act 1968 and that section shall, subject to this section, apply accordingly.

822(3) Any over-deduction to be made good under that section may be made good by a reduction of the amount of tax deducted from the next payment of like nature made on the security in question after the passing of the Act imposing the tax for the year.

822(4) Any amount made good under section 2 of the Provisional Collection of Taxes Act 1968 shall–

(a) in the case of an over-deduction which is made good under subsection (3) above, enure to the benefit of the person entitled to the payment on the occasion of which the over-deduction is made good; and

(b) in any other case, enure to the benefit of the person entitled to the security in question at the date when the amount is made good,

irrespective, in either case, of whether or not he is the person who was entitled to the payment, or to the security at the date when the original deduction was made.

822(5) Subsection (3) above shall not authorise the retention of any part of the amount over-deducted for more than one year from the passing of the Act imposing the tax for the year.

History – In s. 822(1), words "lower rate less" substituted by FA 1996, s. 73 and Sch. 6, para. 23 for 1996–97 and later years of assessment.

Derivations – S. 822(1) (as originally enacted): ICTA 1970, s. 522, as amended by FA 1971, s. 37 and Sch. 6, para. 76; FA 1972, s. 111 and Sch. 24, para. 30.
S. 822(2): ICTA 1970, s. 522(a).
S. 822(3), (4): ICTA 1970, s. 522(b), (c), as amended by FA 1972, s. 111 and Sch. 24, para. 30, Sch. 28, Pt. VI.
S. 822(5): proviso to ICTA 1970, s. 522(b).

Cross references – PCTA 1968, s. 2: deductions in respect of a temporary (e.g. income) tax made prior to its imposition for a year deemed to be legally made.
PCTA 1968, s. 5(2): deductions given provisional statutory effect, application of s. 822.

823 Adjustments of reliefs where given at different times

823 [Omitted by ITA 2007, s. 1027 and Sch. 1, para. 206 and repealed by ITA 2007, s. 1031 and Sch. 3, Pt. 1 with effect for 2007–08 and subsequent tax years.]

824 Repayment supplements: individuals and others

824(1) Subject to the following provisions of this section, a repayment made by the Board or an officer of the Board of any of the following, namely–

(a) an amount paid on account of income tax under section 59A of the Management Act;

(b) any income tax paid by or on behalf of an individual for a year of assessment;

(c) a penalty payable under any paragraph of Schedule 56 to the Finance Act 2009 in respect of an amount falling within any of the following items of the Table in paragraph 1 of that Schedule–

(i) item 1, 12, 18 or 19; or

(ii) insofar as the tax falls within item 1, item 17, 23 or 24; and

(d) a penalty incurred by an individual under any of the provisions of that Act,

shall be increased under this section by an amount (a **"repayment supplement"**) equal to interest on the amount repaid at the rate applicable under section 178 of the Finance Act 1989 for the period (if any) between the relevant time and the date on which the order for the repayment is issued.

824(1A) [Repealed by FA 1989, s. 187 and Sch. 17, Pt. X.]

824(2) [Omitted by FA 2016, s. 5 and Sch. 1, para. 52(3).]

824(2A) Subsection (1) above shall apply to a repayment made in consequence of a claim under section 228 of the Income Tax Act 1952 (relief in respect of income accumulated under trusts) as if the repayment were of income tax paid by the claimant for the year of assessment in which the contingency mentioned in that section happened.

824(2B) Subsection (1) above shall apply to a payment made by the Board under section 375(8) (payment of amount which borrower would have been able to deduct from interest payment under section 369(1)) as if the payment were a repayment falling within that subsection.

824(2C) Subsection (1) above shall apply to a repayment made by the Board as a result of a claim for relief under–

(a) paragraph 2 of Schedule 1B to the Management Act (carry back of loss relief),

(b) paragraph 3 of that Schedule (relief for fluctuating profits of farming etc.), or

(c) Schedule 4A to this Act (relief for fluctuating profits of creative artists etc.),

as if it were a repayment falling within that subsection.

824(2D) Subsection (1) shall apply–

(a) to a repayment made as mentioned in section 270(4) (repayment of excess of life assurance premium relief clawed back over amount of liability) as if the repayment were a repayment of income tax paid for the tax year in which the event concerned happened; and

(b) to a payment made under paragraph 6(1) of Schedule 14 (payment where entitlement to life assurance premium relief has not been given by deduction) as if the payment were a repayment of income tax paid for the tax year in which the entitlement to relief arose.

824(3) For the purposes of subsection (1) above–

(aa) if the repayment is a payment made by the Board under section 375(8), the relevant time is–

(i) if the interest payment was made in the year 1996–97 or a subsequent year of assessment, the 31st January next following that year;

(ii) if the interest payment was made in an earlier year of assessment, the 5th April next following that year;

(ab) if the repayment is a repayment as a result of a claim for relief under any of the provisions mentioned in subsection (2C) above, the relevant time is the 31st January next following the year that is the later year in relation to the claim;

(ac) if the repayment is a repayment as a result of a claim under section 496B of ITA 2007 (relief for payments by discretionary trust taxable as employment income), the relevant time is the 31 January next following the end of the tax year to which the claim relates;

(ad) if the repayment is a payment falling within subsection (2D)(b), the relevant time is 31 January next following the end of the tax year in which the entitlement to relief arose;

(a) if the repayment is–

(i) the repayment of an amount paid in accordance with the requirements of section 59A of the Management Act on account of income tax for a year of assessment, or

(ii) the repayment of income tax for such a year which is not income tax deducted at source,

the relevant time is the date of the payment that is being repaid (other than a repayment within paragraph (ac));

(b) if the repayment is of income tax deducted at source for a year of assessment, the relevant time is the 31st January next following that year; and

(c) if the repayment is of a penalty or surcharge, the relevant time is the date on which the penalty or surcharge was paid.

824(4) For the purposes of subsection (3) above, where a repayment in respect of income tax for a year of assessment is made to any person, that repayment–

(a) shall be attributed first to so much of any payment made by him under section 59B of the Management Act as is a payment in respect of income tax for that year;

(b) in so far as it exceeds the amount (if any) to which it is attributable under paragraph (a) above, shall be attributed in two equal parts to each of the payments made by him under section 59A of the Management Act on account of income tax for that year;

(c) in so far as it exceeds the amounts (if any) to which it is attributable under paragraphs (a) and (b) above, shall be attributed to income tax deducted at source for that year; and

(d) in so far as it is attributable to a payment made in instalments shall be attributed to a later instalment before being attributed to an earlier one.

824(4A) In this section any reference to income tax deducted at source for a year of assessment is a reference to–

(a) income tax deducted or treated as deducted from any income, or treated as paid on any income, in respect of that year,

(b) [omitted by FA 2016, s. 5 and Sch. 1, para. 52(4),]

but does not include a reference to amounts which, in that year, are deducted at source under PAYE regulations in respect of previous years.

824(5) [Repealed by FA 1994, s. 196, Sch. 19, para. 41(3), and s. 258, Sch. 26, Pt. V(23).]

824(6) The Treasury may by order from time to time increase or decrease the rate of interest by reference to which–

(a) repayment supplements are calculated under subsection (1) above; and

(b) repayment supplements are calculated under section 47 of the Finance (No. 2) Act 1975.

824(7) A repayment supplement shall not be payable under this section in respect of a repayment or payment made in consequence of an order or judgment of a court having power to allow interest on the repayment or payment, or in respect of a repayment of a post-war credit within the meaning of the Income Tax (Repayment of Post-War Credits) Act 1959.

824(8) [Omitted by ITTOIA 2005, s. 882 and Sch. 1, para. 331(3) and repealed by s. 884 and Sch. 3.]

824(9) Subsections (1) to (7) above shall apply in relation to the trustees of a settlement, scheme administrators of registered pension schemes, or personal representatives as they apply in relation to an individual.

824(10) [Repealed by FA 1994, s. 196, Sch. 19, para. 41(3), and s. 258, Sch. 26, Pt. V(23).]

Prospective amendments – S. 824(2D)(b) to be repealed by FA 2012, Sch. 39, para. 28(1) with effect on a date to be appointed.
S. 824(3)(ad) to be repealed by FA 2012, Sch. 39, para. 28(1) with effect on a date to be appointed.

History – S. 824(1)(c) substituted by SI 2011/702, art. 11, with effect from 1 April 2011, but subject to SI 2011/702, art. 20, which provides that the substitution does not have effect in relation to a return or other document which is required to be made or delivered to HMRC, or an amount of tax which is payable, in relation to the tax year 2009–10 or any previous tax year.
S. 824(1) and (3) substituted by FA 1994, s. 196 and Sch. 19, para. 41(1), (2), and s. 824(5) and (10) and in s. 824(9) the words "a partnership" and "(within the meaning of section 111 of the Finance Act 1989)" repealed, by FA 1994, s. 196 and Sch. 19, para. 41(3), and s. 258 and Sch. 26, Pt. V(23), with effect for 1996–97 and subsequent years of assessment and, in relation to partnerships whose trades, professions or businesses are set up and commenced before 6 April 1994, with effect for 1997–98 and subsequent years.
In s. 824(1)(a), (b), the words "of not less than £25" repealed by FA 1989, s. 158(2)(b), (5) and s. 187 and Sch. 17, Pt. VIII in relation to repayments of tax made on or after 6 April 1993 by virtue of SI 1993/753.
S. 824(1) amended retrospectively by FA 1988, s. 146 and Sch. 13, para. 7(a) by substituting para. (a) and (b). In s. 824(1), the words "rate applicable under section 178 of the Finance Act 1989" substituted by FA 1989, s. 179(1)(a)(vii), (4) for periods beginning on or after 18 August 1989 (SI 1989/1298 (C. 44)).
The repeal of s. 824(1A) and references to it in s. 824(2), (6) has effect for periods beginning on or after 18 August 1989 (FA 1989, s. 178(7); SI 1989/1298 (C 44)).
S. 824(1A) previously inserted by FA 1988, s. 146 and Sch. 13, para. 7(b).
S. 824(2) omitted by FA 2016, s. 5 and Sch. 1, para. 52(3), with effect in relation to dividends paid or arising (or treated as paid), and other distributions made (or treated as made), in the tax year 2016–17 or at any later time. Former s. 824(2) read as follows:
"**824(2)** Subsection (1) above shall with the necessary modifications apply to a payment of the whole or part of a tax credit as they apply to a repayment falling within subsection (1) of income tax paid in the year of assessment to which the tax credit relates.".
S. 824(2) amended retrospectively by FA 1988, s. 146 and Sch. 13, para. 7(c) by substituting the words "Subsections (1) and (1A)" and "they apply to a repayment falling within subsection (1)". Words "and (1A)" subsequently repealed by FA 1989, s. 187 and Sch. 17, Pt. X.
S. 824(2A) inserted retrospectively by FA 1988, s. 146 and Sch. 13, para. 7(d), to reflect F(No. 2)A 1975, s. 47(3)(b) before its repeal (since revived) by FA 1987, Sch. 16, Pt. VII.
S. 824(2B) and (3)(aa) inserted by FA 1999, s. 41(2), (3), and deemed always to have had effect. Identical amendments are deemed to have been made to corresponding provisions directly or indirectly re-enacted in s. 824 but only if the payments corresponding to payments under s. 375(8) were made in the year 1984–85 or a subsequent year of assessment (FA 1999, s. 41(4)–(6)).
S. 824(2C) and (3)(ab) inserted by FA 2001, s. 90(2), (3) in relation to repayments made after 11 May 2001.
S. 824(2D)(a) omitted by FA 2012, Sch. 39, para. 31(2)(a) in relation to events occurring on or after 6 April 2015.
S. 824(2D) inserted by SI 2011/1037, art. 7(2), with effect in relation to any repayment or (as the case may be) payment made by HMRC on or after 1 April 2011.
S. 842(3)(ac) inserted by SI 2010/157, art. 4(1)(a), with effect for the tax year 2010–11 and subsequent tax years.
S. 824(3)(ad) inserted by SI 2011/1037, art. 7(3), with effect in relation to any repayment or (as thecase may be) payment made by *HMRC on or after 1 April 2011.*
In s. 842(3)(a)(ii), the words "(other than a repayment within paragraph (ac))" inserted by SI 2010/157, art. 4(1)(b), with effect for the tax year 2010–11 and subsequent tax years.
S. 824(3)(a) and (b) substituted by FA 1997, s. 92(2) with effect for 1997–98 and subsequent years and with deemed effect for 1996–97.
In s. 824(3)(c), concluding words from "the relevant time" substituted by FA 1997, s. 92(3) with effect for 1997–98 and subsequent years of assessment and with deemed effect for 1996–97.

S. 824(4) substituted by FA 1997, s. 92(4), with effect for 1997–98 and subsequent years of assessment and with deemed effect for 1996–97.
In s. 824(4A)(b) (and the word "and" preceding it) omitted by FA 2016, s. 5 and Sch. 1, para. 52(4), with effect in relation to dividends paid or arising (or treated as paid), and other distributions made (or treated as made), in the tax year 2016–17 or at any later time. Former s. 824(4A)(b) read as follows:
"(b) amounts which, in respect of that year, are tax credits to which section 397(1) or 397A(1) of ITTOIA 2005 applies,".
In former s. 824(4A)(b), "397A(1)" substituted for "397A(2)" by FA 2009, s. 40 and Sch. 19, para. 10(a), with effect in relation to–
- qualifying distributions arising on or after 22 April 2009,
- cash dividends paid over to a person under paragraph 68(4) of Schedule 2 of ITEPA 2003 on or after 22 April 2009,
- dividends treated under section 407 of ITTOIA 2005 as paid to a person on or after 22 April 2009, and
- manufactured overseas dividends that are representative any of the above distributions.

In former s. 824(4A)(b), "or 397A(2)" inserted by FA 2008, s. 34 and sch. 12, para. 15, with effect for the tax year 2008–09 and subsequent tax years.
In former s. 824(4A)(b) the words "section 397(1) of ITTOIA 2005" substituted by ITTOIA 2005, s. 882(1) and Sch. 1, para. 331(2); effective for income tax purposes for 2005–06 onwards and for corporation tax purposes for accounting periods ending after 5 April 2005 (ITTOIA 2005, s. 883(1)).
In s. 824(4A), the words "PAYE regulations" substituted for the words "section 203" by ITEPA 2003, s. 722 and Sch. 6, para. 104, with effect for income tax purposes, from 2003–04; and for corporation tax purposes, for accounting periods ending after 5 April 2003.
S. 824(4A) inserted by FA 1997, s. 92(4) with effect for 1997–98 and subsequent years and with deemed effect for 1996–97
In s. 824(5), the words "of not less than 25" repealed by FA 1989, s. 158(2)(b), (5) and s. 187 and Sch. 17, Pt. VIII and s. 824(5)(b) repealed by s. 187 and Sch. 17, Pt. VIII of that Act in relation to repayments of tax made on or after 6 April 1993 (SI 1993/753).
S. 824(8) omitted by ITTOIA 2005, s. 882(1) and Sch. 1, para. 331(3) and repealed by s. 884 and Sch. 3; effective for income tax purposes for 2005–06 onwards and for corporation tax purposes for accounting periods ending after 5 April 2005 (ITTOIA 2005, s. 883(1)).
In former s. 824(8), reference to the 1992 Act substituted by TCGA 1992, s. 290 and Sch. 10, para. 14(52).
In s. 824(9) words ", scheme administrators of registered pension schemes" inserted by FA 2004, s. 281 and Sch. 35, para. 33, with effect from 6 April 2006.
In s. 824(9) the words "to (7)" substituted by ITTOIA 2005, s. 882(1) and Sch. 1, para. 331(4); effective for income tax purposes for 2005–06 onwards and for corporation tax purposes for accounting periods ending after 5 April 2005 (ITTOIA 2005, s. 883(1))
S. 824(9) amended by FA 1989, s. 110(5), (6) and s. 111(4), (5) extending previous reference to a UK trust and a UK estate, with effect for 1989–90 and subsequent years of assessment, definitionof UK estate in s. 824(10) repealed accordingly by FA 1989, s. 187 and Sch. 17, Pt. IV.

Derivations – S. 824(1) (as originally enacted): F(No. 2)A 1975, s. 47(1) before its amendment by FA 1987, Sch. 16, Pt. VII.
S. 824(2), as originally enacted: F(No. 2)A 1975, s. 47(3)(a).
S. 824(3), as originally enacted: F(No. 2)A 1975, s. 47(4), before its amendment by FA 1987, Sch. 16, Pt. VII
S. 824(4)–(10), as originally enacted: F(No. 2)A 1975, s. 47(5)–(9), (11), (12).

Cross references – S. 289(15): modification of s. 824 where repayment of tax follows claim for relief under business expansion scheme provisions.
S. 289A(9): modification of s. 824 where repayment of tax follows claim for relief under enterprise investment scheme provisions.
Sch. 15B, para. 1(7): supplement on repayment on claim to relief for subscription to eligible shares in a venture capital trust runs from end of 12 months following year of assessment in which shares were issued.
TMA 1970, s. 30(2), (3): recovery of repayment supplement overpaid, or paid in error.
TMA 1970, s. 70A: when payment of tax by cheque treated as received under self-assessment.
FA 1989, s. 110: UK residence of trustees.
FA 1989, s. 111: UK residence of personal representatives.
FA 1989, s. 178: power of Treasury to set interest rates.
FA 1993, s. 173 and Sch. 19, para. 13(4): disapplication of s. 824 to repayments of tax etc. deducted from investment income of Lloyd's underwriter.
SSCBA 1992, Sch. 2, para. 6: s. 824 applies in relation to Class 4 contributions from 19 April 1993.
SI 1989/1297, reg. 3AB: applicable rate of interest for the purposes of s. 824.
SI 1995/352: application of s. 824 to repayments of tax deducted at source to Lloyd's underwriters.
SI 1995/3225: disapplication of s. 824 to repayments of excessive payments on account to Lloyd's managing agents.
SI 2011/701, art. 5: s. 824 does not apply to any self-assessment amount (as defined in SI 2011/701, art. 2) which becomes payable or repayable on or after 31 October 2011 (the date of the coming into force of FA 2009, s. 101–103).

Extra-statutory concessions – A51 (applicable for repayments and payments made by HMRC before 1 April 2011): repayment supplement and cases where life assurance premium relief given.
A82: repayment supplement payable to individuals and others for year of assessment in which he or she resident in EC member state other than the UK.

Hansard – 2 July 1975, col. 746 and confirmed by ICAEW Technical Release TR 798 (not reproduced): where a taxpayer simultaneously has tax due under one assessment and has overpaid on another and he draws this fact to HMRC's attention and asks for a set off, interest will not be charged on the tax due as of the date that the set off request is made (to the extent that it can be met from the overpayment).

Notes – S. 824(8) rewritten as ITTOIA 2005, s. 749.

825 Repayment supplements: companies

825 [S. 825 superseded by s. 826]

History – S. 825 superseded by s. 826 with effect from 30 September 1993 (see s. 826(8) and (9)).

826 Interest on tax overpaid

826(1) In any case where–

(a) a repayment falls to be made of corporation tax paid by a company for an accounting period which ends after the appointed day; or

(aa) a repayment falls to be made under sections 246N and 246Q of advance corporation tax paid by a company in respect of distributions made by it in such an accounting period; or

(b) a repayment of income tax falls to be made in respect of a payment received by a company in such an accounting period; or

(c) [omitted by FA 2016, s. 5 and Sch. 1, para. 52(6)(a)]

ICTA 1988

(d) a payment of R&D tax credit falls to be made to a company under Chapter 2 or 7 of Part 13 of CTA 2009 in respect of an accounting period; or

(da) [Omitted by CTA 2009, s. 1322 and Sch. 1, para. 267(2)(b) and repealed by CTA 2009, s. 1326 and Sch. 3, Pt. 1.]

(e) a payment of land remediation tax credit or life assurance company tax credit falls to be made to a company under Part 14 of CTA 2009 in respect of an accounting period, or

(f) a payment of film tax credit falls to be made to a company, or

(fa) a payment of television tax credit falls to be made to a company; or

(fb) a payment of video game tax credit falls to be made to a company; or

(fc) a payment of theatre tax credit falls to be made to a company; or

(fd) a payment of orchestra tax credit falls to be made to a company, or

(g) a payment of first-year tax credit falls to be made to a company under Schedule A1 to the Capital Allowances Act.

then, from the material date until the order for repayment or payment is issued, the repayment or payment shall carry interest at the rate applicable under section 178 of the Finance Act 1989.

826(2) Subject to section 826A(2), in relation to corporation tax paid by a company for an accounting period, **"the material date"** for the purposes of this section is the date on which corporation tax was paid or, if it is later, the date on which corporation tax for that accounting period became (or, as the case may be, would have become) due and payable in accordance with section 59D of the Management Act (payment of corporation tax).

826(2A) [Repealed by FA 1998, s. 31 and Sch. 3, para. 38(2); s. 165 and Sch. 27, Pt. III(2)]

826(3) In relation to a repayment of income tax falling within subsection (1)(b) above, **"the material date"** is the day after the end of the accounting period in which the payment referred to in subsection (1)(b) above was received by the company.

826(3A) In relation to a payment of R&D tax credit falling within subsection (1)(d) above the material date is whichever is the later of–

(a) the filing date for the company's company tax return for the accounting period for which the R&D tax credit is claimed, and

(b) the date on which the company tax return or amended company tax return containing the claim for payment of the R&D tax credit is delivered to the Inland Revenue.

For this purpose **"the filing date"**, in relation to a company tax return, has the same meaning as in Schedule 18 to the Finance Act 1998.

826(3AA) [Omitted by CTA 2009, s. 1322 and Sch. 1, para. 267(3) and repealed by CTA 2009, s. 1326 and Sch. 3, Pt. 1.]

826(3B) In relation to a payment of land remediation tax credit or video game tax credit or life assurance company tax credit falling within subsection (1)(e) above the material date is whichever is the later of–

(a) the filing date for the company's company tax return for the accounting period for which the land remediation tax credit or the life assurance company tax credit is claimed, and

(b) the date on which the company tax return or amended company tax return containing the claim for payment of the land remediation tax credit or the life assurance company tax credit is delivered to the Inland Revenue.

For this purpose **"the filing date"**, in relation to a company tax return, has the same meaning as in Schedule 18 to the Finance Act 1998.

826(3C) In relation to a payment of film tax credit, television tax credit, video game tax credit, theatre tax credit or orchestra tax credit the material date is whichever is the later of–

(a) the filing date for the company's company tax return for the accounting period for which the tax credit is payable, and

(b) the date on which the company tax return or amended company tax return containing the claim for payment is delivered to an officer of Revenue and Customs.

For this purpose **"the filing date"**, in relation to a company tax return, has the same meaning as in Schedule 18 to the Finance Act 1998.

826(3D) In relation to a payment of *first-year* tax credit falling within subsection (1)(g) above the material *date is whichever* is the later of–

(a) the filing date for the company's company tax return for the accounting period for which the tax credit is claimed, and

(b) the date on which the company tax return or amended company tax return containing the claim for payment of the tax credit is delivered to the Commissioners for Her Majesty's Revenue and Customs.

For this purpose **"the filing date"**, in relation to a company tax return, has the same meaning as in Schedule 18 to the Finance Act 1998.

826(4) For the purposes of this section a repayment of tax made on a claim under section 458 of CTA 2010 shall be treated as if it were a repayment of corporation tax for the accounting period in which the event giving rise to entitlement to relief under that section occurred but, in relation to such a repayment of tax, **"the material date"** for the purposes of this section is–

(a) the date when the entitlement to relief in respect of the repayment accrued, that is to say–

(i) where the repayment, or the release or writing off, of the loan or advance (or part thereof) occurred on or after the day mentioned in section 458(4) of CTA 2010, the date nine months after the end of that accounting period; and

(ii) in any other case, the date nine months after the end of the accounting period in which the loan or advance was made;

or

(b) if it is later, the date on which the tax which is to be repaid was in fact paid.

826(5)–(5A) [Omitted by CTA 2009, s. 1322 and Sch. 1, para. 267(4) and repealed by CTA 2009, s. 1326 and Sch. 3, Pt. 1.]

826(6) Where a repayment of corporation tax is a repayment of tax paid by a company on different dates, the repayment shall so far as possible be treated for the purposes of this section as a repayment of tax paid on a later rather than an earlier date among those dates.

826(7) [Repealed by FA 1998, s. 31 and Sch. 3, para. 38(3); s. 165 and Sch. 27, Pt. III(2).]

826(7A) In any case where–

(a) a company carrying on a trade incurs a loss in the trade in an accounting period (**"the later period"**),

(b) as a result of a claim under section 37 of CTA 2010, the whole or any part of that loss is relieved (whether under section 37 or 42 of that Act) for the purposes of corporation tax against profits (of whatever description) of an earlier accounting period (**"the earlier period"**) which does not fall wholly within the period of twelve months immediately preceding the later period, and

(c) a repayment falls to be made of corporation tax paid for the earlier period or of income tax in respect of a payment received by the company in that accounting period,

then, in determining the amount of interest (if any) payable under this section on the repayment referred to in paragraph (c) above, no account shall be taken of so much of the amount of that repayment as falls to be made as a result of the claim under section 37 of CTA 2010, except so far as concerns interest for any time after the date on which any corporation tax for the later period became (or, as the case may be, would have become) due and payable, as mentioned in subsection (7D) below.

826(7AA) [Repealed by FA 1998, s. 31 and Sch. 3, para. 38(4); s. 165 and Sch. 27, Pt. III(2).]

826(7B) [Repealed by F(No. 2)A 1997, s. 52 and Sch. 8, Pt. II(4).]

826(7BB) Subject to subsection (7BC) below, in any case where–

(a) within the meaning of section 806D, any relievable underlying tax or relievable withholding tax arises in an accounting period of a company ("the later period"),

(b) pursuant to a claim under section 806G, the whole or any part of that tax is treated as mentioned in section 806D(4)(c) or (5)(c) in relation to the single related dividend or the single unrelated dividend arising in an earlier accounting period ("the earlier period"), and

(c) a repayment falls to be made of corporation tax paid for the earlier period or of income tax in respect of a payment received by the company in that period,

then, in determining the amount of interest (if any) payable under this section on the repayment referred to in paragraph (c) above, no account shall be taken of so much of the amount of the repayment as falls to be made as a result of the claim under section 806G, except so far as concerns interest for any time after the date on which any corporation tax for the later period became due and payable (as mentioned in subsection (7D) below).

826(7BC) [Omitted by FA 2009, s. 34 and Sch. 14, para. 10.]

826(7C) In a case where–

(a) there is for an accounting period of a company (**"the later period"**) a non-trading deficit on the company's loan relationships,

ICTA 1988

(b) as a result of a claim under section 389(1) or 459(1)(b) of CTA 2009 the whole or part of the deficit for the later period is set off against profits of an earlier accounting period (**"the earlier period"**), and

(c) a repayment falls to be made of corporation tax for the earlier period or of income tax in respect of a payment received by the company in that accounting period,

then, in determining the amount of interest (if any) payable under this section on the repayment referred to in paragraph (c) above, no account shall be taken of so much of the amount of the repayment as falls to be made as a result of the claim under section 389(1) or section 459(1)(b) of CTA 2009 except so far as concerns interest for any time after the date on which any corporation tax for the later period became (or, as the case may be, would have become) due and payable, as mentioned in subsection (7D) below.

826(7CA) [Repealed by FA 1998, s. 31 and Sch. 3, para. 38(4); s. 165 and Sch. 27, Pt. III(2).]

826(7D) In subsections (7), (7A), (7B), (7BB) and (7C) above, any reference to the date on which corporation tax for an accounting period became, or would have become, due and payable shall be construed on the basis that corporation tax for an accounting period becomes due and payable on the day following the expiry of nine months from the end of the accounting period.

826(7E) The power conferred by section 59E of the Management Act (alteration of date on which corporation tax becomes due and payable) does not include power to make provision in relation to subsection (7), (7A), (7B), (7BB), (7C) or (7D) above the effect of which would be to change the meaning of references in subsection (7), (7A), (7B), (7BB) or (7C) above to the date on which corporation tax for an accounting period became, or would have become, due and payable (as mentioned in subsection (7D) above).

826(8) In consequence of the preceding provisions of this section, no repayment supplement (within the meaning of section 825) shall be paid in respect of any repayment of tax or payment of tax credit where the relevant accounting period (within the meaning of that section) ends after the appointed day.

826(8A) Where–

(a) interest has been paid to a company under subsection (1)(a) ,(d), (e) (f), (fa), (fb), (fc) or (fd) above,

(b) there is–

(i) a change in the company's assessed liability to corporation tax, or

(ii) a change in the amount of the R&D tax credit, land remediation tax credit or life assurance company tax credit or film tax credit or television tax credit or video game tax credit or theatre tax credit or orchestra tax credit or first-year tax credit under Schedule A1 to the Capital Allowances Act payable to the company (which does not result in a change falling within sub-paragraph (i)),

other than a change which in whole or in part corrects an error made by the Board or an officer of the Board, and

(c) as a result only of that change (and, in particular, not as a result of any error in the calculation of the interest), it appears to an officer of the Board that the interest ought not to have been paid, either at all or to any extent,

the interest that ought not to have been paid may be recovered from the company as if it were interest charged under Part IX of the Management Act (interest on overdue tax).

826(8B) For the purposes of subsection (8A) above, the cases where there is a change in a company's assessed liability to corporation tax are those cases where–

(a) an assessment, or an amendment of an assessment, of the amount of corporation tax payable by the company for the accounting period in question is made, or

(b) a determination of that amount is made under paragraph 36 or 37 of Schedule 18 to the Finance Act 1998 (which until superseded by a self-assessment under that Schedule has effect as if it were one),

whether or not any previous assessment or determination has been made.

826(8BA) For the purposes of subsection (8A)(b) above, the cases where there is a change in the amount of the R&D tax credit, the land remediation tax credit or the life assurance company tax credit or film tax credit or television tax credit or video game tax credit or theatre tax credit or orchestra tax credit or first-year tax credit under Schedule A1 to the Capital Allowances Act payable to the company are those cases where an assessment, or an amendment to an assessment, is made to recover an amount of R&D tax credit, land remediation tax credit or life assurance company tax credit or film tax credit or television tax credit or video game tax credit or theatre tax credit or orchestra tax credit or first-year tax credit under Schedule A1 to the Capital Allowances Act paid to the company for the accounting period in question.

826(8C) In subsection (8A)(b) above "error" includes

(a) any computational error; and

(b) the allowance of a claim or election which ought not to have been allowed.

826(9) In this section **"the appointed day"** means such day or days, not being earlier than 31st March 1992, as the Treasury may by order appoint for the purposes of this section.

History – S. 826(1)(fd) inserted by FA 2016, s. 54 and Sch. 8, para. 2(2), with effect in relation to accounting periods beginning on or after 1 April 2016 (subject to the provisions of Sch. 8, para. 17(2) and (3)).

S. 826(1)(c) (and the word "or" at the end) omitted by FA 2016, s. 5 and Sch. 1, para. 52(6)(a), with effect in relation to dividends paid or arising (or treated as paid), and other distributions made (or treated as made), in the tax year 2016–17 or at any later time. Former s. 826(1)(c) read as follows:

"(c) a payment falls to be made to a company of the whole or part of the tax credit comprised in any franked investment income received by the company in such an accounting period; or".

S. 826(1)(fa) inserted by FA 2013, s. 36 and Sch. 18, para. 1(2) with effect from 19 July 2013 (SI 2013/1817) in relation to accounting periods beginning on or after "the relevant day" (as defined in FA 2013, Sch. 18, para. 23).

S. 826(1)(fb) inserted by FA 2013, s. 36 and Sch. 18, para. 1(2) with effect from 1 April 2014 (SI 2014/1962) in relation to accounting periods beginning on or after "the relevant day" (as defined in FA 2013, Sch. 18, para. 23).

S. 826(1)(fc) inserted by FA 2014, s. 36 and Sch. 4, para. 2(2)with effect from 22 August 2014, in relation to accounting periods beginning on or after 1 September 2014, subject to the transitional provisions in FA 2014, Sch. 4, para. 17.

In s. 826(1)(d), the words "Chapter 2 or 7 of Part 13 of CTA 2009" substituted for "Schedule 20 to the Finance Act 2000" by CTA 2009, s. 1322 and Sch. 1, para. 267(2)(a), with effect for corporation tax purposes for accounting periods ending on or after 1 April 2009, and for income tax and capital gains tax purposes for the tax year 2009–10 and subsequent tax years.

S. 826(1)(da) omitted by CTA 2009, s. 1322 and Sch. 1, para. 267(2)(b) and repealed by CTA 2009, s. 1326 and Sch. 3, Pt. 1, with effect for corporation tax purposes for accounting periods ending on or after 1 April 2009, and for income tax and capital gains tax purposes for the tax year 2009–10 and subsequent tax years.

In s. 826(1)(e), the words "Part 14 of CTA 2009" substituted for "Schedule 22 to the Finance Act 2001" by CTA 2009, s. 1322 and Sch. 1, para. 267(2)(c) , with effect for corporation tax purposes for accounting periods ending on or after 1 April 2009, and for income tax and capital gains tax purposes for the tax year 2009–10 and subsequent tax years.

S. 826(1)(g) inserted by FA 2008, s. 79 and Sch. 25, para. 7(2), with effect in relation to expenditure incurred on or after 1 April 2008.

S. 826(1)(f) inserted by FA 2006, s. 42 and Sch. 5, Pt. 3, para. 26, with effect from 1 January 2007 (FA 2006, s. 53).

S. 826(1) retrospectively amended by FA 1989, s. 178 by substituting the reference to the issuing of the payment order.

In s. 826(1), the words "rate applicable ... Finance Act 1989" inserted by FA 1989, s. 178 where the reference date is after 1 October 1993.

S. 826(1)(da) inserted by FA 2002, s. 54 and Sch. 14, para. 1(2), with effect, by virtue of Sch. 14, para. 5,in relation to tax credits payable under FA 2002, Sch. 13 in respect of expenditure incurred on or after 22 April 2003 which is the day appointed by the Treasury by order made by SI 2003/1472 in accordance with FA 2002, Sch. 13, para. 28(1).

S. 826(1)(e) inserted by FA 2001, s. 70 and Sch. 23, para. 3(2) for accounting periods ending on or after 1 April 2001.

S. 826(1)(aa) and former s. 826(2A) (see History note below for details of repeal) inserted by FA 1994 s. 138 and Sch. 16, para. 20 consequential upon the introduction of the foreign income dividend scheme (s. 246A–246Y).

S. 826(1)(d) inserted by FA 2000, s. 69(2) and Sch. 21, para. 1(2), with effect for accounting periods ending on or after 1 April 2000.

In s. 826(2), the words "section 59D of the Management Act (payment of corporation tax)" substituted for the words "section 10" by FA 1994, s. 196 and Sch. 19, para. 42 with effect in relation to accounting periods ending on or after 1 July 1999, the appointed day for corporation tax self-assessment by virtue of FA 1994, s. 199 and SI 1998/3173 (C. 78).

In s. 826(2), the words "Subject to section 826A(2)," inserted by FA 1998, s. 35 and Sch. 4, para. 1(1).

S. 826(2A) repealed by FA 1998, s. 31 and Sch. 3, para. 38(2); s. 165 and Sch. 27, Pt. III(2), with effect in relation to accounting periods beginning on or after 6 April 1999.

In s. 826(3) the words "or a payment of the whole or part of a tax credit falling within subsection (1)(c) above" (which appeared after the first "above") and the words "or, as the case may be, the franked investment income referred to in subsection (1)(c) above" (which appeared after the second "above") omitted by FA 2016, s. 5 and Sch. 1, para. 52(6)(b), with effect in relation to dividends paid or arising (or treated as paid), and other distributions made (or treated as made), in the tax year 2016–17 or at any later time.

In s. 826(3) the words "is the day after the end of the accounting period" substituted by FA 1998, Sch. 4, para. 2 as respects accounting periods ending on or after 1 July 1999, the appointed day for corporation tax self-assessment by virtue of SI 1998/3173 (FA 1994, s. 199(2)).

S. 826(3A) inserted by FA 2000, s. 69(2) and Sch. 21, para. 1(3), with effect for accounting periods ending on or after 1 April 2000.

S. 826(3AA) omitted by CTA 2009, s. 1322 and Sch. 1, para. 267(3) and repealed by CTA 2009, s. 1326 and Sch. 3, Pt. 1, with effect for corporation tax purposes for accounting periods ending on or after 1 April 2009, and for income tax and capital gains tax purposes for the tax year 2009–10 and subsequent tax years.

Former S. 826(3AA) inserted by FA 2002, s. 54 and Sch. 14, para. 1(3), with effect, by virtue of Sch. 14, para. 5, in relation to tax credits payable under FA 2002, Sch. 13 in respect of expenditureincurred on or after 22 April 2003 which is the day appointed by the Treasury by order made by SI 2003/1472 in accordance with FA 2002, Sch. 13, para. 28(1).

S. 826(3B) inserted by FA 2001, s. 70 and Sch. 23, para. 3(3) for accounting periods ending on or after 1 April 2001.

In s. 826(3C), the words ", theatre tax credit or orchestra tax credit" substituted for the words "or theatre tax credit" by FA 2016, s. 54 and Sch. 8, para. 2(3), with effect in relation to accounting periods beginning on or after 1 April 2016 (subject to the provisions of Sch. 8, para. 17(2) and (3)).

In s. 826(3C), the words ", video game tax credit or theatre tax credit" substituted for the words "or video game tax credit" by FA 2014, s. 36 and Sch. 4, para. 2(3), with effect from 22 August 2014, in relation to accounting periods beginning on or after 1 September 2014, subject to the transitional provisions in FA 2014, Sch. 4, para. 17.

In s. 826(3C), the words "or video game tax credit" inserted after the words "television tax credit" by FA 2013, s. 36 and Sch. 18, para. 1(3) with effect from 1 April 2014 (SI 2014/1962) in relation to accounting periods beginning on or after "the relevant day" (as defined in FA 2013, Sch. 18, para. 23).

In s. 826(3C), the words ", television tax credit" inserted by FA 2013, s. 36 and Sch. 18, para. 1(3) with effect from 19 July 2013 (SI 2013/1817) in relation to accounting periods beginning on or after "the relevant day" (as defined in FA 2013, Sch. 18, para. 23). As the full text to be inserted is partially prospective (see note above) the grammar of the text inserted is wrong.

S. 826(3C) inserted by FA 2006, s. 42 and Sch. 5, Pt. 3, para. 26, with effect from 1 January 2007 (FA 2006, s. 53).

S. 826(3D) inserted by FA 2008, s. 79 and Sch. 25, para. 7(3), with effect in relation to expenditure incurred on or after 1 April 2008.

In s. 826(4), the words "section 458 of CTA 2010" substituted for the words "section 419(4)", and "that section" substituted for the words "section 419(4)", and "section 458(4) of CTA 2010" substituted for the words "section 419(4A)" by CTA 2010, s. 1177 and Sch. 1, para. 117, with effect for corporation tax purposes for accounting periods ending on or after 1 April 2010, and for income and capital gains tax purposes for the tax year 2010–11 and subsequent tax years.

In s. 826(4), words "the event giving rise to entitlement to relief under section 419(4) occurred" substituted for "the repayment of, or of the part in question of, the loan or advance mentioned in section419(4)" and in para. (a) words ", or the release or writing off," inserted by FA 1999, s. 90(1), with effect in relation to the release or writing off of the whole or part of a debt on or after 6 April 1999.

S. 826(4)(a) substituted by FA 1996, s. 173(5) for any loan or advance made in an accounting period ending on or after 31 March 1996.

S. 826(5) and (5A) omitted by CTA 2009, s. 1322 and Sch. 1, para. 267(4) and repealed by CTA 2009, s. 1326 and Sch. 3, Pt. 1, with effect for corporation tax purposes for accounting periods ending on or after 1 April 2009, and for income tax and capital gains tax purposes for the tax year 2009–10 and subsequent tax years.

Former s. 826(5) amended by FA 1998, s. 34(3) with effect where interest is payable under s. 826 in respect of accounting periods ending on or after 1 July 1999, the appointed day for corporation tax self-assessment by virtue of FA 1994, s. 199(2) and SI 1998/3173 (C. 78).
Former s. 826(5A) inserted by FA 1998, s. 34(4) with effect where interest is payable under s. 826 in respect of accounting periods ending on or after 1 July 1999, the appointed day for corporation tax self-assessment by virtue of FA 1994, s. 199(2) and SI 1998/3173 (C. 78).
S. 826(7) repealed by FA 1998, s. 31 and Sch. 3, para. 38(3); s. 165 and Sch. 27, Pt. III(2), with effect where the later period mentioned in s. 826(7) begins on or after 6 April 1999.
In s. 826(7A)(b), the words "section 37 of CTA 2010" substituted for the words "section 393A(1)", and "relieved" substituted for the words "set off ", and "section 37 or 42 of that Act" substituted for the words "section 393A(1) or 393B(3)", by CTA 2010, s. 1177 and Sch. 1, para. 117, with effect for corporation tax purposes for accounting periods ending on or after 1 April 2010, and for income and capital gains tax purposes for the tax year 2010–11 and subsequent tax years.
In s. 826(7A)(b), the words "(whether under section 393A(1) or 393B(3))" inserted by FA 2008, s. 111 and Sch. 35, para. 7, with effect in relation to losses incurred in accounting periods beginning on or after 12 March 2008.
In the words after s. 826(7A)(c), the words "section 37 of CTA 2010" substituted for the words "section 393A(1)" by CTA 2010, s. 1177 and Sch. 1, para. 117, with effect for corporation tax purposes for accounting periods ending on or after 1 April 2010, and for income and capital gains tax purposes for the tax year 2010–11 and subsequent tax years.
In s. 826(7A), words "so much of … to be made" substituted by FA 1993, s. 120 and Sch. 14, para. 10(2) in connection with the introduction of Pay and File.
S. 826(7A) inserted by FA 1991, s. 73 and Sch. 15, para. 23 with effect in relation to losses incurred in accounting periods ending on or after 1 April 1991.
S. 826(7AA) ceases to have effect by FA 1998, s. 31 and Sch.3, para. 38(4), and is repealed by s. 165 and Sch. 27, Pt. III(2), with effect where the earlier period mentioned in that subsection begins on or after 6 April 1999.
Former S. 826(7AA) inserted by FA 1993, s. 120 and Sch. 14, para. 10(3), in relation to any claim made under s. 393A(1) as a result of which there is an amount of surplus ACT in an accounting period ending after 30 September 1993, but subject to the provisions of FA 1993, Sch. 14, para. 10(6) (see cross reference below).
S. 826(7B) repealed by F(No. 2)A 1997, s. 52 and Sch. 8, Pt. II(4), with effect in accordance with F(No. 2)A 1997, s. 20 (broadly, for accounting periods beginning on or after 2 July 1997).
Former S. 826(7BA) inserted by FA 1991, s. 73 and Sch. 15, para. 23 with effect in relation to losses incurred in accounting periods ending on or after 1 April 1991.
S. 826(7BB) inserted by FA 2000, s. 103 and Sch. 30, para. 29(2).
S. 826(7BC) omitted by FA 2009, s. 34 and Sch. 14, para. 10, with effect in relation to distributions paid on or after 1 July 2009.
S. 826(7BC) inserted by FA 2000, s. 103 and Sch. 30, para. 29(2).
In s. 826(7C)(a), words "a non-trading deficit on the company's loan relationships," substituted; in s. 826(7C)(b) words "section 83(2)(c) … set off against profits" substituted; in the words after s. 826(7C)(c) "section 83(2)(c) of that Act … to that Act" substituted by FA 1996, s. 104 and Sch. 14, para. 48(1) for accounting periods ending after 31 March 1996, subject to FA 1996, Sch. 15.
In s. 826(7C)(b), the words "section 389(1) or 459(1)(b) of CTA 2009" substituted for "section 83(2)(c) of the Finance Act 1996 or paragraph 4(3) of Schedule 11 to that Act" by CTA 2009, s. 1322 and Sch. 1, para. 267(5)(a), with effect for corporation tax purposes for accounting periods ending on or after 1 April 2009, and for income tax and capital gains tax purposes for the tax year 2009–10 and subsequent tax years.
In s. 826(7C), in the words following para. (c), the words "section 389(1) or section 459(1)(b) of CTA 2009" substituted for "section 83(2)(c) of that Act or, as the case may be, paragraph 4(3) of Schedule 11 to that Act" by CTA 2009, s. 1322 and Sch. 1, para. 267(5)(b), with effect for corporation tax purposes for accounting periods ending on or after 1 April 2009, and for income tax and capital gains tax purposes for the tax year 2009–10 and subsequent tax years.
In s. 826(7C), words "or of income tax … that accounting period" at end of paragraph (c) added by FA 1995, s. 130 and Sch. 24, para. 11(a) and words "repayment referred to … as a result of" substituted by FA 1995, s. 130 and Sch. 24, para. 11(b) ; both changes deemed to have had effect from the appointed day for FA 1993, s. 165(7)(b), i.e. 23 March 1995.
S. 826(7C) inserted by FA 1993, s. 170 and Sch. 18, para. 5, with effect where a companybecomes entitled to a qualifying asset or to rights and duties under a currency contract, or subject to a qualifying liability on or after 23 March 1995 which is the commencement day for the purposes of FA 1993, s. 165.
S. 826(7CA) ceases to have effect by FA 1998, s. 31 and Sch. 3, para. 38(4), and is repealed by s. 165 and Sch. 27, Pt. III(2), with effect where the earlier period mentioned in that subsection begins on or after 6 April 1999.
Former s. 826(7CA) inserted by FA 1995, s. 130 and Sch. 24, para. 12(2) and deemed to have come into force on the appointed day for FA 1993, s. 165(7)(b), i.e. 23 March 1995.
In s. 826(7D), (7E) references to subs. (7BB) inserted wherever they appear by FA 2000, s. 103 and Sch. 30, para. 29(3) and (4) respectively.
S. 826(7D) and (7E) inserted by FA 1998, Sch. 4, para. 5 where the due and payable date to be determined is for an accounting period ending on or after 1 July 1999, the appointed day for corporation tax self-assessment by virtue of SI 1998/3173 (FA 1994, s. 199(2)).
In s. 826(8A)(a), the words ", (fc) or (fd)" substituted for the words "or (fc)" and in s. 826(8A)(b)(ii), the words "or orchestra tax credit" inserted by FA 2016, s. 54 and Sch. 8, para. 2(4), with effect in relation to accounting periods beginning on or after 1 April 2016 (subject to the provisions of Sch. 8, para. 17(2) and (3)).
In s. 826(8A)(a), "(f), (fa), (fb) or (fc)" substituted for "or (f)" by FA 2014, s. 36 and Sch. 4, para. 2(4)(a), with effect from 22 August 2014, in relation to accounting periods beginning on or after 1 September 2014, subject to the transitional provisions in FA 2014, Sch. 4, para. 17.
In s. 826(8A)(a), ", (d)" substituted for "(d), (da)" by CTA 2009, s. 1322 and Sch. 1, para. 267(6)(a), with effect for corporation tax purposes for accounting periods ending on or after 1 April 2009, and for income tax and capital gains tax purposes for the tax year 2009–10 and subsequent tax years.
In s. 826(8A)(a) the words ", (e) or (f)" substituted for the words "or (e)" and in s. 826(8A)(b)(ii) the words "or film tax credit" inserted by FA 2006, s. 42 and Sch. 5, Pt. 3, para. 26, with effect from 1 January 2007 (FA 2006, s. 53).
In s. 826(8A)(b)(ii), the words "or theatre tax credit" inserted after the words "video game tax credit" by FA 2014, s. 36 and Sch. 4, para. 2(4)(b),with effect from 22 August 2014, in relation to accounting periods beginning on or after 1 September 2014, subject to the transitional provisions in FA 2014, Sch. 4, para. 17.
In s. 826(8A)(b)(ii), the words "or television tax credit" inserted by FA 2013, s. 36 and Sch. 18, para. 1(4) witheffect from 19 July 2013 (SI 2013/1817) in relation to accounting periods beginning on or after "the relevant day" (as defined in FA 2013, Sch. 18, para. 23).
In s. 826(8A)(b)(ii), the words ", tax credit under Schedule 13 to the Finance Act 2002", which appeared after "R&D tax credit", omitted by CTA 2009, s. 1322 and Sch. 1, para. 267(6)(b) and repealed by CTA 2009, s. 1326 and Sch. 3, Pt. 1, with effect for corporation tax purposes for accounting periods ending on or after 1 April 2009, and for income tax and capital gains tax purposes for the tax year 2009–10 and *subsequent tax years.*
In s. 826(8A)(b)(ii), the words "or first-year tax credit under Schedule A1 to the Capital Allowances Act" inserted by FA 2008, s. 79 and Sch. 25, para. 7(4), with effect in relation to expenditure incurred on or after 1 April 2008.
In s. 826(8A)(a), words "(d), (da)" substituted for words "or (d)" by FA 2002, s. 54 and Sch. 14, para. 1(4)(a), with effect, by virtue of Sch. 14, para. 5, in relation to tax credits payable under FA 2002, Sch. 13 in respect of expenditure incurred on or after 22 April 2003 which is the day appointed by the Treasury by order made by SI 2003/1472 in accordance with FA 2002, Sch. 13, para. 28(1).

In s. 826(8A)(a) words "; or" and in s. 826(8A)(b)(ii) words ", land remediation tax credit or life assurance company tax credit" inserted by FA 2001, s. 70 and Sch. 23, para. 3(4) for accounting periods ending on or after 1 April 2001.
In s. 826(8A)(a), words "or (d)" inserted by FA 2000, s. 69(2) and Sch. 21, para. 1(4), with effect for accounting periods ending on or after 1 April 2000.
In s. 826(8A)(b)(ii), the words "or video game tax credit" inserted after the words "or television tax credit" by FA 2013, s. 36 and Sch. 18, para. 1(4) with effect from 1 April 2014 (SI 2014/1962) in relation to accounting periods beginning on or after "the relevant day" (as defined in FA 2013, Sch. 18, para. 23).
In s. 826(8A)(b)(ii), words "tax credit under Schedule 13 to the Finance Act 2002" inserted by FA 2002, s. 54 and Sch. 14, para. 1(4)(b), with effect, by virtue of Sch. 14, para. 5, in relation to tax credits payable under FA 2002, Sch. 13 in respect of expenditure incurred on or after 22 April 2003 which is the day appointed by the Treasury by order made by SI 2003/1472 in accordance with FA 2002, Sch. 13, para. 28(1).
S. 826(8A)(b) substituted, by FA 2000, s. 69(2) and Sch. 21, para. 1(4), with effect for accounting periods ending on or after 1 April 2000.
S. 826(8A) inserted by FA 1998, Sch. 4, para. 3 as respects interest on repayments of corporation tax paid for accounting periods ending on or after 1 July 1999, the appointed day for corporation tax self-assessmentby virtue of SI 1998/3173 (FA 1994, s. 199(2)).
In s. 826(8BA)(a), the words "or orchestra tax credit" inserted (twice) by FA 2016, s. 54 and Sch. 8, para. 2(5), with effect in relation to accounting periods beginning on or after 1 April 2016 (subject to the provisions of Sch. 8, para. 17(2) and (3)).
In s. 826(8BA), the words "or video game tax credit" inserted after the words "or television tax credit" (twice) by FA 2013, s. 36 and Sch. 18, para. 1(5) with effect from 1 April 2014 (SI 2014/1962) in relation to accounting periods beginning on or after "the relevant day" (as defined in FA 2013, Sch. 18, para. 23).
S. 826(8B) inserted by FA 1998, Sch. 4, para. 3 as respects interest on repayments of corporation tax paid for accounting periods ending on or after 1 July 1999, the appointed day for corporation tax self-assessment by virtue of SI 1998/3173 (FA 1994, s. 199(2)).
In s. 826(8BA), the words "or theatre tax credit" inserted after the words "video game tax credit" (in both places) by FA 2014, s. 36 and Sch. 4, para. 2(5), with effect from 22 August 2014, in relation to accounting periods beginning on or after 1 September 2014, subject to the transitional provisions in FA 2014, Sch. 4, para. 17.
In s. 826(8BA), the words "or television tax credit" inserted twice by FA 2013, s. 36 and Sch. 18, para. 1(5) with effect from 19 July 2013 (SI 2013/1817) in relation to accounting periods beginning on or after "the relevant day" (as defined in FA 2013, Sch. 18, para. 23).
In s. 826(8BA), the words ", tax credit under Schedule 13 to the Finance Act 2002", which appeared after the words "R&D tax credit", omitted in both places by CTA 2009, s. 1322 and Sch. 1, para. 267(7) and repealed by CTA 2009, s. 1326 and Sch. 3, Pt. 1, with effect for corporation tax purposes for accounting periods ending on or after 1 April 2009, and for income tax and capital gains tax purposes for the tax year 2009–10 and subsequent tax years.
In s. 826(8BA), the words "or first-year tax credit under Schedule A1 to the Capital Allowances Act" inserted twice by FA 2008, s. 79 and Sch. 25, para. 7(5), with effect in relation to expenditure incurred on or after 1 April 2008.
In s. 826(8BA) the words "or film tax credit" inserted twice by FA 2006, s. 42 and Sch. 5, Pt. 3, para. 26, with effect from 1 January 2007 (FA 2006, s. 53). FA 2006 Sch. 5, para. 26 states that this amendment should be made to s. 826(8B) but as the amendment fits with the wording of s. 826(8BA) rather than (8B) the amendment has been made there.
In s. 826(8BA), words ",tax credit under Schedule 13 to the Finance Act 2002" inserted, in both places after the words "R&D tax credit", by FA 2002, s. 54 and Sch. 14, para. 1(5), with effect, by virtue of Sch. 14, para. 5, in relation to tax credits payable under FA 2002, Sch. 13 in respect of expenditure incurred on or after 22 April 2003 which is the day appointed by the Treasury by order made by SI 2003/1472 in accordance with FA 2002, Sch. 13, para. 28(1).
In s. 826(8BA), the words ", the land remediation tax credit or the life assurance company tax credit" inserted after the words "amount of the R&D tax credit" by FA 2001, s. 70 and Sch. 23, para. 3(5)(a) for accounting periods ending on or after 1 April 2001.
In s. 826(BA), the words ", land remediation tax credit or life assurance tax credit" inserted after the words "amount of R&D tax credit" by FA 2001, s. 70 and Sch. 23, para. 3(5)(b) for accounting periods ending on or after 1 April 2001.
S. 826(8BA) inserted by FA 2000, s. 69(2) and Sch. 21, para. 1(5), with effect for accounting periods ending on or after 1 April 2000.
S. 826(8C) inserted by FA 1998, Sch. 4, para. 3 as respects interest on repayments of corporation tax paid for accounting periods ending on or after 1 July 1999, the appointed day for corporation tax self-assessment by virtue of SI 1998/3173 (FA 1994, s. 199(2)).

Derivations – S. 826(1)–(8) (as originally enacted): F(No. 2)A 1987, s. 87.
S. 826(9): F(No. 2)A 1987, s. 95(2), (3).

Cross references – Sch. 2, para. 56: no liability to corporation tax arises in respect of interest paid under s. 826(1) if the accounting period ends before 1 July 1999.
S. 10: before introduction of corporation tax self-assessment, corporation tax normally payable nine months after the end of an accounting period.
S. 252(2), (4): assessment from the appointed day to recover interest wrongly paid under s. 826.
S. 342A(4): tax on companies in administration – interest received or receivable not exceeding certain limit is not subject to corporation tax.
S. 393A(1): set-off of company trading losses against profits of the same or an earlier accounting period.
S. 419(4): repayment of tax relating to loan to a participator in a close company consequent on repayment of the loan.
S. 434C: s. 826(1) applies to a repayment of ACT paid by a company carrying on life assurance business on distributions made by it with the material date as specified in s. 826(2A).
Sch. 19AB, para. 5(6): effect of s. 826 in relation to provisional repayments of tax credits etc. to life insurance companies carrying on pension business in "transitional" accounting periods between entry into force of Sch. 19AB and the start of Pay and File.
TMA 1970, s. 59D: claim for repayment of corporation tax may be made after the notional date, as defined for the purposes of s. 826.
TMA 1970, s. 70A: when payment of tax by cheque treated as received under self-assessment.
TMA 1970, s. 89(1): prescribed rate of interest for purposes of s. 826.
FA 1989, s. 102(4A): treatment for interest purposes, of amounts surrendered within a group, where s. 826(7)–(7C) apply.
FA 1989, s. 178: power of Treasury to set interest rates.
FA 1993, s. 131(5), (6): claims to carry back unrelieved non-trading exchange losses against non-trading exchange gains of earlier periods.
FA 1993, Sch. 14, para. 10(6): where a claim under s. 393A(1) displaces an amount of surplus ACT which is carried back further under s. 239(3) to an earlier accounting period which ends before the introduction of Pay and File (1 October 1993), s. 826(7AA) does not apply, and instead a modified version of s. 825(4)(a) applies (see corresponding cross reference to s. 825).
FA 1994, s. 221(2): modified application of FA 1993, Sch. 19, para. 13 disapplies s. 826 to repayments of tax deducted etc. from investment income of corporate Lloyd's underwriters.
FA 2002, Sch. 13, para. 18(2)(b): an amount payable in respect of interest under s. 826 on a tax credit for expenditure on vaccine research may be applied in discharging any liability of the company to pay corporation tax.
SI 1989/1297, reg. 3B, 3BA, 3BB: applicable rates of interest on tax overpaid.
SI 1998/3175, reg. 8: modifications of s. 826 as it applies in relation to:

- an amount paid by a large company in respect of its total liability for an accounting period, and
- an amount paid by a company that is not a large company in respect of its total liability for an accounting period where payment is made before the expiry of nine months from the end of the accounting period.

Statutory instruments – SI 1992/3066 (made under s. 826(1), (8) and (9)): the day appointed for the purposes of s. 826 is 30 September 1993 (the day appointed for Pay and File).

HMRC interpretations – IRInt. 140: where trade loss or surplus of ACT in an accounting period ending after 30 September 1993 is relieved by carry-back to an accounting period ending on or before that date, question of whether resulting repayment is s. 825 supplement or s. 826 interest is unaffected by fact that it arises from a relief carry-back.

Other material – Taxline 1994/95 (not reproduced): where there is a corporation tax repayment for an accounting period ending on or before 30 September 1993, s. 825 (and not s. 826) applies for computing interest due.

Notes – S. 826 rewritten as follows:
S. 826(5): CTA 2009, s. Sch. 1, para. 635, Sch. 2, para. 56.
S. 826(5A): not rewritten as unnecessary.

826A Interest on payments in respect of corporation tax and meaning of "the material date"

826A(1) The Treasury may by regulations make provision applying section 826, with such modifications as may be prescribed, for the purpose of conferring on companies of such descriptions as may be prescribed a right to interest–

(a) on such payments made by them in respect of corporation tax as may be prescribed,

(b) at the rate applicable under section 178 of the Finance Act 1989, and

(c) for such period as may be prescribed,

and for treating any such interest for the purposes, or prescribed purposes, of the Tax Acts as interest under section 826(1)(a) on a repayment of corporation tax.

826A(2) The Treasury may by regulations make provision modifying section 826(2) in relation to companies of such description as may be prescribed.

826A(3) Subsections (1) and (2) above do not apply in relation to companies in relation to which section 826(2) is modified or otherwise affected by regulations under section 59E of the Management Act (alteration of date on which corporation tax becomes due and payable) in relation to the accounting period to which the corporation tax in question relates.

826A(4) Where the Treasury make regulations under subsection (2) above in relation to companies of any description, they may also make regulations modifying section 59DA(2) of the Management Act in relation to those companies, or any description of such companies, by varying the date before which the claim there mentioned may not be made.

826A(5) Regulations under this section–

(a) may make different provision in relation to different cases or circumstances or in relation to companies or accounting periods of different descriptions;

(b) may make such supplementary, incidental, consequential or transitional provision as appears to the Treasury to be necessary or expedient.

826A(6) Regulations under this section may not make provision in relation to accounting periods ending before the day appointed under section 199 of the Finance Act 1994 for the purposes of Chapter III of Part IV of that Act (corporation tax self-assessment).

826A(7) In this section **"prescribed"** means prescribed by regulations made under this section.

History – S. 826A inserted by FA 1998, s. 35 and Sch. 4, para. 1(2) as respects interest on repayments of corporation tax paid for accounting periods ending on or after 1 July 1999, the appointed day for corporation tax self-assessment by virtue of FA 1994, s. 199(2) and SI 1998/3173 (C. 78).

Statutory instruments – SI 1998/3175 (as amended): Corporation Tax (Instalment Payments) Regulations 1998.

827 VAT penalties etc.

827 [Omitted by CTA 2009, s. 1322 and Sch. 1, para. 268 and repealed by CTA 2009, s. 1326 and Sch. 3, Pt. 1.]

History – S. 827 omitted by CTA 2009, s. 1322 and Sch. 1, para. 268 and repealed by CTA 2009, s. 1326 and Sch. 3, Pt. 1, with effect for corporation tax purposes for accounting periods ending on or after 1 April 2009, and for income tax and capital gains tax purposes for the tax year 2009–10 and subsequent tax years.

Notes – Rewritten income tax provisions are now located as follows:
S. 827(1): ITTOIA 2005, s. 54(1)–(3), 869(3)–(5) and 872(1).
S. 827(1A): ITTOIA 2005, s. 54(1) and (2), 869(3) and (4) and 872(1).
S. 827(1B): ITTOIA 2005, s. 54(1) and (2), 869(3) and (4) and 872(1).
S. 827(1C): ITTOIA 2005, s. 54(1) and (2), 869(3) and (4) and 872(1).
S. 827(1D): ITTOIA 2005, s. 54(1) and (2), 869(3) and (4) and 872(1).
S. 827(1E): ITTOIA 2005, s. 54(1) and (2), 869(3) and (4) and 872(1).
S. 827(1F): ITTOIA 2005, s. 54(1) and (2), 869(3) and (4) and 872(1).
S. 827 rewritten for corporation tax purposes as follows:
S. 827(1): CTA 2009, s. 1303(1), (2), (3), 1306(1).
S. 827(1A): CTA 2009, s. 1303(1), (2), 1306(1).
S. 827(1B): CTA 2009, s. 1303(1), (2), 1306(1).
S. 827(1C):CTA 2009, s. 1303(1), (2), 1306(1).
S. 827(1D): CTA 2009, s. 1303(1), (2), 1306(1).
S. 827(1E): CTA 2009, s. 1303(1), (2), 1306(1).
S. 827(1F): CTA 2009, s. 1303(1), (2), 1306(1).
S. 827(1G): CTA 2009, s. 1303(1), (2), 1306(1).
S. 827(2): CTA 2009, s. 1286.

827A Territorial scope of charges under certain provisions to which section 836B applies

827A [Omitted by ITA 2007, s. 1027 and Sch. 1, para. 207 and repealed by ITA 2007, Sch. 3, Pt. 1 with effect for 2007–08 and subsequent tax years.]

Notes – S. 827A rewritten as ITA 2007, s. 1015(1), (2), (3), (4), (5).

828 Orders and regulations made by the Treasury or the Board

828(1) Any power of the Treasury or the Board to make any order or regulations under this Act shall be exercisable by statutory instrument.

828(2) [Omitted by CTA 2010, s. 1177 and Sch. 1, para. 118 and repealed by CTA 2010, s. 1181 and Sch. 3, Pt. 1.]

828(3) Subject to subsection (4) below and to any other provision to the contrary, any statutory instrument containing any order or regulations made by the Treasury or the Board under this Act shall be subject to annulment in pursuance of a resolution of the House of Commons.

828(4) Subsection (3) above shall not apply in relation to an order or regulations made under, section 590C(6), or paragraph 7 of Schedule 14 or–

(a) if any other Parliamentary procedure is expressly provided;

(b) if the order in question is an order appointing a day for the purposes of any provision of the Tax Acts, being a day as from which the provision will have effect, with or without amendments, or will cease to have effect.

828(5) [Omitted by CTA 2010, s. 1177 and Sch. 1, para. 118 and repealed by CTA 2010, s. 1181 and Sch. 3, Pt. 1.]

828(6) [Omitted by CTA 2010, s. 1177 and Sch. 1, para. 118 and repealed by CTA 2010, s. 1181 and Sch. 3, Pt. 1.]

History – In s. 828(1), the words "Subject to subsections (2) and (5) below" and the words "or under any provision of the Corporation Tax Acts not contained in this Act (including enactments passed after this Act)", which appeared after the word 'Act", omitted by CTA 2010, s. 1177 and Sch. 1, para. 118 and repealed by CTA 2010, s. 1181 and Sch. 3, Pt. 1, with effect for corporation tax purposes for accounting periods ending on or after 1 April 2010, and for income and capital gains tax purposes for the tax year 2010–11 and subsequent tax years.

In s. 828(1), the former words "provision of the Corporation Tax Acts not contained in this Act" substituted by ITA 2007, s. 1027 and Sch. 1, para. 208(2) with effect for income tax purposes for 2007–08 and subsequent tax years and for corporation tax purposes in relation to accounting periods ending after 5 April 2007.

In s. 828(1), the former words "subsections (2) and (5)" substituted by ITEPA 2003, Sch. 6, para. 105(2) which has effect, for income tax purposes, for the tax year 2003–04 and subsequent tax years, and, for corporation tax purposes, for accounting periods ending after 5 April 2003.

S. 828(2) omitted by CTA 2010, s. 1177 and Sch. 1, para. 118 and repealed by CTA 2010, s. 1181 and Sch. 3, Pt. 1, with effect for corporation tax purposes for accounting periods ending on or after 1 April 2010, and for income and capital gains tax purposes for the tax year 2010–11 and subsequent tax years.

In former s. 828(2) the words "or paragraph 3(3) of Schedule 26 to the Finance Act 2003" inserted by FA 2008, s. 38 and Sch. 16, para. 3(2), with effect from 21 July 2008 (subject to Sch. 16, para. 11(5)).

In former s. 828(2), the words "587B(9ZA) or" inserted by FA 2007, s. 109 and Sch. 26, para. 7(8), with effect from 19 July 2007.

In former s. 828(2), the words "841(1)(b) or" omitted by ITA 2007, s. 1027 and Sch. 1, para. 208(3) and repealed by ITA 2007, s. 1031 and Sch. 3, Pt. 1 with effect for income tax purposes for 2007–08 and subsequent tax years and for corporation tax purposes in relation to accounting periods ending after 5 April 2007.

In former s. 828(2) words "section 841(1)(b) or 841A" substituted by FA 1996, s. 79 and Sch. 7, para. 24 for 1996–97 and later years of assessment (income tax) and accounting periods ending after 31 March 1996 (corporation tax), subject to FA 1996, Sch. 7,para 33–35.

Former s. 828(2) amended by FA 1989, s. 178(6) by inserting the reference to FA 1989, s. 178(5).

In s. 828(3), the words "or under any provision of the Corporation Tax Acts not contained in this Act (including enactments passed after this Act)", which appeared after the words "this Act", omitted by CTA 2010, s. 1177 and Sch. 1, para. 118 and repealed by CTA 2010, s. 1181 and Sch. 3, Pt. 1, with effect for corporation tax purposes for accounting periods ending on or after 1 April 2010, and for income and capital gains tax purposes for the tax year 2010–11 and subsequent tax years.

In s. 828(3), the words "subsection (4)" substituted for the words "subsections (4) and (5)" by CTA 2010, s. 1177 and Sch. 1, para. 118(4)(a), with effect for corporation tax purposes for accounting periods ending on or after 1 April 2010, and for income and capital gains tax purposes for the tax year 2010–11 and subsequent tax years.

In s. 828(3), the former words "provision of the Corporation Tax Acts not contained in this Act" substituted by ITA 2007, s. 1027 and Sch. 1, para. 208(4) with effect for income tax purposes for 2007–08 and subsequent tax years and for corporation tax purposes in relation to accounting periods ending after 5 April 2007.

In s. 828(3), the words "subsections (4) and (5)" substituted by ITEPA 2003, Sch. 6, para. 105(3) which has effect, for income tax purposes, for the tax year 2003–04 and subsequent tax years, and, for corporation tax purposes, for accounting periods ending after 5 April 2003.

In s. 828(4), the words "or 840A(1)(d)", which appeared before the words "or paragraph 7", omitted by CTA 2010, s. 1177 and Sch. 1, para. 118(5) and repealed by CTA 2010, s. 1181 and Sch. 3, Pt. 1, with effect for corporation tax purposes for accounting periods ending on or after 1 April 2010, and for income and capital gains tax purposes for the tax year 2010–11 and subsequent tax years

In s. 828(4), the word "791", which appeared after the word "section 590C(6)", omitted by TIOPA 2010, s. 374 and Sch 8, para. 33 and repealed by TIOPA 2010, s. 378 and Sch. 10, Pt. 1, with effect for corporation tax purposes for accounting periods ending on or after 1 April 2010, for income tax and capital gains tax purposes for the tax year 2010–11 and subsequent tax years, and for petroleum revenue tax purposes for chargeable periods beginning on or after 1 July 2010.

In s. 828(4), "79B(5),", which appeared before "590C(6)", omitted by CTA 2009, s. 1322 and Sch. 1, para. 269(2) and repealed by CTA 2009, s. 1326 and Sch. 3, Pt. 1, with effect for corporation tax purposes for accounting periods ending on or after 1 April 2009, and for income tax and capital gains tax purposes for the tax year 2009–10 and subsequent tax years.

In s. 828(4), "658(3)" omitted by FA 2007, s. 46(4) and repealed by s. 114 and Sch. 27, Pt. 2(13), with effect from 19 July 2007 (FA 2007, s. 46(9)).

In s. 828(4), "1(6),", "257C, 582A(1)," and "or section 82(4)(d) of the Capital Allowances Act" omitted by ITA 2007, s. 1027 and Sch. 1, para. 208(5) and repealed by ITA 2007, s. 1031 and Sch. 3, Pt. 1 with effect for income tax purposes for 2007–08 and subsequent tax years and for corporation tax purposes in relation to accounting periods ending after 5 April 2007.
In s. 828(4), "324" omitted by ITTOIA 2005, s. 882(1) and Sch. 1, para. 334(2) and repealed by s. 884 and Sch. 3; effective for income tax purposes for 2005–06 onwards and for corporation tax purposes for accounting periods ending after 5 April 2005 (ITTOIA 2005, s. 883(1)).
In s. 828(4), "79B(5)" inserted by FA 2003, s. 180(2)], with effect from 10 July 2003.
In s. 828(4), "section 82(4)(d) of the Capital Allowances Act" substituted for "section 22(6)(d) or 36(4)(d) of the 1990 Act" by virtue of CAA 2001, Sch. 2, para. 58, which has effect, as respects allowances and charges falling to be made for chargeable periods ending on or after 6 April 2001 for income tax purposes and 1 April 2001 for corporation tax purposes.
In s. 828(4), reference to s. 377(8) repealed by FA 1999, s. 139 and Sch. 20, Pt. III(7) in accordance with FA 1999, Sch. 4, para. 18 (broadly for any payment of interest made on or after 6 April 2000).
In s. 828(4), former reference to 840A(1)(d) inserted by FA 1996, s. 198 and Sch. 37, para. 1(2).
S. 828(4) amended by FA 1989, s. 75 and Sch. 6, para. 16 inserting the reference to s. 590C(6), and by CAA 1990, s. 164 and Sch. 1, para. 8(34), inserting the reference to s. 22(6)(d), 36(4)(d) of that Act; reference to s. 257C substituted by FA 1990, s. 17(3), for 1990–91 and subsequent years of assessment; reference in s. 828(4) to s. 582A(1) inserted by FA 1991, s. 118(2); reference to s. 376(5) repealed by FA 1994, s. 258 and Sch. 26, Pt. V(19), consequential upon enactment of s. 376A.
S. 828(5) omitted by CTA 2010, s. 1177 and Sch. 1, para. 118 and repealed by CTA 2010, s. 1181 and Sch. 3, Pt. 1, with effect for corporation tax purposes for accounting periods ending on or after 1 April 2010, and for income and capital gains tax purposes for the tax year 2010–11 and subsequent tax years.
In former s. 828(5), the words ", section 717 of ITEPA 2003 or section 1310 of CTA 2009" substituted for "or section 717 of ITEPA 2003" by CTA 2009, s. 1322 and Sch. 1, para. 269(3)(a), with effect for corporation tax purposes for accounting periods ending on or after 1 April 2009, and for income tax and capital gains tax purposes for the tax year 2009–10 and subsequent tax years.
In former s. 828(5)(a), the words ", ITEPA 2003 or CTA 2009" substituted for "or ITEPA 2003" by CTA 2009, s. 1322 and Sch. 1, para. 269(3)(b), with effect for corporation tax purposes for accounting periods ending on or after 1 April 2009, and for income tax and capital gains tax purposes for the tax year 2009–10 and subsequent tax years.
In former s. 828(5)(b), the word "any" substituted for "either" by CTA 2009, s. 1322 and Sch. 1,para. 269(3)(c), with effect for corporation tax purposes for accounting periods ending on or after 1 April 2009, and for income tax and capital gains tax purposes for the tax year 2009–10 and subsequent tax years.
In former s. 828(5), the words "section 570B of the Capital Allowances Act or" and in para. (a), the words "the Capital Allowances Act or" inserted by ITA 2007, s. 1027 and Sch. 1, para. 208(6)(a), (c) with effect for income tax purposes for 2007–08 and subsequent tax years and for corporation tax purposes in relation to accounting periods ending after 5 April 2007.
In former s. 828(5), the words "or section 873 of ITTOIA 2005" and in para. (a), the words "or ITTOIA 2005" omitted by ITA 2007, s. 1027 and Sch. 1, para. 208(6)(b), (d) and repealed by ITA 2007, s. 1031 and Sch. 3, Pt. 1 with effect for income tax purposes for 2007–08 and subsequent tax years and for corporation tax purposes in relation to accounting periods ending after 5 April 2007.
In former s. 828(5) the words "or section 873 of ITTOIA 2005" and "or ITTOIA 2005" inserted and the words "either of those Acts" substituted by ITTOIA 2005, s. 882(1) and Sch. 1, para. 334(3); effective for income tax purposes for 2005–06 onwards and for corporation tax purposes for accounting periods ending after 5 April 2005 (ITTOIA 2005, s. 883(1)).
Former s. 828(5) inserted by ITEPA 2003, Sch. 6, para. 105(4) which has effect, for income tax purposes, for the tax year 2003–04 and subsequent tax years, and, for corporation tax purposes, for accounting periods ending after 5 April 2003.
S. 828(6) omitted by CTA 2010, s. 1177 and Sch. 1, para. 118 and repealed by CTA 2010, s. 1181 and Sch. 3, Pt. 1, with effect for corporation tax purposes for accounting periods ending on or after 1 April 2010, and for income and capital gains tax purposes for the tax year 2010–11 and subsequent tax years.
Former s. 828(6) inserted by FA 2004, s. 281 and Sch. 35, para. 34, with effect from 6 April 2006.

Derivations – S. 828(1) is derived from the following provisions:

- ICTA 1970, s. 65(5), 204(4), 231(3), 335(1), 343(1A) (as inserted by FA 1985, s. 40(3)), 354A(8)(b) (as inserted by FA 1987, s. 39(1), 517(1));
- FA 1970, s. 20(6) (as inserted by F(No. 2)A 1987, s. 58 and Sch. 3, para. 3(5)), 29(6) and Sch. 5, para. 2(3), 10;
- FA 1971, Sch. 3, para. 13(3);
- FA 1972, s. 91(3), 108(4);
- FA 1973, Sch. 16, para. 17(2);
- F(No. 2)A 1975, s. 47(10), 48(6), 69(9), 70(8) (as amended by FA 1980, s. 43 and Sch. 8, para. 3), 70A(3) (as inserted by FA 1982, Sch. 8, para. 5);
- FA 1976, s. 64(4), 64A(4) (as inserted by FA 1981, s. 69), 66(9)(d) and Sch. 4, para. 16(2);
- FA 1978, s. 22(6);
- FA 1980, s. 24(9) and Sch. 10, para. 13(3) (as inserted by FA 1984, s. 39(5));
- FA 1982, s. 28(5), 29(1), (3), 65(5D) (as inserted by F(No. 2)A 1987, s. 67(5)) and Sch. 7, para. 14(2) (as amended by FA 1983, s. 17(4));
- FA 1983, Sch. 5, para. 5A(9) (as inserted by FA 1986, Sch. 9, para. 7), 6(8) (as substituted by FA 1986, Sch. 9, para. 8(4)), 20(6) (as inserted by FA 1986, Sch. 9, para. 21(3));
- FA 1984, s. 26(1), 88(8), 126(1) and Sch. 8, para. 2(1)(f), 3A(1), (2) (as inserted by FA 1985, s. 38(7));
- FA 1985, s. 54(7);
- FA 1986, s. 28(7), 61(8) and Sch. 8, para. 3(1), Sch. 11, para. 11(3), Sch. 12, para. 3(2), 11(3), Sch. 17, para. 6(7);
- F(No. 2)A 1987, s. 20(5), 23(4), 28(2), 42(6), 45(5), 56(3), 73(2) and Sch. 3, para. 20(5), Sch. 6, para. 8(1).

S. 828(2) is a composite provision, added to permit the generalisation made by s. 828(1).
S. 828(3) is derived from the following provisions:

- ICTA 1970, s. 65(5), 204(4), 335(1), 343(1B) (as inserted by FA 1985, s. 40(3)), 354A(8)(b) (as inserted by FA 1987, s. 39(1));
- FA 1970, s. 20(6) (as inserted by F(No. 2)A 1987, s. 58 and Sch. 3, para. 3(5)), 29(8) and Sch. 5, para. 2(3), 10;
- FA 1971, Sch. 3, para. 13(3);
- FA 1973, Sch. 16, para. 17(2);
- F(No. 2)A 1975, s. 47(10), 48(6), 69(9), 70(8) (as amended by FA 1980, s. 43 and Sch. 8, para. 3), 70A(3) (as inserted by FA 1982, Sch. 8, para. 5);
- FA 1976, s. 64(4), 64A(4) (as inserted by FA 1981, s. 69), 66(9)(d);
- FA 1978, s. 22(6);
- FA 1980, Sch. 10, para. 13(3);
- FA 1982, s. 29(5);
- FA 1983, Sch. 5, para. 5A(9) (as inserted by FA 1986, Sch. 9, para. 7), 6(9) (as substituted by FA 1986, Sch. 9, para. 8(4)) and 20(7) (as inserted by FA 1986, Sch. 9, para. 21(3));
- FA 1984, s. 26(6), 88(8) and Sch. 8, para. 2(3), 3A(4) (as inserted by FA 1985, s. 38(7));
- FA 1986, s. 28(7), 61(8) and Sch. 8, para. 3(1), Sch. 11, para. 11(3), Sch. 12, para. 3(2), 11(3), Sch. 17, para. 6(7);
- F(No. 2)A 1987, s. 20(5), 23(4), 28(2), 42(6), 45(5), 56(3), 73(2) and Sch. 6, para. 8(3).

S. 828(4) is a composite provision, added to permit the generalisation made by s. 828(3).

Cross references – S. 1(6): Treasury power to fix higher rate bands.
S. 124(6): power of the Board to designate a recognised clearing system.
S. 257C(3): Treasury power to fix levels of personal allowances.
S. 312(1D): s. 825(1) does not apply for the purposes of s. 312(1B).
S. 324(1): Treasury power to designate as exempt from taxation certain international bodies.
S. 377(8): Treasury power to prescribe qualifying lenders under MIRAS scheme.
S. 582A(1): miscellaneous exemptions for designated international organisations.
S. 590C(6): requirement for Treasury to specify the permitted maximum final remuneration in relation to retirement benefit schemes in accordance with indexation provisions.
S. 658(3): Board's power to make regulations relating to purchased life annuities.
S. 791: Board's power to make regulations in relation to double taxation treaties.
Sch. 3, para. 15(4): power of the Board to make regulations concerning the taxation of certain Irish investment income.
Sch. 14, para. 7(1): Board's power to make regulations relating to life assurance premium relief.
Sch. 28B, para. 2(5): s. 828(1) does not apply to orders made by the Board designating an exchange outside the UK in connection with qualifying holdings in venture capital trusts.
FA 1989, s. 178(5): Board's power to set interest rates.

Notes – S. 828 rewritten for income tax purposes as follows:
S. 828(1): ITA 2007, s. 1014(1), (2), (3), Sch. 1 para. 409.
S. 828(2): ITA 2007, s. 1014(2).
S. 828(3): ITA 2007, s. 1014(4), Sch. 1 para. 409.
S. 828(4): ITA 2007, s. 1014(5), (6), Sch. 1 para. 409.
S. 828(5): ITA 2007, s. 1014(2).
S. 828(6): ITA 2007, s. 1014(2).
S. 828 rewritten for corporation tax purposes as follows:
S. 828(1): CTA 2009, s. 1171(1), (3).
S. 828(2): CTA 2009, s. 1171(2).
S. 828(3): CTA 2009, s. 1171(4), (7).
S. 828(4): CTA 2009, s. 1310(3), 1171(5), (6).
S. 828(5): CTA 2009, s. 1171(2).
S. 828(6): CTA 2009, s. 1171(2).

829 Application of Income Tax Acts to public departments and avoidance of exempting provisions

829 [Omitted by ITA 2007, s. 1027 and Sch. 1, para. 209 and repealed by ITA 2007, s. 1031 and Sch. 3, Pt. 1 with effect for income tax purposes for 2007–08 and subsequent tax years and for corporation tax purposes in relation to accounting periods ending after 5 April 2007.]

Notes – S. 829 rewritten for income tax purposes as follows:
S. 829(1): ITA 2007, s. 978(1).
S. 829(3): ITA 2007, s. 978(2).
S. 829(4): ITA 2007, s. 844(1), (2), (3).

830 Territorial sea

History – In the heading to s. 830, the words "and designated areas", which appeared after "Territorial sea", omitted by SI 2009/2860, art. 3(4)(b), which came into force on 18 November 2009 but was deemed to have come into force on 1 April 2009, with effect for corporation tax purposes for accounting periods ending on or after 1 April 2009, and for income tax and capital gains tax purposes for the tax year 2009–10 and subsequent tax years.

830(1) [Omitted by CTA 2010, s. 1177 and Sch. 1, para. 119 and repealed by CTA 2010, s. 1181 and Sch. 3, Pt. 1.]

830(2-4) [Omitted by CTA 2009, s. 1322 and Sch. 1, para. 270 and repealed by CTA 2009, s. 1326 and Sch. 3, Pt. 1.]

830(5) [Omitted by ITEPA 2003, Sch. 6, para. 106 and repealed by ITEPA 2003, Sch. 8, Pt. 1.]

History – S. 830(1) omitted by CTA 2010, s. 1177 and Sch. 1, para. 119 and repealed by CTA 2010, s. 1181 and Sch. 3, Pt. 1, with effect for corporation tax purposes for accounting periods ending on or after 1 April 2010, and for income and capital gains tax purposes for the tax year 2010–11 and subsequent tax years.
S. 830(2)–(4) omitted by CTA 2009, s. 1322 and Sch. 1, para. 270 and repealed by CTA 2009, s. 1326 and Sch. 3, Pt. 1, with effect for corporation tax purposes for accounting periods ending on or after 1 April 2009, and for income tax and capital gains tax purposes for the tax year 2009–10 and subsequent tax years.
S. 830(5) omitted by ITEPA 2003, Sch. 6, para. 106 and repealed by ITEPA 2003, Sch. 8, Pt. 1 which have effect for the tax year 2003–04 and subsequent tax years.

Derivations – (as originally enacted)FA 1973, s. 38(1), (2)(a), (b), (e), (3), (4), (6), as amended (s. 38(4)) by FA 1984, s. 81(3).

Notes – Rewritten income tax provisions are now located as follows:
S. 830(1): ITA 2007, s. 1013.
S. 830(3): ITTOIA 2005, s. 874(1).
S. 830(5): ITEPA 2003, s. 41(1).
In s. 830(4), the reference to "a branch or agency" is to be read, in relation to a company, as a reference to "a permanent establishment" by virtue of FA 2003, s. 153(2)(a) which has effect in relation to accounting periods beginning on or after 1 January 2003.
S. 830 rewritten for corporation tax purposes as follows:
S. 830(1): CTA 2010, s. 1170.
S. 830(2): CTA 2009, s. 1313(3).
S. 830(3): CTA 2009, s. 1313(1).
S. 830(4): CTA 2009, s. 1313(2).

INTERPRETATION

831 Interpretation of this Act

831(1) In this Act, except so far as the context otherwise requires–

(a) **"the Corporation Tax Acts"** means the enactments relating to the taxation of the income and chargeable gains of companies and of company distributions (including provisions relating also to income tax); and

(b) **"the Income Tax Acts"** means the enactments relating to income tax, including any provisions of the Corporation Tax Acts which relate to income tax.

831(2) In this Act **"the Tax Acts"**, except so far as the context otherwise requires, means this Act and all other provisions of the Income Tax Acts and the Corporation Tax Acts.

831(3) In this Act–

"CTA 2009" means the Corporation Tax Act 2009;

"CTA 2010" means the Corporation Tax Act 2010

"ITEPA 2003" means the Income Tax (Earnings and Pensions) Act 2003;

"ITTOIA 2005" means the Income Tax (Trading and Other Income) Act 2005;

"ITA 2007" means the Income Tax Act 2007;

"the Management Act" means the Taxes Management Act 1970;

"TIOPA 2010"means the Taxation (International and Other Provisions) Act 2010;

"the 1968 Act" means the Capital Allowances Act 1968;

"the 1970 Act" means the Income and Corporation Taxes Act 1970; and

"the 1979 Act" means the Capital Gains Tax Act 1979.

"the 1990 Act" means the Capital Allowances Act 1990.

"the 1992 Act" means the Taxation of Chargeable Gains Act 1992.

831(4) Section 1 of the Family Law Reform Act 1987, the paragraph inserted in Schedule 1 to the Interpretation Act 1978 by paragraph 73 of Schedule 2 to that Act and section 1(3) of the Law Reform (Parent and Child) (Scotland) Act 1986 (legal equality of illegitimate children) shall be disregarded in construing references in this Act to a child or to children (however expressed).

831(5) This Act, so far as it relates to capital gains tax, shall be construed as one with the 1992 Act.

831(6) Any reference in this Act to a section, Part or Schedule is a reference to that section, Part or Schedule of or to this Act, unless the context otherwise requires.

History – In s. 831(3) the definition of "TIOPA 2010" inserted by TIOPA 2010, s. 374 and Sch. 8, para 316, with effect for corporation tax purposes for accounting periods ending on or after 1 April 2010, for income tax and capital gains tax purposes for the tax year 2010–11 and subsequent tax years, and for petroleum revenue tax purposes for chargeable periods beginning on or after 1 July 2010.
In s. 831(3) the definition of "CTA 2010" inserted by CTA 2010, s. 1177 and Sch. 1, para. 121, with effect for corporation tax purposes for accounting periods ending on or after 1 April 2010, and for income and capital gains tax purposes for the tax year 2010–11 and subsequent tax years.
In s. 831(3) the definition of "CTA 2009" inserted by CTA 2009, s. 1322 and Sch. 1, para. 271, with effect for corporation tax purposes for accounting periods ending on or after 1 April 2009, and for income tax and capital gains tax purposes for the tax year 2009–10 and subsequent tax years.
In s. 831(3) the definition of "ITTOIA 2005" inserted by ITTOIA 2005, s. 882(1) and Sch. 1, para. 336; effective for income tax purposes for 2005–06 onwards and for corporation tax purposes for accounting periods ending after 5 April 2005 (ITTOIA 2005, s. 883(1)).
In s. 831(3), the definition of "ITA 2007" inserted by ITA 2007, s. 1027 and Sch. 1, para. 211 with effect for income tax purposes for 2007–08 and subsequent tax years and for corporation tax purposes in relation to accounting periods ending after 5 April 2007.
In s. 831(3), the definition of "ITEPA 2003" inserted by ITEPA 2003, Sch. 6, para. 107 which has effect, for income tax purposes, for the tax year 2003–04 and subsequent tax years, and, for corporation tax purposes, for accounting periods ending after 5 April 2003.
In s. 831(3), the definition of "the 1990 Act" inserted by CAA 1990, s. 164 and Sch. 1, para. 8(35) and continued in effect by CAA 2001, s. 578 and Sch. 2, para. 59.
In s. 831(3), the definition of "the 1992 Act" inserted, and the reference to it in s. 831(5) substituted, by TCGA 1992, s. 290 and Sch. 10, para. 14(53).

Derivations – S. 831(1)(a): Interpretation Act 1978, Sch. 1, as amended by FA 1987, Sch. 15, para. 12.
S. 831(1)(b): ICTA 1970, s. 526(1)(b).
S. 831(2): ICTA 1970, s. 526(2), as amended by Interpretation Act 1978, s. 25 and Sch. 3.
S. 831(5), as originally enacted: ICTA 1970, s. 540(2), as amended by CGTA 1979, s. 157(2) and Sch. 7, para. 8(a).

832 Interpretation of the Corporation Tax Acts etc

832 [Omitted by CTA 2010, s. 1177 and Sch. 1, para. 121 and repealed by CTA 2010, s. 1181 and Sch. 3, *Pt. 1.]*

History – S. 832 omitted by CTA 2010, s. 1177 and Sch. 1, para. 121 and repealed by CTA 2010, s. 1181 and Sch. 3, Pt. 1, with effect for corporation tax purposes for accounting periods ending on or after 1 April 2010, and for income and capital gains tax purposes for the tax year 2010–11 and subsequent tax years.

Notes – Rewritten income tax provisions are now located as follows:
S. 832(1): ITA 2007, s. 4(2), (4), 988(1), 989, 990(1), 992(1), 996(1), (2), (5), (7), 997(1), (2), (3), (4), (5), (6), 1000(1), 1004(1), 1007(1), (2), 1008(1), 1009, 1018(2), Sch. 1 para. 83, 232(2), (4), 233.
S. 832(1): ITTOIA 2005, s. 876(1), (2) and (5).

S. 832(1) ("authorised unit trust"): ITTOIA 2005, s. 375(1), 378, 388(1) and 391.
S. 832(1) ("the Board"): ITTOIA 2005, s. 878(1).
S. 832(1) ("Ulster Savings Certificates"): ITTOIA 2005, s. 693(7).
S. 832(1) ("the year 1988–89"): ITTOIA 2005, s. 878(1).
S. 832(1) ("year of assessment"): ITTOIA 2005, s. 878(1).
ITTOIA 2005 takes a different approach from that in ICTA 1988, 832(1). It defines "farming" explicitly and by referring to the nature of the activities (and not by reference to the land on which it is carried out). (See ITTOIA 2005, Explanatory Notes, Annex 1, Table 1 (Change 158).)
S. 832(2): ITA 2007, s. 992(2), (3).
S. 832(1) rewritten for corporation tax purposes in CTA 2009, s. 1317(1), (2), (5) and Sch. 1, para. 275.
S. 832 rewritten for corporation tax purposes in CTA 2010 as follows:
S. 832(1): CTA 2010, s. 1118(5), 1119, 1121(1), 1125(1), (2), (5), (7), 1126(1), (2), 1127(1), (2), (3), (4), (5), 1136(1), 1140(1), (2), 1166(1), 1167.
S. 832(2): CTA 2010, s. 1118(5), 1121(2).
S. 832(2A): CTA 2010, s. 1169(1).
S. 832(3): CTA 2010, s. 1118(5), 1119.
S. 832(4A): CTA 2010, s. 1126(3), (4).

833 Interpretation of Income Tax Acts

833 [Omitted by ITA 2007, s. 1027 and Sch. 1, para. 213 and repealed by ITA 2007, s. 1031 and Sch. 3, Pt. 1 with effect for 2007–08 and subsequent tax years.]

Notes – S. 833 rewritten as follows:
S. 833(1): ITA 2007, s. 989.
S. 833(2): ITA 2007, s. 989.
S. 833(3): ITA 2007, s. 1012(2), (3), (4), (5), Sch. 1 para. 437, 529.
S. 833(5B): ITA 2007, s. 473(3).
S. 833(5D): ITA 2007, s. 473(4).

834 Interpretation of the Corporation Tax Acts

834 [Omitted by CTA 2010, s. 1177 and Sch. 1, para. 122 and repealed by CTA 2010, s. 1181 and Sch. 3, Pt. 1.]

History – S. 834 omitted by CTA 2010, s. 1177 and Sch. 1, para. 122 and repealed by CTA 2010, s. 1181 and Sch. 3, Pt. 1, with effect for corporation tax purposes for accounting periods ending on or after 1 April 2010, and for income and capital gains tax purposes for the tax year 2010–11 and subsequent tax years.

Notes – S. 834 rewritten for corporation tax purposes in CTA 2010 as follows:
S. 834(1): CTA 2010, s. 1119, Sch. 1, para. 248, 689(3).
S. 834(2): CTA 2010, s. 36(4), 37(3), 62(3), 673(5), 1070(6), 1071(3), (4), (6).
S. 834(3): CTA 2010, s. 1168(1).
S. 834(4): CTA 2010, s. 1172(1), (2).

834A Miscellaneous charges (list for the purposes of certain provisions that formerly referred to Case VI of Schedule D)

834A [Omitted by CTA 2010, s. 1177 and Sch. 1, para. 123 and repealed by CTA 2010, s. 1181 and Sch. 3, Pt. 1.]

History – S. 834A omitted by CTA 2010, s. 1177 and Sch. 1, para. 123 and repealed by CTA 2010, s. 1181 and Sch. 3, Pt. 1, with effect for corporation tax purposes for accounting periods ending on or after 1 April 2010, and for income and capital gains tax purposes for the tax year 2010–11 and subsequent tax years.

Notes – S. 834A rewritten for corporation tax purposes in CTA 2010 as follows:
S. 834A(1): CTA 2010, s. 1173(1).
S. 834A(2): CTA 2010, s. 1173(2).
S. 834A(3): CTA 2010, s. 1173(3).

834B Meaning of "UK property business" and "overseas property business"

834B [Omitted by CTA 2010, s. 1177 and Sch. 1, para. 124 and repealed by CTA 2010, s. 1181 and Sch. 3, Pt. 1.]

History – S. 834B omitted by CTA 2010, s. 1177 and Sch. 1, para. 124 and repealed by CTA 2010, s. 1181 and Sch. 3, Pt. 1, with effect for corporation tax purposes for accounting periods ending on or after 1 April 2010, and for income and capital gains tax purposes for the tax year 2010–11 and subsequent tax years.

Notes – S. 834B rewritten for corporation tax purposes in CTA 2010 as follows:
S. 834B: CTA 2010, s. 1119.

834C Total profits

834C [Omitted by CTA 2010, s. 1177 and Sch. 1, para. 125 and repealed by CTA 2010, s. 1181 and Sch. 3, Pt. 1.]

History – S. 834C omitted by CTA 2010, s. 1177 and Sch. 1, para. 125 and repealed by CTA 2010, s. 1181 and Sch. 3, Pt. 1, with effect for corporation tax purposes for accounting periods ending on or after 1 April 2010, and for income and capital gains tax purposes for the tax year 2010–11 and subsequent tax years.

Notes – S. 834C rewritten for corporation tax purposes in CTA 2010 as follows:
S. 834C(1): CTA 2010, s. 4(3), 1119.
S. 834C(2): CTA 2010, s. 4(3), (4).

835 "Total income" in the Income Tax Acts

835 [Omitted by ITA 2007, s. 1027 and Sch. 1, para. 215 and repealed by ITA 2007, s. 1031 and Sch. 3, Pt. 1 with effect for 2007–08 and subsequent tax years.]

Notes – S. 835 rewritten as follows:
S. 835(1): ITA 2007, s. 23.
S. 835(3): ITA 2007, s. 23, 25(2).
S. 835(4): ITA 2007, s. 23, 25(2), (3).
S. 835(5): ITA 2007, s. 23, 25(2), 58(1), Sch. 1 para. 28.
S. 835(6): ITA 2007, s. 31(1), (2), (3), (4), 449(2), 505(2).
S. 835(7): ITA 2007, s. 31(5).

836 Returns of total income

836 [Omitted by ITA 2007, s. 1027 and Sch. 1, para. 216 and repealed by ITA 2007, s. 1031 and Sch. 3, Pt. 1 with effect for 2007–08 and subsequent tax years.]

836A Generally accepted accounting practice

836A [Ceased to have effect by virtue of FA 2005, s. 80(1) and Sch. 4, para. 25 and repealed by FA 2005, s. 104 and Sch. 11, Pt. 2(7).]

History – S. 836A ceased to have effect by virtue of FA 2005, s. 80(1) and Sch. 4, para. 25 and repealed by FA 2005, s. 104 and Sch. 11, Pt. 2(7), with effect for periods of account beginning on or after 1 January 2005.

836B Table of provisions to which this section applies

836B [Omitted by ITA 2007, s. 1027 and Sch. 1, para. 217 and repealed by ITA 2007, s. 1031 and Sch. 3, Pt. 1 with effect for income tax purposes for 2007–08 and subsequent tax years and for corporation tax purposes in relation to accounting periods ending after 5 April 2007.]

Notes – S. 836B rewritten as ITA 2007, s. 1016(1), (2), (3), (4).

837 "Annual value" of land

837 [Omitted by ITA 2007, s. 1027 and Sch. 1, para. 218 and repealed by ITA 2007, s. 1031 and Sch. 3, Pt. 1 with effect for income tax purposes for 2007–08 and subsequent tax years and for corporation tax purposes in relation to accounting periods ending after 5 April 2007.]

837A Meaning of "research and development"

837A [Omitted by CTA 2010, s. 1177 and Sch. 1, para. 126 and repealed by CTA 2010, s. 1181 and Sch. 3, Pt. 1.]

History – S. 837A omitted by CTA 2010, s. 1177 and Sch. 1, para. 126 and repealed by CTA 2010, s. 1181 and Sch. 3, Pt. 1, with effect for corporation tax purposes for accounting periods ending on or after 1 April 2010, and for income and capital gains tax purposes for the tax year 2010–11 and subsequent tax years.

Notes – S. 837A rewritten for income tax as follows:
S. 837A(1): ITA 2007, s. 1006(1).
S. 837A(2): ITA 2007, s. 1006(2).
S. 837A(3): ITA 2007, s. 1006(3).
S. 837A(4): ITA 2007, s. 1006(4).
S. 837A(6): ITA 2007, s. 1006(5).
S. 837A rewritten for corporation tax as follows:
S. 837A(1): CTA 2010, s. 1138(1).
S. 837A(2): CTA 2010, s. 1138(2).
S. 837A(2A): CTA 2010, s. 1138(3).
S. 837A(2B): CTA 2010, s. 1138(4).
S. 837A(6): CTA 2010, s. 1138(5).

837B Meaning of "oil and gas exploration and appraisal"

837B [Omitted by CTA 2010, s. 1177 and Sch. 1, para. 127 and repealed by CTA 2010, s. 1181 and Sch. 3, Pt. 1.]

History – S. 837B omitted by CTA 2010, s. 1177 and Sch. 1, para. 127 and repealed by CTA 2010, s. 1181 and Sch. 3, Pt. 1, with effect for corporation tax purposes for accounting periods ending on or after 1 April 2010, and for income and capital gains tax purposes for the tax year 2010–11 and subsequent tax years.

Notes – S. 837B rewritten for income tax as follows:
S. 837B(1): ITA 2007, s. 1003(1).
S. 837B(2): ITA 2007, s. 1003(2).
S. 837B rewritten for corporation tax as follows:
S. 837B(1): CTA 2010, s. 1134(1).
S. 837B(2): CTA 2010, s. 1134(2).

837C Meaning of "offshore installation"

837C [Omitted by CTA 2010, s. 1177 and Sch. 1, para. 128 and repealed by CTA 2010, s. 1181 and Sch. 3, Pt. 1.]

History – S. 837C omitted by CTA 2010, s. 1177 and Sch. 1, para. 128 and repealed by CTA 2010, s. 1181 and Sch. 3, Pt. 1, with effect for corporation tax purposes for accounting periods ending on or after 1 April 2010, and for income and capital gains tax purposes for the tax year 2010–11 and subsequent tax years.

Notes – S. 837C rewritten for income tax as follows:
S. 837C(1): ITA 2007, s. 1001(1), (4).
S. 837C(2): ITA 2007, s. 1001(3), (4).
S. 837C(3): ITA 2007, s. 1001(2).
S. 837C(4): ITA 2007, s. 1001(5).
S. 837C(5): ITA 2007, s. 1002(1).
S. 837C(6): ITA 2007, s. 1002(2).
S. 837C rewritten for corporation tax as follows:
S. 837C(1): CTA 2010, s. 1132(1), (4).
S. 837C(2): CTA 2010, s. 1132(3), (4).
S. 837C(3): CTA 2010, s. 1132(2).
S. 837C(4): CTA 2010, s. 1132(5).
S. 837C(5): CTA 2010, s. 1133(1).
S. 837C(6): CTA 2010, s. 1133(2).

838 Subsidiaries

838 [Omitted by CTA 2010, s. 1177 and Sch. 1, para. 129 and repealed by CTA 2010, s. 1181 and Sch. 3, Pt. 1.]

History – S. 838 omitted by CTA 2010, s. 1177 and Sch. 1, para. 129 and repealed by CTA 2010, s. 1181 and Sch. 3, Pt. 1, with effect for corporation tax purposes for accounting periods ending on or after 1 April 2010, and for income and capital gains tax purposes for the tax year 2010–11 and subsequent tax years.

Notes – S. 838(1) rewritten for income tax as ITA 2007, s. 989.
S. 838 rewritten for corporation tax as follows:
S. 838(1): CTA 2010, s. 1154(1), (2), (3), (4).
S. 838(2): CTA 2010, s. 1154(5), 1155(1).
S. 838(3): CTA 2010, s. 1154(6).
S. 838(4): CTA 2010, s. 1155(5).
S. 838(5): CTA 2010, s. 1155(3), (4).
S. 838(6): CTA 2010, s. 1156(1), (2), (3), 1157(1), (2).
S. 838(7): CTA 2010, s. 1156(1), (3).
S. 838(8): CTA 2010, s. 1156(1), (2), (3).
S. 838(9): CTA 2010, s. 1156(1), (2), (3).
S. 838(10): CTA 2010, s. 1156(1), (2).

839 Connected persons

839 [Omitted by CTA 2010, s. 1177 and Sch. 1, para. 130 and repealed by CTA 2010, s. 1181 and Sch. 3, Pt. 1.]

History – S. 839 omitted by CTA 2010, s. 1177 and Sch. 1, para. 130 and repealed by CTA 2010, s. 1181 and Sch. 3, Pt. 1, with effect for corporation tax purposes for accounting periods ending on or after 1 April 2010, and for income and capital gains tax purposes for the tax year 2010–11 and subsequent tax years.

Notes – S. 839 rewritten for income tax as follows:
S. 839(1): ITA 2007, s. 993(1), 994(4), Sch. 1 para. 411.
S. 839(2): ITA 2007, s. 993(2), Sch. 1 para. 411.
S. 839(3): ITA 2007, s. 993(3), 994(1), Sch. 1 para. 411.
S. 839(3A): ITA 2007, s. 993(3).
S. 839(3B): ITA 2007, s. 994(1), (3).
S. 839(4): ITA 2007, s. 993(4), Sch. 1 para. 411.
S. 839(5): ITA 2007, s. 993(5), Sch. 1 para. 411.
S. 839(6): ITA 2007, s. 993(6), Sch. 1 para. 411.
S. 839(7): ITA 2007, s. 993(7), Sch. 1 para. 411.
S. 839(8): ITA 2007, s. 994(1), (2), Sch. 1 para. 411.
S. 839 rewritten for corporation tax as follows:
S. 839(1): CTA 2010, s. 1122(1), 1123(4).
S. 839(2): CTA 2010, s. 1122(5).
S. 839(3): CTA 2010, s. 1122(6), 1123(1).
S. 839(3A): CTA 2010, s. 1122(6).
S. 839(3B): CTA 2010, s. 1123(1), (3).
S. 839(4): CTA 2010, s. 1122(7), (8).
S. 839(5): CTA 2010, s. 1122(2).
S. 839(6): CTA 2010, s. 1122(3).
S. 839(7): CTA 2010, s. 1122(4).
S. 839(8): CTA 2010, s. 34(7), 1123(1), (2).

840 Meaning of "control" in certain contexts

840 [Omitted by CTA 2010, s. 1177 and Sch. 1, para. 131 and repealed by CTA 2010, s. 1181 and Sch. 3, Pt. 1.]

History – S. 840 omitted by CTA 2010, s. 1177 and Sch. 1, para. 131 and repealed by CTA 2010, s. 1181 and Sch. 3, Pt. 1, with effect for corporation tax purposes for accounting periods ending on or after 1 April 2010, and for income and capital gains tax purposes for the tax year 2010–11 and subsequent tax years.

Notes – S. 840 rewritten for income tax as ITA 2007, s. 995(1), (2), (3).
S. 840 rewritten for corporation tax as follows:
S. 840: CTA 2010, s. 1124(1), (2), (3).

840ZA Meaning of "tax advantage"

840ZA [Omitted by CTA 2010, s. 1177 and Sch. 1, para. 132 and repealed by CTA 2010, s. 1181 and Sch. 3, Pt. 1.]

History – S. 840ZA omitted by CTA 2010, s. 1177 and Sch. 1, para. 132 and repealed by CTA 2010, s. 1181 and Sch. 3, Pt. 1, with effect for corporation tax purposes for accounting periods ending on or after 1 April 2010, and for income and capital gains tax purposes for the tax year 2010–11 and subsequent tax years.

Notes – S. 840ZA rewritten for corporation tax as follows:
S. 840ZA(1): CTA 2010, s. 1139(1), (2).
S. 840ZA(2): CTA 2010, s. 1139(3).
S. 840ZA(3): CTA 2010, s. 1139(4).

840A Banks

840A [Omitted by CTA 2010, s. 1177 and Sch. 1, para. 133 and repealed by CTA 2010, s. 1181 and Sch. 3, Pt. 1.]

History – S. 840A omitted by CTA 2010, s. 1177 and Sch. 1, para. 133 and repealed by CTA 2010, s. 1181 and Sch. 3, Pt. 1, with effect for corporation tax purposes for accounting periods ending on or after 1 April 2010, and for income and capital gains tax purposes for the tax year 2010–11 and subsequent tax years.

Notes – S. 840A rewritten for income tax as follows:
S. 840A(1): ITA 2007, s. 991(1), (2), (3).
S. 840A(3): ITA 2007, s. 991(2), (4).
S. 840A rewritten for corporation tax as follows:
S. 840A(1): CTA 2010, s. 1120(1), (2), (3), (5)
S. 840A(3): CTA 2010, s. 1120(2), (4)

841 Meaning of "recognised stock exchange" etc

841 [Omitted by CTA 2010, s. 1177 and Sch. 1, para. 134 and repealed by CTA 2010, s. 1181 and Sch. 3, Pt. 1.]

History – S. 841 omitted by CTA 2010, s. 1177 and Sch. 1, para. 134 and repealed by CTA 2010, s. 1181 and Sch. 3, Pt. 1, with effect for corporation tax purposes for accounting periods ending on or after 1 April 2010, and for income and capital gains tax purposes for the tax year 2010–11 and subsequent tax years.

Notes – S. 841 rewritten for corporation tax as follows:
S. 841(1): CTA 2010, s. 1137(1), (5).
S. 841(2): CTA 2010, s. 1137(2), (3).
S. 841(3): CTA 2010, s. 1137(4).
S. 841(4): CTA 2010, s. 1137(5).

841A Recognised clearing systems

841A [Repealed by FA 2000, s. 156 and Sch. 40, Pt. II(17).]

History – S. 841A repealed by FA 2000, s. 156 and Sch. 40, Pt. II(17), with effect in relation to payments of interest made on or after 1 April 2001.

842 Investment trusts

842 [Omitted by CTA 2010, s. 1177 and Sch. 1, para. 135 and repealed by CTA 2010, s. 1181 and Sch. 3, Pt. 1.]

History – S. 842 omitted by CTA 2010, s. 1177 and Sch. 1, para. 135 and repealed by CTA 2010, s. 1181 and Sch. 3, Pt. 1, with effect for corporation tax purposes for accounting periods ending on or after 1 April 2010, and for income and capital gains tax purposes for the tax year 2010–11 and subsequent tax years.
At the time of repeal by CTA 2010, s. 1181 and Sch. 3, Pt. 1, in s. 824(4), ", 103A" was to be inserted after "sections 99" by FA 2009, s. 44 and Sch. 22, para. 11(2), to come into force in accordance with an order made by the Treasury (FA 2009, Sch. 22, para. 13(2)).

Notes – S. 842 rewritten for income tax as follows:
S. 842(1AB): ITA 2007, s. 276(1), (2).
S. 842(1A): ITA 2007, s. 277(4).
S. 842(2): ITA 2007, s. 277(1).
S. 842(2A): ITA 2007, s. 276(5).
S. 842(2B): ITA 2007, s. 276(6).
S. 842(2C): ITA 2007, s. 276(4).
S. 842(3): ITA 2007, s. 277(1), (2), (3), (5), (6), 278(4), (5), (6).
S. 842(4): ITA 2007, s. 277(5), 278(5), 332.
S. 842 rewritten for corporation tax as follows:
S. 842(1): CTA 2010, s. 1158, 1159(1), 1162(1).
S. 842(1AB): CTA 2010, s. 1160(1), (2).
S. 842(1AC): CTA 2010, s. 1160(5).
S. 842(1A): CTA 2010, s. 1164(3), (4), (5), (6).
S. 842(2): CTA 2010, s. 1162(2), (3), (6).
S. 842(2A): CTA 2010, s. 1161(2).

S. 842(2B): CTA 2010, s. 1161(2), (3).
S. 842(2C): CTA 2010, s. 1161(1).
S. 842(2D): CTA 2010, s. 1160(1), (3).
S. 842(2E): CTA 2010, s. 1160(3).
S. 842(3): CTA 2010, s. 1162(2), 1163(1), (2), 1164(1), (2).
S. 842(3A): CTA 2010, s. 1160(1), (4).
S. 842(4): CTA 2010, s. 1164(7), 1165(1), (2), (3).

842AA Venture capital trusts

842AA [Omitted by ITA 2007, s. 1027 and Sch. 1, para. 229 and repealed by ITA 2007, s. 1031 and Sch. 3, Pt. 1 with effect in relation to accounting periods ending after 5 April 2007.]

Notes – S. 842AA rewritten as follows:
S. 842AA(1): ITA 2007, s. 259(1), 283(1), (2), 989.
S. 842AA(2): ITA 2007, s. 274(1), (2).
S. 842AA(3): ITA 2007, s. 274(1).
S. 842AA(4): ITA 2007, s. 275(1), (2), (3).
S. 842AA(5): ITA 2007, s. 278(1), (2), (3).
S. 842AA(5AA): ITA 2007, s. 279(1), (2).
S. 842AA(5AB): ITA 2007, s. 279(2).
S. 842AA(5AC): ITA 2007, s. 279(3).
S. 842AA(5AD): ITA 2007, s. 279(4).
S. 842AA(5AE): ITA 2007, s. 279(5).
S. 842AA(5A): ITA 2007, s. 280(1).
S. 842AA(5B): ITA 2007, s. 280(2).
S. 842AA(6): ITA 2007, s. 281(1).
S. 842AA(7): ITA 2007, s. 281(2).
S. 842AA(8): ITA 2007, s. 281(3).
S. 842AA(9): ITA 2007, s. 281(4).
S. 842AA(10): ITA 2007, s. 281(5).
S. 842AA(11): ITA 2007, s. 276(1), (2), (4), (5), (6), 277(1), (2), (3), (4), (5), (6), 278(1), (4), (5), (6), 332.
S. 842AA(11A): ITA 2007, s. 285(4).
S. 842AA(11B): ITA 2007, s. 285(5).
S. 842AA(11C): ITA 2007, s. 285(6).
S. 842AA(12): ITA 2007, s. 285(2).
S. 842AA(13): ITA 2007, s. 285(1).
S. 842AA(14): ITA 2007, s. 285(3).

842A Local authorities

842A [Omitted by CTA 2010, s. 1177 and Sch. 1, para. 136 and repealed by CTA 2010, s. 1181 and Sch. 3, Pt. 1.]

History – S. 842A omitted by CTA 2010, s. 1177 and Sch. 1, para. 136 and repealed by CTA 2010, s. 1181 and Sch. 3, Pt. 1, with effect for corporation tax purposes for accounting periods ending on or after 1 April 2010, and for income and capital gains tax purposes for the tax year 2010–11 and subsequent tax years.

Notes – S. 842A rewritten as follows:
S. 842A(1): ITA 2007, s. 999(1), (2), (3).
S. 842A(2): ITA 2007, s. 999(1).
S. 842A(3): ITA 2007, s. 999(2).
S. 842A(4): ITA 2007, s. 999(3).
S. 842A(5): ITA 2007, s. 999(4).
S. 842A rewritten for corporation tax as follows:
S. 842A(1): CTA 2010, s. 1130(1), (2), (3).
S. 842A(2): CTA 2010, s. 1130(1).
S. 842A(3): CTA 2010, s. 1130(2).
S. 842A(4): CTA 2010, s. 1130(3).
S. 842A(5): CTA 2010, s. 1130(4).

842B Meaning of "property investment LLP"

842B [Omitted by CTA 2010, s. 1177 and Sch. 1, para. 137 and repealed by CTA 2010, s. 1181 and Sch. 3, Pt. 1.]

History – S. 842B omitted by CTA 2010, s. 1177 and Sch. 1, para. 137 and repealed by CTA 2010, s. 1181 and Sch. 3, Pt. 1, with effect for corporation tax purposes for accounting periods ending on or after 1 April 2010, and for income and capital gains tax purposes for the tax year 2010–11 and subsequent tax years.

Notes – S. 842B rewritten as follows:
S. 842B(1): ITA 2007, s. 399(6), 1004(1).
S. 842B(2): ITA 2007, s. 399(6), 1004(2).
S. 842B rewritten for corporation tax as follows:
S. 842B(1): CTA 2010, s. 1135(1).
S. 842B(2): CTA 2010, s. 1135(2).

COMMENCEMENT, SAVINGS, REPEALS ETC.

843 Commencement

843(1) Except as otherwise provided by the following provisions of this section, this Act shall come into force in relation to tax for the year 1988–89 and subsequent years of assessment, and for companies' accounting periods ending after 5th April 1988.

843(2) Except as otherwise provided by the following provisions of this section, such of the provisions of this Act as relate to capital gains tax (including the provisions of Part XVIII as applied to capital gains tax by section 277 of the 1992 Act) shall come into force in relation to that tax for the year 1988–89 and subsequent years of assessment.

843(3) The following provisions of this Act, that is to say–

(a) so much of any provision as authorises the making of any Order in Council or regulations or other instrument;

(b) so much of any provision as relates to the making of a return, the furnishing of a certificate or the giving of any other information, including any such provision which imposes a duty on the Board or an officer of the Board as well as any such provision which imposes a duty on any other person;

(c) so much of any provision as imposes any penalty;

(d) except where the tax concerned is all tax for years of assessment before year 1988–89 or accounting periods ending before 6th April 1988, so much of any other provision as confers any power or imposes any duty the exercise or performance of which operates or may operate in relation to tax for more than one chargeable period,

shall come into force for all purposes on 6th April 1988 to the exclusion of the corresponding enactments repealed by this Act.

843(4) This section has effect except as otherwise provided by any other provision of this Act, and in particular except as provided by sections 96, 380 to 384, 393, 400, 703.

History – In s. 843(2), reference to the 1992 Act substituted by TCGA 1992, s. 290 and Sch. 10, para. 14(56) and FA 1994, s. 146 and Sch. 17, para. 8.
In s. 843(4), the words "and 812" repealed by Statute Law (Repeals) Act 2013, s. 1 and Sch. 1, Pt. 10, with effect from 31 January 2013.
In s. 843(4) reference to s. 394 repealed by FA 1991, s. 73 and Sch. 15, para. 24, s. 123 and Sch. 19, Pt. V, with effect in relation to losses incurred in accounting periods ending on or after 1 April 1991.

Cross references – S. 96: relief for fluctuating farming and market gardening profits.
S. 380–384: set-off of trading losses, carry-back of losses in early years of a trade, and extensions of those reliefs to capital allowances.
S. 393: carry-forward of company's trading losses.
S. 400: reduction of loss relief where government investment is written off.
S. 703: cancellation of tax advantage in respect of certain transactions in securities.
S. 812: withdrawal of entitlement to tax credits of certain non-resident companies connected with states (unitary states) taxing companies trading there by reference to their profits made elsewhere.

844 Savings, transitional provisions, consequential amendments and repeals

844(1) Schedule 29, which makes amendments to other enactments consequential on the passing of this Act, shall have effect.

844(2) Schedule 29, section 843 and this section are without prejudice to the provisions of the Interpretation Act 1978 as respects the effect of repeals.

844(3) Schedule 30 which contains savings and transitional provisions shall have effect.

844(4) The enactments mentioned in Schedule 31 are hereby repealed to the extent specified in the third column of that Schedule.

844(5) Subject to subsection (6) below, section 843(3), Schedule 30 and to any other provision of this Act by which any provision is brought into force to the exclusion of the corresponding enactments repealed by this Act, those repeals shall come into force in accordance with subsections (1) and (2) of section 843.

844(6) No provision mentioned in subsection (5) above shall be taken as bringing a repeal into force except to the extent that the repealed enactment is being superseded.

Cross references – Interpretation Act 1978, s. 15–17: subject to exceptions, where an Act repeals a repealing enactment, the repeal does not revive any enactment previously repealed unless expressed to do so. Where an Act repeals a previous enactment and substitutes new provisions the repealed enactment remains in force until substituted provisions come into force. Normally, references to enactments which have been repealed and re-enacted are to be construed as references to the provision as re-enacted.

845 Short title

845 This Act may be cited as the Income and Corporation Taxes Act 1988.

SCHEDULES

SCHEDULE A1 – DETERMINATION OF PROFITS ATTRIBUTABLE TO PERMANENT ESTABLISHMENT: SUPPLEMENTARY PROVISIONS

Section 11AA

[Omitted by CTA 2009, s. 1322 and Sch. 1, para. 278 and repealed by CTA 2009, s. 1326 and Sch. 3, Pt. 1, with effect for corporation tax purposes for accounting periods ending on or after 1 April 2009, and for income tax and capital gains tax purposes for the tax year 2009–10 and subsequent tax years.]

Notes – Sch. A1 rewritten as follows:
Para. 1(2): CTA 2009, s. 21(3)
Para. 2 rewritten as CTA 2009, s. 22.
Para. 3(1): CTA 2009, s. 29(3).
Para. 3(2): CTA 2009, s. 29(4).
Para. 4(1): CTA 2009, s. 31(1).
Para. 4(2): CTA 2009, s. 31(2).
Para. 4(3): CTA 2009, s. 31(3).
Para. 5(1): CTA 2009, s. 32(1).
Para. 5(2): CTA 2009, s. 32(2).
Para. 5(3): CTA 2009, s. 32(3).
Para. 6(1): CTA 2009, s. 23(1).
Para. 6(2): CTA 2009, s. 23(2).
Para. 6(3): CTA 2009, s. 23(3).
Para. 7(1): CTA 2009, s. 25(1), (3), 26(1), 27(1), 28(1).
Para. 7(2): CTA 2009, s. 25(2).
Para. 8(1): CTA 2009, s. 26(1), (2).
Para. 8(2): CTA 2009, s. 26(3), (4).
Para. 9(1): CTA 2009, s. 27(1), (2).
Para. 9(2): not rewritten as unnecessary.
Para. 9(3): CTA 2009, s. 27(3).
Para. 9(4): CTA 2009, s. 27(4).
Para. 9(5): CTA 2009, s. 27(5).
Para. 10(1): CTA 2009, s. 28(1).
Para. 10(2): CTA 2009, s. 28(2).

SCHEDULE A2 – [CORPORATION TAX: THE NON-CORPORATE DISTRIBUTION RATE: SUPPLEMENTARY PROVISIONS]

Section 13AB

[Ceases to have effect by virtue of FA 2006, s. 26(2) and repealed by FA 2006, s. 178 and Sch. 26, Pt. 3(1).]

History – Sch. A2 ceases to have effect by virtue of FA 2006, s. 26(2) and repealed by FA 2006, s. 178 and Sch. 26, Pt. 3(1) with effect for the financial year 2006 and subsequent financial years, subject to the transitional provisions in FA 2006, s. 26(9)–(11) in relation to accounting periods straddling 1 April 2006.

SCHEDULE 1 – RESTRICTIONS ON SCHEDULE A DEDUCTIONS

Section 31

[Repealed by FA 1998, s. 165 and Sch. 27, Pt. III(4).]

History – Sch. 1 repealed by FA 1998, s. 165 and Sch. 27, Pt. III(4), with effect, so far as relating to income tax, for the year 1998–99 and subsequent years of assessment, and so far as relating to corporation tax, from 1 April 1998, subject to the transitional provisions in FA 1998, Sch. 5, Pt. IV.

SCHEDULE 2 – PREMIUMS ETC. TAXABLE UNDER SCHEDULES A AND D: SPECIAL RELIEF FOR INDIVIDUALS

Section 39(3)

1–6 [Repealed by FA 1988, s. 75, 148 and Sch. 14, Pt. IV.]

History – The repeal of Sch. 2 has effect for 1988–89 and subsequent tax years. Sch. 2 never had effect, but its predecessor, ICTA 1970, Sch. 3 accorded top-slicing relief.

ICTA 1988

SCHEDULE 3 – MACHINERY FOR ASSESSMENT, CHARGE AND PAYMENT OF INCOME TAX UNDER SCHEDULE C AND, IN CERTAIN CASES, SCHEDULE D

Section 44(2)

1–15 [Repealed by FA 1996, s. 79 and Sch. 7, para. 27 and s. 205 and Sch. 41, Pt. V(2).]

History – The repeal of Sch. 3 has effect for 1996–97 and subsequent years of assessment (income tax) and accounting periods ending after 31 March 1996 (corporation tax), subject to FA 1996, Sch. 7, para. 33–35.

SCHEDULE 4 – DEEP DISCOUNT SECURITIES

Section 57

[Sch. 4 repealed by FA 1996, s. 104 and Sch. 14, para. 50 and s. 205 and Sch. 41, Pt. V(3).]

History – Sch. 4 was repealed by FA 1996, s. 104 and Sch. 14, para. 50 and s. 205 and Sch. 41, Pt. V(3), with effect for income tax for 1996–97 and subsequent years and for corporation tax for accounting periods ending after 31 March 1996. Where it is of relevance for the transitional provisions at FA 1996, Sch. 15, para. 19 (relating to the charge on accrued interest on certain securities held at 31 March 1996 and disposed of after that date), the text of former Sch. 4 is reproduced in earlier editions of "Tax Statutes and Statutory Instruments".

SCHEDULE 4AA – SHARE INCENTIVE PLANS: CORPORATION TAX DEDUCTIONS

Section 85B

[Omitted by CTA 2009, s. 1322 and Sch. 1, para. 279 and repealed by CTA 2009, s. 1326 and Sch. 3, Pt. 1, with effect for corporation tax purposes for accounting periods ending on or after 1 April 2009, and for income tax and capital gains tax purposes for the tax year 2009–10 and subsequent tax years.]

Notes – Sch. 4AA rewritten as follows:
Para. 1(1): CTA 2009, s. 984(1).
Para. 1(2): CTA 2009, s. 984(2).
Para. 1(3): CTA 2009, s. 985(2).
Para. 1(4): CTA 2009, s. 985(2).
Para. 2(1): CTA 2009, s. 994(1), (2).
Para. 2(2): CTA 2009, s. 994(2), (3), (6).
Para. 2(3): CTA 2009, s. 994(7), (8).
Para. 2(4): CTA 2009, s. 994(4).
Para. 2(5): CTA 2009, s. 994(5).
Para. 2(6): CTA 2009, s. 994(6).
Para. 2(7): CTA 2009, s. 994(9).
Para. 2(8): CTA 2009, s. 994(10).
Para. 3(1): CTA 2009, s. 995(1), (2).
Para. 3(2): CTA 2009, s. 995(2), (3).
Para. 3(3): CTA 2009, s. 995(4), (5).
Para. 3(4): CTA 2009, s. 995(6).
Para. 3(5): CTA 2009, s. 995(7).
Para. 4(1): CTA 2009, s. 996(1).
Para. 4(2): CTA 2009, s. 996(2), (3).
Para. 4(3): CTA 2009, s. 996(2), (3).
Para. 4(4): CTA 2009, s. 996(2), (3).
Para. 4(5): CTA 2009, s. 996(4).
Para. 4(6): CTA 2009, s. 996(5).
Para. 4(7): CTA 2009, s. 996(6).
Para. 4(8): CTA 2009, s. 996(6).
Para.4(9): CTA 2009, s. 996(7).
Para. 5(1): CTA 2009, s. 997(1).
Para. 5(2): CTA 2009, s. 997(2).
Para. 6(1): CTA 2009, s. 984(3), 996(8).
Para. 6(2): CTA 2009, s. 984(4).
Para. 6(3): CTA 2009, s. 996(8).
Para. 7(1): CTA 2009, s. 987(1), (2).
Para. 7(2): CTA 2009, s. 987(3).
Para. 7(3): CTA 2009, s. 987(4).
Para. 7(4): CTA 2009, s. 987(5).
Para. 8(1): CTA 2009, s. 988(1), (2).
Para. 8(2): CTA 2009, s. 988(3), (4).
Para. 8(3): CTA 2009, s. 988(4).
Para. 9(1): CTA 2009, s. 989(1), Sch. 2, para. 105.
Para. 9(2): CTA 2009, s. 989(1), (2), (7).
Para. 9(3): CTA 2009, s. 989(3).
Para. 9(4): CTA 2009, s. 989(4), (5).
Para. 9(5): CTA 2009, s. 989(6), 996(7).
Para. 10(1): CTA 2009, s. 990(1), (2), (3).
Para. 10(2): CTA 2009, s. 986(2), 990(4), (5).
Para. 10(3): CTA 2009, s. 991(1), (2), (3).
Para. 10(4): CTA 2009, s. 991(3), (4).
Para. 10(5): CTA 2009, s. 989(6).

Para. 10(6): CTA 2009, s. 992(1), (2), (3).
Para. 10(7): CTA 2009, s. 992(1), (2), (3).
Para. 10(8): CTA 2009, s. 986(2), 992(4), (6), Sch. 2, para. 106.
Para. 10(9): CTA 2009, s. 992(5).
Para. 10(10): CTA 2009, s. 990(6).
Para. 11(1): CTA 2009, s. 998(1), (2).
Para. 11(2): CTA 2009, s. 986(2), 998(3), (4).
Para. 12(1): CTA 2009, s. 993(1).
Para. 12(2): CTA 2009, s. 986(2), 993(1), (2), (4).
Para. 12(3): CTA 2009, s. 993(3)
Para. 13(1): CTA 2009, s. 985(3), (4).
Para. 13(2): CTA 2009, s. 985(3), (4).
Para. 13(3): CTA 2009, s. 986(4).

SCHEDULE 4A – CREATIVE ARTISTS: RELIEF FOR FLUCTUATING PROFITS

Section 95A

[Omitted by ITTOIA 2005, s. 882 and Sch. 1, para. 342 and repealed by s. 884 and Sch. 3.]

History – Sch. 4A omitted by ITTOIA 2005, s. 882(1) and Sch. 1, para. 342 and repealed by s. 884 and Sch. 3; effective for income tax purposes for 2005–06 onwards and for corporation tax purposes for accounting periods ending after 5 April 2005 (ITTOIA 2005, s. 883(1)).

Notes – Sch. 4A rewritten as follows:
Para. 1: ITTOIA 2005, s. 221(1).
Para. 2(1): ITTOIA 2005, s. 221(2).
Para. 2(2): ITTOIA 2005, s. 221(3).
Para. 3: ITTOIA 2005, s. 222(1).
Para. 4(1): ITTOIA 2005,s. 222(3).
Para. 4(2): ITTOIA 2005, s. 222(4).
Para. 4(3): ITTOIA 2005, s. 222(2).
Para. 5: ITTOIA 2005, s. 222(5) and (6).
Para. 6(1): ITTOIA 2005, s. 223(1).
Para. 6(2): ITTOIA 2005, s. 223(3).
Para. 6(3): ITTOIA 2005, s. 223(4).
Para. 6(4): ITTOIA 2005, s. 224(1).
Para. 8(1): ITTOIA 2005, s. 224(4).
Para. 8(2): ITTOIA 2005, s. 224(5).
Para. 10(1): ITTOIA 2005, s. 225(1)–(3).
Para. 10(2): ITTOIA 2005, s. 225(4).
Para. 11(1): ITTOIA 2005, s. 221(4).
Para. 11(2): ITTOIA 2005, s. 224(3).
Para. 13(1): ITTOIA 2005, s. 224(5).

SCHEDULE 5 – TREATMENT OF FARM ANIMALS ETC. FOR PURPOSES OF CASE I OF SCHEDULE D

Section 97

[Omitted by CTA 2009, s. 1322 and Sch. 1, para. 280 and repealed by CTA 2009, s. 1326 and Sch. 3, Pt. 1, with effect for corporation tax purposes for accounting periods ending on or after 1 April 2009, and for income tax and capital gains tax purposes for the tax year 2009–10 and subsequent tax years.]

Notes – Sch. 5 rewritten for income tax purposes as follows:
Para. 1(1): ITTOIA 2005, s. 30(1).
Para. 1(2): ITTOIA 2005, s. 30(1) and (2) and 111(1) and (2).
Para. 1(3): ITTOIA 2005, s. 111(1).
Para. 2(1): ITTOIA 2005, s. 111(2) and 124(6).
Para. 2(2): ITTOIA 2005, s. 124(1) and (4).
Para. 2(3): ITTOIA 2005, s. 124(2).
Para. 2(4): ITTOIA 2005, s. 124(5) and (7).
Para. 2(5): ITTOIA 2005, s. 124(2).
Para. 2(6): ITTOIA 2005, s. 124(2) and (3).
Para. 3(1): ITTOIA 2005, s. 111(2).
Para. 3(2): ITTOIA 2005, s. 114(1) and (2) and 115(1) and (2).
Para. 3(3): ITTOIA 2005, s. 115(1), (3) and (4) and 120(6).
Para. 3(4): ITTOIA 2005, s. 116(1), (2) and (4). However, ITTOIA 2005 does not replicate the apparent error in para. 3(4)(b) which makes it (and not para. 3(4)(a)) subject to para. 3(6). (See ITTOIA 2005, Explanatory Notes, Annex 1, Table 1 (Change 158).)
Para. 3(5): ITTOIA 2005, s. 116(5).
Para. 3(6): ITTOIA 2005, s. 117(2)–(5).
Para. 3(7): ITTOIA 2005, s. 120(1), (2) and (6).
Para. 3(8): ITTOIA 2005, s. 119(1)–(3), 120(1) and (5) and 122(1) and(4).
Para. 3(9): ITTOIA 2005, s. 120(1), (2), (3) and (5), 121(2)–(4), 122(1)–(3) and 123(2)–(4).
Para. 3(10): ITTOIA 2005, s. 118(1)–(5).
Para. 3(11): ITTOIA 2005, s. 120(4).
Para. 3(12): ITTOIA 2005, s. 113(3) and (4).
Para. 4: ITTOIA 2005, s. 125(1) and (2).
Para. 5(1): ITTOIA 2005, s. 127(1), (2) and (4)–(6).
Para. 5(2): ITTOIA 2005, s. 127(2) and 3) and 878(6).
Para. 6(1): ITTOIA 2005, s. 126(1), (2) and (4).
Para. 6(2): ITTOIA 2005, s. 126(2).

Para. 6(3): ITTOIA 2005, s. 126(3).
Para. 6(4): ITTOIA 2005, s. 126(2).
Para. 6(5): ITTOIA 2005, s. 126(2).
Para. 7: ITTOIA 2005, s. 30(1). But ITTOIA 2005 does not rewrite the rules in para. 7 and 9(5) that prevent working animals from being subject to a herd basis election. These rules are unnecessary as a production herd must be kept wholly or mainly for the sake of the animals' produce. (See ITTOIA 2005, Explanatory Notes, Annex 1, Table 1 (Change 158).)
Para. 8(1): ITTOIA 2005, s. 112(1).
Para. 8(2): ITTOIA 2005, s. 112(3) and (4).
Para. 8(3): ITTOIA 2005, s. 112(5) and (6).
Para. 8(4): ITTOIA 2005, s. 112(1) and 113(5).
Para. 8(5): ITTOIA 2005, s. 112(1) and (2).
Para. 8(6): ITTOIA 2005, s. 113(2).
Para. 9(1): TTOIA 2005, s. 30(1) and (4) and 111(3).
Para. 9(2): ITTOIA 2005, s. 112(1).
Para. 9(3): ITTOIA 2005, s. 113(5).
Para. 9(4): ITTOIA 2005, s. 30(3) and 112(7).
Para. 9(5): ITTOIA 2005, s. 30(1). But ITTOIA 2005 does not rewrite the rules in para. 7 and 9(5) that prevent working animals from being subject to a herd basis election. These rules are unnecessary as a production herd must be kept wholly or mainly for the sake of the animals' produce. (See ITTOIA 2005, Explanatory Notes, Annex 1, Table 1 (Change 158).)
Para. 10: ITTOIA 2005, s. 128(1) and (2).
Para. 11: ITTOIA 2005, s. 129(1) and (2).
Sch. 5 rewritten for corporation tax purposes as follows:
Para. 1(1): CTA 2009, s. 50(1).
Para. 1(2): CTA 2009, s. 50(1), (2), 109(1), (2).
Para. 1(3): CTA 2009, s. 109(1).
Para. 2(1): CTA 2009, s. 109(2), 122(6).
Para. 2(2): CTA 2009, s. 122(1), (4).
Para. 2(3): CTA 2009, s. 122(2).
Para. 2(4): CTA 2009, s. 122(5), (7).
Para. 2(6): CTA 2009, s. 122(3).
Para. 3(1): CTA 2009, s. 109(2).
Para. 3(2): CTA 2009, s. 112(1), (2), 113(1), (2).
Para. 3(3): CTA 2009, s. 113(1), (3), (4), 118(6).
Para. 3(4): CTA 2009, s. 114(1), (2), (4).
Para. 3(5): CTA 2009, s. 114(5).
Para. 3(6): CTA 2009, s. 115(2), (3), (4), (5).
Para. 3(7): CTA 2009, s. 118(1), (2), (6).
Para. 3(8): CTA 2009, s. 117(1), (2), (3), 118(1), (5), 120(1), (4).
Para. 3(9): CTA 2009, s. 118(1), (2), (3), (5), 119(2), (3), (4), 120(1), (2), (3), 121(2), (3), (4).
Para. 3(10): CTA 2009, s. 116(1), (2), (3), (4), (5).
Para. 3(11): CTA 2009, s. 118(4).
Para. 3(12): CTA 2009, s. 111(3), (4).
Para. 4: CTA 2009, s. 123(1), (2).
Para. 5: CTA 2009, s. 164(3).
Para. 5(1): CTA 2009, s. 125(1), (2), (4), (5), (6).
Para. 5(2): CTA 2009, s. 125(2), (3), 1316(2).
Para. 6(1): CTA 2009, s. 124(1), (2), (4).
Para. 6(2): CTA 2009, s. 124(2).
Para. 6(3): CTA 2009, s. 124(3).
Para. 6(4): CTA 2009, s. 124(2).
Para.6(5): CTA 2009, s. 124(2).
Para. 7: CTA 2009, s. 50(1).
Para. 8(1): CTA 2009, s. 110(1).
Para. 8(2): CTA 2009, s. 110(3), (4).
Para. 8(3): CTA 2009, s. 110(5), (6).
Para. 8(4): CTA 2009, s. 110(1), 111(5).
Para. 8(5): CTA 2009, s. 110(1), (2).
Para. 8(6): CTA 2009, s. 111(2).
Para. 8(7): CTA 2009, s. 47(1).
Para. 9(1): CTA 2009, s. 50(1), 109(3).
Para. 9(2): CTA 2009, s. 50(1), 110(1).
Para. 9(3): CTA 2009, s. 111(5).
Para. 9(4): CTA 2009, s. 50(3), 110(7).
Para. 9(5): s. CTA 2009, s. 50(1).
Para. 10: CTA 2009, s. 126(1), (2).
Para. 11: CTA 2009, s. 127(1), (2).

SCHEDULE 5AA – GUARANTEED RETURNS ON TRANSACTIONS IN FUTURES AND OPTIONS

[Section 127A]

[Omitted by ITTOIA 2005, s. 882 and Sch. 1, para. 344 and repealed by s. 884 and Sch. 3.]

History – Sch. 5AA omitted by ITTOIA 2005, s. 882(1) and Sch. 1, para. 344 and repealed by s. 884 and Sch. 3; effective for income tax purposes for 2005–06 onwards and for corporation tax purposes for accounting periods ending after 5 April 2005 (ITTOIA 2005, s. *883(1)*).

Notes – Sch. 5AA: ITTOIA 2005 as follows:
Para. 1(1): ITTOIA 2005, s. 555(1) and (2), 556(2) and 557.
Para. 1(2): ITTOIA 2005, s. 366(1).
Para. 1(4): ITTOIA 2005, s. 556(2).

Para. 1(5): ITTOIA 2005, s. 567(3).
Para. 1(6): ITTOIA 2005, s. 567(1) and (2) and Sch. 1, para. 434.
Para. 1(7): ITTOIA 2005, Sch. 1, para. 434.
Para. 2(1): ITTOIA 2005, s. 559(1)–(3) and (4).
Para. 2(2): ITTOIA 2005, s. 559(5) and (6).
Para. 3(1): ITTOIA 2005, s. 560(1)–(4).
Para. 3(2): ITTOIA 2005, s. 560(5).
Para. 3(3): ITTOIA 2005, s. 560(6).
ITTOIA 2005 does not rewrite para. 4(1) as it adds nothing (except possible confusion). (See ITTOIA 2005, Explanatory Notes, Annex 1, Table 1 (Change 158).)
Para. 4(2): ITTOIA 2005, s. 559(7), 562(1) and 566(5).
Para. 4(3): ITTOIA 2005, s. 562(2)–(4).
Para. 4(4): ITTOIA 2005, s. 563(1)–(5).
Para. 4(5): ITTOIA 2005, s. 563(6).
Para. 4(6): ITTOIA 2005, s. 558(1) and (2) and 562(4).
Para. 4A(1): ITTOIA 2005, s. 564(1)–(3) and (8).
Para. 4A(2): ITTOIA 2005, s. 564(4) and (6).
Para. 4A(3): ITTOIA 2005, s. 564(4), (5) and (6).
Para. 4A(4): ITTOIA 2005, s. 564(7).
Para. 4A(5): ITTOIA 2005, Sch. 1. para. 434.
Para. 4A(6): ITTOIA 2005, Sch. 1. para. 434.
Para. 4A(7): ITTOIA 2005, Sch. 1. para. 434.
Para. 4A(8): ITTOIA 2005, Sch. 1. para. 434.
Para. 4A(9): ITTOIA 2005, Sch. 1. para. 434.
Para. 4A(10): ITTOIA 2005, Sch. 1. para. 434.
Para. 4A(11): ITTOIA 2005, s. 565(1), (3) and (4) and 558(1) and (2).
Para. 4A(11): ITTOIA 2005, s. 565(1), (3) and (4).
Para. 4A(12): ITTOIA 2005, s. 565(2).
Para. 5(1): ITTOIA 2005, s. 561(1).
Para. 5(2): ITTOIA 2005, s. 561(2).
Para. 5(3): ITTOIA 2005, s. 561(3)–(6).
Para. 5(4): ITTOIA 2005, s. 561(7).
Para. 6(1): ITTOIA 2005, s. 566(1).
Para. 6(2): ITTOIA 2005, s. 566(4).
Para. 6(3): ITTOIA 2005, s. 566(2) and (3).
Para. 6(4): ITTOIA 2005, s. 566(6).
Para. 7(1): ITTOIA 2005, s. 568(1) and (5).
Para. 7(2): ITTOIA 2005, s. 568(1)–(4) and Sch. 2, para. 95.
Para. 7(3): ITTOIA 2005, s. 568(6) and (7).
Para. 8: ITTOIA 2005, s. 569(1) and (2).

SCHEDULE 5A – STOCK LENDING: INTEREST ON CASH COLLATERAL

Section 129A

[Repealed by FA 1997, s. 76 and Sch. 10, para. 1(2), s. 113 and Sch. 18, Pt. VI(10).]

History – Sch. 5A repealed by FA 1997, s. 76 and Sch. 10, para. 1(2) and s. 113 and Sch. 18, Pt. VI(10) with effect in relation to, and to transfers under, any arrangement made on or after 1 July 1997, the day appointed by virtue of SI 1997/991 (FA 1997, Sch. 10, para. 7(1)).
Sch. 5A inserted by FA 1995, s. 85(2) for stock lending arrangements entered into after 1 May 1995.

SCHEDULE 6 – TAXATION OF DIRECTORS AND OTHERS IN RESPECT OF CARS

Section 157

[Omitted by ITEPA 2003, s. 722 and Sch. 6, para. 110 and repealed by s. 724 and Sch. 8, Pt. 1.]

CASH EQUIVALENT

1 [Omitted by ITEPA 2003, s. 722 and Sch. 6, para. 110 and repealed by s. 724 and Sch. 8, Pt. 1.]

History – Para. 1 omitted by ITEPA 2003, s. 722 and Sch. 6, para. 110 and repealed by s. 724 and Sch. 8, Pt. 1, with effect for the year 2003–04 and subsequent tax years.

Notes – Para. 1 rewritten as ITEPA 2003, s. 121(1).

THE APPROPRIATE PERCENTAGE

2 [Omitted by ITEPA 2003, s. 722 and Sch. 6, para. 110 and repealed by s. 724 and Sch. 8, Pt. 1.]

History – Para. 2 omitted by ITEPA 2003, s. 722 and Sch. 6, para. 110 and repealed by s. 724 and Sch. 8, Pt. 1, with effect for the year 2003–04 and subsequent tax years.

Notes – Para. 2 rewritten as ITEPA 2003, s. 133(2), (3).

CAR WITH CO_2 EMISSIONS FIGURE

3 [Omitted by ITEPA 2003, s. 722 and Sch. 6, para. 110 and repealed by s. 724 and Sch. 8, Pt. 1.]

History – Para. 3 omitted by ITEPA 2003, s. 722 and Sch. 6, para. 110 and repealed by s. 724 and Sch. 8, Pt. 1, with effect for the year 2003–04 and subsequent tax years.

Notes – Para. 3 rewritten as follows:
Para. 3(1) and 3(2): ITEPA 2003, s. 134, s. 135 and s. 136.
Paras. 3(3), 3(4) and 3(5): ITEPA 2003, s. 139.

THE LOWER THRESHOLD

4 [Omitted by ITEPA 2003, s. 722 and Sch. 6, para. 110 and repealed by s. 724 and Sch. 8, Pt. 1.]

History – Para. 4 omitted by ITEPA 2003, s. 722 and Sch. 6, para. 110 and repealed by s. 724 and Sch. 8, Pt. 1, with effect for the year 2003–04 and subsequent tax years.

Notes – Para. 4 rewritten as follows:
Para. 4(1): ITEPA 2003, s. 139(4).
Para. 4(2): ITEPA 2003, s. 170(3).
Para. 4(3): ITEPA 2003, s. 139(5).

BI-FUEL CARS

5 [Omitted by ITEPA 2003, s. 722 and Sch. 6, para. 110 and repealed by s. 724 and Sch. 8, Pt. 1.]

History – Para. 5 omitted by ITEPA 2003, s. 722 and Sch. 6, para. 110 and repealed by s. 724 and Sch. 8, Pt. 1, with effect for the year 2003–04 and subsequent tax years.

Notes – Para. 5 rewritten as ITEPA 2003, s. 134(1) and (7).

AUTOMATIC CARS MADE AVAILABLE TO DISABLED DRIVERS

5A [Omitted by ITEPA 2003, s. 722 and Sch. 6, para. 110 and repealed by s. 724 and Sch. 8, Pt. 1.]

History – Para. 5A omitted by ITEPA 2003, s. 722 and Sch. 6, para. 110 and repealed by s. 724 and Sch. 8, Pt. 1, with effect for the year 2003–04 and subsequent tax years.

Notes – Para. 5A rewritten as follows:
Para. 5A(1)–(4): ITEPA 2003, s. 138(1)–(5).
Para. 5A(5): ITEPA 2003, s. 171(4).

"EC CERTIFICATE OF CONFORMITY", 'EC TYPE-APPROVAL CERTIFICATE' AND 'UK APPROVAL CERTIFICATE'

5B [Omitted by ITEPA 2003, s. 722 and Sch. 6, para. 110 and repealed by s. 724 and Sch. 8, Pt. 1.]

History – Para. 5B omitted by ITEPA 2003, s. 722 and Sch. 6, para. 110 and repealed by s. 724 and Sch. 8, Pt. 1, with effect for the year 2003–04 and subsequent tax years.

Notes – Para. 5B rewritten as ITEPA 2003, s. 171(1).

CAR WITH NO CO_2 EMISSIONS FIGURE

5C [Omitted by ITEPA 2003, s. 722 and Sch. 6, para. 110 and repealed by s. 724 and Sch. 8, Pt. 1.]

History – Para. 5C omitted by ITEPA 2003, s. 722 and Sch. 6, para. 110 and repealed by s. 724 and Sch. 8, Pt. 1, with effect for the year 2003–04 and subsequent tax years.

Notes – Para. 5C rewritten as follows:
Para. 5C(1): ITEPA 2003, s. 134(2).
Para. 5C(2), (3) and (4): ITEPA 2003, s. 140(2), (3) and (5).

DIESEL CAR SUPPLEMENT

5D [Omitted by ITEPA 2003, s. 722 and Sch. 6, para. 110 and repealed by s. 724 and Sch. 8, Pt. 1.]

History – Para. 5D omitted by ITEPA 2003, s. 722 and Sch. 6, para. 110 and repealed by s. 724 and Sch. 8, Pt. 1, with effect for the year 2003–04 and subsequent tax years.

Notes – Para. 5D rewritten as follows:
Para. 5D(1), (2) and (4): ITEPA 2003, s. 141.
Para. 5D(3): ITEPA 2003, s. 171(1).

DISCOUNTS

5E [Omitted by ITEPA 2003, s. 722 and Sch. 6, para. 110 and repealed by s. 724 and Sch. 8, Pt. 1.]

History – Para. 5E omitted by ITEPA 2003, s. 722 and Sch. 6, para. 110 and repealed by s. 724 and Sch. 8, Pt. 1, with effect for the year 2003–04 and subsequent tax years.

Notes – Para. 5E rewritten as ITEPA 2003, s. 170(4).

CAR REGISTERED BEFORE 1ST JANUARY 1998

5F [Omitted by ITEPA 2003, s. 722 and Sch. 6, para. 110 and repealed by s. 724 and Sch. 8, Pt. 1.]

History – Para. 5F omitted by ITEPA 2003, s. 722 and Sch. 6, para. 110 and repealed by s. 724 and Sch. 8, Pt. 1, with effect for the year 2003–04 and subsequent tax years.

Notes – Para. 5F rewritten as ITEPA 2003, s. 142.

ELECTRICALLY PROPELLED VEHICLE

5G [Omitted by ITEPA 2003, s. 722 and Sch. 6, para. 110 and repealed by s. 724 and Sch. 8, Pt. 1.]

History – Para. 5G omitted by ITEPA 2003, s. 722 and Sch. 6, para. 110 and repealed by s. 724 and Sch. 8, Pt. 1, Pt. 1, with effect for the year 2003–04 and subsequent tax years.

Notes – Para. 5G rewritten as ITEPA 2003, s. 140(4) and s. 142(4).

REDUCTION FOR PERIODS WHEN CAR UNAVAILABLE

6 [Omitted by ITEPA 2003, s. 722 and Sch. 6, para. 110 and repealed by s. 724 and Sch. 8, Pt. 1.]

History – Para. 6 omitted by ITEPA 2003, s. 722 and Sch. 6, para. 110 and repealed by s. 724 and Sch. 8, Pt. 1, with effect for the year 2003–04 and subsequent tax years.

Notes – Para. 6 rewritten as ITEPA 2003, s. 143(1), (3).

REDUCTION FOR PAYMENTS FOR USE OF CAR

7 [Omitted by ITEPA 2003, s. 722 and Sch. 6, para. 110 and repealed by s. 724 and Sch. 8, Pt. 1.]

History – Para. 7 omitted by ITEPA 2003, s. 722 and Sch. 6, para. 110 and repealed by s. 724 and Sch. 8, Pt. 1, with effect for the year 2003–04 and subsequent tax years.

Notes – Para. 7 rewritten as ITEPA 2003, s. 144(1)–(4).

REPLACEMENT CARS

8 [Omitted by ITEPA 2003, s. 722 and Sch. 6, para. 110 and repealed by s. 724 and Sch. 8, Pt. 1.]

History – Para. 8 omitted by ITEPA 2003, s. 722 and Sch. 6, para. 110 and repealed by s. 724 and Sch. 8, Pt. 1, with effect for the year 2003–04 and subsequent tax years.

Notes – Para. 8 is unnecessary and so has not been rewritten into the provisions of ITEPA 2003.

MEANING OF "UNAVAILABLE"

9 [Omitted by ITEPA 2003, s. 722 and Sch. 6, para. 110 and repealed by s. 724 and Sch. 8, Pt. 1.]

History – Para. 9 omitted by ITEPA 2003, s. 722 and Sch. 6, para. 110 and repealed by s. 724 and Sch. 8, Pt. 1, with effect for the year 2003–04 and subsequent tax years.

Notes – Para. 9 rewritten as ITEPA 2003, s. 143(2).

GENERAL

10 [Omitted by ITEPA 2003, s. 722 and Sch. 6, para. 110 and repealed by s. 724 and Sch. 8, Pt. 1.]

History – Para. 10 omitted by ITEPA 2003, s. 722 and Sch. 6, para. 110 and repealed by s. 724 and Sch. 8, Pt. 1 , with effect for the year 2003–04 and subsequent tax years.

Notes – Para. 10 rewritten as ITEPA 2003, s. 116(1), (3).

SCHEDULE 6A – TAXATION OF DIRECTORS AND OTHERS IN RESPECT OF VANS

Section 159AA

[Omitted by ITEPA 2003, s. 722 and Sch. 6, para. 110 and repealed by s. 724 and Sch. 8, Pt 1.]

Part I – Basic Case

CASH EQUIVALENT

1 [Omitted by ITEPA 2003, s. 722 and Sch. 6, para. 110 and repealed by s. 724 and Sch. 8, Pt. 1.]

History – Para. 1 omitted by ITEPA 2003, s. 722 and Sch. 6, para. 110 and repealed by s. 724 and Sch. 8, Pt. 1, with effect for the year 2003–04 and subsequent tax years.

Notes – Para. 1 rewritten as follows:
Para. 1(1): ITEPA 2003, s. 155(2), (4).
Para. 1(2): ITEPA 2003, s. 157.

ICTA 1988

REDUCTIONS FOR PERIODS WHERE VAN UNAVAILABLE

2 [Omitted by ITEPA 2003, s. 722 and Sch. 6, para. 110 and repealed by s. 724 and Sch. 8, Pt. 1.]

History – Para. 2 omitted by ITEPA 2003, s. 722 and Sch. 6, para. 110 and repealed by s. 724 and Sch. 8, Pt. 1, with effect for the year 2003–04 and subsequent tax years.

Notes – Para. 2 rewritten as follows:
Para. 2(1): ITEPA 2003, s. 157 and s. 158(1), (3).
Para. 2(2): ITEPA 2003, s. 158(4).
Para. 2(3): ITEPA 2003, s. 158(2).

REDUCTION FOR PAYMENTS FOR USE OF VAN

3 [Omitted by ITEPA 2003, s. 722 and Sch. 6, para. 110 and repealed by s. 724 and Sch. 8, Pt. 1.]

History – Para. 3 omitted by ITEPA 2003, s. 722 and Sch. 6, para. 110 and repealed by s. 724 and Sch. 8, Pt. 1, with effect for the year 2003–04 and subsequent tax years.

Notes – Para. 3 rewritten as follows:
Para. 3(1): ITEPA 2003, s. 157 and s. 159(1)– (3).
Para. 3(2): ITEPA 2003, s. 159 (1), (2), (3), (5).
Para. 3(3): ITEPA 2003, s. 159(4).

Part II – Shared Vans

INTRODUCTION

4 [Omitted by ITEPA 2003, s. 722 and Sch. 6, para. 110 and repealed by s. 724 and Sch. 8, Pt. 1.]

History – Para. 4 omitted by ITEPA 2003, s. 722 and Sch. 6, para. 110 and repealed by s. 724 and Sch. 8, Pt. 1, with effect for the year 2003–04 and subsequent tax years.

Notes – Para. 4 rewritten as follows:
Para. 4(1): ITEPA 2003, s. 155 (3), (4).
Para. 4(2)–(5): ITEPA 2003, s. 156.

BENEFIT TO EMPLOYEE

5 [Omitted by ITEPA 2003, s. 722 and Sch. 6, para. 110 and repealed by s. 724 and Sch. 8, Pt. 1.]

History – Para. 5 omitted by ITEPA 2003, s. 722 and Sch. 6, para. 110 and repealed by s. 724 and Sch. 8, Pt. 1, with effect for the year 2003–04 and subsequent tax years.

Notes – Para. 5 rewritten as follows:
Para. 5(1), (5): ITEPA 2003, s. 161(1).
Para. 5(2): ITEPA 2003, s. 161(1), (2).
Para. 5(3): ITEPA 2003, s. 162(3).
Para. 5(4): ITEPA 2003, s. 161(2).
Para. 5(5): ITEPA 2003, s. 161(1).
Para. 5(6): ITEPA 2003, s. 155(3), (4), (7).

BASIC VALUE

6 [Omitted by ITEPA 2003, s. 722 and Sch. 6, para. 110 and repealed by s. 724 and Sch. 8, Pt. 1.]

History – Para. 6 omitted by ITEPA 2003, s. 722 and Sch. 6, para. 110 and repealed by s. 724 and Sch. 8, Pt. 1, with effect for the year 2003–04 and subsequent tax years.

Notes – Para. 6 rewritten as ITEPA 2003, s. 163.

LIMIT OF BENEFIT

7 [Omitted by ITEPA 2003, s. 722 and Sch. 6, para. 110 and repealed by s. 724 and Sch. 8, Pt. 1.]

History – Para. 7 omitted by ITEPA 2003, s. 722 and Sch. 6, para. 110 and repealed by s. 724 and Sch. 8, Pt. 1, with effect for the year 2003–04 and subsequent tax years.

Notes – Para. 7 rewritten as ITEPA 2003, s. 161(1).

ALTERNATIVE CALCULATION

8 [Omitted by ITEPA 2003, s. 722 and Sch. 6, para. 110 and repealed by s. 724 and Sch. 8, Pt. 1.]

History – Para. 8 omitted by ITEPA 2003, s. 722 and Sch. 6, para. 110 and repealed by s. 724 and Sch. 8, Pt. 1, with effect for the year 2003–04 and subsequent tax years.

Notes – Para. 8 rewritten as ITEPA 2003, s. 164.

REDUCTION FOR PAYMENTS FOR USE

9 [Omitted by ITEPA 2003, s. 722 and Sch. 6, para. 110 and repealed by s. 724 and Sch. 8, Pt. 1.]

History – Para. 9 omitted by ITEPA 2003, s. 722 and Sch. 6, para. 110 and repealed by s. 724 and Sch. 8, Pt. 1, with effect for the year 2003–04 and subsequent tax years.

Notes – Para. 9 rewritten as follows:
Para. 9(1): ITEPA 2003, s. 161(1), s. 164(2) and s. 165(1)–(3).
Para. 9(2): ITEPA 2003, s. 165(4).
Para. 9(3): ITEPA 2003, s. 165(5).

Part III – General

INTERACTION OF PARTS I AND II

10 [Omitted by ITEPA 2003, s. 722 and Sch. 6, para. 110 and repealed by s. 724 and Sch. 8, Pt. 1.]

History – Para. 10 omitted by ITEPA 2003, s. 722 and Sch. 6, para. 110 and repealed by s. 724 and Sch. 8, Pt. 1, with effect for the year 2003–04 and subsequent tax years.

Notes – Para. 10 rewritten as ITEPA 2003, s. 155(4), (7).

LIMIT OF CASH EQUIVALENT

11 [Omitted by ITEPA 2003, s. 722 and Sch. 6, para. 110 and repealed by s. 724 and Sch. 8, Pt. 1.]

History – Para. 11 omitted by ITEPA 2003, s. 722 and Sch. 6, para. 110 and repealed by s. 724 and Sch. 8, Pt. 1, with effect for the year 2003–04 and subsequent tax years.

Notes – Para. 11 rewritten as ITEPA 2003, s. 166.

INTERPRETATION

12 [Omitted by ITEPA 2003, s. 722 and Sch. 6, para. 110 and repealed by s. 724 and Sch. 8, Pt. 1.]

History – Para. 12 omitted by ITEPA 2003, s. 722 and Sch. 6, para. 110 and repealed by s. 724 and Sch. 8, Pt. 1, with effect for the year 2003–04 and subsequent tax years.

Notes – Para. 12 rewritten as ITEPA 2003, s. 116(1).

SCHEDULE 7 – TAXATION OF BENEFIT FROM LOANS OBTAINED BY REASON OF EMPLOYMENT

Section 160

[Omitted by ITEPA 2003, s. 722 and Sch. 6, para. 110 and repealed by s. 724 and Sch 8, Pt. 1.]

Part I – Meaning of "Obtained by Reason of Employment"

1 [Omitted by ITEPA 2003, s. 722 and Sch. 6, para. 110 and repealed by s. 724 and Sch. 8, Pt. 1]

History – Para. 1 omitted by ITEPA 2003, s. 722 and Sch. 6, para. 110 and repealed by s. 724 and Sch. 8, Pt. 1, with effect for the year 2003–04 and subsequent tax years.

Notes – Para. 1 rewritten as follows:
Para. 1(1): ITEPA 2003, s. 174(1), (2).
Para. 1(2)–(4): ITEPA 2003, s. 174(2).
Para. 1(5): ITEPA 2003, s. 174(5).

2 [Omitted by ITEPA 2003, s. 722 and Sch. 6, para. 110 and repealed by s. 724 and Sch. 8, Pt. 1.]

History – Para. 2 omitted by ITEPA 2003, s. 722 and Sch. 6, para. 110 and repealed by s. 724 and Sch. 8, Pt. 1, with effect for the year 2003–04 and subsequent tax years.

Notes – Para. 2 rewritten as ITEPA 2003, s. 174(2), (3), (4).

Part II – Calculation of Cash Equivalent of Loan Benefit

[Omitted by ITEPA 2003, s. 722 and Sch. 6, para. 110 and repealed by s. 724 and Sch. 8, Pt. 1.]

GENERAL

3 [Omitted by ITEPA 2003, s. 722 and Sch. 6, para. 110 and repealed by s. 724 and Sch. 8, Pt. 1.]

History – Para. 3 omitted by ITEPA 2003, s. 722 and Sch. 6, para. 110 and repealed by s. 724 and Sch. 8, Pt. 1, with effect for the year 2003–04 and subsequent tax years.

Notes – Para. 3 rewritten as follows:
Para. 3(1): ITEPA 2003, s. 175(3), (4).
Paras. 3(2) and 3(3) are not necessary and so have not been rewritten.

NORMAL METHOD OF CALCULATION (AVERAGING)

4 [Omitted by ITEPA 2003, s. 722 and Sch. 6, para. 110 and repealed by s. 724 and Sch. 8, Pt. 1.]

History – Para. 4 omitted by ITEPA 2003, s. 722 and Sch. 6, para. 110 and repealed by s. 724 and Sch 8, Pt. 1, with effect for the year 2003–04 and subsequent tax years.

Notes – Para. 4 rewritten as follows:
Para. 4(1): ITEPA 2003, s. 182.
Para. 4(2), (3): ITEPA 2003, s. 186(1), (2).
Para. 4(4): ITEPA 2003, s. 186(4) and s. 718.

ELECTION FOR ALTERNATIVE METHOD OF CALCULATION

5 [Omitted by ITEPA 2003, s. 722 and Sch. 6, para. 110 and repealed by s. 724 and Sch. 8, Pt. 1.]

History – Para. 5 omitted by ITEPA 2003, s. 722 and Sch. 6, para. 110 and repealed by s. 724 and Sch. 8, Pt. 1, with effect for the year 2003–04 and subsequent tax years.

Notes – Para. 5 rewritten as ITEPA 2003, s. 183(1)–(3).

APPORTIONMENT OF CASH EQUIVALENT IN CASE OF JOINT LOAN ETC.

5A [Omitted by ITEPA 2003, s. 722 and Sch. 6, para. 110 and repealed by s. 724 and Sch. 8, Pt. 1.]

History – Para. 5A omitted by ITEPA 2003, s. 722 and Sch. 6, para. 110 and repealed by s. 724 and Sch. 8, Pt. 1, with effect for the year 2003–04 and subsequent tax years.

Notes – Para. 5A rewritten as follows:
Para. 5A(1): ITEPA 2003, s. 185.
Para. 5A(2): ITEPA 2003, s. 183(4).

Part III – Exceptions Where Interest Eligible for Relief

[Repealed by FA 1994, s. 88(4)(b) and s. 258 and Sch. 26, Pt. V(5) with effect for 1994–95 and subsequent years of assessment.]

Part IV – Interest Eligible for Relief: Consequences of Restriction of Relief to Tax at the Basic Rate only

[Repealed by FA 1994, s. 88(4)(b) and s. 258 and Sch. 26, Pt. V(5), with effect for 1994–95 and subsequent years of assessment.]

Part V – Interpretation

[Repealed by FA 1994, s. 88(4)(b) and s. 258 and Sch. 26, Pt. V(5), with effect for 1994–95 and subsequent years of assessment.]

SCHEDULE 7A – BENEFICIAL LOANS: LOANS ON ORDINARY COMMERCIAL TERMS

[Omitted by ITEPA 2003, s. 722 and Sch. 6, para. 110 and repealed by s. 724 and Sch. 8, Pt. 1.]

INTRODUCTION

1 [Omitted by ITEPA 2003, s. 722 and Sch. 6, para. 110 and repealed by s. 724 and Sch. 8, Pt. 1.]

History – Para. 1 omitted by ITEPA 2003, s. 722 and Sch. 6, para. 110 and repealed by s. 724 and Sch. 8, Pt. 1, with effect for the year 2003–04 and subsequent tax years.

Notes – Para. 1 rewritten as ITEPA 2003, s. 176(2).

REQUIREMENTS RELATING TO ORIGINAL LOAN

2 [Omitted by ITEPA 2003, s. 722 and Sch. 6, para. 110 and repealed by s. 724 and Sch. 8, Pt. 1.]

History – Para. 2 omitted by ITEPA 2003, s. 722 and Sch. 6, para. 110 and repealed by s. 724 and Sch. 8, Pt. 1, with effect for the year 2003–04 and subsequent tax years.

Notes – Para. 2 rewritten as follows:
Para. 2(1)–(4): ITEPA 2003, s. 176(3), (4).
Para. 2(5): ITEPA 2003, s. 176(8).

REQUIREMENTS RELATING TO LOAN VARIED BEFORE 6TH APRIL 2000

3 [Omitted by ITEPA 2003, s. 722 and Sch. 6, para. 110 and repealed by s. 724 and Sch. 8, Pt. 1.]

History – Para. 3 omitted by ITEPA 2003, s. 722 and Sch. 6, para. 110 and repealed by s. 724 and Sch. 8, Pt. 1, with effect for the year 2003–04 and subsequent tax years.

Notes – Para. 3 rewritten as ITEPA 2003, s. 176(5), (7).

REQUIREMENTS RELATING TO LOAN VARIED ON OR AFTER 6TH APRIL 2000

4 [Omitted by ITEPA 2003, s. 722 and Sch. 6, para. 110 and repealed by s. 724 and Sch. 8, Pt. 1.]

History – Para. 4 omitted by ITEPA 2003, s. 722 and Sch. 6, para. 110 and repealed by s. 724 and Sch. 8, Pt. 1, with effect for the year 2003–04 and subsequent tax years.

Notes – Para. 4 rewritten as ITEPA 2003, s. 176(6), (7).

DISREGARD OF CERTAIN PENALTIES, FEES, ETC.

5 [Omitted by ITEPA 2003, s. 722 and Sch. 6, para. 110 and repealed by s. 724 and Sch. 8, Pt. 1.]

History – Para. 5 omitted by ITEPA 2003, s. 722 and Sch. 6, para. 110 and repealed by s. 724 and Sch. 8, Pt. 1, with effect for the year 2003–04 and subsequent tax years.

Notes – Para. 5 rewritten as ITEPA 2003, s. 176(8), (9).

MEANING OF "MEMBER OF THE PUBLIC"

6 [Omitted by ITEPA 2003, s. 722 and Sch. 6, para. 110 and repealed by s. 724 and Sch. 8, Pt. 1.]

History – Para. 6 omitted by ITEPA 2003, s. 722 and Sch. 6, para. 110 and repealed by s. 724 and Sch. 8, Pt. 1, with effect for the year 2003–04 and subsequent tax years.

Notes – Para. 6 rewritten as ITEPA 2003, s. 176(10).

SCHEDULE 8 – PROFIT-RELATED PAY SCHEMES: CONDITIONS FOR REGISTRATION

Section 176(9)

[Sch. 8 repealed by FA 1997, s. 113 and Sch. 18, Pt. VI(3).]

History – Sch. 8 was repealed by FA 1997, s. 113 and Sch. 18, Pt. VI(3), with effect in relation to payments made by reference to profit periods beginning on or after 1 January 2000 (FA 1997, s. 61(2)) but subject to Notes 2 and 3 to Sch. 18, Pt. VI(3). Para. 7 of Sch. 8 is reproduced below because of its continuing application by other legislation notwithstanding repeal.

"**7(1)** The scheme must contain provisions ensuring that no payments are made under it to any person who is employed in the employment unit by a company and who has a material interest in the company.

7(2) For the purposes of this paragraph a person shall be treated as having a material interest in a company, if he, either on his own or with any one or more of his associates, or if any associate of his with or without such other associates,–

(a) is the beneficial owner of, or able, directly or through the medium of other companies, or by any other indirect means, to control, more than 25 per cent of the ordinary share capital of the company, or

(b) in the case of a close company, possesses, or is entitled to acquire, such rights as would, in the event of the winding-up of the company or in any other circumstances, give an entitlement to receive more than 25 per cent of the assets which would then be available for distribution among the participators.

7(3) In this paragraph–

"associate" has the same meaning as in section 417(3) and (4), but subject to sub-paragraph (4) below;

"control" has the meaning given by section 840; and

"participator" has the meaning given by section 417(1);

and the definition of "control" in section 840 applies (with the necessary modifications) in relation to a company which is an unincorporated association as it applies in relation to one that is not.

7(4) For the purposes of this paragraph, where an employee of a company has an interest in shares or obligations of the company as a beneficiary of an employee benefit trust, the trustees shall not be regarded as associates of his by reason only of that interest unless sub-paragraph (8) below applies in relation to him.

7(5) A trust is an employee benefit trust for the purposes of this paragraph if–

(a) all or most of the employees of the company are eligible to benefit under it, and

(b) none of the property subject to it has been disposed of on or after 14th March 1989 (whether by sale, loan or otherwise) except in the ordinary course of management of the trust or in accordance with sub-paragraph (6) below.

7(6) Property is disposed of in accordance with this sub-paragraph if–

(a) it is applied for the benefit of–

(i) individual employees or former employees of the company,

(ii) spouses, former spouses, widows or widowers of employees or former employees of the company,

(iii) relatives, or spouses of relatives, of persons within sub-paragraph (i) or (ii) above, or

(iv) dependants of persons within sub-paragraph (i) above,

(b) it is applied for charitable purposes, or

(c) it is transferred to the trustees of an approved profit sharing scheme (within the meaning of section 187), of another employee benefit trust, or of a qualifying employee share ownership trust (within the meaning of Schedule 5 to the Finance Act 1989),

and the property applied or transferred consists of any of the ordinary share capital of the company or of money paid outright.

7(7) In sub-paragraph (6)(a)(iii) above **"relative"** means parent or remoter forebear, child or remoter issue, brother, sister, uncle, aunt, nephew or niece.

7(8) This sub-paragraph applies in relation to an employee if at any time on or after 14th March 1989–

(a) the employee, either on his own or with any one or more of his associates, or

(b) any associate of his, with or without other such associates,

has been the beneficial owner of, or able (directly or through the medium of other companies or by any other indirect means) to control, more than 25 per cent of the ordinary share capital of the company.

7(9) Where–

(a) on or after 14th March 1989 an employee of a company, or an associate of his, receives a payment (**"the relevant payment"**) from the trustees of an employee benefit trust, and

(b) at any time during the period of three years ending with the day on which the relevant payment is received, the property subject to the trust consists of or includes any part of the ordinary share capital of the company, the employee or associate shall be treated for the purposes of sub-paragraph (8) above as if he were the beneficial owner of the appropriate percentage of the ordinary share capital of the company on the day on which the relevant payment is received (in addition to any percentage of that share capital of which he is actually the beneficial owner on that day).

7(10) For the purposes of sub-paragraph (9) above, the appropriate percentage is–

$$\frac{A \times 100}{B}$$

where–

A is the smaller of–

(a) the aggregate of the relevant payment and any other payments received by the employee or associates of his from the trustees of the trust during the period of 12 months ending with the day on which the relevant payment is received, and

(b) the aggregate of the distributions made to the trustees of the trust by the company in respect of its ordinary share capital during the period of three years ending with the day on which the relevant payment is received; and

B is the aggregate of–

(a) any distributions made by the company in respect of its ordinary share capital during the period of 12 months ending with the day on which the relevant payment is received,

(b) any distributions so made during the period of 12 months immediately preceding that mentioned in paragraph (a) above, and

(c) any distributions so made during the period of 12 months immediately preceding that mentioned in paragraph (b) above,

divided by the number of the periods mentioned in paragraphs (a) to (c) above in which distributions were so made.

7(11) Where–

(a) an employee or associate is treated by sub-paragraph (9) above as if he were the beneficial owner of a percentage of the ordinary share capital of a company by reason of receiving the relevant payment from the trustees of a trust, and

(b) that employee, or an associate of his, has, during the period of 12 months ending with the day on which the relevant payment is received, received one or more payments from trustees of another employee benefit trust or trusts satisfying the requirement in paragraph (b) of sub-paragraph (9) above,

that sub-paragraph shall have effect in relation to the employee or associate mentioned in paragraph (a) above as if he had received the payment from the trustees of the trust or of each of the trusts mentioned in paragraph (b) above (or where more than one payment has been received from the trustees of a trust, the last of the payments) on the day on which the relevant payment is received.

7(12) In sub-paragraphs (8) to (11) above **"associate"**, in relation to an employee, does not include the trustees of an employee benefit trust by reason only that the employee has an interest in shares or obligations of the trust.

History – Reference in para. 7(1) to avoidance of payments to an employee who "is an associate of a person who has" a material interest omitted by FA 1989, Sch. 4, para. 1, 9(1), (2) and Sch. 17, Pt. IV.
Para. 7(4)–(12), and reference thereto in para. 7(3), inserted by FA 1989, Sch. 4, para. 1 and 9(1), (3), (4).
Consequent to the repeal of close company apportionment, para. 7(2) amended by FA 1989, Sch. 12, para. 18, substituting the words after "in a company", effective for accounting periods beginning after 31 March 1989, and the definition of "participator" consequently inserted in para. 7(3).

Derivations – F(No. 2)A 1987, Sch. 1, para. 7.

Cross references – S. 169(1): "profit period" is an accounting period by reference to which PRP is calculated.
S. 360A(5): modified application of meaning of "employee benefit trust" to interest relief on loan to buy interest in close company.
S. 360A(7): para. 7(9)–(12) apply to an individual in relation to interest relief on a loan to buy interest in close company.
S. 832(1): definition of "close company" and "company".
FA 1989, Sch. 5, para. 16(4), (6): modified application of meaning of "employee benefit trust" to employee share ownership trusts and application of para. 7(9)–(12) accordingly.

Other material – ICAEW Technical Release TR 759 (not reproduced): "ordinary course of management" in para. 7(5)(b) means "the sale of investments held by the trustees as part of the normal administration of the trust"."

Notes – S. 832 rewritten for corporation tax purposes as follows:
S. 832(1): CTA 2009, s. 1317(1), (2), (5), Sch. 1, para. 274.

SCHEDULE 9 – APPROVED SHARE OPTION SCHEMES AND PROFIT SHARING SCHEMES

Section 185, 186, 187

Cross references – FA 1989, s. 69(4ZA)(b): chargeable events and employee share ownership trusts.
FA 1989, Sch. 5, para. 4(2A), 9(2ZA), 10: employee share ownership trusts.
FA 1990, s. 117(1): valuation of securities transferred to trustees of a share option scheme or profit sharing scheme approved under Sch. 9 for the purposes of ports levy.
TCGA 1992, s. 238: interaction with capital gains tax.
TCGA 1992, s. 239(6): power to appropriate shares in pursuance of an approved profit sharing scheme does not prevent the no gain, no loss treatment of certain disposals to employee trusts.
FA 1996, s. 116(3): "release date" and profit sharing schemes.
FA 1996, s. 117(3): "appropriate percentage" and profit sharing schemes.
FA 2000, s. 49(1), (2): phasing out of approved profit sharing schemes.
ITEPA 2003, s. 418(3): because of the phasing out of profit sharing schemes, Sch. 9 continues in force so far as it relates to schemes approved under its provisions and is not rewritten in the FA 2003, Sch. 22 amendments to ITEPA 2003.
ITEPA 2003, s. 551(5): conditions for disposals by qualifying employee benefit trusts.
ITEPA 2003, s. 697(4) and s. 701(2): shares acquired under a scheme approved under Sch. 9 not to be treated as readily convertible assets for the purposes of PAYE.

Other material – Taxline 1993/109 (not reproduced): profit-related pay does not form part of relevant emoluments for purposes of approved share option schemes.

Part I – General

[Omitted by ITEPA 2003, s. 722 and Sch. 6, para. 112(2) and repealed by s. 724 and Sch. 8, Pt. 1.]

History – Part. 1 omitted by ITEPA 2003, s. 722 and Sch. 6, para. 112(2) and repealed by s. 724 and Sch. 8, Pt. 1 (except in so far as relating to profit sharing schemes), with effect in relation to schemes approved on or after 6 April 2003, subject to the transitional provisions and savings detailed in ITEPA 2003, Sch. 7. In so far as it continues to apply, former wording is as follows:

"**1(1)** Subject to the provisions of this Schedule, on the application of a body corporate (**"the grantor"**) which has established a share option scheme or a profit sharing scheme, the Board shall approve the scheme if they are satisfied that it fulfils such requirements of Part II and this Part as apply in relation to the scheme in question, and the requirements of Part III, IV or V of this Schedule; and in this Schedule–

"the relevant requirements" means, in relation to any scheme, the requirements of this Schedule by reference to which the scheme is approved; and

"savings-related share option scheme" means a scheme in relation to which the relevant requirements include the requirements of Part III of this Schedule.

1(2) An application under sub-paragraph (1) above shall be made in writing and contain such particulars and be supported by such evidence as the Board may require.

1(3) Where the grantor has control of another company or companies, the scheme may be expressed to extend to all or any of the companies of which it has control and in this Schedule a scheme which is expressed so to extend is referred to as a **"group scheme"**.

1(4) In relation to a group scheme the expression **"participating company"** means the grantor or any other company to which for the time being the scheme is expressed to extend.

Derivations – Para. 1(1): FA 1978, Sch. 9, para. 1(1)(a); FA 1980, Sch. 10, para. 1(1)(a) and FA 1984, Sch. 10, para. 1(1).
Para. 1(2): FA 1978, Sch. 9, para. 1(5); FA 1980, Sch. 10, para. 1(2) and FA 1984, Sch. 10, para. 1(2).
Para. 1(3): FA 1978, Sch. 9, para. 1(2); FA 1980, Sch. 10, para. 1(3) and FA 1984, Sch. 10, para. 1(3).
Para. 1(4): FA 1987, Sch. 9, para. 1(2); FA 1980, Sch. 10, para. 1(3) and FA 1984, Sch. 10, para. 1(4).

Cross references – S. 187(2), 840: definition of "control".
FA 1996, s. 115(5): "relevant requirements" and transitional provisions for share options, profit sharing and employee share ownership.
ICTA 1988, s. 50(7): meaning of "gilt-edged securities".

Extra-statutory concessions – B27: a jointly-owned company (JOC), or companies controlled by a JOC, may join in approved share schemes run by either of the JOC's parent companies.

Other material – IR-decision: IRDec. 5: linkage between approved discretionary share option scheme and "phantom" share scheme.

2(1) The Board shall not approve a scheme under this Schedule if it appears to them that it contains features which are neither essential nor reasonably incidental to the purpose of providing for employees and directors benefits in the nature of rights to acquire shares or, in the case of a profit sharing scheme, in the nature of interests in shares.

2(2) A profit sharing scheme shall not be approved under paragraph 1 above unless the Board are satisfied that, whether under the terms of the scheme or otherwise, every participant in the scheme is bound in contract with the grantor–

(a) to permit his shares to remain in the hands of the trustees throughout the period of retention; and
(b) not to assign, charge or otherwise dispose of his beneficial interest in his shares during that period; and
(c) if he directs the trustees to transfer the ownership of his shares to him at any time before the release date, to pay to the trustees before the transfer takes place a sum equal to income tax at the basic rate on the appropriate percentage of the locked-in value of the shares at the time of the direction; and
(d) not to direct the trustees to dispose of his shares at any time before the release date in any other way except by sale for the best consideration in money that can reasonably be obtained at the time of the sale or, in the case of redeemable shares in a workers' cooperative, by redemption.

2(2A) The Board shall not approve a profit sharing scheme unless they are satisfied–

(a) that the arrangements for the scheme do not make any provision, and are not in any way associated with any provision made, for loans to some or all of the employees of–
  (i) the company that established the scheme, or
  (ii) in the case of a group scheme, any participating company, and
(b) that the operation of the scheme is not in any way associated with such loans.

2(2B) For the purposes of sub-paragraph (2A) above **"arrangements"** includes any scheme, agreement or understanding, whether or not legally enforceable.

2(3) The Board must be satisfied in the case of a savings-related share option scheme or a profit sharing scheme–

(a) that there are no features of the scheme (other than any which are included to satisfy requirements of this Schedule) which have or would have the effect of discouraging any description of employees or former employees who fulfil the conditions in paragraph 26(1) or, as the case may be, 36(1) below from actually participating in the scheme; and
(b) where the grantor is a member of a group of companies, that the scheme does not and would not have the effect of conferring benefits wholly or mainly on directors of companies in the group or on those employees of companies in the group who are in receipt of the higher or highest levels of remuneration.

2(4) For the purposes of sub-paragraph (3) above **"a group of companies"** means a company and any other companies of which it has control.

History – Para. 2(2A) and (2B) inserted by FA 2000, s. 53(1), with deemed effect from 21 March 2000.

Derivations – Para. 2(1): FA 1978, Sch. 9, para. 1(1)(b); FA 1980, Sch. 10, para. 1(1)(b) and FA 1984, Sch. 10, para. 1(1).
Para. 2(2): FA 1978, s. 54(1), as amended by FA 1986, s. 24(3)(a).
Para. 2(3): FA 1978, Sch. 9, para. 2(3) (as amended by FA 1983, s. 25(5)) and FA 1980, Sch. 10, para. 1(1)(aa), (ab) (as inserted by FA 1984, s. 39(2)).
Para. 2(4): FA 1978, Sch. 9, para. 2(4), as inserted by FA 1983, s. 25(5) and from FA 1980, Sch. 10, para. 1(1A), as inserted by FA 1984, s. 39(3).

Cross references – S. 187(2): definition of "participant".
Sch. 10, para. 1: limitations on contractual obligations of participants.
Sch. 10, para. 1(3): breach of obligations in para. 2(2)(b).
Sch. 10, para. 7(2): application of para. 2(2)(c) in the case of personal representatives.
Sch. 10, para. 7(7): trustees to treat sums received by virtue of para. 2(2)(c) as PAYE deducted.
TCGA 1992, s. 238(1): notwithstanding para. 2(2), participant is treated as absolutely entitled as against the trustees to shares appropriated to him.

HMRC Manuals – Employee Share Scheme Unit Manual, ESS 2523: scheme examiners may accept that a discretionary cash payment made as result of non-participation in a profit sharing scheme is not a feature of that scheme, but it is not appropriate or acceptable to refer, in any of the scheme documentation, to the possible availability of cash payments.
Employee Share Scheme Unit Manual, ESS 2534: basis on which Revenue consider whether contributory profit sharing schemes breach the requirement that a scheme should contain only essential or reasonably incidental provisions (para. 2(1)).

3(1) If, at any time after the Board have approved a share option scheme, any of the relevant requirements ceases to be satisfied or the grantor fails to provide information requested by the Board under paragraph 6 below, the Board may withdraw the approval with effect from that time or such later time as the Board may specify; but where rights obtained under a savings-related share option scheme before the withdrawal of approval from the scheme under this paragraph are exercised after the withdrawal, section 185(3) shall apply in respect of the exercise as if the scheme were still approved.
3(2) If at any time after the Board have approved a profit sharing scheme–
(a) a participant is in breach of any of his obligations under paragraph 2(2)(a), (c) and (d) above; or
(b) there is, with respect to the operation of the scheme, any contravention of any of the relevant requirements, Schedule 10, the scheme itself or the terms of the trust referred to in paragraph 30(1)(c) below; or
(c) any shares of a class of which shares have been appropriated to the participants receive different treatment in any respect from the other shares of that class, in particular, different treatment in respect of–
(i) the dividend payable;
(ii) repayment;
(iii) the restrictions attaching to the shares; or
(iv) any offer of substituted or additional shares, securities or rights of any description in respect of the shares; or
(ca) the Board–
(i) cease to be satisfied of the matters mentioned in paragraph 2(2A) above, or
(ii) in the case of a scheme approved before 21st March 2000, are not satisfied of those matters; or
(d) the Board cease to be satisfied that the scheme complies with the requirements of paragraph 2(3) above or paragraph 36 below; or
(e) the trustees, the grantor or, in the case of a group scheme, a company which is or has been a participating company fail or fails to furnish any information which they are or it is required to furnish under paragraph 6 below; or
(f) the trustees appropriate shares to participants, one or more of whom have had free shares appropriated to them, at an earlier time in the same year of assessment, under a relevant share plan,

the Board may, subject to sub-paragraph (3) below, withdraw the approval with effect from that time or from such later time as the Board may specify.
3(3) It shall not be a ground for withdrawal of approval of a profit sharing scheme that shares which have been newly issued receive, in respect of dividends payable with respect to a period beginning before the date on which the shares were issued, treatment which is less favourable than that accorded to shares issued before that date.
3(4) For the purposes of sub-paragraph (2)(f) above the reference to persons having had free shares appropriated to them includes persons who would have had free shares appropriated to them but for their failure to obtain a performance allowance (within the meaning of paragraph 25 of Schedule 8 to the Finance Act 2000).
3(5) In sub-paragraph (2)(f) and (4) above–

"free shares" has the same meaning as in Schedule 8 to the Finance Act 2000;

"relevant share plan", in relation to a profit sharing scheme, means an employee share ownership plan that–
(a) was established by the grantor or a connected company, and
(b) is approved under Schedule 8 to that Act.

3(6) For the purposes of sub-paragraph (5) above **"connected company"** means–
(a) a company which controls or is controlled by the grantor or which is controlled by a company which also controls the grantor, or
(b) a company which is a member of a consortium owning the grantor or which is owned in part by the grantor as a member of a consortium.

History – Para. 3(2)(ca) inserted by FA 2000, s. 53(2), with deemed effect from 21 March 2000.
Para. 3(2)(f) and para. 3(4)–(6) inserted by FA 2000, s. 51(1), (2).

Derivations – Para. 3(1): FA 1980, Sch. 10, para. 3(1), as amended by FA 1987, Sch. 15, para. 13(2)(b) and from FA 1984, Sch. 10, para. 2(1).
Para. 3(2): FA 1978, Sch. 9, para. 3(1), as amended by FA 1983, s. 25(6).
Para. 3(3): FA 1978, Sch. 9, para. 3(3).

4 If an alteration is made in the scheme at any time after the Board have approved the scheme, the approval shall not have effect after the date of the alteration unless the Board have approved the alteration.

Derivations – FA 1978, Sch. 9, para. 3(2); FA 1980, Sch. 10, para. 3(2) and FA 1984, Sch. 10, para. 2(2).

Cross references – Sch. 10, para. 3A: relevant age for purpose of appropriate percentage.
FA 1996, Sch. 16, para. 4: approval of the Board of alterations to share option schemes approved before 29 April 1996.

HMRC Manuals – Employee Share Scheme Unit Manual, ESS 4015: if resolutions make amendments which are expressed not to take effect unless approved by the Board, and Revenue approval is subsequently given to such an amendment, the date from which it takes effect is the earlier date on which it was made by the passing of the relevant resolution. If Revenue approval is never given to such an amendment, it never becomes effective. In these circumstances scheme examiners may accept that it will not cause the scheme to lose its approval.

5 If aggrieved–
(a) in any case, by the failure of the Board to approve the scheme or to approve an alteration in the scheme or by the withdrawal of approval; or
(b) in the case of a savings-related share option scheme, by the failure of the Board to decide that a condition subject to which the approval has been given is satisfied; or
(c) in the case of a profit sharing scheme, by the failure of the Board to approve an alteration in the terms of the trust referred to in paragraph 30(1)(c) below;

the grantor may appeal, by notice given to the Board within 30 days from the date on which it is notified of the Board's decision.

History – In para. 5, the word "appeal" inserted after the word "may" by SI 2009/56, art. 3(1) and Sch. 1, para. 158(a), operative from 1 April 2009, subject to transitional and saving provisions in SI 2009/56, Sch. 3.
In para. 5, the words ", require the matter to be determined by the Special Commissioners, and the Special Commissioners shall hear and determine the matter in like manner as an appeal", which appeared at the end of the paragraph, omitted by SI 2009/56, art. 3(1) and Sch. 1, para. 158(b), operative from 1 April 2009, subject to transitional and saving provisions in SI 2009/56, Sch. 3.

Derivations – FA 1978, Sch. 9, para. 4; FA 1980, Sch. 10, para. 4 and FA 1984, Sch. 10, para. 3.

6 The Board may by notice require any person to furnish them, within such time as the Board may direct (not being less than 30 days), with such information as the Board think necessary for the performance of their functions under the relevant provisions and as the person to whom the notice is addressed has or can reasonably obtain, including in particular information–
(a) *to enable the Board to determine–*
(i) whether to approve a scheme or withdraw an approval already given; or
(ii) the liability to tax, including capital gains tax, of any person who has participated in a scheme; and
(b) in relation to the administration of a scheme and any alteration of the terms of a scheme.

Derivations – FA 1978, s. 53(7); FA 1980, Sch. 10, para. 25 and FA 1984, Sch. 10, para. 14.

Cross references – TMA 1970, s. 98: penalties for failure to comply with notice under para. 6."

Cross references – ITEPA 2003, Sch. 7, paras. 71–72 (transitionals and savings): savings-related share option scheme approved before 6 April 2003 to be treated as a SAYE option scheme under ITEPA 2003, Sch. 3.
ITEPA 2003, Sch. 7, paras. 73–76 (transitionals and savings): discretionary share option scheme approved before 6 April 2003 to be treated as a CSOP scheme under ITEPA 2003, Sch. 4.

Notes – Provisions in Pt. 1 relating to approved profit sharing schemes have been rewritten into the provisions of ITEPA 2003, Sch. 3.

Part II – Requirements Generally Applicable

[Omitted by ITEPA 2003, s. 722 and Sch. 6, para. 112(2) and repealed by s. 724 and Sch. 8, Pt. 1.]

History – Part. 2 omitted by ITEPA 2003, s. 722 and Sch. 6, para. 112(2) and repealed by s. 724 and Sch. 8, Pt. 1 (except in so far as relating to profit sharing schemes), with effect in relation to schemes approved on or after 6 April 2003, subject to the transitional provisions and savings detailed in ITEPA 2003, Sch. 7. In so far as it continues to apply, former wording is as follows:
"**7** The provisions of this Part apply in relation to all schemes unless otherwise stated.

Derivations – Para. 7 is a composite provision introducing the remainder of Pt. II.

8 The scheme must not provide for any person to be eligible to participate in it, that is to say, to obtain and exercise rights under it, or in the case of a profit sharing scheme to have shares appropriated to him, at any time when he has, or has within the preceding 12 months had, a material interest in a close company which is–

(a) a company shares in which, in the case of a profit sharing scheme, are to be appropriated or, in the case of a share option scheme, may be acquired pursuant to the exercise of rights obtained under the scheme; or

(b) a company which has control of such a company or is a member of a consortium which owns such a company.
In determining whether a company is a close company for the purposes of this paragraph, sections 414(1)(a) and 415 shall be disregarded.

Derivations – FA 1978, Sch. 9, para. 11(1), (2); FA 1980, Sch. 10, para. 23 and FA 1984, Sch. 10, para. 4(1)(b), (3).

Cross references – S. 187(2), 840: definition of "control".
S. 187(3), (4) and Sch. 9, para. 37–40: definition of "material interest".
S. 414(1)(a): required residence in the UK.
S. 415: exclusion of certain quoted companies.
Sch. 10, para. 6: provisions concerning excess or unauthorised shares.

8A(1) In the case of a savings-related share option scheme or a profit sharing scheme, the scheme must specify what age is to be the specified age for the purposes of the scheme.

8A(2) The age specified–

(a) must be the same for men and women, and

(b) must be not less than 60 and not more than 75.

History – Para. 8A inserted by FA 1991, s. 38(5), with effect in relation to a scheme not approved before 25 July 1991.

Other material – Taxline 1991, issue 4, p. 12 (not reproduced): Revenue review all new schemes, not just SAYE and profit-sharing schemes, for sex discrimination and will not approve any scheme which has obvious retirement age discrimination.

9(1) A share option scheme must provide for directors and employees to obtain rights to acquire shares (**"scheme shares"**) which satisfy the requirements of paragraphs 10 to 14 below (disregarding paragraph 11A).

9(2) In the case of a profit sharing scheme, the shares to be acquired by the trustees as mentioned in paragraph 30 below (**"scheme shares"**) must satisfy the requirements of paragraphs 10 to 12 and 14 below.

History – In para. 9(1), words "(disregarding paragraph 11A)" inserted by FA 2000, s. 52(2), with deemed effect from 21 March 2000.

Derivations – Para. 9(1): FA 1980, Sch. 10, para. 5(a) and FA 1984, Sch. 10, para. 6.
Para. 9(2) is a composite provision.

Cross references – S. 187(2): "shares" includes stock.

10 Scheme shares must form part of the ordinary share capital of–

(a) the grantor; or

(b) a company which has control of the grantor; or

(c) a company which either is, or has control of, a company which–

  (i) is a member of a consortium owning either the grantor or a company having control of the grantor;

  (ii) [Repealed by FA 1989, s. 64 and Sch. 17, Pt. IV.]

History – Para. 10(c)(ii) and the word "and" preceding it repealed by FA 1989, s. 64 and Sch. 17, Pt. IV.

Derivations – (as originally enacted) – FA 1978, Sch. 9, para. 5; FA 1980, Sch. 10, para. 15 and FA 1984, Sch. 10, para. 7.

Cross references – S. 187(2), 840: definition of "control".
S. 187(7): definition of "member of a consortium".
S. 832(1): definition of "ordinary share capital".

11 Scheme shares must be–

(a) shares of a class listed on a recognised stock exchange; or

(b) shares in a company which is not under the control of another company; or

(c) shares in a company which is under the control of a company (other than a company which is, or would if resident in the United Kingdom be, a close company), whose shares are listed on a recognised stock exchange.

History – In para. 11(a) and (c), the word "listed" was substituted for the word "quoted" by FA 1996, s. 199 and Sch. 38, para. 6(2)(j), in relation to any time falling on or after 1 April 1996.

Derivations – FA 1978, Sch. 9, para. 6 (as amended by FA 1980, s. 46(10)); FA 1980, Sch. 10, para. 16 and FA 1984, Sch. 10, para. 8.

Cross references – S. 187(2), 840: definition of "control".
S. 841: definition of "recognised stock exchange".

11A(1) In the case of a profit sharing scheme, scheme shares must not be shares–

(a) in an employer company, or

(b) in a company that–

  (i) has control of an employer company, and

  (ii) is under the control of a person or persons within sub-paragraph (2)(b)(i) below in relation to an employer company.

11A(2) For the purposes of this paragraph a company is **"an employer company"** if–

(a) the business carried on by it consists substantially in the provision of the services of the persons employed by it, and

(b) the majority of those services are provided to–

  (i) a person who has, or two or more persons who together have, control of the company, or

  (ii) a company associated with the company.

11A(3) For the purposes of sub-paragraph (2)(b)(ii) above a company shall be treated as associated with another company if both companies are under the control of the same person or persons.

ICTA 1988

11A(4) For the purposes of sub-paragraphs (1) to (3) above–
- (a) references to a person include a partnership, and
- (b) where a partner, alone or together with others, has control of a company, the partnership shall be treated as having like control of that company.

11A(5) For the purposes of this paragraph the question whether a person controls a company shall be determined in accordance with section 416(2) to (6).

History – Para. 11A inserted by FA 2000, s. 52(3), with deemed effect from 21 March 2000, but not in relation to shares acquired before 21 March 2000 by the trustees of a profit sharing scheme approved under Sch. 9.

12(1) Scheme shares must be–
- (a) fully paid up;
- (b) not redeemable; and
- (c) not subject to any restrictions other than those permitted by sub-paragraph (1A) below.

Sub-paragraph (b) above does not apply, in the case of a profit sharing scheme, in relation to shares in a workers' cooperative.

12(1A) Subject to sub-paragraph (1B) below, scheme shares may be subject to–
- (a) restrictions which attach to all shares of the same class, or
- (b) a restriction authorised by sub-paragraph (2) below.

(1B) In the case of a profit sharing scheme, scheme shares must not be subject to any restrictions affecting the rights attaching to those shares which relate to–
- (a) dividends, or
- (b) assets on a winding-up of the company,

other than restrictions which attach to all other ordinary shares in the same company.

12(2) Except as provided below, the shares may be subject to a restriction imposed by the company's articles of association–
- (a) requiring all shares held by directors or employees of the company or of any other company of which it has control to be disposed of on ceasing to be so held; and
- (b) requiring all shares acquired, in pursuance of rights or interests obtained by such directors or employees, by persons who are not (or have ceased to be) such directors or employees to be disposed of when they are acquired.

12(3) A restriction is not authorised by sub-paragraph (2) above unless–
- (a) any disposal required by the restriction will be by way of sale for a consideration in money on terms specified in the articles of association; and
- (b) the articles also contain general provisions by virtue of which any person disposing of shares of the same class (whether or not held or acquired as mentioned in sub-paragraph (2) above) may be required to sell them on terms which are the same as those mentioned in paragraph (a) above.

12(4) In the case of a profit sharing scheme, except in relation to redeemable shares in a workers' cooperative, nothing in sub-paragraph (2) above authorises a restriction which would require a person, before the release date, to dispose of his beneficial interest in shares the ownership of which has not been transferred to him.

History – In para. 12(1)(c), words from "other than" to the end substituted, and para. 12(1A), (1B) inserted, by FA 2000, s. 52(4), with deemed effect from 21 March 2000, but not in relation to shares acquired before 21 March 2000 by the trustees of a profit sharing scheme approved under Sch. 9. The former words in para. 12(1)(c) read:

"other than restrictions which attach to all shares of the same class or a restriction authorised by sub-paragraph (2) below."

Derivations – Para. 12(1): FA 1978, Sch. 9, para. 7(1), as amended by FA 1986, s. 22(1), 24(2); FA 1980, Sch. 10, para. 17(1), as amended by FA 1986, s. 22(2); and from FA 1984, Sch. 10, para. 9(1), as amended by FA 1986, s. 22(3).
Para. 12(2), (3): FA 1978, Sch. 9, para. 7(2), (3); FA 1980, Sch. 10, para. 17(2), (3) and FA 1984, Sch. 10, para. 9(2), (3), as inserted by FA 1986, s. 22(1)–(4).
Para. 12(4): FA 1980, Sch. 10, para. 18 and FA 1984, Sch. 10, para. 10(1).

Cross references – S. 187(2), 840: definition of "control".
S. 187(10): definition of "workers' co-operative".

HMRC Manuals – Employee Share Scheme Unit Manual, ESS 12023: in the absence of provisions for the names of participants, and the shares allotted to them, to be registered within 30 days of the option being exercised, the Revenue will usually consider the scheme shares to be restricted.
Employee Share Scheme Unit Manual, ESS 12062: most common examples of employee pre-emption provisions in Articles which fail to meet requirements of para. 12(2) are:
- exclusion of named directors from the employee pre-emption provisions;
- exclusion of cessations for specified reasons (e.g. on retirement);
- being permitted to apply only to part of a holding;
- an "all or nothing" article which provides that if all of a ceasing employee's shares are not sold, the remainder do not have to be offered for sale;
- employee pre-emption to apply at directors' discretion;
- employee pre-emption to apply to shares previously transferred to relatives or family trusts.

IR, Employee Share Scheme Unit Manual, ESS 13008: existence of a "call" option, which gives the holder the right to acquire an employee's scheme shares, restricts employee's freedom to dispose of the shares, but grant of a "put" option to an employee or director, which entitles (but does not compel) him to require the grantor to purchase his shares, is unlikely to constitute such a restriction.

Notes – In relation to profit-sharing schemes redeemable shares in workers' co-operatives were permitted with effect from 25 July 1986. Restrictions under para. 12(2) were permitted with effect from 25 July 1986.

13(1) In determining, in the case of a share option scheme, for the purposes of paragraph 12(1)(c) above whether scheme shares which are or are to be acquired by any person are subject to any restrictions, there shall be regarded as a restriction attaching to the shares any contract, agreement, arrangement or condition by which his freedom to dispose of the shares or of any interest in them or of the proceeds of their sale or to exercise any right conferred by them is restricted or by which such a disposal or exercise may result in any disadvantage to him or to a person connected with him.

13(2) Sub-paragraph (1) does not apply to so much of any contract, agreement, arrangement or condition as contains provisions similar in purpose and effect to any of the provisions of the Model Rules set out in the Model Code for Securities Transactions by Directors of Listed Companies issued by the Stock Exchange in November 1984.

13(3) In the case of schemes other than savings-related share option schemes, sub-paragraph (1) above does not apply in relation to any terms of a loan making provision about how it is to be repaid or the security to be given for it.

History – Para. 13(3) was inserted by FA 1988, s. 69(1) with retrospective effect.

Derivations – Para. 13(1): FA 1980, Sch. 10, para. 18 and FA 1984, Sch. 10, para. 10(1).
Para. *13(2)*: FA 1982, s. 41, as amended by FA 1986, s. 23(4), and from FA 1984, para. 10(2), as amended by FA 1986, s. 23(4).

HMRC Manuals – Employee Share Scheme Unit Manual, ESS 12023: in the absence of provisions for the names of participants, and the shares allotted to them, to be registered within 30 days of the option being exercised, the Revenue will usually consider the scheme shares to be restricted.
Employee Share Scheme Unit Manual, ESS 12062: most common examples of employee pre-emption provisions in Articles which fail to meet requirements of para. 12(2) are:

- exclusion of named directors from the employee pre-emption provisions;
- exclusion of cessations for specified reasons (e.g. on retirement);
- being permitted to apply only to part of a holding;
- an "all or nothing" article which provides that if all of a ceasing employee's shares are not sold, the remainder do not have to be offered for sale;
- employee pre-emption to apply at directors' discretion;
- employee pre-emption to apply to shares previously transferred to relatives or family trusts.

Employee Share Scheme Unit Manual, ESS 13008: existence of a "call option", which gives the holder the right to acquire an employee's scheme shares, restricts employee's freedom to dispose of the shares, but grant of a "put" option to an employee or director, which entitles (but does not compel) him to require the grantor to purchase his shares, is unlikely to constitute such a restriction.

Notes – Before 25 July 1986, para. 13(2) referred to the Model Code issued in April 1981.

14(1) Except where scheme shares are shares in a company the ordinary share capital of which consists of shares of one class only, the majority of the issued shares of the same class either must be employee-control shares or must be held by persons other than–

(a) persons who acquired their shares in pursuance of a right conferred on them or an opportunity afforded to them as a director or employee of the grantor or any other company and not in pursuance of an offer to the public;

(b) trustees holding shares on behalf of persons who acquired their beneficial interests in the shares as mentioned in sub-paragraph (a) above; and

(c) in a case where the shares fall within sub-paragraph (c), but not within sub-paragraph (a), of paragraph 11 above, companies which have control of the company whose shares are in question or of which that company is an associated company.

14(2) In its application to a profit sharing scheme, sub-paragraph (1) above shall have effect with the addition after the words "ordinary share capital of which" of the words "at the time of the acquisition of the shares by the trustees".

14(3) For the purposes of this paragraph, shares in a company are employee-control shares if–

(a) the persons holding the shares are, by virtue of their holding, together able to control the company; and

(b) those persons are or have been employees or directors of the company or of another company which is under the control of the company.

Derivations – Para. 14(1): FA 1978, Sch. 9, para. 8(1), as amended by FA 1980, s. 46(11), (14) and FA 1986, s. 23(2), (3); FA 1980, Sch. 10, para. 19(1), as amended by FA 1986, s. 23(2), (3); and from FA 1984, Sch. 10, para. 11(1), as amended by FA 1986, s. 23(2), (3).

Para. 14(2): FA 1978, Sch. 9, para. 8(1).

Para. 14(3): FA 1978, Sch. 9, para. 8(2) inserted by FA 1986, s. 23(2), (3); FA 1980, Sch. 10, para. 19(2) inserted by FA 1986, s. 23(2), (3); and from FA 1984, Sch. 10, para. 11(2) inserted by FA 1986, s. 23(2), (3).

Cross references – S. 187(2), 416: definition of "associated company".

S. 187(2), 840: definition of "control".

S. 832(1): definition of "ordinary share capital".

Notes – Before 25 July 1986, there was no exception where the majority of shares of the same class were employee-controlled shares.

15(1) Except in the case of a profit sharing scheme, the scheme may provide that if any company (**"the acquiring company"**)–

(a) obtains control of a company whose shares are scheme shares as a result of making a general offer–

(i) to acquire the whole of the issued ordinary share capital of the company which is made on a condition such that if it is satisfied the person making the offer will have control of the company; or

(ii) to acquire all the shares in the company which are of the same class as the scheme shares;

(b) obtains control of a company whose shares are scheme shares in pursuance of a compromise or arrangement sanctioned by the court under section 425 of the Companies Act 1985 or Article 418 of the Companies (Northern Ireland) Order 1986; or

(c) becomes bound or entitled to acquire shares in a company whose shares are scheme shares under sections 428 to 430 of that Act or Articles 421 to 423 of that Order,

any participant in the scheme may at any time within the appropriate period, by agreement with the acquiring company, release his rights under the scheme (in this paragraph referred to as **"the old rights"**) in consideration of the grant to him of rights (in this paragraph referred to as **"the new rights"**) which are equivalent to the old rights but relate to shares in a different company (whether the acquiring company itself or some other company falling within paragraph 10(b) or (c) above).

15(2) In sub-paragraph (1) above **"the appropriate period"** means–

(a) in a case falling within paragraph (a), the period of six months beginning with the time when the person making the offer has obtained control of the company and any condition subject to which the offer is made is satisfied;

(b) in a case falling within paragraph (b), the period of six months beginning with the time when the court sanctions the compromise or arrangement; and

(c) in a case falling within paragraph (c), the period during which the acquiring company remains bound or entitled as mentioned in that paragraph.

15(3) The new rights shall not be regarded for the purposes of this paragraph as equivalent to the old rights unless–

(a) the shares to which they relate satisfy the conditions specified, in relation to scheme shares, in paragraphs 10 to 14 above; and

(b) the new rights will be exercisable in the same manner as the old rights and subject to the provisions of the scheme as it had effect immediately before the release of the old rights; and

(c) the total market value, immediately before the release, of the shares which were subject to the participant's old rights is equal to the total market value, immediately after the grant, of the shares in respect of which the new rights are granted to the participant; and

(d) the total amount payable by the participant for the acquisition of shares in pursuance of the new rights is equal to the total amount that would have been payable for the acquisition of shares in pursuance of the old rights.

15(4) Where any new rights are granted pursuant to a provision included in a scheme by virtue of this paragraph they shall be regarded–

(a) for the purposes of section 185 and this Schedule; and

(b) for the purposes of the subsequent application (by virtue of a condition complying with sub-paragraph (3)(b) above) of the provisions of the scheme,

as having been granted at the time when the corresponding old rights were granted.

15(5) Where a scheme which was approved before 1st August 1987 is altered before 1st August 1989 so as to include such a provision as is mentioned above (**"an exchange provision"**), the scheme as altered may by virtue of this and the following sub-paragraphs apply that provision to rights obtained under the scheme before the date on which the alteration takes effect.

15(6) If an exchange provision is applied as mentioned in sub-paragraph (5) above in a case where, on or after 17th March 1987 but before the date on which the alteration takes effect, an event has occurred by reason of which a person holding rights under the scheme would be able to take advantage of the exchange provision–

(a) the scheme may permit a person who held rights under the scheme immediately before that event to take advantage of the exchange provision; and

(b) in a case where rights then held would otherwise, by reason of the event, have ceased to be exercisable, the scheme may provide that the exchange provision shall apply as if the rights were still exercisable.

15(7) The application of an exchange provision as mentioned in sub-paragraph (5) or (6) above shall not itself be regarded for the purposes of this Schedule as the acquisition of a right.

15(8) Sub-paragraphs (5) and (6) above have effect subject to paragraph 4 above.

Derivations – Para. 15(1): FA 1980, Sch. 10, para. 10A(1) inserted by FA 1987, s. 33 and Sch. 4, para. 1(1), as amended by F(No. 2)A 1987, s. 59(2); and from FA 1984, Sch. 10, para. 4A(1) inserted by FA 1987, s. 33 and Sch. 4, para. 2(1), as amended by F(No. 2)A 1987, s. 59(3)(a).
Para. 15(2): FA 1980, Sch. 10, para. 10A(2) inserted by FA 1987, s. 33 and Sch. 4, para. 1(1); and from FA 1984, Sch. 10, para. 4A(2) inserted by FA 1987, s. 33 and Sch. 4, para. 2(1).
Para. 15(3): FA 1980, Sch. 10, para. 10A(3) inserted by FA 1987, s. 33 and Sch. 4, para. 1(1), as amended by F(No. 2)A 1987, s. 59(2); and from FA 1984, Sch. 10, para. 4A(3) inserted by FA 1987, s. 33 and Sch. 4, para. 2(1), as amended by F(No. 2)A 1987, s. 59(3)(b), (c).
Para. 15(4): FA 1980, Sch. 10, para. 10A(4) inserted by FA 1987, s. 33 and Sch. 4, para. 1(1); and from FA 1984, Sch. 10, para. 4A(4) inserted by FA 1987, s. 33 and Sch. 4, para. 2(1).
Para. 15(5)–(8): FA 1987, Sch. 4, para. 3(1)–(5).

Cross references – S. 187(2): definition of "participant".
S. 187(2), 840: definition of "control".
S. 832(1): definition of "ordinary share capital".
TCGA 1992, s. 238(4): capital gains tax consequences of the substitution of new rights for old.
ITEPA 2003, Sch. 7, para. 71–72 (transitionals and savings): savings-related share option scheme approved before 6 April 2003 to be treated as a SAYE option scheme under ITEPA 2003, Sch. 3.
ITEPA 2003, Sch. 7, para. 73–76 (transitionals and savings): discretionary share option scheme approved before 6 April 2003 to be treated as a CSOP scheme under ITEPA 2003, Sch. 4."

Notes – Provisions in Pt. 2 relating to approved profit sharing schemes have been rewritten into the provisions of ITEPA 2003, Sch. 3.

Part III – Requirements Applicable to Savings-Related Share Option Schemes

[Omitted by ITEPA 2003, s. 722 and Sch. 6, para. 112(3) and repealed by s. 724 and Sch. 8, Pt. 1.]

History – Part 3 omitted by ITEPA 2003, s. 722 and Sch. 6, para. 112(3) and repealed by s. 724 and Sch. 8, Pt. 1, with effect, for income tax purposes, for the year 2003–04 and subsequent years and for the purposes of corporation tax, for accounting periods ending on or after 5 April 2003.

Notes – Part 3 rewritten as ITEPA 2003, Sch. 3.

Part IV – Requirements Applicable to Other Share Option Schemes

[Omitted by ITEPA 2003, s. 722 and Sch. 6, para. 112(3) and repealed by s. 724 and Sch. 8, Pt. 1.]

History – Part 4 omitted by ITEPA 2003, s. 722 and Sch. 6, para. 112(3) and repealed by s. 724 and Sch. 8, Pt. 1, with effect, for income tax purposes, for the year 2003–04 and subsequent years and for the purposes of corporation tax, for accounting periods ending on or after 5 April 2003.

Notes – Part 4 rewritten as ITEPA 2003, Sch. 3.

Part V – Requirements Applicable to Profit Sharing Schemes

30(1) The scheme must provide for the establishment of a body of persons resident in the United Kingdom **("the trustees")**–

(a) who, out of moneys paid to them by the grantor or, in the case of a group scheme, a participating company, are required by the scheme to acquire shares in respect of which the conditions in paragraphs 10 to 12 and 14 above are fulfilled; and

(b) who are under a duty to appropriate shares acquired by them to individuals who participate in the scheme, not being individuals who are ineligible by virtue of paragraph 8 or 35 of this Schedule; and

(c) whose functions with respect to shares held by them are regulated by a trust which is constituted under the law of a part of the United Kingdom and the terms of which are embodied in an instrument which complies with the provisions of paragraphs 31 to 34 below.

30(2) If at any time after the Board have approved the scheme, an alteration is made in the terms of the trust referred to in sub-paragraph (1)(c) above, the approval shall not have effect after the date of the alteration unless the Board have approved the alteration.

30(3) The scheme must provide that the total of the initial market values of the shares appropriated to any one participant in a year of assessment will not exceed the relevant amount.

30(4) In this Part of this Schedule **"initial market value"**, in relation to a participant's shares, means the market value of those shares determined–

(a) except where paragraph (b) below applies, on the date on which the shares were appropriated to him; and

(b) if the Board and the trustees agree in writing, on or by reference to such earlier date or dates as may be provided for in the agreement.

Derivations – Para. 30(1): FA 1978, Sch. 9, para. 1(3).
Para. 30(2): FA 1978, Sch. 9, para. 3(2).
Para. 30(3): FA 1978, Sch. 9, para. 1(4), as amended by FA 1983, s. 25(1).
Para. 30(4): FA 1978, s. 53(4).

HMRC Manuals – Employee Share Scheme Unit Manual, ESS 2523: scheme examiners may accept that discretionary cash payment made as result of non-participation in a profit sharing scheme is not a feature of that scheme, but it is not appropriate or acceptable to refer, in any of the scheme documentation, to the possible availability of cash payments.
Employee Share Scheme Unit Manual, ESS 2534: basis on which Revenue consider whether contributory profit sharing schemes breach the requirement that a scheme should contain only essential or reasonably incidental provisions (para. 2(1)).

Other material – IR booklet IR 96, Approved profit sharing schemes – Explanatory notes (not reproduced) Ch. 2.2 details of mode of application for approval.
IR booklet IR 96, Approved profit-sharing schemes – Explanatory notes (not reproduced) Ch. 4.2: the Revenue will agree the initial market value of shares for the purposes of a profit-sharing scheme.

31 The trust instrument shall provide that, as soon as practicable after any shares have been appropriated to a participant, the trustees will give him notice of the appropriation–

(a) specifying the number and description of those shares; and

(b) stating their initial market value.

Derivations – FA 1978, Sch. 9, para. 12.

32(1) The trust instrument must contain a provision prohibiting the trustees from disposing of any shares, except as mentioned in paragraph 1(1)(a), (b), (c) or (cc) of Schedule 10, during the period of retention (whether by transfer to the participant or otherwise).

32(2) The trust instrument must contain a provision prohibiting the trustees from disposing of any shares after the end of the period of retention and before the release date except–

(a) pursuant to a direction given by or on behalf of the participant or any person in whom the beneficial interest in his shares is for the time being vested; and

(b) by a transaction which would not involve a breach of the participant's obligations under paragraph 2(2)(c) or (d) above.

History – In para. 32(1), reference to para. (cc) added by FA 1994, s. 101(5), in relation to any scheme not approved before 3 May 1994, but subject to FA 1994, s. 101(10).

Derivations – FA 1978, Sch. 9, para. 13, as amended by FA 1980, s. 46(13).

33 The trust instrument must contain a provision requiring the trustees–

(a) subject to their obligations under paragraph 7 of Schedule 10 and to any such direction as is mentioned in paragraph 4(2) of that Schedule to pay over to the participant any money or money's worth received by them in respect of or by reference to any of his shares other than money's worth consisting of new shares within the meaning of paragraph 5 of that Schedule; and

(b) to deal only pursuant to a direction given by or on behalf of the participant or any person in whom the beneficial interest in his shares is for the time being vested with any right conferred in respect of any of his shares to be allotted other shares, securities or rights of any description.

Derivations – FA 1978, Sch. 9, para. 13(2)(a), 14.

Cross references – FA 1994, s. 101(6): reference to Sch. 10, para. 5 to be construed as a reference to para. 5 as applied by para. 5A (retention of QCBs in profit-sharing schemes) in relation to any scheme not approved before 3 May 1994, but subject to FA 1994, s. 101(12), (14).

34 The trust instrument must impose an obligation on the trustees–

(a) to maintain such records as may be necessary to enable the trustees to carry out their obligations under paragraph 7 of Schedule 10; and

(b) where the participant becomes liable to income tax under Schedule E by reason of the occurrence of any event, to inform him of any facts relevant to determining that liability.

Derivations – FA 1978, Sch. 9, para. 15.

35(1) An individual shall not be eligible to have shares appropriated to him under the scheme at any time unless he is at that time or was within the preceding 18 months a director or employee of the grantor or, in the case of a group scheme, of a participating company.

35(2) An individual shall not be eligible to have shares appropriated to him under the scheme at any time if in that year of assessment shares have been appropriated to him under another approved scheme established by the grantor or by–

(a) a company which controls or is controlled by the grantor or which is controlled by a company which also controls the grantor, or

(b) a company which is a member of a consortium owning the grantor or which is owned in part by the grantor as a member of a consortium.

Derivations – FA 1978, Sch. 9, para. 9, 10.

36(1) Subject to paragraphs 8 and 35 above, every person who at any time–

(a) is an employee or a full-time director of the grantor or, in the case of a group scheme, a participating company, and

(b) has been such an employee or director at all times during a qualifying period, not exceeding five years, ending at that time, and

(c) is chargeable to tax in respect of his office or employment under Case I of Schedule E, must then be eligible (subject to paragraphs 8 and 35 of this Schedule) to participate in the scheme on similar terms and those who do participate must actually do so on similar terms.

36(2) For the purposes of sub-paragraph (1) above, the fact that the number of shares to be appropriated to the participants in a scheme varies by reference to the levels of their remuneration, the length of their service or similar factors shall not be regarded as meaning that they are not eligible to participate in the scheme on similar terms or do not actually do so.

History – In para. 36(1)(a), words "an employee" substituted for "a full-time employee" by FA 1995, s. 137 with effect in relation to any scheme not approved before 1 May 1995, subject to FA 1995, s. 137(8).

Derivations – FA 1978, Sch. 9, para. 2(1), (2), as amended by FA 1983, s. 25(4)(a), (b).

Part VI – Material Interest Test

[Omitted by ITEPA 2003, s. 722 and Sch. 6, para. 112(2) and repealed by s. 724 and Sch. 8, Pt. 1.]

History – Part. 6 omitted by ITEPA 2003, s. 722 and Sch. 6, para. 112(2) and repealed by s. 724 and Sch. 8, Pt. 1 (except in so far as relating to profit sharing schemes), with effect in relation to schemes approved on or after 6 April 2003, subject to the transitional provisions and savings detailed in ITEPA 2003, Sch. 7. In so far as it continues to apply, former wording is as follows:

"INTERESTS UNDER TRUSTS

37(1) This paragraph applies in a case where–

(a) the individual (**"the beneficiary"**) was one of the objects of a discretionary trust; and

(b) the property subject to the trust at any time consisted of or included any shares or obligations of the company.

37(2) If neither the beneficiary nor any relevant associate of his had received any benefit under the discretionary trust before 14th November 1986, then, as respects any time before that date, the trustees of the settlement concerned shall not be regarded, by reason only of the matters referred to in sub-paragraph (1) above, as having been associates (as defined in section 417(3) and (4)) of the beneficiary.

37(3) If, on or after 14th November 1986–

(a) the beneficiary ceases to be eligible to benefit under the discretionary trust by reason of–

(i) an irrevocable disclaimer or release executed by him under seal; or

(ii) the irrevocable exercise by the trustees of a power to exclude him from the objects of the trust; and

(b) immediately after he so ceases, no relevant associate of his is interested in the shares or obligations of the company which are subject to the trust; and

(c) during the period of 12 months ending with the date when the beneficiary so ceases, neither the beneficiary nor any relevant associate of his received any benefit under the trust,

the beneficiary shall not be regarded, by reason only of the matters referred to in sub-paragraph (1) above, as having been interested in the shares or obligations of the company as mentioned in section 417(3)(c) at any time during the period of 12 months referred to in paragraph (c) above.

37(4) In sub-paragraphs (2) and (3) above **"relevant associate"** has the meaning given to **"associate"** by subsection (3) of section 417 but with the omission of paragraph (c) of that subsection.

37(5) Sub-paragraph (3)(a)(i) above, in its application to Scotland, shall be construed as if the words "under seal" were omitted.

Derivations – FA 1987, Sch. 4, para. 6.

OPTIONS ETC.

38(1) For the purposes of section 187(3)(a) a right to acquire shares (however arising) shall be taken to be a right to control them.

38(2) Any reference in sub-paragraph (3) below to the shares attributed to an individual is a reference to the shares which, in accordance with section 187(3)(a), fall to be brought into account in his case to determine whether their number exceeds a particular percentage of the company's ordinary share capital.

38(3) In any case where–

(a) the shares attributed to an individual consist of or include shares which he or any other person has a right to acquire; and

(b) the circumstances are such that, if that right were to be exercised, the shares acquired would be shares which were previously unissued and which the company is contractually bound to issue in the event of the exercise of the right;

then, in determining at any time prior to the exercise of that right whether the number of shares attributed to the individual exceeds a particular percentage of the ordinary share capital of the company, that ordinary share capital shall be taken to be increased by the number of unissued shares referred to in paragraph (b) above.

38(4) This paragraph has effect as respects any time after 5th April 1987.

Derivations – FA 1987, Sch. 4, para. 7.

SHARES HELD BY TRUSTEES OF APPROVED PROFIT SHARING SCHEMES

39 In applying section 187(3), as respects any time before or after the passing of this Act, there shall be disregarded–

(a) the interest of the trustees of an approved profit sharing scheme in any shares which are held by them in accordance with the scheme and have not yet been appropriated to an individual; and

(b) any rights exercisable by those trustees by virtue of that interest.

Derivations – FA 1987, Sch. 4, para. 8.

SHARES SUBJECT TO AN EMPLOYEE BENEFIT TRUST

40(1) Where an individual has an interest in shares or obligations of the company as a beneficiary of an employee benefit trust, the trustees shall not be regarded as associates of his by reason only of that interest unless sub-paragraph (3) below applies in relation to him.

40(2) In this paragraph **"employee benefit trust"** has the same meaning as in paragraph 7 of Schedule 8.

40(3) This sub-paragraph applies in relation to an individual if at any time on or after 14th March 1989–

(a) the individual, either on his own or with any one or more of his associates, or

(b) any associate of his, with or without other such associates,

has been the beneficial owner of, or able (directly or through the medium of other companies or by any other indirect means) to control, more than 25 per cent, or in the case of a share option scheme which is not a savings-related share option scheme more than 10 per cent, of the ordinary share capital of the company.

40(4) Sub-paragraphs *(9)* to *(12)* of paragraph 7 of Schedule 8 shall apply for the purposes of this paragraph in relation to an individual as they apply for the purposes of that paragraph in relation to an employee.

History – Para. 40 was inserted by FA 1989, s. 65."

Cross references – ITEPA 2003, Sch. 7, para. 71–72 (transitionals and savings): savings-related share option scheme approved before 6 April 2003 to be treated as a SAYE option scheme under ITEPA 2003, Sch. 3.

ITEPA 2003, Sch. 7, para. 73–76 (transitionals and savings): discretionary share option scheme approved before 6 April 2003 to be treated as a CSOP scheme under ITEPA 2003, Sch. 4.

Notes – Provisions in Pt. 6 relating to approved profit sharing schemes have been rewritten into the provisions of ITEPA 2003, Sch. 3.

SCHEDULE 10 – FURTHER PROVISIONS RELATING TO PROFIT SHARING SCHEMES

Section 186

Cross references – FA 1996, s. 116(3): "release date" and profit sharing schemes.
FA 1996, s. 117(3): "appropriate percentage" and profit sharing schemes.
ITEPA 2003, s. 418(3): because of the phasing-out of profit sharing schemes, Sch. 10 continues in force for schemes approved under Sch. 9 and is not rewritten in the FA 2003, Sch. 22 amendments to ITEPA 2003.
ITEPA 2003, Sch. 7, para. 75: discretionary share option schemes approved before 29 April 1996.

LIMITATIONS ON CONTRACTUAL OBLIGATIONS OF PARTICIPANTS

1(1) Any obligation placed on the participant by virtue of paragraph 2(2) of Schedule 9 shall not prevent the participant from–

(a) directing the trustees to accept an offer for any of his shares (**"the original shares"**) if the acceptance or agreement will result in a new holding being equated with the original shares for the purposes of capital gains tax; or

(b) directing the trustees to agree to a transaction affecting his shares or such of them as are of a particular class, if the transaction would be entered into pursuant to a compromise, arrangement or scheme applicable to or affecting–

(i) all the ordinary share capital of the company in question or, as the case may be, all the shares of the class in question; or

(ii) all the shares, or all the shares of the class in question, which are held by a class of shareholders identified otherwise than by reference to their employment or their participation in an approved scheme; or

(c) directing the trustees to accept an offer of cash, with or without other assets, for his shares if the offer forms part of a general offer which is made to holders of shares of the same class as his or of shares in the same company and which is made in the first instance on a condition such that if it is satisfied the person making the offer will have control of that company, within the meaning of section 416; or

(cc) directing the trustees to accept an offer of a qualifying corporate bond, whether alone or with cash or other assets or both, for his shares if the offer forms part of a general offer which is made as mentioned in paragraph (c) above; or

(d) agreeing after the expiry of the period of retention to sell the beneficial interest in his shares to the trustees for the same consideration as, in accordance with sub-paragraph (d) of paragraph 2(2) of Schedule 9, would be required to be obtained for the shares themselves.

1(2) No obligation placed on the participant by virtue of paragraph 2(2)(c) of Schedule 9 shall be construed as binding his personal representatives to pay any sum to the trustees.

1(3) If, in breach of his obligation under paragraph 2(2)(b) of Schedule 9 a participant assigns, charges or otherwise disposes of the beneficial interest in any of his shares, then, as respects those shares, he shall be treated for the purposes of the relevant provisions as if at the time they were appropriated to him he was ineligible to participate in the scheme; and paragraph 6 below shall apply accordingly.

1(4) In sub-paragraph (1)(cc) above **"qualifying corporate bond"** shall be construed in accordance with section 117 of the 1992 Act.

History – Para. 1(1)(cc) and 1(4) inserted by FA 1994, s. 101(2), (3), with effect where a direction is made on or after 3 May 1994.

Derivations – Para. 1(1) (as originally enacted): FA 1978, s. 54(2), as amended by CGTA 1979, Sch. 7, para. 9.
Para. 1(2): FA 1978, s. 54(1A), as inserted by FA 1980, s. 46(2).
Para. 1(3) (as originally enacted): FA 1978, s. 54(3).

Cross references – TCGA 1992, s. 126–137: provisions concerning share exchanges and reconstruction.
TCGA 1992, s. 238: capital gains tax treatment of approved profit sharing schemes.

Other material – CCAB press release, June 1978 (not reproduced): the Revenue have confirmed that money provided by a close company for the purchase of shares by scheme trustees will not be treated as a distribution.

THE PERIOD OF RETENTION

2 For the purposes of any of the relevant provisions, **"the period of retention"**, in relation to any of a participant's shares, means the period beginning on the date on which they are appropriated to him and ending on the second anniversary of that date or, if it is earlier–

ICTA 1988

(a) the date on which the participant ceases to be a director or employee of the grantor or, in the case of a group scheme, a participating company by reason of injury or disability or on account of his being dismissed by reason of redundancy, within the meaning of the Employment Rights Act 1996 or the Employment Rights (Northern Ireland) Order 1996; or

(b) the date on which the participant reaches the relevant age; or

(c) the date of the participant's death; or

(d) in a case where the participant's shares are redeemable shares in a workers' cooperative, the date on which the participant ceases to be employed by, or by a subsidiary of, the cooperative.

For the purposes of sub-paragraph (a) above, in the case of a group scheme, the participant shall not be treated as ceasing to be a director or employee of a participating company until such time as he is no longer a director or employee of any of the participating companies.

In this paragraph, the reference to the **relevant age** is a reference, in the case of a scheme approved before the day on which the Finance Act 1991 was passed, in the case of a man, to the age of 65, and in the case of a woman, to the age of 60 and, in the case of a scheme approved on or after that day, to the specified age.

History – In para. 2 the words "Employment Rights (Northern Ireland) Order 1996" substituted for "Contracts of Employment and Redundancy Payments Act (Northern Ireland) 1965" by SI 1996/1919, art. 255 and Sch. 1, with effect from 24 September 1996.
In para. 2(a), reference to Employment Rights Act 1996 substituted for former reference to Employment Protection (Consolidation) Act 1978 by Employment Rights Act 1996, s. 240 and Sch. 1, para. 35(4)(b), with effect from 22 August 1996.
In para. 2(b), words "the relevant age" substituted, and words from "In this paragraph ..." to the end inserted by FA 1991, s. 38(3), with effect from 25 July 1991.
Para. 2(c) amended by FA 1988, s. 146 and Sch. 13, para. 9 by adding the word "or", with retrospective effect.
In the endpiece to para. 2, the words "in the case of a man ... to the age of 60" were substituted by Pensions Act 1995, s. 126 and Sch. 4, para. 12(b), with effect from 19 July 1995.

Derivations – FA 1978, s. 54(4) (as amended by FA 1986, s. 24(3); FA 1980, s. 46(3)), 55(4) and Employment Protection (Consolidation) Act 1978, Sch. 15, para. 4.

Notes – The Finance Act 1991 was passed on 25 July 1991.

THE APPROPRIATE PERCENTAGE

3(1) For the purposes of any of the relevant provisions under which an amount counts as employment income of an individual by reason of the occurrence of an event relating to any of his shares, the "appropriate percentage" in relation to those shares is 100 per cent, unless sub-paragraph (2) below applies.

3(2) Where the individual–

(a) ceases to be a director or employee of the grantor or, in the case of a group scheme, a participating company as mentioned in paragraph 2(a) above, or

(b) reaches the relevant age,

before the event occurs, the "appropriate percentage" is 50 per cent, unless paragraph 6(4) below applies.

History – In para. 3(1), words "under which an amount counts as employment income of an individual" substituted for words "charging an individual to income tax under Schedule E" by ITEPA 2003, s. 722 and Sch. 6, para. 113(2), with effect for the year 2003–04 and subsequent years.
Para. 3 substituted by FA 1996, s. 117(1) in relation to events on or after 29 April 1996 giving rise to an income tax charge under ICTA 1988, s. 186, 187 or Sch. 9, 10.

Derivations – FA 1978, s. 54(7), as amended by FA 1985, s. 45(3) and FA 1980, s. 46(5).

Cross references – SSCBA 1992, s. 122(1): "pensionable age" is 65 for men and 60 for women.

Notes – For construction of reference to relevant age, see para. 3A, below.

3A(1) In paragraph 3 above the reference to the relevant age shall be construed as follows.

3A(2) Where the scheme is approved before 25th July 1991 and the event occurs before 30th November 1993, the relevant age is–

(a) in the case of a man, 65 and

(b) in the case of a woman 60.

3A(3) Where–

(a) the scheme is approved before 25th July 1991,

(b) the event occurs on or after 30th November 1993,

(c) the scheme defines the period of retention by reference to the age of 60 for both men and women, and

(d) the reference to that age is incorporated in the definition by virtue of an alteration approved by the Board under paragraph 4 of Schedule 9 before the event occurs,

the relevant age is 60.

3A(4) Where–

(a) the scheme is approved before 25th July 1991,

(b) the event occurs on or after 30th November 1993, and

(c) sub-paragraph (3) above does not apply,

the relevant age is in the case of a man, 65, and in the case of a woman, 60.

3A(5) Where the scheme is approved on or after 25th July 1991, the relevant age is the specified age.

History – In para. 3A(2), the words "(a) in the case of a man … a woman, 60" were substituted by Pensions Act 1995, s. 126 and Sch. 4, para. 12(c), with effect from 19 July 1995.

In para. 3A(4), the words "in the case of a man … a woman, 60" were substituted by Pensions Act 1995, s. 126 and Sch. 4, para. 12(d), with effect from 19 July 1995.

Para. 3A inserted by FA 1994, s. 100(3), with effect from 3 May 1994.

CAPITAL RECEIPTS

4(1) Money or money's worth is not a capital receipt for the purposes of section 186(3) if or, as the case may be, to the extent that–

(a) it constitutes income in the hands of the recipient for the purposes of income tax; or

(b) it consists of the proceeds of a disposal falling within section 186(4); or

(c) it consists of new shares within the meaning of paragraph 5 below.

4(2) If, pursuant to a direction given by or on behalf of the participant or any person in whom the beneficial interest in the participant's shares is for the time being vested, the trustees–

(a) dispose of some of the rights arising under a rights issue, as defined in section 185(8), and

(b) use the proceeds of that disposal to exercise other such rights,

the money or money's worth which constitutes the proceeds of that disposal is not a capital receipt for the purposes of section 186(3).

4(3) If, apart from this sub-paragraph, the amount or value of a capital receipt would exceed the sum which, immediately before the entitlement to the receipt arose, was the locked-in value of the shares to which the receipt is referable, section 186(3) shall have effect as if the amount or value of the receipt were equal to that locked-in value.

4(4) Section 186(3) does not apply in relation to a capital receipt if the entitlement to it arises after the death of the participant to whose shares it is referable.

Derivations – FA 1978, s. 56(2)–(5).

Cross references – S. 186(5): definition of "locked-in value".

COMPANY RECONSTRUCTIONS

5(1) This paragraph applies where there occurs in relation to any of a participant's shares (**"the original holding"**) a transaction which results in a new holding being equated with the original holding for the purposes of capital gains tax; and any such transaction is referred to below as a **"company reconstruction"**.

5(2) Where an issue of shares of any of the following descriptions (in respect of which a charge to income tax arises) is made as part of a company reconstruction, those shares shall be treated for the purposes of this paragraph as not forming part of the new holding, that is to say–

(a) redeemable shares or securities issued as mentioned in condition C or D in section 1000(1) of CTA 2010;

(b) share capital issued in circumstances such that section 1022 of CTA 2010 applies; and

(c) share capital to which section 1049 of CTA 2010 applies.

5(3) In this paragraph–

"corresponding shares", in relation to any new shares, means those shares in respect of which the new shares are issued or which the new shares otherwise represent;

"new shares" means shares comprised in the new holding which were issued in respect of, or otherwise represent, shares comprised in the original holding; and

"original holding" has the meaning given by sub-paragraph (1) above.

5(4) Subject to the following provisions of this paragraph, in relation to a profit sharing scheme, references in the relevant provisions to a participant's shares shall be construed, after the time of the company reconstruction, as being or, as the case may be, as including references to any new shares, and for the purposes of the relevant provisions–

(a) a company reconstruction shall be treated as not involving a disposal of shares comprised in the original holding;

(b) the date on which any new shares are to be treated as having been appropriated to the participant shall be that on which the corresponding shares were appropriated; and

(c) the conditions in paragraphs 10 to 12 and 14 of Schedule 9 shall be treated as fulfilled with respect to any new shares if they were (or were treated as) fulfilled with respect to the corresponding shares.

5(5) In relation to shares comprised in the new holding, section 186(5) shall apply as if the references in that subsection to the initial market value of the shares were references to their locked-in value immediately after the company reconstruction, which shall be determined as follows–

(a) ascertain the aggregate amount of locked-in value immediately before the reconstruction of those shares comprised in the original holding which had at that time the same locked-in value; and

(b) distribute that amount *pro rata* among–

(i) such of those shares as remain in the new holding, and

(ii) any new shares in relation to which those shares are the corresponding shares, according to their market value immediately after the date of their reconstruction;

and section 186(5)(a) shall apply only to capital receipts after the date of the reconstruction.

5(6) For the purposes of the relevant provisions if, as part of a company reconstruction, trustees become entitled to a capital receipt, their entitlement to the capital receipt shall be taken to arise before the new holding comes into being and, for the purposes of sub-paragraph (5) above, before the date on which the locked-in value of any shares comprised in the original holding falls to be ascertained.

5(7) In the context of a new holding, any reference in this paragraph to shares includes securities and rights of any description which form part of the new holding for the purposes of Chapter II of Part IV of the 1992 Act.

History – In para. 5(2)(a), the words "condition C or D in section 1000(1) of CTA 2010" substituted for the words "section 209(2)(c)" by CTA 2010, s. 1177 and Sch. 1, para. 138, with effect for corporation tax purposes for accounting periods ending on or after 1 April 2010, and for income and capital gains tax purposes for the tax year 2010–11 and subsequent tax years.
In para. 5(2)(b), the words "section 1022 of CTA 2010" substituted for the words "section 210(1)" by CTA 2010, s. 1177 and Sch. 1, para. 138, with effect for corporation tax purposes for accounting periods ending on or after 1 April 2010, and for income and capital gains tax purposes for the tax year 2010–11 and subsequent tax years.
In para. 5(2)(c), the words "section 1049 of CTA 2010" substituted for the words "section 249" by CTA 2010, s. 1177 and Sch. 1, para. 138, with effect for corporation tax purposes for accounting periods ending on or after 1 April 2010, and for income and capital gains tax purposes for the tax year 2010–11 and subsequent tax years.
Reference to the 1992 Act in para. 5(7) substituted by TCGA 1992, s. 290 and Sch. 10, para. 14(58), with effect from 6 March 1992.

Derivations – Para. 5(1): FA 1978, s. 57(1), as amended by CGTA 1979, s. 157(2) and Sch. 7, para. 9.
Para. 5(2): FA 1978, s. 57(2).
Para. 5(3)–(6): FA 1978, s. 57(1), (3)–(6).
Para. 5(7): FA 1978, s. 57(7), as amended by CGTA 1979, s. 157(2) and Sch. 7, para. 9.

Cross references – S. 187(2): "shares" include stock.
TCGA 1992, Pt. IV, Ch. II: capital gains tax provisions dealing with company reorganisations, conversions and exchange of securities etc.

5A(1) Paragraph 5(2) to (6) above apply where there occurs in relation to any of a participant's shares (**"the original holding"**) a relevant transaction which would result in a new holding being equated with the original holding for the purposes of capital gains tax, were it not for the fact that what would be the new holding consists of or includes a qualifying corporate bond; and **"relevant transaction"** here means a transaction mentioned in Chapter II of Part IV of the 1992 Act.

5A(2) In paragraph 5(2) to (6) above as applied by this paragraph–

(a) references to a company reconstruction are to the transaction referred to in sub-paragraph (1) above;

(b) references to the new holding are to what would be the new holding were it not for the fact mentioned in sub-paragraph (1) above;

(c) references to the original holding shall be construed in accordance with sub-paragraph (1) above (and not paragraph 5(1));

(d) references to shares, in the context of the new holding, include securities and rights of any description which form part of the new holding.

5A(3) In sub-paragraph (1) above **"qualifying corporate bond"** shall be construed in accordance with section 117 of the 1992 Act.

History – Para. 5A inserted by FA 1994, s. 101(4), with effect where what would be the new holding comes into being on or after 3 May 1994, but subject to FA 1994, s. 101(13).

EXCESS OR UNAUTHORISED SHARES

6(1) This paragraph applies in any case where–

(a) the total amount of the initial market value of all the shares which are appropriated to an individual in any one year of assessment (whether under a single approved profit sharing scheme or under two or more such schemes) exceeds the relevant amount; or

(b) the trustees of an approved profit sharing scheme appropriate shares to an individual at a time when he is ineligible to participate in the scheme by virtue of paragraph 8 or 35 of Schedule 9.

6(2) In this paragraph–

"excess shares" means any share which caused the relevant amount to be exceeded and any share appropriated after that amount was exceeded; and

"unauthorised shares" means any share appropriated as mentioned in sub-paragraph (1)(b) above.

6(3) For the purposes of sub-paragraph (1)(a) above, if a number of shares is appropriated to an individual at the same time under two or more approved profit sharing schemes, the same proportion of the shares appropriated at that time under each scheme shall be regarded as being appropriated before the relevant amount is exceeded.

6(4) For the purposes of any of the relevant provisions under which an amount counts as employment income of an individual by reason of the occurrence of an event relating to any of his shares–

(a) the appropriate percentage in relation to excess or unauthorised shares shall in every case be 100 per cent; and

(b) without prejudice to section 187(8), the event shall be treated as relating to shares which are not excess or unauthorised shares before shares which are.

6(5) Excess or unauthorised shares which have not been disposed of before the release date or, if it is earlier, the date of the death of the participant whose shares they are, shall be treated for the purposes of the relevant provisions as having been disposed of by the trustees immediately before the release date or, as the case may require, the date of the participant's death, for a consideration equal to their market value at that time.

6(6) The locked-in value at any time of any excess or unauthorised shares shall be their market value at that time.

6(7) Where there has been a company reconstruction to which paragraph 5 above applies, a new share (within the meaning of that paragraph) shall be treated as an excess or unauthorised share if the corresponding share (within the meaning of that paragraph) or, if there was more than one corresponding share, each of them was an excess or unauthorised share.

History – In para. 6(4), words "under which an amount counts as employment income of an individual" substituted for words "charging an individual to income tax under Schedule E" by ITEPA 2003, s. 722 and Sch. 6, para. 113(2), with effect for the year 2003–04 and subsequent years.

Derivations – Para. 6(1): FA 1978, s. 58(1), (3), as amended by FA 1983, s. 25(1).
Para. 6(2): FA 1978, s. 58(1), (2), (4)–(7).
Para. 6(3)–(7): FA 1978, s. 58.

P.A.Y.E. DEDUCTION OF TAX

7(1) Subject to sub-paragraphs (4) and (5) below, where the trustees of an approved profit sharing scheme receive a sum of money which constitutes (or forms part of)–

(a) the proceeds of a disposal of shares falling within section 186(4), or

(b) a capital receipt,

in respect of which an amount counts as employment income of the participant in accordance with section 186, the trustees shall pay out of that sum of money to the company specified in sub-paragraph (3) below an amount equal to that on which income tax is so payable; and the company shall then pay over that amount to the participant but in so doing shall make a P.A.Y.E. deduction.

7(2) Where a participant disposes of his beneficial interest in any of his shares to the trustees of the scheme and the trustees are deemed by virtue of section 186(9) to have disposed of the shares in question, this paragraph shall apply as if the consideration payable by the trustees to the participant on the disposal had been received by the trustees as the proceeds of disposal of shares falling within section 186(4).

7(3) The company to which the payment mentioned in sub-paragraph (1) above is to be made is the company–

(a) of which the participant is an employee or director at the time the trustees receive the sum of money referred to in that sub-paragraph, and

(b) whose employees are at that time eligible (subject to the terms of the scheme and Schedule 9) to be participants in the approved profit sharing scheme concerned,

and if there is more than one company which falls within paragraphs (a) and (b) above, such one of those companies as the Board may direct.

7(4) Where the trustees of an approved profit sharing scheme receive a sum of money to which sub-paragraph (1) above applies but–

(a) there is no company which falls within paragraphs (a) and (b) of sub-paragraph (3) above, or

(b) the Board is of opinion that it is impracticable for the company which falls within those paragraphs (or, as the case may be, any of them) to make a P.A.Y.E deduction and accordingly direct that this sub-paragraph shall apply,

then, in paying over to the participant the proceeds of the disposal or the capital receipt, the trustees shall make a P.A.Y.E. deduction in respect of an amount equal to that on which income tax is payable as mentioned in sub-paragraph (1) above as if the participant were a former employee of the trustees.

7(5) Where the trustees of an approved profit sharing scheme receive a sum of money to which sub-paragraph (1) above applies and the Board direct that this sub-paragraph shall apply–

(a) the trustees shall make the payment mentioned in that sub-paragraph to the company specified in the Board's direction; and

(b) that company shall pay over that amount to the participant but in so doing shall make a P.A.Y.E. deduction, and for that purpose if the participant is not an employee of that company he shall be treated as a former employee;

but no such direction shall be given except with the consent of the trustees, the company or companies (if any) specified in sub-paragraph (3) above and the company specified in the direction.

7(6) Where, in accordance with this paragraph any person is required to make a P.A.Y.E. deduction in respect of any amount, that amount shall be treated for the purposes of section 684 of ITEPA 2003 (PAYE regulations) and PAYE regulations as PAYE income payable to the recipient, and, accordingly, such deduction shall be made as is required by those regulations.

7(7) Where, in connection with a transfer of a participant's shares to which sub-paragraph (c) of paragraph 2(2) of Schedule 9 applies, the trustees receive such a sum as is referred to in that sub-paragraph, that sum shall be treated for the purposes of the Income Tax Acts–

(a) as a sum deducted by the trustees pursuant to a requirement to make a P.A.Y.E. deduction under sub-paragraph (4) above; and

(b) as referable to the income tax which, as a result of the transfer, is charged on the participant by virtue of section 186(4).

7(8) Unless the Board otherwise direct, in the application of this paragraph to a sum of money which constitutes or forms part of the proceeds of a disposal of, or a capital receipt referable to, excess or unauthorised shares (within the meaning of paragraph 6 above), the trustees shall determine the amount of the payment mentioned in sub-paragraph (1) above or, as the case may be, the amount of the P.A.Y.E. deduction to be made under sub-paragraph (4) above as if the shares were not excess or unauthorised shares.

History – In para. 7(1), words "an amount counts as employment income of the participant" substituted for words "a participant in the scheme is chargeable to income tax under Schedule E" by ITEPA 2003, s. 722 and Sch. 6, para. 113(3)(a), with effect for the year 2003–04 and subsequent years.

In para. 7(6), words "section 684 of ITEPA 2003 (PAYE regulations) and PAYE regulations as PAYE income payable to the recipient" substituted for words "section 203 and any regulations made under that section as an amount of income payable to the recipient and assessable to income tax under Schedule E" by ITEPA 2003, s. 722 and Sch. 6, para. 113(3)(b), with effect for the year 2003–04 and subsequent years.

Para. 7(7)(b) substituted by ITEPA 2003, s. 722 and Sch. 6, para. 113(3)(c), with effect for the year 2003–04 and subsequent years.

Derivations – Para. 7(1): FA 1978, s. 59(1).
Para. 7(2): FA 1978, s. 59(1A), as inserted by FA 1980, s. 46(8).
Para. 7(3)–(7): FA 1978, s. 59(2)–(6).
Para. 7(8): FA 1978, s. 59(7), as amended by FA 1987, Sch. 15, para. 11(3).

SCHEDULE 11 – PAYMENTS AND OTHER BENEFITS IN CONNECTION WITH TERMINATION OF EMPLOYMENT, ETC.

Section 148

[Omitted by ITEPA 2003, s. 722 and Sch. 6, para. 114 and repealed by s. 724 and Sch. 8, Pt. 1.]

INTRODUCTORY

1 [Omitted by ITEPA 2003, s. 722 and Sch. 6, para. 114 and repealed by s. 724 and Sch. 8, Pt. 1.]

History – Para. 1 omitted by ITEPA 2003, s. 722 and Sch. 6, para. 114 and repealed by s. 724 and Sch. 8, Pt. 1, with effect for the year 2003–04 and subsequent tax years.

Notes – Para. 1 is not necessary and has not been rewritten into the provision of ITEPA 2003.

PAYMENTS AND OTHER BENEFITS TO WHICH SECTION 148 APPLIES

2 [Omitted by ITEPA 2003, s. 722 and Sch. 6, para. 114 and repealed by s. 724 and Sch. 8, Pt. 1.]

History – Para. 2 omitted by ITEPA 2003, s. 722 and Sch. 6, para. 114 and repealed by s. 724 and Sch. 8, Pt. 1, with effect for the year 2003–04 and subsequent tax years.

Notes – Para. 2 rewritten as ITEPA *2003, s. 401(1), (4)*.

PAYMENTS AND OTHER BENEFITS EXCLUDED FROM CHARGE UNDER SECTION 148

3 [Omitted by ITEPA 2003, s. 722 and Sch. 6, para. 114 and repealed by s. 724 and Sch. 8, Pt. 1.]

History – Para. 3 omitted by ITEPA 2003, s. 722 and Sch. 6, para. 114 and repealed by s. 724 and Sch. 8, Pt. 1, with effect for the year 2003–04 and subsequent tax years.

Notes – Para. 3 rewritten as ITEPA 2003, s. 406.

4 [Omitted by ITEPA 2003, s. 722 and Sch. 6, para. 114 and repealed by s. 724 and Sch. 8, Pt. 1.]

History – Para. 4 omitted by ITEPA 2003, s. 722 and Sch. 6, para. 114 and repealed by s. 724 and Sch. 8, Pt. 1, with effect for the year 2003–04 and subsequent tax years.

Notes – Para. 4 rewritten as ITEPA 2003, s. 407.

5 [Omitted by ITEPA 2003, s. 722 and Sch. 6, para. 114 and repealed by s. 724 and Sch. 8, Pt. 1.]

History – Para. 5 omitted by ITEPA 2003, s. 722 and Sch. 6, para. 114 and repealed by s. 724 and Sch. 8, Pt. 1, with effect for the year 2003–04 and subsequent tax years.

Notes – Para. 5 rewritten as ITEPA 2003, s. 411.

6 [Omitted by ITEPA 2003, s. 722 and Sch. 6, para. 114 and repealed by s. 724 and Sch. 8, Pt. 1.]

History – Para. 6 omitted by ITEPA 2003, s. 722 and Sch. 6, para. 114 and repealed by s. 724 and Sch. 8, Pt. 1, with effect for the year 2003–04 and subsequent tax years.

Notes – Para. 6 rewritten as ITEPA 2003, s. 412.

APPLICATION OF £30,000 THRESHOLD

7 [Omitted by ITEPA 2003, s. 722 and Sch. 6, para. 114 and repealed by s. 724 and Sch 8, Pt. 1.]

History – Para. 7 omitted by ITEPA 2003, s. 722 and Sch. 6, para. 114 and repealed by s. 724 and Sch. 8, Pt. 1, with effect for the year 2003–04 and subsequent tax years.

Notes – Para. 7 rewritten as ITEPA 2003, s. 403(4) and s. 404.

8 [Omitted by ITEPA 2003, s. 722 and Sch. 6, para. 114 and repealed by s. 724 and Sch. 8, Pt. 1.]

History – Para. 8 omitted by ITEPA 2003, s. 722 and Sch. 6, para. 114 and repealed by s. 724 and Sch. 8, Pt. 1, with effect for the year 2003–04 and subsequent tax years.

Notes – Para. 8 rewritten as ITEPA 2003, s. 404(2), (3) and s. 719.

EXCLUSION OR REDUCTION OF CHARGE IN CASE OF FOREIGN SERVICE

9 [Omitted by ITEPA 2003, s. 722 and Sch. 6, para. 114 and repealed by s. 724 and Sch. 8, Pt. 1.]

History – Para. 9 omitted by ITEPA 2003, s. 722 and Sch. 6, para. 114 and repealed by s. 724 and Sch. 8, Pt. 1, with effect for the year 2003–04 and subsequent tax years.

Notes – Para. 9 rewritten as follows:
Para. 9(1): ITEPA 2003, s. 413 (1) and s. 414(1)–(5).
Para. 9(2): ITEPA 2003, s. 413(3)–(6).

10 [Omitted by ITEPA 2003, s. 722 and Sch. 6, para. 114 and repealed by s. 724 and Sch. 8, Pt. 1.]

History – Para. 10 omitted by ITEPA 2003, s. 722 and Sch. 6, para. 114 and repealed by s. 724 and Sch. 8, Pt. 1, with effect for the year 2003–04 and subsequent tax years.

Notes – Para. 10 rewritten as ITEPA 2003, s. 413 (1).

11 [Omitted by ITEPA 2003, s. 722 and Sch. 6, para. 114 and repealed by s. 724 and Sch. 8, Pt. 1.]

History – Para. 11 omitted by ITEPA 2003, s. 722 and Sch. 6, para. 114 and repealed by s. 724 and Sch. 8, Pt. 1, with effect for the year 2003–04 and subsequent tax years.

Notes – Para. 11 rewritten as ITEPA 2003, s. 414.

VALUATION OF BENEFITS

12 [Omitted by ITEPA 2003, s. 722 and Sch. 6, para. 114 and repealed by s. 724 and Sch. 8, Pt. 1.]

History – Para. 12 omitted by ITEPA 2003, s. 722 and Sch. 6, para. 114 and repealed by s. 724 and Sch. 8, Pt. 1, with effect for the year 2003–04 and subsequent tax years.

Notes – Para. 12 rewritten as ITEPA 2003, s. 415.

NOTIONAL INTEREST TREATED AS PAID IF AMOUNT CHARGED IN RESPECT OF BENEFICIAL LOAN

13 [Omitted by ITEPA 2003, s. 722 and Sch. 6, para. 114 and repealed by s. 724 and Sch. 8, Pt. 1.]

History – Para. 13 omitted by ITEPA 2003, s. 722 and Sch. 6, para. 114 and repealed by s. 724 and Sch. 8, Pt. 1, with effect for the year 2003–04 and subsequent tax years.

Notes – Para. 13 rewritten as ITEPA 2003, s. 416.

GIVING EFFECT TO THE CHARGE TO TAX

14 [Omitted by ITEPA 2003, s. 722 and Sch. 6, para. 114 and repealed by s. 724 and Sch. 8, Pt. 1.]

History – Para. 14 omitted by ITEPA 2003, s. 722 and Sch. 6, para. 114 and repealed by s. 724 and Sch. 8, Pt. 1, with effect for the year 2003–04 and subsequent tax years.

Notes – Para. 14 rewritten as ITEPA 2003, s. 403(1), (5).

REPORTING REQUIREMENTS

15 [Omitted by ITEPA 2003, s. 722 and Sch. 6, para. 114 and repealed by s. 724 and Sch. 8, Pt. 1.]

History – Para. 15 omitted by ITEPA 2003, s. 722 and Sch. 6, para. 114 and repealed by s. 724 and Sch. 8, Pt. 1, with effect for the year 2003–04 and subsequent tax years.

Notes – Para. 15 rewritten as ITEPA 2003, s. 684(2).

INTERPRETATION

16 [Omitted by ITEPA 2003, s. 722 and Sch. 6, para. 114 and repealed by s. 724 and Sch. 8, Pt. 1.]

History – Para. 16 omitted by ITEPA 2003, s. 722 and Sch. 6, para. 114 and repealed by s. 724 and Sch. 8, Pt. 1, with effect for the year 2003–04 and subsequent tax years.

Notes – Para. 16 rewritten as ITEPA 2003, s. 404(2), (3) s. 413(1), s. 414(3) and s. 721(1).

SCHEDULE 11A – REMOVAL EXPENSES AND BENEFITS

Section 191A

[Omitted by ITEPA 2003, s. 722 and Sch. 6, para. 115 and repealed by s. 724 and Sch. 8, Pt. 1.]

Part I – Tax Relief

1 [Omitted by ITEPA 2003, s. 722 and Sch. 6, para. 115 and repealed by s. 724 and Sch. 8, Pt. 1.]

History – Para. 1 omitted by ITEPA 2003, s. 722 and Sch. 6, para. 115 and repealed by s. 724 and Sch. 8, Pt. 1, with effect for the year 2003–04 and subsequent tax years.

Notes – Para. 1 rewritten as ITEPA 2003, s. 271.

2 [Omitted by ITEPA 2003, s. 722 and Sch. 6, para. 115 and repealed by s. 724 and Sch. 8, Pt. 1.]

History – Para. 2 omitted by ITEPA 2003, s. 722 and Sch. 6, para. 115 and repealed by s. 724 and Sch. 8, Pt. 1, with effect for the year 2003–04 and subsequent tax years.

Notes – Para. 2 is not necessary and has not been rewritten into the provisions of ITEPA 2003.

Part II – Qualifying Expenses and Qualifying Benefits

QUALIFYING REMOVAL EXPENSES

3 [Omitted by ITEPA 2003, s. 722 and Sch. 6, para. 115 and repealed by s. 724 and Sch. 8, Pt. 1.]

History – Para. 3 omitted by ITEPA 2003, s. 722 and Sch. 6, para. 115 and repealed by s. 724 and Sch. 8, Pt. 1, with effect for the year 2003–04 and subsequent tax years.

Notes – Para. 3 rewritten as ITEPA 2003, s. 272(3)..

QUALIFYING REMOVAL BENEFITS

4 [Omitted by ITEPA 2003, s. 722 and Sch. 6, para. 115 and repealed by s. 724 and Sch. 8, Pt. 1.]

History – Para. 4 omitted by ITEPA 2003, s. 722 and Sch. 6, para. 115 and repealed by s. 724 and Sch. 8, Pt. 1, with effect for the year 2003–04 and subsequent tax years.

Notes – Para. 4 rewritten as ITEPA 2003, s. 272(1).

CONNECTION WITH EMPLOYMENT

5 [Omitted by ITEPA 2003, s. 722 and Sch. 6, para. 115 and repealed by s. 724 and Sch. 8, Pt. 1.]

History – Para. 5 omitted by ITEPA 2003, s. 722 and Sch. 6, para. 115 and repealed by s. 724 and Sch. 8, Pt. 1, with effect for the year 2003–04 and subsequent tax years.

Notes – Para. 5 rewritten as ITEPA 2003, s. 273(2)–(4).

THE RELEVANT DAY

6 [Omitted by ITEPA 2003, s. 722 and Sch. 6, para. 115 and repealed by s. 724 and Sch. 8, Pt. 1.]

History – Para. 6 omitted by ITEPA 2003, s. 722 and Sch. 6, para. 115 and repealed by s. 724 and Sch. 8, Pt. 1, with effect for the year 2003–04 and subsequent tax years, subject to the transitional provisions and savings in ITEPA 2003, Sch. 7.

Cross references – ITEPA 2003, Sch. 7, para. 36 (transitionals and savings): direction under former para. 6(2) (meaning of "relevant day", where relevant day is on or after 6 April 2003, not affected by repeal.

Notes – Para. 6 rewritten as ITEPA 2003, s. 274.

Part III – Eligible Removal Expenses

INTRODUCTION

7 [Omitted by ITEPA 2003, s. 722 and Sch. 6, para. 115 and repealed by s. 724 and Sch. 8, Pt. 1.]

History – Para. 7 omitted by ITEPA 2003, s. 722 and Sch. 6, para. 115 and repealed by s. 724 and Sch. 8, Pt. 1, with effect for the year 2003–04 and subsequent tax years.

Notes – Para. 7 rewritten as ITEPA 2003, s. 272(3).

EXPENSES OF DISPOSAL

8 [Omitted by ITEPA 2003, s. 722 and Sch. 6, para. 115 and repealed by s. 724 and Sch. 8, Pt. 1.]

History – Para. 8 omitted by ITEPA 2003, s. 722 and Sch. 6, para. 115 and repealed by s. 724 and Sch. 8, Pt. 1, with effect for the year 2003–04 and subsequent tax years.

Notes – Para. 8 rewritten as ITEPA 2003, s. 272(1), (3)–(5).

EXPENSES OF ACQUISITION

9 [Omitted by ITEPA 2003, s. 722 and Sch. 6, para. 115 and repealed by s. 724 and Sch. 8, Pt. 1.]

History – Para. 9 omitted by ITEPA 2003, s. 722 and Sch. 6, para. 115 and repealed by s. 724 and Sch. 8, Pt. 1.

Notes – Para. 9 rewritten as ITEPA 2003, s. 277.

EXPENSES OF ABORTIVE ACQUISITION

10 [Omitted by ITEPA 2003, s. 722 and Sch. 6, para. 115 and repealed by s. 724 and Sch. 8, Pt. 1.]

History – Para. 10 omitted by ITEPA 2003, s. 722 and Sch. 6, para. 115 and repealed by s. 724 and Sch. 8, Pt. 1, with effect for the year 2003–04 and subsequent tax years.

Notes – Para. 10 rewritten as ITEPA 2003, s. 278.

EXPENSES OF TRANSPORTING BELONGINGS

11 [Omitted by ITEPA 2003, s. 722 and Sch. 6, para. 115 and repealed by s. 724 and Sch. 8, Pt. 1.]

History – Para. 11 omitted by ITEPA 2003, s. 722 and Sch. 6, para. 115 and repealed by s. 724 and Sch. 8, Pt. 1, with effect for the year 2003–04 and subsequent tax years.

Notes – Para. 11 rewritten as ITEPA 2003, s. 280(2), (3).

TRAVELLING AND SUBSISTENCE EXPENSES

12 [Omitted by ITEPA 2003, s. 722 and Sch. 6, para. 115 and repealed by s. 724 and Sch. 8, Pt. 1.]

History – Para. 12 omitted by ITEPA 2003, s. 722 and Sch. 6, para. 115 and repealed by s. 724 and Sch. 8, Pt. 1, with effect for the year 2003–04 and subsequent tax years.

Notes – Para. 12 rewritten as follows:
Para. 12(1)–(3): ITEPA 2003, s. 281(1)–(4), (6).
Para. 12(4): ITEPA 2003, s. 282(1), (2).

BRIDGING LOAN EXPENSES

13 [Omitted by ITEPA 2003, s. 722 and Sch. 6, para. 115 and repealed by s. 724 and Sch. 8, Pt. 1.]

History – Para. 13 omitted by ITEPA 2003, s. 722 and Sch. 6, para. 115 and repealed by s. 724 and Sch. 8, Pt. 1, with effect for the year 2003–04 and subsequent tax years.

Notes – Para. 13 rewritten as ITEPA 2003, s. 284(1)–(3), (6).

DUPLICATE EXPENSES

14 [Omitted by ITEPA 2003, s. 722 and Sch. 6, para. 115 and repealed by s. 724 and Sch. 8, Pt. 1.]

History – Para. 14 omitted by ITEPA 2003, s. 722 and Sch. 6, para. 115 and repealed by s. 724 and Sch. 8, Pt. 1, with effect for the year 2003–04 and subsequent tax years.

Notes – Para. 14 rewritten as follows:
Para. 14(1), (4): ITEPA 2003, s. 285.
Para. 14(2), (3) are not necessary and have not been rewritten into the provisions of ITEPA 2003.

POWER TO AMEND

15 [Omitted by ITEPA 2003, s. 722 and Sch. 6, para. 115 and repealed by s. 724 and Sch. 8, Pt. 1.]

History – Para. 14 omitted by ITEPA 2003, s. 722 and Sch. 6, para. 115 and repealed by s. 724 and Sch. 8, Pt. 1. with effect for the year 2003–04 and subsequent tax years.

Notes – Para. 15 rewritten as follows:
Para. 15(1), (4): ITEPA 2003, s. 285.
Para. 15(2), (3) are not necessary and have not been rewritten into the provisions of ITEPA 2003.

Part IV – Eligible Removal Benefits

INTRODUCTION

16 [Omitted by ITEPA 2003, s. 722 and Sch. 6, para. 115 and repealed by s. 724 and Sch. 8, Pt. 1.]

History – Para. 16 omitted byITEPA 2003, s. 722 and Sch. 6, para. 115 and repealed by s. 724 and Sch. 8, Pt. 1, with effect for the year 2003–04 and subsequent tax years.

Notes – Para. 16 rewritten as ITEPA 2003, s. 272(1).

BENEFITS IN RESPECT OF DISPOSAL

17 [Omitted by ITEPA 2003, s. 722 and Sch. 6, para. 115 and repealed by s. 724 and Sch. 8, Pt. 1.]

History – Para. 17 omitted by ITEPA 2003, s. 722 and Sch. 6, para. 115 and repealed by s. 724 and Sch. 8, Pt. 1, with effect for the year 2003–04 and subsequent tax years.

Notes – Para. 17 rewritten as ITEPA 2003, s. 279.

BENEFITS IN RESPECT OF ACQUISITION

18 [Omitted by ITEPA 2003, s. 722 and Sch. 6, para. 115 and repealed by s. 724 and Sch. 8, Pt. 1.]

History – Para. 18 omitted by ITEPA 2003, s. 722 and Sch. 6, para. 115 and repealed by s. 724 and Sch. 8, Pt. 1, with effect for the year 2003–04 and subsequent tax years.

Notes – Para. 18 rewritten as ITEPA 2003, s. 277.

BENEFITS IN RESPECT OF ABORTIVE ACQUISITION

19 [Omitted by ITEPA 2003, s. 722 and Sch. 6, para. 115 and repealed by s. 724 and Sch. 8, Pt. 1.]

History – Para. 19 omitted by ITEPA 2003, s. 722 and Sch. 6, para. 115 and repealed by s. 724 and Sch. 8, Pt. 1, with effect for the year 2003–04 and subsequent tax years.

Notes – Para. 19 rewritten as ITEPA 2003, s. 278.

BENEFITS IN RESPECT OF THE TRANSPORTING OF BELONGINGS

20 [Omitted by ITEPA 2003, s. 722 and Sch. 6, para. 115 and repealed by s. 724 and Sch. 8, Pt. 1.]

History – Para. 20 omitted by ITEPA 2003, s. 722 and Sch. 6, para. 115 and repealed by s. 724 and Sch. 8, Pt. 1, with effect for the year 2003–04 and subsequent tax years.

Notes – Para. 20 rewritten as ITEPA 2003, s. 280.

TRAVELLING AND SUBSISTENCE BENEFITS

21 [Omitted by ITEPA 2003, s. 722 and Sch. 6, para. 115 and repealed by s. 724 and Sch. 8, Pt. 1.]

History – Para. 21 omitted by ITEPA 2003, s. 722 and Sch. 6, para. 115 and repealed by s. 724 and Sch. 8, Pt. 1, with effect for the year 2003–04 and subsequent tax years.

Notes – Para. 21 rewritten as follows:
Para. 21(1), (3): ITEPA 2003, s. 281.
Para. 21(2), (4)—(6): ITEPA 2003, s. 283.
Para. 21(7), (8): ITEPA 2003, s. 282.

BENEFITS IN RESPECT OF NEW RESIDENCE

22 [Omitted by ITEPA 2003, s. 722 and Sch. 6, para. 115 and repealed by s. 724 and Sch. 8, Pt. 1.]

History – Para. 22 omitted by ITEPA 2003, s. 722 and Sch. 6, para. 115 and repealed by s. 724 and Sch. 8, Pt. 1, with effect for the year 2003–04 and subsequent tax years.

Notes – Para. 22 rewritten as ITEPA 2003, s. 285.

POWER TO AMEND

23 [Omitted by ITEPA 2003, s. 722 and Sch. 6, para. 115 and repealed by s. 724 and Sch. 8, Pt. 1.]

History – Para. 23 omitted by ITEPA 2003, s. 722 and Sch. 6, para. 115 and repealed by s. 724 and Sch. 8, Pt. 1, with effect for the year 2003–04 and subsequent tax years.

Notes – Para. 23 rewritten as ITEPA 2003, s. 286.

Part V – The Qualifying Limit

24 [Omitted by ITEPA 2003, s. 722 and Sch. 6, para. 115 and repealed by s. 724 and Sch. 8, Pt. 1.]

History – Para. 24 omitted by ITEPA 2003, s. 722 and Sch. 6, para. 115 and repealed by s. 724 and Sch. 8, Pt. 1, with effect for the year 2003–04 and subsequent tax years.

Notes – Para. 24 rewritten as ITEPA 2003, s. 287.

Part VI – General

INTERPRETATION

25 [Omitted by ITEPA 2003, s. 722 and Sch. 6, para. 115 and repealed by s. 724 and Sch. 8, Pt. 1.]

History – Para. 25 omitted by ITEPA 2003, s. 722 and Sch. 6, para. 115 and repealed by s. 724 and Sch. 8, Pt. 1, with effect for the year 2003–04 and subsequent tax years.

Notes – Para. 25 rewritten as ITEPA 2003, s. 276.

26 [Omitted by ITEPA 2003, s. 722 and Sch. 6, para. 115 and repealed by s. 724 and Sch. 8, Pt. 1.]

History – Para. 26 omitted by ITEPA 2003, s. 722 and Sch. 6, para. 115 and repealed by s. 724 and Sch. 8, Pt. 1, with effect for the year 2003–04 and subsequent tax years.

Notes – Para. 26 rewritten as ITEPA 2003, s. 721(5).

27 [Omitted by ITEPA 2003, s. 722 and Sch. 6, para. 115 and repealed by s. 724 and Sch. 8, Pt. 1.]

History – Para. 27 omitted by ITEPA 2003, s. 722 and Sch. 6, para. 115 and repealed by s. 724 and Sch. 8, Pt. 1, with effect for the year 2003–04 and subsequent tax years.

Notes – Para. 27 rewritten as ITEPA 2003, s. 5.

28 [Omitted by ITEPA 2003, s. 722 and Sch. 6, para. 115 and repealed by s. 724 and Sch. 8, Pt. 1.]

History – Para. 28 omitted by ITEPA 2003, s. 722 and Sch. 6, para. 115 and repealed by s. 724 and Sch. 8, Pt. 1, with effect for the year 2003–04 and subsequent tax years.

Notes – Para. 28 rewritten as ITEPA 2003, s. 281(6).

COMMENCEMENT

29 [Omitted by ITEPA 2003, s. 722 and Sch. 6, para. 115 and repealed by s. 724 and Sch. 8, Pt. 1.]

History – Para. 29 omitted byITEPA 2003, s. 722 and Sch. 6, para. 115 and repealed by s. 724 and Sch. 8, Pt. 1, with effect for the year 2003–04 and subsequent tax years.

Notes – Para. 29 is unnecessary and has not been rewritten into the provisions of ITEPA 2003.

SCHEDULE 12 – FOREIGN EARNINGS

Section 192A

1 [Omitted by ITEPA 2003, s. 722 and Sch. 6, para. 116 and repealed by s. 724 and Sch. 8, Pt. 1.]

History – Para. 1 omitted by ITEPA 2003, s. 722 and Sch. 6, para. 116 and repealed by s. 724 and Sch. 8, Pt. 1, with effect for the year 2003–04 and subsequent tax years.

Notes – Para. 1 is unnecessary and has not been rewritten into the provisions of ITEPA 2003.

AMOUNT OF EMOLUMENTS

1A [Omitted by ITEPA 2003, s. 722 and Sch. 6, para. 116 and repealed by s. 724 and Sch. 8, Pt. 1.]

History – Para. 1A omitted by ITEPA 2003, s. 722 and Sch. 6, para. 116 and repealed by s. 724 and Sch. 8, Pt. 1, with effect for the year 2003–04 and subsequent tax years.

Notes – Para. 1A rewritten as ITEPA 2003, s. 24(2), (3), s. 329(1), s. 330(1), s. 331 (2) and s. 381.

EMOLUMENTS ELIGIBLE FOR RELIEF

2 [Omitted by ITEPA 2003, s. 722 and Sch. 6, para. 116 and repealed by s. 724 and Sch. 8, Pt. 1.]

History – Para. 2 omitted by ITEPA 2003, s. 722 and Sch. 6, para. 116 and repealed by s. 724 and Sch. 8, Pt. 1, with effect for the year 2003–04 and subsequent tax years.

Notes – Para. 2: ITEPA 2003, s. 24 and s. 380.

QUALIFYING PERIODS

3 [Omitted by ITEPA 2003, s. 722 and Sch. 6, para. 116 and repealed by s. 724 and Sch. 8, Pt. 1.]

History – Para. 3 omitted by ITEPA 2003, s. 722 and Sch. 6, para. 116 and repealed by s. 724 and Sch. 8, Pt. 1, with effect for the year 2003–04 and subsequent tax years.

Notes – Para. 3(1), (2): ITEPA 2003, s. 378.
Para. 3(2A) is not necessary and has not been rewritten into the provisions of ITEPA 2003.
Para. 3(3): ITEPA 2003, s. 379(2).

SUPPLEMENTARY

4 [Omitted by ITEPA 2003, s. 722 and Sch. 6, para. 116 and repealed by s. 724 and Sch. 8, Pt. 1.]

History – Para. 4 omitted by ITEPA 2003, s. 722 and Sch. 6, para. 116 and repealed by s. 724 and Sch. 8, Pt. 1, with effect for the year 2003–04 and subsequent tax years.

Notes – Para. 4 rewritten as ITEPA 2003, s. 378(4).

5 [Omitted by ITEPA 2003, s. 722 and Sch. 6, para. 116 and repealed by s. 724 and Sch. 8, Pt. 1.]

History – Para. 5 omitted by ITEPA 2003, s. 722 and Sch. 6, para. 116 and repealed by s. 724 and Sch. 8, Pt. 1, with effect for the year 2003–04 and subsequent tax years.

Notes – Para. 5 rewritten as ITEPA 2003, s. 40(3)–(5), s. 382(1), (3), (4).

6 [Omitted by ITEPA 2003, s. 722 and Sch. 6, para. 116 and repealed by s. 724 and Sch. 8, Pt. 1.]

History – Para. 6 omitted by ITEPA 2003, s. 722 and Sch. 6, para. 116 and repealed by s. 724 and Sch. 8, Pt. 1, with effect for the year 2003–04 and subsequent tax years.

Notes – Para. 6 rewritten as ITEPA 2003, s. 383.

7 [Omitted by ITEPA 2003, s. 722 and Sch. 6, para. 116 and repealed by s. 724 and Sch. 8, Pt. 1.]

History – Para. 7 omitted by ITEPA 2003, s. 722 and Sch. 6, para. 116 and repealed by s. 724 and Sch. 8, Pt. 1, with effect for the year 2003–04 and subsequent tax years.

Notes – Para. 7 is unnecessary and has not been rewritten into the provisions of ITEPA 2003.

SCHEDULE 12AA – MILEAGE ALLOWANCES: INTERPRETATION

Section 197AH

[Omitted by ITEPA 2003, s. 722 and Sch. 6, para. 117 and repealed by s. 724 and Sch. 8, Pt. 1.]

INTRODUCTION

1 [Omitted by ITEPA 2003, s. 722 and Sch. 6, para. 117 and repealed by s. 724 and Sch. 8, Pt. 1.]

History – Para. 1 omitted by ITEPA 2003, s. 722 and Sch. 6, para. 117 and repealed by s. 724 and Sch. 8, Pt. 1, with effect for the year 2003–04 and subsequent tax years.

Notes – Para. 1 rewritten as follows:
Para. 1(1), (2) is unnecessary and has not been rewritten into the provisions of ITEPA 2003.
Para. 1(3), (2): ITEPA 2003, s. 236(1).

BUSINESS TRAVEL

2 [Omitted by ITEPA 2003, s. 722 and Sch. 6, para. 117 and repealed by s. 724 and Sch. 8, Pt. 1.]

History – Para. 2 omitted by ITEPA 2003, s. 722 and Sch. 6, para. 117 and repealed by s. 724 and Sch. 8, Pt. 1, with effect for the year 2003–04 and subsequent tax years.

Notes – Para. 2 rewritten as ITEPA 2003, s. 236(1).

QUALIFYING VEHICLES

3 [Omitted by ITEPA 2003, s. 722 and Sch. 6, para. 117 and repealed by s. 724 and Sch. 8, Pt. 1.]

History – Para. 3 omitted by ITEPA 2003, s. 722 and Sch. 6, para. 117 and repealed by s. 724 and Sch. 8, Pt. 1, with effect for the year 2003–04 and subsequent tax years.

Notes – Para. 3 rewritten as ITEPA 2003, s. 235.

THE APPROVED AMOUNT: MILEAGE ALLOWANCE PAYMENTS

4 [Omitted by ITEPA 2003, s. 722 and Sch. 6, para. 117 and repealed by s. 724 and Sch. 8, Pt. 1.]

History – Para. 4 omitted by ITEPA 2003, s. 722 and Sch. 6, para. 117 and repealed by s. 724 and Sch. 8, Pt. 1, with effect for the year 2003–04 and subsequent tax years.

Notes – Para. 4 rewritten as ITEPA 2003, s. 230 and s. 719.

THE APPROVED AMOUNT: PASSENGER PAYMENTS

5 [Omitted by ITEPA 2003, s. 722 and Sch. 6, para. 117 and repealed by s. 724 and Sch. 8, Pt. 1.]

History – Para. 5 omitted by ITEPA 2003, s. 722 and Sch. 6, para. 117 and repealed by s. 724 and Sch. 8, Pt. 1, with effect for the year 2003–04 and subsequent tax years.

Notes – Para. 5 rewritten as ITEPA 2003, s. 234.

COMPANY VEHICLES

6 [Omitted by ITEPA 2003, s. 722 and Sch. 6, para. 117 and repealed by s. 724 and Sch. 8, Pt. 1.]

History – Para. 6 omitted by ITEPA 2003, s. 722 and Sch. 6, para. 117 and repealed by s. 724 and Sch. 8, Pt. 1, with effect for the year 2003–04 and subsequent tax years.

Notes – Para. 6 rewritten as ITEPA 2003, s. 236.

EMPLOYMENT

7 [Omitted by ITEPA 2003, s. 722 and Sch. 6, para. 117 and repealed by s. 724 and Sch. 8, Pt. 1.]

History – Para. 7 omitted by ITEPA 2003, s. 722 and Sch. 6, para. 117 and repealed by s. 724 and Sch. 8, Pt. 1, with effect for the year 2003–04 and subsequent tax years.

Notes – Para. 7 rewritten as ITEPA 2003, s. 5.

TAX YEAR

8 [Omitted by ITEPA 2003, s. 722 and Sch. 6, para. 117 and repealed by s. 724 and Sch. 8, Pt. 1.]

History – Para. 8 omitted by ITEPA 2003, s. 722 and Sch. 6, para. 117 and repealed by s. 724 and Sch. 8, Pt. 1, with effect for the year 2003–04 and subsequent tax years.

Notes – Para. 8 rewritten as ITEPA 2003, s. 721(1).

SCHEDULE 12A – ORDINARY COMMUTING AND PRIVATE TRAVEL

Section 198(1A)

[Omitted by ITEPA 2003, s. 722 and Sch. 6, para. 118 and repealed by s. 724 and Sch. 8, Pt. 1.]

INTRODUCTION

1 [Omitted by ITEPA 2003, s. 722 and Sch. 6, para. 118 and repealed by s. 724 and Sch. 8, Pt. 1.]

History – Para. 1 omitted by ITEPA 2003, s. 722 and Sch. 6, para. 118 and repealed by s. 724 and Sch. 8, Pt. 1, with effect for the year 2003–04 and subsequent tax years.

Notes – Para. 1 rewritten as follows:
Para. 1(1) is unnecessary and has not been rewritten into the provisions of ITEPA 2003.
Para. 1(2): ITEPA 2003, s. 5.

ORDINARY COMMUTING AND PRIVATE TRAVEL

2 [Omitted by ITEPA 2003, s. 722 and Sch. 6, para. 118 and repealed by s. 724 and Sch. 8, Pt. 1.]

History – Para. 2 omitted by ITEPA 2003, s. 722 and Sch. 6, para. 118 and repealed by s. 724 and Sch. 8, Pt. 1, with effect for the year 2003–04 and subsequent tax years.

Notes – Para. 2 rewritten as follows:
Para. 2(1), (2): ITEPA 2003, s. 338(3), (5).
Para. 2(3): ITEPA 2003, s. 339(1).

3 [Omitted by ITEPA 2003, s. 722 and Sch. 6, para. 118 and repealed by s. 724 and Sch. 8, Pt. 1.]

History – Para. 3 omitted by ITEPA 2003, s. 722 and Sch. 6, para. 118 and repealed by s. 724 and Sch. 8, Pt. 1, with effect for the year 2003–04 and subsequent tax years.

Notes – Para. 3 rewritten as ITEPA 2003, s. 338(2), (4).

PERMANENT AND TEMPORARY WORKPLACES

4 [Omitted by ITEPA 2003, s. 722 and Sch. 6, para. 118 and repealed by s. 724 and Sch. 8, Pt. 1.]

History – Para. 4 omitted by ITEPA 2003, s. 722 and Sch. 6, para. 118 and repealed by s. 724 and Sch. 8, Pt. 1, with effect for the year 2003–04 and subsequent tax years.

Notes – Para. 4 rewritten as ITEPA 2003, s. 339(2), (3).

THE 24 MONTH RULE AND FIXED TERM APPOINTMENTS

5 [Omitted by ITEPA 2003, s. 722 and Sch. 6, para. 118 and repealed by s. 724 and Sch. 8, Pt. 1.]

History – Para. 5 omitted by ITEPA 2003, s. 722 and Sch. 6, para. 118 and repealed by s. 724 and Sch. 8, Pt. 1, with effect for the year 2003–04 and subsequent tax years.

Notes – Para. 5 rewritten as ITEPA 2003, s. 339(5)–(7).

DEPOTS AND BASES

6 [Omitted by ITEPA 2003, s. 722 and Sch. 6, para. 118 and repealed by s. 724 and Sch. 8, Pt. 1.]

History – Para. 6 omitted by ITEPA 2003, s. 722 and Sch. 6, para. 118 and repealed by s. 724 and Sch. 8, Pt. 1, with effect for the year 2003–04 and subsequent tax years.

Notes – Para. 6 rewritten as ITEPA 2003, s. 339(4).

AREA-BASED EMPLOYEES

7 [Omitted by ITEPA 2003, s. 722 and Sch. 6, para. 118 and repealed by s. 724 and Sch. 8, Pt. 1.]

History – Para. 7 omitted by ITEPA 2003, s. 722 and Sch. 6, para. 118 and repealed by s. 724 and Sch. 8, Pt. 1, with effect for the year 2003–04 and subsequent tax years.

Notes – Para. 7 rewritten as ITEPA 2003, s. 339(8).

SCHEDULE 13 – COLLECTION OF ADVANCE CORPORATION TAX

Section 238(5), 241(4)

[Sch. 13 repealed by FA 1998, s. 31 and Sch. 3, para. 41, s. 165 and Sch. 27, Pt. III(2).]

History – Sch. 13 was repealed by FA 1998, s. 31 and Sch. 3, para. 41, s. 165 and Sch. 27, Pt. III(2) with effect in relation to return periods beginning on or after 6 April 1999 and in relation to accounting periods beginning on or after that date.

SCHEDULE 13A – SURRENDERS OF ADVANCE CORPORATION TAX

Section 240

[Sch. 13A repealed by FA 1998, s. 31 and Sch. 3, para. 42, s. 165 and Sch. 27, Pt. III(2).]

History – Sch. 13A was repealed by FA 1998, s. 31 and Sch. 3, para. 42, s. 165 and Sch. 27, Pt. III(2), with effect in relation to accounting periods of the surrendering company (as defined in s. 240(1)) beginning on or after 6 April 1999.

SCHEDULE 13B – CHILDREN'S TAX CREDIT

Section 257AA(5)

[Sch. 13B repealed by TCA 2002, s. 60 and Sch. 6.]

History – Sch. 13B repealed by TCA 2002, s. 60 and Sch. 6, with effect from 6 April 2003 (SI 2003/962, reg. 2(3)). Sch. 13B originally inserted by FA 1999, s. 30(2) and Sch. 3 with effect for 2001–02 and subsequent years of assessment.

SCHEDULE 14 – PROVISIONS ANCILLARY TO SECTION 266

Section 266(12)

Prospective amendments – Sch. 14 to be repealed by FA 2012, Sch. 39, para. 28(1) with effect on a date to be appointed.

Part I – Modification of Section 266 in Certain Cases

SPOUSES AND CIVIL PARTNERS

History – In the heading before para. 1 the words "Spouses and civil partners" substituted for the words "Husband and wife" by SI 2005/3229, reg. 101(3), with effect from 5 December 2005.

1(1) In section 266–

(a) references to an individual's spouse include any person who–

(i) was that individual's spouse at the time the insurance or contract was made, or

(ii) became that individual's spouse after the insurance or contract was made,

unless the marriage was dissolved before 6th April 1979, and

(b) references to an individual's civil partner include any person who–

(i) was that individual's civil partner at the time the insurance or contract was made, or

(ii) became that individual's civil partner after the insurance or contract was made.

1(1A) But an individual is entitled to relief by virtue of sub-paragraph (1)(a)(ii) or (b)(ii) only in respect of premiums payable after the date on which the person in question became that individual's spouse or civil partner.

1(2) [Repealed by FA 1988, s. 148 and Sch. 14, Pt. VIII.]

1(3) [Repealed by FA 1988, s. 148 and Sch. 14, Pt. VIII.]

History – Para. 1(1) substituted by SI 2011/1037, art. 6(1), with effect in relation to any premium paid on or after 1 April 2011. In former para. *1(1)* the words "In section 266– (a) references" substituted for the words "The references in section 266" and para. 1(1)(b) inserted by SI 2005/3229, reg. 101(2), with effect from 5 December 2005.

Para. 1(2), (3) repealed by FA 1988, s. 148 and Sch. 14, Pt. VIII with effect for 1990–91 and subsequent years of assessment.

Derivations – FA 1976, Sch. 4, para. 8–10.

Extra-statutory concessions – A31: (applicable to premiums paid before 1 April 2011) life assurance premium relief is available also where one party to a dissolved marriage continues to pay premiums in respect of a policy taken out on the life of the other prior to the marriage.

PREMIUMS PAYABLE TO FRIENDLY SOCIETIES AND INDUSTRIAL ASSURANCE COMPANIES

2(1) This paragraph applies to–

(a) a policy issued in the course of an industrial assurance business; and

(b) a policy issued by a friendly society in the course of tax exempt life or endowment business (as defined in section 466).

2(1A) In sub-paragraph (1)(a) **"industrial assurance business"** means any industrial assurance business within the meaning given by–

(a) section 1(2) of the Industrial Assurance Act 1923, or

(b) Article 3(1) of the Industrial Assurance (Northern Ireland) Order 1979,

which was carried on before 1 December 2001.

2(2) Subject to paragraph 3(2) below, if a policy to which this paragraph applies was issued before the passing of the Finance Act 1976 (29th July 1976), section 266 shall have effect in relation to it as if subsections (2)(b), (3)(a), (b) and (d) were omitted; and if a policy to which this paragraph applies was issued after the passing of that Act, subsection (2)(b) of that section shall have effect in relation to it as if it permitted the insurance to be on the life of the individual's parent or grandparent or, subject to sub-paragraph (3) below, on the life of the individual's child or grandchild.

2(3) Relief may be given in respect of premiums under a policy of insurance on the life of an individual's child or grandchild which was or is issued after the passing of the Finance Act 1976 (29th July 1976), as if subsection (3)(d) of section 266 were omitted, but may be given only if the annual amount of the premiums, together with that of any relevant premiums, does not exceed £52 if the policy was issued in respect of an insurance made before 25th March 1982 or £64 in any other case.

2(4) For the purposes of sub-paragraph (3) above, a relevant premium, in relation to an insurance made at any time on the life of an individual's child or grandchild, is any premium under a policy of insurance on the same life, where the insurance is made at the same time or earlier, whether it is made by the individual or any other person.

2(5) In this paragraph **"child"** includes a step-child and an illegitimate child whose parents have married each other after his birth, and **"grandchild"**, **"parent"** and **"grandparent"** have corresponding meanings.

History – Para. 2(1)(b) amended by F(No. 2)A 1992, s. 56 and Sch. 9, para. 18(2) substituting "friendly society" with effect from 19 February 1993 by virtue of SI 1993/236.

Derivations – Para. 2(1)FA 1976, Sch. 4, para. 11(1) and SI 1979/1576, art. 1, 2.
Para. 2(1A) inserted by ITA 2007, s. 1027 and Sch. 1, para. 232(2) with effect for 2007–08 and subsequent tax years.
Para. 2(2): FA 1976, Sch. 4, para. 11(2).
Para. 2(3): FA 1976, Sch. 4, para. 11(3) and FA 1982, s. 35(2), (4).
Para. 2(4): FA 1976, Sch. 4, para. 11(3).
Para. 2(5): ICTA 1970, s. 10(1) and FA 1976, Sch. 4, para. 11(4).

Cross references – S. 832(1): definition of "industrial assurance business".
Civil Partnership Act 2004, Sch. 21, para. 54 (not reproduced): references to an individual's stepchildren to include references to children of that individual's civil partner; in force from 5 December 2005.

Statements of practice – SP 11/79: Revenue practice in according or denying life assurance premium relief in respect of policies taken out on the lives of children under 12 years of age.

3(1) Where a policy is issued or a contract is made by a friendly society or a policy to which paragraph 2 above applies is issued by an industrial assurance company, section 266(4), (5) and (8) shall apply in relation to premiums payable under the policy or contract subject to the following provisions of this paragraph.

3(2) References to the deductions authorised under section 266(5) shall be construed as including references to any amount retained by or refunded to the person paying the premium under any scheme made by the society or company in accordance with regulations made under this paragraph.

3(3) The appropriate authority may make regulations authorising–

(a) the adoption by friendly societies and industrial assurance companies of any prescribed scheme for securing that in the case of policies or contracts to which the scheme applies amounts equal to 12.5 per cent of the premiums payable are retained by or refunded to the person paying the premiums or that, in the case of such policies or contracts issued or made before 6th April 1979, the amounts expressed as the amounts of the premiums payable are treated as amounts arrived at by deducting 12.5 per cent from the amounts payable and that the amounts of the capital sums assured or guaranteed are treated as correspondingly increased; or

(b) the adoption by any such society or company of any special scheme for that purpose which may, in such circumstances as may be prescribed, be approved by the appropriate authority.

3(4) Increases treated as made in pursuance of regulations under this paragraph shall not be treated as variations of a policy or contract and shall be disregarded for the purposes of paragraph 2(3) above, sections 268(6), 460, 461(1) and 464 of, and paragraph 7 of Schedule 15 to this Act.

3(5) The regulations may include such adaptations and modifications of the enactments relating to friendly societies or industrial assurance companies and such other incidental and supplementary provisions as appear to the appropriate authority necessary or expedient for the purpose of enabling such societies or companies to adopt the schemes authorised by the regulations.

3(6) Subsections (4), (5) and (7) to (11) of section 6 of the Decimal Currency Act 1969 shall, with the necessary modifications, apply in relation to regulations made under this paragraph.

History – Para. 3(1), (3)(a) amended by F(No. 2)A 1992, s. 56 and Sch. 9, para. 18 substituting "friendly society" and "friendly societies" with effect from 19 February 1993 by virtue of SI 1993/236.
In para. 3(3)(a), "12.5 per cent" was substituted by FA 1988, s. 29, with effect from 6 April 1989.
In para. 3(4), references at the end to Stamp Act 1891, s. 100, and the heading "Policy of Life Insurance" in Sch. 1 to that Act, were repealed by FA 1989, s. 187 and Sch. 17, Pt. IX, in consequence of the abolition of stamp duty on life policies and superannuation annuities by FA 1989, s. 173.

Derivations – Para. 3(1): FA 1976, Sch. 4, para. 13(1) and FA 1978, Sch. 3, para. 7(1).
Para. 3(2): FA 1976, Sch. 4, para. 13(2).
Para. 3(3)FA 1976, Sch. 4, para. 13(3) and FA 1980, s. 29(2)(c).
Para. 3(4)FA 1976, Sch. 4, para. 13(4); FA 1978, Sch. 3, para. 7(2) and FA 1987, Sch. 15, para. 9. Para. 3(5), (6): FA 1976, Sch. 4, para. 13(4), (5).

Cross references – S. 268(6): some increases treated as pursuant to new policies.
S. 460: tax exemptions for registered friendly societies on certain life and endowment business.
S. 461(1): tax exemption for registered friendly societies on other business.
Sch. 15, para. 7: provisions relating to industrial assurance policies.

Part II – Supplementary Provisions as to Relief under Section 266

4(1) Where it appears to the Board that the relief (if any) to which a person is entitled under section 266 has been exceeded or might be exceeded unless the premiums payable by him under any policy or contract were paid in full, they may, by notice to that person and to the person to whom the payments are made, exclude the application of subsection (5) of that section in relation to any payments due or made after such date as may be specified in the notice and before such date as may be specified in a further notice to those persons.

4(2) Where the application of section 266(5) is so excluded in relation to any payments, the relief (if any) to which the person by whom the payments are made is entitled under section 266 shall be given to him under paragraph 6 below.

Derivations – FA 1976, Sch. 4, para. 14(1), (2) and FA 1978, Sch. 3, para. 8.

5 Where a person is entitled to relief under section 266 in respect of a payment to which section 595 applies, section 386 of ITEPA 2003 (payments to non-approved retirement benefits schemes) shall not apply but the like relief shall be given to him under paragraph 6 below.

History – In para. 5, reference to ITEPA 2003, s. 386 substituted for reference to ICTA 1988, s. 266 by ITEPA 2003, s. 722 and Sch. 6, para. 119, with effect for the year 2003–04 and subsequent tax years.

Derivations – FA 1976, Sch. 4, para. 14A, as inserted by FA 1978, Sch. 3, para. 9.

6(1) Where in any year of assessment the relief to which a person is entitled under section 266 has not been fully given in accordance with that section and the preceding provisions of this Schedule, he may claim relief for the difference, and relief for the difference shall then be given by a payment made by the Board or by discharge or repayment of tax or partly in one such manner and partly in another; and where relief so given to any person exceeds that to which he is entitled under section 266, he shall be liable to make good the excess and an inspector may make such assessments as may in his judgment be required for recovering the excess.

6(2) The Management Act shall apply to any assessment under this paragraph as if it were an assessment to tax for the year of assessment in which the relief was given.

History – In para. 6(1), the words ", otherwise than in accordance with subsection (7) of that section,", which appeared after the words "section 266", omitted by FA 2009, s. 5 and Sch. 1, para. 5, with effect for the tax year 2010–11 and subsequent tax years.
In para. 6(1), the words "subsection (7)" substituted by ITA 2007, s. 1027 and Sch. 1, para. 232(3) with effect for 2007–08 and subsequent tax years.
In para. 6(2), the following words at the end were omitted and repealed by FA 1996, s. 132 and Sch. 18, para. 11(2) and s. 205 and Sch. 41, Pt. V(8), with effect generally for 1996–97 and subsequent years of assessment subject to the transitional provisions in FA 1996, Sch. 18, para. 17(5), (7):
"and as if–
(a) the assessment were among those specified in sections 55(1) (recovery of tax not postponed) and 86(2) (interest on overdue tax) of that Act; and
(b) the sum charged by the assessment were tax specified in paragraph 3 of the Table in section 86(4) of that Act (reckonable date)".

Derivations – FA 1976, Sch. 4, para. 15.

Cross references – FA 2012, Sch. 39, para. 24: no claim for relief under para. 6 may be made after 5 April 2016.

Extra-statutory concessions – A45: if under a term assurance for less than ten years the original sum assured is reduced to less than half, or the term is extended to cover an additional period (but the total term is still less than ten years) any resulting reduction in the rate of premium does not disqualify the policy.

7(1) The Board may make regulations for carrying into effect section 266(4), (5), (8) and (9) and the preceding provisions of this Schedule (**"the relevant provisions"**).

7(2) Regulations under this paragraph may, without prejudice to the generality of sub-paragraph (1) above, provide–

(a) for the furnishing of such information by persons by whom premiums are payable as may be necessary for determining whether they are entitled to make deductions under section 266(5) and for excluding the operation of that subsection in relation to payments made by persons who fail to comply with the regulations;

(b) for rounding to a multiple of one penny any payment which, after a deduction authorised under section 266(5), is not such a multiple;

(c) for the manner in which claims for the recovery of any sum under section 266(5)(b) may be made;

(d) for the furnishing of such information by persons by or to whom premiums are payable as appears to the Board necessary for deciding such claims and for exercising their powers under paragraph 4 or 6 above; and

(e) for requiring persons to whom premiums are paid to make available for inspection by an officer authorised by the Board such books and other documents in their possession or under their control as may reasonably be required for the purposes of determining whether any information given by those persons for the purposes of the relevant provisions is correct and complete.

7(3) The following provisions of the Management Act, that is to say–

(a) section 29(1)(c) (excessive relief) as it has effect apart from section 29(2) to (10) of that Act;

(b) section 30 (recovery of tax repaid in consequence of fraud or negligence etc.) apart from subsection (1B);

(c) section 86 (interest); and

(d) section 95 (incorrect return or accounts);

shall apply in relation to an amount which is paid to any person by the Board as an amount recoverable by virtue of section 266(5)(b) but to which that person is not entitled as if it were income tax which ought not to have been repaid and, where that amount was claimed by that person, as if it had been repaid as respects a chargeable period as a relief which was not due.

7(4) In the application of section 86 of the Management Act by virtue of sub-paragraph (3) above in relation to sums due and payable by virtue of an assessment made for the whole or part of a year of assessment ("the relevant year of assessment") under section 29(1)(c) or 30 of that Act, as applied by that sub-paragraph, the relevant date–

(a) is 1st January in the relevant year of assessment in a case where the person falling within section 266(5)(b) has made a relevant interim claim; and

(b) in any other case, is the later of the following dates, that is to say–

 (i) 1st January in the relevant year of assessment; or

 (ii) the date of the making of the payment by the Board which gives rise to the assessment.

7(5) In this paragraph–

"financial year", in relation to any person, means a financial year of that person for the purposes of the relevant regulations;

"interim claim" means an interim claim within the meaning of the relevant regulations;

"relevant interim claim" means, in relation to an assessment made for a period coterminous with, or falling wholly within, a person's financial year, an interim claim made for a period falling wholly or partly within that financial year;

"the relevant regulations" means regulations made under sub-paragraph (1) above.

History – In para. 7(1), words "and paragraphs 9 and 10 of Schedule 15" omitted by FA 1995, s. 162 and Sch. 29, Pt. VIII(7)), with effect from 5 May 1996.

Para. 7(3)(a) substituted by FA 1996, s. 132 and Sch. 18, para. 11(3)(a), for the purposes of income tax and capital gains tax, with effect for 1996–97 and subsequent years of assessment, for the purposes of corporation tax from 1 July 1999, the date appointed under FA 1994, s. 199 by virtue of SI 1998/3173 (C. 78), and for partnerships set up and commenced before 6 April 1994, with effect for 1997–98 and subsequent years of assessment.

In para. 7(3)(b), words "apart from subsection (1B)" inserted by FA 1996, s. 132 and Sch. 18, para. 11(3)(b), for the purposes of income tax and capital gains tax with effect for 1996–97 and subsequent years of assessment, for the purposes of corporation tax from 1 July 1999, the date appointed by virtue of FA 1994, s. 199 and SI 1998/SI 3173 (C. 78), but for partnerships set up and commenced before 6 April 1994, with effect for 1997–98 and subsequent years of assessment.

In para. 7(3)(c), reference to "section 86" substituted for "section 88" by FA 1996, s. 132 and Sch. 18, para. 11(3)(c), for the purposes of income tax and capital gains tax generally with effect for 1996–97 and subsequent years of assessment, but for partnerships set up and commenced before 6 April 1994, with effect for 1997–98 and subsequent years of assessment, subject to the transitional provisions concerning certain assessments for earlier years in FA 1996, Sch. 18, para. 17(3) and (4).

In para. 7(3), words following para. (d) substituted by FA 1996, s. 132 and Sch. 18, para. 11(3)(d) but only in relation to any payment if the payment, or the claim on which it is made, was made on or after 29 April 1996.

Para. 7(4) and (5) inserted by FA 1996, s. 132 and Sch. 18, para. 11(4), for the purposes of income tax and capital gains tax generally, with effect for 1996–97 and subsequent years of assessment, but for partnerships set up and commenced before 6 April 1994, with effect for 1997–98 and subsequent years of assessment, subject to the transitional provisions concerning certain assessments for earlier years in FA 1996, Sch. 18, para. 17(3) and (4).

Derivations – Para. 7(1): FA 1976, Sch. 4, para. 16(1).
Para. 7(2): FA 1976, Sch. 4, para. 16(2), as amended by FA 1978, Sch. 3, para. 10.
Para. 7(3): FA 1976, Sch. 4, para. 16(4).

Cross references – TMA 1970, s. 98: penalties for failure to furnish information.

Statutory instruments – SI 1978/1159 was made under FA 1976, Sch. 4, para. 16.

8(1) A policy of life insurance issued in respect of an insurance made on or before 19th March 1968 shall be treated for the purposes of section 266(3)(b) as issued in respect of one made after that date if varied after that date so as to increase the benefits secured or to extend the term of the insurance.

8(2) A variation effected before the end of the year 1968 shall be disregarded for the purposes of sub-paragraph (1) above if its only effect was to bring into conformity with paragraph 2 of Schedule 9 to the Finance Act 1968 (qualifying conditions for endowment policies, and now re-enacted as paragraph 2 of Schedule 15 to this Act) a policy previously conforming therewith except as respects the amount guaranteed on death, and no increase was made in the premiums payable under the policy.

8(3) A policy which was issued in the course of industrial assurance business in respect of an insurance made after 13th March 1984 shall be treated for the purposes of section 266(3)(c) and this paragraph as issued in respect of an insurance made on or before that date if–

(a) the proposal form for the policy was completed on or before that date; and

(b) on or before 31st March 1984 the policy was prepared for issue by the company or society concerned; and

(c) on or before 31st March 1984 and in accordance with the normal business practice of the company or society a permanent record of the preparation of the policy was made in any book or by any other means kept or instituted by the company or society for the purpose.

8(3A) In sub-paragraph (3) **"industrial assurance business"** means any industrial assurance business within the meaning given by–

(a) section 1(2) of the Industrial Assurance Act 1923, or

(b) Article 3(1) of the Industrial Assurance (Northern Ireland) Order 1979,

which was carried on before 1 December 2001.

8(4) Subject to sub-paragraph (8) below, for the purposes of section 266(3)(c) a policy of life insurance which was issued in respect of an insurance made on or before 13th March 1984 shall be treated as issued in respect of an insurance made after that date if the policy is varied after that date so as to increase the benefits secured or to extend the term of the insurance.

8(5) If a policy of life insurance which was issued as mentioned in sub-paragraph (4) above confers on the person to whom it was issued an option to have another policy substituted for it or to have any of its terms changed, then, for the purposes of that sub-paragraph and section 266(3)(c), any change in the terms of the policy which is made in pursuance of the option shall be deemed to be a variation of the policy.

8(6) In any case where–

(a) one policy is replaced by another in such circumstances that the provisions of paragraph 20 of Schedule 15 apply; and

(b) the earlier policy was issued in respect of an insurance made on or before 13th March 1984; and

(c) the later policy confers on the life or lives assured thereby benefits which are substantially equivalent to those which would have been enjoyed by the life or lives assured under the earlier policy, if that policy had continued in force;

then, for the purposes of section 266(3)(c), the insurance in respect of which the later policy is issued shall be deemed to have been made before 13th March 1984; and in this sub-paragraph **"the earlier policy"** and **"the later policy"** have the same meaning as in paragraph 20 of Schedule 15.

8(7) In any case where–

(a) there is a substitution of policies falling within paragraph 25(1) or (3) of Schedule 15; and

(b) the old policy was issued in respect of an insurance made on or before 13th March 1984;

then, for the purposes of section 266(3)(c), the insurance in respect of which the new policy is issued shall be deemed to have been made before 13th March 1984; and in this sub-paragraph **"the old policy"** and **"the new policy"** have the same meaning as in paragraph 17 of Schedule 15.

8(8) Sub-paragraph (4) above does not apply in the case of a variation so as to increase the benefits secured, if the variation is made–

(a) on or after such day as the Board may by order appoint, and

(b) in consideration of a change in the method of payment of premiums from collection by a person collecting premiums from house to house to payment by a different method.

History – Para. 8(3A) inserted by ITA 2007, s. 1027 and Sch. 1, para. 232(4) with effect for 2007–08 and subsequent tax years.
In para. 8(4), the words "Subject to sub-paragraph (8) below," at the beginning were inserted by FA 1996, s. 167(5).
Para. 8(8) was inserted by FA 1996, s. 167(6).

Derivations – Para. 8(1), (2): ICTA 1970, s. 19(5).

Para. 8(3)–(5): FA 1984, s. 72(2)–(4).
Para. 8(6), (7): FA 1984, s. 72(6), (7).

Cross references – S. 832(1): definition of "industrial assurance business".

Notes – SI 2001/3643 (C. 118), art. 2(b): the appointed day for the purposes of para. 8(8)(a) is 1 December 2001.

SCHEDULE 15 – QUALIFYING POLICIES

Section 267

Cross references – FA 1995, Sch. 10, para. 4: operation of Sch. 15 modified in relation to certain increases in premium on certain policies issued by friendly societies. See notes to para. 4, 18.

Extra-statutory concessions – A96: benefits from qualifying life assurance policies may be exempt from income tax if an insurer decides to stop collecting premiums.
B42: where the aggregate cost to the insurer of all "free gifts" offered in connection with an insurance does not exceed £30, no account will be taken of the gifts in assessing whether policies are "qualifying" life insurance policies under Sch. 15.

Other material – HMRC guidance: frequently asked questions on the annual premium limit for qualifying life insurance policies effective from 6 April 2013.

Part A1 – Premium Limit for Qualifying Policies

PREMIUM LIMIT FOR QUALIFYING POLICIES TO APPLY FROM 6 APRIL 2013

History – Pt. A1 inserted by FA 2013, s. 25 and Sch. 9, para. 2, with effect from 17 July 2013 (Royal Assent).

A1(1) Sub-paragraph (2) applies if–

(a) an event falling within sub-paragraph (3) occurs,

(b) apart from sub-paragraph (2), the policy to which the event relates would be a qualifying policy after the event, and

(c) an individual who is a beneficiary under that policy is in breach of the premium limit for qualifying policies.

A1(2) That policy is not to be a qualifying policy after the event.

A1(3) The events falling within this sub-paragraph are–

(a) the issue of a policy in respect of an insurance made on or after 6 April 2013;

(b) the variation of a policy on or after 6 April 2013 where as a result of the variation–

  (i) the period over which premiums are payable under the policy is or could be lengthened, or

  (ii) the total amount of the premiums payable under the policy in any relevant period is or could be increased,

or both;

(c) the assignment on or after 6 April 2013 of any rights, or any share in any rights, under a policy where the assignment falls within paragraph B2(3)(c) to (g) or (5) below;

(d) a deceased beneficiary event on or after 6 April 2013;

(e) the conditions in paragraph 24(3) below being fulfilled for the first time in respect of a new non-resident policy where–

  (i) the conditions are fulfilled for the first time on or after 6 April 2013, and

  (ii) but for the conditions being fulfilled, the policy could not be a qualifying policy because of paragraph 24(2).

A1(4) An event does not fall within sub-paragraph (3) if–

(a) the policy to which the event relates is–

  (i) a protected policy,

  (ii) a restricted relief qualifying policy, or

  (iii) a pure protection policy,

(b) the event is the issue of a policy which is a new policy in relation to an earlier policy where–

  (i) the new policy is issued in substitution for the earlier policy (and not on its maturity), and

  (ii) the life assured under the new policy is different to the life assured under the earlier policy but that is the only difference to what the position would have been had the earlier policy continued to run,

(c) paragraph 20ZA below applies to a policy and the event is the reinstatement or replacement of the policy as mentioned in paragraph 20ZA(4),

(d) the event is the issue or variation of a policy in relation to which paragraph 29 of Schedule 39 to the Finance Act 2012 applies, or

(e) the event is an assignment falling within paragraph B2(3)(e) below where the assignment is a mortgage endowment assignment.

A1(5) In sub-paragraph (3)(b)(ii) **"relevant period"** means any period of 12 months beginning at or after the time of the variation.

A1(6) A variation is to be ignored for the purposes of sub-paragraph (3)(b) if its effect is nullified before the end of the period of 3 months after the day on which the variation occurs.

A1(7) Sub-paragraph (4)(a)(i) does not apply in the case of an event mentioned in sub-paragraph (3)(e).

A1(8) Sub-paragraph (4)(a)(ii) does not apply in the case of–

(a) an event mentioned in sub-paragraph (3)(c) or (d) occurring in relation to a restricted relief qualifying policy ("the assigned policy"),

(b) any subsequent event relating to the assigned policy, or

(c) any event relating to–

  (i) a later policy which is a new policy in relation to the assigned policy, or

  (ii) any policy which is a new policy in relation to the later policy,

and so on.

A1(9) In the case of an event mentioned in sub-paragraph (3)(b), sub-paragraph (4)(a)(iii) applies only if the policy is a pure protection policy both before and after the variation.

A1(10) This paragraph is to be applied after all other provisions of this Schedule relevant to the question of whether a policy is a qualifying policy after an event have been applied.

History – Para. A1 inserted by FA 2013, s. 25 and Sch. 9, para. 2, with effect from 17 July 2013 (Royal Assent).

RESTRICTED RELIEF QUALIFYING POLICIES

A2(1) Sub-paragraph (2) applies if–

(a) an event falling within sub-paragraph (3) occurs,

(b) the policy to which the event relates is a qualifying policy after the event, and

(c) an individual who is a beneficiary under that policy is in breach of the premium limit for qualifying policies.

A2(2) That policy is to be a restricted relief qualifying policy after the event.

A2(3) The events falling within this sub-paragraph are–

(a) a premium limit event in relation to a protected policy on or after 21 March 2012;

(b) the issue of a policy as mentioned in paragraph A4(2)(b) below if, assuming that the substitution of the protected policy were instead a variation of that policy, there would be a premium limit event in relation to that policy;

(c) the assignment on or after 6 April 2013 of any rights, or any share in any rights, under a protected policy where the assignment falls within paragraph B2(3)(c) to (g) or (5) below;

(d) a deceased beneficiary event on or after 6 April 2013 where the policy in question is a protected policy;

(e) the issue of a policy in respect of an insurance made on or after 21 March 2012 but before 6 April 2013 otherwise than as mentioned in paragraph A4(2)(b) below;

(f) the variation of a policy, other than a protected policy, on or after 21 March 2012 but before 6 April 2013 where as a result of the variation–

  (i) the period over which premiums are payable under the policy is or could be lengthened, or

  (ii) the total amount of the premiums payable under the policy in any relevant period is or could be increased,

or both;

(g) the conditions in either sub-paragraph (3) or sub-paragraph (4) of paragraph 24 below being fulfilled for the first time in respect of a new non-resident policy where–

  (i) the conditions are fulfilled for the first time on or after 21 March 2012 but before 6 April 2013, and

  (ii) but for the conditions being fulfilled, the policy could not be a qualifying policy because of sub-paragraph (2) of paragraph 24.

A2(4) An event does not fall within sub-paragraph (3) if–

(a) the policy to which the event relates is a pure protection policy,

(b) the event is the issue of a policy which is a new policy in relation to an earlier policy where–

  (i) the new policy is issued in substitution for the earlier policy (and not on its maturity), and

  (ii) the life assured under the new policy is different to the life assured under the earlier policy but that is the only difference to what the position would have been had the earlier policy continued to run,

(c) paragraph 20ZA below applies to a policy and the event is the reinstatement or replacement of the policy as mentioned in paragraph 20ZA(4),

(d) the event is the issue or variation of a policy in relation to which paragraph 29 of Schedule 39 to the Finance Act 2012 applies, or

(e) the event is an assignment falling within paragraph B2(3)(e) below where the assignment is a mortgage endowment assignment.

A2(5) In sub-paragraph (3)(f)(ii) **"relevant period"** means any period of 12 months beginning at or after the time of the variation.

A2(6) A premium limit event or a variation is to be ignored for the purposes of sub-paragraph (3)(a) or (f) if its effect is nullified before 6 July 2013.

A2(7) In the case of a premium limit event which occurs on or after 6 April 2013, in sub-paragraph (6) the reference to 6 July 2013 is to be read as a reference to the end of the period of 3 months after the day on which the premium limit event occurs.

A2(8) In the case of an event mentioned in sub-paragraph (3)(a) or (f), sub-paragraph (4)(a) applies only if the policy is a pure protection policy both before and after the premium limit event or variation.

A2(9) A **"premium limit event"** occurs in relation to a protected policy if–

(a) the policy is varied or a relevant option is exercised so as to change the terms of the policy, and

(b) as a result of the variation or exercise of the relevant option–

  (i) the period over which premiums are payable under the policy is or could be lengthened, or

  (ii) the total amount of the premiums payable under the policy in any relevant period is or could be increased,

or both.

A2(10) A **"premium limit event"** also occurs in relation to a protected policy if on or after 6 April 2013–

(a) the policy is varied or a relevant option is exercised so as to change the terms of the policy, and

(b) as a result of the variation or exercise of the relevant option–

  (i) the period over which premiums are payable under the policy is or could be shortened, or

  (ii) the total amount of the premiums payable under the policy in any relevant period is or could be decreased,

or both.

A2(11) In sub-paragraphs (9)(b)(ii) and (10)(b)(ii) **"relevant period"** means any period of 12 months beginning at or after the time of the variation or exercise of the relevant option.

A2(12) The variation of, or exercise of a relevant option under, a protected policy is not a premium limit event in relation to the policy if–

(a) the policy secures a capital sum payable either–

  (i) on survival for a specified term, or

  (ii) on earlier death or on earlier death or disability,

(b) the policy is issued and maintained for the sole purpose of ensuring that the borrower under an interest-only mortgage will have sufficient funds to repay the principal lent under the mortgage, and

(c) the policy is varied, or the relevant option is exercised, for that sole purpose.

A2(13) In sub-paragraph (3)(g) references to paragraph 24 below are to that paragraph as it has effect before the appointed date for the purposes of section 55 of the Finance Act 1995.

A2(14) A qualifying policy which is a new policy in relation to an earlier policy is a restricted relief qualifying policy if the earlier policy is a restricted relief qualifying policy.

A2(15) A policy which is a restricted relief qualifying policy remains a restricted relief qualifying policy so long as it is a qualifying policy.

A2(16) Paragraph A1 above is to be ignored in determining for the purposes of sub-paragraph (14) or (15) if a policy is a qualifying policy.
This is subject to paragraph A1(8).

A2(17) For further provision about restricted relief qualifying policies, see sections 463A to 463D of ITTOIA 2005.

History – Para. A2 inserted by FA 2013, s. 25 and Sch. 9, para. 2, with effect from 17 July 2013 (Royal Assent).

THE PREMIUM LIMIT FOR QUALIFYING POLICIES

A3(1) For the purposes of paragraphs A1(1)(c) and A2(1)(c) above an individual is in breach of the premium limit for qualifying policies if the total amount of the premiums payable under relevant policies in any relevant period–

(a) exceeds £3,600, or

(b) could exceed £3,600 as a result of–

(i) the exercise of any one or more relevant options conferred by one or more relevant policies, or

(ii) so far as not covered by sub-paragraph (i), the application of one or more terms of one or more relevant policies relating to increases in premiums.

A3(2) For the purposes of sub-paragraph (1)–

(a) so much of a premium payable under a relevant policy as is charged on the grounds that an exceptional risk of death or disability is involved is to be left out of account in determining the premiums payable under the policy,

(b) so much of the first premium payable under a relevant policy the liability for the payment of which–

(i) is discharged in accordance with paragraph 15(2) below, or

(ii) in the case of a policy in relation to which paragraph 3 below applies, is discharged under a provision of the policy falling within paragraph 3(4)(c),

is to be left out of account in determining the premiums payable under the policy (subject to sub-paragraph (3) below),

(c) in determining the premiums payable under a relevant policy any provision for the waiver of premiums by reason of a person's disability is to be ignored, and

(d) **"relevant period"** means any period of 12 months beginning at or after the time when the event falling within paragraph A1(3) or A2(3) above ("the relevant event") occurs.

A3(3) The maximum amount that may be left out of account under sub-paragraph (2)(b) in the case of a relevant policy is–

$$£3,600 \times N$$

where N is the number of complete years for which ran–

(a) the other policy involved, or

(b) if there is more than one other policy involved, the policy which ran for the most number of complete years.

A3(4) For the purposes of this paragraph the following are "relevant policies"–

(a) the policy to which the relevant event relates, and

(b) any other policy–

(i) which is a qualifying policy, and

(ii) under which the individual is a beneficiary.

A3(5) But neither a protected policy nor a pure protection policy is to be a relevant policy by virtue of sub-paragraph (4)(b).

A3(6) Sub-paragraph (7) applies if this paragraph is to be applied in the case of an individual in consequence of two or more events occurring at the same time (including where one or more of the events falls within paragraph A1(3) above and one or more of the events falls within paragraph A2(3) above).

A3(7) For the purpose of applying this paragraph in the case of the individual in consequence of any of the events, sub-paragraph (4)(a) has effect as if the reference to the policy to which the relevant event relates were a reference to all the policies to which the events, taken together, relate.

A3(8) But sub-paragraph (7) does not apply, and sub-paragraph (9) applies instead, if–

(a) all the policies in question are policies issued by the same issuer, and

(b) each of them has an unique identifier in a series of unique identifiers which the issuer gives to policies issued by it.

A3(9) For the purpose of applying this paragraph in the case of the individual in consequence of any of the events, an event relating to a policy ("policy A") is treated as occurring before an event relating to another policy ("policy B") if, in the issuer's series of unique identifiers, policy A's unique identifier comes before policy B's unique identifier.

History – Para. A3 inserted by FA 2013, s. 25 and Sch. 9, para. 2, with effect from 17 July 2013 (Royal Assent).

PROTECTED POLICIES

A4(1) This paragraph applies for the purposes of this Part of this Schedule.

A4(2) A policy is "protected" if–

(a) it is issued in respect of an insurance made before 21 March 2012, or

(b) it is issued in respect of an insurance made on or after 21 March 2012 where–

(i) it is a new policy in relation to an earlier policy,

(ii) it is issued in substitution for the earlier policy (and not on its maturity), and

(iii) the earlier policy is a protected policy (whether by virtue of paragraph (a) or this paragraph).

A4(3) A policy which is protected ceases to be protected if it becomes a restricted relief qualifying policy.

A4(4) A policy issued as mentioned in sub-paragraph (2)(b) is not protected if–

(a) its issue is an event falling within paragraph A2(3) above, and

(b) after that event it is a restricted relief qualifying policy.

History – Para. A4 inserted by FA 2013, s. 25 and Sch. 9, para. 2, with effect from 17 July 2013 (Royal Assent).

HOW TO DETERMINE IF AN INDIVIDUAL IS A BENEFICIARY UNDER A POLICY

A5(1) This paragraph applies for the purposes of this Part of this Schedule in determining if an individual is a beneficiary under a policy.

A5(2) An individual is a beneficiary under a policy if the individual beneficially owns–

(a) any rights under the policy, or

(b) any share in any rights under the policy.

A5(3) An individual is a beneficiary under a policy if–

(a) any rights under the policy are, or any share in any rights under the policy is, held on non-charitable trusts created by the individual, and

(b) those rights are, or that share is, not beneficially owned by any individual.

A5(4) The following provisions of ITTOIA 2005 apply for the purposes of sub-paragraph (3)(a)–

(a) section 465(6), and

(b) the definition of "non-charitable trust" in section 545(1).

A5(5) An individual is a beneficiary under a policy if–

(a) any rights under the policy are, or any share in any rights under the policy is, held as security for a debt of the individual, and

(b) those rights are, or that share is, not beneficially owned by any individual.

History – Para. A5 inserted by FA 2013, s. 25 and Sch. 9, para. 2, with effect from 17 July 2013 (Royal Assent).

FURTHER DEFINITIONS

A6(1) In this Part of this Schedule–

(a) **"new policy"** has the meaning given in paragraph 17 below,

(b) references to the variation of a policy are to a variation in relation to which paragraph 18 below applies,

(c) **"pure protection policy"** means a policy–

(i) which has no surrender value and is not capable of acquiring a surrender value, or

(ii) under which the benefits payable cannot exceed the amount of the premiums paid except on death or in respect of disability, and

(d) **"relevant option"**, in relation to a policy, means an option conferred by the policy on the person to whom it is issued to have another policy substituted for it or to have any of its terms changed.

A6(2) For the purposes of this Part of this Schedule a **"deceased beneficiary event"** occurs if, in connection with the death of an individual ("D") who was a beneficiary under a policy, an individual ("B") becomes a beneficiary under that policy by reference (wholly or partly) to any rights, or to any share in any rights, by reference to which D was a beneficiary (wholly or partly).
For this purpose, it does not matter if B is already a beneficiary under the policy.

A6(3) For the purposes of this Part of this Schedule an assignment is a **"mortgage endowment assignment"** if–

(a) the policy to which the assignment relates secures a capital sum payable either–

(i) on survival for a specified term, or

(ii) on earlier death or on earlier death or disability,

(b) the policy is issued and maintained for the sole purpose of ensuring that the borrower under an interest-only mortgage will have sufficient funds to repay the principal lent under the mortgage, and

(c) when the assignment occurs, it is intended that the policy will continue to be maintained for that sole purpose.

History – Para. A6 inserted by FA 2013, s. 25 and Sch. 9, para. 2, with effect from 17 July 2013 (Royal Assent).

Part I – Qualifying Conditions

RIGHTS TO BE BENEFICIALLY OWNED BY INDIVIDUALS ONLY

B1(1) Sub-paragraph (2) applies in relation to a policy issued in respect of an insurance made on or after 6 April 2013.

B1(2) In order for the policy to be a qualifying policy, when it is issued all the rights under it must be beneficially owned by (and only by)–

(a) one individual, or

(b) two or more individuals taken together.

(This is the case notwithstanding any other provision of this Schedule.)

B1(3) Sub-paragraph (2) does not apply if the policy is protected.

B1(4) A policy is "protected" if it is a new policy (as defined in paragraph 17 below) in relation to–

(a) a policy issued in respect of an insurance made before 21 March 2012, or

(b) a policy which is protected (whether by virtue of paragraph (a) or this paragraph).

History – Para. B1 inserted by FA 2013, s. 25 and Sch. 9, para. 3, with effect from 17 July 2013 (Royal Assent).

ASSIGNMENTS

B2(1) Sub-paragraph (2) applies if any rights under a qualifying policy are, or any share in any rights under a qualifying policy is, assigned on or after 6 April 2013.

B2(2) The policy is not to be a qualifying policy after the assignment (notwithstanding any other provision of this Schedule).

B2(3) Sub-paragraph (2) does not apply if–

(a) the assignment is from an individual by way of security for a debt of the individual,

(b) the assignment is to an individual on the discharge of a debt of the individual secured by the rights or share,

(c) the assignment is from an individual to the individual's spouse or civil partner,

(d) the assignment is to an individual in pursuance of an order made by a court,

(e) the assignment is to an individual in pursuance of a legally enforceable obligation relating to a divorce or the dissolution of a civil partnership,

(f) the assignment is from an individual and, as a result of the assignment, the rights assigned are, or the share assigned is, held on trusts created by the individual,

(g) the assignment is to an individual and, as a result of the assignment, the rights assigned are, or the share assigned is, no longer held on trusts, or

(h) the assignment–

  (i) is to the personal representatives of a deceased individual, or

  (ii) is to an individual where, as a result of the assignment, a deceased beneficiary event (see paragraph A6(2) above) occurs.

B2(4) Section 465(6) of ITTOIA 2005 applies for the purposes of sub-paragraph (3)(f).

B2(5) The Commissioners for Her Majesty's Revenue and Customs may by regulations provide that sub-paragraph (2) does not apply if prescribed conditions are met in relation to the assignment.
"Prescribed" means prescribed by the regulations.

B2(6) Regulations under sub-paragraph (5) may–

(a) make different provision for different cases or circumstances, and

(b) contain incidental, supplementary, consequential, transitional, transitory or saving provision.

B2(7) See *paragraphs* A1 and A2 above which may apply in consequence of an assignment falling within sub-paragraph (3) or (5).

History – Para. B2 inserted by FA 2013, s. 25 and Sch. 9, para. 3, with effect from 17 July 2013 (Royal Assent).

REQUIRED STATEMENTS

B3(1) Sub-paragraph (2) applies if any of the following events occurs–

(a) the issue of a policy in respect of an insurance made on or after 6 April 2013;

(b) the variation of a policy on or after 6 April 2013 where paragraph 18 below applies in relation to the variation and as a result of the variation–

 (i) the period over which premiums are payable under the policy is or could be lengthened, or

 (ii) the total amount of the premiums payable under the policy in any relevant period is or could be increased,

or both;

(c) a premium limit event in relation to a protected policy on or after 6 April 2013 (see paragraph A2(9) to (12) above);

(d) an event on or after 6 April 2013 which would be a premium limit event in relation to a protected policy but for paragraph A2(12) above;

(e) the assignment on or after 6 April 2013 of any rights, or any share in any rights, under a policy where the assignment falls within paragraph B2(3)(c) to (g) or (5) above;

(f) a deceased beneficiary event (see paragraph A6(2) above) on or after 6 April 2013;

(g) the conditions in paragraph 24(3) below being fulfilled for the first time in respect of a new non-resident policy where–

 (i) the conditions are fulfilled for the first time on or after 6 April 2013, and

 (ii) but for the conditions being fulfilled, the policy could not be a qualifying policy because of paragraph 24(2).

B3(2) Each individual who is a beneficiary under the policy must, before the end of the statement period, make to the issuer of the policy a statement dealing with the prescribed matters.

B3(3) If an individual does not comply with sub-paragraph (2) the policy is not to be a qualifying policy after the event (notwithstanding any other provision of this Schedule).

B3(4) In sub-paragraph (1)(b)(ii) **"relevant period"** means any period of 12 months beginning at or after the time of the variation.

B3(5) Sub-paragraph (2)–

(a) does not apply in the case of an event mentioned in sub-paragraph (1)(a), (e), (f) or (g) if the policy is a pure protection policy, and

(b) does not apply in the case of an event mentioned in sub-paragraph (1)(b), (c) or (d) if the policy is a pure protection policy both before and after the event.

"Pure protection policy" has the meaning given by paragraph A6(1)(c) above.

B3(6) Sub-paragraph (2) does not apply in the case of an event mentioned in sub-paragraph (1)(e) where the assignment falls within paragraph B2(3)(e) above and is a mortgage endowment assignment.

"Mortgage endowment assignment" is to be read in accordance with paragraph A6(3) above.

B3(7) The Commissioners for Her Majesty's Revenue and Customs may by regulations provide that an individual is not required to comply with sub-paragraph (2) if prescribed conditions are met.

"Prescribed" means prescribed by the regulations.

B3(8) Accordingly, if by virtue of regulations under sub-paragraph (7) an individual is not required to comply with sub-paragraph (2), sub-paragraph (3) does not apply because that individual does not comply with sub-paragraph (2).

B3(9) In sub-paragraph (2)–

(a) the reference to an individual who is a beneficiary under the policy is to be read in accordance with paragraph A5 above,

(b) **"the statement period"** means–

 (i) the period of 3 months after the day on which the event occurs, or

 (ii) if the event occurs before the day on which the first regulations under paragraph (c) below come into force, the period of 3 months after that day,

or such longer period as an officer of Revenue and Customs may allow, and

(c) **"prescribed"** means prescribed by regulations made by the Commissioners for Her Majesty's Revenue and Customs.

B3(10) An officer of Revenue and Customs may allow a longer period for the purposes of sub-paragraph (9)(b) only if–

(a) the individual in question has made a request in writing to an officer of Revenue and Customs for a longer period to be allowed, and

(b) such an officer is satisfied–

(i) that there is a reasonable excuse for the required statement not having been made within the period mentioned in sub-paragraph (9)(b)(i) or (ii), and

(ii) that the request under paragraph (a) was made without unreasonable delay after the reasonable excuse ceased.

B3(11) Sub-paragraph (12) applies in relation to a policy if the obligations under the policy of its issuer are at any time the obligations of another person ("the transferee") to whom there has been a transfer of the whole or any part of a business previously carried on by the issuer.

B3(12) In relation to that time, in sub-paragraph (2) the reference to the issuer of the policy is to be read as a reference to the transferee.

B3(13) Regulations under sub-paragraph (7) or (9)(c) may–

(a) make different provision for different cases or circumstances, and

(b) contain incidental, supplementary, consequential, transitional, transitory or saving provision.

History – Para. B3 inserted by FA 2013, s. 25 and Sch. 9, para. 3, with effect from 17 July 2013 (Royal Assent).

Cross references – SI 2013/1820: prescribed matters for the purposes of para. B3(2), exceptions to the requirement to make a statement under para. B3(2), applications for the issue of a qualifying policy or statements made under para. B3(2) not in writing and reporting requirements of relevant persons.

Statutory instruments – SI 2013/1820: partly made under para. B3(2), (7) and (9)(c).

GENERAL RULES APPLICABLE TO WHOLE LIFE AND TERM ASSURANCES

1(1) Subject to the following provisions of this Part of this Schedule, if a policy secures a capital sum which is payable only on death, or one payable either on death or on earlier disability, it is a qualifying policy if–

(a) it satisfies the conditions appropriate to it under sub-paragraphs (2) to (5) below, and

(b) except to the extent permitted by sub-paragraph (7) below, it does not secure any other benefits.

1(2) If the capital sum referred to in sub-paragraph (1) above is payable whenever the event in question happens, or if it happens at any time during the life of a specified person–

(a) the premiums under the policy must be payable at yearly or shorter intervals, and either–

(i) until the happening of the event or, as the case may require, until the happening of the event or the earlier death of the specified person, or

(ii) until the time referred to in sub-paragraph (i) above or the earlier expiry of a specified period ending not earlier than ten years after the making of the insurance; and

(b) the total premiums payable in any period of 12 months must not exceed–

(i) twice the amount of the total premiums payable in any other such period, or

(ii) one-eighth of the total premiums which would be payable if the policy were to continue in force for a period of ten years from the making of the insurance, or, in a case falling within sub-paragraph (ii) of paragraph (a) above, until the end of the period referred to in that sub-paragraph.

1(3) If the capital sum referred to in sub-paragraph (1) above is payable only if the event in question happens before the expiry of a specified term ending more than ten years after the making of the insurance, or only if it happens both before the expiry of such a term and during the life of a specified person–

(a) the premiums under the policy must be payable at yearly or shorter intervals, and either–

(i) until the happening of the event or the earlier expiry of that term or, as the case may require, until the happening of the event or, if earlier, the expiry of the term or the death of the specified person, or

(ii) as in sub-paragraph (i) above, but with the substitution for references to the term of references to a specified shorter period being one ending not earlier than ten years after the making of the insurance or, if sooner, the expiry of three-quarters of that term; and

(b) the total premiums payable in any period of 12 months must not exceed–

(i) twice the amount of the total premiums payable in any other such period, or

(ii) one-eighth of the total premiums which would be payable if the policy were to continue in force for the term referred to in sub-paragraph (i) of paragraph (a) above, or, as the case may require, for the shorter period referred to in sub-paragraph (ii) of that paragraph.

1(4) If the capital sum referred to in sub-paragraph (1) above is payable only if the event in question happens before the expiry of a specified term ending not more than ten years after the making of the insurance, or only if it happens both before the expiry of such a term and during the life of a specified person, the policy must provide that any payment made by reason of its surrender during the period is not to exceed the total premiums previously paid under the policy.

1(5) Except where–

(a) the capital sum referred to in sub-paragraph (1) above is payable only in the circumstances mentioned in sub-paragraph (3) or (4) above; and

(b) the policy does not provide for any payment on the surrender in whole or in part of the rights conferred by it; and

(c) the specified term mentioned in sub-paragraph (3) or, as the case may be, (4) above ends at or before the time when the person whose life is insured attains the age of 75 years;

the capital sum, so far as payable on death, must not be less than 75 per cent of the total premiums that would be payable if the death occurred at the age of 75 years, the age being, if the sum is payable on the death of the first to die of two persons, that of the older of them, if on the death of the survivor of them, that of the younger of them, and in any other case, that of the person on whose death it is payable; and if the policy does not secure a capital sum in the event of death occurring before the age of 16 or some lower age, it must not provide for the payment in that event of an amount exceeding the total premiums previously paid under it.

1(6) In determining for the purposes of sub-paragraph (5) above whether a capital sum is less than 75 per cent of the total premiums, any amount included in the premiums by reason of their being payable otherwise than annually shall be disregarded, and if the policy provides for payment otherwise than annually without providing for the amount of the premiums if they are paid annually, 10 per cent of the premiums payable under the policy shall be treated as so included.

1(7) Notwithstanding sub-paragraph (1)(b) above, if a policy secures a capital sum payable only on death, it may also secure benefits (including benefits of a capital nature) to be provided in the event of a person's disability; and no policy is to be regarded for the purposes of that provision as securing other benefits by reason only of the fact that–

(a) it confers a right to participate in profits, or

(b) it provides for a payment on the surrender in whole or in part of the rights conferred by the policy, or

(c) it gives an option to receive payments by way of annuity, or

(d) it makes provision for the waiver of premiums by reason of a person's disability, or for the effecting of a further insurance or insurances without the production of evidence of insurability.

1(8) In applying sub-paragraph (2) or (3) above to any policy–

(a) no account shall be taken of any provision for the waiver of premiums by reason of a person's disability, and

(b) if the term of the policy runs from a date earlier, but not more than three months earlier, than the making of the insurance, the insurance shall be treated as having been made on that date, and any premium paid in respect of the period before the making of the insurance, or in respect of that period and a subsequent period, as having been payable on that date.

1(9) References in this paragraph to a capital sum payable on any event include references to any capital sum, or series of capital sums, payable by reason of that event but where what is so payable is either an amount consisting of one sum or an amount made up of two or more sums, the 75 per cent mentioned in sub-paragraph (5) above shall be compared with the smaller or smallest amount so payable; and a policy secures a capital sum payable either on death or on disability notwithstanding that the amount payable may vary with the event.

1(10) In relation to any policy issued in respect of an insurance made before 1st April 1976 this paragraph shall have effect–

(a) with the omission of sub-paragraphs (5) and (6) and in sub-paragraph (9) the words "but where what is so payable is either an amount consisting of one sum or an amount made up of two or more sums, the 75 per cent mentioned in sub-paragraph (5) above shall be compared with the smaller or smallest amount so payable"; and

(b) with the substitution, for sub-paragraph (7)(b), of–

"(b) it carries a guaranteed surrender value;".

History – In para. 1(6) words "and if the policy provides for payment otherwise than annually without providing for the amount of the premiums if they are paid annually," substituted for "and if the policy is issued in the course of an industrial assurance business" by FA 1996, s. 167(7), with effect from 1 December 2001 in relation to policies issued on or after that date.

Derivations – Para. 1(1): ICTA 1970, Sch. 1, para. 1(1) and FA 1975, Sch. 2, para. 4(2).
Para. 1(2)–(4): ICTA 1970, Sch. 1, para. 1(2)–(4).
Para. 1(5): ICTA 1970, Sch. 1, para. 1, 4A, as inserted by FA 1975, Sch. 2, para. 4(1).
Para. 1(6): FA 1975, Sch. 2, para. 4(4).

Para. 1(7): ICTA 1970, Sch. 1, para. 1(5) and FA 1975, Sch. 2, para. 4(5).
Para. 1(8): ICTA 1970, Sch. 1, para. 1(6).
Para. 1(9): ICTA 1970, Sch. 1, para. 1(7) and FA 1975, Sch. 2, para. 4(6).
Para. 1(10): FA 1975, Sch. 2, para. 4(1) and ICTA 1970, Sch. 1, para. 1(5), (7).

Other material – IR press release, 15 March 1984 (not reproduced): HMRC view of date when life assurance contract made for the purposes of deciding whether a policy was in force before the abolition of life assurance premium relief.

GENERAL RULES APPLICABLE TO ENDOWMENT ASSURANCES

2(1) Subject to the following provisions of this Part of this Schedule, a policy which secures a capital sum payable either on survival for a specified term or on earlier death, or earlier death or disability, including a policy securing the sum on death only if occurring after the attainment of a specified age not exceeding 16, is a qualifying policy if it satisfies the following conditions–

(a) the term must be one ending not earlier than ten years after the making of the insurance;

(b) premiums must be payable under the policy at yearly or shorter intervals, and–

  (i) until the happening of the event in question; or

  (ii) until the happening of that event, or the earlier expiry of a specified period shorter than the term but also ending not earlier than ten years after the making of the insurance; or

  (iii) if the policy is to lapse on the death of a specified person, until one of those times or the policy's earlier lapse;

(c) the total premiums payable under the policy in any period of 12 months must not exceed–

  (i) twice the amount of the total premiums payable in any other such period, or

  (ii) one-eighth of the total premiums which would be payable if the policy were to run for the specified term;

(d) the policy–

  (i) must guarantee that the capital sum payable on death, or on death occurring after the attainment of a specified age not exceeding 16, will, whenever that event may happen, be equal to 75 per cent at least of the total premiums which would be payable if the policy were to run for that term, disregarding any amounts included in those premiums by reason of their being payable otherwise than annually, except that if, at the beginning of that term, the age of the person concerned exceeds 55 years, the capital sum so guaranteed may, for each year of the excess, be less by 2 per cent of that total than 75 per cent thereof, the person concerned being, if the capital sum is payable on the death of the first to die of two persons, the older of them, if on the death of the survivor of them, the younger of them and in any other case the person on whose death it is payable; and

  (ii) if it is a policy which does not secure a capital sum in the event of death before the attainment of a specified age not exceeding 16, must not provide for the payment in that event of an amount exceeding the total premiums previously paid thereunder; and

(e) the policy must not secure the provision (except by surrender in whole or in part of the rights conferred by the policy) at any time before the happening of the event in question of any benefit of a capital nature other than a payment falling within paragraph (d)(ii) above, or benefits attributable to a right to participate in profits or arising by reason of a person's disability.

2(2) For the purposes of sub-paragraph (1)(d)(i) above, 10 per cent of the premiums payable under any policy that provides for the payment of premiums otherwise than annually without providing for the amount of the premiums if they are paid annually, shall be treated as attributable to the fact that they are not paid annually.

2(3) Sub-paragraphs (8) and (9) of paragraph 1 above shall, with any necessary modifications, have effect for the purposes of this paragraph as they have effect for the purposes of that paragraph.

2(4) In relation to any policy issued in respect of an insurance made before 1st April 1976 this paragraph shall have effect with the omission in sub-paragraph (1)(d)(i) of the words from "except that if" to the end, and in sub-paragraph (1)(e) of the words "in whole or in part of the rights conferred by the policy".

History – In para. 2(2) words "that provides for the payment of premiums otherwise than annually without providing for the amount of the premiums if they are paid annually," substituted for "issued in the course of industrial assurance business" by FA 1996, s. 167(7), with effect from 1 December 2001 in relation to policies issued on or after that date.

Derivations – Para. 2(1): ICTA 1970, Sch. 1, para. 2(1) and FA 1975, Sch. 2, para. 4(7), (8).
Para. 2(2), (3): ICTA 1970, Sch. 1, para. 2(2), (3).
Para. 2(4): FA 1975, Sch. 2, para. 4(7), (8) and ICTA 1970, Sch. 1, para. 2(1).

Cross references – S. 832(1): *definition of* "industrial assurance business".

SPECIAL TYPES OF POLICY

(i) Friendly Society policies

3(1) Paragraphs 1 and 2 above do not apply to a policy issued by a friendly society in the course of exempt BLAGAB or eligible PHI business in respect of an insurance made or varied on or after 19th March 1985, but such a policy shall not be a qualifying policy unless–

(a) in the case of a policy for the assurance of a gross sum or annuity, the conditions in sub-paragraph (2) are fulfilled with respect to it; and

(b) in the case of a policy for the assurance of a gross sum, the conditions in sub-paragraphs (5) to (11) below are fulfilled with respect to it;

(c) [Repealed by FA 1991, s. 50 and Sch. 9, para. 4, s. 123 and Sch. 19, Pt. V.]

3(2) The conditions referred to in sub-paragraph (1) above are as follows–

(a) subject to sub-paragraph (3) below, the period (the **"term"** of the policy) between–

(i) the making of the insurance or, where the contract provides for the term to begin on a date not more than three months earlier than the making of the insurance, that date, and

(ii) the time when the gross sum assured is payable (or, as the case may be, when the first instalment of the annuity is payable),

shall be not less than ten years, and must not, on any contingency other than the death, or retirement on grounds of ill health, of the person liable to pay the premiums or whose life is insured, become less than ten years;

(b) subject to sub-paragraph (4) below, the premiums payable under the policy shall be premiums of equal or rateable amounts payable at yearly or shorter intervals over the whole term of the policy of assurance, or over the whole term of the policy of assurance apart from any period after the person liable to pay the premiums or whose life is insured attains a specified age, being an age which he will attain at a time not less than ten years after the beginning of the term of the policy of assurance; and

(c) [Repealed by FA 1995, s. 54 and Sch. 10, para. 3, s. 162 and Sch. 29, Pt. VIII(6).]

3(3) Notwithstanding sub-paragraph (2)(a) above, the policy–

(a) may provide for a payment to a person of an age not exceeding 18 years at any time not less than five years from the beginning of the term of the policy if the premium or premiums payable in any period of 12 months in the term of the policy do not exceed £13;

(b) may provide for a payment at any time not less than five years from the beginning of the term of the policy, if it is one of a series of payments falling due at intervals of not less than five years, and the amount of any payment, other than the final payment, does not exceed four-fifths of the premiums paid in the interval before its payment.

For the purposes of paragraph (a) above, if the term begins on a date earlier than the making of the insurance, any premium paid in respect of a period before the making of the insurance, or in respect of that period and a subsequent period, shall be treated as having been payable on that date.

3(4) Notwithstanding sub-paragraph (2)(b) above, the policy–

(a) may allow a payment at any time after the expiration of one-half of the term of the policy of assurance, or of ten years from the beginning of the term, whichever is the earlier, being a payment in commutation of the liability to pay premiums falling due after that time;

(b) may allow the person liable to pay the premiums to commute any liability for premiums where he ceases to reside in the United Kingdom or gives satisfactory proof of intention to emigrate;

(c) may allow any liability for premiums to be discharged in consideration of surrendering a sum which has become payable on the maturity of any other policy of assurance issued by the same friendly society (or any predecessor of it) to the person liable to pay the premiums, or to his parent, where that other policy of assurance is issued as part of the friendly society's exempt BLAGAB or eligible PHI business; and

(d) may make provision for the waiver of premiums by reason of a person's disability.

3(4A) For the purposes of sub-paragraphs (2) and (4) above–

(a) a friendly society formed on the amalgamation of two or more friendly societies is the successor of each of those societies (and each of those societies was a predecessor of the society so formed), and

(b) an incorporated friendly society that was a registered friendly society before its incorporation is the successor of the registered friendly society (and the registered friendly society was the predecessor of the incorporated friendly society).

ICTA 1988

3(5) Where the policy secures a capital sum which is payable only on death or only on death occurring after the attainment of a specified age not exceeding 16, that capital sum must be not less than 75 per cent of the total premiums which would be payable if the death of the relevant beneficiary occurred at the age of 75.

3(6) Where the policy secures a capital sum which is payable only on survival for a specified term, that capital sum must be not less than 75 per cent of the total premiums which would be payable if the policy were to run for that term.

3(7) Where the policy secures a capital sum which is payable on survival for a specified term or on earlier death, or on earlier death or disability (including a policy securing the sum on death only if occurring after the attainment of a specified age not exceeding 16), the capital sum payable on death, whenever that event occurs, must be not less than 75 per cent of the total premiums which would be payable if the policy were to run for that term, except that if, at the beginning of that term, the age of the relevant beneficiary exceeds 55, that capital sum may, for each year of the excess, be less by 2 per cent of that total than 75 per cent thereof.

3(8) For the purposes of sub-paragraphs (5) to (7) above–

(a) **"the relevant beneficiary"** means–

(i) if the capital sum concerned is payable on the death of the first to die of two persons, the older of them;

(ii) if that capital sum is payable on the death of the survivor of two persons, the younger of them; and

(iii) in any other case, the person on whose death that capital sum is payable; and

(b) in determining the total premiums payable in any circumstances–

(i) where those premiums are payable otherwise than annually, and the policy is issued by a society other than an old society, there shall be disregarded an amount equal to 10 per cent of those premiums;

(ii) where the policy is issued by an old society, there shall be disregarded an amount equal to £10 for each year for which account is taken of those premiums or, where those premiums are payable otherwise than annually, an amount equal to 10 per cent of those premiums if that is greater.

(iii) [Omitted by FA 2003, s. 172(3) and repealed by FA 2003, Sch. 43, Pt. 3(13).]

(c) [Omitted by FA 2003, s. 172(3)] and repealed by FA 2003, Sch. 43, Pt. 3(13).]

3(9) If the policy does not secure a capital sum in the event of death occurring before the age of 16 or some lower age, it must not provide for the payment in that event of an amount exceeding the total premiums previously paid under it.

3(10) References in this paragraph to a capital sum payable on any event include references to a capital sum or series of capital sums payable by reason of that event, but where what is so payable is either an amount consisting of one sum or an amount made up of two or more sums, any reference in sub-paragraphs (5) to (7) above to 75 per cent of the total premiums payable in any circumstances shall be compared with the smaller or smallest amount so payable; and for the purposes of those sub-paragraphs a policy secures a capital sum payable either on death or on disability notwithstanding that the amount may vary with the event.

3(11) For the purposes of sub-paragraphs (5) to (7) and (10) above, in the case of a policy which provides for any such payments as are referred to in sub-paragraph (3) above (**"interim payments"**), the amount of the capital sum which is payable on any event shall be taken to be increased–

(a) in the case of a policy which secures such a capital sum as is referred to in sub-paragraph (5) above, by the total of the interim payments which would be payable if the death of the relevant beneficiary (within the meaning of that sub-paragraph) occurred at the age of 75; and

(b) in the case of a policy which secures such a capital sum as is referred to in sub-paragraph (6) or (7) above, by the total of the interim payments which would be payable if the policy were to run for the specified term referred to in that sub-paragraph.

History – In para. 3(1), the words "exempt BLAGAB or eligible PHI business" substituted for "tax exempt life or endowment business" by FA 2012, s. 176 and Sch. 18, para. 13(2)(a) with effect in relation to accounting periods of companies beginning on or after 1 January 2013, subject to transitional provisions in FA 2012, Sch. 19. For accounting periods straddling 1 January 2013, FA 2012, s. 179 provides for a deemed cessation on 31 December 2012.

In para. 3(1) the words "friendly society" substituted by F(No. 2)A 1992, s. 56 and Sch. 9, para. 19(2) with effect from 19 February 1993 *by virtue of SI 1993/236.*

Para. 3(1)(c) repealed by FA 1991, s. 50 and Sch. 9, para. 4, s. 123 and Sch. 19, Pt. V in relation to policies issued in pursuance of contracts made on or after 25 July 1991.

Para. 3(2)(c) repealed by FA 1995, s. 54 and Sch. 10, para. 3, s. 162 and Sch. 29, Pt. VIII(6) with effect from 1 May 1995.

In former para. 3(2)(c) the words "(or any successor of it)" and in para. 3(4)(c) the words "(or any predecessor of it)" and para. 3(4A) inserted by F(No. 2)A 1992, s. 56 and Sch. 9, para. 19(3), (4), (5) with effect from 19 February 1993 by virtue of SI 1993/236.
In para. 3(4)(c), the words "exempt BLAGAB or eligible PHI business" substituted for "tax exempt life or endowment business" by FA 2012, s. 176 and Sch. 18, para. 13(2)(a) with effect in relation to accounting periods of companies beginning on or after 1 January 2013, subject to transitional provisions in FA 2012, Sch. 19. For accounting periods straddling 1 January 2013, FA 2012, s. 179 provides for a deemed cessation on 31 December 2012.
In para. 3(8)(b)(i), the words "a society other than an old society" substituted for "a new society" by FA 2012, s 176 and Sch. 18, para. 13(2)(b) with effect in relation to accounting periods of companies beginning on or after 1 January 2013, subject to transitional provisions in FA 2012, Sch. 19. For accounting periods straddling 1 January 2013, FA 2012, s. 179 provides for a deemed cessation on 31 December 2012.
In para. 3(8)(b)(ii), the words "an old society" substituted for "a society other than a new society" by FA 2012, s. 176 and Sch. 18, para. 13(2)(c)with effect in relation to accounting periods of companies beginning on or after 1 January 2013, subject to transitional provisions in FA 2012, Sch. 19. For accounting periods straddling 1 January 2013, FA 2012, s. 179 provides for a deemed cessation on 31 December 2012.
In para. 3(8)(b)(ii), the words "or, where those premiums … if that is greater" were inserted by FA 1990, s. 49(5).
Para. 3(8)(b)(iii) and (8)(c) omitted by FA 2003, s. 172(3) and repealed by FA 2003, Sch. 43, Pt. 3(13) (including the word "and" before the omitted text): these omissions and repeals being deemed always to have had effect except that they are to be disregarded to the extent that they would prevent a policy from being a qualifying policy at any time before 9 April 2003. The omissions and repeals followed on amendments to para. 12 and the text omitted was as follows:

"(b)(iii) so much of any premium as is charged on the ground that an exceptional risk of death is involved shall be disregarded; and (c) in determining the capital sum payable on any event, there shall be disregarded any provision of the policy under which, on the ground referred to in paragraph (b)(iii) above, any sum may become chargeable as a debt against that capital sum."

Derivations – Para. 3(1): ICTA 1970, Sch. 1, para. 3(1), as substituted by FA 1985, Sch. 10, Pt. I.
Para. 3(2): ICTA 1970, s. 334(2), 337(5)(a); SI 1979/1576, art. 1(2), 2(1)(a) and FA 1985, s. 41(6)(b).
Para. 3(3): ICTA 1970, s. 334(3) and FA 1985, s. 41(6)(c).
Para. 3(4): ICTA 1970, s. 334(4) and FA 1985, s. 41(6)(d).
Para. 3(5)–(11): ICTA 1970, Sch. 1, para. 3(2)–(8), as substituted by FA 1985, Sch. 10, Pt. I.

Cross references – S. 465: a friendly society other than a "new society" may be treated nevertheless as a new society.
S. 466: provisions as to tax exempt life and endowment business.
S. 466(2): definition of "new society".

4(1) The provisions of this paragraph have effect notwithstanding anything in paragraph 3 above.

4(2) In determining whether a policy–

(a) which affords provision for sickness or other infirmity (whether bodily or mental), and

(b) which also affords assurance for a gross sum independent of sickness or other infirmity, and

(c) under which not less than 60 per cent of the amount of the premiums is attributable to the provision referred to in paragraph (a) above,

is a qualifying policy, the conditions referred to in paragraph 3(1)(b) above shall be deemed to be fulfilled with respect to it.

4(3) A policy shall cease to be a qualifying policy–

(a) if it falls within sub-paragraph (1) of paragraph 3 above and there is such a variation of its terms that any of the conditions referred to in that sub-paragraph ceases to be fulfilled; or

(b) if–

(i) it was effected in the course of the business of effecting or carrying out contracts of insurance which fall within paragraph 1 of Part I or paragraph VI of Part II of Schedule 1 to the Financial Services and Markets Act 2000 (Regulated Activities) Order 2001,

(ii) it was issued by a society other than an old society, and

(iii) the rights conferred by it are surrendered in whole or in part.

History – In para. 4(3)(b)(ii), the words "a society other than an old society" substituted for "a new society" by FA 2012, s. 176 and Sch. 18, para. 13(3) with effect in relation to accounting periods of companies beginning on or after 1 January 2013, subject to transitional provisions in FA 2012, Sch. 19. For accounting periods straddling 1 January 2013, FA 2012, s. 179 provides for a deemed cessation on 31 December 2012.
In para. 4(3)(b)(i), words from "the business of effecting" to "Order 2001" substituted by SI 2001/3629, art. 47(2), with effect from 1 December 2001.
Para. 4(3)(b)(i) substituted by F(No. 2)A 1992, s. 56 and Sch. 9, para. 19(6) with effect from 19 February 1993 by virtue of SI 1993/236.

Derivations – ICTA 1970, Sch. 1, para. 3A, as inserted by FA 1985, Sch. 10, Pt. I.

Cross references – FA 1991, Sch. 9, para. 5: para. 4 modified by the omission of para. 4(3)(a) in its application to certain policies issued by friendly societies between 31 August 1987 and 25 July 1991 which are varied between 25 July 1991 and 31 July 1992, but not so as to breach the limits in s. 464.
FA 1995, Sch. 10, para. 4(2): para. 4 modified by the omission of para. 4(3)(a) in relation to certain policies issued by friendly societies between 31 August 1987 and 1 May 1995 which are varied between 1 May 1995 and 31 March 1996, but not so as to breach the limits in s. 464.

5 [Omitted by FA 2012, s. 176 and Sch. 18, para. 13(4).]

Derivations – ICTA 1970, s. 337(1)(b), as substituted by FA 1985, s. 41(7)(a).

6(1) A policy which was issued by any registered friendly society, or branch of such a society, in the course of exempt BLAGAB or eligible PHI business in respect of insurances made before 19th March 1985 and which has not been varied on or after that date is a qualifying policy notwithstanding that it does not comply with the conditions specified in paragraph 1 or 2 above.

6(2) Notwithstanding paragraphs 3 to 5 or sub-paragraph (1) above, if, on or after 19th March 1985, a person becomes in breach of the limits in section 160 of the Finance Act 2012, the policy effected by that contract which causes those limits to be exceeded shall not be a qualifying policy; and in any case where–

(a) the limits in that section are exceeded as a result of the aggregation of the sums assured or premiums payable under two or more contracts, and

(b) at a time immediately before one of those contracts was entered into (but not immediately after it was entered into) the sums assured by or, as the case may be, the premiums payable under the contract or contracts which were then in existence did not exceed the limits in that section,

only those policies effected by contracts made after that time shall be treated as causing the limits to be exceeded.

History – In para. 6(1), the words "(as defined in section 466)" omitted after "registered friendly society" and before "in respect of insurances" by FA 2012, s. 176 and Sch. 18, para. 13(5)(a)(i) with effect in relation to accounting periods of companies beginning on or after 1 January 2013, subject to transitional provisions in FA 2012, Sch. 19. For accounting periods straddling 1 January 2013, FA 2012, s. 179 provides for a deemed cessation on 31 December 2012.
In para. 6(1), the words "exempt BLAGAB or eligible PHI business" substituted for "tax exempt life or endowment business" by FA 2012, s. 176 and Sch. 18, para. 13(5)(a)(ii) with effect in relation to accounting periods of companies beginning on or after 1 January 2013, subject to transitional provisions in FA 2012, Sch. 19. For accounting periods straddling 1 January 2013, FA 2012, s. 179 provides for a deemed cessation on 31 December 2012.
In para. 6(1) the words "any registered friendly society (as defined in section 466)" and "such a society" substituted by F(No. 2)A 1992, s. 56 and Sch. 9, para. 19(7) with effect from 19 February 1993 by virtue of SI 1993/236.
In para. 6(2), the words "section 160 of the Finance Act 2012" substituted for "section 464" by FA 2012, s. 176 and Sch. 18, para. 13(5)(b) with effect in relation to accounting periods of companies beginning on or after 1 January 2013, subject to transitional provisions in FA 2012, Sch. 19. For accounting periods straddling 1 January 2013, FA 2012, s. 179 provides for a deemed cessation on 31 December 2012.

Derivations – Para. 6(1): ICTA 1970, Sch. 1, para. 3(1) and FA 1985, s. 41(4).
Para. 6(2): Friendly Societies Act 1974, s. 64(2B); FA 1985, s. 41(1) and FA 1987, s. 30(6).

6A Any expression–

(a) which is used in any provision made by any of paragraphs 3 to 6, and

(b) which is used in Part 3 of the Finance Act 2012, has the same meaning in that provision as it has in that Part.

History – Para. 6A inserted by FA 2012, s. 176 and Sch. 18, para. 13(6) with effect in relation to accounting periods of companies beginning on or after 1 January 2013, subject to transitional provisions in FA 2012, Sch. 19. For accounting periods straddling 1 January 2013, FA 2012, s. 179 provides for a deemed cessation on 31 December 2012.

(ii) Industrial assurance policies

7(1) A policy issued in the course of an industrial assurance business, and not constituting a qualifying policy by virtue of paragraph 1 or 2 above, is nevertheless a qualifying policy if–

(a) the sums guaranteed by the policy, together with those guaranteed at the time the assurance is made by all other policies issued in the course of such a business to the same person and not constituting qualifying policies apart from this paragraph, do not exceed £1,000;

(b) it satisfies the conditions with respect to premiums specified in paragraph 1(2) above;

(c) except by reason of death or surrender, no capital sum other than one falling within paragraph (d) below can become payable under the policy earlier than ten years after the making of the assurance; and

(d) where the policy provides for the making of a series of payments during its term–

 (i) the first such payment is due not earlier than five years after the making of the assurance, and the others, except the final payment, at intervals of not less than five years, and

 (ii) the amount of any payment, other than the final payment, does not exceed four-fifths of the premiums paid in the interval before its payment; or

(e) the policy was issued before 6th April 1976, or was issued before 6th April 1979 and is in substantially the same form as policies so issued before 6th April 1976.

7(2) For the purposes of this paragraph, the sums guaranteed by a policy do not include any bonuses, or in the case of a policy providing for a series of payments during its term, any of those payments except the first, or any sum payable on death during the term by reference to one or more of those payments except so far as that sum is referable to the first such payment.

Derivations – Para. 7(1): ICTA 1970, Sch. 1, para. 4(1) and FA 1976, Sch. 4, para. 1, 12.
Para. 7(2): FA 1970, Sch. 1, para. 4(2).

Cross references – S. 832(1): definition of "industrial assurance business".
Sch. 14, para. 3(4): increases in premiums of industrial assurance policies payable to friendly societies to be disregarded for the purposes of para. 7.

8 Where a policy issued in respect of an insurance made after 1st April 1976 in the course of an industrial assurance business is not a qualifying policy by virtue of paragraph 1 or 2 above but is a policy with respect to which the conditions in paragraph 7(1)(b) and (c) above are satisfied, it shall be a qualifying policy whether or not the condition in paragraph 7(1)(a) above is satisfied with respect to it; but where that condition is not satisfied, relief under section 266 in respect of premiums paid under the policy shall be given only on such amount (if any) as would have been the amount of those premiums had that condition been satisfied.

Prospective amendments – In para. 8, the words from "but" on its second occurrence to the end to be repealed by FA 2012, Sch. 39, para. 28(1) with effect on a date to be appointed.

Derivations – FA 1975, Sch. 2, para. 7(1) and FA 1976, Sch. 4, para. 19(4).

Cross references – S. 832(1): definition of "industrial assurance business".

8A(1) Paragraphs 7 and 8 above shall have effect in relation to any policy issued on or after the appointed day as if the references to the issue of a policy in the course of an industrial assurance business were references to the issue of a policy by any company in a case in which–

(a) the company, before that day and in the course of such a business, issued any policy which was a qualifying policy by virtue of either of those paragraphs; and

(b) the policies which on 28th November 1995 were being offered by the company as available to be issued included policies of the same description as the policy issued on or after the appointed day.

8A(2) In this paragraph **"the appointed day"** means such day as the Board may by order appoint.

History – Para. 8A was inserted by FA 1996, s. 167(8).

Notes – SI 2001/3643 (C. 118), art. 2(c): the appointed day for the purposes of para. 8A(2) is 1 December 2001.

(iii) Family income policies and mortgage protection policies

9(1) The following provisions apply to any policy which is not a qualifying policy apart from those provisions, and the benefits secured by which consist of or include the payment on or after a person's death of–

(a) one capital sum which does not vary according to the date of death, plus a series of capital sums payable if the death occurs during a specified period, or

(b) a capital sum, the amount of which is less if the death occurs in a later part of a specified period than if it occurs in an earlier part of that period.

9(2) A policy falling within sub-paragraph (1)(a) above is a qualifying policy if–

(a) it would be one if it did not secure the series of capital sums there referred to, and the premiums payable under the policy were such as would be chargeable if that were in fact the case, and

(b) it would also be one if it secured only that series of sums, and the premiums thereunder were the balance of those actually so payable.

9(3) A policy falling within sub-paragraph (1)(b) above is a qualifying policy if–

(a) it would be one if the amount of the capital sum there referred to were equal throughout the period to its smallest amount, and the premiums payable under the policy were such as would be chargeable if that were in fact the case, and

(b) it would also be one if it secured only that capital sum so far as it from time to time exceeds its smallest amount, and the premiums payable thereunder were the balance of those actually so payable.

Derivations – ICTA 1970, Sch. 1, para. 5.

OTHER SPECIAL PROVISIONS

(i) Short-term assurances

10 A policy which secures a capital sum payable only on death or payable either on death or on earlier disability shall not be a qualifying policy if the capital sum is payable only if the event in question happens before the expiry of a specified term ending less than one year after the making of the insurance.

Derivations – FA 1976, Sch. 4, para. 2.

(ii) Personal accident insurance

11(1) A policy which evidences a contract of insurance to which sub-paragraph (3) below applies shall not be a qualifying policy unless it also evidences–

(a) a contract of insurance on human life; or

(b) a contract to pay annuities on human life.

11(2) A policy which evidences a contract of insurance to which sub-paragraph (4) below applies shall not be a qualifying policy unless it also evidences a contract falling within section 83(2)(a) of the Insurance Companies Act 1974.

11(3) This sub-paragraph applies to contracts of insurance issued in respect of insurances made on or after 25th March 1982 against risks of persons dying as a result of an accident or an accident of a specified class, not being contracts which–

(a) are expressed to be in effect for a period of not less than five years or without limit of time; and

ICTA 1988

(b) either are not expressed to be terminable by the insurer before the expiration of five years from their taking effect or are expressed to be so terminable before the expiration of that period only in special circumstances therein mentioned.

11(4) This sub-paragraph applies to contracts of insurance issued in respect of insurances made before 25th March 1982 against risks of persons dying as a result of an accident or an accident of a specified class, not being contracts falling within section 83(2)(b) of the Insurance Companies Act 1974.

History – In para. 11(1), words "a contract falling" to the end substituted by SI 2001/3629, art. 47(3), with effect from 1 December 2001.

Derivations – Para. 11(1): FA 1976, Sch. 4, para. 2A(1) (as inserted by FA 1978, Sch. 3, para. 4); Insurance Companies Act 1982, Sch. 5, para. 17 and FA 1982, s. 35(1)(a).
Para. 11(2): FA 1976, Sch. 4, para. 2A(1), as inserted by FA 1978, Sch. 3, para. 4.
Para. 11(3): FA 1976, Sch. 4, para. 2A(2) (as inserted by FA 1978, Sch. 3, para. 4) and FA 1982, s. 35(1)(b).
Para. 11(4): FA 1976, Sch. 4, para. 2A(2), as inserted by FA 1978, Sch. 3, para. 4.

(iii) Exceptional risk of death or disability

12 For the purpose of determining whether any policy is a qualifying policy, there shall be disregarded–

(a) so much of any premium thereunder as is charged on the grounds that an exceptional risk of death or disability is involved; and

(b) any provision under which, on those grounds, any sum may become chargeable as a debt against the capital sum guaranteed by the policy on death or disability.

History – In para. 12, the words "or disability" inserted (twice) and, in the heading, the words "risk of death or disability" substituted for "mortality risk" by FA 2003, s. 172(1) and (2): these amendments being deemed always to have had effect except that they are to be disregarded to the extent that they would prevent a policy from being a qualifying policy at any time before 9 April 2003.

Derivations – ICTA 1970, Sch. 1, para. 6.

(iv) Connected policies

13 Subject to paragraph 14 below, where the terms of any policy provide that it is to continue in force only so long as another policy does so, neither policy is a qualifying policy unless, if they had constituted together a single policy issued in respect of an insurance made at the time of the insurance in respect of which the first-mentioned policy was issued, that single policy would have been a qualifying policy.

Derivations – ICTA 1970, Sch. 1, para. 7.

14(1) A policy shall not be a qualifying policy if the policy is connected with another policy and the terms of either policy provide benefits which are greater than would reasonably be expected if any policy connected with it were disregarded.

14(2) For the purposes of this paragraph a policy is connected with another policy if they are at any time simultaneously in force and either of them is issued with reference to the other, or with a view to enabling the other to be issued on particular terms or facilitating its being issued on those terms.

14(3) In this paragraph **"policy"** means a policy evidencing a contract of long-term insurance, and includes any such policy issued outside the United Kingdom.

14(3A) In sub-paragraph (3) **"contract of long-term insurance"** means a contract which falls within Part II of Schedule 1 to the Financial Services and Markets Act 2000 (Regulated Activities) Order 2001.

14(4) Where any person issues a policy–

(a) which by virtue of this paragraph is not a qualifying policy, or

(b) the issue of which causes another policy to cease by virtue of this paragraph to be a qualifying policy,

he shall within three months of issuing the policy give notice of that fact to the Board.

14(5) [Omitted by SI 2009/2035, art. 2 and Sch., para. 24.]

14(6) This paragraph shall apply to policies issued in respect of insurances made before 23rd August 1983 in accordance with sub-paragraphs (7) and (8) below.

14(7) Where–

(a) a policy is issued in respect of an insurance made before 23rd August 1983, and

(b) a policy is issued in respect of an insurance made on or after that date which is connected with it within the meaning of this paragraph,

sub-paragraphs (1) to (6) above shall apply to the policy issued in respect of an insurance made before that date.

14(8) Sub-paragraphs (1) to (7) above shall apply to policies issued in respect of insurances made before 23rd August 1983 (other than policies which, disregarding this paragraph, fall within sub-paragraph (7)) with the substitution–

(a) *in sub-paragraph (1)* for the words "and the terms of either policy" of the words "the terms of which";

(b) in sub-paragraph (3) for the words from "long term business" to "1982" of the words "ordinary long-term insurance business within the meaning of section 83(2) of the Insurance Companies

Act 1974 (as enacted) or, in relation to a policy made after 25th March 1982, section 96(1) of the Insurance Companies Act 1982"; and

(c) in sub-paragraphs (6) and (7) for the words "23rd August 1983" of the words "26th March 1980".

14(9) In any case where payments made–

(a) after 22nd August 1983, and

(b) by way of premium or other consideration in respect of a policy issued in respect of an insurance made before that date,

exceed £5 in any period of 12 months, the policy shall be treated for the purposes of this paragraph as if it were issued in respect of an insurance made after 22nd August 1983; but nothing in this paragraph shall apply with respect to any premium paid in respect of it before that date.

14(10) Sub-paragraphs (8) and (9) above do not apply in relation to policies issued in the course of industrial assurance business.

History – Words in para. 14(3) "evidencing a contract of long-term insurance" substituted by SI 2001/3629, art. 47(4), and para. 14(3A) inserted by SI 2001/3629, art. 14(5), with effect from 1 December 2001.
Para. 14(5) omitted by SI 2009/2035, art. 2 and Sch., para. 24, with effect from 13 August 2009.

Derivations – Para. 14(1): FA 1980, s. 30(1) and FA 1984, s. 74(1).
Para. 14(2): FA 1980, s. 30(2).
Para. 14(3): FA 1980, s. 30(3); Insurance Companies Act 1982, Sch. 5, para. 24 and FA 1984, s. 74(1).
Para. 14(4), (5): FA 1980, s. 30(4), (5).
Para. 14(6), (7): FA 1980, s. 30(6), (7) and FA 1984, s. 74(2).
Para. 14(8): FA 1980, s. 30(1), (3), (6), (7) (as originally enacted) and Insurance Companies Act 1982, Sch. 5, para. 24.
Para. 14(9), (10): FA 1984, s. 74(3), (4).

Cross references – S. 832(1): definition of "industrial assurance business".
TMA 1970, s. 98: penalties for failure to furnish information under para. 14(4) or comply with notice under para. 14(5).

Statements of practice – E4: connected policies will not normally be considered to be associated operations for inheritance tax purposes if the policy is issued on full medical evidence as to the health of the life assured, and issued on the same terms as if the associated annuity had not been bought.

Other material – IR press release, 16 June 1980 (not reproduced): HMRC guidelines as to those features which are not considered as bringing policies within para. 14.

(v) Premiums paid out of sums due under previous policies

15(1) Where, in the case of a policy under which a single premium only is payable, liability for the payment of that premium is discharged in accordance with sub-paragraph (2) below, the policy is a qualifying policy notwithstanding anything in paragraph 1(2) or (3) or paragraph 2(1)(b) or (c) above; and where, in the case of any other policy, liability for the payment of the first premium thereunder, or of any part of that premium, is so discharged, the premium or part shall be disregarded for the purposes of paragraphs 1 (2)(b) and (3)(b) and 2(1)(c) above.

15(2) Liability for the payment of a premium is discharged in accordance with this sub-paragraph if it is discharged by the retention by the company with which the insurance is made of the whole or a part of any sum which has become payable on the maturity of, or on the surrender more than ten years after its issue of the rights conferred by, a policy–

(a) previously issued by the company to the person making the insurance, or, if it is made by trustees, to them or any predecessors in office; or

(b) issued by the company when the person making the insurance was an infant, and securing a capital sum payable either on a specified date falling not more than one month after his attaining 25, or on the anniversary of the policy immediately following his attainment of that age,

being, unless it is a policy falling within paragraph (b) above and the premium in question is a first premium only, a policy which was itself a qualifying policy, or which would have been a qualifying policy had it been issued in respect of an insurance made after 19th March 1968.

Derivations – ICTA 1970, Sch. 1, para. 8.

(vi) Additional premiums under section 72(9) of the Finance Act 1984

16 In determining whether a policy is a qualifying policy, no account shall be taken of any amount recovered, as if it were an additional premium, in pursuance of section 72(9) of the Finance Act 1984.

Derivations – FA 1984, s. 72(9)(a).

Other material – IR press release, 15 March 1984 (not reproduced): HMRC view of the date when a life assurance contract is made for the purpose of determining whether or not a contract was in force before the abolition of life assurance premium relief.

(vii) Substitutions and variations

17(1) Subject to paragraph 19 below, where one policy (**"the new policy"**) is issued in substitution for, or on the maturity of and in consequence of an option conferred by, another policy (**"the old policy"**), the question whether the new policy is a qualifying policy shall, to the extent provided by the rules in sub-paragraph (2) below, be determined by reference to both policies.

17(2) The rules (for the purposes of which, the question whether the old policy was a qualifying policy shall be determined in accordance with this Part of this Schedule, whatever the date of the insurance in respect of which it was issued), are as follows–

(za) the new policy cannot be a qualifying policy if the old policy was not a qualifying policy by virtue of–

(i) paragraph A1(2), B1(2), B2(2) or B3(3) above, or

(ii) sub-paragraph (i) above or this sub-paragraph;

(a) if the new policy would apart from this paragraph be a qualifying policy but the old policy was not and paragraph (za) above does not apply, the new policy is not a qualifying policy unless the person making the insurance in respect of which it is issued was an infant when the old policy was issued, and the old policy was one securing a capital sum payable either on a specified date falling not later than one month after his attaining 25 or on the anniversary of the policy immediately following his attainment of that age;

(b) if the new policy would apart from this paragraph be a qualifying policy, and the old policy was also a qualifying policy, the new policy is a qualifying policy unless–

(i) it takes effect before the expiry of ten years from the making of the insurance in respect of which the old policy was issued, and

(ii) subject to sub-paragraph (4) below, the highest total of premiums payable thereunder for any period of 12 months expiring before that time is less than one half of the highest total paid for any period of 12 months under the old policy, or under any related policy issued less than ten years before the issue of the new policy (**"related policy"** meaning any policy in relation to which the old policy was a new policy within the meaning of this paragraph, any policy in relation to which that policy was such a policy, and so on);

(c) if the new policy would not apart from this paragraph be a qualifying policy, and would fail to be so by reason only of paragraph 1(2) or (3) or 2(1)(a), (b) or (c) above, it is nevertheless a qualifying policy if the old policy was a qualifying policy and–

(i) the old policy was issued in respect of an insurance made more than ten years before the taking effect of the new policy, and, subject to sub-paragraph (4) below, the premiums payable for any period of 12 months under the new policy do not exceed the smallest total paid for any such period under the old policy; or

(ii) the old policy was issued outside the United Kingdom, and the circumstances are as specified in sub-paragraph (3) below.

17(3) The circumstances are–

(a) where the new policy referred to in sub-paragraph (2)(c) above is issued after 22nd February 1984, that the policy holder under the new policy became resident in the United Kingdom during the 12 months ending with the date of its issue;

(b) where paragraph (a) above does not apply, that the person in respect of whom the new insurance is made became resident in the United Kingdom during the 12 months ending with the date of its issue;

(c) that the issuing company certify that the new policy is in substitution for the old, and that the old was issued either by a permanent establishment of theirs outside the United Kingdom or by a company outside the United Kingdom with whom they have arrangements for the issue of policies in substitution for ones held by persons coming to the United Kingdom; and

(d) that the new policy confers on the holder benefits which are substantially equivalent to those which he would have enjoyed if the old policy had continued in force.

17(4) Where the new policy is one issued on or after 1st April 1976 then, in determining under sub-paragraph (2)(a) to (c) above whether that policy would or would not (apart from sub-paragraphs (1) to (3) above) be a qualifying policy, there shall be left out of account so much of the first premium payable thereunder as is accounted for by the value of the old policy.

17(5) In determining under sub-paragraph (2)(a) to (c) above whether the new policy would apart from this paragraph be a qualifying policy, paragraph A1 above is not to be applied in relation to the issue of the new policy; but this does not stop that paragraph being applied in relation to the issue of the new policy after this paragraph has been applied.

History – Para. 17(2)(za) inserted and in para. 17(2)(a), the words "and paragraph (za) above does not apply" inserted by FA 2013, s. 25 and Sch. 9, para. 4(2) and (3), with effect from 17 July 2013 (Royal Assent).

Para. 17(2) amended by FA 1988, s. 146 and Sch. 13, para. 10 by inserting the word "not" after "the old policy was", with retrospective effect.

In para. 17(3)(c) the words "permanent establishment" *substituted* for "branch or agency" by FA 2003, s. 153(1)(a) in relation to accounting periods *beginning on or after 1 January 2003*.

In para. 17(4), the words "(2)(a) to (c)" substituted for the words "(2)" by FA 2013, s. 25 and Sch. 9, para. 4(4), with effect from 17 July 2013 (Royal Assent).

Para. 17(5) inserted by FA 2013, s. 25 and Sch. 9, para. 4(5), with effect from 17 July 2013 (Royal Assent).

Derivations – Para. 17(1), (2): ICTA 1970, Sch. 1, para. 9(1), (2).

Para. 17(3): ICTA 1970, Sch. 1, para. 9(3) and FA 1984, s. 76(3), (6).

Para. 17(4): FA 1975, Sch. 2, para. 5 and SI 1976/70.

Extra-statutory concessions – A45: if under a term assurance for a term of ten years or less the original sum assured is reduced to less than half, or the term is extended to cover an additional period (but the total term still does not exceed ten years), any resulting reduction in the rate of premium to less than half is not treated as leading to disqualification of the policy.

18(1) Subject to paragraph 19 below and to the provisions of this paragraph, where the terms of a policy are varied, the question whether the policy after the variation is a qualifying policy shall be determined in accordance with the rules in paragraph 17 above, with references in those rules to the new policy and the old policy construed for that purpose as references respectively to the policy after the variation and the policy before the variation, and with any other necessary modifications.

18(2) In applying any of those rules by virtue of this paragraph, the question whether a policy after a variation would be a qualifying policy apart from the rule shall be determined as if any reference in paragraphs 1, 2, 3(5) to (11), 4 to 9, 12 and 13 above to the making of an insurance, or to a policy's term, were a reference to the taking effect of the variation or, as the case may be, to the term of the policy as from the variation.

18(3) This paragraph does not apply by reason of–

(a) any variation which, whether or not of a purely formal character, does not affect the terms of a policy in any significant respect, or

(b) any variation effected before the end of the year 1968 for the sole purpose of converting into a qualifying policy any policy issued (but not one treated, by virtue of paragraph 8(1) and (2) of Schedule 1, as issued) in respect of an insurance made after 19th March 1968; or

(c) any variation so as to increase the benefits secured or reduce the premiums payable which is effected–

(i) on or after such day as the Board may by order appoint, and

(ii) in consideration of a change in the method of payment of premiums from collection by a person collecting premiums from house to house to payment by a different method, or

(d) any variation which alters the method for calculating the benefits secured by the policy.

18(4) For the purposes of this paragraph there is no variation in the terms of a policy where–

(a) an amount of premium chargeable on the grounds that an exceptional risk of death or disability is involved becomes or ceases to be payable, or

(b) the policy is amended by the insertion, variation or removal of a provision under which, on those grounds, any sum may become chargeable as a debt against the capital sum guaranteed by the policy on death or disability.

History – Para. 18(2) amended by FA 1988, s. 146 and Sch. 13, para. 11 by substituting "1, 2, 3(5) to (11), 4 to 9" with retrospective effect.

Para. 18(3)(c) and the word "or" at the end of para. 18(3)(b) were inserted by FA 1996, s. 167(9) with effect from 29 April 1996.

In para. 18(3)(c), word "or" at the end and para. 18(3)(d) inserted by FA 2006, s. 87(2) with effect in relation to variations effected on or after 7 October 2005. In the case of a variation effected as part of, or in connection with, an insurance business transfer scheme (within the meaning of FA 2006, s. 87(6), the amendment is deemed always to have had effect (by virtue of FA 2006, s. 87(4)).

Para. 18(4) inserted by FA 2003, s. 172(4): this insertion being deemed always to have had effect except that it is to be disregarded to the extent that it would prevent a policy from being a qualifying policy at any time before 9 April 2003.

Derivations – ICTA 1970, Sch. 1, para. 10.

Cross references – FA 1991, Sch. 9, para. 5: modified application of para. 18(2) to certain policies issued by friendly societies between 31 August 1987 and 25 July 1991 which are varied between 25 July 1991 and 31 July 1992, but not so as to breach the limits in s. 464. FA 1995, Sch. 10, para. 4(2): modified application of para. 18(2) in relation to certain policies issued by friendly societies between 31 August 1987 and 1 May 1995 which are varied between 1 May 1995 and 31 March 1996, but not so as to breach the limits in s. 464.

Extra-statutory concessions – A45: if under a term assurance for a term of ten years or less the original sum assured is reduced to less than half, or the term is extended to cover an additional period (but the total term still does not exceed ten years), any resulting reduction in the rate of premium to less than half is not treated as leading to disqualification of the policy.

Notes – SI 2001/3643 (C. 118), art. 2(c): the appointed day for the purposes of para. 18(3)(c)(i) is 1 December 2001.

19(1) The following provisions of this paragraph shall have effect for determining for the purposes of this Schedule whether a policy has been varied or whether a policy which confers on the person to whom it is issued an option to have another policy substituted for it or to have any of its terms changed is a qualifying policy.

19(2) If the policy is one issued in respect of an insurance made before 1st April 1976–

(a) any such option shall, until it is exercised, be disregarded in determining whether the policy is a qualifying policy; and

(b) any change in the terms of the policy which is made in pursuance of such an option shall be deemed to be a variation of the policy.

19(3) If the policy is one issued in respect of an insurance made on or after 1st April 1976, the policy shall not be a qualifying policy unless it satisfies the conditions applicable to it under this Schedule before any such option is exercised and–

(a) each policy that might be substituted for it in pursuance of such an option would satisfy those conditions under the rules of paragraph 17 above; and

(b) the policy would continue to satisfy those conditions under the rules of that paragraph as applied by paragraph 18 above if each or any of the changes capable of being made in pursuance of such an option had been made and were treated as a variation;

and it shall not be treated as being varied by reason only of any change made in pursuance of such an option.

Derivations – Para. 19(1): FA 1975, Sch. 2, para. 3(1).
Para. 19(2), (3): FA 1975, Sch. 2, para. 3(2), (3) and SI 1976/70.

20(1) Where, as a result of a variation in the life or lives for the time being assured, a qualifying policy (**"the earlier policy"**) is replaced by a new policy (**"the later policy"**) which in accordance with the rules in paragraph 17 above is also a qualifying policy, then, subject to sub-paragraph (2) below, for the purposes of–

(a) sections 268 to 270; and

(b) any second or subsequent application of this paragraph;

the later policy and the earlier policy shall be treated as a single policy issued in respect of an insurance made at the time of the making of the insurance in respect of which the earlier policy was issued; and, accordingly, so long as the later policy continues to be a qualifying policy, the single policy shall also be treated as a qualifying policy for those purposes.

20(2) Sub-paragraph (1) above does not apply unless–

(a) any sum which would otherwise become payable by the insurer on or in connection with the coming to an end of the earlier policy is retained by the insurer and applied in the discharge of some or all of the liability for any premium becoming due under the later policy; and

(b) no consideration in money or money's worth (other than the benefits for which provision is made by the later policy) is receivable by any person on or in connection with the coming to an end of the earlier policy or the coming into existence of the later policy.

20(3) Any sum which is applied as mentioned in sub-paragraph (2)(a) above–

(a) shall be left out of account in determining, for the purposes of sections 268 to 270, the total amount which at any time has been paid by way of premiums under the single policy referred to in sub-paragraph (1) above; and

(b) [Omitted by FA 2008, s. 36 and Sch. 14, para. 9(b).]

20(4) This paragraph applies where the later policy comes into existence on or after 25th March 1982.

History – In para. 20(1)(a), the words "and 540 and 541" which appeared after the words "sections 268 to 270" omitted by FA 2008, s. 36 and Sch. 14, para. 9(a), with effect:

- so far as relating to corporation tax, for accounting periods beginning on or after 1 April 2008;
- so far as relating to income tax, for the tax year 2008–09 and subsequent tax years.

In para. 20(3)(a), the words "and 540 and 541" which appeared after the words "sections 268 to 270" and para. (b) (and the word "and" before it) omitted by FA 2008, s. 36 and Sch. 14, para. 9(b), with effect:

- so far as relating to corporation tax, for accounting periods beginning on or after 1 April 2008;
- so far as relating to income tax, for the tax year 2008–09 and subsequent tax years.

Derivations – Para. 20(1)–(3): FA 1982, s. 34(1)–(4).
Para. 20(4): FA 1982, s. 34(6).

Cross references – S. 268–270: clawback of relief on conversion or surrender of life policies.
S. 540, 541: income tax charge on gains arising in connection with certain life policies on death, maturity, surrender, assignment etc.

Notes – Rewritten income tax provisions are now located as follows:
Para. 20(1): ITTOIA 2005, s. 542(1)–(8).
Para. 20(2): ITTOIA 2005, s. 495(2) and 542(1)–(5).
Para. 20(3): ITTOIA 2005, s. 507(6) and 510(3).
Para. 20(4): ITTOIA 2005, Sch. 2, para. 101.

(viii) Policy reinstated after non-payment of premium

20ZA(1) This paragraph applies to a qualifying policy ("the original policy") if conditions A to D are satisfied.

20ZA(2) Condition A is that one or more premiums due under the original policy are not paid on or before the date on which they become due.

20ZA(3) Condition B is that the original policy, in accordance with its terms, is treated as having lapsed or is converted into a paid-up policy–

(a) by reason only of the failure to pay that premium or those premiums, and

(b) within the period of 12 months beginning with the day following the day on which the earliest unpaid premium becomes due.

20ZA(4) Condition C is that the original policy–

(a) is reinstated *on the same* terms, or

(b) is replaced by another policy in the same terms ("the replacement policy"),

on or before the thirtieth day after the first anniversary of the day following the day on which the earliest unpaid premium becomes due.

20ZA(5) Condition D is that all unpaid premiums due under the original policy are paid on or before the date on which the policy is reinstated or replaced.

20ZA(6) Where condition C is satisfied by virtue of sub-paragraph (4)(b) the replacement policy is to be treated for the purposes of this Schedule as if it were the original policy.

20ZA(7) The policy is to be treated for the purposes of this Schedule as if the premiums payable under it had been paid on their due dates.

History – Para. 20ZA inserted by SI 2011/1037, art. 15, with effect in any case where the policy is reinstated or (as the case may be) replaced on or after 1 April 2011.

20A In this Part of this Schedule **"industrial assurance business"** means any industrial assurance business within the meaning given by–

(a) section 1(2) of the Industrial Assurance Act 1923, or

(b) Article 3(1) of the Industrial Assurance (Northern Ireland) Order 1979,

which was carried on before 1 December 2001.

History – Para. 20A inserted by ITA 2007, s. 1027 and Sch. 1, para. 233 with effect for income tax purposes for 2007–08 and subsequent tax years and for corporation tax purposes in relation to accounting periods ending after 5 April 2007

Part II – Certification of Qualifying Policies

POLICIES ISSUED IN RESPECT OF INSURANCES MADE ON OR AFTER 1st APRIL 1976 OR VARIED ON OR AFTER THAT DATE

21 [Repealed by FA 1995, s. 162 and Sch. 29, Pt. VIII(7).]

History – Para. 21 disapplied by FA 1995, s. 55(1) (as amended by FA 1996, s. 162(1)) and repealed by FA 1995, s. 162 and Sch. 29, Pt. VIII(7), with effect in relation to any time on or after 6 April 2013 (SI 2013/759), for determining whether a policy is or would be a qualifying policy at that time but subject to savings in relation to times before that date. Former para. 21 read as follows:

"**21(1)** A policy of life insurance issued in respect of an insurance made on or after 1st April 1976 or varied on or after that date (other than one to which paragraph 22(2)(c) below applies) shall not be a qualifying policy unless–

(a) it is certified by the Board as being a qualifying policy; or

(b) it conforms with a form which at the time the policy is issued or varied is either–

(i) a standard form certified by the Board as a standard form of qualifying policy; or

(ii) a form varying from a standard form so certified in no other respect than by making such additions thereto as are, at the time the policy is issued, certified by the Board as compatible with a qualifying policy when made to that standard form and satisfy any conditions subject to which they are so certified;

and any certificate issued in pursuance of paragraph (a) above shall be conclusive evidence that the policy is a qualifying policy.

21(2) In issuing a certificate in pursuance of sub-paragraph (1) above the Board may disregard any provision of the policy, standard form or addition which appears to them insignificant.

21(3) Where the Board refuse to certify a policy as being a qualifying policy, the person to whom it is issued may appeal.

21(4) Sub-paragraphs (1) to (3) above do not apply in relation to such a policy as is mentioned in paragraphs 3 to 6 above.".

In former para. 21(3), the words "to the General Commissioners or, if he so elects, to the Special Commissioners", which appeared after "appeal", omitted by SI 2009/56, art. 3(1) and Sch. 1, para. 159, operative from 1 April 2009, subject to transitional and saving provisions in SI 2009/56, Sch. 3.

Derivations – Para. 21(1): FA 1975, Sch. 2, para. 1(1); FA 1976, s. 33(1); SI 1976/70 and FA 1987, Sch. 16, Pt. VII.
Para. 21(2)–(4): FA 1975, Sch. 2, para. 1(2)–(4).

Cross references – FA 1995, s. 55(2): continuing right of appeal under para. 21(3) after the appointed date in relation to events before that day; certificate issued prior to the appointed date continues to prove a qualifying policy after that date.

Other material – IRInt. 266: certification of qualifying life insurance policies: revised requirements.

22 [Repealed by FA 1995, s. 162 and Sch. 29, Pt. VIII(7).]

History – Para. 22 disapplied by FA 1995, s. 55(4) (as amended by FA 1996, s. 162(1)) and repealed by FA 1995, s. 162 and Sch. 29, Pt. VIII(7), with effect in relation to any time on or after 6 April 2013 (SI 2013/759).
In former para. 22(3), word "or" at the end of para. 22(3)(b) and para. 22(3)(c) inserted by FA 2006, s. 87(3) with effect in relation to variations effected on or after 7 October 2005. In the case of a variation effected as part of, or in connection with, an insurance business transfer scheme (within the meaning of FA 2006, s. 87(6)), this amendment is deemed always to have had effect (by virtue of FA 2006, s. 87(4)).

Derivations – Para. 22(1): ICTA 1970, Sch. 1, para. 11(1); FA 1975, Sch. 2, para. 2(1) and FA 1978, Sch 3, para. 13(1)(a), (2).
Para. 22(2): ICTA 1970, Sch. 1, para. 11(2); FA 1975, Sch. 2, para. 2(2); FA 1976, s. 33(2) and FA 1978, Sch. 3, para. 13(1)(b), (2).
Para. 22(3): ICTA 1970, Sch. 1, para. 11(3) and FA 1978, Sch. 3, para. 13(1)(c), (2).

Part III – Policies Issued by Non-Resident Companies

23 In this Part–

(a) any reference to a **"paragraph"** is a reference to that paragraph of this Schedule; and

(b) **"the old policy"** and **"the new policy"** have the same meanings as in paragraph 17.

Derivations – FA 1984, Sch. 15, Pt. II, para. 1.

24(1) This paragraph applies to a policy of life insurance–

(a) which is issued in respect of an insurance made after 17th November 1983; and

(b) which is so issued by a company resident outside the United Kingdom;

and in the following provisions of this paragraph such a policy is referred to as **"a new non-resident policy"** and the company by which it is issued is referred to as **"the issuing company"**.

24(2) Subject to section 55(3) of the Finance Act 1995 (transitional provision for the certification of certain policies), a new non-resident policy that falls outside sub-paragraph (2A) below shall not be a qualifying policy until such time as the conditions in sub-paragraph (3) are fulfilled with respect to it.

24(2A) A policy falls outside this sub-paragraph unless, at the time immediately before the appointed date for the purposes of section 55 of the Finance Act 1995 (removal of certification requirements), it was a qualifying policy by virtue of sub-paragraphs (2)(b) and (4) of this paragraph, as they had effect in relation to that time.

24(3) The conditions referred to in sub-paragraph (2) above are–

(a) that the issuing company is lawfully carrying on in the United Kingdom life assurance business (as defined in section 56 of the Finance Act 2012); and

(b) that the premiums under the policy are payable to a permanent establishment in the United Kingdom of the issuing company, being a permanent establishment through which the issuing company carries on its life assurance business; and

(c) the premiums under the policy form part of those business receipts of the issuing company which arise through that permanent establishment.

24(4) [Omitted by FA 1995, s. 55(5).]

History – Para. 24(2) and (2A) substituted for para. 24(2) by FA 1995, s. 55(5) (as amended by FA 1996, s. 162(1)), with effect in relation to times on or after 6 April 2013 (SI 2013/759).

In para. 24(3) the word "first" after the words "The conditions" omitted by FA 1995, s. 55(5) (as amended by FA 1996, s. 162(1)) and repealed FA 1995, s. 162 and Sch. 29, Pt. VIII(7), with effect in relation to times on or after 6 April 2013 (SI 2013/759).

In para. 24(3)(a), the words "section 56 of the Finance Act 2012" substituted for "section 431(2)" by FA 2012, s. 146 and Sch. 16, para. 45 with effect in relation to accounting periods of companies beginning on or after 1 January 2013, subject to transitional provisions contained in FA 2012, Sch. 17. For accounting periods straddling 1 January 2013, FA 2012, s. 149 provides for a deemed cessation.

In para. 24(3)(b) and (c), the words "permanent establishment" substituted for "branch" (three times) by FA 2003, s. 155 and Sch. 27, para. 1(4) in relation to accounting periods beginning on or after 1 January 2003.

Para. 24(4) omitted by FA 1995, s. 55(5) (as amended by FA 1996, s. 162(1)) and repealed by FA 1995, s. 162 and Sch. 29, Pt. VIII(7), with effect in relation to times on or after 6 April 2013 (SI 2013/759).

Derivations – FA 1975, Sch. 2, para. 1A, as inserted by FA 1984, s. 76(1) and Sch. 15, Pt. I.

Cross references – ITTOIA 2005, Sch. 2, para. 85: gains from contracts for life insurance: foreign policies of life assurance

Notes – Rewritten income tax provisions are now at ITTOIA 2005, s. 476(3) and Sch. 2, para. 103(1) and 111(1).

25(1) In the application of paragraph 17 in any case where–

(a) the old policy was issued in respect of an insurance made after 17th November 1983 and could not be a qualifying policy by virtue of paragraph 24, and

(b) the new policy is not a new non-resident policy as defined in that paragraph,

the rules for the determination of the question whether the new policy is a qualifying policy shall apply with the modifications in sub-paragraph (2) below.

25(2) The modifications are the following–

(a) if, apart from paragraph 24, the old policy or any related policy (within the meaning of paragraph 17(2)(b)) of which account falls to be taken would have been a qualifying policy, that policy shall be assumed to have been a qualifying policy for the purposes of paragraph 17(2); and

(b) if, apart from this paragraph, the new policy would be a qualifying policy, it shall not be such a policy unless the circumstances are as specified in paragraph 17(3); and

(c) in paragraph 17(3)(c) the words "either by a permanent establishment of theirs outside the United Kingdom or" shall be omitted;

and references in this sub-paragraph to being a qualifying policy shall have effect, in relation to any time before the appointed date for the purposes of section 55 of the Finance Act 1995 (removal of certification requirements), as including a reference to being capable of being certified as such a policy.

25(2A) In determining for the purposes of sub-paragraph (2)(a) above whether a policy would, apart from paragraph 24, have been a qualifying policy, paragraphs A1 and B1 to B3 above are to be ignored. (But this does not affect the application of any of those paragraphs in relation to the new policy.)

25(3) In the application of paragraph 17 in any case where–

(a) the old policy is a qualifying policy which was issued in respect of an insurance made on or before 17th November 1983 but, if the insurance had been made after that date, the policy could not have been a qualifying policy by virtue of paragraph 24, and

(b) the new policy is issued after that date and is not a new non-resident policy, as defined in paragraph 24,

the rules for the determination of the question whether the new policy is a qualifying policy shall apply with the modification in sub-paragraph (2)(c) above.

History – In para. 25(2) the words "the appointed date for the purposes of section 55 of the Finance Act 1995 (removal of certification requirements)" were substituted for the words "5th May 1996" by FA 1996 s. 162(2) with effect from 29 April 1996.

Para. 25(2) substituted by FA 1995, s. 55(6) with effect from 1 May 1995.

In the modification made by para. 25(2)(c), the words "permanent establishment" substituted for "branch or agency" by FA 2003, s. 153(1)(a) in relation to accounting periods beginning on or after 1 January 2003.
Para. 25(2A) inserted by FA 2013, s. 25 and Sch. 9, para. 5, with effect from 17 July 2013 (Royal Assent).

Derivations – FA 1984, Sch. 15, Pt. II, para. 2.

Cross references – SI 2013/759 (not reproduced): the appointed date for the purpose of FA 1995, s. 55 is 6 April 2013.

26 If, in the case of a substitution of policies falling within paragraph 25(1) or (3), the new policy confers such an option as results in the application to it of paragraph 19(3), the new policy shall be treated for the purposes of paragraph 19(3) as having been issued in respect of an insurance made on the same day as that on which was made the insurance in respect of which the old policy was issued.

Derivations – FA 1984, Sch. 15, Pt. II, para. 3.

27(1) For the purposes of Part I and paragraph 24, a policy of life insurance which was issued–

(a) in respect of an insurance made on or before 17th November 1983, and

(b) by a company resident outside the United Kingdom,

shall be treated as issued in respect of an insurance made after that date if the policy is varied after that date so as to increase the benefits secured or to extend the term of the insurance.

27(2) If a policy of life insurance which was issued as mentioned in sub-paragraph (1)(a) and (b) above confers on the person to whom it is issued an option to have another policy substituted for it or to have any of its terms changed, then for the purposes of that sub-paragraph any change in the terms of the policy which is made in pursuance of the option shall be deemed to be a variation of the policy.

History – In para. 27(1) the words "paragraph 24" were substituted for the words "paragraphs 21 and 24" by FA 1995, s. 55(7) with effect from 1 May 1995, except so far as it has effect for the purposes of any case where para. 21 applies by virtue of FA 1995, s. 55(1)–(3).

Derivations – FA 1984, Sch. 15, Pt. II, para. 3.

Notes – Rewritten income tax provisions are now at ITTOIA 2005, Sch. 2, para. 103(2) and 103(3) respectively.

SCHEDULE 15A – CONTRACTUAL SAVINGS SCHEMES

Section 326(9)

[Omitted by ITTOIA 2005, s. 882 and Sch. 1, para. 345 and repealed by s. 884 and Sch. 3.]

History – Sch. 15A omitted by ITTOIA 2005, s. 882(1) and Sch. 1, para. 345 and repealed by s. 884 and Sch. 3, effective for income tax purposes for 2005–06 onwards and for corporation tax purposes for accounting periods ending after 5 April 2005 (ITTOIA 2005, s. 883(1)).

Notes – Sch. 15A rewritten as follows:
Para. 2(1): ITTOIA 2005, s. 703(3).
Para. 2(2): ITTOIA 2005, s. 703(3).
Para. 3: ITTOIA 2005, s. 704(6).
Para. 4(1): ITTOIA 2005, s. 705(2).
Para. 4(2): ITTOIA 2005,s. 705(3).
Para. 4(3): ITTOIA 2005, s. 705(4).
Para. 5(1): ITTOIA 2005, s. 706(1) and (2).
Para. 5(2): ITTOIA 2005, s. 706(3).
Para. 5(3): ITTOIA 2005, s. 706(2).
Para. 6(1): ITTOIA 2005, s. 705(1) and 706(1) and (2).
Para. 6(2): ITTOIA 2005, s. 706(3).
Para. 6(3): ITTOIA 2005, s. 706(2).
Para. 7(1): ITTOIA 2005, s. 707(3).
Para. 7(2): ITTOIA 2005, s. 707(4).
Para. 8(1): ITTOIA 2005, s. 708(1)-(3).
Para. 8(2): ITTOIA 2005, s. 708(2) and (4).
Para. 8(3): ITTOIA 2005, s. 708(2) and (4).
Para. 9(1): ITTOIA 2005, s. 708(1) and (2).
Para. 9(2): ITTOIA 2005, s. 708(3).
Para. 9(3): ITTOIA 2005, s. 708(2).
Para. 10(1): ITTOIA 2005, s. 708(1) and (2).
Para. 10(2): ITTOIA 2005, s. 708(3).
Para. 11(1): ITTOIA 2005, s. 708(1) and (3).
Para. 11(2): ITTOIA 2005, s. 708(2).
Para. 12(1): ITTOIA 2005, s. 708(4).
Para. 12(2): ITTOIA 2005, s. 708(4).
Para. 12(3): ITTOIA 2005, s. 708(4).
Para. 12(4): ITTOIA 2005, s. 708(4).

SCHEDULE 15B – VENTURE CAPITAL TRUSTS: RELIEF FROM INCOME TAX

Section 332A

History – Sch. 15B inserted by FA 1995, s. 71(2) and Sch. 15, with effect for the year 1995–96 and subsequent years of assessment.

Part I – Relief on Investment

History – Pt. 1 omitted by ITA 2007, s. 1027 and Sch. 1, para. 234 and repealed by ITA 2007, s. 1031 and Sch. 3, Pt. 1 with effect for 2007–08 and subsequent tax years.

ENTITLEMENT TO CLAIM RELIEF

1 [Omitted by ITA 2007, s. 1027 and Sch. 1, para. 234 and repealed by ITA 2007, s. 1031 and Sch. 3, Pt. 1 with effect for income tax purposes for 2007–08 and subsequent tax years.]

Notes – Para. 1 rewritten as follows:
Para. 1(1): ITA 2007, s. 23, 26(1), 261(1), 262(1), (2).
Para. 1(2): ITA 2007, s. 261(1), (2).
Para. 1(3): ITA 2007, s. 262(3).
Para. 1(4): ITA 2007, s. 261(3).
Para. 1(5): ITA 2007, s. 23, 29(2), 263(1), (2).
Para. 1(6): ITA 2007, s. 23, 27(4), (5).
Para. 1(8): ITA 2007, s. 265.
Para. 1(9): ITA 2007, s. 261(3).
Para. 1(10): ITA 2007, s. 261(4).
Para. 1(11): ITA 2007, s. 271(4).

LOAN-LINKED INVESTMENTS

2 [Omitted by ITA 2007, s. 1027 and Sch. 1, para. 234 and repealed by ITA 2007, s. 1031 and Sch. 3, Pt. 1 with effect for 2007–08 and subsequent tax years.]

Notes – Para. 2 rewritten as follows:
Para. 2(1): ITA 2007, s. 264(1), (3).
Para. 2(2): ITA 2007, s. 264(2), 1008(1).
Para. 2(3): ITA 2007, s. 264(3), 332.

LOSS OF INVESTMENT RELIEF

3 [Omitted by ITA 2007, s. 1027 and Sch. 1, para. 234 and repealed by ITA 2007, s. 1031 and Sch. 3, Pt. 1 with effect for 2007–08 and subsequent tax years.]

Notes – Para. 3 rewritten as follows:
Para. 3(1): ITA 2007, s. 266(1).
Para. 3(2): ITA 2007, s. 266(2).
Para. 3(3): ITA 2007, s. 266(3).
Para. 3(4): ITA 2007, s. 266(4).
Para. 3(5): ITA 2007, s. 267(1).
Para. 3(6): ITA 2007, s. 267(2), (3).
Para. 3(7): ITA 2007, s. 267(4).
Para. 3(8): ITA 2007, s. 266(5), (6), (7).
Para. 3(9): ITA 2007, s. 268(1), (2).

ASSESSMENT ON WITHDRAWAL OR REDUCTION OF RELIEF

4 [Omitted by ITA 2007, s. 1027 and Sch. 1, para. 234 and repealed by ITA 2007, s. 1031 and Sch. 3, Pt. 1 with effect for 2007–08 and subsequent tax years.]

Notes – Para. 4 rewritten as follows:
Para. 4(1): ITA 2007, s. 269, 270(1).
Para. 4(2): ITA 2007, s. 270(1).
Para. 4(3): ITA 2007, s. 270(2).

PROVISION OF INFORMATION

5 [Omitted by ITA 2007, s. 1027 and Sch. 1, para. 234 and repealed by ITA 2007, s. 1031 and Sch. 3, Pt. 1 with effect for 2007–08 and subsequent tax years.]

Notes – Para. 5 rewritten as follows:
Para. 5(1): ITA 2007, s. 271(1).
Para. 5(2): ITA 2007, s. 271(2), (3).
Para. 5(3): ITA 2007, s. 271(5).

INTERPRETATION OF PART I

6 [Omitted by ITA 2007, s. 1027 and Sch. 1, para. 234 and repealed by ITA 2007, s. 1031 and Sch. 3, Pt. 1 with effect for 2007–08 and subsequent tax years.]

Notes – Para. 6 rewritten as follows:
Para. 6(1): ITA 2007, s. 273(1).
Para. 6(2): ITA 2007, s. 332.
Para. 6(3): ITA 2007, s. 273(2).

Part II – Relief on Distributions

7 [Omitted by ITTOIA 2005, s. 882 and Sch. 1, para. 346(3) and repealed by s. 884 and Sch. 3.]

History – Para. 7 omitted by ITTOIA 2005, s. 882(1) and Sch. 1, para. 346(3) and repealed by s. 884 and Sch. 3; effective for income tax purposes for 2005–06 onwards and for corporation tax purposes for accounting periods ending after 5 April 2005 (ITTOIA 2005, s. 883(1)).

Notes – Para. 7: ITTOIA 2005 as follows:
Para. 7(1): ITTOIA 2005, s. 709(1) and (2).
Para. 7(2): ITTOIA 2005, s. 709(3) and (4).
Para. 7(3): ITTOIA 2005, s. 709(1), (2), (4) and (6). But ITTOIA 2005 does not rewrite the words in para. 7(3)(a) "including a capital dividend" as an investor is unlikely to know whether or a dividend received is a capital dividend. (See ITTOIA 2005, Explanatory Notes, Annex 1, Table 1 (Change 158).)

MEANING OF "PERMITTED MAXIMUM"

8 [Omitted by ITTOIA 2005, s. 882 and Sch. 1, para. 346(3) and repealed by s. 884 and Sch. 3.]

History – Para. 8 omitted by ITTOIA 2005, s. 882(1) and Sch. 1, para. 346(3) and repealed by s. 884 and Sch. 3; effective for income tax purposes for 2005–06 onwards and for corporation tax purposes for accounting periods ending after 5 April 2005 (ITTOIA 2005, s. 883(1)).

Notes – Para. 8: ITTOIA 2005 as follows:
Para. 8(1): ITTOIA 2005, s. 709(4) and 710(2).
Para. 8(2): ITTOIA 2005, s. 709(6) and (7).
Para. 8(3): ITTOIA 2005, s. 712(1)–(4).
Para. 8(4): ITTOIA 2005, s. 712(1)–(4).
Para. 8(5): ITTOIA 2005, s. 709(5) and (8).
Para. 8(6): ITTOIA 2005, s. 710(2), (4) and (5) and 711(1)–(4).
Para. 9(1): ITTOIA 2005,s. 709(8).
Para. 9(2): ITTOIA 2005,s. 709(8).

INTERPRETATION OF PART II

9 [Omitted by ITTOIA 2005, s. 882 and Sch. 1, para. 346(3) and repealed by s. 884 and Sch. 3.]

History – Para. 9 omitted by ITTOIA 2005, s. 882(1) and Sch. 1, para. 346(3) and repealed by s. 884 and Sch. 3; effective for income tax purposes for 2005–06 onwards and for corporation tax purposes for accounting periods ending after 5 April 2005 (ITTOIA 2005, s. 883(1)).

Notes – Para. 9: ITTOIA 2005, s. 709(8).

SCHEDULE 16 – COLLECTION OF INCOME TAX ON COMPANY PAYMENTS WHICH ARE NOT DISTRIBUTIONS

Section 350(4)

[Sch. 16 omitted by ITA 2007, s. 1027 and Sch. 1, para. 235 and repealed by ITA 2007, s. 1031 and Sch. 3, Pt. 1 with effect for 2007–08 and subsequent tax years.]

Notes – Sch. 16 rewritten as follows:
Para. 1: ITA 2007, s. 946.
Para. 2(1): ITA 2007, s. 949(1), (2).
Para. 2(2): ITA 2007, s. 947(2), (3), (4), 949(2).
Para. 2(3): ITA 2007, s. 949(3).
Para. 3: ITA 2007, s. 949(4), 950(3).
Para. 4(1): ITA 2007, s. 951(1), (3), 956(1), (2), (3).
Para. 4(2): ITA 2007, s. 957(1), (2), Sch. 1 para. 258.
Para. 5(1): ITA 2007, s. 952(1), (2), (3), (4), (5), 953(1), (2), (3), (7).
Para. 5(2): ITA 2007, s. 953(3), (4).
Para. 6(1): ITA 2007, s. 954(1), (2).
Para. 6(2): ITA 2007, s. 954(3).
Para. 6(3): ITA 2007, s. 955(1), (2).
Para. 6(4): ITA 2007, s. 955(3).
Para. 6(5): ITA 2007, s. 954(4), 955(4).
Para. 7: ITA 2007, s. 953(2), (3), (6).
Para. 7A(1): ITA 2007, s. 958(1), (2).
Para. 7A(3): ITA 2007, s. 958(3), (4).
Para. 9: ITA 2007, s. 950(1), (2), 951(1).
Para. 10(1): ITA 2007, s. 959(1), (2), (3), (4).
Para. 10(2): ITA 2007, s. 960(1).

Para. 10(3): ITA 2007, s. 960(1).
Para. 10(4): ITA 2007, s. 960(2).
Para. 10(5): ITA 2007, s. 960(3).
Para. 11: ITA 2007, s. 959(1), (5), (6), 961.

SCHEDULE 17 – DUAL RESIDENT INVESTING COMPANIES

Section 404

[Omitted by CTA 2010, s. 1177 and Sch. 1, para. 139 and repealed by CTA 2010, s. 1181 and Sch. 3, Pt. 1.]

History – Sch. 17 omitted by CTA 2010, s. 1177 and Sch. 1, para. 139 and repealed by CTA 2010, s. 1181 and Sch. 3, Pt. 1, with effect for corporation tax purposes for accounting periods ending on or after 1 April 2010, and for income and capital gains tax purposes for the tax year 2010–11 and subsequent tax years.

SCHEDULE 17A – GROUP RELIEF: CLAIMS

Section 412

[Sch. 17A repealed by FA 1998, s. 165 and Sch. 27, III(28).]

History – Sch. 17A repealed by FA 1998, s. 165 and Sch. 27, Pt. III(28), with effect in relation to accounting periods ending on or after 1 July 1999, the self-assessment appointed day by virtue of FA 1994, s. 199 and SI 1998/3173 (C. 78), and replaced by the provisions of FA 1998, Sch. 18.

SCHEDULE 18 – GROUP RELIEF: EQUITY HOLDERS AND PROFITS OR ASSETS AVAILABLE FOR DISTRIBUTION

Section 413(10)

[Omitted by CTA 2010, s. 1177 and Sch. 1, para. 140 and repealed by CTA 2010, s. 1181 and Sch. 3, Pt. 1.]

History – Sch. 18 omitted by CTA 2010, s. 1177 and Sch. 1, para. 140 and repealed by CTA 2010, s. 1181 and Sch. 3, Pt. 1, with effect for corporation tax purposes for accounting periods ending on or after 1 April 2010, and for income and capital gains tax purposes for the tax year 2010–11 and subsequent tax years.

Notes – Sch. 18 rewritten as follows:
Para. 1(1): CTA 2010, s. 157(1), 158(1), 167(1).
Para. 1(2): CTA 2010, s. 160(1).
Para. 1(3): CTA 2010, s. 160(2), (3), (4), (5), (6), (7).
Para. 1(4): CTA 2010, s. 158(2).
Para. 1(5): CTA 2010, s. 162(1), (2), (3), (4), (5).
Para. 1(5A): CTA 2010, s. 164(1).
Para. 1(5B): CTA 2010, s. 164(2).
Para. 1(5C): CTA 2010, s. 164(3), (4), (5).
Para. 1(5D): CTA 2010, s. 164(6), (7).
Para. 1(5E): CTA 2010, s. 163(1), (2).
Para. 1(5F): CTA 2010, s. 163(3).
Para. 1(5G): CTA 2010, s. 163(5).
Para. 1(5H): CTA 2010, s. 163(4).
Para. 1(5I): CTA 2010, s. 163(5), (6).
Para. 1(6): CTA 2010, s. 159(1), (2), (3), 167(3).
Para. 1(7): CTA 2010, s. 159(4).
Para. 1(8): CTA 2010, s. 157(2), 1176(1).
Para. 1A(1): CTA 2010, s. 161(1).
Para. 1A(2): CTA 2010, s. 161(2).
Para. 1A(3): CTA 2010, s. 161(3), (5).
Para. 1A(4): CTA 2010, s. 161(4).
Para.1A(5): CTA 2010, s. 161(6).
Para. 1A(6): CTA 2010, s. 161(7).
Para. 1A(7): CTA 2010, s. 161(8).
Para. 1A(8): CTA 2010, s. 157(2).
Para. 2(1): CTA 2010, s. 157(1), 165(1), (2), (3).
Para. 2(1A): CTA 2010, s. 165(4).
Para. 2(2): CTA 2010, s. 165(5).
Para. 2(3): CTA 2010, s. 165(6).
Para. 3(1): CTA 2010, s. 166(1), (2), (3), (4).
Para. 3(2): CTA 2010, s. 166(2).
Para. 3(3): CTA 2010, s. 166(5).
Para. 3(4): CTA 2010, s. 166(6), (7).
Para. 3(5): CTA 2010, s. 157(2), 166(6), 1176(1).
Para. 4(1): CTA 2010, s. 169(2), 170(1), (5).
Para. 4(2): CTA 2010, s. 170(2).
Para. 4(3): *CTA 2010, s. 170(3).*
Para. 4(4): CTA 2010, s. 170(3).
Para. 4(5): CTA 2010, s. 170(6).
Para. 5(1): CTA 2010, s. 169(2), 171(1), (2), (4).
Para. 5(2): CTA 2010, s. 172(1).
Para. 5(3): CTA 2010, s. 169(2), 171(1), (3), (4), 172(2).
Para. 5(4): CTA 2010, s. 172(3).

Para. 5A(1): CTA 2010, s. 175(1).
Para. 5A(2): CTA 2010, s. 175(2).
Para. 5A(3): CTA 2010, s. 175(3).
Para. 5A(4): CTA 2010, s. 175(3).
Para. 5B(1): CTA 2010, s. 169(2), 173(1), (2), 174(1).
Para. 5B(2): CTA 2010, s. 173(3).
Para. 5B(3): CTA 2010, s. 173(4).
Para. 5B(4): CTA 2010, s. 173(5), (6).
Para. 5B(4A): CTA 2010, s. 173(7).
Para. 5B(5): CTA 2010, s. 174(1).
Para. 5B(6): CTA 2010, s. 174(1).
Para. 5B(7): CTA 2010, s. 174(1).
Para. 5B(8): CTA 2010, s. 174(1).
Para. 5B(9): CTA 2010, s. 174(1).
Para. 5B(10): CTA 2010, s. 174(2).
Para. 5C(1): CTA 2010, s. 176(1).
Para. 5C(2): CTA 2010, s. 176(2).
Para. 5C(3): CTA 2010, s. 176(3).
Para. 5C(4): CTA 2010, s. 176(3).
Para. 5C(5): CTA 2010, s. 176(3).
Para. 5D(1): CTA 2010, s. 177(1).
Para. 5D(2): CTA 2010, s. 177(2).
Para. 5D(3): CTA 2010, s. 177(3).
Para. 5D(4): CTA 2010, s. 177(3).
Para. 5D(5): CTA 2010, s. 177(3).
Para. 5E(1): CTA 2010, s. 178(1).
Para. 5E(2): CTA 2010, s. 178(2).
Para. 5E(3): CTA 2010, s. 178(3).
Para. 5E(4): CTA 2010, s. 178(3).
Para. 5E(5): CTA 2010, s. 178(3).
Para. 5F(1): CTA 2010, s. 179(1), (2), (3).
Para. 5F(2): CTA 2010, s. 169(2), 179(4).
Para. 5F(3): CTA 2010, s. 179(4).
Para. 5F(4): CTA 2010, s. 180(1), (2).
Para. 5F(5): CTA 2010, s. 180(1), (2).
Para. 5F(6): CTA 2010, s. 180(1), (3), (4).
Para. 5F(7): CTA 2010, s. 181(1).
Para. 5F(8): CTA 2010, s. 181(1), (2).
Para. 5F(9): CTA 2010, s. 181(1).
Para. 5F(10): CTA 2010, s. 182, 186(1), (2).
Para. 6: CTA 2010, s. 157(1), 167(2).
Para. 7(1): CTA 2010, s. 168(1).
Para. 7(1A): CTA 2010, s. 168(2).
Para. 7(1B): CTA 2010, s. 168(3).
Para. 7(1C): CTA 2010, s. 168(3).
Para. 7(2): CTA 2010, s. 157(2).

SCHEDULE 18A – GROUP RELIEF: OVERSEAS LOSSES OF NON-RESIDENT COMPANIES

Section 403F

[Omitted by CTA 2010, s. 1177 and Sch. 1, para. 141 and repealed by CTA 2010, s. 1181 and Sch. 3, Pt. 1.]

History – Sch. 18A omitted by CTA 2010, s. 1177 and Sch. 1, para. 141 and repealed by CTA 2010, s. 1181 and Sch. 3, Pt. 1, with effect for corporation tax purposes for accounting periods ending on or after 1 April 2010, and for income and capital gains tax purposes for the tax year 2010–11 and subsequent tax years.

Notes – Sch. 18A rewritten as follows:
Para. 2: CTA 2010, s. 114.
Para. 3(1): CTA 2010, s. 115(1).
Para. 3(2): CTA 2010, s. 115(2).
Para. 3(3): CTA 2010, s. 115(3).
Para. 3(4): CTA 2010, s. 115(3).
Para. 3(5): CTA 2010, s. 115(2).
Para. 4(1): CTA 2010, s. 116(1).
Para. 4(2): CTA 2010, s. 116(2).
Para. 4(3): CTA 2010, s. 116(3).
Para. 4(4): CTA 2010, s. 116(4).
Para. 4(5): CTA 2010, s. 116(6).
Para. 4(6): CTA 2010, s. 116(5).
Para. 5(1): CTA 2010, s. 117(2).
Para. 5(2): CTA 2010, s. 117(1).
Para. 6(1): CTA 2010, s. 118(1).
Para. 6(2): CTA 2010, s. 117(3), 118(2).
Para. 6(3): CTA 2010, s. 118(3).
Para. 6(4): CTA 2010, s. 118(4).
Para. 6(5): CTA 2010, s. 117(4).
Para. 7(1): CTA 2010, s. 119(1).
Para. 7(2): CTA 2010, s. 117(3), 119(2).
Para. 7(3): CTA 2010, s. 119(3).
Para. 7(4): CTA 2010, s. 119(4).
Para. 7(5): CTA 2010, s. 117(4).
Para.8(1): CTA 2010, s. 120(1).

Para. 8(2): CTA 2010, s. 120(2).
Para. 8(3): CTA 2010, s. 120(3).
Para. 9(1): CTA 2010, s. 113(2).
Para. 9(2): CTA 2010, s. 121(1).
Para. 9(3): CTA 2010, s. 121(2).
Para. 9(4): CTA 2010, s. 121(3).
Para. 9(5): CTA 2010, s. 121(1).
Para. 10(1): CTA 2010, s. 112.
Para. 10(2): CTA 2010, s. 124(4).
Para. 10(3): CTA 2010, s. 112.
Para. 11(1): CTA 2010, s. 113(2).
Para. 11(2): CTA 2010, s. 113(2).
Para. 11(3): CTA 2010, s. 113(2).
Para. 11(4): CTA 2010, s. 113(2), (3).
Para. 11(5): CTA 2010, s. 113(2).
Para. 12(1): CTA 2010, s. 123(1).
Para. 12(2): CTA 2010, s. 123(2).
Para. 12(3): CTA 2010, s. 123(3).
Para. 13(1): CTA 2010, s. 124(1).
Para. 13(2): CTA 2010, s. 124(2).
Para. 13(3): CTA 2010, s. 124(3).
Para. 14(1): CTA 2010, s. 125(1).
Para. 14(2): CTA 2010, s. 125(2).
Para. 14(3): CTA 2010, s. 125(3).
Para. 14(4): CTA 2010, s. 125(3),(4).
Para. 15(1): CTA 2010, s. 126(1).
Para. 15(2): CTA 2010, s. 126(2).
Para. 15(3): CTA 2010, s. 126(3).
Para. 16(1): CTA 2010, s. 128(1).
Para. 16(2): CTA 2010, s. 128(2).
Para. 16(3): CTA 2010, s. 128(3).
Para. 16(4): CTA 2010, s. 128(4).
Para. 16(5): CTA 2010, s. 128(4).
Para. 17(1): CTA 2010, s. 187(1).
Para. 17(2): CTA 2010, s. 187(1).
Para. 17(3): CTA 2010, s. 187(2).

SCHEDULE 19 – APPORTIONMENT OF INCOME OF CLOSE COMPANIES

Section 423

[Repealed by FA 1989, s. 103, 187 and Sch. 17, Pt. V.]

History – Sch. 19 repealed by FA 1989, s. 103, 187 and Sch. 17, Pt. V in relation to accounting periods beginning after 31 March 1989. The repeal of Sch. 19 took effect subject to saving in so far as Pt. I related to s. 427(4) in any case where the subsequent distribution therein was made before 1 April 1992.

SCHEDULE 19AA – OVERSEAS LIFE ASSURANCE FUND

Section 431

[Omitted by FA 2007, s. 38 and Sch. 7, para. 55.]

History – Sch. 19AA omitted by FA 2007, s. 38 and Sch. 7, para. 55 and repealed by s. 114 and Sch. 27, Pt. 2(7), with effect for the purposes of corporation tax, for periods of account of insurance companies beginning on or after 1 January 2007, and for the purposes of income tax, for the tax year 2007–08 and subsequent tax years (but see transitional provisions at FA 2007, Sch. 7, para. 80–84).

SCHEDULE 19AB – PENSION BUSINESS: PAYMENTS ON ACCOUNT OF TAX CREDITS AND DEDUCTED TAX

Section 438A

[Sch. 19AB repealed by FA 2001, s. 87(1) and s. 110, Sch. 33, Pt. II(12).]

History – Sch. 19AB repealed by FA 2001, s. 87(1) and s. 110, Sch. 33, Pt. II(12) with effect in relation to income tax deducted from payments received after 30 September 2001. For certain purposes in relation to tax credits (exempt business of friendly societies and ISA business of insurance companies and friendly societies), it was deemed to continue to apply, but ceased to apply for these exceptional purposes also in respect of distributions made on or after 6 April 2004 (FA 2001, s. 87(3), (5)).

SCHEDULE 19ABA – MODIFICATION OF LIFE ASSURANCE PROVISIONS OF THE CORPORATION TAX ACTS IN RELATION TO BLAGAB GROUP REINSURERS

Section 44CD

[Omitted by FA 2012, s. 146 and Sch. 16, para. 46.]

History – Sch. 19ABA omitted by FA 2012, s. 146 and Sch. 16, para. 46 with effect in relation to accounting periods of companies beginning on or after 1 January 2013, subject to transitional provisions contained in FA 2012, Sch. 17. For accounting periods straddling 1 January 2013, FA 2012, s. 149 provides for a deemed cessation on 31 December 2012.

SCHEDULE 19AC – MODIFICATION OF ACT IN RELATION TO OVERSEAS LIFE INSURANCE COMPANIES

Section 444B

[Repealed by SI 2006/3271, reg. 43 and Schedule, Pt. 1.]

History – Sch. 19AC repealed by SI 2006/3271, reg. 43 and Schedule, Pt. 1 with effect from 31 December 2006 in relation to accounting periods ending on or after that date.

SCHEDULE 19A – UNDERWRITERS: ASSESSMENT AND COLLECTION OF TAX

Section 450(2A)

1-11 [Repealed for 1992–93 and later years by FA 1993, s. 213 and Sch. 23, Pt. III(12).]

SCHEDULE 19B – PETROLEUM EXTRACTION ACTIVITIES: EXPLORATION EXPENDITURE SUPPLEMENT

Section 496A

History – Sch. 19B inserted by FA 2004, s. 286 and Sch. 38 for claims to supplement in respect of accounting periods ending on or after 1 January 2004 but before 1 January 2006 (see para. 1 for timing provisions).

Part 1 – Introductory

ABOUT THIS SCHEDULE

1(1) This Schedule entitles a company carrying on a ring fence trade, on making a claim in respect of an accounting period ending on or after 1st January 2004 but before 1st January 2006, to a supplement (initially of 6%, but variable by Treasury order) in respect of–

(a) qualifying capital expenditure incurred before the trade is set up and commenced,

(b) losses incurred in the trade, determined by reference to allowances under Part 6 of the Capital Allowances Act (expenditure on research and development) in respect of qualifying capital expenditure, and

(c) some or all of the supplement allowed in respect of earlier periods.

1(2) To qualify, the capital expenditure in question must be incurred on or after 1st January 2004 but before 1st January 2006 in respect of oil and gas exploration and appraisal (as well as satisfying other conditions).

1(3) Part 2 makes provision about the application and interpretation of this Schedule

1(4) Part 3 makes provision about supplement in relation to expenditure incurred by the company–

(a) with a view to carrying on a ring fence trade, but

(b) in an accounting period before the company sets up and commences that trade.

1(5) Part 4 makes provision about supplement in relation to losses incurred in carrying on the ring fence trade.

1(6) There is a limit on the number of accounting periods (6) in respect of which a company may claim supplement.

1(7) In determining the amount of supplement allowable, reductions fall to be made in respect of–

(a) disposal receipts by virtue of section 555 of the Capital Allowances Act (disposal of oil licence with exploitation value),

(b) ring fence losses that could be set off under section 393A or 393B against ring fence profits of earlier periods,

(c) ring fence losses incurred in earlier periods that fall to be set off under section 393 against profits of succeeding periods,

(d) unrelieved group ring fence profits.

History – In para. 1(1), the words "but before 1st January 2006" inserted by FA 2006, s. 154(4)(a) with effect from 19 July 2006.
In para. 1(2), the words "but before 1st January 2006" inserted by FA 2006, s. 154(4)(b) with effect from 19 July 2006.
In para. 1(7)(b), the words "or 393B" inserted by FA 2008, s. 111 and Sch. 35, para. 8(2), with effect in relation to losses incurred in accounting periods beginning on or after 12 March 2008.

Part 2 – Application and Interpretation

QUALIFYING COMPANIES

2 This Schedule applies in relation to any company which–

(a) carries on a ring fence trade, or

(b) is engaged in oil and gas exploration and appraisal (see section 837B of this Act and section 1003 of ITA 2007) with a view to carrying on a ring fence trade,

and in this Schedule any such company is referred to as a "qualifying company".

History – In para. 2(b), the words "of this Act and section 1003 of ITA 2007" inserted by ITA 2007, s. 1027 and Sch. 1, para. 236 with effect in relation to accounting periods ending after 5 April 2007.

ACCOUNTING PERIODS

3(1) In this Schedule, in the case of any qualifying company,–

"the commencement period" means the accounting period in which the company sets up and commences its ring fence trade;

"post-commencement period" means any accounting period ending on or after 1st January 2004 but before 1st January 2006–

(a) which is the commencement period, or

(b) which ends after the commencement period;

"pre-commencement period" means any accounting period ending–

(a) on or after 1st January 2004 but before 1st January 2006, and

(b) before the commencement period.

3(2) For the purposes of this Schedule a company not within the charge to corporation tax which incurs qualifying E&A expenditure is to be treated as having such accounting periods as it would have if–

(a) it carried on a trade consisting of the activities in respect of which the expenditure is incurred, and

(b) it had started to carry on that trade when it started to carry on the research and development on which the expenditure is incurred.

3(3) In the case of an accounting period (a "straddling period") of any qualifying company beginning before 1st January 2006 and ending on or after that date–

(a) so much of the straddling period as falls before 1st January 2006, and

(b) so much of the straddling period as falls on or after that date,

are treated as separate accounting periods for the purposes of this Schedule.

3(4) Special provision is made elsewhere in this Schedule in relation to straddling periods (see paragraphs 16, 18A and 22).

History – In para. 3(1), in the definition of "post-commencement period", the words "but before 1st January 2006" inserted by FA 2006, s. 154(5)(a) with effect from 19 July 2006.
In para. 3(1), in the definition of "pre-commencement period", the words "but before 1st January 2006" inserted by FA 2006, s. 154(5)(b) with effect from 19 July 2006.
Para. 3(3) inserted by FA 2006, s. 154(5)(c) with effect from 19 July 2006.
Para. 3(4) inserted by FA 2006, s. 154(5)(c) with effect from 19 July 2006.

THE RELEVANT PERCENTAGE

4(1) For the purposes of this Schedule, the relevant percentage for any accounting period ending on or after 1st January 2004 is 6%.

4(2) The Treasury may by order vary the percentage for the time being specified in sub-paragraph (1) for such accounting periods as may be specified in the order.

LIMIT ON NUMBER OF ACCOUNTING PERIODS FOR WHICH SUPPLEMENT MAY BE CLAIMED

5(1) A company may claim supplement under this Schedule in respect of no more than 6 accounting periods.

5(2) The accounting periods in respect of which claims are made need not be consecutive.

QUALIFYING E&A EXPENDITURE

6(1) For the purposes of this Schedule **"qualifying E&A expenditure"** is any expenditure as respects which the following conditions are satisfied.

6(2) Condition 1 is that the expenditure is incurred on or after 1st January 2004 but before 1st January 2006.

6(3) Condition 2 is that, for the purposes of Part 6 of the Capital Allowances Act, the expenditure is qualifying expenditure incurred on research and development consisting of oil and gas exploration and appraisal (see section 437(2)(b) of that Act).

6(4) Condition 3 is that an allowance under section 441 of that Act is claimed in respect of the expenditure.

6(5) Condition 4 is that the expenditure is incurred in the course of oil extraction activities.

6(6) Condition 5 is that–

(a) those oil extraction activities are comprised in a ring fence trade, or

(b) after incurring the expenditure, the person incurring it sets up and commences a ring fence trade connected with the research and development or starts to be within the charge to corporation tax in respect of such a ring fence trade.

History – In para. 6(2), the words "but before 1st January 2006" inserted by FA 2006, s. 154(6) with effect from 19 July 2006.
In para. 6(6)(b), the words "or starts to be within the charge to corporation tax in respect of such a ring fence trade." inserted by CTA 2009, s. 1322 and Sch. 1, para. 283, with effect for corporation tax purposes for accounting periods ending on or after 1 April 2009, and for income tax and capital gains tax purposes for the tax year 2009–10 and subsequent tax years.

UNRELIEVED GROUP RING FENCE PROFITS FOR ACCOUNTING PERIODS

7(1) There is an amount of unrelieved group ring fence profits for an accounting period of a qualifying company ("company Q") in any case where–

(a) the company and any other company ("company X") are members of the same group of companies, within the meaning given by section 413(3)(a), and

(b) company X has an amount of taxable ring fence profits (see paragraph 8) for a corresponding accounting period.

7(2) An accounting period of company X corresponds to an accounting period of company Q if–

(a) it coincides with, or falls wholly within, the accounting period of company Q, or

(b) it falls partly within the accounting period of company Q.

7(3) Where an accounting period of company X–

(a) coincides with an accounting period of company Q, or

(b) falls wholly within an accounting period of company Q,

there is, for the accounting period of company Q, an amount of unrelieved group ring fence profits equal to the whole of company X's taxable ring fence profits for its accounting period.

7(4) Where an accounting period of company X falls partly within an accounting period of company Q–

(a) there is an amount of unrelieved group ring fence profits for the accounting period of company Q, and

(b) that amount is an amount equal to the part of company X's taxable ring fence profits for its accounting period that is attributable, on an apportionment in accordance with section 834(4), to the part of that period which falls within the accounting period of company Q.

7(5) This paragraph applies for the purposes of this Schedule.

TAXABLE RING FENCE PROFITS OF AN ACCOUNTING PERIOD

8 For the purposes of this Schedule, a company has taxable ring fence profits for an accounting period if it has an amount of ring fence profits which is chargeable to corporation tax for that accounting period after any group relief claimed under Chapter 4 of Part 10.

Part 3 – Pre-Commencement Supplement

SUPPLEMENT IN RESPECT OF A PRE-COMMENCEMENT ACCOUNTING PERIOD

9(1) Where–

(a) a qualifying company claims an allowance under section 441 of the Capital Allowances Act (research and development allowances) for the commencement period, and

(b) the claim is for an allowance in respect of qualifying E&A expenditure incurred before that period, the company may also claim supplement under this Part of this Schedule ("pre-commencement supplement") in respect of one or more pre-commencement periods.

9(2) Any pre-commencement supplement allowed on a claim in respect of a pre-commencement period shall be treated as an allowance under Part 6 of the Capital Allowances Act for the commencement period in respect of qualifying E&A expenditure incurred by the company.

9(3) The amount of the supplement for any pre-commencement period in respect of which a claim under this paragraph is made is the relevant percentage for that period of the reference amount for that period.

9(4) If the pre-commencement period is a period of less than twelve months, the amount of the supplement for the period (apart from this sub-paragraph) shall be reduced proportionally.

9(5) Paragraphs 10 to 13 have effect for the purpose of determining the reference amount for a pre-commencement period.

THE MIXED POOL OF QUALIFYING E&A EXPENDITURE AND SUPPLEMENT PREVIOUSLY ALLOWED

10(1) For the purpose of determining the amount of any pre-commencement supplement, a qualifying company shall be taken to have had, at all times in the pre-commencement periods of the company, a continuing mixed pool of qualifying E&A expenditure and pre-commencement supplement.

10(2) The pool shall be taken to have consisted of–

(a) the company's qualifying E&A expenditure, allocated to the pool for each pre-commencement period in accordance with sub-paragraph (3), and

(b) the company's pre-commencement supplement, allocated to the pool for each pre-commencement period in accordance with sub-paragraph (4).

10(3) To allocate qualifying E&A expenditure to the pool for any pre-commencement period, take the following steps–

(a) Step 1: count as eligible expenditure for that period so much of the qualifying E&A expenditure mentioned in paragraph 9(1)(b) as was incurred in that period,

(b) Step 2: find the total of all the eligible expenditure for that period (amount E),

(c) Step 3: if paragraph 11 applies, reduce amount E in accordance with that paragraph,

(d) Step 4: if paragraph 12 applies, reduce (or, as the case may be, further reduce) amount E in accordance with that paragraph,

and so much of amount E as remains after making those reductions shall be taken to have been added to the pool in that period.

10(4) If any pre-commencement supplement is allowed on a claim in respect of a pre-commencement period, the amount of that supplement shall be taken to have been added to the pool in that period.

TREATMENT OF DISPOSAL VALUE ON DISPOSAL OF OIL LICENCE WITH EXPLOITATION VALUE

11(1) This paragraph applies in any case where–

(a) the qualifying company disposes of an interest in an oil licence in a pre-commencement period,

(b) part of the value of the interest (the "deductible amount") is attributable to qualifying E&A expenditure incurred by the company, and

(c) section 555 of the Capital Allowances Act (disposal of oil licence with exploitation value) has effect in relation to the disposal.

11(2) For the purpose of allocating qualifying E&A expenditure to the pool for each pre-commencement period–

(a) find the total of the deductible amounts in the case of all such disposals made by the company (amount D), and

(b) taking later periods before earlier periods, reduce (but not below nil) amount E for any pre-commencement period by setting against it so much of amount D as does not fall to be set against amount E for a later pre-commencement period.

11(3) In this paragraph **"oil licence"** has the same meaning as in section 555 of the Capital Allowances Act (see section 552(1) of that Act).

REDUCTION IN RESPECT OF UNRELIEVED GROUP RING FENCE PROFITS

12(1) This paragraph applies if there is an amount of unrelieved group ring fence profits for a pre-commencement period.

12(2) For the purpose of allocating qualifying E&A expenditure to the pool for that period–

(a) find so much (if any) of amount E for that period as remains after any reduction falling to be made under paragraph 11, and

(b) reduce that amount (but not below nil) by setting against it a sum equal to the aggregate of the amounts of unrelieved group ring fence profits for the period.

THE REFERENCE AMOUNT FOR A PRE-COMMENCEMENT PERIOD

13 For the purposes of this Part of this Schedule, the reference amount for a pre-commencement period is the amount in the pool at the end of the period–

(a) after the addition to the pool of any qualifying E&A expenditure allocated to the pool for that period in accordance with paragraph 10(3), but

(b) before determining, and adding to the pool, the amount of any pre-commencement supplement claimed in respect of the period.

14(1) Any claim for pre-commencement supplement in respect of a pre-commencement period must be made at the same time as, and as if it were part of, the claim under section 441 of the Capital Allowances Act mentioned in paragraph 9(1)(a).

14(2) Subsection (3) of that section (claim for reduced amount) applies in relation to any such claim.

ICTA 1988

Part 4 – Post-Commencement Supplement

SUPPLEMENT IN RESPECT OF A POST-COMMENCEMENT PERIOD

15(1) A qualifying company which incurs a qualifying E&A loss (see paragraph 17) in a post-commencement period may claim supplement under this Part of this Schedule ("post-commencement supplement") in respect of–

(a) that period, or

(b) any subsequent accounting period in which it carries on its ring fence trade.

15(2) Any post-commencement supplement allowed on a claim in respect of a post-commencement period shall be treated for the purposes of the Corporation Tax Acts (other than this Part of this Schedule or sections 321 to 329 of CTA 2010) as if it were a loss–

(a) incurred in carrying on the ring fence trade in that period,

(b) which falls in whole to be set off under section 393 against trading income from the ring fence trade in succeeding accounting periods.

15(3) Paragraph 74 of Schedule 18 to the Finance Act 1998 (company tax returns etc: time limit for claims for group relief) shall apply in relation to a claim for post-commencement supplement as it applies in relation to a claim for group relief.

History – In para. 15(2), the words "sections 321 to 329 of CTA 2010" substituted for the words "Part 4 of Schedule 19C" by CTA 2010, s. 1177 and Sch. 1, para. 142(2), with effect for corporation tax purposes for accounting periods ending on or after 1 April 2010, and for income and capital gains tax purposes for the tax year 2010–11 and subsequent tax years.
In para. 15(2), the words "this Schedule or Part 4 of Schedule 19C" substituted for the words "this Schedule" by FA 2006, s. 154(7) with effect from 19 July 2006.

AMOUNT OF POST-COMMENCEMENT SUPPLEMENT FOR A POST-COMMENCEMENT PERIOD

16(1) The amount of the post-commencement supplement for any post-commencement period in respect of which a claim under paragraph 15 is made is the relevant percentage for that period of the reference amount for that period.

16(2) If the post-commencement period is a period of less than twelve months, the amount of the supplement for the period (apart from this sub-paragraph) shall be reduced proportionally.

16(2A) But, if the post-commencement period is the deemed accounting period under paragraph 3(3) ending before 1st January 2006, sub-paragraph (2) has no effect in relation to the amount of the supplement for that period.

16(3) Paragraphs 19 to 24 have effect for the purpose of determining the reference amount for a post-commencement period.

History – Para. 16(2A) inserted by FA 2006, s. 154(8) with effect from 19 July 2006.

RING FENCE LOSSES AND QUALIFYING E&A LOSSES

17(1) Where–

(a) in any post-commencement period ("the period of the loss") a qualifying company carrying on a ring fence trade incurs a loss in the trade, and

(b) some or all of the loss falls to be set off under section 393 against trading income from the trade in succeeding accounting periods,

so much of the loss as falls to be so set off is a "ring fence loss" of the company.

17(2) In determining for the purposes of this Part of this Schedule how much of a loss incurred in a ring fence trade falls to be set off as mentioned in sub-paragraph (1)(b), it shall be assumed

(a) that every claim is made that could be made by the company under section 393A to set losses incurred in the ring fence trade against ring fence profits of earlier post-commencement periods and–

(b) that (where appropriate) section 393B applies in relation to every such claim.

17(3) So much of a ring fence loss as is attributable to qualifying E&A allowances for the period of the loss is a "qualifying E&A loss".

17(4) A ring fence loss is attributable to qualifying E&A allowances to the extent that the amount of the ring fence loss does not exceed the amount of the qualifying E&A allowances for the period of the loss.

17(5) But a claim for post-commencement supplement may include an election for a ring fence loss to be treated–

(a) as attributable to qualifying E&A allowances for the period of the loss to such lesser extent as may be specified in the election, or

(b) as not attributable to such allowances.

17(6) **"Qualifying E&A allowances"**, in the case of an accounting period, means allowances for that period under Part 6 of the Capital Allowances Act in respect of qualifying E&A expenditure incurred by the company (including any pre-commencement supplement treated under paragraph 9(2) as such an allowance)

17(7) This paragraph has effect for the purposes of this Part of this Schedule.

History – In para. 17(2), para. (a) created from existing text and para. (b) inserted by FA 2008, s. 111 and Sch. 35, para. 8(3), with effect in relation to losses incurred in accounting periods beginning on or after 12 March 2008.

RING FENCE LOSSES AND NON-QUALIFYING LOSSES

18(1) So much of a ring fence loss as is not a qualifying E&A loss is a non-qualifying loss.

18(2) Where–

(a) a loss was incurred by a qualifying company in its ring fence trade in an accounting period ending on or before 31st December 2003, and

(b) some or all of that loss falls to be set off under section 393 against profits of that trade in accounting periods ending on or after that date,

so much of the loss as falls to be so set off is a ring fence loss and that loss is a non-qualifying loss.

18(3) This paragraph has effect for the purposes of this Part of this Schedule.

SPECIAL RULE FOR STRADDLING PERIODS

18A(1) This paragraph applies in any case where the period of the loss in which a ring fence loss is incurred is the *deemed accounting period* under paragraph 3(3) ending before 1st January 2006.

18A(2) The following assumption shall be made for the purpose of calculating the amount of the qualifying E&A loss and the amount of the non-qualifying loss.

18A(3) The assumption is that the loss made in the trade is taken to be the loss incurred in the accounting period beginning before 1st January 2006 and ending on or after that date (disregarding paragraph 3(3)).

18A(4) The amount of the non-qualifying loss (found in accordance with that assumption) is then reduced (but not below) by the following amount.

18A(5) The amount is the amount of the ring fence loss in the deemed accounting period beginning on 1st January 2006 determined under section 324 of CTA 2010.

History – In para. 18A(5), the words "section 324 of CTA 2010" substituted for the words "paragraph 18 of Schedule 19C for the purposes of Part 4 of that Schedule" by CTA 2010, s. 1177 and Sch. 1, para. 142(3), with effect for corporation tax purposes for accounting periods ending on or after 1 April 2010, and for income and capital gains tax purposes for the tax year 2010–11 and subsequent tax years.
Para. 18A inserted by FA 2006, s. 154(9) with effect from 19 July 2006.

THE POOL OF QUALIFYING E&A LOSSES AND THE POOL OF NON-QUALIFYING LOSSES

19(1) For the purpose of determining the amount of any post-commencement supplement, a qualifying company shall be taken at all times in its post-commencement periods to have–

(a) a continuing pool of the company's non-qualifying losses (the "non-qualifying pool"), and

(b) a continuing mixed pool of the company's qualifying E&A losses and post-commencement supplement (the "qualifying pool").

19(2) A pool continues even if the amount in it is nil.

THE NON-QUALIFYING POOL

20(1) The non-qualifying pool consists of the company's non-qualifying losses, allocated to the pool in accordance with sub-paragraph (2).

20(2) A non-qualifying loss is allocated to the pool by adding the amount of the non-qualifying loss to the pool in the period of the loss.

20(3) In the case of a non-qualifying loss incurred in an accounting period ending on or before 31st December 2003, the period of the loss shall be taken for the purposes of sub-paragraph (2) to be the first accounting period of the company that ends on or after 1st January 2004.

20(4) The amount in the non-qualifying pool is subject to reductions in accordance with the following provisions of this Part of this Schedule.

20(5) Where a reduction in the amount in the non-qualifying pool falls to be made in any accounting period–

(a) the reduction is to be made after the addition to the pool of any non-qualifying loss allocated to the pool in that period in accordance with sub-paragraph (2), and

(b) references to the amount in the non-qualifying pool shall be construed accordingly.

THE QUALIFYING POOL

21(1) The qualifying pool consists of–

(a) the company's qualifying E&A losses, allocated to the pool in accordance with sub-paragraph (2)(a), and

(b) the company's post-commencement supplement, allocated to the pool in accordance with sub-paragraph (2)(b).

21(2) The allocation of qualifying E&A losses and post-commencement supplement to the pool is as follows–

(a) the amount of a qualifying E&A loss is added to the pool in the period of the loss, and

(b) if any post-commencement supplement is allowed on a claim in respect of a post-commencement period, the amount of that supplement is added to the pool in that period.

21(3) The amount in the qualifying pool is subject to reductions in accordance with the following provisions of this Part of this Schedule.

21(4) Where a reduction in the amount in the qualifying pool falls to be made in any accounting period, the reduction is to be made–

(a) after the addition to the pool of the amount of any qualifying E&A losses allocated to the pool in that period in accordance with sub-paragraph (2)(a), but

(b) before determining, and adding to the pool, the amount of any supplement claimed in respect of the period,

and references to the amount in the pool shall be construed accordingly.

ICTA 1988

REDUCTIONS IN RESPECT OF UTILISED RING FENCE LOSSES

22(1) If one or more ring fence losses are set off under section 393 against any profits of a post-commencement period, reductions shall be made in that period in accordance with this paragraph.

22(2) The amount in the non-qualifying pool shall be reduced (but not below nil) by setting against it a sum equal to the total amount so set off.

22(3) If any of that sum remains after being so set against the amount in the non-qualifying pool, the amount in the qualifying pool shall be reduced (but not below nil) by setting against it so much of that sum as so remains.

22(4) If the post-commencement period is the deemed accounting period under paragraph 3(3) ending before 1st January 2006 ("the deemed accounting period"), the amount of the profits of the deemed accounting period is determined as follows.

22(5) The amount of the profits of the straddling period is apportioned to the deemed accounting period in proportion to the number of days in the deemed accounting period that fall in the straddling period.

22(6) The apportioned amount is taken for the purposes of this paragraph to be the amount of the profits of the deemed accounting period.

22(7) In this paragraph **"the straddling period"**, in relation to a qualifying company, means an accounting period of the company beginning before 1st January 2006 and ending on or after that date (disregarding paragraph 3(3)).

History – Para. 22(4) inserted by FA 2006, s. 154(10) with effect from 19 July 2006.
Para. 22(5) Inserted by FA 2006, s. 154(10) with effect from 19 July 2006.
Para. 22(6) inserted by FA 2006, s. 154(10) with effect from 19 July 2006.
Para. 22(7) inserted by FA 2006, s. 154(10) with effect from 19 July 2006.

REDUCTIONS IN RESPECT OF UNRELIEVED GROUP RING FENCE PROFITS

23(1) If there is an amount of unrelieved group ring fence profits for a post-commencement period, reductions shall be made in that period in accordance with this paragraph.

23(2) In the following provisions of this paragraph, references to the remaining amount in a pool are references to so much (if any) of the amount in the pool as remains after making any reductions that fall to be made in accordance with paragraph 22.

23(3) The remaining amount in the non-qualifying pool shall be reduced (but not below nil) by setting against it a sum equal to the aggregate of the amounts of unrelieved group ring fence profits for the period.

23(4) If any of that sum remains after being so set against the remaining amount in the non-qualifying pool, the remaining amount in the qualifying pool shall be reduced (but not below nil) by setting against it so much of that sum as so remains.

THE REFERENCE AMOUNT FOR A POST-COMMENCEMENT PERIOD

24 For the purposes of this Part of this Schedule the reference amount for a post-commencement period is so much of the amount in the qualifying pool as remains after making any reductions required by paragraph 22 or 23.

SCHEDULE 19C – PETROLEUM EXTRACTION ACTIVITIES: RING FENCE EXPENDITURE SUPPLEMENT

Section 496B

[Omitted by CTA 2010, s. 1177 and Sch. 1, para. 143 and repealed by CTA 2010, s. 1181 and Sch. 3, Pt. 1.]

History – Sch. 19C omitted by CTA 2010, s. 1177 and Sch. 1, para. 143 and repealed by CTA 2010, s. 1181 and Sch. 3, Pt. 1, with effect for corporation tax purposes for accounting periods ending on or after 1 April 2010, and for income and capital gains tax purposes for the tax year 2010–11 and subsequent tax years.

Notes – Sch. 19C rewritten as follows:
Para. 1(1): CTA 2010, s. 157(1), 307(1).
Para. 1(2): CTA 2010, s. 307(2).
Para. 1(3): CTA 2010, s. 307(3).
Para. 1(4): CTA 2010, s. 307(4).
Para. 1(5): CTA 2010, s. 307(5).
Para. 1(6): CTA 2010, s. 307(6).
Para. 2: CTA 2010, s. 308(1), (2).
Para. 3(1): CTA 2010, s. 309(1).
Para. 3(2): CTA 2010, s. 309(2).
Para. 3(3): CTA 2010, s. 309(3).
Para. 3(4): CTA 2010, s. 309(4).

Para. 4(1): CTA 2010, s. 310(1).
Para. 4(2): CTA 2010, s. 310(2).
Para. 5(1): CTA 2010, s. 311(1).
Para. 5(2): CTA 2010, s. 311(2).
Para. 5(3): CTA 2010, s. 311(3).
Para. 5(4): CTA 2010, s. 311(4).
Para. 5(5): CTA 2010, s. 311(5).
Para. 6(1): CTA 2010, s. 312(1).
Para. 6(2): CTA 2010, s. 312(2).
Para. 6(3): CTA 2010, s. 312(3).
Para. 6(4): CTA 2010, s. 312(4).
Para. 6(5): CTA 2010, s. 312(5).
Para. 6(6): CTA 2010, s. 312(6).
Para. 6(7): CTA 2010, s. 312(7).
Para. 6(8): CTA 2010, s. 312(8).
Para. 6(9): CTA 2010, s. 312(9).
Para. 7(1): CTA 2010, s. 313(1), (5).
Para. 7(2): CTA 2010, s. 313(2).
Para. 7(3): CTA 2010, s. 313(3).
Para. 7(4): CTA 2010, s. 313(4).
Para. 7(5): CTA 2010, s. 313(6).
Para. 8: CTA 2010, s. 314.
Para. 9(1): CTA 2010, s. 315(1).
Para. 9(2): CTA 2010, s. 315(2).
Para. 9(3): CTA 2010, s. 315(3).
Para. 9(4): CTA 2010, s. 315(4).
Para. 9(5): CTA 2010, s. 315(5).
Para. 10(1): CTA 2010, s. 316(1).
Para. 10(2): CTA 2010, s. 316(2).
Para. 10(3): CTA 2010, s. 316(3).
Para. 10(4): CTA 2010, s. 316(4).
Para. 10(5): CTA 2010, s. 316(5).
Para. 11(1): CTA 2010, s. 317(1).
Para. 11(2): CTA 2010, s. 317(2).
Para. 11(3): CTA 2010, s. 317(3).
Para. 12(1): CTA 2010, s. 318(1).
Para. 12(2): CTA 2010, s. 318(2).
Para. 13: CTA 2010, s. 319.
Para. 14(1): CTA 2010, s. 320(1).
Para. 14(2): CTA 2010, s. 320(2).
Para. 15(1): CTA 2010, s. 321(1).
Para. 15(2): CTA 2010, s. 321(2), (4).
Para. 15(3): CTA 2010, s. 321(3).
Para. 16(1): CTA 2010, s. 322(1).
Para. 16(2): CTA 2010, s. 322(2).
Para. 16(3): CTA 2010, s. 322(3).
Para. 17(1): CTA 2010, s. 323(1).
Para. 17(2): CTA 2010, s. 321(4), 323(2).
Para. 17(3): CTA 2010, s. 323(3).
Para. 17(3A): CTA 2010, s. 323(4).
Para. 17(4): CTA 2010, s. 323(5).
Para. 17(5): CTA 2010, s. 321(4), 323(6).
Para. 18(1): CTA 2010, s. 324(1).
Para. 18(2): CTA 2010, s. 324(2).
Para. 18(3): CTA 2010, s. 324(3).
Para. 18(4): CTA 2010, s. 324(4).
Para. 18(5): CTA 2010, s. 321(4), 324(5).
Para. 19(1): CTA 2010, s. 325(1).
Para. 19(2): CTA 2010, s. 325(2).
Para. 19(3): CTA 2010, s. 325(3).
Para. 19(4): CTA 2010, s. 325(4).
Para. 19(5): CTA 2010, s. 325(5).
Para. 20(1): CTA 2010, s. 326(1).
Para. 20(2): CTA 2010, s. 326(2).
Para. 20(3): CTA 2010, s. 326(3).
Para. 20(4): CTA 2010, s. 326(4).
Para. 20(5): CTA 2010, s. 326(5).
Para. 21(1): CTA 2010, s. 327(1).
Para. 21(2): CTA 2010, s. 327(2).
Para. 21(3): CTA 2010, s. 327(3).
Para. 21(4): CTA 2010, s. 327(4).
Para. 21(5): CTA 2010, s. 327(5).
Para. 21(6): CTA 2010, s. 327(6).
Para. 21(7): CTA 2010, s. 327(7).
Para. 22(1): CTA 2010, s. 328(1).
Para. 22(2): CTA 2010, s. 328(2).
Para. 22(3): CTA 2010, s. 328(3).
Para. 22(4): CTA 2010, s. 328(4).
Para. 22(5): CTA 2010, s. 328(5).
Para. 23: CTA 2010, s. 329.

SCHEDULE 20 – CHARITABLE COMPANIES: QUALIFYING INVESTMENTS AND LOANS

Section 506

[Omitted by CTA 2010, s. 1177 and Sch. 1, para. 144 and repealed by CTA 2010, s. 1181 and Sch. 3, Pt. 1.]

History – Sch. 20 omitted by CTA 2010, s. 1177 and Sch. 1, para. 144 and repealed by CTA 2010, s. 1181 and Sch. 3, Pt. 1, with effect for corporation tax purposes for accounting periods ending on or after 1 April 2010, and for income and capital gains tax purposes for the tax year 2010–11 and subsequent tax years, subject to transitional provisions (relating to Part 3) in CTA 2010, s. 1180 and Sch. 2, para. 77.

Notes – Sch. 20 rewritten for income tax purposes as follows:
Para. 1: ITA 2007, s. 558.
Para. 2 : ITA 2007, s. 558.
Para. 3 : ITA 2007, s. 558.
Para. 3A: ITA 2007, s. 558.
Para. 4: ITA 2007, s. 558.
Para. 5: ITA 2007, s. 559(1).
Para. 6: ITA 2007, s. 558.
Para. 6A: ITA 2007, s. 559(1).
Para. 7: ITA 2007, s. 558.
Para. 7A: ITA 2007, s. 558.
Para. 8: ITA 2007, s. 558, 1019.
Para. 9: ITA 2007, s. 558.
Para. 10(1): ITA 2007, s. 561(1), (2), (3).
Para. 10(2): ITA 2007, s. 561(4).
Sch. 20 rewritten for corporation tax as follows:
Para. 1: CTA 2010, s. 511.
Para. 2: CTA 2010, s. 511.
Para. 3: CTA 2010, s. 511.
Para. 3A: CTA 2010, s. 511.
Para. 4: CTA 2010, s. 511.
Para. 5: CTA 2010, s. 512(1).
Para. 6: CTA 2010, s. 511.
Para. 6A: CTA 2010, s. 512(1).
Para. 7: CTA 2010, s. 511.
Para. 7A: CTA 2010, s. 511.
Para. 8: CTA 2010, s. 511.
Para. 9: CTA 2010, s. 511.
Para. 10(1): CTA 2010, s. 514(1), (2), (3).
Para. 10(2): CTA 2010, s. 514(4).

SCHEDULE 21 – TAX RELIEF IN CONNECTION WITH SCHEMES FOR RATIONALIZING INDUSTRY AND OTHER REDUNDANCY SCHEMES

Sections 570 and 572

Part I – Preliminary

1(1) In this Schedule–

"scheme" means a scheme which is for the time being certified or has at any time been certified by the Secretary of State under section 568;

"payment" means a payment made under a scheme, being a payment made to a person carrying on a trade to which the scheme relates and not being a payment made by way of repayment of contributions;

"the person chargeable" means, in relation to any such payment, the person liable to pay any tax which may fall to be paid by reason of the receipt of the payment;

"damage" includes any loss, liability, expense or other burden, and references to the amount of any damage are references to the sum which would be fair compensation for that damage;

"contribution" includes part of a contribution, and **"deductible contribution"** means a contribution allowed to be deducted under section 568, any reduction under Part III of this Schedule being left out of account; and

"asset" includes part of an asset.

1(2) For the purposes of this Schedule, a sum received by any person by way of repayment of contributions shall be deemed to be by way of repayment of the last contribution paid by him, and, if the sum exceeds the amount of that contribution, by way of repayment of the penultimate contribution so paid, and so on.

Derivations – ICTA 1970, Sch. 11, para. 1.

Part II – Relief in Respect of Certain Payments

2 The question whether any, and if so, what, relief is to be given shall be determined separately in relation to each payment made under the scheme in respect of the trade, but for the purpose of determining that question regard shall be had, as provided by the following provisions of this Part of this Schedule, to the sum (**"the total payment"**) produced by adding the amount of the payment to the amount of any payments previously so made.

Derivations – ICTA 1970, Sch. 11, para. 2.

3 [Repealed by FA 1996, s. 134 and Sch. 20, para. 43.]

History – Para. 3 repealed by FA 1996, s. 134 and Sch. 20, para. 43 and s. 205 and Sch. 41, Pt. V(10), with effect for income tax and capital gains as respects 1996–97 and subsequent years of assessment and for corporation tax purposes as respects accounting periods ending on or after 1 July 1999, the date appointed under FA 1994, s. 199 by virtue of SI 1998/3173 (C. 78).

Derivations – ICTA 1970, Sch. 11, para. 3.

4 No relief shall be given in respect of the payment unless the total payment, or the amount of the damage in respect of which the total payment has been made, whichever is the smaller, exceeds the aggregate amount of the deductible contributions which have been paid in furtherance of the scheme in respect of the trade in question before the payment is made, exclusive of any contributions which have been repaid before the payment is made.

Derivations – ICTA 1970, Sch. 11, para. 4.

5 The amount of the reduction to be made in respect of the payment shall be arrived at by–

(a) ascertaining the sum which bears to the excess mentioned in paragraph 4 above the same proportion that the amount mentioned in paragraph 3(b) above bears to the amount mentioned in paragraph 3(a); and

(b) deducting from that sum the total amount of any reductions which have been or fall to be made under this Schedule in respect of payments previously made under the scheme in respect of the trade.

Derivations – ICTA 1970, Sch. 11, para. 5.

6(1) For the purposes of this Schedule, and subject to sub-paragraph (2) below, damage shall be deemed to be damage in respect of which relief may be given under the Tax Acts if and only if–

(a) the damage is attributable to any of the following events, that is to say, the demolition, destruction or putting out of use of any asset, or the disposition or termination of an interest in any asset, and, by reason of that event, an allowance falls to be made under Part 2 or 3 of the Capital Allowances Act in calculating the profits of a trade; or

(b) the damage consists of any loss, liability, expense or other burden in respect of which an allowance may be made in computing the profits of the trade for the purposes of the Tax Acts.

6(2) [Repealed by CAA 1990, s. 164 and Sch. 2.]

6(3) Where any event occurs which would give rise to an allowance under the Tax Acts in respect of any asset in taxing, or computing the profits of, a trade but for any of the following matters, that is to say–

(a) that there are no profits against which the allowance could be made, or

(b) that account is required to be taken of allowances previously made or deemed to have been made in respect of the asset; or

(c) that account is required to be taken of any sum which falls to be written off the expenditure incurred on the asset for the purpose of determining whether any and if so what allowance may be given by reason of the event; or

(d) that account is required to be taken of any sum falling to be taken into account as sale, insurance, salvage or compensation moneys, the like consequences shall ensue under this Schedule as if an allowance had fallen to be made by reason of that event.

6(4) Where any damage is attributable to a permanent change in the purposes for which an asset is used, or the temporary or permanent putting out of use of an asset, the question whether the damage is damage in respect of which relief may be given under the Tax Acts shall be determined as if the damage had been attributable to a sale of the asset on the date upon which the change or putting out of use took place.

History – In para. 6(1)(a), the words "Part 2 or 3 of the Capital Allowances Act in calculating the profits of a trade" substituted for "Part I or II of the 1990 Act in taxing the trade" by CAA 2001, s. 578 and Sch. 2, para. 65 with effect as respects allowances and charges falling to be made for chargeable periods ending, for income tax purposes, on or after 6 April 2001, and for corporation tax purposes, on or after 1 April 2001, that reference to CAA 1990, Pt. I or II having itself been substituted in 6(1)(a) by CAA 1990, s. 164 and Sch. 1, para. 8(41) as respects allowances and charges falling to be made for chargeable periods ending after 5 April 1990. Under CAA 2001, Sch. 3, para. 8, where a person is affected by a change in the law brought into effect by CAA 2001, they may elect for the pre-consolidation law to apply for the chargeable period straddling the commencement of CAA 2001.
In para. 6(1)(b), (3), the word "profits" is substituted for "profits or gains" in each place by FA 1998, s. 46(3) and Sch. 7, para. 1.
Para. 6(2) repealed by CAA 1990, s. 164 and Sch. 2 as respects allowances and charges falling to be made for chargeable periods ending after 5 April 1990.

Derivations – ICTA 1970, Sch. 11, para. 6.

Cross references – S. 570: payments under certified schemes which are not repayments of contributions.

Part III – Exclusion of Relief in Respect of Contributions Paid after Relief has been given under Part II

7 The provisions of this Part of this Schedule shall have effect where–

(a) a contribution is paid under a scheme in respect of a trade; and

(b) before the contribution is paid, payments have been made under the scheme to the person carrying on the trade; and

(c) reductions have been made, under Part II of this Schedule, in the amounts which, by reason of those payments, are to be treated as trading receipts of the trade.

Derivations – ICTA 1970, Sch. 11, para. 7.

8 There shall be ascertained–

(a) the total amount of those reductions; and

(b) the sum by which that total would have been decreased if the contribution, and any previous contributions to which this Part of this Schedule applies, had been paid before any of the payments were made.

Derivations – ICTA 1970, Sch. 11, para. 8.

9 For the purpose of determining what deduction is to be made in respect of the contribution under section 568, the contribution shall be deemed to be reduced by the sum specified in paragraph 8(b) above, but–

(a) for the purpose of the application of paragraph 8 above in relation to contributions subsequently paid under the scheme in respect of the trade, the total amount of the reductions referred to in that paragraph shall be treated as decreased by that sum; and

(b) for the purpose of the application of paragraph 5 above in relation to payments subsequently made under the scheme in respect of the trade, the total amount of the reductions referred to in that paragraph shall be treated as decreased by that sum.

Derivations – ICTA 1970, Sch. 11, para. 9.

10 When two or more contributions are paid at the same time, the provisions of this Part of this Schedule shall have effect as if they were a single contribution.

Derivations – ICTA 1970, Sch. 11, para. 10.

SCHEDULE 22 – REDUCTION OF PENSION FUND SURPLUSES

Section 603

[Sch. 22 repealed by FA 2004, s. 326 and Sch. 42, Pt. 3.]

History – Sch. 22 repealed by FA 2004, s. 326 and Sch. 42, Pt. 3, the repeal having effect on 6 April 2006, subject to FA 2004, Sch. 36.

SCHEDULE 23 – OCCUPATIONAL PENSION SCHEMES: SCHEMES APPROVED BEFORE 23rd JULY 1987

Section 609

[Repealed by FA 2004, s. 326 and Sch. 42, Pt. 3.]

History – Sch. 23 repealed by FA 2004, s. 326 and Sch. 42, Pt. 3, with effect from 6 April 2006, subject to FA 2004, Sch. 36.

SCHEDULE 23ZA – CONVERSION OF CERTAIN APPROVED RETIREMENT BENEFITS SCHEMES

Section 631A

[Repealed by FA 2004, s. 326, Sch. 42, Pt. 3.]

History – Sch. 3ZA repealed by FA 2004, s. 326, Sch. 42, Pt. 3, with effect from 6 April 2006, subject to FA 2004, Sch. 36. Former Sch. 23ZA read as follows:

"INTERPRETATION

1(1) In this Schedule–

"the date of the change" *shall* be construed in accordance with paragraph 3(2) below;

"eligible scheme" shall be construed in accordance with paragraph 2(4) below;

"the personal pension provisions of this Act" means this Schedule and the other provisions of Chapter IV of Part XIV;

"prescribed" (except in paragraph 2(3)(c)) means specified in, or determined in accordance with, regulations;

"regulations" means regulations made by the Board.

1(2) Any power conferred by this Schedule to make regulations includes power to make different provision for different cases or different purposes.

ELIGIBLE SCHEMES

2(1) This Schedule applies to any retirement benefits scheme which is for the time being approved under Chapter I of Part XIV.
2(2) Sub-paragraph (1) above is subject to the following provisions of this paragraph.
2(3) This Schedule applies to a retirement benefits scheme only if–
(a) it is an occupational pension scheme, as defined in section 1 of the Pension Schemes Act 1993 or section 1 of the Pensions Schemes (Northern Ireland) Act 1993;
(b) it is a money-purchase scheme, as defined in section 181 of the Pension Schemes Act 1993 or section 176 of the Pensions Schemes (Northern Ireland) Act 1993;
(c) any documents relating to the scheme which are prescribed under section 631(1) are such that, subject to approval under paragraph 3 below, the scheme is capable of being an approved personal pension scheme for the purposes of Chapter IV of Part XIV as from the date of the change; and
(d) such other conditions as may be prescribed are satisfied in the case of the scheme.
2(4) Any retirement benefits scheme to which this Schedule applies is referred to in this Schedule as an "eligible scheme".

Statutory instruments – SI 2001/118: regulations made under Sch. 23ZA, para. 2.

APPROVAL OF ELIGIBLE SCHEMES AS APPROVED PERSONAL PENSION SCHEMES

3(1) The trustees of an eligible scheme may at any time on or after 1st October 2000 apply to the Board for approval of the scheme under this paragraph.
3(2) If an application under sub-paragraph (1) above is granted, the eligible scheme shall, as from such date as the Board may specify in granting the application (the "date of the change"),–
(a) irrevocably cease to be approved, and to be capable of approval, under Chapter I of Part XIV; and
(b) become an approved personal pension scheme (and subject accordingly to section 631(4) and the other provisions of Chapter IV of Part XIV).
3(3) The date of the change must not be earlier than 6th April 2001.
3(4) An application under sub-paragraph (1) above shall be in such form, shall contain such information, and shall be accompanied by such documents, in such form, and prepared as at such time, as the Board may prescribe.
3(5) The Board may at their discretion grant or refuse an application under sub-paragraph (1) above.
3(6) The Board's discretion under sub-paragraph (5) above shall be subject to the restrictions set out in sections 632 to 638A and this Schedule.
3(7) The Board shall give notice to the applicant of the grant or refusal of an application.
3(8) A notice under sub-paragraph (7) above shall, in the case of a refusal, state the grounds for the refusal.
3(9) If, at any time after the making of an application under sub-paragraph (1) above, the eligible scheme concerned ceases to be approved under Chapter I of Part XIV otherwise than by virtue of the operation of sub-paragraph (2)(a) above, the scheme shall not, by virtue of that application, become an approved personal pension scheme.

Cross references – SI 2001/118 reg. 4: documents to accompany application for approval under Sch. 23ZA, para. 3.

EXCESSIVE FUNDING OF CERTAIN INDIVIDUAL MEMBERS

4(1) The Board may refuse or withhold approval under paragraph 3 above in the case of an eligible scheme of a prescribed description if or so long as they are not satisfied that prescribed requirements will be fulfilled with respect to-
(a) the value of any prescribed benefits which may be provided for or in respect of an individual member of a prescribed description, and
(b) the value of the assets held for the purpose of providing benefits for or in respect of that member,
if approval under paragraph 3 above is granted.
4(2) Regulations may make provision for or in connection with cases where the value mentioned in paragraph (b) of sub-paragraph (1) above exceeds, or exceeds by more than a prescribed percentage, the value mentioned in paragraph (a) of that sub-paragraph.
4(3) The provision that may be made by virtue of sub-paragraph (2) above includes provision for or in connection with eliminating or reducing any such excess within a prescribed period by one or more prescribed methods.
4(4) Regulations may make provision for the purposes of this paragraph for or in connection with–
(a) the valuation of benefits; or
(b) the valuation of assets.
4(5) The provision that may be made by virtue of sub-paragraph (4)(a) or (b) above includes provision with respect to, or in connection with,–
(a) the person by whom any such valuation is to be made;
(b) the method or principles of valuation to be used;
(c) certification of any such valuations and of any prescribed matters relating to or connected with them;
(d) any facts, matters or assumptions by reference to which any such valuation is to be made;
(e) any tables to be used for the purpose of making any such valuation;
(f) the basis on which any such tables are to be prepared;
(g) the manner in which any such tables are to be applied.
4(6) The methods or principles of valuation and the tables that may be prescribed by virtue of sub-paragraph (5) above include methods or principles or, as the case may be, tables published by the Government Actuary for any purposes of the personal pension provisions of this Act.

Statutory instruments – SI 2001/118: regulations made under Sch. 23ZA, para. 4.

DIRECTIONS AS TO CONTRIBUTIONS BETWEEN VALUATION AND DATE OF CHANGE ETC.

5(1) The Board may give directions for or in connection with–
(a) prohibiting the making of contributions during the post-valuation period, or
(b) restricting the amount of the contributions that may be made during that period,
by or in respect of members of a converting scheme.
5(2) Directions under sub-paragraph (1) above–
(a) may be given in respect of schemes generally, schemes of a particular description or any particular scheme or schemes; and
(b) may make different provision in relation to different schemes or different members.
5(3) Any directions under sub-paragraph (1) above must be complied with by–
(a) the trustees and managers, or administrators, of any scheme to which the directions relate;
(b) any member of such a scheme to whom the directions relate; and
(c) any person who is the employer of such a member.
5(4) If there is any contravention of, or failure to comply with, directions under sub-paragraph (1) above, the Board may–
(a) refuse or withhold approval of the conversion application in question; or
(b) revoke or vary any approval granted or any conditions pending the satisfaction of which approval is withheld.
5(5) Sub-paragraph (4) above is without prejudice to any other powers of the Board.

5(6) In this paragraph–

"conversion application", in the case of a converting scheme, means the application under paragraph 3(1) above in respect of the scheme;

"converting scheme" means a scheme in respect of which an application under paragraph 3(1) above has been made and not withdrawn or finally refused;

"the post-valuation period", in the case of a converting scheme, means the period which–

(a) begins with the day as at which any valuation for the purposes of paragraph 4 above is made in connection with the conversion application; and

(b) ends with the day preceding the date of the change (or, if earlier, the date on which the conversion application is withdrawn or finally refused).

5(7) For the purposes of this paragraph, an application is "finally refused" when it has been refused by the Board and–

(a) the time for appealing under section 651 against the refusal has expired without such an appeal being made; or

(b) an appeal under that section against the refusal has been withdrawn or finally disposed of in a way which affirms refusal of the application.

5(8) Any directions under this paragraph must be given in writing.

SCHEME RULES TO ALLOW CHANGES FOR PURPOSE OF CONVERSION

6 An approved retirement benefits scheme shall be taken to include provisions allowing the making of changes to any provisions of the scheme for the purpose of enabling the scheme to become an eligible scheme, notwithstanding anything to the contrary in any provision of the scheme.".

Former Sch. 23ZA inserted by FA 2000, s. 61 and Sch. 13, para. 27.

Statutory instruments – SI 2001/118 made under former Sch. 23ZA, para. 2 and 4.

SCHEDULE 23A – MANUFACTURED DIVIDENDS AND INTEREST

Section 736A

[Omitted by CTA 2010, s. 1177 and Sch. 1, para. 145 and repealed by CTA 2010, s. 1181 and Sch. 3, Pt. 1.]

History – Sch. 23A omitted by CTA 2010, s. 1177 and Sch. 1, para. 145 and repealed by CTA 2010, s. 1181 and Sch. 3, Pt. 1, with effect for corporation tax purposes for accounting periods ending on or after 1 April 2010, and for income and capital gains tax purposes for the tax year 2010–11 and subsequent tax years.

Notes – Sch. 23A rewritten for income tax purposes as follows:
Para. 1(1): ITA 2007, s. 566(1), (2), (3), (4), (5), 567(1), (2), (3), (4), 569(3), 591(1), 601(1), 607(1), 921(3), 926(1).
Para. 2(1): ITA 2007, s. 573(1), 591(1), 926(1).
Para. 2(2): ITA 2007, s. 573(1), (2), (3).
Para. 2(3): ITA 2007, s. 573(2), (4).
Para. 2(6): ITA 2007, s. 577(1), (3), (5).
Para. 2(7): ITA 2007, s. 577(4), (6).
Para. 2(8): ITA 2007, s. 577(7).
Para. 2A(1): ITA 2007, s. 24(1), 573(4), 574(1), (2), (3), (10).
Para. 2A(1ZA): ITA 2007, s. 574(4), (6).
Para. 2A(1ZB): ITA 2007, s. 574(5).
Para. 2A(1A): ITA 2007, s. 574(7), (8).
Para. 2A(1B): ITA 2007, s. 575(1), (2), (3).
Para. 2A(4): ITA 2007, s. 574(10).
Para. 3(1): ITA 2007, s. 578(1), 591(1), 919(1), 920(1), 926(1).
Para. 3(2): ITA 2007, s. 24(1), 578(3), 579(1), (2), (3), 919(2), (3), 979(4).
Para. 3(2A): ITA 2007, s. 579(4), (5), (6), (7), (10).
Para. 3(2B): ITA 2007, s. 580(1), (2), (3).
Para. 3(3): ITA 2007, s. 578(2).
Para. 3(4): ITA 2007, s. 919(1), 920(1).
Para. 3(5): ITA 2007, s. 920(1), (2).
Para. 3(6): ITA 2007, s. 920(3), (4).
Para. 3(7): ITA 2007, s. 946.
Para. 3(8): ITA 2007, s. 975(1), (2), (5).
Para. 3(9): ITA 2007, s. 975(6).
Para. 3(10): ITA 2007, s. 579(3), (9).
Para. 3(13): ITA 2007, s. 589(1), (2).
Para. 3A(1): ITA 2007, s. 920(4), 921(1), (2).
Para. 3A(2): ITA 2007, s. 921(1), 1024.
Para. 4(1): ITA 2007, s. 581(1), 591(1), 922(1), 923(1), 926(1).
Para. 4(2): ITA 2007, s. 581(1), 922(1), (2), 923(4), 979(4).
Para. 4(2A): ITA 2007, s. 926(1).
Para. 4(3): ITA 2007, s. 581(1), 922(1), 923(1), (2), (3), 925(3).
Para. 4(3A): ITA 2007, s. 918(5), 923(2).
Para. 4(3B): ITA 2007, s. 924(1), (2).
Para. 4(4): ITA 2007, s. 581(2), (3), (4), (5), (6).
Para. 4(5): ITA 2007, s. 589(1), (3), (4), 590(1), (2).
Para. 4(6): ITA 2007, s. 590(3), (4).
Para. 4(7): ITA 2007, s. 925(1), (2), (5).
Para. 4(7AA): ITA 2007, s. 925(3), (4).
Para. 7(1): ITA 2007, s. 583(1), (2), (3), (4), 589(1), 591(1), 926(1).
Para. 7(3): ITA 2007, s. 584(1), (2), (3).
Para. 7(4): ITA 2007, s. 584(4).
Para. 8(1): ITA 2007, s. 585(1), (2).
Para. 8(1A): ITA 2007, s. 582(1), (2), (3), (4), (5), Sch. 1 para. 339.
Para. 8(2): ITA 2007, s. 586(1).
Para. 8(2A): ITA 2007, s. 586(2).
Para. 8(3): ITA 2007, s. 586(3), (4).
Para. 8(4): ITA 2007, s. 588, 927.

Sch. 23A rewritten for corporation tax purposes as follows:
Para. 1(1): CTA 2010, s. 804(2), 806(1), (2), (3), 813(4), 814(1), (2), (3), (4), (5), (6).
Para. 2(1): CTA 2010, s. 781(1), 782, 784(1).
Para. 2(1A): CTA 2010, s. 783(1).
Para. 2(1B): CTA 2010, s. 783(2).
Para. 2(1C): CTA 2010, s. 783(3), (4).
Para. 2(1D): CTA 2010, s. 783(5).
Para. 2(1E): CTA 2010, s. 783(6).
Para. 2(1F): CTA 2010, s. 783(7).
Para. 2(2): CTA 2010, s. 784(1).
Para. 2(3): CTA 2010, s. 784(1).
Para. 2(3A): CTA 2010, s. 787(1).
Para. 2(3B): CTA 2010, s. 787(2).
Para. 2(6): CTA 2010, s. 788(1), (3), (5).
Para. 2(7): CTA 2010, s. 788(4), (6).
Para. 2(8): CTA 2010, s. 788(7).
Para. 4(1): CTA 2010, s. 781(2), 790, 791(1), 792(1), 794(1).
Para. 4(1A): CTA 2010, s. 791(1).
Para. 4(1B): CTA 2010, s. 791(2).
Para. 4(1C): CTA 2010, s. 791(3).
Para. 4(1D): CTA 2010, s. 791(4).
Para. 4(1E): CTA 2010, s. 791(5), (6).
Para. 4(1F): CTA 2010, s. 791(7).
Para. 4(4): CTA 2010, s. 792(1), (2), (3), (4), 794(1), (2), (3), (4).
Para. 4(4A): CTA 2010, s. 795(1).
Para. 4(4B): CTA 2010, s. 795(2).
Para. 4(5): CTA 2010, s. 813(1), (2), (3).
Para. 4(9): CTA 2010, s. 792(2), 794(2).
Para. 4A(1): CTA 2010, s. 793(1), (2), (3).
Para. 4A(2): CTA 2010, s. 793(2), (3).
Para. 4A(3): CTA 2010, s. 793(4).
Para. 4A(4): CTA 2010, s. 793(5).
Para. 4A(5): CTA 2010, s. 793(7).
Para. 4A(6): CTA 2010, s. 793(7).
Para. 4A(7): CTA 2010, s. 793(6).
Para. 7(1): CTA 2010, s. 796(1), (2), (3), 797(1), (2), (3), 813(1), (3).
Para. 7(1A): CTA 2010, s. 797(4).
Para. 7(3): CTA 2010, s. 798(1), (2), (3).
Para. 7(4): CTA 2010, s. 798(4).
Para. 7A(1): CTA 2010, s. 799(1).
Para. 7A(2): CTA 2010, s. 799(1), (2), (6).
Para. 7A(3): CTA 2010, s. 800(2), (3), (4).
Para. 7A(4): CTA 2010, s. 800(5).
Para. 7A(5): CTA 2010, s. 800(6), (7).
Para. 7A(6): CTA 2010, s. 801(2).
Para. 7A(7): CTA 2010, s. 801(3).
Para.7A(8): CTA 2010, s. 799(1), (4), (5).
Para. 7A(10): CTA 2010, s. 799(3), 800(1), (8), (9), 801(1).
Para. 8(1): CTA 2010, s. 803(1), (2).
Para. 8(1A): CTA 2010, s. 802(1), (2), (3), (4), (5).
Para. 8(2): CTA 2010, s. 789.
Para. 8(4): CTA 2010, s. 804(1).

SCHEDULE 24 – ASSUMPTIONS FOR CALCULATING CHARGEABLE PROFITS, CREDITABLE TAX AND CORRESPONDING UNITED KINGDOM TAX OF FOREIGN COMPANIES

Section 747(6)

Cross references – FA 2000, Sch. 22, para. 54: provisions to which Sch. 24 is subject in relation to tonnage tax companies.

GENERAL

1(1) The company shall be assumed to be resident in the United Kingdom.

1(2) Nothing in sub-paragraph (1) above requires it to be assumed that there is any change in the place or places at which the company carries on its activities.

1(3) For the avoidance of doubt, it is hereby declared that, if any sums forming part of the company's profits for an accounting period have been received by the company without any deduction of or charge to tax and have been so received by virtue of section 1279 of CTA 2009 the effect of the assumption in sub-paragraph (1) above is that those sums are to be brought within the charge to tax for the purposes of calculating the company's chargeable profits or corresponding United Kingdom tax.

(3A) In any case where–

(a) it is at any time necessary for any purpose of Chapter IV of Part XVII to determine in the case of any person the chargeable profits of the company for an accounting period, and

(b) at that time–

(i) it has not been established in the case of that person that that or any earlier accounting period of the company is an accounting period in respect of which an apportionment under section 747(3) falls to be made,

(ii) [Omitted by FA 2009, s. 36 and Sch. 16, para. 2(6)(a).]

in determining the chargeable profits of the company for the accounting period mentioned in paragraph (a) above, it shall be assumed, for the purposes of those provisions of paragraphs 2 and 10 below which refer to the first accounting period in respect of which an apportionment under section 747(3) falls to be made, that that period (but not any earlier period) is an accounting period in respect of which such an apportionment falls to be made.

1(4) In any case where–

(a) it is at any time necessary for any purpose of Chapter IV of Part XVII to determine in the case of any person the chargeable profits of the company for an accounting period, and

(b) at that time it has not been established in the case of that person that that or any earlier accounting period of the company is an accounting period in respect of which an apportionment under section 747(3) falls to be made,

in determining the chargeable profits of the company for the accounting period mentioned in paragraph (a) above, it shall be assumed, for the purposes of those provisions of paragraph 9 below which refer to the first accounting period in respect of which an apportionment under section 747(3) falls to be made, that such an apportionment falls to be made in respect of that period (but not in respect of any earlier period).

1(5) Nothing in this Schedule affects any liability for, or the computation of, corporation tax in respect of a trade which is carried on by a company resident outside the United Kingdom through a permanent establishment in the United Kingdom.

1(6) [Omitted by FA 2009, s. 36 and Sch. 16, para. 2(6)(b).]

History – In para. 1(3), the words "section 1279 of CTA 2009" substituted for "section 154(2) of the Finance Act 1996" by CTA 2009, s. 1322 and Sch. 1, para. 286(2), with effect for corporation tax purposes for accounting periods ending on or after 1 April 2009, and for income tax and capital gains tax purposes for the tax year 2009–10 and subsequent tax years.

In para. 1(3) the words " and have been…Finance Act 1996" were substituted by FA 1996, s. 154(7) and Sch. 28, para. 6, for the purposes of income tax, with effect for 1996–97 and subsequent years of assessment and for the purposes of corporation tax for accounting periods ending after 31 March 1996.

Para. 1(3A)(b)(ii) (and the "and" before it) omitted by FA 2009, s. 36 and Sch. 16, para. 2(6)(a), with effect in relation to accounting periods of controlled foreign companies beginning on or after 1 July 2009, subject to rules for accounting periods straddling 1 July 2009 in FA 2009, Sch. 16, para. 7 and transitional provisions in FA 2009, Sch. 16, para. 8.

In para. 1(3A), the words "or which is an ADP exempt period", which appeared after "falls to be made" in both places, omitted by FA 2009, s. 36 and Sch. 16, para. 2(6)(a), with effect in relation to accounting periods of controlled foreign companies beginning on or after 1 July 2009, subject to rules for accounting periods straddling 1 July 2009 in FA 2009, Sch. 16, para. 7 and transitional provisions in FA 2009, Sch. 16, para. 8.

Para. 1(3A) amended by FA 1998, s. 113 and Sch. 17, para. 17(1)–(5), as respects accounting periods of UK resident companies ending on or after 1 July 1999 (the corporation tax self-assessment appointed day under FA 1994, s. 199 by virtue of SI 1998/3173 (C. 78)), as follows:

- by inserting the words "in the case of any person" in para. 1(3A)(a);
- by substituting para. 1(3A)(b)(i);
- by inserting the words "in the case of that person" in para. 1(3A)(b)(ii); and
- by substituting the words following para. 1(3A)(b).

Para. 1(3A) was inserted by FA 1996, s. 182 and Sch. 36, para. 3(2), in relation to accounting periods of a controlled foreign company beginning on or after 28 November 1995.

Para. 1(4) amended by FA 1998, s. 113 and Sch. 17, para. 17(1), (6)–(9), as respects accounting periods of UK resident companies ending on or after 1 July 1999, the corporation tax self-assessment appointed day (see above), as follows:

- by inserting the words "in the case of any person" in para. 1(4)(a);
- by substituting para. 1(4)(b) and the words following para. 1(4)(b).

In para. 1(4) the words "in determining … paragraph (a) above" inserted by FA 1995, s. 133 and Sch. 25, para. 6(2) and this amendment is deemed always to have had effect.

In para. 1(5) the words "permanent establishment" substituted for "branch or agency" by FA 2003, s. 153(1)(a) in relation to accounting periods beginning on or after 1 January 2003.

Para. 1(6) omitted by FA 2009, s. 36 and Sch. 16, para. 2(6)(b), with effect in relation to accounting periods of controlled foreign companies beginning on or after 1 July 2009, subject to rules for accounting periods straddling 1 July 2009 in FA 2009, Sch. 16, para. 7 and transitional provisions in FA 2009, Sch. 16, para. 8. Former para. 1(6) read as follows:

"**1(6)** Any reference in this Schedule to an "ADP exempt period", in the case of any company, is a reference to an accounting period of the company–

(a) which begins on or after 28th November 1995; and

(b) in respect of which the company pursued, within the meaning of Part I of Schedule 25, an acceptable distribution policy.".

Former para. 1(6) inserted by FA 1996, s. 182 and Sch. 36, para. 3(3), in relation to accounting periods of a controlled foreign company beginning on or after 28 November 1995.

Derivations – FA 1984, Sch. 16, para. 1.

Cross references – S. 47: UK government securities held by non-residents.

S. 48: securities of foreign states.

Pt. XVII, Ch. IV: controlled foreign companies.

S. 750(2)–(4): meaning of "corresponding UK tax".

FA 1998, Sch. 17, para. 37(2)–(4): commencement and transitional provisions – separate determinations and computations to be made, as respects accounting period of a non-resident company which ends before 1 July 1999, in cases where at least one UK-resident company has an accounting period ending on or after that day, and at least one other UK-resident company has an accounting period ending before that day.

2(1) The company shall be assumed to have become resident in the United Kingdom (and, accordingly, within the charge to corporation tax) at the beginning of the first accounting period

(a) in respect of which an apportionment under section 747(3) falls to be made,

(b) [Omitted by FA 2009, s. 36 and Sch. 16, para. 2(6)(c).]

and that United Kingdom residence shall be assumed to continue throughout subsequent accounting periods of the company (whether or not an apportionment falls to be made in respect of all or any of them) until the company ceases to be controlled by persons resident in the United Kingdom.

2(2) Except in so far as the following provisions of this Schedule otherwise provide, for the purposes of calculating a company's chargeable profits or corresponding United Kingdom tax for any accounting period which is not the first such period referred to in sub-paragraph (1) above (and, in particular, for the purpose of applying any relief which is relevant to two or more accounting periods), it shall be assumed that a calculation of chargeable profits or, as the case may be, corresponding United Kingdom tax has been made for every previous accounting period throughout which the company was, by virtue of sub-paragraph (1) above, assumed to have been resident in the United Kingdom.

History – In para. 2(1)(a), words "an apportionment under section 747(3) falls to be made" substituted for "a direction is given under section 747(1)", and in words following para. (b), words "an apportionment falls to be made" substituted for "a direction is given", by FA 1998, s. 113 and Sch. 17, para. 18, as respects accounting periods of UK resident companies ending on or after 1 July 1999, the corporation tax self-assessment appointed day under FA 1994, s. 199 by virtue of SI 1998/3173 (C. 78)).

Para. 2(1)(b) (and the "or" before it) omitted by FA 2009, s. 36 and Sch. 16, para. 2(6)(c), with effect in relation to accounting periods of controlled foreign companies beginning on or after 1 July 2009, subject to rules for accounting periods straddling 1 July 2009 in FA 2009, Sch. 16, para. 7 and transitional provisions in FA 2009, Sch. 16, para. 8.

Para. 2(1)(a) and (b) substituted by FA 1996, s. 182 and Sch. 36, para. 3(4), in relation to accounting periods of a controlled foreign company beginning on or after 28 November 1995.

Derivations – FA 1984, Sch. 16, para. 2.

Cross references – S. 750(2)–(4): meaning of "corresponding UK tax".

S. 751: accounting periods of a company resident outside the UK.

FA 1998, Sch. 17, para. 37(2)–(4): commencement and transitional provisions – separate determinations and computations to be made, as respects accounting period of a non-resident company which ends before 1 July 1999, in cases where at least one UK-resident company has an accounting period ending on or after that day, and at least one other UK-resident company has an accounting period ending before that day.

3 The company shall be assumed not to be a close company.

Derivations – FA 1984, Sch. 16, para. 3.

4(1) Subject to sub-paragraph (2) below, where any relief under the Corporation Tax Acts is dependent upon the making of a claim or election, the company shall be assumed to have made that claim or election which would give the maximum amount of relief and to have made that claim or election within any time limit applicable to it, except that the company shall be assumed not to have made an election under section 18A of CTA 2009.

4(1A) Sub-paragraph (2) below applies to any accounting period of the company–

(a) in respect of which an apportionment under section 747(3) falls to be made; or

(b) [omitted by FA 2009, s. 36 and Sch. 16, para. 2(6)(d).]

4(2) Where this sub-paragraph applies to an accounting period of the company, then if, by notice given to an officer of the Board at any time not later than the expiry of the period of twenty months following the end of the accounting period or within such longer period as the Board may in any particular case allow, the United Kingdom resident company which has or, as the case may be, any two or more United Kingdom resident companies which together have, a majority interest in the company so request, the company shall be assumed–

(a) not to have made any claim or election specified in the notice; or

(b) to have made a claim or election so specified, being different from one assumed by sub-paragraph (1) above but being one which (subject to compliance with any time limit) could have been made in the case of a company within the charge to corporation tax; or

(c) to have disclaimed or required the postponement, in whole or in part, of an allowance if (subject to compliance with any time limit) a company within the charge to corporation tax could have disclaimed the allowance or, as the case may be, required such a postponement.

4(2A) [Repealed by FA 1998, s. 113 and Sch. 17, para. 19(4), s. 165 and Sch. 27, Pt. III(27).]

4(2B) For the purposes of sub-paragraph (1) an election under section 9A of CTA 2010 (designated currency of a UK resident investment company) is not to be regarded as an election upon which relief under the Corporation Tax Acts is dependent, and sub-paragraph (2)(b) does not apply in relation to such an election.

4(2C) But if, by notice given to an officer of the Board, the United Kingdom resident company which has or, as the case may be, any two or more United Kingdom resident companies which together have, a majority interest in the company so request, the company shall be assumed (subject to section 9A(2) of CTA 2010) to have made an election under section 9A of that Act in the form specified in the notice (and accordingly that section and section 9B of that Act apply to determine the effect (if any) of that election).

4(3) For the purposes of this paragraph, a United Kingdom resident company has, or two or more United Kingdom resident companies together have, a **majority interest** in the company if on the apportionment of the company's chargeable profits for the relevant accounting period under section 747(3) more than half of the amount of those profits–

(a) which are apportioned to all United Kingdom resident companies, and

(b) which give rise to any liability on any such companies under subsection (4)(a) of that section,

are apportioned to the United Kingdom resident company or companies concerned.

4(3A) [Omitted by FA 2009, s. 36 and Sch. 16, para. 2(6)(e).]

4(4) In sub-paragraph (3) above **"the relevant accounting period"** means the accounting period or, as the case may be, the first accounting period in which the relief in question is or would be available in accordance with sub-paragraph (1) above.

History – In para. 4(1), the words ", except that the company shall be assumed not to have made an election under section 18A of CTA 2009." inserted by FA 2011, s. 48 and Sch. 13, para. 12, with effect from 19 July 2011.
In para. 4(1A)(a), words "an apportionment under section 747(3) falls to be made" substituted for "a direction is given under section 747(1)" by FA 1998, s. 113 and Sch. 17, para. 19(1), (2), as respects accounting periods of UK resident companies ending on or after 1 July 1999, the corporation tax self-assessment appointed day under FA 1994, s. 199 by virtue of SI 1998/3173 (C. 78).
Para. 4(1A)(b) (and the "or" before it) omitted by FA 2009, s. 36 and Sch. 16, para. 2(6)(d), with effect in relation to accounting periods of controlled foreign companies beginning on or after 1 July 2009, subject to rules for accounting periods straddling 1 July 2009 in FA 2009, Sch. 16, para. 7 and transitional provisions in FA 2009, Sch. 16, para. 8.
Former para. 4(1A) inserted by FA 1996, s. 182 and Sch. 36, para. 3(5), in relation to accounting periods of a controlled foreign company beginning on or after 28 November 1995.
In para. 4(2), words "given to an officer of the Board" substituted for "given to the Board", and "the period of twenty … the accounting period" substituted for "the appropriate period", by FA 1998, s. 113 and Sch. 17, para. 19(1), (3), as respects accounting periods of UK resident companies ending on or after 1 July 1999, the corporation tax self-assessment appointed day (see above).
In para. 4(2), at the beginning the words "Where this sub-paragraph … of the company, then" were inserted by FA 1996, s. 182 and Sch. 36, para. 3(6)(a), in relation to accounting periods of a controlled foreign company beginning on or after 28 November 1995.
In para. 4(2), the words "the appropriate period" were substituted by FA 1996, s. 182 and Sch. 36, para. 3(6)(b), in relation to accounting periods of a controlled foreign company beginning on or after 28 November 1995.
Para. (2B) and (2C) inserted by FA 2011, s. 34 and Sch. 7, para. 5, with effect in relation to periods of account beginning on or after 1 April 2011.
Para. 4(2A) repealed by FA 1998, s. 113 and Sch. 17, para. 19(1), (4), s. 165 and Sch. 27, Pt. III(27), as respects accounting periods of UK resident companies ending on or after 1 July 1999, the corporation tax self-assessment appointed day (see above).
Para. 4(2A) was originally inserted by FA 1996, s. 182 and Sch. 36, para. 3(7), in relationto accounting periods of a controlled foreign company beginning on or after 28 November 1995.
In para. 4(3)(b), words "any liability" substituted for "an assessment" by FA 1998, s. 113 and Sch. 17, para. 19(1), (5), as respects accounting periods of UK resident companies ending on or after 1 July 1999, the corporation tax self-assessment appointed day (see above).
Para. 4(3A) omitted by FA 2009, s. 36 and Sch. 16, para. 2(6)(e), with effect in relation to accounting periods of controlled foreign companies beginning on or after 1 July 2009, subject to rules for accounting periods straddling 1 July 2009 in FA 2009, Sch. 16, para. 7 and transitional provisions in FA 2009, Sch. 16, para. 8.
In former para. 4(3A)(a), words "an apportionment under section 747(3) had fallen to be made" substituted for "a direction had been duly given under section 747(1)", and para. 4(3A)(b) substituted, by FA 1998, s. 113 and Sch. 17, para. 19(1), (6), as respects accounting periods of UK resident companies ending on or after 1 July 1999, the corporation tax self-assessment appointed day (see above).
Former para. 4(3A) inserted by FA 1996, s. 182 and Sch. 36, para. 3(8), in relation to accounting periods of a controlled foreign company beginning on or after 28 November 1995.

Derivations – FA 1984, Sch. 16, para. 4.

Cross references – S. 751: accounting periods of a company resident outside the UK.
S. 753(6): inspector's notice of revised chargeable profits or creditable tax resulting from notice given under para. 4(2) (or para. 12) excludes appeal provisions of s. 753(6).
TMA 1970, s. 115: service of notices.
FA 1998, Sch. 17, para. 37(2)–(4): commencement and transitional provisions – separate determinations and computations to be made, as respects accounting period of a non-resident company which ends before 1 July 1999, in cases where at least one UK-resident company has an accounting period ending on or after that day, and at least one other UK-resident company has an accounting period ending before that day.
FA 2002, Sch. 29, para. 116(3) (assumptions for computing chargeable profits of controlled foreign companies): disapplication of para. 4(1) except where notice given in accordance with para. 4(2).

Other material – ICAEW Technical Release TR 760 (not reproduced): Revenue view that an election etc. must be received within time limit, but accept postage in reasonable expectation of arrival; in cases of dispute inspector will request evidence such as a recorded delivery receipt or well-maintained post book.

4A [Repealed by FA 1995, s. 133 and Sch. 25, para. 6(3), s. 162 and Sch. 29, Pt. VIII(18) and deemed never to have been inserted.]

GROUP RELIEF ETC.

5(1) The company shall be assumed to be neither a member of a group of companies nor a member of a consortium for the purposes of any provision of the Tax Acts.

5(2) Where, under Part 5 of CTA 2010, any relief is in fact surrendered by the company and allowed to another company by way of group relief, it shall be assumed that the chargeable profits of the company, apart from this paragraph, are to be increased by an amount of additional profits equal to the amount of the relief so surrendered and allowed.

History – In para. 5(2), the words "Part 5 of CTA 2010" substituted for the words "Chapter IV of Part X" by CTA 2010, s. 1177 and Sch. 1, para. 146(2), with effect for corporation tax purposes for accounting periods ending on or after 1 April 2010, and for income and capital gains tax purposes for the tax year 2010–11 and subsequent tax years.

Para. 5 made into subpara. 5(1), and para. 5(2) inserted, FA 2000, s. 97 and Sch. 27, para. 10, with effect in relation to accounting periods ending on or after 1 April 2000.

Derivations – FA 1984, Sch. 16, para. 5.

Cross references – FA 2000, Sch. 22, para. 54(4): CFC a member of a tonnage tax group.

6 [Repealed by FA 2001, s. 110 and Sch. 33, Pt. 2(10).]

History – Para. 6 repealed by FA 2001, s. 110 and Sch. 33, Pt. II(10) with effect in relation to payments made after 11 May 2001.

7 [Repealed by FA 1998, s. 31 and Sch. 3, para. 43(1), (3), s. 165 and Sch. 27, Pt. III(2).]

History – Para. 7 repealed by FA 1998, s. 31 and Sch. 3, para. 43(1), (3), s. 165 and Sch. 27, Pt. III(2), with effect in relation to accounting periods of companies resident outside the UK which begin on or after 6 April 1999.

COMPANY RECONSTRUCTIONS

8 Without prejudice to the operation of Chapter 1 of Part 22 of CTA 2010 in a case where the company is the predecessor, within the meaning of that Chapter, and a company resident in the United Kingdom is the successor, within the meaning of that Chapter–

(a) the assumption that the company is resident in the United Kingdom shall not be regarded as requiring it also to be assumed that the company is within the charge to tax in respect of a trade for the purposes of that Chapter, and

(b) except in so far as the company is actually within that charge (by carrying on the trade through a permanent establishment in the United Kingdom), it shall accordingly be assumed that the company can never be the successor, within the meaning of that Chapter, to another company (whether resident in the United Kingdom or not).

History – In para. 8, the words "Chapter 1 of Part 22 of CTA 2010" substituted for the words "section 343", and each reference to "that Chapter" substituted for the words "that section" by CTA 2010, s. 1177 and Sch. 1, para. 146(3), with effect for corporation tax purposes for accounting periods ending on or after 1 April 2010, and for income and capital gains tax purposes for the tax year 2010–11 and subsequent tax years.

In para. 8 the words "permanent establishment" substituted for "branch or agency" by FA 2003, s. 153(1)(a) in relation to accounting periods beginning on or after 1 January 2003.

Derivations – FA 1984, Sch. 16, para. 8.

Cross references – S. 343: company reconstructions without significant change of ownership.

LOSSES IN PRE-DIRECTION ACCOUNTING PERIODS

9(1) This paragraph applies in any case where the company incurred a loss in a trade in an accounting period–

(a) which precedes the first accounting period in respect of which an apportionment under section 747(3) falls to be made (**"the starting period"**); and

(b) which ended less than six years before the beginning of the starting period; and

(c) in which the company was not resident in the United Kingdom;

and in this paragraph any such accounting period is referred to as a **"pre-apportionment period"**.

9(2) [Repealed by FA 1998, s. 113 and Sch. 17, para. 20(4), s. 165 and Sch. 27, Pt. III(27).]

9(3) If a claim is made for the purpose by the United Kingdom resident company or companies referred to in paragraph 4(2) above, the chargeable profits (if any) of the company for accounting periods beginning with that pre-apportionment period which is specified in the claim and in which a loss is incurred as mentioned in sub-paragraph (1) above shall be determined (in accordance with the provisions of this Schedule other than this paragraph) on the assumption that that pre-apportionment period was the first accounting period in respect of which an apportionment under section 747(3) fell to be made.

9(4) A claim under sub-paragraph (3) above shall be made by notice given to an officer of the Board within the period of twenty months following the end of the starting period or within such longer period as the Board may in any particular case allow.

9(5) [Repealed by FA 1998, s. 113 and Sch. 17, para. 20(7), (8), s. 165 and Sch. 27 Pt. III(27).]

9(6) [Repealed by FA 1998, s. 113 and Sch. 17, para. 20(7), (8), s. 165 and Sch. 27, Pt. III(27).]

9(7) Nothing in–

(a) paragraph 10 of Schedule 18 to the Finance Act 1998 (claims or elections in company tax returns), or

(b) Schedule 1A to the Management Act (claims or elections not included in returns),

shall apply, whether by virtue of section 754 or otherwise, to a claim under sub-paragraph (3) above.

History – In para. 9(1), opening words "Subject to sub-paragraph (2) below," repealed, words "an apportionment under section 747(3) falls to be made" substituted for "a direction is given under section 747(1)", and "pre-apportionment" substituted for "pre-direction", by FA 1998, s. 113 and Sch. 17, para. 20(1), (2) and (3), s. 165 and Sch. 27, Pt. III(27), as respects accounting periods of UK resident companies ending on or after 1 July 1999, the corporation tax self-assessment appointed day under FA 1994, s. 199 by virtue of SI 1998/3173 (C. 78).

ICTA 1988

In para. 9(1)(c), the words ", and is not to be assumed by virtue of paragraph 2(1)(b) above to have been resident,", which appeared after "not resident", omitted by FA 2009, s. 36 and Sch. 16, para. 2(6)(f), with effect in relation to accounting periods of controlled foreign companies beginning on or after 1 July 2009, subject to rules for accounting periods straddling 1 July 2009 in FA 2009, Sch. 16, para. 7 and transitional provisions in FA 2009, Sch. 16, para. 8.
In para. 9(1)(c), the words ", and is not to be … to have been resident," were inserted by FA 1996, s. 182 and Sch. 36, para. 3(9), in relation to accounting periods of a controlled foreign company beginning on or after 28 November 1995.
Para. 9(2) repealed by FA 1998, s. 113 and Sch. 17, para. 20(1), (4), s. 165 and Sch. 27, Pt. III(27), as respects accounting periods of UK resident companies ending on or after 1 July 1999, the corporation tax self-assessment appointed day (see above).
In para. 9(3), words "pre-apportionment" substituted for "pre-direction" in both places, and "an apportionment under section 747(3) fell to be made" substituted for "a direction was given under section 747(1)" by FA 1998, s. 113 and Sch. 17, para. 20(1), (2) and (5), as respects accounting periods of UK resident companies ending on or after 1 July 1999, the corporation tax self-assessment appointed day (see above).
Para. 9(4) substituted by FA 1998, s. 113 and Sch. 17, para. 20(1), (6), as respects accounting periods of UK resident companies ending on or after 1 July 1999, the corporation tax self-assessment appointed day (see above).
Para. 9(5), (6) repealed by FA 1998, s. 113 and Sch. 17, para. 20(1), (7) and (1), (8) respectively, s. 165 and Sch. 27, Pt. III(27), as respects accounting periods of UK resident companies ending on or after 1 July 1999, the corporation tax self-assessment appointed day (see above).
Para. 9(7) addedby FA 1998, s. 113 and Sch. 17, para. 20(1), (9), as respects accounting periods of UK resident companies ending on or after 1 July 1999, the corporation tax self-assessment appointed day (see above).

Derivations – FA 1984, Sch. 16, para. 9.

Cross references – S. 751: accounting periods of a company resident outside the UK.
Pt. XVII, Ch. IV: controlled foreign companies.
TMA 1970, s. 42: procedure for making claims.
TMA 1970, s. 115: service of notices.
FA 1998, Sch. 17, para. 37(2)–(4): commencement and transitional provisions – separate determinations and computations to be made, as respects accounting period of a non-resident company which ends before 1 July 1999, in cases where at least one UK-resident company has an accounting period ending on or after that day, and at least one other UK-resident company has an accounting period ending before that day.

CAPITAL ALLOWANCES

10(1) Subject to paragraph 12 below, if, in an accounting period falling before the beginning of the first accounting period

(a) in respect of which an apportionment under section 747(3) falls to be made,

(b) [omitted by FA 2009, s. 36 and Sch. 16, para. 2(6)(g).]

the company incurred any capital expenditure on the provision of plant or machinery for the purposes of its trade, that plant or machinery shall be assumed, for the purposes of Part 2 of the Capital Allowances Act, to have been provided for purposes wholly other than those of the trade and not to have been brought into use for the purposes of that trade until the beginning of that first accounting period, and section 13 of that Act (use for qualifying activity of plant or machinery provided for other purposes) shall apply accordingly.

10(2) This paragraph shall be construed as one with Part 2 of the Capital Allowances Act.

History – In para. 10(1), reference in opening words to para. 12 substituted for references to paras. 11 and 12, and words in para. (a) "an apportionment under section 747(3) falls to be made" substituted for "a direction is given under section 747(1)", by FA 1998, s. 113 and Sch. 17, para. 21, as respects accounting periods of UK resident companies ending on or after 1 July 1999, the corporation tax self-assessment appointed day under FA 1994, s. 199 by virtue of SI 1998/3173 (C. 78)).
Para. 10(1)(b) (and the "or" before it) omitted by FA 2009, s. 36 and Sch. 16, para. 2(6)(g), with effect in relation to accounting periods of controlled foreign companies beginning on or after 1 July 2009, subject to rules for accounting periods straddling 1 July 2009 in FA 2009, Sch. 16, para. 7 and transitional provisions in FA 2009, Sch. 16, para. 8.
Para. 10(1)(a) and (b) and the word "the" which followed were substituted by FA 1996, s. 182 and Sch. 36, para. 3(10), in relation to accounting periods of a controlled foreign company beginning on or after 28 November 1995.
In para. 10(1) the words "plant or machinery for the purposes of its trade, that plant or machinery shall be assumed, for the purposes of Part 2 of the Capital Allowances Act" substituted for "machinery or plant for the purposes of its trade, that machinery or plant shall be assumed, for the purposes of Part II of the 1990 Act", and "section 13 of that Act (use for qualifying activity of plant or machinery provided for other purposes)" substituted for "section 81 of that Act (expenditure treated as equivalent to market value at the time the machinery or plant is brought into use)" and, in para. 10(2), the words "Part 2 of the Capital Allowances Act" substituted for "Part II of the 1990 Act", by CAA 2001, s. 578 and Sch. 2, para. 66(1), (2) with effect as respects allowances and charges falling to be made for chargeable periods ending, for income tax purposes, on or after 6 April 2001, and for corporation tax purposes, on or after 1 April 2001, these references to provisions of CAA 1990 having themselves originally been substituted by s. 164 and Sch. 1, para. 8(42)(a), (b) of that Act. Under CAA 2001, Sch. 3, para. 8, where a person is affected by a change in the law brought into effect by CAA 2001, they may elect for the pre-consolidation law to apply for the chargeable period straddling the commencement of CAA 2001.

Derivations – FA 1984, Sch. 16, para. 10, as amended (para. 10(1)) by FA 1985, Sch. 14, para. 16.

Cross references – S. 751: accounting periods of a company resident outside the UK.
FA 1998, Sch. 17, para. 37(2)–(4): commencement and transitional provisions – separate determinations and computations to be made, as respects accounting period of a non-resident company which ends before 1 July 1999, in cases where at least one UK-resident company has an accounting period ending on or after that day, and at least one other UK-resident company has an accounting period ending before that day.

11 [Repealed by FA 1998, s. 113 and Sch. 17, para. 22, s. 165 and Sch. 27, Pt. III(27).]

History – Para. 11 repealed by FA 1998, s. 113 and Sch. 17, para. 22, s. 165 and Sch. 27, Pt. III(27), with effect as respects accounting periods of UK resident companies ending on or after 1 July 1999, the corporation tax self-assessment appointed day under FA 1994, s. 199 by virtue of SI 1998/3173 *(C. 78))*.

11A [Repealed by FA 2005, s. 104 and Sch. 11, Pt. 2(6).]

History – Para. 11A repealed by FA 2005, s. 104 and Sch. 11, Pt. 2(6), with effect for periods of account beginning on or after 16 March 2005.

Former para. 11A(3) and (6) repealed by FA 1998, s. 113 and Sch. 17, para. 23, s. 165 and Sch. 27, Pt. III(27), with effect as respects accounting periods of UK resident companies ending on or after 1 July 1999, the corporation tax self-assessment appointed day under FA 1994, s. 199 by virtue of SI 1998/3173 (C. 78)).
Former para. 11A inserted by FA 1995, s. 133 and Sch. 25, para. 6(4) with effect in relation to accounting periods affected by s. 747A.

UNREMITTABLE OVERSEAS INCOME

12 For the purposes of the application of Part 18 of CTA 2009 to the company's income it shall be assumed–

(a) that any reference in section 1274(3) or (4) of that Act to the United Kingdom is a reference to both the United Kingdom and the territory in which the company is in fact resident; and

(b) that a claim under section 1275 of that Act (claim for relief for unremittable income) may be made on behalf of the company by the United Kingdom resident company or companies referred to in paragraph 4(2) above.

History – In para. 12, the words "Part 18 of CTA 2009" substituted for "section 584" by CTA 2009, s. 1322 and Sch. 1, para. 286(3)(a), with effect for corporation tax purposes for accounting periods ending on or after 1 April 2009, and for income tax and capital gains tax purposes for the tax year 2009–10 and subsequent tax years.
In para. 12, the words "section 1274(3) or (4) of that Act" substituted for "paragraph (a) or paragraph (b) of subsection (1) of that section" by CTA 2009, s. 1322 and Sch. 1, para. 286(3)(b), with effect for corporation tax purposes for accounting periods ending on or after 1 April 2009, and for income tax and capital gains tax purposes for the tax year 2009–10 and subsequent tax years.
In para. 12, the words "a claim under section 1275 of that Act (claim for relief for unremittable income) may be made" substituted for the words "The references to sections 75 and 76 are references to those provisions as they have effect" by CTA 2009, s. 1322 and Sch. 1, para. 286(3)(c), with effect for corporation tax purposes for accounting periods ending on or after 1 April 2009, and for income tax and capital gains tax purposes for the tax year 2009–10 and subsequent tax years.

Derivations – FA 1984, Sch. 16, para. 13.

Cross references – TMA 1970, s. 115: service of notices.

EXCHANGE GAINS AND LOSSES

13 [Repealed by FA 2002, s. 141 and Sch. 40, Pt. 3(10).]

History – Para. 13 repealed by FA 2002, s. 141 and Sch. 40, Pt. 3(10), with effect relation to accounting periods beginning on or after 1 October 2002, subject to the transitional provisions in FA 2002, s. 79 and Sch. 23, Pt. 3.
Para. 13 originally inserted by FA 1995, s. 133 and Sch. 25, para. 6(5), with effect in relation to accounting periods affected by s. 747A.

14 [Repealed by FA 2002, s. 141 and Sch. 40, Pt. 3(10).]

History – Para. 14 repealed by FA 2002, s. 141 and Sch. 40, Pt. 3(10), with effect relation to accounting periods beginning on or after 1 October 2002, subject to the transitional provisions in FA 2002, s. 79 and Sch. 23, Pt. 3.
Para. 14 inserted by FA 1995, s. 133 and Sch. 25, para. 6(5), with effect in relation to accounting periods affected by s. 747A.

15 [Repealed by FA 2002, s. 141 and Sch. 40, Pt. 3(10).]

History – Para. 15 repealed by FA 2002, s. 141 and Sch. 40, Pt. 3(10), with effect relation to accounting periods beginning on or after 1 October 2002, subject to the transitional provisions in FA 2002, s. 79 and Sch. 23, Pt. 3.
Para. 15 originally inserted by FA 1995, s. 133 and Sch. 25, para. 6(5), with effect in relation to accounting periods affected by s. 747A.

16 [Repealed by FA 2002, s. 141 and Sch. 40, Pt. 3(10).]

History – Para. 16 repealed by FA 2002, s. 141 and Sch. 40, Pt. 3(10), with effect relation to accounting periods beginning on or after 1 October 2002, subject to the transitional provisions in FA 2002, s. 79 and Sch. 23, Pt. 3.
Para. 16 originally inserted by FA 1995, s. 133 and Sch. 25, para. 6(5), with effect in relation to accounting periods affected by s. 747A.

17 [Repealed by FA 2002, s. 141 and Sch. 40, Pt. 3(10).]

History – Para. 17 repealed by FA 2002, s. 141 and Sch. 40, Pt. 3(10), with effect relation to accounting periods beginning on or after 1 October 2002, subject to the transitional provisions in FA 2002, s. 79 and Sch. 23, Pt. 3.
Para. 17 originally inserted by FA 1995, s. 133 and Sch. 25, para. 6(5), with effect in relation to accounting periods affected by s. 747A.

18 [Repealed by FA 2002, s. 141 and Sch. 40, Pt. 3(10).]

History – Para. 18 repealed by FA 2002, s. 141 and Sch. 40, Pt. 3(10), with effect relation to accounting periods beginning on or after 1 October 2002, subject to the transitional provisions in FA 2002, s. 79 and Sch. 23, Pt. 3.
Para. 18 originally inserted by FA 1995, s. 133 and Sch. 25, para. 6(5), with effect in relation to accounting periods affected by s. 747A.

19 [Repealed by FA 2002, s. 141 and Sch. 40, Pt. 3(10).]

History – Para. 19 repealed by FA 2002, s. 141 and Sch. 40, Pt. 3(10), with effect relation to accounting periods beginning on or after 1 October 2002, subject to the transitional provisions in FA 2002, s. 79 and Sch. 23, Pt. 3.
Para. 19 originally inserted by FA 1995, s. 133 and Sch. 25, para. 6(5) with effect in relation to accounting periods affected by s. 747A.

TRANSFER PRICING

20 [Ceased to have effect by virtue of FA 2004, s. 30(9), Sch. 5, para. 4 and repealed by FA 2004, s. 326, Sch. 42, Pt. 2(1).]

History – Para. 20 ceased to have effect by virtue of FA 2004, s. 30(9), Sch. 5, para 4 and was repealed by FA 2004, s. 326, Sch. 42, Pt. 2(1), with effect in relation to chargeable periods beginning on or after 1 April 2004, subject to provisions for periods beginning before, and ending on or after, 1 April 2004 (companies), or 6 April 2004 (persons within the charge to income tax) which effectively split the period into two, separate, periods (corporation tax – FA 2004, s. 37(3): income tax – 37(4)).

SCHEDULE 25 – CASES WHERE SECTION 747(3) DOES NOT APPLY

Section 748

History – Heading to Sch. 25 substituted by FA 1998, s. 113 and Sch. 17, para. 25, with effect as respects accounting periods of companies resident in the UK which end on or after 1 July 1999, the corporation tax self-assessment appointed day.

Cross references – SI 1994/3226: Exchange Gains and Losses (Transitional Provisions) Regulations 1994, reg. 1(5) – treatment where acceptable distribution policy followed.

Other material – HMRC specialist publications: Corporation Tax Guidance: Controlled Foreign Companies.

Part I – Acceptable Distribution Policy

[Omitted by FA 2009, s. 36 and Sch. 16, para. 1(3).]

History – Pt. I omitted by FA 2009, s. 36 and Sch. 16, para. 1(3) with effect in relation to accounting periods of controlled foreign companies beginning on or after 1 July 2009, subject to rules for accounting periods straddling 1 July 2009 in FA 2009, Sch. 16, para. 7 and transitional provisions in FA 2009, Sch. 16, para. 8. Former Pt. I read as follows:

"Part I – Acceptable Distribution Policy

1 The provisions of this Part of this Schedule have effect for the purposes of paragraph (a) of subsection (1) of section 748 and the other provisions of Chapter IV of Part XVII which refer to a company pursuing an acceptable distribution policy.

History – In para. 1, words from "and the other provisions" to the end added by FA 1998, s. 113 and Sch. 17, para. 26, with effect as respects accounting periods of companies resident in the UK which end on or after 1 July 1999, the corporation tax self-assessment appointed day under FA 1994, s. 199 by virtue of SI 1998/3173 (C. 78).

Derivations – FA 1984, Sch. 17, para. 1.

Cross references – FA 1998, Sch. 17, para. 37(2)–(4): commencement and transitional provisions – separate determinations and computations to be made, as respects accounting period of a non-resident company which ends before 1 July 1999, in cases where at least one UK-resident company has an accounting period ending on or after that day, and at least one other UK-resident company has an accounting period ending before that day.

2(1) Subject to paragraph 2A below, a controlled foreign company pursues an acceptable distribution policy in respect of a particular accounting period if, and only if–

(a) a dividend which is not paid out of specified profits is paid for that accounting period; and
(b) the dividend is paid during, or not more than eighteen months after the expiry of, that period or at such later time as the Board may, in any particular case, allow; and
(c) [Repealed by FA 1990, s. 67(3)(a), 132 and Sch. 19, Pt. IV.]
(d) the amount of the dividend or, if there is more than one, of the aggregate of those dividends which is paid to persons resident in the United Kingdom is not less than 90 per cent of the company's net chargeable profits for the accounting period referred to in paragraph (a) above or, where sub-paragraph (4) or (5) below applies, of the appropriate portion of those profits.

2(1A) A payment of dividend to a company shall not fall within sub-paragraph (1)(d) above unless it is taken into account in computing the company's income for corporation tax and–

(a) it is chargeable neither under Chapter 2 of Part 3 of CTA 2009 as profits of a trade carried on wholly or partly in the United Kingdom nor under section 436A (gross roll-up business: separate charge on profits);
(b) if it is chargeable under Chapter 2 of Part 3 of CTA 2009 as profits of a trade carried on wholly or partly in the United Kingdom, or under section 436A, it is not involved in a UK tax avoidance scheme;

and paragraph 2B below has effect for the purposes of paragraph (b) above.

2(1B) A dividend paid by a company shall not fall within sub-paragraph (1)(d) above if, and to the extent that, the profits which are the relevant profits in relation to the dividend derive from dividends or other distributions paid to the company at any time which are dividends or other distributions–

(a) to which section 1285 of CTA 2009 applied; or
(b) to which that section would have applied if the company had been resident in the United Kingdom at that time.

Subsections (3) and (4) of section 799 (double taxation relief: computation of underlying tax) apply for the purposes of this sub-paragraph as they apply for the purposes of subsection (1) of that section.

2(2) [Repealed by FA 1994, s. 134(2) and s. 258 and Sch. 26, Pt. V(15).]

2(3) For the purposes of this paragraph and paragraph 2A below, a dividend which is not paid for the period or periods the profits of which are, in relation to the dividend, the relevant profits for the purposes of section 799 shall be treated (subject to sub-paragraph (3A) below) as so paid.

2(3A) For the purposes of this paragraph and paragraph 2A below–

(a) where a dividend is paid for a period which is not an accounting period but falls wholly within an accounting period it shall be treated as paid for that accounting period, and
(b) where a dividend (**"the actual dividend"**) is paid for a period which falls within two or more accounting periods–
  (i) it shall be treated as if it were a number of separate dividends each of which is paid for so much of the period as falls wholly within an accounting period, and
  (ii) the necessary apportionment of the amount of the actual dividend shall be made to determine the amount of the separate dividends.

2(4) This sub-paragraph applies where–

(a) throughout the accounting period in question all the issued shares of the controlled foreign company are of a single class, and
(b) at the end of that accounting period some of those shares are held by persons resident outside the United Kingdom, and
(c) at no time during that accounting period does any person have an interest in the company other than an interest derived from the issued shares of the company;

and in a case where this sub-paragraph applies the appropriate portion for the purposes of sub-paragraph (1)(d) above is the fraction of which the denominator is the total number of the issued shares of the company at the end of the accounting period in question and, subject to sub-paragraph (8) below, the numerator is the number of those issued shares by virtue of which persons resident in the United Kingdom have interests in the company at that time.

2(5) This sub-paragraph applies where–

(a) throughout the accounting period in question there are only two classes of issued shares of the controlled foreign company and, of those classes, one (**"non-voting shares"**) consists of non-voting fixed-rate preference shares and the other (**"voting shares"**) consists of shares which carry the right to vote in all circumstances at general meetings of the company; and
(b) at the end of that accounting period some of the issued shares of the company are held by persons resident outside the United Kingdom; and

(c) at no time during that accounting period does any person have an interest in the company other than an interest derived from non-voting or voting shares;

and in a case where this sub-paragraph applies the appropriate portion of the profits referred to in sub-paragraph (1)(d) above is the amount determined in accordance with sub-paragraph (6) below.

2(6) The amount referred to in sub-paragraph (5) above is that given by the formula–

$$\frac{P \times Q}{R} + \frac{(X - P) \times Y}{Z}$$

where–

P is the amount of any dividend falling within (a) and (b) of sub-paragraph (1) above which is paid in respect of the non-voting shares or, if there is more than one such dividend, of the aggregate of them;

Q is, subject to sub-paragraph (8) below, the number of the non-voting shares by virtue of which persons resident in the United Kingdom have interests in the company at the end of the accounting period in question;

R is the total number at that time of the issued non-voting shares;

X is the net chargeable profits for the accounting period in question;

Y is, subject to sub-paragraph (8) below, the number of voting shares by virtue of which persons resident in the United Kingdom have interests in the company at the end of that accounting period; and

Z is the total number at that time of the issued voting shares.

2(7) For the purposes of sub-paragraph (5)(a) above, non-voting fixed-rate preference shares are shares–

(a) which are restricted preference shares as defined in section 160(2) to (7) of CTA 2010 as modified by sub-paragraph (7A); and

(b) which either carry no right to vote at a general meeting of the company or carry such a right which is contingent upon the non-payment of a dividend on the shares and which has not in fact become exercisable at any time prior to the payment of a dividend for the accounting period in question.

History – In para. 2(7)(a), the words "section 160(2) to (7) of CTA 2010 as modified by sub-paragraph (7A)" substituted for the words "fixed-rate preference shares as defined in paragraph 1 of Schedule 18" by CTA 2010, s. 1177 and Sch. 1, para. 147(2)(a), with effect for corporation tax purposes for accounting periods ending on or after 1 April 2010, and for income and capital gains tax purposes for the tax year 2010–11 and subsequent tax years.

2(7A) The modification referred to in sub-paragraph (7)(a) is, in section 160 of CTA 2010, the substitution for subsection (6) of–

"**160(6)** Condition D is that the shares do not carry any right to dividends other than dividends which–

(a) are of a fixed amount or are at a fixed percentage rate of the nominal value of the shares, and

(b) represent no more than a reasonable commercial return on the new consideration mentioned in subsection (3)."

History – Para. 2(7A) inserted by CTA 2010, s. 1177 and Sch. 1, para. 147(2)(b), with effect for corporation tax purposes for accounting periods ending on or after 1 April 2010, and for income and capital gains tax purposes for the tax year 2010–11 and subsequent tax years.

2(8) In any case where the immediate interests held by persons resident in the United Kingdom who have indirect interests in a controlled foreign company at the end of a particular accounting period do not reflect the proportion of the shares or, as the case may be, shares of a particular class in the company by virtue of which they have those interests (as in the case where they hold, directly or indirectly, part of the shares in a company which itself holds, directly or indirectly, some or all of the shares in the controlled foreign company) the number of those shares shall be treated as reduced for the purposes of sub-paragraph (4) or (6) above, as the case may be, to such number as may be appropriate having regard to–

(a) the immediate interests held by the persons resident in the United Kingdom; and

(b) any intermediate shareholdings between those interests and the shares in the controlled foreign company.

2(9) The definition of "profits" in section 747(6)(b) does not apply to any reference in this paragraph to specified profits or to relevant profits for the purposes of section 799.

History – In para. 2(1)(d), the words "90 per cent of the company's net chargeable profits" were substituted by FA 1996, s. 182 and Sch. 36, para. 4(2)(a), in relation to accounting periods of a controlled foreign company beginning on or after 28 November 1995.

In para. 2(1), the words "paragraph 2A" substituted; in para. (a), words which appeared at the end of the paragraph, omitted; and in para. (b), the words "that period" substituted and in para. (d) the word "amount" and the words "is not less than" substituted by FA 1994, s. 134(2)(a), in determining whether a company pursues an acceptable distribution policy in respect of accounting periods ending on or after 30 November 1993.

Para. 2(1)(c) repealed by FA 1990, s. 67(3)(a) with application to dividends paid on or after 20 March 1990.

Para. 2(1A)(a) substituted by CTA 2009, s. 1322 and Sch. 1, para. 287(2)(a), with effect for corporation tax purposes for accounting periods ending on or after 1 April 2009, and for income tax and capital gains tax purposes for the tax year 2009–10 and subsequent tax years.

In para. 2(1A)(b), the words "Chapter 2 of Part 3 of CTA 2009 as profits of a trade carried on wholly or partly in the United Kingdom, or under section 436A" substituted for the words "Case I, or under Case VI in the circumstances described in paragraph (a) above" by CTA 2009, s. 1322 and Sch. 1, para. 287(2)(b), with effect for corporation tax purposes for accounting periods ending on or after 1 April 2009, and for income tax and capital gains tax purposes for the tax year 2009–10 and subsequent tax years.

In para. 2(1A)(a), "436A" substituted for "436, 439B or 441" by FA 2007, s. 38 and Sch. 7, para. 56, with effect for the purposes of corporation tax, for periods of account of insurance companies beginning on or after 1 January 2007, and for the purposes of income tax, for the tax year 2007–08 and subsequent tax years (but see transitional provisions at FA 2007, Sch. 7, para. 80–84).

In para. 2(1A), clauses (a) and (b) and words after those clauses at the end of para. 2(1A) inserted by FA 2001, s. 82(2) with application to dividends paid on or after 7 March 2001 by a controlled foreign company for any of its accounting periods which ends on or after that date.

Para. 2(1A) inserted by FA 1990, s. 67(3)(b) with application to dividends paid on or after 20 March 1990.

In para. 2(1B)(a), the words "section 1285 of CTA 2009" substituted for "section 208" by CTA 2009, s. 1322 and Sch. 1, para. 287(3), with effect for corporation tax purposes for accounting periods ending on or after 1 April 2009, and for income tax and capital gains taxpurposes for the tax year 2009–10 and subsequent tax years.

Para. 2(1B) inserted by FA 1999, s. 88(1), with effect for the purpose of determining whether dividends paid on or after 9 March 1999 for accounting periods ending on or after that date fall within para. 2(1)(d) above.

Para. 2(2) repealed by FA 1994, s. 134(2)(b) and by s. 258 and Sch. 26, Pt. V(15), in determining whether a company pursues an acceptable distribution policy in respect of accounting periods ending on or after 30 November 1993.

Para. 2(3), (3A) substituted for former para. 2(3) by FA 1994, s. 134(2)(c), in determining whether a company pursues an acceptable distribution policy in respect of accounting periods ending on or after 30 November 1993.

In para. 2(6), the words "net chargeable profits" were substituted by FA 1996, s. 182 and Sch. 36, para. 4(2)(b), in relation to accounting periods of a controlled foreign company beginning on or after 28 November 1995.

Derivations – FA 1984, Sch. 17, para. 2, and (para. 2(1)) F(No. 2)A 1987, s. 65(2).

Cross references – S. 751: accounting periods of a company resident outside the UK.

S. 799: computation of underlying tax.

S. 834(3): when dividends are paid.

SI 1999/1408: modification of para. 2 in relation to certain companies resident outside the UK which carry on general insurance business (modification does not apply for accounting periods ended on or after 28 October 2008).

ICTA 1988

Other material – IR decision: IRDec. 2: a case summarised where 90 per cent distribution test (see para. 2(2)) appropriate to a company which was acting as a conduit for management fees and the bulk of its net profits came from investments.

2A(1) Paragraph 2 above shall have effect in accordance with this paragraph to determine whether a controlled foreign company pursues an acceptable distribution policy in respect of a particular accounting period (**"the relevant accounting period"**).

2A(2) Subject to sub-paragraphs (4) and (4A) below, where the distribution condition is satisfied in relation to the relevant accounting period, then, in addition to any dividend which falls within paragraph 2(1)(a) above apart from this paragraph–

(a) any dividend which is paid for the accounting period (**"the preceding period"**) immediately preceding the relevant accounting period and which is not an excluded dividend shall be treated as falling within that paragraph, and

(b) if the distribution condition is satisfied in relation to the preceding period, any dividend which is paid for the accounting period immediately preceding the preceding period which is not an excluded dividend shall be treated as falling within that paragraph,

and so on; and in this sub-paragraph **"dividend"** means a dividend not paid out of specified profits.

2A(3) For the purposes of this paragraph, the distribution condition is satisfied in relation to any accounting period if–

(a) a dividend or dividends are paid for the period to persons resident in the United Kingdom,

(b) the amount or, as the case may be, aggregate amount of any dividends falling within paragraph (a) above is not less than–

  (i) the relevant profits for that period, or

  (ii) where paragraph 2(4) or (5) above applies (with the modifications of paragraph 2 made by sub-paragraph (5) below), the appropriate portion of those profits, and

(c) any dividends falling within that paragraph are paid not later than the time by which any dividend paid for the relevant accounting period is required by paragraph 2(1)(b) above to be paid;

or if there are no relevant profits for the period.

2A(4) Where, by reason only of the fact that a company pursued an acceptable distribution policy in respect of any accounting period (**"the earlier period"**) earlier than the relevant accounting period, no apportionment under section 747(3) fell to be made in respect of the earlier period, sub-paragraph (2) above shall apply to any dividend required to be taken into account for the purpose of showing that the company pursued an acceptable distribution policy in respect of the earlier period only to the extent (if any) to which that dividend was not required to be taken into account for that purpose.

2A(4A) Sub-paragraph (2) does not apply where the distribution condition is satisfied in relation to the relevant accounting period, but–

(a) the relevant profits for that period do not include income within sub-paragraph (4B), and

(b) if that income were included, the distribution condition would not be satisfied in relation to that period.

2A(4B) The income within this sub-paragraph is–

(a) any income which accrues during the relevant accounting period to the trustees of a settlement in relation to which the company is a settlor or a beneficiary, and

(b) any income which accrues during that period to a partnership of which the company is a partner, apportioned between the company and the other partners on a just and reasonable basis.

2A(4C) Where there is more than one settlor or beneficiary in relation to the settlement mentioned in sub-paragraph (4B)(a), the income is to be apportioned between the company and the other settlors or beneficiaries on a just and reasonable basis.

2A(4D) In sub-paragraph (4B)(b), **"partnership"** includes an entity established under the law of a country or territory outside the United Kingdom of a similar character to a partnership; and **"partner"** is to be read accordingly.

2A(5) The modifications of paragraph 2 above referred to in sub-paragraph (3)(b) above are that–

(a) the references in sub-paragraphs (4) and (5) to the accounting period in question are to be read as references to the accounting period for which the dividend or dividends are paid,

(b) the references in those sub-paragraphs to sub-paragraph (1)(d) are to be read as references to sub-paragraph (3)(b) above, and

(c) the reference in the definition of "X" in sub-paragraph (6) to net chargeable profits is to be read as a reference to relevant profits.

2A(6)–(7) [Rrepealed by FA 1996, s. 182 and Sch. 36, para. 4(3)(c) and s. 205 and Sch. 41, Pt. V(34).]

2A(8) For the purposes of this paragraph–

(aa) a dividend is an excluded dividend if it is paid, in whole or in part, out of the total profits from which (in accordance with section 747(6)(a)) the chargeable profits for an excluded period are derived,

(a) a period is an excluded period if it is an accounting period in respect of which an apportionment under section 747(3) falls to be made, and

(b) relevant profits for any accounting period are the profits which would be the relevant profits of that period for the purposes of section 799 if a dividend were actually paid for that period.

History – In para. 2A(1), words which appeared after "controlled foreign company" were omitted and repealed by FA 1996, s. 182 and Sch. 36, para. 4(3)(a) and s. 205 and Sch. 41, Pt. V(34), in relation to accounting periods of a controlled foreign company beginning on or after 28 November 1995.

In para. 2A(2), the words "sub-paragraphs (4) and (4A)" substituted for the words "sub-paragraph (4)" by FA 2008, s. 64(4)(a), with effect in relation to any dividend paid on or after 12 March 2008.

In para. 2A(2)(a) and (b), words "immediately preceding" substituted for "which immediately precedes", and "which is not an excluded dividend" substituted for "is not an excluded period", and in para. 2A(4) words "no apportionment under section 747(3) fell to be made in respect of the earlier period" substituted for "no direction could be given in respect of the earlier period under section 747(1)", by FA 1998, s. 113 and Sch. 17, para. 27(1)–(3), with effect as respects accounting periods of companies resident in the UK which end on or after 1 July 1999, the corporation tax self-assessment appointed day under FA 1994, s. 199 by virtue of SI 1998/3173 (C. 78).

Para. 2A(4A) inserted by FA 2008, s. 64(4)(b), with effect in relation to any dividend paid on or after 12 March 2008.

Para. 2A(4B) inserted by FA 2008, s. 64(4)(b), with effect in relation to any dividend paid on or after 12 March 2008.

Para. 2A(4C) inserted by FA 2008, s. 64(4)(b), with effect in relation to any dividend paid on or after 12 March 2008.

Para. 2A(4D) inserted by FA 2008, s. 64(4)(b), with effect in relation to any dividend paid on or after 12 March 2008.

In para. 2A(5)(c), the words "net chargeable profits" were substituted by FA 1996, s. 182 and Sch. 36, para. 4(3)(b), in relation to accounting periods of a controlled foreign company beginning on or after 28 November 1995.

Para. 2A(6) and (7) were omitted and repealed by FA 1996, s. 182 and Sch. 36, para. 4(3)(c) and s. 205 and Sch. 41, Pt. V(34), in relation to accounting periods of a controlled foreign company beginning on or after 28 November 1995.

Para. 2A(8)(aa) inserted, and words in para. 2A(8)(a) "an apportionment under section 747(3) falls to be made" substituted for "a direction is given under section 747(1)", by FA 1998, s. 113 and Sch. 17, para. 27(1), (4) and (5), with effect as respects accounting periods of companies resident in the UK which end on or after 1 July 1999, the corporation tax self-assessment appointed day (see above).

Para.2A inserted by FA 1994, s. 134(3), in determining whether a company pursues an acceptable distribution policy in respect of accounting periods ending on or after 30 November 1993.

Cross references – FA 1998, Sch. 17, para. 37(2)–(4): commencement and transitional provisions – separate determinations and computations to be made, as respects accounting period of a non-resident company which ends before 1 July 1999, in cases where at least one UK-resident company has an accounting period ending on or after that day, and at least one other UK-resident company has an accounting period ending before that day.

2B(1) This paragraph has effect for the purposes of paragraph 2(1A)(b) above.

2B(2) No payment of dividend by a controlled foreign company for an accounting period shall be regarded as involved in a UK tax avoidance scheme by reason only that there is no charge to tax under section 747(4)(a) if the controlled foreign company pursues an acceptable distribution policy for that accounting period.

2B(3) **"UK tax avoidance scheme"** means a scheme or arrangement the purpose, or one of the main purposes, of which is to achieve a reduction in United Kingdom tax.

2B(4) A scheme or arrangement achieves a reduction in United Kingdom tax if, apart from the scheme or arrangement, any company–

(a) would have been liable for any such tax or for a greater amount of any such tax; or

(b) would not have been entitled to a relief from or repayment of any such tax or would have been entitled to a smaller relief from or repayment of any such tax.

2B(5) In this paragraph–

"arrangement" means an arrangement of any kind, whether in writing or not;

"United Kingdom tax" means corporation tax or any tax chargeable as if it were corporation tax.

History – Para. 2B inserted by FA 2001, s. 82(3) with application to dividends paid on or after 7 March 2001 by a controlled foreign company for any of its accounting periods which ends on or after that date.

3(1)–(4) [Omitted and repealed by FA 1996, s. 182 and Sch. 36, para. 4(4)(a) and s. 205 and Sch.41, Pt. V(34).]

3(4A) Subject to sub-paragraph (5) below, for the purposes of this Part of this Schedule, the net chargeable profits of a controlled foreign company for any accounting period are–

(a) its chargeable profits for that period, less

(b) the amount (if any) which, if an apportionment under section 747(3) fell to be made in respect of the period, would be the company's unrestricted creditable tax for that period;

and for the purposes of this sub-paragraph **"unrestricted creditable tax"** in relation to a company's accounting period means the amount which would be its creditable tax for that period if the reference in section 751(6)(a) to Part XVIII did not include section 797.

3(5) In any case where–

(a) a controlled foreign company pays a dividend for any period out of specified profits, and

(b) those profits represent dividends received by the company, directly or indirectly, from another controlled foreign company,

so much of those specified profits as is equal to the dividend referred to in paragraph (a) above shall be left out of account in determining, for the purposes of this Part of this Schedule, the chargeable profits of the controlled foreign company referred to in that paragraph for any accounting period.

History – Para. 3(1)–(4) were omitted and repealed by FA 1996, s. 182 and Sch. 36, para. 4(4)(a) and s. 205 and Sch. 41, Pt. V(34), in relation to accounting periods of a controlled foreign company beginning on or after 28 November 1995.

In para. 3(4A), words "an apportionment under section 747(3) fell to be made" substituted for "a direction were given under section 747(1)" by FA 1998, s. 113 and Sch. 17, para. 28, with effect as respects accounting periods of companies resident in the UK which end on or after 1 July 1999, the corporation tax self-assessment appointed day under FA 1994, s. 199 by virtue of SI 1998/3173 (C. 78).

Para. 3(4A), and in para. 3(5), the words "or, where…chargeable profits", inserted by FA 1994, s. 134(4), in determining whether a controlled foreign company pursues an acceptable distribution policy in respect of accounting periods ending on or after 30 November 1993.

In para. 3(5), words after "Part of this Schedule" were omitted and repealed by FA 1996, s. 182 and Sch. 36, para. 4(4)(b) and s. 205 and Sch. 41, Pt. V(32), in relation to accounting periods of a controlled foreign company beginning on or after 28 November 1995.

Derivations – FA 1984, Sch. 17, para. 3.

Cross references – S. 751: accounting periods of a company resident outside the UK.

S. 753(4), (5): right of appeal to special commissioners and requirement for Board to give notice in relation to declaration made by virtue of para. 3(2).

FA 1998, Sch. 17, para. 37(2)–(4): commencement and transitional provisions – separate determinations and computations to be made, as respects accounting period of a non-resident company which ends before 1 July 1999, in cases where at least one UK-resident company has an accounting period ending on or after that day, and at least one other UK-resident company has an accounting period ending before that day.

4(1) For the purposes of this Part of this Schedule, where–

(a) a controlled foreign company pays a dividend (**"the initial dividend"**) to another company which is also not resident in the United Kingdom, and

(b) that other company or another company which is related to it pays a dividend (**"the subsequent dividend"**) to a United Kingdom resident, and

(c) [Repealed by FA 1990, s. 67(3)(a), 132 and Sch. 19, Pt. IV.]

(d) the subsequent dividend is paid out of profits which are derived, directly or indirectly, from the whole or part of the initial dividend,

so much of the initial dividend as is represented by the subsequent dividend shall be regarded as paid to the United Kingdom resident and shall be taken to satisfy the conditions in paragraph 2(1A) above.

(1A) A payment to a company shall not be a subsequent dividend within the meaning of sub-paragraph (1)(b) above unless it is taken into account in computing the company's income for corporation tax and–

(a) it is chargeable neither under Chapter 2 of Part 3 of CTA 2009 as profits of a trade carried on wholly or partly in the United Kingdom nor under section 436A (gross roll-up business: separate charge on profits);

(b) if it is chargeable under Chapter 2 of Part 3 of CTA 2009 as profits of a trade carried on wholly or partly in the United Kingdom, or under section 436A, it is not involved in a UK tax avoidance scheme;

and paragraph 4A below has effect for the purposes of paragraph (b) above.

4(2) For the purposes of this paragraph, one company is **related** to another if neither is resident in the United Kingdom and the other–

(a) controls directly or indirectly, or

(b) is a subsidiary of a company which controls directly or indirectly,

at least 10 per cent of the voting power in the first-mentioned company; and where one company is so related to another and that other is so related to a third company, the first company is for the purposes of this paragraph related to the third, and so on where there is a chain of companies, each of which is related to the next.

History – Para. 4(1A)(a) substituted by CTA 2009, s. 1322 and Sch. 1, para. 287(4)(a), with effect for corporation tax purposes for accounting periods ending on or after 1 April 2009, and for income tax and capital gains tax purposes for the tax year 2009–10 and subsequent tax years.

In para. 4(1A)(b), the words "Chapter 2 of Part 3 of CTA 2009 as profits of a trade carried on wholly or partly in the United Kingdom, or under section 436A" substituted for the words "Case I, or under Case VI in the circumstances described in paragraph (a) above" by CTA 2009, s. 1322 and Sch. 1, para. 287(4)(b), with effect for corporation tax purposes for accounting periods ending on or after 1 April 2009, and for income tax and capital gains tax purposes for the tax year 2009–10 and subsequent tax years.

Para. 4(1)(c) repealed by FA 1990, s. 67(3)(a) with application to dividends paid on or after 20 March 1990.

In para. 4(1) the words "and shall be taken to satisfy the conditions in paragraph 2(1A) above" inserted by FA 2001, s. 82(4) with application to dividends paid on or after 7 March 2001 by a controlled foreign company for any of its accounting periods which ends on or after that date.

In para. 4(1A), "436A" substituted for "436, 439B or 441" by FA 2008, s. 43 and Sch. 17, para. 29(1), with effect in relation to accounting periods beginning on or after 1 January 2008.

In para. 4(1A), clauses (a) and (b) and the words after those clauses inserted by FA 2001, s. 82(5) with application to dividends paid on or after 7 March 2001 by a controlled foreign company for any of its accounting periods which ends on or after that date.

Para. 4(1A) inserted by FA 1990, s. 67(3)(c) with application to dividends paid on or after 20 March 1990.
In para. 4(2) the words "neither is resident in the United Kingdom and" inserted by FA 2001, s. 82(6) with application to dividends paid on or after 7 March 2001 by a controlled foreign company for any of its accounting periods which ends on or after that date.

Derivations – FA 1984, Sch. 17, para. 4 and (para. 4(1)) F(No. 2)A 1987, s. 65(3).

Cross references – s. 801C: double tax relief – separate streaming of dividend if the whole or any part of it falls to be treated by virtue of Para. 4(1A) as representing an acceptable distribution policy dividend paid by the controlled foreign company to a United Kingdom resident.

4A(1) This paragraph has effect for the purposes of paragraph 4(1A)(b) above.

4A(2) No payment to a company resident in the United Kingdom which represents the whole or part of a dividend paid by a controlled foreign company for an accounting period shall be regarded as involved in a UK tax avoidance scheme by reason only that–

(a) there is no charge to tax under section 747(4)(a) if the controlled foreign company pursues an acceptable distribution policy for that accounting period, and

(b) so much of the dividend as is represented by that payment will (if paragraph 4(1) above has effect) fall to be brought into account in determining whether the controlled foreign company has done so.

4A(3) **"UK tax avoidance scheme"** means a scheme or arrangement the purpose, or one of the main purposes, of which is to achieve a reduction in United Kingdom tax.

4A(4) A scheme or arrangement achieves a reduction in United Kingdom tax if, apart from the scheme or arrangement, any company–

(a) would have been liable for any such tax or for a greater amount of any such tax; or

(b) would not have been entitled to a relief from or repayment of any such tax or would have been entitled to a smaller relief from or repayment of any such tax.

4A(5) In this paragraph–

"arrangement" means an arrangement of any kind, whether in writing or not;

"United Kingdom tax" means corporation tax or any tax chargeable as if it were corporation tax.

History – Para. 4A inserted by FA 2001, s. 82(7) with application to dividends paid on or after 7 March 2001 by a controlled foreign company for any of its accounting periods which ends on or after that date.".

Part II – Exempt Activities

5(1) The provisions of this Part of this Schedule have effect for the purposes of paragraph (b) of subsection (1) of section 748.

5(1A) Except as provided in paragraph 8 below, the provisions of this Part of this Schedule apply in relation to a company which is resident in an EEA territory in the same way as they apply in relation to a company which is resident elsewhere.

5(2) In the case of a controlled foreign company–

(a) which is, by virtue of section 749(5), presumed to be resident in a territory in which it is subject to a lower level of taxation, and

(b) the business affairs of which are, throughout the accounting period in question, effectively managed in a territory outside the United Kingdom other than one in which companies are liable to tax by reason of domicile, residence or place of management,

references in the following provisions of this Part of this Schedule to the territory in which that company is resident shall be construed as references to the territory falling within paragraph (b) above, or, if there is more than one, to that one of them which may be notified to the Board by the United Kingdom resident company or companies referred to in paragraph 4(2) of Schedule 24.

5(3) In the case of a controlled foreign company–

(a) which is, by virtue of section 749(5), presumed to be resident in a territory in which it is subject to a lower level of taxation,

(b) the business affairs of which are, throughout the accounting period in question, effectively managed in a special administrative region, and

(c) which is liable to tax for that period in that region,

references in the following provisions of this Part of this Schedule to the territory in which that company is resident shall be construed as references to that region.

5(4) In sub-paragraph (3) above **"special administrative region"** means the Hong Kong or the Macao Special Administrative Region of the People's Republic of China.

5(5) Where sub-paragraph (3) above applies, it applies in place of sub-paragraph (2).

History – Para. 5(1A) inserted by FA 2007, s. 48 and Sch. 15, para. 7(2), with effect in relation to accounting periods of controlled foreign companies beginning on or after 6 December 2006 (subject to the transitional provisions at FA 2007, Sch. 15, para. 10(2)–(4)).
In para. 5(2)(a), reference to s. 749(5) substituted for reference to s. 749(3) by FA 1998, s. 113 and Sch. 17, para. 29, with effect as respects accounting periods of companies resident in the UK which end on or after 1 July 1999, the corporation tax self-assessment appointed day under FA 1994, s. 199 by virtue of SI 1998/3173 (C. 78).
Para. 5(3)–(5) inserted by FA 2003, s. 201:

(a) as from 1 July 1997, so far as relating to the Hong Kong Special Administrative Region; and

(b) as from 20 December 1999, so far as relating to the Macao Special Administrative Region.

Derivations – *FA 1984, Sch. 17, para. 5.*

Cross references – S. 750(1): meaning of lower level of taxation.
S. 751: accounting periods of a company resident outside the UK.
FA 1998, Sch. 17, para. 37(2)–(4): commencement and transitional provisions – separate determinations and computations to be made, as respects accounting period of a non-resident company which ends before 1 July 1999, in cases where at least one UK-resident company has an accounting period ending on or after that day, and at least one other UK-resident company has an accounting period ending before that day.

6(1) Throughout an accounting period a controlled foreign company is engaged in exempt activities if, and only if, each of the following conditions is fulfilled–

(a) that, throughout that accounting period, the company has a business establishment in the territory in which it is resident; and

(b) that, throughout that accounting period, its business affairs in that territory are effectively managed there; and

(c) that any of sub-paragraphs (2) or (3) below applies to the company.

6(2) This sub-paragraph applies to a company if–

(a) at no time during the accounting period in question does the main business of the company consist of either–

(i) investment business, or

(ii) dealing in goods for delivery to or from the United Kingdom or to or from connected or associated persons; and

(b) in the case of a company which is mainly engaged in wholesale, distributive financial or service business in that accounting period, less than 50 per cent of its gross trading receipts from that business is derived directly or indirectly from persons falling within sub-paragraph (2A) below.

6(2A) Those persons are–

(a) persons who are connected or associated with the company;

(b) persons who have a 25 per cent assessable interest in the company in the case of the accounting period in question;

(c) if the company is a controlled foreign company in that accounting period by virtue of subsection (1A) of section 747, persons who are connected or associated with either or both of the two persons mentioned in that subsection;

(d) persons not falling within paragraphs (a) to (c) above which are companies resident in the United Kingdom;

(e) persons not falling within paragraphs (a) to (c) above which are companies not resident in the United Kingdom which carry on business through a permanent establishment in the United Kingdom;

(f) persons not falling within paragraphs (a) to (c) above who are individuals habitually resident in the United Kingdom;

but where the company is a controlled foreign company falling within sub-paragraph (2B) below, paragraphs (d) to (f) above shall be disregarded.

6(2B) A controlled foreign company falls within this sub-paragraph if either–

(a) its main business is the effecting or carrying out of contracts of long-term insurance, other than protection business; or

(b) it is a member of an insurance group and its main business is insuring or reinsuring large risks.

Paragraph 11A below has effect for the interpretation of this sub-paragraph.

6(2C) For the purposes of sub-paragraph (2)(b) above, a company's gross trading receipts from a business shall be regarded as directly or indirectly derived from a person falling within sub-paragraph (2A)(e) above only to the extent that they are derived directly or indirectly from contracts or other arrangements relating to that person's permanent establishment in the United Kingdom.

6(3) This sub-paragraph applies to a company which is a holding company if at least 90 per cent of its gross income during the accounting period in question is received by it in the territory in which it is resident and is derived directly from companies which it controls and which, throughout that period–

(a) are resident in the territory in which the holding company is resident; and

(b) are not themselves holding companies, but otherwise are, in terms of this Schedule, engaged in exempt activities or are, in terms of sub-paragraph (5A) below, exempt trading companies;

and a holding company to which this sub-paragraph applies is in this Part of this Schedule referred to as a **"local holding company"**.

6(4) [Omitted by FA 2009, s. 36 and Sch. 16, para. 10(2)(c).]

6(4ZA) [Omitted by FA 2009, s. 36 and Sch. 16, para. 10(2)(c).]

6(4A) [Omitted by FA 2009, s. 36 and Sch. 16, para. 10(2)(c).]

6(4AA) [Omitted by FA 2009, s. 36 and Sch. 16, para. 10(2)(c).]

6(4B) [Omitted by FA 2009, s. 36 and Sch. 16, para. 10(2)(c).]

6(4BB) [Omitted by FA 2009, s. 36 and Sch. 16, para. 10(2)(c).]

6(4C) For the purposes of sub-paragraph (2A)(b) above, a person has a 25 per cent assessable interest in a controlled foreign company in the case of an accounting period of the company if, on an apportionment of the chargeable profits and creditable tax (if any) of the company for that accounting period under section 747(3), at least 25 per cent of the controlled foreign company's chargeable profits for the accounting period would be apportioned to that person.

6(5) Any reference in sub-paragraph (3) above to a company which a holding company controls includes a reference to a trading company to which sub-paragraph (5ZA) or (5ZB) below applies.

6(5ZA) This sub-paragraph applies to a trading company in which the holding company holds the maximum amount of ordinary share capital which is permitted under the law of the territory–

(a) in which the trading company is resident; and

(b) from whose laws the trading company derives its status as a company.

6(5ZB) This sub-paragraph applies to a trading company if–

(a) it is a controlled foreign company by virtue of subsection (1A) of section 747; and

(b) the person who satisfies the requirement in paragraph (b) of that subsection in relation to the company also controls the holding company.

6(5A) For the purposes of sub-paragraph (3) above, a company is an exempt trading company throughout any period if–

(a) it is a trading company throughout each of its accounting periods which falls wholly or partly within that period; and

(b) each of those accounting periods is one as regards which–

(i) the condition in section 747(1)(c) is not satisfied; or

(ii) the conditions in section 748(1)(e) are satisfied; or

(iii) the conditions in section 748(3)(a) and (b) are satisfied.

6(5B) [Omitted by FA 2009, s. 36 and Sch. 16, para. 10(2)(h).]

6(5C) For the purposes of this paragraph, the gross income of a holding company during an accounting period includes–

(a) any income which accrues during that period to the trustees of a settlement in relation to which the company is a settlor or a beneficiary, and

(b) any income which accrues during that period to a partnership of which the company is a partner, apportioned between the company and the other partners on a just and reasonable basis.

6(5D) Where there is more than one settlor or beneficiary in relation to the settlement mentioned in sub-paragraph (5C)(a), the income is to be apportioned between the company and the other settlors or beneficiaries on a just and reasonable basis.

6(5E) In sub-paragraph (5C)(b), **"partnership"** includes an entity established under the law of a country or territory outside the United Kingdom of a similar character to a partnership; and **"partner"** is to be read accordingly.

6(6) The following provisions of this Part of this Schedule have effect in relation to this paragraph.

History – In para. 6(1)(c), "(2) or (3)" substituted for "(2), (3), (4) or (4A)" by FA 2009, s. 36 and Sch. 16, para. 10(2)(a), with effect in relation to accounting periods of controlled foreign companies beginning on or after 1 July 2009 (companies other than qualifying holding companies) or 1 July 2011 (qualifying holding companies), subject to rules for accounting periods straddling 1 July 2009 and 1 July 2011 in FA 2009, Sch. 16, para. 14 and 15 and transitional provisions in FA 2009, Sch. 16, para. 17, and subject to anti-avoidance provisions in FA 2009, Sch. 16, para. 19.

In para. 6(1)(c), words "(2), (3), (4) or (4A)" substituted for "(2) to (4A)" by FA 2003, s. 200 and Sch. 42, para. 2, with effect in relation to accounting periods of a controlled foreign company beginning on or after 27 November 2002.

In para. 6(1)(c), reference to sub-paragraph (4A) substituted for reference to sub-paragraph (4) by FA 1998, s. 113 and Sch. 17, para. 30(2), with effect as respects accounting periods of companies resident in the UK which end on or after 1 July 1999, the corporation tax self-assessment appointed day under FA 1994, s. 199 (by virtue of SI 1998/3173 (C. 78)).

In para. 6(2)(b), words "financial or service" substituted for "or financial" and the words "persons falling within" to the end substituted for the words "connected or associated persons or persons who have a 25 per cent. assessable interest in the company in the case of that accounting period" by FA 2000, s. 104 and Sch. 31, para. 5(2), with effect in relation to any accounting period of a controlled foreign company which begins on or after 21 March 2000.

In para. 6(2)(b), words "a 25 per cent. assessable interest in the company in the case of" substituted for "an interest in the company at any time during" by FA 1998, s. 113 and Sch. 17, para. 30(3), with effect as respects accounting periods of companies resident in the UK which end on or after 1 July 1999, the corporation tax self-assessment appointed day under FA 1994, s. 199 (by virtue of SI 1998/3173 (C. 78)).

In para. 6(2)(b), words "or persons who … during that accounting period." were inserted by FA 1996, s. 182 and Sch. 36, para. 4(5), in relation to accounting periods of a controlled foreign company beginning on or after 28 November 1995.

In para. 6(2A), the word "and" immediately preceding paragraph (c) omitted (and repealed by FA 2003, s. 216 and Sch. 43, Pt. 5(2), with effect from 27 November 2002) and (2A)(d)–(f) and the text after (f) added at the end by FA 2003, s. 200 and Sch. 42, para. 2, with effect in relation to accounting periods of a controlled foreign company beginningon or after 27 November 2002.

In para. 6(2A) the words "permanent establishment" substituted for "branch or agency" by FA 2003, s. 153(1)(a) in relation to accounting periods beginning on or after 1 January 2003.

Para. 6(2A) inserted by FA 2000, s. 104 and Sch. 31, para. 5(3), with effect in relation to any accounting period of a controlled foreign company which begins on or after 21 March 2000.

Para. 6(2B) inserted by FA 2003, s. 200 and Sch. 42, para. 2, with effect in relation to accounting periods of a controlled foreign company beginning on or after 27 November 2002.

In para. 6(2C) the words "permanent establishment" substituted for "branch or agency" by FA 2003, s. 153(1)(a) in relation to accounting periods beginning on or after 1 January 2003.

Para. 6(2C) inserted by FA 2003, s. 200 and Sch. 42, para. 2, with effect in relation to accounting periods of a controlled foreign company beginning on or after 27 November 2002.
In para. 6(3)(b), the words "or superior holding companies", which appeared after "holding companies", omitted by FA 2009, s. 36 and Sch. 16, para. 10(2)(b), with effect in relation to accounting periods of controlled foreign companies beginning on or after 1 July 2009 (companies other than qualifying holding companies) or 1 July 2011 (qualifying holding companies), subject to rules for accounting periods straddling 1 July 2009 and 1 July 2011 in FA 2009, Sch. 16, para. 14 and 15 and transitional provisions in FA 2009, Sch. 16, para. 17, and subject to anti-avoidance provisions in FA 2009, Sch. 16, para. 19.
In para. 6(3), words "is received by it" to "resident and" inserted by FA 2000, s. 104 and Sch. 31, para. 6(2), with effect in relation to any accounting period of a controlled foreign company which begins on or after 21 March 2000.
In para. 6(3)(b) and para. 6(4)(b), words "or superior holding companies" and "or are, in terms of sub-paragraph (5A) below, exempt trading companies" inserted by FA 1998, s. 113 and Sch. 17, para. 30(4) and (5), with effect as respects accounting periods of companies resident in the UK which end on or after 1 July 1999, the corporation tax self-assessment appointed day under FA 1994, s. 199 (by virtue of SI 1998/3173 (C. 78)).
Para. 6(4)–(4BB) omitted by FA 2009, s. 36 and Sch. 16, para. 10(2)(c), with effect in relation to accounting periods of controlled foreign companies beginning on or after 1 July 2009 (companies other than qualifying holding companies) or 1 July 2011 (qualifying holding companies), subject to rules for accounting periods straddling 1 July 2009 and 1 July 2011 in FA2009, Sch. 16, para. 14 and 15 and transitional provisions in FA 2009, Sch. 16, para. 17, and subject to anti-avoidance provisions in FA 2009, Sch. 16, para. 19.
In former para. 6(4), words "falls within sub-paragraph (4ZA) below and" inserted by FA 2000, s. 104 and Sch. 31, para. 7(2), with effect in relation to any accounting period of a controlled foreign company which begins on or after 21 March 2000.
Former para. 6(4ZA) inserted by FA 2000, s. 104 and Sch. 31, para. 7(3), with effect in relation to any accounting period of a controlled foreign company which begins on or after 21 March 2000.
Former para. 6(4A)(c) and word "; and" at end of para. (b) inserted by FA 2000, s. 104 and Sch. 31, para. 7(4), with effect in relation to any accounting period of a controlled foreign company which begins on or after 21 March 2000.
Former para. 6(4A) inserted by FA 1998, s. 113 and Sch. 17, para. 30(6), with effect as respects accounting periods of companies resident in the UK which end on or after 1 July 1999, the corporation tax self-assessment appointed day under FA 1994, s. 199 (by virtue of SI 1998/3173 (C. 78)).
Former para. 6(4AA) inserted by FA 2000, s. 104 and Sch. 31, para. 7(5), with effect in relation to any accounting period of a controlled foreign company which begins on or after 21 March 2000.
Former para. 6(4B)(b)(iii), and word "; and" at end of sub-para. (ii), inserted by FA 2000, s. 104 and Sch. 31, para. 7(6), with effect in relation to any accounting period of a controlled foreign company which begins on or after 21 March 2000.
Former para. 6(4BB) inserted by FA 2000, s. 104 and Sch. 31, para. 7(7), with effect in relation to any accounting period of a controlled foreign company which begins on or after 21 March 2000.
Former para. 6(4B) inserted by FA 1998, s. 113 and Sch. 17, para. 30(6), with effect as respects accounting periods of companies resident in the UK which end on or after 1 July 1999, the corporation tax self-assessment appointed day under FA 1994, s 199 (by virtue of SI 1998/3173 (C. 78)).
In para. 6(4C), "(2A)(b)" substituted for "(2)(b)" by FA 2003, s. 200 and Sch. 42, para. 2 with effect in relation to accounting periods of a controlled foreign company beginning on or after 27 November 2002.
Para. 6(4C) inserted by FA 1998, s. 113 and Sch. 17, para. 30(7), with effect as respects accounting periods of companies resident in the UK which end on or after 1 July 1999, the corporation tax self-assessment appointed day under FA 1994, s. 199 (by virtue of SI 1998/3173 (C. 78)).
In para. 6(5), "sub-paragraph (3)" substituted for "sub-paragraphs (3) to (4B)" by FA 2009, s. 36 and Sch. 16, para. 10(2)(d)(i), with effect in relation to accounting periods ofcontrolled foreign companies beginning on or after 1 July 2009 (companies other than qualifying holding companies) or 1 July 2011 (qualifying holding companies), subject to rules for accounting periods straddling 1 July 2009 and 1 July 2011 in FA 2009, Sch. 16, para. 14 and 15 and transitional provisions in FA 2009, Sch. 16, para. 17, and subject to anti-avoidance provisions in FA 2009, Sch. 16, para. 19.
In para. 6(5), the words "or superior holding company", which appeared after "holding company", omitted by FA 2009, s. 36 and Sch. 16, para. 10(2)(d)(ii), with effect in relation to accounting periods of controlled foreign companies beginning on or after 1 July 2009 (companies other than qualifying holding companies) or 1 July 2011 (qualifying holding companies), subject to rules for accounting periods straddling 1 July 2009 and 1 July 2011 in FA 2009, Sch. 16, para. 14 and 15 and transitional provisions in FA 2009, Sch. 16, para. 17, and subject to anti-avoidance provisions in FA 2009, Sch. 16, para. 19.
In para. 6(5), words "to which sub-paragraph (5ZA) or (5ZB) below applies." and sub-para. (5ZA) inserted (effectively sub-para. (5ZA) created out of the remaining text of para. 6(5)) by FA 2000, s. 104 and Sch. 31, para. 7(8)), with effect in relation to any accounting period of a controlled foreign company which begins on or after 21 March 2000.
In para. 6(5), words "sub-paragraphs (3) to (4B)" substituted for "sub-paragraph (3) or (4)", and "or superior holding company" inserted by FA 1998, s. 113 and Sch. 17, para. 30(8), with effect as respects accounting periods of companies resident in the UK which end on or after 1 July 1999, the corporation tax self-assessment appointed day under FA 1994, s. 199 (by virtue of SI 1998/3173 (C. 78)).
In para. 6(5ZA), the words "or superior holding company", which appeared after "holding company", omitted by FA 2009, s. 36 and Sch. 16, para. 10(2)(e), with effect in relation to accounting periods of controlled foreign companies beginning on or after 1 July 2009 (companies other than qualifying holding companies) or 1 July 2011 (qualifying holding companies), subject to rules for accounting periods straddling 1 July 2009 and 1 July 2011 in FA 2009, Sch. 16, para. 14 and 15 and transitional provisions in FA 2009, Sch. 16, para. 17,and subject to anti-avoidance provisions in FA 2009, Sch. 16, para. 19.
In para. 6(5ZB), the words "or superior holding company", which appeared after "holding company", omitted by FA 2009, s. 36 and Sch. 16, para. 10(2)(f), with effect in relation to accounting periods of controlled foreign companies beginning on or after 1 July 2009 (companies other than qualifying holding companies) or 1 July 2011 (qualifying holding companies), subject to rules for accounting periods straddling 1 July 2009 and 1 July 2011 in FA 2009, Sch. 16, para. 14 and 15 and transitional provisions in FA 2009, Sch. 16, para. 17, and subject to anti-avoidance provisions in FA 2009, Sch. 16, para. 19.
Para. 6(5ZB) inserted by FA 2000, s. 104 and Sch. 31, para. 7(9)), with effect in relation to any accounting period of a controlled foreign company which begins on or after 21 March 2000.
In para. 6(5A), the words "sub-paragraph (3)" substituted for "sub-paragraphs (3) to (4B)" by FA 2009, s. 36 and Sch. 16, para. 10(2)(g), with effect in relation to accounting periods of controlled foreign companies beginning on or after 1 July 2009 (companies other than qualifying holding companies) or 1 July 2011 (qualifying holding companies), subject to rules for accounting periods straddling 1 July 2009 and 1 July 2011 in FA 2009, Sch. 16, para. 14 and 15 and transitional provisions in FA 2009, Sch. 16, para. 17, and subject to anti-avoidance provisions in FA 2009, Sch. 16, para. 19.
Para. 6(5A) inserted by FA 1998, s. 113 and Sch. 17, para. 30(9), with effect as respects accounting periods of companies resident in the UK which end on or after 1 July 1999, the corporation tax self-assessment appointed day under FA 1994, s. 199 (by virtue of SI 1998/3173 (C. 78)).
Para. 6(5B) omitted by FA 2009, s. 36 and Sch. 16, para. 10(2)(h), with effect in relation to accounting periods of controlled foreign companies beginning on or after 1 July 2009 (companies other than qualifying holding companies) or 1 July 2011 (qualifying holding companies), subject to rules for accounting periods straddling 1 July 2009 and 1 July 2011 in FA 2009, Sch. 16, para. 14 and 15 and transitional provisions in FA 2009, Sch. 16, para. 17, and subject to anti-avoidance provisions in FA 2009, Sch. 16, para. 19.
Former para. 6(5B) inserted by FA 2000, s. 104 and Sch. 31, para. 7(10), with effect in relation to any accounting period of a controlled foreign company which begins on or after 21 March 2000.
In para. 6(5C), the words "or superior holding company", which appeared after "holding company", omitted by FA 2009, s. 36 and Sch. 16, para. 10(2)(i), with effect in relation to accounting periods of controlled foreign companies beginning on or after 1 July 2009

(companies other than qualifying holding companies) or 1 July 2011 (qualifying holding companies), subject to rules for accounting periods straddling 1 July 2009 and 1 July 2011 in FA 2009, Sch. 16, para. 14 and 15 and transitional provisions in FA 2009, Sch. 16, para. 17, and subject to anti-avoidance provisions in FA 2009, Sch. 16, para. 19. The phrase to be omitted is "or superior holding company" but it is assumed that the words to be omitted are actually "or a superior holding company" as appearing in the statute.
Para. 6(5C) inserted by FA 2008, s. 64(5), with effect in relation to income accruing on or after 12 March 2008.
Para. 6(5D) inserted by FA 2008, s. 64(5), with effect in relation to income accruing on or after 12 March 2008.
Para. 6(5E) inserted by FA 2008, s. 64(5), with effect in relation to income accruing on or after 12 March 2008.
In para 6(6), "this paragraph" substituted for "sub-paragraphs (1) to (4BB) above" by FA 2009, s. 36 and Sch. 16, para. 10(2)(j), with effect in relation to accounting periods of controlled foreign companies beginning on or after 1 July 2009 (companies other than qualifying holding companies) or 1 July 2011 (qualifying holding companies), subject to rules for accounting periods straddling 1 July 2009 and 1 July 2011 in FA 2009, Sch. 16, para. 14 and 15 and transitional provisions in FA 2009, Sch. 16, para. 17, and subject to anti-avoidance provisions in FA 2009, Sch. 16, para. 19.
In para. 6(6), "(4BB)" substituted for "(4)" by FA 2000, s. 104 and Sch. 31, para. 7(11), with effect in relation to any accounting period of a controlled foreign company which begins on or after 21 March 2000.

Derivations – FA 1984, Sch. 17, para. 6.

Cross references – S. 751: accounting periods of a company resident outside the UK.
FA 1998, Sch. 17, para. 37(2)–(4): commencement and transitional provisions – separate determinations and computations to be made, as respects accounting period of a non-resident company which ends before 1 July 1999, in cases where at least one UK-resident company has an accounting period ending on or after that day, and at least one other UK-resident company has an accounting period ending before that day.

HMRC interpretations – IRInt. 215: interaction of Inland Revenue interpretation on income from indefeasible rights to use (a telecommunications cable system) – which is deemed to be "investment business" – with the exempt activities test requirement of para. 6(2)(a)(i).

Other material – TAXline 1998/24 (not reproduced): view of Inland Revenue International Division that exchange differences arising on loans by holding companies to qualifying local holding companies or trading companies form part of the 90 per cent of gross income for CFC purposes, provided that the loan falls within the definition of a "loan relationship" within FA 1996.

7(1) For the purposes of paragraph 6(1)(a) above, a **"business establishment"**, in relation to a controlled foreign company, means premises–

(a) which are, or are intended to be, occupied and used with a reasonable degree of permanence; and

(b) from which the company's business in the territory in which it is resident is wholly or mainly carried on.

7(2) For the purposes of sub-paragraph (1) above the following shall be regarded as premises–

(a) an office, shop, factory or other building or part of a building; or

(b) a mine, an oil or gas well, a quarry or any other place of extraction of natural resources; or

(c) a building site or the site of a construction or installation project;

but such a site as is referred to in paragraph (c) above shall not be regarded as premises unless the building work or the project, as the case may be, has a duration of at least twelve months.

Derivations – FA 1984, Sch. 17, para. 7.

Cross references – S. 749: territory where company construed as resident.

8(1) Subject to sub-paragraph (4) below, the condition in paragraph 6(1)(b) above shall not be regarded as fulfilled in relation to a company which is not resident in an EEA territory unless–

(a) the number of persons employed by the company in the territory in which it is resident is adequate to deal with the volume of the company's business; and

(b) any services provided by the company for persons resident outside that territory are not in fact performed in the United Kingdom.

8(2) For the purposes of sub-paragraph (1)(a) above, persons who are engaged wholly or mainly in the business of the company and whose remuneration is paid by a person connected with, and resident in the same territory as, the company shall be treated as employed by the company.

8(3) In the case of a holding company, sub-paragraph (2) above shall apply with the omission of the words "wholly or mainly".

8(4) For the purposes of sub-paragraph (1)(b) above, no account shall be taken of services–

(a) provided through a permanent establishment of the controlled foreign company if the profits or gains of the business carried on through the permanent establishment are within the charge to tax in the United Kingdom; or

(b) provided through any other person whose profits or gains from the provision of the services are within the charge to tax in the United Kingdom and who provides the services for a consideration which is, or which is not dissimilar from what might reasonably be expected to be, determined under a contract entered into at arm's length; or

(c) which are no more than incidental to services provided outside the United Kingdom.

8(5) *The condition in paragraph 6(1)(b) above shall not be regarded as fulfilled in relation to a company* which is resident in an EEA territory unless there are sufficient individuals working for the company in the territory who have the competence and authority to undertake all, or substantially all, of the company's business.

8(6) For the purposes of sub-paragraph (5) above, individuals are not to be regarded as working for a company in any territory unless–

(a) they are employed by the company in the territory, or

(b) they are otherwise directed by the company to perform duties on its behalf in the territory.

History – In para. 8(1), the words "in relation to a company which is not resident in an EEA territory" inserted by FA 2007, s. 48 and Sch. 15, para. 7(3), with effect in relation to accounting periods of controlled foreign companies beginning on or after 6 December 2006 (subject to the transitional provisions at FA 2007, Sch. 15, para. 10(2)–(4)).

In para. 8(3), the words "or superior holding company", which appeared after "holding company", omitted by FA 2009, s. 36 and Sch. 16, para. 10(3), with effect in relation to accounting periods of controlled foreign companies beginning on or after 1 July 2009 (companies other than qualifying holding companies) or 1 July 2011 (qualifying holding companies), subject to rules for accounting periods straddling 1 July 2009 and 1 July 2011 in FA 2009, Sch. 16, para. 14 and 15 and transitional provisions in FA 2009, Sch. 16, para. 17, and subject to anti-avoidance provisions in FA 2009, Sch. 16, para. 19.

In para. 8(3), words "or superior holding company" inserted by FA 1998, s. 113 and Sch. 17, para. 31, with effect as respects accounting periods of companies resident in the UK which end on or after 1 July 1999, the corporation tax self-assessment appointed day under FA 1994, s. 199 by virtue of SI 1998/3173 (C. 78).

In para. 8(4)(a) the words "permanent establishment" substituted (twice) for "branch or agency" by FA 2003, s. 153(1)(a) in relation to accounting periods beginning on or after 1 January 2003.

Para. 8(5) inserted by FA 2007, s. 48 and Sch. 15, para. 7(4), with effect in relation to accounting periods of controlled foreign companies beginning on or after 6 December 2006 (subject to the transitional provisions at FA 2007, Sch. 15, para. 10(2)–(4)).

Para. 8(6) inserted by FA 2007, s. 48 and Sch. 15, para. 7(4), with effect in relation to accounting periods of controlled foreign companies beginning on or after 6 December 2006 (subject to the transitional provisions at FA 2007, Sch. 15, para. 10(2)–(4)).

Derivations – FA 1984, Sch. 17, para. 8.

Cross references – S. 749: territory where company construed as resident.

FA 1998, Sch. 17, para. 37(2)–(4): commencement and transitional provisions – separate determinations and computations to be made, as respects accounting period of a non-resident company which ends before 1 July 1999, in cases where at least one UK-resident company has an accounting period ending on or after that day, and at least one other UK-resident company has an accounting period ending before that day.

9(1) Subject to sub-paragraph (3) below, for the purposes of paragraph 6(2)(a)(i) above, each of the following activities constitutes investment business–

(a) the holding of securities or intellectual property;

(b) dealing in securities, other than in the capacity of a broker;

(c) the leasing of any description of property or rights; and

(d) the investment in any manner of funds which would otherwise be available, directly or indirectly, for investment by or on behalf of any person (whether resident in the United Kingdom or not) who has, or is connected or associated with a person who has, control, either alone or together with other persons, of the controlled foreign company in question.

9(1A) In sub-paragraph (1)(a) above "intellectual property" includes (in particular)–

(a) any industrial, commercial or scientific information, knowledge or expertise;

(b) any patent, trade mark, registered design, copyright or design right;

(c) any licence or other right in respect of intellectual property;

(d) any rights under the law of a country outside the United Kingdom which correspond or are similar to those falling within paragraph (b) or (c) above.

9(2) In sub-paragraph (1)(b) above **"broker"** includes any person offering to sell securities to, or purchase securities from, members of the public generally.

9(3) For the purposes of paragraph 6(2) above, in the case of a company which is mainly engaged in business falling within paragraph 11(1)(c) below, nothing in sub-paragraph (1) above shall require the main business of the company to be regarded as investment business.

History – In para. 9(1)(a), the words "or intellectual property" were substituted by Copyright, Designs and Patents Act 1988, s. 303(1) and Sch. 7, para. 36(9), with effect from 1 August 1989 (SI 1989/816 (C 21)).

Para. 9(1A) substituted by FA 1998, s. 112(2), with effect in relation to accounting periods of a controlled foreign company, within the meaning of Pt. XVII, Ch. IV, beginning on or after 17 March 1998.

Para. 9(1A) originally inserted by Copyright, Designs and Patents Act 1988, s. 303(1) and Sch. 7, para. 36(9), with effect from 1 August 1989 (SI 1989/816 (C 21)).

In para. 9(3), in consequence of the substitution of para. 11(1)(c), word "business" substituted for "banking or any similar business" by FA 1998, s. 112(4), with effect in relation to accounting periods of a controlled foreign company, within the meaning of Pt. XVII, Ch. IV, beginning on or after 17 March 1998.

Derivations – FA 1984, Sch. 17, para. 9.

Other material – Revenue Tax Bulletin, Issue 50, December 2000: Inland Revenue interpretation on indefeasible rights to use (IRU) (a telecommunications cable system) – comment aside that income from an IRU is deemed to derive from an "investment business" within the definition in para. 9(1)(c) notwithstanding probable Sch. D, Case I treatment if it were taxed in UK.

10 Goods which are actually delivered into the territory in which the controlled foreign company is resident shall not be taken into account for the purposes of paragraph 6(2)(a)(ii) above.

Derivations – FA 1984, Sch. 17, para. 10.

11(1) For the purposes of paragraph 6(2)(b) above, each of the following activities constitutes **wholesale, distributive financial or service business**–

(a) dealing in any description of goods wholesale rather than retail;

(b) the business of shipping or air transport, that is to say, the business carried on by an owner of ships or the business carried on by an owner of aircraft (**"owner"** including, for this purpose, any charterer);

(c) banking, deposit-taking, money-lending or debt-factoring, or any business similar to banking, deposit-taking, money-lending or debt-factoring;

(d) the administration of trusts;

(e) dealing in securities in the capacity of a broker, as defined in paragraph 9(2) above;

(f) dealing in commodity or financial futures;

(g) the effecting or carrying out of contracts of insurance; and

(h) the provision of services not falling within any of the preceding paragraphs.

11(1A) For the purposes of sub-paragraph (1)(g) above **"contract of insurance"** has the meaning given by Article 3(1) of the Financial Services and Markets Act 2000 (Regulated Activities) Order 2001.

11(2) In a case where the gross trading receipts of a company include an amount in respect of the proceeds of sale of any description of property or rights, the cost to the company of the purchase of that property or those rights shall be a deduction in calculating the company's gross trading receipts for the purposes of paragraph 6(2)(b) above.

11(3) In the case of a controlled foreign company engaged in a business falling within sub-paragraph (1)(c) above–

(a) no payment of interest received from a company resident in the United Kingdom which is connected or associated with the controlled foreign company shall be regarded for the purposes of paragraph 6(2)(b) above as a receipt derived directly or indirectly from a person falling within paragraph 6(2A) above, but

(b) it shall be conclusively presumed that the condition in paragraph 6(2)(b) above is not fulfilled if, at any time during the accounting period in question, the amount by which the aggregate value of the capital interests in the company held directly or indirectly by–

(i) the persons who have control of the company, and

(ii) any person connected or associated with those persons,

exceeds the value of the company's fixed assets is 15 per cent or more of the amount by which the company's outstanding capital exceeds that value, and

(c) it shall also be conclusively presumed that the condition in paragraph 6(2)(b) is not fulfilled if 10% or more of the company's gross trading receipts from all businesses carried on by it in the accounting period in question, taken together, are receipts other than interest and are directly or indirectly derived from persons–

(i) which are companies resident in the United Kingdom,

(ii) which are companies not resident in the United Kingdom but which carry on business through a permanent establishment in the United Kingdom, or

(iii) who are individuals habitually resident in the United Kingdom,

but for this purpose a company's gross trading receipts shall be regarded as directly or indirectly derived from a person falling within sub-paragraph (ii) above only to the extent that they are derived directly or indirectly from contracts or other arrangements relating to that person's permanent establishment in the United Kingdom.

11(4) For the purposes of this paragraph, in relation to a controlled foreign company–

(a) **"capital interest"** means an interest in the issued share capital or reserves of the company or in a loan to or deposit with the company or the liability of a guarantor under a guarantee given to or for the benefit of the company;

(b) except in the case of the liability of a guarantor, the value of a capital interest is its value as shown in the company's accounts;

(c) in the case of the liability of a guarantor, the value shall be taken to be the market value of the benefit which the controlled foreign company derives from the provision of the guarantee;

(d) the value of the company's fixed assets means the value, as shown in the company's accounts, of the plant, premises and trade investments employed in the company's business; and

(e) **"outstanding capital"** means the total value of all the capital interests in the company, less the value, as shown in the company's accounts, of any advances made by the company to persons resident outside the United Kingdom and falling within paragraph (i) or paragraph (ii) of sub-paragraph (3)(b) above.

11(5) For the purposes of sub-paragraph (4) above–

(a) **"trade investments"**, in relation to a controlled foreign company, means securities any profit on the sale of which would not be brought into account as a trading receipt in computing the chargeable profits of an accounting period in which that profit arose; and

(b) the reference in paragraph (e) to **advances** made to a person by the controlled foreign company includes, in the case of a company which is a person resident outside the United Kingdom and falling within paragraph (i) or paragraph (ii) of sub-paragraph (3)(b) above, any securities of that company which are held by the controlled foreign company but are not trade investments, as defined in paragraph (a) above;

and in this sub-paragraph **"securities"** includes stocks and shares.

11(6) In the application of paragraph 6(2)(b) above in the case of a controlled foreign company engaged in insurance business of any kind–

(a) the reference to **gross trading receipts** which are derived directly or indirectly from connected or associated persons is a reference to those which, subject to sub-paragraph (7) below, are attributable, directly or indirectly, to liabilities undertaken in relation to any of those persons or their property;

(b) the only receipts to be taken into account are commissions and premiums received under insurance contracts;

(c) so much of any such commission or premium as is returned is not to be taken into account; and

(d) when a liability under an insurance contract is reinsured, in whole or in part, the amount of the premium which is attributable, directly or indirectly, to that liability shall be treated as reduced by so much of the premium under the reinsurance contract as is attributable to that liability.

11(7) In determining, in relation to a controlled foreign company to which sub-paragraph (6) above applies, the gross trading receipts referred to in paragraph (a) of that sub-paragraph, there shall be left out of account any receipts under a local reinsurance contract which are attributable to liabilities which–

(a) are undertaken under an insurance contract made in the territory in which the company is resident; and

(b) are not reinsured under any contract other than a local reinsurance contract; and

(c) relate either to persons who are resident in that territory and are neither connected nor associated with the company or to property which is situated there and belongs to persons who are not so connected or associated;

and in paragraph (a) above **"insurance contract"** does not include a reinsurance contract.

11(8) In sub-paragraph (7) above **"local reinsurance contract"** means a reinsurance contract–

(a) which is made in the territory in which the controlled foreign company is resident; and

(b) the parties to which are companies which are resident in that territory.

11(9) For the purposes of sub-paragraphs (7) and (8) above, any question as to the territory in which a company is resident shall be determined in accordance with section 749 and where appropriate, paragraph 5(2) above; and, for the purpose of the application of those provisions in accordance with this sub-paragraph, the company shall be assumed to be a controlled foreign company.

History – In para. 11(1), words "financial or service" substituted for "or financial", word "and" immediately preceding para. (g) omitted, and para. (h) and word "; and" at the end of para. (g) added, by FA 2000, s. 104 and Sch. 31, para. 8(2), s. 156 and Sch. 40, Pt. II(14), with effect in relation to any accounting period of a controlled foreign company which begins on or after 21 March 2000.

Para. 11(1)(c) substituted, and in para. 11(3) word "business" substituted for "banking or other business", by FA 1998, s. 112(3), s. 112(4)(b), with effect in relation to accounting periods of a controlled foreign company, within the meaning of Pt. XVII, Ch. IV, beginning on or after 17 March 1998.

Para. 11(1)(g) substituted by SI 2001/3629, art. 51(2), and para. 11A(1A) inserted by SI 2001/3629, art. 51(3), with effect from 1 December 2001.

In para. 11(3)(c) the words "permanent establishment" substituted (twice) for "branch or agency" by FA 2003, s. 153(1)(a) in relation to accounting periods beginning on or after 1 January 2003.

Para. 11(3)(a) substituted and 11(3)(c) inserted by FA 2003, s. 200 and Sch. 42, para. 3(2) with effect in relation to accounting periods of a controlled foreign company beginning on or after 27 November 2002.

Derivations – FA 1984, Sch. 17, para. 11 and (para. 11(1)) ICTA 1970, s. 514(1).

11A(1) This paragraph has effect for the interpretation of paragraph 6(2B) above.

11A(2) **"Contract of long-term insurance"** means any contract falling within Part II of Schedule 1 to the Financial Services and Markets Act 2000 (Regulated Activities) Order 2001.

11A(3) **"Protection business"** means contracts of long-term insurance where–

(a) either–

(i) the contract has no surrender value; or

(ii) the consideration consists of a single premium and the surrender value does not exceed the amount of that premium; and

ICTA 1988

(b) the contract makes no provision for its conversion or extension in a manner which would result in its ceasing to fall within paragraph (a) above;

and references to protection business include a reference to reinsurance of protection business.

11A(4) **"Insurance group"** shall be construed in accordance with section 1165(5) of the Companies Act 2006, but does not include such an insurance group if it falls within sub-paragraph (5) below.
but does not include such an insurance group if it falls within sub-paragraph (5) below.

11A(5) Such an insurance group falls within this sub-paragraph if the parent company is a subsidiary undertaking of a parent company which is neither–

(a) the parent company of an insurance group; nor

(b) a subsidiary undertaking of the parent company of an insurance group.

11A(6) A controlled foreign company is, in accordance with sub-paragraphs (4) and (5) above, a **"member of an insurance group"** if (within the meaning of that Part as so read) it is the parent company, or a subsidiary undertaking of the parent company, of an insurance group which is by virtue of sub-paragraph (4) above an insurance group for the purposes of paragraph 6(2B) above.

11A(7) A company's main business is **"insuring or reinsuring large risks"** if (and only if)–

(a) the company's main business is the effecting or carrying out of contracts of insurance; and

(b) 50% or more of its gross trading receipts from that business are derived from insuring or reinsuring large risks.

"Large risks" is defined in paragraph 11B below.

11A(8) In this paragraph–

"contract of insurance" has the meaning given by article 3(1) of the Financial Services and Markets Act 2000 (Regulated Activities) Order 2001;

"contract of long-term insurance" has the meaning given by sub-paragraph (2) above.

History – Para. 11A(4) substituted by SI 2008/954, art. 14(2), with effect from 6 April 2008.
In para. 11A(5) the words "(within the meaning of that Part as so read)" omitted following the words "within this sub-paragraph if" by SI 2008/954, art. 14(2), and art. 3 and Sch., with effect from 6 April 2008.
Para. 11A inserted by FA 2003, s. 200 and Sch. 42, para. 4 with effect in relation to accounting periods of a controlled foreign company beginning on or after 27 November 2002.

11B(1) In paragraph 11A above **"large risks"** means–

(a) risks falling within classes 4, 5, 6, 7, 11 and 12 of Part I of Schedule 1 to the Financial Services and Markets Act 2000 (Regulated Activities) Order 2001;

(b) risks falling within classes 14 and 15 of that Part which relate to a business carried on by the policy holder;

(c) risks falling within classes 3, 8, 9, 10, 13 and 16 of that Part where the policy holder carries on a business in respect of which the condition specified in sub-paragraph (2) below is satisfied.

11B(2) The condition referred to in sub-paragraph (1)(c) above is that, in the case of that business of the policy holder, at least two of the three following criteria were exceeded in the most recent financial year beginning on or after 1st January 1999 for which the information is available–

(a) balance sheet total: 6.2 million euros;

(b) net turnover 12.8 million euros;

(c) number of employees: 250.

11B(3) For the purposes of sub-paragraph (2) above as it applies where the policy holder is a company, within the meaning of section 1 of the Companies Act 2006,–

(a) **"balance sheet total"** has the meaning given by sections 382(5) and 465(5) of the Companies Act 2006;

(b) **"net turnover"** has the meaning given to **"turnover"** by section 474(1) of that Act; and

(c) **"number of employees"** has the meaning given by sections 382(6) and 465(6) of that Act;

and for a financial year which is a company's financial year but not in fact a year, the net turnover of the company shall be proportionately reduced.

11B(4) Where the policy holder is a member of a group for which consolidated accounts (within the meaning of Directive 83/349/EEC) are drawn up, the question whether the condition in sub-paragraph (2) above is met shall be determined by reference to those accounts.

11B(5) For the purposes of sub-paragraph (1)(c) above as it applies where the policy holder is a professional association, joint venture or temporary grouping, the question whether the condition in sub-paragraph (2) above is met shall be determined by reference to the aggregate of the figures of the description in question for all the members of the professional association, joint venture or temporary grouping.

11B(6) In sub-paragraphs (1) to (5) above **"business"** includes a trade or profession and, for the purposes of sub-paragraph (1)(c) above, any activity of a professional association, joint venture or temporary grouping.

11B(7) For the purposes of this paragraph, where an amount is denominated in any accounts in a currency other than the euro, it shall be converted into its equivalent in euros using the London closing exchange rate for that currency and the euro for the last day of the period to which the accounts relate.

11B(8) In this paragraph–

"euro" means the single currency adopted or proposed to be adopted as its currency by a member State in accordance with the Treaty establishing the European Community;

"financial year", in relation to any person, means the period (not exceeding 12 months) for which that person makes up accounts.

History – In para. 11B(3), "1" substituted for "735(1)", "2006" substituted for "1985" and the words "or Article 3 of the Companies (Northern Ireland) Order 1986" omitted by SI 2009/1890, art. 3(5)(c), with effect from 1 October 2009.

In para. 11B(3)(a) the words "sections 382(5) and 465(5) of the Companies Act 2006" substituted for "section 247(5) of that Act or Article 255(5) of that Order" by SI 2008/954, art. 14(3), with effect from 6 April 2008.

In para. 11B(3)(b) the words "section 474(1) of that Act" substituted for "section 262(1) of that Act or Article 270(1) of that Order" by SI 2008/954, art. 14(3), with effect from 6 April 2008.

In para. 11B(3)(c) the words "sections 382(6) and 465(6) of that Act" substituted for "section 247(6) of that Act or Article 255 of that Order" by SI 2008/954, art. 14(3), with effect from 6 April 2008.

Para. 11B inserted by FA 2003, s. 200 and Sch. 42, para. 4 with effect in relation to accounting periods of a controlled foreign company beginning on or after 27 November 2002.

12(1) Subject to sub-paragraph (2) below, in paragraphs 6 and 8(3) above and in sub-paragraphs (4) and (5) below **"holding company"** means–

(a) a company the business of which consists wholly or mainly in the holding of shares or securities of companies which are either local holding companies and its 90 per cent subsidiaries or trading companies and either its 51 per cent subsidiaries or companies falling within paragraph 6(5) above; or

(b) a company which would fall within paragraph (a) above if there were disregarded so much of its business as consists in the holding of property or rights of any description for use wholly or mainly by companies which it controls and which are resident in the territory in which it is resident.

12(2) In determining whether a company is a holding company for the purposes of paragraph 6(3) above (and, accordingly, whether the company is or may be a local holding company), sub-paragraph (1) above shall have effect with the omission from paragraph (a) thereof of the words "either local holding companies and its 90 per cent subsidiaries or".

12(3) In its application for the purposes of this paragraph section 1154 of CTA 2010 has effect with the omission of the following–

(a) in subsection (2), the words "or indirectly", and

(b) subsection (5).

12(4) For the purposes of sub-paragraph (3), of paragraph 6 above, as it applies in relation to a holding company part of whose business consists of activities other than the holding of shares or securities or the holding of property or rights as mentioned in paragraph (a) or (b) of sub-paragraph (1) above, the company's gross income during any accounting period shall be determined as follows–

(a) there shall be left out of account so much of what would otherwise be the company's gross income as is derived from any activity which, if it were the business in which the company is mainly engaged, would be such that paragraph 6(2) above would apply to the company; and

(b) to the extent that the receipts of the company from any other activity include receipts from the proceeds of sale of any description of property or rights, the cost to the company of the purchase of that property or those rights shall (to the extent that the cost does not exceed the receipts) be a deduction in calculating the company's gross income, and no other deduction shall be made in respect of that activity.

12(5) For the purposes of sub-paragraph (3) of paragraph 6 above, so much of the income of a holding company as–

(a) is derived directly from another company which it controls and which is not a holding company or superior holding company but otherwise is, in terms of this Schedule, engaged in exempt activities or, in terms of sub-paragraph (5A) of that paragraph, is an exempt trading company, and

(b) was or could have been paid out of any non-trading income of that other company which is derived directly or indirectly from a third company connected or associated with it,

shall be treated, in relation to the holding company, as if it were not derived directly from companies which it controls.

ICTA 1988

12(6) The reference in sub-paragraph (5) above to the **non-trading income** of a company is a reference to so much of its income as, if the company were carrying on its trade in the United Kingdom, would not be within the charge to corporation tax under section 35 of CTA 2009.

History – In para. 12(1), "in" substituted for "paragraph 12A below and in" by FA 2009, s. 36 and Sch. 16, para. 10(4)(a), with effect in relation to accounting periods of controlled foreign companies beginning on or after 1 July 2009 (companies other than qualifying holding companies) or 1 July 2011 (qualifying holding companies), subject to rules for accounting periods straddling 1 July 2009 and 1 July 2011 in FA 2009, Sch. 16, para. 14 and 15 and transitional provisions in FA 2009, Sch. 16, para. 17, and subject to anti-avoidance provisions in FA 2009, Sch. 16, para. 19.
In para. 12(1), reference to para. 12A inserted, and in para. 12(5)(a), words "or superior holding company" and "or, in terms of sub-paragraph (5A) of that paragraph, is an exempt trading company" inserted, by FA 1998, s. 113 and Sch. 17, para. 32, with effect as respects accounting periods of companies resident in the UK which end on or after 1 July 1999, the corporation tax self-assessment appointed day under FA 1994, s. 199 by virtue of SI 1998/3173 (C. 78).
Para. 12(3) amended by CTA 2010, s. 1177 and Sch. 1, para. 147(3), with effect for corporation tax purposes for accounting periods ending on or after 1 April 2010, and for income and capital gains tax purposes for the tax year 2010–11 and subsequent tax years.
In para. 12(4), the words "or (4), as the case may be,", which appeared after "sub-paragraph (3)", omitted by FA 2009, s. 36 and Sch. 16, para. 10(4)(b), with effect in relation to accounting periods of controlled foreign companies beginning on or after 1 July 2009 (companies other than qualifying holding companies) or 1 July 2011 (qualifying holding companies), subject to rules for accounting periods straddling 1 July 2009 and 1 July 2011 in FA 2009, Sch. 16, para. 14 and 15 and transitional provisions in FA 2009, Sch. 16, para. 17, and subject to anti-avoidance provisions in FA 2009, Sch. 16, para. 19.
In para. 12(5), "sub-paragraph (3)" substituted for "sub-paragraphs (3) and (4)" by FA 2009, s. 36 and Sch. 16, para. 10(4)(c)(i), with effect in relation to accounting periods of controlled foreign companies beginning on or after 1 July 2009 (companies other than qualifying holding companies) or 1 July 2011 (qualifying holding companies), subject to rules for accounting periods straddling 1 July 2009and 1 July 2011 in FA 2009, Sch. 16, para. 14 and 15 and transitional provisions in FA 2009, Sch. 16, para. 17, and subject to anti-avoidance provisions in FA 2009, Sch. 16, para. 19.
In para. 12(5). the words "or superior holding company", which appeared after "holding company", omitted by FA 2009, s. 36 and Sch. 16, para. 10(4)(c)(ii), with effect in relation to accounting periods of controlled foreign companies beginning on or after 1 July 2009 (companies other than qualifying holding companies) or 1 July 2011 (qualifying holding companies), subject to rules for accounting periods straddling 1 July 2009 and 1 July 2011 in FA 2009, Sch. 16, para. 14 and 15 and transitional provisions in FA 2009, Sch. 16, para. 17, and subject to anti-avoidance provisions in FA 2009, Sch. 16, para. 19.
In para. 12(6), the words "section 35 of CTA 2009" substituted for "Case I of Schedule D" by CTA 2009, s. 1322 and Sch. 1, para. 287(5), with effect for corporation tax purposes for accounting periods ending on or after 1 April 2009, and for income tax and capital gains tax purposes for the tax year 2009–10 and subsequent tax years.

Derivations – FA 1984, Sch. 17, para. 12.

Cross references – FA 1998, Sch. 17, para. 37(2)–(4): commencement and transitional provisions – separate determinations and computations to be made, as respects accounting period of a non-resident company which ends before 1 July 1999, in cases where at least one UK-resident company has an accounting period ending on or after that day, and at least one other UK-resident company has an accounting period ending before that day.

12A [Omitted by FA 2009, s. 36 and Sch. 16, para. 10(5).]

History – Para. 12A omitted by FA 2009, s. 36 and Sch. 16, para. 10(5), with effect in relation to accounting periods of controlled foreign companies beginning on or after 1 July 2009 (companies other than qualifying holding companies) or 1 July 2011 (qualifying holding companies), subject to rules for accounting periods straddling 1 July 2009 and 1 July 2011 in FA 2009, Sch. 16, para. 14 and 15 and transitional provisions in FA 2009, Sch. 16, para. 17, and subject to anti-avoidance provisions in FA 2009, Sch. 16, para. 19.

Part 2A – Trading Companies with Limited UK Connection

History – Pt. 2A inserted by FA 2011, s. 47 and Sch. 12, para. 3, with effect in relation to accounting periods of controlled foreign companies beginning on or after 1 January 2011.

INTRODUCTORY

12B(1) For the purposes of section 748(1)(ba), a controlled foreign company ("C") is exempt for an accounting period if the requirements of this Part of this Schedule are satisfied.

12B(2) The requirements are those imposed as to C's–

(a) business establishment (see paragraph 12C),

(b) business activities (see paragraph 12D),

(c) UK connection (see paragraph 12E), and

(d) finance income and relevant IP income (see paragraph 12F).

History – Para. 12B inserted by FA 2011, s. 47 and Sch. 12, para. 3, with effect in relation to accounting periods of controlled foreign companies beginning on or after 1 January 2011.

BUSINESS ESTABLISHMENT

12C(1) The requirement of this paragraph is that throughout the accounting period C has a business establishment in the territory in which it is resident.

12C(2) For the purposes of sub-paragraph (1)–

(a) paragraph 5(2) to (5) (special rules about residence of the company) applies as it applies for the *purposes of Part 2 of this Schedule*, and

(b) paragraph 7 (meaning of "business establishment") applies as it applies for the purposes of paragraph 6(1)(a).

History – Para. 12C inserted by FA 2011, s. 47 and Sch. 12, para. 3, with effect in relation to accounting periods of controlled foreign companies beginning on or after 1 January 2011.

BUSINESS ACTIVITIES

12D(1) The requirement of this paragraph is that–

(a) C's business does not, at any time during the accounting period, include to a substantial extent non-exempt activities, or

(b) if C is wholly engaged in business falling within paragraph 11(1)(c) (banking etc), C's business does not, at any time during the accounting period, include to a substantial extent non-exempt activities which do not constitute investment business.

12D(2) For this purpose–

"non-exempt activities" means–

(a) the holding or managing of shares or securities,

(b) the holding of intellectual property,

(c) dealing in securities, other than in the capacity of a broker,

(d) the leasing of any description of property or rights,

(e) the investment in any manner of funds which would otherwise be available, directly or indirectly, for investment by or on behalf of any person (whether resident in the United Kingdom or not) who has, or is connected or associated with a person who has, control, either alone or together with other persons, of C, and

(f) if C is not a member of an insurance group throughout the accounting period, the effecting or carrying out of contracts of insurance between C and persons related to C;

"investment business" means activities within paragraphs (a) to (d) of paragraph 9(1).

12D(3) For the purposes of sub-paragraph (2)(f), a person is **"related"** to C if–

(a) the person is connected or associated with C,

(b) the person has a 25 per cent assessable interest in C in the case of the accounting period in question (within the meaning of paragraph 6(4C)), or

(c) if C is a controlled foreign company in that accounting period by virtue of subsection (1A) of section 747, the person is connected or associated with either or both of the two persons mentioned in that subsection.

12D(4) In sub-paragraph (2)–

"broker" includes any person offering to sell securities to, or purchase securities from, members of the public generally;

"contract of insurance" has the meaning given by Article 3(1) of the Financial Services and Markets Act 2000 (Regulated Activities) Order 2001;

"insurance group" has the meaning given by paragraph 11A(4);

"intellectual property" is to be construed in accordance with paragraph 9(1A);

"member of an insurance group" has the meaning given by paragraph 11A(6).

History – Para. 12D inserted by FA 2011, s. 47 and Sch. 12, para. 3, with effect in relation to accounting periods of controlled foreign companies beginning on or after 1 January 2011.

UK CONNECTION

12E(1) The requirement of this paragraph is that C does not have a significant connection with the United Kingdom during the accounting period.

12E(2) C has a significant connection with the United Kingdom during the accounting period if Condition A or B is met.

12E(3) Condition A is that–

(a) the UK-connected gross income of C's business for that period exceeds 10% of the gross income of that business for that period, and

(b) sub-paragraph (4) does not apply.

12E(4) This sub-paragraph applies if–

(a) at all times in the accounting period there are sufficient individuals working for C in the territory in which it is resident, or in any other territory outside of the United Kingdom, who have the competence and authority to undertake all, or substantially all, of C's business,

(b) C's relevant profits for the accounting period do not exceed 10% of C's relevant operating expenses for that period, and

(c) the UK-connected gross income of C's business for that period does not exceed 50% of the gross income of that business for that period.

12E(5) Condition B is that–

(a) the UK-connected related-party business expenditure of C's business for that period exceeds 50% of the total related-party business expenditure of C's business for that period, and

(b) during the accounting period C has been involved in a scheme where the main purpose, or one of the main purposes, of any party to the scheme in entering into the scheme is to achieve a reduction in corporation tax or any tax chargeable as if it were corporation tax.

12E(6) For the purposes of sub-paragraph (4)(a), individuals are not to be regarded as working for C in any territory unless–

(a) they are employed by C in the territory, or

(b) they are otherwise directed by C to perform duties on its behalf in the territory.

12E(7) In this paragraph–

"related-party business expenditure" means any expenditure, other than capital expenditure, which gives rise, directly or indirectly, to income of a person related to C;

"relevant profits", for an accounting period, means the total profits of C for that period calculated in accordance with generally accepted accounting practice (disregarding any capital gains or losses), but before any deduction for interest or tax;

"relevant operating expenses" of C means operating expenses of C other than–

(a) the cost of goods sold, and

(b) related-party business expenditure;

"scheme" means any scheme, arrangements or understanding of any kind whatever, whether or not legally enforceable, involving one or more transactions;

"UK-connected gross income" means the gross income derived, directly or indirectly, from persons who are within the charge to United Kingdom tax for all or part of the accounting period;

"UK-connected related-party business expenditure" means related-party business expenditure which gives rise, directly or indirectly, to income of a person within the charge to United Kingdom tax in respect of that income;

"United Kingdom tax" means income tax or corporation tax;

and paragraph 12D(3) (persons "related" to C) applies for the purposes of this paragraph as it applies for the purposes of paragraph 12D(2)(f).

12E(8) In the case of a company which is within the charge to United Kingdom tax only because it carries on a trade in the United Kingdom through a permanent establishment there, for the purposes of sub-paragraph (7)–

(a) the gross income derived from that company is so much of the gross income as is attributable to that establishment, and

(b) the income received by that company is such of its income as is attributable to that establishment.

History – Para. 12E inserted by FA 2011, s. 47 and Sch. 12, para. 3, with effect in relation to accounting periods of controlled foreign companies beginning on or after 1 January 2011.

FINANCE INCOME AND RELEVANT IP INCOME

12F(1) The requirement of this paragraph is that not more than 5% of C's gross income for the accounting period falls within sub-paragraph (2).

12F(2) Gross income falls within this sub-paragraph to the extent that it is–

(a) finance income, or

(b) relevant IP income.

12F(3) **"Finance income"** means–

(a) any amount which in accordance with UK generally accepted accounting practice falls to be recognised as arising from a financial asset, and

(b) any return, in relation to an amount, which–

(i) is produced for C by an arrangement to which C is party, and

(ii) is economically equivalent to interest,

except to the extent that the return is taken into account in determining an amount within paragraph (a).

12F(4) ***"Relevant IP income"*** means royalties and receipts of a similar nature arising from intellectual property.

12F(5) For the purposes of sub-paragraph (3)(b), the amount of a return is the amount which by virtue of the return would, in calculating C's chargeable profits, be treated under section 486B of CTA 2009 (disguised interest to be regarded as profit from loan relationship) as a profit arising to C from a loan relationship.

12F(6) But, in calculating that profit for the purposes of sub-paragraph (5), sections 486B(7) and 486C to 486E of CTA 2009 are to be ignored.

12F(7) In this paragraph–

"economically equivalent to interest" is to be construed in accordance with section 486B(2) and (3) of CTA 2009;

"financial asset" means a financial asset as defined for the purposes of UK generally accepted accounting practice or international accounting standards;

"intellectual property" is to be construed in accordance with paragraph 9(1A).

History – Para. 12F inserted by FA 2011, s. 47 and Sch. 12, para. 3, with effect in relation to accounting periods of controlled foreign companies beginning on or after 1 January 2011.

GROSS INCOME

12G(1) References in this Part of this Schedule to C's gross income are to be construed in accordance with this paragraph.

12G(2) C's gross income for an accounting period does not include–

(a) any distribution that would not be included in C's chargeable profits by reason of it being exempt for the purposes of Part 9A of CTA 2009 (see section 931A of that Act), or

(b) any amount that would be taken into account in computing chargeable gains if C were within the charge to corporation tax.

12G(3) C's gross income for an accounting period includes–

(a) any income which accrues during that period to the trustees of a settlement in relation to which C is a settlor or a beneficiary, and

(b) any income which accrues during that period to a partnership of which C is a partner, apportioned between C and the other partners on a just and reasonable basis.

12G(4) Where there is more than one settlor or beneficiary in relation to the settlement mentioned in sub-paragraph (3)(a), the income is to be apportioned between C and the other settlors or beneficiaries on a just and reasonable basis.

12G(5) In this paragraph–

"distribution" has the same meaning as in the Corporation Tax Acts (see Part 23 of CTA 2010);

"partnership" includes an entity established under the law of a country or territory outside the United Kingdom of a similar character to a partnership; and **"partner"** is to be read accordingly.

History – Para. 12G inserted by FA 2011, s. 47 and Sch. 12, para. 3, with effect in relation to accounting periods of controlled foreign companies beginning on or after 1 January 2011.

Part 2B – Companies Exploiting Intellectual Property with Limited UK Connection

History – Pt. 2B inserted by FA 2011, s. 47 and Sch. 12, para. 3, with effect in relation to accounting periods of controlled foreign companies beginning on or after 1 January 2011.

INTRODUCTORY

12H(1) For the purposes of section 748(1)(bb), a company ("C") is exempt for an accounting period if the requirements of this Part of this Schedule are satisfied.

12H(2) The requirements are those imposed as to C's–

(a) business establishment (see paragraph 12I),

(b) intellectual property business (see paragraph 12J),

(c) other business activities (see paragraph 12K),

(d) UK connection (see paragraph 12L), and

(e) finance income (see paragraph 12M).

History – Para. 12H inserted by FA 2011, s. 47 and Sch. 12, para. 3, with effect in relation to accounting periods of controlled foreign companies beginning on or after 1 January 2011.

BUSINESS ESTABLISHMENT

12I(1) The requirement of this paragraph is that throughout the accounting period C has a business establishment in the territory in which it is resident.

12I(2) For the purposes of sub-paragraph (1)–

(a) paragraph 5(2) to (5) (special rules about residence of the company) applies as it applies for the purposes of Part 2 of this Schedule, and

(b) paragraph 7 (meaning of "business establishment") applies as it applies for the purposes of paragraph 6(1)(a).

History – Para. 12I inserted by FA 2011, s. 47 and Sch. 12, para. 3, with effect in relation to accounting periods of controlled foreign companies beginning on or after 1 January 2011.

INTELLECTUAL PROPERTY BUSINESS

12J(1) The requirement of this paragraph is that C's main business, throughout the accounting period, consists of the exploitation of intellectual property which does not have a relevant UK connection.

12J(2) For the purposes of sub-paragraph (1), if any part of C's main business consists of the exploitation of intellectual property which has a relevant UK connection, that part is to be ignored if it is an insignificant part of C's main business.

12J(3) Intellectual property has a relevant UK connection if–

(a) at any time during the accounting period or the 6 years immediately preceding that period, it has been held by a person resident in the United Kingdom, or

(b) activities relating to the creation, maintenance or enhancement of the intellectual property (other than activities of an incidental or insignificant nature) have been carried on by a person who for some or all of the period–

  (i) beginning when the activities were first carried on by the person, and

  (ii) ending at the end of the accounting period,

was related to C and within the charge to United Kingdom tax.

History – Para. 12J inserted by FA 2011, s. 47 and Sch. 12, para. 3, with effect in relation to accounting periods of controlled foreign companies beginning on or after 1 January 2011.

OTHER BUSINESS ACTIVITIES

12K(1) The requirement of this paragraph is that–

(a) C does not, at any time during the accounting period, carry on any activities otherwise than in the course of its main business, or

(b) if it carries on any such activities ("secondary activities"), the secondary activities condition is met.

12K(2) The secondary activities condition is that either–

(a) the secondary activities do not, at any time during the accounting period, constitute a substantial part of the activities of C's business taken as a whole, or

(b) section 748(1)(b) or (ba) would apply to prevent an apportionment under section 747(3) falling to be made as regards that period, if C's business consisted only of the secondary activities carried on by it during the accounting period.

History – Para. 12K inserted by FA 2011, s. 47 and Sch. 12, para. 3, with effect in relation to accounting periods of controlled foreign companies beginning on or after 1 January 2011.

UK CONNECTION

12L(1) The requirement of this paragraph is that C does not have a significant connection with the United Kingdom during the accounting period.

12L(2) C has a significant connection with the United Kingdom during the accounting period if–

(a) all or a substantial proportion of C's gross income for that period consists of income from the exploitation of intellectual property which derives from persons within the charge to United Kingdom tax, or

(b) during that period C incurs expenditure (other than expenditure of an incidental or insignificant nature) on–

  (i) R&D sub-contractor payments, or

  (ii) the creation, development or maintenance of relevant intellectual property,

and that expenditure forms part of the income of a person who for some or all of that period is related to C and within the charge to United Kingdom tax.

12L(3) In this paragraph–

"R&D sub-contractor payment" means a payment made by C to another person in respect of research and development contracted out by C to that person;

"relevant intellectual property" means intellectual property which does not have a relevant UK connection (see paragraph 12J(3)) and which C exploits in the course of its main business.

History – Para. 12L inserted by FA 2011, s. 47 and Sch. 12, para. 3, with effect in relation to accounting periods of controlled foreign companies beginning on or after 1 January 2011.

FINANCE INCOME

12M The requirement of this paragraph is that not more than 5% of C's gross income for the accounting period consists of finance income (within the meaning of paragraph 12F(3)).

History – Para. 12M inserted by FA 2011, s. 47 and Sch. 12, para. 3, with effect in relation to accounting periods of controlled foreign companies beginning on or after 1 January 2011.

INTERPRETATION OF PART 2B

12N(1) For the purpose of this Part of this Schedule–

"intellectual property" is to be construed in accordance with paragraph 9(1A);

"United Kingdom tax" means corporation tax or income tax;

and paragraph 12G (meaning of "gross income") applies as it applies for the purposes of Part 2A of this Schedule.

12N(2) For the purposes of this Part of this Schedule a person is **"related"** to C at a particular time if at that time–

(a) the person is connected or associated with C,

(b) the person has a 25 per cent assessable interest in C in the case of the accounting period of C in which that time falls (within the meaning of paragraph 6(4C)), or

(c) if C is a controlled foreign company in the accounting period in which that time falls by virtue of subsection (1A) of section 747, the person is connected or associated with either or both of the two persons mentioned in that subsection.

12N(3) In the case of a company which is within the charge to United Kingdom tax only because it carries on a trade in the United Kingdom through a permanent establishment there–

(a) for the purposes of paragraph 12J(3)(b), the activities carried on by the company are such of the activities as are carried on through that establishment,

(b) for the purposes of paragraph 12L(2)(a), the income derived from that company is such of the income so derived as is attributable to that establishment, and

(c) for the purposes of paragraph 12L(2)(b), the income of that company is such of its income as is attributable to that establishment.

History – Para. 12N inserted by FA 2011, s. 47 and Sch. 12, para. 3, with effect in relation to accounting periods of controlled foreign companies beginning on or after 1 January 2011.

Part III – The Public Quotation Condition

[Omitted by FA 2007, s. 48 and Sch. 15, para 8(2).]

History – Pt. III omitted by FA 2007, s. 48 and Sch. 15, para. 8(2) and repealed by s. 114 and Sch. 27, Pt. 2(15), with effect in relation to accounting periods of controlled foreign companies beginning on or after 6 December 2006 (subject to the transitional provisions at FA 2007, Sch. 15, para. 10(2)–(4)).

Part 3A – Exempt Periods

History – Pt. 3A inserted by FA 2011, s. 47 and Sch. 12, para. 8, with effect in relation to accounting periods of controlled foreign companies beginning on or after 1 January 2011.

INTRODUCTORY

15A The provisions of this Part of this Schedule have effect for the purposes of section 748(1)(f).

History – Para. 15A inserted by FA 2011, s. 47 and Sch. 12, para. 8, with effect in relation to accounting periods of controlled foreign companies beginning on or after 1 January 2011.

BEGINNING OF EXEMPT PERIOD

15B(1) An exempt period begins in relation to a company ("X") at a time ("the relevant time") when–

(a) X is resident outside the United Kingdom,

(b) X is controlled by persons resident in the United Kingdom,

(c) there is at least one relevant UK corporate investor in X, and

(d) the requirements of paragraph 15C or 15D are met.

15B(2) There is a **"relevant UK corporate investor in X"** at a particular time if, at that time, there is a company which–

(a) is resident in the United Kingdom, and

(b) would, on the assumptions set out in sub-paragraph (3), be a company to which an apportionment of X's chargeable profits for the relevant accounting period would fall to be made in circumstances where section 747(5) would not prevent tax being chargeable on the company under section 747(4).

15B(3) The assumptions are–

(a) X has chargeable profits for the relevant accounting period,

(b) an apportionment of those profits falls to be made under section 747(3) for that period, and

(c) no reduction of those profits arises under section 751A, 751AA or 751AB.

15B(4) **"The relevant accounting period"** means the accounting period of X in which the time mentioned in sub-paragraph (2) falls.

History – Para. 15B inserted by FA 2011, s. 47 and Sch. 12, para. 8, with effect in relation to accounting periods of controlled foreign companies beginning on or after 1 January 2011.

15C(1) The requirements of this paragraph are that–

(a) no company was, at any time before the relevant time, a relevant UK corporate investor in X,

(b) no asset owned by X, or part of the business carried on by X, at the relevant time was previously owned, or carried on, by a company which–

(i) was under the control of persons resident in the United Kingdom at any time it owned the asset or carried on the part of the business, and

(ii) is or has been related to X,

(c) condition A, B, C or D is met, and

(d) no disqualifying relevant transaction occurs (see paragraph 15E).

15C(2) Condition A is that, immediately before the relevant time, X–

(a) was in existence, but

(b) was not a member of the same group of companies as any person who, at the relevant time, was a controlling UK person.

15C(3) Condition B is that–

(a) at the relevant time X is controlled by a company which is resident in the United Kingdom, and

(b) immediately before that time, X was controlled by that same company but that company was not then resident in the United Kingdom.

15C(4) Condition C is that–

(a) at the relevant time–

(i) X is controlled by a company which is resident in the United Kingdom ("the intermediate parent"), and

(ii) the intermediate parent is controlled by a company which is not resident in the United Kingdom ("the parent"), and

(b) immediately before that time X was controlled by the parent but not the intermediate parent.

15C(5) Condition D is that X–

(a) is a controlled foreign company at the time it is formed, and

(b) is formed by one or more persons for the purpose of controlling one or more companies in circumstances where it is expected that an exempt period will begin in relation to one or more of those companies at the time when X begins to control the company or companies.

15C(6) In this paragraph **"controlling UK person"** means a person resident in the United Kingdom who alone, or together with other such persons, controls X.

History – Para. 15C inserted by FA 2011, s. 47 and Sch. 12, para. 8, with effect in relation to accounting periods of controlled foreign companies beginning on or after 1 January 2011.

15D(1) The requirements of this paragraph are that–

(a) the relevant time falls after 23 March 2011,

(b) X has an accounting period during which 23 March 2011 falls,

(c) no company was, at any time during that accounting period, a relevant UK corporate investor in X,

(d) no company was, immediately before the relevant time, a relevant UK corporate investor in X,

(e) at the relevant time X is controlled by a company which–

(i) is resident in the United Kingdom, and

(ii) is not under the control of another body corporate, or two or more other bodies corporate taken together, and

(f) no disqualifying relevant transaction occurs (see paragraph 15E).

15D(2) In determining for the purposes of sub-paragraph (1)(e)(ii) whether a company is under the control of two or more bodies corporate taken together, a body corporate which holds less than 10% of the issued ordinary shares of that company is to be disregarded.

15D(3) For the purposes of sub-paragraph (2), a body corporate is treated as holding any shares held by persons who are connected or associated with the body corporate.

History – Para. 15D inserted by FA 2011, s. 47 and Sch. 12, para. 8, with effect in relation to accounting periods of controlled foreign companies beginning on or after 1 January 2011.

DISQUALIFYING RELEVANT TRANSACTIONS

15E(1) This paragraph applies for the purposes of paragraph 15C and 15D.

15E(2) A disqualifying relevant transaction occurs if–

(a) a relevant transaction occurs at the relevant time (whether or not the transaction occurs pursuant to an agreement entered into by X before that time), or

(b) a relevant transaction occurs on or after 9 December 2010 but before the relevant time and that transaction forms part of an avoidance scheme.

15E(3) **"Relevant transaction"** means–

(a) the making by X of a loan or advance of an amount (other than a negligible amount) to a person who, at the time it is made, is related to X and subject to United Kingdom tax,

(b) an increase (other than an increase of a negligible amount) in the amount of an existing loan or advance made by X to a person who, at the time of the increase, is related to X and subject to United Kingdom tax,

(c) a change in the terms or conditions of an existing loan or advance made by X where–

(i) the loan or advance is to a person who, at the time the change is made, is related to X and subject to United Kingdom tax, and

(ii) the change has an effect (other than a negligible effect) on the amount of interest payable, or

(d) a transaction to which sub-paragraph (4) applies.

15E(4) This sub-paragraph applies to a transaction if–

(a) it is referable to an activity carried on by X as part, or the whole, of any non-exempt activities carried on by X,

(b) the results of the transaction are reflected in the profits arising in an accounting period of X and are not negligible in value, and

(c) the results of the transaction alone, or together with the results of one or more other transactions, achieves a reduction in United Kingdom tax.

15E(5) A transaction achieves, or two or more transactions together achieve, a reduction in United Kingdom tax if, had the transaction or transactions not been effected, any person–

(a) would have been liable for any such tax or for a greater amount of any such tax, or

(b) would not have been entitled to a relief from or repayment of any such tax or would have been entitled to a smaller relief from or repayment of any such tax.

15E(6) In this paragraph–

"avoidance scheme" means a scheme the main purpose, or one of the main purposes, of any party to which in entering into the scheme is to secure that section 748(1)(f) prevents an apportionment falling to be made under section 747(3) as regards an accounting period, or accounting periods, of X;

"non-exempt activities" has the meaning given by paragraph 12D(2);

"scheme" means any scheme, arrangements or understanding of any kind whatever, whether or not legally enforceable, involving one or more transactions;

"United Kingdom tax" means corporation tax (or any tax chargeable as if it were corporation tax) or income tax.

History – Para. 15E inserted by FA 2011, s. 47 and Sch. 12, para. 8, with effect in relation to accounting periods of controlled foreign companies beginning on or after 1 January 2011.

ENDING OF EXEMPT PERIOD

15F(1) An exempt period ends on the expiry of the period of 24 months which begins immediately after the first accounting period of X to end after the relevant time, unless sub-paragraph (2) applies.

15F(2) If an early termination event occurs after the relevant time but before the time the exempt period would end under sub-paragraph (1), the exempt period ends immediately before that event.

15F(3) An early termination event occurs if and when–

(a) a relevant transaction occurs, whether or not the transaction occurs pursuant to an agreement entered into by X before that time, or

(b) where the exempt period began because Condition D was met, X's business does not consist wholly in the holding of shares of companies which X controls, together with activities incidental to the holding of such shares.

History – Para. 15F inserted by FA 2011, s. 47 and Sch. 12, para. 8, with effect in relation to accounting periods of controlled foreign companies beginning on or after 1 January 2011.

INTERPRETATION OF PART 3A

15G(1) In this Part of this Schedule–

"group" means a company and any other companies it controls;

"the relevant time" has the meaning given by paragraph 15B;

"relevant transaction" has the meaning given by paragraph 15E;

"relevant UK corporate investor in X" has the meaning given by paragraph 15B(2);

"X" is to be construed in accordance with paragraph 15B.

15G(2) For the purposes of this Part of this Schedule a person is **"related"** to X at a particular time if–

(a) the person is connected or associated with X at that time,

(b) the person has a 25 per cent assessable interest in X in the case of the accounting period in which that time falls (within the meaning of paragraph 6(4C)), or

(c) if X is a controlled foreign company in the accounting period in which that time falls by virtue of subsection (1A) of section 747, the person is connected or associated with either or both of the two persons mentioned in that subsection.

History – Para. 15G inserted by FA 2011, s. 47 and Sch. 12, para. 8, with effect in relation to accounting periods of controlled foreign companies beginning on or after 1 January 2011.

Part IV – Reductions in United Kingdom Tax and Diversion of Profits

16(1) The provisions of this Part of this Schedule have effect for the purposes of section 748(3).

16(2) Any reference in paragraphs 17 and 18 below to a **transaction**–

(a) is a reference to a transaction the results of which are reflected in the profits arising in an accounting period of a controlled foreign company; and

(b) includes a reference to two or more transactions taken together, the results of at least one of which are so reflected.

History – In para. 16(2)(a), the words " the results of which are " were inserted by FA 1996, s. 182 and Sch. 36, para. 4(6)(a), in relation to accounting periods of a controlled foreign company beginning on or after 28 November 1995.
In para. 16(2)(b), the words "two or more transactions … which are so reflected" were substituted by FA 1996, s. 182 and Sch. 36, para. 4(6)(b), in relation to accounting periods of a controlled foreign company beginning on or after 28 November 1995.

Derivations – FA 1984, Sch. 17, para. 16.

Cross references – S. 751: accounting periods of a company resident outside the UK.

17(1) A transaction achieves a reduction in United Kingdom tax if, had the transaction not been effected, any person–

(a) would have been liable for any such tax or for a greater amount of any such tax; or

(b) would not have been entitled to a relief from or repayment of any such tax or would have been entitled to a smaller relief from or repayment of any such tax.

17(2) In this Part of this Schedule and section 748(3) **"United Kingdom tax"** means income tax, corporation tax or capital gains tax.

Derivations – *FA 1984, Sch. 17, para. 17.*

18 It is the main purpose or one of the main purposes of a transaction to achieve a reduction in United Kingdom tax if this is the purpose or one of the main purposes–

(a) of the controlled foreign company concerned; or

(b) of a person who has an interest in that company at any time during the accounting period concerned.

Derivations – FA 1984, Sch. 17, para. 18.

19(1) The existence of a controlled foreign company achieves a reduction in United Kingdom tax by a diversion of profits from the United Kingdom in an accounting period if it is reasonable to suppose that, had neither the company nor any company related to it been in existence–

(a) the whole or a substantial part of the receipts which are reflected in the controlled foreign company's profits in that accounting period would have been received by a company or individual resident in the United Kingdom; and

(b) that company or individual or any other person resident in the United Kingdom either–

(i) would have been liable for any United Kingdom tax or for a greater amount of any such tax; or

(ii) would not have been entitled to a relief from or repayment of any such tax or would have been entitled to a smaller relief from or repayment of any such tax.

19(2) For the purposes of sub-paragraph (1) above, a company is **related** to a controlled foreign company if–

(a) it is resident outside the United Kingdom; and

(b) it is connected or associated with the controlled foreign company; and

(c) in relation to any company or companies resident in the United Kingdom, it fulfils or could fulfil, directly or indirectly, substantially the same functions as the controlled foreign company.

19(3) Any reference in sub-paragraph (1) above to a **company resident in the United Kingdom** includes a reference to such a company which, if the controlled foreign company in question were not in existence, it is reasonable to suppose would have been established.

Derivations – FA 1984, Sch. 17, para. 19.

SCHEDULE 26 – RELIEFS AGAINST LIABILITY FOR TAX IN RESPECT OF CHARGEABLE PROFITS

Section 754(5)

TRADING LOSSES AND GROUP RELIEF ETC.

1(1) In any case where–

(a) an amount of chargeable profits is apportioned to a company resident in the United Kingdom, and

(b) the company is entitled, or would on the making of a claim be entitled, in computing its profits for the appropriate accounting period, to a deduction in respect of any relevant allowance,

(c) [Repealed by FA 1998, s. 113 and Sch 17, para 34(2)(a), s. 165 and Sch. 27, Pt. III(27).]

then, on the making of a claim, a sum equal to corporation tax at the appropriate rate on so much of the relevant allowance as is specified in the claim shall be set off against the company's liability to tax under section 747(4)(a) in respect of the chargeable profits apportioned to it.

1(2) In this paragraph–

(a) **"the appropriate accounting period"** means the accounting period for which, by virtue of section 754(2), the company is chargeable to tax by virtue of this Chapter in respect of the chargeable profits concerned; and

(b) **"the appropriate rate"** means the rate of corporation tax applicable to profits of the appropriate accounting period or, if there is more than one such rate, the average rate over the whole accounting period.

1(3) In this paragraph **"relevant allowance"** means–

(a) any loss to which section 37 or 62(1) to (3) of CTA 2010 applies;

(b) any qualifying charitable donation;

(c) any expenses of management to which section 1219(1) of CTA 2009 applies;

(cc) any expenses deduction under section 76(1);

(d) so much of any allowance to which section 74 of the 1968 Act applies as falls within subsection (3) of that section;

(e) any amount available to the company by way of group relief; and

(f) any non-trading deficit on its loan relationships.

1(4) [Repealed by FA 1998, s. 113 and Sch 17, para 34(4), s. 165 and Sch. 27, Pt. III(27).]

1(5) Where, by virtue of sub-paragraph (1) above, a sum is set off against a liability to tax, so much of the relevant allowance as gives rise to the amount set off shall be regarded for the purposes of the Tax Acts as having been allowed as a deduction against the company's profits in accordance with the appropriate provisions of those Acts.

1(6) [Repealed by FA 1998, s. 113 and Sch 17, para. 34(5), s. 165 and Sch. 27, Pt. III(27).]

History – Para. 1(1)(c) and the word "and" immediately preceding it repealed by FA 1998, s. 113 and Sch 17, para 34(2)(a), s. 165 and Sch. 27, Pt. III(27), with effect as respects accounting periods of companies resident in the UK which end on or after 1 July 1999, the corporation tax self-assessment appointed day under FA 1994, s. 199 by virtue of SI 1998/3173 (C. 78).
In para. 1(3)(a), the words "section 37 or 62(1) to (3) of CTA 2010" substituted for the words "section 392A(1) or 393A(1)" by CTA 2010, s. 1177 and Sch. 1, para. 148(2), with effect for corporation tax purposes for accounting periods ending on or after 1 April 2010, and for income and capital gains tax purposes for the tax year 2010–11 and subsequent tax years.
In para. 1(3)(b), the words "qualifying charitable donation" substituted for the words "charge on income to which section 338(1) applies" by CTA 2010, s. 1177 and Sch. 1, para. 148(3), with effect for corporation tax purposes for accounting periods ending on or after 1 April 2010, and for income and capital gains tax purposes for the tax year 2010–11 and subsequent tax years.
In para. 1(3)(c), the words "section 1219(1) of CTA 2009" substituted for "section 75(1)" by CTA 2009, s. 1322 and Sch. 1, para. 288, with effect for corporation tax purposes for accounting periods ending on or after 1 April 2009, and for income tax and capital gains tax purposes for the tax year 2009–10 and subsequent tax years.
Para. 1(3)(cc) inserted by SI 2004/2310, Schedule, para. 38(2), with effect in relation to accounting periods beginning on or after 1 April 2004, subject to transitional provisions at FA 2004, s. 43 and 44.

Derivations – FA 1984, Sch. 18, para. 1.

Cross references – S. 75(1): deductibility of expenses of management in computing total profits.
S. 338(1): charges on income allowable as deductions.
S. 392A(1): set-off of a company's Sch. A loss in an accounting period against company's total profits for that period.
S. 393A(1): set-off of company trading losses against profits of the same or an earlier accounting period.
S. 755A(3), (4): "appropriate rate" for purposes of para. 1 where, in the case of the relevant accounting period, the UK company is not charged to tax under Sch. D, Case I in respect of its profits from life assurance business.
S. 755A(8): set-off against liability to tax of a company carrying on life assurance business in respect of its apportioned profit to be made only against the "eligible part" of such apportioned profit (defined in s. 755A(10)–(14)).
TMA 1970, s. 42: procedure for making claims.
FA 1998, Sch. 17, para. 37(2)–(4): separate determinations and computations to be made, as respects accounting period of a non-resident company which ends before 1 July 1999, in cases where at least one UK-resident company has an accounting period ending on or after that day, and at least one other UK-resident company has an accounting period ending before that day.

Notes – CAA 1968, s. 74(3) referred to in para. 1(3)(d) is repealed and re-enacted as CAA 1990, s. 145(3) which has since become CAA 2001, s. 260(3) (see Interpretation Act 1978, s. 17(2)).

ADVANCE CORPORATION TAX

2 [Repealed by FA 1998, s. 31 and Sch. 3, para. 44(2), s. 165 and Sch. 27, Pt. III(2).]

History – Para. 2 repealed by FA 1998, s. 31 and Sch. 3, para. 44(2), s. 165 and Sch. 27, Pt. III(2), with effect in relation to accounting periods beginning on or after 6 April 1999.

GAINS ON DISPOSAL OF SHARES IN CONTROLLED FOREIGN COMPANIES

3(1) This paragraph applies in any case where–

(a) an accounting period of a controlled foreign company ("the apportionment period") is one in respect of which an apportionment under section 747(3) falls to be made; and

(b) the company's chargeable profits for the apportionment period have been apportioned among the persons in subsection (3) of that section; and

(c) a company resident in the United Kingdom (**"the claimant company"**) disposes of–

(i) shares in the controlled foreign company, or

(ii) shares in another company which, in whole or in part, give rise to the claimant company's interest in the controlled foreign company,

being, in either case, shares acquired before the end of the apportionment period; and

(d) by virtue of the apportionment referred to in paragraph (b) above, a sum is, under section 747(4)(a), chargeable on the claimant company as if it were an amount of corporation tax; and

(e) the claimant company makes a claim for relief under this paragraph;

and in this paragraph the disposal mentioned in paragraph (c) above is referred to as **"the relevant disposal"**.

3(2) Subject to the following provisions of this paragraph, in the computation under Chapter III of Part II of the 1992 Act of the gain accruing on the relevant disposal, the appropriate fraction of the sum referred to in sub-paragraph (1)(d) above shall be allowable as a deduction; but to the extent that any sum has been allowed as a deduction under this sub-paragraph it shall not again be allowed as a deduction on any claim under this paragraph (whether made by the claimant company or another company).

3(3) In relation to the relevant disposal, the appropriate fraction is–

$$\frac{A}{B}$$

where–

A is the average market value in the apportionment period of the shares disposed of, and

B is the average market value in that period of the interest in the controlled foreign company which, in the case of the claimant company, was taken into account in the apportionment referred to in sub-paragraph (1)(b) above.

3(4) Where, before the relevant disposal–

(a) a dividend is paid by the controlled foreign company, and

(b) the profits out of which the dividend is paid are those from which the chargeable profits referred to in sub-paragraph (1)(b) above are derived, and

(c) at least one of the two conditions in sub-paragraph (5) below is fulfilled,

this paragraph does not apply in relation to a sum chargeable under section 747(4)(a) in respect of so much of the chargeable profits as corresponds to the profits which the dividend represents.

3(5) The conditions referred to in sub-paragraph (4) above are–

(a) that the effect of the payment of the dividend is such that the value of the shares disposed of by the relevant disposal is less after the payment than it was before it; and

(b) that, in respect of a dividend paid or payable on the shares disposed of by the relevant disposal, the claimant company is, by virtue of paragraph 4(2) below, entitled under Part 2 of TIOPA 2010 to relief (by way of underlying tax) by reference to sums which include the sum referred to in sub-paragraph (1)(d) above.

3(6) A claim for relief under this paragraph shall be made before the expiry of the period of three months beginning–

(a) at the end of the accounting period in which the relevant disposal occurs; or

(b) if it is later, on the date on which the assessment to tax for which the claimant company is liable by virtue of section 747(4)(a) becomes final and conclusive.

(6A) Nothing in–

(a) paragraph 10 of Schedule 18 to the Finance Act 1998 (claims or elections in company tax returns), or

(b) Schedule 1A to the Management Act (claims or elections not included in returns),

shall apply, whether by virtue of section 754 or otherwise, to a claim under sub-paragraph (6) above.

3(7) In identifying for the purposes of this paragraph shares in a company with shares of the same class which are disposed of by the relevant disposal, shares acquired at an earlier time shall be deemed to be disposed of before shares acquired at a later time.

History – Para. 3(1)(a) substituted, in para. 3(1)(b), (c) "the apportionment period" substituted for "the direction period" in each case, and in para. 3(1)(d) "chargeable on" substituted for "assessed on and recoverable from", by FA 1998, s. 113 and Sch. 17, para. 35(1)–(4), with effect as respects accounting periods of companies resident in the UK which end on or after 1 July 1999, the corporation tax self-assessment appointed day under FA 1994, s. 199 by virtue of SI 1998/3173 (C. 78).

Reference to the 1992 Act in para. 3(2) substituted by TCGA 1992, s. 290 and Sch. 10, para. 14(62).

In para. 3(3), "the apportionment period" substituted for "the direction period"; in para. 3(4), "chargeable under section 747(4)(a)" substituted for "assessed and recoverable", and para. 3(6A) inserted, by FA 1998, s. 113 and Sch. 17, para. 35(1), (5)–(7), with effect as respects accounting periods of companies resident in the UK which end on or after 1 July 1999, the corporation tax self-assessment appointed day (see above).

In para. 3(5)(b), the words "Part 2 of TIOPA 2010" substituted for the words "Part XVIII" by TIOPA 2010, s. 374 and Sch. 8, para. 35(2), with effect for corporation tax purposes for accounting periods ending on or after 1 April 2010, for income tax and capital gains tax purposes for the tax year 2010–11 and subsequent tax years, and for petroleum revenue tax purposes for chargeable periods beginning on or after 1 July 2010.

Derivations – FA 1984, Sch. 18, para. 3.

Cross references – S. 834(3): when dividends are paid.

TMA 1970, s. 42: procedure for making claims.

FA 1998, Sch. 17, para. 37(2)–(4):] separate determinations and computations to be made, as respects accounting period of a non-resident company which ends before 1 July 1999, in cases where at least one UK-resident company has an accounting period ending on or after that day, and at least one other UK-resident company has an accounting period ending before that day.

DIVIDENDS FROM THE CONTROLLED FOREIGN COMPANY

4(1) This paragraph applies in any case where–

(a) an accounting period of a controlled foreign company is one in respect of which an apportionment under subsection (3) of section 747 falls to be made; and

(b) the company's chargeable profits for that period have been apportioned among the persons referred to in that subsection, and

(c) the controlled foreign company pays a dividend in whole or in part out of the total profits from which (in accordance with subsection (6)(a) of that section) those chargeable profits are derived.

4(2) Subject to paragraphs 5 and 6 below, where this paragraph applies, the aggregate of the sums chargeable on companies resident in the United Kingdom in accordance with section 747(4)(a) in respect of the chargeable profits referred to in sub-paragraph (1)(b) above shall be treated for the purposes of Part 2 of TIOPA 2010 (double taxation relief) as if it were an amount of tax paid in respect of the profits concerned under the law of the territory in which the controlled foreign company was resident and, accordingly, as underlying tax for the purposes of Chapter II of that Part.

4(3) In the following provisions of this paragraph and in paragraphs 5 and 6 below, the aggregate of the sums which, under sub-paragraph (2) above, fall to be treated as underlying tax is referred to as the **"gross attributed tax"**.

4(4) If, in the case of a person who receives the dividend, section 36, 40, 41 or 42 of TIOPA 2010 has the effect of reducing the amount which (apart from that section) would have been the amount of the credit for foreign tax which is to be allowed to that person, then, for the purposes of sub-paragraph (5) below, the amount of that reduction shall be determined and so much of it as does not exceed the amount of the foreign tax, exclusive of underlying tax, for which credit is to be allowed in respect of the dividend is in that sub-paragraph referred to as **"the wasted relief"**.

4(5) Except for the purpose of determining the amount of the wasted relief, the gross attributed tax shall be treated as reduced by the aggregate of thewasted relief arising in the case of all the persons falling within sub-paragraph (4) above and, on the making of a claim by any of the companies referred to in sub-paragraph (2) above–

(a) the amount of tax chargeable on the company in accordance with section 747(4)(a) in respect of the chargeable profits referred to in sub-paragraph (1)(b) above shall, where appropriate, be reduced; and

(b) all such adjustments (whether by repayment of tax or otherwise) shall be made as are appropriate to give effect to any reduction under paragraph (a) above.

History – Para. 4(1)(a) substituted, in para. 4(1)(b) "that subsection" substituted for "subsection (3) of that section", and in para. 4(2), (5)(a) "chargeable on" substituted for "assessed on and recoverable from", by FA 1998, s. 113 and Sch. 17, para. 36, with effect as respects accounting periods of companies resident in the UK which end on or after 1 July 1999, the corporation tax self-assessment appointed day under FA 1994, s. 199 by virtue of SI 1998/3173 (C. 78).

In para. 4(2), the words "Part 2 of TIOPA 2010 (double taxation relief)" substituted for the words "Part XVIII" by TIOPA 2010, s. 374 and Sch. 8, para. 35(3), with effect for corporation tax purposes for accounting periods ending on or after 1 April 2010, for income tax and capital gains tax purposes for the tax year 2010-11 and subsequent tax years, and for petroleum revenue tax purposes for chargeable periods beginning on or after 1 July 2010, subject to saving provisions in TIOPA 2010, Sch. 9, para. 27.

In para. 4(4), the words "section 36, 40, 41 or 42 of TIOPA 2010" substituted for the words "section 796 or section 797" by TIOPA 2010, s. 374 and Sch. 8, para. 35(4), with effect for corporation tax purposes for accounting periods ending on or after 1 April 2010, for income tax and capital gains tax purposes for the tax year 2010–11 and subsequent tax years, and for petroleum revenue tax purposes for chargeable periods beginning on or after 1 July 2010.

Derivations – FA 1984, Sch. 18, para. 4.

Cross references – S. 796, 797: limitation of credit relief to tax in respect of the foreign income etc. for income tax and corporation tax respectively.

TMA 1970, s. 42: procedure for making claims.

FA 1998, Sch. 17, para. 37(2)–(4): separate determinations and computations to be made, as respects accounting period of a non-resident company which ends before 1 July 1999, in cases where at least one UK-resident company has an accounting period ending on or after that day, and at least one other UK-resident company has an accounting period ending before that day.

5(1) In so far as any provision of–

(a) arrangements which have effect under section 2(1) of TIOPA 2010 (double taxation relief by agreement with territories outside the United Kingdom), or

(b) unilateral relief arrangements for a territory outside the United Kingdom (as defined by section 8 of that Act),

makes relief which is related to foreign dividends received by a company resident in the United Kingdom conditional upon that company either having a particular degree of control of the company paying the dividend or being a subsidiary of another company which has that degree of control, that condition shall be treated as fulfilled in considering whether any such company is by virtue of paragraph 4(2) above entitled to relief under Part 2 of TIOPA 2010 in respect of any of the gross attributed tax.

5(2) Notwithstanding anything in paragraph 4(2) above, in section 31(2)(b) and (3) of TIOPA 2010 the expression **"underlying tax"** does not include gross attributed tax.

5(3) In a case where the controlled foreign company pays a dividend otherwise than out of specified profits and, on the apportionment referred to in paragraph 4(1) above, less than the whole of the chargeable profits of the controlled foreign company concerned is apportioned to companies which are resident in the United Kingdom and liable for tax thereon as mentioned in section 747(4)(a)–

(a) the gross attributed tax shall be regarded as attributable to a corresponding proportion of the profits in question, and in this sub-paragraph the profits making up that proportion are referred to as **"taxed *profits*"**;

(b) so much of the dividend as is received by, or by a successor in title of, any such company shall be regarded as paid primarily out of taxed profits; and

(c) so much of the dividend as is received by any other person shall be regarded as paid primarily out of profits which are not taxed profits.

5(4) The reference in sub-paragraph (3)(b) above to a successor in title of a company resident in the United Kingdom is a reference to a person who is such a successor in respect of the whole or any part of that interest in the controlled foreign company by virtue of which an amount of its chargeable profits was apportioned to that company.

History – Para. 5(1)(a) and (b) substituted by TIOPA 2010, s. 374 and Sch. 8, para 35(5), with effect for corporation tax purposes for accounting periods ending on or after 1 April 2010, for income tax and capital gains tax purposes for the tax year 2010–11 and subsequent tax years, and for petroleum revenue tax purposes for chargeable periods beginning on or after 1 July 2010.
In para. 5(1), the words "Part 2 of TIOPA 2010" substituted for the words "Part XVIII" by TIOPA 2010, s. 374 and Sch. 8, para 35(6), with effect for corporation tax purposes for accounting periods ending on or after 1 April 2010, for income tax and capital gains tax purposes for the tax year 2010–11 and subsequent tax years, and for petroleum revenue tax purposes for chargeable periods beginning on or after 1 July 2010.
In para. 5(2), the words "section 31(2)(b) and (3) of TIOPA 2010" substituted for the words "section 795(2)(b)" by TIOPA 2010, s. 374 and Sch. 8, para. 35(7), with effect for corporation tax purposes for accounting periods ending on or after 1 April 2010, for income tax and capital gains tax purposes for the tax year 2010–11 and subsequent tax years, and for petroleum revenue tax purposes for chargeable periods beginning on or after 1 July 2010.

Derivations – FA 1984, Sch. 18, para. 5.

Cross references – S. 788: double taxation treaties.
S. 790: unilateral relief for foreign taxes.
S. 795(2)(b): grossing-up for double taxation relief of dividends other than on a remittance basis.

6(1) In any case where–

(a) on a claim for relief under paragraph 3 above, the whole or any part of any sum has been allowed as a deduction on a disposal of shares in any company; and

(b) that sum forms part of the gross attributed tax in relation to a dividend paid by that company; and

(c) a person receiving the dividend in respect of the shares referred to in paragraph (a) above (**"the primary dividend"**) or any other relevant dividend is, by virtue of paragraph 4(2) above, entitled under Part 2 of TIOPA 2010 to relief (by way of underlying tax) by reference to the whole or any part of the gross attributed tax;

the amount which, apart from this paragraph, would be available by way of any such relief to the person referred to in paragraph (c) above shall be reduced or, as the case may be, extinguished by deducting therefrom the amount allowed by way of relief as mentioned in paragraph (a) above.

6(2) For the purposes of sub-paragraph (1)(c) above, in relation to the primary dividend, another dividend is a relevant dividend if–

(a) it is a dividend in respect of shares in a company which is resident outside the United Kingdom; and

(b) it represents profits which, directly or indirectly, consist of or include the primary dividend.

History – In para. 6(1)(c), the words "Part 2 of TIOPA 2010" substituted for the words "Part XVIII" by TIOPA 2010, s. 374 and Sch. 8, para. 35(8), with effect for corporation tax purposes for accounting periods ending on or after 1 April 2010, for income tax and capital gains tax purposes for the tax year 2010–11 and subsequent tax years, and for petroleum revenue tax purposes for chargeable periods beginning on or after 1 July 2010.

Derivations – FA 1984, Sch. 18, para. 6.

SCHEDULE 27 – DISTRIBUTING FUNDS

Section 760

[Sch. 27 repealed by SI 2009/3001, reg. 13 and Sch. 2.]

History – Sch. 27 repealed by SI 2009/3001, reg. 13 and Sch. 2, with effect from 1 December 2009 for various purposes (in accordance with the provisions of SI 2009/3001, reg. 1), subject to transitional and savings provisions in SI 2009/3001, Sch. 1. Former Sch. 27 read as follows:

"SCHEDULE 27 – DISTRIBUTING FUNDS

Section 760

Part I – The Distribution Test

REQUIREMENTS AS TO DISTRIBUTIONS

1(1) For the purposes of this Chapter, an offshore fund pursues a **full distribution policy** with respect to an account period if–

(a) a distribution is made for that account period or for some other period which, in whole or in part, falls within that account period; and

(b) subject to Part II of this Schedule, the amount of the distribution which is paid to the holders of material and other interests in the fund–

  (i) represents at least 85 per cent of the income of the fund for that period, and

  (ii) is not less than 85 per cent of the fund's United Kingdom equivalent profits for that period; and

(c) the distribution is made during that account period or not more than six months, or such longer period as the Board may in any particular case allow, after the expiry of it; and

(d) the form of the distribution is such that–

  (i) if any sum forming part of it were received in the United Kingdom by an individual resident there and did not form part of the profits of a trade, profession or vocation, that sum would fall to be chargeable to tax under a provision specified in section 830(2) of ITTOIA 2005, or

  (ii) if any sum forming part of it were received in the United Kingdom by a company resident there and did not form part of the profits of a trade, profession or vocation, that sum would fall to be chargeable to tax–

    (a) under Part 5 of CTA 2009 (loan relationships) or Chapter 7 of Part 10 of that Act (annual payments not otherwise charged) in respect of income arising from securities out of the United Kingdom or from possessions out of the United Kingdom, or

    (b) under Chapter 2 of Part 10 of CTA 2009 (dividends of non-UK resident companies) or Chapter 8 of that Part (income not otherwise charged);

and any reference in this sub-paragraph to a **distribution made for an account period** includes a reference to any two or more distributions so made or, in the case of paragraph (b), the aggregate of them.

1(2) Subject to sub-paragraph (3) below, with respect to any account period for which–

(a) there is no income of the fund and there are no United Kingdom equivalent profits of the fund, or

(b) the amount of the gross income of the fund does not exceed 1 per cent of the average value of the fund's assets held during the account period,

the fund shall be treated as pursuing a full distribution policy notwithstanding that no distribution is made as mentioned in sub-paragraph (1) above.

1(3) For the purposes of this Chapter, an offshore fund shall be regarded as not pursuing a full distribution policy with respect to an account period for which the fund does not make up accounts.

1(4) For the purposes of this paragraph–

(a) where a period for which an offshore fund makes up accounts includes the whole or part of two or more account periods of the fund, then, subject to paragraph (c) below, income shown in those accounts shall be apportioned between those account periods on a time basis according to the number of days in each period which are comprised in the period for which the accounts are made up;

(b) where a distribution is made for a period which includes the whole or part of two or more account periods of the fund, then, subject to sub-paragraph (5) below, the distribution shall be apportioned between those account periods on a time basis according to the number of days in each period which are comprised in the period for which the distribution is made;

(c) where a distribution is made out of specified income but is not made for a specified period, that income shall be attributed to the account period of the fund in which it in fact arose and the distribution shall be treated as made for that account period; and

(d) where a distribution is made neither for a specified period nor out of specified income, then, subject to sub-paragraph (5) below, it shall be treated as made for the last account period of the fund which ended before the distribution was made.

1(5) If, apart from this sub-paragraph, the amount of a distribution made, or treated by virtue of sub-paragraph (4) above as made, for an account period would exceed the income of that period, then, for the purposes of this paragraph–

(a) if the amount of the distribution was determined by apportionment under sub-paragraph (4)(b) above, the excess shall be re-apportioned, as may be just and reasonable, to any other account period which, in whole or in part, falls within the period for which the distribution was made or, if there is more than one such period, between those periods; and

(b) subject to paragraph (a) above, the excess shall be treated as an additional distribution or series of additional distributions made for preceding account periods in respect of which the distribution or, as the case may be, the aggregate distributions would otherwise be less than the income of the period, applying the excess to later account periods before earlier ones, until it is exhausted.

1(6) In any case where–

(a) for a period which is or includes an account period, an offshore fund is subject to any restriction as regards the making of distributions, being a restriction imposed by the law of any territory outside the United Kingdom; and

(b) the fund is subject to that restriction by reason of an excess of losses over profits (applying the concepts of "profits" and "losses" in the sense in which and to the extent to which they are relevant for the purposes of the law in question);

then in determining for the purposes of the preceding provisions of this paragraph the amount of the fund's income for that account period, there shall be allowed as a deduction any amount which, apart from this sub-paragraph, would form part of the income of the fund for that account period and which cannot be distributed by virtue of the restriction.

History – In para. 1(1)(d)(ii), the words "in accordance with section 18 of ICTA (Schedule D)" omitted by CTA 2009, s. 1322 and Sch. 1, para. 289(2)(a) and repealed by CTA 2009, s. 1326 and Sch. 3, Pt. 1, with effect for corporation tax purposes for accounting periods ending on or after 1 April 2009, and for income tax and capital gains tax purposes for the tax year 2009–10 and subsequent tax years.

In para. 1(1)(d)(ii), the words "Part 5 of CTA 2009 (loan relationships) or Chapter 7 of Part 10 of that Act (annual payments not otherwise charged)" substituted for "Case III of Schedule D" by CTA 2009, s. 1322 and Sch. 1, para. 289(2)(b), with effect for corporation tax purposes for accounting periods ending on or after 1 April 2009, and for income tax and capital gains tax purposes for the tax year 2009–10 and subsequent tax years.

In para. 1(1)(d)(ii), the words "Chapter 2 of Part 10 of CTA 2009 (dividends of non-UK resident companies) or Chapter 8 of that Part (income not otherwise charged)" substituted for "Case V of Schedule D" by CTA 2009, s. 1322 and Sch. 1, para. 289(2)(c), with effect for corporation tax purposes for accounting periods ending on or after 1 April 2009, and for income tax and capital gains tax purposes for the tax year 2009–10 and subsequent tax years.

Para. 1(1)(d) substituted by F(No. 2)A 2005, s. 23(2) with effect from 20 July 2005.

The former para. 1(1)(d)(i) and (ii) inserted and sub-cl. (iii) created from existing text by ITTOIA 2005, s. 882(1) and Sch. 1, para. 350(2); effective for income tax purposes for 2005–06 onwards and for corporation tax purposes for accounting periods ending after 5 April 2005 (ITTOIA 2005, s. 883(1)).

Para. 1(2)(a), (b) substituted by FA 1995, s. 134(4) with effect in relation to account periods ending on or after 29 November 1994.

Derivations – FA 1984, Sch. 19, para. 1 and (para. 1(1)) F(No. 2)A 1987, s. 66(1).

Cross references – S. 760(8)–(10): meaning of "account period".

Transitional – CTA 2009, Sch. 2, para. 55: certain references to CTA 2009, Pt. 5 to include references to FA 1996, Sch. 15 (loan relationships; savings and transitional provisions).

Hansard – Standing Committee A, 19 June 1984, col. 1238 (not reproduced): this is an anti-avoidance provision intended as a deterrent to stop funds from manipulating the computation of income.

Other material – M02/2010: HMRC guidance on late applications for distributing fund status and late distributions.

FUNDS OPERATING EQUALISATION ARRANGEMENTS

2(1) In the case of an offshore fund which throughout any account period operates equalisation arrangements, on any occasion in that period when there is a disposal to which this sub-paragraph applies, the fund shall be treated for the purposes of this Part of this Schedule as making a distribution of an amount equal to so much of the consideration for the disposal as, in accordance with this paragraph, represents income accrued to the date of the disposal.

2(2) Sub-paragraph (1) above applies to a disposal–

(a) which is a disposal of a material interest in the offshore fund concerned; and

(b) which is a disposal to which this Chapter applies (whether by virtue of section 758(3) or otherwise) or is one to which this Chapter would apply if subsections (5) and (6) of that section applied generally and not only for the purpose of determining whether, by virtue of subsection (3) of that section, there is a disposal to which this Chapter applies; and

(c) which is not a disposal with respect to which the conditions in subsection (4) of that section are fulfilled; and

(d) which is a disposal to the fund itself or to the persons concerned in the management of the fund (**"the managers"**) in their capacity as such.

2(3) On a disposal to which sub-paragraph (1) above applies, the part of the consideration which represents income accrued to the date of the disposal is, subject to sub-paragraph (4) and paragraph 4(4) below, the amount which would be credited to the equalisation account of the offshore fund concerned in respect of accrued income if, on the date of the disposal, the material interest which is disposed of were acquired by another person by way of initial purchase.

2(4) If, after the beginning of the period by reference to which the accrued income referred to in sub-paragraph (3) above is calculated, the material interest disposed of by a disposal to which sub-paragraph (1) above applies was acquired by way of initial purchase (whether or not by the person making the disposal)–

(a) there shall be deducted from the amount which, in accordance with sub-paragraph (3) above, would represent income accrued to the date of the disposal, the amount which on that acquisition was credited to the equalisation account of the fund in respect of accrued income; and

(b) if in that period there has been more than one such acquisition of that material interest by way of initial purchase, the deduction to be made under this sub-paragraph shall be the amount so credited to the equalisation account on the latest such acquisition prior to the disposal in question.

2(5) Where, by virtue of this paragraph, an offshore fund is treated for the purposes of this Part of this Schedule as making a distribution on the occasion of a disposal, the distribution shall be treated for those purposes–

(a) as complying with paragraph 1(1)(d) above; and

(b) as made out of the income of the fund for the account period in which the disposal occurs; and

(c) as paid, immediately before the disposal, to the person who was then the holder of the interest disposed of.

2(6) In any case where–

(a) a distribution in respect of an interest in an offshore fund is made to the managers of the fund, and

(b) their holding of that interest is in their capacity as such, and

(c) at the time of the distribution, the fund is operating equalisation arrangements,

the distribution shall not be taken into account for the purposes of paragraph 1(1) above except to the extent that the distribution is properly referable to that part of the period for which the distribution is made during which that interest has been held by the managers of the fund in their capacity as such.

2(7) Subsection (2) of section 758 applies for the purposes of this paragraph as it applies for the purposes of that section.

Derivations – FA 1984, Sch. 19, para. 2.

Cross references – S. 758: definition of "equalisation arrangements".
S. 758(2): definition of "initial purchase".
S. 760(8)–(10): meaning of "account period".

CERTAIN FOREIGN INCOME

History – Heading before para. 3 substituted by CTA 2009, s. 1322 and Sch. 1, para. 289(3), with effect for corporation tax purposes for accounting periods ending on or after 1 April 2009, and for income tax and capital gains tax purposes for the tax year 2009–10 and subsequent tax years.

3(1) Sub-paragraph (2) below applies if any sums which form part of the income of an offshore fund falling within section 756A(1)(b) or (c) are of such a nature that–

(a) the holders of interests in the fund who are individuals domiciled and resident in the United Kingdom–

(i) are chargeable to tax under a provision specified in section 830(2) of ITTOIA 2005 in respect of such of those sums as are referable to their interests; or

(ii) if any of that income is derived from assets within the United Kingdom, would be so chargeable had the assets been outside the United Kingdom;

(aa) the holders of interests in the fund which are companies resident in the United Kingdom–

(i) are chargeable to tax under Part 5 of CTA 2009 (loan relationships) or Chapter 7 of Part 10 of that Act (annual payments not otherwise charged) in respect of income arising from securities out of the United Kingdom or from possessions out of the United Kingdom;

(ii) are chargeable to tax under Chapter 2 of Part 10 of CTA 2009 (dividends of non-UK resident companies) or Chapter 8 of that Part (income not otherwise charged); or

(iii) if any of that income is derived from assets within the United Kingdom, would have been chargeable under sub-paragraph (i) or (ii) had the assets been outside the United Kingdom; and

(b) the holders of interests who are not such companies or individuals would be chargeable as mentioned in paragraph (a) or (aa) above if they were resident in the United Kingdom or, in the case of individuals, if they were domiciled and both resident and ordinarily resident there.

3(2) To the extent that sums falling within sub-paragraph (1) above do not actually form part of a distribution complying with paragraphs 1(1)(c) and (d) above, they shall be treated for the purposes of this Part of this Schedule–

(a) as a distribution complying with those paragraphs and made out of the income of which they form part; and

(b) as paid to the holders of the interests to which they are referable.

History – In para. 3(1)(aa)(i), the words "Part 5 of CTA 2009 (loan relationships) or Chapter 7 of Part 10 of that Act (annual payments not otherwise charged)" substituted for "Case III of Schedule D" by CTA 2009, s. 1322 and Sch. 1, para. 289(4)(a), with effect for corporation tax purposes for accounting periods ending on or after 1 April 2009, and for income tax and capital gains tax purposes for the tax year 2009–10 and subsequent tax years.
In para. 3(1)(aa)(ii), the words "Chapter 2 of Part 10 of CTA 2009 (dividends of non-UK resident companies) or Chapter 8 of that Part (income not otherwise charged)" substituted for "Case V of Schedule D" by CTA 2009, s. 1322 and Sch 1, para. 289(4)(b), with effect for corporation tax purposes for accounting periods ending on or after 1 April 2009, and for income tax and capital gains tax purposes for the tax year 2009–10 and subsequent tax years.
Para. 3(1)(a) substituted and 3(1)(aa) inserted by F(No.2)A 2005, s. 23(3) with effect from 20 July 2005.
In former para. 3(1)(a)(i) the words "Case IV or" omitted (and repealed by s. 884 and Sch. 3) and the words ", or under ITTOIA 2005 on relevant foreign income," inserted by ITTOIA 2005, s. 882(1) and Sch. 1, para. 350(3); effective for income tax purposes for 2005–06 onwards and for corporation tax purposes for accounting periods ending after 5 April 2005 (ITTOIA 2005, s. 883(1)).
In para. 3(1), the reference to "section 756A(1)(b) or (c)" substituted for "section 759(1)(b) or (c)" by FA 2004, s. 145, Sch. 26, para. 8(2) with effect for account periods (within the meaning of Pt. 17, Ch. 5) ending on or after 22 July 2004.
In para. 3(1)(b) the words "paragraph (a) or (aa)" substituted for the former wording "sub-paragraph (i) or (ii)" by F(No.2)A 2005, s. 23(4) with effect from 20 July 2005.

Derivations – FA 1984, Sch. 19, para. 3.

Cross references – S. 756A: general definition of offshore fund.

Transitional – CTA 2009, Sch. 2, para. 55: certain references to CTA 2009, Pt. 5 to include references to FA 1996, Sch. 15 (loan relationships; savings and transitional provisions).

COMMODITY INCOME

4(1) To the extent that the income of an offshore fund for any account period includes profits from dealing in commodities, one half of those profits shall be left out of account in determining for the purposes of paragraphs 1(1)(b) and 5 below–

(a) the income of the fund for that period; and

(b) the fund's United Kingdom equivalent profits for that period;

but in any account period in which an offshore fund incurs a loss in dealing in commodities the amount of that loss shall not be varied by virtue of this paragraph.

4(2) In this paragraph **"dealing in commodities"** shall be construed as follows–
(a) **"commodities"** does not include currency, securities, debts or other assets of a financial nature but, subject to that, means tangible assets which are dealt with on a commodity exchange in any part of the world; and
(b) **"dealing"** includes dealing by way of futures contracts and traded options.

4(3) Where the income of an offshore fund for any account period consists of profits from dealing in commodities and other income, then–
(a) in determining whether the condition in paragraph 1(1)(b) above is fulfilled with respect to that account period, the expenditure of the fund shall be apportioned in such manner as is just and reasonable between the profits from dealing in commodities and the other income; and
(b) in determining whether, and to what extent, any expenditure is deductible under section 1219 of CTA 2009 in computing the fund's United Kingdom equivalent profits for that period, so much of the business of the fund as does not consist of dealing in commodities shall be treated as a business carried on by a separate company.

4(4) Where there is a disposal to which paragraph 2(1) above applies, then, to the extent that any amount which was or would be credited to the equalisation account in respect of accrued income, as mentioned in sub-paragraph (3) or (4) of that paragraph, represents profits from dealing in commodities, one half of that accrued income shall be left out of account in determining under those sub-paragraphs the part of the consideration for the disposal which represents income accrued to the date of the disposal.

History – In para. 4(3)(b), the words "section 1219 of CTA 2009" substituted for "section 75" by CTA 2009, s. 1322 and Sch. 1, para. 289(5), with effect for corporation tax purposes for accounting periods ending on or after 1 April 2009, and for income tax and capital gains tax purposes for the tax year 2009–10 and subsequent tax years.
Para. 4(3)(b) amended retrospectively by FA 1988, s. 146, and Sch. 13, para. 12, by substituting "75".

Derivations – Para. 4(1), (2): FA 1984, Sch. 19, para. 4(1), (2).
Para. 4(3): FA 1984, Sch. 19, para. 4(3).
Para. 4(4): FA 1984, Sch. 19, para. 4(4).

Cross references – S. 760(8)–(10): meaning of "account period".

UNITED KINGDOM EQUIVALENT PROFITS

5(1) Any reference in this Schedule to the United Kingdom equivalent profits of an offshore fund for an account period is a reference to the amount which, on the assumptions in sub-paragraph (3) below, would be the total profits of the fund for that period on which, after allowing for any deductions available against those profits, corporation tax would be chargeable.

5(2) In this paragraph the expression **"profits"** does not include chargeable gains.

5(2A) [Para. 5(2A) repealed in full with effect in relation to FA 1994, s. 159, s. 160 and Sch. 18, para. 1, for accounting periods beginning on or after 1 October 2002. Para. 5(2A)(a) repealed with effect in relation to FA 1993, s. 125–133 for accounting periods beginning on or after 1 October 2002.]

5(3) The assumptions referred to in sub-paragraph (1) above are–
(a) that the offshore fund is a company which, in the account period in question, but not in any other account period, is resident in the United Kingdom; and
(b) that the account period is an accounting period of that company; and
(c) that any dividends or distributions which, by virtue of Chapter 2 or 3 of Part 9A of CTA 2009, should be left out of account in computing income for corporation tax purposes are nevertheless to be brought into account in that computation; and
(d) that the provisions of the Corporation Tax Acts relating to profits, gains or losses arising from a creditor relationship (within the meaning of Part 5 of CTA 2009) apply as if the offshore fund were an authorised unit trust; and
(e) that the provisions of the Corporation Tax Acts relating to profits or losses arising from a derivative contract (within the meaning of Part 7 of CTA 2009) apply as if the offshore fund were an authorised unit trust.

5(4) Without prejudice to any deductions available apart from this sub-paragraph, the deductions referred to in sub-paragraph (1) above include–
(a) a deduction equal to any amount which, by virtue of paragraph 1(6) above, is allowed as a deduction in determining the income of the fund for the account period in question; and
(b) a deduction equal to any amount of tax (paid under the law of a territory outside the United Kingdom) which was taken into account as a deduction in determining the income of the fund for the account period in question but which, because it is referable to capital rather than income, does not fall to be taken into account by virtue of section 811.

5(5) For the avoidance of doubt it is hereby declared that, if any sums forming part of the offshore fund's income for any period have been received by the fund without any deduction of or charge to tax and have been so received by virtue of section 1279 of CTA 2009 or section 714 or 715 of ITTOIA 2005, the effect of the assumption in sub-paragraph (3)(a) above is that those sums are to be brought into account in determining the total profits referred to in sub-paragraph (1) above.

History – Para. 5(2A) repealed by FA 2002, 141 and Sch. 40, Pt. 3(13), with effect in relation to FA 1994, s. 159, s. 160 and Sch. 18, para. 1, for accounting periods beginning on or after 1 October 2002. Para. 5(2A)(a) repealed by FA 2002, 141 and Sch. 40, Pt. 3(10),with effect in relation to FA 1993, s. 125–133 for accounting periods beginning on or after 1 October 2002.
Former para. 5(2A) inserted by FA 1993, s. 170 and Sch. 18, para. 6, and substituted by FA 1994, s. 176(2), with effect where a company becomes entitled to a qualifying asset or to rights and duties under a currency contract, or subject to a qualifying liability, on or after 23 March 1995.
In para. 5(3)(c), "Chapter 2 or 3 of Part 9A" substituted for "section 1285" by FA 2009, s. 34 and Sch. 14, para. 13(a), with effect in relation to distributions paid on or after 1 July 2009.
In para. 5(3)(c), the words "in like manner as if they were dividends or distributions of a company resident outside the United Kingdom", which appeared after "computation", omitted by FA 2009, s. 34 and Sch. 14, para. 13(b), with effect in relation to distributions paid on or after 1 July 2009.
In para. 5(3)(c), the words "section 1285 of CTA 2009" substituted for "section 208" by CTA 2009, s. 1322 and Sch. 1, para. 289(6)(a), with effect for corporation tax purposes for accounting periods ending on or after 1 April 2009, and for income tax and capital gains tax purposes for the tax year 2009–10 and subsequent tax years.
In para. 5(3)(d), the words "Part 5 of CTA 2009" substituted for "Chapter 2 of Part 4 of the Finance Act 1996" by CTA 2009, s. 1322 and Sch. 1, para. 289(6)(b), with effect for corporation tax purposes for accounting periods ending on or after 1 April 2009, and for income tax and capital gains tax purposes for the tax year 2009–10 and subsequent tax years.
Para. 5(3)(d) (together with the word "and" which precedes it) inserted by FA 2004, s. 145, Sch. 26, para. 1(1), with effect for account periods (within the meaning of Pt. 17, Ch. 5) ending on or after 22 July 2004, except that in relation to a fund established on or before that date, the insertion only has effect if an irrevocable election that it should have effect has been made by or on behalf of the fund.
In para. 5(3)(e), the words "Part 7 of CTA 2009" substituted for "Schedule 26 to the Finance Act 2002" by CTA 2009, s. 1322 and Sch. 1, para. 289(6)(c), with effect for corporation tax purposes for accounting periods ending on or after 1 April 2009, and for income tax and capital gains tax purposes for the tax year 2009–10 and subsequent tax years.
Para. 5(3)(e) (together with the word "and" whichprecedes it) inserted by FA 2004, s. 145, Sch. 26, para. 2(1), with effect for account periods (within the meaning of Pt. 17, Ch. 5) ending on or after 22 July 2004, except that in relation to a fund established on or before that date, the insertion only has effect if an irrevocable election that it should have effect has been made by or on behalf of the fund.
In para. 5(5), the words "section 1279 of CTA 2009" substituted for "section 154(2) of the Finance Act 1996" by CTA 2009, s. 1322 and Sch. 1, para. 289(7), with effect for corporation tax purposes for accounting periods ending on or after 1 April 2009, and for income tax and capital gains tax purposes for the tax year 2009–10 and subsequent tax years.

In para. 5(5) the words "or section 714 or 715 of ITTOIA 2005" inserted by ITTOIA 2005, s. 882(1) and Sch. 1, para. 350(4); effective for income tax purposes for 2005–06 onwards and for corporation tax purposes for accounting periods ending after 5 April 2005 (ITTOIA 2005, s. 883(1)).
In para. 5(5) the words "and have been so received by virtue of section 154(2) of the Finance Act 1996" were substituted by FA 1996, s. 154(7) and Sch. 28, para. 6, for the purposes of income tax, with effect for 1996–97 and subsequent years of assessment and for the purposes of corporation tax for accounting periods ending after 31 March 1996.

Derivations – FA 1984, Sch. 19, para. 5.

Cross references – TIOPA 2010, Sch. 9, para. 24: modification of para. 5(4)(b) as it has effect as a result of SI 2009/3001, Sch. 1, para. 3.
S. 47: UK government securities held by non-residents.
S. 48: securities of foreign states.
S. 760(8)–(10): meaning of "account period".
FA 1996, Sch. 10, para. 3: distributing offshore funds and assumptions in para. 5(1).
FA 2002, Sch. 26, para. 35(1) (distributing offshore funds): assumptions to be made for the purposes of para. 5(1).
FA 2004, Sch. 26, para. 1(6) and 2(6): application of para. 5 definition of **"United Kingdom equivalent profits"** for the purpose of determining such profits of an offshore fund for the first account period of the fund in relation to which the insertions made by FA 2004, Sch. 26, para. 1(1) and 2(1) (see History note above) have effect.

Transitional – CTA 2009, Sch. 2, para. 55: certain references to CTA 2009, Pt. 5 to include references to FA 1996, Sch. 15 (loan relationships; savings and transitional provisions).

Statements of practice – SP 2/86: treatment of trading income, interest paid to non-residents, income taxed in the UK and UK tax suffered by direct assessment in computing UK "equivalent profits".

Part II – Modifications of Conditions for Certification in Certain Cases

EXCLUSION OF INVESTMENTS IN DISTRIBUTING OFFSHORE FUNDS

6(1) In any case where–
(a) in an account period of an offshore fund (in this Part of this Schedule referred to as the **"primary fund"**), the assets of the fund consist of or include interests in another offshore fund; and
(b) those interests are such that, by virtue of section 760(3)(a), the primary fund could not, apart from this paragraph, be certified as a distributing fund in respect of that account period; and
(c) that other fund could be certified as a distributing fund in respect of its account period or, as the case may be, each of its account periods which comprises the whole or any part of the account period of the primary fund;

then, in determining whether anything in section 760(3)(a) prevents the primary fund being certified as mentioned in paragraph (b) above, the interests of the primary fund in that other fund shall be left out of account except for the purposes of determining the total value of the assets of the primary fund.

6(2) In this Part of this Schedule an offshore fund falling within sub-paragraph (1)(c) above is referred to as a **"qualifying fund"**.

6(3) In a case falling within sub-paragraph (1) above–
(a) section 760(3)(a) shall have effect in relation to the primary fund with the modification in paragraph 7 below (in addition to that provided for by sub-paragraph (1) above); and
(b) Part I of this Schedule shall have effect in relation to the primary fund with the modification in paragraph 8 below.

History – In para. 6(1)(c), the words "without regard to the provisions of this paragraph," at the start omitted by FA 2007, s. 57(4) and repealed by s. 114 and Sch. 27, Pt. 2(18), with effect in relation to account periods (within the meaning of Chapter 5 of Part 17 of ICTA) beginning on or after 1 January 2007.
In para. 6(1)(b), the words "those interests are such that, by virtue of section 760(3)(a)" substituted for the words "those interests (together with other interests which the primary fund may have) are such that, by virtue of subsection (3)(a) or, if the other fund concerned is a company, subsection (3)(b) or (c) of section 760" and in the words following para. 6(1)(c), the references to "section 760(3)(a)" substituted for those to "section 760(3)(a) to (c)" by FA 2004, s. 145, Sch. 26, para. 14(2), with effect for account periods (within the meaning of Pt. 17, Ch. 5) ending on or after 22 July 2004.
In para. 6(3)(a), the references to "section 760(3)(a)" substituted for those to "section 760(3)(a) to (c)" by FA 2004, s. 145, Sch. 26, para. 14(2), with effect for account periods (within the meaning of Pt. 17, Ch. 5) ending on or after 22 July 2004.

Derivations – FA 1984, Sch. 19, para. 6.

Cross references – S. 760(8)–(10): meaning of "account period".

7 The modification referred to in paragraph 6(3)(a) above is that, in any case where–
(a) at any time in the account period referred to in paragraph 6(1) above, the assets of the primary fund include an interest in an offshore fund or in any company (whether an offshore fund or not); and
(b) that interest falls to be taken into account in determining whether anything in section 760(3)(a) prevents the primary fund being certified as a distributing fund in respect of that account period; and
(c) at any time in that account period the assets of the qualifying fund include an interest in the offshore fund or company referred to in paragraph (a) above;

for the purposes of the application in relation to the primary fund of section 760(3)(a), at any time when the assets of the qualifying fund include the interest referred to in paragraph (c) above, the primary fund's share of that interest shall be treated as an additional asset of the primary fund.

History – In para. 7, the two references to "section 760(3)(a)" substituted for those to "section 760(3)(a) to (c)" by FA 2004, s. 145, Sch. 26, para. 14(3), with effect for account periods (within the meaning of Pt. 17, Ch. 5) ending on or after 22 July 2004.

Derivations – FA 1984, Sch. 19, para. 7.

8(1) The modification referred to in paragraph 6(3)(b) above is that, in determining whether the condition in paragraph 1(1)(b)(ii) above is fulfilled with respect to the account period of the primary fund referred to in paragraph 6(1) above, the United Kingdom equivalent profits of the primary fund for that period shall be treated as increased by the primary fund's share of the excess income (if any) of the qualifying fund which is attributable to that period.

8(2) For the purposes of this paragraph, the excess income of the qualifying fund for any account period of that fund is the amount (if any) by which its United Kingdom equivalent profits for that account period exceed the amount of the distributions made for that period, as determined for the purposes of the application of paragraph 1(1) above to the qualifying fund.

8(3) If an account period of the qualifying fund coincides with an account period of the primary fund, then the excess income (if any) of the qualifying fund for that period is the excess income which is attributable to that period of the primary fund.

8(4) In a case where sub-paragraph (3) above does not apply, the excess income of the qualifying fund which is attributable to an account period of the primary fund is the appropriate fraction of the excess income (if any) of the qualifying fund for any of its account periods which comprises the whole or any part of the account period of the primary fund and, if there is more than one such account period of the qualifying fund, the aggregate of the excess income (if any) of each of them.

8(5) For the purposes of sub-paragraph (4) above, the appropriate fraction is–

$$\frac{A}{B}$$

where–

A is the number of days in the account period of the primary fund which are also days in an account period of the qualifying fund; and

B is the number of days in that account period of the qualifying fund or, as the case may be, in each of those account periods of that fund which comprises the whole or any part of the account period of the primary fund.

Derivations – FA 1984, Sch. 19, para. 8.

9(1) The references in paragraphs 7 and 8(1) above to the primary fund's share of–

(a) an interest forming part of the assets of the qualifying fund, or

(b) the excess income (as defined in paragraph 8 above) of the qualifying fund,

shall be construed as references to the fraction specified in sub-paragraph (2) below of that interest or excess income.

9(2) In relation to any account period of the primary fund, the fraction referred to in sub-paragraph (1) above is–

$$\frac{C}{D}$$

Derivations – FA 1984, Sch. 19, para. 9.

OFFSHORE FUNDS INVESTING IN TRADING COMPANIES

10 [Omitted by FA 2004, s. 145, Sch. 26, para. 14(4) and repealed by s. 326, Sch. 42, Pt. 2(18).]

History – Para. 10 omitted by FA 2004, s. 145, Sch. 26, para. 14(4) and repealed by s. 326, Sch. 42, Pt. 2(18) with effect for account periods (within the meaning of Pt. 17, Ch. 5) ending on or after 22 July 2004.

Derivations – FA 1984, Sch. 19, para. 10.

Cross references – S. 760(3)(b): offshore fund with more than 10 per cent of asset value as interests in a single company not to be certified as a distributing fund.

Statements of practice – SP 2/86: dealing activities etc. not to prevent company ranking as a trading company if incidental to company's business; non-profit making government bodies not to be regarded as companies for purposes of the limit in s. 760(3)(b).

OFFSHORE FUNDS WITH WHOLLY-OWNED SUBSIDIARIES

11(1) In relation to an offshore fund which has a wholly-owned subsidiary which is a company the provisions of Part I of this Schedule shall have effect subject to the modifications in sub-paragraph (4) below.

11(2) Subject to sub-paragraph (3) below, for the purposes of this paragraph, a company is a wholly-owned subsidiary of an offshore fund if and so long as the whole of the issued share capital of the company is–

(a) in the case of an offshore fund falling within section 756A(1)(a), directly and beneficially owned by the fund; and

(b) in the case of an offshore fund falling within section 756A(1)(b), directly owned by the trustees of the fund for the benefit of the fund; and

(c) in the case of an offshore fund falling within section 756A(1)(c), owned in a manner which, as near as may be, corresponds either to paragraph (a) or paragraph (b) above.

11(3) In the case of a company which has only one class of issued share capital, the reference in sub-paragraph (2) above to the whole of the issued share capital shall be construed as a reference to at least 95 per cent of that share capital.

11(4) The modifications referred to in sub-paragraph (1) above are that, for the purposes of Part I of this Schedule–

(a) that percentage of the receipts, expenditure, assets and liabilities of the subsidiary which is equal to the percentage of the issued share capital of the company concerned which is owned as mentioned in sub-paragraph (2) above shall be regarded as the receipts, expenditure, assets and liabilities of the fund; and

(b) there shall be left out of account the interest of the fund in the subsidiary and any distributions or other payments made by the subsidiary to the fund or by the fund to the subsidiary.

History – In para. 11(1), the words "section 760(3) and" omitted and the words "sub-paragraph (4)" substituted for "sub-paragraph (3)" by FA 2004, s. 145, Sch. 26, para. 14(5) and the omitted words repealed by s. 326, Sch. 42, Pt. 2(18) with effect for account periods (within the meaning of Pt. 17, Ch. 5) ending on or after 22 July 2004.

In para. 11(2)(a), (b), (c), references to section 756A(1)(a), (b) and (c) substituted for references to "section 759(1)(a), (b) and (c)" respectively by FA 2004, s. 145, Sch. 26, para. 8(3) with effect for account periods (within the meaning of Pt. 17, Ch. 5) ending on or after 22 July 2004.

In para. 11(4), the words "section 760(3) and" omitted by FA 2004, s. 145, Sch. 26, para. 14(5) and repealed by s. 326, Sch. 42, Pt. 2(18) with effect for account periods (within the meaning of Pt. 17, Ch. 5) ending on or after 22 July 2004.

Derivations – FA 1984, Sch. 19, para. 11, as amended by FA 1986, s. 50(2)–(5).

Cross references – S. 759(1)(a): non-resident companies.
S. 759(1)(b): non-resident unit trust schemes.
S. 759(1)(c): offshore co-ownership arrangements not being non-resident companies or non-resident unit trust schemes.

OFFSHORE FUNDS WITH INTERESTS IN DEALING AND MANAGEMENT COMPANIES

12 [Omitted by FA 2004, s. 145, Sch. 26, para. 14(6) and repealed by s. 326, Sch. 42, Pt. 2(18).]

History – Para. 12 omitted by FA 2004, s. 145, Sch. 26, para. 14(6) and repealed by s. 326, Sch. 42, Pt. 2(18) with effect for account periods (within the meaning of Pt. 17, Ch. 5) ending on or after 22 July 2004.

Derivations – FA 1984, Sch. 19, para. 12.

DISREGARD OF CERTAIN INVESTMENTS FORMING LESS THAN 5 PER CENT OF A FUND

13 [Omitted by FA 2004, s. 145, Sch. 26, para. 14(6) and repealed by s. 326, Sch. 42, Pt. 2(18)]

History – Para. 13 omitted by FA 2004, s. 145, Sch. 26, para. 14(6) and repealed by s. 326, Sch. 42, Pt. 2(18) with effect for account periods (within the meaning of Pt. 17, Ch. 5) ending on or after 22 July 2004.

Derivations – FA 1984, Sch. 19, para. 12A, inserted by FA 1986, s. 50(6).

Cross references – S. 760(8)–*(10): meaning of "account period".*

Hansard – Standing Committee G, 17 June 1986, col. 538 (not reproduced): this provision inserted to ensure that a fund would not be disqualified simply because a de minimis proportion of its assets included a majority holding in a small company.

POWER OF BOARD TO DISREGARD CERTAIN BREACHES OF CONDITIONS

14 If, in the case of any account period of an offshore fund ending after the passing of the Finance (No. 2) Act 1987 (23rd July 1987), it appears to the Board that there has been a failure to comply with the condition in section 760(3)(a) (as modified, where appropriate, by the preceding provisions of this Part of this Schedule) but the Board are satisfied–

(a) that the failure occurred inadvertently; and

(b) that the failure was remedied without unreasonable delay,

the Board may disregard the failure in determining whether to certify the fund as a distributing fund in respect of that account period.

History – In para. 14, the words "the condition in section 760(3)(a)" substituted for "any of the conditions in paragraphs (a) to (c) of section 760(3)" by FA 2004, s. 145, Sch. 26, para. 14(7) with effect for account periods (within the meaning of Pt. 17, Ch. 5) ending on or after 22 July 2004.

Derivations – FA 1984, Sch. 19, para. 12B, inserted by F(No. 2)A 1987, s. 66(2).

Cross references – S. 760(8)–(10): meaning of "account period".

Part III – Certification Procedure

APPLICATION FOR CERTIFICATION

15(1) The Board shall, in such manner as they think appropriate, certify an offshore fund as a distributing fund in respect of an account period if–

(a) an application in respect of that period is made under this paragraph; and

(b) the application is accompanied by the accounts of the fund for, or for a period which includes, the account period to which the application relates; and

(c) there is furnished to the Board such information as they may reasonably require for the purpose of determining whether the fund should be so certified; and

(d) they are satisfied that nothing in section 760(2) or (3) prevents the fund being so certified.

15(2) An application under this paragraph shall be made to the Board by the fund or by a trustee or officer thereof on behalf of the fund and may be so made–

(a) before the expiry of the period of six months beginning at the end of the account period to which the application relates; or

(b) at such later time as the Board may in any particular case allow.

15(3) In any case where, on an application under this paragraph, the Board determine that the offshore fund concerned should not be certified as a distributing fund in respect of the account period to which the application relates, they shall give notice of that fact to the fund.

15(4) If at any time it appears to the Board that the accounts accompanying an application under this paragraph in respect of any account period of an offshore fund or any information furnished to the Board in connection with such an application is or are not such as to make full and accurate disclosure of all facts and considerations relevant to the application, they shall give notice to the fund accordingly, specifying the period concerned.

15(5) Where a notice is given by the Board under sub-paragraph (4) above, any certification by them in respect of the account period in question shall be void.

Derivations – FA 1984, Sch. 19, para. 13.

Cross references – S. 760(8)–(10): meaning of "account period".
TMA 1970, s. 115: service of notices.

Other material – M02/2010: HMRC guidance on late applications for distributing fund status and late distributions.
IR press release, 31 July 1984: application procedure for certification as a distributing fund.

APPEALS

16(1) An appeal–

(a) against such a determination as is referred to in paragraph 15(3) above, or

(b) against a notification under paragraph 15(4) above,

may be made by the offshore fund or on behalf of the fund, and shall be so made by notice specifying the grounds of appeal and given to the Board within 90 days of the date of the notice under paragraph 15(3) or (4), as the case may be.

16(2) The jurisdiction of the tribunal on an appeal under this paragraph shall include jurisdiction to review any decision of the Board which is relevant to a ground of the appeal.

History – In para. 16(1), the words "to the Special Commissioners", which appeared after "An appeal", omitted by SI 2009/56, art. 3(1) and Sch. 1, para. 161(2), operative from 1 April 2009, subject to transitional and saving provisions in SI 2009/56, Sch. 3.
In para. 16(2), the words "tribunal" substituted for "Special Commissioners" by SI 2009/56, art. 3(1) and Sch. 1, para. 161(3), operative from 1 April 2009, subject to transitional and saving provisions in SI 2009/56, Sch. 3.
In para. 16(1), the words "by a trustee or officer thereof" (which appeared after the words "may be made by the offshore fund or" after para. (b)) omitted by FA 2004, s. 145, Sch. 26, para. 14(8) and repealed by s. 326, Sch. 42, Pt. 2(18) with effect for account periods (within the meaning of Pt. 17, Ch. 5) ending on or after 22 July 2004.

Derivations – FA 1984, Sch. 19, para. 14.

Cross references – TMA 1970, s. 115: service of notices.

Part IV – Supplementary

ASSESSMENT: EFFECT OF NON-CERTIFICATION

17 No appeal may be brought against an assessment to tax on the ground that an offshore fund should have been certified as a distributing fund in respect of an account period of the fund.

Derivations – FA 1984, Sch. 19, para. 15.

Cross references – S. 760(8)–(10): meaning of "account period".

18(1) Without prejudice to paragraph 17 above, in any case where no application has been made under paragraph 15 above in respect of an account period of an offshore fund, any person who is assessed to tax for which he would not be liable if the offshore fund were certified as a distributing fund in respect of that period may by notice in writing require the Board to take action under this paragraph with a view to determining whether the fund should be so certified.

18(2) Subject to sub-paragraphs (3) and (5) below, if the Board receive a notice under sub-paragraph (1) above, they shall by notice invite the offshore fund concerned to make an application under paragraph 15 above in respect of the period in question.

18(3) Where sub-paragraph (2) above applies, the Board shall not be required to give notice under that sub-paragraph before the expiry of the account period to which the notice is to relate nor if an application under paragraph 15 above has already been made; but where notice is given under that sub-paragraph, an application under paragraph 15 above shall not be out of time under paragraph 15(2)(a) above if it is made within 90 days of the date of that notice.

18(4) If an offshore fund to which notice is given under sub-paragraph (2) above does not, within the time allowed by sub-paragraph (3) above or, as the case may be, paragraph 15(2)(a) above, make an application under paragraph 15 above in respect of the account period in question, the Board shall proceed to determine the question of certification in respect of that period as if such an application had been made.

18(5) Where the Board receive more than one notice under sub-paragraph (1) above with respect to the same account period of the same offshore fund, their obligations under sub-paragraphs (2) and (4) above shall be taken to be fulfilled with respect to each of those notices if they are fulfilled with respect to any one of them.

18(6) Notwithstanding anything in sub-paragraph (5) above, for the purpose of a determination under sub-paragraph (4) abovewith respect to an account period of an offshore fund, the Board shall have regard to accounts and other information furnished by all persons who have given notice under sub-paragraph (1) above with respect to that account period; and paragraph 15 above shall apply as if accounts and information so furnished had been furnished in compliance with sub-paragraph (1) of that paragraph.

18(7) Without prejudice to sub-paragraph (5) above, in any case where–
- (a) at a time after the Board have made a determination under sub-paragraph (4) above that an offshore fund should not be certified as a distributing fund in respect of an account period, notice is given under sub-paragraph (1) above with respect to that period; and
- (b) the person giving that notice furnishes the Board with accounts or information which had not been furnished to the Board at the time of the earlier determination;

the Board shall reconsider their previous determination in the light of the new accounts or information and, if they consider it appropriate, may determine to certify the fund accordingly.

18(8) Where any person has given notice to the Board under sub-paragraph (1) above with respect to an account period of an offshore fund and no application has been made under paragraph 15 above with respect to that period–
- (a) the Board shall notify that person of their determination with respect to certification under sub-paragraph (4) above; and
- (b) paragraph 16 above shall not apply in relation to that determination.

Derivations – FA 1984, Sch. 19, para. 16.

Cross references – TMA 1970, s. 115: service of notices.

POSTPONEMENT OF TAX PENDING DETERMINATION OF QUESTION AS TO CERTIFICATION

19(1) This paragraph applies where–
- (a) an application has been made under paragraph 15 above with respect to an account period of an offshore fund and that application has not been finally determined; or
- (b) paragraph (a) above does not apply but notice has been given under paragraph 18(1) above in respect of an account period of an offshore fund and the Board have not yet given notice of their decision as to certification under paragraph 18(4) above;

19(1A) Any person who has been assessed to tax and considers that, if the offshore fund were to be certified as a distributing fund in respect of the accounting period in question, he would be overcharged to tax by the assessment may–
- (a) first apply in writing to HMRC within 30 days of the date of the issue of the notice of assessment for a determination by them of the amount of tax the payment of which should be postponed pending the determination of the question whether the fund should be so certified;
- (b) where such a determination is not agreed, refer the application for postponement to the tribunal within 30 days from the date of the document notifying HMRC's decision on the amount to be postponed.

19(2) An application under sub-paragraph (1A) above shall state the amount in which the applicant believes that he is over-charged to tax and his grounds for that belief.

19(3) Subsections (3A) onwards of section 55 of the Management Act (recovery of tax not postponed) shall apply with any necessary modifications in relation to an application under sub-paragraph (1) above as if it were an application under subsection (3) of that section and as if the determination of the question as to certification (whether by the Board or on appeal) were the determination of an appeal.

History – In para. 19(1), the words "This paragraph applies" substituted for "In any case" by SI 2009/56, art. 3(1) and Sch. 1, para. 161(4)(a), operative from 1 April 2009, subject to transitional and saving provisions in SI 2009/56, Sch. 3.
In para. 19, (1A) substituted for the words after (1)(b) by SI 2009/56, art. 3(1) and Sch. 1, para. 161(4)(b), operative from 1 April 2009, subject to transitional and saving provisions in SI 2009/56, Sch. 3.
In para. 19(2), the words "An" and "(1A)" substituted for "A notice of" and "(1)" respectively by SI 2009/56, art. 3(1) and Sch. 1, para. 161(4)(c), operative from 1 April 2009, subject to transitional and saving provisions in SI 2009/56, Sch. 3.

Derivations – FA 1984, Sch. 19, para. 17.

Cross references – S. 760(8)–(10): meaning of "account period".
TMA 1970, s. 115: service of notices.

INFORMATION AS TO DECISIONS ON CERTIFICATION ETC.

20 No obligation as to secrecy imposed by statute or otherwise shall preclude the Board or an inspector from disclosing to any person appearing to have an interest in the matter–
- (a) any determination of the Board or (on appeal) the tribunal whether an offshore fund should or should not be certified as a distributing fund in respect of any account period; or
- (b) the content and effect of any notice given by the Board under paragraph 15(4) above.

History – In para. 20, the words "tribunal" substituted for "Special Commissioners" by SI 2009/56, art. 3(1) and Sch. 1, para. 161(5), operative from 1 April 2009, subject to transitional and saving provisions in SI 2009/56, Sch. 3.

Derivations – FA 1984, Sch. 19, para. 18.

Cross references – TMA 1970, s. 115: service of notices.

APPLICATION OF THIS SCHEDULE IN RELATION TO UMBRELLA FUNDS AND FUNDS COMPRISING MORE THAN ONE CLASS OF INTEREST

21(1) The Treasury may make provision by regulations as to the application of the provisions of this Schedule in relation to–
- (a) a part of an umbrella fund which is treated as an offshore fund under section 756B, or
- (b) a class of interest in an offshore fund which is treated as an offshore fund under section 756C.

21(2) Regulations under this paragraph may–
- (a) make different provision for different cases, and
- (b) include such supplementary, incidental, consequential or transitional provisions (including provisions modifying the effect of other enactments) as appear to the Treasury to be necessary or expedient.

History – Para. 21 inserted by FA 2004, s. 145, Sch. 26, para. 8(4) with effect for account periods (within the meaning of Pt. 17, Ch. 5) ending on or after 22 July 2004 and regulations made under a power conferred by virtue of any of the amendments made by FA 2004 may be made so as to have effect in relation to any such account period.

Statutory instruments – SI 2004/2572: Offshore Funds Regulations 2004 made under para. 21.".

SCHEDULE 28 – COMPUTATION OF OFFSHORE INCOME GAINS

Section 751(1)

[Sch. 28 repealed by SI 2009/3001, reg. 13 and Sch. 2.]

History – Sch. 28 repealed by SI 2009/3001, reg. 13 and Sch. 2, with effect from 1 December 2009 for various purposes (in accordance with the provisions of SI 2009/3001, reg. 1), subject to transitional and savings provisions in SI 2009/3001, Sch. 1. Former Sch. 28 read as follows:

"SCHEDULE 28 – COMPUTATION OF OFFSHORE INCOME GAINS

Section 761(1)

Part I – Disposals of Interests in Non-Qualifying Funds

INTERPRETATION

1 In this Part of this Schedule **"material disposal"** means a disposal to which this Chapter applies, otherwise than by virtue of section 758.

Derivations – FA 1984, Sch. 20, para. 1.

Cross references – S. 758: offshore funds operating equalisation arrangements.

CALCULATION OF UNINDEXED GAIN

2(1) Where there is a material disposal, there shall first be determined for the purposes of this Part of this Schedule the amount (if any) which, in accordance with the provisions of this paragraph, is the unindexed gain accruing to the person making the disposal.

2(2) Subject to section 757(3) to (6) and paragraph 3 below, the **unindexed gain accruing on a material disposal** is the amount which would be the gain on that disposal for the purposes of the 1992 Act if it were computed–

(a) without regard to any charge to income tax or corporation tax by virtue of section 761; and

(b) without regard to any indexation allowance on the disposal under the 1992 Act.

History – References to the 1992 Act substituted by TCGA 1992, s. 290 and Sch. 10, para. 14(63)(a).

Derivations – (as originally enacted) – FA 1984, Sch. 20, para. 2.

Cross references – S. 757(3)–(6): provisions relating to death of investor and exchange of securities involving offshore funds.

3(1) If the amount of any chargeable gain or allowable loss which (apart from section 763) would accrue on the material disposal would fall to be determined in a way which, in whole or in part, would take account of the indexation allowance on an earlier disposal to which section 56(2) of the 1992 Act (disposals on a no gain/no loss basis) applies, the unindexed gain on the material disposal shall be computed as if–

(a) no indexation allowance had been available on any such earlier disposal; and

(b) subject to that, neither a gain nor a loss had accrued to the person making such an earlier disposal.

3(2) If the material disposal forms part of a transfer to which section 162 of the 1992 Act (roll-over relief on transfer of business) applies, the unindexed gain accruing on the disposal shall be computed without regard to any deduction which falls to be made under that section in computing a chargeable gain.

3(3) If the material disposal is made otherwise than under a bargain at arm's length and a claim for relief is made in respect of that disposal under section 165 or 260 of the 1992 Act (relief for gifts) the claim shall not affect the computation of the unindexed gain accruing on the disposal.

3(4) [Repealed by FA 1995, s. 162 and Sch. 29, Pt. VIII(5).]

3(5) Notwithstanding section 16 of the 1992 Act (losses determined in like manner as gains) if, apart from this sub-paragraph, the effect of any computation under the preceding provisions of this Part of this Schedule would be to produce a loss, the unindexed gain on the material disposal shall be treated as nil; and accordingly for the purposes of this Part of this Schedule no loss shall be treated as accruing on a material disposal.

3(6) Section 431 has effect in relation to sub-paragraph (4) above as if it were included in Chapter I of Part XII.

History – In para. 3(3), the words "126 or 147A … the claim" were substituted by FA 1989, s. 124 and Sch. 14, para. 6(6), in relation to disposals on or after 14 March 1989.

Para. 3(4) repealed by FA 1995, s. 162 and Sch. 29, Pt. VIII(5) with effect in relation to accounting periods beginning on or after 1 November 1994, but where the policy or contract for any life assurance business was made before that date the repeal of para. 3(4) does not have effect for determining whether the business is overseas life assurance business (FA 1995, Sch. 8, para. 55(1), (2)). Former para. 3(4) read as follows:

"**3(4)** Where, in the case of an insurance company carrying on life assurance business,–

(a) [Repealed by FA 1991, s. 48 and Sch. 7, para. 10, s. 123 and Sch. 19, Pt. V.]

(b) a profit arising from overseas life assurance business and attributable to a material disposal falls to be taken into account in the computation under section 441,

the unindexed gain, if any, accruing to the company on the disposal shall be computed as if section 37(1) of the 1992 Act (exclusion of certain sums in computing chargeable gain) did not apply."

Former para. 3(4)(a) repealed by FA 1991, s. 48 and Sch. 7, para. 10, s. 123 and Sch. 15, Pt. V with respect to accounting periods beginning on or after 1 January 1992.

In former para. 3(4), the words "life assurance business … unindexed gain," substituted by FA 1990, s. 42 and Sch. 7, para. 7, for accounting periods beginning on or after 1 January 1990.

References to the 1992 Act in para. 3(1)–(5) substituted by TCGA 1992, s. 290 and Sch. 10, para. 14(63)(b).

Derivations – FA 1984, Sch. 20, para. 3.

Cross references – S. 431: interpretations of provisions relating to insurance companies.

S. 436: computation of profits of an insurance company from general annuity or pension business.

S. 437(2): exclusion of offshore income gains from computation of profits of an insurance company from general annuity business.

S. 441: taxation of profits and gains of insurance company from overseas life assurance business.

S. 763: deduction of offshore income gains in determining capital gains.

GAINS SINCE 1ST JANUARY 1984

4(1) This paragraph applies where–

(a) the interest in the offshore fund which is disposed of by the person making a material disposal was acquired by him before 1st January 1984; or

(b) he is treated by virtue of any provision of sub-paragraphs (3) and (4) below as having acquired the interest before that date.

4(2) Where this paragraph applies, there shall be determined for the purposes of this Part of this Schedule the amount which would have been the gain on the material disposal–

(a) on the assumption that, on 1st January 1984, the interest was disposed of and immediately reacquired for a consideration equal to its market value at that time; and

(b) subject to that, on the basis that the gain is computed in like manner as, under paragraphs 2 and 3 above, the unindexed gain on the material disposal is determined;

and that amount is in paragraph 5 below referred to as the **"post-1983 gain"** on the material disposal.

4(3) Where the person making the material disposal acquired the interest disposed of–

(a) on or after 1st January 1984, and

(b) in such circumstances that, by virtue of any enactment other than section 56, 57, 131 or 145 of the 1992 Act (indexation provisions), he and the person from whom he acquired it (**"the previous owner"**) fell to be treated for the purposes of the 1992 Act as if his acquisition were for a consideration of such an amount as would secure that, on the disposal under which he acquired it, neither a gain nor a loss accrued to the previous owner,

the previous owner's acquisition of the interest shall be treated as his acquisition of it.

4(4) If the previous owner acquired the interest disposed of on or after 1st January 1984 and in circumstances similar to those referred to in sub-paragraph (3) above, his predecessor's acquisition of the interest shall be treated for the purposes of this paragraph as the previous owner's acquisition, and so on back through previous acquisitions in similar circumstances until the first such acquisition before 1st January 1984 or, as the case may be, until an acquisition on a material disposal on or after that date.

History – References to the 1992 Act in para. 4(3) substituted by TCGA 1992, s. 290 and Sch. 10, para. 14(63)(c).

Derivations – FA 1984, Sch. 20, para. 4.

THE OFFSHORE INCOME GAIN

5(1) Subject to sub-paragraph (2) below, a material disposal gives rise to an offshore income gain of an amount equal to the unindexed gain on that disposal.

5(2) In any case where–

(a) paragraph 4 above applies, and

(b) the post-1983 gain on the material disposal is less than the unindexed gain on the disposal,

the offshore income gain to which the disposal gives rise is an amount equal to the post-1983 gain.

Derivations – FA 1984, Sch. 20, para. 5.

Part II – Disposals Involving an Equalisation Element

6(1) Subject to paragraph 7 below, a disposal to which this Chapter applies by virtue of section 758(3) gives rise to an offshore income gain of an amount equal to the equalisation element relevant to the asset disposed of.

6(2) Subject to sub-paragraphs (4) to (6) below, the equalisation element relevant to the asset disposed of by a disposal falling within sub-paragraph (1) above is the amount which would be credited to the equalisation account of the offshore fund concerned in respect of accrued income if, on the date of the disposal, the asset which is disposed of were acquired by another person by way of initial purchase.

6(3) In the following provisions of this Part of this Schedule, a disposal falling within sub-paragraph (1) above is referred to as a **"disposal involving an equalisation element"**.

6(4) Where the asset disposed of by a disposal involving an equalisation element was acquired by the person making the disposal after the beginning of the period by reference to which the accrued income referred to in sub-paragraph (2) above is calculated, the amount which, apart from this sub-paragraph, would be the equalisation element relevant to that asset shall be reduced by the following amount, that is to say–

(a) if that acquisition took place on or after 1st January 1984, the amount which, on that acquisition, was credited to the equalisation account of the offshore fund concerned in respect of accrued income or, as the case may be, would have been so credited if that acquisition had been an acquisition by way of initial purchase; and

(b) in any other case, the amount which would have been credited to that account in respect of accrued income if that acquisition had been an acquisition by way of initial purchase taking place on 1st January 1984.

6(5) In any case where–

(a) the asset disposed of by a disposal involving an equalisation element was acquired by the person making the disposal at or before the beginning of the period by reference to which the accrued income referred to in sub-paragraph (2) above is calculated, and

(b) that period began before 1st January 1984 and ends after that date,

the amount which, apart from this sub-paragraph, would be the equalisation element relevant to that asset shall be reduced by the amount which would have been credited to the equalisation account of the offshore fund concerned in respect of accrued income if the acquisition referred to in paragraph (a) above had been an acquisition by way of initial purchase taking place on 1st January 1984.

6(6) Where there is a disposal involving an equalisation element, then, to the extent that any amount which was or would be credited to the equalisation account of the offshore fund in respect of accrued income, as mentioned in any of sub-paragraphs (2) to (5) above, represents profits from dealing in commodities, within the meaning of paragraph 4 of Schedule 27, one half of that accrued income shall be left out of account in determining under those sub-paragraphs the equalisation element relevant to the asset disposed of by that disposal.

Derivations – FA 1984, Sch. 20, para. 6.

Cross references – S. 758(1): definition of "the equalisation account".

S. 758(2): definition of "initial purchase".

7(1) For the purposes of this Part of this Schedule, there shall be determined, in accordance with paragraph 8 below, the Part I gain (if any) on any disposal involving an equalisation element.

7(2) Notwithstanding anything in paragraph 6 above–

(a) if there is no Part I gain on a disposal involving an equalisation element, that disposal shall not give rise to an offshore income gain; and

(b) if, apart from this paragraph, the offshore income gain on a disposal involving an equalisation element would exceed the Part I gain on that disposal, the offshore income gain to which that disposal gives rise shall be reduced to an amount equal to that Part I gain.

Derivations – FA 1984, Sch. 20, para. 7.

8(1) On a disposal involving an equalisation element, the Part I gain is the amount (if any) which, by virtue of Part I of this Schedule (as modified by sub-paragraphs (2) to (5) below), would be the offshore income gain on that disposal if it were a material disposal within the meaning of that Part.

8(2) For the purposes only of the application of Part I of this Schedule to determine the Part I gain (if any) on a disposal involving an equalisation element, subsections (5) and (6) of section 758 shall have effect as if, in subsection (5), the words "by virtue of subsection (3) above" were omitted.

8(3) If a disposal involving an equalisation element is one which, by virtue of any enactment other than section 56, 57, 131 or 145 of the 1992 Act is treated for the purposes of the 1992 Act as one on which neither a gain nor a loss accrues to the person making the disposal, then, for the purpose only of determining the Part I gain (if any) on the disposal, that enactment shall be deemed not to apply to it (but without prejudice to the application of that enactment to any earlier disposal).

8(4), (5) [Repealed by TCGA 1992, s. 290 and Sch. 12.]

History – In para. 8(3), references to the 1992 Act substituted by TCGA 1992, s. 290 and Sch. 10, para. 14(63)(c).
Para. 8(4), (5) repealed by TCGA 1992, s. 290 and Sch. 12, with effect in relation to tax for chargeable periods beginning on or after 6 April 1992.

Derivations – FA 1984, Sch. 20, para. 8.

Part 3 – Supplementary

APPLICATION OF THIS SCHEDULE IN RELATION TO UMBRELLA FUNDS AND FUNDS COMPRISING MORE THAN ONE CLASS OF INTEREST

9(1) The Treasury may make provision by regulations as to the application of the provisions of this Schedule in relation to–
(a) a part of an umbrella fund which is treated as an offshore fund under section 756B, or
(b) a class of interest in an offshore fund which is treated as an offshore fund under section 756C.

9(2) Regulations under this paragraph may–
(a) make different provision for different cases, and
(b) include such supplementary, incidental, consequential or transitional provisions (including provisions modifying the effect of other enactments) as appear to the Treasury to be necessary or expedient.

History – Para. 9 inserted by FA 2004, s. 145 and Sch. 26, para. 9 with effect for account periods (within the meaning of Pt. 17, Ch. 5) ending on or after 22 July 2004 and regulations made under a power conferred by virtue of any of the amendments made by FA 2004 may be made so as to have effect in relation to any such account period.

Statutory instruments – SI 2004/2572: Offshore Fund Regulations 2004 made under para. 9.".

SCHEDULE 28A – CHANGE IN OWNERSHIP OF COMPANY WITH INVESTMENT BUSINESS: DEDUCTIONS

Sections 768B, 768C

[Omitted by CTA 2010, s. 1177 and Sch. 1, para. 149 and repealed by CTA 2010, s. 1181 and Sch. 3, Pt. 1.]

History – Sch. 28A omitted by CTA 2010, s. 1177 and Sch. 1, para. 149 and repealed by CTA 2010, s. 1181 and Sch. 3, Pt. 1, with effect for corporation tax purposes for accounting periods ending on or after 1 April 2010, and for income and capital gains tax purposes for the tax year 2010–11 and subsequent tax years.

Notes – Sch. 28A rewritten as follows:
Para. 1: CTA 2010, s. 688(1).
Para. 2: CTA 2010, s. 688(2).
Para. 3(1): CTA 2010, s. 689(1).
Para. 3(2): CTA 2010, s. 689(2).
Para. 3(3): CTA 2010, s. 689(2).
Para. 3(4): CTA 2010, s. 689(2).
Para. 3(5): CTA 2010, s. 689(2).
Para. 3(6): CTA 2010, s. 689(2).
Para. 3(7): CTA 2010, s. 689(3).
Para. 4(1): CTA 2010, s. 690(1), (2).
Para. 4(2): CTA 2010, s. 690(3).
Para. 5(1): CTA 2010, s. 691(2).
Para. 5(2): CTA 2010, s. 691(3), (5).
Para. 5(3): CTA 2010, s. 691(4).
Para. 6: CTA 2010, s. 685(2), 686(6).
Para. 6A: CTA 2010, s. 686(2), (3).
Para. 7(1): CTA 2010, s. 685(1), (2), 686(4), (5).
Para. 8: CTA 2010, s. 685(3).
Para. 9(1): CTA 2010, s. 679(2).
Para. 9(2): CTA 2010, s. 679(2), (3), (4).
Para. 9(3): CTA 2010, s. 679(4).
Para. 9A(1): CTA 2010, s. 680(2).
Para. 9A(2): CTA 2010, s. 680(3).
Para. 10(1):CTA 2010, s. 696(3).
Para. 10(2): CTA 2010, s. 696(3).
Para. 10(3): CTA 2010, s. 696(4).
Para. 10(4): CTA 2010, s. 696(5).
Para. 10A(1): CTA 2010, s. 697(3).
Para. 10A(2): CTA 2010, s. 697(4).
Para. 11(1): CTA 2010, s. 730(2), (3), (4).
Para. 11(3): CTA 2010, s. 730(5).
Para. 12: CTA 2010, s. 730(6).
Para. 13(1): CTA 2010, s. 702(2), 703(6).
Para. 13(2): CTA 2010, s. 694.
Para. 13A: CTA 2010, s. 703(2), (3).
Para. 14: CTA 2010, s. 702(1).
Para. 15: CTA 2010, s. 702(2).
Para. 16(1): CTA 2010, s. 702(1), (2), 703(4), (5).
Para. 17: CTA 2010, s. 702(3).

SCHEDULE 28AA – PROVISION NOT AT ARM'S LENGTH

Section 770A

[Omitted by TIOPA 2010, s. 374 and Sch. 8, para. 111 and repealed by TIOPA 2010, s. 378 and Sch. 10, Pt. 2.]

History – Sch. 28AA omitted by TIOPA 2010, s. 374 and Sch. 8, para. 111 and repealed by TIOPA 2010, s. 378 and Sch. 10, Pt. 2, with effect for corporation tax purposes for accounting periods ending on or after 1 April 2010, for income tax and capital gains tax purposes for the tax year 2010–11 and subsequent tax years, and for petroleum revenue tax purposes for chargeable periods beginning on or after 1 July 2010.

Notes – Schedule 28AA rewritten as follows:
Para. 1(1): TIOPA 2010, s. 147(1), (2), (4), 148(1), (3).
Para. 1(2): TIOPA 2010, s. 147(1), (2), (3), (4), (5), (6).
Para. 1(3): TIOPA 2010, s. 151(2).
Para. 1A(1): TIOPA 2010, s. 152(1).
Para. 1A(2): TIOPA 2010, s. 152(2), (3).
Para. 1A(3): TIOPA 2010, s. 152(4).
Para. 1A(4): TIOPA 2010, s. 152(5).
Para. 1A(5): TIOPA 2010, s. 152(6).
Para. 1A(6): TIOPA 2010, s. 154(1), (3).
Para. 1A(7): TIOPA 2010, s. 154(1), (4), 175(5), 191(4), 192(6), 197(10), 201(9).
Para. 1A(8): TIOPA 2010, s. 154(1), (5), 204(4).
Para. 1A(9): TIOPA 2010, s. 154(1), (2), (6), 175(3), 181(4), 191(2), 197(8), 199(7), 201(7).
Para. 1A(10): TIOPA 2010, s. 154(1), (7), 175(4), 181(5), 191(3), 197(9), 199(8), 201(8).
Para. 1B(1): TIOPA 2010, s. 153(1).
Para. 1B(2): TIOPA 2010, s. 153(2), (3).
Para. 1B(3): TIOPA 2010, s. 153(4).
Para. 1B(4): TIOPA 2010, s. 153(5).
Para. 1B(5): TIOPA 2010, s. 153(6).
Para. 1B(6): TIOPA 2010, s. 154(1).
Para. 2(1): TIOPA 2010, s. 164(1), (2).
Para. 2(2): TIOPA 2010, s. 164(3).
Para. 2(3): TIOPA 2010, s. 164(4).
Para. 3(1): TIOPA 2010, s. 150(1).
Para. 3(2): TIOPA 2010, s. 150(2).
Para. 3(3): TIOPA 2010, s. 150(3).
Para. 3(4): TIOPA 2010, s. 150(4).
Para. 3(5): TIOPA 2010, s. 150(5).
Para. 4(1): TIOPA 2010, s. 157(1), (2).
Para. 4(2): TIOPA 2010, s. 158(2), (3), (4), 159(1), (2), 160(1), (2).
Para. 4(3): TIOPA 2010, s. 159(3).
Para. 4(4): TIOPA 2010, s. 159(4).
Para. 4(5): TIOPA 2010, s. 159(5).
Para. 4(6): TIOPA 2010, s. 159(6).
Para. 4(7): TIOPA 2010, s. 160(3).
Para. 4(8): TIOPA 2010, s. 160(4).
Para. 4(9): TIOPA 2010, s. 160(5).
Para. 4(10): TIOPA 2010, s. 159(7), 160(6).
Para. 4(11): TIOPA 2010, s. 163(1), (2), (3).
Para. 4(12): TIOPA 2010, s. 163(4).
Para. 4A(1): TIOPA 2010, s. 158(2), 161(1), (2).
Para. 4A(2): TIOPA 2010, s. 158(3), 162(1), (2).
Para. 4A(3): TIOPA 2010, s. 161(3), 162(3).
Para. 4A(4): TIOPA 2010, s. 161(4), 162(4).
Para. 4A(5): TIOPA 2010, s. 161(5), 162(5).
Para. 4A(6): TIOPA 2010, s. 148(4), 161(6), 162(6).
Para. 4A(7): TIOPA 2010, s. 149(3), (4).
Para. 4B(1): TIOPA 2010, s. 148(1), (2).
Para. 4B(2): TIOPA 2010, s. 148(4).
Para. 5(1): TIOPA 2010, s. 155(1), (2), (3), (4).
Para. 5(7): TIOPA 2010, s. 155(5).
Para. 5(8): TIOPA 2010, s. 155(6).
Para. 5(9): TIOPA 2010, s. 155(6).
Para. 5A(1): TIOPA 2010, s. 165(1).
Para. 5A(2): TIOPA 2010, s. 165(2).
Para. 5A(3): TIOPA 2010, s. 165(3).
Para. 5A(4): TIOPA 2010, s. 165(4).
Para. 5B(1): TIOPA 2010, s. 166(1).
Para. 5B(2): TIOPA 2010, s. 166(2), 167(1).
Para. 5B(3): TIOPA 2010, s. 167(2).
Para. 5B(4): TIOPA 2010, s. 167(3).
Para. 5B(5): TIOPA 2010, s. 167(4).
Para. 5B(6): TIOPA2010, s. 167(5).
Para. 5B(7): TIOPA 2010, s. 167(4).
Para. 5C(1): TIOPA 2010, s. 168(1), (2).
Para. 5C(2): TIOPA 2010, s. 169(1), (2).
Para. 5C(3): TIOPA 2010, s. 169(1), (3).
Para. 5C(4): TIOPA 2010, s. 169(1), (4).
Para. 5C(5): TIOPA 2010, s. 170(1).
Para. 5C(6): TIOPA 2010, s. 170(2).
Para. 5C(7): TIOPA 2010, s. 170(3).
Para. 5C(8): TIOPA 2010, s. 171(1).
Para. 5C(9): TIOPA 2010, s. 171(2).

Para. 5C(10): TIOPA 2010, s. 171(3).
Para. 5C(11): TIOPA 2010, s. 171(4).
Para. 5C(12): TIOPA 2010, s. 169(5), 171(5).
Para. 5D(1): TIOPA 2010, s. 172(1), (2).
Para. 5D(2): TIOPA 2010, s. 172(3).
Para. 5D(3): TIOPA 2010, s. 172(4).
Para. 5D(4): TIOPA 2010, s. 172(5).
Para. 5D(5): TIOPA 2010, s. 172(6).
Para. 5D(6): TIOPA 2010, s. 172(7).
Para. 5E(1): TIOPA 2010, s. 173(1).
Para. 5E(2): TIOPA 2010, s. 173(2), (6).
Para. 5E(3): TIOPA 2010, s. 173(3), (6).
Para. 5E(4): TIOPA 2010, s. 173(4), (6).
Para. 5E(5): TIOPA 2010, s. 173(5).
Para. 5E(6): TIOPA 2010, s. 173(7).
Para. 6(1): TIOPA 2010, s. 174(1).
Para. 6(2): TIOPA 2010, s. 174(2), (3), (4).
Para. 6(3): TIOPA 2010, s. 176(1), (2).
Para. 6(4): TIOPA 2010, s. 176(3).
Para. 6(4A): TIOPA 2010, s. 175(1), (3), (4), (5).
Para. 6(4B): TIOPA 2010, s. 175(2).
Para. 6(4C): TIOPA 2010, s. 158(2), (3), 161(1), 162(1).
Para. 6(5): TIOPA 2010, s. 177(1), (2), (3), (6).
Para. 6(6): TIOPA 2010, s. 177(4), (5), (6).
Para. 6(7): TIOPA 2010, s. 178(1), (2), 190.
Para. 6A(1): TIOPA 2010, s. 174(4), 180(1), (2).
Para. 6A(2): TIOPA 2010, s. 180(2).
Para. 6A(3): TIOPA 2010, s. 180(3).
Para. 6B(1): TIOPA 2010, s. 179(1).
Para. 6B(2): TIOPA 2010, s. 179(2).
Para. 6B(3): TIOPA 2010, s. 179(3).
Para. 6B(4): TIOPA 2010, s. 179(4).
Para. 6C(1): TIOPA 2010, s. 181(1), (4), (5).
Para. 6C(2): TIOPA 2010, s. 181(2), (3).
Para. 6C(3): TIOPA 2010, s. 182(1), (2).
Para. 6C(4): TIOPA 2010, s. 182(3).
Para. 6C(5): TIOPA 2010, s. 182(4), (5).
Para. 6C(6): TIOPA 2010, s. 183(1), (2).
Para. 6C(7): TIOPA 2010, s. 183(3).
Para. 6C(8): TIOPA 2010, s. 183(4), 215.
Para. 6C(9): TIOPA 2010, s. 183(5).
Para. 6C(10): TIOPA 2010, s. 184(1), 190.
Para. 6C(11): TIOPA 2010, s. 184(2), (3).
Para. 6C(12): TIOPA 2010, s. 184(4), (5).
Para. 6D(1): TIOPA 2010, s. 191(1), (5).
Para. 6D(2): TIOPA 2010, s. 192(1), (2), (4).
Para. 6D(3): TIOPA 2010, s. 192(3).
Para. 6D(4): TIOPA 2010, s. 193(1).
Para. 6D(5): TIOPA 2010, s. 193(2).
Para. 6D(6): TIOPA 2010, s. 193(3).
Para. 6D(7): TIOPA 2010, s. 193(4).
Para. 6D(8): TIOPA 2010, s. 194(1), (2).
Para. 6D(9): TIOPA 2010, s. 194(3).
Para. 6D(10): TIOPA 2010, s. 191(1), (2), (3), (4), 192(6).
Para. 6D(11): TIOPA 2010, s. 192(5).
Para. 6E: TIOPA 2010, s. 187(1), (2), (3), (4), (5), (6).
Para. 7(1): TIOPA 2010, s. 188(1), (2), (3).
Para. 7(2): TIOPA 2010, s. 188(4), (5).
Para. 7(3): TIOPA 2010, s. 189(1).
Para. 7(4): TIOPA 2010, s. 189(2).
Para. 7(5): TIOPA 2010, s. 188(6), 189(3).
Para. 7(6): TIOPA 2010, s. 188(7).
Para. 7A(1): TIOPA 2010, s. 195(1), (2), (3), (4), (5), 196(1), (2).
Para. 7A(2): TIOPA 2010, s. 196(1), (2).
Para. 7A(3): TIOPA 2010, s. 196(3), (4).
Para. 7B(1): TIOPA 2010, s. 199(1), (2), (3), (4), (5), 204(3).
Para. 7B(2): TIOPA 2010, s. 199(1), 200(1), 201(1), (6), 202(1).
Para. 7B(3): TIOPA 2010, s. 199(6), 204(1).
Para. 7B(4): TIOPA 2010, s. 200(1), 202(1).
Para. 7B(5): TIOPA 2010, s. 203(1), (7).
Para. 7B(6): TIOPA 2010, s. 203(1), (2), (3), (4), (9).
Para. 7B(7): TIOPA 2010, s. 203(1), (5).
Para. 7B(8): TIOPA 2010, s. 203(6).
Para. 7B(9): TIOPA 2010, s. 203(8), 204(2).
Para. 7B(10): TIOPA 2010, s. 199(7), (8), 204(4).
Para. 7C(1): TIOPA 2010, s. 197(1), (2), (3), (4), (5), (6), (7), (8), (9), (10), 198(1).
Para. 7C(2): TIOPA 2010, s. 198(1), (2).
Para. 7D(1): TIOPA 2010, s. 201(1), (2), (3), (4), (5), (7), (8), (9).
Para. 7D(2): TIOPA 2010, s. 201(1), (6), 202(1), 203(1), (2), (3), (4), (5), (6), (7), (8), (9), 204(1).
Para. 7D(3): TIOPA 2010, s. 201(5).
Para. 7D(4): TIOPA 2010, s. 202(1).
Para. 9(1): TIOPA 2010, s. 147(1), 217(3).
Para. 9(2): TIOPA 2010, s. 217(4).
Para. 9(3): TIOPA 2010, s. 217(5).

Para. 9(4): TIOPA 2010, s. 217(3), (6).
Para. 9(5): TIOPA 2010, s. 217(7).
Para. 10: TIOPA 2010, s. 147(7).
Para. 11(1): TIOPA 2010, s. 205(1), 206(1), (2), (3), (4).
Para. 11(3): TIOPA 2010, s. 147(1), 149(2), 205(1), (2), (3).
Para. 11(4): TIOPA 2010, s. 205(4), (5).
Para. 12(1): TIOPA 2010, s. 212(2).
Para. 12(2): TIOPA 2010, s. 212(1).
Para. 12(4): TIOPA 2010, s. 212(3).
Para. 12(5): TIOPA 2010, s. 212(4).
Para. 13(1): TIOPA 2010, s. 213(1), 214(1), (2).
Para. 13(2): TIOPA 2010, s. 213(2), 214(3).
Para. 14(1): TIOPA 2010, s. 149(1), 151(1), 156(1), (2), 164(5), 188(8), 216(1), (2), (3).
Para. 14(2): TIOPA 2010, s. 217(1), (2).
Para. 14(3): TIOPA 2010, s. 188(9).
Para. 14(4): TIOPA 2010, s. 215.
Para. 14(5): TIOPA 2010, s. 207(1), (2), (3), (4), (5).

SCHEDULE 28AB – SECTION 804ZA: PRESCRIBED SCHEMES AND ARRANGEMENTS

[Omitted by TIOPA 2010, s. 374 and Sch. 8, para. 36 and repealed by TIOPA 2010, s. 378 and Sch. 10, Pt. 1.]

History – Sch. 28AB omitted by TIOPA 2010, s. 374 and Sch. 8, para. 36 and repealed by TIOPA 2010, s. 378 and Sch. 10, Pt. 1, with effect for corporation tax purposes for accounting periods ending on or after 1 April 2010, for income tax and capital gains tax purposes for the tax year 2010–11 and subsequent tax years, and for petroleum revenue tax purposes for chargeable periods beginning on or after 1 July 2010.

Notes – Sch. 28AB rewritten as follows:
Para. 1(1): TIOPA 2010, s. 83(1), (2).
Para. 1(2): TIOPA 2010, s. 83(1), (4).
Para. 1(3): TIOPA 2010, s. 83(3), (7).
Para. 1(4): TIOPA 2010, s. 83(5).
Para. 1(5): TIOPA 2010, s. 83(6).
Para. 2: TIOPA 2010, s. 84(1), (2).
Para. 3(1): TIOPA 2010, s. 85(1).
Para. 3(2): TIOPA 2010, s. 85(2), (3).
Para. 3(3): TIOPA 2010, s. 85(3), (4).
Para. 4(1): TIOPA 2010, s. 86(1), (4).
Para. 4(2): TIOPA 2010, s. 86(2).
Para. 4(3): TIOPA 2010, s. 86(3).
Para. 5(1): TIOPA 2010, s. 87(1).
Para. 5(2): TIOPA 2010, s. 87(2).
Para. 5(3): TIOPA 2010, s. 87(3).
Para. 5(4): TIOPA 2010, s. 87(4).
Para. 6(1): TIOPA 2010, s. 88(1).
Para. 6(2): TIOPA 2010, s. 88(2).
Para. 6(3): TIOPA 2010, s. 88(3).
Para. 6(4): TIOPA 2010, s. 88(4).
Para. 6(5): TIOPA 2010, s. 88(5).

SCHEDULE 28B – VENTURE CAPITAL TRUSTS: MEANING OF "QUALIFYING HOLDINGS"

Section 842AA

[Omitted by ITA 2007, s. 1027 and Sch. 1, para. 240 and repealed by ITA 2007, s. 1031 and Sch. 3, Pt. 1 with effect for income tax purposes for 2007–08 and subsequent tax years and for corporation tax purposes in relation to accounting periods ending after 5 April 2007.]

Notes – Sch. 28B rewritten as follows:
Para. 1(1): ITA 2007, s. 286(1), 313(1).
Para. 1(2): ITA 2007, s. 286(2).
Para. 1(3): ITA 2007, s. 286(4), (5).
Para. 2(1): ITA 2007, s. 295(1).
Para. 2(2): ITA 2007, s. 295(2).
Para. 2(3): ITA 2007, s. 295(3).
Para. 2(4): ITA 2007, s. 295(4), (5).
Para. 2(5): ITA 2007, s. 1014(2).
Para. 2(6): ITA 2007, s. 295(6).
Para. 3(2): ITA 2007, s. 290(1), (7).
Para. 3(3): ITA 2007, s. 291(1), (2), (3).
Para. 3(4): ITA 2007, s. 291(4).
Para. 3(5): ITA 2007, s. 291(5).
Para. 3(5A): ITA 2007, s. 291(7).
Para. 3(5B): ITA 2007, s. 291(6).
Para. 3(6): ITA 2007, s. 290(1), (3), 298.
Para. 3(7): ITA 2007, s. 290(1), (7).
Para. 3(8): ITA 2007, s. 290(7).
Para. 3(9): ITA 2007, s. 290(5).

Para. 3(10): ITA2007, s. 290(4).
Para. 3(11): ITA 2007, s. 290(7).
Para. 4(1): ITA 2007, s. 300(1), (2), (3).
Para. 4(2): ITA 2007, s. 300(1), 303(1), 310(1).
Para. 4(3): ITA 2007, s. 304(3), (4), (5).
Para. 4(3A): ITA 2007, s. 308(3), 309(4).
Para. 4(4): ITA 2007, s. 304(6), (7).
Para. 4(5): ITA 2007, s. 306(2), (3).
Para. 4(6): ITA 2007, s. 306(4).
Para. 4(6A): ITA 2007, s. 306(5).
Para. 4(6B): ITA 2007, s. 306(6).
Para. 4(6C): ITA 2007, s. 306(4), (6).
Para. 4(6D): ITA 2007, s. 306(6).
Para. 4(7): ITA 2007, s. 305(1), (3), (4), (7).
Para. 4(8): ITA 2007, s. 305(5), (6).
Para. 4(9): ITA 2007, s. 300(1).
Para. 5(1): ITA 2007, s. 305(8), 307(2), 309(2), (3), 332.
Para. 5(2): ITA 2007, s. 310(3), (4).
Para. 5(3): ITA 2007, s. 310(5).
Para. 5(4): ITA 2007, s. 300(4), 310(5), 313(3).
Para. 5(5): ITA 2007, s. 307(3), 332.
Para. 5(6): ITA 2007, s. 308(2).
Para. 5(7): ITA 2007, s. 307(4).
Para. 5A(1): ITA 2007, s. 301(1).
Para. 5A(2): ITA 2007, s. 301(1), 1021(2).
Para. 5A(3): ITA 2007, s. 301(2).
Para. 5A(4): ITA 2007, s. 301(2).
Para. 5A(5): ITA 2007, s. 301(3).
Para. 5A(6): ITA 2007, s. 301(4).
Para. 6(1): ITA 2007, s. 293(1), (2), (3), (4).
Para. 6(2): ITA 2007, s. 293(1).
Para. 6(2AA): ITA 2007, s. 293(5).
Para. 6(2AB): ITA 2007, s. 294(1), (6).
Para. 6(2AC): ITA 2007, s. 294(2).
Para. 6(2AD): ITA 2007, s. 294(2).
Para. 6(2AE): ITA 2007, s. 294(3).
Para. 6(2AF): ITA 2007, s. 294(4).
Para. 6(2AG): ITA 2007, s. 294(5).
Para. 6(2AH): ITA 2007, s. 331(2), (3).
Para. 6(3): ITA 2007, s. 293(6), (7).
Para. 6(4): ITA 2007, s. 293(8).
Para. 7(1): ITA 2007, s. 287(1).
Para. 7(2): ITA 2007, s. 287(2).
Para. 7(3): ITA 2007, s. 287(4), (5).
Para. 7(4): ITA 2007, s. 287(6), (7).
Para. 7(5): ITA 2007, s. 287(8).
Para. 8(1): ITA 2007, s. 297(1), (2).
Para. 8(2): ITA 2007, s. 297(1), (2), (3).
Para. 8(3): ITA 2007, s. 297(3).
Para. 8(4): ITA 2007, s. 297(2), (3).
Para. 9: ITA 2007, s. 296(1), (2).
Para. 10: ITA 2007, s. 290(5).
Para.10(1): ITA 2007, s. 298, 302(1).
Para. 10(3): ITA 2007, s. 302(2), 1021(2).
Para. 10(4): ITA 2007, s. 302(3).
Para. 10(4A): ITA 2007, s. 302(4).
Para. 10(4B): ITA 2007, s. 302(4).
Para. 10(4C): ITA 2007, s. 302(4), 331(2), (3).
Para. 10(5): ITA 2007, s. 302(5).
Para. 10ZA(1): ITA 2007, s. 299(1).
Para. 10ZA(2): ITA 2007, s. 299(2).
Para. 10ZA(3): ITA 2007, s. 299(3).
Para. 10A(1): ITA 2007, s. 288(1).
Para. 10A(2): ITA 2007, s. 288(2).
Para. 10A(3): ITA 2007, s. 288(3).
Para. 10A(4): ITA 2007, s. 288(4).
Para. 10B(1): ITA 2007, s. 289(1).
Para. 10B(2): ITA 2007, s. 289(2).
Para. 10B(3): ITA 2007, s. 289(3).
Para. 10B(4): ITA 2007, s. 289(4).
Para. 10B(5): ITA 2007, s. 289(5).
Para. 10C(1): ITA 2007, s. 326(1).
Para. 10C(2): ITA 2007, s. 326(2).
Para. 10C(3): ITA 2007, s. 326(3).
Para. 10C(4): ITA 2007, s. 327(2).
Para. 10C(5): ITA 2007, s. 327(3).
Para. 10C(6): ITA 2007, s. 327(4).
Para. 10C(7): ITA 2007, s. 327(5).
Para. 10C(8): ITA 2007, s. 327(6).
Para. 10C(9): ITA 2007, s. 327(7).
Para. 10C(10): ITA 2007, s. 327(8).
Para. 10C(11): ITA 2007, s. 326(4).
Para. 10C(12): ITA 2007, s. 328(4).
Para. 10C(13): ITA 2007, s. 326(5).

Para. 10C(14): ITA 2007, s. 328(1).
Para. 10C(15): ITA 2007, s. 328(2).
Para. 10C(16): ITA 2007, s. 328(3).
Para. 10C(17): ITA 2007, s. 328(5).
Para. 10D(1): ITA 2007, s. 329(1).
Para. 10D(2): ITA 2007, s. 329(3).
Para. 10D(3): ITA 2007, s. 329(4).
Para. 11: ITA 2007, s. 312.
Para. 11A(1): ITA 2007, s. 292(1).
Para. 11A(2): ITA 2007, s. 331(2), (3).
Para. 11A(3): ITA 2007, s. 292(2).
Para. 11B(1): ITA 2007, s. 330(1).
Para. 11B(2): ITA 2007, s. 330(2).
Para. 11B(3): ITA 2007, s. 330(3).
Para. 11B(4): ITA 2007, s. 330(4).
Para. 11B(5): ITA 2007, s. 330(5).
Para. 11B(6): ITA 2007, s. 330(6).
Para. 12: ITA 2007, s. 311.
Para. 13(1): ITA 2007, s. 285(2), 313(2), 1022(1).
Para. 13(2): ITA 2007, s. 313(4).
Para. 13(3): ITA 2007, s. 313(6).
Para. 13(4): ITA 2007, s. 313(5).
Para. 13(5): ITA 2007, s. 313(6).
Para. 13(6): ITA 2007, s. 313(7).

SCHEDULE 29 – CONSEQUENTIAL AMENDMENTS

Section 844

THE CAPITAL ALLOWANCES ACTS

1, 2 [Repealed by CAA 1990, s. 164 and Sch. 2, with respect to allowances and charges falling to be made for chargeable periods ending after 5 April 1990.]

Notes – Para. 1, 2 re-enacted as CAA 1990, s. 161(3) (now part of CAA 2001, s. 27(1) and 468(1)) and s. 74 (now part of CAA 2001, s. 34(1)) respectively.

TAXES MANAGEMENT ACT 1970 C. 9

3 The Taxes Management Act 1970 shall have effect subject to the amendments made by paragraphs 4 to 10 below.

4 [Inserts TMA 1970, s. 8(3A), (3B); repealed by FA 1990, s. 132 and Sch. 19, Pt. V, where a notice to deliver a return was, or falls to be, given after 5 April 1990.]

5 [Amends TMA 1970, s. 16(1)(c), (2)(b); repealed by Copyright, Designs and Patents Act 1988, s. 303(2) and Sch. 8, with effect from 1 August 1989 (SI 1989/816 (C 21).]

6 [Repealed by ITEPA 2003, s. 724 and Sch. 8, Pt. 1.]

7(1) [Amends TMA 1970, s. 18(1).]

7(2) [Amends TMA 1970, s. 18(2), (3).]

7(3) [Inserts TMA 1970, s. 18(4).]

8(1) [Substitutes TMA 1970, s. 55(1)(g).]

8(2) [Inserts TMA 1970, s. 55(6A).]

9 [Substitutes table in TMA 1970, s. 98.]

10(1) The Taxes Management Act 1970, as amended by the Finance (No.2) Act 1987, shall have effect, after the day appointed under section 95 of the 1987 Act for the purposes of the provision in question, subject to the following amendments.

10(2) [Amends TMA 1970, s. 11(8): superseded by FA 1990, s. 91(3).]

10(3) [Amends TMA 1970, s. 30(2A).]

10(4) [Amends provisions as below.]

(a) [Amends TMA 1970, s. 87A(1).]

(b) [Repealed by TCGA 1992, s. 290 and Sch. 12.]

(c) [Repealed by FA 1998, s. 165 and Sch. 27, Pt. III(2).]

(d) *[Amends TMA 1970, s. 87A(5).]*

10(5) [Amends TMA 1970, s. 89.]

10(6) [Amends TMA 1970, s. 91(2A).]

10(7) [Repealed by FA 1998, s. 165 and Sch. 27, Pt. III(2), (28).]

10(8) [Amends provisions as below.]

(a) [Amends TMA 1970, s. 109(3).]

(b) [Amends TMA 1970, s. 109(3A).]

History – Para. 6, which inserted TMA 1970, s. 16A, repealed by ITEPA 2003, s. 724 and Sch. 8, Pt. 1, with effect for income tax purposes, for the year 2003–04 and subsequent tax years and for corporation tax purposes, for accounting periods ending after 5 April 2003.

Para. 10(3), to the extent that it amended TMA 1970, s. 30(3A), repealed by FA 1998, s. 165 and Sch. 27, Pt. III(28), with effect in relation to accounting periods ending on or after 1 July 1999, the self-assessment appointed day under FA 1994, s. 199 by virtue of SI 1998/3173 (C. 78).

Para. 10(4)(c) repealed by FA 1998, s. 165 and Sch. 27, Pt. III(2), with effect where the later period mentioned in TMA 1970, s. 87A(4) begins on or after 6 April 1999.

Para. 10(7), which formerly amended TMA 1970, s. 94(8), repealed by FA 1998, s. 165 and Sch. 27, Pt. III(28), with effect in relation to accounting periods ending on or after 1 July 1999, the self-assessment appointed day (see above) and also by FA 1998, s. 165 and Sch. 27, Pt. III(2) with effect in relation to accounting periods beginning on or after 6 April 1999.

Notes – The day appointed under F(No. 2)A 1987, s. 95 (para. 10(1)) is 30 September 1993 by virtue of SI 1992/3066 (Pay and File).

THE FRIENDLY SOCIETIES ACT (NORTHERN IRELAND) 1970 C. 31 (NI)

11 [Repealed by the Friendly Societies Act 1992, s. 120 and Sch. 22, Pt. I with effect from 1 January 1994 (SI 1993/2213); amended Friendly Societies Act (Northern Ireland) 1970, s. 1(3).]

THE FINANCE ACT 1973 C. 51

12 [Repealed by TCGA 1992, s. 290 and Sch. 12.]

FRIENDLY SOCIETIES ACT 1974 C. 46

13 [Amends Friendly Societies Act 1974, s. 7(3).]

THE SOCIAL SECURITY ACTS

14 In section 9(1) of the Social Security Act 1975 and the Social Security (Northern Ireland) Act 1975 (Class IV contributions) the reference to profits or gains chargeable to income tax under Case I or II of Schedule D shall be taken to include a reference to profits or gains consisting of a payment of enterprise allowance (within the meaning of section 127 of this Act) chargeable to income tax under Case VI of Schedule D.

Derivations – FA 1986, s. 41(4).

Notes – SSA 1975, s. 9(1) repealed and replaced, with effect from 1 July 1992, by SSCBA 1992, s. 15(1).

CAPITAL GAINS TAX ACT 1979 C. 14

15-28 [Repealed by TCGA 1992, s. 290 and Sch. 12.]

FINANCE ACT 1982 C. 39

29 [Amends FA 1982, s. 134(1).]

ADMINISTRATION OF JUSTICE ACT 1985 C. 61

30 [Amends Administration of Justice Act 1985, Sch. 2, para. 36(3).]

LAW REFORM (MISCELLANEOUS PROVISIONS) (SCOTLAND) ACT 1985 C. 73

31 [Amends Law Reform (Miscellaneous Provisions) (Scotland) Act 1985, Sch. 1, para. 41, heading.]

TRANSLATION OF REFERENCES TO ENACTMENTS REPEALED AND RE-ENACTED

32 In the enactments specified in Column 1 of the following Table for the words set out or referred to in Column 2 there shall be substituted the words set out in the corresponding entry in Column 3.

[Table not reproduced: amendments consolidated.]

History – In the Table in para. 32 (not reproduced), entries relating to FA 1973, Sch. 15 repealed by TIOPA 2010, s. 378 and Sch. 10, Pt. 12, with effect for corporation tax purposes for accounting periods ending on or after 1 April 2010, for income tax and capital gains tax purposes for the tax year 2010–11 and subsequent tax years, and for petroleum revenue tax purposes for chargeable periods beginning on or after 1 July 2010

In the Table in para. 32 (not reproduced), entries relating to IHTA 1984, s. 96 and 102(1) repealed by CTA 2010, s. 1181 and Sch. 3, Pt. 1, with effect for corporation tax purposes for accounting periods ending on or after 1 April 2010, and for income and capital gains tax purposes for the tax year 2010–11 and subsequent tax years.

In the Table in para. 32, entries relating to TMA 1970, s. 12(5) and FA 1973, s. 32(1)(b), 32(1)(c), 32(1)(d), 32(2) and 32(3) omitted by SI 2009/2035, art. 2 and Sch., para. 60(b) with effect from 13 August 2009.

In the Table in para. 32, entries relating to IHTA 1984, s. 12(2), 151 and 152 repealed by FA 2004, s. 326 and Sch. 42, Pt.3, with effect from 6 April 2006, subject to FA 2004, Sch. 36.

SCHEDULE 30 – TRANSITIONAL PROVISIONS AND SAVINGS

Section 844

CORPORATION TAX PAYMENT DATES

1 [Spent provision.]

DURATION OF LEASES

2-4 [Omitted by CTA 2009, s. 1322 and Sch. 1, para. 292(2) and repealed by CTA 2009, s. 1326 and Sch. 3, Pt. 1.]

History – Para. 2–4 omitted by CTA 2009, s. 1322 and Sch. 1, para. 292(2) and repealed by CTA 2009, s. 1326 and Sch. 3, Pt. 1, with effect for corporation tax purposes for accounting periods ending on or after 1 April 2009, and for income tax and capital gains tax purposes for the tax year 2009–10 and subsequent tax years

Notes – Para. 2(1): CTA 2009, s. Sch. 2, para. 45(1), 46(1), (2).
Para. 3(1): CTA 2009, Sch. 2, para. 45(1), (2).
Para. 3(2): CTA 2009, Sch. 2, para. 48(1), (2), (3).
Para. 3(3): CTA 2009, Sch. 2, para. 45(1).
Para. 3(4): CTA 2009, Sch. 2, para. 45(1).
Para. 4(1): CTA 2009, Sch. 2, para. 46(1).
Para. 4(2): CTA 2009, Sch. 2, para. 46(1).
Para. 4(3): CTA 2009, Sch. 2, para. 46(1).
Para. 4(4): CTA 2009, Sch. 2, para. 46(1).
Para. 4(5): CTA 2009, Sch. 2, para. 46(1).
Para. 4(6): CTA 2009, Sch. 2, para. 46(1).

REPEAL OF SECTION 136 OF THE INCOME TAX ACT 1952: ALLOWANCE OF ANNUAL VALUE OF LAND AS A BUSINESS EXPENSE

5 [Omitted by CTA 2009, s. 1322 and Sch. 1, para. 292(3) and repealed by CTA 2009, s. 1326 and Sch. 3, Pt. 1.]

History – Para. 5 omitted by CTA 2009, s. 1322 and Sch. 1, para. 292(3) and repealed by CTA 2009, s. 1326 and Sch. 3, Pt. 1, with effect for corporation tax purposes for accounting periods ending on or after 1 April 2009, and for income tax and capital gains tax purposes for the tax year 2009–10 and subsequent tax years.

Notes – Para. 5 is not rewritten by ITTOIA 2005 as it is a transitional measure relating the pre-1963 version of Sch. A and it is thought almost certain that no new claims would be made after 5 April 2005. (See ITTOIA 2005, Explanatory Notes, Annex 1, Table 1 (Change 158).)
In para. 5(12) the expression "another body" denotes in relation to any part of the trade of the London Transport Board transferred under Transport (London) Act 1969, Pt. III, London Country Bus Services Limited or (with effect from 29 June 1984) London Regional Transport: FA 1970, Sch. 3, para. 1.
Para. 5: CTA 2009, not rewritten as unnecessary (see CTA 2009 Explanatory Notes, Annex 1, Change 102).

LOSS RELIEF ETC.

6(1) The substitution of this Act for the corresponding enactments repealed by this Act shall not alter the effect of any provision enacted before this Act (whether or not there is a corresponding provision in this Act) so far as it determines whether and to what extent–

(a) losses or expenditure incurred in, or other amounts referable to, a chargeable period earlier than those to which this Act applies may be taken into account for any tax purposes in a chargeable period to which this Act applies; or

(b) losses or expenditure incurred in, or other amounts referable to, a chargeable period to which this Act applies may be taken into account for any tax purposes in a chargeable period earlier than those to which this Act applies.

6(2) Without prejudice to sub-paragraph (1) above, the repeals made by this Act shall not affect the following enactments (which are not re-enacted)–

(a) section 27(4) of the Finance Act 1952 (restrictions on removal of six year time limit on carry forward of trading losses);

(b) section 29(3) of the Finance Act 1953 (Isles of Scilly);

(c) section 17 of, and Schedule 3 to, the Finance Act 1954 (company reconstructions before corporation tax) so far as in force by virtue of the saving in Part IV of Schedule 22 to the Finance Act 1965, and *section 80(8) of the Finance* Act 1965 (which amends Schedule 3 to the Finance Act 1954);

(d) section 82(4) of the Finance Act 1965 (losses allowable against chargeable gains);

(e) section 85 of the Finance Act 1965 (carry forward of surplus of franked investment income: dividends paid out of pre-1966–67 profits) and the enactments amending that section;

(f) paragraph 25 of Schedule 15 to the Finance Act 1965 (continuity of elections for purposes of corporation tax);

(g) paragraph 7 of Schedule 16 to the Finance Act 1965 (overseas trade corporations);

in so far as those enactments may be relevant to tax for any chargeable period to which this Act applies.

Derivations – ICTA 1970, Sch. 14, para. 9.

7(1) This paragraph shall apply with respect to claims for group relief in respect of any amount which is attributable–

(a) to writing-down allowances, within the meaning of Chapter II of Part I of the 1968 Act, or, as the case may require, Chapter I of Part III of the Finance Act 1971, in respect of expenditure incurred by the surrendering company on the provision of machinery or plant; or

(b) to initial allowances under section 56 of the 1968 Act (expenditure in connection with mines etc.) in respect of expenditure incurred by the surrendering company and falling within section 52(1) of that Act of 1971 (works in a development area or in Northern Ireland); or

(c) to allowances under section 91 of the 1968 Act in respect of expenditure incurred by the surrendering company on scientific research;

where the expenditure is incurred under a contract entered into by the surrendering company before 6th March 1973.

7(2) Notwithstanding anything in section 410(1) to (6) or 413(7) to (10) or in Schedule 18 but subject to sub-paragraph (5) below, group relief may be claimed in respect of any such amount as is referred to in sub-paragraph (1) above if–

(a) immediately before 6th March 1973–

(i) the surrendering company and the company claiming relief were members of a group of companies, and

(ii) throughout the period beginning on that date and ending at the end of the accounting period in respect of which the claim is made, there is no reduction in the rights of the parent company with respect to the matters specified in section 413(7)(a) and (b); or

(b) immediately before 6th March 1973 the company claiming relief was a member of a consortium and, throughout the period beginning on that date and ending at the end of the accounting period in respect of which the claim is made, there is–

(i) no variation in the percentage of the ordinary share capital of the company owned by the consortium which is beneficially owned by that member, and

(ii) no reduction in the rights of that member (in respect of the company owned by the consortium) with respect to the matters specified in section 413(7)(a) and (b);

and in either case no such arrangements as are specified in section 410(1) or (2) have come into existence after 5th March 1973 with respect to any of the companies concerned and no variation is made in any such arrangements which are in existence on that date with respect to any of those companies.

7(3) For the purposes of sub-paragraph (2)(a) above, **"the parent company"** means the company of which another member of the group referred to in that sub-paragraph was, immediately before 6th March 1973, a 75 per cent subsidiary, and the rights of the parent company referred to in that paragraph are–

(a) if the parent company is either the surrendering company or the company claiming relief, its rights in the other company; and

(b) in any other case, its rights in both the surrendering company and the company claiming relief.

7(4) For the purposes of this paragraph an amount which the claimant company claims by way of group relief shall be treated as attributable to an allowance falling within any of paragraphs (a) to (c) of sub-paragraph (1) above to the extent that that amount would not have been available for surrender by the surrendering company if no such allowance had been available to the surrendering company in respect of the expenditure concerned.

7(5) Sub-paragraph (2) above shall not apply if, during the period referred to in that sub-paragraph–

(a) there is a major change in the nature or conduct of a trade or business carried on by the relevant company; or

(b) the relevant company sets up and commences a trade or business, or begins to carry on a trade, which it did not carry on immediately before 6th March 1973.

7(6) In sub-paragraph (5) above–

"a major change in the nature or conduct of a trade or business" has the same meaning as in section 245(1); and

"the relevant company" means, if the machinery or plant to which the allowance relates was brought into use on or before 6th March 1978, the company claiming group relief and in any

ICTA 1988

other case either that company or the company which if sub-paragraph (5) did not apply would be the surrendering company.

7(7) This paragraph shall be construed as if it were contained in Chapter IV of Part X.

History – In para. 7(5)(b), the words ", or begins to carry on a trade," inserted by CTA 2009, s. 1322 and Sch. 1, para. 292(4), with effect for accounting periods ending on or after 1 April 2009.

Derivations – Para. 7(1): FA 1973, Sch. 12, para. 10(1)(b)–(d).
Para. 7(2)–(4): FA 1973, Sch. 12, para. 10(2)–(4).
Para. 7(5): FA 1973, Sch. 12, para. 11(1).
Para. 7(6): FA 1973, Sch. 12, para. 11(3)(c), (4).

CAPITAL ALLOWANCES

8 Without prejudice to paragraphs 6 and 7 above, where a person is, immediately before the commencement of this Act, entitled to a capital allowance by virtue of any enactment repealed by this Act, he shall not cease to be so entitled by reason only of that repeal, notwithstanding that the enactment in question is not re-enacted by this Act; and accordingly the provisions of this Act shall apply, with any necessary modifications, so far as may be necessary to give effect to any such entitlement.

SOCIAL SECURITY BENEFITS

9 [Repealed by Statute Law (Repeals) Act 2013, s. 1 and Sch. 1, Pt. 10.]

History – Para. 9 repealed by Statute Law (Repeals) Act 2013, s. 1 and Sch. 1, Pt. 10, with effect from 31 January 2013.

CHILDREN's SETTLEMENTS: IRREVOCABLE DISPOSITIONS MADE BEFORE 22nd APRIL 1936

10 [Repealed by FA 1995, s. 162 and Sch. 29, Pt. VIII(8) with effect for the year 1995–96 and subsequent years of assessment.]

11 [Repealed by FA 1995, s. 162 and Sch. 29, Pt. VIII(8) with effect for the year 1995–96 and subsequent years of assessment.]

12 [Repealed by FA 1995, s. 162 and Sch. 29, Pt. VIII(8) with effect for the year 1995–96 and subsequent years of assessment.]

GENERAL POWERS OF AMENDMENT IN ACTS RELATING TO OVERSEAS COUNTRIES

13 Where under any Act passed before this Act and relating to a country or territory outside the United Kingdom there is a power to affect Acts passed or in force before a particular time, or instruments made or having effect under such Acts, and the power would but for the passing of this Act, have included power to change the law which is reproduced in, or is made or has effect under, this Act, then that power shall include power to make such provision as will secure the like change in the law reproduced in, or made or having effect under, this Act notwithstanding that it is not an Act passed or in force before that time.

Derivations – ICTA 1970, Sch. 15, para. 10.

DOUBLE TAXATION AGREEMENTS

14 [Repealed by Statute Law (Repeals) Act 2013, s. 1 and Sch. 1, Pt. 10.]

History – Para. 14 repealed by Statute Law (Repeals) Act 2013, s. 1 and Sch. 1, Pt. 10, with effect from 31 January 2013.

SECURITIES

15 [Repealed by Statute Law (Repeals) Act 2013, s. 1 and Sch. 1, Pt. 10.]

History – Para. 15 repealed by Statute Law (Repeals) Act 2013, s. 1 and Sch. 1, Pt. 10, with effect from 31 January 2013.

BUILDING SOCIETIES

16 Any enactment relating to building societies contained in this Act which re-enacts an enactment which was an existing enactment for the purposes of section 121 of the Building Societies Act 1986 shall continue to be an *existing enactment* for those purposes.

Cross references – Building Societies Act 1986, s. 121(4): "existing enactment" for purposes of Building Societies Act 1986 – the enactments in force at the passing of that Act on 25 July 1986.

PENSION BUSINESS

17 Any reference to pension business in any enactment (other than an enactment repealed by this Act) which immediately before the commencement of this Act was such a reference by virtue of paragraph 11(3) of Part III of Schedule 5 to the Finance Act 1970 shall not be affected by the repeal by this Act of that paragraph and accordingly the business in question shall continue to be known as pension business.

STOCK RELIEF

18 [Omitted by ITTOIA 2005, s. 882 and Sch. 1, para. 352(3) and repealed by s. 884 and Sch. 3.]

History – Para. 18 omitted by ITTOIA 2005, s. 882(1) and Sch. 1, para. 352(3) and repealed by s. 884 and Sch. 3; effective for income tax purposes for 2005–06 onwards and for corporation tax purposes for accounting periods ending after 5 April 2005 (ITTOIA 2005, s. 883(1)).

Notes – Para. 18 is not rewritten by ITTOIA 2005 as it is a transitional measure relating to the abolition of stock relief in 1984 and is no longer required. (See ITTOIA 2005, Explanatory Notes, Annex 1, Table 1 (Change 158).)

18A [Omitted by ITTOIA 2005, s. 882 and Sch. 1, para. 352(3) and repealed by s. 884 and Sch. 3.]

History – Para. 18A omitted by ITTOIA 2005, s. 882(1) and Sch. 1, para. 352(3) and repealed by s. 884 and Sch. 3; effective for income tax purposes for 2005–06 onwards and for corporation tax purposes for accounting periods ending after 5 April 2005 (ITTOIA 2005, s. 883(1)).

SCHEDULE E EMOLUMENTS

19 [Repealed by Statute Law (Repeals) Act 2013, s. 1 and Sch. 1, Pt. 10.]

History – Para. 19 repealed by Statute Law (Repeals) Act 2013, s. 1 and Sch. 1, Pt. 10, with effect from 31 January 2013.

UNITARY STATES

20 [Repealed by Statute Law (Repeals) Act 2013, s. 1 and Sch. 1, Pt. 10.]

History – Para. 20 repealed by Statute Law (Repeals) Act 2013, s. 1 and Sch. 1, Pt. 10, with effect from 31 January 2013.

CONTINUITY AND CONSTRUCTION OF REFERENCES TO OLD AND NEW LAW

21(1) The continuity of the operation of the Tax Acts and of the law relating to chargeable gains shall not be affected by the substitution of this Act for the enactments repealed by this Act and earlier enactments repealed by and corresponding to any of those enactments (**"the repealed enactments"**).

21(2) Any reference, whether express or implied, in any enactment, instrument or document (including this Act and any Act amended by this Act) to, or to things done or falling to be done under or for the purposes of, any provision of this Act shall, if and so far as the nature of the reference permits, be construed as including, in relation to the times, years or periods, circumstances or purposes in relation to which the corresponding provision in the repealed enactments has or had effect, a reference to, or as the case may be to things done or falling to be done under or for the purposes of, that corresponding provision.

21(3) Any reference, whether express or implied, in any enactment, instrument or document (including the repealed enactments and enactments, instruments and documents passed or made after the passing of this Act) to, or to things done or falling to be done under or for the purposes of, any of the repealed enactments shall, if and so far as the nature of the reference permits, be construed as including, in relation to the times, years or periods, circumstances or purposes in relation to which the corresponding provision in this Act has effect, a reference to, or as the case may be to things done or falling to be done under or for the purposes of, that corresponding provision.

21(4) Any reference to Case VIII of Schedule D, whether a specific reference or one imported by more general words, in any enactment, instrument or document shall, in relation to the chargeable periods to which section 843(1) applies, be construed as a reference to Schedule A, and for the purposes of sub-paragraph (2) above, Schedule A in this Act shall be treated as corresponding to Case VIII of Schedule D in the repealed enactments, and any provision of this Act or of any Act passed after 12th March 1970 and before this Act referring to Schedule A shall be construed accordingly.

Derivations – See ICTA 1970, s. 539.

SCHEDULE 31 – REPEALS

Section 844

[Not reproduced.]

FINANCE ACT 1988

(1988 Chapter 39)

[*29th July 1988*]

ARRANGEMENT OF SECTIONS

PART III – INCOME TAX, CORPORATION TAX AND CAPITAL GAINS TAX

CHAPTER I – GENERAL

PART III – INCOME TAX, CORPORATION TAX AND CAPITAL GAINS TAX

Chapter I – General

TAX RATES AND PERSONAL RELIEFS

24 Higher and additional rates of income tax

24 [Repealed by ITA 2007, s. 1031 and Sch. 3, Pt. 1.]

History – S. 24 repealed by s. 1031 and Sch. 3, Pt. 1, with effect from 6 April 2007.
S. 24(4), which amended ICTA 1988, s. 832(1), repealed by FA 1997, s. 113 and Sch. 18, Pt. VI(1) with effect in relation to the year 1997–98 and subsequent years of assessment.

Notes – S. 24 rewritten as follows:
S. 24(2): ITA 2007, s. 6(1), 10(3)
S. 24(3): ITA 2007, s. 515.

29 Life assurance premium relief

29(1) [Amends ICTA 1988, s. 266(5)(a), 274(3)(a) and Sch. 14, para. 3(3)(a).]

29(2) This section shall have effect on and after 6th April 1989.

Prospective amendments – S. 29 repealed by FA 2012, s. 227 and Sch. 39, para. 28(1), with effect from a day to be appointed by Treasury order.

30 Additional relief in respect of children

30 [Repealed by FA 1999, s. 139 and Sch. 20, Pt. III(4).]

History – S. 30 repealed by FA 1999, s. 139 and Sch. 20, Pt. III(4), with effect for the year 2000–01 and subsequent years of assessment.

31 Non-residents' personal reliefs

31 [Repealed by Statute Law (Repeals) Act 2013, s. 1 and Sch. 1, Pt. 10.]

History – S. 31 repealed by Statute Law (Repeals) Act 2013, s. 1 and Sch. 1, Pt. 10, with effect from 31 January 2013.
Former s. 31(2) omitted by SI 2005/3229, reg. 60(2), with effect from 5 December 2005.

Post-ICTA 1988

MARRIED COUPLES

33 Personal allowance and married couple's allowance

33 [Omitted by FA 2009, s. 5 and Sch. 1, para. 6(b).]

History – S. 33 omitted by FA 2009, s. 5 and Sch. 1, para. 6(b), with effect for the tax year 2010–11 and subsequent tax years.

34 Jointly held property

34 [Repealed by ITA 2007, s. 1031 and Sch. 3, Pt. 1.]

History – S. 34 repealed by s. 1031 and Sch. 3, Pt. 1, with effect from 6 April 2007.

Notes – S. 34 rewritten as ITA 2007, s. 836(1), (2), (3), 837(1), (2), (3), (4), (5).

35 Minor and consequential provisions

35 Schedule 3 to this Act (which makes provision consequential on sections 32 and 33 above and other minor amendments relating to the treatment for income tax purposes of husbands, wives, widowers and widows) shall have effect.

ANNUAL PAYMENTS

36 Annual payments

36(1) [Repealed by FA 2007, s. 114 and Sch. 27, Pt. 2(3).]

36(2) [Repealed by ITA 2007, s. 1031 and Sch. 3, Pt. 1.]

36(3) [Repealed by ITA 2007, s. 1031 and Sch. 3, Pt. 1.]

36(4) [Repealed by ITA 2007, s. 1031 and Sch. 3, Pt. 1.]

36(5) [Repealed by ITA 2007, s. 1031 and Sch. 3, Pt. 1.]

36(5A) [Repealed by ITA 2007, s. 1031 and Sch. 3, Pt. 1.]

36(6) [Repealed by ITA 2007, s. 1031 and Sch. 3, Pt. 1.]

History – S. 36(1) repealed by FA 2007, s. 114 and Sch. 27, Pt. 2(3) with effect in relation to payments made on or after 6 April 2007.
S. 36(2) repealed by ITA 2007, s. 1031 and Sch. 3, Pt. 1, with effect from 6 April 2007.
S. 36(3) repealed by ITA 2007, s. 1031 and Sch. 3, Pt. 1, with effect from 6 April 2007.
S. 36(4) repealed by ITA 2007, s. 1031 and Sch. 3, Pt. 1, with effect from 6 April 2007.
S. 36(5) repealed by ITA 2007, s. 1031 and Sch. 3, Pt. 1, with effect from 6 April 2007.
S. 36(5A) repealed by ITA 2007, s. 1031 and Sch. 3, Pt. 1, with effect from 6 April 2007.
Former s. 36(5A) inserted by F(No. 2)A 1992, s. 62(2), with effect from 6 April 1993 (SI 1992/2642).
S. 36(6) repealed by ITA 2007, s. 1031 and Sch. 3, Pt. 1, with effect from 6 April 2007.

37 Maintenance payments under existing obligations: 1988–89

37 [Repealed by ITA 2007, s. 1031 and Sch. 3, Pt. 1.]

History – S. 37 repealed by ITA 2007, s. 1031 and Sch. 3, Pt. 1, with effect from 6 April 2007.

38 Maintenance payments under existing obligations: 1989–90 onwards

38 [Repealed by ITA 2007, s. 1031 and Sch. 3, Pt. 1.]

History – S. 38 repealed by ITA 2007, s. 1031 and Sch. 3, Pt. 1, with effect from 6 April 2007.

39 Maintenance payments under existing obligations: election for new rules

39 [Repealed by FA 1999, s. 139 and Sch. 20, Pt. III(6).]

40 Provisions supplementary to sections 37 to 39

40 [Repealed by ITA 2007, s. 1031 and Sch. 3, Pt. 1.]

History – S. 40 repealed by ITA 2007, s. 1031 and Sch. 3, Pt. 1, with effect from 6 April 2007.

RELIEF FOR INTEREST

42 Home loans: restriction of relief

42 [Repealed by FA *1999, s. 139* and Sch. 20, Pt. III(7).]

History – S. 42 repealed by FA 1999, s. 139 and Sch. 20, Pt. III(7), with effect in relation to any payment of interest falling within FA 1999, s. 38(3) or (4) (broadly, a payment made on or after 6 April 2000, or made on or after 9 March 1999 and before 6 April 2000 but not falling due until on or after 6 April 2000).

43 Home improvement loans

43 [Repealed by FA 1999, s. 139 and Sch. 20, Pt. III(7).]

History – S. 43 repealed by FA 1999, s. 139 and Sch. 20, Pt. III(7), with effect in relation to any payment of interest falling within FA 1999, s. 38(3) or (4) (broadly, a payment made on or after 6 April 2000, or made on or after 9 March 1999 and before 6 April 2000 but not falling due until on or after 6 April 2000).

44 Loans for residence of dependent relative etc.

44 [Repealed by FA 1999, s. 139 and Sch. 20, Pt. III(7).]

History – S. 44 repealed by FA 1999, s. 139 and Sch. 20, Pt. III(7), with effect in relation to any payment of interest falling within FA 1999, s. 38(3) or (4) (broadly, a payment made on or after 6 April 2000, or made on or after 9 March 1999 and before 6 April 2000 but not falling due until on or after 6 April 2000).

BENEFITS IN KIND

46 Car parking facilities

46 [Repealed by ITEPA 2003, Pt. 1.]

History – S. 46 repealed by ITEPA 2003, Pt. 1 with effect for the tax year 2003–04 and subsequent tax years.

47 Entertainment: non-cash vouchers

47(1) [Repealed by ITEPA 2003, Sch. 8, Pt. 1.]

47(2), (3) [Spent.]

47(4) [Spent.]

History – S. 47(1) repealed by ITEPA 2003, Sch. 8, Pt. 1 with effect for the tax year 2003–04 and subsequent tax years.

48 Entertainment: credit-tokens

48(1) [Repealed by ITEPA 2003, Sch. 8, Pt. 1.]

48(2) [Spent.]

48(3) [Spent.]

History – S. 48(1) repealed by ITEPA 2003, Sch. 8, Pt. 1 with effect for the tax year 2003–04 and subsequent tax years.

49 Entertainment of directors and higher-paid employees

49(1) [Repealed by ITEPA 2003, Sch. 8, Pt. 1.]

49(2) [Spent.]

49(3) [Spent.]

History – S. 49(1) repealed by ITEPA 2003, Sch. 8, Pt. 1 with effect for the tax year 2003–04 and subsequent tax years.

BUSINESS EXPANSION SCHEME

50 Private rented housing

50 [Repealed by FA 1994, s. 258 and Sch. 26, Pt. V(17).]

History – S. 50 repealed in respect of shares issued after 31 December 1993.

51 Restriction of relief

51(1) [Amends ICTA 1988, s. 289(12)(b) and inserts s. 290A.]

51(2) [Spent.]

52 Valuation of interests in land

52(1) [Inserts ICTA 1988, s. 294(5A).]

52(2) This section shall have effect in relation to valuations which fall to be made after the passing of this Act.

53 Approved investment funds

53 [Repealed by ITA 2007, s. 1031 and Sch. 3, Pt. 2.]

History – S. 53 repealed by ITA 2007, s. 1031 and Sch. 3, Pt. 2, with effect in relation to shares issued after 5 April 2007.

Notes – S. 53 rewritten as ITA 2007, s. 250(3), 251(1), (2), (3).

PENSIONS ETC.

54 Personal pension schemes: commencement

54 [Repealed by FA 2004, s. 326 and Sch. 42, Pt. 3.]

History – S. 54 repealed by FA 2004, s. 326 and Sch. 42, Pt. 3 with effect from 6 April 2006 but subject to FA 2004, Sch. 36 (Pension schemes etc.: transitional provisions and savings). Former s. 54 amended ICTA 1988, s. 655(4) and ICTA 1988, s. 618(1), (2), 632(3), 655(2), (3), (5).

55 Personal pension schemes: other amendments

55 [Repealed by FA 2004, s. 326 and Sch. 42, Pt. 3.]

History – S. 55 repealed by FA 2004, s. 326 and Sch. 42, Pt. 3 with effect from 6 April 2006 but subject to FA 2004, Sch. 36 (Pension schemes etc.: transitional provisions and savings). Former s. 55 amended ICTA 1988, s. 630 and substituted ICTA 1988, s. 638(7) and (8) and ICTA 1988, s. 686(2)(c).

56 Occupational pension schemes

56 [Repealed by FA 2004, s. 326 and Sch. 42, Pt. 3.]

History – S. 56 repealed by FA 2004, s. 326 and Sch. 42, Pt. 3 with effect from 6 April 2006 but subject to FA 2004, Sch. 36 (Pension schemes etc.: transitional provisions and savings). Former s. 56 substituted ICTA 1988, Sch. 23, para. 1(2).

57 Lump sum benefits paid otherwise than on retirement

57 [Repealed by ITEPA 2003, Sch. 8, Pt. 1.]

History – S. 57 repealed by ITEPA 2003, Sch. 8, Pt. 1 with effect for the tax year 2003–04 and subsequent tax years.

UNDERWRITERS

58 Assessment and collection

58 [Repealed by Statute Law (Repeals) Act 2013, s. 1 and Sch. 1, Pt. 10.]

History – S. 58 repealed by Statute Law (Repeals) Act 2013, s. 1 and Sch. 1, Pt. 10, with effect from 31 January 2013. Former s. 58(1) substituted ICTA 1988, s. 450(2) (subsequently repealed) and former s. 58(2)–(5) were spent.

59 Reinsurance: general

59(1) [Substitutes ICTA 1988, s. 450(4)(b) (now repealed).]

59(2) [Spent.]

59(3) [Spent.]

60 Reinsurance to close

60(1) [Substitutes ICTA 1988, s. 450(5) (now repealed).]

60(2) [Spent.]

60(3) [Spent.]

61 Minor and consequential amendments

61(1) [Repealed by Statute Law (Repeals) Act 2013, s. 1 and Sch. 1, Pt. 10.]

61(2)–(4) [Spent.]

61(5) [Spent.]

History – S. 61(1) repealed by Statute Law (Repeals) Act 2013, s. 1 and Sch. 1, Pt. 10, with effect from 31 January 2013. Former s. 61(1) substituted ICTA 1988, s. 451(1)(a) and inserted (1A), and amended ICTA 1988, s. 452(8) (all subsequently repealed).
Former s. 61(1)(a) (which inserted words into ICTA 1988, s. 20(2)) repealed by ITTOIA 2005, s. 884 and Sch. 3 effective for income tax purposes for 2005–06 onwards (ITTOIA 2005, s. 883(1)).
In s. 61(5), the words "Subsection (1) above shall have effect for the year 1988–89 and subsequent years of assessment; and" repealed by Statute Law (Repeals) Act 2013, s. 1 and Sch. 1, Pt. 10, with effect from 31 January 2013.

MISCELLANEOUS

65 Commercial woodlands

65 [Omitted by CTA 2009, s. 1322 and Sch. 1, para. 331 and repealed by CTA 2009, s. 1326 and Sch. 3, Pt. 1.]

History – S. 65 omitted by CTA 2009, s. 1322 and Sch. 1, para. 331 and repealed by CTA 2009, s. 1326 and Sch. 3, Pt. 1, with effect, for corporation tax purposes, for accounting periods ending on or after 1 April 2009 and, for income tax and capital gains tax purposes, for the tax year 2009–10 and subsequent years.

66 Company residence

66 [Omitted by CTA 2009, s. 1322 and Sch. 1, para. 332 and repealed by CTA 2009, s. 1326 and Sch. 3, Pt. 1.]

History – S. 66 omitted by CTA 2009, s. 1322 and Sch. 1, para. 332 and repealed by CTA 2009, s. 1326 and Sch. 3, Pt. 1, with effect, for corporation tax purposes, for accounting periods ending on or after 1 April 2009 and, for income tax and capital gains tax purposes, for the tax year 2009–10 and subsequent years.

Notes – S. 66 rewritten as follows:
S. 66(2): CTA 2009, s. 15(2)–(4).
S. 66(3): CTA 2009, Sch. 1, para. 309.
S. 66(4): Spent.

66A Residence of SE

66A [Omitted by CTA 2009, s. 1322 and Sch. 1, para. 333 and repealed by CTA 2009, s. 1326 and Sch. 3, Pt. 1.]

History – S. 66A omitted by CTA 2009, s. 1322 and Sch. 1, para. 333 and repealed by CTA 2009, s. 1326 and Sch. 3, Pt. 1, with effect, for corporation tax purposes, for accounting periods ending on or after 1 April 2009 and, for income tax and capital gains tax purposes, for the tax year 2009–10 and subsequent years.

Notes – S. 66A rewritten as follows:
S. 66A(1): CTA 2009, s. 16(1), s. 17(1).
S. 66A(2): CTA 2009, s. 16(2) and (3), s. 17(2) and (3).
S. 66A(3): CTA 2009, s. 16(4), s. 17(4).
S. 66A(4): CTA 2009, Sch. 1, para. 309.

68 Priority share allocations for employees etc.

68 [Repealed by ITEPA 2003, Sch. 8, Pt. 1.]

History – S. 68 repealed by ITEPA 2003, Sch. 8, Pt. 1 with effect for the tax year 2003–04 and subsequent tax years.

Notes – S. 68 rewritten as follows:
S. 68(1): ITEPA 2003, s. 542(1), (2), s. 544(1) and (2).
S. 68(1ZA): ITEPA 2003, s. 544(1).
S. 68(1ZB): ITEPA 2003, s. 544(1), (2), (3), (4), s. 545(1) and s. 547(2).
S. 68(1A): ITEPA 2003, s. 543(1), (2), s. 545(1) and (2).
S. 68(2): ITEPA 2003, s. 542(3), (5), (6), s. 544(3), (5) and (6).
S. 68(2A): ITEPA 2003, s. 542(3) and s. 544(3).
S. 68(2B): ITEPA 2003, s. 542(3), (4), s. 544(3) and (4).
S. 68(2C): s. 544(3) and (4).
S. 68(3): ITEPA 2003, s. 546(2).
S. 68(3A): ITEPA 2003, s. 546(3), (4), (5), (6) and (7).
S. 68(5) ("director", "employee", "the employee offer", "the public offer"): ITEPA 2003, s. 548(1) .
S. 68(5A): ITEPA 2003, s. 547.
S. 68(5B): ITEPA 2003, s. 545(3) and (5).
S. 68(5C): ITEPA 2003, s. 545(4) and (6).

69 Share options: loans

69 [Repealed by ITEPA 2003, Sch. 8, Pt. 1.]

History – S. 69 repealed by ITEPA 2003, Sch. 8, Pt. 1 with effect for the tax year 2003–04 and subsequent tax years.

71 Unit trusts: relief on certain payments

71 [Repealed by ITA 2007, s. 1031 and Sch. 3, Pt. 1.]

History – S. 71 repealed by ITA 2007, s. 1031 and Sch. 3, Pt. 1, with effect from 6 April 2007.

Notes – S. 71 rewritten as ITA 2007, s. 942(4), (5), 943(1), (2), (3).

72 Entertainment of overseas customers

72 [Repealed by CTA 2009, s. 1326 and Sch. 3, Pt. 1.]

History – S. 72 repealed by CTA 2009, s. 1326 and Sch. 3, Pt. 1, with effect, for corporation tax purposes, for accounting periods ending on or after 1 April 2009 and, for income tax and capital gains tax purposes, for the tax year 2009–10 and subsequent years.

73 Consideration for certain restrictive undertakings

73(1) [Repealed by ITEPA 2003, Sch. 8, Pt. 1.]

73(2) [Omitted by CTA 2009, s. 1322 and Sch. 1, para. 334 and repealed by CTA 2009, s. 1326 and Sch. 3, Pt. 1.]

73(3) [Omitted by CTA 2009, s. 1322 and Sch. 1, para. 334 and repealed by CTA 2009, s. 1326 and Sch. 3, Pt. 1.]

73(4) [Omitted by CTA 2009, s. 1322 and Sch. 1, para. 334 and repealed by CTA 2009, s. 1326 and Sch. 3, Pt. 1.]

History – S. 73(1) repealed by ITEPA 2003, Sch. 8, Pt. 1 with effect for the tax year 2003–04 and subsequent tax years.

S. 73(2)–(4) omitted by CTA 2009, s. 1322 and Sch. 1, para. 334 and repealed by CTA 2009, s. 1326 and Sch. 3, Pt. 1, with effect, for corporation tax purposes, for accounting periods ending on or after 1 April 2009 and, for income tax and capital gains tax purposes, for the tax year 2009–10 and subsequent years.

Notes – S. 73 rewritten for income tax purposes as ITTOIA 2005, s. 69.
S. 73 rewritten for corporation tax purposes as follows:
S. 73(2): CTA 2009, s. 51(1) and (2), s. 69(1) and (2).
S. 73(3): CTA 2009, s. 1232, s. 1234(1) and (2).
S. 73(4): Spent.

75 Premiums for leases etc.

75 [Repealed by Statute Law (Repeals) Act 2013, s. 1 and Sch. 1, Pt. 10.]

History – S. 75 repealed by Statute Law (Repeals) Act 2013, s. 1 and Sch. 1, Pt. 10, with effect from 31 January 2013.

Chapter II – Unapproved Employee Share Schemes

PRELIMINARY

77 Scope of Chapter

77 [Repealed by ITEPA 2003, Sch. 8, Pt. 1.]

History – S. 77 repealed by ITEPA 2003, Sch. 8, Pt. 1 which has effect for the tax year 2003–04 and subsequent tax years.

Notes – S. 77 rewritten as follows:
S. 77(1): ITEPA 2003, s. 447(1), (4), s. 452(2), s. 456(2) and Sch. 7, para. 55 (Sch. 7: transitionals and savings).
S. 77(2): ITEPA 2003, s. 448(1).
S. 77(3): ITEPA 2003, s. 448(2).
S. 77(4): ITEPA 2003, s. 448(3), (4) and Sch. 7, para. 58 (Sch. 7: transitionals and savings).

CHARGES TO TAX

78 Charge where restrictions removed etc.

78 [Repealed by ITEPA 2003, Sch. 8, Pt. 1.]

History – S. 78 repealed by ITEPA 2003, Sch. 8, Pt. 1 which has effect for the tax year 2003–04 and subsequent tax years.

Notes – S. 78 rewritten as follows:
S. 78(1): ITEPA 2003, s. 449(1) and s. 452(4).
S. 78(2): ITEPA 2003, s. 449(5), s. 450(2) and (3).
S. 78(3): ITEPA 2003, s. 7(6), s. 10(3), s. 449(2), (3) and s. 451.
S. 78(4): ITEPA 2003, s. 452(3).
S. 78(5): ITEPA 2003, s. 450(4).
S. 78(6): ITEPA 2003, s. 450(4), (5) and s. 469.
S. 78(7): ITEPA 2003, s. 450(6).

79 Charge for shares in dependent subsidiaries

79 [Repealed by ITEPA 2003, Sch. 8, Pt. 1.]

History – S. 79 repealed by ITEPA 2003, Sch. 8, Pt. 1 which has effect for the tax year 2003–04 and subsequent tax years.

Notes – S. 79 rewritten as follows:
S. 79(1): ITEPA 2003, s. 453(1).
S. 79(2): ITEPA 2003, s. 454(2) and (3).
S. 79(3): ITEPA 2003, s. 453(5), s. 454(4) and (5).
S. 79(4): ITEPA 2003, s. 7(6), s. 10(3), s. 453(2), (3), s. 455(1) and (4).
S. 79(5): ITEPA 2003, s. 455(2).
S. 79(6): ITEPA 2003, s. 455(3).
S. 79(6A): ITEPA 2003, s. 455(2).
S. 79(6B): ITEPA 2003, s. 455(2).
S. 79(7): ITEPA 2003, s. 456(3).

80 Charge on special benefits

80 [Repealed by ITEPA 2003, Sch. 8, Pt. 1.]

History – S. 80 repealed by ITEPA 2003, Sch. 8, Pt. 1 which has effect for the tax year 2003–04 and subsequent tax years.

Notes – S. 80 rewritten as follows:
S. 80(1): ITEPA 2003, s. 457(1) and (2).
S. 80(1A): ITEPA 2003, s. 458(4).
S. 80(2): ITEPA 2003, s. 458(3) and (5).
S. 80(3): ITEPA 2003, s. 458(6) and s. 469.
S. 80(3A): ITEPA 2003, s. 458(7).
S. 80(4): ITEPA 2003, s. 7(6), s. 10(3), s. 457(3), (4) and s. 459.
S. 80(5): ITEPA 2003, s. 460.
S. 80(6): ITEPA 2003, s. 457(6).

MISCELLANEOUS

81 Changes in interest

81 [Repealed by ITEPA 2003, Sch. 8, Pt. 1.]

History – S. 81 repealed by ITEPA 2003, Sch. 8, Pt. 1 which has effect for the tax year 2003–04 and subsequent tax years.

Notes – S. 81 rewritten into the provisions of ITEPA 2003, s. 464.

82 Company reorganisations etc.

82 [Repealed by ITEPA 2003, Sch. 8, Pt. 1.]

History – S. 82 repealed by ITEPA 2003, Sch. 8, Pt. 1 which has effect for the tax year 2003–04 and subsequent tax years.

Notes – S. 82 rewritten as follows:
S. 82(1): ITEPA 2003, s. 461(1).
S. 82(2): ITEPA 2003, s. 461(2) and (3).
S. 82(3): ITEPA 2003, s. 462.

83 Connected persons etc.

83 [Repealed by ITEPA 2003, Sch. 8, Pt. 1.]

History – S. 83 repealed by ITEPA 2003, Sch. 8, Pt. 1 which has effect for the tax year 2003–04 and subsequent tax years.

Notes – S. 83 rewritten as follows:
S. 83(1): ITEPA 2003, s. 447(5).
S. 83(2): ITEPA 2003, s. 463.
S. 83(3): ITEPA 2003, s. 463.
S. 83(4): ITEPA 2003, s. 457(2) and s. 460.

84 Capital gains tax

84 [Repealed by ITEPA 2003, Sch. 8, Pt. 1.]

History – S. 84 repealed by ITEPA 2003, Sch. 8, Pt. 1 which has effect for the tax year 2003–04 and subsequent tax years.

85 Information

85 [Repealed by ITEPA 2003, Sch. 8, Pt. 1.]

History – S. 85 repealed by ITEPA 2003, Sch. 8, Pt. 1 which has effect for the tax year 2003–04 and subsequent tax years.

Notes – S. 85 rewritten as follows:
S. 85(1): ITEPA 2003, s. 465(1), (3) and (4).
S. 85(2): ITEPA 2003, s. 466.
S. 85(3) amended TMA 1970, s. 98 and so it has not been rewritten.

SUPPLEMENTARY

86 Meaning of "dependent subsidiary"

86 [Repealed by ITEPA 2003, Sch. 8, Pt. 1.]

History – S. 86 repealed by ITEPA 2003, Sch. 8, Pt. 1 which has effect for the tax year 2003–04 and subsequent tax years.

Notes – S. 86 rewritten as follows:
S. 86(1): ITEPA 2003, s. 467(1), (2), (3), (4) and (5).
S. 86(2): ITEPA 2003, s. 467(6) and (7).
S. 86(3): ITEPA 2003, s. 467(8).

87 Other interpretation provisions

87 [Repealed by ITEPA 2003, Sch. 8, Pt. 1.]

History – S. 87 repealed by ITEPA 2003, Sch. 8 which has effect for the tax year 2003–04 and subsequent tax years.

Notes – S. 87 rewritten as follows:
S. 87(1): ITEPA 2003, s. 448(2), s. 450(4), s. 458(7), s. 459, s. 467(8) and s. 470(1).
S. 87(2): ITEPA 2003, s. 468 and s. 718.
S. 87(3): ITEPA 2003, s. 719.
S. 87(4): ITEPA 2003, s. 447(4).

88 Transitional provisions

88 [Repealed by ITEPA 2003, Sch. 8, Pt. 1.]

History – S. 88 repealed by ITEPA 2003, Sch. 8, Pt. 1 which has effect for the tax year 2003–04 and subsequent tax years.

Notes – S. 88 rewritten as follows:
S. 88(1): ITEPA 2003, Sch. 7, para. 57.
S. 88(2) is spent and so has not been rewritten.
S. 88(3): ITEPA 2003, Sch. 7, para. 55.
S. 88(4): ITEPA 2003, Sch. 7, para. 56.

89 Consequential amendments

89 [Amends ICTA 1988, s. 186(2).]

History – In s. 89, the words "section 185(3)(a) (approved share option schemes) and" and paragraph "(b)" of ICTA 1988, s. 186(2) were repealed by ITEPA 2003, Sch. 8, Pt. 1 which has effect for the tax year 2003–04 and subsequent tax years.

Chapter IV – Capital Gains

COMPANY MIGRATION

105 Deemed disposal of assets on company ceasing to be resident in UK

105(1)–(5) [Repealed by TCGA 1992, s. 290 and Sch. 12.]

105(6) [Omitted by FA 2009, s. 37 and Sch. 17, para. 3(a).]

105(7) This section … shall be deemed to have come into force on 15th March 1988.

History – S. 105(6) omitted by FA 2009, s. 37 and Sch. 17, para. 3(a) with effect for events taking place and transactions carried out on or after 1 July 2009.
Former s. 105(6) repealed ICTA 1988, s. 765(1)(a) and amended ICTA 1988, s. 765(1)(c).

MISCELLANEOUS

117 Definition of "investment trust"

117(1) [Repealed by CTA 2010, s. 1181 and Sch. 3, Pt. 1.]

117(2) [Spent.]

117(3) [Repealed by CA 2006, s. 1295 and Sch. 16.]

117(4) Subsection (2) above shall have effect for companies' accounting periods ending on or before that date.

History – S. 117(1) repealed by CTA 2010, s. 1181 and Sch. 3, Pt. 1, with effect for corporation tax purposes for accounting periods ending on or after 1 April 2010, and for income tax and capital gains tax purposes for the tax year 2010–11 and subsequent tax years.
S. 117(3) repealed by CA 2006, s. 1295 and Sch. 16, with effect from 6 April 2008, by virtue of SI 2007/3495.
In s. 117(4), the words "Subsections (1) above shall have effect for companies' accounting periods ending after 5th April 1988 and" (which preceded the words "subsection (2) above") repealed by CTA 2010, s. 1181 and Sch. 3, Pt. 1, with effect for corporation tax purposes for accounting periods ending on or after 1 April 2010, and for income tax and capital gains tax purposes for the tax year 2010–11 and subsequent tax years.
In s. 117(4), the words "and (3)" after the words "Subsections (1)" repealed by CA 2006, s. 1295 and Sch. 16, with effect from 6 April 2008, by virtue of SI 2007/3495.

Chapter V – Management

ASSESSMENT

119 Current year assessments

119 [Repealed by Statute Law (Repeals) Act 2013, s. 1 and Sch. 1, Pt. 10.]

History – S. 119 repealed by Statute Law (Repeals) Act 2013, s. 1 and Sch. 1, Pt. 10, with effect from 31 January 2013. Former s. 119 amended TMA 1970, s. 29.

RETURNS OF INCOME AND GAINS

120 Notice of liability to income tax

120 [Repealed by Statute Law (Repeals) Act 2013, s. 1 and Sch. 1, Pt. 10.]

History – S. 120 repealed by Statute Law (Repeals) Act 2013, s. 1 and Sch. 1, Pt. 10, with effect from 31 January 2013. Former s. 120 amended TMA 1970, s. 7.

122 Notice of liability to capital gains tax

122 [Repealed by Statute Law (Repeals) Act 2013, s. 1 and Sch. 1, Pt. 10.]

History – S. 122 repealed by Statute Law (Repeals) Act 2013, s. 1 and Sch. 1, Pt. 10, with effect from 31 January 2013.

OTHER RETURNS AND INFORMATION

123 Three year time limit

123(1) [Inserts TMA 1970, s. 13(3).]

123(2) [Amends TMA 1970, s. 17(1).]

123(3) [Inserts TMA 1970, s. 18(3A).]

123(4) [Inserts TMA 1970, s. 19(4).]

123(5) This section has effect with respect to notices given after the passing of this Act.

124 Returns of fees, commissions etc.

124(1) [Inserts TMA 1970, s. 16(8).]

124(2) This section has effect with respect to payments made in the year 1988–89 or any subsequent year of assessment.

125 Other payments and licences etc.

125 [Inserts TMA 1970, s. 18A.]

PRODUCTION OF ACCOUNTS, BOOKS ETC.

126 Production of documents relating to a person's tax liability

126 [Repealed by FA 2008, s. 113 and Sch. 36, para. 92.]

History – S. 126 repealed by FA 2008, s. 113 and Sch. 36, para. 92, with effect from 1 April 2009 (SI 2009/404, art. 2, subject to savings at SI 2009/404, art. 3). Former s. 126 amended TMA 1970, s. 20(7), (8A), (8B), 20B(1), (2), (4), (8) and (9) and National Savings Bank Act 1971, s. 2, 12(3).

127 Production of computer records etc.

127 [Omitted by FA 2008, s. 114(8)(b).]

History – S. 127 omitted by FA 2008, s. 114(8)(b), with effect from 21 July 2008.

INTEREST AND PENALTIES

128 Interest on overdue or overpaid PAYE

128 [Repealed by ITEPA 2003, Sch. 8, Pt. 1.]

History – S. 128 repealed by ITEPA 2003, Sch. 8, Pt. 1 which has effect for the tax year 2003–04 and subsequent tax years.

129 Two or more tax-geared penalties in respect of same tax

129(1) [Inserts TMA 1970, s. 97A.]

129(2) Section 97(A)(a) of that Act has effect with respect to the year 1988–89 or any subsequent year of assessment; and section 97A(b) has effect with respect to accounting periods ending after 31st March 1989.

COMPANY MIGRATION

130 Provisions for securing payment by company of outstanding tax

130 [Omitted by TIOPA 2010, s. 371 and Sch. 7, para. 56 and repealed by TIOPA 2010, s. 378 and Sch. 10, Pt. 12.]

History – S. 130 omitted by TIOPA 2010, s. 371 and Sch. 7, para. 56 and repealed by TIOPA 2010, s. 378 and Sch. 10, Pt. 12, with effect for corporation tax purposes for accounting periods ending on or after 1 April 2010, for income tax and capital gains tax purposes for the tax year 2010–11 and subsequent tax years, and for petroleum revenue tax purposes for chargeable periods beginning on or after 1 July 2010.

Notes – S. 130 rewritten in TIOPA 2010 as follows:
S. 130(1): TIOPA 2010, Sch. 7, para. 54.
S. 130(2): TIOPA 2010, Sch. 7, para. 54.
S. 130(3): TIOPA 2010, Sch. 7, para. 54.
S. 130(4): TIOPA 2010, Sch. 7, para. 54.
S. 130(5): TIOPA 2010, Sch. 7, para. 54.
S. 130(7): TIOPA 2010, Sch. 7, para. 54.
S. 130(8): TIOPA 2010, Sch. 7, para. 54.

131 Penalties for failure to comply with section 130

131 [Omitted by TIOPA 2010, s. 371 and Sch. 7, para. 56 and repealed by TIOPA 2010, s. 378 and Sch. 10, Pt. 12.]

History – S. 131 omitted by TIOPA 2010, s. 371 and Sch. 7, para. 56 and repealed by TIOPA 2010, s. 378 and Sch. 10, Pt. 12, with effect for corporation tax purposes for accounting periods ending on or after 1 April 2010, for income tax and capital gains tax purposes for the tax year 2010–11 and subsequent tax years, and for petroleum revenue tax purposes for chargeable periods beginning on or after 1 July 2010.

Notes – S. 131 rewritten in TIOPA 2010 as follows:
S. 131(1): TIOPA 2010, Sch. 7, para. 54.
S. 131(2): TIOPA 2010, Sch. 7, para. 54.

S. 131(3): TIOPA 2010, Sch. 7, para. 54.
S. 131(4): TIOPA 2010, Sch. 7, para. 54.
S. 131(5): TIOPA 2010, Sch. 7, para. 54.
S. 131(6): TIOPA 2010, Sch. 7, para. 54.

132 Liability of other persons for unpaid tax

132 [Omitted by TIOPA 2010, s. 371 and Sch. 7, para. 56 and repealed by TIOPA 2010, s. 378 and Sch. 10, Pt. 12.]

History – S. 132 omitted by TIOPA 2010, s. 371 and Sch. 7, para. 56 and repealed by TIOPA 2010, s. 378 and Sch. 10, Pt. 12, with effect for corporation tax purposes for accounting periods ending on or after 1 April 2010, for income tax and capital gains tax purposes for the tax year 2010–11 and subsequent tax years, and for petroleum revenue tax purposes for chargeable periods beginning on or after 1 July 2010.

Notes – S. 132 rewritten in TIOPA 2010 as follows:
S. 132(1): TIOPA 2010, Sch. 7, para. 54.
S. 132(2): TIOPA 2010, Sch. 7, para. 54.
S. 132(3): TIOPA 2010, Sch. 7, para. 54.
S. 132(4): TIOPA 2010, Sch. 7, para. 54.
S. 132(5): TIOPA 2010, Sch. 7, para. 54.
S. 132(6): TIOPA 2010, Sch. 7, para. 54.

APPEALS ETC.

133 Jurisdiction of General Commissioners

133 [Omitted by SI 2009/56, art. 3 and Sch. 1, para. 165.]

History – S. 133 omitted by SI 2009/56, art. 3 and Sch. 1, para. 165, with effect from 1 April 2009, subject to transitional and saving provisions in SI 2009/56, Sch. 3.

134 General Commissioners for Northern Ireland

134 [Omitted by SI 2009/56, art. 3 and Sch. 1, para. 165.]

History – S. 134 omitted by SI 2009/56, art. 3 and Sch. 1, para. 165, with effect from 1 April 2009, subject to transitional and saving provisions in SI 2009/56, Sch. 3.

135 Cases stated in Northern Ireland

135 [Omitted by SI 2009/56, art. 3 and Sch. 1, para. 165.]

History – S. 135 omitted by SI 2009/56, art. 3 and Sch. 1, para. 165, with effect from 1 April 2009, subject to transitional and saving provisions in SI 2009/56, Sch. 3.

PART IV – MISCELLANEOUS AND GENERAL

MISCELLANEOUS

145 Building societies: change of status

145 Schedule 12 to this Act (which makes provision in connection with the transfer of a building society's business to a company in accordance with the Building Societies Act 1986) shall have effect.

146 Post-consolidation amendments

146 The enactments specified in Schedule 13 to this Act shall have effect subject to the amendments specified in that Schedule (being amendments to correct errors in the Taxes Act 1988 and in the amendments made by the Finance Act 1987 for the purposes of the consolidation effected by the Taxes Act 1988).

147 Interpretation etc.

147(1) In this Act **"the Taxes Act 1970"** means the Income and Corporation Taxes Act 1970 and **"the Taxes Act 1988"** means the Income and Corporation Taxes Act 1988.

147(2) [Not relevant to income, corporation or capital gains taxes.]

147(3) Part III of this Act, so far as it relates to income tax, shall be construed as one with the Income Tax Acts, so far as it relates to corporation tax, shall be construed as one with the Corporation Tax Acts …

149 Short title

149 This Act may be cited as the Finance Act 1988.

SCHEDULES

SCHEDULE 3 – MARRIED COUPLES: MINOR AND CONSEQUENTIAL PROVISIONS

Section 35

Part I – Amendments of the Taxes Act 1988

INTRODUCTORY

1 The Taxes Act 1988 shall have effect subject to the following amendments.

COMMENCEMENT OF TRADE ETC.

2 [Repealed by ITTOIA 2005, s. 884 and Sch. 3.]

History – Para. 2 repealed by ITTOIA 2005, s. 884 and Sch. 3 effective for income tax purposes for 2005–06 onwards (ITTOIA 2005, s. 883(1)).

DISCONTINUANCE OF TRADE ETC.

3 [Repealed by ITTOIA 2005, s. 884 and Sch. 3.]

History – Para. 3 repealed by ITTOIA 2005, s. 884 and Sch. 3 effective for income tax purposes for 2005–06 onwards (ITTOIA 2005, s. 883(1)).

UNDERPAYMENTS

4 [Repealed by ITEPA 2003, Sch. 8, Pt. 1.]

History – Para. 4 repealed by ITEPA 2003, Sch. 8, Pt. 1 which has effect for the tax year 2003–04 and subsequent tax years.

ADDITIONAL RELIEF IN RESPECT OF CHILDREN

5 [Repealed by FA 1999, s. 139 and Sch. 20, Pt. III(4).]

History – Para. 5 repealed by FA 1999, s. 139 and Sch. 20, Pt. III(4), with effect for the year 2000–01 and subsequent years of assessment.

6 [Repealed FA 1999, s. 139 and Sch. 20, Pt. III(4).]

History – Para. 6 repealed by FA 1999, s. 139 and Sch. 20, Pt. III(4), with effect for the year 2000–01 and subsequent years of assessment.

WIDOW'S BEREAVEMENT ALLOWANCE

7 [Spent: amended ICTA 1988, s. 262 (now repealed).]

History – Para. 7(3) repealed by FA 1999, s. 139 and Sch. 20, Pt. III(5), with effect in relation to deaths occurring on or after 6 April 2000.

BLIND PERSON'S ALLOWANCE

8 [Omitted by FA 2009, s. 5 and Sch. 1, para. 6(b).]

History – Para. 8 omitted by FA 2009, s. 5 and Sch. 1, para. 6(b), with effect for the tax year 2010–11 and subsequent tax years. Former para. 8 substituted ICTA 1988, s. 265.

LIFE ASSURANCE PREMIUMS

9 [Amends ICTA 1988, s. 266(9), (11)(a) for 1990–91 and subsequent years.]

Prospective amendments – Para. 9 repealed by FA 2012, s. 227 and Sch. 39, para. 28(1), with effect from a day to be appointed by Treasury order.

PAYMENTS SECURING ANNUITIES

10 [Omitted by FA 2009, s. 5 and Sch. 1, para. 6(b).]

History – Para. 10 omitted by FA 2009, s. 5 and Sch. 1, para. 6(b), with effect for the tax year 2010–11 and subsequent tax years. Former para. 10 substituted ICTA 1988, s. 273.

MARRIED COUPLES LIVING TOGETHER

11 [Repealed by ITA 2007, s. 1031 and Sch. 3, Pt. 1.]

History – Para. 11 repealed by ITA 2007, s. 1031 and Sch. 3, Pt. 1, with effect from 6 April 2007.

Notes – Para. 11 rewritten as ITA 2007, s. 1011.

BUSINESS EXPANSION SCHEME

12(1)–(3) [Spent.]

QUALIFYING MAINTENANCE PAYMENTS

13 [Repealed by Statute Law (Repeals) Act 2013, s. 1 and Sch. 1, Pt. 10.]

History – Para. 13 repealed by Statute Law (Repeals) Act 2013, s. 1 and Sch. 1, Pt. 10, with effect from 31 January 2013. Former para. 13 amended ICTA 1988, s. 347B(3).

HOME LOANS

14 [Repealed by FA 1999, s. 139 and Sch. 20, Pt. III(7).]

History – Para. 14 repealed by FA 1999, s. 139 and Sch. 20, Pt. III(7), with effect in relation to any payment of interest falling within FA 1999, s. 38(3) or (4) (broadly, a payment made on or after 6 April 2000, or made on or after 9 March 1999 and before 6 April 2000 but not falling due until on or after 6 April 2000).

LOANS FOR SHARES IN EMPLOYEE-CONTROLLED COMPANY

15(1) [Repealed by ITA 2007, s. 1031 and Sch. 3, Pt. 1.]

History – Sch. 3, para. 15 repealed by ITA 2007, s. 1031 and Sch. 3, Pt. 1, with effect from 6 April 2007.

Notes – Para. 15 rewritten as follows:
Para. 15(1): ITA 2007, s. 396(4), Sch. 2, para. 95(1).
Para. 15(2): ITA 2007, Sch. 2, para. 95(1).
Para. 15(3): ITA 2007, Sch. 2, para. 95(2).

CLOSE COMPANY LOANS

16 [Repealed by CTA 2010, s. 1181 and Sch. 3, Pt. 1.]

History – Para. 16 repealed by CTA 2010, s. 1181 and Sch. 3, Pt. 1, with effect for corporation tax purposes for accounting periods ending on or after 1 April 2010, and for income tax and capital gains tax purposes for the tax year 2010–11 and subsequent tax years. Former para. 16 amended ICTA 1988, s. 420(2)(a)(i).

TRADE UNIONS AND EMPLOYERS' ASSOCIATIONS

17 [Repealed by CTA 2010, s. 1181 and Sch. 3, Pt. 1.]

History – Para. 17 repealed by CTA 2010, s. 1181 and Sch. 3, Pt. 1, with effect for corporation tax purposes for accounting periods ending on or after 1 April 2010, and for income tax and capital gains tax purposes for the tax year 2010–11 and subsequent tax years. Former para. 17 amended ICTA 1988, s. 467(2).

RETIREMENT BENEFIT SCHEMES

18 [Repealed by FA 2004, s. 326 and Sch. 42, Pt. 3.]

History – Para. 18 repealed by FA 2004, s. 326 and Sch. 42, Pt. 3 with effect from 6 April 2006 but subject to FA 2004, Sch. 36 (Pension schemes etc.: transitional provisions and savings).

PARTNERSHIP RETIREMENT ANNUITIES

19 [Amends ICTA 1988, s. 628(1) for 1990–91 and subsequent years.]

20 [Repealed by FA 1995, s. 162 and Sch. 29, Pt. VIII(8), with effect for 1995–96 and subsequent years of assessment.]

EARNED INCOME

21 [Repealed by TIOPA 2010, s. 378 and Sch. 10, Pt. 13.]

History – Para. 21 repealed by TIOPA 2010, s. 378 and Sch. 10, Pt. 13, with effect for corporation tax purposes for accounting periods ending on or after 1 April 2010, for income tax and capital gains tax purposes for the tax year 2010–11 and subsequent tax years, and for petroleum revenue tax purposes for chargeable periods beginning on or after 1 July 2010. Former para. 21 amended ICTA 1988, s. 833(4)(a).

TOTAL INCOME

22 [Repealed by ITA 2007, s. 1031 and Sch. 3, Pt. 1.]

History – Para. 22 repealed by ITA 2007, s. 1031 and Sch. 3, Pt. 1, with effect from 6 April 2007.

Notes – Para. 22 rewritten as ITA 2007, s. 58(1), Sch. 1, para. 28.

Part II – Other Provisions

THE TRANSITION

25 The operation of section 279(1) of the Taxes Act 1988 for a year of assessment earlier than the year 1990–91 in the case of a married woman shall not affect the question whether there is any income of hers chargeable to income tax for the year 1990–91 or any subsequent year of assessment or, if there is, what is to be taken to be its amount for income tax purposes.

Cross references – ICTA 1988, s. 279(1): aggregation of income of spouses (effective only for years prior to 1990–91).

RETURNS

26–28 [Spent.]

TIME LIMITS FOR ASSESSMENTS

29 [Repealed by FA 1989, s. 187 and Sch. 17, Pt. VIII; but not affecting the making of assessments for years of assessment before 1983–84 or for accounting periods which ended before 1 April 1983.]

TRANSFERS OF ALLOWANCES

30 [Inserts TMA 1970, s. 37A for 1990–91 and subsequent years.]

CLASS 4 SOCIAL SECURITY CONTRIBUTIONS

31 [Substitutes SSA 1975, Sch. 2, para. 3(3) (SSCBA 1992, Sch. 2, para. 3(3)) for 1990–91 and subsequent years.]

ANNUAL PAYMENTS

32 Section 36 of this Act shall have effect in relation to a payment which is due from a husband to his wife or from a wife to her husband at a time after 5th April 1990 when they are living together, notwithstanding that the payment is made in pursuance of an obligation which is an existing obligation for the purposes of subsection (3) of that section.

Cross references – S. 36: annual payments after 15 March 1988 or in pursuance of existing obligations.

MAINTENANCE PAYMENTS

33 [Repealed by FA 1994, s. 258 and Sch. 26, Pt. V(1) in relation to payments becoming due on or after 6 April 1994.]

SCHEDULE 4 – BUSINESS EXPANSION SCHEME: PRIVATE RENTED HOUSING

Section 50

[Sch. 4 repealed by FA 1994, s. 258 and Sch. 26, Pt. V(17) in relation to shares issued after 31 December 1993.]

SCHEDULE 5 – UNDERWRITERS: ASSESSMENT AND COLLECTION OF TAX

Section 58

[Repealed by Statute Law (Repeals) Act 2013, s. 1 and Sch. 1, Pt. 10.]

History – Sch. 5 repealed by Statute Law (Repeals) Act 2013, s. 1 and Sch. 1, Pt. 10, with effect from 31 January 2013.

SCHEDULE 6 – COMMERCIAL WOODLANDS

Section 65

[Omitted by CTA 2009, s. 1322 and Sch. 1, para. 335 and repealed by CTA 2009, s. 1326 and Sch. 3, Pt. 1.]

History – Sch. 6 omitted by CTA 2009, s. 1322 and Sch. 1, para. 335 and repealed by CTA 2009, s. 1326 and Sch. 3, Pt. 1, with effect, for corporation tax purposes, for accounting periods ending on or after 1 April 2009 and, for income tax and capital gains tax purposes, for the tax year 2009–10 and subsequent years.

Notes – Sch. 6 rewritten as follows:
Para. 2(1): CTA 2009, s. 980(1) and (2).
Para. 2(2): Spent.
Para. 2(3): Spent.
Para. 3(2): CTA 2009, s. 37(1), CTA 2009, s. 980(1).
Para. 3(7): Spent.

SCHEDULE 7 – EXCEPTIONS TO RULE IN SECTION 66(1)

Section 66

[Omitted by CTA 2009, s. 1322 and Sch. 1, para. 336 and repealed by CTA 2009, s. 1326 and Sch. 3, Pt. 1.]

History – Sch. 7 omitted by CTA 2009, s. 1322 and Sch. 1, para. 336 and repealed by CTA 2009, s. 1326 and Sch. 3, Pt. 1, with effect, for corporation tax purposes, for accounting periods ending on or after 1 April 2009 and, for income tax and capital gains tax purposes, for the tax year 2009–10 and subsequent years.

Notes – Sch. 7 rewritten as follows:
Para. 1(1): CTA 2009, Sch. 2, para. 13(1).
Para. 1(2): CTA 2009, Sch. 2, para. 13(2).
Para. 1(3): CTA 2009, Sch. 2, para. 13(2).
Para. 2(1): CTA 2009, Sch. 2, para. 14(1)
Para. 2(2): CTA 2009, Sch. 2, para. 14(2).
Para. 2(3): CTA 2009, Sch. 2, para. 14(2).
Para. 3(1): Spent.
Para. 3(2): Spent.
Para. 4(1): Spent.
Para. 4(2): Spent.
Para. 5(1): CTA 2009, Sch. 2, para. 15(1).
Para. 5(2): CTA 2009, Sch. 2, para. 15(2).
Para. 5(3): Unnecessary.

SCHEDULE 12 – BUILDING SOCIETIES: CHANGE OF STATUS

Section 145

INTRODUCTORY

1 Paragraphs 3 to 7 below apply where there is a transfer of the whole of a building society's business to a company (**"the successor company"**) in accordance with section 97 and the other applicable provisions of the Building Societies Act 1986.

History – In para. 1 "3" substituted for "2" by FA 2002, s. 105(2)(a) with effect from 24 July 2002.

GILT-EDGED SECURITIES AND OTHER FINANCIAL TRADING STOCK

2 [Repealed by FA 2002, s. 105(2)(b), s. 141 and Sch. 40, Pt. 3(17).]

History – Para. 2 repealed by FA 2002, s. 105(2)(b), s. 141 and Sch. 40, Pt. 3(17) with effect from 24 July 2002.

CAPITAL ALLOWANCES

3(1) [Omitted by CTA 2009, s. 1322 and Sch. 1, para. 337(a) and repealed by CTA 2009, s. 1326 and Sch. 3, Pt. 1.]

3(2) There shall be made to or on the successor company in accordance with the Capital Allowances Act 2001 all such allowances and charges as would, if the society had continued to carry on the trade, have fallen to be made to or on it, and the amount of any such allowance or charge shall be computed as if the successor company had been carrying on the trade since the society began to do so and as if everything done to or by the society had been done to or by the successor company.

3(3) No transfer of assets from the society to the successor company effected by section 97 of the Building Societies Act 1986 shall be treated as giving rise to any such allowance or charge.

History – Para. 3(1) omitted by CTA 2009, s. 1322 and Sch. 1, para. 337(a) and repealed by CTA 2009, s. 1326 and Sch. 3, Pt. 1, with effect, for corporation tax purposes, for accounting periods ending on or after 1 April 2009 and, for income tax and capital gains tax purposes, for the tax year 2009–10 and subsequent years.

In para. 3(2) the words "the Capital Allowances Act 2001" substituted for the words "those Acts" by CTA 2009, s. 1322 and Sch. 1, para. 337(b) and repealed by CTA 2009, s. 1326 and Sch. 3, Pt. 1, with effect, for corporation tax purposes, for accounting periods ending on or after 1 April 2009 and, for income tax and capital gains tax purposes, for the tax year 2009–10 and subsequent years.

DISTRIBUTIONS

6(1) Where, in connection with the transfer, qualifying benefits are conferred by the society or the successor company on members of the society, the conferring of those benefits shall not be regarded as–

(a) the making of a distribution, within the meaning of the Corporation Tax Acts;

(b) [omitted by FA 2016, s. 39 and Sch. 6, para. 19(b);]

6(2) Sub-paragraph (1) above does not preclude any qualifying benefit (and, in particular, any qualifying benefit which in the hands of the recipient would, apart from that sub-paragraph, constitute income for the purposes of income tax) from being a capital distribution for the purposes of section 122 of the Taxation of Chargeable Gains Act 1992, and in that section **"distribution"** shall be construed accordingly.

6(3) In this paragraph **"qualifying benefits"** means–

(a) any such rights as are mentioned in paragraph 5(1)(a), (b) or (c) above, and any property obtained by the exercise of those rights;

(b) any shares issued or disposed of as mentioned in paragraph 5(2) above;

(c) any shares issued or disposed of, or to which a member becomes entitled, as mentioned in paragraph 5(3) or (4) above, and any interest in the settled property constituted by those shares;

(d) any payment in lieu of a qualifying benefit falling within paragraphs (a) to (c) above;

(e) any distribution made in pursuance of section 100(2)(b) of the Building Societies Act 1986.

6(4) **"Member"** has the same meaning in this paragraph as in paragraph 5 above.

History – Para. 6(1)(b) omitted (with the word "or" preceding it and the word "either" preceding para. 6(1)(a)) by FA 2016, s. 39 and Sch. 6, para. 19, with effect in relation to benefits conferred on or after 6 April 2016. Former para. 6(1)(b) read as follows:

"(b) the payment or crediting of a dividend for the purposes of Chapter 2 of Part 15 of the Income Tax Act 2007 (deduction of income tax at source: deposit-takers and building societies).".

In former para. 6(1)(b) the words "Chapter 2 of Part 15 of the Income Tax Act 2007 (deduction of income tax at source: deposit-takers and building societies)" substituted for the words "section 477A of the Taxes Act 1988 or any regulations under that section (building society interest etc.)" by ITA 2007, s. 1027 and Sch. 1, para. 277, with effect from 6 April 2007.

In former para. 6(1)(b) reference to ICTA 1988, s. 477A substituted by FA 1991, s. 79, applicable where qualifying benefits (see para. 6(3)) are conferred on or after 6 April 1991.

Reference to TCGA 1992 in para. 6(2) substituted by TCGA 1992, s. 290 and Sch. 10, para. 16(7).

Cross references – TCGA 1992, s. 122 distribution which is not a new holding on reorganisation, conversion etc.

Notes – ICTA 1988, s. 209: principal meaning of "distribution".

SI 1990/2231: regulations under ICTA 1988, s. 477A (see para. 6(1)(b)).

CERTIFIED SAYE SAVINGS ARRANGEMENTS

7 Section 702 of the Income Tax (Trading and Other Income) Act 2005 (interest under certified SAYE savings arrangements to be exempt from income tax) shall have effect in relation to any interest (or bonus) payable after the transfer under a savings arrangement which immediately before the transfer was a certified SAYE savings arrangement (within the meaning of section 703(1) of that Act) in relation to the society despite the fact that it ceased to be such an arrangement by reason of the transfer.

History – The whole of para. 7 (including the heading) substituted by ITTOIA 2005, s. 882(1) and Sch. 1, para. 404; effective for income tax purposes for 2005–06 onwards and for corporation tax purposes for accounting periods ending after 5 April 2005 (ITTOIA 2005, s. 883(1)).

STAMP DUTY

8 [Not reproduced here.]

SCHEDULE 13 – POST-CONSOLIDATION AMENDMENTS

Section 146

[Retrospective amendments of ICTA 1988, CGTA 1979, FA 1980, FA 1981, FA 1984, FA 1986 and FA 1987. In so far as they remain relevant these are consolidated in the relevant enactments and are not reproduced here.]

HOUSING ACT 1988

(1988 Chapter 50) [*15th November 1988*]

PART II – HOUSING ASSOCIATIONS

GRANTS: FUNCTIONS OF SECRETARY OF STATE

54 Tax relief grants

54(1) If a housing association makes a claim to the Secretary of State in respect of a period and satisfies him that throughout the period it was a housing association to which this section applies and its functions either–

(a) consisted exclusively of the function of providing or maintaining housing accommodation for letting or hostels and activities incidental to that function, or

(b) included that function and activities incidental to that function,

the Secretary of State may make grants to the association for affording relief from tax chargeable on the association.

54(2) This section applies to a housing association at any time if, at that time–

(a) it is a relevant housing association;

(b) it does not trade for profit; and

(c) it is not approved for the purposes of Chapter 7 of Part 13 of the Corporation Tax Act 2010 (tax treatment of co-operative housing associations).

54(3) References in this section to tax chargeable on an association are to income tax (other than income tax which the association is entitled to deduct on making any payment) and corporation tax.

54(4) A grant under this section may be made–

(a) in a case falling within subsection (1)(a) above, for affording relief from any tax chargeable on the association for the period in respect of which the claim is made; and

(b) in a case falling within subsection (1)(b) above, for affording relief from such part of any tax so chargeable as the Secretary of State considers appropriate having regard to the other functions of the association;

and in any case shall be of such amount, shall be made at such times and shall be subject to such conditions as the Secretary of State thinks fit.

54(5) The conditions may include conditions for securing the repayment in whole or in part of a grant made to an association–

(a) in the event of tax in respect of which it was made being found not to be chargeable; or

(b) in such other events (including the association beginning to trade for profit) as the Secretary of State may determine.

54(6) A claim under this section shall be made in such manner and shall be supported by such evidence as the Secretary of State may direct.

54(7) The Commissioners of Inland Revenue and their officers may disclose to the Secretary of State such particulars as he may reasonably require for determining whether a grant should be made on a claim or whether a grant should be repaid or the amount of such grant or repayment.

54(8) In this section "letting" includes–

(a) in England and Wales, the grant of a shared ownership lease or a licence to occupy;

(b) in Scotland, disposal under a shared ownership agreement or the grant of a right or permission to occupy.

Prospective amendments – S. 54 is repealed by the Housing (Scotland) Act 2001, s. 112, 113 and Sch. 10, para. 15(5) with effect from such date as Scottish Ministers appoint.

History – In s. 54(2)(a), the words "a relevant housing association" substituted for the words "a registered social landlord" by the Housing and Regeneration Act 2008, s. 56 and Sch. 8, para. 49, with effect from 1 April 2010 (SI 2010/862).

In s. 54(2)(a), the words "a registered social landlord" substituted for the word "registered" by SI 1996/2325, art. 5 and Sch. 2, para. 18(7), with effect from 1 October 1996.

In s. 54(2)(c), the words "Chapter 7 of Part 13 of the Corporation Tax Act 2010" substituted for the words "section 488 of the Income and Corporation Taxes Act 1988" by CTA 2010, s. 1177 and Sch. 1, para. 211, with effect for corporation tax purposes for accounting periods ending on or after 1 April 2010, and for income tax and capital gains tax purposes for the tax year 2010–11 and subsequent tax years.

Notes – S. 54 has effect from 1 April 1989 by virtue of SI 1989/404.

FINANCE ACT 1989

(1989 Chapter 26)

[*27th July 1989*]

ARRANGEMENT OF SECTIONS

PART II – INCOME TAX, CORPORATION TAX AND CAPITAL GAINS TAX

CHAPTER I – GENERAL

INCOME TAX RATES AND ALLOWANCES

RECEIPTS BASIS ETC.

INTEREST

BENEFITS IN KIND

MEDICAL INSURANCE

CHARITIES

PROFIT-RELATED PAY, SHARE SCHEMES ETC.

EMPLOYEE SHARE OWNERSHIP TRUSTS

PART II – INCOME TAX, CORPORATION TAX AND CAPITAL GAINS TAX

Chapter I – General

INCOME TAX RATES AND ALLOWANCES

33 Married couples

33(1) Sections 257 to 257F and 265 of the Taxes Act 1988, as inserted for the year 1990–91 and subsequent years by the Finance Act 1988, shall be amended as follows.

33(2) [Spent.]

33(3) [Spent.]

(a) [Omitted by FA 2009, s. 5 and Sch. 1, para. 6(c).]

(b) [Spent.]

(a) [Spent.]

(b) [Omitted by FA 2009, s. 5 and Sch. 1, para. 6(c).]

33(6), (7) [Spent.]

(a) [Omitted by FA 2009, s. 5 and Sch. 1, para. 6(c).]

(b) [Spent.]

(a) [Spent.]

(b) [Omitted by FA 2009, s. 5 and Sch. 1, para. 6(c).]

33(10) [Inserts ICTA 1988, s. 257D(8)(c), and 265(3)(c); partially repealed by F(No. 2)A 1992, s. 82 and Sch. 18, Pt. VII(1), and FA 1999, s. 139 and Sch. 20, Pt. III(3).]

33(11)–(13) [Amends ICTA 1988, s. 257E(1)(b), (2)(a), (b), and FA 1999, s. 139 and Sch. 20, Pt. III(3).]

History – S. 33(4)(a), (5)(b), (8)(a) and (9)(b) omitted by FA 2009, s. 5 and Sch. 1, para. 6(c), with effect for the tax year 2010–11 and subsequent tax years.

S. 33(6), (10) (partially) and (11)–(13) repealed by FA 1999, s. 139 and Sch. 20, Pt. III(3), with effect for the year 2000–01 and subsequent years of assessment.

S. 33(10) inserted ICTA 1988, s. 257B(2)(c); reference to ICTA 1988, s. 257B(2) repealed by F(No. 2)A 1992, s 82 and Sch. 18, Pt. VII(1) in relation to tax for 1993–94 and subsequent years of assessment.

RECEIPTS BASIS ETC.

36 Schedule E: revised Cases

36 [Repealed by ITEPA 2003, Sch. 8, Pt. 1.]

History – S. 36 repealed by ITEPA 2003, Sch. 8, Pt. 1 which has effect for the tax year 2003–04 and subsequent tax years.

37 Schedule E: assessment on receipts basis

37 [Repealed by ITEPA 2003, Sch. 8, Pt. 1 with effect for 2003–04 and subsequent tax years.]

38 Schedule E: unpaid emoluments

38 [Repealed by ITEPA 2003, Sch. 8, Pt. 1 with effect for 2003–04 and subsequent tax years.]

39 Schedule E: unremitted emoluments

39 [Repealed by ITEPA 2003, Sch. 8, Pt. 1 with effect for 2003–04 and subsequent tax years.]

Notes – S. 39 has been rewritten into the provision of ITEPA 2003, Sch. 7, para. 8(3) (Sch. 7: transitionals and savings) which has effect for the tax year 2003–04 and subsequent tax years.

40 Schedule E: emoluments already paid

40 [Repealed by ITEPA 2003, Sch. 8, Pt. 1 with effect for 2003–04 and subsequent tax years.]

41 Schedule E: pensions etc.

41 [Repealed by ITEPA 2003, Sch. 8, Pt. 1 with effect for 2003–04 and subsequent tax years.]

Notes – S. 41 rewritten as follows:
S. 41(1): ITEPA 2003, s. 571, s. 578, s. 581, s. 616, s. 634(2) and s. 661.
S. 41(2): ITEPA 2003, s. 571, s. 578, s. 581, s. 616, s. 634(2) and s. 661.

42 Schedule E: supplementary

42 [Repealed by ITEPA 2003, Sch. 8, Pt. 1 with effect for 2003–04 and subsequent tax years.]

43 Schedule D: computation

43 [Omitted by CTA 2009, s. 1322 and Sch. 1, para. 339 and repealed by CTA 2009, s. 1326 and Sch. 3, Pt. 1.]

History – S. 43 omitted by CTA 2009, s. 1322 and Sch. 1, para. 339 and repealed by CTA 2009, s. 1326 and Sch. 3, Pt. 1, with effect, for corporation tax purposes, for accounting periods ending on or after 1 April 2009 and, for income tax and capital gains tax purposes, for the tax year 2009–10 and subsequent years.

Notes – The income tax rules formerly within s. 43 are principally rewritten at ITTOIA 2005, s. 36, s. 37 and s. 865.
S. 43 rewritten for corporation tax purposes as follows:
S. 43(1): CTA 2009, s. 1288(1) and (3).
S. 43(2): CTA 2009, s. 1289(1).
S. 43(3): CTA 2009, s. 1289(2).
S. 43(4): CTA 2009, s. 1289(2).
S. 43(5): CTA 2009, s. 1289(3).
S. 43(6): CTA 2009, s. 1289(4).
S. 43(7): CTA 2009, s. 1289(5).

44 Companies with investment business and insurance companies: computation

44 [Omitted by CTA 2009, s. 1322 and Sch. 1, para. 340 and repealed by CTA 2009, s. 1326 and Sch. 3, Pt. 1.]

History – S. 44 omitted by CTA 2009, s. 1322 and Sch. 1, para. 340 and repealed by CTA 2009, s. 1326 and Sch. 3, Pt. 1, with effect, for corporation tax purposes, for accounting periods ending on or after 1 April 2009 and, for income tax and capital gains tax purposes, for the tax year 2009–10 and subsequent years.

Notes – The income tax rules formerly within s. 43 are principally rewritten at ITTOIA 2005, s. 36, s. 37 and s. 865.
S. 44 rewritten for corporation tax purposes as follows:
S. 44(1): CTA 2009, s. 1249(1) and (3).
S. 44(2): CTA 2009, s. 1250(1).
S. 44(3): CTA 2009, s. 1250(2).
S. 44(4): CTA 2009, s. 1249(2).
S. 44(5): CTA 2009, s. 1250(3).
S. 44(6): CTA 2009, s. 1250(4).
S. 44(7): CTA 2009, Sch. 1, para. 42.
S. 44(8): CTA 2009, s. 1250(5).

45 PAYE: meaning of payment

45 [Repealed by ITEPA 2003, Sch. 8, Pt. 1 with effect for 2003–04 and subsequent tax years.]

INTEREST

47 Close company loans: business expansion scheme

47 [Repealed by ITA 2007, s. 1031 and Sch. 3, Pt. 1.]

History – S. 47 repealed by ITA 2007, s. 1031 and Sch. 3, Pt. 1, with effect from 6 April 2007.

Notes – S. 47 rewritten as ITA 2007, s. 392(3).

48 Close company loans: material interest

48 [Repealed by ITA 2007, s. 1031 and Sch. 3, Pt. 1.]

History – S. 48 repealed by ITA 2007, s. 1031 and Sch. 3, Pt. 1, with effect from 6 April 2007.

Notes – S. 48 rewritten as follows:
S. 48(1): ITA 2007, s. 392(4).
S. 48(2): ITA 2007, s. 394(1), (2), (3), (4), (5), 395(1), (2), (3), (4), (5), (6), Sch. 2, para. 93(1), (2), (3), (4), (5).

BENEFITS IN KIND

50 Security assets and services

50 [Repealed by ITEPA 2003, Sch. 8, Pt. 1 with effect for 2003–04 and subsequent tax years.]

Notes – S. 50 rewritten as follows:
S. 50(1): ITEPA 2003, s. 377(1).
S. 50(2): ITEPA 2003, s. 328(1), s. 329(1), s. 369(1), s. 377(1), (2) and (6).
S. 50(3): ITEPA 2003, s. 328(1), s. 329(1), s. 369(1), s. 377(1), (2) and (6).
S. 50(4): ITEPA 2003, s. 377(1).
S. 50(5): ITEPA 2003, s. 377(1).
S. 50(6): ITEPA 2003, s. 377(6).
S. 50(7): ITEPA 2003, s. 377(2).

51 Assets used partly for security

51 [Repealed by ITEPA 2003, Sch. 8, Pt. 1 with effect for 2003–04 and subsequent tax years.]

Notes – S. 51(1), (2), (3) and (4) have been rewritten into the provision of ITEPA 2003, s. 377(4).

52 Security: supplementary

52 [Repealed by ITEPA 2003, Sch. 8, Pt. 1 with effect for 2003–04 and subsequent tax years.]

Notes – S. 52 rewritten as follows:
S. 52(1): ITEPA 2003, s. 377(3).
S. 52(2): ITEPA 2003, s. 377(7).
S. 52(3): ITEPA 2003, s. 377(8).
S. 52(4): ITEPA 2003, s. 377(5).
S. 52(5): ITEPA 2003, s. 377(5).

53 Employees earning £8,500 or more and directors

53(1) [Repealed by ITEPA 2003, Sch. 8, Pt. 1.]

53(2) [Repealed, except subsection (2)(f) so far as relating to ICTA 1988, s. 418(3), by ITEPA 2003, Sch. 8, Pt. 1.]

(f) [Amends ICTA 1988, s. 332(2)(c), 418(3)(a).]

(g) [Amends TMA 1970, s. 15(3)(a).]

History – S. 53(1) repealed by ITEPA 2003, Sch. 8, Pt. 1 which has effect for the tax year 2003–04 and subsequent tax years.
S. 53(2), except subsection (2)(f) so far as relating to ICTA 1988, s. 418(3), has been repealed by ITEPA 2003, Sch. 8, Pt. 1 which has effect for the tax year 2003–04 and subsequent tax years.
In s. 53(2)(f) (amendments consequential on the substitution of a new ICTA 1988, s. 167), the words "section 418(3)(a)" were substituted for the words "sections 332(2)(c) and 418(3)(a)" by ITEPA 2003, Sch. 6, para. 159 which has effect, for income tax purposes, for the tax year 2003–04 and subsequent tax years and, for corporation tax purposes, for accounting periods ending after 5 April 2003.

MEDICAL INSURANCE

54 Relief

54 [Repealed by F(No. 2)A 1997, s. 52 and Sch. 8, Pt. II(2).]

History – S. 54 repealed by F(No. 2)A 1997, s. 52 and Sch. 8, Pt. II(2), with effect for the year 1997–98 and subsequent years of assessment except in relation to the cases in which relief that has been or may be given under s. 54 in respect of any payment, is unaffected by the provisions of F(No. 2)A 1997, s. 17(1).

Cross references – F(No. 2)A 1997, s. 17: withdrawal of relief on medical insurance premiums paid on or after 5 April 1997; saving for certain premiums paid before 6 April 1999.

55 Eligible contracts

55 [Repealed by F(No. 2)A 1997, s. 52 and Sch. 8, Pt. II(2).]

History – S. 55 repealed by F(No. 2)A 1997, s. 52 and Sch. 8, Pt. II(2), with effect for the year 1997–98 and subsequent years of assessment except in relation to the cases in which relief that has been or may be given under FA 1989, s. 54 in respect of any payment, is unaffected by the provisions of F(No. 2)A 1997, s. 17(1) (see Cross reference note to s. 54).

56 Certification of contracts

56 [Repealed by F(No. 2)A 1997, s. 52 and Sch. 8, Pt. II(2).]

History – S. 56 repealed by F(No. 2)A 1997, s. 52 and Sch. 8, Pt. II(2), with effect for the year 1997–98 and subsequent years of assessment except in relation to the cases in which relief that has been or may be given under FA 1989, s. 54 in respect of any payment, is unaffected by the provisions of F(No. 2)A 1997, s. 17(1) (see Cross reference note to s. 54).

57 Medical insurance: supplementary

57 [Repealed by F(No. 2)A 1997, s. 52 and Sch. 8, Pt. II(2).]

History – S. 57(2) repealed by SI 2009/2035, art. 2 and Schedule, para. 60(c), with effect from 13 August 2009, despite the whole of s. 57 having been previously repealed (see below).
S. 57 repealed by F(No. 2)A 1997, s. 52 and Sch. 8, Pt. II(2), with effect for the year 1997–98 and subsequent years of assessment except in relation to the cases in which relief that has been or may be given under FA 1989, s. 54 in respect of any payment, is unaffected by the provisions of F(No. 2)A 1997, s. 17(1) (see Cross reference note to s. 54).

CHARITIES

58 Payroll deduction scheme

58(1) [Amends ICTA 1988, s. 202(7).]

58(2) This section shall have effect for the year 1989–90 and subsequent years of assessment.

59 Covenanted subscriptions

59 [Repealed by FA 2000, s. 41(7) and Sch. 40, Pt. II(1).]

History – S. 59 repealed by FA 2000, s. 41(7) and Sch. 40, Pt. II(1) in relation to covenanted payments falling to be made by individuals on or after 6 April 2000; or made by companies on or after 1 April 2000.

60 British Museum and Natural History Museum

60(1) [Repealed by CTA 2010, s. 1181 and Sch. 3. Pt. 1.]

60(2) [Repealed by CTA 2010, s. 1181 and Sch. 3. Pt. 1.]

60(3) [Repealed by FA 1995, s. 74 and Sch. 17, para. 25 and s. 162 and Sch. 2, Pt. VIII(8).]

60(4) [Repealed by CTA 2010, s. 1181 and Sch. 3. Pt. 1.]

History – S. 60(1) repealed by CTA 2010, s. 1181 and Sch. 3. Pt. 1, with effect for corporation tax purposes for accounting periods ending on or after 1 April 2010, and for income tax and capital gains tax purposes for the tax year 2010–11 and subsequent tax years.
S. 60(2) repealed by CTA 2010, s. 1181 and Sch. 3. Pt. 1, with effect for corporation tax purposes for accounting periods ending on or after 1 April 2010, and for income tax and capital gains tax purposes for the tax year 2010–11 and subsequent tax years.
S. 60(3) repealed by FA 1995, s. 74 and Sch. 17, para. 25 and s. 162 and Sch. 29, Pt. VIII(8) with effect for 1995–96 and subsequent years of assessment.
S. 60(4) repealed by CTA 2010, s. 1181 and Sch. 3. Pt. 1, with effect for corporation tax purposes for accounting periods ending on or after 1 April 2010, and for income tax and capital gains tax purposes for the tax year 2010–11 and subsequent tax years.
In s. 60(4) "subsection (2)" substituted by FA 1995, s. 74 and Sch. 17, para. 25 with effect for 1995–96 and subsequent years of assessment.

PROFIT-RELATED PAY, SHARE SCHEMES ETC.

61 Profit-related pay

61 [Repealed by FA 1997, s. 113 and Sch. 18, Pt. VI(3).]

History – S. 61 repealed by FA 1997, s. 113 and Sch. 18, Pt. VI(3) in relation to any payment made by reference to a profit period beginning on or after 1 January 2000.

62 Savings-related share option schemes

62 [Repealed by ITEPA 2003, Sch. 8, Pt. 1.]

History – S. 62 repealed by ITEPA 2003, Sch. 8, Pt. 1 which has effect for the tax year 2003–04 and subsequent tax years.

64 Share option and profit sharing schemes: shares of consortium member

64 [Repealed by ITEPA 2003, Sch. 8, Pt. 1.]

History – S. 64 repealed by ITEPA 2003, Sch. 8, Pt. 1 which has effect for the tax year 2003–04 and subsequent tax years.

65 Employee share schemes: material interest

65 [Inserts ICTA 1988, Sch. 9, para. 40(1)–(4).]

66 Priority share allocations for employees etc.

66 [Repealed by ITEPA 2003, Sch. 8, Pt. 1]

History – S. 66 repealed by ITEPA 2003, Sch. 8, Pt. 1 which has effect for the tax year 2003–04 and subsequent tax years.

EMPLOYEE SHARE OWNERSHIP TRUSTS

Notes – S. 67 does not apply in relation to sums expended by a company in an accounting period beginning on or after 1 January 2003. See cross reference note below for authority.

67 Tax relief

67(1) This section applies where–

(a) a company expends a sum in making a payment by way of contribution to the trustees of a trust which is a qualifying employee share ownership trust at the time the sum is expended,

(b) at that time, the company or a company which it then controls has employees who are eligible to benefit under the terms of the trust deed,

(c) at that time the company is resident in the United Kingdom,

(d) before the expiry of the expenditure period the sum is expended by the trustees for one or more of the qualifying purposes, and

(e) before the end of the claim period a claim for relief under this section is made.

67(2) In such a case the sum–

(a) shall be deducted in computing for the purposes of Schedule D the profits of a trade carried on by the company,

(b) if the company is an investment company, shall be treated as expenses of management, or

(c) if the company is a company in relation to which the I – E rules apply and the sum is referable, in accordance with Chapter 4 of Part 2 of the Finance Act 2012, to the company's basic life assurance and general annuity business, shall be treated for the purposes of section 76 of that Act as ordinary BLAGAB management expenses of the company.

67(3) For the purposes of subsection (1)(b) above, the question whether one company is **"controlled"** by another shall be construed in accordance with section 840 of the Taxes Act 1988.

67(4) For the purposes of subsection (1)(d) above each of the following is a **"qualifying purpose"**–

(a) the acquisition of shares in the company which established the trust;

(b) the repayment of sums borrowed;

(c) the payment of interest on sums borrowed;

(d) the payment of any sum to a person who is a beneficiary under the terms of the trust deed;

(e) the meeting of expenses.

67(5) For the purposes of subsection (1)(d) above the **"expenditure period"** is the period of nine months beginning with the day following the end of the period of account in which the sum is charged as an expense of the company, or such longer period as the Board may allow by notice given to the company.

67(6) For the purposes of subsection (1)(e) above the **"claim period"** is the period of two years beginning with the day following the end of the period of account in which the sum is charged as an expense of the company.

67(7) For the purposes of this section the trustees of an employee share ownership trust shall be taken to expend sums paid to them in the order in which the sums are received by them (irrespective of the number of companies making payments).

History – In s. 67(2)(a), the word "profits" substituted for "profits or gains" by FA 1998, s. 46(3) and Sch. 7, para. 3.
S. 67(2)(b) substituted and (c) inserted, by FA 2012, s. 146 and Sch. 16, para. 48, in relation to accounting periods beginning on or after 1 January 2013 (FA 2012, s. 148) but subject to transitional provisions in FA 2012, Sch. 17. Where an accounting period would otherwise straddle 1 January 2013, it is deemed to end on 31 December 2012 (FA 2012, s. 149).

Cross references – ICTA 1988, s. 76: application of s. 75 (relief for expenses of management) to insurance companies.
ICTA 1988, s. 85A: deduction for costs of establishing qualifying ESOT.
TCGA 1992, s. 227–236: roll-over relief for disposal of shares to qualifying ESOT.
FA 2003, s. 142(1)(ending of relief for contributions to employee share trusts): s. 67 does not apply in relation to sums expended by a company in an accounting period of the company beginning on or after 1 January 2003.
FA 2003, Sch. 24, para. 8(f): FA 2003, Sch. 24 (restrictions on deductions for employee benefit contributions) does not apply to any deduction that is allowable under FA 1989, s. 67.

Hansard – 6 June 1989, col. 305: in Standing Committee on the 1989 Finance Bill the Financial Secretary to the Treasury confirmed that payments to non-qualifying ESOTs would potentially still be able to attract a deduction under general Sch. D principles.

Other material – IR press release, 9 May 1990: procedure for obtaining Revenue clearance for a qualifying ESOT.
IR press release, 14 December 1990: extension of clearance procedure to draft trust deeds.
Law Society's Gazette, 4 October 1989 (not reproduced): Revenue consider s. 43 (deduction for emoluments, including those paid through an intermediary) will not generally prevent the deduction of a company contribution to non-statutory trust.

68 Principal charges to tax

68(1) This section applies where a chargeable event (within the meaning of section 69 below) occurs in relation to the trustees of an employee share ownership trust.

68(2) In such a case–

(a) the trustees shall be treated as receiving, when the event occurs, income of an amount that is equal to the chargeable amount (within the meaning of section 70 below),

(b) that income shall be chargeable to income tax for the year of assessment in which the event occurs,

(ba) the tax so chargeable shall be charged on the full amount of the income the trustees are treated as receiving in the year of assessment, and

(bb) the trustees are liable for any tax so chargeable

(c) [Ceases to have effect by virtue of FA 2006, s. 89 and Sch. 13, para. 28(2)(a) and repealed by FA 2006, s. 178 and Sch. 26, Pt. 3(15).]

68(3) If the whole or any part of the tax assessed on the trustees is not paid before the expiry of the period of six months beginning with the day on which the assessment becomes final and conclusive, a notice of liability to tax under this subsection may be served on a qualifying company and the tax or the part unpaid (as the case may be) shall be payable by the company on service of the notice.

68(4) Where a notice of liability is served under subsection (3) above–

(a) any interest which is due on the tax or the part (as the case may be) and has not been paid by the trustees, and

(b) any interest accruing due on the tax or the part (as the case may be) after the date of service,

shall be payable by the company.

68(5) Where a notice of liability is served under subsection (3) above and any amount payable by the company (whether on account of tax or interest) is not paid by the company before the expiry of the period of three months beginning with the date of service, the amount unpaid may be recovered from the trustees (without prejudice to the right to recover it instead from the company).

68(6) For the purposes of this section each of the following is a **"qualifying company"**–

(a) the company which established the employee share ownership trust;

(b) any company falling within subsection (7) below.

68(7) A company falls within this subsection if, before it is sought to serve a notice of liability on it under subsection (3) above–

(a) it has paid a sum to the trustees, and

(b) the sum has been deducted as mentioned in section 67(2)(a) above or treated as mentioned in section 67(2)(b) above.

History – In s. 68(2), the word "and" inserted at the end of para. (ba) by FA 2006, s. 89 and Sch. 13, para. 28(3) with effect from 6 April 2006. FA 2006 inserted an additional comma before the word "and" at the end of para. (ba). This has not been reproduced.
In s. 68(2), the word "and" at the end of para. (bb) omitted by FA 2006, s. 89 and Sch. 13, para. 28(3) and repealed by FA 2006, s. 178 and Sch. 26, Pt. 3(15) with effect from 6 April 2006.
S. 68(2)(c) ceases to have effect by virtue of FA 2006, s. 89 and Sch. 13, para. 28(2)(a) and repealed by FA 2006, s. 178 and Sch. 26, Pt. 3(15) in relation to payments made on or after 6 April 2006.

In s. 68(2), the words "income of an amount that" substituted for the former wording ("annual profits or gains whose amount") by ITTOIA 2005, s. 882(1) and Sch. 1, para. 407(a); effective for income tax purposes for 2005–06 onwards (ITTOIA 2005, s. 883(1)).
In s. 68(2), para. (b), (ba) and (bb) substituted for the former para. (b) by ITTOIA 2005, s. 882(1) and Sch. 1, para. 407(b); effective for income tax purposes for 2005–06 onwards (ITTOIA 2005, s. 883(1)).
In s. 68(2)(c), the words "the rate applicable to trusts" substituted by FA 1993, s. 79 and Sch. 6, para. 20 in relation to 1993–94 and subsequent years of assessment.

Cross references – ICTA 1988, s. 686A(2)(h): where trustees receive a payment of the kind mentioned in s. 68(2) it is treated as if it were income to which ICTA 1988, s. 686 applies.

Other material – ICAEW Technical Release TR 759 (not reproduced): Revenue state sum regarded as deducted for s. 68(7)(b) when claim for relief determined.

69 Chargeable events

69(1) For the purposes of section 68 above each of the following is a **"chargeable event"** in relation to the trustees of an employee share ownership trust–

(a) the transfer of securities by the trustees, if the transfer is not a qualifying transfer;

(b) the transfer of securities by the trustees to persons who are at the time of the transfer beneficiaries under the terms of the trust deed, if the terms on which the transfer is made are not qualifying terms;

(c) the retention of securities by the trustees at the expiry of the qualifying period beginning with the date on which they acquired them;

(d) the expenditure of a sum by the trustees for a purpose other than a qualifying purpose.

(e) where–

(i) the trustees make a qualifying transfer within subsection (3AA) below for a consideration, and

(ii) they do not, during the period specified in subsection (5A) below, expend a sum of not less than the amount of that consideration for one or more qualifying purposes,

the expiry of that period.

69(2) For the purposes of subsection (1)(a) above a transfer is a **"qualifying transfer"** if it is made to a person who at the time of the transfer is a beneficiary under the terms of the trust deed.

69(3) For the purposes of subsection (1)(a) above a transfer is also a **"qualifying transfer"** if–

(a) it is made to the trustees of a scheme which at the time of the transfer is a profit sharing scheme approved under Schedule 9 to the Taxes Act 1988, and

(b) it is made for a consideration which is not less than the price the securities might reasonably be expected to fetch on a sale in the open market.

69(3AA) For the purposes of subsection (1)(a) above a transfer is also a qualifying transfer if–

(a) it is a transfer of relevant shares made to the trustees of the plan trust of a share incentive plan,

(b) the plan is approved under Schedule 2 to the Income Tax (Earnings and Pensions) Act 2003 when the transfer is made, and

(c) the consideration (if any) for which the transfer is made does not exceed the market value of the shares.

69(3AB) For the purpose of determining whether a transfer by the trustees is a qualifying transfer within subsection (3AA) above, where on or after 21st March 2000–

(a) the trustees transfer or dispose of part of a holding of shares (whether by way of a qualifying transfer or otherwise), and

(b) the holding includes any relevant shares,

the relevant shares shall be treated as transferred or disposed of before any other shares included in that holding.

For this purpose **"holding"** means any number of shares of the same class held by the trustees, growing or diminishing as shares of that class are acquired or disposed of.

69(3AC) For the purposes of subsections (3AA) and (3AB) above–

"market value" has the same meaning as it has for the purposes of the SIP code (see paragraph 92 of Schedule 2 to the Income Tax (Earnings and Pensions) Act 2003); and

"relevant shares" means–

(i) *shares that are held* by the trustees of the employee share ownership trust at midnight on 20th March 2000, and

(ii) shares purchased by those trustees with original funds after that time.

69(3AD) For the purposes of subsection (3AC) above–

(a) **"original funds"** means any money held by the trustees of the employee share ownership trust in a bank or building society account at midnight on 20th March 2000, and;

(b) any payment made by the trustees after that time (whether to acquire shares or otherwise) shall be treated as made out of original funds (and not out of money received after that time) until those funds are exhausted.

69(3A) For the purposes of subsection (1)(a) above a transfer is also a qualifying transfer if it is made by way of exchange in circumstances mentioned in section 85(1) of the Capital Gains Tax Act 1979 or section 135(1) of the Taxation of Chargeable Gains Act 1992.

69(4) For the purposes of subsection (1)(b) above a transfer of securities is made on **"qualifying terms"** if–

(a) all the securities transferred at the same time other than those transferred on a transfer such as is mentioned in subsection (4ZA) below are transferred on similar terms,

(b) securities have been offered to all the persons who are beneficiaries under the terms of the trust deed by virtue of a rule which conforms with paragraph 4(2), (3) or (4) of Schedule 5 to this Act when the transfer is made, and

(c) securities are transferred to all such persons who have accepted.

69(4ZA) For the purposes of subsection (1)(b) above a transfer of securities is also made on qualifying terms if–

(a) it is made to a person exercising a right to acquire shares, and

(b) that right was obtained in accordance with the provisions of an SAYE option scheme within the meaning of the SAYE code (see section 516(4) of the Income Tax (Earnings and Pensions) Act 2003)–

(i) which was established by, or by a company controlled by, the company which established the trust, and

(ii) which is approved under Schedule 3 to that Act, and

(c) that right is being exercised in accordance with the provisions of that scheme, and

(d) the consideration for the transfer is payable to the trustees.

69(4A) For the purposes of subsection (1)(c) above the **"qualifying period"** is–

(a) seven years, in the case of trusts established on or before the day on which the Finance Act 1994 was passed;

(b) twenty years, in the case of other trusts;

and for this purpose a trust is established when the deed under which it is established is executed.

69(5) For the purposes of subsection (1)(d) or (e) above each of the following is a **"qualifying purpose"**–

(a) the acquisition of shares in the company which established the trust;

(b) the repayment of sums borrowed;

(c) the payment of interest on sums borrowed;

(d) the payment of any sum to a person who is a beneficiary under the terms of the trust deed;

(e) the meeting of expenses.

69(5A) The period referred to in paragraph (e) of subsection (1) above is the period–

(a) beginning with the qualifying transfer mentioned in that paragraph, and

(b) ending nine months after the end of the period of account in which that qualifying transfer took place.

For this purpose the **"period of account"** means the period of account of the company that established the employee share ownership trust.

69(6) For the purposes of subsection (4) above, the fact that terms vary according to the levels of remuneration of beneficiaries, the length of their service, or similar factors, shall not be regarded as meaning that the terms are not similar.

69(7) In ascertaining for the purposes of this section whether particular securities are retained, securities acquired earlier by the trustees shall be treated as transferred by them before securities acquired by them later.

69(8) For the purposes of this section trustees–

(a) acquire securities when they become entitled to them (subject to the exceptions in subsection (9) below);

(b) transfer securities to another person when that other becomes entitled to them;

(c) retain securities if they remain entitled to them.

69(9) The exceptions are these–

(a) if securities are issued to trustees in exchange in circumstances mentioned in section 135(1) of the Taxation of Chargeable Gains Act 1992, they shall be treated as having acquired them when they became entitled to the securities for which they are exchanged;

(b) if trustees become entitled to securities as a result of a reorganisation, they shall be treated as having acquired them when they became entitled to the original shares which those securities represent (construing **"reorganisation"** and **"original shares"** in accordance with section 126 of that Act).

69(10) If trustees agree to take a transfer of securities, for the purposes of this section they shall be treated as becoming entitled to them when the agreement is made and not on a later transfer made pursuant to the agreement.

69(11) If trustees agree to transfer securities to another person, for the purposes of this section the other person shall be treated as becoming entitled to them when the agreement is made and not on a later transfer made pursuant to the agreement.

69(12) For the purposes of this section the following are **"securities"**–

(a) shares;

(b) debentures.

History – S. 69(1)(e) inserted by FA 2000, s. 55(2) with effect from 21 March 2000.
In s. 69(1)(c), the words "qualifying period" substituted by FA 1994, s. 102 and Sch. 13, para. 1, 6(1), (2), with effect from 3 May 1994.
In s. 69(3AA)(a), the words "a share incentive" substituted for the words "an employee share ownership" by ITEPA 2003, Sch. 6, para. 160(2)(a) which has effect for the tax year 2003–04 and subsequent tax years.
In s. 69(3AA)(b), the words "Schedule 2 to the Income Tax (Earnings and Pensions) Act 2003" substituted for the words "Schedule 8 to the Finance Act 2000" by ITEPA 2003, Sch. 6, para. 160(2)(b) which has effect for the tax year 2003–04 and subsequent tax years.
S. 69(3AA)–(3AD) inserted by FA 2000, s. 55(3) with effect from 21 March 2000.
In s. 69(3AC), in the definition of "market value", the words "it has for the purposes of the SIP code (see paragraph 92 of Schedule 2 to the Income Tax (Earnings and Pensions) Act 2003)" are substituted for the words "in Schedule 8 to the Finance Act 2000", by ITEPA 2003, Sch. 6, para. 160(3) with effect for the tax year 2003–04 and subsequent tax years.
S. 69(3A) (including reference to CGTA 1979, s. 85(1)) inserted by F(No. 2)A 1992, s. 36 in relation to exchanges made on or after 1 January 1992.
In s. 69(4)(a) "other than…below" inserted, in s. 69(4)(b) "by virtue…this Act" inserted, and in s. 69(4)(c) "persons" substituted for "beneficiaries" by FA 1996, s. 120(3), with effect in relation to trusts established on or after 29 April 1996.
S. 69(4ZA) inserted by FA 1996, s. 120(4), with effect in relation to trusts established on or after 29 April 1996.
In s. 69(4ZA)(b), the words "an SAYE option scheme within the meaning of the SAYE code (see section 516(4) of the Income Tax (Earnings and Pensions) Act 2003)" substituted for the words "a savings-related share option scheme within the meaning of Schedule 9 to the Taxes Act 1988", by ITEPA 2003, Sch. 6, para. 160(4)(a) which has effect for the tax year 2003–04 and subsequent tax years.
In s. 69(4ZA)(b)(ii), the words "Schedule 3 to that Act" substituted for the words "that Schedule" by ITEPA 2003, Sch. 6, para. 160(4)(b) which has effect for the tax year 2003–04 and subsequent tax years.
S. 69(4A) inserted by FA 1994, s. 102 and Sch. 13, para. 1, 6(1), (3), with effect from 3 May 1994.
In s. 69(5) words "or (e)" inserted by FA 2000, s. 55(4) with effect from 21 March 2000.
S. 69(5A) inserted by FA 2000, s. 55(5) with effect from 21 March 2000.
References to TCGA 1992 in s. 69(9) substituted by TCGA 1992, s. 290 and Sch. 10, para. 19(1).

Cross references – ITEPA 2003, Sch. 2, para. 78(2): acquisition by trustees of shares from employee share ownership trust.
TCGA 1992, s. 135(1): exchange of securities for those in another company (CGTA 1979, s. 85(1) was the predecessor provision).
TCGA 1992, s. 228(7): restriction of relief for disposals of shares to an ESOT by reference to a chargeable event.
TCGA 1992, s. 232(9): effective clawback of roll-over relief on share disposal to ESOT where chargeable event in relation to trustees.
FA 2003, s. 142(2) (ending of relief for contributions to employee share trusts): the definitions in s. 69(3AC) and (3AD) have effect in relation to 26 November 2002 as they had effect in relation to 20 March 2000; in relation to shares that are relevant shares by virtue of FA 2003, s. 142(2)(a), subsection s. 69(3AB) has effect as if the reference to 21 March 2000 were to 27 November 2002; and the other provisions of s. 69 have effect accordingly.

European material – Directive 90/434, art. 8 (s. 69(3A)).

70 Chargeable amounts

70(1) This section has effect to determine the chargeable amount for the purposes of section 68 above.

70(2) If the chargeable event falls within section 69(1)(a), (b) or (c) above the following rules shall apply–

(a) if the event constitutes a disposal of the securities by the trustees for the purposes of the Taxation of Chargeable Gains Act 1992, the chargeable amount is an amount equal to the sums allowable under section 38(1)(a) and (b) of that Act;

(b) if the event does not constitute such a disposal, the chargeable amount is an amount equal to the sums which would be so allowable had the trustees made a disposal of the securities for the purposes of that Act at the time the chargeable event occurs.

70(3) If the chargeable event falls within section 69(1)(d) above the chargeable amount is an amount equal to the sum concerned.

70(4) *If the chargeable event falls within section 69(1)(e) above the chargeable amount is an amount equal to–*

(a) the amount of the consideration received for the qualifying transfer mentioned in section 69(1)(e) above, less

(b) the amount of any expenditure by the trustees for a qualifying purpose during the period mentioned in section 69(5A) above.

History – References to TCGA 1992 in s. 70(2) substituted by TCGA 1992, s. 290 and Sch. 10, para. 19(2). s. 70(4) inserted by FA 2000, s. 55(6) with effect from 21 March 2000.

Cross references – TCGA 1992, s. 38(1)(a), (b): allowance for acquisition cost, enhancement expenditure and cost of establishing etc. title.

71 Further charges to tax: borrowing

71(1) This section applies where–

(a) a chargeable event (within the meaning of section 69 above) occurs in relation to the trustees of an employee share ownership trust,

(b) at the time the event occurs anything is outstanding in respect of the principal of an amount or amounts borrowed at any time by the trustees, and

(c) the chargeable event is one as regards which section 72(2)(b) below applies.

71(2) In the following provisions of this section–

(a) **"the initial chargeable event"** means the event referred to in subsection (1)(a) above, and

(b) **"the total outstanding amount"** means the total amount outstanding, at the time the initial chargeable event occurs, in respect of the principal of an amount or amounts borrowed at any time by the trustees.

71(3) If any of the total outstanding amount is repaid after the initial chargeable event occurs, a further chargeable event shall occur in relation to the trustees at the end of the year of assessment in which the repayment is made.

71(4) In such a case–

(a) the trustees shall be treated as receiving, when the further event occurs, income of an amount that is equal to the chargeable amount,

(b) that income shall be chargeable to income tax for the year of assessment at the end of which the further event occurs,

(ba) the tax so chargeable shall be charged on the full amount of the income the trustees are treated as receiving in the year of assessment, and

(bb) the trustees are liable for any tax so chargeable

(c) [Ceases to have effect by virtue of FA 2006, s. 89 and Sch. 13, para. 28(2)(b) and repealed by FA 2006, s. 178 and Sch. 26, Pt. 3(15).]

71(5) Subject to subsection (6) below, for the purposes of subsection (4) above the chargeable amount is an amount equal to the aggregate of the total outstanding amount repaid in the year of assessment.

71(6) In a case where section 72(2)(b) below had effect in the case of the initial chargeable event, for the purposes of subsection (4) above the chargeable amount is an equal to the smaller of–

(a) the aggregate of the total outstanding amount repaid in the year of assessment, and

(b) an amount found by applying the formula A–B–C.

71(7) For the purposes of subsection (6) above–

(a) A is the amount which would be the chargeable amount for the initial chargeable event apart from section 72(2) below,

(b) B is the chargeable amount for the initial chargeable event, and

(c) C is the amount (if any) found under subsection (8) below.

71(8) If, before the further chargeable event occurs, one or more prior chargeable events have occurred in relation to the trustees by virtue of the prior repayment of any of the total outstanding amount found for the time the initial chargeable event occurs, the amount found under this subsection is an amount equal to the chargeable amount for the prior chargeable event or to the aggregate of the chargeable amounts for the prior chargeable events (as the case may be).

71(9) In a case where–

(a) a chargeable event (within the meaning of section 69 above) occurs in relation to the trustees in circumstances mentioned in subsection (1) above,

(b) a sum falls to be included in the total outstanding amount found for the time the event occurs,

(c) another chargeable event (within the meaning of that section) occurs in relation to the trustees in circumstances mentioned in subsection (1) above, and

(d) the same sum or a part of it would (apart from this subsection) fall to be included in the total outstanding amount found for the time the event occurs,

the sum or part (as the case may be) shall not be included in the total outstanding amount found for the time the other chargeable event occurs.

71(10) In ascertaining for the purposes of this section whether a repayment is in respect of a particular amount, amounts borrowed earlier shall be taken to be repaid before amounts borrowed later.

71(11) Subsections (3) to (7) of section 68 above shall apply where tax is assessed by virtue of this section as they apply where tax is assessed by virtue of that section.

History – In s. 71(4), the word "and" inserted at the end of para. (ba) by FA 2006, s. 89 and Sch. 13, para. 28(4) with effect from 6 April 2006. FA 2006 inserted an additional comma before the word "and" at the end of para. (ba). This has not been reproduced.
In s. 71(4), the word "and" at the end of para. (bb) omitted by FA 2006, s. 89 and Sch. 13, para. 28(4) and repealed by FA 2006, s. 178 and Sch. 26, Pt. 3(15) with effect from 6 April 2006.
S. 71(4)(c) ceases to have effect by virtue of FA 2006, s. 89 and Sch. 13, para. 28(2)(a) and repealed by FA 2006, s. 178 and Sch. 26, Pt. 3(15) in relation to payments made on or after 6 April 2006.
In s. 71(4), the words "income of an amount that" substituted for the former wording ("annual profits or gains whose amount") by ITTOIA 2005, s. 882(1) and Sch. 1, para. 408(a); effective for income tax purposes for 2005–06 onwards (ITTOIA 2005, s. 883(1)).
In s. 71(4), para. (b), (ba) and (bb) substituted for the former para. (b) by ITTOIA 2005, s. 882(1) and Sch. 1, para. 408(b); effective for income tax purposes for 2005–06 onwards (ITTOIA 2005, s. 883(1)).
In s. 71(4)(c), the words "the rate applicable to trusts" substituted by FA 1993, s. 79 and Sch. 6, para. 20 in relation to 1993–94 and subsequent years of assessment.

Cross references – ICTA 1988, s. 686A(2)(h): where trustees receive a payment of the kind mentioned in s. 71(4) it is treated as if it were income to which ICTA 1988, s. 686 applies.

72 Limit on chargeable amount

72(1) For the purposes of this section each of the following is a **"chargeable event in relation to the trustees of an employee share ownership trust"**–

(a) an event which is a chargeable event by virtue of section 69 above;

(b) an event which is a chargeable event by virtue of section 71 above.

72(2) If a chargeable event (**"the event in question"**) occurs in relation to the trustees of an employee share ownership trust, the following rules shall apply–

(a) the amount which would (apart from this subsection) be the chargeable amount for the event in question shall be aggregated, for the purposes of paragraph (b) below, with the chargeable amounts for other chargeable events (if any) occurring in relation to the trustees before the event in question,

(b) if the amount which would (apart from this subsection) be the chargeable amount for the event in question (or the aggregate found under paragraph (a) above, if there is one) exceeds the deductible amount, the chargeable amount for the event in question shall be the amount it would be apart from this subsection less an amount equal to the excess, and

(c) section 70(2) and (3) and section 71(5) above shall have effect subject to paragraph (b) above.

72(3) For the purposes of subsection (2) above the **"deductible amount"** (as regards the event in question) is an amount equal to the total of the sums falling within subsection (4) below.

72(4) A sum falls within this subsection if it has been received by the trustees before the occurrence of the event in question and–

(a) it has been deducted as mentioned in section 67(2)(a) above, or treated as mentioned in section 67(2)(b) above, before the occurrence of that event, or

(b) it would fall to be so deducted or treated if a claim for relief under section 67 above had been made immediately before the occurrence of that event.

73 Information

73(1) An inspector may by notice in writing require a return to be made by the trustees of an employee share ownership trust if they have at any time received a sum which has been deducted as mentioned in section 67(2)(a) above or treated as mentioned in section 67(2)(b) above.

73(2) Where he requires such a return to be made the inspector shall specify the information to be contained in it.

73(3) The information which may be specified is information the inspector needs for the purposes of sections 68 to 72 above, and may include information about–

(a) sums received (including sums borrowed) by the trustees;

(b) expenditure incurred by them;

(c) assets acquired by them;

(d) transfers of assets made by them.

73(4) The information which may be required under subsection (3)(a) above may include the persons from whom the sums were received.

73(5) The information which may be required under subsection (3)(b) above may include the purpose of the expenditure and the persons receiving any sums.

73(6) The information which may be specified under subsection (3)(c) above may include the persons from whom the assets were acquired and the consideration furnished by the trustees.

73(7) The information which may be included under subsection (3)(d) above may include the persons to whom assets were transferred and the consideration furnished by them.

73(8) In a case where a sum has been deducted as mentioned in section 67(2)(a) above, or treated as mentioned in section 67(2)(b) above, the inspector shall send to the trustees to whom the payment was made a certificate stating–

(a) that a sum has been so deducted or so treated, and

(b) what sum has been so deducted or so treated.

73(9) [Amends TMA 1970, s. 98.]

74 Interpretation

74 Schedule 5 to this Act shall have effect to determine whether, for the purposes of sections 67 to 73 above, a trust is at a particular time–

(a) an employee share ownership trust;

(b) a qualifying employee share ownership trust.

PENSIONS ETC.

75 Retirement benefits schemes

75 [Repealed by FA 2004, s. 326 and Sch. 42, Pt. 3.]

History – S. 75 repealed by FA 2004, s. 326 and Sch. 42, Pt. 3 with effect from 6 April 2006 but subject to FA 2004, Sch. 36. Former s. 75 read as follows:

"Retirement benefits schemes

75 Schedule 6 to this Act (which relates to retirement benefits schemes) shall have effect.".

76 Non-approved retirement benefits schemes

76 [Repealed by FA 2004, s. 326 and Sch. 42, Pt. 3.]

History – S. 76 repealed by FA 2004, s. 326 and Sch. 42, Pt. 3 with effect from 6 April 2006 but subject to FA 2004, Sch. 36. Former s. 76 read as follows:

"Non-approved retirement benefits schemes

76(1) In computing the amount of the profits to be charged under Case I or Case II of Schedule D or under Part 2 of the Income Tax (Trading and Other Income) Act 2005, no sum shall be deducted in respect of any expenses falling within subsection (2) or (3) below; and no expenses falling within either of those subsections shall be treated–

(a) for the purposes of section 75 of the Taxes Act 1988 (companies with investment business) as expenses of management, or

(b) for the purposes of section 76 of that Act (companies carrying on life assurance business) as expenses payable.

76(2) Subject to subsection (6A) below, expenses fall within this subsection if–

(a) they are expenses of providing benefits pursuant to a relevant retirement benefits scheme, and

(b) the benefits are not ones in respect of which a person is on receipt chargeable to income tax.

76(3) Subject to subsection (6A) below, expenses fall within this subsection if–

(a) they are expenses of paying any sum pursuant to a relevant retirement benefits scheme with a view to the provision of any benefits, and

(b) the sum is not one which when paid counts as employment income of a person by virtue of section 386(1) of the Income Tax (Earnings and Pensions) Act 2003 (charge on payments to non-approved retirement benefit schemes).

76(4) No sum shall be deducted in respect of any expenses falling within subsection (5) or (6) below–

(a) in computing the amount of the profits to be charged under Case I or Case II of Schedule D or under Part 2 of the Income Tax (Trading and Other Income) Act 2005, or

(b) under section 75 or 76 of the Taxes Act 1988,

unless the sum has actually been expended.

76(4A) The reference in subsection (4) above to a sum being deducted shall be construed, so far as relating to section 76 of the Taxes Act 1988, as a reference to an amount being brought into account under that section as expenses payable.

76(5) Subject to subsection (6A) below, expenses fall within this subsection if–

(a) they are expenses of providing benefits pursuant to a relevant retirement benefits scheme, and

(b) the benefits are ones in respect of which a person is on receipt chargeable to income tax.

76(6) Subject to subsection (6A) below, expenses fall within this subsection if–

(a) they are expenses of paying any sum pursuant to a relevant retirement benefits scheme with a view to the provision of any benefits, and

(b) the sum is one which when paid counts as employment income of a person by virtue of section 386(1) of the Income Tax (Earnings and Pensions) Act 2003 (charge on payments to non-approved retirement benefit schemes).

76(6A) Expenses to which subsection (6B) or (6C) below applies shall be treated as not falling within any of subsections (2), (3), (5) or (6) above.

76(6B) This subsection applies to expenses of paying any sum, or of providing benefits, pursuant to a superannuation fund which satisfies the requirements of section 615(6) of the Taxes Act 1988.

76(6C) This subsection applies to expenses of paying any sum, or of providing benefits, pursuant to a retirement benefits scheme which is established outside the United Kingdom and which the Board are satisfied corresponds to such a scheme as is mentioned in section 387(2) of the Income Tax (Earnings and Pensions) Act 2003, where the expenses are incurred for the benefit of:

(a) employees whose earnings are earnings and amounts treated as earnings to which subsection (6D) applies, or

(b) employees who are not resident in the United Kingdom and whose duties are performed wholly outside the United Kingdom (and for this purpose duties performed in the United Kingdom the performance of which is merely incidental to the performance of other duties outside the United Kingdom shall be treated as performed outside the United Kingdom).

76(6D) This subsection applies to earnings and amounts treated as earnings for a year of assessment if–
(a) the employee or office-holder is not domiciled in the United Kingdom in that year, and
(b) the employment is with a foreign employer.
76(6E) If there is a dispute as to whether the employee or office-holder is not domiciled in the United Kingdom, sections 42 and 43 of the Income Tax (Earnings and Pensions) Act 2003 (Board to determine dispute as to domicile) apply to the dispute as they apply to a dispute mentioned in section 42(1) of that Act.
76(7) In this section–

"earnings and amounts treated as earnings" means earnings and amounts treated as earnings which constitute employment income (see section 7(2)(a) or (b) of ITEPA 2003);

"foreign employer" has the meaning given by section 721 of that Act;

"retirement benefits scheme" has the same meaning as in Chapter I of Part XIV of the Taxes Act 1988, and

references to a **"relevant retirement benefits scheme"** are references to a retirement benefits scheme which is not of a description mentioned in section 387(2) of the Income Tax (Earnings and Pensions) Act 2003.

76(8) This section has effect in relation to expenses incurred on or after the day on which this Act is passed.".

In former s. 76(1) the words "or under Part 2 of the Income Tax (Trading and Other Income) Act 2005" inserted by ITTOIA 2005, s. 882(1) and Sch. 1, para. 409(2); effective for income tax purposes for 2005–06 onwards and for corporation tax purposes for accounting periods ending after 5 April 2005 (ITTOIA 2005, s. 883(1)).
In former s. 76(1) the words from "and no expenses" to the end substituted by SI 2004/2310, Schedule, para. 43(2), with effect in relation to accounting periods beginning on or after 1 April 2004, subject to the transitional provisions at FA 2004, s. 43 and 44.
In former s. 76(4)(a) the words "or under Part 2 of the Income Tax (Trading and Other Income) Act 2005" inserted by ITTOIA 2005, s. 882(1) and Sch. 1, para. 409(3); effective for income tax purposes for 2005–06 onwards and for corporation tax purposes for accounting periods ending after 5 April 2005 (ITTOIA 2005, s. 883(1)).
Former s. 76(4)(b) substituted by SI 2004/2310, Schedule, para. 43(3), with effect in relation to accounting periods beginning on or after 1 April 2004, subject to the transitional provisions at FA 2004, s. 43 and 44.
Former s. 76(4A) inserted by SI 2004/2310, Schedule, para. 43(4), with effect in relation to accounting periods beginning on or after 1 April 2004, subject to the transitional provisions at FA 2004, s. 43 and 44.
In former s. 76(1) and s. 76(4)(a), the word "profits" substituted for "profits or gains" by FA 1998 s. 46(3) and Sch. 5, para. 3.
In former s. 76(2), (3), (5) and (6), the words before "expenses", and s. 76(6A)–(6C), inserted by FA 1996, Sch. 39, para. 2, in relation to expenses incurred on or after 29 April 1996.
In former s. 76(3)(b), the words "counts as employment income of a person by virtue of section 386(1) of the Income Tax (Earnings and Pensions) Act 2003 (charge on payments to non-approved retirement benefit schemes)" substituted for "is treated as the income of a person by virtue of section 595(1) of the Taxes Act 1988 (sum paid with a view to the provision of any related benefits for an employee)" by FA 2004, s. 92 and Sch. 17, para. 10(4)(a) with effect from 22 July 2004.
In former s. 76(6)(b), the words "countsas employment income of a person by virtue of section 386(1) of the Income Tax (Earnings and Pensions) Act 2003 (charge on payments to non-approved retirement benefit schemes)" substituted for "is treated as the income of a person by virtue of section 595(1) of the Taxes Act 1998" by FA 2004, s. 92 and Sch. 17, para. 10(4)(a) with effect from 22 July 2004.
In former s. 76(6C)(a) the words "of the Taxes Act 1988" omitted by ITTOIA 2005, s. 882(1) and Sch. 1, para. 409(4) and ITTOIA 2005, s. 884 and Sch. 3; effective for income tax purposes for 2005–06 onwards and for corporation tax purposes for accounting periods ending after 5 April 2005 (ITTOIA 2005, s. 883(1)). These words, originally occurring after the former phrase "foreign emoluments within the meaning of section 192", should have been omitted by ITEPA 2003, Sch. 6, para. 161(2)(c) which limited the scope of its substitution to that phrase only (see below).
In former s. 76(6C), the words "section 387(2) of the Income Tax (Earnings and Pensions) Act 2003" substituted for the words "paragraphs (a), (b) or (c) of section 596(1) of the Taxes Act 1988" by ITEPA 2003, Sch. 6, para. 161(2)(a) which has effect, for income tax purposes, for the tax year 2003–04 and subsequent tax years and, for corporation tax purposes, for accounting periods ending after 5 April 2003.
In former s. 76(6C), the word "earnings" substituted for the word "emoluments" in the first place where it occurs, by ITEPA 2003, Sch. 6, para. 161(2)(b) which has effect, for income tax purposes, for the tax year 2003–04 and subsequent tax years and, for corporation tax purposes, for accounting periods ending after 5 April 2003.
In former s. 76(6C), the words "earnings and amounts treated as earnings to which subsection (6D) applies" substituted for the words "foreign emoluments within the meaning of section 192" by ITEPA 2003, Sch. 6, para. 161(2)(c) which has effect, for income tax purposes, for the tax year 2003–04 and subsequent tax years and, for corporation tax purposes, for accounting periods ending after 5 April 2003.
In former s. 76(6D)(a), the word "employee" substituted for "employer" by FA 2004, s. 92 and Sch. 17, para. 10(4)(b) with effect from 22 July 2004.
S. 76(6D) and s. 76(6E) inserted by ITEPA 2003, Sch. 6, para. 161(3) which has effect, for income tax purposes, for the tax year 2003–04 and subsequent tax years and, for corporation tax purposes, for accounting periods ending after 5 April 2003.
In former s. 76(7), after the words "this section", definitions of "earnings and amounts treated as earnings" and "foreign employer" were inserted by ITEPA 2003, Sch. 6, para. 161(4)(a) which has effect, for income taxpurposes, for the tax year 2003–04 and subsequent tax years and, for corporation tax purposes, for accounting periods ending after 5 April 2003.
In former s. 76(7), in the definition of "relevant retirement benefits scheme", the words "section 387(2) of the Income Tax (Earnings and Pensions) Act 2003" were substituted for the words "section 596(1)(a), (b) or (c) of the Taxes Act 1988" by ITEPA 2003, Sch. 6, para. 161(4)(b) which has effect, for income tax purposes, for the tax year 2003–04 and subsequent tax years and, for corporation tax purposes, for accounting periods ending after 5 April 2003.

Cross references – ICTA 1988, s. 21A: amounts chargeable in respect of a Sch. A business.
FA 2002, Sch. 29, para. 112: expenditure which is "not generally deductible for tax purposes".
FA 2002, Sch. 29, para. 114: meaning of "pension contributions".
ITEPA 2003, Sch. 7, para. 12(2)(a) (Sch. 7: transitionals and savings): disputes as to domicile or ordinary residence.

77 Personal pension schemes

77 [Repealed by FA 2004, s. 326 and Sch. 42, Pt. 3.]

History – S. 77 repealed by FA 2004, s. 326 and Sch. 42, Pt. 3 with effect from 6 April 2006 but subject to FA 2004, Sch. 36. Former s. 77 read as follows:

"Personal pension schemes

77 *Schedule 7 to this Act (which relates to personal pension schemes) shall have effect.".*

UNIT TRUSTS ETC.

80 Gilt unit trusts

80 [Repealed by FA 1998, s. 165 and Sch. 27, Pt. III(23).]

History – S. 80 repealed by FA 1998, s. 165 and Sch. 27, Pt. III(23) with effect from 31 July 1998.

Cross references – ICTA 1988, s. 67: basis of assessment for Sch. D, Case III etc. where source of income disposed of or ceases, including (s. 67(1)(b)) charge to tax for year preceding final year by reference to amount arising if greater.
ICTA 1988, s. 468(5): certain fixed interest trusts excluded from authorised unit trust tax regime (repealed for distribution periods beginning after 31 December 1990).
SI 1997/1154, reg. 5(3)(g): open-ended investment companies.

European material – For Directive 85/611 see OJ 1985 L375/3.

81 Offshore funds operating equalisation arrangements

81(1) [Amends ICTA 1988, s. 758(6).]

81(2) This section shall apply where a conversion of securities occurs on or after 14th March 1989; and **"conversion of securities"** here has the same meaning as in section 82 of the Capital Gains Tax Act 1979.

Notes – CGTA 1979, s. 82 was repealed by TCGA 1992, s. 290 and Sch. 12 in relation to chargeable periods beginning on or after 6 April 1992; see now TCGA 1992, s. 132 for meaning of "conversion of securities" (Interpretation Act 1978, s. 17(2)).

LIFE ASSURANCE

82 Calculation of profits: bonuses etc.

82 [Omitted by FA 2012, s. 146 and Sch. 16, para. 49.]

History – S. 82 omitted by FA 2012, s. 146 and Sch. 16, para. 49 in relation to accounting periods beginning on or after 1 January 2013 (FA 2012, s. 148) but subject to transitional provisions in FA 2012, Sch. 17. Where an accounting period would otherwise straddle 1 January 2013, it is deemed to end on 31 December 2012 (FA 2012, s. 149).

82A Calculation of profits: policy holders' tax

82A [Omitted by FA 2012, s. 146 and Sch. 16, para. 50.]

History – S. 82A omitted by FA 2012, s. 146 and Sch. 16, para. 50 in relation to accounting periods beginning on or after 1 January 2013 (FA 2012, s. 148) but subject to transitional provisions in FA 2012, Sch. 17. Where an accounting period would otherwise straddle 1 January 2013, it is deemed to end on 31 December 2012 (FA 2012, s. 149).
Former s. 82, 82A and 82B substituted for former s. 82 by FA 2003, Sch. 33, para. 1 with effect for accounting periods beginning on or after 1 January 2003.

82B Unappropriated surplus on valuation

82B [Omitted by FA 2012, s. 146 and Sch. 16, para. 51.]

History – S. 82B omitted by FA 2012, s. 146 and Sch. 16, para. 51 in relation to accounting periods beginning on or after 1 January 2013 (FA 2012, s. 148) but subject to transitional provisions in FA 2012, Sch. 17. Where an accounting period would otherwise straddle 1 January 2013, it is deemed to end on 31 December 2012 (FA 2012, s. 149).
Former s. 82, 82A and 82B substituted for former s. 82 by FA 2003, Sch. 33, para. 1 with effect for accounting periods beginning on or after 1 January 2003.

82C Relevant financial reinsurance contracts

82C [Omitted by FA 2007, s. 40 and Sch. 9, para. 9 and repealed by FA 2007, s. 114 and Sch. 27, Pt. 2(9).]

History – S. 82C omitted by FA 2007, s. 40 and Sch. 9, para. 9 and repealed by FA 2007, s. 114 and Sch. 27, Pt. 2(9) in relation to contracts entered into in a period of account beginning on or after 1 January 2008, by virtue of FA 2007, Sch. 9, para. 17, as amended by FA 2008, s. 43 and Sch. 17, para. 38. See also Note below.
S. 82C inserted by FA 2004, s. 47 and Sch. 7, para. 5(2) with effect in relation to periods of account ending on or after 17 March 2004 (whether the insurance business transfer scheme takes place, or the relevant financial reinsurance contract is entered into, before or on or after that date).

Notes – Before FA 2007, Sch. 9, para. 17 was amended by FA 2008, s. 43 and Sch. 17, para. 38, the omission of s. 82C was made with effect from 11 March 2008, in relation to transfers of business taking place on or after 1 July 2008, and subject to any provision made by an order under Sch. 9, para. 16 on or after 11 March 2008, by virtue of SI 2008/379.

82D Treatment of profits: life assurance – adjustment consequent on change in Insurance Prudential Sourcebook

82D [Omitted by FA 2012, s. 146 and Sch. 16, para. 52.]

History – S. 82D omitted by FA 2012, s. 146 and Sch. 16, para. 52 in relation to accounting periods beginning on or after 1 January 2013 (FA 2012, s. 148) but subject to transitional provisions in FA 2012, Sch. 17. Where an accounting period would otherwise straddle 1 January 2013, it is deemed to end on 31 December 2012 (FA 2012, s. 149).
Former s. 82D inserted by SI 2006/3387, art. 5, with effect from 8 January 2007 for periods of account ending on or after 31 December 2006.

82E Section 82D: treatment of transferors under insurance business transfer schemes

82E [Omitted by FA 2012, s. 146 and Sch. 16, para. 52.]

History – S. 82E omitted by FA 2012, s. 146 and Sch. 16, para. 52 in relation to accounting periods beginning on or after 1 January 2013 (FA 2012, s. 148) but subject to transitional provisions in FA 2012, Sch. 17. Where an accounting period would otherwise straddle 1 January 2013, it is deemed to end on 31 December 2012 (FA 2012, s. 149).
Former s. 82E inserted by SI 2007/1031, art. 13, with effect from 17 April 2007, in relation to accounting periods ending on or after 31 December 2006, whenever beginning.

82F Section 82D: treatment of transferees under insurance business transfer schemes

82F [Omitted by FA 2012, s. 146 and Sch. 16, para. 52.]

History – S. 82F omitted by FA 2012, s. 146 and Sch. 16, para. 52 in relation to accounting periods beginning on or after 1 January 2013 (FA 2012, s. 148) but subject to transitional provisions in FA 2012, Sch. 17. Where an accounting period would otherwise straddle 1 January 2013, it is deemed to end on 31 December 2012 (FA 2012, s. 149).
Former s. 82F inserted by SI 2007/1031, art. 13, with effect from 17 April 2007, in relation to accounting periods ending on or after 31 December 2006, whenever beginning.

83 Receipts to be taken into account

83 [Omitted by FA 2012, s. 146 and Sch. 16, para. 53.]

History – S. 83 omitted by FA 2012, s. 146 and Sch. 16, para. 53 in relation to accounting periods beginning on or after 1 January 2013 (FA 2012, s. 148) but subject to transitional provisions in FA 2012, Sch. 17. Where an accounting period would otherwise straddle 1 January 2013, it is deemed to end on 31 December 2012 (FA 2012, s. 149).
Former s. 83, 83A substituted for former s. 83 by FA 1995, s. 51 and Sch. 8, para. 16, with effect in relation to accounting periods beginning on or after 1 January 1995.

83XA Structural assets

83XA [Omitted by FA 2012, s. 146 and Sch. 16, para. 54.]

History – S. 83XA omitted by FA 2012, s. 146 and Sch. 16, para. 54 in relation to accounting periods beginning on or after 1 January 2013 (FA 2012, s. 148) but subject to transitional provisions in FA 2012, Sch. 17. Where an accounting period would otherwise straddle 1 January 2013, it is deemed to end on 31 December 2012 (FA 2012, s. 149).
Former s. 83XA inserted by FA 2007, s. 41 and Sch. 10, para. 2(1) with effect in relation to periods of account beginning on or after 1 January 2007.

83YA Changes in value of assets brought into account: non-profit companies

83YA [Omitted by FA 2012, s. 146 and Sch. 16, para. 55.]

History – S. 83YA omitted by FA 2012, s. 146 and Sch. 16, para. 55 in relation to accounting periods beginning on or after 1 January 2013 (FA 2012, s. 148) but subject to transitional provisions in FA 2012, Sch. 17. Where an accounting period would otherwise straddle 1 January 2013, it is deemed to end on 31 December 2012 (FA 2012, s. 149).
Former s. 83YA inserted by FA 2006, s. 86 and Sch. 11, para. 7(1) in relation to periods of account ending on or after 29 September 2005; subject to the modifications in FA 2006, Sch. 11, para. 7(4)–(11) in the case of any period of account that begins before 29 September 2005 and ends on or after that date.

83YB Meaning of "appropriate line 51 amount" for purposes of s. 83YA

83YB [Omitted by FA 2012, s. 146 and Sch. 16, para. 55.]

History – S. 83YB omitted by FA 2012, s. 146 and Sch. 16, para. 55 in relation to accounting periods beginning on or after 1 January 2013 (FA 2012, s. 148) but subject to transitional provisions in FA 2012, Sch. 17. Where an accounting period would otherwise straddle 1 January 2013, it is deemed to end on 31 December 2012 (FA 2012, s. 149).
Former s. 83YB inserted by FA 2006, s. 86 and Sch. 11, para. 7(1) in relation to periods of account ending on or after 29 September 2005 subject to the modifications in FA 2006, Sch. 11, para. 7(4)–(11) in the case of any period of account that begins before 29 September 2005 and ends on or after that date.

83YC FAFTS: charge in relevant period of account

83YC [Omitted by FA 2012, s. 146 and Sch. 16, para. 56.]

History – S. 83YC omitted by FA 2012, s. 146 and Sch. 16, para. 56 in relation to accounting periods beginning on or after 1 January 2013 (FA 2012, s. 148) but subject to transitional provisions in FA 2012, Sch. 17. Where an accounting period would otherwise straddle 1 January 2013, it is deemed to end on 31 December 2012 (FA 2012, s. 149).
Former s. 83YC inserted by FA 2008, s. 43 and Sch. 17, para. 1(3), with effect in relation to periods of account beginning on or after 1 January 2008, subject to the transitional provisions in FA 2008, Sch. 17, para. 4.

83YD FAFTS: deduction in subsequent periods of account

83YD [Omitted by FA 2012, s. 146 and Sch. 16, para. 56.]

History – S. 83YD omitted by FA 2012, s. 146 and Sch. 16, para. 56 in relation to accounting periods beginning on or after 1 January 2013 (FA 2012, s. 148) but subject to transitional provisions in FA 2012, Sch. 17. Where an accounting period would otherwise straddle 1 January 2013, it is deemed to end on 31 December 2012 (FA 2012, s. 149).
Former s. 83YD inserted by FA 2008, s. 43 and Sch. 17, para. 1(3), with effect in relation to periods of account beginning on or after 1 January 2008, subject to the transitional provisions in FA 2008, Sch. 17, para. 4.

83YE Regulations: apportionment and redefining "financial reinsurance arrangement"

83YE [Omitted by FA 2012, s. 146 and Sch. 16, para. 56.]

History – S. 83YE omitted by FA 2012, s. 146 and Sch. 16, para. 56 in relation to accounting periods beginning on or after 1 January 2013 (FA 2012, s. 148) but subject to transitional provisions in FA 2012, Sch. 17. Where an accounting period would otherwise straddle 1 January 2013, it is deemed to end on 31 December 2012 (FA 2012, s. 149).
Former s. 83YE inserted by FA 2008, s. 43 and Sch. 17, para. 1(3), with effect in relation to periods of account beginning on or after 1 January 2008.

83YF Financial reinsurance arrangements: further provision

83YF [Omitted by FA 2012, s. 146 and Sch. 16, para. 56.]

History – S. 83YF omitted by FA 2012, s. 146 and Sch. 16, para. 56 in relation to accounting periods beginning on or after 1 January 2013 (FA 2012, s. 148) but subject to transitional provisions in FA 2012, Sch. 17. Where an accounting period would otherwise straddle 1 January 2013, it is deemed to end on 31 December 2012 (FA 2012, s. 149).
Former s. 83YF inserted by FA 2008, s. 43 and Sch. 17, para. 1(3), with effect in relation to periods of account beginning on or after 1 January 2008.

83ZA Contingent loans

83ZA(1) For the purposes of this section a contingent loan is made to an insurance company if–

(a) a deposit is received by the company from a reinsurer or arises out of insurance operations of the company,

(b) a debenture loan is made to the company, or

(c) an amount is borrowed by the company from a credit institution,

and the deposit, debenture loan or amount borrowed is taken into account as a receipt of the company under section 83(2) above.

83ZA(2) For the purposes of this section the time when a contingent loan is made to an insurance company is the time when the assets constituting the deposit, debenture loan or amount borrowed are received by the company.

83ZA(3) For the purposes of this section an insurance company has unrepaid contingent loan liabilities at any time if–

(a) one or more contingent loans have been made to the company at or before that time, and

(b) amounts will or may at some later time become repayable by the company in respect of the contingent loan or contingent loans.

83ZA(4) Where, at any time during a period of account of an insurance company (**"the period of account in question"**), the company has unrepaid contingent loan liabilities–

(a) subsection (5) below applies if the company did not have unrepaid contingent loan liabilities at the end of the period of account immediately preceding the period of account in question, and

(b) subsection (6) below applies if it did.

83ZA(5) Where this subsection applies, the appropriate amount for the period of account in question is allowed as a deduction in calculating the profits of the company for the period of account in question.

83ZA(6) Where this subsection applies–

(a) if the appropriate amount for the period of account in question exceeds the appropriate amount for the immediately preceding period of account, the excess is allowed as a deduction in calculating the profits for the period of account in question, but

(b) if the appropriate amount for the immediately preceding period of account exceeds the appropriate amount for the period of account in question, the excess is to be taken into account as a receipt of the period of account in question.

83ZA(7) For the purposes of subsections (5) and (6) above the appropriate amount for a period of account is the amount of the unrepaid contingent loan liabilities at the end of the period of account reduced (but not below nil) by–

(a) any relevant net transfers to shareholders,

(b) [omitted by FA 2006, s. 86 and Sch. 11, para. 8(2)(b) and repealed by FA 2006, s. 178 and Sch. 26 Pt. 3(14).]

83ZA(8) In subsection (7)(a) above **"relevant net transfers to shareholders"** means the aggregate of the positive amounts brought into account as transfers to non-technical account for–

(a) the period of account,

(b) the period of account in which the relevant contingent loan was made to the company, and

(c) any period of account falling between the periods of account mentioned in paragraphs (a) and (b) above, as reduced in accordance with subsection (9) below.

83ZA(9) The reduction to be made from the positive amount brought into account as a transfer to non-technical account for any of the periods of account mentioned in subsection (8) above is so much of the positive amount as does not exceed 12% of the amount allocated to policy holders as bonuses in relation to the period of account.

83ZA(10) [Omitted by FA 2006, s. 86 and Sch. 11, para. 8(3) and repealed by FA 2006, s. 178 and Sch. 26, Pt. 3(14).]

83ZA(11) In subsection (8) above **"the relevant contingent loan"** means–

(a) if amounts will or may at some later time become repayable by the company in respect of only one contingent loan, that contingent loan, and

(b) if amounts will or may at some later time become repayable by the company in respect of more than one contingent loan, whichever of those contingent loans was made to the company first.

83ZA(12) [Omitted by FA 2006, s. 86 and Sch. 11, para. 8(5) and repealed by FA 2006, s. 178 and Sch. 26, Pt. 3(14).]

83ZA(13) Where in a period of account of an insurance company–

(a) an amount becomes repayable under a contingent loan made to the company, and

(b) the amount repayable is brought into account as other expenses for the period of account,

so much of the amount repayable as does not exceed the amount specified in subsection (14) below is allowed as a deduction in calculating the profits of the company for the period of account.

83ZA(14) The amount referred to in subsection (13) above is the amount arrived at by deducting from the amount taken into account as a receipt of the company under section 83(2) above in relation to the contingent loan the aggregate of any amounts which–

(a) have become repayable in respect of the contingent loan in any earlier period of account, and

(b) have been allowed as a deduction in calculating the profits of the company for any such period.

83ZA(15) The references in subsections (8) and (13) above to an amount being brought into account–

(a) in a case where the amount taken into account as a receipt of the company under section 83(2) above in relation to the contingent loan or loans in question is an amount brought into account in an account concerned wholly with non-participating business, are to its being brought into account in that account or in any other account concerned wholly with non-participating business, and

(b) in a case where the amount so taken into account is an amount brought into account in an account concerned wholly or partly with participating business, are to its being brought into account in that account or in any other account concerned wholly or partly with participating business.

83ZA(16) Where–

(a) a transfer to another fund brought into account for a period of account as other expenditure in any account concerned wholly with non- participating business is brought into account as other income in an account concerned wholly or partly with participating business, or

(b) a transfer to another fund brought into account for a period of account as other expenditure in any account concerned wholly or partly with participating business is brought into account as other income in an account concerned wholly with non-participating business,

subsection (8) above has effect as if it were a positive amount brought into account as transfers to non-technical account for that period of account in the account in which it is brought into account as other expenditure.

83ZA(17) For the purposes of subsections (15) and (16) above–

(a) an account is concerned wholly with non-participating business if it relates exclusively to policies or contracts under which the policy holders or annuitants are not eligible to participate in surplus, and

(b) an account is concerned wholly or partly with participating business if it relates wholly or partly to other policies or contracts.

History – In s. 83ZA(4), the words "any time during a" substituted for "the end of the" by FA 2007, s. 41 and Sch. 10, para. 1 with effect on and after 10 May 2007. See also Note below.

In s. 83ZA(7), the words "the aggregate of" at the end of the opening words, the word "and" before para. (b) and para. (b) itself omitted by FA 2006, s. 86 and Sch. 11, para. 8(2) and repealed by FA 2006, s. 178 and Sch. 26, Pt. 3(14), with effect in relation to transfers taking place on or after 2 December 2004.

S. 83ZA(10) *omitted by FA 2006*, s. 86 and Sch. 11, para. 8(3) and repealed by FA 2006, s. 178 and Sch. 26, Pt. 3(14), with effect in relation to transfers taking place on or after 2 December 2004.

In former s. 83ZA(10)(b), the words "line 31 figure" substituted for the words "line 15 figure" by SI 2004/3266, art. 9(2), with effect in relation to periods of account beginning on or after 1 January 2005.

In s. 83ZA(11), the words "subsection (8)" substituted for the former wording ("subsections (8) and (10)") by FA 2006, s. 86 and Sch. 11, para. 8(4), with effect in relation to transfers taking place on or after 2 December 2004.

S. 83ZA(12) omitted by FA 2006, s. 86 and Sch. 11, para. 8(5) and repealed by FA 2006, s. 178 and Sch. 26, Pt. 3(14), with effect in relation to transfers taking place on or after 2 December 2004.

In former s. 83ZA(12), the words "line 31 figure" substituted for the words "line 15 figure" by SI 2004/3266, art. 9(2), with effect in relation to periods of account beginning on or after 1 January 2005.
In former s. 83ZA(12), the words "as business transfers-in" substituted for the words "as other income" by SI 2004/3266, art. 9(3), with effect in relation to periods of account beginning on or after 1 January 2005.
In s. 83ZA(15), the reference to s. 83ZA(12) omitted by FA 2006, s. 86 and Sch. 11, para. 8(6) and repealed by FA 2006, s. 178 and Sch. 26, Pt. 3(14), with effect in relation to transfers taking place on or after 2 December 2004.
S. 83ZA inserted by FA 2003, s. 170 and Sch. 33, para. 3(1) with effect in relation to contingent loans made to an insurance company in a period of account beginning on or after 1 January 2003.

Cross references – S. 90A: expressions used in s. 82–90 have the same meaning as in ICTA 1988, Pt. XII, Ch. 1.
Sch. 8A: modification of s. 83–83A in relation to overseas life insurance companies.
ICTA 1988, s. 444AE: transfers of business: modification of s. 83ZA.
FA 1996, Sch. 11, para. 2: debt under a contingent loan within s. 83ZA regarded for loan relationship purposes as not arising from a transaction for the lending of money.
SI 2006/3271, reg. 23: modification of s. 83ZA with effect from 31 December 2006 in relation to periods of account ending on or after that date.

Notes – In s. 83ZA(4), the words "any time during a" substituted for "the end of the" by FA 2007, s. 41 and Sch. 10, para. 1 with effect on and after 10 May 2007. The text above has been presented on the basis that the occurrence of the words "the end of the" in s. 83ZA(4)(a) was not within the scope of the amendment.

83AA Amounts added to long-term insurance fund of a company in excess of that company's loss

83AA [Omitted by FA 2007, s. 40 and Sch. 9, para. 11(2)(b) and repealed by FA 2007, s. 114 and Sch. 27, Pt. 2(9).]

History – S. 83AA omitted by FA 2007, s. 40 and Sch. 9, para. 11(2)(b) and repealed by FA 2007, s. 114 and Sch. 27, Pt. 2(9), with effect in relation to periods of account beginning on or after 1 January 2007 where the transfer of business or demutualisation concerned took place before 21 March 2007, and with effect in relation periods of account ending after 30 June 2008 where the transfer of business or demutualisation concerned took place on or after 21 March 2007 and before 1 July 2008. For other purposes, the omissions and repeals take effect from 11 March 2008, in relation to transfers of business taking place on or after 1 July 2008, and subject to any provision made by an order under Sch. 9, para. 16 on or after 11 March 2008, by virtue of SI 2008/379. These commencement rules are by virtue of FA 2007, Sch. 9, para. 17, as amended by FA 2008, s. 43 and Sch. 17, para. 38.

83AB Treatment of surplus where there is a subsequent transfer of business from the company etc.

83AB [Omitted by FA 2007, s. 40 and Sch. 9, para. 11(2)(c) and repealed by FA 2007, s. 114 and Sch. 27, Pt. 2(9).]

History – S. 83AB omitted by FA 2007, s. 40 and Sch. 9, para. 11(2)(c) and repealed by FA 2007, s. 114 and Sch. 27, Pt. 2(9), with effect in relation to periods of account beginning on or after 1 January 2007 where the transfer of business or demutualisation concerned took place before 21 March 2007, and with effect in relation periods of account ending after 30 June 2008 where the transfer of business or demutualisation concerned took place on or after 21 March 2007 and before 1 July 2008. For other purposes, the omissions and repeals take effect from 11 March 2008, in relation to transfers of business taking place on or after 1 July 2008, and subject to any provision made by an order under Sch. 9, para. 16 on or after 11 March 2008, by virtue of SI 2008/379. These commencement rules are by virtue of FA 2007, Sch. 9, para. 17, as amended by FA 2008, s. 43 and Sch. 17, para. 38. See also Note below.

83A Meaning of "brought into account"

83A [Omitted by FA 2012, s. 146 and Sch. 16, para. 57.]

History – S. 83A omitted by FA 2012, s. 146 and Sch. 16, para. 57 in relation to accounting periods beginning on or after 1 January 2013 (FA 2012, s. 148) but subject to transitional provisions in FA 2012, Sch. 17. Where an accounting period would otherwise straddle 1 January 2013, it is deemed to end on 31 December 2012 (FA 2012, s. 149).

83B Changes in recognised accounts: attribution of amounts carried forward under s. 432F of Taxes Act 1988

83B [Omitted by FA 2012, s. 146 and Sch. 16, para. 58.]

History – S. 83B omitted by FA 2012, s. 146 and Sch. 16, para. 58 in relation to accounting periods beginning on or after 1 January 2013 (FA 2012, s. 148) but subject to transitional provisions in FA 2012, Sch. 17. Where an accounting period would otherwise straddle 1 January 2013, it is deemed to end on 31 December 2012 (FA 2012, s. 149).

84 Interpretation of sections 85 to 89 and further provisions about insurance companies

84(1) [Repealed by FA 2003, s. 216 and Sch. 43, Pt. 3(12).]

84(2)–(3) [Omitted by FA 2007, s. 41 and Sch. 10, para. 16(4)(a) and repealed by FA 2007, s. 114 and Sch. 27, Pt. 2(10).]

84(4) [Omitted by FA 2012, s. 146 and Sch. 16, para. 247(a).]

84(5)–(6) [Omitted by FA 2007, s. 41 and Sch. 10, para. 16(4)(a) and repealed by FA 2007, s. 114 and Sch. 27, Pt. 2(10).]

History – S. 84(1) repealed by FA 2003, s. 216 and Sch. 43, Pt. 3(12) with effect from 10 July 2003.

85 Charge of certain receipts of basic life assurance business

85 [Omitted by FA 2012, s. 146 and Sch. 16, para. 59.]

History – S. 85 omitted by FA 2012, s. 146 and Sch. 16, para. 59 in relation to accounting periods beginning on or after 1 January 2013 (FA 2012, s. 148) but subject to transitional provisions in FA 2012, Sch. 17. Where an accounting period would otherwise straddle 1 January 2013, it is deemed to end on 31 December 2012 (FA 2012, s. 149).

85A Excess adjusted life assurance trade profits

85A [Omitted by FA 2012, s. 146 and Sch. 16, para. 60.]

History – S. 85A omitted by FA 2012, s. 146 and Sch. 16, para. 60 in relation to accounting periods beginning on or after 1 January 2013 (FA 2012, s. 148) but subject to transitional provisions in FA 2012, Sch. 17. Where an accounting period would otherwise straddle 1 January 2013, it is deemed to end on 31 December 2012 (FA 2012, s. 149).

86 Spreading of relief for acquisition expenses

86 [Omitted by FA 2012, s. 146 and Sch. 16, para. 61.]

History – S. 86 omitted by FA 2012, s. 146 and Sch. 16, para. 61 in relation to accounting periods beginning on or after 1 January 2013 (FA 2012, s. 148) but subject to transitional provisions in FA 2012, Sch. 17. Where an accounting period would otherwise straddle 1 January 2013, it is deemed to end on 31 December 2012 (FA 2012, s. 149).

87 Management expenses

87 [Omitted by FA 2007, s. 41 and Sch. 10, para. 16(4)(d) and repealed by FA 2007, s. 114 and Sch. 27, Pt. 2(10).]

History – S. 87 omitted by FA 2007, s. 41 and Sch. 10, para. 16(4)(d) and repealed by FA 2007, s. 114 and Sch. 27, Pt. 2(10) with effect from Royal Assent (19 July 2007).

88 Corporation tax: policy holders' share of profits

88 [Omitted by FA 2012, s. 146 and Sch. 16, para. 62.]

History – S. 88 omitted by FA 2012, s. 146 and Sch. 16, para. 62 in relation to accounting periods beginning on or after 1 January 2013 (FA 2012, s. 148) but subject to transitional provisions in FA 2012, Sch. 17. Where an accounting period would otherwise straddle 1 January 2013, it is deemed to end on 31 December 2012 (FA 2012, s. 149).

88A Lower corporation tax rate on certain insurance company profits

88A [Omitted by FA 2003, s. 170 and Sch. 33, para. 13(3) and repealed by FA 2003, s. 216 and Sch. 43, Pt. 3(12)]

History – S. 88A omitted by FA 2003, s. 170 and Sch. 33, para. 13(3) and repealed by FA 2003, s. 216 and Sch. 43, Pt. 3(12) with effect for the financial year 2003 and subsequent financial years.

89 Policy holders' share of profits

89 [Omitted by FA 2012, s. 146 and Sch. 16, para. 63.]

History – S. 89 omitted by FA 2012, s. 146 and Sch. 16, para. 63 in relation to accounting periods beginning on or after 1 January 2013 (FA 2012, s. 148) but subject to transitional provisions in FA 2012, Sch. 17. Where an accounting period would otherwise straddle 1 January 2013, it is deemed to end on 31 December 2012 (FA 2012, s. 149).

89A Modification of sections 83 and 89 in relation to overseas life insurance companies

89A [Repealed by SI 2006/3271, reg. 43 and Sch., Pt. 1.]

History – S. 89A repealed by SI 2006/3271, reg. 43 and Sch., Pt. 1 with effect from 31 December 2006 in relation to periods of account ending on or after that date. S. 89A previously gave effect to Sch. 8A.

90 Life policies etc. held by companies

90 [Omitted by FA 2008, s. 36 and Sch. 14, para. 17(a).]

History – S. 90 omitted by FA 2008, s. 36 and Sch. 14, para. 17(a), with effect:

- so far as relating to corporation tax, for accounting periods beginning on or after 1 April 2008, and
- so far as relating to income tax, for the tax year 2008–09 and subsequent tax years.

90A Interpretation

90A [Omitted by FA 2007, s. 41 and Sch. 10, para. 14(3)(c) and repealed by FA 2007, s. 114 and Sch. 27, Pt. 2(10).]

History – S. 90A omitted by FA 2007, s. 41 and Sch. 10, para. 14(3)(c) and repealed by FA 2007, s. 114 and Sch. 27, Pt. 2(10) with effect in relation to periods of account beginning on or after 1 January 2007.

UNDERWRITERS

91 Premiums trust funds: stock lending

91 [Repealed by Statute Law (Repeals) Act 2013, s. 1 and Sch. 1, Pt. 10.]

History – S. 91 repealed by Statute Law (Repeals) Act 2013, s. 1 and Sch. 1, Pt. 10, with effect from 31 January 2013.

Cross references – ICTA 1988, s. 129(6): stock lending, regulations for which specify a date of 18 August 1989.

92 Regulations about underwriters etc.

92(1), (2) [Repealed by Statute Law (Repeals) Act 2013, s. 1 and Sch. 1, Pt. 10.]

92(3) [Repealed by TCGA 1992, s. 290 and Sch. 12.]

92(4)–(7) [Repealed by FA 1993, s. 213 and Sch. 23, Pt. III(12).]

History – S. 91(1) and (2) repealed by Statute Law (Repeals) Act 2013, s. 1 and Sch. 1, Pt. 10, with effect from 31 January 2013.
S. 92(3), and reference in s. 92(4) to CGTA 1979 and other enactments relating to capital gains tax, repealed by TCGA 1992, s. 290 and Sch. 12.
S. 92(4)–(7) repealed by FA 1993, s. 213 and Sch. 23, Pt. III(12) in relation to 1992–93 and subsequent years of assessment.

Cross references – FA 1993, s. 182(5)(b): regulations made under s. 92(5) in force immediately before 6 April 1992 continue in force for 1992–93 and subsequent years of assessment notwithstanding repeal of s. 92(5).

SECURITIES

96 Securities: miscellaneous

96(1) [Repealed by Statute Law (Repeals) Act 2013, s. 1 and Sch. 1, Pt. 10.]

96(2) [Repealed by ITA 2007, s. 1031 and Sch. 3, Pt. 1.]

96(3) [Repealed by TCGA 1992, s. 290 and Sch. 12.]

96(4) [Repealed by Statute Law (Repeals) Act 2013, s. 1 and Sch. 1, Pt. 10.]

History – S. 96(1) repealed by Statute Law (Repeals) Act 2013, s. 1 and Sch. 1, Pt. 10, with effect from 31 January 2013.
S. 96(2) repealed by ITA 2007, s. 1031 and Sch. 3, Pt. 1, with effect from 6 April 2007.
S. 96(4) repealed by Statute Law (Repeals) Act 2013, s. 1 and Sch. 1, Pt. 10, with effect from 31 January 2013.
In former s. 96(4) the words "and subsection (2) above" repealed by ITA 2007, s. 1031 and Sch. 3, Pt. 1, with effect from 6 April 2007. Additional comma following "above" removed as it is assumed this was left in error.

Notes – S. 96(2) rewritten as ITA 2007, s. 498(1).

GROUPS OF COMPANIES

97 Set-off of ACT where companies remain in same group

97(1) [Repealed by FA 1998, s. 165 and Sch. 27, Pt. III(2).]

97(2) [Repealed by FA 1998, s. 165 and Sch. 27, Pt. III(2).]

History – S. 97 repealed by FA 1998 s. 165 and Sch. 27, Pt. III(2), with effect in relation to accounting periods of the surrendering company (as defined in ICTA 1988, s. 240(1)) beginning on or after 6 April 1999.

98 Restriction on set-off of ACT

98(1)–(2) [Repealed by FA 1998, s. 165 and Sch. 27, Pt. III(2).]

History – S. 98 repealed by FA 1998, s. 165 and Sch. 27, Pt. III(2), with effect in relation to changes of ownership on or after 6 April 1999.

99 Dividends etc. paid by one member of a group to another

99(1) [Repealed by FA 2001, Sch. 33, Pt. 2(10).]

99(2) [Repealed by FA 1998, s. 165 and Sch. 27, Pt. III(2).]

99(3)–(7) [Repealed by FA 2001, Sch. 33, Pt. 2(10).]

History – S. 99 repealed by FA 2001, Sch. 33, Pt. 2(10) with effect from 11 May 2001.
Former s. 99(2) (which substituted ICTA 1988, s. 247(1)(b)) repealed by FA 1998, s. 165 and Sch 27 with effect in relation to distributions made on or after 6 April 1999.

100 Change in ownership of company

100 [Repealed by CTA 2010, s. 1181 and Sch. 3, Pt. 1.]

History – S. 100 repealed by CTA 2010, s. 1181 and Sch. 3, Pt. 1, with effect for corporation tax purposes for accounting periods ending on or after 1 April 2010, and for income tax and capital gains tax purposes for the tax year 2010–11 and subsequent tax years.

101 Treatment of convertible shares or securities for purposes relating to group relief etc.

101 [Repealed by CTA 2010, s. 1181 and Sch. 3, Pt. 1.]

History – S. 101 repealed by CTA 2010, s. 1181 and Sch. 3, Pt. 1, with effect for corporation tax purposes for accounting periods ending on or after 1 April 2010, and for income tax and capital gains tax purposes for the tax year 2010–11 and subsequent tax years.

102 Surrender of company tax refund etc. within group

102 [Omitted by CTA 2010, s. 1177 and Sch. 1, para. 215 and repealed by CTA 2010, s. 1181 and Sch. 3, Pt. 1.]

History – S. 102 omitted by CTA 2010, s. 1177 and Sch. 1, para. 215 and repealed by CTA 2010, s. 1181 and Sch. 3, Pt. 1, with effect for corporation tax purposes for accounting periods ending on or after 1 April 2010, and for income tax and capital gains tax purposes for the tax year 2010–11 and subsequent tax years.

Notes – S. 102 rewritten in CTA 2010 as follows:
S. 102(1): CTA 2010, s. 963(1), (2).
S. 102(2): CTA 2010, s. 963(2), (3).
S. 102(3): CTA 2010, s. 963(2), (4).
S. 102(4): CTA 2010, s. 964(2), (4), (5).
S. 102(4A): CTA 2010, s. 965(1), (2), (3), (4), (5).
S. 102(5): CTA 2010, s. 964(6).
S. 102(6): CTA 2010, s. 964(3).
S. 102(7): CTA 2010, s. 966(1), (2).
S. 102(8): CTA 2010, s. 963(5).

CLOSE COMPANIES

103 Repeal of apportionment provisions

103 [Spent.]

104 Meaning of "close company"

104 [Repealed by CTA 2010, s. 1181 and Sch. 3, Pt. 1.]

History – S. 104 repealed by CTA 2010, s. 1181 and Sch. 3, Pt. 1, with effect for corporation tax purposes for accounting periods ending on or after 1 April 2010, and for income tax and capital gains tax purposes for the tax year 2010–11 and subsequent tax years.

105 Small companies' rate not available to certain close companies

105 [Repealed by CTA 2010, s. 1181 and Sch. 3, Pt. 1.]

History – S. 105 repealed by CTA 2010, s. 1181 and Sch. 3, Pt. 1, with effect for corporation tax purposes for accounting periods ending on or after 1 April 2010, and for income tax and capital gains tax purposes for the tax year 2010–11 and subsequent tax years.

106 Restriction on payment of tax credits

106 [Repealed by F(No. 2)A 1997, s. 52 and Sch. 8, Pt. II(9) with effect in relation to distributions made on or after 6 April 1999.]

107 Close companies: consequential amendments

107 Schedule 12 to this Act (in which Part I contains administrative provisions relating to close companies and Part II makes amendments connected with section 103 above) shall have effect.

SETTLEMENTS ETC.

108 Outright gifts etc. between husband and wife

108(1)–(5) [Repealed by FA 1995, s. 162 and Sch. 29, Pt. VIII(8), for 1995–96 and subsequent years of assessment.]

109 Settlements where settlor retains interest in settled property

109(1)–(3) [Repealed by FA 1995, s. 162 and Sch. 29, Pt. VIII(8), for 1995–96 and subsequent years of assessment.]

109(4) [Repealed by ITTOIA 2005, s. 884 and Sch. 3 with effect for income tax purposes from 2005–06 onwards and for corporation tax purposes for accounting periods ending after 5 April 2005 (ITTOIA 2005, *s. 883(1).]*

110 Residence of trustees

110 [Repealed by FA 2006, s. 89 and Sch. 13, para. 28(2)(c) and FA 2006, s. 178 and Sch. 26, Pt. 3(15).]

History – S. 110 ceases to have effect from 6 April 2007 by virtue of FA 2006, s. 89 and Sch. 13, para. 28(2)(c) and FA 2006, s. 178 and Sch. 26, Pt. 3(15) in relation to settlements whenever created.

111 Residence of personal representatives

111(1) [Omitted by ITA 2007, s. 1027 and Sch. 1, para. 280(a), and repealed by s. 1031 and Sch. 3, Pt. 1.]

111(2) [Omitted by ITA 2007, s. 1027 and Sch. 1, para. 280(a), and repealed by s. 1031 and Sch. 3, Pt. 1.]

111(3) [Omitted by ITA 2007, s. 1027 and Sch. 1, para. 280(a), and repealed by s. 1031 and Sch. 3, Pt. 1.]

111(4) [Amends ICTA 1988, s. 824(9).]

111(5) This section shall apply for the year 1989–90 and subsequent years of assessment.

111(6) [Omitted by ITA 2007, s. 1027 and Sch. 1, para. 280(a), and repealed by s. 1031 and Sch. 3, Pt. 1.]

111(7) [Omitted by ITA 2007, s. 1027 and Sch. 1, para. 280(a), and repealed by s. 1031 and Sch. 3, Pt. 1.]

111(8) [Omitted by ITA 2007, s. 1027 and Sch. 1, para. 280(a), and repealed by s. 1031 and Sch. 3, Pt. 1.]

History – S. 111(1) omitted by ITA 2007, s. 1027 and Sch. 1, para. 280(a), and repealed by s. 1031 and Sch. 3, Pt 1, with effect from 6 April 2007.
S. 111(2) omitted by ITA 2007, s. 1027 and Sch. 1, para. 280(a), and repealed by s. 1031 and Sch. 3, Pt. 1, with effect from 6 April 2007.
S. 111(3) omitted by ITA 2007, s. 1027 and Sch. 1, para. 280(a), and repealed by s. 1031 and Sch. 3, Pt. 1, with effect from 6 April 2007.
In s. 111(5) the opening words "Subject to subsections (6) to (8) below," omitted by ITA 2007, s. 1027 and Sch. 1, para. 280(b), and repealed by s. 1031 and Sch. 3, Pt. 1, with effect from 6 April 2007.
S. 111(6) omitted by ITA 2007, s. 1027 and Sch. 1, para. 280(a), and repealed by s. 1031 and Sch. 3, Pt. 1, with effect from 6 April 2007.
S. 111(7) omitted by ITA 2007, s. 1027 and Sch. 1, para. 280(a), and repealed by s. 1031 and Sch. 3, Pt. 1, with effect from 6 April 2007.
S. 111(8) omitted by ITA 2007, s. 1027 and Sch. 1, para. 280(a), and repealed by s. 1031 and Sch. 3, Pt. 1, with effect from 6 April 2007.

Cross references – ICTA 1988, s. 739: liability to income tax of transferor where attempt to avoid tax through transfer of assets abroad.
ICTA 1988, s. 740: liability to income tax on non-transferors where attempt to avoid tax through transfer of assets abroad.
ICTA 1988, s. 824(9): eligibility for repayment supplement of UK-resident personal representatives.
TCGA 1992, s. 62: residence of personal representatives for capital gains tax purposes.

Other material – Law Society's Gazette, 25 April 1990 (not reproduced): where a person dies leaving separate wills for UK and non-UK property, Revenue confirm s. 111 applies to each estate separately.

Notes – S. 111 rewritten as follows:
S. 111(1): ITA 2007, s. 718(2), 834(1), (2), (4).
S. 111(2): ITA 2007, s. 834(3).
S. 111(3): ITA 2007, s. 989.
S. 111(7): ITA 2007, Sch. 2, para. 136(1), (2), (3), (4).
S. 111(8): ITA 2007, Sch. 2, para. 137(1), (2), (3), (4), (5).

MISCELLANEOUS

112 Security: trades etc.

112 [Omitted by ITTOIA 2005, s. 882(1) and Sch. 1, para. 410; and repealed by ITTOIA 2005, s. 884 and Sch. 3.]

History – S. 112 omitted by ITTOIA 2005, s. 882(1) and Sch. 1, para. 410; and repealed by ITTOIA 2005, s. 884 and Sch. 3 effective for income tax purposes for 2005–06 onwards (ITTOIA 2005, s. 883(1)).

113 Security: trades etc. (supplementary)

113 [Omitted by ITTOIA 2005, s. 882(1) and Sch. 1, para. 410; and repealed by ITTOIA 2005, s. 884 and Sch. 3.]

History – S. 113 omitted by ITTOIA 2005, s. 882(1) and Sch. 1, para. 410; and repealed by ITTOIA 2005, s. 884 and Sch. 3 effective for income tax purposes for 2005–06 onwards (ITTOIA 2005, s. 883(1)).

Notes – The income tax provisions rewritten at ITTOIA 2005, s. 81.

114 Relief for pre-trading expenditure

114 [Repealed by CTA 2009, s. 1326 and Sch. 3, Pt. 1 and Statute Law (Repeals) Act 2013, s. 1 and Sch. 1, Pt. 10.]

History – S. 114 repealed by CTA 2009, s. 1326 and Sch. 3, Pt. 1 with effect, for corporation tax purposes, for accounting periods ending on or after 1 April 2009 and, for income tax and capital gains tax purposes, for the tax year 2009–10 and subsequent years and by Statute Law (Repeals) Act 2013, s. 1 and Sch. 1, Pt. 10, with effect from 31 January 2013.

115 Double taxation: tax credits

115 [Omitted by FA 2016, s. 5 and Sch. 1, para. 54(a).]

History – S. 115 omitted by FA 2016, s. 5 and Sch. 1, para. 54(a), with effect in relation to dividends paid or arising (or treated as paid) and other distributions made (or treated as made) in the tax year 2016–17 or at any later time. Former s. 115 read as follows:

"Double taxation: tax credits

115(1) Where any arrangements which have effect under section 2(1) of the Taxation (International and Other Provisions) Act 2010 provide–

(a) for persons who are resident outside the United Kingdom and who receive distributions from companies resident in the United Kingdom to be entitled to tax credits, and

(b) for the amount paid to such a person by way of tax credit to be determined by reference to the amount to which an individual resident in the United Kingdom would have been entitled, subject to a deduction calculated by reference to the aggregate of the amount or value of the distribution and the amount of the tax credit paid,

the arrangements shall be construed as providing for that deduction to be calculated by reference to the gross amount or value of the distribution and tax credit, without any allowance for the deduction itself.

115(2) This section shall have effect in relation to payments made before the passing of this Act as well as those made after that time, except that it shall not affect–

(a) the judgment of any court given before 25th October 1988, or

(b) the law to be applied in proceedings on appeal to the Court of Appeal or the House of Lords where the judgment of the High Court or the Court of Session which is in issue was given before that date.

History – In s. 115(1), the words "which have effect under section 2(1) of the Taxation (International and Other Provisions) Act 2010" substituted for the words "having effect by virtue of section 788 of the Taxes Act 1988" by TIOPA 2010, s. 374 and Sch. 8, para. 38, with effect for corporation tax purposes for accounting periods ending on or after 1 April 2010, for income tax and capital gains tax purposes for the tax year 2010–11 and subsequent tax years, and for petroleum revenue tax purposes for chargeable periods beginning on or after 1 July 2010."

Chapter II – Capital Allowances

121 Miscellaneous amendments

121 [Repealed by CAA 2001, s. 580 and Sch. 4.]

History – S. 121 (which introduced Sch. 13) repealed by CAA 2001, s. 580 and Sch. 4, with effect as respects allowances and charges falling to be made for chargeable periods ending, for income tax purposes, on or after 6 April 2001, and for corporation tax purposes, on or after 1 April 2001.

Chapter III – Capital Gains

EXEMPTIONS

123 Increase of chattel exemption

123(1) [Amends provisions as below.]

(a) [Repealed by TCGA 1992, s. 290 and Sch. 12.]

(b) [Omitted by SI 2009/2035, art. 2 and Schedule, para. 60(c).]

(c) [Amends TMA 1970, s. 25(7).]

123(2) This section applies to disposals on or after 6th April 1989 and accordingly, in relation to subsection (1)(b) above, acquired on or after that date.

History – S. 123(1)(b) omitted by SI 2009/2035, art. 2 and Schedule, para. 60(c), with effect from 13 August 2009.

Chapter IV – Management

INFORMATION

142 Power to call for documents and information

142(1) Section 20 of the Taxes Management Act 1970 (power to call for documents of taxpayer and others) shall be amended in accordance with subsections (2) to (8) below.

142(2) [Omitted by FA 2008, s. 113 and Sch. 36, para. 92(b).]

142(3) [Omitted by FA 2008, s. 113 and Sch. 36, para. 92(b).]

142(4) [Omitted by FA 2008, s. 113 and Sch. 36, para. 92(b).]

142(5) [Omitted by FA 2008, s. 113 and Sch. 36, para. 92(b).]

142(6) [Omitted by FA 2008, s. 113 and Sch. 36, para. 92(b).]

142(7) [Omitted by FA 2008, s. 113 and Sch. 36, para. 92(b).]

142(8) [Omitted by FA 2008, s. 113 and Sch. 36, para. 92(b).]

142(9) [Omitted by FA 2008, s. 113 and Sch. 36, para. 92(b).]

142(10) This section shall apply with respect to notices given on or after the day on which this Act is passed.

History – S. 142(2), (3), (4), (6)(a), (7), (8) and (9) omitted by FA 2008, s. 113 and Sch. 36, para. 92(b), with effect from 1 April 2009 (SI 2009/404, art. 2, subject to savings at SI 2009/404, art. 3).

143 Power to call for papers of tax accountant

143(1) [Substitutes TMA 1970, s. 20A(1A), (1B).]

143(2) This section shall apply with respect to notices given on or after the day on which this Act is passed.

144 Restrictions on powers under TMA ss. 20 and 20A

144(1) Section 20B of the Taxes Management Act 1970 (restrictions on powers under sections 20 and 20A) shall be amended as follows.

144(2) [Amended TMA 1970, s. 20B(1).]

144(3) [Omitted by FA 2008, s. 113 and Sch. 36, para. 92(b).]

144(4) [Amended TMA 1970, s. 20(2).]

144(5) [Omitted by FA 2008, s. 113 and Sch. 36, para. 92(b).]

144(6) [Amends TMA 1970, s. 20(7).]

144(7) [Omitted by FA 2008, s. 113 and Sch. 36, para. 92(b).]

144(8) This section shall apply with respect to notices given on or after the day on which this Act is passed.

History – S. 144(3), (5) and (7) omitted by FA 2008, s. 113 and Sch. 36, para. 92(b), with effect from 1 April 2009 (by virtue of SI 2009/404).

145 Falsification etc. of documents

145(1) [Inserts TMA 1970, s. 20BB.]

145(2) This section shall apply to any falsification, concealment, destruction or disposal of a document occurring on or after the day on which this Act is passed.

146 Entry with warrant to obtain documents

146 [Repealed by FA 2007, s. 114 and Sch. 27, Pt. 5(1).]

History – S. 146 repealed by FA 2007, s. 114 and Sch. 27, Pt. 5(1), with effect from 8 November 2007 by virtue of SI 2007/3166, art. 2(c), in accordance with FA 2007, s. 84(5).

147 Procedure where documents etc. are removed

147 [Repealed by FA 2007, s. 114 and Sch. 27, Pt. 5(1).]

History – S. 147 repealed by FA 2007, s. 114 and Sch. 27, Pt. 5(1), with effect from 8 November 2007 by virtue of SI 2007/3166, art. 2(c), in accordance with FA 2007, s. 84(5).

148 Interpretation

148(1) Section 20D of the Taxes Management Act 1970 shall be amended as follows.

148(2) [Amends TMA 1970, s. 20D(2).]

148(3) [Substitutes TMA 1970, s. 20D(3).]

148(4) [Omitted by FA 2007, s. 84(4) and Sch. 22, para. 7; repealed by FA 2007, s. 114 and Sch. 27, Pt. 5(1).]

History – S. 148(4) omitted by FA 2007, s. 84(4) and Sch. 22, para. 7 with effect from 1 December 2007 by virtue of SI 2007/3166, art. 3(a), and repealed by FA 2007, s. 114 and Sch. 27, Pt. 5(1), with effect from 8 November 2007 by virtue of SI 2007/3166, art. 2(c), in accordance with FA 2007, s. 84(5).

ASSESSMENTS, CLAIMS ETC.

149 Assessments founded on fraudulent or negligent conduct

149(1) [Substitutes TMA 1970, s. 36.]

149(2) [Repeals TMA 1970, s. 37–39 and s. 41.]

149(3) [Amends provisions as below.]

(a) [Amends TMA 1970, s. 30(6).]

(b) [Amends TMA 1970, s. 118(3).]

(c) [Repealed by FA 1998, s. 165 and Sch. 27, Pt. III(2).]

(d) [Repealed by ITA 2007, s. 1031 and Sch. 3, Pt. 1.]

149(4) [Amends provisions as below.]

(a) [Amends provisions as below.]

  (i) [Omitted by FA 2008, s. 118 and Sch. 39, para. 65(a).]

  (ii) [Omitted by FA 2008, s. 118 and Sch. 39, para. 65(a).]

  (iii) [Amends FA 1973, Sch. 16A, para. 9 and ICTA 1988, Sch. 19A, para. 9.]

(b) [Repealed by ITA 2007, s. 1031 and Sch. 3, Pt. 2.]

149(5) [Amends TMA 1970, s. 105.]

149(6) [Amends FA 1973, Sch. 16A, para. 9 and ICTA 1988, Sch. 19A, para. 9.]

149(7) Nothing in this section shall affect the making of assessments–

(a) for years of assessment before the year 1983–84, or

(b) for accounting periods which ended before 1st April 1983.

History – S. 149(3)(c) repealed by FA 1998, s. 165 and Sch. 27, Pt. III(2), with effect in relation to return periods beginning on or after 6 April 1999 and in relation to accounting periods beginning on or after that date.

S. 149(3)(d) repealed by s. 1031 and Sch. 3, Pt. 1, with effect from 6 April 2007.

S. 149(4)(a)(i) and (ii) omitted by FA 2008, s. 118 and Sch. 39, para. 65(a), with effect from 1 April 2010 (SI 2009/403, art. 2(2) subject to SI 2009/403, art. 3–10 – in particular art. 10). Former s. 149(4)(a) amended TMA 1970, s. 37A and former s. 149(4)(a)(ii) amended TMA 1970, s. 40(2).

S. 149(4)(b) repealed by ITA 2007, s. 1031 and Sch. 3, Pt. 2, with effect in relation to shares issued after 5 April 2007. Former s. 149(4)(b) amended ICTA 1988, s. 307(5).

Notes – S. 149 rewritten as follows:

S. 149(3): ITA 2007, s. 959(4).

S. 149(4): ITA 2007, s. 237(3).

150 Further assessments: claims etc.

150(1) [Inserts TMA 1970, s. 43A, 43B.]

150(2) This section shall apply in relation to any assessment notice of which is issued on or after the day on which this Act is passed.

151 Assessment of trustees etc.

151 [Omitted by TIOPA 2010, s. 371 and Sch. 7, para. 60 and repealed by TIOPA 2010, s. 378 and Sch. 10, Pt. 12.]

History – S. 151 omitted by TIOPA 2010, s. 371 and Sch. 7, para. 60 and repealed by TIOPA 2010, s. 378 and Sch. 10, Pt. 12, with effect for corporation tax purposes for accounting periods ending on or after 1 April 2010, for income tax and capital gains tax purposes for the tax year 2010–11 and subsequent tax years, and for petroleum revenue tax purposes for chargeable periods beginning on or after 1 July 2010.

Notes – S. 151 rewritten in TIOPA 2010 as follows:

S. 151(1): TIOPA 2010, Sch. 7, para. 58.

S. 151(2): TIOPA 2010, Sch. 7, para. 58.

DISTRESS AND POINDING ETC.

152 Distress for non-payment of tax

152(1) Section 61 of the Taxes Management Act 1970 (distress) shall be amended as follows.

152(2) [Amends TMA 1970, s. 61(1).]

152(3) [Amends TMA 1970, s. 61(2).]

152(4) [Amends TMA 1970, s. 61(4).]

152(5) [Amends TMA 1970, s. 61(5).]

152(6) [Inserts TMA 1970, s. 61(6).]

152(7) This section shall come into force on such day as the Treasury may by order made by statutory instrument appoint.

153 Priority in cases of distraint by others

153(1)–(4) [Amends TMA 1970, s. 62(1), (2); inserts s. 62(1A).]

154 Recovery of tax from debtor in Scotland

154(1)–(3) [Amends TMA 1970, s. 63(3); inserts s. 63(4).]

155 Priority in cases of poinding etc. by others in Scotland

155(1)–(4) [Amends TMA 1970, s. 64(1), (2); inserts s. 64(1A).]

INTEREST ETC.

156 Interest on overdue tax

156(1) [Substitutes TMA 1970, s. 86(3), (4) (the words preceding the Table); inserts s. 86(3A).]

156(2) [Amends TMA 1970, s. 55(2); substitutes s. 55(6)(a), (b), (9).]

156(3) [Amends TMA 1970, s. 56(9).]

156(4) This section shall apply to tax charged by any assessment notice of which is issued after 30th July 1982.

158 Small amounts of interest

158(1) [Amends provisions as below.]

(a) [Repeals TMA 1970, s. 86(6).]

(b) [Repeals TMA 1970, s. 87(4).]

158(2) [Amends provisions as below.]

(a) [Partially repeals TCGA 1992, s. 283(1).]

(b) [Partially repeals ICTA 1988, s. 824(1)(a), (b), (5); partially repeals ICTA 1988, s. 825(2).]

158(3) Paragraph (a) of subsection (1) above shall have effect–

(a) in relation to income tax under Schedule E, where the demand for the tax is made on or after the appointed day, and

(b) in any other case, where the tax is charged by an assessment notice of which is issued on or after the appointed day.

158(4) Paragraph (b) of that subsection shall have effect where the tax is charged by an assessment relating to an accounting period beginning on or after the appointed day.

158(5) Subsection (2) above shall have effect in relation to repayments of tax made on or after the appointed day.

158(6) In this section **"the appointed day"** means such day as the Treasury may by order made by statutory instrument appoint; and different days may be appointed for different enactments or for different purposes of the same enactment.

Statutory instruments – SI 1994/3230: made under s. 158(3)–(6).

159 Interest on tax in case of failure or error

159 [Repealed by FA 1996, Sch. 41, Pt. V(8).]

History – S. 159 repealed by FA 1996, Sch. 41, Pt. V(8), with effect in accordance with FA 1996, Sch. 18, para. 17(3), (4).

160 Determinations under TMA s. 88

160(1) [Repealed by FA 1996, Sch. 41, Pt. V(8).]

160(2) [Repealed by FA 1996, Sch. 41, Pt. V(8).]

160(3) [Repealed by Statute Law (Repeals) Act 2013, s. 1 and Sch. 1, Pt. 10.]

160(4) [Repealed by FA 1996, Sch. 41, Pt. V(8).]

160(5) [Amends TMA 1970, s. 114.]

160(6) [Repealed by FA 1996, Sch. 41, Pt. V(12).]

History – S. 160(1), (2), (4) repealed by FA 1996, Sch. 41, Pt. V(8), with effect as provided by FA 1996, Sch. 18, para. 17.
S. 160(3) repealed by Statute Law (Repeals) Act 2013, s. 1 and Sch. 1, Pt. 10, with effect from 31 January 2013.
S. 160(6) (which amended TMA 1970, Sch. 3, para. 5) repealed by FA 1996, Sch. 41, Pt. V(12), with effect in relation to proceedings relating to any tax year after 1995–96 or any accounting period ending on or after the day appointed under FA 1994, s. 199.

161 Tax carrying interest under TMA ss. 86 and 88

161 [Repealed by FA 1996, Sch. 41, Pt. V(8).]

History – S. 161 repealed by FA 1996, Sch. 41, Pt. V(8), with effect in accordance with FA 1996, Sch. 18, para. 17(3), (4).

PENALTIES

162 Failure to make return

162 [Repealed by Statute Law (Repeals) Act 2013, s. 1 and Sch. 1, Pt. 10.]

History – S. 162 repealed by Statute Law (Repeals) Act 2013, s. 1 and Sch. 1, Pt. 10, with effect from 31 January 2013.

163 Incorrect return, accounts etc.

163(1) [Amends provisions as below.]

(a) [Repealed by FA 2007, s. 114 and Sch. 27, Pt. 5(5).]

(b) [Amends TMA 1970, s. 96(1).]

163(2) This section shall apply in relation to returns, statements, declarations or accounts delivered, made or submitted on or after the day on which this Act is passed.

History – S. 163(1)(a) (which amended TMA 1970, s. 95(1)) repealed by FA 2007, s. 114 and Sch. 27, Pt. 5(5), with effect from a number of different dates, but the latest date being 1 April 2009, by virtue of SI 2008/568, art. 2.

164 Special returns, information etc.

164(1)–(5) [Amends TMA 1970, s. 98(1), (2) and Table; substitutes s. 98(3); inserts s. 98(4). S. 164(5)(b) repealed by TIOPA 2010, s. 378 and Sch. 10, Pt.12]

164(6) [Repeals TMA 1970, s. 16(6).]

164(7) This section shall apply in relation to–

(a) any failure to comply with a notice or to furnish information, give a certificate or produce a document or record beginning on or after the day on which this Act is passed, and

(b) the furnishing, giving, producing or making of any incorrect information, certificate, document, record or declaration on or after that day.

History – S. 164(5)(b) repealed by TIOPA 2010, s. 378 and Sch. 10, Pt. 12, with effect for corporation tax purposes for accounting periods ending on or after 1 April 2010, for income tax and capital gains tax purposes for the tax year 2010–11 and subsequent tax years, and for petroleum revenue tax purposes for chargeable periods beginning on or after 1 July 2010.

165 Special penalties in the case of certain returns

165(1) [Inserts TMA 1970, s. 98A but s. 98A(2)(a) is not effective in the form prescribed by this section until repeal of s. 165(2) below.]

165(2) [Repealed by FA 1989, s. 187 and Sch. 17, Pt. VIII.]

History – S. 165(2) repealed by FA 1989, s. 187 and Sch. 17, Pt. VIII, with effect from 20 May 1995 (the appointed day for the purpose of s. 165(2) by virtue of SI 1994/2508 (C 50)).

166 Assisting in preparation of incorrect return etc.

166(1) [Substitutes TMA 1970, s. 99.]

166(2) This section shall apply in relation to assistance and inducements occurring on or after the day on which this Act is passed.

167 Determination of penalties

167 [Substitutes TMA 1970, s. 100; inserts s. 100A–100D.]

168 Amendments consequential on section 167

168(1) In consequence of the amendment made by section 167 above the Taxes Management Act 1970 shall be amended in accordance with subsections (2) to (8) below.

168(2) [Amends TMA 1970, s. 20A(1), (2), (4).]

168(3) [Amends TMA 1970, s. 53(1)–(3).]

168(4) [Amends TMA 1970, s. 102.]

168(5) [Substitutes TMA 1970, s. 105(1)(a); amends s. 105(2)(b); inserts s. 105(2)(c).]

168(6) [Inserts TMA 1970, s. 112(3).]

168(7) [Inserts TMA 1970, s. 113(1D); amends s. 113(3).]

168(8) [Repealed by FA 1996, Sch. 41, Pt. V(12).]

168(9) [Amends provisions not reproduced.]

History – S. 168(8) (which amended TMA 1970, Sch. 3, para. 5) repealed by FA 1996, Sch. 41, Pt. V(12), with effect in relation to proceedings relating to any tax year after 1995–96 or any accounting period ending on or after 1 July 1999, the day appointed under FA 1994, s. 199 (SI 1998/3173 (C. 78)).

169 Time limits

169(1) [Substitutes TMA 1970, s. 103.]

169(2) [Spent.]

170 Up-rating of certain penalties

170(1) [Repealed by FA 1995, s. 162 and Sch. 29, Pt. VIII(1).]

170(2) [Repealed by F(No. 2)A 1992, s. 82 and Sch. 18, Pt. VII(4).]

170(3) [Repealed by ITA 2007, s. 1031 and Sch. 3, Pt. 2.]

170(4) [Amends provisions as below.]

(a) [Repealed by FA 2004, s. 326 and Sch. 42, Pt. 3.]

(b) [Repealed by FA 2004, s. 326 and Sch. 42, Pt. 3.]

(c) [Amends ICTA 1988, s. 658(5).]

170(5) [Amends ICTA 1988, Sch. 19A, para. 2(4) and FA 1973, Sch. 16A, para. 2(4).]

170(6) This section shall apply in relation to things done or omitted on or after the day on which this Act is passed.

History – S. 170(1) repealed by FA 1995, s. 162 and Sch. 29, Pt. VIII(1) with effect for 1995–96 and subsequent tax years and, for the purpose of corporation tax, in relation to accounting periods ending on or after 31 March 1995. The repeal of s. 170(1) (which amended ICTA 1988, s. 23(8)) does not apply for 1995–96 to a source where:

- that source is a source in respect of the profits or gains from which that person is chargeable to tax for the year 1994–95 under Sch. A or Sch. D, Case VI; and
- that source ceases, in the course of the year 1995–96, to be a source from which any such profits or gains arise to that or any other person as would be chargeable to tax under Sch. A or Sch. D, Case VI if the amendments for which FA 1995, s. 39 and Sch. 6 provide were to be disregarded; and
- that person is not a person who sets up and commences a Sch. A business in the course of the year 1995–96.

S. 170(3) repealed by ITA 2007, s. 1031 and Sch. 3, Pt. 2, with effect in relation to shares issued after 5 April 2007. Former s. 170(3) amended ICTA 1988, s. 306(6).

S. 170(4)(a) and (b) repealed by FA 2004, s. 326 and Sch. 42, Pt. 3 with effect from 6 April 2006 but subject to FA 2004, Sch. 36 (Pension schemes etc.: transitional provisions and savings). Former s. 170(4)(a) and (b) amended ICTA 1988, s. 619(7) and ICTA 1988, s. 653 respectively.

Notes – S. 170(3) rewritten as ITA 2007, s. 207.

PART III – MISCELLANEOUS AND GENERAL

INTEREST ETC.

178 Setting of rates of interest

178(1) The rate of interest applicable for the purposes of an enactment to which this section applies shall be the rate which for the purposes of that enactment is provided for by regulations made by the Treasury under this section.

178(2) This section applies to–

(aa) section 15A of the Stamp Act 1891;

(a) section 8(9) of the Finance Act 1894,

(b) section 18 of the Finance Act 1896,

(c) section 61(5) of the Finance (1909–10) Act 1910,

(d) section 17(3) of the Law of Property Act 1925,

(e) [Repealed by Land Registration Act 2002, s. 135 and Schedule 13.]

(f) sections 86, 86A, 87, 87A and 103A of the Taxes Management Act 1970,

(g) paragraph 3 of Schedule 16A to the Finance Act 1973,

(ga) section 48(1) of the Finance Act 1975,

(gg) paragraph 6 of Schedule 1 to the Social Security Contributions and Benefits Act 1992,

(gh) section 71(8A) of the Social Security Administration Act 1992, and section 69(8A) of the Social Security Administration (Northern Ireland) Act 1992, as they have effect in any case where the overpayment was made in respect of working families' tax credit or disabled person's tax credit;

(h) paragraphs 15 and 16 of Schedule 2, and paragraph 8 of Schedule 5, to the Oil Taxation Act 1975,

(i) section 283 of the Taxation of Chargeable Gains Act 1992,

(j) paragraph 59 of Schedule 8 to the Development Land Tax Act 1976,

(k) sections 233, 235(1) and 236(3) and (4) of the Inheritance Tax Act 1984,

(l) section 92 of the Finance Act 1986, [and]

(m) sections 824, 825, 826 and 826A of, and paragraph 3 of Schedule 19A to, the Taxes Act 1988, and

(n) [Repealed by FA 1995, s. 153 and Sch. 29, Pt. XII, and]

(o) section 14(4) of the Ports Act 1991,

(p) paragraph 8 of Schedule 4 to the Tax Credits Act 1999,

(q) section 110 of the Finance Act 1999,

(r) paragraph 8 of Schedule 1 to the Employment Act 2002,

(s) Chapter 7 of Part 3 of the Income Tax (Earnings and Pensions) Act 2003, and

(t) sections 87, 88 and 89 of the Finance Act 2003,

(u) paragraph 11 of Schedule 35 to the Finance Act 2014, and

(v) section 79 of FA 2015.

178(3) Regulations under this section may–

(a) make different provision for different enactments or for different purposes of the same enactment,

(b) either themselves specify a rate of interest for the purposes of an enactment or make provision for any such rate to be determined by reference to such rate or the average of such rates as may be referred to in the regulations,

(c) provide for rates to be reduced below, or increased above, what they otherwise would be by specified amounts or by reference to specified formulae,

(d) provide for rates arrived at by reference to averages to be rounded up or down,

(e) provide for circumstances in which alteration of a rate of interest is or is not to take place, and

(f) provide that alterations of rates are to have effect for periods beginning on or after a day determined in accordance with the regulations in relation to interest running from before that day as well as from or from after that day.

178(4) The power to make regulations under this section shall be exercisable by statutory instrument which shall be subject to annulment in pursuance of a resolution of the House of Commons.

178(5) [Omitted by FA 2009, s. 105(6)(a).]

178(6) [Repealed by CTA 2010, s. 1181 and Sch. 3, Pt. 1.]

178(7) Subsection (1) shall have effect for periods beginning on or after such day as the Treasury may by order made by statutory instrument appoint and shall have effect in relation to interest running from before that day as well as from or from after that day; and different days may be appointed for different enactments.

History – S. 178(2)(aa) inserted by FA 1999, s. 109(2), with effect for instruments executed on or after 1 October 1999.
S. 178(2)(e) repealed by Land Registration Act 2002, s. 135 and Sch. 13, with effect from 13 October 2003 (SI 2003/1725).
In s. 178(2)(f), "59C,", which appeared after "sections", omitted by SI 2011/702, art. 12, with effect from 1 April 2011, but subject to SI 2011/702, art. 20, which provides that the omission does not have effect in relation to a return or other document which is required to be made or delivered to HMRC, or an amount of tax which is payable, in relation to the tax year 2009–10 or any previous tax year.
In s. 178(2)(f), the references to s. 59C and 103A inserted by FA 1994, s. 196 and Sch. 19, para. 44, in so far as it applies to income tax and capital gains tax as respects years after 1995–96, and in so far as it applies to corporation tax, as respects accounting periods ending on or after 1 July 1999, the appointed day for corporation tax self-assessment by virtue of FA 1994, s. 199(3) and SI 1998/3173 (C. 78); and the former reference to s. 88 omitted by FA 1996, Sch. 18, para. 13; and FA 1996, Sch. 41, Pt. V(8); with effect in accordance with FA 1996, Sch. 18, para. 17(3).
S. 178(2)(ga) inserted by FA 2009, s. 105(5)(a), with effect from 21 July 2009.
In s. 178(2)(gg), the words "paragraph 6 …Benefits Act 1992" substituted by SS(CP)A 1992, s. 4 and Sch. 2, para. 107, with effect from 1 July 1992.
S. 178(2)(gg) inserted by SSA 1990, s. 17(10) and SI 1992/632, with effect from 6 April 1992.
S. 178(2)(gh) inserted by Tax Credits Act 1999, s. 2 and Sch. 2, para. 10(2), with effect from 5 October 1999.
In s. 178(2)(k), the words ", 235(1)" inserted by FA 2009, s. 105(5)(b), with effect from 21 July 2009.
Reference to TCGA 1992 in s. 178(2)(i) substituted by TCGA 1992, s. 290 and Sch. 10, para. 19(4).
In s. 178(2)(m), the words "160" omitted by ITEPA 2003, Sch. 6, para. 162(a) and Sch. 8, Pt. 1 which have effect for the tax year 2003–04 and subsequent tax years.
In s. 178(2)(m), the reference to 118F was inserted by FA 1996, Sch. 29, para. 8, with effect from 29 April 1996 and omitted by FA 2000, Sch. 40, Pt. II(17) with effect for chargeable dates on or after 1 April 2000.
In s. 178(2)(m), the reference to ICTA 1988, s. 826A inserted by FA 1998, s. 35 and Sch. 4, para. 1(3) with effect in relation to accounting periods ending on or after 1 July 1999 (the date appointed for the purposes of self assessment to corporation tax – see above).
In s.178(2)(m), the words "and paragraph 6B of Schedule 3 to," (inserted by F(No. 2)A 1992, s. 63 and Sch. 11, para. 5, in relation to transactions effected on or after 1 October 1992) repealed by FA 1996, s. 79 and Sch. 7, para. 30 and s. 205 and Sch. 41, Pt. V(2), with effect for years after 1995–96;
S. 178(2)(n), which was inserted by FA 1990, s. 118(8), repealed by FA 1995, s. 162 and Sch. 29, Pt. XII, with effect from 1 May 1995.
S. 178(2)(o) and word "and" preceding it inserted by Ports Act 1991, s. 14(5), with effect from 15 July 1991.
S. 178(2)(p), inserted by Tax Credits Act 1999, s. 10(4) and Sch. 4, para. 8, with effect from 5 October 1999.
At the end of s. 178(2)(q), the word "and" omitted by ITEPA 2003, Sch. 6, para. 162(b) and Sch. 8, Pt. 1 which have effect for the tax year 2003–04 and subsequent tax years.
S. 178(2)(q), and word "and" preceding it, added by FA 1999, s. 110(9), with effect for instruments executed on or after 1 October 1999. The para. was originally designated para. (p) by FA 1999, but this error was corrected by ITEPA 2003, Sch. 6, para. 162(d),as later amended by a correction slip issued in December 2003. The correction has effect for 2003–04 and subsequent tax years.
At the end of s. 178(2)(r), the word "and" inserted by ITEPA 2003, Sch. 6, para. 162(d) which has effect for the tax year 2003–04 and subsequent tax years.
S. 178(2)(s) inserted by ITEPA 2003, Sch. 6, para. 162(c), which has effect for the tax year 2003–04 and subsequent tax years. This para. was originally designated para. (r) by ITEPA 2003, but that error was corrected by a correction slip issued in December 2003.
S. 178(2)(r) inserted by Employment Act 2002, s. 11, s. 12, and Sch. 1, para. 8 with effect from 8 December 2002. This para. was originally designated para. (q) by the Employment Act 2002, but by inference, based on the correction slip issued in December 2003 for ITEPA 2003, Sch. 6, para. 162(d), it should correctly be para. (r).
S. 178(2)(s) inserted by ITEPA 2003, Sch. 6, para. 162(d) which has effect for the tax year 2003–04 and subsequent tax years. This para. was originally designated para. (r), but this error was corrected by a correction slip issued in December 2003 This para. was originally designated para. (r) by FA 2003, but this error was corrected by a correction slip issued in December 2003.
S. 178(2)(t), inserted by FA 2003, s. 123 and Sch. 18, para. 4 with effect from 10 July 2003 (date of Royal Assent to FA 2003) for transactions which are within the charge to stamp duty land tax from 1 December 2003 (the appointed day by virtue of SI 2003/2899 (C. 106)).
S. 178(2)(u) inserted by FA 2014, s. 274 and Sch. 35, para. 11(2), with effect from 17 July 2014.
S. 178(2)(v) (and the word ", and" preceding it) inserted and the word "and" at the end of s. 178(2)(t) omitted by FA 2015, s. 115(4),with effect in relation to accounting periods beginning on or after 1 April 2015 (subject to provisions of FA 2015, s. 116(2)–(5)).
S. 178(5) omitted by FA 2009, s. 105(6)(a), with effect from 21 July 2009.
S. 178(6) repealed by CTA 2010, s. 1181 and Sch. 3, Pt. 1, with effect for corporation tax purposes for accounting periods ending on or after 1 April 2010, and for income tax and capital gains tax purposes for the tax year 2010–11 and subsequent tax years.

Cross references – ICTA 1988, s. 824 (as amended by FA 1994, s. 196 and Sch. 19, para. 41(1) in relation to self-assessment): repayment supplement paid at rate applicable under s. 178.
ICTA 1988, s. 826A: interest on payments of corporation tax at the rate applicable under s. 178
ICTA 1988, s. 828(2): power to make orders which are not exercisable by statutory instrument.
ICTA 1988, Sch. 19AB, para. 3: interest at the rate applicable under s. 178 on excess provisional repayments to insurance companies.
TMA 1970, s. 59C: surcharge under s. 59(2) or (3) imposed at rate applicable under s. 178.
TMA 1970, s. 86 interest on overdue income and capital gains tax charged at rate applicable under s. 178.
TMA 1970, s. 103A: interest on penalties.
FA 1990, s. 118(7): interest at the rate applicable under s. 178 applies to unpaid ports levy.
SSCBA 1992, Sch. 1, para. 6(3): power to combine collection of contributions with tax; interest rate to be applied as prescribed by s. 178.
FA 1993, s. 173 and Sch. 19, para. 11(4): application to Lloyd's underwriters.
FA 1995, s. 178(6): application to certificates of tax deposit withdrawn for cash on or after 6 April 1990.
F(No. 2)A 1997, Sch. 2, para 12(4): interest at the rate applicable under s. 178 applies to unpaid windfall tax.
ITEPA 2003, s. 181: the official rate of interest.
FA 2003, s. 87, 88 and 89: stamp duty land tax – interest on unpaid tax, on penalties and on repayment of tax overpaid respectively.
FA 2003, s. 114(2): disapplication of FA 2003, s. 114(1) (stamp duty land tax – power to make regulations) in relation to the powers conferred under FA 1989, s. 178.
FA 2003, Sch. 5, para. 8(2), (3): application of s. 178(3)(b) to (f) and (5) to regulations for setting temporal discount rate used in calculation of stamp duty land tax where chargeable consideration consists of or includes rent.
SI 1992/2326, reg. 6(3): rate of interest where a provisional repayment to an insurance company in respect of its pension business exceeds its maximum reduced entitlement for a provisional repayment period.
SI 2003/2682, reg. 82(7), 83(4): application to PAYE.
SI 2004/674, reg. 23(1): equivalent treatment of foreign claims corresponding to UK claims.

Statutory instruments – SI 1989/1297, made under s. 178.
SI 2008/778: made under s. 178(1)–(3).
SI 2008/3234: partly made under s. 178(1)–(3).
SI 2009/199: partly made under s. 178(1) and (2)(s).

179 Provisions consequential on section 178

179(1) The words "rate applicable under section 178 of the Finance Act 1989" shall be substituted–

(a)

(i)–(iii) [Amends provisions not reproduced.]

(iv) [Repealed by LRA 2002, s. 135 and Sch. 13.]

(v) [Amends OTA 1975, Sch. 2, para. 15(1), 16 and Sch. 5, para. 8(4).]

(vi) [Repealed by TCGA 1992, s. 290 and Sch. 12.]

(vii) [Amends ICTA 1988, s. 824(1), 825(2).]

(b) for the words "prescribed rate" in–

(i) sections …87A(1) …of the Taxes Management Act 1970, (Otherwise amends TMA 1970, s. 86(1), 86A(1) and 87(1).)

(ii) [Amends FA 1973, Sch. 16A, para. 3(4).]

(iii) [Amends ICTA 1988, Sch. 19A, para. 3(4).]

(c) for the words "rate which" onwards in–

(i) [Amends provisions not reproduced.]

(ii) section 826(1) of the Taxes Act 1988,

(d) [Amends IHTA 1984, s. 233(1).]

(e) [Amends IHTA 1984, s. 236(3), (4).]

(f) [Amends FA 1986, s. 92(2).]

(g) [Repealed by ITEPA 2003, Sch. 8, Pt. 1.]

179(2) [Amends provisions not reproduced.]

179(3) [Amends IHTA 1984, s. 236(4).]

179(4) Any amendment made by subsection (1), (2) or (3) above shall have effect in relation to any period for which section 178(1) above has effect for the purposes of the enactment concerned.

179(5) [Repealed by ITEPA 2003, Sch. 8, Pt. 1.]

History – S. 179(1)(a)(iv) repealed by LRA 2002, s. 135 and Sch. 13, with effect from 13 October 2003 by virtue of SI 2003/1725, art. 2(1).
In s. 179(1)(b)(i), the words "and (5)" (which appeared after "87A(1)") omitted by FA 2016, s. 5 and Sch. 1, para. 54(b), with effect in relation to dividends paid or arising (or treated as paid) and other distributions made (or treated as made) in the tax year 2016–17 or at any later time.
In s. 179(1)(b)(i), the words "and 88(1)" repealed by FA 1996, Sch. 41 Pt. V(8), with effect in accordance with FA 1996, Sch. 18, para. 17(3), (4).
S. 179(1)(g) repealed by ITEPA 2003, Sch. 8, Pt. 1 which has effect for the tax year 2003–04 and subsequent tax years.
S. 179(5) repealed by ITEPA 2003, Sch. 8, Pt. 1 which has effect for the tax year 2003–04 and subsequent tax years.

Notes – The substitutions contained in s. 179(1)(b)(i) (in respect of TMA 1970, s. 87A(1) and (5) and s. 179(1)(c)(ii)) have yet to take effect (see s. 179(4) and "Statutory instruments" under s. 178).

180 Repayment interest: period of accrual

180(1) [Amends provisions not reproduced.]

180(2) [Amends provisions as below.]

(a) [Amends OTA 1975, Sch. 2, para. 16.]

(b-d) [Spent.]

180(3) [Spent.]

180(4) [Amends IHTA 1984, s. 235(1); otherwise spent.]

180(5) [Amends FA 1986, s. 92(2).]

180(6) [Amends ICTA 1988, s. 826(1).]

180(7) The amendments made by this section shall be deemed always to have had effect.

MISCELLANEOUS

182 Disclosure of information

182(1) A person who discloses any information which he holds or has held in the exercise of tax functions, tax credit functions, child trust fund functions or social security functions is guilty of an offence if it is information about any matter relevant, for the purposes of any of those functions–

(a) to tax or duty in the case of any identifiable person,

(aa) to a tax credit in respect of any identifiable person,

(ab) to a child trust fund of any identifiable person,

(b) to contributions payable by or in respect of any identifiable person, or

(c) to statutory sick pay or statutory maternity pay, statutory paternity pay, statutory adoption pay or statutory shared parental pay in respect of any identifiable person.

182(2) In this section **"tax functions"** means functions relating to tax or duty–

(a) of the Commissioners, the Board and their officers,

(b) of any person carrying out the administrative work of the First-tier Tribunal or Upper Tribunal, and

(c) of any other person providing, or employed in the provision of, services to any person mentioned in paragraph (a) or (b) above.

182(2ZA) In this section **"tax credit functions"** means the functions relating to tax credits–

(a) of the Board,

(b) of any person carrying out the administrative work of the First-tier Tribunal or Upper Tribunal, and

(c) of any other person providing, or employed in the provision of, services to the Board or to any person mentioned in paragraph (b) above.

182(2ZB) In this section **"child trust fund functions"** means the functions relating to child trust funds–

(a) of the Board and their officers,

(b) of any person carrying out the administrative work of the First-tier Tribunal or an appeal tribunal constituted under Chapter 1 of Part 2 of the Social Security (Northern Ireland) Order 1998, or

(c) of any person providing, or employed in the provision of, services to the Board or any person mentioned in paragraph (b) above.

182(2A) In this section **"social security functions"** means–

(a) the functions relating to contributions, child benefit, guardian's allowance, statutory sick pay or statutory maternity pay, statutory paternity pay, statutory adoption pay or statutory shared parental pay–

  (i) of the Board and their officers,

  (ii) of any person carrying out the administrative work of the First-tier Tribunal or Upper Tribunal, and

  (iii) of any other person providing, or employed in the provision of, services to any person mentioned in sub-paragraph (i) or (ii) above, and

(b) the functions under Part III of the Pension Schemes Act 1993 or Part III of the Pension Schemes (Northern Ireland) Act 1993 of the Board and their officers and any other person providing, or employed in the provision of, services to the Board or their officers.

182(3) [Omitted by SI 2009/56, art. 3 and Sch. 1, para. 167(e).]

182(4) A person who discloses any information which–

(a) he holds or has held in the exercise of functions–

(i) of the Comptroller and Auditor General, of the National Audit Office and any member or employee of that Office or of any member of the staff of the National Audit Office that was established by section 3 of the National Audit Act 1983,

(ia) of the Comptroller and Auditor General for Northern Ireland and any member of the staff of the Northern Ireland Audit Office,

(ii) of the Parliamentary Commissioner for Administration and his officers,

(iii) of the Auditor General for Wales and any member of his staff,

(iv) of the Public Services Ombudsman for Wales and any member of his staff, or

(v) of the Scottish Public Services Ombudsman and any member of his staff,

(b) is, or is derived from, information which was held by any person in the exercise of tax functions, tax credit functions, child trust fund functions or social security functions, and

(c) is information about any matter relevant, for the purposes of tax functions, tax credit functions, child trust fund functions or social security functions–

(i) to tax or duty in the case of any identifiable person,

(ia) to a tax credit in respect of any identifiable person,'

(ib) to a child trust fund of any identifiable person,"

(ii) to contributions payable by or in respect of any identifiable person, or

(iii) to child benefit, guardian's allowance, statutory sick pay or statutory maternity pay, statutory paternity pay, statutory adoption pay or statutory shared parental pay in respect of any identifiable person,

is guilty of an offence.

182(5) Subsections (1) and (4) above do not apply to any disclosure of information–

(a) with lawful authority,

(b) with the consent of any person in whose case the information is about a matter relevant to tax or duty, to a tax credit or to a child trust fund or to contributions, statutory sick pay or statutory maternity pay, statutory paternity pay, statutory adoption pay or statutory shared parental pay, or

(c) which has been lawfully made available to the public before the disclosure is made.

182(6) For the purposes of this section a disclosure of any information is made with lawful authority if, and only if, it is made–

(a) by a Crown servant in accordance with his official duty,

(b) by any other person for the purposes of the function in the exercise of which he holds the information and without contravening any restriction duly imposed by the person responsible,

(c) to, or in accordance with an authorisation duly given by, the person responsible,

(d) in pursuance of any enactment or of any order of a court, or

(e) in connection with the institution of or otherwise for the purposes of any proceedings relating to any matter within the general responsibility of the Commissioners or, as the case requires, the Board,

and in this subsection **"the person responsible"** means the Commissioners, the Board, the Comptroller and Auditor General, the Comptroller and Auditor General for Northern Ireland, the Parliamentary Commissioner, the Auditor General for Wales, the Public Services Ombudsman for Wales or the Scottish Public Services Ombudsman, as the case requires.

182(7) It is a defence for a person charged with an offence under this section to prove that at the time of the alleged offence–

(a) he believed that he had lawful authority to make the disclosure in question and had no reasonable cause to believe otherwise, or

(b) he believed that the information in question had been lawfully made available to the public before the disclosure was made and had no reasonable cause to believe otherwise.

182(8) A person guilty of an offence under this section is liable–

(a) on conviction on indictment, to imprisonment for a term not exceeding two years or a fine or both, and

(b) on summary conviction, to imprisonment for a term not exceeding six months or a fine not exceeding the statutory maximum or both.

182(9) No prosecution for an offence under this section shall be instituted in England and Wales or in Northern Ireland except–

(a) by the Commissioners or the Board, as the case requires, or

(b) by or with the consent of the Director of Public Prosecutions or, in Northern Ireland, the Director of Public Prosecutions for Northern Ireland.

182(10) In this section–

"the Board" means the Commissioners of Inland Revenue,

"child trust fund" has the same meaning as in the Child Trust Funds Act 2004,

"the Commissioners" means the Commissioners of Customs and Excise,

"contributions" means contributions under Part I of the Social Security Contributions and Benefits Act 1992 or Part I of the Social Security Contributions and Benefits (Northern Ireland) Act 1992;

"Crown servant" has the same meaning as in the Official Secrets Act 1989,

"tax credit" means a tax credit under the Tax Credits Act 2002, and

"tax or duty" means any tax or duty within the general responsibility of the Commissioners or the Board.

182(10A) In this section, in relation to the disclosure of information "identifiable person" means a person whose identity is specified in the disclosure or can be deduced from it.

182(11) In this section–

(a) [omitted by the Budget Responsibility and National Audit Act 2011, s. 26 and Sch. 5, para. 14(4),]

(b) [omitted by the Budget Responsibility and National Audit Act 2011, s. 26 and Sch. 5, para. 14(4),]

(c) references to the Parliamentary Commissioner for Administration include the Health Service Commissioner for England, the Northern Ireland Parliamentary Commissioner for Administration and the Northern Ireland Commissioner for Complaints.

182(11A) In this section, references to statutory paternity pay, statutory adoption pay or statutory shared parental pay include statutory pay under Northern Ireland legislation corresponding to Part 12ZA, Part 12ZB or Part 12ZC of the Social Security Contributions and Benefits Act 1992 (c. 4).

182(12) This section shall come into force on the repeal of section 2 of the Official Secrets Act 1911.

History – In s. 182(1)(c), the words " statutory paternity pay, " substituted for the words "ordinary statutory paternity pay, additional statutory paternity pay or" by Children and Families Act 2014, s. 126(1) and Sch. 7, para. 5(2)(a), with effect from 5 April 2015, subject to the transitional and saving provisions in SI 2014/1640, art. 16 (amendments do not have effect in relation to– (a) children whose expected week of birth ends on or before 4 April 2015; (b) children placed for adoption on or before 4 April 2015) and 17 (transitional and saving provisions applicable where Northern Ireland legislation contains provision on additional statutory paternity pay) (SI 2014/1640, art. 6 and 7).

In s. 182(1) the words ", child trust fund functions" inserted after "tax credit functions" and para. (ab) inserted by CTFA 2004, s. 18, with effect from 1 January 2005 by virtue of SI 2004/2422, reg. 2.

In s. 182(1), (4)(b) and (4)(c) the words ", tax credit functions" inserted by Tax Credits Act 1999, s. 12(2)(a), (4)(a) and (4)(b) respectively, with effect from 5 October 1999 (TCA 1999, s. 20(2)), and continued by TCA 2002, s. 59 and Sch. 5, para. 11(2)(a) with effect for the purposes of TCA 2002 from 1 August 2002 by virtue of SI 2002/1727 (C. 52).

In s. 182(1), words "social security functions" inserted, words from "any of those functions" to the end substituted, and s. 182(2A) inserted, by Social Security (Transfer of Functions, etc.) Act 1999, s. 6 and Sch. 6, para. 9(2), (3), with effect from 1 April 1999 by virtue of SI 1999/527 (C. 11), art. 2(b) and Sch. 2.

S. 182(1)(aa) substituted by TCA 2002, s. 59 and Sch. 5, para. 11(2)(b) with effect for the purposes of TCA 2002 from 1 August 2002 by virtue of SI 2002/1727 (C. 52).

Former s. 182(1)(aa) and (4)(c)(ia) inserted by TCA 1999, s. 12(2)(b) and (4)(b) respectively, with effect from 5 October 1999 (TCA 1999, s. 20(2)).

In s. 182(1)(c), the words " or statutory shared parental pay" inserted (after the words "statutory adoption pay") by Children and Families Act 2014, s. 126(1) and Sch. 7, para. 5(2)(b), with effect from 1 December 2014 (SI 2014/1640, art. 5).

In s. 182(1)(c), (2A)(a), (4)(c)(iii), (5)(b) and (11A) the words "ordinary statutory paternity pay, additional statutory paternity pay" substituted for the words "statutory paternity pay" by the Work and Families Act 2006, s. 11 and Sch. 1, para. 2, with effect from 6 April 2010 (SI 2010/495, art. 4).

In s. 182(1)(c), (2A)(a), (4)(c)(iii) and (5)(b) the words "statutory maternity pay, statutory paternity pay or statutory adoption pay" substituted by Employment Act 2002, s. 53 and Sch. 7, para. 1(3) with effect from 8 December 2002.

In s. 182(2)(b) the words "the First-tier Tribunal or Upper Tribunal" substituted for the words "anytribunal mentioned in subsection (3) below" by SI 2009/56, art. 3 and Sch. 1, para. 167(a), with effect from 1 April 2009, subject to transitional and saving provisions in SI 2009/56, Sch. 3.

In s. 182(2A)(a), the words "statutory paternity pay," substituted for the words "ordinary statutory paternity pay, additional statutory paternity pay or" by Children and Families Act 2014, s. 126(1) and Sch. 7, para. 5(3)(a), with effect from 5 April 2015, subject to the transitional and saving provisions in SI 2014/1640, art. 16 (amendments do not have effect in relation to– (a) children whose expected week of birth ends on or before 4 April 2015; (b) children placed for adoption on or before 4 April 2015) and 17 (transitional and saving provisions applicable where Northern Ireland legislation contains provision on additional statutory paternity pay) (SI 2014/1640, art. 6 and 7).

In s. 182(2ZA)(b) the words "the First-tier Tribunal or Upper Tribunal" substituted for the words "General Commissioners or the Special Commissioners" by SI 2009/56, art. 3 and Sch. 1, para. 167(b), with effect from 1 April 2009, subject to transitional and saving provisions in SI 2009/56, Sch. 3.

S. 182(2ZA) substituted for s. 182(2AA) by TCA 2002, s. 59 and Sch. 5, para. 11(3), with effect for the purposes of TCA 2002 from 1 August 2002 by virtue of SI 2002/1727 (C. 52).

Former s. 182(2AA) inserted by Tax Credits Act 1999, s. 12(3), with effect from 5 October 1999.

In s. 182(2ZB)(b) the words "First-tier Tribunal or an appeal tribunal constituted under Chapter 1 of Part 2 of the Social Security (Northern Ireland) Order 1998" substituted for the words "General Commissioners or the Special Commissioners" by SI 2009/56, art. 3 and Sch. 1, para. 167(c), with effect from 1 April 2009, subject to transitional and saving provisions in SI 2009/56, Sch. 3.
S. 182(2ZB) inserted by CTFA 2004, s. 18, (temporary modification contained in s. 24), with effect from 1 January 2005 by virtue of SI 2004/2422, reg. 2.
In s. 182(2A)(a), the words " or statutory shared parental pay " inserted (after the words "statutory adoption pay") by Children and Families Act 2014, s. 126(1) and Sch. 7, para. 5(3)(b), with effect from 1 December 2014 (SI 2014/1640, art. 5).
In s. 182(2A)(a)(ii) the words "the First-tier Tribunal or Upper Tribunal" substituted for the words "General Commissioners or the Special Commissioners" by SI 2009/56, art. 3 and Sch. 1, para. 167(d), with effect from 1 April 2009, subject to transitional and saving provisions in SI 2009/56, Sch. 3.
In s. 182(2A), words "child benefit, guardian's allowance," inserted by TCA 2002, s. 59 and Sch.5, para. 11(4), with effect for the purposes of TCA 2002 from 1 August 2002 by virtue of SI 2002/1727 (C. 52).
S. 182(3) omitted by SI 2009/56, art. 3 and Sch. 1, para. 167(e), with effect from 1 April 2009, subject to transitional and saving provisions in SI 2009/56, Sch. 3.
In former s. 182(3) the words "or section 704 of the Income Tax Act 2007" inserted by ITA 2007, s. 1027 and Sch. 1, para. 282, with effect from 6 April 2007.
Former s. 182(3)(c) repealed by the Statute Law (Repeals) Act 2004, s. 1 and Sch. 1, Pt. 5, Grp. 18, with effect from 22 July 2004.
In former s. 182(3)(c), the words "for the purposes of section 80(3) of the Taxes Management Act 1970 or" which followed the word "appointed" repealed by FA 1995, s. 162 and Sch. 29, Pt. VIII(16) for the purposes of income tax and capital gains tax in relation to 1996–97 and subsequent years of assessment and for the purposes of corporation tax, in relation to accounting periods beginning after 31 March 1996.
In s. 182(4)(a)(i), the words ", of the National Audit Office and any member or employee of that Office or any member of the staff of the National Audit Office that was established by section 3 of the National Audit Act 1983" substituted for the words "and any member of the staff of the National Audit Office" by the Budget Responsibility and National Audit Act 2011, s. 26 and Sch. 5, para. 14(2)(a), with effect from 1 April 2012 (SI 2011/2576, art. 5).
S. 182(4)(a)(ia) inserted by the Budget Responsibility and National Audit Act 2011, s. 26 and Sch. 5, para. 14(2)(b), with effect from 1 April 2012 (SI 2011/2576, art. 5).
S. 182(4)(a)(iii), (iv) inserted by Government of Wales Act 1998, s. 125 and Sch. 12, para. 31, and word "or" in s. 182(4)(a)(i) repealed by s. 152 and Sch. 18, Pt. I of that Act, with effect from 1 February 1999 by virtue of SI 1999/118.
S. 182(4)(a)(iv) substituted by the Public Services Ombudsman (Wales) Act 2005, s. 39 and Sch. 6, para. 22(a), with effect from 1 April 2006 (by virtue of SI 2005/2800).
S. 182(4)(a)(v) inserted (and the "or" after (iii) omitted) by SI 2004/1823, art. 10, with effect from 14 July 2004.
In s. 182(4)(b), words "social security functions" inserted, and in s. 182(4)(c), words "tax functions" to the end of para. (c) substituted by Social Security (Transfer of Functions, etc.) Act 1999, s. 6 and Sch. 6, para. 9(4), with effect from 1 April 1999 by virtue of SI 1999/527 (C. 11), art. 2(b) and Sch. 2.
In s. 182(4)(b) and (c) the words ", child trust fund functions" inserted after "tax credit functions" by CTFA 2004, s. 18, with effect from 1 January 2005 by virtue of SI 2004/2422, reg. 2.
In s. 182(4)(b), words "social security functions" inserted, and in s. 182(4)(c), words "tax functions" to the end of para. (c) substituted by SSTFA 1999,s. 6 and Sch. 6, para. 9(4), with effect from 1 April 1999 by virtue of SI 1999/527 (C. 11), art. 2(b) and Sch. 2. In s. 182(4)(b) and (c), words ", tax credit functions" continued in force by TCA 2002, s. 59 and Sch. 5, para. 11(5)(a), (b), with effect for the purposes of TCA 2002 from 1 August 2002 by virtue of SI 2002/1727 (C. 52)
In s. 182(4)(c), the words "statutory paternity pay," substituted for the words "ordinary statutory paternity pay, additional statutory paternity pay or" by Children and Families Act 2014, s. 126(1) and Sch. 7, para. 5(4)(a), with effect from 5 April 2015, subject to the transitional and saving provisions in SI 2014/1640, art. 16 (amendments do not have effect in relation to– (a) children whose expected week of birth ends on or before 4 April 2015; (b) children placed for adoption on or before 4 April 2015) and 17 (transitional and saving provisions applicable where Northern Ireland legislation contains provision on additional statutory paternity pay) (SI 2014/1640, art. 6 and 7).
S. 182(4)(c)(ia) substituted by TCA 2002, s. 59 and Sch. 5, para. 11(5)(c), with effect for the purposes of TCA 2002 from 1 August 2002 by virtue of SI 2002/1727 (C. 52).
In s. 182(4)(c)(ib) inserted by CTFA 2004, s. 18, with effect from 1 January 2005 by virtue of SI 2004/2422, reg. 2.
In s. 182(4)(c)(iii), the words " or statutory shared parental pay " inserted (after the words "statutory adoption pay") by Children and Families Act 2014, s. 126(1) and Sch. 7, para. 5(4)(b), with effect from 1 December 2014 (SI 2014/1640, art. 5).
In s. 182(4)(c)(iii), words "child benefit, guardian's allowance," inserted by TCA 2002, s. 59 and Sch. 5, para. 11(d), with effect for the purposes of TCA 2002 from 1 August 2002 by virtue of SI 2002/1727 (C. 52).
In s. 182(5)(b), the words " or statutory shared parental pay " inserted (after the words "statutory adoption pay") by Children and Families Act 2014, s. 126(1) and Sch. 7, para. 5(5)(b), with effect from 1 December 2014 (SI 2014/1640, art. 5).
In s. 182(5)(b) the words "to a tax credit or to a child trust fund" substituted for "or to a tax credit" by CTFA 2004, s. 18, with effect from 1 January 2005 by virtue of SI 2004/2422, reg. 2.
In s. 182(5)(b), words "or to a tax credit" substituted for ", to working families' tax credit or disabled person's tax credit" by TCA 2002, s. 59 and Sch. 5, para. 11(6), with effect for the purposes of TCA 2002 from 1 August 2002 by virtue of SI 2002/1727 (C. 52).
In s. 182(5)(b), former words ", to working families' tax credit or disabled person's tax credit" inserted by Tax Credits Act 1999, s. 12(5), with effect from 5 October 1999.
In s. 182(5)(b), words "or to contributions, statutory sick pay or statutory maternity pay", and in s. 182(10) the definition of "contributions", inserted by Social Security(Transfer of Functions, etc.) Act 1999, s. 6 and Sch. 6, para. 9(5) (6), with effect from 1 April 1999 by virtue of SI 1999/527 (C. 11), art. 2(b) and Sch. 2.
In s. 182(5)(b), the words "statutory paternity pay," substituted for the words "ordinary statutory paternity pay, additional statutory paternity pay or" by Children and Families Act 2014, s. 126(1) and Sch. 7, para. 5(5)(a), with effect from 5 April 2015, subject to the transitional and saving provisions in SI 2014/1640, art. 16 (amendments do not have effect in relation to– (a) children whose expected week of birth ends on or before 4 April 2015; (b) children placed for adoption on or before 4 April 2015) and 17 (transitional and saving provisions applicable where Northern Ireland legislation contains provision on additional statutory paternity pay) (SI 2014/1640, art. 6 and 7).
In s. 182(6), the words "and Auditor General, the Comptroller and Auditor General for Northern Ireland" inserted after the word "Comptroller" by the Budget Responsibility and National Audit Act 2011, s. 26 and Sch. 5, para. 14(3), with effect from 1 April 2012 (SI 2011/2576, art. 5).
In s. 182(6), the words "the Public Services Ombudsman for Wales" were substituted for the words "the Welsh Administration Ombudsman" by the Public Services Ombudsman (Wales) Act 2005, s. 39 and Sch. 6, para. 22, with effect from 1 April 2006 (by virtue of SI 2005/2800).
In s. 182(6), the words ", the Welsh Administration Ombudsman or the Scottish Public Services Ombudsman" substituted for the words "or the Welsh Administration Ombudsman" by SI 2004/1823, art. 10(c), with effect from 14 July 2004.
In s. 182(6), the words ", the Parliamentary Commissioner, the Auditor General for Wales or the Welsh Administration Ombudsman," were substituted for the words "or the Parliamentary Commissioner," by the Government of Wales Act 1998, s. 125 and Sch. 12, para. 31(3), with effect from 1 February 1999 (SI 1999/118).
In s. 182(10) the definition of "child trust fund" inserted after the definition of "the Board" by CTFA 2004, s. 18, with effect from 1 January 2005 by virtue of SI 2004/2422, reg. 2.

In s. 182(10), definition of "tax credit" inserted by TCA 2002, s. 59 and Sch. 5, para. 11(7), with effect for the purposes of TCA 2002 from 1 August 2002 by virtue of SI 2002/1727 (C. 52).
S. 182(10A) inserted by CRCA 2005, s. 50 and Sch. 4, para. 39, from 18 April 2005 (by virtue of SI 2005/1126, reg. 2(2)).
S. 182(11)(a) and (b) omitted by the Budget Responsibility and National Audit Act 2011, s. 26 and Sch. 5, para. 14(4), with effect from 1 April 2012 (SI 2011/2576, art. 5).
In s. 182(11)(c), the words "the Health Service Commissioner for Wales" omitted by the Public Services Ombudsman (Wales) Act 2005, s. 39 and Sch. 6, para. 22, and repealed by s. 39 and Sch. 7 of the same Act, with effect from 1 April2006 (by virtue of SI 2005/2800).
In s. 182(11)(c), the words "the Health Service Commissioner for Scotland" omitted by SI 2004/1823, art. 10(d), with effect from 14 July 2004.
In s. 182(11A), the words "statutory paternity pay," substituted for the words "ordinary statutory paternity pay, additional statutory paternity pay or"; the words "or statutory shared parental pay" inserted (after the words "statutory adoption pay") and the words ", Part 12ZB or Part 12ZC" substituted for the words "or Part 12ZB" by Children and Families Act 2014, s. 126(1) and Sch. 7, para. 5(6), with effect from 15 March 2015 (the day on which Northern Ireland legislation containing provision corresponding to SSCBA 1992, Pt. 12ZC (the Statutory Shared Parental Pay (General) Regulations (Northern Ireland) 2015 (S.R.(N.I.) 2015/94)) comes into force), subject to the transitional and saving provisions in SI 2014/1640, art. 18 (amendments do not have effect in relation to– (a) children whose expected week of birth ends on or before 4 April 2015; (b) children placed for adoption on or before 4 April 2015) (SI 2014/1640, art. 8).
S. 182(11A) inserted by EA 2002, s. 53 and Sch. 7, para. 1(3) with effect from 8 December 2002.

Cross references – TMA 1970, s. 80(3): disputes where profits of non-resident assessed with reference to percentage of turnover.
ICTA 1988, s. 706: tribunal in respect of disputes relating to application of ICTA 1988, s. 703 (cancellation of tax advantage from certain transactions in securities.
SSAA 1992, s. 122: disclosure of information by Inland Revenue.
SSAA 1992, s. 123: disclosure of information by DSS.
SI 1992/12, reg. 12(2): para. 1 of the regulations shall not be construed as preventing any disclosure of information under s. 182(5).

Notes – Official Secrets Act 1911, s. 2 (see s. 182(12)) is repealed by Official Secrets Act 1989, s. 16(4), (6) and Sch. 2, with effect from 1 March 1990 (SI 1990/199 (C 8)).
FA 1969, s. 58: disclosure for statistical purposes of information regarding employment.
TMA 1970, s. 6: declarations by HMRC officials etc.
HMRC may also disclose personal information to other government departments under:

- Land Registration Act 1925, s. 129;
- Parliamentary Commissioner Act 1967, s. 8;
- FA 1972, s. 127;
- SSPA 1975, s. 59K(6) (from 18 July 1990, by virtue of SI 1990/1446);
- FA 1978, s. 77;
- Tenant's Rights etc. (Scotland) Act 1980, s. 1;
- SSHBA 1982, s. 25;
- National Audit Act 1983, s. 8;
- Data Protection Act 1984, s. 17;
- Housing Associations Act 1985, s. 62;
- SSA 1986, s. 59;
- ICTA 1988, s. 375(9), (10), 816;
- SSAA 1992, s. 122.
- Charities Act 1993, s. 10(2).

HMRC may also disclose personal information to the police under:

- Drug Trafficking Offences Act 1986, s. 30;
- Prevention of Terrorism (Temporary Provisions) Act 1989, s. 17 and Sch. 17.

182A Double taxation: disclosure of information

182A(1) A person who discloses any information acquired by him in the exercise of his functions as a member of an advisory commission set up under the Arbitration Convention is guilty of an offence.

182A(2) Subsection (1) above does not apply to any disclosure of information–

(a) with the consent of the person who supplied the information to the commission, or

(b) which has been lawfully made available to the public before the disclosure is made.

182A(3) It is a defence for a person charged with an offence under this section to prove that at the time of the alleged offence he believed that the information in question had been lawfully made available to the public before the disclosure was made and had no reasonable cause to believe otherwise.

182A(4) A person guilty of an offence under this section is liable–

(a) on conviction on indictment, to imprisonment for a term not exceeding two years or a fine or both;

(b) on summary conviction, to imprisonment for a term not exceeding six months or a fine not exceeding the statutory maximum or both.

182A(5) No prosecution for an offence under this section shall be instituted in England and Wales or in Northern Ireland except–

(a) by the Board, or

(b) by or with the consent of the Director of Public Prosecutions or, in Northern Ireland, the Director of Public Prosecutions for Northern Ireland.

182A(6) In this section–

"the Arbitration Convention" has the meaning given by section 126 of the Taxation (International and Other Provisions) Act 2010;

"the Board" means the Commissioners of Inland Revenue.

History – In s. 182A(6), the words "section 126 of the Taxation (International and Other Provisions) Act 2010" substituted for the words "section 815B(4) of the Taxes Act 1988" by TIOPA 2010, s. 374 and Sch. 8, para. 39, with effect for corporation tax purposes

for accounting periods ending on or after 1 April 2010, for income tax and capital gains tax purposes for the tax year 2010–11 and subsequent tax years, and for petroleum revenue tax purposes for chargeable periods beginning on or after 1 July 2010.
S. 182A inserted by F(No. 2)A 1992, s. 51(3).

European material – Convention 90/436, art. 9(6).

Notes – For Convention 90/436 (the "Arbitration Convention"), see the European Material division in this volume. The convention entered into force on 1 January 1995.
See also ICTA 1988, s. 815B and s. 816(2A).

GENERAL

186 Interpretation etc.

186(1) In this Act **"the Taxes Act 1970"** means the Income and Corporation Taxes Act 1970 and **"the Taxes Act 1988"** means the Income and Corporation Taxes Act 1988.

186(2) Chapter II of Part I of this Act shall be construed as one with the Value Added Tax Act 1983.

186(3) Part II of this Act, so far as it relates to capital gains tax, shall be construed as one with the Capital Gains Tax Act 1979.

Notes – The Capital Gains Tax Act 1979 repealed by TCGA 1992, s. 290 and Sch. 12 in relation to chargeable periods beginning after 5 April 1992. References to the 1979 Act to be construed as references to the Taxation of Chargeable Gains Act 1992 (Interpretation Act 1978, s. 17(2)).

188 Short title

188 This Act may be cited as the Finance Act 1989.

SCHEDULES

SCHEDULE 4 – PROFIT-RELATED PAY

Section 61

1 [Repealed by FA 1997, s. 113 and Sch. 18, Pt. VI(3).]

History – Sch. 4 repealed by FA 1997, s. 113 and Sch. 18, Pt. VI(3) in relation to any payment made by reference to a profit period beginning on or after 1 January 2000.

SCHEDULE 5 – EMPLOYEE SHARE OWNERSHIP TRUSTS

Section 74

QUALIFYING TRUSTS

1 A trust is a qualifying employee share ownership trust at the time it is established if the conditions set out in paragraphs 2 to 11 below are satisfied in relation to the trust at that time.

Cross references – ICTA 1988, s. 85A(4): in relation to relief for costs of establishment, qualifying ESOT determined in accordance with Sch. 5.
TCGA 1992, s. 228(7): in relation to roll-over relief for share disposals, qualifying ESOT determined in accordance with Sch. 5.
TCGA 1992, s. 235(8): in relation to an inspector's power to require trustees to supply information, qualifying ESOT determined in accordance with Sch. 5.

GENERAL

2(1) The trust must be established under a deed (the trust deed).

2(2) The trust must be established by a company (the founding company) which, at the time the trust is established, is resident in the United Kingdom and not controlled by another company.

TRUSTEES

3(1) The trust deed must provide for the establishment of a body of trustees.

3(2) The trust deed must–

(a) appoint the initial trustees;

(b) contain rules for the retirement and removal of trustees;

(c) contain rules for the appointment of replacement and additional trustees.

Post-ICTA 1988

3(3) The trust deed must provide that at any time while the trust subsists (the relevant time)–

(a) the number of trustees must not be less than three;

(b) all the trustees must be resident in the United Kingdom;

(c) the trustees must include one person who is a trust corporation, a solicitor, or a member of such other professional body as the Board may from time to time allow for the purposes of this paragraph;

(d) most of the trustees must be persons who are not and have never been directors of any company which falls within the founding company's group at the relevant time;

(e) most of the trustees must be persons who are employees of companies which fall within the founding company's group at the relevant time, and who do not have and have never had a material interest in any such company;

(f) the trustees falling within paragraph (e) above must, before being appointed as trustees, have been selected by a majority of the employees of the companies falling within the founding company's group at the time of the selection or by persons elected to represent those employees.

3(4) For the purposes of sub-paragraph (3) above a company falls within the founding company's group at a particular time if–

(a) it is the founding company, or

(b) it is at that time resident in the United Kingdom and controlled by the founding company.

3(5) This paragraph applies in relation to trusts established on or before the day on which the Finance Act 1994 was passed.

History – Para. 3(5) inserted by FA 1994, s. 102 and Sch. 13, para. 1, 2, with effect from 3 May 1994.

Other material – ICAEW Technical Release TR 759 (not reproduced): Revenue confirm full-time working director can be a trustee – the only stipulation is that most of the trustees must be "employees", i.e. not directors.

3A Where a trust is established after the day on which the Finance Act 1994 was passed, the trust deed must make provision as mentioned in one of paragraphs (a) to (c) below–

(a) provision for the establishment of a body of trustees and complying with paragraph 3(2) to (4) above;

(b) provision for the establishment of a body of trustees and complying with paragraph 3B(2) to (9) below;

(c) provision that at any time while the trust subsists there must be a single trustee.

History – Para. 3A inserted by FA 1994, s. 102 and Sch. 13, para. 1, 3, with effect in relation to trusts established after 3 May 1994.

3B(1) The following are the provisions that must be complied with under paragraph 3A(b) above.

3B(2) The trust deed must–

(a) appoint the initial trustees;

(b) contain rules for the retirement and removal of trustees;

(c) contain rules for the appointment of replacement and additional trustees.

3B(3) The trust deed must be so framed that at any time while the trust subsists the conditions set out in sub-paragraph (4) below are fulfilled as regards the persons who are then trustees; and in that sub-paragraph **"the relevant time"** means that time.

3B(4) The conditions are that–

(a) the number of trustees is not less than three;

(b) all the trustees are resident in the United Kingdom;

(c) the trustees include at least one person who is a professional trustee and at least two persons who are non-professional trustees;

(d) at least half of the non-professional trustees were, before being appointed as trustees, selected in accordance with sub-paragraph (7) or (8) below;

(e) all the trustees so selected are persons who are employees of companies which fall within the founding company's group at the relevant time, and who do not have and have never had a material interest in any such company.

3B(5) For the purposes of this paragraph a trustee is a professional trustee at a particular time if–

(a) the trustee is then a trust corporation, a solicitor, or a member of such other professional body as the Board may at that time allow for the purposes of this sub-paragraph.

(b) the trustee is not then an employee or director of any company then falling within the founding company's group, and

(c) the trustee meets the requirements of sub-paragraph (6) below;

and for the purposes of this paragraph a trustee is a non-professional trustee at a particular time if the trustee is not then a professional trustee for those purposes.

3B(6) A trustee meets the requirements of this sub-paragraph if–

(a) he was appointed as an initial trustee and, before being appointed as trustee, was selected by (and only by) the persons who later became the non-professional initial trustees, or

(b) he was appointed as a replacement or additional trustee and, before being appointed as a trustee, was selected by (and only by) the persons who were the non-professional trustees at the time of the selection.

3B(7) Trustees are selected in accordance with this sub-paragraph if the process of selection is one under which–

(a) all the persons who are employees of the companies which fall within the founding company's group at the time of the selection, and who do not have and have never had a material interest in any such company, are (so far as is reasonably practicable) given the opportunity to stand for selection,

(b) all the employees of the companies falling within the founding company's group at the time of the selection are (so far as is reasonably practicable) given the opportunity to vote, and

(c) persons gaining more votes are preferred to those gaining less.

3B(8) Trustees are selected in accordance with this sub-paragraph if they are selected by persons elected to represent the employees of the companies falling within the founding company's group at the time of the selection.

3B(9) For the purposes of this paragraph a company falls within the founding company's group at a particular time if–

(a) it is at that time resident in the United Kingdom, and

(b) it is the founding company or it is at that time controlled by the founding company.

History – Para. 3B inserted by FA 1994, s. 102 and Sch. 13, para. 1, 3, with effect in relation to trusts established after 3 May 1994.

3C(1) This paragraph applies where the trust deed provides that at any time while the trust subsists there must be a single trustee.

3C(2) The trust deed must–

(a) be so framed that at any time while the trust subsists the trustee is a company which at that time is resident in the United Kingdom and controlled by the founding company;

(b) appoint the initial trustee;

(c) contain rules for the removal of any trustee and for the appointment of a replacement trustee.

3C(3) The trust deed must be so framed that at any time while the trust subsists the company which is then the trustee is a company so constituted that the conditions set out in sub-paragraph (4) below are then fulfilled as regards the persons who are then directors of the company; and in that sub-paragraph **"the relevant time"** is that time and **"the trust company"** is that company.

3C(4) The conditions are that–

(a) the number of directors is not less than three;

(b) all the directors are resident in the United Kingdom;

(c) the directors include at least one person who is a professional director and at least two persons who are non-professional directors;

(d) at least half of the non-professional directors were, before being appointed as directors, selected in accordance with sub-paragraph (7) or (8) below;

(e) all the directors so selected are persons who are employees of companies which fall within the founding company's group at the relevant time, and who do not have and have never had a material interest in any such company.

3C(5) For the purposes of this paragraph a director is a professional director at a particular time if–

(a) the director is then a solicitor or a member of such other professional body as the Board may at that time allow for the purposes of this sub-paragraph,

(b) the director is not then an employee of any company then falling within the founding company's group,

(c) the director is not then a director of any such company (other than the trust company), and

(d) the director meets the requirements of sub-paragraph (6) below;

and for the purposes of this paragraph a director is a non-professional director at a particular time if the director is not then a professional director for those purposes.

3C(6) A director meets the requirements of this sub-paragraph if–

(a) he was appointed as an initial director and, before being appointed as director, was selected by (and only by) the persons who later became the non-professional initial directors, or

(b) he was appointed as a replacement or additional director and, before being appointed as director, was selected by (and only by) the persons who were the non-professional directors at the time of the selection.

3C(7) Directors are selected in accordance with this sub-paragraph if the process of selection is one under which–

(a) all the persons who are employees of the companies which fall within the founding company's group at the time of the selection, and who do not have and have never had a material interest in any such company, are (so far as is reasonably practicable) given the opportunity to stand for selection,

(b) all the employees of the companies falling within the founding company's group at the time of the selection are (so far as is reasonably practicable) given the opportunity to vote, and

(c) persons gaining more votes are preferred to those gaining less.

3C(8) Directors are selected in accordance with this sub-paragraph if they are selected by persons elected to represent the employees of the companies falling within the founding company's group at the time of the selection.

3C(9) For the purposes of this paragraph a company falls within the founding company's group at a particular time if–

(a) it is at that time resident in the United Kingdom, and

(b) it is the founding company or it is at that time controlled by the founding company.

History – Para. 3C inserted by FA 1994, s. 102 and Sch. 13, para. 1, 3, with effect in relation to trusts established after 3 May 1994.

BENEFICIARIES

4(1) The trust deed must contain provision as to the beneficiaries under the trust, in accordance with the following rules.

4(2) The trust deed must provide that a person is a beneficiary at a particular time (**"the relevant time"**) if–

(a) he is at the relevant time an employee or director of a company which at that time falls within the founding company's group,

(b) at each given time in a qualifying period he was an employee or director of a company falling within the founding company's group at that given time, and

(c) in the case of a director, at that given time he worked as a director of the company concerned at the rate of at least 20 hours a week (ignoring such matters as holidays and sickness).

4(2A) The trust deed may provide that a person is a beneficiary at a given time if at that time he is eligible to participate in an SAYE option scheme–

(a) which was established by a company within the founding company's group, and

(b) which is approved under Schedule 3 to the Income Tax (Earnings and Pensions) Act 2003.

4(2B) Where a trust deed contains a rule conforming with sub-paragraph (2A) above it must provide that the only powers and duties which the trustees may exercise in relation to persons who are beneficiaries by virtue only of that rule are those which may be exercised in accordance with the provisions of a scheme such as is mentioned in that sub-paragraph.

4(3) The trust deed may provide that a person is a beneficiary at a particular time (**"the relevant time"**) if–

(a) he has at each given time in a qualifying period been an employee or director of a company falling within the founding company's group at that given time,

(b) he has ceased to be an employee or director of the company or the company has ceased to fall within that group, and

(c) at the relevant time a period of not more than eighteen months has elapsed since he so ceased or the company so ceased (as the case may be).

4(4) The trust deed may provide for a person to be a beneficiary if the person is a charity and the circumstances are such that–

(a) there is no person who is a beneficiary within any rule which is included in the deed and conforms with sub-paragraph (2), (2A) or (3) above, and

(b) the trust is in consequence being wound up.

4(5) For the purposes of sub-paragraph (2) above a qualifying period is a period–

(a) whose length is not more than five years,

(b) whose length is specified in the trust deed, and

(c) which ends with the relevant time (within the meaning of that sub-paragraph).

4(6) For the purposes of sub-paragraph (3) above a qualifying period is a period–

(a) whose length is equal to that of the period specified in the trust deed for the purposes of a rule which conforms with sub-paragraph (2) above, and

(b) which ends when the person or company (as the case may be) ceased as mentioned in sub-paragraph (3)(b) above.

4(7) The trust deed must not provide for a person to be a beneficiary unless he falls within any rule which is included in the deed and conforms with sub-paragraph (2), (2A), (3) or (4) above.

4(8) The trust deed must provide that, notwithstanding any other rule which is included in it, a person cannot be a beneficiary at a particular time (the relevant time) by virtue of a rule which conforms with sub-paragraph (2), (3) or (4) above if–

(a) at that time he has a material interest in the founding company, or

(b) at any time in the period of one year preceding the relevant time he has had a material interest in that company.

4(9) For the purposes of this paragraph a company falls within the founding company's group at a particular time if–

(a) it is at that time resident in the United Kingdom, and

(b) it is the founding company or it is at that time controlled by the founding company.

4(10) [Omitted by FA 2010, s. 30 and Sch. 6, para. 12.]

History – In para. 4(2)(c), the words "in the case of…worked as a", substituted for the words "at that given time he worked as an employee or", by FA 1995, s. 137(5), with effect in relation to trusts established on or after 1 May 1995 (a trust is established for this purpose when the deed under which it is established is executed – FA 1995, s. 137(9)).
In para. 4(2A), the words "an SAYE option scheme" substituted for the words "a savings-related share option scheme within the meaning of Schedule 9 to the Taxes Act 1988" by ITEPA 2003, Sch. 6, para. 163(2)(a) which has effect for the tax year 2003–04 and subsequent tax years.
In para. 4(2A)(b), the words "Schedule 3 to the Income Tax (Earnings and Pensions) Act 2003" substituted for the words "that Schedule" ITEPA 2003, Sch. 6, para. 163(2)(b) which has effect for the tax year 2003–04 and subsequent tax years.
Para. 4(2A), (2B), the references in para. 4(4) and 4(7) to "(2A)", and the words in para. 4(8) "by virtue … above", inserted by FA 1996, s. 120(1), (5)-(7), with effect in relation to trusts established on or after 29 April 1996.
In para. 4(5)(a), the words "not less than one year and" omitted by FA 1996, s. 119, s. 205 and Sch. 41, Pt. V(5), with effect in relation to trusts established on or after 29 April 1996.
Para. 4(10) omitted by FA 2010, s. 30 and Sch. 6, para. 12, with effect in relation to trusts established on or after 6 April 2012 (SI 2012/736, art. 7).

TRUSTEES' FUNCTIONS

5(1) The trust deed must contain provision as to the functions of the trustees.

5(2) The functions of the trustees must be so expressed that it is apparent that their general functions are–

(a) to receive sums from the founding company and other sums (by way of loan or otherwise);

(b) to acquire securities;

(c) to transfer securities or sums (or both) to persons who are beneficiaries under the terms of the trust deed;

(cc) to grant rights to acquire shares to persons who are beneficiaries under the terms of the trust deed;

(d) to transfer securities to the trustees of profit sharing schemes approved under Schedule 9 to the Taxes Act 1988, for a price not less than the price the securities might reasonably be expected to fetch on a sale in the open market;

(e) pending transfer, to retain the securities and to manage them (whether by exercising voting rights or otherwise).

History – Para. 5(2)(cc) inserted by FA 1996, s. 120(8), with effect in relation to trusts established on or after 29 April 1996.

SUMS

6(1) The trust deed must require that any sum received by the trustees–

(a) must be expended within the relevant period,

(b) may be expended only for one or more of the qualifying purposes, and

(c) must, while it is retained by them, be kept as cash or be kept in an account with a bank or building society.

6(2) For the purposes of sub-paragraph (1) above the relevant period is the period of nine months beginning with the day found as follows–

(a) in a case where the sum is received from the founding company, or a company which is controlled by that company at the time the sum is received, the day following the end of the period of account in which the sum is charged as an expense of the company from which it is received;

(b) in any other case, the day the sum is received.

6(3) For the purposes of sub-paragraph (1) above each of the following is a qualifying purpose–

(a) the acquisition of shares in the founding company;

(b) the repayment of sums borrowed;

(c) the payment of interest on sums borrowed;

(d) the payment of any sum to a person who is a beneficiary under the terms of the trust deed;

(e) the meeting of expenses.

6(4) The trust deed must provide that, in ascertaining for the purposes of a relevant rule whether a particular sum has been expended, sums received earlier by the trustees shall be treated as expended before sums received by them later; and a relevant rule is one which is included in the trust deed and conforms with sub-paragraph (1) above.

6(5) The trust deed must provide that, where the trustees pay sums to different beneficiaries at the same time, all the sums must be paid on similar terms.

6(6) For the purposes of sub-paragraph (5) above, the fact that terms vary according to the levels of remuneration of beneficiaries, the length of their service, or similar factors, shall not be regarded as meaning that the terms are not similar.

SECURITIES

7(1) Subject to paragraph 8 below, the trust deed must provide that securities acquired by the trustees must be shares in the founding company which–

(a) form part of the ordinary share capital of the company,

(b) are fully paid up,

(c) are not redeemable, and

(d) are not subject to any restrictions other than restrictions which attach to all shares of the same class or a restriction authorised by sub-paragraph (2) below.

7(2) Subject to sub-paragraph (3) below, a restriction is authorised by this sub-paragraph if–

(a) it is imposed by the founding company's articles of association,

(b) it requires all shares held by directors or employees of the founding company, or of any other company which it controls for the time being, to be disposed of on ceasing to be so held, and

(c) it requires all shares acquired, in pursuance of rights or interests obtained by such directors or employees, by persons who are not (or have ceased to be) such directors or employees to be disposed of when they are acquired.

7(3) A restriction is not authorised by sub-paragraph (2) above unless–

(a) any disposal required by the restriction will be by way of sale for a consideration in money on terms specified in the articles of association, and

(b) the articles also contain general provisions by virtue of which any person disposing of shares of the same class (whether or not held or acquired as mentioned in sub-paragraph (2) above) may be required to sell them on terms which are the same as those mentioned in paragraph (a) above.

7(4) The trust deed must provide that shares in the founding company may not be acquired by the trustees at a price exceeding the price they might reasonably be expected to fetch on a sale in the open market.

7(5) The trust deed must provide that shares in the founding company may not be acquired by the trustees at a time when that company is controlled by another company.

Cross references – TCGA 1992, s. 227(3)(e): exclusion for authorised restrictions from the condition for roll-over relief on disposals of shares to ESOT that the shares are not subject to any restrictions.

TCGA 1992, s. 228(5)(a): exclusion for arrangements arising from authorised restrictions from condition for roll-over relief (TCGA 1992, s. 227(6)) that no potential reacquisition by claimant.

Other material – ICAEW Technical Release TR 759 (not reproduced): Revenue confirm where trustees take out loan to buy shares, *charge of shares as security to lender not regarded as a restriction for para. 7(1)(d).*

8 The trust deed may provide that the trustees may acquire securities other than shares in the founding company–

(a) if they are securities issued to the trustees in exchange in circumstances mentioned in section 135(1) of the Taxation of Chargeable Gains Act 1992, or

(b) if they are securities acquired by the trustees as a result of a reorganisation, and the original shares the securities represent are shares in the founding company (construing "reorganisation" and "original shares" in accordance with section 126 of that Act).

History – References to TCGA 1992 substituted by TCGA 1992, s. 290 and Sch. 10, para. 19(5).

9(1) The trust deed must provide that–

(a) where the trustees transfer securities to a beneficiary, they must do so on qualifying terms;

(b) the trustees must transfer securities before the expiry of the qualifying period beginning with the date on which they acquired them.

9(2) For the purposes of sub-paragraph (1) above a transfer of securities is made on qualifying terms if–

(a) all the securities transferred at the same time other than those transferred on a transfer such as is mentioned in sub-paragraph (2ZA) below are transferred on similar terms,

(b) securities have been offered to all the persons who are beneficiaries under the terms of the trust deed by virtue of a rule which conforms with paragraph 4(2), (3) or (4) above when the transfer is made, and

(c) securities are transferred to all such persons who have accepted.

9(2ZA) For the purposes of sub-paragraph (1) above a transfer of securities is also made on qualifying terms if–

(a) it is made to a person exercising a right to acquire shares, and

(b) that right was obtained in accordance with the provisions of an SAYE option scheme–

 (i) which was established by, or by a company controlled by, the founding company, and

 (ii) which is approved under Schedule 3 to the Income Tax (Earnings and Pensions) Act 2003, and

(c) that right is being exercised in accordance with the provisions of that scheme, and

(d) the consideration for the transfer is payable to the trustees.

9(2A) For the purposes of sub-paragraph (1) above the qualifying period is–

(a) seven years, in the case of trusts established on or before the day on which the Finance Act 1994 was passed;

(b) twenty years, in the case of other trusts.

9(3) For the purposes of sub-paragraph (2) above, the fact that terms vary according to the levels of remuneration of beneficiaries, the length of their service, or similar factors, shall not be regarded as meaning that the terms are not similar.

9(4) The trust deed must provide that, in ascertaining for the purposes of a relevant rule whether particular securities are transferred, securities acquired earlier by the trustees shall be treated as transferred by them before securities acquired by them later; and a relevant rule is one which is included in the trust deed and conforms with sub-paragraph (1) above.

History – In para. 9(1)(b), the words "qualifying period" substituted by FA 1994, s. 102 and Sch. 13, para. 1, 7(1), (2), with effect from 3 May 1994.
In para. 9(2)(a), "other than … below" inserted, in para. 9(2)(b) " by virtue … above" inserted, and in para. 9(2)(c) "persons" substituted for "beneficiaries", by FA 1996, s. 120(9), with effect in relation to trusts established on or after 29 April 1996.
In para. 9(2ZA)(b), the words "an SAYE option scheme" substituted for the words "a savings-related share option scheme within the meaning of Schedule 9 to the Taxes Act 1988" by ITEPA 2003, Sch. 6, para. 163(3)(a) which has effect for the tax year 2003–04 and subsequent tax years.
In para. 9(2ZA)(b)(ii), the words "Schedule 3 to the Income Tax (Earnings and Pensions) Act 2003" substituted for the words "that Schedule" by ITEPA 2003, Sch. 6, para. 163(3)(b) which has effect for the tax year 2003–04 and subsequent tax years.
Para. 9(2ZA) inserted by FA 1996, s. 120(10), with effect in relation to trusts established on or after 29 April 1996.
Para. 9(2A) inserted by FA 1994, s. 102 and Sch. 13, para. 1, 7, with effect from 3 May 1994.

OTHER FEATURES

10 The trust deed must not contain features which are not essential or reasonably incidental to the purpose of acquiring sums and securities, granting rights to acquire shares to persons who are eligible to participate in SAYE option schemes approved under Schedule 3 to the Income Tax (Earnings and Pensions) Act 2003, transferring shares to such persons, transferring sums and securities to employees and directors, and transferring securities to the trustees of profit sharing schemes approved under Schedule 9 to the Taxes Act 1988.

History – In para. 10, the words "SAYE option schemes approved under Schedule 3 to the Income Tax (Earnings and Pensions) Act 2003" substituted for the words "savings-related share option schemes approved under Schedule 9 to the Taxes Act 1988" by ITEPA 2003, Sch. 6, para. 163(4)(a) which has effect for the tax year 2003–04 and subsequent tax years.
In para. 10, the words "Schedule 9 to the Taxes Act 1988" substituted for the words "that Schedule" by ITEPA 2003, Sch. 6, para. 163(4)(b) which has effect for the tax year 2003–04 and subsequent tax years.
In para. 10, the words "granting rights … such persons" inserted, and "that Schedule" substituted for "Schedule 9 to the Taxes Act 1988", by FA 1996, s. 120(11), with effect in relation to trusts established on or after 29 April 1996.

RULES ABOUT ACQUISITION ETC.

11(1) The trust deed must provide that, for the purposes of the deed, the trustees–

(a) acquire securities when they become entitled to them;

(b) transfer securities to another person when that other becomes entitled to them;

(c) retain securities if they remain entitled to them.

11(2) But if the deed provides as mentioned in paragraph 8 above, it must provide for the following exceptions to any rule which is included in it and conforms with sub-paragraph (1)(a) above, namely, that–

(a) if securities are issued to the trustees in exchange in circumstances mentioned in section 135(1) of the Taxation of Chargeable Gains Act 1992, they shall be treated as having acquired them when they became entitled to the securities for which they are exchanged;

(b) if the trustees become entitled to securities as a result of a reorganisation, they shall be treated as having acquired them when they became entitled to the original shares which those securities represent (construing "reorganisation" and "original shares" in accordance with section 126 of that Act).

11(3) The trust deed must provide that–

(a) if the trustees agree to take a transfer of securities, for the purposes of the deed they become entitled to them when the agreement is made and not on a later transfer made pursuant to the agreement;

(b) if the trustees agree to transfer securities to another person, for the purposes of the deed the other person becomes entitled to them when the agreement is made and not on a later transfer made pursuant to the agreement.

History – References to TCGA 1992 in para. 11(2) substituted by TCGA 1992, s. 290 and Sch. 10, para. 19(5).

POSITION AFTER TRUST'S ESTABLISHMENT

12 A trust which was at the time it was established a qualifying employee share ownership trust shall continue to be one, except that it shall not be such a trust at any time when the requirements mentioned in paragraph 3(3)(a) to (f) above are not satisfied.

This paragraph applies in relation to trusts established on or before the day on which the Finance Act 1994 was passed.

History – Final sentence inserted by FA 1994, s. 102 and Sch. 13, para. 1, 4, with effect from 3 May 1994.

12A(1) Subject to sub-paragraphs (2) and (3) below, a trust which was at the time it was established a qualifying employee share ownership trust shall continue to be one.

12A(2) If the trust deed makes provision under paragraph 3A(a) above, the trust shall not be a qualifying employee share ownership trust at any time when the requirements mentioned in paragraph 3(3)(a) to (f) above are not satisfied.

12A(3) If the trust deed makes provision under paragraph 3A(b) above, the trust shall not be a qualifying employee share ownership trust at any time when the conditions mentioned in paragraph 3B(4)(a) to (e) above are not satisfied.

12A(4) If the trust deed makes provision under paragraph 3A(c) above, the trust shall not be a qualifying employee share ownership trust at any time when–

(a) there is not a single trustee,

(b) the trustee is not a company which is resident in the United Kingdom and controlled by the founding company, or

(c) the conditions mentioned in paragraph 3C(4)(a) to (e) above are not satisfied as regards the directors of the trustee.

12A(5) This paragraph applies in relation to trusts established after the day on which the Finance Act 1994 was passed.

History – Para. 12A inserted by FA 1994, s. 102 and Sch. 13, para. 1, 5, "the day on which the Finance Act 1994 was passed" being 3 May 1994.

13 A trust is an employee share ownership trust at a particular time (the relevant time) if it was a qualifying employee share ownership trust at the time it was established; and it is immaterial whether or not it is a qualifying employee share ownership trust at the relevant time.

INTERPRETATION

14 For the purposes of this Schedule the following are securities–

(a) shares;

(b) debentures.

15 For the purposes of this Schedule, the question whether one company is controlled by another shall be construed in accordance with section 995 of the Income Tax Act 2007.

History – In para. 15 the words "section 995 of the Income Tax Act 2007" substituted for the words "section 840 of the Taxes Act 1988" by ITA 2007, s. 1027 and Sch. 1, para. 283(2), with effect from 6 April 2007.

16(1) For the purposes of this Schedule a person shall be treated as having a material interest in a company if he, either on his own or with one or more of his associates, or if any associate of his with or without other such associates,–

(a) is the beneficial owner of, or able (directly or through the medium of other companies or by any other indirect means) to control, more than 5 per cent of the ordinary share capital of the company, or

(b) possesses, or is entitled to acquire, such rights as would, in the event of the winding-up of the company or in any other circumstances, give an entitlement to receive more than 5 per cent of the assets which would then be available for distribution among the participators.

16(2) In this paragraph–

(a) **"associate"** has the meaning given by section 448 of the Corporation Tax Act 2010, but subject to sub-paragraph (3) below,

(b) **"control"** has the meaning given by section 995 of the Income Tax Act 2007, and

(c) **"participator"** has the meaning given by section 454 of the Corporation Tax Act 2010.

16(3) Where a person has an interest in shares or obligations of the company as a beneficiary of an employee benefit trust, the trustees shall not be regarded as associates of his by reason only of that interest unless sub-paragraph (5) below applies in relation to him.

16(4) In sub-paragraph (3) above **"employee benefit trust"** has the same meaning as in paragraph 7 of Schedule 8 to the Taxes Act 1988, except that in its application for this purpose paragraph 7(5)(b) of that Schedule shall have effect as if it referred to the day on which this Act was passed instead of to 14th March 1989.

16(5) This sub-paragraph applies in relation to a person if at any time on or after the day on which this Act was passed–

(a) he, either on his own or with any one or more of his associates, or

(b) any associate of his, with or without other such associates,

has been the beneficial owner of, or able (directly or through the medium of other companies or by any other indirect means) to control, more than 5 per cent of the ordinary share capital of the company.

16(6) Sub-paragraphs (9) to (12) of paragraph 7 of Schedule 8 to the Taxes Act 1988 shall apply for the purposes of sub-paragraph (5) above as they apply for the purposes of that paragraph.

History – In para. 16(2)(a), the words "meaning given by section 448 of the Corporation Tax Act 2010" substituted for the words "same meaning as in section 417(3) and (4) of the Taxes Act 1988" by CTA 2010, s. 1177 and Sch. 1, para. 216(a), with effect for corporation tax purposes for accounting periods ending on or after 1 April 2010, and for income tax and capital gains tax purposes for the tax year 2010–11 and subsequent tax years.

In para. 16(2)(b) the words "section 995 of the Income Tax Act 2007" substituted for the words "section 840 of that Act" by ITA 2007, s. 1027 and Sch. 1, para. 283(3)(a), with effect from 6 April 2007.

In para. 16(2)(c), the words "meaning given by section 454 of the Corporation Tax Act 2010" substituted for the words "same meaning as in Part XI of the Taxes Act 1988" by CTA 2010, s. 1177 and Sch. 1, para. 216(b), with effect for corporation tax purposes for accounting periods ending on or after 1 April 2010, and for income tax and capital gains tax purposes for the tax year 2010–11 and subsequent tax years.

In para. 16(2)(c) the words "the Taxes Act 1988" substituted for the words "that Act" by ITA 2007, s. 1027 and Sch. 1, para. 283(3)(a), with effect from 6 April 2007.

17 For the purposes of this Schedule a trust is established when the deed under which it is established is executed.

History – Para. 17 inserted by FA 1994, s. 102 and Sch. 13, para. 1, 8, with effect from 3 May 1994.

18 For the purposes of this Schedule "SAYE option scheme" has the same meaning as in the SAYE code (see section 516 of the Income Tax (Earnings and Pensions) Act 2003) (approved SAYE option schemes).

History – Para. 18 inserted by ITEPA 2003, Sch. 6, para. 163(5) which has effect for the tax year 2003–04 and subsequent tax years.

SCHEDULE 6 – RETIREMENT BENEFITS SCHEMES

Section 75

1-35 [Repealed by FA 2004, s. 326 and Sch. 42, Pt. 3.]

History – Sch. 6 repealed by FA 2004, s. 326 and Sch. 42, Pt. 3 with effect from 6 April 2006 but subject to FA 2004, Sch. 36. Former Sch. 6 read as follows:

"SCHEDULE 6 – RETIREMENT BENEFITS SCHEMES

Section 75

Part I – Amendments of Taxes Act

PRELIMINARY

1 The Taxes Act 1988 shall be amended as mentioned in the following provisions of this Part of this Schedule.

AMENDMENTS

2 [Repealed by FA 1995, s. 162 and Sch. 29, Pt. VIII(5).]

History – Para. 2 repealed by FA 1995, s. 162 and Sch. 29, Pt. VIII(5) in relation to accounting periods beginning on or after 1 January 1995. Para. 2 formerly substituted ICTA 1988, s. 431(4)(d)(ii).

3(1)–(4) [Amends ICTA 1988, s. 590(3)(d); substitutes s. 590(3)(e)–(h), (7); inserts s. 590(8)–(11).]

4 [Inserts ICTA 1988, s. 590A–590C.]

5(1)–(4) [Inserts ICTA 1988, s. 592(8A)–(8E).]

6 [Amends provisions as below.]

6(1)–(5) [Amends ICTA 1988, s. 594(1), (2); inserts s. 594(3)–(7).]

7 [Repealed by ITEPA 2003, Sch. 8, Pt. 1.]

History – Para. 7 repealed by ITEPA 2003, Sch. 8, Pt. 1 which has effect for the tax year 2003–04 and subsequent tax years.

8 [Repealed by ITEPA 2003, Sch. 8, Pt. 1.]

History – Para. 8 repealed by ITEPA 2003, Sch. 8, Pt. 1 which has effect for the tax year 2003–04 and subsequent tax years.

9 [Repealed by ITEPA 2003, Sch. 8, Pt. 1.]

History – Para. 9 repealed by ITEPA 2003, Sch. 8, Pt. 1 which has effect for the tax year 2003–04 and subsequent tax years.

10 [Amends ICTA 1988, s. 598(1)(b).]

11 [Amends provisions as below.]

11(1)–(3) [Amends ICTA 1988, s. 599(2); inserts s. 599(10)–(12).]

12(1) [Inserts ICTA 1988, s. 599A.]

Notes – This provision has been designated para. 12(1) presumably in error, as it is not followed by a para. 12(2).

13 [Repealed by ITEPA 2003, Sch. 8, Pt. 1.]

History – Para. 13 repealed by ITEPA 2003, Sch. 8, Pt. 1 which has effect for the tax year 2003–04 and subsequent tax years.

14 [Amends ICTA 1988, s. 605(2), (3)(a), (b)(i) and (4).]

15 [Inserts ICTA 1988, s. 611A.]

16 [Amends ICTA 1988, s. 828(4).]

17 [Repeals ICTA 1988, Sch. 23, para. 8.]

EFFECT OF AMENDMENTS

18(1) Paragraphs 2, 6(2), 10, 11(2), 14 and 15 above shall be deemed to have come into force on 14th March 1989.

18(2) Paragraphs 3(2) and (3) and 4 above shall have effect in relation to a scheme not approved by the Board before the day on which this Act is passed; but if the scheme came into existence before 14th March 1989 those provisions shall not have effect as regards an employee who became a member of the scheme before 1st June 1989.

18(3) Paragraph 3(4) above shall have effect where a determination is made on or after the day on which this Act is passed.

18(4) Paragraphs 5 and 6(3), (4) and (5) above shall have effect for the year 1989–90 and subsequent years of assessment, but paragraphs 5(4) and 6(5) above shall not have effect as regards a person's remuneration in respect of an office or employment in such circumstances as the Board may by regulations prescribe for the purposes of this sub-paragraph.

18(5) [Repealed by ITEPA 2003, Sch. 8, Pt. 1.]

18(6) [Repealed by ITEPA 2003, Sch. 8, Pt. 1.]

18(7) [Repealed by ITEPA 2003, Sch. 8, Pt. 1.]

18(8) Paragraph 11(3) above shall have effect where the charge to tax under section599 arises on or after 14th March 1989, but not where the scheme came into existence before that date and the employee became a member of it before 1st June 1989.

18(9) Paragraphs 12 and 13 above shall have effect in relation to payments made on or after the day on which this Act is passed.

18(10) Paragraph 17 above shall have effect in relation to benefits provided on or after the day on which this Act is passed.

History – In para. 18(1), the words "8(2)(b)" repealed by ITEPA 2003, Sch. 8, Pt. 1 which has effect for the tax year 2003–04 and subsequent tax years.

Para. 18(5) repealed by ITEPA 2003, Sch. 8, Pt. 1 which has effect for the tax year 2003–04 and subsequent tax years.

Para. 18(6) repealed by ITEPA 2003, Sch. 8, Pt. 1 which has effect for the tax year 2003–04 and subsequent tax years.

Para. 18(7) repealed by ITEPA 2003, Sch. 8, Pt. 1 which has effect for the tax year 2003–04 and subsequent tax years.

Cross references – ICTA 1988, s. 595(2): charge on amounts equal to cost of benefits provided by third parties (now repealed).
ICTA 1988, s. 599: charge on commutation of entire pension in special circumstances.

Part II – Approved Schemes: General

PRELIMINARY

19(1) This Part of this Schedule shall be deemed to have come into force on 14th March 1989 and, subject to sub-paragraphs (2) to (4) below, applies in relation to any retirement benefits scheme (within the meaning of Chapter I of Part XIV of the Taxes Act 1988) approved by the Board before the day on which this Act is passed.

19(2) The Board may by regulations provide that, in circumstances prescribed in the regulations, this Part of this Schedule or any provision of it shall not apply or shall apply with such modifications as may be so prescribed.

19(3) Regulations under sub-paragraph (2) above–

(a) may include provision authorising the Board to direct that this Part of this Schedule or any provision of it shall not apply in any particular case where in the opinion of the Board the facts are such that its application would not be appropriate;

(b) may take effect (and may authorise any direction given under them to take effect) as from 14th March 1989 or any later date;

(c) may make such supplementary provision as appears to the Board to be necessary or expedient.

19(4) This Part of this Schedule shall not apply to a scheme if, before the end of 1989, the administrator of the scheme gives written notice to the Board that it is not to apply.

19(5) Where a notice is given to the Board under sub-paragraph (4) above, the scheme shall cease to be approved–
(a) if it came into existence before 14th March 1989, with effect from 1st June 1989 or (if later) the date with effect from which it was approved;
(b) if it came into existence on or after 14th March 1989, with effect from the date with effect from which it was approved.

REMUNERATION

20(1) This paragraph applies–
(a) where the scheme came into existence before 14th March 1989, as regards an employee who became a member of the scheme on or after 1st June 1989;
(b) where the scheme came into existence on or after 14th March 1989, as regards any employee who is a member of the scheme (whenever he became a member).

20(2) The rules of the scheme shall have effect (notwithstanding anything in them to the contrary and notwithstanding the effect of anything in Schedule 23 to the Taxes Act 1988) as if, in arriving at the employee's relevant annual remuneration for the purposes of calculating benefits, any excess of what would be his relevant annual remuneration (apart from this paragraph) over the permitted maximum for the year of assessment in which his participation in the scheme ceases shall be disregarded.

20(3) The rules of the scheme shall have effect (notwithstanding anything in them to the contrary) as if, in arriving at the employee's remuneration for the year 1988–89 or any subsequent year of assessment for the purposes of any restriction on the aggregate amount of contributions payable under the scheme by the employee and the employer, there were disregarded any excess of what would be his remuneration for the year (apart from this paragraph) over the permitted maximum for the year.

20(4) In this paragraph **"the permitted maximum"**, in relation to a year of assessment, means the figure found for that year by virtue of sub-paragraphs (5) and (6) below.

20(5) For the years 1988–89 and 1989–90 the figure is £60,000.

20(6) For any subsequent year of assessment the figure is the figure found for that year, for the purposes of section 590C of the Taxes Act 1988, by virtue of section 590C(4) to (5A).

History – In para. 20(6), the words "to (5A)" substituted by FA 1993, s. 107(7) with effect for 1994–95 and subsequent years of assessment.

Cross references – ICTA 1988, s. 590C: earnings cap.
FA 2004, Sch. 36, para. 16: post-commencement earnings limit for capped individuals.

21(1) The rules of the scheme shall have effect (notwithstanding anything in them to the contrary) as if the amount of contributions payable under the scheme by an employee in the year 1989–90 or any subsequent year of assessment were limited to 15 per cent of his remuneration for the year in respect of the employment.

21(2) Where in relation to any year of assessment a percentage higher than 15 per cent applies for the purposes of section 592(8) or (8A) of the Taxes Act 1988 (relief in respect of contributions) as regards any employee, sub-paragraph (1) above, as regards him, shall have effect in relation to that year with the substitution for 15 per cent of that higher percentage.

22(1) This paragraph applies–
(a) where the scheme came into existence before 14th March 1989, as regards an employee who became a member of the scheme on or after 1st June 1989;
(b) where the scheme came into existence on or after 14th March 1989, as regards any employee who is a member of the scheme (whenever he became a member).

22(2) For the purposes of paragraph 21(1) above, in arriving at the employee's remuneration for the year any excess of what would be his remuneration for the year (apart from this sub-paragraph) over the permitted maximum for the year shall be disregarded.

22(3) In sub-paragraph (2) above **"the permitted maximum"**, in relation to a year of assessment, means the figure found for that year by virtue of sub-paragraphs (4) and (5) below.

22(4) For the year 1989–90 the figure is £60,000.

22(5) For any subsequent year of assessment the figure is the figure found for that year, for the purposes of section 590C of the Taxes Act 1988, by virtue of section 590C(4) to (5A).

History – In para. 22(5), the words "to (5A)" substituted by FA 1993, s. 107(6) with effect for 1994–95 and subsequent years of assessment.

ACCELERATED ACCRUAL

23(1) This paragraph applies where the scheme allows a member to commute his pension or part of it for a lump sum or sums and–
(a) where the scheme came into existence before 14th March 1989, applies as regards an employee who became a member of the scheme on or after 1st June 1989, and
(b) where the scheme came into existence on or after 14th March 1989, applies as regards any employee who is a member of the scheme (whenever he became a member).

23(2) The rules of the scheme shall have effect (notwithstanding anything in them to the contrary and notwithstanding the effect of paragraph 3 of Schedule 23 to the Taxes Act 1988) as if they did not allow the employee to obtain by way of commutation a lump sum or sums exceeding in all the greater of the following sums–
(a) a sum of three-eightieths of his relevant annual remuneration for each year of service up to a maximum of 40,
(b) a sum of the pension payable under the scheme to the employee for the first year in which it is payable multiplied by 2.25.

23(3) The following rules shall apply in calculating, for the purposes of sub-paragraph (2) above, the pension payable under the scheme to the employee for the first year in which it is payable–
(a) if the pension payable for the year changes, the initial pension payable shall be taken;
(b) it shall be assumed that the employee will survive for the year;
(c) the effect of commutation, and of any allocation of pension to provide benefits for survivors, shall be ignored.

Cross references – ICTA 1988, Sch. 23: occupational pension schemes approved before 23 July 1987.

24(1) This paragraph applies where the scheme provides a lump sum or sums for a member otherwise than by commutation of his pension or part of it and–
(a) where the scheme came into existence before 14th March 1989, applies as regards an employee who became a member of the scheme on or after 1st June 1989, and
(b) where the scheme came into existence on or after 14th March 1989, applies as regards any employee who is a member of the scheme (whenever he became a member).

24(2) The rules of the scheme shall have effect (notwithstanding anything in them to the contrary and notwithstanding the effect of paragraph 4 of Schedule 23 to the Taxes Act 1988) as if they did not allow the payment to the employee, otherwise than by way of commutation, of a lump sum or sums exceeding in all the greater of the following sums–
(a) a sum of three-eightieths of his relevant annual remuneration for each year of service up to a maximum of 40;
(b) a sum of the relevant number of eightieths of his relevant annual remuneration.

24(3) For the purposes of sub-paragraph (2) above the relevant number shall be found by taking the number of eightieths (of relevant annual remuneration) by reference to which the pension payable under the scheme to the employee is calculated, multiplying that number by three, and treating the resulting number as 120 if it would otherwise exceed 120.

Cross references – ICTA 1988, Sch. 23: occupational pension schemes approved before 23 July 1987.

ASSOCIATED EMPLOYMENTS

25(1) This paragraph applies–

(a) where the scheme came into existence before 14th March 1989, as regards an employee who became a member of the scheme on or after 1st June 1989;

(b) where the scheme came into existence on or after 14th March 1989, as regards any employee who is a member of the scheme (whenever he became a member).

25(2) Where the employee is a member of the scheme by virtue of two or more relevant associated employments, the rules of the scheme shall have effect as mentioned in sub-paragraph (3) below.

25(3) The rules of the scheme shall have effect (notwithstanding anything in them to the contrary) as if they prohibited the amount payable by way of pension in respect of service in any of the relevant associated employments, when aggregated with any amount payable by way of pension in respect of service in the other such employment or employments, from exceeding the relevant amount.

25(4) For the purposes of sub-paragraph (3) above the relevant amount, in relation to the employee, shall be found by applying the following formula–

$$\frac{A \times C}{30}$$

25(5) For the purposes of this paragraph–

(a) section 590B(5) and (6) of the Taxes Act 1988 shall apply for the purpose of defining A, and

(b) section 590B(9) to (11) of that Act shall apply for the purpose of defining C,

as they apply for the purposes of section 590B of that Act, except that for the purposes of this paragraph A shall not exceed 20.

25(6) The reference to two or more relevant associated employments shall be construed in accordance with section 590A of the Taxes Act 1988.

CONNECTED SCHEMES

26(1) This paragraph applies–

(a) where the scheme came into existence before 14th March 1989, as regards an employee who became a member of the scheme on or after 1st June 1989;

(b) where the scheme came into existence on or after 14th March 1989, as regards any employee who is a member of the scheme (whenever he became a member).

26(2) Where in relation to the employee the scheme is connected with another scheme which is (or other schemes each of which is) an approved scheme, the rules of the scheme shall have effect as mentioned in sub-paragraph (3) below.

26(3) The rules of the scheme shall have effect (notwithstanding anything in them to the contrary) as if they prohibited the amount payable by way of pension under the scheme, when aggregated with any amount payable by way of pension under the other scheme or schemes, from exceeding the relevant amount.

26(4) For the purposes of sub-paragraph (3) above the relevant amount, in relation to the employee, shall be found by applying the following formula–

$$\frac{B \times C}{30}$$

26(5) For the purposes of this paragraph–

(a) section 590B(7) and (8) of the Taxes Act 1988 shall apply for the purpose of defining B, and

(b) section 590B(9) to (11) of that Act shall apply for the purpose of defining C,

as they apply for the purposes of section 590B of that Act, except that for the purposes of this paragraph B shall not exceed 20.

26(6) References in this paragraph to the scheme being connected with another scheme in relation to the employee shall be construed in accordance with section 590A of the Taxes Act 1988.

AUGMENTATION

27(1) This paragraph applies–

(a) where the scheme came into existence before 14th March 1989, as regards an employee who became a member of the scheme on or after 1st June 1989;

(b) where the scheme came into existence on or after 14th March 1989, as regards any employee who is a member of the scheme (whenever he became a member).

27(2) Where in addition to being a member of the scheme (the main scheme) the employee is also a member of an approved scheme (the voluntary scheme) which provides additional benefits to supplement those provided by the main scheme and to which no contributions are made by any employer of his, sub-paragraph (3) below shall apply in relation to any augmentation of the benefits provided for him by the main scheme after he has ceased to participate in it.

27(3) Any rules of the main scheme imposing a limit on the amount of a benefit provided for the employee shall have effect (notwithstanding anything in them to the contrary) as if they provided for the limit to be reduced by the amount of any like benefit provided for the employee by the voluntary scheme.

CENTRALISED SCHEMES

28(1) Where the scheme is a centralised scheme, sub-paragraph (1)(a) and (b) of each of paragraphs 20 and 22 to 27 above shall have effect with the substitution for the reference to the coming into existence of the scheme of a reference to the commencement of the employer's participation in the scheme.

28(2) For the purposes of this paragraph a centralised scheme is a retirement benefits scheme (within the meaning of Chapter I of Part XIV of the Taxes Act 1988) established for the purpose of enabling any employer, other than an employer associated with the person by whom the scheme is established, to participate in it as regards his employees.

28(3) For the purposes of sub-paragraph (2) above one person is associated with another if (directly or indirectly) one is controlled by the other or if both are controlled by a third person.

28(4) In sub-paragraph (3) above the reference to control, in relation to a body corporate, shall be construed–

(a) where the body corporate is a close company, in accordance with section 416 of the Taxes Act 1988, and

(b) where it is not, in accordance with section 840 of that Act.

ELECTION

29(1) In a case where–

(a) an employee became a member of the scheme on or after 17th March 1987 and before 1st June 1989, and

(b) he gives written notice to the administrator of the scheme that this Part of this Schedule is to apply in his case,

he shall be deemed for the purposes of this Part of this Schedule to have become a member of the scheme on 1st June 1989.

29(2) A notice under this paragraph shall be given in such form as the Board may prescribe.

SUPPLEMENTARY

30 In this Part of this Schedule **"relevant annual remuneration"** means final remuneration or, if the scheme provides for benefits to be calculated by reference to some other annual remuneration, that other annual remuneration.

Part III – Approved Schemes: Additional Voluntary Contributions

PRELIMINARY

31(1) Subject to sub-paragraphs (2) to (4) below, this Part of this Schedule applies in relation to any retirement benefits scheme which was approved by the Board before the day on which this Act is passed and which makes provision for the payment by an employee of voluntary contributions.

31(2) Paragraph 32 below only applies where–

(a) the provision for the payment of voluntary contribution is freestanding, and

(b) the scheme is not one to which contributions are made by any employer of the employee.

31(3) The Board may by regulations provide that, in circumstances prescribed in the regulations, this Part of this Schedule or any provision of it shall not apply or shall apply with such modifications as may be so prescribed.

31(4) Regulations under sub-paragraph (3) above–

(a) may include provision authorising the Board to direct that this Part of this Schedule or any provision of it shall not apply in any particular case where in the opinion of the Board the facts are such that its application would not be appropriate;

(b) may make such supplementary provision as appears to the Board to be necessary or expedient.

ABATEMENT OF BENEFITS

32(1) The scheme shall have effect (notwithstanding anything in it to the contrary) as if its rules included a rule imposing, in the case of each benefit provided for the employee, such a limit on the amount of the benefit as is mentioned in sub-paragraph (2) below.

32(2) The limit referred to above is a limit of such an amount as is found by–

(a) taking the amount of the limit imposed by the main scheme on the provision of any like benefit for the employee by that scheme, and

(b) subtracting from that amount an amount equal to the relevant amount.

32(3) For the purposes of sub-paragraph (2) above the relevant amount is–

(a) where the employee is not a member of any other relevant scheme, the amount of any like benefit provided for the employee by the main scheme, and

(b) where the employee is a member of another relevant scheme or schemes, an amount equal to the aggregate of the amount mentioned in paragraph (a) above and the amount of any like benefit provided for the employee by the other relevant scheme or schemes.

32(4) In sub-paragraph (3) above, references to the employee being a member of another relevant scheme are references to his being a member of any approved scheme, other than the scheme, which provides additional benefits for him to supplement those provided by the main scheme.

32(5) This paragraph shall have effect in relation to benefits provided on or after the day on which this Act is passed.

RETURN OF SURPLUS FUNDS

33(1) The scheme shall have effect (notwithstanding anything in it to the contrary) as if its rules included a rule requiring the administrator, in the circumstances mentioned in sub-paragraph (2) or (3) below, as the case may be, to make to the employee or his personal representatives a payment of an amount equal to the prescribed amount out of funds which are or have been held for the purposes of the scheme.

33(2) Where the provision for payment of voluntary contributions is freestanding, the circumstances referred to above are that the amount of any benefit provided for the employee by the scheme would have been greater had the amount of any like benefit provided for him by the main scheme, or any other relevant scheme of which he is a member, been less.

33(3) Where the provision for the payment of voluntary contributions is not freestanding, the circumstances referred to above are that the amount of any benefit provided for the employee by virtue of the voluntary contributions would have been greater had the amount of any like benefit provided for him by the principal provisions of the scheme, or any other relevant scheme of which he is a member, been less.

33(4) In sub-paragraph (1) above, the reference to the prescribed amount is to an amount calculated in accordance with the method for the time being specified in regulations made for the purposes of section 591 of the Taxes Act 1988 as the method to be used for calculating the amount of any surplus funds.

33(5) In sub-paragraph (2) above, the reference to the employee being a member of another relevant scheme is a reference to his being a member of any approved scheme, other than the scheme, which provides additional benefits for him to supplement those provided by the main scheme.

33(6) In sub-paragraph (3) above, the reference to the employee being a member of another relevant scheme is a reference to his being a member of any approved scheme, other than the scheme, which provides additional benefits for him to supplement those provided by the principal provisions of the scheme.

Cross references – ITEPA 2003, s. 583(3)(b)(ii): unauthorised payments.

ITEPA 2003, s. 593(1)(b)(ii): application of section 583 with regards to unauthorised payments.

34 The scheme shall have effect (notwithstanding anything in it to the contrary) as if its rules included a rule enabling the administrator, before making any payment by virtue of paragraph 33 above, to deduct the amount of any tax to which he is charged by section 599A of the Taxes Act 1988 by virtue of making the payment.

SUPPLEMENTARY

35 In this Part of this Schedule–

(a) **"administrator"**, **"approved scheme"**, **"employee"** and **"retirement benefits scheme"** have the same meanings as in Chapter I of Part XIV of the Taxes Act 1988,

(b) **"freestanding"**, in relation to provision for the payment of voluntary contributions, means provision which is contained in a retirement benefits scheme other than the one which provides the benefits which the voluntary contributions are intended to supplement,

(c) **"the main scheme"**, in relation to provision for the payment of voluntary contributions which is freestanding, means the retirement benefits scheme which provides the benefits which the voluntary contributions are intended to supplement,

(d) **"principal provisions"**, in relation to a retirement benefits scheme which makes provision for the payment of voluntary contributions which is not freestanding, means the provisions of the scheme concerning the provision of the benefits which the voluntary contributions are intended to supplement,

(e) references to the provision of a benefit for an employee shall, in relation to a deceased employee, be construed as references to the provision of a benefit in respect of him, and

(f) references to an employee being (or not being) a member of a scheme shall, in relation to a deceased employee, be construed as references to his having been (or not having been) a member of a scheme immediately before the time of his death.".

SCHEDULE 7 – PERSONAL PENSION SCHEMES

Section 77

1–12 [Repealed by FA 2004, s. 326 and Sch. 42, Pt. 3.]

History – Sch. 7 repealed by FA 2004, s. 326 and Sch. 42, Pt. 3 with effect from 6 April 2006 but subject to FA 2004, Sch. 36. Former Sch. 7 read as follows:

"SCHEDULE 7 – PERSONAL PENSION SCHEMES

Section 77

Part I – Amendments of Taxes Act

1 Chapter IV of Part XIV of the Taxes Act 1988 (personal pension schemes) shall be amended as mentioned in the following provisions of this Part of this Schedule.
2(1), (3) [Substitutes ICTA 1988, s. 635(3); repeals s. 635(4).]
2(4) This paragraph shall have effect in relation to the approval of a scheme on or after the day on which this Act is passed; but if the scheme came into existence before that day sub-paragraph (2) above shall not have effect as regards arrangements made by a member in accordance with the scheme before that day.
3(1) [Substitutes ICTA 1988, s. 640A(2), Table.]
3(2) This paragraph shall have effect for the year 1989–90 and subsequent years of assessment.
4(1) [Inserts ICTA 1988, s. 640A.]
4(2) This paragraph shall have effect for the year 1989–90 and subsequent years of assessment.
5(1)–(3) [Amends ICTA 1988, s. 644(2); inserts s. 644(6A)–(6F).]
5(4) This paragraph shall be deemed to have come into force on 6th April 1989.
6(1)–(5) [Amends ICTA 1988, s. 645(1)(c); inserts s. 645(3)(c), (4A); repeals s. 645(5).]
6(6) This paragraph shall be deemed to have come into force on 6th April 1989.
7(1) [Amends ICTA 1988, s. 646(1).]
7(2) This paragraph shall have effect for the year 1989–90 and subsequent years of assessment.
8(1) [Inserts ICTA 1988, s. 646A.]
8(2) This paragraph shall have effect for the year 1989–90 and subsequent years of assessment.
9 [Amends ICTA 1988, s. 655(5).]

Part II – Schemes Approved Before Passing of This Act

INTERPRETATION

10 In this Part of this Schedule–
(a) **"personal pension scheme"** has the same meaning as in Chapter IV of Part XIV of the Taxes Act 1988, and
(b) references to approval of such a scheme do not include references to provisional approval under regulations made under section 655(5) of that Act.

LUMP SUM TO MEMBER

11(1) This paragraph applies as regards arrangements made by a member of a personal pension scheme approved by the Board before the day on which this Act is passed, if the arrangements are made by the member in accordance with the scheme on or after that day.
11(2) The rules of the scheme shall have effect (notwithstanding anything in them to the contrary) as if any limitation imposed on the maximum amount payable to the member by way of lump sum, and imposed by reference to a fraction of the total value of the benefits for him provided for by the arrangements, were imposed by reference to the same fraction of the difference between–
(a) the total value, at the time when the lump sum is paid, of the benefits provided for by the arrangements, and
(b) the value, at that time, of such of his rights under the scheme as are protected rights for the purposes of the Pension Schemes Act 1993 or the Pension Schemes (Northern Ireland) Act 1993.

History – In para. 11(2)(b), the words "Pension Schemes Act 1993" substituted by the Pension Schemes Act 1993, s. 190 and Sch. 8, para. 22, with effect from 7 February 1994 (SI 1994/86 (C 3)).
In para. 11(2)(b), the words "Pension Schemes (Northern Ireland) Act 1993" substituted by the Pension Schemes (Northern Ireland) Act 1993, s. 184 and Sch. 7, para. 24, with effect from 7 February 1994 (SI 1994/17 (C 1)).

12(1) This paragraph applies where on or after the day on which this Act is passed a lump sum becomes payable under a personal pension scheme approved by the Board before that day.
12(2) The rules of the scheme shall have effect (notwithstanding anything in them to the contrary) as if any limitation imposed on the maximum amount payable to a member by way of lump sum, and imposed by reference to a figure, did not apply.
12(3) The reference in sub-paragraph (2) above to a limitation imposed on the maximum amount payable to a member by way of lump sum does not include a reference to a limitation imposed on the maximum amount so payable out of a transfer payment.".

SCHEDULE 8 – AMENDMENTS OF CHAPTER I OF PART XII OF TAXES ACT 1988(INSURANCE COMPANIES)

Section 84

[Sch. 8 omitted by FA 2012, s. 146 and Sch. 16, para. 247(a).]

History – Sch. 8 omitted by FA 2012, s. 146 and Sch. 16, para. 247(a) in relation to accounting periods beginning on or after 1 January 2013 (FA 2012, s. 148) but subject to transitional provisions in FA 2012, Sch. 17. Where an accounting period would otherwise straddle 1 January 2013, it is deemed to end on 31 December 2012 (FA 2012, s. 149).

SCHEDULE 8A – MODIFICATION OF SECTIONS 83 TO 83A AND 89 IN RELATION TO OVERSEAS LIFE INSURANCE COMPANIES

Section 89A

[Repealed by SI 2006/3271, reg. 43 and Sch., Pt. 1.]

History – Sch. 8A repealed bySI 2006/3271, reg. 43 and Sch., Pt. 1 with effect from 31 December 2006 in relation to periods of account ending on or after that date. Sch. 8A previously modified s. 83 to 83A and s. 89.

Heading to Sch. 8A amended by FA 1996, s. 163 and Sch. 31, para. 8(2) by insertion of words "to 83A".

Cross references – S. 90A: expressions used in Sch. 8A have the same meaning as in ICTA 1988, Pt. XII, Ch. 1.

SCHEDULE 9 – LIFE POLICIES ETC. HELD BY COMPANIES

Section 90

[Omitted by FA 2008, s. 36 and Sch. 14, para 17(a).]

History – Sch. 9 omitted by FA 2008, s. 36 and Sch. 14, para. 17(a), with effect–

- so far as relating to corporation tax, for accounting periods beginning on or after 1 April 2008, and
- so far as relating to income tax, for the tax year 2008–09 and subsequent tax years.

SCHEDULE 10 – DEEP DISCOUNT SECURITIES: AMENDMENTS

Section 93

[Repealed by FA 1996, s. 205 and Sch. 41, Pt. V(3) for accounting periods ending after 31 March 1996 (corporation tax) and for 1996–97 (income tax), subject to FA 1996, Sch. 15.]

SCHEDULE 11 – DEEP GAIN SECURITIES

Section 94

[Sch. 11 repealed by FA 1996, Sch 41, Pt. V(3).]

History – Sch. 11 repealed by FA 1996, Sch 41, Pt. V(3) with effect, for corporation tax purposes, in relation to accounting periods ending after 31 March 1996 and, for income tax purposes in relation to tax years after 1995–96.

SCHEDULE 12 – CLOSE COMPANIES: CONSEQUENTIAL AMENDMENTS

Section 107

Part I – Administrative Provisions

INTERPRETATION

1 [Omitted by CTA 2010, s. 1177 and Sch. 1, para. 217 and repealed by CTA 2010, s. 1181 and Sch. 3, Pt. 1.]

History – Para. 1 omitted by CTA 2010, s. 1177 and Sch. 1, para. 217 and repealed by CTA 2010, s. 1181 and Sch. 3, Pt. 1, with effect for corporation tax purposes for accounting periods ending on or after 1 April 2010, and for income tax and capital gains tax purposes for the tax year 2010–11 and subsequent tax years.

Notes – Para. 1 rewritten as CTA 2010, s. 31(1), (3), (4), 465(1), (3), (4), 1109(4), Sch. 1 para. 450, 458.

PROVISION OF INFORMATION BY COMPANY

2 [Omitted by SI 2009/2035, art. 2 and Schedule, para. 25.]

History – Para. 2 omitted by SI 2009/2035, art. 2 and Schedule, para. 25, with effect from 13 August 2009.

PROVISION OF INFORMATION BY SHAREHOLDERS

3 [Omitted by CTA 2010, s. 1177 and Sch. 1, para. 217, repealed by CTA 2010, s. 1181 and Sch. 3, Pt. 1 and omitted by FA 2011, s. 86 and Sch. 23, para. 56.]

History – Para. 3, so far as it continues to have effect (see CTA 2010, s. 1184), omitted by FA 2011, s. 86 and Sch. 23, para. 56, with effect from 1 April 2012, subject to transitional provisions in FA 2011, Sch. 23, para. 65.

Para. 3 omitted by CTA 2010, s. 1177 and Sch. 1, para. 217 and repealed by CTA 2010, s. 1181 and Sch. 3, Pt. 1, with effect for corporation tax purposes for accounting periods ending on or after 1 April 2010, and for income tax and capital gains tax purposes for the tax year 2010–11 and subsequent tax years.

Notes – Para. 3 rewritten in CTA 2010 as follows:
Para. 3(1): CTA 2010, s. 31(1), 465(1), 1102(2), 1109(4), Sch. 1, para. 450, 458.
Para. 3(2): CTA 2010, s. 31(1), 465(1), 1102(2).

INFORMATION ABOUT BEARER SECURITIES

4 [Omitted by CTA 2010, s. 1177 and Sch. 1, para. 217 and repealed by CTA 2010, s. 1181 and Sch. 3, Pt. 1.]

History – Para. 4 omitted by CTA 2010, s. 1177 and Sch. 1, para. 217 and repealed by CTA 2010, s. 1181 and Sch. 3, Pt. 1, with effect for corporation tax purposes for accounting periods ending on or after 1 April 2010, and for income tax and capital gains tax purposes for the tax year 2010–11 and subsequent tax years.

Notes – Para. 4 rewritten in CTA 2010 as follows:
Para. 4(1): CTA 2010, s. 31(2), (3), (4), 465(2), (3), (4), 1102(3), (4), (5), 1109(4), Sch. 1, para. 450, 458
Para. 4(2): CTA 2010, s. 31(5), 465(5), 1102(6), 1109(4), Sch. 1, para. 450, 458

Part II – Amendments Connected With Repeal of Chapter III of Part XI of Taxes Act 1988

THE TAXES MANAGEMENT ACT 1970(C. 9)

5 [Omitted by SI 2009/2035, art. 2 and Schedule, para. 60(c).]

History – Para. 5 omitted by SI 2009/2035, art. 2 and Schedule, para. 60(c), with effect from 13 August 2009.

THE INCOME AND CORPORATION TAXES ACT 1988(C. 1)

7 [Amends ICTA 1988, s. 13(9).]

8 [Repealed by ITEPA 2003, Sch. 8, Pt. 1.]

History – Para. 8 repealed by ITEPA 2003, Sch. 8, Pt. 1 which has effect, for income tax purposes, for the tax year 2003–04 and subsequent tax years and, for corporation tax purposes, for accounting periods ending after 5 April 2003.

9(1) [Amends ICTA 1988, s. 187(3).]

9(2) This paragraph shall have effect in relation to accounting periods beginning after 31st March 1989.

10(1) [Amends ICTA 1988, s. 214(1)(c).]

10(2) This paragraph shall have effect in relation to accounting periods beginning after 31st March 1989, except in any case where section 427(4) of the Taxes Act 1988 has effect by virtue of section 103(2) of this Act.

Cross references – ICTA 1988, s. 427(4): exclusion from income for higher-rate tax of distributions where amount previously treated as deemed income by apportionment (now repealed).

11 [Repealed by CTA 2010, s. 1181 and Sch. 3, Pt. 1.]

History – Para. 11 repealed by CTA 2010, s. 1181 and Sch. 3, Pt. 1, with effect for corporation tax purposes for accounting periods ending on or after 1 April 2010, and for income tax and capital gains tax purposes for the tax year 2010–11 and subsequent tax years.

12 [Repealed by CTA 2010, s. 1181 and Sch. 3, Pt. 1.]

History – Para. 12 repealed by CTA 2010, s. 1181 and Sch. 3, Pt. 1, with effect for corporation tax purposes for accounting periods ending on or after 1 April 2010, and for income tax and capital gains tax purposes for the tax year 2010–11 and subsequent tax years. Para. 12(1)–(3) also previously repealed by ITA 2007, s. 1031 and Sch. 3, Pt. 1, with effect from 6 April 2007.

Notes – Para. 12(1) rewritten as ITA 2007, s. 392(2).

13(1)–(3) [Repealed by ITA 2007, s. 1031 and Sch. 3, Pt. 1.]

13(4) This paragraph shall have effect in relation to accounting periods beginning after 31st March 1989.

History – Para. 13(1) repealed by ITA 2007, s. 1031 and Sch. 3, Pt. 1, with effect from 6 April 2007.
Para. 13(2) repealed by ITA 2007, s. 1031 and Sch. 3, Pt. 1, with effect from 6 April 2007.
Para. 13(3) repealed by ITA 2007, s. 1031 and Sch. 3, Pt. 1, with effect from 6 April 2007.

14(1) [Substitutes ICTA 1988, s. 576(5)(a).]

14(2) This paragraph shall have effect in relation to disposals made after 31st March 1989.

15 [Repealed by FA 2004, s. 326 and Sch. 42, Pt. 3 .]

History – Para. 15 repealed by FA 2004, s. 326 and Sch. 42, Pt. 3 with effect from 6 April 2006 but subject to FA 2004, Sch. 36 (Pension schemes etc.: transitional provisions and savings).

16 [Repealed by FA 2004, s. 326 and Sch. 42, Pt. 3.]

History – Para. 16 repealed by FA 2004, s. 326 and Sch. 42, Pt. 3 with effect from 6 April 2006 but subject to FA 2004, Sch. 36 (Pension schemes etc.: transitional provisions and savings).

17 [Repealed by ITA 2007, s. 1031 and Sch. 3, Pt. 1.]

History – Para. 17 repealed by ITA 2007, s. 1031 and Sch. 3, Pt. 1, with effect from 6 April 2007.

Notes – Para. 17 rewritten as ITA 2007, s. 749(6).

18 [Repealed by FA 1997, s.113 and Sch. 18, Pt. VI(3).]

History – Para. 18 repealed by FA 1997, s. 113 and Sch. 18, Pt. VI(3) in relation to any payment made by reference to a profit period beginning on or after 1 January 2000.

SCHEDULE 13 – CAPITAL ALLOWANCES: MISCELLANEOUS AMENDMENTS

Section 121

PATENT RIGHTS

27 [*Repealed by CAA 2001*, s. 580 and Sch. 4.]

History – Sch. 13, para. 27 (which amended ICTA 1988, s. 521) repealed by CAA 2001, s. 580 and Sch. 4, with effect as respects allowances and charges falling to be made for chargeable periods ending, for income tax purposes, on or after 6 April 2001, and for corporation tax purposes, on or after 1 April 2001.

FINANCE ACT 1990

(1990 Chapter 29)

[*26th July 1990*]

ARRANGEMENT OF SECTIONS

PART II – INCOME TAX, CORPORATION TAX AND CAPITAL GAINS TAX

CHAPTER I – GENERAL

PART II – INCOME TAX, CORPORATION TAX AND CAPITAL GAINS TAX

Chapter I – General

INCOME TAX RATES AND ALLOWANCES

17 Rates and main allowances

17 [Repealed by ITA 2007, s. 1031 and Sch. 3, Pt. 1.]

History – S. 17 repealed by ITA 2007, s. 1031 and Sch. 3, Pt. 1, with effect from 6 April 2007.

18 Relief for blind persons

18 [Repealed by ITA 2007, s. 1031 and Sch. 3, Pt. 1.]

History – S. 18 repealed by ITA 2007, s. 1031 and Sch. 3, Pt. 1, with effect from 6 April 2007.

BENEFITS IN KIND

21 Care for children

21 [Repealed by ITEPA 2003, Sch. 8, Pt.1 with effect from 6 April 2003.]

History – S.21 repealed by ITEPA 2003, Sch. 8, Pt.1 which has effect for the tax year 2003–04 and subsequent tax years

MILEAGE ALLOWANCES

23 Limit on chargeable mileage profit

23 [Repealed by FA 2001, Sch. 33, Pt. 2(1). with effect for 2002-03 and subsequent tax years.]

CHARITIES

25 Donations to charity by individuals

25(1)–(9A) [Omitted by ITA 2007, s. 1027 and Sch. 1, para. 284(2), and repealed by s. 1031 and Sch. 3, Pt. 1.]

25(10) [Omitted by CTA 2010, s. 1177 and Sch. 1, para. 220 and repealed by CTA 2010, s. 1181 and Sch. 3, Pt. 1.]

25(10A) [Repealed by CTA 2010, s. 1181 and Sch. 3, Pt. 1.]

25(11) [Omitted by ITA 2007, s. 1027 and Sch. 1, para. 284(2), and repealed by s. 1031 and Sch. 3, Pt. 1.]

25(12) [Omitted by CTA 2010, s. 1177 and Sch. 1, para. 220 and repealed by CTA 2010, s. 1181 and Sch. 3, Pt. 1.]

25(13) [Omitted by ITA 2007, s. 1027 and Sch. 1, para. 284(2), and repealed by s. 1031 and Sch. 3, Pt. 1.]

History – S. 25(1)–(9A) omitted by ITA 2007, s. 1027 and Sch. 1, para. 284(2), and repealed by s. 1031 and Sch. 3, Pt. 1, with effect from 6 April 2007. See ITA 2007, Sch. 2, para. 98–100 for saving provisions.
S. 25(10) omitted by CTA 2010, s. 1177 and Sch. 1, para. 220 and repealed by CTA 2010, s. 1181 and Sch. 3, Pt. 1, with effect for corporation tax purposes for accounting periods ending on or after 1 April 2010, and for income tax and capital gains tax purposes for the tax year 2010–11 and subsequent tax years.
In former s. 25(10) the words "charitable company" substituted for "charity" twice, the words "for the purposes of Chapter 2 of Part 8 of the Income Tax Act 2007 (gift aid)" inserted, and the words "Corporation Tax Acts" substituted for the words "Tax Acts" by ITA 2007, s. 1027 and Sch. 1, para. 284(3), with effect from 6 April 2007. See ITA 2007, Sch. 2, para. 98–100 for saving provisions.
S. 25(10A) repealed by CTA 2010, s. 1181 and Sch. 3, Pt. 1, with effect for corporation tax purposes for accounting periods ending on or after 1 April 2010, and for income tax and capital gains tax purposes for the tax year 2010–11 and subsequent tax years.
Former s. 25(10A) inserted by FA 2008, s. 53 and Sch. 19, para. 8, with effect from 21 July 2008.
S. 25(11) omitted by ITA 2007, s. 1027 and Sch. 1, para. 284(2), and repealed by s. 1031 and Sch. 3, Pt. 1, with effect from 6 April 2007. See ITA 2007, Sch. 2, para. 98–100 for saving provisions.
S. 25(12) omitted by CTA 2010, s. 1177 and Sch. 1, para. 220 and repealed by CTA 2010, s. 1181 and Sch. 3, Pt. 1, with effect for corporation tax purposes for accounting periods ending on or after 1 April 2010, and for income tax and capital gains tax purposes for the tax year 2010–11 and subsequent tax years.
In former s. 25(12)(a) the words "charitable company" substituted for "charity" by ITA 2007, s. 1027 and Sch. 1, para. 284(4), with effect from 6 April 2007. See ITA 2007, Sch. 2, para. 98–100 for saving provisions.
Former s. 25(12)(b), (e) repealed by FA 2000, s. 39(7) and Sch. 40, Pt. II(1)) with effect for gifts or covenanted payments made on or after 6 April 2000.
S. 25(13) omitted by ITA 2007, s. 1027 and Sch. 1, para. 284(2) and repealed by s. 1031 and Sch. 3, Pt. 1, with effect from 6 April 2007. See ITA 2007, Sch. 2, para. 98–100 for saving provisions.

Cross references – ICTA 1988, s. 339: qualifying donations to charity made by companies treated as charges on income for CT purposes.
ICTA 1988, s. 349(1): s. 349(1) (payments not out of profits or gains brought into charge to income tax, and annual interest) does not apply to a donation which is a qualifying donation for the purposes of FA 1990, s. 25.

ICTA 1988, s. 506B(7): benefits etc. provided to a donor that are within the limits set by s. 25 are to be disregarded when applying ICTA 1988, s. 506A (designation of certain payments by a charity to a "substantial donor" as being non-charitable expenditure of the charity).
ICTA 1988, s. 839: connected persons.
FA 1998, s. 48(4A): millennium gift aid (gifts of money for relief in poor countries): application of s. 25(10) where aggregated gifts, including gifts made in different years of assessment, are treated as a single qualifying donation made to the charity.
FA 2002, s. 98: Gift aid: election to be treated as if gift made in previous tax year: a donor may elect to have a gift which is a qualifying donation treated as if it were made by him in the previous year of assessment.
FA 2002, s. 98(5): Gift aid: election to be treated as gift made in previous tax year: reference to the relevant year of assessment in s. 25(10) to be construed as a reference to the year of assessment in which the gift is actually made.
FA 2002, Sch. 18, para. 5(3)(b): Exemption for interest and gift aid income: application of s. 25(10) to determine gift aid income in respect of a club.
FA 2002, Sch. 18, para. 9(1): s. 25 has effect as if a registered club were a charity.
FA 2004, s. 83: giving through the self assessment return.

Statutory instruments – SI 2000/2074: Donations to Charity by Individuals (Appropriate Declarations) Regulations 2000.

Other material – IR press release, 28 February 1998: following introduction of Scottish variable rate (SVR), tax relief to continue to apply at the UK basic rate, regardless of the tax position of the donor.

Notes – S. 25 rewritten in ITA 2007 as follows:
S. 25(1): ITA 2007, s. 416(1).
S. 25(2): ITA 2007, s. 416(2), (3), (4), (6), (7), (8), 417, 418(1), (2), (3), 422(2), (3), (4), (5), 427(1), (2), (3), (4), 1025(2), (3), 1026.
S. 25(3): ITA 2007, s. 428(1).
S. 25(3A): ITA 2007, s. 428(2), (3).
S. 25(4): ITA 2007, s. 417, 418(2).
S. 25(5): ITA 2007, s. 418(3), (4).
S. 25(5A): ITA 2007, s. 418(2).
S. 25(5B): ITA 2007, s. 419(1), (2), (3), (4), (6)
S. 25(5C): ITA 2007, s. 419(1), (5), (7).
S. 25(5D): ITA 2007, s. 419(6), (7), (8).
S. 25(5E): ITA 2007, s. 420(1), (3)
S. 25(5F): ITA 2007, s. 420(4).
S. 25(5G): ITA 2007, s420(5), (6).
S. 25(5H): ITA 2007, s. 420(7), (8).
S. 25(5I): ITA 2007, s. 420(2), 421(5).
S. 25(5J): ITA 2007, s. 421(2), (3), (4).
S. 25(6): ITA 2007, s. 23, 414(1), (2), 423(1), (2), (4), (5), Sch. 1, para. 536.
S. 25(7): ITA 2007, s. 23.
S. 25(8): ITA 2007, s. 23, 30(1), 424(1), (2), (4), (5), (6), 425(2).
S. 25(9): ITA 2007, s. 23, 30(1), 424(3), 425(2), (3), (4), (5).
S. 25(9A): ITA 2007, s. 58(1), 423(5), Sch. 1, para. 28.
S. 25(10): ITA 2007, s. 520(1), (2), (4), 521(1), (2), (3), (4), (6)
S. 25(11): ITA 2007, s. 1021(1).
S. 25(12): ITA 2007, s. 415, 430(1), 520(2), (3), 521(2), (5).
S. 25 rewritten in CTA 2010 as follows:
S. 25(10): CTA 2010, s. 471(1), (2), (4), 472(1), (2), 475(1), (2), (4), (5).
S. 25(12): CTA 2010, s. 467, 471(3), 472(3), 475(1), (2), (3), (4), 1128(1).

26 Company donations to charity

26 [Repealed by CTA 2010, s. 1181 and Sch. 3, Pt. 1.]

History – S. 26 repealed by CTA 2010, s. 1181 and Sch. 3, Pt. 1, with effect for corporation tax purposes for accounting periods ending on or after 1 April 2010, and for income tax and capital gains tax purposes for the tax year 2010–11 and subsequent tax years.

27 Maximum qualifying company donations

27(1) [Repealed by FA 1991, s. 123 and Sch. 19, Pt. V.]

27(2) [Repealed by CTA 2010, s. 1181 and Sch. 3, Pt. 1.]

27(3) [Repealed by FA 1991, s. 123 and Sch. 19, Pt. V.]

27(4) [Repealed by CTA 2010, s. 1181 and Sch. 3, Pt. 1.]

History – S. 27(1), (3) repealed by FA 1991, s. 123 and Sch. 19, Pt. V effectively in relation to accounting periods beginning on or after 19 March 1991 (see FA 1991, s. 71(3); see also s. 71(4)).
S. 27(2) repealed by CTA 2010, s. 1181 and Sch. 3, Pt. 1, with effect for corporation tax purposes for accounting periods ending on or after 1 April 2010, and for income tax and capital gains tax purposes for the tax year 2010–11 and subsequent tax years.
S. 27(4) repealed by CTA 2010, s. 1181 and Sch. 3, Pt. 1, with effect for corporation tax purposes for accounting periods ending on or after 1 April 2010, and for income tax and capital gains tax purposes for the tax year 2010–11 and subsequent tax years.

SAVINGS

28 Tax-exempt special savings accounts

28(1) [Repealed by ITTOIA 2005, s. 884 and Sch. 3, s. 28(1).]

28(2) [Repealed by ITTOIA 2005, s. 884 and Sch. 3, s. 28(2).]

28(3) [Repealed by *ITTOIA 2005*, s. 884 and Sch. 3, also repealed by TCGA 1992, s. 290 and Sch. 12; *s. 29(3).]*

History – S. 28(1), (2) and (3) repealed by ITTOIA 2005, s. 884 and Sch. 3 (notwithstanding that s. 28(3) was repealed by TCGA 1992, see below); effective for income tax purposes for 2005–06 onwards and for corporation tax purposes for accounting periods ending after 5 April 2005 (ITTOIA 2005, s. 883(1)).
S. 28(3) repealed by TCGA 1992, s. 290 and Sch. 12 in relation to tax for 1992–93 and subsequent years of assessment.

29 Extension of SAYE

29 [Repealed by ITTOIA 2005, s. 884 and Sch. 3.]

History – Repealed by ITTOIA 2005, s. 884 and Sch. 3; effective for income tax purposes for 2005–06 onwards and for corporation tax purposes for accounting periods ending after 5 April 2005 (ITTOIA 2005, s. 883(1)).

Notes – The amendments originally introduced by s. 29, at ICTA 1988, s. 326, are rewritten at ITTOIA 2005, s. 702 to s. 708

30 Building societies and deposit-takers

30 Schedule 5 to this Act (which contains provisions relating to building societies, deposit-takers and investors) shall have effect.

INSURANCE COMPANIES AND FRIENDLY SOCIETIES

41 Apportionment of income etc.

41 [Omitted by FA 2012, s. 146 and Sch. 16, para. 247(b)(i).]

History – S. 41 omitted by FA 2012, s. 146 and Sch. 16, para. 247(b)(i), with effect in relation to accounting periods beginning on or after 1 January 2013 (FA 2012, s. 148) but subject to transitional provisions in FA 2012, Sch. 17. Where an accounting period would otherwise straddle 1 January 2013, it is deemed to end on 31 December 2012 (FA 2012, s. 149).

42 Overseas life assurance business

42 [Omitted by FA 2012, s. 146 and Sch. 16, para. 247(b)(i).]

History – S. 42 omitted by FA 2012, s. 146 and Sch. 16, para. 247(b)(i), with effect in relation to accounting periods beginning on or after 1 January 2013 (FA 2012, s. 148) but subject to transitional provisions in FA 2012, Sch. 17. Where an accounting period would otherwise straddle 1 January 2013, it is deemed to end on 31 December 2012 (FA 2012, s. 149).

43 Deduction for policy holders' tax

43 [Repealed by FA 2003, s. 216 and Sch. 43, Pt. 3(12).]

History – S. 43 repealed by FA 2003, s. 216 and Sch. 43, Pt. 3(12) with effect for periods of account beginning on or after 1 January 2003.

44 Reinsurance commissions

44 [Repealed by FA 2004, s. 326 and Sch. 42, Pt. 2(3).]

History – S. 44 repealed by FA 2004, s. 326 and Sch. 42, Pt. 2(3) with effect for accounting periods beginning on or after 1 April 2004, but subject to transitional provisions in FA 2004, s. 43, 44, and Sch. 6.

45 Policy holders' share of profits etc.

45(1) [Omitted by FA 2012, s. 146 and Sch. 16, para. 247(b)(ii).]

45(2) [Omitted by FA 2012, s. 146 and Sch. 16, para. 247(b)(ii).]

45(3) [Omitted by FA 2012, s. 146 and Sch. 16, para. 247(b)(ii).]

45(4) [Omitted by FA 2012, s. 146 and Sch. 16, para. 247(b)(ii).]

45(5) [Repealed by FA 2003, s. 216 and Sch. 43, Pt. 3(12) and omitted by FA 2012, s. 146 and Sch. 16, para. 247(b)(ii).]

45(6) [Repealed by FA 1998, s. 165 and Sch. 27, Pt. III(2) and omitted by FA 2012, s. 146 and Sch. 16, para. 247(b)(ii).]

45(7) [Omitted by FA 2012, s. 146 and Sch. 16, para. 247(b)(ii).]

45(8) [Repealed by FA 1995, s. 162 and Sch. 29, Pt. VIII(5).]

45(9) [Repealed by F(No. 2)A 1997, s. 52 and Sch. 8, Pt. II(6) and omitted by FA 2012, s. 146 and Sch. 16, para. 247(b)(ii).]

45(10) [Omitted by FA 2012, s. 146 and Sch. 16, para. 247(b)(ii).]

45(11) [Omitted by FA 2012, s. 146 and Sch. 16, para. 247(b)(ii).]

History – S. 45(1) to (7) omitted by FA 2012, s. 146 and Sch. 16, para. 247(b)(ii), with effect in relation to accounting periods beginning on or after 1 January 2013 (FA 2012, s. 148) but subject to transitional provisions in FA 2012, Sch. 17. Where an accounting period would otherwise straddle 1 January 2013, it is deemed to end on 31 December 2012 (FA 2012, s. 149). Note that s. 45(5) and (6) had previously been repealed (see history notes below).
Former s. 45(5) repealed by FA 2003, s. 216 and Sch. 43, Pt. 3(12) in relation to distributions on or after 9 April 2003.
Former s. 45(6), repealed by FA 1998, s. 165 and Sch. 27, Pt. III(2), with effect in relation to accounting periods beginning on or after 6 April 1999.
S. 45(8) repealed by FA 1995, s. 162 and Sch. 29, Pt. VIII(5) for accounting periods beginning on or after 1 January 1995.
S. 45(9) to (11) omitted by FA 2012, s. 146 and Sch. 16, para. 247(b)(ii), with effect in relation to accounting periods beginning on or after 1 January 2013 (FA 2012, s. 148) but subject to transitional provisions in FA 2012, Sch. 17. Where an accounting period would otherwise straddle 1 January 2013, it is deemed to end on 31 December 2012 (FA 2012, s. 149).
Former s. 45(9) repealed by F(No. 2)A 1997, s. 52 and Sch. 8, Pt. II(6) (in accordance with Sch. 3, para. 6(5) and (8)) with effect for accounting periods beginning on or after 2 July 1997.

48 Transfers of long term business

48 Schedule 9 to this Act (which makes provision about the tax consequences of certain transfers of long term business by insurance companies) shall have effect.

48 [Omitted by FA 2012, s. 146 and Sch. 16, para. 247(b)(iii).]

History – S. 48 omitted by FA 2012, s. 146 and Sch. 16, para. 247(b)(iii), with effect in relation to accounting periods beginning on or after 1 January 2013 (FA 2012, s. 148) but subject to transitional provisions in FA 2012, Sch. 17. Where an accounting period would otherwise straddle 1 January 2013, it is deemed to end on 31 December 2012 (FA 2012, s. 149).

49 Friendly societies: increased tax exemption

49(1) [Omitted by FA 2012, s. 176 and Sch. 18, para. 23(a)(i).]

49(2) [Omitted by FA 2012, s. 176 and Sch. 18, para. 23(a)(i).]

49(3) [Omitted by FA 2012, s. 176 and Sch. 18, para. 23(a)(i).]

49(4) [Omitted by FA 2012, s. 176 and Sch. 18, para. 23(a)(i).]

49(5) [Amends ICTA 1988, Sch. 15, para. 3(8)(b)(ii).]

History – S. 49(1) to (4) omitted by FA 2012, s. 176 and Sch. 18, para. 23(a)(i), with effect in relation to accounting periods beginning on or after 1 January 2013 (FA 2012, s. 178) but subject to transitional provisions in FA 2012, Sch. 19. Where an accounting period would otherwise straddle 1 January 2013, it is deemed to end on 31 December 2012 (FA 2012, s. 179).

50 Friendly societies: application of enactments

50 [Omitted by FA 2012, s. 176 and Sch. 18, para. 23(a)(ii).]

History – S. 50 omitted by FA 2012, s. 176 and Sch. 18, para. 23(a)(ii), with effect in relation to accounting periods beginning on or after 1 January 2013 (FA 2012, s. 178) but subject to transitional provisions in FA 2012, Sch. 19. Where an accounting period would otherwise straddle 1 January 2013, it is deemed to end on 31 December 2012 (FA 2012, s. 179).

UNIT AND INVESTMENT TRUSTS ETC.

52 Unit trusts: repeals

52(1) The Taxes Act 1988 shall have effect subject to the following provisions of this section.

52(2) [Repeals ICTA 1988, s. 468(5).]

52(3) Where a particular distribution period is by virtue of subsection (2) above the last distribution period as regards which section 468(5) applies in the case of a trust, the trustees' liability to income tax in respect of any source of income chargeable under Case III of Schedule D shall be assessed as if they had ceased to possess the source of income on the last day of that distribution period.

52(4) But where section 67 of the Taxes Act 1988 applies by virtue of subsection (3) above, it shall apply with the omission from subsection (1)(b) of the words from "and shall" to "this provision".

52(5) [Repeals ICTA 1988, s. 468B.]

52(6) [Repeals ICTA 1988, s. 468C.]

52(7) [Repeals ICTA 1988, s. 468D.]

52(8) In this section **"distribution period"** has the same meaning as in section 468 of the Taxes Act 1988.

Cross references – ICTA 1988, s. 67: special rules where source of income disposed of or yield ceases.

55 Investment trusts

55 [Repealed by CTA 2010, s. 1181 and Sch. 3, Pt. 1.]

History – S. 55 repealed by CTA 2010, s. 1181 and Sch. 3, Pt. 1, with effect for corporation tax purposes for accounting periods ending on or after 1 April 2010, and for income tax and capital gains tax purposes for the tax year 2010–11 and subsequent tax years.

OIL INDUSTRY

60 Allowance for abandonment expenditure related to offshore machinery or plant

60 [Repealed by CAA 2001, s. 580 and Sch. 4.]

History – S. 60, repealed by CAA 2001, s. 580 and Sch. 4, with effect as respects allowances and charges falling to be made for chargeable periods ending, for income tax purposes, on or after 6 April 2001, and for corporation tax purposes, on or after 1 April 2001.

62 CT treatment of *PRT* repayment

62(1) [Repealed by CTA 2010, s. 1181 and Sch. 3, Pt. 1.]

62(2) [Repealed by CTA 2010, s. 1181 and Sch. 3, Pt. 1.]

62(3) [Repealed by CTA 2010, s. 1181 and Sch. 3, Pt. 1 and TIOPA 2010, s. 378 and Sch. 10, Pt. 6.]

History – S. 62(1) repealed by CTA 2010, s. 1181 and Sch. 3, Pt. 1, with effect for corporation tax purposes for accounting periods ending on or after 1 April 2010, and for income tax and capital gains tax purposes for the tax year 2010–11 and subsequent tax years.
S. 62(2) repealed by CTA 2010, s. 1181 and Sch. 3, Pt. 1, with effect for corporation tax purposes for accounting periods ending on or after 1 April 2010, and for income tax and capital gains tax purposes for the tax year 2010–11 and subsequent tax years.
Para. 62(3) repealed by CTA 2010, s. 1181 and Sch. 3, Pt. 2, with effect for accounting periods ending on or after 1 April 2010 and TIOPA 2010, s. 378 and Sch. 10, Pt. 6, with effect for corporation tax purposes for accounting periods ending on or after 1 April 2010, for income tax and capital gains tax purposes for the tax year 2010–11 and subsequent tax years, and for petroleum revenue tax purposes for chargeable periods beginning on or after 1 July 2010.

INTERNATIONAL

67 Dual resident companies: controlled foreign companies

67(1) [Repealed by FA 1994, s. 258 and Sch. 26, Pt. VIII(1).]

67(2) [Repealed by FA 1994, s. 258 and Sch. 26, Pt. VIII(1).]

67(3) [Amends provisions as below.]

(a) [Repeals ICTA 1988, Sch. 25, para. 2(1)(c), 4(1)(c).]

(b) [Omitted by FA 2009, s. 36 and Sch. 16, para. 5(a).]

(c) [Omitted by FA 2009, s. 36 and Sch. 16, para. 5(a).]

67(4) Subsections (1) and (2) above shall apply on and after 20th March 1990 and subsection (3) above shall apply to dividends paid on or after that date.

History – S. 67(1), (2) repealed by FA 1994, s. 251, s. 258 and Sch. 26, Pt. VIII(1), with effect from 30 November 1993.
S. 67(3)(b) and (c) omitted by FA 2009, s. 36 and Sch. 16, para. 5(a) with effect in relation to accounting periods of controlled foreign companies beginning on or after 1 July 2009, subject to rules in FA 2009, Sch. 16, para. 7 for accounting periods straddling that date and transitional rules in FA 2009, Sch. 16, para. 8.

68 Movements of capital between residents of member States

68(1) [Omitted by FA 2009, s. 37 and Sch. 17, para. 3(b).]

68(2) [Omitted by FA 2009, s. 37 and Sch. 17, para. 3(b).]

68(3) [Amends provisions as below.]

(a) [Amends TMA 1970, s. 98(1).]

(b) [Omitted by FA 2009, s. 37 and Sch. 17, para. 3(b).]

(c) [Omitted by FA 2009, s. 37 and Sch. 17, para. 3(b).]

(d) [Omitted by FA 2009, s. 37 and Sch. 17, para. 3(b).]

68(4) This section shall apply to transactions carried out on or after 1st July 1990.

History – S. 68(1), (2) and (3)(b)–(d) omitted by FA 2009, s. 37 and Sch. 17, para. 3(b) with effect in relation to events taking place and transactions carried out on or after 1 July 2009.

69 European Economic Interest Groupings

69 Schedule 11 to this Act (which makes provision about the taxation of income and gains in the case of European Economic Interest Groupings) shall have effect.

Other material – HMRC press release, 9 February 1994: provisions introduced by s. 69 apply to all European Economic Interest Groupings established within the European Economic Area.

Post-ICTA 1988

MISCELLANEOUS

76 Training and enterprise councils and local enterprise companies

76 [Repealed by CTA 2009, s. 1326 and Sch. 3, Pt. 1.]

History – S. 76 repealed by CTA 2009, s. 1326 and Sch. 3, Pt. 1, with effect, for corporation tax purposes, for accounting periods ending on or after 1 April 2009 and, for income tax and capital gains tax purposes, for the tax year 2009–10 and subsequent years.

77 Expenses of entertainers

77 [Repealed by ITEPA 2003, Sch. 8, Pt. 1 with effect for 2003-04 and subsequent tax years.]

78 Waste disposal

78 [Repealed by CTA 2009, s. 1326 and Sch. 3, Pt. 1.]

History – S. 78 repealed by CTA 2009, s. 1326 and Sch. 3, Pt. 1, with effect, for corporation tax purposes for accounting periods ending on or after 1 April 2009 and, for income tax and capital gains tax purposes, for the tax year 2009–10 and subsequent years.

79 Priority share allocations for employees etc.

79 [Repealed by ITEPA 2003, Sch. 8, Pt. 1 with effect for 2003-04 and subsequent tax years.]

81 Futures and options: exemptions

81(1) [Repealed by FA 2002, s. 141 and Sch. 40, Pt. 3(13).]

81(2) [Inserts ICTA 1988, s. 659A.]

81(3) [Repealed by TCGA 1992, s. 290 and Sch. 12.]

81(4) [Repeals ICTA 1988, s. 659.]

81(5) Subsections (1) and (2) above apply in relation to income derived after the day on which this Act is passed.

81(6) [Repealed by TCGA 1992, s. 290 and Sch. 12.]

81(7) Insofar as section 659 of the Taxes Act 1988 relates to provisions of that Act, subsection (4) above applies in relation to income derived after the day on which this Act is passed.

81(8) Insofar as section 659 of the Taxes Act 1988 relates to section 149B of the Capital Gains Tax Act 1979, subsection (4) above applies in relation to disposals made after the day on which this Act is passed.

History – S. 81(1) repealed by FA 2002, s. 141 and Sch. 40, Pt. 3(13), with effect in relation to accounting periods beginning on or after 1 October 2002. S. 81(1) .
S. 81(3), (6) repealed by TCGA 1992, s. 290 and Sch. 12, in relation to tax for 1992–93 and subsequent years of assessment and tax for other chargeable periods beginning on or after 6 April 1992.

87 Capital allowances: vehicles provided by employees

87 [Repealed by CAA 2001, s. 580 and Sch. 4.]

History – S. 87, repealed by CAA 2001, s. 580 and Sch. 4, with effect as respects allowances and charges falling to be made for chargeable periods ending, for income tax purposes, on or after 6 April 2001.

88 Capital allowances: miscellaneous amendments

88 Schedule 13 to this Act shall have effect.

89 Correction of errors in Taxes Act 1988

89 Schedule 14 to this Act shall have effect.

Chapter II – Management

RETURNS AND INFORMATION

90 Income tax returns

90(1) [Substitutes TMA 1970, s. 8, 8A, 9.]

90(2) [Amends provisions as below.]

(a) [Amends TMA 1970, s. 12(1).]

(b) [Omitted by SI 2009/2035, art. 2 and Schedule, para. 60(d).]

(c) [Amends TMA 1970, s. 12(4).]

90(3) [Amends TMA 1970, s. 93(1).]

90(4) [Amends TMA 1970, s. 95(1)(a).]

90(5) This section applies where a notice to deliver a return was, or falls to be, given after 5th April 1990.

History – S. 90(2)(b) omitted by SI 2009/2035, art. 2 and Schedule, para. 60(d), with effect from 13 August 2009.

91 Corporation tax returns

91 [Repealed by FA 1998, s. 165 and Sch. 27, Pt. III(28).]

History – S. 91 repealed by FA 1998, s. 165 and Sch. 27, Pt. III(28) with effect in relation to accounting periods ending on or after 1 July 1999 (the self-assessment appointed day under FA 1994, s. 199 by virtue of SI 1998/3173 (C. 78)).

92 Information powers relating to interest

92(1) [Amends TMA 1970, s. 17 as below.]

92(2) [Amends TMA 1970, s. 17(1).]

92(3) [Inserts TMA 1970, s. 17(5), (6).]

92(4) [Amends TMA 1970, s. 18 as below.]

92(5) [Amends TMA 1970, s. 18(1).]

92(6) [Inserts TMA 1970, s. 18(3B), (3C).]

92(7) Subsections (1) to (3) above shall have effect as regards a case where interest is paid or credited in the year 1991–92 or a subsequent year of assessment.

92(8) Subsections (4) to (6) above shall have effect as regards a case where interest is paid in the year 1991–92 or a subsequent year of assessment.

93 Restrictions on Board's power to call for information

93(1) [Inserts TMA 1970, s. 20(7A).]

93(2) This section shall apply with respect to notices given on or after the day on which this Act is passed.

CORPORATION TAX DETERMINATIONS

95 Determinations

95 [Repealed by FA 1998, s. 165 and Sch. 27, Pt. III(28).]

History – S. 95 repealed by FA 1998, s. 165 and Sch. 27, Pt. III(28) with effect in relation to accounting periods ending on or after 1 July 1999 (the self-assessment appointed day under FA 1994, s. 199 by virtue of SI 1998/3173 (C. 78)).

96 Consequential group relief adjustments

96 [Repealed by FA 1999, s. 92(6), 139 and Sch. 20, Pt. III(20).]

History – S. 96 repealed by FA 1999, s. 92(6), 139 and Sch. 20, Pt. III(20), with effect in relation to accounting periods ending on or after 1 July 1999.

CLAIMS BY COMPANIES

97 Payment of tax credits

97 [Repealed by F(No. 2)A 1997, s. 52 and Sch. 8, Pt. II(9).]

History – S. 97 repealed by F(No. 2)A 1997, s. 52 and Sch. 8, Pt. II(9) (in accordance with Sch. 4, para. 2) with effect in relation to tax credits in respect of distributions made on or after 6 April 1999.

98 Repayment of income tax deducted at source

98(1) The Taxes Act 1988 shall be amended as follows.

98(2) [Partially repeals ICTA 1988, s. 7(2).]

98(3) [Repealed by FA 1998, s. 165 and Sch. 27, Pt. III(28).]

98(4) [Partially repeals ICTA 1988, s. 11(3).]

98(5) This section applies in relation to income tax falling to be set off against corporation tax for accounting periods ending after the day appointed for the purposes of section 10 of the Taxes Act 1988 (pay and file).

History – S. 98(3) repealed by FA 1998, s. 165 and Sch. 27, Pt. III(28) with effect in relation to accounting periods ending on or after 1 July 1999 (the self-assessment appointed day under FA 1994, s. 199 by virtue of SI 1998/3173 (C. 78)).

Notes – The day appointed for the purposes of ICTA 1988, s. 10 was 30 September 1993 (SI 1992/3066).

99 Loss relief

99 [Repealed by CTA 2010, s. 1181 and Sch. 3, Pt. 1.]

History – S. 99 repealed by CTA 2010, s. 1181 and Sch. 3, Pt. 1, with effect for corporation tax purposes for accounting periods ending on or after 1 April 2010, and for income tax and capital gains tax purposes for the tax year 2010–11 and subsequent tax years.

100 Group relief: general

100 [Repealed by FA 1998, s. 165 and Sch. 27, Pt. III(28).]

History – S. 100 repealed by FA 1998, s. 165 and Sch. 27, Pt. III(28) with effect in relation to accounting periods ending on or after 1 July 1999 (the self-assessment appointed day under FA 1994, s. 199 by virtue of SI 1998/3173 (C. 78)).

101 Group relief: relieved losses

101 [Repealed by FA 1999, s. 139 and Sch. 20, Pt. III(21).]

History – S. 101 repealed by FA 1999, s. 139 and Sch. 20, Pt. III(21), with effect in relation to accounting periods ending on or after 1 July 1999.

102 Capital allowances: general

102 [Repealed by FA 1998, s. 165 and Sch. 27, Pt. III(28).]

History – S. 102 repealed by FA 1998, s. 165 and Sch. 27, Pt. III(28) with effect in relation to accounting periods ending on or after 1 July 1999 (the self-assessment appointed day under FA 1994, s. 199 by virtue of SI 1998/3173 (C. 78)).

103 Capital allowances: assimilation to claims by individuals

103 [Repealed by CAA 2001, s. 580 and Sch. 4.]

History – S. 103 repealed by CAA 2001, s. 580 and Sch. 4, with effect as respects allowances and charges falling to be made for chargeable periods ending, for income tax purposes, on or after 6 April 2001, and for corporation tax purposes, on or after 1 April 2001.

MISCELLANEOUS

104 Officers

104(1) [Inserts TMA 1970, s. 1(2A), (2B).]

104(2) [Amends provisions as below.]

(a) [Amends TMA 1970, s. 55(7).]

(b) [Repealed by FA 2001, Sch. 33, Pt. 2(13).]

104(3) The amendment made by subsection (1) above shall be deemed always to have had effect.

104(4) The amendments made by subsection (2) above shall apply where notice of appeal is given on or after the day on which this Act is passed.

History – S. 104(2)(b) repealed by FA 2001, Sch. 33, Pt. 2(13), with effect from 11 May 2001.

105 Recovery of excessive repayments of tax

105(1) [Inserts TMA 1970, s. 30(1A).]

105(2) This section applies in relation to amounts of tax repaid on or after the day on which this Act is passed.

106 Corporation tax: collection

106 [Substitutes ICTA 1988, s. 10(2).]

PART IV – MISCELLANEOUS AND GENERAL

MISCELLANEOUS

125 Information for tax authorities in other member States

125(1) [Omitted by FA 2008, s. 113 and Sch. 36, para. 83(a).]

125(2) [Omitted by FA 2008, s. 113 and Sch. 36, para. 83(a).]

125(3) [Omitted by SI 2009/2035, art. 2 and Schedule, para. 26.]

125(4) [Omitted by SI 2009/2035, art. 2 and Schedule, para. 26.]

125(5) [Repealed by FA 2003, s. 216 and Sch. 43, Pt. 5(1).]

125(6) [Omitted by SI 2009/2035, art. 2 and Schedule, para. 26.]

History – S. 125(1) omitted by FA 2008, s. 113 and Sch. 36, para. 83(a), with effect from 1 April 2009 (SI 2009/404, art. 2, subject to savings at SI 2009/404, art. 3).

S. 125(2) omitted by FA 2008, s. 113 and Sch. 36, para. 83(a), with effect from 1 April 2009 (SI 2009/404, art. 2, subject to savings at SI 2009/404, art. 3).

S. 125(3) omitted by SI 2009/2035, art. 2 and Schedule, para. 26, with effect from 13 August 2009.

In former s. 125(3), the words "the Directive of the Council of the European Communities dated 19 December 1977 No. 77/799/EEC (the "1977 Directive")" substituted for the words "the Directive mentioned in subsection (1) above" by FA 2008, s. 113 and Sch. 36, para. 83(b), with effect from 1 April 2009 (SI 2009/404, art. 2, subject to savings at SI 2009/404, art. 3).

S. 125(4) omitted by SI 2009/2035, art. 2 and Schedule, para. 26, with effect from 13 August 2009.

In former s. 125(4), the words "which is covered by the provisions for the exchange of information under the 1977 Directive" substituted for the words "such as is mentioned in subsection (1) above" by FA 2008, s. 113 and Sch. 36, para. 83(c), with effect from 1 April 2009 (SI 2009/404, art. 2, subject to savings at SI 2009/404, art. 3).

S. 125(5) repealed by FA 2003, s. 216 and Sch. 43, Pt. 5(1) with effect from 10 July 2003 (Royal Assent to Finance Act 2003).

S. 125(6) omitted by SI 2009/2035, art. 2 and Schedule, para. 26, with effect from 13 August 2009.

In former s. 125(6), the words "Subsections (1) and (2) above shall apply with respect to notices given on or after the day on which this Act is passed," omitted by FA 2008, s. 113 and Sch. 36, para. 83(d), with effect from 1 April 2009 (SI 2009/404, art. 2, subject to savings at SI 2009/404, art. 3).

In s. 125(6), the words "and subsection (5) above shall come into force on that day" (which appeared after the word "appoint") repealed by FA 2003, s. 216 and Sch. 43, Pt. 5(1) with effect from 10 July 2003 (Royal Assent to Finance Act 2003).

European material – Directive 77/799 deals with mutual assistance between the revenue authorities of member states (OJ 1977, L336/15).

Other material – ICAEW Technical Release TR 812 (not reproduced): nature of assurances as to confidentiality sought by Revenue from foreign tax authority *before releasing* information.

126 Pools payments for football ground improvements

126 [Repealed by FA 2012, s. 227 and Sch. 39, para. 19(1).]

History – S. 126 repealed by FA 2012, s. 227 and Sch. 39, para. 19(1), with effect, for corporation tax purposes, in relation to payments made on or after 1 April 2013, and for income tax purposes, in relation to payments made on or after 6 April 2013.

127 Definition of "local authority" for certain tax purposes

127(1) [Repealed by CTA 2010, s. 1181 and Sch. 3, Pt. 1.]

127(2) [Repealed by TCGA 1992, s. 290 and Sch. 12.]

127(3) Schedule 18 to this Act (consequential amendments) shall have effect.

127(4) This section shall be deemed to have come into force on 1st April 1990.

History – S. 127(1) repealed by CTA 2010, s. 1181 and Sch. 3, Pt. 1, with effect for corporation tax purposes for accounting periods ending on or after 1 April 2010, and for income tax and capital gains tax purposes for the tax year 2010–11 and subsequent tax years.

GENERAL

131 Interpretation etc.

131(1) In this Act **"the Taxes Act 1970"** means the Income and Corporation Taxes Act 1970 and **"the Taxes Act 1988"** means the Income and Corporation Taxes Act 1988.

131(2) Chapter II of Part I of this Act shall be construed as one with the Value Added Tax Act 1983.

131(3) Part II of this Act, so far as it relates to capital gains tax, shall be construed as one with the Capital Gains Tax Act 1979.

Notes – The Capital Gains Tax Act 1979 was repealed by TCGA 1992, s. 290 and Sch. 12 in relation to chargeable periods beginning after 5 April 1992. References to the 1979 Act to be construed as references to the Taxation of Chargeable Gains Act 1992 (Interpretation Act 1978, s. 17(2)).

133 Short title

133 This Act may be cited as the Finance Act 1990.

SCHEDULES

SCHEDULE 4 – LIMIT ON CHARGEABLE MILEAGE PROFIT

Section 23

[Repealed by FA 2001, Sch. 33, Pt. 2(1).]

History – Sch. 4 repealed by FA 2001, Sch. 33, Pt. 2(1), with effect for 2002–03 and subsequent years of assessment.

SCHEDULE 5 – BUILDING SOCIETIES AND DEPOSIT-TAKERS

Section 30

INTRODUCTION

1 The Taxes Act 1988 shall be amended as mentioned in paragraphs 2 to 14 below.

BUILDING SOCIETIES

2(1) [Repeals ICTA 1988, s. 476.]

2(2) This paragraph shall apply as regards the year 1991–92 and subsequent years of assessment.

3(1) [Repeals ICTA 1988, s. 477.]

3(2) This paragraph shall apply as regards any time falling on or after 6th April 1991.

4 [Repealed by CTA 2010, s. 1181 and Sch. 3, Pt. 1.]

History – Para. 4 repealed by CTA 2010, s. 1181 and Sch. 3, Pt. 1, with effect for corporation tax purposes for accounting periods ending on or after 1 April 2010, and for income tax and capital gains tax purposes for the tax year 2010–11 and subsequent tax years.

DEPOSIT-TAKERS

5(1) [Repeals ICTA 1988, s. 479.]

5(2) This paragraph shall apply as regards interest paid or credited on or after 6th April 1991.

6(1) [Repeals ICTA 1988, s. 480.]

6(2) This paragraph shall apply as regards any time falling on or after 6th April 1991.

7–11 [Repealed by ITA 2007, s. 1031 and Sch. 3, Pt. 1.]

History – Para. 7–11 repealed by ITA 2007, s. 1031 and Sch. 3, Pt. 1, with effect from 6 April 2007.

Notes – Para. 7–11 rewritten as follows:
Para. 7(1): ITA 2007, s. 850(6), 851(1), (2), 852(1), (2), (3), 855(1), 946, 948(1), 953(6), (7).
Para. 8(3): ITA 2007, s. 853(4).
Para. 8(4): ITA 2007, s. 872(1), (2), (4)
Para. 9(2): ITA 2007, s. 985(1), 986(1).
Para. 9(3): ITA 2007, s. 866(2).
Para. 9(4): ITA 2007, s. 871(1).
Para. 9(5): ITA 2007, s. 871(3)
Para. 10(1): ITA 2007, s. 876(1), (2).
Para. 10(2): ITA 2007, s. 876(1), (2).
Para. 10(3): ITA 2007, s. 889(7), 891.
Para. 11: ITA 2007, s. 495(1).

GENERAL

12(1) [Repeals ICTA 1988, s. 483(1)–(3), (5).]

12(2) This paragraph shall apply where the first year of assessment mentioned in section 483(1) is 1990–91 or a subsequent year of assessment.

13(1) [Repeals ICTA 1988, s. 686(5).]

13(2) This paragraph shall apply as regards a sum paid or credited on or after 6th April 1991.

14(1) [Repeals ICTA 1988, s. 687(3), endwords.]

14(2) This paragraph shall apply as regards an amount paid or credited on or after 6th April 1991.

MANAGEMENT

15 [Amends TMA 1970, s. 98, Table.]

TRANSITIONAL PROVISION

16 [Repealed by ITA 2007, s. 1031 and Sch. 3, Pt. 1.]

History – Para. 7–11 repealed by ITA 2007, s. 1031 and Sch. 3, Pt. 1, with effect from 6 April 2007.
Para. 16 repealed by ITA 2007, s. 1031 and Sch. 3, Pt. 1, with effect from 6 April 2007.

SCHEDULE 6 – LIFE ASSURANCE: APPORTIONMENT OF INCOME ETC.

Section 41

1 [Omitted by FA 2012, s. 146 and Sch. 16, para. 247(b)(iv).]

History – Para. 1 omitted by FA 2012, s. 146 and Sch. 16, para. 247(b)(iv), with effect in relation to accounting periods beginning on or after 1 January 2013 (FA 2012, s. 148) but subject to transitional provisions in FA 2012, Sch. 17. Where an accounting period would otherwise straddle 1 January 2013, it is deemed to end on 31 December 2012 (FA 2012, s. 149).
Former para. 1(2)(b) partially repealed by FA 2007, s. 114 and Sch. 27, Pt. 2(7) with effect:
- for the purposes of corporation tax, for periods of account of insurance companies beginning on or after 1 January 2007; and
- for the purposes of income tax, for the 2007–08 tax year and subsequent tax years.

Former para. 1(2) partially repealed by F(No. 2)A 2005, s. 70 and Sch. 11, Pt. 2(10) in relation to periods of account ending on or after 31 December 2004.
Former para. 1(3), (4) repealed, and para. 1(2) partially repealed by FA 1995, s. 162 and Sch. 29, Pt. VIII(5), mostly in relation to accounting periods beginning on or after 1 January 1995.

2 [Inserts ICTA 1988, s. 431A: repealed by F(No. 2)A 2005, s. 70 and Sch. 11, Pt. 2(10).]

History – Para. 2 repealed by F(No. 2)A 2005, s. 70 and Sch. 11, Pt. 2(10) with effect from 20 July 2005 (Royal Assent).

3 [Repealed by FA 1996, s. 205 and Sch. 41, Pt. V(26) for accounting periods beginning on or after 1 January 1996.]

4 [Omitted by FA 2012, s. 146 and Sch. 16, para. 247(b)(iv).]

History – Para. 4 omitted by FA 2012, s. 146 and Sch. 16, para. 247(b)(iv), with effect in relation to accounting periods beginning on or after 1 January 2013 (FA 2012, s. 148) but subject to transitional provisions in FA 2012, Sch. 17. Where an accounting period would otherwise straddle 1 January 2013, it is deemed to end on 31 December 2012 (FA 2012, s. 149).

5 [Repealed by F(No. 2)A 1997, s. 52 and Sch. 8, Pt. II(6).]

History – Para. 5 repealed by F(No. 2)A 1997, s. 52 and Sch. 8, Pt. II(6) (in accordance with Sch. 3, para. 5) with effect in relation to distributions made on or after 2 July 1997.

6 [Repealed by FA 1991, s. 123 and Sch. 19, Pt. V, with effect for accounting periods beginning on or after 1 January 1992.]

7 [*Repealed by FA 2007*, s. *114* and Sch. 27, Pt. 2(7).]

History – Para. 7 repealed by FA 2007, s. 114 and Sch. 27, Pt. 2(7) with effect:
- for the purposes of corporation tax, for periods of account of insurance companies beginning on or after 1 January 2007; and
- for the purposes of income tax, for the 2007–08 tax year and subsequent tax years.

8 [Omitted by FA 2012, s. 146 and Sch. 16, para. 247(b)(iv).]

History – Para. 8 omitted by FA 2012, s. 146 and Sch. 16, para. 247(b)(iv), with effect in relation to accounting periods beginning on or after 1 January 2013 (FA 2012, s. 148) but subject to transitional provisions in FA 2012, Sch. 17. Where an accounting period would otherwise straddle 1 January 2013, it is deemed to end on 31 December 2012 (FA 2012, s. 149).

9 [Repealed by ITA 2007, s. 1031 and Sch. 3, Pt. 1.]

History – Para. 9 repealed by ITA 2007, s. 1031 and Sch. 3, Pt. 1, with effect from 6 April 2007.

Notes – Para. 9 rewritten as ITA 2007, s. 623(2), (3), (4), 624(2), (3), 674(5).

10 [Repealed by TCGA 1992, s. 290 and Sch. 12.]

11(1)

(a) in so far as it relates to determinations of profits in accordance with section 83 of the Finance Act 1989, this Schedule shall apply in relation to any period for which such a determination falls to be made, other than a period for which it falls to be made only by virtue of an election under section 83(5) of the Finance Act 1989, and

(b) in so far as it relates to section 432A of the Taxes Act 1988, this Schedule shall apply to income arising, and disposals occurring, on or after 1st January 1990.

11(2) Subject to sub-paragraph (1) above, this Schedule shall be deemed to have come into force on 1st January 1990.

11(3) The preceding provisions of this paragraph shall have effect subject to paragraph 12 below.

History – Para. 11(1) repealed by ITA 2007, s. 1031 and Sch. 3, Pt. 1, with effect from 6 April 2007 but reinstated by FA 2007, s. 41 and Sch. 10, para. 7 except for the opening words before the paragraphs which are deemed to have been repealed by ITA 2007, Sch. 3. In para. 11(2) the words "Subject to sub-paragraph (1) above," repealed by ITA 2007, s. 1031 and Sch. 3, Pt. 1, with effect from 6 April 2007 but reinstated by FA 2007, s. 41 and Sch. 10, para. 7.

12(1) Where at the end of 1989 the assets of an insurance company include securities of a class some of which are regarded as a single 1982 holding, and the rest of which are regarded as a single new holding, for the purposes of corporation tax on chargeable gains–

(a) at the beginning of 1990 there shall be both a 1982 holding and a new holding of the description mentioned in any paragraph of section 440A(2) of the Taxes Act 1988 within which any of the securities fall at that time (whether or not there would be apart from this sub-paragraph), and

(b) the 1982 holding and the new holding of the description mentioned in any such paragraph shall at that time bear to one another the same proportions as the single 1982 holding and the single new holding at the end of 1989.

12(2) For the period beginning with 1st January 1990 and ending with 19th March 1990, section 440(4) of the Taxes Act 1988 (as substituted by paragraph 8 of this Schedule) and section 440A(2) of that Act shall have effect with the omission of paragraph (d) (so that all assets not within paragraphs (a) to (c) fall within paragraph (e)).

12(3) Sub-paragraph (4) below applies where–

(a) at the end of 19th March 1990 the assets of an insurance company include securities of a class some of which are regarded as a relevant 1982 holding, and others of which are regarded as a relevant new holding, for the purposes of corporation tax on chargeable gains, and

(b) some of the securities are included in the company's long term business fund but others are not;

and for the purposes of this sub-paragraph a holding is a "relevant" holding if it is not linked to pension business or basic life assurance business and is not an asset of the overseas life assurance fund.

Post-ICTA 1988

12(4) Where this sub-paragraph applies–

(a) at the beginning of 20th March 1990 there shall be both a 1982 holding and a new holding of each of the descriptions mentioned in paragraphs (d) and (e) of section 440A(2) of the Taxes Act 1988 (whether or not there would be apart from this sub-paragraph), and

(b) the 1982 holding and the new holding of each of those descriptions shall at that time bear to one another the same proportions as the 1982 holding and the new holding mentioned in sub-paragraph (3)(a) above at the end of 19th March 1990.

12(5) Except for the purposes of determining the assets of a company which are linked solely to basic life assurance business, the amendments made by this Schedule shall have effect in relation to a company with the omission of references to overseas life assurance business as respects any time before the provisions of Schedule 7 to this Act have effect in relation to the company.

12(6) Sub-paragraph (7) below applies where–

(a) the first accounting period of an insurance company beginning on or after 1st January 1990 begins after 20th March 1990,

(b) at some time during the accounting period the company carries on overseas life assurance business, and

(c) immediately before the beginning of the accounting period the assets of the long term business fund of the company include both a relevant 1982 holding and a relevant new holding of securities of the same class;

and for the purposes of this sub-paragraph a holding is a "relevant" holding if it is not linked to pension business or basic life assurance business.

12(7) Where this sub-paragraph applies–

(a) at the beginning of the accounting period there shall be both a 1982 holding and a new holding of each of the descriptions mentioned in paragraphs (c) and (d) of section 440A(2) of the Taxes Act 1988 (whether or not there would be apart from this sub-paragraph), and

(b) the 1982 holding and the new holding of each of those descriptions shall at that time bear to one another the same proportions as the 1982 holding and the new holding mentioned in sub-paragraph (6)(c) above immediately before the beginning of the period.

12(8) No disposal or re-acquisition shall be deemed to occur by virtue of section 440 of the Taxes Act 1988 (as substituted by paragraph 8 of this Schedule) by reason only of the coming into force (in accordance with the provisions of paragraph 11 of this Schedule and this paragraph) of any provision of section 440A of that Act.

12(9) The substitution made by paragraph 8 of this Schedule shall not affect–

(a) the operation of section 440 of the Taxes Act 1988 (as it has effect before the substitution) before 20th March 1990, or

(b) the operation of subsections (6) and (7) of that section (as they have effect before the substitution) in relation to the disposal of an asset which has not been deemed to be disposed of by virtue of section 440 (as it has effect after the substitution) before the time of the disposal.

12(10) In this paragraph–

"1982 holding" has the meaning given by Part II of Schedule 19 to the Finance Act 1985;

"new holding" has the meaning given by Part III of that Schedule; and

"securities" has the same meaning as in section 65 of the Capital Gains Tax Act 1979.

Cross references – ICTA 1988, s. 440A: securities.

Notes – Provisions of CGTA 1979 repealed and re-enacted in TCGA 1992 for accounting periods beginning on or after 6 April 1992.

SCHEDULE 7 – OVERSEAS LIFE ASSURANCE BUSINESS

Section 42

[Omitted by FA 2012, s. 146 and Sch. 16, para. 247(b)(v).]

History – Sch. 7 omitted by FA 2012, s. 146 and Sch. 16, para. 247(b)(v), with effect in relation to accounting periods beginning on or after 1 January 2013 (FA 2012, s. 148) but subject to transitional provisions in FA 2012, Sch. 17. Where an accounting period would otherwise straddle 1 January 2013, it is deemed to end on 31 December 2012 (FA 2012, s. 149).

SCHEDULE 9 – INSURANCE COMPANIES: TRANSFERS OF LONG TERM BUSINESS

Section 48

ACCOUNTING PERIODS

3 [Repealed by SI 2008/381, art. 31 and Sch., Pt. 1.]

History – Para. 3 repealed by SI 2008/381, art. 31 and Sch., Pt. 1, with effect in relation to transfers of business taking place on or after 19 February 2008.

EXPENSES OF MANAGEMENT AND LOSSES

4 [Omitted by FA 2012, s. 146 and Sch. 16, para. 247(b)(vi).]

History – Para. 4 omitted by FA 2012, s. 146 and Sch. 16, para. 247(b)(vi), with effect in relation to accounting periods beginning on or after 1 January 2013 (FA 2012, s. 148) but subject to transitional provisions in FA 2012, Sch. 17. Where an accounting period would otherwise straddle 1 January 2013, it is deemed to end on 31 December 2012 (FA 2012, s. 149).

CAPITAL ALLOWANCES

5 [Repealed by CAA 2001, s. 580 and Sch. 4.]

History – Para. 5, repealed by CAA 2001, s. 580 and Sch. 4, with effect as respects allowances and charges falling to be made for chargeable periods ending, for income tax purposes, on or after 6 April 2001, and for corporation tax purposes, on or after 1 April 2001.

TRANSFER TO FRIENDLY SOCIETY

6 [Omitted by FA 2012, s. 176 and Sch. 18, para. 23(a)(iii).]

History – Para. 6 omitted by FA 2012, s. 176 and Sch. 18, para. 23(a)(iii), with effect in relation to accounting periods beginning on or after 1 January 2013 (FA 2012, s. 178) but subject to transitional provisions in FA 2012, Sch. 19. Where an accounting period would otherwise straddle 1 January 2013, it is deemed to end on 31 December 2012 (FA 2012, s. 179).

COMMENCEMENT

7 [Omitted by FA 2012, s. 146 and Sch. 16, para. 247(b)(vi).]

History – Para. 7 omitted by FA 2012, s. 146 and Sch. 16, para. 247(b)(vi), with effect in relation to accounting periods beginning on or after 1 January 2013 (FA 2012, s. 148) but subject to transitional provisions in FA 2012, Sch. 17. Where an accounting period would otherwise straddle 1 January 2013, it is deemed to end on 31 December 2012 (FA 2012, s. 149).

SCHEDULE 10 – CONVERTIBLE SECURITIES

Section 56

[Sch. 10 repealed by FA 1996, s. 104 and Sch. 14, para. 58 as respects accounting periods ending after 31 March 1996 and, as respects income tax, for years after 1995–96]

History – Para. 29(2), (3) repealed by TCGA 1992, s. 290 and Sch. 12 in relation to tax for 1992–93 and subsequent years of assessment and tax for other chargeable periods beginning after 6 April 1992.

SCHEDULE 11 – EUROPEAN ECONOMIC INTEREST GROUPINGS

Section 69

TAXATION

1 [Repealed by CTA 2010, s. 1181 and Sch. 3, Pt. 1.]

History – Para. 1 repealed by CTA 2010, s. 1181 and Sch. 3, Pt. 1, with effect for corporation tax purposes for accounting periods ending on or after 1 April 2010, and for income tax and capital gains tax purposes for the tax year 2010–11 and subsequent tax years.

MANAGEMENT

2 [Inserts TMA 1970, s. 12A.]

3(1) [Inserts TMA 1970, s. 98B.]

3(2) [Inserts TMA 1970, s. 100(2)(e).]

4(1) [Inserts TMA 1970, s. 36(4).]

4(2) [Inserts TMA 1970, s. 40(3).]

COMMENCEMENT

5 This Schedule shall be deemed to have come into force on 1st July 1989.

SCHEDULE 13 – CAPITAL ALLOWANCES: MISCELLANEOUS AMENDMENTS

Section 88

History – Sch. 13, para. 1–6, repealed by CAA 2001, s. 580 and Sch. 4, with effect as respects allowances and charges falling to be made for chargeable periods ending, for income tax purposes, on or after 6 April 2001, and for corporation tax purposes, on or after 1 April 2001.

HOTELS IN ENTERPRISE ZONES: INITIAL ALLOWANCES

1(1)–(3) [Repealed by CAA 2001, s. 580 and Sch. 4, see History note above.]

SCIENTIFIC RESEARCH ALLOWANCE: WRITING OFF OF EXPENDITURE

2(1)–(2) [Repealed by CAA 2001, s. 580 and Sch. 4, see History note above.]

DISPOSAL VALUE OF MACHINERY OR PLANT AFTER SUCCESSION TO TRADE

3(1)–(2) [Repealed by CAA 2001, s. 580 and Sch. 4, see History note above.]

NON-RESIDENT COMPANIES: USE OF ALLOWANCES

4(1)–(2) [Repealed by CAA 2001, s. 580 and Sch. 4, see History note above.]

CONTRIBUTIONS: MACHINERY AND PLANT

5(1)–(2) [Repealed by CAA 2001, s. 580 and Sch. 4, see History note above.]

SALE OF MACHINERY OR PLANT

6(1)–(2) [Repealed by CAA 2001, s. 580 and Sch. 4, see History note above.]

ASSURED TENANCIES ALLOWANCE

7(1) [Amends ICTA 1988, s. 832(1).]

7(2) This paragraph shall apply for chargeable periods beginning on or after 6th April 1990.

SCHEDULE 14 – AMENDMENTS CORRECTING ERRORS IN THE TAXES ACT 1988

Section 89

Part I – Amendments of the Taxes Act 1988

1 The Taxes Act 1988 shall have effect, and shall be deemed always to have had effect, subject to the amendments made by this Part of this Schedule.

2 [Repealed by FA 1998, s. 165 and Sch. 27, Pt. III(4) and omitted by CTA 2009, s. 1322 and Sch. 1, para. 354 and repealed by CTA 2009, s. 1326 and Sch. 3, Pt. 1.]

History – Para. 2 omitted by CTA 2009, s. 1322 and Sch. 1, para. 354 and repealed by CTA 2009, s. 1326 and Sch. 3, Pt. 1, with effect, for corporation tax purposes, for accounting periods ending on or after 1 April 2009 and, for income tax and capital gains tax purposes, for the tax year 2009–10 and subsequent years.

Para. 2 (which amended ICTA 1988, s. 37(1)) repealed by FA 1998, s. 165 and Sch. 27, Pt. III(4) with effect for income tax for the year 1998–99 and subsequent years of assessment and, for corporation tax, from 1 April 1998 (subject to the transitional provisions in FA 1998, Sch. 5, Pt. IV).

3 [Repealed by CTA 2010, s. 1181 and Sch. 3, Pt. 1.]

History – Para. 3 repealed by CTA 2010, s. 1181 and Sch. 3, Pt. 1, with effect for corporation tax purposes for accounting periods ending on or after 1 April 2010, and for income tax and capital gains tax purposes for the tax year 2010–11 and subsequent tax years.

4(1) [Repealed by ITTOIA 2005, s. 884 and Sch. 3.]

4(2) [Repealed by ITEPA 2003, Sch. 8, Pt. 1.]

History – Para. 4(1) repealed by ITTOIA 2005, s. 884 and Sch. 3; effective for income tax purposes for 2005–06 onwards and for corporation tax purposes for accounting periods ending after 5 April 2005 (ITTOIA 2005, s. 883(1)).

Para. 4(2) omitted and repealed by ITEPA 2003, Sch. 6, para. 167(3) and Sch. 8, Pt. 1 respectively; both of which have effect for the tax year 2003–04 and subsequent tax years.

5 [Repealed by ITTOIA 2005, s. 884 and Sch. 3. Para. 5.]

History – Para. 5 repealed by ITTOIA 2005, s. 884 and Sch. 3; effective for income tax purposes for 2005–06 onwards and for corporation tax purposes for accounting periods ending after 5 April 2005 (ITTOIA 2005, s. 883(1)).

6 [Repealed by FA 1999, s. 139 and Sch. 20, Pt. III(7).]

History – Para. 6 repealed by FA 1999, s. 139 and Sch. 20, Pt. III(7), with effect in relation to any payment of interest falling within FA 1999, s. 38(3) or (4) (broadly, a payment made on or after 6 April 2000, or on or after 9 March 1999 and before 6 April 2000, but not due until on or after 6 April 2000).

7 [Repealed by FA 1991, s. 123 and Sch. 19, Pt. V, in relation to losses incurred in accounting periods ending on or after 1 April 1991.]

8 [Amends ICTA 1988, s. 478(3).]

9 [Amends ICTA 1988, s. 751(1)(a).]

10 [Repealed by SI 2009/3001, reg. 13(2) and Sch. 2.]

History – Para. 10 repealed by SI 2009/3001, reg. 13(2) and Sch. 2, with effect from 1 December 2009 for various purposes (in accordance with the provisions of SI 2009/3001, reg. 1), subject to transitional and savings provisions in SI 2009/3001, Sch. 1.

At the time of its repeal by SI 2009/3001, para. 10 was to have been omitted prospectively by FA 2008, s. 41(7), with effect from a day which was to have been appointed.

11 [Repealed by SI 2009/3001, reg. 13(2) and Sch. 2.]

History – Para. 11 repealed by SI 2009/3001, reg. 13(2) and Sch. 2, with effect from 1 December 2009 for various purposes (in accordance with the provisions of SI 2009/3001, reg. 1), subject to transitional and savings provisions in SI 2009/3001, Sch. 1.

At the time of its repeal by SI 2009/3001, para. 11 was to have been omitted prospectively by FA 2008, s. 41(7), with effect from a day which was to have been appointed.

12 [Repealed by FA 1998, s. 165 and Sch. 27, Pt. III(25).]

History – Para. 12 repealed by FA 1998, s. 165 and Sch. 27, Pt. III(25) with effect, for the purposes of corporation tax, as respects accounting periods ending on or after 1 July 1999 (the day appointed by FA 1994, s. 199 by virtue of SI 1998/3173 (C. 78)) and, for the purposes of income tax, as respects any year of assessment ending on or after that day.

13 [Repealed by FA 1999, s. 139 and Sch. 20, Pt. III(19).]

History – Para. 13 (which amended ICTA 1988, Sch. 16, para. 4(1)) repealed by FA 1999, s. 139 and Sch. 20, Pt. III(19), with effect in relation to return periods beginning on or after 6 April 1999.

Part II – Amendments of Other Enactments

THE TAXES MANAGEMENT ACT 1970 (C. 9)

14 [Amends TMA 1970, s. 31(3).]

15 [Omitted by SI 2009/2035, art. 2 and Schedule, para. 60(d).]

History – Para. 15 omitted by SI 2009/2035, art. 2 and Schedule, para. 60(d), with effect from 13 August 2009.

THE OIL TAXATION ACT 1975 (C. 22)

16 [Amends Oil Taxation Act 1975, Sch. 3, para. 5(2).]

COMMENCEMENT

19(1) Subject to the following provisions of this paragraph, the amendments made by this Part of this Schedule shall be treated for the purposes of their commencement as if they had been made by the Taxes Act 1988.

19(2)–(4) [Repealed by TCGA 1992, s. 290 and Sch. 12.]

History – Para. 19(2)–(4) repealed by TCGA 1992, s. 290 and Sch. 12 in relation to tax for 1992–93 and subsequent years of assessment and other chargeable periods beginning after 6 April 1992.

SCHEDULE 15 – CLAIMS FOR GROUP RELIEF

Section 100

[Repealed by FA 1998, s. 165 and Sch. 27, Pt. III(28).]

History – Sch. 15 repealed by FA 1998, s. 165 and Sch. 27, Pt. III(28) with effect in relation to accounting periods ending on or after 1 July 1999 (the self-assessment appointed day under FA 1994, s. 199 by virtue of SI 1998/3173 (C. 78)).

SCHEDULE 16 – CAPITAL ALLOWANCES: CLAIMS BY COMPANIES

Section 102

[Repealed by FA 1998, s. 165 and Sch. 27, Pt. III(28).]

History – Sch. 16 repealed by FA 1998, s. 165 and Sch. 27, Pt. III(28) with effect in relation to accounting periods ending on or after 1 July 1999 (the self-assessment appointed day under FA 1994, s. 199 by virtue of SI 1998/3173 (C. 78)).

SCHEDULE 17 – CAPITAL ALLOWANCES: ASSIMILATION OF CLAIMS BY COMPANIES TO CLAIMS BY INDIVIDUALS

Section 103

[Repealed by CAA 2001, s. 580 and Sch. 4.]

History – Sch. 17, repealed by CAA 2001, s. 580 and Sch. 4, with effect as respects allowances and charges falling to be made for chargeable periods ending, for income tax purposes, on or after 6 April 2001, and for corporation tax purposes, on or after 1 April 2001.

SCHEDULE 18 – DEFINITION OF "LOCAL AUTHORITY"

Section 127

1 [Amends FA 1952, s. 74(4).]

2 [Repeals FA 1974, s. 52.]

4 [Omitted by SI 2013/463, art. 2(2).]

5 [Repealed by CTA 2010, s. 1181 and Sch. 3, Pt. 1.]

History – Para. 4 omitted by SI 2013/463, art. 2(2), with effect from 1 April 2013.
Para. 5 repealed by CTA 2010, s. 1181 and Sch. 3, Pt. 1, with effect for corporation tax purposes for accounting periods ending on or after 1 April 2010, and for income tax and capital gains tax purposes for the tax year 2010–11 and subsequent tax years.

FINANCE ACT 1991

(1991 Chapter 31) *[25th July 1991]*

ARRANGEMENT OF SECTIONS

PART II – INCOME TAX, CORPORATION TAX AND CAPITAL GAINS TAX

CHAPTER I – GENERAL

CAPITAL ALLOWANCES

59. Interaction with VAT capital goods scheme
60. Toll roads
61. Hiring motor cars

OIL INDUSTRY

62. Expenditure on and under abandonment guarantees
63. Relief for reimbursement expenditure under abandonment guarantees
64. Relief for expenditure incurred by a participator in meeting defaulter's abandonment expenditure
65. Reimbursement by defaulter in respect of certain abandonment expenditure
66. Restriction on setting ACT against liability to corporation tax on profits from oil extraction activities etc.

MISCELLANEOUS

68. Gifts to educational establishments
69. Expenses of entertainers
70. Personal equity plans
71. Donations to charity
72. Deduction of trading losses
73. Relief for company trading losses
74. Trade unions and employers' associations
75. Audit powers in relation to non-residents
76. Capital element in annuities
77. Definition of "normal commercial loan"
78. Sharing of transmission facilities
79. Abolition of CRT: consequential amendment
80. Interest on certain debentures
82. Certificates of non-liability to tax

PART V – MISCELLANEOUS AND GENERAL

MISCELLANEOUS

118. Designated international organisations: miscellaneous exemptions
121. Pools payments to support games etc.

GENERAL

122. Interpretation etc.
124. Short title

SCHEDULES

6. RESTRICTION OF HIGHER RATE RELIEF: BENEFICIAL LOANS ETC.
7. BASIC LIFE ASSURANCE AND GENERAL ANNUITY BUSINESS
8. PENSION BUSINESS: PAYMENTS ON ACCOUNT OF TAX CREDITS AND DEDUCTED TAX
9. FRIENDLY SOCIETIES
10. BUILDING SOCIETIES: QUALIFYING SHARES
11. BUILDING SOCIETIES: MARKETABLE SECURITIES
12. SECURITIES: NEW ISSUES
13. MANUFACTURED DIVIDENDS AND INTEREST
14. CAPITAL ALLOWANCES: VAT CAPITAL GOODS SCHEME
15. RELIEF FOR COMPANY TRADING LOSSES

PART II – INCOME TAX, CORPORATION TAX AND CAPITAL GAINS TAX

Chapter I – General

CORPORATION TAX RATES

24 Charge and rate of corporation tax for 1991

24 [Spent.]

25 Small companies

25 [Repealed by CTA 2010, s. 1181 and Sch. 3, Pt. 1.]

History – S. 25 repealed by CTA 2010, s. 1181 and Sch. 3, Pt. 1, with effect for corporation tax purposes for accounting periods ending on or after 1 April 2010, and for income tax and capital gains tax purposes for the tax year 2010–11 and subsequent tax years.

Notes – S. 25 not rewritten in CTA 2010, as spent.

INTEREST

27 Abolition of higher rate relief on certain mortgage interest etc.

27(1)–(5) [Repealed by FA 1994, s. 258 and Sch. 26, Pt. V(2).]

27(6) [Repealed by Statute Law (Repeals) Act 2013, s. 1 and Sch. 1, Pt. 10.]

27(7) [Repealed by FA 1994, s. 258 and Sch. 26, Pt. V(2).]

History – The repeal of s. 27(1)–(5), (7) has effect:

- in relation to payments of interest made on or after 6 April 1994 (whenever falling due); and
- in relation to payments of relevant loan interest, as regards payments of interest becoming due on or after 6 April 1994 which have been made before 6 April 1994, but on or after 30 November 1993.

S. 27(6) repealed by Statute Law (Repeals) Act 2013, s. 1 and Sch. 1, Pt. 10, with effect from 31 January 2013.

28 Mortgage interest relief: caravans

28(1) [Repeals ICTA 1988, s. 354(3).]

28(2) This section shall have effect for the year 1991–92 and subsequent years of assessment.

BENEFITS IN KIND

30 Mobile telephones

30 [Repealed by FA 1999, s. 139 and Sch. 20, Pt. III(9), with effect for the year 1999–2000 and subsequent years of assessment.]

VOCATIONAL TRAINING

32 Relief

32 [Repealed by FA 1999, s. 59(2), 139 and Sch. 20, Pt. III(15)]

History – S. 32 repealed by FA 1999, s. 59(2), 139 and Sch. 20, Pt. III(15), with effect in relation to payments made on or after 1 September 2000, the appointed day (SI 2000/2004 (C.53)).

33 Section 32: supplementary

33 [Repealed by FA 1999, s. 59(2), 139 and Sch. 20, Pt. III(15)]

History – S. 33(2) repealed by SI 2009/2035, art. 2 and Schedule, para. 60(e), with effect from 13 August 2009, despite the whole of s. 33 having been repealed previously (see below).

S. 33 repealed by FA 1999, s. 59(2), 139 and Sch. 20, Pt. III(15), with effect in relation to payments made on or after 1 September 2000, the appointed day (SI 2000/2004 (C.53)).

RETIREMENT BENEFITS SCHEMES

34 Conditions for approval: amendments

34 *[Repealed by FA 2004, s. 326 and Sch. 42, Pt. 3.]*

History – S. 34 repealed by FA 2004, s. 326 and Sch. 42, Pt. 3 with effect from 6 April 2006 but subject to FA 2004, Sch. 36 (Pension schemes etc.: transitional provisions and savings).

35 Cessation of approval

35 [Repealed by FA 2004, s. 326 and Sch. 42, Pt. 3.]

History – S. 35 repealed by FA 2004, s. 326 and Sch. 42, Pt. 3 with effect from 6 April 2006 but subject to FA 2004, Sch. 36 (Pension schemes etc.: transitional provisions and savings).

36 Cessation of approval: general provisions

36 [Repealed by FA 2004, s. 326 and Sch. 42, Pt. 3.]

History – S. 36 repealed by FA 2004, s. 326 and Sch. 42, Pt. 3 with effect from 6 April 2006 but subject to FA 2004 Sch. 36 (Pension schemes etc.: transitional provisions and savings). Former s. 36 read as follows:

"Cessation of approval: general provisions

36(1) [Inserts ICTA 1988, s. 591B.]
36(2) [Repeals ICTA 1988, s. 590(5) and (6).]
36(3) The amendments made by subsections (1) and (2) above shall be deemed always to have had effect.
36(4) The Finance Act 1970 shall be deemed always to have had effect–
(a) with the omission of section 19(3) and (4), and
(b) with the insertion after section 20 of a section 20A in the same form as section 591B of the Taxes Act 1988 (with the omission before 17th March 1987 of the words from "(which shall not" to "whichever is the later)").".

PROFIT-RELATED PAY, SHARE SCHEMES ETC.

37 Profit-related pay: increased relief

37(1)–(2) [Repealed by FA 1997, s. 113 and Sch. 18, Pt. VI(3).]

Notes – S. 37 repealed by FA 1997, s. 113 and Sch. 18, Pt. VI(3). This repeal does not affect the operation of the repealed provisions, or prevent the exercise of any power under the provisions, in relation to profit periods or other connected purposes, beginning before 1 January 2000.

38 Employee share schemes: non-discrimination

38(1) The Taxes Act 1988 shall be amended as follows.

38(2) [Repealed by ITEPA 2003, Sch. 8, Pt. 1.]

38(3) [Amends ICTA 1988, Sch. 10, para. 2(b), para. 3(c)(ii).]

38(4) [Amends ICTA 1988, s. 187(2).]

38(5) [Inserts ICTA 1988, Sch. 9, para. 8A.]

38(6) Subsection (5) above shall have effect in relation to a scheme not approved before the day on which this Act is passed.

History – S. 38(2) omitted and repealed by ITEPA 2003, Sch. 6, para. 168(2) and ITEPA 2003, Sch. 8, Pt. 1 respectively; both of which have effect for the tax year 2003–04 and subsequent tax years.
In s. 38(6), the word "Subsection" substituted for the words "Subsections (2) and" by ITEPA 2003, Sch. 6, para. 168(3) which has effect for the tax year 2003–04 and subsequent tax years.

Post-ICTA 1988

39 Approved share option schemes: price at which shares may be acquired

39 [Repealed by ITEPA 2003, Sch. 8, Pt. 1.]

History – S. 39 repealed by ITEPA 2003, Sch. 8, Pt. 1 which has effect for the tax year 2003–04 and subsequent tax years.

40 Savings-related share option schemes

40 [Repealed by ITEPA 2003, Sch. 8, Pt. 1.]

History – S. 40 repealed by ITEPA 2003, Sch. 8, Pt. 1 which has effect for the tax year 2003–04 and subsequent tax years.

41 Profit sharing schemes

41(1) [Amends ICTA 1988, s. 187(2).]

41(2) This section shall apply for the year 1991–92 and subsequent years of assessment.

42 Costs of establishing share option or profit sharing schemes: relief

42 [Repealed by TIOPA 2010, s. 378 and Sch. 10, Pt. 12.]

History – S. 42 repealed by TIOPA 2010, s. 378 and Sch. 10, Pt. 12, with effect for corporation tax purposes for accounting periods ending on or after 1 April 2010, for income tax and capital gains tax purposes for the tax year 2010–11 and subsequent tax years, and for petroleum revenue tax purposes for chargeable periods beginning on or after 1 July 2010.

43 Costs of establishing employee share ownership trusts: relief

43 [Repealed by CTA 2009, s. 1326 and Sch. 3, Pt. 1.]

History – S. 43 repealed by CTA 2009, s. 1326 and Sch. 3, Pt. 1, with effect, for corporation tax purposes, for accounting periods ending on or after 1 April 2009 and, for income tax and capital gains tax purposes, for the tax year 2009–10 and subsequent years.

44 Priority share allocations for employees etc.

44 [Repealed by ITEPA 2003, Sch. 8, Pt. 1.]

History – S. 44 repealed by ITEPA 2003, Sch. 8, Pt. 1 which has effect for the tax year 2003–04 and subsequent tax years.

FOREIGN EARNINGS

45 Seafarers

45 [Repealed by FA 1998, s. 165 and Sch. 27, Pt. III(11).]

History – S. 45 repealed by FA 1998, s. 165 and Sch. 27, Pt. III(11) with effect in relation to emoluments attributable to qualifying periods beginning on or after 17 March 1998, and emoluments attributable to qualifying periods beginning before 17 March 1998 and received before that date.

46 Workers in Kuwait or Iraq

46 [Repealed by Statute Law (Repeals) Act 2013, s. 1 and Sch. 1, Pt. 10.]

History – S. 46 repealed by Statute Law (Repeals) Act 2013, s. 1 and Sch. 1, Pt. 10, with effect from 31 January 2013.

Other material – IR press release, 19 March 1991 (not reproduced): Revenue will consider sympathetically requests for extra time to pay tax liabilities by former hostages and others returned from the Gulf who have difficulty paying on time.

INSURANCE COMPANIES AND FRIENDLY SOCIETIES

47 Investor protection schemes

47 [Repealed by FA 2004, s. 326 and Sch. 42, Pt. 2(3).]

History – S. 47 repealed by FA 2004, s. 326 and Sch. 42, Pt. 2(3) with effect for accounting periods beginning on or after 1 April 2004, but subject to transitional provisions in FA 2004, sections 43 and 44, and Sch. 6.
S. 47(1), (2), (4) repealed by FSMA 2000 s. 432(3) and Sch. 22 with effect from 1 December 2001 (SI 2001/3538).

48 Assimilation of basic life assurance business and general annuity business

48 Schedule 7 to this Act shall have effect.

49 Pension business: payments on account of tax credits and deducted tax

49 [Repealed by FA 2001, Sch. 33 Pt. 2(12) in accordance with the dates set out in FA 2001, s. 87.]

History – S. 49 repealed by FA 2001, Sch. 33, Pt. 2(12), in relation to income tax borne by deduction from payments received after 30 September 2001 and in relation to tax credits in respect of distributions made on or after 6 April 2004.
Statutory instruments – SI 1992/1746 (C. 58): s. 49 has effect in relation to accounting periods beginning on or after 2 October 1992.

50 Friendly societies

50 Schedule 9 to this Act (which makes provision about friendly societies) shall have effect.

BUILDING SOCIETIES

51 Qualifying shares

51 Schedule 10 to this Act (which makes provision about certain kinds of building society share) shall have effect.

52 Marketable securities

52(1) Schedule 11 to this Act (which makes provision about the deduction of income tax in the case of marketable securities issued by building societies) shall have effect.

52(2) [Repealed by FA 1996, Sch. 41, Pt. V(3).]

52(3) [Repealed by FA 1996, Sch. 41, Pt. V(3).]

History – S. 52(2), (3) repealed by FA 1996, Sch. 41, Pt. V(3), for corporation tax purposes in relation to accounting periods ending after 31 March 1996, and for income tax purposes for years after 1995–96.

53 Income Tax (Building Societies) Regulations 1986

53 *[Omitted by ITA 2007, s. 1027 and Sch. 1, para. 286 and repealed by s. 1031 and Sch. 3, Pt. 1.]*

History – S. 53 omitted by ITA 2007, s. 1027 and Sch. 1, para. 286 and repealed by s. 1031 and Sch. 3, Pt. 1, with effect from 6 April 2007.

SECURITIES

54 New issues

54 Schedule 12 to this Act (which contains provisions about securities issued after an issue of securities of the same kind) shall have effect.

55 Purchase and sale of securities: options

55 [Omitted by FA 2008, s. 66(4).]

History – S. 55 omitted by FA 2008, s. 66(4), with effect in relation to cases where the purchase by the first buyer (within the meaning of s. 731(2) of ICTA 1988) is made on or after 1 April 2008.

57 Stock lending

57 [Repealed by FA 1997, s. 113 and Sch. 18, Pt. VI(10), with effect from 1 July 1997, the day appointed under FA 1997, Sch. 10, para. 7(1) by virtue of SI 1997/991 (C. 33).]

58 Manufactured dividends and interest

58(1) [Inserts ICTA 1988, s. 736A.]

58(2) The enactments mentioned in Schedule 13 to this Act shall have effect with the amendments there specified.

58(3) This section shall have effect in relation to payments made on or after such day as the Treasury may specify for this purpose by regulations made by statutory instrument and different days may be so appointed for different provisions or different purposes.

Statutory instruments – SI 1992/173 and SI 1992/1346 (made under s. 58(3)).
SI 1993/933 (C. 17) (made under s. 58(3).

CAPITAL ALLOWANCES

59 Interaction with VAT capital goods scheme

59 [Repealed by CAA 2001, s. 580 and Sch. 4.]

History – S. 59 repealed by CAA 2001, s. 580 and Sch. 4, with effect as respects allowances and charges falling to be made for chargeable periods ending, for income tax purposes, on or after 6 April 2001, and for corporation tax purposes, on or after 1 April 2001.

60 Toll roads

60 [Repealed by CAA 2001, s. 580 and Sch. 4.]

History – S. 60 repealed by CAA 2001, s. 580 and Sch. 4, with effect as respects allowances and charges falling to be made for chargeable periods ending, for income tax purposes, on or after 6 April 2001, and for corporation tax purposes, on or after 1 April 2001.

61 Hiring motor cars

61 [Repealed by CAA 2001, s. 580 and Sch. 4.]

History – S. 61 repealed by CAA 2001, s. 580 and Sch. 4, with effect as respects allowances and charges falling to be made for chargeable periods ending, for income tax purposes, on or after 6 April 2001, and for corporation tax purposes, on or after 1 April 2001.

OIL INDUSTRY

62 Expenditure on and under abandonment guarantees

62 [Omitted by CTA 2010, s. 1177 and Sch. 1, para. 222 and repealed by CTA 2010, s. 1181 and Sch. 3, Pt. 2; also omitted by TIOPA 2010, s. 374 and Sch. 8, para. 186 and repealed by TIOPA 2010, s. 378 and Sch. 10, Pt. 6.]

History – S. 62 omitted by CTA 2010, s. 1177 and Sch. 1, para. 222 and repealed by CTA 2010, s. 1181 and Sch 3, Pt. 2, for corporation tax purposes only, with effect for accounting periods ending on or after 1 April 2010. S. 62 also omitted by TIOPA 2010, s. 374 and Sch. 8, para. 186 and repealed by TIOPA 2010, s. 378 and Sch. 10, Pt. 6, with effect for corporation tax purposes for accounting periods ending on or after 1 April 2010, for income tax and capital gains tax purposes for the tax year 2010–11 and subsequent tax years, and for petroleum revenue tax purposes for chargeable periods beginning on or after 1 July 2010.

Notes – S. 62 rewritten for income tax purposes in TIOPA 2010, Sch. 1, para. 2.
S. 62 rewritten for corporation tax purposes as follows:
S. 62(1): CTA 2010, s. 292(1), (2).
S. 62(2): CTA 2010, s. 275, 278.
S. 62(3): CTA 2010, s. 292(3), (4).
S. 62(4): CTA 2010, s. 294(1), (2).
S. 62(5): CTA 2010, s. 292(6).

63 Relief for reimbursement expenditure under abandonment guarantees

63 [Omitted by CTA 2010, s. 1177 and Sch. 1, para. 222 and repealed by CTA 2010, s. 1181 and Sch. 3, Pt. 2; also omitted by TIOPA 2010, s. 374 and Sch. 8, para. 186 and repealed by TIOPA 2010, s. 378 and Sch. 10, Pt. 6.]

History – S. 63 omitted by CTA 2010, s. 1177 and Sch. 1, para. 222 and repealed by CTA 2010, s. 1181 and Sch. 3, Pt. 2, for corporation tax purposes only, with effect for accounting periods ending on or after 1 April 2010. S. 62 also omitted by TIOPA 2010, s. 374 and Sch. 8, para. 186 and repealed by TIOPA 2010, s. 378 and Sch. 10, Pt. 6, with effect for corporation tax purposes for accounting periods ending on or after 1 April 2010, for income tax and capital gains tax purposes for the tax year 2010–11 and subsequent tax years, and for petroleum revenue tax purposes for chargeable periods beginning on or after 1 July 2010.

Notes – S. 63 rewritten for income tax purposes in TIOPA 2010, Sch. 1, para. 2.
S. 63 rewritten for corporation tax purposes as follows:
S. 63(1): CTA 2010, s. 293(1).
S. 63(2): CTA 2010, s. 295(1), (2), (3).
S. 63(3): CTA 2010, s. 293(2).
S. 63(4): CTA 2010, s. 293(3).
S. 63(5): CTA 2010, s. 293(4).
S. 63(6): CTA 2010, s. 293(5), (6).
S. 63(7): CTA 2010, s. 293(7).
S. 63(8): CTA 2010, s. 292(6).

64 Relief for expenditure incurred by a participator in meeting defaulter's abandonment expenditure

64 [Omitted by CTA 2010, s. 1177 and Sch. 1, para. 222 and repealed by CTA 2010, s. 1181 and Sch. 3, Pt. 2; also omitted by TIOPA 2010, s. 374 and Sch. 8, para. 186 and repealed by TIOPA 2010, s. 378 and Sch. 10, Pt. 6.]

History – S. 64 omitted by CTA 2010, s. 1177 and Sch. 1, para. 222 and repealed by CTA 2010, s. 1181 and Sch. 3, Pt. 2, for corporation tax purposes only, with effect for accounting periods ending on or after 1 April 2010. S. 62 also omitted by TIOPA 2010, s. 374 and Sch. 8, para. 186 and repealed by TIOPA 2010, s. 378 and Sch. 10, Pt. 6, with effect for corporation tax purposes for accounting periods ending on or after 1 April 2010, for income tax and capital gains tax purposes for the tax year 2010–11 and subsequent tax years, and for petroleum revenue tax purposes for chargeable periods beginning on or after 1 July 2010.

Notes – S. 64 rewritten for income tax purposes in TIOPA 2010, Sch. 1, para. 2.
S. 64 rewritten for corporation tax purposes as follows:
S. 64(1): CTA 2010, s. 296(1).
S. 64(2): CTA 2010, s. 296(3).
S. 64(3): CTA 2010, s. 296(2).
S. 64(4): CTA 2010, s. 297(1).
S. 64(5): CTA 2010, s. 297(2), (3).

65 Reimbursement by defaulter in respect of certain abandonment expenditure

65 [Omitted by CTA 2010, s. 1177 and Sch. 1, para. 222 and repealed by CTA 2010, s. 1181 and Sch. 3, Pt. 2; also omitted by TIOPA 2010, s. 374 and Sch. 8, para. 186 and repealed by TIOPA 2010, s. 378 and Sch. 10, Pt. 6.]

History – S. 65 omitted by CTA 2010, s. 1177 and Sch. 1, para. 222 and repealed by CTA 2010, s. 1181 and Sch. 3, Pt. 2, for corporation tax purposes only, with effect for accounting periods ending on or after 1 April 2010. S. 62 also omitted by TIOPA 2010, s. 374 and Sch. 8, para. 186 and repealed by TIOPA 2010, s. 378 and Sch. 10, Pt. 6, with effect for corporation tax purposes for accounting periods ending on or after 1 April 2010, for income tax and capital gains tax purposes for the tax year 2010–11 and subsequent tax years, and for petroleum revenue tax purposes for chargeable periods beginning on or after 1 July 2010.

Notes – S. 65 rewritten for income tax purposes in TIOPA 2010, Sch. 1, para. 2.
S. 65 rewritten for corporation tax purposes as follows:
S. 65(1): CTA 2010, s. 296(1), (3), 298(1).
S. 65(2): CTA 2010, s. 298(2).
S. 65(3): CTA 2010, s. 298(3).
S. 65(4): CTA 2010, s. 298(4).
S. 65(5): CTA 2010, s. 298(8).
S. 65(6): CTA 2010, s. 298(5).
S. 65(7): CTA 2010, s. 298(6).
S. 65(8): CTA 2010, s. 298(7).

66 Restriction on setting ACT against liability to corporation tax on profits from oil extraction activities etc.

66 [Repealed by Statute Law (Repeals) Act 2013, s. 1 and Sch. 1, Pt. 10.]

History – S. 66 repealed by Statute Law (Repeals) Act 2013, s. 1 and Sch. 1, Pt. 10, with effect from 31 January 2013.

MISCELLANEOUS

68 Gifts to educational establishments

68 [Repealed by CTA 2009, s. 1326 and Sch. 3, Pt. 1.]

History – S. 68 repealed by CTA 2009, s. 1326 and Sch. 3, Pt. 1, with effect, for corporation tax purposes, for accounting periods ending on or after 1 April 2009 and, for income tax and capital gains tax purposes, for the tax year 2009–10 and subsequent years.

69 Expenses of entertainers

69 [Repealed by ITEPA 2003, Sch. 8, Pt. 1.]

History – S. 69 repealed by ITEPA 2003, Sch. 8, Pt. 1 which has effect for the tax year 2003–04 and subsequent tax years.

70 Personal equity plans

Notes – S. 70 is repealed by ITTOIA 2005. See the History note for details. The amendments originally introduced by s. 70, at ICTA 1988, s. 333(3), are rewritten at ITTOIA 2005, s. 694(4) and s. 695(4).

70 [Repealed by ITTOIA 2005, s. 884 and Sch. 3.]

History – Repealed by ITTOIA 2005, s. 884 and Sch. 3; effective for income tax purposes for 2005–06 onwards and for corporation tax purposes for accounting periods ending after 5 April 2005 (ITTOIA 2005, s. 883(1)).

71 Donations to charity

71(1) [Repeals ICTA 1988, s. 339A.]

71(2) [Repealed by CTA 2010, s. 1181 and Sch. 3, Pt. 1.]

71(3) Subsections (1) and (2) above shall apply in relation to accounting periods beginning on or after 19th March 1991.

71(4) In its application to accounting periods beginning before 19th March 1991 and ending on or after that date, section 339A of the Taxes Act 1988 shall have effect as if–

(a) [Amends ICTA 1988, s. 339A(1), (2).]

(b) [Amends ICTA 1988, s. 339A(3)(b).]

71(5) [Repeals FA 1990, s. 25(2)(h).]

71(6) Subsection (5) above shall apply in relation to gifts made on or after 19th March 1991.

History – S. 71(2) repealed by CTA 2010, s. 1181 and Sch. 3, Pt. 1, with effect for corporation tax purposes for accounting periods ending on or after 1 April 2010, and for income tax and capital gains tax purposes for the tax year 2010–11 and subsequent tax years.

72 Deduction of trading losses

72 [Omitted by ITA 2007, s. 1027 and Sch. 1, para. 287 and repealed by s. 1031 and Sch. 3, Pt. 1.]

History – S. 72 omitted by ITA 2007, s. 1027 and Sch. 1, para. 287 and repealed by s. 1031 and Sch. 3, Pt. 1, with effect from 6 April 2007.

73 Relief for company trading losses

73(1) [Repealed by CTA 2010, s. 1181 and Sch. 3, Pt. 1.]

73(2) [Repeals ICTA 1988, s. 393(2)–(6), 394.]

73(3) Schedule 15 to this Act shall have effect.

73(4) This section shall have effect only in relation to losses incurred in accounting periods ending on or after 1st April 1991.

73(5) Any enactment amended by this section or that Schedule shall, in its application in relation to losses so incurred, be deemed to have had effect at all times with that amendment; and where any such enactment is the re-enactment of a repealed enactment, the repealed enactment shall, in its application in relation to losses so incurred, be deemed to have had effect at all times with a corresponding amendment

History – S. 73(1) repealed by CTA 2010, s. 1181 and Sch. 3, Pt. 1, with effect for corporation tax purposes for accounting periods ending on or after 1 April 2010, and for income tax and capital gains tax purposes for the tax year 2010–11 and subsequent tax years.

74 Trade unions and employers' associations

74 [Repealed by CTA 2010, s. 1181 and Sch. 3, Pt. 1.]

History – S. 74 repealed by CTA 2010, s. 1181 and Sch. 3, Pt. 1, with effect for corporation tax purposes for accounting periods ending on or after 1 April 2010, and for income tax and capital gains tax purposes for the tax year 2010–11 and subsequent tax years.

75 Audit powers in relation to non-residents

75 [Repealed by Statute Law (Repeals) Act 2013, s. 1 and Sch. 1, Pt. 10.]

History – S. 75 repealed by Statute Law (Repeals) Act 2013, s. 1 and Sch. 1, Pt. 10, with effect from 31 January 2013.

76 Capital element in annuities

76(1) [Omitted by FA 2008, s. 36 and Sch. 14, para. 17.]

76(2) Section 230 of the Income and Corporation Taxes Act 1970 (from which section 656 of the Taxes Act 1988 is derived) shall be deemed always to have had effect as if the subsections (7) to (9) set out in subsection (1) above had been contained in that section as subsections (8) to (10) respectively, but with the substitution for "(2)(a)" and "(4)(c)", in each place where they occur, of "(2A)(a)" and "(3)(c)" respectively.

76(3) Section 27 of the Finance Act 1956 (from which section 230 of the Income and Corporation Taxes Act 1970 was derived) shall be deemed always to have had effect as if the subsections (7) and (9) set out in subsection (1) above had been contained in that section as subsections (8A) and (8B) respectively, but with the omission in subsection (7) of paragraph (a) and with the substitution of "(3)(c)" for "(4)(c)" in both places where it occurs.

History – S. 76(1) omitted by FA 2008, s. 36 and Sch. 14, para. 17, with effect for corporation tax for accounting periods beginning on or after 1 April 2008, and with effect for income tax for the tax year 2008–09 and subsequent tax years.

77 Definition of "normal commercial loan"

77(1) [Inserts ICTA 1988, Sch. 18, para. 1(5E)–(5I).]

77(2) [Repealed by TCGA 1992, s. 290 and Sch. 12.]

77(3) Except as provided by subsection (2) above, this section shall be deemed to have come into force on 1st April 1991.

History – S. 77(2) repealed by TCGA 1992, s. 290 and Sch. 12 in relation to tax for 1992–93 and subsequent years of assessment or for other chargeable periods beginning on or after 6 April 1992.

78 Sharing of transmission facilities

78(1) This section applies to any agreement relating to the sharing of transmission facilities–

(a) to which the parties are national broadcasting companies,

(b) which is entered into on or after the day on which this Act is passed and before 1st January 1992 or such later date as may be specified for the purposes of this paragraph by the Secretary of State, and

(c) in relation to which the Secretary of State has certified that it is expedient that this section should apply.

78(2), (3) [Repealed by TCGA 1992, s. 290 and Sch. 12.]

78(4) Where under an agreement to which this section applies one party to the agreement disposes of plant or machinery to another party to the agreement, the Capital Allowances Act shall apply–

(a) in the case of the party making the disposal, as if the disposal value of the plant or machinery for the purposes of section 60 of that Act were equal to the capital expenditure incurred by that party on its provision, and

(b) in the case of the party to whom the disposal is made, as if the amount expended by that party in acquiring the plant or machinery were equal to the capital expenditure so incurred.

78(5) In subsection (4) above, references to plant or machinery include a share in plant or machinery.

78(6), (7) [Repealed by TCGA 1992, s. 290 and Sch. 12.]

78(8) In this section, **"national broadcasting company"** means a body corporate engaged in the broadcasting for general reception by means of wireless telegraphy of radio or television services or both on a national basis.

History – In s. 78(4) reference to CAA 1990 removed and words "section 60 of that Act" substituted for "section 24 of that Act" by CAA 2001, s. 578 and Sch. 2, para. 74 with effect as respects allowances and charges falling to be made for chargeable periods ending, for income tax purposes, on or after 6 April 2001, and for corporation tax purposes, on or after 1 April 2001.
In s. 78(4), (5), words "plant or machinery" substituted for "machinery and plant" by CAA 2001, s. 578 and Sch. 2, para. 74, with effect as respects allowances and charges falling to be made for chargeable periods ending, for income tax purposes, on or after 6 April 2001, and for corporation tax purposes, on or after 1 April 2001.
S. 78(2), (3), (6), (7) repealed by TCGA 1992, s. 290 and Sch. 12 in relation to tax for 1992–93 and subsequent years of assessment or for other chargeable periods beginning on or after 6 April 1992.

79 Abolition of CRT: consequential amendment

79(1) [Amends FA 1988, Sch. 12, para. 6(1)(b).]

79(2) This section shall apply where qualifying benefits are conferred on or after 6th April 1991.

80 Interest on certain debentures

80 [Amends Electricity Act 1989, Sch. 11, para. 8(2).]

82 *Certificates of* non-liability to tax

82(1) [Inserts TMA 1970, s. 99A.]

82(2) So far as relating to the giving of a certificate, this section shall apply in relation to certificates given on or after the day on which this Act is passed.

82(3) So far as relating to failure to comply with an undertaking contained in a certificate, this section shall apply in relation to certificates whenever given, but not so as to impose liability for a failure occurring before the day on which this Act is passed.

PART V – MISCELLANEOUS AND GENERAL

MISCELLANEOUS

118 Designated international organisations: miscellaneous exemptions

118(1) [Repealed by s. 1031 and Sch. 3, Pt. 1.]

118(2) [Amends ICTA 1988, s. 828(4).]

History – S. 118(1) repealed by ITA 2007, s. 1031 and Sch. 3, Pt. 1, with effect from 6 April 2007.

121 Pools payments to support games etc.

121 [Repealed by FA 2012, s. 227 and Sch. 39, para. 20(1).]

History – S. 121 repealed by FA 2012, s. 227 and Sch. 39, para. 20(1), with effect from 6 April 2013 (in relation to payments wherever made).
Former s. 121(2) omitted by CTA 2009, s. 1322 and Sch. 1, para. 357 and repealed by CTA 2009, s. 1326 and Sch. 3, Pt. 1, with effect, for corporation tax purposes, for accounting periods ending on or after 1 April 2009 and, for income tax and capital gains tax purposes, for the tax year 2009–10 and subsequent years.
In former s. 121(2) the word "company" substituted for the former word ("person") and the words "corporation tax purposes" substituted for the former words ("tax purposes"), by ITTOIA 2005, s. 882(1) and Sch. 1, para. 418(2); effective for income tax purposes for 2005–06 onwards and for corporation tax purposes for accounting periods ending after 5 April 2005 (ITTOIA 2005, s. 883(1)).
In former s. 121(2), the word "profits" substituted for the words "profits or gains" by FA 1998, s. 46(3) and Sch. 7, para. 6.
Former s. 121(3) omitted by CTA 2009, s. 1322 and Sch. 1, para. 357 and repealed by CTA 2009, s. 1326 and Sch. 3, Pt. 1, with effect, for corporation tax purposes, for accounting periods ending on or after 1 April 2009 and, for income tax and capital gains tax purposes, for the tax year 2009–10 and subsequent years.
In former s. 121(3) the words ", for corporation tax purposes," inserted by ITTOIA 2005, s. 882(1) and Sch. 1, para. 418(3); effective for income tax purposes for 2005–06 onwards and for corporation tax purposes for accounting periods ending after 5 April 2005 (ITTOIA 2005, s. 883(1)).

Cross references – IHTA 1984, Pt. III, Ch. III: settlements without interests in possession.

Notes – The income tax provisions are principally rewritten at ITTOIA 2005, s. 162 and s. 748.
S. 121(2) and (3) rewritten for corporation tax purposes as follows:
S. 121(2): CTA 2009, s. 138(3).
S. 121(3): CTA 2009, s. 978(1).
S. 5 provides for a reduction in the rate of pool betting duty from 40 per cent to 37.5 per cent in relation to bets made at any time by reference to an event taking place on or after 17 August 1991.

GENERAL

122 Interpretation etc.

122(1) In this Act **"the Taxes Act 1988"** means the Income and Corporation Taxes Act 1988.

122(2) Part II of this Act, so far as it relates to capital gains tax, shall be construed as one with the Capital Gains Tax Act 1979.

122(3) Part III of this Act shall be construed as one with Part I of the Oil Taxation Act 1975 and in that Part of this Act **"the principal Act"** means that Act.

124 Short title

124 This Act may be cited as the Finance Act 1991.

SCHEDULES

SCHEDULE 6 – RESTRICTION OF HIGHER RATE RELIEF: BENEFICIAL LOANS ETC.

Section 27

TAXATION OF BENEFICIAL LOAN ARRANGEMENTS

1 [Repealed by ITEPA 2003, Sch. 8, Pt. 1]

History – Para. 1 repealed by ITEPA 2003, Sch. 8, Pt. 1 with effect for the tax year 2003–04 and subsequent tax years.

2 [Repealed by FA 1994, s. 258 and Sch. 26, Pt. V(5) with effect for 1994–95 and subsequent years of assessment.]

3 [Para. 3 repealed by ITEPA 2003, Sch. 8, Pt. 1]

History – Para. 3 repealed by ITEPA 2003, Sch. 8, Pt. 1 with effect for the tax year 2003–04 and subsequent tax years.

4(1) [Repealed by Statute Law (Repeals) Act 2013, s. 1 and Sch. 1, Pt. 10.]

History – Para. 4 repealed by Statute Law (Repeals) Act 2013, s. 1 and Sch. 1, Pt. 10, with effect from 31 January 2013.

5 [Repealed by FA 1994, s. 258 and Sch. 26, Pt. V(5) with effect for 1994–95 and subsequent years of assessment.]

SCHEDULE 7 – BASIC LIFE ASSURANCE AND GENERAL ANNUITY BUSINESS

Section 48

MANAGEMENT EXPENSES

1(1) [Amends ICTA 1988, s. 76(1)(ca), (d).]

History – The former extension of the amendment made by para. 1 to include ICTA 1988, s. 76(1)(e) was repealed by FA 2003, s. 216 and Sch. 43, Pt. 3(12) (following the substitution of ICTA 1988, s. 76(1)(e) by FA 2003, Sch. 33, para. 8(1)) with effect for accounting periods beginning on or after 1 January 2003 except those ending before 9 April 2003.

INTERPRETATION OF CHAPTER I OF PART XII

2 [Repealed by FA 1995, s. 162 and Sch. 29, Pt. VIII(5).]

History – Para. 2 repealed by FA 1995, s. 162 and Sch. 29, Pt. VIII(5) for accounting periods beginning on or after 1 January 1995.

APPORTIONMENT OF INCOME AND GAINS

3(1)–(6) [Repealed by FA 1995, s. 162 and Sch. 29, Pt. VIII(5).]

History – Para. 3 repealed by FA 1995, s. 162 and Sch. 29, Pt. VIII(5) for accounting periods beginning on or after 1 January 1995.

COMPUTATION OF TRADING PROFIT

4(1) [Amends ICTA 1988, s. 436(1). Partially repealed by FA 2007, s. 114 and Sch. 27, Pt. 2(7).]

4(2) [Amends ICTA 1988, s. 436(3)(c), (e).]

4(3) [Amends ICTA 1988, s. 436(4).]

4(4) [Repeals ICTA 1988, s. 437(2)–(5).]

History – Para. 4(1)(b) repealed by FA 2007, s. 114 and Sch. 27, Pt. 2(7) with effect:
- for the purposes of corporation tax, for periods of account of insurance companies beginning on or after 1 January 2007; and
- for the purposes of income tax, for the 2007–08 tax year and subsequent tax years.

DEDUCTION FOR ANNUITIES REFERABLE TO BASIC LIFE ASSURANCE AND GENERAL ANNUITY BUSINESS

5 [Omitted by FA 2012, s. 146 and Sch. 16, para. 247(c)(i).]

History – Para. 5 omitted by FA 2012, s. 146 and Sch. 16, para. 247(c)(i), with effect in relation to accounting periods beginning on or after 1 January 2013 (FA 2012, s. 148) but subject to transitional provisions in FA 2012, Sch. 17. Where an accounting period would otherwise straddle 1 January 2013, it is deemed to end on 31 December 2012 (FA 2012, s. 149).

TRANSFER OF ASSETS BETWEEN CLASSES OF BUSINESS

6(1)–(4) [Repealed by FA 1995, s. 162 and Sch. 29, Pt. VIII(5).]

History – Para. 6 repealed by FA 1995, s. 162 and Sch. 29, Pt. VIII(5) for accounting periods beginning on or after 1 January 1995.

UNITED KINGDOM BRANCHES OF OVERSEAS LIFE ASSURANCE COMPANIES

7(1) [Repealed by FA 1993, s. 213 and Sch. 23, Pt. III(9).]

7(2) [Repealed by FA 1993, s. 213 and Sch. 23, Pt. III(9).]

7(3) [Repeals ICTA 1988, s. 447(3).]

7(4) [Repealed by FA 1993, s. 213 and Sch. 23, Pt. III(9).]

7(5) [Repealed by FA 1993, s. 213 and Sch. 23, Pt. III(9).]

History – Para. 7(1)(a), (2), (4) and (5) repealed by FA 1993, s. 213 and Sch. 23, Pt. III(9) in relation to accounting periods beginning after 31 December 1992.

TREATMENT OF TAX-FREE INCOME

8 [Amends ICTA 1988, s. 474(1)(b).]

LIFE ANNUITY CONTRACTS: TAXATION OF GAIN ON CHARGEABLE EVENT

9 [Repealed by ITTOIA 2005, s. 884 and Sch. 3.]

History – Para. 9 repealed by ITTOIA 2005, s. 884 and Sch. 3; effective for income tax purposes for 2005–06 onwards and for corporation tax purposes for accounting periods ending after 5 April 2005 (ITTOIA 2005, s. 883(1)).

Notes – The amendments originally made by para. 9, at ICTA 1988, s. 547, are rewritten at ITTOIA 2005, s. 531.

COMPUTATION OF OFFSHORE INCOME GAINS

10 [Repealed by FA 1995, s. 162 and Sch. 29, Pt. VIII(5).]

History – Para. 10 repealed by FA 1995, s. 162 and Sch. 29, Pt. VIII(5) as prescribed by FA 1995, Sch. 8, para. 55.

INTERPRETATION OF SECTIONS 85 TO 89 OF FINANCE ACT 1989

11 [Repealed by FA 2003, s. 216 and Sch. 43, Pt. 3(12).]

History – Para. 11 repealed by FA 2003, s. 216 and Sch. 43, Pt. 3(12) (following the repeal of FA 1989, s. 84(1) by the same provision of Finance Act 2003) with effect from 10 July 2003 (Royal Assent to Finance Act 2003).

MISCELLANEOUS RECEIPTS

12 [Omitted by FA 2012, s. 146 and Sch. 16, para. 247(c)(i).]

History – Para. 12 omitted by FA 2012, s. 146 and Sch. 16, para. 247(c)(i), with effect in relation to accounting periods beginning on or after 1 January 2013 (FA 2012, s. 148) but subject to transitional provisions in FA 2012, Sch. 17. Where an accounting period would otherwise straddle 1 January 2013, it is deemed to end on 31 December 2012 (FA 2012, s. 149).

SPREADING OF RELIEF FOR ACQUISITION EXPENSES

13(1) [Repealed by FA 2004, s. 326 and Sch. 42, Pt. 2(3).]

13(2) [Repealed by FA 2007, s. 114 and Sch. 27, Pt. 2(7).]

13(3) [Inserts FA 1989, s. 86(4)(b).]

History – Para. 13(1) repealed by FA 2004, s. 326 and Sch. 42, Pt. 2(3) with effect for accounting periods beginning on or after 1 April 2004, but subject to transitional provisions in FA 2004, s. 43, 44 and Sch. 6.
Para. 13(2) repealed by FA 2007, s. 114 and Sch. 27, Pt. 2(10) with effect from Royal Assent 19 July 2007.

TRANSITIONAL RELIEF FOR OLD GENERAL ANNUITY CONTRACTS

16(1) In the application of the I – E rules in relation to an accounting period of an insurance company, an amount equal to the lesser of the following amounts is to be treated (if it is not nil) for the purposes of section 76 of the Finance Act 2012 as a deemed BLAGAB management expense for the accounting period, that is to say–

(a) A, and

(b) A – (R1 – R2 + C – SV – DB),

and if the result of the formula in paragraph (b) above is a negative amount, it shall be taken to be nil.

16(2) For the purposes of sub-paragraph (1) above–

A Is the gross amount of any annuities paid in the accounting period so far as referable to old annuity contracts;

R1 is the amount of the company's opening liabilities for the accounting period in respect of old annuity contracts but taking that amount as nil if it would otherwise be below nil;

R2 is the amount of the company's closing liabilities for the accounting period in respect of old annuity contracts but taking that amount as nil if it would otherwise be below nil;

C is the amount of any consideration received in the accounting period in respect of old annuity contracts;

SV is the amount of any sums paid in the accounting period by reason of the surrender of rights conferred by old annuity contracts;

DB is the amount of any death benefits paid in the accounting period in respect of old annuity contracts.

16(3) [Repealed by FA 1997, s. 113 and Sch. 18, Pt. VI(6).]

16(4) [Repealed by FA 1997, s. 113 and Sch. 18, Pt. VI(6).]

16(5) If, in the case of an annuity under a group annuity contract made by an insurance company in an accounting period beginning before 1st January 1992–

(a) the company's liabilities first include an amount in respect of that annuity in an accounting period beginning on or after that date, and

(b) the company's liability in respect of that annuity is referable to its basic life assurance and general annuity business,

the group annuity contract, so far as relating to that annuity, shall be treated for the purposes of this paragraph, other than this sub-paragraph, as if it had been made in an accounting period beginning on or after 1st January 1992 (and were, accordingly, not an old annuity contract).

16(6) If, in the case of an annuity which is subject to a reinsurance treaty made by the reinsurer in an accounting period beginning before 1st January 1992–

(a) the reinsurer's liabilities first include an amount in respect of that annuity in an accounting period beginning on or after that date; and

(b) the reinsurer's liability in respect of that annuity is referable to its basic life assurance and general annuity business,

the reinsurance treaty, as respects the reinsurer and so far as relating to that annuity, shall be treated for the purposes of this paragraph, other than this sub-paragraph, as if it had been made in an accounting period beginning on or after 1st January 1992 (and were, accordingly, not an old annuity contract).

16(7) In this paragraph–

"general annuity contract" means an annuity contract so far as referable to general annuity business;

"group annuity contract" means a contract between an insurance company and some other person under which the company undertakes to become liable to pay annuities to or in respect of such persons as may subsequently be specified or otherwise ascertained under or in accordance with the contract (whether or not annuities under the contract are also payable to or in respect of persons who are specified or ascertained at the time the contract is made);

"old annuity contract" means a general annuity contract made by an insurance company in an accounting period beginning before 1st January 1992 (including one forming part of the business transferred to another insurance company by an insurance business transfer scheme);

"reinsurance treaty" means a contract under which one insurance company is obliged to cede, and another (in this paragraph referred to as a **"reinsurer"**) to accept, the whole or part of a risk of a class or description to which the contract relates;

16(8) Where–

(a) business is transferred to an insurance company by an insurance business transfer scheme during an accounting period of the company, and

(b) the business transferred consists of or includes old annuity contracts ("the transferred contracts"), the reference in the definition of R1 in sub-paragraph (2) above to the company's opening liabilities for the accounting period is, in relation to the transferred contracts, a reference to the company's liabilities in respect of the transferred contracts immediately after the transfer.

History – In para. 16(1), the words "application of the I – E rules in relation to an accounting period of an insurance company, an amount equal to the lesser of the following amounts is to be treated (if it is not nil) for the purposes of section 76 of the Finance Act 2012 as a deemed BLAGAB management expense for the accounting period" substituted for the words "computation under the I minus E basis of the relevant profits (within the meaning of section 88(1) of the Finance Act 1989) of an insurance company for any accounting period, an amount equal to the lesser of the following amounts shall be treated (if it is not nil) as expenses payable which fall to be brought into account for that period at Step 3 in section 76(7) of the Taxes Act 1988" by FA 2012 s. 146 and Sch. 16, para. 71, with effect in relation to accounting periods beginning on or after 1 January 2013 (FA 2012, s. 148) but subject to transitional provisions in FA 2012, Sch. 17. Where an accounting period would otherwise straddle 1 January 2013, it is deemed to end on 31 December 2012 (FA 2012, s. 149).

In para. 16(1), the words, "under the I minus E basis" substituted for ", otherwise than in accordance with the provisions applicable to Case I of Schedule D," by FA 2007, s. 39(1) and Sch. 8, para. 17 with effect for the purposes of corporation tax, for periods of insurance companies beginning on or after 1 January 2007 (subject to any transitional provisions contained in FA 2007, Sch. 8, Pt. 2 (FA 2007, s. 39(2))).

In para. 16(1), the words "expenses payable which fall to be brought into account for that period at Step 3 in section 76(7) of the Taxes Act 1988" substituted for the words "a sum disbursed as expenses of management of the company for that period" by SI 2004/2310, Schedule, para. 47(2), with effect in relation to accounting periods beginning on or after 1 April 2004, subject to the transitional provisions at FA 2004, s. 43 and 44.

In para. 16(1), the words "relevant profits (within the meaning of section 88(1) of the Finance Act 1989) of an insurance company for any accounting period" substituted for the words "profits for any accounting period of an insurance company's life assurance business" by FA 2003, s. 170 and Sch. 33, para. 6(10) with effect for accounting periods ending on or after 9 April 2003.

In para. 16(1), the words, "In this computation … that is to say–" substituted by FA 1997,s. 67(6) with effect from accounting periods beginning after 5 March 1997.

In para. 16(2), the words "but taking that amount as nil if it would otherwise be below nil" inserted in both places by SI 2007/1031, art. 14(2), with effect from 17 April 2007, in relation to accounting periods ending on or after 31 December 2006, whenever beginning.

Para. 16(3) repealed by FA 1997, s. 113 and Sch. 18, Pt. VI(6), in relation to accounting periods beginning after 5 March 1997.

Para. 16(4) repealed by FA 1997, s. 113 and Sch. 18, Pt. VI(6), in relation to accounting periods beginning after 5 March 1997.

In para. 16(7), in the definition of "old annuity contract", the parenthetical words at the end inserted by FA 2007, s. 40 and Sch. 9, para. 13(2) with effect in relation to periods of account beginning on or after 1 January 2007.

In para. 16(7), the closing words "and, subject to that, expressions used in this paragraph and in Chapter I of Part XII of the Taxes Act 1988 have the same meaning in this paragraph as they have in that Chapter" omitted by FA 2007, s. 41 and Sch. 10, para. 14(4) and repealed by FA 2007, s. 114 and Sch. 27, Pt. 2(10) with effect in relation to periods of account beginning on or after 1 January 2007.

Para. 16(8) inserted by FA 2007, s. 40 and Sch. 9, para. 13(3) with effect in relation to periods of account beginning on or after 1 January 2007.

Cross references – SI 2012/3008, reg. 3: modification of para. 16(7), with effect in relation to accounting periods beginning on or after 1 January 2013, in specified circumstances where the Corporation Tax Acts apply to the life assurance business and other long-term business carried on by a friendly society; where any part of the business of an insurance company is exempt from corporation tax as a result of a transfer of business from a friendly society, or as a result of a conversion by a friendly society to a company under Friendly Societies Act 1992, s. 91.
FA 1995, Sch. 29, Pt. VIII(5), Note 3: repeal of definitions of "general annuity business" and "basic life assurance business" in ICTA 1988, Pt. XII, Ch. I by FA 1995 does not affect the meaning of those expressions in para. 16.
SI 2005/2014, reg. 33: modification of para. 16 so as to make it applicable to friendly societies carrying on life insurance business (which is not entirely tax exempt).

TRANSITIONAL PROVISIONS FOR CHARGEABLE GAINS AND UNRELIEVED GENERAL ANNUITY LOSSES

17(1) An insurance company's unrelieved general annuity losses shall be relieved under this paragraph by setting them against the relevant part of any chargeable gains arising to the company in accounting periods beginning on or after 1st January 1992.

17(2) Any relief under this paragraph shall be given as far as possible for the first accounting period of the company beginning on or after 1st January 1992 and, so far as it cannot be so given, for the next accounting period, and so on.

17(3) For the purposes of this paragraph an insurance company's **"unrelieved general annuity losses"** are so much of any losses–

(a) arising from the company's general annuity business in an accounting period or year of assessment beginning before 1st January 1992, and

(b) computed as mentioned in paragraph (c) of subsection (3) of section 436 of the Taxes Act 1988 as it applied in relation to such accounting periods,

as, by virtue only of an insufficiency of profits, cannot be relieved under that subsection (or any previous enactment which it re-enacts) by setting them off against the profits of such an accounting period or year of assessment.

17(4) For the purposes of this paragraph the relevant part of the chargeable gains arising to a company in an accounting period is so much of the chargeable gains arising to the company in the accounting period as are referable to its basic life assurance and general annuity business.

17(4A) [Omitted by FA 2007, s. 41 and Sch, 10, para. 15(4)(b) and repealed by FA 2007, s. 114 and Sch. 27, Pt. 2(7).]

17(5) [Omitted by FA 2007, s. 41 and Sch, 10, para. 15(4)(b) and repealed by FA 2007, s. 114 and Sch. 27, Pt. 2(7).]

History – In para. 17(4) the words "is so much of the chargeable gains arising to the company in the accounting period as are referable to its basic life assurance and general annuity business" substituted by FA 2007, s. 41] and Sch, 10, para. 15(4)(a) with effect in relation to periods of account beginning on or after 1 January 2007.
In para. 17(4) the words "(but taking that mean to be nil if it would otherwise be below nil)" inserted by SI 2007/1031, art. 14(4), with effect from 17 April 2007, in relation to accounting periods ending on or after 31 December 2006, whenever beginning.
Para. 17(4A) omitted by FA 2007, s. 41 and Sch, 10, para. 15(4)(b) and repealed by FA 2007, s. 114 and Sch. 27, Pt. 2(10) with effect in relation to periods of account beginning on or after 1 January 2007.
Para. 17(4A) inserted by SI 2007/1031, art. 14(3), and the words "This is subject to sub-paragraph (4A)." inserted, with effect from 17 April 2007, in relation to accounting periods ending on or after 31 December 2006, whenever beginning.
Para. 17(5) omitted by FA 2007, s. 41 and Sch, 10, para. 15(4)(b) and repealed by FA 2007, s. 114 and Sch. 27, Pt. 2(10) with effect in relation to periods of account beginning on or after 1 January 2007.

Cross references – FA 1995, Sch. 29, Pt. VIII(5), Note 3: repeal of definitions of "general annuity business" and "basic life assurance business" in ICTA 1988, Pt. XII, Ch. I by FA 1995 does not affect the meaning of those expressions in para. 17.
SI 2005/2014, reg. 34: modification of para. 17 so as to make it applicable to friendly societies carrying on life insurance business (which is not entirely tax exempt).

Extra-statutory concessions – ESC C29: in transfers of long term insurance business, permits the carry forward of unrelieved losses incurred by the transferring company in general annuity business prior to 1992.

APPLICATION OF THIS SCHEDULE

18 Paragraphs 1, 3, 4, 5, 6(1) and (2), 7, 8, 10 to 14, 16 and 17 above have effect with respect only to accounting periods beginning on or after 1st January 1992.

SCHEDULE 8 – PENSION BUSINESS: PAYMENTS ON ACCOUNT OF TAX CREDITS AND DEDUCTED TAX

Section 49

[Sch. 8 repealed by FA 2001, Sch. 33, Pt. 2(12).]

History – Repealed by FA 2001, Sch. 33, Pt. 2(12), in relation to income tax borne by deduction from payments received after 30 September 2001 and in relation to tax credits in respect of distributions made on or after 6 April 2004 (FA 2001, s. 87).

SCHEDULE 9 – FRIENDLY SOCIETIES

Section 50

TAX EXEMPT LIFE OR ENDOWMENT BUSINESS

1 [Omitted by FA 2012, s. 176 and Sch. 18, para. 23(b).]

History – Para. 1 omitted by FA 2012, s. 176 and Sch. 18, para. 23(b), with effect in relation to accounting periods beginning on or after 1 January 2013 (FA 2012, s. 178) but subject to transitional provisions in FA 2012, Sch. 19. Where an accounting period would otherwise straddle 1 January 2013, it is deemed to end on 31 December 2012 (FA 2012, s. 179).

2 [Omitted by FA 2008, s. 44 and Sch. 18, para. 5 and by FA 2012, s. 176 and Sch. 18, para. 23(b).]

History – Para. 2 omitted by FA 2012, s. 176 and Sch. 18, para. 23(b), with effect in relation to accounting periods beginning on or after 1 January 2013 (FA 2012, s. 178) but subject to transitional provisions in FA 2012, Sch. 19. Where an accounting period would otherwise straddle 1 January 2013, it is deemed to end on 31 December 2012 (FA 2012, s. 179). Para. 2 had previously been omitted by FA 2008 (see below).
Para. 2 formerly omitted by FA 2008, s. 44 and Sch. 18, para. 5, with effect from 21 July 2008.

MAXIMUM BENEFITS PAYABLE TO MEMBERS

3(1) [Omitted by FA 2012, s. 176 and Sch. 18, para. 23(b).]

History – Para. 3 omitted by FA 2012, s. 176 and Sch. 18, para. 23(b), with effect in relation to accounting periods beginning on or after 1 January 2013 (FA 2012, s. 178) but subject to transitional provisions in FA 2012, Sch. 19. Where an accounting period would otherwise straddle 1 January 2013, it is deemed to end on 31 December 2012 (FA 2012, s. 179).

QUALIFYING POLICIES

4(1) [Omits ICTA 1988, Sch. 15, para. 3(1)(c).]

4(2) This paragraph shall apply in relation to policies issued in pursuance of contracts made on or after the day on which this Act is passed.

5(1) This paragraph applies to any policy–

(a) issued by a friendly society, or branch of a friendly society, in the course of tax exempt life or endowment business (as defined in section 466 of the Taxes Act 1988), and

(b) effected by a contract made after 31st August 1987 and before the day on which this Act is passed.

5(2) Where–

(a) the amount payable by way of premium under a policy to which this paragraph applies is increased by virtue of a variation made in the period beginning with the day on which this Act is passed and ending with 31st July 1992, and

(b) the variation is not such as to cause a person to become in breach of the limits in section 464 of the Taxes Act 1988,

Schedule 15 to that Act, in its application to the policy, shall have effect, in relation to that variation, with the modifications mentioned in sub-paragraph (3) below.

5(3) The modifications are the omission of paragraph 4(3)(a) and the insertion at the end of paragraph 18(2) of

"and as if for paragraph 3(2)(b) above there were substituted–

(b) subject to sub-paragraph (4) below, the premiums payable under the policy shall be premiums of equal or rateable amounts payable at yearly or shorter intervals over the whole of the term of the policy as from the variation, or, where premiums are not payable for any period after the person liable to pay them or whose life is insured has attained a specified age, being an age attained at a time not less than ten years after the beginning of the term of the policy, over the whole of the remainder of the period for which premiums are payable."

SCHEDULE 10 – BUILDING SOCIETIES: QUALIFYING SHARES

Section 51

ACCRUED INCOME SCHEME: INCLUSION

2 [Repealed by ITA 2007, s. 1031 and Sch. 3, Pt. 1.]

History – Para. 2 repealed by ITA 2007, s. 1031 and Sch. 3, Pt. 1, with effect from 6 April 2007.

INCIDENTAL COSTS OF ISSUE

3 [Repealed by CTA 2009, s. 1326 and Sch. 3, Pt. 1.]

History – Para. 3 repealed by CTA 2009, s. 1326 and Sch. 3, Pt. 1, with effect, for corporation tax purposes, for accounting periods ending on or after 1 April 2009 and, for income tax and capital gains tax purposes, for the tax year 2009–10 and subsequent years.

SCHEDULE 11 – BUILDING SOCIETIES: MARKETABLE SECURITIES

Section 52

DEDUCTION OF INCOME TAX

1 [Repealed by ITA 2007, s. 1031 and Sch. 3, Pt. 1.]

History – Para. 1 repealed by ITA 2007, s. 1031 and Sch. 3, Pt. 1, with effect from 6 April 2007.

2(1) [Repealed by TIOPA 2010, s. 378 and Sch. 10, Pt. 13.]

2(2) [Repealed by ITA 2007, s. 1031 and Sch. 3, Pt. 1.]

2(3) [Repealed by TIOPA 2010, s. 378 and Sch. 10, Pt. 13.]

History – Para. 2(1) repealed by TIOPA 2010, s. 378 and Sch. 10, Pt. 13, with effect for corporation tax purposes for accounting periods ending on or after 1 April 2010, for income tax and capital gains tax purposes for the tax year 2010–11 and subsequent tax years, and for petroleum revenue tax purposes for chargeable periods beginning on or after 1 July 2010.
Para. 2(2) repealed by ITA 2007, s. 1031 and Sch. 3, Pt. 1, with effect from 6 April 2007.
Para. 2(3) repealed by TIOPA 2010, s. 378 and Sch. 10, Pt. 13, with effect for corporation tax purposes for accounting periods ending on or after 1 April 2010, for income tax and capital gains tax purposes for the tax year 2010–11 and subsequent tax years, and for petroleum revenue tax purposes for chargeable periods beginning on or after 1 July 2010.

COLLECTION

3 [Repealed by ITA 2007, s. 1031 and Sch. 3, Pt. 1.]

History – Para. 3 repealed by ITA 2007, s. 1031 and Sch. 3, Pt. 1, with effect from 6 April 2007.

4 [Repealed by ITA 2007, s. 1031 and Sch. 3, Pt. 1.]

History – Para. 4 repealed by ITA 2007, s. 1031 and Sch. 3, Pt. 1, with effect from 6 April 2007.

INFORMATION

5(1) [Inserts TMA 1970, s. 18(3D).]

5(2) This paragraph shall have effect as regards a case where the payment is made on or after the day on which this Act is passed.

SCHEDULE 12 – SECURITIES: NEW ISSUES

Section 54

GENERAL TREATMENT OF EXTRA RETURN

1 [Repealed by ITA 2007, s. 1031 and Sch. 3, Pt. 1.]

History – Para. 1 repealed by ITA 2007, s. 1031 and Sch. 3, Pt. 1, with effect from 6 April 2007.

ACCRUED INCOME SCHEME

2 [Repealed by ITA 2007, s. 1031 and Sch. 3, Pt. 1.]

History – Para. 2 repealed by ITA 2007, s. 1031 and Sch. 3, Pt. 1, with effect from 6 April 2007.

DEEP DISCOUNT SECURITIES

3 [Para. 3 repealed by FA 1996, s. 205 and Sch. 41, Pt. V(3), for corporation tax purposes in relation to accounting periods ending after 31 March 1996, and for income tax purposes for years after 1995–96, subject to FA 1996, Sch. 15.]

DEEP GAIN SECURITIES

4 [Para. 4 repealed by FA 1996, s. 205 and Sch. 41, Pt. V(3), for corporation tax purposes in relation to accounting periods ending after 31 March 1996, and for income tax purposes for years after 1995–96, subject to FA 1996, Sch. 15.]

GENERAL

5 This Schedule applies if the new securities are issued on or after 19th March 1991 (whether the old securities are issued before or on or after that day).

SCHEDULE 13 – MANUFACTURED DIVIDENDS AND INTEREST

Section 58

THE NEW ARRANGEMENTS

1 [Inserts ICTA 1988, Sch. 23A.]

Cross references – SI 1993/933 (C. 17).

POWER TO OBTAIN INFORMATION IN CONNECTION WITH DEALINGS IN SECURITIES

2 [Repealed by FA 1997, s. 113 and Sch. 18, Pt. VI(10).]

History – Para. 2 repealed by FA 1997, s. 113 and Sch. 18, Pt. VI(10), with effect from 1 July 1997, the day appointed under FA 1997, Sch. 10, para. 7(1) by virtue of SI 1997/991.

MANUFACTURED DIVIDENDS ETC: AMENDMENTS OF SECTION 737

3 [Repealed by FA 1997, s. 113 and Sch. 18, Pt. VI(10).]

History – Para. 3 repealed by FA 1997, s. 113 and Sch. 18, Pt. VI(10), with effect from 1 July 1997, the day appointed under FA 1997, Sch. 10, para. 7(1) by virtue of SI 1997/991.

CONSEQUENTIAL PROVISIONS

4 [Repealed by FA 1997, s. 113 and Sch. 18, Pt. VI(10).]

History – Para. 4 repealed by FA 1997, s. 113 and Sch. 18, Pt. VI(10), with effect from 1 July 1997, the day appointed under FA 1997, Sch. 10, para. 7(1) by virtue of SI 1997/991.

SCHEDULE 14 – CAPITAL ALLOWANCES: VAT CAPITAL GOODS SCHEME

Section 59

[Sch. 14 repealed by CAA 2001, s. 580 and Sch. 4.]

History – Sch. 14 repealed by CAA 2001, s. 580 and Sch. 4, with effect as respects allowances and charges falling to be made for chargeable periods ending, for income tax purposes, on or after 6 April 2001, and for corporation tax purposes, on or after 1 April 2001.

SCHEDULE 15 – RELIEF FOR COMPANY TRADING LOSSES

Section 73

THE TAXES MANAGEMENT ACT 1970 (C. 9)

1(1) [Inserts TMA 1970, s. 86(2A).]

1(2) The subsection (2A) inserted by sub-paragraph (1) above shall be omitted where the accounting period referred to in that subsection as the earlier period ends after the appointed day for the purposes of section 86 of the Finance (No. 2) Act 1987 so far as relating to the omission of section 86(2)(d) of the Taxes Management Act 1970.

Notes – The day appointed for the purposes of F(No. 2)A 1987, s. 86 is 30 September 1993 (SI 1992/3066).

2 [Repealed by FA 1993, s. 212 and Sch. 23, Pt. III(11).]

History – Para. 2 repealed by FA 1993, s. 213 and Sch. 23, Pt. III(11) in relation to accounting periods ending after 30 September 1993 (appointed day for Pay and File by virtue of SI 1992/3066).

THE INCOME AND CORPORATION TAXES ACT 1988 (C. 1)

3 [Repealed by CTA 2009, s. 1326 and Sch. 3, Pt. 1.]

History – Para. 3 repealed by CTA 2009, s. 1326 and Sch. 3, Pt. 1, with effect, for corporation tax purposes, for accounting periods ending on or after 1 April 2009 and, for income tax and capital gains tax purposes, for the tax year 2009–10 and subsequent years.

4 [Repealed by CTA 2010, s. 1181 and Sch. 3, Pt. 1.]

History – Para. 4 repealed by CTA 2010, s. 1181 and Sch. 3, Pt. 1, with effect for corporation tax purposes for accounting periods ending on or after 1 April 2010, and for income tax and capital gains tax purposes for the tax year 2010–11 and subsequent tax years.

5 [Repealed by F(No. 2)A 1997, s. 52 and Sch. 8, Pt. II(4).]

History – Para. 5 repealed by F(No. 2)A 1997, s. 52 and Sch. 8, Pt. II(4) (in accordance with s. 20) with effect for any accounting period beginning on or after 2 July 1997.

6 [Repealed by F(No. 2)A 1997, s. 52 and Sch. 8, Pt. II(4).]

History – Para. 6 repealed by F(No. 2)A 1997, s. 52 and Sch. 8, Pt. II(4) (in accordance with s. 20) with effect for any accounting period beginning on or after 2 July 1997.

7 [Repealed by CTA 2010, s. 1181 and Sch. 3, Pt. 1.]

History – Para. 7 repealed by CTA 2010, s. 1181 and Sch. 3, Pt. 1, with effect for corporation tax purposes for accounting periods ending on or after 1 April 2010, and for income tax and capital gains tax purposes for the tax year 2010–11 and subsequent tax years.

8 [Repealed by CTA 2010, s. 1181 and Sch. 3, Pt. 1.]

History – Para. 8 repealed by CTA 2010, s. 1181 and Sch. 3, Pt. 1, with effect for corporation tax purposes for accounting periods ending on or after 1 April 2010, and for income tax and capital gains tax purposes for the tax year 2010–11 and subsequent tax years.

9 [Repealed by FA 1993, s. 213 and Sch. 23, Pt. III(11) in relation to accounting periods ending after 30 September 1993 (appointed day for Pay and File by virtue of SI 1992/3066).]

10 [Repealed by CTA 2010, s. 1181 and Sch. 3, Pt. 1.]

History – Para. 10 repealed by CTA 2010, s. 1181 and Sch. 3, Pt. 1, with effect for corporation tax purposes for accounting periods ending on or after 1 April 2010, and for income tax and capital gains tax purposes for the tax year 2010–11 and subsequent tax years.

11 [Repealed by CTA 2010, s. 1181 and Sch. 3, Pt. 1.]

History – Para. 11 repealed by CTA 2010, s. 1181 and Sch. 3, Pt. 1, with effect for corporation tax purposes for accounting periods ending on or after 1 April 2010, and for income tax and capital gains tax purposes for the tax year 2010–11 and subsequent tax years.

12 [Repealed by CTA 2010, s. 1181 and Sch. 3, Pt. 1.]

History – Para. 12 repealed by CTA 2010, s. 1181 and Sch. 3, Pt. 1, with effect for corporation tax purposes for accounting periods ending on or after 1 April 2010, and for income tax and capital gains tax purposes for the tax year 2010–11 and subsequent tax years.

13 [Repealed by FA 1998, s. 165 and Sch 27, Pt. III(4).]

History – Para. 13 repealed by FA 1998, s. 165 and Sch. 27, Pt. III(4) with effect, so far as relating to income tax, for the year 1998–99 and subsequent years and, so far as relating to corporation tax, from 1 April 1998 (subject to the transitional provisions in Sch. 5, Pt. IV).

14 [Repealed by CTA 2010, s. 1181 and Sch. 3, Pt. 1.]

History – Para. 14 repealed by CTA 2010, s. 1181 and Sch. 3, Pt. 1, with effect for corporation tax purposes for accounting periods ending on or after 1 April 2010, and for income tax and capital gains tax purposes for the tax year 2010–11 and subsequent tax years.

15 [Omitted by FA 2012, s. 146 and Sch. 16, para. 247(c)(ii).]

History – Para. 15 omitted by FA 2012, s. 146 and Sch. 16, para. 247(c)(ii), with effect in relation to accounting periods beginning on or after 1 January 2013 (FA 2012, s. 148) but subject to transitional provisions in FA 2012, Sch. 17. Where an accounting period would otherwise straddle 1 January 2013, it is deemed to end on 31 December 2012 (FA 2012, s. 149).

16 [Repealed by FA 2007, s. 114 and Sch. 27, Pt. 2(7).]

History – Para. 16 repealed by FA 2007, s. 114 and Sch. 27, Pt. 2(7) with effect (FA 2007, s. 38(2)):

- for the purposes of corporation tax, for periods of account of insurance companies beginning on or after 1 January 2007; and
- for the purposes of income tax, for the 2007–08 tax year and subsequent tax years.

17 [Repealed by CTA 2010, s. 1181 and Sch. 3, Pt. 1.]

History – Para. 17 repealed by CTA 2010, s. 1181 and Sch. 3, Pt. 1, with effect for corporation tax purposes for accounting periods ending on or after 1 April 2010, and for income tax and capital gains tax purposes for the tax year 2010–11 and subsequent tax years.

18 [Repealed by FA 1995, s. 162 and Sch. 29, Pt. VIII(1) with effect in accordance with FA 1995, s. 39(4).]

19 [Repealed by CTA 2010, s. 1181 and Sch. 3, Pt. 1.]

History – Para. 19 repealed by CTA 2010, s. 1181 and Sch. 3, Pt. 1, with effect for corporation tax purposes for accounting periods ending on or after 1 April 2010, and for income tax and capital gains tax purposes for the tax year 2010–11 and subsequent tax years.

20 [Repealed by CTA 2010, s. 1181 and Sch. 3, Pt. 1.]

History – Para. 20 repealed by CTA 2010, s. 1181 and Sch. 3, Pt. 1, with effect for corporation tax purposes for accounting periods ending on or after 1 April 2010, and for income tax and capital gains tax purposes for the tax year 2010–11 and subsequent tax years.

21 [Repealed by CTA 2010, s. 1181 and Sch. 3, Pt. 1.]

History – Para. 21 repealed by CTA 2010, s. 1181 and Sch. 3, Pt. 1, with effect for corporation tax purposes for accounting periods ending on or after 1 April 2010, and for income tax and capital gains tax purposes for the tax year 2010–11 and subsequent tax years.

22 [Inserts ICTA 1988, s. 825(c), (d).]

23 [Inserts ICTA 1988, s. 826(7A), (7B).]

24 [Amends ICTA 1988, s. 843(4).]

25 [Amends ICTA 1988, Sch. 5, para. 2(3)(a).]

26 [Repealed by FA 1998, s. 165 and Sch 27, Pt. III(4).]

History – Para. 26 (which amends ICTA 1988, Sch. 26, para. 1(3)(a)) repealed by FA 1998, s. 165 and Sch. 27, Pt. III(4) with effect, so far as relating to income tax, for the year 1998–99 and subsequent years and, so far as relating to corporation tax, from 1 April 1998 (subject to the transitional provisions in Sch. 5, Pt. IV).

27(1) [Amends ICTA 1988, Sch. 30, para. 2(2)(a).]

27(2) [Amends ICTA 1988, Sch. 30, para. 3(1)(b).]

THE CAPITAL ALLOWANCES ACT 1990 (C. 1)

28 [Repealed by CAA 2001, s. 580 and Sch. 4.]

History – Para. 28, repealed by CAA 2001, s. 580 and Sch. 4, with effect as respects allowances and charges falling to be made for chargeable periods ending, for income tax purposes, on or after 6 April 2001, and for corporation tax purposes, on or after 1 April 2001.

TAXATION OF CHARGEABLE GAINS ACT 1992

(1992 Chapter 12)

[*6th March 1992*]

ARRANGEMENT OF SECTIONS

PART I – CAPITAL GAINS TAX AND CORPORATION TAX ON CHARGEABLE GAINS

PART II – GENERAL PROVISIONS RELATING TO COMPUTATION OF GAINS AND ACQUISITIONS AND DISPOSALS OF ASSETS

CHAPTER I – INTRODUCTORY

CHAPTER II – ASSETS AND DISPOSALS OF ASSETS

GENERAL PROVISIONS

VALUE SHIFTING

CHAPTER III – COMPUTATION OF GAINS: GENERAL PROVISIONS

RE-BASING TO 1982, AND ASSETS HELD ON 6TH APRIL 1965

ALLOWABLE DEDUCTIONS

CHAPTER II – SETTLEMENTS

GENERAL PROVISIONS

CHAPTER III – COLLECTIVE INVESTMENT SCHEMES AND INVESTMENT TRUSTS ETC

CHAPTER 4 – COLLECTIVE INVESTMENT SCHEMES: EXCHANGES, MERGERS AND SCHEMES OF RECONSTRUCTION

CHAPTER 5 – CARRIED INTEREST

PART IV – SHARES, SECURITIES, OPTIONS ETC.

CHAPTER I – GENERAL

SHARE POOLING, IDENTIFICATION OF SECURITIES, AND INDEXATION

TRANSFERS CONCERNING COMPANIES OF DIFFERENT MEMBER STATES

MERGERS WITHIN EUROPEAN COMMUNITY

TRANSPARENT ENTITIES: DISAPPLICATION OF RELIEFS RELATED TO MERGERS DIRECTIVE

CHAPTER III – MISCELLANEOUS PROVISIONS RELATING TO COMMODITIES, FUTURES, OPTIONS AND OTHER SECURITIES

CHAPTER 4 – ALTERNATIVE FINANCE ARRANGEMENTS

INTRODUCTION

ARRANGEMENTS THAT ARE ALTERNATIVE FINANCE ARRANGEMENTS

MEANING OF "ALTERNATIVE FINANCE RETURN"

SPECIAL RULES FOR INVESTMENT BOND ARRANGEMENTS

OTHER RULES

PART V – TRANSFER OF BUSINESS ASSETS, ENTREPRENEURS' RELIEF AND INVESTORS' RELIEF

CHAPTER I – TRANSFER OF BUSINESS ASSETS: GENERAL PROVISIONS

REPLACEMENT OF BUSINESS ASSETS

CHAPTER 4 – ENTREPRENEURS' RELIEF WHERE HELD-OVER GAINS BECOME CHARGEABLE

CHAPTER 5 – INVESTORS' RELIEF

OVERVIEW

QUALIFYING SHARES

THE RELIEF

TRUSTEES OF A SETTLEMENT: SPECIAL PROVISION

DISPOSALS OF INTERESTS IN SHARES

CAP ON RELIEF

CLAIMS FOR RELIEF

REORGANISATIONS

SUPPLEMENTAL

PART VI – COMPANIES, OIL, INSURANCE ETC.

CHAPTER I – COMPANIES

CHAPTER III – INSURANCE

CHAPTER IV – MISCELLANEOUS CASES

RE-ORGANISATIONS OF MUTUAL BUSINESSES

BUILDING SOCIETIES ETC.

FRIENDLY SOCIETIES

REGISTERED SOCIETIES AND CO-OPERATIVES

THE REGULATOR OF SOCIAL HOUSING, THE SECRETARY OF STATE, SCOTTISH HOMES AND HOUSING ASSOCIATIONS

OTHER BODIES

PART VII – OTHER PROPERTY, BUSINESSES, INVESTMENTS ETC.

PRIVATE RESIDENCES

PART VIII – SUPPLEMENTAL

SCHEDULES

PART I – CAPITAL GAINS TAX AND CORPORATION TAX ON CHARGEABLE GAINS

GENERAL

1 The charge to tax

1(1) Tax shall be charged in accordance with this Act in respect of capital gains, that is to say chargeable gains computed in accordance with this Act and accruing to a person on the disposal of assets.

1(2) Companies shall be chargeable to corporation tax in respect of chargeable gains accruing to them in accordance with section 2 of CTA 2009 and the other provisions of the Corporation Tax Acts, subject to the exception in subsection (2A).

1(2A) But companies are chargeable to capital gains tax, and not corporation tax, in respect of chargeable gains accruing to them to the extent that those gains are–

(a) ATED-related gains in respect of which the companies are chargeable to capital gains tax under section 2B, or

(b) NRCGT gains in respect of which the companies are chargeable to capital gains tax under section 14D or 188D.

1(3) Without prejudice to subsections (2) and (2A), capital gains tax shall be charged for all years of assessment in accordance with the following provisions of this Act.

History – In s. 1(2), the words ", subject to the exception in subsection (2A)" inserted by FA 2013, s. 65 and Sch. 25, para. 2(2), with effect in relation to disposals occurring on or after 6 April 2013.
In s. 1(2) the words "section 2 of CTA 2009" substituted for the words "section 6 of the Taxes Act" by CTA 2009, s. 1322 and Sch. 1, para. 359, with effect for corporation tax purposes for accounting periods ending on or after 1 April 2009, and for income tax and capital gains tax purposes for the tax year 2009–10 and subsequent tax years.
In s. 1(2A), the words "gains are–" and para. (a) and (b) substituted for the words "gains are ATED-related gains in respect of which the companies are chargeable to capital gains tax under section 2B." by FA 2015, s. 37 and Sch. 7, para. 2, with effect in relation to disposals made on or after 6 April 2015.
S. 1(2A) inserted by FA 2013, s. 65 and Sch. 25, para. 2(3), with effect in relation to disposals occurring on or after 6 April 2013.
In s. 1(3), the words "subsections (2) and (2A)" substituted for the words "subsection (2)" by FA 2013, s. 65 and Sch. 25, para. 2(4), with effect in relation to disposals occurring on or after 6 April 2013.

Derivations – CGTA 1979, s. 1.

Cross references – ICTA 1988, s. 6: the charge to corporation tax and consequent exclusion of income tax and capital gains tax.

Notes – S. 15(2): definition of "chargeable gain".
S. 21–34: general meaning of "disposal" and "asset".
TMA 1970, s. 119(4): TMA 1970, so far as it relates to chargeable gains, to be construed as one with this Act.
Interpretation Act 1978, s. 5 and Sch. 1: the Corporation Tax Acts means the enactments relating to the taxation of income and chargeable gains of companies and of company distributions.

CAPITAL GAINS TAX

2 Persons and gains chargeable to capital gains tax, and allowable losses

2(1) Subject to any exceptions provided by this Act, and without prejudice to sections 10 and 276, a person shall be chargeable to capital gains tax in respect of chargeable gains accruing to him in a year of assessment if the residence condition is met.

2(1A) The residence condition is–

(a) in the case of an individual, that the individual is resident in the United Kingdom for the year in question,

(b) in the case of personal representatives of a deceased person, that the single and continuing body mentioned in section 62(3) is resident in the United Kingdom,

(c) in the case of the trustees of a settlement, that the single person mentioned in section 69(1) is resident in the United Kingdom during any part of the year in question, and

(d) in any other case, that the person is resident in the United Kingdom when the gain accrues.

2(1B) If the year is a split year as respects an individual, the individual is not chargeable to capital gains tax in respect of any chargeable gains accruing to the individual in the overseas part of that year.

2(1C) But subsection (1B)–

(a) does not apply to chargeable gains in respect of which the individual would have been chargeable to capital gains tax under section 10, had the individual been not resident in the UK for the year, and

(b) is without prejudice to section 10A.

2(2) Capital gains tax shall be charged on the total amount of chargeable gains accruing to the person chargeable in the year of assessment or, where subsection (1B) applies, the UK part of that year, after deducting–

(a) any allowable losses accruing to that person in that year of assessment or that part (as the case may be), and

(b) so far as they have not been allowed as a deduction from chargeable gains accruing in any previous year of assessment, any allowable losses accruing to that person in any previous year of assessment (not earlier than the year 1965–66).

2(2A) Where subsection (1B) applies, the amounts that may be deducted under subsection (2)(a) include any allowable NRCGT losses accruing to the person in the overseas part of the tax year concerned (see section 14B(4)).

2(2B) The amounts that may be deducted under subsection (2)(b) include any allowable NRCGT losses (other than group losses, as defined in section 188E(4)) accruing to the person in a tax year ("year P") previous to the year mentioned in subsection (2)(a) (so far as those losses have not been allowed as a deduction from chargeable gains accruing in year P or any previous year).

2(3) Except as provided by section 62, an allowable loss accruing in a year of assessment shall not be allowable as a deduction from chargeable gains accruing in any earlier year of assessment, and relief shall not be given under this Act more than once in respect of any loss or part of a loss, and shall not be given under this Act if and so far as relief has been or may be given in respect of it under the Income Tax Acts.

2(4) If chargeable gains are treated by virtue of section 87 or 89(2) as accruing to a person in a tax year ("the relevant deemed gains")–

(a) subsection (2) has effect as if the relevant deemed gains had not accrued, and

(b) the amount on which the person is charged to capital gains tax for that year is the sum of–

(i) the amount given by subsection (2) as it has effect by virtue of paragraph (a), and

(ii) the amount of the relevant deemed gains.

2(5) In subsection (4) the reference to section 87 or 89(2) is to that section read, where appropriate, with section 10A.

2(6) [Effectively omitted by FA 1998, Sch. 21, para. 2.]

2(7) Where in any year of assessment–

(a) there are amounts treated as accruing to a person by virtue of section 86,

(b) two or more of those amounts, or elements of them–

(i) relate to different settlements,

(ii) [omitted by FA 2008, s. 8 and Sch. 2, para. 24(3)(a).]

(c) losses are deductible from the amounts or elements mentioned in paragraph (b) above but are not enough to exhaust them all,

the deduction applicable to each of the amounts shall be the appropriate proportion of the aggregate of those losses.

The **"appropriate proportion"** is that given by dividing the amount in question by the total of the amounts.

2(7A) Nothing in this section applies in relation to an ATED-related gain chargeable to, or an ATED-related loss allowable for the purposes of, capital gains tax by virtue of section 2B.

2(7B) Except where otherwise specified (see subsections (2A) and (2B)), nothing in this section applies in relation to an NRCGT gain chargeable to, or an NRCGT loss allowable for the purposes of, capital gains tax by virtue of section 14D or 188D.

2(8) [Omitted by FA 2008, s. 8 and Sch. 2, para. 24(4).]

History – In s. 2(1), the words "if the residence condition is met" substituted for the words "during any part of which he is resident in the United Kingdom, or during which he is ordinarily resident in the United Kingdom" by FA 2013, s. 219 and Sch. 46, para 75(2), with effect in relation to a person's liability to capital gains tax for the tax year 2013–14 or any subsequent tax year, without prejudice to any provision in FA 2013, Sch. 46, Pt. 3 about the application of a particular amendment.
S. 2(1A) inserted by FA 2013, s. 219 and Sch. 46, para. 75(3), with effect in relation to a person's liability to capital gains tax for the tax year 2013–14 or any subsequent tax year, without prejudice to any provision in FA 2013, Sch. 46, Pt. 3 about the application of a particular amendment.
S. 2(1B) and s. 2(1C) inserted by FA 2013, s. 218 and Sch. 45, para. 93(2), with effect in calculating an individual's liability to income tax or capital gains tax for the tax year 2013–14 or any subsequent tax year, subject to the transitional and saving provision in FA 2013, Sch. 45, para. 154–159.
In s. 2(2), the words "or, where subsection (1B) applies, the UK part of that year" inserted by FA 2013, s. 218 and Sch. 45, para. 93(3)(a), with effect in calculating an individual's liability to income tax or capital gains tax for the tax year 2013–14 or any subsequent tax year, subject to the transitional and saving provision in FA 2013, Sch. 45, para. 154–159.
In s. 2(2), the words "or that part (as the case may be)" inserted by FA 2013, s. 218 and Sch. 45, para. 93(3)(b), with effect in calculating an individual's liability to income tax or capital gains tax for the tax year 2013–14 or any subsequent tax year, subject to the transitional and saving provision in FA 2013, Sch. 45, para. 154–159.
S. 2(2A) and (2B) inserted by FA 2015, s. 37 and Sch. 7, para. 3(2), with effect in relation to disposals made on or after 6 April 2015.
S. 2(4) and (5) substituted for former s. 2(4)–(6) by FA 2008, s. 8 and Sch. 2, para. 24(2) with effect in relation to chargeable gains accruing or treated as accruing in the tax year 2008–09 or any subsequent tax year (FA 2008, Sch. 2, para. 56(3)).
Former s. 2(4) inserted by FA 1998, Sch. 21, para. 2, with effect for the year 1998–99 and subsequent years of assessment.
At the end of former s. 2(5)(a), the word "and" omitted by FA 2002, Sch.11, para. 2(2) and Sch. 40, Pt. 3(4), with effect for the year 2003–04 and subsequent years of assessment or, if the person so elects in accordance with FA 2002, Sch. 11, para. 8, in relation to chargeable gains so accruing to a person in any of the years of assessment 2000–01, 2001–02 and 2002–03.
Former s. 2(5)(aa), and the word "and" appearing immediately thereafter, inserted by FA 2002, Sch. 11, para. 2(2) with effect for the year 2003–04 and subsequent years of assessment or, if the person so elects in accordance with FA 2002, Sch. 11, para. 8, in relation to chargeable gains so accruing to a person in any of the years of assessment 2000–01, 2001–02 and 2002–03.
In former s. 2(5)(b), the words "sections 87 and 89(2)" substituted for the words "sections 77, 86, 87 and 89(2)" by FA 2002, Sch. 11, para. 2(3) with effect for the year 2003–04 and subsequent years of assessment or, if the person so elects in accordance with FA 2002, Sch. 11, para. 8, in relation to chargeable gains so accruing to a person in any of the years of assessment 2000–01, 2001–02 and 2002–03.
S. 2(5) originally inserted by FA 1998, Sch. 21, para. 2, with effect for the year 1998–99 and subsequent years of assessment.
S. 2(6) originally inserted by FA 2002, Sch. 11, para. 2(4) with effect for the year 2003–04 and subsequent years of assessment or, if the person so elects in accordance with FA 2002, Sch. 11, para. 8, in relation to chargeable gains so accruing to a person in any of the years of assessment 2000–01, 2001–02 and 2002–03.
In s. 2(7)(a), reference to s. 77 omitted by FA 2008, s. 8 and Sch. 2, para. 2 with effect from 2008–09 (FA 2008, Sch. 2, para. 22).
S. 2(7)(b)(ii) and preceding word "and" omitted by FA 2008, s. 8 and Sch. 2, para. 24(3)(a) with effect in relation to chargeable gains accruing or treated as accruing in the tax year 2008–09 or any subsequent tax year (FA 2008, Sch. 2, para. 56(3)).
In s. 2(7)(c), the words "(the equal tapered amounts)" omitted by FA 2008, s. 8 and Sch. 2, para. 24(3)(b) with effect in relation to chargeable gains accruing or treated as accruing in the tax year 2008–09 or any subsequent tax year (FA 2008, Sch. 2, para. 56(3)).
In s. 2(7), in the words following para. (c), the words "equal-tapered" omitted byFA 2008, s. 8 and Sch. 2, para. 24(3)(c) with effect in relation to chargeable gains accruing or treated as accruing in the tax year 2008–09 or any subsequent tax year (FA 2008, Sch. 2, para. 56(3)).
S. 2(7) inserted by FA 2002, Sch. 11, para. 2(4) with effect for the year 2003–04 and subsequent years of assessment or, if the person so elects in accordance with FA 2002, Sch. 11, para. 8, in relation to chargeable gains so accruing to a person in any of the years of assessment 2000–01, 2001–02 and 2002–03.
S. 2(7A) inserted by FA 2013, s. 65 and Sch. 25, para. 3, with effect in relation to disposals occurring on or after 6 April 2013.
S. 2(7B) inserted by FA 2015, s. 37 and Sch. 7, para. 3(3), with effect in relation to disposals made on or after 6 April 2015.
S. 2(8) omitted by FA 2008, s. 8 and Sch. 2, para. 24(4) with effect in relation to chargeable gains accruing or treated as accruing in the tax year 2008–09 or any subsequent tax year (FA 2008, Sch. 2, para. 56(3)).
Former s. 2(8) inserted by FA 2002, Sch. 11, para. 2(4) with effect for the year 2003–04 and subsequent years of assessment or, if the person so elects in accordance with FA 2002, Sch. 11, para. 8, in relation to chargeable gains so accruing to a person in any of the years of assessment 2000–01, 2001–02 and 2002–03.

Derivations – S. 2(1): CGTA 1979, s. 2.
S. 2(2): CGTA 1979, s. 4(1).
S. 2(3): CGTA 1979, s. 29(5).

Cross references – S. 2A: application of taper relief.
S. 10: extent of charge on non-resident with UK branch or agency.
S. 10A: extent of charge on temporary non-residents.
S. 62: relief by carry-back on death.
S. 77: charge on settlor who retains an interest rather than the trustees in respect of net gains.
S. 86(1): attribution of net gains to settlor with an interest in a non-resident or dual resident settlement.
S. 87(2), 88(3): attribution of certain net gains to beneficiaries of non-resident or dual resident settlements.
S. 276: extent of charge in respect of the UK territorial shelf and the continental sea.
S. 279A–D: deferred unascertainable consideration – election for treatment of loss.
Sch. 5, para. 1(2): as regards the attribution of certain gains to settlors in non-resident or dual resident settlements, deductions provided for by s. 2(2) are made in respect of disposals of any of the settled property originating from the settlor.
FA 1995, s. 90(5): brought forward losses disregarded in computing available excess relief for post-cessation expenditure.
FA 1995, s. 92(8): brought forward losses disregarded in computing maximum amount of excess relief for post-employment deductions.
FA 2003, s. 195: companies acquiring their own shares.
FA 2004, s. 109: capital gains tax credit etc. for special withholding tax under the EU Savings Directive or similar provisions.
SI 2009/3001, reg. 22: application of s. 2(1) for income tax or corporation tax purposes in relation to offshore income gains.

Extra-statutory concessions – A19: proportion of arrears waived where arises through official error.
D2: person arriving in UK generally taxable only on gains arising from date of arrival; person leaving UK and becoming non-resident and not ordinarily resident not chargeable on disposals arising after date of departure, subject to exceptions.
D18: election by vendor to disregard disposal to extent that purchaser defaults on outstanding balance so that interest in the property reverts to vendor.
D35: when trustees of employee trust within IHTA 1984, s. 86 transfer assets to employees who pay income tax on the benefit, the trustees are not charged to capital gains tax.

Statements of practice – SP 2/99: simplified CGT computation where individuals dispose of shares or units in investment funds which they acquired through monthly savings schemes before 6 April 1999 (superseding SP 2/97).

Notes – S. 9(1): meaning of "resident" and "ordinarily resident".
S. 59: charge to tax on partners.
S. 65: charge in the name of one or more trustees or personal representatives.

S. 69: charge in the name of the trustees in respect of unpaid tax on trust gains on a person receiving the proceeds of sale.
S. 71: unused losses or trustees transferred to person becoming absolutely entitled to settled property.
S. 79B: attribution to trustees of gains of non-resident companies
S. 137(4): charge for unpaid tax where equation of original and new holdings on an exchange, reconstruction etc. nullified by a finding that not effected for bona fide commercial reasons etc.
S. 164K: disapplication of relief for re-investment provisions in relation to foreign residents.
S. 206(2): charge on trustees of premiums trust fund for Lloyd's underwriter, notwithstanding that the underwriter is treated as absolutely entitled to investments in the fund.
S. 271(3), (4): exemption from capital gains tax for a local authority, local authority association, a health service body, trustees to various museums, scientific research organisations, public bodies and certain signatories to INMARSAT or in respect of stock lending, certified contractual savings scheme bonuses and tax-exempt special savings accounts bonuses.
S. 277: double tax relief, applying the provisions of ICTA 1988, s. 788–806.
S. 279: charge in respect of foreign assets delayed until gains become remittable.
S. 282: charge on the donee in the name of the donor in respect of unpaid tax on a gift etc.
ICTA 1988, s. 574(1): no deduction available for loss on disposal of shares in unquoted trading company relieved against income.
TMA 1970, s. 8, 8A, 12: tax returns and information for capital gains tax purposes.
TMA 1970, s. 84: administrative arrangements for charging gains from a UK branch or agency.
Interpretation Act 1978, s. 5 and Sch. 1: the Income Tax Acts mean the enactments relating to income tax.
IHTA 1984, s. 165: in some cases, where a chargeable transfer includes a disposal, capital gains tax borne by the donee is treated as reducing the value transferred.
SI 1990/237, reg. 4: European School exempt from taxes on capital gains.
SI 1991/757, reg. 7 : European Bank for Reconstruction and Development exempt from tax in respect of property, assets etc. within the scope of its Official Activities.

2A Taper relief

2A [Omitted by FA 2008, s. 8 and Sch. 2, para. 25.]

History – S. 2A omitted by FA 2008, s. 8 and Sch. 2, para. 25 with effect in relation to chargeable gains accruing or treated as accruing in the tax year 2008–09 or any subsequent tax year (FA 2008, Sch. 2, para. 56(3)).

2B Persons chargeable to capital gains tax on ATED-related gains

2B(1) A person (other than an excluded person) ("P") is chargeable to capital gains tax in respect of any ATED-related chargeable gain accruing to P in a tax year on a relevant high value disposal.

2B(2) A person is **"excluded"** if the person is an individual, the trustees of a settlement or the personal representatives of a deceased person and–

(a) the gain accrues on a disposal of any partnership assets and the person is a member of the partnership, or

(b) the gain accrues on a disposal of any property held for the purposes of a relevant collective investment scheme and the person is a participant in relation to the scheme.

2B(3) Capital gains tax is charged on the total amount of ATED-related chargeable gains accruing to P in the tax year on relevant high value disposals, after deducting ring-fenced ATED-related allowable losses in relation to that year.

2B(4) Subsections (5) to (7) apply in relation to an ATED-related allowable loss accruing to P in a tax year on a relevant high value disposal.

2B(5) The loss is not allowable as a deduction from ATED-related chargeable gains accruing in any earlier tax year on relevant high value disposals.

2B(6) Relief is not to be given under this Act more than once in respect of the loss or any part of the loss.

2B(7) Relief is not to be given under this Act in respect of the loss if, and so far as, relief has been or may be given in respect of it under the Tax Acts.

2B(8) The only deductions which can be made from ATED-related chargeable gains are those permitted by this section.

2B(9) See section 57A and Schedule 4ZZA for how to compute–

(a) the ATED-related gain or loss accruing on a relevant high value disposal, and

(b) the gain or loss accruing on a relevant high value disposal which is not ATED-related.

2B(10) In this section–

"participant", in relation to a relevant collective investment scheme, is to be read in accordance with section 235 of the Financial Services and Markets Act 2000;

"relevant collective investment scheme" means a collective investment scheme within the meaning of Part 17 of that Act (see section 235 of that Act) other than–

(a) a unit trust scheme within the meaning of that Part (see section 237(1) of that Act), or

(b) an open-ended investment company within the meaning of that Part (see section 236(1) of that Act);

"ring-fenced ATED-related allowable losses", in relation to a tax year, means–

(a) any ATED-related allowable losses accruing to P in the tax year on relevant high value disposals, and

(b) so far as they have not been allowed as a deduction from chargeable gains accruing in any previous tax year, any ATED-related allowable losses accruing to P in any previous tax year (not earlier than the tax year 2013–14) on such disposals.

History – In s. 2B(10), in paragraph (b) of the definition of "ring-fenced ATED-related allowable losses", the words "from chargeable gains accruing in any previous tax year," substituted for the words "from ATED-related chargeable gains accruing in any previous tax year on relevant high value disposals," by FA 2015, s. 37 and Sch. 7, para. 4, with effect in relation to disposals made on or after 6 April 2015.

S. 2B inserted by FA 2013, s. 65 and Sch. 25, para. 4, with effect in relation to disposals occurring on or after 6 April 2013.

2C "Relevant high value disposal"

2C(1) A disposal on which a gain or loss accrues to P is a **"relevant high value disposal"** if conditions A to D are met.

2C(2) Condition A is that the disposal is of the whole or part of a chargeable interest ("the disposed of interest").

2C(3) Condition B is that the disposed of interest has, at any time during the relevant ownership period, been or formed part of a single-dwelling interest.

2C(4) Condition C is that–

(a) P, or

(b) if the disposed of interest is a partnership asset, the responsible partners, or

(c) if the disposed of interest is held for the purposes of a relevant collective investment scheme, the person who has day-to-day control over the management of the property subject to the scheme,

has or have been within the charge to annual tax on enveloped dwellings with respect to that single-dwelling interest on one or more days in the relevant ownership period which are not relievable days in relation to the interest.

2C(5) Condition D is that the amount or value of the consideration for the disposal exceeds the threshold amount (see section 2D).

2C(6) In this section and section 2D–

"chargeable interest" has the same meaning as in Part 3 of the Finance Act 2013 (annual tax on enveloped dwellings) (see section 107 of that Act (chargeable interest));

"dwelling" has the same meaning as in that Part (see section 112 of that Act);

"relevant collective investment scheme" has the same meaning as in section 2B;

"the relevant ownership period" means the period which begins–

(a) if an election has been made under paragraph 5 of Schedule 4ZZA, with the day on which P acquired the chargeable interest or, if later, 31 March 1982, and

(b) in any other case, with the day on which P acquired the chargeable interest or, if later, 6 April in the relevant year,

and ends with the day before the day on which the disposal occurs;

"the relevant year" means–

(a) in Case 1 in paragraph 2 of Schedule 4ZZA, 2013;

(b) in Case 2 in that paragraph, 2015;

(c) in Case 3 in that paragraph, 2016;

"relievable day" means a day which is **"relievable"** by virtue of any of the provisions mentioned in section 132 of the Finance Act 2013 (ATED: effect of reliefs) and in respect of which a claim has been made under section 106(3) of that Act;

"the responsible partners" has the same meaning as in section 96 of that Act;

"single-dwelling interest" has the same meaning as in Part 3 of that Act;

and a reference to being **"within the charge"** to annual tax on enveloped dwellings with respect to a single-dwelling interest is to be read in accordance with section 170(2) of that Act.

2C(7) For the purposes of Condition C–

(a) Part 3 of the Finance Act 2013 applies, in relation to any part of the relevant ownership period falling before 1 April 2013, as if section 94(8)(a) of that Act (first chargeable period for ATED) read "the period beginning with 31 March 1982 and ending with 31 March 1983", and

(b) when determining whether any day falling before 1 April in the relevant year is a relievable day, the definition of **"relievable day"** in subsection (6) above is to read as if the words "and in respect of which a claim has been made under section 106(3) of that Act" were omitted.

History – In s. 2C(6), in the definition of "the relevant ownership period", the words "6 April in the relevant year" substituted for the words "6 April 2013" by FA 2015, s. 38 and Sch. 8, para. 2(2), with effect from 26 March 2015.

In s. 2C(6), the definition of "the relevant year" inserted by FA 2015, s. 38 and Sch. 8, para. 2(3), with effect from 26 March 2015.

In s. 2C(7)(b), the words "1 April in the relevant year" substituted for the words "1 April 2013" by FA 2015, s. 38 and Sch. 8, para. 2(4), with effect from 26 March 2015.
S. 2C inserted by FA 2013, s. 65 and Sch. 25, para. 4, with effect in relation to disposals occurring on or after 6 April 2013.

2D "The threshold amount"

2D(1) This section applies to determine "the threshold amount" in relation to a disposal which meets Conditions A to C in section 2C ("the current disposal").

2D(2) If–

(a) the current disposal is not a part disposal of an asset, and

(b) P has not made any relevant related disposals,

the threshold amount is £500,000, subject to subsection (5) (joint interests).

2D(3) If paragraphs (a) and (b) of subsection (2) do not both apply, the threshold amount is the relevant fraction of £500,000, subject to subsection (5) (joint interests).

2D(4) **"The relevant fraction"** is–

$$\frac{C}{TMV}$$

where–

"C" is the amount or value of the consideration for the current disposal;

"TMV" is what would be the market value, at the time of the current disposal, of a notional asset comprising–

(a) the disposed of interest (see section 2C(2)),

(b) if the current disposal is a part disposal, any part of the chargeable interest held by P that remains undisposed of immediately following that part disposal,

(c) any chargeable interest (or part of a chargeable interest) which was the subject of a relevant related disposal, and

(d) any chargeable interest (or part of a chargeable interest) held by P at the time of the current disposal which, if P had disposed of it at that time, would have been the subject of a relevant related disposal.

2D(5) If the disposed of interest is a share of the whole of–

(a) a chargeable interest, or

(b) a part of a chargeable interest,

subsections (2) and (3) have effect as if the references to **"£500,000"** were to the joint share fraction of that amount.

2D(6) The joint share fraction is the fraction of the whole of the chargeable interest or part represented by the disposed of interest.

2D(7) **"Relevant related disposal"**, in relation to the current disposal, means any disposal by P which–

(a) meets Conditions A to C in section 2C in circumstances where the single-dwelling interest referred to in Condition C is–

(i) the single-dwelling interest by virtue of which Condition C is met in relation to the current disposal, or

(ii) another single-dwelling interest in the same dwelling as that interest, and

(b) was made in the period of 6 years ending with the day on which the current disposal occurs, but not before 6 April 2013.

History – In s. 2D(2), the figure "£500,000" substituted for the figure "£1 million" by FA 2015, s. 38 and Sch. 8, para. 4(2), with effect in relation to disposals occurring on or after 6 April 2016.
In s. 2D(2), the figure "£1 million" substituted for the figure "£2 million" by FA 2015, s. 38 and Sch. 8, para. 3(2), with effect in relation to disposals occurring in the tax year 2015–16.
In s. 2D(3), the figure "£500,000" substituted for the figure "£1 million" by FA 2015, s. 38 and Sch. 8, para. 4(3), with effect in relation to disposals occurring on or after 6 April 2016.
In s. 2D(3), the figure "£1 million" substituted for the figure "£2 million" by FA 2015, s. 38 and Sch. 8, para. 3(3), with effect in relation to disposals occurring in the tax year 2015–16.
In s. 2D(5), the figure "£500,000" substituted for the figure "£1 million" by FA 2015, s. 38 and Sch. 8, para. 4(4), with effect in relation to disposals occurring on or after 6 April 2016.
In s. 2D(5), the figure "£1 million" substituted for the figure "£2 million" by FA 2015, s. 38 and Sch. 8, para. 3(4), with effect in relation to disposals occurring in the tax year 2015–16.
S. 2D inserted by FA 2013, s. 65 and Sch. 25, para. 4, with effect in relation to disposals occurring on or after 6 April 2013.

2E Restriction of losses

2E(1) This section applies where (ignoring this section)–

(a) a disposal would be a relevant high value disposal, but for a failure to meet condition D in section 2C,

(b) if it were a relevant high value disposal, an ATED-related loss would accrue to a person (other than an excluded person) in a tax year on the disposal, and

(c) the total of the sums allowable as a deduction under section 38 in relation to the disposal exceeds the threshold amount in relation to the disposal.

2E(2) For the purposes of this Act–

(a) the disposal is to be treated as a relevant high value disposal (and section 57A and Schedule 4ZZA apply accordingly), and

(b) the ATED-related loss which accrues on the disposal is to be restricted to the amount which would have been that loss had the consideration for the disposal been £1 greater than the threshold amount in relation to the disposal.

2E(3) In a case where paragraph 2 of Schedule 4ZZA applies (calculation of gains or losses on disposals of assets held on 5 April 2013 etc), the reference in subsection (1)(c) to the disposal is to be read as a reference to the notional disposal referred to in paragraph 3(2) of that Schedule (disposal on which notional post-commencement gain or loss accrues).

2E(4) Nothing in subsection (2)(b) restricts any loss which is not ATED-related, or affects any gain (whether or not ATED-related), accruing on the relevant high value disposal.

2E(5) In this section–

"excluded" has the meaning given by section 2B(2);

"the threshold amount" has the meaning given by section 2D.

History – In s. 2E(3), the word "etc" inserted, and the words "post-commencement" substituted for the words "post-April 2013" by FA 2015, s. 38 and Sch. 8, para. 5, with effect from 26 March 2015.
S. 2E inserted by FA 2013, s. 65 and Sch. 25, para. 4, with effect in relation to disposals occurring on or after 6 April 2013.

2F Tapering relief for gains

2F(1) This section applies to an ATED-related gain which accrues on a relevant high value disposal and is chargeable to capital gains tax by virtue of section 2B.

2F(2) There is excluded from the gain so much of it as exceeds five-thirds of the difference between–

(a) the amount or value of the consideration, and

(b) the threshold amount (within the meaning of section 2D) in relation to the disposal.

2F(3) But where the relevant fraction is less than 1, subsection (2) has effect as if the amount determined under that subsection were the relevant fraction of that amount.

2F(4) **"The relevant fraction"**–

(a) in a case where the ATED-related gain is determined in accordance with paragraph 3 of Schedule 4ZZA, has the meaning given by paragraph 3(4) of that Schedule, and

(b) in a case where the ATED-related gain is determined in accordance with paragraph 6 of that Schedule, has the same meaning as in paragraph 6(5)(a) of that Schedule.

2F(5) Nothing in this section restricts any gain which is not ATED-related, or affects any loss (whether or not ATED-related), accruing on the relevant high value disposal.

History – S. 2F inserted by FA 2013, s. 65 and Sch. 25, para. 4, with effect in relation to disposals occurring on or after 6 April 2013.

3 Annual exempt amount

3(1) An individual shall not be chargeable to capital gains tax in respect of so much of his taxable amount for any year of assessment as does not exceed the exempt amount for the year.

3(1A) Subsection (1) does not apply to an individual for a tax year if section 809B of ITA 2007 (claim for remittance basis to apply) applies to the individual for that year.

3(2) The exempt amount for a tax year is £11,100.

3(3) If there is a relevant increase in CPI in relation to a tax year–

(a) the exempt amount is to be increased in accordance with Steps 1 and 2, and

(b) subsection (2) has effect from then on (for that and subsequent tax years) as if it referred to the increased amount,

unless Parliament otherwise determines.

3(3A) There is a relevant increase in CPI in relation to a tax year if the consumer prices index for the September before the start of the tax year is higher than it was for the previous September.

3(3B) Steps 1 and 2 are–

Step 1

Increase the exempt amount for the previous tax year by the same percentage as the percentage of the relevant increase in CPI.

Step 2

If the result of Step 1 is not a multiple of £100, round it up to the nearest multiple of £100.

3(4) If there is a relevant increase in CPI in relation to a tax year, the Treasury must before the start of that tax year make an order showing the amount arrived at as a result of Steps 1 and 2.

3(5) For the purposes of this section an individual's taxable amount for any year of assessment is (what would apart from this section be) the total of the amounts for that year on which that individual is chargeable to capital gains tax in accordance with either (or both) of–

(a) section 2 (gains, other than ATED-related gains and NRCGT gains, chargeable to capital gains tax), and

(b) section 14D (NRCGT gains chargeable to capital gains tax).

3(5A) Where, in the case of any individual, the amount of the adjusted net gains for any year of assessment is equal to or less than the exempt amount for that year, no deduction shall be made for that year in respect of–

(a) any allowable losses carried forward from a previous year; or

(b) any allowable losses carried back from a subsequent year in which the individual dies.

3(5B) Where, in the case of any individual, the amount of the adjusted net gains for any year of assessment exceeds the exempt amount for the year, the deductions made for that year in respect of allowable losses falling within subsection (5A)(a) or (b) above shall not be greater than the excess.

3(5BA) In this section, **"adjusted net gains"**, in relation to a tax year and an individual, means–

(a) if the residence condition is met (see section 2(1A)) and the year is not a split year as respects the individual, the section 2 adjusted net gains;

(b) if the residence condition is not met, the section 14D adjusted net gains;

(c) if the residence condition is met and the year is a split year as respects the individual, the total of the section 2 adjusted net gains (if any) and the section 14D adjusted net gains (if any).

3(5C) In subsection (5BA) **"section 2 adjusted net gains"**, in relation to an individual and a tax year, means the amount given in the individual's case by–

(a) taking the amount for that year from which the deductions for which section 2(2)(a) and (b) provides are to be made;

(aa) if section 16ZB (certain chargeable gains charged on remittance basis) applies for that year, deducting the amount of the relevant gains (within the meaning of that section),

(b) deducting (from the amount mentioned in paragraph (a), as reduced under paragraph (aa)) only the amounts falling to be deducted in accordance with section 2(2)(a); and

(c) if section 2(4) applies for that year[,], adding whichever is the smaller of the exempt amount for that year and the amount mentioned in section 2(4)(b)(ii).

3(5D) In subsection (5BA) **"section 14D adjusted net gains"**, in relation to an individual and a tax year, means the amount given in the individual's case by–

(a) taking the amount from which the deductions provided for by paragraphs (a) and (b) of subsection (2) of section 14D are to be made, and

(b) deducting only the amounts falling to be deducted in accordance with paragraph (a) of that subsection.

3(6) [Omitted by FA 2003, Sch. 28, para. 3(2) and repealed by FA 2003, Sch. 43, Pt. 3(7).]

3(7) For the year of assessment in which an individual dies and for the next 2 following years, subsections (1) to (5D) above shall apply to his personal representatives as they apply to an individual.

3(7A) As they apply by virtue of subsection (7) above–

(a) subsection (5A) has effect with the omission of paragraph (b), and

(b) subsection (5B) has effect with the omission of the words "or (b)".

3(8) Schedule 1 shall have effect as respects the application of this section to trustees.

History – S. 3(1A) inserted by FA 2008, s. 25 and Sch. 7, para. 56(2) with effect from 2008–09 (FA 2008, Sch. 7, para. 81).
In s. 3(2), the figure "£11,100" substituted for "£11,000" by FA 2014, s. 9(1), with effect for the tax year 2015–16 and subsequent tax years.

In s. 3(2), the figure "£11,000" substituted for "£10,900" by FA 2014, s. 8(1), with effect for the tax year 2014–15.
In s. 3(2), the exempt amount for the tax year 2013–14 is £10,900, by virtue of SI 2013/662, art. 2.
In s. 3(2), "£10,600" substituted for "£11,200" by FA 2012, s. 34(2), with effect for 2012–13 and subsequent tax years.
In s. 3(2), the exempt amount for 2012–13 is £11,200, by virtue of SI 2012/881.
S. 3(2) substituted by FA 2011, s. 8(2), with effect for the tax year 2011–12 and subsequent tax years.
In s. 3(2), the exempt amount for 2011–12 is £10,600, by virtue of SI 2011/899.
In s. 3(2), the exempt amount for 2010–11 is £10,100, by virtue of SI 2010/923.
In s. 3(2), the exempt amount for 2009–10 is £10,100, by virtue of SI 2009/824.
In s. 3(2), the exempt amount for 2008–09 is £9,600, by virtue of SI 2008/708.
In s. 3(2), the exempt amount for 2007–08 is £9,200, by virtue of SI 2007/942.
In s. 3(2), the exempt amount for 2006–07 is £8,800, by virtue of SI 2006/871. Previous amount of £8,500 substituted for the year 2005–06 by SI 2005/721.
In s. 3(3), (3A), (3B) and (4), "CPI" substituted for "RPI" by FA 2012, s. 34(3)(a), with effect for the tax year 2013–14 and subsequent tax years.
S. 3(3), (3A), (3B) and (4) substituted for s. 3(3) and (4) by FA 2011, s. 8(3), with effect for the tax year 2012–13 and subsequent tax years. S. 3(3) does not apply in relation to the tax year 2012–13 (FA 2012, s. 34(6)).
In former s. 3(3), the word "September" substituted (in each place) for "December" by FA 1993, s. 83, in relation to 1994–95 and subsequent years of assessment.
In s. 3(3A), "consumer prices index" substituted for "retail prices index" by FA 2012, s. 34(3)(b), with effect for the tax year 2013–14 and subsequent tax years.
In s. 3(5), the words "is (what would apart from this section be)" and para. (a) and (b), substituted for the words "is the amount which is (apart from this section) the amount for that year on which that individual is chargeable to capital gains tax in accordance with section 2." by FA 2015, s. 37 and Sch. 7, para. 5(2), with effect in relation to disposalsmade on or after 6 April 2015.
S. 3(5) amended (by removal of order of adjustments in former para. (a)–(c)) by FA 2008, s. 8 and Sch. 2, para. 26(2) with effect in relation to chargeable gains accruing or treated as accruing in the tax year 2008–09 or any subsequent tax year (FA 2008, Sch. 2, para. 56(3)).
S. 3(5), (5A) and (5B) (together with (5C)) substituted for former s. 3(5) by FA 1998, Sch. 21, para. 3 with effect for the year 1998–99 and subsequent years of assessment.
S. 3(5BA) inserted by FA 2015, s. 37 and Sch. 7, para. 5(3), with effect in relation to disposals made on or after 6 April 2015.
In s. 3(5C), the words "In subsection (5BA) **"section 2 adjusted net gains"**, in relation to an individual and a tax year, means the amount given in the individual's case by–" substituted for the words "In subsections (5A) and (5B) above the references, in relation to any individual's case, to the adjusted net gains for any year are references to the amount given in his case by–" by FA 2015, s. 37 and Sch. 7, para. 5(4), with effect in relation to disposals made on or after 6 April 2015.
S. 3(5C)(aa) inserted by FA 2008, s. 25 and Sch. 7, para. 56(3)(a) with effect from 2008–09 (FA 2008, Sch. 7, para. 81).
In s. 3(5C)(b), the words "(from the amount mentioned in paragraph (a), as reduced under paragraph (aa))" inserted by FA 2008, s. 25 and Sch. 7, para. 56(3)(b) with effect from 2008–09 (FA 2008, Sch. 7, para. 81).
In s. 3(5C)(c), the words "if section 2(4) applies for that year," and "mentioned in section 2(4)(b)(ii)" substituted for "in a year in which any amount falls to be brought into account by virtue of section 2(5)(b)" and "falling to be so brought into account" respectively by FA 2008, s. 8 and Sch. 2, para. 26(3) with effect in relation to chargeable gains accruing or treated as accruing in the tax year 2008–09 or any subsequent tax year (FA 2008, Sch. 2, para. 56(3)).
S. 3(5C) (together with s. 3(5), (5A) and (5B) substituted for former s. 3(5) by FA 1998, Sch. 21, para. 3 with effect for the year 1998–99 and subsequent years of assessment.
S. 3(5D) inserted by FA 2015, s. 37 and Sch. 7, para. 5(5), with effect in relation to disposals made on or after 6 April 2015
S. 3(6) omitted by FA 2003, s. 159 and Sch. 28, para. 3(2), and repealed by FA 2003, s. 216 and Sch. 43, Pt. 3(7), which apply, by virtue of FA 2003, Sch. 28, para. 3(7), in relation to any notice given under section 8 or 8A of the Taxes Management Act 1970 in relation to the year 2003–04 or any subsequent year of assessment.
In s. 3(7), "(5D)" substituted for "(5C)" by FA 2015, s. 37 and Sch. 7, para. 5(6), with effect in relation to disposals made on or after 6 April 2015.
In s. 3(7), the words "subsections (1) to (5C)" substituted for the words "subsections (1) to (6)" by FA 2003, s. 159 and Sch. 28, para. 3(3) which apply, by virtue of FA 2003, Sch. 28, para. 3(7), in relation to any notice given under section 8 or 8A of the Taxes Management Act 1970 in relation to the year 2003–04 or any subsequent year of assessment.
S. 3(7A) inserted by FA 2003, s. 159 and Sch. 28, para. 3(4) which, by virtue of FA 2003, Sch. 28, para. 3(8), shall be deemed always to have had effect.

Derivations – S. 3(1): CGTA 1979, s. 5(1), as substituted by FA 1980, s. 77(2) and amended by FA 1982, s. 80(1)(a).
S. 3(2) (as originally enacted): CGTA 1979, s. 5(1A), as inserted by FA 1982, s. 80(2) and amended by SI 1991/736.
Former s. 3(3) (as originally enacted), (4): CGTA 1979, s. 5(1B), (1C), as inserted by FA 1982, s. 80(2).
S. 3(5): CGTA 1979, s. 5(4), as amended by FA 1982, s. 80(1)(a).
S. 3(6): CGTA 1979, s. 5(5), as amended by FA 1982, s. 80(1)(b).
S. 3(7): CGTA 1979, Sch. 1, para. 4.
S. 3(8): CGTA 1979, s. 5(6).

Cross references – S. 77: charge on settlor who retains an interest rather than the trustees in respect of net gains disregarding s. 3.
S. 279B(1): deferred unascertainable consideration – election for treatment of loss.
S. 287(4): negative resolution procedure of House of Commons not to apply to statutory instrument effecting order under s. 3(4).
Sch. 1, para. 1: application of exempt amount in cases involving settled property.
Sch. 5, para. 1: as regards the attribution of certain gains to settlors in non-resident or dual resident settlements, the effect of s. 3 is ignored.
TMA 1970, s. 8: personal income tax return requirements, adapted to capital gains tax by s. 12 of that Act.
FA 1991, s. 72(4): maximum amount of trading loss treated as allowable loss preserves loss in favour of using the annual exemption.
FA 1995, s. 90(5): annual exempt amount disregarded in computing available excess relief for post-cessation expenditure.
FA 1995, s. 92(8): annual exempt amount disregarded in computing maximum amount of excess relief for post-employment deductions.
FA 2004, s. 109: capital gains tax credit etc. for special withholding tax under the EU Savings Directive or similar provisions.
FA 2014, s. 8(2): s. 3(3) does not apply for the tax year 2014–15.
FA 2014, s. 9(2): s. 3(3) does not apply in relation to the tax year 2015–16.

Notes – Former s. 3(3) does not apply for the tax year 2011–12 (FA 2011, s. 8(5)).
In s. 3(5C)(c), the amendment by FA 2008, s. 8 and Sch. 2, para. 26(3)(a) appears to have left in a surplus comma.

3A Reporting limits

3A(1) Where in the case of an individual–

(a) the amount of chargeable gains accruing to him in any year of assessment or, if that year is a split year as respects the individual, the UK part of that year does not exceed the exempt amount for that year, and

(b) the aggregate amount or value of the consideration for all chargeable disposals of assets made by him in that year or, as the case may be, that part of the year does not exceed four times the exempt amount for that year,

a statement to that effect is sufficient compliance with so much of any notice under section 8 of the Management Act as requires information for the purposes of establishing the amount in which he is chargeable to capital gains tax for that year.

3A(2) For the purposes of subsection (1)(a) above–

(a) [omitted by FA 2008, s. 8 and Sch. 2, para. 27(a);]

(b) the amount of chargeable gains accruing to an individual in a year of assessment (or the UK part of such a year) for which a deduction falls to be made in respect of allowable losses is the amount before the deduction.

3A(3) For the purposes of subsection (1)(b) above a **"chargeable disposal"** is any disposal other than–

(a) a disposal on which any gain accruing is not a chargeable gain, or

(b) a disposal the consideration for which is treated by virtue of section 58 (spouses and civil partners) as being such that neither a gain nor a loss would accrue.

3A(4) Subsection (1) above applies to personal representatives (for the year of assessment in which the individual in question dies and for the next 2 following years) as it applies to an individual.

3A(5) Subsection (1) above applies to the trustees of a settlement in accordance with Schedule 1.

3A(5A) Subsection (1) does not apply to an individual for a tax year if–

(a) section 809B of ITA 2007 (claim for remittance basis to apply), or

(b) section 16ZB below (certain chargeable gains charged on remittance basis),

applies to the individual for that year.

3A(6) In this section **"exempt amount"** has the meaning given by section 3 (read, where appropriate, with Schedule 1).

History – In s. 3A(1)(a) the words "or, if that year is a split year as respects the individual, the UK part of that year" inserted by FA 2013, s. 218 and Sch. 45, para. 94(2)(a), with effect in calculating an individual's liability to income tax or capital gains tax for the tax year 2013–14 or any subsequent tax year, subject to the transitional and saving provision in FA 2013, Sch. 45, para. 154–159.
In s. 3A(1)(b) the words "or, as the case may be, that part of the year" inserted by FA 2013, s. 218 and Sch. 45, para. 94(2)(b), with effect in calculating an individual's liability to income tax or capital gains tax for the tax year 2013–14 or any subsequent tax year, subject to the transitional and saving provision in FA 2013, Sch. 45, para. 154–159.
S. 3A(2)(a) omitted by FA 2008, s. 8 and Sch. 2, para. 27(a) with effect in relation to chargeable gains accruing or treated as accruing in the tax year 2008–09 or any subsequent tax year (FA 2008, Sch. 2, para. 56(3)).
In s. 3A(2)(b) the words "(or the UK part of such a year)" inserted by FA 2013, s. 218 and Sch. 45, para. 94(3), with effect in calculating an individual's liability to income tax or capital gains tax for the tax year 2013–14 or any subsequent tax year, subject to the transitional and saving provision in FA 2013, Sch. 45, para. 154–159.
In s. 3A(2)(b), the words "a deduction falls to be made in respect of allowable losses is the amount before the deduction" substituted for "such a deduction does fall to be made is the amount before deduction of losses or any reduction for taper relief" amended by FA 2008, s. 8 and Sch. 2, para. 27(b) with effect in relation to chargeable gains accruing or treated as accruing in the tax year 2008–09 or any subsequent tax year (FA 2008, Sch. 2, para. 56(3)).
In s. 3A(3)(b) the words "(spouses and civil partners)" substituted for the words "(husband and wife)" by SI 2005/3229, reg. 106, with effect from 5 December 2005.
S. 3A(5A) inserted by FA 2008, s. 25 and Sch. 7, para. 57 with effect from 2008–09 (FA 2008, Sch. 7, para. 81).
S. 3A inserted by FA 2003, s. 159 and Sch. 28, para. 1 which apply, by virtue of FA 2003, Sch. 28, para. 7, in relation to any notice under s. 8, or as the case may be, s.8A, of the Taxes Management Act 1970 given in relation to the year 2003–04 or any subsequent year of assessment.

Cross references – Sch. 1, para. 1(5A) and 2(6A): when applied to the trustees of a settlement the reference to TMA 1970, s. 8 in s. 3A(1) above shall be read as a reference to TMA 1970, s. 8A.
Sch. 1: application of exempt amount and reporting limits in cases involving settled property.

4 Rates of capital gains tax

4(1) This section makes provision about the rates at which capital gains tax is charged, but is subject to section 169N (rate in case of claim for entrepreneurs' relief) and section 169VC (rate in case of claim for investors' relief).

4(2) Subject to the following provisions of this section and section 4BA, the rate of capital gains tax–

(a) in respect of upper rate gains accruing to a person in a tax year, is 18%, and

(b) in respect of gains accruing to a person in a tax year which are not upper rate gains, is 10%.

4(2A) In this section **"upper rate gains"** means–

(a) residential property gains (see section 4BB),

(b) NRCGT gains (see section 14D), and

(c) carried interest gains (see subsections (12) and (13)).

4(3) The rate of capital gains tax in respect of gains accruing in a tax year to the trustees of a settlement or the personal representatives of a deceased person–

(a) in respect of upper rate gains, is 28%, and

(b) in respect of gains which are not upper rate gains, is 20%.

4(3A) The rate of capital gains tax in respect of gains chargeable under section 2B accruing to a person in a tax year is 28%.

4(3B) The rate of capital gains tax is 20% in respect of–

(a) gains chargeable under section 14D accruing to a company in a tax year, and

(b) gains chargeable under section 188D accruing in a tax year to the relevant body of an NRCGT group (as defined in that section).

4(4) If income tax is chargeable at the higher rate, the Scottish higher rate or the dividend upper rate in respect of any part of the income of an individual for a tax year, the rate of capital gains tax–

(a) in respect of upper rate gains accruing to the individual in the tax year, is 28%, and

(b) in respect of gains accruing to the individual in the tax year which are not upper rate gains, is 20%.

4(5) If no income tax is chargeable at the higher rate, the Scottish higher rate or the dividend upper rate in respect of the income of an individual for a tax year, but the amount on which the individual is chargeable to capital gains tax exceeds the unused part of the individual's basic rate band, the rate of capital gains tax on the excess is (subject to section 4BA) 20%.

4(6) Subsection (6A) applies for the purposes of subsection (5) where–

(a) there is an excess as mentioned in that subsection ("the higher-rate excess"), and

(b) the amount on which the individual is chargeable to capital gains tax for the tax year includes any special rate gains, that is, gains which are–

(i) chargeable to capital gains tax at the rate in section 169N(3), or

(ii) chargeable to capital gains tax at the rate in section 169VC(2).

4(6A) Where this subsection applies–

(a) if the total amount of the special rate gains exceeds the unused part of the individual's basic rate band, the higher-rate excess is to be treated as reduced by the amount by which the special rate gains exceed that unused part;

(b) if not, the higher-rate excess is to be treated as consisting of gains other than the special rate gains.

4(7) Any reference in this section to the unused part of an individual's basic rate band is a reference to the amount by which the basic rate limit exceeds the individual's Step 3 income.

4(8) For the purposes of this section, **"the Step 3 income"** of an individual means the individual's net income less allowances deducted at Step 3 of the calculation in section 23 of ITA 2007 for the purpose of calculating the individual's income tax liability.

4(9) Section 989 of ITA 2007 (the definitions) applies for the purposes of this section and section 4BA as it applies for income tax purposes.

4(10) [Prospectively inserted – see note below.]

4(11) [Prospectively inserted – see note below.]

4(12) In subsection (2A)(c) "carried interest gains" means–

(a) gains treated as accruing under section 103KA(2) or (3), and

(b) gains accruing to an individual as a result of carried interest arising to the individual where–

(i) the individual performs investment management services directly or indirectly in respect of an investment scheme under arrangements not involving a partnership,

(ii) the carried interest arises to the individual under the arrangements, and

(iii) the carried interest does not constitute a co-investment repayment or return.

4(13) For the purposes of subsection (12)(b)–

(a) "carried interest", in relation to any arrangements, has the same meaning as in section 809EZB of ITA 2007 (see sections 809EZC and 809EZD of that Act);

(b) carried interest "arises" to an individual if it arises to him or her for the purposes of Chapter 5E of Part 13 of ITA 2007;

(c) "arrangements", "investment management services" and "investment scheme" have the same meanings as in that Chapter (see sections 809EZA(6) and 809EZE of that Act);

(d) "co-investment repayment or return" has the same meaning as in section 103KA.

Prospective amendments – In s. 4(4) and (5) the words ", the default higher rate, the savings higher rate" inserted after the words "at the higher rate" by FA 2016, s. 6(23), with effect for the tax year appointed under SCA 2016, s. 13(15) and for subsequent tax years. In s. 4(4), the words ", the Welsh higher rate" inserted before the words "or the dividend" by WA 2014, s. 9(14), with effect from a date to be appointed under s. 14.

In s. 4(4), the words ", the Scottish higher rate" omitted by SCA 2016, s. 15(3), with effect in relation to the tax year appointed by the Treasury under SCA 2016, s. 13(15) and subsequent tax years.

In s. 4(5), the words ", the Welsh higher rate" inserted before the words "or the dividend" by WA 2014, s. 9(14), with effect from a date to be appointed under s. 14.
In s. 4(5), the words ", the Scottish higher rate" omitted by SCA 2016, s. 15(3), with effect in relation to the tax year appointed by the Treasury under SCA 2016, s. 13(15) and subsequent tax years.
S. 4(10) (as amended by FA 2016, s. 83(11)) and (11) inserted by SCA 2016, s. 15(4), with effect in relation to the tax year appointed by the Treasury under SCA 2016, s. 13(15) and subsequent tax years.

History – In s. 4(1), the words "and section 169VC (rate in case of claim for investors' relief)" inserted by FA 2016, s. 83(2), with effect in relation to gains accruing on or after 6 April 2016.
In s. 4(2), the words "and section 4BA" inserted and para. (a) and (b) substituted for the words "in respect of gains accruing to a person in a tax year is 18%" by FA 2016, s. 83(3), with effect in relation to gains accruing on or after 6 April 2016.
S. 4(2A) inserted by FA 2016, s. 83(4), with effect in relation to gains accruing on or after 6 April 2016.
S. 4(3) substituted by FA 2016, s. 83(5), with effect in relation to gains accruing on or after 6 April 2016. Former s. 4(3) read as follows:
"**4(3)** The rate of capital gains tax in respect of gains accruing to–
(a) the trustees of a settlement, or
(b) the personal representatives of a deceased person,
in a tax year is 28%.".
S. 4(3A) inserted by FA 2013, s. 65 and Sch. 25, para. 5, with effect in relation to disposals occurring on or after 6 April 2013.
S. 4(3B) inserted by FA 2015, s. 37 and Sch. 7, para. 6, with effect in relation to disposals made on or after 6 April 2015.
In s. 4(4), para. (a) and (b) substituted for the words "in respect of gains accruing to the individual in the year is 28%" by FA 2016, s. 83(6), with effect in relation to gains accruing on or after 6 April 2016.
In s. 4(4), the words ", the Scottish higher rate" inserted after the words "the higher rate" by FA 2014, s. 296 and Sch. 38, para. 15(2), with effect in relation to the tax year 2016-17 and subsequent tax years (SI 2015/2000, art. 3).
In s. 4(5), the words "(subject to section 4BA) 20%" substituted for the words "28%" by FA 2016, s. 83(7), with effect in relation to gains accruing on or after 6 April 2016.
In s. 4(5), the words ", the Scottish higher rate" inserted after the words "the higher rate" by FA 2014, s. 296 and Sch. 38, para. 15(2), with effect in relation to the tax year 2016-17 and subsequent tax years (SI 2015/2000, art. 3).
S. 4(6) and (6A) substituted for former s. 4(6) by FA 2016, s. 83(8), with effect in relation to gains accruing on or after 6 April 2016. Former s. 4(6) read as follows:
"**4(6)** For the purposes of subsection (5), gains which are chargeable to capital gains tax at the rate in section 169N(3) are to be treated as forming the lowest part of the amount on which an individual is chargeable to capital gains tax.".
In s. 4(7), the words "Any reference in this section" substituted for the words "The reference in subsection (5)" by FA 2016, s. 83(9), with effect in relation to gains accruing on or after 6 April 2016.
In s. 4(9), the words "and section 4BA" inserted by FA 2016, s. 83(10), with effect in relation to gains accruing on or after 6 April 2016.
S. 4(12) inserted by FA 2016, s. 83(12), with effect in relation to gains accruing on or after 6 April 2016.
S. 4(13) inserted by FA 2016, s. 83(12), with effect in relation to gains accruing on or after 6 April 2016.
S. 4 and 4A substituted for former s. 4 by F(No. 2)A 2010, s. 2 and Sch. 1, para. 2, with effect in relation to gains accruing on or after 23 June 2010, subject to transitional provisions in F(No. 2)A 2010, Sch. 1, para. 18–22.
S. 4 previously substituted by FA 2008, s. 8(1) with effect from 2008–09.

Derivations – FA 1988, s. 98.

Other material – IR press release, 28 February 1998: Scottish variable rate (SVR) not to be extended to capital gains tax.

4A Section 4: special cases

4A(1) Subsection (2) applies if for a tax year–

(a) a person is entitled, by virtue of section 539 of ITTOIA 2005 (gains from contracts for life insurance etc), to relief by reference to the amount of a deficiency, or

(b) the residuary income of an estate is treated, by virtue of section 669(1) and (2) of that Act (reduction in residuary income: inheritance tax on accrued income), as reduced so as to reduce a person's income by any amount for the purposes of extra liability.

4A(2) Section 4(7) is to have effect as if the person's Step 3 income for the year were reduced by the amount of the deficiency mentioned in subsection (1)(a) or the amount mentioned in subsection (1)(b) (as the case may be).

4A(3) Subsections (4) and (5) apply if, by virtue of section 465 of ITTOIA 2005 (gains from contracts for life insurance etc), a person's total income for a tax year is deemed to include any amount or amounts.

4A(4) Section 4(7) is to have effect as if the person's Step 3 income for the year included not the whole of the amount or amounts concerned but only the annual equivalent within the meaning of section 536(1) of that Act or the total annual equivalent within the meaning of section 537 of that Act (as the case may be).

4A(5) If–

(a) relief is given under section 535 of that Act, and

(b) the calculation under section 536(1) or 537 of that Act (as the case may be) does not involve the higher rate of income tax,

section 4(4) and (5) and section 4BA(1) are to have effect as if no income tax were chargeable at the higher rate, the Scottish higher rate or the dividend upper rate in respect of the person's income.

Prospective amendments – In s. 4A(5), the words ", the Welsh higher rate" inserted before the words "or the dividend" by WA 2014, s. 9(15), with effect from a date to be appointed under s. 14.
In s. 4A(5), the words ", the Scottish higher rate" omitted by SCA 2016, s. 15(5), with effect in relation to the tax year appointed by the Treasury under SCA 2016, s. 13(15) and subsequent tax years.

History – In s. 4A(5) the words "and section 4BA(1)" inserted by FA 2016, s. 83(13), with effect in relation to gains accruing on or after 6 April 2016.
In s. 4A(5), the words ", the Scottish higher rate" inserted after the words "at the higher rate" by FA 2014, s. 296 and Sch. 38, para. 15(3), with effect in relation to the tax year 2016–17 and subsequent tax years (SI 2015/2000, art.3).
S. 4 and 4A substituted for former s. 4 by F(No. 2)A 2010, s. 2 and Sch. 1, para. 2, with effect in relation to gains accruing on or after 23 June 2010, subject to transitional provisions in F(No. 2)A 2010, Sch. 1, para. 18–22.

4B Deduction of losses etc in most beneficial way

4B(1) Where it is necessary to determine–

(a) from which chargeable gains an allowable loss accruing to a person is to be deducted, or

(b) which allowable losses are to be deducted from any chargeable gains accruing to a person,

(including in a case falling within subsection (2)), the losses concerned may be used in whichever way is most beneficial to that person.

4B(2) Where the gains accruing to a person in a tax year are (apart from this section) chargeable to capital gains tax at different rates, the exempt amount under section 3 may be used in respect of those gains in whichever way is most beneficial to that person.

4B(3) This section is subject to any enactment which contains a limitation on the gains from which allowable losses may be deducted.

History – S. 4B substituted by FA 2015, s. 37 and Sch. 7, para. 7, with effect in relation to disposals made on or after 6 April 2015.

4BA Rates, and use of unused basic rate band, in certain cases

4BA(1) This section applies where an individual is chargeable to capital gains tax in respect of gains accruing in a tax year and–

(a) no income tax is chargeable at the higher rate, the Welsh higher rate or the dividend upper rate in respect of the income of the individual for the tax year,

(b) the amount on which the individual is chargeable to capital gains tax for the tax year ("the chargeable gains amount") exceeds the unused part of the individual's basic rate band, and

(c) all or part of the chargeable gains amount consists of upper rate gains.

4BA(2) In the following provisions of this section **"the available gains"** means the gains on which the individual is chargeable to capital gains tax for the tax year, excluding any special rate gains.

4BA(3) The available gains not used by the individual under subsection (4) are to be charged to capital gains tax–

(a) to the extent that they consist of upper rate gains, at the rate in section 4(4)(a);

(b) to the extent that they consist of gains which are not upper rate gains, at the rate in section 4(5).

4BA(4) The individual may, subject to subsection (5) (which limits the overall amount that can be used under this subsection)–

(a) use any of the available gains that are upper rate gains to be charged at the rate in section 4(2)(a);

(b) use any of the available gains that are not upper rate gains to be charged at the rate in section 4(2)(b).

4BA(5) The total amount of gains used under subsection (4) must equal the qualifying amount.

4BA(6) The **"qualifying amount"** is the unused part of the individual's basic rate band less the total amount of any special rate gains.

4BA(7) If special rate gains are included in the chargeable gains amount, subsection (4) applies only if the unused part of the individual's basic rate band exceeds the total amount of the special rate gains.

4BA(8) In this section–

"upper rate gains" has the same meaning as in section 4;

"special rate gains" has the same meaning as in section 4(6);

"the unused part of the individual's basic rate band" has the same meaning as in section 4.

Prospective amendments – In s. 4BA(1) the words ", the default higher rate, the savings higher rate" inserted after the words "at the higher rate" by FA 2016, s. 6(23) with effect for the tax year appointed under SCA 2016, s. 13(15) and for subsequent tax years.

History – S. 4BA inserted by FA 2016, s. 83(14), with effect in relation to gains accruing on or after 6 April 2016.

Cross references – FA 2016, s. 83(18): transitional rules as regards Wales.
FA 2016, s. 83(19): transitional rules as regards Scotland.

4BB Residential property gain or loss

4BB(1) For the purposes of the charge to capital gains tax, a residential property gain or loss is a gain or loss which accrues on the disposal of a residential property interest.

4BB(2) But a residential property gain or loss does not accrue on a non-resident CGT disposal.

4BB(3) In this Act **"disposal of a residential property interest"** means–

(a) a disposal of a UK residential property interest, or

(b) a disposal of a non-UK residential property interest.

4BB(4) Schedule B1 gives the meaning in this Act of **"disposal of a UK residential property interest"**.

4BB(5) Schedule BA1 gives the meaning in this Act of **"disposal of a non-UK residential property interest"**.

4BB(6) See section 57C and Schedule 4ZZC for how to compute–

(a) the residential property gain or loss accruing on the disposal of a residential property interest, and

(b) the gain or loss accruing on the disposal of a residential property interest which is not a residential property gain or loss.

History – S. 4BB inserted by FA 2016, s. 83(14), with effect in relation to gains accruing on or after 6 April 2016.

5 Accumulation and discretionary settlements

5 [Repealed by FA 1998, s. 165 and Sch. 27, Pt. III(29) with effect for the year 1998–99 and subsequent years of assessment.]

6 Other special cases

6 [Omitted by FA 2008, s. 8 and Sch. 2, para. 3.]

History – S. 6 omitted by FA 2008, s. 8 and Sch. 2, para. 3 with effect from 2008–09 (FA 2008, Sch. 2, para. 22).

7 Time for payment of tax

7 [Repealed by FA 1995, s. 115(12).]

History – S. 7 repealed by FA 1995, s. 115(12), s. 162 and Sch. 29, Pt. VIII(14) for years after 1995–96.

CORPORATION TAX

8 Company's total profits to include chargeable gains

8(1) Subject to the provisions of this section and Chapter 7 of Part 4 of CTA 2010, the amount to be included in respect of chargeable gains in a company's total profits for any accounting period shall be the total amount of chargeable gains accruing to the company in the accounting period after deducting–

(a) any allowable losses accruing to the company in the period, and

(b) so far as they have not been allowed as a deduction from chargeable gains accruing in any previous accounting period–

(i) any allowable losses previously accruing to the company while it has been within the charge to corporation tax, and

(ii) any allowable NRCGT losses previously accruing to the company.

8(2) For the purposes of corporation tax in respect of chargeable gains, **"allowable loss"** does not include a loss accruing to a company in such circumstances that if a gain accrued the company would be exempt from corporation tax in respect of it.

8(2A) [Omitted by FA 2007, s. 27(2)(b); and repealed by FA 2007, s. 114 and Sch. 27, Pt. 2(2).]

8(2B) [Omitted by FA 2007, s. 27(2)(b); and repealed by FA 2007, s. 114 and Sch. 27, Pt. 2(2).]

8(2C) [Omitted by FA 2007, s. 27(2)(b); and repealed by FA 2007, s. 114 and Sch. 27, Pt. 2(2).]

8(3) Except as otherwise provided by this Act or any other provision of the Corporation Tax Acts, the total amount of the chargeable gains to be included in respect of chargeable gains in a company's total profits for any accounting period shall for purposes of corporation tax be computed in accordance with the principles applying for capital gains tax, all questions–

(a) as to the amounts which are or are not to be taken into account as chargeable gains or as allowable losses, or in computing gains or losses, or charged to tax as a person's gain; or

(b) as to the time when any such amount is to be treated as accruing,

being determined in accordance with the provisions relating to capital gains tax as if accounting periods were years of assessment.

8(4) Subject to subsection (5) below, where the enactments relating to capital gains tax contain any reference to income tax or to the Income Tax Acts the reference shall, in relation to a company, be construed as a reference to corporation tax or to the Corporation Tax Acts; but–

(a) this subsection shall not affect the references to income tax in section 39(2); and

(b) in so far as those enactments operate by reference to matters of any specified description, account shall for corporation tax be taken of matters of that description which are confined to companies, but not of any which are confined to individuals.

8(4A) Nothing in this section applies in relation to an ATED-related gain chargeable to, or an ATED-related loss allowable for the purposes of, capital gains tax by virtue of section 2B.

8(4B) Subject to subsection (1)(b)(ii), nothing in this section applies in relation to an NRCGT gain chargeable to, or an NRCGT loss allowable for the purposes of, capital gains tax by virtue of section 14D or 188D.

8(5) This Act as it has effect in accordance with this section shall not be affected in its operation by the fact that capital gains tax and corporation tax are distinct taxes but, so far as is consistent with the Corporation Tax Acts, shall apply in relation to capital gains tax and corporation tax on chargeable gains as if they were one tax, so that, in particular, a matter which in a case involving 2 individuals is relevant for both of them in relation to capital gains tax shall in a like case involving an individual and a company be relevant for him in relation to that tax and for it in relation to corporation tax.

8(6) Where assets of a company are vested in a liquidator under section 145 of the Insolvency Act 1986 or Article 123 of the Insolvency (Northern Ireland) Order 1989 or otherwise, this section and the enactments applied by this section shall apply as if the assets were vested in, and the acts of the liquidator in relation to the assets were the acts of, the company (acquisitions from or disposals to him by the company being disregarded accordingly).

History – In s. 8(1), the words "Chapter 7 of Part 4 of CTA 2010" substituted for "section 400 of the Taxes Act" by CTA 2010, s. 1177 and Sch. 1, para. 226, with effect for corporation tax purposes for accounting periods ending on or after 1 April 2010, and for income tax and capital gains tax purposes for the tax year 2010–11 and subsequent tax years.
In s. 8(1)(b), the word "period–" and para. (a) and (b) substituted for the words "period, any allowable losses previously accruing to the company while it has been within the charge to corporation tax." by FA 2015, s. 37 and Sch. 7, para. 8(2), with effect in relation to disposals made on or after 6 April 2015.
In s. 8(2), the words: "does not include a loss accruing to a company in such circumstances that if a gain accrued the company would be exempt from corporation tax in respect of it." substituted for the former wording by FA 2007, s.27(2)(a), with effect in relation to losses accruing on disposals made on or after 6 December 2006 (FA 2007, s. 27(6)).
In s. 8(2), the words "does not include– (a) a loss" substituted for "does not include a loss". (so that the end of the original text becomes para. (a)), para. (b) (and the preceding word "or") inserted by FA 2006, s. 69(2), with effect in relation to any loss accruing on a disposal made on or after 5 December 2005.
S. 8(2A), (2B) and (2C) omitted by FA 2007, s. 27(2)(b); and repealed by FA 2007, s. 114 and Sch. 27, Pt. 2(2), with effect in relation to losses accruing on disposals made on or after 6 December 2006 (FA 2007, s. 27(6)).
S. 8(2A), (2B) and (2C) inserted by FA 2006, s. 69(3), with effect in relation to any loss accruing on a disposal made on or after 5 December 2005.
S. 8(4A) inserted by FA 2013, s. 65 and Sch. 25, para. 6, with effect in relation to disposals occurring on or after 6 April 2013.
S. 8(4B) inserted by FA 2015, s. 37 and Sch. 7, para. 8(3), with effect in relation to disposals made on or after 6 April 2015.

Derivations – S. 8(1): ICTA 1988, s. 345(1).
S. 8(2): ICTA 1988, s. 834(1).
S. 8(3)–(6): ICTA 1988, s. 345(2)–(5), as amended (subs. (5)) by SI 1989/2405 (NI 19).

Cross references – S. 39(2): restriction on allowable deduction for expenditure which would be allowable for income tax if asset used for notional trade chargeable to that tax.
S. 184–184I: restrictions on uses of losses where losses or gains bought or income converted to capital.
S. 210A: in the application of s. 8(1) to insurance companies, ring-fencing of losses subject to s. 210A.
ICTA 1988, s. 400(2)(e): losses to be reduced by corresponding amounts of any government investment written off.
ICTA 1988, s. 768C: restriction to set-off of management expenses and charges defrayed and paid by an investment company before a change in ownership against chargeable gains on disposal of assets acquired intra-group in three years following the change.
FA 1996, Sch. 15, para. 8(7): loan relationships, savings and transitional provisions.
FA 2000, Sch. 22, para. 66: tonnage tax election does not affect the deduction under s. 8(1)
FA 2004, s. 133: companies in partnership: relationship with chargeable gains.
British Technology Group Act 1991, s. 12(2): application to successor company to National Research Development Corporation and National Enterprise Board without regard to any allowable losses of the Corporation or the Board.
SI 1994/3226, reg. 9(3): treatment of assets held by a company on its commencement day (for the purposes of FA 1993, Pt. II, Ch. II) where the company was non-resident at any time before its commencement day.
SI 1994/3226, reg. 16(4): a company's pre-commencement day (for the purposes of FA 1993, Pt. II, Ch. II) losses are not available for set off against exchange gains if deductible under s. 8(1).
SI 1994/3226, reg. 16(6): computation of available losses on assets held by a company on its commencement day (for the purposes of FA 1993, Pt. II, Ch. II) where the company was non-resident at any time before its commencement day.
SI 1994/3226, reg. 16(12): losses specified in an election to set available losses against exchange gains not deductible under s. 8(1).

Notes – S. 15(2): definition of "chargeable gain".
S. 16: computation of losses.
S. 137(4): charge for unpaid tax where equation of original and new holdings on an exchange, reconstruction etc. nullified by a finding that not effected for bona fide commercial reasons etc.
S. 139(6), (7): charge for unpaid tax on transferee (or subsequent transferee etc.) in a reconstruction or amalgamation involving the transfer of business at no gain, no loss where nullified by a finding that not effected for bona fide commercial reasons etc. if transferor company wound up or undue delay.
S. 178(9), 179(11): charge for unpaid tax on principal company of a group where company leaves a group with an asset transferred intra-group.
S. 189(2): charge for unpaid tax on recipient of capital distribution emanating from the disposal of assets in respect of which the gain arose.
S. 190(1): charge for unpaid tax as the principal company of the chargeable company's group or as a fellow group member previously owning the asset.
S. 191(1): charge for unpaid tax where gain forms part of chargeable profits of non-resident under s. 10(3) on a fellow group company or a controlling director of the chargeable company or a company controlling that company.
S. 277: double tax relief, applying the provisions of ICTA 1988, s. 788–806.
Sch. 7A, para. 6(1): restrictions on the deduction of pre-entry losses.
ICTA 1988, s. 6: charge to corporation tax on profits.
ICTA 1988, s. 12, 834(1): meaning of "accounting period".
ICTA 1988, s. 438: exemption from tax on chargeable gains in respect of investments referable to pension business.
ICTA 1988, s. 832(1): company within the charge to corporation tax by reference to a source from which any income would be charged to that tax.
Interpretation Act 1978, s. 5 and Sch. 1: the Corporation Tax Acts means the enactments relating to the taxation of income and chargeable gains of companies and of company distributions.

SI 1990/237, reg. 4: European School exempt from taxes on capital gains.
SI 1991/757, reg. 7: European Bank for Reconstruction and Development exempt from tax in respect of property, assets etc. within the scope of its Official Activities.

RESIDENCE ETC.

9 Residence, including temporary residence

9 [Omitted by FA 2013, s. 218 and Sch. 45, para. 148(2).]

History – S. 9 omitted by FA 2013, s. 218 and Sch. 45, para. 148(2), with effect from 17 July 2013.
Former s. 9(2) omitted by FA 2008, s. 25 and Sch. 7, para. 58 with effect from 2008–09 (FA 2008, Sch. 7, para. 81).

Derivations – CGTA 1979, s. 18(1)–(3).

10 Non-resident with United Kingdom branch or agency

10(1) Subject to any exceptions provided by this Act, a person shall be chargeable to capital gains tax in respect of chargeable gains accruing to him in a year of assessment if the residence condition is not met (see section 2(1A)) but the person is carrying on a trade in the United Kingdom through a branch or agency, and shall be so chargeable on chargeable gains accruing on the disposal–

(a) of assets situated in the United Kingdom and used in or for the purposes of the trade at or before the time when the capital gain accrued, or

(b) of assets situated in the United Kingdom and used or held for the purposes of the branch or agency at or before that time, or assets acquired for use by or for the purposes of the branch or agency.

10(2) Subsection (1) above does not apply unless the disposal is made at a time when the person is carrying on the trade in the United Kingdom through a branch or agency.

10(3) [Omitted by FA 2003, s. 155 and Sch. 27, para. 2(2)(a), and repealed by FA 2003, s. 216 and Sch. 43, Pt. 3(6).]

10(4) This section shall not apply to a person who, by virtue of Part 2 of TIOPA 2010 (double taxation relief), is exempt from income tax chargeable for the chargeable period in respect of the profits or gains of the branch or agency.

10(5) This section shall apply as if references in subsections (1) and (2) above to a trade included references to a profession or vocation, but subsection (1) shall not apply in respect of chargeable gains accruing on the disposal of assets only used in or for the purposes of the profession or vocation before 14th March 1989 or only used or held for the purposes of the branch or agency before that date.

10(6) In this Act, unless the context otherwise requires, **"branch or agency"** means any factorship, agency, receivership, branch or management, but does not include any person within the exemptions in section 82 of the Management Act (general agents and brokers).

History – In s. 10(1), the words "if the residence condition is not met (see section 2(1A)) but the person" substituted for the words "in which he is not resident and not ordinarily resident in the United Kingdom but" by FA 2013, s. 219 and Sch. 46, para. 76, with effect in relation to a person's liability to capital gains tax for the tax year 2013–14 or any subsequent tax year, without prejudice to any provision in FA 2013, Sch. 46, Pt. 3 about the application of a particular amendment.
S. 10(3) omitted by FA 2003, s. 155 and Sch. 27, para. 2(2)(a), and repealed by FA 2003, s. 216 and Sch. 43, Pt. 3(6), which have effect in relation to accounting periods beginning on or after 1 January 2003 (FA 2003, s. 155(2)).
In s. 10(4), the words "Part 2 of TIOPA 2010 (double taxation relief)" substituted for "Part XVIII of the Taxes Act (double taxation relief agreements)" by TIOPA 2010, s. 374 and Sch. 8, para. 41, with effect for corporation tax purposes for accounting periods ending on or after 1 April 2010, for income tax and capital gains tax purposes for the tax year 2010–11 and subsequent tax years, and for petroleum revenue tax purposes for chargeable periods beginning on or after 1 July 2010.
In s. 10(4), immediately after the words "income tax", the words "or corporation tax" omitted by FA 2003, s. 155 and Sch. 27, para. 2(2)(b), and repealed by FA 2003, s. 216 and Sch. 43, Pt. 3(6), which have effect in relation to accounting periods beginning on or after 1 January 2003.

Derivations – S. 10(1), (2): CGTA 1979, s. 12(1), (1A), the latter as inserted by FA 1989, s. 128(2).
S. 10(3): ICTA 1988, s. 11(2)(b), 6(4).
S. 10(4): CGTA 1979, s. 12(2).
S. 10(5): CGTA 1979, s. 12(2A), as inserted by FA 1989, s. 126(2); FA 1989, s. 126(6).
S. 10(6): CGTA 1979, s. 12(3).

Cross references – S. 2(1): persons and gains chargeable to capital gains tax.
S. 16(3): parallel treatment of allowable losses.
S. 25: deemed disposals by non-residents of chargeable assets within s. 10.
S. 191(1): charge for unpaid tax where gain forms part of chargeable profits of non-resident under s. 10(3) on a fellow group company or a controlling director of the chargeable company or a company controlling that company.
S. 199(5): deemed disposals by non-residents of assets ceasing to be chargeable assets within s. 10(1), (3) by virtue of ceasing to be dedicated to an oil field etc. and of assets which do not continue to be used for UK exploration or exploitation activities on cessation of a UK branch etc.
S. 228([illegible]): asset chargeable within s. 10 satisfies condition for relief on disposal of shares to an employee share ownership trust that proceeds suitably reinvested.
ICTA 1988, s. 11(2): the chargeable profits of a non-resident company are to include such chargeable gains as are specified in s. 10(3).
ICTA 1988, s. 715(1)(f), (h), (4), (5), (8): certain exemptions in relation to the accrued income scheme, for persons not resident or not domiciled in the UK, provided not within s. 10.
TMA 1970, s. 82: exemptions for non-residents in respect of sales or transactions carried out through a broker or agent.

FA 1995, s. 126(2)(c): branch or agency of non-resident carrying on trade in UK through the branch or agency to be non-resident's UK representative in respect of gains chargeable under s. 10 for 1996–97 and later years of assessment and accounting periods beginning after 31 March 1996.
FA 1995, s. 127: persons not treated as UK representatives.
FA 1995, Sch. 23: obligations etc. imposed on UK representatives.
SI 1994/3226, reg. 9(3): treatment of assets held by a company on its commencement day (for the purposes of FA 1993, Pt. II, Ch. II) where the company was non-resident at any time before its commencement day.
SI 2009/3001, reg. 22: modified application of s. 10 for income tax or corporation tax purposes in relation to offshore income gains.

Extra-statutory concessions – B40: Revenue do not seek to tax non-residents in respect of transactions carried out through an exempt UK investment manager or broker.
D2: years of commencement and cessation of UK residence.

Statements of practice – SP 4/92: time limit for election to rebase to 31 March 1982 value where person becomes resident in the UK after 6 April 1988.

Notes – S. 15(2): definition of "chargeable gain".
S. 21–34: general meaning of "disposal" and "asset".
S. 80: assets which remain within the charge to tax by virtue of s. 10 are not subject to the deemed disposal rules on trustees ceasing to be resident and ordinarily resident.
S. 265: security issued by designated international organisations taken to be situated outside the UK.
S. 266: security issued by the Inter-American Development Bank taken as situated outside the UK.
S. 275: location of assets (see also s. 265, 266, 276).
S. 276: territorial sea of the UK deemed to be part of the UK, certain exploration or exploitation rights effectively deemed to be UK assets and certain gains in respect thereof treated as if on assets used for a UK trade etc.
TMA 1970, s. 84: administrative arrangements for charging gains from a UK branch or agency.

10A Temporary non-residents

10A(1) This section applies if an individual ("the taxpayer") is temporarily non-resident.

10A(2) The taxpayer is chargeable to capital gains tax as if gains and losses within subsection (3) were chargeable gains or, as the case may be, losses accruing to the taxpayer in the period of return.

10A(3) The gains and losses within this subsection are–

(a) chargeable gains and losses that accrued to the taxpayer in the temporary period of non-residence,

(b) chargeable gains that would be treated under section 13 as having accrued to the taxpayer in that period if the residence assumption were made,

(c) losses that would be allowable in the taxpayer's case under section 13(8) in that period if that assumption were made, and

(d) chargeable gains that would be treated under section 86 as having accrued to the taxpayer in a tax year falling wholly in that period if the taxpayer had been resident in the United Kingdom for that year.

10A(4) The residence assumption is–

(a) that the taxpayer had been resident in the United Kingdom for the tax year in which the gain or loss accrued to the company, or

(b) if that tax year was a split year as respects the taxpayer, that the gain or loss had accrued to the company in the UK part of it.

10A(5) But–

(a) a gain is not within subsection (3) if, ignoring this section, the taxpayer is chargeable to capital gains tax in respect of it (and could not cease to be so chargeable by making a claim under section 6 of TIOPA 2010), and

(b) a loss is not within subsection (3) if the test in paragraph (a) would be met if it were a gain.

10A(6) Subsection (2) is subject to sections 10AA and 86A.

10A(7) To determine the losses mentioned in subsection (3)(c)–

(a) calculate separately, for each tax year falling wholly or partly in the temporary period of non-residence, the portion of sum A that does not exceed sum B, and

(b) add up all those portions.

10A(8) For the purposes of subsection (7)–

"sum A" is the aggregate of the losses that were not available in accordance with section 13(8) for reducing gains accruing to the taxpayer by virtue of section 13 in the relevant tax year, but would have been available if the residence assumption had been made, and

"sum B" is the amount of the gains that did not accrue to the taxpayer by virtue of section 13 in that tax year but would have so accrued if that assumption had been made.

10A(9) If section 809B, 809D or 809E of ITA 2007 (remittance basis) applies to the taxpayer for the year of return, any foreign chargeable gains falling within subsection (3) by virtue of paragraph (a) of that subsection that were remitted to the United Kingdom at any time in the temporary period of non-residence are to be treated as remitted to the United Kingdom in the period of return.

10A(10) Part 4 of Schedule 45 to the Finance Act 2013 (statutory residence test: anti-avoidance) explains–

(a) when an individual is to be regarded as "temporarily non-resident", and

(b) what **"the temporary period of non-residence"** and **"the period of return"** mean.

10A(11) In this section–

"foreign chargeable gains" has the meaning given by section 12(4);

"remitted to the United Kingdom" has the same meaning as in Chapter A1 of Part 14 of ITA 2007;

"the year of return" means the tax year that consists of or includes the period of return.

History – S. 10A substituted by FA 2013, s. 218 and Sch. 45, para. 119, with effect if the year of departure (as defined in FA 2013, Sch. 45, Pt. 4) is the tax year 2013–14 or a subsequent tax year, subject to the transitional and saving provision in FA 2013, Sch. 45, para. 154–159. Former s. 10A read as follows:

"Temporary non-residents

10A(1) This section applies in the case of any individual ("the taxpayer") if–

(a) he satisfies the residence requirements for any year of assessment ("the year of return");

(b) he did not satisfy those requirements for one or more years of assessment immediately preceding the year of return but there are years of assessment before that year for which he did satisfy those requirements;

(c) there are fewer than five years of assessment falling between the year of departure and the year of return; and

(d) four out of the seven years of assessment immediately preceding the year of departure are also years of assessment for each of which he satisfied those requirements.

10A(2) Subject to the following provisions of this section and section 86A, the taxpayer shall be chargeable to capital gains tax as if–

(a) all the chargeable gains and losses which (apart from this subsection) would have accrued to him in an intervening year,

(b) all the chargeable gains which under section 13 or 86 would be treated as having accrued to him in an intervening year if he had been resident in the United Kingdom throughout that intervening year, and

(c) any losses which by virtue of section 13(8) would have been allowable in his case in any intervening year if he had been resident in the United Kingdom throughout that intervening year,

were gains or, as the case may be, losses accruing to the taxpayer in the year of return.

10A(3) Subject to subsection (4) below, the gains and losses which by virtue of subsection (2) above are to be treated as accruing to the taxpayer in the year of return shall not include any gain or loss accruing on the disposal by the taxpayer of any asset if–

(a) that asset was acquired by the taxpayer at a time in the year of departure or any intervening year when

(i) he was neither resident nor ordinarily resident in the United Kingdom, or

(ii) he was resident or ordinarily resident in the United Kingdom but was Treaty non-resident;

(b) that asset was so acquired otherwise than by means of a relevant disposal which by virtue of section 58, 73 or 258(4) is treated as having been a disposal on which neither a gain nor a loss accrued;

(c) that asset is not an interest created by or arising under a settlement; and

(d) the amount or value of the consideration for the acquisition of that asset by the taxpayer does not fall, by reference to any relevant disposal, to be treated as reduced under section 23(4)(b) or (5)(b), 152(1)(b), 153(1)(b), 162(3)(b), or 247(2)(b) or 247(3)(b).

10A(4) Where–

(a) any chargeable gain that has accrued or would have accrued on the disposal of any asset ("the first asset") is a gain falling (apart from this section) to be treated by virtue of section 116(10) or (11), 134 or 154(2) or (4) as accruing on the disposal of the whole or any part of another asset, and

(b) the other asset is an asset falling within paragraphs (a) to (d) of subsection (3) above but the first asset is not,

subsection (3) above shall not exclude that gain from the gains which by virtue of subsection (2) above are to be treated as accruing to the taxpayer in the year of return.

10A(5) The gains and losses which by virtue of subsection (2) above are to be treated as accruing to the taxpayer in the year of return shall not include any chargeable gain or allowable loss accruing to the taxpayer in an intervening year which, in the taxpayer's case, has fallen to be brought into account for that year by virtue of section 10, 14D or 16(3).

10A(6) The reference in subsection (2)(c) above to losses allowable in an individual's case in an intervening year is a reference to only so much of the aggregate of the losses that would have been available in accordance with subsection (8) of section 13 for reducing gains accruing by virtue of that section to that individual in that year as does not exceed the amount of the gains that would have accrued to him in that year if it had been a year throughout which he was resident in the United Kingdom.

10A(7) Where this section applies in the case of any individual, nothing in any enactment imposing any limit on the time within which an assessment to capital gains tax may be made shall prevent any such assessment for the year of departure from being made in the taxpayer's case at any time before the end of two years after the 31st January next following the year of return.

10A(8) In this section–

"intervening year" means any year of assessment which, in a case where the conditions in paragraphs (a) to (d) of subsection (1) above are satisfied, falls between the year of departure and the year of return;

"relevant disposal", means a disposal of an asset acquired by the person making the disposal at a time when that person was resident or ordinarily resident in the United Kingdom and was not Treaty non-resident; and

"the year of departure" means the last year of assessment before the year of return for which the taxpayer satisfied the residence requirements.

10A(9) For the purposes of this section an individual satisfies the residence requirements for a year of assessment–

(a) if, during any part of that year of assessment, he is resident in the United Kingdom and not Treaty non-resident, or

(b) if he is ordinarily resident in the United Kingdom during that year of assessment, unless he is Treaty non-resident during that year of assessment.

10A(9ZA) If–

(a) section 809B, 809D or 809E of ITA 2007 (remittance basis) applies to the taxpayer for the year of return, and

(b) the taxpayer is not domiciled in the United Kingdom in that year,

any foreign chargeable gains falling within subsection (2)(a) which were remitted in an intervening year are treated as remitted in the year of return.

For this purpose **"foreign chargeable gains"** has the meaning given by section 12(4).

10A(9A) *[Omitted by FA 2006, s. 74(4)(a) and repealed by FA 2006, s. 178 and Sch. 26, Pt. 3(11).]*

10A(9B) Where this section applies in the case of any individual in circumstances in which one or more intervening years would, but for his being Treaty non-resident during some or all of that year or those years, not be an intervening year, this section shall have effect in the taxpayer's case–

(a) as if subsection (2)(a) above did not apply in the case of any amount treated by virtue of section 87 or 89(2) as an amount of chargeable gains accruing to the taxpayer in any such intervening year, and

(b) as if any such intervening year were not an intervening year for the purposes of subsections (2)(b) and (c) and (6) above.

10A(9C) Nothing in any double taxation relief arrangements shall be read as preventing the taxpayer from being chargeable to capital gains tax in respect of any of the chargeable gains treated by virtue of subsection (2)(a) above as accruing to the taxpayer in the year of return (or as preventing a charge to that tax from arising as a result).

10A(10) [Omitted by F(No. 2)A 2005, s. 32(6) and repealed by F(No. 2)A 2005, s. 70 and Sch. 11, Pt. 2(4).]".

In former s. 10A(3), words "(i) he was neither resident nor ordinarily resident in the United Kingdom, or (ii) he was resident or ordinarily resident in the United Kingdom but was Treaty non-resident;" substituted for words "he was neither resident nor ordinarily resident in the United Kingdom;" by F(No. 2)A 2005, s. 32(2)(a) with effect, in accordance with F(No. 2)A 2005, s 32(7).

In former s. 10A(3), the words ", 153(1)(b)" inserted by F(No. 2)A 2005, s. 32(2)(b) with effect, in accordance with F(No. 2)A 2005, s. 32(8), in relation to relevant disposals made on or after 16 March 2005.

In former s. 10A(5), as that section has effect where the year of departure (as defined in FA 2013, Sch. 45, Pt. 4) is the tax year 2012–13 or an earlier tax year, the words ", 14D" inserted by FA 2015, s. 37 and Sch. 7, para. 9 with effect in relation to disposals made on or after 6 April 2015.

In former s. 10A(8) in definition of "relevant disposal", words "and was not Treaty non-resident" inserted by F(No. 2)A 2005, s. 32(3) with effect, in accordance with F(No. 2)A 2005, s. 32(9), for determining whether a disposal of an asset is a relevant disposal for the purposes of s. 10A in any case in which the person making the disposal acquired the asset on or after 16 March 2005.

Former s. 10A(9) substituted by F(No. 2)A 2005, s. 32(4) with effect, in accordance with F(No. 2)A 2005, s. 32(7).

Former s. 10A(9ZA) inserted by FA 2008, s. 25 and Sch. 7, para. 59 with effect from 2008–09 (FA 2008, Sch. 7, para. 81).

Former s. 10A(9A) omitted by FA 2006, s. 74(4)(a) and repealed by FA 2006, s. 178 and Sch. 26, Pt. 3(11), with effect in relation to any time on or after 22 March 2006.

Former s. 10A(9A) inserted by F(No. 2)A 2005, s. 32(4), with effect, in accordance with F(No. 2)A 2005, s. 32(7).

Former s. 10A(9B) inserted by F(No. 2)A 2005, s. 32(4), with effect, in accordance with F(No. 2)A 2005, s. 32(7).

Former s. 10A(9C) inserted by F(No. 2)A 2005, s. 32(5), with effect, in accordance with F(No. 2)A 2005, s. 32(7).

Former s. 10A(10) omitted by F(No. 2)A 2005, s. 32(6) and repealed by F(No. 2)A 2005, s. 70 and Sch. 11, Pt. 2(4), with effect, in accordance with F(No. 2)A 2005, s. 32(7).

Former s. 10A inserted by FA 1998, s. 127(1), with effect in any case where the year of departure is the year 1998–99 or a subsequent year of assessment, and where 1997–98 is the year of departure and the taxpayer was resident or ordinarily resident in the UK at a time in that year on or after 17 March 1998.

Cross references – S. 86A: attribution of gains to settlor in s. 10A cases.

S. 279A, s. 279B, s. 279C and s. 279D: deferred unascertainable consideration – election for treatment of loss.

Sch. 4C, para. 6: gains attributed to settlor.

Sch. 4C, para. 12: Sch. 4B trust gains – attribution of gains to settlor in section 10A cases.

Sch. 4C, para. 12A: attribution of gains to beneficiaries in section 10A cases.

FA 2002, Sch. 11, para. 5: amendment of s. 86A with effect for the year 2003–04 and subsequent years of assessment or, if the person so elects in accordance with FA 2002, Sch. 11, para. 8, in relation to chargeable gains so accruing to a person in any of the years of assessment 2000–01, 2001–02 and 2002–03.

FA 2003, s. 162(3): deferred unascertainable consideration – election for treatment of loss; timing of insertion of s. 279A, s. 279B, s. 279C and s. 279D.

FA 2008, Sch. 7, para. 84(3): nothing in s. 10A applies in relation to any part of the gain remitted to the UK in any tax year before 2008–09.

SI 2009/3001, reg. 23: modified application of s. 10A in relation to offshore income gains.

Other material – Tax Bulletin TB04/05-3: the taxation of share options: internationally mobile employees – commentary on the interaction of provisions of UK domestic legislation on share options and EMI withdouble taxation agreements.

10AA Section 10A: supplementary

10AA(1) Section 10A(2) does not apply to a gain or loss accruing on the disposal by the taxpayer of an asset if–

(a) the asset was acquired by the taxpayer in the temporary period of non-residence,

(b) it was so acquired otherwise than by means of a relevant disposal that by virtue of section 58, 73 or 258(4) is treated as having been a disposal on which neither a gain nor a loss accrued,

(c) the asset is not an interest created by or arising under a settlement, and

(d) the amount or value of the consideration for the acquisition of the asset by the taxpayer does not fall, by reference to any relevant disposal, to be treated as reduced under section 23(4)(b) or (5)(b), 152(1)(b), 153(1)(b), 162(3)(b) or 247(2)(b) or (3)(b).

10AA(2) **"Relevant disposal"** means a disposal of an asset acquired by the person making the disposal at a time when that person was resident in the United Kingdom and was not Treaty non-resident.

10AA(3) Subsection (1) does not apply if–

(a) the gain is one that (ignoring section 10A) would fall to be treated by virtue of section 116(10) or (11), 134 or 154(2) or (4) as accruing on the disposal of the whole or part of another asset, and

(b) that other asset meets the requirements of paragraphs (a) to (d) of subsection (1), but the asset in respect of which the gain actually accrued or would actually accrue does not.

10AA(4) Nothing in any double taxation relief arrangements is to be read as preventing the taxpayer from being chargeable to capital gains tax in respect of any chargeable gains treated under section 10A as accruing to the taxpayer in the period of return (or as preventing a charge to that tax from arising as a result).

10AA(5) Nothing in any enactment imposing any limit on the time within which an assessment to capital gains tax may be made prevents any assessment for the year of departure from being made in the taxpayer's case at any time before the end of the second anniversary of the 31 January next following the year of return (as defined in section 10A).

History – S. 10AA inserted by FA 2013, s. 218 and Sch. 45, para. 119, with effect if the year of departure (as defined in FA 2013, Sch. 45, Pt. 4) is the tax year 2013–14 or a subsequent tax year, subject to the transitional and saving provision in FA 2013, Sch. 45, para. 154–159.

10B Non-resident company with United Kingdom permanent establishment

10B(1) Subject to any exceptions provided by this Act, the chargeable profits for the purposes of corporation tax of a company not resident in the United Kingdom but carrying on a trade in the United Kingdom through a permanent establishment there include chargeable gains accruing to the company on the disposal of–

(a) assets situated in the United Kingdom and used in or for the purposes of the trade at or before the time the gain accrued, or

(b) assets situated in the United Kingdom and used or held for the purposes of the permanent establishment at or before the time the gain accrued or acquired for use by or for the purposes of the permanent establishment.

10B(2) Subsection (1) does not apply unless the disposal is made at a time when the company is carrying on a trade in the United Kingdom through a permanent establishment there.

10B(3) This section does not apply to a company that, by virtue of Part 2 of TIOPA 2010 (double taxation relief), is exempt from corporation tax for the chargeable period in respect of the profits of the permanent establishment.

10B(3A) This section applies to an overseas life insurance company in the case of its long-term business with the omission from subsection (1)(b) of the words "situated in the United Kingdom and".

10B(4) In this section–

(a) references to a trade include an office, and

(b) references to carrying on a trade include holding an office.

History – In s. 10B(3), the words "Part 2 of TIOPA 2010 (double taxation relief)" substituted for "Part 18 of the Taxes Act (double taxation relief agreements)" by TIOPA 2010, s. 374 and Sch. 8, para. 42, with effect for corporation tax purposes for accounting periods ending on or after 1 April 2010, for income tax and capital gains tax purposes for the tax year 2010–11 and subsequent tax years, and for petroleum revenue tax purposes for chargeable periods beginning on or after 1 July 2010.

S. 10B(3A) inserted by FA 2012, s. 146 and Sch. 16, para. 73 in relation to accounting periods beginning on or after 1 January 2013 (FA 2012, s. 148) but subject to transitional provisions in FA 2012, Sch. 17. Where an accounting period would otherwise straddle 1 January 2013, it is deemed to end on 31 December 2012 (FA 2012, s. 149).

S. 10B(4) substituted by CTA 2009, s. 1322 and Sch. 1, para. 360, with effect for corporation tax purposes for accounting periods ending on or after 1 April 2009, and for income tax and capital gains tax purposes for the tax year 2009–10 and subsequent tax years.

S. 10B inserted by FA 2003, s. 149(4) with effect in relation to accounting periods (of the non-resident company) beginning on or after 1 January 2003.

Cross references – S. 179A(12): definition of "chargeable asset".

S. 288(1): definition of "permanent establishment" (taken from FA 2003, s. 148).

Sch. 7AC, para. 3(2): one of conditions for exemption that company's chargeable gain constitutes part of profits chargeable to corporation tax.

ICTA 1988, s. 11(2A)(c): profits attributable to a permanent establishment for the purposes of corporation tax.

FA 1996, Sch. 15, para. 8(6): loan relationships, savings and transitional provisions.

FA 2000, Sch. 15, para. 79(5): a chargeable gain accruing on a chargeable event under that paragraph is treated as if it was a gain accruing on the disposal of an asset to which s. 10B applies.

FA 2003, s. 148: definition of "permanent establishment".

SI 2006/3271, reg. 27: modification of s. 10B with effect from 31 December 2006 in relation to periods of account ending on or after that day.

SI 2009/3001, reg. 22: modified application of s. 10B for income tax or corporation tax purposes in relation to offshore income gains.

Notes – S. 288(1): meaning of "permanent establishment" as taken from FA 2003, s. 148.

11 Visiting forces and official agents

11(1) If section 833 of ITA 2007 (visiting forces and staff of designated allied headquarters) applies to an individual throughout a period, the period is not treated for capital gains tax purposes as–

(a) a period of residence in the United Kingdom, or

(b) creating a change of the individual's residence or domicile.

11(2) If an individual is entitled to immunity from income tax by virtue of section 841 of ITA 2007 (which provides immunity from income tax for official agents of Commonwealth countries or the Republic of Ireland etc), the individual is entitled to the same immunity from capital gains tax as that to which a member of the staff of a mission is entitled under the Diplomatic Privileges Act 1964.

11(3) **"A member of the staff of a mission"** is to be read in accordance with the Diplomatic Privileges Act 1964.

History – S. 11 substituted by ITA 2007, Sch. 1, para. 297, with effect from 6 April 2007.

Cross references – ICTA 1988, s. 320, 323: exemption from income tax in respect of certain staff of Agents-General etc., visiting forces, civilian component or persons attached to allied headquarters.

Statutory instruments – SI 1961/580; SI 1964/924; SI 1998/1514: designation of countries and allied headquarters for the purposes of s. 11(1).

Notes – S. 276: territorial sea of the UK deemed to be part of the UK.

12 Non-UK domiciled individuals to whom remittance basis applies

12(1) This section applies to foreign chargeable gains accruing to an individual in a tax year ("the foreign chargeable gains") if section 809B, 809D or 809E of ITA 2007 (remittance basis) applies to the individual for that year.

12(1A) But it does not apply to foreign chargeable gains accruing to an individual in the overseas part of a split year as respects that individual, regardless of the part of the year (the overseas part or the UK part) in which the foreign chargeable gains are remitted.

12(2) Chargeable gains are treated as accruing to the individual in any tax year in which any of the foreign chargeable gains are remitted to the United Kingdom.

12(2A) If that tax year is a split year as respects the individual, the chargeable gains are treated as accruing to the individual in the part of the year (the overseas part or the UK part) in which the foreign chargeable gains are so remitted.

12(3) The amount of chargeable gains treated as accruing is equal to the full amount of the foreign chargeable gains so remitted in that year or, where applicable, that part of the year.

12(4) In this section **"foreign chargeable gains"** means chargeable gains accruing from the disposal of an asset which is situated outside the United Kingdom.

12(5) See Chapter A1 of Part 14 of ITA 2007 for the meaning of **"remitted to the United Kingdom"** etc.

History – S. 12(1) substituted by FA 2013, s. 219 and Sch. 46, para. 17, with effect in relation to an individual's foreign income and gains for the tax year 2013–14 or any subsequent tax year, subject to the savings provision in FA 2013, Sch. 46, para. 26. Former s. 12(1) read as follows:

"**12(1)** This section applies to foreign chargeable gains accruing to an individual in a tax year ("the foreign chargeable gains") if–

(a) section 809B, 809D or 809E of ITA 2007 (remittance basis) applies to the individual for that year, and

(b) the individual is not domiciled in the United Kingdom in that year.".

s. 12(1A) inserted by FA 2014, s. 59(2), with effect in relation to gains accruing on or after 6 April 2013.

S. 12(2A) inserted by FA 2013, s. 218 and Sch. 45, para. 95(2), with effect in calculating an individual's liability to income tax or capital gains tax for the tax year 2013–14 or any subsequent tax year, subject to the transitional and saving provision in FA 2013, Sch. 45, para. 154–159.

In s. 12(3), the words "or, where applicable, that part of the year" inserted by FA 2013, s. 218 and Sch. 45, para 95(3), with effect in calculating an individual's liability to income tax or capital gains tax for the tax year 2013–14 or any subsequent tax year, subject to the transitional and saving provision in FA 2013, Sch. 45, para. 154–159.

S. 12 substituted by FA 2005, s. 25 and Sch. 7, para. 60 with effect from 2008–09 (FA 2008, Sch. 7, para. 81) but see transitional provision at Sch. 7, para. 84.

In former s. 12(2), words ", and sections 833 and 834 of ITTOIA 2005 shall apply as they would apply for the purposes of section 832 of that Act (remittance basis) if the gain were relevant foreign income." substituted for words ", and subsections (6) to (9) of section 65 of the Taxes Act (under which income applied outside the United Kingdom in payment of debts is, in certain cases, treated as received in the United Kingdom) shall apply as they would apply for the purposes of subsection (5) of that section if the gain were income arising from possessions out of the United Kingdom." by virtue of ITTOIA 2005, s. 882 and Sch. 1, para. 429 which, in accordance with ITTOIA 2005, s. 883, have effect, for income tax purposes, for tax year 2005–06 and subsequent tax years, and, for corporation tax purposes, for accounting periods ending after 5 April 2005.

Derivations – CGTA 1979, s. 14.

Cross references – S. 16(4): parallel treatment of allowable losses.
Sch. A1: application of taper relief to postponed gains treated, by virtue of s. 12(1), as accruing after the time of disposal.
ICTA 1988, s. 65(6)–(9): constructive remittances.
SI 2009/3001, reg. 20: offshore income gains of non-resident settlements: modified application of s. 12 where s 87 applies.

Other material – IR booklet CGT 8, para. 50 (not reproduced and currently withdrawn): in practice, where an individual comes to the UK to take up permanent residence, any remittances in respect of gains arising before arrival are normally ignored. But see Taxation, 6 June 1991, p. 257 for Revenue's attitude to remittance of gains following change of domicile.
Tax Bulletin TB04/05-3: the taxation of share options: internationally mobile employees – commentary on the interaction of provisions of UK domestic legislation on share options and EMI withdouble taxation agreements.

Notes – S. 15(2): definition of "chargeable gain".
S. 21–34: general meaning of "disposal" and "asset".
S. 275: location of assets (see also s. 276).
S. 276: territorial sea of the UK deemed to be part of the UK and certain exploration or exploitation rights effectively deemed to be UK assets.
S. 288: interpretation, including "the Taxes Act" as being ICTA 1988 and "year of assessment" as being 6 April to the following 5 April.

13 Attribution of gains to members of non-resident companies

13(1) This section applies as respects chargeable gains accruing to a company–

(a) which is not resident in the United Kingdom, and

(b) which would be a close company if it were resident in the United Kingdom.

13(1A) But this section does not apply if the gain is

(a) an ATED-related gain chargeable to capital gains tax by virtue of section 2B (capital gains tax on ATED-related gains), or

(b) an NRCGT gain chargeable to capital gains tax by virtue of section 14D or 188D (capital gains tax on NRCGT gains).

13(2) Subject to this section, every person who at the time when the chargeable gain accrues to the company is resident in the United Kingdom and is a participator in the company, shall be treated for the purposes of this Act as if a part of the chargeable gain had accrued to him.

13(3) That part shall be equal to the proportion of the gain that corresponds to the extent of the participator's interest as a participator in the company.

13(3A) Subsection (2) does not apply in the case of a participator who is an individual if–

(a) the tax year in which the chargeable gain accrues to the company is a split year as respects the participator, and

(b) the chargeable gain accrues to the company in the overseas part of that year.

13(4) Subsection (2) above shall not apply in the case of any participator in the company to which the gain accrues where the aggregate amount falling under that subsection to be apportioned to him and to persons connected with him does not exceed one quarter of the gain.

13(5) This section shall not apply in relation to–

(a) [repealed by FA 1996, s. 174(4) and s. 205 and Sch. 41, Pt. V(30),]

(b) a chargeable gain accruing on the disposal of an asset used, and used only–

- (i) for the purposes of a trade carried on by the company wholly outside the United Kingdom, or
- (ii) for the purposes of the part carried on outside the United Kingdom of a trade carried on by the company partly within and partly outside the United Kingdom,

(ca) a chargeable gain accruing on the disposal of an asset used, and used only, for the purposes of economically significant activities carried on by the company wholly or mainly outside the United Kingdom, or

(cb) a chargeable gain accruing to the company on a disposal of an asset where it is shown that neither–

- (i) the disposal of the asset by the company, nor
- (ii) the acquisition or holding of the asset by the company, formed part of a scheme or arrangements of which the main purpose, or one of the main purposes, was avoidance of liability to capital gains tax or corporation tax, or

(c) [omitted by FA 2012, s. 35(2).]

(d) to a chargeable gain in respect of which the company is chargeable to tax by virtue of section 10B.

13(5A) Where–

(a) an amount of tax is paid by a person in pursuance of subsection (2) above, and

(b) an amount in respect of the chargeable gain is distributed (either by way of dividend or distribution of capital or on the dissolution of the company) before the end of the period specified in subsection (5B) below,

the amount of tax (so far as neither reimbursed by the company nor applied as a deduction under subsection (7) below) shall be applied for reducing or extinguishing any liability of that person to income tax, capital gains tax or corporation tax in respect of the distribution.

13(5B) The period referred to in subsection (5A)(b) above is the period of three years from–

(a) the end of the period of account of the company in which the chargeable gain accrued, or

(b) the end of the period of twelve months beginning with the date on which the chargeable gain accrued,

whichever is earlier.

13(6) [Repealed by FA 1996, s. 205 and Sch. 41, Pt. V(30).]

13(7) The amount of capital gains tax paid by a person in pursuance of subsection (2) above (so far as neither reimbursed by the company nor applied under subsection (5A) above for reducing any liability to tax) shall be allowable as a deduction in the computation under this Act of a gain accruing on the disposal by him of any asset representing his interest as a participator in the company.

13(7A) In ascertaining for the purposes of subsection (5A) or (7) above the amount of capital gains tax or income tax chargeable on any person for any year on or in respect of any chargeable gain or distribution–

(a) any such distribution as is mentioned in subsection (5A)(b) above and falls to be treated as income of that person for that year shall be regarded as forming the highest part of the income on which he is chargeable to tax for the year;

(b) [omitted by FA 2008, s. 8 and Sch. 2, para. 4;]

(c) [omitted by FA 2008, s. 8 and Sch. 2, para. 4;]

(d) [omitted by FA 2008, s. 8 and Sch. 2, para. 4;]

13(8) So far as it would go to reduce or extinguish chargeable gains accruing by virtue of this section to a person in a year of assessment this section shall apply in relation to a loss accruing to the company on the disposal of an asset in that year of assessment as it would apply if a gain instead of a loss had accrued to the company on the disposal, but shall only so apply in relation to that person; and subject to the preceding provisions of this subsection this section shall not apply in relation to a loss accruing to the company.

13(9) If a person who is a participator in the company at the time when the chargeable gain accrues to the company is itself a company which is not resident in the United Kingdom but which would be a close company if it were resident in the United Kingdom, an amount equal to the amount apportioned under subsection (3) above out of the chargeable gain to the participating company's interest as a participator in the company to which the gain accrues shall be further apportioned among the participators in the participating company according to the extent of their respective interests as participators, and subsection (2) above shall apply to them accordingly in relation to the amounts further apportioned, and so on through any number of companies.

13(10) The persons treated by this section as if a part of a chargeable gain accruing to a company had accrued to them shall include the trustees of a settlement who are participators in the company, or in any company amongst the participators in which the gain is apportioned under subsection (9) above, if when the gain accrues to the company the trustees are not resident in the United Kingdom.

13(10A) [Omitted by FA 2008, s. 8 and Sch. 2, para. 28.]

13(10B) A chargeable gain that would be treated as accruing to a person under subsection (2) above shall not be so treated if–

(a) it would be so treated only if assets that are assets of a pension scheme were taken into account in ascertaining that person's interest as a participator in the company, and

(b) at the time the gain accrues a gain arising on a disposal of those assets would be exempt from tax by virtue of section 271(1)(c) or (1A).

In paragraph (a) above **"assets of a pension scheme"** means assets held for the purposes of a fund or scheme to which any of the provisions mentioned in paragraph (b) above applies.

13(11) If any tax payable by any person by virtue of subsection (2) above is paid by the company to which the chargeable gain accrues, or in a case under subsection (9) above is paid by any such other company, the amount so paid shall not for the purposes of income tax, capital gains tax or corporation tax be regarded as a payment to the person by whom the tax was originally payable.

13(11A) For the purposes of this section the amount of the gain or loss accruing at any time to a company that is not resident in the United Kingdom shall be computed (where it is not the case) as if that company were within the charge to corporation tax on capital gains.

13(12) In this section **"participator"**, in relation to a company, has the meaning given by section 454 of CTA 2010.

13(13) In this section–

(a) references to a person's interest as a participator in a company are references to the interest in the company which is represented by all the factors by reference to which he falls to be treated as such a participator; and

(b) references to the extent of such an interest are references to the proportion of the interests as participators of all the participators in the company (including any who are not resident in the United Kingdom) which on a just and reasonable apportionment is represented by that interest.

13(14) For the purposes of this section, where–

(a) the interest of any person in a company is wholly or partly represented by an interest which he has under any settlement ("his beneficial interest"), and

(b) his beneficial interest is the factor, or one of the factors, by reference to which that person would be treated (apart from this subsection) as having an interest as a participator in that company,

the interest as a participator in that company which would be that person's shall be deemed, to the extent that it is represented by his beneficial interest, to be an interest of the trustees of the settlement (and not of that person), and references in this section, in relation to a company, to a participator shall be construed accordingly.

13(15) [Omitted by SI 2009/56, art. 3(1) and Sch. 1, para. 178.]

History – S. 13(1A)(a) and (b) substituted for the words "an ATED-related gain chargeable to capital gains tax by virtue of section 2B (capital gains tax on ATED-related gains)." by FA 2015, s. 37 and Sch. 7, para. 10, with effect in relation to disposals made on or after 6 April 2015.

S. 13(1A) inserted by FA 2013, s. 65 and Sch. 25, para. 7, with effect in relation to disposals occurring on or after 6 April 2013.

In s. 13(2), the word "and" substituted for ", who, if an individual, is domiciled in the United Kingdom, and who" by FA 2008, s. 25 and Sch. 7, para. 103 with effect in relation to chargeable gains accruing on or after 6 April 2008 (FA 2008, Sch. 7, para. 105).

In s. 13(2), the words "or ordinarily resident" omitted by FA 2013, s. 219 and Sch. 46, para. 77(2), with effect in relation to a person's liability to capital gains tax for the tax year 2013–14 or any subsequent tax year, without prejudice to any provision in FA 2013, Sch. 46, Pt. 3 about the application of a particular amendment.

S. 13(3A) inserted by FA 2013, s. 218 and Sch. 45, para. 96, with effect in calculating an individual's liability to income tax or capital gains tax for the tax year 2013–14 or any subsequent tax year, subject to the transitional and saving provision in FA 2013, Sch. 45, para. 154–159.

In s. 13(4), the words "one quarter" substituted for the words "one tenth" by FA 2013, s. 62(2) with effect in relation to disposals made on or after 6 April 2012 (subject to provisions in FA 2013, s. 62(6) and (7) in relation to disposals made on or after that date but before 6 April 2013: election for s. 13 to apply without FA 2013, s. 62 amendments).

S. 13(5)(ca) and (cb) inserted by FA 2013 s. 62(3) with effect in relation to disposals made on or after 6 April 2012 (subject to provisions in FA 2013, s. 62(6) and (7) in relation to disposals made on or after that date but before 6 April 2013: election for s. 13 to apply without FA 2013, s. 62 amendments).
S. 13(5)(c) omitted by FA 2012, s. 35(2) with effect in relation to disposals occurring on or after 6 April 2012.
In s. 13(5)(d), the words "10B" substituted for the words "10(3)" by FA 2003, s. 155 and Sch. 27, para. 2(3) which have effect in relation to accounting periods beginning on or after 1 January 2003.
In s. 13(5), para. (a), and s. 13(6) repealed by FA 1996, s. 174(4) and s. 205 and Sch. 41, Pt. V(30) with effect in relation to gains accruing on or after 28 November 1995.
In s. 13(5B), second sentence (which defined "period of account") repealed by FA 2002, s. 141 and Sch. 40, Pt. 3(16). "Period of account" is now defined in CTA 2010, s. 1119.
S. 13(7A)(b)–(d) omitted by FA 2008, s. 8 and Sch. 2, para. 4 with effect from 2008–09 (FA 2008, Sch. 2, para. 22).
In s. 13(10), the words "not resident" substituted for the words "neither resident nor ordinarily resident" by FA 2013, s. 219 and Sch. 46, para. 77(3), with effect in relation to a person's liability to capital gains tax for the tax year 2013–14 or any subsequent tax year, without prejudice to any provision in FA 2013, Sch. 46, Pt. 3 about the application of a particular amendment.
In s. 13(10), the words "the trustees of a settlement who are participators" substituted for "trustees who are participators" by FA 2006, s. 88 and Sch. 12, para. 8(1) with effect in relation to gains accruing on or after 6 April 2006.
S. 13(10A) omitted by FA 2008, s. 8 and Sch. 2, para. 28 with effect in relation to chargeable gains accruing or treated as accruing in the tax year 2008–09 or any subsequent tax year (FA 2008, Sch. 2, para. 56(3)).
Former s. 13(10A) inserted by FA 1998, Sch. 21, para. 4, with effect for the year 1998–99 and subsequent years of assessment.
In s. 13(10B)(b), the words "section 271(1)(c) or (1A)" substituted for the words "section 271(1)(b), (c), (d), (g) or (h) or (2)" by FA 2004, s. 281 and Sch. 35, para. 39 which, by virtue of FA 2004, s. 284(1), came into force on 6 April 2006.
S. 13(11A) inserted by FA 1998, s. 122(4), with effect in relation to disposals on or after 6 April 1998.
In s. 13(12), the words "section 454 of CTA 2010" substituted for "section 417(1) of the Taxes Act for the purposes of Part XI of that Act (close companies)" by CTA 2010, s. 1177 and Sch. 1, para. 227, with effect for corporation tax purposes for accounting periods ending on or after 1 April 2010, and for income tax and capital gains tax purposes for the tax year 2010–11 and subsequent tax years.
In s. 13(13)(b), the words "or ordinarily resident" omitted by FA 2013, s. 219 and Sch. 46, para. 77(4), with effect in relation to a person's liability to capital gains tax for the tax year 2013–14 or any subsequent tax year, without prejudice to any provision in FA 2013, Sch. 46, Pt. 3 about the application of a particular amendment.
S. 13(15) omitted by SI 2009/56, art. 3(1) and Sch. 1, para. 178, operative from 1 April2009, subject to transitional and saving provisions in SI 2009/56, Sch. 3.
In s. 13:

- in s. 13(2) "is a participator" substituted for "holds shares";
- in s. 13(3), (4) substituted;
- s. 13(5A) inserted;
- in s. 13(7) "neither reimbursed … tax" substituted for "not reimbursed by the company", and "any asset … the company" substituted for "the shares by reference to which the tax was paid";
- s. 13(7A) inserted;
- in s. 13(9) "a person who is a participator" substituted for "the person owning any of the shares", and "participating company's …further apportioned" substituted for " to the shares so owned shall be apportioned among the issued shares of the second-mentioned company, and the holders of those shares shall be treated in accordance with subsection (2) above";
- in s. 13(10) "who are …subsection (9) above" substituted for "owning shares in the company";
- s. 13(12)–(15) inserted;

by FA 1996, s. 174(1)–(9) with effect in relation to gains accruing on or after 28 November 1995.
In s. 13 the following are amended by FA 2001, s. 80 with effect for gains accruing as mentioned in s. 13(1) on or after 7 March 2001:

- in s. 13(4) "one tenth" substituted for "one twentieth";
- s. 13(5)(b) substituted;
- s. 13(5A) substituted;
- s. 13(5B) inserted; and
- s. 13(10B) inserted;

Derivations – S. 13(1)–(9): CGTA 1979, s. 15(1)–(9).
S. 13(10): FA 1981, s. 85.
S. 13(11): CGTA 1979, s. 15(10).

Cross references – S. 79B: attribution to trustees of gains of non-resident companies.
S. 252(1): debts owed by a bank which are not in sterling and which are represented by sums standing to the credit of persons in accounts in the bank.
Sch. 4C, para. 12A: attribution of gains to beneficiaries in section 10A cases.
Sch. 5, para. 1(3): as regards the attribution of certain gains to settlors in non-resident or dual resident settlements, gains or losses attributed to the trustees under s. 13 are taken into account.
Sch. 7B, para. 2: modification of s. 13(5)(d) in relation to overseas life insurance companies applying in relation to chargeable gains accruing to companies in accounting periods beginning after 31 December 1992.
FA 2005, s. 30(4): special capital gains treatment for trusts with vulnerable beneficiaries: defining qualifying trusts gains.
TMA 1970, s. 28: power of Board to demand information from a person holding shares or securities in a non-resident company for the purposes of s. 13.
SI 2009/3001, reg. 24: modified application of s. 13 in relation to offshore income gains.

Statements of practice – D23: credit or deduction available for overseas tax on gain apportioned.
SP 10/84: all bank accounts in taxpayer's name containing a particular foreign currency may be treated as one account and direct transfers disregarded for capital gains tax purposes (s. 13(5)(c)).
SP 6/88: credit for overseas taxes available so long as they relate to the same source; credit remains available notwithstanding that liabilities arise at different times or charged on different persons.

Other material – ICAEW Technical Release TR 500 (not reproduced): no charge under s. 13 where an overseas subsidiary falls under double tax agreement providing exemption from charge on UK capital gains.

Notes – S. 15(2): definition of "chargeable gain".
S. 21–34: general meaning of "disposal" and "asset".
S. 276: territorial sea of the UK deemed to be part of the UK.
S. 288: interpretation, including when shares are issued, the meaning of "company", "close company", shares as including stock.
TMA 1970, s. 29: assessing procedure.

13A Section 13(5): interpretation

13A(1) For the purposes of section 13(5)(b) a disposal of an asset is to be regarded as a disposal of an asset used for the purposes of a trade carried on wholly outside the United Kingdom by a company if–

(a) the asset is accommodation, or an interest or right in accommodation, which is situated outside the United Kingdom, and

(b) the accommodation has for each relevant period been furnished holiday accommodation of which a person has made a commercial letting.

13A(2) For the purposes of subsection (1)(b) each of the following is **"a relevant period"**–

(a) the period of 12 months ending with the date of the disposal and each of the two preceding periods of 12 months, or

(b) if the company has been the beneficial owner of the accommodation (or interest or right) for a period longer than 36 months, the period of 12 months ending with the date of the disposal and each of the preceding periods of 12 months throughout which the company has been the beneficial owner of the accommodation (or interest or right).

13A(3) The reference in subsection (1)(b) to the commercial letting of furnished holiday accommodation is to be read in accordance with Chapter 6 of Part 4 of CTA 2009, but–

(a) as if sections 266, 268 and 268A were omitted, and

(b) as if, in section 267(1), the reference to an accounting period were a reference to a relevant period as defined by subsection (2) above.

13A(4) For the purposes of section 13(5)(ca) activities carried on by a company are **"economically significant activities"** if they are activities which consist of the provision by the company of goods or services to others on a commercial basis and involve–

(a) the use of staff in numbers, and with competence and authority,

(b) the use of premises and equipment, and

(c) the addition of economic value, by the company, to those to whom the goods or services are provided,

commensurate with the size and nature of those activities.

13A(5) In subsection (4) **"staff"** means employees, agents or contractors of the company.

History – S. 13A inserted by FA 2013 s. 62(4) with effect in relation to disposals made on or after 6 April 2012 (subject to provisions in FA 2013, s. 62(6) and (7) in relation to disposals made on or after that date but before 6 April 2013: election for s. 13 to apply without FA 2013, s. 62 amendments).

14 Non-resident groups of companies

14(1) This section has effect for the purposes of section 13.

14(2) The following provisions–

(a) section 41(8),

(b) section 171 (except subsections (1)(b) and (1A)),

(c) section 173 (with the omission of the words "to which this section applies" in subsections (1)(a) and (2)(a) and "such" in subsections (1)(c) and (2)(c) and with the omission of subsection (3)),

(d) section 174(4) (with the substitution of "at a time when both were members of the group" for "in a transfer to which section 171(1) applied"), and

(e) section 175(1) (with the omission of the words "to which this section applies"),

shall apply in relation to non-resident companies which are members of a non-resident group of companies as they apply in relation to companies which are members of a group of companies.

14(3) Section 179 (except subsections (1)(b) and (1A)) shall apply for the purposes of section 13 as if for any reference therein to a group of companies there were substituted a reference to a non-resident group of companies, and as if references to companies were references to companies not resident in the United Kingdom.

14(4) For the purposes of this section–

(a) a **"non-resident group"** of companies–

(i) in the case of a group, none of the members of which are resident in the United Kingdom, means that group, and

(ii) in the case of a group, 2 or more members of which are not resident in the United Kingdom, means the members which are not resident in the United Kingdom;

(b) **"group"** shall be construed in accordance with section 170.

History – S. 14(2) substituted by FA 2000, Sch. 29, para. 16(2), with effect in accordance with FA 2000, Sch. 29, para. 16(5) (broadly, for acquisitions and disposals on or after 1 April 2000).

In s. 14(3), words "Section 179 (except subsections (1)(b) and (1A))" substituted for "Sections 178 to 180" by FA 2000, Sch. 29, para. 16(3), with effect in accordance with FA 2000, Sch. 29, para. 16(5) (broadly, for acquisitions and disposals on or after 1 April 2000).

In s. 14(4)(b), words at end "without subsections (2)(a), (9) and (12) to (14)" repealed by FA 2000, Sch. 29, para. 16(4)), s. 156 and Sch. 40, Pt. II(12), with effect in accordance with FA 2000, Sch. 29, para. 16(5) (broadly, for acquisitions and disposals on or after 1 April 2000).

Derivations – CGTA 1979, s. 16.

Cross references – S. 41(8): restriction of losses by reference to capital allowances and renewals allowances.
S. 170: determination of group by reference to 75 per cent subsidiary relationships.
S. 171–174, 175(1): deemed no gain, no loss on transfers of capital assets within group (with or without deemed appropriation to or from trading stock) or on domestication of UK branch and treatment of group effectively as if single company for interaction with capital allowances, 1965 assets and replacement of business assets.
S. 178–180: crystallisation of gains where company ceases to be member of group and holds asset transferred intra-group.

HMRC interpretations – IRInt. 43: where group provisions are imported in s. 14 they apply whether within charge to corporation tax or capital gains tax and are not limited to those transactions otherwise within the charge to corporation tax.

Notes – S. 276: territorial sea of the UK deemed to be part of the UK.

14A Section 13: non-UK domiciled individuals

14A(1) This section applies if–

(a) by virtue of section 13, part of a chargeable gain that accrues to a company on the disposal of an asset is treated as accruing to an individual in a tax year, and

(b) the individual is not domiciled in the United Kingdom in that year.

14A(2) The part of the chargeable gain treated as accruing to the individual ("the deemed chargeable gain") is a foreign chargeable gain within the meaning of section 12 if (and only if) the asset is situated outside the United Kingdom.

14A(3) For the purposes of Chapter A1 of Part 14 of ITA 2007 (remittance basis)–

(a) treat any consideration obtained by the company on the disposal of the asset as deriving from the deemed chargeable gain, and

(b) unless the consideration so obtained is of an amount at least equal to the market value of the asset, treat the asset as deriving from the deemed chargeable gain.

14A(4) If–

(a) the deemed chargeable gain is a foreign chargeable gain (within the meaning of section 12),

(b) section 809B, 809D or 809E of ITA 2007 (remittance basis) applies to the individual for the year mentioned in subsection (1), and

(c) any of the deemed chargeable gain is remitted to the United Kingdom in a tax year after that year,

the chargeable gain treated under section 12(2) as accruing may not be reduced or extinguished under section 13(8).

History – In s. 14A(3)(b) the words "at least" inserted by FA 2009, s. 51 and Sch. 27, para. 12 with effect from 22 April 2009.
S. 14A inserted by FA 2008, s. 25 and Sch. 7, para. 104 with effect in relation to chargeable gains accruing on or after 6 April 2008 (FA 2008, Sch. 7, para. 105).

UK RESIDENTIAL PROPERTY: NON-RESIDENT CGT

Other material – HMRC guidance: "capital gains tax for non-residents: UK residential property" is available at https://www.gov.uk/capital-gains-tax-for-non-residents-uk-residential-property.
Misc. 05/2015: capital gains tax for non-UK residents: sales and disposals of UK residential property FAQs.

14B Meaning of "non-resident CGT disposal"

14B(1) For the purposes of this Act a disposal made by a person is a "non-resident CGT disposal" if–

(a) it is a disposal of a UK residential property interest (within the meaning given by Schedule B1), and

(b) condition A or B is met.

But see also subsections (5) and (6).

14B(2) Condition A is–

(a) in the case of an individual, that the individual is not resident in the United Kingdom for the tax year in question (see subsection (3)),

(b) in the case of personal representatives of a deceased person, that the single and continuing body mentioned in section 62(3) is not resident in the United Kingdom,

(c) in the case of the trustees of a settlement, that the single person mentioned in section 69(1) is not resident in the United Kingdom during any part of the tax year in question, and

(d) in any other case, that the person is not resident in the United Kingdom at the relevant time.

14B(3) In subsection (2)–

(a) **"the tax year in question"** means the tax year in which any gain on the disposal accrues (or would accrue were there to be such a gain);

(b) **"the relevant time"** means the time at which any gain on the disposal accrues (or would accrue were there to be such a gain).

14B(4) Condition B is that–

(a) the person is an individual, and

(b) any gain accruing to the individual on the disposal would accrue in the overseas part of a tax year which is a split year as respects the individual.

14B(5) A disposal by a person of a UK residential property interest is not a non-resident CGT disposal so far as any chargeable gains accruing to the person on the disposal–

(a) would be gains in respect of which the person would be chargeable to capital gains tax–

(i) under section 10(1) (non-resident with UK branch or agency), or

(ii) under section 2 as a result of subsection (1C) of that section (corresponding provision relating to the overseas part of a split year), or

(b) would be gains forming part of the person's chargeable profits for corporation tax purposes by virtue of section 10B (non-resident company with UK permanent establishment).

14B(6) A disposal of a UK residential property interest is not a non-resident CGT disposal if section 356OC(1) of CTA 2010 (gains etc on certain disposals treated as trading profits for corporation tax purposes) or section 517C of ITA 2007 (gains etc on certain disposals treated as trading profits for income tax purposes) applies in relation to it.

History – In s. 14B(1)(a), the words "(within the meaning given by Schedule B1)" inserted by FA 2016, s. 83 and Sch. 11, para. 2, with effect in relation to gains accruing on or after 6 April 2016.
In s. 14B(1), the words "subsections (5) and (6)" substituted for the words "subsection (5)" by FA 2016, s. 77(6)(a), with effect from 15 September 2016 (Royal Assent).
S. 14B(6) inserted by FA 2016, s. 77(6)(b), with effect from 15 September 2016 (Royal Assent).
S. 14B inserted by FA 2015, s. 37 and Sch. 7, para. 11, with effect in relation to disposals made on or after 6 April 2015.

14C Meaning of "disposal of a UK residential property interest"

14C [Omitted by FA 2016, s. 83 and Sch. 11, para. 3.]

History – S. 14C omitted by FA 2016, s. 83 and Sch. 11, para. 3, with effect in relation to gains accruing on or after 6 April 2016. Former s. 14C read as follows:

"Meaning of "disposal of a UK residential property interest"

14C Schedule B1 gives the meaning in this Act of "disposal of a UK residential property interest".

History – S. 14C inserted by FA 2015, s. 37 and Sch. 7, para. 11, with effect in relation to disposals made on or after 6 April 2015.".

14D Persons chargeable to capital gains tax on NRCGT gains

14D(1) A person is chargeable to capital gains tax in respect of any chargeable NRCGT gain accruing to the person in the tax year on a non-resident CGT disposal.

See also section 188D(1).

14D(2) Capital gains tax is charged on the total amount of chargeable NRCGT gains accruing to the person in the tax year, after deducting–

(a) any allowable losses accruing to the person in the tax year on disposals of UK residential property interests, and

(b) so far as they have not been allowed as a deduction from chargeable gains accruing in any previous tax year, any allowable losses accruing to the person in any previous tax year (not earlier than the tax year 1965–66) on disposals of UK residential property interests.

14D(3) In subsection (2), the reference to chargeable NRCGT gains does not include any such gains which accrue to a member of an NRCGT group.

14D(4) The only deductions that can be made from chargeable NRCGT gains to which subsection (2) applies are those permitted by this section.

This is subject to section 62(2AA) (carry-back of losses accruing in year of death).

14D(5) See section 57B and Schedule 4ZZB for how to determine–

(a) whether an NRCGT gain (or loss) accrues on a non-resident CGT disposal, and

(b) the amount of any NRCGT gain (or loss) so accruing.

History – S. 14D inserted by FA 2015, s. 37 and Sch. 7, para. 11, with effect in relation to disposals made on or after 6 April 2015.

14E Further provision about use of NRCGT losses

14E(1) Subsections (2) to (4) apply in relation to an allowable NRCGT loss accruing to a person in a tax year on a non-resident CGT disposal.

14E(2) The loss is not allowable as a deduction from chargeable gains accruing in any earlier tax year.

This is subject to section 62(2) and (2AA) (carry-back of losses accruing in year of death).

14E(3) Relief is not to be given under this Act more than once in respect of the loss or any part of the loss.

14E(4) Relief is not to be given under this Act in respect of the loss if, and so far as, relief has been or may be given in respect of it under the Tax Acts.

History – S. 14E inserted by FA 2015, s. 37 and Sch. 7, para. 11, with effect in relation to disposals made on or after 6 April 2015.

14F Persons not chargeable under section 14D if a claim is made

14F(1) A person is not chargeable to capital gains tax under section 14D in respect of a chargeable NRCGT gain accruing to the person on a non-resident CGT disposal if the person–

(a) is an eligible person in relation to the disposal, and

(b) makes a claim under this section with respect to the disposal.

14F(2) A diversely-held company which makes a non-resident CGT disposal is an eligible person in relation to the disposal.

14F(3) A scheme (see subsection (7)) which makes a non-resident CGT disposal is an eligible person in relation to the disposal if condition A or B is met.

14F(4) Condition A is that the scheme is a widely-marketed scheme throughout the relevant ownership period.

14F(5) Condition B is that–

(a) an investor in the scheme is an offshore fund, an open-ended investment company or an authorised unit trust ("the feeder fund"),

(b) the scheme is a widely-marketed scheme throughout the alternative period, after taking into account–

 (i) the scheme documents relating to the feeder fund, and

 (ii) the intended investors in the feeder fund, and

(c) the scheme and the feeder fund have the same manager.

14F(6) A company carrying on life assurance business (as defined in section 56 of the Finance Act 2012) which makes a non-resident CGT disposal is an eligible person if immediately before the time of the disposal the interest in UK land which is the subject of that disposal is held for the purpose of providing benefits to policyholders in the course of that business.

14F(7) In this section **"scheme"** means any of the following–

(a) a unit trust scheme;

(b) a company which is an open-ended investment company incorporated by virtue of regulations under section 262 of the Financial Services and Markets Act 2000;

(c) a company incorporated under the law of a territory outside the United Kingdom which is, under that law, the equivalent of an open-ended investment company.

14F(8) In this section **"the relevant ownership period"**, in relation to a scheme, means–

(a) the period beginning with the day on which the scheme acquired the interest in UK land which (or part of which) is the subject of the non-resident CGT disposal and ending with the day on which that disposal occurs, or

(b) if shorter, the period of 5 years ending with the day on which that disposal occurs.

14F(9) For the purposes of subsection (5), the **"alternative period"**, in relation to a scheme, is the shorter of–

(a) the relevant ownership period, and

(b) the period beginning when the feeder fund first became an investor in the scheme and ending with the date of the disposal.

14F(10) In this section–

"diversely-held company" means a company which is not a closely-held company;

"interest in UK land" has the same meaning as in Schedule B1;

"open-ended investment company" has the same meaning as in Part 17 of the Financial Services and Markets Act 2000 (see section 236 of that Act).

14F(11) In Schedule C1–

(a) Part 1 sets out the rules for determining whether or not a company is a closely-held company;

(b) Part 2 sets out how to determine whether or not a scheme is a widely-marketed scheme at any time.

History – S. 14F inserted by FA 2015, s. 37 and Sch. 7, para. 11, with effect in relation to disposals made on or after 6 April 2015.

14G Section 14F: divided companies

14G(1) This section applies where a company which makes a non-resident CGT disposal–

(a) is a divided company, and

(b) would, without this section, be an eligible person for the purposes of section 14F in relation to the disposal.

14G(2) In determining for the purposes of section 14F whether or not the company is an eligible company in relation to the disposal, the company is to be treated as if it were a closely-held company if the conditions in subsection (3) are met.

14G(3) The conditions are that–

(a) the gain or loss accruing on the disposal is primarily or wholly attributable to a particular division of the company, and

(b) if that division were a separate company, that separate company would be a closely-held company.

14G(4) For the purposes of this section a company is a **"divided company"** if, under the law under which the company is formed, under the company's articles of association or other document regulating the company or under arrangements entered into by or in relation to the company–

(a) some or all of the assets of the company are available primarily, or only, to meet particular liabilities of the company, and

(b) some or all of the members of the company, and some or all of its creditors, have rights primarily, or only, in relation to particular assets of the company.

14G(5) References in this section to a **"division"** of a divided company are to an identifiable part of the company that carries on distinct business activities and to which particular assets and liabilities of the company are primarily or wholly attributable.

History – S. 14G inserted by FA 2015, s. 37 and Sch. 7, para. 11, with effect in relation to disposals made on or after 6 April 2015.

14H Section 14F: arrangements for avoiding tax

14H(1) Subsection (2) applies where–

(a) arrangements are entered into, and

(b) the main purpose, or one of the main purposes, of any party entering into them (or any part of them) is to avoid capital gains tax being charged under section 14D as a result of a person not being an eligible person in relation to the disposal by virtue of subsection (2) (diversely-held companies) or, as the case may be, subsection (3) (widely-marketed schemes) of section 14F (persons not chargeable under section 14D if a claim is made).

14H(2) The arrangements (or that part of the arrangements) are to be disregarded in determining whether or not the company is an eligible person by virtue of that subsection.

14H(3) In this section **"arrangements"** includes any agreement, understanding, scheme, transaction or series of transactions (whether or not legally enforceable).

History – S. 14H inserted by FA 2015, s. 37 and Sch. 7, para. 11, with effect in relation to disposals made on or after 6 April 2015.

PART II – GENERAL PROVISIONS RELATING TO COMPUTATION OF GAINS AND ACQUISITIONS AND DISPOSALS OF ASSETS

Chapter I – Introductory

15 Computation of gains

15(1) The amount of the gains accruing on the disposal of assets shall be computed in accordance with this Part, subject to the other provisions of this Act.

15(2) Every gain shall, except as otherwise expressly provided, be a **chargeable gain**.

Derivations – CGTA 1979, s. 28(1), (2), 30, and see also FA 1982, s. 86.

Extra-statutory concessions – D39: extension of a lease by surrender of the old lease and grant of a new lease will not be regarded as a disposal.

Statements of practice – D7: treatment of VAT.

SP 2/97: simplified tax scheme for individuals investing regular sums in monthly savings schemes of authorised unit trusts and approved investment trusts.

Notes – S. 21–34: general meaning of "disposal" and "asset".

S. 35–52: general provisions for computation of gains, including (s. 38) allowable acquisition, enhancement and title expenditure.

S. 82(5): tax paid by past trustee of emigrating trust on resulting deemed disposals is not deductible.

S. 144(2): addition to disposal consideration in respect of any option consideration.
S. 152–157: adjustment of gain where proceeds reinvested in replacement assets.
S. 168(1): chargeable gain deemed to accrue to emigrating transferee in respect of gift for which gain held-over under s. 168 or 260.
S. 194(2): consideration for disposal of oil licence relating to an undeveloped area is deemed nil to extent that it consists of a similar licence or an obligation to undertake certain work.
S. 197: to ring fence certain oil results, chargeable gains on disposals of certain interests in oil fields etc. are left out of account in favour of a net chargeable gain or allowable loss on a notional disposal.
S. 212, 213: spreading of gains from annual deemed disposal by insurance company of holdings of unit trusts and relevant interests in offshore funds.
S. 217(4)(d), (5): notwithstanding s. 76(1), gain on disposal by member of an interest in a settlement comprising shares issued on incorporation of a building society is a chargeable gain but gain on disposal by former society of shares in the successor is not a chargeable gain.
S. 229(3): reduction in gain where partial roll-over for disposal of shares to employee share ownership trust.
S. 232–236: clawback by reference to deemed disposal and reacquisition or deemed chargeable gain where chargeable event occursfollowing roll-over on disposal of shares to qualifying share ownership trust.
S. 250(2), (5): certain sums received for the disposal of trees are excluded from the computation of the gain if the disponor is the occupier of the woodlands in point; consideration attributable to trees growing on the land is excluded from the gain on disposal of woodlands.
S. 253(5)–(8), 254(8), (9): deemed chargeable gain by way of clawback of relief given for losses in respect of loans to traders or guarantees therefor and of qualifying corporate bonds.
S. 260(3): chargeable gain reduced by held-over gain where gift on which inheritance tax chargeable.
S. 279: charge in respect of foreign assets crystallises when gains become remittable by reference to deemed chargeable gains.
ICTA 1988, s. 442: profit on transfer of overseas insurance business of UK branch to non-resident company is a chargeable gain rather than income.
TMA 1970, s. 11(1)(b): power of the Board to require particulars of disposals giving rise to chargeable gains.
For no gain, no loss enactments, see list in s. 35(3)(d) and see inability in some cases to substitute a gain for a loss or vice versa by using re-basing to 31 March 1982 (s. 35(4)), oil industry assets (s. 200(6)), member becoming absolutely entitled to settled property comprising shares issued on incorporation of a building society (s. 217(4)(c)), roll-over relief on disposal of shares to an employee share ownership trust (s. 229(1)), gifts etc. to employee trusts (s. 239(2)), roll-over relief on replacement of land compulsorily purchased (s. 247), gifts to charities etc. (s. 257(2)), gifts to housing associations etc.(s. 259(2)), inability to substitute a gain for a loss or vice versa using 6 April 1965 value (Sch. 2, para. 2(1), 9(4), 17(2)).
Apart from the partial effect of provisions above, the following gains are not chargeable gains:

- s. 45(1): certain tangible movable property which is a wasting asset;
- s. 51: winnings and damages for personal injury;
- s. 62(4), (5): transfer by personal representatives to legatee or disposal by way of donatio mortis causa;
- s. 72, 73: death of life tenant;
- s. 76: interest created by or arising under a settlement, except where acquired for money etc.;
- s. 115: gilt-edged securities, qualifying corporate bonds or options in respect thereof;
- s. 121: government non-marketable securities, including savings certificates, premium bonds, etc.;
- s. 150(2): gains in respect of certain BES shares;
- s. 150A(2): gains in respect of certain enterprise investment scheme shares.
- s. 176(6): subsequent relief where loss restricted by reference to a depreciatory transaction;
- s. 204: rights of insurer under policy of insurance and rights of insured excluding those relating to assets on disposal of which a gain could accrue.
- s. 210(2): life assurance policies etc., unless purchased from a third party;
- s. 223: gain to extent that relief provided for only or main residence;
- s. 237: payments out of superannuation funds, annuities and annual payments under covenant;
- s. 251: disposal of a debt in the hands of the original creditor, except a debt on a security;
- s. 256: subject to possible restriction, gains accruing to a charity which are applicable and applied for charitable purposes but subject to clawback where the proceeds cease to be subject to charitable trusts;
- s. 258(1): gifts of property falling to be treated for inheritance tax purposes as gifts for the public benefit under IHTA 1984, s. 26(2);
- s. 262: tangible movable property to extent that consideration does not exceed given limit and partial relief thereafter;
- s. 263: private cars etc.;
- s. 268: disposal of a decoration awarded for valour or gallant conduct acquired otherwise than for consideration in money or money's worth;
- s. 269: disposal of foreign currency acquired for personal use outside the UK;
- s. 271: gains on certain pension scheme investments, stocks held by the Bank of England, non-UK assets of consular officials etc.;
- Sch. 2, para. 16: gain apportioned to period before 6 April 1965;
- Sch. 6, para. 6–12: gains qualifying for retirement relief;
- Sch. 7AC: certain gains from disposals by company with substantial shareholding;
- SI 1989/469, reg. 17: shares held in a personal equity plan.
- SI 1998/1870, reg. 22: individual savings account investments.

16 Computation of losses

16(1) Subject to sections 261B, 261D and 263ZA and except as otherwise expressly provided, the amount of a loss accruing on a disposal of an asset shall be computed in the same way as the amount of a gain accruing on a disposal is computed.

16(2) Except as otherwise expressly provided, all the provisions of this Act which distinguish gains which are chargeable gains from those which are not, or which make part of a gain a chargeable gain, and part not, shall apply also to distinguish losses which are allowable losses from those which are not, and to make part of a loss an allowable loss, and part not; and references in this Act to an **allowable loss** shall be construed accordingly.

16(2A) A loss accruing to a person in a year of assessment shall not be an allowable loss for the purposes of this Act unless, in relation to that year, he gives a notice to an officer of the Board quantifying the amount of that loss; and sections 42 and 43 of the Management Act shall apply in relation to such a notice as if it were a claim for relief.

16(3) A loss accruing to a person in a year of assessment where the residence condition is not met (see section 2(1A)) shall not be an allowable loss for the purposes of this Act unless, under section 2B,10, 10B, 14D or 188D, he would be chargeable to tax in respect of a chargeable gain if there had been a gain instead of a loss on that occasion.

16(3A) If the person is an individual and the year is a split year as respects that individual, subsection (3) also applies to a loss accruing to the individual in the overseas part of that year.

16(4) [Omitted by FA 2008, s. 25 and Sch. 7, para. 61.]

History – In s. 16(1), the reference to TCGA 1992, s. 261B, s. 261D and s. 265ZA substituted for a reference to FA 1991, s. 72, by ITA 2007, s. 1027, Sch. 1, para. 298, with effect from 6 April 2007.
S. 16(2A) inserted by FA 1995, s. 113(1) for 1996–97 and later years of assessment; and for corporation tax for accounting periods ending on or after 1 July 1999, the appointed day under FA 1994, s. 199, by virtue of SI 1998/3173 (C. 78).
In s. 16(3), ", 10B, 14D or 188D" substituted for "or 10B" by FA 2015, s. 37 and Sch. 7, para. 12, with effect in relation to disposals made on or after 6 April 2015.
In s. 16(3), the words "where the residence condition is not met (see section 2(1A))" substituted for the words "during no part of which he is resident or ordinarily resident in the United Kingdom" by FA 2013, s. 219 and Sch. 46, para. 78, with effect in relation to a person's liability to capital gains tax for the tax year 2013–14 or any subsequent tax year, without prejudice to any provision in FA 2013, Sch. 46, Pt. 3 about the application of a particular amendment.
In s. 16(3), the words "2B," inserted by FA 2013, s. 65 and Sch. 25, para. 8, with effect in relation to disposals occurring on or after 6 April 2013.
In s. 16(3), words "or 10B" inserted by F(No. 2)A 2005, s. 34 and Sch. 4, para. 7(2) with effect, in accordance with F(No. 2)A 2005, Sch. 4, para. 10(2), in relation to any loss accruing to a company in an accounting period ending on or after 16 March 2005.
S. 16(3A) inserted by FA 2013, s. 218 and Sch. 45, para. 97, with effect in calculating an individual's liability to income tax or capital gains tax for the tax year 2013–14 or any subsequent tax year, subject to the transitional and saving provision in FA 2013, Sch. 45, para. 154–159.
S. 16(4) omitted by FA 2008, s. 25 and Sch. 7, para. 61 with effect from 2008–09 (FA 2008, Sch. 7, para. 81).

Derivations – CGTA 1979, s. 29(1)–(4).

Cross references – S. 10: extent of charge in respect of non-resident with UK branch or agency.
S. 10A(5): losses within s. 16(3) excluded from charge to CGT on temporary non-residents.
S. 53(2A): indexation may not be used to create or augment a loss on a disposal made on or after 30 November 1993 (subject to transitional relief for individuals and trustees by virtue of FA 1994, s. 93 and Sch. 12).
S. 12(1): charge to capital gains tax on remittance basis in respect of foreign assets of person with foreign domicile.
S. 97(6): notwithstanding s. 16(3), deduction for losses accruing to trustees in a tax year for which s. 87 (or CGTA 1979, s. 17) applied to attribute trust gains to a beneficiary.
S. 150A(2A): loss on a disposal of eligible shares issued on or after 1 January 1994 is an allowable loss.
Sch. 5, para. 1(2): as regards the attribution of certain gains to settlors in non-resident or dual resident settlements, losses are not prevented from being carried forward by s. 16(3).
Sch. 7B, para. 3: modification of s. 16(3) in relation to overseas life insurance companies applying in relation to accounting periods beginning after 31 December 1992.
FA 1991, s. 72: relevant amount of unrelieved trading loss can be claimed as allowable capital gains tax loss. The amount of allowable trading loss is calculated disregarding taper relief in respect of losses sustained in the trading year 2004–05 and subsequent years, but election may be made for earlier treatment in accordance with this rule.
FA 1996, Sch. 13, para. 13D: corporate strips: manipulation of price: associated payment giving rise to CGT loss: conditions for loss being disallowable for CGT purposes.
SI 2009/3001, reg. 42: certain offshore funds: no loss to be treated as arising on disposals of interests, notwithstanding s. 16.

Extra-statutory concessions – A94: losses by theatre backers ("angels") may be treated as Sch. D, Case VI losses, rather than capital losses (Revenue press release, 18 February 1996).

Statements of practice – SP 2/97: simplified tax scheme for individuals investing regular sums in monthly savings schemes of authorised unit trusts and approved investment trusts.

Notes – S. 9–14: residence etc.
S. 21–34: general meaning of "disposal" and "asset".
S. 71: unused losses of trustees transferred to person becoming absolutely entitled to settled property.
S. 176: restriction of allowable loss on a disposal following a depreciatory transaction.
S. 197: to ring fence certain oil results, allowable losses on disposals of certain interests in oil fields etc. are left out of account in favour of a net chargeable gain or allowable loss on a notional disposal.
S. 200(5): limitation of losses on disposal of certain oil industry assets.
S. 202: claim to crystallise a loss in respect of an interest in land subject to a type of mineral lease or agreement.
S. 212, 213: spreading of losses from annual deemed disposal by insurance company of holdings of unit trusts and relevant interests in offshore funds.
S. 253, 254: deemed allowable loss in respect of certain loans to traders or guarantees in respect thereof and of qualifying corporate bonds.
S. 262(3): losses on tangible movable property restricted by reference to floor on disposal consideration.
S. 275: location of assets (see also s. 276).
S. 276: territorial sea of the UK deemed to be part of the UK and certain exploration or exploitation rights effectively deemed to be UK assets.
Sch. 11, para. 12: unrelieved Sch. D, Case VII loss treated as an allowable loss.
ICTA 1988, s. 442: loss on transfer of overseas insurance business of UK branch to non-resident company is an allowable loss for tax on chargeable gains rather than income.
ICTA 1988, s. 573–576: losses on unquoted shares in trading companies set against income.
TMA 1970, s. 11(1)(b): power of the Board to requireparticulars of disposals giving rise to allowable losses.
FA 1990, Sch. 12, para. 6: apportionment of unallowed capital losses on reorganisation of the undertakings of the Independent Broadcasting Authority and Cable Authority.
F(No. 2)A 1992, s. 77 and Sch. 17, para. 3: treatment of unallowed capital losses on privatisation of Northern Ireland Electricity.
FA 1995, s. 113(2): priority of allowable losses:

- losses accruing in 1996–97 set off before losses accruing in earlier years of assessment;
- losses accruing to a company in an accounting period ending on or after 1 July 1999 set off before losses accruing in an accounting period ending before that date.

Electricity Act 1989, Sch. 11, para. 4 (not reproduced): treatment of unallowed capital losses on privatisation.
For no gain, no loss enactments, see list in s. 35(3)(d) and see inability in some cases to substitute a gain for a loss or vice versa by using re-basing to 31 March 1982 (s. 35(4)), oil industry assets (s. 200(6)), member becoming absolutely entitled to settled property comprising shares issued on incorporation of a building society (s. 217(4)(c)), roll-over relief on disposal of shares to an employee

share ownership trust (s. 229(1)), gifts etc. to employee trusts (s. 239(2)), roll-over relief on replacement of land compulsorily purchased (s. 247), gifts to charities etc. (s. 257(2)), gifts to housing associations etc. (S. 259(2)), loss accruing to a former port authority on a disposal attracting ports levy (Ports Act 1991, s. 35(3)), inability to substitute a gain for a loss or vice versa by using 6 April 1965 value (Sch. 2, para. 2(1), 9(4), 17(2)).

Apart from provisions relating to the computation of gains, which indirectly apply to losses, there are special provisions for computation of allowable losses as follows:

- s. 30(5), (6): just and reasonable determination of disposal consideration where tax-free benefit from value shifting;
- s. 41: allowable expenditure restricted by reference to capital allowances;
- s. 176: reduction by reference to a depreciatory transaction.

Losses which are specifically not allowable losses (see also notes to s. 15 on gains which are not chargeable gains):

- s. 8(2): loss accruing to a company where if a gain accrued the company would be exempt from corporation tax in respect of it;
- s. 29(3): loss attributable to value having been shifted out of shares etc. which are thereby deemed to be disposed of;
- s. 51: disposal of rights to winnings;
- s. 62(2A): losses on death cannot be set against gains brought into account by s. 2(5)(b);
- s. 150(2): losses in respect of certain BES shares;
- s. 150A(1): losses in respect of certain enterprise investment scheme shares.
- s. 251(4): disposal of debt acquired from the original creditor by a connected person;
- ICTA 1988, s. 574: loss on unquoted shares in trading company relieved against income;
- SI 1989/469, reg. 17(1): losses in respect of personal equity plan investments.
- SI 1998/1870, reg. 22(1)(b): losses in respect of individual savings account investments.

16ZA Losses: non-UK domiciled individuals

16ZA(1) In this section **"the relevant tax year"**, in relation to an individual, means the first tax year for which–

(a) section 809B of ITA 2007 (claim for remittance basis) applies to the individual, and

(b) the individual is not domiciled in the United Kingdom.

16ZA(2) An individual may make an election under this section for the relevant tax year (in which case sections 16ZB and 16ZC have effect in relation to the individual for the relevant tax year and all subsequent tax years).

16ZA(3) If an individual does not make such an election, foreign losses accruing to the individual in–

(a) the relevant tax year, or

(b) any subsequent tax year except one in which the individual is domiciled in the United Kingdom,

are not allowable losses.

16ZA(4) Sections 42 and 43 of the Management Act (procedure and time limit for making claims), except section 42(1A) of that Act, apply in relation to an election under this section as they apply in relation to a claim for relief.

16ZA(5) An election under this section is irrevocable.

16ZA(6) In this section **"foreign loss"** means a loss accruing from the disposal of an asset situated outside the United Kingdom.

History – S. 16ZA inserted by FA 2008, s. 25 and Sch. 7, para. 62 with effect from 2008–09 (FA 2008, Sch. 7, para. 81).

16ZB Individual who has made election under section 16ZA: foreign chargeable gains remitted in tax year after tax year in which accrue

16ZB(1) This section applies to an individual for a tax year ("the applicable tax year") if–

(a) the individual has made an election under section 16ZA,

(b) foreign chargeable gains accrued to the individual in or after the relevant tax year (within the meaning of section 16ZA) but before the applicable tax year, and

(c) by reason of the remission of any of the foreign chargeable gains to the United Kingdom, chargeable gains are treated under section 12 as accruing to the individual in the applicable tax year or a part of the applicable tax year ("the relevant gains").

16ZB(2) Section 2(2) or (4) has effect for the applicable tax year as if the relevant gains had not accrued.

16ZB(3) The amount on which the individual is charged to capital gains tax for the applicable tax year is (instead of the amount given by section 2(2) or (4)(b), as reduced under section 3) the sum of–

(a) the adjusted taxable amount, and

(b) the amount of the relevant gains.

16ZB(4) **"The adjusted taxable amount"** is–

(a) if section 3(1) (annual exempt amount) does not apply to the individual for the applicable tax year, the amount given by section 2(2) or (4)(b) as it has effect by virtue of subsection (2), and

(b) otherwise, so much of that amount as exceeds the exempt amount for the applicable tax year (within the meaning of section 3).

16ZB(5) In subsection (1) **"foreign chargeable gains"** has the meaning given by section 12(4).

16ZB(6) For the purposes of subsection (1)(c) foreign chargeable gains are remitted to the United Kingdom if they are regarded as so remitted for the purposes of section 12.

History – In s. 16ZB(1)(c), the words "or a part of the applicable tax year" inserted by FA 2013, s. 218 and Sch. 45, para. 98, with effect in calculating an individual's liability to income tax or capital gains tax for the tax year 2013–14 or any subsequent tax year, subject to the transitional and saving provision in FA 2013, Sch. 45, para. 154–159.
S. 16ZB inserted by FA 2008, s. 25 and Sch. 7, para. 62 with effect from 2008–09 (FA 2008, Sch. 7, para. 81).

16ZC Individual who has made election under section 16ZA and to whom remittance basis applies

16ZC(1) This section applies to an individual for a tax year if–

(a) the individual has made an election under section 16ZA for the tax year or any earlier tax year,

(b) section 809B, 809D or 809E of ITA 2007 (remittance basis) applies to the individual for the tax year, and

(c) the individual is not domiciled in the United Kingdom in the tax year.

16ZC(2) The following steps apply for the purpose of calculating the amount on which the individual is to be charged to capital gains tax for the tax year.

Step 1

Deduct any relevant allowable losses from the chargeable gains referred to in subsection (3) in the order in which they appear there (starting with paragraph (a) of that subsection).

If allowable losses are deductible from the chargeable gains referred to in subsection (3)(b) but are not enough to exhaust them all–

(a) those chargeable gains are to be ordered according to the day on which they accrued,

(b) the losses are to be deducted from those gains in reverse chronological order (starting with the last chargeable gain to accrue), and

(c) if allowable losses are deductible from chargeable gains that accrued on a particular day but are not enough to exhaust all of the chargeable gains that accrued on that day, the amount deducted from each of those chargeable gains is the appropriate proportion of the losses.

In paragraph (c) **"the appropriate proportion"**, in relation to a chargeable gain, is the amount of that gain divided by the total amount of the chargeable gains that accrued on the day in question.

Step 2

Treat the amount referred to in section 2(2) or (4)(a) or 16ZB(3)(a) as being equal to–

(a) the amount it would be if there were no relevant allowable losses, minus

(b) the total amount deducted under Step 1 from chargeable gains within subsection (3)(a) or (c).

16ZC(3) The chargeable gains are–

(a) foreign chargeable gains accruing to the individual in the tax year, to the extent that they are remitted to the United Kingdom in that year or, if that year is a split year as respects the individual, in the UK part of that year,

(b) foreign chargeable gains accruing to the individual in that year, to the extent that they are not so remitted in that year or they are so remitted in that year but it is a split year as respects the individual and they are so remitted in the overseas part of the year, and

(c) chargeable gains accruing to the individual in that year (other than foreign chargeable gains).

16ZC(4) Chargeable gains treated as accruing under section 87 or 89(2) (read, where appropriate, with section 10A) are not within any paragraph of subsection (3).

16ZC(5) Chargeable gains treated as accruing under section 12 are not within subsection (3)(c).

16ZC(6) For the purposes of subsection (3) foreign chargeable gains are remitted to the United Kingdom if they are regarded as so remitted for the purposes of section 12.

16ZC(7) In this section–

"relevant allowable losses" means the allowable losses that section 2(2) provides may be deducted from chargeable gains accruing to the individual in the tax year or a part of the tax year, and

"foreign chargeable gains" has the meaning given by section 12(4).

History – In s. 16ZC(3)(a), the words "or, if that year is a split year as respects the individual, in the UK part of that year" inserted by FA 2013, s. 218 and Sch. 45, para. 99(2)(a), with effect in calculating an individual's liability to income tax or capital gains tax for the tax year 2013–14 or any subsequent tax year, subject to the transitional and saving provision in FA 2013, Sch. 45, para. 154–159.
In s. 16ZC(3)(b), the words "or they are so remitted in that year but it is a split year as respects the individual and they are so remitted in the overseas part of the year" inserted by FA 2013, s. 218 and Sch. 45, para. 99(2)(b), with effect in calculating an individual's liability to income tax or capital gains tax for the tax year 2013–14 or any subsequent tax year, subject to the transitional and saving provision in FA 2013, Sch. 45, para. 154–159.

In s. 16ZC(7), in the definition of "relevant allowable losses", the words "or a part of the tax year" inserted by FA 2013, s. 218 and Sch. 45, para. 99(3), with effect in calculating an individual's liability to income tax or capital gains tax for the tax year 2013–14 or any subsequent tax year, subject to the transitional and saving provision in FA 2013, Sch. 45, para. 154–159.
S. 16ZC inserted by FA 2008, s. 25 and Sch. 7, para. 62 with effect from 2008-09 (FA 2008, Sch. 7, para. 81).

16ZD Section 16ZC: supplementary

16ZD(1) This section applies if section 16ZC applies to an individual for a tax year.

16ZD(2) Any allowable loss deducted under step 1 of section 16ZC(2) is to be regarded (for the purposes of section 2(2)(b)) as allowed as a deduction from chargeable gains accruing to the individual in the tax year.

16ZD(3) If a deduction is made under step 1 of section 16ZC(2) from a foreign chargeable gain within section 16ZC(3)(b), the amount of the foreign chargeable gain is reduced by the amount deducted.

History – S. 16ZD inserted by FA 2008, s. 25 and Sch. 7, para. 62 with effect from 2008-09 (FA 2008, Sch. 7, para. 81).

16A Restrictions on allowable losses

16A(1) For the purposes of this Act, "allowable loss" does not include a loss accruing to a person if–

(a) it accrues to the person directly or indirectly in consequence of, or otherwise in connection with, any arrangements, and

(b) the main purpose, or one of the main purposes, of the arrangements is to secure a tax advantage.

16A(2) For the purposes of subsection (1)–

"arrangements" includes any agreement, understanding, scheme, transaction or series of transactions (whether or not legally enforceable), and

"tax advantage" means–

(a) relief or increased relief from tax,

(b) repayment or increased repayment of tax,

(c) the avoidance or reduction of a charge to tax or an assessment to tax, or

(d) the avoidance of a possible assessment to tax,

and for the purposes of this definition **"tax"** means capital gains tax, corporation tax or income tax.

16A(3) For the purposes of subsection (1) it does not matter–

(a) whether the loss accrues at a time when there are no chargeable gains from which it could otherwise have been deducted, or

(b) whether the tax advantage is secured for the person to whom the loss accrues or for any other person.

History – S. 16A inserted by FA 2007, s. 27(3) with effect in relation to losses accruing on disposals made on or after 6 December 2006 (FA 2007, s. 27(6)).

17 Disposals and acquisitions treated as made at market value

17(1) Subject to the provisions of this Act, a person's acquisition or disposal of an asset shall for the purposes of this Act be deemed to be for a consideration equal to the market value of the asset–

(a) where he acquires or, as the case may be, disposes of the asset otherwise than by way of a bargain made at arm's length, and in particular where he acquires or disposes of it by way of gift or on a transfer into settlement by a settlor or by way of distribution from a company in respect of shares in the company, or

(b) where he acquires or, as the case may be, disposes of the asset wholly or partly for a consideration that cannot be valued, or in connection with his own or another's loss of office or employment or diminution of emoluments, or otherwise in consideration for or recognition of his or another's services or past services in any office or employment or of any other service rendered or to be rendered by him or another.

17(2) Subsection (1) shall not apply to the acquisition of an asset if–

(a) there is no corresponding disposal of it, and

(b) there is no consideration in money or money's worth or the consideration is of an amount or value lower than the market value of the asset.

Derivations – CGTA 1979, s. 29A(1), (2), as inserted by FA 1981, s. 90(1), and as amended (s. 29A(2)) by FA 1984, s. 66(1).

Cross references – S. 62(5): priority of provision deeming there to be no chargeable gain on a disposal by donatio mortis causa.
S. 142: *person absolutely entitled* as against the trustee to shares issued as a stock dividend treated as acquiring them for the appropriate amount in cash, notwithstanding s. 17(1).
S. 144ZA: application of market value rule in case of exercise of option.
S. 149A: disapplication of s. 17(1) in respect of certain options granted on or after 16 March 1993.
S. 149B: disapplication of s. 17(1) in respect of conditional interests in shares granted under employee incentive schemes.
S. 165(7): hold-over gain on gifts of business assets, reduced by reference to any actual consideration outside s. 17.
S. 239(2): disapplication of s. 17(1) to certain disposals by a company or an individual to an employee trust.

S. 257(2): disapplication of s. 17(1) to certain disposals to a charity or for national purposes.
S. 259(2): disapplication of s. 17(1) to certain disposals to housing associations.
ICTA 1988, s. 185(3)(b): disapplication in calculating the consideration for acquisition of shares by an employee etc. on exercise of rights under an approved share option scheme (and any corresponding disposal of them).
FA 1988, s. 68(4): disapplication to acquisition of shares on a priority allocation for employees etc. exempt from certain charges to income tax.
FA 2005, s. 53: determining consideration for sale and purchase of asset where FA 2005, s. 47 applies to alternative finance arrangements.
SI 2013/2242, art. 3(b): in relation to a disposal constituted by a relevant transfer from BRB (Residuary) Limited ("BRB Residuary") to Network Rail Infrastructure Limited ("Network Rail"), s. 17 is not to have effect and the disposal is to be treated as made:
(i) in a case where consideration in money or money's worth is given by Network Rail or on its behalf for a consideration equal to the amount or value of that consideration, or
(ii) in a case where no such consideration is given, for a consideration of nil.

HMRC interpretations – IRInt. 91: HMRC will use market value to compute chargeable gain on employer transferring an asset to an employee at undervalue.

Notes – S. 21–34: general meaning of "disposal" and "asset".
S. 70: transfers into settlement as disposals of the entire property in point.
S. 122, 123: capital distributions in respect of shares etc.
S. 125: apportionment to shareholders of close company effectively reducing base cost where company transfers asset otherwise than by bargain made at arm's length.
S. 165–169: relief for gifts of business assets.
S. 256–261: charities and relief for gifts of non-business assets etc.
S. 272–274 and Sch. 11: meaning of "market value".
S. 288: interpretation, including shares as encompassing stock.
See notes to s. 38 for other deemed market value transactions.

18 Transactions between connected persons

18(1) This section shall apply where a person acquires an asset and the person making the disposal is connected with him.

18(2) Without prejudice to the generality of section 17(1) the person acquiring the asset and the person making the disposal shall be treated as parties to a transaction otherwise than by way of a bargain made at arm's length.

18(3) Subject to subsection (4) below, if on the disposal a loss accrues to the person making the disposal, it shall not be deductible except from a chargeable gain accruing to him on some other disposal of an asset to the person acquiring the asset mentioned in subsection (1) above, being a disposal made at a time when they are connected persons.

18(4) Subsection (3) above shall not apply to a disposal by way of gift in settlement if the gift and the income from it is wholly or primarily applicable for educational, cultural or recreational purposes, and the persons benefiting from the application for those purposes are confined to members of an association of persons for whose benefit the gift was made, not being persons all or most of whom are connected persons.

18(5) Where the asset mentioned in subsection (1) above is an option to enter into a sale or other transaction given by the person making the disposal a loss accruing to the person acquiring the asset shall not be an allowable loss unless it accrues on a disposal of the option at arm's length to a person who is not connected with him.

18(6) Subject to subsection (7) below, in a case where the asset mentioned in subsection (1) above is subject to any right or restriction enforceable by the person making the disposal, or by a person connected with him, then (where the amount of the consideration for the acquisition is, in accordance with subsection (2) above, deemed to be equal to the market value of the asset) that market value shall be–

(a) what its market value would be if not subject to the right or restriction, minus–

(b) the market value of the right or restriction or the amount by which its extinction would enhance the value of the asset to its owner, whichever is the less.

18(7) If the right or restriction is of such a nature that its enforcement would or might effectively destroy or substantially impair the value of the asset without bringing any countervailing advantage either to the person making the disposal or a person connected with him or is an option or other right to acquire the asset or, in the case of incorporeal property, is a right to extinguish the asset in the hands of the person giving the consideration by forfeiture or merger or otherwise, the market value of the asset shall be determined, and the amount of the gain accruing on the disposal shall be computed, as if the right or restriction did not exist.

18(8) Subsections (6) and (7) above shall not apply to a right of forfeiture or other right exercisable on breach of a covenant contained in a lease of land or other property, and shall not apply to any right or restriction under a mortgage or other charge.

Derivations – CGTA 1979, s. 62, as amended by FA 1981, s. 90(3).

Cross references – S. 197(6), (7): material disposals involving certain interests in oil fields etc. to connected persons left out the ring fence provisions but generally s. 18(3) applies.
Sch. 11, para. 12: unrelieved Sch. D, Case VII loss treated as an allowable loss subject to s. 18.
FA 2004, s. 133: companies in partnership: relationship with chargeable gains.

HMRC interpretations – IRInt. 38: connected persons in relation to settlements, application of s. 18(3).

Other material – Taxline 1995/86 (not reproduced): contract can provide that sale price of property is to be adjusted to figure agreed with District Valuer.

Notes – S. 21–34: general meaning of "disposal" and "asset", including the time of certain disposals.
S. 58: priority of no gain, no loss rule for transfers between spouses.
S. 68: meaning of "settled property".
S. 143–149: treatment of certain options.
S. 286: meaning of "connected" in references to persons being connected with one another.

19 Deemed consideration in certain cases where assets disposed of in a series of transactions

19(1) For the purposes of this Act, in any case where–

(a) by way of 2 or more material transactions which are linked (a series of linked transactions), one person disposes of assets to another person with whom he is connected or to 2 or more other persons with each of whom he is connected, and

(b) the original market value of the assets disposed of by any of the transactions in the series as determined under section 20, is less than the appropriate portion of the aggregate market value of the assets disposed of by all the transactions in the series, as so determined,

then, subject to subsection (2) below, the disposal effected by any linked transaction in the series in respect of which the condition in paragraph (b) above is fulfilled shall be deemed to be for a consideration equal to the appropriate portion referred to in that paragraph.

19(2) Where the disposal effected by a material transaction is one to which section 58 applies, nothing in subsection (1) above shall affect the amount which, for the purposes of this Act, is the consideration for that disposal.

19(3) Subject to subsection (5) below, any reference in this section to a material transaction is a reference to a transaction by way of gift or otherwise; and, for the purposes of this section, 2 or more material transactions are linked if they occur within the period of 6 years ending on the date of the last of them.

19(4) This section shall apply or, as the case may be, shall again apply–

(a) when a second material transaction causes a series of linked transactions to come into being; and

(b) whenever, on the occurrence of a further material transaction, an existing series is extended by the inclusion of that transaction (whether or not an earlier transaction ceases to form part of the series);

and all such assessments and adjustments of assessments shall be made as may be necessary to give effect to this section on each such occasion.

19(5) Where a member of a group of companies disposes of an asset to another member of the group in circumstances such that, by virtue of section 171, both companies are treated, so far as relates to corporation tax on chargeable gains, as if the consideration for the disposal were of such an amount as would secure that neither a gain nor a loss would accrue, the transaction by which that disposal is effected is not a material transaction; and a disposal in these circumstances is in this section referred to as an **"inter-group transfer"**.

19(6) In any case where–

(a) a company (**"company A"**) disposes of an asset by way of a material transaction, and

(b) company A acquired the asset after 19th March 1985 by way of an inter-group transfer, and

(c) the disposal by company A is to a person who is connected with another company (**"company B"**) which at some time after 19th March 1985 disposed of the asset by way of an inter-group transfer, and

(d) either the disposal by way of inter-group transfer which is referred to in paragraph (c) above was the occasion of the acquisition referred to in paragraph (b) above or, between that disposal and that acquisition, there has been no disposal of the asset which was not an inter-group transfer,

then, for the purpose of determining whether subsection (1) above applies in relation to a series of linked transactions, the disposal by company A shall be treated as having been made by company B; but any increase in the consideration for that disposal resulting from the application of subsection (1) above shall have effect with respect to company A.

Derivations – FA 1985, s. 71(1)–(4), (6), (7).

Cross references – S. 58: deemed no gain, no loss on transfers between spouses.
S. 171: deemed no gain, no loss transfers of capital assets within a group.
Sch. 11, para. 2: transitional provisions for gifts and transactions between connected persons before 20 March 1985.

Notes – S. 21–34: general meaning of "disposal" and "asset".
S. 286: meaning of "connected" in references to persons being connected with one another.
S. 288: interpretation, including the meaning of "company" and reference to sections being those of this Act.
TMA 1970, s. 29: assessing procedure.

20 Original market value and aggregate market value for purposes of section 19

20(1) This section has effect for determining the original market value of assets and the aggregate market value of assets as mentioned in subsection (1)(b) of section 19.

20(2) Expressions used in this section have the same meaning as in that section.

20(3) Where there is a series of linked transactions, the original market value of the assets disposed of by each transaction in the series shall be determined as follows–

(a) if at the time in question the transaction is the most recent in the series, the original market value of the assets disposed of by that transaction is the market value which, apart from section 19, would be deemed to be the consideration for that transaction for the purposes of this Act; and

(b) in the case of any other transaction in the series, the original market value of the assets disposed of by that transaction is the value which, prior to the occurrence of the most recent transaction in the series, was or would have been deemed for the purposes of this Act to be the consideration for the transaction concerned (whether by virtue of the previous operation of section 19, or by virtue of any other provision of this Act).

20(4) Subject to subsections (6) to (9) below, in relation to any transaction in a series of linked transactions–

(a) any reference in this section or section 19 to the aggregate market value of the assets disposed of by all the transactions in the series is a reference to what would have been the market value of all those assets for the purposes of this Act if, considering all the assets together, they had been disposed of by one disposal occurring at the time of the transaction concerned; and

(b) any reference in section 19 to the appropriate portion of the aggregate market value of the assets disposed of by all the transactions in the series is a reference to that portion of the market value determined in accordance with paragraph (a) above which it is reasonable to apportion to those of the assets which were actually disposed of by the transaction concerned.

20(5) The reference in subsection (4)(a) above to considering all the assets together includes a reference not only to considering them as a group or holding or collection of assets retaining their separate identities but also (if it gives a higher market value) to considering them as brought together, physically or in law, so as to constitute either a single asset or a number of assets which are distinct from those which were comprised in each of the transactions concerned.

20(6) If any of the assets disposed of by all the transactions in a series of linked transactions were acquired after the time of the first of those transactions, then, in the application of subsections (4) and (5) above in relation to each of the transactions in the series–

(a) no account shall be taken of any assets which were acquired after the time of that transaction unless they were acquired by way of an inter-group transfer; and

(b) subject to subsection (7) below, the number of assets of which account is to be taken shall be limited to the maximum number which were held by the person making the disposal at any time in the period beginning immediately before the first of the transactions in the series and ending immediately before the last.

20(7) If, before the first of the transactions referred to in paragraph (b) of subsection (6) above, the person concerned (being a company) disposed of any assets by way of an inter-group transfer, the maximum number of assets referred to in that paragraph shall be determined as if the inter-group transfer had occurred after that first transaction.

20(8) In the application of subsection (6) above in a case where the assets disposed of are securities, the assets disposed of by any of the transactions in a series of linked transactions shall be identified with assets acquired on an earlier date rather than with assets acquired on a later date.

20(9) In subsection (8) above **"securities"** includes any assets which are of a nature to be dealt in without identifying the particular assets disposed of or acquired.

Derivations – FA 1985, Sch. 21.

Notes – S. 21–34: general meaning of "disposal" and "asset", including the time of certain disposals.
S. 272–274 and Sch. 11: meaning of "market value".
S. 288: interpretation, including the meaning of "company" and reference to sections being those of this Act.

Chapter II – Assets and Disposals of Assets

GENERAL PROVISIONS

21 Assets and disposals

21(1) All forms of property shall be **assets** for the purposes of this Act, whether situated in the United Kingdom or not, including–

(a) options, debts and incorporeal property generally, and

(b) currency, with the exception (subject to express provision to the contrary) of sterling,

(c) any form of property created by the person disposing of it, or otherwise coming to be owned without being acquired.

21(2) For the purposes of this Act–

(a) references to a **disposal** of an asset include, except where the context otherwise requires, references to a part disposal of an asset, and

(b) there is a **part disposal** of an asset where an interest or right in or over the asset is created by the disposal, as well as where it subsists before the disposal, and generally, there is a part disposal of an asset where, on a person making a disposal, any description of property derived from the asset remains undisposed of.

History – S. 21(1)(b) substituted by FA 2006, s. 88 and Sch. 12, para. 9, with effect from 19 July 2006.

Derivations – CGTA 1979, s. 19(1), (2).

Cross references – S. 144(1): grant of an option is a disposal of an option except in certain circumstances when it can be treated as part of a larger transaction, without prejudice to s. 21.
FA 2003, s. 195: companies acquiring their own shares.

Extra-statutory concessions – D39: extension of a lease by surrender of the old lease and grant of a new lease will not be regarded as a disposal.

Statements of practice – SP 2/97: simplified tax scheme for individuals investing regular sums in monthly savings schemes of authorised unit trusts and approved investment trusts.

HMRC interpretations – IRInt. 11: grantor of option over land thereby disposes of an equitable interest in the land but this is treated as a separate disposal, although roll-over relief on replacement of business assets may be available by reference to the underlying land.
IRInt. 202: HMRC view that the right to occupy a "pitch" at a particular racecourse is an asset for CGT purposes, with no market value under the pre-October 1998 system of allocation.

Other material – Tax Bulletin TB04/98-1: building society and other windfalls: free shares and cash bonuses.
HMRC "Working Together" Bulletin, issue 6, August 2001: windfall payments made to Scottish Widows joint life policy holders: cash payments treated as immediate capital gain with no expenditure to set against the gain; payment in loan notes a chargeable gain in year in which loan notes redeemed or sold.

Notes – S. 42: apportionment of allowable expenditure on a part disposal.
S. 56: calculation of indexation allowance on a part disposal.
S. 70: transfer into settlement is a disposal.
S. 71: deemed disposal when person becomes absolutely entitled to settled property.
S. 72, 73: deemed disposal on death of life tenant.
S. 76: deemed disposal when person who acquired an interest in settled property becomes absolutely entitled to any of the settled property.
S. 80: deemed disposal where trustees cease to be resident and ordinarily resident.
S. 122: except in certain circumstances, capital distributions treated as part disposals of shares.
S. 126(3): deemed disposal by shareholder on redemption of shares otherwise than by the issue of shares or debentures and otherwise than in a liquidation.
S. 127: reorganisation not to be treated as involving a disposal, except in relation to consideration other than any new holding; also extended to conversions (s. 132), exchanges (s. 135) and reconstructions involving the issue of shares (s. 136).
S. 134: compulsory acquisition of shares in exchange for gilt-edged stock not to involve a disposal.
S. 143–149: treatment of certain options, commodity deals and financial futures.
S. 185–188: deemed disposal where a company ceases to be resident or becomes dual resident, unless assets remain chargeable, or where a company, being dual resident, becomes exempt.
S. 199: deemed disposals by non-residents of assets ceasing to be chargeable assets by virtue of ceasing to be dedicated to an oil field etc. and of assets which do not continue to be used for UK exploration or exploitation activities on cessation of a UK branch etc. (or later when such assets as do so continue cease to be used in that way).
S. 210: paymentof sums assured, transfer of investments etc. to the assured, surrender of assurance policy, payment of the first instalment of a deferred annuity and the surrender of rights under a contract for a deferred annuity are occasions of disposal.
S. 212–214: annual deemed disposal by insurance company of holdings of unit trusts and relevant interests in offshore funds, subject to transitional provisions permitting the company to effect certain exchanges on a tax-free basis.
S. 232–234: clawback by reference to deemed disposal and reacquisition or deemed chargeable gain where chargeable event occurs following roll-over on disposal of shares to qualifying share ownership trust.
S. 238(4): switching of certain rights in approved share option and profit sharing schemes on a takeover does not involve a disposal and the replacement right is treated as the same asset as the original right.
S. 242–244: claims for small part disposals of land not to be treated as disposals.
S. 245: deemed part disposal where land compulsorily acquired and the consideration includes an amount for splitting a larger holding.
S. 249: grants for giving up agricultural land are not treated as consideration for the disposal of any asset.
S. 251–255: treatment of certain debts.
S. 256(2): deemed disposal and reacquisition where property ceases to be subject to charitable trusts.
S. 258(5): deemed market value disposal where sale or failure to observe undertaking as regards designated property.
S. 269: exemption in respect of foreign currency for personal expenditure.
S. 275: location of assets (see also s. 276).
S. 276: territorial sea of the UK deemed to be part of the UK and certain exploration or exploitation rights effectively deemed to be UK assets.

22 Disposal where capital sums derived from assets

22(1) Subject to sections 23 and 26(1), and to any other exceptions in this Act, there is for the purposes of this Act a **disposal** of assets by their owner where any capital sum is derived from assets notwithstanding that no asset is acquired by the person paying the capital sum, and this subsection applies in particular to–

(a) capital sums received by way of compensation for any kind of damage or injury to assets or for the loss, destruction or dissipation of assets or for any depreciation or risk of depreciation of an asset,

(b) capital sums received under a policy of insurance of the risk of any kind of damage or injury to, or the loss or depreciation of, assets,

(c) capital sums received in return for forfeiture or surrender of rights, or for refraining from exercising rights, and

(d) capital sums received as consideration for use or exploitation of assets.

22(2) In the case of a disposal within paragraph (a), (b), (c) or (d) of subsection (1) above, the time of the disposal shall be the time when the capital sum is received as described in that subsection.

22(3) In this section **"capital sum"** means any money or money's worth which is not excluded from the consideration taken into account in the computation of the gain.

22(4) Subsection (1) does not apply where a company receives, or becomes entitled to receive–

(a) a capital distribution within the meaning of section 122 (see instead subsection (1) of that section), or

(b) a distribution to which the charge to corporation tax on income under Part 9A of CTA 2009 (company distributions) applies or would apply were the distribution not exempt for the purposes of that Part.

History – S. 22(4) inserted by F(No. 3)A 2010, s. 9 and Sch. 3, para. 4(2), with effect in relation to distributions made on or after 1 July 2009, subject to any election made under F(No. 3)A 2010, Sch. 3, para. 7 in respect of distributions made before 22 June 2010. See cross-reference note below for treatment of certain distributions of UK resident companies made before 1 July 2009.

Derivations – CGTA 1979, s. 20.

Cross references – S. 204(2): notwithstanding the limitation of gains for disposal of rights under a policy for risk to assets by reference to the nature of the assets insured, receipts under such a policy are sums derived from assets.
S. 214C(1): taper relief not available on gains accruing on certain re-organisations (e.g. reconstructions or amalgamations of mutual companies, building societies or friendly societies).
S. 245(1): in considering need for apportionment of compulsory acquisition consideration so as to treat part as a capital sum within s. 22(1)(a), disregard of the compulsory nature thereof and of any statutory provision treating the consideration as being for land itself.
S. 250(2): certain sums received under a policy of insurance relating to woodlands are excluded from the computation of the gain if the disponor is the occupier.
Sch. 2, para. 10(8): in relation to land held at 6 April 1965, the current use value of land from which a receipt within s. 22(1)(a), (c) or (d) is derived is determined without reference to the circumstances causing the receipt.
F(No. 3)A 2010, Sch. 3, para. 6(3): retrospective disapplication of s. 22(1) where a company receives or becomes entitled to receive a capital distribution within the meaning of s. 122 made before 1 July 2009 or a distribution that is exempt from corporation tax under CTA 2009, s. 1285 or ICTA 1988, s. 208 as modified by F(No. 3)A 2010, Sch. 3, para. 6(1). This is subject to any election made under F(No. 3)A 2010, Sch. 3, para. 7 in respect of distributions made before 22 June 2010.

Extra-statutory concessions – D33: compensation or damages arising from a right of action treated as if arising from underlying asset.
D50: exempts from capital gains tax certain compensation payments in respect of property which has been lost or confiscated.

Statements of practice – SP 4/97, para. 35: HMRC view that a cashback (as defined) does not derive from a chargeable asset for capital gains tax purposes.

HMRC interpretations – IRInt. 138: payments made to agricultural or business tenants pursuant to early surrender agreement following service of notice to quit not chargeable to CGT to extent that they represent statutory compensation.
IR Int. 219: a lump sum under a *Matrimonial Causes Act* 1973 court order is derived from the exercise of a court's discretion under the Act and therefore is not a capital payment derived from an asset.

Other material – IR press release, 21 March 1996 (not reproduced): CGT treatment of "cashbacks" and certain lump sum payments received from banks or building societies, e.g. on conversions or takeovers.
IR press release, 27 March 1997: capital gains tax treatment of cash payments to investors in Cheltenham and Gloucester Building Society on takeover by Lloyd's Bank.
Tax Bulletin TB10/02–2: calculation of reliefs when a capital sum is derived from an asset and when ESC D33 is applied, particularly situations where taper relief is due (also examples of interaction with roll-over relief and private residence relief).

Notes – S. 37: exclusion from the consideration for a disposal of amounts chargeable to tax as income.
S. 171(4): where compensation within terms of s. 22(1)(a) is money or money's worth, the deemed no gain, no loss on transfer of capital assets within a group applies by reference to the acquirer as the person who ultimately bears the burden.
Circumstances in which there is no disposal of assets where a capital sum is derived from assets:

- s. 23(1): receipt of compensation or insurance used to restore asset;
- s. 122(2): receipt of a small capital distribution;
- s. 133(2): receipt of a small premium on conversion of securities;
- s. 244: small part disposal of land;
- s. 249: grants for giving up agricultural land.

23 Receipt of compensation and insurance money not treated as a disposal

23(1) If the recipient so claims, receipt of a capital sum within paragraph (a), (b), (c) or (d) of section 22(1) derived from an asset which is not lost or destroyed shall not be treated for the purposes of this Act as a disposal of the asset if–

(a) the capital sum is wholly applied in restoring the asset, or

(b) (subject to subsection (2) below), the capital sum is applied in restoring the asset except for a part of the capital sum which is not reasonably required for the purpose and which is small as compared with the whole capital sum, or

(c) (subject to subsection (2) below), the amount of the capital sum is small, as compared with the value of the asset,

but, if the receipt is not treated as a disposal, all sums which would, if the receipt had been so treated, have been brought into account as consideration for that disposal in the computation of the gain shall be deducted from any expenditure allowable under Chapter III of this Part as a deduction in computing a gain on the subsequent disposal of the asset.

23(2) If the allowable expenditure is less than the consideration for the disposal constituted by the receipt of the capital sum (or is nil)–

(a) paragraphs (b) and (c) of subsection (1) above shall not apply, and

(b) if the recipient so elects (and there is any allowable expenditure)–

(i) the amount of the consideration for the disposal shall be reduced by the amount of the allowable expenditure, and

(ii) none of that expenditure shall be allowable as a deduction in computing a gain accruing on the occasion of the disposal or any subsequent occasion.

In this subsection **"allowable expenditure"** means expenditure which immediately before the disposal, was attributable to the asset under paragraphs (a) and (b) of section 38(1).

23(3) If, in a case not falling within subsection (1)(b) above, a part of a capital sum within paragraph (a) or paragraph (b) of section 22(1) derived from an asset which is not lost or destroyed is applied in restoring the asset, then if the recipient so claims, that part of the capital sum shall not be treated as consideration for the disposal deemed to be effected on receipt of the capital sum but shall be deducted from any expenditure allowable under Chapter III of this Part as a deduction in computing a gain on the subsequent disposal of the asset.

23(4) If an asset is lost or destroyed and a capital sum received by way of compensation for the loss or destruction, or under a policy of insurance of the risk of the loss or destruction, is within one year of receipt, or such longer period as the inspector may allow, applied in acquiring an asset in replacement of the asset lost or destroyed the owner shall if he so claims be treated for the purposes of this Act–

(a) as if the consideration for the disposal of the old asset were (if otherwise of a greater amount) of such amount as would secure that on the disposal neither a gain nor a loss accrues to him, and

(b) as if the amount of the consideration for the acquisition of the new asset were reduced by the excess of the amount of the capital sum received by way of compensation or under the policy of insurance, together with any residual or scrap value, over the amount of the consideration which he is treated as receiving under paragraph (a) above.

23(5) A claim shall not be made under subsection (4) above if part only of the capital sum is applied in acquiring the new asset but if all of that capital sum except for a part which is less than the amount of the gain (whether all chargeable gain or not) accruing on the disposal of the old asset is so applied, then the owner shall if he so claims be treated for the purposes of this Act–

(a) as if the amount of the gain so accruing were reduced to the amount of the said part (and, if not all chargeable gain, with a proportionate reduction in the amount of the chargeable gain), and

(b) as if the amount of the consideration for the acquisition of the new asset were reduced by the amount by which the gain is reduced under paragraph (a) of this subsection.

23(6) If a building ("the old building") is destroyed or irreparably damaged, and all or part of a capital sum received by way of compensation for the destruction or damage, or under a policy of insurance of the risk of the destruction or damage, is applied by the recipient in constructing or otherwise acquiring a replacement building situated on other land ("the new building"), then for the purposes of subsections (4) and (5) above each of the old building and the new building shall be regarded as an asset separate from the land on which it is or was situated and the old building shall be treated as lost or destroyed.

23(7) For the purposes of subsection (6) above:

(a) references to a building include references to any permanent or semi-permanent structure in the nature of a building; and

(b) the reference to a sum applied in acquiring the new building does not include a reference to a sum applied in acquiring the land on which the new building is situated; and

(c) all necessary apportionments shall be made of any expenditure, compensation or consideration, and the method of apportionment shall be such as is just and reasonable.

23(8) This section shall apply in relation to a wasting asset with the following modifications:

(a) paragraphs (b) and (c) of subsection (1) above, and subsection (2) above, shall not apply; and

(b) in subsections (1) and (3) above, the amount of the expenditure from which the deduction is to be made shall be the amount which would have been allowable under Chapter III of this Part if the asset had been disposed of immediately after the application of the capital sum.

History – S. 23(6)–(8) substituted for former s. 23(6) by FA 1996, Sch. 39, para. 3, with effect in relation to capital sums received after 5 April 1996.

Derivations – CGTA 1979, s. 21.

Cross references – S. 38(1)(a) and (b): acquisition, enhancement or title expenditure and incidental costs.
Sch. 2, para. 23: modification of s. 23(4), (5) where gain on asset held at 6 April 1965 is time apportioned.
Sch. 3, para. 4(2): corresponding reduction in reacquisition expenditure to effect re-basing where original expenditure would be disallowed under s. 23(2) in respect of a disposal between 31 March 1982 and 6 April 1988.
Sch. 4, para. 2: reduction of one half in the amount to be deducted under s. 21(4), (5) in computing gains arising from disposal of a replacement asset in relation to deferral before 6 April 1988 where original asset held on 31 March 1982 (or acquired in a chain of no gain, no loss disposals from that date).
Broadcasting Act 1996, Sch. 7, para. 10: compensation or insurance money received by BBC, or to which BBC entitled, becoming available to, or received by, successor organisation to BBC under privatisation scheme.
SI 1992/58, Sch. 2, para. 2: disapplication of s. 23(4) in relation to reorganisation of port authorities.

Extra-statutory concessions – D33: compensation or damages arising from a right of action treated as if arising from underlying asset.
D50: gains arising on compensation from an overseas government for property lost or confiscated, paid under a statutory order under the Foreign Compensation Act 1950 is not a chargeable gain, subject to conditions.

HMRC interpretations – IR Int. 157: Revenue now take view that "small" can mean 5 per cent or less of value of asset etc., or receipt of £3,000 or less whether or not falling within the 5 per cent test; exceptionally taxpayers may suggest different limits in the context of their particular circumstances (*O'Rourke v Binks* [1992] BTC 460).

Notes – The changes made to s. 23 by FA 1996 enact ESC D1 (and broadens its scope by permitting s. 23 to be applied to wasting assets generally and to all capital sums, not just insurance policies) and ESC D19.
S. 15–20: certain general provisions relating to computation of gains, including the meaning of "chargeable gain".
S. 44–47: treatment of wasting assets (see also s. 288(1)).
S. 288: interpretation, including "inspector" as being any inspector of taxes and reference to sections being those of this Act.
TMA 1970, s. 42–43B: procedures and time limits for making claims.

24 Disposals where assets lost or destroyed, or become of negligible value

24(1) Subject to the provisions of this Act and, in particular to sections 140A(1D), 140E(7) and 144, the occasion of the entire loss, destruction, dissipation or extinction of an asset shall, for the purposes of this Act, constitute a **disposal** of the asset whether or not any capital sum by way of compensation or otherwise is received in respect of the destruction, dissipation or extinction of the asset.

24(1A) A negligible value claim may be made by the owner of an asset ("P") if condition A or B is met.

24(1B) Condition A is that the asset has become of negligible value while owned by P.

24(1C) Condition B is that–

(a) the disposal by which P acquired the asset was a no gain/no loss disposal,

(b) at the time of that disposal the asset was of negligible value, and

(c) between the time when the asset became of negligible value and the disposal by which P acquired it, each other disposal (if any) of the asset was a no gain/no loss disposal.

24(2) Where a negligible value claim is made:

(a) this Act shall apply as if the claimant had sold, and immediately reacquired, the asset at the time of the claim or (subject to paragraphs (b) and (c) below) at any earlier time specified in the claim, for a consideration of an amount equal to the value specified in the claim.

(b) An earlier time may be specified in the claim if:

(i) the claimant owned the asset at the earlier time; and

(ii) the asset had become of negligible value at the earlier time; and either

(iii) for capital gains tax purposes the earlier time is not more than two years before the beginning of the year of assessment in which the claim is made; or

(iv) for corporation tax purposes the earlier time is on or after the first day of the earliest accounting period ending not more than two years before the time of the claim.

(c) Section 93 of and Schedule 12 to the Finance Act 1994 (indexation losses and transitional relief) shall have effect in relation to an asset to which this section applies as if the sale and reacquisition occurred at the time of the claim and not at any earlier time.

24(3) For the purposes of this section, a building and any permanent or semi-permanent structure in the nature of a building may be regarded as an asset separate from the land on which it is situated, but where a building or structure is so regarded, the person deemed to make the disposal of the building or structure shall be treated as if he had also sold and immediately reacquired, the site of the building or structure (including in the site any land occupied for purposes ancillary to the use of the building or structure) for a consideration equal to its market value at that time.

24(4) For the purposes of subsection (1C), a no gain/no loss disposal is one which, by virtue of any of the no gain/no loss provisions, neither a gain nor a loss accrues to the person making the disposal.

History – In s. 24(1) the words "sections 140A(1D), 140E(7) and 144" substituted for "section 144" by SI 2007/3186, reg. 3(2) and Sch. 2, para. 3, in relation to mergers relating to the formation of an SE or SCE which take place on or after 18 August 2006, and in relation to all other mergers which take place on or after 1 January 2007.

S. 24(1A), (1B) and (1C) inserted by SI 2009/730, art. 4(2), with effect on and after 6 April 2009 (no matter whether the conditions for making a negligible value claim were met before or after that date).

In s. 24(2), the words "Where a negligible value claim is made:" substituted for the words "Where the owner of an asset which has become of negligible value makes a claim to that effect:" by SI 2009/730, art. 4(3), with effect on and after 6 April 2009 (no matter whether the conditions for making a negligible value claim were met before or after that date).

S. 24(2) substituted by FA 1996, Sch. 39, para. 4, with effect in relation to claims made after 5 April 1996.

In s. 24(3), the words "this section" substituted for the words "subsections (1) and (2) above" by SI 2009/730, art. 4(4)(a), with effect on and after 6 April 2009 (no matter whether the conditions for making a negligible value claim were met before or after that date).

In s. 24(3), the words "where a building or structure is so regarded," substituted for the words "where either of those subsections applies in accordance with this subsection," by SI 2009/730, art. 4(4)(b), with effect on and after 6 April 2009 (no matter whether the conditions for making a negligible value claim were met before or after that date).

S. 24(4) inserted by SI 2009/730, art. 4(5), with effect on and after 6 April 2009 (no matter whether the conditions for making a negligible value claim were met before or after that date).

Derivations – CGTA 1979, s. 22.

Cross references – S. 144: treatment of certain options and forfeited deposits.

S. 176(8): occasion of negligible value claim is a disposal as regards the restriction in allowable losses in respect of depreciatory transactions.

Sch. 7AC, para. 33: time when an option under s. 24(2) can be made by a company subject to this schedule where a loss accruing to the company on a disposal of shares at the time of the claim would not be an allowable loss.

Sch. 7AD, para. 8: insurance companies subject to this schedule may not make a claim under s. 24(2) in relation to the single asset.

ICTA 1988, s. 575(1)(c): relief against income for loss on unquoted shares in trading company is available on a deemed disposal under s. 24(2).

FA 1999, s. 82(9): operation of s. 24(1) in relation to syndicate rights held by a member of Lloyd's under a members' agent pooling arrangement not affected by special rules in FA 1999, s. 82.

FA 2002, Sch. 16, para. 28(2): disposal of loan made to community development finance institution will not result in loss of relief if a disposal within s. 24(1) or (2).

Extra-statutory concessions – D33: compensation or damages arising from a right of action treated as if arising from underlying asset.

Other material – Taxline 1996/113 (not reproduced): where a person contracts to purchase an asset and then discovers the asset does not exist, the contract (a chose in action) has become worthless and a loss on it can be claimed.

HMRC Brief 48/14: making a negligible value claim for an asset affected by Common Agricultural Policy reform.

Notes – The changes made to s. 24 by FA 1996 enact ESC D28.

S. 272–274 and Sch. 11: meaning of "market value".

S. 288: interpretation, including "inspector" as being any inspector of taxes, meaning of "land" and reference to sections being those of this Act.

TMA 1970, s. 42–43B: procedures and time limits for making claims.

25 Non-residents: deemed disposals

Notes – In s. 25(2), (3) and (5), any reference to a "branch or agency" shall be read, in relation to a company, as if it were a reference to a "permanent establishment" (FA 2003, s. 153(2)(b); with effect in relation to accounting periods beginning on or after 1 January 2003).

25(1) Where an asset ceases by virtue of becoming situated outside the United Kingdom to be a chargeable asset in relation to a person, he shall be deemed for all purposes of this Act–

(a) to have disposed of the asset immediately before the time when it became situated outside the United Kingdom, and

(b) immediately to have reacquired it,

at its market value at that time.

25(2) Subsection (1) above does not apply–

(a) where the asset becomes situated outside the United Kingdom contemporaneously with the person there mentioned ceasing to carry on a trade in the United Kingdom through a branch or agency, or

(b) where the asset is an exploration or exploitation asset.

25(3) Where an asset ceases to be a chargeable asset in relation to a person by virtue of his ceasing to carry on a trade in the United Kingdom through a branch or agency, he shall be deemed for all purposes of this Act–

(a) to have disposed of the asset immediately before the time when he ceased to carry on the trade in the United Kingdom through a branch or agency, and

(b) immediately to have reacquired it,

at its market value at that time.

25(3A) Subsection (3) above shall not apply if–

(a) the person ceasing to carry on the trade is a company, and

(b) the trade is transferred to another company in circumstances in which section 139 or 171 applies in relation to the assets transferred.

25(4) [Repealed by FA 2000, s. 102 and Sch. 29, para. 6(3), s. 156 and Sch. 40, Pt. II(12).]

25(5) Subsection (3) above does not apply to an asset which is a chargeable asset in relation to the person there mentioned at any time after he ceases to carry on the trade in the United Kingdom through a branch or agency and before the end of the chargeable period in which he does so.

25(6) In this section–

"exploration or exploitation asset" means an asset used in connection with exploration or exploitation activities carried on in the United Kingdom or a designated area, and

"designated area" and

"exploration or exploitation activities" have the same meanings as in section 276.

25(7) For the purposes of this section an asset is at any time a chargeable asset in relation to a person if, were it to be disposed of at that time, any chargeable gains accruing to him on the disposal–

(a) would be gains in respect of which he would be chargeable to capital gains tax under section 10(1), or

(b) would form part of his chargeable profits for corporation tax purposes by virtue of section 10B.

25(8) This section shall apply as if references to a trade include, references to a profession or vocation.

History – S. 25(3A) inserted by FA 2000, s. 102 and Sch. 29, para. 6(2) with effect for disposals made on or after 1 April 2000 in cases where s. 139 or s. 171 have effect.

S. 25(4) repealed by FA 2000, s. 102 and Sch. 29, para. 6(3), s. 156 and Sch. 40, Pt. II(12), with effect for disposals made on or after 1 April 2000 in cases where s. 139 has effect.

In s. 25(7)(b), the words "10B" substituted for the words "10(3)" by FA 2003, s. 155 and Sch. 27, para. 2(3), which have effect in relation to accounting periods beginning on or after 1 January 2003.

Derivations – FA 1989, s. 127(1)–(6), (9); FA 1990, Sch. 9, para. 2.

Cross references – S. 10: charge on non-residents in respect of UK branch or agency.

S. 139, 211: deemed no gain, no loss on transfers of business under scheme sanctioned by the court.

S. 172(2): priority of deemed no gain, no loss provision on domestication of UK branch.

S. 276: activities involving the seabed or subsoil and their natural resources situated in the UK (deemed to include its territorial sea) or in an area designated by Order under the Continental Shelf Act 1964; rights to assets produced effectively deemed UK assets.

Sch. 7B, para. 4: modification of s. 25 by substitution of s. 25(7) (as set out in para. 4) in relation to overseas life insurance companies applying in relation to accounting periods beginning after 31 December 1992.

FA 2003, s. 153(2)(b): when dealing with a company; requirement to read any reference to a "branch or agency" (in s. 25(2), (3) and (5)), as if it were a reference to a "permanent establishment", (effective for accounting periods beginning on or after 1 January 2003).

Notes – S. 272–274 and Sch. 11: meaning of "market value".

S. 275: location of assets (see also s. 276, above).

S. 288: interpretation, including "chargeable period" as being a tax year or accounting period and reference to sections being those of this Act.

25ZA Deemed disposal of UK residential property interest under section 25(3)

25ZA(1) This section applies if, ignoring subsections (3) and (4)–

(a) a gain or loss would accrue to a person on a disposal of a UK residential property interest deemed to have been made by virtue of section 25(3), and

(b) on the assumptions in subsection (2), that gain or loss would be an NRCGT gain chargeable to, or an NRCGT loss allowable for the purposes of, capital gains tax by virtue of section 14D (see section 57B and Schedule 4ZZB).

25ZA(2) The assumptions are–

(a) the disposal is a non-resident CGT disposal, and

(b) if the person is a company, any claim which the company could make under section 14F is made.

25ZA(3) No gain or loss accrues to the person on that disposal.

25ZA(4) But, on a subsequent disposal of the whole or part of the interest in UK land which is the subject of the disposal mentioned in subsection (1)(a), the whole or a corresponding part of the gain or loss which would have accrued to the person were it not for subsection (3)–

(a) is deemed to accrue to the person (in addition to any gain or loss that actually accrues on that subsequent disposal), and

(b) (if that would not otherwise be the case) is to be treated as an NRCGT gain chargeable to, or an NRCGT loss allowable for the purposes of, capital gains tax by virtue of section 14D accruing on a non-resident CGT disposal.

25ZA(5) A person may make an election for subsections (3) and (4) not to apply in relation to the disposal mentioned in subsection (1)(a).

25ZA(6) If the person is a company, such an election must be made within 2 years after the day on which the company ceases to carry on a trade in the United Kingdom through a branch or agency.

25ZA(7) In this section, **"interest in UK land"** has the meaning given by paragraph 2 of Schedule B1.

History – S. 25ZA inserted by FA 2015, s. 37 and Sch. 7, para. 13, with effect in relation to disposals made on or after 6 April 2015.

25A Long funding leases of plant or machinery: deemed disposals

25A(1) This section applies where plant or machinery is used for the purpose of leasing under a long funding lease.

25A(2) The lessor shall be deemed for all purposes of this Act–

(a) to have disposed of the plant or machinery at the commencement of the term of the lease at the relevant disposal value, and

(b) to have immediately reacquired it at the same value.

25A(3) The lessor shall also be deemed for all purposes of this Act–

(a) to have disposed of the plant or machinery on the termination of the lease for a consideration equal to the termination amount, and

(b) to have immediately reacquired it for the same consideration.

25A(4) **"Relevant disposal value"** means–

(a) in relation to a long funding finance lease, the disposal value described in item 5A of the table in section 61(2) of the Capital Allowances Act (disposal values), and

(b) in relation to a long funding operating lease, the disposal value described in item 5B of that table.

25A(5) For the purposes of this section, the following expressions have the meaning given in Chapter 6A of Part 2 of the Capital Allowances Act (interpretation of provisions about long funding leases)–

"commencement", in relation to the term of a lease,

"lessor",

"long funding lease",

"long funding finance lease",

"long funding operating lease",

"the term", in relation to a lease,

"termination",

"termination amount".

History – In s. 25A(2)(a) the words "the relevant disposal value" substituted for the words "the value described in subsection (4)(a) or (b)" by FA 2009, s. 64 and Sch. 32, para. 3(2), with effect in relation to leases whose inception is on or after 22 April 2009.

S. 25A(4) substituted for former s. 25A(4)–(4D) by FA 2009, s. 64 and Sch. 32, para. 3(3), with effect in relation to leases whose inception is on or after 22 April 2009. Former s. 25A(4)–(4D) read as follows:

"**25A(4)** The value mentioned in subsection (2)(a) is–

(a) where the lease is a long funding finance lease, an amount equal to that which would fall to be recognised as the lessor's net investment in the lease if accounts were prepared in accordance with generally accepted accounting practice on the date on which the lessor's net investment in the lease is first recognised in the books or other financial records of the lessor ("the relevant date"), or

(b) where the lease is a long funding operating lease, an amount equal to the market value of the plant or machinery at the commencement of the term of the lease.

25A(4A) The following provisions apply for the purposes of subsection (4)(a).

25A(4B) Treat any rentals under the lease made (or due) on or before the relevant date as made (and due) on the day after that date.

25A(4C) Treat the lessor as having no liabilities of any kind at any time on the relevant date (but only if the effect of doing so would be to increase the amount calculated under subsection (4)(a)).

25A(4D) For the purposes of subsection (4C) **"liabilities"** includes, where the lessor is a company, any share capital issued by the company which falls to be treated for accounting purposes as a liability."

In former s. 25A(4)(a), the words "("the relevant date")" inserted by FA 2008, s. 55 and Sch. 20, para. 5(2) with effect in relation to leases granted on or after 13 December 2007.

Former s. 25A(4A) inserted by FA 2008, s. 55 and Sch. 20, para. 5(3) with effect in relation to leases granted on or after 13 December 2007.

Former s. 25A(4B) inserted by FA 2008, s. 55 and Sch. 20, para. 5(3) with effect in relation to leases granted on or after 13 December 2007.

Former s. 25A(4C) inserted by FA 2008, s. 55 and Sch. 20, para. 5(4) with effect in relation to leases granted on or after 12 March 2008.

Former s. 25A(4D) inserted by FA 2008, s. 55 and Sch. 20, para. 5(4) with effect in relation to leases granted on or after 12 March 2008.

In s. 25A(5) the words ""market value"" omitted by FA 2009, s. 64 and Sch. 32, para. 3(4), with effect in relation to leases whose inception is on or after 22 April 2009.

S. 25A inserted by FA 2006, s. 81 and Sch. 9, para. 4(1) with effect where the commencement of the lease term is on or after 1 April 2006.

26 Mortgages and charges not to be treated as disposals

26(1) The conveyance or transfer by way of security of an asset or of an interest or right in or over it, or transfer of a subsisting interest or right by way of security in or over an asset (including a retransfer on redemption of the security), shall not be treated for the purposes of this Act as involving any acquisition or disposal of the asset.

26(2) Where a person entitled to an asset by way of security or to the benefit of a charge or incumbrance on an asset deals with the asset for the purpose of enforcing or giving effect to the security, charge or incumbrance, his dealings with it shall be treated for the purposes of this Act as if they were done through him as nominee by the person entitled to it subject to the security, charge or incumbrance; and this subsection shall apply to the dealings of any person appointed to enforce or give effect to the security, charge or incumbrance as receiver and manager or judicial factor as it applies to the dealings of the person entitled as aforesaid.

26(3) An asset shall be treated as having been acquired free of any interest or right by way of security subsisting at the time of any acquisition of it, and as being disposed of free of any such interest or right subsisting at the time of the disposal; and where an asset is acquired subject to any such interest or right the full amount of the liability thereby assumed by the person acquiring the asset shall form part of the consideration for the acquisition and disposal in addition to any other consideration.

Derivations – CGTA 1979, s. 23.

Cross references – FA 1996, s. 91A(10): shares subject to outstanding third party obligations.

Notes – S. 15: general provisions for computation of chargeable gains.

26A Transfer of dormant bank or building society account

26A(1) This section applies where the balance of a dormant account held by a person with a bank or building society is transferred–

(a) to an authorised reclaim fund, with the result that section 1 of the Dormant Bank and Building Society Accounts Act 2008 applies in relation to the account, or

(b) to an authorised reclaim fund and one or more charities, with the result that section 2 of that Act applies in relation to the account.

26A(2) For the purposes of this Act–

(a) the transfer is not to be treated as involving any acquisition or disposal of an asset, and

(b) the person's rights under Part 1 of that Act are to be treated as the same asset as the original rights, acquired as the original rights were acquired and having the same characteristics as those rights.

26A(3) **"The original rights"** are the person's rights against the bank or building society immediately before the transfer.

26A(4) Terms used in this section and in the Dormant Bank and Building Society Accounts Act 2008 have the same meaning in this section as in that Act.

History – S. 26A inserted by FA 2008, s. 39(7), with effect from 1 February 2011 (SI 2011/23).

27 Disposals in cases of hire-purchase and similar transactions

27 A hire-purchase or other transaction under which the use and enjoyment of an asset is obtained by a person for a period at the end of which the property in the asset will or may pass to that person shall be treated for the purposes of this Act, both in relation to that person and in relation to the person from whom he obtains the use and enjoyment of the asset, as if it amounted to an entire disposal of the asset to that person at the beginning of the period for which he obtains the use and enjoyment of the asset, but subject to such adjustments of tax, whether by way of repayment or discharge of tax or otherwise, as may be required where the period for which that person has the use and enjoyment of the asset terminates without the property in the asset passing to him.

Derivations – CGTA 1979, s. 24.

Notes – CAA 2001, s. 67: treatment of machinery or plant on hire purchase as belonging to hirer etc. for the purposes of capital allowances.

28 Time of disposal and acquisition where asset disposed of under contract

28(1) Subject to section 22(2), and subsection (2) below, where an asset is disposed of and acquired under a contract the time at which the disposal and acquisition is made is the time the contract is made (and not, if different, the time at which the asset is conveyed or transferred).

28(2) If the contract is conditional (and in particular if it is conditional on the exercise of an option) the time at which the disposal and acquisition is made is the time when the condition is satisfied.

Derivations – CGTA 1979, s. 27.

Cross references – Sch. 7AC, para. 3(7), 18(5), 19(3): application of s. 28 to provisions on exemption for disposals by companies with substantial shareholding.
HMRC Brief 26/07: alternative finance arrangements – diminishing shared ownership cases – implications for capital gains.

HMRC interpretations – IRInt. 202: given HMRC view that the right to occupy a "pitch" at a particular racecourse is an asset for CGT purposes, when a pitch is auctioned, the date of disposal is the date on which the purchaser's bid is accepted rather than the date on which the new owner takes possession of it at the next race meeting.

Notes – S. 143–149: treatment of certain options.
S. 288: interpretation, including reference to sections being those of this Act.

VALUE SHIFTING

29 General provisions

29(1) Without prejudice to the generality of the provisions of this Act as to the transactions which are disposals of assets, any transaction which under the following subsections is to be treated as a disposal of an asset–

(a) shall be so treated (with a corresponding acquisition of an interest in the asset) notwithstanding that there is no consideration, and

(b) so far as, on the assumption that the parties to the transaction were at arm's length, the party making the disposal could have obtained consideration, or additional consideration, for the disposal, shall be treated as not being at arm's length and the consideration so obtainable, or the additional consideration so obtainable added to the consideration actually passing, shall he treated as the market value of what is acquired.

29(2) If a person having control of a company exercises his control so that value passes out of shares in the company owned by him or a person with whom he is connected, or out of rights over the company exercisable by him or by a person with whom he is connected, and passes into other shares in or rights over the company, that shall be a disposal of the shares or rights out of which the value passes by the person by whom they were owned or exercisable.

29(3) A loss on the disposal of an asset shall not be an allowable loss to the extent to which it is attributable to value having passed out of other assets, being shares in or rights over a company which by virtue of the passing of value are treated as disposed of under subsection (2) above.

29(4) If, after a transaction which results in the owner of land or of any description of property becoming the lessee of the property there is any adjustment of the rights and liabilities under the lease, whether or not involving the grant of a new lease, which is as a whole favourable to the lessor, that shall be a disposal by the lessee of an interest in the property.

29(5) If an asset is subject to any description of right or restriction the extinction or abrogation, in whole or in part, of the right or restriction by the person entitled to enforce it shall be a disposal by him of the right or restriction.

Derivations – CGTA 1979, s. 25.

Cross references – TCGA 1992, s. 30: tax-free benefits.
TCGA 1992, s. 176: depreciatory transactions within a group.
TCGA 1992, s. 177: dividend stripping.

Notes – S. 16: priority over general rules for determining allowable losses.
S. 240 and Sch. 8, para. 10: meaning of "lease", and cognate expressions.
S. 286: meaning of "connected" in references to persons being connected with one another.
S. 288: interpretation, including meaning of "company", "shares" as including stock and the interpretation of "control".

30 Tax-free benefits

30(1) This section has effect as respects the disposal of an asset if a scheme has been effected or arrangements have been made (whether before or after the disposal) whereby–

(a) the value of the asset has been materially reduced, and

(b) a tax-free benefit has been or will be conferred–

(i) on the person making the disposal or a person with whom he is connected, or

(ii) subject to subsection (4) below, on any other person.

30(2) But, for the purposes of corporation tax, this section does not have effect if the disposal of the asset is a disposal by a company of shares in, or securities of, another company (as to which see section 31).

30(3) For the purposes of subsection (1)(b) above a benefit is conferred on a person if he becomes entitled to any money or money's worth or the value of any asset in which he has an interest is increased or he is wholly or partly relieved from any liability to which he is subject; and a benefit is tax-free unless it is required, on the occasion on which it is conferred on the person in question, to be brought into account in computing his income, profits or gains for the purposes of income tax, capital gains tax or corporation tax.

30(4) This section shall not apply by virtue of subsection (1)(b)(ii) above in a case where avoidance of tax was not the main purpose or one of the main purposes of the scheme or arrangements in question.

30(5) Where this section has effect in relation to any disposal, any allowable loss or chargeable gain accruing on the disposal shall be calculated as if the consideration for the disposal were increased by such amount as is just and reasonable having regard to the scheme or arrangements and the tax-free benefit in question.

30(6) Where–

(a) by virtue of subsection (5) above the consideration for the disposal of an asset has been treated as increased, and

(b) the benefit taken into account under subsection (1)(b) above was an increase in the value of another asset,

any allowable loss or chargeable gain accruing on the first disposal of the other asset after the increase in its value shall be calculated as if the consideration for that disposal were reduced by such amount as is just and reasonable having regard to the scheme or arrangements in question and the increase made in relation to the disposal mentioned in paragraph (a) above.

30(7) References in this section to a disposal do not include references to any disposal falling within section 58(1), 62(4) or 171(1).

30(8) [Omitted by FA 2011, s. 44 and Sch. 9, para. 1(c).]

30(9) In relation to a case in which the disposal of an asset precedes its acquisition the references in subsections (1)(a) and (2) above to a reduction shall be read as including a reference to an increase.

History – In s. 30(1)(a), the words " or a relevant asset" (which followed the words "the value of the asset") omitted by FA 2011, s. 44 and Sch. 9, para. 1(a), with effect in relation to disposals of shares or securities by companies made on or after 19 July 2011. But see also the transitional provision in FA 2011, Sch. 9, para. 6(2) regarding disposals under TCGA 1992, s. 30 to which TCGA 1992, s. 31A refers that occurred before 19 July 2011 ("the commencement day").
S. 30(2) substituted by FA 2011, s. 44 and Sch. 9, para. 1(b), with effect in relation to disposals of shares or securities by companies made on or after 19 July 2011. But see also the transitional provision in FA 2011, Sch. 9, para. 6(2) regarding disposals under TCGA 1992, s. 30 to which TCGA 1992, s. 31A refers that occurred before 19 July 2011 ("the commencement day").
In former s. 30(2)(b) words "178 or" repealed by FA 2000, s. 156 and Sch. 40. Pt. II(12).
In s. 30(4) the words "in a case where" substituted for "if it is shown that", and in s. 30(5), (6) the word "is" substituted by FA 1996, Sch. 20, para. 46, 47, with effect for the purposes of income tax and capital gains tax as respects 1996–97 and subsequent years of assessment and, for corporation tax purposes, accounting periods ending on or after 1 July 1999, the day appointed under FA 1994, s. 199 by virtue of SI 1998/3173 (C. 78).
S. 30(8) omitted by FA 2011, s. 44 and Sch. 9, para. 1(c), with effect in relation to disposals of shares or securities by companies made on or after 19 July 2011. But see also the transitional provision in FA 2011, Sch. 9, para. 6(2) regarding disposals under TCGA 1992, s. 30 to which TCGA 1992, s. 31A refers that occurred before 19 July 2011 ("the commencement day").

Derivations – S. 30(1): CGTA 1979, s. 26(1), as amended by FA 1989, s. 135(1).
S. 30(2): CGTA 1979, s. 26(1A), as inserted by FA 1989, s. 135(1).
S. 30(3)–(7): CGTA 1979, s. 26(2)–(6).
S. 30(8): CGTA 1979, s. 26(7) as substituted by FA 1989, s. 135(2).
S. 30(9): CGTA 1979, s. 26(8), as amended by FA 1989, s. 135(3).

Cross references – S. 31: distributions within a group followed by a disposal of shares.
S. 31A: asset-holding company leaving the group.
S. 32: disposals within a group followed by a disposal of shares.
S. 33: provisions supplementary to TCGA 1992, s. 30–32.
S. 33A: modification of s. 30–33 in relation to chargeable intangible assets.
S. 58(1): deemed no gain, no loss on transfers between spouses.
S. 62(4): no chargeable gain on the personal representatives where a person acquires an asset as legatee.
S. 132: definition of security by reference to any loan stock or similar security.
S. 171(1): deemed no gain, no loss on transfer of capital asset within a group.
S. 176: depreciatory transactions within a group.
S. 177: dividend stripping.
S. 179: crystallisation of gain where company leaves group holding asset transferred intra-group.
Sch. 11, para. 10(1): application restricted to reductions after 29 March 1977.
ICTA 1988, s. 576(2): modification of s. 30(1)(b), (5) to refer to any benefit, whether tax-free or not, where claim is made for relief against income for loss on unquoted shares in a trading company.
Broadcasting Act 1996, Sch. 7, para. 9: transactions etc. forming part of certain privatisation schemes involving BBC undertakings not to be regarded as a scheme or arrangement for purpose of value-shifting provisions.
SI 2002/653, art. 6 (not reproduced): nothing in the Water Industry (Scotland) Act 2002, Part 3, or in the Scottish Water (Transfer of Functions, etc.) (Tax Provisions) Order 2002/653, and nothing done under those provisions, is to be regarded as a scheme or arrangement for the purposes of s. 30.

Statements of practice – D18: sale of agricultural freehold where proceeds reduced by lease at rack rent not to fall within s. 30.

Notes – S. 15: priority over general rules for determining chargeable gains.
S. 16: priority over general rules for determining allowable losses.
S. 286: meaning of "connected" in references to persons being connected with one another (for associated, see s. 33(9)).
S. 288: interpretation, including meaning of "company", "inspector" as being any inspector and reference to sections being those of this Act.

31 Disposal of shares or securities by a company

31(1) For the purposes of corporation tax, subsection (2) has effect as respects the disposal by a company ("the disposing company") of shares in, or securities of, another company if–

(a) arrangements have been made whereby the value of those shares or securities, or any relevant asset, is materially reduced,

(b) the main purpose, or one of the main purposes, of the arrangements is to obtain a tax advantage, and

(c) the arrangements do not consist solely of the making of an exempt distribution.

31(2) Any allowable loss or chargeable gain accruing on the disposal is to be calculated as if the consideration for the disposal were increased by such amount as is just and reasonable having regard to–

(a) the arrangements, and

(b) any charge to, or relief from, corporation tax that, in the absence of this section, would arise in consequence of the disposal or the arrangements.

31(3) For the purposes of subsection (1)–

(a) an asset is a relevant asset if, at the time of the disposal, it is owned by a company which is a member of the same group as the disposing company, and

(b) it does not matter whether the tax advantage is obtained for the disposing company or any other person.

31(4) In relation to a case in which the disposal of the shares or securities precedes their acquisition, the reference in subsection (1)(a) to a reduction is to be read as including a reference to an increase.

31(5) Where, but for arrangements to which subsection (6) applies, a transaction would, by virtue of section 29(2), be treated as a disposal of shares by a company, that transaction is to be treated as if it were, by virtue of section 29(2), a disposal of those shares.

31(6) The arrangements to which this subsection applies are arrangements–

(a) whereby the value of the shares or securities is materially reduced, and

(b) the main purpose, or one of the main purposes, of which is to obtain a tax advantage (whether for the company or any other person).

31(7) In this section–

"arrangements" includes any agreement, understanding, scheme, transaction or series of transactions (whether or not legally enforceable);

"exempt distribution" means a distribution which–

(a) for the purposes of section 931D of CTA 2009 (exemption from charge to tax: distributions received by companies that are not small), falls within an exempt class by virtue of section 931H of that Act (dividends derived from transactions not designed to reduce tax), or

(b) would be within paragraph (a) but for the recipient being a small company (within the meaning of section 931S of that Act) in the accounting period of the recipient in which the distribution was received;

"group" is to be construed in accordance with section 170;

"securities" has the same meaning as in section 132;

"tax advantage" means the avoidance of a liability to corporation tax in respect of chargeable gains.

History – S. 31 substituted by FA 2011, s. 44 and Sch. 9, para. 2, with effect in relation to disposals of shares or securities by companies made on or after 19 July 2011. But see also the transitional provision in FA 2011, Sch. 9, para. 6(2) regarding disposals under TCGA 1992, s. 30 to which TCGA 1992, s. 31A refers that occurred before 19 July 2011 ("the commencement day").

Former s. 31(6)(b) substituted by FA 2002, s. 45 and Sch. 9, para. 5(2), with effect in relation to shares and debentures issued on or after 17 April 2002.

In former s. 31(7)(b) words "178 or" repealed by FA 2000, s. 156 and Sch. 40, Pt. II(12).

Derivations – CGTA 1979, s. 26A, as inserted by FA 1989, s. 136(1).

Cross references – Former s. 33A(3),:s. 31(6) does not apply to a revaluation where the profit on the revaluation is wholly taken into account as a credit under FA 2002, Sch. 29.

Former s. 33A: modification of s. 30–33 in relation to chargeable intangible assets.

Former s. 33A(4): s. 31(9) cannot be satisfied where an asset with enhanced value is a chargeable intangible asset within the meaning of FA 2002, Sch. 29.

S. 135, 136: exchange of securities for those in another company so as to defer chargeable gains and applied to a scheme of reconstruction or amalgamation involving the issue of securities by treatment as an exchange.

S 171(1): deemed no gain, no loss on transfer of capital asset within a group.

S 179: crystallisation of gain where company leaves group holding asset transferred intra-group.

Sch. 11, para. 10(2): application restricted to reductions after 13 March 1989.

FA 2002, Sch. 9, para. 7(2): references above to shares or debentures includes any interests falling to be treated as shares or debentures for the purposes of TCGA 1992, s. 135 or 136 as substituted by FA 2002, Sch. 9, para. 1, 2.

Notes – S. 288: interpretation, including meaning of "company", "class" as being a class of shares, securities, etc. of any one company, "shares" as embracing stock and reference to section being those of this Act.

31A Asset-holding company leaving the group

31A [Effectively omitted by FA 2011, s. 44 and Sch. 9, para. 2.]

History – S. 31A effectively omitted by FA 2011, s. 44 and Sch. 9, para. 2, which substitutes s. 31 for former s. 31–34, with effect in relation to disposals of shares or securities by companies made on or after 19 July 2011. But see also the transitional provision in FA 2011, Sch. 9, para. 6(2) regarding disposals under TCGA 1992, s. 30 to which TCGA 1992, s. 31A refers that occurred before 19 July 2011 ("the commencement day").

In former s. 31A(9)(b) words "any other company which–

(i) is a member of that group immediately before that event, and

(ii) is designated as the chargeable company for the purposes of this section in a notice served on the company by an officer of the Board,"

substituted for "the principal company of that group" by FA 2000, s. 102 and Sch. 29, para.17(3), with effect in relation to disposals made on or after 1 April 2000.

Former s. 31A(11) inserted by FA 2000, s. 102 and Sch. 29, para.17(3), with effect in relation to disposals made on or after 1 April 2000.

Former s. 31A inserted by FA 1999, s. 74 and Sch. 9, para. 2, with effect in relation to any disposal of an asset which occurs on or after 9 March 1999.

Cross references – Former s. 33A: modification of s. 30–33 in relation to chargeable intangible assets.
S. 179: company ceasing to be a member of a group.

32 Disposals within a group followed by a disposal of shares

32 [Effectively omitted by FA 2011, s. 44 and Sch. 9, para. 2.]

History – S. 32 effectively omitted by FA 2011, s. 44 and Sch. 9, para. 2, which substitutes s. 31 for former s. 31–34, with effect in relation to disposals of shares or securities by companies made on or after 19 July 2011. But see also the transitional provision in FA 2011, Sch. 9, para. 6(2) regarding disposals under TCGA 1992, s. 30 to which TCGA 1992, s. 31A refers that occurred before 19 July 2011 ("the commencement day").

Derivations – CGTA 1979, s. 26B, as inserted by FA 1989, s. 136(1).

33 Provisions supplementary to sections 30 to 32

33 [Effectively omitted by FA 2011, s. 44 and Sch. 9, para. 2.]

History – S. 33 effectively omitted by FA 2011, s. 44 and Sch. 9, para. 2, which substitutes s. 31 for former s. 31–34, with effect in relation to disposals of shares or securities by companies made on or after 19 July 2011. But see also the transitional provision in FA 2011, Sch. 9, para. 6(2) regarding disposals under TCGA 1992, s. 30 to which TCGA 1992, s. 31A refers that occurred before 19 July 2011 ("the commencement day").

Derivations – CGTA 1979, s. 26C, as inserted by FA 1989, s. 136(1).

33A Modification of sections 30 to 33 in relation to chargeable intangible asset

33A [Effectively omitted by FA 2011, s. 44 and Sch. 9, para. 2.]

History – S. 33A effectively omitted by FA 2011, s. 44 and Sch. 9, para. 2, which substitutes s. 31 for former s. 31–34, with effect in relation to disposals of shares or securities by companies made on or after 19 July 2011. But see also the transitional provision in FA 2011, Sch. 9, para. 6(2) regarding disposals under TCGA 1992, s. 30 to which TCGA 1992, s. 31A refers that occurred before 19 July 2011 ("the commencement day").

34 Transactions treated as a reorganisation of share capital

34 [Effectively omitted by FA 2011, s. 44 and Sch. 9, para. 2.]

History – S. 34 effectively omitted by FA 2011, s. 44 and Sch. 9, para. 2, which substitutes s. 31 for former s. 31–34, with effect in relation to disposals of shares or securities by companies made on or after 19 July 2011. But see also the transitional provision in FA 2011, Sch. 9, para. 6(2) regarding disposals under TCGA 1992, s. 30 to which TCGA 1992, s. 31A refers that occurred before 19 July 2011 ("the commencement day").

Derivations – CGTA 1979, s. 26D, as inserted by FA 1989, s. 137(1).

Chapter III – Computation of Gains: General Provisions

RE-BASING TO 1982, AND ASSETS HELD ON 6TH APRIL 1965

35 Assets held on 31st March 1982 (including assets held on 6th April 1965)

35(1) This section applies to a disposal of an asset which was held on 31st March 1982 by the person making the disposal.

35(2) In computing for the purpose of this Act the gain or loss accruing on the disposal it shall be assumed that the asset was on 31st March 1982 sold by the person making the disposal, and immediately reacquired by that person, at its market value on that date.

35(2A) For the purposes of corporation tax, subsection (2) above has effect subject to subsections (3) to (8) below (and see also subsections (9) and (10)).

35(3) Subject to subsection (5) below, subsection (2) above shall not apply to a disposal–

(a) where a gain would accrue on the disposal to the person making the disposal if that subsection did apply, and either a smaller gain or a loss would so accrue if it did not,

(b) where a loss would so accrue if that subsection did apply, and either a smaller loss or a gain would accrue if it did not,

(c) where, either on the facts of the case or by virtue of Schedule 2, neither a gain nor a loss would accrue if that subsection did not apply,

(ca) where, by virtue of section 195B, 195C or 195E, neither a gain nor a loss accrues to the person making the disposal, or

(d) where neither a gain nor a loss would accrue by virtue of any of the no gain/no loss provisions–

(i) sections 58, 73, 139, 140A, 140E, 171, 211, 215, 216, 217A, 218 to 221, 257(3), 258(4), 264 and 267(2) of this Act;
(ii) section 148 of the 1979 Act;
(iii) section 148 of the Finance Act 1982;
(iv) paragraph 2 of Schedule 2 to the Trustee Savings Banks Act 1985;
(v) section 130(3) of the Transport Act 1985;
(vi) section 486(8) of the Taxes Act;
(vii) paragraph 2(1) of Schedule 12 to the Finance Act 1990;
(viii) paragraph 5(3) of Schedule 17 to the Finance (No 2) Act 1992;
(ix) paragraphs 2(1), 7(2), 11(3) and (4) and 25(2) of Schedule 24 to the Finance Act 1994;
(x) paragraph 4(2) of Schedule 25 to the Finance Act 1994;
(xi) paragraph 2(1) of Schedule 4 to the Coal Industry Act 1994;
(xii) paragraph 2(1) of Schedule 7 to the Broadcasting Act 1996;
(xiii) paragraph 2(1) of Schedule 7 to the Transport Act 2000;
(xiv) paragraphs 3 and 9 of Schedule 26 to the Transport Act 2000;
(xv) paragraph 3, 18, 29 or 32 of Schedule 9 to the Energy Act 2004;
(xvi) paragraph 5 or 16 of Schedule 10 to the Railways Act 2005;
(xvii) paragraph 9 of Schedule 4 to the Consumers, Estate Agents and Redress Act 2007;
(xviii) paragraph 11 or 22 of Schedule 13 to the Crossrail Act 2008.

35(4) Where in the case of a disposal of an asset–
(a) the effect of subsection (2) above would be to substitute a loss for a gain or a gain for a loss, but
(b) the application of subsection (2) is excluded by subsection (3),
it shall be assumed in relation to the disposal that the asset was acquired by the person making the disposal for a consideration such that, on the disposal, neither a gain nor a loss accrues to that person.

35(5) If a person so elects, disposals made by that person (including any made by that person before the election) shall fall outside subsection (3) above (so that subsection (2) above is not excluded by that subsection).

35(6) An election by a person under subsection (5) above shall be irrevocable and shall be made by notice to an officer of the Board at any time before 6th April 1990 or at any time during the period beginning with the day of the first relevant disposal and ending–
(a) [omitted by FA 2008, s. 8 and Sch. 2, para. 58(7)(a).]
(aa) 2 years after the end of the accounting period in which the disposal is made; or
(b) at such later time as the Board may allow;
and **"the first relevant disposal"** means the first disposal to which this section applies which is made by the person making the election.

35(7) An election made by a person under subsection (5) above in one capacity does not cover disposals made by that person in another capacity.

35(8) All such adjustments shall be made, whether by way of discharge or repayment of tax, the making of assessments or otherwise, as are required to give effect to an election under subsection (5) above.

35(9) Schedule 2 shall have effect for the purposes of corporation tax in relation to disposals of assets owned on 6th April 1965 in cases where neither subsection (2) nor subsection (4) above applies.

35(10) Schedule 3, which contains provisions supplementary to subsections (1) to (8) above, shall have effect for the purposes of capital gains tax and corporation tax.

History – In s. 35(2), the words "In" and "that person" substituted for "Subject to the following provisions of this section, in" and "him" respectively by FA 2008, s. 8 and Sch. 2, para. 58(2) with effect in relation to disposals on or after 6 April 2008 (FA 2008, Sch. 2, para. 71).
S. 35(2A) inserted by FA 2008, s. 8 and Sch. 2, para. 58(3) with effect in relation to disposals on or after 6 April 2008 (FA 2008, Sch. 2, para. 71).
In s. 35(3)(c) the word "or" at the end omitted and para. (ca) inserted by FA 2009, s. 86 and Sch. 40, para. 2 with effect in relation to disposals made on or after 22 April 2009.
In s. 35(3)(d), the words "the no gain/no loss provisions." substituted for a list of provisions which effected no gain/no loss transfers by FA 2008, s. 8 and Sch. 2, para. 58(4) with effect in relation to disposals on or after 6 April 2008 (FA 2008, Sch. 2, para. 71).
In s. 35(3)(d)(i) the reference to s. 211 inserted by FA 2007, s. 40 and Sch. 9, para. 14(3), with effect in relation to periods of account beginning on or after 1 January 2007 (Sch. 9, para. 17(1)).
In s. 35(3)(d)(i), reference to s. 140E inserted by F(No. 2)A 2005, s. 59(2) with effect from 20 July 2005 (Royal Assent).
In s. 35(3)(d)(i), reference to s. 172 repealed by FA 2000, s 156 and Sch. 40, Pt. II(12), with effect for disposals made on or after 1 April 2000.
In s. 35(3)(d)(i), reference to s. 140A inserted by F(No. 2)A 1992, s. 46(2), and deemed always to have had effect; a similar amendment was made to FA 1988, Sch. 8, para. 1(3) (the predecessor provision) with respect to any disposal by way of transfer where the transfer takes effect on or after 1 January 1992 (F(No. 2)A 1992, s. 49(7)).

In s. 35(3)(d)(i), reference to s. 217A inserted by F(No. 2)A 1992, s. 56 and Sch. 9, para. 21(2) with effect from 19 February 1993.
S. 35(3)(d)(viii) inserted by F(No. 2)A 1992, s. 77 and Sch. 17, para. 5(9), and word "and" following para. (vi) repealed by F(No. 2)A 1992, s. 82 and Sch. 18, Pt. X, with these amendments deemed always to have had effect.
In s. 35(3)(d), the word "and" immediately preceding para. (viii) repealed by FA 1994, s. 258 and Sch. 26, Pt. VIII(2) with effect from 11 January 1994.
S. 35(3)(d)(ix) inserted by FA 1994, s. 250 and Sch. 24, para. 2(2) with effect from 11 January 1994.
S. 35(3)(d)(x) inserted by FA 1994, s. 253 and Sch. 25, para. 4(3).
S. 35(3)(d)(xi) inserted by the Coal IndustryAct 1994, s. 21 and Sch. 4, para. 2(3), with effect from 19 September 1994.
S. 35(3)(d)(xii) inserted by the Broadcasting Act 1996, Sch. 7, para. 3 with effect from 24 July 1996.
S. 35(3)(d)(xiii) inserted by the Transport Act 2000, Sch. 7, para. 2 with effect from 1 February 2001 by virtue of SI 2001/57, art. 2 and Sch. 2, Pt. I.
S. 35(3)(d)(xiv) inserted by the Transport Act 2000, Sch. 26, para. 37 with effect from 1 February 2001 by virtue of SI 2001/57, art. 2 and Sch. 2, Pt. I.
S. 35(3)(d)(xv) inserted by the Energy Act 2004, s. 47 and Sch. 9, para. 36, with effect from 4 October 2004 by virtue of SI 2004/2575).
S. 35(3)(d)(xvi) inserted by the Railways Act 2005, s. 53 and Sch. 10, para. 33 with effect for some purposes from 8 June 2005 by virtue of SI 2005/1444 and with effect for other purposes from 24 July 2005 by virtue of SI 2005/1909.
S. 35(3)(d)(xvii) inserted by the Consumers, Estate Agents and Redress Act 2007, s. 63 and Sch. 7, para 11, with effect from 21 December 2007 by virtue of SI 2007/3546.
S. 35(3)(d)(xviii) inserted by Crossrail Act 2008, s. 37 and Sch. 13, para. 46, with effect from 22 July 2008 (even though this date is before the repeal of the former s. 35(d)(xviii)).
Former s. 35(3)(d)(xviii) omitted by SI 2008/3002, art. 4 and Sch. 1, para. 42, with effect from 1 December 2008.
Former s. 35(3)(d)(xviii) inserted by the Housing and Regeneration Act 2008, Sch. 7, para. 9, with effect from 8 September 2008 (by virtue of SI 2008/2358).
In s. 35(4), the words "that person" substituted for "him" by FA 2008, s. 8 and Sch. 2, para. 58(5) with effect in relation to disposals on or after 6 April 2008 (FA 2008, Sch. 2, para. 71).
In s. 35(5), the words "that person" substituted twice for "him" by FA 2008, s. 8 and Sch. 2, para. 58(6) with effect in relation to disposals on or after 6 April 2008 (FA 2008, Sch. 2, para. 71).
S. 35(6)(a) omitted by FA 2008, s. 8 and Sch. 2, para. 58(7)(a) with effect in relation to disposals on or after 6 April 2008 (FA 2008, Sch. 2, para. 71).
In s. 35(6)(aa), the opening words (reference to a corporation tax election) omitted by FA 2008, s. 8 and Sch. 2, para. 58(7)(b) with effect in relation to disposals on or after 6 April 2008 (FA 2008, Sch. 2, para. 71).
In s. 35(6)(b), the opening words (reference to elections) omitted by FA 2008, s. 8 and Sch. 2, para. 58(7)(c) with effect in relation to disposals on or after 6 April 2008 (FA 2008, Sch. 2, para. 71).
In s. 35(6) the words "an officer of the Board" substitutedand para. (a)–(b) substituted by FA 1996, s. 135 and Sch. 21, para. 35 for 1996–97 and later years of assessment and accounting periods ending on or after 1 July 1999, the appointed day for self-assessment to corporation tax (FA 1994, s. 199 by virtue of SI 1998/3173 (C. 78)).
In s. 35(7), the words "that person" substituted for "him" by FA 2008, s. 8 and Sch. 2, para. 58(8) with effect in relation to disposals on or after 6 April 2008 (FA 2008, Sch. 2, para. 71).
In s. 35(9), the "for the purposes of corporation tax" inserted by FA 2008, s. 8 and Sch. 2, para. 58(9) with effect in relation to disposals on or after 6 April 2008 (FA 2008, Sch. 2, para. 71).
In s. 35(10), the words "for the purposes of capital gains tax and corporation tax" inserted by FA 2008, s. 8 and Sch. 2, para. 58(10) with effect in relation to disposals on or after 6 April 2008 (FA 2008, Sch. 2, para. 71).

Derivations – S. 35(1), (2): FA 1988, s. 96(1), (2).
S. 35(3) (as originally enacted): FA 1988, s. 96(3); Sch. 8, para. 1(3), as amended by FA 1989, s. 141 and Sch. 15, para. 4(2), FA 1990, s. 70(7)(b) and Sch. 12, para. 2(2), FA 1991, s. 78(7).
S. 35(4)–(8): FA 1988, s. 96(4)–(8).
S. 35(9): CGTA 1979, s. 28(3); see also s. 21(6).
S. 35(10): FA 1988, s. 96(9).

Cross references – S. 55(2): except where election made for simplified scheme, indexation allowance calculated by reference to original cost etc. notwithstanding s. 35(2) or s. 55(1).
S. 55(7): treatment of indexation losses in relation to no gain/no loss disposals.
S. 58: transfers between spouses.
S. 73: death of life tenant.
S. 125(5): where s. 35(2) does not apply, allowable acquisition cost of shares in close company reduced by reference to transfers at an undervalue by the company since 6 April 1965.
S. 139: reconstruction or amalgamation involving the transfer of business.
S. 140A: intra-Community transfer of a UK trade.
S. 164FF: reinvestment relief reductions under s. 164A(2)(b) or s. 164F(10A)(b) not defeated by anything in s. 35 in respect of disposals on or after 20 June 1994 following no gain/no loss disposals.
S. 171: transfers of capital assets within a group.
S. 172: transfers of trade from UK branches or agencies to UK companies (domestication).
S. 175(2C): no roll-over relief where the new assets are acquired on or after 29 November 1994 by a company in a group in a transaction listed in s. 35(3)(d).
S. 176(9): where disposal outside s. 35(2), loss restriction by reference to depreciatory transactions effected after 5 April 1965.
S. 177(4): where disposal outside s. 35(2), loss restriction by reference to dividend stripping effected after 30 April 1969.
S. 200: limitation of losses on disposal of certain oil industry assets held or treated as held on 31 March 1982 but for which re-basing disapplied by reference to a smaller loss or a gain otherwise arising.
S. 215: amalgamation etc. of building societies.
S. 216: incorporation of building societies.
S. 217A: transfer of assets on incorporation of registered friendly society.
S. 218–221: disposals involving housing associations and transfer of trade to harbour authority etc.
S. 257(3): charity etc. becoming entitled to settled property.
S. 258(4): gifts etc. of works of art subject to undertaking as to preservation etc.
S. 264: reorganisation of political constituencies.
S. 267(2), (3): sharing of broadcasting transmission facilities.
Sch. 7A, para. 12: treatment of losses for the purpose of restriction of pre-entry losses where no gain/no loss by virtue of enactment listed in s. 35(3)(d).
TMA 1970, s. 43A: further assessments – the general extension of the time limit to make elections does not apply to an election under s. 35, with effect for further assessment notices issued after 10 July 2003.
FA 1982, s. 148: transfer of assets of Hops Marketing Board.
ICTA 1988, s. 486(8): amalgamation etc. of registered industrial and provident societies.
FA 1997, s. 89(8): use of earn-out rights for exchange of securities.
FA 1997, Sch. 12, para. 7: assignment of lessor's interest under a lease.
Trustee Savings Banks Act 1985, Sch. 2, para. 2: reorganisation of the TSB.

Transport Act 1985, s. 130(3): transfer of an asset from a Passenger Transport Executive to a Passenger Transport Authority.
SI 1992/58, Sch. 2, para. 13: disapplication of s. 35 in relation to reorganisation of port authorities.
SI 1994/3226, reg. 9(4): deemed disposal immediately before commencement day (for FA 1993, Pt. II, Ch. II) of assets held by a company on that day not a no gain/no loss disposal.
SI 1994/3226, reg. 14(8), (9): application of rules in FA 1993, Pt. II, Ch. II to assets held on a company's commencement day and not acquired in a no gain/no loss disposal.
SI 1994/3226, reg. 16(7): computation of available losses on assets held on its commencement day (for FA 1993, Pt. II, Ch. II) by a company non-resident at any time before that day.

European material – Directive 90/434, art. 4 (amendment to s. 35(3)(d)(i) by F(No. 2)A 1992).

Extra-statutory concessions – D34: valuation for purposes of re-basing of shares or securities of the same class where some acquired before 6 April 1965 and other acquired between 6 April 1965 and 31 March 1982.

Statements of practice – SP 5/89: shares or securities acquired on a relevant no gain, no loss transfer (see s. 35(3)(d)) added to any existing holding before 1982 valuation, the proportion taken on a disposal being on the basis of the number of shares or securities.
SP 4/92: description of the range of disposals in relation to which HMRC exercise their discretion (see s. 35(6)) to extend the time limit for making an election.

HMRC interpretations – IRInt. 9: an election under s. 35(5) by a person in one capacity does not cover disposals in another capacity – clarification in connection with partners, jointly owned assets, sole traders and assets held in a fiduciary capacity.
IRInt. 26: person deemed to have held an asset at 31 March 1982 for indexation or rebasing purposes can be treated as having incurred expenditure incurred after that date by a previous holder of the asset.

Other material – ICAEW Technical Release TR 831 (not reproduced): Revenue confirmation that, for the purpose of valuing a partner's share in an asset at 31 March 1982 under re-basing where the partnership held the asset at that date, SP D12, para. (1) applies (share valued as a fraction of the total value with no discount for size).
Taxline 1993/41 (not reproduced): taxpayers who invested in small workshops, claimed IBAs and sold their interest by creating long leaseholds may be able to claim capital losses through making a re-basing election.

Notes – S. 21–34: general meaning of "disposal" and "asset".
S. 272–274 and Sch. 11: meaning of "market value".
S. 288: interpretation, including the 1979 Act as CGTA 1979, "inspector" as being any inspector of taxes, "notice" as being one in writing and reference to sections being those of this Act.

35A Disposal of asset acquired on no gain/no loss disposal

35A(1) This section applies for the purposes of capital gains tax in relation to a disposal of an asset if–

(a) the person making the disposal acquired the asset after 31 March 1982 and before 6 April 2008,

(b) the disposal by which the person acquired the asset ("the relevant disposal"), and any previous disposal of the asset after 31 March 1982, was a disposal on which, by virtue of any enactment, neither a gain nor a loss accrued to the person making the disposal, and

(c) section 35(2) did not apply to the relevant disposal.

35A(2) It is be assumed that section 35(2) did apply to the relevant disposal (and that section 56(2) applied to the relevant disposal accordingly).

History – S. 35A inserted by FA 2008, s. 8 and Sch. 2, para. 59 with effect in relation to disposals on or after 6 April 2008 (FA 2008, Sch. 2, para. 71).

36 Deferred charges on gains before 31st March 1982

36 Schedule 4 which provides for the reduction of a deferred charge to corporation tax in respect of chargeable gains where the charge is wholly or partly attributable to an increase in the value of an asset before 31st March 1982, shall have effect.

History – In s. 36, the words "corporation tax in respect of chargeable gains" substituted for the word "tax" by FA 2008, s. 8 and Sch. 2 para. 73 with effect in relation to disposals on or after 6 April 2008 and to which Sch. 4 would otherwise apply (FA 2008, Sch. 2, para. 76).

Derivations – FA 1988, s. 97.

Cross references – SI 1992/58, Sch. 2, para. 13: disapplication of s. 36 in relation to reorganisation of port authorities.

Notes – S. 21–34: general meaning of "asset".

ALLOWABLE DEDUCTIONS

37 Consideration chargeable to tax on income

37(1) There shall be excluded from the consideration for a disposal of assets taken into account in the computation of the gain any money or money's worth charged to income tax as income of, or taken into account as a receipt in computing income or profits or gains or losses of, the person making the disposal for the purposes of the Income Tax Acts.

37(2) Subsection (1) above shall not be taken as excluding from the consideration so taken into account any money or money's worth which is–

(a) taken into account in the making of a balancing charge under the Capital Allowances Act but excluding Part 10 of that Act,

(b) brought into account as the disposal value of plant or machinery under Part 2 of that Act, or

(c) brought into account as the disposal value of an asset representing qualifying expenditure under Part 6 of that Act.

See also section 37A(4) and (5) (consideration on disposal of certain leases).

37(2A) Subsection (1) is not to be taken as excluding from the consideration so taken into account any money or money's worth which is, or is taken into account in computing, a return on which income tax is charged under Chapter 2A of Part 4 of ITTOIA 2005 (disguised interest) (but see section 381D of that Act).

37(3) This section shall not preclude the taking into account in a computation of the gain, as consideration for the disposal of an asset, of the capitalised value of a rentcharge (as in a case where a rentcharge is exchanged for some other asset) or of the capitalised value of a ground annual or feu duty, or of a right of any other description to income or to payments in the nature of income over a period, or to a series of payments in the nature of income.

37(4) [Repealed by SI 2004/2310, Schedule, para. 48(2).]

37(5) If–

(a) because section 517G(4) or (6) of ITA 2007 (transactions in land: the chargeable person) applies, an amount is charged to income tax as income of a person other than the person ("A") by whom the gain was realised, and

(b) the income tax has been paid,

for the purposes of this section the amount charged to that tax is regarded as having been charged as the income of A.

37(5A) If–

(a) because section 356OG(4) or (6) of CTA 2010 (transactions in land: the chargeable company) applies, an amount is charged to corporation tax as profits of a person other than the person ("C") by whom the gain was realised, and

(b) the corporation tax has been paid,

for the purposes of this section the amount charged to that tax is regarded as having been charged as the income of C.

37(6) If–

(a) because section 777(5) of that Act applies, the person charged to tax under Chapter 4 of Part 13 of that Act (sales of occupation income) is a person other than the person ("B")–

(i) for whom the capital amount was obtained, or

(ii) in the case of income treated as arising under section 779 of that Act, by whom the property or right was sold or realised, and

(b) the income tax has been paid,

for the purposes of this section the amount charged to that tax is regarded as having been charged as the income of B.

37(7) In subsection (6) **"capital amount"** has the same meaning as in Chapter 4 of Part 13 of that Act (sales of occupation income) (see section 777(7) of that Act).

History – In s. 37(2), the words "See also section 37A(4) and (5) (consideration on disposal of certain leases)." inserted by TIOPA 2010, s. 374 and Sch. 8, para. 231, with effect for corporation tax purposes for accounting periods ending on or after 1 April 2010, for income tax and capital gains tax purposes for the tax year 2010–11 and subsequent tax years, and for petroleum revenue tax purposes for chargeable periods beginning on or after 1 July 2010.
S. 37(2)(a)–(c) substituted for s. 37(2)(a), (b) by CAA 2001, s. 578 and Sch. 2, para 77, with effect as respects allowances and charges falling to be made for chargeable periods ending, for income tax purposes, on or after 6 April 2001, and for corporation tax purposes, on or after 1 April 2001.
S. 37(2A) inserted by FA 2013, s. 28 and Sch. 12, para. 6, with effect for the tax year 2013–14 and subsequent tax years, subject to the transitional provision in FA 2013, Sch. 12, para. 18.
S. 37(4) repealed by SI 2004/2310, Schedule, para. 48(2), with effect in relation to accounting periods beginning on or after 1 April 2004, subject to the transitional provisions at FA 2004, s. 43 and 44.
In s. 37(5)(a), the words "517G(4) or (6) of ITA 2007 (transactions in land: the chargeable person) applies, an amount is charged to income tax as income of" substituted for the words "759(4) or (6) of ITA 2007 applies, the person charged to tax under Chapter 3 of Part 13 of that Act (transactions in land) is" by FA 2016, s. 79(8), with effect from 15 September 2016 (Royal Assent).
S. 37(5) inserted by ITA 2007, s. 1027 and Sch. 1, para. 299, with effect from 6 April 2007.
In s. 37(5A), the words "356OG(4) or (6) of CTA 2010 (transactions in land: the chargeable company) applies, an amount is charged to corporation tax as profits of a person other than" substituted for the words "821(3) or (5) of CTA 2010 applies, the company charged to tax under Part 18 of that Act (transactions in land) is not" by FA 2016, s. 77(7), with effect from 15 September 2016 (Royal Assent).
S. 37(5A) inserted by CTA 2010, s. 1177 and Sch. 1, para. 228, with effect for corporation tax purposes for accounting periods ending on or after 1 April 2010, and for income tax and capital gains tax purposes for the tax year 2010–11 and subsequent tax years.
S. 37(6) inserted by ITA 2007, s. 1027 and Sch. 1, para. 299, with effect from 6 April 2007.
S. 37(7) inserted by ITA 2007, s. 1027 and Sch. 1, para. 299, with effect from 6 April 2007.

Derivations – CGTA 1979, s. 31, as amended (subs. (2)) by CAA 1990, s. 164 and Sch. 1, para. 3, and subs. (4) as inserted by ICTA 1988, s. 844 and Sch. 29, para. 17.

Cross references – S. 119: disapplication to disposals of securities to which accrued income scheme applies, in favour of special rules.
S. 195(5): clawback of scientific research allowances in respect of certain expenditure on searching or testing for oil treated as a balancing charge.
S. 210(7): life insurance and deferred annuities, situation where s. 37 is disregarded.
Sch. 8, para. 5, 6: disapplication to amounts determined under Sch. A or associated Sch. D charges (see note to the said para. 5) and to amounts on which tax is charged on assignment of a lease granted at an undervalue.

ICTA 1988, s. 76(2): relief for expenses of management of an insurance company restricted by reference to a notional Sch. D, Case I computation.
ICTA 1988, s. 450(6): consideration in respect of assets forming part of an underwriter's premiums trust fund not excluded by s. 37.
ICTA 1988, s. 763(2): disapplication of s. 37(1) to disposal giving rise to an offshore income gain in favour of special provisions.
ICTA 1988, s. 777(12): for s. 37, in respect of quasi-dealing transactions in land, person for whom the capital amount was obtained or by whom the gains was realised treated as the person upon whom the charge as income arose.
ICTA 1988, Sch. 5AA, para. 4A: disapplication of s. 37 to disposals of guaranteed futures and options.
F(No. 2)A 1992, s. 65(2)(e): s. 37(1) is relevant provision for the purposes of s. 65 – life assurance business I minus E basis.
FA 1993, s. 176(2): costs of acquisition or consideration for disposal of assets forming part of Lloyd's underwriter's ancillary trust fund are not excluded from s. 37.
FA 1997, Sch. 12, para. 12(3), (4): disapplication to disposals under leasing arrangements where any of the return on investment is in capital form.
FA 2004, s. 133: companies in partnership: relationship with chargeable gains.
SI 1992/58, Sch. 2, para. 3: disapplication of s. 37(1) in relation to reorganisation of port authorities.
SI 2009/3001, reg. 45: applies instead of s. 37(1) for offshore income gains.

Statements of practice – SP 4/89: distribution element on a purchase of own shares from a corporate vendor shareholder not excluded from consideration for chargeable gains purposes.

Notes – S. 8(4): reference to income tax and the Income Tax Acts construed in relation to a company as reference to corporation tax and the Corporation Tax Acts.
S. 21–34: general meaning of "disposal" and "asset".
S. 288: interpretation, including the Taxes Act as ICTA 1988.
Interpretation Act 1978, s. 5 and Sch. 1: the Income Tax Acts mean the enactments relating to income tax.

37A Consideration on disposal of certain leases

37A(1) This section applies if–

(a) a disposal occurs that is within section 614BP of ITA 2007 (including that section as it has effect as a result of section 614CD of that Act), and

(b) for the purposes of Chapter 2 or 3 of Part 11A of that Act there is any cumulative accountancy rental excess in relation to the lease for the period of account of the current lessor in which the disposal takes place.

37A(2) This section also applies if–

(a) a disposal occurs that is within section 915 of CTA 2010 (including that section as it has effect as a result of section 929 of that Act), and

(b) for the purposes of Chapter 2 or 3 of Part 21 of that Act there is any cumulative accountancy rental excess in relation to the lease for the period of account of the current lessor in which the disposal takes place.

37A(3) In determining for the purposes of this Act the amount of any gain accruing to the person making the disposal, the consideration for the disposal is treated as reduced by setting against it that excess (but not so as to reduce the amount of that consideration below nil).

37A(4) Subsection (3) only affects section 37 so far as subsection (5) provides.

37A(5) Section 37 does not exclude any money or money's worth from the consideration for a disposal so far as it is represented by any such cumulative accountancy rental excess that, in accordance with subsection (3)–

(a) falls to be set against the consideration for the disposal, or

(b) has fallen to be set against the consideration for a previous disposal made by the person making the disposal in question or a person connected with that person.

37A(6) Subsections (7) to (9) apply if the disposal mentioned in subsection (1) or (2) is a part disposal of the asset in question.

37A(7) The cumulative accountancy rental excess mentioned in subsection (3) must be apportioned between–

(a) the property disposed of, and

(b) the property that remains undisposed of.

37A(8) That apportionment must be made in the same proportions as those in which the sums that under section 38(1)(a) or (b) are attributable to the asset fall to be apportioned under section 42.

37A(9) Only so much of the cumulative accountancy rental excess as is so apportioned to the property disposed of is set against the consideration for the part disposal in accordance with subsection (3).

37A(10) If subsection (3) applies in a case where two or more disposals within subsection (1) or (2) are made at the same time, the cumulative accountancy rental excess mentioned in subsection (3) must be apportioned, subject to subsections (7) to (9), between the disposals in such proportions as are just and reasonable.

37A(11) Section 614DC of ITA 2007 (connected persons) applies for the purposes of this section in its application as a result of any leasing arrangements (within the meaning of that section) as it applies for the purposes mentioned in that section.

History – S. 37A inserted by TIOPA 2010, s. 367 and Sch. 3, para. 7, with effect for corporation tax purposes for accounting periods ending on or after 1 April 2010, for income tax and capital gains tax purposes for the tax year 2010–11 and subsequent tax years, and for petroleum revenue tax purposes for chargeable periods beginning on or after 1 July 2010.

38 Acquisition and disposal costs etc.

38(1) Except as otherwise expressly provided, the sums allowable as a deduction from the consideration in the computation of the gain accruing to a person on the disposal of an asset shall be restricted to–

(a) the amount or value of the consideration, in money or money's worth, given by him or on his behalf wholly and exclusively for the acquisition of the asset, together with the incidental costs to him of the acquisition or, if the asset was not acquired by him, any expenditure wholly and exclusively incurred by him in providing the asset,

(b) the amount of any expenditure wholly and exclusively incurred on the asset by him or on his behalf for the purpose of enhancing the value of the asset, being expenditure reflected in the state or nature of the asset at the time of the disposal, and any expenditure wholly and exclusively incurred by him in establishing, preserving or defending his title to, or to a right over, the asset,

(c) the incidental costs to him of making the disposal.

38(2) For the purposes of this section and for the purposes of all other provisions of this Act, the incidental costs to the person making the disposal of the acquisition of the asset or of its disposal shall consist of expenditure wholly and exclusively incurred by him for the purposes of the acquisition or, as the case may be, the disposal, being fees, commission or remuneration paid for the professional services of any surveyor or valuer, or auctioneer, or accountant, or agent or legal adviser and costs of transfer or conveyance (including stamp duty or stamp duty land tax) together–

(a) in the case of the acquisition of an asset, with costs of advertising to find a seller, and

(b) in the case of a disposal, with costs of advertising to find a buyer and costs reasonably incurred in making any valuation or apportionment required for the purposes of the computation of the gain, including in particular expenses reasonably incurred in ascertaining market value where required by this Act.

38(3) Except as provided by section 40, no payment of interest shall be allowable under this section.

38(4) Any provision in this Act introducing the assumption that assets are sold and immediately reacquired shall not imply that any expenditure is incurred as incidental to the sale or reacquisition.

History – In s. 38(2), the words "or stamp duty land tax" inserted after "stamp duty" by FA 2003, s. 123(1) and Sch. 18, para. 5 with effect for transactions within the charge to SDLT: broadly from 1 December 2003 (SI 2003/2899), subject to transitional rules.

Derivations – CGTA 1979, s. 32.

Cross references – S. 23(2): election for allowable expenditure within s. 38(1)(a), (b) to be wholly deductible from deemed proceeds where part disposal on receipt of compensation or insurance.

S. 53, 54: indexation allowance by reference to expenditure within s. 38(1)(a), (b).

S. 55(10), (11): proportion of allowable expenditure to be calculated in arriving at consideration for a no gain/no loss disposal or part disposal.

S. 99B: calculation of cost of disposal by unit holder of units in unit trust scheme.

S. 106(8): transfer of items of allowable expenditure where shares disposed by one company identified with shares acquired by another.

S. 109(6): for the purposes of determining the deemed date expenditure incurred for indexation allowance (s. 54(4)), relevant allowable expenditure on a "1982 holding" falls within s. 38(1)(a).

S. 119A(2): increase in expenditure by reference to tax charged in relation to employment-related securities.

S. 120(2): acquisition consideration deemed to be increased by amounts chargeable to tax in respect of gains from certain share options etc.

S. 122: small capital distribution deducted from allowable expenditure or, where excess, election for whole of allowable expenditure to reduce the consideration received.

S. 125(2): allowable acquisition cost of shares in close company reduced by reference to transfers at an undervalue by the company.

S. 133: small premium on conversion of securities deducted from allowable expenditure or, where excess, election for whole of allowable expenditure to reduce the consideration received.

S. 142(3): person absolutely entitled as against the trustee to shares issued as a stock dividend treated as acquiring them for the appropriate amount in cash.

S. 144A: cash-settled options – cost of acquisition treated as allowable expenditure for purpose of s. 38(1)(a).

S. 162(3): allowable acquisition expenditure reduced by rolled-over gain on incorporation of a business.

S. 165: acquisition consideration reduced by held-over gain on gift of business assets; held-over gains reduced by reference to actual consideration in excess of allowable sums within s. 38.

S. 195(1): certain capital expenditure on scientific research on searching or testing for oil allowable within s. 38(1)(b) on disposal of an oil licence.

S. 225A: private residence held by personal representatives.

S. 242–244: claims where small part disposal of land (by reference to market value) for consideration to be deducted from allowable expenditure on remainder or, where the consideration exceeds allowable expenditure, vice versa.

S. 257(2): disposals to charity or for national purposes etc. for consideration up to the amount of allowable expenditure treated as no gain, no loss disposals.

S. 259(2): disposals to housing associations for consideration up to the amount of allowable expenditure treated as no gain, no loss disposals.

Sch. 2, para. 10(4)–(6), 12: in relation to land held at 6 April 1965, current use value of an interest in land which has been disposed of by part disposal is determined on the same basis as the apportionment of expenditure within s. 38(1)(a), (b) on such part disposal, ignoring any wholly attributable expenditure but as reduced in the case of a lease under the curved line restriction.

Sch. 2, para. 16: expenditure within s. 38(1)(a) and (b) treated as separate items to permit time apportionment where asset held at 6 April 1965.

Sch. 7A, para. 2(9), 4(12): in relation to restriction of losses on pre-entry assets (and "pooled assets"), amounts allowed as deduction of relevant allowable expenditure computed in accordance with s. 38(1)(a), (b).
Sch. 8, para. 1(2): a lease does not become a wasting asset until the end of any sublease if it is estimated that its value will be greater than expenditure within s. 38(1)(a).
Sch. 8, para. 3(5): consideration in lieu of rent or to vary or waive any of the terms of a lease (but not for surrendering it), where the landlord is himself a tenant of a short lease, is within s. 38(1)(b).
Sch. 8, para. 4: disapplication of normal part disposal rules to the grant of a sublease out of a short lease and apportionment of expenditure within s. 38(1)(a), (b) by reference to the curved line write-off of expenditure.
Sch. 8, para. 7: amount charged as rent (or Sch. D, Case VI profits) for the value of any obligation on a tenant under a lease to carry out work to the extent that a deduction would not have been available to the landlord had he carried out the work is deemed expenditure within s. 38(1)(b).
Sch. 11, para. 13(2), 14: on disposal of designated securities etc. representing a foreign currency loan taken out before 19 November 1967 or certain trust funds, the sums allowable under s. 38(1)(a) are increased to seven-sixths their amount.
Sch. 11, para. 17: allowance for betterment levy.
FA 1988, s. 84: certain amounts chargeable to income tax in respect of unapproved shares schemes deductible as if acquisition expenditure.
FA 1989, s. 70(2): clawback of relief for disposal of securities to a qualifying employee share ownership trust by reference to a charge equal to the amount allowable under s. 38(1)(a), (b) on a subsequent disposal.
FA 1993, Sch. 20A, para. 3: Lloyd's underwriters: conversion to limited liability underwriting: rollover relief on disposal of syndicate capacity.
FA 1993, Sch. 20A, para. 4: Lloyd's underwriters: conversion to limited liability underwriting: rollover relief on disposal of assets of ancillary trust fund.
FA 1994, s. 173(4): interest rates and currency contracts – sums falling within s. 173(4) not to be taken into account for the purposes of s. 38.
FA 1996, s. 92(5D): incidental costs of disposal where exchange gains from disposal of convertible security etc.
FA 1996, Sch. 15, para. 8(8): loan relationships, savings and transitional provisions.
FA 1997, Sch. 12, para. 12(2): consideration in relation to disposals under leasing arrangements where any of the return on investment is in capital form.
FA 1999, Sch. 6: revenue, as opposed to capital, treatment of receipts by way of reverse premium.
CTA 2009, Sch. 2, para. 93(3) and (4): rules for deduction under s. 38(1)(a) when calculating gain on disposal of a plain vanilla contract which became a derivative contract before 30 December 2006.
SI 1992/58, Sch. 2, para. 4(1), 5(1), (2): modification of s. 38(1) in relation to reorganisation of port authorities.
SI 2002/653, art. 4(5)(b): Scottish Water takes on the acquisition costs etc. of the East of Scotland Water Authority, West of Scotland Water Authority and North of Scotland Water Authority on any disposal of assets acquired by Scottish Water from those authorities by virtue of the Water Industry (Scotland) Act 2002, s. 22.

Statements of practice – D7: irrecoverable VAT included in cost.
D24: expenditure on initial property repairs not allowable for Sch. A and undertaken to make property fit to let to be regarded as allowable under s. 38(1)(a).
SP 02/04: allowable expenditure: expenses incurred by personal representatives and corporate trustees – in relation to certain expenses incurred by the personal representatives of deceased persons where the death in question occurred on or after 6 April 2004, and to expenses incurred by corporate trustees in making transfers and disposals on or after 6 April 2004.

HMRC interpretations – IRInt. 26: person deemed to have held an asset at 31 March 1982 for indexation or rebasing purposes can be treated as having incurred expenditure incurred after that date by a previous holder of the asset. Provided general conditions met, that expenditure may be taken into account on eventual disposal.
IRInt. 27: allowable deductions in respect of a sale of shares acquired before 19 March 1986 where BES relief claimed.

Other material – CCAB press release, 1968 (not reproduced): where on a reorganisation of share capital any share issue treated as income, amount of dividend allowed as cost of bonus issue.
ICAEW Technical Release TR 713 (not reproduced): capital contribution by shareholders to a company paid on acquisition of shares might be in the nature of a share premium, but otherwise unlikely to fall within s. 38(1)(b).
Taxline, 1992/18 (not reproduced): HMRC confirmation that, on disposal by a surviving spouse of an asset previously jointly owned, the survivor's acquisition cost is half of the couple's original cost/March 1982 value plus the probate value of the other half interest.
Taxline 1994/25 (not reproduced): HMRC view that only reasonable costs incurred in making the valuation in first instance, so that gain can be calculated and returned, are allowable under s. 38(2)(b); costs incurred subsequently e.g. negotiating with District Valuer, Shares Valuation Division, or litigating, are not.

Notes – FA 2003, Pt. 4: SDLT (not stamp duty) applies to transfers of property with effect from 1 December 2003. Stamp duty is abolished from 1 December 2003 other than on transfers of stock or marketable securities – FA 2003, s. 125.
S. 21–34: general meaning of "disposal" and "asset".
S. 82(5): tax paid by past trustee of emigrating trust on resulting deemed disposals is not deductible.
S. 143(5), (6): payment in the course of dealing in commodity or financial futures to close out the contract or on expiry is treated as incidental costs of disposal of asset constituting the outstanding obligations.
S. 144(2), (3): consideration for put option (binding grantor to buy) reduces the cost of grantor's acquisition thereunder and is an incidental cost of disposal for the disponor; consideration for call option (binding grantor to sell) is part of the disponor's acquisition cost.
S. 148(3): incidental costs of disposal in respect of the grant of a traded option are increased by the costs of acquiring a second traded option to close out the first contract.
S. 150(3), (10): reduction in BES relief by reference to market value of original shares following an allotment of new shares effectively transfers allowable costs after 18 March 1986 from the original shares to the newly allotted shares; allowable deductions exceeding BES relief in respect of shares issued before 19 March 1986 generally reduced by reference to that relief.
S. 152(1): acquisition consideration reduced by rolled-over gain on replacement of business assets.
S. 161(2): deemed acquisition at trade price where asset appropriated from trading stock.
S. 191(6): in respect of a non-resident company, tax paid by a fellow group company or a controlling director of the chargeable company or a company controlling that company is not deductible.
S. 201(3): no deductions allowed from the part of mineral royalties deemed to be capital.
S. 217(2), (4): in connection with the incorporation of a building society, shares acquired by the member treated as acquired for any new consideration given and, where acquired by trustees for free distribution to members, the shares and the interest of the members in the settlement are treated as acquired for nil consideration and when the member becomes absolutely entitled that is deemed to be on a no gain, no loss basis.
S. 229(3): reduction of consideration for acquisition where partial roll-over for disposals of shares to an employee share ownership trust.
S. 232–234: clawback by reference to deemed disposal and reacquisition or deemed chargeable gain where chargeable event occurs following roll-over on disposal of shares to qualifying share ownership trust.
S. 250(4): cost of woodland attributable to trees growing on the land is not allowable.
S. 260(3): acquisition consideration reduced by held-over gain where gift subject to inheritance tax.
S. 272–274 and Sch. 11: meaning of "market value".

For no gain, no loss enactments determining acquisition expenditure, see list in s. 35(3)(d) and see inability in some cases to substitute a gain for a loss or vice versa by using re-basing to 31 March 1982 (s. 35(4)), member becoming absolutely entitled to settled property comprising shares issued on incorporation of a building society (s. 217(4)(c)), roll-over relief on disposal of shares to an employee share ownership trust (s. 229(1)), roll-over relief on replacement of land compulsorily purchased (s. 247), gifts etc. to employee trusts (s. 239(2)), gifts to charities etc. (s. 257(2)), gifts to housing associations etc. (s. 259(2)), inability to substitute a gain for a loss or vice versa by using 6 April 1965 value (Sch. 2, para. 2(1), 9(4), para. 17(2)).

Express provisions permitting sums as deductions (in addition to specific cross references to s. 38, above):

- s. 64: expenditure on transfer of assets by personal representatives or trustees to beneficiaries;
- s. 67: inheritance tax on acquisition for which general gifts relief claimed;
- s. 124: higher rate income tax paid by an individual or personal representatives in respect of a close company apportionment;
- s. 260(7): on disposal by the transferee, inheritance tax on a chargeable transfer for which the transferee's acquisition cost is reduced by hold-over relief;
- s. 278: foreign tax chargeable where relief from double taxation not otherwise in point;
- ICTA 1988, s. 763(3): disposal giving rise to offshore income gain;
- ICTA 1988, Sch. 26, para. 3(2): claim for relief on a relevant disposal of shares in a controlled foreign company (or in a company through which the recipient's interest in a CFC is held);
- Ports Act 1991, s. 18(2): ports levy payable on disposal by successor company to former port authority.

Provisions specifying disposal and reacquisition at market value and provisions otherwise requiring the ascertainment of market value:

- s. 17: bargains otherwise than at arm's length or where consideration cannot be valued or in connection with payment for services;
- s. 19: assets disposed of in a series of transactions;
- s. 24: deemed disposal of site of building in respect of which negligible value or loss, destruction claim made;
- s. 25: assets of non-resident ceasing to be chargeable assets;
- s. 32: value shifting by reference to certain disposals within a group followed by a disposal of shares;
- s. 35: re-basing to 31 March 1982 and valuation of assets held at 6 April 1965;
- s. 42: part disposals;
- s. 55: indexation allowance by reference to 31 March 1982 value;
- s. 62, 63: uplift on death;
- s. 71(1): person becoming absolutely entitled to settled property;
- s. 72(1): death of life tenant;
- s. 80: trustees ceasing to be resident and ordinarily resident;
- s. 83: trustees ceasing to be liable to UK tax;
- s. 85: person disposing of an interest in a non-resident trust, where s. 80, 83 applies;
- s. 101(1): company becoming an investment trust with assets transferred at no gain, no loss on reconstruction or amalgamation;
- s. 103(3): restriction on availability of indexation allowance for deposit-based unit trusts etc.;
- s. 116(10): reorganisation, conversion or reconstruction where qualifying corporate bonds form part of the new holding but not the original holding;
- s. 125: apportionment of notional gains to shareholders of close company;
- s. 128: disregard of certain consideration given on a reorganisation;
- s. 129, 130: apportionment of cost of original shares to new holding following a reorganisation;
- s. 140(3): transfer of overseas branch assets to overseas company partly in exchange for securities;
- s. 140A(4): transfers of UK trade between companies in different EU member states;
- s. 161: appropriations to and from trading stock;
- s. 162(3): apportionment of rolled over gains between composite holdings transferred to an individual on incorporation of a business;
- s. 176: losses attributable to depreciatory transactions;
- s. 185(2), 186(2), 188(2): company ceasing to be resident, becoming dual resident or, by virtue of being dual resident, becomes exempt;
- s. 199: assets of non-residents ceasing to be dedicated to an oil field etc. and assets which do not continue to be used for UK exploration or exploitation activities on cessation of a UK branch etc. (or later such assets as do so continue ceasing to be used in that way);
- s. 202(3): claims in respect of relevant interests in land to which certain mineral leases or agreements relate;
- s. 204(3): transfer to life policy holder of investments etc.;
- s. 210(4): payment of the first instalment of a deferred annuity or surrender of rights under a contract therefor;
- s. 212(1): annual deemed disposal by insurance company of holdings of unit trusts or relevant interests in offshore funds;
- s. 242, 243: claims where small part disposal of land for consideration to be deducted from allowable expenditure on remainder;
- s. 256(2): property ceasing to be subject to charitable trusts;
- s. 258(5): sale or failure to observe undertaking as regards designated property;
- Sch. 2, para. 1(2), 9(2), 16(7), (8), 17(1), 19: assets held at 6 April 1965;
- SI 1989/469, reg. 27(1): transfer of personal equity plan investments to investor;
- Water Act 1989, s. 95(4), (5): succession to undertaking of a water authority.

39 Exclusion of expenditure by reference to tax on income

39(1) There shall be excluded from the sums allowable under section 38 as a deduction in the computation of the gain any expenditure allowable as a deduction in computing the profits or losses of a trade, profession or vocation for the purposes of income tax or allowable as a deduction in computing any other income or profits or gains or losses for the purposes of the Income Tax Acts and any expenditure which, although not so allowable as a deduction in computing any losses, would be so allowable but for an insufficiency of income or profits or gains; and this subsection applies irrespective of whether effect is or would be given to the deduction in computing the amount of tax chargeable or by discharge or repayment of tax or in any other way.

39(2) Without prejudice to the provisions of subsection (1) above, there shall be excluded from the sums allowable under section 38 as a deduction in the computation of the gain any expenditure which, if the assets, or all the assets to which the computation relates, were, and had at all times been, held or used as part of the fixed capital of a trade the profits of which were (irrespective of whether the person making the disposal is a company or not) chargeable to income tax would be allowable as a deduction in computing the profits or losses of the trade for the purposes of income tax.

39(3) No account shall be taken of any relief under Chapter II of Part IV of the Finance Act 1981 or under Schedule 5 to the Finance Act 1983, in so far as it is not withdrawn and relates to shares issued before 19th March 1986, in determining whether any sums are excluded by virtue of subsection (1) or (2) above from the sums allowable as a deduction in the computation of gains or losses for the purposes of this Act.

39(3A) This section is not to be taken as excluding, from the sums allowable under section 38 as a deduction in the computation of the gain, expenditure allowable as a deduction in computing a return on which income tax is charged under Chapter 2A of Part 4 of ITTOIA 2005 (disguised interest) (but see section 381D of that Act).

39(4) If–

(a) because section 517G(4) or (6) of ITA 2007(transactions in land: the chargeable person) applies, an amount is charged to income tax as income of a person other than the person ("A") by whom the gain was realised, and

(b) the income tax has been paid,

for the purposes of this section the amount charged to that tax is regarded as having been charged as the income of A.

39(5) If–

(a) because section 356OG(4) or (6) of CTA 2010 (transactions in land: the chargeable company) applies, an amount is charged to corporation tax as profits of a person other than the person ("B") by whom the gain was realised, and

(b) the corporation tax has been paid,

for the purposes of this section the amount charged to that tax is regarded as having been charged as the income of B.

History – In s. 39(1) and (2), the word "profits" substituted for the words "profits or gains" by FA 1998, s. 46(3) and Sch. 7, para. 7.
S. 39(3A) inserted by FA 2013, s. 28 and Sch. 12, para. 7, with effect for the tax year 2013–14 and subsequent tax years, subject to the transitional provision in FA 2013, Sch. 12, para. 18.
In s. 39(4)(a), the words "517G(4) or (6) of ITA 2007 (transactions in land: the chargeable person) applies, an amount is charged to income tax as income of" substituted for the words "759(4) or (6) of ITA 2007 applies, the person charged to tax under Chapter 3 of Part 13 of that Act (transactions in land) is" by FA 2016, s. 79(9), with effect from 15 September 2016 (Royal Assent).
S. 39(4) inserted by ITA 2007, s. 1027 and Sch. 1, para. 300, with effect from 6 April 2007.
In s. 39(5)(a), the words "356OG(4) or (6) of CTA 2010 (transactions in land: the chargeable company) applies, an amount is charged to corporation tax as profits of a person other than" substituted for the words "821(3) or (5) of CTA 2010 applies, the company charged to tax under Part 18 of that Act (transactions in land) is not" by FA 2016, s. 77(8), with effect from 15 September 2016 (Royal Assent).
S. 39(5) inserted by CTA 2010, s. 1177 and Sch. 1, para. 229, with effect for corporation tax purposes for accounting periods ending on or after 1 April 2010, and for income tax and capital gains tax purposes for the tax year 2010–11 and subsequent tax years.

Derivations – CGTA 1979, s. 33(3) as inserted by ICTA 1988, s. 844 and Sch. 29, para. 19.

Cross references – S. 8(4): general application of s. 8 disapplied in respect of references to income tax in s. 39(2).
TCGA 1992, s. 41: restriction of losses by reference to capital allowances and renewals allowances.
S. 119: disapplication to disposals of securities to which accrued income scheme applies, in favour of special rules.
S. 205: without prejudice to s. 39, insurance premiums for risk to assets are not deductible.
S. 210(7): life insurance and deferred annuities, situation where s. 39 is disregarded.
ICTA 1988, s. 450(6): consideration in respect of assets forming part of an underwriter's premiums trust fund not excluded by s. 39.
ICTA 1988, s. 777(12): for s. 39, person for whom the capital amount was obtained or by whom the gains was realised treated as the person upon whom the charge as income arose in respect of quasi-dealing transactions in land.
ICTA 1988, Sch. 5AA, para. 4A: disapplication of s. 39 to disposals of guaranteed futures and options.
FA 1981, Pt. IV, Ch. II and FA 1983, Sch. 5: the Business Start-up Scheme and BES (see ICTA 1988, s. 289–312 in relation to shares issued on or before 31 December 1993). BES replaced by EIS in relation to shares issued on or after 1 January 1994.
FA 1993, s. 176(2): costs of acquisition or consideration for disposal of assets forming part of Lloyd's underwriter's ancillary trust fund are not excluded from s. 39.
FA 2001, Sch. 22 para. 19: Certain qualifying land remediation expenditure excluded for purposes of capital gains.
FA 2001, Sch. 22 para. 28: Certain qualifying expenditure excluded for purposes of capital gains.
FA 2004, s. 133: companies in partnership: relationship with chargeable gains.
SI 1992/58, Sch. 2, para. 6: disapplication of s. 39(1), (2) in relation to reorganisation of port authorities.

Statements of practice – SP 5/81: certain capital expenditure on farm drainage allowed as revenue expenditure.

Notes – S. 8(4): reference to income tax and the Income Tax Acts construed in relation to a company as reference to corporation tax and the Corporation Tax Acts.
S. 21–34: general meaning of "disposal" and "asset".
S. 288: interpretation, including reference to sections being those of this Act.
Interpretation Act 1978, s. 5 and Sch. 1: the Income Tax Acts means the enactments relating to income tax.

40 Interest charged to capital

40(1) Where–

(a) a company incurs expenditure on the construction of any building, structure or works, being expenditure allowable as a deduction under section 38 in computing a gain accruing to the company on the disposal of the building, structure or work, or of any asset comprising it, and

(b) that expenditure was defrayed out of borrowed money,

the sums so allowable under section 38 shall, subject to subsection (2) below, include the amount of any interest on that borrowed money which is referable to a period or part of a period ending on or before the disposal.

40(2) Subsection (1) above has effect subject to section 39 and does not apply to interest which is a charge on income.

40(3) In relation to interest paid in any accounting period ending before 1st April 1981 subsection (1) above shall have effect with the substitution for all following paragraph (b) of–

(c) the company charged to capital all or any of the interest on that borrowed money referable to a period or part of a period ending on or before the disposal,

and the sums so allowable under section 38 shall include the amount of that interest charged to capital.;

and subsection (2) above shall not apply.

40(4) In consequence of Chapter 2 of Part 4 of the Finance Act 1996 (loan relationships) and CTA 2009 (Part 5 of which re-enacts that Chapter) this section does not have effect in relation to interest referable to an accounting period ending on or after 1st April 1996.

History – In s. 40(4) the words "and CTA 2009 (Part 5 of which re-enacts that Chapter)" inserted by CTA 2009, s. 1322 and Sch. 1, para. 362, with effect for corporation tax purposes for accounting periods ending on or after 1 April 2009, and for income tax and capital gains tax purposes for the tax year 2009–10 and subsequent tax years.
S. 40(4) inserted by FA 2002, s. 82 and Sch. 25, para. 60(2).

Derivations – S. 40(1), (2): ICTA 1970, s. 269, as amended by FA 1981, s. 38(3).
S. 40(3): ICTA 1970, s. 269(1)(c) and endpiece as enacted.

Notes – S. 21–34: general meaning of "disposal" and "asset".
S. 288: interpretation, including meaning of "company" and reference to sections being those of this Act.
ICTA 1988, s. 12, 834(1): meaning of "accounting period".
ICTA 1988, s. 338: meaning of "charge on income".

41 Restriction of losses by reference to capital allowances and renewals allowances

41(1) Section 39 shall not require the exclusion from the sums allowable as a deduction in the computation of the gain of any expenditure as being expenditure in respect of which a capital allowance or renewals allowance is made, but the amount of any losses accruing on the disposal of an asset shall be restricted by reference to capital allowances and renewals allowances as follows.

41(2) In the computation of the amount of a loss accruing to the person making the disposal, there shall be excluded from the sums allowable as a deduction any expenditure to the extent to which any capital allowance or renewals allowance has been or may be made in respect of it.

41(3) If the person making the disposal acquired the asset–

(a) by a transfer by way of sale in relation to which an election under section 569 of the Capital Allowances Act was made, or

(b) by a transfer to which section 268 of that Act applies,

(being enactments under which a transfer is treated for the purposes of capital allowances as being made at written down value), the preceding provisions of this section shall apply as if any capital allowance made to the transferor in respect of the asset had (except so far as any loss to the transferor was restricted under those provisions) been made to the person making the disposal (that is the transferee); and where the transferor acquired the asset by such a transfer, capital allowances which by virtue of this subsection can be taken into account in relation to the transferor shall also be taken into account in relation to the transferee (that is the person making the disposal), and so on for any series of transfers before the disposal.

41(4) In this section **"capital allowance"** means–

(a) any allowance under the Capital Allowances Act,

(aa) any deduction under section 311A of ITTOIA 2005 or section 250A of CTA 2009 (replacement domestic items relief),

(b) any deduction under section 315 of ITTOIA 2005 or section 254 of CTA 2009 (expenditure on sea walls), and

(c) any deduction in computing profits allowable under section 170 of ITTOIA 2005 or section 147 of CTA 2009 (cemeteries).

41(5) In this section **"renewals allowance"** means a deduction allowable in computing the profits of a trade, profession or vocation for the purpose of income tax by reference to the cost of acquiring an asset for the purposes of the trade, profession or vocation in replacement of another asset, and for the purposes of this Chapter a renewals allowance shall be regarded as a deduction allowable in respect of the expenditure incurred on the asset which is being replaced.

41(6) The amount of capital allowances to be taken into account under this section in relation to a disposal include any allowances falling to be made by reference to the event which is the disposal, and there shall be deducted from the amount of the allowances the amount of any balancing charge to which effect has been or is to be given by reference to the event which is the disposal, or any earlier event.

41(7) Where the disposal is of plant or machinery in relation to expenditure on which allowances or charges have been made under Part 2 of the Capital Allowances Act, and neither Chapter 15 (assets provided or used only partly for qualifying activity) nor Chapter 16 (partial depreciation subsidies) of that Part applies, the capital allowances to be taken into account under this section are to be regarded as equal to the difference between the qualifying expenditure incurred, or treated as incurred, under that Part on the provision of the plant or machinery by the person making the disposal and the disposal value required to be brought into account in respect of the plant or machinery.

41(8) Where there is a disposal of an asset acquired in circumstances in which–

(a) section 140A applies, or

(b) section 171 applies or would apply but for subsection (2) of that section,

this section has effect in relation to capital allowances made to the person from which it was acquired (so far as not taken into account in relation to a disposal of the asset by that person), and so on as respects previous transfers of the asset in such circumstances.

This does not affect the consideration for which an asset is deemed under section 140A or 171 to be acquired.

History – In s. 41(3), references to CAA 2001, s. 569 and s. 268 substituted for former references to CAA 1990, s. 158 and s. 78 by CAA 2001, s. 578 and Sch. 2, para. 78, with effect as respects allowances and charges falling to be made for chargeable periods ending, for income tax purposes, on or after 6 April 2001, and for corporation tax purposes, on or after 1 April 2001.
S. 41(4)(aa) inserted by FA 2016, s. 73(3), with effect in relation to expenditure on or after 1 April 2016 (corporation tax) and 6 April 2016 (income tax).
In s. 41(4)(b) the words "any relief given under section 30 of the Taxes Act or" omitted (and repealed by CTA 2009, s. 1326 and Sch. 3, Pt. 1) and the words "or section 254 of CTA 2009" inserted, and in para. (c) the words "section 91 of the Taxes Act or" omitted (and repealed by CTA 2009, s. 1326 and Sch. 3, Pt. 1) and the words "or section 147 of CTA 2009" inserted by CTA 2009, s. 1322 and Sch. 1, para. 363, with effect for corporation tax purposes for accounting periods ending on or after 1 April 2009, and for income tax and capital gains tax purposes for the tax year 2009–10 and subsequent tax years.
S. 41(4)(a) substituted by CAA 2001, s. 578 and Sch. 2, para. 78, Sch. 4, with effect as respects allowances and charges falling to be made for chargeable periods ending, for income tax purposes, on or after 6 April 2001, and for corporation tax purposes, on or after 1 April 2001.
In s. 41(4)(b), words "or any deduction under section 315 of ITTOIA 2005" inserted by ITTOIA 2005, s. 882 and Sch. 1, para. 430(a) which, in accordance with ITTOIA 2005, s. 883, have effect, for income tax purposes, for tax year 2005–06 and subsequent tax years, and, for corporation tax purposes, for accounting periods ending after 5 April 2005.
In s. 41(4)(c), words "or section 170 of ITTOIA 2005" inserted by ITTOIA 2005, s. 882 and Sch. 1, para. 430(b) which, in accordance with ITTOIA 2005, s. 883, have effect, for income tax purposes, for tax year 2005–06 and subsequent tax years, and, for corporation tax purposes, for accounting periods ending after 5 April 2005.
In s. 41(4) and (5), the word "profit" substituted for the words "profits or gains" by FA 1998, s. 46(3) and Sch. 7, para. 7.
In s. 41(7), words "plant or machinery" substituted for "machinery or plant", and "Part 2 of the Capital Allowances Act, and neither Chapter 15 (assets provided or used only partly for qualifying activity) nor Chapter 16 (partial depreciation subsidies) of that Part" substituted for "Part II of the 1990 Act, and neither section 79 (assets used only partly for trade purposes) nor section 80 (wear and tear subsidies) of that Act",and "qualifying expenditure" substituted for "capital expenditure" by CAA 2001, s. 578 and Sch. 2, para. 78, with effect as respects allowances and charges falling to be made for chargeable periods ending, for income tax purposes, on or after 6 April 2001, and for corporation tax purposes, on or after 1 April 2001.
S. 41(8) inserted by FA 2000, s. 102 and Sch. 29, para. 12(1), with effect in relation to disposals made on or after 1 April 2000.

Derivations – CGTA 1979, s. 34, as amended by CAA 1990, s. 164 and Sch. 1, para. 3.

Cross references – S. 55(3): application by reference to capital allowances in respect of actual expenditure where deemed disposal and reacquisition to effect indexation allowance on 31 March 1982 value irrespective of re-basing exclusions.
S. 174(1): application to allowances made to previous owners in any chain of transactions for which no gain, no loss deemed on domestication of UK branch or on transfer of capital assets within a group (or would be so deemed but for certain exclusions).
S. 195(5): clawback of scientific research allowances in respect of certain expenditure on searching or testing for oil treated as a balancing charge.
S. 276(9): application of the 1992 Act to the territorial sea and the continental shelf.
Sch. 2, para. 20: application by reference to capital allowances in respect of actual expenditure where deemed disposal and reacquisition to effect the rules for assets held at 6 April 1965.
Sch. 3, para. 3: application by reference to capital allowances in respect of actual expenditure where deemed disposal and reacquisition to effect re-basing.
ICTA 1988, s. 30: expenditure on sea walls deductible over 21-year period.
ICTA 1988, s. 33(1): allowance for excess expenditure on maintenance of agricultural land on an estate.
ICTA 1988, s. 91: trading deduction in respect of capital expenditure on land and certain buildings as a cemetery.

Other material – Taxline 1993/42 (not reproduced): arguable that on a disposal of an asset that has qualified for capital allowances, the loss restriction applies to the unindexed loss.

Notes – S. 21–34: general meaning of "disposal" and "asset".
S. 288: interpretation.

41A Restriction of losses: long funding leases of plant or machinery

41A(1) This section applies where a person disposes of an asset–

(a) which includes plant or machinery which is a fixture for the purposes of Chapter 6A of Part 2 of the Capital Allowances Act, and

(b) which he has used for the purpose of leasing under one or more long funding leases.

41A(2) In the computation of the amount of a loss accruing to the person on the disposal there shall be excluded from the sums allowable as a deduction by virtue of section 38(1)(a) and (b) (acquisition and enhancement costs) an amount determined in accordance with subsection (3) or (4).

41A(3) Where the person has used the plant or machinery for the purpose of leasing under one long funding lease, the amount is equal to the fall in value of the plant or machinery during the period of the lease.

41A(4) Where the person has used the plant or machinery for the purpose of leasing under more than one long funding lease, the amount is equal to the sum of the fall in value of the plant or machinery during the period of each lease.

41A(5) In this section, references to the fall in value of plant or machinery during the period of a lease are references to the amount (if any) by which–

(a) the market value of the plant or machinery at the commencement of the term of the lease,

exceeds

(b) its market value at the termination of the lease.

41A(6) For the purposes of this section, the following expressions have the meaning given in Chapter 6A of Part 2 of the Capital Allowances Act (interpretation of provisions about long funding leases)–

"commencement", in relation to the term of a lease,

"long funding lease",

"market value",

"the term", in relation to a lease,

"termination".

History – S. 41A inserted by FA 2006, s. 81 and Sch. 9, para. 5(1), with effect in relation to disposals on or after 1 April 2006.

42 Part disposals

42(1) Where a person disposes of an interest or right in or over an asset, and generally wherever on the disposal of an asset any description of property derived from that asset remains undisposed of, the sums which under paragraphs (a) and (b) of section 38(1) are attributable to the asset shall, both for the purposes of the computation of the gain accruing on the disposal and for the purpose of applying this Part in relation to the property which remains undisposed of, be apportioned.

42(2) The apportionment shall be made by reference–

(a) to the amount or value of the consideration for the disposal on the one hand (call that amount or value A), and

(b) to the market value of the property which remains undisposed of on the other hand (call that market value B),

and accordingly the fraction of the said sums allowable as a deduction in the computation of the gain accruing on the disposal shall be–

$$\frac{A}{A + B}$$

and the remainder shall be attributed to the property which remains undisposed of.

42(3) Any apportionment to be made in pursuance of this section shall be made before operating the provisions of section 41 and if, after a part disposal, there is a subsequent disposal of an asset the capital allowances or renewals allowances to be taken into account in pursuance of that section in relation to the subsequent disposal shall, subject to subsection (4) below, be those referable to the sums which under paragraphs (a) and (b) of section 38(1) are attributable to the asset whether before or after the part disposal, but those allowances shall be reduced by the amount (if any) by which the loss on the earlier disposal was restricted under the provisions of section 41.

42(4) This section shall not be taken as requiring the apportionment of any expenditure which, on the facts, is wholly attributable to what is disposed of, or wholly attributable to what remains undisposed of.

42(5) It is hereby declared that this section, and all other provisions for apportioning on a part disposal expenditure which is deductible in computing a gain, are to be operated before the operation of, and without regard to, section 58(1), sections 152 to 158 (but without prejudice to section 152(10)), section 171(1) or any other enactment making an adjustment to secure that neither a gain nor a loss occurs on a disposal.

Derivations – CGTA 1979, s. 35.

Cross references – S. 56: indexation allowance on part disposals – s. 42 applied before indexation provisions.
S. 58(1): deemed no gain, no loss on transfers between spouses.
S. 152–157: deferral of chargeable gains on replacement of business assets, including determination of the consideration before application of the deferral (s. 152(10)).
S. 164A(10): application of s. 42(5) to adjustments under s. 164A (relief on re-investment) of consideration for the acquisition of any shares.
S. 164F(4A): calculation of part disposal where there is a held-over gain on re-investment.
S. 171(1): deemed no gain, no loss on transfers of capital assets within a group.

S. 194(4), (5): application to a disposal of an oil licence relating to an undeveloped area partly for a further licence or an obligation to undertake certain work (consideration for which is deemed to be nil) only if there would otherwise be a gain (before incidental costs of disposal) and in modified form.
S. 195(7): allowance as if it were enhancement expenditure etc. of certain expenditure on searching or testing for oil is wholly attributable to any part disposed of.
S. 242–244: claims where small part disposal of land (by reference to market value) for consideration to be deducted from allowable expenditure on remainder or, where the consideration exceeds allowable expenditure, vice versa.
S. 267(3): where, as regards the sharing of transmission facilities, an asset is returned to a person having made a part disposal in relation to the transfer of it to the disponor, s. 42 is deemed to have had effect without s. 42(4).
Sch. 2, para. 10(5): in relation to land held at 6 April 1965, current use value of an interest in land which has been disposed of by part disposal is determined on the same basis as the apportionment of expenditure on such part disposal, but ignoring any wholly attributable expenditure.
Sch. 2, para. 16(7), (8): on a part disposal of an asset held at 6 April 1965 there is a deemed market value disposal and reacquisition for the purposes of time apportionment.
Sch. 3, para. 4: on a part disposal before 6 April 1988 of an asset held on 31 March 1982, the amount carried forward as expenditure for a subsequent disposal after that date is recalculated using re-basing.
Sch. 7A, para. 2(9), 4(12): in relation to restriction of losses on pre-entry assets (and "pooled assets"), amounts allowed as deduction of relevant allowable expenditure computed (where appropriate) in accordance with s. 42.
Sch. 7AD, para. 6: valuation of remaining property when disposal of part of relevant single asset by insurance company.
Sch. 8, para. 2: the grant of a lease for a premium is a part disposal of the interest out of which it is granted and the property which remains undisposed of includes the right to any rent, etc.
Sch. 8, para. 4: disapplication of s. 42 to the grant of a lease out of a sublease in favour of special rules.
Sch. 8, para. 5: the part of any lease premium which is charged as rent etc. and the charge on sale of land with a right to reconveyance are excluded from the consideration to be brought into account in the computation of the gain except in the denominator, (A + B), in s. 42 or, in the case of a sublease out of a short lease, any charge as rent by reference to the premium is deducted from the gain arising from that premium.
Sch. 11, para. 5(2): part disposal before 6 July 1973 recalculated by reference to change in basis of ascertaining market value.
ICTA 1988, s. 763(4): modification to disposal giving rise to an offshore income gain.
FA 1997, Sch. 12, para. 12(2): consideration in relation to disposals under leasing arrangements where any of the return on investment is in capital form.

Statements of practice – D1: fair and reasonable alternative to cost apportionment method in s. 42 is acceptable on part disposal of land.
D3: reasonable, rather than strict, valuations acceptable where first or subsequent interim distributions during liquidation of unquoted company.

Other material – CCAB press release, 1968 (not reproduced): elaboration as to what constitutes a single asset for the purposes of s. 42 (land and buildings).

Notes – S. 21–34: general meaning of "disposal" and "asset", including (s. 21(2)) part disposals as disposals.
S. 104(6): a disposal of securities in a "new holding", other than a disposal of the whole of it, is a part disposal.
S. 122: small capital distribution as part disposal of shares deducted from allowable expenditure or, where excess, election for whole of allowable expenditure to reduce the consideration received.
S. 245: deemed part disposal where land compulsorily acquired and the consideration includes an amount for splitting a larger holding.
S. 272–274 and Sch. 11: meaning of "market value".
S. 288: interpretation, including reference to sections being those of this Act.
For no gain, no loss enactments, see list in s. 35(3)(d) and see inability in some cases to substitute a gain for a loss or vice versa by using re-basing to 31 March 1982 (s. 35(4)), member becoming absolutely entitled to settled property comprising shares issued on incorporation of a building society (s. 217(4)(c)), roll-over relief on disposal of shares to an employee share ownership trust (s. 229(1)), roll-over relief on replacement of land compulsorily purchased (s. 247), gifts etc. to employee trusts (s. 239(2)), gifts to charities etc. (s. 257(2)), gifts to housing associations etc. (S. 259(2)), inability to substitute a gain for a loss or vice versa by using 6 April 1965 value (Sch. 2, para. 2(1), 9(4), 17(2)).

43 Assets derived from other assets

43 If and so far as, in a case where assets have been merged or divided or have changed their nature or rights or interests in or over assets have been created or extinguished, the value of an asset is derived from any other asset in the same ownership, an appropriate proportion of the sums allowable as a deduction in the computation of a gain in respect of the other asset under paragraphs (a) and (b) of section 38(1) shall, both for the purpose of the computation of a gain accruing on the disposal of the first-mentioned asset and, if the other asset remains in existence, on a disposal of that other asset, be attributed to the first-mentioned asset.

Derivations – CGTA 1979, s. 36.

Cross references – S. 55(4): for indexation allowance, s. 43 applies to division etc. after 31 March 1982 of asset held on that date by reference to value on that date if advantageous.
Sch. 2, para. 16(9): time apportionment of gain where asset held at 6 April 1965 takes into account period of ownership of the other asset within s. 43.
Sch. 3, para. 5: modifications to re-basing where asset not held on 31 March 1982 but which derived value from an asset so held.
Sch. 4, para. 8: modifications of 50 per cent relief where charge deferred in respect of gain before 31 March 1982 where original asset not held on that date but derived its value from an asset so held.

Notes – S. 21–34: general meaning of "disposal" and "asset".
S. 288: interpretation, including reference to sections being those of this Act.

WASTING ASSETS

44 Meaning of "wasting asset"

44(1) In this Chapter **"wasting asset"** means an asset with a predictable life not exceeding 50 years but so that–

(a) freehold land shall not be a wasting asset whatever its nature, and whatever the nature of the buildings or works on it;

(b) **"life"**, in relation to any tangible movable property, means useful life, having regard to the purpose for which the tangible assets were acquired or provided by the person making the disposal;

(c) plant and machinery shall in every case be regarded as having a predictable life of less than 50 years, and in estimating that life it shall be assumed that its life will end when it is finally put out of use as being unfit for further use, and that it is going to be used in the normal manner and to the normal extent and is going to be so used throughout its life as so estimated;

(d) a life interest in settled property shall not be a wasting asset until the predictable expectation of life of the life tenant is 50 years or less, and the predictable life of life interests in settled property and of annuities shall be ascertained from actuarial tables approved by the Board.

44(2) In this Chapter **"the residual or scrap value"**, in relation to a wasting asset, means the predictable value, if any, which the wasting asset will have at the end of its predictable life as estimated in accordance with this section.

44(3) The question what is the predictable life of an asset, and the question what is its predictable residual or scrap value at the end of that life, if any, shall, so far as those questions are not immediately answered by the nature of the asset, be taken, in relation to any disposal of the asset, as they were known or ascertainable at the time when the asset was acquired or provided by the person making the disposal.

Derivations – CGTA 1979, s. 37.

Cross references – S. 146: special rules for certain quoted options, traded options, financial options and trade use options but application of s. 44 to options which are not within those rules.
S. 154(7): a wasting asset (or one that will become one within ten years) is a depreciating asset for the purposes of hold-over relief on replacement of business assets.
FA 2004, s. 241(3): registered pension schemes: scheme chargeable payment; meaning of "wasting asset".

HMRC interpretations – IRInt. 42: depreciating assets in the context of roll-over relief.
IRInt. 200: whether wines and spirits are wasting assets for the purposes of capital gains tax.
IRInt. 206 (shotguns in issue 45): whether guns are machinery, and whether they have a predictable life not exceeding 50 years.

Notes – S. 21–34: general meaning of "disposal" and "asset".
S. 68: meaning of "settled property".
S. 240: leases.
S. 288: interpretation, including meaning of "land" and reference to sections being those of this Act.
Sch. 8: leases.

45 Exemption for certain wasting assets

45(1) Subject to the provisions of this section, no chargeable gain shall accrue on the disposal of, or of an interest in, an asset which is tangible movable property and which is a wasting asset.

45(2) Subsection (1) above shall not apply to a disposal of, or of an interest in, an asset–

(a) if, from the beginning of the period of ownership of the person making the disposal to the time when the disposal is made, the asset has been used and used solely for the purposes of a trade, profession or vocation and if that person has claimed or could have claimed any capital allowance in respect of any expenditure attributable to the asset or interest under paragraph (a) or paragraph (b) of section 38(1); or

(b) if the person making the disposal has incurred any expenditure on the asset or interest which has otherwise qualified in full for any capital allowance.

45(3) In the case of the disposal of, or of an interest in, an asset which, in the period of ownership of the person making the disposal, has been used partly for the purposes of a trade, profession or vocation and partly for other purposes, or has been used for the purposes of a trade, profession or vocation for part of that period, or which has otherwise qualified in part only for capital allowances–

(a) the consideration for the disposal, and any expenditure attributable to the asset or interest by virtue of section 38(1)(a) and (b), shall be apportioned by reference to the extent to which that expenditure qualified for capital allowances, and

(b) the computation of the gain shall be made separately in relation to the apportioned parts of the expenditure and consideration, and

(c) subsection (1) above shall not apply to any gain accruing by reference to the computation in relation to the part of the consideration apportioned to use for the purposes of the trade, profession or vocation, or to the expenditure qualifying for capital allowances.

45(3A) But subsection (3) does not apply in the case of a disposal in relation to which subsection (3B) disapplies subsection (1).

45(3B) Subsection (1) does not apply to a disposal of, or of an interest in, an asset if–

(a) at any time in the period of ownership of the person making the disposal, the asset is used for the purposes of a trade, profession or vocation carried on by another person,

(b) as a result of that use, the asset becomes plant,

(c) but for the asset therefore being regarded under section 44(1)(c) as having a predictable life of less than 50 years, the disposal would not be of, or of an interest in, a wasting asset, and

(d) the disposal is not within subsection (3C).

45(3C) A disposal of, or of an interest in, an asset is within this subsection if the asset is plant used for the purpose of leasing under a long funding lease and–

(a) the disposal takes place after the commencement of the term of the lease but before the termination of the lease, or

(b) the disposal is the deemed disposal of the asset under section 25A(3)(a) on the termination of the lease.

45(3D) Section 25A(5) applies for the purposes of subsection (3C).

45(4) Subsection (1) above shall not apply to a disposal of commodities of any description by a person dealing on a terminal market or dealing with or through a person ordinarily engaged in dealing on a terminal market.

History – S. 45(3A)–(3D) inserted by FA 2015, s. 40(1), with effect for corporation tax purposes, in relation to disposals on or after 1 April 2015, and for capital gains tax purposes, in relation to disposals on or after 6 April 2015.

Derivations – CGTA 1979, s. 127.

Cross references – S. 146: special rules for certain quoted options, traded options, financial options and trade use options but application of s. 45 to options which are not within those rules.

HMRC interpretations – IRInt. 86: antique clocks and watches, motor vehicles (not normal private passenger vehicles) and motor propelled vessels are machinery and constitute wasting assets if not used for a trade, profession or vocation.
IRInt. 200: considerations in determining whether "fine" wines and spirits are wasting assets for purposes of s. 45.

Other material – Taxline 1993/67 (not reproduced): the Capital Taxes Office have informed Christies that clocks and watches constitute machinery and so are wasting assets.
Taxline 1996/15 (not reproduced): assets which may be wasting assets include clocks, watches, road vehicles other than normal motor cars, railway locomotives, tramway engines and certain yachts and dinghies.

Notes – S. 15: meaning of "chargeable gain".
S. 21–34: general meaning of "disposal" and "asset", including the time of certain disposals.
SI 1973/173: the VAT (Terminal Markets) Order 1973 includes reference to the term "terminal market".

46 Straightline restriction of allowable expenditure

46(1) In the computation of the gain accruing on the disposal of a wasting asset it shall be assumed–

(a) that any expenditure attributable to the asset under section 38(1)(a) after deducting the residual or scrap value, if any, of the asset, is written off at a uniform rate from its full amount at the time when the asset is acquired or provided to nothing at the end of its life, and

(b) that any expenditure attributable to the asset under section 38(1)(b) is written off from the full amount of that expenditure at the time when that expenditure is first reflected in the state or nature of the asset to nothing at the end of its life,

so that an equal daily amount is written off day by day.

46(2) Thus, calling the predictable life of a wasting asset at the time when it was acquired or provided by the person making the disposal L, the period from that time to the time of disposal T(1), and, in relation to any expenditure attributable to the asset under section 38(1)(b), the period from the time when that expenditure is first reflected in the state or nature of the asset to the said time of disposal T(2), there shall be excluded from the computation of the gain–

(a) out of the expenditure attributable to the asset under section 38(1)(a) a fraction–

$$\frac{T(1)}{L}$$

of an amount equal to the amount of that expenditure minus the residual or scrap value, if any, of the asset, and

(b) out of the expenditure attributable to the asset under section 38(1)(b) a fraction–

$$\frac{T(2)}{L - (T(1) - T(2))}$$

of the amount of the expenditure.

46(3) *If any expenditure attributable* to the asset under section 38(1)(b) creates or increases a residual or scrap value of the asset, the provisions of subsection (1)(a) above shall be applied so as to take that into account.

Derivations – CGTA 1979, s. 38.

Cross references – S. 143(7): disapplication of s. 46 in relation to certain commodity or financial futures contracts.

S. 146: special rules for certain quoted options, traded options, financial options and trade use options but application of s. 46 to options which are not within those rules.
Sch. 8, para. 1(3): priority of curved line write-off of expenditure on leases.
Notes – S. 21–34: general meaning of "disposal" and "asset", including the time of certain disposals.

47 Wasting assets qualifying for capital allowances

47(1) Section 46 shall not apply in relation to a disposal of an asset–

(a) which, from the beginning of the period of ownership of the person making the disposal to the time when the disposal is made, is used and used solely for the purposes of a trade, profession or vocation and in respect of which that person has claimed or could have claimed any capital allowance in respect of any expenditure attributable to the asset under paragraph (a) or paragraph (b) of section 38(1), or

(b) on which the person making the disposal has incurred any expenditure which has otherwise qualified in full for any capital allowance.

47(2) In the case of the disposal of an asset which, in the period of ownership of the person making the disposal, has been used partly for the purposes of a trade, profession or vocation and partly for other purposes, or has been used for the purposes of a trade, profession or vocation for part of that period, or which has otherwise qualified in part only for capital allowances–

(a) the consideration for the disposal, and any expenditure attributable to the asset by paragraph (a) or paragraph (b) of section 38(1) shall be apportioned by reference to the extent to which that expenditure qualified for capital allowances, and

(b) the computation of the gain shall be made separately in relation to the apportioned parts of the expenditure and consideration, and

(c) section 46 shall not apply for the purposes of the computation in relation to the part of the consideration apportioned to use for the purposes of the trade, profession or vocation, or to the expenditure qualifying for capital allowances, and

(d) if an apportionment of the consideration for the disposal has been made for the purposes of making any capital allowance to the person making the disposal or for the purpose of making any balancing charge on him, that apportionment shall be employed for the purposes of this section, and

(e) subject to paragraph (d) above, the consideration for the disposal shall be apportioned for the purposes of this section in the same proportions as the expenditure attributable to the asset is apportioned under paragraph (a) above.

Derivations – CGTA 1979, s. 39.

Cross references – S. 55(3): application by reference to capital allowances in respect of actual expenditure where deemed disposal and reacquisition to effect indexation allowance on 31 March 1982 value irrespective of re-basing exclusions.
S. 146: special rules for certain quoted options, traded options, financial options and trade use options but application of s. 46 to options which are not within those rules.
Sch. 2, para. 20: application by reference to capital allowances in respect of actual expenditure where deemed disposal and reacquisition to effect the rules for assets held at 6 April 1965.
Sch. 3, para. 3: application by reference to capital allowances in respect of actual expenditure where deemed disposal and reacquisition to effect re-basing.
Sch. 8, para. 1(6): application to leases.
Notes – S. 21–34: general meaning of "disposal" and "asset", including the time of certain disposals.

CASH BASIS ACCOUNTING

47A Exemption for disposals by persons using cash basis

47A(1) No chargeable gain shall accrue on the disposal of, or of an interest in, an asset if conditions A to D are met in relation to the asset.

47A(2) Condition A is that the asset is–

(a) tangible movable property, and

(b) a wasting asset.

47A(3) Condition B is that, at any time during the period of ownership of the person making the disposal, the asset has been used for the purposes of a trade, profession or vocation carried on by the person.

47A(4) Condition C is that an election under section 25A of ITTOIA 2005 (cash basis for small businesses) has effect in relation to the trade, profession or vocation at the time of the disposal.

47A(5) Condition D is that–

(a) any expenditure attributable to the asset or interest under paragraph (a) or (b) of section 38(1) has been brought into account in calculating the profits of the trade, profession or vocation on the cash basis, or

(b) any of that expenditure would have been so brought into account if an election under section 25A of ITTOIA 2005 had had effect in relation to the trade, profession or vocation at the time the expenditure was paid.

47A(6) Subsection (7) applies in the case of the disposal of, or of an interest in, an asset which, in the period of ownership of the person making the disposal–

(a) has been used partly for the purposes of the trade, profession or vocation and partly for other purposes, or

(b) has been used for the purposes of the trade, profession or vocation for part of that period.

47A(7) In such a case–

(a) the consideration for the disposal, and any expenditure attributable to the asset or interest by virtue of section 38(1)(a) and (b), shall be apportioned by reference to the extent to which that expenditure was, or (as the case may be) would have been, brought into account as mentioned in subsection (5) above,

(b) the computation of the gain shall be made separately in relation to the apportioned parts of the expenditure and consideration, and

(c) subsection (1) above shall apply to any gain accruing by reference to the computation in relation to the part of the consideration apportioned to use for the purposes of the trade, profession or vocation.

History – S. 47A inserted by FA 2013, s. 17 and Sch. 4, para. 45, with effect for the tax year 2013–14 and subsequent tax years, subject to the transitional provision in FA 2013, Sch. 4, para. 57.

47B Disposals made by persons after leaving cash basis

47B(1) This section applies where–

(a) a person disposes of, or of an interest in, an asset that has been used for the purposes of a trade, profession or vocation carried on by the person, and

(b) conditions A and B are met in relation to the trade, profession or vocation.

47B(2) Condition A is that–

(a) any expenditure attributable to the asset or interest under paragraph (a) or (b) of section 38(1) was incurred at a time when an election under section 25A of ITTOIA 2005 (cash basis for small businesses) had effect in relation to the trade, profession or vocation, and

(b) that expenditure ("the relevant expenditure") has been brought into account in calculating the profits of the trade, profession or vocation on the cash basis.

47B(3) Condition B is that no such election has effect in relation to the trade, profession or vocation at the time of the disposal.

47B(4) Section 39 (exclusion of expenditure by reference to tax on income) does not apply in relation to the relevant expenditure.

47B(5) Section 41 (restriction of losses by reference to capital allowances and renewals allowances) has effect as if–

(a) the election mentioned in subsection (2)(a) above had not had effect at the time the relevant expenditure was incurred, and

(b) the reference in subsection (7) to qualifying expenditure included a reference to expenditure which, if that election had not had effect at that time, would have been qualifying expenditure.

47B(6) Section 45 (exemption for certain wasting assets) and section 47 (wasting assets qualifying for capital allowances) have effect as if the election mentioned in subsection (2)(a) above had not had effect at the time the relevant expenditure was incurred.

Accordingly, any reference in those sections to expenditure qualifying for capital allowances is to be read as a reference to expenditure that would, in the absence of the election, have qualified for such allowances.

History – S. 47B inserted by FA 2013, s. 17 and Sch. 4, para. 45, with effect for the tax year 2013–14 and subsequent tax years, subject to the transitional provision in FA 2013, Sch. 4, para. 57.

MISCELLANEOUS PROVISIONS

48 Consideration due after time of disposal

48(1) In the computation of the gain consideration for the disposal shall be brought into account without any discount for postponement of the right to receive any part of it and, in the first instance, without regard to a risk of any part of the consideration being irrecoverable or to the right to receive any part of the consideration being contingent; and if any part of the consideration so brought into account subsequently proves to be irrecoverable, there shall be made, on a claim being made to that effect, such adjustment, whether by way of discharge or repayment of tax or otherwise, as is required in consequence.

48(2) Subsection (1) above does not apply in relation to so much of any consideration as consists of rights under a creditor relationship to which a company becomes a party as a result of the disposal.

48(3) In the computation of the gain in a case where subsection (2) above has effect in relation to any consideration, the amount to be brought into account in respect of that consideration is the fair value of the creditor relationship.

48(4) In this section–

(a) **"creditor relationship"**, and

(b) **"fair value"**, in relation to a creditor relationship,

each have the same meaning as in Part 5 of CTA 2009 (see sections 302(5) and 313(6)).

History – Former s. 48 became s. 48(1) by virtue of F(No. 2)A 2005, s. 39 and Sch. 7, para. 7(2) with effect from 20 July 2005 (Royal Assent).
In former s. 48 "subsequently proves … in consequence" substituted by FA 1996, Sch. 20, para. 48, with effect in relation to years after 1995–96 and, for corporation tax purposes, accounting periods ending on or after 1 July 1999, the day appointed under FA 1994, s. 199 by virtue of SI 1998/3173 (C. 78).
S. 48(2) inserted by F(No. 2)A 2005, s. 39 and Sch. 7, para. 7(3) with effect from 20 July 2005 (Royal Assent).
S. 48(3) inserted by F(No. 2)A 2005, s. 39 and Sch. 7, para. 7(3) with effect from 20 July 2005 (Royal Assent).
In s. 48(4) the words "Part 5 of CTA 2009 (see sections 302(5) and 313(6))" substituted for the words "Chapter 2 of Part 4 of the Finance Act 1996 (see section 103(1) of that Act)" by CTA 2009, s. 1322 and Sch. 1, para. 364, with effect for corporation tax purposes for accounting periods ending on or after 1 April 2009, and for income tax and capital gains tax purposes for the tax year 2009–10 and subsequent tax years.
S. 48(4) inserted by F(No. 2)A 2005, s. 39 and Sch. 7, para. 7(3) with effect from 20 July 2005 (Royal Assent).
Derivations – CGTA 1979, s. 40(2).

Cross references – S. 279A–279D: treatment of loss on realisation of deferred unascertainable consideration.
S. 280: consideration payable by instalments.
ICTA 1988, s. 587B(7)(b): application of s. 48 in case of disposal of shares or securities to a charity at an undervalue.
SI 1992/58, Sch. 2, para. 7: modification of s. 48 in relation to reorganisation of port authorities.
Notes – S. 21–34: general meaning of "disposal".
S. 280: payment of tax by instalments in cases of hardship where consideration due in instalments.
S. 288: interpretation, including "inspector" as being any inspector of taxes.

48A Unascertainable consideration

48A(1) This section applies where–

(a) a person ("P") has made a non-resident CGT disposal in relation to which there accrued to P an NRCGT gain chargeable to, or an NRCGT loss allowable for the purposes of, capital gains tax by virtue of section 14D or 188D ("the original disposal"),

(b) P acquired a right as the whole or part of the consideration for that disposal,

(c) on P's acquisition of the right, there was no corresponding disposal of it, and

(d) the right is a right to unascertainable consideration (see subsections (4) to (6)).

48A(2) If P subsequently receives consideration ("the ascertained consideration") representing the whole or part of the consideration referred to in subsection (1)(d) and condition A in section 14B would have been met in relation to the original disposal had a gain on that disposal accrued at the time of the receipt of the ascertained consideration–

(a) the ascertained consideration is treated as not accruing on the disposal of the right,

(b) the costs of P's acquisition of the right (or, in the case of a part disposal of the right, those costs so far as referable to the part disposed of) are taken to be nil, and

(c) the following steps are taken.

Step 1

Any amount by which the ascertained consideration exceeds the relevant original consideration is treated as consideration (or further consideration) accruing on the original disposal.

If the relevant original consideration exceeds the ascertained consideration, the consideration accruing on the original disposal is treated as reduced by the amount of the excess.

Step 2

Compute the difference that the adjustment under step 1 makes to what (if any) NRCGT gain or loss, ATED-related gain or loss or other gain or loss accrues on the original disposal (computing this separately for each type of gain or loss).

The difference is "positive" if a loss is decreased (to nil or otherwise) or a gain created or increased.

The difference is "negative" if a gain is reduced (to nil or otherwise) or a loss created or increased.

Step 3

Any positive amount computed under step 2 is treated for the purposes of this Act and the Management Act as a gain (of the type appropriate to the computation) accruing to P at the time of the receipt of the ascertained consideration.

Any negative amount computed under step 2 is treated for the purposes of this Act and the Management Act as a loss (of the type appropriate to the computation) accruing to P at the time of the receipt of the ascertained consideration.

48A(3) In step 1 in subsection (2), **"the relevant original consideration"** means the consideration accruing on the original disposal, so far as referable to the right mentioned in subsection (1)(b) (or, in the case of a part disposal of the right, referable to the part disposed of).

48A(4) A right is a right to unascertainable consideration if, and only if–

(a) it is a right to consideration the amount or value of which is unascertainable at the time when the right is conferred, and

(b) that amount or value is unascertainable at that time on account of its being referable, in whole or in part, to matters which are uncertain at that time because they have not yet occurred.

This subsection is subject to subsections (5) and (6).

48A(5) The amount or value of any consideration is not to be regarded as being unascertainable by reason only–

(a) that the right to receive the whole or any part of the consideration is postponed or contingent, if the consideration or, as the case may be, that part of it is, in accordance with section 48, brought into account in the computation of the gain accruing to a person on the disposal of an asset, or

(b) in a case where the right to receive the whole or any part of the consideration is postponed and is to be, or may be, to any extent satisfied by the receipt of property of one description or property of some other description, that some person has a right to select the property, or the description of property, that is to be received.

48A(6) A right is not to be taken to be a right to unascertainable consideration by reason only that either the amount or the value of the consideration has not been fixed, if–

(a) the amount will be fixed by reference to the value, and the value is ascertainable, or

(b) the value will be fixed by reference to the amount, and the amount is ascertainable.

History – S. 48A inserted by FA 2015, s. 37 and Sch. 7, para. 14, with effect in relation to disposals made on or after 6 April 2015.

49 Contingent liabilities

49(1) In the first instance no allowance shall be made in the computation of the gain–

(a) in the case of a disposal by way of assigning a lease of land or other property, for any liability remaining with, or assumed by, the person making the disposal by way of assigning the lease which is contingent on a default in respect of liabilities thereby or subsequently assumed by the assignee under the terms and conditions of the lease,

(b) for any contingent liability of the person making the disposal in respect of any covenant for quiet enjoyment or other obligation assumed as vendor of land, or of any estate or interest in land, or as a lessor,

(c) for any contingent liability in respect of a warranty or representation made on a disposal by way of sale or lease of any property other than land.

49(2) If any such contingent liability subsequently becomes enforceable and is being or has been enforced, there shall be made, on a claim being made to that effect, such adjustment, whether by way of discharge or repayment of tax or otherwise, as is required in consequence.

49(3) Subsection (2) above also applies where the disposal in question was before the commencement of this section.

History – S. 49(2) substituted by FA 1996, Sch. 20, para. 49, with effect in relation to years after 1995–96 and, for corporation tax purposes, accounting periods ending on or after 1 July 1999, the day appointed under FA 1994, s. 199 by virtue of SI 1998/3173 (C. 78).

Derivations – CGTA 1979, s. 41.

Cross references – SI 1992/58, Sch. 2, para. 7: modification of s. 49(2) in relation to reorganisation of port authorities.

Extra-statutory concessions – D33: s. 49 applies to adjust the sale proceeds on a subsequent sale where contractual indemnity or warranty payments have been made by the vendor of an asset to its purchaser, rather than the compensation being treated as if arising from an underlying asset.

D52: payments incurred in respect of certain contingent liabilities arising from share exchange or company reconstruction or amalgamation.

Notes – S. 21–34: general meaning of "disposal".

S. 288: interpretation, including meaning of "land" and "inspector" as being any inspector of taxes.

50 Expenditure reimbursed out of public money

50 There shall be excluded from the computation of a gain any expenditure which has been or is to be met directly or indirectly by the Crown or by any Government, public or local authority whether in the United Kingdom or elsewhere.

Derivations – CGTA 1979, s. 42.

Cross references – ICTA 1988, s. 400(6): expenditure not treated as met by the Crown by reason only of the writing-off of a government investment.
CAA 2001, s. 532: capital allowances not given on expenditure which is met directly or indirectly out of public funds.

Extra-statutory concessions – D53: where expenditure met out of a grant would otherwise fall to be disregarded in computing any gain, the amount to be disregarded will be treated as reduced by any amount of the grant repaid.

Notes – S. 288: interpretation, including meaning of "local authority".

51 Exemption for winnings and damages etc.

51(1) It is hereby declared that winnings from betting, including pool betting, or lotteries or games with prizes are not chargeable gains, and no chargeable gain or allowable loss shall accrue on the disposal of rights to winnings obtained by participating in any pool betting or lottery or game with prizes.

51(2) It is hereby declared that sums obtained by way of compensation or damages for any wrong or injury suffered by an individual in his person or in his profession or vocation are not chargeable gains.

Derivations – CGTA 1979, s. 19(4), (5).

Cross references – TMA 1970, s. 12(2): assets within s. 51(1) are excluded from the requirements to divulge information about assets for purposes of capital gains tax.

Extra-statutory concessions – D33: exemption in s. 51(2) extends to compensation for professional negligence in relation to any action in respect of the wrong or injury; explanation of the terms "in his person", "in his profession or vocation"; application to compensation received by person other than individual suffering the wrong or injury etc.

Notes – S. 15: meaning of "chargeable gain".
S. 16: allowable losses.

52 Supplemental

52(1) No deduction shall be allowable in a computation of the gain more than once from any sum or from more than one sum.

52(2) References in this Chapter to sums taken into account as receipts or as expenditure in computing profits or gains or losses for the purposes of income tax shall include references to sums which would be so taken into account but for the fact that any profits or gains of a trade, profession, employment or vocation are not chargeable to income tax or that losses are not allowable for those purposes.

52(3) In this Chapter references to income or profits charged or chargeable to tax include references to income or profits taxed or as the case may be taxable by deduction at source.

52(4) For the purposes of any computation of the gain any necessary apportionments shall be made of any consideration or of any expenditure and the method of apportionment adopted shall, subject to the express provisions of this Chapter, be just and reasonable.

52(5) In this Chapter **"capital allowance"** and **"renewals allowance"** have the meanings given by subsections (4) and (5) of section 41.

History – In s. 52(4), words before "just and reasonable" omitted by FA 1996, Sch. 20, para. 50 and Sch. 41, Pt. V(10), with effect for years after 1995–96 and accounting periods ending on or after 1 July 1999, the day appointed under FA 1994, s. 199 by virtue of SI 1998/3173 (C. 78).

Derivations – CGTA 1979, s. 43.

Cross references – S. 152(11): without prejudice to s. 52(4), apportionment in respect of assets some or part of which are subject to a roll-over relief claim on replacement of business assets in just and reasonable manner.
S. 164A(12): without prejudice to s. 52(4) where consideration given for acquisition of assets including shares in respect of which claim under s. 164A made (deferral of gain on re-investment) consideration is to be apportioned in just and reasonable manner between shares to which claim relates and others.
S. 245(1): in considering need for apportionment under s. 52(4) of compulsory acquisition consideration, disregard of the compulsory nature thereof and of any statutory provision treating the consideration as being for land itself.
Sch. 11 para. 11(4): notwithstanding s. 52(4), part disposals chargeable under the former Sch. D, Case VII.
SI 1992/58, Sch. 2, para. 8: modification of s. 52(4) in relation to reorganisation of port authorities.

HMRC interpretations – IRInt. 39: apportionment of base cost where consideration on a share exchange is partly in the form of qualifying corporate bonds.
IRInt. 145: where principle in *Gray (Exor of Lady Fox dec'd) v IR Commrs* [1994] BTC 8,034 is followed (i.e. two or more different assets treated as single unit of property if disposal as one unit is the course a prudent hypothetical vendor would adopt), and valuation of assets when valued collectively is greater than when valued singly, apportionment under s. 52 must be on just and reasonable basis and reflect the value of each of the assets.

Other material – HMRC Practice Note: apportioning the price paid for a business transferred as a going concern.

Notes – S. 8(4): reference to income tax and the Income Tax Acts construed in relation to a company as reference to corporation tax and the Corporation Tax Acts.
S. 288: interpretation, including "inspector" as being any inspector of taxes and reference to sections being those of this Act.
TMA 1970, s. 44–58 and Sch. 3: appeals procedures and rules for assigning proceedings.

Chapter IV – Computation of Gains: The Indexation Allowance

Notes – In relation to disposals made on or after 30 November 1993 indexation may not generally be used to create or increase a capital loss.

52A Chapter to apply only for corporation tax purposes

52A This Chapter applies only for the purposes of corporation tax.

History – S. 52A inserted by FA 2008, s. 8 and Sch. 2, para. 78 with effect in computing gains on disposals made on or after 6 April 2008 (FA 2008, Sch. 2, para. 83).

GENERAL

53 The indexation allowance and interpretative provisions

53(1) Subject to any provision to the contrary, if on the disposal of an asset there is an unindexed gain, an allowance (**"the indexation allowance"**) shall be allowed against the unindexed gain–

(a) so as to give the gain for the purposes of this Act, or

(b) if the indexation allowance equals or exceeds the unindexed gain, so as to extinguish it (in which case the disposal shall be one on which, after taking account of the indexation allowance, neither a gain nor a loss accrues)

and any reference in this Act to an indexation allowance or to the making of an indexation allowance shall be construed accordingly.

53(1A) [Omitted by FA 2008, s. 8 and Sch. 2, para. 79(a).]

53(2) For the purposes of this Chapter, in relation to any disposal of an asset–

(a) **"unindexed gain"** means the amount of the gain on the disposal computed in accordance with this Part; and

(b) **"relevant allowable expenditure"** means, subject to subsection (3) below, any sum which, in the computation of the unindexed gain was taken into account by virtue of paragraph (a) or paragraph (b) of section 38(1).

53(2A) Notwithstanding anything in section 16 of this Act, this section shall not apply to a disposal on which a loss accrues.

53(3) In determining what sum (if any) was taken into account as mentioned in subsection (2)(b) above, account shall be taken of any provision of any enactment which, for the purpose of the computation of the gain, increases, excludes or reduces the whole or any part of any item of expenditure falling within section 38 or provides for it to be written-down.

53(4) Sections 54 and 108 and this section have effect subject to sections 56, 57, 109, 110, 113, 131 and 145.

History – In s. 53(1), the words "if on the disposal … nor a loss accrues)" substituted by FA 1994, s. 93(1) in relation to disposals made on or after 30 November 1993.

S. 53(1A) omitted by FA 2008, s. 8 and Sch. 2, para. 79(a) with effect in computing gains on disposals made on or after 6 April 2008 (FA 2008, Sch. 2, para. 83).

Former s. 53(1A), inserted by FA 1998, s. 122(1), with effect in relation to disposals on or after 6 April 1998.

In s. 53(2), the words "this Chapter" substituted, para. (a) substituted, and in para. (b) the word "gain" substituted by FA 1994, s. 93(2) in relation to disposals made on or after 30 November 1993.

S. 53(2A) inserted by FA 1994, s. 93(3) in relation to disposals made on or after 30 November 1993.

In s. 53(4), the reference to s. 110A omitted by FA 2008, s. 8 and Sch. 2, para. 79(b) with effect in computing gains on disposals made on or after 6 April 2008 (FA 2008, Sch. 2, para. 83).

In s. 53(4), reference to s. 110A inserted by FA 1998, s. 125(3), with effect in relation to disposals on or after 6 April 1998.

Derivations – S. 53(1)–(3) (as originally enacted): FA 1982, s. 86(2)–(4), as amended by FA 1985, s. 68(1), (2) and Sch. 19, para. 1. S. 53(4): FA 1982, s. 86(6).

Cross references – FA 1998, s. 122(7): disapplication of s. 53(1A) where a gain is treated as chargeable on or after 6 April 1998 in relation to an actual or deemed disposal occurring before that date.

FA 1998, s. 123(5): in s. 53(4), reference to s. 110A omitted where a gain is treated as chargeable after 6 April 1998 in relation to an actual or deemed disposal occurring before that date.

S. 38: allowable expenditure, including acquisition expenditure and incidental costs thereof (s. 38(1)(a)) and enhancement or title expenditure (s. 38(1)(b)).

S. 104: pooling of "new holdings" of shares by reference to relevant allowable expenditure, as defined in s. 53(2)(b), (3).

S. 108: identification of securities within accrued income scheme, qualifying corporate bonds or material interests in non-qualifying offshore funds.

S. 109: determination of indexation allowance in respect of pre-1982 share pools.

S. 110: calculation of indexation allowance in respect of a "new holding" of shares by reference to an indexed pool of expenditure.

S. 113: indexation allowance from date of actual consideration where call on shares results in consideration given more than 12 months after issue.

S. 131: indexation allowance from date of actual consideration notwithstanding the equation of a new holding with the original shares on a reorganisation.

S. 145: indexation allowance from date of actual consideration notwithstanding the treatment of a call option and the resulting acquisition as a single transaction.

S. 194(4), (5): application of part disposal apportionment of expenditure etc. to a disposal of an oil licence relating to an undeveloped area partly for a further licence or an obligation to undertake certain work (consideration for which is deemed to be nil) only if there would otherwise be a gain by reference to relevant allowable expenditure and indexation allowance and then in modified form.
S. 208: adaptation in relation to assets forming part of a premiums trust fund for a Lloyd's underwriter.

HMRC interpretations – IRInt. 27: computation of relevant allowable expenditure in respect of a sale of shares acquired before 19 March 1986 where BES relief claimed.

Notes – S. 21–34: general meaning of "disposal" and "asset".
S. 197: indexation allowance in respect of the provisions to ring fence certain gains and losses from disposals of interests in oil fields etc.
S. 288: interpretation, including reference to sections being those of this Act.
Provisions denying indexation allowance:

- s. 103: rights in deposit-based unit trust schemes etc.;
- s. 111: shares in a building society or a registered industrial and provident society;
- s. 182: linked company debt on a security;
- s. 183: in part, redeemable preference shares in a linked company, linked company shares or a new holding received on a reorganisation and equated therewith or with a linked company debt; and
- ICTA 1988, Sch. 28, para. 2(2): interest in a non-qualifying offshore fund (to extent gain taxed as income).

In relation to disposals made on or after 30 November 1993 indexation may not generally be used to create or increase a capital loss.

54 Calculation of indexation allowance

54(1) Subject to any provision to the contrary, the indexation allowance is the aggregate of the indexed rise in each item of relevant allowable expenditure; and, in relation to any such item of expenditure, the indexed rise is a sum produced by multiplying the amount of that item by a figure expressed as a decimal and determined, subject to subsections (2) and (3) below, by the formula–

$$\frac{(RD - RI)}{RI}$$

where–

RD is the retail prices index for the month in which the disposal occurs; and

RI is the retail prices index for March 1982 or the month in which the expenditure was incurred, whichever is the later.

54(1A) [Omitted by FA 2008, s. 8 and Sch. 2, para. 80(3).]

54(2) If, in relation to any item of expenditure–

(a) the expenditure is attributable to the acquisition of relevant securities, within the meaning of section 108, which are disposed of within the period of 10 days beginning on the day on which the expenditure was incurred, or

(b) RD, as defined in subsection (1) above, is equal to or less than RI, as so defined,

the indexed rise in that item is nil.

54(3) If, in relation to any item of expenditure, the figure determined in accordance with the formula in subsection (1) above would, apart from this subsection, be a figure having more than 3 decimal places, it shall be rounded to the nearest third decimal place.

54(4) For the purposes of this section–

(a) relevant allowable expenditure falling within paragraph (a) of subsection (1) of section 38 shall be assumed to have been incurred at the time when the asset in question was acquired or provided; and

(b) relevant allowable expenditure falling within paragraph (b) of that subsection shall be assumed to have been incurred at the time when that expenditure became due and payable.

History – In s. 54(1), the words "the month in which the disposal occurs" substituted for "the relevant month" by FA 2008, s. 8 and Sch. 2, para. 80(2) with effect in computing gains on disposals made on or after 6 April 2008 (FA 2008 Sch. 2, para. 83).
In s. 54(1), the words "the relevant month" substituted for the former words "the month in which the disposal occurs" by FA 1998, s. 122(2), with effect in relation to disposals on or after 6 April 1998.
S. 54(1A) omitted by FA 2008, s. 8 and Sch. 2, para. 80(3) with effect in computing gains on disposals made on or after 6 April 2008 (FA 2008, Sch. 2, para. 83).
Former s. 54(1A) inserted by FA 1998, s. 122(3), with effect in relation to disposals on or after 6 April 1998.

Derivations – FA 1982, s. 87, as amended by FA 1985, s. 68(1), (2) and Sch. 19, para. 2.

Cross references – FA 1998, s. 122(7): disapplication of revised definition of "RD" in s. 54(1), with effect in relation to gain treated as chargeable after 6 April 1998 where actual or deemed disposal occurred before that date.
S. 38: allowable expenditure, including acquisition expenditure and incidental costs thereof (s. 38(1)(a)) and enhancement or title expenditure (s. 38(1)(b)).
S. 107(6): securities otherwise within a "new holding" where any disposal within ten days of an acquisition treated for s. 54(2) as relevant securities within s. 108.
S. 108: identification of securities within accrued income scheme, deep discount securities or material interests in non-qualifying offshore funds.
S. 109(6): for s. 54(4), relevant allowable expenditure on a "1982 holding" falls within s. 38(1)(a).
S. 110: special provisions for calculating indexation allowance on a "new holding" of securities (replaced by s. 110A with effect in relation to disposals by individuals on or after 6 April 1998).
S. 113: disapplication of s. 54(4), certain calls on shares after 12-month delay being treated as incurred when actually given.
S. 182(2): for disposal of a debt on a security outstanding between linked companies, RD taken as RPI for the first month after acquisition in which they were linked.
S. 208: adaptation in relation to assets forming part of a premiums trust fund for a Lloyd's underwriter.

SI 1992/58, Sch. 2, para. 12(1): modification of s. 54(2) in relation to reorganisation of port authorities.
Notes – S. 21–34: general meaning of "disposal" and "asset", including the time of certain disposals.
S. 183: reduction in relation to a disposal of redeemable preference shares in a linked company, linked company shares or a new holding received on a reorganisation and equated therewith or with a linked company debt.
S. 288: interpretation, including the meaning of "retail prices index".
In relation to disposals on or after 30 November 1993 indexation may not generally be used to create or increase a capital loss.

55 Assets owned on 31st March 1982 or acquired on a no gain/no loss disposal

55(1) For the purpose of computing the indexation allowance on a disposal of an asset where, on 31st March 1982, the asset was held by the person making the disposal, it shall be assumed that on that date the asset was sold by the person making the disposal and immediately reacquired by him at its market value on that date.

55(2) Except where an election under section 35(5) has effect, neither subsection (1) above nor section 35(2) shall apply for the purpose of computing the indexation allowance in a case where that allowance would be greater if they did not apply.

55(3) If under subsection (1) above it is to be assumed that any asset was on 31st March 1982 sold by the person making the disposal and immediately reacquired by him, sections 41 and 47 shall apply in relation to any capital allowance or renewals allowance made in respect of the expenditure actually incurred by him in providing the asset as if it were made in respect of expenditure which, on that assumption, was incurred by him in reacquiring the asset on 31st March 1982.

55(4) Where, after 31st March 1982, an asset which was held on that date has been merged or divided or has changed its nature or rights in or over the asset have been created, then, subject to subsection (2) above, subsection (1) above shall have effect to determine for the purposes of section 43 the amount of the consideration for the acquisition of the asset which was so held.

55(5) Subsection (6) below applies to a disposal of an asset which is not a no gain/no loss disposal if–

(a) the person making the disposal acquired the asset after 31st March 1982; and

(b) the disposal by which he acquired the asset and any previous disposal of the asset after 31st March 1982 was a no gain/no loss disposal;

and for the purposes of this subsection a no gain/no loss disposal is one on which, by virtue of section 257(2) or 259(2) or any of the no gain/no loss provisions, neither a gain nor a loss accrues (or accrued) to the person making the disposal.

55(5A) For the purposes of subsection (5), a disposal is also a no gain/no loss disposal if it is one on which, by virtue of section 195B, 195C or 195E, neither a gain nor a loss accrues to the person making the disposal; but, in such a case, subsection (6)(b) below does not apply.

55(6) Where this subsection applies to a disposal of an asset–

(a) the person making the disposal shall be treated for the purpose of computing the indexation allowance on the disposal as having held the asset on 31st March 1982;

(aa) in the case of a disposal to which paragraph 1A of Schedule 3 applies (certain holdings of shares or securities), the market value of the asset on that date is to be determined in accordance with that paragraph; and

(b) for the purpose of determining any gain or loss on the disposal, the consideration which, apart from this subsection, that person would be treated as having given for the asset shall be taken to be reduced by deducting therefrom any indexation allowance brought into account by virtue of section 56(2) on any disposal falling within subsection (5)(b) above.

55(7) The rules in subsection (8) below apply (after the application of section 53 but before the application of section 35(3) or (4)) to give the gain or loss for the purposes of this Act where–

(a) subsection (6) above applies to the disposal (the **"disposal in question"**) of an asset by any person (the **"transferor"**), and

(b) but for paragraph (b) of that subsection, the consideration the transferor would be treated as having given for the asset would include an amount or amounts of indexation allowance brought into account by virtue of section 56(2) on any disposal made before 30th November 1993.

55(8) The rules are as follows–

(a) where (apart from this subsection) there would be a loss, an amount equal to the rolled-up indexation shall be added to it so as to increase it,

(b) where (apart from this subsection) the unindexed gain or loss would be nil, there shall be a loss of an amount equal to the rolled-up indexation, and

(c) where (apart from this subsection)–

(i) there would be an unindexed gain, and

(ii) the gain or loss would be nil but the amount of the indexation allowance used to extinguish the gain would be less than the rolled-up indexation,

the difference shall constitute a loss.

55(9) In this section the **"rolled-up indexation"** means, subject to subsections (10) and (11) below, the amount or, as the case may be, the aggregate of the amounts referred to in subsection (7)(b) above; and subsections (10) and (11) below shall, as well as applying on the disposal in question, be treated as having applied on any previous part disposal by the transferor.

55(10) Where, for the purposes of any disposal of the asset by the transferor, any amount falling within any, or any combination of, paragraphs (a) to (c) of section 38(1) is required by any enactment to be excluded, reduced or written down, the amount or aggregate referred to in subsection (9) above (or so much of it as remains after the application of this subsection and subsection (11) below on a previous part disposal) shall be reduced in proportion to any reduction made in the amount falling within the paragraph, or the combination of paragraphs, in question.

55(11) Where the transferor makes a part disposal of the asset at any time, then, for the purposes of that and any subsequent disposal, the amount or aggregate referred to in subsection (9) above (or so much of it as remains after the application of this subsection and subsection (10) above on a previous part disposal by him or after the application of subsection (10) above on the part disposal) shall be apportioned between the property disposed of and the property which remains in the same proportions as the sums falling within section 38(1)(a) and (b).

History – In s. 55(5), the words "no gain/no loss provisions" substituted for the words "enactments specified in section 35(3)(d)" by FA 2008, s. 8 and Sch. 2, para. 60 with effect in relation to disposals on or after 6 April 2008 (FA 2008, Sch. 2, para. 71).
S. 55(5A) inserted by FA 2009, s. 86 and Sch. 40, para. 3, with effect in relation to disposals made on or after 22 April 2009
S. 55(7) inserted by FA 1994, s. 93(4), in relation to disposals made on or after 30 November 1993.
S. 55(6)(aa) inserted (and the "and" at the end of s. 55(6)(a) omitted) by SI 2010/157, art. 7(1), with effect in relation to disposals made on or after 1 April 2010.
S. 55(8) inserted by FA 1994, s. 93(4), in relation to disposals made on or after 30 November 1993.
S. 55(9) inserted by FA 1994, s. 93(4), in relation to disposals made on or after 30 November 1993.
S. 55(10) inserted by FA 1994, s. 93(4), in relation to disposals made on or after 30 November 1993.
S. 55(11) inserted by FA 1994, s. 93(4), in relation to disposals made on or after 30 November 1993.

Derivations – S. 55(1): FA 1985, s. 68(4).
S. 55(2): FA 1985, s. 68(5), as substituted by FA 1988, s. 96 and Sch. 8, para. 11.
S. 55(3): FA 1985, s. 68(5A), as inserted by FA 1988, s. 118(2).
S. 55(4): FA 1985, s. 68(6).
S. 55(5): FA 1985, s. 68(7), as amended by FA 1988, s. 118(4); FA 1985, s. 68(7A), as inserted by FA 1988, s. 118(4) and amended by FA 1989, s. 141 and Sch. 15, para. 4, FA 1990, s. 70(7), FA 1991, s. 78(6), 99(1).
S. 55(6): FA 1985, s. 68(8).

Cross references – S. 35: potential re-basing to 31 March 1982 (s. 35(2)) subject to excluded disposals such as (s. 35(3)(d)) various no gain, no loss disposals, with election (s. 35(5)) for simplified scheme to ignore such exclusions.
S. 41: restriction of losses by reference to capital allowances.
S. 43: attribution of allowable expenditure where the value of an asset is derived from another asset.
S. 47: straightline restriction of allowable expenditure on wasting asset limited to extent asset qualifies for capital allowances etc.
S. 164FF: reinvestment relief reductions under s. 164A(2)(b) or s. 164F(10A)(b) not defeated by anything in s. 55 in respect of disposals on or after 20 June 1994 following no gain/no loss disposals.
S. 208: adaptation in relation to assets forming part of a premiums trust fund for a Lloyd's underwriter.
S. 257(2): gifts or certain partial gifts to charity or for national purposes.
S. 259(2): claims in respect of gifts or certain partial gifts to housing associations.
Sch. 7A, para. 2(8A): calculation of any restriction on pre-entry losses where any part of the loss is attributable to an amount of rolled-up indexation.
SI 1992/58, Sch. 2, para. 12(2): disapplication of s. 55(1) in relation to reorganisation of port authorities.

Extra-statutory concessions – D34: valuation for purposes of re-basing of shares or securities of the same class where some acquired before 6 April 1965 and others acquired between 6 April 1965 and 31 March 1982.

HMRC interpretations – IRInt. 26: person deemed to have held an asset at 31 March 1982 for indexation or rebasing purposes can be treated as having incurred expenditure incurred after that date by a previous holder of the asset.

Notes – S. 21–34: general meaning of "disposal" and "asset", including the timing of certain disposals.
S. 246: time of disposal in cases of compulsory purchase of land as being when compensation etc. agreed or, if earlier, when the authority enter upon the land.
S. 272–274 and Sch. 11: meaning of "market value".
S. 288: interpretation, including reference to sections being those of this Act.
In relation to disposals on or after 30 November 1993 indexation may not generally be used to create or increase a capital loss.

56 Part disposals and disposals on a no-gain/no-loss basis

56(1) For the purpose of determining the indexation allowance (if any) on the occasion of a part disposal of an asset, the apportionment under section 42 of the sums which make up the relevant allowable expenditure shall be effected before the application of section 54 and, accordingly, in relation to a part disposal–

(a) references in section 54 to an item of expenditure shall be construed as references to that part of that item which is so apportioned for the purposes of the computation of the unindexed gain on the part disposal; and

(b) no indexation allowance shall be determined by reference to the part of each item of relevant allowable expenditure which is apportioned to the property which remains undisposed of.

56(2) On a no gain/no loss disposal by any person (**"the transferor"**)–

(a) the amount of the consideration shall be calculated for the purposes of this Act on the assumption that, on the disposal, an unindexed gain accrues to the transferor which is equal to the indexation allowance on the disposal, and

(b) the disposal shall accordingly be one on which, after taking account of the indexation allowance, neither a gain nor a loss accrues;

and for the purposes of the application of sections 53 and 54 there shall be disregarded so much of any enactment as provides that, on the subsequent disposal of the asset by the person acquiring the asset on the disposal (**"the transferee"**), the transferor's acquisition of the asset is to be treated as the transferee's acquisition of it.

56(3) Where apart from this subsection–

(a) a loss would accrue on the disposal of an asset, and

(b) the sums allowable as a deduction in computing that loss would include an amount attributable to the application of the assumption in subsection (2) above on any no gain/no loss disposal made on or after 30th November 1993,

those sums shall be determined as if that subsection had not applied on any such disposal made on or after that date and the loss shall be reduced accordingly or, if those sums are then equal to or less than the consideration for the disposal, the disposal shall be one on which neither a gain nor a loss accrues.

56(4) For the purposes of this section **a no gain/no loss disposal** is one which, by virtue of any enactment other than section 35(4), 53(1) or this section, is treated as a disposal on which neither a gain nor a loss accrues to the person making the disposal.

History – In s. 56(1)(a), the words "or loss" which appeared after "unindexed gain" repealed by FA 1994, s. 258 and Sch. 26, Pt. V(8) in relation to disposals made on or after 30 November 1993.
In s. 56(2), the words preceding para. (a) were substituted by FA 1994, s. 93(5)(a) in relation to disposals made on or after 30 November 1993.
S. 56(3) inserted by FA 1994, s. 93(5)(b) in relation to disposals made on or after 30 November 1993.
S. 56(4) inserted by FA 1994, s. 93(5)(b) in relation to disposals made on or after 30 November 1993.

Derivations – As originally enacted: FA 1982, Sch. 13, para. 1, 2, as amended (respectively) by FA 1985, s. 68(1), (2) and Sch. 19, para. 5(1), (2).

Cross references – S. 35A: explicit application of s. 56(2) in respect of transfers between spouses or civil partners between 1 April 1982 and 5 April 2008.
S. 42: attribution of allowable expenditure on part disposals.
S. 110: disapplication of s. 56(2) in certain circumstances relating to indexation allowance on share pools.
Sch. 7A, para. 2(6): disapplication of s. 56(2) in relation to pre-entry losses and assets.
ICTA 1988, Sch. 28, para. 2, 3(1), 4(3), 8(3): offshore income gain which is taxed as income is calculated by reference to gain using principles of this Act but if acquired on a no gain, no loss basis as if no allowance had been available under s. 56(2) and generally as if transferee's acquisition of it had been the disponor's; a gain on a disposal involving an equalisation element is calculated ignoring no gain, no loss provisions (although reference to s. 56 in para. 4(3) and 8(3) appears to be an error, the previous reference reflecting the exclusion of no gain, no loss indexation provisions aimed at preventing losses from indexation before 1985).

HMRC interpretations – IRInt. 26: person deemed to have held an asset at 31 March 1982 for indexation or rebasing purposes can be treated as having incurred expenditure incurred after that date by a previous holder of the asset.

Notes – S. 21–34: general meaning of "disposal" and "asset", including (s. 21(2)) part disposals as disposals.
S. 104(6): a disposal of securities in a "new holding", other than a disposal of the whole of it, is a part disposal.
For no gain, no loss enactments, see list in s. 35(3)(d) and see inability in some cases to substitute a gain for a loss or vice versa by using re-basing to 31 March 1982 (s. 35(4)), oil industry assets, member becoming absolutely entitled to settled property comprising shares issued on incorporation of a building society (s. 217(4)(c)), roll-over relief on disposal of shares to an employee share ownership trust (s. 229(1)), roll-over relief on replacement of land compulsorily purchased (s. 247), gifts etc. to employee trusts (s. 239(2)), gifts to charities etc. (s. 257(2)), gifts to housing associations etc. (s. 259(2)), inability to substitute a gain for a loss or vice versa by using 6 April 1965 value (Sch. 2, para. 2(1), 9(4), 17(2)).
In relation to disposals on or after 30 November 1993 indexation may not generally be used to create or increase a capital loss.

57 Receipts etc. which are not treated as disposals but affect relevant allowable expenditure

57(1) This section applies where, in determining the relevant allowable expenditure in relation to a disposal of an asset, account is required to be taken, as mentioned in section 53(3), of any provision of any enactment which, by reference to a relevant event, reduces the whole or any part of an item of expenditure as mentioned in that subsection.

57(2) For the purpose of determining, in a case where this section applies, the indexation allowance (if any) to which the person making the disposal is entitled, no account shall in the first instance be taken of the provision referred to in subsection (1) above in calculating the indexed rise in the item of expenditure to which that provision applies but, from that indexed rise as so calculated, there shall be deducted a sum equal to the indexed rise (determined as for the purposes of the actual disposal) in a notional item of expenditure which–

(a) is equal to the amount of the reduction effected by the provision concerned; and

(b) was incurred on the date of the relevant event referred to in subsection (1) above.

57(3) In this section **"relevant event"** means any event which does not fall to be treated as a disposal for the purposes of this Act.

Derivations – FA 1982, Sch. 13, para. 4.

Cross references – S. 208: adaptation in relation to assets forming part of a premiums trust fund for a Lloyd's underwriter. ICTA 1988, Sch. 28, para. 2, 3(1), 4(3), 8(3): offshore income gain which is taxed as income is calculated by reference to gain using principles of this Act but if acquired on a no gain, no loss basis as if no allowance had been available under s. 56(2) and generally as if transferee's acquisition of it had been the disponor's; a gain on a disposal involving an equalisation element is calculated ignoring no gain, no loss provisions (although reference to s. 57 in para. 4(3) and 8(3) appears to be an error, the previous reference reflecting the exclusion of no gain, no loss indexation provisions aimed at preventing losses from indexation before 1985).

Notes – S. 21–34: general meaning of "disposal" and "asset".
S. 288: interpretation, including reference to sections as being those of this Act.
Provisions reducing allowable expenditure otherwise than on a disposal:

- s. 23(1): allowable expenditure reduced by deemed proceeds where otherwise part disposal on receipt of compensation or insurance;
- s. 122(2): allowable expenditure reduced by deemed proceeds where otherwise part disposal on receipt of a capital distribution;
- s. 133(2): allowable expenditure reduced by deemed proceeds where otherwise part disposal on receipt of a premium on conversion of securities; and
- s. 244: allowable expenditure reduced by deemed proceeds where otherwise small part disposal of land.

Chapter 5 – Computation of Gains and Losses: Relevant High Value Disposals

History – Ch. 5 inserted by FA 2013, s. 65 and Sch. 25, para. 9, with effect in relation to disposals occurring on or after 6 April 2013.

57A Gains and losses on relevant high value disposals

57A(1) Schedule 4ZZA makes provision about the computation of gains and losses on relevant high value disposals, including provision about whether a gain or loss is ATED-related or not.

57A(2) But if the effect of Schedule 4ZZA applying in relation to a disposal would be that no ATED-related gain or loss accrues on the disposal, for the purposes of this Act the gain or loss on the disposal is to be computed ignoring that Schedule (and is not ATED-related).

57A(3) Subsection (2) does not apply where–

(a) Part 4 of Schedule 4ZZB applies (non-resident CGT disposals which are or involve relevant high value disposals) or,

(b) Part 3 of Schedule 4ZZC applies (other disposals of residential property interests which are or involve relevant high value disposals).

History – S. 57A(3)(a) created from the existing text and s. 57A(3(b) (and the word "or," preceding it) inserted by FA 2016, s. 83 and Sch. 12, para. 2, with effect in relation to gains accruing on or after 6 April 2016.
S. 57A(3) inserted by FA 2015, s. 37 and Sch. 7, para. 15, with effect in relation to disposals made on or after 6 April 2015.
S. 57A inserted by FA 2013, s. 65 and Sch. 25, para. 9, with effect in relation to disposals occurring on or after 6 April 2013.

Chapter 6 – Computation of Gains and Losses: Non-resident CGT Disposals

History – Ch. 6 inserted by FA 2015, s. 37 and Sch. 7, para. 16, with effect in relation to disposals made on or after 6 April 2015.

57B Gains and losses on non-resident CGT disposals

57B(1) Schedule 4ZZB makes provision about the computation of–

(a) NRCGT gains or losses, and

(b) other gains or losses,

on non-resident CGT disposals.

57B(2) For further provision about non-resident CGT disposals and NRCGT gains and losses see sections 14B to 14H and 188D and 188E.

History – S. 57B inserted by FA 2015, s. 37 and Sch. 7, para. 16, with effect in relation to disposals made on or after 6 April 2015.

Chapter 7 – Computation of Gains and Losses: Disposals of Residential Property Interests

History – Ch. 7 inserted by FA 2016, s. 83 and Sch. 12, para. 3, with effect in relation to gains accruing on or after 6 April 2016.

57C Gains and losses on disposals of residential property interests

57C Schedule 4ZZC makes provision about the computation of–

(a) residential property gains or losses, and

(b) other gains or losses,

on disposals of residential property interests which are not non-resident CGT disposals.

History – S. 57C inserted by FA 2016, s. 83 and Sch. 12, para. 3, with effect in relation to gains accruing on or after 6 April 2016.

PART III – INDIVIDUALS, PARTNERSHIPS, TRUSTS AND COLLECTIVE INVESTMENT SCHEMES ETC

History – In the heading to Pt. III, "Etc" inserted by FA 2009, s. 44 and Sch. 22, para. 9, with effect in relation to the acquisition, holding and disposal of rights in a relevant offshore fund on or after 1 December 2009 (capital gains tax) and subject to FA 2009, Sch. 22, para. 13 and 15.

Chapter I – Miscellaneous Provisions

58 Spouses and civil partners

History – The wording of the heading to s. 58 substituted for "Husband and wife" by SI 2005/3229, reg. 107(3), with effect from 5 December 2005.

58(1) If, in any year of assessment,–

(a) an individual is living with his spouse or civil partner, and

(b) one of them disposes of an asset to the other,

both shall be treated as if the asset was acquired from the one making the disposal for a consideration of such amount as would secure that on the disposal neither a gain nor a loss would accrue to the one making the disposal.

58(2) This section shall not apply–

(a) if until the disposal the asset formed part of trading stock of a trade carried on by the one making the disposal, or if the asset is acquired as trading stock for the purposes of a trade carried on by the one acquiring the asset,

(b) if the disposal is by way of donatio mortis causa, or

(c) if the disposal is a relevant disposal of exempt employee shareholder shares (see sections 236B to 236D),

but this section shall have effect notwithstanding the provisions of section 18 or 161, or of any other provisions of this Act fixing the amount of the consideration deemed to be given on a disposal or acquisition.

58(3) For the purposes of subsection (2) a disposal of exempt employee shareholder shares is a "relevant disposal" if (apart from this section)–

(a) a gain would accrue on the disposal, and

(b) no part of the gain would be a chargeable gain.

58(4) Subsection (5) applies where the disposal is of exempt employee shareholder shares and (apart from this section)–

(a) a gain would accrue on the disposal, and

(b) part (but not the whole) of the gain would be a chargeable gain by virtue of section 236B(1A).

58(5) Where this subsection applies, subsection (1) has effect in relation to the disposal as if–

(a) for "such amount as" there were substituted "the maximum amount, not exceeding the market value of the asset, that", and

(b) for "neither a gain nor a loss" there were substituted "no chargeable gain".

History – In s. 58(1) the words from the beginning to the word "both" substituted for the words "If, in any year of assessment, and in the case of a woman who in that year of assessment is a married woman living with her husband, the man disposes of an asset to the wife, or the wife disposes of an asset to the man, both " by SI 2005/3229, reg. 107(2), with effect from 5 December 2005.
In s. 58(2)(c) the words "a relevant disposal" inserted by FA 2016, s. 88(8), with effect in relation to disposals made after 16 March 2016.
S. 58(2)(c) (and the "or" before it) inserted (and the "or" after (a) omitted) by FA 2013, s. 55 and Sch. 23, para. 18, with effect from 1 September 2013 (SI 2013/1755).
S. 58(3) inserted by FA 2016, s. 88(9), with effect in relation to disposals made after 16 March 2016.
S. 58(4) inserted by FA 2016, s. 88(9), with effect in relation to disposals made after 16 March 2016.
S. 58(5) inserted by FA 2016, s. 88(9), with effect in relation to disposals made after 16 March 2016.

Derivations – CGTA 1979, s. 44.

Cross references – S. 3A: transfers between spouses and civil partnersnot to be treated as disposals for the purposes of determining the reporting limits.
S. 10A: transfers between spouses not to be treated as relevant disposals for the purposes of the charge to CGT on temporary residents.
S. 18: transactions between connected persons treated as otherwise than at arm's length, so that market value generally applies.
S. 19(2): priority over deemed consideration in certain cases where assets disposed of in a series of transactions.
S. 30(7): priority over value shifting provisions.
S. 35(3)(d), (5): re-basing not to apply to disposal under these provisions unless an election exists for the simplified scheme (re-basing of all assets held at 31 March 1982 irrespective of matters in s. 35(3)).
S. 42: application of part disposal rules.
S. 116(11): disapplication to a transfer within s. 58(1) of provisions deeming there to be no disposal but so that any market value gain or loss crystallises at subsequent disposal on a reorganisation, conversion or reconstruction where qualifying corporate bonds form part of the new holding but not the original holding.
S. 134(4): there is no crystallisation of a deferred gain on disposal of gilt-edged stock obtained on a compulsory acquisition of securities until the first disposal outside s. 58(1) etc.

S. 137(4): charge for unpaid tax by reference to acquisition within s. 58(1) etc. where equation of original and new holdings on an exchange, reconstruction etc. nullified by a finding that not effected for bona fide commercial reasons etc.
S. 150(3), (7): where disposal within s. 58(1), exclusion from chargeable gains, allowable losses for BES shares issued after 18 March 1986 applies to transferee's disposal; disapplication of reduction in allowable deductions exceeding BES relief in respect of shares issued before 19 March 1986 by reference to that relief.
S. 161: appropriations to trading stock treated as disposals at market value (subject to election) and from trading stock as acquisitions at trade value.
S. 162A(5): disregard transfers between husband and wife when calculating relevant date for election to forego roll-over relief.
S. 164F(5): treatment of acquired holding in relation to relief for re-investment where disposal to spouse (circumstances where relief fails).
S. 164FF(4): reinvestment relief reductions under s. 164A(2)(b) or s. 164F(10A)(b) not defeated by anything in s. 35, s. 55 or Sch. 3, para. 1 in respect of s. 58 disposals on or after 20 June 1994 following no gain/no loss disposals.
S. 168(3): subsequent disposal within s. 58 does not prevent emigrating donee from being deemed to have realised a chargeable gain equal to the held-over gain under s. 168 or s. 260.
S. 242: claim where small part disposal of land (by reference to market value) which is not a transfer within s. 58 for consideration to be deducted from allowable expenditure on remainder.
S. 288(3): meaning of "an individual living with his spouse or civil partner".
Sch. A1, para. 15: application of taper relief to transfers between spouses.
Sch. 2, para. 4(9), 22: transferor's acquisition of assets treated as transferee's for rules in respect of assets held at 6 April 1965 but only an election by transferor for pooling of quoted securities held at that date has effect in relation to subsequent disposal by transferee.
Sch. 3, para. 1: person disposing of asset acquired through disposal under these provisions after 31 March 1982 treated as holding asset at 31 March 1982 for purposes of re-basing.
Sch. 3, para. 2, 3: where there is any acquisition of an asset after 5 April 1985 within these provisions, any election to re-base using the simplified scheme, above, is by reference to the holder on that date or to the last person acquiring it thereafter on a disposal outside these provisions and the group transfer provisions (s. 171).
Sch. 5C, para. 6(2): a disposal of relevant shares following a qualifying investment in a venture capital trust not a chargeable event if the disposal is one to which s. 58 applies.
ICTA 1988, s. 282: construction of references to husband and wife living together.
ICTA 1988, s. 299: disposal of shares acquired through disposal under these provisions treated as acquired on the date of issue for the purposes of withdrawal of EIS relief.
FA 1996, Sch. 15, para. 26(3): loan relationships, savings and transitional provisions.

Extra-statutory concessions – D44: where individual disposes of shares acquired on a no gain/no loss transfer from spouse who held shares at 31 March 1982, by concession, a more favourable basis of valuation at that date may be adopted.
D50: transfers under s. 58 ignored in determining applicability of this concession to any person.

Other material – HMRC press release, 21 November 1990: capital gains tax on jointly-owned assets under independent taxation.

Notes – S. 21–34: general meaning of "disposal" and "asset".
S. 56(2): no gain, no loss calculated after applying indexation allowance.
S. 288: interpretation, including meaning of "trade", of "trading stock" and of "individual living with his spouse or civil partner" and reference to sections being those of this Act.

59 Partnerships

59(1) Where 2 or more persons carry on a trade or business in partnership–

(a) tax in respect of chargeable gains accruing to them on the disposal of any partnership assets shall, in Scotland as well as elsewhere in the United Kingdom, be assessed and charged on them separately, and

(b) any partnership dealings shall be treated as dealings by the partners and not by the firm as such;

(c) [repealed by FA 1995, s. 162 and Sch. 29, Pt. VIII(16).]

59(2) Subsection (3) applies if–

(a) a person resident in the United Kingdom ("the resident partner") is a member of a partnership which resides outside the United Kingdom or which carries on any trade, profession or business the control and management of which is situated outside the United Kingdom, and

(b) by virtue of any arrangements that have effect under section 2(1) of TIOPA 2010 ("the arrangements") any of the capital gains of the partnership are relieved from capital gains tax or corporation tax in the United Kingdom.

59(3) The arrangements (so far as providing for that relief) do not affect any liability to capital gains tax or corporation tax in respect of the resident partner's share of any capital gains of the partnership.

59(4) For the purposes of subsections (2) and (3) the members of a partnership include any person entitled to a share of capital gains of the partnership.

History – The existing text of s. 59 was renumbered s. 59(1) by ITTOIA 2005, s. 882 and Sch. 1, para. 431(2) which, in accordance with ITTOIA 2005, s. 883, came into force on 6 April 2005 and have effect, for income tax purposes, for tax year 2005–06 and subsequent tax years, and, for corporation tax purposes, for accounting periods ending after 5 April 2005.
S. 59(1)(c) and word "and" immediately preceding it repealed by FA 1995, s. 162 and Sch. 29, Pt. VIII(16) for 1995–96 and subsequent years of assessment as regards partnerships whose trade etc. was set up and commenced on or after 6 April 1994. In relation to other partnerships the repeal has effect for 1997–98 and subsequent years.
In s. 59(1)(c), the words "that have effect under section 2(1) of TIOPA 2010" substituted for "falling within section 788 of the Taxes Act" by TIOPA 2010, s. 374 and Sch. 8, para. 43, with effect for corporation tax purposes for accounting periods ending on or after 1 April 2010, for income tax and capital gains tax purposes for the tax year 2010–11 and subsequent tax years, and for petroleum revenue tax purposes for chargeable periods beginning on or after 1 July 2010.
In s. 59(2)(b) the words "or corporation tax" inserted by CTA 2009, s. 1322 and Sch. 1, para. 365(2), with effect for corporation tax purposes for accounting periods ending on or after 1 April 2009, and for income tax and capital gains tax purposes for the tax year 2009–10 and subsequent tax years.
S. 59(2) inserted by ITTOIA 2005, s. 882 and Sch. 1, para. 431(3) which, in accordance with ITTOIA 2005, s. 883, have effect, for income tax purposes, for tax year 2005–06 and subsequent tax years, and, for corporation tax purposes, for accounting periods ending after 5 April 2005.

In s. 59(3) the words "(so far as providing for that relief)" and the words "or corporation tax" inserted by CTA 2009, s. 1322 and Sch. 1, para. 365(3), with effect for corporation tax purposes for accounting periods ending on or after 1 April 2009, and for income tax and capital gains tax purposes for the tax year 2009–10 and subsequent tax years.
S. 59(3) inserted by ITTOIA 2005, s. 882 and Sch. 1, para. 431(3) which, in accordance with ITTOIA 2005, s. 883, have effect, for income tax purposes, for tax year 2005–06 and subsequent tax years, and, for corporation tax purposes, for accounting periods ending after 5 April 2005.
S. 59(4) inserted by FA 2008, s. 58(2), such change treated as always having had effect.

Derivations – (as originally enacted) – CGTA 1979, s. 60.

Cross references – S. 59A: limited liability partnerships.
Sch. 7AD, para. 3(1): s. 59 does not apply to make a company liable on its share of gains of relevant partnership assets where that Schedule applies.
Partnership Act 1890, s. 1 and s. 2: defining a partnership.
ICTA 1988, s. 112(1), (2): partnership trade or business controlled etc. abroad deemed to be carried on by non-residents; partnership deemed to be non-resident and extent of charge on the firm in respect of UK operations.

Statements of practice – D11: application of roll-over relief for replacement of assets to partner in respect of assets owned by him and used by the partnership.
D12: general practice on the capital gains tax treatment of partnerships.
SP 1/79: extension of SP D12 in cases in which a lump sum is paid to a retiring partner.
SP 1/89: extension of SP D12 to encompass re-basing to 31 March 1982.

HMRC interpretations – IRInt. 9: elections for the simplified re-basing scheme under s. 35(5) in relation to partners.

Other material – Tax Bulletin TB10/02-3: treatment of partnership goodwill when calculating taper relief on disposal of business, partnership merger, or partners joining and leaving.

Notes – S. 2: charge to capital gains tax in respect of chargeable gains.
S. 8: company's total profits to include chargeable gains.
S. 15: meaning of "chargeable gains".
S. 21–34: general meaning of "disposal" and "asset".
S. 163(8), 164(6), (7) and Sch. 6, para. 10: application of retirement relief to disposal of partnership assets, of partners' interests in the partnership or of assets used by the partnership but owned by partners outside the partnership.
S. 276: territorial sea of the UK deemed to be part of the UK.
S. 288: interpretation, including the Taxes Act as ICTA 1988.
TMA 1970, s. 29: assessing procedure.

59A Limited liability partnerships

59A(1) Where a limited liability partnership carries on a trade or business with a view to profit–

(a) assets held by the limited liability partnership are treated for the purposes of tax in respect of chargeable gains as held by its members as partners, and

(b) any dealings by the limited liability partnership are treated for those purposes as dealings by its members in partnership (and not by the limited liability partnership as such),

and tax in respect of chargeable gains accruing to the members of the limited liability partnership on the disposal of any of its assets shall be assessed and charged on them separately.

59A(2) For all purposes, except as otherwise provided, in the enactments relating to tax in respect of chargeable gains–

(a) references to a partnership include a limited liability partnership in relation to which subsection (1) above applies,

(b) references to members of a partnership include members of such a limited liability partnership,

(c) references to a company do not include such a limited liability partnership, and

(d) references to members of a company do not include members of such a limited liability partnership.

59A(3) Subsection (1) above continues to apply in relation to a limited liability partnership which no longer carries on any trade or business with a view to profit–

(a) if the cessation is only temporary, or

(b) during a period of winding up following a permanent cessation, provided–

 (i) the winding up is not for reasons connected in whole or in part with the avoidance of tax, and

 (ii) the period of winding up is not unreasonably prolonged,

but subject to subsection (4) below.

59A(4) Subsection (1) above ceases to apply in relation to a limited liability partnership–

(a) on the appointment of a liquidator or (if earlier) the making of a winding-up order by the court, or

(b) on the occurrence of any event under the law of a country or territory outside the United Kingdom corresponding to an event specified in paragraph (a) above.

59A(5) Where subsection (1) above ceases to apply in relation to a limited liability partnership with the effect that tax is assessed and charged–

(a) on the limited liability partnership (as a company) in respect of chargeable gains accruing on the disposal of any of its assets, and

(b) on the members in respect of chargeable gains accruing on the disposal of any of their capital interests in the limited liability partnership, it shall be assessed and charged on the limited liability partnership as if subsection (1) above had never applied in relation to it.

59A(6) Neither the commencement of the application of subsection (1) above nor the cessation of its application in relation to a limited liability partnership shall be taken as giving rise to the disposal of any assets by it or any of its members.

History – S. 59A inserted by Limited Liability Partnerships Act 2000, s. 10(3), and substituted by FA 2001 s. 75(2) with effect from 6 April 2001.

Cross references – S. 156A: crystallising of certain rolled over gains on permanent cessation of trade by limited liability partnership. S. 169A: crystallising of certain held-over gains on permanent cessation of trade by limited liability partnership.

Statements of practice – D12 – general practice on the capital gains tax treatment of partnerships.

Other material – Tax Bulletin TB10/02-3: article (with examples) on the treatment of partnership goodwill when calculating taper relief on disposal of business, partnership merger, or partners joining and leaving.

59B Alternative investment fund managers (1)

59B(1) Subsection (2) applies if–

(a) under section 863I of ITTOIA 2005, a partner ("P") in a partnership allocates to the partnership an amount of profit ("the allocated profit") representing variable remuneration which, if it vests in P, will vest in the form of instruments,

(b) there is a disposal to P of instruments which are partnership assets of the partnership for the purposes of section 59, and

(c) by virtue of that disposal the variable remuneration vests in P.

59B(2) Both the persons making the disposal and P are to be treated as if the instruments were acquired by P from those persons for a consideration of an amount equal to the allocated profit net of the income tax for which the partnership is liable by virtue of section 863I of ITTOIA 2005 in respect of the allocated profit.

59B(3) Terms used in this section which are also used in section 863I or 863J of ITTOIA 2005 have the same meaning as in that section.

History – S. 59B inserted by FA 2014, s. 74 and Sch. 17, para. 17, with effect for the tax year 2014–15 and subsequent tax years.

59C Alternative investment managers (2)

59C(1) Subsection (2) applies if–

(a) under section 863I of ITTOIA 2005, a partner ("P") in a partnership allocates to the partnership an amount of profit ("the allocated profit") representing variable remuneration which, if it vests in P, will vest in the form of instruments,

(b) there is a disposal to P of instruments by a company which is a partner in the partnership,

(c) by virtue of that disposal the variable remuneration vests in P, and

(d) the company would, as a partner in the partnership, have been charged to tax on the allocated profit but for adjustments made in the case of the company under section 1264A(2) of CTA 2009 or section 850C(5) of ITTOIA 2005.

59C(2) Both the company and P are to be treated as if the instruments were acquired by P from the company for a consideration of an amount equal to the allocated profit net of the income tax for which the partnership is liable by virtue of section 863I of ITTOIA 2005 in respect of the allocated profit.

59C(3) Terms used in this section which are also used in section 863I or 863J of ITTOIA 2005 have the same meaning as in that section.

History – S. 59C inserted by FA 2014, s. 74 and Sch. 17, para. 17, with effect for the tax year 2014–15 and subsequent tax years.

60 Nominees and bare trustees

60(1) In relation to property held by a person as nominee for another person or as trustee for another person absolutely entitled as against the trustee, or for any person who would be so entitled but for being an infant or other person under disability (or for 2 or more persons who are or would be jointly so entitled), this Act shall apply as if the property were vested in, and the acts of the nominee or trustee in relation to the property were the acts of, the person or persons for whom he is the nominee or trustee (acquisitions from or disposals to him by that person or persons being disregarded accordingly).

60(2) It is hereby declared that references in this Act to any property held by a person as trustee for another person absolutely entitled as against the trustee are references to a case where that other person has the exclusive right, subject only to satisfying any outstanding charge, lien or other right of the trustees to resort to the property for payment of duty, taxes, costs or other outgoings, to direct how that property shall be dealt with.

History – In s. 60(1), the word "property" substituted for "assets" in each place it occurred by FA 2006, s. 88 and Sch. 12, para. 10(1) with effect from 6 April 2006.
In s. 60(2), the word "property" substituted for "asset" in each place it occurred by FA 2006, s. 88 and Sch. 12, para. 10(2) with effect from 6 April 2006.

Derivations – CGTA 1979, s. 46.

Cross references – S. 68: property to which s. 60 applies is not "settled property".
S. 71(1): deemed market value disposal by trustee and reacquisition as bare trustee when person becomes absolutely entitled to the settled property.
S. 97(2): capital payment, for the purposes of the attribution of gains of certain non-resident or dual resident settlements, by reference to the inclusion as a payment of any occasion when settled property becomes subject to s. 60.
S. 217(4): deemed no gain, no loss where disposal by trustee on member becoming absolutely entitled to settled property comprising shares issued on incorporation of a building society.

Statements of practice – SP 4/94: enhanced stock dividends received by trustees of interest in possession trusts.

Notes – S. 21–34: general meaning of "disposal" and "asset".
S. 206(1): an underwriting member of Lloyd's is treated as absolutely entitled as against the trustees to the investments of his premiums trust fund, his special reserve fund and other required funds.
S. 238(1): participant in an approved profit sharing scheme treated as absolutely entitled as against the trustees to the shares.

61 Funds in court

61(1) For the purposes of section 60, funds in court held by the Accountant General shall be regarded as held by him as nominee for the persons entitled to or interested in the funds, or as the case may be for their trustees.

61(2) Where funds in court standing to an account are invested or, after investment, are realised, the method by which the Accountant General effects the investment or the realisation of investments shall not affect the question whether there is for the purposes of this Act an acquisition, or as the case may be a disposal, of an asset representing funds in court standing to the account, and in particular there shall for those purposes be an acquisition or disposal of shares in a court investment fund notwithstanding that the investment in such shares of funds in court standing to an account, or the realisation of funds which have been so invested, is effected by setting off, in the Accountant General's accounts, investment in one account against realisation of investments in another.

61(3) In this section **"funds in court"** means–

(a) money in the Supreme Court, money in the county court and statutory deposits described in section 40 of the Administration of Justice Act 1982, and

(b) money in the Supreme Court of Judicature of Northern Ireland and money in a county court in Northern Ireland,

and investments representing such money; and references in this section to the Accountant General are references to the Accountant General of the Supreme Court of Judicature in England and, in relation to money within paragraph (b) above and investments representing such money, include references to the Accountant General of the Supreme Court of Judicature of Northern Ireland or any other person by whom such funds are held.

History – In s. 61(3)(a), the words "the county court" substituted for the words "county courts" by Crime and Courts Act 2013, s. 17 and Sch. 9, para. 131, with effect from 22 April 2014 (SI 2014/954, art. 2).

Derivations – CGTA 1979, s. 99, as amended by the Administration of Justice Act 1982, s. 46(2).

Cross references – ICTA 1988, s. 469A: income tax treatment of court common investment funds (as if the common investment funds were authorised unit trusts and those entitled to an interest were unit holders).

Notes – S. 21–34: general meaning of "disposal" and "asset".
S. 100(3): meaning of "court investment fund".

62 Death: general provisions

62(1) For the purposes of this Act the assets of which a deceased person was competent to dispose–

(a) shall be deemed to be acquired on his death by the personal representatives or other person on whom they devolve for a consideration equal to their market value at the date of the death, but

(b) shall not be deemed to be disposed of by him on his death (whether or not they were the subject of a testamentary disposition).

62(2) Allowable losses sustained by an individual in the year of assessment in which he dies may, so far as they cannot be deducted from chargeable gains accruing in that year, be deducted from chargeable gains accruing to the deceased in the 3 years of assessment preceding the year of assessment in which the death occurs taking chargeable gains accruing in a later year before those accruing in an earlier year.

62(2A) Amounts deductible from chargeable gains for any year in accordance with subsection (2) above shall not be so deductible from any such gains so far as they are–

(a) gains that are treated as accruing by virtue of section 87 or 89(2) (read, where appropriate, with section 10A), or

(b) NRCGT gains (see section 57B and Schedule 4ZZB).

62(2AA) Where allowable NRCGT losses (see section 57B and Schedule 4ZZB) are sustained by an individual in the year of assessment in which the individual dies, the losses may, so far as they cannot be deducted from chargeable gains accruing to the individual in that year, be deducted from any gains such as are mentioned in subsection (2A)(b) that accrued to the deceased in the 3 years of assessment preceding the year of assessment in which the death occurs, taking chargeable gains accruing in a later year before those accruing in an earlier year.

62(2B) [Omitted by FA 2008, s. 8 and Sch. 2, para. 29(3).]

62(3) In relation to property forming part of the estate of a deceased person the personal representatives shall for the purposes of this Act be treated as being a single and continuing body of persons (distinct from the persons who may from time to time be the personal representatives), and that body shall be treated as having the deceased's residence and domicile at the date of death.

62(4) On a person acquiring any asset as legatee (as defined in section 64)–

(a) no chargeable gain shall accrue to the personal representatives, and

(b) the legatee shall be treated as if the personal representatives' acquisition of the asset had been his acquisition of it.

62(4A) The Treasury may by regulations make provision having effect in place of subsection (4)(b) above in a case where there has been a time when the personal representatives–

(a) held the asset acquired by the legatee, and

(b) would, if they had disposed of the asset at that time–

(i) by way of a bargain at arm's length, and

(ii) otherwise than to a legatee,

have been entitled as a result of regulations under section 151 (investments under plans) to relief from capital gains tax in respect of any chargeable gain accruing on the disposal.

62(4B) Provision made by regulations under subsection (4A) above may (in particular) treat a person who acquires an asset as legatee as doing so at a time or for a consideration, or at a time and for a consideration, ascertained as specified by the regulations.

62(5) Notwithstanding section 17(1) no chargeable gain shall accrue to any person on his making a disposal by way of donatio mortis causa.

62(6) Subject to subsections (7) and (8) below, where within the period of 2 years after a person's death any of the dispositions (whether effected by will, under the law relating to intestacy or otherwise) of the property of which he was competent to dispose are varied, or the benefit conferred by any of those dispositions is disclaimed, by an instrument in writing made by the persons or any of the persons who benefit or would benefit under the dispositions–

(a) the variation or disclaimer shall not constitute a disposal for the purposes of this Act, and

(b) this section shall apply as if the variation had been effected by the deceased or, as the case may be, the disclaimed benefit had never been conferred.

62(7) Subsection (6) above does not apply to a variation unless the instrument contains a statement by the persons making the instrument to the effect that they intend the subsection to apply to the variation.

62(8) Subsection (6) above does not apply to a variation or disclaimer made for any consideration in money or money's worth other than consideration consisting of the making of a variation or disclaimer in respect of another of the dispositions.

62(9) Subsection (6) above applies whether or not the administration of the estate is complete or the property has been distributed in accordance with the original dispositions.

62(10) In this section references to assets of which a deceased person was competent to dispose are references to assets of the deceased which (otherwise than in right of a power of appointment or of the testamentary power conferred by statute to dispose of entailed interests) he could, if of full age and capacity, have disposed of by his will, assuming that all the assets were situated in England and, if he was not domiciled in the United Kingdom, that he was domiciled in England, and include references to his severable share in any assets to which, immediately before his death, he was beneficially entitled as a joint tenant.

History – In s. 62(2A), the words "are–" and para. (a) and (b) substituted for the words "are gains that are treated as accruing by virtue of section 87 or 89(2) (read, where appropriate, with section 10A)." by FA 2015, s. 37 and Sch. 7, para. 17(2), with effect in relation to disposals made on or after 6 April 2015.

In s. 62(2A), the words the words "treated as accruing by virtue of section 87 or 89(2) (read, where appropriate, with section 10A)" substituted for "brought into account for that year by virtue of section 2(5)(b)" by FA 2008, s. 8 and Sch. 2, para. 29(2) with effect in relation to chargeable gains accruing or treated as accruing in the tax year 2008–09 or any subsequent tax year (FA 2008, Sch. 2, para. 56(3)).

S. 62(2A) inserted by FA 1998, Sch. 21, para. 5, with effect for the year 1998–99 and subsequent years of assessment.

S. 62(2AA) inserted by FA 2015, s. 37 and Sch. 7, para. 17(3), with effect in relation to disposals made on or after 6 April 2015.

S. 62(2B) omitted by FA 2008, s. 8 and Sch. 2, para. 29(3) with effect in relation to chargeable gains accruing or treated as accruing in the tax year 2008–09 or any subsequent tax year (FA 2008, Sch. 2, para. 56(3)).

Former s. 62(2B) inserted by FA 1998, Sch. 21, para. 5, with effect for the year 1998–99 and subsequent years of assessment.
In s. 62(3), the words ", ordinary residence," omitted by FA 2013, s. 219 and Sch. 46, para. 79, with effect in relation to a person's liability to capital gains tax for the tax year 2013–14 or any subsequent tax year, without prejudice to any provision in FA 2013, Sch. 46, Pt. 3 about the application of a particular amendment.
S. 62(4A) inserted by FA 2016, s. 27(3), with effect from 15 September 2016 (Royal Assent).
S. 62(4B) inserted by FA 2016, s. 27(3), with effect from 15 September 2016 (Royal Assent).
S. 62(7) substituted by FA 2002, s. 52(1) with effect in relation to instruments made on or after 1 August 2002.

Derivations – CGTA 1979, s. 49, as amended (subs. (5)) by FA 1981, s. 90(3).

Cross references – S. 2(3): priority over general prevention of deduction by carry-back.
S. 17(1): acquisitions and disposals deemed to be at market value where bargains otherwise than at arm's length or where consideration cannot be valued or in connection with payment for services.
S. 30(7): priority over value shifting provisions.
S. 64(2): definition of legatee, and date of donee's acquisition by donatio mortis causa deemed to be on date of donor's death.
S. 116(11): disapplication to a transfer within s. 62(4) of provisions deeming there to be no disposal but so that any market value gain or loss crystallises at subsequent disposal on a reorganisation, conversion or reconstruction where qualifying corporate bonds form part of the new holding but not the original holding.
S. 134(4): there is no crystallisation of a deferred gain on disposal of gilt-edged stock obtained on a compulsory acquisition of securities until the first disposal outside s. 62(4) etc.
TMA 1970, s. 40: assessment on personal representatives.
SI 2009/3001, reg. 34: special provisions for application of s. 62 in relation to disposals of interests in non-reporting offshore funds.

HMRC interpretations – IRInt. 36: HMRC view that where qualifying corporate bonds (QCBs) issued in exchange for shares or securities the held-over gain which would be released on a later disposal of the QCBs is, in the event of the death of the holder, in effect wiped-out.
IRInt. 145: principle in *Gray (Exor of Lady Fox dec'd) v IR Commrs* [1994] BTC 8,034 (i.e. two or more different assets treated as single unit of property if disposal as one unit is the course a prudent hypothetical vendor would adopt) extended to CGT valuations in which statutory hypothesis deems two or more assets to be disposed of together, including s. 62.
IRInt. 202: Revenue view that where a bookmaker's pitch has been acquired by inheritance after October 1998 changes to the allocation rules, it has a market value and forms part of the assets of which the deceased was competent to dispose.
IRInt. 1003: where one of the beneficiaries to a will dies before the expiry of the time limit for varying the will, personal representatives of the deceased beneficiary may enter into a variation and sign an election.

Other material – Tax Bulletin TB08/02-5: procedures for dealing with instruments of variation following changes in FA 2002.

Notes – S. 2(2): offset of allowable losses against chargeable gains in same year.
S. 3: preservation of loss by reference to use of annual exempt amount.
S. 9: meaning of residence and ordinary residence.
S. 15: meaning of "chargeable gains".
S. 16: meaning of "allowable loss".
S. 272–274 and Sch. 11: meaning of "market value", including agreed inheritance tax value taken as market value.
S. 288: interpretation, including meaning of "personal representatives" and reference to sections as being those of this Act.

63 Death: application of law in Scotland

63(1) The provisions of this Act, so far as relating to the consequences of the death of a proper liferenter of any property, shall have effect subject to the provisions of this section.

63(2) [O]n the death of any such liferenter the person (if any) who, on the death of the liferenter, becomes entitled to possession of the property as fiar shall be deemed to have acquired all the assets forming part of the property at the date of the deceased's death for a consideration equal to their market value at that date.

History – In s. 63(1), the words "an heir of entail in possession of any property in Scotland subject to an entail, whether sui juris or not, or of" (after "death of") omitted by FA 2006, s. 88 and Sch. 12, para. 11(1)(a) and repealed by FA 2006, s. 178 and Sch. 26, Pt. 3(15), with effect in relation to a death occurring on or after 6 April 2006.
In s. 63(2):

- the opening words "For the purposes of this Act,";
- the words "heir or" before "liferenter"; and
- the words "the heir of entail next entitled to the entailed property under the entail or, as the case may be," after "liferenter"; and

omitted by FA 2006, s. 88 and Sch. 12, para. 11(1)(b) and repealed by FA 2006, s. 178 and Sch. 26, Pt. 3(15), with effect in relation to a death occurring on or after 6 April 2006.

Derivations – CGTA 1979, s. 50.

Notes – S. 272–274 and Sch. 11: meaning of "market value", including agreed inheritance tax value taken as market value.

63A Death: application of law in Northern Ireland

63A(1) The provisions of this Act, so far as relating to the consequences of the death of a person to whom property in Northern Ireland stands limited for life ("the deceased"), shall have effect subject to the provisions of this section.

63A(2) A person who acquires property in fee simple absolute or fee tail in possession as a consequence of the deceased's death shall be deemed to have acquired all the assets forming part of the property at the date of the deceased's death for a consideration equal to their market value at that date.

History – S. 63A inserted by FA 2006, s. 88 and Sch. 12, para. 11(2), with effect in relation to a death occurring on or after 6 April 2006.

64 Expenses in administration of estates and trusts

64(1) In the case of a gain accruing to a person on the disposal of, or of a right or interest in or over, an asset held by another person as trustee, or as a personal representative of a deceased person, to which he became absolutely entitled as legatee or as against the trustee–

(a) any expenditure within section 38(2) incurred by him in relation to the transfer of the asset to him by the personal representative or trustee, and

(b) any such expenditure incurred in relation to the transfer of the asset by the personal representative or trustee,

shall be allowable as a deduction in the computation of the gain accruing to that person on the disposal.

64(2) In this Act, unless the context otherwise requires, **"legatee"** includes any person taking under a testamentary disposition or on an intestacy or partial intestacy, whether he takes beneficially or as trustee, and a person taking under a donatio mortis causa shall be treated (except for the purposes of section 62) as a legatee and his acquisition as made at the time of the donor's death.

64(3) For the purposes of the definition of **"legatee"** above, and of any reference in this Act to a person acquiring an asset **"as legatee"**, property taken under a testamentary disposition or on an intestacy or partial intestacy includes any asset appropriated by the personal representatives in or towards satisfaction of a pecuniary legacy or any other interest or share in the property devolving under the disposition or intestacy.

History – In s. 64(1), the words "an asset held by another person as trustee, or as a personal representative of a deceased person, to which he became absolutely entitled as legatee or as against the trustee" substituted by FA 2006, s. 88 and Sch. 12, para. 12(1)(a), with effect in relation to disposals made on or after 6 April 2006.
In s. 64(1)(a) and (b), the words "personal representative or trustee" substituted for "personal representatives or trustees" by FA 2006, s. 88 and Sch. 12, para. 12(1)(b), with effect in relation to disposals made on or after 6 April 2006.

Derivations – CGTA 1979, s. 47.

Cross references – S. 38(2): incidental costs etc. of disposal and acquisition.
Sch. A1, para. 5(5): conditions for assets other than shares to qualify as business assets for the purpose of taper relief.

Statements of practice – SP 8/94: scale of expenditure for disposal by personal representatives in respect of establishing title to assets – in relation to certain expenses incurred by the personal representatives of deceased persons where the death in question occurred before 6 April 2004, and to expenses incurred by corporate trustees in making transfers and disposals before 6 April 2004.
SP 02/04: allowable expenditure: expenses incurred by personal representatives and corporate trustees – in relation to certain expenses incurred by the personal representatives of deceased persons where the death in question occurred on or after 6 April 2004, and to expenses incurred by corporate trustees in making transfers and disposals on or after 6 April 2004.

Notes – S. 21–34: general meaning of "disposal" and "asset".
S. 68: meaning of "settled property".
S. 288: interpretation, including meaning of "personal representatives".

65 Liability for tax of trustees or personal representatives

65(1) Subject to subsection (3) below, capital gains tax chargeable in respect of chargeable gains accruing to the trustees of a settlement or capital gains tax due from the personal representatives of a deceased person may be assessed and charged on and in the name of any one or more of the relevant trustees or the relevant personal representatives.

65(2) Subject to section 60 and any other express provision to the contrary, chargeable gains accruing to the trustees of a settlement or to the personal representatives of a deceased person, and capital gains tax chargeable on or in the name of such trustees or personal representatives, shall not be regarded for the purposes of this Act as accruing to, or chargeable on, any other person, nor shall any trustee or personal representative be regarded for the purposes of this Act as an individual.

65(3) Where section 80 applies as regards the trustees of a settlement (**"the migrating trustees"**), nothing in subsection (1) above shall enable any person–

(a) who ceased to be a trustee of the settlement before the end of the relevant period, and

(b) who shows that, when he ceased to be a trustee of the settlement, there was no proposal that the trustees might cease to be resident in the United Kingdom,

to be assessed and charged to any capital gains tax which is payable by the migrating trustees by virtue of section 80(2).

65(4) In this section–

"the relevant period" has the same meaning as in section 82;

"the relevant trustees", in relation to any chargeable gains, means the trustees in the year of assessment in which the chargeable gains accrue and any subsequent trustees of the settlement, and "the relevant personal representatives" has a corresponding meaning.

History – S. 65(1) substituted by FA 1995, s. 114(1) and s. 65(3) for 1996–97 and later years of assessment.
In s. 65(3)(b), the words "cease to be resident" substituted for the words "become neither resident nor ordinarily resident" by FA 2013, s. 219 and Sch. 46, para. 80, with effect in relation to a person's liability to capital gains tax for the tax year 2013–14 or any subsequent tax year, without prejudice to any provision in FA 2013, Sch. 46, Pt. 3 about the application of a particular amendment.
S. 65(4) inserted by FA 1995, s. 114(2) for 1996–97 and later years of assessment.

Derivations – CGTA 1979, s. 48, as originally enacted.

Cross references – S. 80: applies if the trustees become neither resident nor ordinarily resident in the UK.
S. 82: "relevant period" is 12 months ending with the time when the trustees become neither resident nor ordinarily resident in the UK.

Notes – S. 2: charge to capital gains tax in respect of chargeable gains.
S. 9: meaning of residence and ordinary residence.
S. 15: meaning of "chargeable gains".

S. 68: meaning of "settled property".
S. 288: interpretation, including meaning of "personal representatives".
TMA 1970, s. 29: assessing procedure.
TMA 1970, s. 77(2): management provisions relating to persons chargeable in representative capacity not to affect question of who is chargeable or to whom gains accrue for purposes of exemptions and applicable tax rate.

66 Insolvents' assets

66(1) In relation to assets held by a person as trustee or assignee in bankruptcy or under a deed of arrangement this Act shall apply as if the assets were vested in, and the acts of the trustee or assignee in relation to the assets were the acts of, the bankrupt or debtor (acquisitions from or disposals to him by the bankrupt or debtor being disregarded accordingly), and tax in respect of any chargeable gains which accrue to any such trustee or assignee shall be assessable on and recoverable from him.

66(2) Assets held by a trustee or assignee in bankruptcy or under a deed of arrangement at the death of the bankrupt or debtor shall for the purposes of this Act be regarded as held by a personal representative of the deceased and–

(a) subsection (1) above shall not apply after the death, and

(b) section 62(1) shall apply as if any assets held by a trustee or assignee in bankruptcy or under a deed of arrangement at the death of the bankrupt or debtor were assets of which the deceased was competent to dispose and which then devolved on the trustee or assignee as if he were a personal representative.

66(3) Assets vesting in a trustee in bankruptcy after the death of the bankrupt or debtor shall for the purposes of this Act be regarded as held by a personal representative of the deceased, and subsection (1) above shall not apply.

66(4) The definition of **"settled property"** in section 68 shall not include any property as being property held by a trustee or assignee in bankruptcy or under a deed of arrangement.

66(5) In this section–

"deed of arrangement" means a deed of arrangement to which an enactment forming part of the law of Scotland or Northern Ireland which corresponds to the Deeds of Arrangement Act 1914 applies, and

"trustee in bankruptcy" includes a permanent trustee within the meaning of the Bankruptcy (Scotland) Act 1985.

History – In s. 66(5), the words "an enactment forming part of the law of Scotland or Northern Ireland which corresponds to the Deeds of Arrangement Act 1914 applies" substituted for the words "the Deeds of Arrangement Act 1914 or any corresponding enactment forming part of the law of Scotland or Northern Ireland applies" by Deregulation Act 2015, s. 19 and Sch. 6, para. 2(12), with effect from 1 October 2015 (SI 2015/1732, art. 2(e)).

Derivations – CGTA 1979, s. 61.

Notes – S. 15: meaning of "chargeable gains".
S. 21–34: general meaning of "disposal" and "asset".
S. 288: interpretation, including meaning of "personal representatives".
TMA 1970, s. 29: assessing procedure.

67 Provisions applicable where section 79 of the Finance Act 1980 has applied

67(1) In this section **"a claim"** means a claim under section 79 of the Finance Act 1980 ("section 79") and **"relief"** means relief under that section (which provided general relief for gifts).

67(2) Where a disposal in respect of which a claim is or has been made is or proves to be a chargeable transfer for inheritance tax purposes, there shall be allowed as a deduction in computing (for capital gains tax purposes) the chargeable gain accruing to the transferee on the disposal of the asset in question an amount equal to whichever is the lesser of–

(a) the inheritance tax attributable to the value of the asset; and

(b) the amount of the chargeable gain as computed apart from this subsection;

and in the case of a disposal which, being a potentially exempt transfer, proves to be a chargeable transfer, all necessary adjustments shall be made, whether by the discharge or repayment of capital gains tax or otherwise.

67(3) Where an amount of inheritance tax–

(a) falls to be redetermined in consequence of the transferor's death within 7 years of making the chargeable transfer in question; or

(b) is otherwise varied,

after it has been taken into account under subsection (2) above (or under section 79(5)), all necessary adjustments shall be made, whether by the making of an assessment to capital gains tax or by the discharge or repayment of such tax.

67(4) Where–

(a) a claim for relief has been made in respect of the disposal of an asset to a trustee, and

(b) the trustee is deemed to have disposed of the asset, or part of it, by virtue of section 71(1) or 72(1)(a),

sections 72(1)(b) and 73(1)(a) shall not apply to the disposal of the asset, or part by the trustee, but any chargeable gain accruing to the trustee on the disposal shall be restricted to the amount of the held-over gain (or a corresponding part of it) on the disposal of the asset to him.

67(5) Subsection (4) above shall not have effect in a case within section 73(2) but in such a case the reduction provided for by section 73(2) shall be diminished by an amount equal to the proportion there mentioned of the held-over gain.

67(6) Section 168 shall apply where relief has been given–

(a) with the substitution for subsection (1) of the following–

"**168(1)** If–

(a) relief has been given under section 79 of the Finance Act 1980 in respect of a disposal made after 5th April 1981 to an individual (**"the relevant disposal"**); and

(b) at a time when he has not disposed of the asset in question, the transferee ceases to be resident in the United Kingdom,

then, subject to the following provisions of this section, a chargeable gain shall be deemed to have accrued to the transferee immediately before that time, and its amount shall be equal to the held-over gain (within the meaning of section 67) on the relevant disposal."; and

(b) with the substitution in subsections (2), (6) and (10) for the references to section 165(4)(b) of references to section 79(1)(b).

67(7) In this section **"held-over gain"**, in relation to a disposal, means the chargeable gain which would have accrued on that disposal apart from section 79, reduced where applicable in accordance with subsection (3) of that section and references to inheritance tax include references to capital transfer tax.

History – In s. 67(6)(a), in the substituted s. 168(1)(b), the words "ceases to be resident" substituted for the words "becomes neither resident nor ordinarily resident" by FA 2013, s. 219 and Sch. 46, para. 81, with effect in relation to a person's liability to capital gains tax for the tax year 2013–14 or any subsequent tax year, without prejudice to any provision in FA 2013, Sch. 46, Pt. 3 about the application of a particular amendment.

Derivations – S. 67(1)–(3): FA 1980, s. 79(5), (6) as amended by FA 1986, s. 101(2).
S. 67(4), (5): CGTA 1979, s. 56A, as inserted by FA 1982, s. 84(3).
S. 67(6): FA 1989, s. 124(3); FA 1981, s. 79 as enacted.
S. 67(7): FA 1980, s. 79(2), (3).

Cross references – S. 71(1): person becoming absolutely entitled to settled property.
S. 72(1): termination of life interest on death of person entitled (s. 72(1)(a)) but no chargeable gain to accrue (s. 72(1)(b)).
S. 73: where person becomes absolutely entitled to settled property on the death of the life tenant, no chargeable gain if interest in whole of property (s. 73(1)(a)) or such gain reduced to extent interest in part of property (s. 73(2)).
S. 168: deemed disposal where donee becomes neither resident nor ordinarily resident, in relation to deferral on gifts of business assets (s. 165(4)) or on gifts on which inheritance tax chargeable (s. 260(3)).
FA 1980, s. 79: on a claim, chargeable gain otherwise arising on a gift before 14 March 1989 effectively held-over until disposal by the transferee, s. 79(5), (6) providing the reliefs now in s. 67(2), (3). S. 79(1)–(3) is reproduced earlier in this volume.

Notes – S. 21–34: general meaning of "disposal" and "asset".
S. 38: allowable deductions generally.
S. 288: interpretation, including reference to sections as being those of this Act (but note "section 79" in s. 67(1)).
TMA 1970, s. 29: assessing procedure.
IHTA 1984, s. 2: meaning of "chargeable transfer".
IHTA 1984, s. 3A: potentially exempt transfers.

Chapter II – Settlements

GENERAL PROVISIONS

68 Meaning of "settled property"

68 In this Act, unless the context otherwise requires, **"settled property"** means any property held in trust other than property to which section 60 applies (and references, however expressed, to property comprised in a settlement are references to settled property).

History – In s. 68, the definition of "settled property" substituted by FA 2006, s. 88 and Sch. 12, para. 1(1), with effect from 6 April 2006 (in relation to settlements whenever created).

Derivations – CGTA 1979, s. 51.

Cross references – S. 60: property held by a person as nominee or as trustee for another person absolutely entitled as against the trustee or for any person who would be so entitled but for being an infant or other person under disability.

Notes – TCGA 1992, s. 72, 73: death of life tenant, etc.
TMA 1970, s. 27: power of Board to demand information from a party to a settlement for the purposes of tax on chargeable gains.

68A Meaning of "settlor"

68A(1) In this Act, unless the context otherwise requires–

(a) **"settlor"** in relation to a settlement means the person, or any of the persons, who has made, or is treated for the purposes of this Act as having made, the settlement, and

(b) a person is a settlor of property which–

(i) is settled property by reason of his having made the settlement (or by reason of an event which causes him to be treated under this Act as having made the settlement), or

(ii) derives from property to which sub-paragraph (i) applies.

68A(2) A person is treated for the purposes of this Act as having made a settlement if–

(a) he has made or entered into the settlement, directly or indirectly, or

(b) the settled property, or property from which the settled property is derived, is or includes property of which he was competent to dispose immediately before his death, and the settlement arose on his death, whether by will, on his intestacy, or otherwise.

68A(3) A person is, in particular, treated for the purposes of this Act as having made a settlement if–

(a) he has provided property directly or indirectly for the purposes of the settlement, or

(b) he has undertaken to provide property directly or indirectly for the purposes of the settlement.

68A(4) Where one person (A) makes or enters into a settlement in accordance with reciprocal arrangements with another person (B), for the purposes of this Act–

(a) B shall be treated as having made the settlement, and

(b) A shall not be treated as having made the settlement by reason only of the reciprocal arrangements.

68A(5) In subsection (2)(b) **"property of which he was competent to dispose immediately before his death"** shall be construed in accordance with section 62(10) (reading each reference to "assets" as a reference to "property").

68A(6) A person who has been a settlor in relation to a settlement shall be treated for the purposes of this Act as having ceased to be a settlor in relation to the settlement if–

(a) no property of which he is a settlor is comprised in the settlement,

(b) he has not undertaken to provide property directly or indirectly for the purposes of the settlement in the future, and

(c) he has not made reciprocal arrangements with another person for that other person to enter into the settlement in the future.

68A(7) For the purpose of this section and sections 68B and 68C property is derived from other property–

(a) if it derives (directly or indirectly and wholly or partly) from that property or any part of it, and

(b) in particular, if it derives (directly or indirectly and wholly or partly) from income from that property or any part of it.

68A(8) In this section **"arrangements"** includes any scheme, agreement or understanding, whether or not legally enforceable.

History – S. 68A inserted by FA 2006, s. 88 and Sch. 12, para. 1(2), with effect from 6 April 2006 (in relation to settlements whenever created).

68B Transfer between settlements: identification of settlor

68B(1) This section applies in relation to a transfer of property from the trustees of one settlement ("Settlement 1") to the trustees of another ("Settlement 2") otherwise than–

(a) for full consideration, or

(b) by way of a bargain made at arm's length.

68B(2) In this section **"transfer of property"** means–

(a) a disposal of property by the trustees of Settlement 1, and

(b) the acquisition by the trustees of Settlement 2 of–

(i) property disposed of by the trustees of Settlement 1, or

(ii) property created by the disposal;

and a reference to transferred property is a reference to property acquired by the trustees of Settlement 2 on the disposal.

68B(3) For the purposes of this Act, except where the context otherwise requires–

(a) the settlor (or each settlor) of the property disposed of by the trustees of Settlement 1 shall be treated from the time of the disposal as having made Settlement 2, and

(b) if there is more than one settlor of the property disposed of by the trustees of Settlement 1, each settlor shall be treated in relation to Settlement 2 as the settlor of a proportionate part of the transferred property.

68B(4) For the purposes of this Act, except where the context otherwise requires, if and to the extent that the property disposed of by the trustees of Settlement 1 was provided for the purposes of Settlement 1, or is derived from property provided for the purposes of Settlement 1, the transferred property shall be treated from the time of the disposal as having been provided for the purposes of Settlement 2.

68B(5) If transferred property is treated by virtue of subsection (4) as having been provided for the purposes of Settlement 2–

(a) the person who provided the property disposed of by the trustees of Settlement 1, or property from which it was derived, for the purposes of Settlement 1 shall be treated as having provided the transferred property, and

(b) if more than one person provided the property disposed of by the trustees of Settlement 1, or property from which it was derived, for the purposes of Settlement 1, each of them shall be treated as having provided a proportionate part of the transferred property.

68B(6) But subsections (3) and (4) do not apply in relation to a transfer of property–

(a) which occurs by reason only of the assignment or assignation by a beneficiary under Settlement 1 of an interest in that settlement to the trustees of Settlement 2,

(b) which occurs by reason only of the exercise of a general power of appointment, or

(c) to which section 68C(6) applies.

68B(7) In determining whether this section applies in relation to a transfer of property between settlements, section 18(2) shall be disregarded.

History – S. 68B inserted by FA 2006, s. 88 and Sch. 12, para. 1(2), with effect from 6 April 2006 (in relation to settlements whenever created).

68C Variation of will or intestacy, etc: identification of settlor

68C(1) This section applies where–

(a) a disposition of property following a person's death is varied, and

(b) section 62(6) applies in respect of the variation.

68C(2) Where property becomes settled property in consequence of the variation (and would not, but for the variation, have become settled property), a person mentioned in subsection (3) shall be treated for the purposes of this Act, except where the context otherwise requires–

(a) as having made the settlement, and

(b) as having provided the property for the purposes of the settlement.

68C(3) Those persons are–

(a) a person who immediately before the variation was entitled to the property, or to property from which it derives, absolutely as legatee,

(b) a person who would have become entitled to the property, or to property from which it derives, absolutely as legatee but for the variation,

(c) a person who immediately before the variation would have been entitled to the property, or to property from which it derives, absolutely as legatee but for being an infant or other person under a disability, and

(d) a person who would, but for the variation, have become entitled to the property, or to property from which it derives, absolutely as legatee if he had not been an infant or other person under a disability.

68C(4) In subsection (3) references to a person being entitled to property absolutely as legatee shall be construed in accordance with section 64(3) (reading the references to "an asset" and "any asset" as references to "property").

68C(5) Where–

(a) property would have become comprised in a settlement–

  (i) which arose on the deceased person's death (whether in accordance with his will, on his intestacy or otherwise), or

  (ii) which was already in existence on the deceased person's death (whether or not the deceased person was a settlor in relation to that settlement), but

(b) in consequence of the variation the property, or property derived from it, becomes comprised in another settlement,

the deceased person shall be treated for the purposes of this Act, except where the context otherwise requires, as having made the other settlement.

68C(6) Where–

(a) immediately before the variation property is comprised in a settlement and is property of which the deceased person is a settlor, and

(b) immediately after the variation the property, or property derived from it, becomes comprised in another settlement,

the deceased person shall be treated for the purposes of this Act, except where the context otherwise requires, as having made the other settlement.

68C(7) If a person is treated as having made a settlement under subsection (5) or (6), for the purposes of this Act he shall be treated as having made the settlement immediately before his death.

68C(8) But subsection (7) does not apply in relation to a settlement which arose on the person's death.

History – S. 68C inserted by FA 2006, s. 88 and Sch. 12, para. 1(2), with effect in respect of variations occurring on or after 6 April 2006 (irrespective of the date the deceased died).

69 Trustees of settlements

69(1) For the purposes of this Act the trustees of a settlement shall, unless the context otherwise requires, together be treated as if they were a single person (distinct from the persons who are trustees of the settlement from time to time).

69(2) The deemed person referred to in subsection (1) shall be treated for the purposes of this Act as resident in the United Kingdom at any time when a condition in subsection (2A) or (2B) is satisfied.

69(2A) Condition 1 is that all the trustees are resident in the United Kingdom.

69(2B) Condition 2 is that–

(a) at least one trustee is resident in the United Kingdom,

(b) at least one is not resident in the United Kingdom, and

(c) a settlor in relation to the settlement was resident or domiciled in the United Kingdom at a time which is a relevant time in relation to him.

69(2C) In subsection (2B)(c) **"relevant time"** in relation to a settlor–

(a) means, where the settlement arose on the settlor's death (whether by will, intestacy or otherwise), the time immediately before his death, and

(b) in any other case, means a time when the settlor made the settlement (or was treated for the purposes of this Act as making the settlement);

and, in the case of a transfer of property from Settlement 1 to Settlement 2 in relation to which section 68B applies, **"relevant time"** in relation to a settlor of the transferred property in respect of Settlement 2 includes any time which, immediately before the time of the disposal by the trustees of Settlement 1, was a relevant time in relation to that settlor in respect of Settlement 1.

69(2D) A trustee who is not resident in the United Kingdom shall be treated for the purposes of subsections (2A) and (2B) as if he were resident in the United Kingdom at any time when he acts as trustee in the course of a business which he carries on in the United Kingdom through a branch, agency or permanent establishment there.

69(2DA) A trustee who is resident in the United Kingdom for a tax year is to be treated for the purposes of subsections (2A) and (2B) as if he or she were not resident in the United Kingdom for that year if–

(a) the trustee is an individual,

(b) the individual becomes or ceases to be a trustee of the settlement during the tax year,

(c) that year is a split year as respects the individual, and

(d) in that year, the only period when the individual is a trustee of the settlement falls wholly within the overseas part of the year.

69(2DB) Subsection (2DA) is subject to subsection (2D) and, accordingly, an individual who is treated under subsection (2DA) as not resident is, in spite of that, to be regarded as resident whenever the individual acts as mentioned in subsection (2D).

69(2E) If the deemed person referred to in subsection (1) is not treated for the purposes of this Act as resident in the United Kingdom, then for the purposes of this Act it is treated as being not resident in the United Kingdom.

69(3) For the purposes of this section, and of sections 71(1) and 72(1), where part of the property comprised in a settlement is vested in one trustee or set of trustees and part in another (and in particular where settled land within the meaning of the Settled Land Act 1925 is vested in the tenant for life and investments representing capital money are vested in the trustees of the settlement), they shall be treated as together constituting and, in so far as they act separately, as acting on behalf of a single body of trustees.

69(4) If tax assessed on the trustees, or any one trustee, of a settlement in respect of a chargeable gain accruing to the trustees is not paid within 6 months from the date when it becomes payable by the trustees or trustee, and before or after the expiration of that period of 6 months the asset in respect of which the chargeable gain accrued, or any part of the proceeds of sale of that asset, is transferred by the trustees to a person who as against the trustees is absolutely entitled to it, that person may at any time within 2 years from the time when the tax became payable be assessed and charged (in the name of the trustees) to an amount of capital gains tax not exceeding tax chargeable on an amount equal to the amount of the chargeable gain and, where part only of the asset or of the proceeds was transferred, not exceeding a proportionate part of that amount.

History – In s. 69(2), the words "and ordinarily resident" omitted by FA 2013, s. 219 and Sch. 46, para. 82(2), with effect in relation to a person's liability to capital gains tax for the tax year 2013–14 or any subsequent tax year, without prejudice to any provision in FA 2013, Sch. 46, Pt. 3 about the application of a particular amendment.
In s. 69(2B)(c), the words ", ordinarily resident" omitted by FA 2013, s. 219 and Sch. 46, para. 82(3), with effect in relation to a person's liability to capital gains tax for the tax year 2013–14 or any subsequent tax year, without prejudice to any provision in FA 2013, Sch. 46, Pt. 3 about the application of a particular amendment.
S. 69(2DA) and (2DB) inserted by FA 2013, s. 218 and Sch. 45, para. 102, with effect in calculating an individual's liability to income tax or capital gains tax for the tax year 2013–14 or any subsequent tax year, subject to the transitional and saving provision in FA 2013, Sch. 45, para. 154–159.
In s. 69(2E), the words "in the United Kingdom, then for the purposes of this Act it is treated as being not resident in the United Kingdom" substituted for the words " and ordinarily resident in the United Kingdom, then for the purposes of this Act it shall be treated as neither resident nor ordinarily resident in the United Kingdom" by FA 2013, s. 219 and Sch. 46, para. 82(4), with effect in relation to a person's liability to capital gains tax for the tax year 2013–14 or any subsequent tax year, without prejudice to any provision in FA 2013, Sch. 46, Pt. 3 about the application of a particular amendment.
S. 69(1)–(2E) substituted for former s. 69(1)–(2) by FA 2006, s. 88 and Sch. 12, para. 2(1). The substitution has effect from 6 April 2006 for most purposes. However, for the purposes of determining the residence status of trustees of a settlement (whenever created), the substitution has effect only from 6 April 2007.

Derivations – CGTA 1979, s. 52.

Cross references – S. 169: gifts into dual resident trusts prevented from benefiting from hold-over relief under s. 165 or s. 260, if any gains exempt under double tax treaty.
Sch. 1, para. 2: the annual exempt amount for certain trustees is spread over the settlements in a group, determined by reference to qualifying settlements which do not encompass those with non-resident trustees within s. 69.
ICTA 1988, s. 220(2): as regards condition for relief on purchase of own shares that vendor be resident and ordinarily resident, the case of trustees is determined as under s. 69.
M08/2009: HMRC guidance on the application of the test in s. 69D(2D).

Extra-statutory concessions – D35: when trustees of employee trust within IHTA 1984, s. 86 transfer assets to employees who pay Sch. E income tax on the benefit, the trustees are not charged to capital gains tax.

HMRC interpretations – IRInt. 9: an election under s. 35(5) by the single body formed by all the trustees of a settlement applies only to that one settlement.
IRInt. 38: settlements – connected persons.

Notes – S. 2: charge to capital gains tax in respect of chargeable gains.
S. 5: rate of tax payable by trustees of accumulation or discretionary settlement is equivalent to the sum of the basic and additional rates of income tax.
S. 7: time for payment of capital gains tax.
S. 9: general meaning of resident and ordinarily resident.
S. 15: meaning of "chargeable gains".
S. 21–34: general meaning of "disposal" and "asset".
S. 166(1): gifts to non-residents prevented from benefiting from hold-over relief under s. 165 or s. 260.
S. 168: deemed chargeable gain on emigration of transferee in respect of a gift for which gain held-over under s. 165 or s. 260.
S. 281: election for payment in instalments of tax on certain gifts or deemed disposals under s. 71(1) or s. 72(1).
TMA 1970, s. 29: assessing procedure.

69A Sub-fund settlements

69A Schedule 4ZA (which makes provision about sub-fund settlements) shall have effect.

History – S. 69A inserted by FA 2006, s. 88 and Sch. 12, para. 6(1), with effect in relation to years of assessment beginning on or after 6 April 2006.

Cross references – FA 2006, s. 88 and Sch. 12, para. 6(3): a sub-fund election may not be treated as having taken place before 6 April 2006.

70 Transfers into settlement

70 A transfer into settlement, whether revocable, or irrevocable, is a disposal of the entire property thereby becoming settled property notwithstanding that the transferor has some interest as a beneficiary under the settlement and notwithstanding that he is a trustee, or the sole trustee, of the settlement.

Derivations – CGTA 1979, s. 53, as amended by FA 1981, s. 86.

Notes – S. 17: deemed market value disposal on transfer into settlement by a settlor.
S. 21–34: general meaning of "disposal" and "asset".

71 Person becoming absolutely entitled to settled property

71(1) On the occasion when a person becomes absolutely entitled to any settled property as against the trustee all the assets forming part of the settled property to which he becomes so entitled shall be deemed to have been disposed of by the trustee, and immediately reacquired by him in his capacity as a trustee within section 60(1), for a consideration equal to their market value.

71(2) Where, in any case in which a person (**"the beneficiary"**) becomes absolutely entitled to any settled property as against the trustee, an allowable loss would (apart from this subsection) have accrued to the trustee on the deemed disposal under subsection (1) above of an asset comprised in that property–

(a) that loss shall be treated, to the extent only that it cannot be deducted from pre-entitlement gains of the trustee, as an allowable loss accruing to the beneficiary (instead of to the trustee); but

(b) any allowable loss treated as accruing to the beneficiary under this subsection shall be deductible under this Act from chargeable gains accruing to the beneficiary to the extent only that it can be deducted from gains accruing to the beneficiary on the disposal by him of–

   (i) the asset on the deemed disposal of which the loss accrued; or

   (ii) where that asset is an estate, interest or right in or over land, that asset or any asset deriving from that asset.

71(2A) In subsection (2) above **"pre-entitlement gain"**, in relation to an allowable loss accruing to a trustee on the deemed disposal of any asset comprised in any settled property, means a chargeable gain accruing to that trustee on–

(a) a disposal which, on the occasion on which the beneficiary becomes absolutely entitled as against the trustee to that property, is deemed under subsection (1) above to have taken place; or

(b) any other disposal taking place before that occasion but in the same year of assessment.

71(2B) For the purposes of subsection (2)(b)(ii) above an asset (**"the relevant asset"**) derives from another if, in a case where–

(a) assets have merged,

(b) an asset has divided or otherwise changed its nature, or

(c) different rights or interests in or over any asset have been created or extinguished at different times,

the value of the relevant asset is wholly or partly derived (through one or more successive events falling within paragraphs (a) to (c) above but not otherwise) from the other asset.

71(2C) The rules set out in subsection (2D) below shall apply (notwithstanding any other rules contained in this Act or in section 113(2) of the Finance Act 1995 (order of deduction))–

(a) for determining for the purposes of this section whether an allowable loss accruing to the trustee, or treated as accruing to the beneficiary, can be deducted from particular chargeable gains for any year of assessment; and

(b) for the making of deductions of allowable losses from chargeable gains in cases where it has been determined that such an allowable loss can be deducted from particular chargeable gains.

71(2D) Those rules are as follows–

(a) allowable losses accruing to the trustee on a deemed disposal under subsection (1) above shall be deducted before any deduction is made in respect of any other allowable losses accruing to the trustee in that year;

(b) allowable losses treated as accruing to the beneficiary under this section, so far as they cannot be deducted in a year of assessment as mentioned in subsection (2)(b) above, may be carried forward from year to year until they can be so deducted; and

(c) allowable losses treated as accruing to the beneficiary for any year of assessment under this section, and allowable losses carried forward to any year of assessment under paragraph (b) above–

   (i) shall be deducted before any deduction is made in respect of any allowable losses accruing to the beneficiary in that year otherwise than by virtue of this section; and

   (ii) in the case of losses carried forward to any year, shall be deductible as if they were losses actually accruing in that year.

71(3) References in this section to the case where a person becomes absolutely entitled to settled property as against the trustee shall be taken to include references to the case where a person would become so entitled but for being an infant or other person under disability.

History – S. 71(2)–(2D) substituted for former s. 71(2) by FA 1999, s. 75(1), in relation to any occasion on or after 16 June 1999 on which a person becomes absolutely entitled to settled property as against the trustee.

Derivations – CGTA 1979, s. 54, as amended by FA 1981, s. 87(1).

Cross references – S. 60: trustees as nominees or bare trustees (s. 60(1)) and meaning of "absolutely entitled as against the trustee" (s. 60(2)).
S. 67(4), (5): elimination or reduction of chargeable gain on disposal under s. 71(1) of asset gifted into trust (s. 73(1)(a), (2)) restricted by reference to any held-over gain.
S. 217(4): disapplication to disposal by trustees when member becomes absolutely entitled to settled property comprising shares issued on incorporation of a building society.
S. 257(3): deemed no gain, no loss where person becoming entitled (otherwise than on the termination of a life interest) is a charity or body established for national purposes and no other person receives consideration in connection with the transaction.
S. 260(9): where disposal under s. 71(1), held-over gain on gift for which inheritance tax chargeable is not restricted by reference to actual consideration.
S. 281(1): election for payment of tax in respect of certain assets in instalments.

Sch. 7, para. 2(3): in relation to hold-over relief on gifts of business assets by trustees deemed to have arisen under s. 71(1), the restriction on the amount to be held-over by reference to actual consideration does not apply.

Extra-statutory concessions – D43: capital gains tax treatment of life interests in possession in settled property on death of life tenant extended to other interests in possession on death of person entitled.

Statements of practice – D10: HMRC practice on termination of life interest.
SP 7/84: application of s. 71(1) on exercise of power of appointment or advancement when continuing trusts are declared.

HMRC interpretations – IRInt. 38: settlements – connected persons; transfer of losses from trustees to beneficiaries.
IRInt. 145: principle in *Gray (Exor of Lady Fox dec'd) v IR Commrs* [1994] BTC 8,034 (i.e. two or more different assets treated as single unit of property if disposal as one unit is the course a prudent hypothetical vendor would adopt) extended to CGT valuations in which statutory hypothesis deems two or more assets to be disposed of together, including s. 71(1).

Notes – S. 2(2): current year deduction and carry-forward of allowable losses.
S. 16: meaning of "allowable losses".
S. 238(2)(d): gain accruing on appropriation of shares under approved profit sharing scheme not chargeable in certain circumstances.
S. 272–274 and Sch. 11: meaning of "market value".
S. 288: interpretation, including reference to sections as being those of this Act.
TMA 1970, s. 27: Board may demand certain particulars from a party to a settlement.

72 Termination of life interest on death of person entitled

72(1) On the termination, on the death of the person entitled to it, of an interest in possession in all or any part of settled property–

(a) the whole or a corresponding part of each of the assets forming part of the settled property and not ceasing at that time to be settled property shall be deemed for the purposes of this Act at that time to be disposed of and immediately reacquired by the trustee for a consideration equal to the whole or a corresponding part of the market value of the asset; but

(b) no chargeable gain shall accrue on that disposal.

For the purposes of this subsection an interest which is a right to part of the income of settled property shall be treated as an interest in a corresponding part of the settled property.

72(1A) Where the interest in possession mentioned in subsection (1) above is one to which the person becomes entitled on or after 22nd March 2006, the first sentence of that subsection applies in relation to that interest only if,

(a) immediately before the person's death, the interest falls within subsection (1B) below, or

(b) the person dies under the age of 18 years and, immediately before the person's death, section 71D of the Inheritance Tax Act 1984 (age 18-to-25 trusts) applies to the property in which the interest subsists.

72(1B) An interest falls within this subsection if–

(a) the interest is–

(i) an immediate post-death interest, within the meaning given by section 49A of the Inheritance Tax Act 1984, or

(ii) a transitional serial interest, within the meaning given by section 49B of that Act, or

(iii) a disabled person's interest , within the meaning given by section 89B of that Act, or

(b) section 71A of that Act (trusts for bereaved minors) applies to the property in which the interest subsists.

Subsection (1A) above does not have effect in relation to the operation of subsection (1) above as applied by subsection (2) below (but see subsection (2A) below).

72(1C) Subsection (1A) above does not have effect in relation to the operation of subsection (1) above as applied by subsection (2) below (but see subsection (2) below).

72(2) Subsection (1) above shall apply where the person entitled to an interest in possession in all or any part of settled property dies (although the interest does not then terminate) as it applies on the termination of such an interest.

72(2A) Where the interest in possession mentioned in subsection (2) above is one to which the person becomes entitled on or after 22nd March 2006–

(a) subsection (2) above, and

(b) the first sentence of subsection (1) above as applied by subsection (2) above,

apply in relation to that interest only if, immediately before the person's death, the interest falls within subsection (1B)(a) above.

72(3) This section shall apply on the death of the person entitled to any annuity payable out of or charged on, settled property or the income of settled property as it applies on the death of a person whose interest in possession in the whole or any part of settled property terminates on his death.

72(4) Where, in the case of any entitlement to an annuity created by a settlement some of the settled property is appropriated by the trustees as a fund out of which the annuity is payable, and there is no right of recourse to, or to the income of, settled property not so appropriated, then without prejudice to subsection (5) below, the settled property so appropriated shall, while the annuity is payable, and on the occasion of the death of the person entitled to the annuity, be treated for the purposes of this section as being settled property under a separate settlement.

72(5) If there is an interest in a part of the settled property and, where that is an interest in income, there is no right of recourse to, or to the income of, the remainder of the settled property, the part of the settled property in which the interest subsists shall while it subsists be treated for the purposes of this section as being settled property under a separate settlement.

72(6) An interest which is a disabled person's interest by virtue of section 89B(1)(a) or (b) of the Inheritance Tax Act 1984 is to be treated as an interest in possession for the purposes of this section.

History – In s. 72(1), (2) and (5), the word "an" substituted for "a life"; in s. 72(5) the word "life" (occurring before "interest subsists") omitted; and s. 72(3), (4) substituted above by FA 1996, Sch. 39, para. 6 and Sch. 41, Pt. VIII(4), with effect in relation to deaths occurring after 5 April 1996.

In s. 72(1B)(a)(iii), the words ", within the meaning given by section 89B" substituted for the words "within section 89B(1)(c) or (d)" by FA 2014, s. 60(2)(a), with effect in relation to deaths occurring on or after 5 December 2013.

S. 72(1A)–(1C) inserted by FA 2006, s. 156 and Sch. 20, para. 30(2), with effect from 22 March 2006.

S. 72(2A) inserted by FA 2006, s. 156 and Sch. 20, para. 30(3), with effect from 22 March 2006.

S. 72(6) inserted by FA 2014, s. 60(2)(b), with effect in relation to deaths occurring on or after 5 December 2013.

Derivations – CGTA 1979, s. 55(1), (3)–(6), as amended by FA 1982, s. 84(1).

Cross references – S. 67(4), (5): elimination of chargeable gain on disposal under s. 72(1)(a) of asset gifted into trust restricted by reference to any gain held over under FA 1980, s. 79.

S. 260(9): where disposal under s. 72(1), held-over gain on gift for which inheritance tax chargeable is not restricted by reference to actual consideration.

S. 281(1): election for payment of tax in respect of certain assets in instalments.

Sch. 7, para. 2: in relation to hold-over relief on gifts of business assets by trustees deemed to have arisen under s. 71(1), the restriction on the amount to be held-over by reference to actual consideration does not apply.

Statements of practice – D10: Revenue will accept that there is no deemed disposal and re-acquisition under s. 72(1) of any of the settled property not directly involved in any release etc. of the life interest in point.

Notes – The changes made to s. 72 and s. 73 by FA 1996 enact ESC D43.

TMA 1970, s. 27: Board may demand certain particulars from a party to a settlement.

73 Death of life tenant: exclusion of chargeable gain

73(1) Where, by virtue of section 71(1), the assets forming part of any settled property are deemed to be disposed of and reacquired by the trustee on the occasion when a person becomes (or would but for a disability become) absolutely entitled thereto as against the trustee, then, if that occasion is the death of a person entitled to an interest in possession in the settled property–

(a) no chargeable gain shall accrue on the disposal, and

(b) if on the death the property reverts to the disponer, the disposal and reacquisition under that subsection shall be deemed to be for such consideration as to secure that neither a gain nor a loss accrues to the trustee, and shall, if the trustee had first acquired the property at a date earlier than 31 March 1982, be deemed to be at that earlier date.

73(1A) Subsection (1)(b) above shall be treated as having effect in relation to a sub-fund settlement if the property does not revert to the trustees of the principal settlement in relation to that sub-fund settlement by reason only that–

(a) a sub-fund election is or has been made in respect of another sub-fund of the principal settlement, and

(b) the property becomes comprised in that other sub-fund settlement on the death of the person entitled to the interest in possession.

73(2) Where the interest referred to in subsection (1) above is an interest in part only of the settled property to which section 71 applies, subsection (1)(a) above shall not apply but any chargeable gain accruing on the disposal shall be reduced by a proportion corresponding to that represented by the part.

73(2A) Where the interest in possession referred to in subsection (1) above is one to which the person becomes entitled on or after 22nd March 2006, subsections (1) and (2) above apply in relation to that interest only if–

(a) immediately before the person's death, the interest falls within section 72(1B), or

(b) the person dies under the age of 18 years and, immediately before the person's death, section 71D of the Inheritance Tax Act 1984(age 18-to-25 trusts) applies to the property in which the interest subsists.

73(3) The last sentence of subsection (1) of section 72 and subsections (3) to (6) of that section shall apply for the purposes of this section as they apply for the purposes of section 72(1).

History – In s. 73(1), the words "31 March 1982" substituted for the words "6th April 1965" by FA 2008, s. 8 and Sch. 2, para. 61 with effect in relation to disposals on or after 6 April 2008 (FA 2008, Sch. 2, para. 71).

In s. 73(1), the words "death of … settled property" substituted for " termination of a life interest (within the meaning of section 72) by the death of the person entitled to that interest"; in s. 73(2) the word "life" omitted; in s. 73(3) the words "subsections (3) … this section" substituted for "subsection (5) of that section shall apply for the purposes of subsection (2) above"; by FA 1996, Sch. 39, para. 6 and Sch. 41, Pt. VIII(4), with effect in relation to deaths occurring after 5 April 1996.

S. 73(1A) inserted by FA 2006, s. 88 and Sch. 12, para. 42, with effect for years of assessment beginning on or after 6 April 2006.
S. 73(2A) inserted by FA 2006, s. 156 and Sch. 20, para. 31, with effect from 22 March 2006.
In s. 73(3), the words "to (6)" substituted for the words "to (5)" by FA 2014, s. 60(3), with effect in relation to deaths occurring on or after 5 December 2013.

Derivations – S. 73(1): CGTA 1979, s. 56(1) as amended by FA 1981, s. 87(2).
S. 73(2), (3): CGTA 1979, s. 56(1A), (1B), as inserted by FA 1982, s. 84(2).
S. 10A: charge to CGT on temporary non-residents does not apply to disposals under these provisions.
S. 35(3)(d), (5): re-basing not to apply to disposal under these provisions unless an election exists for the simplified scheme (re-basing of all assets held at 31 March 1982 irrespective of matters in s. 35(3)).
S. 67(4), (5): elimination or reduction of chargeable gain on disposal under s. 71(1) of asset gifted into trust (s. 73(1)(a), (2)) restricted by reference to any held-over gain.

Cross references – Sch. 1A, para. (3): disregard of s. 73(1)(b), so far as relating to pre-6 April 1965 acquisitions.
Sch. 3, para. 1: person disposing of asset acquired through disposal under these provisions after 31 March 1982 treated as holding asset at 31 March 1982 for purposes of re-basing.

Notes – S. 56(2): no gain, no loss calculated after applying indexation allowance.
S. 288: interpretation, including reference to sections as being those of this Act.
TMA 1970, s. 27: Board may demand certain particulars from a party to a settlement.
The changes made to s. 72 and s. 73 by FA 1996 enact ESC D43.

74 Effect on sections 72 and 73 of relief under section 165 or 260

74(1) This section applies where–

(a) a claim for relief was made under section 165 or 260 in respect of the disposal of an asset to a trustee, and

(b) the trustee is deemed to have disposed of the asset, or part of it, by virtue of section 71(1) or 72(1)(a).

74(2) Sections 72(1)(b) and 73(1)(a) shall not apply to the disposal of the asset or part by the trustee, but any chargeable gain accruing to the trustee on the disposal shall be restricted to the amount of the held-over gain (or corresponding part of it) on the disposal of the asset to him.

74(3) Subsection (2) above shall not have effect in a case within section 73(2) but in such a case the reduction provided for by section 73(2) shall be diminished by an amount equal to the proportion there mentioned of the held-over gain.

74(4) In this section **"held-over gain"** has the same meaning as in section 165 or, as the case may be, 260.

Derivations – CGTA 1979, s. 56A, as inserted by FA 1982, s. 84(3) and amended by FA 1989, s. 124 and Sch. 14, para. 6(1).

Cross references – S. 165: deferral on gifts of business assets.
S. 260: deferral on gifts on which inheritance tax chargeable.

Notes – S. 15: meaning of "chargeable gains".
S. 21–34: general meaning of "disposal".
S. 288: interpretation, including reference to sections as being those of this Act.

75 Death of annuitant

75 [Repealed by FA 1996, Sch. 41, Pt. VIII(4), in relation to deaths occurring after 5 April 1996.]

76 Disposal of interests in settled property

76(1) Subject to subsection (1A) below no chargeable gain shall accrue on the disposal of an interest created by or arising under a settlement (including, in particular, an annuity or life interest and the reversion to an annuity or life interest) by the person for whose benefit the interest was created by the terms of the settlement or by any other person except one who acquired, or derives his title from one who acquired, the interest for a consideration in money or money's worth, other than consideration consisting of another interest under the settlement.

76(1A) Subject to subsection (3) below, subsection (1) above does not apply if–

(a) the settlement falls within subsection (1B) below; or

(b) the property comprised in the settlement is or includes property deriving directly or indirectly from a settlement falling within that subsection.

76(1B) A settlement falls within this subsection if there has been a time when the trustees of that settlement–

(a) were not resident in the United Kingdom; or

(b) fell to be regarded for the purposes of any double taxation relief arrangements as resident in a territory outside the United Kingdom.

76(2) Subject to subsection (1) above, where a person who has acquired an interest in settled property (including in particular the reversion to an annuity or life interest) becomes, as the holder of that interest, absolutely entitled as against the trustee to any settled property, he shall be treated as disposing of the interest in consideration of obtaining that settled property (but without prejudice to any gain accruing to the trustee on the disposal of that property deemed to be effected by him under section 71(1)).

76(3) Subsection (1A) above shall not prevent subsection (1) above from applying where the disposal in question is a disposal in consideration of obtaining settled property that is treated as made under subsection (2) above.

History – In s. 76(1) the words "Subject to subsection (1A) below" inserted at the beginning by FA 1998, s. 128(1), with effect in relation to any disposal on or after 6 March 1998.
In s. 76(1B)(a), the words "not resident" substituted for the words "neither resident nor ordinarily resident" by FA 2013, s. 219 and Sch. 46, para. 83, with effect in relation to a person's liability to capital gains tax for the tax year 2013–14 or any subsequent tax year, without prejudice to any provision in FA 2013, Sch. 46, Pt. 3 about the application of a particular amendment.
S. 76(1A), (1B) and (3) inserted by FA 1998, s. 128(2), (3), with effect in relation to any disposal on or after 6 March 1998.
In s. 76(1B)(a), the words "neither resident nor ordinarily resident in the United Kingdom" substituted for "not resident or ordinarily resident in the United Kingdom" by FA 2006, s. 88 and Sch. 12, para. 30(1), (2)(a), with effect from 6 April 2007 (in relation to settlements whenever created).

Derivations – CGTA 1979, s. 58.

Cross references – S. 85: disposal of interests in non-resident settlements.
S. 217(4)(d): notwithstanding s. 76(1), gain on disposal by member of an interest in a settlement comprising shares issued on incorporation of a building society is a chargeable gain.

Notes – S. 15: meaning of "chargeable gains".
S. 21–34: general meaning of "disposal".
S. 60(2): meaning of "absolutely entitled as against the trustee".
S. 288: interpretation, including reference to sections as being those of this Act.
TMA 1970, s. 27: Board may demand certain particulars from a party to a settlement.

76A Disposal of interest in settled property: deemed disposal of underlying assets

76A Schedule 4A to this Act has effect with respect to disposals for consideration of an interest in settled property.

History – S. 76A inserted by FA 2000, s. 91(1), with effect in relation to any disposal of an interest in settled property made, or the effective completion of which falls, on or after 21 March 2000.

76B Transfers of value by trustees linked with trustee borrowing

76B Schedule 4B to this Act has effect with respect to transfers of value by trustees that are, in accordance with the Schedule, treated as linked with trustee borrowing.

History – S. 76B inserted by FA 2000, s. 92(1), with effect in relation to any transfer of value in relation to which the material time is on or after 21 March 2000.

77 Charge on settlor with interest in settlement

77 [Omitted by FA 2008, s. 8 and Sch. 2, para. 5.]

History – S. 77 omitted by FA 2008, s. 8 and Sch. 2, para. 5 with effect from 2008–09 (FA 2008, Sch. 2, para. 22).

78 Right of recovery

78 [Omitted by FA 2008, s. 8 and Sch. 2, para. 5.]

History – S. 78 omitted by FA 2008, s. 8 and Sch. 2, para. 5 with effect from 2008–09 (FA 2008, Sch. 2, para. 22).

79 Provisions supplemental to sections 77 and 78

79 [Omitted by FA 2008, s. 8 and Sch. 2, para. 5.]

History – S. 79 omitted by FA 2008, s. 8 and Sch. 2, para. 5 with effect from 2008–09 (FA 2008, Sch. 2, para. 22).

79A Restriction on set-off of trust losses

79A(1) This section applies to a chargeable gain accruing to the trustees of a settlement where–

(a) in computing the gain, the allowable expenditure is reduced in consequence, directly or indirectly, of a claim to gifts relief in relation to an earlier disposal to the trustees;

(b) the transferor on that earlier disposal, or any person connected with the transferor, has at any time–

(i) acquired an interest in the settled property, or

(ii) entered into an arrangement to acquire such an interest; and

(c) in connection with that acquisition or arrangement any person has at any time received, or become entitled to receive, any consideration.

79A(2) Where this section applies to a chargeable gain, no allowable losses accruing to the trustees (in the year in which the gain accrues or any earlier year) may be set against the gain.

This applies to the whole of the chargeable gain (and not just the element deferred as a result of the claim to gifts relief).

79A(3) In this section–

(a) **"gifts relief"** means relief under section 165 or 260; and

(b) references to losses not being allowed to be set against a chargeable gain are to the losses not being allowed as a deduction against chargeable gains to the extent that they include that gain.

79A(4) The references in subsection (1)(b) above to an interest in settled property have the same meaning as in Schedule 4A.

History – S. 79A inserted by FA 2000, s 93(1), with effect for gains which accrue on or after 21 March 2000.

Notes – S. 2: extent of charge to capital gains tax in respect of any year of assessment.
S. 16: meaning of "allowable loss".

79B Attribution to trustees of gains of non-resident companies

79B(1) This section applies where the trustees of a settlement are participators–

(a) in a close company, or

(b) in a company that is not resident in the United Kingdom but would be a close company if it were resident in the United Kingdom.

For this purpose **"participator"** has the same meaning as in section 13.

79B(2) Where this section applies, nothing in any double taxation relief arrangements shall be read as preventing a charge to tax arising by virtue of the attribution to the trustees under section 13, by reason of their participation in the company mentioned in subsection (1) above, of any part of a chargeable gain accruing to a company that is not resident in the United Kingdom.

79B(3) Where this section applies and–

(a) a chargeable gain accrues to a company that is not resident in the United Kingdom but would be a close company if it were resident in the United Kingdom, and

(b) all or part of the chargeable gain is treated under section 13(2) as accruing to a close company which is not chargeable to corporation tax in respect of the gain by reason of double taxation arrangements, and

(c) had the company mentioned in paragraph (b) (and any other relevant company) not been resident in the United Kingdom, all or part of the chargeable gain would have been attributed to the trustees by reason of their participation in the company mentioned in subsection (1) above,

section 13(9) shall apply as if the company mentioned in paragraph (b) above (and any other relevant company) were not resident in the United Kingdom.

79B(4) The references in subsection (3) above to "any other relevant company" are to any other company which if it were not resident in the United Kingdom would be a company in relation to which section 13(9) applied with the result that all or part of the chargeable gain was attributed to the trustees as mentioned in that subsection.

History – In s. 79B(1), the word "the" inserted before "trustees of a settlement" by FA 2006, s. 88 and Sch. 12, para. 14(1), with effect in relation to gains accruing on or after 6 April 2006.
S. 79B inserted by FA 2000, s. 94(1), with effect for chargeable gains which accrue on or after 21 March 2000 to companies which are not resident in the UK.

Notes – S. 2: extent of charge to capital gains tax in respect of any year of assessment.
S. 15: meaning of "chargeable gains".
S. 288: interpretation, including meaning of "close company".

MIGRATION OF SETTLEMENTS, NON-RESIDENT SETTLEMENTS AND DUAL RESIDENT SETTLEMENTS

80 Trustees ceasing to be resident in UK

Notes – In s. 80(4)(a), (b) and (7)(b) (but not, apparently, (7)(a)), any reference to a "branch or agency" shall be read, in relation to a company, as if it were a reference to a "permanent establishment" (FA 2003, s. 153(2)(b); with effect in relation to accounting periods beginning on or after 1 January 2003).

80(1) This section applies if the trustees of a settlement become at any time (**"the relevant time"**) not resident in the United Kingdom.

80(2) The trustees shall be deemed for all purposes of this Act–

(a) to have disposed of the defined assets immediately before the relevant time, and

(b) immediately to have reacquired them,

at their market value at that time.

80(3) Subject to subsections (4) and (5) below, the defined assets are all assets constituting settled property of the settlement immediately before the relevant time.

80(4) If immediately after the relevant time–

(a) the trustees carry on a trade in the United Kingdom through a branch or agency, and

TCGA 1992

(b) any assets are situated in the United Kingdom and either used in or for the purposes of the trade or used or held for the purposes of the branch or agency,

the assets falling within paragraph (b) above shall not be defined assets.

80(5) Assets shall not be defined assets if–

(a) they are of a description specified in any double taxation relief arrangements, and

(b) were the trustees to dispose of them immediately before the relevant time, the trustees would fall to be regarded for the purposes of the arrangements as not liable in the United Kingdom to tax on gains accruing to them on the disposal.

80(6) Section 152 shall not apply where the trustees–

(a) have disposed of the old assets, or their interest in them, before the relevant time, and

(b) acquire the new assets, or their interest in them, after that time,

unless the new assets are excepted from this subsection by subsection (7) below.

80(7) If at the time when the new assets are acquired–

(a) the trustees carry on a trade in the United Kingdom through a branch or agency, and

(b) any new assets are situated in the United Kingdom and either used in or for the purposes of the trade or used or held for the purposes of the branch or agency,

the assets falling within paragraph (b) above shall be excepted from subsection (6) above.

80(8) In this section **"the old assets"** and **"the new assets"** have the same meanings as in section 152.

History – In s. 80(1), the words "not resident" substituted for the words "neither resident nor ordinarily resident" by FA 2013, s. 219 and Sch. 46, para. 84, with effect in relation to a person's liability to capital gains tax for the tax year 2013–14 or any subsequent tax year, without prejudice to any provision in FA 2013, Sch. 46, Pt. 3 about the application of a particular amendment.

Derivations – FA 1991, s. 83(1)–(8).

Cross references – S. 65(3): a person may not be charged and assessed under s. 65(1) (as substituted by FA 1995, s. 114(1) for 1996–97 and later years of assessment) on gains of a migrating trust if he ceases to be a trustee before the migration was proposed.
S. 83: trustees ceasing to be liable to UK tax.
S. 84: prevention of rollover relief if new assets acquired when trustees are not UK-resident.
S. 152: deferral on replacement of business assets.
FA 2003, s. 153(2)(b): when dealing with a company; requirement to read any reference to a "branch or agency" (in s. 80(4)(a), (b) and (7)(b)), as if it were a reference to a "permanent establishment" (effective for accounting periods beginning on or after 1 January 2003).

Statements of practice – SP 5/92: trustees who became not resident and not ordinarily resident in the UK between 6 April 1990 and 18 March 1991 and remained so until after 5 April 1992 are not liable to a s. 80 charge.

Notes – S. 9: general meaning of "resident" and "ordinarily resident" but as applied by s. 69.
S. 10: charge on non-residents by reference to UK branch or agency.
S. 21–34: general meaning of "disposal" and "asset".
S. 272–274 and Sch. 11: meaning of "market value".
S. 288: interpretation, including meaning of "trade", "double taxation relief arrangements" and reference to sections as being those of this Act.

80A Deemed disposal of UK residential property interest under section 80

80A(1) Subsection (2) applies if, ignoring subsections (2) to (4)–

(a) a gain or loss would accrue to the trustees of a settlement on a disposal of a UK residential property interest deemed to have been made by virtue of section 80(2), and

(b) on the assumption that the disposal is a non-resident CGT disposal, that gain or loss would be a chargeable NRCGT gain or an allowable NRCGT loss (see section 57B and Schedule 4ZZB).

80A(2) The trustees may elect for subsections (3) and (4) to have effect.

80A(3) No gain or loss accrues to the trustees on that disposal.

80A(4) But, on a subsequent disposal of the whole or part of the interest in UK land which is the subject of the disposal mentioned in subsection (1)(a), the whole or a corresponding part of the gain or loss which would have accrued to the trustees were it not for subsection (3)–

(a) is deemed to accrue to the trustees (in addition to any gain or loss that actually accrues on that subsequent disposal), and

(b) (if that would not otherwise be the case) is to be treated as a chargeable NRCGT gain or an allowable NRCGT loss accruing on a non-resident CGT disposal.

80A(5) In this section, **"interest in UK land"** has the meaning given by paragraph 2 of Schedule B1.

History – S. 80A inserted by FA 2015, s. 37 and Sch. 7, para. 18, with effect in relation to disposals made on or after 6 April 2015.

81 Death of trustee: special rules

81(1) Subsection (2) below applies where–

(a) section 80 applies as a result of the death of a trustee of the settlement, and

(b) within the period of 6 months beginning with the death, the trustees of the settlement become resident in the United Kingdom.

81(2) That section shall apply as if the defined assets were restricted to such assets (if any) as–

(a) would be defined assets apart from this section, and

(b) fall within subsection (3) or (4) below.

81(3) Assets fall within this subsection if they were disposed of by the trustees in the period which–

(a) begins with the death, and

(b) ends when the trustees become resident in the United Kingdom.

81(4) Assets fall within this subsection if–

(a) they are of a description specified in any double taxation relief arrangements,

(b) they constitute settled property of the settlement at the time immediately after the trustees become resident in the United Kingdom, and

(c) were the trustees to dispose of them at that time, the trustee would fall to be regarded for the purposes of the arrangements as not liable in the United Kingdom to tax on gains accruing to them on the disposal.

81(5) Subsection (6) below applies where–

(a) at any time the trustees of a settlement become resident in the United Kingdom as a result of the death of a trustee of the settlement, and

(b) section 80 applies as regards the trustees of the settlement in circumstances where the relevant time (within the meaning of that section) falls within the period of 6 months beginning with the death.

81(6) That section shall apply as if the defined assets were restricted to such assets (if any) as–

(a) would be defined assets apart from this section, and

(b) fall within subsection (7) below.

81(7) Assets fall within this subsection if–

(a) the trustees acquired them in the period beginning with the death and ending with the relevant time, and

(b) they acquired them as a result of a disposal in respect of which relief is given under section 165 or in relation to which section 260(3) applies.

History – In s. 81(1)(b), the words "and ordinarily resident" omitted by FA 2013, s. 219 and Sch. 46, para. 85(2), with effect in relation to a person's liability to capital gains tax for the tax year 2013–14 or any subsequent tax year, without prejudice to any provision in FA 2013, Sch. 46, Pt. 3 about the application of a particular amendment.
In s. 81(3)(b), the words "and ordinarily resident" omitted by FA 2013, s. 219 and Sch. 46, para. 85(3), with effect in relation to a person's liability to capital gains tax for the tax year 2013–14 or any subsequent tax year, without prejudice to any provision in FA 2013, Sch. 46, Pt. 3 about the application of a particular amendment.
In s. 81(4)(b), the words "and ordinarily resident" omitted by FA 2013, s. 219 and Sch. 46, para. 85(4), with effect in relation to a person's liability to capital gains tax for the tax year 2013–14 or any subsequent tax year, without prejudice to any provision in FA 2013, Sch. 46, Pt. 3 about the application of a particular amendment.
In s. 81(5)(a), the words "and ordinarily resident" omitted by FA 2013, s. 219 and Sch. 46, para. 85(5), with effect in relation to a person's liability to capital gains tax for the tax year 2013–14 or any subsequent tax year, without prejudice to any provision in FA 2013, Sch. 46, Pt. 3 about the application of a particular amendment.

Derivations – FA 1991, s. 84(1)–(7).

Cross references – S. 165: deferral on gifts of business assets.
S. 260(3): deferral on gifts on which inheritance tax chargeable.

Notes – S. 9: general meaning of "resident" and "ordinarily resident" but as applied by s. 69.
S. 21–34: general meaning of "disposal" and "asset".
S. 288: interpretation, including meaning of "double taxation relief arrangements" and reference to sections as being those of this Act.

82 Past trustees: liability for tax

82(1) This section applies where–

(a) section 80 applies as regards the trustees of a settlement (**"the migrating trustees"**), and

(b) any capital gains tax which is payable by the migrating trustees by virtue of section 80(2) is not paid within 6 months from the time when it became payable.

82(2) The Board may, at any time before the end of the period of 3 years beginning with the time when the amount of the tax is finally determined, serve on any person to whom subsection (3) below applies a notice–

(a) stating particulars of the tax payable, the amount remaining unpaid and the date when it became payable;

(b) stating particulars of any interest payable on the tax, any amount remaining unpaid and the date when it became payable;

(c) requiring that person to pay the amount of the unpaid tax, or the aggregate amount of the unpaid tax and the unpaid interest, within 30 days of the service of the notice.

82(3) This subsection applies to any person who, at any time within the relevant period, was a trustee of the settlement, except that it does not apply to any such person if–

(a) he ceased to be a trustee of the settlement before the end of the relevant period, and

(b) he shows that, when he ceased to be a trustee of the settlement, there was no proposal that the trustees might cease to be resident in the United Kingdom.

82(4) Any amount which a person is required to pay by a notice under this section may be recovered from him as if it were tax due and duly demanded of him; and he may recover any such amount paid by him from the migrating trustees.

82(5) A payment in pursuance of a notice under this section shall not be allowed as a deduction in computing any income, profits or losses for any tax purposes.

82(6) For the purposes of this section–

(a) where the relevant time (within the meaning of section 80) falls within the period of 12 months beginning with 19th March 1991, **the relevant period** is the period beginning with that date and ending with that time;

(b) in any other case, **the relevant period** is the period of 12 months ending with the relevant time.

History – In s. 82(3)(b), the words "cease to be resident" substituted for the words "become neither resident nor ordinarily resident" by FA 2013, s. 219 and Sch. 46, para. 86, with effect in relation to a person's liability to capital gains tax for the tax year 2013–14 or any subsequent tax year, without prejudice to any provision in FA 2013, Sch. 46, Pt. 3 about the application of a particular amendment.

Derivations – FA 1991, s. 85.

Cross references – S. 65(4): as respects liability for tax of trustees or personal representatives "relevant period" defined as in s. 82(6).

Statements of practice – SP 5/92: in seeking payment of tax from former trustees, the Revenue will generally first pursue those persons who resigned as trustees immediately before the trust migrated, and then earlier trustees. An amount recovered from present trustees by a former trustee under this section is not treated as a capital payment under s. 97.

Notes – S. 7: time for payment of capital gains tax.
S. 288: interpretation, including reference to sections as being those of this Act.
TMA 1970, s. 86: interest on overdue capital gains tax.
TMA 1970, s. 115: service of notices.

83 Trustees ceasing to be liable to UK tax

83(1) This section applies if the trustees of a settlement, while continuing to be resident in the United Kingdom, become at any time (**"the time concerned"**) trustees who fall to be regarded for the purposes of any double taxation relief arrangements–

(a) as resident in a territory outside the United Kingdom, and

(b) as not liable in the United Kingdom to tax on gains accruing on disposals of assets (**"relevant assets"**) which constitute settled property of the settlement and fall within descriptions specified in the arrangements.

83(2) The trustees shall be deemed for all purposes of this Act–

(a) to have disposed of their relevant assets immediately before the time concerned, and

(b) immediately to have reacquired them,

at their market value at that time.

History – In s. 83(1), the words "and ordinarily resident" omitted by FA 2013, s. 219 and Sch. 46, para. 87, with effect in relation to a person's liability to capital gains tax for the tax year 2013–14 or any subsequent tax year, without prejudice to any provision in FA 2013, Sch. 46, Pt. 3 about the application of a particular amendment.

Derivations – FA 1991, s. 86(1), (2).

Notes – S. 9: general meaning of "resident" and "ordinarily resident" but as applied by s. 69.
S. 272–274 and Sch. 11: meaning of "market value".
S. 288: interpretation, including meaning of "double taxation relief arrangements".

83A Trustees both resident and non-resident in a year of assessment

83A(1) This section applies if a chargeable gain accrues to the trustees of a settlement on the disposal by them of an asset in a year of assessment and the trustees–

(a) are within the charge to capital gains tax in that year of assessment, but

(b) are non-UK resident at the time of the disposal.

83A(2) Where this section applies, nothing in any double taxation relief arrangements shall be read as preventing the trustees from being chargeable to capital gains tax (or as preventing a charge to tax arising, whether or not on the trustees) by virtue of the accrual of that gain.

83A(3) For the purposes of this section the trustees of a settlement are within the charge to capital gains tax in a year of assessment–

(a) if, during any part of that year of assessment, they are resident in the United Kingdom and not Treaty non-resident,

(b) [omitted by FA 2006, s. 88 and Sch. 12, para. 32(b) and repealed by FA 2006, s. 178 and Sch. 26, Pt. 3(15).]

83A(4) For the purposes of this section the trustees of a settlement are non-UK resident at a particular time if, at that time,–

(a) they are not resident in the United Kingdom, or

(b) they are resident in the United Kingdom but are Treaty non-resident.

83A(5) [Omitted by FA 2006, s. 74(4)(b) and repealed by FA 2006, s. 178 and Sch. 26, Pt. 3(11).]

History – In s. 83A(3)(a), the words "and ordinarily resident" omitted by FA 2013, s. 219 and Sch. 46, para. 88(2), with effect in relation to a person's liability to capital gains tax for the tax year 2013–14 or any subsequent tax year, without prejudice to any provision in FA 2013, Sch. 46, Pt. 3 about the application of a particular amendment.

In s. 83A(3)(a), the words "and ordinarily resident" inserted after "resident" by FA 2006, s. 88 and Sch. 12, para. 32(a)(i), with effect from 6 April 2007 (in relation to settlements whenever created).

In s. 83A(3)(a), the word "or" at the end omitted by FA 2006, s. 88 and Sch. 12, para. 32(a)(ii) and by FA 2006, s. 178 and Sch. 26, Pt. 3(15), with effect from 6 April 2007 (in relation to settlements whenever created).

S. 83A(3)(b) omitted by FA 2006, s. 88 and Sch. 12, para. 32(b) and repealed by FA 2006, s. 178 and Sch. 26, Pt. 3(15), with effect from 6 April 2007 (in relation to settlements whenever created).

In s. 83A(4)(a), the words "not resident" substituted for the words "neither resident nor ordinarily resident" by FA 2013, s. 219 and Sch. 46, para. 88(3)(a), with effect in relation to a person's liability to capital gains tax for the tax year 2013–14 or any subsequent tax year, without prejudice to any provision in FA 2013, Sch. 46, Pt. 3 about the application of a particular amendment.

In s. 83A(4)(b), the words "and ordinarily resident" omitted by FA 2013, s. 219 and Sch. 46, para. 88(3)(b), with effect in relation to a person's liability to capital gains tax for the tax year 2013–14 or any subsequent tax year, without prejudice to any provision in FA 2013, Sch. 46, Pt. 3 about the application of a particular amendment.

In s. 83A(4)(b), the words "resident and ordinarily resident in the United Kingdom" substituted for "resident or ordinarily resident in the United Kingdom" by FA 2006, s. 88 and Sch. 12, para. 34(1), (2)(a), with effect from 6 April 2007 (in relation to settlements whenever created).

S. 83A(5) omitted by FA 2006, s. 74(4)(b) and repealed by FA 2006, s. 178 and Sch. 26, Pt. 3(11), with effect in relation to any time on or after 22 March 2006.

S. 83A inserted by F(No. 2)A 2005, s. 33(1), with effect in relation to disposals made on or after 16 March 2005.

84 Acquisition by dual resident trustees

84(1) Section 152 shall not apply where–

(a) the new assets are, or the interest in them is, acquired by the trustees of a settlement,

(b) at the time of the acquisition the trustees are resident in the United Kingdom and fall to be regarded for the purposes of any double taxation relief arrangements as resident in a territory outside the United Kingdom,

(c) the assets are of a description specified in the arrangements, and

(d) were the trustees to dispose of the assets immediately after the acquisition, the trustees would fall to be regarded for the purposes of the arrangements as not liable in the United Kingdom to tax on gains accruing to them on the disposal.

84(2) In this section **"the new assets"** has the same meaning as in section 152.

History – In s. 84(1)(b), the words "and ordinarily resident" omitted by FA 2013, s. 219 and Sch. 46, para. 89, with effect in relation to a person's liability to capital gains tax for the tax year 2013–14 or any subsequent tax year, without prejudice to any provision in FA 2013, Sch. 46, Pt. 3 about the application of a particular amendment.

Derivations – FA 1991, s. 87(1), (2).

Cross references – S. 65(4): as respects liability for tax of trustees or personal representatives "relevant period" defined as in s. 82(6). S. 152: deferral on replacement of business assets.

Notes – S. 9: general meaning of "resident" and "ordinarily resident" but as applied by s. 69.
S. 288: interpretation, including meaning of "double taxation relief arrangements" and reference to sections as being those of this Act.

85 Disposal of interests in non-resident settlements

85(1) Subsection (1) of section 76 shall not apply to the disposal of an interest in settled property, other than one treated under subsection (2) of that section as made in consideration of obtaining the settled property, if at the time of the disposal the trustees are not resident in the United Kingdom.

85(2) Subject to subsections (4) (9) and (10) below, subsection (3) below applies where–

(a) section 80 applies as regards the trustees of a settlement,

(b) after the relevant time (within the meaning of that section) a person disposes of an interest created by or arising under the settlement and the circumstances are such that subsection (1) above prevents section 76(1) applying, and

(c) the interest was created for his benefit, or he otherwise acquired it, before the relevant time.

85(3) For the purpose of calculating any chargeable gain accruing on the disposal of the interest, the person disposing of it shall be treated as having–

(a) disposed of it immediately before the relevant time, and

(b) immediately reacquired it,

at its market value at that time.

85(4) Subsection (3) above shall not apply if section 83 applied as regards the trustees in circumstances where the time concerned (within the meaning of that section) fell before the time when the interest was created for the benefit of the person disposing of it or when he otherwise acquired it.

85(5) Subject to subsection (10) below, subsection (7) below applies where–

(a) section 80 applies as regards the trustees of a settlement,

(b) after the relevant time (within the meaning of that section) a person disposes of an interest created by or arising under the settlement and the circumstances are such that subsection (1) above prevents section 76(1) applying,

(c) the interest was created for his benefit, or he otherwise acquired it, before the relevant time, and

(d) section 83 applied as regards the trustees in circumstances where the time concerned (within the meaning of that section) fell in the relevant period.

85(6) The relevant period is the period which–

(a) begins when the interest was created for the benefit of the person disposing of it or when he otherwise acquired it, and

(b) ends with the relevant time.

85(7) For the purpose of calculating any chargeable gain accruing on the disposal of the interest, the person disposing of it shall be treated as having–

(a) disposed of it immediately before the time found under subsection (8) below, and

(b) immediately reacquired it,

at its market value at that time.

85(8) The time is–

(a) the time concerned (where there is only one such time), or

(b) the earliest time concerned (where there is more than one because section 83 applied more than once).

85(9) Subsection (3) above shall not apply where subsection (7) above applies.

85(10) Subsection (3) or (7) above does not apply to the disposal of an interest created by or arising under a settlement which has relevant offshore gains at the material time.

The material time is–

(a) in relation to subsection (3) above, the relevant time within the meaning of section 80;

(b) in relation to subsection (7) above, the time found under subsection (8) above.

85(11) For the purposes of subsection (10) above, a settlement has relevant offshore gains at any time if, were the year of assessment to end at that time, chargeable gains would be treated under section 89(2) or paragraph 8 of Schedule 4C as accruing in the following year of assessment to a beneficiary who received a capital payment from the trustees of the settlement in that year.

History – In s. 85(1), the words "not resident" substituted for the words "neither resident nor ordinarily resident" by FA 2013, s. 219 and Sch. 46, para. 90, with effect in relation to a person's liability to capital gains tax for the tax year 2013–14 or any subsequent tax year, without prejudice to any provision in FA 2013, Sch. 46, Pt. 3 about the application of a particular amendment.

In s. 85(2) words "Subject to subsections (4), (9) and (10) below" substituted for "Subject to subsections (4) and (9) below" by FA 2000, s. 95(2), with effect in relation to any disposal of interest in a non-resident settlement in relation to which the material time is on or after 21 March 2000.

In s. 85(5) words "Subject to subsections 10) below" inserted by FA 2000, s. 95(3), with effect in relation to any disposal of interest in a non-resident settlement in relation to which the material time is on or after 21 March 2000.

S. 85(9) inserted by FA 2000, s. 95(4), with effect in relation to any disposal of interest in a non-resident settlement in relation to which the material time is on or after 21 March 2000.

S. 85(10) inserted by FA 2000, s. 95(4), with effect in relation to any disposal of interest in a non-resident settlement in relation to which the material time is on or after 21 March 2000.

In s. 85(11), the words "chargeable gains would be treated under section 89(2) or paragraph 8 of Schedule 4C as accruing in the following year of assessment to a beneficiary who received a capital payment from the trustees of the settlement in that year" substituted for "there would be an amount of trust gains which by virtue of section 89(2) or paragraph 8(3) of Schedule 4C would be available to be treated as chargeable gains accruing to any beneficiaries of the settlement receiving capital payments in the following year of assessment" by FA 2008, s. 25 and Sch. 7, para. 107 with effect from 2008–09 (FA 2008, Sch. 7, para. 115).

Derivations – S. 85(1): FA 1981, s. 88(1).

S. 85(2)–(9): FA 1991, s. 88.

Notes – S. 9: general meaning of "resident" and "ordinarily resident" but as applied by s. 69.

S. 15: meaning of "chargeable gains".

S. 272–274 and Sch. 11: meaning of "market value".

S. 288 *interpretation, including reference to sections as being those of this Act.*

85A Transfers of value: attribution of gains to beneficiaries and treatment of losses

85A(1) Schedule 4C to this Act has effect with respect to the attribution of gains to beneficiaries where there has been a transfer of value to which Schedule 4B applies.

85A(2) Sections 86A to 95 have effect subject to the provisions of Schedule 4C.

85A(2A) For the purposes of sections 87 to 89, no account is to be taken of any section 2(2) amount in a Schedule 4C pool (see paragraph 1 of Schedule 4C).

85A(3) When calculating the section 2(2) amount for a settlement for a tax year (within the meaning of section 87), no account is to be taken of any chargeable gains or allowable losses accruing by virtue of Schedule 4B.

Nothing in this subsection affects any increase in a section 2(2) amount by virtue of paragraph 1(3A) or 7B(2)(b) of Schedule 4C.

85A(4) No account shall be taken of any chargeable gains or allowable losses to which sections 87 to 89 apply in computing the gains or losses accruing by virtue of Schedule 4B.

History – S. 85A(2A) inserted by FA 2008, s. 25 and Sch. 7, para. 129(2) with effect in relation to transfers of value to which Sch. 4B applies that are made on or after 6 April 2008 (FA 2008, Sch. 7, para. 147).

S. 85A(3) substituted by FA 2008, s. 25 and Sch. 7, para. 129(3) with effect in relation to transfers of value to which Sch. 4B applies that are made on or after 6 April 2008 (FA 2008, Sch. 7, para. 147).

In former s. 85A(3), the words "resident and ordinarily resident in the United Kingdom" substituted for "resident or ordinarily resident in the United Kingdom" by FA 2006, s. 88 and Sch. 12, para. 34(1), (2)(b) with effect from 6 April 2007 (in relation to settlements whenever created).

S. 85A substituted by FA 2003, s. 163(1) which came into force in accordance with FA 2003, s. 163(4).

Former s. 85A inserted by FA 2000, s. 92(3), with effect in relation to any transfer of value in relation to which the material time is on or after 21 March 2000.

86 Attribution of gains to settlors with interest in non-resident or dual resident settlements

86(1) This section applies where the following conditions are fulfilled as regards a settlement in a particular year of assessment–

(a) the settlement is a qualifying settlement in the year;

(b) the trustees of the settlement fulfil the condition as to residence specified in subsection (2) below;

(c) a person who is a settlor in relation to the settlement (**"the settlor"**) is domiciled in the United Kingdom at some time in the year and is resident in the United Kingdom for the year;

(d) at any time during the year the settlor has an interest in the settlement;

(e) by virtue of disposals of any of the settled property originating from the settlor, there is an amount on which the trustees would be chargeable to tax for the year under section 2(2) if the assumption as to residence specified in subsection (3) below were made,

(f) paragraph 3, 4 or 5 of Schedule 5 does not prevent this section applying.

86(2) The condition as to residence is that–

(a) there is no time in the year when the trustees are resident in the United Kingdom, or

(b) there is such a time but, whenever the trustees are resident in the United Kingdom during the year, they fall to be regarded for the purposes of any double taxation relief arrangements as resident in a territory outside the United Kingdom.

86(3) Where subsection (2)(a) above applies, the assumption as to residence is that the trustees are resident in the United Kingdom throughout the year; and where subsection (2)(b) above applies, the assumption as to residence is that the double taxation relief arrangements do not apply.

86(4) Where this section applies–

(a) chargeable gains of an amount equal to that referred to in subsection (1)(e) above shall be treated as accruing to the settlor in the year or if, as respects the settlor, the year is a split year, in the UK part of that year, and

(b) those gains shall be treated as forming the highest part of the amount on which he is chargeable to capital gains tax for the year.

86(4ZA) Where a disposal of any settled property (which would apart from this subsection meet the condition in subsection (1)(e) with respect to the tax year) is a non-resident CGT disposal–

(a) any chargeable gain or allowable loss accruing on the disposal, other than an NRCGT gain chargeable to, or an NRCGT loss allowable for the purposes of, capital gains tax by virtue of section 14D, is to be treated as if it were a chargeable gain or (as the case requires) allowable loss falling to be taken into account in calculating the amount mentioned in subsection (1)(e) for the tax year, and

(b) the disposal is otherwise to be disregarded for the purposes of subsection (1)(e).

86(4A) [Repealed by FA 2002, s. 141 and Sch. 40, Pt. 3(4).]

86(5) Schedule 5 (which contains provisions supplementary to this section) shall have effect.

History – In s. 86(1)(c), the words "resident in the United Kingdom for the year" substituted for the words "either resident in the United Kingdom during any part of the year or ordinarily resident in the United Kingdom during the year" by FA 2013, s. 219 and Sch. 46, para. 91(2), with effect in relation to a person's liability to capital gains tax for the tax year 2013–14 or any subsequent tax year, without prejudice to any provision in FA 2013, Sch. 46, Pt. 3 about the application of a particular amendment.
In s. 86(1)(e), the words "if the assumption as to residence specified in subsection (3) below were made;" substituted by FA 2008, s. 8 and Sch. 2, para. 30 with effect in relation to chargeable gains accruing or treated as accruing in the tax year 2008–09 or any subsequent tax year (FA 2008, Sch. 2, para. 56(3)).
In s. 86(1)(e), the words from "if" to the end of paragraph (e) substituted for the words "if the assumption as to residence specified in subsection (3) below were made;" by FA 2002, s. 51 and Sch. 11, para. 4 with effect for the year 2003–04 and subsequent years of assessment or, if the person so elects in accordance with FA 2002, Sch. 11, para. 8, in relation to chargeable gains so accruing to a person in any of the years of assessment 2000–01, 2001–02 and 2002–03.
S. 86(2) substituted by FA 2013, s. 219 and Sch. 46, para. 91(3), with effect in relation to a person's liability to capital gains tax for the tax year 2013–14 or any subsequent tax year, without prejudice to any provision in FA 2013, Sch. 46, Pt. 3 about the application of a particular amendment.
In s. 86(2)(a), the words "neither resident nor ordinarily resident in the United Kingdom" substituted for "not resident or ordinarily resident in the United Kingdom" by FA 2006, s. 88 and Sch. 12, para. 30(1), (2)(b) with effect from 6 April 2007 (in relation to settlements whenever created).
In s. 86(2)(b), the words "resident and ordinarily resident in the United Kingdom during any part of the year" substituted for "resident in the United Kingdom during any part of the year or ordinarily resident in the United Kingdom during the year" and the words "such residence and ordinary residence" substituted for "such residence or ordinary residence" by FA 2006, s. 88 and Sch. 12, para. 35(1), (2)(a) with effect from 6 April 2007 (in relation to settlements whenever created) (FA 2006, s. 88 and Sch. 12, para. 41).
In s. 86(3), the words "and ordinarily resident" omittedby FA 2013, s. 219 and Sch. 46, para. 91(4), with effect in relation to a person's liability to capital gains tax for the tax year 2013–14 or any subsequent tax year, without prejudice to any provision in FA 2013, Sch. 46, Pt. 3 about the application of a particular amendment.
In s. 86(3), the words "resident and ordinarily resident in the United Kingdom" substituted for "resident or ordinarily resident in the United Kingdom" by FA 2006, s. 88 and Sch. 12, para. 34(1), (2)(c) with effect from 6 April 2007 (in relation to settlements whenever created).
In s. 86(4)(a), the words "or if, as respects the settlor, the year is a split year, in the UK part of that year" inserted by FA 2013, s. 218 and Sch. 45, para. 100, with effect in calculating an individual's liability to income tax or capital gains tax for the tax year 2013–14 or any subsequent tax year, subject to the transitional and saving provision in FA 2013, Sch. 45, para. 154–159.
S. 86(4ZA) inserted by FA 2015, s. 37 and Sch. 7, para. 19, with effect in relation to disposals made on or after 6 April 2015.
S. 86(4A), which was inserted by FA 1998, Sch. 21, para. 6(2) with effect for the year 1998–99 and subsequent years of assessment, repealed by FA 2002, s. 141 and Sch. 40, Pt. 3(4) with effect for the year 2003–04 and subsequent years of assessment or, if the person so elects in accordance with FA 2002, Sch. 11, para. 8, in relation to chargeable gains so accruing to a person in any of the years of assessment 2000–01, 2001–02 and 2002–03.

Derivations – S. 86(1)–(3): FA 1991, Sch. 16, para. 1(1)–(3).
S. 86(4): FA 1991, Sch. 16, para. 2.

Cross references – S. 2: extent of charge to capital gains tax in respect of any year of assessment, by reference to deduction from chargeable gains in the year of current-year and brought-forward losses.
FA 1998, s. 132(5): disposals made before 6 April 1999 disregarded when construing s. 86(1)(e) in relation to certain pre-19 March 1991 settlements.
FA 1998, Sch. 23: charges on settlors of pre-19 March 1991 settlements; transitional provisions for pre-6 April 1999 gains and losses.
FA 2004, Sch. 15, para. 9(1): charge to income tax on benefits received by former owner of property: intangible property comprised in settlement where settlor retains an interest.

HMRC interpretations – IRInt. 227: HMRC now accept that net capital losses incurred by non-resident trustees between 17 March 1998 and 5 April 1999 ("the transitional period") may be set against 1999–2000 gains, and that net losses in 1999–2000 can be set against gains arising in the transitional period in respect of which a settlor is chargeable under s. 86.

Other material – Taxline 1994/18 (not reproduced): oral suggestion by Inland Revenue (Claims Branch) that trustees of a pre-19 March 1991 non-resident trust who elect to receive an enhanced scrip dividend from a large plc with many shareholders will not be regarded as bringing the trust within s. 86, irrespective of whether the trustees decide the scrip belongs to income or capital. However, if the company only has a small number of shareholders, the trust may in these circumstances be "tainted".
Taxline 1994/31 (not reproduced): although Claims Branch still take the view that a loan by the settlor to the trustees on fully commercial terms does not taint a pre-19 March 1991 non-resident trust, there has been an apparent change as to what they regard as a "commercial loan".
Taxline 2003/4 (not reproduced): these losses form part of the s. 87 pool going forward. No carry back loss can be made.

Notes – S. 9: general meaning of "resident" and "ordinarily resident" but as applied by s. 69 to trustees.
S. 15: meaning of "chargeable gains".
S. 21–34: general meaning of "disposal".
S. 288: interpretation, including meaning of "double taxation relief arrangements".
Sch. 4C: transfers of value – attribution of gains to beneficiaries.

86A Attribution of gains to settlor in section 10A cases

86A(1) Subsection (3) applies if–

(a) chargeable gains of an amount equal to the amount referred to in section 86(1)(e) for a tax year ("year A") are treated under section 10A as accruing to a settlor under section 86 in the period of return,

(b) there are amounts on which beneficiaries of the settlement are charged to tax under section 87 or 89(2) for one or more tax years, each of which is earlier than the year of return, and

(c) those amounts are in respect of matched capital payments received by the beneficiaries.

86A(2) A **"matched"** capital payment is a capital payment, all or part of which is matched under section 87A with the section 2(2) amount for year A.

86A(3) The amount of the chargeable gains mentioned in subsection (1)(a) for year A that are treated under section 10A as accruing to the settlor under section 86 in the period of return is to be reduced by the appropriate amount.

86A(4) The appropriate amount is–

(a) the sum of the amounts mentioned in subsection (1)(c) to the extent that the matched capital payments are matched under section 87A with the section 2(2) amount for year A, or

(b) if the property comprised in the settlement has at any time included property not originating from the settlor, so much (if any) of that sum as, on a just and reasonable apportionment, is properly referable to the settlor.

86A(5) If a reduction falls to be made under subsection (3) for the year of return, the deduction to be made in accordance with section 87(4)(b) for the settlement for that year must not be made until–

(a) all the reductions to be made under subsection (3) for that year for each settlor have been made, and

(b) those reductions are to be made starting with the year immediately preceding the year of return and working backwards.

86A(6) Subsection (7) applies if, with respect to year A, an amount remains to be treated under section 10A as accruing to any of the settlors in the period of return after having made the reductions under subsection (3) with respect to year A.

86A(7) The aggregate of the amounts remaining to be so treated (for all of the settlors) is to be applied in reducing so much of the section 2(2) amount for year A as has not already been matched with a capital payment under section 87A for any year prior to the year of return (but not so as to reduce the section 2(2) amount below zero).

86A(8) In this section–

(a) **"the settlement"** means the settlement in relation to which the settlor mentioned in subsection (1)(a) is a settlor,

(b) a reference to **"the settlors"** or **"each settlor"** is to the settlors or each settlor in relation to the settlement,

(c) **"period of return"** and **"year of return"** have the same meanings as in section 10A, and

(d) paragraph 8 of Schedule 5 applies in construing the reference to property originating from the settlor.

History – S. 86A substituted by FA 2013. s. 218 and Sch. 45, para. 120, with effect if the year of departure (as defined in FA 2013, Sch. 45, Pt. 4) is the tax year 2013–14 or a subsequent tax year, subject to the transitional and saving provision in FA 2013, Sch. 45, para. 154–159. Former s. 86A read as follows:

"Attribution of gains to settlor in section 10A cases

86A(1) Subsection (2) below applies in the case of a person who is a settlor in relation to any settlement (**"the relevant settlement"**) where–

(a) by virtue of section 10A, amounts falling within section 86(1)(e) for any intervening year or years would (apart from this section) be treated as accruing to the settlor in the year of return; and

(b) there is an excess of the relevant chargeable amounts for the non-residence period over the amount of the section 87 pool at the end of the year of departure.

86A(2) Only so much (if any) of–

(a) the amount falling within section 86(1)(e) for the intervening year, or

(b) if there is more than one intervening year, the aggregate of the amounts falling within section 86(1)(e) for those years,

as exceeds the amount of the excess mentioned in subsection (1)(b) above shall fall in accordance with section 10A to be attributed to the settlor for the year of return.

86A(2A) [Omitted by FA 2008, s. 8 and Sch. 2, para. 31(3).]

86A(2B) [Omitted by FA 2008, s. 8 and Sch. 2, para. 31(4).]

86A(3) In subsection (1) above, the reference to the relevant chargeable amounts for the non-residence period is (subject to subsection (5) below) a reference to the aggregate of the amounts on which beneficiaries of the relevant settlement are charged to tax under section 87 or 89(2) for the intervening year or years in respect of any capital payments received by them.

86A(4) In subsection (1) above, the reference to the section 87 pool at the end of the year of departure is (subject to subsection (5) below) a reference to the amount (if any) which, in accordance with subsection (2) of that section, fell in relation to the relevant settlement to be carried forward from the year of departure to be included in the amount of the trust gains for the year of assessment immediately following the year of departure.

86A(5) Where the property comprised in the relevant settlement has at any time included property not originating from the settlor, only so much (if any) of any capital payment or amount carried forward in accordance with section 87(2) as, on a just and reasonable apportionment, is properly referable to property originating from the settlor shall be taken into account for the purposes of subsections (3) and (4) above.

86A(6) Where any reduction falls to be made by virtue of subsection (2) above in any amount to be attributed in accordance with section 10A to any settlor for any year of assessment, the reduction to be treated as made for that year in accordance with section 87(3) in the case of the settlement in question shall not be made until–

(a) the reduction (if any) falling to be made by virtue of that subsection has been made in the case of every settlor to whom any amount is so attributed; and

(b) effect has been given to any reduction required to be made under subsection (7) below.

86A(7) Where in the case of any settlement there is (after the making of any reduction or reductions in accordance with subsection (2) above) any amount or amounts falling in accordance with section 10A to be attributed for any year of assessment to settlors of the settlement, the amount (or aggregate amount) falling in accordance with that section to be so attributed shall be applied in reducing the amount carried forward to that year in accordance with section 87(2).

86A(7A) [Omitted by FA 2008, s. 8 and Sch. 2, para. 31(6).]

86A(8) Where an amount has been applied, in accordance with subsection (7) above, in reducing the amount which in the case of any settlement is carried forward to any year in accordance with section 87(2), that amount (or, as the case may be, so much of it as does not exceed the amount which it is applied in reducing) shall be deducted from the amount used for that year for making the reduction under section 87(3) in the case of that settlement.

86A(9) Expressions used in this section and section 10A have the same meanings in this section as in that section; and paragraph 8 of Schedule 5 shall apply for the construction of the references in subsection (5) above to property originating from the settlor as it applies for the purposes of that Schedule.".

In former s. 86A(2), the words "the amount falling within section 86(1)(e)" and "the amounts falling within section 86(1)(e)" substituted by FA 2008, s. 8 and Sch. 2, para. 31(2)(a), (b) with effect where the intervening year is 2008–09 or later (FA 2008, Sch. 2, para. 56(1)).

In former s. 86A(2)(a), the words "the tapered section 86(1)(e) amount" substituted for the words "the amount falling within section 86(1)(e)" by FA 2002, s. 51 and Sch. 11, para. 5(2)(a), with effect for the year 2003–04 and subsequent years of assessment or, if the person so elects in accordance with FA 2002, Sch. 11, para. 8, in relation to chargeable gains so accruing to a person in any of the years of assessment 2000–01, 2001–02 and 2002–03.

In former s. 86A(2)(b), the words "the tapered section 86(1)(e) amounts" substituted for the words "the amounts falling within section 86(1)(e)" by FA 2002, s. 51 and Sch. 11, para. 5(2)(b), with effect for the year 2003–04 and subsequent years of assessment or, if the person so elects in accordance with FA 2002, Sch. 11, para. 8, in relation to chargeable gains so accruing to a person in any of the years of assessment 2000–01, 2001–02 and 2002–03.

Former s. 86A(2A) omitted by FA 2008, s. 8 and Sch. 2, para. 31(3) with effect where the intervening year is 2008–09 or later (FA 2008, Sch. 2, para. 56(1)).

Former s. 86A(2A) inserted by FA 2002, s. 51 and Sch. 11, para. 5(3), with effect for the year 2003–04 and subsequent years of assessment or, if the person so elects in accordance with FA 2002, Sch. 11, para. 8, in relation to chargeable gains so accruing to a person in any of the years of assessment 2000–01, 2001–02 and 2002–03.

Former s.. 86A(2B) omitted by FA 2008, s. 8 and Sch. 2, para. 31(4) with effect in relation to chargeable gains accruing or treated as accruing in the tax year 2008–09 or any subsequent tax year (FA 2008, Sch. 2, para. 56(3)).

Former s. 86A(2B) inserted by FA 2002, s. 51 and Sch. 11, para. 5(3), with effectfor the year 2003–04 and subsequent years of assessment or, if the person so elects in accordance with FA 2002, Sch. 11, para. 8, in relation to chargeable gains so accruing to a person in any of the years of assessment 2000–01, 2001–02 and 2002–03.

In former s. 86A(7), the words "the amount (or aggregate amount) falling in accordance with that section to be so attributed" substituted by FA 2008, s. 8 and Sch. 2, para. 31(5) with effect in relation to chargeable gains accruing or treated as accruing in the tax year 2008–09 or any subsequent tax year (FA 2008, Sch. 2, para. 56(3)).

In former s. 86A(7), the words "the tapered section 10A amount" substituted for the words "the amount or (as the case may be) aggregate amount falling in accordance with that section to be so attributed" by FA 2002, s. 51 and Sch. 11, para. 5(4), with effect for the year 2003–04 and subsequent years of assessment or, if the person so elects in accordance with FA 2002, Sch. 11, para. 8, in relation to chargeable gains so accruing to a person in any of the years of assessment 2000–01, 2001–02 and 2002–03.

Former s. 86A(7A) omitted by FA 2008, s. 8 and Sch. 2, para. 31(6) with effect in relation to chargeable gains accruing or treated as accruing in the tax year 2008–09 or any subsequent tax year (FA 2008, Sch. 2, para. 56(3)).

Former s. 86A(7A) inserted by FA 2002, s. 51 and Sch. 11, para. 5(5), with effect for the year 2003–04 and subsequent years of assessment or, if the person so elects in accordance with FA 2002, Sch. 11, para. 8, in relation to chargeable gains so accruing to a person in any of the years of assessment 2000–01, 2001–02 and 2002–03.

In former s. 86A(8), the words "or aggregate amount" repealed by FA 2002, s. 141 and Sch. 40, Pt. 3(4), with effect for the year 2003–04 and subsequent years of assessment or, if the person so elects in accordance with FA 2002, Sch. 11, para. 8, in relation to chargeable gains so accruing to a person in any of the years of assessment 2000–01, 2001–02 and 2002–03.

Former s. 86A inserted by FA 1998, s. 127(1), with effect where the year of departure is 1997–98 or any subsequent year of assessment.

Cross references – S. 10A: effect of temporary non-residence in UK on charge to capital gains tax.
Sch. 4C: transfers of value – attribution of gains to beneficiaries.

87 Non-UK resident settlements: attribution of gains to beneficiaries

87(1) This section applies to a settlement for a tax year ("the relevant tax year") if there is no time in that year when the trustees are resident in the United Kingdom.

87(2) Chargeable gains are treated as accruing in the relevant tax year to a beneficiary of the settlement who has received a capital payment from the trustees in the relevant tax year or any earlier tax year if all or part of the capital payment is matched (under section 87A as it applies for the relevant tax year) with the section 2(2) amount for the relevant tax year or any earlier tax year.

87(3) The amount of chargeable gains treated as accruing is equal to–

(a) the amount of the capital payment, or

(b) if only part of the capital payment is matched, the amount of that part.

87(4) The section 2(2) amount for a settlement for a tax year for which this section applies to the settlement is–

(a) the amount upon which the trustees of the settlement would be chargeable to tax under section 2(2) for that year if they were resident in the United Kingdom in that year, or

(b) if section 86 applies to the settlement for that year, the amount mentioned in paragraph (a) minus the total amount of chargeable gains treated under that section as accruing in that year.

87(5) The section 2(2) amount for a settlement for a tax year for which this section does not apply to the settlement is nil.

87(5A) For the purpose of determining the section 2(2) amount for a settlement for a tax year–

(a) any chargeable gain or allowable loss accruing in that tax year on a non-resident CGT disposal made (or treated as made) by the trustees, other than an NRCGT gain chargeable to, or an NRCGT loss allowable for the purposes of, capital gains tax by virtue of section 14D, is to be treated as if it were a chargeable gain or (as the case requires) allowable loss falling to be taken into account in calculating the amount mentioned in subsection (4)(a), and

(b) such a disposal is otherwise to be disregarded.

87(6) For the purposes of this section a settlement arising under a will or intestacy is treated as made by the testator or intestate at the time of death.

87(7) If the relevant tax year is a split year as respects a beneficiary of the settlement–

(a) the amount on which the beneficiary is chargeable to capital gains tax by virtue of this section for that year (in respect of the settlement) is a portion of the amount on which the beneficiary would have been so chargeable if the relevant tax year had not been a split year, and

(b) the portion is the portion attributable to the UK part of the relevant tax year calculated on a time apportionment basis.

History – In s. 87(1), the words "there is no time in that year when the trustees are resident in the United Kingdom" substituted for the words "the trustees are neither resident nor ordinarily resident in the United Kingdom in that year" by FA 2013, s. 219 and Sch. 46, para. 92(2), with effect in relation to a person's liability to capital gains tax for the tax year 2013–14 or any subsequent tax year, without prejudice to any provision in FA 2013, Sch. 46, Pt. 3 about the application of a particular amendment.
In s. 87(4)(a), the words "and ordinarily resident" omitted by FA 2013, s. 219 and Sch. 46, para. 92(3), with effect in relation to a person's liability to capital gains tax for the tax year 2013–14 or any subsequent tax year, without prejudice to any provision in FA 2013, Sch. 46, Pt. 3 about the application of a particular amendment.
S. 87(5A) inserted by FA 2015, s. 37 and Sch. 7, para. 20, with effect in relation to disposals made on or after 6 April 2015.
S. 87(7) inserted by FA 2013, s. 218 and Sch. 45, para. 101, with effect in calculating an individual's liability to income tax or capital gains tax for the tax year 2013–14 or any subsequent tax year, subject to the transitional and saving provision in FA 2013, Sch. 45, para. 154–159.
S. 87 (together with s. 87A, 87B, 87C) substituted for former s. 87 by FA 2008, s. 25 and Sch. 7, para. 108 with effect from 2008–09 (FA 2008, Sch. 7, para. 115) but see also Sch. 7, para. 116–127.

87A Section 87: matching

87A(1) This section supplements section 87.

87A(2) The following steps are to be taken for the purposes of matching capital payments with section 2(2) amounts.

Step 1

Find the section 2(2) amount for the relevant tax year.

Step 2

Find the total amount of capital payments received by the beneficiaries from the trustees in the relevant tax year.

Step 3

The section 2(2) amount for the relevant tax year is matched with–

(a) if the total amount of capital payments received in the relevant tax year does not exceed the section 2(2) amount for the relevant tax year, each capital payment so received, and

(b) otherwise, the relevant proportion of each of those capital payments.

"The relevant proportion" is the section 2(2) amount for the relevant tax year divided by the total amount of capital payments received in the relevant tax year.

Step 4

If paragraph (a) of Step 3 applies–

(a) reduce the section 2(2) amount for the relevant tax year by the total amount of capital payments referred to there, and

(b) reduce the amount of those capital payments to nil.

If paragraph (b) of that Step applies–

(a) reduce the section 2(2) amount for the relevant tax year to nil, and

(b) reduce the amount of each of the capital payments referred to there by the relevant proportion of that capital payment.

Step 5

Start again at Step 1 (unless subsection (3) applies).

If the section 2(2) amount for the relevant tax year (as reduced under Step 4) is not nil, read references to capital payments received in the relevant tax year as references to capital payments received in the latest tax year which–

(a) is before the last tax year for which Steps 1 to 4 have been undertaken, and

(b) is a tax year in which capital payments (the amounts of which have not been reduced to nil) were received by beneficiaries.

If the section 2(2) amount for the relevant tax year (as so reduced) is nil, read references to the section 2(2) amount for the relevant tax year as the section 2(2) amount for the latest tax year–

(a) which is before the last tax year for which Steps 1 to 4 have been undertaken, and

(b) for which the section 2(2) amount is not nil.

87A(3) This subsection applies if–

(a) all of the capital payments received by beneficiaries from the trustees in the relevant tax year or any earlier tax year have been reduced to nil, or

(b) the section 2(2) amounts for the relevant tax year and all earlier tax years have been reduced to nil.

87A(4) The effect of any reduction under Step 4 of subsection (2) is to be taken into account in any subsequent application of this section.

History – S. 87A (together with s. 87, 87B, 87C) substituted for former s. 87 by FA 2008, s. 25 and Sch. 7, para. 108 with effect from 2008–09 (FA 2008, Sch. 7, para. 115).

Cross references – FA 2008, Sch. 7, para. 116: for the purposes of s. 87 and 87A, no account to be taken of:
- any capital payment received before 10 March 1981; or
- any capital payment received on or after that date but before 6 April 1984 so far as it represents a chargeable gain which accrued to the trustees before 6 April 1981.

FA 2008, Sch. 7, para. 122: reduction of capital payment if all or part of a capital payment would (in 2008–09) have been left out of account by virtue of s. 87(6) (as originally enacted).
FA 2008, Sch. 7, para. 124: application of s. 87 in or after 2008–09 where individual not domiciled in the UK: individual not to be charged in respect of certain amounts arising before 6 April 2008.
FA 2008, Sch. 7, para. 125: application of s. 87–89 where individual not domiciled in UK received capital payment on or after 12 March 2008 and before 6 April 2008.
SI 2009/3001, reg. 20: offshore income gains of non-resident settlements: modified application of s. 87–90A.

87B Section 87: remittance basis

87B(1) This section applies if–

(a) chargeable gains are treated under section 87 as accruing to an individual in a tax year, and

(b) section 809B, 809D or 809E (remittance basis) applies to the individual for that year,

(c) [omitted by FA 2013, s. 219 and Sch. 46, para. 18.]

87B(2) The chargeable gains are foreign chargeable gains within the meaning of section 12 (non-UK domiciled beneficiaries to whom remittance basis applies).

87B(3) For the purposes of Chapter A1 of Part 14 of ITA 2007 (remittance basis), treat relevant property or benefits as deriving from the chargeable gains.

87B(4) For the purposes of subsection (3) property or a benefit is "relevant" if the capital payment by reason of which the chargeable gains are treated as accruing consists of–

(a) the payment or transfer of the property or its becoming property to which section 60 applies, or

(b) the conferring of the benefit.

History – S. 87B(1)(c) (and the word "and" before it) omitted (and the word "and" after (a) inserted) by FA 2013, s. 219 and Sch. 46, para. 18, with effect in relation to an individual's foreign income and gains for the tax year 2013–14 or any subsequent tax year, subject to the savings provision in FA 2013, Sch. 46, para. 26.
S. 87B (together with s. 87, 87A, 87C) substituted for former s. 87 by FA 2008, s. 25 and Sch. 7, para. 108 with effect from 2008–09 (FA 2008, Sch. 7, para. 115).

Cross references – FA 2008, Sch. 7, para. 125: application of s. 87–89 where individual not domiciled in UK received capital payment on or after 12 March 2008 and before 6 April 2008.
SI 2009/3001, reg. 20: offshore income gains of non-resident settlements: modified application of s. 87–90A.

87C Sections 87 and 87A: disregard of certain capital payments

87C(1) For the purposes of sections 87 and 87A as they apply in relation to a settlement no account is to be taken of a capital payment (or a part of a capital payment) within subsection (2).

87C(2) A capital payment is within this subsection if (and to the extent that) it is received (or treated as received) in a tax year from the trustees of the settlement by a company that–

(a) is not resident in the United Kingdom in that year, and

(b) would be a close company if it were resident in the United Kingdom,

(and is not treated under any of subsections (3) to (5) of section 96 as received by another person).

History – S. 87C (together with s. 87, 87A, 87B) substituted for former s. 87 by FA 2008, s. 25 and Sch. 7, para. 108 with effect from 2008–09 (FA 2008, Sch. 7, para. 115).

Cross references – FA 2008, Sch. 7, para. 119: s. 87C not to apply in relation to any capital payment received before 6 April 2008.
FA 2008, Sch. 7, para. 125: application of s. 87–89 where individual not domiciled in UK received capital payment on or after 12 March 2008 and before 6 April 2008.
SI 2009/3001, reg. 20: offshore income gains of non-resident settlements: modified application of s. 87–90A.

88 Gains of dual resident settlements

88(1) Section 87 also applies to a settlement for any year of assessment beginning on or after 6th April 1991 if–

(a) the trustees are resident in the United Kingdom during any part of the year, and

(b) at any time of such residence they fall to be regarded for the purposes of any double taxation relief arrangements as resident in a territory outside the United Kingdom.

88(2) The section 2(2) amount for a tax year for which section 87 applies by virtue of this section is what it would be if the amount mentioned in section 87(4)(a) were the assumed chargeable amount.

88(3) For the purposes of subsection (2) above the assumed chargeable amount in respect of a year of assessment is the lesser of the following 2 amounts–

(a) the amount on which the trustees would be chargeable to tax for the year under section 2(2) on the assumption that the double taxation relief arrangements did not apply;

(b) the amount on which, by virtue of disposals of protected assets, the trustees would be chargeable to tax for the year under section 2(2) on the assumption that those arrangements did not apply.

88(4) For the purposes of subsection (3)(b) above assets are **protected assets** if–

(a) they are of a description specified in the double taxation relief arrangements, and

(b) were the trustees to dispose of them at any relevant time, the trustees would fall to be regarded for the purposes of the arrangements as not liable in the United Kingdom to tax on gains accruing to them on the disposal.

88(5) For the purposes of subsection (4) above–

(a) the assumption specified in subsection (3)(b) above shall be ignored;

(b) a relevant time is any time, in the year of assessment concerned, when the trustees fall to be regarded for the purposes of the arrangements as resident in a territory outside the United Kingdom;

(c) if different assets are identified by reference to different relevant times, all of them are protected assets.

88(6) [Omitted by FA 2008, s. 8 and Sch. 2, para. 6.]

88(7) [Omitted by FA 2008, s. 25 and Sch. 7, para. 109(3).]

History – In s. 88(1)(a) and (b), the words "and ordinarily resident" omitted by FA 2013, s. 219 and Sch. 46, para. 93, with effect in relation to a person's liability to capital gains tax for the tax year 2013–14 or any subsequent tax year, without prejudice to any provision in FA 2013, Sch. 46, Pt. 3 about the application of a particular amendment.

In s. 88(1), the words "resident and ordinarily resident in the United Kingdom during any part of the year" substituted for "resident in the United Kingdom during any part of the year or ordinarily resident in the United Kingdom during the year" and the words "such residence and ordinary residence" substituted for "such residence or ordinary residence" by FA 2006, s. 88 and Sch. 12, para. 35(1), (2)(b) with effect from 6 April 2007 (in relation to settlements whenever created) (FA 2006, s. 88 and Sch. 12, para. 41).

In s. 88(1), the word "and" inserted, s. 88(1)(c) and the word "and" immediately preceding it repealed by FA 1998, s. 130(2), s. 165 and Sch. 27, Pt. III(30), with effect for the year 1998–99 and subsequent years of assessment and with effect for 1997–98 subject to s. 130(4).

S. 88(2) substituted by FA 2008, s. 25 and Sch. 7, para. 109(2) with effect from 2008–09 (FA 2008, Sch. 7, para. 115).

S. 88(6) omitted by FA 2008, s. 8 and Sch. 2, para. 6 with effect from 2008–09 (FA 2008, Sch. 2, para. 22).

S. 88(7) omitted by FA 2008, s. 25 and Sch. 7, para. 109(3) with effect from 2008–09 (FA 2008, Sch. 7, para. 115).

Derivations – FA 1981, s. 80A, as inserted by FA 1991, s. 91 and Sch. 18, para. 2.

Cross references – S. 2: extent of charge to capital gains tax in respect of any year of assessment, by reference to deduction from chargeable gains in the year of current-year and brought-forward losses.

FA 2008, Sch. 7, para. 125: application of s. 87–89 where individual not domiciled in UK received capital payment on or after 12 March 2008 and before 6 April 2008.

SI 2009/3001, reg. 20: offshore income gains of non-resident settlements: modified application of s 87–90A.

Notes – S. 9: general meaning of "resident" and "ordinarily resident" but as applied by s. 69 to trustees.

S. 21–34: general meaning of "disposal" and "assets".

S. 288: interpretation, including meaning of "double taxation relief arrangements" reference to sections as being those of this Act.

89 Migrant settlements etc.

89(1) Where a period of one or more years of assessment for which section 87 applies to a settlement (**"a non-resident period"**) succeeds a period of one or more years of assessment for each of which section 87 does not apply to the settlement (**"a resident period"**), a capital payment received by a beneficiary in the resident period shall be disregarded for the purposes of sections 87 and 87A if it was not made in anticipation of a disposal made by the trustees in the non-resident period.

89(1A) Subsection (2) applies to a settlement if–

(a) a non-resident period is succeeded by a resident period, and

(b) in relation to the last tax year in the non-resident period ("the last non-resident tax year"), section 87A(3) applied by virtue of paragraph (a) of that provision (exhaustion of capital payments).

89(2) Chargeable gains are treated as accruing in a tax year (in the resident period) to a beneficiary of the settlement who receives a capital payment from the trustees in that year if all or part of the capital payment is matched (under section 87A as it applies for that year) with the section 2(2) amount for the last non-resident tax year or any earlier tax year.

89(3) Section 87(3) and (4) and sections 87A to 87C apply for the purposes of subsection (2) as if the relevant tax year were the tax year mentioned in subsection (2).

89(4) Section 87B (remittance basis) applies in relation to chargeable gains treated under subsection (2) as accruing as it applies in relation to chargeable gains treated under section 87 as accruing.

History – In s. 89(1), the words "sections 87 and 87A if" substituted for "section 87 if" by FA 2008, s. 25 and Sch. 7, para. 110(2) with effect from 2008–09 (FA 2008, Sch. 7, para. 115).
S. 89(1A) (together with s. 89(2), (3), (4)) substituted for former s. 89(2), (3) by FA 2008, s. 25 and Sch. 7, para. 110(3) with effect from 2008–09 (FA 2008, Sch. 7, para. 115).
S. 89(2) (together with s. 89(1A), (3), (4)) substituted for former s. 89(2), (3) by FA 2008, s. 25 and Sch. 7, para. 110(3) with effect from 2008–09 (FA 2008, Sch. 7, para. 115).
S. 89(3) (together with s. 89(1A), (2), (4)) substituted for former s. 89(2), (3) by FA 2008, s. 25 and Sch. 7, para. 110(3) with effect from 2008–09 (FA 2008, Sch. 7, para. 115).
S. 89(4) (together with s. 89(1A), (2), (3)) substituted for former s. 89(2), (3) by FA 2008, s. 25 and Sch. 7, para. 110(3) with effect from 2008–09 (FA 2008, Sch. 7, para. 115).

Derivations – FA 1981, s. 81, as amended by FA 1991, s. 81 and Sch. 18, para. 3.

Cross references – S. 10A: temporary non-residents.
S. 91: supplementary charge.
Sch. 4C: transfers of value – attribution of gains to beneficiaries.
FA 2008, Sch. 7, para. 120: calculation of s. 2(2) amount where s. 87 applied to a settlement for the tax year 2007–08 or any earlier tax year.
FA 2008, Sch. 7, para. 123: application of s. 89(2) (as substituted) if s. 89(2) (as originally enacted) would (but for the amendments in FA 2008, Sch. 7) have applied for 2008–09.
FA 2008, Sch. 7, para. 124: application of s. 89(2) in or after 2008–09 where individual not domiciled in the UK: individual not to be charged in respect of certain amounts arising before 6 April 2008.
FA 2008, Sch. 7, para. 125: application of s. 87–89 where individual not domiciled in UK received capital payment on or after 12 March 2008 and before 6 April 2008.
SI 2009/3001, reg. 20: offshore income gains of non-resident settlements: modified application of s. 87–90A.

Notes – S. 15: meaning of "chargeable gains".
S. 288: interpretation, including reference to sections as being those of this Act.

90 Sections 87 and 89(2): transfers between settlements

90(1) This section applies if the trustees of a settlement ("the transferor settlement") transfer all or part of the settled property to the trustees of another settlement ("the transferee settlement").

90(2) In this section **"the year of transfer"** means the tax year in which the transfer occurs.

90(3) Treat the section 2(2) amount for the transferee settlement for any tax year (not later than the year of transfer) as increased by–

(a) the section 2(2) amount for the transferor settlement for that year (as reduced under section 87A as it applies in relation to that settlement for the year of transfer and all earlier tax years), or

(b) if part only of the settled property is transferred, the relevant proportion of the amount mentioned in paragraph (a).

90(4) **"The relevant proportion"** is–

(a) the market value of the property transferred, divided by

(b) the market value of the property comprised in the transferor settlement immediately before the transfer.

90(5) Treat the section 2(2) amount for the transferor settlement for any tax year as reduced by the amount by which the section 2(2) amount for the transferee settlement for that year is increased under subsection (3).

90(6) If neither section 87 nor section 89(2) would otherwise apply to the transferee settlement for the year of transfer –

(a) section 89(2) to (4) apply to the settlement for that year (and subsequent tax years), and

(b) for this purpose, references there to the last non-resident tax year are to be read as the year of transfer.

90(7) The increase under subsection (3) has effect for the year of transfer and subsequent tax years.

90(8) The reduction under subsection (5) has effect for tax years after the year of transfer.

90(9) When calculating the market value of property for the purposes of this section or section 90A in a case where the property is subject to a debt, reduce the market value by the amount of the debt.

90(10) This section does not apply to–

(a) a transfer to which Schedule 4B applies, or

(b) any section 2(2) amount that is in a Schedule 4C pool (see paragraph 1 of Schedule 4C).

History – S. 90 (together with s. 90A) substituted for former s. 90 by FA 2008, s. 25 and Sch. 7, para. 111 with effect from 2008–09 (FA 2008, Sch. 7, para. 115) but see also Sch. 7, para. 116–127. Former s. 90 read as follows:

"Transfers between settlements

90(1) If in a year of assessment for which section 87 or 89(2) applies to a settlement (**"the transferor settlement"**) the trustees transfer all or part of the settled property to the trustees of another settlement (**"the transferee settlement"**) then, subject to the following provisions–

(a) if section 87 applies to the transferee settlement for the year, its trust gains for the year shall be treated as increased by an amount equal to the outstanding trust gains for the year of the transferor settlement or, where part only of the settled property is transferred, to a proportionate part of those trust gains;

(b) if subsection (2) of section 89 applies to the transferee settlement for the year (otherwise than by virtue of paragraph (c) below), the trust gains referred to in that subsection shall be treated as increased by the amount mentioned in paragraph (a) above;

(c) if (apart from this paragraph) neither section 87 nor section 89(2) applies to the transferee settlement for the year, subsection (2) of section 89 shall apply to it as if the year were the first year of a resident period succeeding a non-resident period and the trust gains referred to in that subsection were equal to the amount mentioned in paragraph (a) above.

90(2) Subject to subsection (3) below, the reference in subsection (1)(a) above to the outstanding trust gains for the year of the transferor settlement is a reference to the amount of its trust gains for the year so far as they are not treated under section 87(4) as chargeable gains accruing to beneficiaries in that year.

90(3) Where section 89(2) applies to the transferor settlement for the year, the reference in subsection (1)(a) above to the outstanding trust gains of the settlement is a reference to the trust gains referred to in section 89(2) so far as not treated as chargeable gains accruing to beneficiaries in that or an earlier year.

90(4) This section shall not apply to a transfer so far as it is made for consideration in money or money's worth.

90(5) This section does not apply–

(a) to a transfer to which Schedule 4B applies, or

(b) to gains to which Schedule 4C applies (that is, to "Schedule 4C gains" within the meaning of that Schedule).

History – S. 90(5) substituted by FA 2003, s. 163(3) which came into force in accordance with FA 2003, s. 163(4).
Former s. 90(5) inserted by FA 2000, s. 92(4) and Sch. 26, para. 2 with effect for any transfer of value in relation to which the material time is on or after 21 March 2000.

Derivations – FA 1981, s. 82.

Cross references – Sch. 4C: transfers of value – attribution of gains to beneficiaries.
ICTA 1988, s. 740(6)(a): interaction with charge on non-transferors where assets transferred abroad.
SI 2009/3001, reg. 20: offshore income gains of non-resident settlements: modified application of s. 87–90A.

Notes – S. 15: meaning of "chargeable gains".
S. 288: interpretation, including "year of assessment" as being 6 April to the following 5 April and reference to sections as being those of this Act."

90A Section 90: transfers made for consideration in money or money's worth

90A(1) Section 90 does not apply to a transfer of settled property made for consideration in money or money's worth if the amount (or value) of that consideration is equal to or exceeds the market value of the property transferred.

90A(2) The following provisions apply if–

(a) section 90 applies to a transfer of settled property made for consideration in money or money's worth, and

(b) the amount (or value) of that consideration is less than the market value of the property transferred.

90A(3) If the transfer is of all of the settled property, for the purposes of section 90 treat the transfer as being of part only of the settled property.

90A(4) Deduct the amount (or value) of the consideration from the amount of the market value referred to in section 90(4)(a).

History – S. 90A (together with s. 90) substituted for former s. 90 by FA 2008, s. 25 and Sch. 7, para. 111 with effect from 2008–09 (FA 2008, Sch. 7, para. 115).

Cross references – SI 2009/3001, reg. 20: offshore income gains of non-resident settlements: modified application of s. 87–90A.

91 Increase in tax payable under section 87 or 89(2)

91(1) This section applies if–

(a) chargeable gains are treated under section 87 or 89(2) as accruing to a beneficiary by virtue of the matching (under section 87A) of all or part of a capital payment with the section 2(2) amount for a tax year ("the relevant tax year"),

(b) the beneficiary is charged to tax by virtue of that matching, and

(c) the capital payment was made more than one year after the end of the relevant tax year.

91(1A) Where part of a capital payment is matched, references in subsections (2) and (3) to the capital payment are to the part matched.

91(2) The tax payable by the beneficiary in respect of the payment shall be increased by the amount found under subsection (3) below, except that it shall not be increased beyond the amount of the payment; and an assessment may charge tax accordingly.

91(3) The amount is one equal to the interest that would be yielded if an amount equal to the tax which would be payable by the beneficiary in respect of the payment (apart from this section) carried interest for the chargeable period at the rate of 10 per cent per annum.

91(4) **The chargeable period** is the period which–

(a) begins with the later of the 2 days specified in subsection (5) below, and

(b) ends with 30th November in the year of assessment following that in which the capital payment is made.

91(5) The 2 days are–

(a) 1st December in the tax year immediately after the relevant tax year, and

(b) 1st December falling 6 years before 1st December in the year of assessment following that in which the capital payment is made.

91(6) The Treasury may by order substitute for the percentage specified in subsection (3) above (whether as originally enacted or as amended at any time under this subsection) such other percentage as they think fit.

91(7) An order under subsection (6) above may provide that an alteration of the percentage is to have effect for periods beginning on or after a day specified in the order in relation to interest running for chargeable periods beginning before that day (as well as interest running for chargeable periods beginning on or after that day).

91(8) [Omitted by FA 2008, s. 25 and Sch. 7, para. 112(4).]

History – S. 91(1) (together with s. 91(1A)) substituted for former s. 91(1) by FA 2008, s. 25 and Sch. 7, para. 112(2) with effect from 2008–09 (FA 2008, Sch. 7, para. 115).

S. 91(1A) (together with s. 91(1)) substituted for former s. 91(1) by FA 2008, s. 25 and Sch. 7, para. 112(2) with effect from 2008–09 (FA 2008, Sch. 7, para. 115).

In s. 91(5)(a), the words "tax year immediately after the relevant tax year," substituted for "year of assessment following that for which the qualifying amount mentioned in subsection (1)(c) above is the qualifying amount," by FA 2008, s. 25 and Sch. 7, para. 112(3) with effect from 2008–09 (FA 2008, Sch. 7, para. 115).

S. 91(8) omitted by FA 2008, s. 25 and Sch. 7, para. 112(4) with effect from 2008–09 (FA 2008, Sch. 7, para. 115).

Derivations – FA 1991, Sch. 17, para. 4(1)–(7).

Other material – Taxline 1996/137 (not reproduced): Revenue confirmation that where a beneficiary receives a capital payment from a non-resident trust which is subject to a supplementary charge under s. 91, and the beneficiary also has personal capital gains, the personal annual exemption and any allowable losses will first be set against the trust gains that are subject to the supplementary charge.

Notes – S. 288: interpretation, including reference to sections as being those of this Act.

92 Qualifying amounts and matching

92 [Omitted by FA 2008, s. 25 and Sch. 7, para. 113.]

History – S. 92 omitted by FA 2008, s. 25 and Sch. 7, para. 113 with effect from 2008–09 (FA 2008, Sch. 7, para. 115).

93 Matching: special cases

93 [Omitted by FA 2008, s. 25 and Sch. 7, para. 113.]

History – S. 93 omitted by FA 2008, s. 25 and Sch. 7, para. 113 with effect from 2008–09 (FA 2008, Sch. 7, para. 115).

94 Transfers of settled property where qualifying amounts not wholly matched

94 [Omitted by FA 2008, s. 25 and Sch. 7, para. 113.]

History – S. 94 omitted by FA 2008, s. 25 and Sch. 7, para. 113 with effect from 2008–09 (FA 2008, Sch. 7, para. 115).

95 Matching after transfer

95 [Omitted by FA 2008, s. 25 and Sch. 7, para. 113.]

History – S. 95 omitted by FA 2008, s. 25 and Sch. 7, para. 113 with effect from 2008–09 (FA 2008, Sch. 7, para. 115).

96 Payments by and to companies

96(1) Where a capital payment is received from a qualifying company which is controlled by the trustees of a settlement at the time it is received, for the purposes of sections 87 to 90 and Schedule 4C it shall be treated as received from the trustees.

96(2) Where a capital payment is received from the trustees of a settlement (or treated as so received by virtue of subsection (1) above) and it is received by a non-resident qualifying company, the rules in subsections (3) to (6) below shall apply for the purposes of sections 87 to 90 and Schedule 4C.

96(3) If the company is controlled by one person alone at the time the payment is received, and that person is then resident in the United Kingdom, it shall be treated as a capital payment received by that person.

96(4) If the company is controlled by 2 or more persons (taking each one separately) at the time the payment is received, then–

(a) if one of them is then resident in the United Kingdom, it shall be treated as a capital payment received by *that person;*

(b) if 2 or more of them are then resident in the United Kingdom (**"the residents"**) it shall be treated as being as many equal capital payments as there are residents and each of them shall be treated as receiving one of the payments.

96(5) If the company is controlled by 2 or more persons (taking them together) at the time the payment is received–

(a) it shall be treated as being as many capital payments as there are participators in the company at the time it is received, and

(b) each such participator (whatever his residence) shall be treated as receiving one of the payments, quantified on the basis of a just and reasonable apportionment,

but where (by virtue of the preceding provisions of this subsection and apart from this provision) a participator would be treated as receiving less than one-twentieth of the payment actually received by the company, he shall not be treated as receiving anything by virtue of this subsection.

96(6) For the purposes of subsection (1) above a qualifying company is a close company or a company which would be a close company if it were resident in the United Kingdom.

96(7) For the purposes of subsection (1) above a company is controlled by the trustees of a settlement if it is controlled by the trustees alone or by the trustees together with a person who (or persons each of whom) falls within subsection (8) below.

96(8) A person falls within this subsection if–

(a) he is a settlor in relation to the settlement, or

(b) he is connected with a person falling within paragraph (a) above.

96(9) For the purposes of subsection (2) above **a non-resident qualifying company** is a company which is not resident in the United Kingdom and would be a close company if it were so resident.

96(9A) For the purposes of this section an individual shall be deemed to have been resident in the United Kingdom at any time in any year of assessment for which he or she was not so resident if–

(a) section 10A applies to him or her, and

(b) the year falls within the temporary period of non-residence.

96(9B) If–

(a) it appears after the end of any year of assessment that any individual is to be treated by virtue of subsection (9A) above as having been resident in the United Kingdom at any time in that year, and

(b) as a consequence, any adjustments fall to be made to the amounts of tax taken to have been chargeable by virtue of this section on any person,

nothing in any enactment limiting the time for the making of any claim or assessment shall prevent the making of those adjustments (whether by means of an assessment, an amendment of an assessment, a repayment of tax or otherwise).

96(10) For the purposes of this section–

(a) the question whether a company is controlled by a person or persons shall be construed in accordance with sections 450 and 451 of CTA 2010, but in deciding that question for those purposes no rights or powers of (or attributed to) an associate or associates of a person shall be attributed to him under section 451(4) to (6) of CTA 2010 if he is not a participator in the company;

(b) **"participator"** has the meaning given by section 454 of CTA 2010.

96(11) This section shall apply to payments received on or after 19th March 1991.

History – In s. 96(1) and (2) words "and Schedule 4C" inserted by FA 2000, s. 92(4) and Sch. 26, para. 3, with effect for any transfer of value in relation to which the material time is on or after 21 March.

In s. 96(3), the words "or ordinarily resident" omitted by FA 2013, s. 219 and Sch. 46, para. 94(2), with effect in relation to a person's liability to capital gains tax for the tax year 2013–14 or any subsequent tax year, without prejudice to any provision in FA 2013, Sch. 46, Pt. 3 about the application of a particular amendment.

In s. 96(4)(a) and (b), the words "or ordinarily resident" omitted by FA 2013, s. 219 and Sch. 46, para. 94(3), with effect in relation to a person's liability to capital gains tax for the tax year 2013–14 or any subsequent tax year, without prejudice to any provision in FA 2013, Sch. 46, Pt. 3 about the application of a particular amendment.

In s. 96(5)(b), the words "or ordinary residence" omitted by FA 2013, s. 219 and Sch. 46, para. 94(4), with effect in relation to a person's liability to capital gains tax for the tax year 2013–14 or any subsequent tax year, without prejudice to any provision in FA 2013, Sch. 46, Pt. 3 about the application of a particular amendment.

In s. 96(5) words "and each of them is then resident or ordinarily resident in the United Kingdom" in the opening words repealed by FA 2000, s. 96(1) with effect for payments received on or after 21 March 2000.

In s. 96(9A), the words "for which he or she was not so resident if … period of non-residence" substituted for the words "which in his case is an intervening year for the purposes of section 10A" by FA 2013, s. 218 and Sch. 45, para. 121, with effect if the year of departure (as defined in FA 2013, Sch. 45, Pt. 4) is the tax year 2013–14 or a subsequent tax year, subject to the transitional and saving provision in FA 2013, Sch. 45, para. 154–159.

S. 96(9A) inserted by FA 1998, s. 127(3), with effect in relation to departures from the UK in the year 1998–99 and subsequent years of assessment, and where 1997–98 is the year of departure and the taxpayer was resident or ordinarily resident in the UK at a time in that year on or after 17 March 1998.

S. 96(9B) inserted by FA 1998, s. 127(3), with effect in relation to departures from the UK in the year 1998–99 and subsequent years of assessment, and where 1997–98 is the year of departure and the taxpayer was resident or ordinarily resident in the UK at a time in that year onor after 17 March 1998.

In s. 96(10)(a), the words "sections 450 and 451 of CTA 2010" substituted for "section 416 of the Taxes Act" by CTA 2010, s. 1177 and Sch. 1, para. 230(a)(i), with effect for corporation tax purposes for accounting periods ending on or after 1 April 2010 and for income tax and capital gains tax purposes for the tax year 2010–11 and subsequent tax years.

In s. 96(10)(a), the words "section 451(4) to (6) of CTA 2010" substituted for "section 416(6)" by CTA 2010, s. 1177 and Sch. 1, para. 230(a)(ii), with effect for corporation tax purposes for accounting periods ending on or after 1 April 2010, and for income tax and capital gains tax purposes for the tax year 2010–11 and subsequent tax years.
In s. 96(10)(b), the words "section 454 of CTA 2010" substituted for "section 417(1) of the Taxes Act" by CTA 2010, s. 1177 and Sch. 1, para. 230(b), with effect for corporation tax purposes for accounting periods ending on or after 1 April 2010, and for income tax and capital gains tax purposes for the tax year 2010–11 and subsequent tax years.

Derivations – FA 1981, s. 82A, as inserted by FA 1991, s. 91 and Sch. 18, para. 4.

Cross references – ICTA 1988, s. 416, 417: control by reference to the company's affairs but, in particular, entitlement etc. to the majority of share capital, issued share capital, voting power, income or assets; participator as a person having a share or interest in the capital or income of the company etc.
SI 2009/3001, reg. 20: offshore income gains of non-resident settlements: modified application of s. 96–98.

Extra-statutory concessions – D40: in applying s. 96 and Sch. 5, para. 8, a trust beneficiary is not regarded as a participator in a company solely because of his beneficiary status.

Statements of practice – SP 5/92: intra-group payments which are not capital payments do not fall under s. 96.

Notes – S. 9: general meaning of "resident" and "ordinarily resident".
S. 288: interpretation, including meaning of "company", "close company", "the Taxes Act" as ICTA 1988 and reference to sections as being those of this Act.

97 Supplementary provisions

97(1) In sections 86A to 96 and Schedule 4C and this section **"capital payment"**–

(a) means any payment which is not chargeable to income tax on the recipient or, in the case of a recipient who is not resident in the United Kingdom, any payment received otherwise than as income, but

(b) does not include a payment under a transaction entered into at arm's length if it is received on or after 19th March 1991.

97(2) In subsection (1) above references to a payment include references to the transfer of an asset and the conferring of any other benefit, and to any occasion on which settled property becomes property to which section 60 applies.

97(3) The fact that the whole or part of a benefit is by virtue of section 733 of ITA 2007 treated as the recipient's income for a year of assessment after that in which it is received–

(a) shall not prevent the benefit or that part of it being treated for the purposes of sections 86A to 96 and Schedule 4C as a capital payment in relation to any year of assessment earlier than that in which it is treated as his income; but

(b) shall preclude its being treated for those purposes as a capital payment in relation to that or any later year of assessment.

97(4) For the purposes of sections 86A to 96 and Schedule 4C the amount of a capital payment made by way of loan, and of any other capital payment which is not an outright payment of money, shall be taken to be equal to the value of the benefit conferred by it.

97(5) For the purposes of sections 86A to 90 and Schedule 4C a capital payment shall be regarded as received by a beneficiary from the trustees of a settlement if–

(a) he receives it from them directly or indirectly, or

(b) it is directly or indirectly applied by them in payment of any debt of his or is otherwise paid or applied for his benefit, or

(c) it is received by a third person at the beneficiary's direction.

97(6) Section 16(3) shall not prevent losses accruing to trustees in a year of assessment for which section 87 of this Act or section 17 of the 1979 Act applied to the settlement from being allowed as a deduction from chargeable gains accruing in any later year (so far as they have not previously been set against gains for the purposes of a computation under either of those sections or otherwise).

97(7) In sections 86A to 96 and Schedule 4C and in this section–

"settlement" has the meaning given by section 620 of ITTOIA 2005, and

"settled property" and references (however expressed) to property comprised in a settlement shall be construed accordingly.

97(7A) In this section, sections 86A to 96 and Schedule 4C **"trustee"**, in relation to a settlement in relation to which there would be no trustees apart from this subsection, means any person in whom the settled property or its management is for the time being vested (and a person who is treated as a trustee of the settlement by virtue of this subsection shall be treated as a trustee of the settlement for the purposes of section 69).

97(8) In a case where–

(a) at any time on or after 19th March 1991 a capital payment is received from the trustees of a settlement or is treated as so received by virtue of section 96(1),

(b) it is received by a person, or treated as received by a person by virtue of section 96(2) to (5),

(c) at the time it is received or treated as received, the person is not (apart from this subsection) a beneficiary of the settlement, and

(d) subsection (9) or (10) below does not prevent this subsection applying,

for the purposes of sections 86A to 90 and Schedule 4C the person shall be treated as a beneficiary of the settlement as regards events occurring at or after that time.

97(9) Subsection (8) above shall not apply where a payment mentioned in paragraph (a) is made in circumstances where it is treated (otherwise than by subsection (8) above) as received by a beneficiary.

97(10) Subsection (8) above shall not apply so as to treat–

(a) the trustees of the settlement referred to in that subsection, or

(b) the trustees of any other settlement,

as beneficiaries of the settlement referred to in that subsection.

History – In s. 97(1)(a), the words "not resident" substituted for the words "neither resident nor ordinarily resident" by FA 2013, s. 219 and Sch. 46, para. 95, with effect in relation to a person's liability to capital gains tax for the tax year 2013–14 or any subsequent tax year, without prejudice to any provision in FA 2013, Sch. 46, Pt. 3 about the application of a particular amendment.
In s. 97(1), (3)(a), (4), (5), (7) and (8), words "and Schedule 4C" inserted by FA 2000, s. 92(4) and Sch. 26, para. 4, with effect for any transfer of value in relation to which the material time is on or after 21 March 2000.
In s. 97(1)–(5), (7) and (8), references to s. 87 substituted by references to s. 86A by FA 1998, s. 129(2), with effect where the year of departure is the year 1997–98 or any subsequent year of assessment.
In s. 97(3), the words "section 733 of ITA 2007" substituted for the words "section 740(2)(b) of the Taxes Act" by ITA 2007, s. 1027, Sch. 1, para. 302, with effect from 6 April 2007.
In s. 97(7), the words "the preceding provisions of" (before "this section") omitted by FA 2006, s. 88 and Sch. 12, para. 15(1)(a) and repealed by FA 2006, s. 178 and Sch. 26, Pt. 3(15) with effect from 6 April 2006 (in relation to settlements whenever created).
In s. 97(7), the definitions "settlement" and "settled property" substituted in place of the former definitions for the terms "settlement" and "settlor" (which also provided for how the term "settled property" should be construed) by FA 2006, s. 88 and Sch. 12, para. 15(1)(b), with effect from 6 April 2006 (in relation to settlements whenever created). TCGA 1992, s. 68A provides for a TCGA 1992-wide definition of the term "settlor", with effect from 6 April 2006.
In s. 97(7), words "section 660G(1) and (2) of the Taxes Act" substituted by words "section 620 of ITTOIA 2005" by virtue of ITTOIA 2005, s. 882 and Sch. 1, para. 432 which, in accordance with ITTOIA 2005, s. 883, have effect, for income tax purposes, for tax year 2005–06 and subsequent tax years, and, for corporation tax purposes, for accounting periods ending after 5 April 2005.
In s. 97(7), words "section 660G(1) and (2)" substituted for "section 681(4)" by FA 1995, s. 74 and Sch. 17, para. 30, with effect for 1995–96 and subsequent years of assessment.
S. 97(7A) inserted by FA 2006, s. 88 and Sch. 12, para. 15(2) with effect from 6 April 2006 (in relation to settlements whenever created).

Derivations – S. 97(1)(a): FA 1981, s. 83(1) (as amended by FA 1991, s. 91 and Sch. 18, para. 6(2)), s. 83(11) (as inserted by FA 1991, s. 91 and Sch. 18, para. 5) and FA 1991, Sch. 17, para. 1(c).
S. 97(1)(b): FA 1981, s. 83(1A) as inserted by FA 1991, s. 91 and Sch. 18, para. 6(3).
S. 97(2)–(6): FA 1981, s. 83(2)–(6), as amended by FA 1991, s. 91 and Sch. 18, para. 6(4), (5).
S. 97(7): FA 1981, s. 83(7), as inserted by FA 1984, s. 71(1) and amended by FA 1991, s. 91 and Sch. 18, para. 6(5).
S. 97(8)–(10): FA 1981, s. 83(8)–(10), as inserted by FA 1991, s. 91 and Sch. 18, para. 5.

Cross references – TCGA 1992, s. 68A: (inserted by FA 2006, Sch. 12, para. 1(2)) provides for a TCGA 1992-wide definition of the term "settlor" with effect from 6 April 2006.
S. 16(3): losses of tax years for no part of which the person is resident or ordinarily resident are not allowable losses except to the extent they relate to a UK branch etc.
ICTA 1988, s. 60: assets held by persons as nominee or bare trustee.
ICTA 1988, s. 660G(1), (2): "settlement" includes any disposition, trust, covenant, agreement, arrangement or transfer of assets and "settlor" means any person by whom the settlement was made.
ICTA 1988, s. 740(2)(b): liability of non-transferors in respect of transfers of assets abroad by reference to the first subsequent year for which it becomes relevant income.
SI 2009/3001, reg. 20: offshore income gains of non-resident settlements: modified application of s. 96–98.

Statements of practice – SP 5/92: an amount recovered from present trustees by a former trustee in respect of tax under s. 82 is not regarded as a capital payment under s. 97.

Notes – S. 9: general meaning of "resident" and "ordinarily resident".
S. 288: interpretation, including "the Taxes Act" as ICTA 1988, the "1979 Act" as CGTA 1979 and reference to other sections as being those of this Act.
CGTA 1979, s. 17 (now repealed): attribution of trust gains to beneficiaries, although capital gains tax could be postponed by certain persons until they become absolutely entitled to the property or dispose of their interest (see Sch. 11, para 18(a) to this Act).

98 Power to obtain information for purposes of sections 87 to 90

98(1) The Board may by notice require any person to furnish them within such time as they may direct, not being less than 28 days, with such particulars as they think necessary for the purposes of sections 87 to 90.

98(2) Sections 748(3) to (5), 749 and 750 of ITA 2007 shall have effect in relation to subsection (1) above as they have effect in relation to section 748(1) and (2) of that Act, but in their application by virtue of this subsection–

(a) references to Chapter 2 of Part 13 of that Act shall be construed as references to sections 87 to 90;

(b) [omitted by FA 2006, s. 88 and Sch. 12, para. 16(1)(c) and repealed by FA 2006, s. 178 and Sch. 26, Pt. 3(15).]

98(3) The provisions of subsections (1) and (2) above have effect as if the references to sections 87 to 90 included references to Schedule 4C.

History – In s. 98(2), the words "Sections 748(3) to (5), 749 and 750 of ITA 2007 shall have effect in relation to subsection (1) above as they have effect in relation to section 748(1) and (2) of that Act" substituted for the words "Subsections (2) to (6) of section 745 of

the Taxes Act shall have effect in relation to subsection (1) above as they have effect in relation to section 745(1)" by ITA 2007, s. 1027, Sch. 1, para. 303(a), with effect from 6 April 2007.
In s. 98(2)(a), the words "Chapter 2 of Part 13 of the Act" substituted for the words "Chapter III of Part XVII of the Taxes Act" by ITA 2007, s. 1027, Sch. 1, para. 303(b), with effect from 6 April 2007.
S. 98(2)(b) and the word "and" preceding it omitted by FA 2006, s. 88 and Sch. 12, para. 16(1)(b), (c) and repealed by FA 2006, s. 178 and Sch. 26, Pt. 3(15) with effect from 6 April 2006 (in relation to settlements whenever created).

Derivations – FA 1981, s. 84.

Cross references – ICTA 1988, s. 745(2)–(5): details of required particulars, subject to certain exclusions in relation to solicitors and banks.
section 98(3) inserted by FA 2000, s. 92(4) and Sch. 26, para. 5 with effect for any transfer of value in relation to which the material time is on or after 21 March 2000.
SI 2009/3001, reg. 20: offshore income gains of non-resident settlements: modified application of s. 96–98.

Notes – S. 288: interpretation, including "the Taxes Act" as ICTA 1988 and reference to other sections as being those of this Act.
TMA 1970, s. 27(1): power of Board to demand information generally from a party to a settlement for the purposes of tax on chargeable gains.
TMA 1970, s. 115: service of notices.

98A Settlements with foreign element: information

98A Schedule 5A to this Act (which contains general provisions about information relating to settlements with a foreign element) shall have effect.

History – S. 98A inserted by FA 1994, s. 97(2), with effect from 3 May 1994.

Chapter III – Collective Investment Schemes and Investment Trusts Etc

History – In the heading to Ch. III, "Etc" inserted by FA 2009, s. 44 and Sch. 22, para. 9, with effect in relation to the acquisition, holding and disposal of rights in a relevant offshore fund on or after 1 December 2009 (capital gains tax) or 1 April 2010 (corporation tax, by virtue of SI 2010/670) and subject to FA 2009, Sch. 22, para. 13 and 15.

99 Application of Act to unit trust schemes

99(1) This Act shall apply in relation to any unit trust scheme as if–

(a) the scheme were a company,

(b) the rights of the unit holders were shares in the company, and

(c) in the case of an authorised unit trust, the company were resident in the United Kingdom,

except that nothing in this section shall be taken to bring a unit trust scheme within the charge to corporation tax on chargeable gains.

99(2) Subject to subsection (3) and sections 99A and 151W(a) below, in this Act–

(a) **"unit trust scheme"** has the meaning given by section 237(1) of the Financial Services and Markets Act 2000,

(aa) **"unit holder"** means a person entitled to a share of the investments subject to the trusts of a unit trust scheme;

(b) **"authorised unit trust"** means, as respects an accounting period, a unit trust scheme in the case of which an order under section 243 of the Financial Services and Markets Act 2000 is in force during the whole or part of that period.

99(3) The Treasury may by regulations provide that any scheme of a description specified in the regulations shall be treated as not being a unit trust scheme for the purposes of this Act; and regulations under this section may contain such supplementary and transitional provisions as appear to the Treasury to be necessary or expedient.

History – In s. 99(1)(c), the words "and ordinarily resident" omitted by FA 2013, s. 219 and Sch. 46, para. 96, with effect in relation to a person's liability to capital gains tax for the tax year 2013–14 or any subsequent tax year, without prejudice to any provision in FA 2013, Sch. 46, Pt. 3about the application of a particular amendment.
In s. 99(2), the words "sections 99A and 151W(a)" substituted for "section 99A" by TIOPA 2010, s. 374 and Sch. 8, para. 199, with effect for corporation tax purposes for accounting periods ending on or after 1 April 2010, for income tax and capital gains tax purposes for the tax year 2010–11 and subsequent tax years, and for petroleum revenue tax purposes for chargeable periods beginning on or after 1 July 2010.
In s. 99(2)(a), the words "and section 99A" inserted after the words "Subject to subsection (3)" by FA 2004, s. 118(2)(a), with effect, by virtue of FA 2004, s. 118(5), in relation to years of assessment and accounting periods beginning on or after 1 April 2004.
In s. 99(2)(a), the words "same meaning as in the Financial Services Act 1986" substituted for the words "meaning given by section 237(1) of the Financial Services and Markets Act 2000" by SI 2001/3629, art. 62(1) operative from 1 December 2001.
S. 99(2)(aa) and (b) substituted for the former s. 99(2)(b) by FA 2004, s. 118(2)(b), with effect, by virtue of FA 2004, s. 118(5), in relation to years of assessment and accounting periods beginning on or after 1 April 2004.

Derivations – S. 99(1): CGTA 1979, s. 93.
S. 99(2): CGTA 1979, s. 92(1)(a), (b), as amended (para. (a)) by FA 1987, s. 40(3).
S. 99(3): CGTA 1979, s. 92(2), (3)(a), as inserted by FA 1987, s. 40(4).

Cross references – TIOPA 2010, s. 363A: where an offshore fund to which TIOPA 2010, s. 363A applies is treated by TCGA 1992, s. 99 as if it were a company, it is to be treated for the purposes of TCGA 1992 as a company that is neither resident nor ordinarily resident in the UK.
FA 2005, s. 48B(5): alternative finance investment bonds within FA 2005, s. 48A are not to be treated as unit trust schemes.

S. 135(4)(a): for the purposes of the share exchange provisions, "ordinary share capital" includes rights in relation to a unit trust scheme treated as shares in a company.
Sch. A1, para. 6(6): companies which are qualifying companies.
ICTA 1988, s. 468: similar deeming provisions in relation to income and relief for capital expenditure, "authorised unit trust scheme" being a unit trust scheme in the case of which an order under Financial Services Act 1986, s. 78 is in force.
ICTA 1988, s. 472A: trading profits etc. from securities: taxation of amounts taken to reserves.
ICTA 1988, s. 473: equation of securities, including units within s. 99, for purposes of taxes on income where reorganisation and assets represent trading stock of a bank, insurance company or dealer.
TMA 1970, s. 25: returns of information which may be required from issuing houses, stockbrokers, auctioneers etc. by reference to transactions involving companies within s. 99.
Financial Services Act 1986, s. 75(8): a "unit trust scheme" is a collective investment scheme under which the property in point is held on trust for the participants.
SI 1997/1154, reg. 5(3)(k), 7(4)(f), 20: modifications of s. 99 in relation to open-ended investment companies, holdings in and assets of such companies, and transactions involving such companies.
SI 2006/964, reg. 105: modification of s. 99 for the purposes of authorised investment funds.

Statutory instruments – SI 1988/266 and SI 1996/1583: regulations under s. 99.

HMRC interpretations – IRInt. 161: HMRC view of application of s. 99 to umbrella scheme: that each sub-fund is a separate company, and the unit-holder's interest is as a deemed shareholder in a company corresponding to the sub-fund.

Other material – Tax Bulletin TB10/04-2: background to FA 2004 changes.

Notes – S. 1, 8 (and ICTA 1988, s. 6): the charge to corporation tax in respect of chargeable gains.
S. 287: regulations to be by statutory instrument, subject to the negative resolution procedure of the House of Commons.
S. 288: interpretation, including "the Taxes Act" as ICTA 1988.

99A Treatment of umbrella schemes

99A(1) In this section an **"umbrella scheme"** means a relevant collective investment scheme–

(a) which provides arrangements for separate pooling of the contributions of the participants and the profits or income out of which payments are to be made to them, and

(b) under which the participants are entitled to exchange rights in one pool for rights in another,

and any reference to a part of an umbrella scheme is a reference to such of the arrangements as relate to a separate pool.

99A(2) For the purposes of this Act (except subsection (1) and section 103C)–

(a) each of the parts of an umbrella scheme shall itself be regarded as a collective investment scheme of the same form as the umbrella scheme as a whole, and

(b) the umbrella scheme as a whole shall not be regarded as a collective investment scheme of that form or as any other form of collective investment scheme,

and the participants in the umbrella scheme are to be treated accordingly.

99A(2A) Subsection (2)–

(a) does not prevent gains or losses accruing to an umbrella scheme which is a unit trust scheme (other than an authorised unit trust) being regarded as gains or losses accruing to the umbrella scheme as a whole, and

(b) does not apply for the purposes of section 100(2).

99A(3) [Omitted by SI 2013/1400, reg. 8(c).]

99A(4) Nothing in subsection (2) shall prevent–

(a) gains accruing to an umbrella scheme being regarded as gains accruing to an authorised unit trust for the purposes of section 100(1) (exemption for authorised unit trusts etc);

(b) a transfer of business to an umbrella scheme being regarded as a transfer to a unit trust scheme for the purposes of section 139(4) (exclusion of transfers to authorised unit trusts etc);

(c) [Repealed by FA 2004, s. 326 and Sch. 42, Pt. 3.]

99A(5) For the purposes of subsection (1), **"arrangements"** includes arrangements provided in a company's instrument of incorporation.

99A(6) In this section, **"relevant collective investment scheme"** means a collective investment scheme which is–

(a) an authorised contractual scheme which is a co-ownership scheme,

(b) a unit trust scheme, or

(c) an offshore fund.

History – Heading to s. 99A substituted by SI 2013/1400, reg. 8(f), with effect in relation to disposals on or after 8 June 2013.
In s. 99A(1), the words "a relevant collective investment scheme" substituted for the words "an authorised unit trust" by SI 2013/1400, reg. 8(a), with effect in relation to disposals on or after 8 June 2013.
S. 99A(2) and (2A) substituted for (2) by SI 2013/1400, reg. 8(b), with effect in relation to disposals on or after 8 June 2013.
In s. 99A(2), the words "and section 103C" inserted by FA 2012, s. 36(2) with effect from 17 July 2012.
S. 99A(3) omitted by SI 2013/1400, reg. 8(c), with effect in relation to disposals on or after 8 June 2013.
In s. 99A(4), the words "subsection (2)" substituted for the words "subsections (2) or (3)" by SI 2013/1400, reg. 8(d)(i), with effect in relation to disposals on or after 8 June 2013.
In s. 99A(4)(b), the words "a unit trust scheme" substituted for the words "an authorised unit trust" by SI 2013/1400, reg. 8(d)(ii), with effect in relation to disposals on or after 8 June 2013.

S. 99A(4)(c) repealed by FA 2004, s. 326 and Sch. 42, Pt. 3, with effect from 6 April 2006 (but subject to FA 2004, Sch. 36).
S. 99(5) and (6) inserted by SI 2013/1400, reg. 8(e), with effect in relation to disposals on or after 8 June 2013.
S. 99A inserted by FA 2004, s. 118(3), with effect, by virtue of FA 2004, s. 118(5), in relation to years of assessment and accounting periods beginning on or after 1 April 2004.

Cross references – S. 99(2): definitions of terms used for the purposes of s. 99 are subject to s. 99A.
S. 288: definition of "collective investment scheme" subject to s. 99A.

Other material – Tax Bulletin TB10/04-2: background to FA 2004 changes.

99B Calculation of the disposal cost of accumulation units

99B(1) For the purposes of computing the gain accruing on a disposal by a unit holder of units in a unit trust scheme and for the purposes of all other provisions of this Act, an amount shall be treated as expenditure falling within section 38(1)(b) if–

(a) it represents income from the investments subject to the unit trust scheme,

(b) it has been reinvested in respect of the units on behalf of the unit holder (without an issue of new units), and

(c) it is either–

(i) charged to income tax as income of the unit holder (or would be charged to income tax as his income but for a relief which has effect in respect of it) for the purposes of the Income Tax Acts, or

(ii) taken into account as a receipt in calculating profits, gains or losses of the unit holder for the purposes of the Income Tax Acts.

99B(2) Where an amount is treated as expenditure by virtue of subsection (1), the expenditure shall be treated for the purposes of this Act as having been incurred–

(a) in relation to an authorised unit trust, on the distribution date for the distribution period in respect of which the amount is reinvested, and

(b) in relation to any other unit trust scheme, on the date on which the amount is reinvested.

99B(3) In subsection (2)(a) **"distribution date"** and **"distribution period"** shall have the meaning given by regulations made under section 17(3) of the Finance (No. 2) Act 2005 (as at 1st April 2006, see regulation 15 of the Authorised Investment Funds (Tax) Regulations 2006 (S.I. 2006/964)).

History – In s. 99B(3) the words "regulations made under section 17(3) of the Finance (No. 2) Act 2005 (as at 1 April 2006, see regulation 15 of the Authorised Investment Funds (Tax) Regulations 2006 (S.I. 2006/964))" substituted for the words "section 468H of the Taxes Act" by SI 2006/964, reg. 89(2), with effect:

- for the purposes of income tax for the tax year 2006–07 and subsequent tax years, for distributions made on or after 6 April 2006;
- for the purposes of corporation tax on income, for accounting periods beginning on or after 1 April 2006 and on chargeable gains, in relation to disposals made on or after 1 April 2006, and for distributions made on or after 1 April 2006; and
- for the purposes of capital gains tax, in relation to disposals made on or after 6 April 2006.

S. 99B inserted by F(No. 2)A 2005, s. 21(1), with effect in relation to a disposal of units on or after 16 March 2005.

100 Exemption for authorised unit trusts etc.

100(1) Gains accruing to an authorised unit trust, an investment trust, a venture capital trust or a court investment fund shall not be chargeable gains.

100(2) [Omitted by SI 2013/2819, reg. 34, with effect from 6 April 2014.]

100(2A) [Omitted by SI 2013/2819, reg. 34, with effect from 6 April 2014.]

100(2B) [Omitted by SI 2013/2819, reg. 34, with effect from 6 April 2014.]

100(3) In this Act **"court investment fund"** means a fund established under section 42 of the Administration of Justice Act 1982.

History – In s. 100(1), words "a venture capital trust" inserted by FA 1995, s. 72(2), with effect in relation to gains accruing on or after 6 April 1995.
S. 100(2)–(2B) omitted by SI 2013/2819, reg. 34, with effect from 6 April 2014.
Former s. 100(2A) inserted by F(No. 2)A 2005, s. 20(2), with effect for 2005–06 and subsequent years of assessment.
In former s. 100(2B)(a) the words "section 65 of the Finance Act 2012" substituted for the words "section 431 of the Taxes Act" by FA 2012, s. 146 and Sch. 16, para. 74 in relation to accounting periods beginning on or after 1 January 2013 (FA 2012, s. 148) but subject to transitional provisions in FA 2012, Sch. 17. Where an accounting period would otherwise straddle 1 January 2013, it is deemed to end on 31 December 2012 (FA 2012, s. 149).
In former s. 100(2B)(b) the words "section 172 of the Finance Act 2012" substituted for the words "section 466(2) of the Taxes Act" by FA 2012, s. 176 and Sch. 18, para. 15 in relation to accounting periods beginning on or after 1 January 2013 (FA 2012, s. 178). Where an accounting period would otherwise straddle 1 January 2013, it is deemed to end on 31 December 2012 (FA 2012, s. 179).
Former s. 100(2B) inserted by F(No. 2)A 2005, s. 20(2) with effect for 2005–06 and subsequent years of assessment.

Derivations – S. 100(1): FA 1980, s. 81(1), as originally enacted.
S. 100(2): CCTA 1979, s. 96.
S. 100(3): CCTA 1979, s. 92(1)(d).

Cross references – S. 99A: authorised unit trusts: treatment of umbrella schemes.
S. 139(4): deemed no gain, no loss provisions for reconstructions or amalgamations involving the transfer of business not to apply to a unit trust scheme within s. 100(2).
ICTA 1988, s. 842: investment trusts.
ICTA 1988, s. 842AA(7): a company ceases to be a venture capital trust if Board's approval is withdrawn.

SI 1997/1154, reg. 5(3)(k): open-ended investment companies.
SI 2004/2199, reg. 5: treatment of pre-winding-up gains and losses of a VCT-in-liquidation.

Extra-statutory concessions – D17: exemption under s. 100(2) not withheld because of such temporary holding by trust managers as is necessary under ordinary arrangements of the trust for the issue and redemption of units.

Notes – S. 15: meaning of "chargeable gains".
S. 21–34: general meaning of "disposal" and "assets".
S. 288: interpretation.

100A Exemption for certain EEA UCITS

100A(1) ATED-related gains accruing on relevant high value disposals made by an EEA UCITS which is not an open-ended investment company or a unit trust scheme are not chargeable gains under section 2B.

100A(2) In this section–

"EEA UCITS" has the same meaning as in Part 17 of the Financial Services and Markets Act 2000 (see section 237 of that Act);

"unit trust scheme" has same meaning as in that Part (see section 237(1) of that Act);

"open-ended investment company" has the same meaning as in that Part (see section 236(1) of that Act).

History – S. 100A inserted by FA 2013, s. 65 and Sch. 25, para. 10, with effect in relation to disposals occurring on or after 6 April 2013.

101 Transfer of company's assets to investment trust

101(1) Where section 139 has applied on the transfer of a company's business (in whole or in part) to a company which at the time of the transfer was not an investment trust, then if–

(a) at any time after the transfer the company becomes for an accounting period an investment trust, and

(b) at the beginning of that accounting period the company still owns any of the assets of the business transferred,

the company shall be treated for all the purposes of this Act as if immediately after the transfer it had sold, and immediately reacquired, the assets referred to in paragraph (b) above at their market value at that time.

101(1A) Any chargeable gain or allowable loss which, apart from this subsection, would accrue to the company on the sale referred to in subsection (1) above shall be treated as accruing to the company immediately before the end of the last accounting period to end before the beginning of the accounting period mentioned in that subsection.

101(1B) This section does not apply if at the time at which the company becomes an investment trust there has been an event by virtue of which it falls by virtue of section 101B(1) to be treated as having sold, and immediately reacquired, the assets immediately after the transfer referred to in subsection (1) above.

101(2) Notwithstanding any limitation on the time for making assessments, an assessment to corporation tax chargeable in consequence of subsection (1) above may be made at any time within 6 years after the end of the accounting period referred to in subsection (1) above, and where under this section a company is to be treated as having disposed of, and reacquired, an asset of a business, all such recomputations of liability in respect of other disposals and all such adjustments of tax, whether by way of assessment or by way of discharge or repayment of tax, as may be required in consequence of the provisions of this section shall be carried out.

History – S 101(1A) inserted by FA 1996, s. 140 for accounting periods ending on or after 1 July 1999, the appointed day for self-assessment to corporation tax underFA 1994, s. 199 by virtue of SI 1998/3173 (C. 78).
S. 101(1B) inserted by FA 1998, s. 134(3) as respects companies with VCT approval under ICTA 1988, s. 842AA that has effect as from a time falling on or after 17 March 1998.

Derivations – CGTA 1979, s. 98, as amended by FA 1980, s. 81(3).

Cross references – S. 139: reconstruction or amalgamation involving the transfer of business.

Notes – S. 272–274 and Sch. 11: meaning of "market value".
S. 288: interpretation, including meaning of "investment trust" as respects any accounting period and reference to sections being those of this Act.
ICTA 1988, s. 12: meaning of "accounting period".
TMA 1970, s. 29–36: assessing procedure and general time limits.

101A Transfer within group to investment trust

101A(1) This section applies where–

(a) an asset has been disposed of to a company (the "acquiring company") and the disposal has been treated by virtue of section 171(1) as giving rise to neither a gain nor a loss,

(b) at the time of the disposal the acquiring company was not an investment trust, and

(c) the conditions set out in subsection (2) below are satisfied by the acquiring company.

101A(2) Those conditions are satisfied by the acquiring company if–

(a) it becomes an investment trust for an accounting period beginning not more than 6 years after the time of the disposal,

(b) at the beginning of that accounting period, it owns, otherwise than as trading stock–

(i) the asset, or

(ii) property to which a chargeable gain has been carried forward from the asset on a replacement of business assets,

(c) it has not been an investment trust for any earlier accounting period beginning after the time of the disposal, and

(d) at the time at which it becomes an investment trust, there has not been an event by virtue of which it falls by virtue of section 179(3) or 101C(3) to be treated as having sold, and immediately reacquired, the asset at the time specified in subsection (3) below.

101A(3) The acquiring company shall be treated for all the purposes of this Act as if immediately after the disposal it had sold, and immediately reacquired, the asset at its market value at that time.

101A(4) Any chargeable gain or allowable loss which, apart from this subsection, would accrue to the acquiring company on the sale referred to in subsection (3) above shall be treated as accruing to it immediately before the end of the last accounting period to end before the beginning of the accounting period for which the acquiring company becomes an investment trust.

101A(5) For the purposes of this section a chargeable gain is carried forward from an asset to other property on a replacement of business assets if–

(a) by one or more claims under sections 152 to 158, the chargeable gain accruing on a disposal of the asset is reduced, and

(b) as a result an amount falls to be deducted from the expenditure allowable in computing a gain accruing on the disposal of the other property.

101A(6) For the purposes of this section an asset acquired by the acquiring company shall be treated as the same as an asset owned by it at a later time if the value of the second asset is derived in whole or in part from the first asset; and, in particular, assets shall be so treated where–

(a) the second asset is a freehold and the first asset was a leasehold; and

(b) the lessee has acquired the reversion.

101A(7) Where under this section a company is to be treated as having disposed of and reacquired an asset–

(a) all such recomputations of liability in respect of other disposals, and

(b) all such adjustments of tax, whether by way of assessment or by way of discharge or repayment of tax,

as may be required in consequence of the provisions of this section shall be carried out.

101A(8) Notwithstanding any limitation on the time for making assessments, any assessment to corporation tax chargeable in consequence of this section may be made at any time within 6 years after the end of the accounting period referred to in subsection (2)(a) above.

History – S. 101A inserted by FA 1998, s. 133(1) as respects any company that becomes an investment trust for an accounting period beginning on or after 17 March 1998.

Cross references – S. 179(2C): disapplication of s. 179 where s. 101A(3) applies.

101B Transfer of company's assets to venture capital trust

101B(1) Where section 139 has applied on the transfer of a company's business (in whole or in part) to a company which at the time of the transfer was not a venture capital trust, then if–

(a) at any time after the transfer the company becomes a venture capital trust by virtue of an approval for the purposes of Part 6 of ITA 2007; and

(b) at the time as from which the approval has effect the company still owns any of the assets of the business transferred,

the company shall be treated for all the purposes of this Act as if immediately after the transfer it had sold, and immediately reacquired, the assets referred to in paragraph (b) above at their market value at that time.

101B(2) Any chargeable gain or allowable loss which, apart from this subsection, would accrue to the company on the sale referred to in subsection (1) above shall be treated as accruing to the company immediately before the time mentioned in subsection (1)(b) above.

101B(3) This section does not apply if at the time mentioned in subsection (1)(b) above there has been an event by virtue of which the company falls by virtue of section 101(1) to be treated as having sold, and immediately reacquired, the assets immediately after the transfer referred to in subsection (1) above.

101B(4) Notwithstanding any limitation on the time for making assessments, any assessment to corporation tax chargeable in consequence of this section may, in a case in which the approval mentioned in subsection (1)(a) above has effect as from the beginning of an accounting period, be made at any time within 6 years after the end of that accounting period.

101B(5) Where under this section a company is to be treated as having disposed of, and reacquired, an asset of a business, all such recomputations of liability in respect of other disposals and all such adjustments of tax, whether by way of assessment or by way of discharge or repayment of tax, as may be required in consequence of the provisions of this section shall be carried out.

History – S. 101B inserted by FA 1998, s. 134(2), with effect as respects companies with VCT approval under ICTA 1988, s. 842AA that has effect as from a time falling on or after 17 March 1998.
In s. 101B(1)(a), the words "Part 6 of ITA 2007" substituted for the words "section 842AA of the Taxes Act" by ITA 2007, s. 1027, Sch. 1, para. 304, with effect from 6 April 2007.

Notes – S. 101: similar provision to TCGA 1992, s. 101B for investment trusts.
S. 151A–B: provisions on venture capital trusts.

101C Transfer within group to venture capital trust

101C(1) This section applies where–

(a) an asset has been disposed of to a company (the **"acquiring company"**) and the disposal has been treated by virtue of section 171(1) as giving rise to neither a gain nor a loss,

(b) at the time of the disposal the acquiring company was not a venture capital trust, and

(c) the conditions set out in subsection (2) below are satisfied by the acquiring company.

101C(2) Those conditions are satisfied by the acquiring company if–

(a) it becomes a venture capital trust by virtue of an approval having effect as from a time (the "time of approval") not more than 6 years after the time of the disposal,

(b) at the time of approval the company owns, otherwise than as trading stock–
  (i) the asset, or
  (ii) property to which a chargeable gain has been carried forward from the asset on a replacement of business assets,

(c) it has not been a venture capital trust at any earlier time since the time of the disposal, and

(d) at the time of approval, there has not been an event by virtue of which it falls by virtue of section 179(3) or 101A(3) to be treated as having sold, and immediately reacquired, the asset at the time specified in subsection (3) below.

101C(3) The acquiring company shall be treated for all the purposes of this Act as if immediately after the disposal it had sold, and immediately reacquired, the asset at its market value at that time.

101C(4) Any chargeable gain or allowable loss which, apart from this subsection, would accrue to the acquiring company on the sale referred to in subsection (3) above shall be treated as accruing to it immediately before the time of approval.

101C(5) Subsections (5) to (7) of section 101A apply for the purposes of this section as they apply for the purposes of that section.

101C(6) Notwithstanding any limitation on the time for making assessments, any assessment to corporation tax chargeable in consequence of this section may, in a case in which the time of approval is the time at which an accounting period of the company begins, be made at any time within 6 years after the end of that accounting period.

101C(7) Any reference in this section to an approval is a reference to an approval for the purposes of Part 6 of ITA 2007.

History – In s. 101C(7), the words "Part 6 of ITA 2007" substituted for the words "section 842AA of the Taxes Act" by ITA 2007, s. 1027, Sch. 1, para. 305, with effect from 6 April 2007.
S. 101C inserted by FA 1998, s. 135(2), with effect as respects companies with VCT approval under ICTA 1988, s. 842AA that has effect as from a time falling on or after 17 March 1998.

Notes – S. 101A: similar provision to TCGA 1992, s. 101C for investment trusts.
S. 151A–B: provisions on venture capital trusts.

102 Collective investment schemes with property divided into separate parts

102 [Omitted by SI 2013/1400, reg. 9.]

History – S. 102 omitted by SI 2013/1400, reg. 9, with effect in relation to disposals on or after 8 June 2013.
In former s. 102(3), the words "section 235 of the Financial Services and Markets Act 2000" substituted for the words "the Financial Services Act 1986" by SI 2001/3629, art. 62(2), operative from 1 December 2001.
In former s. 102(3), words "or 136" added by FA 2002, s. 45 and Sch. 9, para. 5(4), with effect in relation to shares or debentures issued on or after 17 April 2002.

Derivations – FA 1989, s. 140(1)–(4).

Cross references – S. 127: equation of original shares and new holding on a reorganisation.

HMRC interpretations – IRInt. 161: HMRC view that former s. 102 does not apply where an investor switches between income units and accumulation units in the same sub-fund of an authorised unit trust umbrella scheme.

Notes – S. 288: interpretation, including reference to sections as being those of this Act.

103 Restriction on availability of indexation allowance

103 [Repealed by FA 1994, s. 93(7) and s. 258 and Sch. 26, Pt. V(8), in relation to disposals made on or after 30 November 1993.]

103A Application of Act to certain offshore funds

103A(1) This Act applies in relation to a relevant offshore fund as if–

(a) the fund were a company, and

(b) the rights of the participants in the fund were shares in the company.

103A(2) An offshore fund is a relevant offshore fund if–

(a) it is not constituted by a company or by two or more persons carrying on a trade or business in partnership, and

(b) it is not a unit trust scheme (see section 99).

103A(3) In this section and section 103B, **"participant"**, in relation to an offshore fund which is not a collective investment scheme, has the meaning given in section 362(1) of TIOPA 2010.

History – In s. 103A(2)(a), the words "or by two or more persons carrying on a trade or business in partnership" inserted by SI 2011/1211, reg. 44(2)(a), with effect in relation to disposals made on or after 27 May 2011.

In s. 103A(3), the words "section 103B, **"participant"**, in relation to an offshore fund which is not a collective investment scheme, has the meaning given in section 362(1) of TIOPA 2010." substituted for the words"section 103B–

> **"offshore fund"** has the meaning given in section 355 of TIOPA 2010;
>
> **"participant"**, in relation to a fund, has the meaning given in section 362(1) of that Act."

by SI 2013/1400, reg. 10, with effect in relation to disposals on or after 8 June 2013.

S. 103A(3) substituted by SI 2011/1211, reg. 44(2)(b), with effect in relation to disposals made on or after 27 May 2011.

S. 103A inserted by FA 2009, s. 44 and Sch. 22, para. 8, with effect in relation to the acquisition, holding and disposal of rights in a relevant offshore fund on or after 1 December 2009 (capital gains tax) or 1 April 2010 (corporation tax, by virtue of SI 2010/670) and subject to FA 2009, Sch. 22, para. 13 and 15.

Cross references – TIOPA 2010, s. 363A: where an offshore fund to which TIOPA 2010, s. 363A applies is treated by TCGA 1992, s. 103A as if it were a company, it is to be treated for the purposes of TCGA 1992 as a company that is neither resident nor ordinarily resident in the UK.

103B Application of section 99B to transparent funds

103B(1) This section applies in relation to an offshore fund which is a transparent fund but is not a unit trust scheme ("the fund").

103B(2) Section 99B applies for the purposes of computing the gain accruing on a disposal by a participant of an interest in the fund and for all other provisions of this Act as if–

(a) the fund were a unit trust scheme,

(b) the interest in the fund were units in a unit trust scheme (but not an authorised unit trust), and

(c) the participant were a unit holder.

103B(3) In this section **"transparent fund"** has the meaning given by the Offshore Funds (Tax) Regulations 2009 (S.I. 2009/3001) (see regulation 11).

History – S. 103B inserted by SI 2011/1211, reg. 44(3), with effect in relation to disposals made on or after 27 May 2011.

103C Power to make regulations about collective investment schemes

103C(1) The Treasury may by regulations make provision about the treatment of participants in collective investment schemes for the purposes of this Act.

103C(2) The regulations may, in particular, specify descriptions of collective investment scheme in relation to which they are to apply.

103C(3) Regulations under this section may make different provision for different cases or different purposes.

103C(4) Regulations under this section–

(a) may modify this Act or any other enactment or instrument (whenever passed or made), and

(b) may include incidental, consequential, supplementary or transitional provision.

103C(5) A statutory instrument containing regulations under this section must be laid before the House of Commons after being made.

103C(6) The regulations cease to have effect at the end of the period of 40 days beginning with the day on which the instrument is made unless before the end of that period the instrument is approved by a resolution of the House of Commons.

103C(7) After an instrument containing regulations under this section has been approved under subsection (6), subsections (5) and (6) do not apply to any subsequent such instrument (and accordingly section 287(3) applies to any such instrument).

103C(8) If regulations cease to have effect as a result of subsection (6), that does not–

(a) affect anything previously done under the regulations, or

(b) prevent the making of new regulations to the same or similar effect.

103C(9) In calculating the period of 40 days for the purposes of subsection (6), no account is to be taken of any time during which Parliament is dissolved or prorogued or during which the House of Commons is adjourned for more than 4 days.

103C(10) In this section–

"modify" includes amend, repeal or revoke, and

"participant", in relation to a collective investment scheme, is to be read in accordance with section 235 of the Financial Services and Markets Act 2000.

History – S. 103C inserted by FA 2012, s. 36(3) with effect from 17 July 2012.

103D Co-ownership schemes

103D(1) This section applies in relation to an authorised contractual scheme which is a co-ownership scheme and is not a relevant offshore fund.

103D(2) Subject to what follows, a participant's interests in the property subject to the scheme are to be disregarded for the purposes of this Act.

103D(3) A unit in the scheme is to be treated as an asset for the purposes of this Act.

103D(4) Section 99B applies for the purpose of computing the gain accruing on the disposal by a participant of such a unit (but for no other purpose) as if–

(a) the scheme were a unit trust scheme,

(b) the unit were a unit in a unit trust scheme (but not an authorised unit trust), and

(c) the participant were a unit holder.

103D(5) For the purposes of this Act–

"authorised contractual scheme" has the meaning given by section 237(3) of the Financial Services and Markets Act 2000;

"co-ownership scheme" has the meaning given by section 235A of the Financial Services and Markets Act 2000.

103D(6) In subsection (1), **"relevant offshore fund"** has the same meaning as in section 103A.

History – S. 103D inserted by SI 2013/1400, reg. 3, with effect in relation to disposals on or after 8 June 2013.

Chapter 4 – Collective Investment Schemes: Exchanges, Mergers and Schemes of Reconstruction

History – Ch. 4 inserted by SI 2013/1400, reg. 11, with effect in relation to disposals on or after 8 June 2013.

103E Application of Chapter

103E(1) In this Chapter (except this section) references to a collective investment scheme are to a collective investment scheme falling within any of the following paragraphs–

(a) an authorised contractual scheme which is a co-ownership scheme,

(b) a unit trust scheme, or

(c) an offshore fund.

103E(2) Sections 126 to 138A (reorganisation of share capital, conversion of securities etc) do not apply for the purposes of the treatment of participants in collective investment schemes falling within subsection (1)(a) to (c) except as applied by this Chapter.

103E(3) But sections 135 to 138A (company reconstructions) may apply for those purposes where either company A or company B is not a collective investment scheme falling within subsection (1)(a) to (c).

103E(4) In subsection (3), **"company A"** and **"company B"** have the meaning given by section 135 or 136 as the case may be.

103E(5) In this Chapter, **"units"** includes shares in a company.

History – S. 103E inserted by SI 2013/1400, reg. 11, with effect in relation to disposals on or after 8 June 2013.

103F Exchanges of units for units in the same scheme

103F(1) This section applies in the following cases.

Case 1

Where–

(a) a participant in a collective investment scheme exchanges units in the scheme for other units in the scheme ("new units") of substantially the same value, and

(b) the property subject to the scheme and the rights of participants to share in the capital and income in relation to that property are the same immediately before and immediately after the event (ignoring any changes as a result of a variation in management charges).

Case 2

Where there is a reorganisation of the units in a collective investment scheme in which all the participants holding units in the scheme or, where there are different classes of unit in the scheme, all the participants holding units in the same class, exchange all their units for other units ("new units") in the scheme.

103F(2) Where this section applies–

(a) sections 127 to 131 (share reorganisations etc) apply with the necessary adaptations as if the collective investment scheme were a company and the event mentioned in subsection (1) were a reorganisation of its share capital, and

(b) any distribution in relation to any new units is to be treated for the purposes of capital gains tax, corporation tax or income tax on the basis set out in section 127 (as adapted).

103F(3) In subsection (1), **"management charges"** mean the costs charged to the property subject to the scheme in respect of remunerating the parties operating the scheme, administrating the scheme or investing or safeguarding the property subject to the scheme.

History – S. 103F inserted by SI 2013/1400, reg. 11, with effect in relation to disposals on or after 8 June 2013.

103G Exchange of units for those in another collective investment scheme

103G(1) This section applies in the following cases where units in a collective investment scheme ("collective investment scheme B") are issued to a person in exchange for units in another collective investment scheme ("collective investment scheme A").

103G(2) The cases are–

Case 1

Where units in collective investment scheme B are issued in exchange for units as the result of a general offer–

(a) made to participants in collective investment scheme A or any class of them, and

(b) made in the first instance on a condition such that if it were satisfied the property subject to collective investment scheme B would include units in collective investment scheme A giving rights to more than 50% of the capital, and more than 50% of the income, of collective investment scheme A.

Case 2

Where–

(a) under an arrangement, participants in collective investment scheme A exchange units in that scheme for units of substantially the same value in collective investment scheme B, and

(b) in consequence of the exchanges under the arrangement, 85% or more of the property subject to collective investment scheme B is constituted by units in collective investment scheme A.

103G(3) Where this section applies, sections 127 to 131 (share reorganisations etc) apply with the necessary adaptations as if collective investment scheme A and collective investment scheme B were the same company and the exchange were a reorganisation of its share capital.

103G(4) This section has effect subject to section 103K(1)(exchange must be for bona fide commercial reasons and not part of tax avoidance scheme).

History – S. 103G inserted by SI 2013/1400, reg. 11, with effect in relation to disposals on or after 8 June 2013.

103H Scheme of reconstruction involving issue of units

103H(1) This section applies where–

(a) for the purposes of, or in connection with, a scheme of reconstruction an arrangement is entered into by all the participants holding units in an original collective investment scheme ("scheme A"), or where there are different classes of units in the scheme, all the participants holding any class of those units, and

(b) under the arrangement–

(i) units in a successor collective investment scheme or feeder fund ("scheme B") are issued to those participants in respect of and in proportion to (or as nearly as may be in proportion to) their relevant holdings in scheme A, and

(ii) the units in scheme A comprised in relevant holdings are retained by those participants or are cancelled or otherwise extinguished.

103H(2) Where this section applies–

(a) those participants are treated as exchanging their relevant holdings in scheme A for the units held by them in consequence of the arrangement, and

(b) sections 127 to 131 (share reorganisations etc) apply with the necessary adaptations as if scheme A and scheme B were the same company and the exchange were a reorganisation of its share capital.

For this purpose units in scheme A comprised in relevant holdings that are retained are treated as if they had been cancelled and replaced by a new issue.

103H(3) Where a reorganisation within case 2 of section 103F(1) of the units in scheme A is carried out for the purposes of the scheme of reconstruction, the provisions of subsections (1) and (2) apply in relation to the position after the reorganisation.

103H(4) In this section, references to **"relevant holdings"** of units are–

(a) where there is only one class of units in scheme A, to holdings of units in the scheme, and

(b) where there are different classes of units in scheme A, to holdings of a class of units that is involved in the scheme of reconstruction (within the meaning of paragraph 3 of Schedule 5AZA).

103H(5) This section has effect subject to section 103K(1) (scheme of reconstruction must be for bona fide commercial reasons and not part of tax avoidance scheme).

History – S. 103H inserted by SI 2013/1400, reg. 11, with effect in relation to disposals on or after 8 June 2013.

103I Scheme of reconstruction involving conversion scheme

103I(1) This section applies where–

(a) a scheme of reconstruction is entered into and given effect to, and

(b) for the purposes of, or in connection with, the scheme of reconstruction, units in a collective investment scheme ("the conversion scheme") are issued to participants in another collective investment scheme ("scheme C") in exchange for and in proportion to (or as nearly as may be in proportion to) their conversion holdings in accordance with regulation 12(1)(b) of the Undertakings for Collective Investment in Transferable Securities Regulations 2011 (S.I. 2011/1613).

103I(2) Where this section applies sections 127 to 131 apply with the necessary adaptations as if scheme C and the conversion scheme were the same company and the exchange were a reorganisation of its share capital.

103I(3) In this section **"conversion holdings"** means the units in scheme C to be converted in accordance with regulation 12(1)(b) of the Undertakings for Collective Investment in Transferable Securities Regulations 2011 into units in the conversion scheme for the purposes of, or in connection with, the scheme of reconstruction.

103I(4) This section has effect subject to section 103K(1) (scheme of reconstruction must be for bona fide commercial reasons and not part of tax avoidance scheme).

History – S. 103I inserted by SI 2013/1400, reg. 11, with effect in relation to disposals on or after 8 June 2013.

103J Supplementary provisions

103J In sections 103H and 103I–

(a) **"feeder fund"** has the meaning given by paragraph 3(2) of Schedule 5AZA to this Act;

(b) **"scheme of reconstruction"** has the meaning given by paragraph 1 of Schedule 5AZA;

(c) **"original collective investment scheme"** and **"successor collective investment scheme"** must be construed in accordance with paragraph 2(2) of Schedule 5AZA; and

(d) references to units being retained include their being retained with altered rights or in an altered form, whether as the result of reduction, consolidation, division or otherwise.

History – S. 103J inserted by SI 2013/1400, reg. 11, with effect in relation to disposals on or after 8 June 2013.

103K Restriction on application of sections 103G, 103H and 103I

103K(1) Subject to subsection (2) below, and section 138, section 103G, 103H or 103I shall not apply to any issue of units in a collective investment scheme in exchange for or in respect of units in another scheme unless the exchange or scheme of reconstruction in question is effected for bona fide commercial reasons and does not form part of a scheme or arrangements of which the main purpose, or one of the main purposes, is avoidance of liability to capital gains tax, corporation tax or income tax.

103K(2) Subsection (1) above shall not affect the operation of section 103G, 103H or 103I in any case where the participant to whom the units are issued does not hold more than 5 per cent of, or of any class of, the units in the second scheme mentioned in subsection (1) above.

103K(3) For the purposes of subsection (2) above units held by participants connected with the participant there mentioned shall be treated as held by that participant.

103K(4) If any tax assessed on a participant ("the chargeable participant") by virtue of subsection (1) above is not paid within 6 months from the date determined under subsection (5) below, any other participant who–

(a) holds all or any part of the units that were issued to the chargeable participant, and

(b) has acquired them without there having been, since their acquisition by the chargeable participant, any disposal of them not falling within section 58(1) or 171,

may, at any time within 2 years from that date, be assessed and charged (in the name of the chargeable participant) to all or, as the case may be, a corresponding part of the unpaid tax; and a participant paying any amount of tax under this subsection shall be entitled to recover from the chargeable participant a sum equal to that amount together with any interest paid by him under section 87A of the Management Act on that amount.

103K(5) The date referred to in subsection (4) above is whichever is the later of–

(a) the date when the tax becomes due and payable by the chargeable participant; and

(b) the date when the assessment was made on the chargeable participant.

103K(6) Section 138 (procedure for clearance in advance) applies to this section as it applies to section 137 (with any necessary modifications).

History – S. 103K inserted by SI 2013/1400, reg. 11, with effect in relation to disposals on or after 8 June 2013.

Chapter 5 – Carried Interest

History – Ch. 5 inserted by F(No. 2)A 2015, s. 43(1), with effect in relation to carried interest arising on or after 8 July 2015 under any arrangements, unless the carried interest arises in connection with the disposal of an asset or assets of a partnership or partnerships before that date and subject to F(No. 2)A 2015, s. 43(3)–(5).

103KA Carried interest

103KA(1) This section applies where–

(a) an individual ("A") performs investment management services directly or indirectly in respect of an investment scheme under arrangements involving at least one partnership, and

(b) carried interest arises to A under the arrangements.

103KA(2) If the carried interest arises to A in connection with the disposal of one or more assets of the partnership or partnerships–

(a) a chargeable gain equal to the amount of the carried interest less any permitted deductions (and no other chargeable gain or loss) is to be treated as accruing to A on the disposal, and

(b) the chargeable gain is to be treated as accruing to A at the time the carried interest arises.

103KA(3) If the carried interest arises to A in circumstances other than those specified in subsection (2), a chargeable gain of an amount equal to the amount of the carried interest less any permitted deductions is to be treated as accruing to A at the time the carried interest arises.

103KA(4) Subsections (2) and (3) do not apply in relation to carried interest to the extent that–

(a) it is brought into account in calculating the profits of a trade of A for the purposes of income tax for any tax year, or

(b) it constitutes a co-investment repayment or return.

103KA(5) For the purpose of subsections (2) and (3) **"permitted deductions"** in relation to A means such parts of the amounts specified in subsection (6) as is just and reasonable.

103KA(6) The amounts referred to in subsection (5) are–

(a) the amount of any consideration in money given to the scheme by or on behalf of A wholly and exclusively for entering into the arrangements referred to in subsection (1)(a) (but not consideration in respect of co-investments),

(b) any amount that constituted earnings of A under Chapter 1 of Part 3 of ITEPA 2003 (earnings) in respect of A's entering into those arrangements (but not any earnings in respect of co-investments or any amount of exempt income within the meaning of section 8 of that Act), and

(c) any amount which, by reason of events occurring no later than the time the carried interest arises, counts as income of A under the enactments referred to in section 119A(3) in respect of A's participation in the arrangements referred to in subsection (1)(a) (but not an amount counting as income of A in respect of co-investments) (and section 119A(5) applies for the purposes of this paragraph as it applies for the purposes of section 119A(4)).

For the purposes of this Act no other deduction may be made from the amount of the carried interest referred to in subsection (2) or (3).

103KA(7) Where the carried interest arises to A by virtue of his or her acquisition of a right to it from another person for consideration given in money by or on behalf of A, the amount of the chargeable gain accruing to A under subsection (2) or (3) is, on the making of a claim by A under this subsection, to be regarded as reduced by the amount of the consideration.

103KA(8) In this section–

"co-investment", in relation to A, means an investment made directly or indirectly by A in the scheme, where there is no return on the investment which is not an arm's length return within the meaning of section 809EZB(2) of ITA 2007;

"co-investment repayment or return" means a repayment in whole or in part of, or a return on, a co-investment;

"trade" includes profession or vocation.

History – S. 103KA inserted by F(No. 2)A 2015, s. 43(1), with effect in relation to carried interest arising on or after 8 July 2015 under any arrangements, unless the carried interest arises in connection with the disposal of an asset or assets of a partnership or partnerships before that date and subject to F(No. 2)A 2015, s. 43(3)–(5).

103KB Carried interest: consideration on disposal etc of right

103KB(1) For the purposes of section 103KA, consideration received or receivable by an individual for the disposal, variation, loss or cancellation of a right to carried interest is to be treated as carried interest arising to that individual at the time of the disposal, variation, loss or cancellation.

103KB(2) But subsection (1) does not apply if and to the extent that the consideration is a disguised fee arising to the individual for the purposes of section 809EZA of ITA 2007.

History – S. 103KB inserted by F(No. 2)A 2015, s. 43(1), with effect in relation to carried interest arising on or after 8 July 2015 under any arrangements, unless the carried interest arises in connection with the disposal of an asset or assets of a partnership or partnerships before that date and subject to F(No. 2)A 2015, s. 43(3)–(5).

103KC Carried interest: foreign chargeable gains

103KC In a case where section 103KA applies, a chargeable gain accruing or treated as accruing to an individual in respect of carried interest is a foreign chargeable gain within the meaning of section 12 only to the extent that the individual performs the services referred to in section 103KA(1)(a) outside the United Kingdom.

History – S. 103KC inserted by F(No. 2)A 2015, s. 43(1), with effect in relation to carried interest arising on or after 8 July 2015 under any arrangements, unless the carried interest arises in connection with the disposal of an asset or assets of a partnership or partnerships before that date and subject to F(No. 2)A 2015, s. 43(3)–(5).

103KD Carried interest: anti-avoidance

103KD In determining whether section 103KA applies in relation to an individual, no regard is to be had to any arrangements the main purpose, or one of the main purposes, of which is to secure that that section does not to any extent apply in relation to–

(a) the individual, or

(b) the individual and one or more other individuals.

History – S. 103KD inserted by F(No. 2)A 2015, s. 43(1), with effect in relation to carried interest arising on or after 8 July 2015 under any arrangements, unless the carried interest arises in connection with the disposal of an asset or assets of a partnership or partnerships before that date and subject to F(No. 2)A 2015, s. 43(3)–(5).

103KE Carried interest: avoidance of double taxation

103KE(1) This section applies where–

(a) capital gains tax is charged on an individual by virtue of section 103KA in respect of any carried interest, and

(b) Condition A or Condition B is met.

103KE(2) Condition A is that–

(a) at any time, tax (whether income tax or another tax) charged on the individual in relation to the carried interest has been paid by the individual (and has not been repaid), and

(b) the amount on which tax is charged as specified in subsection (1)(a) is not a permissible deduction under section 103KA(6)(b) or (c).

103KE(3) Condition B is that at any time tax (whether income tax or another tax) charged on another person in relation to the carried interest has been paid by that other person (and has not been repaid).

103KE(4) In order to avoid a double charge to tax, the individual may make a claim for one or more consequential adjustments to be made in respect of the capital gains tax charged as mentioned in subsection (1)(a).

103KE(5) On a claim under this section an officer of Revenue and Customs must make such of the consequential adjustments claimed (if any) as are just and reasonable.

103KE(6) The value of any consequential adjustments made must not exceed the lesser of–

(a) the capital gains tax charged as mentioned in subsection (1)(a), and

(b) the tax charged as mentioned in subsection (2)(a) or (3).

103KE(7) Consequential adjustments may be made–

(a) in respect of any period,

(b) by way of an assessment, the modification of an assessment, the amendment of a claim, or otherwise, and

(c) despite any time limit imposed by or under an enactment.

103KE(8) Where–

(a) an individual makes a claim under this section in respect of a year of assessment, and

(b) apart from this subsection, an amount falls to be deducted under section 2(2)(b) from the total amount of chargeable gains accruing to the individual in that year,

the individual may elect that the amount to be so deducted be reduced by any amount not exceeding the amount on which tax is charged as specified in subsection (2)(a) or (3).

History – S. 103KE inserted by F(No. 2)A 2015, s. 43(1), with effect in relation to carried interest arising on or after 8 July 2015 under any arrangements, unless the carried interest arises in connection with the disposal of an asset or assets of a partnership or partnerships before that date and subject to F(No. 2)A 2015, s. 43(3)–(5).

103KF Relief for external investors on disposal of partnership asset

103KF(1) If–

(a) a chargeable gain accrues to an external investor in an investment scheme on the disposal of one or more partnership assets, and

(b) the external investor makes a claim for relief under this section,

then subsection (2) applies in relation to the disposal.

103KF(2) The amount of the chargeable gain is to be reduced by an amount equal to–

$$I - C$$

where–

(a) I is an amount equal to such part of the sum invested in the fund by the external investor which on a just and reasonable basis is referable to the asset or assets disposed of, and

(b) C is the amount deducted under section 38(1)(a) in respect of consideration given wholly and exclusively for the acquisition of the asset or assets.

History – S. 103KF inserted by F(No. 2)A 2015, s. 43(1), with effect in relation to carried interest arising on or after 8 July 2015 under any arrangements, unless the carried interest arises in connection with the disposal of an asset or assets of a partnership or partnerships before that date and subject to F(No. 2)A 2015, s. 43(3)–(5).

103KG Meaning of "arise" in Chapter 5

103KG(1) For the purposes of this Chapter, carried interest "arises" to an individual ("A") if, and only if, it arises to him or her for the purposes of Chapter 5E of Part 13 of ITA 2007.

103KG(2) But section 809EZDB of ITA 2007 (sums arising to connected company or unconnected person) does not apply in relation to a sum of carried interest arising to–

(a) a company connected with A, or

(b) a person not connected with A,

where the sum is deferred carried interest in relation to A.

103KG(3) In this section, "deferred carried interest", in relation to A–

(a) means a sum of carried interest where the provision of the sum to A or a person connected with A is deferred (whether pending the meeting of any conditions (including conditions which may never be met) or otherwise), and

(b) includes A's share (as determined on a just and reasonable basis) of any carried interest the provision of which to A and one or more other persons, taken together, has been deferred (whether pending the meeting of any conditions (including conditions which may never be met) or otherwise).

In this subsection, in a case where the sum referred to in subsection (2) arises to a company connected with A, the reference to a person connected with A does not include that company.

103KG(4) Where–

(a) section 809EZDB of ITA 2007 has been disapplied in relation to a sum of deferred carried interest by virtue of subsection (2),

(b) the sum ceases to be deferred carried interest in relation to A, and

(c) the sum does not in any event arise to A apart from this subsection,

the sum is to be regarded as arising to A at the time it ceases to be deferred carried interest.

103KG(5) But subsection (4) does not apply if–

(a) none of the enjoyment conditions is met in relation to the sum when it ceases to be deferred carried interest, and

(b) there is no reasonable likelihood that any of those conditions will ever be met in relation to the sum.

103KG(6) The enjoyment conditions are–

(a) the sum, or part of the sum, is in fact so dealt with by any person as to be calculated at some time to enure for the benefit of A or a person connected with A;

(b) the sum's ceasing to be deferred carried interest in relation to A operates to increase the value to A or a person connected with A of any assets which–

  (i) A or the connected person holds, or

  (ii) are held for the benefit of A or the connected person;

(c) A or a person connected with A receives or is entitled to receive at any time any benefit provided or to be provided out of the sum or part of the sum;

(d) A or a person connected with A may become entitled to the beneficial enjoyment of the sum or part of the sum if one or more powers are exercised or successively exercised (and for these purposes it does not matter who may exercise the powers or whether they are exercisable with or without the consent of another person);

(e) A or a person connected with A is able in any manner to control directly or indirectly the application of the sum or part of the sum.

In this subsection, in a case where the sum referred to in subsection (2) arises to a company connected with A, references to a person connected with A do not include that company.

103KG(7) In determining whether any of the enjoyment conditions is met in relation to a sum or part of a sum–

(a) regard must be had to the substantial result and effect of all the relevant circumstances, and

(b) all benefits which may at any time accrue to a person as a result of the sum ceasing to be deferred carried interest in relation to A must be taken into account, irrespective of–

  (i) the nature or form of the benefits, or

  (ii) whether the person has legal or equitable rights in respect of the benefits.

103KG(8) The enjoyment condition in subsection (6)(b), (c) or (d) is to be treated as not met if it would be met only by reason of A holding shares or an interest in shares in a company.

103KG(9) The enjoyment condition in subsection (6)(a) or (e) is to be treated as not met if the sum referred to in subsection (2) arises to a company connected with A and–

(a) the company is liable to pay corporation tax in respect of its profits and the sum is included in the computation of those profits, or

(b) paragraph (a) does not apply but–

  (i) the company is a CFC and the exemption in Chapter 14 of Part 9A of TIOPA 2010 applies for the accounting period in which the sum arises, or

  (ii) the company is not a CFC but, if it were, that exemption would apply for that period.

In this subsection **"CFC"** has the same meaning as in Part 9A of TIOPA 2010.

103KG(10) But subsections (8) and (9) do not apply if the sum referred to in subsection (2) arises to the company referred to in subsection (2)(a) or the person referred to in subsection (2)(b) as part of arrangements where–

(a) it is reasonable to assume that in the absence of the arrangements the sum or part of the sum would have arisen to A or an individual connected with A, and

(b) it is reasonable to assume that the arrangements have as their main purpose, or one of their main purposes, the avoidance of a liability to pay income tax, capital gains tax, inheritance tax or corporation tax.

103KG(11) The condition in subsection (10)(b) is to be regarded as met in a case where the sum is applied directly or indirectly as an investment in a collective investment scheme.

103KG(12) Subsection (2) does not apply in relation to any sum in relation to which the condition in subsection (8)(b) of section 809EZDB is met by virtue of subsection (9) of that section.

103KG(13) Subsection (2) also does not apply if–

(a) it is reasonable to assume that the deferral referred to in subsection (3)(a) or (b) is not the effect of genuine commercial arrangements, or

(b) that deferral is the effect of such arrangements but it is reasonable to assume that the arrangements have as their main purpose, or one of their main purposes, the avoidance of a liability to pay income tax, capital gains tax, corporation tax or inheritance tax.

103KG(14) In subsection (13), **"genuine commercial arrangements"** means arrangements involving A (alone or jointly with others performing investment management services) and external investors in the investment scheme.

103KG(15) Section 993 of ITA 2007 (meaning of "connected") applies for the purposes of this section but as if–

(a) subsection (4) of that section were omitted, and

(b) partners in a partnership in which A is also a partner were not "associates" of A for the purposes of sections 450 and 451 of CTA 2010 ("control").

History – S. 103KG inserted by F(No. 2)A 2015, s. 43(1), with effect in relation to carried interest arising on or after 8 July 2015 under any arrangements, unless the carried interest arises in connection with the disposal of an asset or assets of a partnership or partnerships before that date and subject to F(No. 2)A 2015, s. 43(3)–(5).

103KH Interpretation of Chapter 5

103KH(1) In this Chapter–

"arrangements" has the same meaning as in Chapter 5E of Part 13 of ITA 2007 (see 809EZE of that Act);

"carried interest", in relation to arrangements referred to in section 103KA(1)(a), has the same meaning as in section 809EZB of ITA 2007 (see sections 809EZC and 809EZD of that Act);

"investment scheme", **"investment management services"** and **"external investor"** have the same meanings as in Chapter 5E of Part 13 of ITA 2007 (see sections 809EZA(6) and 809EZE of that Act).

History – S. 103KH inserted by F(No. 2)A 2015, s. 43(1), with effect in relation to carried interest arising on or after 8 July 2015 under any arrangements, unless the carried interest arises in connection with the disposal of an asset or assets of a partnership or partnerships before that date and subject to F(No. 2)A 2015, s. 43(3)–(5).

PART IV – SHARES, SECURITIES, OPTIONS ETC.

Chapter I – General

Cross references – S. 263B(3) (as inserted by FA 1997, s. 76 and Sch. 10, para. 5(1), with effect from 1 July 1997 (para. 7(1))): identification rules under stock lending arrangements.

Sch. 8, para. 100 shares within an employee share ownership plan are treated as a different class of shares from any shares held outside the plan.

Sch. 8B, para. 6(6): investments in social enterprises: Pt. 4, Ch. 1 has effect subject to Sch. 8B, para. 6(3)–(5).

Sch. 15, para. 93(5) share pooling does not apply to investment relief shares acquired under the CVS.

FA 2002, Sch. 16, para. 47(5), (6): where investment is made in a community development finance institution this chapter is subject to FA 2002, Sch. 16 for the purposes of the identification of securities or shares on a disposal. S. 104 to 107 do not apply to such securities or shares where relief is attributable to them.

Notes – FA 2005, s. 21(8): Treasury may modify, by way of regulations, Part 4 of TCGA 1992.

SHARE POOLING, IDENTIFICATION OF SECURITIES, AND INDEXATION

104 Share pooling: general interpretative provisions

104(1) Any number of securities of the same class acquired by the same person in the same capacity shall for the purposes of this Act (subject to express provision to the contrary) be regarded as indistinguishable parts of a single asset growing or diminishing on the occasions on which additional securities of the same class are acquired or some of the securities of that class are disposed of.

104(2) For the purposes of corporation tax, subsection (1) does not apply to any securities acquired by a company before 1 April 1982.

104(2A) See also sections 105 to 105B and–

(a) section 106A in the case of capital gains tax, or

(b) sections 107 to 114 in the case of corporation tax.

104(3) For the purposes of this section and sections 105, 107, 110 and 114–

"a section 104 holding" is a holding of securities which, by virtue of subsection (1) above, is to be regarded as a single asset;

"securities" does not include relevant securities as defined in section 108 but, subject to that, means–

(i) shares or securities of a company; and

(ii) any other assets where they are of a nature to be dealt in without identifying the particular assets disposed of or acquired; and

"relevant allowable expenditure" has the meaning assigned to it by section 53(2)(b) and (3);

but shares or securities of a company shall not be treated as being of the same class unless they are so treated by the practice of a recognised stock exchange or would be so treated if dealt with on a recognised stock exchange.

104(3A) For the purposes of capital gains tax section 35(2) applies in relation to a section 104 holding as if the reference to an asset were to any of the securities constituting or forming part of the section 104 holding which were held by the person making the disposal on 31 March 1982.

104(4) For the purposes of this Chapter securities of a company which are held–

(a) by a person who acquired them as an employee of the company or of any other person, and

(b) on terms which for the time being restrict his right to dispose of them,

shall (notwithstanding that they would otherwise fall to be treated as of the same class) be treated as of a different class from any securities acquired by him otherwise than as an employee of the company or of any other person and also from any shares that are not held subject to restrictions, or the same restrictions, on disposal or in the case of which the restrictions are no longer in force.

104(4A) For the purposes of this Chapter, securities of a company which are held by the trustees of a settlement, having been last acquired or deemed to be acquired by them in circumstances where section 236H or 236Q applied, shall (notwithstanding that they would otherwise fall to be treated as of the same class) be treated as of a different class from any other securities of the company acquired by those trustees.

104(5) Nothing in this section or sections 110 and 114 shall be taken as affecting the manner in which the market value of any securities is to be ascertained.

104(6) Without prejudice to the generality of subsections (1) and (2) above, a disposal of securities in a section 104 holding, other than a disposal of the whole of it, is a disposal of part of an asset and the provisions of this Act relating to the computation of a gain accruing on a disposal of part of an asset shall apply accordingly.

History – In s. 104(1), the words "(subject to express provision to the contrary)" inserted by FA 2006, s. 88 and Sch. 12, para. 17(1), with effect from 6 April 2006.

S. 104(2) substituted (with s. 104(2A)) for former s. 104(2), (2A) by FA 2008, s. 8 and Sch. 2, para. 85(2) with effect in relation to disposals made on or after 6 April 2008 (FA 2008, Sch. 2, para. 100).

S. 104(2)(aa) inserted by FA 1998, s. 123(1) as respects any disposal of securities on or after 6 April 1998.

In s. 104(2)(b), the reference to s. 106 omitted by FA 2006, s. 72(2)(a) and repealed by FA 2006, s. 178 and Sch. 26, Pt. 3(9), with effect in relation to any disposal made on or after 5 December 2005.

S. 104(2A) substituted (with s. 104(2)) for former s. 104(2), (2A) by FA 2008, s. 8 and Sch. 2, para. 85(2) with effect in relation to disposals made on or after 6 April 2008 (FA 2008, Sch. 2, para. 100).

S. 104(2A) originally inserted by FA 1998, s. 123(2) as respects any disposal of securities on or after 6 April 1998.

In s. 104(3), the reference to s. 110A omitted by FA 2008, s. 8 and Sch. 2, para. 85(3) with effect in relation to disposals made on or after 6 April 2008 (FA 2008, Sch. 2, para. 100).

In s. 104(3), the reference to s. 110A inserted by FA 1998, s. 125(3) as respects disposals on or after 6 April 1998.

S. 104(3A) inserted by FA 2008, s. 8 and Sch. 2, para. 85(4) with effect in relation to disposals made on or after 6 April 2008 (FA 2008, Sch. 2, para. 100).

S. 104(4) substituted by FA 1998, s. 123(4) as respects any disposal of securities on or after 6 April 1998.

S. 104(4A) inserted by FA 2014, s. 290 and Sch. 37, para. 18(1), with effect in relation to any disposal on or after 6 April 2014 of any securities (whenever acquired).
In s. 104(3), references to a "section 104 holding" substituted by FA 1998, s. 123(3) and (5) for references to a "new holding", as respects any disposal of securities on or after 6 April 1998.
In s. 104(5), the reference to s. 110A omitted by FA 2008, s. 8 and Sch. 2, para. 85(5) with effect in relation to disposals made on or after 6 April 2008 (FA 2008, Sch. 2, para. 100).
In s. 104(5), the reference to s. 110A inserted by FA 1998, s. 125(3) as respects disposals on or after 6 April 1998.
In s. 104(6), references to a "section 104 holding" substituted by FA 1998, s. 123(3) and (5) for references to a " new holding", as respects any disposal of securities on or after 6 April 1998.

Derivations – S. 104(1): FA 1985, Sch. 19, para. 9(1).
S. 104(2): FA 1985, Sch. 19, para. 9(1)(b), 17(1)(a), (b).
S. 104(3): CGTA 1979, s. 66(4), FA 1985, s. 68(9) ("securities"); CGTA 1979, s. 66(3), FA 1985, s. 68(10) (endpiece); Sch. 19, para. 8(1)(c) ("relevant allowable expenditure"), 9(3) ("new holding").
S. 104(4), (5): FA 1985, Sch. 19, para. 8(2), (3).
S. 104(6): FA 1985, Sch. 19, para. 10.

Cross references – S. 53(2)(b), (3): acquisition expenditure (including incidental costs) and enhancement or title expenditure, by reference to s. 38(1)(a), (b), after adjusting for specified increases, exclusions, reductions and write-offs.
S. 105B(3): effect of shares ceasing to be treated as shares of a different class under s. 104(4) when election made under section s. 105A.
S. 150(4): priority of special identification rules for BES shares (applies in relation to shares issued on or before 31 December 1993).
S. 150A(5): s. 104 disapplied in relation to shares to which relief is attributable under the enterprise investment scheme (applies to shares issued on or after 1 January 1994).
S. 151B(1): s. 104 does not apply to shares in a venture capital trust eligible for relief under s. 151A.
S. 151B(7): s. 104 applies to deemed reacquisition of shares in a venture capital trust following disposal deemed to occur on a withdrawal of approval.
Sch. 5B, para. 4(4C): s. 104 does not apply to shares to which CGT deferral relief, but not EIS or BES relief, is attributable.
Sch. 5C, para. 4(2): identification rules for disposal of shares in venture capital trusts following postponement of a gain.
Sch. 8B, para. 6(7): investments in social enterprises: s. 104, 105 and 106A do not apply to assets to which relief under Sch. 8B is attributable if SI relief under ITA 2007, Pt. 5B of ITA 2007 is not also attributable to them.
ICTA 1988, s. 440A(6): application to subpools of securities in respect of different categories of business of insurance company.
ICTA 1988, s. 576(5): shares held as in s. 104(4) so treated in relation to relief against income for a loss on unquoted shares in a trading company.
FA 1998, s. 125(5): in s. 104(3) and (5) reference to s. 110A omitted where a gain is treated as chargeable after 6 April 1998 in relation to an actual or deemed disposal occurring before that date.
FA 2000, Sch. 15, para. 93(6) share pooling does not apply to investment relief shares acquired under the CVS.
SI 2009/3001, reg. 43: special application of s. 104 in relation to interests in offshore funds.

Statements of practice – SP 2/99: simplified tax scheme for individuals investing regular sums in monthly savings schemes of investing funds (supersedes SP 3/89 and SP 2/97).

Notes – S. 21–34: general meaning of "disposal" and "assets".
S. 42: attribution of allowable expenditure on a part disposal.
S. 56: indexation allowance on a part disposal.
S. 288: interpretation, including meaning of "company", "recognised stock exchange", reference to shares as including stock, "class" in relation to securities as being in one company and reference to sections as being those of this Act.
TMA 1970, s. 25: returns of information which may be required from issuing houses, stockbrokers, auctioneers etc.

105 Disposal on or before day of acquisition of shares and other unidentified assets

105(1) Paragraphs (a) and (b) below shall apply where securities of the same class are acquired or disposed of by the same person on the same day and in the same capacity–

(a) all the securities so acquired shall be treated as acquired by a single transaction and all the securities so disposed of shall be treated as disposed of by a single transaction, and

(b) all the securities so acquired shall, so far as their quantity does not exceed that of the securities so disposed of, be identified with those securities.

105(2) Where the quantity of securities disposed of by any person exceeds the aggregate quantity of–

(a) the securities (if any) which are required by subsection (1) above to be identified with securities acquired on the day of the disposal,

(b) the securities (if any) which are required by section 106A(5) to be identified with securities acquired after the day of the disposal, and

(c) the securities (if any) which are required by any of the provisions of sections 104, 106A or 107, or of Schedule 2, to be identified with securities acquired before the day of the disposal,

the disposal shall be treated as diminishing a quantity of securities subsequently acquired, and as so diminishing any quantity so acquired at an earlier date, rather than one so acquired at a later date.

105(3) None of the securities which, by virtue of this section, are identified with other securities shall be regarded as forming part of an existing section 104 holding or as constituting a section 104 holding.

105(4) Subsection (5) applies if an individual–

(a) *acquires shares* ("*the relevant shares*") of the same class, on the same day and in the same capacity, and

(b) some of the relevant shares are relevant EMI shares (as defined by section 169I(7C) to (7G)).

105(5) This section has effect as if–

(a) paragraph (a) of subsection (1) required the relevant EMI sharesto be treated as acquired by the individual by a single transaction separate from the remainder of the relevant shares (which are also to be treated by virtue of that paragraph as acquired by the individual by a single transaction), and

(b) subsection (1) required the relevant EMI sharesto be treated as disposed of after the remainder of the relevant shares.

History – Words at beginning of s. 105(1) "Paragraphs (a) and (b) below" substituted by FA 1998, s. 124(2) as respects any disposal on or after 6 April 1998.

In s. 105(2)(b), the word "section" substituted for "any of the provisions of section 106 or" by FA 2006, s. 72(2)(b)(i), in relation to any disposal made on or after 5 December 2005.

In s. 105(2)(c), the reference to s. 106 omitted by FA 2006, s. 72(2)(b)(ii) and repealed by FA 2006, s. 178 and Sch. 26, Pt. 3(9), in relation to any disposal made on or after 5 December 2005.

S. 105(2) substituted by FA 1998, s. 124(2) as respects any disposal on or after 6 April 1998.

S. 105(3) inserted by FA 2008, s. 8 and Sch. 2, para. 86 with effect in relation to disposals made on or after 6 April 2008 (FA 2008, Sch. 2, para. 100).

S. 105(4) inserted by FA 2013, s. 64 and Sch. 24, para. 3, with effect in relation to disposals of shares on or after 6 April 2013, subject to the transitional provisions in FA 2013, Sch. 24, para. 6.

S. 105(5) inserted by FA 2013, s. 64 and Sch. 24, para. 3, with effect in relation to disposals of shares on or after 6 April 2013, subject to the transitional provisions in FA 2013, Sch. 24, para. 6.

Derivations – CGTA 1979, s. 66(1), (2); FA 1985, Sch. 19, para. 17(2).

Cross references – FA 2012, s. 121: s. 105 applies if applicable pooling rules apply in relation to UK life assurance companies carrying on long-term business.

S. 105A: shares acquired on same day: election for alternative treatment.

S. 108: s. 105 does not apply to relevant securities as defined in s. 108 – instead, s. 108 applies to those securities.

S. 150(4): priority of special identification rules for BES shares (applies in relation to shares issued on or before 31 December 1993).

S. 150A(5): s. 105 disapplied in relation to shares to which relief is attributable under the enterprise investment scheme (applies to shares issued on or after 1 January 1994).

S. 151B(1): s. 105 does not apply to shares in a venture capital trust eligible for relief under s. 151A.

S. 151B(7): s. 105 applies to deemed reacquisition of shares in a venture capital trust following disposal deemed to occur on a withdrawal of approval.

Sch. 2, para. 2(3), 18(3): priority over rules for determining shares held on 6 April 1965 where disposals matched with acquisitions on a LIFO basis.

Sch. 5B, para. 4(4C): s. 105 does not apply to shares to which CGT deferral relief, but not EIS or BES relief, is attributable.

Sch. 5C, para. 4(2): identification rules for disposal of shares in venture capital trusts following postponement of a gain.

Sch. 8B, para. 6(7): investments in social enterprises: s. 104, 105 and 106A do not apply to assets to which relief under Sch. 8B is attributable if SI relief under ITA 2007, Pt. 5B of ITA 2007 is not also attributable to them.

ICTA 1988, s. 440A(5): application as if different securities with regard to those held in separate subpools in respect of different categories of business of insurance company.

FA 1998, s. 124(8): identification rules for capital gains tax (but not corporation tax) where disposals occur between 17 March 1998 and 5 April 1998 (inclusive).

FA 2000, Sch. 15 para. 93(6): shares pooling does not apply to investment relief shares acquired under the CVS.

HMRC interpretations – IR Int. 218: application of the FA 1998 rules for share pooling.

IR Int. 224: share pooling where shares are transferred between a married couple at no gain/no loss.

Notes – S. 21–34: general meaning of "disposal".

S. 288: interpretation, including "class" in relation to securities as being in one company and reference to sections as being those of this Act.

105A Shares acquired on same day: election for alternative treatment

105A(1) Subsection (2) below applies where an individual–

(a) acquires shares ("the relevant shares") of the same class, on the same day and in the same capacity, and

(b) some of the relevant shares ("the tax-advantaged-scheme shares") are shares acquired by him as a result of–

(i) the exercise of a qualifying option within the meaning given by section 527(4) of ITEPA 2003 (enterprise management incentives) in circumstances where section 530 or 531 of that Act (exercise of option to acquire shares) applies, or

(ii) the exercise of an option to which Chapter 7 or 8 of Part 7 of that Act (share option schemes) applies in circumstances where section 519(1) or 524(1) of that Act applies.

105A(2) Where the individual first makes a disposal of any of the relevant shares, he may elect for subsections (3) to (5) below to have effect in relation to that disposal and all subsequent disposals of any of those shares.

105A(3) In circumstances where section 105 applies, that section shall have effect as if–

(a) paragraph (a) of subsection (1) of that section required the tax-advantaged-scheme shares to be treated as acquired by the individual by a single transaction separate from the remainder of the relevant shares (which shall also be treated by virtue of that paragraph as acquired by the individual by a single transaction), and

(b) subsection (1) of that section required the tax-advantaged-scheme shares to be treated as disposed of after the remainder of the relevant shares.

105A(4) If the relevant shares include shares to which relief under Chapter 3 of Part 7 of the Taxes Act, relief under Part 5 of ITA 2007 or deferral relief (within the meaning of Schedule 5B to this Act) is attributable–

(a) paragraph 4(4) of that Schedule has effect as if it required the tax-advantaged-scheme shares falling within paragraph (a), (b), (c) or (d) of that provision to be treated as disposed of after the remainder of the relevant shares falling within the paragraph in question, and

(b) section 299 of the Taxes Act or section 246 of ITA 2007 has effect for the purposes of section 150A(4) below as if it required–

  (i) the tax-advantaged-scheme shares falling within paragraph (a), (b), (c) or (d) of subsection (6A) of section 299 of the Taxes Act or subsection (3) of section 246 of ITA 2007 to be treated as disposed of after the remainder of the relevant shares falling within the paragraph in question, and

  (ii) the tax-advantaged-scheme shares to which subsection (6B) of section 299 of the Taxes Act or subsection (4) of section 246 of ITA 2007 applies to be treated as disposed of after the remainder of the relevant shares to which that subsection applies.

105A(5) Where section 127 applies in relation to any of the relevant shares ("the reorganisation shares"), that section shall apply separately to such of those shares as are tax-advantaged-scheme shares and to the remainder of the reorganisation shares (so that those tax-advantaged-scheme shares and the remainder of the reorganisation shares are treated as comprised in separate holdings of original shares and identified with separate new holdings).

105A(6) In subsection (5)–

(a) the reference to section 127 includes a reference to that section as it is applied by virtue of any enactment relating to chargeable gains, and

(b) **"original shares"** and **"new holding"** have the same meaning as in section 127 or (as the case may be) that section as applied by virtue of the enactment in question.

105A(7) For the purposes of subsection (1) above–

(a) any shares to which relief under Chapter 3 of Part 7 of the Taxes Act or relief under Part 5 of ITA 2007 is attributable and which were transferred to an individual as mentioned in section 304 of the Taxes Act or section 245 of ITA 2007, and

(b) any shares to which deferral relief (within the meaning of Schedule 5B to this Act), but not relief under that Chapter or relief under that Part, is attributable and which were acquired by an individual on a disposal to which section 58 above applies,

shall be treated as acquired by the individual on the day on which they were issued.

105A(8) In this section the references to Chapter 3 of Part 7, section 299 and section 304 of the Taxes Act shall be read as references to those provisions as they apply to shares issued after 31st December 1993 (enterprise investment scheme).

105A(9) In this section references to Part 5 of ITA 2007 or any provision of that Part are to a Part or provision that applies only in relation to shares issued after 5 April 2007.

History – In s. 105A, in all places, the words "tax-advantaged-scheme" substituted for the words "approved-scheme" by FA 2014, s. 51 and Sch. 8, para. 122(2), which is treated as having come into force on 6 April 2014, subject to the transitional provisions in FA 2014, Sch. 8, para. 147 to 157.

In s. 105A(1)(b)(ii), the word "approved", which appeared before the words "share option schemes", omitted by FA 2014, s. 51 and Sch. 8, para. 122(3), which is treated as having come into force on 6 April 2014, subject to the transitional provisions in FA 2014, Sch. 8, para. 147 to 157.

S. 105A(1)(b)(i) and (ii) substituted by F(No. 2)A 2005, s. 35 and Sch. 5, para. 3(2) with effect, in accordance with F(No. 2)A 2005, Sch. 5, para. 6(1), in relation to cases where option concerned, whenever acquired, is exercised on or after 2 December 2004.

In s. 105A(4), the words ", relief under Part 5 of ITA 2007" inserted by ITA 2007, s. 1027 and Sch. 1, para. 306(2)(a), with effect from 6 April 2007.

In s. 105A(4)(a), the words "or section 246 of ITA 2007" inserted by ITA 2007, s. 1027 and Sch. 1, para. 306(2)(b), with effect from 6 April 2007.

In s. 105A(4)(b)(i), the words "of the Taxes Act or subsection (3) of section 246 of ITA 2007" substituted for "of that Act" by ITA 2007, s. 1027 and Sch. 1, para. 306(2)(c), with effect from 6 April 2007.

In s. 105A(4)(b)(ii), the words "section 299 of the Taxes Act or subsection (4) of section 246 of ITA 2007" substituted for "that section" by ITA 2007, s. 1027 and Sch. 1, para. 306(2)(d), with effect from 6 April 2007.

In s. 105A(7)(a), the words "or relief under Part 5 of ITA 2007" inserted by ITA 2007, s. 1027 and Sch. 1, para. 306(3)(a) and the words "the Taxes Act or section 245 of ITA 2007" substituted for "that Act" by ITA 2007, s. 1027, Sch. 1, para. 306(3)(b), both with effect from 6 April 2007.

In s. 105A(7)(b), the words "or relief under that Part" inserted by ITA 2007, s. 1027 and Sch. 1, para. 306(3)(c), with effect from 6 April 2007.

S. 105A(9) inserted by ITA 2007, s. 1027 and Sch. 1, para. 306(4), with effect from 6 April 2007.

S. 105A inserted by FA 2002, s. 50(1) with effect in relation to shares acquired by an individual on or after 6 April 2002.

Cross references – FA 2002, s. 50(3): for purposes of commencement of s. 105A, any shares to which relief is attributable under ICTA 1988, Pt. 7, Ch. 3 and which were transferred to an individual as mentioned in ICTA 1988, s. 304, and shares to which deferral relief (see Sch. 5B) is attributable and which were acquired by an individual on a disposal to which s. 58 applies, are treated as acquired by the individual on the day on which they were issued.

105B Provision supplementary to section 105A

105B(1) The provisions of section 105A have effect in the case of any disposal notwithstanding that some or all of the securities disposed of are otherwise identified–

(a) by the disposal, or

(b) by a transfer or delivery giving effect to it.

105B(2) An election must be made, by a notice given to an officer of the Board, on or before the first anniversary of the 31st January next following the year of assessment in which the individual first makes a disposal of any of the relevant shares.

105B(3) Where–

(a) an election is made in respect of the relevant shares, and

(b) any shares (**"the other shares"**) acquired by the individual on the same day and in the same capacity as the relevant shares cease to be treated under section 104(4) as shares of a different class from the relevant shares,

the election shall have effect in respect of the other shares from the time they cease to be so treated.

105B(4) In determining for the purposes of section 105A(2) and subsection (2) above whether the individual has made a disposal of any of the relevant shares, sections 122(1) and 128(3) shall be disregarded.

105B(5) No election may be made in respect of ordinary shares in a venture capital trust

For this purpose **"ordinary shares"** has the meaning given in section 151A(7).

105B(6) For the purposes of section 105A, shares in a company shall not be treated as being of the same class unless they are so treated by the practice of a recognised stock exchange, or would be so treated if dealt with on that recognised stock exchange.

105B(7) In section 105A(2) to (5) and subsections (2) to (4) above, any reference to the relevant shares or to the tax-advantaged-scheme shares includes a reference to the securities (if any) directly or indirectly derived from the shares in question by virtue of one or more applications of section 127 (including that section as applied by virtue of any enactment relating to chargeable gains).

105B(8) In this section–

"the tax-advantaged-scheme shares" has the same meaning as in section 105A;

"election" means an election under that section;

"the relevant shares" has the same meaning as in that section; and

"securities" has the meaning given in section 104(3)and in subsection (4) the reference to section 128(3) includes a reference to that provision as it is applied by virtue of any enactment relating to chargeable gains.

History – In s. 105B(7), the words "tax-advantaged-scheme" substituted for the words "approved-scheme" by FA 2014, s. 51 and Sch. 8, para. 123, which is treated as having come into force on 6 April 2014, subject to the transitional provisions in FA 2014, Sch. 8, para. 147 to 157.

In s. 105B(8), the words "tax-advantaged-scheme" substituted for the words "approved-scheme" by FA 2014, s. 51 and Sch. 8, para. 123, which is treated as having come into force on 6 April 2014, subject to the transitional provisions in FA 2014, Sch. 8, para. 147 to 157.

S. 105B inserted by FA 2002, s. 50(1) with effect in relation to shares acquired by an individual on or after 6 April 2002.

Cross references – FA 2002, s. 50(3): for purposes of commencement of s. 105B, any shares to which relief is attributable under ICTA 1988, Pt. 7, Ch. 3 and which were transferred to an individual as mentioned in ICTA 1988, s. 304, and shares to which deferral relief (see Sch. 5B) is attributable and which were acquired by an individual on a disposal to which s. 58 applies, are treated as acquired by the individual on the day on which they were issued.

106 Disposal of shares and securities by company within prescribed period of acquisition

106 [Ceased to have effect by virtue of FA 2006, s. 72(1) and repealed by FA 2006, s. 178 and Sch. 26, Pt. 3(9).]

History – S. 106 ceased to have effect by virtue of FA 2006, s. 72(1) and repealed by FA 2006, s. 178 and Sch. 26, Pt. 3(9) in relation to any disposal made on or after 5 December 2005.

106A Identification of securities: capital gains tax

History – In the heading, the words "general rules for" omitted by FA 2008, s. 8 and Sch. 2, para. 87(7) with effect in relation to disposals made on or after 6 April 2008 (FA 2008, Sch. 2, para. 100).

106A(1) This section has effect for the purposes of capital gains tax (but not corporation tax) where any securities are disposed of by any person.

106A(2) The securities disposed of shall be identified in accordance with the following provisions of this section with securities of the same class that have been acquired by the person making the disposal.

106A(3) The provisions of this section have effect in the case of any disposal notwithstanding that some or all of the securities disposed of are otherwise identified–

(a) by the disposal, or

(b) by a transfer or delivery giving effect to it;

but where a person disposes of securities in one capacity, they shall not be identified under those provisions with any securities which he holds, or can dispose of, only in some other capacity.

106A(4) Securities disposed of on an earlier date shall be identified before securities disposed of on a later date; and, accordingly, securities disposed of by a later disposal shall not be identified with securities already identified as disposed of by an earlier disposal.

106A(5) Subject to subsection (4) above, if within the period of thirty days after the disposal the person making it acquires securities of the same class, the securities disposed of shall be identified–

(a) with securities acquired by him within that period, rather than with other securities;

(aa) with securities acquired by him within that period which are not relevant EMI shares, rather than with securities acquired by him within that period which are relevant EMI shares; and

(b) subject to paragraph (aa), with securities acquired at an earlier time within that period, rather than with securities acquired at a later time within that period.

106A(5ZA) None of the securities which, by virtue of subsection (5) above, are identified with other securities shall be regarded as forming part of an existing section 104 holding or as constituting a section 104 holding.

106A(5A) Subsection (5) above shall not require securities to be identified with securities which the person making the disposal acquires at a time when–

(a) he is not resident in the United Kingdom, or

(b) he is resident in the United Kingdom but is Treaty non-resident.

106A(6) Subject to subsections (4) and (5) above, relevant securities disposed of shall be identified with relevant securities acquired at a later time, rather than with relevant securities acquired at an earlier time.

106A(6A) Subject to subsections (4) and (5) above, a company's shares which are disposed of shall be identified–

(a) with relevant EMI shares, rather than with other shares, and

(b) with relevant EMI sharesacquired at an earlier time rather than with relevant EMI sharesacquired at a later time.

106A(6B) No shares identified with relevant EMI sharesby virtue of subsection (6A)(a) or (b) above shall be regarded as forming part of an existing section 104 holding or as constituting a section 104 holding.

106A(7) [Omitted by FA 2008, s. 8 and Sch. 2, para. 87(4).]

106A(8) [Omitted by FA 2008, s. 8 and Sch. 2, para. 87(5).]

106A(9) The identification rules set out in the preceding provisions of this section have effect subject to subsection (1) of section 105, and securities disposed of shall not be identified with securities acquired after the disposal except in accordance with that section or subsection (5) above.

106A(10) In this section–

"relevant EMI shares" has the meaning given by section 169I(7C) to (7G),

"securities" means any securities within the meaning of section 104 or any relevant securities, and

"relevant securities" means–

(a) securities within the meaning of Chapter 2 of Part 12 of ITA 2007 (accrued income profits),

(b) qualifying corporate bonds, and

(c) securities which are interests in a non-reporting fund, within the meaning of the Offshore Funds (Tax) Regulations 2009 (S.I. 2009/3001) (see regulation 4(2)).

106A(11) For the purposes of this section securities of a company shall not be treated as being of the same class unless they are so treated by the practice of a recognised stock exchange, or would be so treated if dealt with on that recognised stock exchange.

History – S. 106A(5)(aa) inserted (and the word "and" before it omitted) by FA 2013, s. 64 and Sch. 24, para. 4(2)(a) and (b), with effect in relation to disposals of shares on or after 6 April 2013, subject to the transitional provisions in FA 2013, Sch. 24, para. 6.
In s. 106A(5)(b), the words "subject to paragraph (aa)," inserted by FA 2013, s. 64 and Sch. 24, para. 4(2)(c), with effect in relation to disposals of shares on or after 6 April 2013, subject to the transitional provisions in FA 2013, Sch. 24, para. 6.
S. 106A(5ZA) inserted by FA 2008, s. 8 and Sch. 2, para. 87(2) with effect in relation to disposals made on or after 6 April 2008 (FA 2008, Sch. 2, para. 100).
In s. 106A(5A)(a), the words "not resident" substituted for the words "neither resident nor ordinarily resident" by FA 2013, s. 219 and *Sch. 46, para. 97(a), with effect in relation* to a person's liability to capital gains tax for the tax year 2013–14 or any subsequent tax year, without prejudice to any provision in FA 2013, Sch. 46, Pt. 3 about the application of a particular amendment.
In s. 106A(5A)(b), the words "or ordinarily resident" omitted by FA 2013, s. 219 and Sch. 46, para. 97(b), with effect in relation to a person's liability to capital gains tax for the tax year 2013–14 or any subsequent tax year, without prejudice to any provision in FA 2013, Sch. 46, Pt. 3 about the application of a particular amendment.
S. 106A(5A) inserted by FA 2006, s. 74(2), with effect in relation to any acquisition made on or after 22 March 2006.

In s. 106A(6), the word "relevant" inserted before "securities" three times by FA 2008, s. 8 and Sch. 2, para. 87(3) with effect in relation to disposals made on or after 6 April 2008 (FA 2008, Sch. 2, para. 100).
S. 106A(6A) and (6B) inserted by FA 2013, s. 64 and Sch. 24, para. 4(3), with effect in relation to disposals of shares on or after 6 April 2013, subject to the transitional provisions in FA 2013, Sch. 24, para. 6.
S. 106A(7) omitted by FA 2008, s. 8 and Sch. 2, para. 87(4) with effect in relation to disposals made on or after 6 April 2008 (FA 2008, Sch. 2, para. 100).
S. 106A(8) omitted by FA 2008, s. 8 and Sch. 2, para. 87(5) with effect in relation to disposals made on or after 6 April 2008 (FA 2008, Sch. 2, para. 100).
In s. 106A(10), the definition of "relevant EMI shares" inserted by FA 2013, s. 64 and Sch. 24, para. 4(4), with effect in relation to disposals of shares on or after 6 April 2013, subject to the transitional provisions in FA 2013, Sch. 24, para. 6.
In s. 106A(10), in the definition of "relevant securities", para. (c) substituted by SI 2011/1211, reg. 44(4), with effect in relation to disposals made on or after 27 May 2011.
S. 106A(10) substituted by FA 2008, s. 8 and Sch. 2, para. 87(6) with effect in relation to disposals made on or after 6 April 2008 (FA 2008, Sch. 2, para. 100).
S. 106A inserted by FA 1998, s. 124(1), as respects any disposal on or after 6 April 1998.

Cross references – S. 150A(5): s. 106A disapplied in relation to shares to which relief is attributable under the enterprise investment scheme in respect of shares issued on or after 6 April 1998.
Sch. 5B, para. 4(4C): s. 106A does not apply to shares to which CGT deferral relief, but not EIS or BES relief, is attributable.
Sch. 8B, para. 6(7): investments in social enterprises: s. 104, 105 and 106A do not apply to assets to which relief under Sch. 8B is attributable if SI relief under ITA 2007, Pt. 5B of ITA 2007 is not also attributable to them.
FA 1998, s. 124(8): identification rules for capital gains tax (but not corporation tax) where disposals occur between 17 March 1998 and 5 April 1998 (inclusive).
SI 1989/469, reg. 27(2), (3): modifications of s. 106A for pooling and identifying personal equity plan investments or for identifying securities which are eligible to become plan investments.
FA 2013, Sch. 24, para. 6: modifications of s. 106A(6A) and (6B) for identification of shares disposed of where an election under FA 2013, Sch. 24, para. 6(3) has been made.

HMRC interpretations – IR Int. 218: application of the FA 1998 rules for share pooling.
IR Int. 224: share pooling where shares are transferred between a married couple at no gain/no loss.

107 Identification of securities etc: general rules for corporation tax

History – In the heading, the words "for corporation tax" inserted by FA 2008, s. 8 and Sch. 2, para. 88 with effect in relation to disposals made on or after 6 April 2008 (FA 2008, Sch. 2, para. 100).

107(1) This section has effect for the purposes of corporation tax where any securities are disposed of by a company.

107(1A) The securities disposed of shall be identified in accordance with the following provisions of this section with securities of the same class that have been acquired by the company making the disposal and could be comprised in that disposal.

107(2) The provisions of this section have effect in the case of any disposal notwithstanding that some or all of the securities disposed of are otherwise identified–

(a) by the disposal, or

(b) by a transfer or delivery giving effect to it;

but where a company disposes of securities in one capacity, they shall not be identified with securities which it holds, or can dispose of, only in some other capacity.

107(3) Without prejudice to section 105 if, within a period of 10 days, a number of securities are acquired and subsequently a number of securities disposed of and, apart from this subsection–

(a) the securities acquired would increase the size of, or constitute a section 104 holding, and

(b) the securities disposed of would decrease the size of, or extinguish, the same section 104 holding,

then, subject to subsections (4) and (5) below, the securities disposed of shall be identified with the securities acquired and none of them shall be regarded as forming part of an existing section 104 holding or constituting a section 104 holding.

107(4) If, in a case falling within subsection (3) above, the number of securities acquired exceeds the number disposed of–

(a) the excess shall be regarded as forming part of an existing section 104 holding or, as the case may be, as constituting a section 104 holding; and

(b) if the securities acquired were acquired at different times (within the 10 days referred to in subsection (3) above) the securities disposed of shall be identified with securities acquired at an earlier time rather than with securities acquired at a later time.

107(5) If, in a case falling within subsection (3) above, the number of securities disposed of exceeds the number acquired, the excess shall not be identified in accordance with that subsection.

107(6) Securities which, by virtue of subsection (3) above, do not form part of or constitute a section 104 holding shall be treated for the purposes of section 54(2) as relevant securities within the meaning of section 108.

107(7) The identification rules set out in subsections (8) and (9) below have effect subject to section 105 but, subject to that, have priority according to the order in which they are so set out.

107(8) Securities disposed of shall be identified with securities forming part of a section 104 holding rather than with other securities.

107(9) Securities disposed of shall be identified with securities forming part of a 1982 holding, within the meaning of section 109, rather than with other securities and, subject to that, shall be identified with securities acquired at a later time rather than with securities acquired at an earlier time.

History – S. 107(1), (1A) and (2) substituted by FA 1998, s. 124(3) as respects any disposal of securities on or after 6 April 1998. In s. 107(3), (4), (6) and (8) references to a "section 104 holding" substituted for references to a "new holding" by FA 1998, s. 123(5), with effect in relation to any disposal on or after 6 April 1998 of any securities (whenever acquired).

Derivations – S. 107(1), (2): FA 1985, Sch. 19, para. 16(1), (2).
S. 107(3)–(6): FA 1985, Sch. 19, para. 18.
S. 107(7)–(9): FA 1985, Sch. 19, para. 19.

Cross references – S. 54(2): in determining indexation allowance, the indexed rise in expenditure on the acquisition of relevant securities disposed of within ten days is nil.
S. 150(4): priority of special identification rules for BES shares, s. 107 being disapplied (applies in relation to shares issued on or before 31 December 1993 but not in relation to disposals made on or after 6 April 1998).
S. 150A(5): s. 107 disapplied in relation to shares to which relief is attributable under the enterprise investment scheme (applies in relation to shares issued on or after 1 January 1994 but before 6 April 1998).
S. 151B(1): s. 107 does not apply to shares in a venture capital trust eligible for relief under s. 151A.
S. 151B(7): s. 107 applies to deemed reacquisition of shares in a venture capital trust following disposal deemed to occur on a withdrawal of approval.
Sch. 5C para. 4(2): identification rules for disposal of shares in venture capital trust following postponement of a gain.
FA 2000, Sch. 15 para. 93(6): shares pooling does not apply to investment relief shares acquired under the CVS.

Notes – S. 21–34: general meaning of "disposal".
S. 288: interpretation, including "class" in relation to securities as being in one company and reference to sections as being those of this Act.

108 Identification of relevant securities for corporation tax

History – In the heading, the words "for corporation tax" inserted by FA 2008, s. 8 and Sch. 2, para. 89 with effect in relation to disposals made on or after 6 April 2008 (FA 2008, Sch. 2, para. 100).

108(A1) This section has effect for the purposes of corporation tax where any relevant securities are disposed of by a company.

108(1) In this section **"relevant securities"** means–

(a) securities, within the meaning of Chapter 2 of Part 12 of ITA 2007 (accrued income profits);

(aa) qualifying corporate bonds;

(b) [Repealed by FA 1996, s. 205 and Sch. 41, Pt. V(3).]

(c) securities which are interests in a non-reporting fund, within the meaning of regulations under section 354(1) of TIOPA 2010 (see Part 2 of the Offshore Funds (Tax) Regulations 2009 (S.I. 2009/3001));

and shares or securities of a company shall not be treated for the purposes of this section as being of the same class unless they are so treated by the practice of a recognised stock exchange or would be so treated if dealt with on a recognised stock exchange.

108(2) Where a company disposes of relevant securities, the securities disposed of shall be identified in accordance with the rules contained in this section with the securities of the same class acquired by the company which could be comprised in that disposal, and shall be so identified notwithstanding that they are otherwise identified by the disposal or by a transfer or delivery giving effect to it (but so that where a company disposes of securities in one capacity, they shall not be identified with securities which it holds or can dispose of only in some other capacity).

108(3) Relevant securities disposed of on an earlier date shall be identified before securities disposed of on a later date, and the identification of the securities first disposed of shall accordingly determine the securities which could be comprised in the later disposal.

108(4) Relevant securities disposed of for transfer or delivery on a particular date or in a particular period–

(a) shall not be identified with securities acquired for transfer or delivery on a later date or in a later period; and

(b) shall be identified with securities acquired for transfer or delivery on or before that date or in or before that period, but on or after the date of the disposal, rather than with securities not so acquired.

108(5) The relevant securities disposed of shall be identified–

(a) with securities acquired within the 12 months preceding the disposal rather than with securities not so acquired, and with securities so acquired on an earlier date rather than with securities so acquired on a later date, and

(b) subject to paragraph (a) above, with securities acquired on a later date rather than with securities acquired on an earlier date; and

(c) with securities acquired at different times on any one day in as nearly as may be equal proportions.

108(6) The rules contained in the preceding subsections shall have priority according to the order in which they are so contained.

108(7) Notwithstanding anything in subsections (3) to (5) above, where, under arrangements designed to postpone the transfer or delivery of relevant securities disposed of, a company by a single bargain acquires securities for transfer or delivery on a particular date or in a particular period and disposes of them for transfer or delivery on a later date or in a later period, then–

(a) the securities disposed of by that bargain shall be identified with the securities thereby acquired; and

(b) securities previously disposed of which, but for the operation of paragraph (a) above in relation to acquisitions for transfer or delivery on the earlier date or in the earlier period, would have been identified with the securities acquired by that bargain–

  (i) shall, subject to subsection (3) above, be identified with any available securities acquired for such transfer or delivery (that is to say, any securities so acquired other than securities to which paragraph (a) above applies and other than securities with which securities disposed of for such transfer or delivery would be identified apart from this subsection); and

  (ii) in so far as they cannot be so identified shall be treated as disposed of for transfer or delivery on the later date, or in the later period, mentioned above.

108(8) This section shall not apply–

(a) where the disposal is of quoted securities (within the meaning of paragraph 8 of Schedule 2), unless an election has been made with respect to the securities under paragraph 4 of that Schedule or under section 109(4), or

(b) where the disposal is of securities as respects which paragraph 17 or 18 of Schedule 2 has effect.

History – S. 108(A1) inserted by FA 1998, s. 124(4), as respects any disposal on or after 6 April 1998.
In s. 108(1)(a), the words "Chapter 2 of Part 12 of ITA 2007 (accrued income profits)" substituted for the words "section 710 of the Taxes Act" by ITA 2007, s. 1027 and Sch. 1, para. 307, with effect from 6 April 2007.
S. 108(1)(aa) inserted by FA 1996, Sch. 14, para. 59, and s. 108(1)(b) repealed by FA 1996, s. 205 and Sch. 41, Pt. V(3), with effect for corporation tax purposes, for accounting periods ending after 31 March 1996 and, for income tax, in relation to years after 1995–1996.
In s. 108(1)(c), the words "under section 354(1) of TIOPA 2010" substituted for "made under section 41(1) of the Finance Act 2008" by TIOPA 2010, s. 374 and Sch. 8, para. 164, with effect for corporation tax purposes for accounting periods ending on or after 1 April 2010, for income tax and capital gains tax purposes for the tax year 2010–11 and subsequent tax years, and for petroleum revenue tax purposes for chargeable periods beginning on or after 1 July 2010.
In s. 108(1)(c), the words", or have at any time been,", which appeared after the words "securities which are", omitted by SI 2009/3001, reg. 127(2)(a), and repealed by SI 2009/3001, reg. 13(2) and Sch. 2, with effect from 1 December 2009 for various purposes (in accordance with the provisions of SI 2009/3001, reg. 1), subject to transitional and savings provisions in SI 2009/3001, Sch. 1.
In s. 108(1)(c), the words "interests in a non-reporting fund, within the meaning of regulations made under section 41(1) of the Finance Act 2008 (see Part 2 of the Offshore Funds (Tax) Regulations 2009 (S.I. 2009/3001))" substituted for the words "material interests in a non-qualifying offshore fund, within the meaning of Chapter V of Part XVII of that Act" by SI 2009/3001, reg. 127(2)(b), with effect from 1 December 2009 for various purposes (in accordance with the provisions of SI 2009/3001, reg. 1), subject to transitional and savings provisions in SI 2009/3001, Sch. 1.
In s. 108(2) and (7) references to a "company", "the company" and "it" substituted for references to, respectively, "person", "him" and "he" by FA 1998, s. 124(5) as respects any disposal on or after 6 April 1998.
In s. 108(8), the words "shall have effect subject to section 106 but" (after "This section") omitted by FA 2006, s. 72(2)(c) and repealed by FA 2006, s. 178 and Sch. 26, Pt. 3(9), in relation to any disposal made on or after 5 December 2005.

Derivations – FA 1982, s. 88.

Cross references – S. 53(4): s. 108 is subject to the following indexation allowance provisions:

- s. 56: part disposals and no gain, no loss disposals;
- s. 57: receipts etc. which are not treated as disposals but affect relevant allowable expenditure;
- s. 109: pre-1982 share pools;
- s. 110: "new holding" of shares;
- s. 113: call on shares resulting in consideration given more than 12 months after issue;
- s. 131: consideration given for a new holding on a reorganisation;
- s. 145: consideration given for both a call option and the resulting acquisition.

S. 54(2): for indexation allowance, the indexed rise in expenditure attributable to the acquisition of relevant securities disposed of within ten days is nil.
S. 104(3): acquisitions of relevant shares are not pooled.
S. 105: provisions of s. 105 do not apply to relevant securities.
S. 150(4): priority of special identification rules for BES shares (applies in relation to shares issued on or before 31 December 1993).
Sch. 2, para. 1, 2, 4, 8, 17, 18: in relation to assets held on 6 April 1965, election for pooling of quoted securities (defined by reference to quotation in six-year period to 6 April 1965 but including unit trust rights and excluding employee shares), election for budget day value and identification rules for remaining shares. ICTA 1988, s. 710: definition of security by reference to loan stock or similar security but not shares (other than certain shares in a building society) and excluding certain quasi-equity foreign-held securities, savings certificates and premium-only redemption securities. ICTA 1988, Pt. XVII, Ch. V (s. 757–764): definition of material interest in a non-qualifying offshore fund by reference to an interest in a non-resident company, unit trust scheme or arrangement the value of which is realisable within seven years.
FA 1998, s. 124(8): identification rules for capital gains tax (but not corporation tax) where disposals occur between 17 March 1998 and 5 April 1998 (inclusive).

Notes – S. 21–34: general meaning of "disposal" and the timing of certain disposals.
S. 288: interpretation, including the meaning of "company", "recognised stock exchange", "the Taxes Act" as ICTA 1988, "shares" as including stock, "class" in relation to securities as being in one company and reference to sections as being those of this Act.

109 Corporation tax: pre-April 1982 share pools

History – In the heading, the words "Corporation tax: pre-April" substituted for the words "Pre-April" by FA 2008, s. 8 and Sch. 2, para. 90(3) with effect in relation to disposals made on or after 6 April 2008 (FA 2008, Sch. 2, para. 100).

109(1) For the purposes of corporation tax, this section has effect in relation to any 1982 holding, and in this section **"1982 holding"** means a holding which, immediately before the coming into force of this section, was a 1982 holding for the purposes of Part II of Schedule 19 to the Finance Act 1985.

109(2) Subject to subsections (3) to (5) below–

(a) the holding shall continue to be regarded as a single asset for the purposes of this Act (subject to express provision to the contrary), but one which cannot grow by the acquisition of additional securities of the same class, and

(b) every sum, which on a disposal of the holding, would be an item of relevant allowable expenditure shall be regarded for the purposes of section 54 as having been incurred at such a time that the month which determines RI in the formula in subsection (1) of that section is March 1982.

Securities of a company shall not be treated for the purposes of this section as being of the same class unless they are so treated by the practice of a recognised stock exchange or would be so treated if dealt with on a recognised stock exchange.

109(3) Nothing in subsection (2) above affects the operation of section 127 in relation to the holding, but without prejudice to section 131.

109(4) If a person so elects, quoted securities, as defined in paragraph 8 of Schedule 2 which are covered by the election–

(a) shall be treated as an accretion to an existing 1982 holding or, as the case may be, as constituting a new 1982 holding; and

(b) shall be excluded from paragraph 2 of that Schedule;

and the relevant allowable expenditure which is attributable to that 1982 holding shall be adjusted or determined accordingly.

109(5) Paragraphs 4(8) to (13) and 5 to 8 of Schedule 2 shall apply in relation to an election under subsection (4) above as they apply in relation to an election under paragraph 4(2) of that Schedule, but with the substitution for any reference to 19th March 1968 of a reference to 31st March 1985 in the case of holdings or disposals by companies and 5th April 1985 in any other case.

109(6) For the purpose of computing the indexation allowance (if any) on a disposal of a 1982 holding, the relevant allowable expenditure attributable to the holding on the coming into force of this section shall be the amount which, if the holding had been disposed of immediately before the coming into force of this section, would have been the relevant allowable expenditure in relation to that holding on that disposal, and for the purposes of section 54(4) relevant allowable expenditure attributable to a 1982 holding shall be deemed to be expenditure falling within section 38(1)(a).

History – In s. 109(1), the words "For the purposes of corporation tax, this" substituted for the word "This" by FA 2008, s. 8 and Sch. 2, para. 90(2) with effect in relation to disposals made on or after 6 April 2008 (FA 2008, Sch. 2, para. 100).
In s. 109(2)(a), the words "(subject to express provision to the contrary)" inserted by FA 2006, s. 88 and Sch. 12, para. 18(1), with effect from 6 April 2006.

Derivations – S. 109(1): FA 1982, Sch. 13, para. 8(1) (and see FA 1985, Sch. 19, para. 6(1), (2): "1982 holding").
S. 109(2): FA 1982, Sch. 13, para. 8(2)(a), (c), s. 88(9); FA 1985, Sch. 19, para. 7.
S. 109(3): FA 1982, Sch. 13, para. 8(3).
S. 109(4), (5): FA 1985, Sch. 19, para. 6(3), (4).
S. 109(6): FA 1985, Sch. 19, para. 7.

Cross references – S. 38(1)(a): allowable acquisition expenditure.
S. 53(4): priority over general indexation allowance provisions (s. 53 and s. 54 below) and identification of certain securities (s. 108).
S. 54: calculation of indexation allowance, including (s. 54(4)) time expenditure deemed incurred.
S. 127: equation of original shares and new holding on a reorganisation.
S. 131: indexation allowance on a reorganisation from date of actual expenditure.
S. 150(4): priority of special identification rules for BES shares (applies in relation to shares issued on or before 31 December 1993).
Sch. 2, para. 1, 2, 8: quoted securities defined by reference to quotation in six-year period to 6 April 1965 but including unit trust rights and excluding employee shares; special rules for basing to 6 April 1965.
Sch. 2, para. 4(8)–(13), 5–8: as regards elections for pooling at 6 April 1965 (para. 4(2)), timing of separate elections for fixed interest etc. and other securities by reference to first disposal after 19 March 1968 and modification in relation to groups, exchange of securities or underwriters.
ICTA 1988, s. 440A(6): application to subpools of securities in respect of different categories of business of insurance company.

Notes – S. 288: interpretation, including meaning of "company", "recognised stock exchange", "shares" as including stock, "class" in relation to securities as being in one company and reference to sections as being those of this Act.

110 Indexation for section 104 holdings for corporation tax

History – The heading substituted by FA 2008, s. 8 and Sch. 2, para. 91 with effect in relation to disposals made on or after 6 April 2008 (FA 2008, Sch. 2, para. 100).

110(1) For the purposes of corporation tax this section and section 114–

(a) apply in place of section 54 in relation to a disposal of a section 104 holding for the purpose of computing the indexation allowance;

(b) have effect subject to section 105.

110(2) On any disposal of a section 104 holding, other than a disposal of the whole of it–

(a) the qualifying expenditure and the indexed pool of expenditure shall each be apportioned between the part disposed of and the remainder in the same proportions as, under this Act, the relevant allowable expenditure is apportioned; and

(b) the indexation allowance is the amount by which the portion of the indexed pool which is attributed to the part disposed of exceeds the portion of the qualifying expenditure which is attributed to that part.

110(3) On a disposal of the whole of a section 104 holding, the indexation allowance is the amount by which the indexed pool of expenditure at the time of the disposal exceeds the qualifying expenditure at that time.

110(4) In relation to a section 104 holding, the qualifying expenditure is at any time the amount which would be the aggregate of the relevant allowable expenditure in relation to a disposal of the whole of the holding occurring at that time.

110(5) Subject to subsection (6) below and section 114 the indexed pool of expenditure shall come into being at the time that the holding comes into being or, if it is earlier, when any of the qualifying expenditure is incurred and shall at the time it comes into being be the same as the qualifying expenditure at that time.

110(6) In relation to a section 104 holding which was in existence immediately before the coming into force of this section, the indexed pool of expenditure on the coming into force of this section shall be the same as it was for the purposes of Part III of Schedule 19 to the Finance Act 1985 immediately before then.

110(6A) Where a disposal to a person acquiring or adding to a section 104 holding is treated by virtue of any enactment as one on which neither a gain nor a loss accrues to the person making the disposal–

(a) section 56(2) shall not apply to the disposal (and, accordingly, the amount of the consideration shall not be calculated on the assumption that a gain of an amount equal to the indexation allowance accrues to the person making the disposal), but

(b) an amount equal to the indexation allowance on the disposal shall be added to the indexed pool of expenditure for the holding acquired or, as the case may be, held by the person to whom the disposal is made (and, where it is added to the indexed pool of expenditure for a holding so held, it shall be added after any increase required by subsection (8)(a) below).

110(7) Any reference below to an operative event is a reference to any event (whether a disposal or otherwise) which has the effect of reducing or increasing the qualifying expenditure referable to the section 104 holding.

110(8) Whenever an operative event occurs–

(a) there shall be added to the indexed pool of expenditure the indexed rise, as calculated under subsection (10) or (11) below, in the value of the pool since the last operative event or, if there has been no previous operative event, since the pool came into being; and

(b) if the operative event results in an increase in the qualifying expenditure then, in addition to any increase under paragraph (a) above, the same increase shall be made to the indexed pool of expenditure; and

(c) if the operative event is a disposal resulting in a reduction in the qualifying expenditure, the indexed pool of expenditure shall be reduced in the same proportion as the qualifying expenditure is reduced; and

(d) if the operative event results in a reduction in the qualifying expenditure but is not a disposal, the same reduction shall be made to the indexed pool of expenditure.

110(9) Where the operative event is a disposal–

(a) any addition under subsection (8)(a) above shall be made before the calculation of the indexation allowance under subsection (2) above; and

(b) the reduction under subsection (8)(c) above shall be made after that calculation.

110(10) At the time of any operative event, the indexed rise in the indexed pool of expenditure is a sum produced by multiplying the value of the pool immediately before the event by a figure expressed as a decimal and determined, subject to subsection (11) below, by the formula–

$$\frac{RE - RL}{RL}$$

where–

RE is the retail prices index for the month in which the operative event occurs; and

RL is the retail prices index for the month in which occurred the immediately preceding operative event or, if there has been no such event, in which the indexed pool of expenditure came into being.

110(11) If RE, as defined in subsection (10) above, is equal to or less than RL, as so defined, the indexed rise is nil.

History – In s. 110, references to a "section 104 holding" substituted for references to a "new holding" by FA 1998, s. 123(5), with effect in relation to any disposal on or after 6 April 1998 of any securities (whenever acquired).
In s. 110(1)(b), the words "section 105" substituted for "sections 105 and 106" by FA 2006, s. 72(2)(d) in relation to any disposal made on or after 5 December 2005.
In s. 110(1), the words "For the purposes of corporation tax" inserted by FA 1998, s. 125(1), with effect in relation to disposals on or after 6 April 1998, but not affecting certain gains which are treated as chargeable after 6 April 1998 in relation to an actual or deemed disposal occurring before that date (FA 1998, s. 125(5)).
S. 110(6A) inserted by FA 1994, s. 93(6) with effect in relation to disposals made on or after 30 November 1993.

Derivations – S. 110(1)–(3): FA 1985, Sch. 19, para. 11, and see (s. 110(1)(b)) para. 17(1)(b).
S. 110(4): FA 1985, Sch. 19, para. 12.
S. 110(5)–(9) as originally enacted: FA 1985, Sch. 19, para. 13.
S. 110(10), (11): FA 1985, Sch. 19, para. 14.

Cross references – S. 54: calculation of indexation allowance.
S. 113: calls on shares.
S. 114: consideration for options.
S. 150(4): priority of special identification rules for BES shares (applies in relation to shares issued on or before 31 December 1993).

Notes – S. 21–34: general meaning of "disposal" and the timing of certain disposals.
S. 42: general provisions for apportioning expenditure on a part disposal.
S. 246: time of disposal in cases of compulsory purchase of land as being when compensation etc. agreed or, if earlier, when the authority enter upon the land.

110A Indexation for section 104 holdings: capital gains tax

110A [Omitted by FA 2008, s. 8 and Sch. 2, para. 92.]

History – S. 110A omitted by FA 2008, s. 8 and Sch. 2, para. 92 with effect in relation to disposals made on or after 6 April 2008 (FA 2008, Sch. 2, para. 100).

111 Indexation: building society etc. shares

111 [Repealed by FA 1994, s. 93(7) and s. 258 and Sch. 26, Pt. V(8).]

History – S. 111 repealed by FA 1994, s. 93(7) and s. 258 and Sch. 26, Pt. V(8), in relation to disposals made on or after 30 November 1993.

112 Parallel pooling regulations: corporation tax

History – In the heading, the words ": corporation tax" inserted by FA 2008, s. 8 and Sch. 2, para. 93 with effect in relation to disposals made on or after 6 April 2008 (FA 2008, Sch. 2, para. 100).

112(1) The Capital Gains Tax (Parallel Pooling) Regulations 1986 made by the Treasury under paragraph 21 of Schedule 19 to the Finance Act 1985 shall continue to have effect notwithstanding the repeal by this Act of that Schedule, and for the purposes of section 14 of the Interpretation Act 1978 that paragraph shall be deemed not to have been repealed.

112(2) An election under Schedule 6 to the Finance Act 1983 which has not been revoked before 6th April 1992 shall not have effect in relation to any disposal after 5th April 1992 and may, if the Board allow, be revoked by notice to the inspector.

112(3) All such adjustments shall be made, whether by way of discharge or repayment of tax, or the making of assessments or otherwise, as are required in consequence of a revocation under subsection (2) above.

Derivations – S. 112(1), (2): see FA 1985, Sch. 19, para. 20, 21(2), (3), and SI 1986/387.
S. 112(3): FA 1985, Sch. 19, para. 20(3).

Cross references – S. 150(4): priority of special identification rules for BES shares (applies in relation to shares issued on or before 31 December 1993).
Interpretation Act 1978, s. 14: implied power to amend regulations.

Statutory instruments – SI 1986/387: the aforementioned regulations for identification of disposals after 31 March 1985 of parallel pooled securities.

Notes – S. 21–34: general meaning of "disposal" and the timing of certain disposals.
S. 288: interpretation, including "notice" as being in writing and "inspector" as any inspector of taxes.
TMA 1970, s. 29: assessing procedure.

113 Calls on shares: corporation tax

History – In the heading, the words ": corporation tax" inserted by FA 2008, s. 8 and Sch. 2, para. 94(3) with effect in relation to disposals made on or after 6 April 2008 (FA 2008, Sch. 2, para. 100).

113(A1) This section has effect for the purposes of corporation tax.

113(1) Subsection (2) below applies where–

(a) on a disposal to which section 53 applies, the relevant allowable expenditure is or includes the amount or value of the consideration given for the issue of shares or securities in, or debentures of, a company; and

(b) the whole or some part of that consideration was given after the expiry of the period of 12 months beginning on the date of the issue of the shares, securities or debentures.

113(2) For the purpose of computing the indexation allowance (if any) on the disposal referred to in subsection (1)(a) above–

(a) so much of the consideration as was given after the expiry of the period referred to in subsection (1)(b) above shall be regarded as an item of expenditure separate from any consideration given during that period; and

(b) section 54(4) shall not apply to that separate item of expenditure which, accordingly, shall be regarded as incurred at the time the consideration in question was actually given.

History – S. 113(A1) inserted by FA 2008, s. 8 and Sch. 2, para. 94(2) with effect in relation to disposals made on or after 6 April 2008 (FA 2008, Sch. 2, para. 100).

Derivations – FA 1982, Sch. 13, para. 6.

Cross references – S. 53(4): priority over general indexation allowance provisions (s. 53, 54) and identification of certain securities (s. 108).
S. 54(4): time expenditure deemed incurred for indexation allowance.
S. 150(4): priority of special identification rules for BES shares (applies in relation to shares issued on or before 31 December 1993).

Other material – Taxline 1992/125 (not reproduced): HMRC confirmation that, where shares issued as fully paid but with the sale price payable by instalments (as in certain privatisation issues), indexation allowance can be based on the full acquisition cost and runs from issue/purchase; this contrasts with issue of shares partly paid.

Notes – S. 21–34: general meaning of "disposal".
S. 288: interpretation, including the meaning of "company", "shares" as embracing stock, issue by reference to letters of allotment and references to sections being those of this Act.

114 Consideration for options: corporation tax

History – In the heading, the words ": corporation tax" inserted by FA 2008, s. 8 and Sch. 2, para. 95(3) with effect in relation to disposals made on or after 6 April 2008 (FA 2008, Sch. 2, para. 100).

114(A1) This section has effect for the purposes of corporation tax.

114(1) If, in a case where section 110(8)(b) applies, the increase in the qualifying expenditure is, in whole or in part, attributable to the cost of acquiring an option binding the grantor to sell (**"the option consideration"**), then, in addition to any increase under section 110(8)(a) or (b), the indexed pool of expenditure shall be increased by an amount equal to the indexed rise in the option consideration, as determined under subsection (2) below.

114(2) The indexed rise in the option consideration is a sum produced by multiplying the consideration by a figure expressed as a decimal and determined, subject to subsection (3) below, by the formula–

$$\frac{RO - RA}{RA}$$

where–

RO is the retail prices index for the month in which falls the date on which the option is exercised; and

RA is the retail prices index for the month in which falls the date in which the option was acquired or, if it is later, March 1982.

114(3) If RO, as defined in subsection (2) above, is equal to or less than RA, as so defined, the indexed rise is nil.

History – S. 114(A1) inserted by FA 2008, s. 8 and Sch. 2, para. 95(2) with effect in relation to disposals made on or after 6 April 2008 (FA 2008, Sch. 2, para. 100).

Derivations – FA 1985, Sch. 19, para. 15.

Cross references – S. 145: general provisions for calculating indexation allowance on most call options not to apply where s. 114 in point.
S. 150(4): priority of special identification rules for BES shares (applies in relation to shares issued on or before 31 December 1993).

Other material – Taxline 1992/75 (not reproduced): strictly, s. 114 covers only options to purchase shares, but the Board operates an unpublished concession which covers warrants (i.e. options to subscribe for, rather than purchase, shares).

Notes – S. 288: interpretation, including the meaning of "retail prices index" and references to sections being those of this Act.

GILT-EDGED SECURITIES AND QUALIFYING CORPORATE BONDS

115 Exemptions for gilt-edged securities and qualifying corporate bonds etc.

115(1) A gain which accrues on the disposal by any person of–

(a) gilt-edged securities or qualifying corporate bonds, or

(b) any option or contract to acquire or dispose of gilt-edged securities or qualifying corporate bonds,

shall not be a chargeable gain.

115(2) In subsection (1) above the reference to the disposal of a contract to acquire or dispose of gilt-edged securities or qualifying corporate bonds is a reference to the disposal of the outstanding obligations under such a contract.

115(3) Without prejudice to section 143(5), where a person who has entered into any such contract as is referred to in subsection (1)(b) above closes out that contract by entering into another contract with obligations which are reciprocal to those of the first-mentioned contract, that transaction shall for the purposes of this section constitute the disposal of an asset, namely, his outstanding obligations under the first-mentioned contract.

Derivations – CGTA 1979, s. 67, as substituted by FA 1986, s. 59.

Cross references – S. 15: meaning of "chargeable gains".
S. 21–34: general meaning of "disposal".
S. 108: qualifying corporate bonds, being relevant securities as defined in s. 108, are identified therefore in accordance with s. 108.
S. 117: meaning of "qualifying corporate bond".
S. 134(2): exemption does not apply in respect of the deferred gain crystallising on disposal of gilt-edged stock obtained on compulsory acquisition of securities.
S. 143(5): commodity or financial futures dealer closing out an option etc. deemed to dispose of his outstanding obligations under that option for any money received, any money given being incidental costs of the disposal.
S. 150(4): priority of special identification rules for BES shares (applies in relation to shares issued on or before 31 December 1993).
S. 260(6): hold-over relief on gift where inheritance tax chargeable not applicable to disposal of asset within s. 115(1) on which a gain is deemed to accrue by virtue of s. 116(10)(b).
Sch. 9, Pt. I, para. 1: meaning of "gilt-edged securities".
Sch. 9, Pt. II: list of gilt-edged securities, the disposals of which give rise to non-chargeable gains for the purposes of capital gains tax and corporation tax.

116 Reorganisations, conversions and reconstructions

116(1) This section shall have effect in any case where a transaction occurs of such a description that, apart from the provisions of this section–

(a) sections 127 to 130 would apply by virtue of any provision of Chapter II of this Part; and

(b) either the original shares would consist of or include a qualifying corporate bond and the new holding would not, or the original shares would not and the new holding would consist of or include such a bond;

and in paragraph (b) above **"the original shares"** and **"the new holding"** have the same meaning as they have for the purposes of sections 127 to 130.

116(2) In this section references to a transaction include references to any conversion of securities (whether or not effected by a transaction) within the meaning of section 132 and **"relevant transaction"** means a reorganisation, conversion of securities or other transaction such as is mentioned in subsection (1) above, and, in addition to its application where the transaction takes place after the coming into force of this section, subsection (10) below applies where the relevant transaction took place before the coming into force of this section so far as may be necessary to enable any gain or loss deferred under paragraph 10 of Schedule 13 to the Finance Act 1984 to be taken into account on a subsequent disposal.

116(3) Where the qualifying corporate bond referred to in subsection (1)(b) above would constitute the original shares for the purposes of sections 127 to 130, it is in this section referred to as **"the old asset"** and the shares or securities which would constitute the new holding for those purposes are referred to as **"the new asset"**.

116(4) Where the qualifying corporate bond referred to in subsection (1)(b) above would constitute the new holding for the purposes of sections 127 to 130, it is in this section referred to as **"the new asset"** and the shares or securities which would constitute the original shares for those purposes are referred to as **"the old asset"**.

116(4A) In determining for the purposes of subsections (1) to (4) above, as they apply for the purposes of corporation tax–

(a) whether sections 127 to 130 would apply in any case, and

(b) what, in a case where they would apply, would constitute the original shares and the new holding,

it shall be assumed that every asset representing a loan relationship of a company is a security within the meaning of section 132.

116(5) So far as the relevant transaction relates to the old asset and the new asset, sections 127 to 130 shall not apply in relation to it.

116(6) In accordance with subsection (5) above, the new asset shall not be treated as having been acquired on any date other than the date of the relevant transaction or, subject to subsections (7) and (8) below, for any consideration other than the market value of the old asset as determined immediately before that transaction.

116(7) If, on the relevant transaction, the person concerned receives, or becomes entitled to receive, any sum of money which, in addition to the new asset, is by way of consideration for the old asset, that sum shall be deducted from the consideration referred to in subsection (6) above.

116(8) If, on the relevant transaction, the person concerned gives any sum of money which, in addition to the old asset, is by way of consideration for the new asset, that sum shall be added to the consideration referred to in subsection (6) above.

116(8A) Where subsection (6) above applies for the purposes of corporation tax in a case where the old asset consists of a qualifying corporate bond, Part 5 of CTA 2009 (loan relationships) shall have effect, subject to subsection (8B) below, so as to require such debits and credits to be brought into account for the purposes of that Part in relation to the relevant transaction as would have been brought into account if the transaction had been a disposal of the old asset at the market value mentioned in subsection (6) above. This subsection does not apply in relation to a relevant loan relationship transaction.

116(8AA) In subsection (8A) **"relevant loan relationship transaction"** means a transaction to which any of the following provisions applies–

section 342 of CTA 2009 (continuity of treatment on transfers within groups or reorganisations: issues of new securities on reorganisations: disposal at notional carrying value),

section 343 of that Act (continuity of treatment on transfers within groups or reorganisations: receiving company using fair value accounting),

section 424 of that Act (European cross-border transfers of business: reorganisations involving loan relationships),

section 425 of that Act (European cross-border transfers of business: original holder using fair value accounting),

section 435 of that Act (European cross-border mergers: reorganisations involving loan relationships),

section 436 of that Act (European cross-border mergers: original holder using fair value accounting).

116(8B) Subsection (8A) above does not apply where the relevant transaction is a conversion of securities occurring in consequence of the operation of the terms of any security or of any debenture which is not a security.

116(9) In any case where the old asset consists of a qualifying corporate bond, then, so far as it relates to the old asset and the new asset, the relevant transaction shall be treated for the purposes of this Act as a disposal of the old asset and an acquisition of the new asset.

116(10) Except in a case falling within subsection (9) above, so far as it relates to the old asset and the new asset, the relevant transaction shall be treated for the purposes of this Act as not involving any disposal of the old asset but–

(a) there shall be calculated the chargeable gain or allowable loss that would have accrued if, at the time of the relevant transaction, the old asset had been disposed of for a consideration equal to its market value immediately before that transaction; and

(b) subject to subsections (12) to (14) below, the whole or a corresponding part of the chargeable gain or allowable loss mentioned in paragraph (a) above shall be deemed to accrue on a subsequent disposal of the whole or part of the new asset (in addition to any gain or loss that actually accrues on that disposal); and

(c) on that subsequent disposal, section 115 shall have effect only in relation to any gain or loss that actually accrues and not in relation to any gain or loss which is deemed to accrue by virtue of paragraph (b) above.

116(11) Subsection (10)(b) and (c) above shall not apply to any disposal falling within section 58(1), 62(4), 139, 140A, 140E, or 171(1), but a person who has acquired the new asset on a disposal falling within any of those sections (and without there having been a previous disposal not falling within any of those sections or a devolution on death) shall be treated for the purposes of subsection (10)(b) and (c) above as if the new asset had been acquired by him at the same time and for the same consideration as, having regard to subsections (5) to (8) above, it was acquired by the person making the disposal.

116(12) In any case where–

(a) on the calculation under subsection (10)(a) above, a chargeable gain would have accrued, and

(b) the consideration for the old asset includes such a sum of money as is referred to in subsection (7) above,

then, subject to subsection (13) below, the proportion of that chargeable gain which that sum of money bears to the market value of the old asset immediately before the relevant transaction shall be deemed to accrue at the time of that transaction.

116(13) If the sum of money referred to in subsection (12)(b) above is small, as compared with the market value of the old asset immediately before the relevant transaction, subsection (12) above shall not apply.

116(14) In a case where subsection (12) above applies, the chargeable gain which, apart from that subsection, would by virtue of subsection (10)(b) above be deemed to accrue on a subsequent disposal of the whole or part of the new asset shall be reduced or, as the case may be, extinguished by deducting therefrom the amount of the chargeable gain which, by virtue of subsection (12) above, is deemed to accrue at the time of the relevant transaction.

116(15) In any case where–

(a) the new asset mentioned in subsections (10) and (11) above is a qualifying corporate bond in respect of which an allowable loss is treated as accruing under section 254(2), and

(b) the loss is treated as accruing at a time falling after the relevant transaction but before any actual disposal of the new asset subsequent to the relevant transaction,

then for the purposes of subsections (10) and (11) above a subsequent disposal of the new asset shall be treated as occurring at (and only at) the time the loss is treated as accruing.

116(16) This section has effect for the purposes of corporation tax notwithstanding anything in section 464(1) of CTA 2009 (matters to be brought into account in the case of loan relationships only under Part 5 of that Act).

History – In s. 116(2) the words "references to a transaction … within the meaning of section 132 and" inserted by FA 1997, s. 88(4), with effect for disposals on or after 26 November 1996 and earlier conversions (FA 1997, s. 88(6)).
S. 116(4A) inserted by FA 1996, s. 104 and Sch. 14 para. 60 for accounting periods ending after 31 March 1996 (corporation tax) and for 1996–97 (income tax), subject to FA 1996, Sch. 15.
In s. 116(8A) the words "Part 5 of CTA 2009" substituted for the words "Chapter II of Part IV of the Finance Act 1996", the words "that Part" substituted for the words "that Chapter" and the words "relevant loan relationship transaction" substituted for the words "transaction to which paragraph 12G of Schedule 9 to the Finance Act 1996 (c. 8) (exchanges etc: treatment of loan relationships) applies" by CTA 2009, s. 1322 and Sch. 1, para. 366(2), with effect for corporation tax purposes for accounting periods ending on or after 1 April 2009, and for income tax and capital gains tax purposes for the tax year 2009–10 and subsequent tax years.
In s. 116(8A), the words "This subsection does not apply in relation to a transaction to which paragraph 12G of Schedule 9 to the Finance Act 1996 (c. 8) (exchanges etc: treatment of loan relationships) applies." inserted by SI 2008/1579, reg. 3(1) and Sch. 1, para. 2, with effect in relation to cross-border mergers that relate to the formation of an SE (Societas Europaea) or an SCE (Societas Cooperativa Europaea) which take place on or after 18 August 2006 and in relation to other cross-border mergers and cross-border transfers of business which take place on or after 1 January 2007.
In s. 116(8A), words ", subject to subsection (8B) below," inserted and words "subsection (6) above" substituted for words "that subsection" by F(No. 2)A 2005, s. 37 and Sch. 6, para. 8(1), with effect in relation to transactions occurring after 26 May 2005.
S. 116(8A) inserted by FA 1996, s. 104 and Sch. 14 para. 60 for accounting periods ending after 31 March 1996 (corporation tax) and for 1996–97 (income tax), subject to FA 1996, Sch. 15.
S. 116(8AA) inserted by CTA 2009, s. 1322 and Sch. 1, para. 366(3), with effect for corporation tax purposes for accounting periods ending on or after 1 April 2009, and for income tax and capital gains tax purposes for the tax year 2009–10 and subsequent tax years.
S. 116(8B) inserted by F(No. 2)A 2005, s. 37 and Sch. 6, para. 8(2), with effect in relation to transactions occurring after 26 May 2005.
In s. 116(11), reference to s. 140E inserted by F(No. 2)A 2005, s. 64(1) with effect, in relation to formation of SE (Societas Europaea) under Article 2 of Council Regulation (EC) 2157/2001 on the Statute for a European Company (Societas Europaea) which occurs on or after 1 April 2005.
In s. 116(11), reference to s. 140A inserted by F(No.2)A 1992, s. 46(3), and deemed always to have had effect. (A corresponding amendment was made to FA 1984, Sch. 13, para. 10(2) (the predecessor provision) with respect to any disposal by way of transfer where the transfer takes effect on or after 1 January 1992 (F(No. 2)A 1992, s. 49(5)).) Reference to s. 172 effectively repealed by FA 2000, s. 102 and Sch. 29, para. 19 in relation to disposals made on or after 1 April 2000.
In s. 116(13) words "the inspector is satisfied that" and "and so directs," repealed by FA 1996, s. 134 and Sch. 20, para. 51 for 1996–97 and later years of assessment (income tax and capital gains tax) and accounting periods ending on or after 1 July 1999, the appointed day for self-assessment in relation to corporation tax (FA 1994, s. 199 and SI 1998/3173 (C. 78)).
In s. 116(16) the words "section 464(1) of CTA 2009" substituted for the words "section 80(5) of the Finance Act 1996" and the words "Part 5" substituted for the words "Chapter II of Part IV" by CTA 2009, s. 1322 and Sch. 1, para. 366(4), with effect for corporation tax purposes for accounting periods ending on or after 1 April 2009, and for income tax and capital gains tax purposes for the tax year 2009–10 and subsequent tax years.
S. 116(16) inserted by FA 1996, s. 104 and Sch. 14 para. 60 for accounting periods ending after 31 March 1996 (corporation tax) and for 1996–97 (income tax), subject to FA 1996, Sch. 15.

Derivations – S. 116(1): FA 1984, s. 64(7).
S. 116(2)–(4) (as originally enacted): FA 1984, Sch. 13, para. 7.
S. 116(5)–(8): FA 1984, Sch. 13, para. 8.
S. 116(9): FA 1984, Sch. 13, para. 9.
S. 116(10), (11) (as originally enacted): FA 1984, Sch. 13, para. 10, as amended by FA 1985, s. 67(2)(c), FA 1989, s. 139(6), and FA 1990, s. 70(6).
S. 116(12)–(14) (as originally enacted): FA 1984, Sch. 13, para. 11.
S. 116(15): FA 1984, Sch. 13, para. 12, as inserted by FA 1990, s. 85.

Cross references – S. 58(1): deemed no gain, no loss on transfers between spouses.
S. 62(4): no chargeable gain on transfer of asset by personal representatives to legatee.
S. 127–130: equation of original and new holdings on a reorganisation and provisions for dealing with consideration given or received, part disposals and composite new holdings, as extended by other parts of Ch. II of this Part to conversion of securities (s. 132–134) and exchanges of securities or company reconstructions and amalgamations involving the issue of securities (s. 135–136).
S. 139: deemed no gain, no loss on reconstruction or amalgamation involving the transfer of business.
S. 140A: intra-Community transfer of a non-UK trade.
S. 150(4): priority of special identification rules for BES shares (applies in relation to shares issued on or before 31 December 1993).
S. 151BB: disapplication of s. 116(10) in cases of rights issues and Community Investment Tax Relief.
S. 151BC: application of s. 116 to be subject to s. 151BC.
S. 164A(2A): reinvestment relief on disposal of a qualifying corporate bond.
S. 164F(2): crystallisation of held-over gain in respect of shares in acquired holding (following re-investment) being the subject of transaction within s. 116.

S. 165(3): where gain accrues under s. 116(10)(b), disapplication of hold-over relief for gifts of business assets to disposal of qualifying corporate bond.
S. 171(1): deemed no gain, no loss on transfer of capital assets within a group.
S. 172: deemed no gain, no loss on transfer of UK branch to resident company by way of a scheme of domestication.
S. 234(2): clawback on a chargeable event following roll-over on disposal of shares to a qualifying share ownership trust where further relief under s. 116(10) between the disposal and the chargeable event.
S. 254(2): special relief for debts on qualifying corporate bonds.
Sch. 4, para. 4: 50 per cent reduction in gain crystallising under s. 116(10), (11) where attributable to the deferral before 6 April 1988 if original securities held at 31 March 1982 (or acquired in a chain of no gain, no loss disposals from that date).
Sch. 5C, para. 3(1): chargeable events in relation to shares in a venture capital trust following the making of a qualifying investment.
Sch. 7A, para. 1(9): in relation to pre-entry losses for the purpose of determining whether a loss accrued before a company became a group member a loss is deemed to accrue at the time of the relevant transaction within the meaning of s. 116(2).
Sch. 7A, para. 2(8): pre-entry proportion of losses on pre-entry assets.
Sch. 7A, para. 7(5), (6): gains from which pre-entry losses deductible include those accruing under s. 116(10) where bond acquired post-entry but the old asset was held pre-entry.
Sch. 7AC, para. 4(1) and 34(1): question of exemption for disposal by company with large shareholding determined without reference to s. 116(10) unless deemed accrual of gain or loss held over on earlier transaction.
FA 1996, s. 91G: shares beginning or ceasing to be subject to FA 1996, s. 91A or 91B.
FA 1996, Sch. 10, para. 5: application of s. 116 to loan relationships of collective investment schemes.
FA 1996, Sch. 15, para. 8, 9, 30: transitional rules for the application of s. 116 to loan relationships.
FA 1997, s. 89(8)(b): a claim under ESC D27 (in respect of an earn-out right acquired before 26 April 1988) will enable TCGA 1992, s. 138A to have effect in the case of a disposal on or after 26 November 1996 of any asset acquired prior to that date which is a qualifying corporate bond and was acquired under a relevant transaction within s. 116.
FA 1999, s. 66: treatment of accrued gain from security which was not a relevant discounted security (RDS) before 15 February 1999 but became one as a result of changes to definition of RDS in FA 1996, Sch. 13 brought about by FA 1999, s. 65.
FA 2000, Sch. 15, para. 80(1): share reoganisation rules apply separately to investment relief shares acquired under the CVS.
FA 2000, Sch. 15, para. 81(2): s. 116(10) does not apply to CVS shares with investment relief which have been held continously from the date of issue.
FA 2002, Sch. 16, para. 40(2), (4) and 41(4): s. 116(10) disapplied in certain circumstances where community development finance institution restructured. S. 116 otherwise applies subject to the schedule.
FA 2008, Sch. 3, para. 7: application of Pt. 5, Ch. 3 (entrepreneurs' relief) in cases where a chargeable gain is deemed (by s. 116(10)(b)) to accrue on or after 6 April 2008 by reason of a relevant transaction taking place before that date.
Broadcasting Act 1996, Sch. 7, para. 7 (not reproduced): provisions applying where a company issues shares or debentures to the BBC in exchange for shares in or debentures of a successor company; disapplication of s. 116.
SI 1994/3226, reg. 9(1): no attribution of pre-commencement day (for FA 1993, Pt. II, Ch. II) gains or losses to former capital gains tax assets a disposal of which would fall within s. 116(10)(b).
SI 1994/3226, reg. 16(3): attribution of pre-commencement day (for FA 1993, Pt. II, Ch. II) losses to assets subject to reorganisations to which TCGA 1992, s. 127 applied.
SI 1994/3227, reg. 9: computation and deferral of gain or loss under foreign exchange matching rules in respect of assets which are replaced in a transaction to which s. 116 applies.
SI 2002/1970, reg. 10: a special rule for bringing into account amounts of exchange gains or losses where, but for s. 116, s. 127 would apply in relation to a transaction involving original shares.

European material – Council Regulation (EC) 2157/2001 on the Statute for a European Company (Societas Europaea).
Directive 90/434, art. 4 (amendment to s. 116(11) by F(No. 2)A 1992).

Extra-statutory concessions – D38 (losses on irrecoverable loans in the form of certain post-1989 qualifying corporate bonds): where that concession applies, any gain or loss on sale of original (pre-1989) shares or securities treated as accruing at same time as the loss on the bonds.

HMRC interpretations – IRInt. 36: HMRC view that where qualifying corporate bonds (QCBs) issued in exchange for shares or securities the held-over gain which would be released on a later disposal of the QCBs is, in the event of the death of the holder, in effect wiped out.
IRInt. 39: where consideration on a share exchange is partly in the form of qualifying corporate bonds the base cost of the original shares is apportioned between new shares and qualifying corporate bonds according to their respective market values at the time of the exchange.
IRInt. 152: HMRC view that no gain/no loss rule (TCGA 1992, s. 171(1)) does not apply to C's acquisition where a group company A exchanges shares in company B for a new issue of QCBs in another group company C.
IRInt. 157: Revenue now take view that "small" can mean 5 per cent or less of value of asset etc., or receipt of £3,000 or less whether or not falling within the 5 per cent test; exceptionally taxpayers may suggest different limits in the context of their particular circumstances (O'Rourke v Binks [1992] BTC 460).

Other material – ICAEW Technical Release TR 551 (not reproduced): "small" in s. 116(13) clarified as 5 per cent or less.

Notes – S. 15: meaning of "chargeable gains".
S. 16: meaning of "allowable loss".
S. 21–34: general meaning of "disposal".
S. 272–274 and Sch. 11: meaning of "market value".
S. 288: interpretation, including "inspector" as any inspector of taxes and reference to sections as being those of this Act.

116A Holding beginning or ceasing to fall within section 490 of CTA 2009

116A(1) Section 116 applies in accordance with the following assumptions if–

(a) a holding that is a relevant holding for the purposes of section 490 of CTA 2009 (holdings in OEICs, unit trusts and offshore funds treated as creditor relationship rights) is held by a company both at the end of one accounting period and at the beginning of the next, and

(b) that section applies to the holding for one of those periods but not for the other.

116A(2) The assumptions in subsections (3) and (4) apply for the purposes of this Act if the accounting period for which section 490 of CTA 2009 applies to the relevant holding is the first of those periods.

116A(3) The relevant holding is assumed to have ceased to be a relevant holding for the second of those periods as a result of a transaction such as is mentioned in section 116(1) ("the reorganisation transaction") occurring at the beginning of that period.

116A(4) In relation to the reorganisation transaction within subsection (3), for the purposes of section 116–

(a) the relevant holding immediately before the beginning of the second of those periods is assumed to be the old asset, and

(b) the relevant holding immediately after the beginning of that period is assumed to be the new asset.

116A(5) The assumptions in subsections (6) and (8) apply for the purposes of this Act if the accounting period for which section 490 of CTA 2009 applies to the relevant holding is the second of those periods.

116A(6) The holding is assumed to have become a relevant holding for the second of those periods as a result of the occurrence at the end of first period of a transaction such as is mentioned in section 116(1).

116A(7) But subsection (6) does not apply if the first of those periods is a period at the end of which a disposal of the relevant holding is treated as having occurred under section 212 (annual deemed disposal of holdings of unit trusts etc by insurance companies).

116A(8) In relation to the reorganisation transaction within subsection (6), for the purposes of section 116–

(a) the relevant holding immediately before the beginning of the second of those periods is assumed to be the old asset, and

(b) the relevant holding immediately after the beginning of that period is assumed to be the new asset.

History – S. 116A inserted by CTA 2009, s. 1322 and Sch. 1, para. 367, with effect for corporation tax purposes for accounting periods ending on or after 1 April 2009, and for income tax and capital gains tax purposes for the tax year 2009–10 and subsequent tax years.

116B Shares beginning or ceasing to be shares to which section 521B of CTA 2009 applies

History – In the heading to s. 116B "521B" substituted for "523" (though incorrectly stated as "522" in the amending provision) by FA 2009, s. 48 and Sch. 24, para. 5(2), with effect from 22 April 2009.

116B(1) If at any time section 521B of CTA 2009 (application of Part 5 of that Act to certain shares as rights under a creditor relationship) begins or ceases to apply in the case of a share held by the investing company it is treated for the purposes of this Act–

(a) as having disposed of the share immediately before that time for consideration of an amount equal to the notional carrying value of the share at that time, and

(b) as having immediately reacquired it for consideration of the same amount.

116B(2) In this section–

"notional carrying value" has the same meaning as in subsection (2) of section 521F of CTA 2009 (see subsection (3) of that section),

"investing company" has the same meaning as it has for the purposes of Chapter 6A of Part 6 of that Act (shares accounted for as liabilities) (see section 521A(3) of that Act).

History – In s. 116B(1) "521B" substituted for "523" (though incorrectly stated as "522" in the amending provision) by FA 2009, s. 48 and Sch. 24, para. 5(2), with effect from 22 April 2009.

In s. 116B(1)(a) (though incorrectly stated as "(1)(b)" in the amending provision), the words "the notional carrying value of the share" substituted for the words "its fair value" by FA 2009, s. 48 and Sch. 24, para. 5(3), with effect from 22 April 2009.

In s. 116B(2), the definition of "notional carrying value" substituted for the definition of "fair value" by FA 2009, s. 48 and Sch. 24, para. 5(4), with effect from 22 April 2009.

In s. 116B(2), in the definition of "investing company", "6A" substituted for "7" and "accounted for as liabilities) (see section 521A(3)" substituted for "with guaranteed returns) (see section 522(3)" by FA 2009, s. 48 and Sch. 24, para. 5(5), with effect from 22 April 2009.

S. 116B inserted by CTA 2009, s. 1322 and Sch. 1, para. 367, with effect for corporation tax purposes for accounting periods ending on or after 1 April 2009, and for income tax and capital gains tax purposes for the tax year 2009–10 and subsequent tax years.

117 Meaning of "qualifying corporate bond"

117(A1) For the purposes of corporation tax **"qualifying corporate bond"** means any asset representing a loan relationship of a company; and for purposes other than those of corporation tax references to a qualifying corporate bond shall be construed in accordance with the following provisions of this section.

117(1) For the purposes of this section, a **"corporate bond"** is a security, as defined in section 132(3)(b)–

(a) the debt on which represents and has at all times represented a normal commercial loan; and

(b) which is expressed in sterling and in respect of which no provision is made for conversion into, or redemption in, a currency other than sterling,

and in paragraph (a) above **"normal commercial loan"** has the meaning which would be given by section 162 of CTA 2010 if for paragraphs (a) to (c) of subsection (2) of that section there were substituted the words "corporate bonds (within the meaning of section 117 of TCGA 1992)".

117(2) For the purposes of subsection (1)(b) above–

(a) a security shall not be regarded as expressed in sterling if the amount of sterling falls to be determined by reference to the value at any time of any other currency or asset; and

(b) a provision for redemption in a currency other than sterling but at the rate of exchange prevailing at redemption shall be disregarded.

117(2AA) For the purposes of this section **"corporate bond"** also includes any asset which is not included in the definition in subsection (1) above and which is a deeply discounted security for the purposes of Chapter 8 of Part 4 of ITTOIA 2005 (see section 430).

117(2A) [Repealed by FA 1996, s. 205 and Sch. 41, Pt. V(3).]

117(3) [Repealed by FA 1996, s. 205 and Sch. 41, Pt. V(3).]

117(4) For the purposes of this section **"corporate bond"** also includes a share in a building society–

(a) which is a qualifying share,

(b) which is expressed in sterling, and

(c) in respect of which no provision is made for conversion into, or redemption in, a currency other than sterling.

117(5) For the purposes of subsection (4) above, a share in a building society is **a qualifying share** if–

(a) it is a permanent interest bearing share, or

(b) it is of a description specified in regulations made by the Treasury for the purposes of this paragraph.

117(6) Subsection (2) above applies for the purposes of subsection (4) above as it applies for the purposes of subsection (1)(b) above, treating the reference to a security as a reference to a share.

117(6A) For the purposes of this section **"corporate bond"** also includes, except in relation to a person who acquires it on or after a disposal in relation to which section 115 has or has had effect in accordance with section 116(10)(c), any debenture issued on or after 16th March 1993 which is not a security (as defined in section 132) but–

(a) is issued in circumstances such that it would fall by virtue of section 251(6) to be treated for the purposes of section 251 as such a security; and

(b) would be a corporate bond if it were a security as so defined.

117(6B) An excluded indexed security issued on or after 6th April 1996 is not a corporate bond for the purposes of this section; and an excluded indexed security issued before that date shall be taken to be such a bond for the purposes of this section only if–

(a) it would be so taken apart from this subsection; and

(b) the question whether it should be so taken arises for the purposes of section 116(10).

117(6C) In subsection (6B) above **"excluded indexed security"** has the same meaning as in Chapter 8 of Part 4 of ITTOIA 2005 (profits from deeply discounted securities) (see section 433).

117(6D) Section 151T provides for arrangements to which section 151N (alternative finance arrangements: investment bond arrangements) applies also to be a corporate bond for the purposes of this section.

117(7) Subject to subsections (9) and (10) below, for the purposes of this Act, a corporate bond–

(a) is a **"qualifying"** corporate bond if it is issued after 13th March 1984; and

(b) becomes a **"qualifying"** corporate bond if, having been issued on or before that date, it is acquired by any person after that date and that acquisition is not as a result of a disposal which is excluded for the purposes of this subsection, or which was excluded for the purposes of section 64(4) of the Finance Act 1984.

117(8) Where a person disposes of a corporate bond which was issued on or before 13th March 1984 and, before the disposal, the bond had not become a qualifying corporate bond, the disposal is excluded for the purposes of subsection (7) above if, by virtue of any enactment–

(a) the disposal is treated for the purposes of this Act as one on which neither a gain nor a loss accrues to the person making the disposal; or

(b) the consideration for the disposal is treated for the purposes of this Act as reduced by an amount equal to the held-over gain on that disposal, as defined for the purposes of section 165 or 260.

117(8A) A corporate bond falling within subsection (2AA) above is a qualifying corporate bond whatever its date of issue.

117(9) [Repealed by FA 1996, s. 205 and Sch. 41, Pt. V(3).]

117(10) [Repealed by FA 1996, s. 205 and Sch. 41, Pt. V(3).]

117(11) For the purposes of this section–

(a) where a security is comprised in a letter of allotment or similar instrument and the right to the security thereby conferred remains provisional until accepted, the security shall not be treated as issued until there has been acceptance; and

(b) **"permanent interest bearing share"** means a share which is a permanent interest bearing share for the purposes of the General Prudential Sourcebook made by the Financial Services Authority under the Financial Services and Markets Act 2000 as that Sourcebook applies in relation to shares issued on the date that the share is issued.

117(12) The Treasury may by regulations provide that for the definition of the expression **"permanent interest bearing share"** in subsection (11) above (as it has effect for the time being) there shall be substituted a different definition of that expression, and regulations under this subsection or subsection (5)(b) above may contain such supplementary, incidental, consequential or transitional provision as the Treasury thinks fit.

117(13) This section shall have effect for the purposes of section 254 with the omission of subsections (4) to (6), (11) and (12).

History – In s. 117(A1), words "(subject to sections 117A and 117B below)" which appeared between "means" and "any asset" repealed by FA 2002, s. 141 and Sch. 40, Pt. 3(10), with effect in relation to accounting periods beginning on or after 1 October 2002.
S. 117(A1) inserted by FA 1996, s. 104 and Sch. 14 para. 61; for accounting periods ending after 31 March 1996 (corporation tax) and for 1996–97 (income tax), subject to FA 1996, Sch. 15.
In s. 117(1), the words "section 162 of CTA 2010 if for paragraphs (a) to (c) of subsection (2) of that section there were substituted the words "corporate bonds (within the meaning of section 117 of TCGA 1992)"" substituted for the words "sub-paragraph (5) of paragraph 1 of Schedule 18 to the Taxes Act if for paragraph (a)(i) to (iii) of that sub-paragraph there were substituted the words "corporate bonds (within the meaning of section 117 of the 1992 Act)"" by CTA 2010, s. 1177 and Sch. 1, para. 231, with effect for corporation tax purposes for accounting periods ending on or after 1 April 2010, and for income tax and capital gains tax purposes for the tax year 2010–11 and subsequent tax years.
S. 117(2A), repealed by FA 1996, s. 205 and Sch. 41, Pt. V(3) in accordance with FA 1996, Pt. IV, Ch. II.
S. 117(2A) inserted by FA 1995, s. 50.
In s. 117(2AA), words "deeply discounted security for the purposes of Chapter 8 of Part 4 of ITTOIA 2005 (see section 430)" substituted for "relevant discounted security for the purposes of Schedule 13 to the Finance Act 1996" by virtue of ITTOIA 2005, s. 882 and Sch. 1, para. 433(2) which, in accordance with ITTOIA 2005, s. 883, have effect, for income tax purposes, for tax year 2005–06 and subsequent tax years, and, for corporation tax purposes, for accounting periods ending after 5 April 2005.
S. 117(2AA) inserted by FA 1996, s. 104 and Sch. 14 para. 61; for accounting periods ending after 31 March 1996 (corporation tax) and for 1996–97 (income tax), subject to FA 1996, Sch. 15.
S. 117(3) repealed by FA 1996, s. 205 and Sch. 41, Pt. V(3) in accordance with FA 1996, Pt. IV, Ch. II.
S. 117(6A) inserted by FA 1993, s. 84(1) in relation to chargeable periods ending on or after 16 March 1993; in relation to any accounting period which began before 6 April 1992 the corresponding predecessor provision shall be treated as amended and apply accordingly.
S. 117(6B) inserted by FA 1996, s. 104 and Sch. 14, para. 61; for accounting periods ending after 31 March 1996 (corporation tax) and for 1996–97 (income tax), subject to FA 1996, Sch. 15.
In s. 117(6C), words "Chapter 8 of Part 4 of ITTOIA 2005 (profits from deeply discounted securities) (see section 433)" substituted for "Schedule 13 to the Finance Act 1996 (relevant discounted securities)" by virtue of ITTOIA 2005, s. 882 and Sch. 1, para. 433(3) which, in accordance with ITTOIA 2005, s. 883, have effect, for income tax purposes, for tax year 2005–06 and subsequent tax years, and, for corporation tax purposes, for accounting periods ending after 5 April 2005.
S. 117(6C) inserted by FA 1996, s. 104 and Sch. 14 para. 61; for accounting periods ending after 31 March 1996 (corporation tax) and for 1996–97 (income tax), subject to FA 1996, Sch. 15.
In s. 117(6D) the words "of that Act or section 507 of CTA 2009" inserted by CTA 2009, s. 1322 and Sch. 1, para. 368, with effect for corporation tax purposes for accounting periods ending on or after 1 April 2009, and for income tax and capital gains tax purposes for the tax year 2009–10 and subsequent tax years.
S. 117(6D) substituted by TIOPA 2010, s. 374 and Sch. 8, para. 200, with effect for corporation tax purposes for accounting periods ending on or after 1 April 2010, for income tax and capital gains tax purposes for the tax year 2010–11 and subsequent tax years, and for petroleum revenue tax purposes for chargeable periods beginning on or after 1 July 2010.
Former s. 117(6D) inserted by FA 2007, s. 53(10) with effect in relation to:

(1) alternative finance arrangements entered into on or after 1 April 2007 (for corporation tax); or on or after 6 April 2007 (for income tax and capital gains tax); and
(2) to the extent provided by FA 2005, s. 56(3)–(6), to alternative finance arrangements entered into before 1 April 2007 (for corporation tax); or before 6 April 2007 (for income tax and capital gains tax) where the profit share return is payable on or after those dates.

The commencement provisions of FA 2005, s. 56 are applied to the insertion of s. 117(6D), with amendment, by virtue of FA 2007, s. 53(13). For the purposes of income tax and capital gains tax, in relation to disposals after 6 April 2007 to which the newly inserted FA 2005, s. 48A applies, that section and FA 2005, s. 48B are to be treated as having always having had effect (FA 2007, s. 53(14)(a)).
S. 117(8A) inserted by FA 1996, s. 104 and Sch. 14 para. 61; for accounting periods ending after 31 March 1996 (corporation tax) and for 1996–97 (income tax), subject to FA 1996, Sch. 15.
S. 117(9) repealed by FA 1996, s. 205 and Sch. 41, Pt. V(3) in accordance with FA 1996, Pt. IV, Ch. II.
S. 117(10) repealed by FA 1996, s. 205 and Sch. 41, Pt. V(3) in accordance with FA 1996, Pt. IV, Ch. II.
In s. 117(11)(b) the words "for the purposes of" substituted for "within the meaning of, and is eligible for inclusion in the calculation for capital adequacy requirements in accordance with," by SI 2006/3291, reg. 2 with effect from 1 January 2007.
In s. 117(11)(b) the end words omitted after para. (b) by SI 2006/3291, reg. 2 with effect from 1 January 2007.
S. 117(11)(b) and the endpiece substituted for former s. 117(11)(b) by SI 2001/3629, art. 63(1) operative in relation to shares in a building society issued on or after 1 December 2001.
In former s. 117(11)(b), words "as if that Order" to the end added by SI 1999/1953, reg. 2, with effect from 29 July 1999.

Derivations – S. 117(1): FA 1984, s. 64(2)(b), (c), (2A) as inserted by FA 1991, s. 98(3).
S. 117(2): FA 1984, s. 64(3).
S. 117(3): FA 1984, s. 64(3A)–(3C) as inserted by FA 1989, s. 139(3), and s. 64(3D) as inserted by FA 1990, s. 56 and Sch. 10, para. 28.
S. 117(4)–(6): FA 1984, s. 64(3E)–(3G), as inserted by FA 1991, s. 51 and Sch. 10, para. 1.
S. 117(7), (8): FA 1984, s. 64(4), (5) as amended (subs. (5)) by FA 1989, s. 124 and Sch. 14 para. 6(4)
S. 117(9): FA 1984, s. 64(5A)–(5C) as inserted by FA 1989, s. 139(4), and s. 64(5D) as inserted by FA 1990, s. 56 and Sch. 10, para. 28.
S. 117(10): FA 1984, s. 64(6) as amended by FA 1989, s. 139(5).
S. 117(11)(a): FA 1984, s. 64(8).
S. 117(11)(b), (12): FA 1984, s. 64(9)–(11), as inserted by FA 1991, s. 51 and Sch. 10, para. 1.

S. 117(13): FA 1991, Sch. 10, para. 1(5).

Cross references – SI 2013/460 (not reproduced): "core capital deferred shares" are not qualifying corporate bonds under s. 117, with effect in relation to shares issued, and securities converted into shares, on or after 1 March 2013. SI 2013/460, reg. 2, defines "core capital deferred shares" as "shares that form part of the core tier one capital of a building society" (for the purposes of which ""building society" and "deferred shares" have the same meanings as in the Building Societies Act 1986, and the reference to "core tier one capital" is to be read in accordance with the Handbook of Rules and Guidance made by the Financial Services Authority (as that handbook has effect from time to time)").
S. 132(3)(b): definition of security by reference to loan stock or similar security.
S. 150(4): priority of special identification rules for BES shares (applies to shares issued on or before 31 December 1993).
S. 165: deferral on gifts of business assets.
S. 170: group defined by reference to 75 per cent subsidiary relationships.
S. 251(6): certain debentures issued on or after 16 March 1993 deemed to be securities.
S. 254: special relief for debts on qualifying corporate bonds.
S. 260: deferral on gifts on which inheritance tax chargeable.
ICTA 1988, s. 477B: allowable deduction for costs of issuing permanent interest bearing shares (PIBS) and similarly recognised securities.
ICTA 1988, s. 710(2A): accrued income scheme includes securities which are permanent interest bearing securities (PIBS) and similarly recognised securities issued by building societies.
ICTA 1988, Sch. 10, para. 1(4), 5A(3): definition of qualifying corporate bond contained in s. 117 to apply in relation to profit sharing schemes.
ICTA 1988, Sch. 18, para. 1(5): definition of normal commercial loan by reference to a loan of or including new consideration which satisfies certain conditions as to conversion (into specified shares or securities: para. 1(5)(a)(i)–(iii)), rate of interest and premium on redemption.
FA 1993, Sch. 17, para. 5, 6: definition of a qualifying corporate bond broadened where a right to settlement under a debt on a security is a qualifying asset for FA 1993, Pt. II, Ch. II.
FA 1999, s. 65(11): for the purposes of s. 117(2AA), the definition of "relevant discounted security" in FA 1996, Sch. 13 which was substituted by FA 1999, s. 65 has effect in relation to any disposal (in whole or in part) of an asset on or after 15 February 1999.
ITEPA 2003, Sch. 2, para. 99: approved share incentive plans.
FA 2005, s. 48A: arrangements falling within s. 48A (alternative finance investment bonds) are a corporate bond, for the purposes of s. 117, provided certain conditions are met (FA 2005, s. 48B(4)).

Extra-statutory concessions – D38: recipient of bonds which became qualifying corporate bonds as a result of FA 1989 may claim an allowable capital loss if the bonds become of negligible value or give rise to losses on or after their redemption date.

Other material – Taxline 2004/8 (not reproduced): even though a corporate bond (CB) may not hold the right to convert into ordinary shares if it has the right to convert into other CB's which then have the right to covert into ordinary shares it will not be a qualifying "normal commercial loan" and therefore cannot be a "qualifying corporate bond".

Notes – S. 21–34: general meaning of "disposal".
S. 287: Board's power to make regulations is exercisable by statutory instrument, subject to the negative resolution procedure of the House of Commons.
SI 1991/702: the aforementioned order relating to permanent interest bearing shares.
For no gain, no loss enactments, see list in s. 35(3)(d) and see inability in some cases to substitute a gain for a loss or vice versa by using re-basing to 31 March 1982 (s. 35(4)), oil industry assets (s. 200(6)), member becoming absolutely entitled to settled property comprising shares issued on incorporation of a building society (s. 217(4)(c)), roll-over relief on disposal of shares to an employee share ownership trust (s. 229(1)), roll-over relief on replacement of land compulsorily purchased (s. 247), gifts etc. to employee trusts (s. 239(2)), gifts to charities etc. (s. 257(2)), gifts to housing associations etc. (s. 259(2)), inability to substitute a gain for a loss or vice versa by using 6 April 1965 value (Sch. 2, para. 2(1), 9(4), 17(2)).

117A Assets that are not qualifying corporate bonds for corporation tax purposes

117A [Repealed by FA 2002, s. 141 and Sch. 40, Pt. 3(10).]

History – S. 117A repealed by FA 2002, s. 141 and Sch. 40, Pt. 3(10), with effect in relation to accounting periods beginning on or after 1 October 2002.

117B Holdings in unit trusts and offshore funds excluded from treatment as qualifying corporate bonds

117B [Repealed by FA 2002, s. 141 and Sch. 40, Pt. 3(10).]

History – S. 117B repealed by FA 2002, s. 141 and Sch. 40, Pt. 3(10) with effect in relation to accounting periods beginning on or after 1 October 2002.

DEEP DISCOUNT SECURITIES, THE ACCRUED INCOME SCHEME ETC.

118 Amount to be treated as consideration on disposal of deep discount securities etc.

118 [Repealed by FA 1996, Sch. 41, Pt. V(3).]

History – S. 118 repealed by FA 1996, Sch. 41, Pt. V(3), with effect in relation to accounting periods ending after 31 March 1996 and tax years after 1995–96, but subject to transitional provisions and savings contained in FA 1996, Sch. 15.

119 Transfers of securities subject to the accrued income scheme

119(1) Where there is a transfer of securities within the meaning of Chapter 2 of Part 12 of ITA 2007 (accrued income profits)–

(a) if a payment is treated as made to the transferor under section 632 of that Act or by the transferor under section 633 of that Act, section 37 shall be disregarded in computing the gain accruing on the disposal concerned;

(b) if a payment is treated as made by the transferee under section 632 of that Act or to the transferee under section 633 of that Act, section 39 shall be disregarded in computing the gain accruing to the transferee if he disposes of the securities;

but subsections (2) and (3) below shall apply.

119(2) Where the securities are transferred with accrued interest (within the meaning of that Chapter)–

(a) if a payment is treated as made to the transferor under section 632 of ITA 2007, an amount equal to the amount of that payment shall be excluded from the consideration mentioned in subsection (8) below;

(b) if a payment is treated as made by the transferee under that section, an amount equal to the amount of that payment shall be excluded from the sums mentioned in subsection (9) below.

119(3) Where the securities are transferred without accrued interest (within the meaning of that Chapter)–

(a) if a payment is treated as made by the transferor under section 633 of ITA 2007, an amount equal to the amount of that payment shall be added to the consideration mentioned in subsection (8) below;

(b) if a payment is treated as made to the transferee under that section, an amount equal to the amount of that payment shall be added to the sums mentioned in subsection (9) below.

119(3A) Subsections (3B) and (3C) below apply where there is a transfer of variable rate securities (within the meaning of that Chapter) and–

(a) the transferor is treated as making accrued income profits under section 630(2) of ITA 2007, or

(b) a payment is treated as made to the transferor under section 635 of that Act.

119(3B) Section 37 shall be disregarded in computing the gain accruing on the disposal concerned.

119(3C) An amount equal to the amount of the profits or payment shall be excluded from the consideration mentioned in subsection (8) below.

119(4) Where there is a transfer of securities with unrealised interest (within the meaning of Chapter 2 of Part 12 of ITA 2007)–

(a) if section 630 of that Act applies or a payment is treated as made to the transferor under section 634 of that Act, section 37 shall be disregarded in computing the gain accruing on the disposal concerned, but the relevant amount shall be excluded from the consideration mentioned in subsection (8) below;

(b) if section 681 of that Act applies, section 39 shall be disregarded in computing the gain accruing on the disposal concerned, but the relevant amount shall be excluded from the sums mentioned in subsection (9) below.

119(5) In subsection (4) above **"the relevant amount"** means an amount equal to–

(a) if paragraph (b) below does not apply, the amount of the unrealised interest in question (within the meaning of Chapter 2 of Part 12 of ITA 2007);

(b) if section 660 of that Act applies–

(i) in a case falling within subsection (4)(a) above, the amount taken, by virtue of section 660 or 661 of that Act (as the case may be), to be the unrealised interest value for the purposes of section 660(2) or (3) of that Act;

(ii) in a case falling within subsection (4)(b) above, the amount of income that is exempt from liability to income tax under section 681 of that Act.

119(6) In relation to any securities which by virtue of subsection (7) below are treated for the purposes of this subsection as having been transferred, subsections (2) and (3) above shall have effect as if for "is treated as made", in each place where it occurs, there were substituted "would, if the disposal were a transfer, be treated as made".

119(7) Where there is a disposal of securities for the purposes of this Act which is not a transfer (within the meaning of Chapter 2 of Part 12 of ITA 2007) but, if it were such a transfer, a payment would be treated as made under section 632 or 633 of that Act, the securities shall be treated–

(a) for the purposes of subsection (6) above, as transferred on the day of the disposal, and

(b) for the purposes of subsections (2) and (3) above, as transferred with accrued interest if, had the disposal been a transfer within the meaning of that Chapter, it would have been a transfer with accrued interest and as transferred without accrued interest if, had the disposal been such a transfer, it would have been a transfer without accrued interest.

119(7A) In relation to any securities which by virtue of subsection (7B) below are treated for the purposes of this subsection as having been transferred, subsection (3A) above shall have effect as if–

(a) for "is treated as making" there were substituted "would, if the disposal were a transfer, be treated as making", and

(b) for "is treated as made" there were substituted "would, if the disposal were a transfer, be treated as made".

119(7B) Where there is a disposal of securities for the purposes of this Act which is not a transfer (within the meaning of Chapter 2 of Part 12 of ITA 2007) but, if it were such a transfer, the transferor would be treated as making accrued income profits under section 630(2) of that Act in respect of a transfer of variable rate securities or a payment would be treated as made under section 635 of that Act–

(a) the securities shall be treated, for the purposes of subsection (7A) above, as transferred on the day of the disposal, and

(b) the transfer shall be treated, for the purposes of subsection (3A) above, as a transfer of variable rate securities.

119(8) The consideration is the consideration for the disposal of the securities transferred which is taken into account in the computation of the gain accruing on the disposal.

119(9) The sums are the sums allowable to the transferee as a deduction from the consideration in the computation of the gain accruing to him if he disposes of the securities.

119(10) Where on a conversion or exchange of securities a payment is treated as made to a person under section 632 or 635 of ITA 2007, or a person is treated as making accrued income profits under section 630(2) of that Act in respect of a transfer of variable rate securities, an amount equal to the amount of the payment or profits shall, for the purposes of this Act, be treated as follows–

(a) to the extent that it does not exceed the amount of any consideration which the person receives (or is deemed to receive) or becomes entitled to receive on the conversion or exchange (other than his new holding), it shall be treated as reducing that consideration; and

(b) to the extent that it does exceed that amount, it shall be treated as consideration which the person gives on the conversion or exchange;

and where on a conversion or exchange of securities a payment is treated as made by a person under section 633 of that Act an amount equal to the amount of the payment shall, for the purposes of the computation of the gain, be treated as consideration which the person receives on the conversion or exchange.

119(11) In subsection (10) above **"conversion"** means conversion within the meaning of section 132 and **"exchange"** means an exchange which by virtue of Chapter II of this Part does not involve a disposal.

History – S. 119(1)–(5) substituted by ITA 2007, s. 1027 and Sch. 1, para. 308(2), with effect from 6 April 2007.
In s. 119(6), the words "as if for "is treated as made", in each place where it occurs, there were substituted "would, if the disposal were a transfer, be treated as made"" substituted for "as if for "applies" (in each place where it occurs) there were substituted "would apply if the disposal were a transfer"" by ITA 2007, s. 1027 and Sch. 1, para. 308(3), with effect from 6 April 2007.
S. 119(7), (7A) and (7B) substituted for the former s. 119(7) by ITA 2007, s. 1027 and Sch. 1, para. 308(4), with effect from 6 April 2007.
In s. 119(10), the words "a payment is treated as made to a person under section 632 or 635 of ITA 2007, or a person is treated as making accrued income profits under section 630(2) of that Act in respect of a transfer of variable rate securities, an amount equal to the amount of the payment or profits" substituted for "a person is treated as entitled to a sum under subsection (2)(a) of section 713 of the Taxes Act an amount equal to the accrued amount (determined under that section)" by ITA 2007, s. 1027 and Sch. 1, para. 308(5), with effect from 6 April 2007.
In s. 119(10), the words "a payment is treated as made by a person under section 633 of that Act an amount equal to the amount of the payment" substituted for "a person is treated as entitled to relief under subsection (3)(a) of that section an amount equal to the rebate amount (determined under that section)" by ITA 2007, s. 1027 and Sch. 1, para. 308(6), with effect from 6 April 2007.

Derivations – CGTA 1979, s. 33A, as inserted by ICTA 1988, s. 844 and Sch. 29, para. 20.

Cross references – S. 37: general provision that amounts charged to tax as income are excluded from consideration for the purpose of taxing chargeable gains.
S. 39: general provision that sums allowed as deduction in computing profits for income purposes are not also allowed for the purpose of computing chargeable gains.
S. 132: equation of original and new holdings on a conversion of securities.
ICTA 1988, s. 710–728: accrued income scheme, whereby transferor deemed entitled to accrued amount and transferee entitled to corresponding relief (s. 713(2)(a), (b)) or transferor entitled to relief for rebate amount and transferee entitled to corresponding receipt (s. 713(3)(a), (b)); on the transfer of securities with the right to unrealised interest, the transferor is treated as entitled thereto (s. 716(2), (3)) and it is left out of account for the transferee (s. 716(4)) but where the interest is in default such amounts are reduced to reflect the value of the right (s. 719).

Notes – S. 135–136: application of provisions (of Chapter II of this Part) equating the original and new holdings on an exchange of securities or scheme of reconstruction involving issue of securities.
S. 150(4): priority of special identification rules for BES shares (applies to shares issued on or before 31 December 1993).
S. 288: interpretation, including "the Taxes Act" as ICTA 1988 and reference to other sections being those of this Act.

119A Increase in expenditure by reference to tax charged in relation to employment-related securities

119A(1) This section applies to a disposal of an asset consisting of employment-related securities if the disposal–

(a) is an event giving rise to a relevant income tax charge, or

(b) is the first disposal after an event, other than a disposal, giving rise to a relevant income tax charge.

119A(2) Section 38(1)(a) applies as if the relevant amount had formed part of the consideration given by the person making the disposal for his acquisition of the employment-related securities.

119A(3) For the purposes of this section an event gives rise to a relevant income tax charge if it results in an amount counting as employment income in respect of the employment-related securities–

(a) under section 426 of ITEPA 2003 (restricted securities),

(b) under section 438 of ITEPA 2003 by virtue of section 439(3)(a) of that Act (conversion of convertible securities),

(c) under section 446U of ITEPA 2003 (securities acquired for less than market value: discharge of notional loan),

(ca) under section 447 of ITEPA 2003 (receipt of benefit) in a case where the benefit is an increase in the market value of the employment-related securities,

(d) under section 476 of ITEPA 2003 by virtue of section 477(3)(a) of that Act (acquisition of securities pursuant to employment-related securities option), or

(e) under subsection (3) of section 21 of the Finance Act 2005 (transitional charge in relation to shares in spin-out companies) by virtue of subsection (4)(b) of that section (election by employee).

119A(4) For the purposes of this section **"the relevant amount"** is the aggregate of the amounts counting as employment income as mentioned in subsection (3) above by reason of events occurring–

(a) not later than the disposal, and

(b) where this section has applied to an earlier disposal of the employment-related securities, after the last disposal to which this section applied.

119A(5) In determining for the purposes of subsection (4) the amount counting as employment income–

(a) in the case of an amount counting as employment income under section 476 of ITEPA 2003 any amounts deducted under section 480(5)(a), (b) or (d) of that Act shall be added back, and

(b) no account shall be taken of any relief under section 428A, 442A, 481 or 482 of that Act (relief for secondary Class 1 contributions or special contribution met by employee).

119A(5A) See also section 119B (unchargeable, and unremitted chargeable, foreign securities income) and section 119C (unremitted Part 7A income).

119A(6) Where securities or interests in securities cease to be employment-related securities–

(a) by reason of subsection (6) of section 421B of ITEPA in circumstances in which, immediately before the employee's death, the employment-related securities are held otherwise than by the employee, or

(b) by reason of subsection (7) of that section,

they are to be regarded for the purposes of this section as remaining employment-related securities until the next occasion on which they are disposed of.

119A(7) In this section–

"employment-related securities", and

"employee", in relation to employment-related securities,

have the same meaning as in Chapters 1 to 4 of Part 7 of ITEPA 2003.

119A(8) [Omitted by FA 2004, s. 85 and Sch. 16, para. 6(3) and repealed by FA 2004, s. 326 and Sch. 42, Pt. 2(10), all of which came into force on 1 September 2004.]

History – In s. 119A(3), immediately after words "employment income", the words "in respect of the employment-related securities" inserted by FA 2005, s. 22(2)(a) with effect in relation to any disposal, whether before or after 7 April 2005 (date of Royal Assent to FA 2005).

S. 119A(3)(ca), substituted for the word "or" at the end of para. (c) by FA 2005, s. 22(2)(b) with effect in relation to disposals on or after 6 April 2005.

In s. 119A(3)(e), and the word "or" immediately before it inserted by FA 2005, s. 22(2)(c) with effect in relation to any disposal, whether before or after 7 April 2005 (date of Royal Assent to FA 2005).

In s. 119A(3), words "in respect of the employment related securities", which followed the paragraphs omitted by FA 2005, s. 22(2)(d) and repealed by FA 2005, s. 104 and Sch. 11, Pt. 2(2), with effect in relation to any disposal, whether before or after 7 April 2005 (date of Royal Assent to FA 2005).

In s. 119A(5)(a), the words ", (b) or (d)" substituted for the words "or (b)" by FA 2011, s. 26 and Sch. 2, para. 49(2)(a), with effect where ITEPA 2003, Pt. 7A has effect, which is namely in relation to "relevant steps" taken on or after 6 April 2011 (FA 2011, Sch. 2, para. 52(1)), subject to the provisions of Sch. 2, para. 52(2).

S. 119A(5) substituted by FA 2004, s. 85 and Sch. 16, para. 6(2) which came into force on 1 September 2004, by virtue of SI 2004/1945 that was made on 22 July 2004. However, in accordance with FA 2004, Sch. 16, para. 6(4), nothing in FA 2004, Sch. 16, para. 6 affects the operation of s. 119A(5), as inserted by FA 2003, Sch. 22, para. 50(1), in relation to amounts deducted under ITEPA 2003, s. 481 or s. 482 before the amendment of those sections by FA 2004, Sch. 16.

In s. 119A(5A), the words "unchargeable, and unremitted chargeable, foreign securities income" substituted for the words "unremitted foreign securities income" by FA 2014, s. 52 and Sch. 9, para. 23, with effect from 6 April 2015 in relation to employment-related securities and employment-related securities options irrespective of the date of the acquisition.

In s. 119A(5A), the words "and section 119C (unremitted Part 7A income)" inserted at the end by FA 2011, s. 26 and Sch. 2, para. 49(2)(b), with effect where ITEPA 2003, Pt. 7A has effect, which is namely in relation to "relevantsteps" taken on or after 6 April 2011 (FA 2011, Sch. 2, para. 52(1)), subject to the provisions of Sch. 2, para. 52(2).
S. 119A(5A) inserted by FA 2008, s. 25 and Sch. 7, para. 63 with effect from 2008–09 (FA 2008, Sch. 7, para. 81).
S. 119A(8) omitted by FA 2004, s. 85 and Sch. 16, para. 6(3) which came into force on 1 September 2004, by virtue of SI 2004/1945 that was made on 22 July 2004. Also, s. 119A(8) was repealed by FA 2004, s. 326 and Sch. 42, Pt. 2(10) which, in accordance with FA 2004, s. 85(2), came into force on 1 September 2004 by virtue of SI 2004/1945 that was made on 22 July 2004. Furthermore, the repeal of s. 119A(8) has effect subject to FA 2004, Sch. 16, para. 6(4), by virtue of FA 2004, Sch. 42, Pt. 2(10). FA 2004, Sch. 16, para. 6(4) states that nothing in FA 2004, Sch. 16, para. 6 affects the operation of s. 119A(5), as inserted by FA 2003, Sch. 22, para. 50(1), in relation to amounts deducted under ITEPA 2003, s. 481 or s. 482 before the amendment of those sections by FA 2004, Sch. 16.
S. 119A inserted by FA 2003, s. 140 and Sch. 22, para. 50(1) which, by virtue of FA 2003, Sch. 22, para. 50(2), have effect in relation to disposals on or after 16 April 2003.

Cross references – FA 2004, Sch. 16, para. 6(4): relief where national insurance contributions met by employee: transitional provision.

119B Section 119A: unchargeable, and unremitted chargeable, foreign securities income

History – In the heading to s. 119B, the words "unchargeable, and unremitted chargeable, foreign securities income" substituted for the words "unremitted foreign securities income" by FA 2014, s. 52 and Sch. 9, para. 24(2), with effect from 6 April 2015 in relation to employment-related securities and employment-related securities options irrespective of the date of the acquisition.

119B(1) For the purposes of section 119A reduce the amount that counts as employment income by so much of that amount (if any) as is–

(a) unchargeable foreign securities income, or

(b) unremitted chargeable foreign securities income.

119B(1A) In this section **"unchargeable foreign securities income"** means unchargeable foreign securities income for the purposes of section 41F of ITEPA 2003 (taxable specific income: internationally mobile employees etc) (see sections 41H to 41L of that Act).

119B(2) In this section **"unremitted chargeable foreign securities income"** means income that–

(a) is chargeable foreign securities income for the purposes of section 41F of ITEPA 2003, and

(b) has not been remitted to the United Kingdom by the end of the tax year in which the disposal mentioned in section 119A(1) occurs.

119B(3) The following provisions apply if any of the unremitted chargeable foreign securities income is remitted to the United Kingdom after the end of the tax year referred to in subsection (2)(b).

119B(4) The person liable for the capital gains tax on any chargeable gains arising on the disposal may make a claim for section 119A(2) to have effect as if the remitted income had been remitted before the end of that tax year.

119B(5) All adjustments (by way of repayment of tax, assessment or otherwise) are to be made which are necessary to give effect to a claim under subsection (4).

119B(6) Those adjustments may be made at any time, despite anything to the contrary in any enactment relating to capital gains tax.

History – In s. 119B(1), words from "as is–" to end substituted for the words "unremitted foreign securities income" by FA 2014, s. 52 and Sch. 9, para. 24(3), with effect from 6 April 2015 in relation to employment-related securities and employment-related securities options irrespective of the date of the acquisition.
S. 119B(1A) inserted by FA 2014, s. 52 and Sch. 9, para. 24(4), with effect from 6 April 2015 in relation to employment-related securities and employment-related securities options irrespective of the date of the acquisition.
In s. 119B(2), the word "chargeable" inserted after the word "unremitted" by FA 2014, s. 52 and Sch. 9, para. 24(5)(a), with effect from 6 April 2015 in relation to employment-related securities and employment-related securities options irrespective of the date of the acquisition.
S. 199B(2)(a) substituted by FA 2014, s. 52 and Sch. 9, para. 24(5)(b), with effect from 6 April 2015 in relation to employment-related securities and employment-related securities options irrespective of the date of the acquisition.
In s. 119B(3), the word "chargeable" inserted after the word "unremitted" by FA 2014, s. 52 and Sch. 9, para. 24(6), with effect from 6 April 2015 in relation to employment-related securities and employment-related securities options irrespective of the date of the acquisition.
S. 119B inserted by FA 2008, s. 25 and Sch. 7, para. 64 with effect in relation to employment-related securities and employment-related securities options where the date of acquisition is on or after 6 April 2008 (except those securities acquired under an option acquired before that date) (FA 2008, Sch. 7, para. 80).

119C Section 119A: unremitted Part 7A income

119C(1) This section applies for the purposes of section 119A if an amount deducted under section 480(5)(d) of ITEPA 2003, which (apart from this section) would by virtue of section 119A(5)(a) be added back to an amount counting as employment income, is or includes unremitted Part 7A income.

119C(2) So much of the amount deducted as is unremitted Part 7A income is not to be added back.

119C(3) In this section **"unremitted Part 7A income"** means an amount counting as employment income under Chapter 2 of Part 7A of ITEPA 2003–

(a) to which section 554Z9(2) or 554Z10(2) of that Act applies, and

(b) which has not been remitted to the United Kingdom by the end of the tax year in which the disposal mentioned in section 119A(1) occurs.

119C(4) Section 119B(4) to (6) applies if any of the unremitted Part 7A income is remitted to the United Kingdom after the end of the tax year referred to in subsection (3)(b).

History – S. 119C inserted by FA 2011, s. 26 and Sch. 2, para. 49(3), with effect where ITEPA 2003, Pt. 7A has effect, which is namely in relation to "relevant steps" taken on or after 6 April 2011 (FA 2011, Sch. 2, para. 52(1)), subject to the provisions of Sch. 2, para. 52(2).

120 Increase in expenditure by reference to tax charged in relation to shares etc.

120(1) Subsection (1A) applies where–

(a) a person (**"the employee"**) has acquired shares or an interest in shares as mentioned in section 447(1) of ITEPA 2003, and

(b) an amount counts as employment income of the employee under Chapter 4 of Part 7 of that Act in respect of the shares.

120(1A) On the first disposal of the shares after the acquisition occurs, the employment income amount shall be treated for the purposes of section 38(1)(a) as consideration given by the person making the disposal for the acquisition of the shares.

120(1B) For the purposes of subsections (1) and (1A)–

(a) the **"employment income amount"** means the amount counting as employment income of the employee under that Chapter in respect of the shares, and

(b) it is immaterial whether the disposal of the shares mentioned in subsection (1A) is made by the employee or another person.

120(2) Section 38(1)(a) applies as if the relevant amount as defined in the following provisions of this section in the cases there specified had formed part of the consideration given by the person making the disposal for his acquisition of the assets in question.

120(3) Where an amount is treated as earnings under section 195(2) of ITEPA 2003 in respect of shares or an interest in shares, then–

(a) on a disposal of the shares or interest, where that is the event giving rise to the charge; or

(b) in any case, on the first disposal of the shares or interest after the event,

the relevant amount is a sum equal to the amount so treated as earnings.

120(4) If a gain counting as employment income under section 476 or 477 of ITEPA 2003 is realised by the exercise of a right to acquire shares, the relevant amount is a sum equal to the amount of the gain so counting as employment income.

120(5) Where an amount is chargeable to tax under section 138 of the Taxes Act on a person acquiring any shares or interest in shares, then on the first disposal (whether by him or another person) of the shares after his acquisition, the relevant amount is an amount equal to the amount so chargeable.

120(5A) Where an amount counts as employment income under Chapter 2 of Part 7 of ITEPA 2003 in respect of–

(a) the acquisition or disposal of any interest in shares, or

(b) any interest in shares ceasing to be only conditional,

the relevant amount is a sum equal to the amount so counting as employment income.

120(5B) Where an amount counts as employment income under Chapter 3 of Part 7 of ITEPA 2003 in respect of the conversion of shares, the relevant amount is a sum equal to the amount so counting as employment income.

120(6) [Omitted by ITEPA 2003, Sch. 6, para 210(7) and repealed by ITEPA 2003, Sch. 8, Pt. 1.]

120(7) Each of the provisions of this section mentioned in the first column of the following table is to be construed as if it were contained in the Chapter of ITEPA 2003 specified in the corresponding entry in the second column–

Provision of this section	Chapter of ITEPA 2003
subsections (1), (1A) and (1B)	Chapter 4 of Part 7
subsection (3)	Chapter 8 of Part 3
subsection (4)	Chapter 5 of Part 7
subsection (5A)	Chapter 2 of Part 7
subsection (5B)	Chapter 3 of Part 7

and subsection (5) of this section is to be construed as one with section 138 of the Taxes Act.

120(7A) In relation to events that gave rise to amounts chargeable to income tax before 6th April 2003, this section is to be read as if any reference to an amount mentioned in the first column of the following table included a reference to an amount mentioned in the corresponding entry in the second column–

Amount mentioned in this section	Amount chargeable before 6th April 2003
an amount counting as employment income under Chapter 4 of Part 7 of ITEPA 2003	an amount chargeable to tax under Chapter 2 of Part 3 of the Finance Act 1988
an amount treated as earnings under section 195(2) of ITEPA 2003	an amount chargeable to tax under section 162(5) of the Taxes Act
an amount counting as employment income under section 476 or 477 of ITEPA 2003	an amount chargeable to tax under section 135(1) or (6) of the Taxes Act
an amount counting as employment income under Chapter 2 of Part 7 of ITEPA 2003	an amount chargeable to tax under section 140A of the Taxes Act
an amount counting as employment income under Chapter 3 of Part 7 of ITEPA 2003	an amount chargeable to tax under section 140D of the Taxes Act.

120(8) For the purposes of subsection (5A) above this section shall have effect as if references in this section to shares included anything referred to as shares in Chapter 2 of Part 7 of ITEPA 2003.

120(9) References in this section to ITEPA 2003 are to that Act as originally enacted.

History – S. 120(1), (1A), (1B) substituted for previous s. 120(1) by ITEPA 2003, Sch. 6, para. 210(2) with effect for 2003–04 and subsequent tax years.

In s. 120(3), the words "is treated as earnings under section 195(2) of ITEPA 2003" substituted for the words "is chargeable to tax by virtue of section 162(5) of the Taxes Act" by ITEPA 2003, Sch. 6, para. 210(3)(a) with effect for 2003–04 and subsequent tax years.

In s. 120(3), the words "so treated as earnings" substituted for the words "so chargeable" by ITEPA 2003, Sch. 6, para. 210(3)(b) with effect for 2003–04 and subsequent tax years.

In s. 120(4), the words "counting as employment income under section 476 or 477 of ITEPA 2003" substituted for the words "chargeable to tax under section 135(1) or (6) of the Taxes Act" by ITEPA 2003, Sch. 6, para. 210(4)(a) with effect for 2003–04 and subsequent tax years.

In s. 120(4), the words "so counting as employment income" substituted for the words "so chargeable to tax" by ITEPA 2003, Sch. 6, para. 210(4)(b) with effect for 2003–04 and subsequent tax years.

In s. 120(5A), the words "counts as employment income under Chapter 2 of Part 7 of ITEPA 2003" substituted for the words "is chargeable to tax under section 140A of the Taxes Act" by ITEPA 2003, Sch. 6, para. 210(5)(a) with effect for 2003–04 and subsequent tax years.

In s. 120(5A), the words "so counting as employment income" substituted for the words "so chargeable to tax" by ITEPA 2003, Sch. 6, para. 210(5)(b) with effect for 2003–04 and subsequent tax years.

S. 120(5A) inserted by FA 1998, s. 54(2) and (4) as respects disposals of shares, or interests in shares, on or after 17 March 1998 where the shares, or the interests in shares, were also acquired on or after that date.

In s. 120(5B), the words "counts as employment income under Chapter 3 of Part 7 of ITEPA 2003" substituted for the words "is chargeable to tax under section 140D of the Taxes Act" by ITEPA 2003, Sch. 6, para. 210(6)(a) with effect for 2003–04 and subsequent tax years.

In s. 120(5B), the words "so counting as employment income" substituted for the words "so chargeable to tax" by ITEPA 2003, Sch. 6, para. 210(6)(b) with effect for 2003–04 and subsequent tax years.

S. 120(5B) inserted by FA 1998, s. 54(2) and (4) as respects disposals of shares, or interests in shares, on or after 17 March 1998 where the shares, or the interests in shares, were also acquired on or after that date.

S. 120(6) omitted by ITEPA 2003, Sch. 6, para. 210(7) and repealed by ITEPA 2003, Sch. 8, Pt. 1 with effect for 2003–04 and subsequent tax years.

S. 120(7) substituted by ITEPA 2003, Sch. 6, para. 210(8) with effect for 2003–04 and subsequent tax years.

S. 120(7A) inserted by ITEPA 2003, Sch. 6, para. 210(9) with effectfor 2003–04 and subsequent tax years.

In s. 120(8), the words "Chapter 2 of Part 7 of ITEPA 2003" substituted for the words "section 140A of the Taxes Act" by ITEPA 2003, Sch. 6, para. 210(10) with effect for 2003–04 and subsequent tax years.

S. 120(8), inserted by FA 1998, s. 54(2) and (4) as respects disposals of shares, or interests in shares, on or after 17 March 1998 where the shares, or the interests in shares, were also acquired on or after that date.

S. 120(9) inserted by FA 2003, s. 140 and Sch. 22, para. 51 which came into force on 10 July 2003 (i.e. date of Royal Assent of FA 2003).

Derivations – S. 120(1): FA 1988, s. 84.

S. 120(2)–(7): CGTA 1979, s. 32A, as inserted by ICTA 1988, s. 844 and Sch. 29, para. 18.

Cross references – S. 38(1)(a): deduction for allowable acquisition expenditure including incidental costs.

S. 150(4): priority of special identification rules for BES shares (applies to shares issued on or before 31 December 1993).

ICTA 1988, s. 135(1), (6): charges under Sch. E on an individual in respect of gains realised by him from exercise of rights to acquire shares obtained as a director or employee or in respect of certain such gains realised by another person from exercise of rights granted by reason of the individual's office or employment.

ICTA 1988, s. 138, 139(14): in relation to acquisitions before 26 October 1987, charge on any increase in market value of shares or units in an authorised unit trust received in pursuance of rights etc. conferred as director or employee (the "growth in value charge").

ICTA 1988, s. 162(5): charge to income tax on termination of notional interest-free loan in respect of shares acquired at an undervalue etc. where disposal, surrender etc. or credit to partly-paid shares.

ICTA 1988, s. 185(6A): charge on obtaining option under an approved share option scheme (not savings-related) on difference between market value of shares and the aggregate of the option price and the option consideration.

ICTA 1988, s. 187A(5)(b): relief for contributions in respect of share option gains given by deduction from chargeable gain does not affect the amount of the gain for the purposes of s. 120(4).

FA 1988, Pt. III, Ch. II (s. 77–89): unapproved employee share schemes, including rights conferred by virtue of being a person connected with an employee or director, certain disposals to connected persons and benefits received thereby.

ITEPA 2003, Pt. 3, Ch. 8: taxable benefits: notional loans in respect of acquisitions of shares.

ITEPA 2003, s. 195(2): discharge of notional loan in respect of shares acquired at an undervalue etc: amount treated as earnings.

ITEPA 2003, Pt. 7, Ch. 2: conditional interests in shares.

ITEPA 2003, Pt. 7, Ch. 3: convertible shares.

ITEPA 2003, Pt.7, Ch. 4: post-acquisition benefits in respect of shares.
ITEPA 2003, s. 447: post-acquisition benefits from shares
ITEPA 2003, Pt. 7, Ch. 5: share options.
ITEPA 2003, s. 476: charge on exercise, assignment or release of option by employee.
ITEPA 2003, s. 477: charge on employee where option exercised, assigned or released by another person.
Notes – S. 120 applies only to disposals between 6 April 2003 and 16 April 2003 (by virtue of the reference in s. 120(9) to ITEPA 2003 as originally enacted) it is now effectively superseded by s. 119A.
S. 21–34: general meaning of "disposal" and "assets".
S. 288: interpretation, including "the Taxes Act" as ICTA 1988 and reference to other sections being those of this Act.

SAVINGS CERTIFICATES ETC.

121 Exemption for government non-marketable securities

121(1) Savings certificates and non-marketable securities issued under the National Loans Act 1968 or the National Loans Act 1939, or any corresponding enactment forming part of the law of Northern Ireland, shall not be chargeable assets, and accordingly no chargeable gain shall accrue on their disposal.

121(2) In this section–

(a) **"savings certificates"** means savings certificates issued under section 12 of the National Loans Act 1968, or section 7 of the National Debt Act 1958, or section 59 of the Finance Act 1920 and any war savings certificates as defined in section 9(3) of the National Debt Act 1972, together with any savings certificates issued under any enactment forming part of the law of Northern Ireland and corresponding to the said enactments, and

(b) **"non-marketable securities"** means securities which are not transferable, or which are transferable only with the consent of some Minister of the Crown, or the consent of a department of the Government of Northern Ireland, or only with the consent of the National Debt Commissioners.

Derivations – CGTA 1979, s. 71.

Cross references – S. 150(4): priority of special identification rules for BES shares (applies to shares issued on or before 31 December 1993).
TMA 1970, s. 12(2): assets within s. 121 are excluded from the requirements to divulge information about assets for purposes of capital gains tax.
Notes – S. 15: meaning of "chargeable gains".
S. 21–34: general meaning of "disposal" and "assets".

CAPITAL DISTRIBUTION IN RESPECT OF SHARES ETC.

122 Distribution which is not a new holding within Chapter II

122(1) Where a person receives or becomes entitled to receive in respect of shares in a company any capital distribution from the company (other than a new holding as defined in section 126) he shall be treated as if he had in consideration of that capital distribution disposed of an interest in the shares.

122(1A) Subsection (1) is subject to the provisions of section 140A(1D) and section 140E(7).

122(2) If the amount distributed is small, as compared with the value of the shares in respect of which it is distributed –

(a) the occasion of the capital distribution shall not be treated for the purposes of this Act as a disposal of the asset, and

(b) the amount distributed shall be deducted from any expenditure allowable under this Act as a deduction in computing a gain or loss on the disposal of the shares by the person receiving or becoming entitled to receive the distribution of capital.

122(3) [Repealed by FA 1996, Sch. 20, para. 52(2).]

122(4) Where the allowable expenditure is less than the amount distributed (or is nil)–

(a) subsection (2) above shall not apply, and

(b) if the recipient so elects (and there is any allowable expenditure)–

(i) the amount distributed shall be reduced by the amount of the allowable expenditure, and

(ii) none of that expenditure shall be allowable as a deduction in computing a gain accruing on the occasion of the capital distribution, or on any subsequent occasion.

In this subsection **"allowable expenditure"** means the expenditure which immediately before the occasion of the capital distribution was attributable to the shares under paragraphs (a) and (b) of section 38(1).

122(5) In this section–

(a) the **"amount distributed"** means the amount or value of the capital distribution,

(b) **"capital distribution"** means any distribution from a company, including a distribution in the course of dissolving or winding up the company, in money or money's worth except a distribution which in the hands of the recipient constitutes income for the purposes of income tax.

122(5A) The reference in subsection (5)(b) to a distribution in the course of dissolving a company includes a reference to a distribution to which section 1030A(3) of CTA 2010 (distributions prior to dissolution of company) applies.

122(6) The reference in subsection (5)(b) to a distribution which in the hands of the recipient constitutes income for the purposes of income tax includes, where the recipient is a company, a distribution to which the charge to corporation tax on income under Part 9A of CTA 2009 (company distributions) would apply were the distribution not exempt for the purposes of that Part.

History – S. 122(1A) inserted by SI 2007/3186, reg. 3(2) and Sch. 2, para. 4, in relation to mergers relating to the formation of an SE or SCE which take place on or after 18 August 2006, and in relation to all other mergers which take place on or after 1 January 2007.
In s. 122(2) the words "the inspector is satisfied that" and "and so directs" repealed by FA 1996, Sch. 20, para. 52 and s. 205 and Sch. 41, Pt. V(10), as respects years after 1995–96 (capital gains tax) and accounting periods ending on or after 1 July 1999, the day appointed under FA 1994, s. 199 by virtue of SI 1998/3173 (C. 78) (corporation tax).
S. 122(3) repealed by FA 1996, Sch. 20, para. 52 and s. 205 and Sch. 41, Pt. V(10), as respects years after 1995–96 (capital gains tax) and accounting periods ending on or after 1 July 1999, the day appointed under FA 1994, s. 199 by virtue of SI 1998/3173 (C. 78) (corporation tax).
In s. 122(4)(a) a reference to subs. (3) omitted, by FA 1996, Sch. 20, para. 52 and s. 205 and Sch. 41, Pt. V(10), as respects years after 1995–96 (capital gains tax) and accounting periods ending on or after 1 July 1999, the day appointed under FA 1994, s. 199 by virtue of SI 1998/3173 (C. 78) (corporation tax).
S. 122(5A) inserted by SI 2012/266, art. 17, with effect in relation to distributions made on or after 1 March 2012.
S. 122(6) inserted by F(No. 3)A 2010, s. 9 and Sch. 3, para. 4(3), with effect in relation to distributions made on or after 1 July 2009, subject to any election made under F(No. 3)A 2010, Sch. 3, para. 7 in respect of distributions made before 22 June 2010. See cross-reference note below for retrospective modification of s. 122 by F(No. 3)A 2010, Sch. 3 in respect of certain distributions of UK resident companies.

Derivations – CGTA 1979, s. 72.

Cross references – S. 38: sums allowable in relation to acquisition and disposal costs.
S. 57: determining relevant allowable expenditure for the purposes of indexation allowance.
S. 105B(4): s. 122(1) disregarded in determining whether disposal of relevant shares for purpose of s. 105A.
S. 110(8)(d): reduction of pool of qualifying expenditure and pool of indexed expenditure where shares are held in a section 104 holding.
S. 123: disposal of provisional letter of allotment (sale of rights nil paid) treated as a capital distribution.
S. 128(3): where disposal under s. 122 in a reorganisation, recipient treated as if the new holding resulted from his having disposed of an interest in the original shares for that consideration.
S. 150(4): priority of special identification rules for BES shares (applies to shares issued on or before 31 December 1993).
S. 171(2): priority over no gain, no loss on transfers of capital assets within a group.
S. 189: recovery of unpaid tax from recipient shareholder of a capital distribution within s. 122 (except on a reduction of capital) where the capital derives from a source from which the gain arose.
S. 192(2): on a demerger, an exempt distribution consisting of the transfer to all or any of its members by a company of shares in one or more companies which are its 75 per cent subsidiaries is not a capital distribution for s. 122.
S. 238(2)(b): charge to income tax under Sch. E in respect of any capital receipt in money or money's worth by a trustee or recipient of an approved profits sharing scheme (ICTA 1988, s. 186(3)) disregarded in determining a capital distribution.
Sch. 3, para. 4(2): corresponding reduction in reacquisition expenditure to effect re-basing where original expenditure would be disallowed under s. 122(4) in respect of a disposal between 31 March 1982 and 6 April 1988.
Sch. 6, para. 11: capital distribution within s. 122 does not qualify for retirement relief if it consists wholly of chargeable business assets (or to the extent that it does so where it consists of such assets and money or money's worth).
ICTA 1988, s. 209: distributions which for the recipient constitute income for the purposes of income tax.
ICTA 1988, s. 734(2): interest on certain short term buying and selling of securities is treated as a capital distribution within s. 122(5)(b).
FA 1988, Sch. 12, para. 6(2): on incorporation of a building society, priority rights given to members may be a capital distribution for s. 122.
F(No. 3)A 2010, Sch. 3, para. 6(4): s. 122 treated as always having had effect as if references in it to a capital distribution did not include a distribution that is exempt from corporation tax under CTA 2009, s. 1285 or ICTA 1988, s. 208 as modified by F(No. 3)A 2010, Sch. 3, para. 6(1). This is subject to any election made under F(No. 3)A 2010, Sch. 3, para. 7 in respect of distributions made before 22 June 2010.

HMRC interpretations – IR Int. 157: HMRC now take view that "small" can mean 5 per cent or less of value of asset etc., or receipt of £3,000 or less whether or not falling within the 5 per cent test; exceptionally taxpayers may suggest different limits in the context of their particular circumstances (*O'Rourke v Binks* [1992] BTC 460).

Notes – S. 38: deduction for allowable acquisition expenditure (including incidental costs), enhancement or title expenditure and incidental cost of disposal.
S. 288: interpretation, including meaning of "company", "shares" as embracing stock, "inspector" as being any inspector of taxes and reference to sections being those of this Act.
TMA 1970, s. 44–59 and Sch. 3: procedure and rules for assigning appeals.

123 Disposal of right to acquire shares or debentures

123(1) Where a person receives or becomes entitled to receive in respect of any shares in a company a provisional allotment of shares in or debentures of the company and he disposes of his rights, section 122 shall apply as if the amount of the consideration for the disposal were a capital distribution received by him from the company in respect of the first-mentioned shares, and as if that person had, instead of disposing of the rights, disposed of an interest in those shares.

123(2) This section shall apply in relation to rights obtained in respect of debentures of a company as it applies in relation to rights obtained in respect of shares in a company.

Derivations – CGTA 1979, s. 73(1), (3).

Cross references – S. 150(4): priority of special identification rules for BES shares (applies to shares issued on or before 31 December 1993).

Notes – S. 21–34: general meaning of "disposal".
S. 288: interpretation, including meaning of "company", "shares" as embracing stock and reference to sections being those of this Act; shares or debentures comprised in a letter of allotment are treated as issued unless the right is provisional.

CLOSE COMPANIES

124 Disposal of shares: relief in respect of income tax consequent on shortfall in distributions

124(1) If in pursuance of section 426 of the Taxes Act (consequences for income tax of apportionment of income etc. of close company) a person is assessed to income tax, then, in the computation of the gain accruing on a disposal by him of any shares forming part of his interest in the company to which the relevant apportionment relates, the amount of the income tax paid by him, so far as attributable to those shares, shall be allowable as a deduction.

124(2) Subsection (1) above shall not apply in relation to tax charged in respect of undistributed income which has, before the disposal, been subsequently distributed and is then exempt from tax by virtue of section 427(4) of the Taxes Act or in relation to tax treated as having been paid by virtue of section 426(2)(b) of that Act.

124(3) For the purposes of this section the income assessed to tax shall be the highest part of the individual's income for the year of assessment in question, but so that if the highest part of the said income is taken into account under this section in relation to an assessment to tax the next highest part shall be taken into account in relation to any other relevant assessment, and so on.

124(4) For the purpose of identifying shares forming part of an interest in a company with shares subsequently disposed of which are of the same class, shares bought at an earlier time shall be deemed to have been disposed of before shares bought at a later time.

Derivations – CGTA 1979, s. 74(1)–(4).

Cross references – S. 150(4): priority of special identification rules for BES shares (applies to shares issued on or before 31 December 1993).

Notes – S. 38: allowable deductions generally restricted to acquisition and incidental costs, enhancement expenditure and incidental costs of disposal.
S. 288: interpretation, including meaning of "close company", "the Taxes Act" as ICTA 1988 and reference to other sections being those of this Act.

125 Shares in close company transferring assets at an undervalue

125(1) If a company which is a close company transfers, or has after 31st March 1982 transferred, an asset to any person otherwise than by way of a bargain made at arm's length and for a consideration of an amount or value less than the market value of the asset, an amount equal to the difference shall be apportioned among the issued shares of the company, and the holders of those shares shall be treated in accordance with the following provisions of this section.

125(2) For the purposes of the computation of the gain accruing on the disposal of any of those shares by the person owning them on the date of transfer, an amount equal to the amount so apportioned to that share shall be excluded from the expenditure allowable as a deduction under section 38(1)(a) from the consideration for the disposal.

125(3) If the person owning any of the shares at the date of transfer is itself a close company an amount equal to the amount apportioned to the shares so owned under subsection (1) above to that close company shall be apportioned among the issued shares of that close company, and the holders of those shares shall be treated in accordance with subsection (2) above, and so on through any number of close companies.

125(4) This section does not apply in the following cases.

Case 1

Case 1 is where the transfer of the asset is a disposal to which section 171(1) applies (transfers within a group: general provisions).

Case 2

Case 2 is where the transferee is a participator, or an associate of a participator, in the company and an amount equal to the undervalue amount is treated as–

(a) a distribution within section 209(2)(b) or (4) of the Taxes Act (meaning of "distribution"), or

(b) a capital distribution within section 122 of this Act (distribution which is not a new holding within Chapter 2).

Case 3

Case 3 is where the transferee is an employee of the company and–

(a) an amount equal to the undervalue amount is treated as the employee's employment income, and

(b) no part of that amount is treated as exempt income.

125(5) In relation to a disposal to which section 35(2) does not apply, subsection (1) above shall have effect with the substitution of "6th April 1965" for "31st March 1982".

125(6) In this section–

"associate" has the meaning given by section 448 of CTA 2010;

"employee" has the meaning given by section 4 of ITEPA 2003 (as read with section 5(2) of that Act);

"employment income" has the meaning given by section 7(2) of ITEPA 2003;

"exempt income" has the meaning given by section 8 of ITEPA 2003;

"participator" has the meaning given by section 454 of CTA 2010;

"undervalue amount" means the amount by which the amount or value of the consideration for the transfer is less than the market value of the asset transferred.

History – S. 125(4) substituted by SI 2009/730, art. 5(2), with effect for the purposes of computing the gain accruing on any disposal of shares in a close company on or after 6 April 2009.
In s. 125(6), in the definition of "associate", the words "section 448 of CTA 2010" substituted for "section 417 of the Taxes Act" by CTA 2010, s. 1177 and Sch. 1, para. 232(a), with effect for corporation tax purposes for accounting periods ending on or after 1 April 2010, and for income tax and capital gains tax purposes for the tax year 2010–11 and subsequent tax years.
In s. 125(6), in the definition of "participator", the words "section 454 of CTA 2010" substituted for "section 417 of the Taxes Act" by CTA 2010, s. 1177 and Sch. 1, para. 232(b), with effect for corporation tax purposes for accounting periods ending on or after 1 April 2010, and for income tax and capital gains tax purposes for the tax year 2010–11 and subsequent tax years.
S. 125(6) inserted by SI 2009/730, art. 5(3), with effect for the purposes of computing the gain accruing on any disposal of shares in a close company on or after 6 April 2009.

Derivations – S. 125(1)–(4): CGTA 1979, s. 75, as amended by FA 1988, s. 96(9) and Sch. 8, para. 7.
S. 125(5): CGTA 1979, s. 75 as enacted.

Cross references – S. 35(2): re-basing to 31 March 1982.
S. 38(1)(a): allowable acquisition expenditure.
S. 150(4): priority of special identification rules for BES shares (applies to shares issued on or before 31 December 1993).
S. 171(1): deemed no gain, no loss on transfers of capital assets within a group.
S. 239(3): modification to certain disposals by a close company to employee trusts by substitution of allowable expenditure for market value where lower.

Extra-statutory concessions – D51: HMRC will not seek to apply s. 125 if the transfer has already been taxed as income or a distribution, or where the transferee is an employee of the company and has already been taxed under Sch. E on the difference between the market value of the asset and the amount actually paid for it.

Other material – ICAEW Tax Faculty technical release TAX 7/95, section C: Revenue confirmation that, in principle, post-incorporation partnership annuity payments can be relieved as an annual charge under ICTA 1988, s. 338, and that s. 125 should not apply.

Notes – S. 17: disposals and acquisitions treated as made at market value by reference to bargains otherwise than at arm's length.
S. 272–274 and Sch. 11: meaning of "market value".
S. 288: interpretation, including meaning of "close company", "issue" of shares by reference to letters of allotment, "shares" as embracing stock and reference to sections being those of this Act.

SHARE LOSS RELIEF

125A Effect of share loss relief

125A(1) If loss relief under Chapter 6 of Part 4 of ITA 2007 or Chapter 5 of Part 4 of CTA 2010 ("share loss relief") is obtained in respect of a loss or any part of a loss, no deduction is to be made in respect of the loss or (as the case may be) the part under this Act.

125A(2) If a claim is made for share loss relief in respect of a loss accruing on the disposal of shares, section 30 has effect in relation to the disposal as if for the references in subsections (1)(b) and (5) to a tax-free benefit there were substituted references to any benefit whether tax-free or not.

125A(3) All such adjustments of corporation tax on chargeable gains or capital gains tax are to be made, whether by way of assessment or by way of discharge or repayment of tax, as may be required in consequence of–

(a) share loss relief being obtained in respect of an allowable loss, or

(b) such relief not being obtained in respect of the whole or part of such a loss in respect of which a claim is made.

History – In s. 125A(1), the words "section 573 of the Taxes Act or", which appeared after "relief under", omitted by CTA 2010, s. 1177 and Sch. 1, para. 233(a) and repealed by CTA 2010, s. 1181 and Sch. 3, Pt. 1, with effect for corporation tax purposes for accounting periods ending on or after 1 April 2010, and for income tax and capital gains tax purposes for the tax year 2010–11 and subsequent tax years.
In s. 125A(1). the words "or Chapter 5 of Part 4 of CTA 2010" inserted by CTA 2010, s. 1177 and Sch. 1, para. 233(b), with effect for corporation tax purposes for accounting periods ending on or after 1 April 2010, and for income tax and capital gains tax purposes for the tax year 2010–11 and subsequent tax years.
S. 125A inserted by ITA 2007, s. 1027 and Sch. 1, para. 309, with effect from 6 April 2007.

Chapter II – Reorganisation of Share Capital, Conversion of Securities etc.

REORGANISATION OR REDUCTION OF SHARE CAPITAL

Cross references – TCGA 1992, s. 151BC (Community Investment Tax Relief): Application of this Chapter to be subject to that section.

126 Application of sections 127 to 131

126(1) For the purposes of this section and sections 127 to 131 **"reorganisation"** means a reorganisation or reduction of a company's share capital, and in relation to the reorganisation–

(a) **"original shares"** means shares held before and concerned in the reorganisation,

(b) **"new holding"** means, in relation to any original shares, the shares in and debentures of the company which as a result of the reorganisation represent the original shares (including such, if any, of the original shares as remain).

126(2) The reference in subsection (1) above to the reorganisation of a company's share capital includes–

(a) any case where persons are, whether for payment or not, allotted shares in or debentures of the company in respect of and in proportion to (or as nearly as may be in proportion to) their holdings of shares in the company or of any class of shares in the company, and

(b) any case where there are more than one class of share and the rights attached to shares of any class are altered.

126(3) The reference in subsection (1) above to a reduction of share capital does not include the paying off of redeemable share capital, and where shares in a company are redeemed by the company otherwise than by the issue of shares or debentures (with or without other consideration) and otherwise than in a liquidation, the shareholder shall be treated as disposing of the shares at the time of the redemption.

Derivations – CGTA 1979, s. 77 and FA 1982, Sch. 13, para. 5(3) ("reorganisation", "original shares", "new holding").

Cross references – S. 99: application of TCGA 1992 to unit trust schemes.
S. 142: issue of shares as stock dividend to trustees for person absolutely entitled thereto is not a reorganisation.
S. 150(6), (9): where reorganisation affects BES shares (applies to shares issued on or before 31 December 1993) forming part of a larger holding, s. 127 applies as if separate holdings; s. 127–130 do not apply to allotment after 18 March 1986 within s. 126(2)(a) if relief applicable to the original holding or the allotted shares.
S. 150A(6), (7): where reorganisation affects EIS shares (applies to shares issued on or after 1 January 1994) forming part of a larger holding, s. 127 applies as if separate holdings: s. 127–130 do not apply to allotment within s. 126(2)(a) if relief is attributable, immediately after the reorganisation, to the existing holding or the allotted shares.
S. 151B(2): where reorganisation affects ordinary shares in a venture capital trust, s. 127 applies separately to each category of such shares listed in s. 151B(3).
S. 151B(4): s. 127–130 do not apply to an allotment within s. 126(2)(a) if immediately after the reorganisation the shares or the allotted holding are shares falling within s. 151B(3)(a)–(c).
S. 192(2): on a demerger, an exempt distribution consisting of the transfer to all or any of its members by a company of shares in one or more companies which are its 75 per cent subsidiaries is deemed to be a reorganisation.
S. 251(6): circumstances in which a debenture issued by a company after 15 March 1993 shall be deemed to be a security.
Sch. 3, para. 7(3): provisions unaffected by exclusion from simplified re-basing scheme of unquoted shares deriving value from oil exploration etc.
ICTA 1988, s. 187(2): application of s. 126(1)(b) to income tax charges and reliefs for approved share schemes in respect of any new holding.
ICTA 1988, s. 299, 305: identification of EIS shares (shares issued on or after 1 January 1994) (and formerly BES shares (shares issued on or before 31 December 1993)) on a disposal or reorganisation.
ICTA 1988, s. 762A: offshore income gains: exchange of interests of different classes in offshore funds.
IHTA 1984, s. 107(4), 113A(6), 124A(6): business and agricultural property relief given in relation to the new holding on satisfaction of certain conditions by reference to the original holding.
IHTA 1984, s. 135: original and new holdings treated as one for purposes of ascertaining any charge in respect of transfers within seven years before death.
IHTA 1984, s. 183: equation of original and new holdings in relation to relief for loss in value of shares etc. between probate and sale within 12 months of death.
FA 1989, s. 69(9) and Sch. 5, para. 8, 11: power of trustees to acquire exchange securities in company other than founding company and in determining the occasion of a chargeable event on the trustees of an employee share ownership trust following a disposal to them of securities, time of acquisition of new holding treated as that of the original holding.
FA 1999, s. 66(1)): reorganisation before 15 February 1999, resulting in new holding which is not a qualifying corporate bond under the former definition of "relevant discounted security" in FA 1996, Sch. 13, para. 3, becomes one after 15 February 1999 as a result of amendments made to that definition by FA 1999, s. 65(1), (2)).
FA 2000, Sch. 15 para. 81(1): allotment of shares effecting a holding of CVS shares with investment relief which have been held continously from the date of issue.
FA 2002, Sch. 16, para. 40: effect of allotment of shares as in s. 126(2)(a), where investment in community development finance institution.
FA 2003, s. 195: companies acquiring their own shares.
SI 1989/469, reg. 27(3): s. 127–130 do not apply to shares held in a personal equity plan if there is a reorganisation affecting those shares by virtue of an allotment for payment under s. 126(2).

HMRC interpretations – IRInt. 72: HMRC will treat any subscription for shares, under an open offer, which is equal to or less than the shareholder's minimum entitlement as a share reorganisation. Any shares subscribed for in excess of the minimum entitlement will be treated as a separate acquisition.
IRInt. 161: Capital gains tax: authorised unit trust umbrella schemes.

Other material – Taxline 1993/137 (not reproduced): HMRC regard an "open offer" as a reorganisation within s. 126 as the shares are not allotted but offered in proportion to existing shareholdings.

Taxline 1997/20 (not reproduced): interaction of reinvestment relief rules with those on a rights issue.

Notes – S. 288: interpretation, including "shares" as embracing stock, "class" in relation to shares being in one company and reference to sections being those of this Act.
HMRC Capital Gains Manual, CG 51781: Inland Revenue accept that an alteration of rights is a "reorganisation" under TCGA 1992, s. 126(2)(b) even if there is only one class of shares.

127 Equation of original shares and new holding

127 Subject to sections 128 to 130, a reorganisation shall not be treated as involving any disposal of the original shares or any acquisition of the new holding or any part of it, but the original shares (taken as a single asset) and the new holding (taken as a single asset) shall be treated as the same asset acquired as the original shares were acquired.

Derivations – CGTA 1979, s. 78.

Cross references – S. 34: circumstances in which value shifting provisions override application of s. 135 and 136 to a reorganisation involving an exchange of shares in or debentures of a subsidiary company with those of a non-group member.
S. 99: application of TCGA 1992 to unit trust schemes.
S. 102: exchange of rights in one part of a unit trust scheme etc. for those in another part may be a disposal and acquisition notwithstanding s. 127, including its application to conversions of securities (s. 132) but not to company reconstructions and amalgamations (s. 135–136).
S. 105A: application of s. 127 in relation to "approved-scheme shares" and other reorganisation shares.
S. 109(3): priority over treatment of relevant allowable expenditure on a "1982 holding" as incurred in March 1982.
S. 116: disapplication to the extent that reorganisation involves a qualifying corporate bond.
S. 135: s. 127–131 apply to share exchanges within this section as if the exchange were a reorganisation.
S. 136: s. 127–131 apply to schemes of reconstruction within this section as if the exchange were a reorganisation.
S. 142: issue of shares as stock dividend to trustees for person absolutely entitled thereto is not a reorganisation.
S. 150(6), (9): where reorganisation affects BES shares (applies to shares issued on or before 31 December 1993) forming part of a larger holding, s. 127 applies as if separate holdings; s. 127–130 do not apply to allotment after 18 March 1986 within s. 126(2)(a) if relief applicable to the original holding or the allotted shares.
S. 150A(6), (7): where reorganisation affects EIS shares (applies to shares issued on or after 1 January 1994) forming part of a larger holding, s. 127 applies as if separate holdings: s. 127–130 do not apply to allotment within s. 126(2)(a) if relief is attributable, immediately after the reorganisation, to the existing holding or the allotted shares.
S. 151B(2): where reorganisation affects ordinary shares in a venture capital trust, s. 127 applies separately to each category of such shares listed in s. 151B(3).
S. 151B(4): s. 127–130 do not apply to an allotment within s. 126(2)(a) if immediately after the reorganisation the shares or the allotted holding are shares falling within s. 151B(3)(a)–(c).
S. 162A(9): effect where election to forego roll-over relief on transfer of business.
S. 164F: crystallisation of held-over gain (on reinvestment) where acquired shares are included in original shares in relation to transaction within s. 116.
S. 169Q: election to disapply s. 127 in order to claim entrepreneurs relief.
S. 171(2): priority over no gain, no loss on transfers of capital assets within a group.
S. 192(2): on a demerger, an exempt distribution consisting of the transfer to all or any of its members by a company of shares in one or more companies which are its 75 per cent subsidiaries is deemed to be a reorganisation.
Sch. 2, para. 19: shares held on 6 April 1965 and forming part of a new holding are deemed to have been disposed of and reacquired at market value on that date; for time apportionment, where reorganisation after 5 April 1965, new holding deemed to have been disposed of and reacquired at market value immediately after the reorganisation.
Sch. 3, para. 7(3): provisions unaffected by exclusion from simplified re-basing scheme of unquoted shares deriving value from oil exploration etc.
Sch. 7AC, para. 4(1)(b): provision for exemption for disposals by company with substantial shareholding. Question of exemption for such disposal determined without reference to s. 127.
ICTA 1988, s. 220(9): as regards condition as to residence and period of ownership for relief on purchase of own shares, time of acquisition determined as under s. 127 unless allotment for payment or part of stock dividend.
ICTA 1988, s. 299, 305: identification of EIS shares (shares issued on or after 1 January 1994) (and formerly BES shares (shares issued on or before 31 December 1993)) on a disposal or reorganisation.
ICTA 1988, s. 473: equation of securities for purposes of taxes on income where reorganisation and assets represent trading stock of a bank, insurance company or dealer.
ICTA 1988, s. 575(2): relief for loss on unquoted shares in a trading company restricted where shares acquired on reorganisation within s. 127 by reference to new consideration for the new holding.
IHTA 1984, s. 107(4), 113A(6), 124A(6): business and agricultural property relief given in relation to the new holding on satisfaction of certain conditions by reference to the original holding.
IHTA 1984, s. 135: original and new holdings treated as one for purposes of ascertaining any charge in respect of transfers within seven years before death.
IHTA 1984, s. 183: equation of original and new holdings in relation to relief for loss in value of shares etc. between probate and sale within 12 months of death.
FA 1997, s. 89(8)(c): a claim under ESC D27 (in respect of an earn-out right acquired before 26 April 1988) will enable TCGA 1992, s. 138A to have effect in the case of a disposal on or after 26 November 1996 of any asset acquired prior to that date as a result of a reorganisation within s. 127.
FA 2000, Sch. 15, para. 80: s. 127 applies separately to CVS shares with investment relief which have been held continously from the date of issue.
FA 2000, Sch. 15, para. 81(1): s. 127 does not apply to CVS shares with investment relief which have been held continously from the date of issue.
FA 2000, Sch. 15, para. 84: an exchange of shares to which investment relief is applicable is not treated as a disposal of old shares and acquisition of new shares.
FA 2000, Sch. 15 para. 93(7): the new holding of CVS shares with investment relief are treated as having been acquired when the original shares were acquired.
ITEPA 2003, s. 462: as regards charges to income tax on unapproved employee share schemes, s. 127–130 adapted to apply to reorganisations of the shares.
ITEPA 2003, s. 702: meaning of "readily convertible asset".
ITEPA 2003, Sch. 2, para. 88(5): s. 127–130 do not apply to shares acquired by a rights issue which are not treated as approved SIP shares.
ITEPA 2003, Sch. 5, para. 40(4): qualifying exchange of shares for the purposes of the EMI code.

SI 1989/469, reg. 27(4): s. 127–131 do not apply to ordinary shares, qualifying EC shares, other qualifying shares, shares in securities companies, units in funds of funds, units in securities funds or qualifying securities held in a personal equity plan if there is a reorganisation affecting those shares or securities etc. by virtue of an allotment for payment under s. 126(2).
SI 1994/3226, reg. 14: application of rules in FA 1993, Pt. II, Ch. II to assets held on a company's commencement day and to which s. 127 has applied.
FA 1996, s. 93B(3): effect of deemed disposal and re-acquisition where loan relationship ceases to be within FA 1996, s. 93.
FA 2002, Sch. 16, para. 40 and 47: s. 127–130 disapplied for certain rights issues where investment in community development finance institution. Where s. 127 does apply, shares in new holding treated as acquired when original shares acquired.
SI 1994/3227, reg. 9: computation and deferral of gain or loss under foreign exchange matching rules in respect of assets which are replaced in a transaction to which s. 127 applies.
SI 2002/1970, regs. 10 to 12: special rules for bringing into account amounts of exchange gains or losses.
SI 2004/1450, reg. 36(2): disapplication of s. 127 to 131 in relation to certain qualifying investments.
SI 2009/3001, reg. 37: special provisions for application of s. 127 in relation to disposals of interests in non-reporting offshore funds.

HMRC interpretations – IRInt. 39: treatment of base cost where consideration on a share exchange is partly in the form of qualifying corporate bonds.
IRInt. 152: HMRC view that no gain/no loss rule (TCGA 1992, s. 171(1)) does not apply to C's acquisition where a group company A exchanges shares in company B for a new issue of QCBs in another group company C.
IRInt. 161: possible application of s. 127 where an investor switches between income units and accumulation units in a single sub-fund of an umbrella scheme.

Other material – Taxline 1997/20 (not reproduced): interaction of reinvestment relief rules with those on a rights issue.
Taxline 1998/6 (not reproduced): Revenue view that s. 127 should be applied literally, so that a rights issue investment is taken as having been made when the underlying shares were acquired, and that the tests of eligibility as at that date are the ones used.

128 Consideration given or received by holder

128(1) Subject to subsection (2) below, where, on a reorganisation, a person gives or becomes liable to give any consideration for his new holding or any part of it, that consideration shall in relation to any disposal of the new holding or any part of it be treated as having been given for the original shares, and if the new holding or part of it is disposed of with a liability attaching to it in respect of that consideration, the consideration given for the disposal shall be adjusted accordingly.

128(2) There shall not be treated as consideration given for the new holding or any part of it–

(a) any surrender, cancellation or other alteration of the original shares or of the rights attached thereto, or

(b) any consideration consisting of any application, in paying up the new holding or any part of it, of assets of the company or of any dividend or other distribution declared out of those assets but not made,

and, in the case of a reorganisation on or after 10th March 1981, any consideration given for the new holding or any part of it otherwise than by way of a bargain made at arm's length shall be disregarded to the extent that its amount or value exceeds the relevant increase in value; and for this purpose **"the relevant increase in value"** means the amount by which the market value of the new holding immediately after the reorganisation exceeds the market value of the original shares immediately before the reorganisation.

128(3) Where on a reorganisation a person receives (or is deemed to receive), or becomes entitled to receive, any consideration, other than the new holding, for the disposal of an interest in the original shares, and in particular–

(a) where under section 122 he is to be treated as if he had in consideration of a capital distribution disposed of an interest in the original shares, or

(b) where he receives (or is deemed to receive) consideration from other shareholders in respect of a surrender of rights derived from the original shares,

he shall be treated as if the new holding resulted from his having for that consideration disposed of an interest in the original shares (but without prejudice to the original shares and the new holding being treated in accordance with section 127 as the same asset).

128(4) Where for the purpose of subsection (3) above it is necessary in computing the gain or loss accruing on the disposal of the interest in the original shares mentioned in that subsection to apportion the cost of acquisition of the original shares between what is disposed of and what is retained, the apportionment shall be made in the like manner as under section 129.

Derivations – S. 128(1): CGTA 1979, s. 79(1).
S. 128(2): CGTA 1979, s. 79(1), provisos, 2nd proviso as added by FA 1981, s. 91(1).
S. 128(3), (4): CGTA 1979, s. 79(2), (3).

Cross references – S. 34(1): circumstances in which value shifting provisions override application of s. s. 135 and 136 to a reorganisation involving an exchange of shares in or debentures of a subsidiary company with those of a non-group member: amount brought into charge under s. 128(3).
S. 99: application of TCGA 1992 to unit trust schemes.
S. 105B(4): s. 128(3) disregarded in determining whether disposal of relevant shares for purpose of s. 105A (shares acquired on the same day: election for alternative treatment).S. 116: disapplication to the extent that reorganisation involves a qualifying corporate bond.
S. 122: receipt of a capital distribution is a part disposal except in certain cases in which the amount is small.
S. 141: appropriate amount in cash of a stock dividend allowed as consideration given for s. 128(1), notwithstanding s. 128(2).
S. 142: issue of shares as stock dividend to trustees for person absolutely entitled thereto is not a reorganisation.
S. 150(9): disapplication to allotment after 18 March 1986 within s. 126(2)(a) if BES relief applicable to the original holding or the allotted shares (applies to shares issued on or before 31 December 1993).

S. 150A(7): disapplication of s. 128 to allotment within s. 126(2)(a) if EIS relief is applicable to the original holding or the allotted shares (applies to shares issued on or after 1 January 1994).
S. 151B(4): s. 127–130 do not apply to an allotment within s. 126(2)(a) if immediately after the reorganisation the shares or the allotted holding are shares falling within s. 151B(3)(a)–(c).
S. 164F: crystallisation of held-over gain (on re-investment) where acquired shares are included in original shares in relation to transaction within s. 116.
S. 171(2): priority over no gain, no loss on transfers of capital assets within a group.
S. 192(2): on a demerger, an exempt distribution consisting of the transfer to all or any of its members by a company of shares in one or more companies which are its 75 per cent subsidiaries is deemed to be a reorganisation.
S. 272: determining market values.
Sch. 3, para. 7(3): provisions unaffected by exclusion from simplified re-basing scheme of unquoted shares deriving value from oil exploration etc.
ICTA 1988, s. 576(5): new consideration in relation to relief against income for a loss on shares in an unquoted trading company excludes the items specified in the proviso to s. 128(1)(a), (b).
FA 2000, Sch. 15, para. 81(1): s. 128 does not apply to CVS shares with investment relief which have been held continously from the date of issue.
ITEPA 2003, s. 462: as regards charges to income tax on unapproved employee share schemes, s. 127–130 adapted to apply to reorganisations of the shares.
ITEPA 2003, s. 702: meaning of "readily convertible asset".
ITEPA 2003, Sch. 2, para. 88(5): s. 127–130 do not apply to shares acquired by a rights issue which are not treated as approved SIP shares.
ITEPA 2003, Sch. 5, para. 40(4): qualifying exchange of shares for the purposes of the EMI code.
SI 1989/469, reg. 27(4): s. 127–131 do not apply to ordinary shares, qualifying EC shares, other qualifying shares, shares in securities companies, units in funds of funds, units in securities funds or qualifying securities held in a personal equity plan if there is a reorganisation affecting those shares or securities etc. by virtue of an allotment for payment under s. 126(2).
SI 2004/1450, reg. 36(2): disapplication of s. 127 to 131 in relation to certain qualifying investments.
SI 2009/3001, reg. 47: application of s. 128 in relation to offshore income gains.

HMRC interpretations – IRInt. 39: treatment of base cost where consideration on a share exchange is partly in the form of qualifying corporate bonds.

Notes – S. 272–274 and Sch. 11: meaning of "market value".

129 Part disposal of new holding

129 Subject to section 130(2), where for the purpose of computing the gain or loss accruing to a person from the acquisition and disposal of any part of the new holding it is necessary to apportion the cost of acquisition of any of the original shares between what is disposed of and what is retained, the apportionment shall be made by reference to market value at the date of the disposal (with such adjustment of the market value of any part of the new holding as may be required to offset any liability attaching thereto but forming part of the cost to be apportioned).

Derivations – CGTA 1979, s. 80.

Cross references – S. 99: application of TCGA 1992 to unit trust schemes.
S. 116: disapplication to the extent that reorganisation involves a qualifying corporate bond.
S. 150(9): disapplication to allotment after 18 March 1986 within s. 126(2)(a) if BES relief applicable to the original holding or the allotted shares (applies to shares issued on or before 31 December 1993).
S. 150A(7): disapplication of s. 129 to allotment within s. 126(2)(a) if EIS relief is applicable to the original holding or the allotted shares (applies to shares issued on or after 1 January 1994).
S. 151B(4): s. 127–130 do not apply to an allotment within s. 126(2)(a) if immediately after the reorganisation the shares or the allotted holding are shares falling within s. 151B(3)(a)–(c).
S. 164F: crystallisation of held-over gain (on re-investment) where acquired shares are included in original shares in relation to transaction within s. 116.
S. 171(3): priority over no gain, no loss on transfers of capital assets within a group.
S. 192(2): on a demerger, an exempt distribution consisting of the transfer to all or any of its members by a company of shares in one or more companies which are its 75 per cent subsidiaries is deemed to be a reorganisation.
Sch. 3, para. 7(3): provisions unaffected by exclusion from simplified re-basing scheme of unquoted shares deriving value from oil exploration etc.
Sch. 7A, para. 3(9): disapplication of s. 129 in relation to pooled "pre-entry" assets.
FA 2000, Sch. 15, para. 81(1): s. 129 does not apply to CVS shares with investment relief which have been held continously from the date of issue.
ITEPA 2003, s. 462: as regards charges to income tax on unapproved employee share schemes, s. 127–130 adapted to apply to reorganisations of the shares.
ITEPA 2003, s. 702: meaning of "readily convertible asset".
ITEPA 2003, Sch. 2, para. 88(5): s. 127–130 do not apply to shares acquired by a rights issue which are not treated as approved SIP shares.
ITEPA 2003, Sch. 5, para. 40(4): qualifying exchange of shares for the purposes of the EMI code.
SI 1989/469, reg. 27(4): s. 127–131 do not apply to ordinary shares, qualifying EC shares, other qualifying shares, shares in securities companies, units in funds of funds, units in securities funds or qualifying securities held in a personal equity plan if there is a reorganisation affecting those shares or securities etc. by virtue of an allotment for payment under s. 126(2).
SI 2004/1450, reg. 36(2): disapplication of s. 127 to 131 in relation to certain qualifying investments.

Other material – Taxline 1997/20 (not reproduced): interaction of reinvestment relief rules with those on a rights issue.

Notes – S. 21–34: general meaning of "disposal" and the timing of certain disposals.
S. 42: apportionment of base cost on a part disposal.
S. 246: time of disposal in cases of compulsory purchase of land as being when compensation etc. agreed or, if earlier, when the authority enter upon the land.
S. 272–274 and Sch. 11: meaning of "market value".

130 Composite new holdings

130(1) This section shall apply to a new holding–

(a) if it consists of more than one class of shares in or debentures of the company and one or more of those classes is of shares or debentures which, at any time not later than the end of the period of

3 months beginning with the date on which the reorganisation took effect, or of such longer period as the Board may by notice allow, were listed on a recognised stock exchange, or

(b) if it consists of more than one class of rights of unit holders and one or more of those classes is of rights the prices of which were published daily by the managers of the scheme at any time not later than the end of that period of 3 months (or longer if so allowed).

130(2) Where for the purpose of computing the gain or loss accruing to a person from the acquisition and disposal of the whole or any part of any class of shares or debentures or rights of unit holders forming part of a new holding to which this section applies it is necessary to apportion costs of acquisition between what is disposed of and what is retained, the cost of acquisition of the new holding shall first be apportioned between the entire classes of shares or debentures or rights of which it consists by reference to market value on the first day (whether that day fell before the reorganisation took effect or later) on which market values or prices were quoted or published for the shares, debentures or rights as mentioned in subsection (1)(a) or (1)(b) above (with such adjustment of the market value of any class as may be required to offset any liability attaching thereto but forming part of the cost to be apportioned).

130(3) For the purposes of this section the day on which a reorganisation involving the allotment of shares or debentures or unit holders' rights takes effect is the day following the day on which the right to renounce any allotment expires.

History – In s. 130(1)(a) the words "were listed" substituted for the former wording ("had quoted market values") by FA 2007, s. 109 and Sch. 26, para. 8(2)(a), with effect from 19 July 2007 (Royal Assent).
In s. 130(1)(a) the words at the end; "in the United Kingdom or elsewhere"; omitted by FA 2007, s. 109 and Sch. 26, para. 8(2)(b) and repealed by FA 2007, s. 114 and Sch. 27, Part 6(5), with effect from 19 July 2007 (Royal Assent).

Derivations – CGTA 1979, s. 81.

Cross references – S. 99: application of TCGA 1992 to unit trust schemes.
S. 116: disapplication to the extent that reorganisation involves a qualifying corporate bond.
S. 150(9): disapplication to allotment after 18 March 1986 within s. 126(2)(a) if BES relief applicable to the original holding or the allotted shares (applies to shares issued on or before 31 December 1993).
S. 150A(7): disapplication of s. 129 to allotments within s. 126(2)(a) if EIS relief is applicable to the original holding or the allotted shares (applies to shares issued on or after 1 January 1994).
S. 151B(4): s. 127–130 do not apply to an allotment within s. 126(2)(a) if immediately after the reorganisation the shares or the allotted holding are shares falling within s. 151B(3)(a)–(c).
S. 164F: crystallisation of held-over gain (on re-investment) where acquired shares are included in original shares in relation to transaction within s. 116.
S. 171(2): priority over no gain, no loss on transfers of capital assets within a group.
S. 192(2): on a demerger, an exempt distribution consisting of the transfer to all or any of its members by a company of shares in one or more companies which are its 75 per cent subsidiaries is deemed to be a reorganisation.
Sch. 3, para. 7(3): provisions unaffected by exclusion from simplified re-basing scheme of unquoted shares deriving value from oil exploration etc.
Sch. 7A, para. 3(9): disapplication of s. 130 in relation to pooled "pre-entry" assets.
FA 2000, Sch, 15 para. 81(1): s. 130 does not apply to CVS shares with investment relief which have been held continously from the date of issue.
ITEPA 2003, s. 462: as regards charges to income tax on unapproved employee share schemes, s. 127–130 adapted to apply to reorganisations of the shares.
ITEPA 2003, s. 702: meaning of "readily convertible asset".
ITEPA 2003, Sch. 2, para. 88(5): s. 127–130 do not apply to shares acquired by a rights issue which are not treated as approved SIP shares.
ITEPA 2003, Sch. 5, para. 40(4): qualifying exchange of shares for the purposes of the EMI code.
SI 1989/469, reg. 27(4): s. 127–131 do not apply to ordinary shares, qualifying EC shares, other qualifying shares, shares in securities companies, units in funds of funds, units in securities funds or qualifying securities held in a personal equity plan if there is a reorganisation affecting those shares or securities etc. by virtue of an allotment for payment under s. 126(2).
SI 2004/1450, reg. 36(2): disapplication of s. 127 to 131 in relation to certain qualifying investments.

Other material – Taxline 1997/20 (not reproduced): interaction of reinvestment relief rules with those on a rights issue.

Notes – S. 42: apportionment of base cost on a part disposal.
S. 272–274 and Sch. 11: meaning of "market value".
S. 288: interpretation, including meaning of recognised stock exchange and "notice" as being in writing.
TMA 1970, s. 115: service of notices.

131 Indexation allowance

131(1) This section applies where–

(a) by virtue of section 127, on a reorganisation the original shares (taken as a single asset) and the new holding (taken as a single asset) fall to be treated as the same asset acquired as the original shares were acquired; and

(b) on the reorganisation, a person gives or becomes liable to give any consideration for his new holding or any part of it.

131(2) Where this section applies, so much of the consideration referred to in subsection (l)(b) above as, *on a disposal to which section* 53 applies of the new holding, will, by virtue of section 128(1), be treated as having been given for the original shares, shall be treated for the purposes of section 54 as an item of relevant allowable expenditure incurred not at the time the original shares were acquired but at the time the person concerned gave or became liable to give the consideration (and, accordingly, section 54(4) shall not apply in relation to that item of expenditure).

Derivations – FA 1982, Sch. 13, para. 5(1), (2).

Cross references – S. 53(4): priority over general indexation allowance provisions (s. 53, 54) and identification of certain securities (s. 108).
S. 99: application of TCGA 1992 to unit trust schemes.
S. 109(3): notwithstanding the priority of the reorganisation provisions of s. 127 over the deeming of expenditure on a "1982 holding" as incurred in March 1982, s. 131 applies.
S. 171(2): priority over no gain, no loss on transfers of capital assets within a group.
ICTA 1988, Sch. 28, para. 2, 3(1), 4(3), 8(3): offshore income gain which is taxed as income is calculated by reference to gain using principles of this Act but if acquired on a no gain, no loss basis as if no allowance had been available under s. 56(2) and generally as if transferee's acquisition of it had been the disponor's; a gain on a disposal involving an equalisation element is calculated ignoring no gain, no loss provisions.
SI 1989/469, reg. 27(4): s. 127–131 do not apply to ordinary shares, qualifying EC shares, other qualifying shares, shares in securities companies, units in funds of funds, units in securities funds or qualifying securities held in a personal equity plan if there is a reorganisation affecting those shares or securities etc. by virtue of an allotment for payment under s. 126(2).
SI 2004/1450, reg. 36(2): disapplication of s. 127 to 131 in relation to certain qualifying investments.

Notes – S. 288: interpretation, including reference to sections being those of this Act.

CONVERSION OF SECURITIES

132 Equation of converted securities and new holding

132(1) Sections 127 to 131 shall apply with any necessary adaptations in relation to the conversion of securities as they apply in relation to a reorganisation (that is to say, a reorganisation or reduction of a company's share capital).

132(2) This section has effect subject to sections 133 and 134.

132(3) For the purposes of this section and section 133–

(a) **"conversion of securities"** includes any of the following, whether effected by a transaction or occurring in consequence of the operation of the terms of any security or of any debenture which is not a security, that is to say –

- (i) a conversion of securities of a company into shares in the company, and
- (ia) a conversion of a security which is not a qualifying corporate bond into a security of the same company which is such a bond, and
- (ib) a conversion of a qualifying corporate bond into a security which is a security of the same company but is not such a bond, and
- (ii) a conversion at the option of the holder of the securities converted as an alternative to the redemption of those securities for cash, and
- (iii) any exchange of securities effected in pursuance of any enactment (including an enactment passed after this Act) which provides for the compulsory acquisition of any shares or securities and the issue of securities or other securities instead,

(b) **"security"** includes any loan stock or similar security whether of the Government of the United Kingdom or of any other government, or of any public or local authority in the United Kingdom or elsewhere, or of any company, and whether secured or unsecured.

132(4) In subsection (3)(a)(ia) above the reference to the conversion of a security of a company into a qualifying corporate bond includes a reference to–

(a) any such conversion of a debenture of that company that is deemed to be a security for the purposes of section 251 as produces a security of that company which is a qualifying corporate bond; and

(b) any such conversion of a security of that company, or of a debenture that is deemed to be a security for those purposes, as produces a debenture of that company which, when deemed to be a security for those purposes, is such a bond.

132(5) In subsection (3)(a)(ib) above the reference to the conversion of a qualifying corporate bond into a security of the same company which is not such a bond includes a reference to any conversion of a qualifying corporate bond which produces a debenture which–

(a) is not a security; and

(b) when deemed to be a security for the purposes of section 251, is not such a bond.

History – In s. 132(3)(a) the words "any of the following … that is to say" and subpara. (ia) and (ib) inserted by FA 1997, s. 88(2) with effect in relation to disposals on or after 26 November 1996 and earlier conversions (FA 1997, s. 88(6)).
S. 132(4) inserted by FA 1997, s. 88(3) with effect in relation to disposals on or after 26 November 1996 and earlier conversions (FA 1997, s. 88(6)).
S. 132(5) inserted by FA 1997, s. 88(3) with effect in relation to disposals on or after 26 November 1996 and earlier conversions (FA 1997, s. 88(6).

Derivations – CGTA 1979, s. 82; FA 1982, Sch. 13, para. 5(3).

Cross references – S. 30(2): determination of value shift via a relevant asset where disposal is of securities in another company.
S. 99: application of TCGA 1992 to unit trust schemes.

S. 102: exchange of rights in one part of a unit trust scheme etc. for those in another part may be a disposal and acquisition notwithstanding s. 127, including its application to conversions of securities (s. 132) but not to company reconstructions and amalgamations (s. 135–136).
S. 106(12): securities, as defined in s. 132, are subject to the special identification rules for disposals by companies within the prescribed period of acquisition.
S. 116: disapplication to the extent that conversion involves a qualifying corporate bond.
S. 117(1): securities, as defined in s. 132, are corporate bonds if the debt represents a normal commercial loan, is expressed in sterling and is not convertible into another currency.
S. 118(2): where conversion within s. 132 involves a deep discount security, the accrued income reduces any capital consideration received in addition to the new holding and any excess is treated as allowable enhancement expenditure.
S. 119(10), (11): where conversion within s. 132 involves a security to which the accrued income scheme applies, any amount to which the transferor is deemed entitled (income credit) reduces any capital consideration received in addition to the new holding and any excess is treated as consideration given while any income relief is treated as increasing the capital consideration received.
S. 171(2): priority over no gain, no loss on transfers of capital assets within a group.
S. 251: debenture issued on a reorganisation or in exchange for shares deemed to be a security.
S. 251(1): exclusion of a debt on a "security" from provisions deeming there to be non-chargeable gain on a debt in the hands of the original creditor.
S. 251(6): debenture which results from a conversion of securities within the meaning of s. 132 deemed to be a security.
S. 253(1), 254(1): application of "security" in determining a debt on a security for the purposes of relief for losses on loans to traders and on qualifying corporate bonds.
Sch. 2, para. 8: securities within s. 132 are "fixed interest securities" for the purpose of the pooling of quoted securities held at 6 April 1965.
ICTA 1988, s. 56(5): application to special charge in relation to certain transactions in deposits.
ICTA 1988, s. 220(9): as regards condition as to residence and period of ownership for relief on purchase of own shares, time of acquisition determined as under s. 127 unless allotment for payment or part of stock dividend.
ICTA 1988, s. 473: equation of securities for purposes of taxes on income where reorganisation and assets represent trading stock of a bank, insurance company or dealer.
ICTA 1988, s. 710(13): for the accrued income scheme, where there is a conversion of securities there is a deemed transfer of them if there is not otherwise an actual transfer.
ICTA 1988, s. 757–764: special provisions for treating as income disposals of material interests in non-qualifying offshore funds.
ICTA 1988, Sch. 4, para. 2(4): charge to tax after acquisition of deep discount securities by issue on a conversion; event within s. 132 is effectively a disposal for the purposes of the charge.
IHTA 1984, s. 107(4), 113A(6), 124A(6): business and agricultural property relief given in relation to the new holding on satisfaction of certain conditions by reference to the original holding.
IHTA 1984, s. 135: original and new holdings treated as one for purposes of ascertaining any charge in respect of transfers within seven years before death.
IHTA 1984, s. 183: equation of original and new holdings in relation to relief for loss in value of shares etc. between probate and sale within 12 months of death.

HMRC interpretations – IRInt. 39: treatment of base cost where consideration on a share exchange is partly in the form of qualifying corporate bonds.

Other material – IR press release, 11 June 1970: definition of "security" in s. 132(3)(b) regarded as exhaustive; elaboration of term "loan stock".

Notes – S. 288: interpretation, including "shares" as embracing stock and reference to sections being those of this Act.

133 Premiums on conversion of securities

133(1) This section applies where, on a conversion of securities, a person receives, or becomes entitled to receive, any sum of money (**"the premium"**) which is by way of consideration (in addition to his new holding) for the disposal of the converted securities.

133(2) If the premium is small, as compared with the value of the converted securities–

(a) receipt of the premium shall not be treated for the purposes of this Act as a disposal of part of the converted securities, and

(b) the premium shall be deducted from any expenditure allowable under this Act as a deduction in computing a gain or loss on the disposal of the new holding by the person receiving or becoming entitled to receive the premium.

133(3) [Repealed by FA 1996, Sch. 20, para. 53(2) and s. 205 and Sch. 41, Pt. V(10).]

133(4) Where the allowable expenditure is less than the premium (or is nil)–

(a) subsection (2) above shall not apply, and

(b) if the recipient so elects (and there is any allowable expenditure)–

(i) the amount of the premium shall be reduced by the amount of the allowable expenditure, and

(ii) none of that expenditure shall be allowable as a deduction in computing a gain accruing on the occasion of the conversion, or on any subsequent occasion.

133(5) In subsection (4) above **"allowable expenditure"** means expenditure which immediately before the conversion was attributable to the converted securities under paragraphs (a) and (b) of section 38(1).

History – In s. 133(2) the words "the inspector is satisfied that" and "and so directs" repealed by FA 1996, Sch. 20, para. 53 and Sch. 41, Pt. V(10), as respects years of assessment after 1995–96 and accounting periods ending on or after 1 July 1999, the day appointed under FA 1994, s. 199 by virtue of SI 1998/3173 (C. 78).
S. 133(3) repealed by FA 1996, Sch. 20, para. 53 and Sch. 41, Pt. V(10), as respects years of assessment after 1995–96 and accounting periods ending on or after 1 July 1999, the day appointed under FA 1994, s. 199 by virtue of SI 1998/3173 (C. 78).
In s. 133(4)(a) a reference to subs. (3) omitted, by FA 1996, Sch. 20, para. 53 and Sch. 41, Pt. V(10), as respects years of assessment after 1995–96 and accounting periods ending on or after 1 July 1999, the day appointed under FA 1994, s. 199 by virtue of SI 1998/3173 (C. 78).

Derivations – CGTA 1979, s. 83.

Cross references – S. 38(1)(a), (b): deduction for allowable acquisition expenditure including incidental costs and enhancement of title expenditure.
S. 99: application of TCGA 1992 to unit trust schemes.
S. 116: disapplication to the extent that conversion involves a qualifying corporate bond.
S. 171(2): priority over no gain, no loss on transfers of capital assets within a group.
Sch. 3, para. 4(2): corresponding reduction in reacquisition expenditure to effect re-basing where original expenditure would be disallowed under s. 133(4) in respect of a disposal between 31 March 1982 and 6 April 1988.

HMRC interpretations – IR Int. 157: HMRC now take view that "small" can mean 5 per cent or less of value of asset etc., or receipt of £3,000 or less whether or not falling within the 5 per cent test; exceptionally taxpayers may suggest different limits in the context of their particular circumstances (*O'Rourke v Binks* [1992] BTC 460).

Notes – S. 288: interpretation, including "inspector" as being any inspector of taxes.
TMA 1970, s. 44–59 and Sch. 3: appeals procedures and rules for assigning proceedings.

134 Compensation stock

134(1) This section has effect where gilt-edged securities are exchanged for shares in pursuance of any enactment (including an enactment passed after this Act) which provides for the compulsory acquisition of any shares and the issue of gilt-edged securities instead.

134(2) The exchange shall not constitute a conversion of securities within section 132 and shall be treated as not involving any disposal of the shares by the person from whom they were compulsorily acquired but–

(a) there shall be calculated the gain or loss that would have accrued to him if he had then disposed of the shares for a consideration equal to the value of the shares as determined for the purpose of the exchange, and

(b) on a subsequent disposal of the whole or part of the gilt-edged securities by the person to whom they were issued–

(i) there shall be deemed to accrue to him the whole or a corresponding part of the gain or loss mentioned in paragraph (a) above, and

(ii) section 115(1) shall not have effect in relation to any gain or loss that is deemed to accrue as aforesaid.

134(3) Where a person to whom gilt-edged securities of any kind were issued as mentioned in subsection (1) above disposes of securities of that kind, the securities of which he disposes–

(a) shall, so far as possible, be identified with securities which were issued to him as mentioned in subsection (1) above rather than with other securities of that kind, and

(b) subject to paragraph (a) above, shall be identified with securities issued at an earlier time rather than those issued at a later time.

134(4) Subsection (2)(b) above shall not apply to any disposal falling within the provisions of section 58(1), 62(4) or 171(1) but a person who has acquired the securities on a disposal falling within those provisions (and without there having been a previous disposal not falling within those provisions or a devolution on death) shall be treated for the purposes of subsections (2)(b) and (3) above as if the securities had been issued to him.

134(5) Where the gilt-edged securities to be exchanged for any shares are not issued until after the date on which the shares are compulsorily acquired but on that date a right to the securities is granted, this section shall have effect as if the exchange had taken place on that date, as if references to the issue of the securities and the person to whom they were issued were references to the grant of the right and the person to whom it was granted and references to the disposal of the securities included references to disposals of the rights.

134(6) In this section **"shares"** includes securities within the meaning of section 132.

134(7) This section does not apply where the compulsory acquisition took place before 7th April 1976.

Derivations – S. 134(1): CGTA 1979, s. 84(1).
S. 134(2): CGTA 1979, s. 84(2), (3).
S. 134(3): CGTA 1979, s. 84(4), as amended by FA 1985, s. 67(2).
S. 134(4)–(6): CGTA 1979, s. 84(5)–(7).

Cross references – S. 58(1): deemed no gain, no loss on transfers between spouses.
S. 62(4): no chargeable gain arises on transfers by personal representatives to legatees.
S. 99: application of TCGA 1992 to unit trust schemes.
S. 115(1): gains on disposal of gilt-edged securities are not chargeable gains.
S. 116(10): operation of gains being held-over where qualifying corporate bonds (exempt) are issued in exchange for shares or securities (chargeable) under TCGA 1992, s. 116(10) is similar to operation of gains being held-over under s. 134(2) where gilt-edged securities (exempt) are issued as compensation for compulsory purchase of shares or securities (chargeable).
S. 171(1), (2): deemed no gain, no loss on transfer of capital assets within a group; priority of s. 134 over such provisions.
Sch. A1, para. 16: taper relief and special rules for postponed gains.
Sch. 4, para. 4: 50 per cent reduction in gain crystallising under s. 134 where attributable to the deferral before 6 April 1988 if original securities held at 31 March 1982 (or acquired in a chain of no gain, no loss disposals from that date).
ICTA 1988, s. 220(9): as regards condition as to residence and period of ownership for relief on purchase of own shares, time of acquisition determined as under s. 127 unless allotment for payment or part of stock dividend.
IHTA 1984, s. 135: original and new holdings treated as one for purposes of ascertaining any charge in respect of transfers within seven years before death.

Notes – S. 288: interpretation, including "shares" as embracing stock and reference to sections being those of this Act.
Sch. 9: meaning of gilt-edged securities.

COMPANY RECONSTRUCTIONS

History – In the heading, words "and amalgamations" which followed "reconstructions" repealed by FA 2002, s. 141 and Sch. 40, Pt. 3(2), with effect in relation to shares or debentures issued on or after 17 April 2002.

135 Exchange of securities for those in another company

135(1) This section applies in the following circumstances where a company ("company B") issues shares or debentures to a person in exchange for shares in or debentures of another company ("company A").

135(2) The circumstances are:

Case 1

Where company B holds, or in consequence of the exchange will hold, more than 25% of the ordinary share capital of company A.

Case 2

Where company B issues the shares or debentures in exchange for shares as the result of a general offer–

(a) made to members of company A or any class of them (with or without exceptions for persons connected with company B), and

(b) made in the first instance on a condition such that if it were satisfied company B would have control of company A.

Case 3

Where company B holds, or in consequence of the exchange will hold, the greater part of the voting power in company A.

135(3) Where this section applies, sections 127 to 131 (share reorganisations etc.) apply with the necessary adaptations as if company A and company B were the same company and the exchange were a reorganisation of its share capital.

135(4) In this section **"ordinary share capital"** has the meaning given by section 1119 of CTA 2010 and also includes–

(a) in relation to a unit trust scheme, any rights that are treated by section 99(1)(b) of this Act (application of Act to unit trust schemes) as shares in a company, and

(b) in relation to a company that has no share capital, any interests in the company possessed by members of the company.

135(5) This section applies in relation to a company that has no share capital as if references to shares in or debentures of the company included any interests in the company possessed by members of the company.

135(6) This section has effect subject to section 137(1) (exchange must be for bona fide commercial reasons and not part of tax avoidance scheme).

History – In s. 135(4), the words "section 1119 of CTA 2010" substituted for "section 832(1) of the Taxes Act" by CTA 2010, s. 1177 and Sch. 1, para. 234, with effect for corporation tax purposes for accounting periods ending on or after 1 April 2010, and for income tax and capital gains tax purposes for the tax year 2010–11 and subsequent tax years.
S. 135 substituted by FA 2002, s. 45(1) and Sch. 9, para. 1, with effect in relation to shares or debentures issued on or after 17 April 2002.

Derivations – CGTA 1979, s. 85; FA 1982, Sch. 13, para. 5(3).

Cross references – S. 31(6): exclusion from value shifting provisions of reductions caused by certain dividends except to the extent that payable out of particular profits, including those out of profits and treated by virtue of section 135 or 136 as a reorganisation of share capital.
S. 34: circumstances in which value shifting provisions override application of s. 135 and 136 to a reorganisation involving an exchange of shares in or debentures of a subsidiary company with those of a non-group member.
S. 99: application of TCGA 1992 to unit trust schemes.
S. 102: exchange of rights in one part of a unit trust scheme etc. for those in another part may be a disposal and acquisition notwithstanding s. 127, including its application to conversions of securities (s. 132) but not to company reconstructions and amalgamations (s. 135).
S. 116: TCGA 1992, s. 135 is subordinate to TCGA 1992, s. 116 where qualifying corporate bonds are issued in exchange for shares or debentures that are not qualifying corporate bonds.
S. 119(10), (11): where exchange within s. 135 involves a security to which the accrued income scheme applies, any amount to which the transferor is deemed entitled (income credit) reduces any capital consideration received in addition to the new holding and any excess is treated as consideration given while any income relief is treated as increasing the capital consideration received.
S. 150(8): application to BES shares issued after 18 March 1986 only if relief is withdrawn (applies to shares issued on or before 31 December 1993).
S. 150(8A): disapplication of s. 135 by s. 150(8) overridden for shares issued after 29 November 1994 where condition in s. 150(8B) is satisfied.
S. 150A(8): s. 135 does not apply to shares to which EIS relief is attributable (applies to shares issued on or after 1 January 1994).
S. 150A(8A): disapplication of s. 135 by s. 150A(8) overridden for shares issued after 29 November 1994 where condition in s. 150A(8B) is satisfied.
S. 151B(5), (8): s. 135 disapplied where shares in a venture capital trust eligible for relief under s. 151A(1) are exchanged for a holding not consisting of ordinary shares in a venture capital trust.

S. 171(3): priority over no gain, no loss on transfers of capital assets within a group.
S. 251(2), (3): priority over the deemed disposal on satisfaction or part satisfaction of a debt and over the provisions where property is accepted in satisfaction of a debt; certain debentures deemed securities (s. 251(6)).
S. 288: interpretation of certain words and expressions (e.g., "company", "control" and "shares") within TCGA 1992.
Sch. 7AC, para. 14: exemption for disposals by company with substantial shareholding: position where earlier company reconstruction etc.
ICTA 1988, s. 220(9): as regards condition as to residence and period of ownership for relief on purchase of own shares, time of acquisition determined as under s. 127 unless allotment for payment or part of stock dividend.
ICTA 1988, s. 416: meaning of "control".
ICTA 1988, s. 472A: trading profits etc. from securities: taxation of amounts taken to reserves.
ICTA 1988, s. 473: equation of securities for purposes of taxes on income where reorganisation and assets represent trading stock of a bank, insurance company or dealer.
ICTA 1988, s. 575(3): no relief against income for loss on unquoted shares in trading company where disposal within s. 135.
ICTA 1988, s. 832(1): ordinary share capital means all the issued share capital other than capital the holders of which have a right to a dividend at a fixed rate but have no other right to share in profits.
IHTA 1984, s. 107(4), 113A(6), 124A(6): business and agricultural property relief given in relation to the new holding on satisfaction of certain conditions by reference to the original holding.
IHTA 1984, s. 135: original and new holdings treated as one for purposes of ascertaining any charge in respect of transfers within seven years before death.
IHTA 1984, s. 183: equation of original and new holdings in relation to relief for loss in value of shares etc. between probate and sale within 12 months of death.
FA 1989, s. 69(3A): a transfer made by way of exchange in circumstances mentioned in s. 135(1) (or its predecessor) does not give rise to a charge to tax on the trustees of an ESOP trust.
FA 1989, s. 69(9) and Sch. 5, para. 8, 11: power of trustees to acquire exchange securities in company other than founding company and in determining the occasion of a chargeable event on the trustees of an employee share ownership trust following a disposal to them of securities, time of acquisition of new holding treated as that of the original holding.
Broadcasting Act 1996, Sch. 7, para. 7: provisions applying where a company issues shares or debentures to the BBC in exchange for shares in or debentures of a successor company; disapplication of s. 127–131.
FA 2000, Sch. 15, para. 82(1): s. 135 does not apply in respect of the existing holding of CVS shares.
FA 2000, Sch. 15, para. 84: s 127 is applied through s 135 so an exchange of shares to which investment relief is applicable is not treated as a disposal of old shares and acquisition of new shares.
FA 2002, Sch. 16, para. 41: s. 135–136 disapplied for certain company reconstructions and amalgamations where investment in community development finance institution.
ITEPA 2003, Sch. 5, para. 40: meaning of "qualifying exchange of shares" for the purposes of the enterprise management incentives (EMI) code.
FA 2007, s. 109(1)(d): where s. 135 applies, the Treasury may make Regulations about the tax consequences for share for share exchanges involving companies that are resident in different EU member states.
SI 2009/3001, reg. 35: special provisions for application of s. 135 in relation to disposals of interests in non-reporting offshore funds.

European material – Directive 90/434, art. 2(d), 8 (s. 135(1)(c)).

Extra-statutory concessions – D52: incidental costs of acquisition or disposal and payments in respect of contingent liabilities attributable to the new holding of shares or debentures may be treated as consideration given for the shares or debentures.

HMRC interpretations – IRInt. 39: consideration on a share exchange partly in the form of qualifying corporate bonds.
IRInt. 152: HMRC view that no gain/no loss rule (TCGA 1992, s. 171(1)) does not apply to C's acquisition where a group company A exchanges shares in company B for a new issue of QCBs in another group company C.
IRInt. 216: HMRC view that a Delaware Limited Liability Company may be a party to share exchanges.

Other material – ICAEW Technical Release TR 657 (not reproduced): s. 138 clearance procedure does not as a rule confirm s. 135 will apply to the relevant transactions, only that conditions of s. 137(1) satisfied.

Notes – S. 116: disapplication to the extent that reconstruction involves a qualifying corporate bond.
S. 286: meaning of "connected" in references to persons being connected with one another.
S. 288: interpretation, including meaning of "company", "control", "shares" as embracing stock and reference to sections being those of this Act.
ICTA 1988, s. 416: by virtue of TCGA 1992, s. 288, "control" is construed in accordance with ICTA 1988, s. 416.

136 Scheme of reconstruction involving issue of securities

136(1) This section applies where–

(a) an arrangement between a company ("company A") and–

(i) the persons holding shares in or debentures of the company, or

(ii) where there are different classes of shares in or debentures of the company, the persons holding any class of those shares or debentures,

is entered into for the purposes of, or in connection with, a scheme of reconstruction, and

(b) under the arrangement–

(i) another company ("company B") issues shares or debentures to those persons in respect of and in proportion to (or as nearly as may be in proportion to) their relevant holdings in company A, and

(ii) the shares in or debentures of company A comprised in relevant holdings are retained by those persons or are cancelled or otherwise extinguished.

136(2) Where this section applies–

(a) those persons are treated as exchanging their relevant holdings in company A for the shares or debentures held by them in consequence of the arrangement, and

(b) sections 127 to 131 (share reorganisations etc) apply with the necessary adaptations as if company A and company B were the same company and the exchange were a reorganisation of its share capital.

For this purpose shares in or debentures of company A comprised in relevant holdings that are retained are treated as if they had been cancelled and replaced by a new issue.

136(3) Where a reorganisation of the share capital of company A is carried out for the purposes of the scheme of reconstruction, the provisions of subsections (1) and (2) apply in relation to the position after the reorganisation.

136(4) In this section–

(a) **"scheme of reconstruction"** has the meaning given by Schedule 5AA to this Act;

(b) references to **"relevant holdings"** of shares in or debentures of company A are–

(i) where there is only one class of shares in or debentures of the company, to holdings of shares in or debentures of the company, and

(ii) where there are different classes of shares in or debentures of the company, to holdings of a class of shares or debentures that is involved in the scheme of reconstruction (within the meaning of paragraph 2 of Schedule 5AA);

(c) references to shares or debentures being retained include their being retained with altered rights or in an altered form, whether as the result of reduction, consolidation, division or otherwise; and

(d) any reference to a reorganisation of a company's share capital is to a reorganisation within the meaning of section 126.

136(5) This section applies in relation to a company that has no share capital as if references to shares in or debentures of the company included any interests in the company possessed by members of the company.

136(6) This section has effect subject to section 137(1) (scheme of reconstruction must be for bona fide commercial reasons and not part of tax avoidance scheme).

History – S. 136 substituted by FA 2002, s. 45(1) and FA 2002, Sch. 9, para. 2, with effect in relation to shares or debentures issued on or after 17 April 2002.

Derivations – CGTA 1979, s. 86.

Cross references – S. 34: value shifting on transactions treated as a reorganisation of share capital.
S. 99: application of TCGA 1992 to unit trust schemes.
S. 118(2): where reconstruction within s. 136 involves a deep discount security, the accrued income reduces any consideration received in addition to the new holding and any excess is treated as allowable enhancement expenditure.
S. 139: s. 136 is usually accompanied by s. 139 (reconstruction involving transfer of business): s. 136 relates to the shareholder and s. 139 relates to the company.
S. 150(8): application to BES shares issued after 18 March 1986 only if relief is withdrawn (applies to shares issued on or before 31 December 1993).
S. 150(8A): disapplication of s. 136 by s. 150(8) overridden for shares issued after 29 November 1994 where condition in s. 150(8B) is satisfied.
S. 150A(8): s. 136 does not apply to shares to which EIS relief is attributable (applies to shares issued on or after 1 January 1994).
S. 150A(8A): disapplication of s. 136 by s. 150A(8) overidden for shares issued after 29 November 1994 where condition in s. 150A(8B) is satisfied.
S. 151B(5), (8): s. 136 disapplied where shares in a venture capital trust eligible for relief under s. 151A(1) are exchanged for a holding not consisting of ordinary shares in a venture capital trust.
S. 251(6): certain debentures deemed securities.
Sch. A1, para. 18: taper relief and special rules for assets acquired in the reconstruction of a mutual business.
ICTA 1988, s. 220(9): as regards condition as to residence and period of ownership for relief on purchase of own shares, time of acquisition determined as under s. 127 unless allotment for payment or part of stock dividend.
ICTA 1988, s. 312(3): exchange by virtue of s. 136(1) is a disposal for purposes of EIS (applies to shares issued on or after 1 January 1994) and previously BES.
ICTA 1988, s. 472A: trading profits etc. from securities: taxation of amounts taken to reserves.
ICTA 1988, s. 473: equation of securities for purposes of taxes on income where reorganisation and assets represent trading stock of a bank, insurance company or dealer.
ICTA 1988, s. 575(3): no relief against income for loss on unquoted shares in trading company where disposal within s. 136.
IHTA 1984, s. 107(4), 113A(6), 124A(6): business and agricultural property relief given in relation to the new holding on satisfaction of certain conditions by reference to the original holding.
IHTA 1984, s. 135: original and new holdings treated as one for purposes of ascertaining any charge in respect of transfers within seven years before death.
IHTA 1984, s. 183: equation of original and new holdings in relation to relief for loss in value of shares etc. between probate and sale within 12 months of death.
FA 2000, Sch. 15, para. 82(1): s. 136 does not apply in respect of the existing holding of CVS shares.
FA 2002, Sch. 16, para. 48: investment in community development finance institution: exchange treated as disposal.
FA 2002, Sch. 29, para. 84: transfer of intangible assets as part of scheme of reconstruction: tax neutral in certain circumstances.
SI 1994/3226, reg. 14: computation and deferral of gain or loss under foreign exchange matching rules on assets exchanged within meaning of s. 136 where TCGA 1992, s. 127 applies.
SI 2009/3001, reg. 36: special provisions for application of s. 136 in relation to disposals of interests in non-reporting offshore funds.

Statements of practice – 2/99, para. 32, 33: where s. 136 applies to an investor's holding with an AUT, AIT or OEIC on a transfer or merger, and the investor continues to make the same regular monthly payments to the new fund, HMRC will apply SP 2/99 as if no transfer or merger had taken place.

HMRC interpretations – *IRInt.* 39: consideration on a share exchange partly in the form of qualifying corporate bonds.
IRInt. 161: HMRC view that, if relevant conditions are satisfied, paper for paper rollover treatment is available where, in an authorised unit trust umbrella scheme, one sub-fund disappears on being merged with another sub-fund.
IRInt. 216: HMRC view that a Delaware Limited Liability Company may be a party to share exchanges.

Notes – S. 116: disapplication to the extent that reconstruction involves a qualifying corporate bond.

S. 119(10), (11): where reconstruction within s. 136 involves a security to which the accrued income scheme applies, any amount to which the transferor is deemed entitled (income credit) reduces any capital consideration received in addition to the new holding and any excess is treated as consideration given while any income relief is treated as increasing the capital consideration received.
S. 184(4): as regards the restriction of indexation allowance on a disposal of shares representing a new holding on a reorganisation when similar restriction would otherwise have applied to the original holding, reorganisation defined by reference to s. 126, as extended to other cases in which s. 127, 128 apply.
S. 288: interpretation, including meaning of "company", "shares" as embracing stock and reference to sections being those of this Act. The substitution of s. 136 by FA 2002 gives statutory effect to SP 5/85.

137 Restriction on application of sections 135 and 136

137(1) Subject to subsection (2) below, and section 138, neither section 135 nor section 136 shall apply to any issue by a company of shares in or debentures of that company in exchange for or in respect of shares in or debentures of another company unless the exchange or scheme of reconstruction in question is effected for bona fide commercial reasons and does not form part of a scheme or arrangements of which the main purpose, or one of the main purposes, is avoidance of liability to capital gains tax or corporation tax.

137(2) Subsection (1) above shall not affect the operation of section 135 or 136 in any case where the person to whom the shares or debentures are issued does not hold more than 5 per cent of, or of any class of, the shares in or debentures of the second company mentioned in subsection (1) above.

137(3) For the purposes of subsection (2) above shares or debentures held by persons connected with the person there mentioned shall be treated as held by him.

137(4) If any tax assessed on a person (the chargeable person) by virtue of subsection (1) above is not paid within 6 months from the date determined under subsection (4A) below, any other person who–

(a) holds all or any part of the shares or debentures that were issued to the chargeable person, and

(b) has acquired them without there having been, since their acquisition by the chargeable person, any disposal of them not falling within section 58(1) or 171,

may, at any time within 2 years from that date, be assessed and charged (in the name of the chargeable person) to all or, as the case may be, a corresponding part of the unpaid tax; and a person paying any amount of tax under this subsection shall be entitled to recover from the chargeable person a sum equal to that amount together with any interest paid by him under section 87A of the Management Act on that amount.

137(4A) The date referred to in subsection (4) above is whichever is the later of–

(a) the date when the tax becomes due and payable by the chargeable person; and

(b) the date when the assessment was made on the chargeable person.

137(5) [Amends subsection (4) above and inserts subsection (4A) above: see history note.]

137(6) In this section references to shares or debentures include references to any interests or options to which this Chapter applies by virtue of section 135(5), section 136(5) or 147.

History – In s. 137(1), words "or scheme of reconstruction" substituted for ", reconstruction or amalgamation" by FA 2002, s. 45 and Sch. 9, para. 5(5) with effect in relation to shares or debentures issued on or after 17 April 2002.
In s. 137(4), the words "the date determined under subsection (4A) below" were substituted for the words "the date when it is payable", the words "that date" were substituted for the words "the time when the tax became payable" and the words "from the chargeable person a sum equal to that amount together with any interest paid by him under section 87A of the Management Act on that amount." were substituted for the words "a sum of that amount from the chargeable person.", by TCGA 1992, s. 137(5) with effect for chargeable gains accruing in chargeable periods ending after 30 September 1993 (i.e. ending after the day appointed by the Treasury under article 2 of the Order that may be cited as the SI 1992/3066 and that was made on 7 December 1992).
S. 137(4A) inserted by TCGA 1992, s. 137(5) with effect for chargeable gains accruing in chargeable periods ending after 30 September 1993 (i.e. ending after the day appointed by the Treasury under article 2 of the Order that may be cited as the SI 1992/3066 and that was made on 7 December 1992).
S. 137(5) amends s. 137(4) and inserts s. 137(4A) with respect to chargeable gains accruing in chargeable periods ending after such day as the Treasury may appoint by order; 30 September 1993 is the day appointed by the Treasury under article 2 of the Order that may be cited as the SI 1992/3066 and that was made on 7 December 1992.
In s. 137(6), words "section 135(5), 136(5)" substituted for "section 136(3)" by FA 2002, s. 45 and Sch. 9, para. 5(5), with effect in relation to shares or debentures issued on or after 17 April 2002.

Derivations – S. 137(1)–(4), (6): CGTA 1979, s. 87.
S. 137(5): CGTA 1979, s. 87(4), (4A), as amended and inserted by F(No. 2)A 1987, s. 95(4) and Sch. 6, para. 5.

Cross references – S. 58(1): deemed no gain, no loss on transfers between spouses.
S. 147: certain quoted options are treated as part of new holdings.
S. 171(1): deemed no gain, no loss on transfer of capital assets within a group.
TMA 1970, s. 87A: interest on overdue corporation tax under Pay and File, from the date when tax becomes payable on the company even when assessed on another person under s. 137(4).

Statutory instruments – SI 1992/3066: the day appointed for the purposes of s. 137(5) is 30 September 1993 (the day appointed for Pay and File).

Other material – ICAEW Technical Release TR 657 (not reproduced): s. 138 clearance procedure does not as a rule confirm s. 135 will apply to the relevant transactions, only that conditions of s. 137(1) satisfied.

Notes – S. 7: time for payment of capital gains tax.
S. 15: meaning of "chargeable gains".
S. 286: meaning of "connected" in references to persons being connected with one another.
S. 287: power to make order exercisable by statutory instrument and negative resolution procedure of House of Commons not to apply.

S. 288: interpretation, including meaning of "company", "shares" as embracing stock, "chargeable period" as being an accounting period or tax year, the "Management Act" as TMA 1970 and reference to other sections being those of this Act.
ICTA 1988, s. 10: time for payment of corporation tax.
TMA 1970, s. 29: assessing procedure.

138 Procedure for clearance in advance

138(1) Section 137 shall not affect the operation of section 135 or 136, in any case where, before the issue is made, the Board have, on the application of either company mentioned in section 137(1), notified the company that the Board are satisfied that the exchange or scheme of reconstruction will be effected for bona fide commercial reasons and will not form part of any such scheme or arrangements as are mentioned in section 137(1).

138(2) Any application under subsection (1) above shall be in writing and shall contain particulars of the operations that are to be effected and the Board may, within 30 days of the receipt of the application or of any further particulars previously required under this subsection, by notice require the applicant to furnish further particulars for the purpose of enabling the Board to make their decision; and if any such notice is not complied with within 30 days or such longer period as the Board may allow, the Board need not proceed further on the application.

138(3) The Board shall notify their decision to the applicant within 30 days of receiving the application or, if they give a notice under subsection (2) above, within 30 days of the notice being complied with.

138(4) If the Board notify the applicant that they are not satisfied as mentioned in subsection (1) above or do not notify their decision to the applicant within the time required by subsection (3) above, the applicant may within 30 days of the notification or of that time require the Board to transmit the application, together with any notice given and further particulars furnished under subsection (2) above, to the tribunal; and in that event any notification by the tribunal shall have effect for the purposes of subsection (1) above as if it were a notification by the Board.

138(5) If any particulars furnished under this section do not fully and accurately disclose all facts and considerations material for the decision of the Board or the tribunal, any resulting notification that the Board or the tribunal are satisfied as mentioned in subsection (1) above shall be void.

History – In s. 138(1), words "or scheme of reconstruction" substituted for ", reconstruction or amalgamation" by FA 2002, s. 45 and Sch. 9, para. 5(6) with effect in relation to shares or debentures issued on or after 17 April 2002.
In s. 138(4) the word "tribunal" substituted for the words "Special Commissioners" twice by SI 2009/56, art. 3(1) and Sch. 1, para. 179, operative from 1 April 2009, subject to transitional and saving provisions in SI 2009/56, Sch. 3.
In s. 138(5) the words "the tribunal" substituted for the words "the Special Commissioners" and the words "Commissioners" by SI 2009/56, art. 3(1) and Sch. 1, para. 179, operative from 1 April 2009, subject to transitional and saving provisions in SI 2009/56, Sch. 3.

Derivations – CGTA 1979, s. 88.

Cross references – SI 2009/275, art. 3(d): any decision under s. 138(4) is an excluded decision for the purposes of TCEA 2007, s. 11(1) and 13(1).
ICTA 1988, s. 444A(8): application of s. 138(2)–(5) to application for clearance in respect of the transfer of long term business of an insurance company under a court-approved scheme.

Statements of practice – SP 13/80: use of a single application for clearance under s. 138 and clearance under ICTA 1988, s. 215(1) (demergers).

Other material – IR press release, 9 August 1989: procedure for clearance and addresses to which applications should be sent.
IR press release, 27 July 1990: insurance companies and friendly societies – clearance procedure for proposed transfers of long term business.
ICAEW Technical Release TR 657 (not reproduced): Board would not normally refuse clearance under s. 138 where consideration is in form of short-dated stock and stock has life of more than six months; s. 138 clearance procedure does not as a rule confirm s. 135 will apply to the relevant transactions, only that conditions of s. 137(1) satisfied.
Law Society's Gazette, 27 March 1991: in cases of extreme urgency, Revenue will consider making available for collection at Somerset House a faxed notification of the s. 138 clearance, or, where applications are submitted from outside London, faxing notification directly to the applicant.

Notes – S. 288: interpretation, including "notice" as being in writing.
TMA 1970, s. 115: service of notices.

138A Use of earn-out rights for exchange of securities

138A(1) For the purposes of this section an earn-out right is so much of any right conferred on any person (**"the seller"**) as–

(a) constitutes the whole or any part of the consideration for the transfer by him of shares in or debentures of a company (**"the old securities"**);

(b) consists in a right to be issued with shares in or debentures of another company (**"the new company"**);

(c) is such that the value or quantity of the shares or debentures to be issued in pursuance of the right (**"the new securities"**) is unascertainable at the time when the right is conferred; and

(d) is not capable of being discharged in accordance with its terms otherwise than by the issue of the new securities.

138A(2) Where–

(a) there is an earn-out right, and

(b) the exchange of the old securities for the earn-out right is an exchange to which section 135 would apply, in a manner unaffected by section 137, if the earn-out right were an ascertainable amount of shares in or debentures of the new company,

(c) [omitted by FA 2003, s. 161(2) and repealed by FA 2003, s. 216 and Sch. 43, Pt. 3(8)]

this Act shall have effect, in the case of the seller and every other person who from time to time has the earn-out right, in accordance with the assumptions specified in subsection (3) below.

138A(2A) Subsection (2) above does not have effect if the seller elects under this section for the earn-out right not to be treated as a security of the new company.

138A(3) Those assumptions are–

(a) that the earn-out right is a security within the definition in section 132;

(b) that the security consisting in the earn-out right is a security of the new company and is incapable of being a qualifying corporate bond for the purposes of this Act;

(c) that references in this Act (including those in this section) to a debenture include references to a right that is assumed to be a security in accordance with paragraph (a) above; and

(d) that the issue of shares or debentures in pursuance of such a right constitutes the conversion of the right, in so far as it is discharged by the issue, into the shares or debentures that are issued.

138A(4) For the purposes of this section where–

(a) any right which is assumed, in accordance with this section, to be a security of a company (**"the old right"**) is extinguished,

(b) the whole of the consideration for the extinguishment of the old right consists in another right (**"the new right"**) to be issued with shares in or debentures of that company,

(c) the new right is such that the value or quantity of the shares or debentures to be issued in pursuance of the right (**"the replacement securities"**) is unascertainable at the time when the old right is extinguished, and

(d) the new right is not capable of being discharged in accordance with its terms otherwise than by the issue of the replacement securities,

(e) [omitted by FA 2003, s. 161(4)(b) and repealed by FA 2003, s. 216 and Sch. 43, Pt. 3(8)]

the assumptions specified in subsection (3) above shall have effect in relation to the new right, in the case of the person on whom the new right is conferred and every other person who from time to time has the new right, as they had effect in relation to the old right.

138A(4A) Subsection (4) above does not have effect if the person on whom the new right is conferred elects under this section for it not to be treated as a security of the new company.

138A(5) An election under this section in respect of any right must be made, by a notice given to an officer of the Board–

(a) in the case of an election by a company within the charge to corporation tax, within the period of two years from the end of the accounting period in which the right is conferred; and

(b) in any other case, on or before the first anniversary of the 31st January next following the year of assessment in which that right is conferred.

138A(6) An election under this section shall be irrevocable.

138A(7) Subject to subsections (8) to (10) below, where any right to be issued with shares in or debentures of a company is conferred on any person, the value or quantity of the shares or debentures to be issued in pursuance of that right shall be taken for the purposes of this section to be unascertainable at a particular time if, and only if–

(a) it is made referable to matters relating to any business or assets of one or more relevant companies; and

(b) those matters are uncertain at that time on account of future business or future assets being included in the business or assets to which they relate.

138A(8) Where a right to be issued with shares or debentures is conferred wholly or partly in consideration for the transfer of other shares or debentures or the extinguishment of any right, the value and quantity of the shares or debentures to be issued shall not be taken for the purposes of this section to be unascertainable in any case where, if–

(a) the transfer or extinguishment were a disposal, and

(b) a gain on that disposal fell to be computed in accordance with this Act,

the shares or debentures to be issued would, in pursuance of section 48, be themselves regarded as, or as included in, the consideration for the disposal.

138A(9) Where any right to be issued with shares in or debentures of a company comprises an option to choose between shares in that company and debentures of that company, the existence of that option shall not, by itself, be taken for the purposes of this section either–

(a) to make unascertainable the value or quantity of the shares or debentures to be issued; or

(b) to prevent the requirements of subsection (1)(b) and (d) or (4)(b) and (d) above from being satisfied in relation to that right.

138A(10) For the purposes of this section the value or quantity of shares or debentures shall not be taken to be unascertainable by reason only that it has not been fixed if it will be fixed by reference to the other and the other is ascertainable.

138A(11) In subsection (7) above **"relevant company"**, in relation to any right to be issued with shares in or debentures of a company, means–

(a) that company or any company which is in the same group of companies as that company; or

(b) the company for whose shares or debentures that right was or was part of the consideration, or any company in the same group of companies as that company;

and in this subsection the reference to a group of companies shall be construed in accordance with section 170(2) to (14).

History – In s. 138A(2), at the end of paragraph (a), the word "and" inserted by FA 2003, s. 161(2)(a) with effect in relation to rights conferred on or after 10 April 2003.
S. 138A(2)(c), and the word "and" immediately preceding s. 138A(2)(c), omitted by FA 2003, s. 161(2)(b) and repealed by FA 2003, s. 216 and Sch. 43, Pt. 3(8), which have effect in relation to rights conferred on or after 10 April 2003.
S. 138A(2A) inserted by FA 2003, s. 161(3) with effect in relation to rights conferred on or after 10 April 2003.
In s. 138A(4)(c), the word "and" inserted by FA 2003, s. 161(4)(a) with effect in relation to rights conferred on or after 10 April 2003.
S. 138A(4)(e), and the word "and" immediately preceding s. 138A(4)(e), omitted by FA 2003, s. 161(4)(b) and repealed by FA 2003, s. 216 and Sch. 43, Pt. 3(8) with effect in relation to rights conferred on or after 10 April 2003.
In s. 138A(4), the words "the person on whom the new right is conferred" substituted for the words "that person" by FA 2003, s. 161(4)(c) with effect in relation to rights conferred on or after 10 April 2003.
S. 138A(4A) inserted by FA 2003, s. 161(5) with effect in relation to rights conferred on or after 10 April 2003.
S. 138A inserted by FA 1997, s. 89(1), and deemed always to have had effect by virtue of FA 1997, s. 89(2) which is subject to FA 1997, s. 89(3) to (8).

Cross references – S. 48: consideration due after time of disposal.
S. 170(2)–(14): interpretation provisions in relation to (groups of) companies.
FA 1997, s. 89(3), (5), (6): timing of election under s. 138A.
FA 1997, s. 89(7), (8): particular provisions in relation to claims under ESC D27 in respect of earn-out rights acquired before 26 April 1988.
FA 2000, Sch. 29, para. 22: chargeable gains of non resident companies and groups – rights conferred on or after 1 April 2000.

139 Reconstruction involving transfer of business

139(1) Subject to the provisions of this section, where–

(a) any scheme of reconstruction involves the transfer of the whole or part of a company's business to another company, and

(b) the conditions in subsection (1A) below are met in relation to the assets included in the transfer, and

(c) the first-mentioned company receives no part of the consideration for the transfer (otherwise than by the other company taking over the whole or part of the liabilities of the business),

then, so far as relates to corporation tax on chargeable gains, the 2 companies shall be treated as if any assets included in the transfer were acquired by the one company from the other company for a consideration of such amount as would secure that on the disposal by way of transfer neither a gain nor a loss would accrue to the company making the disposal, and for the purposes of Schedule 2 the acquiring company shall be treated as if the respective acquisitions of the assets by the other company had been the acquiring company's acquisition of them.

139(1A) The conditions referred to in subsection (1)(b) above are–

(a) that the company acquiring the assets is resident in the United Kingdom at the time of the acquisition, or the assets are chargeable assets or NRCGT assets in relation to that company immediately after that time, and

(b) that the company from which the assets are acquired is resident in the United Kingdom at the time of the acquisition, or the assets are chargeable assets or NRCGT assets in relation to that company immediately before that time.

For this purpose an asset is a "chargeable asset" in relation to a company at any time if, were the asset to be disposed of by the company at that time, any gain accruing to the company would be a chargeable gain and would by virtue of section 10B form part of its chargeable profits for corporation tax purposes.

139(1AA) For the purposes of subsection (1A), an asset is an "NRCGT asset" in relation to a company at any time if–

(a) the disposal of the asset by the company at that time would be a non-resident CGT disposal, and

(b) the company would not be, in relation to that disposal, an eligible person (as defined in section 14F).

139(1B) Nothing in section 179(3D) prevents the two companies being treated as mentioned in subsection (1).

139(2) This section does not apply in relation to an asset which, until the transfer, formed part of trading stock of a trade carried on by the company making the disposal, or in relation to an asset which is acquired as trading stock for the purposes of a trade carried on by the company acquiring the asset.

Section 170(1) applies for the purposes of this subsection.

139(3) [Repealed by FA 1994, s. 251(5) and s. 258 and Sch. 26, Pt. VIII(1).]

139(4) This section does not apply in the case of a transfer of the whole or part of a company's business to a unit trust scheme to which section 100(2) applies or which is an authorised unit trust or to an investment trust or a venture capital trust.

139(5) This section does not apply unless the reconstruction is effected for bona fide commercial reasons and does not form part of a scheme or arrangements of which the main purpose, or one of the main purposes, is avoidance of liability to corporation tax, capital gains tax or income tax; but the foregoing provisions of this subsection shall not affect the operation of this section in any case where, before the transfer, the Board have, on the application of the acquiring company, notified the company that the Board are satisfied that the reconstruction will be effected for bona fide commercial reasons and will not form part of any such scheme or arrangements as aforesaid.

Subsections (2) to (5) of section 138 shall have effect in relation to this subsection as they have effect in relation to subsection (1) of that section.

139(6) Where, if the company making the disposal had not been wound up, tax could have been assessed on it by virtue of subsection (5) above, that tax may be assessed and charged (in the name of the company making the disposal) on the company to which the disposal is made.

139(7) If any tax assessed on a company (**"the chargeable company"**) by virtue of subsection (5) or (6) above is not paid within 6 months from the date when it is due and payable or, if later, the date when the assessment is made on the company, any other person who–

(a) holds all or any part of the assets in respect of which the tax is charged; and

(b) either is the company to which the disposal was made or has acquired the assets without there having been any subsequent disposal not falling within this section or section 171,

may, within 2 years from the later of those dates, be assessed and charged (in the name of the chargeable company) to all or, as the case may be, a corresponding part of the unpaid tax; and a person paying any amount of tax under this section shall be entitled to recover from the chargeable company a sum equal to that amount together with any interest paid by him under section 87A of the Management Act on that amount.

139(8) [Amends subsection (7) above: see history note.]

139(9) In this section **"scheme of reconstruction"** has the same meaning as in section 136.

History – In s. 139(1)(a), words "or amalgamation" which followed "reconstruction" repealed by FA 2002, s. 141 and Sch. 40, Pt. 3(2), with effect in relation to shares or debentures issued on or after 17 April 2002.

S. 139(1)(b) substituted by FA 2000, s. 102 and Sch. 29, para. 5(2) with effect in relation to disposals made on or after 1 April 2000.

In s. 139(1A)(a) and (b), the words "or NRCGT assets" inserted by FA 2015, s. 37 and Sch. 7, para. 21(2), with effect in relation to disposals made on or after 6 April 2015.

S. 139(1A) inserted by FA 2000, s. 102 and Sch. 29, para. 5(3) with effect in relation to disposals made on or after 1 April 2000.

In s. 139(1A), the reference "10B" substituted for the reference "10(3)" by FA 2003, s. 155 and Sch. 27, para. 2(3) which have effect in relation to accounting periods beginning on or after 1 January 2003.

S. 139(1AA) inserted by FA 2015, s. 37 and Sch. 7, para. 21(3), with effect in relation to disposals made on or after 6 April 2015.

S. 139(1B) inserted by FA 2011, s. 45 and Sch. 10, para. 1, with effect in relation to any disposal of an asset by one company (B) to another company (A) made at a time when B is a member of a group if either A ceases to be a member of the group on or after 19 July 2011 or ceased to be so before 19 July 2011 in circumstances where TCGA 1992, s. 179(6)–(8) applied and ceases to satisfy the conditions in TCGA 1992, s. 179(7) on or after 19 July 2011 (see FA 2011, Sch. 10, para. 9(1)). But references to 19 July 2011 may be replaced by references to 1 April 2011 if an "early commencement election" is made (see FA 2011, Sch. 10, para. 9(4)–(8)).

S. 139(3) repealed by FA 1994, s. 251(5) and s. 258 and Sch. 26, Pt. VIII(1), in relation to acquisitions on or after 30 November 1993.

The words "or a venture capital trust" inserted in s. 139(4) by FA 1998, s. 134(1), with effect for transfers made on or after 17 March 1998.

In s. 139(5), words "or amalgamation" which followed "reconstruction" in both places repealed by FA 2002, s. 141 and Sch. 40, Pt. 3(2), with effect in relation to shares or debentures issued on or after 17 April 2002.

In s. 139(7), the words "when it is due and payable or, if later, the date when the assessment is made on the company" were substituted for the words "when it is payable", the words "the later of those dates" were substituted for the words "the time when the tax became payable" and the words "from the chargeable person a sum equal to that amount together with any interest paid by him under section 87Aof the Management Act on that amount." were substituted for the words "a sum of that amount from the chargeable person.", by TCGA 1992, s. 139(8) with effect for chargeable gains accruing in chargeable periods ending after 30 September 1993 (i.e. ending after the day appointed by the Treasury under article 2 of the Order that may be cited as SI 1992/3066 and that was made on 7 December 1992).

S. 139(8) amends s. 139(7) with respect to chargeable gains accruing in chargeable periods ending after such day as the Treasury may by order appoint; 30 September 1993 is the day appointed by the Treasury under article 2 of the Order that may be cited as SI 1992/3066 and that was made on 7 December 1992.

S. 139(9) substituted by FA 2002, s. 45 and Sch. 9, para. 5(7) with effect in relation to shares or debentures issued on or after 17 April 2002.

Derivations – S. 139(1), (2): ICTA 1970, s. 267(1), (2); s. 238(4).
S. 139(3): ICTA 1970, s. 267(2A), as inserted by FA 1990, s. 65(1).
S. 139(4): ICTA 1970, s. 267(3), as amended by FA 1980, s. 81(2).
S. 139(5)–(7): ICTA 1970, s. 267(3A)–(3C), as inserted by FA 1977, s. 41.
S. 139(8): ICTA 1970, s. 267(3C) as amended by F(No. 2)A 1987, s. 95(4) and Sch. 6, para. 2.
S. 139(9): ICTA 1970, s. 267(4).

Cross references – S. 25(4): priority over deemed market value disposal rules for cessation of trade by UK branch or agency in accordance with court-approved insurance company transfer scheme.
S. 35(3)(d), (5): re-basing not to apply to disposal under these provisions unless an election exists for the simplified scheme (re-basing of all assets held at 31 March 1982 irrespective of matters in s. 35(3)).
S. 99A: authorised unit trusts: treatment of umbrella schemes.
S. 100(2): unit trusts for exempt unit holders.
S. 101(1): transferee later becoming an investment trust deemed to dispose of assets at market value.
S. 101B: transferee later becoming a venture capital trust deemed to dispose of assets at market value.
S. 116(11): disapplication to a transfer within s. 139 of provisions deeming there to be no disposal but so that any market value gain or loss crystallises at subsequent disposal on a reorganisation, conversion or reconstruction where qualifying corporate bonds form part of the new holding but not the original holding.
S. 170(1): "trade" defined to include, until 6 April 1993, the occupation of woodlands in certain circumstances.
S. 171: deemed no gain, no loss on transfer of capital assets within a group.
S. 211: relaxation of conditions for the transfer of long term business of an insurance company under a court-approved scheme.
Sch. 2: assets held on 6 April 1965.
Sch. 3, para. 1: person disposing of asset acquired through disposal under these provisions after 31 March 1982 treated as holding asset at 31 March 1982 for purposes of re-basing.
ICTA 1988, s. 220(9): as regards condition as to residence and period of ownership for relief on purchase of own shares, time of acquisition determined as under s. 127 unless allotment for payment or part of stock dividend.
TMA 1970, s. 87A: interest on overdue corporation tax under Pay and File, from the date when tax becomes payable on the company even when assessed on another person under s. 139(7).
FA 1993, Sch. 17, para. 7: disapplication of s. 139 where that paragraph (exchange gains and losses: chargeable gains – reconstructions) applies.
FA 1995, s. 131(2): s. 139 disapplied where a qualifying company (for FA 1993, Pt. II, Ch. II) transfers before its commencement day a qualifying asset to another qualifying company on or after the second company's commencement day.
SI 1992/58, Sch. 2, para. 1: disapplication of s. 139 in relation to reorganisation of port authorities.
SI 1994/3227, reg. 8: deferral of gain or loss deemed to accrue on disposal, which is a no gain/no loss transaction under s. 139, of a matched asset by one company to another.

Statutory instruments – SI 1992/3066: the day appointed for the purposes of s. 139(8) is 30 September 1993 (the day appointed for Pay and File).

Statements of practice – 13/80: procedure for clearance application under ICTA 1988, s. 215(1) (demergers) where clearance also sought under s. 139(5) (but see also IR press release, below).

Other material – HMRC press release, 9 August 1989: clearance applications under s. 139(5) following relocation of Revenue work.
HMRC press release, 27 July 1990: clearance applications in respect of proposed transfers of long term business of insurance company or friendly society.
Law Society's Gazette, 27 March 1991: in cases of extreme urgency, Revenue will consider making available for collection at Somerset House a faxed notification of the s. 139(5) clearance, or, where applications are submitted from outside London, faxing notification directly to the applicant.

Notes – S. 9: meaning of residence.
S. 21–34: general meaning of "disposal" and "asset".
S. 56(2): no gain, no loss calculated after applying indexation allowance.
S. 288: interpretation, including meaning of "company", "double taxation relief arrangements", "trading stock", the "Management Act" as TMA 1970 and reference to other sections as being those of this Act.
ICTA 1988, s. 10: time for payment of corporation tax.
FA 1994, s. 249: companies treated as resident in the UK for tax purposes, but resident abroad for the purposes of any double taxation relief arrangements ("dual resident companies"), are with effect from 30 November 1993 to be treated as non-UK resident for all tax purposes, even if they are incorporated in the UK.

140 Postponement of charge on transfer of assets to non-resident company

140(1) This section applies where a company resident in the United Kingdom carries on a trade outside the United Kingdom through a permanent establishment and–

(a) that trade, or part of it, together with the whole assets of the company used for the purposes of the trade or part (or together with the whole of those assets other than cash) is transferred to a company not resident in the United Kingdom;

(b) the trade or part is so transferred wholly or partly in exchange for securities consisting of shares, or of shares and loan stock, issued by the transferee company to the transferor company;

(c) the shares so issued, either alone or taken together with any other shares in the transferee company already held by the transferor company, amount in all to not less than one quarter of the ordinary share capital of the transferee company; and

(d) either no allowable losses accrue to the transferor company on the transfer or the aggregate of the chargeable gains so accruing exceeds the aggregate of the allowable losses so accruing;

and also applies in any case where section 268A of the Income and Corporation Taxes Act 1970 applied unless the deferred gain had been wholly taken into account in accordance with that section before the coming into force of this section.

Section 170(1) shall apply for the purposes of this section.

140(2) In any case to which this section applies the transferor company may claim that this Act shall have effect in accordance with the following provisions.

140(3) Any allowable losses accruing to the transferor company on the transfer shall be set off against the chargeable gains so accruing and the transfer shall be treated as giving rise to a single chargeable gain equal to the aggregate of those gains after deducting the aggregate of those losses and–

(a) if the securities are the whole consideration for the transfer, the whole of that gain shall be treated as not accruing to the transferor company on the transfer but an equivalent amount (**"the deferred gain"**) shall be brought into account in accordance with subsections (4) and (5) below;

(b) if the securities are not the whole of that consideration–

  (i) paragraph (a) above shall apply to the appropriate proportion of that gain; and

  (ii) the remainder shall be treated as accruing to the transferor company on the transfer.

In paragraph (b)(i) above "**the appropriate proportion**" means the proportion that the market value of the securities at the time of the transfer bears to the market value of the whole of the consideration at that time.

140(4) If at any time after the transfer the transferor company disposes of the whole or part of the securities held by it immediately before that time, there shall be deemed to accrue to the transferor company as a chargeable gain on that occasion the whole or the appropriate proportion of the deferred gain so far as not already taken into account under this subsection or subsection (5) below.

In this subsection "**the appropriate proportion**" means the proportion that the market value of the part of the securities disposed of bears to the market value of the securities held immediately before the disposal.

140(4A) A chargeable gain which is deemed to accrue under subsection (4) is in addition to any gain or loss that actually accrues to the transferor company on the disposal of the securities.

140(5) If at any time within 6 years after the transfer the transferee company disposes of the whole or part of the relevant assets held by it immediately before that time there shall be deemed to accrue to the transferor company as a chargeable gain on that occasion the whole or the appropriate proportion of the deferred gain so far as not already taken into account under this subsection or subsection (4) above.

In this subsection **"relevant assets"** means assets the chargeable gains on which were taken into account in arriving at the deferred gain and "**the appropriate proportion**" means the proportion which the chargeable gain so taken into account in respect of the part of the relevant assets disposed of bears to the aggregate of the chargeable gains so taken into account in respect of the relevant assets held immediately before the time of the disposal.

140(6) There shall be disregarded–

(a) for the purposes of subsection (4) above any disposal to which section 171 applies; and

(b) for the purposes of subsection (5) above any disposal to which that section would apply if subsections (1)(b) and (1A) of that section and section 170(9) were disregarded;

and where a person acquires securities or an asset on a disposal disregarded for the purposes of subsection (4) or (5) above (and without there having been a previous disposal not so disregarded) a disposal of the securities or asset by that person shall be treated as a disposal by the transferor or, as the case may be, transferee company.

140(6A) No claim may be made under this section as regards a transfer in relation to which a claim is made under section 140C.

140(6AA) If securities are transferred by a transferor company as part of the process of the transfer of a business to which section 140A or 140C applies–

(a) the transfer shall be disregarded for the purposes of subsection (4), and

(b) the transferee company shall be treated as if it were the transferor company in relation to–

  (i) any subsequent disposal of the securities, and

  (ii) any subsequent disposal by the transferee of assets to which subsection 5 applies.

140(6B) If securities are transferred by a transferor as part of the process of a merger to which section 140E applies–

(a) the transfer shall be disregarded for the purposes of subsection (4), and

(b) the transferee shall be treated as if it were the transferor in relation to–

  (i) any subsequent disposal of the securities, and

  (ii) any subsequent disposal by the transferee of assets to which subsection (5) applies.

140(6C) In subsection (6B) **"transferor"** and **"transferee"** have the meaning given by section 140E(9).

140(7) If in the case of any such transfer as was mentioned in section 268(1) of the Income and Corporation Taxes Act 1970 there were immediately before the coming into force of this section chargeable gains which by virtue of section 268(2) and 268A(8) of that Act were treated as not having accrued to the transferor company, subsection (4) above shall (without any claim in that behalf) apply to the aggregate of those gains as if references to the deferred gain were references to that aggregate and as if references to the transfer and the securities were references to the transfer and the shares, or shares and loan stock, mentioned in section 268(1).

140(8) If in the case of any such transfer as was mentioned in section 268A(1) of the Income and Corporation Taxes Act 1970 there were immediately before the coming into force of this section deferred gains which by virtue of section 268A(3) were treated as not having accrued to the transferor company, subsections (4) and (5) above shall (without any claim in that behalf) apply to those deferred gains as they apply to gains deferred by virtue of subsection (3) above (as if the references to the transfer and the securities were references to the transfer and securities mentioned in section 268A(1)).

History – In s. 140(1), the words "permanent establishment" substituted for the words "branch or agency" by FA 2003, s. 153(1)(b) with effect in relation to accounting periods beginning on or after 1 January 2003.
In s. 140(4), the words "there shall be deemed to accrue to the transferor company as a chargeable gain on that occasion" substituted for "the consideration received by it on the disposal shall be treated as increased by" by FA 2010, s. 37(1)(a), with effect in relation to disposals of securities on or after 6 January 2010.
S. 140(4A) inserted by FA 2010, s. 37(1)(b), with effect in relation to disposals of securities on or after 6 January 2010.
In s. 140(6)(b), words "if subsections (1)(b) and … were disregarded" substituted for words "apart from section 170(2)(a) and (9)" by FA 2000, s. 102 and Sch. 29, para. 23(1) with effect in relation to disposals on or after 1 April 2000.
S. 140(6A) inserted by F(No. 2)A 1992, s. 46(4), and deemed always to have had effect. (A corresponding provision was inserted into ICTA 1970, s. 268A (the predecessor provision), as s. 268A(6), by F(No. 2)A 1992, s. 49(2)).
S. 140(6AA) inserted by SI 2007/3186, reg. 3(1) and Sch. 1, para. 7, with effect in relation to transfers which take place on or after 1 January 2007, and in relation to cross-border mergers taking place on or after that date, but in the case of mergers relating to the formation of an SE or SCE, in relation to those taking place on or after 18 August 2006 (see SI 2008/1579, reg. 4(1)).
S. 140(6B) and (6C) substituted for s. 140(6B) by SI 2007/3186, reg. 3(2) and Sch. 2, para. 5, in relation to mergers relating to the formation of an SE or SCE which take place on or after 18 August 2006, and in relation to all other mergers which take place on or after 1 January 2007.
S. 140(6B) inserted by F(No. 2)A 2005, s. 64(2) with effect in relation to the formation of an SE (i.e. Societas Europaea) under Article 2 of Council Regulation (EC) 2157/2001 on the Statute for a European Company (Societas Europaea) which occurs on or after 1 April 2005.

Derivations – ICTA 1970, s. 268A, as inserted by FA 1977, s. 42; and (subs. (1)) ICTA 1970, s. 238(4).

Cross references – S. 35(3)(d): re-basing not to apply to disposal under these provisions unless election for universal rebasing (of all assets at 31 March 1982) made.
S. 171: deemed no gain, no loss on transfer of capital assets within a group.
Sch. 4, para. 4, 5: 50 per cent reduction in gain crystallising under s. 140 where attributable to the deferral before 6 April 1988 if original assets held at 31 March 1982 (or acquired in a chain of no gain, no loss disposals from that date).
Sch. 7AC, para. 35: disposal of shares by company with substantial shareholding where s. 140(4) applies.
ICTA 1988, s. 220(9): as regards condition as to residence and period of ownership for relief on purchase of own shares, time of acquisition determined as under s. 127 unless allotment for payment or part of stock dividend.
FA 2002, Sch. 29, para. 127: treatment of certain intangible assets acquired on transfer of business as existing assets in the hands of the transferee company.
SI 1992/58, Sch. 2, para. 1: disapplication of s. 140 in relation to reorganisation of port authorities.
SI 1994/3227, reg. 8: adjustment of consideration for transfers which include the disposal of a matched asset on which a deemed gain or loss would otherwise accrue.

European material – Council Regulation (EC) 2157/2001 of 8 October 2001 on the Statute for a European Company (Societas Europaea).
Directive 90/434, art. 10 (s. 140(6A)).

Notes – S. 9: meaning of residence.
S. 10(6): meaning of "branch or agency".
S. 15: meaning of "chargeable gains".
S. 16: meaning of "allowable losses".
S. 21–34: general meaning of "disposal" and "asset".
S. 272–274 and Sch. 11: meaning of "market value".
S. 276: UK territorial sea deemed to be part of the UK.
S. 288: interpretation, including meaning of "company", "shares" as embracing stock and reference to sections as being those of this Act.
TMA 1970, s. 42–43B: procedures and time limits for claims.

TRANSFERS CONCERNING COMPANIES OF DIFFERENT MEMBER STATES

140A Transfer or division of UK business

140A(1) This section applies where–

(a) a company resident in one member State (**the transferor**) transfers the whole or part of a business carried on by it in the United Kingdom to a company resident in another member State (**the transferee**),

(b) the transfer is wholly in exchange for shares or debentures issued by the transferee to the transferor,

(c) a claim is made under this section by the transferor and the transferee,

(d) section 140B does not prevent this section applying, and

(e) the appropriate condition is met in relation to the transferee immediately after the time of the transfer.

140A(1A) This section also applies where a company transfers part of its business to one or more companies if–

(a) the transferor is resident in one member State,

(b) the part of the transferor's business which is to be transferred is carried on by the transferor in the United Kingdom,

(c) at least one transferee is resident in a member State other than that in which the transferor is resident,

(d) the transferor company continues to carry on a business after the transfer,

(e) the conditions in subsection (1)(c) to (e) are satisfied (for which purpose references to the transferee shall be taken as references to each of the transferees), and

(f) either of the following conditions is satisfied.

140A(1B) Condition 1 is that the transfer is made in exchange for the issue of shares in or debentures of each transferee company to the persons holding shares in or debentures of the transferor.

140A(1C) Condition 2 is that the transfer is not made in exchange for the issue of shares in or debentures of each transferee by reason only, and to the extent only, that a transferee is prevented from complying with Condition 1 by section 658 of the Companies Act 2006 (rule against limited company acquiring own shares) or by a corresponding provision of the law of another member State preventing the issue of shares or debentures to itself.

140A(1D) If Condition 2 applies in relation to the whole or part of a transfer, sections 24 and 122 do not apply in relation to the transfer.

140A(2) Where immediately after the time of the transfer the transferee (or each of the transferees) is not resident in the United Kingdom, the appropriate condition is that were it to dispose of the assets included in the transfer any chargeable gains accruing to it on the disposal would form part of its chargeable profits for corporation tax purposes by virtue of section 10B.

140A(3) Where immediately after the time of the transfer the transferee (or each of the transferees) is resident in the United Kingdom, the appropriate condition is that none of the assets included in the transfer is one in respect of which, by virtue of the asset being of a description specified in double taxation relief arrangements, the company falls to be regarded for the purposes of the arrangements as not liable in the United Kingdom to tax on gains accruing to it on a disposal.

140A(4) Where this section applies–

(a) the transferor and the transferee (or each of the transferees) shall be treated, so far as relates to corporation tax on chargeable gains, as if any assets included in the transfer were acquired by the transferee (or each of the transferees) from the transferor for a consideration of such amount as would secure that on the disposal by way of transfer neither a gain nor a loss would accrue to the transferor;

(b) section 25(3) shall not apply to any such assets by reason of the transfer (if it would apply apart from this paragraph).

140A(5) [Omitted by SI 2007/3186, reg. 3(1) and Sch. 1, para. 2(6).]

140A(6) [Omitted by SI 2007/3186, reg. 3(1) and Sch. 1, para. 2(6).]

140A(7) [Omitted by SI 2007/3186, reg. 3(1) and Sch. 1, para. 2(6).]

History – The heading to s. 140A substituted for "Transfer of a UK trade" by SI 2007/3186, reg. 3(1) and Sch. 1, para. 2(7), with effect in relation to transfers which take place on or after 1 January 2007, and in relation to cross-border mergers taking place on or after that date, but in the case of mergers relating to the formation of an SE or SCE, in relation to those taking place on or after 18 August 2006 (see SI 2008/1579, reg. 4(1)).

In s. 140A(1) the words "the transferor" substituted for "company A", "the transferee" substituted for "company B", "company" substituted for "qualifying company", and "business" substituted for "trade" by SI 2007/3186, reg. 3(1) and Sch. 1, para. 2(2), with effect in relation to transfers which take place on or after 1 January 2007, and in relation to cross-border mergers taking place on or after that date, but in the case of mergers relating to the formation of an SE or SCE, in relation to those taking place on or after 18 August 2006 (see SI 2008/1579, reg. 4(1)).

In s. 140A(1)(b), words "shares or debentures" substituted for word "securities" by F(No. 2)A 2005, s. 59(5)(a) with effect in relation to an issue effected on or after 1 April 2005.

S. 140A(1A)–(1D) inserted by SI 2007/3186, reg. 3(1) and Sch. 1, para. 2(3), with effect in relation to transfers which take place on or after 1 January 2007, and in relation to cross-border mergers taking place on or after that date, but in the case of mergers relating to the formation of an SE or SCE, in relation to those taking place on or after 18 August 2006 (see SI 2008/1579, reg. 4(1)).

In s. 140A(2)–(4) the words "the transferor" substituted for "company A", "the transferee (or each of the transferees)" substituted for "company B" by SI 2007/3186, reg. 3(1) and Sch. 1, para. 2(4), with effect in relation to transfers which take place on or after 1 January 2007, and in relation to cross-border mergers taking place on or after that date, but in the case of mergers relating to the formation of an SE or SCE, in relation to those taking place on or after 18 August 2006 (see SI 2008/1579, reg. 4(1)).

In s. 140A(2), the reference "10B" substituted for the reference "10(3)" by FA 2003, s. 155 and Sch. 27, para. 2(3) which have effect in relation to accounting periods beginning on or after 1 January 2003.

In s. 140A(4) the words "the transferor and the transferee (or each of the transferees)" substituted for "the two companies" by SI 2007/3186, reg. 3(1) and Sch. 1, para. 2(5), with effect in relation to transfers which take place on or after 1 January 2007, and in relation to cross-border mergers taking place on or after that date, but in the case of mergers relating to the formation of an SE or SCE, in relation to those taking place on or after 18 August 2006 (see SI 2008/1579, reg. 4(1)).

S. 140A(5), (6) and (7)omitted by SI 2007/3186, reg. 3(1) and Sch. 1, para. 2(6), with effect in relation to transfers which take place on or after 1 January 2007, and in relation to cross-border mergers taking place on or after that date, but in the case of mergers relating to the formation of an SE or SCE, in relation to those taking place on or after 18 August 2006 (see SI 2008/1579, reg. 4(1)).
Previously in s. 140A(7), definition of "securities" omitted by F(No. 2)A 2005, s. 59(3)(b) and repealed by F(No. 2)A 2005, s. 70 and Sch. 11, Pt. 4 with effect in relation to an issue effected on or after 1 April 2005; definition of "securities" was "securities includes shares".
S. 140A inserted by F(No. 2)A 1992, s. 44, and deemed always to have had effect; corresponding provisions were inserted by F(No. 2)A 1992, s. 47 as ICTA 1970, s. 269A and 269B in relation to transfers taking effect on or after 1 January 1992.

Cross references – S. 10(3): company not resident in the UK but carrying on a trade, profession or vocation in the UK through a branch or agency – chargeable profits include chargeable gains accruing on disposal of assets situated in the UK as charged by s. 10.
S. 25(3): deemed disposal where asset ceases to be a chargeable asset in relation to non-resident by virtue of his ceasing to carry on a trade etc. through UK branch or agency.
S. 35(3)(d)(i): re-basing not to apply to disposal under s. 140A unless election exists for simplified universal re-basing scheme.
S. 116(11): reorganisations etc., modification of s. 116(10)(b), (c) in relation to disposals within s. 140A.
S. 177(2): application of provisions (s. 176) relating to depreciatory transactions within groups.
Sch. 7B, para. 5: modification of s. 140A(2) in respect of overseas life insurance companies in relation to transfers taking place in accounting periods of company B after 31 December 1992.
CAA 2001, s. 561(1) (formerly CAA 1990, s. 152B): where immediately after the transfer company B carries on the transferred trade in the UK through a branch or agency, the transfer itself will not give rise to any capital allowances or charges, and everything done to or by company A before the transfer in relation to the assets transferred is treated, after the transfer, as having been done to or by company B.
FA 1995, s. 131(2): s. 140A disapplied where a qualifying company (for FA 1993, Pt. II, Ch. II) transfers before its commencement day a qualifying asset to another qualifying company on or after the second company's commencement day.
FA 2002, Sch. 29, para. 127: treatment of certain intangible assets acquired on transfer of business as existing assets in the hands of the transferee company.
SI 1994/3227, reg. 8: deferral of gain or loss deemed to accrue on disposal, which is a no gain/no loss transaction under s. 140A, of a matched asset by one company to another.

Transitional – Until s. 658 of the Companies Act 2006 (rule against limited company acquiring own shares) comes into force, the reference to that section in s. 140A(1C) has effect as if it were a reference to s. 143 of the Companies Act 1985 (general rule against companies acquiring own shares) (SI 2008/1579, reg. 6(1) and Sch. 4, para. 2(a)).

European material – Directive 90/434, art. 4.

140B Section 140A: anti-avoidance

140B(1) Section 140A shall not apply unless the transfer of the business or part is effected for bona fide commercial reasons and does not form part of a scheme or arrangements of which the main purpose, or one of the main purposes, is avoidance of liability to income tax, corporation tax or capital gains tax.

140B(2) Subsection (1) above shall not apply where, before the transfer, the Board have on the application of the transferor and the transferee (or each of the transferees) notified those companies that the Board are satisfied that the transfer will be effected for bona fide commercial reasons and will not form part of any such scheme or arrangements as are mentioned in that subsection.

140B(3) Subsections (2) to (5) of section 138 shall have effect in relation to subsection (2) above as they have effect in relation to subsection (1) of that section.

History – In s. 140B the words "the transferor" substituted for "company A", "the transferee (or each of the transferees)" substituted for "company B", and "business" substituted for "trade" by SI 2007/3186, reg. 3(1) and Sch. 1, para. 3, with effect in relation to transfers which take place on or after 1 January 2007, and in relation to cross-border mergers taking place on or after that date, but in the case of mergers relating to the formation of an SE or SCE, in relation to those taking place on or after 18 August 2006 (see SI 2008/1579, reg. 4(1)).
S. 140B inserted by F(No. 2)A 1992, s. 44, and deemed always to have had effect; corresponding provisions were inserted by F(No. 2)A 1992, s. 47 as ICTA 1970, s. 269A and 269B in relation to transfers taking effect on or after 1 January 1992.

European material – Directive 90/434, art. 4.

140C Transfer or division of non-UK business

140C(1) This section applies where–

(a) a company resident in the United Kingdom (**the transferor**) transfers to a company resident in another member State (**the transferee**) the whole or part of a business which, immediately before the time of the transfer, the transferor carried on in a member State other than the United Kingdom through a permanent establishment,

(b) the transfer includes the whole of the assets of the transferor used for the purposes of the business or part (or the whole of those assets other than cash),

(c) the transfer is wholly or partly in exchange for shares or debentures issued by the transferee to the transferor,

(d) the aggregate of the chargeable gains accruing to the transferor on the transfer exceeds the aggregate of the allowable losses so accruing,

(e) a claim is made under this section by the transferor, and

(f) section 140D does not prevent this section applying.

140C(1A) This section also applies where a company resident in the United Kingdom transfers part of its business to one or more companies if–

(a) the part of the transferor's business which is to be transferred is carried on, immediately before the time of the transfer, by the transferor in a member State other than the United Kingdom through a permanent establishment,

(b) at least one transferee is resident in a member State other than the United Kingdom,

(c) the transferor company continues to carry on a business after the transfer,

(d) the conditions in subsection (1)(b), (d), (e) and (f) are satisfied, and

(e) either of the following conditions is satisfied.

140C(1B) Condition 1 is that the transfer is made in exchange for the issue of shares in or debentures of each transferee company to the persons holding shares in or debentures of the transferor.

140C(1C) Condition 2 is that the transfer is not made in exchange for the issue of shares in or debentures of each transferee by reason only, and to the extent only, that a transferee is prevented from complying with Condition 1 by section 658 of the Companies Act 2006 (rule against limited company acquiring own shares) or by a corresponding provision of the law of another member State preventing the issue of shares or debentures to itself.

140C(2) In a case where this section applies, this Act shall have effect in accordance with subsection (3) below.

140C(3) The allowable losses accruing to the transferor on the transfer shall be set off against the chargeable gains so accruing and the transfer shall be treated as giving rise to a single chargeable gain equal to the aggregate of those gains after deducting the aggregate of those losses.

140C(4) No claim may be made under this section as regards a transfer in relation to which a claim is made under section 140.

140C(5) In a case where this section applies, section 122 of TIOPA 2010 (tax treated as chargeable in respect of gains on transfer of non-UK business) shall also apply.

140C(6) [Omitted by SI 2007/3186, reg. 3(1) and Sch. 1, para. 4(5).]

140C(7) [Omitted by SI 2007/3186, reg. 3(1) and Sch. 1, para. 4(5).]

140C(8) [Omitted by FA 2012, s. 146 and Sch. 16, para. 75.]

140C(9) [Omitted by SI 2007/3186, reg. 3(1) and Sch. 1, para. 4(5).]

History – The heading to s. 140C substituted for "Transfer of a non-UK trade", by SI 2007/3186, reg. 3(1) and Sch. 1, para. 4(6), with effect in relation to transfers which take place on or after 1 January 2007, and in relation to cross-border mergers taking place on or after that date, but in the case of mergers relating to the formation of an SE or SCE, in relation to those taking place on or after 18 August 2006 (see SI 2008/1579, reg. 4(1)).
In s. 140C(1) the words "the transferor" substituted for "company A", "the transferee" substituted for "company B", "company" substituted for "qualifying company", and "business" substituted for "trade" by SI 2007/3186, reg. 3(1) and Sch. 1, para. 4(2), with effect in relation to transfers which take place on or after 1 January 2007, and in relation to cross-border mergers taking place on or after that date, but in the case of mergers relating to the formation of an SE or SCE, in relation to those taking place on or after 18 August 2006 (see SI 2008/1579, reg. 4(1)).
In s. 140C(1)(a), the words "permanent establishment" substituted for the words "branch or agency" by FA 2003, s. 153(1)(b) with effect in relation to accounting periods beginning on or after 1 January 2003.
In s. 140C(1)(c), words "shares or debentures" substituted for word "securities" by F(No. 2)A 2005, s. 59(4)(a) with effect in relation to an issue effected on or after 1 April 2005.
S. 140C(1A)–(1C) inserted by SI 2007/3186, reg. 3(1) and Sch. 1, para. 4(3), with effect in relation to transfers which take place on or after 1 January 2007, and in relation to cross-border mergers taking place on or after that date, but in the case of mergers relating to the formation of an SE or SCE, in relation to those taking place on or after 18 August 2006 (see SI 2008/1579, reg. 4(1)).
In s. 140C(3) and former (8) the words "the transferor" substituted for "company A" by SI 2007/3186, reg. 3(1) and Sch. 1, para. 4(4), with effect in relation to transfers which take place on or after 1 January 2007, and in relation to cross-border mergers taking place on or after that date, but in the case of mergers relating to the formation of an SE or SCE, in relation to those taking place on or after 18 August 2006 (see SI 2008/1579, reg. 4(1)).
In s. 140C(5), the words "section 122 of TIOPA 2010 (tax treated as chargeable in respect of gains on transfer of non-UK business)" substituted for the words "section 815A of the Taxes Act" by SI 2013/463, art. 5, with effect from 1 April 2013.
S. 140C(6) and (7) omitted by SI 2007/3186, reg. 3(1) and Sch. 1, para. 4(5), with effect in relation to transfers which take place on or after 1 January 2007, and in relation to cross-border mergers taking place on or after that date, but in the case of mergers relatingto the formation of an SE or SCE, in relation to those taking place on or after 18 August 2006 (see SI 2008/1579, reg. 4(1)).
S. 140C(8) omitted by FA 2012, s. 146 and Sch. 16, para. 75 in relation to accounting periods beginning on or after 1 January 2013 (FA 2012, s. 148) but subject to transitional provisions in FA 2012, Sch. 17. Where an accounting period would otherwise straddle 1 January 2013, it is deemed to end on 31 December 2012 (FA 2012, s. 149).
S. 140C(9) omitted by SI 2007/3186, reg. 3(1) and Sch. 1, para. 4(5), with effect in relation to transfers which take place on or after 1 January 2007, and in relation to cross-border mergers taking place on or after that date, but in the case of mergers relating to the formation of an SE or SCE, in relation to those taking place on or after 18 August 2006 (see SI 2008/1579, reg. 4(1)).
In former s. 140C(9), definition of "securities" omitted by F(No. 2)A 2005, s. 59(4)(b) and repealed by F(No. 2)A 2005, s. 70 and Sch. 11, Pt. 4 with effect in relation to an issue effected on or after 1 April 2005; definition of "securities" was "securities includes shares".
S. 140C inserted by F(No. 2)A 1992, s. 45, and deemed always to have had effect; corresponding provisions were inserted by F(No. 2)A 1992, s. 48 as ICTA 1970, s. 269C and 269D, in relation to transfers taking effect on or after 1 January 1992.

Cross references – ICTA 1988, s. 815A: arrangements for double taxation relief with other member states.

Transitional – Until s. 658 of the Companies Act 2006 (rule against limited company acquiring own shares) comes into force, the reference to that section in s. 140C(1C) has effect as if it were a reference to s. 143 of the Companies Act 1985 (general rule against companies acquiring own shares) (SI 2008/1579, reg. 6(1) and Sch. 4, para. 2(b)).

European material – Directive 90/434, art. 10.

140D Section 140C: anti-avoidance

140D(1) Section 140C shall not apply unless the transfer of the business or part is effected for bona fide commercial reasons and does not form part of a scheme or arrangements of which the main purpose, or one of the main purposes, is avoidance of liability to income tax, corporation tax or capital gains tax.

140D(2) Subsection (1) above shall not apply where, before the transfer, the Board have on the application of the transferor notified that company that the Board are satisfied that the transfer will be effected for bona fide commercial reasons and will not form part of any such scheme or arrangements as are mentioned in that subsection.

140D(3) Subsections (2) to (5) of section 138 shall have effect in relation to subsection (2) above as they have effect in relation to subsection (1) of that section.

History – In s. 140D the words "the transferor" substituted for "company A", and "business" substituted for "trade" by SI 2007/3186, reg. 3(1) and Sch. 1, para. 5, with effect in relation to transfers which take place on or after 1 January 2007, and in relation to cross-border mergers taking place on or after that date, but in the case of mergers relating to the formation of an SE or SCE, in relation to those taking place on or after 18 August 2006 (see SI 2008/1579, reg. 4(1)).
S. 140D inserted by F(No. 2)A 1992, s. 45, and deemed always to have had effect. (Corresponding provisions were inserted by F(No. 2)A 1992, s. 48 as ICTA 1970, s. 269C, 269D, in relation to transfers taking effect on or after 1 January 1992.)

European material – Directive 90/434, art. 10.

140DA Securities issued on division of business

140DA(1) This section applies where–

(a) a transfer of assets to which section 140A(1A) or 140C(1A)(a) applies has taken place,

(b) the transferor and the transferee (or each of the transferees) are each resident in a member State,

(c) they are not all resident in the same State, and

(e) the transfer does not constitute or form part of a scheme of reconstruction within the meaning of section 136.

140DA(2) Where this section applies, the transfer shall be treated for the purposes of section 136 as if it were a scheme of reconstruction.

140DA(3) Where section 136 applies by virtue of subsection (2) above section 136(6) (and section 137) shall not apply.

History – S. 140DA inserted by SI 2007/3186, reg. 3(1) and Sch. 1, para. 6, with effect in relation to transfers which take place on or after 1 January 2007, and in relation to cross-border mergers taking place on or after that date, but in the case of mergers relating to the formation of an SE or SCE, in relation to those taking place on or after 18 August 2006 (see SI 2008/1579, reg. 4(1)).

MERGERS WITHIN EUROPEAN COMMUNITY

European material – Council Regulation (EC) No 2157/2001 of 8 October 2001 on the Statute for a European Company (Societas Europaea).

140E Merger leaving assets within UK tax charge

140E(1) This section applies on a merger which satisfies the conditions specified in subsection (2), where–

(a) an SE is formed by the merger of two or more companies in accordance with Articles 2(1) and 17(2)(a) or (b) of Council Regulation (EC) 2157/2001 on the Statute for a European Company (Societas Europaea),

(b) an SCE is formed by the merger of two or more cooperative societies, at least one of which is a registered society within the meaning of the Co-operative and Community Benefit Societies Act 2014 or a society registered or treated as registered under the Industrial and Provident Societies Act (Northern Ireland) 1969, in accordance with Articles 2(1) and 19 of Council Regulation (EC) 1435/2003 on the Statute for a European Cooperative Society (SCE),

(c) the merger is effected by the transfer by one or more companies of all their assets and liabilities to a single existing company, or

(d) the merger is effected by the transfer by two or more companies of all their assets and liabilities to a single new company (other than an SE or an SCE) in exchange for the issue by the transferee, to each person holding shares in or debentures of a transferor, of shares or debentures.

140E(2) The conditions mentioned in subsection (1) are that–

(a) each of the merging companies is resident in a member State,

(b) the merging companies are not all resident in the same State,

(c) section 139 does not apply to any qualifying transferred assets,

(d) in the case of a merger to which subsection (1)(a), (b) or (c) applies, either–

(i) the transfer of assets and liabilities is made in exchange for the issue by the transferee, to each person holding shares in or debentures of a transferor, of shares or debentures, or

(ii) sub-paragraph (i) is not satisfied by reason only, and to the extent only, that the transferee is prevented from complying with sub-paragraph (i) by section 658 of the Companies Act 2006 (rule against limited company acquiring own shares) or a corresponding provision of the law of another member State preventing the issue of shares or debentures to itself, and

(e) in the case of a merger to which subsection (1)(c) or (d) applies, in the course of the merger each transferor ceases to exist without being in liquidation (within the meaning given by section 247 of the Insolvency Act 1986).

140E(3) Where this section applies, qualifying transferred assets shall be treated for the purposes of corporation tax on chargeable gains as if acquired by the transferee for a consideration resulting in neither gain nor loss for the transferor.

140E(4) For the purposes of subsections (2) and (3) an asset is a qualifying transferred asset if–

(a) it is transferred to the transferee as part of the process of the merger, and

(b) subsections (5) and (6) are satisfied in respect of it.

140E(5) This subsection is satisfied in respect of a transferred asset if–

(a) the transferor is resident in the United Kingdom at the time of the transfer, or

(b) any gain that would have accrued to the transferor, had it disposed of the asset immediately before the time of the transfer, would have been a chargeable gain forming part of the transferor's chargeable profits in accordance with section 10B.

140E(6) This subsection is satisfied in respect of a transferred asset if–

(a) the transferee is resident in the United Kingdom at the time of the transfer, or

(b) any gain that would accrue to the transferee were it to dispose of the asset immediately after the transfer would be a chargeable gain forming part of the transferee's chargeable profits in accordance with section 10B.

140E(7) If subsection (2)(d)(ii) applies in relation to a transfer of assets and liabilities on a merger (in whole or in part), sections 24 and 122 do not apply.

140E(8) This section does not apply in relation to a merger if–

(a) it is not effected for bona fide commercial reasons, or

(b) it forms part of a scheme or arrangements of which the main purpose, or one of the main purposes, is avoiding liability to corporation tax, capital gains tax or income tax,

and section 138 (clearance in advance) shall apply to this subsection as it applies to section 137 (with any necessary modifications).

140E(9) In this section–

(a) **"cooperative society"** means a registered society within the meaning of the Co-operative and Community Benefit Societies Act 2014, a society registered or treated as registered under the Industrial and Provident Societies Act (Northern Ireland) 1969 or a similar society established in accordance with the law of a member State other than the United Kingdom,

(b) **"transferor"** means–

(i) in relation to a merger to which subsection (1)(a) applies, each company merging to form the SE,

(ii) in relation to a merger to which subsection (1)(b) applies, each cooperative society merging to form the SCE, and

(iii) in relation to a merger to which subsection (1)(c) or (d) applies, each company transferring all of its assets and liabilities,

(c) **"transferee"** means–

(i) in relation to a merger to which subsection (1)(a) applies, the SE,

(ii) in relation to a merger to which subsection (1)(b) applies, the SCE, and

(iii) in relation to a merger to which subsection (1)(c) or (d) applies, the company to which assets and liabilities are transferred, and

(d) references in subsections (1)(c) and (2) to (7) to a company include references to a cooperative society.

History – In s. 140E(1)(b), the words "registered society within the meaning of the Co-operative and Community Benefit Societies Act 2014 or a society registered or treated as registered under the Industrial and Provident Societies Act (Northern Ireland) 1969" substituted for the words "society registered under the Industrial and Provident Societies Act 1965" by Co-operative and Community Benefit Societies Act 2014, s. 151 and Sch. 4, para. 47(2), with effect from 1 August 2014.

In s. 140E(9)(a), the words "registered society within the meaning of the Co-operative and Community Benefit Societies Act 2014, a society registered or treated as registered under the Industrial and Provident Societies Act (Northern Ireland) 1969" substituted for

the words "society registered under the Industrial and Provident Societies Act 1965" by Co-operative and Community Benefit Societies Act 2014, s. 151 and Sch. 4, para. 47(3), with effect from 1 August 2014.
S. 140E substituted by SI 2007/3186, reg. 3(2) and Sch. 2, para. 2, in relation to mergers relating to the formation of an SE or SCE which take place on or after 18 August 2006, and in relation to all other mergers which take place on or after 1 January 2007.
S. 140E originally inserted by F(No. 2)A 2005, s. 51(1) with effect in relation to formation of SE (i.e. Societas Europaea) which occurs on or after 1 April 2005.

Cross references – S. 140(6B): postponement of charge on transfer of assets to non-resident company.
S. 154(2A) and (2B): held-over gains on depreciating assets.
CAA 2001, s. 561A: no capital allowance or charge arises where transfer of qualifying asset is part of process of merger to which s. 140E applies (or would apply but for s. 140E(1)(d)).

Transitional – Until s. 658 of the Companies Act 2006 (rule against limited company acquiring own shares) comes into force, the reference to that section in s. 140E(2)(d) has effect as if it were a reference to s. 143 of the Companies Act 1985 (general rule against companies acquiring own shares) (SI 2008/1579, reg. 6(1) and Sch. 4, para. 2(c)).

140F Merger: assets outside UK tax charge

140F(1) This section applies on a merger which satisfies the conditions specified in subsection (2), where–

(a) an SE is formed by the merger of two or more companies in accordance with Articles 2(1) and 17(2)(a) or (b) of Council Regulation (EC) 2157/2001 on the Statute for a European Company (Societas Europaea),

(b) an SCE is formed by the merger of two or more cooperative societies, at least one of which is a registered society within the meaning of the Co-operative and Community Benefit Societies Act 2014 or a society registered or treated as registered under the Industrial and Provident Societies Act (Northern Ireland) 1969, in accordance with Articles 2(1) and 19 of Council Regulation (EC) 1435/2003 on the Statute for a European Cooperative Society (SCE),

(c) the merger is effected by the transfer by one or more companies of all their assets and liabilities to a single existing company, or

(d) the merger is effected by the transfer by two or more companies of all their assets and liabilities to a single new company (other than an SE or an SCE) in exchange for the issue by the transferee, to each person holding shares in or debentures of a transferor, of shares or debentures.

140F(2) The conditions mentioned in subsection (1) are that–

(a) each merging company is resident in a member State,

(b) the merging companies are not all resident in the same State,

(c) in the course of the merger a company resident in the United Kingdom ("company A") transfers to a company resident in another member State ("company B") all assets and liabilities relating to a business which company A carried on in a member State other than the United Kingdom through a permanent establishment,

(d) the aggregate of the chargeable gains accruing to company A on the transfer exceeds the aggregate of any allowable losses so accruing,

(e) in the case of a merger to which subsection (1)(a), (b) or (c) applies, either–

  (i) the transfer of assets and liabilities is made in exchange for the issue by the transferee, to each person holding shares in or debentures of a transferor, of shares or debentures, or

  (ii) sub-paragraph (i) is not satisfied by reason only, and to the extent only, that the transferee is prevented from complying with sub-paragraph (i) by section 658 of the Companies Act 2006 (rule against limited company acquiring own shares) or a corresponding provision of the law of another member State preventing the issue of shares or debentures to itself, and

(f) in the case of a merger to which subsection (1)(c) or (d) applies, in the course of the merger each transferor ceases to exist without being in liquidation (within the meaning given by section 247 of the Insolvency Act 1986 (c.55)).

140F(3) Where this section applies, for the purposes of this Act–

(a) the allowable losses accruing to company A on the transfer shall be set off against the chargeable gains so accruing, and

(b) the transfer shall be treated as giving rise to a single chargeable gain equal to the aggregate of those gains after deducting the aggregate of those losses.

140F(4) Where this section applies, section 122 of TIOPA 2010 (tax treated as chargeable in respect of gains on transfer of non-UK business) shall also apply.

140F(5) Subsections (8) and (9) of section 140E apply for the purposes of this section as they apply for the purposes of that section.

History – In s. 140F(1)(b), the words "registered society within the meaning of the Co-operative and Community Benefit Societies Act 2014 or a society registered or treated as registered under the Industrial and Provident Societies Act (Northern Ireland) 1969" substituted for the words "society registered under the Industrial and Provident Societies Act 1965" by Co-operative and Community Benefit Societies Act 2014, s. 151 and Sch. 4, para. 48, with effect from 1 August 2014.

S. 140F(2)(f) and the word "and" preceding that paragraph inserted by SI 2008/1579, reg. 3(1) and Sch. 1, para 3, with effect in relation to cross-border mergers that relate to the formation of an SE (Societas Europaea) or an SCE (Societas Cooperativa Europaea) which take place on or after 18 August 2006 and in relation to other cross-border mergers and cross-border transfers of business which take place on or after 1 January 2007.
In s. 140F(4), the words "section 122 of TIOPA 2010 (tax treated as chargeable in respect of gains on transfer of non-UK business)" substituted for the words "section 815A of the Taxes Act (transfer of a non-UK trade)" by SI 2013/463, art. 6, with effect from 1 April 2013.
S. 140F substituted by SI 2007/3186, reg. 3(2) and Sch. 2, para. 2, in relation to mergers relating to the formation of an SE or SCE which take place on or after 18 August 2006, and in relation to all other mergers which take place on or after 1 January 2007.
S. 140F originally inserted by F(No. 2)A 2005, s. 51(1) with effect in relation to formation of SE (i.e. Societas Europaea) which occurs on or after 1 April 2005.

Transitional – Until s. 658 of the Companies Act 2006 (rule against limited company acquiring own shares) comes into force, the reference to that section in s. 140F(2)(e) has effect as if it were a reference to s. 143 of the Companies Act 1985 (general rule against companies acquiring own shares) (SI 2008/1579, reg. 6(1) and Sch. 4, para. 2(d)).

140G Treatment of securities issued on merger

140G(1) This section applies on a merger which satisfies the conditions specified in subsection (2), where–

(a) an SE is formed by the merger of two or more companies in accordance with Articles 2(1) and 17(2)(a) or (b) of Council Regulation (EC) 2157/2001 on the Statute for a European Company (Societas Europaea),

(b) an SCE is formed by the merger of two or more cooperative societies, at least one of which is a registered society within the meaning of the Co-operative and Community Benefit Societies Act 2014 or a society registered or treated as registered under the Industrial and Provident Societies Act (Northern Ireland) 1969, in accordance with Articles 2(1) and 19 of Council Regulation (EC) 1435/2003 on the Statute for a European Cooperative Society (SCE),

(c) the merger is effected by the transfer by one or more companies of all their assets and liabilities to a single existing company in exchange for the issue by the transferee, to each person holding shares in or debentures of a transferor, of shares or debentures, or

(d) the merger is effected by the transfer by two or more companies of all their assets and liabilities to a single new company (other than an SE or an SCE) in exchange for the issue by the transferee, to each person holding shares in or debentures of a transferor, of shares or debentures.

140G(2) The conditions mentioned in subsection (1) are that–

(a) each of the merging companies is resident in a member State,

(b) the merging companies are not all resident in the same State, and

(c) the merger does not constitute or form part of a scheme of reconstruction within the meaning of section 136.

140G(3) Where this section applies, the merger shall be treated for the purposes of section 136 as if it were a scheme of reconstruction.

140G(4) Where section 136 applies by virtue of subsection (3) above section 136(6) (and section 137) shall not apply.

140G(5) Subsections (8) and (9) of section 140E apply for the purposes of this section as they apply for the purposes of that section.

History – In s. 140G(1)(b), the words "registered society within the meaning of the Co-operative and Community Benefit Societies Act 2014 or a society registered or treated as registered under the Industrial and Provident Societies Act (Northern Ireland) 1969" substituted for the words "society registered under the Industrial and Provident Societies Act 1965" by Co-operative and Community Benefit Societies Act 2014, s. 151 and Sch. 4, para. 49, with effect from 1 August 2014.
S. 140G substituted by SI 2007/3186, reg. 3(2) and Sch. 2, para. 2, in relation to mergers relating to the formation of an SE or SCE which take place on or after 18 August 2006, and in relation to all other mergers which take place on or after 1 January 2007.
S. 140G originally inserted by F(No. 2)A 2005, s. 51(1) with effect in relation to formation of SE (i.e. Societas Europaea) which occurs on or after 1 April 2005.

140GA Disapplication of sections 24 and 122 where subsidiary merges with its parent

140GA Sections 24 and 122 do not apply if–

(a) a merger is effected by the transfer by a company ("the transferor company") of all of its assets and liabilities to a single company that holds the whole of the ordinary share capital in the transferor company,

(b) each merging company is resident in a member State,

(c) the merging companies are not all resident in the same State,

(d) section 139 does not apply in relation to the transfer, and

(e) in the course of the merger the transferor company ceases to exist without being in liquidation (within the meaning given by section 247 of the Insolvency Act 1986 (c. 55).

History – S. 140GA inserted by SI 2008/1579, reg. 3(1) and Sch. 1, para. 4, with effect in relation to cross-border mergers that relate to the formation of an SE (Societas Europaea) or an SCE (Societas Cooperativa Europaea) which take place on or after 18 August 2006 and in relation to other cross-border mergers and cross-border transfers of business which take place on or after 1 January 2007.

TRANSPARENT ENTITIES: DISAPPLICATION OF RELIEFS RELATED TO MERGERS DIRECTIVE

140H Share exchanges

140H(1) This section applies if–

(a) a company ("company B") issues shares or debentures to a person in exchange for shares in or debentures of another company ("company A"),

(b) the exchange falls within one of the cases specified in section 135(2), and

(c) either company B or company A or both is a transparent entity.

140H(2) Where this section applies–

(a) **"company"** in section 135 shall be treated as meaning an entity listed in Part A of Annex I to the Mergers Directive, and

(b) section 135(3) does not apply.

140H(3) If, as a result of an exchange in relation to which this section applies, a gain accruing to a person holding shares in or debentures of company A on the exchange would, but for the Mergers Directive, have been chargeable to tax under the law of a member State other than the United Kingdom, Part 2 of TIOPA 2010 (double taxation relief), including any double taxation relief arrangements, shall apply as if that tax, calculated in accordance with subsection (4), had been chargeable.

140H(4) Tax is calculated in accordance with this subsection if–

(a) so far as permitted under the law of the relevant member State, losses arising on the exchange are set against gains arising on the exchange, and

(b) any relief available to company A under that law has been claimed.

History – In s. 140H(2)(a), the words "Part A of Annex I" substituted for the words "the Annex" by SI 2011/1431, reg. 2(2), with effect from 1 July 2011.
In s. 140H(3), the words "Part 2 of TIOPA 2010" substituted for "Part 18 of the Taxes Act" by TIOPA 2010, s. 374 and Sch. 8, para. 44(a), with effect for corporation tax purposes for accounting periods ending on or after 1 April 2010, for income tax and capital gains tax purposes for the tax year 2010–11 and subsequent tax years, and for petroleum revenue tax purposes for chargeable periods beginning on or after 1 July 2010, subject to transitional provisions in TIOPA 2010, Sch. 9, para. 27.
In s. 140H(3), the words "double taxation relief arrangements" substituted for "arrangements having effect by virtue of section 788 of that Act (bilateral relief)" by TIOPA 2010, s. 374 and Sch. 8, para. 44(b), with effect for corporation tax purposes for accounting periods ending on or after 1 April 2010, for income tax and capital gains tax purposes for the tax year 2010–11 and subsequent tax years, and for petroleum revenue tax purposes for chargeable periods beginning on or after 1 July 2010, subject to transitional provisions in TIOPA 2010, Sch. 9, para. 27.
S. 140H inserted by SI 2007/3186, reg. 3(3) and Sch. 3, para. 1, with effect in relation to mergers relating to the formation of an SE or SCE which take place on or after 18 August 2006, and in relation to all other mergers and cross-border transfers of business (see SI 2008/1579, reg. 4(2)) which take place on or after 1 January 2007.

140I Division of business or transfer of assets

140I(1) This section applies in relation to a transfer of a business, or part of a business, where–

(a) the transfer is of a kind mentioned in section 140A(1) or (1A) (or which would be of such a kind if the business, or the part of the business, transferred were carried on by the transferor in the United Kingdom and the condition mentioned in section 140A(1)(e) were satisfied in relation to the transferee, or each of the transferees), and

(b) either the transferor or the transferee, or one of the transferees, is a transparent entity.

140I(2) Where this section applies–

(a) if the transferor is a transparent entity, sections 140A and 140DA do not apply in relation to the transfer;

(b) if a transferee is a transparent entity, section 140DA does not apply in relation to the transfer to it.

140I(3) If, as a result of a transfer in relation to which this section applies, a transfer gain would, but for the Mergers Directive, have been chargeable to tax under the law of a member State other than the United Kingdom, Part 2 of TIOPA 2010 (double taxation relief), including any double taxation relief arrangements, shall apply as if that tax, calculated in accordance with subsection (5), had been chargeable.

140I(4) In subsection (3) **"transfer gain"** means a gain accruing to a transparent entity (or which would be treated as accruing to that entity were it not transparent) by reason of the transfer of assets by the transparent entity to the transferee.

140I(5) Tax is calculated in accordance with this subsection if–

(a) so far as permitted under the law of the relevant member State, losses arising on the transfer are set against gains arising on the transfer, and

(b) any relief available under that law has been claimed.

History – In s. 140I(1)(a), the words "mentioned in section 140A(1) or (1A) (or which would be of such a kind" substituted for "to which section 140A(1) or 140A(1A) applies (or to which either of those provisions would apply" by SI 2008/1579, reg. 3(1) and Sch. 1, para. 5, with effect in relation to cross-border mergers that relate to the formation of an SE (Societas Europaea) or an SCE (Societas Cooperativa Europaea) which take place on or after 18 August 2006 and in relation to other cross-border mergers and cross-border transfers of business which take place on or after 1 January 2007.
In s. 140I(3), the words "Part 2 of TIOPA 2010" substituted for "Part 18 of the Taxes Act" by TIOPA 2010, s. 374 and Sch. 8, para. 44(a), with effect for corporation tax purposes for accounting periods ending on or after 1 April 2010, for income tax and capital gains tax purposes for the tax year 2010–11 and subsequent tax years, and for petroleum revenue tax purposes for chargeable periods beginning on or after 1 July 2010, subject to transitional provisions in TIOPA 2010, Sch. 9, para. 27.
In s. 140I(3), the words "double taxation relief arrangements" substituted for "arrangements having effect by virtue of section 788 of that Act (bilateral relief)" by TIOPA 2010, s. 374 and Sch. 8, para. 44(b), with effect for corporation tax purposes for accounting periods ending on or after 1 April 2010, for income tax and capital gains tax purposes for the tax year 2010–11 and subsequent tax years, and for petroleum revenue tax purposes for chargeable periods beginning on or after 1 July 2010, subject to transitional provisions in TIOPA 2010, Sch. 9, para. 27.
S. 140I inserted by SI 2007/3186, reg. 3(3) and Sch. 3, para. 1, with effect in relation to mergers relating to the formation of an SE or SCE which take place on or after 18 August 2006, and in relation to all other mergers and cross-border transfers of business (see SI 2008/1579, reg. 4(2)) which take place on or after 1 January 2007.

140J Mergers

140J(1) This section applies in relation to a merger if–

(a) the merger is of a kind mentioned in section 140E(1),

(b) the conditions in section 140E(2) are satisfied in relation to the merger, and

(c) one or more of the merging companies is a transparent entity.

140J(2) Where this section applies–

(a) if the assets and liabilities of a transparent entity are transferred to another company by reason of the merger, sections 140E and 140G shall not apply;

(b) if the assets and liabilities of one or more other companies are transferred to a transparent entity by reason of the merger section 140G shall not apply.

140J(3) If, as a result of a merger in relation to which this section applies, a merger gain would, but for the Mergers Directive, have been chargeable to tax under the law of a member State other than the United Kingdom, Part 2 of TIOPA 2010 (double taxation relief), including any double taxation relief arrangements shall apply as if that tax, calculated in accordance with subsection (5), had been chargeable.

140J(4) In subsection (3) **"merger gain"** means a gain accruing to a transparent entity (or which would be treated as accruing to that entity were it not transparent) by reason of the transfer of assets by the transparent entity to another company on the merger.

140J(5) Tax is calculated in accordance with this subsection if–

(a) so far as permitted under the law of the relevant member State, losses arising on the merger are set against gains arising on the merger, and

(b) any relief available under that law has been claimed.

History – In s. 140J(1)(a), the words "mentioned in section 140E(1)" substituted for "to which section 140E(1) applies" by SI 2008/1579, reg. 3(1) and Sch. 1, para. 6, with effect in relation to cross-border mergers that relate to the formation of an SE (Societas Europaea) or an SCE (Societas Cooperativa Europaea) which take place on or after 18 August 2006 and in relation to other cross-border mergers and cross-border transfers of business which take place on or after 1 January 2007.
In s. 140J(3), the words "Part 2 of TIOPA 2010" substituted for "Part 18 of the Taxes Act" by TIOPA 2010, s. 374 and Sch. 8, para. 44(a), with effect for corporation tax purposes for accounting periods ending on or after 1 April 2010, for income tax and capital gains tax purposes for the tax year 2010–11 and subsequent tax years, and for petroleum revenue tax purposes for chargeable periods beginning on or after 1 July 2010, subject to transitional provisions in TIOPA 2010, Sch. 9, para. 27.
In s. 140J(3), the words "double taxation relief arrangements" substituted for "arrangements having effect by virtue of section 788 of that Act (bilateral relief)" by TIOPA 2010, s. 374 and Sch. 8, para. 44(b), with effect for corporation tax purposes for accounting periods ending on or after 1 April 2010, for income tax and capital gains tax purposes for the tax year 2010–11 and subsequent tax years, and for petroleum revenue tax purposes for chargeable periods beginning on or after 1 July 2010, subject to transitional provisions in TIOPA 2010, Sch. 9, para. 27.
S. 140J inserted by SI 2007/3186, reg. 3(3) and Sch. 3, para. 1, with effect in relation to mergers relating to the formation of an SE or SCE which take place on or after 18 August 2006, and in relation to all other mergers and cross-border transfers of business (see SI 2008/1579, reg. 4(2)) which take place on or after 1 January 2007.

140K Transparent entities: taxation after merger, &c

140K(1) This section applies if–

(a) a transparent entity ("company A") is a transferee for the purposes of section 140A(1A) or 140E,

(b) a person ("X") with an interest in company A was or is also a shareholder or debenture holder of a company ("company B"),

(c) X became entitled to an interest, or an increased interest, in company A in exchange for a disposal of shares in, or debentures of, company B on a merger to which section 140E applied or on a transfer to which section 140A(1A) applied,

(d) a chargeable gain accrued to X on the disposal of shares in or debentures of company B,

(e) in calculating the gain on the shares or debentures account was taken of the value of an asset of company B, and

(f) X makes a disposal of his interest in the asset.

140K(2) In computing the gain accruing to X on a disposal to which subsection (1)(f) applies, the sum allowable as a deduction in accordance with section 38(1)(a) in relation to the interest, or the proportion of the interest, which X acquired on the merger or transfer shall be the value taken into account in computing the gain on the disposal of his shares in, or debentures of, company B.

140K(3) In this section a reference to an interest in company A includes–

(a) an interest in the assets of company A,

(b) shares in company A, and

(c) debentures of company A.

History – S. 140K inserted by SI 2007/3186, reg. 3(3) and Sch. 3, para. 1, with effect in relation to mergers relating to the formation of an SE or SCE which take place on or after 18 August 2006, and in relation to all other mergers and cross-border transfers of business (see SI 2008/1579, reg. 4(2)) which take place on or after 1 January 2007.

140L Interpretation

140L(1) In sections 140A to 140K and in this section, unless the contrary intention appears–

(a) **"the Mergers Directive"** means Council Directive 2009/133/EC,

(b) **"company"** means an entity listed as a company in Part A of Annex I to the Mergers Directive, and

(c) **"transparent entity"** means an entity which is resident in a member State other than the United Kingdom and is listed as a company in Part A of Annex I to the Mergers Directive, but–

(i) does not have an ordinary share capital (within the meaning given by section 1119 of CTA 2010), and

(ii) if it were resident in the United Kingdom, would not be capable of being a company within the meaning given by the Companies Act 2006.

140L(2) For the purposes of those sections and subsection (1) above, a company is resident in a member State if–

(a) it is within a charge to tax under the law of the State as being resident for that purpose, and

(b) it is not regarded, for the purpose of any double taxation relief arrangements to which the State is a party, as resident in a territory not within a member State.

History – In s. 140L(1)(a), "2009/133/EC," substituted for the words "90/434/EEC of 23rd July 1990 on mergers, transfers &c.," by SI 2011/1431, reg. 2(3)(a), with effect from 1 July 2011.
In s. 140L(1)(a) and (c), the words "Part A of Annex I" substituted for the words "the Annex" by SI 2011/1431, reg. 2(3)(b), with effect from 1 July 2011.
In s. 140L(1)(c)(i), the words "section 1119 of CTA 2010" substituted for "section 832 of the Taxes Act" by CTA 2010, s. 1177 and Sch. 1, para. 235, with effect for corporation tax purposes for accounting periods ending on or after 1 April 2010, and for income tax and capital gains tax purposes for the tax year 2010–11 and subsequent tax years.
In s. 140L(1), the words "and in this section" inserted after "140K" by SI 2008/1579, reg. 3(1) and Sch. 1, para. 7, with effect in relation to cross-border mergers that relate to the formation of an SE (Societas Europaea) or an SCE (Societas Cooperativa Europaea) which take place on or after 18 August 2006 and in relation to other cross-border mergers and cross-border transfers of business which take place on or after 1 January 2007.
S. 140L inserted by SI 2007/3186, reg. 3(3) and Sch. 3, para. 1, with effect in relation to mergers relating to the formation of an SE or SCE which take place on or after 18 August 2006, and in relation to all other mergers and cross-border transfers of business (see SI 2008/1579, reg. 4(2)) which take place on or after 1 January 2007.

Chapter III – Miscellaneous Provisions Relating to Commodities, Futures, Options and Other Securities

141 Stock dividends: consideration for new holding

141 [S. 141 superseded by new s. 142 as respects any share capital issued on or after 6 April 1998 (FA 1998, s. 126(1) and (2)).]

History – In relation to share capital issued before 6 April 1998, s. 141 provides as follows:
"**141(1)** *In applying section 128(1) in relation to the issue of any share capital to which section 249 of the Taxes Act (stock dividends) applies as involving a reorganisation of the company's share capital, there shall be allowed, as consideration given for so much of the new holding as was issued as mentioned in subsection (4), (5) or (6) of section 249 (read in each case with subsection (3) of that section) an amount equal to what is, for that much of the new holding, the appropriate amount in cash within the meaning of section 251(2) of the Taxes Act.*
141(2) *This section shall have effect notwithstanding section 128(2).*"

142 Capital gains on stock dividends

142(1) This section applies where any share capital to which section 410(2), (3) or (4) of ITTOIA 2005 applies in respect of shares in the company held by any person.

142(2) The case shall not constitute a reorganisation of the company's share capital for the purposes of sections 126 to 128.

142(3) The person who acquires the share capital by means of its issue shall (notwithstanding section 17(1)) be treated for the purposes of section 38(1)(a) as having acquired that asset for a consideration equal to the cash equivalent of the share capital in accordance with section 412 of ITTOIA 2005.

History – In s. 142(1), words "section 410(2), (3) or (4) of ITTOIA 2005 applies" substituted for "section 249 of the Taxes Act applies is issued as mentioned in subsection (4), (5) or (6) of that section" by ITTOIA 2005, s. 882 and Sch. 1, para. 434(2) which, in accordance with ITTOIA 2005, s. 883, have effect, for income tax purposes, for tax year 2005–06 and subsequent tax years, and, for corporation tax purposes, for accounting periods ending after 5 April 2005.

In s. 142(3), words "the cash equivalent of the share capital in accordance with section 412 of ITTOIA 2005" substituted for "the appropriate amount in cash (within the meaning of section 251(2) to (4) of the Taxes Act)" by ITTOIA 2005, s. 882 and Sch. 1, para. 434(3) which, in accordance with ITTOIA 2005, s. 883, have effect, for income tax purposes, for tax year 2005–06 and subsequent tax years, and, for corporation tax purposes, for accounting periods ending after 5 April 2005.

S. 142 substituted for former s. 141 and 142 by FA 1998, s. 126(1) as respects share capital issued on or after 6 April 1998. In relation to share capital issued before that date, s. 142 provides as follows:

"**142(1)** This section applies where a company issues any share capital to which section 249 of the Taxes Act applies in respect of shares in the company held by a person as trustee, and another person is at the time of the issue absolutely entitled thereto as against the trustee or would be so entitled but for being an infant or other person under disability (or 2 or more other persons are or would be jointly so entitled thereto).

142(2) Notwithstanding paragraph (a) of section 126(2) the case shall not constitute a reorganisation of the company's share capital for the purposes of sections 126 to 128.

142(3) Notwithstanding section 171(1), the person who is or would be so entitled to the share capital (or each of the persons who are or would be jointly so entitled thereto) shall be treated for the purposes of section 38(1)(a) as having acquired that share capital, or his interest in it, for a consideration equal to the appropriate amount in cash within the meaning of section 251(2) to (4) of the Taxes Act.".

Cross references – S. 17(1): acquisition or disposal generally treated as made at market value on a distribution in respect of shares etc.

S. 38(1)(a): allowable acquisition expenditure, including incidental costs.

S. 126–128: equation of original and new holdings on a reorganisation with special treatment of other consideration given or received; reorganisation generally includes a case where a person is allotted shares etc. in respect of or in proportion to existing holdings (s. 126(2)).

ICTA 1988, s. 249: certain stock dividends treated as income of the recipient for some purposes.

Statements of practice – SP 4/94: application of s. 142 to enhanced stock dividends received by transfers of interest in possession trusts.

Notes – S. 288: interpretation, including "the Taxes Act" as ICTA 1988 and reference to other sections being those of this Act.

142A REITs: chargeable gains on stock dividends

142A(1) This section applies if share capital issued in lieu of a cash dividend by–

(a) a company UK REIT, or

(b) the principal company of a group UK REIT,

is attributed as mentioned in section 550(2)(a), (c) or (d) of CTA 2010 (attribution of distributions).

142A(2) The case shall not constitute a reorganisation of the company's share capital for the purposes of sections 126 to 128.

142A(3) The person who acquires the share capital by means of its issue shall (notwithstanding section 17(1)) be treated for the purposes of section 38(1)(a) as having acquired that asset for a consideration equal to the cash equivalent of the share capital.

142A(4) Section 414A(2) to (4) of ITTOIA 2005 (meaning of "share capital issued in lieu of a cash dividend") applies for the purposes of this section as it applies for the purposes of Chapter 5 of Part 4 of that Act.

142A(5) Section 412(1), (2), (4) and (5) of that Act (meaning of "cash equivalent of share capital") applies for the purposes of this section as it applies in relation to share capital issued as mentioned in section 410(1)(a) of that Act.

142A(6) In this section **"company UK REIT"** and **"principal company of a group UK REIT"** are to be read in accordance with Part 12 of CTA 2010 (Real Estate Investment Trusts).

History – S. 142A inserted by F(No. 3)A 2010, s. 10 and Sch. 4, para. 1, with effect in relation to distributions made on or after 16 December 2010.

143 Commodity and financial futures and qualifying options

143(1) If, apart from section 981 of CTA 2009 and section 779 of ITTOIA 2005, gains arising to any person in the course of dealing in commodity or financial futures or in qualifying options would constitute, for the purposes of the Tax Acts, profits or gains chargeable to tax–

(a) under Chapter 8 of Part 10 of CTA 2009, or

(b) under Chapter 8 of Part 5 of ITTOIA 2005,

then his outstanding obligations under any futures contract entered into in the course of that dealing and any qualifying option granted or acquired in the course of that dealing shall be regarded as assets to the disposal of which this Act applies.

143(2) In subsection (1) above–

(a) **"commodity or financial futures"** means commodity futures or financial futures which are for the time being dealt in on a recognised futures exchange; and

(b) **"qualifying option"** means a traded option or financial option as defined in section 144(8).

143(3) Notwithstanding the provisions of subsection (2)(a) above, where, otherwise than in the course of dealing on a recognised futures exchange–

(a) an authorised person enters into a commodity or financial futures contract with another person, or

(b) the outstanding obligations under a commodity or financial futures contract to which an authorised person is a party are brought to an end by a further contract between the parties to the futures contract,

then, except in so far as any gain or loss arising to any person from that transaction arises in the course of a trade, that gain or loss shall be regarded for the purposes of subsection (1) above as arising to him in the course of dealing in commodity or financial futures.

143(4) [Repealed by FA 1994, s. 95(1) and s. 258 and Sch. 26, Pt. V(9).]

143(5) For the purposes of this Act, where, in the course of dealing in commodity or financial futures, a person who has entered into a futures contract closes out that contract by entering into another futures contract with obligations which are reciprocal to those of the first-mentioned contract, that transaction shall constitute the disposal of an asset (namely, his outstanding obligations under the first-mentioned contract) and, accordingly–

(a) any money or money's worth received by him on that transaction shall constitute consideration for the disposal; and

(b) any money or money's worth paid or given by him on that transaction shall be treated as incidental costs to him of making the disposal.

143(6) In any case where, in the course of dealing in commodity or financial futures, a person has entered into a futures contract and–

(a) he has not closed out the contract (as mentioned in subsection (5) above), and

(b) he becomes entitled to receive or liable to make a payment, whether under the contract or otherwise, in full or partial settlement of any obligations under the contract,

then, for the purposes of this Act, he shall be treated as having disposed of an asset (namely, that entitlement or liability) and the payment received or made by him shall be treated as consideration for the disposal or, as the case may be, as incidental costs to him of making the disposal.

143(7) Section 46 shall not apply to obligations under–

(a) a commodity or financial futures contract which is entered into by a person in the course of dealing in such futures on a recognised futures exchange; or

(b) a commodity or financial futures contract to which an authorised person is a party.

143(8) In this section **"authorised person"** means a person who–

(a) falls within section 31(1)(a), (b) or (c) of the Financial Services and Markets Act 2000, and

(b) has permission under that Act to carry on one or more of the activities specified in Article 14 and, in so far as it applies to that Article, Article 64 of the Financial Services and Markets Act 2000 (Regulated Activities) Order 2001.

History – In s. 143(1) the words "section 981 of CTA 2009" substituted for the words "section 128 of the Taxes Act" and in para. (a) the words "Chapter 8 of Part 10 of CTA 2009" substituted for the words "Schedule D otherwise than as the profits of a trade" by CTA 2009, s. 1322 and Sch. 1, para. 369, with effect for corporation tax purposes for accounting periods ending on or after 1 April 2009, and for income tax and capital gains tax purposes for the tax year 2009–10 and subsequent tax years.

In s. 143(1) the words "and section 779 of ITTOIA 2005" inserted and the words "chargeable to tax–" and para. (a) and (b) substituted for the words "chargeable to tax under Schedule D otherwise than as the profits of a trade, then" by SI 2006/959, art. 3(2), with effect for income tax purposes for the tax year 2006–07 and subsequent tax years, and for corporation tax purposes, for accounting periods ending after 5 April 2006. The changes also had deemed effect for income tax purposes, for the tax year 2005–06, and for corporation tax purposes, for accounting periods ending after 5 April 2005 and before 6 April 2006.

In s. 143(3)(a) and (b), the words "or listed institution" which appeared after the words "an authorised person" omitted by SI 2001/3629, art. 64(2) operative from 1 December 2001.

S. 143(4) repealed by FA 1994, s. 95(1) and s. 258 and Sch. 26, Pt. V(9) in relation to contracts entered into on or after 30 November 1993.

S. 143(6) substituted by FA 1994, s. 95(1) in relation to contracts entered into on or after 30 November 1993.

In s. 143(7)(b), the words "or listed institution" which appeared after the words "an authorised person" omitted by SI 2001/3629, art. 64(2) operative from 1 December 2001.

S. 143(7) inserted by FA 1994, s. 95(1) in relation to contracts entered into on or after 30 November 1993.

S. 143(8) substituted by SI 2001/3629, art. 64(3) operative from 1 December 2001.

S. 143(8) inserted by FA 1994, s. 95(1) in relation to contracts entered into on or after 30 November 1993.

Derivations – S. 143(1), (2): FA 1985, s. 72(1), (2), as amended by F(No. 2)A 1987, s. 81(1), (2).

S. 143(3), (4) (as originally enacted): FA 1985, s. 72(2A), (2B), as inserted by F(No. 2)A 1987, s. 81(3).
S. 143(5), (6) (as originally enacted): FA 1985, s. 72(3), (4).

Cross references – S. 21–34: general meaning of "disposal" and "asset".
S. 38(1)(c): deduction for incidental costs of disposal.
S. 115(3): without prejudice to s. 143(5), person closing out option etc. to acquire or dispose of gilt-edged stock or qualifying corporate bonds deemed to dispose of his outstanding obligations under that option.
ICTA 1988, s. 128: non-trading gains from dealing in commodities, financial futures or qualifying options exempt from tax under Sch. D.
S. 288: interpretation, including meaning of "recognised futures exchange", "the Taxes Act" as ICTA 1988 and reference to other sections being those of this Act.
ICTA 1988, s. 399(1), (5): prevention of loss relief against Sch. D income in respect of losses from dealing in commodity futures, financial futures or qualifying options.
ICTA 1988, Sch. 5AA: guaranteed transactions in futures and options.
FA 2002, Sch. 26, para. 37 and 45, and Sch. 28, para. 4(9): taxation of profits from derivative contracts: the Schedules apply to obligations under futures contracts which s. 143 treats as assets the disposal of which constitutes a chargeable gain.
SI 1994/3226, reg. 16: election, to be made in the 92 days following commencement day or by 21 September 1995 if later, to set against exchange gains pre-commencement day (for FA 1993, Pt. II, Ch. II and FA 1994, Pt. IV, Ch. II) losses accrued under s. 143 on certain instruments.

Statements of practice – SP 3/02: tax treatment of transactions in financial futures and options.

HMRC interpretations – IRInt. 253: swaps held by non-corporates.

Hansard – Statement by Financial Secretary to the Treasury, 28 November 1985 (not reproduced): a taxpayer would not be regarded as trading in respect of transactions which were relatively infrequent or intended as a hedge against specific investments, and an individual is unlikely to be regarded as trading as a result of purely speculative transactions in financial futures.

144 Options and forfeited deposits

144(1) Without prejudice to section 21, the grant of an option, and in particular–

(a) the grant of an option in a case where the grantor binds himself to sell what he does not own, and because the option is abandoned, never has occasion to own, and

(b) the grant of an option in a case where the grantor binds himself to buy what, because the option is abandoned, he does not acquire,

is the disposal of an asset (namely of the option), but subject to the following provisions of this section as to treating the grant of an option as part of a larger transaction.

144(2) If an option is exercised, the grant of the option and the transaction entered into by the grantor in fulfilment of his obligations under the option shall be treated as a single transaction and accordingly–

(a) if the option binds the grantor to sell, the consideration for the option is part of the consideration for the sale, and

(b) if the option binds the grantor to buy, the consideration for the option shall be deducted from the cost of acquisition incurred by the grantor in buying in pursuance of his obligations under the option.

144(3) The exercise of an option by the person for the time being entitled to exercise it shall not constitute the disposal of an asset by that person, but, if an option is exercised then the acquisition of the option (whether directly from the grantor or not) and the transaction entered into by the person exercising the option in exercise of his rights under the option shall be treated as a single transaction and accordingly–

(a) if the option binds the grantor to sell, the cost of acquiring the option shall be part of the cost of acquiring what is sold, and

(b) if the option binds the grantor to buy, the cost of the option shall be treated as a cost incidental to the disposal of what is bought by the grantor of the option.

144(4) The abandonment of–

(a) a quoted option to subscribe for shares in a company, or

(b) a traded option or financial option, or

(c) an option to acquire assets exercisable by a person intending to use them, if acquired, for the purpose of a trade carried on by him,

shall constitute the disposal of an asset (namely of the option); but the abandonment of any other option by the person for the time being entitled to exercise it shall not constitute the disposal of an asset by that person.

144(5) This section shall apply in relation to an option binding the grantor both to sell and to buy as if it were 2 separate options with half the consideration attributed to each.

144(6) In this section references to an option include references to an option binding the grantor to grant a lease for a premium, or enter into any other transaction which is not a sale, and references to buying and selling in pursuance of an option shall be construed accordingly.

144(7) This section shall apply in relation to a forfeited deposit of purchase money or other consideration money for a prospective purchase or other transaction which is abandoned as it applies in relation to the consideration for an option which binds the grantor to sell and which is not exercised.

144(8) In subsection (4) above and sections 146 and 147–

(a) **"quoted option"** means an option which, at the time of the abandonment or other disposal, is listed on a recognised stock exchange;

(b) **"traded option"** means an option which, at the time of the abandonment or other disposal, is listed on a recognised stock exchange or a recognised futures exchange; and

(c) **"financial option"** means an option which is not a traded option, as defined in paragraph (b) above, but which, subject to subsection (9) below–

(i) relates to currency, shares, securities or an interest rate and is granted (otherwise than as agent) by a member of a recognised stock exchange, by an authorised person within the meaning given by section 143(8); or

(ii) relates to shares or securities which are dealt in on a recognised stock exchange and is granted by a member of such an exchange, acting as agent; or

(iii) relates to currency, shares, securities or an interest rate and is granted to such an authorised person as is referred to in sub-paragraph (i) above and concurrently and in association with an option falling within that sub-paragraph which is granted by that authorised person to the grantor of the first-mentioned option; or

(iv) relates to shares or securities which are dealt in on a recognised stock exchange and is granted to a member of such an exchange, including such a member acting as agent.

144(9) If the Treasury by order so provide, an option of a description specified in the order shall be taken to be within the definition of **"financial option"** in subsection (8)(c) above.

History – In s. 144(8)(a) the words "listed on" substituted for the words "quoted on" by FA 2007, s. 109 and Sch. 26, para. 8(3), with effect from 19 July 2007 (Royal Assent).

In s. 144(8)(c)(i), the words "authorised person within the meaning given by section 143(8)" substituted for the words "authorised person within the meaning of the Financial Services Act 1986 or by a listed institution within the meaning of section 43 of that Act" by SI 2001/3629, art. 65(a) operative from 1 December 2001.

In s. 144(8)(c)(iii), the words "or institutution" which had appeared after the words "authorised person" in two places omitted by SI 2001/3629, art. 65(b) operative from 1 December 2001.

Derivations – S. 144(1)–(4): CGTA 1979, s. 137(1)–(4), as amended (subs. (4)) by F(No. 2)A 1987, s. 81(4).
S. 144(5)–(9): CGTA 1979, s. 137(6)–(10), subs.(9) as substituted by F(No. 2)A 1987, s. 81(5).
S. 144(8)(b): "listed" substituted for "quoted" by FA 1996, s. 199 and Sch. 38, para. 10 in relation to disposals on or after 1 April 1996.

Cross references – S. 17: disposals and acquisitions treated as made at market value.
S. 21: general meaning of "disposal" and "asset".
S. 24(1): priority over deemed disposal on the occasion of the entire loss, destruction, dissipation or extinction of an asset.
S. 144A: cash-settled options.
S. 217(1): on incorporation of a building society, priority rights to shares and rights to shares at an undervalue are regarded as options within the meaning of s. 144.
ICTA 1988, s. 731(4B): application of special provisions for certain short term buying and selling of securities determined by reference to traded or financial options on certain assumptions.
ICTA 1988, Sch. 5AA: guaranteed returns on transactions in futures and options.

HMRC interpretations – IRInt. 11: roll-over relief on replacement of business assets available in respect of gains on grant of an option over land by reference to the underlying land.
IRInt. 254: claims to increase capital losses following judgment in case of *Mansworth (HMIT) v Jelley* [2003] BTC 3.

Other material – IR/Customs press release, 29 July 1998: continuity of treatment for capital gains purposes for assets and derivatives on introduction of single currency or redenomination of derivative or the underlying asset in euro.

Notes – S. 15: except as otherwise provided, every "gain" is a chargeable gain.
S. 38: deductions for allowable acquisition expenditure including incidental costs, enhancement expenditure and incidental costs of disposal.
S. 287: power of Board exercisable by statutory instrument, subject to the negative resolution procedure of the House of Commons.
S. 288: interpretation, including meaning of "recognised stock exchange", "recognised futures exchange", "shares" as embracing stock and reference to sections being those of this Act.

144ZA Application of market value rule in case of exercise of option

144ZA(1) Subject to section 144ZB, this section applies where–

(a) an option is exercised, so that by virtue of section 144(2) or (3) the grant or acquisition of the option and the transaction resulting from its exercise are treated as a single transaction, and

(b) section 17(1) (**"the market value rule"**) applies, or would apply but for this section, in relation to–

(i) the grant of the option,

(ii) the acquisition of the option (whether directly from the grantor or not) by the person exercising it, or

(iii) the transaction resulting from its exercise.

144ZA(2) If the option binds the grantor to sell–

(a) the market value rule does not apply for determining the consideration for the sale, except, where the rule applies for determining the consideration for the option, to that extent (in accordance with section 144(2)(a));

(b) the market value rule does not apply for determining the cost to the person exercising the option of acquiring what is sold, except, where the rule applies for determining the cost of acquiring the option, to that extent (in accordance with section 144(3)(a)).

144ZA(3) If the option binds the grantor to buy–

(a) the market value rule does not apply for determining the cost of acquisition incurred by the grantor, but without prejudice to its application (in accordance with section 144(2)(b)) where the rule applies for determining the consideration for the option;

(b) the market value rule does not apply for determining the consideration for the disposal of what is bought, but without prejudice to its application (in accordance with section 144(3)(b)) where the rule applies for determining the cost of the option.

144ZA(4) To the extent that, by virtue of this section, the market value rule does not apply for determining an amount or value, the amount or value to be taken into account is (subject to section 119A) the exercise price.

144ZA(4A) In subsection (4) above **"exercise price"**, in relation to an option, means the amount or value of the consideration which, under the terms of the option, is–

(a) receivable (if the option binds the grantor to buy), or

(b) payable (if the option binds the grantor to sell),

as a result of the exercise of the option (and does not include the amount or value of any consideration for the acquisition of the option (whether directly from the grantor or not)).

144ZA(5) Subsections (5) and (6) of section 144 shall apply for the purposes of this section and sections 144ZB to 144ZD as they apply for the purposes of that section.

History – In s. 144ZA(1), words "Subject to section 144ZB" inserted by F(No. 2)A 2005, s. 35 and Sch. 5, para. 1(2) with effect, in accordance with F(No. 2)A 2005, Sch. 5, para. 6(1), in relation to cases where option concerned, whenever acquired, is exercised on or after 2 December 2004.

In s. 144ZA(4), words "(subject to section 119A) the exercise price" substituted for words "(subject to section 120) the actual amount or value" by F(No. 2)A 2005, s. 35 and Sch. 5, para. 1(3) with effect, in accordance with F(No. 2)A 2005, Sch. 5, para. 6(1), in relation to cases where option concerned, whenever acquired, is exercised on or after 2 December 2004.

S. 144ZA(4A) inserted by F(No. 2)A 2005, s. 35 and Sch. 5, para. 1(4) with effect, in accordance with F(No. 2)A 2005, Sch. 5, para. 6(1), in relation to cases where option concerned, whenever acquired, is exercised on or after 2 December 2004.

S. 144ZA(5) substituted by F(No. 2)A 2005, s. 35 and Sch. 5, para. 1(5) with effect, in accordance with F(No. 2)A 2005, Sch. 5, para. 6(1), in relation to cases where option concerned, whenever acquired, is exercised on or after 2 December 2004.

S. 144ZA inserted by FA 2003, 158(1) which applies in relation to the exercise of an option on or after 10 April 2003.

Cross references – S. 149A: share option schemes obtained from individual's employment.

144ZB Exception to rule in section 144ZA

144ZB(1) This section applies where–

(a) section 144ZA would apply but for this section in relation to an option, and

(b) the exercise of the option is non-commercial (see section 144ZC).

144ZB(2) But this section does not apply if–

(a) the option is a securities option within the meaning of Chapter 5 of Part 7 of ITEPA 2003 (see section 420(8) of that Act) to which that Chapter applies (see section 471 of that Act), or

(b) section 144ZD of this Act (value of underlying subject matter of option altered with a view to obtaining a tax advantage) applies in relation to the option.

144ZB(3) Where this section applies, neither section 144ZA nor the following provisions of section 144 shall apply in relation to the option–

(a) in subsection (2), the words from "and accordingly" to the end of that subsection, and

(b) in subsection (3), the words from "and accordingly" to the end of that subsection;

but subsection (4) or (5) below shall instead have effect (subject to subsection (6) below).

144ZB(4) If the option binds the grantor to buy–

(a) the cost of acquisition incurred by the grantor in buying in pursuance of his obligations under the option, and

(b) the consideration for the disposal of what is bought by the grantor,

shall be deemed for the purposes of tax in respect of chargeable gains to be the market value, at the time the option is exercised, of what is bought.

144ZB(5) If the option binds the grantor to sell–

(a) the consideration for the sale, and

(b) the cost to the person exercising the option of acquiring what is sold,

shall be deemed for the purposes of tax in respect of chargeable gains to be the market value, at the time the option is exercised, of what is sold.

144ZB(6) But if the whole or any part of the underlying subject matter of the option (see subsection (7)) is subject to any right or restriction which is enforceable by the person disposing of the underlying subject matter or a person connected with him–

(a) the market value of the underlying subject matter shall be determined for the purposes of subsection (4) or (5) above as if the right or restriction did not exist, and

(b) to the extent that subsection (6) or (7) of section 18 would apply apart from this paragraph, it shall be disregarded.

144ZB(7) In this section **"underlying subject matter"**, in relation to an option, means–

(a) if the option binds the grantor to sell, what falls to be sold on exercise of the option;

(b) if the option binds the grantor to buy, what falls to be bought on exercise of the option.

History – In s. 144ZB(2)(a), the words "or would, apart from section 474 of that Act, apply" omitted by FA 2014, s. 52 and Sch. 9, para. 25, with effect from 6 April 2015 in relation to employment-related securities and employment-related securities options irrespective of the date of the acquisition.

S. 144ZB inserted by F(No. 2)A 2005, s. 35 and Sch. 5, para. 2 with effect, in accordance with F(No. 2)A 2005, Sch. 5, para. 6(1), in relation to cases where option concerned, whenever acquired, is exercised on or after 2 December 2004.

144ZC Section 144ZB: non-commercial exercise of option

144ZC(1) For the purposes of section 144ZB, the exercise of an option which binds the grantor to buy is non-commercial if the exercise price for the option (see subsection (3)) is less than the open market price (see subsection (4)) of what is bought.

144ZC(2) For the purposes of section 144ZB, the exercise of an option which binds the grantor to sell is non-commercial if the exercise price for the option is greater than the open market price of what is sold.

144ZC(3) In this section **"exercise price"**, in relation to an option, means the amount or value of the consideration which, under the terms of the option, is–

(a) receivable (if the option binds the grantor to buy), or

(b) payable (if the option binds the grantor to sell),

as a result of the exercise of the option (and does not include the amount or value of any consideration for the acquisition of the option (whether directly from the grantor or not)).

144ZC(4) In this section **"open market price"**, in relation to the underlying subject matter of an option (see section 144ZB(7)), means the price which the underlying subject matter might reasonably be expected to fetch on a sale in the open market at the time the option is exercised; and subsections (5) to (7) below apply for the purposes of this subsection.

144ZC(5) If the whole or any part of the underlying subject matter of the option is subject to any right or restriction which is enforceable by–

(a) the person disposing of the underlying subject matter, or

(b) a person connected with him,

the open market price of the underlying subject matter shall be determined as if the right or restriction did not exist.

144ZC(6) Section 272(2) (no reduction in estimated market value on account of assumption that whole of assets are placed on market at one time) shall apply in estimating the open market price of the underlying subject matter of an option as it applies in estimating the market value of any assets.

144ZC(7) Where the underlying subject matter of an option comprises or includes assets to which section 273 applies (unquoted shares and securities), subsection (3) of that section (assumption that relevant information is available) shall apply in determining the open market price of those assets as it applies for the purposes of a determination falling within subsection (1) of that section.

144ZC(8) This section is to be construed as one with section 144ZB.

History – S. 144ZC inserted by F(No. 2)A 2005, s. 35 and Sch. 5, para. 2 with effect, in accordance with F(No. 2)A 2005, Sch. 5, para. 6(1), in relation to cases where option concerned, whenever acquired, is exercised on or after 2 December 2004.

144ZD Section 144ZB: alteration of value to obtain tax advantage

144ZD(1) This section applies in relation to an option if each of the following conditions is satisfied (as to the effect of this section applying, see section 144ZB(2)(b)).

144ZD(2) Condition 1 is that section 144ZB would, apart from subsection (2)(b) of that section, apply in relation to the option.

144ZD(3) Condition 2 is that, at the time the option is exercised, the open market price (see section 144ZC(4)) of the underlying subject matter of the option (see section 144ZB(7)) differs from the open market price of the underlying subject matter of the option at the time the option was granted.

144ZD(4) Condition 3 is that some or all of that change in the open market price of the underlying subject matter of the option results to any extent, directly or indirectly, from arrangements (see subsection (8)) ("the relevant arrangements")–

(a) to which a relevant person is or has been a party, or

(b) which include one or more transactions to which a relevant person is or has been a party.

144ZD(5) In subsection (4) above **"relevant person"** means any of the following–

(a) the grantor of the option;

(b) any person who at any time holds the option;

(c) a person connected with one or more of the persons mentioned in paragraph (a) or (b) above.

144ZD(6) Condition 4 is that, if there were to be disregarded so much of that change in the open market price of the underlying subject matter of the option as results to any extent, directly or indirectly, from the relevant arrangements, the exercise of the option would not be non-commercial (see section 144ZC).

144ZD(7) Condition 5 is that (apart from this section) as a result, directly or indirectly, of the relevant arrangements–

(a) the grantor of the option, or

(b) the person exercising the option,

would obtain or might be expected to obtain an advantage (see subsection (9)) in relation to capital gains tax or corporation tax in respect of chargeable gains directly or indirectly in consequence of, or otherwise in connection with, the exercise of the option.

144ZD(8) In this section **"arrangements"** includes any agreement, understanding, scheme, transaction or series of transactions (whether or not legally enforceable).

144ZD(9) In this section **"advantage"**, in relation to capital gains tax or corporation tax in respect of chargeable gains, means–

(a) relief or increased relief from, or repayment or increased repayment of, that tax, or the avoidance or reduction of a charge to that tax or an assessment to that tax or the avoidance of a possible assessment to that tax, or

(b) the deferral of any payment of that tax or the advancement of any repayment of that tax.

144ZD(10) This section is to be construed as one with sections 144ZB and 144ZC.

History – S. 144ZD inserted by F(No. 2)A 2005, s. 35 and Sch. 5, para. 2 with effect, in accordance with F(No. 2)A 2005, Sch. 5, para. 6(1), in relation to cases where option concerned, whenever acquired, is exercised on or after 2 December 2004.

144A Cash-settled options

144A(1) In any case where–

(a) an option is exercised; and

(b) the nature of the option (or its exercise) is such that the grantor of the option is liable to make, and the person exercising it is entitled to receive, a payment in full settlement of all obligations under the option,

subsections (2) and (3) below shall apply in place of subsections (2) and (3) of section 144.

144A(2) As regards the grantor of the option–

(a) he shall be treated as having disposed of an asset (namely, his liability to make the payment) and the payment made by him shall be treated as incidental costs to him of making the disposal; and

(b) the grant of the option and the disposal shall be treated as a single transaction and the consideration for the option shall be treated as the consideration for the disposal.

144A(3) As regards the person exercising the option–

(a) he shall be treated as having disposed of an asset (namely, his entitlement to receive the payment) and the payment received by him shall be treated as the consideration for the disposal;

(b) the acquisition of the option (whether directly from the grantor or not) and the disposal shall be treated as a single transaction and the cost of acquiring the option shall be treated as expenditure allowable as a deduction under section 38(1)(a) from the consideration for the disposal; and

(c) for the purpose of computing the indexation (if any) on the disposal, the cost of the option shall be treated (notwithstanding paragraph (b) above) as incurred when the option was acquired.

144A(4) In any case where subsections (2) and (3) above would apply as mentioned in subsection (1) above if the reference in that subsection to full settlement included a reference to partial settlement, those subsections and subsections (2) and (3) of section 144 shall both apply but with the following modifications–

(a) for any reference to the grant or acquisition of the option there shall be substituted a reference to the grant or acquisition of so much of the option as relates to the making and receipt of the payment or, as the case may be, the sale or purchase by the grantor; and

(b) for any reference to the consideration for, or the cost of or of acquiring, the option there shall be substituted a reference to the appropriate proportion of that consideration or cost.

144A(5) In this section **"appropriate proportion"** means such proportion as may be just and reasonable in all the circumstances.

History – S. 144A inserted by FA 1994, s. 96(1) in relation to options granted on or after 30 November 1993.

Cross references – S. 38(1)(a): allowable expenditure on a disposal.
S. 144: options and forfeited deposits.

145 Call options: indexation allowance

145(1) This section applies where, on a disposal to which section 53 applies, the relevant allowable expenditure includes both–

(a) the cost of acquiring an option binding the grantor to sell (**"the option consideration"**); and

(b) the cost of acquiring what was sold as a result of the exercise of the option (**"the sale consideration"**),

but does not apply in any case where section 114 applies.

145(1A) [Omitted by FA 2008, s. 8 and Sch. 2, para. 81(3).]

145(2) For the purpose of computing the indexation allowance (if any) on the disposal referred to in subsection (1) above–

(a) the option consideration and the sale consideration shall be regarded as separate items of expenditure; and

(b) subsection (4) of section 54 shall apply to neither of those items and, accordingly, they shall be regarded as incurred when the option was acquired and when the sale took place, respectively.

145(3) This section has effect notwithstanding section 144, but expressions used in this section have the same meaning as in that section and subsection (5) of that section applies for the purpose of determining the cost of acquiring an option binding the grantor to sell.

History – In s. 145(1), the reference to s. 145(1A) omitted by FA 2008, s. 8 and Sch. 2, para. 81(2) with effect in computing gains on disposals made on or after 6 April 2008 (FA 2008, Sch. 2, para. 83).
In s. 145(1), the former reference to s. 145(1A) inserted by FA 1998, s. 122(5) with effect for disposals on or after 6 April 1998.
S. 145(1A) omitted by FA 2008, s. 8 and Sch. 2, para. 81(3) with effect in computing gains on disposals made on or after 6 April 2008 (FA 2008, Sch. 2, para. 83).
Former s. 145(1A) inserted by FA 1998, s. 122(5) with effect for disposals on or after 6 April 1998.

Derivations – FA 1982, Sch. 13, para. 7.

Cross references – S. 53(4): priority over general indexation allowance provisions (s. 53, 54) and identification of certain securities (s. 108).
S. 114: consideration for option which increases the qualifying expenditure on a "new holding" of securities as defined in s. 104.
ICTA 1988, Sch. 28, para. 2, 3(1), 4(3), 8(3): offshore income gain which is taxed as income is calculated by reference to gain using principles of this Act but if acquired on a no gain, no loss basis as if no allowance had been available under s. 56(2) and generally as if transferee's acquisition of it had been the disponor's; a gain on a disposal involving an equalisation element is calculated ignoring no gain, no loss provisions.
FA 1998, s. 122(7): s. 145(1A) disapplied where a gain is treated as chargeable after 6 April 1998 in relation to an actual or deemed disposal occurring before that date.

Notes – S. 21–34: general meaning of "disposal".

146 Options: application of rules as to wasting assets

146(1) Section 46 shall not apply–

(a) to a quoted option to subscribe for shares in a company, or

(b) to a traded option, or financial option, or

(c) to an option to acquire assets exercisable by a person intending to use them, if acquired, for the purpose of a trade carried on by him.

146(2) In relation to the disposal by way of transfer of an option (other than an option falling within subsection (1)(a) or (b) above) binding the grantor to sell or buy quoted shares or securities, the option shall be regarded as a wasting asset the life of which ends when the right to exercise the option ends, or when the option becomes valueless, whichever is the earlier.

Subsections (5) and (6) of section 144 shall apply in relation to this subsection as they apply in relation to that section.

146(3) The preceding provisions of this section are without prejudice to the application of sections 44 to 47 to options not within those provisions.

146(4) In this section–

(a) **"financial option"**, **"quoted option"** and **"traded option"** have the meanings given by section 144(8), and

(b) **"quoted shares or securities"** means shares or securities which are listed on a recognised stock exchange.

History – In s. 146(4)(b) the words at the end ("in the United Kingdom or elsewhere") omitted by FA 2007, s. 109 and Sch. 26, para. 8(4); and repealed by FA 2007, s. 114 and Sch. 27, Pt. 6(5) with effect from 19 July 2007 (Royal Assent).
In s. 144(4)(b) the words "are listed" substituted for "have a quoted market value" by FA 1996, s. 199 and Sch. 38, para. 11 in relation to disposals of options on or after 1 April 1996.

Derivations – CGTA 1979, s. 138, as amended by FA 1980, s. 84(5), (6), and F(No. 2)A 1987, s. 81(6), (7).

Cross references – S. 44–47: meaning of "wasting asset", exemption for wasting assets which are tangible movable property, straight line restriction of allowable expenditure on a wasting asset (s. 46) and adjustments where wasting asset qualifies for capital allowances.

Notes – S. 288: interpretation, including meaning of "recognised stock exchange", "shares" as embracing stock and reference to sections being those of this Act.

147 Quoted options treated as part of new holdings

147(1) If a quoted option to subscribe for shares in a company is dealt in (on the stock exchange where it is quoted) within 3 months after the taking effect, with respect to the company granting the option, of any reorganisation, reduction, conversion, exchange or scheme of reconstruction to which Chapter II of this Part applies, or within such longer period as the Board may by notice allow–

(a) the option shall, for the purposes of that Chapter be regarded as the shares which could be acquired by exercising the option, and

(b) section 272(3) shall apply for determining its market value.

147(2) In this section **"quoted option"** has the meaning given by section 144(8) and **"scheme of reconstruction"** has the same meaning as in section 136.

History – In s. 147(1), words ", exchange or scheme of reconstruction" substituted for "amalgamation", and in s. 147(2), words "and scheme of reconstruction" to the end inserted by FA 2002, s. 45 and Sch. 9, para. 5(8) with effect in relation to shares or debentures issued on or after 17 April 2002.

Derivations – CGTA 1979, s. 139.

Cross references – S. 137(6): restriction on equation of original and new holdings on an exchange, reconstruction etc. by reference to bona fide nature etc. applies equally to options within s. 147.
Pt. IV, Ch. II (s. 126–140): equation of original and new holdings on a reorganisation, reduction, conversion or amalgamation (and provisions applied to certain other transactions) and effective deferral of tax in certain other reconstructions.
S. 272(3): market value of quoted shares is generally the lower of the "quarter-up" and "mid-market" prices.
ICTA 1988, s. 473: equation of securities, including option within s. 147, for purposes of taxes on income where reorganisation and assets represent trading stock of a bank, insurance company or dealer.

Notes – S. 288: interpretation, including meaning of "company", "notice" as being in writing, "shares" as embracing stock and reference to sections being those of this Act.
TMA 1970, s. 115: service of notices.

148 Traded options: closing purchases

148(1) This section applies where a person (**"the grantor"**) who has granted a traded option (**"the original option"**) closes it out by acquiring a traded option of the same description (**"the second option"**).

148(2) Any disposal by the grantor involved in closing out the original option shall be disregarded for the purposes of capital gains tax or, as the case may be, corporation tax on chargeable gains.

148(3) The incidental costs to the grantor of making the disposal constituted by the grant of the original option shall be treated for the purposes of the computation of the gain as increased by an amount equal to the aggregate of–

(a) the amount or value of the consideration, in money or money's worth, given by him or on his behalf wholly and exclusively for the acquisition of the second option, and

(b) the incidental costs to him of that acquisition.

148(4) In this section **"traded option"** has the meaning given by section 144(8).

Derivations – FA 1991, s. 102.

Notes – S. 21–34: general meaning of "disposal".
S. 38(1)(c): deduction for incidental costs of disposal.
S. 288: interpretation, including reference to sections being those of this Act.

148A Futures and options involving guaranteed returns

148A [Omitted by FA 2013, s. 28 and Sch. 12, para. 8.]

History – S. 148A omitted by FA 2013, s. 28 and Sch. 12, para. 8, with effect for the tax year 2013–14 and subsequent tax years, subject to FA 2013, Sch. 12, para. 18(2).

148B Deemed disposals at a gain under section 564(4) of ITTOIA 2005

148B [Omitted by FA 2013, s. 28 and Sch. 12, para. 8.]

History – S. 148B omitted by FA 2013, s. 28 and Sch. 12, para. 8, with effect for the tax year 2013–14 and subsequent tax years, subject to FA 2013, Sch. 12, para. 18(2).

148C Deemed disposals at a loss under section 564(4) of ITTOIA 2005

148C [Omitted by FA 2013, s. 28 and Sch. 12, para. 8.]

History – S. 148C omitted by FA 2013, s. 28 and Sch. 12, para. 8, with effect for the tax year 2013–14 and subsequent tax years, subject to FA 2013, Sch. 12, para. 18(2).

149 Rights to acquire qualifying shares

149(1) This section applies where on or after 25th July 1991 (the day on which the Finance Act 1991 was passed) a building society confers–

(a) on its members, or

(b) on any particular class or description of its members,

any rights to acquire, in priority to other persons, shares in the society which are qualifying shares.

149(2) Any such right so conferred shall be regarded for the purposes of capital gains tax as an option granted to, and acquired by, the member concerned for no consideration and having no value at the time of that grant and acquisition.

149(3) In this section–

"member" includes a former member, and

"qualifying share" has the same meaning as in section 117(4).

Derivations – FA 1991, Sch. 10, para. 4.

Cross references – S. 117(4): a corporate bond includes a qualifying share in a building society, defined (s. 117(5)) as a permanent interest bearing share (PIBS) or one specified as such by Treasury regulations.
S. 144: options and forfeited deposits.

Notes – S. 288: interpretation, including reference to sections being those of this Act.

149A Employment-related securities options

History – Heading of s. 149A, which was "Share option schemes", became "Employment-related securities options" by F(No. 2)A 2005, s. 35 and Sch. 5, para. 4(4) with effect, in accordance with F(No. 2)A 2005, Sch. 5, para. 6(2), in relation to options granted on or after 2 December 2004.

149A(1) This section applies where–

(a) an option is granted on or after 16th March 1993,

(b) the option is a securities option within the meaning of Chapter 5 of Part 7 of ITEPA 2003 (see section 420(8) of that Act) to which that Chapter applies (see section 471 of that Act), and

(c) section 17(1) of this Act would (apart from this section) apply for the purposes of calculating the consideration for the grant of the option.

149A(2) Both the grantor of the option and the person to whom the option is granted shall be treated for the purposes of this Act as if section 17(1) did not apply for the purposes of calculating the consideration and, accordingly, as if the amount or value of the consideration was its actual amount or value.

149A(3) Where the option is granted wholly or partly in recognition of services or past services in any office or employment, the value of those services shall not be taken into account in calculating the actual amount or value of the consideration.

149A(4) [Repealed by FA 1996, s. 111(4) and s. 205 and Sch. 41, Pt. V(5).]

History – In s. 149A(1)(b), the words "or would, apart from section 474 of that Act, apply" omitted by FA 2014, s. 52 and Sch. 9, para. 26, with effect from 6 April 2015 in relation to employment-related securities and employment-related securities options irrespective of the date of the acquisition.
S. 149A(1)(b) substituted by F(No. 2)A 2005, s. 35 and Sch. 5, para. 4(2) with effect, in accordance with F(No. 2)A 2005, Sch. 5, para. 6(2), in relation to options granted on or after 2 December 2004.
In former s. 149A(1)(b) words "by an individual by reason of his office or employment as a director or employee of that or any other body corporate" substituted; in s. 149A(2) words "Both the grantor of the option and the person to whom the option is granted" substituted; s. 149A(4) repealed; and heading amended by FA 1996, s. 111 and s. 205 and Sch. 41, Pt. V(5) in relation to any right to acquire shares in a body corporate obtained on or after 28 November 1995 by an individual by reason of his office or employment as a director or employee of a body corporate.
In s. 149A(1)(c), after reference "section 17(1)", words "of this Act" inserted by F(No. 2)A 2005, s. 35 and Sch. 5, para. 4(3) with effect, in accordance with F(No. 2)A 2005, Sch. 5, para. 6(2), in relation to options granted on or after 2 December 2004.
S. 149A inserted by FA 1993, s. 104.

Cross references – S. 17: disposals and acquisitions treated as made at market value.

149AA Restricted and convertible employment-related securities and employee shareholder shares

History – In the heading to s. 149AA, the words "and employee shareholder shares" inserted by FA 2013, s. 55 and Sch. 23, para. 19(7), *with effect from 1 September 2013 (SI 2013/1755).*

149AA(1) Subject to subsection (1A), where an individual has acquired an asset consisting of employment-related securities which are–

(a) restricted securities or a restricted interest in securities, or

(b) convertible securities or an interest in convertible securities, the consideration for the acquisition shall (subject to section 119A) be taken to be equal to the aggregate of the actual amount or value given for the employment-related securities and any amount that constituted earnings under Chapter 1 of Part 3 of ITEPA 2003 (earnings) in respect of the acquisition.

149AA(1A) Where an individual has acquired an asset consisting of shares which, on acquisition, became employee shareholder shares–

(a) the consideration for the acquisition is (subject to section 119A) to be taken to be equal to any amount that constituted earnings under Chapter 1 of Part 3 of ITEPA 2003 (earnings) or section 226A of that Act (employee shareholder shares), and

(b) no other consideration is to be treated as having been given for the acquisition of the shares.

149AA(2) Subsections (1) and (1A) apply only to the individual making the acquisition and, accordingly, are to be disregarded in calculating the consideration received by the person from whom the employment-related securities are acquired.

149AA(3) This section has effect in relation to acquisitions on or after the day appointed under paragraph 3(2) of Schedule 22 to the Finance Act 2003.

149AA(4) In this section **"employment-related securities"** has the same meaning as in Chapters 1 to 4 of Part 7 of ITEPA 2003 (as substituted by Schedule 22 to the Finance Act 2003).

149AA(5) In this section–

"restricted interest in securities", and

"restricted securities",

have the same meaning as in Chapter 2 of that Part of ITEPA 2003 (as so substituted).

149AA(6) In this section **"convertible securities"** has the same meaning as in Chapter 3 of that Part of ITEPA 2003 (as so substituted).

149AA(6A) For the purposes of subsection (1A)–

"employee shareholder share" has the meaning given in section 236B(3) (exemption for employee shareholder shares), and

shares are **"acquired"** by an individual if the individual becomes beneficially entitled to them (and they are so acquired at the time when the individual becomes so entitled).

149AA(7) In subsections (1) and (1A) a reference to any amount that constituted earnings under Chapter 1 of Part 3 of ITEPA 2003 or was treated as earnings under section 226A of that Act does not include–

(a) any amount of exempt income (within the meaning of section 8 of that Act), and

(b) in a case in which the amount that constituted, or was treated as, earnings was not an amount of general earnings to which any of the charging provisions of Chapters 4 and 5 of Part 2 of ITEPA 2003 applied, any amount that would have been an amount of such exempt income if any of those charging provisions had applied.

History – In s. 149AA(1), the words "Subject to subsection (1A), where" substituted for the word "Where" by FA 2013, s. 55 and Sch. 23, para. 19(2), with effect from 1 September 2013 (SI 2013/1755).
S. 149AA(1A) inserted by FA 2013, s. 55 and Sch. 23, para. 19(3), with effect from 1 September 2013 (SI 2013/1755).
In s. 149AA(2), the words "Subsections (1) and (1A) apply" substituted for the words "Subsection (1) above applies" by FA 2013, s. 55 and Sch. 23, para. 19(4)(a), with effect from 1 September 2013 (SI 2013/1755).
In s. 149AA(2), the word "are" substituted for the word "is" by FA 2013, s. 55 and Sch. 23, para. 19(4)(b), with effect from 1 September 2013 (SI 2013/1755).
S. 149AA(6A) inserted by FA 2013, s. 55 and Sch. 23, para. 19(5), with effect from 1 September 2013 (SI 2013/1755)
In s. 149AA(7), existing text used to form para. (a) and para. (b) inserted by FA 2014, s. 52 and Sch. 9, para. 27, with effect from 6 April 2015 in relation to employment-related securities and employment-related securities options irrespective of the date of the acquisition:
In s. 149AA(7), the words "In subsections (1) and (1A) a" substituted for the words "In subsection (1) the" and the words "or was treated as earnings under section 226A of that Act" inserted after the words "ITEPA 2003" by FA 2013, s. 55 and Sch. 23, para. 19(6), with effect from 1 September 2013 (SI 2013/1755).
S. 149AA(7) inserted by FA 2008, s. 49(1) with effect in relation to disposals made on or after 12 March 2008.
S. 149AA inserted by FA 2003, s. 140 and Sch. 22, para. 52(1) with effect in relation to acquisitions on and after 1 September 2003 (SI 2003/1997).

149AB Shares in research institution spin-out companies

149AB(1) Where an individual has acquired shares (or an interest in shares) in circumstances where section 452(1) and (2)(a) of ITEPA 2003 (shares in research institution spin-out companies: market value on acquisition) apply (and section 149AA does not apply in relation to those shares (or interest in shares)) the consideration for the acquisition shall (subject to section 119A) be taken to be equal to the aggregate of–

(a) the actual amount or value given for the shares (or interest in shares), and

(b) any amount that constituted earnings under Chapter 1 of Part 3 of ITEPA 2003 (earnings) in respect of the acquisition.

149AB(2) Subsection (1) above applies only to the individual making the acquisition and, accordingly, is to be disregarded in calculating the consideration received by the person from whom the shares (or interest in shares) are (or is) acquired.

History – S. 149AB inserted by FA 2005, s. 22(3) with effect in relation to any acquisition, whether before or after 7 April 2005 (date of Royal Assent to FA 2005).

149B Employee incentive schemes: conditional interests in shares

149B(1) Where–

(a) an individual has acquired an interest in any shares or securities which is only conditional,

(b) that interest is one which for the purposes of Chapter 2 of Part 7 of ITEPA 2003 (conditional interests in shares) is taken to have been acquired by him as a director or employee of a company, and

(c) by virtue of section 17(1)(b) the acquisition of that interest would, apart from this section, be an acquisition for a consideration equal to the market value of the interest,

section 17 shall not apply for calculating the consideration.

149B(2) Instead, the consideration for the acquisition shall be taken (subject to section 120) to be equal to the actual amount or value of the consideration given for that interest as computed in accordance with section 429 of ITEPA 2003.

149B(3) This section shall apply in relation only to the individual making the acquisition and, accordingly, shall be disregarded in calculating the consideration received by the person from whom the interest is acquired.

149B(4) Expressions used in this section and in Chapter 2 of Part 7 of ITEPA 2003 have the same meanings in this section as in that Chapter.

149B(5) This section does not apply to acquisitions on or after the day appointed under paragraph 3(2) of Schedule 22 to the Finance Act 2003.

149B(6) References in this section to ITEPA 2003 are to that Act as originally enacted.

History – In s. 149B(1), the words "Chapter 2 of Part 7 of ITEPA 2003" substituted for the words "section 140A of the Taxes Act" by ITEPA 2003, Sch. 6, para. 211(2) with effect for 2003–04 and subsequent tax years.

In s. 149B(2), the words "section 429 of ITEPA 2003" substituted for the words "section 140B of the Taxes Act" by ITEPA 2003, Sch. 6, para. 211(3) with effect for 2003–04 and subsequent tax years.

In s. 149B(4), the words "Chapter 2 of Part 7 of ITEPA 2003" substituted for the words "section 140A of the Taxes Act" by ITEPA 2003, Sch. 6, para. 211(4)(a) with effect for 2003–04 and subsequent tax years.

In s. 149B(4), the words "that Chapter" substituted for the words "that section" by ITEPA 2003, Sch. 6, para. 211(4)(b) with effect for 2003–04 and subsequent tax years.

S. 149B(5) inserted by FA 2003, s. 140 and Sch. 22, para. 53 which came into force on 10 July 2003 [i.e. date of passing of FA 2003].

S. 149B(6) inserted by FA 2003, s. 140 and Sch. 22, para. 53 which came into force on 10 July 2003 [i.e. date of passing of FA 2003].

S. 149B inserted by FA 1998, s. 54(5), with effect in relation to disposals on or after 17 March 1998 of interests and shares acquired on or after that date.

Notes – As s. 149B applies only to acquisitions before 1 September 2003 (by virtue of s. 149B(5) and (6)), it is now effectively spent.

149C Priority share allocations

149C Section 17(1) shall not apply to an acquisition of shares if section 542 or 544 of ITEPA 2003 applies in relation to it.

History – S. 149C inserted by ITEPA 2003, Sch. 6, para. 212 with effect for 2003–04 and subsequent tax years.

150 Business expansion schemes

150(1) In this section **"relief"** means relief under Chapter III of Part VII of the Taxes Act, Schedule 5 to the Finance Act 1983 (**"the 1983 Act"**) or Chapter II of Part IV of the Finance Act 1981 (**"the 1981 Act"**) and **"eligible shares"** has the meaning given by section 289(4) of the Taxes Act and references in this section to Chapter III of Part VII of the Taxes Act or any provision of that Chapter are to that Chapter or provision as it applies in relation to shares issued before 1st January 1994.

150(2) A gain or loss which accrues to an individual on the disposal of any shares issued after 18th March 1986 in respect of which relief has been given to him and not withdrawn shall not be a chargeable gain or allowable loss for the purposes of capital gains tax.

150(3) The sums allowable as deductions from the consideration in the computation for the purposes of capital gains tax of the gain or loss accruing to an individual on the disposal of shares issued before 19th March 1986 in respect of which relief has been given and not withdrawn shall be determined without regard to that relief, except that where those sums exceed the consideration they shall be reduced by an amount equal to–

(a) the amount of that relief; or

(b) the excess,

whichever is the less, but the foregoing provisions of this subsection shall not apply to a disposal falling within section 58(1).

150(4) Any question–

(a) as to which of any shares acquired by an individual at different times, being shares in respect of which relief has been given and not withdrawn, a disposal relates to, or

(b) whether a disposal relates to shares in respect of which relief has been given and not withdrawn or to other shares,

shall for the purposes of capital gains tax be determined as for the purposes of section 299 of the Taxes Act, or section 57 of the Finance Act 1981 if the relief has only been given under that Act; and Chapter I of this Part shall have effect subject to the foregoing provisions of this subsection.

150(5) Sections 104, 105 and 106A do not apply to shares in respect of which relief has been given and not withdrawn.

150(6) Where an individual holds shares which form part of the ordinary share capital of a company and the relief has been given (and not withdrawn) in respect of some but not others, then, if there is within the meaning of section 126 a reorganisation affecting those shares, section 127 shall apply separately to the shares in respect of which the relief has been given (and not withdrawn) and to the other shares (so that shares of each kind are treated as a separate holding of original shares and identified with a separate new holding).

150(7) Where section 58 has applied to any shares in respect of which relief has been given and not withdrawn disposed of by an individual to his or her spouse or civil partner (**"the transferee"**), subsection (2) above shall apply in relation to the subsequent disposal of the shares by the transferee to a third party.

150(8) Where section 135 or 136 would, but for this subsection, apply in relation to shares issued after 18th March 1986 in respect of which in individual has been given relief, that section shall apply only if the relief is withdrawn.

150(8A) Subsection (8) above shall not have effect to disapply section 135 or 136 where–

(a) the new holding consists of new ordinary shares carrying no present or future preferential right to dividends or to a company's assets on its winding up and no present or future right to be redeemed,

(b) the new shares are issued on or after 29th November 1994 and after the end of the relevant period, and

(c) the condition in subsection (8B) below is fulfilled.

150(8B) The condition is that at some time before the issue of the new shares–

(a) the company issuing them issued eligible shares, and

(b) a certificate in relation to those eligible shares was issued by the company for the purposes of subsection (2) of section 306 of the Taxes Act and in accordance with that section.

150(8C) In subsection (8A) above–

(a) **"new holding"** shall be construed in accordance with sections 126, 127, 135 and 136;

(b) **"relevant period"** means the period found by applying section 289(12)(a) of the Taxes Act by reference to the company issuing the shares referred to in subsection (8) above and by reference to those shares.

150(8D) Where shares in respect of which relief has been given and not withdrawn are exchanged for other shares in circumstances such that section 304A of the Taxes Act (acquisition of share capital by new company) applies–

(a) subsection (8) above shall not have effect to disapply section 135; and

(b) subsections (2)(b), (3) and (4) of section 304A of the Taxes Act, and subsection (5) of that section so far as relating to section 306(2) of that Act, shall apply for the purposes of this section as they apply for the purposes of Chapter III of Part VII of that Act.

150(9) Sections 127 to 130 shall not apply in relation to any shares in respect of which relief (other than relief under the 1981 Act) has been given and which form part of a company's ordinary share capital if–

(a) there is, by virtue of any such allotment for payment as is mentioned in section 126(2)(a), a reorganisation occurring after 18th March 1986 affecting those shares; and

(b) immediately following the reorganisation, the relief has not been withdrawn in respect of those shares or relief has been given in respect of the allotted shares and not withdrawn.

150(10) Where relief is reduced by virtue of subsection (2) of section 305 of the Taxes Act–

(a) the sums allowable as deductions from the consideration in the computation, for the purposes of capital gains tax, of the gain or loss accruing to an individual on the disposal, after 18th March 1986, of any of the allotted shares or debentures shall be taken to include the amount of the reduction apportioned between the allotted shares or (as the case may be) debentures in a way which is just and reasonable; and

(b) the sums so allowable on the disposal (in circumstances in which subsections (2) to (8) above do not apply) of any of the shares referred to in section 305(2)(a) shall be taken to be reduced by the amount mentioned in paragraph (a) above, similarly apportioned between those shares.

150(11) There shall be made all such adjustments of capital gains tax, whether by way of assessment or by way of discharge or repayment of tax, as may be required in consequence of the relief being given or withdrawn.

150(12) In this section–

"ordinary share capital" has the same meaning as in the Taxes Act;

"ordinary shares", in relation to a company, means shares forming part of its ordinary share capital.

History – In s. 150(1), the words "and references in ... 1st January 1994" which appear at the end inserted by FA 1994, s. 137 and Sch. 15, para. 29.
In s. 150(4)(a), the words "acquired by an individual" substituted for the words "issued to a person", and word "to" inserted after "relates", by FA 1998, s. 74(1) and Sch. 13, para. 42(1), with effect in relation to disposals made on or after 6 April 1998.
In s. 150(5) the words "Sections 104, 105 and 106A do not apply" substituted for the words "Notwithstanding anything in section 107(1) and (2), section 107 does not apply" by FA 1998, s. 74(1) and Sch. 13, para. 42(2), with effect in relation to disposals made on or after 6 April 1998.
In s. 150(7) the words "or civil partner" inserted by SI 2005/3229, reg. 109, with effect from 5 December 2005.
In s. 150(7) the words "shares in respect of which relief has been given and not withdrawn" substituted for the words "eligible shares" by FA 1998, s. 74(1) and Sch. 13, para. 42(3), with effect in relation to "subsequent disposals" made on or after 6 April 1998.
In s. 150(8) the word "eligible", which appeared between "in relation to" and "shares", repealed by FA 1998, s. 74(1) and Sch. 13, para. 42(4), s. 165 and Sch. 27, Pt. III(14), with effect in relation to events occurring on or after 6 April 1998.
In s. 150(8A)(a) the word "preferential", in the second place where it appeared (between "no present or future" and "right to be redeemed"), repealed by FA 1998, s. 74(1) and Sch. 13, para. 42(5), s. 165 and Sch. 27, Pt. III(17), with effect in relation to new shares (within the meaning of s. 150(8A) issued on or after 6 April 1998.
S. 150(8A)–(8C) inserted by FA 1995, s. 69 in relation to shares issued before 1 January 1994.
S. 150(8D) inserted by FA 1998, s. 74(1) and Sch. 13, para. 42(6), with effect in relation to new shares (within the meaning of ICTA 1988, s. 304A) issued on or after 6 April 1998.
In s. 150(10)(a) words "a way which is" substituted for "such a way as appears to the inspector, or on appeal to the Commissioners concerned, to be" by FA 1996, s. 134 and Sch. 20, para. 54 for 1996–97 and later years of assessment.
S. 150(12) inserted by FA 1998, s. 74(1) and Sch. 13, para. 42(7), with effect in relation to events occurring on or after 6 April 1998.

Derivations – S. 150(1)–(4), (6)–(11): CGTA 1979, s. 149C, as inserted by ICTA 1988, s. 844 and Sch. 29, para. 26.
S. 150(5): FA 1985, Sch. 19, para. 16(3), as amended by FA 1991, s. 99(2).

Cross references – S. 58: deemed no gain, no loss on transfers between spouses.
S. 104–125 (Pt. IV, Ch. I): identification rules etc. for shares and securities, including (s. 107) general rules.
S. 126: "reorganisation" embraces a reorganisation or reduction of share capital.
S. 127–130: equation of original and new holdings on a reorganisation; consideration given or received, part disposal of new holding and composite new holdings in relation to reorganisations.
S. 135, 136: equation of original and new holdings on an exchange or a company reconstruction involving the issue of securities.
ICTA 1988, Pt. VII, Ch. III (and formerly FA 1983, Sch. 5, FA 1981, Pt. IV, Ch. II): business expansion scheme (as it applies in relation to shares issued on or before 31 December 1993, and its predecessor the business start-up scheme), eligible shares being defined (s. 289(4)) by reference to new ordinary shares with no preferential rights for five years and identification being determined (s. 299(3), (4)) with relieved shares before others, with start-up shares before expansion shares and on a first-in, first-out (FIFO) basis; EIS company becoming wholly-owned subsidiary without losing income tax relief for its investors (s. 304A); reduction of relief on a reorganisation by reference to the market value of the original shares (s. 305(2)). The enterprise investment scheme is the successor relief applying in relation to shares issued on or after 1 January 1994 (see s. 150A).

HMRC interpretations – IRInt. 27: allowable deductions (s. 38) and computation of relevant allowable expenditure (s. 150) in respect of a sale of shares acquired before 19 March 1986 where BES relief claimed.

Notes – S. 15: meaning of "chargeable gains".
S. 16: meaning of "allowable losses".
S. 21–34: general meaning of "disposal".
S. 38: allowable deductions for acquisition expenditure, including incidental costs, enhancement or title expenditure and incidental costs of disposal.
S. 288: interpretation, including "the Taxes Act" as ICTA 1988 and reference to other sections being those of this Act.
TMA 1970, s. 29: assessing procedure.

150A Enterprise investment schemes

150A(1) For the purpose of determining the gain or loss on any disposal of shares by an individual where–

(a) an amount of EIS relief is attributable to the shares, and

(b) apart from this subsection there would be a loss,

the consideration given by him for the shares shall be treated as reduced by the amount of the EIS relief.

150A(2) Subject to subsection (3) below, if on any disposal of shares by an individual after the end of the *period referred to in section 312(1A)(a) of the Taxes Act or section 159(2) of ITA 2007* where an amount of EIS relief is attributable to the shares, there would (apart from this subsection) be a gain, the gain shall not be a chargeable gain.

150A(2A) Notwithstanding anything in section 16(2), subsection (2) above shall not apply to a disposal on which a loss accrues.

150A(3) Where–

(a) an individual's liability to income tax has been reduced (or treated by virtue of section 304 of the Taxes Act or section 245 of ITA 2007 (spouses and civil partners) as reduced) for any year of assessment under section 289A of the Taxes Act or section 158 of ITA 2007 in respect of any issue of shares,

(b) the amount of the reduction ("A") is less than the amount ("B") which is equal to tax at the EIS original rate for that year on the amount subscribed for the issue, and

(c) A is not found under section 289A(2)(b) of the Taxes Act or (as the case may require) is not within paragraph (b) solely by virtue of section 29(2) and (3) of ITA 2007,

then, if there is a disposal of the shares on which there is a gain, subsection (2) above shall apply only to so much of the gain as is found by multiplying it by the fraction–

$$\frac{A}{B}$$

150A(3A) In subsection (3) **"EIS original rate"** has the meaning given by section 256A of ITA 2007, except that where the year mentioned in subsection (3)(b) is the tax year 2007–08 or an earlier year, it means 20%.

150A(4) Any question as to–

(a) which of any shares acquired by an individual at different times a disposal relates to, being shares to which EIS relief is attributable, or

(b) whether a disposal relates to shares to which EIS relief is attributable or to other shares,

shall for the purposes of capital gains tax be determined as for the purposes of section 299 of the Taxes Act or as provided by section 246 of ITA 2007; and Chapter I of this Part shall have effect subject to the foregoing provisions of this subsection.

150A(5) Sections 104, 105 and 106A shall not apply to shares to which EIS relief is attributable.

150A(6) Where an individual holds shares which form part of the ordinary share capital of a company and include shares of more than one of the following kinds, namely–

(a) shares to which EIS relief is attributable and to which subsection (6A) below applies;

(b) shares to which EIS relief is attributable and to which that subsection does not apply;

(ba) shares to which SEIS relief is attributable; and

(c) shares to which neither EIS nor SEIS relief is attributable,

then, if there is within the meaning of section 126 a reorganisation affecting those shares, section 127 shall apply (subject to the following provisions of this section) separately to shares falling within paragraph (a), (b), (ba) or (c) above (so that shares of each kind are treated as a separate holding of original shares and identified with a separate new holding).

150A(6A) This subsection applies to any shares if–

(a) expenditure on the shares has been set under Schedule 5B to this Act against the whole or part of any gain; and

(b) in relation to the shares there has been no chargeable event for the purposes of that Schedule.

150A(7) Where–

(a) an individual holds shares (**"the existing holding"**) which form part of the ordinary share capital of a company,

(b) there is, by virtue of any such allotment for payment as is mentioned in section 126(2)(a), a reorganisation affecting the existing holding, and

(c) immediately following the reorganisation, EIS relief is attributable to the existing holding or the allotted shares,

sections 127 to 130 shall not apply in relation to the existing holding.

150A(8) Sections 135 and 136 shall not apply in respect of shares to which EIS relief is attributable.

150A(8A) Subsection (8) above shall not have effect to disapply section 135 or 136 where–

(a) the new holding consists of new ordinary shares carrying no present or future preferential right to dividends or to a company's assets on its winding up and no present or future right to be redeemed,

(b) the new shares are issued on or after 29th November 1994 and after the end of the relevant period, and

(c) the condition in subsection (8B) below is satisfied.

150A(8B) The condition is that at some time before the issue of the new shares–

(a) the company issuing them issued eligible shares, and

(b) a certificate in relation to those eligible shares was issued by the company for the purposes of section 306(2) of the Taxes Act or section 203(1) of ITA 2007 and in accordance with section 306 of the Taxes Act or sections 204 and 205 of ITA 2007.

150A(8C) In subsection (8A) above–

(a) **"new holding"** shall be construed in accordance with sections 126, 127, 135 and 136;

(b) **"relevant period"** means the period found by applying section 312(1A)(a) of the Taxes Act or section 159(2) of ITA 2007 by reference to the company issuing the shares referred to in subsection (8) above and by reference to those shares.

150A(8D) Where shares to which EIS relief is attributable are exchanged for other shares in circumstances such that section 304A of the Taxes Act or section 247 of ITA 2007 (acquisition of share capital by new company) applies–

(a) subsection (8) above shall not have effect to disapply section 135; and

(b) the following–

(i) subsections (2)(b), (3) and (4) of section 304A of the Taxes Act and subsection (5) of that section so far as relating to section 306(2) of that Act, or

(ii) sections 247(3)(b), 248(2)(a) and 249 of ITA 2007,

shall apply for the purposes of this section as they apply for the purposes of Chapter 3 of Part 7 of the Taxes Act or Part 5 of ITA 2007.

150A(9) Where the EIS relief attributable to any shares is reduced by virtue of section 305(2) of the Taxes Act–

(a) the sums allowable as deductions from the consideration in the computation, for the purposes of capital gains tax, of the gain or loss accruing to an individual on the disposal of any of the allotted shares or debentures shall be taken to include the amount of the reduction apportioned between the allotted shares or (as the case may be) debentures in a way which is just and reasonable, and

(b) the sums so allowable on the disposal (in circumstances in which the preceding provisions of this section do not apply) of any of the shares referred to in section 305(1)(a) shall be taken to be reduced by the amount mentioned in paragraph (a) above, similarly apportioned between those shares.

150A(10) There shall be made all such adjustments of capital gains tax, whether by way of assessment or by way of discharge or repayment of tax, as may be required in consequence of EIS relief being given or withdrawn.

150A(10A) In this section–

"EIS relief" means relief under Chapter 3 of Part 7 of the Taxes Act or Part 5 of ITA 2007;

"ordinary share capital" has the meaning given in section 989 of ITA 2007;

"ordinary shares", in relation to a company, means shares forming part of its ordinary share capital;

"SEIS relief" means relief under Part 5A of ITA 2007.

150A(11) Chapter III of Part VII of the Taxes Act or Part 5 of ITA 2007 (enterprise investment scheme) applies for the purposes of this section to determine whether EIS relief is attributable to any shares and, if so, the amount of EIS relief so attributable; and **"eligible shares"** has the same meaning as in that Chapter or means shares that meet the requirements of section 173(2) of ITA 2007.

150A(12) References in this section to Chapter III of Part VII of the Taxes Act or any provision of that Chapter are to that Chapter or provision as it applies in relation to shares issued on or after 1st January 1994.

150A(13) References in this section to Part 5 of ITA 2007 or any provision of that Part are to a Part or provision that applies only in relation to shares issued after 5 April 2007.

History – In s. 150A "EIS relief" substituted for "relief" in each place it occurred (except subsections (6)(c) and (10)) by FA 2012, s. 38 and Sch. 6, para. 20(2) with effect in relation to shares issued on or after 6 April 2012.

In s. 150A(1) and (2) the word "eligible", where it appeared between "any disposal of" and "shares by an individual", repealed by FA 1998, s. 74(1) and Sch. 13, para. 24(1), s. 165 and Sch. 27, Pt. III(14), with effect in relation to disposals made on or after 6 April 1998.

In s. 150A(2) the words "or section 159(2) of ITA 2007" inserted by ITA 2007, s. 1027 and Sch. 1, para. 311(2), with effect from 6 April 2007.

S. 150A(2A) inserted by FA 1995, s. 67 and Sch. 13, para. 2(2) in relation to shares issued on or after 1 January 1994.

In s. 150A(3)(b), "EIS original rate" substituted for "basic rate" by FA 2012, s. 39 and Sch. 7, para. 27(a) with effect in relation to shares issued on or after 6 April 2012, regardless of whether the disqualifying arrangements were entered into before or on or after that date.

In s. 150A(3)(b), reference to "basic rate" substituted for "savings rate" by FA 2008, s. 5 and Sch. 1, para. 48 with effect from 2008–09.

In s. 150A(3), paragraphs (a), (b) and (c) substituted for the former paragraphs (a), (aa) and (b) by ITA 2007, s. 1027 and Sch. 1, para. 311(3), with effect from 6 April 2007.

S. 150A(3A) inserted by FA 2012, s. 39 and Sch. 7, para. 27(b) with effect in relation to shares issued on or after 6 April 2012, regardless of whether the disqualifying arrangements were entered into before or on or after that date.

In s. 150A(4)(a) the words "shares acquired by an individual at different times a disposal relates to" substituted for the words "issued to a person at different times a disposal relates" by FA 1998, s. 74(1) and Sch. 13, para. 24(2), with effect in relation to disposals made on or after 6 April 1998.
In s. 150A(4), the words "or as provided by section 246 of ITA 2007" inserted by ITA 2007, s. 1027 and Sch. 1, para. 311(4) with effect from 6 April 2007.
In s. 150A(5) reference to s. 106A substituted for s. 107 by FA 1998, s. 74(1) and Sch. 13, para. 24(3), with effect in relation to disposals made on or after 6 April 1998.
In s. 150A(6) the word "and" at the end of s. 150A(6)(b), and s. 150A(6)(ba) inserted, by FA 2012, s. 38 and Sch. 6, para 20(3)(a) with effect in relation to shares issued on or after 6 April 2012.
In s. 150A(6)(c) the words "neither EIS nor SEIS relief is" substituted for the words "relief is not" by FA 2012, s. 38 and Sch. 6, para. 20(3)(b) with effect in relation to shares issued on or after 6 April 2012.
In s. 150A(6) the words ", (ba)" inserted by FA 2012, s. 38 and Sch. 6, para. 20(3)(c) with effect in relation to shares issued on or after 6 April 2012.
S. 150A(6) and (6A)substituted for former s. 150A(6) by FA 1998, s. 74(1) and Sch. 13, para. 24(4), with effect in relation to reorganisations taking place on or after 6 April 1998.
In s. 150A(8A)(a) the word "preferential", in the second place where it occurred (between "no present or future" and "right to be redeemed"), repealed by FA 1998, s. 74(1) and Sch. 13, para. 24(5), s. 165 and Sch. 27, Pt. III(14), with effect in relation to new shares (within the meaning of s. 150A(8A)) issued on or after 6 April 1998.
S. 150(8A) inserted by FA 1995, s. 67 and Sch. 13, para. 2(4).
In s. 150A(8B), the words "section 306(2) of the Taxes Act or section 203(1) of ITA 2007 and in accordance with section 306 of the Taxes Act or sections 204 and 205 of ITA 2007" substituted for "subsection (2) of section 306 of the Taxes Act and in accordance with that section" by ITA 2007, s. 1027 and Sch. 1, para. 311(5), with effect from 6 April 2007.
S. 150(8B) inserted by FA 1995, s. 67 and Sch. 13, para. 2(4).
In s. 150A(8C), the words "or section 159(2) of ITA 2007" inserted by ITA 2007, s. 1027 and Sch. 1, para. 311(6), with effect from 6 April 2007.
S. 150(8C) inserted by FA 1995, s. 67 and Sch. 13, para. 2(4).
In s. 150A(8D), the words "or section 247 of ITA 2007" inserted by ITA 2007, s. 1027 and Sch. 1, para. 311(7)(a); and s. 150A(8D)(b) substituted by ITA 2007, s. 1027 and Sch. 1, para. 311(7)(b), both with effect from 6 April 2007.
S. 150A(8D) inserted by FA 1998, s. 74(1) and Sch. 13, para. 24(6), with effect in relation to new shares (within the meaning of ICTA 1988, s. 304A) issued on or after 6 April 1998.
In s. 150A(9)(a) words "a way which is" substituted for "such a way as appears to the inspector, or on appeal to the Commissioners concerned, to be" by FA 1996, s. 134 and Sch. 20, para. 54 for 1996–97 and later years of assessment.
In s. 150A(10) "EIS relief" substituted for "the relief" by FA 2012, s. 38 and Sch. 6, para. 20(4) with effect in relation to shares issued on or after 6 April 2012.
In s. 150A(10) definitions of "EIS relief" and "SEIS relief" inserted by FA 2012, s. 38 and Sch. 6, para. 20(5) with effect in relation to shares issued on or after 6 April 2012.
In s. 150A(10A), the words "the meaning given in section 989 of ITA 2007" substituted for "the same meaning as in the Taxes Act" by ITA 2007, s. 1027 and Sch. 1, para. 311(8), with effect from 6 April 2007.
S. 150A(10A) inserted by FA 1998, s. 74(1) and Sch. 13, para. 24(7), with effect in relation to events occurring on or after 6 April 1998.
In s. 150A(11), the words "or Part 5 of ITA 2007" and "or means shares that meet the requirements of section 173(2) of ITA 2007" inserted by ITA 2007, s. 1027 and Sch. 1, para. 311(9), with effect from 6 April 2007.
S. 150A(13) inserted by ITA 2007, s. 1027 and Sch. 1, para. 311(10),with effect from 6 April 2007.
S. 150A inserted by FA 1994, s. 137 and Sch. 15, para. 30.

Cross references – S. 104: share pooling – interpretative provisions.
S. 105: identification rules applying to shares disposed of on or before the day of acquisition.
S. 107: general identification rules in respect of securities.
S. 126: "reorganisation" embraces a reorganisation or reduction of share capital.
S. 127: equation of original shares and new holding on a reorganisation.
S. 135, s. 136: equation of original and new holdings on an exchange or company reconstruction involving the issue of securities.
Sch. 5B, para. 1(4)(b): interaction of double tax treaty relief with postponement of gains on disposal of EIS shares.
ICTA 1988, s. 289A: form of relief to income tax for investment in enterprise investment scheme.
ICTA 1988, s. 299: disposal of shares acquired under the enterprise investment scheme.
ICTA 1988, s. 304A: EIS company becoming wholly-owned subsidiary without losing income tax relief for its investors.
ICTA 1988, s. 312(1A)(a): "relevant period" is the period of five years ending five years after the later of the company's incorporation and the date which falls two years before the issue of the shares.

Other material – Tax Bulletin TB06/95-1: no exemption from capital gains tax on a merger of an EIS company with a BES company.

150B Enterprise investment scheme: reduction of EIS relief

150B(1) This section has effect where section 150A(2) applies on a disposal of shares, and before the disposal but on or after 29th November 1994–

(a) value is received in circumstances where EIS relief attributable to the shares is reduced by an amount under section 300(1A)(a) of the Taxes Act, or section 213(2)(a) of ITA 2007

(b) there is a repayment, redemption, repurchase or payment in circumstances where EIS relief attributable to the shares is reduced by an amount under section 303(1A)(a) of the Taxes Act or section 224(2)(a) of ITA 2007, or

(c) paragraphs (a) and (b) above apply.

150B(2) If section 150A(2) applies on the disposal but section 150A(3) does not, section 150A(2) shall apply only to so much of the gain as remains after deducting so much of it as is found by multiplying it by the fraction–

(a) whose numerator is equal to the amount by which the EIS relief attributable to the shares is reduced as mentioned in subsection (1) above, and

(b) whose denominator is equal to the amount of the EIS relief attributable to the shares.

150B(3) If section 150A(2) and (3) apply on the disposal, section 150A(2) shall apply only to so much of the gain as is found by–

(a) taking the part of the gain found under section 150A(3), and

(b) deducting from that part so much of it as is found by multiplying it by the fraction mentioned in subsection (2) above.

150B(4) Where the EIS relief attributable to the shares is reduced as mentioned in subsection (1) above by more than one amount, the numerator mentioned in subsection (2) above shall be taken to be equal to the aggregate of the amounts.

150B(5) The denominator mentioned in subsection (2) above shall be found without regard to any reduction mentioned in subsection (1) above.

150B(5A) In this section **"EIS relief"** means relief under Chapter 3 of Part 7 of the Taxes Act or Part 5 of ITA 2007.

150B(6) Subsections (11) to (13) of section 150A apply for the purposes of this section as they apply for the purposes of that section.

History – In s. 150B "EIS relief" substituted for "relief" in each place it occurred by FA 2012, s. 38 and Sch. 6, para. 21(2) with effect in relation to shares issued on or after 6 April 2012.
In s. 150B(1) the words "or section 213(2)(a) of ITA 2007" inserted by ITA 2007, s. 1027 and Sch. 1, para. 312(2)(a) and the words "the Taxes Act or section 224(2)(a) of ITA 2007" substituted for "that Act" by ITA 2007, s. 1027 and Sch. 1, para. 312(2)(b), both with effect from 6 April 2007.
S. 150B(5A) inserted by FA 2012, s. 38 and Sch. 6, para. 21(3) with effect in relation to shares issued on or after 6 April 2012.
In s. 150B(6), the words "Subsections (11) to (13)" substituted for "Subsections (11) and (12)" by ITA 2007, s. 1027 and Sch. 1, para. 312(3), with effect from 6 April 2007.
S. 150B inserted by FA 1995, s. 67 and Sch. 13, para. 3.

Cross references – ICTA 1988, s. 300(1A)(a): amount of the reduction is tax at the lower rate for the year of assessment for which the relief was given on the amount of the value received.
ICTA 1988, s. 303(1A)(a): amount of the reduction is tax at the lower rate for the year of assessment for which the relief was given on the amount of the value receivable.

150C Enterprise investment scheme: re-investment

150C Schedule 5B to this Act (which provides relief in respect of re-investment under the enterprise investment scheme) shall have effect.

History – S. 150C inserted by FA 1995, s. 67 and Sch. 13, para. 4(1) in relation to gains accruing and events occurring on or after 29 November 1994.

150D Enterprise investment scheme: application of taper relief

150D [Omitted by FA 2008, s. 8 and Sch. 2, para. 32.]

History – S. 150D omitted by FA 2008, s. 8 and Sch. 2, para. 32 with effect in relation to chargeable gains accruing or treated as accruing in the tax year 2008–09 or any subsequent tax year (FA 2008, Sch. 2, para. 56(3)).

150E Seed enterprise investment scheme

150E(1) For the purpose of determining the gain or loss on any disposal of shares by an individual where–

(a) an amount of SEIS relief is attributable to the shares, and

(b) apart from this subsection there would be a loss,

the consideration given by the individual for the shares is to be treated as reduced by the amount of the relief.

150E(2) Where–

(a) shares are disposed of by an individual after the end of the period referred to in section 257AC(2) of ITA 2007,

(b) an amount of SEIS relief is attributable to the shares, and

(c) (apart from this subsection) there would be a gain, the gain is not a chargeable gain.

150E(3) Despite section 16(2), subsection (2) does not apply to a disposal on which a loss accrues.

150E(4) Subsection (5) applies where–

(a) an individual's liability to income tax has been reduced (or treated by virtue of section 257H of ITA 2007 (spouses and civil partners) as reduced) for any tax year under section 257AB of that Act in respect of an issue of shares,

(b) the amount of the reduction ("R") is less than the amount ("T") which is equal to tax at the SEIS rate on the amount subscribed for the issue, and

(c) R is not within paragraph (b) solely by virtue of section 29(2) and (3) of ITA 2007.

150E(5) If there is a disposal of the shares on which there is a gain, subsection (2) applies only to so much of the gain as is found by multiplying it by the fraction–

$$\frac{R}{T}$$

150E(6) Any question as to–

(a) which of any shares that–

(i) are acquired by an individual at different times, and

(ii) are shares to which SEIS relief is attributable,

a disposal relates to, or

(b) whether a disposal relates to shares to which SEIS relief is attributable,

is to be determined for the purposes of capital gains tax as for the purposes of section 257HA of ITA 2007. Chapter 1 of this Part has effect subject to this subsection.

150E(7) Sections 104, 105 and 106A do not apply to shares to which SEIS relief is attributable.

150E(8) Where–

(a) an individual holds shares ("the existing holding") which form part of the ordinary share capital of a company,

(b) there is, by virtue of any such allotment for payment as is mentioned in section 126(2)(a), a reorganisation affecting the existing holding, and

(c) immediately following the reorganisation, SEIS relief is attributable to the existing holding or the allotted shares,

sections 127 to 130 do not apply in relation to the existing holding.

150E(9) Sections 135 and 136 do not apply in respect of shares to which SEIS relief is attributable.

150E(10) Subsection (9) does not have effect to disapply section 135 or 136 where–

(a) the new holding consists of new ordinary shares carrying no present or future preferential right to dividends or to a company's assets on its winding up and no present or future right to be redeemed,

(b) the new shares are issued after the end of the relevant period, and

(c) the condition in subsection (11) is satisfied.

150E(11) The condition is that at some time before the issue of the new shares–

(a) the company issuing them issued eligible shares, and

(b) a certificate in relation to those eligible shares was issued by the company for the purposes of section 257EB(1) of ITA 2007 and in accordance with sections 257EC and 257ED of that Act.

150E(12) All such adjustments of capital gains tax are to be made, whether by way of assessment or by way of discharge or repayment of tax, as may be required in consequence of the SEIS relief being given or withdrawn.

150E(13) Where shares to which SEIS relief is attributable are exchanged for other shares in circumstances such that section 257HB of ITA 2007 (acquisition of share capital by new company) applies–

(a) subsection (9) above does not have effect to disapply section 135, and

(b) sections 257HB(3)(b), 257HC(2)(a) and 257HD of ITA 2007 apply for the purposes of this section as they apply for the purposes of Part 5A of that Act.

150E(14) For the purposes of this section–

"eligible shares" means shares that meet the requirements of section 257CA(2);

"new holding" is to be construed in accordance with sections 126, 127, 135 and 136;

"ordinary share capital" has the meaning given in section 989 of ITA 2007;

"ordinary shares" in relation to a company, means shares forming part of its ordinary share capital;

"relevant period" means the period found by applying section 257AC(2) of ITA 2007 by reference to the company issuing the shares referred to in subsection (9) and by reference to those shares;

"the SEIS rate" has the meaning given by section 257AB(3) of ITA 2007;

"SEIS relief" means relief under Part 5A of ITA 2007 (seed enterprise investment scheme);

and that Part applies to determine whether SEIS relief is attributable to any shares and, if so, the amount of SEIS relief so attributable.

History – S. 150E inserted by FA 2012, s. 38 and Sch. 6, para. 3 in relation to shares issued on or after 6 April 2012.

150F Seed enterprise investment scheme: reduction of relief

150F(1) This section has effect where–

(a) section 150E(2) applies on a disposal of shares, and

(b) before the disposal, value is received in circumstances where SEIS relief attributable to the shares is reduced by an amount under section 257FE(2)(a) of ITA 2007.

150F(2) If section 150E(2) applies on the disposal but section 150E(5) does not, section 150E(2) applies only to so much of the gain as remains after deducting so much of it as is found by multiplying it by the fraction–

$$\frac{A}{B}$$

where–

A is the amount by which the SEIS relief attributable to the shares is reduced as mentioned in subsection (1), and

B is the amount of the relief attributable to the shares.

150F(3) If section 150E(2) and (5) apply on the disposal, section 150E(2) applies only to so much of the gain as is found by–

(a) taking the part of the gain found under section 150E(5), and

(b) deducting from that part so much of it as is found by multiplying it by the fraction mentioned in subsection (2) above.

150F(4) Where the SEIS relief attributable to the shares is reduced as mentioned in subsection (1) by more than one amount, "A" in subsection (2) is to be taken to be equal to the aggregate of the amounts.

150F(5) The amount which is "B" in subsection (2) is to be found without regard to any reduction mentioned in subsection (1).

150F(6) For the purposes of this section, Part 5A of ITA 2007 (seed enterprise investment scheme) applies to determine whether SEIS relief is attributable to any shares and, if so, the amount of SEIS relief so attributable.

History – S. 150F inserted by FA 2012, s. 38 and Sch. 6, para. 3 in relation to shares issued on or after 6 April 2012.

150G Seed enterprise investment scheme: re-investment

150G Schedule 5BB to this Act (which provides relief in respect of reinvestment under the seed enterprise investment scheme) has effect.

History – In s. 150G, the words "in the tax years 2012–13 and 2013–14", which appeared after the word "scheme", omitted by FA 2014, s. 55(2), with effect from 17 July 2014.
In s. 150G, the words "tax years 2012–13 and 2013–14" substituted for the words "tax year 2012–13" by FA 2013, s. 57(5) with effect from 17 July 2013.
S. 150G inserted by FA 2012, s. 38 and Sch. 6, para. 3 with effect from 17 July 2012.

151 Personal equity plans

151(1) The Treasury may make regulations providing that an individual who invests under a plan shall be entitled to relief from capital gains tax in respect of the investments.

151(2) The provisions of Chapter 3 of Part 6 of ITTOIA 2005 (income from individual investment plans), except section 694(1) to (2) and 694A(1), shall apply in relation to regulations made under subsection (1) as they apply to regulations made under section 694(1), but with the following modifications–

(a) any reference to income tax is to be read as a reference to capital gains tax,

(aa) section 694A(2) applies also for the purposes of subsection (1) of this section,

(ab) the reference in section 694A(3) to section 694A(1) is to be read as a reference to paragraph (aa) of this subsection,

(ac) the reference in section 694A(4)(b)(iii) to the individual's income from investments under the plan being exempt from income tax is to be read as a reference to the individual being entitled to relief from capital gains tax in respect of the investments,

(b) the reference in section 695A(1) to the case where regulations provide that income of a child from investments under a plan is exempt from income tax is to be read as a reference to the case where regulations provide that a child who invests under a plan is entitled to relief from capital gains tax in respect of the investments,

(c) the reference in section 695A(4) to that Chapter is to be read as a reference to this section, and

(d) that Chapter has effect as if sections 699(9) and 701(6) were omitted.

151(3) Regulations under this section may include provision securing that losses are disregarded for the purposes of capital gains tax where they accrue on the disposal of investments on or after 18th January 1988.

151(4) Regulations under this section may include provision which, for cases where a person subscribes to a plan by transferring or renouncing shares or rights to shares–

(a) modifies the effect of this Act in relation to their acquisition and their transfer or renunciation; and

(b) makes consequential modifications of the effect of this Act in relation to anything which (apart from the regulations) would have been regarded on or after their acquisition as an indistinguishable part of the same asset.

History – In s. 151(2), the words "section 694(1) to (2) and 694A(1)" substituted for the words "section 694(1) to (2)" and s. 151(2)(aa), (ab) and (ac) inserted by FA 2016, s. 27(2), with effect from 15 September 2016 (Royal Assent).
In s. 151(2), the words "section 694(1) to (2)" substituted for the words "section 694(1) and (2)" by FA 2011, s. 40(6)(a), with effect from 19 July 2011.
S. 151(2)(a), (b), (c) and (d) and the preceding words "but with the following modifications–" substituted for the words "but with the substitution for any reference to income tax of a reference to capital gains tax." by FA 2011, s. 40(6)(b), with effect from 19 July 2011.
S. 151(2) substituted for former s. 151(2) and (2A) by ITTOIA 2005, s. 882 and Sch. 1, para. 436 which, in accordance with ITTOIA 2005, s. 883, have effect, for income tax purposes, for tax year 2005–06 and subsequent tax years, and, for corporation tax purposes, for accounting periods ending after 5 April 2005.
In former s. 151(2), reference to ICTA 1988, s. 333(1A) substituted for s. 333(2) by FA 1998, s. 75(6).
In former s. 151(2) and (2A), references to personal equity plans, which followed references to ICTA 1988, s. 333, repealed by FA 1998,, s. 165 and Sch. 27, Pt. III(15).
Former s. 151(2A) inserted by FA 1995, s. 64(2).
S. 151(4) inserted by FA 1993, s. 85.

Derivations – S. 151(1), former (2): CGTA 1979, s. 149D(1), (2), as inserted by ICTA 1988, Sch. 29, para. 26.
S. 151(3): CGTA 1979, s. 149D(2A), as inserted by FA 1988, s. 116.

Cross references – FA 1998, s. 123(7): power of Treasury to issue regulations regarding relief from capital gains tax on investments may be exercised to make rules that are of retrospective action with effect from 17 March 1998 onwards.
ICTA 1988, s. 333: power of Board to make regulations providing exemption from income tax in respect of investments in a personal equity plan and (s. 333(2)–(5)) permitted nature of regulations.

Statutory instruments – SI 1998/1870 (as amended).
SI 2008/704: made partly under s. 151.
SI 2008/3025: made partly under s. 151.

Notes – S. 16: allowable losses.
S. 287: power of Board exercisable by statutory instrument, subject to negative resolution of the House of Commons.
S. 288: interpretation, including "the Taxes Act" as ICTA 1988 and reference to other sections being those of this Act.

151A Venture capital trusts: reliefs

151A(1) A gain or loss accruing to an individual on a qualifying disposal of any ordinary shares in a company which–

(a) was a venture capital trust at the time when he acquired the shares, and

(b) is still such a trust at the time of the disposal,

shall not be a chargeable gain or, as the case may be, an allowable loss.

151A(2) For the purposes of this section a disposal of shares is a qualifying disposal in so far as–

(a) it is made by an individual who has attained the age of eighteen years;

(b) the shares disposed of were not acquired in excess of the permitted maximum for any year of assessment; and

(c) that individual acquired those shares for bona fide commercial purposes and not as part of a scheme or arrangement the main purpose of which, or one of the main purposes of which, is the avoidance of tax.

151A(3) [Repealed by FA 2004, s. 326 and Sch. 42, Pt. 2(13) and ceases to have effect by FA 2004, s. 94 and Sch. 19, para. 4, but see History Notes below.]

151A(4) In determining for the purposes of this section whether a disposal by any person of shares in a venture capital trust relates to shares acquired in excess of the permitted maximum for any year of assessment, it shall be assumed (subject to subsection (5) below)–

(a) as between shares acquired by the same person on different days, that those acquired on an earlier day are disposed of by that person before those acquired on a later day; and

(b) as between shares acquired by the same person on the same day, that those acquired in excess of the permitted maximum are disposed of by that person before he disposes of any other shares acquired on that day.

151A(5) It shall be assumed for the purposes of subsection (1) above that a person who disposes of shares in a venture capital trust disposes of shares acquired at a time when it was not such a trust before he disposes of any other shares in that trust.

151A(6) References in this section to shares in a venture capital trust acquired in excess of the permitted maximum for any year of assessment shall be construed as references to shares not acquired within the limit in section 709(4) of ITTOIA 2005; and the question whether shares are acquired within that limit shall be determined as it is for the purposes of Chapter 5 of Part 6 of that Act.

151A(7) In this section and section 151B **"ordinary shares"**, in relation to a company, means any shares forming part of the company's ordinary share capital (within the meaning given in section 989 of ITA 2007).

History – S. 151A(3) (introducing TCGA 1992, Sch. 5C) ceases to have effect by virtue of FA 2004, s. 94 and Sch. 19, para. 4 and is repealed by FA 2004, s. 326 and Sch. 42, Pt. 2(13); which have effect, by FA 2004, Sch. 19, para. 7(1), in relation to shares issued on or

after 6 April 2004 that are shares by reference to which an individual is given relief under ICTA 1988, Sch. 15B, Pt. 1 (venture capital trust: relief on investment). However, by virtue of FA 2004, Sch. 19, para. 7(2), nothing in FA 2004 affects the continuing operation of TCGA 1992, Sch. 5C for the purposes of TCGA 1992, s. 151B(8)(b)(ii).
In s. 151A(6), words "as references to shares not acquired within the limit in section 709(4) of ITTOIA 2005; and the question whether shares are acquired within that limit shall be determined as it is for the purposes of Chapter 5 of Part 6 of that Act" substituted for "in accordance with the provisions of Part II of Schedule 15B to the Taxes Act; and the provisions of that Part of that Schedule shall apply (with subsections (4) and (5) above) for identifying the shares which are, in any case, to be treated as representing shares acquired in excess of the permitted maximum" by virtue of ITTOIA 2005, s. 882 and Sch. 1, para. 437 which, in accordance with ITTOIA 2005, s. 883, have effect, for income tax purposes, for tax year 2005–06 and subsequent tax years, and, for corporation tax purposes, for accounting periods ending after 5 April 2005.
In s. 151A(7), the words "the meaning given in section 989 of ITA 2007 " substituted for "the meaning of the Taxes Act" by ITA 2007, s. 1027 and Sch. 1, para. 314, with effect from 6 April 2007.
S. 151A inserted by FA 1995, s. 72(3).

Cross references – S. 105A: no election under this section may be made in respect of ordinary shares in a venture capital trust.
S. 257(1) (disposals otherwise than at arm's length to charities or bodies listed in IHTA 1984, Sch. 3): does not apply to disposals in relation to which s. 151A(1) has effect.
Sch. 5C, para. 1(4)(b): interaction of double tax treaty relief with postponement of gains on disposal of shares in a venture capital trust.
Sch. 5C, para. 3(1), (2): chargeable event where relevant shares (as there defined) are exchanged for shares which are not ordinary shares in a venture capital trust.
Sch. 5C, para. 4(2): identification rules for disposal of shares in venture capital trusts following postponement of a gain.
ICTA 1988, Sch. 15B, para. 8(6): former provision giving meaning of "permitted maximum" (rewritten into ITTOIA 2005, s. 709ff.).
ITTOIA 2005, s. 709–712: venture capital trust dividends.
SI 2004/2199: modified application of s. 151A and 151B for VCTs in liquidation and where there is a merger of VCTs.

151B Venture capital trusts: supplementary

151B(1) Sections 104, 105 and 106A shall not apply to any shares in a venture capital trust which are eligible for relief under section 151A(1).

151B(2) Subject to the following provisions of this section, where–

(a) an individual holds any ordinary shares in a venture capital trust,

(b) some of those shares fall within one of the paragraphs of subsection (3) below, and

(c) others of those shares fall within at least one other of those paragraphs,

then, if there is within the meaning of section 126 a reorganisation affecting those shares, section 127 shall apply separately in relation to the shares (if any) falling within each of the paragraphs of that subsection (so that shares of each kind are treated as a separate holding of original shares and identified with a separate new holding).

151B(3) The kinds of shares referred to in subsection (2) above are–

(a) any shares in a venture capital trust which are eligible for relief under section 151A(1) and by reference to which any person hasobtained or is entitled to claim relief under Chapter 2 of Part 6 of ITA 2007

(b) any shares in a venture capital trust which are eligible for relief under section 151A(1) but by reference to which no person has obtained, or is entitled to claim, any relief under that Chapter of that Part;

(c) any shares in a venture capital trust by reference to which any person has obtained, or is entitled to claim, any relief under that Chapter of that Part but which are not shares that are eligible for relief under section 151A(1); and

(d) any shares in a venture capital trust that do not fall within any of paragraphs (a) to (c) above.

151B(4) Where–

(a) an individual holds ordinary shares in a company (**"the existing holding"**),

(b) there is, by virtue of any such allotment for payment as is mentioned in section 126(2)(a), a reorganisation affecting the existing holding, and

(c) immediately following the reorganisation, the shares or the allotted holding are shares falling within any of paragraphs (a) to (c) of subsection (3) above,

sections 127 to 130 shall not apply in relation to the existing holding.

151B(5) Sections 135 and 136 shall not apply where–

(a) the exchanged holding consists of shares falling within paragraph (a) or (b) of subsection (3) above; and

(b) that for which the exchanged holding is or is treated as exchanged does not consist of ordinary shares in a venture capital trust.

151B(6) *Where–*

(a) the approval of any company as a venture capital trust is withdrawn, and

(b) the withdrawal of the approval is not one to which section 281(3) of ITA 2007 applies,

any person who at the time when the withdrawal takes effect is holding shares in that company which (apart from the withdrawal) would be eligible for relief under section 151A(1) shall be deemed for the purposes of this Act, at that time, to have disposed of and immediately re-acquired those shares for a consideration equal to their market value at that time.

151B(7) The disposal that is deemed to take place by virtue of subsection (6) above shall be deemed for the purposes of section 151A to take place while the company is still a venture capital trust; but, for the purpose of applying sections 104, 105 and 106A to the shares that are deemed to be re-acquired, it shall be assumed that the re-acquisition for which that subsection provides takes place immediately after the company ceases to be such a trust.

151B(8) For the purposes of this section–

(a) shares are eligible for relief under section 151A(1) at any time when they are held by an individual whose disposal of the shares at that time would (on the assumption, where it is not the case, that the individual attained the age of eighteen years before that time) be a disposal to which section 151A(1) would apply; and

(b) shares shall not, in relation to any time, be treated as shares by reference to which relief has been obtained under Chapter 2 of Part 6 of ITA 2007 if that time falls after–

(i) any relief given by reference to those shares has been reduced or withdrawn,

(ii) any chargeable event (within the meaning of Schedule 5C) has occurred in relation to those shares, or

(iii) the death of a person who held those shares immediately before his death; and

(c) a reference to the exchanged holding is, in relation to section 135 or 136, to the shares in the company referred to in that section as company A.

History – In s. 151B(1) the reference to s. 106A substituted for reference to s. 107 by FA 1998, s. 124(6), with effect in relation to any disposal on or after 6 April 1998.
In s. 151B(3)(a), the word "obtained" substituted for "been given" and the words "Chapter 2 of Part 6 of ITA 2007" substituted for the words "Part 1 of Schedule 15B to the Taxes Act" by ITA 2007, s. 1027 and Sch. 1, para. 315(2)(a), with effect from 6 April 2007.
In s. 151B(3)(b) and (c), the word "obtained" substituted for "been given" and the words "that Chapter of that Part" substituted for "that Part of that Schedule" by ITA 2007, s. 1027 and Sch. 1, para. 315(2)(b), with effect from 6 April 2007.
In s. 151(6)(b), the words "section 281(3) of ITA 2007" substituted for the words "section 842AA of the Taxes Act" by ITA 2007, s. 1027, Sch. 1, para. 315(3) with effect from 6 April 2007.
In s. 151B(7) the reference to s. 106A substituted for a reference to s. 107 by FA 1998, s. 124(6), with effect in relation to any disposal on or after 6 April 1998.
In s. 151B(8)(b), the word "obtained" substituted for "given" and the reference to ITA 2007, Pt. 6, Ch. 2 substituted for a reference to ICTA 1988, Sch. 15B, Part I, by ITA 2007, s. 1027 and Sch. 1, para. 315(4), with effect from 6 April 2007.
S. 151B(8)(c) substituted by FA 2002, s. 45 and Sch. 9, para. 5(9) with effect in relation to shares or debentures issued on or after 17 April 2002.
S. 151B inserted by FA 1995, s. 72(3).

Cross references – FA 1998, s. 124(8): identification rules for capital gains tax (but not corporation tax) where disposals occur between 17 March 1998 and 5 April 1998 (inclusive).
S. 104: all securities of same class acquired by same person in same capacity to be regarded as indistinguishable parts of a single asset.
S. 105: matching of disposals of securities of same class acquired by same person in same capacity with same-day acquisitions.
S. 107: matching of disposals of securities of same class acquired by same person in same capacity with acquisitions in the preceding ten days.
S. 126: "reorganisation" embraces a reorganisation or a reduction of share capital.
S. 127–130: equation of original and new holdings on a reorganisation; consideration given or received, part disposal of new holding and composite new holdings in relation to reorganisations.
S. 135, 136: equation of original and new holdings on an exchange or a company reconstruction involving the issue of securities.
Sch. 5C: postponement, on reinvestment, of chargeable gains on disposals of shares in venture capital trusts
Sch. 5C, para. 3(1)(c): actual or deemed exchanges of shares within s. 151B(3)(c) for shares which are not ordinary shares of a venture capital trust are, after making of a qualifying investment, chargeable events.
Sch. 5C, para. 3(6): references to disposals in connection with chargeable events following the making of a qualifying investment do not include deemed disposals under s. 151B(6).
Sch. 5C, para. 4(2): identification rules for disposal of shares in venture capital trusts following postponement of a gain.
ICTA 1988, s. 842AA(8): if approval given in expectation that conditions for approval would be fulfilled within specified times is withdrawn, approval is deemed never to have been given.
ICTA 1988, Sch. 15B, Pt. I: income tax relief for investment in venture capital trusts.
FA 2004, Sch. 19, para. 7(2): nothing in FA 2004 affects the continuing operation of TCGA 1992, Sch. 5C for the purposes of s. 151B(8)(b)(ii).
SI 2004/2199: modified application of s. 151A and 151B for VCTs in liquidation and where there is a merger of VCTs.

151BA CITR: identification of securities or shares on a disposal

151BA(1) This section applies for the purpose of identifying the securities or shares disposed of in any case where–

(a) an individual or company ("the investor") disposes of part of a holding of securities or shares ("the holding"), and

(b) the holding includes securities or shares to which CITR is attributable in respect of one or more years of assessment or accounting periods that have been held by the investor continuously from the time they were issued until the disposal.

151BA(2) Any disposal by the investor of securities or shares included in the holding which have been acquired by the investor on different days is treated as relating to those acquired on an earlier day rather than to those acquired on a later day.

151BA(3) If there is a disposal by the investor of securities or shares included in the holding which have been acquired by the investor on the same day, any of those securities or shares–

(a) to which CITR is attributable, and

(b) which have been held by the investor continuously from the time they were issued until the time of disposal,

are treated as disposed of after any other securities or shares included in the holding which were acquired by the investor on that day.

151BA(4) For the purposes of this section a holding of securities is any number of securities of a company which–

(a) carry the same rights,

(b) were issued under the same terms, and

(c) are held by the investor in the same capacity.

It does not matter for this purpose that the number of the securities grows or diminishes as securities carrying those rights and issued under those terms are acquired or disposed of.

151BA(5) For the purposes of this section a holding of shares is any number of shares in a company which–

(a) are of the same class, and

(b) are held by the investor in the same capacity.

It does not matter for this purpose that the number of the shares grows or diminishes as shares of that class are acquired or disposed of.

151BA(6) Chapter 1 of Part 4 (share pooling, etc) has effect subject to this section.

151BA(7) Sections 104 to 107 (which make provision for the identification of securities and shares on a disposal) do not apply to securities or shares to which CITR is attributable.

151BA(8) In a case to which section 127 (equation of original shares and new holding) applies, shares included in the new holding are treated for the purposes of subsections (2) and (3) as acquired when the original shares were acquired.

151BA(9) In subsection (8)–

(a) the reference to section 127 includes a reference to that section as it is applied by virtue of any enactment relating to chargeable gains, and

(b) **"original shares"** and **"new holding"** have the same meaning as in section 127, or (as the case may be) that section as applied by virtue of the enactment in question.

151BA(10) In this section and sections 151BB and 151BC–

(a) if the investor is an individual–

  (i) **"CITR"** has the meaning given by section 333 of ITA 2007,

  (ii) references to CITR being attributable to securities, shares or debentures are to be read in accordance with section 357 of that Act, and

  (iii) references to securities, shares or debentures having been held by the investor continuously are to be read in accordance with section 380 of that Act,

(b) if the investor is a company–

  (i) **"CITR"** means relief under Part 7 of CTA 2010,

  (ii) references to CITR being attributable to securities, shares or debentures are to be read in accordance with section 240 of that Act, and

  (iii) references to securities, shares or debentures having been held by the investor continuously are to be read in accordance with section 267 of that Act.

History – In s. 151BA(10)(b)(i), the words "Part 7 of CTA 2010" substituted for "Part 5 of Schedule 16 to the Finance Act 2002" by CTA 2010, s. 1177 and Sch. 1, para. 236(a), with effect for corporation tax purposes for accounting periods ending on or after 1 April 2010, and for income tax and capital gains tax purposes for the tax year 2010–11 and subsequent tax years.

In s. 151BA(10)(b)(ii), the words "attributable to securities, shares or debentures" substituted for "so attributable" by CTA 2010, s. 1177 and Sch. 1, para. 236(b)(i), with effect for corporation tax purposes for accounting periods ending on or after 1 April 2010, and for income tax and capital gains tax purposes for the tax year 2010–11 and subsequent tax years.

In s. 151BA(10)(b)(ii), the words "section 240 of that Act" substituted for "paragraph 26 of that Schedule" by CTA 2010, s. 1177 and Sch. 1, para. 236(b)(ii), with effect for corporation tax purposes for accounting periods ending on or after 1 April 2010, and for income tax and capital gains tax purposes for the tax year 2010–11 and subsequent tax years.

In s. 151BA(10)(b)(iii), the words "section 267 of that Act" substituted for "paragraph 49 of that Schedule" by CTA 2010, s. 1177 and Sch. 1, para. 236(c), with effect for corporation tax purposes for accounting periods ending on or after 1 April 2010, and for income tax and capital gains tax purposes for the tax year 2010–11 and subsequent tax years.

S. 151BA inserted by ITA 2007, s. 1027 and Sch. 1, para. 316, with effect from 6 April 2007.

151BB CITR: rights issues etc

151BB(1) If–

(a) an individual or company ("the investor") holds shares in the CDFI which are of the same class and held in the same capacity ("the existing holding"),

(b) there is a reorganisation affecting the existing holding as a result of an allotment which–

(i) falls within section 126(2)(a) (an allotment of shares or debentures in respect of and in proportion to an original holding), and

(ii) is not an allotment of corresponding bonus shares,

(c) immediately after the reorganisation, CITR is attributable to the shares included in the existing holding or the shares or debentures allotted in respect of those shares, in respect of one or more years of assessment or accounting periods, and

(d) if CITR is attributable to the shares included in the existing holding at that time, those shares have been held by the investor continuously from the time they were issued until the reorganisation,

sections 127 to 130 (treatment of share capital following a reorganisation) do not apply in relation to the existing holding.

151BB(2) Section 116(10) (reorganisations, conversions and reconstructions) does not apply in any case where the old asset consists of shares held (in the same capacity) by the investor–

(a) that have been held by the investor continuously from the time they were issued until the relevant transaction, and

(b) to which CITR is attributable immediately before that transaction.

In this subsection **"old asset"** and **"the relevant transaction"** have the meaning given by section 116.

151BB(3) For the purposes of subsection (1)–

"corresponding bonus shares" means bonus shares that–

(a) are issued in respect of shares included in the existing holding, and

(b) are in the same company, are of the same class, and carry the same rights as, those shares,

"reorganisation" has the meaning given in section 126.

151BB(4) The following provisions of this Act have effect subject to this section–

section 116 (reorganisations, conversions and reconstructions);

Chapter 2 of Part 4 (reorganisation of share capital, conversion of securities etc).

151BB(5) In this section **"the CDFI"** is to be read–

(a) if the investor is an individual, in accordance with section 334(2) of ITA 2007,

(b) if the investor is a company, in accordance with section 219(2) of CTA 2010.

History – In s. 151BB(5)(b), the words "section 219(2) of CTA 2010" substituted for "paragraph 1(2) of Schedule 16 to the Finance Act 2002" by CTA 2010, s. 1177 and Sch. 1, para. 237, with effect for corporation tax purposes for accounting periods ending on or after 1 April 2010, and for income tax and capital gains tax purposes for the tax year 2010–11 and subsequent tax years.
S. 151BB inserted by ITA 2007, s. 1027 and Sch. 1, para. 317, with effect from 6 April 2007.

151BC CITR: company reconstructions etc

151BC(1) If–

(a) an individual or company ("the investor") holds shares in or debentures of a company ("company A"),

(b) there is a reconstruction or amalgamation affecting that holding ("the existing holding"),

(c) immediately before the reconstruction or amalgamation, CITR is attributable to the shares or debentures included in the existing holding in respect of one or more years of assessment or accounting periods, and

(d) the shares or debentures included in the existing holding have been held by the investor continuously from the time they were issued until the reconstruction or amalgamation,

sections 135 and 136 (share exchanges and company reconstructions) do not apply in respect of the existing holding.

151BC(2) Subsection (1)(a) applies only if the shares or debentures are held by the investor in the same capacity.

151BC(3) For the purposes of subsection (1) a **"reconstruction or amalgamation"** means an issue by a company of shares in or debentures of that company in exchange for or in respect of shares in or debentures of company A.

151BC(4) The following provisions of this Act have effect subject to this section–

section 116 (reorganisations, conversions and reconstructions),

Chapter 2 of Part 4 (reorganisation of share capital, conversion of securities etc).

151BC(5) The investor is treated as disposing of any securities or shares which but for subsection (1) the investor–

(a) would be treated as exchanging for other securities or shares by virtue of section 136, or

(b) would be so treated but for section 137(1) (which restricts section 136 to genuine reconstructions).

History – S. 151BC inserted by ITA 2007, s. 1027 and Sch. 1, para. 318 with effect from 6 April 2007.

151C Strips: manipulation of price: associated payment giving rise to loss

151C(1) This section applies if–

(a) as a result of any scheme or arrangement which has an unallowable purpose, the circumstances are, or might have been, as mentioned in paragraph (a), (b) or (c) of section 449(2) of ITTOIA 2005,

(b) under the scheme or arrangement, a payment falls to be made otherwise than in respect of the acquisition or disposal of a strip, and

(c) as a result of that payment or the circumstances in which it is made, a loss accrues to any person.

151C(2) The loss shall not be an allowable loss.

151C(3) For the purposes of this section a scheme or arrangement has an unallowable purpose if the main benefit, or one of the main benefits that might have been expected to result from, or from any provision of, the scheme or arrangement (apart from section 449 of ITTOIA 2005 and this section) is–

(a) the obtaining of a tax advantage by any person, or

(b) the accrual to any person of an allowable loss.

151C(4) The reference in subsection (1)(b) to the acquisition or disposal of a strip shall be construed as if it were in Chapter 8 of Part 4 of ITTOIA 2005 (profits from deeply discounted securities) (see, in particular, sections 437 and 445 of that Act for the meaning of **"disposal"** and **"acquisition"** and section 444 of that Act for the meaning of "strip").

151C(5) In subsection (3)(a) **"tax advantage"** has the meaning given by section 1139 of CTA 2010.

151C(6) This section applies to losses accruing on or after 17th March 2004.

History – In s. 151C(5), the words "section 1139 of CTA 2010" substituted for "section 840ZA of the Taxes Act" by CTA 2010, s. 1177 and Sch. 1, para. 238, with effect for corporation tax purposes for accounting periods ending on or after 1 April 2010, and for income tax and capital gains tax purposes for the tax year 2010–11 and subsequent tax years.

In s. 151C(5), the words "section 840ZA" substituted for the words "section 709(1)" by ITA 2007, s. 1027, Sch. 1, para. 319, with effect from 6 April 2007.

S. 151C inserted by ITTOIA 2005, s. 882 and Sch. 1, para. 438 which, in accordance with ITTOIA 2005, s. 883, have effect, for income tax purposes, for tax year 2005–06 and subsequent tax years, and, for corporation tax purposes, for accounting periods ending after 5 April 2005.

151D Corporate strips: manipulation of price: associated payment giving rise to loss

151D(1) This section applies if–

(a) as a result of any scheme or arrangement which has an unallowable purpose, the circumstances are, or might have been, as mentioned in paragraph (a), (b) or (c) of section 452G(2) of ITTOIA 2005,

(b) under the scheme or arrangement, a payment falls to be made otherwise than in respect of the acquisition or disposal of a corporate strip, and

(c) as a result of that payment or the circumstances in which it is made, a loss accrues to any person.

151D(2) The loss shall not be an allowable loss.

151D(3) For the purposes of this section a scheme or arrangement has an unallowable purpose if the main benefit, or one of the main benefits, that might have been expected to result from, or from any provision of, the scheme or arrangement (apart from section 452G of ITTOIA 2005 and this section) is–

(a) the obtaining of a tax advantage by any person, or

(b) the accrual to any person of an allowable loss.

151D(4) The reference in subsection (1)(b) above to the acquisition or disposal of a corporate strip shall be construed as if it were in Chapter 8 of Part 4 of ITTOIA 2005 (profits from deeply discounted securities) (see, in particular, sections 437 and 452F of that Act for the meaning of "disposal" and section 452E of that Act for the meaning of "corporate strip").

151D(5) In subsection (3)(a) above **"tax advantage"** has the meaning given by section 1139 of CTA 2010.

151D(6) This section applies to losses accruing on or after 6th April 2005.

History – In s. 151D(5), the words "section 1139 of CTA 2010" substituted for "section 840ZA of the Taxes Act" by CTA 2010, s. 1177 and Sch. 1, para. 239, with effect for corporation tax purposes for accounting periods ending on or after 1 April 2010, and for income tax and capital gains tax purposes for the tax year 2010–11 and subsequent tax years.
In s. 151D(5), the words "section 840ZA" substituted for the words "section 709(1)" by ITA 2007, s. 1027, Sch. 1, para. 320, with effect from 6 April 2007.
S. 151D inserted by F(No. 2)A 2005, s. 39 and Sch. 7, para. 8, with effect from 20 July 2005 (Royal Assent).

151E Exchange gains and losses from loan relationships: regulations

151E(1) The Treasury may by regulations make provision for or in connection with bringing into account in prescribed circumstances for the purposes of this Act exchange gains or losses (as defined by section 475 of CTA 2009) to which section 328(1) of CTA 2009 does not apply because of section 328(3) of that Act or because of regulations under section 328(4) of that Act.

151E(1A) The regulations may make provision as to the way in which, including the currency by reference to which, the amounts to be brought into account are to be calculated.

151E(2) The regulations may–

(a) make different provision for different cases, and

(b) make provision subject to an election or to other prescribed conditions.

History – In s. 151E(1) the words "exchange gains or losses (as defined by section 475 of CTA 2009)" substituted for the word "amounts" and the words "of that Act or because of regulations under section 328(4) of that Act" substituted for the words "or (4) of that Act" by F(No. 2)A 2015, s. 32 and Sch. 7, para. 98(2), with effect in relation to accounting periods beginning on or after 1 January 2016 (subject to the provisions of F(No. 2)A 2015, Sch. 7 para. 106–129).
S. 151E(1A) inserted by F(No. 2)A 2015, s. 32 and Sch. 7, para. 98(3), with effect in relation to accounting periods beginning on or after 1 January 2016 (subject to the provisions of F(No. 2)A 2015, Sch. 7 para. 106–129).
S. 151E inserted by CTA 2009, s. 1322 and Sch. 1, para. 370, with effect for corporation tax purposes for accounting periods ending on or after 1 April 2009, and for income tax and capital gains tax purposes for the tax year 2009–10 and subsequent tax years.

Notes – S. 151E was to cease to have effect by virtue of CTA 2009, s. 1325 and Sch. 2, para. 71(1)(f) and (2) (as amended by SI 2009/2860, art. 6(7)(a)) and repealed by CTA 2009, s. 1326 and Sch. 3, Pt. 2 (as amended by SI 2009/2860, art. 6(8)) from a day to be appointed under CTA 2009, s. 1329(3) but those provisions were repealed before coming into effect.

151F Treatment of alternative finance arrangements

151F [Omitted by TIOPA 2010, s. 374 and Sch. 8, para. 201 and repealed by TIOPA 2010, s. 378 and Sch. 10, Pt. 7.]

History – S. 151F omitted by TIOPA 2010, s. 374 and Sch. 8, para. 201 and repealed by TIOPA 2010, s. 378 and Sch. 10, Pt. 7, with effect for corporation tax purposes for accounting periods ending on or after 1 April 2010, for income tax and capital gains tax purposes for the tax year 2010–11 and subsequent tax years, and for petroleum revenue tax purposes for chargeable periods beginning on or after 1 July 2010.

Notes – S. 151F rewritten as follows:
S. 151F(1): TIOPA 2010, Sch. 2, para. 44.
S. 151F(2): TIOPA 2010, Sch. 2, para. 44.
S. 151F(3): TIOPA 2010, Sch. 2, para. 44.

151G Regulations where non-qualifying shares conditions altered

151G(1) If the Treasury make regulations under section 533 of CTA 2009 (power to change conditions for non-qualifying shares) adding, varying or removing such a condition as is mentioned in subsection (1) of that section, they may also by regulations amend this Act so as to make provision for or in connection with taxation in the case of any asset or transaction that is or was mentioned in the condition.

151G(2) Regulations under this section may–

(a) make different provision for different cases, and

(b) make incidental, supplemental, consequential and transitional provisions and savings.

151G(3) Regulations made under subsection (2)(b) may, in particular, include provision amending any enactment or any instrument made under an enactment.

History – S. 151G inserted by CTA 2009, s. 1322 and Sch. 1, para. 370, with effect for corporation tax purposes for accounting periods ending on or after 1 April 2009, and for income tax and capital gains tax purposes for the tax year 2009–10 and subsequent tax years.

Chapter 4 – Alternative Finance Arrangements

History – Ch. 4 inserted by TIOPA 2010, s. 365 and Sch. 2, para. 28, with effect for corporation tax purposes for accounting periods ending on or after 1 April 2010, for income tax and capital gains tax purposes for the tax year 2010–11 and subsequent tax years, and for petroleum revenue tax purposes for chargeable periods beginning on or after 1 July 2010.

Transitional – Ch. 4 does not apply to purchase and resale arrangements entered into before 6 April 2005 or diminishing shared ownership arrangements entered into before the relevant date (TIOPA 2010, Sch. 9, para. 37(1)).
If deposit arrangements, profit share agency arrangements or investment bond arrangements were entered into before the "relevant date", the alternative finance provisions apply only if alternative finance return is payable under the arrangements on or after the relevant date and then–

(a) apply for the purposes of income tax in relation to payments of alternative finance return under the arrangements to a person other than a company on or after the relevant date (so far as relevant to the tax year 2010–11 and subsequent tax years), and

(b) if a company is a party to the arrangements, apply in relation to the company in respect of the arrangements with effect from the relevant date (so far as relevant to those tax years or, as the case may be, any accounting period ending on or after 1 April 2010) (TIOPA 2010, Sch. 9, para. 37(2)).

For the purposes of income tax and capital gains tax in relation to the disposal after 6 April 2007 of investment bond arrangements (whenever entered into), TCGA 1992, s. 151N, 151S(3) and (4) and 151T to 151W are treated as always having had effect. (TIOPA 2010, Sch. 9, para. 37(4)).

The "relevant date" means:

(a) in the case of deposit arrangements, 6 April 2005,

(b) in the case of diminishing shared ownership arrangements or profit share agency arrangements, for income tax purposes 6 April 2006, and

(c) in the case of investment bond arrangements, for corporation tax purposes 1 April 2007 and for income tax and capital gains tax purposes 6 April 2007. (TIOPA 2010, Sch. 9, para. 37(6)).

INTRODUCTION

151H Introduction

151H(1) This Chapter makes provision about the treatment of alternative finance arrangements with financial institutions and alternative finance return under such arrangements for the purposes of this Act (see sections 151T to 151Y).

151H(2) In this Chapter **"alternative finance arrangements"** means–

(a) purchase and resale arrangements,

(b) diminishing shared ownership arrangements,

(c) deposit arrangements,

(d) profit share agency arrangements, and

(e) investment bond arrangements.

151H(3) In this Chapter–

(a) **"purchase and resale arrangements"** means arrangements to which section 151J applies,

(b) **"diminishing shared ownership arrangements"** means arrangements to which section 151K applies,

(c) **"deposit arrangements"** means arrangements to which section 151L applies,

(d) **"profit share agency arrangements"** means arrangements to which section 151M applies, and

(e) **"investment bond arrangements"** means arrangements to which section 151N applies.

151H(4) For the meaning of **"alternative finance return"**, see sections 151P to 151S.

151H(5) For the meaning of **"financial institution"**, see section 151I.

151H(6) Also, see–

(a) section 366 of TIOPA 2010 (power to extend this Chapter and other provisions to other arrangements by order), and

(b) Schedule 61 to FA 2009 (alternative finance investment bonds) which makes further provision about the treatment of investment bond arrangements for the purposes of this Act.

History – S. 151H inserted by TIOPA 2010, s. 365 and Sch. 2, para. 28, with effect for corporation tax purposes for accounting periods ending on or after 1 April 2010, for income tax and capital gains tax purposes for the tax year 2010–11 and subsequent tax years, and for petroleum revenue tax purposes for chargeable periods beginning on or after 1 July 2010, subject to transitional provisions in TIOPA 2010, Sch. 9, para. 37.

151I Meaning of "financial institution"

151I(1) In this Chapter **"financial institution"** means–

(a) a bank, as defined by section 1120 of CTA 2010,

(b) a building society,

(c) a wholly-owned subsidiary–

(i) of a bank within paragraph (a), or

(ii) of a building society,

(d) a person authorised by a licence under Part 3 of the Consumer Credit Act 1974 to carry on a consumer credit business or consumer hire business within the meaning of that Act,

(e) a bond-issuer, within the meaning of section 151N, but only in relation to any bond assets which are rights under purchase and resale arrangements, diminishing shared ownership arrangements or profit share agency arrangements,

(f) a person authorised in a jurisdiction outside the United Kingdom–

(i) to receive deposits or other repayable funds from the public, and

(ii) to grant credits for its own account,

(g) an insurance company as defined in section 65 of the Finance Act 2012, or

(h) a person who is authorised in a jurisdiction outside the United Kingdom to carry on a business which consists of effecting or carrying out contracts of insurance or substantially similar business but not an insurance special purpose vehicle as defined in section 139(1) of the Finance Act 2012.

151I(2) For the purposes of subsection (1)(c) a company is a wholly-owned subsidiary of a bank or building society ("the parent") if it has no members except–

(a) the parent or persons acting on behalf of the parent, and

(b) the parent's wholly-owned subsidiaries or persons acting on behalf of the parent's wholly-owned subsidiaries.

History – In s. 151I(1)(g) the words "section 65 of the Finance Act 2012" substituted for the words "section 431(2) of ICTA" by FA 2012, s. 146 and Sch. 16, para. 76(a) in relation to accounting periods beginning on or after 1 January 2013 (FA 2012, s. 148) but subject to transitional provisions in FA 2012, Sch. 17. Where an accounting period would otherwise straddle 1 January 2013, it is deemed to end on 31 December 2012 (FA 2012, s. 149).

In s. 151I(1)(h) the words "section 139(1) of the Finance Act 2012" substituted for the words "section 431(2) of ICTA" by FA 2012, s. 146 and Sch. 16, para. 76(b) in relation to accounting periods beginning on or after 1 January 2013 (FA 2012, s. 148) but subject to transitional provisions in FA 2012, Sch. 17. Where an accounting period would otherwise straddle 1 January 2013, it is deemed to end on 31 December 2012 (FA 2012, s. 149).

S. 151I inserted by TIOPA 2010, s. 365 and Sch. 2, para. 29, with effect for corporation tax purposes for accounting periods ending on or after 1 April 2010, for income tax and capital gains tax purposes for the tax year 2010–11 and subsequent tax years, and for petroleum revenue tax purposes for chargeable periods beginning on or after 1 July 2010, subject to transitional provisions in TIOPA 2010, Sch. 9, para. 37.

Transitional – TIOPA 2010, Sch. 9, para. 40(2): modifications of s. 151I(1) in relation to arrangements entered into before 15 October 2009.

ARRANGEMENTS THAT ARE ALTERNATIVE FINANCE ARRANGEMENTS

151J Purchase and resale arrangements

151J(1) This section applies to arrangements if–

(a) they are entered into between two persons ("the first purchaser" and "the second purchaser"), one or both of whom are financial institutions, and

(b) under the arrangements–

(i) the first purchaser purchases an asset and sells it to the second purchaser,

(ii) the sale occurs immediately after the purchase or in the circumstances mentioned in subsection (2),

(iii) all or part of the second purchase price is not required to be paid until a date later than that of the sale,

(iv) the second purchase price exceeds the first purchase price, and

(v) the excess equates, in substance, to the return on an investment of money at interest.

151J(2) The circumstances are that–

(a) the first purchaser is a financial institution, and

(b) the asset referred to in subsection (1)(b)(i) was purchased by the first purchaser for the purpose of entering into arrangements within this section.

151J(3) In this section–

"the first purchase price" means the amount paid by the first purchaser in respect of the purchase, and

"the second purchase price" means the amount payable by the second purchaser in respect of the sale.

151J(4) This section is subject to section 151O (provision not at arm's length: exclusion of arrangements from this section and sections 151K to 151N).

History – S. 151J inserted by TIOPA 2010, s. 365 and Sch. 2, para. 30, with effect for corporation tax purposes for accounting periods ending on or after 1 April 2010, for income tax and capital gains tax purposes for the tax year 2010–11 and subsequent tax years, and for petroleum revenue tax purposes for chargeable periods beginning on or after 1 July 2010, subject to transitional provisions in TIOPA 2010, Sch. 9, para. 37.

151K Diminishing shared ownership arrangements

151K(1) This section applies to arrangements if under them–

(a) a financial institution ("the first owner") acquires a beneficial interest in an asset,

(b) another person ("the eventual owner") also acquires a beneficial interest in it,

(c) the eventual owner is to make payments to the first owner amounting in aggregate to the consideration paid for the acquisition of the first owner's beneficial interest (but subject to any adjustment required for such a reduction as is mentioned in subsection (5)),

(d) the eventual owner is to acquire the first owner's beneficial interest (whether or not in stages) as a result of those payments,

(e) the eventual owner is to make other payments to the first owner (whether under a lease forming part of the arrangements or otherwise),

(f) the eventual owner has the exclusive right to occupy or otherwise to use the asset, and

(g) the eventual owner is exclusively entitled to any income, profit or gain arising from or attributable to the asset (including, in particular, an increase in its value).

151K(2) For the purposes of subsection (1)(a) it does not matter if–

(a) the first owner acquires its beneficial interest from the eventual owner,

(b) the eventual owner, or another person who is not the first owner, also has a beneficial interest in the asset, or

(c) the first owner also has a legal interest in it.

151K(3) Subsection (1)(f) does not prevent the eventual owner from granting an interest or right in relation to the asset if the conditions in subsection (4) are met.

151K(4) The conditions are that–

(a) the grant is not to–

(i) the first owner,

(ii) a person controlled by the first owner, or

(iii) a person controlled by a person who also controls the first owner, and

(b) the grant is not required by the first owner or arrangements to which the first owner is a party.

151K(5) Subsection (1)(g) does not prevent the first owner from–

(a) having responsibility for any reduction in the asset's value, or

(b) having a share in a loss arising out of any such reduction.

151K(6) Section 1124 of CTA 2010 (meaning of "control") applies for the purposes of this section.

151K(7) This section is subject to section 151O (provision not at arm's length: exclusion of arrangements from section 151J, this section and sections 151L to 151N).

History – S. 151K inserted by TIOPA 2010, s. 365 and Sch. 2, para. 31, with effect for corporation tax purposes for accounting periods ending on or after 1 April 2010, for income tax and capital gains tax purposes for the tax year 2010–11 and subsequent tax years, and for petroleum revenue tax purposes for chargeable periods beginning on or after 1 July 2010, subject to transitional provisions in TIOPA 2010, Sch. 9, para. 37.

151L Deposit arrangements

151L(1) This section applies to arrangements if under them–

(a) a person ("the depositor") deposits money with a financial institution,

(b) the money, together with money deposited with the institution by other persons, is used by it with a view to producing a profit,

(c) from time to time the institution makes or credits a payment to the depositor out of profit resulting from the use of the money,

(d) the payment is in proportion to the amount deposited by the depositor, and

(e) the payments so made or credited by the institution equate, in substance, to the return on an investment of money at interest.

151L(2) This section is subject to section 151O (provision not at arm's length: exclusion of arrangements from sections 151J, 151K, this section and sections 151M and 151N).

History – S. 151L inserted by TIOPA 2010, s. 365 and Sch. 2, para. 32, with effect for corporation tax purposes for accounting periods ending on or after 1 April 2010, for income tax and capital gains tax purposes for the tax year 2010–11 and subsequent tax years, and for petroleum revenue tax purposes for chargeable periods beginning on or after 1 July 2010, subject to transitional provisions in TIOPA 2010, Sch. 9, para. 37.

151M Profit share agency arrangements

151M(1) This section applies to arrangements if under them–

(a) a person ("the principal") appoints an agent,

(b) one or both of the principal and agent is a financial institution,

(c) the agent uses money provided by the principal with a view to producing a profit,

(d) the principal is entitled, to a specified extent, to profits resulting from the use of the money,

(e) the agent is entitled to any additional profits resulting from its use (and may also be entitled to a fee paid by the principal), and

(f) payments made because of the principal's entitlement to profits equate, in substance, to the return on an investment of money at interest.

151M(2) This section is subject to section 151O (provision not at arm's length: exclusion of arrangements from sections 151J to 151L, this section and section 151N).

History – S. 151M inserted by TIOPA 2010, s. 365 and Sch. 2, para. 33, with effect for corporation tax purposes for accounting periods ending on or after 1 April 2010, for income tax and capital gains tax purposes for the tax year 2010–11 and subsequent tax years, and for petroleum revenue tax purposes for chargeable periods beginning on or after 1 July 2010, subject to transitional provisions in TIOPA 2010, Sch. 9, para. 37.

Transitional – TIOPA 2010, Sch. 9, para. 40(3): modifications of s. 151I(1) in relation to arrangements entered into before 15 October 2009.

151N Investment bond arrangements

151N(1) This section applies to arrangements if–

(a) they provide for one person ("the bond-holder") to pay a sum of money ("the capital") to another ("the bond-issuer"),

(b) they identify assets, or a class of assets, which the bond-issuer will acquire for the purpose of generating income or gains directly or indirectly ("the bond assets"),

(c) they specify a period at the end of which they cease to have effect ("the bond term"),

(d) the bond-issuer undertakes under the arrangements –

(i) to dispose at the end of the bond term of any bond assets which are still in the bond-issuer's possession,

(ii) to make a repayment of the capital ("the redemption payment") to the bond-holder during or at the end of the bond-term (whether or not in instalments), and

(iii) to pay to the bond-holder other payments on one or more occasions during or at the end of the bond term ("additional payments"),

(e) the amount of the additional payments does not exceed an amount which would be a reasonable commercial return on a loan of the capital,

(f) under the arrangements the bond-issuer undertakes to arrange for the management of the bond assets with a view to generating income sufficient to pay the redemption payment and additional payments,

(g) the bond-holder is able to transfer the rights under the arrangements to another person (who becomes the bond-holder because of the transfer),

(h) the arrangements are a listed security on a recognised stock exchange, and

(i) the arrangements are wholly or partly treated in accordance with international accounting standards as a financial liability of the bond-issuer, or would be if the bond-issuer applied those standards.

151N(2) For the purposes of subsection (1)–

(a) the bond-issuer may acquire bond assets before or after the arrangements take effect,

(b) the bond assets may be property of any kind, including rights in relation to property owned by someone other than the bond-issuer,

(c) the identification of the bond assets mentioned in subsection (1)(b) and the undertakings mentioned in subsection (1)(d) and (f) may (but need not) be described as, or accompanied by a document described as, a declaration of trust,

(d) a reference to the management of assets includes a reference to disposal,

(e) the bond-holder may (but need not) be entitled under the arrangements to terminate them, or participate in terminating them, before the end of the bond term,

(f) the amount of the additional payments may be–

(i) fixed at the beginning of the bond term,

(ii) determined wholly or partly by reference to the value of or income generated by the bond assets, or

(iii) determined in some other way,

(g) if the amount of the additional payments is not fixed at the beginning of the bond term, the reference in subsection (1)(e) to the amount of the additional payments is a reference to the maximum amount of the additional payments,

(h) the amount of the redemption payment may (but need not) be subject to reduction in the event of a fall in the value of the bond assets or in the rate of income generated by them, and

(i) entitlement to the redemption payment may (but need not) be capable of being satisfied (whether or not at the option of the bond-issuer or the bond-holder) by the issue or transfer of shares or other securities.

151N(3) This section is subject to section 151O (provision not at arm's length: exclusion of arrangements from sections 151J to 151M and this section).

History – S. 151N inserted by TIOPA 2010, s. 365 and Sch. 2, para. 34, with effect for corporation tax purposes for accounting periods ending on or after 1 April 2010, for income tax and capital gains tax purposes for the tax year 2010–11 and subsequent tax years, and for petroleum revenue tax purposes for chargeable periods beginning on or after 1 July 2010, but subject to TIOPA 2010, Sch. 9, para. 37(4).

Cross references – TIOPA 2010, Sch. 9, para. 37(4): disapplication of transitional provisions in para. 37(2).

151O Provision not at arm's length: exclusion of arrangements from sections 151J to 151N

151O(1) Arrangements to which this section applies are not–

(a) purchase and resale arrangements,

(b) diminishing shared ownership arrangements,

(c) deposit arrangements,

(d) profit share agency arrangements, or

(e) investment bond arrangements.

151O(2) This section applies to arrangements if –

(a) apart from this section they would be alternative finance arrangements,

(b) subsection (3) or (5) of section 147 of TIOPA 2010 (tax calculations to be based on arm's length, not actual, provision) requires the profits and losses of a person who is a party to the arrangements to be calculated for tax purposes as if the arm's length provision (within the meaning of that section) had been made or imposed rather than in accordance with the arrangements,

(c) any person who is an affected person for the purposes of Part 4 of that Act ("the affected person") is entitled to–

(i) relevant return in relation to the arrangements, or

(ii) an amount representing relevant return in relation to them, and

(d) the affected person is not subject–

(i) to income tax or corporation tax, or

(ii) to any corresponding tax under the law of a territory outside the United Kingdom,

on the relevant return or the amount representing it.

151O(3) In this section **"relevant return"**, in relation to arrangements, means any amount which would be alternative finance return if the arrangements were alternative finance arrangements.

History – S. 151O inserted by TIOPA 2010, s. 365 and Sch. 2, para. 35, with effect for corporation tax purposes for accounting periods ending on or after 1 April 2010, for income tax and capital gains tax purposes for the tax year 2010–11 and subsequent tax years, and for petroleum revenue tax purposes for chargeable periods beginning on or after 1 July 2010, subject to transitional provisions in TIOPA 2010, Sch. 9, para. 37.

MEANING OF "ALTERNATIVE FINANCE RETURN"

151P Purchase and resale arrangements

151P(1) In the case of purchase and resale arrangements, so much of the second purchase price as is specified under the following provisions of this section is alternative finance return for the purposes of this Chapter.

151P(2) If under the arrangements the whole of the second purchase price is paid on one day, the alternative finance return equals the amount by which the second purchase price exceeds the first purchase price.

151P(3) If under the arrangements the second purchase price is paid by instalments, the alternative finance return in each instalment equals the appropriate amount.

151P(4) The appropriate amount is an amount equal to the interest which would have been included in the instalment on the assumptions in subsection (5).

151P(5) The assumptions are that–

(a) interest is payable on a loan by the first purchaser to the second purchaser of an amount equal to the first purchase price,

(b) the total interest payable on the loan is equal to the amount by which the second purchase price exceeds the first purchase price,

(c) the instalment is a part repayment of the principal of the loan with interest, and

(d) the loan is made on arm's length terms and accounted for under generally accepted accounting practice.

151P(6) In this section expressions used in section 151J have the same meaning as in that section.

History – S. 151P inserted by TIOPA 2010, s. 365 and Sch. 2, para. 36, with effect for corporation tax purposes for accounting periods ending on or after 1 April 2010, for income tax and capital gains tax purposes for the tax year 2010–11 and subsequent tax years, and for petroleum revenue tax purposes for chargeable periods beginning on or after 1 July 2010, subject to transitional provisions in TIOPA 2010, Sch. 9, para. 37.

151Q Purchase and resale arrangements where return in foreign currency

151Q(1) If, in the case of purchase and resale arrangements, alternative finance return is paid in a currency other than sterling–

(a) by or to a person other than a company, and

(b) otherwise than for the purposes of a trade, profession or vocation or a property business,

subsections (2) and (3) apply as respects that person.

151Q(2) The amount of the excess referred to in section 151P(2) and (5)(b) and the appropriate amount for the purposes of section 151P(3) and (4) are to be calculated in that other currency.

151Q(3) The amount of each payment of alternative finance return is to be translated into sterling at a spot rate of exchange for the day on which the payment is made.

History – S. 151Q inserted by TIOPA 2010, s. 365 and Sch. 2, para. 37, with effect for corporation tax purposes for accounting periods ending on or after 1 April 2010, for income tax and capital gains tax purposes for the tax year 2010–11 and subsequent tax years, and for petroleum revenue tax purposes for chargeable periods beginning on or after 1 July 2010, subject to transitional provisions in TIOPA 2010, Sch. 9, para. 37.

151R Diminishing shared ownership arrangements

151R(1) In the case of diminishing shared ownership arrangements, payments by the eventual owner under the arrangements are alternative finance return for the purposes of this Chapter, except so far as subsection (2) or (3) applies to them.

151R(2) This subsection applies to the payments so far as they amount to payments of the kind described in section 151K(1)(c) (payments to be made by the eventual owner to the institution, amounting to the consideration paid for the acquisition of the institution's beneficial interest).

151R(3) This subsection applies to the payments so far as they amount to payments in respect of any arrangement fee or legal or other expenses which the eventual owner is required under the arrangements to pay.

151R(4) In this section **"the eventual owner"** has the same meaning as in section 151K.

History – S. 151R inserted by TIOPA 2010, s. 365 and Sch. 2, para. 38, with effect for corporation tax purposes for accounting periods ending on or after 1 April 2010, for income tax and capital gains tax purposes for the tax year 2010–11 and subsequent tax years, and for petroleum revenue tax purposes for chargeable periods beginning on or after 1 July 2010, subject to transitional provisions in TIOPA 2010, Sch. 9, para. 37.

151S Other arrangements

151S(1) In the case of deposit arrangements, amounts paid or credited as mentioned in section 151L(1)(c) by a financial institution under the arrangements (payments to depositor out of profits resulting from use of money) are alternative finance return for the purposes of this Chapter.

151S(2) In the case of profit share agency arrangements, amounts paid or credited by a financial institution in accordance with such an entitlement as is mentioned in section 151M(1)(d) (principal's entitlement to profits under the arrangements) are alternative finance return for the purposes of this Chapter.

151S(3) In the case of investment bond arrangements, the additional payments under the arrangements are alternative finance return for the purposes of this Chapter.

151S(4) In this section **"additional payments"** has the same meaning as in section 151N (see subsection (1)(d)(iii) of that section).

History – S. 151S inserted by TIOPA 2010, s. 365 and Sch. 2, para. 39, with effect for corporation tax purposes for accounting periods ending on or after 1 April 2010, for income tax and capital gains tax purposes for the tax year 2010–11 and subsequent tax years, and for petroleum revenue tax purposes for chargeable periods beginning on or after 1 July 2010, but subject to TIOPA 2010, Sch. 9, para. 37(4).

Cross references – TIOPA 2010, Sch. 9, para. 37(4): disapplication of transitional provisions in para. 37(2) in so far as s. 151S(3) and (4).

SPECIAL RULES FOR INVESTMENT BOND ARRANGEMENTS

151T Investment bond arrangements are qualifying corporate bonds

151T(1) For the purposes of section 117, investment bond arrangements are a corporate bond, issued on the date on which the arrangements are entered into, if each of conditions A to D is met.

151T(2) Condition A is that the capital is expressed in sterling.

151T(3) Condition B is that the arrangements do not include provision for the redemption payment to be in a currency other than sterling.

151T(4) Condition C is that entitlement to the redemption payment is not capable of conversion (directly or indirectly) into an entitlement to the issue of securities apart from other arrangements to which section 151N applies.

151T(5) Condition D is that the additional payments are not determined wholly or partly by reference to the value of the bond assets.

151T(6) Section 117(2) applies for the purposes of this section as it applies for the purposes of section 117(1).

151T(7) Expressions used in this section have the same meaning as in section 151N.

History – S. 151T(7) inserted by SI 2010/2901, art. 2 (effective from 1 January 2011 but with deemed effect from 1 April 2010). S. 151T(7) is deemed to have come into force for corporation tax purposes for accounting periods ending on or after 1 April 2010, and for income tax and capital gains tax purposes for the tax year 2010–11 and subsequent tax years.
S. 151T inserted by TIOPA 2010, s. 365 and Sch. 2, para. 40, with effect for corporation tax purposes for accounting periods ending on or after 1 April 2010, for income tax and capital gains tax purposes for the tax year 2010–11 and subsequent tax years, and for petroleum revenue tax purposes for chargeable periods beginning on or after 1 July 2010, but subject to TIOPA 2010, Sch. 9, para. 37(4).

Cross references – TIOPA 2010, Sch. 9, para. 37(4): disapplication of transitional provisions in para. 37(2).

151U Treatment of bond-holder and bond-issuer

151U(1) This section applies for the purposes of this Act and any other enactment about capital gains tax and irrespective of the position for other purposes.

151U(2) The bond-holder under investment bond arrangements is not treated as having a legal or beneficial interest in the bond assets.

151U(3) The bond-issuer under such arrangements is not treated as a trustee of the bond assets.

151U(4) Gains accruing to the bond-issuer in connection with the bond assets are gains of the bond-issuer and not of the bond-holder (and do not arise to the bond-issuer in a fiduciary or representative capacity).

151U(5) Payments made by the bond-issuer by way of redemption payment or additional payment are not made in a fiduciary or representative capacity.

151U(6) The bond-holder is not entitled to relief for capital expenditure in connection with the bond assets.

151U(7) Expressions used in this section have the same meaning as in section 151N.

History – S. 151U inserted by TIOPA 2010, s. 365 and Sch. 2, para. 41, with effect for corporation tax purposes for accounting periods ending on or after 1 April 2010, for income tax and capital gains tax purposes for the tax year 2010–11 and subsequent tax years, and for petroleum revenue tax purposes for chargeable periods beginning on or after 1 July 2010, but subject to TIOPA 2010, Sch. 9, para. 37(4).

Cross references – TIOPA 2010, Sch. 9, para. 37(4): disapplication of transitional provisions in para. 37(2).

151V Treatment as securities

151V(1) Investment bond arrangements are securities for the purposes of this Act and any other enactment about capital gains tax.

151V(2) For those purposes–

(a) a reference in an enactment to redemption is to be taken as a reference to making the redemption payment, and

(b) a reference in an enactment to interest is to be taken as a reference to alternative finance return.

151V(3) In subsection (2) **"the redemption payment"** has the same meaning as in section 151N (see subsection (1)(d)(ii) of that section).

History – S. 151V inserted by TIOPA 2010, s. 365 and Sch. 2, para. 42, with effect for corporation tax purposes for accounting periods ending on or after 1 April 2010, for income tax and capital gains tax purposes for the tax year 2010–11 and subsequent tax years, and for petroleum revenue tax purposes for chargeable periods beginning on or after 1 July 2010, but subject to TIOPA 2010, Sch. 9, para. 37(4).

Cross references – TIOPA 2010, Sch. 9, para. 37(4): disapplication of transitional provisions in para. 37(2).

151W Investment bond arrangements not unit trust scheme or offshore fund

151W Investment bond arrangements are not–

(a) a unit trust scheme for the purposes of this Act, or

(b) an offshore fund for the purposes of section 354 of TIOPA 2010 so far as relating to capital gains tax.

History – S. 151W inserted by TIOPA 2010, s. 365 and Sch. 2, para. 43, with effect for corporation tax purposes for accounting periods ending on or after 1 April 2010, for income tax and capital gains tax purposes for the tax year 2010–11 and subsequent tax years, and for petroleum revenue tax purposes for chargeable periods beginning on or after 1 July 2010, but subject to TIOPA 2010, Sch. 9, para. 37(4).

Cross references – TIOPA 2010, Sch. 9, para. 37(4): disapplication of transitional provisions in para. 37(2).

Transitional – TIOPA 2010, Sch. 9, para. 38: references to TIOPA 2010, s. 354 in s. 151W(b) are to be read as references to ICTA 1988, Ch. 5, Pt. 17.

OTHER RULES

151X Exclusion of some alternative finance return from sale consideration

151X(1) If under purchase and resale arrangements an asset is sold by one party to the arrangements to the other party, the alternative finance return is excluded in determining the consideration for the sale and purchase of the asset for the purposes of this Act so far as it applies for capital gains tax (apart from section 151J).

151X(2) If under diminishing shared ownership arrangements an asset is sold by one party to the arrangements to the other party, the alternative finance return is excluded in determining the consideration for the sale and purchase of the asset for the purposes of this Act so far as it applies for capital gains tax (apart from section 151K).

151X(3) If under investment bond arrangements an asset is sold by one party to the arrangements to the other party, the alternative finance return is excluded in determining the consideration for the sale and purchase of the asset for the purposes of this Act so far as it applies for capital gains tax (apart from section 151N).

151X(4) Subsections (1) to (3) do not affect the operation of any provision of this Act or the Tax Acts that provides that the consideration for a sale or purchase is taken for any purpose to be an amount other than the actual consideration.

History – S. 151X inserted by TIOPA 2010, s. 365 and Sch. 2, para. 44, with effect for corporation tax purposes for accounting periods ending on or after 1 April 2010, for income tax and capital gains tax purposes for the tax year 2010–11 and subsequent tax years, and for petroleum revenue tax purposes for chargeable periods beginning on or after 1 July 2010, subject to transitional provisions in TIOPA 2010, Sch. 9, para. 37.

151Y Diminishing shared ownership arrangements not partnerships

151Y Diminishing shared ownership arrangements are not treated as a partnership for capital gains tax purposes.

History – S. 151Y inserted by TIOPA 2010, s. 365 and Sch. 2, para. 45, with effect for corporation tax purposes for accounting periods ending on or after 1 April 2010, for income tax and capital gains tax purposes for the tax year 2010–11 and subsequent tax years, and for petroleum revenue tax purposes for chargeable periods beginning on or after 1 July 2010, subject to transitional provisions in TIOPA 2010, Sch. 9, para. 37.

PART V – TRANSFER OF BUSINESS ASSETS, ENTREPRENEURS' RELIEF AND INVESTORS' RELIEF

History – In the heading, the words ", ENTREPRENEURS' RELIEF AND INVESTORS' RELIEF" inserted by FA 2016, s. 87 and Sch. 14, para. 1(1), with effect from 15 September 2016 (Royal Assent).

Chapter I – Transfer of Business Assets: General Provisions

History – In the heading, the words "Transfer of Business Assets:" inserted by FA 2016, s. 87 and Sch. 14, para. 1(2), with effect from 15 September 2016 (Royal Assent).

REPLACEMENT OF BUSINESS ASSETS

152 Roll-over relief

152(1) If the consideration which a person carrying on a trade obtains for the disposal of, or of his interest in, assets (**"the old assets"**) used, and used only, for the purposes of the trade throughout the period of ownership is applied by him in acquiring other assets, or an interest in other assets (**"the new**

assets") which on the acquisition are taken into use, and used only, for the purposes of the trade, and the old assets and new assets are within the classes of assets listed in section 155, then the person carrying on the trade shall, on making a claim as respects the consideration which has been so applied, be treated for the purposes of this Act–

(a) as if the consideration for the disposal of, or of the interest in, the old assets were (if otherwise of a greater amount or value) of such amount as would secure that on the disposal neither a gain nor a loss accrues to him, and

(b) as if the amount or value of the consideration for the acquisition of, or of the interest in, the new assets were reduced by the excess of the amount or value of the actual consideration for the disposal of, or of the interest in, the old assets over the amount of the consideration which he is treated as receiving under paragraph (a) above,

but neither paragraph (a) nor paragraph (b) above shall affect the treatment for the purposes of this Act of the other party to the transaction involving the old assets, or of the other party to the transaction involving the new assets.

152(2) Where subsection (1)(a) above applies to exclude a gain which, in consequence of Schedule 2, is not all chargeable gain, the amount of the reduction to be made under subsection (1)(b) above shall be the amount of the chargeable gain, and not the whole amount of the gain.

152(3) Subject to subsection (4) below, this section shall only apply if the acquisition of, or of the interest in, the new assets takes place, or an unconditional contract for the acquisition is entered into, in the period beginning 12 months before and ending 3 years after the disposal of, or of the interest in, the old assets, or at such earlier or later time as the Board may by notice allow.

152(4) Where an unconditional contract for the acquisition is so entered into, this section may be applied on a provisional basis without waiting to ascertain whether the new assets, or the interest in the new assets, is acquired in pursuance of the contract, and, when that fact is ascertained, all necessary adjustments shall be made by making or amending assessments or by repayment or discharge of tax, and shall be so made notwithstanding any limitation on the time within which assessments or amendments may be made.

152(5) This section shall not apply unless the acquisition of, or of the interest in, the new assets was made for the purpose of their use in the trade, and not wholly or partly for the purpose of realising a gain from the disposal of, or of the interest in, the new assets.

152(6) If, over the period of ownership or any substantial part of the period of ownership, part of a building or structure is, and part is not, used for the purposes of a trade, this section shall apply as if the part so used, with any land occupied for purposes ancillary to the occupation and use of that part of the building or structure, were a separate asset, and subject to any necessary apportionments of consideration for an acquisition or disposal of, or of an interest in, the building or structure and other land.

152(7) If the old assets were not used for the purposes of the trade throughout the period of ownership this section shall apply as if a part of the asset representing its use for the purposes of the trade having regard to the time and extent to which it was, and was not, used for those purposes, were a separate asset which had been wholly used for the purposes of the trade, and this subsection shall apply in relation to that part subject to any necessary apportionment of consideration for an acquisition or disposal of, or of the interest in, the asset.

152(8) This section shall apply in relation to a person who, either successively or at the same time, carries on 2 or more trades as if both or all of them were a single trade.

152(9) In this section **"period of ownership"** does not include any period before 31st March 1982.

152(10) The provisions of this Act fixing the amount of the consideration deemed to be given for the acquisition or disposal of assets shall be applied before this section is applied.

152(11) Without prejudice to section 52(4), where consideration is given for the acquisition or disposal of assets some or part of which are assets in relation to which a claim under this section applies, and some or part of which are not, the consideration shall be apportioned in such manner as is just and reasonable.

History – In s. 152(4) the words "or amending" and "or amendments" added by FA 1996, s. 141(1) with effect as respects the year 1996–1997 and subsequent years of assessment and, for corporation tax purposes, as respects accounting periods ending on or after 1 July 1999, the day appointed for corporation tax self-assessment under FA 1994, s. 199 by virtue of SI 1998/3173 (C. 78).

Derivations – S. 152(1), (2): CGTA 1979, s. 115(1), (2).
S. 152(3), (4) (as originally enacted): CGTA 1979, s. 115(3).
S. 152(5)–(8): CGTA 1979, s. 115(4)–(7).
S. 152(9): CGTA 1979, s. 115(7A), as inserted by FA 1988, s. 96(9) and Sch. 8, para. 9.
S. 152(10), (11): CGTA 1979, s. 115(8), (9).

Cross references – S. 10A(3): temporary non-residents.
S. 52(4): necessary apportionments for the purposes of computing any gain as determined by the inspector or, on appeal, the commissioners.
S. 80(6): disapplication where trustees dispose of old assets before becoming not resident and not ordinarily resident and acquire new assets after emigration, unless the new assets are within the charge to tax.
S. 84: disapplication where trustees are dual resident at the time of the acquisition of the new assets.
S. 175(1): all trades carried by members of a group treated as a single trade, except in relation to intra-group transfers.

S. 175(2A): where disposal and acquisition are made by different companies in a group, s. 152 applies as though the companies were the same person, if each was in the group when it made its disposal or, as the case may be, its acquisition.
S. 175(2B): non-trading companies treated as trading companies for the purpose of s. 152 if they acquire or dispose of assets used for the purposes of a trade carried by other companies in the same group.
S. 175(2C): s. 152 not to apply if acquisition of new assets is made by a member of a group of companies in a no gain/no loss transaction.
S. 179B(2), (4) and Sch. 7AB, para 2, 3: modification of s. 152 and 153 where roll-over relief claimed where company treated by virtue of s. 179(3) or s. 179(6) as having sold and immediately re-acquired an asset at market value.
S. 185, 186: disapplication where a company disposes of old assets before ceasing to be resident or becoming dual resident and acquires new assets after emigration etc., unless the new assets are within the charge to tax.
S. 198: notwithstanding s. 152(8), relief on replacement of assets used in connection with oil fields restricted by reference to ring fence assets.
S. 233: clawback on a chargeable event in relation to the roll-over on disposal of shares to a qualifying share ownership trust where further relief under s. 152–158 between the disposal and the clawback.
S. 236: gain charged by way of clawback on a chargeable event in relation to the roll-over on disposal of shares to a qualifying share ownership trust cannot be rolled over under s. 152–158.
S. 241(3), (6): commercial lettings of furnished holiday accommodation chargeable under Sch. D, Case VI are treated as a trade and where, as a result, the consideration for acquisition of a dwelling-house is reduced under s. 152, 153, the gain to which principal private residence relief applies is similarly reduced.
S. 247(5): application of s. 152(2), (3) to roll-over relief on replacement of land compulsorily acquired.
S. 264(6): certain land disposed of by former parliamentary constituency association treated as if it had been held by the successor association if the proceeds were transferred.
Sch. 2: assets held on 6 April 1965.
Sch. 4, para. 2, 5: reduction of one half in the amount to be deducted under s. 152 in computing gains arising from disposal of a new asset in relation to deferral before 6 April 1988 where old asset held on 31 March 1982 (or acquired in a chain of no gain, no loss disposals from that date).
F(No. 2)A 1992, s. 77 and Sch. 17, para. 3: s. 152–156 apply in relation to any disposal by Northern Ireland Electricity of trade assets, before transfer to successor companies under Electricity (Northern Ireland) Order 1992, as if Northern Ireland Electricity and the successor company were the same person.
FA 2000, Sch. 22, para. 67(1): s. 152 does not apply if the new assets are tonnage tax assets.
FA 2002, Sch. 29, para. 132: method of claiming roll-over relief where an asset is both specified in s. 155 and an intangible fixed asset: interaction of the Schedule and s. 152–153.
SI 1992/58, Sch. 2, para. 10: disapplication of s. 152 in relation to reorganisation of port authorities.

Extra-statutory concessions – D15: roll-over relief extended to assets of a company owned by an unincorporated association or its members (see s. 158(1)(e)).
D16: s. 152 applies to repurchase of same asset for purely commercial reasons.
D22: roll-over relief applies where consideration for “old assets” used to improve existing assets, subject to certain conditions.
D23: partition of land on the dissolution of a partnership.
D24: roll-over relief applies where “new assets” not immediately used in the trade, subject to certain conditions.
D25: acquisition of an interest in an asset already used for the purposes of a trade treated as a “new asset”.

Statements of practice – D6: extension of time limit for roll-over relief under s. 152 where land compulsorily acquired and leased back to previous owner.
D11: roll-over relief for assets let to partnership.
D12: roll-over relief on partnership merger.
D19: to obtain benefit of s. 175 (see above), company acquiring “new assets” need not have been a member of the group at the time the “old assets” disposed of, nor must company disposing of “old assets” be such a member when “new assets” acquired.
8/81: availability of roll-over relief where an interval between cessation of one trade and commencement of another (see s. 152(8)).
5/86: application of roll-over relief to employees and office holders (see s. 158(1)(c)).

HMRC interpretations – IRInt. 5: in exercising its discretion to extend time-limit for replacement length of the extension is a factor; a taxpayer prevented from meeting reinvestment intention by circumstances beyond his control will be treated sympathetically.
IRInt. 7: meaning of the phrase “on the acquisition are taken into use”.
IRInt. 11: roll-over relief available in respect of a gain on grant of an option over land by reference to the underlying land.
IRInt. 28: provided requirements of ICTA 1988, s. 503, 504 met during main holiday period a longer letting in the same year of assessment should not preclude roll-over relief.
IRInt. 42: roll-over relief and fixed plant/machinery or buildings on short leasehold land as depreciating assets.
IRInt. 85: allowance of relief on acquisition of a building or structure used only partly for business purposes is statutory, not concessionary.

Other material – ICAEW Technical Release TR 291 (not reproduced): roll-over relief not available on sale of houses acquired or built for a company’s workers unless occupiers in representative capacity.
ICAEW Technical Release TR 488, 508 (not reproduced): roll-over relief available where assets exchanged.
ICAEW Technical Release TR 546, 551 (not reproduced): roll-over relief and furnished holiday lettings (ICTA 1988, s. 503–504) – extension of period qualifying for treatment as a trade.
ICAEW Technical Release TR 831 (not reproduced): Revenue confirm roll-over relief available where the sale proceeds from the “old assets” are not in cash but comprise further chargeable assets which are not themselves qualifying (see s. 155).
Taxline 1991/26 (not reproduced): Revenue view that roll-over relief takes priority over any retirement relief (see s. 163, 164 and Sch. 6) otherwise available; not possible, for example, to limit a roll-over claim to an amount equal to the balance after retirement relief, though where gain not fully rolled over retirement relief can be used to reduce any gain remaining after acceptance of roll-over claim.
Taxline 1992/50 (not reproduced): Revenue confirmation that roll-over relief under s. 152 can be claimed in respect of asset disposals between husband and wife, provided all other conditions for relief satisfied.
IoT Technical Information Release, October 1991 (not reproduced): the words “If the consideration which a person … obtains for the disposal of … assets … is applied by him in acquiring other assets” simply requires the taxpayer to reinvest an amount equal to the proceeds received; gifts of assets are within s. 152(10); relief is not available where there is a deemed disposal and reacquisition of the same asset; there is no reason, in principle, why relief should not be available where the consideration is satisfied by an issue of shares; relief under s. 152 if preferred to incorporation relief (s. 162); in addition to the first new trade, second or subsequent new trades commenced after the cessation of the old trade could be regarded as a successor for s. 152(8).
Taxline 1994/35 (not reproduced): although relief under TCGA 1992, s. 162 (roll-over relief on transfer of a business) is mandatory where a business is incorporated under that section, the Revenue will usually allow claims under s. 152 to take precedence over s. 162 relief if that is what the taxpayer wants.

Notes – S. 15: meaning of “chargeable gains”.
S. 21–34: general meaning of “disposal” and “asset”, including the timing of certain disposals.
S. 38(1)(a): allowable acquisition expenditure generally.
S. 288: interpretation, including “notice” as being in writing, “land” by reference to messuages, tenements, hereditaments etc. and reference to sections being those of this Act.

TMA 1970, s. 29: assessing procedure.
TMA 1970, s. 42–43B: procedure for making claims.
For provisions of this Act fixing the amount of the consideration given, see notes to s. 15.

153 Assets only partly replaced

153(1) Section 152(1) shall not apply if part only of the amount or value of the consideration for the disposal of, or of the interest in, the old assets is applied as described in that subsection, but if all of the amount or value of the consideration except for a part which is less than the amount of the gain (whether all chargeable gain or not) accruing on the disposal of, or of the interest in, the old assets is so applied, then the person carrying on the trade, on making a claim as respects the consideration which has been so applied, shall be treated for the purposes of this Act–

(a) as if the amount of the gain so accruing were reduced to the amount of the said part (and, if not all chargeable gain, with a proportionate reduction in the amount of the chargeable gain), and

(b) as if the amount or value of the consideration for the acquisition of, or of the interest in, the new assets were reduced by the amount by which the gain is reduced (or as the case may be the amount by which the chargeable gain is proportionately reduced) under paragraph (a) of this subsection,

but neither paragraph (a) nor paragraph (b) above shall affect the treatment for the purposes of this Act of the other party to the transaction involving the old assets, or of the other party to the transaction involving the new assets.

153(2) Subsections (3) to (11) of 152 shall apply as if this section formed part of that section.

Derivations – CGTA 1979, s. 116.

Cross references – S. 10A(3): temporary non-residents.
S. 175(1): all trades carried on by members of a group treated as a single trade, except in relation to intra-group transfers.
S. 179B(2), (4) and Sch. 7AB: modification of s. 153 where roll-over relief claimed where company treated by virtue of s. 179(3) or (6) as having sold and immediately re-acquired an asset at market value.
S. 198: relief on replacement of assets used in connection with oil fields restricted by reference to ring fence assets.
S. 233: clawback on a chargeable event in relation to the roll-over on disposal of shares to a qualifying share ownership trust where further relief under s. 152–158 between the disposal and the clawback.
S. 236: gain charged by way of clawback on a chargeable event in relation to the roll-over on disposal of shares to a qualifying share ownership trust cannot be rolled over under s. 152–158.
S. 241(3), (6): commercial lettings of furnished holiday accommodation chargeable under Sch. D, Case VI are treated as a trade and where, as a result, the consideration for acquisition of a dwelling-house is reduced under s. 152, 153, the gain to which principal private residence relief applies is similarly reduced.
S. 264(6): certain land disposed of by former parliamentary constituency association treated as if it had been held by the successor association if the proceeds were transferred.
FA 1990, Sch. 12, para. 7: continuation of roll-over relief from Independent Broadcasting Authority (IBA) to nominated company on transfer of undertakings.
F(No. 2)A 1992, Sch. 17, para. 3: s. 152–156 apply in relation to any disposal by Northern Ireland Electricity of trade assets, before transfer to successor companies under Electricity (Northern Ireland) Order 1992, as if Northern Ireland Electricity and the successor company were the same person.
FA 1994, Sch. 24, para. 6: application of s. 152–160 in relation to railways privatisation.
FA 1994, Sch. 25, para. 3(2): s. 152–156 apply in relation to disposal by Northern Ireland Airports Limited (NIAL) before transfer to successor company under Airports (Northern Ireland) Order 1994, as if NIAL and successor were the same person.
FA 2000, Sch. 22, para. 67(1): s. 153 does not apply if the new assets are tonnage tax assets.
FA 2002, Sch. 29, para. 132: method of claiming roll-over relief where an asset is both specified in s. 155 and an intangible fixed asset: interaction of the Schedule and s. 152–153.
SI 1992/58, Sch. 2, para. 10: disapplication of s. 153 in relation to reorganisation of port authorities.

Statements of practice – D12: roll-over relief on partnership merger.

Notes – S. 15: meaning of "chargeable gains".
S. 21–34: general meaning of "disposal".
S. 38(1)(a): allowable acquisition expenditure generally.
S. 178(3): crystallisation of gain where company leaves a group holding asset replacing asset transferred intra-group (or associated company holding asset also leaves the group).
S. 288: interpretation, including reference to sections being those of this Act.

153A Provisional application of sections 152 and 153

153A(1) This section applies where a person carrying on a trade who for a consideration disposes of, or of his interest in, any assets (**"the old assets"**) declares, in his return for the chargeable period in which the disposal takes place–

(a) that the whole or any specified part of the consideration will be applied in the acquisition of, or of an interest in, other assets (**"the new assets"**) which on the acquisition will be taken into use, and used only, for the purposes of the trade;

(b) that the acquisition will take place as mentioned in subsection (3) of section 152; and

(c) that the new assets will be within the classes listed in section 155.

153A(2) Until the declaration ceases to have effect, section 152 or, as the case may be, section 153 shall apply as if the acquisition had taken place and the person had made a claim under that section.

153A(3) The declaration shall cease to have effect as follows–

(a) if and to the extent that it is withdrawn before the relevant day, or is superseded before that day by a valid claim made under section 152 or 153, on the day on which it is so withdrawn or superseded; and

(b) if and to the extent that it is not so withdrawn or superseded, on the relevant day.

153A(4) On the declaration ceasing to have effect in whole or in part, all necessary adjustments–

(a) shall be made by making or amending assessments or by repayment or discharge of tax; and

(b) shall be so made notwithstanding any limitation on the time within which assessments or amendments may be made.

153A(5) In this section **"the relevant day"** means–

(a) in relation to capital gains tax, the third anniversary of the 31st January next following the year of assessment in which the disposal of, or of the interest in, the old assets took place;

(b) in relation to corporation tax, the fourth anniversary of the last day of the accounting period in which that disposal took place.

153A(6) Subsections (6), (8), (10) and (11) of section 152 shall apply for the purposes of this section as they apply for the purposes of that section.

History – S. 153A inserted by FA 1996, s. 141(2) with effect as respects the year 1996–97 and subsequent years of assessment and, for corporation tax purposes, as respects accounting periods ending on or after the day appointed under FA 1994, s. 199.

Cross references – S. 179B(2), (4) and Sch. 7AB: modification of s. 153A where roll-over relief claimed where company treated by virtue of s. 179(3) or (6) as having sold and immediately re-acquired an asset at market value.

Other material – Tax Bulletin TB08/96-2: procedure for claiming and withdrawing claim for provisional roll-over relief.

154 New assets which are depreciating assets

154(1) Sections 152, 153 and 229 shall have effect subject to the provisions of this section in which–

(a) the **"held-over gain"** means the amount by which, under those sections, and apart from the provisions of this section, any chargeable gain on one asset (**"asset No. 1"**) is reduced, with a corresponding reduction of the expenditure allowable in respect of another asset (**"asset No. 2"**), and

(b) any reference to a gain of any amount being carried forward to any asset is a reference to a reduction of that amount in a chargeable gain coupled with a reduction of the same amount in expenditure allowable in respect of that asset.

154(2) If asset No. 2 is a depreciating asset, the held-over gain shall not be carried forward, but the claimant shall be treated as if so much of the chargeable gain on asset No. 1 as is equal to the held-over gain did not accrue until–

(a) the claimant disposes of asset No. 2, or

(b) he ceases to use asset No. 2 for the purposes of a trade carried on by him, or

(c) the expiration of a period of 10 years beginning with the acquisition of asset No. 2,

whichever event comes first.

154(2A) If asset No 2 or shares in a company which holds asset No 2 are transferred as part of the process of a merger to which section 140E applies, the transfer shall be disregarded for the purpose of subsection (2), and for that purpose–

(a) if the transferee holds asset No 2 it shall be treated for the purpose of subsection (2), in relation to asset No 2, as if it were the claimant, or

(b) if the transferee holds shares in the company which holds asset No 2 section 175 shall apply in relation to the group of which the transferee is a member as if it were the same group as any group of which the claimant was a member before the merger.

154(2B) If, as part of the process of a merger to which section 140E applies, the transferee becomes a member (whether or not as the principal company) of a group of which the claimant is also a member, for the purposes of subsection (2) section 175 shall apply in relation to the trade carried on by the claimant as if the group of which the transferee is a member were the same group as the group of which the claimant was a member before the merger.

154(2C) In subsections (2A) and (2B), **"transferor"** and **"transferee"** have the meaning given by section 140E(9).

154(2D) Subsections (2A) and (2B) shall apply in relation to the transfer of an asset in circumstances where section 140A applies as they apply in relation to the transfer of an asset on a merger to which section 140E applies, and for that purpose–

(a) references to the merger shall be treated as references to the transfer,

(b) references to section 140E shall be treated as references to section 140A, and

(c) references to the transferor and the transferee shall be treated as references to the transferor and the transferee in relation to the asset.

154(3) Where section 229 has effect subject to the provisions of this section, subsection (2)(b) above shall have effect as if it read–

"(b) section 232(3) applies as regards asset No. 2 (whether or not by virtue of section 232(5)), or".

154(4) If, in the circumstances specified in subsection (5) below, the claimant acquires an asset (**"asset No. 3"**) which is not a depreciating asset, and claims under section 152 or 153–

(a) the gain held-over from asset No. 1 shall be carried forward to asset No. 3, and

(b) the claim which applies to asset No. 2 shall be treated as withdrawn (so that subsection (2) above does not apply).

154(5) The circumstances are that asset No. 3 is acquired not later than the time when the chargeable gain postponed under subsection (2) above would accrue and, assuming–

(a) that the consideration for asset No. 1 was applied in acquiring asset No. 3, and

(b) that the time between the disposal of asset No. 1 and the acquisition of asset No. 3 was within the time limited by section 152(3),

the whole amount of the postponed gain could be carried forward from asset No. 1 to asset No. 3; and the claim under subsection (4) above shall be accepted as if those assumptions were true.

154(6) If part only of the postponed gain could be carried forward from asset No. 1 to asset No. 3, and the claimant so requires, that and the other part of the postponed gain shall be treated as derived from 2 separate assets, so that, on that claim–

(a) subsection (4) above applies to the first-mentioned part, and

(b) the other part remains subject to subsection (2) above.

154(7) For the purposes of this section, an asset is a depreciating asset at any time if–

(a) at that time it is a wasting asset, as defined in section 44 or

(b) within the period of 10 years beginning at that time it will become a wasting asset (so defined).

History – S. 154(2A)–(2C) substituted for s. 154(2A) and (2B) by SI 2007/3186, reg. 3(2) and Sch. 2, para. 6, in relation to mergers relating to the formation of an SE or SCE which take place on or after 18 August 2006, and in relation to all other mergers which take place on or after 1 January 2007.
S. 154(2A) inserted by F(No. 2)A 2005, s. 64(3) with effect in relation to the formation of an SE (Societas Europaea) under Article 2 of Council Regulation (EC) 2157/2001 on the Statute for a European Company (Societas Europaea) which occurs on or after 1 April 2005.
S. 154(2B) inserted by F(No. 2)A 2005, s. 64(3) with effect in relation to the formation of an SE (Societas Europaea) under Article 2 of Council Regulation (EC) 2157/2001 on the Statute for a European Company (Societas Europaea) which occurs on or after 1 April 2005.
S. 154(2D) inserted by SI 2007/3186, reg. 3(1) and Sch. 1, para. 8,with effect in relation to transfers which take place on or after 1 January 2007, and in relation to cross-border mergers taking place on or after that date, but in the case of mergers relating to the formation of an SE or SCE, in relation to those taking place on or after 18 August 2006 (see SI 2008/1579, reg. 4(1)).

Derivations – S. 154(1): CGTA 1979, s. 117(1), as amended by FA 1990, s. 40(2).
S. 154(2): CGTA 1979, s. 117(2).
S. 154(3): CGTA 1979, s. 117(2A), as inserted by FA 1990, s. 40(3).
S. 154(4): CGTA 1979, s. 117(3), as amended by FA 1990, s. 40(4).
S. 154(5)–(7): CGTA 1979, s. 117(4)–(6).

Cross references – S. 44: "wasting asset" defined by reference to an asset with a predictable life not exceeding 50 years, but specifically including machinery and plant while excluding freehold land.
S. 175(1): all trades carried on by members of a group treated as a single trade, except in relation to intra-group transfers.
S. 198: relief on replacement of assets used in connection with oil fields restricted by reference to ring fence assets but the trade in s. 154(2)(b) becomes the ring fence trade and s. 154(4)–(7) are disapplied.
S. 229, 232(2): roll-over relief in respect of disposals of shares to certain employee share ownership trusts with a deemed disposal and reacquisition of the replacement assets if certain chargeable events occur in relation to the trustees.
S. 233: clawback on a chargeable event in relation to the roll-over on disposal of shares to a qualifying share ownership trust where further relief under s. 152–158 between the disposal and the clawback.
S. 236: gain charged by way of clawback on a chargeable event in relation to the roll-over on disposal of shares to a qualifying share ownership trust cannot be rolled over under s. 152–158.
S. 241(3): commercial lettings of furnished holiday accommodation chargeable under Sch. D, Case VI are treated as a trade.
S. 248(3): modified application for purposes of roll-over relief on replacement of land compulsorily acquired.
S. 264(6): certain land disposed of by former parliamentary constituency association treated as if it had been held by the successor association if the proceeds were transferred.
Sch. A1, para. 16: taper relief and special rules for postponed gains.
Sch. 4, para. 2–5: 50 per cent reduction in a gain treated as accruing under s. 154(2) where the hold-over was effected before 6 April 1988 and the old asset was held at 31 March 1982 (or acquired in a chain of no gain, no loss disposals from that date); the 50 per cent reduction in the deduction from acquisition consideration for a disposal in respect of rolled-over gains referable to periods before 31 March 1982 does not apply where the substituted non-depreciating asset within s. 154(4) was acquired after 18 March 1991 unless the 50 per cent hold-over relief would have applied, essentially, if the held-over gain had continued but crystallised on that disposal.
SI 1992/58, Sch. 2, para. 10: disapplication of s. 154 in relation to reorganisation of port authorities.
Electricity Act 1989, Sch. 11, para. 3: where, but for these provisions, a held-over gain would have been carried forward to a depreciating asset which is then transferred on privatisation, s. 154 has effect as if the gain had accrued to, and the claim for it to be held-over had been made by the transferor company.

European material – Council Regulation (EC) 2157/2001 of 8 October 2001 on the Statute for a European Company (Societas Europaea).

Extra-statutory concessions – D45: charge to tax under s. 154(2)(b) does not arise where asset ceases to be used in claimant's trade on death of claimant.

HMRC interpretations – IRInt. 42,: treatment of building constructed on leasehold land where lease has 60 years or less to run and items of fixed plant and machinery which have become part of a building.

Notes – S. 15: meaning of "chargeable gains".
S. 21–34: general meaning of "disposal" and "assets".
S. 38(1)(a): allowable acquisition expenditure generally.
S. 178(3): crystallisation of gain where company leaves a group holding asset replacing asset transferred intra-group (or associated company holding asset also leaves the group).
S. 288: interpretation, including reference to sections being those of this Act.

155 Relevant classes of assets

155 The classes of assets for the purposes of section 152(1) are as follows.

CLASS 1

Assets within heads A and B below.

Head A

1. Any building or part of a building and any permanent or semi-permanent structure in the nature of a building, occupied (as well as used) only for the purposes of the trade.

2. Any land occupied (as well as used) only for the purposes of the trade.

Head A has effect subject to section 156.

Head B

Fixed plant or machinery which does not form part of a building or of a permanent or semi-permanent structure in the nature of a building.

CLASS 2

Ships, aircraft and hovercraft (**"hovercraft"** having the same meaning as in the Hovercraft Act 1968).

CLASS 3

Satellites, space stations and spacecraft (including launch vehicles).

CLASS 4

Goodwill.

CLASS 5

Milk quotas (that is, rights to sell dairy produce without being liable to pay milk levy or to deliver dairy produce without being liable to pay a contribution to milk levy) and potato quotas (that is, rights to produce potatoes without being liable to pay more than the ordinary contribution to the Potato Marketing Board's fund).

CLASS 6

Ewe and suckler cow premium quotas (that is, rights in respect of any ewes or suckler cows to receive payments by way of any subsidy entitlement to which is determined by reference to limits contained in a Community instrument).

CLASS 7

Fish quota (that is, an allocation of quota to catch fish stocks, which derives from the Total Allowable Catches set in pursuance of Article 8(4) of Council Regulation (EEC) No. 3760/92 and under annual Council Regulations made in accordance with that Article, or under any replacement Community Instruments).

CLASS 7A

Assets within heads A and B below.

Head A

Payment entitlements under the single payment scheme (that is, the scheme of income support for farmers in pursuance of Title III of Council Regulation (EC) No 73/2009).

Head B

Payment entitlements under the basic payment scheme (that is, the scheme of income support for farmers in pursuance of Regulation (EU) No 1307/2013 of the European Parliament and of the Council).

CLASS 8

Assets within heads A and B below.

Head A

Rights of a member of Lloyd's under a syndicate within the meaning of Chapter III of Part II of the Finance Act 1993.

Head B

An asset which a member of Lloyd's is treated as having acquired by virtue of section 82 of the Finance Act 1999.

History – Class 6 inserted by FA 1993, s. 86 in relation to disposals of old assets (or interests therein) or acquisitions of new assets (or interests therein) on or after 1 January 1993 (in relation to accounting periods which began before 6 April 1992 the insertion has effect as if it were Class 5 under CGTA 1979, s. 118).

Class 7 inserted by SI 1999/564, art. 3, with effect–

(a) in a case where the old assets (but not the new assets), referred to in TCGA 1992, s. 152(1), are fish quota, where the disposal of the old assets takes place on or after 29 March 1999;

(b) in a case where the new assets (but not the old assets), referred to in TCGA 1992, s. 152(1), are fish quota, where the acquisition of the new assets takes place on or after 29 March 1999; and

(c) in a case where both the old assets and the new assets referred to in TCGA 1992, s. 152(1), are fish quota, where both the disposal of the old assets and the acquisition of the new assets takes place on or after 29 March 1999.

In the entry for Class 7A, the descriptions "Assets within heads A and B below." and "Head A" inserted by FA 2014, s. 61(2), and the description "Head B" and the text below it inserted by FA 2014, s. 61(3), with effect where the disposal of the old assets (or an interest in them) or the acquisition of the new assets (or an interest in them) is on or after 20 December 2013.

In the entry for Class 7A, "Council Regulation (EC) No 73/2009" substituted for "Council Regulation (EC) No. 1782/2003" by FA 2012, s. 37(1) with effect where the disposal of the old assets (or an interest in them) or the acquisition of the new assets (or an interest in them) is on or after 1 January 2009.

Class 7A inserted by SI 2005/409, art. 2, with effect–

(a) in a case where the old assets (but not the new assets), referred to in TCGA 1992, s. 152(1), are rights to receive payments (hereafter, referred to as "payment entitlements") under the single payment scheme as set-out under Title III of EC Council Regulation No. 1782/2003 (hereafter, referred to as "the single payment scheme"), where the disposal of the old assets (or of the interest in them) takes place on or after 22 March 2005;

(b) in a case where the new assets (but not the old assets), referred to in TCGA 1992, s. 152(1), are payment entitlements under the single payment scheme, where the acquisition of the new assets (or of the interest in them) takes place on or after 22 March 2005; and

(c) in a case where both the old assets and the new assets, referred to in TCGA 1992, s. 152(1), are payment entitlements under the single payment scheme, where the disposal of the old assets (or of the interest in them) and the acquisition of the new assets (or of the interest in them) both take place on or after 22 March 2005.

Class 8 inserted by FA 1999, s. 84(1), with effect in relation to–

(a) assets (or interests in them) disposed of on or after 6 April 1999;

(b) assets (or interests in them) acquired on or after 6 April 1999.

Derivations – CGTA 1979, s. 118, as amended by FA 1988, s. 112.

Cross references – S. 175(1): all trades carried on by members of a group treated as a single trade, except in relation to intra-group transfers.

S. 179B(2) and Sch. 7AB: modification of Head A of Class 1 where roll-over relief claimed where company treated by virtue of s. 179(3) or (6) as having sold and immediately re-acquired an asset at market value.

S. 193: oil licences are not within s. 155.

S. 233: clawback on a chargeable event in relation to the roll-over on disposal of shares to a qualifying share ownership trust where further relief under s. 152–158 between the disposal and the clawback.

S. 236: gain charged by way of clawback on a chargeable event in relation to the roll-over on disposal of shares to a qualifying share ownership trust cannot be rolled over under s. 152–158.

S. 241(3): commercial lettings of furnished holiday accommodation chargeable under Sch. D, Case VI are treated as a trade.

S. 264(6): certain land disposed of by former parliamentary constituency association treated as if it had been held by the successor association if the proceeds were transferred.

FA 1993, s. 86(2): Treasury power to add further classes of assets to the classes specified in s. 155.

FA 2002, Sch. 29, para. 132: method of claiming roll-over relief where an asset is both specified in s. 155 and an intangible fixed asset: interaction of the Schedule ands. 152–153. Classes 4 to 7 do not have effect for the purposes of corporation tax as regards the acquisition of new assets that are chargeable intangible assets.

SI 1992/58, Sch. 2, para. 10: disapplication of s. 155 in relation to reorganisation of port authorities.

Statements of practice – D11: roll-over relief for assets let to partnership.

HMRC interpretations – IRInt. 11: roll-over relief available in respect of a gain on grant of an option over land by reference to the underlying land.

Other material – ICAEW Technical Release TR 291 (not reproduced): roll-over relief not available on sale of houses acquired or built for a company's workers unless occupiers in representative capacity.
ICAEW Technical Release TR 831 (not reproduced): HMRC confirm roll-over relief available where the sale proceeds from the "old assets" are not in cash but comprise further chargeable assets which are not themselves within the categories in s. 155
Taxline 1995/133 (not reproduced): roll-over relief on disposal of a musical instrument by a self-employed musician.

Notes – S. 178(3), s. 179(3): crystallisation of gain where company leaves a group holding asset replacing asset transferred intra-group (or associated company holding asset also leaves the group).
S. 288: interpretation, including "land" by reference to messuages, tenements, hereditaments etc. and reference to sections being those of this Act.

156 Assets of Class 1

156(1) This section has effect as respects head A of Class 1 in section 155.

156(2) Head A shall not apply where the trade is a trade–

(a) of dealing in or developing land, or

(b) of providing services for the occupier of land in which the person carrying on the trade has an estate or interest.

156(3) Where the trade is a trade of dealing in or developing land, but a profit on the sale of any land held for the purposes of the trade would not form part of the trading profits, then, as regards that land, the trade shall be treated for the purposes of subsection (2)(a) above as if it were not a trade of dealing in or developing land.

156(4) Where section 19 of ITTOIA 2005 or section 42 of CTA 2009 applies (tied premises receipts and expenses treated as those of trade) the trader shall be treated, to the extent that the conditions in subsection (1) of that section are met in relation to premises, as occupying as well as using the premises for the purposes of the trade.

History – In s. 156(4) the words "section 98 of the Taxes Act or" omitted (and repealed by CTA 2009, s. 1326 and Sch. 3, Pt. 1) and the words "or section 42 of CTA 2009" inserted by CTA 2009, s. 1322 and Sch. 1, para. 371, with effect for corporation tax purposes for accounting periods ending on or after 1 April 2009, and for income tax and capital gains tax purposes for the tax year 2009–10 and subsequent tax years.
In s. 156(4), words "or section 19 of ITTOIA 2005" inserted by ITTOIA 2005, s. 882 and Sch. 1, para. 439 which, in accordance with ITTOIA 2005, s. 883, have effect, for income tax purposes, for tax year 2005–06 and subsequent tax years, and, for corporation tax purposes, for accounting periods ending after 5 April 2005.
S. 156(4) substituted by FA 1998, s. 41(2), with effect on and after 17 March 1998, subject to the transitional provisions in FA 1998, s. 41(4)–(7).

Derivations – CGTA 1979, s. 119.

Cross references – S. 175(1): all trades carried on by members of a group treated as a single trade, except in relation to intra-group transfers.
S. 233: clawback on a chargeable event in relation to the roll-over on disposal of shares to a qualifying share ownership trust where further relief under s. 152–158 between the disposal and the clawback.
S. 236: gain charged by way of clawback on a chargeable event in relation to the roll-over on disposal of shares to a qualifying share ownership trust cannot be rolled over under s. 152–158.
S. 241(3): commercial lettings of furnished holiday accommodation chargeable under Sch. D, Case VI are treated as a trade.
S. 264(6): certain land disposed of by former parliamentary constituency association treated as if it had been held by the successor association if the proceeds were transferred.
ICTA 1988, s. 98(2): meaning of "tied premises" by reference to the supply as principle or agent of goods sold or used on the premises; "the relevant trade" is determined accordingly.
FA 1990, Sch. 12, para. 7: continuation of roll-over relief from Independent Broadcasting Authority (IBA) to nominated company on transfer of undertakings.
F(No. 2)A 1992, Sch. 17, para. 3: s. 152–156 apply in relation to any disposal by Northern Ireland Electricity of trade assets, before transfer to successor companies under Electricity (Northern Ireland) Order 1992, as if Northern Ireland Electricity and the successor company were the same person.
FA 1994, Sch. 24, para. 6: application of s. 152–160 in relation to railways privatisation.
FA 1994, Sch. 25, para. 3(2): s. 152–156 apply in relation to disposal by Northern Ireland Airports Limited (NIAL) before transfer to successor company under Airports (Northern Ireland) Order 1994 as if NIAL and successor were the same person.
SI 1992/58, Sch. 2, para. 10: disapplication of s. 156 in relation to reorganisation of port authorities.

Notes – S. 178(3), s. 179(3): crystallisation of gain where company leaves a group holding asset replacing asset transferred intra-group (or associated company holding asset also leaves the group).
S. 288: interpretation, including "land" by reference to messuages, tenements, hereditaments etc., the "Taxes Act" as ICTA 1988 and reference to other sections being those of this Act.
Sch. 8, para. 10(1): meaning of "lease" and cognate expressions.

156ZA Intangible fixed assets: roll-over relief

156ZA(1) This section applies if a company is entitled to relief under Chapter 7 of Part 8 of CTA 2009 (roll-over relief in case of realisation and reinvestment) as a result of–

(a) section 898 of that Act (roll-over relief where pre-FA 2002 assets disposed of on or after 1 April 2002), or

(b) section 899 of that Act (roll-over relief where degrouping charge on pre-FA 2002 asset arises on or after 1 April 2002).

156ZA(2) The company is treated for the purposes of this Act as if the consideration for the disposal of the old asset were reduced by the amount available for relief.

156ZA(3) Subsection (2) does not affect the treatment for any purpose of the Taxes Acts of the other party to any transaction involved in the disposal of the old asset or the expenditure on other assets.

156ZA(4) In this section–

"the old asset" has the same meaning as in Chapter 7 of Part 8 of CTA 2009 (see section 754(2)), and

"the Taxes Acts" means the enactments relating to income tax, corporation tax or chargeable gains.

History – S. 156ZA inserted by CTA 2009, s. 1322 and Sch. 1, para. 372, with effect for corporation tax purposes for accounting periods ending on or after 1 April 2009, and for income tax and capital gains tax purposes for the tax year 2009–10 and subsequent tax years.

156ZB Intangible fixed assets: interaction with relief under Chapter 7 of Part 8 of CTA 2009

156ZB(1) Subsection (2) applies if there is a disposal on or after 1 April 2002 of an asset that is both–

(a) an asset of a class specified in section 155, and

(b) an intangible fixed asset for the purposes of Part 8 of CTA 2009.

156ZB(2) The period specified in section 152(3)–

(a) does not include any period beginning on or after 1 April 2002, and

(b) may not be extended so as to include any such period.

156ZB(3) Classes 4 to 7A in section 155 do not apply for the purposes of corporation tax as respects the acquisition of new assets that are chargeable intangible assets for the purposes of Part 8 of CTA 2009 (see section 741 of that Act).

156ZB(4) In the case of an acquisition before 22 March 2005, subsection (3) applies as if it referred to Classes 4 to 7, instead of Classes 4 to 7A.

History – In s. 156ZB(1), the words "Subsection (2)" substituted for the words "This section" by FA 2014, s. 62(1), with effect in relation to claims for relief under s. 152 or 153 made on or after 19 March 2014.
S. 156ZB inserted by CTA 2009, s. 1322 and Sch. 1, para. 372, with effect for corporation tax purposes for accounting periods ending on or after 1 April 2009, and for income tax and capital gains tax purposes for the tax year 2009–10 and subsequent tax years.

156A Cessation of trade by limited liability partnership

156A(1) Where, immediately before the time of cessation of trade, a member of a limited liability partnership holds an asset, or an interest in an asset, acquired by him for a consideration treated as reduced under section 152 or 153, he shall be treated as if a chargeable gain equal to the amount of the reduction accrued to him immediately before that time.

156A(2) Where, as a result of section 154(2), a chargeable gain on the disposal of an asset, or an interest in an asset, by a member of a limited liability partnership has not accrued before the time of cessation of trade, the member shall be treated as if the chargeable gain accrued immediately before that time.

156A(3) In this section **"the time of cessation of trade"**, in relation to a limited liability partnership, means the time when section 59A(1) ceases to apply in relation to the limited liability partnership.

History – S. 156A inserted by Limited Liability Partnerships Act 2000, s. 11(4), with effect from 6 April 2001 by virtue of SI 2000/3316 (C. 108).

157 Trade carried on by personal company: business assets dealt with by individual

157 In relation to a case where–

(a) the person disposing of, or of his interest in, the old assets and acquiring the new assets, or an interest in them, is an individual, and

(b) the trade or trades in question are carried on not by that individual but by a company which, both at the time of the disposal and at the time of the acquisition referred to in paragraph (a) above, is his personal company, that is to say, a company the voting rights in which are exercisable, as to not less than 5 per cent, by him,

any reference in sections 152 to 156 to the person carrying on the trade (or the 2 or more trades) includes a reference to that individual.

History – Heading to section amended by CCH, to reflect altered content, by substitution of word "personal" for "family".
In s. 157(b) the words "personal company" substituted for "family company" by FA 1993, s. 87 and Sch. 7, para. 1(1) in relation to any disposal made on or after 16 March 1993.
In s. 157(b), the words "that is to say, a company the voting rights in which are exercisable, as to not less than 5 per cent, by him" substituted for the words "within the meaning of Schedule 6" by FA 1998, s. 140(3) which has effect in relation to the year 2003–04 and subsequent years of assessment.

Derivations – (as originally enacted) – CGTA 1979, s. 120, as amended by FA 1985, s. 70(9).

Cross references – S. 175(1): all trades carried on by members of a group treated as a single trade for corporation tax purposes, except in relation to intra-group transfers.

S. 233: clawback on a chargeable event in relation to the roll-over on disposal of shares to a qualifying share ownership trust where further relief under s. 152–158 between the disposal and the clawback.
S. 236: gain charged by way of clawback on a chargeable event in relation to the roll-over on disposal of shares to a qualifying share ownership trust cannot be rolled over under s. 152–158.
S. 241(3): commercial lettings of furnished holiday accommodation chargeable under Sch. D, Case VI are treated as a trade
S. 264(6): certain land disposed of by former parliamentary constituency association treated as if it had been held by the successor association if the proceeds were transferred.
Sch. 6, para. 1: for retirement relief, "personal company" defined, in relation to an individual, by reference to his rights to exercise at least 5 per cent of the votes ("family company" was 25 per cent or 5 per cent if his family held another 45 per cent).
FA 1994, Sch. 24, para. 6: application of s. 152–160 to railways privatisation.
SI 1992/58, Sch. 2, para. 10: disapplication of s. 157 in relation to reorganisation of port authorities.

Statements of practice – D11: roll-over relief for assets let to partnership.

Other material – Taxline 1991/26 (not reproduced): Revenue view that the new asset must be used by the same family (now personal) company, and not, for example, by a subsidiary of the family company.
IoT Technical Information Release, October 1991 (not reproduced): Revenue confirm both old and new assets to be used by family (now personal) company; notwithstanding that group trades treated as one (s. 175), relief not available where asset used by 100 per cent subsidiary of a holding company since it is not a family company; payment of rent does not preclude claim.

Notes – S. 178(3): crystallisation of gain where company leaves a group holding asset replacing asset transferred intra-group (or associated company holding asset also leaves the group).
S. 288: interpretation, including meaning of "company" and reference to sections being those of this Act.

158 Activities other than trades, and interpretation

158(1) Sections 152 to 157 shall apply with the necessary modifications–

(a) in relation to the discharge of the functions of a public authority, and

(b) in relation to the occupation of woodlands where the woodlands are managed by the occupier on a commercial basis and with a view to the realisation of profits, and

(c) in relation to a profession, vocation, office or employment, and

(d) in relation to such of the activities of a body of persons whose activities are carried on otherwise than for profit and are wholly or mainly directed to the protection or promotion of the interests of its members in the carrying on of their trade or profession as are so directed, and

(e) in relation to the activities of an unincorporated association or other body chargeable to corporation tax, being a body not established for profit whose activities are wholly or mainly carried on otherwise than for profit, but in the case of assets within head A of class 1 only if they are both occupied and used by the body, and in the case of other assets only if they are used by the body, and

(f) in relation to the activities of a company owned by such an unincorporated association or other body ("the parent body"), but in the case of any assets within head A of class 1 only if they are both occupied and used by the parent body, and in the case of any other assets only if they are used by the parent body,

as they apply in relation to a trade.

158(1A) For the purposes of subsection (1)(f) the parent body owns the company if–

(a) it holds not less than 90% of the company's ordinary share capital,

(b) it is beneficially entitled to not less than 90% of the profits available for distribution to the equity holders of the company, and

(c) it would be beneficially entitled on a winding up to not less than 90% of the assets of the company available for distribution to equity holders.

158(1B) For the purposes of subsection (1A)–

(a) **"ordinary share capital"** has the meaning given by section 832(1) of the Taxes Act and also includes, in relation to a company that has no share capital, any interests in the company possessed by members of the company, and

(b) the meaning of **"equity holder"** and method of determination of profits or assets available for distribution shall be that prescribed for the purposes of paragraph 8 of Schedule 7AC by sub-paragraphs (2) and (3) of that paragraph.

158(2) In sections 152 to 157 and this section the expressions **"trade"**, **"profession"**, **"vocation"**, **"office"** and **"employment"** have the same meanings as in the Income Tax Acts.

158(3) Sections 152 to 157 and this section shall be construed as one.

History – S. 158(1)(f) (and the "and" at the end of s. 158(1)(e)) inserted by SI 2009/730, art. 6(2), with effect in relation to disposals on or after 6 April 2009.
S. 158(1A) and (1B) inserted by SI 2009/730, art. 6(3), with effect in relation to disposals on or after 6 April 2009.
In s. 158(2) the words ", but not so as to apply the provisions of the Income Tax Acts as to the circumstances in which, on a change in the persons carrying on a trade, a trade is to be regarded as discontinued, or as set up and commenced" omitted by CTA 2009, s. 1322 and Sch. 1, para. 373 and repealed by CTA 2009, s. 1326 and Sch. 3, Pt. 1, with effect for corporation tax purposes for accounting periods ending on or after 1 April 2009, and for income tax and capital gains tax purposes for the tax year 2009–10 and subsequent tax years.

Derivations – CGTA 1979, s. 121.

Cross references – S. 175(1): all trades carried on by members of a group treated as a single trade, except in relation to intra-group transfers.
S. 233: clawback on a chargeable event in relation to the roll-over on disposal of shares to a qualifying share ownership trust where further relief under s. 152–158 between the disposal and the clawback.
S. 236: gain charged by way of clawback on a chargeable event in relation to the roll-over on disposal of shares to a qualifying share ownership trust cannot be rolled over under s. 152–158.
S. 264(6): certain land disposed of by former parliamentary constituency association treated as if it had been held by the successor association if the proceeds were transferred.
FA 1994, Sch. 24, para. 6: application of s. 152–160 to railways privatisation.
SI 1992/58, Sch. 2, para. 10: disapplication of s. 158 in relation to reorganisation of port authorities.

Extra-statutory concessions – D15: roll-over relief extended to assets owned by an unincorporated association or its members.

Statements of practice – 5/86: application of roll-over relief to employees and office holders.

Other material – IoT Technical Information Release, October 1991 (not reproduced): HMRC confirm that s. 158 requires both the old and the new assets to be used by the family (now personal) company; notwithstanding that group trades treated as one (s. 175), relief not available where asset used by 100 per cent subsidiary of a holding company since it is not a family company; payment of rent does not preclude a claim.

Notes – S. 8: charge to corporation tax in respect of chargeable gains.
S. 10(4): reference to the Income Tax Acts is construed as a reference also to the Corporation Tax Acts.
S. 178(3), s. 179(3): crystallisation of gain where company leaves a group holding asset replacing asset transferred intra-group (or associated company holding asset also leaves the group).
S. 288: interpretation, including reference to sections being those of this Act.
Interpretation Act 1978, s. 5 and Sch. 1: the Income Tax Acts mean the enactments relating to income tax.

159 Non-residents: roll-over relief

159(1) Section 152 shall not apply in the case of a person if the old assets are chargeable assets in relation to him at the time they are disposed of, unless the new assets are chargeable assets in relation to him immediately after the time they are acquired.

159(2) Subsection (1) above shall not apply where–

(a) the person acquires the new assets after he has disposed of the old assets, and

(b) immediately after the time they are acquired the person is resident in the United Kingdom.

159(3) Subsection (2) above shall not apply where immediately after the time the new assets are acquired–

(a) the person is a dual resident, and

(b) the new assets are prescribed assets.

159(4) For the purposes of this section an asset is at any time a **chargeable asset** in relation to a person if, were it to be disposed of at that time, any chargeable gains accruing to him on the disposal–

(a) would be gains in respect of which he would be chargeable to capital gains tax under section 10(1), or

(b) would form part of his chargeable profits for corporation tax purposes by virtue of section 10B.

159(5) In this section–

"dual resident" means a person who is resident in the United Kingdom and falls to be regarded for the purposes of any double taxation relief arrangements as resident in a territory outside the United Kingdom; and

"prescribed asset", in relation to a dual resident, means an asset in respect of which, by virtue of the asset being of a description specified in any double taxation relief arrangements, he falls to be regarded for the purposes of the arrangements as not liable in the United Kingdom to tax on gains accruing to him on a disposal.

159(6) In this section–

(a) **"the old assets"** and **"the new assets"** have the same meanings as in section 152,

(b) references to disposal of the old assets include references to disposal of an interest in them, and

(c) references to acquisition of the new assets include references to acquisition of an interest in them or to entering into an unconditional contract for the acquisition of them.

159(7) Where the acquisition of the new assets took place before 14th March 1989 and the disposal of the old assets took place, or takes place, on or after that date, this section shall not apply if the disposal of the old assets took place, or takes place, within 12 months of the acquisition of the new assets or such longer period as the Board may by notice allow.

History – In s. 159(2)(b), the words "or ordinarily resident" omitted by FA 2013, s. 219 and Sch. 46, para. 98(2), with effect in relation to a person's liability to capital gains tax for the tax year 2013–14 or any subsequent tax year, without prejudice to any provision in FA 2013, Sch. 46, Pt. 3 about the application of a particular amendment.
In s. 159(4)(b), the reference "10B" substituted for the reference "10(3)" by FA 2003, s. 155 and Sch. 27, para. 2(3) which have effect in relation to accounting periods beginning on or after 1 January 2003.
In s. 159(5), in the definition of "dual resident", the words "or ordinarily resident" omitted by FA 2013, s. 219 and Sch. 46, para. 98(3), with effect in relation to a person's liability to capital gains tax for the tax year 2013–14 or any subsequent tax year, without prejudice to any provision in FA 2013, Sch. 46, Pt. 3 about the application of a particular amendment.

Derivations – FA 1989, s. 129.

Cross references – Sch. 7B, para. 6: modification of s. 159(4)(b) in respect of overseas life insurance companies in relation to disposals or acquisitions made in accounting periods beginning after 31 December 1992.

Notes – S. 9: meaning of "resident" and "ordinarily resident".
S. 10: extent of charge to tax on a non-resident by reference to assets held or used etc. for the purposes of a UK branch or agency.
S. 15: meaning of "chargeable gains".
S. 21–34: general meaning of "disposal" and "assets", including the timing of certain disposals.
S. 288: interpretation, including meaning of "double taxation relief arrangements", "notice" as being in writing and reference to sections being those of this Act.
S. 179B(2), (4) and Sch. 7AB: modification of s. 159 where roll-over relief claimed where company treated by virtue of s. 179(3) or (6) as having sold and immediately re-acquired an asset at market value.
FA 1994, Sch. 24, para. 6: application of s. 152–160 to railways privatisation.

159A Non-resident CGT disposals: roll-over relief

159A(1) Section 152 does not apply in relation to a person who would (apart from that section) be chargeable to capital gains tax under section 14D or 188D in respect of NRCGT gains accruing on the disposal of the old assets, unless the new assets are qualifying residential property interests immediately after the time they are acquired.

159A(2) For the purposes of this section an asset is a **"qualifying residential property interest"** at any time if it–

(a) is an interest in UK land, and

(b) consists of or includes a dwelling.

159A(3) In this section–

(a) **"dwelling"** has the meaning given by paragraph 4 of Schedule B1;

(b) **"interest in UK land"** has the meaning given by paragraph 2 of Schedule B1;

(c) **"the old assets"** and **"the new assets"** have the same meaning as in section 152;

(d) the reference to disposal of the old assets includes a reference to disposal of an interest in them;

(e) the reference to acquisition of the new assets includes a reference to acquisition of an interest in them or entering into an unconditional contract for the acquisition of them.

History – S. 159A inserted by FA 2015, s. 37 and Sch. 7, para. 22, with effect in relation to disposals made on or after 6 April 2015.

160 Dual resident companies: roll-over relief

160 [Repealed by FA 1994, s. 251(6) and Sch. 26, Pt. VIII(1).]

History – S. 160 repealed by FA 1994, s. 251(6) and s. 258 and Sch. 26, Pt. VIII(1), where the disposal of the old assets or the interest in them is made, or where the unconditional contract for their acquisition is entered into on or after 30 November 1993.

Derivations – FA 1989, s. 133.

Notes – S. 9: meaning of "resident".
S. 21–34: general meaning of "disposal" and "assets", including the timing of certain disposals.
S. 288: interpretation, including meaning of "company", "double taxation relief arrangements", "notice" as being in writing and reference to sections being those of this Act.

STOCK IN TRADE

161 Appropriations to and from stock

161(1) Subject to subsections (3) to (3ZB) below, where an asset acquired by a person otherwise than as trading stock of a trade carried on by him is appropriated by him for the purposes of the trade as trading stock (whether on the commencement of the trade or otherwise) and, if he had then sold the asset for its market value, a chargeable gain or allowable loss would have accrued to him, he shall be treated as having thereby disposed of the asset by selling it for its then market value.

161(2) If at any time an asset forming part of the trading stock of a person's trade is appropriated by him for any other purpose, or is retained by him on his ceasing to carry on the trade, he shall be treated as having acquired it at that time for a consideration equal to the amount brought into the accounts of the trade in respect of it for tax purposes on the appropriation or on his ceasing to carry on the trade, as the case may be.

161(3) Subject to subsection (4) below, subsection (1) above shall not apply in relation to a person's appropriation of an asset for the purposes of a trade if–

(a) he is chargeable to corporation tax in respect of the profits of the trade under Chapter 2 of Part 3 of CTA 2009 and the trade is carried on wholly or partly in the United Kingdom, or

(b) he is chargeable to income tax in respect of the profits of the trade under Chapter 2 of Part 2 of ITTOIA 2005 and the trade is carried on wholly or partly in the United Kingdom,

and he elects that instead the market value of the asset at the time of the appropriation shall, in computing the profits of the trade for purposes of tax, be treated as reduced by the amount of the chargeable gain or increased by the amount of the allowable loss referred to in subsection (1), and where that subsection does not apply by reason of such an election, the profits of the trade shall be computed accordingly.

161(3ZA) But if the person–

(a) meets the requirement of paragraph (a) or (b) of subsection (3), and

(b) (ignoring any election under this section) would be treated under subsection (1) as making a relevant high value disposal on which an ATED-related gain chargeable to, or loss allowable for the purposes of, capital gains tax under section 2B would accrue,

the person may not elect under subsection (3) but may elect for subsection (3ZB) to apply.

161(3ZB) Subject to subsection (4), where an election is made for this subsection to apply–

(a) a gain or loss accruing on the disposal under subsection (1) which is not ATED-related is not a chargeable gain or an allowable loss,

(b) the market value of the asset at the time of the appropriation is, for the purposes of computing the profits of the trade for the purposes of tax, to be treated as reduced by the amount of any gain, or increased by the amount of any loss, which would be a chargeable gain or allowable loss but for paragraph (a), and

(c) the chargeable gain or allowable loss which accrues on that disposal and is ATED-related is unaffected by the election.

161(3A) An election under subsection (3) or (3ZA) above shall be made–

(a) for the purposes of capital gains tax, on or before the first anniversary of the 31st January next following the year of assessment in which ends the period of account in which the asset is appropriated for the purposes of the trade as trading stock;

(b) for the purposes of corporation tax, within 2 years after the end of the accounting period in which the asset is appropriated for the purposes of the trade as trading stock.

161(4) If a person making an election under subsection (3) or (3ZA) is at the time of the appropriation carrying on the trade in partnership with others, the election shall not have effect unless concurred in by the others.

161(5) If–

(a) any person is charged to income tax by virtue of sections 517B and 517C of CTA 2010 (certain profits or gains on a disposal of land treated as trading profits) on the realisation of a profit or gain because the condition in section 517B(7) of that Act is met, and.

(b) the gain is calculated on the basis that any property was appropriated as trading stock,

the property shall be treated on that basis also for the purposes of this section.

161(6) If–

(a) any person is charged to corporation tax by virtue of sections 356OB and 356OC of CTA 2010 (certain profits or gains on a disposal of land treated as trading profits) on the realisation of a profit or gain because the condition in section 356OB(7) of that Act is met, and

(b) the gain is calculated on the basis that any property was appropriated as trading stock,

the property shall be treated on that basis also for the purposes of this section.

History – In s. 161(1), the words "subsections (3) to (3ZB)" substituted for the words "subsection (3)" by FA 2013, s. 65 and Sch. 25, para. 11(2), with effect in relation to disposals occurring on or after 6 April 2013.

In s. 161(3)(a) the words "under Chapter 2 of Part 3 of CTA 2009 and the trade is carried on wholly or partly in the United Kingdom" substituted for the words "under Case I of Schedule D" by CTA 2009, s. 1322 and Sch. 1, para. 374, with effect for corporation tax purposes for accounting periods ending on or after 1 April 2009, and for income tax and capital gains tax purposes for the tax year 2009–10 and subsequent tax years.

In s. 161(3) the word "if–" and para. (a) and (b) and the words "and he elects" following them substituted for the words "if he is chargeable to income tax in respect of the profits of the trade under Case I of Schedule D, and elects" by SI 2006/959, art. 3(3), with effect for income tax purposes for the tax year 2006–07 and subsequent tax years, and for corporation tax purposes, for accounting periods ending after 5 April 2006. The changes also had deemed effect for income tax purposes, for the tax year 2005–06, and for corporation tax purposes, for accounting periods ending after 5 April 2005 and before 6 April 2006.

S. 161(3ZA) and (3ZB) inserted by FA 2013, s. 65 and Sch. 25, para. 11(3), with effect in relation to disposals occurring on or after 6 April 2013.

In s. 161(3A), the words "or (3ZA)" inserted by FA 2013, s. 65 and Sch. 25, para. 11(4), with effect in relation to disposals occurring on or after 6 April 2013.

In s. 161(3A), endpiece (which defined "period of account") repealed by FA 2002, s. 141 and Sch. 40, Pt. 3(16). "Period of account" is defined in ICTA 1988, s. 832(1).

S. 161(3A) inserted by FA 1996, s. 135 and Sch. 21, para. 36 for 1996–97 and later years of assessment and accounting periods ending on or after 1 July 1999, the appointed day for self-assessment to corporation tax (FA 1994, s. 199 and SI 1998/3173 (C. 78)).

In s. 161(4), the words "or (3ZA)" inserted by FA 2013, s. 65 and Sch. 25, para. 11(5), with effect in relation to disposals occurring on or after 6 April 2013.

S. 161(5)(a) substituted by FA 2016, s. 79(10), with effect from 15 September 2016 (Royal Assent). Former s. 161(5)(a) read as follows:

"(a) any person is charged to income tax under section 755 of ITA 2007 (charge to tax from transactions in land) on the realisation of a gain because the condition in section 756(3)(d) is met, and".

S. 161(5) inserted by ITA 2007, s. 1027 and Sch. 1, para. 321, with effect from 6 April 2007.

S. 161(6)(a) substituted by FA 2016, s. 77(9), with effect from 15 September 2016 (Royal Assent). Former s. 161(6)(a) read as follows:

"(a) any person is charged to corporation tax under section 818 of CTA 2010 (charge to tax on gains from transactions in land) on the realisation of a gain because the condition in section 819(2)(d) of that Act is met, and".

S. 161(6) inserted by CTA 2010, s. 1177 and Sch. 1, para. 240, with effect for corporation tax purposes for accounting periods ending on or after 1 April 2010, and for income tax and capital gains tax purposes for the tax year 2010–11 and subsequent tax years.

Derivations – CGTA 1979, s. 122.

Cross references – S. 15: meaning of "chargeable gains".
S. 16: meaning of "allowable losses".
S. 21–34: general meaning of "disposal" and "assets", including the timing of certain disposals.
S. 38(1)(a): allowable acquisition expenditure.
S. 58: priority of no gain, no loss rule for transfers between spouses.
S. 173: transfers within a group of asset which is trading stock for one but not the other, treated as appropriation by the member for which it is trading stock.
S. 272–274 and Sch. 11: meaning of "market value".
S. 288: interpretation, including meaning of "trading stock".
Sch. 7A, para. 10: adjustment for pre-entry losses where but for election under s. 161(3) there is a deemed disposal of asset by a company.
ICTA 1988, s. 18: charge under Sch. D, Case I.
ICTA 1988, s. 777(11): where land treated as appropriated as trading stock for purposes of the treatment as income of certain gains from quasi-dealing transactions, that also applies for s. 161.
FA 1994, Sch. 12, para. 3: elections under s. 161(3) are ignored for the purpose of computing transitional relief in respect of indexation losses on an appropriation to trading stock.
FA 2002, Sch. 26, para. 45: application of s. 161 to provisions on derivative contracts where certain contracts become held for purposes of trade.

Statements of practice – A32: goods taken for own consumption.

TRANSFER OF BUSINESS TO A COMPANY

162 Roll-over relief on transfer of business

162(1) This section shall apply for the purposes of this Act where a person who is not a company transfers to a company a business as a going concern, together with the whole assets of the business, or together with the whole of those assets other than cash, and the business is so transferred wholly or partly in exchange for shares issued by the company to the person transferring the business.

Any shares so received by the transferor in exchange for the business are referred to below as **"the new assets"**.

162(2) The amount determined under subsection (4) below shall be deducted from the aggregate of the chargeable gains less allowable losses ("the amount of the gain on the old assets").

162(3) For the purpose of computing any chargeable gain accruing on the disposal of any new asset–

(a) the amount determined under subsection (4) below shall be apportioned between the new assets as a whole, and

(b) the sums allowable as a deduction under section 38(1)(a) shall be reduced by the amount apportioned to the new asset under paragraph (a) above;

and if the shares which comprise the new assets are not all of the same class, the apportionment between the shares under paragraph (a) above shall be in accordance with their market values at the time they were acquired by the transferor.

162(4) The amount referred to in subsections (2) and (3)(a) above shall not exceed the cost of the new assets but, subject to that, it shall be the fraction–

$$\frac{A}{B}$$

of the amount of the gain on the old assets where–

A is the cost of the new assets, and

B is the value of the whole of the consideration received by the transferor in exchange for the business;

and for the purposes of this subsection **"the cost of the new assets"** means any sums which would be allowable as a deduction under section 38(1)(a) if the new assets were disposed of as a whole in circumstances giving rise to a chargeable gain.

162(5) References in this section to the business, in relation to shares or consideration received in exchange for the business, include references to such assets of the business as are referred to in subsection (1) above.

Derivations – CGTA 1979, s. 123.

Cross references – S. 38(1)(a): allowable acquisition expenditure, including incidental costs.
Sch. 4, para. 2, 5: reduction of one half in the amount to be deducted under s. 162 in computing gains arising from disposal of a new asset in relation to deferral before 6 April 1988 where old asset held on 31 March 1982 (or acquired in a chain of no gain, no loss disposals from that date).
SI 2009/3001, reg. 46: modification of s. 162 in relation to offshore income gains.

Extra-statutory concessions – D32: HMRC prepared not to treat liabilities taken over by transferee company as consideration; relief not precluded if some or all the liabilities of the business are not taken over by the company.

Other material – ICAEW Tax Faculty technical release TAX 7/95: HMRC confirmation, in relation to incorporation of professional partnerships, that an undertaking to pay an annuity involves taking on a liability and in strictness s. 162(4) will apply, although relief is available by virtue of ESC D32.
ICAEW Tax Faculty technical release TAX 7/95: Revenue confirmation that where the whole of the business of a partnership is transferred to a company, the HMRC will, for the purposes of s. 162, view each partner separately so that individual partners are not denied relief.
Taxline 1994/35 (not reproduced): although relief under s. 162 (roll-over relief on transfer of a business) is mandatory where a business is incorporated under that section, the Revenue will usually allow claims under TCGA 1992, s. 152 (roll-over relief on replacement of business assets) to take precedence over s. 162 relief if that is what the taxpayer wants.
Taxline 1997/57 (not reproduced): prior to 26 November 1996 reinvestment relief could be claimed under s. 164A where the reinvestment was the transfer of a business to a company in return for shares under s. 162. Somerset House has confimed that s. 164FA(3)(c) (inserted by FA 1997) overrules reinvestment relief and requires money to be used in the relevant trade within twelve months.

Notes – S. 15: meaning of "chargeable gains".
S. 16: meaning of "allowable losses".
S. 21–34: general meaning of "disposal" and "assets".
S. 272–274 and Sch. 11: meaning of "market value".
S. 288: interpretation, including meaning of "company" and "shares" as embracing stock.

162A Election for section 162 not to apply

162A(1) Section 162 shall not apply where the transferor makes an election under this section.

162A(2) An election under this section must be made by a notice given to an officer of the Board no later than the relevant date.

162A(3) Except where subsection (4) below applies, the relevant date is the second anniversary of the 31st January next following the year of assessment in which the transfer of the business took place.

162A(4) Where, by the end of the year of assessment following the one in which the transfer of the business took place, the transferor has disposed of all the new assets, the relevant date is the first anniversary of the 31st January next following the year of assessment in which the transfer of the business took place.

162A(5) For the purposes of subsection (4) above–

(a) a disposal of any of the new assets by the transferor shall be disregarded if it falls within section 58(1) (transfers between spouses and civil partners); but

(b) where a disposal of any assets to a person is disregarded by virtue of paragraph (a) above, a subsequent disposal by that person of any of those assets (other than a disposal to the transferor) shall be regarded as a disposal by the transferor.

162A(6) All such adjustments shall be made, whether by way of discharge or repayment of tax, the making of assessments or otherwise, as are required to give effect to an election under this section.

162A(7) Where, immediately before it was transferred, the business was owned by two or more persons–

(a) each of them has a separate entitlement to make an election under this section;

(b) an election made by a person by virtue of paragraph (a) above shall apply only to–

(i) the share of the amount of the gain on the old assets, and

(ii) the share of the new assets,

that is attributable to that person for the purposes of this Act.

162A(8) The reference in subsection (7) above to ownership by two or more persons includes, in Scotland as well as elsewhere in the United Kingdom, a reference to ownership by a partnership consisting of two or more persons.

162A(9) Expressions used in this section and in section 162 have the same meaning in this section as in that one.

But references in this section to new assets also include any shares or debentures that are treated by virtue of one or more applications of section 127 (including that section as applied by virtue of any enactment relating to chargeable gains) as the same asset as the new assets.

History – In s. 162A(5)(a) the words "spouses and civil partners" substituted for the words "husband and wife" by SI 2005/3229, reg. 111, with effect from 5 December 2005.
S. 162A inserted by FA 2002, s. 49(1) in relation to a transfer of a business on or after 6 April 2002.

TRANSFER OF BUSINESS FROM COMPANY TO SHAREHOLDERS

162B Disincorporation relief: assets (including pre-FA 2002 goodwill)

162B(1) This section applies where–

(a) a company transfers its business to some or all of the shareholders of the company, and

(b) a claim for disincorporation relief in respect of the transfer has been made under section 58 of the Finance Act 2013.

162B(2) The disposal and acquisition of any qualifying asset of the business included in the transfer is to be deemed to be for a consideration equal to the lower of–

(a) the sums allowable under section 38 as a deduction in the computation of the gain accruing to the company on the disposal of the asset in question, and

(b) the market value of the asset.

162B(3) In subsection (2) a **"qualifying asset"** means–

(a) goodwill, or

(b) an interest in land which is not held as trading stock.

162B(4) But subsection (2) does not apply to the goodwill of the business if section 162C applies to it.

History – S. 162B inserted by FA 2013, s. 61(1), with effect in relation to a transfer of a business with a business transfer date of 1 April 2013 or a later date.

Other material – HMRC guidance: disincorporation relief.

162C Disincorporation relief: post-FA 2002 goodwill

162C(1) This section applies where–

(a) a company transfers its business to some or all of the shareholders of the company,

(b) a claim for disincorporation relief in respect of the transfer has been made under section 58 of the Finance Act 2013, and

(c) section 849A of CTA 2009 (disincorporation relief: transfer values for post-FA 2002 goodwill) applies to the transfer of the goodwill of the business.

162C(2) The acquisition of the goodwill of the business is deemed to be for a consideration equal to the value at which the goodwill is treated as transferred by virtue of section 849A of CTA 2009.

History – S. 162C inserted by FA 2013, s. 61(1), with effect in relation to a transfer of a business with a business transfer date of 1 April 2013 or a later date.

RETIREMENT RELIEF

163 Relief for disposals by individuals on retirement

163 [Repealed by FA 1998, s. 140(2)(b), s. 165 and Sch. 27, Pt. III(31).]

History – Heading amended by CCH to reflect altered content by the omission of the words "from family business" which appeared at the end.
S. 163 repealed by FA 1998, s. 140(2)(a), s. 165 and Sch. 27, Pt. III(31), with effect in relation to disposals in the year 2003–04 and subsequent years of assessment.

164 Other retirement relief

164 [Repealed by FA 1998, s. 140(2)(b), s. 165 and Sch. 27, Pt. III(31).]

History – S. 164 repealed by FA 1998, s. 140(2)(a), s. 165 and Sch. 27, Pt. III(31), with effect in relation to disposals in the year 2003–04 and subsequent years of assessment.

Chapter IA – Roll-Over Relief on Re-Investment

History – Part V, Chapter IA repealed by FA 1998, s. 165 and Sch. 27, Pt. III(32), with effect in relation to acquisitions made on or after 6 April 1998.

164A Relief on re-investment for individuals

164A [Repealed by FA 1998, s. 165 and Sch. 27, Pt. III(32).]

History – S. 164A repealed by FA 1998, s. 165 and Sch. 27, Pt. III(32), with effect in relation to acquisitions made on or after 6 April 1998.

164B Roll-over relief on re-investment by trustees

164B [Repealed by FA 1998, Sch. 27, Pt. III(32).]

History – S. 164B repealed by FA 1998, Sch. 27, Pt. III(32) as respects acquisitions made on or after 6 April 1998.

164BA Interaction with retirement relief

164BA [Repealed by FA 1998, s. 165 and Sch. 27, Pt. III(32).]

History – S. 164BA repealed by FA 1998, s. 165 and Sch. 27, Pt. III(32), with effect in relation to acquisitions made on or after 6 April 1998.

164C Restriction applying to retirement relief and roll-over relief on re-investment

164C [Repealed by FA 1994, s. 91, Sch. 11, para. 4 and s. 258 and Sch. 26, Pt. V(7).]

History – S. 164C repealed by FA 1994, s. 91, Sch. 11, para. 4 and s. 258 and Sch. 26, Pt. V(7) in relation to disposals made on or after 30 November 1993.

164D Relief carried forward into replacement shares

164D [Repealed by FA 1994, s. 91, Sch. 11, para. 4, and s. 258 and Sch. 26, Pt. V(7).]

History – S. 164D repealed by FA 1994, s. 91, Sch. 11, para. 4 and s. 258 and Sch. 26, Pt. V(7) in relation to disposals made on or after 30 November 1993.

164E Applications of Chapter in cases of an exchange of shares

164E [Repealed by FA 1994, s. 91 and Sch. 11, para. 4, and s. 258 and Sch. 26, Pt. V(7).]

History – S. 164E repealed by FA 1994, s. 91, Sch. 11, para. 4 and s. 258 and Sch. 26, Pt. V(7) in relation to disposals made on or after 30 November 1993.

164F Failure of conditions of relief

164F [Repealed by FA 1998, s. 165 and Sch. 27, Pt. III(32).]

History – S. 164F repealed by FA 1998, s. 165 and Sch. 27, Pt. III(32), with effect in relation to acquisitions made on or after 6 April 1998.

164FA Loss of relief in cases where shares acquired on being issued

164FA [Repealed by FA 1998, s. 165 and Sch. 27, Pt. III(32).]

History – S. 164FA repealed by FA 1998, s. 165 and Sch. 27, Pt. III(32) , with effect in relation to acquisitions made on or after 6 April 1998.

164FF Qualifying investment acquired from husband or wife

164FF [Repealed by FA 1998, s. 165, Sch. 27, Pt. III(32).]

History – S. 164FF repealed by FA 1998, s. 165, Sch. 27, Pt. III(32), with effect in relation to acquisitions made on or after 6 April 1998.

164FG Multiple claims

164FG [Repealed by FA 1998, s. 165 and Sch. 27, Pt. III(32).]

History – S. 164FG repealed by FA 1998, s. 165 and Sch. 27, Pt. III(32), with effect in relation to acquisitions made on or after 6 April 1998.

164G Meaning of "qualifying company"

164G [Repealed by FA 1998, s. 165 and Sch. 27, Pt. III(32).]

History – S. 164G repealed by FA 1998, s. 165 and Sch. 27, Pt. III(32), with effect in relation to acquisitions made on or after 6 April 1998.

164H Property companies etc. not to be qualifying companies

164H [Repealed by FA 1998, s. 165, Sch. 27, Pt. III(32).]

History – S. 164H repealed by FA 1998, s. 165, Sch. 27, Pt. III(32), with effect in relation to acquisitions made on or after 6 April 1998.

164I Qualifying trades

164I [Repealed by FA 1998, s. 165, Sch. 27, Pt. III(32).]

History – S. 164I repealed by FA 1998, s. 165, Sch. 27, Pt. III(32), with effect in relation to acquisitions made on or after 6 April 1998.

164J Provisions supplementary to section 164I

164J [Repealed by FA 1998, s. 165 Sch. 27, Pt. III(32).]

History – S. 164J repealed by FA 1998, s. 165 Sch. 27, Pt. III(32), with effect in relation to acquisitions made on or after 6 April 1998.

164K Foreign residents

164K [Repealed by FA 1998, s. 165 and Sch. 27, Pt. III(32).]

History – S. 164K repealed by FA 1998, s. 165 and Sch. 27, Pt. III(32), with effect in relation to acquisitions made on or after 6 April 1998.

164L Anti-avoidance provisions

164L [Repealed by FA 1998, s. 165 and Sch. 27, Pt. III(32).]

History – S. 164L repealed by FA 1998, s. 165 and Sch. 27, Pt. III(32), with effect in relation to acquisitions made on or after 6 April 1998.

164M Exclusion of double relief

164M [Repealed by FA 1998, s. 165 and Sch. 27, Pt. III(32).]

History – S. 164M repealed by FA 1998, s. 165 and Sch. 27, Pt. III(32), with effect in relation to acquisitions made on or after 6 April 1998.

164MA Exclusion of double relief

164MA [Repealed by FA 1998, s. 165 and Sch. 27, Pt. III(32), with effect in relation to acquisitions made on or after 6 April 1998.]

History – S. 164MA repealed by FA 1998, s. 165 and Sch. 27, Pt. III(32), with effect in relation to acquisitions made on or after 6 April 1998.

164N Interpretation of Chapter IA

164N [Repealed by FA 1998, s. 165 and Sch. 27, Pt. III(32).]

History – S. 164N repealed by FA 1998, s. 165 and Sch. 27, Pt. III(32), with effect in relation to acquisitions made on or after 6 April 1998.

Chapter II – Gifts of Business Assets

165 Relief for gifts of business assets

165(1) If–

(a) an individual (**"the transferor"**) makes a disposal otherwise than under a bargain at arm's length of an asset within subsection (2) below, and

(b) a claim for relief under this section is made by the transferor and the person who acquires the asset (**"the transferee"**) or, where the trustees of a settlement are the transferee, by the transferor alone,

then, subject to subsection (3) and sections 166, 167, 167A, 169, 169B and 169C, subsection (4) below shall apply in relation to the disposal.

165(2) An asset is within this subsection if–

(a) it is, or is an interest in, an asset used for the purposes of a trade, profession or vocation carried on by–

  (i) the transferor, or

  (ii) his personal company, or

  (iii) a member of a trading group of which the holding company is his personal company, or

(b) it consists of shares or securities of a trading company, or of the holding company of a trading group, where–

  (i) the shares or securities are not listed on a recognised stock exchange, or

  (ii) the trading company or holding company is the transferor's personal company.

165(3) Subsection (4) below does not apply in relation to a disposal if–

(a) [repealed by FA 1998, s. 165 and Sch. 27, Pt. III(31)], or

(b) [repealed by FA 1998, s. 165 and Sch. 27, Pt. III(31)], or

(ba) in the case of a disposal of shares or securities, the transferee is a company,

(c) in the case of a disposal of qualifying corporate bonds, a gain is deemed to accrue by virtue of section 116(10)(b), or

(d) subsection (3) of section 260 applies in relation to the disposal (or would apply if a claim for relief were duly made under that section).

165(4) Where a claim for relief is made under this section in respect of a disposal–

(a) the amount of any chargeable gain which, apart from this section, would accrue to the transferor on the disposal, and

(b) the amount of the consideration for which apart from this section, the transferee would be regarded for the purposes of capital gains tax as having acquired the asset or, as the case may be, the shares or securities,

shall each be reduced by an amount equal to the held-over gain on the disposal.

165(5) Part I of Schedule 7 shall have effect for extending the relief provided for by virtue of subsections (1) to (4) above in the case of agricultural property and for applying it in relation to settled property.

165(6) Subject to Part II of Schedule 7 and subsection (7) below, the reference in subsection (4) above to the held-over gain on a disposal is a reference to the chargeable gain which would have accrued on that disposal apart from subsection (4) above, and in subsection (7) below that chargeable gain is referred to as the unrelieved gain on the disposal.

165(7) In any case where–

(a) there is actual consideration (as opposed to the consideration equal to the market value which is deemed to be given by virtue of section 17(1)) for a disposal in respect of which a claim for relief is made under this section, and

(b) that actual consideration exceeds the sums allowable as a deduction under section 38,

the **held-over gain** on the disposal shall be the amount by which the unrelieved gain on the disposal exceeds the excess referred to in paragraph (b) above.

165(7A) Subsections (7B) and (7C) apply in any case where–

(a) the disposal is a non-resident CGT disposal, and

(b) the transferee is resident in the United Kingdom.

165(7B) Subsections (4) and (6) have effect in relation to the disposal as if the references to "chargeable gain" were references to "chargeable NRCGT gain".

165(7C) Subsection (7) has effect in relation to the disposal as if the reference to "the excess referred to in paragraph (b) above" were a reference to "the chargeable NRCGT gain which, ignoring this section and section 17(1), would accrue to the transferor on the disposal".

165(8) Subject to subsection (9) below, in this section and Schedule 7–

(a) **"personal company"**, in relation to an individual, means a company the voting rights in which are exercisable, as to not less than 5 per cent, by that individual;

(aa) **"holding company"**, **"trading company"** and **"trading group"** have the meaning given by section 165A; and

(b) **"trade"**, **"profession"** and **"vocation"** have the same meaning as in the Income Tax Acts.

165(9) In this section and Schedule 7 and in determining whether a company is a trading company for the purposes of this section and that Schedule, the expression **"trade"** shall be taken to include the occupation of woodlands where the woodlands are managed by the occupier on a commercial basis and with a view to the realisation of profits.

165(10) Where a disposal in relation to which subsection (4) above applies is (or proves to be) a chargeable transfer for inheritance tax purposes, there shall be allowed as a deduction in computing (for capital gains tax purposes) the chargeable gain accruing to the transferee on the disposal of the asset in question an amount equal to whichever is the lesser of–

(a) the inheritance tax attributable to the value of the asset, and

(b) the amount of the chargeable gain as computed apart from this subsection,

and, in the case of a disposal which, being a potentially exempt transfer, proves to be a chargeable transfer, all necessary adjustments shall be made, whether by the discharge or repayment of capital gains tax or otherwise.

165(11) Where an amount of inheritance tax–

(a) falls to be redetermined in consequence of the transferor's death within 7 years of making the chargeable transfer in question, or

(b) is otherwise varied,

after it has been taken into account under subsection (10) above, all necessary adjustments shall be made, whether by the making of an assessment to capital gains tax or by the discharge or repayment of such tax.

History – In s. 165(1), "167A," inserted by FA 2015, s. 37 and Sch. 7, para. 23(2), with effect in relation to disposals made on or after 6 April 2015.

In s. 165(1), the words "and 169" substituted by the words "169, 169B and 169C" by FA 2004, s. 116 and Sch. 21, para. 3(2) with effect, by virtue of FA 2004, Sch. 21, para. 10(4), in relation to disposals on or after 10 December 2003 (whenever any earlier disposal as mentioned in section 169B(3)(b) or 169C(3)(b) was made).

In s. 165(1) reference to s. 169 inserted by FA 2000, s. 90(1) with effect in relation to disposals made on or after 9 November 1999.

S. 165(2)(b)(i): "listed" substituted for "quoted" by FA 1996, s. 199 and Sch. 38, para. 10 for disposals on or after 1 April 1996. Words "not listed on a recognised stock exchange" substituted for "neither listed on a recognised stock exchange nor dealt in on the Unlisted Securities Market" by FA 2000, s. 90(3) with effect in relation to disposals made on or after 9 November 1999.

In s. 165(2) references to "personal company" substituted by FA 1993, s. 87 and Sch. 7, para. 1 in relation to disposals on or after 16 March 1993.

S. 165(3)(a) and (b) repealed by FA 1998, s. 165 and Sch. 27, Pt. III(31) which have effect in relation to disposals in the year 2003–04 and subsequent years of assessment.

In s. 165(3)(b) words "the transferee is a company or" inserted by FA 2000, s. 90(4) with effect in relation to disposals made on or after 9 November 1999.

S. 165(3)(ba) inserted by FA 2004, s. 116 and Sch. 21, para. 3(3) with effect, by virtue of FA 2004, Sch. 21, para. 10(5), in relation to disposals on or after 21 October 2003.

In s. 165(6), the words "and (in appropriate cases) Schedule 6" repealed by FA 1998, s. 165 and Sch. 27, Pt. III(31) which have effect *in relation to disposals in the year 2003–04* and subsequent years of assessment.

S. 165(7A), (7B) and (7C) inserted by FA 2015, s. 37 and Sch. 7, para. 23(3), with effect in relation to disposals made on or after 6 April 2015.

S. 165(8)(aa) substituted by FA 2008, s. 8 and Sch. 2, para. 33 with effect in relation to chargeable gains accruing or treated as accruing in the tax year 2008–09 or any subsequent tax year (FA 2008, Sch. 2, para. 56(3)).

S. 165(8)(aa) substituted for former s. 165(8)(aa) by FA 2004, s. 116 and Sch. 21, para. 3(4) with effect, by virtue of FA 2004, Sch. 21, para. 10(6), in relation to the year 2004–05 and subsequent years of assessment.

In s. 165(8) references to "personal company" substituted by FA 1993, s. 87 and Sch. 7, para. 1 in relation to disposals on or after 16 March 1993.
S.165(8)(a) and (aa) substituted for former s. 165(8)(a) by FA 1998, s. 140(4) which have effect in relation to the year 2003–04 and subsequent years of assessment.
In s. 165(10), the words "after 13th March 1989, in respect of which a claim is made under this section," substituted by the words "in relation to which subsection (4) above applies" by FA 2004, s. 116 and Sch. 21, para. 3(5) with effect, by virtue of FA 2004, Sch. 21, para. 10(7), in relation to disposals on or after 10 December 2003.

Derivations – S. 165(1), (2) as originally enacted: CGTA 1979, s. 126(1), (1A), as (respectively) substituted and inserted by FA 1989, s. 124 and Sch. 14, para. 1.
S. 165(3): CGTA 1979, s. 126(2), as amended by FA 1985, s. 70(9)(a) and FA 1989, s. 124 and Sch. 14, para. 1.
S. 165(4)–(6): CGTA 1979, s. 126(3)–(5).
S. 165(7): CGTA 1979, s. 126(6), as amended by FA 1981, s. 90(3)(a).
S. 165(8) (as originally enacted): CGTA 1979, s. 126(7), as amended by FA 1985, s. 70(9)(b) and FA 1989, s. 124 and Sch. 14, para. 1.
S. 165(9): CGTA 1979, s. 126(8).
S. 165(10), (11): CGTA 1979, s. 126(9), (10), as inserted by FA 1989, s. 124 and Sch. 14, para. 1.

Cross references – S. 17(1): acquisitions and disposals otherwise than in bargains made at arm's length generally at market value.
S. 38: deduction for allowable acquisition expenditure, including incidental costs, enhancement or title expenditure and incidental costs of disposal.
S. 74: elimination or reduction (s. 72(1)(b), 73(1)(a), (2)) of chargeable gain on disposal under s. 71(1) or s. 72(1)(a) of asset gifted into trust restricted by reference to any held-over gain.
S. 81(7): deemed market value disposal of certain trust assets continues to apply to assets gifted into trust for which relief under s. 165 given, notwithstanding restriction where emigration results from the death of a trustee within the previous six months.
S. 116(10)(b): crystallisation of notional market value gain in respect of original shares or securities on disposal of certain qualifying corporate bonds acquired on reorganisation etc. of the shares or securities.
S. 117(8): disposal within s. 165 does not result in a corporate bond issued before 14 March 1984 becoming a qualifying corporate bond.
S. 169A(2)(b): cessation of trade by limited liability partnership.
S. 169B: disapplication of s. 165(4) in the case of gifts to certain settlor-interested settlements.
S. 169C: clawback of relief given under s. 165(4), in the case of gifts to certain settlements that become "settlor-interested".
S. 241(3): commercial lettings of furnished holiday accommodation treated as a trade.
S. 260(3): hold-over of gains in respect of gifts on which inheritance tax chargeable.
S. 281(1): election for payment of tax by instalments is not available to disposals within s. 165(4) unless the held-over gain is less than the chargeable gain otherwise accruing.
Sch. 4, para. 2, 5: reduction of one half in the amount to be deducted under s. 165 in computing gains arising from disposal of the gifted asset in relation to deferral before 6 April 1988 where asset held by donor etc. on 31 March 1982 (or acquired in a chain of no gain, no loss disposals from that date).
Sch. 6: retirement relief.
Sch. 7: relief for gifts of business assets.
Sch. 7AC, para. 3: substantial shareholding requirement exemption conditions no longer satisfied: effect on disposal where gift relief previously claimed by company in which shares sold.
Sch. 7AC, para. 37: exemption for companies with substantial shareholding: effect of earlier claim for relief under s. 165.
FA 2002, Sch. 29, para. 92(4C): gains and losses from intangible fixed assets: exception to transfer between company and related party as being at market value.

Statements of practice – SP 8/92: HMRC's practice for dealing with valuation of assets where a claim to gifts hold-over relief has been made.

HMRC interpretations – IRInt. 8: the fact that agricultural property transferred has "hope" or "development" value does not preclude or restrict relief under TCGA 1992, s. 165 as extended by Sch. 7, para. 1.
IRInt. 214: HMRC view that it is possible to claim hold-over relief under s. 165 in respect of disposals of shares or securities to a trust with a corporate trustee occurring on or after 9 November 1999: trust with corporate trustee is not a company per se: transfer to a bare trust is regarded as transfer to underlying beneficiaries.
IRInt. 250: HMRC view, with effect from 31 July 2002, that spouse who is provided with asset through court order made under Matrimonial Causes Act 1973 or Family Law (Scotland) Act 1985 has not given actual consideration by surrendering rights to alternative financial provision: transfer of asset to spouse arises from statute instead of any exchange.

Other material – HMRC press release, 20 February 1995: shares or securities of companies listed on the Alternative Investment Market will be not be regarded as quoted on a recognised stock exchange.
ICAEW Technical Release TR 759 (not reproduced): HMRC confirm that, by virtue of s. 59, relief available for Scottish partnerships.

Notes – S. 15: meaning of "chargeable gains".
S. 21–34: general meaning of "disposal" and "assets".
S. 288: interpretation, including meaning of "company", "recognised stock exchange" and "shares" as embracing stock.
TMA 1970, s. 29: assessing procedure.
TMA 1970, s. 42–43B: procedure for making claims.
FA 1980, s. 79: general gifts relief for disposals before 14 March 1989 (see cross reference to s. 67).
IHTA 1984, s. 2: meaning of "chargeable transfer".
IHTA 1984, s. 3A: potentially exempt transfers.

165A Meaning of "holding company", 'trading company' and 'trading group'

165A(1) This section has effect for the interpretation of section 165 (and this section).

165A(2) **"Holding company"** means a company that has one or more 51% subsidiaries.

165A(3) **"Trading company"** means a company carrying on trading activities whose activities do not include to a substantial extent activities other than trading activities.

165A(4) For the purposes of subsection (3) above **"trading activities"** means activities carried on by the company–

(a) in the course of, or for the purposes of, a trade being carried on by it,

(b) for the purposes of a trade that it is preparing to carry on,

(c) with a view to its acquiring or starting to carry on a trade, or

(d) with a view to its acquiring a significant interest in the share capital of another company that–
   (i) is a trading company or the holding company of a trading group, and
   (ii) if the acquiring company is a member of a group of companies, is not a member of that group.

165A(5) Activities do not qualify as trading activities under subsection (4)(c) or (d) above unless the acquisition is made, or the company starts to carry on the trade, as soon as is reasonably practicable in the circumstances.

165A(6) The reference in subsection (4)(d) above to the acquisition of a significant interest in the share capital of another company is to an acquisition of ordinary share capital in the other company–

(a) such as would make that company a 51% subsidiary of the acquiring company, or

(b) such as would give the acquiring company a qualifying shareholding in a joint venture company without making the two companies members of the same group of companies.

165A(7) For the purpose of determining whether a company which has a qualifying shareholding in a joint venture company is a trading company–

(a) any holding by it of shares in the joint venture company is to be disregarded, and

(b) it is to be treated as carrying on an appropriate proportion of the activities of the joint venture company or, where the joint venture company is the holding company of a trading group, of the activities of that group;

and in paragraph (b) above **"appropriate proportion"** means a proportion corresponding to the percentage of the ordinary share capital of the joint venture company held by the company.

165A(8) **"Trading group"** means a group of companies–

(a) one or more of whose members carry on trading activities, and

(b) the activities of whose members, taken together, do not include to a substantial extent activities other than trading activities.

165A(9) For the purposes of subsection (8) above **"trading activities"** means activities carried on by a member of the group–

(a) in the course of, or for the purposes of, a trade being carried on by any member of the group,

(b) for the purposes of a trade that any member of the group is preparing to carry on,

(c) with a view to any member of the group acquiring or starting to carry on a trade, or

(d) with a view to any member of the group acquiring a significant interest in the share capital of another company that–
   (i) is a trading company or the holding company of a trading group, and
   (ii) is not a member of the same group of companies as the acquiring company.

165A(10) Activities do not qualify as trading activities under subsection (9)(c) or (d) above unless the acquisition is made, or the group member in question starts to carry on the trade, as soon as is reasonably practicable in the circumstances.

165A(11) The reference in subsection (9)(d) above to the acquisition of a significant interest in the share capital of another company is to an acquisition of ordinary share capital in the other company–

(a) such as would make that company a member of the same group of companies as the acquiring company, or

(b) such as would give the acquiring company a qualifying shareholding in a joint venture company without making the joint venture company a member of the same group of companies as the acquiring company.

165A(12) For the purpose of determining whether a group of companies is a trading group in a case where any one or more members of the group has a qualifying shareholding in a joint venture company which is not a member of the group–

(a) every holding of shares in the joint venture company by a member of the group having a qualifying shareholding in it is to be disregarded, and

(b) each member of the group having such a qualifying shareholding is to be treated as carrying on an appropriate proportion of the activities of the joint venture company or, where the joint venture company is a holding company of a trading group, of the activities of that group;

and in paragraph (b) above **"appropriate proportion"** means a proportion corresponding to the percentage of the ordinary share capital of the joint venture company held by the member of the group.

165A(13) For the purposes of this section the activities of the members of a group of companies are to be treated as one business (with the result that activities are disregarded to the extent that they are intra-group activities).

165A(14) In this section–

"51% subsidiary" has the meaning given by Chapter 3 of Part 24 of CTA 2010,

"group of companies" means a company which has one or more 51% subsidiaries together with those subsidiaries,

"joint venture company" means a company–

(a) which is a trading company or the holding company of a trading group, and

(b) 75% or more of the ordinary share capital of which (in aggregate) is held by not more than 5 persons (the shareholdings of members of a group of companies being regarded for the purposes of this paragraph as held by a single company),

"ordinary share capital" has the meaning given by section 989 of ITA 2007,

"qualifying shareholding", in relation to a company and a joint venture company, means–

(a) the holding by the company of 10% or more of the ordinary share capital of the joint venture company, or

(b) (where the company is a member of a group of companies) the holding by the company and the other members of the group (between them) of 10% or more of that ordinary share capital, and

"trade" means (subject to section 241(3)) anything which–

(a) is a trade, profession or vocation, within the meaning of the Income Tax Acts, and

(b) is conducted on a commercial basis and with a view to the realisation of profits.

History – In s. 165A(14), in the definition of "51% subsidiary" the words "Chapter 3 of Part 24 of CTA 2010" substituted for "section 838 of the Taxes Act" by CTA 2010, s. 1177 and Sch. 1, para. 241, with effect for corporation tax purposes for accounting periods ending on or after 1 April 2010, and for income tax and capital gains tax purposes for the tax year 2010–11 and subsequent tax years.

S. 165A inserted by FA 2008, s. 8 and Sch. 2, para. 34 with effect in relation to chargeable gains accruing or treated as accruing in the tax year 2008–09 or any subsequent tax year (FA 2008, Sch. 2, para. 56(3)).

166 Gifts to non-residents

166(1) Subject to section 167A, section 165(4) shall not apply where the transferee is not resident in the United Kingdom.

166(2) Section 165(4) shall not apply where the transferee is an individual if that individual–

(a) though resident in the United Kingdom, is regarded for the purposes of any double taxation relief arrangements as resident in a territory outside the United Kingdom, and

(b) by virtue of the arrangements would not be liable in the United Kingdom to tax on a gain arising on a disposal of the asset occurring immediately after its acquisition.

History – In s. 166(1), the words "Subject to section 167A, section 165(4)" substituted for the words "Section 165(4)" by FA 2015, s. 37 and Sch. 7, para. 24, with effect in relation to disposals made on or after 6 April 2015.

In s. 166(1), the words "not resident" substituted for the words "neither resident nor ordinarily resident" by FA 2013, s. 219 and Sch. 46, para. 99(2), with effect in relation to a person's liability to capital gains tax for the tax year 2013–14 or any subsequent tax year, without prejudice to any provision in FA 2013, Sch. 46, Pt. 3 about the application of a particular amendment.

In s. 166(2)(a), the words "or ordinarily resident" omitted by FA 2013, s. 219 and Sch. 46, para. 99(3), with effect in relation to a person's liability to capital gains tax for the tax year 2013–14 or any subsequent tax year, without prejudice to any provision in FA 2013, Sch. 46, Pt. 3 about the application of a particular amendment.

In s. 166(2), the words "or a company" and "or company" which appeared after the references to "an individual" and "that individual" respectively, omitted by FA 1994, s. 251(7) and s. 258 and Sch. 26, Pt. VIII(1) in relation to disposals made on or after 30 November 1993.

Derivations – CGTA 1979, s. 126A, as inserted by FA 1989, s. 124 and Sch. 14, para. 2.

Cross references – FA 1994, s. 249: companies treated as resident in the UK for tax purposes, but resident abroad for the purposes of any double taxation relief arrangements ("dual resident companies"), are with effect from 30 November 1993 to be treated as non-UK resident for all tax purposes, even if they are incorporated in the UK.

Notes – S. 9: meaning of "resident" and "ordinarily resident".

S. 21–34: general meaning of "disposal" and "assets", including the timing of certain disposals.

S. 288: interpretation, including meaning of "double taxation relief arrangements" and reference to sections being those of this Act.

167 Gifts to foreign-controlled companies

167(1) Subject to section 167A, section 165(4) shall not apply where the transferee is a company which is within subsection (2) below.

167(2) A company is within this subsection if it is controlled by a person who, or by persons each of whom–

(a) is not resident in the United Kingdom, and

(b) is connected with the person making the disposal.

167(3) For the purposes of subsection (2) above, a person who (either alone or with others) controls a company by virtue of holding assets relating to that or any other company and who is resident in the United Kingdom is to be regarded as not resident there if–

(a) he is regarded for the purposes of any double taxation relief arrangements as resident in a territory outside the United Kingdom, and

(b) by virtue of the arrangements he would not be liable in the United Kingdom to tax on a gain arising on a disposal of the assets.

History – In s. 167(1), the words "Subject to section 167A, section 165(4)" substituted for "Section 165(4)" by FA 2015, s. 37 and Sch. 7, para. 25, with effect in relation to disposals made on or after 6 April 2015.
In s. 167(2)(a), the words "not resident" substituted for the words "neither resident nor ordinarily resident" by FA 2013, s. 219 and Sch. 46, para. 100(2), with effect in relation to a person's liability to capital gains tax for the tax year 2013–14 or any subsequent tax year, without prejudice to any provision in FA 2013, Sch. 46, Pt. 3 about the application of a particular amendment.
In s. 167(3), the words "in the United Kingdom is to be regarded as not resident" substituted for the words " or ordinarily resident in the United Kingdom shall be regarded as neither resident nor ordinarily resident" by FA 2013, s. 219 and Sch. 46, para. 100(3), with effect in relation to a person's liability to capital gains tax for the tax year 2013–14 or any subsequent tax year, without prejudice to any provision in FA 2013, Sch. 46, Pt. 3 about the application of a particular amendment.

Derivations – CGTA 1979, s. 126B, as inserted by FA 1989, s. 124 and Sch. 14, para. 2.

Notes – S. 9: meaning of "resident" and "ordinarily resident".
S. 286: meaning of "connected" in references to persons being connected with one another.
S. 288: interpretation, including meaning of "company", "double taxation relief arrangements", "control" and reference to sections being those of this Act.

167A Gifts of UK residential property interests to non-residents

167A(1) This section applies where the disposal in relation to which a claim could be made under section 165 is a disposal of a UK residential property interest to a transferee who is not resident in the United Kingdom and, ignoring section 165–

(a) a gain would accrue to the transferor on the disposal, and

(b) on the assumption that the disposal is a non-resident CGT disposal (whether or not that is the case), that gain would be a chargeable NRCGT gain (see section 57B and Schedule 4ZZB).

167A(2) Section 165(4) has effect in relation to the disposal as if it read–

"**165(4)** Where a claim for relief is made under this section in respect of the disposal, the amount of any chargeable gain which, apart from this section, would accrue to the transferor on the disposal, shall be reduced by an amount equal to the heldover gain on the disposal."

167A(3) Where the disposal is a non-resident CGT disposal–

(a) section 165(4), as modified by subsection (2) of this section, has effect in relation to the disposal as if the reference to "chargeable gain" were a reference to "chargeable NRCGT gain",

(b) section 165(6) has effect in relation to the disposal as if the references to "chargeable gain" were references to "chargeable NRCGT gain", and

(c) section 165(7) has effect in relation to the disposal as if the reference to "the excess referred to in paragraph (b) above" were a reference to "the chargeable NRCGT gain which, ignoring this section and section 17(1), would accrue to the transferor on the disposal".

167A(4) Where a claim for relief is made under section 165 in relation to the disposal mentioned in subsection (1), on a subsequent disposal by the transferee of the whole or part of the interest in UK land which is the subject of the disposal mentioned in subsection (1), the whole or a corresponding part of the held-over gain (see section 165(6))–

(a) is deemed to accrue to the transferee (in addition to any gain or loss that actually accrues on that subsequent disposal), and

(b) (if that would not otherwise be the case) is to be treated as an NRCGT gain chargeable to capital gains tax by virtue of section 14D accruing on a non-resident CGT disposal.

167A(5) Where the subsequent disposal mentioned in subsection (4) is (or proves to be) a chargeable transfer for inheritance tax purposes, section 165(10) has effect in relation to the disposal as if–

(a) the reference to **"the chargeable gain accruing to the transferee on the disposal of the asset"** were a reference to the chargeable gain accruing on the disposal as computed apart from subsection (4), and

(b) the reference in section 165(10)(b) to **"the chargeable gain"** were a reference to–

(i) the chargeable gain chargeable to capital gains tax by virtue of any provision of this Act accruing on the disposal, and

(ii) the held-over gain deemed to accrue under subsection (4).

167A(6) In this section, **"interest in UK land"** has the meaning given by paragraph 2 of Schedule B1.

History – S. 167A inserted by FA 2015, s. 37 and Sch. 7, para. 26 with effect in relation to disposals made on or after 6 April 2015.

168 Emigration of donee

168(1) If–

(a) relief is given under section 165 in respect of a disposal to an individual or under section 260 in respect of a disposal to an individual (**"the relevant disposal"**); and

(aa) the transferee is resident in the United Kingdom at the time of that disposal; and

(b) at a time when he has not disposed of the asset in question, the transferee ceases to be resident in the United Kingdom,

then, subject to the following provisions of this section, a chargeable gain shall be deemed to have accrued to the transferee immediately before that time, and its amount shall be equal to the held-over gain (within the meaning of section 165 or 260) on the relevant disposal.

168(2) For the purposes of subsection (1) above the transferee shall be taken to have disposed of an asset before the time there referred to only if he has made a disposal or disposals in connection with which the whole of the held-over gain on the relevant disposal was represented by reductions made in accordance with section 165(4)(b) or 260(3)(b) and where he has made a disposal in connection with which part of that gain was so represented, the amount of the chargeable gain deemed by virtue of this section to accrue to him shall be correspondingly reduced.

168(3) The disposals by the transferee that are to be taken into account under subsection (2) above shall not include any disposal to which section 58 applies; but where any such disposal is made by the transferee, disposals by his spouse or civil partner shall be taken into account under subsection (2) above as if they had been made by him.

168(4) Subsection (1) above shall not apply by reason of a person ceasing to be resident more than 6 years after the end of the year of assessment in which the relevant disposal was made.

168(5) Subsection (1) above shall not apply in relation to a disposal made to an individual if–

(a) the reason for his ceasing to be resident in the United Kingdom is that he works in an employment or office all the duties of which are performed outside the United Kingdom, and

(b) he again becomes resident in the United Kingdom within the period of 3 years from the time when he ceases to be so, without having meanwhile disposed of the asset in question;

and accordingly no assessment shall be made by virtue of subsection (1) above before the end of that period in any case where the condition in paragraph (a) above is, and the condition in paragraph (b) above may be, satisfied.

168(6) For the purposes of subsection (5) above a person shall be taken to have disposed of an asset if he has made a disposal in connection with which the whole or part of the held-over gain on the relevant disposal would, had he been resident in the United Kingdom, have been represented by a reduction made in accordance with section 165(4)(b) or 260(3)(b) and subsection (3) above shall have effect for the purposes of this subsection as it has effect for the purposes of subsection (2) above.

168(7) Where an amount of tax assessed on a transferee by virtue of subsection (1) above is not paid within the period of 12 months beginning with the date when the tax becomes payable then, subject to subsection (8) below, the transferor may be assessed and charged (in the name of the transferee) to all or any part of that tax.

168(8) No assessment shall be made under subsection (7) above more than 6 years after the end of the year of assessment in which the relevant disposal was made.

168(9) Where the transferor pays an amount of tax in pursuance of subsection (7) above, he shall be entitled to recover a corresponding sum from the transferee.

168(10) Gains on disposals made after a chargeable gain has under this section been deemed to accrue by reference to a held-over gain shall be computed without any reduction under section 165(4)(b) or 260(3)(b) in respect of that held-over gain.

History – S. 168(1)(aa) inserted by FA 2015, s. 37 and Sch. 7, para. 27, with effect in relation to disposals made on or after 6 April 2015.
In s. 168(1)(b), the words "ceases to be resident" substituted for the words "becomes neither resident nor ordinarily resident" by *FA 2013, s. 219 and Sch. 46, para. 101(2)*, with effect in relation to a person's liability to capital gains tax for the tax year 2013–14 or any subsequent tax year, without prejudice to any provision in FA 2013, Sch. 46, Pt. 3 about the application of a particular amendment.
In s. 168(3) the words "or civil partner" substituted for the words "husband and wife" by SI 2005/3229, reg. 112, with effect from 5 December 2005.
In s. 168(4), the words "ceasing to be resident" substituted for the words "becoming neither resident nor ordinarily resident" by FA 2013, s. 219 and Sch. 46, para. 101(3), with effect in relation to a person's liability to capital gains tax for the tax year 2013–14 or any subsequent tax year, without prejudice to any provision in FA 2013, Sch. 46, Pt. 3 about the application of a particular amendment.
In s. 168(5)(a), the words "ceasing to be resident" substituted for the words "becoming neither resident nor ordinarily resident" by FA 2013, s. 219 and Sch. 46, para. 101(4)(a), with effect in relation to a person's liability to capital gains tax for the tax year 2013–14 or any subsequent tax year, without prejudice to any provision in FA 2013, Sch. 46, Pt. 3 about the application of a particular amendment.
In s. 168(5)(b), the words "or ordinarily resident" omitted by FA 2013, s. 219 and Sch. 46, para. 101(4)(b), with effect in relation to a person's liability to capital gains tax for the tax year 2013–14 or any subsequent tax year, without prejudice to any provision in FA 2013, Sch. 46, Pt. 3 about the application of a particular amendment.

Derivations – FA 1981, s. 79, as amended by FA 1989, s. 124 and Sch. 14, para. 6(3); FA 1991, s. 92(2).

Cross references – S. 58: deemed no gain, no loss on transfers between spouses.
S. 67(6): modification in relation to general gifts relief for disposals before 14 March 1989.
S. 260: gifts on which inheritance tax chargeable.
Sch. 4, para. 4: 50 per cent reduction in gain crystallising under s. 168 as modified by s. 67(6) where attributable to the deferral before 6 April 1988 if gifted asset held at 31 March 1982.

Extra-statutory concessions – D2: person leaving UK treated as neither resident nor ordinarily resident on date of departure not charged to tax on gains accruing from disposal made after departure; the concession does not apply to settlors of non-resident trusts where the gains are chargeable on the settlor under s. 86 and Sch. 5.

Notes – S. 9: meaning of "resident" and "ordinarily resident".
S. 15: meaning of "chargeable gains".
S. 276: UK territorial sea deemed to be part of the UK.
S. 288: interpretation.
TMA 1970, s. 29: assessing procedure.

168A Deemed disposal of UK residential property interest under section 168

168A(1) Subsection (2) applies if, ignoring subsections (2) to (4)–

(a) a gain would accrue to a transferee on a disposal of a UK residential property interest deemed to have been made by virtue of section 168(1), and

(b) on the assumption that the disposal is a non-resident CGT disposal, that gain would be an NRCGT gain chargeable to capital gains tax by virtue of section 14D (see section 57B and Schedule 4ZZB).

168A(2) The transferee may elect for subsections (3) and (4) to have effect.

168A(3) The held-over gain (within the meaning of section 165 or 260) does not accrue to the transferee on that disposal.

168A(4) But, on a subsequent disposal of the whole or part of the interest in UK land which is the subject of the disposal mentioned in subsection (1)(a), the whole or a corresponding part of the held-over gain which would have accrued to the transferee were it not for subsection (3)–

(a) is deemed to accrue to the transferee (in addition to any gain or loss that actually accrues on that subsequent disposal), and

(b) (if that would not otherwise be the case) is to be treated as an NRCGT gain chargeable to capital gains tax by virtue of section 14D accruing on a non-resident CGT disposal.

168A(5) In this section, **"interest in UK land"** has the meaning given by paragraph 2 of Schedule B1.

History – S. 168A inserted by FA 2015, s. 37 and Sch. 7, para. 28, with effect in relation to disposals made on or after 6 April 2015.

169 Gifts into dual resident trusts

169(1) This section applies where there is or has been a disposal of an asset to the trustees of a settlement in such circumstances that, on a claim for relief, section 165 or 260 applies, or would but for this section apply, so as to reduce the amounts of the chargeable gain and the consideration referred to in section 165(4) or 260(3).

169(2) In this section **"a relevant disposal"** means such a disposal as is referred to in subsection (1) above.

169(3) Relief under section 165 or 260 shall not be available on a relevant disposal if–

(a) at the material time the trustees to whom the disposal is made are resident in the United Kingdom; and

(b) on a notional disposal of the asset concerned occurring immediately after the material time, the trustees would be regarded for the purposes of any double taxation relief arrangements–

  (i) as resident in a territory outside the United Kingdom; and

  (ii) as not liable in the United Kingdom to tax on a gain accruing on that disposal.

169(4) In subsection (3) above–

(a) **"the material time"** means the time of the relevant disposal; and

(b) a **"notional disposal"** means a disposal by the trustees of the asset which was the subject of the relevant disposal.

History – In s. 169(3)(a), the words "and ordinarily resident" omitted by FA 2013, s. 219 and Sch. 46, para. 102, with effect in relation to a person's liability to capital gains tax for the tax year 2013–14 or any subsequent tax year, without prejudice to any provision in FA 2013, Sch. 46, Pt. 3 about the application of a particular amendment.
In s. 169(3)(a), the word "are" substituted for "fall to be treated, under section 69, as" by FA 2006, s. 88 and Sch. 12, para. 37(1)(a), with effect in relation to relevant disposals (within the meaning of s. 169(2)) made on or after 6 April 2007 (in relation to settlements whenever created).
In s. 169(3)(a), the words at the end of the paragraph ", although the general administration of the trust is ordinarily carried on outside the United Kingdom" omitted by FA 2006, s. 88 and Sch. 12, para. 37(1)(b) and repealed by FA 2006, s. 178 and Sch. 26, Pt. 3(15), with effect in relation to relevant disposals (within the meaning of s. 169(2)) made on or after 6 April 2007 (in relation to settlements whenever created). It is not clear from the repeal instructions whether the word "and" which occurs at the end of paragraph (a) is omitted and repealed along with the other text. To omit it completely would make the remaining provisions less clear.
In s. 169(3)(b)(ii), the word "accruing" substituted for "arising" by FA 2006, s. 88 and Sch. 12, para. 37(2), with effect in relation to relevant disposals (within the meaning of s. 169(2)) made on or after 6 April 2007 (in relation to settlements whenever created).

Derivations – FA 1986, s. 58, as amended by FA 1989, s. 124 and Sch. 14, para. 6(5).

Cross references – S. 69(1): trustees as a body treated as resident and ordinarily resident in the UK unless the general administration of the trusts is ordinarily carried on outside the UK and a majority of trustees are not resident or not ordinarily resident.
S. 165(1): relief for gifts of business assets.
S. 260: gifts on which inheritance tax chargeable.
Sch. 7, para. 2(1): relief for gifts of business assets: settled property.

Notes – S. 288: interpretation, including meaning of "double taxation relief arrangements" and reference to sections being those of this Act.

169A Cessation of trade by limited liability partnership

169A(1) This section applies where section 59A(1) ceases to apply to a limited liability partnership.

169A(2) A member of the partnership who immediately before the time at which section 59A(1) ceases to apply holds an asset, or an interest in an asset, acquired by him–

(a) on a disposal to members of a partnership, and

(b) for a consideration which is treated as reduced under section 165(4)(b) or 260(3)(b),

shall be treated as if a chargeable gain equal to the amount of the reduction accrued to him immediately before that time.

History – s. 169A inserted by FA 2001, s. 75(3) with effect from 3 May 2001 and applies where section 59A(1) ceased or ceases to apply as mentioned in this section.

GIFTS TO SETTLOR-INTERESTED SETTLEMENTS ETC

169B Gifts to settlor-interested settlements etc

169B(1) Neither section 165(4) nor section 260(3) shall apply in relation to a disposal ("the relevant disposal")–

(a) made by a person ("the transferor") to the trustees of a settlement, and

(b) in respect of which Condition 1 or Condition 2 below is satisfied.

169B(2) Condition 1 is that, immediately after the making of the relevant disposal,–

(a) there is a settlor (see section 169E) who has an interest in the settlement (see section 169F), or

(b) an arrangement (see section 169G) subsists under which such an interest will or may be acquired by a settlor.

169B(3) Condition 2 is that–

(a) a chargeable gain would (assuming that neither section 165(4) nor section 260(3) applied in relation to the relevant disposal) accrue to the transferor on that disposal,

(b) in computing the gain, the allowable expenditure would to any extent fall to be reduced in consequence, directly or indirectly, of a claim under section 165 or 260 in respect of an earlier disposal made by an individual (whether or not to the transferor), and

(c) immediately after the making of the relevant disposal,–

  (i) that individual has an interest in the settlement, or

  (ii) an arrangement subsists under which such an interest will or may be acquired by him.

169B(4) This section is subject to section 169D (exception for maintenance funds for historic buildings and certain settlements for disabled persons).

History – S. 169B inserted by FA 2004, s. 116 and Sch. 21, para. 4 with effect, by virtue of FA 2004, Sch. 21, para. 10(4), in relation to disposals on or after 10 December 2003 (whenever any earlier disposal as mentioned in section 169B(3)(b) or 169C(3)(b) was made).

Cross references – S. 165(1): relief for gifts of business assets.
Sch. 7, para. 2(1): relief for gifts of business assets: settled property.

169C Clawback of relief if settlement becomes settlor-interested etc

169C(1) This section applies in relation to a disposal ("the relevant disposal")–

(a) made by a person ("the transferor") to the trustees of a settlement,

(b) in relation to which section 165(4) or 260(3) applies, or would apart from this section apply, and

(c) in respect of which Condition 1 or Condition 2 below is satisfied.

169C(2) Condition 1 is that, at any time during the clawback period,–

(a) there is a settlor who has an interest in the settlement, or

(b) an arrangement subsists under which such an interest will or may be acquired by a settlor.

169C(3) Condition 2 is that–

(a) in computing the chargeable gain which would (assuming that neither section 165(4) nor section 260(3) applied in relation to the relevant disposal) accrue to the transferor on that disposal, the allowable expenditure would fall to be reduced,

(b) that reduction would to any extent fall to be made in consequence, directly or indirectly, of a claim under section 165 or 260 in respect of an earlier disposal made by an individual (whether or not to the transferor), and

(c) at any time during the clawback period,–

(i) that individual has an interest in the settlement, or

(ii) an arrangement subsists under which such an interest will or may be acquired by him.

169C(4) If no claim for relief under section 165 or 260 in respect of the relevant disposal is made before the material time, neither section 165(4) nor section 260(3) shall apply in relation to that disposal.

169C(5) Subsections (7) to (9) below apply if a claim for relief under section 165 or 260 in respect of the relevant disposal is made before the material time.

169C(6) But those subsections do not apply if–

(a) the transferor is an individual, and

(b) he dies before the material time.

169C(7) A chargeable gain, of an amount equal to the amount of the held-over gain (within the meaning of section 165 or 260) on the relevant disposal, shall be treated for the purposes of tax in respect of chargeable gains as accruing to the transferor at the material time.

169C(8) For any chargeable period ending after the making of the relevant disposal, the chargeable gains and allowable losses of–

(a) the trustees of the settlement, or

(b) any person whose title to any property to any extent derives, directly or indirectly, from them,

shall be determined on the assumption that neither section 165(4)(b) nor section 260(3)(b) ever applied in relation to that disposal.

169C(9) All such adjustments shall be made, whether by discharge or repayment of tax, the making of assessments or otherwise, as are required to give effect to subsection (8) above (notwithstanding any limitation on the time within which any adjustment may be made).

169C(10) If a claim for relief under section 165 or 260 in respect of the relevant disposal is revoked, this section shall apply as if the claim had never been made.

169C(11) In this section **"the clawback period"** means the period–

(a) beginning immediately after the making of the relevant disposal, and

(b) ending six years after the end of the year of assessment in which that disposal was made.

169C(12) In this section **"the material time"** means the time at which subsection (1)(c) above first becomes satisfied.

169C(13) This section is subject to section 169D.

History – S. 169C inserted by FA 2004, s. 116 and Sch. 21, para. 4 with effect, by virtue of FA 2004, Sch. 21, para. 10(4), in relation to disposals on or after 10 December 2003 (whenever any earlier disposal as mentioned in section 169B(3)(b) or 169C(3)(b) was made).

Cross references – S. 165(1): relief for gifts of business assets.
S. 281(8): application of rules for payment of tax by instalments in s. 281 to charges under 169C(7).
S. 282(4): application of rules for recovery of tax from donee (trustees of settlement) in s. 282 to charges under 169C(7).
Sch. A1, para. 16(2)(da): application of special taper relief rules, where there is a postponed gain, to charges under 169C(7).
Sch. 7, para. 2(1): relief for gifts of business assets: settled property.

169D Exceptions to sections 169B and 169C

169D(1) Sections 169B and 169C shall not apply in relation to a disposal to the trustees of a settlement in a year of assessment if the trustees have elected, or could have elected, that section 508 of ITA 2007 (trustees' election in respect of income arising from heritage maintenance property) shall have effect in the case of–

(a) the settlement, or

(b) any part of the settlement,

in relation to that year of assessment.

169D(2) Sections 169B and 169C shall not apply in relation to a disposal to the trustees of a settlement if the following conditions are satisfied.

169D(3) The first condition is that, immediately after the making of the disposal, the settled property is held on trusts which secure that, during the lifetime of a disabled person–

(a) if any of the property is applied for the benefit of a beneficiary, it is applied for the disabled person's benefit, and

(b) either–

(i) the disabled person is entitled to all of the income (if there is any) arising from any of the property, or

(ii) if any such income is applied for the benefit of a beneficiary, it is applied for the disabled person's benefit.

169D(4) The second condition is that if, immediately after the making of the disposal, one or more settlors is an interested settlor, each such settlor must at that time be a disabled beneficiary.

169D(4A) Where the income arising from the settled property is held on trusts of the kind described in section 33 of the Trustee Act 1925 (protective trusts), subsection (3) has effect as if the reference to the lifetime of a disabled person were a reference to the period during which the income is held on trust for the disabled person.

169D(4B) The trusts on which the settled property is held are not to be treated as falling outside subsection (3) by reason only of–

(a) the trustees' having powers that enable them to apply in any tax year otherwise than for the benefit of the disabled person amounts (whether consisting of income or capital, or both) not exceeding the annual limit,

(b) the trustees' having the powers conferred by section 32 of the Trustee Act 1925 (powers of advancement),

(c) the trustees' having those powers but free from, or subject to a less restrictive limitation than, the limitation imposed by proviso (a) of subsection (1) of that section,

(d) the trustees' having the powers conferred by section 33 of the Trustee Act (Northern Ireland) 1958 (corresponding provision for Northern Ireland),

(e) the trustees' having those powers but free from, or subject to a less restrictive limitation than, the limitation imposed by subsection (1)(a) of that section, or

(f) the trustees' having powers to the like effect as the powers mentioned in any of paragraphs (b) to (e).

169D(4C) For the purposes of this section, the **"annual limit"** for a tax year is whichever is the lower of the following amounts–

(a) £3,000, and

(b) 3% of the amount that is the maximum value of the settled property during the tax year in question.

169D(4D) The Treasury may by order–

(a) specify circumstances in which subsection (4B)(a) is, or is not, to apply in relation to a trust, and

(b) amend the definition of **"the annual limit"** in subsection (4C).

169D(4E) An order under subsection (4D) may–

(a) make different provision for different cases, and

(b) contain transitional and saving provision.

169D(4F) A statutory instrument containing an order under subsection (4D) may not be made unless a draft of the instrument has been laid before, and approved by a resolution of, the House of Commons.

169D(5) For the purposes of subsection (4) above a settlor is an **"interested settlor"** in relation to a settlement if–

(a) he has an interest in the settlement, or

(b) an arrangement subsists under which such an interest will or may be acquired by him;

and for this purpose, the references to an individual's spouse or civil partner in section 169F(2) and (3) and to an individual's dependent child in section 169F(2A) shall be disregarded.

169D(6) In subsection (4) above **"disabled beneficiary"**, in relation to a settlement, means a disabled person who–

(a) is a beneficiary under the settlement, or

(b) would be such a beneficiary if he had the interest in the settlement by virtue of which subsection (5)(b) above applies in relation to him.

169D(7) In this section **"disabled person"** has the meaning given by Schedule 1A to the Finance Act 2005

169D(8) [Effectively omitted by FA 2013, s. 216 and Sch. 44, para. 12(4).]

169D(9) [Effectively omitted by FA 2013, s. 216 and Sch. 44, para. 12(4).]

169D(10) [Omitted by FA 2013, s. 216 and Sch. 44, para. 12(5).]

169D(11) The references in subsection (3) above to the lifetime of a person shall, where the income from the settled property is held for his benefit on trusts of the kind described in section 33 of the Trustee

Act 1925 (protective trusts), be construed as references to the period during which the income is held on trust for him.

History – In s. 169D(1), the words ", or could have elected," inserted by FA 2013, s. 63(1) with effect for the tax year 2012–13 and subsequent tax years.
In s. 169D(1), the words "508 of ITA 2007 (trustees' election in respect of income arising from heritage maintenance property)" substituted for "691(2) of the Taxes Act (certain income of maintenance funds for historic buildings not to be income of settlor etc)" by ITA 2007, s. 1027 and Sch. 1, para. 322, with effect from 6 April 2007.
S. 169D(3) substituted by FA 2013, s. 216 and Sch. 44, para. 12(2), with effect in relation to disposals to the trustees of a settlement on or after 8 April 2013 (but if the settlement is a relevant settlement, nothing in Sch. 44, para. 12 is to be read as preventing s. 169D(2) from applying in relation to the disposal).
S. 169D(4A)–(4F) inserted by FA 2013, s. 216 and Sch. 44, para. 12(3), with effect in relation to disposals to the trustees of a settlement on or after 8 April 2013 (but if the settlement is a relevant settlement, nothing in Sch. 44, para. 12 is to be read as preventing s. 169D(2) from applying in relation to the disposal).
In s. 169D(5), the words "and to an individual's dependent child in section 169F(2A)" inserted by FA 2006, s. 88 and Sch. 12, para. 19(1), with effect from 6 April 2006.
In s. 169D(5) the words "or civil partner" inserted by SI 2005/3229, reg. 113, with effect from 5 December 2005.
S. 169D(7) substituted for s. 169D(7)–(9) by FA 2013, s. 216 and Sch. 44, para. 12(4), with effect in relation to disposals to the trustees of a settlement on or after 8 April 2013 (but if the settlement is a relevant settlement, nothing in Sch. 44, para. 12 is to be read as preventing s. 169D(2) from applying in relation to the disposal).
S. 169D(10) omitted by FA 2013, s. 216 and Sch. 44, para. 12(5), with effect in relation to disposals to the trustees of a settlement on or after 8 April 2013 (but if the settlement is a relevant settlement, nothing in Sch. 44, para. 12 is to be read as preventing s. 169D(2) from applying in relation to the disposal).
S. 169D inserted by FA 2004, s. 116 and Sch. 21, para. 4 with effect, by virtue of FA 2004, Sch. 21, para. 10(4), in relation to disposals on or after 10 December 2003 (whenever any earlier disposal as mentioned in section 169B(3)(b) or 169C(3)(b) was made).

169E Meaning of "settlor" in sections 169B to 169D and 169G

169E(1) For the purposes of this section, and sections 169B to 169D, a person is a settlor in relation to a settlement if–

(a) he is an individual, and

(b) the settled property consists of, or includes, property originating from him.

169E(2) In subsection (1) above, the reference to property originating from a settlor is a reference to–

(a) property which that settlor has provided directly or indirectly for the purposes of the settlement, and

(b) property which wholly or partly represents that property or any part of it.

169E(3) In subsection (2) above, the references to property which a settlor has provided directly or indirectly–

(a) include references to property which has been provided directly or indirectly by another person in pursuance of reciprocal arrangements with that settlor, but

(b) do not include references to property which that settlor has provided directly or indirectly in pursuance of reciprocal arrangements with another person.

169E(4) In subsection (2) above, the reference to property which represents other property includes a reference to property which represents accumulated income from that other property.

History – In s. 169E(1), the word "and" inserted after the words "this section" by SI 2009/2035, art. 2 and Schedule, para. 30(i), with effect from 13 August 2009.
In s. 169E(1), the words "and section 169G", which appeared after "169D", omitted by SI 2009/2035, art. 2 and Schedule, para. 30(ii), with effect from 13 August 2009.
S. 169E inserted by FA 2004, s. 116 and Sch. 21, para. 4 with effect, by virtue of FA 2004, Sch. 21, para. 10(4), in relation to disposals on or after 10 December 2003 (whenever any earlier disposal as mentioned in section 169B(3)(b) or 169C(3)(b) was made).

169F Meaning of "interest in a settlement" in sections 169B to 169D

169F(1) For the purposes of this section and sections 169B to 169D, an individual is to be regarded as having an interest in a settlement if subsection (2), (3) or (3A) below applies.

169F(2) This subsection applies if–

(a) any property which is or may at any time be comprised in the settlement, or

(b) any derived property,

is, or will or may become, payable to or applicable for the benefit of the individual or his spouse or civil partner in any circumstances whatsoever.

169F(3) This subsection applies if the individual or his spouse or civil partner enjoys a benefit deriving directly or indirectly from–

(a) any property which is comprised in the settlement, or

(b) any derived property.

169F(3A) This subsection applies if–

(a) any property which is or may at any time be comprised in the settlement, or any derived property, is, or will or may become, payable to or applicable for the benefit of a child of the individual, at a time when that child is a dependent child of his, in any circumstances whatsoever, or

(b) a dependent child of the individual enjoys a benefit deriving directly or indirectly from any property which is comprised in the settlement or any derived property.

169F(4) The references in subsections (2) and (3) above to the spouse or civil partner of the individual do not include–

(a) a spouse or civil partner from whom the individual is separated–

(i) under an order of a court,

(ii) under a separation agreement, or

(iii) in such circumstances that the separation is likely to be permanent, or

(b) the widow or widower or surviving civil partner of the individual.

169F(4A) In this section–

(a) **"dependent child"** means a child who is–

(i) under the age of 18 years,

(ii) unmarried, and

(iii) does not have a civil partner, and

(b) **"child"** includes a stepchild.

169F(4B) For the purposes of subsection (3A) above no account shall be taken of a term of a settlement relating to dependent children of an individual in respect of any time at which he has no dependent child.

169F(5) An individual is not to be regarded as having an interest in a settlement by virtue of subsection (2) above if and so long as none of the property which may at any time be comprised in the settlement, and no derived property, can become payable or applicable as mentioned in that provision except in the event of–

(a) in the case of a marriage settlement or civil partnership settlement, the death of both parties to the marriage or civil partnership and of all or any of the children of the family of the parties to the marriage or civil partnership, or

(b) the death of a child of the individual where the child had become beneficially entitled to the property or any derived property at an age not exceeding 25.

169F(5A) In subsection (5) **"child of the family"**, in relation to parties to a marriage or civil partnership, means a child of one or both of them.

169F(6) In this section **"derived property"**, in relation to any property, means–

(a) income from that property,

(b) property directly or indirectly representing–

(i) proceeds of that property, or

(ii) proceeds of income from that property, or

(c) income from property which is derived property by virtue of paragraph (b) above.

History – In s. 169F(1), the words ", (3) or (3A)" substituted for "or (3)" by FA 2006, s. 88 and Sch. 12, para. 4(1)(a), with effect for the purpose of determining whether an individual is regarded as having an interest in a settlement (whenever created) on or after 6 April 2006 but not, for the purposes of s. 169C, if the relevant disposal is made on or before 5 April 2006.
In s. 169F(2)(a), the words "is or" inserted by FA 2006, s. 88 and Sch. 12, para. 4(1)(b), with effect for the purpose of determining whether an individual is regarded as having an interest in a settlement (whenever created) on or after 6 April 2006 but not, for the purposes of s. 169C, if the relevant disposal is made on or before 5 April 2006.
In s. 169F(2) the words "or civil partner" inserted by SI 2005/3229, reg. 114(2), with effect from 5 December 2005.
In s. 169F(3) the words "or civil partner" inserted by SI 2005/3229, reg. 114(3), with effect from 5 December 2005.
S. 169F(3A) inserted by FA 2006, s. 88 and Sch. 12, para. 4(1)(c), with effect for the purpose of determining whether an individual is regarded as having an interest in a settlement (whenever created) on or after 6 April 2006 but not, for the purposes of s. 169C, if the relevant disposal is made on or before 5 April 2006.
In s. 169F(4) the words "or civil partner" inserted twice and the words "or surviving civil partner" inserted by SI 2005/3229, reg. 114(4), with effect from 5 December 2005.
S. 169F(4A) inserted by FA 2006, s. 88 and Sch. 12, para. 4(1)(d), with effect for the purpose of determining whether an individual is regarded as having an interest in a settlement (whenever created) on or after 6 April 2006 but not, for the purposes of s. 169C, if the relevant disposal is made on or before 5 April 2006.
S. 169F(4B) inserted by FA 2006, s. 88 and Sch. 12, para. 4(1)(d), with effect for the purpose of determining whether an individual is regarded as having an interest in a settlement (whenever created) on or after 6 April 2006 but not, for the purposes of s. 169C, if the relevant disposal is made on or before 5 April 2006.
S. 169F(5)(a) substituted by SI 2005/3229, reg. 114(5), with effect in relation to disposals made on or after 5 December 2005.
S. 169F(5A) inserted by SI 2005/3229, reg. 114(6), with effect in relation to disposals made on or after 5 December 2005.
S. 169F inserted by FA 2004, s. 116 and Sch. 21, para. 4 with effect, by virtue of FA 2004, Sch. 21, para. 10(4), in relation to disposals on or after 10 December 2003 (whenever any earlier disposal as mentioned in section 169B(3)(b) or 169C(3)(b) was made).

169G Meaning of "arrangement" in sections 169B to 169E and information power

169G(1) In sections 169B to 169E **"arrangement"** or **"arrangements"** includes any scheme, agreement or understanding, whether or not legally enforceable.

169G(2-5) [Omitted by SI 2009/2035, art. 2 and Schedule, para. 31.]

History – S. 169G(2)–(5) omitted by SI 2009/2035, art. 2 and Schedule, para. 31, with effect from 13 August 2009.
In former s. 169G(4)(a) and (b) the words "or civil partner" inserted by SI 2005/3229, reg. 115, with effect from 5 December 2005.
S. 169G inserted by FA 2004, s. 116 and Sch. 21, para. 4 with effect, by virtue of FA 2004, Sch. 21, para. 10(4), in relation to disposals on or after 10 December 2003 (whenever any earlier disposal as mentioned in section 169B(3)(b) or 169C(3)(b) was made).

Cross references – TMA 1970, s. 98: s. 169G(2) entered into first column of Table: daily and continuing penalties for failures to furnish particulars and penalty for negligent etc. provision of particulars.

Chapter 3 – Entrepreneurs' Relief

History – Ch. 3 inserted by FA 2008, s. 9 and Sch. 3, para. 2 with effect in relation to disposals, reorganisations (within the meaning of s. 169Q) and relevant transactions (within the meaning of s. 116) taking place on or after 6 April 2008 (FA 2008, Sch. 3, para. 5).

Cross references – FA 2008, Sch. 3, para. 7: application of Ch. 3 in cases where a chargeable gain is deemed (by s. 116(10)(b)) to accrue on or after 6 April 2008 by reason of a relevant transaction taking place before that date.
FA 2008, Sch. 3, para. 8: interaction of Ch. 3 rules in cases where the original gain would have accrued before 6 April 2008, but for the provisions of Sch. 5B (enterprise investment scheme) or 5C (venture capital trusts).

Statements of practice – D12: partnerships and entrepreneurs' relief.

169H Introduction

169H(1) This Chapter provides for a lower rate of capital gains tax in respect of qualifying business disposals (to be known as "entrepreneurs' relief").

169H(2) The following are qualifying business disposals–

(a) a material disposal of business assets: see section 169I,

(b) a disposal of trust business assets: see section 169J, and

(c) a disposal associated with a relevant material disposal: see section 169K.

169H(3) But in the case of certain qualifying business disposals, entrepreneurs' relief is given only in respect of disposals of relevant business assets comprised in the qualifying business disposal: see sections 169L and 169LA.

169H(4) Section 169M makes provision requiring the making of a claim for entrepreneurs' relief.

169H(5) Sections 169N to 169P make provision as to the amount of entrepreneurs' relief.

169H(6) Section 169Q and 169R make provision about reorganisations.

169H(7) Sections 169S and 169SA contain interpretative provisions for the purposes of this Chapter.

History – In s. 169H(3), "sections 169L and 169LA" substituted for "section 169L" by FA 2015, s. 42(2), with effect in relation to qualifying business disposals made on or after 3 December 2014.
In s. 169H(1), the words "for a lower rate of capital gains tax" substituted for the words "relief from capital gains tax" by F(No. 2)A 2010, s. 2 and Sch. 1, para. 4, with effect in relation to qualifying business disposals occurring on or after 23 June 2010, subject to transitional provisions in F(No. 2)A 2010, Sch. 1, para. 18–22.
In s. 169H(7), the words "Sections 169S and 169SA contain" substituted for the words "Section 169S contains" by FA 2016, s. 86 and Sch. 13, para. 2, with effect in relation to disposals made on or after 18 March 2015, but only for the purposes of determining what is a trading company or trading group at times on or after that date.
S. 169H inserted by FA 2008, s. 9 and Sch. 3, para. 2 with effect in relation to disposals, reorganisations (within the meaning of s. 169Q) and relevant transactions (within the meaning of s. 116) taking place on or after 6 April 2008 (FA 2008, Sch. 3, para. 5).

169I Material disposal of business assets

169I(1) There is a material disposal of business assets where–

(a) an individual makes a disposal of business assets (see subsection (2)), and

(b) the disposal of business assets is a material disposal (see subsections (3) to (7)).

169I(2) For the purposes of this Chapter a disposal of business assets is–

(a) a disposal of the whole or part of a business,

(b) a disposal of (or of interests in) one or more assets in use, at the time at which a business ceases to be carried on, for the purposes of the business, or

(c) a disposal of one or more assets consisting of (or of interests in) shares in or securities of a company.

169I(3) A disposal within paragraph (a) of subsection (2) is a material disposal if the business is owned by the individual throughout the period of 1 year ending with the date of the disposal.

169I(4) A disposal within paragraph (b) of that subsection is a material disposal if–

(a) the business is owned by the individual throughout the period of 1 year ending with the date on which the business ceases to be carried on, and

(b) that date is within the period of 3 years ending with the date of the disposal.

169I(5) A disposal within paragraph (c) of subsection (2) is a material disposal if condition A, B, C or D is met.

169I(6) Condition A is that, throughout the period of 1 year ending with the date of the disposal–

(a) the company is the individual's personal company and is either a trading company or the holding company of a trading group, and

(b) the individual is an officer or employee of the company or (if the company is a member of a trading group) of one or more companies which are members of the trading group.

169I(7) Condition B is that the conditions in paragraphs (a) and (b) of subsection (6) are met throughout the period of 1 year ending with the date on which the company–

(a) ceases to be a trading company without continuing to be or becoming a member of a trading group, or

(b) ceases to be a member of a trading group without continuing to be or becoming a trading company,

and that date is within the period of 3 years ending with the date of the disposal.

169I(7A) Condition C is that–

(a) the assets disposed of are relevant EMI shares,

(b) the option grant date is, or is before, the first date of the period of 1 year ending with the date of the disposal, and

(c) throughout that period of 1 year–

(i) the company is either a trading company or the holding company of a trading group, and

(ii) the individual is an officer or employee of the company or (if the company is a member of a trading group) of one or more companies which are members of the trading group.

169I(7B) Condition D is that–

(a) the assets disposed of are relevant EMI sharesacquired by the individual before the cessation date,

(b) the option grant date is, or is before, the first date of the period of 1 year ending with the cessation date,

(c) the conditions in paragraph (c) of subsection (7A) are met throughout that period of 1 year, and

(d) the cessation date is within the period of 3 years ending with the date of the disposal.

169I(7C) In this section **"relevant EMI shares"** means–

(a) shares of a company acquired by an individual to which subsection (7D) applies, or

(b) shares of a company to which subsection (7F) applies.

169I(7D) This subsection applies to shares of a company acquired by an individual if the individual–

(a) acquires them on or after 6 April 2013, and

(b) acquires them as a result of the exercise of a qualifying option within the meaning given by section 527(4) of ITEPA 2003 (enterprise management incentives) where the option is exercised on or before the tenth anniversary of the date mentioned in section 529(2) of that Act.

169I(7E) Subsection (7D) does not apply to shares acquired as a result of the exercise of a qualifying option if–

(a) a disqualifying event (see section 533 of ITEPA 2003) occurs in relation to the option before its exercise, and

(b) it is exercised later than the period mentioned in section 532(1)(b) of ITEPA 2003.

169I(7F) This subsection applies to shares of a company if–

(a) the shares are the new holding in a case in which section 127 applies in relation to an individual,

(b) the original shares in that case are relevant EMI shares(whether by virtue of subsection (7D) or this subsection), and

(c) that case is one in which section 127 applies by virtue only of–

(i) section 126, or

(ii) subject to subsection (7G), section 135(3).

169I(7G) Subsection (7F)(c)(ii) applies only if–

(a) the exchange of shares in question is a qualifying exchange of shares as defined in paragraph 40 of Schedule 5 to ITEPA 2003, and

(b) when the exchange occurs, the independence requirement (see paragraph 9 of Schedule 5 to ITEPA 2003) and the trading activities requirement (see paragraphs 13 and 14 of that Schedule) are met in relation to the new company (see paragraph 40(1)(a) of that Schedule).

169I(7H) In this section **"the original relevant EMI shares"**, in relation to shares which are relevant EMI sharesby virtue of subsection (7F), means the shares originally acquired by the individual to which subsection (7D) applied.

169I(7I) If the shares disposed of are relevant EMI sharesby virtue of subsection (7F), in relation to times before the reorganisation mentioned in section 127, in subsection (7A)(c) references to the company are to be read as references to (if different)–

(a) the company whose shares are the original relevant EMI shares, or

(b) if there has been more than one reorganisation since the original relevant EMI shareswere acquired–

(i) the company whose shares are the original relevant EMI shares, or

(ii) if at the time in question the individual is holding relevant EMI shareswhich are shares of another company, that other company.

This subsection is subject to subsection (7N).

169I(7J) If the shares disposed of are relevant EMI sharesby virtue of subsection (7F), the question of whether the requirement of subsection (7B)(a) is met is to be determined by reference to the date of the acquisition of the original relevant EMI shares.

169I(7K) Subject to what follows, in subsections (7A)(b) and (7B)(b) **"the option grant date"** means the date on which the qualifying option in question was granted.

169I(7L) Subsections (7M) and (7N) apply if the qualifying option is a replacement option for the purposes of the EMI code(see paragraph 41 of Schedule 5 to ITEPA 2003).

169I(7M) In subsections (7A)(b) and (7B)(b) **"the option grant date"** means–

(a) the date on which the old option was granted, or

(b) if the old option was also a replacement option, the date on which the earlier old option was granted,

and so on.

169I(7N) In relation to any time during the currency of an old option taken into account under subsection (7M), in subsection (7A)(c) references to the company are to be read as references to the company whose shares were the subject of the old option.

169I(7O) In subsection (7B) **"the cessation date"** means the date on which the company–

(a) ceases to be a trading company without continuing to be or becoming a member of a trading group, or

(b) ceases to be a member of a trading group without continuing to be or becoming a trading company.

169I(7P) Subsections (7Q) and (7R) apply in relation to a disposal of relevant EMI sharesif–

(a) the shares were acquired as a result of the exercise of a qualifying option where–

(i) a disqualifying event (see section 533 of ITEPA 2003) occurs in relation to the option before its exercise, but

(ii) it is exercised within the period mentioned in section 532(1)(b) of ITEPA 2003, or

(b) if the shares are relevant EMI sharesby virtue of subsection (7F), the original relevant EMI shareswere acquired as mentioned in paragraph (a).

169I(7Q) Subsection (7A)(b) has effect as if the reference to the date of the disposal were a reference to the date of the disqualifying event.

169I(7R) If the disqualifying event is within section 534(1)(c) of ITEPA 2003, subsection (7B)(a) has effect as if the reference to the cessation date were a reference to the first day after the period mentioned in section 532(1)(b) of that Act if that day is later than the cessation date.

169I(8) For the purposes of this section–

(a) an individual who disposes of (or of interests in) assets used for the purposes of a business carried on by the individual on entering into a partnership which is to carry on the business is to be treated as disposing of a part of the business,

(b) the disposal by an individual of the whole or part of the individual's interest in the assets of a partnership is to be treated as a disposal by the individual of the whole or part of the business carried on by the partnership, and

(c) at any time when a business is carried on by a partnership, the business is to be treated as owned by each individual who is at that time a member of the partnership.

History – In s. 169I(5), the words ", B, C or D" substituted for the words "or B" by FA 2013, s. 64 and Sch. 24, para. 1(2), with effect in relation to disposals of shares on or after 6 April 2013, subject to the transitional provisions in FA 2013, Sch. 24, para. 6.

S. 169I(7A)–(7R) inserted by FA 2013, s. 64 and Sch. 24, para. 1(3), with effect in relation to disposals of shares on or after 6 April 2013, subject to the transitional provisions in FA 2013, Sch. 24, para. 6.

S. 169I inserted by FA 2008, s. 9 and Sch. 3, para. 2 with effect in relation to disposals, reorganisations (within the meaning of s. 169Q) and relevant transactions (within the meaning of s. 116) taking place on or after 6 April 2008 (FA 2008, Sch. 3, para. 5).

Cross references – FA 2016, Sch. 13, para. 6(2): For the purposes of conditions B and D, any reference to a company ceasing to be a trading company or ceasing to be a member of a trading group does not include a case where a company ceases to be a trading company or ceases to be a member of a trading group by virtue only of the coming into force of FA 2016, Sch. 13.

FA 2015, s. 43(4): For the purposes of conditions B and D, any reference to a company ceasing to be a trading company or ceasing to be a member of a trading group does not include a case where a company ceases to be a trading company or ceases to be a member of a trading group by virtue only of the coming into force of FA 2015, s. 43(2) and (3).

169J Disposal of trust business assets

169J(1) There is a disposal of trust business assets where–

(a) the trustees of a settlement make a disposal of settlement business assets (see subsection (2)),

(b) there is an individual who is a qualifying beneficiary (see subsection (3)), and

(c) the relevant condition is met (see subsections (4) and (5)).

169J(2) In this Chapter **"settlement business assets"** means–

(a) assets consisting of (or of interests in) shares in or securities of a company, or

(b) assets (or interests in assets) used or previously used for the purposes of a business,

which are part of the settled property.

169J(3) An individual is a qualifying beneficiary if the individual has, under the settlement, an interest in possession (otherwise than for a fixed term) in–

(a) the whole of the settled property, or

(b) a part of it which consists of or includes the settlement business assets disposed of.

169J(4) In relation to a disposal of settlement business assets within paragraph (a) of subsection (2) the relevant condition is that, throughout a period of 1 year ending not earlier than 3 years before the date of the disposal–

(a) the company is the qualifying beneficiary's personal company and is either a trading company or the holding company of a trading group, and

(b) the qualifying beneficiary is an officer or employee of the company or (if the company is a member of a group of companies) of one or more companies which are members of the trading group.

169J(5) In relation to a disposal of settlement business assets within paragraph (b) of that subsection, the relevant condition is that–

(a) the settlement business assets are used for the purposes of the business carried on by the qualifying beneficiary throughout the period of 1 year ending not earlier than 3 years before the date of the disposal, and

(b) the qualifying beneficiary ceases to carry on the business on the date of the disposal or within the period of three years before that date.

169J(6) In subsection (5)–

(a) the reference to a business carried on by the qualifying beneficiary includes a business carried on by a partnership of which the qualifying beneficiary is a member, and

(b) the reference to the qualifying beneficiary ceasing to carry on the business includes the qualifying beneficiary ceasing to be a member of the partnership or the partnership ceasing to carry on the business.

History – S. 169J inserted by FA 2008, s. 9 and Sch. 3, para. 2 with effect in relation to disposals, reorganisations (within the meaning of s. 169Q) and relevant transactions (within the meaning of s. 116) taking place on or after 6 April 2008 (FA 2008, Sch. 3, para. 5).

169K Disposal associated with relevant material disposal

169K(1) There is a disposal associated with a relevant material disposal if–

(a) condition A1, A1A, A2 or A3 is met, and

(b) conditions B, C and D are met.

169K(1A) Condition A1 is that an individual (**"P"**) makes a material disposal of business assets which consists of the disposal of the whole or part of P's interest in the assets of a partnership, and–

(a) P's disposed of interest is at least a 5% interest in the partnership's assets, and

(b) at the date of the disposal, no partnership purchase arrangements exist.

169K(1AA) Condition A1A is that P makes a material disposal of business assets which consists of the disposal of the whole of P's interest in the assets of a partnership, and–

(a) that interest is an interest of less than 5%,

(b) P holds at least a 5% interest in the partnership's assets throughout a continuous period of at least 3 years in the 8 years ending with the date of the disposal, and

(c) at the date of the disposal, no partnership purchase arrangements exist.

169K(1AB) Subject to subsection (6A), for the purposes of conditions A1 and A1A, in relation to the disposal of an interest in the assets of a partnership, **"partnership purchase arrangements"** means arrangements (other than the material disposal itself) under which P or a person connected with P is entitled to acquire any interest in, or increase that person's interest in, the partnership (including a share of the profits or assets of the partnership or an interest in such a share).

169K(1B) Condition A2 is that P makes a material disposal of business assets which consists of the disposal of shares in a company, all or some of which are ordinary shares, and at the date of the disposal–

(a) the ordinary shares disposed of–

(i) constitute at least 5% of the company's ordinary share capital, and

(ii) carry at least 5% of the voting rights in the company, and

(b) no share purchase arrangements exist.

169K(1C) But condition A2 is not met if the disposal of shares is a disposal by virtue of section 122, other than such a disposal treated as made in consideration of a capital distribution from a company which is made in the course of dissolving or winding up the company.

169K(1D) Condition A3 is that P makes a material disposal of business assets which consists of the disposal of securities of a company, and at the date of the disposal–

(a) the securities disposed of constitute at least 5% of the value of the securities of the company, and

(b) no share purchase arrangements exist.

169K(1E) Subject to subsection (6A), for the purposes of conditions A2 and A3, in relation to the disposal of shares in or securities of a company **("company A")**, **"share purchase arrangements"** means arrangements (other than the material disposal itself) under which P or a person connected with P is entitled to acquire shares in or securities of–

(a) company A, or

(b) a company which is a member of a trading group of which company A is a member.

169K(2) For the purposes of subsection (1E)(b), a company is treated as a member of a trading group of which company A is a member if, at the date of the disposal mentioned in condition A2 or A3, arrangements exist which it is reasonable to assume will result in the company and company A becoming members of the same trading group.

169K(3) Condition B is that P makes the disposal as part of P's withdrawal from participation in the business carried on by the partnership or by the company or (if the company is a member of a trading group) a company which is a member of the trading group.

169K(3A) The disposal mentioned in condition B is not treated as part of P's withdrawal from participation in the business carried on by a partnership if at the date of that disposal there exist any partnership purchase arrangements.

169K(3AA) Subject to subsection (6A), for the purposes of condition B, in relation to a disposal mentioned in that condition and a partnership, **"partnership purchase arrangements"** means arrangements under which P or a person connected with P is entitled to acquire any interest in, or increase that person's interest in, the partnership (including a share of the profits or assets of the partnership or an interest in such a share), but does not include any arrangements in connection with a material disposal in relation to which condition A1 or A1A is met.

169K(3B) The disposal mentioned in condition B is not treated as part of P's withdrawal from participation in the business carried on by a company ("company A") if at the date of that disposal there exist any share purchase arrangements.

169K(3BA) Subject to subsection (6A), for the purposes of condition B, in relation to a disposal mentioned in that condition and company A, **"share purchase arrangements"** means arrangements under which P or a person connected with P is entitled to acquire shares in or securities of–

(a) company A, or

(b) a company which is a member of a trading group of which company A is a member,

but does not include any arrangements in connection with a material disposal in relation to which condition A2 or A3 is met.

169K(3C) For the purposes of subsection (3BA)(b), a company is treated as a member of a trading group of which company A is a member if, at the date of the disposal mentioned in condition B, arrangements exist which it is reasonable to assume will result in the company and company A becoming members of the same trading group.

169K(4) Condition C is that, throughout the period of 1 year ending with the earlier of–

(a) the date of the material disposal of business assets, and

(b) the cessation of the business of the partnership or company,

the assets which (or interests in which) are disposed of are in use for the purposes of the business.

169K(4A) Condition D is that the disposal mentioned in condition B is of an asset which P owns throughout the period of 3 years ending with the date of that disposal.

169K(5) For the purposes of this Chapter the disposal mentioned in Condition B is the disposal associated with a relevant material disposal.

169K(6) [Omitted by FA 2016, s. 84(10).]

169K(6A) For the purposes of this section, in relation to a material disposal of business assets and a disposal mentioned in condition B, arrangements are not partnership purchase arrangements or share purchase arrangements if they were made before both disposals and without regard to either of them.

169K(7) In this section–

> **"arrangements"** includes any agreement, understanding, scheme, transaction or series of transactions (whether or not legally enforceable);
>
> **"securities"** includes an interest in securities, and an **"interest in securities"** includes (in particular) an option to acquire securities;
>
> **"shares"** includes an interest in shares, and an **"interest in shares"** includes (in particular) an option to acquire shares.

169K(8) For the purposes of this section, a person is treated as entitled to acquire anything which the person–

(a) is entitled to acquire at a future date, or

(b) will at a future date be entitled to acquire.

169K(9) For the purposes of this section the assets of–

(a) a Scottish partnership, or

(b) a partnership under the law of any other country or territory under which assets of a partnership are regarded as held by or on behalf of the partnership as such,

are to be treated as held by the members of the partnership in the proportions in which they are entitled to share in the capital profits of the partnership.

References in this section to an individual's interest in the partnership's assets are to be construed accordingly.

History – In s. 169K(1)(a), the words" A1A," inserted by FA 2016, s. 84(2)(a), with effect in relation to disposals made on or after 18 March 2015.
In s. 169K(1)(b), the words ", C and D" substituted for the words "and C" by FA 2016, s. 84(2)(b), with effect in relation to disposals of assets which are acquired on or after 13 June 2016.
S. 169K(1) and (2) substituted, and (1A) to (1E) inserted, by FA 2015, s. 41(2), with effect in relation to disposals made on or after 18 March 2015.
S. 169K(1AA) inserted by FA 2016, s. 84(3), with effect in relation to disposals made on or after 18 March 2015.
S. 169K(1AB) inserted by FA 2016, s. 84(3), with effect in relation to disposals made on or after 18 March 2015.
In s. 169K(1E), the words "Subject to subsection (6A)," and "(other than the material disposal itself)" inserted by FA 2016, s. 84(4), with effect in relation to disposals made on or after 18 March 2015.
In s. 169K(3), "P" substituted for the words "the individual", and the words "P's withdrawal" substituted for the words "the withdrawal of the individual", by FA 2015, s. 41(3), with effect in relation to disposals made on or after 18 March 2015.
S. 169K(3A) to (3C) inserted by FA 2015, s. 41(4), with effect in relation to disposals made on or after 18 March 2015.
S. 169K(3AA) inserted by FA 2016, s. 84(5), with effect in relation to disposals made on or after 18 March 2015.
In s. 169K(3B), the words "share purchase arrangements" substituted for the words below by FA 2016, s. 84(6), with effect in relation to disposals made on or after 18 March 2015. The substituted words read as follows:

> "arrangements under which P or a person connected with P is entitled to acquire shares in or securities of–
> (a) company A, or
> (b) a company which is a member of a trading group of which company A is a member.".

S. 169K(3BA) inserted by FA 2016, s. 84(7), with effect in relation to disposals made on or after 18 March 2015.
In s. 169K(3C), the words "(3BA)" substituted for the words "(3B)" by FA 2016, s. 84(8), with effect in relation to disposals made on or after 18 March 2015.
S. 169K(4A) inserted by FA 2016, s. 84(9), with effect in relation to disposals of assets which are acquired on or after 13 June 2016.
S. 169K(6) omitted by FA 2016, s. 84(10), with effect in relation to disposals made on or after 18 March 2015. Former s. 169K(6) read as follows:
"**(6)** In this section, in relation to a partnership, **"partnership purchase arrangements"** means arrangements under which P or a person connected with P is entitled to acquire any interest in, or increase that person's interest in, the partnership (including a share of the profits or assets of the partnership or an interest in such a share).".
S. 169K(6A) inserted by FA 2016, s. 84(11), with effect in relation to disposals made on or after 18 March 2015.
In s. 169K(9), the word "capital" inserted by FA 2016, s. 84(12), with effect in relation to disposals made on or after 18 March 2015.
S. 169K(6) to (9) inserted by FA 2015, s. 41(5), with effect in relation to disposals made on or after 18 March 2015.
S. 169K inserted by FA 2008, s. 9 and Sch. 3, para. 2 with effect in relation to disposals, reorganisations (within the meaning of s. 169Q) and relevant transactions (within the meaning of s. 116) taking place on or after 6 April 2008 (FA 2008, Sch. 3, para. 5).

169L Relevant business assets

169L(1) If a qualifying business disposal is one which does not consist of the disposal of (or of interests in) shares in or securities of a company, entrepreneurs' relief is given only in respect of the disposal of relevant business assets comprised in the qualifying business disposal.

169L(2) In this Chapter **"relevant business assets"** means assets (including, subject to section 169LA, goodwill) which are, or are interests in, assets to which subsection (3) applies, other than excluded assets (see subsection (4) below).

169L(3) This subsection applies to assets which–

(a) in the case of a material disposal of business assets, are assets used for the purposes of a business carried on by the individual or a partnership of which the individual is a member,

(b) in the case of a disposal of trust business assets, are assets used for the purposes of a business carried on by the qualifying beneficiary or a partnership of which the qualifying beneficiary is a member, or

(c) in the case of a disposal associated with a relevant material disposal, are assets used for the purposes of a business carried on by the partnership or company.

169L(4) The following are excluded assets–

(a) shares and securities, and

(b) assets, other than shares or securities, which are held as investments.

History – In s. 169L(2), the words ", subject to section 169LA," inserted by FA 2015, s. 42(3), with effect in relation to qualifying business disposals made on or after 3 December 2014.

S. 169L inserted by FA 2008, s. 9 and Sch. 3, para. 2 with effect in relation to disposals, reorganisations (within the meaning of s. 169Q) and relevant transactions (within the meaning of s. 116) taking place on or after 6 April 2008 (FA 2008, Sch. 3, para. 5).

169LA Relevant business assets: goodwill transferred to a close company

History – In the heading, the words "close company" substituted for the words "related party etc" by FA 2016, s. 85(8), with effect in relation to disposals made on or after 3 December 2014.

169LA(1) Subject to subsection (1A), subsection (4) applies if–

(a) as part of a qualifying business disposal, a person ("P") disposes of goodwill directly or indirectly to a close company ("C"), and

(aa) immediately after the disposal–

(i) P and any relevant connected person together own 5% or more of the ordinary share capital of C or of any company which is a member of a group of companies of which C is a member, or

(ii) P and any relevant connected person together hold 5% or more of the voting rights in C or in any company which is a member of a group of companies of which C is a member.

(b) [omitted by FA 2016, s. 85(2),]

(c) [omitted by FA 2016, s. 85(2).]

169LA(1A) Where–

(a) subsection (1)(aa) applies by virtue of P's ownership, or any relevant connected person's ownership, of C's ordinary share capital, and

(b) the conditions mentioned in subsection (1B) are met,

subsection (4) does not apply.

169LA(1B) The conditions referred to in subsection (1A)(b) are–

(a) P and any relevant connected person dispose of C's ordinary share capital to another company ("A") such that, immediately before the end of the relevant period, neither P nor any relevant connected person own any of C's ordinary share capital, and

(b) where A is a close company, immediately before the end of the relevant period–

(i) P and any relevant connected person together own less than 5% of the ordinary share capital of A or of any company which is a member of a group of companies of which A is a member, and

(ii) P and any relevant connected person together hold less than 5% of the voting rights in A or in any company which is a member of a group of companies of which A is a member.

169LA(1C) In subsection (1B) **"the relevant period"** means the period of 28 days beginning with the date of the qualifying business disposal, or such longer period as the Commissioners for Her Majesty's Revenue and Customs may by notice allow.

169LA(2) [Omitted by FA 2016, s. 85(4).]

169LA(3) [Omitted by FA 2016, s. 85(4).]

169LA(4) For the purposes of this Chapter, the goodwill is not one of the relevant business assets comprised in the qualifying business disposal.

169LA(5) If a company–

(a) is not resident in the United Kingdom, but

(b) would be a close company if it were resident in the United Kingdom,

the company is to be treated as being a close company for the purposes of this section.

169LA(6) If a person–

(a) disposes of goodwill as part of a qualifying business disposal, and

(b) is party to relevant avoidance arrangements,

subsection (4) applies (if it would not otherwise do so).

169LA(7) In subsection (6) **"relevant avoidance arrangements"** means arrangements the main purpose, or one of the main purposes, of which is to secure–

(a) that subsection (4) does not apply in relation to the goodwill,

(b) [omitted by FA 2016, s. 85(6).]

169LA(8) In this section–

"arrangements" includes any agreement, understanding, scheme, transaction or series of transactions (whether or not legally enforceable);

"group" is to be construed in accordance with section 170;

"relevant connected person" means–

(a) a company connected with P, and

(b) trustees connected with P.

History – In s. 169LA(1), the words "Subject to subsection (1A)," and para. (aa) (and the word "and" preceding it) inserted and para. (b) and (c) omitted by FA 2016, s. 85(2), with effect in relation to disposals made on or after 3 December 2014.
S. 169LA(1A) inserted by FA 2016, s. 85(3), with effect in relation to disposals made on or after 3 December 2014.
S. 169LA(1B) inserted by FA 2016, s. 85(3), with effect in relation to disposals made on or after 3 December 2014.
S. 169LA(1C) inserted by FA 2016, s. 85(3), with effect in relation to disposals made on or after 3 December 2014.
S. 169LA(2) omitted by FA 2016, s. 85(4), with effect in relation to disposals made on or after 3 December 2014.
S. 169LA(3) omitted by FA 2016, s. 85(4), with effect in relation to disposals made on or after 3 December 2014.
In s. 169LA(5), the words "(including for the purposes of determining whether a person is a related party in relation to the company for the purposes of this section)" at the end omitted by FA 2016, s. 85(5), with effect in relation to disposals made on or after 3 December 2014.
S. 169LA(7)(b) (and the word "or" at the end of para. (a)) omitted by FA 2016, s. 85(6), with effect in relation to disposals made on or after 3 December 2014.
In s. 169LA(8) the definition of "group" inserted and the definition of "relevant connected person" substituted for the definitions of "associate", "control", "major interest" and "participator" by FA 2016, s. 85(7), with effect in relation to disposals made on or after 3 December 2014.
S. 169LA inserted by FA 2015, s. 42(4), with effect in relation to qualifying business disposals made on or after 3 December 2014.

169M Relief to be claimed

169M(1) Entrepreneurs' relief is to be given only on the making of a claim.

169M(2) A claim for entrepreneurs' relief in respect of a qualifying business disposal must be made–

(a) in the case of a disposal of trust business assets, jointly by the trustees and the qualifying beneficiary, and

(b) otherwise, by the individual.

169M(3) A claim for entrepreneurs' relief in respect of a qualifying business disposal must be made on or before the first anniversary of the 31 January following the tax year in which the qualifying business disposal is made.

169M(4) A claim for entrepreneurs' relief in respect of a qualifying business disposal may only be made if the amount resulting under section 169N(1) is a positive amount.

History – S. 169M inserted by FA 2008, s. 9 and Sch. 3, para. 2 with effect in relation to disposals, reorganisations (within the meaning of s. 169Q) and relevant transactions (within the meaning of s. 116) taking place on or after 6 April 2008 (FA 2008, Sch. 3, para. 5).

169N Amount of relief: general

169N(1) Where a claim is made in respect of a qualifying business disposal–

(a) the relevant gains (see subsection (5)) are to be aggregated, and

(b) any relevant losses (see subsection (6)) are to be aggregated and deducted from the aggregate arrived at under paragraph (a).

169N(2) The resulting amount is to be treated for the purposes of this Act as a chargeable gain accruing at the time of the disposal to the individual or trustees by whom the claim is made.

169N(3) The rate of capital gains tax in respect of that gain is 10%, but this is subject to subsections (4) to (4B).

169N(4) Subsections (4A) and (4B) apply if the aggregate of–

(a) the gain mentioned in subsection (2), and

(b) the total of so much of each amount resulting under subsection (1) by virtue of its operation in relation to earlier relevant qualifying business disposals (if any) as was–
 (i) charged at the rate in subsection (3), or
 (ii) subject to reduction under subsection (2) of this section as originally enacted,

exceeds £10 million.

169N(4A) The rate in subsection (3) is to apply only to so much (if any) of the gain mentioned in subsection (2) as (when added to the total mentioned in subsection (4)(b)) does not exceed £10 million.

169N(4B) Section 4 (rates of capital gains tax) is to apply to so much of the gain mentioned in subsection (2) as is not subject to the rate in subsection (3).

169N(5) In subsection (1)(a) **"relevant gains"** means–

(a) if the qualifying business disposal is of (or of interests in) shares in or securities of a company (or both), the gains accruing on the disposal (computed in accordance with the provisions of this Act fixing the amount of chargeable gains), and

(b) otherwise, the gains accruing on the disposal of any relevant business assets comprised in the qualifying business disposal (so computed).

169N(6) In subsection (1)(b) **"relevant losses"** means–

(a) if the qualifying business disposal is of (or of interests in) shares in or securities of a company (or both), any losses accruing on the disposal (computed in accordance with the provisions of this Act fixing the amount of allowable losses, on the assumption that notice has been given under section 16(2A) in respect of them), and

(b) otherwise, any losses accruing on the disposal of any relevant business assets comprised in the qualifying business disposal (so computed, on that assumption).

169N(7) In subsection (4) **"earlier relevant qualifying business disposals"** means–

(a) where the qualifying business disposal is made by an individual, earlier qualifying business disposals made by the individual and earlier disposals of trust business assets in respect of which the individual is the qualifying beneficiary, and

(b) where the qualifying business disposal is a disposal of trust business assets in respect of which an individual is the qualifying beneficiary, earlier disposals of trust business assets in respect of which that individual is the qualifying beneficiary and earlier qualifying business disposals made by that individual.

169N(8) If, on the same day, there is both a disposal of trust business assets in respect of which an individual is the qualifying beneficiary and a qualifying business disposal by the individual, this section applies as if the disposal of trust business assets were later.

169N(9) Any gain or loss taken into account under subsection (1) is not to be taken into account under this Act as a chargeable gain or an allowable loss.

History – S. 169N(2)–(4B) substituted for former s. 169N(2)–(4) by F(No. 2)A 2010, s. 2 and Sch. 1, para. 5(2), with effect in relation to qualifying business disposals occurring on or after 23 June 2010, subject to transitional provisions in F(No. 2)A 2010, Sch. 1, para. 18–22.
In former s. 169N(3), the words "£2 million" substituted for "£1 million" in both places by FA 2010, s. 4(1)(a), with effect in relation to qualifying business disposals occurring on or after 6 April 2010.
In former s. 169N(3)(b), the words "so much of" inserted after "total of" and the words "as was subject to reduction under subsection (2)" inserted by FA 2010, s. 4(1)(b), with effect in relation to qualifying business disposals occurring on or after 6 April 2010.
In s. 169N(4), the words "£10 million" substituted for the words "£5 million" by FA 2011, s. 9(1)(a), with effect in relation to qualifying business disposals occurring on or after 6 April 2011.
In s. 169N(4A), the words "£10 million" substituted for the words "£5 million" by FA 2011, s. 9(1)(b), with effect in relation to qualifying business disposals occurring on or after 6 April 2011.
In s. 169N(7), the words "subsection (4)" substituted for the words "subsection (3)" by F(No. 2)A 2010, s. 2 and Sch. 1, para. 5(3), with effect in relation to qualifying business disposals occurring on or after 23 June 2010, subject to transitional provisions in F(No. 2)A 2010, Sch. 1, para. 18–22.
S. 169N inserted by FA 2008, s. 9 and Sch. 3, para. 2 with effect in relation to disposals, reorganisations (within the meaning of s. 169Q) and relevant transactions (within the meaning of s. 116) taking place on or after 6 April 2008 (FA 2008, Sch. 3, para. 5).

169O Amount of relief: special provisions for certain trust disposals

169O(1) This section applies where, on a disposal of trust business assets, there is (in addition to the qualifying beneficiary) at least one other beneficiary who, at the material time, has an interest in possession in–

(a) the whole of the settled property, or

(b) a part of it which consists of or includes the shares or securities (or interests in shares or securities) or assets (or interests in assets) disposed of.

169O(2) Only the relevant proportion of the amount which would otherwise result under subsection (1) of section 169N is to be treated as so resulting.

169O(3) And the balance of that amount is accordingly a chargeable gain for the purposes of this Act.

169O(4) For the purposes of this section **"the relevant proportion"** of an amount is the same proportion of the amount as that which, at the material time–

(a) the qualifying beneficiary's interest in the income of the part of the settled property comprising the shares or securities (or interests in shares or securities) or assets (or interests in assets) disposed of, bears to

(b) the interests in that income of all the beneficiaries (including the qualifying beneficiary) who then have interests in possession in that part of the settled property.

169O(5) In subsection (4) **"the qualifying beneficiary's interest"** means the interest by virtue of which he is the qualifying beneficiary (and not any other interest the qualifying beneficiary may have).

169O(6) In this section **"the material time"** means the end of the latest period of 1 year which ends not earlier than 3 years before the date of the disposal and–

(a) in the case of a disposal of settlement business assets within paragraph (a) of subsection (2) of section 169J, throughout which the conditions in paragraphs (a) and (b) of subsection (4) of that section are met, and

(b) in the case of a disposal of settlement business assets within paragraph (b) of subsection (2) of that section, throughout which the business is carried on by the qualifying beneficiary.

History – In s. 169O(3), the words "with no reduction under subsection (2) of that section", which appeared after "that amount,", omitted by F(No. 2)A 2010, s. 2 and Sch. 1, para. 6, with effect in relation to qualifying business disposals occurring on or after 23 June 2010, subject to transitional provisions in F(No. 2)A 2010, Sch. 1, para. 18–22. F(No. 2)A 2010, Sch. 1, para. 6 omits the words but it is assumed that the intention was also to omit the commas which appeared immediately before and after these words and the CCH text reflects this assumption.

S. 169O inserted by FA 2008, s. 9 and Sch. 3, para. 2 with effect in relation to disposals, reorganisations (within the meaning of s. 169Q) and relevant transactions (within the meaning of s. 116) taking place on or after 6 April 2008 (FA 2008, Sch. 3, para. 5).

169P Amount of relief: special provision for certain associated disposals

169P(1) This section applies where, on a disposal associated with a relevant material disposal, any of the conditions in subsection (4) is met.

169P(2) Only such part of the amount which would otherwise result under subsection (1) of section 169N as is just and reasonable is to be treated as so resulting.

169P(3) And the balance of that amount is accordingly a chargeable gain for the purposes of this Act.

169P(4) The conditions referred to in subsection (1) are–

(a) that the assets which (or interests in which) are disposed of are in use for the purposes of the business for only part of the period in which they are in the ownership of the individual,

(b) that only part of the assets which (or interests in which) are disposed of are in use for the purposes of the business for that period,

(c) that the individual is concerned in the carrying on of the business (whether personally, as a member of a partnership or as an officer or employee of a company which is the individual's personal company) for only part of the period in which the assets which (or interests in which) are disposed of are in use for the purposes of the business, and

(d) that, for the whole or any part of the period for which the assets which (or interests in which) are disposed of are in use for the purposes of the business, their availability is dependent on the payment of rent.

169P(5) In determining how much of an amount it is just and reasonable to bring into account under subsection (1) regard is to be had to–

(a) in a case within paragraph (a) of subsection (4), the length of the period for which the assets are in use as mentioned in that paragraph,

(b) in a case within paragraph (b) of that subsection, the part of the assets that are in use as mentioned in that paragraph,

(c) in a case within paragraph (c) of that subsection, the length of the period for which the individual is concerned in the carrying on of the business as mentioned in that paragraph, and

(d) in a case within paragraph (d) of that subsection, the extent to which any rent paid is less than the amount which would be payable in the open market for the use of the assets.

History – In s. 169P(3), the words "with no reduction under subsection (2) of that section", which appeared after "that amount,", omitted by F(No. 2)A 2010, s. 2 and Sch. 1, para. 7, with effect in relation to qualifying business disposals occurring on or after 23 June 2010, subject to transitional provisions in F(No. 2)A 2010, Sch. 1, para. 18–22. F(No. 2)A 2010, Sch. 1, para. 7 omits the words but it is assumed that the intention was also to omit the commas which appeared immediately before and after these words and the CCH text reflects this assumption.

S. 169P inserted by FA 2008, s. 9 and Sch. 3, para. 2 with effect in relation to disposals, reorganisations (within the meaning of s. 169Q) and relevant transactions (within the meaning of s. 116) taking place on or after 6 April 2008 (FA 2008, Sch. 3, para. 5).

Cross references – FA 2008, Sch. 3, para. 6: disapplication of s. 169P(4)(d) in respect of periods before 6 April 2008.

169Q Reorganisations: disapplication of section 127

169Q(1) This section applies where–

(a) there is a reorganisation (within the meaning of section 126), and

(b) the original shares and the new holding (within the meaning of that section) would fall to be treated by virtue of section 127 as the same asset.

169Q(2) If an election is made under this section, a claim for entrepreneurs' relief may be made as if the reorganisation involved a disposal of the original shares; and if such a claim is made section 127 does not apply.

169Q(3) An election under this section must be made–

(a) if the reorganisation would (apart from section 127) involve a disposal of trust business assets, jointly by the trustees and the qualifying beneficiary, and

(b) otherwise, by the individual.

169Q(4) An election under this section must be made on or before the first anniversary of the 31 January following the tax year in which the reorganisation takes place.

169Q(5) The references in this section to a reorganisation (within the meaning of section 126) includes an exchange of shares or securities which is treated as such a reorganisation by virtue of section 135 or 136.

History – S. 169Q inserted by FA 2008, s. 9 and Sch. 3, para. 2 with effect in relation to disposals, reorganisations (within the meaning of s. 169Q) and relevant transactions (within the meaning of s. 116) taking place on or after 6 April 2008 (FA 2008, Sch. 3, para. 5).

169R Reorganisations involving acquisition of qualifying corporate bonds

169R(1) This section applies where the calculation under section 116(10)(a) would (apart from this section) have effect to produce a chargeable gain for an individual by reason of a relevant transaction.

169R(2) If an election is made under this section, a claim for entrepreneurs' relief may be made as if the relevant transaction involved a disposal of the old asset; and if such a claim is made section 116(10) does not apply.

169R(3) An election under this section must be made–

(a) if the relevant transaction, so far as it relates to the old asset, would (apart from section 116(10)) involve a disposal of trust business assets, jointly by the trustees and the qualifying beneficiary, and

(b) otherwise, by the individual.

169R(4) An election under this section must be made on or before the first anniversary of the 31 January following the tax year in which the relevant transaction takes place.

169R(5) In this section, **"old asset"** and **"relevant transaction"** have the meaning given by section 116.

History – S. 169R substituted by F(No. 2)A 2010, s. 2 and Sch. 1, para. 8, with effect in relation to relevant transactions occurring on or after 23 June 2010, subject to transitional provisions in F(No. 2)A 2010, Sch. 1, para. 18–22.

Former s. 169R inserted by FA 2008, s. 9 and Sch. 3, para. 2 with effect in relation to disposals, reorganisations (within the meaning of s. 169Q) and relevant transactions (within the meaning of s. 116) taking place on or after 6 April 2008 (FA 2008, Sch. 3, para. 5).

169S Interpretation of Chapter

169S(1) For the purposes of this Chapter **"a business"** means anything which–

(a) is a trade, profession or vocation, and

(b) is conducted on a commercial basis and with a view to the realisation of profits.

169S(2) References in this Chapter to a disposal of an interest in shares in a company include a disposal of an interest in shares treated as made by virtue of section 122.

169S(3) For the purposes of this Chapter **"personal company"**, in relation to an individual, means a company–

(a) at least 5% of the ordinary share capital of which is held by the individual, and

(b) at least 5% of the voting rights in which are exercisable by the individual by virtue of that holding.

169S(4) For the purposes of subsection (3) if the individual holds any shares in the company jointly or in common with one or more other persons, the individual is to be treated as sole holder of so many of them as is proportionate to the value of the individual's share (and as able to exercise voting rights by virtue of that holding).

169S(4A) [Omitted by FA 2016, s. 86 and Sch. 13, para. 3.]

169S(5) In this Chapter–

"disposal associated with a relevant material disposal" has the meaning given by section 169K,

"disposal of business assets" has the meaning given by section 169I(2),

"disposal of trust business assets" has the meaning given by section 169J,

"employment" has the meaning given by section 4 of ITEPA 2003,

"entrepreneurs' relief" has the meaning given by section 169H(1),

"holding company" has the same meaning as in section 165 (see section 165A),

"material disposal of business assets" has the meaning given by section 169I,

"office" has the meaning given by section 5(3) of ITEPA 2003,

"ordinary share capital" has the same meaning as in the Income Tax Acts (see section 989 of ITA 2007),

"qualifying business disposal" has the meaning given by section 169H(2),

"relevant business asset" has the meaning given by section 169L,

"rent", in relation to an asset, includes any form of consideration given for the use of the asset,

"securities", in relation to a company, includes any debentures of the company which are deemed by subsection (6) of section 251 to be securities for the purposes of that section,

"settlement business assets" has the meaning given by section 169J(2),

"trade" has the same meaning as in the Income Tax Acts (see section 989 of ITA 2007).

History – S. 169S(4A) omitted by FA 2016, s. 86 and Sch. 13, para. 3 and is treated as never having had effect.
Former s. 169S(4A) inserted by FA 2015, s. 43(2), with effect from 18 March 2015.
In s. 169S(5), entry relating to ""trading company" and "trading group"" (and the word "and" before it), omitted by FA 2015, s. 43(3), with effect from 18 March 2015.
S. 169S inserted by FA 2008, s. 9 and Sch. 3, para. 2 with effect in relation to disposals, reorganisations (within the meaning of s. 169Q) and relevant transactions (within the meaning of s. 116) taking place on or after 6 April 2008 (FA 2008, Sch. 3, para. 5).

169SA Meaning of "trading company" and "trading group"

169SA Schedule 7ZA gives the meaning in this Chapter of "trading company" and "trading group".

History – S. 169SA inserted by FA 2016, s. 86 and Sch. 13, para. 4, with effect in relation to disposals made on or after 18 March 2015, but only for the purposes of determining what is a trading company or trading group at times on or after that date.

Chapter 4 – Entrepreneurs' Relief Where Held-over Gains Become Chargeable

History – Ch. 4 inserted by FA 2015, s. 44(1), with effect in relation to cases where the disposal mentioned in s. 169U(4)(a) or (b) is made on or after 3 December 2014.

169T Overview of Chapter

169T This Chapter makes provision about claiming entrepreneurs' relief in certain cases where, in relation to held-over gains that originally arose on a business disposal, there is a chargeable event for the purposes of Schedule 5B or 8B (relief for gains invested under the enterprise investment scheme or in social enterprises).

History – S. 169T inserted by FA 2015, s. 44(1), with effect in relation to cases where the disposal mentioned in s. 169U(4)(a) or (b) is made on or after 3 December 2014.

169U Eligibility conditions for deferred entrepreneurs' relief

169U(1) Section 169V applies if, ignoring the operation of section 169V(2)(b), each of the following conditions is met.

169U(2) The first condition is that a chargeable gain (**"the first eventual gain"**) accrues as a result of the operation of–

paragraph 4 of Schedule 5B (enterprise investment scheme), or

paragraph 5 of Schedule 8B (investments in social enterprises).

169U(3) If the first condition is met, the paragraph and Schedule mentioned in subsection (2) that apply in the case are referred to in this section, and section 169V, as **"the relevant paragraph"** and **"the applicable Schedule"**.

169U(4) The second condition is–

(a) that the first eventual gain accrues in a case in which the original gain would, but for the operation of the applicable Schedule, have accrued on a relevant business disposal, or

(b) where the first eventual gain accrues in a case in which the original gain would, but for the operation of the applicable Schedule, have accrued as a result of the operation of either of the paragraphs mentioned in subsection (2), that the underlying disposal is a relevant business disposal.

169U(5) The third condition is that a claim for entrepreneurs' relief in respect of the first eventual gain is made, on or before the first anniversary of the 31 January following the tax year in which the first eventual gain accrues, by the individual who made the disposal mentioned in subsection (4)(a) or (b).

169U(6) The fourth condition is that the first eventual gain is the first gain to accrue in the case as a result of the operation of the relevant paragraph.

169U(7) In subsection (4) **"the underlying disposal"** means the disposal (not being a disposal within paragraph 3 of Schedule 5B or paragraph 6 of Schedule 8B) by virtue of which Schedule 5B or 8B has effect.

169U(8) For the purposes of subsection (4), whether the disposal on which the original gain would have accrued is a relevant business disposal, or whether the underlying disposal is a relevant business disposal, is to be decided according to the law applicable to disposals made at the time the disposal was made.

169U(9) In this section–

"the original gain", in relation to a particular case, has the same meaning as in the applicable Schedule,

"relevant business asset" has the meaning given by section 169L, and

"relevant business disposal" means–

(a) a disposal–

(i) within section 169H(2)(a) or (c) (qualifying business disposals), and

(ii) consisting of the disposal of (or of interests in) shares in or securities of a company, or

(b) a disposal of relevant business assets which is comprised in a disposal–

(i) within section 169H(2)(a) or (c), and

(ii) not consisting of the disposal of (or of interests in) shares in or securities of a company.

History – S. 169U inserted by FA 2015, s. 44(1), with effect in relation to cases where the disposal mentioned in s. 169U(4)(a) or (b) is made on or after 3 December 2014.

169V Operation of deferred entrepreneurs' relief

169V(1) Where this section applies, the following rules have effect.

169V(2) The gain mentioned in section 169U(2) (**"the first eventual gain"**)–

(a) is treated for ER purposes as the amount resulting from a calculation under section 169N(1) carried out–

(i) in respect of a qualifying business disposal made when the first eventual gain accrues, and

(ii) because of the claim mentioned in section 169U(5), and

(b) except for ER purposes, is not to be taken into account under this Act as a chargeable gain.

169V(3) If the first eventual gain is a part only of the original gain in the case concerned, each part of the original gain that subsequently accrues as a chargeable gain as a result of the operation of the relevant paragraph–

(a) is treated for ER purposes as the amount resulting from a calculation under section 169N(1) carried out–

(i) in respect of a qualifying business disposal made when that chargeable gain so accrues, and

(ii) because of the claim mentioned in section 169U(5), and

(b) except for ER purposes, is not to be taken into account under this Act as a chargeable gain.

169V(4) If the disposal mentioned in paragraph (a) or (b) of section 169U(4) is a disposal within section 169H(2)(c) (qualifying business disposal: disposal associated with a relevant material disposal)–

(a) a disposal mentioned in subsection (2) or (3) of this section is treated for the purposes of section 169P(1) as a disposal associated with a relevant material disposal, but

(b) section 169P applies in relation to that disposal as if the disposal referred to in section 169P(4) were the disposal mentioned in section 169U(4)(a) or (b).

169V(5) In this section **"ER purposes"** means the purposes of–

(a) section 169N(2) to (4B), (7) and (8), and

(b) section 169P.

History – S. 169V inserted by FA 2015, s. 44(1), with effect in relation to cases where the disposal mentioned in s. 169U(4)(a) or (b) is made on or after 3 December 2014.

Chapter 5 – Investors' Relief

History – Ch. 5 inserted by FA 2016, s. 87 and Sch. 14, para. 2, with effect from 15 September 2016 (Royal Assent).

OVERVIEW

169VA Overview of Chapter

169VA(1) This Chapter provides for a relief, in the form of a lower rate of capital gains tax, in respect of disposals of (and disposals of interests in) certain ordinary shares in unlisted companies.

169VA(2) Section 169VB defines "qualifying shares", "potentially qualifying shares" and "excluded shares".

169VA(3) Section 169VC creates the relief, and relief under that section is to be known as "investors' relief".

169VA(4) Section 169VD makes provision about disposals from holdings consisting partly of qualifying shares.

169VA(5) Sections 169VE to 169VG contain rules for cases where there have been previous disposals from a holding, to determine which shares remain in the holding.

169VA(6) Sections 169VH and 169VI make provision about disposals by trustees of a settlement.

169VA(7) Section 169VJ makes provision about disposals of interests in shares.

169VA(8) Sections 169VK and 169VL provide for a cap on the amount of investors' relief that can be claimed.

169VA(9) Section 169VM makes provision about claims for investors' relief.

169VA(10) Sections 169VN to 169VT make provision about how investor's relief applies following a company's reorganisation of its share capital, an exchange of shares or securities or a scheme of reconstruction.

169VA(11) Sections 169VU to 169VY contain definitions for the purposes of this Chapter.

History – S. 169VA inserted by FA 2016, s. 87 and Sch. 14, para. 2, with effect from 15 September 2016 (Royal Assent).

QUALIFYING SHARES

169VB Qualifying shares, potentially qualifying shares and excluded shares

169VB(1) Where there is a disposal of all or part of (or of an interest in) a holding of shares in a company, this section applies to determine whether a share which is in the holding at the time immediately before the disposal ("the relevant time") is, for the purposes of this Chapter–

(a) a qualifying share,

(b) a potentially qualifying share, or

(c) an excluded share.

169VB(2) The share is a **"qualifying share"** at the relevant time if–

(a) the share was subscribed for, within the meaning given by section 169VU, by the person making the disposal ("the investor"),

(b) the investor has held the share continuously for the period beginning with the issue of the share and ending with the relevant time ("the share-holding period"),

(c) the share was issued on or after 17 March 2016,

(d) at the time the share was issued, none of the shares or securities of the company that issued it were listed on a recognised stock exchange,

(e) the share was an ordinary share when issued and is an ordinary share at the relevant time,

(f) the company that issued the share–

(i) was a trading company or the holding company of a trading group (as defined by section 169VV) when the share was issued, and

(ii) has been so throughout the share-holding period,

(g) at no time in the share-holding period was the investor or a person connected with the investor a relevant employee in respect of that company (within the meaning given by section 169VW), and

(h) the period beginning with the date the share was issued and ending with the date of the disposal is at least 3 years.

169VB(3) The share is a **"potentially qualifying share"** at the relevant time if–

(a) the conditions in subsection (2)(a) to (g) are met, but

(b) the period beginning with the date the share was issued and ending with the date of the disposal is less than 3 years.

169VB(4) The share is an **"excluded share"** at the relevant time if it is, at that time–

(a) not a qualifying share, and

(b) not a potentially qualifying share.

169VB(5) This section is subject to Schedule 7ZB (disqualification of share where value received by investor).

169VB(6) In relation to a share issued on or after 17 March 2016 but before 6 April 2016, any reference in subsection (2)(h) or (3) to **"3 years"** is to be read as a reference to the minimum period.

169VB(7) In subsection (6) **"the minimum period"** means the period of 3 years extended by a period equal in length to the period beginning with the date the share was issued and ending with 5 April 2016.

History – S. 169VB inserted by FA 2016, s. 87 and Sch. 14, para. 2, with effect from 15 September 2016 (Royal Assent).

THE RELIEF

169VC Investors' relief

169VC(1) This section applies where–

(a) a qualifying person disposes of a holding, or part of a holding, of shares in a company, and

(b) immediately before that disposal some or all of the shares in the holding are qualifying shares.

169VC(2) If–

(a) a chargeable gain accrues to the qualifying person on the disposal, and

(b) a claim for relief under this section is made,

the rate of capital gains tax in respect of the relevant gain is 10 per cent.

169VC(3) In subsection (2) **"the relevant gain"** means–

(a) where immediately before the disposal all the shares in the holding are qualifying shares, the chargeable gain on the disposal;

(b) where at that time only some of the shares in the holding are qualifying shares, the appropriate part of that chargeable gain (defined by section 169VD).

169VC(4) In this section–

(a) subsection (1) is subject to section 169VH (disposals by trustees of a settlement: further conditions for relief), and

(b) subsection (2) is subject to–

section 169VI (reduction of relief for certain disposals by trustees of a settlement), and

sections 169VK and 169VL (cap on investors' relief).

169VC(5) A reference in subsection (3) to the chargeable gain on the disposal, or to the appropriate part of that gain, is a reference to that chargeable gain, or (as the case may be) that part, after any deduction of allowable losses which is made in accordance with this Act from that chargeable gain or from that part.

169VC(6) For the application of this section to disposals of interests in shares, see section 169VJ.

169VC(7) In this Chapter a **"qualifying person"** means–

(a) an individual, or

(b) the trustees of a settlement.

History – S. 169VC inserted by FA 2016, s. 87 and Sch. 14, para. 2, with effect from 15 September 2016 (Royal Assent).

169VD Disposal where holding consists partly of qualifying shares

169VD(1) This section applies where–

(a) a disposal ("the disposal concerned") is made as mentioned in section 169VC(1), and

(b) at the time immediately before the disposal, only some of the shares in the holding are qualifying shares.

169VD(2) *Where this section applies, for the purposes of section 169VC(3)* **"the appropriate part"** of the chargeable gain on the disposal is so much of that chargeable gain as is found by multiplying it by the appropriate fraction.

169VD(3) The appropriate fraction is–

$$\frac{Q}{T}$$

where–

Q is the number of qualifying shares found under subsection (4), and

T is the total number of shares disposed of in the disposal concerned.

169VD(4) The number of qualifying shares found under this subsection is–

(a) all the qualifying shares in the holding at the time immediately before the disposal concerned, or

(b) if less, such number of those qualifying shares as equals the number of shares disposed of in that disposal.

History – S. 169VD inserted by FA 2016, s. 87 and Sch. 14, para. 2, with effect from 15 September 2016 (Royal Assent).

169VE Which shares are in holding immediately before disposal

169VE(1) This section applies where–

(a) a particular disposal is made as mentioned in section 169VC(1)(a) ("the current disposal"),

(b) there have been one or more previous disposals of shares from the holding mentioned in section 169VC(1) before the current disposal, and

(c) it is necessary to determine for the purposes of this Chapter which shares are to be treated as in the holding immediately before the current disposal (and, accordingly, which shares are to be treated as having been disposed of in those previous disposals).

169VE(2) In the case of a previous disposal as regards which investors' relief has been claimed or is being claimed, the shares to be treated as disposed of in that previous disposal are to be determined in accordance with the rules in section 169VF.

169VE(3) In the case of a previous disposal not falling within subsection (2), the shares to be treated as disposed of in that previous disposal are to be determined in accordance with the rules in section 169VG.

History – S. 169VE inserted by FA 2016, s. 87 and Sch. 14, para. 2, with effect from 15 September 2016 (Royal Assent).

169VF Shares treated as disposed of in previous disposal where claim made

169VF(1) The rules referred to in section 169VE(2) are as follows; and in this section **"the disposal concerned"** means the previous disposal mentioned in section 169VE(2).

169VF(2) There are to be treated as having been disposed of in the disposal concerned–

(a) all the qualifying shares in the holding at the time immediately before that disposal ("the material time"), or

(b) if less, such number of those qualifying shares as equals the number of shares disposed of in that disposal.

169VF(3) If–

(a) the number of qualifying shares in the holding at the material time was less than the total number of shares disposed of, and

(b) excluded shares were in the holding at the material time,

the available excluded shares are also to be treated as having been disposed of.

169VF(4) **"The available excluded shares"** means–

(a) all the excluded shares in the holding at the material time, or

(b) if less, such number of those excluded shares as is equal to the difference between–

(i) the total number of shares disposed of, and

(ii) the number of qualifying shares in the holding at the material time.

169VF(5) If the number of shares treated under subsections (2) to (4) as disposed of in the disposal concerned is less than the total number of shares disposed of, such number of the potentially qualifying shares in the holding at the material time as is equal to the difference are also to be treated as having been disposed of.

169VF(6) Where the number of potentially qualifying shares in the holding at the material time exceeds the difference mentioned in subsection (5), under that subsection potentially qualifying shares acquired later are to be treated as disposed of in preference to ones acquired earlier.

169VF(7) In this section **"disposed of"** (without more) means disposed of in the disposal concerned.

History – S. 169VF inserted by FA 2016, s. 87 and Sch. 14, para. 2, with effect from 15 September 2016 (Royal Assent).

169VG Shares treated as disposed of in previous disposal: no claim made

169VG(1) The rules referred to in section 169VE(3) are as follows; and in this section **"the disposal concerned"** means the previous disposal mentioned in section 169VE(3).

169VG(2) If any excluded shares were in the holding at the time immediately before the disposal concerned ("the material time"), the maximum number of excluded shares are to be treated as having been disposed of in the disposal concerned.

169VG(3) **"The maximum number of excluded shares"** means–

(a) all the excluded shares in the holding at the material time, or

(b) if less, such number of those excluded shares as is equal to the number of shares disposed of.

169VG(4) If–

(a) there were no excluded shares in the holding at the material time, or the number of such shares was less than the total number of shares disposed of, and

(b) potentially qualifying shares were in the holding at the material time,

the available potentially qualifying shares are to be treated as having been disposed of.

169VG(5) **"The available potentially qualifying shares"** means–

(a) all the potentially qualifying shares in the holding at the material time, or

(b) if less, such number of those potentially qualifying shares as is equal to the difference between–

(i) the total number of shares disposed of, and

(ii) the number of excluded shares in the holding at the material time.

169VG(6) Where the number of potentially qualifying shares in the holding at the material time exceeds the difference mentioned in subsection (5), potentially qualifying shares acquired later are to be treated as disposed of in preference to ones acquired earlier.

169VG(7) If the number of shares treated under subsections (2) to (5) as disposed of in the disposal concerned is less than the total number of shares disposed of, such number of the qualifying shares in the holding at the material time as is equal to the difference are to be treated as having been disposed of.

169VG(8) In this section **"disposed of"** (without more) means disposed of in the disposal concerned.

History – S. 169VG inserted by FA 2016, s. 87 and Sch. 14, para. 2, with effect from 15 September 2016 (Royal Assent).

TRUSTEES OF A SETTLEMENT: SPECIAL PROVISION

169VH Disposals by trustees: further conditions for relief

169VH(1) Where a disposal falling within section 169VC(1)(a) and (b) is made by the trustees of a settlement, section 169VC does not apply to the disposal unless there is at least one individual who is an eligible beneficiary in respect of the disposal.

169VH(2) For the purposes of this section, an individual is an **"eligible beneficiary"** in respect of the disposal if–

(a) at the time immediately before the disposal, the individual has under the settlement an interest in possession in settled property that includes or consists of the holding of shares mentioned in section 169VC(1),

(b) the individual has had such an interest in possession under the settlement throughout the period of 3 years ending with the date of the disposal,

(c) at no time in that period has the individual been a relevant employee in respect of the company that issued the shares (within the meaning given by section 169VW), and

(d) the individual has (by the time of the claim under section 169VC in respect of the disposal) elected to be treated as an eligible beneficiary in respect of the disposal.

169VH(3) For the purposes of subsection (2)(d), an individual elects to be treated as an eligible beneficiary in respect of a disposal if the individual tells the trustees (by whatever means) that he or she wishes to be so treated; and an election under subsection (2)(d) may be withdrawn by the individual at any time until the claim is made.

169VH(4) In this section **"interest in possession"** does not include an interest in possession for a fixed term.

169VH(5) In relation to a disposal made by the trustees of a settlement, any reference in section 169VB(2)(g) to the investor is to be read as a reference to any trustee of the settlement.

History – S. 169VH inserted by FA 2016, s. 87 and Sch. 14, para. 2, with effect from 15 September 2016 (Royal Assent).

169VI Disposals by trustees: relief reduced in certain cases

169VI(1) Subsection (2) applies where–

(a) a disposal falling within section 169VC(1)(a) and (b) is made by the trustees of a settlement,

(b) section 169VC applies to the disposal by reason of there being at least one individual who is an eligible beneficiary in respect of the disposal (see section 169VH), and

(c) at the time immediately before the disposal, there are two or more persons each of whom has under the settlement an interest in possession in the settled property.

169VI(2) In such a case the reference in section 169VC(2) to the relevant gain is to be read as a reference–

(a) to the eligible beneficiary's share of the relevant gain (see subsections (3) to (6)), or

(b) if there is more than one individual who is an eligible beneficiary in respect of the disposal, to so much of the relevant gain as is equal to the aggregate of the eligible beneficiaries' shares of that gain.

169VI(3) In this section–

"eligible beneficiary" has the meaning given by section 169VH(2);

"relevant gain" has the meaning given by section 169VC(3);

"the settled property" means settled property that includes or consists of the holding of shares mentioned in section 169VC(1).

169VI(4) Subsection (5) applies to determine for the purposes of this Chapter, in relation to any individual who is an eligible beneficiary in respect of a disposal within section 169VC(1) made by the trustees of a settlement, that individual's share of the relevant gain.

169VI(5) That individual's share of the relevant gain on the disposal is so much of the relevant gain on the disposal as bears to the whole of that gain the same proportion as X bears to Y, where–

X is the interest in possession (other than for a fixed term) which, at the time immediately before the disposal, that individual has under the settlement in the income from the holding of shares mentioned in section 169VC(1), and

Y is all the interests in that income that persons (including that individual) with interests in possession in that holding have under the settlement at that time.

History – S. 169VI inserted by FA 2016, s. 87 and Sch. 14, para. 2, with effect from 15 September 2016 (Royal Assent).

DISPOSALS OF INTERESTS IN SHARES

169VJ Disposals of interests in shares: joint holdings etc

169VJ(1) In section 169VC(1)(a), the reference to the case where a qualifying person disposes of a holding, or part of a holding, of shares in a company includes the case where a qualifying person disposes of an interest in a relevant holding.

169VJ(2) In this section a **"relevant holding"** means either–

(a) a number of shares in a company which are of the same class and were acquired in the same capacity jointly by the same two or more persons including the qualifying person, or

(b) a number of shares in a company which are of the same class and were acquired in the same capacity by the qualifying person solely.

169VJ(3) In this section–

(a) **"an interest"** in a relevant holding means any interests of the qualifying person, in any of the shares in the relevant holding, which are by virtue of section 104 to be regarded as a single asset, and

(b) references to an interest include part of an interest.

169VJ(4) Where section 169VC(1) applies by reason of this section, section 169VD(3) and (4) have effect as if any reference to the number of shares disposed of were a reference to the number of shares an interest in which is disposed of.

169VJ(5) In relation to a disposal by the trustees of a settlement of an interest in a relevant holding falling within subsection (2)(a), sections 169VH(2) and 169VI(3) and (5) have effect as if any reference to the holding of shares mentioned in section 169VC(1) were to the interest disposed of.

169VJ(6) In accordance with subsection (1)–

(a) in sections 169VN(1)(d), 169VP(1)(d) and 169VS(1)(d) (reorganisations), any reference to a disposal of all or part of a holding includes a disposal by the qualifying person of an interest in the holding, and

(b) the reference in section 169VT(2) to a disposal of the original shares is to be read, in relation to a case where the original shares fall within subsection (2)(a) above, as a reference to a disposal of the qualifying person's interest in those shares.

History – S. 169VJ inserted by FA 2016, s. 87 and Sch. 14, para. 2, with effect from 15 September 2016 (Royal Assent).

CAP ON RELIEF

169VK Cap on relief for disposal by an individual

169VK(1) This section applies if, on a disposal within section 169VC(1) made by an individual ("the individual concerned"), the aggregate of–

(a) the amount of the relevant gain on the disposal ("the gain in question"),

(b) the total amount of any gains that, in relation to earlier disposals by the individual concerned, were charged at the rate in section 169VC(2), and

(c) the total amount of any reckonable trust gains that, on any previous trust disposals in respect of which the individual concerned was an eligible beneficiary, were charged at the rate in section 169VC(2),

exceeds £10 million.

169VK(2) The rate in section 169VC(2) applies only to so much (if any) of the gain in question as, when added to the aggregate of the total amounts mentioned in subsection (1)(b) and (c), does not exceed £10 million.

169VK(3) Section 4 (rates of capital gains tax) applies to so much of the gain in question as is not subject to the rate in section 169VC(2).

169VK(4) In this section–

"eligible beneficiary", in relation to a disposal, is to be read in accordance with section 169VH(2);

"reckonable trust gain", in relation to a trust disposal in respect of which the individual concerned was an eligible beneficiary, means–

(a) if section 169VI(1)(c) applied in relation to the disposal, that individual's share of the relevant gain on that disposal, within the meaning given by section 169VI(4) and (5);

(b) otherwise, the relevant gain on that disposal;

"the relevant gain", in relation to a disposal, has the meaning given by section 169VC(3);

"trust disposal" means a disposal by the trustees of a settlement.

History – S. 169VK inserted by FA 2016, s. 87 and Sch. 14, para. 2, with effect from 15 September 2016 (Royal Assent).

169VL Cap on relief for disposal by trustees of a settlement

169VL(1) This section applies where–

(a) a disposal ("the disposal in question") is made by the trustees of a settlement,

(b) that disposal is within section 169VC(1), and

(c) there is an excess amount in relation to an individual who is an eligible beneficiary in respect of the disposal in question ("the individual concerned").

169VL(2) For the purposes of this section there is an **"excess amount"** in relation to the individual concerned if the aggregate of–

(a) the amount of the current gain,

(b) the total amount of any gains that, in relation to earlier disposals made by the individual concerned, were charged at the rate in section 169VC(2), and

(c) the total amount of any reckonable trust gains that, on any previous trust disposals in respect of which the individual concerned was an eligible beneficiary, were charged at the rate in section 169VC(2),

exceeds £10 million.

169VL(3) The rate in section 169VC(2) applies to the current gain only to the extent (if any) that the current gain when added to the aggregate of the total amounts mentioned in subsection (2)(b) and (c) does not exceed £10 million.

169VL(4) Section 4 (rates of capital gains tax) applies to so much of the current gain as is not subject to the rate in section 169VC(2).

169VL(5) In this section–

"the current gain" means the reckonable trust gain on the disposal in question;

"eligible beneficiary", in relation to a disposal, is to be read in accordance with section 169VH(2);

"reckonable trust gain", in relation to any trust disposal in respect of which the individual concerned is an eligible beneficiary, means–

(a) if section 169VI(1)(c) applies in relation to the disposal, that individual's share of the relevant gain on that disposal, within the meaning given by section 169VI(4) and (5);

(b) otherwise, the relevant gain on that disposal;

"the relevant gain", in relation to a disposal, has the meaning given by section 169VC(3);

"trust disposal" means a disposal by the trustees of a settlement.

History – S. 169VL inserted by FA 2016, s. 87 and Sch. 14, para. 2, with effect from 15 September 2016 (Royal Assent).

CLAIMS FOR RELIEF

169VM Claims for relief

169VM(1) Any claim for investors' relief must be made–

(a) in the case of a disposal by an individual, by that individual;

(b) in the case of a disposal by the trustees of a settlement, jointly by–

(i) the trustees, and

(ii) the eligible beneficiary in respect of the disposal, within the meaning given by section 169VH(2) (or, if more than one, all those eligible beneficiaries).

169VM(2) Any claim for investors' relief in respect of a disposal must be made on or before the first anniversary of the 31 January following the tax year in which the disposal is made.

History – S. 169VM inserted by FA 2016, s. 87 and Sch. 14, para. 2, with effect from 15 September 2016 (Royal Assent).

REORGANISATIONS

169VN Reorganisations where no consideration given

169VN(1) This section applies where–

(a) there is a reorganisation within the meaning of section 126,

(b) immediately before the reorganisation, a qualifying person holds ordinary shares which, in relation to that reorganisation, are original shares within the meaning of section 126,

(c) on the reorganisation that person does not give or become liable to give any consideration for, or for any part of, a new holding, and

(d) at a time after the reorganisation, there is a disposal of all or part of a new holding.

169VN(2) In this section a **"new holding"** means–

(a) the holding that immediately after the reorganisation is (in relation to the original shares) the new holding within the meaning of section 126, or

(b) where the new holding within the meaning of section 126 consists of two or more actual holdings, any of those actual holdings.

169VN(3) Subsections (4) and (5) apply for the purposes of determining (for any purpose of this Chapter) the status of shares that immediately before the disposal mentioned in subsection (1)(d) are in the new holding mentioned there ("the new holding concerned").

169VN(4) Where a number of the original shares were–

(a) subscribed for by the qualifying person,

(b) issued on a particular date ("the relevant issue date"), and

(c) held continuously by that person for a particular period ending immediately before the reorganisation ("the period concerned"),

the following assumption is to be made.

169VN(5) That assumption is that an appropriate number of the new shares were–

(a) subscribed for by the qualifying person,

(b) issued on the relevant issue date, and

(c) had by the time immediately after the reorganisation already been held continuously by that person for the period concerned.

169VN(6) In subsections (4) and (5)–

"the appropriate number" has the meaning given by section 169VO;

"the original shares" means the shares held by the qualifying person immediately before the reorganisation that were original shares in relation to the reorganisation;

"the new shares" means the shares that immediately after the reorganisation were in the new holding concerned (including such, if any, of the original shares as remained after the reorganisation and were in that holding).

169VN(7) In this section a reference to the **"status"** of a share is to whether it is qualifying, potentially qualifying or excluded.

169VN(8) Section 169VE applies to determine, for the purposes of this Chapter, which shares are included in a holding immediately before a reorganisation as it applies for the purposes of determining which shares are included in a holding immediately before a particular disposal.

169VN(9) References in this section to consideration are to be read in accordance with section 128(2).

History – S. 169VN inserted by FA 2016, s. 87 and Sch. 14, para. 2, with effect from 15 September 2016 (Royal Assent).

169VO The appropriate number

169VO(1) The **"appropriate number"** for the purposes of section 169VN(5) is the number found by multiplying the number of shares that are in the new holding concerned immediately after the reorganisation by the fraction–

$$\frac{A}{B}$$

where–

A is the number of the original shares that were–

(a) subscribed for by the qualifying person,

(b) issued on the relevant issue date, and

(c) continuously held by that person for the period concerned, and

B is the total number of the original shares.

169VO(2) In this section–

"the new holding concerned" has the meaning given by section 169VN(3);

"the original shares" has the meaning given by section 169VN(6);

"the relevant issue date" has the meaning given by section 169VN(4);

"the period concerned" has the meaning given by section 169VN(4).

History – S. 169VO inserted by FA 2016, s. 87 and Sch. 14, para. 2, with effect from 15 September 2016 (Royal Assent).

169VP Reorganisations where consideration given

169VP(1) This section applies where–

(a) there is a reorganisation within the meaning of section 126,

(b) immediately before the reorganisation, a qualifying person holds ordinary shares which, in relation to that reorganisation, are original shares within the meaning of section 126,

(c) on the reorganisation that person gives or becomes liable to give consideration for shares ("shares issued for consideration") which–

(i) are issued to that person on the reorganisation, and

(ii) immediately after the reorganisation are in a new holding, and

(d) at a time after the reorganisation, there is a disposal of all or part of that new holding.

169VP(2) In this section a **"new holding"** means–

(a) the holding that immediately after the reorganisation is (in relation to the original shares) the new holding within the meaning of section 126, or

(b) where the new holding within the meaning of section 126 consists of two or more actual holdings, any of those actual holdings.

169VP(3) In determining, for any purpose of this Chapter, the status of shares that immediately before the disposal mentioned in subsection (1)(d) are in the new holding mentioned there–

(a) the date of issue of the shares issued for consideration is to be taken to be their actual date of issue (rather than the date of issue of any of the original shares), and

(b) *in relation to any part of the* new holding for which consideration was not given, sections 169VN(3) to (6) and 169VO apply but as if any reference to the new holding concerned were to that part of the new holding.

169VP(4) Section 169VN(3) to (6) and 169VO also apply in relation to any other holding which is a new holding in relation to the reorganisation and as respects which the person did not, on the reorganisation, give or become liable to give any consideration.

169VP(5) In this section a reference to the **"status"** of a share is to whether it is qualifying, potentially qualifying or excluded.

169VP(6) References in this section to consideration are to be read in accordance with section 128(2).

History – S. 169VP inserted by FA 2016, s. 87 and Sch. 14, para. 2, with effect from 15 September 2016 (Royal Assent).

169VQ Exchange of shares for those in another company

169VQ(1) This section applies where section 135 applies in relation to an issue of shares in a company ("company B") in exchange for shares in another company ("company A").

169VQ(2) For the purposes of sections 169VN to 169VP–

(a) companies A and B are to be treated as if they were the same company, and

(b) the exchange of shares is to be treated as if it were a reorganisation of that company's share capital.

History – S. 169VQ inserted by FA 2016, s. 87 and Sch. 14, para. 2, with effect from 15 September 2016 (Royal Assent).

169VR New shares issued on scheme of reconstruction

169VR(1) This section applies where–

(a) section 136 applies in relation to an arrangement between a company ("company A") and the persons holding shares, or any class of shares, in company A, under which another company ("company B") issues shares to those persons, and

(b) under section 136(2)(a) those persons are treated as exchanging shares in company A for the shares held by them in consequence of the arrangement.

169VR(2) For the purposes of sections 169VN to 169VP–

(a) companies A and B are to be treated as if they were the same company, and

(b) the exchange of shares is to be treated as if it were a reorganisation of that company's share capital.

169VR(3) In the following provisions of this Chapter, any reference to an exchange of shares includes anything that section 136(2)(a) treats as an exchange of shares.

History – S. 169VR inserted by FA 2016, s. 87 and Sch. 14, para. 2, with effect from 15 September 2016 (Royal Assent).

169VS Modification of conditions for being a qualifying share

169VS(1) This section applies where–

(a) an ordinary share ("the original share") is subscribed for by a qualifying person ("the investor");

(b) the conditions in section 169VB(2)(c) and (d) are met in relation to the original share,

(c) the share is involved in an exchange of shares treated under section 169VQ or 169VR as a reorganisation of share capital, and accordingly is included in the original shares within the meaning of section 169VN(6), and

(d) subsequently there is a disposal of all or part of a holding of shares that in relation to that exchange is a new holding within the meaning given by section 169VI(2).

169VS(2) As respects a share which is in that holding immediately before that disposal, the conditions in section 169VB(2)(f) and (g) are to be regarded as met if (and only if)–

(a) in relation to the period beginning with the issue of the original share and ending with the exchange of shares, those conditions were met by the original share, and

(b) in relation to the period beginning with the exchange of shares and ending with the disposal, those conditions were met by a share representing the original share.

169VS(3) Accordingly–

(a) in section 169VB(2)(f) and (g) as they apply to the original share, any reference to the share-holding period is to be read as to the period mentioned in subsection (2)(a) above, and

(b) in section 169VB(2)(f) and (g) as they apply to a share representing the original share, any reference to the share-holding period is to be read as to the period mentioned in subsection (2)(b) above.

169VS(4) In subsection (1)(c) **"the share"** includes a share that, following a reorganisation or following an exchange of shares in relation to which section 169VQ or 169VR applies, represents the original share, and subsections (2) and (3) apply in such a case with the necessary modifications.

History – S. 169VS inserted by FA 2016, s. 87 and Sch. 14, para. 2, with effect from 15 September 2016 (Royal Assent).

169VT Election to disapply section 127

169VT(1) This section applies where–

(a) there is–

  (i) a reorganisation (within the meaning of section 126), or

(ii) an exchange of shares which is treated as such a reorganisation by virtue of section 135 or 136, and

(b) the original shares and the new holding would fall to be treated by virtue of section 127 as the same asset.

169VT(2) If an election is made under this section, a claim for investors' relief may be made as if the reorganisation or exchange of shares involved a disposal of the original shares; and if such a claim is made section 127 and sections 169VN to 169VS do not apply.

169VT(3) Any election under this section must be made–

(a) if the reorganisation or exchange of shares would (apart from section 127) involve a disposal by the trustees of a settlement, jointly by–

(i) the trustees, and

(ii) the person who if the disposal were made would be the eligible beneficiary in respect of the disposal, within the meaning given by section 169VH(2) (or, if more than one, all the persons who would be such eligible beneficiaries);

(b) otherwise, by the individual concerned.

169VT(4) Any election under this section must be made on or before the first anniversary of the 31 January following the tax year in which the reorganisation or exchange of shares takes place.

169VT(5) In this section **"the original shares"** and **"the new holding"** have the meaning given by section 126.

History – S. 169VT inserted by FA 2016, s. 87 and Sch. 14, para. 2, with effect from 15 September 2016 (Royal Assent).

SUPPLEMENTAL

169VU "Subscribe" etc

169VU(1) For the purposes of this Chapter (other than this subsection) a person **"subscribes for"** a share in a company if–

(a) that person subscribes for the share,

(b) the share is issued to that person by the company for consideration consisting wholly of cash,

(c) the share is fully paid up at the time it is issued,

(d) the share is subscribed for, and issued, for genuine commercial reasons and not as part of arrangements the main purpose, or one of the main purposes, of which is to secure a tax advantage to any person, and

(e) the share is subscribed for, and issued, by way of a bargain at arm's length.

169VU(2) In subsection (1) **"arrangements"** and **"tax advantage"** have the same meaning as in section 16A.

169VU(3) If–

(a) an individual ("A") subscribed for, or is treated under this subsection as having subscribed for, any shares,

(b) A transferred the shares to another individual ("B") during their lives, and

(c) A was living together with B as B's spouse or civil partner at the time of the transfer,

B is to be treated for the purposes of this Chapter as having subscribed for the shares.

169VU(4) Accordingly, for the purposes of this Chapter any period for which A held the shares continuously is to be added to, and treated as part of, the period for which B held the shares continuously.

169VU(5) In this Chapter, apart from subsections (3) and (4), references to a person's having subscribed for a share include the person's having subscribed for the share jointly with any other person (and references to a person's holding a share or to a share being issued to a person are to be read accordingly).

History – S. 169VU inserted by FA 2016, s. 87 and Sch. 14, para. 2, with effect from 15 September 2016 (Royal Assent).

169VV "Trading company" etc

169VV(1) In this Chapter **"trading company"** and **"the holding company of a trading group"** have the same meaning as in section 165 (see section 165A).

169VV(2) *For the purposes of this Chapter* a company is not to be regarded as ceasing to be a trading company, or the holding company of a trading group, merely because of anything done in consequence of–

(a) the company, or any of its subsidiaries, being in administration or receivership, or

(b) a resolution having been passed, or an order made, for the winding up of the company or any of its subsidiaries.

169VV(3) But subsection (2) applies only if–

(a) the entry into administration or receivership, or the resolution or order for winding up, and

(b) everything done as a result of the company concerned being in administration or receivership, or as a result of that resolution or order,

is for genuine commercial reasons and is not part of a scheme or arrangement the main purpose or one of the main purposes of which is the avoidance of tax.

History – S. 169VV inserted by FA 2016, s. 87 and Sch. 14, para. 2, with effect from 15 September 2016 (Royal Assent).

169VW "Relevant employee"

169VW(1) This section applies to determine for the purposes of–

(a) section 169VB(2)(g), or

(b) section 169VH(2)(c),

whether a particular person has at any time in the relevant period been a **"relevant employee"** in respect of the issuing company.

169VW(2) A person who has at any time in the relevant period been an officer or employee of–

(a) the issuing company, or

(b) a connected company,

is to be regarded as having at that time been a relevant employee in respect of the issuing company, but this is subject to subsections (3) and (5).

169VW(3) If–

(a) a person is an unremunerated director of the issuing company or a connected company at any time in the relevant period, and

(b) the condition in subsection (4) is met,

the fact that the person holds that directorship at that time does not make the person a relevant employee in respect of the issuing company at that time.

169VW(4) The condition referred to in subsection (3) is that at no time before the relevant period had the person mentioned in that subsection, or a person connected with that person, been–

(a) connected with the issuing company, or

(b) involved in carrying on (whether on the person's own account or as a partner, director or employee) the whole or any part of the trade, business or profession carried on by the issuing company or a company connected with that company.

169VW(5) If–

(a) a person becomes an employee of the issuing company or a connected company at a time which is–

(i) within the relevant period, but

(ii) not within the first 180 days of that period,

(b) at the beginning of the relevant period, there was no reasonable prospect that the person would become such an employee within the relevant period, and

(c) the person is not at any time in the relevant period a director of the issuing company or a connected company,

that employment of the person does not make the person a relevant employee in respect of the issuing company at any time in the relevant period.

169VW(6) For the purposes of subsection (5) there is a **"reasonable prospect"** of a thing if it is more likely than not.

169VW(7) In this section–

"director" is to be read in accordance with section 452 of CTA 2010,

"connected company" means a company which at any time in the relevant period is connected with the issuing company (and it does not matter for this purpose whether that time is a time when the person in question is an officer or employee of either company);

"the issuing company" means the company mentioned in (as the case may be) section 169VB(2)(g) or 169VH(2)(c);

"the relevant period" means the period mentioned in (as the case may be) section 169VB(2)(g) or section 169VH(2)(c);

"unremunerated director" has the meaning given by section 169VX.

History – S. 169VW inserted by FA 2016, s. 87 and Sch. 14, para. 2, with effect from 15 September 2016 (Royal Assent).

169VX "Unremunerated director"

169VX(1) For the purposes of section 169VW a person ("the person concerned") is an **"unremunerated director"** of the issuing company or a connected company at a particular time in the relevant period if that person is a director of that company at that time and–

(a) does not receive in the relevant period any disqualifying payment from the issuing company or a related person, and

(b) is not entitled to receive any such payment in respect of that period or any part of it.

169VX(2) In this section **"disqualifying payment"** means any payment other than–

(a) a payment or reimbursement of travelling or other expenses wholly, exclusively and necessarily incurred by the person concerned in the performance of his or her duties as a director,

(b) any interest which represents no more than a reasonable commercial return on money lent to the issuing company or a related person,

(c) any dividend or other distribution which does not exceed a normal return on the investment to which the dividend or distribution relates,

(d) any payment for the supply of goods which does not exceed their market value,

(e) any payment of rent for any property occupied by the issuing company or a related person which does not exceed a reasonable and commercial rent for the property, or

(f) any necessary and reasonable remuneration which is–

(i) paid for qualifying services that are provided to the issuing company or a related person in the course of a trade or profession carried on wholly or partly in the United Kingdom, and

(ii) taken into account in calculating for tax purposes the profits of that trade or profession.

169VX(3) In this section a **"related person"** means–

(a) a connected company of which the person concerned is a director, or

(b) any person connected with the issuing company or with a company within paragraph (a).

169VX(4) In this section any reference to a payment to the person concerned includes a payment made to that person indirectly or to that person's order or for that person's benefit.

169VX(5) In this section **"qualifying services"** means services which are–

(a) not secretarial or managerial services, and

(b) not services of a kind provided by the person to whom they are provided.

169VX(6) In this section the following expressions have the same meaning as in section 169VW–

"connected company";

"director";

"issuing company";

"relevant period".

History – S. 169VX inserted by FA 2016, s. 87 and Sch. 14, para. 2, with effect from 15 September 2016 (Royal Assent).

169VY General definitions

169VY In this Chapter–

"employee" (except in the expression "relevant employee", which is to be read in accordance with section 169VW) has the meaning given by section 4 of ITEPA 2003;

"employment" has the meaning given by section 4 of ITEPA 2003;

"exchange of shares" is to be read in accordance with section 169VR(3);

"excluded share" has the meaning given by section 169VB;

a **"holding"** of shares in a company means a holding of such shares which by virtue of section 104(1) is to be regarded as a single asset;

"investors' relief" has the meaning given by section 169VA(3);

"office" has the meaning given by section 5(3) of ITEPA 2003;

"ordinary shares", in relation to a company, means any shares forming part of the company's ordinary share capital (within the meaning given by section 989 of ITA 2007);

"*potentially qualifying share*" has the meaning given by section 169VB;

"qualifying person" has the meaning given by section 169VC(7);

"qualifying share" has the meaning given by section 169VB;

"subscribe" is to be read in accordance with section 169VU;

"trading company" and **"the holding company of a trading group"** are to be read in accordance with section 169VV.

History – S. 169VY inserted by FA 2016, s. 87 and Sch. 14, para. 2, with effect from 15 September 2016 (Royal Assent).

PART VI – COMPANIES, OIL, INSURANCE ETC.

Chapter I – Companies

Cross references – Commonwealth Development Corporation Act 1999, Sch. 3, para. 4(1): the Corporation cannot be a member of a group of companies for the purposes of Pt. VI, Ch. I at any time during its exempt period.

GROUPS OF COMPANIES

170 Interpretation of sections 171 to 181

170(1) This section has effect for the interpretation of sections 171 to 181 except in so far as the context otherwise requires, and in those sections–

(a) **"profits"** means income and chargeable gains, and

(b) **"trade"** includes **"vocation"**, and includes also an office or employment.

Until 6th April 1993 paragraph (b) shall have effect with the addition at the end of the words "or the occupation of woodlands in any context in which the expression is applied to that in the Income Tax Acts".

170(2) Except as otherwise provided–

(a) [Repealed by FA 2000, s. 102 and Sch. 29, para. 1(1), s. 156 and Sch. 40, Pt. II(12).]

(b) subsections (3) to (6) below apply to determine whether companies form a group and, where they do, which is the principal company of the group;

(c) in applying section 1154(3) of CTA 2010 (meaning of "75% subsidiary") any share capital of a registered society (see section 1119 of that Act) shall be treated as ordinary share capital; and

(d) **"group"** and **"subsidiary"** shall be construed with any necessary modifications where applied to a company incorporated under the law of a country outside the United Kingdom.

170(3) Subject to subsections (4) to (6) below–

(a) a company (referred to below and in sections 171 to 181 as the **"principal company of the group"**) and all its 75 per cent subsidiaries form a group and, if any of those subsidiaries have 75 per cent subsidiaries, the group includes them and their 75 per cent subsidiaries, and so on, but

(b) a group does not include any company (other than the principal company of the group) that is not an effective 51 per cent subsidiary of the principal company of the group.

170(4) A company cannot be the principal company of a group if it is itself a 75 per cent subsidiary of another company.

170(5) Where a company (**"the subsidiary"**) is a 75 per cent subsidiary of another company but those companies are prevented from being members of the same group by subsection (3)(b) above, the subsidiary may, where the requirements of subsection (3) above are satisfied, itself be the principal company of another group notwithstanding subsection (4) above unless this subsection enables a further company to be the principal company of a group of which the subsidiary would be a member.

170(6) A company cannot be a member of more than one group; but where, apart from this subsection, a company would be a member of 2 or more groups (the principal company of each group being referred to below as the **"head of a group"**), it is a member only of that group, if any, of which it would be a member under one of the following tests (applying earlier tests in preference to later tests)–

(a) it is a member of the group it would be a member of if, in applying subsection (3)(b) above, there were left out of account any amount to which a head of a group is or would be beneficially entitled of any profits available for distribution to equity holders of a head of another group or of any assets of a head of another group available for distribution to its equity holders on a winding-up,

(b) it is a member of the group the head of which is beneficially entitled to a percentage of profits available for distribution to equity holders of the company that is greater than the percentage of those profits to which any other head of a group is so entitled,

(c) it is a member of the group the head of which would be beneficially entitled to a percentage of any assets of the company available for distribution to its equity holders on a winding-up that is greater than the percentage of those assets to which any other head of a group would be so entitled,

(d) it is a member of the group the head of which owns directly or indirectly a percentage of the company's ordinary share capital that is greater than the percentage of that capital owned directly or indirectly by any other head of a group (interpreting this paragraph as if it were included in section 1154(2) of CTA 2010).

170(7) For the purposes of this section and sections 171 to 181, a company ("the subsidiary") is an effective 51 per cent subsidiary of another company ("the parent") at any time if and only if–

(a) the parent is beneficially entitled to more than 50 per cent of any profits available for distribution to equity holders of the subsidiary; and

(b) the parent would be beneficially entitled to more than 50 per cent of any assets of the subsidiary available for distribution to its equity holders on a winding-up.

170(8) Chapter 6 of Part 5 of CTA 2010 (group relief: equity holders and profits or assets available for distribution) applies for the purposes of subsections (6) and (7) as if–

(a) references to section 151(4)(a) and (b) of that Act were references to subsections (6) and (7) above,

(aa) in section 158 of that Act after subsection (2) there were inserted–

"**158(2A)** But for those purposes a person carrying on a business of banking is not treated as a loan creditor of a company in respect of any loan capital or debt issued or incurred by the company for money lent by the person to the company in the ordinary course of that business.", and

(b) sections 171(1)(b) and (3), 173, 174 and 176 to 178 of that Act were omitted.

170(9) For the purposes of this section and sections 171 to 181, references to a **company** apply only to–

(a) a company as defined in section 1(1) of the Companies Act 2006 (c. 46), and

(b) a company (other than a limited liability partnership) which is constituted under any other Act or a Royal Charter or letters patent or is formed under the law of a country or territory outside the United Kingdom, and

(c) a registered society (see section 1119 of CTA 2010); and

(cc) an incorporated friendly society within the meaning of the Friendly Societies Act 1992; and

(d) a building society.

170(10) For the purposes of this section and sections 171 to 181, a group remains the same group so long as the same company remains the principal company of the group, and if at any time the principal company of a group becomes a member of another group, the first group and the other group shall be regarded as the same, and the question whether or not a company has ceased to be a member of a group shall be determined accordingly.

170(10A) Where the principal company of a group (Group 1)–

(a) becomes an SE by reason of being the acquiring company in the formation of an SE by merger by acquisition (in accordance with Articles 2(1), 17(2)(a) and 29(1) of Council Regulation (EC) 2157/2001 on the Statute for a European Company (Societas Europaea)),

(b) becomes a subsidiary of a holding SE (formed in accordance with Article 2(2) of that Regulation), or

(c) is transformed into an SE (in accordance with Article 2(4) of that Regulation),

Group 1 and any group of which the SE is a member on formation shall be regarded as the same; and the question whether or not a company has ceased to be a member of a group shall be determined accordingly.

170(11) For the purposes of this section and sections 171 to 181, the passing of a resolution or the making of an order, or any other act, for the winding-up of a member of a group of companies shall not be regarded as the occasion of that or any other company ceasing to be a member of the group.

170(12) Sections 171 to 181, except in so far as they relate to recovery of tax, shall also have effect in relation to bodies from time to time established by or under any enactment for the carrying on of any industry or part of an industry, or of any undertaking, under national ownership or control as if they were companies within the meaning of those sections, and as if any such bodies charged with related functions (and in particular the Boards and Holding Company established under the Transport Act 1962 and the new authorities within the meaning of the Transport Act 1968 established under that Act of 1968) and subsidiaries of any of them formed a group, and as if also any 2 or more such bodies charged at different times with the same or related functions were members of a group.

170(13) Subsection (12) shall have effect subject to any enactment by virtue of which property, rights, liabilities or activities of one such body fall to be treated for corporation tax as those of another, including in particular any such enactment in Chapter VI of Part XII of the Taxes Act.

170(14) Sections 171 to 181, except in so far as they relate to recovery of tax, shall also have effect in relation to the Executive for a designated area within the meaning of section 9(1) of the Transport Act 1968 as if that Executive were a company within the meaning of those sections.

History – S. 170(2)(b) repealed by FA 2000, s. 102 and Sch. 29, para. 1(1), s. 156 and Sch. 40, Pt. II(12), with effect in relation to disposals on or after 1 April 2000.

In s. 170(2)(c), the words "registered society (see section 1119 of that Act)" substituted for the words "registered industrial and provident society" by Co-operative and Community Benefit Societies Act 2014, s. 151 and Sch. 4, para. 50(2), with effect from 1 August 2014.
In s. 170(2)(c), the words "section 1154(3) of CTA 2010 (meaning of "75% subsidiary")" substituted for "the definition of "75 per cent subsidiary" in section 838 of the Taxes Act" by CTA 2010, s. 1177 and Sch. 1, para. 242(2), with effect for corporation tax purposes for accounting periods ending on or after 1 April 2010, and for income tax and capital gains tax purposes for the tax year 2010–11 and subsequent tax years.
In s. 170(6)(d), the words "section 1154(2) of CTA 2010" substituted for "section 838(1)(a) of the Taxes Act" by CTA 2010, s. 1177 and Sch. 1, para. 242(3), with effect for corporation tax purposes for accounting periods ending on or after 1 April 2010, and for income tax and capital gains tax purposes for the tax year 2010–11 and subsequent tax years.
S. 170(8)(aa) inserted (and the "and" at the end of s. 170(8)(a) omitted) by SI 2010/2902, art. 2(2) (effective from 1 January 2011 but with deemed effect from 1 April 2010). These amendments are deemed to have come into force for corporation tax purposes for accounting periods ending on or after 1 April 2010, and for income tax and capital gains tax purposes for the tax year 2010–11 and subsequent tax years.
S. 170(8) substituted by CTA 2010, s. 1177 and Sch. 1, para. 242(4), with effect for corporation tax purposes for accounting periods ending on or after 1 April 2010, and for income tax and capital gains tax purposes for the tax year 2010–11 and subsequent tax years.
In former s. 170(8), reference to omission of para. 5B to 5E in applying ICTA 1988, Sch. 18 inserted by F(No. 2)A 1992, s. 24 and Sch. 6, para. 5, and words "or subsection (7) to (9)" which followed "subsection (7)" repealed by FA 2000, s. 156 and Sch. 40, Pt. II(11) and deemed always to have had effect.
In s. 170(9)(a), the words "as defined in section 1(1) of the Companies Act 2006 (c. 46)" substituted for the words "within the meaning of the Companies Act 1985 or the corresponding enactment in Northern Ireland" by SI 2009/1890, art. 3(2)(c), with effect from 1 October 2009.
In s. 170(9)(c) the words "within the meaning of section 486 of the Taxes Act" omitted by CTA 2009, s. 1322 and Sch. 1, para. 375 and repealed by CTA 2009, s. 1326 and Sch. 3, Pt. 1, with effect for corporation tax purposes for accounting periods ending on or after 1 April 2009, and for income tax and capital gains tax purposes for the tax year 2009–10 and subsequent tax years.
In s. 170(9)(b) words "(although resident in the United Kingdom)" between "letters patent or" and "is formed" repealed by FA 2000, s. 102 and Sch. 29, para. 1(1), s. 156 and Sch. 40, Pt. II(12), with effect in relation to disposals on or after 1 April 2000.
In s. 170(9)(b) words "(other than a limited liability partnership)" inserted by FA 2001, s. 75(4) with effect from 6 April 2001.
In s. 170(9)(c), the words "registered society (see section 1119 of CTA 2010)" substituted for the words "registered industrial and provident society" by Co-operative and Community Benefit Societies Act 2014, s. 151 and Sch. 4, para. 50(3), with effect from 1 August 2014.
S. 170(10A) inserted by F(No. 2)A 2005, s. 62(1) with effect in relation to formation of SE (including its formation by transformation) which occurs on or after 1 April 2005.

Derivations – S. 170(1): ICTA 1970, s. 238(4); FA 1988, Sch. 14, Pt. V.
S. 170(9)(cc) inserted by FA 1998 s. 136(1) for the purpose of determining whether a friendly society is a company within the meaning of s. 170–181 in relation to times on or after 17 March 1998.
S. 170(2): ICTA 1970, s. 272(1), as amended by FA 1989, s. 138(1).
S. 170(3)–(8) (as originally enacted): ICTA 1970, s. 272(1A)–(1F), as inserted by FA 1989, s. 138(2) and amended by FA 1990, s. 86(1).
S. 170(9): ICTA 1970, s. 272(2)(a)–(c) ((a) as amended by the Companies Consolidation (Consequential Provisions) Act 1985), (e) as inserted by F(No. 2)A 1987, s. 79.
S. 170(10), (11): ICTA 1970, s. 272(3), (4), as amended by FA 1989, s. 138(3), (4).
S. 170(12), (13): ICTA 1970, s. 272(5).
S. 170(14): ICTA 1970, s. 272(6), as amended by London Regional Transport Act 1984, Sch. 6, para. 7.

Cross references – S. 14: as regards attribution to members of gains of non-resident companies, s. 170 adapted to any non-resident group.
S. 33(10): application of s. 170(2)–(11) for purposes of value shifting provisions.
S. 106(10): application of s. 170 for purposes of the special rules for identifying securities disposed of by a company within the prescribed period of acquisition by the group.
S. 117(10): application of s. 170 for purposes of the exclusion from qualifying corporate bonds of intra-group funding.
S. 138A(11): use of earn-out rights for exchange of securities.
S. 139(2): asset forming part of trade within s. 170(1) on acquisition or disposal not subject to the deemed transfer at no gain, no loss on reconstruction involving the transfer of business.
S. 140(6): no crystallisation of deferred gain on transfer of foreign branch to foreign company where disposal of resulting securities is within s. 171 ignoring s. 170(1), (2)(a), (9).
S. 164N: application of s. 170 to s. 164G and s. 164I (in relation to disposal of shares or securities and re-investment in other shares).
S. 216(7): application of s. 170 for purposes of the no gain, no loss relief and relief from crystallisation of gains on leaving a group on incorporation of a building society.
S. 228(8): application of s. 170 for purposes of the relief for disposals of shares to an employee share ownership trust established by a suitable company.
S. 253(14): application of s. 170 for purposes of relief for losses in respect of loans to traders.
S. 276(8): application of s. 171–174 and s. 178–181 to certain transfers of exploration or exploitation rights or assets by a non-resident, as if s. 170(2)(a), (9) ignored.
Sch. 3, para. 8, 9: as regards elections for the simplified scheme of re-basing, in so far as an election must be made by the principal company, group is defined by reference to s. 170.
Sch. 7A, para. 1(6), 9(6): modification of application of s. 170(6) in relation to pre-entry loss restrictions and, subject to that, where a group becomes part of another group its members are deemed to join the enlarged group at that time notwithstanding s. 170(10).
ICTA 1988, s. 209(8E): definition of "effective 51 per cent subsidiary" in s. 170(7) applies for determining "relevant connection" and "UK grouping" in relation to the treatment as qualifying distributions of interest or other distributions out of assets.
ICTA 1988, s. 486: registered industrial and provident society means a society registered or deemed to be registered under the Industrial and Provident Societies Act 1965 or under the Industrial and Provident Societies Act (Northern Ireland) 1969.
ICTA 1988, s. 503–519A (Pt. XII, Ch. VI): miscellaneous businesses and bodies.
ICTA 1988, s. 838: definition of "75 per cent subsidiary" by reference to beneficial ownership, directly or indirectly, of at least 75 per cent of ordinary share capital.
ICTA 1988, Sch. 18: for s. 413(7)–(9) (group relief), "equity holder" defined by reference to any person who holds ordinary shares or is a creditor for a loan which is not a normal commercial loan, with the omission of certain bank lending (para. 1(4) proviso) and deemed effect being given to certain arrangements for increasing an equity holder's entitlements (para. 5(3)); the relevant accounting period in point in relation to a consortium is irrelevant (para. 7(1)(b)).
FA 1988, s. 132(6): liability of other members of a group (as the term is modified) for unpaid tax of a migrating company.
FA 1989, s. 83XA(7): application of s. 170 for the purposes of interpreting FA 1989, s. 83XA.
FA 1993, s. 136: in applying arm's length test for purposes of foreign exchange gains and losses the test in s 170 applies to establish whether companies are members of the same group.
FA 1993, s. 136A(10): in applying arm's length test for purposes of exchange gains and losses on debts of varying amounts the test in s. 170 applies for determining whether companies are members of the same group.

FA 1993, s. 141 (as modified by SI 1994/3228, reg. 4): claim to defer unrealised exchange gain by a company which is a member of a group for TCGA 1992, s. 171–181 by virtue of s. 170.
British Aerospace Act 1980, s. 12(2) (not reproduced): certain aerospace companies not to be treated as bodies within s. 170(12).
FA 1999, s. 81(7): application of s. 170 for construing references to groups of companies in FA 1999, s. 81(1)–6.
FA 2000, Sch. 29, para. 47: definition and application of "old section 170" and "new section 170" concerning the de-grouping charge.
CAA 2001, s. 220(7): s. 170 applies to determine for the purposes of s. 220 whether a company is a member of a group and which company is the principal member.
FA 2002, Sch. 26, para. 28(6): application of s. 170 to provisions on derivative contracts.
FA 2002, Sch. 29, para. 54(2): application of s. 170(10)–(12) to provisions on gains and losses from intangible fixed assets.
FA 2004, s. 51(3): use of different accounting practices within a group of companies, where the provisions of s. 170(3) to (6) are used for determining whether companies are in the same group.
FA 2004, s. 307(4): disclosure of tax avoidance schemes: meaning of promoter.
FA 2006, s. 134(5): s. 170(6) applies to determine, where it is uncertain, which group a company is member of for the purposes of REITs.
Telecommunications Act 1984, s. 72(2) (not reproduced): certain telecommunications companies not to be treated as bodies within s. 170(12).
Airports Act 1986, s. 77(2) (not reproduced): certain airport management companies not to be treated as bodies within s. 170(12).
Gas Act 1986, s. 60(2) (not reproduced): certain gas companies not to be treated as bodies within s. 170(12).
British Steel Act 1988, s. 11(2) (not reproduced): successor companies to British Steel Corporation not to be treated as a bodies falling within s. 170(12).
Health and Medicines Act 1988, s. 6(2) (not reproduced): certain health organisations not to be treated as bodies within s. 170(12).
Greater London Authority Act 1999, s. 419 (not reproduced): references in s.170 to a company do not apply to Transport for London.
Commonwealth Development Corporation Act 1999, Sch. 3 para. 4(1) (not reproduced): the Corporation cannot be a member of a group of companies for the purposes of Pt. VI Ch. I at any time during its exempt period.
SI 1994/3228, reg. 4: modification of FA 1993, s. 139, 141 for claim to defer unrealised exchange gain by a company which is a member of a group for TCGA 1992, s. 171–181 by virtue of s. 170.
SI 1994/3229, reg. 3: relief for a company's unrelievable non-exchange loss cancelled if loss is recovered by a company in the same group for TCGA 1992, s. 171–181 by virtue of s. 170.
SI 2006/575, reg. 37: Pension Protection Fund etc. are not members of a group.
SI 2006/964, reg. 107: modification of s. 170 for the purposes of authorised investment funds.
Council Regulation (EC) 2157/2001: Statute for a European Company (Societas Europaea).

Statements of practice – SP 10/91: HMRC interpretation of "major change in the nature or conduct of a trade (or business)".

HMRC interpretations – IRInt. 216: HMRC view that a Delaware Limited Liability Company may be a member of a capital gains group.

Other material – CCAB press release, 1968 (not reproduced): Revenue confirmation that the passing of a resolution or the making of an order for the winding up of a company is not regarded as the occasion of a company leaving the group for these purposes.

Notes – S. 9: meaning of "resident".
S. 10(4): reference to the Income Tax Acts is construed as a reference also to the Corporation Tax Acts.
S. 288: interpretation, including the "Taxes Act" as ICTA 1988 and reference to other sections being those of this Act.
Interpretation Act 1978, s. 5 and Sch. 1: the Income Tax Acts means the enactments relating to income tax.

TRANSACTIONS WITHIN GROUPS

171 Transfers within a group: general provisions

171(1) Where–

(a) a company ("company A") disposes of an asset to another company ("company B") at a time when both companies are members of the same group, and

(b) the conditions in subsection (1A) below are met,

company A and company B are treated for the purposes of corporation tax on chargeable gains as if the asset were acquired by company B for a consideration of such amount as would secure that neither a gain nor a loss would accrue to company A on the disposal.

171(1A) The conditions referred to in subsection (1)(b) above are–

(a) that company A is resident in the United Kingdom at the time of the disposal, or the asset is a chargeable asset in relation to that company immediately before that time, and

(b) that company B is resident in the United Kingdom at the time of the disposal, or the asset is a chargeable asset in relation to that company immediately after that time.

For this purpose an asset is a "chargeable asset" in relation to a company at any time if, were the asset to be disposed of by the company at that time, any gain accruing to the company would be a chargeable gain and would by virtue of section 10B form part of its chargeable profits for corporation tax purposes.

171(2) Subsection (1) above shall not apply where the disposal is–

(a) a disposal of a debt due from company B effected by satisfying the debt or part of it; or

(b) a disposal of redeemable shares in a company on the occasion of their redemption; or

(ba) a relevant high value disposal on which (ignoring subsection (1)) there accrues to company A an ATED-related gain chargeable to, or an ATED-related loss allowable for the purposes of, capital gains tax by virtue of section 2B; or

(c) a disposal by or to an investment trust; or

(cc) a disposal by or to a venture capital trust; or

(cd) a disposal by or to a qualifying friendly society; or

(d) a disposal to a dual resident investing company; or

(da) a disposal by or to a company which is, or is a member of, a UK REIT within the meaning of Part 12 of CTA 2010 (Real Estate Investment Trusts); or

(db) a disposal by company A in fulfilment of its obligations under an option granted to company B at a time when those companies were not members of the same group;

(e) [repealed by FA 1994, s. 251(7) and s. 258 and Sch. 26, Pt. VIII(1).]

and the reference in subsection (1) above to company A disposing of an asset shall not apply to anything which under section 122 is to be treated as a disposal of an interest in shares in a company in consideration for a capital distribution (as defined in that section) from that company, whether or not involving a reduction of capital.

171(3) Subsection (1) above shall not apply to a transaction treated by section 127 as it applies by virtue of section 135 as not involving a disposal by company A.

171(3A) [Omitted by FA 2009, s. 48 and Sch. 24, para. 9(b).]

171(4) For the purposes of subsection (1) above, so far as the consideration for the disposal consists of money or money's worth by way of compensation for any kind of damage or injury to assets, or for the destruction or dissipation of assets or for anything which depreciates or might depreciate an asset, the disposal shall be treated as being to the person who, whether as an insurer or otherwise, ultimately bears the burden of furnishing that consideration.

171(5) In subsection (2)(cd) above **"qualifying friendly society"** means a company which is a qualifying society for the purposes of section 165 of the Finance Act 2012 (incorporated friendly societies entitled to exemption from income tax and corporation tax on certain profits).

171(6) Subsection (1) above applies notwithstanding any provision in this Act fixing the amount of the consideration deemed to be received on a disposal or given on an acquisition.

But where it is assumed for any purpose that a member of a group of companies has sold or acquired an asset, it shall be assumed also that it was not a sale or acquisition to which this section applies.

History – S. 171(1) substituted by FA 2000, s. 102 and Sch. 29, para. 2(2) with effect in relation to disposals made on or after 1 April 2000.

S. 171(1A) inserted by FA 2000, s. 102 and Sch. 29, para. 2(2) with effect in relation to disposals made on or after 1 April 2000.

In s. 171(1A), the reference "10B" substituted for the reference "10(3)" by FA 2003, s. 155 and Sch. 27, para. 2(3) which have effect in relation to accounting periods beginning on or after 1 January 2003.

In s. 171(2)(a), words "company B" substituted for "a member of a group of companies" and in the closing sentence words, "company A" substituted for "a member of a group of companies" by FA 2000, s. 102 and Sch. 29, para. 2(3) as respects disposals made on or after 1 April 2000.

S. 171(2)(ba) inserted by FA 2013, s. 65 and Sch. 25, para. 12, with effect in relation to disposals occurring on or after 6 April 2013.

S. 171(2)(cc) inserted by FA 1998, s. 135(1) as respects disposals made on or after 17 March 1998.

S. 171(2)(cd) inserted by FA 1998, s. 136(2) as respects disposals made on or after 17 March 1998.

In s. 171(2)(da), the words "which is, or is a member of, a UK REIT within the meaning of Part 12 of CTA 2010" substituted for "to which Part 4 of the Finance Act 2006 applies" by CTA 2010, s. 1177 and Sch. 1, para. 243, with effect for corporation tax purposes for accounting periods ending on or after 1 April 2010, and for income tax and capital gains tax purposes for the tax year 2010–11 and subsequent tax years.

S. 171(2)(da) and the preceding word "or" inserted by FA 2006, s. 135 with effect from 19 July 2006 but in relation to provisions that effectively come into force for accounting periods beginning on or after 1 January 2007.

S. 171(2)(db) and the preceding word "or" inserted by FA 2007, s. 30 and Sch. 5, para. 10(1), with effect in relation to cases where an option is exercised on or after 6 March 2007 (whatever the date of grant) (Sch. 5, para. 10(2)).

S. 171(2)(e) and the word "or" immediately preceding it were omitted by FA 1994, s. 258 and s. 251(7) and Sch. 26, Pt. VIII(1) in relation to disposals made on or after 30 November 1993.

In s. 171(2), words "company A" substituted for "a member of a group of companies" by FA 2000, s. 102 and Sch. 29, para. 2(4) as respects disposals made on or after 1 April 2000.

In s. 171(3), words "by section 127 as it applies by virtue of section 135" substituted for "by virtue of sections 127 and 135" by FA 2002, s. 45 and Sch. 9, para. 5(10) with effect in relation to shares or debentures issued on or after 17 April 2002.

S. 171(3A) omitted by FA 2009, s. 48 and Sch. 24, para. 9(b), with effect from 22 April 2009.

In former s. 171(3A) the words "section 524 of CTA 2009" substitutedfor the words "section 91A of the Finance Act 1996" by CTA 2009, s. 1322 and Sch. 1, para. 376, with effect for corporation tax purposes for accounting periods ending on or after 1 April 2009, and for income tax and capital gains tax purposes for the tax year 2009–10 and subsequent tax years.

Former s. 171(3A) inserted by F(No. 2)A 2005, s. 39 and Sch. 7, para. 9(2) with effect in any case where disposal is on or after 16 March 2005.

In s. 171(5) the words "section 165 of the Finance Act 2012" substituted for the words "section 461B of the Taxes Act" by FA 2012, s. 176 and Sch. 18, para. 16 in relation to accounting periods beginning on or after 1 January 2013 (FA 2012, s. 178). Where an accounting period would otherwise straddle 1 January 2013, it is deemed to end on 31 December 2012 (FA 2012, s. 179).

Former s. 171(5) inserted by FA 1998, s. 136(3) as respects disposals made on or after 17 March 1998.

S. 171(6) inserted by FA 2000, s. 102 and Sch. 29, para. 2(5) as respects disposals made on or after 1 April 2000.

Derivations – (as originally enacted) S. 171(1): ICTA 1970, s. 273(1).

S. 171(2): ICTA 1970, s. 273(2), as amended by FA 1980, s. 81(4), F(No. 2)A 1987, s. 64(3), and FA 1990, s. 65(2).

S. 171(3): ICTA 1970, s. 273(2A), as inserted by FA 1988, s. 115.

S. 171(4): ICTA 1970, s. 273(3).

Cross references – S. 14: as regards attribution to members of gains made by non-resident companies, s. 171 adapted to any non-resident group.

S. 19(5): transfer within s. 171 is not a material transaction for purposes of the deemed consideration where assets disposed of in a series of such transactions.

S. 30(2), (7): priority over value shifting provisions and determination of value shift via a relevant asset where reduction in value not realised by reference to a disposal outside s. 171(1).

S. 31(6), (7): exclusion from value shifting provisions of reductions caused by certain dividends except to the extent that payable out of particular profits (including those out of profits from transactions within s. 171(1)) unrealised by reference to a disposal outside s. 171(1).
S. 32(1): exclusion from value shifting provisions of reductions caused by the disposal of an asset within s. 171(1).
S. 33(3B), (3C): operation of value shifting provisions where asset with enhanced value transferred within group before being disposed of outside group.
S. 35(3)(d), (5): re-basing not to apply to disposal under these provisions unless an election exists for the simplified scheme (re-basing of all assets held at 31 March 1982 irrespective of matters in s. 35(3)).
S. 42(5): application of apportionment in relation to part disposals without prejudice to s. 171.
S. 116(11): disapplication to a transfer within s. 171(1) of provisions deeming there to be no disposal but so that any market value gain or loss crystallises at subsequent disposal on a reorganisation, conversion or reconstruction where qualifying corporate bonds form part of the new holding but not the original holding.
S. 122: capital distribution in respect of shares treated as a part disposal.
S. 125(4): apportionment to shareholders of close companies in respect of undervalue transfers does not apply to transfers within s. 171(1).
S. 127–135: equation of original and new holdings on a reorganisation, conversion, exchange etc. and treatment of consideration given or received in addition to the new holding; there is no crystallisation of a deferred gain on disposal of gilt-edged stock obtained on a compulsory acquisition of securities until the first disposal outside s. 171 etc. (s. 134(4)).
S. 137(4): charge for unpaid tax by reference to acquisition within s. 171 etc. where equation of original and new holdings on an exchange, reconstruction etc. nullified by a finding that not effected for bona fide commercial reasons etc.
S. 139(7): charge for unpaid tax by reference to acquisition within s. 171 etc. where no gain, no loss on transfer of business in a reconstruction or amalgamation nullified by a finding that not effected for bona fide commercial reasons etc.
S. 140(6): no crystallisation of deferred gain on transfer of foreign branch to foreign company where disposal of resulting securities is within s. 171 ignoring s. 170(1), (2)(a), (9).
S. 179A(7): disapplication of reallocation within group provisions where either company qualifying friendly society as defined in s. 171(5).
S. 242: claim where small part disposal of land (by reference to market value) which is not a transfer within s. 171 for consideration to be deducted from allowable expenditure on remainder.
S. 276(8): application of s. 171 to certain transfers of exploration or exploitation rights or assets by a non-resident company.
Sch. 2, para. 4(9): election by transferor company for pooling of quoted securities held at 6 April 1965 has effect in relation to subsequent disposal by the transferee.
Sch. 3, para. 1: person disposing of asset acquired through disposal under these provisions after 31 March 1982 treated as holding asset at 31 March 1982 for purposes of re-basing.
Sch. 3, para. 2, 3: where there is any acquisition of an asset after 5 April 1985 within these provisions, any election to re-base using the simplified scheme, above, is by reference to the holder on that date or to the last person acquiring it thereafter on a disposal outside these provisions and the inter- spouse transfer provisions (s. 58).
Sch. 7A, para. 1(4): an asset is not a "pre-entry asset" if disposed of otherwise than by a disposal to which s. 171 applies.
Sch. 7AC, para. 10: no gain/no loss treatment applies for purposes of provisions on companies with substantial shareholding notwithstanding s. 171(3).
Sch. 7AC, para. 18: requirements to be met in relation to investing company to qualify for exemption for substantial shareholding can be satisfied by another group member.
Sch. 7B, para. 6A: modified application of s. 171(1A) to overseas life insurance companies.
ICTA 1988, s. 440: disapplication to disposal or acquisition where asset directly allocated to individual category of business of insurance company.
ICTA 1988, s. 768C(1)(d): restriction to set-off of management expenses and charges defrayed and paid by an investment company before a change in ownership against chargeable gains on disposal of assets acquired intra-group in three years following the change.
IHTA 1984, s. 97: minority participators in a close company who are only marginally affected by a disposal within s. 171(1) which is a transfer of value are excluded in apportioning the value transferred.
FA 1993, s. 169 and Sch. 17, para. 7: disapplication of s. 171 where that paragraph (exchange gains and losses: chargeable gains reconstructions) applies.
FA 1994, s. 249: companies treated as resident in the UK for tax purposes, but resident abroad for the purposes of any double taxation relief arrangements ("dual resident companies") are with effect from 30 November 1993 to be treated as non-UK resident for all tax purposes, even if they are incorporated in the UK.
FA 2002, Sch. 29, para. 86(6): disposal within s. 171 disregarded for purposes of realisation of postponed charge where assets have been transferred to non-resident company in exchange for certain securities.
FA 2006, s. 136: for accounting periods beginning on or after 1 January 2007; a group of investment trust companies carrying on property rental businesses that meet specific requirements can elect to be regarded as a group of Real Estate Investment Trusts (REIT). In such circumstances; the group (in so far as it is subject to the REIT rules) is to be treated as if it were a separate group distinct from the group: (i) prior to the time that the REIT rules began to apply; (ii) after the time that the REIT rules ceased to apply; and (iii) in so far as it carries on activities that are not within the REIT rules.
Broadcasting Act 1996, Sch. 7, para. 2(2) (not reproduced): s. 171(1) does not apply where disposal in question is a "preparatory transfer" within meaning of that Act.
Greater London Authority Act 1999, s. 419 (not reproduced): references in s. 171 to a company do not apply to transport for London.
SI 1994/3227, reg. 8: deferral of gain or loss deemed to accrue on disposal, which is a no gain/no loss transaction under s. 171, of a matched asset by one company to another.
SI 1999/358, reg. 18: restriction on set-off of unrelieved surplus ACT (as at 6 April 1999) against liability to corporation tax where there is a change in ownership of a company, that company acquires an asset from another group member and the asset is disposed of within three years of the change in ownership.
SI 2004/2199, reg. 12: disapplication of s. 171(2)(cc) in certain circumstances where there is a merger of VCTs.
SI 2007/3402, reg. 9: Taxation of Insurance Securitisation Companies Regulations 2007, disapplication of s. 171.
Budget Responsibility and National Audit Act 2001, Sch. 4, para. 4 (not reproduced): transfers between Comptroller and Auditor General and NAO treated as no gain/no loss transfers.

Extra-statutory concessions – D44: where company disposes of shares acquired on a no gain/no loss transfer from group company which held the shares at 31 March 1982 by concession a more favourable basis of valuation at that date may be adopted.
D50: transfer under s. 171 ignored in determining the applicability of this concession to any person.

HMRC interpretations – IRInt. 43: no gain/no loss rule applies whether the shareholder is assessable to capital gains tax or to corporation tax.
IRInt. 152: Revenue view that no gain/no loss rule (s. 171(1)) does not apply to C's acquisition where a group company A exchanges shares in company B for a new issue of QCBs in another group company C.
IRInt. 216: Delaware Limited Liability Company may be a member of a capital gains group.

Hansard – 10 April 1984, col. 254 (not reproduced): Chief Secretary to the Treasury stated that the Revenue would not invoke the principles of *Furniss v Dawson* to challenge the tax treatment of straightforward transfers of assets between members of the same group.

Other material – ICAEW Technical Release TR 172 (not reproduced): relief generally available where an asset distributed by a liquidator in specie.
ICAEW Technical Release TR 588 (not reproduced): limited application of the principles of Furniss v Dawson where benefit of capital losses effectively transferred from one group to another.

Notes – S. 8: charge to corporation tax in respect of chargeable gains.
S. 9: meaning of "residence".
S. 15: meaning of "chargeable gains".
S. 21–34: general meaning of "disposal" and "assets", including deemed disposals where receipt of a capital sum by way of compensation for any kind of damage or injury to assets or for the loss, destruction of dissipation of assets or for any depreciation or risk of depreciation of an asset (s. 22), except in some circumstances where it is small and the asset is not lost or destroyed (s. 23).
S. 56(2): no gain, no loss calculated after applying indexation allowance.
S. 288: interpretation, including meaning of "investment trust", "company", "double taxation relief arrangements", "dual resident investing company" and reference to sections being those of this Act.

171A Election to reallocate gain or loss to another member of the group

171A(1) This section applies where–

(a) a chargeable gain or an allowable loss accrues to a company ("company A") in respect of an asset (or would so accrue but for an election under this section),

(b) at the time of accrual, company A and another company ("company B") are members of the same group, and

(c) had company A disposed of the asset to company B immediately before the time of accrual, section 171(1) would have applied.

171A(2) In determining for the purposes of subsection (1)(c) whether subsection (1) of section 171 would have applied, it is to be assumed that subsection (1A)(b) of that section read–

"(b) that, at the time of the disposal, company B is resident in the United Kingdom, or carrying on a trade in the United Kingdom through a permanent establishment there.".

171A(3) In this section **"the time of accrual"** means the time the chargeable gain or allowable loss accrues to company A (or would so accrue but for an election under this section).

171A(4) Companies A and B may make a joint election to transfer the chargeable gain or allowable loss, or such part of it as is specified in the election, from company A to company B (but see subsection (4A)).

171A(4A) An election may not be made under this section to transfer the whole or part of a ring fence chargeable gain from a company carrying on a ring fence trade to a company not carrying on such a trade.

171A(4B) In subsection (4A)–

"ring fence chargeable gain", in relation to a company, means–

(a) a chargeable gain accruing to the company on a material disposal within the meaning of section 197 (disposals of interests in oil fields etc: ring fence provisions), or

(b) a chargeable gain treated as accruing to the company by virtue of section 197(4);

"ring fence trade" has the same meaning as in Part 8 of CTA 2010 (see section 277 of that Act).

171A(5) An election under this section must be made–

(a) by notice to an officer of Revenue and Customs, and

(b) no later than two years after the end of the accounting period of company A in which the time of accrual falls.

171A(6) An election, or two or more elections made simultaneously, is or are of no effect if, taken together with each earlier election (if any) made in respect of the same gain or loss, it or they would (apart from this subsection) have effect in relation to an amount exceeding the gain or loss.

171A(7) [Omitted by FA 2011, s. 45 and Sch. 10, para. 2.]

171A(8) For the effect of an election under this section, see section 171B.

History – In s. 171A(4), the words "(but see subsection (4A))" inserted by FA 2012, s. 181(2) in relation to chargeable gains accruing, or treated by virtue of TCGA 1992, s. 197(4) as accruing, in chargeable periods ending on or after 6 December 2011, but subject to transitional provisions in FA 2012, s . 181(5).
S. 171A(4A) and (4B) inserted by FA 2012, s. 181(3) in relation to chargeable gains accruing, or treated by virtue of TCGA 1992, s. 197(4) as accruing, in chargeable periods ending on or after 6 December 2011, but subject to transitional provisions in FA 2012, s. 181(5).
S. 171A(7) omitted by FA 2011, s. 45 and Sch. 10, para. 2, with effect in relation to any disposal of an asset by one company (B) to another company (A) made at a time when B is a member of a group if either A ceases to be a member of the group on or after 19 July 2011 or ceased to be so before 19 July 2011 in circumstances where TCGA 1992, s. 179(6)–(8) applied and ceases to satisfy the conditions in TCGA 1992, s. 179(7) on or after 19 July 2011 (see FA 2011, Sch. 10, para. 9(1)). But references to 19 July 2011 may be replaced by references to 1 April 2011 if an "early commencement election" is made (see FA 2011, Sch. 10, para. 9(4)–(8)).
S. 171A (with s. 171B and 171C) substituted for former s. 171A by FA 2009, s. 31 and Sch. 12, para. 1, with effect in relation to chargeable gains and allowable losses accruing on or after 21 July 2009 (Royal Assent).
Former s. 171A(2)(d) inserted by FA 2001, s. 77(2) and deemed to have effect from 1 April 2000.
Former s. 171A(3ZA) inserted by F(No. 2)A 2005, s. 36(2) with effect in relation to disposals made on or after 16 March 2005.
Former s. 171A(3A) inserted by FA 2003, s. 170 and Sch. 33, para. 17(2) which, by virtue of Sch. 33, para. 17(4), have effect in relation to disposals on or after 23 December 2002.
In former s. 171A(4), words "subsection (2) above" substituted for the words "that subsection" by FA 2003, s. 170 and Sch. 33, para. 17(3) which, by virtue of Sch. 33, para. 17(4), have effect in relation to disposals on or after 23 December 2002.

In former s. 171A(4), words "on or before" substituted for "before" by FA 2001, s. 77(3) and deemed to have effect from 1 April 2000.
In former s. 171A(5)(b), words "or acharge on income", that immediately followed words "regarded as a distribution", were repealed by F(No. 2)A 2005, s. 70 and Sch. 11, Pt. 2(7), with effect, in accordance with F(No. 2)A 2005, s. 38, in relation to payments made on or after 16 March 2005.
Former s. 171A inserted by FA 2000, s. 101(1) with effect in relation to disposals made on or after 1 April 2000.

Cross references – IHTA 1984, s. 97: minority participators in a close company who are only marginally affected by an election under s. 171A(2) are excluded in apportioning the deemed value transferred.
FA 2006, s. 136: for accounting periods beginning on or after 1 January 2007; a group of investment trust companies carrying on property rental businesses that meet specific requirements can elect to be regarded as a group of Real Estate Investment Trusts (REIT). In such circumstances; the group (in so far as it is subject to the REIT rules) is to be treated as if it were a separate group distinct from the group: (i) prior to the time that the REIT rules began to apply; (ii) after the time that the REIT rules ceased to apply; and (iii) in so far as it carries on activities that are not within the REIT rules.

HMRC interpretations – IRInt. 216: Delaware Limited Liability Company may be a member of a capital gains group.

171B Election under section 171A: effect

171B(1) This section applies where an election is made under section 171A.

171B(2) The effect of the election is that the chargeable gain or allowable loss, or such amount of it as is specified in the election, is treated as accruing not to company A but to company B.

171B(3) The gain or loss treated as accruing to company B is to be taken to accrue at the time that, had the election not been made, it would have accrued to company A.

171B(4) Where company B is not resident in the United Kingdom, the gain or loss treated as accruing to it is to be taken to accrue in respect of a chargeable asset held by it.

171B(5) For this purpose an asset is a **"chargeable asset"** in relation to a company at any time if any gain accruing to the company on a disposal of the asset by the company at that time would be a chargeable gain and would by virtue of section 10B form part of its chargeable profits for corporation tax purposes.

171B(6) Any payment made by company A to company B or by company B to company A, in pursuance of an agreement between them in connection with the election–

(a) is not to be taken into account in computing profits or losses of either company for corporation tax purposes, and

(b) is not for any purposes of the Corporation Tax Acts to be regarded as a distribution,

provided it does not exceed the amount of the chargeable gain or allowable loss that is treated, as a result of the election, as accruing to company B.

History – S. 171B (with s. 171A and 171C) substituted for former s. 171A by FA 2009, s. 31 and Sch. 12, para. 1, with effect in relation to chargeable gains and allowable losses accruing on or after 21 July 2009 (Royal Assent).

171C Elections under section 171A: insurance companies

171C(1) This section applies where–

(a) an election is made under section 171A in relation to a gain or loss, and

(b) company B is an insurance company.

171C(2) For the purposes of section 171A(1)(c), section 118 of the Finance Act 2012 (disposals of certain assets by and to insurance companies to fall outside the rule in section 171) is to be disregarded.

171C(3) Subsection (2) does not apply if–

(a) company A is an insurance company, and

(b) the gain or loss arose in respect of the disposal of an asset that, immediately before the disposal, was held for the purposes of the company's long-term business.

171C(4) The chargeable gain or allowable loss treated as accruing to company B as a result of the election is to be treated for the purposes of section 210A (ring-fencing of losses) as a non-BLAGAB chargeable gain or (as the case may be) a non-BLAGAB allowable loss.

171C(5) [Omitted by FA 2012, s. 146 and Sch. 16, para. 77(5).]

History – In s. 171C(2) the words "section 118 of the Finance Act 2012" substituted for the words "section 440(3) of the Taxes Act" by FA 2012, s. 146 and Sch. 16, para. 77(2) in relation to accounting periods beginning on or after 1 January 2013 (FA 2012, s. 148) but subject to transitional provisions in FA 2012, Sch. 17. Where an accounting period would otherwise straddle 1 January 2013, it is deemed to end on 31 December 2012 (FA 2012, s. 149).
In s. 171C(3)(b) the words "held for the purposes of the company's long-term business" substituted for the words "part of that company's long-term insurance fund" by FA 2012, s. 146 and Sch. 16, para. 77(3) in relation to accounting periods beginning on or after 1 January 2013 (FA 2012, s. 148) but subject to transitional provisions in FA 2012, Sch. 17. Where an accounting period would otherwise straddle 1 January 2013, it is deemed to end on 31 December 2012 (FA 2012, s. 149).
In s. 171C(4) the words "for the purposes of section 210A (ring-fencing of losses) as a non-BLAGAB chargeable gain or (as the case may be) a *non-BLAGAB allowable loss*" substituted for the words "as arising in respect of an asset that is not part of company B's long-term insurance fund" by FA 2012, s. 146 and Sch. 16, para. 77(4) in relation to accounting periods beginning on or after 1 January 2013 (FA 2012, s. 148) but subject to transitional provisions in FA 2012, Sch. 17. Where an accounting period would otherwise straddle 1 January 2013, it is deemed to end on 31 December 2012 (FA 2012, s. 149).
S. 171C(5) omitted by FA 2012, s. 146 and Sch. 16, para. 77(5) in relation to accounting periods beginning on or after 1 January 2013 (FA 2012, s. 148) but subject to transitional provisions in FA 2012, Sch. 17. Where an accounting period would otherwise straddle 1 January 2013, it is deemed to end on 31 December 2012 (FA 2012, s. 149).

Former s. 171C (with s. 171A and 171B) substituted for former s. 171A by FA 2009, s. 31 and Sch. 12, para. 1, with effect in relation to chargeable gains and allowable losses accruing on or after 21 July 2009 (Royal Assent).

172 Transfer of United Kingdom branch or agency

172 [Repealed by FA 2000, s. 102 and Sch. 29, para 3, s. 156 and Sch. 40, Pt. II(12).]

History – S. 172 repealed by FA 2000, s. 102 and Sch. 29, para 3, s. 156 and Sch. 40, Pt. II(12), in relation to disposals made on or after 1 April 2000.

173 Transfers within a group: trading stock

173(1) Where–

(a) a company ("company A") acquires an asset as trading stock of a trade to which this section applies,

(b) the acquisition is from a company ("company B") that at the time of the acquisition is a member of the same group of companies, and

(c) the asset did not form part of the trading stock of any such trade carried on by company B,

company A is treated for the purposes of section 161 as having acquired the asset otherwise than as trading stock and immediately appropriated it for the purposes of the trade as trading stock.

173(2) Where–

(a) a company ("company C") disposes of an asset forming part of the trading stock of a trade to which this section applies carried on by that company,

(b) the disposal is to another company ("company D") that at the time of the disposal is a member of the same group of companies, and

(c) the asset is acquired by company D otherwise than as trading stock of any such trade carried on by it,

company C is treated for the purposes of section 161 as having appropriated the asset immediately before the disposal for some purpose other than the purpose of use as trading stock.

173(3) The trades to which this section applies are–

(a) any trade carried on by a company resident in the United Kingdom, and

(b) any trade carried on in the United Kingdom through a permanent establishment by a company not so resident.

History – In s. 173(3)(b), the words "permanent establishment" substituted for the words "branch or agency' by FA 2003, s. 153(1) (b) with effect in relation to accounting periods beginning on or after 1 January 2003.
S. 173 substituted by FA 2000, s. 102 and Sch. 29, para 11(1) with effect in relation to acquisitions and disposals made on or after 1 April 2000.

Cross references – S. 14: as regards non resident members of a non-resident group, s. 173 applies to any trade carried on in the UK by a non resident company and any trade carried on by a UK resident company.
S. 161: deemed disposal at market value where asset acquired otherwise than as trading stock appropriated to trading stock, subject to election to reduce for income tax the acquisition cost and for capital gains tax the disposal consideration by the notional gain; deemed acquisition at trade price where asset forming part of trading stock appropriated for another purpose.
S. 276(8): application of s. 173 to certain transfers of exploration or exploitation rights or assets by a non-resident, as if s. 173(3), and certain other words are ignored.
Sch. 7AC, para. 36(2): s. 173 applies in relation to provisions on exemption for disposals by company with substantial shareholding as it applies in relation to s. 161.
Greater London Authority Act 1999, s. 419, references in s.173 to a company do not apply to Transport for London.

HMRC interpretations – IRInt. 216: Delaware Limited Liability Company may be a member of a capital gains group.

Hansard – 10 April 1984, col. 254: the Revenue would not seek to apply the Ramsay/Furniss principle to "straightforward transfers of assets between members of the same group of companies".

Notes – S. 21–34: general meaning of "disposal" and "assets", including the timing of certain disposals.
S. 288: interpretation, including meaning of "trading stock" and reference to sections being those of this Act.

174 Disposal or acquisition outside a group

174(1)–(3) [Repealed by FA 2000, s. 156 and Sch. 40, Pt. II (12).]

174(4) Schedule 2 shall apply in relation to a disposal of an asset by a company which is or has been a member of a group of companies, and which acquired the asset from another member of the group in a transfer to which section 171(1)) applied, as if all members of the group for the time being were the same person, and as if the acquisition or provision of the asset by the group, so taken as a single person, had been the acquisition or provision of it by the member disposing of it.

174(5) [Repealed by FA 2000, s. 156 and Sch. 40, Pt. II (12).]

History – In s. 174, (1), (2), (3) repealed by FA 2000, s. 156 and Sch. 40, Pt. II (12) with effect in relation to acquisitions or disposals made on or after 1 April 2000.
In s. 174(4) words "in a transfer to which section 171(1)) applied" substituted for "at a time when both were members of the group", by FA 2000, s. 102 and Sch. 29, para 13(2) with effect in relation to acquisitions made on or after 1 April 2000.
S. 174(5) repealed by FA 2000, s. 102 and Sch. 29, para. 13(3), s. 156 and Sch. 40, Pt. II(12), with effect in relation to acquisitions made on or after 1 April 2000.

Derivations – S. 174(1)–(3): ICTA 1970, s. 275(1), (1A), (1B), as (respectively) substituted and inserted by FA 1990, s. 70(3).

S. 174(4): ICTA 1970, s. 275(2).
S. 174(5): ICTA 1970, s 275(3), as inserted by FA 1980, s. 81(5).

Cross references – S. 14: as regards attribution to members of gains of non-resident companies, s. 174 adapted to any non-resident group.
S. 41: restriction of allowable losses in respect of assets qualifying for capital allowances.
S. 140A: transfer of UK trade involving companies of different member states.
S. 276(8): application of s. 174 to certain transfers of exploration or exploitation rights or assets by a non-resident.
Sch. 2: assets held on 6 April 1965.
FA 1994, Sch. 24, para. 5: application of s. 174 in connection with railways privatisation.
FA 2000, Sch. 29, para. 13(5): any question whether a company was, in relation to times before 1 April 2000, a member of a group is to be determined in accordance with s. 170 as it stood before the amendments made by FA 2000, s. 102 and Sch. 29, para. 1.
Broadcasting Act 1996, Sch. 7, para. 4: s. 174(1) has effect where there has been a "preparatory transfer" within the meaning of that Act as if the asset to which the preparatory transfer relates had thereby been transferred and acquired in relevant circumstances.
Greater London Authority Act 1999, s. 419, references in s. 174 to a company do not apply to Transport for London.

Notes – S. 21–34: general meaning of "disposal" and "assets".
S. 288: interpretation, including reference to sections being those of this Act.

175 Replacement of business assets by members of a group

175(1) Subject to subsection (2) below, for the purposes of sections 152 to 158 all the trades to which this section applies carried on by members of a group of companies shall, for the purposes of corporation tax on chargeable gains, be treated as a single trade.

175(1A) The trades to which this section applies are–

(a) any trade carried on by a company that is resident in the United Kingdom, and

(b) any trade carried on in the United Kingdom through a permanent establishment by a company not so resident.

175(2) Subsection (1) above does not apply where so much of the consideration for the disposal of the old assets as is applied in acquiring the new assets or the interest in them is so applied by a member of the group which is a dual resident investing company and in this subsection **"the old assets"** and **"the new assets"** have the same meanings as in section 152.

175(2A) Section 152 or 153 shall apply where–

(a) the disposal is by a company which, at the time of the disposal, is a member of a group of companies,

(b) the acquisition is by another company which, at the time of the acquisition, is a member of the same group, and

(ba) the conditions in subsection (2AA) below are met, and

(c) the claim is made by both companies,

as if both companies were the same person.

175(2AA) The conditions referred to in subsection (2A)(ba) above are–

(a) that the company making the disposal is resident in the United Kingdom at the time of the disposal, or the assets are chargeable assets in relation to that company immediately before that time, and

(b) that the acquiring company is resident in the United Kingdom at the time of the acquisition, or the assets are chargeable assets in relation to that company immediately after that time.

For this purpose an asset is a "chargeable asset" in relation to a company at any time if, were the asset to be disposed of by the company at that time, any gain accruing to the company would be a chargeable gain and would by virtue of section 10B form part of its chargeable profits for corporation tax purposes.

175(2B) Section 152 or 153 shall apply where a company which is a member of a group of companies but is not carrying on a trade–

(a) disposes of assets (or an interest in assets) used, and used only, for the purposes of the trade which (in accordance with subsection (1) above) is treated as carried on by the members of the group which carry on a trade, or

(b) acquires assets (or an interest in assets) taken into use, and used only, for those purposes,

as if the first company were carrying on that trade.

175(2C) Neither section 152 nor section 153 shall apply if the acquisition of, or of the interest in, the new assets–

(a) is made by a company which is a member of a group of companies, and

(b) is one to which any of the no gain/no loss provisions applies or is one where, by virtue of section 195B, 195C or 195E, neither a gain nor a loss accrues to the person making the disposal.

175(3) Section 154(2) applies where the company making the claim is a member of a group of companies–

(a) as if all members of the group for the time being carrying on a trade to which this section applies were the same person, and

(b) in accordance with subsection (1) above, as if all those trades were the same trade;

so that the gain accrues to the member of the group holding the asset concerned on the occurrence of the event mentioned in section 154(2).

175(4) Subsection (2) above shall apply where the acquisition took place before 20th March 1990 and the disposal takes place within the period of 12 months beginning with the date of the acquisition or such longer period as the Board may by notice allow with the omission of the words from "or a company" to "the acquisition".

History – In s. 175(1), words "to which this section applies" inserted by FA 2000, s. 102 and Sch. 29, para. 10(2) with effect in relation to cases in which either the disposal or acquisition is on or after 1 April 2000, or both the disposal and acquisition are on or after that date.
In s. 175(1) the words "(unless it is a case of one member of the group acquiring, or acquiring the interest in, the new assets from another or disposing of, or of the interest in, the old assets to another)" repealed by FA 1995, s. 162 and Sch. 29, Pt. VIII(4) for acquisitions on or after 29 November 1994.
In s. 175(1A)(b), the words "permanent establishment" substituted for the words "branch or agency" by FA 2003, s. 153(1)(b) with effect in relation to accounting periods beginning on or after 1 January 2003.
S. 175(1A) inserted by FA 2000, s. 102 and Sch. 29, para 10(3) with effect in relation to cases in which either the disposal or acquisition is on or after 1 April 2000, or both the disposal and acquisition are on or after that date.
In s. 175(2C)(b), the words "or is one where, by virtue of section 195B, 195C or 195E, neither a gain nor a loss accrues to the person making the disposal" inserted by FA 2009, s. 86 and Sch. 40, para. 4, with effect in relation to disposals made on or after 22 April 2009.
S. 175(2)(a) and (b) and the words immediately preceding them omitted by FA 1994, s. 251(8) and s. 258 and Sch. 26, Pt. VIII(1), with effect where the disposal of the old assets (or of the interest in them), or the acquisition of the new assets (or of the interest in them) took place on or after 30 November 1993.
S. 175(2A) inserted by FA 1995, s. 48(1) and deemed always to have had effect except paragraph (c) which applies only where the claim is made on or after 29 November 1994. The predecessor enactments are deemed to have contained provision to the same effect as s. 175(2A) (FA 1995, s. 48(3)(b)).
S. 175(2A)(ba) inserted by FA 2000, Sch. 29, para 10(4) with effect in relation to cases in which either the disposal or acquisition is on or after 1 April 2000, or both the disposal and acquisition are on or after that date.
S. 175(2AA) inserted by FA 2000, Sch. 29, para 10(5) with effect in relation to cases in which either the disposal or acquisition is on or after 1 April 2000, or both the disposal and acquisition are on or after that date.
In s. 175(2AA), the reference "10B" substituted for the reference "10(3)" by FA 2003, s. 155 and Sch. 27, para. 2(3) which have effect in relation to accounting periods beginning on or after 1 January 2003.
S. 175(2B) inserted by FA 1995, s. 48(1) for disposals or acquisitions on or after 29 November 1994.
In s. 175(2C), the words "no gain/no loss provisions" substitutedfor the words "enactments specified in section 35(3)(d)" by FA 2008, s. 8 and Sch. 2, para. 62 with effect in relation to disposals on or after 6 April 2008 (FA 2008, Sch. 2, para. 71).
S. 175(2C) inserted by FA 1995, s. 48(1) for acquisitions on or after 29 November 1994.
In s. 175(2A), (2B), (2C), references to s. 153 inserted by FA 1996, s. 141(3) as respects accounting periods ending on or after 1 July 1999, the day appointed under FA 1994, s. 199 by virtue of SI 1998/3173 (C. 78).
S. 175(3) substituted by FA 2000, Sch. 29, para 10(6) with effect in relation to cases in which either the disposal or acquisition is on or after 1 April 2000, or both the disposal and acquisition are on or after that date.

Derivations – S. 175(1): ICTA 1970, s. 276(1), as amended by F(No. 2)A 1987, s. 64(4).
S. 175(2): ICTA 1970, s. 276(1A), as inserted by F(No. 2)A 1987, s. 64(4), and amended by FA 1990, s. 65(3).
S. 175(3): ICTA 1970, s. 276(2).
S. 175(4): ICTA 1970, s. 276(1A) as enacted; FA 1990, s. 65(6).

Cross references – S. 14: as regards attribution to members of gains of non-resident companies, s. 175(1) applies with the omission of the words "to which this section applies".
S. 152–158: roll-over relief on replacement of business assets, including (s. 154(2)) crystallisation of the held-over gain where the new asset is a depreciating asset on disposal, cessation of trade use or effluxion of time.
S. 179B(2), (4) and Sch. 7AB: modification of s. 175 where roll-over relief claimed where company treated by virtue of s. 179(3) or s. 179(6) as having sold and immediately re-acquired an asset at market value.
S. 198(4): modification to replacement of business assets used in connection with oil fields.
S. 247(5A): s. 175(2A), (2C) apply for roll-over relief on compulsory acquisitions of land.
Sch. 7B para. 6B: s. 175(2AA) applies in relation to overseas life insurance companies with the words "section 11(2)(b), (c), (d) or (e) of the Taxes Act" treated as substituted for "section (10(3))".
FA 1994, s. 249: companies treated as resident in the UK for tax purposes, but resident abroad for the purposes of any double taxation relief arrangements ("dual resident companies"), are with effect from 30 November 1993 to be treated as non-UK resident for all tax purposes, even if they are incorporated in the UK.
Greater London Authority Act 1999, s. 419, references in s. 175 to a company do not apply to Transport for London.

Statements of practice – D19: acquiring company and disponor company must be members of "the group" at the time of their respective transactions but not necessarily at the same time.
8/81: interpretation where one member makes a disposal and another makes the acquisition and in particular on commencement and cessation of trade.

HMRC interpretations – IRInt. 216: Delaware Limited Liability Company may be a member of a capital gains group.

Other material – CCAB press release, June 1965 (not reproduced): Revenue confirmation that what is now ESC D22, treating improvement expenditure as incurred in acquiring assets if used for the trade, extends to a group holding company.

Notes – S. 9: meaning of "resident".
S. 288: interpretation, including meaning of "dual resident investing company", "double taxation relief arrangements", "notice" as being in writing and reference to sections being those of this Act.

LOSSES ATTRIBUTABLE TO DEPRECIATORY TRANSACTIONS

176 Depreciatory transactions within a group

176(1) This section has effect as respects a disposal of shares in, or securities of, a company (**"the ultimate disposal"**) if the value of the shares or securities has been materially reduced by a depreciatory transaction effected within the period of 6 years ending with the disposal; and for this purpose **"depreciatory transaction"** means–

(a) any disposal of assets at other than market value by one member of a group of companies to another, or

(b) any other transaction satisfying the conditions of subsection (2) below,

except that a transaction shall not be treated as a depreciatory transaction to the extent that it consists of a payment which is required to be or has been brought into account, for the purposes of corporation tax on chargeable gains, in computing a chargeable gain or allowable loss accruing to the person making the ultimate disposal.

176(2) The conditions referred to in subsection (1)(b) above are–

(a) that the company, the shares in which, or securities of which, are the subject of the ultimate disposal, or any 75 per cent subsidiary of that company, was a party to the transaction, and

(b) that the parties to the transaction were or included 2 or more companies which at the time of the transaction were members of the same group of companies.

176(3) Without prejudice to the generality of subsection (1) above, the cancellation of any shares in or securities of one member of a group of companies under section 641 of the Companies Act 2006 shall, to the extent that immediately before the cancellation those shares or securities were the property of another member of the group, be taken to be a transaction fulfilling the conditions in subsection (2) above.

176(4) If the person making the ultimate disposal is, or has at any time been, a member of the group of companies referred to in subsection (1) or (2) above, any allowable loss accruing on the disposal shall be reduced to such extent as is just and reasonable having regard to the depreciatory transaction, but if the person making the ultimate disposal is not a member of that group when he disposes of the shares or securities, no reduction of the loss shall be made by reference to a depreciatory transaction which took place when that person was not a member of that group.

176(5) A reduction under subsection (4) above shall be made on the footing that the allowable loss ought not to reflect any diminution in the value of the company's assets which was attributable to a depreciatory transaction, but allowance may be made for any other transaction on or after 31st March 1982 which has enhanced the value of the company's assets and depreciated the value of the assets of any other member of the group.

176(6) If, under subsection (4) above, a reduction is made in an allowable loss, any chargeable gain accruing on a disposal of the shares or securities of any other company which was a party to the depreciatory transaction by reference to which the reduction was made, being a disposal not later than 6 years after the depreciatory transaction, shall be reduced to such extent as is just and reasonable having regard to the effect of the depreciatory transaction on the value of those shares or securities at the time of their disposal, but the total amount of any one or more reductions in chargeable gains made by reference to a depreciatory transaction shall not exceed the amount of the reductions in allowable losses made by reference to that depreciatory transaction.

All such adjustments, whether by way of discharge or repayment of tax, or otherwise, as are required to give effect to the provisions of this subsection may be made at any time.

176(7) For the purposes of this section–

(a) **"securities"** includes any loan stock or similar security whether secured or unsecured,

(b) references to the disposal of assets include references to any method by which one company which is a member of a group appropriates the goodwill of another member of the group;

(c) [repealed by FA 2000, s. 102 and Sch. 29, para. 24(1), s. 156 and Sch. 40, Pt. II(12).]

176(8) References in this section to the disposal of shares or securities include references to the occasion of the making of a claim under section 24(2) that the value of shares or securities has become negligible, and references to a person making a disposal shall be construed accordingly.

176(9) In any case where the ultimate disposal is not one to which section 35(2) applies, the references above to 31st March 1982 shall be read as references to 6th April 1965.

History – In s. 176(1), the words "within the period of 6 years ending with the disposal" substituted for the words "on or after 31st March 1982", with effect in relation to disposals of shares or securities by companies made on or after 19 July 2011.
In s. 176(3), "641" substituted for "135", and "2006" substituted for "1985" by SI 2009/1890, art. 9, with effect from 1 October 2009.
In s. 176(4), (6) the word "is" substituted; and in s. 176(5) the words "A reduction under subsection (4) above shall be made" substituted by FA 1996, s. 134 and Sch. 20, para. 57 for accounting periods ending on or after 1 July 1999, the appointed day for self-assessment in relation to corporation tax (FA 1994, s. 199 and SI 1998/3173 (C. 78)).
S. 176(7)(c) and the preceding word "and" repealed by FA 2000, s. 102 and Sch. 29, para. 24(1)), s. 156 and Sch. 40, Pt. II(12), with effect in relation to cases where the depreciatory transaction is on or after 1 April 2000.

Derivations – S. 176(1)–(8): ICTA 1970, s. 280, as amended by Companies Consolidation (Consequential Provisions) Act 1985, and FA 1988, s. 96 and Sch. 8, para. 6.
S. 176(9): ICTA 1970, s. 280 prior to amendment by FA 1988 as above.

Cross references – S. 24(2): deemed disposal and reacquisition on negligible value claim.
S. 35(2): re-basing to 31 March 1982.

HMRC interpretations – IRInt. 216: Delaware Limited Liability Company may be a member of a capital gains group.

Other material – ICAEW Technical Release TR 588 (not reproduced): Furniss v Dawson principle not normally applied to dividends paid out of distributable reserves by subsidiary to parent company before sale of subsidiary, or annually; and no depreciatory transaction where dividends are paid out of post-acquisition reserves.

Notes – S. 8: charge to corporation tax in respect of chargeable gains.

S. 9: meaning of "resident".
S. 15: meaning of "chargeable gains".
S. 16: meaning of "allowable losses".
S. 21–34: general meaning of "disposal" and "assets".
S. 272–274 and Sch. 11: meaning of "market value".
S. 288: interpretation, including meaning of "company", "shares" as embracing stock, "inspector" as being any inspector of taxes and reference to sections being those of this Act.
TMA 1970, s. 44–58 and Sch. 3: appeals procedures and rules for assigning proceedings.
Greater London Authority Act 1999, s. 419 , references in s. 176 to a company do not apply to Transport for London.
SI 1994/3226, reg. 9(6): in attributing to former CGT assets a pre-commencement day (for FA 1993, Pt. II, Ch. II) loss on a disposal which would have been a depreciatory transaction, loss computed under s. 176.
SI 1994/3226, reg. 14(4): s. 176 applies, if appropriate, for computing the amount of a loss to be set against a gain on an asset held on a company's commencement day (for FA 1993, Pt. II, Ch. II).

177 Dividend stripping

177(1) The provisions of this section apply where one company ("the first company") has a holding in another company ("the second company") and the following conditions are fulfilled–

(a) that the holding amounts to, or is an ingredient in a holding amounting to, 10 per cent of all holdings of the same class in the second company,

(b) that the first company is not a dealing company in relation to the holding,

(c) that a distribution is or has been made to the first company in respect of the holding, and

(d) that the effect of the distribution is that the value of the holding is or has been materially reduced.

177(2) Where this section applies in relation to a holding, section 176 shall apply, subject to subsection (3) below, in relation to any disposal of any shares or securities comprised in the holding, whether the disposal is by the first company or by any other company to which the holding is transferred by a transfer to which section 140A, or 171 applies, as if the distribution were a depreciatory transaction and, if the companies concerned are not members of a group of companies, as if they were.

177(3) The distribution shall not be treated as a depreciatory transaction to the extent that it consists of a payment which is required to be or has been brought into account, for the purposes of corporation tax on chargeable gains, in computing a chargeable gain or allowable loss accruing to the person making the ultimate disposal.

177(4) This section shall be construed as one with section 176, and in any case where the ultimate disposal is not one to which section 35(2) applies, the reference in subsection (1)(c) above to a distribution does not include a distribution made before 30th April 1969.

177(5) For the purposes of this section a company is **"a dealing company"** in relation to a holding if a profit on the sale of the holding would be taken into account in computing the company's trading profits.

177(6) References in this section to a holding in a company refer to a holding of shares or securities by virtue of which the holder may receive distributions made by the company, but so that–

(a) a company's holdings of different classes in another company shall be treated as separate holdings, and

(b) holdings of securities which differ in the entitlements or obligations they confer or impose shall be regarded as holdings of different classes.

177(7) For the purposes of subsection (1) above–

(a) all a company's holdings of the same class in another company are to be treated as ingredients constituting a single holding, and

(b) a company's holding of a particular class shall be treated as an ingredient in a holding amounting to 10 per cent of all holdings of that class if the aggregate of that holding and other holdings of that class held by connected persons amounts to 10 per cent of all holdings of that class,

and section 286 shall have effect in relation to paragraph (b) above as if, in subsection (7) of that section, after the words "or exercise control of" in each place where they occur there were inserted the words "or to acquire a holding in".

History – In s. 177(2) reference to s. 140A inserted by F(No. 2)A 1992, s. 46(6), and deemed always to have had effect. Reference to s. 172 effectively repealed by FA 2000, s. 102 and Sch. 29, para. 25(1) with effect in relation to disposals on or after 1 April 2000.

Derivations – ICTA 1970, s. 281, as amended by FA 1990, s. 70(4).

Cross references – S. 35(2): re-basing to 31 March 1982.
S. 140A: transfer of UK trade involving companies of different member states.
S. 286: "connected" in references to persons being connected with one another, including (s. 286(7)) treatment of two or more persons acting together etc. to secure or exercise control as connected.

HMRC interpretations – IRInt. 216: Delaware Limited Liability Company may be a member of a capital gains group.

Other material – Taxline 1992/106 (not reproduced): guidance from Insurance and Specialist Division (Capital Gains) on interaction with re-basing provisions.

Notes – S. 15: meaning of "chargeable gains".
S. 16: meaning of "allowable losses".
S. 21–34: general meaning of "disposal" and "assets".

S. 288: interpretation, including meaning of "company", "shares" as embracing stock and reference to sections being those of this Act. Greater London Authority Act 1999, s. 419, references in s. 177 to a company do not apply to Transport for London.

177A Restriction on set-off of pre-entry losses

177A Schedule 7A to this Act (which makes provision in relation to losses accruing to a company before the time when it becomes a member of a group of companies) shall have effect.

History – In s. 177A, the words "and losses accruing on assets held by any company at such a time" omitted by FA 2011, s. 46 and Sch. 11, para. 1, with effect on and after 19 July 2011 in relation to the deduction of any allowable loss that has accrued to a company at a time before it became a member of the relevant group (FA 2011, Sch. 11, para. 11), subject to a transitional provision concerning the pre-entry proportion of an allowable loss accruing to a company on the disposal of a pre-entry asset (FA 2011, Sch. 11, para. 12). S. 177A inserted by FA 1993, s. 88 in respect of chargeable gains in a company's total profits for any accounting period ending on or after 16 March 1993 but to apply only in respect of carried forward pre-entry losses accruing to a company which joined a group on or after 1 April 1987. (In relation to accounting periods beginning before 6 April 1992, s. 177A takes effect as if inserted in CGTA 1979.) Greater London Authority Act 1999, s. 419, references in s. 177A to a company do not apply to Transport for London.

HMRC interpretations – IRInt. 216: Delaware Limited Liability Company may be a member of a capital gains group.

[PRE-ENTRY GAINS]

History – The cross-heading ("PRE-ENTRY GAINS", which is reproduced in italics in the official Stationery Office version of the Act) is repealed by FA 2006, s. 178 and Sch. 26, Pt. 3(9) in respect of any accounting period ending on or after 5 December 2005 (but not in relation to the deduction of a loss arising before that date from a chargeable gain accruing before that date).

177B Restrictions on setting losses against pre-entry gains

177B [Ceased to have effect by virtue of FA 2006, s. 70(4) and repealed by FA 2006, s. 178 and Sch. 26, Pt. 3(9).]

History – S. 177B ceased to have effect by virtue of FA 2006, s. 70(4) and repealed by FA 2006, s. 178 and Sch. 26, Pt. 3(9) in respect of any accounting period ending on or after 5 December 2005 (but not in relation to the deduction of a loss arising before that date from a chargeable gain accruing before that date).

COMPANIES LEAVING GROUPS

178 Company ceasing to be member of group: pre-appointed day cases

178 [Repealed by FA 2000, s. 102 and Sch. 29, para 26, s. 156 and Sch. 40, Pt. II(12).]

History – S. 178 repealed by FA 2000, s. 102 and Sch. 29, para 26, s. 156 and Sch. 40, Pt. II(12), in relation to companies which left a group during an accounting period ending after 30 September 1993.

179 Company ceasing to be member of group: post-appointed day cases

179(1) This section applies where–

(a) a company ("company A") acquires an asset from another company ("company B") at a time when company A and company B are members of the same group,

(b) the conditions in subsection (1A) below are met, and

(c) company A ceases to be a member of that group within the period of six years after the time of the acquisition.

References in this section to a company ceasing to be a member of a group of companies do not apply to cases where a company ceases to be a member of a group in consequence of another member of the group ceasing to exist.

179(1A) The conditions referred to in subsection (1)(b) above are–

(a) that company A is resident in the United Kingdom at the time it acquires the asset, or the asset is a chargeable asset in relation to that company immediately after that time, and

(b) that company B is resident in the United Kingdom at the time of that acquisition, or the asset is a chargeable asset in relation to that company immediately before that time.

179(1AA) If shares in a company are transferred as part of the process of the transfer of a business to which section 140A or 140C applies and in consequence of the transfer the company ceases to be a member of a group ("Group 1")–

(a) the company shall not be treated for the purposes of this section as having left Group 1, and

(b) if the transferee is a member of a group ("Group 2") and in consequence of the transfer the company becomes a member of Group 2 it shall be treated, for the purposes of this section, as if Group 1 and Group 2 were the same.

179(1B) Where, as part of the process of a merger to which section 140E applies, a company which is a member of a group ("Group 1") ceases to exist and in consequence of that cessation–

(a) assets are transferred to the transferee, or

(b) shares in one or more companies which were also members of the group are transferred to the transferee,

a company which has ceased to exist, or the shares in which have been transferred to the transferee, shall not be treated for the purposes of this section as having left Group 1.

179(1C) If subsection (1B) applies in relation to a company then for the purposes of this section–

(a) the transferee and a company which has ceased to exist in consequence of the merger shall be treated as the same entity, and

(b) if the transferee is a member of a group ("Group 2") following the merger (whether or not as the principal company of the group) a company which was a member of Group 1 and became a member of Group 2 in consequence of the merger shall be treated, for the purposes of this section, as if Group 1 and Group 2 were the same.

179(1D) In subsections (1B) and (1C), **"transferor"** and **"transferee"** have the meaning given by section 140E(9).

179(2) Where two companies cease to be members of the group at the same time, subsection (1) does not have effect as respects the acquisition of an asset by one of the companies from the other if condition A or B is met.

179(2ZA) Condition A is that the companies–

(a) are both 75 per cent subsidiaries and effective 51 per cent subsidiaries of another company on the date of the acquisition, and

(b) remain both 75 per cent subsidiaries and effective 51 per cent subsidiaries of that other company until immediately after they cease to be members of the group.

179(2ZB) Condition B is that one of the companies–

(a) is both a 75 per cent subsidiary and an effective 51 per cent subsidiary of the other on the date of the acquisition, and

(b) remains both a 75 per cent subsidiary and an effective 51 per cent subsidiary of the other until immediately after the companies cease to be members of the group.

179(2A) Subsection (2AA) applies where

(a) a company ("company A") acquired an asset from another company ("company B") at a time when both company A and company B were members of the same group ("the first group"),

(aa) company A has ceased to be a member of the first group,

(b) subsection (2) above applies in the case of company A's ceasing to be a member of the first group so that subsection (1) above does not have effect as respects the acquisition of that asset,

(c) at the time company A ceases to be a member of the first group there is a connection between that group and the group of companies of which company A becomes a member on leaving the first group ("the second group"), and

(d) subsequently–

  (i) company A ceases to be a member of the second group, or

  (ii) (before sub-paragraph (i) applies) there ceases to be a connection between the two groups.

179(2AA) Where this subsection applies–

(a) in a case within subsection (2A)(d)(ii), for the purposes of this section (other than subsection (2A)) as it applies as respects the acquisition, company A and any associated company are to be treated as having ceased to be members of the second group at the time the connection between the two groups ceases,

(b) subsection (1) has effect in relation to company A's ceasing to be a member of the second group as if it had been the second group of which both companies had been members at the time of the acquisition, and

(c) subsection (2) may operate to prevent subsection (1) applying by virtue of paragraph (b), unless subsection (2AB) applies.

179(2AB) This subsection applies if company A's ceasing to be a member of the first group at the same time as one or more associated companies forms part of arrangements the main purpose, or one of the main purposes, of which is the avoidance of a liability to corporation tax.

179(2B) For the purposes of subsection (2A) above there is a **connection** between the first group and the second group at a particular time if, at that time, the company which is the principal company of that group is under the control of–

(a) the company which is the principal company of the first group or, if that group no longer exists, which was the principal company of that group when company A ceased to be a member of it;

(b) any person or persons who control the company mentioned in paragraph (a) above or who have had it under their control at any time in the period since company A ceased to be a member of the first group; or

(c) any person or persons who have, at any time in that period, had under their control either–

(i) a company which would have been a person falling within paragraph (b) above if it had continued to exist, or

(ii) a company which would have been a person falling within this paragraph (whether by reference to a company which would have been a person falling within that paragraph or to a company or series of companies falling within this sub-paragraph).

179(2C) This section shall not have effect as respects any asset if, before the time when company A ceases to be a member of the group or, as the case may be, the second group, an event has already occurred by virtue of which the company falls by virtue of section 101A(3) to be treated as having sold and immediately reacquired the asset at the time specified in subsection (3) below.

179(2D) This section shall not have effect as respects any asset if, before the time when company A ceases to be a member of the group or, as the case may be, the second group, an event has already occurred by virtue of which the company falls by virtue of section 101C(3) to be treated as having sold and immediately reacquired the asset at the time specified in subsection (3) below.

179(3) If, when company A ceases to be a member of the group, company A, or an associated company also leaving the group, owns, otherwise than as trading stock–

(a) the asset, or

(b) property to which a chargeable gain has been carried forward from the asset on a replacement of business assets,

then, subject to subsection (4) below, company A shall be treated for all the purposes of this Act as if immediately after its acquisition of the asset it had sold, and immediately reacquired, the asset at market value at that time.

179(3A) Any chargeable gain or allowable loss which would otherwise accrue to company A on the sale referred to in subsection (3) does not so accrue if–

(a) company A ceases to be a member of the group in consequence of–

(i) a disposal of shares in company A or another member of the group made by a member of the group, or

(ii) two or more such disposals,

(b) either–

(i) subsection (3B) applies to the disposal or, if there is more than one disposal, to at least one of them, or

(ii) sub-paragraph (i) does not apply but had subsection (3B) applied to the disposal or, if there is more than one disposal, to each of them, any gain arising on the disposal or disposals would not have been a chargeable gain by virtue of Schedule 7AC, and

(c) in the absence of this subsection, section 535 of CTA 2010 (UK REITS: exemption of gains) would not apply to the chargeable gain or allowable loss which would accrue to company A on the sale.

179(3B) This subsection applies to a disposal of shares if–

(a) the company making the disposal is resident in the United Kingdom at the time of the disposal,

(b) the shares are chargeable assets in relation to that company immediately before that time, or

(c) any part of the chargeable gain or allowable loss accruing on the disposal is treated as a gain or loss accruing to a person by virtue of section 13(2) (attribution of gains to members of non-resident companies).

In this section **"group disposal"** means a disposal within subsection (3A)(a) to which this subsection applies and the company making the disposal is referred to as **"the transferor company"**.

179(3C) For the purposes of subsections (3A) and (3B), the question whether there is a disposal is to be determined ignoring section 127 (share reorganisations etc treated as not involving disposal).

179(3D) If subsection (3A) applies, any chargeable gain or allowable loss accruing to the transferor company on a group disposal (other than a group disposal to which section 127 applies) is to be calculated–

(a) where a chargeable gain would accrue to company A in the absence of subsection (3A), as if the amount of the consideration for the group disposal were increased by the amount of the gain, and

(b) where an allowable loss would accrue to company A in the absence of subsection (3A), as if an amount equal to the amount of the loss were a sum allowable under section 38 as a deduction in the computation of the gain or loss accruing on the group disposal.

179(3E) If subsection (3A) applies, and section 127 applies to a group disposal, any chargeable gain or allowable loss accruing to the transferor company on a disposal of the new holding arising from the group disposal (or any part of that holding) is to be calculated–

(a) where a chargeable gain would accrue to company A in the absence of subsection (3A)–

(i) as if an amount equal to the amount of the gain were excluded from the expenditure allowable as a deduction under section 38 in the computation of the gain or loss accruing on the disposal (but not so as to reduce that expenditure below nil), and

(ii) where (ignoring sub-paragraph (i)) the amount of the gain exceeds the expenditure allowable as such a deduction, as if a gain equal to that excess accrued on the disposal of the new holding (or, if the disposal is of a part of the new holding, a gain equal to the corresponding part of that excess accrued on that disposal), in addition to any gain or loss that actually accrues on the disposal of the new holding or part, and

(b) where an allowable loss would accrue to company A in the absence of subsection (3A), as if an amount equal to the amount of the loss were a sum allowable under section 38 as a deduction in the computation of the gain or loss accruing on the disposal.

In this subsection **"new holding"** has the meaning given by section 126.

179(3F) If there is more than one group disposal, the references in subsections (3D) and (3E) to the amount of the gain or loss which would accrue to company A in the absence of subsection (3A) are to be read, in relation to each disposal, as references to–

(a) such proportion of that amount as the transferor companies in relation to the group disposals jointly elect as the appropriate proportion in relation to the disposal in question, or

(b) where no election is made, the proportion of that amount attributable to that disposal if that amount is divided equally between the group disposals.

179(3G) An election under subsection (3F) must–

(a) specify the appropriate proportion in relation to each group disposal, and

(b) be made, by notice to an officer of Revenue and Customs, no later than 2 years after the end of the first accounting period of a company in which any chargeable gain or allowable loss on a group disposal accrues.

179(3H) If a group disposal by a company consists of shares of more than one class, then, for the purposes of subsections (3D) and (3E), the company may apportion any increase or deduction to be made between the classes of shares in such manner as it considers appropriate.

179(4) Any chargeable gain or allowable loss accruing to company A on the sale referred to in subsection (3) above shall be treated as accruing to company A at whichever is the later of the following, that is to say–

(a) the time immediately after the beginning of the accounting period of that company in which or, as the case may be, at the end of which the company ceases to be a member of the group; and

(b) the time when under subsection (3) above it is treated as having reacquired the asset;

and sections 138 to 142 of CTA 2010 have effect accordingly as if the actual circumstances were as they are treated as having been.

179(5) Subsections (6) to (8) apply where–

(a) in the absence of subsection (6), company A would be treated by virtue of subsection (3) as selling an asset at any time, by reason of ceasing to be a member of the group, and

(b) company A ceases to be a member of the group by reason only of the fact that the principal company of that group becomes a member of another group.

179(6) Subsection (3) does not apply to treat company A as selling the asset at that time; but if–

(a) within 6 years of that time the company A ceases at any time ("the relevant time") to satisfy the following conditions, and

(b) at the relevant time, the company A, or a company in the same group as that company, owns otherwise than as trading stock the asset or property to which a chargeable gain has been carried forward from the asset on a replacement of business assets,

the company A shall be treated for all the purposes of this Act as if, immediately after its acquisition of the asset, it had sold and immediately reacquired the asset at the value that, at the time of acquisition, was its market value.

179(7) Those conditions are–

(a) that company A is a 75 per cent subsidiary of one or more members of the other group referred to in subsection (5) above, and

(b) that company A is an effective 51 per cent subsidiary of one or more of those members.

179(7A) Any chargeable gain or allowable loss which would otherwise accrue to company A on the sale referred to in subsection (6) does not so accrue if–

(a) company A ceases at the relevant time to satisfy the conditions in subsection (7) in consequence of–

(i) a disposal of shares in company A, or another member of the other group mentioned in subsection (5)(b), made by a member of that other group, or

(ii) two or more such disposals,

(b) either–

(i) subsection (3B) applies to the disposal or, if there is more than one disposal, to at least one of them, or

(ii) sub-paragraph (i) does not apply but had subsection (3B) applied to the disposal or, if there is more than one disposal, to each of them, any gain arising on the disposal or disposals would not have been a chargeable gain by virtue of Schedule 7AC, and

(c) in the absence of this subsection, section 535 of CTA 2010 (UK REITS: exemption of gains) would not apply to the chargeable gain or allowable loss which would accrue to company A on the sale.

179(7B) Where subsection (7A) applies, subsections (3C) to (3H) apply to the calculation of any chargeable gain or allowable loss accruing on a disposal within subsection (7A)(a) to which subsection (3B) applies (a "relevant disposal") with the following modifications–

(a) in subsections (3C) to (3H) for the references to a group disposal substitute references to a relevant disposal, and

(b) in subsections (3C), (3D) and (3E) for the references to subsection (3A) substitute references to subsection (7A).

179(8) Any chargeable gain or allowable loss accruing to company A on the sale referred to in subsection (6) is to be treated as accruing immediately before the relevant time.

179(9) Where–

(a) by virtue of this section a company is treated as having sold an asset at any time, and

(b) if at that time the company had in fact sold the asset at market value at that time, then, by virtue of section 30 or 31, any allowable loss or chargeable gain accruing on the disposal would have been calculated as if the consideration for the disposal were increased by an amount,

subsections (3) and (6) above shall have effect as if the market value at that time had been that amount greater.

179(9A) Sections 450 and 451 of CTA 2010 (meaning of control) shall have effect for the purposes of subsection (2B) above as they have effect for the purposes of Part 10 of CTA 2010; but a person carrying on a business of banking shall not for the purposes of that subsection be regarded as having control of any company by reason only of having, or of the consequences of having exercised, any rights of that person in respect of loan capital or debt issued or incurred by the company for money lent by that person to the company in the ordinary course of that business.

179(10) For the purposes of this section–

(a) two companies are associated with each other if one is a 75 per cent subsidiary of the other or both are 75 per cent subsidiaries of another company.

(b) a chargeable gain is carried forward from an asset to other property on a replacement of business assets if, by one or more claims under sections 152 to 158, the chargeable gain accruing on a disposal of the asset is reduced, and as a result an amount falls to be deducted from the expenditure allowable in computing a gain accruing on the disposal of the other property,

(c) an asset acquired by company A shall be treated as the same as an asset owned at a later time by that company or an associated company if the value of the second asset is derived in whole or in part from the first asset, and in particular where the second asset is a freehold, and the first asset was a leasehold and the lessee has acquired the reversion.

179(10A) For the purposes of this section an asset is a **"chargeable asset"** in relation to a company at any time if any gain accruing to the company on a disposal of the asset by the company at that time–

(a) would be a chargeable gain and would by virtue of section 10B form part of its chargeable profits for corporation tax purposes, or

(b) would, but for Schedule 7AC (exemptions for disposals by companies with substantial *shareholdings*), be within paragraph (a).

179(11,12) [Repealed by FA 2000, s. 102 and Sch. 29, para. 4(5), s. 153 and Sch. 40, Pt. II(12).]

179(13) Where under this section company A is to be treated as having disposed of, and reacquired, an asset, all such recomputations of liability in respect of other disposals, and all such adjustments of tax, whether by way of assessment or by way of discharge or repayment of tax, as may be required in consequence of the provisions of this section shall be carried out.

History – In s. 179(1)(a), the words "company A and company B are members of the same group" substituted for the words "company B is a member of a group" by FA 2011, s. 45 and Sch. 10, para. 3(2), with effect in relation to any disposal of an asset by one company (B) to another company (A) made at a time when B is a member of a group if either A ceases to be a member of the group on or after 19 July 2011 or ceased to be so before 19 July 2011 in circumstances where TCGA 1992, s. 179(6)–(8) applied and ceases to satisfy the conditions in TCGA 1992, s. 179(7) on or after 19 July 2011 (see FA 2011, Sch. 10, para. 9(1)). But references to 19 July 2011 may be replaced by references to 1 April 2011 if an "early commencement election" is made (see FA 2011, Sch. 10, para. 9(4)–(8)).
S. 179(1) substituted by FA 2000, s. 102 and Sch. 29, para. 4(2) with effect in relation to assets acquired on or after 1 April 2000.
In s. 179(1A), the words "For this purpose an asset is a "chargeable asset" in relation to a company at any time if, were the asset to be disposed of by the company at that time, any gain accruing to the company would be a chargeable gain and would by virtue of section 10B form part of its chargeable profits for corporation tax purposes. " omitted by FA 2011, s. 45 and Sch. 10, para. 3(3), with effect in relation to any disposal of an asset by one company (B) to another company (A) made at a time when B is a member of a group if either A ceases to be a member of the group on or after 19 July 2011 or ceased to be so before 19 July 2011 in circumstances where TCGA 1992, s. 179(6)–(8) applied and ceases to satisfy the conditions in TCGA 1992, s. 179(7) on or after 19 July 2011 (see FA 2011, Sch. 10, para. 9(1)). But references to 19 July 2011 may be replaced by references to 1 April 2011 if an "early commencement election" is made (see FA 2011, Sch. 10, para. 9(4)–(8)).
In s. 179(1A), the reference "10B" substituted for the reference "10(3)" by FA 2003, s. 155 and Sch. 27, para. 2(3) which have effect in relation to accounting periods beginning on or after 1 January 2003.
S. 179(1A) inserted by FA 2000, s. 102 and Sch. 29, para. 4(2) with effect in relation to assets acquired on or after 1 April 2000.
S. 179(AA) inserted by SI 2007/3186, reg.3(1) and Sch. 1, para. 9,with effect in relation to transfers which take place on or after 1 January 2007, and in relation to cross-border mergers taking place on or after that date, but in the case of mergers relating to the formation of an SE or SCE, in relation to those taking place on or after 18 August 2006 (see SI 2008/1579, reg. 4(1)).
S. 179(1B)–(1D) substituted for s. 179(1B) and (1C) by SI 2007/3186, reg. 3(2) and Sch. 2, para. 7, in relation to mergers relating to the formation of an SE or SCE which take place on or after 18 August 2006, and in relation to all other mergers which take place on or after 1 January 2007.
S. 179(1B) originally inserted by F(No. 2)A 2005, s. 64(4) with effect in relation to formation of an SE (Societas Europaea) under Article 2 of Council Regulation (EC) 2157/2001 on the Statute for a European Company (Societas Europaea) which occurs on or after 1 April 2005.
S. 179(1C) inserted by F(No. 2)A 2005, s. 64(4) with effect in relation to formation of an SE (Societas Europaea) under Article 2 of Council Regulation (EC) 2157/2001 on the Statute for a European Company (Societas Europaea) which occurs on or after 1 April 2005.
S. 179(2), (2ZA) and (2ZB) substituted for former s. 179(2) by FA 2011, s. 45 and Sch. 10, para. 3(4), with effect in relation to any disposal of an asset by one company (B) to another company (A) made at a time when B is a member of a group if either A ceases to be a member of the group on or after 19 July 2011 or ceased to be so before 19 July 2011 in circumstances where TCGA 1992, s. 179(6)–(8) applied and ceases to satisfy the conditions in TCGA 1992, s. 179(7) on or after 19 July 2011 (see FA 2011, Sch. 10, para. 9(1)). But references to 19 July 2011 may be replaced by references to 1 April 2011 if an "early commencement election" is made (see FA 2011, Sch. 10, para. 9(4)–(8)).
In s. 179(2A), the words "Subsection (2AA) applies where" substituted for the word "Where" by FA 2011, s. 31(2)(a), with effect in relation to a company in any case in which the time of the company's ceasing to be a member of the first group is on or after 23 March 2011.
S. 179(2A)(a) and (aa) substituted for s. 179(2A)(a) by FA 2011, s. 45 and Sch. 10, para. 3(5), with effect in relation to any disposal of an asset by one company (B) to another company (A) made at a time when B is a member of a group if either A ceases to be a member of the group on or after 19 July 2011 or ceased to be so before 19 July 2011 in circumstances where TCGA 1992, s. 179(6)–(8) appliedand ceases to satisfy the conditions in TCGA 1992, s. 179(7) on or after 19 July 2011 (see FA 2011, Sch. 10, para. 9(1)). But references to 19 July 2011 may be replaced by references to 1 April 2011 if an "early commencement election" is made (see FA 2011, Sch. 10, para. 9(4)–(8)).
In s. 179(2A)(a) the words "(company A)" and "(company B)" inserted, and "company A's" substituted in s. 179(2A)(b) for "that company's", in s. 179(2A)(c) for and "the company that made the acquisition", and in the closing words for "that company's", by FA 2000, s. 102 and Sch. 29, para. 4(3) with effect in relation to assets acquired on or after 1 April 2000.
S. 179(2A)(c) and (d) substituted for the former s. 179(2A)(c) and (d) and the words following those two paragraphs by FA 2011, s. 31(2)(b), with effect in relation to a company in any case in which the time of the company's ceasing to be a member of the first group is on or after 23 March 2011.
S. 179(2AA) inserted by FA 2011, s. 31(3), with effect in relation to a company in any case in which the time of the company's ceasing to be a member of the first group is on or after 23 March 2011.
S. 179(2AB) inserted by FA 2011, s. 31(3), with effect in relation to a company in any case in which the time of the company's ceasing to be a member of the first group is on or after 23 March 2011.
In s. 179(2B), the words "at a particular time if, at that time," substituted for the words "if, at the time when company A ceases to be a member of the second group," by FA 2011, s. 31(4), with effect in relation to a company in any case in which the time of the company's ceasing to be a member of the first group is on or after 23 March 2011.
In s. 179(2B)(b) the words "person or persons who control the company mentioned in paragraph (a) above or who have had it under their" substituted by FA 1998, s. 139(1)(a) with effect for any company for which the time of its ceasing to be a member of the second group is on or after 17 March 1998.
In s. 179(2B)(c) the words "person or persons who have, at any time in that period, had under their" substituted by FA 1998, s. 139(1)(b) with effect for any company for which the time of its ceasing to be a member of the second group is on or after 17 March 1998.
In s. 179(2B)(c) the words "been a person falling" substituted by FA 1998, s. 137(1)(c) with effect for any company for which the time of its ceasing to be a member of the second group is on or after 17 March 1998.
S. 179(2A), (2B) inserted by FA 1995, s. 49(1) with effect for any company for which the time of its ceasing to be a member of the secondgroup is on or after 29 November 1994.
S. 179(2C) inserted by FA 1998, s. 133(2) as respects any company which becomes an investment trust for an accounting period beginning on or after 17 March 1998.
S. 179(2D) inserted by FA 1998, s. 135(3) as respects companies with VCT approval under ICTA 1988, s. 842AA that has effect on or after 17 March 1998.
S. 179(3A)–(3H) inserted by FA 2011, s. 45 and Sch. 10, para. 3(6), with effect in relation to any disposal of an asset by one company (B) to another company (A) made at a time when B is a member of a group if either A ceases to be a member of the group on or after 19 July 2011 or ceased to be so before 19 July 2011 in circumstances where TCGA 1992, s. 179(6)–(8) applied and ceases to satisfy the conditions in TCGA 1992, s. 179(7) on or after 19 July 2011 (see FA 2011, Sch. 10, para. 9(1)). But references to 19 July 2011 may be replaced by references to 1 April 2011 if an "early commencement election" is made (see FA 2011, Sch. 10, para. 9(4)–(8)).
In s. 179(4), the words "and sections 138 to 142 of CTA 2010 have effect accordingly as if the actual circumstances were as they are treated as having been" substituted for the words "and sections 403A and 403B of the Taxes Act (limits on group relief) shall have effect accordingly as if the actual circumstances were as they are treated as having been" by CTA 2010, s. 1177 and Sch. 1, para. 244(2), with effect for corporation tax purposes for accounting periods ending on or after 1 April 2010, and for income tax and capital gains tax purposes for the tax year 2010–11 and subsequent tax years.

In s. 179(4), the words after paragraph (b) substituted by F(No. 2)A 1997, s. 41 and Sch. 7, para. 8 with effect, subject to F(No. 2)A 1997, s. 41 and Sch. 7, para. 9 in relation to any claim for group relief if–

(a) the accounting period of the claimant company for which relief is claimed, or

(b) the accounting period of the surrendering company to which that claim relates,

is an accounting period ending on or after 2 July 1997.

In s. 179(4) the words "at whichever is the later … true accounting period" substituted by FA 1993, s. 89 in relation to accounting periods ending after 30 September 1993 (the appointed day for Pay and File).

In s. 179(4) the word "accruing" substituted for "which, apart from this subsection, would accrue" by FA 2002, s. 44(2) and Sch. 8, para. 2, with effect where the company in question ceases to be a member of the group in question on or after 1 April 2002.

S. 179(5) substituted by FA 2011, s. 45 and Sch. 10, para. 3(7), with effect in relation to any disposal of an asset by one company (B) to another company (A) made at a time when B is a member of a group if either A ceases to be a member of the group on or after 19 July 2011 or ceased to be so before 19 July 2011 in circumstances where TCGA 1992, s. 179(6)–(8) applied and ceases to satisfy the conditions in TCGA 1992, s. 179(7) on or after 19 July 2011 (see FA 2011, Sch. 10, para. 9(1)). But references to 19 July 2011 may be replaced by references to 1 April 2011 if an "early commencement election" is made (see FA 2011, Sch. 10, para. 9(4)–(8)).

In s. 179(6), the words "Subsection (3) does not apply to treat company A as selling the asset at that time; but" substituted for the words "The company in question shall not be treated as selling the asset at that time; but" and the words "company A" substituted for the words "the company in question" (in each place) by FA 2011, s. 45 and Sch. 10, para. 3(8), with effect in relation to any disposal of an asset by one company (B) to another company (A) made at a time when B is a member of a group if either A ceases to be a member of the group on or after 19 July 2011 or ceased to be so before 19 July 2011 in circumstances where TCGA 1992, s. 179(6)–(8) applied and ceases to satisfy the conditions in TCGA 1992, s. 179(7) on or after 19 July 2011 (see FA 2011, Sch. 10, para. 9(1)). But references to 19 July 2011 may be replaced by references to 1 April 2011 if an "early commencement election" is made (see FA 2011, Sch. 10, para. 9(4)–(8)).

In s. 179(7), the words "company A" substituted for the words "the company" (in both places) by FA 2011, s. 45 and Sch. 10, para. 3(9),with effect in relation to any disposal of an asset by one company (B) to another company (A) made at a time when B is a member of a group if either A ceases to be a member of the group on or after 19 July 2011 or ceased to be so before 19 July 2011 in circumstances where TCGA 1992, s. 179(6)–(8) applied and ceases to satisfy the conditions in TCGA 1992, s. 179(7) on or after 19 July 2011 (see FA 2011, Sch. 10, para. 9(1)). But references to 19 July 2011 may be replaced by references to 1 April 2011 if an "early commencement election" is made (see FA 2011, Sch. 10, para. 9(4)–(8)).

S. 179(7A) and (7B) inserted by FA 2011, s. 45 and Sch. 10, para. 3(10), with effect in relation to any disposal of an asset by one company (B) to another company (A) made at a time when B is a member of a group if either A ceases to be a member of the group on or after 19 July 2011 or ceased to be so before 19 July 2011 in circumstances where TCGA 1992, s. 179(6)–(8) applied and ceases to satisfy the conditions in TCGA 1992, s. 179(7) on or after 19 July 2011 (see FA 2011, Sch. 10, para. 9(1)). But references to 19 July 2011 may be replaced by references to 1 April 2011 if an "early commencement election" is made (see FA 2011, Sch. 10, para. 9(4)–(8)).

In s. 179(8), the words "company A on the sale referred to in subsection (6) is to be treated as accruing immediately before the relevant time" substituted for the words "the company on that sale shall be treated as accruing at the relevant time" by FA 2011, s. 45 and Sch. 10, para. 3(11), with effect in relation to any disposal of an asset by one company (B) to another company (A) made at a time when B is a member of a group if either A ceases to be a member of the group on or after 19 July 2011 or ceased to be so before 19 July 2011 in circumstances where TCGA 1992, s. 179(6)–(8) applied and ceases to satisfy the conditions in TCGA 1992, s. 179(7) on or after 19 July 2011 (see FA 2011, Sch. 10, para. 9(1)). But references to 19 July 2011 may be replaced by references to 1 April 2011 if an "early commencement election" ismade (see FA 2011, Sch. 10, para. 9(4)–(8)).

In s. 179(9), the words "or 31" inserted by FA 2011, s. 44 and Sch. 9, para. 4, with effect in relation to disposals of shares or securities treated under TCGA 1992, s. 179 as taking place on or after 19 July 2011.

In s. 179(9A), the words "Sections 450 and 451 of CTA 2010" substituted for "Section 416(2) to (6) of the Taxes Act" by CTA 2010, s. 1177 and Sch. 1, para. 244(3)(a), with effect for corporation tax purposes for accounting periods ending on or after 1 April 2010, and for income tax and capital gains tax purposes for the tax year 2010–11 and subsequent tax years.

In s. 179(9A), the words "they have" substituted for "it has" by CTA 2010, s. 1177 and Sch. 1, para. 244(3)(b), with effect for corporation tax purposes for accounting periods ending on or after 1 April 2010, and for income tax and capital gains tax purposes for the tax year 2010–11 and subsequent tax years.

In s. 179(9A), the words "Part 10 of CTA 2010" substituted for "Part XI of that Act" by CTA 2010, s. 1177 and Sch. 1, para. 244(3)(c), with effect for corporation tax purposes for accounting periods ending on or after 1 April 2010, and for income tax and capital gains tax purposes for the tax year 2010–11 and subsequent tax years.

S. 179(9A) inserted by FA 1995, s. 49(2) with effect for any company for which the time of its ceasing to be a member of the second group is on or after 29 November 1994.

S. 179(10)(a) substituted by FA 2011, s. 45 and Sch. 10, para. 3(12), with effect in relation to any disposal of an asset by one company (B) to another company (A) made at a time when B is a member of a group if either A ceases to be a member of the group on or after 19 July 2011 or ceased to be so before 19 July 2011 in circumstances where TCGA 1992, s. 179(6)–(8) applied and ceases to satisfy the conditions in TCGA 1992, s. 179(7) on or after 19 July 2011 (see FA 2011, Sch. 10, para. 9(1)). But references to 19 July 2011 may be replaced by references to 1 April 2011 if an "early commencement election" is made (see FA 2011, Sch. 10, para. 9(4)–(8)).

S. 179(10A) inserted by FA 2011, s. 45 and Sch. 10, para. 3(13), with effect in relation to any disposal of an asset by one company (B) to another company (A) made at a time when B is a member of a group if either A ceases to be a member of the group on or after 19 July 2011 or ceased to be so before 19 July 2011 in circumstances where TCGA 1992, s. 179(6)–(8) applied and ceases to satisfy the conditions in TCGA 1992, s. 179(7) on or after 19 July 2011 (see FA 2011, Sch. 10, para. 9(1)). But references to 19 July 2011 may be replaced by references to 1 April 2011 if an "early commencement election" is made (see FA 2011, Sch. 10, para. 9(4)–(8)).

S. 179(11) and (12) repealed by FA 2000, s. 102 and Sch. 29, para. 4(5), s. 156 and Sch. 40, Pt. II(12), with effect in relation to gains accruing on or after 1 April 2000, being superseded by TCGA 1992, s. 190 and 191 as substituted by FA 2000, s. 102 and Sch. 29, para. 9.

In s. 179 words "company A" substituted for "the chargeable company" wherever they occur by FA 2000, s. 102 and Sch. 29, para. 4 with effect in relation to assets acquired on or after 1 April 2000.

Derivations – S. 179(1), (2): ICTA 1970, s. 278(1), (2).

S. 179(3): ICTA 1970, s. 278(3), as amended by F(No. 2)A 1987, s. 95 and Sch. 6, para. 4(2).

S. 179(4): ICTA 1970, s. 278(3A), as inserted by F(No. 2)A 1987, s. 95 and Sch. 6, para. 4(2).

S. 179(5)–(9): ICTA 1970, s. 278(3B)–(3F), as inserted by FA 1989, s. 138(5).

S. 179(10): ICTA 1970, s. 278(4).

S. 179(11): ICTA 1970, s. 278(5), as amended by F(No. 2)A 1987, s. 95, Sch. 6, para. 4(3).

S. 179(12): ICTA 1970, s. 278(5A), as inserted by F(No. 2)A 1987, s. 95 and Sch. 6, para. 4(4).

S. 179(13): ICTA 1970, s. 278(6), as amended by F(No. 2)A 1987, s. 95 and Sch. 6, para. 4(5).

Cross references – S. 14: as regards attribution to members of gains of non-resident companies, s. 178–180 adapted to any non-resident group.

S. 30: adjustment of consideration where value shifting in point and (s. 30(2)) determination of value shift via a relevant asset where reduction in value not realised by reference to disposal under s. 179.

S. 31(7): exclusion from value shifting provisions of reductions caused by certain dividends except to the extent that payable out of particular profits unrealised by reference to a disposal under s. 179.

S. 31A(6): company holding asset with enhanced value leaving group within six years of value shifting transaction.

S. 33(3B), (3C): operation of value shifting provisions where asset with enhanced value transferred within group before being disposed of outside group.
S. 152–158: roll-over relief on replacement of business assets.
S. 197(2): the sale of an asset within s. 179(3) which was acquired on a disposal of an interest in oil to be won from a field or of an asset used in connection with the field is a material disposal in respect of which any gain or loss is to be ring fenced.
S. 276(8): application of s. 179 except subsections (1)b) to (1A), to certain transfers of exploration or exploitation rights or assets by a non-resident.
ICTA 1988, s. 416(2)–(6): definition of control by reference to interests in a company's affairs, capital, income and assets on a winding-up.
TMA 1970, s. 87A: interest on unpaid corporation tax under Pay and File, from the date when tax becomes payable by the company even where it is assessed on another person under s. 179(11).
FA 1994, s. 250(2): references in s. 179 to a company ceasing to be a member of a group do not apply where the company leaves the group by virtue solely of the coming into force of FA 1994, s. 249 (certain companies treated as non-residents).
FA 1994, Sch. 24: in connection with railways privatisation a company degrouped by virtue of a qualifying transaction shall not be treated as having sold and immediately reacquired any asset received from a company which was a group member at the time of acquisition.
FA 2000, Sch. 29, para. 47: definition and application of "old section 179" and "new section 179" concerning the de-grouping charge.
FA 2002, Sch. 29, para. 131: modification of roll-over relief in relation to degrouping charge on existing asset arising after commencement in cases of realisation and reinvestment.
TGGA 1992, Sch. 7AB: modifying roll-over of degrouping charge and inserted by FA 2002, s. 43 and Sch. 7.
TCGA 1992, s. 179A: reallocation within group of gain or loss accruing under section 179 as inserted by FA 2002, s. 42(1) and s. 179B: roll-over of degrouping charge on business assets inserted by FA 2002, s. 43(1).
TSBA 1985, Sch. 2, para. 4: application of s. 178 to cessation of membership of successor group(s) to Trustee Savings Bank group rather than to cessation of membership of the latter.
Electricity Act 1989, Sch. 11, para. 2 (not reproduced): if, when an electricity company transfers assets on privatisation which it acquired from another group company, it thereby ceases to be a member of the same group as the transferee, s. 179 applies as if any assets so acquired at any time had been acquired by the company at that time.
Ports Act 1991, s. 17 (not reproduced): ports levy chargeable in circumstances where property, rights, liabilities and functions of a relevant port authority transferred to a company which disposes of land etc. within ten years of ceasing to be a wholly owned subsidiary of the relevant port authority (see s. 179(3), (6)).
Ports Act 1991, s. 35(6) (not reproduced): exception to above where company formed by Port of London Authority ceases to be a member of the group of which that Authority is the principal company.
Broadcasting Act 1996, Sch. 7, para. 6 (not reproduced): circumstances in which sale by BBC of successor company does not trigger deemed sale and acquisition of asset acquired from another group company.
Greater London Authority Act 1999, s. 419 (not reproduced): references in s. 179 to a company do not apply to Transport for London.
Greater London Authority Act 1999, Sch 33 para 3 (not reproduced): company leaving London Regional Transport group of companies and joining Transport for London group - no deemed disposal and reacquisition of any asset acquired from member of former group.
Greater London Authority Act 1999, Sch. 33 para 9 (not reproduced): treatment under s. 179 of company leaving London Regional Transport group of companies to join public-private partnership.
Commonwealth Development Corporation Act 1999 Sch. 3 para 3(4)(a), (4(2) (not reproduced): disapplication of s. 179 during its exempt period, and where the Corporation ceases to be resident in the UK within a certain time following its exempt period
SI 2009/2971, reg. 6, 7: building societies: company ceasing to be member of group: disapplication of s. 179.
SI 2009/2971, reg. 17, 18: industrial and provident societies: company ceasing to be member of group: disapplication of s. 179.

Statutory instruments – SI 1992/3066: the day appointed for the effective commencement of s. 179 is 30 September 1993.

European material – Council Regulation (EC) 2157/2001 of 8 October 2001 on the Statute for a European Company (Societas Europaea).

HMRC interpretations – IRInt. 63: Revenue view that s. 179 (and not s. 178) applies to companies leaving groups in accounting periods ending on or after 1 October 1993, and s. 178 (and not s. 179) applies to companies leaving groups in accounting periods ending before 1 October 1993.
IRInt. 216: Delaware Limited Liability Company may be a member of a capital gains group.

Other material – ICAEW Technical Releases TR 366, 386 (not reproduced): Revenue will not normally seek to apply s. 179 to assets transferred to a holding company of a group consisting of that company and one subsidiary when the subsidiary leaves the group, except where the parent company emigrates.
ICAEW Technical Release TR 713 (not reproduced): Revenue sympathetic to loss carry-back against gain arising under s. 179 and would consider specific cases.
ICAEW Technical Release TR 831 (not reproduced): s. 179 applies where a company makes an intra-group transfer, the asset is transferred back, and the company leaves the group within six years; also where two companies (not themselves a group) leave a group, in respect of assets transferred between them before leaving (even if both companies are acquired by the same group).
Taxline 1994/26 (not reproduced): even if company leaves group on or after 30 November 1993, restrictions on availability of indexation allowance will not apply if loss triggered by reference to intra-group transfer before that date.

Notes – S. 15: meaning of "chargeable gains".
S. 16: meaning of "allowable losses".
S. 21–34: general meaning of "disposal" and "assets", including the timing of certain disposals.
S. 272–274 and Sch. 11: meaning of "market value".
S. 288: interpretation, including meaning of "trading stock", the "Management Act" as TMA 1970 and reference to other sections as being those of this Act.
ICTA 1988, s. 10: time for payment of corporation tax.
TMA 1970, s. 29: assessing procedure.
TMA 1970, s. 34: time limits for making assessments generally.

179ZA Claim for adjustment of calculations under section 179

179ZA(1) This section applies where–

(a) a gain accrues to a company ("company A") on a sale referred to in subsection (3) or (6) of section 179, or

(b) a gain would so accrue but for subsection (3A) or (7A) of that section.

179ZA(2) If subsection (3D) or (3E) of that section applies in relation to one or more group disposals (within the meaning of that section)–

(a) the company making the disposal, or

(b) if there is more than one disposal, the companies making those disposals acting jointly,

may make a claim for the amount of the gain to be treated for the purposes of the subsection in question as reduced by an amount specified in the claim.

179ZA(3) In any other case, company A may make a claim for the amount of the gain to be treated for all purposes of this Act as reduced by an amount specified in the claim.

179ZA(4) Where a claim is made under subsection (2) or (3), the gain must be treated, for the purposes mentioned in the subsection in question, as reduced by such amount (if any) as is just and reasonable.

179ZA(5) In determining the amount which is just and reasonable regard must be had, in particular, to any transaction as a direct or indirect result of which company A or any associated company (within the meaning of section 179(10)) acquired the asset to which the gain relates.

179ZA(6) Where under this section the gain accruing to company A on a sale referred to in subsection (3) or (6) of section 179 is treated as reduced by an amount ("the permitted deduction"), the subsection in question has effect, so far as it provides for the immediate reacquisition of the asset by company A, as if the reference to market value of the asset were to its market value less the permitted deduction.

History – S. 179ZA inserted by FA 2011, s. 45 and Sch. 10, para. 4, with effect in relation to any disposal of an asset by one company (B) to another company (A) made at a time when B is a member of a group if either A ceases to be a member of the group on or after 19 July 2011 or ceased to be so before 19 July 2011 in circumstances where TCGA 1992, s. 179(6)–(8) applied and ceases to satisfy the conditions in TCGA 1992, s. 179(7) on or after 19 July 2011 (see FA 2011, Sch. 10, para. 9(1)). But references to 19 July 2011 may be replaced by references to 1 April 2011 if an "early commencement election" is made (see FA 2011, Sch. 10, para. 9(4)–(8)).

179A Reallocation within group of gain or loss accruing under section 179

179A [Repealed by FA 2011, s. 45 and Sch. 10, para. 5(a).]

History – S. 179A repealed by FA 2011, s. 45 and Sch. 10, para. 5(a), with effect in relation to any disposal of an asset by one company (B) to another company (A) made at a time when B is a member of a group if either A ceases to be a member of the group on or after 19 July 2011 or ceased to be so before 19 July 2011 in circumstances where TCGA 1992, s. 179(6)–(8) applied and ceases to satisfy the conditions in TCGA 1992, s. 179(7) on or after 19 July 2011 (see FA 2011, Sch. 10, para. 9(1)). But references to 19 July 2011 may be replaced by references to 1 April 2011 if an "early commencement election" is made (see FA 2011, Sch. 10, para. 9(4)–(8)).

179B Roll-over of degrouping charge on business assets

179B [Repealed by FA 2011, s. 45 and Sch. 10, para. 5(b).]

History – S. 179B repealed by FA 2011, s. 45 and Sch. 10, para. 5(b), with effect in relation to any disposal of an asset by one company (B) to another company (A) made at a time when B is a member of a group if either A ceases to be a member of the group on or after 19 July 2011 or ceased to be so before 19 July 2011 in circumstances where TCGA 1992, s. 179(6)–(8) applied and ceases to satisfy the conditions in TCGA 1992, s. 179(7) on or after 19 July 2011 (see FA 2011, Sch. 10, para. 9(1)). But references to 19 July 2011 may be replaced by references to 1 April 2011 if an "early commencement election" is made (see FA 2011, Sch. 10, para. 9(4)–(8)).

180 Transitional provisions

180 [Repealed by FA 2000, s. 102 and Sch. 29, para. 27, s. 156 and Sch. 40, Pt. II(12).]

History – S. 180 repealed by FA 2000, s. 102 and Sch. 29, para. 27, s. 156 and Sch. 40, Pt. II(12), in relation to companies which left a group during an accounting period ending after 30 September 1993.

181 Exemption from charge under section 178 or 179 in the case of certain mergers

Notes – In the title to s. 181, the word "section" was omitted apparently by error and has been inserted by CCH.

181(1) Subject to the following provisions of this section, section 179 shall not apply in a case where–

(a) as part of a merger, a company (**"company A"**) ceases to be a member of a group of companies (**"the A group"**); and

(b) the merger was carried out for bona fide commercial reasons and the avoidance of liability to tax was not the main or one of the main purposes of the merger.

181(2) In this section **"merger"** means an arrangement (which in this section includes a series of arrangements)–

(a) whereby one or more companies ("the acquiring company" or, as the case may be, "the acquiring companies") none of which is a member of the A group acquires or acquire, otherwise than with a view to their disposal, one or more interests in the whole or part of the business which, before the arrangement took effect, was carried on by company A; and

(b) whereby one or more members of the A group acquires or acquire, otherwise than with a view to their disposal, one or more interests in the whole or part of the business or each of the businesses which, before the arrangement took effect, was carried on either by the acquiring company or acquiring companies or by a company at least 90 per cent of the ordinary share capital of which was then beneficially owned by 2 or more of the acquiring companies; and

(c) in respect of which the conditions in subsection (4) below are fulfilled.

181(3) For the purposes of subsection (2) above, a member of a group of companies shall be treated as carrying on as one business the activities of that group.

181(4) The conditions referred to in subsection (2)(c) above are–

(a) that not less than 25 per cent by value of each of the interests acquired as mentioned in paragraphs (a) and (b) of subsection (2) above consists of a holding of ordinary share capital, and the remainder of the interest, or as the case may be of each of the interests, acquired as mentioned in subsection (2)(b), consists of a holding of share capital (of any description) or debentures or both; and

(b) that the value or, as the case may be, the aggregate value of the interest or interests acquired as mentioned in subsection (2)(a) above is substantially the same as the value or, as the case may be, the aggregate value of the interest or interests acquired as mentioned in subsection (2)(b) above; and

(c) that the consideration for the acquisition of the interest or interests acquired by the acquiring company or acquiring companies as mentioned in subsection (2)(a) above, disregarding any part of that consideration which is small by comparison with the total, either consists of, or is applied in the acquisition of, or consists partly of and as to the balance is applied in the acquisition of, the interest or interests acquired by members of the A group as mentioned in subsection (2)(b) above;

and for the purposes of this subsection the value of an interest shall be determined as at the date of its acquisition.

181(5) [Repealed by FA 2000, s. 102 and Sch. 29, para. 28(1), s. 156 and Sch. 40, Pt. II(12).]

History – In s. 181(1)(b), words "it is shown that" and second occurrence of "that" repealed by FA 1996, s. 134 and Sch. 20, para. 58 and s. 205 and Sch. 41, Pt. V(10), for accounting periods ending on or after 1 July 1999, the appointed day for corporation tax self-assessment (FA 1994, s. 199 and SI 1998/3173 (C. 78)).

In s. 181(1)(b), words "section 179 shall not" substituted for "neither section 178 nor section 179 shall", and s. 181(5) repealed by FA 2000, s. 102 and Sch. 29, para. 28(1), s. 156 and Sch. 40, Pt. II(12), with effect in relation to companies which cease to be a member of a group on or after 1 April 2000.

Derivations – ICTA 1970, s. 278A, as inserted by FA 1970, s. 27.

Cross references – S. 276(8): application of s.181 to certain transfers of exploration or exploitation rights or assets by a non-resident. Greater London Authority Act 1999, s. 419, references in s. 181 to a company do not apply to Transport for London.

HMRC interpretations – IRInt. 216: Delaware Limited Liability Company may be a member of a capital gains group.

Notes – S. 9: meaning of "resident".
S. 21–34: general meaning of "disposal".
S. 288: interpretation, including reference to sections being those of this Act.

RESTRICTION ON INDEXATION ALLOWANCE FOR GROUPS AND ASSOCIATED COMPANIES

182 Disposals of debts

182 [Repealed by FA 1994, s. 93(7) and s. 258 and Sch. 26, Pt. V(8) in relation to disposals made on or after 30 November 1993.]

183 Disposals of shares

183 [Repealed by FA 1994, s. 93(7) and s. 258 and Sch. 26, Pt. V(8), in relation to disposals made on or after 30 November 1993.]

184 Definitions and other provisions supplemental to sections 182 and 183

184 [Repealed by FA 1994, s. 93(7) and s. 258 and Sch. 26, Pt. V(8), in relation to disposals made on or after 30 November 1993.]

RESTRICTIONS ON BUYING LOSSES OR GAINS ETC

Notes – S. 184A–184F (and the cross heading above) inserted by FA 2006, s. 70(2) in respect of any accounting period ending on or after 5 December 2005 (but not in relation to the deduction of a loss arising before that date from a chargeable gain accruing before that date).

184A Restrictions on buying losses: tax avoidance schemes

184A(1) This section applies for the purposes of corporation tax in respect of chargeable gains if–

(a) at any time ("the relevant time") there is a qualifying change of ownership in relation to a company ("the relevant company") (see section 184C),

(b) a loss (a "qualifying loss") accrues to the relevant company or any other company on a disposal of a pre-change asset (see subsection (3)),

(c) the change of ownership occurs directly or indirectly in consequence of, or otherwise in connection with, any arrangements the main purpose, or one of the main purposes, of which is to secure a tax advantage (see section 184D), and

(d) the advantage involves the deduction of a qualifying loss from any chargeable gains (whether or not it also involves anything else).

184A(2) A qualifying loss accruing to a company is not to be deductible from chargeable gains accruing to the company.

184A(3) In this section a **"pre-change asset"** means an asset which was held by the relevant company before the relevant time (but see also sections 184E and 184F).

184A(4) In this section **"arrangements"** includes any agreement, understanding, scheme, transaction or series of transactions (whether or not legally enforceable).

184A(5) For the purposes of this section it does not matter–

(a) whether a qualifying loss accrues before, after or at the relevant time,

(b) whether a qualifying loss accrues at a time when there are no chargeable gains from which it could be deducted (or could otherwise have been deducted), or

(c) whether the tax advantage is secured for the company to which a qualifying loss accrues or for any other company.

History – In s. 184A(2) the words at the end ("unless the gains accrue to the company on a disposal of a pre-change asset") omitted by FA 2007, s. 32(2) and repealed by FA 2007 s. 114 and Sch. 27, Pt 2(4); with effect in relation to gains accruing on disposals made on or after 21 March 2007 (FA 2007, s. 32(7)).

S. 184A inserted by FA 2006, s. 70(2) in respect of any accounting period ending on or after 5 December 2005 (but not in relation to the deduction of a loss arising before that date from a chargeable gain accruing before that date).

Cross references – FA 2006, s. 70(9)–(10): application of s. 184A in relation to qualifying changes of ownership before 5 December 2005.

184B Restrictions on buying gains: tax avoidance schemes

184B(1) This section applies for the purposes of corporation tax in respect of chargeable gains if–

(a) at any time ("the relevant time") there is a qualifying change of ownership in relation to a company ("the relevant company") (see section 184C),

(b) a gain (a "qualifying gain") accrues to the relevant company or any other company on a disposal of a pre-change asset (see subsection (3)),

(c) the change of ownership occurs directly or indirectly in consequence of, or otherwise in connection with, any arrangements the main purpose, or one of the main purposes, of which is to secure a tax advantage, and

(d) the advantage involves the deduction of a loss from a qualifying gain (whether or not it also involves anything else).

184B(2) In the case of a qualifying gain accruing to a company, a loss accruing to the company is not to be deductible from the gain.

184B(3) In this section a **"pre-change asset"** means an asset which was held by the relevant company before the relevant time (but see also sections 184E and 184F).

184B(4) In this section **"arrangements"** includes any agreement, understanding, scheme, transaction or series of transactions (whether or not legally enforceable).

184B(5) For the purposes of this section it does not matter–

(a) whether a qualifying gain accrues before, after or at the relevant time,

(b) whether a qualifying gain accrues at a time when there are no losses which could be deducted (or could otherwise have been deducted) from the gain, or

(c) whether the tax advantage is secured for the company to which a qualifying gain accrues or for any other company.

History – In s. 184B(2) the words at the end ("unless the loss accrues to the company on a disposal of a pre-change asset") omitted by FA 2007, s. 32(3) and repealed by FA 2007 s. 114 and Sch. 27, Pt. 2(4); with effect in relation to losses accruing on disposals made on or after 21 March 2007 (FA 2007, s. 32(8)).

S. 184B inserted by FA 2006, s. 70(2) in respect of any accounting period ending on or after 5 December 2005 (but not in relation to the deduction of a loss arising before that date from a chargeable gain accruing before that date).

Cross references – FA 2006, s. 70(9)–(10): application of s. 184B in relation to qualifying changes of ownership before 5 December 2005.

184C Sections 184A and 184B: meaning of "qualifying change of ownership"

184C(1) For the purposes of sections 184A and 184B, there is a qualifying change of ownership in relation to a company at any time if any one or more of the following occur at that time–

(a) the company joins a group of companies (see subsections (2) to (5)),

(b) the company ceases to be a member of a group of companies,

(c) the company becomes subject to different control (see subsections (6) to (9)).

184C(2) Whether a company is a member of a group of companies at any time is determined in accordance with section 170.

184C(3) But, apart from in the excepted case, nothing in section 170(10) or (10A) is to prevent all the companies of one group from being regarded as joining another group when the principal company of the first group becomes a member of the other group at any time.

184C(4) The excepted case is the case where–

(a) the persons owning the shares of the principal company of the first group immediately before that time are the same as the persons owning the shares of the principal company of the other group immediately after that time,

(b) the principal company of the other group was not the principal company of any group immediately before that time, and

(c) immediately after that time the principal company of the other group had assets consisting entirely (or almost entirely) of shares of the principal company of the first group.

184C(5) For this purpose, references to shares of a company are to the shares comprised in the issued share capital of the company.

184C(6) The general rule is that a company becomes subject to different control at any time if any one or more of the following occur–

(a) a person has control of the company at that time (whether alone or together with one or more others) and the person did not previously have control of the company,

(b) a person has control of the company at that time together with one or more others and the person previously had control of the company alone,

(c) a person ceases to have control of the company at that time (whether the person had control alone or together with one or more others).

184C(7) The general rule is subject to the following exceptions.

184C(8) A company does not become subject to different control in any case where it joins a group of companies and the case is the excepted case mentioned above.

184C(9) A company ("the subsidiary") does not become subject to different control at any time in any case where–

(a) immediately before that time the subsidiary is the 75 per cent. subsidiary of another company, and

(b) (although there is a change in the direct ownership of the subsidiary) that other company continues immediately after that time to own it as a 75 per cent. subsidiary.

History – S. 184C inserted by FA 2006, s. 70(2) in respect of any accounting period ending on or after 5 December 2005 (but not in relation to the deduction of a loss arising before that date from a chargeable gain accruing before that date).

Cross references – FA 2006, s. 70(11): transitional application of s. 184A–184B in relation to qualifying changes of ownership before 5 December 2005.

184D Sections 184A and 184B: meaning of "tax advantage"

184D For the purposes of sections 184A and 184B, **"tax advantage"** means–

(a) relief or increased relief from corporation tax,

(b) repayment or increased repayment of corporation tax,

(c) the avoidance or reduction of a charge to corporation tax or an assessment to corporation tax, or

(d) the avoidance of a possible assessment to corporation tax.

History – S. 184D inserted by FA 2006, s. 70(2) in respect of any accounting period ending on or after 5 December 2005 (but not in relation to the deduction of a loss arising before that date from a chargeable gain accruing before that date).

184E Sections 184A and 184B: "pre-change assets": basic rules

184E(1) If–

(a) a company other than the relevant company makes a disposal of an asset, and

(b) the asset has been disposed of at any time after the relevant time by a disposal to which section 171(1) does not apply (a "non-section 171(1) transfer"),

the asset ceases to be regarded as a pre-change asset for the purposes of sections 184A and 184B (but see also subsections (10) and (11)).

184E(2) But (without affecting the generality of the provision made by the following subsection) if, on a non-section 171(1) transfer,–

(a) an asset would cease to be regarded as a pre-change asset as a result of subsection (1), and

(b) the company making the non-section 171(1) transfer retains any interest in or over the asset,

that interest is to be regarded as a pre-change asset for the purposes of sections 184A and 184B.

184E(3) If–

(a) the relevant company or any other company holds an asset ("the new asset") at or after the relevant time,

(b) the value of the new asset derives in whole or in part from a pre-change asset, and

(c) the new asset is not acquired by the company concerned as a result of a non-section 171(1) transfer,

the new asset is also to be regarded as a pre-change asset for the purposes of sections 184A and 184B.

184E(4) For this purpose the cases in which the value of an asset may be derived from any other asset include any case where–

(a) assets have been merged or divided,

(b) assets have changed their nature, or

(c) rights or interests in or over assets have been created or extinguished.

184E(5) If a pre-change asset is **"the old asset"** for the purposes of section 116 (reorganisations, conversions and reconstructions), **"the new asset"** for the purposes of that section is also to be regarded as a pre-change asset for the purposes of sections 184A and 184B.

184E(6) If a pre-change asset is the **"original shares"** for the purposes of sections 127 to 131 (reorganisation or reduction of share capital), the **"new holding"** for the purposes of those sections is also to be regarded as a pre-change asset for the purposes of sections 184A and 184B.

184E(7) The following subsection applies if, as a result of the application of a relevant deferral provision in the case of a disposal of a pre-change asset ("the original disposal"),–

(a) a gain or loss that would otherwise accrue to a company does not so accrue, or

(b) any part of any such gain is treated as forming part of a single chargeable gain which does not accrue to the company on the original disposal,

and a gain or loss does, wholly or partly in consequence of the application of that provision in the case of the original disposal, accrue to the company or any other company on a subsequent occasion.

184E(8) So much of the gain or loss accruing on the subsequent occasion as accrues in consequence of the application of the relevant deferral provision in the case of the original disposal is to be regarded for the purposes of sections 184A and 184B as accruing on a disposal of a pre-change asset (so far as it would not otherwise be so regarded).

184E(9) A **"relevant deferral provision"** means any of the following–

(a) section 139 (reconstruction involving transfer of business),

(b) section 140 (postponement of charge on transfer of assets to non-resident company),

(c) section 140A (transfer of a UK trade),

(d) section 140E (merger leaving assets within UK tax charge),

(e) sections 152 and 153 (replacement of business assets),

(f) section 187 (postponement of charge on deemed disposal under section 185).

184E(10) If–

(a) a pre-change asset of the relevant company is transferred to another company ("the transferee company"),

(b) any of sections 139, 140A and 140E apply to the companies in the case of the asset, and

(c) the transfer of the asset is made directly or indirectly in consequence of, or otherwise in connection with, the arrangements mentioned in section 184A or 184B,

the asset is to be regarded as a "pre-change asset" in the hands of the transferee company for the purposes of sections 184A and 184B.

184E(11) In such a case, subsection (1) applies as if the reference in paragraph (a) of that subsection to the relevant company were to the transferee company.

History – S. 184E inserted by FA 2006, s. 70(2) in respect of any accounting period ending on or after 5 December 2005 (but not in relation to the deduction of a loss arising before that date from a chargeable gain accruing before that date).

184F Sections 184A and 184B: "pre-change assets": pooling rules

184F(1) This section applies, in the case of any pre-change asset of the relevant company or any pre-change asset of any company which is acquired on a disposal to which section 171(1) applies, if–

(a) the pre-change asset consists of a holding of securities which falls as a result of any provision of Chapter 1 of Part 4 to be regarded as a single asset ("the pre-change pooled asset"), and

(b) as a result of any disposal or acquisition at any time after the relevant time, any securities ("the other securities") would (but for this section) be regarded as forming part of the pre-change pooled asset.

184F(2) None of the other securities are to be regarded for the purposes of this Act as forming part of the pre-change pooled asset.

184F(3) But this does not prevent the other securities from being regarded, as a result of any provision of that Chapter, as forming part of or constituting a different, single asset ("the other pooled asset").

184F(4) Securities of the same class as the other securities which are disposed of at or after the relevant time–

(a) are to be identified first with the other securities or securities forming part of the other pooled asset,

(b) are to be identified next with securities forming part of the pre-change pooled asset (if the number of securities disposed of exceeds the number identified in accordance with paragraph (a)), and

(c) subject to paragraphs (a) and (b), are to be identified in accordance with the provisions applicable apart from those paragraphs.

184F(5) The above identification rules apply even if some or all of the securities disposed of are otherwise identified–

(a) by the disposal, or

(b) by a transfer or delivery giving effect to it;

but where a company disposes of securities in one capacity, they are not to be identified with securities which it holds, or can dispose of, only in some other capacity.

184F(6) Chapter 1 of Part 4 has effect subject to this section.

184F(7) In this section–

"pre-change asset" means an asset which is pre-change asset for the purposes of section 184A or 184B,

"securities" does not include relevant securities as defined in section 108 but, subject to that, means–

(a) shares or securities of a company, and

(b) any other assets where they are of a nature to be dealt in without identifying the particular assets disposed of or acquired.

184F(8) For the purposes of this section, shares or securities of a company are not to be treated as being of the same class unless–

(a) they are so treated by the practice of a recognised stock exchange, or

(b) they would be so treated if dealt with on a recognised stock exchange.

History – S. 184F inserted by FA 2006, s. 70(2) in respect of any accounting period ending on or after 5 December 2005 (but not in relation to the deduction of a loss arising before that date from a chargeable gain accruing before that date).

184G Avoidance involving losses: schemes converting income to capital

184G(1) This section applies for the purposes of corporation tax in respect of chargeable gains if conditions A to D are satisfied.

184G(2) Condition A is that a receipt or other amount arises to a company directly or indirectly in consequence of, or otherwise in connection with, any arrangements.

184G(3) Condition B is that–

(a) that amount falls to be taken into account in calculating a chargeable gain (the "relevant gain") which accrues to a company ("the relevant company"), and

(b) losses accrue (or have accrued) to the relevant company (whether before or after or as part of the arrangements).

184G(4) Condition C is that, but for the arrangements, an amount would have fallen to be taken into account wholly or partly instead of the amount mentioned in subsection (2) in calculating the income chargeable to corporation tax–

(a) of the relevant company, or

(b) of a company which, at any qualifying time, is a member of the same group as the relevant company.

184G(5) Condition D is that–

(a) the main purpose of the arrangements, or

(b) one of the main purposes of the arrangements,

is to secure a tax advantage that involves the deduction of any of the losses from the relevant gain (whether or not it also involves anything else).

184G(6) If the Board consider, on reasonable grounds, that conditions A to D are or may be satisfied, they may give the relevant company a notice in respect of the arrangements (but see also section 184I).

184G(7) If, when the notice is given, conditions A to D are satisfied, no loss accruing to the relevant company at any time is to be deductible from the relevant gain.

184G(8) A notice under this section must–

(a) specify the arrangements,

(b) specify the accounting period in which the relevant gain accrues, and

(c) inform the relevant company of the effect of this section.

184G(9) If relevant gains accrue in more than one accounting period, a single notice under this section may specify all the accounting periods concerned.

184G(10) In this section–

"arrangements" includes any agreement, understanding, scheme, transaction or series of transactions (whether or not legally enforceable),

"group", in relation to companies, means a group determined in accordance with section 170,

"qualifying time", in relation to any arrangements, means any time which falls in the period–

(a) beginning with the time at which the arrangements are made, and

(b) ending with the time at which the matters (other than any tax advantage) intended to be secured by the arrangements are secured,

"tax advantage" has the meaning given by section 184D.

History – S. 184G(2) and (3) substituted by FA 2014, s. 63(1)(a), with effect in relation to arrangements entered into on or after 30 January 2014, and in relation to arrangements entered into before that date but only to the extent that any chargeable gain accrues on a disposal which occurs on or after that date.

In s. 184G(4), the words "the amount mentioned in subsection (2)" substituted for the words "the receipt" by FA 2014, s. 63(1)(b), with effect in relation to arrangements entered into on or after 30 January 2014, and in relation to arrangements entered into before that date but only to the extent that any chargeable gain accrues on a disposal which occurs on or after that date.

S. 184G inserted by FA 2006, s. 71(1), with effect in relation to chargeable gains accruing on any disposal made on or after 5 December 2005.

Cross references – FA 1998, Sch. 18, para. 25(1): extension of enquiry scope to cover notices under s. 184G.

FA 1998, Sch. 18, para. 42: limit on restriction of powers to make a discovery assessment or determination where notice given under s. 184G.

184H Avoidance involving losses: schemes securing deductions

184H(1) This section applies for the purposes of corporation tax in respect of chargeable gains if conditions A to D are satisfied.

184H(2) Condition A is that–

(a) a chargeable gain (the "relevant gain") accrues to a company ("the relevant company") directly or indirectly in consequence of, or otherwise in connection with, any arrangements, and

(b) losses accrue (or have accrued) to the relevant company (whether before or after or as part of the arrangements).

184H(3) Condition B is that the relevant company, or a company connected with the relevant company, becomes entitled to an income deduction directly or indirectly in consequence of, or otherwise in connection with, the arrangements.

184H(4) Condition C is that the main purpose, or one of the main purposes, of the arrangements is to secure a tax advantage that involves both–

(a) that income deduction, and

(b) the deduction of any of the losses from the relevant gain,

whether or not it also involves anything else.

184H(5) Condition D is that the arrangements are not excluded arrangements.

For this purpose arrangements are excluded arrangements if–

(a) the arrangements are made in respect of land or any estate or interest in land,

(b) the arrangements fall within section 835(1) or 836(1) of CTA 2010 (sale and lease-back: limitation on tax reliefs),

(c) the person to whom the payment mentioned in that subsection is payable is not a company connected with the relevant company, and

(d) the arrangements are made between persons dealing at arm's length.

184H(6) If the Board consider, on reasonable grounds, that conditions A to D are or may be satisfied, they may give the company a notice in respect of the arrangements (but see also section 184I).

184H(7) If, when the notice is given, conditions A to D are satisfied, no loss accruing to the company at any time is to be deductible from the relevant gain.

184H(8) A notice under this section must–

(a) specify the arrangements,

(b) specify the accounting period in which the relevant gain accrues, and

(c) inform the relevant company of the effect of this section.

184H(9) If relevant gains accrue in more than one accounting period, a single notice under this section may specify all the accounting periods concerned.

184H(10) In this section–

"arrangements" includes any agreement, understanding, scheme, transaction or series of transactions (whether or not legally enforceable),

"income deduction" means–

(a) a deduction in calculating income for corporation tax purposes, or

(b) a deduction from total profits,

"tax advantage" has the meaning given by section 184D.

184H(11) For the purposes of this section it does not matter whether the tax advantage is secured for the relevant company or for any other company.

History – In s. 184H(2)(b), the words "on any disposal of any asset", which appeared after the words "the relevant company", omitted by FA 2014, s. 63(2)(a), with effect in relation to arrangements entered into on or after 30 January 2014, and in relation to arrangements entered into before that date but only to the extent that any chargeable gain accrues on a disposal which occurs on or after that date.

S. 184H(3) substituted by FA 2014, s. 63(2)(b), with effect in relation to arrangements entered into on or after 30 January 2014, and in relation to arrangements entered into before that date but only to the extent that any chargeable gain accrues on a disposal which occurs on or after that date.

S. 184H(4)(a) substituted by FA 2014, s. 63(2)(c), with effect in relation to arrangements entered into on or after 30 January 2014, and in relation to arrangements entered into before that date but only to the extent that any chargeable gain accrues on a disposal which occurs on or after that date.

In s. 184H(5)(b), the words "section 835(1) or 836(1) of CTA 2010" substituted for "section 779(1) or (2) of the Taxes Act" by CTA 2010, s. 1177 and Sch. 1, para. 245, with effect for corporation tax purposes for accounting periods ending on or after 1 April 2010, and for income tax and capital gains tax purposes for the tax year 2010–11 and subsequent tax years.

In s. 184H(10), the definition of "income deduction" inserted by FA 2014, s. 63(2)(d), with effect in relation to arrangements entered into on or after 30 January 2014, and in relation to arrangements entered into before that date but only to the extent that any chargeable gain accrues on a disposal which occurs on or after that date.

S. 184H inserted by FA 2006, s. 71(1) with effect in relation to chargeable gains accruing on any disposal made on or after 5 December 2005.

Cross references – FA 1998, Sch. 18, para. 2591): extension of enquiry scope to cover notices under s. 184H.

FA 1998, Sch. 18, para. 42: limit on restriction of powers to make a discovery assessment or determination where notice given under s. 184H.

184I Notices under sections 184G and 184H

184I(1) Subsection (2) applies if–

(a) the Board give a notice under section 184G or 184H (a "relevant notice") to a company that specifies an accounting period, and

(b) the notice is given before the company has made its company tax return for that accounting period.

184I(2) If the company makes its return for that period before the end of the applicable 90 day period (see subsection (12)), it may–

(a) make a return that disregards the notice, and

(b) at any time after making the return and before the end of the applicable 90 day period, amend the return for the purpose of complying with the provision referred to in the notice.

184I(3) If a company has made a company tax return for an accounting period, the Board may give the company a relevant notice in relation to that period only if a notice of enquiry has been given to the company in respect of its return for that period.

184I(4) After any enquiries into the return for that period have been completed, the Board may give the company a relevant notice only if requirements A and B are met.

184I(5) Requirement A is that at the time the enquiries into the return were completed, the Board could not have been reasonably expected, on the basis of information made available–

(a) to them before that time, or

(b) to an officer of theirs before that time,

to have been aware that the circumstances were such that a relevant notice could have been given to the company in relation to that period.

184I(6) For the purposes of requirement A, paragraph 44(2) and (3) of Schedule 18 to the Finance Act 1998 (information made available) applies as it applies for the purposes of paragraph 44(1).

184I(7) Requirement B is that–

(a) the company or any other person was requested to produce or provide information during an enquiry into the return for that period, and

(b) if the request had been duly complied with, the Board could reasonably have been expected to give the company a relevant notice in relation to that period.

184I(8) If–

(a) a company makes a company tax return for an accounting period, and

(b) the company is subsequently given a relevant notice that specifies that period,

it may amend the return for the purpose of complying with the provision referred to in the notice at any time before the end of the applicable 90 day period.

184I(9) If the relevant notice is given to the company after it has been given a notice of enquiry in respect of its return for the period, no closure notice may be given in relation to its company tax return until–

(a) the end of the applicable 90 day period, or

(b) the earlier amendment of its company tax return for the purpose of complying with the provision referred to in the notice.

184I(10) If the relevant notice is given to the company after any enquiries into the return for the period are completed, no discovery assessment may be made as regards the chargeable gain to which the notice relates until–

(a) the end of the applicable 90 day period, or

(b) the earlier amendment of the company tax return for the purpose of complying with the provision referred to in the notice.

184I(11) Subsections (2)(b) and (8) do not prevent a company tax return for a period becoming incorrect if–

(a) a relevant notice is given to the company in relation to that period,

(b) the return is not amended in accordance with subsection (2)(b) or (8) for the purpose of complying with the provision referred to in the notice, and

(c) the return ought to have been so amended.

184I(12) In this section–

"the applicable 90 day period", in relation to a relevant notice, means the period of 90 days beginning with the day on which the notice is given,

"closure notice" means a notice under paragraph 32 of Schedule 18 to the Finance Act 1998,

"company tax return" means the return required to be delivered pursuant to a notice under paragraph 3 of that Schedule, as read with paragraph 4 of that Schedule,

"discovery assessment" means an assessment under paragraph 41 of that Schedule,

"notice of enquiry" means a notice under paragraph 24 of that Schedule.

History – S. 184I inserted by FA 2006, s. 71(1) with effect in relation to chargeable gains accruing on any disposal made on or after 5 December 2005.

NON-RESIDENT AND DUAL RESIDENT COMPANIES

185 Deemed disposal of assets on company ceasing to be resident in UK

185(1) This section and section 187 apply to a company if, at any time (**"the relevant time"**), the company ceases to be resident in the United Kingdom.

185(2) The company shall be deemed for all purposes of this Act–

(a) to have disposed of all its assets, other than assets excepted from this subsection by subsection (4) below, immediately before the relevant time; and

(b) immediately to have reacquired them,

at their market value at that time.

185(3) Section 152 shall not apply where the company–

(a) has disposed of the old assets, or of its interest in those assets, before the relevant time; and

(b) acquires the new assets, or its interest in those assets, after that time,

unless the new assets are excepted from this subsection by subsection (4) below.

185(4) If at any time after the relevant time the company carries on a trade in the United Kingdom through a permanent establishment–

(a) any assets which, immediately after the relevant time, are situated in the United Kingdom and are used in or for the purposes of the trade, or are used or held for the purposes of the permanent establishment, shall be excepted from subsection (2) above; and

(b) any new assets which, after that time are so situated and are so used or so held shall be excepted from subsection (3) above;

and references in this subsection to assets situated in the United Kingdom include references to exploration or exploitation assets and to exploration or exploitation rights.

185(4A) Subsection (4) applies to an overseas life insurance company in the case of its long-term business with–

(a) the omission from paragraph (a) of the words "are situated in the United Kingdom and", and

(b) the omission from paragraph (b) of the words "are so situated and".

185(5) In this section–

(a) **"designated area"**, **"exploration or exploitation activities"** and **"exploration or exploitation rights"** have the same meanings as in section 276;

(b) **"exploration or exploitation assets"** means assets used or intended for use in connection with exploration or exploitation activities carried on in the United Kingdom or a designated area;

(c) **"the old assets"** and **"the new assets"** have the same meanings as in section 152;

and a company shall not be regarded for the purposes of this section as ceasing to be resident in the United Kingdom by reason only that it ceases to exist.

History – In s. 185(4), the words "permanent establishment" substituted for the words "branch or agency" by FA 2003, s. 153(1)(b) with effect in relation to accounting periods beginning on or after 1 January 2003.
S. 185(4A) inserted by FA2012, s. 146 and Sch. 16, para. 78 in relation to accounting periods beginning on or after 1 January 2013 (FA 2012, s. 148) but subject to transitional provisions in FA 2012, Sch. 17. Where an accounting period would otherwise straddle 1 January 2013, it is deemed to end on 31 December 2012 (FA 2012, s. 149).

Derivations – FA 1988, s. 105(1)–(5).

Cross references – S. 152: roll-over relief on replacement of business assets.
S. 276: UK includes the territorial sea of the UK, "designated area" is an area designated under the Continental Shelf Act 1964, "exploration or exploitation activities" are given by reference to the seabed, subsoil and their natural resources located therein and "exploration or exploitation rights" are to assets to be consequently produced.
S. 179B(2), (4) and Sch. 7AB: modification of s. 185 where roll-over relief claimed where company treated by virtue of s. 179(3) or s. 179(6) as having sold and immediately re-acquired an asset at market value.
Sch. 7B, para. 8: modification of s. 185(2)(a), (3) and modification of s. 185(4), (5) by the deemed insertion of s. 185(4A), (4B) and s. 185(5)(ba) in respect of overseas life insurance companies in relation to accounting periods beginning after 31 December 1992.
FA 1994, s. 250(3): certain companies treated as non-resident after 30 November 1993.
SI 2006/3271, reg. 29: modification of s. 185 with effect from 31 December 2006 in relation to periods of account ending on or after that day.

Other material – Taxline 1994/32 (not reproduced): confirmation by Inland Revenue International Division that "exit charge" under TCGA 1992, s. 185 on assets held by certain dual resident companies, which became non-resident for tax purposes on 30 November 1993, will apply subject to any relevant tax treaty.
Taxline 1994/46 (not reproduced): exemption for gains from alienation of certain property under relevant double tax treaty applies to s. 185 exit charge where company ceased to be resident at 30 November 1993 by virtue of FA 1994, s. 249.

Notes – S. 9: meaning of "resident".
S. 10: extent of charge on non-resident by reference to assets used or held for a UK branch or agency.
S. 21–34: general meaning of "disposal" and "assets".
S. 272–274 and Sch. 11: meaning of "market value".
S. 275: location of assets.
S. 288: interpretation, including meaning of "company" and reference to sections being those of this Act.
Commonwealth Development Corporation Act 1999 Sch. 3 para 3(4)(b): disapplication of s. 179 where the Corporation ceases to be resident in the UK within a certain time folowing its exempt period.

186 Deemed disposal of assets on company ceasing to be liable to UK taxation

186 [Repealed by FA 1994, s. 251(9) and Sch. 26, Pt. VIII(1).]

History – S. 186 repealed by FA 1994, s. 251(9) and s. 258 and Sch. 26, Pt. VIII(1) with effect where the company concerned becomes on or after 30 November 1993 a company which falls to be regarded as mentioned in s. 186(1).
As it continues to have effect (e.g. for the purposes of s. 187(3)), s. 186(1) provides as follows:
"**186(1)** This section and section 187 apply to a company if, at any time (**"the relevant time"**), the company, while continuing to be resident in the United Kingdom, becomes a company which falls to be regarded for the purposes of any double taxation relief arrangements–

(a) as resident in a territory outside the United Kingdom; and

(b) as not liable in the United Kingdom to tax on gains arising on disposals of assets of descriptions specified in the arrangements (**"prescribed assets"**).

186(2) The company shall be deemed for all purposes of this Act –

(a) to have disposed of all its prescribed assets immediately before the relevant time; and

(b) immediately to have reacquired them,

at their market value at that time.

186(3) Section 152 shall not apply where the new assets are prescribed assets and the company–

(a) has disposed of the old assets, or of its interest in those assets, before the relevant time; and

(b) acquires the new assets, or its interest in those assets, after that time,

and in this section **"the old assets"** and **"the new assets"** have the same meaning as in section 152.".

Derivations – FA 1988, s. 106.

Cross references – S. 152: roll-over relief on replacement of business assets.

Notes – S. 9: meaning of **"resident"**.

S. 10: extent of charge on non-resident by reference to assets used or held for a UK branch or agency.

S. 21–34: general meaning of **"disposal"** and **"assets"**.

S. 272–274 and Sch. 11: meaning of **"market value"**.

S. 288: interpretation, including meaning of **"company"**, **"double taxation relief arrangements"** and reference to sections being those of this Act.

187 Postponement of charge on deemed disposal under section 185 or 186

187(1) If–

(a) immediately after the relevant time, a company to which this section applies by virtue of section 185 (**"the company"**) is a 75 per cent subsidiary of another company (**"the principal company"**) which is resident in the United Kingdom; and

(b) the principal company and the company so elect, by notice given to the inspector within 2 years after that time,

this Act shall have effect in accordance with the following provisions.

187(2) Any allowable losses accruing to the company on a deemed disposal of foreign assets shall be set off against the chargeable gains so accruing and–

(a) that disposal shall be treated as giving rise to a single chargeable gain equal to the aggregate of those gains after deducting the aggregate of those losses; and

(b) the whole of that gain shall be treated as not accruing to the company on that disposal but an equivalent amount (**"the postponed gain"**) shall be brought into account in accordance with subsections (3) and (4) below.

187(3) If at any time within 6 years after the relevant time the company disposes of any assets (**"relevant assets"**) the chargeable gains on which were taken into account in arriving at the postponed gain, there shall be deemed to accrue to the principal company as a chargeable gain on that occasion the whole or the appropriate proportion of the postponed gain so far as not already taken into account under this subsection or subsection (4) below.

In this subsection **"the appropriate proportion"** means the proportion which the chargeable gain taken into account in arriving at the postponed gain in respect of the part of the relevant assets disposed of bears to the aggregate of the chargeable gains so taken into account in respect of the relevant assets held immediately before the time of the disposal.

187(4) If at any time after the relevant time–

(a) the company ceases to be a 75 per cent subsidiary of the principal company on the disposal by the principal company of ordinary shares of the company;

(b) after the company has ceased to be such a subsidiary otherwise than on such a disposal, the principal company disposes of such shares; or

(c) the principal company ceases to be resident in the United Kingdom,

there shall be deemed to accrue to the principal company as a chargeable gain on that occasion the whole of the postponed gain so far as not already taken into account under this subsection or subsection (3) above.

187(5) If at any time–

(a) the company has allowable losses which have not been allowed as a deduction from chargeable gains; and

(b) a chargeable gain accrues to the principal company under subsection (3) or (4) above,

then, if and to the extent that the principal company and the company so elect by notice given to the inspector within 2 years after that time, those losses shall be allowed as a deduction from that gain.

187(6) In this section–

"deemed disposal" means a disposal which, by virtue of section 185(2) is deemed to have been made;

"foreign assets" means any assets of the company which, immediately after the relevant time, are situated outside the United Kingdom and are used in or for the purposes of a trade carried on outside the United Kingdom;

"ordinary share" means a share in the ordinary share capital of the company;

"the relevant time" has the meaning given by section 185(1).

187(7) For the purposes of this section a company is a **75 per cent subsidiary** of another company if and so long as not less than 75 per cent of its ordinary share capital is owned directly by that other company.

History – In s. 187(1)(a), the words "or 186" which appeared after "section 185" omitted by FA 1994, s. 251(9) and s. 258 and Sch. 26, Pt. VIII(1) with effect where a company becomes, on or after 30 November 1993, a company which falls to be regarded as mentioned in s. 186(1).

In s. 187(6), in the definition of "deemed disposal" and "the relevant time" respectively, the words "or, as the case may be, section 186(2)" and "or, as the case may be, section 186(1)" which appeared after "185(2)" and "185(1)" respectively omitted by FA 1994, s. 251(9) and s. 258 and Sch. 26, Pt. VIII(1) with effect where a company becomes, on or after 30 November 1993, a company which falls to be regarded as mentioned in s. 186(1).

Derivations – (as originally enacted) – FA 1988, s. 107.

Cross references – FA 1994, s. 249: companies treated as resident in the UK for tax purposes, but resident abroad for the purposes of any double taxation relief arrangements ("dual resident companies"), are with effect from 30 November 1993 to be treated as non-UK resident for all tax purposes, even if they are incorporated in the UK.

Notes – S. 9: meaning of "resident".
S. 15: meaning of "chargeable gains".
S. 16: meaning of "allowable losses".
S. 21–34: general meaning of "disposal" and "assets", including the timing of certain disposals.
S. 275: location of assets.
S. 276: UK territorial sea is part of the UK.
S. 288: interpretation, including "inspector" as being any inspector of taxes, "notice" as being in writing and reference to sections being those of this Act.

187A Deemed disposal under section 185: ATED-related gains and losses

187A(1) This section applies if–

(a) (ignoring subsections (2) and (3)) a gain or loss would accrue to a company on a disposal of an asset deemed to have been made by virtue of section 185(2), and

(b) that gain or loss is an ATED-related gain chargeable to, or an ATED-related loss allowable for the purposes of, capital gains tax under section 2B.

187A(2) That gain or loss does not accrue to the company on that disposal.

187A(3) But, on a subsequent disposal of the whole or part of the asset, the whole or a corresponding part of the gain or loss–

(a) is deemed to accrue to the company (in addition to any gain or loss that actually accrues on that subsequent disposal), and

(b) (if that would not otherwise be the case) is to be treated as an ATED-related gain or loss accruing on a relevant high value disposal.

187A(4) Nothing in this section affects the treatment, for the purposes of this Act, of any gain or loss which is not ATED-related and accrues on the disposal of the asset deemed to have been made by virtue of section 185(2).

History – S. 187A inserted by FA 2013, s. 65 and Sch. 25, para. 13, with effect in relation to disposals occurring on or after 6 April 2013.

187B Deemed disposal of UK residential property interest under section 185

187B(1) This section applies if, ignoring subsections (3) and (4)–

(a) a gain or loss would accrue to a company on a disposal of a UK residential property interest deemed to have been made by virtue of section 185(2), and

(b) on the assumptions in subsection (2), that gain or loss would be an NRCGT gain chargeable to, or an NRCGT loss allowable for the purposes of, capital gains tax by virtue of section 14D or 188D (see section 57B and Schedule 4ZZB).

187B(2) The assumptions are that–

(a) the disposal is a non-resident CGT disposal, and

(b) any claim which the company could make under section 14F is made.

187B(3) No gain or loss accrues to the company on that disposal.

187B(4) But, on a subsequent disposal of the whole or part of the interest in UK land which is the subject of the disposal mentioned in subsection (1)(a), the whole or a corresponding part of the gain or loss which would have accrued to the company were it not for subsection (3)–

(a) is deemed to accrue to the company (in addition to any gain or loss that actually accrues on that subsequent disposal), and

(b) (if that would not otherwise be the case) is to be treated as an NRCGT gain chargeable to, or an NRCGT loss allowable for the purposes of, capital gains tax by virtue of section 14D accruing on a non-resident CGT disposal.

187B(5) A company may make an election for subsections (3) and (4) not to apply in relation to the disposal mentioned in subsection (1)(a).

187B(6) Such an election must be made within 2 years after the day on which the company ceases to be resident in the United Kingdom.

187B(7) In this section, **"interest in UK land"** has the meaning given by paragraph 2 of Schedule B1.

History – S. 187B inserted by FA 2015, s. 37 and Sch. 7, para. 29 with effect in relation to disposals made on or after 6 April 2015.

188 Dual resident companies: deemed disposal of certain assets

188 [Repealed by FA 1994, s. 251(10) and s. 258 and Sch. 26, Pt. VIII(1) with effect from 30 November 1993.]

POOLING OF NRCGT GAINS AND LOSSES

188A Election for pooling

188A(1) A **"pooling election"** is an election which–

(a) specifies the date from which the election is to have effect (the "effective date" of the election), and

(b) is made by all those members of a group (the "potential pooling group") which are qualifying members.

188A(2) For this purpose the **"qualifying members"** of a group are all the companies which are members of that group and meet the qualifying conditions on the effective date of the election.

188A(3) The **"qualifying conditions"** are met by a company at any time when it–

(a) is not resident in the United Kingdom,

(b) is a closely-held company,

(c) is not a company carrying on life assurance business (as defined in section 56 of the Finance Act 2012),

(d) does not hold any chargeable residential assets, and

(e) holds an asset the disposal of which would be a disposal of a UK residential property interest.

188A(4) For the purposes of subsection (3), an asset is a **"chargeable residential asset"** at any time if a disposal of the asset at that time would be a non-resident CGT disposal but for section 14B(5) (gains forming part of chargeable profits for corporation tax purposes by virtue of section 10B etc) or section 14B(6) (gains on certain disposals treated as trading profits).

188A(5) The day on which a pooling election is made must not be later than the 30th day after the day specified as its effective date.

188A(6) A pooling election is irrevocable.

188A(7) In this section–

"closely-held company" is to be interpreted in accordance with Part 1 of Schedule C1;

"group" is to be interpreted in accordance with section 170.

History – In s. 188A(4), the words "or section 14B(6) (gains on certain disposals treated as trading profits)" inserted by FA 2016, s. 77(10), with effect from 15 September 2016 (Royal Assent).
S. 188A inserted by FA 2015, s. 37 and Sch. 7, para. 30, with effect in relation to disposals made on or after 6 April 2015.

188B Meaning of "NRCGT group"

188B(1) The companies which make a pooling election form an NRCGT group.

188B(2) An NRCGT group continues to exist as long as at least one member of the NRCGT group continues to be a member of the potential pooling group and to meet the conditions in paragraphs (a) to (d) of section 188A(3).

188B(3) See also section 188F (companies becoming eligible to join NRCGT group) and section 188G (company ceasing to be a member of an NRCGT group).

History – S. 188B inserted by FA 2015, s. 37 and Sch. 7, para. 30, with effect in relation to disposals made on or after 6 April 2015.

188C Transfers within an NRCGT group

188C(1) *This section applies* where a company ("company A") makes a non-resident CGT disposal to another company ("company B") at a time when both companies are members of the same NRCGT group.

188C(2) In subsections (3) to (5) **"the asset"** means the asset which is the subject of that disposal.

188C(3) For the relevant purposes (see subsection (4))–

(a) company A's acquisition of the asset is treated as company B's acquisition of the asset,

(b) everything done by company A in relation to the asset in the period of company A's ownership of the asset is accordingly treated as done by company B, and

(c) the disposal mentioned in subsection (1) is accordingly disregarded.

188C(4) The **"relevant purposes"** means the purposes of–

(a) the determination of whether or not an NRCGT gain or loss accrues on the disposal mentioned in subsection (1) or any subsequent disposal of the asset;

(b) the determination of the amount of any such gain or loss;

(c) the treatment for capital gains tax purposes of any such gain or loss.

188C(5) Accordingly, references in subsection (3) to an acquisition made by, or anything else done by, company A include anything that company A is treated as having done as a result of the application of this section in relation to an earlier disposal of the asset.

188C(6) Nothing in this section affects the treatment of the disposal in question for any other purposes (including the computation of any gains or losses, other than NRCGT gains or losses, that may accrue on the disposal).

History – S. 188C inserted by FA 2015, s. 37 and Sch. 7, para. 30, with effect in relation to disposals made on or after 6 April 2015.

188D Person chargeable to capital gains tax on NRCGT gains accruing to members of an NRCGT group

188D(1) The relevant body for a tax year ("year Y") of an NRCGT group (see subsection (4)) is chargeable to capital gains tax in respect of chargeable NRCGT gains accruing to members of the group in the tax year on non-resident CGT disposals (and section 14D(1) does not apply to such gains).

188D(2) Capital gains tax is charged on the total amount of chargeable NRCGT gains accruing in year Y to members of the NRCGT group, after deducting–

(a) any allowable NRCGT losses accruing in year Y to any member of the NRCGT group,

(b) so far as they have not been allowed as a deduction from chargeable gains accruing in any previous tax year, any allowable NRCGT losses which in any previous tax year (not earlier than the tax year 2015–16) accrued to any member of the NRCGT group, and

(c) so far as they have not been allowed as a deduction from chargeable gains accruing in any previous tax year, any allowable losses (not falling within paragraph (b)) on disposals of UK residential property interests which in any previous tax year (not earlier than the tax year 1965–66) accrued to any company which is, at any time in year Y, a member of the NRCGT group.

188D(3) The only deductions that can be made in calculating the total amount of chargeable NRCGT gains accruing as mentioned in subsection (2) are those permitted by this section.

188D(4) The **"relevant body"** of an NRCGT group for a tax year is the body constituted by all the companies which are members of that NRCGT group at any time in that tax year.

188D(5) This Act and the Management Act have effect with any modifications that may be necessary in relation to cases where the relevant body of an NRCGT group is chargeable to capital gains tax in accordance with this section.

History – S. 188D inserted by FA 2015, s. 37 and Sch. 7, para. 30, with effect in relation to disposals made on or after 6 April 2015.

188E Further provision about group losses

188E(1) Relief is not to be given under this Act more than once in respect of a group loss or any part of a group loss.

188E(2) Relief is not to be given under this Act in respect of a group loss if, and so far as, relief has been or may be given in respect of it under the Tax Acts.

188E(3) No relief is to be given otherwise than in accordance with this section for group losses.

188E(4) In this section **"group loss"** means an NRCGT loss accruing to a member of an NRCGT group.

History – S. 188E inserted by FA 2015, s. 37 and Sch. 7, para. 30, with effect in relation to disposals made on or after 5 April 2015.

188F Companies becoming eligible to join an NRCGT group

188F(1) A company which is not a member of an NRCGT group and is eligible to become a member of that group may elect to do so.

188F(2) A company is eligible to become a member of an NRCGT group at any time when it–

(a) is a member of the potential pooling group, and

(b) meets the qualifying conditions.

But see subsections (3) and (4).

188F(3) Subsection (4) applies if, throughout a period of 12 months, a company–

(a) holds a UK residential asset, and

(b) is eligible to become a member of an NRCGT group.

188F(4) If the company has not elected to become a member of the NRCGT group by the end of that period of 12 months, the company is not eligible to become a member of the NRCGT group at any time after the end of that period of 12 months.

188F(5) The effect of subsection (4) in relation to a company expires if at any time the company–

(a) no longer holds the whole or part of any UK residential asset that was held by the company at any time in the 12 month period referred to in subsection (3), but

(b) holds another UK residential asset.

188F(6) For the purposes of this section a person holds a **"UK residential asset"** at any time when the person holds an interest in UK land the disposal of which would be a disposal of a UK residential property interest.

History – S. 188F inserted by FA 2015, s. 37 and Sch. 7, para. 30, with effect in relation to disposals made on or after 6 April 2015.

188G Company ceasing to be a member of an NRCGT group

188G(1) A company ceases to be a member of an NRCGT group if it ceases–

(a) to be a member of the potential pooling group, or

(b) to meet the any of the conditions in paragraphs (a) to (d) of section 188A(3).

188G(2) Where a company ceases to be a member of an NRCGT group, the company is treated for the purposes of this Act and the Management Act as having–

(a) disposed of the relevant assets immediately before the company ceased to be a member of the NRCGT group, and

(b) immediately re-acquired them,

at their market value at that time.

188G(3) References in subsection (2) to a company ceasing to be a member of an NRCGT group do not apply to cases where a company ceases to be a member of the potential pooling group in consequence of another member of that group ceasing to exist.

188G(4) Subsection (2) does not apply in a case where all the companies which are members of an NRCGT group cease to be members of that NRCGT group by reason only of an event which causes–

(a) the principal company of the potential pooling group to cease to be a closely-held company, or

(b) the head of a sub-group of which they are members, to cease to be a closely-held company or to become a member of another group (as defined in section 170).

188G(5) Subsection (2) does not apply where a company which is a member of an NRCGT group ceases to be a member of the potential pooling group by reason only of the fact that the principal company of the potential pooling group becomes a member of another group (as defined in section 170).

188G(6) In subsection (2) **"the relevant assets"** means any assets the company holds immediately before it ceases to be a member of the NRCGT group the disposal of which would be a disposal of a UK residential property interest (see Schedule B1).

188G(7) For the purposes of this section–

"sub-group" means anything that would be a group (as defined in section 170) in the absence of subsections (4) and (6) of section 170;

the **"head"** of a sub-group is the company which is not a 75% subsidiary of any other member of the sub-group;

references to the **"principal company"** of the potential pooling group are to be interpreted in accordance with section 170.

History – S. 188G inserted by FA 2015, s. 37 and Sch. 7, para. 30, with effect in relation to disposals made on or after 6 April 2015.

188H The responsible members of an NRCGT group

188H(1) Anything required or authorised to be done under this Act or the Management Act by or in relation to the relevant body of an NRCGT group is required or authorised to be done by or in relation to all the responsible members of that NRCGT group for that tax year.

188H(2) The "responsible members" of an NRCGT group for a tax year are–

(a) all the companies which are members of the NRCGT group at any time in that tax year, and

(b) any companies which have subsequently become members of the NRCGT group.

188H(3) This section is subject to section 188J (representative company).

History – S. 188H inserted by FA 2015, s. 37 and Sch. 7, para. 30, with effect in relation to disposals made on or after 6 April 2015.

188I Joint and several liability of responsible members

188I Where the responsible members of an NRCGT group are liable, in connection with their responsibility under section 188H to make a payment of tax or interest on unpaid tax, or pay any other amount, that liability is a joint and several liability of those responsible members.

History – S. 188I inserted by FA 2015, s. 37 and Sch. 7, para. 30, with effect in relation to disposals made on or after 6 April 2015.

188J The representative company of an NRCGT group

188J(1) Anything required or authorised to be done under this Act or the Management Act by or in relation to the relevant body of an NRCGT group may instead be done by or in relation to the company which is for the time being the representative company of the group.

188J(2) This includes the making of the declaration required by section 9(2) or 12ZB(4)(b) of the Management Act (declaration that return is correct and complete).

188J(3) The **"representative company"** means a member of the NRCGT group nominated by all the members of that group for the purposes of this section.

188J(4) A nomination under subsection (3), or the revocation of such a nomination, has effect only after written notice of the nomination or revocation has been given to an officer of Revenue and Customs.

History – S. 188J inserted by FA 2015, s. 37 and Sch. 7, para. 30, with effect in relation to disposals made on or after 6 April 2015.

188K Interpretation of sections 188A to 188J

188K(1) In sections 188A to 188J–

(a) references to the "relevant body" of an NRCGT group are to be interpreted in accordance with section 188D(4);

(b) references to an NRCGT gain or loss accruing to a member of an NRCGT group are to such a gain or loss accruing to a company at a time when the company is a member of the NRCGT group.

188K(2) In sections 188A to 188J and this section–

"company" is to be interpreted in accordance with section 170(9);

"interest in UK land" has the same meaning as in Schedule B1;

"pooling election" has the meaning given by section 188A(1);

"potential pooling group", in relation to an NRCGT group, is to be interpreted in accordance with section 188A(1)(b);

"qualifying conditions" has the meaning given by section 188A(3).

History – S. 188K inserted by FA 2015, s. 37 and Sch. 7, para. 30, with effect in relation to disposals made on or after 6 April 2015.

RECOVERY OF TAX OTHERWISE THAN FROM TAX-PAYER COMPANY

189 Capital distribution of chargeable gains: recovery of tax from shareholder

189(1) This section applies where a person who is connected with a company resident in the United Kingdom receives or becomes entitled to receive in respect of shares in the company any capital distribution from the company, other than a capital distribution representing a reduction of capital, and–

(a) the capital so distributed derives from the disposal of assets in respect of which a chargeable gain accrued to the company; or

(b) the distribution constitutes such a disposal of assets;

and that person is referred to below as **"the shareholder"**.

189(2) If the corporation tax assessed on the company for the accounting period in which the chargeable gain accrues included any amount in respect of chargeable gains, and any of the tax assessed on the company for that period is not paid within 6 months from the date determined under subsection (3) below, the shareholder may by an assessment made within 2 years from that date be assessed and charged (in the name of the company) to an amount of that corporation tax–

(a) not exceeding the amount or value of the capital distribution which the shareholder has received or become entitled to receive; and

(b) not exceeding a proportion equal to the shareholder's share of the capital distribution made by the company of corporation tax on the amount of that gain at the rate in force when the gain accrued.

189(3) The date referred to in subsection (2) above is whichever is the later of–

(a) the date when the tax becomes due and payable by the company; and

(b) the date when the assessment was made on the company.

189(4) Where the shareholder pays any amount of tax under this section, he shall be entitled to recover from the company a sum equal to that amount together with any interest paid by him under section 87A of the Management Act on that amount.

189(5) The provisions of this section are without prejudice to any liability of the shareholder in respect of a chargeable gain accruing to him by reference to the capital distribution as constituting a disposal of an interest in shares in the company.

189(6) With respect to chargeable gains accruing in accounting periods ending on or before such day as the Treasury may by order appoint this section shall have effect–

(a) with the substitution for the words in subsection (3) after "above" of the words "is the date when the tax becomes payable by the company"; and

(b) with the omission of the words in subsection (4) from "together" to the end of the subsection.

189(7) In this section **"capital distribution"** has the same meaning as in section 122.

History – In s. 189(3), the words "is the date when the tax becomes payable by the company" are substituted for the words "is whichever is the later of–

(a) the date when the tax becomes due and payable by the company; and

(b) the date when the assessment was made on the company"

by TCGA 1992, s. 189(6)(a) with respect to chargeable gains accruing in accounting periods ending **on or before** the day appointed by order of the Treasury; 30 September 1993 is the day appointed by the Treasury under article 2 of the Order that may be cited as SI 1992/3066 and that was made on 7 December 1992.

In s. 189(4), the words "together with any interest paid by him under section 87A of the Management Act on that amount" are omitted by TCGA 1992, s. 189(6)(b) with respect to chargeable gains accruing in accounting periods ending **on or before** the day appointed by order of the Treasury; 30 September 1993 is the day appointed by the Treasury under article 2 of the Order that may be cited as SI 1992/3066 and that was made on 7 December 1992.

Derivations – ICTA 1988, s. 346.

Cross references – S. 122: a distribution, including one in the course of dissolving or winding up, in money or money's worth represents a part disposal unless it is taxable as income.
TMA 1970, s. 87A: interest on unpaid corporation tax under Pay and File.

Statutory instruments – SI 1992/3066: the day appointed for the purposes of s. 189 was 30 September 1993 (the day appointed for Pay and File).

Notes – S. 9: meaning of "resident".
S. 21–34: general meaning of "disposal" and "assets".
S. 286: "connected" in references to persons being connected with one another.
S. 287: power of Treasury exercisable by statutory instrument but not subject to the negative resolution procedure of the House of Commons.
S. 288: interpretation, including meaning of "company", the "Management Act" as TMA 1970 and reference to sections being those of this Act.
ICTA 1988, s. 10: time for payment of corporation tax.
ICTA 1988, s. 12: meaning of "accounting period".
TMA 1970, s. 29: assessing procedure.

190 Tax recoverable from another group company or controlling director

190(1) This section applies where–

(a) a chargeable gain has accrued to a company ("the taxpayer company"),

(b) the condition in subsection (2) below is met, and

(c) the whole or part of the corporation tax assessed on the company for the accounting period in which the gain accrued ("the relevant accounting period") is unpaid at the end of the period of six months after it became payable.

190(2) The condition referred to in subsection (1)(b) above is–

(a) that the taxpayer company is resident in the United Kingdom at the time when the gain accrued, or

(b) that the gain forms part of the taxpayer company's chargeable profits for corporation tax purposes by virtue of section 10B.

190(3) The following persons may, by notice under this section, be required to pay the unpaid tax–

(a) if the taxpayer company was a member of a group at the time when the gain accrued–

(i) a company which was at the time the principal company of the group, and

(ii) any other company which in any part of the period of 12 months ending with that time was a member of that group and owned the asset disposed of, or any part of it, or where that asset is an interest or right in or over another asset, owned either asset or any part of either asset; and

(b) if the gain forms part of the chargeable profits of the taxpayer company for corporation tax purposes by virtue of section 10B, any person who is, or during that period of twelve months ending with the time when the gain accrued was, a controlling director of the taxpayer company or of a company which has, or within that period had, control over the taxpayer company.

190(4) The Board may serve a notice on a person within subsection (3) above requiring him, within 30 days of the service of the notice, to pay–

(a) the amount which remains unpaid of the corporation tax assessed on the taxpayer company for the relevant accounting period, or

(b) if less, an amount equal to corporation tax on the amount of the chargeable gain at the rate in force when the gain accrued.

190(5) The notice must state–

(a) the amount of corporation tax assessed on the taxpayer company for the relevant accounting period that remains unpaid,

(b) the date when it first became payable, and

(c) the amount required to be paid by the person on whom the notice is served.

190(6) The notice has effect–

(a) for the purposes of the recovery from that person of the amount required to be paid and of interest on that amount, and

(b) for the purposes of appeals,

as if it were a notice of assessment and that amount were an amount of tax due from that person.

190(7) Any notice under this section must be served before the end of the period of three years beginning with the date on which the liability of the taxpayer company to corporation tax for the relevant accounting period is finally determined.

190(8) Where the unpaid tax is charged in consequence of a determination under paragraph 36 or 37 of Schedule 18 to the Finance Act 1998 (determination where no return delivered or return incomplete), the date mentioned in subsection (7) above shall be taken to be the date on which the determination was made.

190(9) Where the unpaid tax is charged in a self-assessment, including a self-assessment that supersedes a determination (see paragraph 40 of Schedule 18 to the Finance Act 1998), the date mentioned in subsection (7) above shall be taken to be the latest of–

(a) the last date on which notice of enquiry may be given into the return containing the self-assessment;

(b) if notice of enquiry is given, 30 days after the enquiry is completed;

(c) if more than one notice of enquiry is given, 30 days after the last notice of completion;

(d) if after such an enquiry the Inland Revenue amend the return, 30 days after notice of the amendment is issued;

(e) if an appeal is brought against such an amendment, 30 days after the appeal is finally determined.

190(10) If the unpaid tax is charged in a discovery assessment, the date mentioned in subsection (7) above shall be taken to be–

(a) where there is no appeal against the assessment, the date when the tax becomes due and payable;

(b) where there is such an appeal, the date on which the appeal is finally determined.

190(11) A person who has paid an amount in pursuance of a notice under this section may recover that amount from the taxpayer company.

190(12) A payment in pursuance of a notice under this section is not allowed as a deduction in computing any income, profits or losses for any tax purposes.

190(13) In this section–

"director", in relation to a company, has the meaning given by section 67(1) and (2) of ITEPA 2003 and includes any person falling within section 452(1) of CTA 2010;

"controlling director", in relation to a company, means a director of the company who has control of it (construing control in accordance with sections 450 and 451 of CTA 2010);

"group" and

"principal company" have the meaning which would be given by section 170 if in that section for references to 75 per cent. subsidiaries there were substituted references to 51 per cent. subsidiaries.

History – In s. 190(2)(b), the reference "10B" substituted for the reference "10(3)" by FA 2003, s. 155 and Sch. 27, para. 2(3) which have effect in relation to accounting periods beginning on or after 1 January 2003.

In s. 190(3)(b), the reference "10B" substituted for the reference "10(3)" by FA 2003, s. 155 and Sch. 27, para. 2(3) which have effect in relation to accounting periods beginning on or after 1 January 2003.

In s. 190(13), the definition of "director" substituted by CTA 2010, s. 1177 and Sch. 1, para. 246(a), with effect for corporation tax purposes for accounting periods ending on or after 1 April 2010, and for income tax and capital gains tax purposes for the tax year 2010–11 and subsequent tax years.

In s. 190(13), in the definition of "controlling director", the words "sections 450 and 451 of CTA 2010" substituted for "section 416 of the Taxes Act" by CTA 2010, s. 1177 and Sch. 1, para. 246(b), with effect for corporation tax purposes for accounting periods ending on or after 1 April 2010, and for income tax and capital gains tax purposes for the tax year 2010–11 and subsequent tax years.

S. 190 substituted for former s. 190 and 191 by FA 2000, s. 102 and Sch. 29, para. 9(1) with effect in relation to gains accruing on or after 1 April 2000.

Derivations – ICTA 1988, s. 347.

Cross references – TMA 1970, s. 87A: interest on unpaid corporation tax.

Notes – S. 21–34: general meaning of "disposal" and "assets".
S. 288: interpretation, including meaning of "company", the "Management Act" as TMA 1970 and reference to sections being those of this Act.
ICTA 1988, s. 10: time for payment of corporation tax.
ICTA 1988, s. 12: meaning of "accounting period".
TMA 1970, s. 29: assessing procedure.

191 Tax on non-resident company recoverable from another member of group or from controlling director

191 [Superseded by s. 190 as substituted by FA 2000, s. 102 and Sch. 29, para. 9(1).]

History – S. 191 superseded by s. 190 as substituted by FA 2000, s. 102 and Sch. 29, para. 9(1) with effect in relation to gains accruing on or after 1 April 2000.

DEMERGERS

192 Tax exempt distributions

192(1) This section has effect for facilitating certain transactions whereby trading activities carried on by a single company or group are divided so as to be carried on by 2 or more companies not belonging to the same group or by 2 or more independent groups.

192(2) Where a company makes a distribution which is exempt by virtue of section 1076 of CTA 2010–

(a) the distribution shall not be a capital distribution for the purposes of section 122; and

(b) sections 126 to 130 shall, with the necessary modifications, apply as if that company and the subsidiary whose shares are transferred were the same company and the distribution were a reorganisation of its share capital.

192(3) Subject to subsection (4) below, section 179 shall not apply in a case where a company ceases to be a member of a group by reason only of an exempt distribution.

192(4) Subsection (3) does not apply if within 5 years after the making of the exempt distribution there is chargeable payment; and the time for making an assessment under 179 by virtue of this subsection shall not expire before the end of 3 years after the making of the chargeable payment.

192(5) In this section–

"chargeable payment" has the meaning given in section 1088 of CTA 2010;

"exempt distribution" means a distribution which is exempt by virtue of section 1076 or 1077 of CTA 2010; and

"group" means a company which has one or more 75 per cent subsidiaries together with that or those subsidiaries.

192(6) In determining for the purposes of this section whether one company is a 75 per cent subsidiary of another, the other company shall be treated as not being the owner of–

(a) any share capital which it owns directly in a body corporate if a profit on a sale of the shares would be treated as a trading receipt of its trade; or

(b) any share capital which it owns indirectly and which is owned directly by a body corporate for which a profit on the sale of the shares would be a trading receipt.

History – In s. 192(2), the words "a distribution which is exempt by virtue of section 1076 of CTA 2010" substituted for "an exempt distribution which falls within section 213(3)(a) of the Taxes Act" by CTA 2010, s. 1177 and Sch. 1, para. 247(2), with effect for corporation tax purposes for accounting periods ending on or after 1 April 2010, and for income tax and capital gains tax purposes for the tax year 2010–11 and subsequent tax years.
In s. 192(3)(b), words "section 179 shall not" substituted for "neither section 178 nor section 179 shall", and in s. 178(4) reference to s. 178 repealed, by FA 2000, s. 102 and Sch. 29, para 29, s. 156 and Sch. 40, Pt. II(12).
In s. 192(5), in the definition of "chargeable payment", the words "section 1088 of CTA 2010" substituted for "section 214(2) of the Taxes Act" by CTA 2010, s. 1177 and Sch. 1, para. 247(3)(a), with effect for corporation tax purposes for accounting periods ending on or after 1 April 2010, and for income tax and capital gains tax purposes for the tax year 2010–11 and subsequent tax years.
In s. 192(5), in the definition of "exempt distribution", the words "section 1076 or 1077 of CTA 2010" substituted for "section 213(2) of that Act" by CTA 2010, s. 1177 and Sch. 1, para. 247(3)(b), with effect for corporation tax purposes for accounting periods ending on or after 1 April 2010, and for income tax and capital gains tax purposes for the tax year 2010–11 and subsequent tax years.

Derivations – FA 1980, s. 117, Sch. 18, para. 9, 10, 15, 23(1), (3).

Cross references – S. 122: a capital distribution represents a part disposal unless it is taxable as income.
S. 126–130: equation of original and new holdings on a reorganisation and treatment of other consideration given or received.
ICTA 1988, s. 213(3)(a): on a demerger, an exempt distribution consisting of the transfer to all or any of its members by a company of shares in one or more companies which are its 75 per cent subsidiaries.
ICTA 1988, s. 214(2): following an exempt distribution on a demerger, a chargeable payment is determined by reference to a share-related payment to avoid tax or otherwise than for bona fide commercial reasons to a member of that company or another company concerned and which is not a distribution, an exempt distribution or an intra-group payment.

Statements of practice – 13/80: clarification of demerger provisions and clearance procedure.

Notes – S. 288: interpretation, including meaning of "company", the "Taxes Act" as ICTA 1988 and reference to other sections being those of this Act.

DISPOSALS BY COMPANIES WITH SUBSTANTIAL SHAREHOLDING

192A Exemptions for gains or losses on disposal of shares etc

192A Schedule 7AC (exemptions for disposal of shares etc by companies with substantial shareholding) has effect.

History – S. 192A added by FA 2002, s. 44(1), with effect in relation to disposals on or after 1 April 2002 (FA 2002 s. 44(3)).

Chapter II – Oil and Mining Industries

OIL EXPLORATION AND EXPLOITATION

193 Roll-over relief not available for gains on oil licences

193 [Repealed by FA 1999, s. 103, s. 139 and Sch. 20, Pt. IV(2).]

History – S. 193 repealed by FA 1999, s. 103, s. 139 and Sch. 20, Pt. IV(2), with effect in relation to–

(a) a disposal of a licence or an interest in a licence which occurs on or after 1 July 1999;

(b) an acquisition of a licence or an interest in a licence which occurs on or after 1 July 1999.

Derivations – F(No. 2)A 1987, s. 80.

Cross references – S. 155: classes of asset eligible for roll-over relief on replacement of business assets.

Notes – S. 288: interpretation, including reference to other sections being those of this Act.

194 Disposals of oil licences relating to undeveloped areas

194(1) In this section any reference to a disposal (including a part disposal) is a reference to a disposal made by way of a bargain at arm's length.

194(2) If, at the time of the disposal, the licence relates to an undeveloped area, then, to the extent that the consideration for the disposal consists of–

(a) another licence which at that time relates to an undeveloped area or an interest in another such licence, or

(b) an obligation to undertake exploration work or appraisal work in an area which is or forms part of the licensed area in relation to the licence disposed of,

the value of that consideration shall be treated as nil for the purposes of this Act.

194(3) If the disposal of a licence which, at the time of the disposal, relates to an undeveloped area is part of a larger transaction under which one party makes to another disposals of 2 or more licences, each of which at the time of the disposal relates to an undeveloped area, the reference in subsection (2)(b) above to the licensed area in relation to the licence disposed of shall be construed as a reference to the totality of the licensed areas in relation to those 2 or more licences.

194(4) In relation to a disposal of a licence which, at the time of the disposal, relates to an undeveloped area, being a disposal–

(a) which is a part disposal of the licence in question, and

(b) part but not the whole of the consideration for which falls within paragraph (a) or paragraph (b) of subsection (2) above,

section 42 shall not apply unless the amount or value of the part of the consideration which does not fall within one of those paragraphs is less than the aggregate of the amounts which, if the disposal were a disposal of the whole of the licence rather than a part disposal, would be–

(i) the relevant allowable expenditure, as defined in section 53; and

(ii) the indexation allowance on the disposal.

194(5) Where section 42 has effect in relation to such a disposal as is referred to in subsection (4) above, it shall have effect as if, for subsection (2) thereof, there were substituted the following subsection–

"**42(2)** The apportionment shall be made by reference to–

(a) the amount or value of the consideration for the disposal on the one hand (call that amount or value A), and

(b) the aggregate referred to in section 194(4) on the other hand (call that aggregate C),

and the fraction of the said sums allowable as a deduction in computing the amount of the gain (if any) accruing on the disposal shall be–

$$\frac{A}{C}$$

and the remainder shall be attributed to the part of the property which remains undisposed of."

Derivations – FA 1988, s. 62.

Cross references – S. 42: apportionment of base cost on a part disposal.
S. 53: relevant allowable expenditure eligible for indexation allowance determined by reference to the acquisition cost, including incidental costs and enhancement or title expenditure.

Notes – S. 15: except as otherwise specified, any gain is a chargeable gain.
S. 21–34: general meaning of "disposal".
S. 288: interpretation, including reference to other sections being those of this Act.

195 Allowance of certain drilling expenditure etc.

195(1) On the disposal of a licence, relevant qualifying expenditure incurred by the person making the disposal–

(a) in searching for oil anywhere in the licensed area, or

(b) in ascertaining the extent or characteristics of any oil-bearing area the whole or part of which lies in the licensed area or what the reserves of oil of any such oil-bearing area are,

shall be treated as expenditure falling within section 38(1)(b).

195(2) Expenditure incurred as mentioned in subsection (1) above is relevant expenditure if, and only if–

(a) it is expenditure of a capital nature on research and development; and

(b) either it is expenditure in respect of which the person was entitled to an allowance under section 441 of the Capital Allowances Act (research and development allowances) for a relevant chargeable period which began before the date of the disposal or it would have been such expenditure if the trading condition had been fulfilled, and

(c) on the disposal, section 443 of that Act (disposal values) applies in relation to the expenditure or would apply if the trading condition had been fulfilled (and the expenditure had accordingly been qualifying expenditure under Part 6 of that Act).

195(3) In subsection (2) above and subsection (4) below, the expression "if the trading condition had been fulfilled" means, in relation to expenditure of a capital nature on research and development, if, after the expenditure was incurred but before the disposal concerned was made, the person incurring the expenditure had set up and commenced a trade connected with that research and development; and in subsection (2)(b) above–

"relevant chargeable period" has the same meaning as in section 441 of the Capital Allowances Act;

195(4) Relevant expenditure is qualifying expenditure only to the extent that it does not exceed the disposal value which, by reason of the disposal–

(a) is required to be bought into account under section 443 of the Capital Allowances Act; or

(b) would be required to be so bought into account if the trading condition had been fulfilled (and the expenditure had accordingly been qualifying expenditure under Part 6 of that Act).

195(5) [Repealed by CAA 2001, s. 578 and Sch. 2, para. 79 and s. 580 and Sch. 4.]

195(6) Where, on the disposal of a licence, subsection (1) above has effect in relation to any relevant qualifying expenditure in respect of which the person had not in fact been entitled to an allowance as mentioned in subsection (2)(b) above–

(a) no allowance shall be made in respect of that expenditure under section 441 of the Capital Allowances Act;

(b) [Repealed by CAA 2001, s. 578 and Sch. 2, para. 79 and s. 580 and Sch. 4.]

195(7) Where, on the disposal of a licence which is a part disposal, subsection (1) above has effect in relation to any relevant qualifying expenditure, then, for the purposes of section 42, that expenditure shall be treated as wholly attributable to what is disposed of (and, accordingly, shall not be apportioned as mentioned in that section).

195(8) In this section **"research and development"** has the same meaning as in Part 6 of the Capital Allowances Act (research and development allowances).

History – *S. 195(2)(b), (c), substituted by* CAA 2001, s. 578 and Sch. 2, para. 79, with effect as respects allowances and charges falling to be made for chargeable periods ending, for income tax purposes, on or after 6 April 2001, and for corporation tax purposes, on or after 1 April 2001.
In s. 195(2) and (3) words "research and development" substituted for "scientific research" and words "and development" inserted by FA 2000, s. 68 and Sch. 19, para. 12(2), (3), with effect for 2000-01 and subsequent years of assessment and for accounting periods ending on or after 1 April 2000.

In s. 195(3) reference to CAA 2001, s. 441, substituted by CAA 2001, s. 578 and Sch. 2, para. 79 with effect as respects allowances and charges falling to be made for chargeable periods ending, for income tax purposes, on or after 6 April 2001, and for corporation tax purposes, on or after 1 April 2001.
In s. 195(3) words from "basis year" to the end, and the word "and" before the definition, repealed by CAA 2001, s. 578 and Sch. 2, para. 79 and s. 580 and Sch. 4, with effect as respects allowances and charges falling to be made for chargeable periods ending, for income tax purposes, on or after 6 April 2001, and for corporation tax purposes, on or after 1 April 2001.
In s. 195(4) words "disposal value" substituted for the words "trading receipt" and para. (a) and (b) substituted by CAA 2001, s. 578 and Sch. 2, para. 79 with effect as respects capital allowances falling to be made for chargeable periods ending on or after 1 April 2001.
S. 195(5) repealed by CAA 2001, s. 578 and Sch. 2, para. 79 and s. 580 and Sch. 4, with effect as respects allowances and charges falling to be made for chargeable periods ending, for income tax purposes, on or after 6 April 2001, and for corporation tax purposes, on or after 1 April 2001.
In s. 195(6) words "in respect of which the person had not in fact been entitled to an allowance" substituted for the words "which had not in fact been allowed or become allowable", and words "section 441 of the Capital Allowances Act" substituted for "section 137 of the 1990 Act" by CAA 2001, s. 578 and Sch. 2, para. 79, with effect as respects allowances and charges falling to be made for chargeable periods ending, for income tax purposes, on or after 6 April 2001, and for corporation tax purposes, on or after 1 April 2001.
S. 195(6)(b) and the word "and" before it, repealed by CAA 2001, s. 578 and Sch. 2, para. 79 and s. 580 and Sch. 4, with effect as respects allowances and charges falling to be made for chargeable periods ending, for income tax purposes, on or after 6 April 2001, and for corporation tax purposes, on or after 1 April 2001.
In s. 195(8) words "Part 6 of the Capital Allowances Act (research and development allowances)" substituted for the words "Part VII of the Capital Allowances Act 1990 (allowances for researchand development expenditure)", by CAA 2001, s. 578 and Sch. 2, para. 79, with effect as respects allowances and charges falling to be made for chargeable periods ending, for income tax purposes, on or after 6 April 2001, and for corporation tax purposes, on or after 1 April 2001.
S. 195(8) inserted by FA 2000, s. 68 and Sch. 19, para. 12(4) with effect for 2000-01 and subsequent years of assessment and for accounting periods ending on or after 1 April 2000.

Derivations – FA 1988, s. 63.

Cross references – S. 37: amounts taken into account in the making of balancing charges are not excluded from the consideration for a disposal by virtue of being chargeable to tax as income.
S. 38(1)(b): allowable enhancement or title expenditure.
S. 41: restriction of allowable losses by reference to amounts qualifying for capital allowances.
S. 42: apportionment of base cost on a part disposal to the part disposed of and the remainder.
CAA 1990, s. 137, 138: allowance for capital expenditure on scientific research in taxing a trade by reference to the accounting period in which the expenditure was incurred or the tax year during the income tax basis period for which it was incurred (except as adjusted for commencement and cessation) and clawback by way of trading receipt where the asset ceases to belong to the taxpayer in point.

Notes – S. 21–34: general meaning of "disposal", including the timing of certain disposals.
S. 288: interpretation, including reference to other sections as being those of this Act.

195A Oil licence swaps

195A(1) Sections 195B to 195F apply for the purposes of corporation tax on chargeable gains.

195A(2) In those sections–

"licence-consideration swap" means a case where conditions A, B, C and D are met;

"mixed-consideration swap" means a case where conditions A, B, C and E are met.

195A(3) Condition A is that a company ("company A") disposes of one or more UK licences to another company ("company B"), by way of a bargain at arm's length ("disposal A").

195A(4) Condition B is that company B disposes of one or more UK licences to company A, by way of a bargain at arm's length ("disposal B").

195A(5) Condition C is that either or both of the following paragraphs applies–

(a) the licence, or at least one of the licences, comprised in disposal A relates to a developed area;

(b) the licence, or at least one of the licences, comprised in disposal B relates to a developed area.

195A(6) Condition D is that both–

(a) disposal A is the only consideration given for disposal B, and

(b) disposal B is the only consideration given for disposal A.

195A(7) Condition E is that either–

(a) disposal A is the only consideration given for disposal B, or

(b) disposal B is the only consideration given for disposal A,

(and accordingly one of the disposals is part of the consideration given for the other disposal).

195A(8) In this section and sections 195B to 196 a reference to disposal of a UK licence includes–

(a) a disposal of an interest in a UK licence, and

(b) a disposal of a UK licence, or an interest in a UK licence, only so far as the licence relates to part of the licensed area.

History – In s. 195A(1), the word "195F" substituted for the word "195E" by FA 2011, s. 64 and Sch. 15, para. 1, with effect in relation to disposals made on or after 23 March 2011.
S. 195A inserted by FA 2009, s. 86 and Sch. 40, para. 5, with effect in relation to disposals made on or after 22 April 2009.

195B Licence-consideration swap

195B(1) This section applies to a licence-consideration swap.

195B(2) Each company participating in the swap is to be treated as follows.

195B(3) As regards the licence, or each licence, which the company disposes of, the company is to be treated as if it had disposed of that licence for a consideration of such amount as to secure that on the disposal neither a gain nor a loss accrues to the company.

195B(4) In a case where the company acquires only one licence, the company is to be treated as if it had acquired the licence for a consideration of the same amount as the deemed disposal consideration.

195B(5) In a case where the company acquires two or more licences, as regards each licence acquired, the company is to be treated as if it had acquired that licence for a consideration of–

$$DDC \times \frac{A}{TA}$$

where–

DDC is the deemed disposal consideration;

A is the value of the licence acquired;

TA is total value of all the licences acquired.

195B(6) In this section **"deemed disposal consideration"**, in relation to a company participating in the swap, means–

(a) the amount of the consideration for which the company is, under subsection (3), treated as having disposed of its licence (if the company disposes of only one licence), or

(b) the aggregate of all such amounts (if the company disposes of two or more licences).

History – S. 195B inserted by FA 2009, s. 86 and Sch. 40, para. 5, with effect in relation to disposals made on or after 22 April 2009.

195C Company that receives mixed consideration: N exceeds C

195C(1) This section applies to a mixed-consideration swap if–

(a) the no gain/no loss amount ("N") of the company that receives the mixed consideration ("company R") exceeds

(b) the amount of non-licence consideration ("C") which company R receives.

195C(2) In a case where company R acquires only one licence, company R is to be treated as if it had acquired the licence for a consideration of–

$$N - C$$

195C(3) In a case where company R acquires two or more licences, as regards each licence acquired, company R is to be treated as if it had acquired the licence for a consideration of–

$$(N - C) \times \frac{A}{TA}$$

where–

A is the value of the licence acquired;

TA is total value of all the licences acquired.

195C(4) The disposal by company R of a licence under the swap is to be taken to be one on which neither a gain nor a loss accrues.

195C(5) But (despite subsection (4)), the disposal by company R is not a no gain/no loss disposal for the purposes of section 56.

195C(6) For the purposes of the application of sections 53 and 54, any enactment is to be disregarded insofar as it provides that, if the other company which acquires a licence under the swap ("company G") subsequently disposes of the licence, company R's acquisition of the licence is to be treated as company G's acquisition of it.

195C(7) In this section the reference to the no gain/no loss amount of company R is a reference to–

(a) in a case where company R disposes of only one licence, company R's no gain/no loss amount in relation to that disposal, or

(b) in a case where company R disposes of two or more licences, the aggregate of company R's no gain/no loss amounts in relation to all of those disposals.

History – S. 195C inserted by FA 2009, s. 86 and Sch. 40, para. 5, with effect in relation to disposals made on or after 22 April 2009.

195D Company that receives mixed consideration: N does not exceed C

195D(1) This section applies to a mixed-consideration swap if–

(a) the no gain/no loss amount ("N") of the company that receives the mixed consideration ("company R") does not exceed

(b) the amount of non-licence consideration ("C") which company R receives.

195D(2) As regards the licence, or each licence, which company R acquires, company R is to be treated as if it had acquired the licence for nil consideration.

195D(3) In a case where company R disposes of only one licence, company R is to be treated as if, on the disposal of the licence, there had arisen a gain of–

$$C - N$$

195D(4) In a case where company R disposes of two or more licences, as regards each licence disposed of, company R is to be treated as if, on the disposal of the licence, there had arisen a gain of–

$$(C - N) \times \frac{D}{TD}$$

where–

D is the value of the licence disposed of;

TD is total value of all the licences disposed of.

History – S. 195D inserted by FA 2009, s. 86 and Sch. 40, para. 5, with effect in relation to disposals made on or after 22 April 2009.

195E Company that gives mixed consideration

195E(1) This section applies to a mixed-consideration swap–

(a) whatever the no gain/no loss amount ("N") of the company that gives the mixed consideration ("company G"), and

(b) whatever the amount of the non-licence consideration ("C") which company G gives.

195E(2) In a case where company G acquires only one licence, company G is to be treated as if it had acquired the licence for a consideration of–

$$N + C$$

195E(3) In a case where company G acquires two or more licences, as regards each licence acquired, company G is to be treated as if it had acquired the licence for a consideration of–

$$(N + C) \times \frac{A}{TA}$$

where–

A is the value of the licence acquired;

TA is total value of all the licences acquired.

195E(4) The disposal by company G of a licence under the swap is to be taken to be one on which neither a gain nor a loss accrues.

195E(5) But (despite subsection (4)), the disposal by company G is not a no gain/no loss disposal for the purposes of section 56.

195E(6) For the purposes of the application of sections 53 and 54, any enactment is to be disregarded insofar as it provides that, if the other company which acquires a licence under the swap ("company R") subsequently disposes of the licence, company G's acquisition of the licence is to be treated as company R's acquisition of it.

195E(7) In this section the reference to the no gain/no loss amount of company G is a reference to–

(a) in a case where company G disposes of only one licence, company G's no gain/no loss amount in relation to that disposal, or

(b) in a case where company G disposes of two or more licences, the aggregate of company G's no gain/no loss amounts in relation to all of those disposals.

History – S. 195E inserted by FA 2009, s. 86 and Sch. 40, para. 5, with effect in relation to disposals made on or after 22 April 2009.

195F Reimbursed expenditure

195F(1) This section applies if–

(a) expenditure is incurred by company A or company B (see section 195A) on a licence disposed of by it under a licence-consideration swap or mixed-consideration swap,

(b) the expenditure is incurred before the disposal,

(c) the expenditure falls within section 38(1)(b), and

(d) the expenditure is reimbursed or effectively reimbursed (whether by way of adjustment of the non-licence consideration (if any) or otherwise) by the company ("the other company") to whom the disposal is made (whether before, on or after the date of the disposal).

195F(2) The expenditure is to be treated for the purposes of this Act as expenditure–

(a) incurred by the other company on the licence immediately after the disposal, and

(b) which falls within section 38(1)(b).

History – S. 195F inserted by FA 2011, s. 64 and Sch. 15, para. 2, with effect in relation to disposals made on or after 23 March 2011.

196 Interpretation of sections 194 to 195F

History – In the heading to s. 196 , "to 195E" substituted for "and 195" by FA 2009, s. 86 and Sch. 40, para. 6(2), with effect in relation to disposals made on or after 22 April 2009.

196(1) For the purposes of section 194 and this section, a UK licence relates to an undeveloped area at any time if–

(a) for no part of the licensed area has consent for development been granted to the licensee by the Oil and Gas Authority on or before that time; and

(b) for no part of the licensed area has a programme of development been served on the licensee or approved by the Oil and Gas Authority on or before that time.

196(1A) For the purposes of section 194 a licence other than a UK licence relates to an undeveloped area at any time if, at that time–

(a) no development has actually taken place in any part of the licensed area; and

(b) no condition for the carrying out of development anywhere in that area has been satisfied–

(i) by the grant of any consent by the authorities of a country or territory exercising jurisdiction in relation to the area; or

(ii) by the approval or service on the licensee, by any such authorities, of any programme of development.

196(1B) In sections 195A to 195F, a reference to a UK licence that relates to a developed area is a reference to any UK licence apart from one that relates to an undeveloped area.

196(2) Subsections (4) and (5) of section 36 of the Finance Act 1983 (meaning of "development") shall have effect in relation to subsections (1) to (1B) above as they have effect in relation to subsection (2) of that section.

196(3) In relation to a licence under the Petroleum (Production) Act (Northern Ireland) 1964 any reference in subsection (1) or (1B) above to the Oil and Gas Authority shall be construed as a reference to the Department of Economic Development.

196(4) In relation to a disposal to which section 194 applies of a licence under which the buyer acquires an interest in the licence only so far as it relates to part of the licensed area, any reference in subsection (1) or subsection (3) of that section or subsection (1) above to the licensed area shall be construed as a reference only to that part of the licensed area to which the buyer's acquisition relates.

196(5) In sections 194 to 195F and this section–

"foreign oil concession" means any right to search for or win overseas petroleum, being a right conferred or exercisable (whether or not by virtue of a licence) in relation to a particular area;

"interest" in relation to a licence, includes, where there is an agreement which–

(a) relates to oil from the whole or any part of the licensed area, and

(b) was made before the extraction of the oil to which it relates,

any entitlement under that agreement to, or to a share of, either that oil or the proceeds of its sale;

"licence" means any UK licence or foreign oil concession;

"licence-consideration swap" has the meaning given in section 195A(2);

"licensed area" (subject to subsection (4) above)–

(a) in relation to a UK licence, has the same meaning as in Part I of the Oil Taxation Act 1975; and

(b) in relation to a foreign oil concession, means the area to which the concession applies;

"licensee"–

(a) in relation to a UK licence, has the same meaning as in Part I of the Oil Taxation Act 1975; and

(b) in relation to a foreign oil concession, means the person with the concession or any person having an interest in it;

"mixed consideration" means consideration that consists partly of disposal of a UK licence;

"mixed-consideration swap" has the meaning given in section 195A(2);

"no gain/no loss amount", in relation to a company that disposes of a UK licence, means the amount that would be taken to be the consideration for the disposal if section 56(2) applied to the disposal;

"non-licence consideration" means consideration that does not consist of disposal of a UK licence;

"oil"–

(a) except in relation to a UK licence, means any petroleum (within the meaning of the Petroleum (Production) Act 1934); and

(b) in relation to such a licence, has the same meaning as in Part I of the Oil Taxation Act 1975;

"overseas petroleum" means any oil that exists in its natural condition at a place to which neither the Petroleum (Production) Act 1934 nor the Petroleum (Production) Act (Northern Ireland) 1964 applies; and

"swap arrangements", in relation to a licence-consideration swap or a mixed-consideration swap, means the arrangements under which the swap takes place;

"UK licence" means a licence within the meaning of Part I of the Oil Taxation Act 1975.

196(5A) References in sections 194 and 195 to a part disposal of a licence shall include references to the disposal of any interest in a licence.

196(5B) Subsections (5C) to (5F) apply for the purposes of sections 195A to 195F.

196(5C) Any determination–

(a) of the consideration given for disposal A or disposal B,

(b) of the non-licence consideration, or

(c) of the value of a licence comprised in disposal A or disposal B,

is to be made as at the time the swap arrangements are entered into. But this is subject to subsections (5D) to (5F).

196(5D) Subsections (5E) and (5F) apply if, under the swap arrangements, economic benefits and liabilities under the licences concerned are treated as passing at a time ("the effective time") which falls before or after the day on which the arrangements are entered into.

196(5E) Any determination–

(a) of the consideration given for disposal A or disposal B,

(b) of the non-licence consideration, or

(c) of the value of a licence comprised in disposal A or disposal B,

is to be made as at the effective time.

196(5F) But if the swap arrangements make provision for an increase in the non-licence consideration to reflect the period between the effective time and the time it is payable, the non-licence consideration is to be treated as if it were the amount found by making a corresponding increase in the amount determined under subsection (5E).

196(6) In section 194–

(a) **"exploration work"**, in relation to any area, means work carried out for the purpose of searching for oil anywhere in that area;

(b) **"appraisal work"**, in relation to any area, means work carried out for the purpose of ascertaining the extent or characteristics of any oil-bearing area the whole or part of which lies in the area concerned or what the reserves of oil of any such oil-bearing area are.

History – In the heading to s. 196, the word "195F" substituted for the word "195E" by FA 2011, s. 64 and Sch. 15, para. 3(2), with effect in relation to disposals made on or after 23 March 2011.

In s. 196(1), the words "Oil and Gas Authority" substituted for the words "Secretary of State" by SI 2016/898, reg. 12, with effect from 1 October 2016 (as the 21st day after being made on 10 September 2016).

In s. 196(1), the words "and this section" inserted by FA 2009, s. 86 and Sch. 40, para. 6(3), with effect in relation to disposals made on or after 22 April 2009.

In s. 196(1) reference to "UK licence" substituted; s. 196(1A), and reference to it in s. 196(2) inserted; and s. 196(5), (5A) substituted for former s. 196(5) by FA 1996, s. 181, in relation to any disposal on or after 13 September 1995 and the substitution of s. 196(5), (5A) is deemed always to have had effect, for the construction of s. 195 and its predecessors in its application to disposals before that date.

S. 196(1A) inserted by FA 2009, s. 86 and Sch. 40, para. 6(4), with effect in relation to disposals made on or after 22 April 2009.

In s. 196(1B), the word "195F" substituted for the word "195E" by FA 2011, s. 64 and Sch. 15, para. 3(3), with effect in relation to disposals made on or after 23 March 2011.

In s. 196(2), "to (1B)" substituted for "and (1A)" by FA 2009, s. 86 and Sch. 40, para. 6(5), with effect in relation to disposals made on or after 22 April 2009.

In s. 196(3), the words "Oil and Gas Authority" substituted for the words "Secretary of State" by SI 2016/898, reg. 12, with effect from 1 October 2016 (as the 21st day after being made on 10 September 2016).

In s. 196(3), "or (1B)" inserted by FA 2009, s. 86 and Sch. 40, para. 6(6), with effect in relation to disposals made on or after 22 April 2009.
In s. 196(5), the word "195F" substituted for the word "195E" and the words "as determined at the time the swap arrangements are entered into" omitted from the definition of "non-licence consideration" by FA 2011, s. 64 and Sch. 15, para. 3(4), with effect in relation to disposals made on or after 23 March 2011.
In s. 196(5), "to 195E" substituted for "and 195" by FA 2009, s. 86 and Sch. 40, para. 6(7)(a), with effect in relation to disposals made on or after 22 April 2009.
In s. 196(5), the definition of "licence-consideration swap" inserted by FA 2009, s. 86 and Sch. 40, para. 6(7)(b), with effect in relation to disposals made on or after 22 April 2009.
In s. 196(5), the definition of "mixed consideration" inserted by FA 2009, s. 86 and Sch. 40, para. 6(7)(c), with effect in relation to disposals made on or after 22 April 2009.
In s. 196(5), the definition of "mixed-consideration swap" inserted by FA 2009, s. 86 and Sch.40, para. 6(7)(c), with effect in relation to disposals made on or after 22 April 2009.
In s. 196(5), the definition of "no gain/no loss amount" inserted by FA 2009, s. 86 and Sch. 40, para. 6(7)(c), with effect in relation to disposals made on or after 22 April 2009.
In s. 196(5), the definition of "non-licence consideration" inserted by FA 2009, s. 86 and Sch. 40, para. 6(7)(c) with effect in relation to disposals made on or after 22 April 2009.
In s. 196(5), the definition of "swap arrangements" inserted by FA 2009, s. 86 and Sch. 40, para. 6(7)(c), with effect in relation to disposals made on or after 22 April 2009. Note that CCH has inserted this definition in its correct alphabetical location rather than after the definition of "non-licence consideration" as required by the amending provision.
S. 196(5B)–(5F) substituted for former s. 196(5B) by FA 2011, s. 64 and Sch. 15, para. 3(5), with effect in relation to disposals made on or after 23 March 2011.
Former s. 196(5B) inserted by FA 2009, s. 86 and Sch. 40, para. 6(8), with effect in relation to disposals made on or after 22 April 2009.

Derivations – FA 1988, s. 64.

Cross references – FA 1983, s. 36(4), (5): for petroleum revenue tax, "development" is defined by reference to the winning of oil or erection or carrying out of certain permanent works for getting oil or conveying oil won.
OTA 1975, s. 12(1): definitions of "oil", "licence" and cognate expressions by reference to substances other than methane gas won in the course of operations for making and keeping mines safe and licences authorising the winning thereof.

Notes – S. 288: interpretation, including reference to sections other than those separately identified as being those of this Act.

197 Disposals of interests in oil fields etc.: ring fence provisions

197(1) This section applies where in pursuance of a transfer by a participator in an oil field of the whole or part of his interest in the field, there is–

(a) a disposal of an interest in oil to be won from the oil field; or

(b) a disposal of an asset used in connection with the field;

and section 12 of the Oil Taxation Act 1975 (interpretation of Part I of that Act) applies for the interpretation of this subsection and the reference to the transfer by a participator in an oil field of the whole or part of his interest in the field shall be construed in accordance with paragraph 1 of Schedule 17 to the Finance Act 1980.

197(2) In this section **"material disposal"** means–

(a) a disposal falling within paragraph (a) or paragraph (b) of subsection (1) above; or

(b) the sale of an asset referred to in section 179(3) where the asset was acquired by the chargeable company (within the meaning of that section) on a disposal falling within one of those paragraphs.

197(3) For any chargeable period in which a chargeable gain or allowable loss accrues to any person (**"the chargeable person"**) on a material disposal (whether taking place in that period or not), subject to subsection (6) below there shall be aggregated–

(a) the chargeable gains accruing to him in that period on such disposals, and

(b) the allowable losses accruing to him in that period on such disposals,

and the lesser of the 2 aggregates shall be deducted from the other to give an aggregate gain or, as the case may be, an aggregate loss for that chargeable period.

197(4) For the purposes of tax in respect of chargeable gains–

(a) the several chargeable gains and allowable losses falling within paragraphs (a) and (b) of subsection (3) above shall be left out of account; and

(b) the aggregate gain or aggregate loss referred to in that subsection shall be treated as a single chargeable gain or allowable loss accruing to the chargeable person in the chargeable period concerned on the notional disposal of an asset; and

(c) if in any chargeable period there is an aggregate loss, then, except as provided by subsection (5) below, it shall not be allowable as a deduction against any chargeable gain arising in that or any later period, other than an aggregate gain treated as accruing in a later period by virtue of paragraph (b) above (so that the aggregate gain of that later period shall be reduced or extinguished accordingly); and

(d) if in any chargeable period there is an aggregate gain, no loss shall be deducted from it except in accordance with paragraph (c) above; and

(e) without prejudice to any indexation allowance which was taken into account in determining an aggregate gain or aggregate loss under subsection (3) above, no further indexation allowance shall be allowed on a notional disposal referred to in paragraph (b) above.

197(5) In any case where–

(a) by virtue of subsection (4)(b) above, an aggregate loss is treated as accruing to the chargeable person in any chargeable period, and

(b) before the expiry of the period of 2 years beginning at the end of the chargeable period concerned, the chargeable person makes a claim under this subsection,

the whole, or such portion as is specified in the claim, of the aggregate loss shall be treated for the purposes of this Act as an allowable loss arising in that chargeable period otherwise than on a material disposal.

197(6) In any case where a loss accrues to the chargeable person on a material disposal made to a person who is connected with him–

(a) the loss shall be excluded from those referred to in paragraph (b) of subsection (3) above and, accordingly, shall not be aggregated under that subsection; and

(b) except as provided by subsection (7) below, section 18 shall apply in relation to the loss as if, in subsection (3) of that section, any reference to a disposal were a reference to a disposal which is a material disposal; and

(c) to the extent that the loss is set against a chargeable gain by virtue of paragraph (b) above, the gain shall be excluded from those referred to in paragraph (a) of subsection (3) above and, accordingly, shall not be aggregated under that subsection.

197(7) In any case where–

(a) the losses accruing to the chargeable person in any chargeable period on material disposals to a connected person exceed the gains accruing to him in that chargeable period on material disposals made to that person at a time when they are connected persons, and

(b) before the expiry of the period of 2 years beginning at the end of the chargeable period concerned, the chargeable person makes a claim under this subsection,

the whole, or such part as is specified in the claim, of the excess referred to in paragraph (a) above shall be treated for the purposes of section 18 as if it were a loss accruing on a disposal in that chargeable period, being a disposal which is not a material disposal and which is made by the chargeable person to the connected person referred to in paragraph (a) above.

197(8) Where a claim is made under subsection (5) or subsection (7) above, all such adjustments shall be made whether by way of discharge or repayment of tax or otherwise, as may be required in consequence of the operation of that subsection.

History – In s. 197(2)(b) words "178 or" repealed by FA 2000, s. 156 and Sch. 40 Pt. II(12) with effect in relation to companies which left a group during an accounting period ending after 30 September 1993.

Derivations – FA 1984, s. 79(1)–(4), (6)–(9).

Cross references – S. 18(3): loss accruing on a disposal to a connected person only to be deductible from a chargeable gain on a disposal to the same person.
S. 179(3): crystallisation of gain where company leaves a group with an asset transferred intra-group.
ICTA 1988, s. 502(1A): ring fence profits by reference to inclusion of ring fence net gains.
OTA 1975, s. 12: interpretation, including meaning of "oil", "oil field", "participator" and "asset used in connection with the field".
FA 1980, Sch. 17, para. 1: there is a transfer by a participator of an interest in an oil field when a share in the oil to be won and saved becomes the share of another person who is or becomes a participator, except on a re-determination under a unitisation agreement or certain agreements between associated companies.

Notes – S. 15: meaning of "chargeable gains".
S. 16: meaning of "allowable losses".
S. 21–34: general meaning of "disposal".
S. 286: "connected" in references to persons being connected with one another.
S. 288: interpretation, including "chargeable period" as an accounting period or tax year and reference to sections being those of this Act.
TMA 1970, s. 42–43B: procedures for making claims.

198 Replacement of business assets used in connection with oil fields

198(1) If the consideration which a person obtains on a material disposal is applied, in whole or in part, as mentioned in subsection (1) of section 152 or 153, that section shall not apply unless the new assets are taken into use, and used only, for the purposes of the ring fence trade.

198(2) Subsection (1) above has effect notwithstanding subsection (8) of section 152.

198(2A) But subsection (1) is subject to section 198A(3)(a).

198(3) Where–

(a) section 152 or 153 applies in relation to any of the consideration on a material disposal, and

(b) the asset which constitutes the new assets for the purposes of that section is a depreciating asset, section 154(2)(b) is to have effect as if the reference to a trade carried on by the claimant were a reference solely to the claimant's ring fence trade.

198(4) In any case where sections 152 to 154 have effect in accordance with subsections (1) to (3) above, the operation of section 175 shall be modified as follows–

(a) only those members of a group which actually carry on a ring fence trade shall be treated for the purposes of those sections as carrying on a single trade which is a ring fence trade; and

(b) only those activities which, in relation to each individual member of the group, constitute its ring fence trade shall be treated as forming part of that single trade.

198(5) In this section–

(a) **"material disposal"** has the meaning assigned to it by section 197; and

(b) **"ring fence trade"** means a trade consisting of activities falling within the definition of "oil-related activities" in section 16(2) of ITTOIA 2005 or section 274 of CTA 2010.

History – S. 198(2A) inserted by FA 2009, s. 86 and Sch. 40, para. 11, with effect in relation to disposals made on or after 22 April 2009 (whether the acquisition in which the consideration is reinvested takes place before, on or after that date).
S. 198(3) substituted by FA 2009, s. 86 and Sch. 40, para. 10, with effect in relation to disposals made on or after 22 April 2009 (whether the acquisition in which the consideration is reinvested takes place before, on or after that date).
In s. 198(5)(b), the words "activities falling within the definition of "oil-related activities" in section 16(2) of ITTOIA 2005 or section 274 of CTA 2010" substituted for the words "either or both of the activities mentioned in paragraphs (a) and (b) of subsection (1) of section 492 of the Taxes Act or defined as **"oil-related activities"** in section 16(2) of ITTOIA 2005" by CTA 2010, s. 1177 and Sch. 1, para. 248, with effect for corporation tax purposes for accounting periods ending on or after 1 April 2010, and for income tax and capital gains tax purposes for the tax year 2010–11 and subsequent tax years.
In s. 198(5)(b), words "or defined as **"oil-related activities"** in section 16(2) of ITTOIA 2005" inserted by ITTOIA 2005, s. 882 and Sch. 1, para. 440 which, in accordance with ITTOIA 2005, s. 883, have effect, for income tax purposes, for tax year 2005–06 and subsequent tax years, and, for corporation tax purposes, for accounting periods ending after 5 April 2005.

Derivations – FA 1984, s. 80.

Cross references – S. 152–154: roll-over relief on replacement of business assets, including (s. 152(8)) application to person who carries on multiple trades as if they were one and (s. 154(2)(b), (4)–(7)) crystallisation of held-over gain where depreciating asset ceases to be used for a trade purpose, substitution of roll-over claim for hold-over claim and definition of depreciating asset.
S. 175: group trades treated as one for roll-over relief on replacement of business assets.
S. 179B(2), (4) and Sch. 7AB, para. 9: modification of s. 198 where roll-over relief claimed where company treated by virtue of s. 179(3) or s. 179(6) as having sold and immediately re-acquired an asset at market value.
ICTA 1988, s. 492(1)(a), (b): oil extraction activities and the acquisition, enjoyment or exploitation of oil rights.

Notes – S. 288: interpretation, including the "Taxes Act" as ICTA 1988 and reference to other sections as being those of this Act.

198A Ring fence reinvestment: whole consideration reinvested

198A(1) This section applies if a person ("P") makes a disposal and acquisition which–

(a) is a ring fence reinvestment, and

(b) qualifies for roll-over relief.

198A(2) P may make a claim under this section in relation to the disposal and acquisition.

198A(3) If P makes a claim under this section–

(a) section 152 does not apply to any of the disposal consideration, and

(b) any gain accruing to P on the disposal is not a chargeable gain.

198A(4) In this section **"disposal consideration"** means the whole of the consideration obtained on the disposal made by P.

History – S. 198A inserted by FA 2009, s. 86 and Sch. 40, para. 12, with effect in relation to disposals made on or after 22 April 2009 (whether the acquisition in which the consideration is reinvested takes place before, on or after that date).

198B Ring fence reinvestment: part of consideration reinvested

198B(1) This section applies if a person ("P") makes a disposal and acquisition which–

(a) is a ring fence reinvestment, and

(b) qualifies for section 153 relief.

198B(2) P may make a claim under this section in relation to the disposal and acquisition.

198B(3) If P makes a claim under this section–

(a) section 153(1)(a) applies in relation to P and the disposal, but

(b) section 153(1)(b) does not apply to P and the acquisition.

History – S. 198B inserted by FA 2009, s. 86 and Sch. 40, para. 12, with effect in relation to disposals made on or after 22 April 2009 (whether the acquisition in which the consideration is reinvested takes place before, on or after that date).

198C Provisional application of sections 198A and 198B

198C(1) This section applies where a person ("P") carrying on a ring fence trade who for a consideration disposes of, or of an interest in, any assets ("the old assets") declares, in P's return for the chargeable period in which the disposal takes place–

(a) that the whole or any specified part of the consideration will be applied in the acquisition of, or of an interest in, other assets ("the new assets"),

(b) that the acquisition will take place as mentioned in section 152(3),

(c) that the disposal and acquisition will be a ring fence reinvestment,

(d) that P intends to make a claim under section 198A or 198B in relation to the disposal and acquisition, and

(e) that P has not made, and will not make, a declaration under section 153A in relation to the disposal and acquisition.

198C(2) Until the declaration ceases to have effect, section 198A or 198B applies as if the acquisition had taken place and the person had made a claim under that section.

198C(3) The declaration ceases to have effect as follows–

(a) if and to the extent that it is withdrawn before the relevant day, or is superseded before that day by a valid claim made under section 198A or 198B, on the day on which it is so withdrawn or superseded, and

(b) if and to the extent that it is not so withdrawn or superseded, on the relevant day.

198C(4) On the declaration ceasing to have effect in whole or in part, all necessary adjustments–

(a) are to be made by making or amending assessments or by repayment or discharge of tax, and

(b) are to be so made despite any limitation on the time within which assessments or amendments may be made.

198C(5) If–

(a) P makes a declaration under this section, and

(b) the disposal and acquisition is not a ring fence reinvestment, but qualifies for roll-over relief or section 153 relief,

on P making a claim, the declaration is to have effect as also a declaration under section 153A.

198C(6) In this section **"the relevant day"** means–

(a) in relation to capital gains tax, the third anniversary of the 31st January next following the year of assessment in which the disposal of, or of the interest in, the old assets took place, and

(b) in relation to corporation tax, the fourth anniversary of the last day of the accounting period in which that disposal took place.

198C(7) Section 152(6), (10) and (11) apply for the purposes of this section as they apply for the purposes of section 152.

History – S. 198C inserted by FA 2009, s. 86 and Sch. 40, para. 12, with effect in relation to disposals made on or after 22 April 2009 (whether the acquisition in which the consideration is reinvested takes place before, on or after that date).

198D No double claims

198D(1) If P makes a claim under section 198A or 198B, no other relevant claim may be made in respect of the relevant acquisition.

198D(2) P may make a claim under section 198A or 198B ("the new claim"), if P has previously made a claim under section 152 or 153 ("the previous claim") in respect of the relevant acquisition.

198D(3) But P may make the new claim only if the previous claim is withdrawn at or before the time the new claim is made.

198D(4) If the new claim is made in accordance with subsections (2) and (3), all necessary adjustments–

(a) are to be made by making or amending assessments or by repayment or discharge of tax, and

(b) are to be so made despite any limitation on the time within which assessments or amendments may be made.

198D(5) In this section–

"relevant acquisition" means the acquisition of the new assets that is comprised in the disposal and acquisition to which a claim under section 198A or 198B or declaration under section 198C relates;

"relevant claim" means a claim under section 152, 153, 198A or 198B.

History – S. 198D inserted by FA 2009, s. 86 and Sch. 40, para. 12, with effect in relation to disposals made on or after 22 April 2009 (whether the acquisition in which the consideration is reinvested takes place before, on or after that date).

198E Ring fence reinvestments and disposal consideration

198E(1) This section applies for the purposes of sections 198A to 198G.

198E(2) A disposal and acquisition is a ring fence reinvestment if–

(a) the disposal was–

(i) a material disposal, or

(ii) a disposal of a UK licence which relates to an undeveloped area,

(b) the old assets were used only for the purposes of P's ring fence trade,

(c) the new assets are taken into use, and used only, for one or more of the following trades–

(i) P's ring fence trade;

(ii) if P is a member of a group of companies (within the meaning given in section 170), a ring fence trade of another member of that group, and

(d) the new assets are oil assets.

198E(3) If the disposal consists of–

(a) disposal of a licence to which section 195D(3) applies, or

(b) disposal of two or more licences to which section 195D(4) applies,

the consideration for the disposal is to be taken to be the whole of the non-licence consideration obtained on the disposal (which is referred to as "C" in section 195D).

198E(4) Accordingly, in sections 198A to 198G (including section 198A(4)), any reference to the consideration obtained on the disposal has effect subject to subsection (2A).

198E(5) Each of the following is an **"oil asset"** for the purposes of this section–

(a) an interest in oil to be won from an oil field,

(b) an asset used in connection with an oil field,

(c) a structure which is to be placed on the seabed of the United Kingdom continental shelf,

(d) an asset used wholly in the winning of oil, or in the measuring of oil won, in the United Kingdom otherwise than from an oil field,

(e) an asset used for the initial treatment or storage of oil in the United Kingdom,

(f) an asset used for the transportation of oil from an oil field to the United Kingdom, and

(g) a UK licence which relates to an undeveloped area.

198E(6) Section 12 of the Oil Taxation Act 1975 (interpretation of Part 1 of that Act) applies for the interpretation of subsection (3)(a) to (f).

198E(7) Expressions used in this section and in section 152 have the same meanings in this section as in section 152.

198E(8) In this section a reference to a UK licence which relates to an undeveloped area has the same meaning as in section 194 (see section 196).

198E(9) In this section–

"material disposal" has the meaning given in section 197;

"ring fence trade" has the meaning given in section 198.

History – S. 198E inserted by FA 2009, s. 86 and Sch. 40, para. 12, with effect in relation to disposals made on or after 22 April 2009 (whether the acquisition in which the consideration is reinvested takes place before, on or after that date).

198F Qualification for roll-over relief

198F(1) This section applies for the purposes of sections 198A and 198B and section 198G.

198F(2) A disposal and acquisition qualifies for roll-over relief if–

(a) the consideration for the disposal is applied in an acquisition as mentioned in section 152(1), and

(b) section 152(1)(a) and (b) would apply to the disposal and acquisition if the appropriate claim were made.

198F(3) Subsections (4) to (6) apply in deciding whether a disposal and acquisition is one that qualifies for roll-over relief.

198F(4) Section 152(8) is to be disregarded.

198F(5) Section 198A is to be disregarded.

198F(6) Subject to subsections (4) to (5), all the circumstances are to be taken into account, including section 153(1) and section 198(1) and (2).

History – S. 198F inserted by FA 2009, s. 86 and Sch. 40, para. 12, with effect in relation to disposals made on or after 22 April 2009 (whether the acquisition in which the consideration is reinvested takes place before, on or after that date).

198G Qualification for section 153 relief

198G(1) This section applies for the purposes of sections 198B and 198C.

198G(2) A disposal and acquisition qualifies for section 153 relief if–

(a) section 153(1) applies to part of the amount or value of the consideration for the disposal,

(b) section 153(1)(a) and (b) would apply to the disposal and acquisition if the appropriate claim were made, and

(c) the disposal and acquisition would qualify for roll-over relief but for the disapplication of section 152(1) by section 153(1).

198G(3) Subsections (4) to (6) apply in deciding whether a disposal and acquisition is one that qualifies for section 153 relief.

198G(4) Section 153(2) has effect subject to section 198F(4) and (5).

198G(5) Section 198B is to be disregarded.

198G(6) Subject to subsections (4) and (5), all the circumstances are to be taken into account, including section 198(1).

History – S. 198G inserted by FA 2009, s. 86 and Sch. 40, para. 12, with effect in relation to disposals made on or after 22 April 2009 (whether the acquisition in which the consideration is reinvested takes place before, on or after that date).

198H Acquisition by member of same group

198H Section 198A or 198B is to apply where–

(a) the disposal is by a company which, at the time of the disposal, is a member of a group of companies (within the meaning given in section 170),

(b) the acquisition is by another company which, at the time of the acquisition, is a member of the same group, and

(c) the claim under that section is made by both companies,

as if both companies were the same person.

History – S. 198H inserted by F(No. 3)A 2010, s. 17(1), with effect in relation to disposals made on or after 22 April 2009 (whether the acquisition takes place before, on or after that date).

198I Exploration, appraisal and development expenditure

198I(1) The incurring of exploration, appraisal and development expenditure in the course of a ring fence trade is to be treated for the purposes of sections 198A to 198H as the acquisition of assets–

(a) which are the new assets mentioned in section 152,

(b) which are taken into use, and used only, for the purposes of the ring fence trade,

(c) which are oil assets, and

(d) which fall within the classes of assets listed in section 155.

198I(2) The reference in subsection (1) to sections 198A to 198H includes sections 152, 153, 175 and 198(1) so far as they apply for the purpose of determining whether a disposal and acquisition qualifies for rollover relief or section 153 relief (within the meaning given in section 198F or 198G).

198I(3) Section 198C has effect in relation to expenditure within subsection (1) of this section as if subsection (5) of that section were omitted.

198I(4) References in this section to exploration, appraisal and development expenditure are to expenditure on oil and gas exploration, appraisal and development activities which is treated as such under generally accepted accounting practice.

198I(5) Nothing in this section affects sections 152, 153, 175 and 198(1) so far as they apply otherwise than for the purposes of sections 198A to 198H.

198I(6) In this section–

"oil asset" has the meaning given in section 198E(5);

"ring fence trade" has the meaning given in section 198.

History – S. 198I inserted by FA 2011, s. 64 and Sch. 15, para. 5, with effect in relation to disposals made on or after 23 March 2010 (whether the deemed acquisition takes place before, on or after that date).

198J Oil and gas: reinvestment after pre-trading disposal

198J(1) This section applies if a company which is an E&A company makes a disposal of, or of the company's interest in, relevant E&A assets and that disposal is–

(a) a disposal of, or of an interest in, a UK licence which relates to an undeveloped area, or

(b) a disposal of an asset used in an area covered by a licence under Part 1 of the Petroleum Act 1998 or the Petroleum (Production) Act (Northern Ireland) 1964 which authorises the company to undertake E&A activities.

198J(2) If–

(a) the consideration which the company obtains for the disposal is applied by the company, within the permitted reinvestment period–
  (i) on E&A expenditure at a time when the company is an E&A company, or
  (ii) on oil assets taken into use, and used only, for the purposes of a ring fence trade carried on by it, and

(b) the company makes a claim under this subsection in relation to the disposal,

any gain accruing to the company on the disposal is not a chargeable gain.

198J(3) If part only of the amount or value of the consideration for the disposal is applied as described in subsection (2)(a)–

(a) subsection (2) does not apply, but

(b) subsection (4) applies if all of the amount or value of the consideration is so applied except for a part which is less than the amount of the gain (whether all chargeable gain or not) accruing on the disposal.

198J(4) If the company makes a claim under this subsection in relation to the disposal, the company is to be treated for the purposes of this Act as if the amount of the gain accruing on the disposal were reduced to the amount of the part mentioned in subsection (3)(b) (and, if not all chargeable gain, with a proportionate reduction in the amount of the chargeable gain).

198J(5) The incurring of expenditure is within **"the permitted reinvestment period"** if the expenditure is incurred in the period beginning 12 months before and ending 3 years after the disposal, or at such earlier or later time as the Commissioners for Her Majesty's Revenue and Customs may by notice allow.

198J(6) Subsections (6), (7), (10) and (11) of section 152 apply for the purposes of this section as they apply for the purposes of section 152, except that–

(a) in subsection (6) the reference to a trade is to be read as a reference to E&A activities or a ring fence trade,

(b) in subsection (7), the reference to the old assets is to be read as a reference to the assets disposed of as mentioned in subsection (1) of this section, and

(c) in subsection (7), the references to the trade are to be read as references to the E&A activities.

198J(7) In this section–

"E&A activities" means oil and gas exploration and appraisal in the United Kingdom or an area designated by Order in Council under section 1(7) of the Continental Shelf Act 1964;

"E&A company" means a company which carries on E&Aactivities and does not carry on a ring fence trade;

"E&A expenditure" means expenditure on E&A activities which is treated as such under generally accepted accounting practice;

"oil asset" has the same meaning as in section 198E, and section 198I applies for the purposes of this section as it applies for the purposes of section 198E;

"relevant E&A assets" means assets which–

(a) are used, and used only, for the purposes of E&A activities carried on by the company throughout the period of ownership, and

(b) are within the classes of assets listed in section 155 (with references to "the trade" in that section being read as references to the E&A activities);

"ring fence trade" has the meaning given by section 277 of CTA 2010;

"UK licence" means a licence within the meaning of Part 1 of the Oil Taxation Act 1975;

and a reference to a UK licence which relates to an undeveloped area has the same meaning as in section 194 (see section 196).

History – S. 198J inserted by FA 2014, s. 71(1), with effect in relation to disposals made on or after 1 April 2014.

198K Provisional application of section 198J

198K(1) This section applies where a company for a consideration disposes of, or of an interest in, any assets at a time when it is an E&A company and declares, in the company's return for the chargeable period in which the disposal takes place–

(a) that the whole or any specified part of the consideration will be applied, within the permitted reinvestment period–
  (i) on E&A expenditure at a time when the company is an E&A company, or
  (ii) on expenditure on oil assets which are taken into use, and used only, for the purposes of the company's ring fence trade, and

(b) that the company intends to make a claim under section 198J(2) or (4) in relation to the disposal.

198K(2) Until the declaration ceases to have effect, section 198J applies as if the expenditure had been incurred and the person had made such a claim.

198K(3) The declaration ceases to have effect as follows–

(a) if and to the extent that it is withdrawn before the relevant day, or is superseded before that day by a valid claim under section 198J, on the day on which it is so withdrawn or superseded, and

(b) if and to the extent that it is not so withdrawn or superseded, on the relevant day.

198K(4) On the declaration ceasing to have effect in whole or in part, all necessary adjustments–

(a) are to be made by making or amending assessments or by repayment or discharge of tax, and

(b) are to be so made despite any limitation on the time within which assessments or amendments may be made.

198K(5) In this section **"the relevant day"** means the fourth anniversary of the last day of the accounting period in which the disposal took place.

198K(6) For the purposes of this section–

(a) sections (6), (10) and (11) of section 152 apply as they apply for the purposes of that section, except that in subsection (6) the reference to a trade is to be read as a reference to E&A activities or a ring fence trade, and

(b) terms used in this section which are defined in section 198J have the meaning given by that section.

History – S. 198K inserted by FA 2014, s. 71(1), with effect in relation to disposals made on or after 1 April 2014.

198L Expenditure by member of same group

198L(1) Section 198J applies where–

(a) the disposal is by a company which, at the time of the disposal, is a member of a group of companies (within the meaning of section 170),

(b) the E&A expenditure or expenditure on oil assets is by another company which, at the time the expenditure is incurred, is a member of the same group, and

(c) the claim under section 198J is made by both companies,

as if both companies were the same person.

198L(2) **"E&A company"**, **"E&A expenditure"** and **"oil assets"** have the meaning given by section 198J.

History – S. 198L inserted by FA 2014, s. 71(1), with effect in relation to disposals made on or after 1 April 2014.

199 Exploration or exploitation assets: deemed disposals

Notes – In s. 199(2) and (4); any reference to a "branch or agency" shall be read, in relation to a company, as if it were a reference to a "permanent establishment" (FA 2003, s. 153(2)(b); with effect in relation to accounting periods beginning on or after 1 January 2003).

199(1) Where an exploration or exploitation asset which is a mobile asset ceases to be chargeable in relation to a person by virtue of ceasing to be dedicated to an oil field in which he, or a person connected with him, is or has been a participator, he shall be deemed for all purposes of this Act–

(a) to have disposed of the asset immediately before the time when it ceased to be so dedicated, and

(b) immediately to have reacquired it,

at its market value at that time.

199(2) Where a person in respect of whom the residence condition (see section 2(1A)) is not met ceases to carry on a trade in the United Kingdom through a branch or agency, he shall be deemed for all purposes of this Act–

(a) to have disposed immediately before the time when he ceased to carry on the trade in the United Kingdom through a branch or agency of every asset to which subsection (3) below applies, and

(b) immediately to have reacquired every such asset,

at its market value at that time.

199(3) This subsection applies to any exploration or exploitation asset, other than a mobile asset, used in or for the purposes of the trade at or before the time of the deemed disposal.

199(4) A person shall not be deemed by subsection (2) above to have disposed of an asset if, immediately after the time when he ceases to carry on the trade in the United Kingdom through a branch or agency, the asset is used in or for the purposes of exploration or exploitation activities carried on by him in the United Kingdom or a designated area.

199(5) Where in a case to which subsection (4) above applies the person ceases to use the asset in or for the purposes of exploration or exploitation activities carried on by him in the United Kingdom or a designated area, he shall be deemed for all purposes of this Act–

(a) to have disposed of the asset immediately before the time when he ceased to use it in or for the purposes of such activities, and

(b) immediately to have reacquired it,

at its market value at that time.

199(6) For the purposes of this section an asset is at any time a chargeable asset in relation to a person if, were it to be disposed of at that time, any chargeable gains accruing to him on the disposal–

(a) would be gains in respect of which he would be chargeable to capital gains tax under section 10(1), or

(b) would form part of his chargeable profits for corporation tax purposes by virtue of section 10B.

199(7) In this section–

(a) **"exploration or exploitation asset"** means an asset used in connection with exploration or exploitation activities carried on in the United Kingdom or a designated area;

(b) **"designated area"** and **"exploration or exploitation activities"** have the same meanings as in section 276; and

(c) the expressions **"dedicated to an oil field"** and **"participator"** shall be construed as if this section were included in Part I of the Oil Taxation Act 1975.

History – In s. 199(2), the words "in respect of whom the residence condition (see section 2(1A)) is not met" substituted for the words "who is not resident and not ordinarily resident in the United Kingdom" by FA 2013, s. 219 and Sch. 46, para. 103, with effect in relation to a person's liability to capital gains tax for the tax year 2013–14 or any subsequent tax year, without prejudice to any provision in FA 2013, Sch. 46, Pt. 3 about the application of a particular amendment.
In s. 199(6)(b), the reference "section 10B" substituted for the reference "10(3)" by FA 2003, s. 155 and Sch. 27, para. 2(3) with effect in relation to accounting periods beginning on or after 1 January 2003.

Derivations – FA 1989, s. 131(1)–(7).

Cross references – S. 10: extent of charge on non-resident in respect of assets used or held for a UK branch or agency.
S. 276: UK includes the territorial sea of the UK, "designated area" is an area designated under the Continental Shelf Act 1964 and "exploration or exploitation activities" are given by reference to the seabed, subsoil and their natural resources.
OTA 1975, Pt. I: petroleum revenue tax, including (s. 12) interpretation of "oil", "oil field", "participator" and when an asset is "dedicated to an oil field".
FA 2003, s. 153(2)(b): when dealing with a company; requirement to read any reference to a "branch or agency" (in s. 199(2) and (4)), as if it were a reference to a "permanent establishment" (effective for accounting periods beginning on or after 1 January 2003).

Notes – S. 9: meaning of "resident" and "ordinarily resident".
S. 15: meaning of "chargeable gains".
S. 21–34: general meaning of "disposal" and "asset".
S. 272–274 and Sch. 11: meaning of "market value".
S. 286: "connected" in references to persons being connected with one another.
S. 288: interpretation, including reference to sections as being those of this Act.

200 Limitation of losses on disposal of oil industry assets held on 31st March 1982

200 [Repealed by FA 1994, s. 93(7) and s. 258 and Sch. 26, Pt. V(8) in relation to disposals made on or after 30 November 1993.]

History – S. 200 repealed by FA 1994, s. 93(7) and s. 258 and Sch. 26, Pt. V(8) in relation to disposals made on or after 30 November 1993.

MINERAL LEASES

201 Royalties

201 [Repealed by FA 2012, s. 227 and Sch. 39, para. 45(1).]

History – S. 201 repealed by FA 2012, s. 227 and Sch. 39, para. 45(1), for the purposes of capital gains tax, in relation to mineral royalties which a person is entitled to receive on or after 6 April 2013, and for the purposes of corporation tax in respect of chargeable gains, in relation to mineral royalties which a company is entitled to receive on or after 1 April 2013.
Former s. 201(2) omitted by CTA 2009, s. 1322 and Sch. 1, para. 377 and repealed by CTA 2009, s. 1326 and Sch. 3, Pt. 1, with effect for corporation tax purposes for accounting periods ending on or after 1 April 2009, and for income tax and capital gains tax purposes for the tax year 2009–10 and subsequent tax years.

202 Capital losses

202(1) This section has effect in relation to capital losses which accrue during the currency of a mineral lease or agreement entered into before the relevant date, and applies in any case where, at the time of the occurrence of a relevant event in relation to a mineral lease or agreement entered into before that date, the person who immediately before that event occurred was entitled to receive mineral royalties under the lease or agreement ("the taxpayer") has an interest in the land to which the mineral lease or agreement relates (**"the relevant interest"**).

202(1A) For the purposes of this section **"the relevant date"** means–

(a) for the purposes of capital gains tax, 6 April 2013; and

(b) for the purposes of corporation tax in respect of chargeable gains, 1 April 2013.

202(2) For the purposes of this section, a **relevant event** occurs in relation to a mineral lease or agreement–

(a) on the expiry or termination of the mineral lease or agreement;

(b) if the relevant interest is disposed of, or is treated as having been disposed of by virtue of any provision of this Act.

202(3) On the expiry or termination of a mineral lease or agreement entered into before the relevant date the taxpayer shall, if he makes a claim in that behalf, be treated for purposes of tax in respect of chargeable gains as if he had disposed of and immediately reacquired the relevant interest for a consideration equal to its market value, but a claim may not be made under this subsection–

(a) if the expiry or termination of the mineral lease or agreement is also a relevant event falling within subsection (2)(b) above; nor

(b) unless, on the notional disposal referred to above, an allowable loss would accrue to the taxpayer.

202(4) In this section **"the terminal loss"**, in relation to a relevant event in respect of which a claim is made under subsection (3) above, means the allowable loss which accrues to the taxpayer by virtue of the notional disposal occurring on that relevant event by virtue of that subsection.

202(5) On making a claim under subsection (3) above, the taxpayer shall specify whether he requires the terminal loss to be dealt with in accordance with subsection (6) or subsections (9) to (11) below.

202(6) Where the taxpayer requires the loss to be dealt with in accordance with this subsection it shall be treated as an allowable loss accruing to him in the chargeable period in which the mineral lease or agreement expires.

202(7) If on the occurrence of a relevant event falling within subsection (2)(b) above, an allowable loss accrues to the taxpayer on the disposal or notional disposal which constitutes that relevant event, the taxpayer may make a claim under this subsection requiring the loss to be dealt with in accordance with subsections (9) to (11) below and not in any other way.

202(8) In subsections (9) to (11) below **"the terminal loss"** in relation to a relevant event in respect of which a claim is made under subsection (7) above means the allowable loss which accrues to the taxpayer as mentioned in that subsection.

202(9) Where, as a result of a claim under subsection (3) or (7) above, the terminal loss is to be dealt with in accordance with this subsection, then, subject to subsection (10) below, it shall be deducted from or set off against the amount on which the taxpayer was chargeable to capital gains tax, or as the case may be corporation tax, for chargeable periods preceding that in which the relevant event giving rise to the terminal loss occurred and falling wholly or partly within the period of 15 years ending with the date of that event.

202(10) The amount of the terminal loss which, by virtue of subsection (9) above, is to be deducted from or set off against the amount on which the taxpayer was chargeable to capital gains tax, or as the case may be corporation tax, for any chargeable period shall not exceed the amount of the gain which in that period was treated, by virtue of section 201(1), as accruing to the taxpayer in respect of mineral royalties under the mineral lease or agreement in question; and subject to this limit any relief given to the taxpayer by virtue of subsection (9) above shall be given as far as possible for a later rather than an earlier chargeable period.

202(11) If in any case where relief has been given to the taxpayer in accordance with subsections (9) and (10) above there remains an unexpended balance of the terminal loss which cannot be applied in accordance with those subsections, there shall be treated as accruing to the taxpayer in the chargeable period in which the relevant event occurs an allowable loss equal to that unexpended balance.

History – In s. 202(1) "entered into before the relevant date" inserted after "currency of a mineral lease or agreement", and "entered into before that date" inserted after "in relation to a mineral lease or agreement" by FA 2012, s. 227 and Sch. 39, para. 46(2), for the purposes of capital gains tax, in relation to mineral royalties which a person is entitled to receive on or after 6 April 2013, and for the purposes of corporation tax in respect of chargeable gains, in relation to mineral royalties which a company is entitled to receive on or after 1 April 2013.

S. 202(1A) inserted by FA 2012, s. 227 and Sch. 39, para. 46(3), for the purposes of capital gains tax, in relation to mineral royalties which a person is entitled to receive on or after 6 April 2013, and for the purposes of corporation tax in respect of chargeable gains, in relation to mineral royalties which a company is entitled to receive on or after 1 April 2013.

In s. 202(3) "entered into before the relevant date" inserted after "termination of a mineral lease or agreement" by FA 2012, s. 227 and Sch. 39, para. 46(4), for the purposes of capital gains tax, in relation to mineral royalties which a person is entitled to receive on or after 6 April 2013, and for the purposes of corporation tax in respect of chargeable gains, in relation to mineral royalties which a company is entitled to receive on or after 1 April 2013.

Derivations – S. 202(1): FA 1970, s. 29(5) and Sch. 6, para. 3(1).
S. 202(2): FA 1970, Sch. 6, para. 3(2).
S. 202(3), (4): FA 1970, Sch. 6, para. 4.
S. 202(5), (6): FA 1970, Sch. 6, para. 5.
S. 202(7), (8): FA 1970, Sch. 6, para. 6.
S. 202(9)–(11): FA 1970, Sch. 6, para. 7.

Notes – S. 2: charge to capital gains tax.
S. 8: charge to corporation tax on chargeable gains.
S. 16: meaning of "allowable loss".

S. 21–34: general meaning of "disposal".
S. 272–274 and Sch. 11: meaning of "market value".
S. 288: interpretation, including "chargeable period" as an accounting period or tax year and reference to sections being those of this Act.
TMA 1970, s. 32–33B: procedures and normal time limits for making claims (but see s. 203(2)).

203 Provisions supplementary to section 202

203(1) Sections 274 to 276 of CTA 2009 (meaning of **"mineral royalties"** etc) apply for the interpretation of this section and section 202 (despite their repeal by paragraph 44(1)(c) of Schedule 39 to the Finance Act 2012).

203(2) No claim under section 202(3) or (7) shall be allowed unless it is made within 4 years from the date of the relevant event by virtue of which the taxpayer is entitled to make the claim.

203(3) All such repayments of tax shall be made as may be necessary to give effect to any such claim.

History – In s. 203(1) "(despite their repeal by paragraph 44(1)(c) of Schedule 39 to the Finance Act 2012)" substituted for "as they apply for the interpretation of Chapter 7 of Part 4 of CTA 2009" by FA 2012, s. 227 and Sch. 39, para. 47, for the purposes of capital gains tax, in relation to mineral royalties which a person is entitled to receive on or after 6 April 2013, and for the purposes of corporation tax in respect of chargeable gains, in relation to mineral royalties which a company is entitled to receive on or after 1 April 2013.
In s. 203(1) "section 202" substituted for "sections 201 and 202", and in the heading "section 202" substituted for "sections 201 and 202" by FA 2012, s. 227 and Sch. 39, para. 45(2), for the purposes of capital gains tax, in relation to mineral royalties which a person is entitled to receive on or after 6 April 2013, and for the purposes of corporation tax in respect of chargeable gains, in relation to mineral royalties which a company is entitled to receive on or after 1 April 2013.
S. 203(1) substituted by CTA 2009, s. 1322 and Sch. 1, para. 378, with effect for corporation tax purposes for accounting periods ending on or after 1 April 2009, and for income tax and capital gains tax purposes for the tax year 2009–10 and subsequent tax years.
In s. 203(2), the words "4 years" substituted for words "6 years" by FA 2008, s. 118(1) and Sch. 39, para. 29, with effect from 1 April 2010 (SI 2009/403, art. 2(2) subject to SI 2009/403, art. 3–10 – in particular art. 10).

Derivations – S. 203(1): FA 1970, s. 29(6), (7), (9).
S. 203(2), (3): FA 1970, Sch. 6, para. 8.

Cross references – ICTA 1988, s. 122(5)–(7): "mineral royalties" defined by reference to periodical payments in the nature of rent and relating to the winning and working of "minerals".

Notes – S. 288: interpretation, including "the Taxes Act" as ICTA 1988 and reference to other sections being those of this Act.

Chapter III – Insurance

204 Policies of insurance and non-deferred annuities

204(1) A gain accruing on a disposal of, or of an interest in, the rights conferred by a non-life policy of insurance is not a chargeable gain (but see subsection (2)).

204(2) If a disposal is of, or of an interest in, the rights conferred by a non-life policy of insurance of the risk of–

(a) any kind of damage to assets, or

(b) the loss or depreciation of assets,

the exemption under subsection (1) does not apply so far as those rights relate to chargeable assets.

204(3) For this purpose **"chargeable assets"** means assets on the disposal of which a chargeable gain–

(a) may accrue, or

(b) might have accrued.

204(4) Nothing in subsections (1) and (2) prevents sums received under a non-life policy of insurance of the risk of–

(a) any kind of damage to assets, or

(b) the loss or depreciation of assets,

from being sums derived from the assets for the purposes of this Act (and, in particular, for the purposes of section 22).

204(5) A gain accruing on a disposal of, or of an interest in, the rights conferred by a contract for an annuity is not a chargeable gain if the annuity is–

(a) a non-deferred annuity, or

(b) an annuity granted (or deemed to be granted) under the Government Annuities Act 1929.

204(6) If any investments or other assets are, in accordance with a policy issued in the course of life assurance business carried on by an insurance company, transferred to the policy holder–

(a) the policy holder's acquisition of the assets, and

(b) the disposal of the assets to the policy holder,

are to be taken for the purposes of this Act to be for a consideration equal to the market value of the assets.

204(7) In this section **"interest"**, in relation to any rights, means an interest as a co-owner of the rights.

204(8) It does not matter–

(a) whether the rights are owned jointly or in common, or

(b) whether or not the interests of the co-owners are equal.

204(9) In this section a **"non-deferred annuity"** means an annuity–

(a) which is not granted under a contract for a deferred annuity, and

(b) which is granted in the ordinary course of a business of granting annuities on the life of any person,

and it does not matter whether the annuity includes instalments of capital.

204(10) In this section a **"non-life policy of insurance"** means–

(a) a contract made in the course of a capital redemption business, within the meaning of section 56(3) of the Finance Act 2012, and

(b) any policy of insurance which is not a policy of insurance on the life of any person.

History – In s. 204(10)(a) the words "section 56(3) of the Finance Act 2012" substituted for the words "Chapter 1 of Part 12 of the Taxes Act" by FA 2012, s. 146 and Sch. 16, para. 79 in relation to accounting periods beginning on or after 1 January 2013 (FA 2012, s. 148) but subject to transitional provisions in FA 2012, Sch. 17. Where an accounting period would otherwise straddle 1 January 2013, it is deemed to end on 31 December 2012 (FA 2012, s. 149).

In former s. 204(10)(a) the words "within the meaning of Chapter 1 of Part 12" substituted for the words "as defined in section 458(3)" by FA 2007, s. 38 and Sch. 7, para. 61(a) with effect; for income tax purposes from 2007–08 onwards; and for corporation tax purposes of insurance companies for periods of account beginning on or after 1 January 2007, subject to the transitional provisions in Sch. 7, Part 2 (FA 2007, s. 38(2), (3)).

In s. 204(10)(b) the word "other" (in the phrase "any other policy of insurance") omitted by FA 2007, s. 38 and Sch. 7, para. 61(b) and repealed by FA 2007, s. 114 and Sch. 27, Pt. 2(7) with effect; for income tax purposes from 2007–08 onwards; and for corporation tax purposes of insurance companies for periods of account beginning on or after 1 January 2007, subject to the transitional provisions in Sch. 7, Part 2 (FA 2007, s. 38(2), (3)).

S. 204 substituted by FA 2006, s. 73(2) with effect in relation to disposals made on or after 5 December 2005.

Derivations – CGTA 1979, s. 140, 149A(2) as inserted by ICTA 1988, s. 844 and Sch. 29, para. 26, for the former, original version of s. 204.

Cross references – ICTA 1988, Pt. 12, Ch. 1: in s. 204(10)(a) the reference to "Chapter 1 of Part 12" appears to be a reference to that Part of ICTA 1988.

S. 22: deemed disposal of assets where a capital sum is received under a policy of insurance of the risk to assets.

HMRC interpretations – IRInt. 257: assignment on divorce of life insurance policies, capital redemption policies and purchased life annuities.

Notes – S. 15(2): "chargeable gains" determined by reference to gains generally.

S. 21–34: general meaning of "disposal" and "asset".

S. 288: interpretation, including reference to sections as being those of this Act.

ICTA 1988, s. 545, 547: charge to tax as income on certain benefits under capital redemption policies.

205 Disallowance of insurance premiums as expenses

205 Without prejudice to the provisions of section 39, there shall be excluded from the sums allowable as a deduction in the computation of the gain accruing on the disposal of an asset any premiums or other payments made under a policy of insurance of the risk of any kind of damage or injury to, or loss or depreciation of, the asset.

Derivations – CGTA 1979, s. 141.

Cross references – S. 39: expenditure taken into account in computing taxes on income is not deductible.

Notes – S. 15(2): "chargeable gains" determined by reference to gains generally.

S. 21–34: general meaning of "disposal" and "asset".

S. 288: interpretation, including reference to sections as being those of this Act.

206 Underwriters

206 [Repealed by FA 1993, s. 213 and Sch. 23, Pt. III(12).]

History – S. 206 repealed by FA 1993, s. 213 and Sch. 23, Pt. III(12) with effect for 1992–93 and subsequent years of assessment (s. 206(1)) and with effect for 1994–95 and subsequent years of assessment (s. 206(2)–(5)).

207 Disposal of assets in premiums trust fund etc.

207 [Repealed by FA 1993, s. 213 and Sch. 23, Pt. III(12).]

History – S. 207 repealed by FA 1993, s. 213 and Sch. 23, Pt. III(12) with effect for 1994 and subsequent underwriting years (1994 underwriting year assessable 1997–98).

208 Premiums trust funds: indexation

208 [Repealed by FA 1993, s. 213 and Sch. 23, Pt. III(12).]

History – S. 208 repealed by FA 1993, s. 213 and Sch. 23, Pt. III(12) with effect for 1994 and subsequent underwriting years (1994 underwriting year assessable 1997–98).

209 Interpretation, regulations about underwriters etc.

209 [Repealed by FA 1993, s. 213 and Sch. 23, Pt. III(12).]

History – Repealed by FA 1993, s. 213 and Sch. 23, Pt. III(12) with effect for 1992–93 and subsequent years of assessment (s. 209(3)–(5)) and with effect for 1994–95 and subsequent years of assessment (s. 209(1),(2),(6)).

210 Life insurance and deferred annuities

210(1) This section has effect in relation to any policy of insurance or contract for a deferred annuity on the life of any person.

210(2) A gain accruing on a disposal of, or of an interest in, the rights conferred by the policy of insurance or contract for a deferred annuity is not a chargeable gain unless subsection (3) below applies.

210(3) This subsection applies if–

(a) (in the case of a disposal of the rights) the rights or any interest in the rights, or

(b) (in the case of a disposal of an interest in the rights) the rights, the interest or any interest from which the interest directly or indirectly derives (in whole or in part),

have or has at any time been acquired by any person for actual consideration (as opposed to consideration deemed to be given by any enactment relating to the taxation of chargeable gains).

210(4) For the purposes of subsection (3) above–

(a) (in the case of a policy of insurance) amounts paid under the policy by way of premiums, and

(b) (in the case of a contract for a deferred annuity) amounts paid under the contract, whether by way of premiums or as lump sum consideration,

do not constitute actual consideration.

210(5) And for those purposes actual consideration for–

(a) a disposal which is made by one spouse or civil partner to the other or is an approved post-marriage disposal or an approved post-civil partnership disposal, or

(b) a disposal to which section 171(1) applies,

is to be treated as not constituting actual consideration.

210(6) For the purposes of subsection (5)(a) above a disposal is an approved post-marriage disposal or an approved post-civil partnership disposal if–

(a) it is made in consequence of the dissolution or annulment of a marriage or civil partnership by one person who was a party to the marriage or civil partnership to the other,

(b) it is made with the approval, agreement or authority of a court (or other person or body) having jurisdiction under the law of any country or territory or pursuant to an order of such a court (or other person or body), and

(c) the rights disposed of were, or the interest disposed of was, held by the person by whom the disposal is made immediately before the marriage or civil partnership was dissolved or annulled.

210(7) Subsection (8) below applies for the purposes of tax on chargeable gains where–

(a) (if that subsection did not apply) a loss would accrue on a disposal of, or of an interest in, the rights conferred by the policy of insurance or contract for a deferred annuity, but

(b) if sections 37 and 39 were disregarded, there would accrue on the disposal a loss of a smaller amount, a gain or neither a loss nor a gain.

210(8) If (disregarding those sections) a loss of a smaller amount would accrue, that smaller amount is to be taken to be the amount of the loss accruing on the disposal; and in any other case, neither a loss nor a gain is to be taken to accrue on the disposal.

210(9) But subsection (8) above does not affect the treatment for the purposes of tax on chargeable gains of the person who acquired rights, or an interest in rights, on the disposal.

210(10) The occasion of–

(a) the receipt of the sum or sums assured by the policy of insurance,

(b) the transfer of investments or other assets to the owner of the policy of insurance in accordance with the policy, or

(c) the surrender of the policy of insurance,

is for the purposes of tax on chargeable gains an occasion of a disposal of the rights (or of all of the interests in the rights) conferred by the policy of insurance.

210(11) The occasion of–

(a) the receipt of the first instalment of the annuity under the contract for a deferred annuity, or

(b) the surrender of the rights conferred by the contract for a deferred annuity,

is for the purposes of tax on chargeable gains an occasion of a disposal of the rights (or of all of the interests in the rights) conferred by the contract for a deferred annuity.

210(12) Where there is a disposal on the occasion of the receipt of the first instalment of the annuity under the contract for a deferred annuity–

(a) in the case of a disposal of the rights conferred by the contract, the consideration for the disposal is the aggregate of the amount or value of the first instalment and the market value at the time of the disposal of the right to receive the further instalments of the annuity, and

(b) in the case of a disposal of an interest in the rights, the consideration for the disposal is such proportion of that aggregate as is just and reasonable;

and no gain accruing on any subsequent disposal of, or of any interest in, the rights is a chargeable gain (even if subsection (3) above applies).

210(13) In this section **"interest"**, in relation to rights conferred by a policy of insurance or contract for a deferred annuity, means an interest as a co-owner of the rights (whether the rights are owned jointly or in common and whether or not the interests of the co-owners are equal).

History – In s. 210(5)(a) the words "or civil partner" and "or an approved post-civil partnership disposal" inserted by SI 2005/3229, reg. 116(2), with effect from 5 December 2005.
In s. 210(6) the words "or an approved post-civil partnership disposal" inserted and the words "or civil partnership" inserted three times by SI 2005/3229, reg. 116(3), with effect from 5 December 2005.
S. 210 substituted by FA 2003, s. 157(1) with effect in relation to disposals on or after 9 April 2003.

Derivations – CGTA 1979, s. 143.

HMRC interpretations – IRInt. 257: assignment on divorce of life insurance policies, capital redemption policies and purchased life annuities.

Notes – S. 15: meaning of "chargeable gain".
S. 21–34: general meaning of "disposal" and "asset".
S. 272–274 and Sch. 11: meaning of "market value".

210A Ring-fencing of losses

Notes – In s. 210A(10), a substitution of certain words has been made by FA 2004, s. 47 and Sch. 7, para. 6(1) which only has effect in relation to accounting periods beginning on or after 17 March 2004. See the History Note below for the substitution concerned.

210A(1) Section 8(1) has effect in relation to insurance companies subject to the provisions of this section.

210A(2) Non-BLAGAB allowable losses accruing to an insurance company are allowable as a deduction from the shareholders' share (if any) of the BLAGAB chargeable gains accruing to the company (but are not otherwise allowable as a deduction from the BLAGAB chargeable gains accruing to the company).

210A(3) BLAGAB allowable losses accruing to an insurance company are allowable as a deduction from non-BLAGAB chargeable gains accruing to the company as permitted by the following provisions of this section (and not otherwise).

210A(4) They are allowable as a deduction from only so much of non-BLAGAB chargeable gains accruing to the company in an accounting period as exceeds the aggregate of–

(a) non-BLAGAB allowable losses accruing to the company in the accounting period, and

(b) non-BLAGAB allowable losses previously accruing to the company which have not been allowed as a deduction from chargeable gains accruing in any previous accounting period.

210A(5) And they are allowable as a deduction from non-BLAGAB chargeable gains accruing to the company in an accounting period only to the extent that they do not exceed the permitted amount for the accounting period.

210A(6) The permitted amount for the first accounting period of an insurance company in relation to which this section has effect is the aggregate of–

(a) the amount by which shareholders' share for that accounting period of BLAGAB allowable losses accruing to the company in the accounting period exceeds the shareholders' share of BLAGAB chargeable gains so accruing, and

(b) the shareholder's share for the immediately preceding accounting period of BLAGAB allowable losses previously accruing to the company which have not been allowed as a deduction from chargeable gains accruing in that immediately preceding accounting period or any earlier accounting period.

210A(7) The permitted amount for any subsequent accounting period of the company is arrived at by–

(a) deducting from the permitted amount for the immediately preceding accounting period the amount of any BLAGAB allowable losses allowed as a deduction from non-BLAGAB chargeable gains accruing to the company in the immediately preceding accounting period, and

(b) adjusting the result in accordance with subsection (8) or (9) below.

210A(8) If the BLAGAB chargeable gains accruing to the company in the subsequent accounting period exceed the BLAGAB allowable losses so accruing, the amount arrived at under subsection (7)(a) above is reduced by a fraction of which–

(a) the denominator is the BLAGAB allowable losses accruing to the company in any previous accounting period which have not been allowed as a deduction from chargeable gains accruing to the company in any previous accounting period, and

(b) the numerator is so many of those allowable losses as are allowed as a deduction from BLAGAB chargeable gains accruing to the company in the accounting period.

210A(9) If the BLAGAB allowable losses accruing to the company in the subsequent accounting period exceed the BLAGAB chargeable gains so accruing, the amount arrived at under subsection (7)(a) above is increased by the shareholders' share of the amount by which those allowable losses exceed those chargeable gains.

210A(10) For the purposes of this section the **"shareholders' share"** of BLAGAB chargeable gains or BLAGAB allowable losses accruing to an insurance company in an accounting period is determined as follows.

210A(10A) If the company has an I – E profit for the accounting period–

(a) find the percentage (including, if applicable, nil) of the I – E profit that is not represented by the policyholders' share of that profit as determined in accordance with section 103 of the Finance Act 2012, and

(b) then multiply that percentage by the amount of the BLAGAB chargeable gains or BLAGAB allowable losses.

The result is the shareholder's share of the BLAGAB chargeable gains or BLAGAB allowable losses.

210A(10B) If the company does not have an I – E profit for the accounting period, the shareholders' share of the BLAGAB chargeable gains or BLAGAB allowable losses is nil.

210A(10C) In determining for the purposes of subsections (10A) and (10B) whether or not the company has an I – E profit for an accounting period, assume that non-BLAGAB allowable losses cannot be deducted to any extent from BLAGAB chargeable gains (and, accordingly, assume that section 95 is not included in the Finance Act 2012).

210A(11) In arriving at the shareholders' share of chargeable gains accruing to an insurance company under subsections (10) to (10C) above there is to be ignored–

(a) any deduction under section 202(9) (mineral leases: capital losses),

(b) any reduction section 213(3) (spreading of losses from deemed disposal of holdings of unit trust etc.), and

(c) any amount carried back under section 389(1) of CTA 2009 (non-trading deficit on loan relationships).

210A(12) [Omitted by FA 2012, s. 146 and Sch. 16, para. 80(5).]

210A(13) In this section–

"BLAGAB allowable losses", in relation to an insurance company, means allowable losses referable, in accordance with Chapter 4 of Part 2 of the Finance Act 2012, to the company's basic life assurance and general annuity business,

"BLAGAB chargeable gains", in relation to an insurance company, means chargeable gains referable, in accordance with Chapter 4 of Part 2 of the Finance Act 2012, to the company's basic life assurance and general annuity business,

"non-BLAGAB allowable losses", in relation to an insurance company, means allowable losses of the company which are not BLAGAB allowable losses, and

"non-BLAGAB chargeable gains", in relation to an insurance company, means chargeable gains of the company which are not BLAGAB chargeable gains.

History – S. 210A(2) substituted by FA 2012, s. 146 and Sch. 16, para. 80(2) in relation to accounting periods beginning on or after 1 January 2013 (FA 2012, s. 148) but subject to transitional provisions in FA 2012, Sch. 17. Where an accounting period would otherwise straddle 1 January 2013, it is deemed to end on 31 December 2012 (FA 2012, s. 149).

In s. 210A(10)(a), the words "(within the meaning of section 89(1B) of the Finance Act 1989)" omitted by FA 2008, s. 43 and Sch. 17, para. 18(5)(b) with effect in relation to accounting periods beginning on or after 1 January 2008.

In s. 210A(10), the words "for the accounting period bears to those BLAGAB profits" substituted for the words "of the company for the accounting period bears to those relevant profits" by FA 2004, s. 47 and Sch. 7, para. 6(1) which has effect, by virtue of FA 2004, Sch. 7, para. 6(2), in relation to accounting periods beginning on or after 17 March 2004.

In s. 210A(10A) the words "life assurance trade profits" substituted for the words "Case I profits" twice and the words "life assurance trade profits provisions" substituted for the words "provisions applicable to Case I of Schedule D" by CTA 2009, s. 1322 and Sch. 1, para. 379(2), with effect for corporation tax purposes for accounting periods ending on or after 1 April 2009, and for income tax and capital gains tax purposes for the tax year 2009–10 and subsequent tax years.

S. 210A(10A) inserted by FA 2008, s. 43 and Sch. 17, para. 13 with effect in relation to accounting periods beginning on or after 1 January 2008 and ending on or after 12 March 2008.

S. 210A(10) and (10A) substituted (and s. 210A(10B) and (10C) inserted) by FA 2012, s. 146 and Sch. 16, para. 80(3) in relation to accounting periods beginning on or after 1 January 2013 (FA 2012, s. 148) but subject to transitional provisions in FA 2012, Sch. 17. Where an accounting period would otherwise straddle 1 January 2013, it is deemed to end on 31 December 2012 (FA 2012, s. 149).

In s. 210A(11) the words "the shareholders' share" substituted for the words "the policy holders' share" by FA 2012, s. 146 and Sch. 16, para. 80(4)(a) in relation to accounting periods beginning on or after 1 January 2013 (FA 2012, s. 148) but subject to transitional provisions in FA 2012, Sch. 17. Where an accounting period would otherwise straddle 1 January2013, it is deemed to end on 31 December 2012 (FA 2012, s. 149).

In s. 210A(11) the words "subsections (10) to (10C)" substituted for the words "subsection (10)" by FA 2012, s. 146 and Sch. 16, para. 80(4)(b) in relation to accounting periods beginning on or after 1 January 2013 (FA 2012, s. 148) but subject to transitional

provisions in FA 2012, Sch. 17. Where an accounting period would otherwise straddle 1 January 2013, it is deemed to end on 31 December 2012 (FA 2012, s. 149).
In s. 210A(11)(c) the words "section 389(1) of CTA 2009" substituted for the words "paragraph 4(3) of Schedule 11 to the Finance Act 1996" by CTA 2009, s. 1322 and Sch. 1, para. 379(3), with effect for corporation tax purposes for accounting periods ending on or after 1 April 2009, and for income tax and capital gains tax purposes for the tax year 2009–10 and subsequent tax years.
S. 210A(12) omitted by FA 2012, s. 146 and Sch. 16, para. 80(5) in relation to accounting periods beginning on or after 1 January 2013 (FA 2012, s. 148) but subject to transitional provisions in FA 2012, Sch. 17. Where an accounting period would otherwise straddle 1 January 2013, it is deemed to end on 31 December 2012 (FA 2012, s. 149).
In s. 210A(13), in the definitions of "BLAGAB allowable losses" and "BLAGAB chargeable gains", the words ", in accordance with Chapter 4 of Part 2 of the Finance Act 2012," substituted for the words "(in accordance with section 432A of the Taxes Act)" by FA 2012, s. 146 and Sch. 16, para. 80(6)(a) in relation to accounting periods beginning on or after 1 January 2013 (FA 2012, s. 148) but subject to transitional provisions in FA 2012, Sch. 17. Where an accounting period would otherwise straddle 1 January 2013, it is deemed to end on 31 December 2012 (FA 2012, s. 149).
S. 210A(13) definitions of "the relevant profits" and "the policy holders' share of the relevant profits" (together with the "and" before the definition of "the relevant profits") omitted by FA 2012, s. 146 and Sch. 16, para. 80(6)(b) in relation to accounting periods beginning on or after 1 January 2013 (FA 2012, s. 148) but subject to transitional provisions in FA 2012, Sch. 17. Where an accounting period would otherwisestraddle 1 January 2013, it is deemed to end on 31 December 2012 (FA 2012, s. 149).
In s. 210A(13), in the definition of "BLAGAB allowable losses" the words "(in accordance with section 432A of the Taxes Act)" have been inserted by FA 2004, s. 47 and Sch. 7, para. 9(3)(a) with effect from 22 July 2004.
In s. 210A(13), in the definition of "BLAGAB chargeable gains" the words "(in accordance with section 432A of the Taxes Act)" have been inserted by FA 2004, s. 47 and Sch. 7, para. 9(3)(a) with effect from 22 July 2004.
S. 210A inserted by FA 2003, s. 170 and Sch. 33, para. 14(1) which, by virtue of Sch. 33, para. 14(2), have the effect of limiting the deductions that may be made from chargeable gains accruing in: (a) any accounting period of an insurance company beginning on or after 23 December 2002, and (b) any accounting period of an insurance company beginning before 23 December 2002 but ending on or after that date, in respect of allowable losses accruing in any accounting period (whenever beginning or ending); furthermore, where (b) applies, the limitations imposed by s. 210A apply only as respects chargeable gains accruing on or after 23 December 2002 (Sch. 33, para. 14(3)).

Cross references – S. 211ZA: transfers of business – transfer of unused losses.
ICTA 1988, s. 431A: Treasury may by order amend s. 210A.

Statutory instruments – SI 1997/473, reg. 40A: has effect for the purposes of s. 210A in relation to any accounting period of a company if it is necessary under that section to determine the company's taxable basic life assurance and general annuity business profits for the period.

Notes – ICTA 1988, s. 431A(3), (4) and (5): Treasury may by order amend s. 210A so as to have effect in relation to periods of account beginning on or after 1 January 2005 and ending before 1 October 2006 (Treasury may by order change from 1 October 2006 to another date provided it is not later than 1 October 2007).

210B Disposal and acquisition of section 119 or 120 securities

210B(1) Subsections (2) to (4) below apply in a case where, within a period of 10 days, an insurance company disposes of a number of section 119 or 120 securities and (whether subsequently or previously) acquires a number of section 119 or 120 securities if–

(a) the securities disposed of decrease the size of a chargeable section 119 or 120 holding,

(b) the securities acquired increase the size of the same chargeable section 119 or 120 holding, and

(c) (apart from this section) an allowable loss would accrue on the disposal.

210B(2) The securities disposed of shall be identified with the securities acquired.

210B(3) The securities disposed of shall be identified with securities acquired before the disposal rather than securities acquired after the disposal and–

(a) in the case of securities acquired before the disposal, with those acquired later rather than those acquired earlier, and

(b) in the case of securities acquired after the disposal, with those acquired earlier rather than those acquired later.

210B(4) Where securities acquired could be identified with securities disposed of either at an earlier or at a later date, they shall be identified with the former rather than the latter; and the identification of securities acquired with securities disposed of on any occasion shall preclude their identification with securities comprised in a later disposal.

210B(5) Subsections (2) to (4) above have effect subject to section 105(1).

210B(6) Subsections (2) to (4) above do not apply to–

(a) securities which are assets within section 212(1).

(b) [omitted by FA 2007, s. 38 and Sch. 7, para. 62(a), and repealed by FA 2007, s. 114 and Sch. 27, Pt. 2(7)]

210B(7) Subsections (2) to (4) above do not apply if–

(a) the securities disposed of are assets wholly matched to BLAGAB liabilities and the assets are appropriated to a BLAGAB internal linked fund,

(b) the securities acquired are, on acquisition, appropriated to that or another internal linked fund, and

(c) the disposal and acquisition are made with a view to adjusting the value of the assets of that fund, or of those funds, in order to match its or their liabilities.

210B(8) In this section–

"BLAGAB internal linked fund" means an internal linked fund all the assets appropriated to which are matched wholly to BLAGAB liabilities,

"chargeable section 119 or 120 holding" means a holding which is a separate holding as a result of section 119(1)(a), (c) or (d) or section 120(1)(a), (c) or (d) of the Finance Act 2012 (and section 121(1) and (2) of that Act),

"internal linked fund", in relation to an insurance company, means an account–

(a) to which assets matched to the company's life assurance liabilities are appropriated by the company, and

(b) which may be divided into units the value of which is determined by the company by reference to the value of those assets, and

"section 119 or 120 securities" means securities within the meaning of section 119 or 120 of the Finance Act 2012 (see section 121(6)).

History – In the heading to s. 210B the words "section 119 or 120 securities" substituted for the words "section 440A securities" by FA 2012, s. 146 and Sch. 16, para. 81(5) in relation to accounting periods beginning on or after 1 January 2013 (FA 2012, s. 148) but subject to transitional provisions in FA 2012, Sch. 17. Where an accounting period would otherwise straddle 1 January 2013, it is deemed to end on 31 December 2012 (FA 2012, s. 149).

In s. 210B(1) the words "section 119 or 120 securities" substituted for the words "section 440A securities" (in both places) by FA 2012, s. 146 and Sch. 16, para. 81(2)(a) in relation to accounting periods beginning on or after 1 January 2013 (FA 2012, s. 148) but subject to transitional provisions in FA 2012, Sch. 17. Where an accounting period would otherwise straddle 1 January 2013, it is deemed to end on 31 December 2012 (FA 2012, s. 149).

In s. 210B(1)(a) the words "chargeable section 119 or 120 holding" substituted for the words "chargeable section 440A holding" by FA 2012, s. 146 and Sch. 16, para. 81(2)(b) in relation to accounting periods beginning on or after 1 January 2013 (FA 2012, s. 148) but subject to transitional provisions in FA 2012, Sch. 17. Where an accounting period would otherwise straddle 1 January 2013, it is deemed to end on 31 December 2012 (FA 2012, s. 149).

In s. 210B(1)(b) the words "chargeable section 119 or 120 holding" substituted for the words "chargeable section 440A holding" by FA 2012, s. 146 and Sch. 16, para. 81(2)(b) in relation to accounting periods beginning on or after 1 January 2013 (FA 2012, s. 148) but subject to transitional provisions in FA 2012, Sch. 17. Where an accounting period would otherwise straddle 1 January 2013, it is deemed to end on 31 December 2012 (FA 2012, s. 149).

In s. 210B(7)(a) the words "assets wholly matched to BLAGAB liabilities and the assets are" substituted for the words "linked assets" by FA 2012, s. 146 and Sch. 16, para. 81(3) in relation to accounting periods beginning on or after 1 January 2013 (FA 2012, s. 148) but subject to transitional provisions in FA 2012, Sch. 17.Where an accounting period would otherwise straddle 1 January 2013, it is deemed to end on 31 December 2012 (FA 2012, s. 149).

In s. 210B(6)(a) the words "assets within section 212(1)" substituted for the former wording ("section 212 assets within the meaning of section 214(1) (rights under authorised unit trusts and interests in offshore funds)") by FA 2007, s. 41 and Sch. 10, para. 5(2), with effect in relation to periods of account beginning on or after 1 January 2007.

In s. 210B(6)(b) and the word "or" immediately preceding it omitted by FA 2007, s. 38 and Sch. 7, para. 62(a) and repealed by FA 2007, s. 114 and Sch. 27, Pt. 2(7) with effect; for income tax purposes from 2007–08 onwards; and for corporation tax purposes of insurance companies for periods of account beginning on or after 1 January 2007, subject to the transitional provisions in Sch. 7, Part 2 (FA 2007, s. 38(2), (3)).

S. 210B(8) substituted by FA 2012, s. 146 and Sch. 16, para. 81(4) in relation to accounting periods beginning on or after 1 January 2013 (FA 2012, s. 148) but subject to transitional provisions in FA 2012, Sch. 17. Where an accounting period would otherwise straddle 1 January 2013, it is deemed to end on 31 December 2012 (FA 2012, s. 149).

In s. 210B(8), in the definition for "chargeable section 440A holding" the reference to"subsection (2)(a)(i)" substituted for the former reference ("subsection (2)(a)(iii)") by FA 2007, s. 38 and Sch. 7, para. 62(b) with effect; for income tax purposes from 2007–08 onwards; and for corporation tax purposes of insurance companies for periods of account beginning on or after 1 January 2007 (FA 2007, s. 38(2)).

In s. 210B(8) the definition of "internal linked fund" omitted by FA 2007, s. 41 and Sch. 10, para. 9(2)(c) and repealed by FA 2007, s. 114 and Sch. 27, Pt. 2(10) with effect for periods of account beginning on or after 1 January 2007 (FA 2007, Sch. 10, para. 17(2)).

S. 210B inserted by FA 2003, s. 170 and Sch. 33, para. 15(1) which, by virtue of Sch. 33, para. 15(2), have effect in relation to disposals on or after 23 December 2002; but, by virtue of Sch. 33, para. 15(3), s. 210B has effect in relationto disposals made by an insurance during the period beginning with 23 December 2002 and ending with 31 December 2002, only if the amount of the allowable losses referable to the company's life assurance business which would have accrued to the company on the disposals (i.e. based on ignoring the operation of s. 210B) were at least £10 million.

Cross references – SI 2005/2014, reg. 35: modification of s. 210B so as to make it applicable to friendly societies carrying on life insurance business (which is not entirely tax exempt).

210C Losses on disposal of authorised investment fund assets to connected manager

210C(1) Section 18(3) does not apply in relation to a loss accruing on the disposal by an insurance company of authorised investment fund assets to the manager of the authorised investment fund.

210C(2) In this section–

"authorised investment fund assets" means assets held by the company for the purposes of its long-term business that consist of rights under an authorised unit trust or shares in an open-ended investment company,

"the manager of the authorised investment fund" means–

(a) in the case of an authorised unit trust, the person who is the manager of the unit trust scheme for the purposes of Chapter 3 of Part 17 of the Financial Services and Markets Act 2000, and

(b) in the case of an open-ended investment company, a director or other person having responsibility for the management of its scheme property, and

"open-ended investment company" means a company incorporated in the United Kingdom to which section 236 of the Financial Services and Markets Act 2000 applies.

History – S. 210C inserted by FA 2007, s. 40 and Sch. 10, para. 3 with effect in relation to losses accruing in a period of account beginning on or after 1 January 2007 (FA 2007, Sch. 10, para. 17(4)).
In s. 210C(2) in the definition of "authorised investment fund assets", the words "held by the company for the purposes of its long-term business that consist of" substituted for the words "of the company's long-term insurance fund consisting of" by FA 2012, s. 146 and Sch. 16, para. 82 in relation to accounting periods beginning on or after 1 January 2013 (FA 2012, s. 148) but subject to transitional provisions in FA 2012, Sch. 17. Where an accounting period would otherwise straddle 1 January 2013, it is deemed to end on 31 December 2012 (FA 2012, s. 149).

211 Transfers of business

211(1) This section applies where an insurance business transfer scheme has effect to transfer business which consists of the effecting or carrying out of contracts of long-term insurance from one person ("the transferor") to another ("the transferee").

211(1A) [Repealed by FA 2003, s. 216 and Sch. 43, Pt. 3(12).]

211(2) Where this section applies the transferor and the transferee are treated for the purposes of corporation tax on chargeable gains as if any assets included in the transfer which–

(a) immediately before they are acquired by the transferee, were assets held by the transferor for the purposes of its long-term business, and

(b) immediately after they are so acquired are assets held by the transferee for the purposes of its long-term business,

were acquired for a consideration of such amount as would secure that neither a gain nor a loss would accrue to the transferor on the disposal.

211(2A) The reference in subsection (2) above to assets included in the transfer does not include assets which formed part of the long-term business fixed capital of the company in question.

211(3) [Repealed by FA 2000, s. 102 and Sch. 29, para. 30(4), s. 156 and Sch. 40, Pt. II(12).]

211(4) Subsection (2) does not apply in relation to assets which are referable to the long-term business of the transferor if all the income of the transferor's long-term business is chargeable to corporation tax on income under section 35 of CTA 2009.

History – S. 211(1A) repealed by FA 2003, s. 216 and Sch. 43, Pt. 3(12) which, by virtue of FA 2003, s. 216(2), came into force on 10 July 2003 (i.e. date of Royal Assent of FA 2003).
S. 211(1) and (1A) substituted for former s. 211(1) by SI 2001/3629, art. 66(1) operative in relation to any transfer under a scheme falling within section 105 of the Financial Services and Markets Act 2000, including an excluded scheme falling within Case 2, 3 or 4 of subsection (3) of that section.
In s. 211(2)(a) the words "held by the transferor for the purposes of its long-term business" substituted for the words "of the transferor's long-term insurance fund" by FA 2012, s. 146 and Sch. 16, para. 83(2)(a) in relation to accounting periods beginning on or after 1 January 2013 (FA 2012, s. 148) but subject to transitional provisions in FA 2012, Sch. 17. Where an accounting period would otherwise straddle 1 January 2013, it is deemed to end on 31 December 2012 (FA 2012, s. 149).
In s. 211(2)(b) the words "held by the transferee for the purposes of its long-term business" substituted for the words "of the transferee's long-term insurance fund" by FA 2012, s. 146 and Sch. 16, para. 83(2)(b) in relation to accounting periods beginning on or after 1 January 2013 (FA 2012, s. 148) but subject to transitional provisions in FA 2012, Sch. 17. Where an accounting period would otherwise straddle 1 January 2013, it is deemed to end on 31 December 2012 (FA 2012, s. 149).
Former s. 211(2) and (3) substituted for former subsections (2) and (2A) by FA 2007, s. 40 and Sch. 9, para. 14(2), with effect in relation to accounting periods beginning on or after 1 January 2007 (FA 2007, Sch. 9, para. 17(1)).
In former s. 211(2) words "Subject to subsection (3) below" repealed, and after paragraph (a) word "or" inserted by FA 2000, s. 102 and Sch. 29, para. 30(2)(a), (b), s. 156 and Sch. 40, Pt. II(12), with effect in relation to disposals made on or after 1 April 2000.
Former s. 211(2)(a) words "within the meaning of that section" inserted by FA 2002, s. 45 and Sch. 9, para. 5(11), with effect in relation to shares or debentures issued on or after 17 April 2002.
In former s. 211(2)(a) and in the closing words, "or amalgamation" which occurredafter "reconstruction" repealed by FA 2002, s. 141 and Sch. 40, Pt. 3(2), with effect in relation to shares or debentures issued on or after 17 April 2002.
Former s. 211(2)(b) and word "or" following it repealed by FA 2000, s. 102 and Sch. 29, para. 30(2)(c), s. 156 and Sch. 40, Pt. II(12), with effect in relation to disposals made on or after 1 April 2000.
In s. 211(2A) the words "assets which formed part of the long-term business fixed capital of the company in question" substituted for the words "structural assets within the meaning of section 83XA of the Finance Act 1989" by FA 2012, s. 146 and Sch. 16, para. 83(3) in relation to accounting periods beginning on or after 1 January 2013 (FA 2012, s. 148) but subject to transitional provisions in FA 2012, Sch. 17. Where an accounting period would otherwise straddle 1 January 2013, it is deemed to end on 31 December 2012 (FA 2012, s. 149).
New s. 211(2A) inserted by FA 2007, s. 41 and Sch. 10, para. 2(4) with effect in relation to accounting periods beginning on or after 1 January 2007 (FA 2007, Sch. 10, para. 17(1)).
Former s. 211(2A) inserted by FA 2000, s. 102 and Sch. 29, para. 30(3) with effect in relation to disposals made on or after 1 April 2000.
Former s. 211(3) repealed by s. 102 and FA 2000, Sch. 29 para. 30(4), s. 156 and Sch. 40, Pt. II(12), with effect in relation to disposals made on or after 1 April 2000.
S. 211(4) inserted by FA2012, s. 146 and Sch. 16, para. 83(4) in relation to accounting periods beginning on or after 1 January 2013 (FA 2012, s. 148) but subject to transitional provisions in FA 2012, Sch. 17. Where an accounting period would otherwise straddle 1 January 2013, it is deemed to end on 31 December 2012 (FA 2012, s. 149).

Derivations – ICTA 1970, s. 267A, as inserted by FA 1990, s. 48 and Sch. 9, para. 1.

Cross references – S. 25(4): priority of no gain, no loss provisions (s. 139) over deemed market value disposal rules for cessation of trade by UK branch or agency in accordance with court-approved insurance company transfer scheme.
S. 139: no gain, no loss etc. on reconstruction or amalgamation involving the transfer of business where the transferor company receives no part of the consideration (s. 139(1)(c)) but excluding trading stock (s. 139(2)), provided it is done for bona fide commercial arrangements and not to avoid tax (s. 139(5)).
Sch. 7B, para. 9A: transfers in s. 211(1) sanctioned or authorised after 30 June 1994 include "qualifying overseas transfers" (as defined in ICTA 1988, Sch. 19AC, para. 4A).

FA 1994, s. 249: companies treated as resident in the UK for tax purposes, but resident abroad for the purposes of any double taxation relief arrangements ("dual resident companies"), are with effect from 30 November 1993 to be treated as non-UK resident for all tax purposes, even if they are incorporated in the UK.

Statutory instruments – SI 1997/473, reg. 44: modification of s. 211 in relation to specified transactions that take place on or after 1 January 1995; in accordance with SI 1997/473, reg. 2, specified transactions mean: (a) the transfer of the whole or part of the business of a friendly society to another friendly society, (b) the amalgamation of two or more friendly societies, (c) the transfer of the whole or part of the business of a friendly society to a company which is not a friendly society, and (d) the conversion of a friendly society into a company which is not a friendly society.

SI 1995/171, reg. 4(1), (2): modification of s. 211(1), s. 213(5), s. 214(11) and s. 214A(7) in certain cases of transfers of business of friendly societies.

Other material – HMRC press release, 27 July 1990: clearance applications in respect of proposed transfers of long term business.

Notes – S. 15: meaning of "chargeable gain".
S. 21–34: general meaning of "disposal" and "asset".
S. 288: interpretation, including reference to sections being those of this Act.

211ZA Transfers of business: transfer of unused losses

211ZA(1) This section applies where–

(a) an insurance business transfer scheme has effect to transfer business consisting of or including basic life assurance and general annuity business from one person (**"the transferor"**) to another (**"the transferee"**) or more than one others (**"the transferees"**), and

(b) the transferor has relevant unused losses.

211ZA(2) For the purposes of subsection (1)(b) above the transferor has relevant unused losses if–

(a) BLAGAB allowable losses accrue to the transferor in the accounting period ending with the day of the transfer or have so accrued in any earlier accounting period, and

(b) they are not deducted from chargeable gains accruing to the transferor in that accounting period and have not been deducted from chargeable gains so accruing in any previous accounting period.

211ZA(2A) For the purposes of subsection (2) above, where there is no accounting period of the transferor ending with the day of the transfer–

(a) there is deemed to be such an accounting period,

(b) BLAGAB allowable losses which would have accrued to the transferor in that accounting period are deemed to have accrued to the transferor in that accounting period, and

(c) if those BLAGAB allowable losses would not have been deducted from chargeable gains accruing to the transferor in that accounting period, they are deemed to be relevant unused losses.

211ZA(3) Subject as follows–

(a) for the purposes of ascertaining the transferor's total profits for any accounting period ending after that in which the transfer takes place, the relevant unused losses are deemed not to have accrued to the transferor, but

(b) (instead) they are treated as accruing to the transferee (in accordance with subsection (4) below).

211ZA(4) The losses treated as accruing to the transferee under subsection (3)(b) above shall be deemed to be BLAGAB allowable losses accruing to the transferee in the accounting period of the transferee in which the transfer takes place.

211ZA(5) But those losses are not allowable as a deduction from chargeable gains accruing before the transfer takes place.

211ZA(6) For the purposes of section 210A (ring-fencing of losses), the shareholders' share of those losses is to be taken to be the same proportion as would be the shareholders' share of them if they had remained losses of the transferor.

211ZA(7) If only part of the transferor's basic life assurance and general annuity business is transferred, subsection (3) above applies as if the references to the relevant unused losses were to such part of the relevant unused losses as is appropriate.

211ZA(8) If the transfer is to more than one others, subsection (3)(b) above applies as if the reference to the relevant unused losses being treated as accruing to the transferee were to such part of the relevant unused losses as is appropriate being treated as accruing to each of the transferees.

211ZA(9) Any question arising as to the operation of subsection (7) or (8) above shall be determined in the same manner as an appeal, and both the transferor and the transferee shall be entitled to be a party to any proceedings.

211ZA(10) *In this section* **"BLAGAB allowable losses"** means allowable losses referable in accordance with Chapter 4 of Part 2 of the Finance Act 2012, to the transferor's basic life assurance and general annuity business.

History – S. 211ZA(2A) inserted by SI 2008/381, art. 28(2), with effect from 19 February 2008 in relation to transfers of business taking place on or after that date.
In s. 211ZA(3)(a), the word "ending" inserted by SI 2008/381, art. 28(3), with effect from 19 February 2008 in relation to transfers of business taking place on or after that date.

In s. 211ZA(9) the words "in the same manner as an appeal, and both the transferor and the transferee shall be entitled to be a party to any proceedings" substituted for the words "by the Special Commissioners who shall determine the question in the same manner as they determine appeals; but both the transferor and the transferee (or the one of the transferees concerned) shall be entitled to appear and be heard or to make representations in writing" by SI 2009/56, art. 3(1) and Sch. 1, para. 180, operative from 1 April 2009, subject to transitional and saving provisions in SI 2009/56, Sch. 3.
In s. 211ZA(10) the words "in accordance with Chapter 4 of Part 2 of the Finance Act 2012," substituted for the words "(in accordance with section 432A of the Taxes Act)" by FA 2012, s. 146 and Sch. 16, para. 84 in relation to accounting periods beginning on or after 1 January 2013 (FA 2012, s. 148) but subject to transitional provisions in FA 2012, Sch. 17. Where an accounting period would otherwise straddle 1 January 2013, it is deemed to end on 31 December 2012 (FA 2012, s. 149).
In former s. 211ZA(10), the words "(in accordance with section 432A of the Taxes Act)" have been inserted after the word "referable" by FA 2004, s. 47 and Sch. 7, para. 9(3)(b) with effect from 22 July 2004.
S. 211ZA inserted by FA 2003, s. 170 and Sch. 33, para. 21(1) which, by virtue of Sch. 33, para. 21(2), have effect in relation to insurance business transfer schemes taking place on or after 1 January 2003.

Cross references – SI 2005/2014, reg. 36: modification of s. 211ZA so as to make it applicable to friendly societies carrying on life insurance business (which is not entirely tax exempt).

211A Gains of insurance company from venture capital investment partnership

211A Schedule 7AD to this Act has effect with respect to the gains of an insurance company from a venture capital investment partnership.

History – S. 211A inserted by FA 2002, s. 85(1).

211B Transfers of assets to certain collective investment schemes

211B(1) Subsection (2) applies if–

(a) an asset of an insurance company is made subject to a collective investment scheme which is–

 (i) an authorised contractual scheme which is a co-ownership scheme, or

 (ii) a relevant offshore fund,

(b) that is wholly in exchange for the company being issued with units in the scheme, and

(c) the condition in subsection (3) is met.

211B(2) For the purposes of corporation tax on chargeable gains, the company is to be treated–

(a) as having disposed of the asset mentioned in subsection (1)(a) for a consideration of such amount as would secure that on the disposal neither a gain nor a loss would accrue to the company, and

(b) as having acquired the units mentioned in subsection (1)(b) for a consideration of the same amount.

211B(3) The condition is that–

(a) immediately before the asset mentioned in subsection (1)(a) is made subject to the scheme, the asset was an asset held by the company for the purposes of its long-term business within one of the long-term business categories, and

(b) immediately after the asset is made subject to the scheme, the units mentioned in subsection (1)(b) are assets held by the company for the purposes of its long-term business within the same category.

211B(4) For the purposes of subsection (3), a **"long-term business category"** is–

(a) if the company is a UK life insurance company, a long-term business category set out in section 116(2) of the Finance Act 2012 (subject to section 116(3)), or

(b) if the company is an overseas life insurance company, a UK long-term business category set out in section 117(2) of that Act (subject to section 117(3)).

211B(5) In subsection (1), **"relevant offshore fund"** has the same meaning as in section 103A (application of Act to certain offshore funds).

211B(6) In this section, in relation to a relevant offshore fund, **"units"** means rights in the fund which are treated as shares under section 103A.

History – S. 211B inserted by SI 2013/1400, reg. 4, with effect in relation to disposals on or after 8 June 2013.

212 Annual deemed disposal of holdings of unit trusts etc.

212(1) Where at the end of an accounting period the assets held by an insurance company for the purposes of its long-term business include –

(a) rights under an authorised unit trust, or

(b) interests in an offshore fund, or

(ba) units in an authorised contractual scheme which is a co-ownership scheme, or

(c) shares in a company which is, or is a member of, a UK REIT within the meaning of Part 12 of CTA 2010 (Real Estate Investment Trusts), then, subject to the following provisions of this section and to section 213, the company shall be deemed for the purposes of corporation tax on capital gains to have disposed of and immediately reacquired each of the assets concerned at its market value at that time.

212(2) [Omitted by FA 2012, s. 146 and Sch. 16, para. 85(3).]

212(2A) [Omitted by FA 2007, s. 41 and Sch. 10, para. 5(3)(a); and repealed by FA 2007, s. 114 and Sch. 27, Pt. 2(10)]

212(3) [Repealed by FA 1993, s. 91(2)(b), s. 213 and Sch. 23, Pt. III(8).]

212(4) [Repealed by FA 1993, s. 91(2)(b), s. 213 and Sch. 23, Pt. III(8).]

212(5) [Omitted by SI 2009/3001, reg. 127(3)(b) and repealed by SI 2009/3001, reg. 13(2) and Sch. 2.]

212(6) [Repealed by FA 1993, s. 91(2)(b), s. 213 and Sch. 23, Pt. III(8).]

212(6A) [Omitted by SI 2009/3001, reg. 127(3)(b) and repealed by SI 2009/3001, reg. 13(2) and Sch. 2.]

212(7) [Omitted by SI 2009/3001, reg. 127(3)(b) and repealed by SI 2009/3001, reg. 13(2) and Sch. 2.]

212(7A) [Omitted by FA 2007, s. 39 and Sch. 8, para. 18 and repealed by FA 2007, s. 114 and Sch. 27, Pt. 2(8).]

212(8) [Repealed by FA 1993, s. 213 and Sch. 23, Pt. III(8).]

212(9) This section applies to an overseas life insurance company as if references in subsection (1) to assets were to such of the assets concerned as are UK assets.

212(10) Assets (whether situated in the United Kingdom or elsewhere) are **"UK assets"** if, in accordance with the provision made by or under Chapter 4 of Part 2 of CTA 2009, they fall to be attributed to the permanent establishment in the United Kingdom through which the company carries on life assurance business.

History – In s. 212(1) the words "held by an insurance company for the purposes of its long-term business" substituted for the words "of an insurance company's long-term insurance fund" by FA 2012, s. 146 and Sch. 16, para. 85(2) in relation to accounting periods beginning on or after 1 January 2013 (FA 2012, s. 148) but subject to transitional provisions in FA 2012, Sch. 17. Where an accounting period would otherwise straddle 1 January 2013, it is deemed to end on 31 December 2012 (FA 2012, s. 149).

In s. 212(1)(b), the words "within the meaning of section 355 of TIOPA 2010" omitted by SI 2013/1400, reg. 5(a), with effect in relation to disposals on or after 8 June 2013.

S. 212(1)(ba) inserted by SI 2013/1400, reg. 5(b), with effect in relation to disposals on or after 8 June 2013.

In s. 212(1)(b), the words "section 355 of TIOPA 2010" substituted for "section 40A of the Finance Act 2008" by TIOPA 2010, s. 374 and Sch. 8, para. 165, with effect for corporation tax purposes for accounting periods ending on or after 1 April 2010, for income tax and capital gains tax purposes for the tax year 2010–11 and subsequent tax years, and for petroleum revenue tax purposes for chargeable periods beginning on or after 1 July 2010.

In s. 212(1)(b), the words "interests in an offshore fund within the meaning of section 40A of the Finance Act 2008" substituted for the words "relevant interests in an offshore fund" by SI 2009/3001, reg. 127(3)(a), with effect from 1 December 2009 for various purposes (in accordance with the provisions of SI 2009/3001, reg. 1), subject to transitional and savings provisions in SI 2009/3001, Sch. 1.

In s. 212(1)(c), the words "which is, or is a member of, a UK REIT within the meaning of Part 12 of CTA 2010" substituted for "to which Part 4 of the Finance Act 2006 applies" by CTA 2010, s. 1177 and Sch. 1, para. 249, with effect for corporation tax purposes for accounting periods ending on or after 1 April 2010, and for income tax and capital gains tax purposes for the tax year 2010–11 and subsequent tax years.

S. 212(1)(c) and the preceding word ", or" inserted by FA 2006, s. 137, with effect from 19 July 2005 but in relation to provisions that effectively come into force for accounting periods beginning on or after 1 January 2007.

In s. 212(1), the words "long-term insurance" substituted for the words "long term business" by SI 2001/3629, art. 73(1)(a) operative from 1 December 2001.

S. 212(2) omitted by FA 2012, s. 146 and Sch. 16, para. 85(3) in relation to accounting periods beginning on or after 1 January2013 (FA 2012, s. 148) but subject to transitional provisions in FA 2012, Sch. 17. Where an accounting period would otherwise straddle 1 January 2013, it is deemed to end on 31 December 2012 (FA 2012, s. 149).

In former s. 212(2) the words "gross roll-up business" substituted for the former wording ("pension business or life reinsurance business or to assets of the overseas life assurance fund") by FA 2007, s. 38 and Sch. 7, para. 63, with effect for income tax purposes from 2007–08 onwards; and for corporation tax purposes of insurance companies for periods of account beginning on or after 1 January 2007, subject to the transitional provisions in Sch. 7, Part 2 (FA 2007, s. 38(2), (3)).

In former s. 212(2), the former words which appeared at the end repealed by FA 1993, s. 91(2)(b), s. 213 and Sch. 23, Pt. III(8) in relation to any accounting period beginning on or after 1 January 1993; words "or life reinsurance business" inserted by FA 1995, s. 51 and Sch. 8, para. 9(2) in relation to accounting periods beginning on or after 1 January 1995.

S. 212A(2A) omitted by FA 2007, s. 41 and Sch. 10, para. 5(3)(a), and repealed by FA 2007, s. 114 and Sch. 27, Pt. 2(10) with effect for periods of account beginning on or after 1 January 2007 (Sch. 10, para. 17(2)).

S. 212(2A) inserted by FA 1996, s. 104 and Sch. 14 para. 63 for accounting periods ending after 31 March 1996, subject to FA 1996, Sch. 15.

S. 212(3), (4) and (6) repealed by FA 1993, s. 91(2), s. 213 and Sch. 23, Pt. III(8) and in s. 212(7) the word "214A" substituted by FA 1993, s. 91(3) in relation to any accounting period beginning on or after 1 January 1993.

S. 212(5)–(7) omitted by SI 2009/3001, reg. 127(3)(b) and repealed by SI 2009/3001, reg. 13(2) and Sch. 2, with effect from 1 December 2009 for various purposes (in accordance with the provisions of SI 2009/3001, reg. 1), subject to transitional and savings provisions in SI 2009/3001, Sch. 1.

Former s. 212(5)(b) substituted by FA 1995, s. 134(6) for deciding on or after 29 November 1994 whether an interest is a relevant interest in an offshore fund.

In former s. 212(6A)(a), the words "paragraphs (a) to (c) of subsection (1) of section 756A" substitutedfor the words "paragraphs (a) to (c) of subsection (1) of section 759" by FA 2004, s. 145 and Sch. 26, para. 11(a) with effect, by virtue of FA 2004, s. 145(2)(a), for account periods (within the meaning of ICTA 1988, Pt. 17, Ch. 5) ending on or after 22 July 2004.

In former s. 212(6A)(b), the words "section 759 of that Act" substituted for the words "that section" by FA 2004, s. 145 and Sch. 26, para. 11(b) with effect, by virtue of FA 2004, s. 145(2)(a), for account periods (within the meaning of ICTA 1988, Pt. 17, Ch. 5) ending on or after 22 July 2004.

Former s. 212(6A) inserted by FA 1995, s. 134(7) for deciding on or after 29 November 1994 whether an interest is a relevant interest in an offshore fund.

In former s. 212(7), immediately after paragraph (b), the words "; and in this section and sections 213 to 214A other expressions have the same meanings as in Chapter I of Part XII of the Taxes Act" repealed by FA 2003, s. 216 and Sch. 43, Pt. 3(12) which, by virtue of FA 2003, s. 216(2), came into force on 10 July 2003 (i.e. date of Royal Assent of FA 2003).
S. 212(7A) omitted by FA 2007, s. 39 and Sch. 8, para. 18, and repealed by FA 2007, s. 114 and Sch. 27, Pt. 2(8) with effect for periods of account for insurance companies beginning on or after 1 January 2007, subject to the transitional provisions in Sch. 8, Part 2.
S. 212(7A) inserted by FA 1995, s. 51 and Sch. 8, para. 28(5) in relation to accounting periods beginning on or after 1 January 1995.
S. 212(8) repealed by FA 1993, s. 213 and Sch. 23, Pt. III(8), with effect, in accordance with FA 1993, s. 91(1), in relation to accounting periods beginning on or after 1 January 1991 or, where the Treasury by order appoint a later day, in relation to accounting periods beginning on or after that day (and not in relation to any earlier accounting period, even if the order is made after 1 January 1991 and the period has ended before it is made).
S. 212(9) and (10) inserted by FA 2012, s. 146 and Sch. 16, para. 85(4) in relation to accounting periods beginning on or after 1 January 2013 (FA 2012, s. 148) but subject to transitional provisions in FA 2012, Sch. 17. Where an accounting period would otherwise straddle 1 January 2013, it is deemed to end on 31 December 2012 (FA 2012, s. 149).
Former s. 212 has effect in relation to accounting periods beginning on or after 1 January 1993 (FA 1993, s. 91(1), and see cross reference below).

Derivations – FA 1990, s. 46(1)–(7), (9), as amended by FA 1991, s. 48 and Sch. 7, para. 14.

Cross references – Sch. 7A, para. 1(10): in relation to pre-entry losses determining whether loss under s. 212 accrued before a company became a group member, s. 213 is disregarded.
Sch. 7B, para. 10(1): modification of s. 212 in relation to overseas life insurance companies by deemed insertion of s. 212(5A) in relation to accounting periods beginning after 31 December 1992.
ICTA 1988, s. 431–458 (Pt. XII, Ch. I) insurance companies etc., including meaning of "basic life assurance and general annuity business", "overseas life assurance fund" etc. and (s. 432A(8), (9)) determination of the appropriate part of the investment reserve for the apportionment of income.
ICTA 1988, s. 440B: s. 212(1) does not apply, for accounting periods beginning on or after 1 January 1995 where the profits of a life assurance business taxed under Sch. D, Case I, but without prejudice to bringing into account amounts deferred under TCGA 1992, s. 213(1) or s. 214A(2) from accounting periods beginning before 1 January 1995.
ICTA 1988, s. 757–764 (Pt. XVII, Ch. V): offshore funds, including a material interest in an offshore fund as not embracing shares in certain ten per cent overseas companies necessary or desirable for the maintenance and development of a trade carried on by the company or an associated company nor an interest permitting the holder to wind up the fund company with an entitlement to more than 50 per cent of the assets.
FA 1989, s. 85: charge of receipts which would be trading receipts under Sch. D, Case VI if they are referable to basic life assurance or general annuity business with limited exceptions.
FA 1993, s. 91(1): s. 212 has effect in relation to accounting periods beginning on or after 1 January 1993, and neither it nor its predecessor has effect in relation to any earlier accounting periods.
SI 1992/1655, reg. 21: modifications of s. 212 so far as it applies to the life or endowment business carried on (a) by registered friendly societies, (b) by directive societies within SI 1992/1655, reg. 5(2), and (c) non-directive societies for accounting periods beginning on or after 6 April 1992.
SI 1998/1871, reg. 23: modification of s. 212(2)(a) so far as concerns individual savings account business of insurance companies.
SI 2005/2014, reg. 37: modification of s. 212 so as to make it applicable to friendly societies carrying on life insurance business (which is not entirely tax exempt).
SI 2006/3271, reg. 30: modification of s. 212 with effect from 31 December 2006 in relation to periods of account ending on or after that day.
SI 2007/2145, reg. 13: modification of s. 212(2) where any part of the business of a company is business which is exempt from corporation tax under ICTA 1988, s. 460(11) or (12), s. 461(4) or (4A) or s. 461B(5) or (6A).
SI 2012/3044, reg. 6: modification of s. 212, with effect in relation to accounting periods beginning on or after 1 January 2013, to avoid a double charge where an insurance company is deemed to dispose of an interest in a CFC under s. 212.

Notes – S. 21–34: general meaning of "disposal" and "asset".
S. 99: meaning of "authorised unit trust".
S. 287: power of Treasury exercisable by statutory instrument but not subject to the negative resolution procedure of the House of Commons.
S. 288: interpretation, including the "Taxes Act" as ICTA 1988 and reference to other sections as being those of this Act.
ICTA 1988, s. 12: meaning of "accounting period".

213 Spreading of gains and losses under section 212

213(1) Any chargeable gains or allowable losses which would otherwise accrue on disposals deemed by virtue of section 212 to have been made at the end of a company's accounting period shall be treated as not accruing to it, but instead–

(a) there shall be ascertained the difference (**"the net amount"**) between the aggregate of those gains and the aggregate of those losses, and

(b) one-seventh of the net amount shall be treated as a chargeable gain or, where it represents an excess of losses over gains, as an allowable loss accruing to the company at the end of the accounting period, and

(c) a further one-seventh shall be treated as a chargeable gain or, as the case may be, as an allowable loss accruing at the end of each succeeding accounting period until the whole amount has been accounted for.

213(1A) Subsection (1) above shall not apply to chargeable gains or allowable losses except so far as they are gains or losses which–

(a) are referable, in accordance with Chapter 4 of Part 2 of the Finance Act 2012, to basic life assurance and general annuity business.

(b) [omitted by s. 38 and Sch. 7, para. 64, and repealed by s. 114 and Sch. 27, Part 2(7).]

213(2) For any accounting period of less than one year, the fraction of one-seventh referred to in subsection (1)(c) above shall be proportionately reduced; and where this subsection has had effect in relation to any accounting period before the last for which subsection (1)(c) above applies, the fraction treated as accruing at the end of that last accounting period shall also be adjusted appropriately.

213(3) Subject to subsection (8H) below, where–

(a) the net amount for an accounting period of an insurance company represents an excess of gains over losses,

(b) the net amount for either of the next two accounting periods (after taking account of any reductions made by virtue of this section) represents an excess of losses over gains,

(c) there is (after taking account of any such reductions) no net amount for the intervening accounting period (if there is one),

(ca) the intervening accounting period (if there is one) is not an accounting period in which the company joined a group of companies, and

(d) within 2 years after the end of the later accounting period the company makes a claim for the purpose in respect of the whole or part of the net amount for that period,

the net amounts for both the earlier and the later period shall be reduced by the amount in respect of which the claim is made.

213(3A) [Omitted by FA 2003, s. 170 and Sch. 33, para. 16(3) and repealed by FA 2003, s. 216 and Sch. 43, Pt. 3(12)]

213(3B) [Omitted by FA 2003, s. 170 and Sch. 33, para. 16(3) and repealed by FA 2003, s. 216 and Sch. 43, Pt. 3(12)]

213(4) Subject to subsection (5) below, where a company ceases to carry on long-term business before the end of the last of the accounting periods for which subsection (1)(c) above would apply in relation to a net amount, the fraction of that amount that is treated as accruing at the end of the accounting period ending with the cessation shall be such as to secure that the whole of the net amount has been accounted for.

213(4ZA) Subsection (4) applies in relation to an overseas life insurance company with the insertion after "long-term business" of the words "in the United Kingdom through a permanent establishment".

213(4ZB) Subject to subsection (5) below, where a company–

(a) acquired units in a collective investment scheme where section 211B(2) applied in relation to that acquisition, and

(b) other than by virtue of section 212, disposes of some or all of those units during the period of three years after the end of the accounting period of the company in which the acquisition took place,

the fraction of any net amount that is treated as accruing at the end of the accounting period of the company in which the disposal occurs is to be adjusted so as to secure that the whole of the chargeable gain or allowable loss attributable to the units disposed of which has been taken into account in determining the net amount has been accounted for; and fractions of the net amount treated as accruing at the end of subsequent accounting periods are to be adjusted accordingly.

213(4ZC) For the purposes of subsection (4ZB) (notwithstanding the provisions of Chapter 1 of Part 4 (shares, securities, options etc))–

(a) units in a collective investment scheme acquired as mentioned in subsection (4ZB)(a) are treated as being disposed of before other units in the scheme or, where there are different classes of unit in the scheme, units of the same class held by the company, and

(b) where units are acquired as mentioned in subsection (4ZB)(a) at different times, units acquired at a later time are treated as disposed of before units acquired at an earlier time or, where there are different classes of unit in the scheme, units of the same class acquired at an earlier time.

213(4ZD) In subsections (4ZB) and (4ZC), in relation to a relevant offshore fund, **"units"** means rights in the fund which are treated as shares under section 103A (application of Act to certain offshore funds).

213(4ZE) In subsection (4ZD), **"relevant offshore fund"** has the same meaning as in section 103A.

213(4A) The following provisions apply where an insurance business transfer scheme has effect to transfer business which consists of the effecting or carrying out of contracts of long-term insurance from one person ("the transferor") to another ("the transferee").

213(5) Subject to subsections (5A) to (7) below, any chargeable gain or allowable loss which (making the assumptions in subsection (5ZA) below) would have accrued to the transferor by virtue of *subsection (1) above after the transfer* shall instead be deemed to accrue to the transferee.

213(5ZA) The assumptions referred to in subsection (5) above are–

(a) that the transferor had continued to carry on the business transferred after the transfer, and

(b) where there is no accounting period of the transferor ending with the day of the transfer, that for the purposes of section 212 and this section, there was such an accounting period.

213(5A) Subsection (5) above shall not apply where the transferee is resident outside the United Kingdom unless the business to which the transfer relates is carried on by the transferee, for a period beginning with the time when the transfer takes effect, through a permanent establishment in the United Kingdom.

213(6) Where subsection (5) above has effect, the amount of the gain or loss accruing at the end of the first accounting period of the transferee ending after the day when the transfer takes place shall be calculated as if that accounting period began with the day after the transfer.

213(7) Where the transfer is of part only of the transferor's long-term business, subsection (5) above shall apply only to such part of any amount to which it would otherwise apply as is appropriate.

213(8) Any question arising as to the operation of subsection (7) above shall be determined in the same manner as an appeal, and both the transferor and the transferee shall be entitled to be a party to any proceedings.

213(8A) Subsection (8B) below applies where–

(a) [omitted by SI 2008/381, art. 29(4)]

(b) the transferor and the transferee are, at the time of the transfer, members of the same group,

(c) the transferred assets net amount for the accounting period of the transferor ending with the day of the transfer, or for the immediately preceding accounting period of the transferor, ("the relevant pre-transfer period of the transferor") represents an excess of gains over losses,

(d) the transferred assets net amount for the accounting period of the transferee in which the transfer takes place, or for the immediately following accounting period of the transferee, ("the relevant post-transfer period of the transferee") represents an excess of losses over gains (after taking account of any reductions made by virtue of this section), and

(e) within 2 years after the end of the relevant post-transfer period of the transferee, the transferor and the transferee make a joint election in respect of the whole or part of the net amount for that period by notice to an officer of the Board.

213(8B) Subject to subsections (8C) to (8E) and (8H) below, the transferred assets net amounts for both the relevant pre-transfer period of the transferor and the relevant post-transfer period of the transferee shall be reduced by the amount in respect of which the election is made.

213(8C) Subsection (8B) above does not apply if–

(a) the relevant post-transfer period of the transferee is the accounting period immediately following that in which the transfer takes place, and

(b) the relevant pre-transfer period of the transferor is the accounting period immediately preceding that ending with the day of the transfer.

213(8D) If–

(a) the relevant post-transfer period of the transferee is the accounting period immediately following that in which the transfer takes place, and

(b) the relevant pre-transfer period of the transferor is the accounting period ending with the day of the transfer,

subsection (8B) above applies only if the conditions in subsection (8F) below are satisfied in relation to the accounting period of the transferee in which the transfer takes place.

213(8E) If–

(a) the relevant post-transfer period of the transferee is the accounting period in which the transfer takes place, and

(b) the relevant pre-transfer period of the transferor is the accounting period immediately preceding that ending with the day of the transfer,

subsection (8B) above applies only if the conditions in subsection (8F) below are satisfied in relation to the accounting period of the transferor ending with the day of the transfer.

213(8F) The conditions referred to in subsections (8D) and (8E) above are that–

(a) there is (after taking account of any reductions made by virtue of this section) no transferred assets net amount for the accounting period, and

(b) the company whose accounting period it is did not join a group of companies in the accounting period.

213(8G) A copy of the notice containing an election under subsection (8A)(e) above must accompany the tax return for the relevant post-transfer period of the transferee; and paragraphs 54 to 60 of Schedule 18 to the Finance Act 1998 (claims and elections for corporation tax purposes) do not apply to such an election.

213(8H) Subsection (3) above has effect where the company, or the transferee, in question joins a group of companies in the accounting period for which the net amount represents an excess of losses over gains as if a claim or election could not be made in respect of that net amount except to the extent (if any) that the net amount would still arise even if losses accruing after the date on which the company or transferee joined the group of companies were disregarded.

213(8HA) Subsections (8A) and (8B) above have effect where the company, or the transferee, in question joins a group of companies in the accounting period for which the transferred assets net amount represents an excess of losses over gains as if a claim or election could not be made in respect of that net amount except to the extent (if any) that the transferred assets net amount would still arise even if losses accruing after the date on which the company or transferee joined the group of companies were disregarded.

213(8I) References in this section to a company joining a group of companies are to be construed in accordance with section 184C as if those references were contained in that section; and in subsection (8A) (b) above **"group"** has the same meaning as in that section.

213(8J) **"Transferred assets net amount"** means a net amount ascertained in accordance with section 213(1)(a) but only in relation to those assets referred to in section 212(1) which are transferred by the insurance business transfer scheme from the transferor to the transferee.

213(9) [Repealed by FA 1993, s. 213 and Sch. 23, Pt. III(8).]

213(10) [Omitted by SI 2008/381, art. 29(10).]

History – In s. 213(1A), the words ", in accordance with Chapter 4 of Part 2 of the Finance Act 2012," substituted for the words "(in accordance with section 432A of the Taxes Act)" by FA 2012, s. 146 and Sch. 16, para. 86(2) in relation to accounting periods beginning on or after 1 January 2013 (FA 2012, s. 148) but subject to transitional provisions in FA 2012, Sch. 17. Where an accounting period would otherwise straddle 1 January 2013, it is deemed to end on 31 December 2012 (FA 2012, s. 149).

In s. 213(1A) the whole of the text that follows the words "general annuity business" (which included para. (b) and the words following that paragraph) omitted by FA 2007, s. 38 and Sch. 7, para. 64, and repealed by s. 114 and Sch. 27, Part 2(7) with effect; for income tax purposes from 2007–08 onwards; and for corporation tax purposes of insurance companies for periods of account beginning on or after 1 January 2007, subject to the transitional provisions in Sch. 7, Part 2 (FA 2007, s. 38(2), (3)).

In s. 213(1A)(a), the words "(in accordance with section 432A of the Taxes Act)" have been inserted after the word "referable" by FA 2004, s. 47 and Sch. 7, para. 9(3)(c), with effect from 22 July 2004.

S. 213(1A) inserted by FA 1993, s. 91(4) in relation to accounting periods beginning on or after 1 January 1993.

In s. 213(3) the reference to subsection (8H) substituted for the former reference (to "subsection (3A)" by FA 2003, s. 170 and Sch. 33, para. 16(2)(a); with effect where the accounting period for which the net amount represents an excess of losses over gains is an accounting period beginning on or after 1 January 2003 (FA 2003, Sch. 33, para. 16(6)).

In s. 213(3)(b) the words "either of the next two" substituted for the former wording ("one of the next 6"), and the word "section" substituted for the word "subsection" by FA 2003, s. 170 and Sch. 33, para. 16(2)(b); with effect where the accounting period for which the net amount represents an excess of losses over gains is an accounting period beginning on or after 1 January 2003 (FA 2003, Sch. 33, para. 16(6)).

In s. 213(3)(c) the words "the intervening accounting period (if there is one)" substituted for the former wording ("any intervening accounting period") by FA 2003, s. 170 and Sch. 33, para. 16(2)(c); with effect where the accounting period for which the net amount represents an excess of losses over gains is an accountingperiod beginning on or after 1 January 2003 (FA 2003, Sch. 33, para. 16(6)).

S. 213(3)(ca) inserted by FA 1998, s. 137(3)(b) as respects any intervening period ending on or after 17 March 1998.

In s. 213(3)(ca) the words "the intervening accounting period (if there is one) is not" substituted for the former wording ("none of the intervening accounting periods is") by FA 2003, s. 170 and Sch. 33, para. 16(2)(d); with effect where the accounting period for which the net amount represents an excess of losses over gains is an accounting period beginning on or after 1 January 2003 (FA 2003, Sch. 33, para. 16(6)).

S. 213(3A) and (3B) omitted by FA 2003, s. 170 and Sch. 33, para. 16(3); and repealed by FA 2003, s. 216 and Sch. 43, Pt. 3(12); with effect where the accounting period for which the net amount represents an excess of losses over gains is an accounting period beginning on or after 1 January 2003 (FA 2003, Sch. 33, para. 16(6)).

Former s. 213(3A) and (3B) inserted by FA 1998, s. 137(4) as respects any case where the earlier accounting period ends on or after 17 March 1998.

In s. 213(3) the words "Subject to subsection (3A) below," inserted by FA 1998, s. 137(3)(a) as respects any intervening period ending on or after 17 March 1998.

In s. 213(4), the words "long-term" substituted for the words "long term" by SI 2001/3629, art. 73(2)(a) operative from 1 December 2001.

S. 213(4ZA) inserted by FA2012, s. 146 and Sch. 16, para. 86(3) in relation to accounting periods beginning on or after 1 January 2013 (FA 2012, s. 148) but subject to transitional provisions in FA 2012, Sch. 17. Where an accounting period would otherwise straddle 1 January 2013, it is deemed to end on 31 December 2012 (FA 2012, s. 149).

S. 213(4ZB)–(4ZE) inserted by SI 2013/1400, reg. 6, with effect in relation to disposals on or after 8 June 2013.

S. 213(4A) inserted by FA 2003, s. 170 and Sch. 33, para. 16(4); with effect where the accounting period for which the net amount represents an excess of losses over gains is an accounting period beginning on or after 1 January 2003 (FA 2003, Sch. 33, para. 16(6)).

In s. 213(5), the words in square brackets "making the assumptions in subsection (5ZA) below" substituted for "assuming that the transferor had continued to carry on the business transferred" by SI 2008/381, art. 29(2), with effect from 19 February 2008 in relation to transfers of business taking placeon or after that date. The text of s. 213(5) was incorrectly stated in the substituting article, but this was corrected by FA 2008, s. 43 and Sch. 17, para. 39(2), the correction being treated as always having had effect.

S. 213(5) substituted by FA 2003, s. 170 and Sch. 33, para. 16(4); with effect where the accounting period for which the net amount represents an excess of losses over gains is an accounting period beginning on or after 1 January 2003 (FA 2003, Sch. 33, para. 16(6)).

In the former s. 213(5) the words "Subject to subsections (5A) to (7) below" inserted by FA 1995, s. 53 and Sch. 9, para. 4 and words "Part I of Schedule 2C to the Insurance Companies Act 1982" substituted for "section 49 of the Insurance Companies Act 1982" by FA 1995, s. 53 and Sch. 9, para. 1(2)(d); both amendments have effect for transfers sanctioned or authorised after 30 June 1994.

In the former s. 213(5), the words "an insurance business transfer scheme has … another ("the transferee")" substituted for the words "there is a transfer of the whole or part of the long term business of an insurance company (**"the transferor"**) to another company (**"the transferee"**) in accordance with a scheme sanctioned by a court under Part I of Schedule 2C to the Insurance Companies Act 1982" by SI 2001/3629, art. 67(1) operative in relation to any transfer under a scheme falling within section 105 of the Financial Services and Markets Act 2000, including an excluded scheme falling within Case 2, 3 or 4 of subsection (3) of that section.

S. 213(5ZA) inserted by SI 2008/381, art. 29(3), with effect from 19 February 2008 in relation to transfers of business taking place on or after that date.

In s. 213(5A), the words "permanent establishment" substituted for the words "branch or agency" by FA 2003, s. 153(1)(b) with effect in relation to accounting periods beginning on or after 1 January 2003.

S. 213(5A) inserted by FA 1995, s. 53 and Sch. 9, para. 4, with effect in relation to any transfers sanctioned on or authorised after 30 June 1994.

In s. 213(7), the words "long-term" substituted for the words "long term" by SI 2001/3629, art. 73(2)(a) operative from 1 December 2001.

In s. 213(8), the words "in the same manner as an appeal, and both the transferor and the transferee shall be entitled to be a party to any proceedings" substituted for the words "by the Special Commissioners who shall determine the question in the same manner as

they determine appeals; but both the transferor and the transferee shall be entitled to appear and be heard or to make representations in writing" bySI 2009/56, art. 3(1) and Sch. 1, para. 181, operative from 1 April 2009, subject to transitional and saving provisions in SI 2009/56, Sch. 3.
S. 213(8A)(a) omitted by SI 2008/381, art. 29(4), with effect from 19 February 2008 in relation to transfers of business taking place on or after that date.
In s. 213(8A)(c) and (d) the words "transferred assets" inserted by SI 2008/381, art. 29(4), with effect from 19 February 2008 in relation to transfers of business taking place on or after that date.
In s. 213(8B) the words "transferred assets" inserted by SI 2008/381, art. 29(5), with effect from 19 February 2008 in relation to transfers of business taking place on or after that date.
In s. 213(8F)(a) the words "transferred assets" inserted by SI 2008/381, art. 29(6), with effect from 19 February 2008 in relation to transfers of business taking place on or after that date.
In s. 213(8H) the words "Subsection (3) above has" substituted for "Subsections (3) and (8A) and (8B) above have" by SI 2008/381, art. 29(7), with effect from 19 February 2008 in relation to transfers of business taking place on or after that date.
S. 213(8HA) inserted by SI 2008/381, art. 29(8), with effect from 19 February 2008 in relation to transfers of business taking place on or after that date.
In s. 213(8H), the words "that the net amount would still arise even if losses accruing after the date on which the company or transferee joined the group of companies were disregarded" substituted for "that the net amount is an amount which, assuming there to be gains accruing to the company or transferee immediately after the beginning of that period, would fall to be treated under paragraph 4 of Schedule 7AA as a qualifying loss in relation to those gains" by FA 2006, s. 70(5)(a), with effect where the accounting period for which the net amount represents an excess of losses over gains is an accounting period ending on or after 5 December 2005.
In s. 213(8I), the words "section 184C as if those references were contained in that section; and in subsection (8A)(b) above **"group"** has the same meaning as in that section" substituted for "paragraph 1 of Schedule 7AA as if those references were contained in that Schedule; and in subsection (8A)(b) above "group" has the same meaning as in that Schedule" by FA 2006, s. 70(5)(b), with effect where the accounting period for which the net amount represents an excess of losses over gains is an accounting period ending on or after 5 December 2005.
S. 213(8A)–(8I) inserted by FA 2003, s. 170 and Sch. 33, para. 16(5); with effect where the accounting period for which the net amount represents an excess of losses over gains is an accounting period beginning on or after 1 January 2003 (FA 2003, Sch. 33, para. 16(6)).
S. 213(8J) inserted by SI 2008/381, art. 29(9), with effect from 19 February 2008 in relation to transfers of business taking place on or after that date.
S. 213(9) repealed by FA 1993, s. 213 and Sch. 23, Pt. III(8) in relation to accounting periods beginning on or after 1 January 1993.
S. 213(10) omitted by SI 2008/381, art. 29(10), with effect from 19 February 2008 in relation to transfers of business taking place on or after that date.
In former s. 213(10) the words "before the relevant transfer date (within the meaning of that section)" substituted for the former wording ("before the transfer.") by FA 2007, s. 40 and Sch. 9, para. 3(4) with effect for periods of account beginning on or after 1 January 2007 (FA 2007, Sch. 9, para. 17).
S. 213(10) inserted by F(No. 2)A 2005, s. 42 and Sch. 9, para. 20(6) with effect where accounting period, for which net amount represents excess of losses over gains, is an accounting period beginning on or after 1 January 2003.

Derivations – (as originally enacted) – FA 1990, s. 47.

Cross references – ICTA 1988, s. 458: capital redemption business.
Sch. 7A, para. 1(10): in relation to pre-entry losses determining whether loss under s. 212 accrued before a company became a group member, s. 213 is disregarded.
Sch. 7B, para. 11: modification of s. 213(4) in respect of overseas life insurance companies in relation to events occurring in accounting periods beginning after 31 December 1992.
Sch. 7B, para. 11(1A): transfers in s. 213(5) sanctioned or authorised after 30 June 1994 include "qualifying overseas transfers" (as defined in ICTA 1988, Sch. 19AC, para. 4A).
ICTA 1988, s. 440B: s. 212(1) does not apply, for accounting periods beginning on or after 1 January 1995 where the profits of a life assurance business taxed under Sch. D, Case I, but without prejudice to bringing into account amounts deferred under s. 213(1) or s. 214A(2) from accounting periods beginning before 1 January 1995.
SI 1995/171, reg. 4(1), (2): modification of TCGA 1992, s. 211(1), s. 213(5), s. 214(11) and s. 214A(7) in certain cases of transfers of business of friendly societies.
SI 1999/498, reg. 11: modification of s. 213 in relation to the capital redemption business carried on by insurance companies.
SI 2005/2014, reg. 38: modification of s. 213 so as to make it applicable to friendly societies carrying on life insurance business (which is not entirely tax exempt).
SI 2006/3271, reg. 31: modification of s. 213 with effect from 31 December 2006 in relation to periods of account ending on or after that day.

Notes – S. 15: meaning of "chargeable gains".
S. 16: meaning of "allowable losses".
S. 288: interpretation, including reference to sections as being those of this Act.
ICTA 1988, s. 12: meaning of "accounting period".

213A Power to modify ss.212 and 213 etc in case of CFCs that are offshore funds

213A(1) The Treasury may make regulations for the purpose mentioned in subsection (2) in any case where–

(a) an insurance company to which the I – E rules apply is deemed to make a disposal under section 212 of an interest in an offshore fund,

(b) the offshore fund is a CFC, and

(c) there is (or, but for the regulations, would be) a CFC charge on the insurance company referable to its relevant interest in the CFC for the accounting period in which the disposal is deemed to have been made.

213A(2) The regulations are to be made for the purpose of modifying the operation of–

(a) section 212 or 213,

(b) the CFC rules, or

(c) the I – E rules,

in relation to any accounting period of the insurance company so as to reduce the charge to tax.

213A(3) The regulations may–

(a) make different provision for different cases or circumstances, and

(b) contain incidental, supplementary, consequential, transitional, transitory or saving provision.

213A(4) The provision that may be made as a result of subsection (3)(b) includes provision modifying any other provision of the Corporation Tax Acts.

213A(5) In this section–

"CFC" and **"CFC charge"** have the same meanings as in Part 9A of TIOPA 2010 (see section 371VA),

"the CFC rules" means the rules contained in that Part, and

"offshore fund" has the meaning given by section 355 of TIOPA 2010.

History – S. 213A inserted by FA2012, s. 146 and Sch. 16, para. 87 in relation to accounting periods beginning on or after 1 January 2013 (FA 2012, s. 148) but subject to transitional provisions in FA 2012, Sch. 17. Where an accounting period would otherwise straddle 1 January 2013, it is deemed to end on 31 December 2012 (FA 2012, s. 149).

Statutory instruments – SI 2012/3044: Insurance Companies and CFCs (Avoidance of Double Charge) Regulations 2012: made under s. 231A.

214 Transitional provisions

214 [Omitted by FA 2007, s. 41 and Sch. 10, para. 5(3)(b) and repealed by FA 2007, s. 114 and Sch. 27, Pt. 2(10).]

History – S. 214 omitted by FA 2007, s. 41 and Sch. 10, para. 5(3)(b) and repealed by FA 2007, s. 114 and Sch. 27, Pt. 2(10) with effect for periods of account beginning on or after 1 January 2007 (Sch. 10, para. 17(2)).

214A Further transitional provisions

214A [Omitted by FA 2007, s. 41 and Sch. 10, para. 5(3)(c) and repealed by FA 2007, s. 114 and Sch. 27, Pt. 2(10).]

History – S. 214A omitted by FA 2007, s. 41 and Sch. 10, para. 5(3)(c) and repealed by FA 2007, s. 114 and Sch. 27, Pt. 2(10) with effect for periods of account beginning on or after 1 January 2007 (Sch. 10, para. 17(2)).

214B Modification of Act in relation to overseas life insurance companies

214B [Repealed by SI 2006/3271, reg. 43 and Schedule, Pt. 2.]

History – S. 214B repealed by SI 2006/3271, reg. 43 and Schedule, Pt. 2, with effect from 31 December 2006 in relation to accounting periods ending on or after that day.

214BA Interpretation

214BA [Omitted by FA 2007, s. 41 and Sch. 10, para. 14(5)(a) and repealed by FA 2007, s. 114 and Sch. 27, Pt. 2(10).]

History – S. 214BA omitted by FA 2007, s. 41 and Sch. 10, para. 14(5)(a) and repealed by FA 2007, s. 114 and Sch. 27, Pt. 2(10) with effect for periods of account beginning on or after 1 January 2007 (Sch. 10, para. 17(2)).

Chapter IV – Miscellaneous Cases

RE-ORGANISATIONS OF MUTUAL BUSINESSES

214C Gains not eligible for taper relief

214C [Omitted by FA 2008, s. 8 and Sch. 2, para. 35.]

History – S. 214C omitted by FA 2008, s. 8 and Sch. 2, para. 35 with effect in relation to chargeable gains accruing or treated as accruing in the tax year 2008–09 or any subsequent tax year (FA 2008, Sch. 2, para. 56(3)).

BUILDING SOCIETIES ETC.

215 Disposal of assets on amalgamation of building societies etc.

215 If, in the course of or as part of an amalgamation of 2 or more building societies or a transfer of engagements from one building society to another, there is a disposal of an asset by one society to another, both shall be treated for the purposes of corporation tax on chargeable gains as if the asset were acquired from the one making the disposal for a consideration of such amount as would secure that on the disposal neither a gain nor a loss would accrue to the one making the disposal.

Derivations – CGTA 1979, s. 149A(1), as inserted by ICTA 1988, s. 844 and Sch. 29, para. 26.

Cross references – S. 35(3)(d), (5): re-basing not to apply to disposal under these provisions unless an election exists for the simplified scheme (re-basing of all assets held at 31 March 1982 irrespective of matters in s. 35(3)).

Sch. 3, para. 1: person disposing of asset acquired through disposal under these provisions after 31 March 1982 treated as holding asset at 31 March 1982 for purposes of re-basing.

FA 1995, s. 131(2): s. 215 disapplied where a qualifying company (for FA 1993, Pt. II, Ch. II) transfers before its commencement day a qualifying asset to another qualifying company on or after the second company's commencement day.
SI 1994/3227, reg. 8: deferral of gain or loss deemed to accrue on disposal, which is a no gain/no loss transaction under s. 215, of a matched asset by one company to another.

Notes – S. 21–34: general meaning of "disposal" and "asset".
S. 56(2): no gain, no loss calculated after applying indexation allowance.
ICTA 1988, s. 476: treatment of building societies generally.

216 Assets transferred from society to company

216(1) This section and section 217 apply where there is a transfer of the whole of a building society's business to a company (**"the successor company"**) in accordance with section 97 and the other applicable provisions of the Building Societies Act 1986.

216(2) Where the society and the successor company are not members of the same group at the time of the transfer–

(a) they shall be treated for the purposes of corporation tax on capital gains as if any asset disposed of as part of the transfer were acquired by the successor company for a consideration of such amount as would secure that on the disposal neither a gain nor a loss would accrue to the society, and

(b) if because of the transfer any company ceases to be a member of the same group as the society, that event shall not cause section 179 to have effect as respects any asset acquired by the company from the society or any other member of the same group.

216(3) Where the society and the successor company are members of the same group at the time of the transfer but later cease to be so, that later event shall not cause section 179 to have effect as respects–

(a) any asset acquired by the successor company on or before the transfer from the society or any other member of the same group, or

(b) any asset acquired from the society or any other member of the same group by any company other than the successor company which is a member of the same group at the time of the transfer.

216(4) Subject to subsection (6) below, where a company which is a member of the same group as the society at the time of the transfer–

(a) ceases to be a member of that group and becomes a member of the same group as the successor company, and

(b) subsequently ceases to be a member of that group,

Section 179 shall have effect on that later event as respects any relevant asset acquired by the company otherwise than from the successor company as if it had been acquired from the successor company.

216(5) In subsection (4) above **"relevant asset"** means any asset acquired by the company–

(a) from the society, or

(b) from any other company which is a member of the same group at the time of the transfer,

when the company and the society, or the company, the society and the other company, were members of the same group.

216(6) Subsection (4) above shall not apply if the company which acquired the asset and the company from which it was acquired (one being a 75 per cent subsidiary of the other) cease simultaneously to be members of the same group as the successor company but continue to be members of the same group as one another.

216(7) For the purposes of this section **"group"** shall be construed in accordance with section 170.

History – In s. 216(2)(b), (3) and (4) words "178 or" repealed by FA 2000, s. 156 and Sch. 40, Pt. II(12).

Derivations – S. 216(1): FA 1988, Sch. 12, para. 1.
S. 216(2)–(7): FA 1988, Sch. 12, para. 4.

Cross references – S. 35(3)(d), (5): re-basing not to apply to disposal under these provisions unless an election exists for the simplified scheme (re-basing of all assets held at 31 March 1982 irrespective of matters in s. 35(3)).
S. 170: groups of companies by reference to 75 per cent subsidiary relationships.
S. 178, 179: crystallisation of gain where company leaves a group with asset transferred intra-group.
S. 271(4): exemption from capital gains tax in respect of a savings scheme bonus is not affected by the loss of certification resulting from a s. 216 transfer.
Sch. 3, para. 1: person disposing of asset acquired through disposal under these provisions after 31 March 1982 treated as holding asset at 31 March 1982 for purposes of re-basing.
FA 1995, s. 131(2): s. 216 disapplied where a qualifying company (for FA 1993, Pt. II, Ch. II) transfers before its commencement day a qualifying asset to another qualifying company on or after the second company's commencement day.
FA 2000, Sch. 29, para. 31: the amendments of TCGA 1992, s. 170 by para. 1 of that Schedule (repealing the provision which stated that references to a company applied only to companies resident in the UK) have effect for the purposes of s. 216 in relation to transfers on or after 1 April 2000.
SI 1994/3227, reg. 8: deferral of gain or loss deemed to accrue on disposal, which is a no gain/no loss transaction under s. 216, of a matched asset by one company to another.

Notes – S. 21–34: general meaning of "disposal" and "asset".
S. 56(2): no gain, no loss calculated after applying indexation allowance.
S. 288: interpretation, including reference to sections as being those of this Act.

217 Shares, and rights to shares, in successor company

217(1) Where, in connection with the transfer, there are conferred on members of the society–

(a) any rights to acquire shares in the successor company in priority to other persons, or

(b) any rights to acquire shares in that company for consideration of an amount or value lower than the market value of the shares, or

(c) any rights to free shares in that company,

any such right so conferred on a member shall be regarded for the purposes of tax on chargeable gains as an option (within the meaning of section 144) granted to, and acquired by, him for no consideration and having no value at the time of that grant and acquisition.

217(2) Where, in connection with the transfer, shares in the successor company are issued by that company, or disposed of by the society, to a member of the society, those shares shall be regarded for the purposes of tax on chargeable gains–

(a) as acquired by the member for a consideration of an amount or value equal to the amount or value of any new consideration given by him for the shares (or, if no new consideration is given, as acquired for no consideration); and

(b) as having, at the time of their acquisition by the member, a value equal to the amount or value of the new consideration so given (or, if no new consideration is given, as having no value);

but this subsection is without prejudice to the operation of subsection (1) above, where applicable.

217(3) Subsection (4) below applies in any case where–

(a) in connection with the transfer, shares in the successor company are issued by that company, or disposed of by the society, to the trustees of a settlement on terms which provide for the transfer of those shares to members of the society for no new consideration;

(b) [Omitted by FA 2006, s. 88 and Sch. 12, para. 20(1)(b) and repealed by FA 2006, s. 178 and Sch. 26, Pt. 3(15).]

217(4) Where this subsection applies, then, for the purposes of tax on chargeable gains–

(a) the shares shall be regarded as acquired by the trustees for no consideration;

(b) the interest of any member in the settled property constituted by the shares shall be regarded as acquired by him for no consideration and as having no value at the time of its acquisition;

(c) where a member becomes absolutely entitled as against the trustees to any of the settled property, both the trustees and the member shall be treated as if, on his becoming so entitled, the shares in question had been disposed of and immediately reacquired by the trustees, in their capacity as trustees within section 60(1), for a consideration of such an amount as would secure that on the disposal neither a gain nor a loss would accrue to the trustees (and accordingly section 71 shall not apply in relation to that occasion); and

(d) on the disposal by a member of an interest in the settled property, other than the disposal treated as occurring for the purposes of paragraph (c) above, any gain accruing shall be a chargeable gain (and accordingly section 76(1) shall not apply in relation to the disposal).

217(5) Where, in connection with the transfer, the society disposes of any shares in the successor company, then, for the purposes of this Act, any gains accruing on the disposal shall not be chargeable gains.

217(6) In this section–

"free shares", in relation to a member of the society, means any shares issued by the successor company, or disposed of by the society, to that member in connection with the transfer but for no new consideration;

"member", in relation to the society, means a person who is or has been a member of it, in that capacity, and any reference to a member includes a reference to a member of any particular class or description;

"new consideration" means consideration other than–

(a) consideration provided directly or indirectly out of the assets of the society; or

(b) consideration derived from a member's shares or other rights in the society.

217(7) References in this section to the case where a member becomes absolutely entitled to settled property as against the trustees shall be taken to include references to the case where he would become so entitled but for being an infant or otherwise under disability.

History – In s. 217(3)(a), the words "the trustees of a settlement" substituted for "trustees" by FA 2006, s. 88 and Sch. 12, para. 20(1)(a)(i) with effect in relation to a transfer falling within s. 216(1) effected on or after 6 April 2006.

S. 217(3)(b) and the word "and" preceding it omitted by FA 2006, s. 88 and Sch. 12, para. 20(1)(a)(ii), (b) and repealed by FA 2006, s. 178 and Sch. 26, Pt. 3(15) with effect in relation to a transfer falling within s. 216(1) effected on or after 6 April 2006.

In s. 217(5), the word "accruing" substituted for "arising" by FA 2006, s. 88 and Sch. 12, para. 20(1)(c) with effect in relation to a transfer falling within s. 216(1) effected on or after 6 April 2006.

Derivations – FA 1988, Sch. 12, para. 5.

Cross references – S. 60: bare trustees and nominees; meaning of "absolutely entitled as against the trustee".
S. 71: deemed market value disposal and reacquisition by trustees on occasion of person becoming absolutely entitled to trust property as against the trustees.
S. 76(1): no chargeable gain generally accrues on the disposal of an interest created by or arising under a settlement.
S. 144: the grant, exercise, abandonment etc. of options as separate disposals or part of larger transactions.

Notes – S. 68: meaning of "settled property".
S. 21–34: general meaning of "disposal".
S. 288: interpretation, including "shares" as embracing stock and reference to sections as being those of this Act.

FRIENDLY SOCIETIES

217A Transfer of assets on incorporation of registered friendly society

217A(1) This section and section 217B apply where a registered friendly society is incorporated under the Friendly Societies Act 1992 (**"the 1992 Act"**).

217A(2) In this section and section 217B–

(a) **"the registered society"** means the society before the incorporation, and

(b) **"the incorporated society"** means the society after the incorporation.

217A(3) For the purposes of corporation tax on chargeable gains–

(a) any asset of the registered society that by virtue of section 6(2) or (3) of the 1992 Act is transferred to the incorporated society,

(b) any asset of a branch of the registered society that by virtue of section 6(4) of the 1992 Act is transferred to the incorporated society, and

(c) any asset of a branch of the registered society that is identified in a scheme under section 6(5) of the 1992 Act,

shall be taken to be disposed of by the registered society or branch and acquired by the incorporated society on the incorporation for a consideration of such amount as to secure that on the disposal neither a gain nor a loss accrues to the registered society or branch.

History – S. 217A inserted by F(No. 2)A 1992, s. 56 and Sch. 9, para. 21(3), with effect from 19 February 1993 by virtue of SI 1993/236. (Subject to the repeals made by TCGA 1992, CGTA 1979, s. 143A inserted in identical terms to s. 217A by F(No. 2)A 1992, s. 56 and Sch. 9, para. 20(1).)

Cross references – S. 35(3)(d), (5): re-basing not to apply to disposal under these provisions unless an election exists for the simplified scheme (re-basing of all assets held at 31 March 1982 irrespective of matters in s. 35(3)).
FA 1995, s. 131(2): s. 217A disapplied where a qualifying company (for FA 1993, Pt. II, Ch. II) transfers before its commencement day a qualifying asset to another qualifying company on or after the second company's commencement day.

Notes – Sch. 3, para. 1: person disposing of asset acquired through disposal under these provisions sometimes treated as holding asset at 31 March 1982 for purposes of re-basing.

217B Rights of members in registered society equated with rights in incorporated society

217B(1) In this section, **"change of membership"** means a change effected by Schedule 4 to the 1992 Act whereby a member of the registered society or of a branch of the registered society becomes a member of the incorporated society or of a branch of the incorporated society.

217B(2) For the purposes of this Act, a change of membership shall not be taken to involve any disposal or acquisition of an asset by the member concerned, but all the interests and rights in the incorporated society or a branch of the incorporated society that he has immediately after the change, taken together, shall be treated as a single asset which–

(a) was acquired by the first relevant acquisition, and

(b) was added to by any subsequent relevant acquisitions.

217B(3) In subsection (2) above, **"relevant acquisition"** means an acquisition by which the member acquired any interest or right in the registered society or a branch of the registered society that he had immediately before the change of membership.

History – S. 217B inserted by F(No. 2)A 1992, s. 56 and Sch. 9, para. 21(3), with effect from 19 February 1993 by virtue of SI 1993/236.

217C Subsequent disposal of assets by incorporated society, etc.

217C(1) Where any asset acquired on a disposal to which section 217A(3) applies is subsequently disposed of by the incorporated society, section 41 shall apply as if any capital allowance made to the registered society in respect of the asset had been made to the incorporated society.

217C(2) If the disposal by the incorporated society is in the circumstances mentioned in subsection (8) of section 41, the disposal to which section 217A(3) applies shall for the purposes of that subsection be taken to have been a previous transfer of the asset in such circumstances.

History – S. 217C(2) substituted by FA 2000, s. 102 and Sch. 29, para. 32 with effect in relation to cases in which the disposal by the incorporated society is on or after 1 April 2000.
S. 217C inserted by F(No. 2)A 1992, s. 56 and Sch. 9, para. 21(3), with effect from 19 February 1993 by virtue of SI 1993/236. (Subject to the repeals made by TCGA 1992, CGTA 1979, s. 143B inserted in identical terms to s. 217C by F(No. 2)A 1992, s. 56 and Sch. 9, para. 20(1).)
Cross references – S. 41: restriction of losses by reference to capital allowances.
S. 174(1): extension of s. 41 to capital allowances made to previous owners that transfer the asset in relevant circumstances.

REGISTERED SOCIETIES AND CO-OPERATIVES

History – In the heading, the words "Registered societies" substituted for the words "Industrial and provident societies" by Co-operative and Community Benefit Societies Act 2014, s. 151 and Sch. 4, para. 51, with effect from 1 August 2014.

217D Disposal of assets on union, amalgamation or transfer of engagements

217D(1) Subsection (2) applies if–

(a) there is a union or amalgamation of two or more relevant bodies or a transfer of engagements from one relevant body to another, and

(b) in the course of, or as part of, that union, amalgamation or transfer there is a disposal of an asset by one relevant body to another.

217D(2) Both bodies are treated for the purposes of corporation tax on chargeable gains as if the asset were acquired from the body making the disposal for a consideration which is of the amount needed to secure that on the disposal neither a gain nor a loss accrues to the body making the disposal.

217D(3) In this section **"relevant body"** means–

(a) a registered society within the meaning of the Co-operative and Community Benefit Societies Act 2014 or a society registered or treated as registered under the Industrial and Provident Societies Act (Northern Ireland) 1969,

(aa) a society registered as a credit union under the Credit Unions (Northern Ireland) Order 1985 (S.I. 1985/1205 (N.I. 12)),

(b) an SCE formed in accordance with Council Regulation (EC) No 1435/2003 on the Statute for a European Co-Operative Society, or

(c) a UK agricultural or fishing co-operative, as defined in section 1058 of CTA 2010.

History – S. 217D(3)(a) substituted by Co-operative and Community Benefit Societies Act 2014, s. 151 and Sch. 4, para. 52, with effect from 1 August 2014.
S. 217D(3)(aa) inserted by FA 2014, s. 298 and Sch. 39, para. 1, with effect from 1 August 2014.
S. 217D inserted by CTA 2010, s. 1177 and Sch. 1, para. 250, with effect for corporation tax purposes for accounting periods ending on or after 1 April 2010, and for income tax and capital gains tax purposes for the tax year 2010–11 and subsequent tax years.

THE REGULATOR OF SOCIAL HOUSING, THE SECRETARY OF STATE, SCOTTISH HOMES AND HOUSING ASSOCIATIONS

History – In the heading the words "Regulator of Social Housing," substituted for the words "Housing Corporation," by the Housing and Regeneration Act 2008, Sch. 9, para. 17, with effect from 1 April 2010 (SI 2010/862).
In the heading, "Secretary of State" substituted for "Housing for Wales" by Government of Wales Act 1998, s. 140 and Sch. 16, para. 80, with effect from 1 November 1998 by virtue of SI 1998/2244.

218 Disposals of land between the Regulator of Social Housing, the Secretary of State or Scottish Homes and housing associations

History – In the heading to s. 218, the words "Regulator of Social Housing," substituted for the words "Housing Corporation," by the Housing and Regeneration Act 2008, Sch. 9, para. 17, with effect from 1 April 2010 (SI 2010/862).

218(1) Where–

(a) in accordance with a scheme approved under section 5 of the Housing Act 1964 or paragraph 5 of Schedule 7 to the Housing Associations Act 1985, or in accordance with a requirement imposed under section 253 of the Housing and Regeneration Act 2008, the Regulator of Social Housing acquires from a housing association the association's interest in all the land held by the association for carrying out its objects, or

(b) after the Regulator of Social Housing has so acquired from a housing association all the land so held by it the Corporation disposes to a single housing association of the whole of that land (except any part previously disposed of or agreed to be disposed of otherwise than to a housing association), together with all related assets,

then both parties to the disposal of the land to or, as the case may be, by the Regulator of Social Housing shall be treated for the purposes of corporation tax in respect of chargeable gains as if the land and any related assets disposed of therewith (and each part of that land and those assets) were acquired from the party making the disposal for a consideration of such an amount as would secure that on the disposal neither a gain nor a loss accrued to that party.

218(2) In subsection (1) above, **"housing association"** has the same meaning as in the Housing Associations Act 1985, and **"related assets"** means, in relation to an acquisition of land by the Regulator of Social Housing, assets acquired by the Regulator in accordance with the same scheme as that land, and in relation to a disposal of land by the Regulator of Social Housing, assets held by the Regulator for the purposes of the same scheme as that land.

218(3) This section shall also have effect with the substitution of the words "the Secretary of State" for the words "the Regulator of Social Housing" and "the Regulator" in each place where they occur

218(4) This section shall also have effect with the substitution of the words " Scottish Homes" for the words "the Regulator of Social Housing" and "the Regulator" in each place where they occur.

History – In s. 218(1)(a) the words ", or in accordance with a requirement imposed under section 253 of the Housing and Regeneration Act 2008," inserted by the Housing and Regeneration Act 2008, Sch. 9, para. 17, with effect from 1 April 2010 (SI 2010/862).
In s. 218 the words "the Regulator of Social Housing" substituted for the words "the Housing Corporation" and the words "the Regulator" substituted for the words "the Corporation" by the Housing and Regeneration Act 2008, Sch. 9, para. 17, with effect from 1 April 2010 (SI 2010/862).
In the heading and in s. 218(3), "Secretary of State" substituted for "Housing for Wales" by Government of Wales Act 1998, s. 140 and Sch. 16, para. 78, 80, with effect from 1 November 1998 (SI 1998/2244).

Derivations – ICTA 1970, s. 342, as amended by FA 1991, s. 95(1)–(4), 96(1), and Housing (Consequential Provisions) Act 1985, Sch. 2, para. 18(4).

Cross references – S. 35(3)(d), (5): re-basing not to apply to disposal under these provisions unless an election exists for the simplified scheme (re-basing of all assets held at 31 March 1982 irrespective of matters in s. 35(3)).
Sch. 3, para. 1: person disposing of asset acquired through disposal under these provisions after 31 March 1982 treated as holding asset at 31 March 1982 for purposes of re-basing.

Notes – S. 21–34: general meaning of "disposal" and "assets".
S. 56(2): no gain, no loss calculated after applying indexation allowance.
S. 288: interpretation, including "land" as embracing messuages, tenements, and hereditaments, houses and buildings of any tenure.

219 Disposals by housing related bodies

History – The heading to s. 219 substituted by the Housing and Regeneration Act 2008, Sch. 9, para. 18, with effect from 1 April 2010 (SI 2010/862).
In the former heading to s. 219, "Secretary of State" substituted for "Housing for Wales" by Government of Wales Act 1998, s. 140 and Sch. 16, para. 79, 80, with effect from 1 November 1998 (SI 1998/2244).

219(1) In any case where–

(a) a housing regulator, the Homes and Communities Agency or the Greater London Authority disposes of any land to a relevant housing provider, or

(b) a relevant housing provider disposes of any land to another relevant housing provider, or

(c) in pursuance of a direction of a housing regulator given under section 167 of the Housing and Regeneration Act 2008, section 106 of the Housing (Scotland) Act 2010, Part I of the Housing Act 1996 or Part I of the Housing Associations Act 1985 (as the case may be) requiring it to do so, a relevant housing provider disposes of any of its property, other than land, to another relevant housing provider, or

(d) a relevant housing provider or an unregistered self-build society disposes of any land to a housing regulator or the Homes and Communities Agency,

both parties to the disposal shall be treated for the purposes of tax on chargeable gains as if the land or property disposed of were acquired from the housing regulator, the Home and Community Agency, relevant housing provider or unregistered self-build society making the disposal for a consideration of such an amount as would secure that on the disposal neither a gain nor a loss accrued to the housing regulator, the Homes and Communities Agency or, as the case may be, that relevant housing provider or society.

219(2) In this section–

"housing regulator" means the Regulator of Social Housing, the Scottish Housing Regulator, the Secretary of State or Scottish Homes;

"relevant housing provider" means–

(a) a non-profit registered provider of social housing,

(b) a registered social landlord within the meaning of Part 1 of the Housing Act 1996, or

(c) a body registered in the register maintained under section 20(1) of the Housing (Scotland) Act 2010;

"unregistered self-build society" has the same meaning as in the Housing Associations Act 1985.

Prospective amendments – In s. 219(2), in the definition of "housing regulator" (formerly the definition of "the Corporation"), the words "or the Secretary of State" substituted for the words "the secretary of State or Scottish Homes" by the Housing (Scotland) Act 2001, s. 112 and Sch. 10, para. 18(2), with effect from a day to be appointed.

History – In s. 219(1) (wherever occurring) the words "relevant housing provider" substituted for the words "relevant housing association" and "association" by the Housing and Regeneration Act 2008, Sch. 9, para. 18, with effect from 1 April 2010 (SI 2010/862).
In s. 219(1)(a), the words ", the Homes and Communities Agency or the Greater London Authority" substituted for the words "or the Homes and Communities Agency" by the Localism Act 2011, s. 195 and Sch. 19, para. 32, with effect from 1 April 2012 (SI 2012/628).

In s. 219(1)(a) the words "a housing regulator" substituted for the words "the Corporation" and in s. 219(1) (wherever occurring) the words "relevant housing provider" substituted for the words "relevant housing association" and "association" by the Housing and Regeneration Act 2008, Sch. 9, para. 18, with effect from 1 April 2010 (SI 2010/862).
In s. 219(1)(a) the words "or the Homes and Communities Agency" by the Housing and Regeneration Act 2008, Sch. 8, para. 62, with effect from 1 December 2008 (SI 2008/3068).
In s. 219(1)(c), the words ", section 106 of the Housing (Scotland) Act 2010" inserted by SI 2012/700, art. 4 and Schedule, para. 4(2), with effect from 1 April 2012.
In s. 219(1)(c) the words "section 167 of the Housing and Regeneration Act 2008," inserted by the Housing and Regeneration Act 2008, Sch. 9, para. 18, with effect from 1 April 2010 (SI 2010/862).
In s. 219(1)(c) the words "a housing regulator" substituted for the words "the Corporation" by the Housing and Regeneration Act 2008, Sch. 9, para. 18, with effect from 1 April 2010 (SI 2010/862).
In s. 219(1)(d) the words "a housing regulator" substituted for the words "the Corporation" by the Housing and Regeneration Act 2008, Sch. 9, para. 18, with effect from 1 April 2010 (SI 2010/862).
In s. 219(1)(d) the words "or the Homes and Communities Agency" inserted at end by the Housing and Regeneration Act 2008, Sch. 8, para. 62, with effect from 1 December 2008 (SI 2008/3068).
In the words after s. 219(1)(d) the words "the housing regulator" substituted for the words "the Corporation" by the Housing and Regeneration Act 2008, Sch. 9, para. 18, with effect from 1 April 2010 (SI 2010/862).
In the words after s. 219(1)(d) the words "the Homes and Communities Agency" inserted twice by the Housing and Regeneration Act 2008, Sch. 8, para. 62, with effect from 1 December 2008 (SI 2008/3068).
In s. 219(2), in the definition of "housing regulator", the words ", the Scottish Housing Regulator" inserted by SI 2012/700, art. 4 and Schedule, para. 4(3)(a), with effect from 1 April 2012.
In s. 219(2), in the definition of "relevant housing provider", the words "section 20(1) of the Housing (Scotland) Act 2010" substituted for the words "section 57 of the Housing (Scotland) Act 2001" bySI 2012/700, art. 4 and Schedule, para. 4(3)(b), with effect from 1 April 2012.
In s. 219(2) the words ""housing regulator" means the Regulator of Social Housing" substituted for the words ""the Corporation" means the Housing Corporation" by the Housing and Regeneration Act 2008, Sch. 9, para. 18, with effect from 1 April 2010 (SI 2010/862).
In s. 219(2), in the former definition of "the Corporation", the words "Secretary of State" substituted for "Housing for Wales" by Government of Wales Act 1998, s. 140 and Sch. 16, para. 79, 80, with effect from 1 November 1998 (SI 1998/2244).
In s. 219(2) the definition of "relevant housing provider" substituted for the definition of "relevant housing association" by the Housing and Regeneration Act 2008, Sch. 9, para. 18, with effect from 1 April 2010 (SI 2010/862).
S. 219 substituted by SI 1996/2325, art. 5 and Sch. 2, para. 20(2), with effect from 1 October 1996.

Derivations – ICTA 1970, s. 342A, as inserted by Housing Act 1974, s. 11, as amended by FA 1991, s. 95(5), 96(2), and Housing (Consequential Provisions) Act 1985, Sch. 2, para. 18(5).

Cross references – S. 35(3)(d), (5): re-basing not to apply to disposal under these provisions unless an election exists for the simplified scheme (re-basing of all assets held at 31 March 1982 irrespective of matters in s. 35(3)).
Sch. 3, para. 1: person disposing of asset acquired through disposal under these provisions after 31 March 1982 treated as holding asset at 31 March 1982 for purposes of re-basing.

Notes – S. 21–34: general meaning of "disposal".
S. 56(2): no gain, no loss calculated after applying indexation allowance.
S. 288: interpretation, including "land" as embracing messuages, tenements, and hereditaments, houses and buildings of any tenure.
ICTA 1988, s. 488(5): exemption from corporation tax on chargeable gains on disposal by approved housing association of property occupied by tenant.

220 Disposals by Northern Ireland housing associations

220(1) In any case where–

(a) a registered Northern Ireland housing association disposes of any land to another such association, or

(b) in pursuance of a direction of the Department of the Environment for Northern Ireland given under Chapter II of Part VII of the Housing (Northern Ireland) Order 1981 requiring it to do so, a registered Northern Ireland housing association disposes of any of its property, other than land, to another such association,

both parties to the disposal shall be treated for the purposes of tax on chargeable gains as if the land or property disposed of were acquired from the association making the disposal for a consideration of such an amount as would secure that on the disposal neither a gain nor a loss accrued to that association.

220(2) In subsection (1) above **"registered Northern Ireland housing association"** means a registered housing association within the meaning of Part VII of the Order referred to in paragraph (b) of that subsection.

Derivations – ICTA 1970, s. 342B, as inserted by FA 1984, s. 56(3).

Cross references – S. 35(3)(d), (5): re-basing not to apply to disposal under these provisions unless an election exists for the simplified scheme (re-basing of all assets held at 31 March 1982 irrespective of matters in s. 35(3)).
Sch. 3, para. 1: person disposing of asset acquired through disposal under these provisions after 31 March 1982 treated as holding asset at 31 March 1982 for purposes of re-basing.

Notes – S. 21–34: general meaning of "disposal".
S. 56(2): no gain, no loss calculated after applying indexation allowance.
S. 288: interpretation, including "land" as embracing messuages, tenements, and hereditaments, houses and buildings of any tenure.

OTHER BODIES

221 Harbour authorities

221 [Repealed by FA 2012, s. 227 and Sch. 39, para. 15.]

History – S. 221 repealed by FA 2012, s. 227 and Sch. 39, para. 15 in relation to any transfer occurring on or after 1 April 2013.

Derivations – CGTA 1979, s. 123A, as inserted by ICTA 1988, s. 844 and Sch. 29, para. 22.

PART VII – OTHER PROPERTY, BUSINESSES, INVESTMENTS ETC.

PRIVATE RESIDENCES

222 Relief on disposal of private residence

222(1) This section applies to a gain accruing to an individual so far as attributable to the disposal of, or of an interest in–

(a) a dwelling-house or part of a dwelling-house which is, or has at any time in his period of ownership been, his only or main residence, or

(b) land which he has for his own occupation and enjoyment with that residence as its garden or grounds up to the permitted area.

222(2) In this section **"the permitted area"** means, subject to subsections (3) and (4) below, an area (inclusive of the site of the dwelling-house) of 0.5 of a hectare.

222(3) Where the area required for the reasonable enjoyment of the dwelling-house (or of the part in question) as a residence, having regard to the size and character of the dwelling-house, is larger than 0.5 of a hectare, that larger area shall be the permitted area.

222(4) Where part of the land occupied with a residence is and part is not within subsection (1) above, then (up to the permitted area) that part shall be taken to be within subsection (1) above which, if the remainder were separately occupied, would be the most suitable for occupation and enjoyment with the residence.

222(5) So far as it is necessary for the purposes of this section to determine which of 2 or more residences is an individual's **main residence** for any period–

(a) the individual may conclude that question by notice to an officer of the Board given within 2 years from the beginning of that period but subject to a right to vary that notice by a further notice to an officer of the Board as respects any period beginning not earlier than 2 years before the giving of the further notice.

(b) [repealed by FA 1996, s. 134 and Sch. 20, para. 59(3) and s. 205 and Sch. 41, Pt. V(10).]

222(6) In the case of an individual living with his spouse or civil partner–

(a) there can only be one residence or main residence for both, so long as living together and, where a notice under subsection (5)(a) above affects both the individual and his spouse or civil partner, it must be given by both.

(b) [Repealed by FA 1996, s. 134 and Sch. 20, para. 59(4) and s. 205 and Sch. 41, Pt. V(10).]

222(6A) Where an individual has determined, by giving notice under subsection (5)(a), that a residence is the individual's main residence, that determination does not cease to be effective at any time by reason only of the fact that, at that time, another of the individual's residences is treated by section 222B(1) as not being occupied as a residence (or, having been so treated, is no longer so treated).

222(7) In this section and sections 222A to 226, **"the period of ownership"** where the individual has had different interests at different times shall be taken to begin from the first acquisition taken into account in arriving at the expenditure which under Chapter III of Part II is allowable as a deduction in the computation of the gain to which this section applies, and in the case of an individual living with his spouse or civil partner–

(a) if the one disposes of, or of his or her interest in, the dwelling-house or part of a dwelling-house which is their only or main residence to the other, and in particular if it passes on death to the other as legatee, the other's period of ownership shall begin with the beginning of the period of ownership of the one making the disposal, and

(b) if paragraph (a) above applies, but the dwelling-house or part of a dwelling-house was not the only or main residence of both throughout the period of ownership of the one making the disposal, account shall be taken of any part of that period during which it was his only or main residence as if it was also that of the other.

222(8) If at any time during an individual's period of ownership of a dwelling-house or part of a dwelling-house he–

(a) resides in living accommodation which is for him job-related, and

(b) intends in due course to occupy the dwelling-house or part of a dwelling-house as his only or main residence,

this section and sections 223 to 226 shall apply as if the dwelling-house or part of a dwelling-house were at that time occupied by him as a residence.

222(8A) Subject to subsections (8B), (8C) and (9) below, for the purposes of subsection (8) above living accommodation is job-related for a person if–

(a) it is provided for him by reason of his employment, or for his spouse or civil partner by reason of the spouse's or civil partner's employment, in any of the following cases–

(i) where it is necessary for the proper performance of the duties of the employment that the employee should reside in that accommodation;

(ii) where the accommodation is provided for the better performance of the duties of the employment, and it is one of the kinds of employment in the case of which it is customary for employers to provide living accommodation for employees;

(iii) where, there being a special threat to the employee's security, special security arrangements are in force and the employee resides in the accommodation as part of those arrangements;

or

(b) under a contract entered into at arm's length and requiring him or his spouse or civil partner to carry on a particular trade, profession or vocation, he or his spouse or civil partner is bound–

(i) to carry on that trade, profession or vocation on premises or other land provided by another person (whether under a tenancy or otherwise); and

(ii) to live either on those premises or on other premises provided by that other person.

222(8B) If the living accommodation is provided by a company and the employee is a director of that or an associated company, subsection (8A)(a)(i) or (ii) above shall not apply unless–

(a) the company of which the employee is a director is one in which he or she has no material interest; and

(b) either–

(i) the employment is as a full-time working director, or

(ii) the company is non-profit making, that is to say, it does not carry on a trade nor do its functions consist wholly or mainly in the holding of investments or other property, or

(iii) the company is a charitable company.

222(8C) Subsection (8A)(b) above does not apply if the living accommodation concerned is in whole or in part provided by–

(a) a company in which the borrower or his spouse or civil partner has a material interest; or

(b) any person or persons together with whom the borrower or his spouse or civil partner carries on a trade or business in partnership.

222(8D) For the purposes of this section–

(a) a company is an associated company of another if one of them has control of the other or both are under the control of the same person; and

(b) **"employment"**, **"director"**, **"full-time working director"**, **"material interest"** and **"control"**, in relation to a body corporate, have the meanings given by Chapter 2 of Part 3 of ITEPA 2003.

222(9) Subsections (8A)(b) and (8C) above shall apply for the purposes of subsection (8) above only in relation to residence on or after 6th April 1983 in living accommodation which is job-related for the purposes of that subsection.

222(10) Apportionments of consideration shall be made wherever required by this section or sections 223 to 226 and, in particular, where a person disposes of a dwelling-house only part of which is his only or main residence.

History – S. 222(3) substituted by FA 1996, s. 134 and Sch. 20, para. 59(2) for 1996–97 and later years of assessment.

In s. 222(5)(a), the words "an officer of the Board" substituted, on both occasions, for the words "the inspector" by FA 2004, s. 117 and Sch. 22, para. 1(2) with effect, by virtue of FA 2004, Sch. 22, para. 7(1), in relation to any notice given on or after 10 December 2003.

S. 222(5)(b) and its endpiece repealed by FA 1996, s. 134 and Sch. 20, para. 59 and s. 205 and Sch. 41, Pt. V(10) for 1996–97 and later years of assessment.

In s. 222(6) the words "an individual living with his spouse or civil partner" substituted for the words "a man and his wife living with him" and the words "the individual and his spouse or civil partner" substituted for the words "the husband and the wife" by SI 2005/3229, reg. 117(2), with effect from 5 December 2005.

S. 222(6)(b) and the word "and" immediately preceding it repealed by FA 1996, s. 134 and Sch. 20, para. 59 and s. 205 and Sch. 41, Pt. V(10) for 1996–97 and later years of assessment.

S. 222(6A) inserted by FA 2015, s. 39 and Sch. 9, para. 2(a), with effect in relation to disposals made on or after 6 April 2015.

In s. 222(7), "222A" substituted for "223" by FA 2015, s. 39 and Sch. 9, para. 2(b), with effect in relation to disposals made on or after 6 April 2015.

In s. 222(7) the words "an individual living with his spouse or civil partner" substituted for the words "a man and his wife living with him" by SI 2005/3229, reg. 117(3), with effect from 5 December 2005.

S. 222(8) amended by removing references to ICTA 1988, s. 356 and inserting references to s. 222(8A)(b) and (8C) by FA 1999, s. 38 and Sch. 4, para. 17, s. 139 and Sch. 20, Pt. III(7), with effect for the year 2000–01 and subsequent years of assessment.

In s. 222(8A) the words "or civil partner" inserted three times and the words "the spouse's or civil partner's" substituted for the word "her" by SI 2005/3229, reg. 117(4), with effect from 5 December 2005.

S. 222(8A) inserted by FA 1999, s. 38 and Sch. 4, para. 17, s. 139 and Sch. 20, Pt. III(7), with effect for the year 2000–01 and subsequent years of assessment.

In s. 222(8B)(b)(iii), the words "a charitable company" substituted for the words "established for charitable purposes only" by FA 2010, s. 30 and Sch. 6, para. 13(2), with effect in relation to living accommodation provided for a director (as defined at TCGA 1992, s. 222(8D)) on or after 6 April 2012 if that accommodation was not already provided for the director immediately before that date (SI 2012/736, art. 8).
S. 222(8B) inserted by FA 1999, s. 38 and Sch. 4, para. 17, s. 139 and Sch. 20, Pt. III(7), with effect for the year 2000–01and subsequent years of assessment.
In s. 222(8C) the words "or civil partner" inserted twice by SI 2005/3229, reg. 117(5), with effect from 5 December 2005.
S. 222(8C) inserted by FA 1999, s. 38 and Sch. 4, para. 17, s. 139 and Sch. 20, Pt. III(7), with effect for the year 2000–01 and subsequent years of assessment.
S. 222(8D) inserted by FA 1999, s. 38 and Sch. 4, para. 17, s. 139 and Sch. 20, Pt. III(7), with effect for the year 2000–01 and subsequent years of assessment.
In s. 222(8D)(b), the words "the meanings given by Chapter 2 of Part 3 of ITEPA 2003" substituted for the words "the same meanings as they have for the purposes of Chapter II of Part V of the Taxes Act" by ITEPA 2003, Sch. 6, para. 213 with effect for 2003–04 and subsequent tax years.
S. 222(9) amended by removing references to ICTA 1988, s. 356 and inserting references to s. 222(8A)(b) and (8C) by FA 1999, s. 38 and Sch. 4, para. 17, s. 139 and Sch. 20, Pt. III(7), with effect for the year 2000–01 and subsequent years of assessment.

Derivations – CGTA 1979, s. 101, as amended by FA 1991, s. 93 and ICTA 1988, s. 844 and Sch. 29, para. 21.

Cross references – S. 35–52 (Pt. II, Ch. III): general provisions as to computation of gains.
S. 241(6): gain to which s. 222 applies is reduced by the amount of any reduction in the acquisition consideration on the roll-over of business assets by virtue of the treatment of commercial lettings of furnished holiday accommodation as a trade.
S. 248(1): roll-over relief on replacement of land compulsorily acquired not available where replacement land is a dwelling-house subject to relief under s. 222–226.
Sch. 7C, para. 6: relief for transfers to approved share plans – operation of relief where disposal within s. 222(1).
Sch. 11, para. 19: reference in s. 222(5)(a) includes a notice given before the end of 1966–67 if later.
ICTA 1988, s. 356: except in relation to certain directors (s. 356(4)) and partners or persons with material interests (s. 356(5)), job-related determined by reference to (s. 356(3)(a)) provision by reason of employment where necessary for proper performance, customary for better performance or as special security or (s. 356(3)(b)) to an arm's length contract requiring a trade etc. to be carried on there on a live-in basis.
ICTA 1988, s. 776(9): disapplication of provisions treating as income certain quasi-dealing transactions in land where gain exempt within s. 222.

Extra-statutory concessions – D6: application of s. 222–224 to disposal of residence as part of financial settlement between a separated couple.
D21: election under s. 222(5)(a) permitted late in case where all residences but one have negligible open market value.
D26: joint beneficial owners becoming sole owners on exchange of joint interests.
D37: exemption for employee's right to share in profits from a sale of his home by a relocation business.
D49: short delay by owner-occupier in taking up residence treated as period of occupation for purposes of s. 222.

Statements of practice – 14/80: interaction of letting relief (s. 223(4)) and exemption for only or main residence.

HMRC interpretations – IRInt. 22 in general, joint owner-occupiers of a property who are not husband and wife are entitled to full private residence relief.
IRInt. 87: elections or determinations under s. 222(5) are not appropriate where an individual has a legal or equitable interest in only one property but occupies another property under licence.
IRInt. 114: meaning of garden or grounds.

Other material – Taxline 1995/72 (not reproduced): s. 222(5)(a) time limit where second property becomes taxpayer's residence after acquisition.
Taxline 1995/137 (not reproduced): where s. 222(3) reasonable enjoyment test may be met if part of land is sold.

Notes – S. 21–34: general meaning of "disposal".
S. 64(2), (3): meaning of "legatee".
S. 288: interpretation, including "inspector" as being any inspector of taxes, "notice" as being in writing, the "Taxes Act" as ICTA 1988, interpretation of reference to a married woman living with her husband and reference to other sections as being those of this Act.
TMA 1970, s. 115: service of notices.
For disposals before 21 March 1991, the area in s. 222(2), (3) was one acre.

222A Determination of main residence: non-resident CGT disposals

222A(1) This section applies where–

(a) an individual ("P") makes a disposal of, or of an interest in–

(i) a dwelling-house, or part of a dwelling-house, which was at any time in P's period of ownership occupied by P as a residence, or

(ii) land (as mentioned in section 222(1)(b)) which P had for P's own occupation and enjoyment with that residence as its garden or grounds, and

(b) the disposal is a non-resident CGT disposal (see section 14B).

In the remainder of this section the residence concerned is referred to as "the dwelling-house".

222A(2) So far as it is necessary for the purposes of section 222, P may determine, by a notice under this section, which of 2 or more residences (of which one is the dwelling-house) was P's main residence for any period within P's period of ownership of the dwelling-house.

222A(3) A notice under this section may vary, as respects any period within P's period of ownership of the dwelling-house, a notice previously given under section 222(5)(a).

See also subsections (4) and (7).

222A(4) A notice under this section may not vary a notice previously given under section 222(5)(a) as respects any period for which the previous notice had the effect of determining whether or not a disposed of residence was P's main residence.

222A(5) In subsection (4) **"disposed of residence"** means one of P's residences which was disposed of (in whole or in part) before the date of the disposal mentioned in subsection (1)(a).

222A(6) A notice under this section–

(a) must be given in the NRCGT return in respect of the disposal mentioned in subsection (1)(a), and

(b) may not subsequently be varied, whether by a notice under this section or section 222(5)(a).

222A(7) Where a notice under this section affects both P and an individual ("X") who was, in the period to which the notice relates ("the relevant period"), P's spouse or civil partner living with P–

(a) in a case where each of P and X is required to make an NRCGT return in respect of the disposal of an interest in the dwelling-house, notice given by P under this section is effective as respects any part of the relevant period when P and X were living together as spouses or civil partners only if notice to the same effect is also given under this section by X in respect of that period;

(b) in any other case, notice given by P under this section is effective as respects any part of the relevant period when P and X were living together as spouses or civil partners only if it is accompanied by written notification from X agreeing to the terms of the notice in respect of that period.

222A(8) Nothing in subsection (2) affects the application of section 222(5) in relation to P.

History – S. 222A inserted by FA 2015, s. 39 and Sch. 9, para. 3, with effect in relation to disposals made on or after 6 April 2015.

222B Non-qualifying tax years

222B(1) For the purposes of sections 222 to 226 the dwelling-house or part of a dwelling-house mentioned in section 222(1) is treated as not being occupied as a residence by the individual so mentioned ("P") at any time in P's period of ownership which falls within–

(a) a non-qualifying tax year, or

(b) a non-qualifying partial tax year.

In the remainder of this section the dwelling-house or part of a dwelling-house is referred to as **"the dwelling-house"**.

222B(2) Except where the disposal mentioned in section 222(1) is a non-resident CGT disposal, subsection (1) does not have effect in respect of any tax year or partial tax year before the tax year 2015–16.

222B(3) A tax year the whole of which falls within P's period of ownership is **"a non-qualifying tax year"** in relation to the dwelling-house if–

(a) neither P nor P's spouse or civil partner was resident for that tax year in the territory in which the dwelling-house is situated, and

(b) the day count test was not met by P with respect to the dwelling-house for that tax year (see section 222C).

222B(4) A partial tax year is **"a non-qualifying partial tax year"** in relation to the dwelling-house if–

(a) neither P nor P's spouse or civil partner was resident for the tax year in question in the territory in which the dwelling-house is situated, and

(b) the day count test was not met by P with respect to the dwelling-house for that partial tax year.

222B(5) Where part only of a tax year falls within P's period of ownership, that part is a **"partial tax year"** for the purposes of this section.

222B(6) For the purposes of this section an individual is resident in a territory outside the United Kingdom ("the overseas territory") for a tax year ("year X") in relation to which condition A or B is met.

222B(7) Condition A is that the individual is, in respect of a period or periods making up more than half of year X, liable to tax in the overseas territory under the law of that territory by reason of the individual's domicile or residence.

222B(8) Condition B is that the individual would be resident in the overseas territory for year X in accordance with the statutory residence test in Part 1 of Schedule 45 to the Finance Act 2013, if in Parts 1 and 2 of that Schedule–

(a) any reference to the United Kingdom (however expressed) were read as a reference to the overseas territory,

(b) "overseas" meant anywhere outside that territory, and

(c) in paragraph 26 (meaning of "work"), sub-paragraphs (2) to (4), (6) and (7) were disregarded.

222B(9) *In applying the* statutory residence test in accordance with subsection (8), any determination of whether–

(a) the individual was resident in the overseas territory for a tax year preceding year X, or

(b) another individual is resident in the overseas territory for year X,

is to be made in accordance with the statutory residence test, as modified by subsection (8).

222B(10) Section 11(1)(a) (visiting forces etc) is to be disregarded in determining for the purposes of this section whether or not an individual is resident in the United Kingdom.

222B(11) Subsection (1) is subject to–

(a) section 222(8) (job-related accommodation), and

(b) section 223(3) (absence reliefs).

History – S. 222B inserted by FA 2015, s. 39 and Sch. 9, para. 3, with effect in relation to disposals made on or after 6 April 2015.

222C Day count test

222C(1) This section explains how P meets the day count test (see section 222B) with respect to the dwelling-house or part of a dwelling-house mentioned in section 222(1) for a full or partial tax year.

In the remainder of this section the dwelling-house or part of a dwelling-house is referred to as **"the dwelling-house"**.

222C(2) P meets that test for a tax year with respect to the dwelling-house if, during that year, P spends at least 90 days in one or more qualifying houses.

222C(3) P meets that test for a partial tax year with respect to the dwelling-house if, during that partial tax year, P spends at least the relevant number of days in one or more qualifying houses.

222C(4) To find the relevant number of days for the purposes of subsection (3), multiply 90 days by the relevant fraction and round up the result to the nearest whole number of days if necessary.

222C(5) The relevant fraction is–

$$\frac{X}{Y}$$

where–

"X" is the number of days in the partial tax year;

"Y" is the number of days in the tax year.

222C(6) For the purposes of subsections (2) and (3) the days need not be consecutive, and days spent in different qualifying houses may be aggregated.

222C(7) A day spent by P's spouse or civil partner in a dwelling-house or part of a dwelling-house which is a qualifying house in relation to P counts as a day spent by P in the qualifying house (but no day is to be counted twice as a result of this subsection).

222C(8) For the purposes of this section, a day counts as a day spent by an individual in a qualifying house if–

(a) the individual is present at the house at the end of the day, or

(b) the individual–

 (i) is present in the house for some period during the day, and

 (ii) the next day, has stayed overnight in the house.

222C(9) For the purposes of this section–

(a) the dwelling-house is a qualifying house in relation to P, and

(b) any other dwelling-house or part of a dwelling-house which is situated in the same territory as the dwelling-house is a qualifying house in relation to P at any particular time if at that time any of the following has an interest in it–

 (i) P,

 (ii) an individual who is P's spouse or civil partner at that time, and

 (iii) an individual who is P's spouse or civil partner at the time of disposal of the dwelling-house.

222C(10) In this section **"partial tax year"** has the meaning given by section 222B(5).

History – S. 222C inserted by FA 2015, s. 39 and Sch. 9, para. 3, with effect in relation to disposals made on or after 6 April 2015.

223 Amount of relief

223(1) No part of a gain to which section 222 applies shall be a chargeable gain if the dwelling-house or part of a dwelling-house has been the individual's only or main residence throughout the period of ownership, or throughout the period of ownership except for all or any part of the last 18 months of that period.

223(2) Where subsection (1) above does not apply, a fraction of the gain shall not be a chargeable gain, and that fraction shall be–

(a) the length of the part or parts of the period of ownership during which the dwelling-house or the part of the dwelling-house was the individual's only or main residence, but inclusive of the last 18 months of the period of ownership in any event, divided by

(b) the length of the period of ownership.

223(3) For the purposes of sections 222(5) and 222A and subsections (1) and (2) above–

(a) a period of absence not exceeding 3 years (or periods of absence which together did not exceed 3 years), and in addition

(b) any period of absence throughout which the individual worked in an employment or office all the duties of which were performed outside the United Kingdom or lived with a spouse or civil partner who worked in such an employment or office, and in addition

(c) any period of absence not exceeding 4 years (or periods of absence which together did not exceed 4 years) throughout which the individual was prevented from residing in the dwelling-house or part of the dwelling-house in consequence of the situation of his place of work or in consequence of any condition imposed by his employer requiring him to reside elsewhere, being a condition reasonably imposed to secure the effective performance by the employee of his duties, and in addition,

(d) any period of absence not exceeding 4 years (or periods of absence which together did not exceed 4 years) throughout which the individual lived with a spouse or civil partner in respect of whom paragraph (c) applied in respect of that period (or periods),

shall be treated as if in that period of absence the dwelling-house or the part of the dwelling-house were occupied by the individual as a residence if conditions A and B are met.

223(3A) Condition A is that before the period there was a time when the dwelling-house was the individual's only or main residence.

223(3B) Condition B is that after the period–

(a) in a case falling within paragraph (a), (b), (c) or (d) of subsection (3), there was a time when the dwelling-house was the individual's only or main residence,

(b) in a case falling within paragraph (b), (c) or (d) of that subsection, the individual was prevented from resuming residence in the dwelling-house in consequence of the situation of the individual's place of work or a condition imposed by the terms of the individual's employment requiring the individual to reside elsewhere, being a condition reasonably imposed to secure the effective performance by the employee of his duties, or

(c) in a case falling within paragraph (b), (c) or (d) of that subsection, the individual lived with a spouse or civil partner to whom paragraph (b) of this subsection applied.

223(4) Where a gain to which section 222 applies accrues to any individual and the dwelling-house in question or any part of it is or has at any time in his period of ownership been wholly or partly let by him as residential accommodation, the part of the gain, if any, which (apart from this subsection) would be a chargeable gain by reason of the letting, shall be such a gain only to the extent, if any, to which it exceeds whichever is the lesser of–

(a) the part of the gain which is not a chargeable gain by virtue of the provisions of subsection (1) to (3) above; and

(b) £40,000.

223(5) [Omitted by FA 2014, s. 58(2)(b).]

223(6) [Omitted by FA 2014, s. 58(2)(b).]

223(7) In this section **"period of ownership"**–

(a) does not include any period before 31 March 1982, and

(b) where the whole or part of the gain to which section 222 applies is an NRCGT gain chargeable to capital gains tax by virtue of section 14D, does not include any period before 6 April 2015 (but see subsection (7A)).

223(7A) Paragraph (b) of the definition of **"period of ownership"** does not apply in a case where paragraph 9 of Schedule 4ZZB applies by virtue of sub-paragraph (1)(b) of that paragraph (the individual has made an election for the retrospective basis of computation to apply).

223(7B) In this section **"period of absence"** means a period during which the dwelling-house or the part of the dwelling-house was not occupied by the individual as a residence.

223(8) *This section is subject to–*

(a) section 224 (amount of relief: further provisions),

(aa) section 225D (private residence of adult placement carer),

(ab) section 225E (disposals by disabled persons or persons in care homes etc), and

(b) section 226A (private residence relief: cases where relief obtained under section 260).

History – In s. 223(1), the words "18 months" substituted for the words "36 months" by FA 2014, s. 58(2)(a), with effect in relation to disposals made on or after 6 April 2014.
In s. 223(2)(a), the words "18 months" substituted for the words "36 months" by FA 2014, s. 58(2)(a), with effect in relation to disposals made on or after 6 April 2014.
In s. 223(3), the words "sections 222(5) and 222A and" inserted by FA 2015, s. 39 and Sch. 9, para. 4(2)(a) with effect in relation to disposals made on or after 6 April 2015.
In s. 223(3)(b), the words "or lived with a spouse or civil partner who worked in such an employment or office" inserted by SI 2009/730, art. 7(2), with effect in relation to disposals on or after 6 April 2009.
In s. 223(3)(c), the words "and in addition," inserted by SI 2009/730, art. 7(3), with effect in relation to disposals on or after 6 April 2009.
S. 223(3)(d) inserted by SI 2009/730, art. 7(4), with effect in relation to disposals on or after 6 April 2009.
In s. 223(3), the words "were occupied by the individual as a residence" substituted for the words "was the individual's only or main residence" by FA 2015, s. 39 and Sch. 9, para. 4(2)(b), with effect in relation to disposals made on or after 6 April 2015.
In s. 223(3) the words "if conditions A and B are met." substituted for the words "if both before and after the period there was a time when the dwelling-house was the individual's only or main residence." by SI 2009/730, art. 8(2), with effect in relation to disposals on or after 6 April 2009.
S. 223(3A) and (3B) inserted by SI 2009/730, art. 8(3), with effect in relation to disposals on or after 6 April 2009.
In s. 223(4)(a), the words "or those provisions as applied by section 225" omitted by FA 2004, s. 117 and Sch. 22, para. 2(2), and repealed by FA 2004, s. 326 and Sch. 42, Pt. 2(15), with effect, by virtue of FA 2004, Sch. 22, para. 7(2), in relation to disposals made on or after 10 December 2003.
S. 223(5) and (6) omitted by FA 2014, s. 58(2)(b), with effect in relation to disposals made on or after 6 April 2014.
S. 223(7) substituted, and s. 223(7A) and (7B) inserted, by FA 2015, s. 39 and Sch. 9, para. 4(3), with effect in relation to disposals made on or after 6 April 2015.
S. 223(8)(aa) inserted by F(No. 3)A 2010, s. 16(1), with effect in relation to disposals made on or after 9 December 2009.
S. 223(8)(ab) inserted (and the "and " at the end of s. 223(8)(aa) omitted) by FA 2014, s. 58(2)(c), with effect in relation to disposals made on or after 6 April 2014.
S. 223(8) inserted by FA 2004, s. 117 and Sch. 22, para. 2(3) with effect, by virtue of FA 2004, Sch. 22, para. 7(3) and subject to the transitional provision of FA 2004, Sch. 22, para. 8 which makes modifications to TCGA 1992, s. 226A thatwas inserted by FA 2004, Sch. 22, para. 6, in relation to gains or parts of gains accruing on later disposals (within the meaning of the section 226A inserted by FA 2004, Sch. 22, para. 6) made on or after 10 December 2003 (whenever any relevant earlier disposal was made); the transitional provision of FA 2004, Sch. 22, para. 8 has effect where TCGA 1992, s. 226A (as inserted by FA 2004, Sch. 22, para. 6) applies in circumstances in which either (a) the relevant earlier disposal or (b) each of the relevant earlier disposals (if there were more than one such disposal) was made before 10 December 2003.

Derivations – S. 223(1)–(3): CGTA 1979, s. 102(1)–(3), as amended by FA 1991, s. 94(1).
S. 223(4): FA 1980, s. 80(1), as amended by FA 1991, s. 94(3).
S. 223(5), (6): CGTA 1979, s. 102(5), (6), as inserted by FA 1991, s. 94(2).
S. 223(7): CGTA 1979, s. 102(3), (4) as amended by FA 1988, s. 96(9) and Sch. 8, para. 8.

Cross references – S. 248(1): roll-over relief on replacement of land compulsorily acquired not available where replacement land is a dwelling-house subject to relief under s. 222–226.
Sch. 2, para. 16(10): fraction in s. 223(2) applies in relation to assets held at 6 April 1965 after any time apportionment.
ICTA 1988, s. 776(9): disapplication of provisions treating as income certain quasi-dealing transactions in land where gain exempt within s. 223.

Extra-statutory concessions – D3: in relation to absence through employment under s. 223(3), condition, if satisfied for one spouse, is also regarded as satisfied for the other spouse.
D4: inability to resume residence because of employment does not lead to denial of relief under s. 223(3)(b), (c).
D6: application of s. 222–224 to disposal of residence as part of financial settlement between a separated couple.
D26: joint beneficial owners becoming sole owners on exchange of joint interests.

Statements of practice – 14/80: relief for owner occupiers.

Other material – ICAEW Technical Release TR 500 (not reproduced): for absences exceeding limit in s. 223(3), only the excess does not qualify for exemption.

Notes – S. 15: meaning of "chargeable gain".
S. 276: UK territorial sea is part of the UK.
S. 287: power of Treasury exercisable by statutory instrument, subject to the negative resolution procedure of the House of Commons.
S. 288: interpretation, including reference to sections being those of this Act.
For disposals before 19 March 1991, the period in s. 223(1), (2)(a) was 24 months and the limit in s. 223(4) was £20,000.

223A Amount of relief: non-resident CGT disposals

223A(1) This section applies where–

(a) the individual mentioned in section 223(1) ("P") acquired the asset to which the gain mentioned in section 222(1) is attributable before 6 April 2015, and

(b) P's period of ownership for the purposes of section 223 begins on that date because of section 223(7)(b).

223A(2) Times before 6 April 2015 are to be ignored in determining whether or not condition A in section 223 is met in relation to a period of absence, unless P elects that this subsection is not to apply in relation to the period.

223A(3) An election under subsection (2)–

(a) must specify which day before 6 April 2015 P relies on in relation to the period of absence for the purpose of meeting condition A in section 223, and

(b) must be made in the NRCGT return in respect of the disposal.

223A(4) Where P has made an election under subsection (2), section 223 applies as if relevant prior periods of absence counted against the maximum periods (and maximum aggregate periods) specified in subsection (3)(a), (c) and (d) of that section.

223A(5) In relation to a maximum period (or maximum aggregate period) specified in paragraph (a), (c) or (d) of section 223(3), **"relevant prior period of absence"** means a period of absence which would have counted against that maximum period (or maximum aggregate period) if the bridge period were included in the period of ownership.

223A(6) In subsection (5) **"the bridge period"** means the period beginning with the day specified in the election and ending with 5 April 2015.

223A(7) In this section **"period of absence"** has the same meaning as in section 223.

History – S. 223A inserted by FA 2015, s. 39 and Sch. 9, para. 5, with effect in relation to disposals made on or after 6 April 2015.

224 Amount of relief: further provisions

224(1) If the gain accrues on the disposal of a dwelling-house or part of a dwelling-house part of which is used exclusively for the purpose of a trade or business, or of a profession or vocation, the gain shall be apportioned and section 223 shall apply in relation to the part of the gain apportioned to the part which is not exclusively used for those purposes.

224(2) If at any time in the period of ownership there is a change in what is occupied as the individual's residence, whether on account of a reconstruction or conversion of a building or for any other reason, or there have been changes as regards the use of part of the dwelling-house for the purpose of a trade or business, or of a profession or vocation, or for any other purpose, the relief given by section 223 may be adjusted in a manner which is just and reasonable.

224(3) Section 223 shall not apply in relation to a gain if the acquisition of, or of the interest in, the dwelling-house or the part of a dwelling-house was made wholly or partly for the purpose of realising a gain from the disposal of it, and shall not apply in relation to a gain so far as attributable to any expenditure which was incurred after the beginning of the period of ownership and was incurred wholly or partly for the purpose of realising a gain from the disposal.

224(4) This section is subject to section 225D (private residence of adult placement carer).

History – In s. 224(1), the words "accrues on" were substituted for the words "accrues from" by FA 2004, s. 117 and Sch. 22, para. 3(2) with effect, by virtue of FA 2004, Sch. 22, para. 7(2), in relation to disposals made on or after 10 December 2003.
In s. 224(2) words "may be adjusted in a manner which is just and reasonable" substituted for "may be adjusted in such manner as the Commissioners concerned may consider to be just and reasonable" by FA 1996, s. 134 and Sch. 20, para. 60 for 1996–97 and later years of assessment.
S. 224(4) inserted by F(No. 3)A 2010, s. 16(2), with effect in relation to disposals made on or after 9 December 2009.

Derivations – CGTA 1979, s. 103.

Cross references – S. 248(1): roll-over relief on replacement of land compulsorily acquired not available where replacement land is a dwelling-house subject to relief under s. 222–226.
ICTA 1988, s. 776(9): disapplication of provisions treating as income certain quasi-dealing transactions in land where gain exempt or would be exempt but for s. 224(3).

Extra-statutory concessions – D6: application of s. 222–224 to disposal of residence as part of financial settlement between a separated couple.

Notes – S. 288: meaning of "trade" and reference to sections being those of this Act.

225 Private residence occupied under terms of settlement

225(1) Sections 222 to 224 shall also apply in relation to a gain accruing to the trustees of a settlement on a disposal of settled property being an asset within section 222(1) where, during the period of ownership of the trustees, the dwelling-house or part of the dwelling-house mentioned in that subsection has been the only or main residence of a person ("B") entitled to occupy it under the terms of the settlement, and in those sections as so applied–

(a) references to the individual shall be taken as references to the trustees except in relation to the matters dealt with in subsection (2), and

(b) the notice which may be given to an officer of the Board under section 222(5)(a) shall be a joint notice by the trustees and B, and;

(c) the notice which may be given by the trustees under section 222A is effective only if it is accompanied by written notification from B agreeing to the terms of the notice;

but section 223 (as so applied) shall apply only on the making of a claim by the trustees.

225(2) In sections 222 to 224, as applied by subsection (1), references to the individual, in relation to–

(a) the occupation of the dwelling-house or part of the dwelling-house,

(b) residence in a territory, or

(c) meeting the day count test,

are to be taken as references to B.

History – S. 225(1) created from existing text by FA 2015, s. 39 and Sch. 9, para. 6(2), with effect in relation to disposals made on or after 6 April 2015.
In s. 225(1), the words "("B")" inserted by FA 2015, s. 39 and Sch. 9, para. 6(3)(a), with effect in relation to disposals made on or after 6 April 2015.

In the opening words of s. 225(1) , the words "the trustees of a settlement" were substituted for the words "a trustee", and the words "the trustees" were substituted for the words "the trustee" by FA 2004, s. 117 and Sch. 22, para. 4(2) with effect, by virtue of FA 2004, Sch. 22, para. 7(2), in relation to disposals made on or after 10 December 2003.
In s. 225(1)(a), the words "the matters dealt with in subsection (2)," substituted for the words "the occupation of the dwelling-house or part of the dwelling-house, and" by FA 2015, s. 39 and Sch. 9, para. 6(3)(b), with effect in relation to disposals made on or after 6 April 2015.
In s. 225(1)(a), the words "the trustees" were substituted for the words "the trustee" by FA 2004, s. 117 and Sch. 22, para. 4(3) with effect, by virtue of FA 2004, Sch. 22, para. 7(2), in relation to disposals made on or after 10 December 2003.
In s. 225(1)(b), the words "B, and" substituted for the words "the person entitled to occupy the dwelling-house or part of the dwelling-house;" by FA 2015, s. 39 and Sch. 9, para. 6(3)(c), with effect in relation to disposals made on or after 6 April 2015.
In s. 225(1)(b), the words "an officer of the Board" were substituted for the words "the inspector" by FA 2004, s. 117 and Sch. 22, para. 4(4)(a) with effect, by virtue of FA 2004, Sch. 22, para. 7(1), in relation to any notice given on or after 10 December 2003.
In s. 225(1)(b), the words "the trustees" were substituted for the words "the trustee" by FA 2004, s. 117 and Sch. 22, para. 4(4)(b) with effect, by virtue of FA 2004, Sch. 22, para. 7(2), in relation to disposals made on or after 10 December 2003.
In s. 225(1)(b), the words "; but section 223 (as so applied) shall apply only on the making of a claim by the trustees." were inserted by FA 2004, s. 117 and Sch. 22, para. 4(5) with effect, by virtue of FA 2004, Sch. 22, para. 7(2), in relation to disposals made on or after 10 December 2003.
S. 225(1)(c) inserted by FA 2015, s. 39 and Sch. 9, para. 6(3)(d), with effect in relation to disposals made on or after 6 April 2015.
S. 225(2) inserted by FA 2015, s. 39 and Sch. 9, para. 6(4), with effect in relation to disposals made on or after 6 April 2015.

Derivations – CGTA 1979, s. 104.

Cross references – S. 248(1): roll-over relief on replacement of land compulsorily acquired not available where replacement land is a dwelling-house subject to relief under s. 222–226.
ICTA 1988, s. 776(9): disapplication of provisions treating as income certain quasi-dealing transactions in land where gain exempt within s. 222–226.

Extra-statutory concessions – D5: relief extended to personal representatives disposing of a deceased's residence in certain circumstances.

Statements of practice – SP 10/79: as regards inheritance tax, power for trustees to allow a beneficiary to occupy a dwelling-house.

Notes – S. 68: meaning of "settled property".
S. 21–34: general meaning of "disposal".
S. 288: interpretation, including reference to sections being those of this Act.

225A Private residence held by personal representatives

225A(1) Sections 222 to 224 shall also apply in relation to a gain accruing to the personal representatives of a deceased person on a disposal of an asset within section 222(1) if the following conditions are satisfied.

225A(2) The first condition is that, immediately before and immediately after the death of the deceased person, the dwelling-house or part of the dwelling-house mentioned in section 222(1) was the only or main residence of one or more individuals.

225A(3) The second condition is that–

(a) that individual or one of those individuals has a relevant entitlement, or two or more of those individuals have relevant entitlements, and

(b) the relevant entitlement accounts for, or the relevant entitlements together account for, 75% or more of the net proceeds of disposal;

and for this purpose **"relevant entitlement"** means an entitlement as legatee of the deceased person to, or to an interest in possession in, the whole or any part of the net proceeds of disposal.

225A(4) In subsection (3) above **"net proceeds of disposal"** means–

(a) the proceeds of the disposal of the asset realised by the personal representatives, less

(b) any incidental costs allowable as a deduction in accordance with section 38(1)(c) in computing the gain accruing to the personal representatives on that disposal,

but on the assumption that none of the proceeds is required to meet the liabilities of the deceased person's estate (including any liability to inheritance tax).

225A(5) In sections 222 to 224 as applied by this section–

(a) references to the individual shall be taken as references to the personal representatives except in relation to the matters dealt with in paragraph (aa),

(aa) in relation to the occupation of the dwelling-house or part of the dwelling-house, residence in a territory, or meeting the day count test, references to the individual are to be taken as references to a qualifying individual,

(b) the notice which may be given to an officer of the Board under section 222(5)(a) shall be a joint notice by the personal representatives and the individual or individuals entitled to occupy the dwelling-house or part of the dwelling-house, and

(c) the notice which may be given by the personal representatives under section 222A is effective only if it is accompanied by written notification from the individual or individuals entitled to occupy the dwelling-house or part of the dwelling-house agreeing to the terms of the notice.

225A(6) But section 223 (as so applied) shall apply only on the making of a claim by the personal representatives.

225A(7) In subsection (5)(aa) **"a qualifying individual"** means an individual–

(a) who has a relevant entitlement, and

(b) by virtue of whom the first condition is met.

History – In s. 225A(5)(a), the words "the matters dealt with in paragraph (aa)," substituted for the words "the occupation of the dwelling-house or part of the dwelling-house, and" by FA 2015, s. 39 and Sch. 9, para. 7(2)(a), with effect in relation to disposals made on or after 6 April 2015.

S. 225A(5)(aa) inserted by FA 2015, s. 39 and Sch. 9, para. 7(2)(b), with effect in relation to disposals made on or after 6 April 2015.

S. 225A(5)(c), and the word "and" before it, inserted by FA 2015, s. 39 and Sch. 9, para. 7(2)(c), with effect in relation to disposals made on or after 6 April 2015.

S. 225A(7) inserted by FA 2015, s. 39 and Sch. 9, para. 7(3), with effect in relation to disposals made on or after 6 April 2015.

S. 225A inserted by FA 2004, s. 117 and Sch. 22, para. 5 with effect, by virtue of FA 2004, Sch. 22, para. 7(2), in relation to disposals made on or after 10 December 2003.

225B Disposals in connection with divorce, etc

225B(1) Where an individual–

(a) ceases to live with his spouse or civil partner in a dwelling-house or part of a dwelling-house which is their only or main residence, and

(b) subsequently disposes of, or of an interest in, the dwelling-house or part to the spouse or civil partner,

then, if conditions A to C are met, sections 222 to 224 shall apply as if the dwelling-house or part continued to be the individual's only or main residence until the disposal.

225B(2) Condition A is that the disposal mentioned in subsection (1)(b) is pursuant to–

(a) an agreement between the individual and his spouse or civil partner made in contemplation of or otherwise in connection with the dissolution or annulment of the marriage or civil partnership, their judicial separation or the making of a separation order in respect of them, or their separation in other circumstances such that the separation is likely to be permanent, or

(b) an order of a court–

(i) made on granting an order or a decree of divorce or nullity of marriage, for the dissolution or annulment of the civil partnership, or for judicial separation,

(ii) made in connection with the dissolution or annulment of the marriage or civil partnership or the parties' judicial separation and which is made at any time after the granting of such an order or decree,

(iii) made at any time under section 22A, 23, 23A, 24 or 24A of the Matrimonial Causes Act 1973,

(iv) made at any time under article 25 or 26 of the Matrimonial Causes (Northern Ireland) Order 1978,

(v) made under section 8 of the Family Law (Scotland) Act 1985, including incidental orders made by virtue of section 14 of that Act, or

(vi) made at any time under any provision of Schedule 5 to the Civil Partnership Act 2004 that corresponds to any of the provisions mentioned in paragraphs (iii) and (iv).

225B(3) Condition B is that in the period between the individual ceasing to reside in the dwelling-house or part of the dwelling-house and the disposal to the spouse or civil partner, the dwelling-house or part continues to be the only or main residence of the spouse or civil partner.

225B(4) Condition C is that the individual has not given notice under section 222(5) or 222A that another dwelling-house or part of a dwelling-house is to be treated as the individual's main residence for any part of that period.

225B(5) Section 223 (as applied by this section) shall apply only on the making of a claim by the individual.

History – In s. 225B(4), the words "or 222A" inserted by FA 2015, s. 39 and Sch. 9, para. 8, with effect in relation to disposals made on or after 6 April 2015.

S. 225B inserted by SI 2009/730, art. 9(1), with effect in relation to disposals on or after 6 April 2009.

225C Sale of private residence under certain agreements with employer, etc

225C(1) This section applies where–

(a) an individual disposes of, or of an interest in, a dwelling-house or a part of a dwelling-house which is the individual's only or main residence ("the initial disposal"),

(b) the individual does so as a consequence of a change to the situation of the individual's place of work or that of a co-owner of the dwelling-house or the interest, being a change that is required by the employer of the individual or the co-owner, and

(c) the initial disposal is under a home purchase agreement.

225C(2) If–

(a) under the terms of the agreement the individual receives, within three years of the initial disposal, a share of any profit made by the purchaser upon the purchaser's disposal of, or of an interest in, the dwelling-house or part of the dwelling-house, and

(b) the receipt of that sum would be treated (apart from this section) as a disposal falling within section 22 (disposal where capital sums derived from assets),

that receipt shall be treated for the purposes of this Act as a gain attributable to the initial disposal but accruing to the individual at the time the sum is received.

225C(3) In this section–

"home purchase agreement" means an agreement–

(a) made with the employer or a person operating under an agreement with the employer ("the purchaser"),

(b) which includes a term entitling the individual to receive a share of any such profit as is mentioned in subsection (2)(a);

"co-owner", in relation to any individual ("A"), means another individual who holds an interest jointly or in common with A, whether or not the interests of the co-owners are equal.

History – S. 225C inserted by SI 2009/730, art. 10(1), with effect in relation to disposals on or after 6 April 2009.

225D Private residence of adult placement carer

225D(1) This section applies where a gain to which section 222 applies accrues to an individual ("A") and, at any time during A's period of ownership, part of the dwelling-house was occupied by another person ("B")–

(a) in England and Wales, pursuant to an adult placement scheme,

(b) in Scotland, pursuant to arrangements which constitute or form part of an adult placement service involving the provision of accommodation for B, or

(c) in Northern Ireland, pursuant to arrangements made with an adult placement agency for the provision of accommodation for B.

225D(2) For the purposes of this Part, in determining the periods during which the dwelling-house, or any part of the dwelling-house, was A's only or main residence, B's occupation of part of the dwelling-house pursuant to the scheme or arrangement is to be disregarded.

225D(3) For the purposes of section 224, the occupation of the part of the dwelling-house by B pursuant to the scheme or arrangement does not amount to the use of that part of the dwelling-house by A exclusively for the purpose of a trade, business, profession or vocation.

225D(4) In this section–

"adult placement agency" means an organisation or undertaking–

(a) that arranges for the provision of care and support (including accommodation) for persons in need, and

(b) in respect of which a requirement to register arises under Article 12 of the Health and Personal Social Services (Quality, Improvement and Regulation) (Northern Ireland) Order 2003,

"adult placement scheme" means a scheme–

(a) under which an individual agrees with the person carrying on the scheme to provide care and support (including accommodation) to an adult who is in need of it, and

(b) in respect of which a requirement to register arises under section 11 of the Care Standards Act 2000, and

"adult placement service" has the meaning given by paragraph 11 of schedule 12 to the Public Services Reform (Scotland) Act 2010.

History – S. 225D inserted by F(No. 3)A 2010, s. 16(3), with effect in relation to disposals made on or after 9 December 2009, subject to the transitional modification of s. 225D(4) made by F(No. 3)A 2010, s. 16(5).

225E Disposals by disabled persons or persons in care homes etc

225E(1) This section applies where a gain to which section 222 applies accrues to an individual and–

(a) the conditions in subsection (2) are met, or

(b) the conditions in subsection (3) are met.

225E(2) The conditions mentioned in subsection (1)(a) are that at the time of the disposal–

(a) the individual is a disabled person or a long-term resident in a care home, and

(b) the individual does not have any other relevant right in relation to a private residence.

225E(3) The conditions mentioned in subsection (1)(b) are that at the time of the disposal–

(a) the individual's spouse or civil partner is a disabled person or a long-term resident in a care home, and

(b) neither the individual nor the individual's spouse or civil partner has any other relevant right in relation to a private residence.

225E(4) Where this section applies, the references in section 223(1) and (2)(a) to 18 months are treated as references to 36 months.

225E(5) An individual is a **"long-term resident"** in a care home at the time of the disposal if at that time the individual–

(a) is resident there, and

(b) has been resident there, or can reasonably be expected to be resident there, for at least three months.

225E(6) An individual has **"any other relevant right in relation to a private residence"** at the time of the disposal if–

(a) at that time–

(i) the individual owns or holds an interest in a dwelling-house or part of a dwelling-house other than that in relation to which the gain accrued, or

(ii) the trustees of a settlement own or hold an interest in a dwelling-house or part of a dwelling-house other than that in relation to which the gain accrued, and the individual is entitled to occupy that dwelling-house or part under the terms of the settlement, and

(b) section 222 would have applied to any gain accruing to the individual or trustees on the disposal at that time of, or of that interest in, that dwelling house or part (or would have applied if a notice under subsection (5) of that section or under section 222A had been given).

225E(7) In the application of this section in relation to a gain to which section 222 applies by virtue of section 225 (private residence occupied under terms of settlement)–

(a) the reference in subsection (1) of this section to an individual is to the trustees of the settlement;

(b) the references in subsections (2) to (6) of this section to the individual are to the person entitled under the terms of the settlement, as mentioned in section 225.

225E(8) In this section–

"care home" means an establishment that provides accommodation together with nursing or personal care;

"disabled person" has the meaning given by Schedule 1A to FA 2005.

History – In s. 225E(6)(b), the words "or under section 222A" inserted by FA 2015, s. 39 and Sch. 9, para. 9, with effect in relation to disposals made on or after 6 April 2015.

S. 225E inserted by FA 2014, s. 58(3), with effect in relation to disposals made on or after 6 April 2014.

226 Private residence occupied by dependent relative before 6th April 1988

226(1) Subject to subsection (3) below, this section applies to a gain accruing to an individual so far as attributable to the disposal of, or of an interest in, a dwelling-house or part of a dwelling-house which, on 5th April 1988 or at any earlier time in his period of ownership, was the sole residence of a dependent relative of the individual, provided rent-free and without any other consideration.

226(2) If the individual so claims, such relief shall be given in respect of it and its garden or grounds as would be given under sections 222 to 224 if the dwelling-house (or part of the dwelling-house) had been the individual's only or main residence in the period of residence by the dependent relative, and shall be so given in addition to any relief available under those sections apart from this section.

226(3) If in a case within subsection (1) above the dwelling-house or part ceases, whether before 6th April 1988 or later, to be the sole residence (provided as mentioned above) of the dependent relative, any subsequent period of residence beginning on or after that date by that or any other dependent relative shall be disregarded for the purposes of subsection (2) above.

226(4) Not more than one dwelling-house (or part of a dwelling-house) may qualify for relief as being the residence of a dependent relative of the claimant at any one time nor, in the case of an individual and his spouse or civil partner living with him, as being the residence of a dependent relative of the claimant or of the claimant's spouse or civil partner at any one time.

226(5) *[Repealed by FA 1996, s. 134 and Sch. 20, para. 61 and s. 205 and Sch. 41, Pt. V(10).]*

226(6) In this section **"dependent relative"** means, in relation to an individual–

(a) any relative of his or of his wife who is incapacitated by old age or infirmity from maintaining himself, or

(b) his or his wife's mother who, whether or not incapacitated, is either widowed, or living apart from her husband, or a single woman in consequence of dissolution or annulment of marriage.

226(7) If the individual mentioned in subsection (6) above is a woman the references in that subsection to the individual's wife shall be construed as references to the individual's husband.

History – In s. 226(4) the words "an individual and his spouse or civil partner living with him" substituted for the words "a man and his wife living with him" and the words "spouse or civil partner" substituted for the words "husband or wife" by SI 2005/3229, reg. 118, with effect from 5 December 2005.

S. 226(5) repealed by FA 1996, Sch. 20, para. 61 and s. 205 and Sch. 41, Pt. V(10), with effect as respects years after 1995–96.

Derivations – S. 226(1), (2): CGTA 1979, s. 105; FA 1988, s. 111(2).

S. 226(3): FA 1988, s. 111(3).

S. 226(4)–(7): CGTA 1979, s. 105(3)–(6).

Cross references – S. 248(1): roll-over relief on replacement of land compulsorily acquired not available where replacement land is a dwelling-house subject to relief under s. 222–226.

ICTA 1988, s. 776(9): disapplication of provisions treating as income certain quasi-dealing transactions in land where gain exempt within s. 222–226.

Notes – S. 288: interpretation, including "inspector" as being any inspector of taxes and reference to sections being those of this Act.

TMA 1970, s. 42–43B: procedure for making claims.

226A Private residence relief: cases where relief obtained under section 260

Notes – S. 226A has effect subject to certain modifications when FA 2004, Sch. 22, para. 8 has effect. For further information on the modifications that apply, reference should be made to the **Notes** in the legislation annotation at the end of s. 226A.

226A(1) This section applies where–

(a) section 223 applies, or would apart from this section apply, in relation to a gain or part of a gain accruing to an individual or the trustees of a settlement ("the transferor") on a disposal (the "later disposal"),

(b) in computing the chargeable gain which would, apart from section 223, accrue to the transferor on the later disposal, the allowable expenditure would fall to be reduced, and

(c) that reduction would to any extent fall to be made in consequence, directly or indirectly, of a claim or claims under section 260 in respect of one or more earlier disposals (whether or not made to the transferor).

226A(2) If a claim for relief under section 260 in respect of–

(a) the earlier disposal, or

(b) if there were two or more such disposals, any of them,

is made on or before the making of the later disposal, section 223 shall not apply in relation to the gain or part of a gain accruing on the later disposal.

226A(3) If a claim for relief under section 260 in respect of–

(a) the earlier disposal, or

(b) if there were two or more such disposals, any of them,

is made after the making of the later disposal and subsection (2) above does not apply, it is to be assumed for the purposes of capital gains tax that section 223 never applied in relation to the gain or part of a gain accruing on the later disposal.

226A(4) All such adjustments shall be made, whether by discharge or repayment of tax, the making of assessments or otherwise, as are required to give effect to subsection (3) above (notwithstanding any limitation on the time within which any adjustment may be made).

226A(5) Where the later disposal is made by the trustees of a settlement, the references in subsections (2) and (3) above to the making of the later disposal shall be read as references to the making of a claim for relief under section 223 in respect of the gain or part of a gain accruing on that disposal.

226A(6) If a claim for relief under section 260 in respect of an earlier disposal is revoked, this section shall apply as if the claim had never been made.

226A(7) This section is subject to section 226B (exception for maintenance funds for historic buildings).

History – S. 226A inserted by FA 2004, s. 117 and Sch. 22, para. 6 with effect, by virtue of FA 2004, Sch. 22, para. 7(3) and subject to the transitional provision of FA 2004, Sch. 22, para. 8 which makes modifications to s. 226A that was inserted by FA 2004, Sch. 22, para. 6, in relation to gains or parts of gains accruing on later disposals (within the meaning of the s. 226A inserted by FA 2004, Sch. 22, para. 6) made on or after 10 December 2003 (whenever any relevant earlier disposal was made); the transitional provision of FA 2004, Sch. 22, para. 8 has effect where s. 226A (as inserted by FA 2004, Sch. 22, para. 6) applies in circumstances in which either (a) the relevant earlier disposal or (b) each of the relevant earlier disposals (if there were more than one such disposal) was made before 10 December 2003.

Cross references – FA 2004, Sch. 22, para. 8: transitional provision modifying s. 226A.

Notes – S. 226A has effect subject to modifications where FA 2004, Sch. 22, para. 8 has effect.

"**8(1)** This paragraph has effect where section 226A of the Taxation of Chargeable Gains Act 1992 (c. 12) (as inserted by paragraph 6 of this Schedule) ("section 226A") applies in circumstances in which–

(a) the relevant earlier disposal, or

(b) if there were two or more such disposals, each of them, was made before 10th December 2003.

8(2) Section 226A shall have effect subject to the following modifications.
8(3) In subsection (2), omit "not" and at the end insert "subject to the modifications set out in subsections (2A) to (2C) below".
8(4) After subsection (2) insert–
"**226A(2A)** Section 223(1) shall not apply.
226A(2B) For the purposes of section 223(2)(a) and (3)–
(a) the dwelling-house or the part of the dwelling-house in question is to be taken not to have been the individual's only or main residence during the post-commencement period or any part of that period, and
(b) the words "but inclusive of the last 36 months of the period of ownership in any event" shall not have effect in respect of so much of that period of 36 months as falls within the post-commencement period.
226A(2C) In subsection (2B) above **"post-commencement period"** means the period beginning on 10th December 2003 and ending on the date of the later disposal.".
8(5) In subsection (3), omit "never" and at the end insert "subject to the modifications set out in subsections (2A) to (2C) above".
8(6) In this paragraph **"relevant earlier disposal"**, in relation to a later disposal, means an earlier disposal in respect of which a claim mentioned in subsection (1)(c) of section 226A is made.
8(7) This paragraph is to be construed as one with section 226A.
8(8) Subsections (5) and (6) of section 223 of the Taxation of Chargeable Gains Act 1992 apply in relation to the subsection (2B) (b) treated as inserted by sub-paragraph (4) above as they apply in relation to subsections (1) and (2)(a) of that section.".

226B Exception to section 226A

226B(1) Section 226A shall not apply in relation to a later disposal made by the trustees of a settlement if the trustees have elected that section 508 of ITA 2007 (trustees' election in respect of income arising from heritage maintenance property) shall have effect in the case of–

(a) the settlement, or

(b) any part of the settlement,

in relation to each year of assessment in which a relevant earlier disposal is made.

226B(2) In this section **"relevant earlier disposal"**, in relation to a later disposal, means an earlier disposal in respect of which a claim mentioned in section 226A(1)(c) is made.

226B(3) This section is to be construed as one with section 226A.

History – In s. 226B(1), the words "508 of ITA 2007 (trustees' election in respect of income arising from heritage maintenance property)" substituted for "691(2) of the Taxes Act (certain income of maintenance funds for historic buildings not to be income of settlor etc)" by ITA 2007, s. 1027 and Sch. 1, para. 323, with effect from 6 April 2007.
S. 226B inserted by FA 2004, s. 117 and Sch. 22, para. 6 with effect, by virtue of FA 2004, Sch. 22, para. 7(3) and subject to the transitional provision of FA 2004, Sch. 22, para. 8 which makes modifications to s. 226A that was inserted by FA 2004, Sch. 22, para. 6, in relation to gains or parts of gains accruing on later disposals (within the meaning of the s. 226A inserted by FA 2004, Sch. 22, para. 6) made on or after 10 December 2003 (whenever any relevant earlier disposal was made); the transitional provision of FA 2004, Sch. 22, para. 8 has effect where s. 226A (as inserted by FA 2004, Sch. 22, para. 6) applies in circumstances in which either (a) the relevant earlier disposal or (b) each of the relevant earlier disposals (if there were more than one such disposal) was made before 10 December 2003.

EMPLOYEE SHARE OWNERSHIP TRUSTS

227 Conditions for roll-over relief

227(1) Relief is available under section 229(1) where each of the 6 conditions set out in subsections (2) to (7) below is fulfilled.

227(2) The first condition is that a person ("the claimant") makes a disposal of shares, or his interest in shares, to the trustees of a settlement which–

(a) is a qualifying employee share ownership trust at the time of the disposal, and

(b) was established by a company (**"the founding company"**) which immediately after the disposal is a trading company or the holding company of a trading group.

227(3) The second condition is that the shares–

(a) are shares in the founding company,

(b) form part of the ordinary share capital of the company,

(c) are fully paid up,

(d) are not redeemable, and

(e) are not subject to any restrictions other than restrictions which attach to all shares of the same class or a restriction authorised by paragraph 7(2) of Schedule 5 to the Finance Act 1989.

227(4) The third condition is that, at any time in the entitlement period, the trustees–

(a) are beneficially entitled to not less than 10 per cent of the ordinary share capital of the founding company,

(b) are beneficially entitled to not less than 10 per cent of any profits available for distribution to equity holders of the founding company, and

(c) would be beneficially entitled to not less than 10 per cent of any assets of the founding company available for distribution to its equity holders on a winding-up.

227(5) The fourth condition is that the claimant obtains consideration for the disposal and, at any time in the acquisition period, all the amount or value of the consideration is applied by him in making an acquisition of assets or an interest in assets (**"replacement assets"**) which–

(a) are, immediately after the time of the acquisition, chargeable assets in relation to the claimant, and

(b) are not shares in, or debentures issued by, the founding company or a company which is (at the time of the acquisition) in the same group as the founding company;

but the preceding provisions of this subsection shall have effect without the words ", at any time in the acquisition period," if the acquisition is made pursuant to an unconditional contract entered into in the acquisition period.

227(6) The fifth condition is that, at all times in the proscribed period, there are no unauthorised arrangements under which the claimant or a person connected with him may be entitled to acquire any of the shares, or an interest in or right deriving from any of the shares, which are the subject of the disposal by the claimant.

227(7) The sixth condition is that no chargeable event occurs in relation to the trustees in–

(a) the chargeable period in which the claimant makes the disposal,

(b) the chargeable period in which the claimant makes the acquisition, or

(c) any chargeable period falling after that mentioned in paragraph (a) above and before that mentioned in paragraph (b) above.

History – In s. 227(2), the words "the trustees of a settlement" substituted for "the trustees of a trust" by FA 2006, s. 88 and Sch. 12, para. 21(1) with effect in relation to disposals made on or after 6 April 2006.

Derivations – FA 1990, s. 31(1)–(7).

Cross references – FA 1989, Sch. 5, para. 7(2): authorisation of restriction in relation to employee share ownership trusts by reference to imposition under the company's articles and requirements to dispose of shares so as not to be held by persons who are not directors or employees.

Notes – S. 21–34: general meaning of "disposal" and "assets" and the timing of certain disposals.
S. 286: "connected" in references to persons being connected with one another.
S. 288: interpretation, including meaning of "company", "shares" as embracing stock, "chargeable period" by reference to a tax year and reference to sections being those of this Act.

228 Conditions for relief: supplementary

228(1) This section applies for the purposes of section 227.

228(2) The entitlement period is the period beginning with the disposal and ending on the expiry of 12 months beginning with the date of the disposal.

228(3) The acquisition period is the period beginning with the disposal and ending on the expiry of 6 months beginning with–

(a) the date of the disposal, or

(b) if later, the date on which the third condition (set out in section 227(4)) first becomes fulfilled.

228(4) The proscribed period is the period beginning with the disposal, and ending on–

(a) the date of the acquisition, or

(b) if later, the date on which the third condition (set out in section 227(4)) first becomes fulfilled.

228(5) All arrangements are unauthorised unless–

(a) they arise wholly from a restriction authorised by paragraph 7(2) of Schedule 5 to the Finance Act 1989, or

(b) they only allow one or both of the following as regards shares, interests or rights, namely, acquisition by a beneficiary under the settlement and appropriation under an approved profit sharing scheme.

228(6) An asset is a chargeable asset in relation to the claimant at a particular time if, were the asset to be disposed of at that time, any gain accruing to him on the disposal would be a chargeable gain, and either–

(a) at that time he is resident or ordinarily resident in the United Kingdom, or

(b) he would be chargeable to capital gains tax under section 10(1) in respect of the gain, or it would form part of his chargeable profits for corporation tax purposes by virtue of section 10B,

unless (were he to dispose of the asset at that time) the claimant would fall to be regarded for the purposes of any double taxation relief arrangements as not liable in the United Kingdom to tax on any gains accruing to him on the disposal.

228(7) The question whether a settlement is at a particular time a qualifying employee share ownership trust shall be determined in accordance with Schedule 5 to the Finance Act 1989; and **"chargeable event"** in relation to trustees has the meaning given by section 69 of that Act.

228(8) The expressions **"holding company"**, **"trading company"** and **"trading group"** have the same meaning as in section 165 (see section 165A); and **"group"** (except in the expression **"trading group"**) shall be construed in accordance with section 170.

228(9) **"Ordinary share capital"** in relation to the founding company means all the issued share capital (by whatever name called) of the company, other than capital the holders of which have a right to a dividend at a fixed rate but have no other right to share in the profits of the company.

228(10) Chapter 6 of Part 5 of CTA 2010 (group relief: equity holders and profits or assets available for distribution) applies for the purposes of section 227(4) as if–

(a) the trustees were a company, and

(b) references to section 151(4)(a) and (b) of that Act were references to section 227(4) above.

History – In s. 228(5)(b), the words "a beneficiary under the settlement" substituted for "a beneficiary under the trust" by FA 2006, s. 88 and Sch. 12, para. 22(1) with effect in relation to arrangements which allow an acquisition to be made on or after 6 April 2006 (irrespective of when the arrangements were made).
In s. 228(6)(b), the reference "10B" substituted for the reference "10(3)" by FA 2003, s. 155 and Sch. 27, para. 2(3); with effect in relation to accounting periods beginning on or after 1 January 2003.
In s. 228(7), the words "whether a settlement is" substituted for "whether a trust is" by FA 2006, s. 88 and Sch. 12, para. 22(2) with effect for the purposes of determining what constitutes a qualifying share ownership trust for the purpose of s. 227 on or after 6 April 2006.
In s. 228(8), words "same meaning as in section 165 (see section 165A)" substituted by FA 2008, s. 8 and Sch. 2, para. 36 with effect in relation to chargeable gains accruing or treated as accruing in the tax year 2008–09 or any subsequent tax year (FA 2008, Sch. 2, para. 56(3)).
In s. 228(8), reference "paragraph 22 of Schedule A1" substituted for reference "paragraph 1 of Schedule 6" by FA 1998, s. 140(5)(a) which has effect in relation to the year 2003–04 and subsequent years of assessment by virtue of FA 1998, s. 140(6).
S. 228(10) substituted by CTA 2010, s. 1177 and Sch. 1, para. 252, with effect for corporation tax purposes for accounting periods ending on or after 1 April 2010, and for income tax and capital gains tax purposes for the tax year 2010–11 and subsequent tax years.
In former s. 228(10)(b) words "to (9)" repealed by FA 2000, s. 153 and Sch. 40 Pt. II(11) and deemed always to have had effect.

Derivations – FA 1990, s. 32.

Cross references – S. 10: extent of charge on non-resident by reference to assets used or held for a UK branch or agency.
S. 170: groups of companies by reference to 75 per cent subsidiary relationships.
Sch. 6, para. 1: determination of "holding company", "trading company" and "trading group" by reference to business wholly or mainly of holding shares in 51 per cent subsidiaries, of carrying on a trade or trades (by company or group, as appropriate).
Sch. 7B, para. 14: modification of s. 228(6)(b) in respect of overseas life insurance companies in relation to acquisitions made in chargeable periods beginning after 31 December 1992.
ICTA 1988, Sch. 18: for s. 413(7)–(9) (group relief), "equity holder" defined by reference to any person who holds ordinary shares or is a creditor for a loan which is not a normal commercial loan; the relevant accounting period in point is that by reference to that current at the time in question (para. 7(2)(a)) while that in relation to a consortium is irrelevant (para. 7(1)(b)).
FA 1989, s. 69: "chargeable event" by reference to the following in relation to the trustees: a non-qualifying transfer, a transfer not on qualifying terms, retention of shares for more than seven years or expenditure for a non-qualifying purpose.
FA 1989, Sch. 5, para. 7(2): authorisation of restriction in relation to employee share ownership trusts by reference to imposition under the company's articles and requirements to dispose of shares so as not to be held by persons who are not directors or employees.
FA 2000, Sch. 29, para. 33: the amendments of TCGA 1992, s. 170 by para. 1 of that Schedule (repealing the provision which stated that references to a company applied only to companies resident in the UK) have effect for the purposes of s. 233 in relation to disposals on or after 1 April 2000.

Notes – S. 9: meaning of "resident" and "ordinarily resident".
S. 15: meaning of "chargeable gain".
S. 21–34: general meaning of "disposal" and "assets" and the timing of certain disposals.
S. 288: interpretation, including meaning of "double taxation relief arrangements", "shares" as embracing stock and reference to sections being those of this Act.

229 The relief

229(1) In a case where relief is available under this subsection the claimant shall, on making a claim in the period of 2 years beginning with the acquisition, be treated for the purposes of this Act–

(a) as if the consideration for the disposal were (if otherwise of a greater amount or value) of such amount as would secure that on the disposal neither a gain nor a loss accrues to him, and

(b) as if the amount or value of the consideration for the acquisition were reduced by the excess of the amount or value of the actual consideration for the disposal over the amount of the consideration which the claimant is treated as receiving under paragraph (a) above.

229(2) Relief is available under subsection (3) below where–

(a) relief would be available under subsection (1) above but for the fact that part only of the amount or value mentioned in section 227(5) is applied as there mentioned, and

(b) all the amount or value so mentioned except for a part which is less than the amount of the gain (whether all chargeable gain or not) accruing on the disposal is so applied.

229(3) In a case where relief is available under this subsection the claimant shall, on making a claim in *the period of 2 years beginning* with the acquisition, be treated for the purposes of this Act–

(a) as if the amount of the gain accruing on the disposal were reduced to the amount of the part mentioned in subsection (2)(b) above, and

(b) as if the amount or value of the consideration for the acquisition were reduced by the amount by which the gain is reduced under paragraph (a) above.

229(4) Nothing in subsection (1) or (3) above shall affect the treatment for the purposes of this Act of the other party to the disposal or of the other party to the acquisition.

229(5) The provisions of this Act fixing the amount of the consideration deemed to be given for a disposal or acquisition shall be applied before the preceding provisions of this section are applied.

Derivations – FA 1990, s. 33(1)–(5).

Cross references – S. 154: effect of provisions for crystallisation of held-over gain on acquisition of depreciating assets
FA 2000, s. 54: no rollover for disposals made to employee share ownership trust on or after 6 April 2001.

Notes – TMA 1970, s. 42–43B: procedure for making claims.

230 Dwelling-houses: special provision

230(1) Subsection (2) below applies where–

(a) a claim is made under section 229,

(b) immediately after the time of the acquisition mentioned in section 227(5) and apart from this section, any replacement asset was a chargeable asset in relation to the claimant,

(c) the asset is a dwelling-house or part of a dwelling-house or land, and

(d) there was a time in the period beginning with the acquisition and ending with the time when section 229(1) or (3) falls to be applied such that, if the asset (or an interest in it) were disposed of at that time, it would be within section 222(1) and the individual there mentioned would be the claimant or the claimant's spouse or civil partner.

230(2) In such a case the asset shall be treated as if, immediately after the time of the acquisition mentioned in section 227(5), it was not a chargeable asset in relation to the claimant.

230(3) Subsection (4) below applies where–

(a) the provisions of section 229(1) or (3) have been applied,

(b) any replacement asset which, immediately after the time of the acquisition mentioned in section 227(5) and apart from this section, was a chargeable asset in relation to the claimant consists of a dwelling-house or part of a dwelling-house or land, and

(c) there is a time after section 229(1) or (3) has been applied such that, if the asset (or an interest in it) were disposed of at that time, it would be within section 222(1) and the individual there mentioned would be the claimant or the claimant's spouse or civil partner.

230(4) In such a case–

(a) the asset shall be treated as if, immediately after the time of the acquisition mentioned in section 227(5), it was not a chargeable asset in relation to the claimant and adjustments shall be made accordingly, but

(b) any gain treated as accruing in consequence of the application of paragraph (a) above shall be treated as accruing at the time mentioned in subsection (3)(c) above or, if there is more than one such time, at the earliest of them.

230(5) Subsection (6) below applies where–

(a) a claim is made under section 229,

(b) immediately after the time of the acquisition mentioned in section 227(5) and apart from this section, any replacement asset was a chargeable asset in relation to the claimant,

(c) the asset was an option to acquire (or to acquire an interest in) a dwelling-house or part of a dwelling-house or land,

(d) the option has been exercised, and

(e) there was a time in the period beginning with the exercise of the option and ending with the time when section 229(1) or (3) falls to be applied such that, if the asset acquired on exercise of the option were disposed of at that time, it would be within section 222(1) and the individual there mentioned would be the claimant or the claimant's spouse or civil partner.

230(6) In such a case the option shall be treated as if, immediately after the time of the acquisition mentioned in section 227(5), it was not a chargeable asset in relation to the claimant.

230(7) Subsection (8) below applies where–

(a) the provisions of section 229(1) or (3) have been applied,

(b) any replacement asset which, immediately after the time of the acquisition mentioned in section 227(5) and apart from this section, was a chargeable asset in relation to the claimant consisted of an option to acquire (or to acquire an interest in) a dwelling-house or part of a dwelling-house or land,

(c) the option has been exercised, and

(d) there is a time after section 229(1) or (3) has been applied such that, if the asset acquired on exercise of the option were disposed of at that time, it would be within section 222(1) and the individual there mentioned would be the claimant or the claimant's spouse or civil partner.

230(8) In such a case–

(a) the option shall be treated as if, immediately after the time of the acquisition mentioned in section 227(5), it was not a chargeable asset in relation to the claimant and adjustments shall be made accordingly, but

(b) any gain treated as accruing in consequence of the application of paragraph (a) above shall be treated as accruing at the time mentioned in subsection (7)(d) above or, if there is more than one such time, at the earliest of them.

230(9) References in this section to an individual include references to a person entitled to occupy under the terms of a settlement.

History – In s. 230(1)(d), (3)(c), (5)(e) and (7)(d) the words "or civil partner" inserted by SI 2005/3229, reg. 119, with effect from 5 December 2005.

Derivations – FA 1990, s. 34.

Notes – S. 288: interpretation, including references to sections being those of this Act.

231 Shares: special provision

231(1) Subsection (2) below applies where–

(a) a claim is made under section 229,

(b) immediately after the time of the acquisition mentioned in section 227(5) and apart from this section, any replacement asset was a chargeable asset in relation to the claimant,

(c) the asset consists of shares, and

(d) in the period beginning with the acquisition and ending when section 229(1) or (3) falls to be applied relief is claimed under Chapter III of Part VII of the Taxes Act or Part 5 of ITA 2007 in respect of the asset.

231(2) In such a case the asset shall be treated as if, immediately after the time of the acquisition mentioned in section 227(5), it was not a chargeable asset in relation to the claimant.

231(3) Subsection (4) below applies where–

(a) the provisions of section 229(1) or (3) have been applied,

(b) any replacement asset which, immediately after the time of the acquisition mentioned in section 227(5) and apart from this section, was a chargeable asset in relation to the claimant consists of shares, and

(c) after section 229(1) or (3) has been applied relief is claimed under Chapter III of Part VII of the Taxes Act or Part 5 of ITA 2007 in respect of the asset.

231(4) In such a case the asset shall be treated as if, immediately after the time of the acquisition mentioned in section 227(5), it was not a chargeable asset in relation to the claimant and adjustments shall be made accordingly.

231(5) Subsection (4) above shall also apply where section 33(1) or (3) of the Finance Act 1990 has applied and the claimant acquired the replacement asset in a chargeable period beginning before 6th April 1992.

History – In s. 231(1), the words "or Part 5 of ITA 2007" inserted by ITA 2007, s. 1027 and Sch. 1, para. 324, with effect from 6 April 2007.

In s. 231(1)(d) the words "(business expansion scheme)" occurring immediately after the words "Taxes Act" omitted by FA 1994, s. 137 and Sch. 15, para. 34, s. 258 and Sch. 26, Pt. V(17) in relation to shares issued on or after 1 January 1994.

In s. 231(3), the words "or Part 5 of ITA 2007" inserted by ITA 2007, s. 1027 and Sch. 1, para. 324, with effect from 6 April 2007.

Derivations – FA 1990, s. 35.

Cross references – ICTA 1988, s. 289–312 (Pt. VII, Ch. III): business expansion scheme relief for subscription to certain issues of shares.

FA 1990, s. 33: see derivation of s. 229.

Notes – S. 288: interpretation, including the "Taxes Act" as ICTA 1988 and reference to other sections as being those of this Act.

232 Chargeable event when replacement assets owned

232(1) Subsection (3) below applies where–

(a) the provisions of section 229(1) or (3) are applied,

(b) a *chargeable event occurs in relation to the trustees on or after the date on which the disposal is* made (and whether the event occurs before or after the provisions are applied),

(c) the claimant was neither an individual who died before the chargeable event occurs nor trustees of a settlement which ceased to exist before the chargeable event occurs, and

(d) the condition set out below is fulfilled.

232(2) The condition is that, at the time the chargeable event occurs, the claimant or a person then connected with him is beneficially entitled to all the replacement assets.

232(3) In a case where this subsection applies, the claimant or connected person (as the case may be) shall be deemed for all purposes of this Act–

(a) to have disposed of all the replacement assets immediately before the time when the chargeable event occurs, and

(b) immediately to have reacquired them,

at the relevant value.

232(4) The **relevant value** is such value as secures on the deemed disposal a chargeable gain equal to–

(a) the amount by which the amount or value of the consideration mentioned in section 229(1)(b) was treated as reduced by virtue of that provision (where it applied), or

(b) the amount by which the amount or value of the consideration mentioned in section 229(3)(b) was treated as reduced by virtue of that provision (where it applied).

232(5) In a case where subsection (3) above would apply if "all" read "any of" in subsection (2) above, subsection (3) shall nevertheless apply, but as if–

(a) in subsection (3)(a) "all the replacement assets" read "the replacement assets concerned", and

(b) the relevant value were reduced to whatever value is just and reasonable.

232(6) Subsection (7) below applies where–

(a) subsection (3) above applies (whether or not by virtue of subsection (5) above), and

(b) before the time when the chargeable event occurs anything has happened as regards any of the replacement assets such that it can be said that a charge has accrued in respect of any of the gain carried forward by virtue of section 229(1) or (3).

232(7) If in such a case it is just and reasonable for subsection (3) above to apply as follows, it shall apply as if–

(a) the relevant value were reduced (or further reduced) to whatever value is just and reasonable, or

(b) the relevant value were such value as secures that on the deemed disposal neither a gain nor a loss accrues (if that is just and reasonable);

but paragraph (a) above shall not apply so as to reduce the relevant value below that mentioned in paragraph (b) above.

232(8) For the purposes of subsection (6)(b) above the gain carried forward by virtue of section 229(1) or (3) is the gain represented by the amount which by virtue of either of those provisions falls to be deducted from the expenditure allowable in computing a gain accruing on the disposal of replacement assets (that is, the amount found under subsection (4)(a) or (b) above, as the case may be).

232(9) In this section **"chargeable event"** in relation to trustees has the meaning given by section 69 of the Finance Act 1989.

Derivations – FA 1990, s. 36.

Cross references – FA 1989, s. 69: "chargeable event" by reference to the following in relation to the trustees: a non-qualifying transfer, a transfer not on qualifying terms, retention of shares for more than seven years or expenditure for a non-qualifying purpose.

Notes – S. 286: "connected" in references to persons being connected with one another.

233 Chargeable event when replacement property owned

233(1) Subsection (3) below applies where–

(a) paragraphs (a) to (c) of section 232(1) are fulfilled, and

(b) the condition set out below is fulfilled.

233(2) The condition is that–

(a) before the time when the chargeable event occurs, all the gain carried forward by virtue of section 229(1) or (3) was in turn carried forward from all the replacement assets to other property on a replacement of business assets, and

(b) at the time the chargeable event occurs, the claimant or a person then connected with him is beneficially entitled to all the property.

233(3) In a case where this subsection applies, the claimant or connected person (as the case may be) shall be deemed for all purposes of this Act–

(a) to have disposed of all the property immediately before the time when the chargeable event occurs, and

(b) immediately to have reacquired it,

at the relevant value.

233(4) The relevant value is such value as secures on the deemed disposal a chargeable gain equal to–

(a) the amount by which the amount or value of the consideration mentioned in section 229(1)(b) was treated as reduced by virtue of that provision (where it applied), or

(b) the amount by which the amount or value of the consideration mentioned in section 229(3)(b) was treated as reduced by virtue of that provision (where it applied).

233(5) In a case where subsection (3) above would apply if "all the" in subsection (2) above (in one or more places) read "any of the", subsection (3) shall nevertheless apply, but as if–

(a) in subsection (3)(a) "all the property" read "the property concerned", and

(b) the relevant value were reduced to whatever value is just and reasonable.

233(6) Subsection (7) below applies where –

(a) subsection (3) above applies (whether or not by virtue of subsection (5) above), and

(b) before the time when the chargeable event occurs anything has happened as regards any of the replacement assets, or any other property, such that it can be said that a charge has accrued in respect of any of the gain carried forward by virtue of section 229(1) or (3).

233(7) If in such a case it is just and reasonable for subsection (3) above to apply as follows, it shall apply as if–

(a) the relevant value were reduced (or further reduced) to whatever value is just and reasonable, or

(b) the relevant value were such value as secures that on the deemed disposal neither a gain nor a loss accrues (if that is just and reasonable);

but paragraph (a) above shall not apply so as to reduce the relevant value below that mentioned in paragraph (b) above.

233(8) For the purposes of subsections (2) and (6)(b) above the gain carried forward by virtue of section 229(1) or (3) is the gain represented by the amount which by virtue of either of those provisions falls to be deducted from the expenditure allowable in computing a gain accruing on the disposal of replacement assets (that is, the amount found under subsection (4)(a) or (b) above, as the case may be).

233(9) For the purposes of subsection (2) above a gain is carried forward from assets to other property on a replacement of business assets if, by one or more claims under sections 152 to 158, the chargeable gain accruing on a disposal of the assets is reduced, and as a result an amount falls to be deducted from the expenditure allowable in computing a gain accruing on the disposal of the other property.

Derivations – FA 1990, s. 37(1)–(9).

Cross references – S. 152–158: deferral of chargeable gains on replacement of business assets.

Notes – S. 288: interpretation, including reference to sections being those of this Act.

234 Chargeable events when bonds owned

234(1) Subsection (3) below applies where–

(a) paragraphs (a) to (c) of section 232(1) are fulfilled, and

(b) the condition set out below is fulfilled.

234(2) The condition is that–

(a) all the replacement assets were shares (new shares) in a company or companies,

(b) there has been a transaction to which section 116(10) applies and as regards which all the new shares constitute the old asset and qualifying corporate bonds constitute the new asset, and

(c) at the time the chargeable event occurs, the claimant or a person then connected with him is beneficially entitled to all the bonds.

234(3) In a case where this subsection applies, a chargeable gain shall be deemed to have accrued to the claimant or connected person (as the case may be); and the gain shall be deemed to have accrued immediately before the time when the chargeable event occurs and to be of an amount equal to the relevant amount.

234(4) The **relevant amount** is an amount equal to the lesser of–

(a) the first amount, and

(b) the second amount.

234(5) The **first amount** is–

(a) the amount of the chargeable gain that would be deemed to accrue under 116(10)(b) if there were a disposal of all the bonds at the time the chargeable event occurs, or

(b) nil, if an allowable loss would be so deemed to accrue if there were such a disposal.

234(6) The **second amount** is an amount equal to–

(a) the amount by which the amount or value of the consideration mentioned in section 229(1)(b) was treated as reduced by virtue of that provision (where it applied), or

(b) the amount by which the amount or value of the consideration mentioned in section 229(3)(b) was treated as reduced by virtue of that provision (where it applied).

234(7) In a case where subsection (3) above would apply if "all the" in subsection (2) above (in one or more places) read "any of the", subsection (3) shall nevertheless apply, but as if–

(a) in subsection (5) above " all the bonds" read "the bonds concerned",

(b) the second amount were reduced to whatever amount is just and reasonable, and

(c) the relevant amount were reduced accordingly.

234(8) Subsection (9) below applies where–

(a) subsection (3) above applies (whether or not by virtue of subsection (7) above), and

(b) before the time when the chargeable event occurs anything has happened as regards any of the new shares, or any of the bonds, such that it can be said that a charge has accrued in respect of any of the gain carried forward by virtue of section 229(1) or (3).

234(9) If in such a case it is just and reasonable for subsection (3) above to apply as follows, it shall apply as if–

(a) the second amount were reduced (or further reduced) to whatever amount is just and reasonable, and

(b) the relevant amount were reduced (or further reduced) accordingly (if the second amount is less than the first amount),

but nothing in this subsection shall have the effect of reducing the second amount below nil.

234(10) For the purposes of subsection (8)(b) above the gain carried forward by virtue of section 229(1) or (3) is the gain represented by the amount which by virtue of either of those provisions falls to be deducted from the expenditure allowable in computing a gain accruing on the disposal of replacement assets (that is, the amount found under subsection (6)(a) or (b) above, as the case may be).

Derivations – FA 1990, s. 38.

Cross references – S. 116(10): reorganisation, conversion or reconstruction where qualifying corporate bonds form part of the new holding but not the original holding, including crystallisation of the notional market value gain or loss calculated on the reorganisation etc. when the new holding is realised (s. 116(10)(b)).

Notes – S. 15: meaning of "chargeable gain".
S. 16: meaning of "allowable loss".
S. 286: "connected" in references to persons being connected with one another.
S. 288: interpretation, including meaning of "company", "shares" as embracing stock and reference to sections being those of this Act.
In s. 234(5)(a), the word "section" was omitted apparently by error.

235 Information

235 [Omitted by SI 2009/2035, art. 2 and Schedule, para. 32.]

History – S. 235 omitted by SI 2009/2035, art. 2 and Schedule, para. 32, with effect from 13 August 2009.

236 Prevention of double charge

236(1) Where a charge can be said to accrue by virtue of section 232 or 233 in respect of any of the gain carried forward by virtue of section 229(1) or (3), so much of the gain charged shall not be capable of being carried forward (from assets to other property or from property to other property) under sections 152 to 158 on a replacement of business assets.

236(2) For the purpose of construing subsection (1) above–

(a) what of the gain has been charged shall be found in accordance with what is just and reasonable;

(b) section 233(8) and (9) shall apply.

236(3) In a case where–

(a) section 234 applies in the case of bonds,

(b) subsequently a disposal of the bonds occurs as mentioned in section 116(10)(b), and

(c) a chargeable gain is deemed to accrue under section 116(10)(b),

the chargeable gain shall be reduced by the relevant amount found under section 234 or (if the amount exceeds the gain) shall be reduced to nil.

236(4) The relevant amount shall be apportioned where the subsequent disposal is of some of the bonds mentioned in subsection (3)(a) above; and subsection (3) shall apply accordingly.

Derivations – FA 1990, s. 40(5)–(8).

Cross references – S. 116(10): reorganisation, conversion or reconstruction where qualifying corporate bonds form part of the new holding but not the original holding, including crystallisation of the notional market value gain or loss calculated on the reorganisation etc. when the new holding is realised (s. 116(10)(b)).

S. 152–158: deferral of chargeable gains on replacement of business assets.
Notes – S. 288: interpretation, including reference to sections being those of this Act.

SHARE INCENTIVE PLANS

History – The heading "Share Incentive Plans" substituted for the heading "Employee Share Ownership Plans" by ITEPA 2003, Sch. 6, para. 214 with effect for 2003–04 and subsequent tax years.

236A Relief for transfers to share incentive plans

History – In the heading for s. 236A the words "share incentive" substituted for the words "employee share ownership" by ITEPA 2003, Sch. 6, para. 214 with effect for 2003–04 and subsequent tax years.

Schedule 7C (which makes provision for roll-over relief where shares are transferred to a Schedule 2 share incentive plan) shall have effect.

History – In s. 236A, the words "a Schedule 2" substituted for the words "an approved" by FA 2014, s. 51 and Sch. 8, para. 34, which is treated as having come into force on 6 April 2014, subject to the transitional provisions in FA 2014, Sch. 8, para. 90 to 96.
In s. 236A, the words "share incentive" substituted for the words "employee share ownership" by ITEPA 2003, Sch. 6, para. 214 with effect for 2003–04 and subsequent tax years.
S. 236A inserted by FA 2000, s. 48(1).

EMPLOYEE SHAREHOLDERS

History – Heading inserted by FA 2013, s. 55 and Sch. 23, para. 20, with effect from 1 September 2013 (SI 2013/1755).

236B Exemption for employee shareholder shares

236B(1) A gain which accrues on the first disposal of an exempt employee shareholder share is not a chargeable gain.

236B(1A) Where a gain accrues to a person ("P") on the first disposal of a post-16 March 2016 exempt employee shareholder share (the "relevant disposal"), subsection (1) applies only to so much of the gain as, when added to the total amount of previous potentially chargeable gains, does not exceed £100,000.

236B(1B) For the purposes of subsection (1A), **"previous potentially chargeable gain"** means a gain accruing to P on the first disposal of a post-16 March 2016 exempt employee shareholder share at any time before the relevant disposal.

236B(1C) Where a single transaction disposes of more than one post-16 March 2016 exempt employee shareholder share, the reference in subsection (1A) to the first disposal of a share is to be treated as a reference to the disposal of all of the post-16 March 2016 exempt employee shareholder shares first disposed of by that transaction.

236B(2) A share is an exempt employee shareholder share if it is–

(a) an employee shareholder share, and

(b) exempt in accordance with sections 236C and 236D.

236B(2A) Subsection (1) does not apply in relation to a gain accruing on a disposal where the proceeds of the disposal, in relation to any individual, constitute–

(a) a disguised fee for the purposes of Chapter 5E of Part 13 of ITA 2007 (see section 809EZA(3) of that Act), or

(b) carried interest within the meaning given by section 809EZC of that Act.

236B(3) In this section and sections 236C to 236G–

shares are **"acquired"** by an employee if the employee becomes beneficially entitled to them (and they are acquired at the time when the employee becomes so entitled);

"employee shareholder share" means a share acquired in consideration of an employee shareholder agreement and held by the employee;

"employee shareholder agreement" means an agreement by virtue of which an employee is an employee shareholder (see section 205A(1)(a) to (d) of the Employment Rights Act 1996);

"employee" and **"employer company"**, in relation to an employee shareholder agreement, mean the individual and the company which enter into the agreement.

236B(3A) In this section, **"post-16 March 2016 exempt employee shareholder share"** means an exempt employee shareholder share acquired in consideration of an employee shareholder agreement entered into after 16 March 2016.

History – S. 236B(1A) inserted by FA 2016, s. 88(2), with effect in relation to disposals made after 16 March 2016.
S. 236B(1B) inserted by FA 2016, s. 88(2), with effect in relation to disposals made after 16 March 2016.
S. 236B(1C) inserted by FA 2016, s. 88(2), with effect in relation to disposals made after 16 March 2016.
S. 236B(2A) inserted by FA 2016, s. 89(1), with effect in relation to gains accruing on or after 6 April 2016.
S. 236B(3A) inserted by FA 2016, s. 88(3), with effect in relation to disposals made after 16 March 2016.
S. 236B inserted by FA 2013, s. 55 and Sch. 23, para. 20, with effect from 1 September 2013 (SI 2013/1755).
Other material – HMRC guidance on the capital gains tax treatment of employee shareholder shares.

236C Only first £50,000 of shares under associated agreements to be exempt

236C(1) An employee shareholder share acquired in consideration of an employee shareholder agreement ("the relevant agreement") is exempt for the purposes of section 236B only if, immediately after its acquisition, the total value of qualifying shares which have been acquired by the employee does not exceed £50,000.

236C(2) **"Qualifying share"** means an employee shareholder share in–

(a) the employer company in relation to the relevant agreement, or

(b) an associated company of that company,

which is acquired by the employee in consideration of an agreement within subsection (3).

236C(3) An agreement is within this subsection if it is–

(a) the relevant agreement,

(b) another employee shareholder agreement with the same employer company, or

(c) an employee shareholder agreement with an associated company of that company.

236C(4) For the purposes of this section–

(a) a company is an **"associated company"** of another if–

(i) one of the two has control of the other, or

(ii) both are under the control of the same person or persons, and

(b) if a company controls another when an employee shareholder agreement is entered into with the employee, paragraph (a) applies as if that continued to be the case (in addition to any other circumstances) when any subsequent employee shareholder agreement is entered into with that employee.

236C(5) But subsection (4)(b) does not apply as between two companies if–

(a) one of the companies has been dissolved,

(b) the period of two years beginning with the date of the dissolution has passed, and

(c) the employee has not, at any time in that period, been engaged in any office or employment (including engagement under a contract for services) with any company which is an associated company of the dissolved company.

236C(6) If a number of qualifying shares are acquired by an employee on a day and–

(a) before that day, the value of qualifying shares that have been acquired by the employee does not exceed £50,000, and

(b) at the end of that day, that value does exceed that sum,

the appropriate proportion of the shares (rounded down, if necessary, to the nearest share) is to be treated for the purposes of subsection (1) as having been acquired separately and before the others.

236C(7) The **"appropriate proportion"** is the following–

$$\frac{50000 - B}{T}$$

where–

B is the value of qualifying shares acquired before the day;

T is the total value of qualifying shares acquired on the day.

236C(8) For the purposes of this section, the value of a share (at any time) is its unrestricted market value at the time when it was acquired by the employee.

236C(9) The unrestricted market value of a share when it is acquired by an employee is what the market value of the share would be immediately after the acquisition, but for any restriction.

For this purpose **"restriction"** has the meaning given by section 432(8) of ITEPA 2003 (restricted securities for the purposes of Chapter 2 of Part 7 of that Act).

History – S. 236C inserted by FA 2013, s. 55 and Sch. 23, para. 20, with effect from 1 September 2013 (SI 2013/1755).

Other material – HMRC guidance on the capital gains tax treatment of employee shareholder shares.

236D Shares not exempt if shareholder or connected person has material interest in company

236D(1) An employee shareholder share is not exempt for the purposes of section 236B if, on the date on which the share is acquired–

(a) the employee has a material interest in the employer company or a relevant parent undertaking, or

(b) the employee is connected with an individual who has a material interest in the employer company or a relevant parent undertaking.

236D(2) An employee shareholder share is not exempt for the purposes of section 236B if–

(a) at any time in the period of one year ending with the date on which the share is acquired, the employee had a material interest in the employer company or a relevant parent undertaking, or

(b) on the date on which the share is acquired, the employee is connected with an individual who, at any time in the period of one year ending with that date, had a material interest in the employer company or a relevant parent undertaking.

236D(3) Subsections (4) and (5) define **"material interest"** for the purposes of this section. Those subsections must be read together with subsections (6) to (8).

236D(4) An individual ("A") has a material interest in a company if at least 25% of the voting rights in the company are exercisable–

(a) by A,

(b) by persons connected with A, or

(c) by A and persons connected with A together.

236D(5) If a company is a close company, an individual ("A") has a material interest in it if–

(a) A,

(b) persons connected with A, or

(c) A and persons connected with A together,

possess such rights as would, in the event of the winding up of the company or in any other circumstances, give an entitlement to receive at least 25% of the assets that would then be available for distribution among the participators.

236D(6) For the purposes of subsection (1), A is to be treated as having a material interest in a company at any time if either of the following conditions is met.

236D(7) The first condition is that–

(a) A,

(b) persons connected with A, or

(c) A and persons connected with A together,

have an entitlement to acquire such rights as would (together with any existing rights) give A a material interest in the company.

236D(8) The second condition is that there are arrangements in place between–

(a) the employer company or a relevant parent undertaking, and

(b) A, or persons connected with A, or A and persons connected with A together,

which enable A or those persons to acquire such rights as would (together with any existing rights) give A a material interest in the company.

236D(9) In this section–

"arrangements" includes any agreement, understanding, scheme, transaction or series of transactions (whether or not legally enforceable);

"close company" includes a company that would be a close company but for–

(a) section 442(a) of CTA 2010 (exclusion of companies not resident in the United Kingdom), or

(b) sections 446 and 447 of CTA 2010 (exclusion of certain quoted companies);

"relevant parent undertaking" means any parent undertaking of the employer company and for this purpose **"parent undertaking"** is to be read in accordance with section 1162 of the Companies Act 2006.

History – S. 236D inserted by FA 2013, s. 55 and Sch. 23, para. 20, with effect from 1 September 2013 (SI 2013/1755).

Other material – HMRC guidance on the capital gains tax treatment of employee shareholder shares.

236E Identification of exempt employee shareholder shares

236E(1) Sections 104 (share pooling), 105 (disposal on or before acquisition) and 106A (identification of securities) do not apply to exempt employee shareholder shares.

236E(2) Subsection (3) applies where–

(a) an employee holds shares of the same class in a company,

(b) some, but not all, of the shares are exempt employee shareholder shares, and

(c) the employee disposes of some, but not all, of the shares in that holding.

236E(3) Where this subsection applies–

(a) the employee may determine what proportion of the shares disposed of are to be treated as exempt employee shareholder shares (up to the number of such shares which the employee holds), and

(b) the consideration received for the shares disposed of is to be apportioned accordingly.

236E(4) For the purposes of this section shares in a company are not to be treated as being of the same class unless they are so treated by the practice of a recognised stock exchange or would be so treated if dealt with on a recognised stock exchange.

History – S. 236E inserted by FA 2013, s. 55 and Sch. 23, para. 20, with effect from 1 September 2013 (SI 2013/1755).

Other material – HMRC guidance on the capital gains tax treatment of employee shareholder shares.

236F Reorganisation of share capital involving employee shareholder shares

236F(1) Section 127 (equation of original shares and new holding on reorganisation) does not apply to exempt employee shareholder shares.

236F(1A) Subsection (1B) applies where–

(a) an exempt employee shareholder share ("the original EES share") is held by a person ("P") before, and is concerned in, a reorganisation, and

(b) the original EES share is disposed of on the reorganisation.

236F(1B) P is to be treated as if the original EES share were disposed of for consideration of an amount determined in accordance with subsections (1D) to (1H) (the "relevant amount").

236F(1C) In this section **"notional gain"** means the gain, if any, that would accrue to P if the original EES share were disposed of on the reorganisation for consideration of an amount equal to the market value of the share.

236F(1D) Subsections (1E) to (1G) apply where a notional gain would accrue to P on the disposal of the original EES share.

236F(1E) Where the whole of the notional gain would be a chargeable gain by virtue of section 236B(1A), the relevant amount is the amount that would secure that on the disposal neither a gain nor a loss would accrue to P.

236F(1F) Where part (but not the whole) of the notional gain would be a chargeable gain by virtue of section 236B(1A), the relevant amount is the maximum amount, not exceeding the market value of the share, that would secure that on the disposal no chargeable gain would accrue to P.

236F(1G) Where no part of the notional gain would be a chargeable gain by virtue of section 236B(1A), the relevant amount is equal to the market value of the original EES share at the time of the disposal.

236F(1H) Where no notional gain would accrue to P on the disposal of the original EES share, the relevant amount is the amount that would secure that on the disposal neither a gain nor a loss would accrue to P.

236F(1I) In determining for the purposes of this section whether any part of a notional gain is a chargeable gain by virtue of section 236B(1A), subsection (1B) is to be disregarded.

236F(1J) Where more than one original EES share is disposed of by P on a reorganisation, references in this section to the disposal of the original EES share are to be treated as references to the disposal of all of the original EES shares disposed of on the reorganisation.

236F(1K) In this section **"reorganisation"** has the same meaning as in section 127.

236F(2) The references in this section to section 127 include that section as applied by sections 135 and 136 (other company reconstructions).

History – S. 236F(1A) inserted by FA 2016, s. 88(5), with effect in relation to disposals made after 16 March 2016.
S. 236F(1B) inserted by FA 2016, s. 88(5), with effect in relation to disposals made after 16 March 2016.
S. 236F(1C) inserted by FA 2016, s. 88(5), with effect in relation to disposals made after 16 March 2016.
S. 236F(1D) inserted by FA 2016, s. 88(5), with effect in relation to disposals made after 16 March 2016.
S. 236F(1E) inserted by FA 2016, s. 88(5), with effect in relation to disposals made after 16 March 2016.
S. 236F(1F) inserted by FA 2016, s. 88(5), with effect in relation to disposals made after 16 March 2016.
S. 236F(1G) inserted by FA 2016, s. 88(5), with effect in relation to disposals made after 16 March 2016.
S. 236F(1H) inserted by FA 2016, s. 88(5), with effect in relation to disposals made after 16 March 2016.
S. 236F(1I) inserted by FA 2016, s. 88(5), with effect in relation to disposals made after 16 March 2016.
S. 236F(1J) inserted by FA 2016, s. 88(5), with effect in relation to disposals made after 16 March 2016.
S. 236F(1K) inserted by FA 2016, s. 88(5), with effect in relation to disposals made after 16 March 2016.
In s. 236F(2), the words "references in this section to section 127 include" substituted for the words "reference in subsection (1) to section 127 includes" by FA 2016, s. 88(6), with effect in relation to disposals made after 16 March 2016.
S. 236F inserted by FA 2013, s. 55 and Sch. 23, para. 20, with effect from 1 September 2013 (SI 2013/1755).

Other material – HMRC guidance on the capital gains tax treatment of employee shareholder shares.

236G Relinquishment of employment rights is not disposal of an asset

236G(1) This section applies where an individual has acquired shares in consideration of entering into an employee shareholder agreement.

236G(2) The individual is not to be regarded as disposing of an asset by reason of the individual ceasing to have, or not acquiring, the rights mentioned in section 205A of the Employment Rights Act 1996 (rights which an employee shareholder does not have) in consequence of entering into the agreement.

History – S. 236G inserted by FA 2013, s. 55 and Sch. 23, para. 20, with effect from 1 September 2013 (SI 2013/1755).

Other material – HMRC guidance on the capital gains tax treatment of employee shareholder shares.

EMPLOYEE-OWNERSHIP TRUSTS

236H Disposals to employee-ownership trusts

236H(1) This section applies where–

(a) a person other than a company ("P") disposes of any ordinary share capital of a company ("C") to the trustees of a settlement,

(b) the relief requirements are met, and

(c) P makes a claim under this section.

236H(2) Section 17(1) (disposals and acquisitions treated as made at market value) does not apply to the disposal.

236H(3) The disposal, and the acquisition by the trustees, are to be treated for the purposes of this Act as being made for such consideration as to secure that neither a gain nor a loss accrues on the disposal.

236H(4) **"The relief requirements"** are–

(a) that C meets the trading requirement (see section 236I) at the time of the disposal and continues to meet that requirement for the remainder of the tax year in which that time falls,

(b) that the settlement meets the all-employee benefit requirement at the time of the disposal and continues to meet that requirement for the remainder of the tax year in which that time falls (see sections 236J to 236L and subsection (5) of this section),

(c) that the settlement does not meet the controlling interest requirement (see section 236M) immediately before the beginning of the tax year in which the disposal occurs, but–

  (i) it meets that requirement at the end of that tax year, and

  (ii) if it met the requirement at an earlier time in that tax year (whether before or after the time of the disposal) it continued to meet it throughout the remainder of that tax year,

(d) that the limited participation requirement is met (see section 236N), and

(e) that this section does not apply in relation to any related disposal by P or a person connected with P which occurs in an earlier tax year.

236H(5) For the purposes of subsection (4)(b)–

(a) unless the settlement met the all-employee benefit requirement by virtue of section 236L (cases in which all-employee benefit requirement treated as met) at the time of the disposal, that section does not apply for the purposes of determining whether the settlement continues to meet that requirement after the disposal, and

(b) if, at the time of the disposal, the settlement met that requirement by virtue of section 236L and later continues to meet it otherwise than by virtue of that section, it may not again meet the requirement by virtue of that section.

236H(6) A disposal in an earlier tax year is **"related"** to the disposal in question if–

(a) both disposals are of ordinary share capital of the same company, or

(b) the disposal in the earlier tax year is of ordinary share capital of a company which is, or at the time of that disposal was, a member of the same group as the company whose ordinary share capital is the subject of the disposal in question.

236H(7) A claim under this section must include–

(a) information to identify the settlement,

(b) C's name and the address of its registered office, and

(c) the date of the disposal and the number of shares disposed of.

236H(8) Section 236O makes provision about events which prevent a claim being made under this section and circumstances in which a claim is revoked.

History – S. 236H inserted by FA 2014, s. 290 and Sch. 37, para. 1, with effect in relation to disposals made on or after 6 April 2014, subject to the transitional provisions in FA 2014, Sch. 37, para. 3.

236I Trading requirement

236I(1) C meets the trading requirement if C is–

(a) a trading company which is not a member of a group, or

(b) the principal company of a trading group.

236I(2) **"Trading company"** means a company carrying on trading activities whose activities do not include to a substantial extent activities other than trading activities.

236I(3) **"Trading group"** means a group–

(a) one or more of whose members carry on trading group activities, and

(b) the activities of whose members, taken together, do not include to a substantial extent activities other than trading group activities.

236I(4) In this section–

"trading activities" means activities carried on by the company in the course of, or for the purposes of, a trade being carried on by it;

"trading group activities" means activities carried on by a member of the group in the course of, or for the purposes of, a trade being carried on by any member of the group.

236I(5) For the purposes of determining whether C is a trading company or the principal company of a trading group–

(a) the activities of the members of a group are to be treated as one business (with the result that activities are disregarded to the extent that they are intra-group activities), and

(b) a business carried on by a company in partnership with one or more other persons is to be treated as not being a trading activity or a trading group activity.

History – S. 236I inserted by FA 2014, s. 290 and Sch. 37, para. 1, with effect in relation to disposals made on or after 6 April 2014, subject to the transitional provisions in FA 2014, Sch. 37, para. 3.

236J All-employee benefit requirement

236J(1) A settlement meets the all-employee benefit requirement if the trusts of the settlement–

(a) do not permit any of the settled property to be applied, at any time, otherwise than for the benefit of all the eligible employees on the same terms,

(b) do not permit the trustees at any time to apply any of the settled property–

(i) by creating a trust, or

(ii) by transferring property to the trustees of any settlement other than by an authorised transfer,

(c) do not permit the trustees at any time to make loans to beneficiaries of the trusts, and

(d) do not permit the trustees or any other person at any time to amend the trusts in a way such that the amended trusts would not comply with one or more of paragraphs (a) to (c).

236J(2) Section 236K makes provision about the requirement in subsection (1)(a).

236J(3) **"Eligible employee"** means–

(a) if C meets the trading requirement by virtue of section 236I(1)(a), any individual who is employed by, or is an office-holder of, C, and

(b) if C meets the trading requirement by virtue of section 236I(1)(b), any individual who is employed by, or is an office-holder of, a relevant group company,

but does not include an excluded participator.

236J(4) But where–

(a) C has ceased to meet the trading requirement or the trustees have ceased to hold any shares in C (or both), and

(b) a person was an eligible employee at any time during the period of two years ending immediately before that event (or, where both have occurred, the earlier of them),

that person continues to be an "eligible employee".

236J(5) **"Excluded participator"** means–

(a) a person who is a participator in C, or, where C meets the trading requirement by virtue of section 236I(1)(b), in any relevant group company,

(b) any other person who is a participator in any close company that has made a disposition whereby property became comprised in the same settlement, being a disposition which but for section 13 or 13A of the Inheritance Tax Act 1984 (dispositions by close companies for benefit of employees or to employee-ownership trusts) would have been a transfer of value for the purposes of inheritance tax,

(c) any other person who has been a participator in any company mentioned in paragraph (a) or (b) at any time on or after the look-back date, or

(d) any person who is connected with any person within paragraph (a), (b) or (c).

236J(6) The participators in a company who are referred to in subsection (5) do not include any participator who–

(a) is not beneficially entitled to, or to rights entitling the participator to acquire, 5% or more of, or of any class of the shares comprised in, the company's share capital, and

(b) on a winding-up of the company would not be entitled to 5% or more of its assets.

236J(7) In this section–

"authorised transfer" means a transfer of property consisting of or including any ordinary share capital of a company ("the transferred company") where–

(a) the transferred company meets the trading requirement, and

(b) the transfer is made to the trustees of a settlement which–

(i) meets the controlling interest requirement with respect to the transferred company immediately after the transfer, and

(ii) meets the all-employee benefit requirement with respect to the transferred company (ignoring section 236L),

and for this purpose references to "C" in sections 236I, 236M and 236T and this section are to be read as references to the transferred company,

"close company" and **"participator"** have the same meaning as in Part 4 of the Inheritance Tax Act 1984 (see section 102 of that Act), and references to a participator in a company are, in the case of a company which is not a close company, to be construed as references to a person who would be a participator in the company if it were a close company,

"the look-back date" means the first day of the period of 10 years ending with whichever is later of–

(a) 10 December 2013, and

(b) the day on which any property first became comprised in the settlement, and

"relevant group company" means C or any other company which is a member of the group of which C is the principal company.

236J(8) In this section references to the settled property include references to any income arising from it.

236J(9) See section 236L for cases where the all-employee benefit requirement is treated as met.

History – S. 236J inserted by FA 2014, s. 290 and Sch. 37, para. 1, with effect in relation to disposals made on or after 6 April 2014, subject to the transitional provisions in FA 2014, Sch. 37, para. 3.

236K Further provision about the equality requirement

236K(1) The requirement in section 236J(1)(a) ("the equality requirement") is not infringed by the trusts by reason only that they–

(a) permit the settled property to be applied, where an eligible employee has died, as if a surviving spouse, civil partner or dependant of the deceased person were the eligible employee (and continued to be employed) for a period of 12 months, or such shorter period as the trusts may provide, starting with the time of death,

(b) prevent the settled property being applied for the benefit of persons who have not been eligible employees for a continuous period of 12 months or such shorter period as the trusts may provide,

(c) permit the trustees to comply with a written request from a person that the trustees do not apply any of the settled property for the benefit of that person, or

(d) prevent the settled property being applied for the benefit of all persons who are eligible employees by reason only that they are office-holders.

236K(2) The equality requirement is not infringed by the trusts by reason only that, in addition to requiring the settled property to be applied for the benefit of all the eligible employees on the same terms, they also permit the settled property to be applied for charitable purposes.

236K(3) Subject to subsections (1) and (2), the equality requirement is infringed by the trusts if they permit the settled property to be applied by reference to factors other than those mentioned in subsection (4).

236K(4) The equality requirement is not infringed by the trusts by reason only that they permit the settled property to be applied for the benefit of all the eligible employees by reference to–

(a) an eligible employee's remuneration,

(b) an eligible employee's length of service, or

(c) hours worked by an eligible employee;

but this is subject to subsections (5) and (6).

236K(5) The equality requirement is infringed by the trusts if they permit any of the settled property to be applied on terms such that some (but not all) eligible employees receive no benefits (other than by virtue of subsection (1)(b), (c) and (d)).

236K(6) If any of the settled property is applied by reference to more than one of the factors mentioned in subsection (4), the equality requirement is infringed unless–

(a) each factor gives rise to a separate entitlement related to the level of remuneration, length of service or (as the case may be) hours worked, and

(b) the total entitlement is the sum of those separate entitlements.

236K(7) **"Eligible employee"** has the same meaning as in section 236J.

236K(8) In this section, references to the settled property include references to any income arising from it.

History – S. 236K inserted by FA 2014, s. 290 and Sch. 37, para. 1, with effect in relation to disposals made on or after 6 April 2014, subject to the transitional provisions in FA 2014, Sch. 37, para. 3.

236L Cases in which all-employee benefit requirement treated as met

236L(1) A settlement which would not otherwise meet the all-employee benefit requirement at any time is treated as meeting that requirement at that time if–

(a) the settlement was created before 10 December 2013,

(b) on that date–

(i) section 86 of the Inheritance Tax Act 1984 (trusts for the benefit of employees) applied to the settled property,

(ii) the trustees held a significant interest in C, and

(iii) the settlement did not meet the all-employee benefit requirement (ignoring this section), and

(c) the trustees of the settlement do not, during the period of 12 months ending with the time in question, do any of the following–

(i) apply any of the settled property otherwise than for the benefit of all eligible employees on the same terms,

(ii) apply any of the settled property by creating a trust,

(iii) apply any of the settled property by transferring property to the trustees of any settlement other than by an authorised transfer, or

(iv) make loans to beneficiaries of the trusts of the settlement.

236L(2) The trustees held a significant interest in C on 10 December 2013 if on that date–

(a) they–

(i) held 10% or more of the ordinary share capital of C, and

(ii) had powers of voting on all questions affecting C as a whole which, if exercised, would have yielded 10% or more of the votes capable of being exercised on them,

(b) they were entitled to 10% or more of the profits available for distribution to the equity holders of C,

(c) they would have been entitled, on a winding up of C, to 10% or more of the assets of C available for distribution to equity holders, and

(d) there were no provisions in any agreement or instrument affecting C's constitution or management or its shares or securities whereby the condition in paragraph (a), (b) or (c) could cease to be satisfied without the consent of the trustees.

See 236T for further provision relating to the holding of a significant interest.

236L(3) Subsections (3) to (8) of section 236J apply for the purposes of this section.

236L(4) The requirement in subsection (1)(c)(i) ("the behaviour requirement") is not infringed by reason only that the trustees of the settlement–

(a) apply any of the settled property, where an eligible employee has died, as if a surviving spouse, civil partner or dependant of the deceased person were the eligible employee (and continued to be employed) for a period of 12 months, or such shorter period as the trustees may determine, starting with the time of death,

(b) only apply the settled property for the benefit of persons who have been eligible employees for a continuous period of 12 months or such shorter period as the trustees may determine,

(c) comply with a written request from a person that the trustees do not apply any of the settled property for the benefit of that person, or

(d) have complied with the terms of the trusts of the settlement which prevent the settled property being applied for the benefit of some or all of the persons who are eligible employees by reason only that they are office-holders.

236L(5) The behaviour requirement is not infringed by reason only that, in addition to applying any of the settled property for the benefit of all the eligible employees on the same terms, the trustees also apply any of it for charitable purposes.

236L(6) Subject to subsections (4) and (5), the behaviour requirement is infringed by the trustees if they apply the settled property by reference to factors other than those mentioned in subsection (7).

236L(7) The behaviour requirement is not infringed by the trustees applying the settled property for the benefit of all the eligible employees by reference to–

(a) an eligible employee's remuneration,

(b) an eligible employee's length of service, or

(c) hours worked by an eligible employee;

but this is subject to subsections (8) and (9).

236L(8) The behaviour requirement is infringed if any of the settled property is applied by the trustees on terms such that some (but not all) eligible employees receive no benefits (other than as mentioned in subsection (4)(b), (c) and (d)).

236L(9) If the trustees apply any of the settled property by reference to more than one of the factors mentioned in subsection (7), the behaviour requirement is infringed unless–

(a) each factor gives rise to a separate entitlement related to the level of remuneration, length of service or (as the case may be) hours worked, and

(b) the total entitlement is the sum of those separate entitlements.

History – S. 236L inserted by FA 2014, s. 290 and Sch. 37, para. 1, with effect in relation to disposals made on or after 6 April 2014, subject to the transitional provisions in FA 2014, Sch. 37, para. 3.

Cross references – FA 2014, Sch. 37, para. 4(a): for the purposes of determining if the requirement of s. 236L(1)(c) is met, anything done by the trustees before 10 December 2013 is to be disregarded, subject to the exception in FA 2014, Sch. 37, para. 4(b).

236M Controlling interest requirement

236M(1) A settlement meets the controlling interest requirement if–

(a) the trustees–

(i) hold more than 50% of the ordinary share capital of C, and

(ii) have powers of voting on all questions affecting C as a whole which, if exercised, would yield a majority of the votes capable of being exercised on them,

(b) the trustees are entitled to more than 50% of the profits available for distribution to the equity holders of C,

(c) the trustees would be entitled, on a winding up of C, to more than 50% of the assets of C available for distribution to equity holders, and

(d) there are no provisions in any agreement or instrument affecting C's constitution or management or its shares or securities whereby the condition in paragraph (a), (b) or (c) can cease to be satisfied without the consent of the trustees.

236M(2) See section 236T for further provision relating to the controlling interest requirement.

History – S. 236M inserted by FA 2014, s. 290 and Sch. 37, para. 1, with effect in relation to disposals made on or after 6 April 2014, subject to the transitional provisions in FA 2014, Sch. 37, para. 3.

236N Limited participation requirement

236N(1) The limited participation requirement is met if Conditions A and B are met.

236N(2) Condition A is that there was no time in the period of 12 months ending immediately after the disposal mentioned in section 236H(1) when–

(a) P was a participator in C, and

(b) the participator fraction exceeded 2/5.

236N(3) Condition B is that the participator fraction does not exceed 2/5 at any time in the period beginning with that disposal and ending at the end of the tax year in which it occurs.

236N(4) But a time which falls in a period during which the participator fraction exceeded 2/5 is to be disregarded for the purposes of subsection (2)(b) and (3) if–

(a) that period lasts no more than 6 months, and

(b) the fraction exceeded 2/5 during that period by reason of events outside the reasonable control of the trustees.

236N(5) **"The participator fraction"** means–

$$\frac{NP}{NE}$$

where–

NP is the sum of–

(a) the number of persons who at the time in question are both–

(i) participators in C, and

(ii) employees of, or office-holders in, C, and

(b) the number of other persons who at that time are both–

(i) employees of, or office-holders in, C or, if C is the principal company of a trading group, any member of the group, and

(ii) connected with persons within paragraph (a);

NE is the number of persons who at that time are employees of C or, if C is the principal company of a trading group, any member of the group.

236N(6) The participators in C who are referred to in subsections (2) and (5) do not include any participator who–

(a) is not beneficially entitled to, or to rights entitling the participator to acquire, 5% or more of, or of any class of the shares comprised in, C's share capital, and

(b) on a winding-up of C would not be entitled to 5% or more of its assets.

236N(7) In this section–

(a) **"participator"** has the meaning given by section 454 of CTA 2010, and

(b) references to a participator in a company are, in the case of a company which is not a close company (within the meaning of Chapter 2 of Part 10 of that Act), to be construed as references to a person who would be a participator in the company if it were a close company.

History – S. 236N inserted by FA 2014, s. 290 and Sch. 37, para. 1, with effect in relation to disposals made on or after 6 April 2014, subject to the transitional provisions in FA 2014, Sch. 37, para. 3.

236O No section 236H relief if disqualifying event in next tax year

236O(1) This section applies where–

(a) a disposal is made in circumstances where paragraphs (a) and (b) of section 236H(1) are satisfied, and

(b) one or more disqualifying events occur in relation to the disposal in the tax year following the tax year in which the disposal occurs.

236O(2) A **"disqualifying event"** occurs in relation to the disposal if and when–

(a) C ceases to meet the trading requirement,

(b) the settlement ceases to meet the all-employee benefit requirement,

(c) the settlement ceases to meet the controlling interest requirement,

(d) the participator fraction exceeds 2/5, or

(e) the trustees act in a way which the trusts, as required by the all-employee benefit requirement, do not permit.

236O(3) No claim for relief under section 236H may be made in respect of the disposal on or after the day on which the disqualifying event (or, if more than one, the first of them) occurs.

236O(4) Any claim for relief under section 236H made in respect of the disposal before that day is revoked, and the chargeable gains and allowable losses of any person for any chargeable period are to be calculated as if that claim had never been made.

236O(5) Such adjustments must be made in relation to any person, whether by the making of assessments or otherwise, as are required to give effect to subsection (4) (regardless of any limitation on the time within which any adjustment may be made).

236O(6) Section 236H(5) (restrictions on application of section 236L) applies for the purposes of subsection (2)(b).

236O(7) Section 236N(4) applies for the purposes of subsection (2)(b) as it applies in relation to section 236N(2)(b) and (3).

History – S. 236O inserted by FA 2014, s. 290 and Sch. 37, para. 1, with effect in relation to disposals made on or after 6 April 2014, subject to the transitional provisions in FA 2014, Sch. 37, para. 3.

236P Events which trigger deemed disposal and reacquisition by trustees

236P(1) Where the trustees of a settlement acquire any ordinary share capital in a tax year in circumstances where section 236H applies, subsection (3) applies on the first occasion, after the end of the tax year following the tax year in which the acquisition occurs, when a disqualifying event occurs in relation to the acquisition.

236P(2) A **"disqualifying event"** occurs in relation to the acquisition if and when–

(a) C ceases to meet the trading requirement,

(b) the settlement ceases to meet the all-employee benefit requirement,

(c) the settlement ceases to meet the controlling interest requirement,

(d) the participator fraction exceeds 2/5, or

(e) the trustees act in a way which the trusts, as required by the all-employee benefit requirement, do not permit.

236P(3) The trustees are treated as having, immediately before the disqualifying event–

(a) disposed of any ordinary share capital of C held by the trustees which comprises shares acquired in circumstances where section 236H applied (and not subsequently disposed of and reacquired), and

(b) immediately reacquired that ordinary share capital,

at its market value at that time.

236P(4) For the purposes of subsection (2)(b)–

(a) unless the settlement met the all-employee benefit requirement at the time of the acquisition by virtue of section 236L, that section does not apply for the purposes of determining whether the settlement continues to meet that requirement after the acquisition, and

(b) if, at the time of the acquisition, the settlement met that requirement by virtue of section 236L and later continues to meet it otherwise than by virtue of that section, it may not again meet the requirement by virtue of that section.

236P(5) Section 236N(4) applies for the purposes of subsection (2)(b) as it applies in relation to section 236N(2)(b) and (3).

History – S. 236P inserted by FA 2014, s. 290 and Sch. 37, para. 1, with effect in relation to disposals made on or after 6 April 2014, subject to the transitional provisions in FA 2014, Sch. 37, para. 3.

236Q Relief for deemed disposals under section 71

236Q(1) This section applies where–

(a) a deemed disposal arises under section 71(1) by reason of the trustees of a settlement ("the acquiring settlement") becoming absolutely entitled to settled property as against the trustee of that settled property ("the transferring trustee"),

(b) that settled property consists of ordinary share capital of a company,

(c) the relief requirements in section 236H(4)(a) to (d) are met, and

(d) the transferring trustee makes a claim under this section.

236Q(2) Section 17(1) (disposals and acquisitions treated as made at market value) does not apply to the disposal.

236Q(3) The deemed disposal and acquisition by the transferring trustee under section 71(1) are to be treated for the purposes of this Act as being made for such consideration as to secure that neither a gain nor a loss accrues on the disposal.

236Q(4) For the purposes of section 236P the trustees of the acquiring settlement are treated as acquiring the ordinary share capital from the transferring trustee, at the time of the deemed disposal, in circumstances where section 236H applies.

236Q(5) In applying sections 236H(4), 236I to 236P and 236T for the purposes of this section–

(a) references in those provisions to the settlement are to be read as references to the acquiring settlement, and

(b) references in those provisions to C are to be read as references to the company mentioned in subsection (1)(b).

236Q(6) A claim under this section must include–

(a) information to identify the acquiring settlement,

(b) the name of the company mentioned in subsection (1)(b) and the address of its registered office, and

(c) the date of the deemed disposal and the number of shares deemed to have been disposed of.

236Q(7) Section 236R makes provision about events which prevent a claim being made under this section and circumstances in which a claim is revoked.

History – S. 236Q inserted by FA 2014, s. 290 and Sch. 37, para. 1, with effect in relation to disposals made on or after 6 April 2014, subject to the transitional provisions in FA 2014, Sch. 37, para. 3.

236R No section 236Q relief if disqualifying event in next tax year

236R(1) This section applies where–

(a) a deemed disposal arises in circumstances where paragraphs (a) to (c) of section 236Q(1) are satisfied, and

(b) one or more disqualifying events occur in relation to the disposal in the tax year following the tax year in which the deemed disposal arises.

236R(2) No claim for relief under section 236Q may be made in respect of the deemed disposal on or after the day on which the disqualifying event (or, if more than one, the first of them) occurs.

236R(3) Any claim for relief under section 236Q made in respect of the deemed disposal before that day is revoked, and the chargeable gains and allowable losses of any person for any chargeable period are to be calculated as if that claim had never been made.

236R(4) Such adjustments must be made in relation to any person, whether by the making of assessments or otherwise, as are required to give effect to subsection (3) (regardless of any limitation on the time within which any adjustment may be made).

236R(5) **"Disqualifying event"** is to be construed in accordance with subsections (2), (6) and (7) of section 236O except that–

(a) references in those subsections to the disposal are to be read as references to the deemed disposal, and

(b) in applying sections 236I to 236P and 236T for this purpose–

(i) references in those provisions to the settlement are to be read as references to the acquiring settlement (within the meaning of section 236Q(1)), and

(ii) references in those provisions to C are to be read as references to the company mentioned in section 236Q(1)(b).

History – S. 236R inserted by FA 2014, s. 290 and Sch. 37, para. 1, with effect in relation to disposals made on or after 6 April 2014, subject to the transitional provisions in FA 2014, Sch. 37, para. 3.

236S Identification of shares where section 236H or 236Q applies

236S(1) This section applies where the trustees of a settlement hold–

(a) shares which were–

(i) acquired in circumstances where section 236H applied, or

(ii) the subject of a deemed acquisition under section 71(1) in circumstances where section 236Q applied,

and not subsequently disposed of and reacquired ("EOT exempt shares"), and

(b) other shares which, but for section 104(4A), would be shares of the same class as those shares.

236S(2) If the trustees dispose of some, but not all, of the shares so held, they may determine what proportion of the shares disposed of are EOT exempt shares (up to the number of such shares held).

236S(3) For the purposes of this section shares in a company are not to be treated as being of the same class unless they are so treated by the practice of a recognised stock exchange or would be so treated if dealt with on a recognised stock exchange.

236S(4) Nothing in subsection (2) applies in relation to a disposal by virtue of section 236P(3).

History – S. 236S inserted by FA 2014, s. 290 and Sch. 37, para. 1, with effect in relation to disposals made on or after 6 April 2014, subject to the transitional provisions in FA 2014, Sch. 37, para. 3.

236T Further provision about significant and controlling interests

236T(1) This section applies for the purposes of–

(a) section 236L(2) (trustees hold a significant interest in C), and

(b) section 236M (controlling interest requirement).

236T(2) Chapter 6 of Part 5 of CTA 2010 (group relief: equity holders and profits or assets available for distribution) applies as it applies for the purposes of the provisions mentioned in section 157(1) of that Act.

236T(3) The trustees are to be treated, for the purposes of section 236L(2)(b) or 236M(1)(b), as entitled to dividends on shares even if the trustees are required, or permitted, by the trusts of the settlement to waive their entitlement to those dividends.

236T(4) In determining whether section 236L(2)(d) or 236M(1)(d) applies, ignore any provision of–

(a) a mortgage or charge (or, in Scotland, a charge or security) granted by the trustees to a third party to secure any debt, or

(b) an agreement in respect of a loan made to the trustees by a third party,

which confers any entitlement on the third party in the event of a default by the trustees in performing their obligations in relation to that debt or loan.

236T(5) In this section–

"third party" means a person other than–

(a) C or a member of a group of which C is the principal company,

(b) a person who is, or has at any time in the preceding 12 months been, a participator in C or in a member of such a group, or

(c) a person connected with a person within paragraph (b);

"close company" and **"participator"** have the same meaning as in Part 4 of the Inheritance Tax Act 1984 (see section 102 of that Act), and a reference to a participator in a company is, in the case of a company which is not a close company, to be construed as a reference to a person who would be a participator in the company if it were a close company.

History – S. 236T inserted by FA 2014, s. 290 and Sch. 37, para. 1, with effect in relation to disposals made on or after 6 April 2014, subject to the transitional provisions in FA 2014, Sch. 37, para. 3.

236U Interpretation of sections 236H to 236U

236U(1) In sections 236H to 236T and this section–

"company" has the meaning given by section 170(9);

"ordinary share capital" has the meaning given by section 1119 of CTA 2010;

"trade" means any trade which is conducted on a commercial basis and with a view to the realisation of profits.

236U(2) In those sections–

(a) references to a group, to membership of a group or to the principal company of a group, are to be construed in accordance with section 170, and

(b) references to a group are to be construed with any necessary modifications where applied to a company incorporated under the law of a country or territory outside the United Kingdom.

236U(3) In determining whether a person is connected with another for the purposes of those sections, section 286 applies as if subsection (8) of that section also mentioned uncle, aunt, nephew and niece.

History – S. 236U inserted by FA 2014, s. 290 and Sch. 37, para. 1, with effect in relation to disposals made on or after 6 April 2014, subject to the transitional provisions in FA 2014, Sch. 37, para. 3.

SUPERANNUATION FUNDS, PROFIT SHARING SCHEMES, EMPLOYEE TRUSTS ETC.

237 Superannuation funds, annuities and annual payments

237 No chargeable gain shall accrue to any person on the disposal of a right to, or to any part of–

(a) any allowance, annuity or capital sum payable out of any superannuation fund, or under any superannuation scheme, established solely or mainly for persons employed in a profession, trade, undertaking or employment, and their dependants, or

(b) [Omitted by FA 2006, s. 73(3)(b) and repealed by FA 2006, s. 178 and Sch. 26, Pt. 3(10).]

(c) annual payments which are due under a covenant made by any person and which are not secured on any property.

History – In s. 237(a), the word "or" at the end inserted by FA 2006, s. 73(3)(a) with effect in relation to disposals made on or after 5 December 2005.

S. 237(b) omitted by FA 2006, s. 73(3)(b) and repealed by FA 2006, s. 178 and Sch. 26, Pt. 3(10) with effect in relation to disposals made on or after 5 December 2005.

Derivations – CGTA 1979, s. 144.

HMRC interpretations – IRInt. 257: assignment on divorce of life insurance policies, capital redemption policies and purchased life annuities.

Notes – S. 15: meaning of "chargeable gain".
S. 21–34: general meaning of "disposal".
S. 210: gains in respect of deferred annuities.

237A Share option schemes: release and replacement of options

237A(1) This section applies in any case where a right to acquire shares in a body corporate (**"the old right"**) which was obtained by an individual by reason of his office or employment as a director or employee of that or any other body corporate is released in whole or in part for a consideration which consists of or includes the grant to that individual of another right (**"the new right"**) to acquire shares in that or any other body corporate.

237A(2) As respects the person to whom the new right is granted–

(a) without prejudice to subsection (1) above, the new right shall not be regarded for the purposes of capital gains tax as consideration for the release of the old right;

(b) the amount or value of the consideration given by him or on his behalf for the acquisition of the new right shall be taken for the purposes of section 38(1) to be the amount or value of the consideration given by him or on his behalf for the old right; and

(c) any consideration paid for the acquisition of the new right shall be taken to be expenditure falling within section 38(1)(b).

237A(3) As respects the grantor of the new right, in determining for the purposes of this Act the amount or value of the consideration received for the new right, the release of the old right shall be disregarded.

History – S. 237A inserted by FA 1996, s. 112(1) in relation to transactions effected on or after 28 November 1995.

238 Approved profit sharing and share option schemes

238(1) Notwithstanding anything in a profit sharing scheme approved under Schedule 9 of the Taxes Act or in paragraph 2(2) of that Schedule or in the trust instrument relating to that scheme, for the purposes of capital gains tax a person who is a participant in relation to that scheme shall be treated as absolutely entitled to his shares as against the trustees of the scheme.

238(2) For the purposes of capital gains tax–

(a) no deduction shall be made from the consideration for the disposal of any shares by reason only that an amount determined under section 186 or 187 of or Schedule 9 or 10 to the Taxes Act counts as employment income (or was chargeable to income tax for 2002–03 or an earlier year of assessment) under section 186(3) or (4) of that Act;

(b) any charge to income tax by virtue of section 186(3) of that Act shall be disregarded in determining whether a distribution is a capital distribution within the meaning of section 122(5)(b);

(c) nothing in any provision of section 186 or 187 of or Schedule 9 or 10 to that Act with respect to–

  (i) the order in which any of a participant's shares are to be treated as disposed of for the purposes of those provisions as they have effect in relation to profit sharing schemes, or

  (ii) the shares in relation to which an event is to be treated as occurring for any such purpose,

shall affect the rules applicable to the computation of a gain accruing on a part disposal of a holding of shares or other securities which were acquired at different times; and

(d) a gain accruing on an appropriation of shares to which section 186(11) of that Act applies shall not be a chargeable gain.

238(3) In this section **"participant"** and **"the trust instrument"** have the meanings given by section 187 of the Taxes Act.

238(4) [Repealed by FA 1996, s. 112(2) and 205 and Sch. 41, Pt. V(5).]

History – In s. 238(2)(a), the words "counts as employment income (or was chargeable to income tax for 2002–03 or an earlier year of assessment)" substituted for the words "is chargeable to income tax" by ITEPA 2003, Sch. 6, para. 215 with effect for 2003–04 and subsequent tax years.

S. 238(4) superseded by s. 237A and repealed by FA 1996, s. 112(2) and 205 and Sch. 41, Pt. V(5), with effect in relation to transactions effected after 27 November 1995.

Derivations – CGTA 1979, s. 144A, as inserted by ICTA 1988, s. 844 and Sch. 29, para. 25.

Cross references – S. 122(5)(b): "capital distribution" by reference to a distribution in money or money's worth except one constituting income for income tax purposes.

ICTA 1988, s. 185–187: charges and reliefs in respect of approved share option and profit sharing schemes the terms of which are set out in a formal "trust instrument", including the charge under Sch. E in respect of any capital receipt in money or money's worth (s. 186(3)) and relief from additional rate tax in respect of dividends relating to shares appropriated to persons who thereby become "participants" within 18 months of acquisition (s. 186(11)); rights in respect of a savings-related scheme obtained as director or employee after 14 November 1980 (s. 185(1)).

ICTA 1988, Sch. 9, 10: approval by the Board of share option and profit sharing schemes and obligations of trustees and participants, including requirement for profit sharing schemes that every participant is bound to keep his beneficial interest in the shares which the trustees hold for the period of retention and that the trustees can, before the release date, only dispose of shares on a best-price sale or transfer them to the participant on payment of an amount equivalent to basic rate tax on the locked-in value (Sch. 9, para. 2(2)); switching of rights on a takeover (Sch. 9, para. 15).

Notes – S. 21–34: general meaning of "disposal".

S. 60(1): treatment of trust property and of the acts of the trustees where person absolutely entitled as against the trustees.

S. 288: interpretation, including the "Taxes Act" as ICTA 1988 and reference to other sections being those of this Act.

238A Share schemes and share incentives

238A(1) Schedule 7D (share schemes and share incentives) shall have effect.

238A(2) Schedule 7D relates–

(a) in Part 1, to Schedule 2 share incentive plans (SIPs) (see section 488 of ITEPA 2003),

(b) in Part 2, to Schedule 3 SAYE option schemes (see section 516 of that Act),

(c) in Part 3, to Schedule 4 CSOP schemes (CSOPs) (see section 521 of that Act),

(d) [omitted by FA 2016, s. 16 and Sch. 3, para. 9(1).]

History – In the heading to s. 238A, the word "Approved" omitted from the beginning by FA 2014, s. 51 and Sch. 8, para. 35(2), which is treated as having come into force on 6 April 2014, subject to the transitional provisions in FA 2014, Sch. 8, para. 90 to 96.

In s. 238A(1), the word "approved" (which appeared before the words "share schemes") omitted by FA 2014, s. 51 and Sch. 8, para. 35(3), which is treated as having come into force on 6 April 2014, subject to the transitional provisions in FA 2014, Sch. 8, para. 90 to 96.

In s. 238A(2)(a), the words "Schedule 2" substituted for the word "approved" by FA 2014, s. 51 and Sch. 8, para. 35(4), which is treated as having come into force on 6 April 2014, subject to the transitional provisions in FA 2014, Sch. 8, para. 90 to 96.

In s. 238A(2)(b), the words "Schedule 3" substituted for the word "approved" by FA 2014, s. 51 and Sch. 8, para. 124, which is treated as having come into force on 6 April 2014, subject to the transitional provisions in FA 2014, Sch. 8, para. 147 to 157.

In s. 238A(2)(c), the words "Schedule 4" substituted for the word "approved" by FA 2014, s. 51 and Sch. 8, para. 184, which is treated as having come into force on 6 April 2014, subject to the transitional provisions in FA 2014, Sch. 8, para. 205 to 215.

S. 238A(2)(d) (and the word "and" preceding it) omitted by FA 2016, s. 16 and Sch. 3, para. 9(1), with effect from 15 September 2016 (Royal Assent). Former s. 238A(2)(d) read as follows:

"(d) in Part 4, to enterprise management incentives (see section 527 of that Act).".

S. 238A inserted by ITEPA 2003, Sch. 6, para. 216 with effect for 2003–04 and subsequent tax years.

239 Disposals to trustees of employee trusts

History – Heading to s. 239 substituted by SI 2009/730, art. 11(2), with effect in relation to disposals on or after 6 April 2009. Former heading read "Employee trusts".

239(1) Where–

(a) a close company disposes of an asset to trustees in circumstances such that the disposal is a disposition which by virtue of section 13 of Inheritance Tax Act 1984 (employee trusts) is not a transfer of value for the purposes of inheritance tax, or

(b) an individual disposes of an asset to trustees in circumstances such that the disposal is an exempt transfer by virtue of section 28 of that Act (employee trusts: inheritance tax),

this Act shall have effect in relation to the disposal in accordance with subsections (2) and (3) below.

239(2) Section 17(1) shall not apply to the disposal; and if the disposal is by way of gift or is for a consideration not exceeding the sums allowable as a deduction under section 38–

(a) the disposal, and the acquisition by the trustees, shall be treated for the purposes of this Act as being made for such consideration as to secure that neither a gain nor a loss accrues on the disposal, and

(b) where the trustees dispose of the asset, its acquisition by the company or individual shall be treated as its acquisition by the trustees.

Paragraph (b) above also applies where section 149(1) of the 1979 Act applied on the disposal of an asset to trustees who have not disposed of it before the coming into force of this section.

239(3) Where the disposal is by a close company, section 125(1) shall apply to the disposal as if for the reference to market value there were substituted a reference to market value or the sums allowable as a deduction under section 38, whichever is the less.

239(4) Subject to subsection (5) below, this Act shall also have effect in accordance with subsection (2) above in relation to any disposal made by a company other than a close company if–

(a) the disposal is made to trustees otherwise than under a bargain made at arm's length, and

(b) the property disposed of is to be held by them on trusts of the description specified in section 86(1) of the Inheritance Tax Act 1984 (that is to say, those in relation to which the said section 13 of that Act has effect) and the persons for whose benefit the trusts permit the property to be applied include all or most of either–

(i) the persons employed by or holding office with the company, or

(ii) the persons employed by or holding office with the company or any one or more subsidiaries of the company.

239(5) Subsection (4) above does not apply if the trusts permit any of the property to be applied at any time (whether during any such period as is referred to in the said section 86(1) or later) for the benefit of–

(a) a person who is a participator in the company (**"the donor company"**), or

(b) any other person who is a participator in any other company that has made a disposal of property to be held on the same trusts as the property disposed of by the donor company, being a disposal in relation to which this Act has had effect in accordance with subsection (2) above, or

(c) any other person who has been a participator in the donor company or any such company as is mentioned in paragraph (b) above at any time after, or during the 10 years before, the disposal made by that company, or

(d) any person who is connected with a person within paragraph (a), (b) or (c) above.

239(6) The participators in a company who are referred to in subsection (5) above do not include any participator who–

(a) is not beneficially entitled to, or to rights entitling him to acquire, 5 per cent or more of, or of any class of the shares comprised in, its issued share capital, and

(b) on a winding-up of the company would not be entitled to 5 per cent or more of its assets;

and in determining whether the trusts permit property to be applied as mentioned in that subsection, no account shall be taken–

(i) of any power to make a payment which is the income of any person for any of the purposes of income tax, or would be the income for any of those purposes of a person not resident in the United Kingdom if he were so resident, or

(ii) if the trusts are those of a profit sharing scheme approved under Schedule 9 to the Taxes Act of any power to appropriate shares in pursuance of the scheme.

239(7) In subsection (4) above **"subsidiary"** has the meaning given by section 1159 of and Schedule 6 to the Companies Act 2006 and in subsections (5) and (6) above **"participator"** has the meaning given by section 454 of CTA 2010, except that it does not include a loan creditor.

239(8) In this section **"close company"** includes a company which, if resident in the United Kingdom, would be a close company as defined in section 288.

History – In s. 239(7), the words "by section 454 of CTA 2010" substituted for "in section 417(1) of the Taxes Act" by CTA 2010, s. 1177 and Sch. 1, para. 253, with effect for corporation tax purposes for accounting periods ending on or after 1 April 2010, and for income tax and capital gains tax purposes for the tax year 2010–11 and subsequent tax years.
In s. 239(7), the words "1159 of and Schedule 6 to" substituted for the words "736 of", and "2006" substituted for "1985" by SI 2009/1890, art. 4(1)(i), with effect from 1 October 2009.

Derivations – CGTA 1979, s. 149, as amended by FA 1981, s. 90(3), and Companies Consolidation (Consequential Provisions) Act 1985, Sch. 2.

Cross references – S. 17(1): acquisitions and disposals at market value where bargains otherwise than at arm's length or where consideration cannot be valued or in connection with payment for services.
S. 38: deduction for acquisition expenditure, including incidental costs, enhancement or title expenditure and incidental costs of disposal.
S. 125(1): apportionment of notional market value gain to shareholders so as to reduce their allowable expenditure in respect of the appropriate shares.
ICTA 1988, s. 417(1): participator as a person having a share or interest in the capital or income of the company etc.
ICTA 1988, Sch. 9: approval by the Board of share option and profit sharing schemes.
IHTA 1984, s. 13: certain dispositions by close companies to employee trusts for the benefit of employees etc are not transfers of value.
IHTA 1984, s. 28: transfers of value by individuals beneficially entitled to shares are exempt transfers to the extent that the value transferred is attributable to securities which become comprised in an employee trust.
IHTA 1984, s. 86(1): trusts where settled property to be applied indefinitely or for a determinable period only for the benefit of persons of a class defined by reference to employment or to marriage to, relationship to or dependence on such persons.

Notes – S. 9: meaning of "resident".
S. 21–34: general meaning of "disposal".
S. 286: "connected" in references to persons being connected with one another.
S. 288: interpretation, including meaning of "close company" by reference to ICTA 1988, s. 414, 415 and reference to sections as being those of this Act.

239ZA Relief for disposals by trustees of employee trusts

239ZA(1) Any gain accruing to trustees on the disposal of an asset comprised in the settled property of an employee trust shall not be a chargeable gain where the disposal is–

(a) a disposal to a beneficiary, or

(b) a deemed disposal under section 71(1),

if the conditions in subsection (2) are satisfied.

239ZA(2) The conditions are that–

(a) an amount that is equal to or exceeds the market value of the asset is chargeable to income tax as employment income within the meaning of section 7 of ITEPA 2003 (meaning of "employment income" etc);

(b) neither the beneficiary nor (if different) the person who is liable for the income tax is an excluded person;

(c) no actual consideration (as opposed to consideration deemed to be given by any enactment relating to the taxation of chargeable gains) is given directly or indirectly to the trustees for the asset; and

(d) Schedule 7D does not to any extent prevent the gain being a chargeable gain.

239ZA(3) The following are excluded persons–

(a) a participator in a company, shares in or securities of which are comprised in the settled property;

(b) a participator in a close company that has provided any property that has become comprised in the settled property;

(c) a person who was a participator in a company within paragraph (a) or (b) at any time during the 10 years before the shares, securities or other property concerned became comprised in the settled property;

(d) a person connected with a person within any of paragraphs (a) to (c).

239ZA(4) For the purposes of subsection (3)–

(a) **"participator"** has the same meaning as in section 239 and shall, in the case of a company which is not a close company, be construed as a person who would be a participator in the company if it were a close company, but

(b) a person is not a participator unless either–

(i) that person is entitled to, or entitled to rights enabling the acquisition of, 5% or more of the share capital of the company or any class of shares in the company, or

(ii) that person would be entitled to 5% or more of the company's assets on winding-up.

239ZA(5) In determining whether a person is connected with another for the purposes of this section, section 286 shall apply as if subsection (8) of that section also mentioned uncle, aunt, nephew and niece.

239ZA(6) In this section–

"beneficiary" means a person within paragraph (a) or (b) of section 86(1) of the Inheritance Tax Act 1984 (trusts for benefit of employees);

"close company" includes a company which, if resident in the United Kingdom, would be a close company as defined in section 288;

"employee trust" means a settlement of property to which section 86 of the Inheritance Tax Act 1984 applies or would apply but for subsection (3) of that section;

"market value" means the market value for the purposes of capital gains tax (as to which see section 272).

History – S. 239ZA inserted by SI 2009/730, art. 11(3), with effect in relation to disposals on or after 6 April 2009.

REGISTERED PENSION SCHEMES

239A De-registration of registered pension schemes

239A(1) This section applies where tax is charged in accordance with section 242 of the Finance Act 2004 (de-registration charge) where the registration of a registered pension scheme is withdrawn.

239A(2) For the purposes of this Act the assets which at the relevant time are held for the purposes of the pension scheme–

(a) are treated as having been acquired at the relevant time for a consideration equal to the amount on which tax is charged by virtue of section 242 of the Finance Act 2004 by the person who would be chargeable in respect of a chargeable gain accruing on a disposal of the assets at the relevant time, and

(b) are not to be treated as having been disposed of by any person at the relevant time.

239A(3) In subsection (2) **"the relevant time"** means the time immediately before the date of withdrawal of registration of the pension scheme.

History – S. 239A substituted for former s. 239A and s. 239B by FA 2004, s. 281 and Sch. 35, para. 40 which, by virtue of FA 2004, s. 284(1), come into force on 6 April 2006.

Former s. 239A inserted by FA 1995, s. 61(2) in relation to any approval of a retirement benefits scheme ceasing to have effect on or after 2 November 1994 other than an approval ceasing to have effect by virtue of a notice given before that day under ICTA 1988, s. 591B(1).

Cross references – ICTA 1988, s. 591C: tax charged under Sch. D, Case VI at 40 per cent on value of scheme's assets immediately before the scheme ceased to be approved.

PERSONAL PENSION SCHEMES

239B Withdrawal of approval of approved arrangements

239B [Effectively omitted by FA 2004, s. 281 and Sch. 35, para. 40.]

History – S. 239B effectively omitted by FA 2004, s. 281 and Sch. 35, para. 40 which, by virtue of FA 2004, s. 284(1), come into force on 6 April 2006.

LEASES

240 Leases of land and other assets

240 Schedule 8 shall have effect as respects leases of land and, to the extent specified in paragraph 9 of that Schedule, as respects leases of property other than land.

Derivations – CGTA 1979, s. 106, 129.

Notes – S. 288: interpretation, including "land" as embracing messuages, tenements, and hereditaments, houses and buildings of any tenure.

241 UK furnished holiday lettings

241(1) The following provisions of this section shall have effect with respect to the treatment for the purposes of tax on chargeable gains of the commercial letting of furnished holiday accommodation in the United Kingdom.

241(2) For the purposes of this section as it applies to capital gains tax the **"commercial letting of furnished holiday accommodation"** has the same meaning as it has for the purposes of Chapter 6 of Part 3 of ITTOIA 2005.

For the purposes of this section as it applies to corporation tax in respect of chargeable gains the **"commercial letting of furnished holiday accommodation"** has the same meaning as it has for the purposes of Chapter 6 of Part 4 of CTA 2009.

241(3) Subject to subsections (4) to (8) below, for the purposes of the provisions mentioned in subsection (3A) below–

(a) any UK property business which consists of, or so far as it consists of, the commercial letting of furnished holiday accommodation shall be treated as a trade, and

(b) all such lettings made by a particular person or partnership or body of persons shall be treated as one trade.

241(3A) The provisions referred to in subsection (3) above are–

sections 152 to 157 (roll-over relief on replacement of business asset),

section 165 (gifts relief),

section 169S(1) (entrepreneur's relief),

section 253 (relief for loans to traders),

Schedule 7AC (exemptions for disposals by companies with substantial shareholding).

241(4) Subject to subsection (5) below, for the purposes of the provisions mentioned in subsection (3A) above as they apply by virtue of this section, where in any chargeable period a person makes a commercial letting of furnished holiday accommodation in the United Kingdom–

(a) the accommodation shall be taken to be used in that period only for the purposes of the trade of making such lettings; and

(b) that trade shall be taken to be carried on throughout that period.

241(5) Subsection (4) above does not apply to any part of a chargeable period during which the accommodation is neither let commercially nor available to be so let unless it is prevented from being so let or available by any works of construction or repair.

241(6) Where–

(a) a gain to which section 222 applies accrues to any individual on the disposal of an asset; and

(b) by virtue of subsection (3) above the amount or value of the consideration for the acquisition of the asset is treated as reduced under section 152 or 153,

the gain to which section 222 applies shall be reduced by the amount of the reduction mentioned in paragraph (b) above.

241(7) Where there is a letting of accommodation only part of which is holiday accommodation such apportionments shall be made for the purposes of this section as are just and reasonable.

241(8) Where a person has been charged to tax in respect of chargeable gains otherwise than in accordance with the provisions of this section, such assessment, reduction or discharge of an assessment or, where a claim for repayment is made, such repayment, shall be made as may be necessary to give effect to those provisions.

History – In the heading to s. 241, the words "UK furnished" substituted for the word "Furnished" by FA 2011, s. 52 and Sch. 14, para. 14(2)(a), with effect in relation to disposals made in accounting periods beginning on or after 1 April 2011 (corporation tax) or made on or after 6 April 2011 (capital gains tax).

In s. 241(2) the words "has the same meaning as it has for the purposes of Chapter 6 of Part 4 of CTA 2009" substituted for the words "has the meaning given by section 504 of the Taxes Act" by CTA 2009, s. 1322 and Sch. 1, para. 380(2), with effect for corporation tax purposes for accounting periods ending on or after 1 April 2009, and for income tax and capital gains tax purposes for the tax year 2009–10 and subsequent tax years.

S. 241(2) substituted by ITTOIA 2005, s. 882 and Sch. 1, para. 441(2) which, in accordance with ITTOIA 2005, s. 883, have effect, for income tax purposes, for tax year 2005–06 and subsequent tax years, and, for corporation tax purposes, for accounting periods ending after 5 April 2005.
In s. 241(3) the words "(within the meaning of the Income Tax Acts), or any Schedule A business (within the meaning of the Taxes Act)," omitted by CTA 2009, s. 1322 and Sch. 1, para. 380(2) and repealed by CTA 2009, s. 1326 and Sch. 3, Pt. 1, with effect for corporation tax purposes for accounting periods ending on or after 1 April 2009, and for income tax and capital gains tax purposes for the tax year 2009–10 and subsequent tax years.
In s. 241(3), opening words substituted by FA 2002, s. 44(2) and Sch. 8, para. 3(2), effectively adding TCGA 1992, Sch. 7AC to the list of provisions that is now set out in s. 241(3A), with effect in relation to disposals on or after 1 April 2002. This substitution makes redundant the repeal of the words "and Schedule 6", which were within s. 241(3), as made by FA 1998, s. 165 and Sch. 27, Pt. III(31) with effect for disposals in the year 2003–04 and subsequent years of assessment.
In s. 241(3)(a), the words "the Income Tax Acts), or any Schedule A business (within the meaning of the Taxes Act)" substituted for "the Taxes Act), or any Schedule A business (within the meaning of that Act)" by ITA 2007, s. 1027 and Sch. 1, para. 325, with effect from 6 April 2007.
In s. 241(3)(a), the words "UK property business (within the meaning of the Taxes Act), or any Schedule A business (within the meaning of that Act), which consists of, or so far as it consists of, the commercial letting of furnished holiday accommodation" substituted for "Schedule A business (within the meaning of the Taxes Act) which consists in the commercial letting of furnished holiday accommodation in the United Kingdom" by virtue of ITTOIA 2005, s. 882 and Sch. 1, para. 441(3) which, in accordance with ITTOIA 2005, s. 883, have effect, for income tax purposes,for tax year 2005–06 and subsequent tax years, and, for corporation tax purposes, for accounting periods ending after 5 April 2005.
S. 241(3)(a) substituted by FA 1995, s. 39 and Sch. 6, para. 36 as respects capital gains tax purposes only, for 1995–96 and subsequent years of assessment, and by FA 1998, s. 38 and Sch. 5, para. 61 for the purposes of capital gains chargeable to corporation tax with effect from 1 April 1998 (subject to transitional provisions in FA 1998, Sch. 5, Pt. IV).
In s. 241(3A), the words "Schedule 6 (retirement relief etc)" omitted from the list of sections and Schedules by FA 2011, s. 52 and Sch. 14, para. 14(2)(b), with effect in relation to disposals made in accounting periods beginning on or after 1 April 2011 (corporation tax) or made on or after 6 April 2011 (capital gains tax).
In s. 241(3A), reference to s. 169S(1) inserted by FA 2008, s. 9 and Sch. 3, para. 3, with effect in relation to disposals, reorganisations (within the meaning of s. 169Q) and relevant transactions (within the meaning of s. 116) taking place on or after 6 April 2008 (FA 2008, Sch. 3, para. 5).
In s. 241(3A), the words "Schedule A1 (taper rellief)," omitted by FA 2008, s. 8 and Sch. 2, para. 37 with effect in relation to chargeable gains accruing or treated as accruing in the tax year 2008–09 or any subsequent tax year (FA 2008, Sch. 2, para. 56(3)).
S. 241(3A) inserted by FA 2002, s. 44(2) and Sch. 8, para. 3(3), and reference to it in s. 241(4) substituted by FA 2002, s. 44(2) and Sch. 8, para. 3(4), with effect in relation to disposals on or after 1 April 2002.
In s. 241(4), the words "in the United Kingdom" inserted by FA 2011, s. 52 and Sch. 14, para. 14(2)(c), with effect in relation to disposals made in accounting periods beginning on or after 1 April 2011 (corporation tax) or made on or after 6 April 2011 (capital gains tax).
In s. 241(7) the word "are" substituted by FA 1996, s. 134 and Sch. 20, para. 62 for capital gains tax purposes for 1996–97 and later tax years , and for corporation tax purposes for accounting periods ending on or after 1 July 1999, the appointed day for self-assessment to corporation tax (FA 1994, s. 199 and SI 1998/3173 (C. 78)).

Derivations – S. 241(1): FA 1984, s. 50(1).
S. 241(2): FA 1984, s. 50(2)–(9).
S. 241(3): FA 1984, Sch. 11, para. 1, as amended by FA 1985, s. 70(10).
S. 241(4)–(8): FA 1984, Sch. 11, para. 4–7.

Cross references – S. 152–157: roll-over relief on replacement of business assets.
S. 165: deferral of tax on gifts of business assets.
S. 222: relief for disposal of dwelling-house by reference to use as an only or main residence.
S. 253: relief for loans to traders.
Sch. A1: taper relief.
Sch. 7AC: exemptions for disposals by companies with substantial shareholding.
ICTA 1988, s. 504: interpretation for purposes of the treatment of the commercial letting of furnished holiday letting as a trade for certain purposes in respect of taxes on income (s. 503), including the meaning of "commercial letting", "furnished accommodation" and "holiday accommodation".

Notes – In s. 241(3A), although the reference to "Schedule 6 (retirement relief etc.)" has not been repealed, this reference is redundant effectively because Schedule 6 was repealed by FA 1998, s. 140(2)(c), s. 165 and Sch. 27, Pt. III(31) with effect in relation to disposals in the year 2003–04 and subsequent years of assessment. The repeal of the words "and Schedule 6", which was made by FA 1998, s. 140(2)(c), s. 165 and Sch. 27, Pt. III(31) with effect for disposals in the year 2003–04 and subsequent years of assessment, relates to s. 241(3).

241A EEA furnished holiday lettings

241A(1) The following provisions of this section shall have effect with respect to the treatment for the purposes of tax on chargeable gains of the commercial letting of furnished holiday accommodation in EEA states other than the United Kingdom.

241A(2) For the purposes of this section as it applies to capital gains tax, the "commercial letting of furnished holiday accommodation" has the same meaning as it has for the purposes of Chapter 6 of Part 3 of ITTOIA 2005.

241A(3) For the purposes of this section as it applies to corporation tax in respect of chargeable gains, the **"commercial letting of furnished holiday accommodation"** has the same meaning as it has for the purposes of Chapter 6 of Part 4 of CTA 2009.

241A(4) Subject to subsections (6) to (10) below, for the purposes of the provisions mentioned in subsection (5) below–

(a) any overseas property business which consists of, or so far as it consists of, the commercial letting of furnished holiday accommodation in one or more EEA states shall be treated as a trade, and

(b) all such lettings made by a particular person or partnership or body of persons shall be treated as one trade.

241A(5) The provisions referred to in subsection (4) above are–

sections 152 to 157 (roll-over relief on replacement of business assets),
section 165 (gifts relief),
section 169S(1) (entrepreneurs' relief),
section 253 (relief for loans to traders), and
Schedule 7AC (exemptions for disposals by companies with substantial shareholdings).

241A(6) Subject to subsection (7) below, for the purposes of the provisions mentioned in subsection (5) above as they apply by virtue of this section, where in any chargeable period a person makes a commercial letting of furnished holiday accommodation in an EEA state other than the United Kingdom–

(a) the accommodation shall be taken to be used in that period only for the purposes of the trade of making such lettings, and

(b) that trade shall be taken to be carried on throughout that period.

241A(7) Subsection (6) does not apply to any part of a chargeable period during which the accommodation is neither let commercially nor available to be so let unless it is prevented from being so let or available by any works of construction or repair.

241A(8) Where–

(a) a gain to which section 222 applies accrues to any individual on the disposal of an asset, and

(b) by virtue of subsection (4) above the amount or value of the consideration for the acquisition of the asset is treated as reduced under section 152 or 153,

the gain to which section 222 applies shall be reduced by the amount of the reduction mentioned in paragraph (b) above.

241A(9) Where there is a letting of accommodation only part of which is holiday accommodation such apportionments shall be made for the purposes of this section as are just and reasonable.

241A(10) Where a person has been charged to tax in respect of chargeable gains otherwise than in accordance with the provisions of this section, such assessment, reduction or discharge of an assessment, or, where a claim for repayment is made, such repayment, shall be made as may be necessary to give effect to those provisions.

241A(11) In this section **"overseas property business"** means–

(a) an overseas property business within the meaning of the Income Tax Acts (see section 989 of ITA 2007), or

(b) a overseas property business within the meaning of the Corporation Tax Acts (see section 1119 of CTA 2010).

History – S. 241A inserted by FA 2011, s. 52 and Sch. 14, para. 14 (3), with effect in relation to disposals made in accounting periods beginning on or after 1 April 2011 (corporation tax) or made on or after 6 April 2011 (capital gains tax) but, insofar as s. 241A applies for the purposes of TCGA 1992, s. 253 (relief for loans to traders), with effect in relation to claims made on or after 1 April 2011 (corporation tax) or on or after 6 April 2011 (capital gains tax). See FA 2011, Sch. 14, para. 17 for circumstances in which s. 241A is to be treated as having had effect before those dates.

PART DISPOSALS

242 Small part disposals

242(1) This section applies to a transfer of land forming part only of a holding of land, where–

(a) the amount or value of the consideration for the transfer does not exceed one-fifth of the market value of the holding as it subsisted immediately before the transfer, and

(b) the transfer is not one which, by virtue of section 58 or 171(1), is treated as giving rise to neither a gain nor a loss.

242(2) Subject to subsection (3) below, if the transferor so claims, the transfer shall not be treated for the purposes of this Act as a disposal, but all sums which, if it had been so treated, would have been brought into account as consideration for that disposal in the computation of the gain shall be deducted from any expenditure allowable under Chapter III of Part II as a deduction in computing a gain on any subsequent disposal of the holding.

242(2A) A claim under subsection (2) above shall be made–

(a) for the purposes of capital gains tax, on or before the first anniversary of the 31st January next following the year of assessment in which the transfer is made;

(b) for the purposes of corporation tax, within 2 years after the end of the accounting period in which the transfer is made.

242(3) This section shall not apply–

(a) if the amount or value of the consideration for the transfer exceeds £20,000, or

(b) where in the year of assessment in which the transfer is made, the transferor made any other disposal of land, if the total amount or value of the consideration for all disposals of land made by the transferor in that year exceeds £20,000.

242(4) No account shall be taken under subsection (3) above of any transfer of land to which section 243 applies.

242(5) In relation to a transfer which is not for full consideration in money or money's worth **"the amount or value of the consideration"** in this section shall mean the market value of the land transferred.

242(6) For the purposes of this section the holding of land shall comprise only the land in respect of which the expenditure allowable under paragraphs (a) and (b) of section 38(1) would be apportioned under section 42 if the transfer had been treated as a disposal (that is, as a part disposal of the holding).

242(7) In this section references to a **holding of land** include references to any estate or interest in a holding of land, not being an estate or interest which is a wasting asset, and references to part of a holding shall be construed accordingly.

History – S. 242(2A) inserted by FA 1996, s. 135 and Sch. 21, para. 37 as respects capital gains tax for 1996–97 and later years of assessment and for corporation tax accounting periods ending on or after 1 July 1999, the appointed day for self-assessment to corporation tax (FA 1994, s. 199 and SI 1998/3173 (C. 78)).

Derivations – CGTA 1979, s. 107, as amended by FA 1986, s. 60 and FA 1984, s. 63.

Cross references – S. 35–52 (Pt. II, Ch. III): general provisions as to the computation of gains, including the apportionment on a part disposal (s. 42) of allowable acquisition expenditure, including incidental costs, and of enhancement or title expenditure (s. 38(1)(a), (b)).
S. 58: deemed no gain, no loss on transfers between spouses.
S. 171(1): deemed no gain, no loss on transfers of capital assets within a group.

Statements of practice – D1: alternative method of calculating cost basis on a part disposal of land.

Notes – S. 272–274 and Sch. 11: meaning of "market value".
S. 288: interpretation, including meaning of "wasting asset", "land" as embracing messuages, tenements, and hereditaments, houses and buildings of any tenure, "year of assessment" as being 6 April to the following 5 April and reference to sections being those of this Act.
TMA 1970, s. 42–43B: procedures and time limits for making claims.

243 Part disposal to authority with compulsory powers

243(1) This section applies to a transfer of land forming part only of a holding of land to an authority exercising or having compulsory powers where–

(a) the amount or value of the consideration for the transfer, or if the transfer is not for full consideration in money or money's worth, the market value of the land transferred, is small, as compared with the market value of the holding as it subsisted immediately before the transfer, and

(b) the transferor had not taken any steps by advertising or otherwise to dispose of any part of the holding or to make his willingness to dispose of it known to the authority or others.

243(2) If the transferor so claims, the transfer shall not be treated for the purposes of this Act as a disposal, but all sums which if it had been so treated, would have been brought into account as consideration for that disposal in the computation of the gain shall be deducted from any expenditure allowable under Chapter III of Part II as a deduction in computing a gain on any subsequent disposal of the holding.

243(2A) A claim under subsection (2) above shall be made–

(a) for the purposes of capital gains tax, on or before the first anniversary of the 31st January next following the year of assessment in which the transfer is made;

(b) for the purposes of corporation tax, within 2 years after the end of the accounting period in which the transfer is made.

243(3) For the purposes of this section the holding of land shall comprise only the land in respect of which the expenditure allowable under paragraphs (a) and (b) of section 38(1) would be apportioned under section 42 if the transfer had been treated as a disposal (that is, as a part disposal of the holding).

243(4) In this section references to a **holding of land** include references to an estate or interest in a holding of land, not being an estate or interest which is a wasting asset, and references to part of a holding shall be construed accordingly.

243(5) In this section **"authority exercising or having compulsory powers"** means, in relation to the land transferred, a person or body of persons acquiring it compulsorily or who has or have been, or could be, authorised to acquire it compulsorily for the purposes for which it is acquired, or for whom another person or body of persons has or have been, or could be, authorised so to acquire it.

History – S. 243(2A) inserted by FA 1996, s. 135 and Sch. 21, para. 38 as respects capital gains tax for 1996–97 and later years of assessment and for corporation tax accounting periods ending on or after 1 July 1999, the appointed day for self-assessment to corporation tax (FA 1994, s. 199 and SI 1998/3173 (C. 78)).

Derivations – CGTA 1979, s. 108.

Cross references – S. 35–52 (Pt. II, Ch. III): general provisions as to the computation of gains, including the apportionment on a part disposal (s. 42) of allowable acquisition expenditure, including incidental costs, and of enhancement or title expenditure (s. 38(1)(a), (b)).
SI 1992/58, Sch. 2, para. 9: modification of s. 243(4) in relation to reorganisation of port authorities.

Statements of practice – 13/93: relief under s. 247 where landlord disposes of land to an "authority exercising or having compulsory powers" and acquires replacement land.

HMRC interpretations – IR Int. 157: Revenue now take view that "small" can mean 5 per cent or less of value of asset etc., or receipt of £3,000 or less whether or not falling within the 5 per cent test; exceptionally taxpayers may suggest different limits in the context of their particular circumstances (*O'Rourke v Binks* [1992] BTC 460).

Notes – S. 272–274 and Sch. 11: meaning of "market value".
S. 288: interpretation, including meaning of "wasting asset", "land" as embracing messuages, tenements, and hereditaments, houses and buildings of any tenure and reference to sections as being those of this Act.
TMA 1970, s. 42–43B: procedures and time limits for making claims.

244 Part disposal: consideration exceeding allowable expenditure

244(1) The provisions of sections 242(2) and 243(2) shall have effect subject to this section.

244(2) Where the allowable expenditure is less than the consideration for the part disposal (or is nil)–

(a) the said provisions shall not apply, and

(b) if the recipient so elects (and there is any allowable expenditure)–

(i) the consideration for the part disposal shall be reduced by the amount of the allowable expenditure, and,

(ii) none of that expenditure shall be allowable as a deduction in computing a gain accruing on the occasion of the part disposal or on any subsequent occasion.

In this subsection **"allowable expenditure"** means expenditure which, immediately before the part disposal, was attributable to the holding of land under paragraphs (a) and (b) of section 38(1).

244(3) An election under subsection (2)(b) above shall be made–

(a) for the purposes of capital gains tax, on or before the first anniversary of the 31st January next following the year of assessment in which the part disposal is made;

(b) for the purposes of corporation tax, within 2 years after the end of the accounting period in which the part disposal is made.

History – S. 244(3) inserted by FA 1996, s. 135 and Sch. 21, para. 39 as respects capital gains tax for 1996–97 and later years of assessment and for corporation tax accounting periods ending on or after 1 July 1999, the appointed day for self-assessment to corporation tax (FA 1994, s. 199 and SI 1998/3173 (C. 78)).

Derivations – CGTA 1979, s. 109.

Cross references – S. 38(1)(a), (b): allowable acquisition expenditure, including incidental costs, and of enhancement or title expenditure.
Sch. 3, para. 4(2): corresponding reduction in reacquisition expenditure to effect re-basing where original expenditure would be disallowed under s. 244 in respect of a disposal between 31 March 1982 and 6 April 1988.

Notes – S. 21: part disposals as disposals.
S. 42: apportionment of allowable expenditure on a part disposal.
S. 288: interpretation, including reference to sections as being those of this Act.

COMPULSORY ACQUISITION

245 Compensation paid on compulsory acquisition

245(1) Where land or an interest in or right over land is acquired and the acquisition is, or could have been, made under compulsory powers, then in considering whether, under section 52(4), the purchase price or compensation or other consideration for the acquisition should be apportioned and treated in part as a capital sum within section 22(1)(a), whether as compensation for loss of goodwill or for disturbance or otherwise, or should be apportioned in any other way, the fact that the acquisition is or could have been made compulsorily, and any statutory provision treating the purchase price or compensation or other consideration as exclusively paid in respect of the land itself, shall be disregarded.

245(2) In any case where land or an interest in land is acquired as mentioned in subsection (1) above from any person and the compensation or purchase price includes an amount in respect of severance of the land comprised in the acquisition or sale from other land in which that person is entitled in the same capacity to an interest, or in respect of that other land as being injuriously affected, there shall be deemed for the purposes of this Act to be a part disposal of that other land.

Derivations – CGTA 1979, s. 110.

Cross references – S. 22(1)(a): disposal where capital sum received by way of compensation for damage to or loss of assets etc.
S. 52(4): necessary apportionments by such method as appears to the inspector or on appeal the commissioners concerned to be just and reasonable.

Extra-statutory concessions – D33: damages or compensation treated as derived from underlying asset and taxed accordingly.

Statements of practice – 8/79: compensation for temporary loss of profits taxable as income.

Other material – Ryde's scale (not reproduced): reimbursement of surveyor's fees to a claimant, by an acquiring or compensating authority, in respect of a claim for compensation following the exercise of powers of compulsory purchase. Obtainable from Valuation Office Agency.

Notes – S. 21: part disposals as disposals.
S. 42: apportionment of allowable expenditure on a part disposal.

S. 288: interpretation, including "land" as embracing messuages, tenements, and hereditaments, houses and buildings of any tenure and reference to sections as being those of this Act.

246 Time of disposal and acquisition

246 Where an interest in land is acquired, otherwise than under a contract, by an authority possessing compulsory purchase powers, the time at which the disposal and acquisition is made is the time at which the compensation for the acquisition is agreed or otherwise determined (variations on appeal being disregarded for this purpose).

History – The concluding words "or, if earlier (but after 20th April 1971), the time when the authority enter on the land in pursuance of their powers)" repealed by FA 1996, s. 141(4) and 205 and Sch. 41, Pt. V(6), with effect as respects years after 1995–96 and, for corporation tax purposes, as respects accounting periods ending on or after 1 July 1999, the day appointed under FA 1994, s. 199 and SI 1998/3173 (C. 78).

Derivations – CGTA 1979, s. 111.

Statements of practice – D6: extension of time limit for roll-over relief under s. 152 where land compulsorily acquired and leased back to previous owner.

Notes – S. 28: time of disposal and acquisition where asset disposed of under contract.
S. 288: interpretation, including "land" as embracing messuages, tenements, and hereditaments, houses and buildings of any tenure.

247 Roll-over relief on compulsory acquisition

247(1) This section applies where–

(a) land (**"the old land"**) is disposed of by any person (**"the landowner"**) to an authority exercising or having compulsory powers; and

(b) the landowner did not take any steps, by advertising or otherwise, to dispose of the old land or to make his willingness to dispose of it known to the authority or others; and

(c) the consideration for the disposal is applied by the landowner in acquiring other land (**"the new land"**) not being land excluded from this paragraph by section 248.

247(2) Subject to section 248, in a case where the whole of the consideration for the disposal was applied as mentioned in subsection (1)(c) above, the landowner, on making a claim as respects the consideration so applied, shall be treated for the purposes of this Act–

(a) as if the consideration for the disposal of the old land were (if otherwise of a greater amount or value) of such amount as would secure that on the disposal neither a gain nor a loss accrues to him; and

(b) as if the amount or value of the consideration for the acquisition of the new land were reduced by the excess of the amount or value of the actual consideration for the disposal of the old land over the amount of the consideration which he is treated as receiving under paragraph (a) above.

247(3) If part only of the consideration for the disposal of the old land was applied as mentioned in subsection (1)(c) above, then, subject to section 248, if the part of the consideration which was not so applied (**"the unexpended consideration"**) is less than the amount of the gain (whether all chargeable gain or not) accruing on the disposal of the old land, the landowner, on making a claim as respects the consideration which was so applied, shall be treated for the purposes of this Act–

(a) as if the amount of the gain so accruing were reduced to the amount of the unexpended consideration (and, if not all chargeable gain, with a proportionate reduction in the amount of the chargeable gain); and

(b) as if the amount or value of the consideration for the acquisition of the new land were reduced by the amount by which the gain is reduced (or, as the case may be, the amount by which the chargeable gain is proportionately reduced) under paragraph (a) above.

247(4) Nothing in subsection (2) or subsection (3) above affects the treatment for the purposes of this Act of the authority by whom the old land was acquired or of the other party to the transaction involving the acquisition of the new land.

247(5) For the purposes of this section–

(a) subsection (2) of section 152 shall apply in relation to subsection (2)(a) and subsection (2)(b) above as it applies in relation to subsection (1)(a) and subsection (1)(b) of that section; and

(b) subsections (3) and (4) of that section shall apply as if any reference to the new assets were a reference to the new land, any reference to the old assets were a reference to the old land and any reference to that section were a reference to this.

247(5A) Subsections (2A) and (2C) of section 175 shall apply in relation to this section as they apply in relation to section 152 (but as if the reference in subsection (2C) to the new assets were a reference to the new land).

247(6) Where this section applies, any such amount as is referred to in subsection (2) of section 245 shall be treated as forming part of the consideration for the disposal of the old land and, accordingly, so much of that subsection as provides for a deemed disposal of other land shall not apply.

247(7) The provisions of this Act fixing the amount of the consideration deemed to be given for the acquisition or disposal of assets shall be applied before this section is applied.

247(8) In this section–

"land" includes any interest in or right over land; and

"authority exercising or having compulsory powers" shall be construed in accordance with section 243(5).

History – In s. 247(5)(b) reference to s. 152(4) added by FA 1996, s. 141(5) with effect as respects the year 1996–97 and subsequent years of assessment and, for corporation tax purposes, as respects accounting periods ending on or after 1 July 1999, the day appointed under FA 1994, s. 199 and SI 1998/3173 (C. 78)).
S. 247(5A) inserted by FA 1995, s. 48(2) for disposals or acquisitions on or after 29 November 1994, so far as it relates to TCGA 1992, s. 175(2A), and acquisitions on or after 29 November 1994, so far as it relates to TCGA 1992, s. 175(2C).

Derivations – CGTA 1979, s. 111A, as inserted by FA 1982, s. 83.

Cross references – S. 152(2), (3): for roll-over relief on replacement of business assets (s. 152(1)), where a gain is time apportioned etc. to provide the chargeable gain in respect of an asset held on 6 April 1965, the reduction in point is the amount of the chargeable gain and not the whole gain; the new assets must generally be acquired in the period beginning 12 months before and ending three years after the disposal of the old assets.
S. 175(2A): where disposal and acquisition are made by different companies in a group, s. 152 applies as though the companies were the same person, if each was in the group when it made its disposal or, as the case may be, its acquisition.
S. 175(2C): s. 152 not to apply if acquisition of new assets is made by a member of a group of companies in a no gain/no loss transaction.
Sch. 4, para. 2: reduction of one half in the amount to be deducted under s. 247 in computing gains arising from disposal of a replacement asset in relation to deferral before 6 April 1988 where original asset held on 31 March 1982 (or acquired in a chain of no gain, no loss disposals from that date).
SI 1992/58, Sch. 2, para. 10: disapplication of s. 247 in relation to reorganisation of port authorities.

Extra-statutory concessions – D26: joint beneficial owners becoming sole owners on exchange of joint interests.

Statements of practice – 13/93 (as amended – see IRInt. 196): relief under s. 247 is available to the landlord where a tenant acquires the freehold reversion under the Leasehold Reform Act 1967 or the Housing and Urban Development Act 1993, or acquires the freehold or an extension of the lease under the Housing Acts 1995 to 1996.

HMRC interpretations – IRInt. 196: extension of SP 13/93 to cover tenant's right to buy under Housing Acts 1985 to 1996 as preserved following transfer of housing stock into private sector.

Other material – ICAEW Technical Releases TR 467, 477 (not reproduced): for purposes of the condition in s. 247(1)(b), in practice any event more than three years prior to the disposal is ignored.
Taxline 2005/2 (not reproduced): "an authority" is defined to include "any person requiring it compulsorily" (SP 13/93).

Notes – S. 15: meaning of "chargeable gain".
S. 21–34: general meaning of "disposal".
S. 288: interpretation, including "land" as embracing messuages, tenements, and hereditaments, houses and buildings of any tenure.
TMA 1970, s. 42–43B: procedures and time limits for making claims.

247A Provisional application of section 247

247A(1) This section applies where a person who disposes of land (**"the old land"**) to an authority exercising or having compulsory powers declares, in his return for the chargeable period in which the disposal takes place–

(a) that the whole or any specified part of the consideration for the disposal will be applied in the acquisition of other land (**"the new land"**);

(b) that the acquisition will take place as mentioned in subsection (3) of section 152; and

(c) that the new land will not be land excluded from section 247(1)(c) by section 248.

247A(2) Until the declaration ceases to have effect, section 247 shall apply as if the acquisition had taken place and the person had made a claim under that section.

247A(3) For the purposes of this section, subsections (3) to (5) of section 153A shall apply as if the reference to section 152 or 153 were a reference to section 247 and the reference to the old assets were a reference to the old land.

247A(4) In this section **"land"** and **"authority exercising or having compulsory powers"** have the same meaning as in section 247.

History – S. 247A inserted by FA 1996, s. 141(6) with effect as respects years after 1995–96 and, for corporation tax purposes, as respects accounting periods ending on or after 1 July 1999, the day appointed under FA 1994, s. 199 by virtue of SI 1998/3173 (C. 78).

Other material – Tax Bulletin TB08/96-2: procedure for claiming and withdrawing claim for provisional roll-over relief.

248 Provisions supplementary to section 247

248(1) Land is excluded from paragraph (c) of subsection (1) of section 247 if–

(a) it is a dwelling-house or part of a dwelling-house (or an interest in or right over a dwelling-house), and

(b) by virtue of, or of any claim under, any provision of sections 222 to 226 the whole or any part of a gain accruing on a disposal of it by the landowner at a material time would not be a chargeable gain;

and for the purposes of this subsection **"a material time"** means any time during the period of 6 years beginning on the date of the acquisition referred to in the said paragraph (c).

248(2) If, at any time during the period of 6 years referred to in subsection (1) above, land which at the beginning of that period was not excluded from section 247(1)(c) by virtue of that subsection becomes so excluded, the amount of any chargeable gain accruing on the disposal of the old land shall be redetermined without regard to any relief previously given under section 247 by reference to the amount or value of the consideration for the acquisition of that land; and all such adjustments of capital gains tax, whether by way of assessment or otherwise, may be made at any time, notwithstanding anything in section 34 of the Management Act (time limit for assessments).

This subsection also applies where the period of 6 years referred to above began before the commencement of this section (and accordingly the references to section 247 include references to section 111A of the 1979 Act).

248(3) Where the new land is a depreciating asset, within the meaning of section 154, that section has effect as if–

(a) any reference in subsection (1) or subsection (4) to section 152 or 153 were a reference to subsection (2) or subsection (3) respectively of section 247; and

(b) paragraph (b) of subsection (2) were omitted; and

(c) the reference in subsection (5) to section 152(3) were a reference to that provision as applied by section 247(5).

248(4) No claim may be made under section 243 in relation to a transfer which constitutes a disposal in respect of which a claim is made under section 247.

248(5) Expressions used in this section have the same meaning as in section 247.

Derivations – CGTA 1979, s. 111B, as inserted by FA 1982, s. 83.

Cross references – S. 154: modification of roll-over relief on replacement of business asset (s. 152, 153) so as to hold-over gain until disposal, cessation of trade use (s. 154(2)(b)) or the expiration of ten years where replacement is a "depreciating asset" defined by reference to an asset which is or will become within ten years a wasting asset.

S. 222–226: relief on disposal of dwelling-house by reference to use as an only or main residence.

Sch. 4, para. 4: 50 per cent reduction in gain crystallising under s. 248(3) where attributable to the deferral before 6 April 1988 of land held at 31 March 1982 (or acquired in a chain of no gain, no loss disposals from that date).

TMA 1970, s. 34: ordinary time limit for making assessments of six years from the end of the chargeable period in point.

Extra-statutory concessions – D26: joint beneficial owners becoming sole owners on exchange of joint interests.

Notes – S. 288: interpretation, including "land" as embracing messuages, tenements, and hereditaments, houses and buildings of any tenure.

TMA 1970, s. 29: assessing procedure.

JOINT INTERESTS IN LAND

248A Roll-over relief on disposal of joint interests in land: conditions

248A(1) Section 248B applies where conditions A to E are met.

248A(2) Condition A is that a person ("the landowner") and one or more other persons jointly hold–

(a) a holding of land, or

(b) two or more separate holdings of land.

248A(3) Condition B is that the landowner disposes of an interest ("the relinquished interest") in–

(a) the holding, or

(b) one or more of the holdings,

to the co-owner or to one or more of the co-owners.

248A(4) Condition C is that the consideration for the disposal is or includes an interest ("the acquired interest") in a holding of land held jointly by the landowner and one or more of the co-owners.

248A(5) Condition D is that as a consequence of the disposal (taken together with any related disposals) the landowner and each of the co-owners become–

(a) in a case falling within subsection (2)(a), the sole owner of part of the holding, or

(b) in a case falling within subsection (2)(b), the sole owner of one or more of the holdings.

248A(6) Condition E is that the acquired interest is not an interest in excluded land (see section 248C).

248A(7) For the purposes of this section–

(a) references to a holding of land include references to an estate or interest in a holding of land, and are to be read in accordance with section 243(3);

(b) references to holding land jointly are to holding land–
  (i) in England and Wales, as joint tenants or tenants in common,
  (ii) in Scotland, as joint owners or owners in common, or
  (iii) in Northern Ireland, as joint tenants, tenants in common or coparceners;

(c) **"co-owner"** means any person who holds a holding of land jointly with the landowner;

(d) a related disposal (in relation to a disposal mentioned in condition B) is a disposal of an interest in the holding, or in one or more of the holdings, which is made–
  (i) by the landowner to a co-owner, or
  (ii) by a co-owner to the landowner or another co-owner,

  at the same time as the disposal mentioned in that condition;

(e) spouses who are living together, or civil partners who are living together, are together treated as a landowner or a co-owner.

History – S. 248A inserted by SI 2010/157, art. 8(1), with effect in relation to disposals made on or after 6 April 2010.

248B Calculation of relief

248B(1) If the amount or value of the consideration for the disposal of the relinquished interest is equal to or less than the amount or value of the consideration for the acquired interest, the landowner, on making a claim, is to be treated for the purposes of this Act–

(a) as if the consideration for the disposal of the relinquished interest were of such amount as would secure that on the disposal neither a gain nor a loss accrues to the landowner, and

(b) as if the amount or value of the consideration for the acquired interest were reduced by the excess of the amount or value of the consideration for the disposal of the relinquished interest over the amount of the consideration which the landowner is treated as receiving under paragraph (a).

248B(2) Where the amount or value of the consideration for the disposal of the relinquished interest exceeds the amount or value of the consideration for the acquired interest, then if the excess ("the unexpended consideration") is less than the amount of the gain (whether all chargeable gain or not) accruing on the disposal of the relinquished interest, the landowner on making a claim is to be treated for the purposes of this Act–

(a) as if the amount of the gain so accruing were reduced to the amount of the unexpended consideration (and, if not all chargeable gain, with a proportionate reduction in the amount of the chargeable gain), and

(b) as if the amount or value of the consideration for the acquired interest were reduced by the amount by which the gain is reduced (or, as the case may be, the amount by which the chargeable gain is proportionately reduced) under paragraph (a).

248B(3) Subsections (1) and (2) are subject to section 248C(3).

248B(4) Nothing in subsection (1) or (2) affects the treatment for the purposes of this Act of a co-owner (within the meaning given by section 248A(7)).

248B(5) Where subsection (1)(a) applies to exclude a gain which, in consequence of Schedule 2 (assets held on 6th April 1965) is not all chargeable gain, the amount of the reduction to be made under subsection (1)(b) shall be the amount of the chargeable gain, and not the whole amount of the gain.

History – S. 248B(1) and (2) substituted by SI 2013/234, art. 2(1), with effect in relation to disposals on or after 1 March 2013.
S. 248B inserted by SI 2010/157, art. 8(1), with effect in relation to disposals made on or after 6 April 2010.

248C Excluded land

248C(1) Land is excluded land to the extent that–

(a) it is a dwelling-house or part of a dwelling-house (or an interest in or right over a dwelling-house), and

(b) by virtue of, or of any claim under, any provision of sections 222 to 226 (private residences) the whole or any part of a gain accruing on a disposal of it by the landowner at a material time would not be a chargeable gain.

248C(2) In subsection (1)(b), "a material time" means any time during the period of 6 years beginning on the date of the acquisition of the acquired interest.

248C(3) If land was not excluded land at the date of the acquisition of the acquired interest but becomes excluded land within 6 years of the acquisition, the amount of any chargeable gain accruing on the disposal of the relinquished interest shall be re-determined without regard to any relief previously given under section 248B by reference to the amount or value of the consideration for the acquisition of the interest in that land.

248C(4) Any adjustments of capital gains tax in accordance with subsection (3), whether by way of assessment or otherwise, may be made at any time, despite anything in section 34 of the Management Act (time limit for assessments).

248C(5) Expressions used in this section have the same meaning as in section 248A.

History – S. 248C inserted by SI 2010/157, art. 8(1), with effect in relation to disposals made on or after 6 April 2010.

248D Milk quotas

248D(1) This section applies where–

(a) section 248B applies to a holding (or holdings) of land, and

(b) milk quota is associated with the holding in which the relinquished interest is held and with the holding in which the acquired interest is held.

248D(2) Section 248B(1), (2) and (4) apply–

(a) to the disposal of quota associated with the holding in which the relinquished interest is held as they apply to the disposal of that interest, and

(b) to the acquisition of quota associated with the holding in which the acquired interest is held as they apply to the acquisition of that interest.

History – S. 248D inserted by SI 2010/157, art. 8(1), with effect in relation to disposals made on or after 6 April 2010.

248E Relief on disposal of joint interests in private residence

248E(1) This section applies where conditions A to E are met.

248E(2) Condition A is that a person ("the landowner") and one or more other persons jointly hold an interest in two or more dwelling-houses.

248E(3) Condition B is that the landowner disposes of an interest ("the relinquished interest") in one or more of the dwelling-houses to the co-owner or to one or more of the co-owners.

248E(4) Condition C is that the consideration for the disposal is or includes an interest ("the acquired interest") in one of the other dwelling-houses.

248E(5) Condition D is that as a consequence of the disposal (taken together with any related disposals)–

(a) the dwelling-house in which the landowner acquires an interest becomes the only or main residence of the landowner, and

(b) each of the other dwelling-houses becomes the only or main residence of one (and only one) of the co-owners.

248E(6) Condition E is that if each dwelling-house were disposed of immediately after the disposal (or disposals) mentioned in subsection (5) then by virtue of sections 222 and 223 (private residences) no part of the gain accruing on each of those disposals would be a chargeable gain.

248E(7) The landowner, on making a claim jointly with the co-owner or co-owners, shall be treated for the purposes of this Act–

(a) as if the consideration for the disposal of the relinquished interest were of such amount as would secure that on the disposal neither a gain nor a loss accrues, and

(b) as if the acquired interest were acquired by the landowner–

 (i) at the time it was acquired jointly by the landowner and the co-owner or co-owners, and

 (ii) for a consideration equal to the amount of the sums that would have been allowable under section 38(1)(a) and (b) (acquisition and disposal costs etc) as a deduction in the computation of any gain on a disposal of the acquired interest by the co-owner or co-owners.

248E(8) For the purposes of this section–

(a) **"co-owner"** means any person who holds an interest in a dwelling-house jointly with the landowner;

(b) references to holding land jointly are to holding land–

 (i) in England and Wales, as joint tenants or tenants in common,

 (ii) in Scotland, as joint owners or owners in common, or

 (iii) in Northern Ireland, as joint tenants, tenants in common or coparceners;

(c) a related disposal (in relation to a disposal mentioned in condition B) is a disposal of an interest in a dwelling-house which is made–

 (i) by the landowner to a co-owner, or

 (ii) by a co-owner to the landowner or another co-owner,

at the same time as the disposal mentioned in that condition;

(d) spouses who are living together, or civil partners who are living together, are together treated as a landowner or a co-owner.

History – S. 248D inserted by SI 2010/157, art. 8(1), with effect in relation to disposals made on or after 6 April 2010.

WOODLANDS

History – Heading before s. 249 amended by FA 2012, s. 227 and Sch. 39, para. 49(2) with effect in relation to disposals made on or after 6 April 2013. Former heading read as follows: "AGRICULTURAL LAND AND WOODLANDS".

249 Grants for giving up agricultural land

249 [Repealed by FA 2012, s. 227 and Sch. 39, para. 49(1).]

History – S. 249 repealed by FA 2012, s. 227 and Sch. 39, para. 49(1), with effect in relation to disposals made on or after 6 April 2013.
Derivations – CGTA 1979, s. 112.
Notes – S. 21–34: general meaning of "disposal" and "asset".

250 Woodlands

250(1) Consideration for the disposal of trees standing or felled or cut on woodlands managed by the occupier on a commercial basis and with a view to the realisation of profits shall be excluded from the computation of the gain if the person making the disposal is the occupier.

250(2) Capital sums received under a policy of insurance in respect of the destruction of or damage or injury to trees by fire or other hazard on such woodlands shall be excluded from the computation of the gain if the, person making the disposal is the occupier.

250(3) Subsection (2) above has effect notwithstanding section 22(1).

250(4) In the computation of the gain so much of the cost of woodland in the United Kingdom shall be disregarded as is attributable to trees growing on the land.

250(5) In the computation of the gain accruing on a disposal of woodland in the United Kingdom so much of the consideration for the disposal as is attributable to trees growing on the land shall be excluded.

250(6) References in this section to trees include references to saleable underwood.

Derivations – CGTA 1979, s. 113, as amended by FA 1988, s. 65 and Sch. 6, para. 6(5).

Cross references – S. 22(1): disposal where capital sums received under policy of insurance of risk to assets etc.
SI 1992/58, Sch. 2, para. 11: disapplication of s. 250 in relation to reorganisation of port authorities.

Notes – S. 21–34: general meaning of "disposal".
S. 288: interpretation, including reference to sections being those of this Act.
FA 1988, Sch. 6: provisions taking the commercial occupation of woodlands outside the scope of taxes on income.

DEBTS

251 General provisions

251(1) Where a person incurs a debt to another, whether in sterling or in some other currency, no chargeable gain shall accrue to that (that is the original) creditor or his personal representative or legatee on a disposal of the debt, except in the case of the debt on a security (as defined in section 132).

251(2) Subject to the provisions of sections 132, 135 and 136 and subject to subsection (1) above, the satisfaction of a debt or part of it (including a debt on a security as defined in section 132) shall be treated as a disposal of the debt or of that part by the creditor made at the time when the debt or that part is satisfied.

251(3) Where property is acquired by a creditor in satisfaction of his debt or part of it, then subject to the provisions of sections 132, 135 and 136 the property shall not be treated as disposed of by the debtor or acquired by the creditor for a consideration greater than its market value at the time of the creditor's acquisition of it; but if under subsection (1) above (and in a case not falling within section 132, 135 or 136) no chargeable gain is to accrue on a disposal of the debt by the creditor (that is the original creditor), and a chargeable gain accrues to him on a disposal by him of the property, the amount of the chargeable gain shall (where necessary) be reduced so as not to exceed the chargeable gain which would have accrued if he had acquired the property for a consideration equal to the amount of the debt or that part of it.

251(4) A loss accruing on the disposal of a debt acquired by the person making the disposal from the original creditor or his personal representative or legatee at a time when the creditor or his personal representative or legatee is a person connected with the person making the disposal, and so acquired either directly or by one or more purchases through persons all of whom are connected with the person making the disposal, shall not be an allowable loss.

251(5) Where the trustees of a settlement are the original creditor, subsections (1) and (4) above shall apply as if for the references to the original creditors personal representative or legatee there were substituted references to any person becoming absolutely entitled, as against the trustees, to the debt on its ceasing to be settled property, and to that person's personal representative or legatee.

251(5A) References in this section to the disposal of a debt include the disposal of an interest in a debt (and, in the case of an interest in a debt, the reference in subsection (3) to the amount of the debt is to the amount of the person's interest in the debt).

251(6) For the purposes of this section a debenture issued by any company on or after 16th March 1993 shall be deemed to be a security (as defined in section 132) if–

(a) it is issued on a reorganisation (as defined in section 126(1)) or in pursuance of its allotment on any such reorganisation;

(b) it is issued in exchange for shares in or debentures of another company and in a case to which section 135 applies and which is unaffected by section 137(1);

(c) it is issued under any such arrangements as are mentioned in subsection (1)(a) of section 136 and in a case unaffected by section 137 where section 136 requires shares or debentures in another company to be treated as exchanged for, or for anything that includes, that debenture; or

(d) it is issued in pursuance of rights attached to any debenture issued on or after 16th March 1993 and falling within paragraph (a), (b) or (c) above.

and any debenture which results from a conversion of securities within the meaning of section 132, or is issued in pursuance of rights attached to such a debenture, shall be deemed for the purposes of this section to be a security (as defined in that section).

251(7) Where any instrument specified in subsection (8) below is not a security (as defined in section 132), that instrument shall be deemed to be such a security for the purposes of this section, other than the purposes of determining what is or is not an allowable loss in any case.

251(8) The instruments mentioned in subsection (7) above are–

(a) [Omitted by CTA 2009, s. 1322 and Sch. 1, para. 381;]

(b) any instrument which is not a loan relationship of a company but which would be a deeply discounted security for the purposes of Chapter 8 of Part 4 of ITTOIA 2005 if section 432(2) of that Act (excluded indexed securities) were omitted.

History – In s. 251(2), references to TCGA 1992, s. 132, 135 and 136 substituted for former references to s. 132 and 135 by FA 2002, s. 45 and Sch. 9, para. 12(a), (b), with effect in relation to shares or debentures issued on or after 17 April 2002.
In s. 251(3), references to TCGA 1992, s. 132, 135 and 136 substituted for former references to s. 132 and 135 by FA 2002, s. 45 and Sch. 9, para. 12(a), (b), with effect in relation to shares or debentures issued on or after 17 April 2002.
In s. 251(5), the words "Where the trustees of a settlement are the original creditor" substituted for "Where the original creditor is a trustee and the debt, when created, is settled property" by FA 2006, s. 88 and Sch. 12, para. 23(1)(a) with effect in relation to debts created on or after 6 April 2006.
In s. 251(5), the words "as against the trustees" substituted for "as against the trustee" by FA 2006, s. 88 and Sch. 12, para. 23(1)(b) with effect in relation to debts created on or after 6 April 2006.
S. 251(5A) inserted by FA 2012, s. 35(3) with effect in relation to disposals occurring on or after 6 April 2012.
S. 251(6) inserted by FA 1993, s. 84(2) in relation to any chargeable period ending on or after 16 March 1993. (In relation to any accounting period beginning before 6 April 1992, FA 1993, s. 84(2) treated as referring to and amending the predecessor Act.)
In s. 251(6) words "and any debenture … (as defined in that section)" inserted by FA 1997, s. 88(5) with effect in relation to disposals on or after 26 November 1996 and earlier conversions (FA 1997, s. 88(6)).
In s. 251(6)(b) words "to which section 135 applies and which is unaffected by section 137(1)" substituted for "unaffected by section 137 where one or more of the conditions mentioned in paragraphs (a) to (c) of section 135(1) is satisfied in relation to the exchange", by FA 2002, s. 45 and Sch. 9, para. 12(c), with effect in relation to shares or debentures issued on or after 17 April 2002.
S. 251(7) inserted by FA 1996, s. 104 and Sch. 14 para. 64 for accounting periods ending after 31 March 1996, subject to FA 1996, Sch. 15.
S. 251(8)(a) omitted and in para. (b) the words "(even apart from those provisions)" omitted by CTA 2009, s. 1322 and Sch. 1, para. 381 and repealed by CTA 2009, s. 1326 and Sch. 3, Pt. 1, with effect for corporation tax purposes for accounting periods ending on or after 1 April 2009, and for income tax and capital gains tax purposes for the tax year 2009–10 and subsequent tax years.
In s. 251(8)(b), words "deeply discounted security for the purposes of Chapter 8 of Part 4 of ITTOIA 2005 if section 432(2) of that Act" substituted for "relevantdiscounted security for the purposes of Schedule 13 to that Act if paragraph 3(2)(c) of that Schedule" by ITTOIA 2005, s. 882 and Sch. 1, para. 442 which, in accordance with ITTOIA 2005, s. 883, have effect, for income tax purposes, for tax year 2005–06 and subsequent tax years, and, for corporation tax purposes, for accounting periods ending after 5 April 2005.
S. 251(8) inserted by FA 1996, s. 104 and Sch. 14 para. 64 for accounting periods ending after 31 March 1996, subject to FA 1996, Sch. 15.

Derivations – CGTA 1979, s. 134.

Cross references – S. 126: reorganisation of share capital etc.
S. 132: equation of original and new holdings on a conversion of securities, defined by reference to loan stocks or similar securities.
S. 135–137: equation of original and new holdings on an exchange of securities in one company for those in another or certain reconstructions and amalgamations, but restricted in cases of tax avoidance etc.
FA 1990, Sch. 12, para. 2: where a debt, in relation to which Independent Broadcasting Authority (IBA) would have been the original creditor is transferred to nominated company on transfer of undertakings, the successor is to be treated as the original creditor.
FA 1994, Sch. 24, para. 9: where a debt is transferred from the predecessor to transferee by virtue of a "relevant transfer" in connection with the railways privatisation, the transferee is treated as the original creditor for s. 251 purposes.
FA 1999, s. 65(11): for the purposes of s. 251(8), the definition of "relevant discounted security" in FA 1996, Sch. 13 which was substituted by FA 1999, s. 65 has effect in relation to any disposal (in whole or in part) of an asset on or after 15 February 1999.
TSBA 1985, Sch. 2, para. 4: transferee on reorganisation of the Trustee Savings Banks is treated as the original creditor in relation to certain debts.
Water Act 1989, s. 95(6): where a debt, in relation to which a water authority would have been the original creditor is transferred to a successor company, the successor is to be treated as the original creditor.

Extra-statutory concessions – D18: default on mortgage granted by vendor.

Statements of practice – 10/84: all taxpayer's bank accounts of same foreign currency treated as one account and transfers disregarded for capital gains tax purposes.

Other material – IR press release, 11 June 1970: definition of "security" regarded as exhaustive.
Law Society's Gazette, 26 April 1995: Revenue view that s. 251(4) does not apply to debts which are debts on a security.
Taxline 1995/136 (not reproduced): Revenue may not apply s. 251(4) to debts on security.

Notes – S. 15: meaning of "chargeable gain".
S. 60: meaning of "absolutely entitled as against the trustee".
S. 64(2), (3): meaning of "legatee".
S. 68: meaning of "settled property".
S. 132: meaning of "security" (s. 132 does not define the phrase "the debt on a security").
S. 286: "connected" in references to persons being connected with one another.

252 Foreign currency bank accounts

252(1) Section 251(1) does not apply in relation to a gain accruing to a person on a disposal of a foreign currency debt (or an interest in such a debt) unless that person is–

(a) an individual,

(b) the trustees of a settlement, or

(c) the personal representatives of a deceased person.

252(2) A **"foreign currency debt"** is a debt–

(a) owed by a bank in a currency other than sterling, and

(b) represented by a sum standing to the credit of an account-holder in an account in that bank.

History – S. 252 substituted by FA 2012, s. 35(4) with effect in relation to disposals occurring on or after 6 April 2012.

Derivations – CGTA 1979, s. 135.

Cross references – S. 13(5)(c): disapplication of provisions attributing gains to members of non-resident companies for debts within s. 252(1).

Statements of practice – SP 10/84: all taxpayer's bank accounts of same foreign currency treated as one account and transfers disregarded for capital gains tax purposes.

252A Foreign currency bank accounts and the remittance basis

252A [Omitted by FA 2012, s. 35(5).]

History – S. 252A omitted by FA 2012, s. 35(5) with effect in relation to disposals occurring on or after 6 April 2012.

253 Relief for loans to traders

253(1) In this section **"a qualifying loan"** means a loan in the case of which–

(a) the money lent is used by the borrower wholly for the purposes of a trade carried on by him, not being a trade which consists of or includes the lending of money, and

(b) the borrower is resident in the United Kingdom, and

(c) the borrower's debt is not a debt on a security as defined in section 132;

and for the purposes of paragraph (a) above money used by the borrower for setting up a trade which is subsequently carried on by him shall be treated as used for the purposes of that trade.

253(2) In subsection (1) above references to a **trade** include references to a profession or vocation; and where money lent to a company is lent by it to another company in the same group, being a trading company, that subsection shall apply to the money lent to the first-mentioned company as if it had used it for any purpose for which it is used by the other company while a member of the group.

253(3) Where a person who has made a qualifying loan makes a claim and at that time–

(a) any outstanding amount of the principal of the loan has become irrecoverable, and

(b) the claimant has not assigned his right to recover that amount, and

(c) the claimant and the borrower were not each other's spouses or civil partners, or companies in the same group, when the loan was made or at any subsequent time,

then, to the extent that that amount is not an amount which, in the case of the claimant, falls to be brought into account as a debit given for the purposes of Part 5 of CTA 2009 (loan relationships), this Act: shall have effect as if an allowable loss equal to that amount had accrued to the claimant at the time of the claim or (subject to subsection (3A) below) any earlier time specified in the claim.

253(3A) For the purposes of subsection (3) above, an earlier time may be specified in the claim if:

(a) the amount to which that subsection applies was also irrecoverable at the earlier time; and either

(b) for capital gains tax purposes the earlier time falls not more than two years before the beginning of the year of assessment in which the claim is made; or

(c) for corporation tax purposes the earlier time falls on or after the first day of the earliest accounting period ending not more than two years before the time of the claim.

253(4) Where a person who has guaranteed the repayment of a loan which is, or but for subsection (1)(c) above would be, a qualifying loan makes a claim and at that time–

(a) any outstanding amount of, or of interest in respect of, the principal of the loan has become irrecoverable from the borrower, and

(b) the claimant has made a payment under the guarantee (whether to the lender or a co-guarantor) in respect of that amount, and

(c) the claimant has not assigned any right to recover that amount which has accrued to him (whether by operation of law or otherwise) in consequence of his having made the payment, and

(d) the lender and the borrower were not each other's spouses or civil partners, or companies in the same group, when the loan was made or at any subsequent time and the claimant and the borrower were not each other's spouses or civil partners, and the claimant and the lender were not companies in the same group, when the guarantee was given or at any subsequent time,

this Act shall have effect as if an allowable loss had accrued to the claimant when the payment was made; and the loss shall be equal to the payment made by him in respect of the amount mentioned in paragraph (a) above less any contribution payable to him by any co-guarantor in respect of the payment so made.

253(4A) A claim under subsection (4) above shall be made–

(a) for the purposes of capital gains tax, not more than 4 years after the end of the year of assessment in which the payment was made;

(b) for the purposes of corporation tax, within 4 years after the end of the accounting period in which the payment was made.

253(5) Where an allowable loss has been treated under subsection (3) or (4) above as accruing to any person and the whole or any part of the outstanding amount mentioned in subsection (3)(a) or, as the case may be, subsection (4)(a) is at any time recovered by him, this Act shall have effect as if there had accrued to him at that time a chargeable gain equal to so much of the allowable loss as corresponds to the amount recovered.

253(6) Where–

(a) an allowable loss has been treated under subsection (4) above as accruing to any person, and

(b) the whole or any part of the amount of the payment mentioned in subsection (4)(b) is at any time recovered by him,

this Act shall have effect as if there had accrued to him at that time a chargeable gain equal to so much of the allowable loss as corresponds to the amount recovered.

253(7) Where–

(a) an allowable loss has been treated under subsection (3) above as accruing to a company (**"the first company"**), and

(b) the whole or any part of the outstanding amount mentioned in subsection (3)(a) is at any time recovered by a company (**"the second company"**) in the same group as the first company,

this Act shall have effect as if there had accrued to the second company at that time a chargeable gain equal to so much of the allowable loss as corresponds to the amount recovered.

253(8) Where–

(a) an allowable loss has been treated under subsection (4) above as accruing to a company (**"the first company"**), and

(b) the whole or any part of the outstanding amount mentioned in subsection (4)(a), or the whole or any part of the amount of the payment mentioned in subsection (4)(b), is at any time recovered by a company (**"the second company"**) in the same group as the first company,

this Act shall have effect as if there had accrued to the second company at that time a chargeable gain equal to so much of the allowable loss as corresponds to the amount recovered.

253(9) For the purposes of subsections (5) to (8) above, a person shall be treated as recovering an amount if he (or any other person by his direction) receives any money or money's worth in satisfaction of his right to recover that amount or in consideration of his assignment of the right to recover it; and where a person assigns such a right otherwise than by way of a bargain made at arm's length he shall be treated as receiving money or money's worth equal to the market value of the right at the time of the assignment.

253(10) No amount shall be treated under this section as giving rise to an allowable loss or chargeable gain in the case of any person if it falls to be taken into account in computing his income for the purposes of income tax or corporation tax.

253(11) Where an allowable loss has been treated as accruing to a person under subsection (4) above by virtue of a payment made by him at any time under a guarantee–

(a) no chargeable gain shall accrue to him otherwise than under subsection (5) above, and

(b) no allowable loss shall accrue to him under this Act,

on his disposal of any rights that have accrued to him (whether by operation of law or otherwise) in consequence of his having made any payment under the guarantee at or after that time.

253(12) References in this section to an amount having become irrecoverable do not include references to cases where the amount has become irrecoverable in consequence of the terms of the loan, of any arrangements of which the loan forms part, or of any act or omission by the lender or, in a case within subsection (4) above, the guarantor.

253(13) For the purposes of subsections (7) and (8) above, 2 companies are in the same group if they were in the same group when the loan was made or have been in the same group at any subsequent time.

253(14) In this section–

(a) **"spouses"** means spouses who are living together (construed in accordance with section 288(3)),

(aa) **"civil partners"** means civil partners who are living together (construed in accordance with section 288(3)),

(b) **"trading company"** has the same meaning as in section 165 (see section 165A), and

(c) **"group"** shall be construed in accordance with section 170.

253(15) Subsection (3) above does not apply where the loan was made before 12th April 1978 and subsection (4) above does not apply where the guarantee was given before that date.

History – In s. 253(3) the words "Part 5 of CTA 2009" substituted for the words "Chapter II of Part IV of the Finance Act 1996" by CTA 2009, s. 1322 and Sch. 1, para. 382, with effect for corporation tax purposes for accounting periods ending on or after 1 April 2009, and for income tax and capital gains tax purposes for the tax year 2009–10 and subsequent tax years.
In s. 253(3)(c) the words "or civil partners" inserted by SI 2005/3229, reg. 120(2), with effect from 5 December 2005.
In s. 253(3) words "Where a person who has made a qualifying loan makes a claim and at that time" and "at the time of the claim or (subject to subsection (3A) below) any earlier time specified in the claim." substituted by FA 1996, s. 201 and Sch. 39, para. 8, in relation to claims made on or after 6 April 1996.
In s. 253(3) words "then, to the extent that that amount is not an amount which, in the case of the claimant, falls to be brought into account as a debit given for the purposes of Chapter II of Part IV of the Finance Act 1996 (loan relationships)," inserted at beginning of endpiece by FA 1996, s. 104 and Sch. 14, para. 65 for accounting periods ending after 31 March 1996, subject to FA 1996, Sch. 15, para. 7.
S. 253(3A) inserted by FA 1996, s. 201 and Sch. 39, para. 8, in relation to claims made on or after 6 April 1996.
In s. 253(4)(d) the words "or civil partners" inserted twice by SI 2005/3229, reg. 120(3), with effect from 5 December 2005.
In s. 253(4A), the words "not more than 4 years after the end of" and "4 years" substituted for "on or before the fifth anniversary of the 31st January next following" and "6 years" (respectively) by FA 2008, s. 118(1) and Sch. 39, para. 30, with effect from 1 April 2010 (SI 2009/403, art. 2(2) subject to SI 2009/403, art. 3–10 – in particular art. 10).
S. 253(4A) inserted by FA 1996, s. 135 and Sch. 21, para. 40 for 1996–97 and later years of assessment and accounting periods ending on or after 1 July 1999, the appointed day for self-assessment to corporation tax (FA 1994, s. 199 and SI 1998/3173 (C. 78)).
In s. 253(14)(b), the words "same meaning as in section 165 (see section 165A)" substituted for the words "meaning given by paragraph 22 of Schedule A1" by FA 2008, s. 8 and Sch. 2, para. 38 with effect in relation to chargeable gains accruing or treated as accruing in the tax year 2008–09 or any subsequent tax year (FA 2008, Sch. 2, para. 56(3)).
S. 253(14)(aa) inserted by SI 2005/3229, reg. 120(4), with effect from 5 December 2005.
In s. 253(14)(b) reference to "paragraph 22 of Schedule A1" substituted for a reference to "paragraph 1 of Schedule 6" by FA 1998, s. 140(5)(b) which has effect in relation to the year 2003–04 and subsequent years of assessment by virtue of FA 1998, s. 140(6).

Derivations – S. 253(1)–(5): CGTA 1979, s. 136(1)–(5).
S. 253(6)–(8): CGTA 1979, s. 136(5A)–(5C), as inserted by FA 1990, s. 83.
S. 253(9): CGTA 1979, s. 136(6), as amended by FA 1990, s. 83.
S. 253(10)–(12): CGTA 1979, s. 136(7)–(9).
S. 253(13): CGTA 1979, s. 136(9A), as inserted by FA 1990, s. 83.
S. 253(14): CGTA 1979, s. 136(10), as amended by FA 1989, s. 107 and Sch. 12, para. 6.
S. 253(15): CGTA 1979, s. 136(11).

Cross references – S. 132: definition of "security" by reference to loan stock or similar security.
S. 170 with (2)(a) and (9)(b)omitted: groups of companies by reference to 75 per cent subsidiary relationships (i.e. as amended by FA 2000, Sch. 29, para. 34 in relation to loans made on or after 1 April 2000 and guarantees given on or after that date).
S. 241(3), (3A): commercial lettings of furnished holiday accommodation treated as a trade.
S. 288(3): reference to an individual living with his spouse or civil partner construed in accordance with ITA 2007, s. 1011.
Sch. 6, para. 1: trading company means a company whose business consists wholly or mainly of the carrying on of a trade or trades.
FA 1994, Sch. 24, para. 9: where by virtue of a "relevant transfer" in connection with railways privatisation obligations under a guarantee of repayment of a loan are transferred, transferee is treated as guarantor for the purposes of s. 253. S. 253 is also modified by para. 9(4).

Other material – IR press release, 11 June 1970: definition of "security" regarded as exhaustive.
ICAEW Technical Release TR 308 (not reproduced): "guarantee" (s. 253(4)) covers case where person's property charged as security for qualifying loan; an indemnity as such is not a guarantee; s. 253(4) applies to overdrafts but not to hire purchase agreements.
Taxline 1993/43 (not reproduced): it is important to ensure that any payment is made "under the guarantee" and not otherwise.
Taxline 1995/4 (not reproduced): Revenue interpret irrecoverability requirement in s. 253(3) such that, if loan is irrecoverable ab initio (eg because loan is to near-insolvent business) relief is not available.
Taxline 2004/7 (not reproduced): no need to waive the loan before rather than after the claim for the relief to be valid.

Notes – S. 9: meaning of "resident".
S. 15: meaning of "chargeable gain".
S. 16: meaning of "allowable loss".
S. 288: interpretation, including meaning of "trade", "company", "inspector" as being any inspector of taxes and reference to sections being those of this Act.
TMA 1970, s. 42–43B: procedures and time limits for making claims.
FA 1996, Sch. 39, para. 8, 9: amendments to s. 253 and 254 enact (see history notes) ESC D36.

254 Relief for debts on qualifying corporate bonds

254 [Repealed by FA 1998, s. 141(1)(b), s. 165 and Sch. 27, Pt. III(32).]

History – S. 254 repealed by FA 1998, s. 141(1)(b), s. 165 and Sch. 27, Pt. III(32) as respects loans made on or after 17 March 1998.

255 Provisions supplementary to section 254

255 [Repealed by FA 1998, s. 141(1)(b), s. 165 and Sch. 27, Pt. III(32).]

History – S. 255 repealed by FA 1998, s. 141(1)(b), s. 165 and Sch. 27, Pt. III(32) as respects loans made on or after 17 March 1998.

INVESTMENTS IN SOCIAL ENTERPRISES

History – S. 255A–255E inserted by FA 2014, s. 57 and Sch. 12, para. 2, with effect from 17 July 2014.

255A Hold-over relief for gains re-invested in social enterprises

255A Schedule 8B to this Act (which provides relief in respect of gains re-invested in social enterprises) has effect.

History – S. 255A inserted by FA 2014, s. 57 and Sch. 12, para. 2, with effect from 17 July 2014.

Other material – Misc. 22/2014: Social Investment Tax Relief (Sitr): Guide For Social Enterprises.
Misc. 23/2014: Social Investment Tax Relief (Sitr) – Investors.
Misc. 24/2014: Social Investment Tax Relief (Sitr): Guidance For Social Enterprises – Process To Follow.
Misc. 25/2014: Social Investment Tax Relief (Sitr): Guidance For Investors – How To Claim Tax Relief.
Misc. 26/2014: Social Investment Tax Relief Compliance Statement Sitr(2014).

255B Gains and losses on investments in social enterprises

255B(1) For the purpose of determining the gain or loss on any disposal of an asset by an individual where–

(a) an amount of SI relief is attributable to the asset, and

(b) apart from this subsection there would be a loss,

treat the consideration given by the individual for the acquisition of the asset as reduced by the amount of the SI relief.

255B(2) If–

(a) an individual disposes of an asset,

(b) an amount of SI relief is attributable to the asset,

(c) the disposal takes place after the end of the 3 years beginning with the day when the individual acquired the asset, and

(d) apart from this subsection, there would be a gain on the disposal,

the gain is not a chargeable gain, subject to section 255C.

255B(3) Despite section 16(2), subsection (2) above does not apply to a disposal on which a loss accrues.

255B(4) Any question as to–

(a) which of any assets acquired by an individual at different times a disposal relates to, being assets to which SI relief is attributable, or

(b) whether a disposal relates to assets to which SI relief is attributable or to other assets,

is to be determined for the purposes of capital gains tax as provided by section 257TA of ITA 2007.

255B(5) Chapter 1 of this Part has effect subject to subsection (4).

255B(6) Sections 104, 105 and 106A do not apply to assets to which SI relief is attributable.

255B(7) There are to be made all such adjustments of capital gains tax, whether by way of assessment or by way of discharge or repayment of tax, as may be required in consequence of SI relief being given or withdrawn.

255B(8) In this section and sections 255C to 255E **"SI relief"** means relief under Part 5B of ITA 2007 (income tax relief for investments in social enterprises).

255B(9) That Part applies for the purposes of this section and sections 255C to 255E to determine whether SI relief is attributable to any asset and, if so, the amount of SI relief so attributable.

History – S. 255B inserted by FA 2014, s. 57 and Sch. 12, para. 2, with effect from 17 July 2014.

255C Application of section 255B(2) where maximum SI relief not obtained

255C(1) Subsection (2) applies if–

(a) an individual's liability to income tax has been reduced (or treated by virtue of section 257T of ITA 2007 (spouses or civil partners) as reduced) for any tax year under section 257JA of ITA 2007 (SI relief) in respect of the acquisition of an asset,

(b) the amount of the reduction ("D") is less than the amount given by–

$$I \times R$$

where–

I is the amount on which the individual has SI relief in the case of the asset, and

R is the SI rate for the tax year for which the SI relief was obtained, and

(c) D is not within paragraph (b) solely by virtue of section 29(2) and (3) of ITA 2007.

255C(2) If the individual disposes of the asset and there is a gain on the disposal, section 255B(2) has effect in relation to the gain as if it were reduced by multiplying it by–

$$\frac{D}{I \times R}$$

255C(3) In this section **"SI rate"** has the meaning given by section 257JA(5) of ITA 2007.

History – S. 255C inserted by FA 2014, s. 57 and Sch. 12, para. 2, with effect from 17 July 2014.

255D Application of section 255B(2) where SI relief has been reduced

255D(1) Subsection (2) applies if before a disposal of an asset–

(a) value is received in circumstances where SI relief attributable to the asset is reduced by an amount under section 257Q(1)(a) of ITA 2007, or

(b) there is a repayment, redemption, repurchase or payment in circumstances where SI relief attributable to the asset is reduced by an amount under section 257QJ(2)(a) of ITA 2007, or

(c) paragraphs (a) and (b) both apply.

255D(2) If section 255B(2) applies on the disposal but section 255C does not, section 255B(2) applies only to so much of the gain as remains after deducting so much of it as is found by multiplying it by the fraction–

$$\frac{A}{B}$$

where–

A is equal to the amount by which the SI relief given in respect of the asset is reduced as mentioned in subsection (1) above, and

B is equal to the amount of the SI relief given in respect of the asset.

255D(3) If sections 255B(2) and 255C apply on the disposal, section 255B(2) applies only to so much of the gain as is found by–

(a) taking the part of the gain found under section 255C, and

(b) deducting from that part so much of it as is found by multiplying it by the fraction mentioned in subsection (2).

255D(4) If the SI relief given in respect of the asset is reduced as mentioned in subsection (1) by more than one amount, the amount referred to as A in subsection (2) is to be taken to be equal to the aggregate of those amounts.

255D(5) The amount referred to in subsection (2) as B is to be found without regard to any reduction mentioned in subsection (1).

History – S. 255D inserted by FA 2014, s. 57 and Sch. 12, para. 2, with effect from 17 July 2014.

255E Reorganisations involving shares to which SI relief is attributable

255E(1) Subsection (2) applies if an individual holds shares which form part of the ordinary share capital of a company and include shares of more than one of the following kinds–

(a) shares to which SI relief is attributable and to which subsection (3) applies,

(b) shares to which SI relief is attributable and to which subsection (3) does not apply, and

(c) shares to which SI relief is not attributable and to which subsection (3) does not apply.

255E(2) If there is a reorganisation within the meaning of section 126 affecting the shares listed in subsection (1), section 127 applies separately to those shares so that shares of each kind are treated as a separate holding of original shares and identified with a separate new holding.

255E(3) This subsection applies to any shares if–

(a) expenditure on the shares has been set under Schedule 8B to this Act against the whole or part of any gain, and

(b) in relation to the shares there has been no chargeable event for the purposes of that Schedule.

255E(4) If–

(a) an individual holds shares ("the existing holding") which form part of the ordinary share capital of a company,

(b) there is, by virtue of any such allotment for payment as is mentioned in section 126(2)(a), a reorganisation affecting the existing holding, and

(c) immediately following the reorganisation, SI relief is attributable to the existing holding or the allotted shares,

sections 127 to 130 do not apply in relation to the existing holding.

255E(5) Subject to subsection (6), sections 135 and 136 do not apply in respect of shares to which SI relief is attributable.

255E(6) Subsection (5) does not have effect to disapply section 135 or 136 in a case where the original shares are shares to which SI relief is attributable if–

(a) the new holding consists of new ordinary shares which meet conditions A and B of section 257L of ITA 2007,

(b) the new shares are issued after the end of three years beginning with the day on which the original shares were acquired,

(c) before issuing the new shares, the company had issued shares which met conditions A and B of section 257L of ITA 2007, and

(d) the company issued a compliance certificate in relation to those earlier shares for the purposes of section 257PA(1) of ITA 2007 and in accordance with sections 257PB and 257PC of ITA 2007.

255E(7) In subsection (6) **"new holding"** is to be construed in accordance with sections 126, 127, 135 and 136.

255E(8) In this section–

"ordinary share capital" has the meaning given in section 989 of ITA 2007;

"ordinary shares", in relation to a company, means shares forming part of its ordinary share capital.

History – S. 255E inserted by FA 2014, s. 57 and Sch. 12, para. 2, with effect from 17 July 2014.

CHARITIES AND GIFTS OF NON-BUSINESS ASSETS ETC.

256 Charities

256(1) Subject to the following provisions of this section, a gain shall not be a chargeable gain if it accrues to a charity and is applicable and applied for charitable purposes.

256(2) If property held on charitable trusts ceases to be subject to charitable trusts–

(a) the trustees shall be treated as if they had disposed of, and immediately reacquired, the property for a consideration equal to its market value, any gain on the disposal being treated as not accruing to a charity, and

(b) if and so far as any of that property represents, directly or indirectly, the consideration for the disposal of assets by the trustees, any gain accruing on that disposal shall be treated as not having accrued to a charity,

and an assessment to capital gains tax chargeable by virtue of paragraph (b) above may be made at any time not more than 3 years after the end of the year of assessment in which the property ceases to be subject to charitable trusts.

256(3) Subsection (4) below applies if a charitable trust has a non-exempt amount under section 540 of ITA 2007 for a year of assessment.

256(3A) Subsection (4) below also applies if a charitable company has a non-exempt amount under section 493 of CTA 2010 for an accounting period.

256(4) Gains accruing–

(a) to the charitable trust in the year of assessment, or

(b) to the charitable company in the accounting period,

are treated as being, and always having been, chargeable gains so far as they are attributed to the non-exempt amount under section 256A (in the case of a charitable trust) or section 256C (in the case of a charitable company).

256(5) For restrictions on exemptions under Part 10 of ITA 2007 (special rules about charitable trusts etc) see section 539 of that Act.

256(6) [Omitted by FA 2010, s. 30 and Sch. 6, para. 13(3).]

256(7) For restrictions on exemptions under Part 11 of CTA 2010 (charitable companies etc) see section 492 of that Act.

256(8) [Omitted by FA 2010, s. 30 and Sch. 6, para. 13(3).]

History – In s. 256(1), the words "section 505(4) of the Taxes Act and", which appeared after "subject to", omitted by CTA 2010, s. 1177 and Sch. 1, para. 254(2) and repealed by CTA 2010, s. 1181 and Sch. 3, Pt. 1, with effect for corporation tax purposes for accounting periods ending on or after 1 April 2010, and for income tax and capital gains tax purposes for the tax year 2010–11 and subsequent tax years.
In s. 256(1), the words "the following provisions of this section" substituted for "subsection 2 below" by ITA 2007, s. 1027 and Sch. 1, para. 326(2), with effect from 6 April 2007.
In s. 256(1) the words "section 505(4)" substituted for the words "section 505(3)" by FA 2006, s. 55(4) with effect in relation to chargeable periods beginning on or after 22nd March 2006 (s. 55(5)).
S. 256(3) inserted by ITA 2007, s. 1027 and Sch. 1, para. 326(3), with effect from 6 April 2007.
S. 256(3A) inserted by CTA 2010, s. 1177 and Sch. 1, para. 254(3), with effect for corporation tax purposes for accounting periods ending on or after 1 April 2010, and for income tax and capital gains tax purposes for the tax year 2010–11 and subsequent tax years.
S. 256(4) substituted by CTA 2010, s. 1177 and Sch. 1, para. 254(4), with effect for corporation tax purposes for accounting periods ending on or after 1 April 2010, and for income tax and capital gains tax purposes for the tax year 2010–11 and subsequent tax years.
Former s. 256(4) inserted by ITA 2007, s. 1027 and Sch. 1, para. 326(3), with effect from 6 April 2007.
S. 256(5) inserted by ITA 2007, s. 1027 and Sch. 1, para. 326(3), with effect from 6 April 2007.
S. 256(6) omitted by FA 2010, s. 30 and Sch. 6, para. 13(3), with effect for corporation tax purposes for accounting periods beginning on or after 1 April 2012 and for capital gains tax purposes for the tax year 2012–13 and subsequent tax years (SI 2012/736, art. 9).
Former s. 265(6) inserted by SI 2009/23, art. 3, with effect for income and capital gains tax purposes for the tax year 2007–08 and subsequent tax years, and with effect for corporation tax purposes for accounting periods ending after 5 April 2007.
S. 256(7) inserted by CTA 2010, s. 1177 and Sch. 1, para. 254(5), with effect for corporation tax purposes for accounting periods ending on or after 1 April 2010, and for income tax and capital gains tax purposes for the tax year 2010–11 and subsequent tax years.
S. 256(8) omitted by FA 2010, s. 30 and Sch. 6, para. 13(3), with effect for corporation tax purposes for accounting periods beginning on or after 1 April 2012 and for capital gains tax purposes for the tax year 2012–13 and subsequent tax years (SI 2012/736, art. 9).
Former s. 256(8) inserted by CTA 2010, s. 1177 and Sch. 1, para. 254(5), with effect for corporation tax purposes for accounting periods ending on or after 1 April 2010, andfor income tax and capital gains tax purposes for the tax year 2010–11 and subsequent tax years.

Derivations – CGTA 1979, s. 145.

Cross references – ICTA 1988, s. 505(4), (5), (6) and (7): restriction of relief for certain charities by reference to non-qualifying expenditure.

Extra-statutory concessions – D47: removal of CGT charge, in certain circumstances, where disposal occurs during period of temporary loss of charitable status.

HMRC interpretations – IRInt. 180: HMRC view that s. 256 may exempt gains of offshore trusts which might otherwise be chargeable on UK charitable beneficiaries under s. 87, in relation to capital payments made to charities on or after 10 August 1998, and any such payments made before that date where the tax liability was still open on that date.

Notes – S. 15: meaning of "chargeable gain".
S. 21–34: general meaning of "disposal" and "asset".
S. 288: interpretation, including the "Taxes Act" as ICTA 1988.
ICTA 1988, s. 505, 506: restriction of tax exemptions for certain charities where they incur non-qualifying expenditure.
TMA 1970, s. 29–41: assessing procedures.

256A Attributing gains to the non-exempt amount: charitable trusts

256A(1) This section applies if a charitable trust has a non-exempt amount under section 540 of ITA 2007 for a year of assessment.

256A(2) Attributable gains of the charitable trust for the year of assessment may be attributed to the non-exempt amount but only so far as the non-exempt amount has not been used up.

256A(3) The non-exempt amount can be used up (in whole or in part) by–

(a) attributable gains being attributed to it under this section, or

(b) attributable income being attributed to it under section 541 of ITA 2007.

256A(4) The whole of the non-exempt amount must be used up by–

(a) attributable gains being attributed to the whole of it under this section,

(b) attributable income being attributed to the whole of it under section 541 of ITA 2007, or

(c) a combination of attributable gains being attributed to some of it under this section and attributable income being attributed to the rest of it under section 541 of ITA 2007.

256A(5) See section 256B for the way in which gains are to be attributed to the non-exempt amount under this section.

256A(6) In this section and section 256B a charitable trust's **"attributable income"**, and **"attributable gains"**, for a tax year have the same meaning as in Part 10 of ITA 2007 (see section 540 of that Act).

History – In s. 256A, in the title, the words ": charitable trusts" inserted by CTA 2010, s. 1177 and Sch. 1 para. 255, with effect for corporation tax purposes for accounting periods ending on or after 1 April 2010, and for income tax and capital gains tax purposes for the tax year 2010–11 and subsequent tax years.
S. 256A inserted by ITA 2007, s. 1027 and Sch. 1, para. 327, with effect from 6 April 2007.

256B How gains are attributed to the non-exempt amount: charitable trusts

256B(1) This section is about the ways in which attributable gains can be attributed to a non-exempt amount under section 256A.

256B(2) The trustees of the charitable trust may specify the attributable gains that are to be attributed to the non-exempt amount.

256B(3) A specification under subsection (2) is made by notice to an officer of Revenue and Customs.

256B(4) Subsection (6) applies if–

(a) an officer of Revenue and Customs requires the trustees of a charitable trust to make a specification under this section, and

(b) the trustees have not given notice under subsection (3) of the specification before the end of the required period.

256B(5) The required period is 30 days beginning with the day on which the officer made the requirement.

256B(6) An officer of Revenue and Customs may determine the attributable gains that are to be attributed to the non-exempt amount.

History – In s. 256B in the title, the words ": charitable trusts" inserted by CTA 2010, s. 1177 and Sch. 1, para. 256, with effect for corporation tax purposes for accounting periods ending on or after 1 April 2010, and for income tax and capital gains tax purposes for the tax year 2010–11 and subsequent tax years.
S. 256B inserted by ITA 2007, s. 1027 and Sch. 1, para. 327 with effect from 6 April 2007.

256C Attributing gains to the non-exempt amount: charitable companies

256C(1) This section applies if a charitable company has a non-exempt amount under section 493 of CTA 2010 for an accounting period.

256C(2) Attributable gains of the charitable company for the period may be attributed to the non-exempt amount but only so far as the non-exempt amount has not been used up.

256C(3) The non-exempt amount can be used up (in whole or in part) by–

(a) attributable gains being attributed to it under this section, or

(b) attributable income being attributed to it under section 494 of CTA 2010.

256C(4) The whole of the non-exempt amount must be used up by–

(a) attributable gains being attributed to the whole of it under this section,

(b) attributable income being attributed to the whole of it under section 494 of CTA 2010, or

(c) a combination of attributable gains being attributed to some of it under this section and attributable income being attributed to the rest of it under section 494 of CTA 2010.

256C(5) In this section and section 256D a charitable company's **"attributable income"** and **"attributable gains"** for an accounting period have the same meaning as in Part 11 of CTA 2010 (see section 493 of that Act).

256C(6) [Omitted by FA 2010, s. 30 and Sch. 6, para. 13(4).]

History – S. 256C(6) omitted by FA 2010, s. 30 and Sch. 6, para. 13(4), with effect for corporation tax purposes for accounting periods beginning on or after 1 April 2012 and for capital gains tax purposes for the tax year 2012–13 and subsequent tax years (SI 2012/736, art. 9).
S. 256C inserted by CTA 2010, s. 1177 and Sch. 1, para. 257, with effect for corporation tax purposes for accounting periods ending on or after 1 April 2010, and for income tax and capital gains tax purposes for the tax year 2010–11 and subsequent tax years.

256D How gains are attributed to the non-exempt amount: charitable companies

256D(1) This section is about the ways in which attributable gains can be attributed to a non-exempt amount under section 256C.

256D(2) The charitable company may specify the attributable gains that are to be attributed to the non-exempt amount.

256D(3) A specification under subsection (2) is made by notice to an officer of Revenue and Customs.

256D(4) Subsection (6) applies if–

(a) an officer of Revenue and Customs requires a charitable company to make a specification under this section, and

(b) the charitable company has not given notice under subsection (3) of the specification before the end of the required period.

256D(5) The required period is 30 days beginning with the day on which the officer made the requirement.

256D(6) An officer of Revenue and Customs may determine the attributable gains that are to be attributed to the non-exempt amount.

256D(7) [Omitted by FA 2010, s. 30 and Sch. 6, para. 13(5).]

History – S. 256D(7) omitted by FA 2010, s. 30 and Sch. 6, para. 13(5), with effect for corporation tax purposes for accounting periods beginning on or after 1 April 2012 and for capital gains tax purposes for the tax year 2012–13 and subsequent tax years (SI 2012/736, art. 9).

S. 256D inserted by CTA 2010, s. 1177 and Sch. 1, para. 257, with effect for corporation tax purposes for accounting periods ending on or after 1 April 2010, and for income tax and capital gains tax purposes for the tax year 2010–11 and subsequent tax years.

257 Gifts to charities etc.

257(1) Subsection (2) below shall apply where a disposal of an asset is made otherwise than under a bargain at arm's length–

(a) to a charity or a registered club, or

(b) to any bodies mentioned in Schedule 3 to the Inheritance Tax Act 1984 (gifts for national purposes, etc)

and the disposal is not one in relation to which section 151A(1) has effect.

257(2) Sections 17(1) and 258(3) shall not apply; but if the disposal is by way of gift (including a gift in settlement) or for a consideration not exceeding the sums allowable as a deduction under section 38, then–

(a) the disposal and acquisition shall be treated for the purposes of this Act as being made for such consideration as to secure that neither a gain nor a loss accrues on the disposal, and

(b) where, after the disposal, the asset is disposed of by the person who acquired it under the disposal, its acquisition by the person making the earlier disposal shall be treated for the purposes of this Act as the acquisition of the person making the later disposal.

257(2A) Subsection (2B) applies if relief is available under Chapter 3 of Part 8 of ITA 2007 or as a result of Chapter 3 of Part 6 of CTA 2010 (gifts of shares, securities and real property to charities) in relation to the disposal of a qualifying investment to a charity (whether or not a claim for relief is actually made).

257(2B) The consideration for which the charity's acquisition of the qualifying investment is treated by virtue of subsection (2) above as having been made–

(a) is reduced by the relievable amount within the meaning of Chapter 3 of Part 8 of ITA 2007 if relief in relation to the disposal is available only under that Chapter,

(b) is reduced by the relievable amount within the meaning of Chapter 3 of Part 6 of CTA 2010 if relief in relation to the disposal is available only as a result of that Chapter,

(c) is reduced by the relievable amount within the meaning of Chapter 3 of Part 8 of ITA 2007 if relief in relation to the disposal is available both under that Chapter and as a result of Chapter 3 of Part 6 of CTA 2010 because of section 442 of ITA 2007 and section 214 of CTA 2010, or

(d) is reduced to nil if that consideration is less than the amount referred to in paragraph (a), (b) or (c) (as the case may be).

257(2C) In subsections (2A) and (2B)–

"qualifying investment" has the same meaning as in Chapter 3 of Part 8 of ITA 2007 (see section 432 of that Act),

257(3) Where–

(a) otherwise than on the termination of a life interest (within the meaning of section 72) by the death of the person entitled thereto, any assets or parts of any assets forming part of settled property are, under section 71, deemed to be disposed of and reacquired by the trustee, and

(b) the person becoming entitled as mentioned in section 71(1) is a charity, a registered club or a body mentioned in Schedule 3 to the Inheritance Tax Act 1984 (gifts for national purposes, etc),

then, if no consideration is received by any person for or in connection with any transaction by virtue of which the charity, registered club or other body becomes so entitled, the disposal and reacquisition of the assets to which the charity, registered club or other body becomes so entitled shall, notwithstanding section 71, be treated for the purposes of this Act as made for such consideration as to secure that neither a gain nor a loss accrues on the disposal.

257(4) In subsection (2)(b) above the first reference to a disposal includes a disposal to which section 146(2) of the 1979 Act applied where the person who acquired the asset on that disposal disposes of the asset after the coming into force of this section.

257(5) For the purposes of this section **"registered club"** has the same meaning as in Chapter 9 of Part 13 of CTA 2010.

History – In s. 257(1)(a). the words "or a registered club" inserted by CTA 2010, s. 1177 and Sch. 1, para. 258(2), with effect for corporation tax purposes for accounting periods ending on or after 1 April 2010, and for income tax and capital gains tax purposes for the tax year 2010–11 and subsequent tax years.

In s. 257(1) the words "and the disposal is not one in relation to which section 151A(1) has effect" following para. (b) added by FA 1995, s. 72(5), with effect for 1995–96 and subsequent years of assessment.
In s. 257(2A), the words "as a result of Chapter 3 of Part 6 of CTA 2010" substituted for "section 587B of the Taxes Act" by CTA 2010, s. 1177 and Sch. 1, para. 258(3), with effect for corporation tax purposes for accounting periods ending on or after 1 April 2010, and for income tax and capital gains tax purposes for the tax year 2010–11 and subsequent tax years.
S. 257(2A) inserted by ITA 2007, s. 1027 and Sch. 1, para. 328 with effect from 6 April 2007.
S. 257(2B)(a)–(c) substituted by CTA 2010, s. 1177 and Sch. 1, para. 258(4), with effect for corporation tax purposes for accounting periods ending on or after 1 April 2010, and for income tax and capital gains tax purposes for the tax year 2010–11 and subsequent tax years.
Former s. 257(2B) inserted by ITA 2007, s. 1027 and Sch. 1, para. 328 with effect from 6 April 2007.
In s. 257(2C), the definitions of "relevant amount" and "relievable amount" omitted by CTA 2010, s. 1177 and Sch. 1, para. 258(5) and repealed by CTA 2010, s. 1181 and Sch. 3, Pt. 1, with effect for corporation tax purposes for accounting periods ending on or after 1 April 2010, and for income tax and capital gains tax purposes for the tax year 2010–11 and subsequent tax years.
S. 257(2C) inserted by ITA 2007, s. 1027 and Sch. 1, para. 328 with effect from 6 April 2007.
In s. 257(3). the words "a registered club" inserted by CTA 2010, s. 1177 and Sch. 1, para. 258(6)(a), with effect for corporation tax purposes for accounting periods ending on or after 1 April 2010, and for income tax and capital gains tax purposes for the tax year 2010–11 and subsequent tax years.
In s. 257(3). the words ", registered club" inserted , in both places where it occurs, by CTA 2010, s. 1177 and Sch. 1, para. 258(6)(b), with effect for corporation tax purposes for accounting periods ending on or after 1 April 2010, and for income tax and capital gains tax purposes for the tax year 2010–11 and subsequent tax years.
S. 257(5) inserted by CTA 2010, s. 1177 and Sch. 1, para. 258(7), with effect for corporation tax purposes for accounting periods ending on or after 1 April 2010, and for income tax and capital gains tax purposes for the tax year 2010–11 and subsequent tax years.

Derivations – (as originally enacted) – CGTA 1979, s. 146, as amended by FA 1981, s. 90(3).

Cross references – S. 17(1): acquisition and disposals deemed to be at market value where bargains otherwise than at arm's length or where consideration cannot be valued or in connection with payment for services.
S. 35(3)(d), (5): re-basing not to apply to disposal under s. 257(3) unless an election exists for the simplified scheme (re-basing of all assets held at 31 March 1982 irrespective of matters in s. 35(3)).
S. 38: deduction for allowable acquisition expenditure, including incidental costs, enhancement or title expenditure and incidental costs of disposal.
S. 55(5): for potential indexation allowance on 31 March 1982 value, asset treated as held on that date if all acquisitions since were on no gain, no loss disposals.
S. 71: deemed disposal where person becomes absolutely entitled to settled property as against the trustee.
S. 72: uplift to market value on termination by death of a life interest, defined by reference to the inclusion of a right to income or the use or occupation of settled property for the life or lives of another person or persons and certain annuities, but excluding rights contingent upon the discretion of the trustees.
S. 151A(1): an individual's gain or loss on qualifying disposal of ordinary shares in a company not chargeable or allowable if it was a venture capital trust both when the individual acquired and disposed of the shares.
Sch. 3, para. 1: person disposing of asset acquired through disposal under s. 257(3) after 31 March 1982 treated as holding asset at 31 March 1982 for purposes of re-basing.
ICTA 1988, S. 587B(3): consideration for gifts of shares to charities.
IHTA 1984, Sch. 3: list of bodies such as The National Gallery, The British Museum etc. to which gifts are deemed to be for national purposes etc.
FA 2002, Sch. 18, para. 3(b): s. 257 has effect as if a registered community amateur sports club were a charity.

Extra-statutory concessions – D47: removal of CGT charge, in certain circumstances, where disposal occurs during period of temporary loss of charitable status.

HMRC interpretations – IRInt. 23: if a disposal of qualifying corporate bonds, previously acquired in exchange for shares subject to s. 116(10), is to a charity such as to come within s. 257, there will be no charge on the deferred gain either on the donor or on the charity on a subsequent disposal of the bonds.

Notes – S. 257(2C) not rewritten in CTA 2010 because of amendment to TCGA 1992, s. 257(2B).
S. 21–34: general meaning of "disposal" and "asset".
S. 56(2): no gain, no loss calculated after applying indexation allowance.
S. 288: interpretation, including reference to sections as being those of this Act.

257A Tainted charity donations

257A(1) Section 257 does not apply in relation to–

(a) a tainted donation made by a person, or

(b) any associated donation.

257A(2) For the purposes of this section–

(a) **"tainted donation"** means a tainted donation within the meaning of Chapter 8 of Part 13 of ITA 2007 (tainted charity donations: removal of income tax reliefs etc) or Part 21C of CTA 2010 (tainted charity donations: removal of corporation tax relief), and

(b) **"associated donation"** means an associated donation within the meaning of section 809ZM of ITA 2010 or section 939F of CTA 2010.

History – S. 257A inserted by FA 2011, s. 27 and Sch. 3, para. 3, with effect in relation to relievable charity donations made on or after 1 April 2011.

258 Works of art etc.

258(1) [Repealed by FA 1998, s. 165 and Sch. 27, Pt. IV as respects any disposal on or after 17 March 1998.]

258(1A) A gain is not a chargeable gain if it accrues on a disposal made in the circumstances described in paragraph 1 of Schedule 14 to the Finance Act 2012 (gifts to the nation).

258(2) A gain shall not be a chargeable gain if it accrues on the disposal of an asset which is property which has been or could be designated under section 31 of the Inheritance Tax Act 1984 ("the 1984 Act") (designation and undertakings) and–

(a) the disposal is by way of sale by private treaty to a body mentioned in Schedule 3 to the 1984 Act (museums, etc.), or is to such a body otherwise than by sale, or

(b) the disposal is to the Board in pursuance of section 230 of the 1984 Act (acceptance of property in satisfaction of tax).

258(3) Subsection (4) below shall have effect in respect of the disposal of any asset which is property which has been or could be designated under section 31 of the 1984 Act, being–

(a) a disposal by way of gift, including a gift in settlement, or

(b) a disposal of settled property by the trustee on an occasion when, under section 71(1), the trustee is deemed to dispose of and immediately reacquire settled property (other than any disposal on which by virtue of section 73 no chargeable gain or allowable loss accrues to the trustee),

if the requisite undertaking described in section 31 of the 1984 Act (maintenance, preservation and access) is given by such person as the Board think appropriate in the circumstances of the case.

258(4) The person making a disposal to which subsection (3) above applies and the person acquiring the asset on the disposal shall be treated for all the purposes of this Act as if the asset was acquired from the one making the disposal for a consideration of such an amount as would secure that on the disposal neither a gain nor a loss would accrue to the one making the disposal.

258(5) If–

(a) there is a sale of the asset and inheritance tax is chargeable under section 32 of the 1984 Act (or would be chargeable if an inheritance tax undertaking as well as an undertaking under this section had been given), or

(b) the Board are satisfied that at any time during the period for which any such undertaking was given it has not been observed in a material respect,

the person selling that asset or, as the case may be, the owner of the asset shall be treated for the purposes of this Act as having sold the asset for a consideration equal to its market value, and, in the case of a failure to comply with the undertaking, having immediately reacquired it for a consideration equal to its market value.

258(6) The period for which an undertaking under this section is given shall be until the person beneficially entitled to the asset dies or it is disposed of, whether by sale or gift or otherwise; and if the asset subject to the undertaking is disposed of–

(a) otherwise than on sale, and

(b) without a further undertaking being given under this section,

subsection (5) above shall apply as if the asset had been sold to an individual.

References in this subsection to a disposal shall be construed without regard to any provision of this Act under which an asset is deemed to be disposed of.

258(7) Where under subsection (5) above a person is treated as having sold for a consideration equal to its market value any asset within section 31(1)(c), (d) or (e) of the 1984 Act, he shall also be treated as having sold and immediately reacquired for a consideration equal to its market value any asset associated with it; but the Board may direct that the preceding provisions of this subsection shall not have effect in any case in which it appears to them that the entity consisting of the asset and any assets associated with it has not been materially affected.

For the purposes of this subsection 2 or more assets are associated with each other if one of them is a building falling within section 31(1)(c) of the 1984 Act and the other or others such land or objects as, in relation to that building, fall within section 31(1)(d) or (e) of the 1984 Act.

258(8) If in pursuance of subsection (5) above a person is treated as having on any occasion sold an asset and inheritance tax becomes chargeable on the same occasion, then, in determining the value of the asset for the purposes of that tax, an allowance shall be made for the capital gains tax chargeable on any chargeable gain accruing on that occasion.

258(8A) Section 35A of the 1984 Act (variation of undertakings) shall have effect in relation to an undertaking given under this section as it has effect in relation to an undertaking given under section 30 of that Act.

258(9) In this section **"inheritance tax undertaking"** means an undertaking under Chapter II of Part II or section 78 of, or Schedule 5 to, the 1984 Act.

History – S. 258(1) repealed by FA 1998, s. 165 and Sch. 27, Pt. IV as respects any disposal on or after 17 March 1998.
S. 258(1A) inserted by FA 2012, s. 49 and Sch. 14. para. 34, with effect from 17 July 2012.
In s. 258(2), the words "which is property which has been or could be designated under section 31 of the Inheritance Tax Act 1984 ("the 1984 Act") (designation and undertakings)" substituted for the words "with respect to which an inheritance tax undertaking or

an undertaking under the following provisions of this section has been given" by SI 2009/730, art. 12(1)(a), with effect in relation to disposals on or after 6 April 2009.
In s. 258(2)(a), the words "the 1984 Act" substituted for the words "the Inheritance Tax Act 1984 ("the 1984 Act")" by SI 2009/730, art. 12(1)(b), with effect in relation to disposals on or after 6 April 2009.
In s. 258(2)(b), the words "or in accordance with directions given by the Treasury under section 50 or 51 of the Finance Act 1946", which appeared before "(acceptance of property", omitted by SI 2009/730, art. 12(1)(c), with effect in relation to disposals on or after 6 April 2009.
In s. 258(2)(b) the words "Inheritance Tax Act 1984 ("the 1984 Act")" substituted by FA 1998, s. 143(7) as respects any disposals on or after 17 March 1998.
S. 258(8A) inserted by FA 1998, s. 142 and Sch. 25, para. 9(1) as respects undertakings given on or after 31 July 1998, subject to retrospective effect of FA 1998, Sch. 25, para. 10.

Derivations – CGTA 1979, s. 147; FA 1985, s. 95(1)(b).

Cross references – FA 1998, Sch. 25, para. 10: validity of IHTA 1984 s. 35A undertakings given prior to 31 July 1998.
S. 35(3)(d), (5): re-basing not to apply to disposal under s. 258(4) unless an election exists for the simplified scheme (re-basing of all assets held at 31 March 1982 irrespective of matters in s. 35(3)).
S. 71(1), 73: deemed disposal where person becomes absolutely entitled to settled property as against the trustee, no chargeable gain accruing if the occasion is the death of the life tenant.
Sch. 3, para. 1: person disposing of asset acquired through disposal under s. 258(4) after 31 March 1982 treated as holding asset at 31 March 1982 for purposes of re-basing.
IHTA 1984, s. 26(2): land, buildings and artistic works etc.
IHTA 1984, s. 30–35 (Pt. II, Ch. II): designation by the Treasury of property, including buildings of outstanding architectural or historical significance and related land or objects (s. 31(1)(c)–(e) in respect of which a transfer of value is conditionally exempt (s. 30), becoming chargeable by reference to certain chargeable events (s. 32)).
IHTA 1984, s. 78: conditionally exempt occasions in relation to settlements without an interest in possession.
IHTA 1984, s. 79(2): exemption from ten-yearly charge on discretionary trusts etc.
IHTA 1984, s. 230: acceptance of property in satisfaction of inheritance tax and interest on overdue inheritance tax.
IHTA 1984, Sch. 3: list of bodies such as The National Gallery, The British Museum etc. to which gifts are deemed to be for national purposes etc.
IHTA 1984, Sch. 5: conditional exemption for deaths before 7 April 1976.
VATA 1994, Sch. 9, Grp. 11: VAT exemption for assets in respect of which any gain accruing is not a chargeable gain by virtue of s. 258(2).

Notes – S. 15: meaning of "chargeable gain".
S. 21–34: general meaning of "disposal" and "asset".
S. 56(2): no gain, no loss calculated after applying indexation allowance.
S. 68: meaning of "settled property".

259 Gifts to housing associations

259(1) Subsection (2) below shall apply where–

(a) a disposal of an estate or interest in land in the United Kingdom is made to a relevant housing provider otherwise than under a bargain at arm's length, and

(b) a claim for relief under this section is made by the transferor and the relevant housing provider.

259(2) Section 17(1) shall not apply; but if the disposal is by way of gift or for a consideration not exceeding the sums allowable as a deduction under section 38, then–

(a) the disposal and acquisition shall be treated for the purposes of this Act as being made for such consideration as to secure that neither a gain nor a loss accrues on the disposal, and

(b) where, after the disposal, the estate or interest is disposed of by the relevant housing provider, its acquisition by the person making the earlier disposal shall be treated for the purposes of this Act as the acquisition of the relevant housing provider.

259(3) In this section **"relevant housing provider"** means–

(a) a non-profit registered provider of social housing,

(b) a registered social landlord within the meaning of Part 1 of the Housing Act 1996,

(c) a body registered in the register maintained under section 20(1) of the Housing (Scotland) Act 2010, or

(d) a registered housing association within the meaning of Part 2 of the Housing (Northern Ireland) Order 1992.

259(4) In subsection (2)(b) above the first reference to a disposal includes a disposal to which section 146A(2) of the 1979 Act applied where the association which acquired the estate or interest in land on that disposal disposes of it after the coming into force of this section.

History – In s. 259(1)(a), the words "relevant housing provider" substituted for the words "relevant housing association" by the Housing and Regeneration Act 2008, Sch. 9, para. 19, with effect from 1 April 2010 (SI 2010/862).
In s. 259(1)(a) the word "relevant" substituted for the word "registered" by SI 1996/2325, art. 5 and Sch. 2, para. 20(3)(a), with effect from 1 October 1996.
In s. 259(1)(b), the words "relevant housing provider" substituted for the words "association" by the Housing and Regeneration Act 2008, Sch. 9, para. 19, with effect from 1 April 2010 (SI 2010/862).
In s. 259(2), the words "relevant housing provider" substituted for the words "association" (twice) by the Housing and Regeneration Act 2008, Sch. 9, para. 19, with effect from 1 April 2010 (SI 2010/862).
In s. 259(3)(c) the words "section 20(1) of the Housing (Scotland) Act 2010" substituted for the words "section 57 of the Housing (Scotland) Act 2001" by SI 2012/700, art. 4 and Schedule, para. 4(4), with effect from 1 April 2012.
S. 259(3) substituted by the Housing and Regeneration Act 2008, Sch. 9, para. 19, with effect from 1 April 2010 (SI 2010/862).
S. 259(3) substituted by SI 1996/2325, art. 5 and Sch. 2, para. 20(3)(b), with effect from 1 October 1996.

Derivations – CGTA 1979, s. 146A, as inserted by FA 1989, s. 125.

Cross references – S. 17(1): acquisition and disposals deemed to be at market value where bargains otherwise than at arm's length or where consideration cannot be valued or in connection with payment for services.
S. 38: deduction for allowable acquisition expenditure, including incidental costs, enhancement or title expenditure and incidental costs of disposal.
S. 55(5): for potential indexation allowance on 31 March 1982 value, asset treated as held on that date if all acquisitions since were on no gain, no loss disposals.

Notes – S. 21–34: general meaning of "disposal".
S. 56(2): no gain, no loss calculated after applying indexation allowance.
S. 288: interpretation, including reference to sections as being those of this Act.
TMA 1970, s. 42–43B: procedures and time limits for making claims.

260 Gifts on which inheritance tax is chargeable etc.

260(1) If–

(a) an individual or the trustees of a settlement (**"the transferor"**) make a disposal within subsection (2) below of an asset,

(b) the asset is acquired by an individual or the trustees of a settlement (**"the transferee"**), and

(c) a claim for relief under this section is made by the transferor and the transferee or, where the trustees of a settlement are the transferee, by the transferor alone,

then, subject to subsection (6) below and sections 169, 169B, 169C, 261 and 261ZA, subsection (3) below shall apply in relation to the disposal.

260(2) A disposal is within this subsection if it is made otherwise than under a bargain at arm's length and–

(a) is a chargeable transfer within the meaning of the Inheritance Tax Act 1984 (or would be but for section 19 of that Act) and is not a potentially exempt transfer (within the meaning of that Act),

(b) is an exempt transfer by virtue of–

  (i) section 24 of that Act (transfers to political parties),

  (ii) [Repealed by FA 1998, s. 165 and Sch. 27, Pt. IV as respects any disposal on or after 17 March 1998.]

  (iii) section 27 of that Act (transfers to maintenance funds for historic buildings etc.), or

  (iv) section 30 of that Act (transfers of designated property),

(c) is a disposition to which section 57A of that Act applies and by which the property disposed of becomes held on trusts of the kind referred to in subsection (1)(b) of that section (maintenance funds for historic buildings etc.),

(d) by virtue of subsection (4) of section 71 of that Act (accumulation and maintenance trusts) does not constitute an occasion on which inheritance tax is chargeable under that section,

(da) by virtue of subsection (2) of section 71B of that Act (trusts for bereaved minors) does not constitute an occasion on which inheritance tax is chargeable under that section,

(db) by virtue of subsection (2) of section 71E of that Act (age 18-to-25 trusts) does not constitute an occasion on which inheritance tax is charged under that section,

(e) by virtue of section 78(1) of that Act (transfers of works of art etc.) does not constitute an occasion on which tax is chargeable under Chapter III of Part III of that Act, or

(f) is a disposal of an asset comprised in a settlement where, as a result of the asset or part of it becoming comprised in another settlement, there is no charge, or a reduced charge, to inheritance tax by virtue of paragraph 9, 16 or 17 of Schedule 4 to that Act (transfers to maintenance funds for historic buildings etc.).

260(3) Where this subsection applies in relation to a disposal–

(a) the amount of any chargeable gain which, apart from this section, would accrue to the transferor on the disposal, and

(b) the amount of the consideration for which, apart from this section, the transferee would be regarded for the purposes of capital gains tax as having acquired the asset in question,

shall each be reduced by an amount equal to the held-over gain on the disposal.

260(4) Subject to subsection (5) below, the reference in subsection (3) above to the held-over gain on a disposal is a reference to the chargeable gain which would have accrued on that disposal apart from this section.

260(5) In any case where–

(a) there is actual consideration (as opposed to the consideration equal to the market value which is deemed to be given by virtue of any provision of this Act) for a disposal in respect of which a claim for relief is made under this section, and

(b) that actual consideration exceeds the sums allowable as a deduction under section 38, the held-over gain on the disposal shall be reduced by the excess referred to in paragraph (b) above.

260(6) Subsection (3) above does not apply in relation to a disposal of assets within section 115(1) on which a gain is deemed to accrue by virtue of section 116(10)(b).

260(6ZA) Subsections (6ZB) and (6ZC) apply in any case where–

(a) the disposal is a non-resident CGT disposal, and

(b) the transferee is resident in the United Kingdom.

260(6ZB) Subsections (3) and (4) have effect in relation to the disposal as if the reference to "chargeable gain" were a reference to "chargeable NRCGT gain".

260(6ZC) Subsection (5) has effect in relation to the disposal as if the reference to "the excess referred to in paragraph (b) above" were a reference to "the chargeable NRCGT gain which, ignoring this section and section 17(1), would accrue to the transferor on the disposal".

260(6A) [Omitted by FA 2004, s. 116 and Sch. 21, para. 5(3) and repealed by FA 2004, s. 326 and Sch. 42, Pt. 2(14).]

260(6B) [Omitted by FA 2004, s. 116 and Sch. 21, para. 5(4) and repealed by FA 2004, s. 326 and Sch. 42, Pt. 2(14).]

260(7) In the case of a disposal within subsection (2)(a) above (whether or not subsection (3) above applies in relation to it) there shall be allowed as a deduction in computing the chargeable gain accruing to the transferee on the disposal of the asset in question an amount equal to whichever is the lesser of–

(a) the inheritance tax attributable to the value of the asset; and

(b) the amount of the chargeable gain as computed apart from this subsection.

260(8) Where an amount of inheritance tax is varied after it has been taken into account under subsection (7) above, all necessary adjustments shall be made, whether by the making of an assessment to capital gains tax or by the discharge or repayment of such tax.

260(9) Where subsection (3) above applies in relation to a disposal which is deemed to occur by virtue of section 71(1) or 72(1), subsection (5) above shall not apply.

260(10) Where a disposal is partly within subsection (2) above, or is a disposal within paragraph (f) of that subsection on which there is a reduced charge such as is mentioned in that paragraph, the preceding provisions of this section shall have effect in relation to an appropriate part of the disposal.

History – In s. 260(1), the words ", 261 and 261ZA" substituted for the words "and 261" by FA 2015, s. 37 and Sch. 7, para. 31(2), with effect in relation to disposals made on or after 6 April 2015.
In s. 260(1), the references ",169B, 169C" were inserted after "169" by FA 2004, s. 116 and Sch. 21, para. 5(2) with effect, by virtue of FA 2004, Sch. 21, para. 10(4), in relation to disposals on or after 10 December 2003 (whenever any earlier disposal as mentioned in section 169B(3)(b) or 169C(3)(b) was made).
In s. 260(1) words "sections 169 and 261" substituted for "section 261" by FA 2000, s. 90(2) with effect in relation to disposals made on or after 9 November 1999.
S. 260(2)(b)(ii) repealed by FA 1998, s. 165 and Sch. 27, Pt. IV as respects any disposal on or after 17 March 1998.
S. 260(2)(da) inserted by FA 2006, s. 156 and Sch. 20, para. 32 with effect from 22 March 2006.
S. 260(2)(db) inserted by FA 2006, s. 156 and Sch. 20, para. 32 with effect from 22 March 2006.
In s. 260(5), the words " or, if part of the gain on the disposal is relieved under Schedule 6, by so much, if any, of that excess as exceeds the part so relieved" repealed by FA 1998, s. 165 and Sch. 27, Pt. III(31) which have effect in relation to disposals in the year 2003–04 and subsequent years of assessment.
S. 260(6ZA), (6ZB), and (6ZC) inserted by FA 2015, s. 37 and Sch. 7, para. 31(3), with effect in relation to disposals made on or after 6 April 2015.
S. 260(6A) omitted by FA 2004, s. 116 and Sch. 21, para. 5(3), and repealed by FA 2004, s. 326 and Sch. 42, Pt. 2(14), with effect, by virtue of FA 2004, Sch. 21, para. 10(8), in relation to gains accruing on or after 6 April 2004.
S. 260(6A) inserted by FA 1995, s. 67 and Sch. 13, para. 4(2) in relation to gains accruing and events occurring on or after 29 November 1994.
S. 260(6B) omitted by FA 2004, s. 116 and Sch. 21, para. 5(4), and repealed by FA 2004, s. 326 and Sch. 42, Pt. 2(14), with effect, by virtue of FA 2004, Sch. 21, para. 10(8), in relation to gains accruing on or after 6 April 2004.
S. 260(6B) inserted by FA 1995, s. 72(6) with effect for 1995–96 and subsequent years of assessment.
In s. 260(7), the words "(whether or not subsection (3) above applies in relation to it)" were inserted after the words "subsection (2)(a) above" by FA 2004, s. 116 and Sch. 21, para. 5(5) with effect, by virtue of FA 2004, Sch. 21, para. 10(9)], in relation to disposals on or after 6 April 2004.

Derivations – (as originally enacted) – CGTA 1979, s. 147A, as inserted by FA 1989, s. 124 and Sch. 14, para. 4.

Cross references – S. 74: elimination or reduction under s. 72(1)(b), 73(1)(a), (2) of chargeable gain on disposal where person becomes absolutely entitled to settled property or a life interest terminates on death (s. 71(1) or s. 72(1)) of asset gifted into trust restricted by reference to any held-over gain.
S. 81(7): deemed market value disposal of certain trust assets continues to apply to assets gifted into trust where s. 260(3) applied, notwithstanding restriction where emigration results from the death of a trustee within the previous six months.
S. 115(1), 116(10)(b): disposal of qualifying corporate bond obtained on a reorganisation etc. crystallises a notional market value gain by reference to the original holding.
S. 117(8): disposal within s. 260 does not result in a corporate bond issued before 14 March 1984 becoming a qualifying corporate bond.
S. 165(3): priority over hold-over relief for gifts of business assets.
S. 168: deemed chargeable gain where transferee emigrates.
S. 169A(2)(b): Cessation of trade by limited liability partnership.
S. 281(1): election for payment of tax by instalments not available to disposals within s. 260(3) unless held-over gain is less than the chargeable gain otherwise accruing.
Sch. 5B: postponement of gains on disposal of enterprise investment scheme shares following the making of a qualifying investment.
Sch. 5C: postponement of gains on disposal of shares in a venture capital trust following the making of a qualifying investment.

Sch. 6: retirement relief.
IHTA 1984, s. 19: annual exemption for inheritance tax.

Statements of practice – 8/92: HMRC's practice for dealing with valuation of assets where a claim to gifts hold-over relief has been made.

Other material – HMRC press release, 30 September 1996 (withdrawing SP E8): following *Begg-McBrearty (HMIT) v Stilwell* [1996] BTC 269, where Trustee Act 1925, s. 31 applies to property appointed after the commencement date of the Family Reform Act 1969 (1 January 1970) out of a settlement created before that date, the beneficiary's interest in possession is regarded as arising at age 18.

Notes – S. 15: meaning of "chargeable gain".
S. 21–34: general meaning of "disposal".
S. 68: meaning of "settled property".
TMA 1970, s. 29: assessing procedure.
TMA 1970, s. 42–43B: procedures and time limits for making claims.
IHTA 1984, s. 2: meaning of "chargeable transfer".
IHTA 1984, s. 3A: potentially exempt transfers.

261 Section 260 relief: gifts to non-residents

261(1) Subject to section 261ZA, section 260(3), shall not apply where the transferee is not resident in the United Kingdom.

261(2) Section 260(3) shall not apply where the transferee is an individual who–

(a) though resident in the United Kingdom, is regarded for the purposes of any double taxation relief arrangements as resident in a territory outside the United Kingdom, and

(b) by virtue of the arrangements would not be liable in the United Kingdom to tax on a gain arising on a disposal of the asset occurring immediately after its acquisition.

History – In s. 261(1), the words "Subject to section 261ZA, section 260(3)" substituted for the words "Section 260(3)" by FA 2015, s. 37 and Sch. 7, para. 32, with effect in relation to disposals made on or after 6 April 2015.
In s. 261(1), the words "not resident" substituted for the words "neither resident nor ordinarily resident" by FA 2013, s. 219 and Sch. 46, para. 104(2), with effect in relation to a person's liability to capital gains tax for the tax year 2013–14 or any subsequent tax year, without prejudice to any provision in FA 2013, Sch. 46, Pt. 3 about the application of a particular amendment.
In s. 261(2)(a), the words "or ordinarily resident" omitted by FA 2013, s. 219 and Sch. 46, para. 104(3), with effect in relation to a person's liability to capital gains tax for the tax year 2013–14 or any subsequent tax year, without prejudice to any provision in FA 2013, Sch. 46, Pt. 3 about the application of a particular amendment.

Derivations – CGTA 1979, s. 147B, as inserted by FA 1989, s. 124 and Sch. 14, para. 4.

Notes – S. 9: meaning of "resident" and "ordinarily resident".
S. 288: interpretation, including meaning of "double taxation relief arrangements".

261ZA Gifts of UK residential property interests to non-residents

261ZA(1) This section applies where the disposal in relation to which a claim could be made under section 260 is a disposal of a UK residential property interest to a transferee who is not resident in the United Kingdom and, ignoring section 260–

(a) a gain would accrue to the transferor on the disposal, and

(b) on the assumption that the disposal is a non-resident CGT disposal (whether or not that is the case), that gain would be a chargeable NRCGT gain (see section 57B and Schedule 4ZZB).

261ZA(2) Section 260(3) has effect in relation to the disposal as if it read–

> "**260(3)** Where this subsection applies in relation to a disposal, the amount of any chargeable gain which, apart from this section, would accrue to the transferor on the disposal, shall be reduced by an amount equal to the held-over gain on the disposal."

261ZA(3) Where the disposal is a non-resident CGT disposal–

(a) section 260(3), as modified by subsection (2) of this section, and section 260(4) have effect in relation to the disposal as if the references to "chargeable gain" were references to "chargeable NRCGT gain", and

(b) section 260(5) has effect in relation to the disposal as if the reference to "the excess referred to in paragraph (b) above" were a reference to "the chargeable NRCGT gain which, ignoring this section and section 17(1), would accrue to the transferor on the disposal".

261ZA(4) Where a claim for relief is made under section 260 in relation to the disposal mentioned in subsection (1), on a subsequent disposal by the transferee of the whole or part of the interest in UK land which is the subject of the disposal mentioned in subsection (1), the whole or a corresponding part of the held-over gain (see section 260(4))–

(a) is deemed to accrue to the transferee (in addition to any gain or loss that actually accrues on that subsequent disposal), and

(b) (if that would not otherwise be the case) is to be treated as a chargeable NRCGT gain accruing on a non-resident CGT disposal.

261ZA(5) Where the subsequent disposal mentioned in subsection (4) is a disposal within section 260(2)(a), subsection (7) of that section has effect in relation to the disposal as if–

TCGA 1992

(a) the reference to "the chargeable gain accruing to the transferee on the disposal of the asset" were a reference to the chargeable gain accruing on the disposal as computed apart from subsection (4), and

(b) the reference in section 260(7)(b) to "the chargeable gain" were a reference to–

(i) the chargeable gain (or, where the disposal is a non-resident CGT disposal, the chargeable NRCGT gain) accruing on the disposal, and

(ii) the held-over gain deemed to accrue under subsection (4).

261ZA(6) In this section, **"interest in UK land"** has the meaning given by paragraph 2 of Schedule B1.

History – S. 261ZA inserted by FA 2015, s. 37 and Sch. 7, para. 33, with effect in relation to disposals made on or after 6 April 2015.

KNOW-HOW

261A Disposal of know-how as part of disposal of all or part of a trade

261A(1) This section applies if–

(a) a person carrying on a trade receives consideration for the disposal of know-how which has been used in the trade, and

(b) the know-how is disposed of as part of the disposal of all or part of the trade.

261A(2) If, as a result of section 194 of ITTOIA 2005, the consideration is treated for income tax purposes as–

(a) a capital receipt for goodwill (in relation to the person disposing of the know-how), or

(b) a capital payment for goodwill (in relation to the person acquiring the know-how),

the consideration is treated for capital gains tax purposes in the same way.

261A(3) This section has effect as if it were contained in Chapter 14 of Part 2 of ITTOIA 2005.

History – S. 261A inserted by ITTOIA 2005, s. 882 and Sch. 1, para. 444 which, in accordance with ITTOIA 2005, s. 883, have effect, for income tax purposes, for tax year 2005–06 and subsequent tax years, and, for corporation tax purposes, for accounting periods ending after 5 April 2005.

DEDUCTION OF TRADING LOSSES OR POST-CESSATION EXPENDITURE ETC

261B Treating trade loss etc as CGT loss

261B(1) A person may make a claim under this section if–

(a) relief is available to the person under section 64 or 128 of ITA 2007 (trade or employment loss relief against general income) for a tax year in relation to an amount of loss, and

(b) the person makes a claim under that section for the amount to be deducted in calculating the person's net income for the tax year.

261B(2) A person may also make a claim under this section if–

(a) relief is available to the person as mentioned in subsection (1)(a) for a tax year in relation to an amount of loss, but

(b) the person's total income for the tax year is nil or does not include any income from which the amount can be deducted.

261B(3) A claim under this section is for determining so much of the amount of the loss ("the relevant amount") as–

(a) is not deducted in calculating the person's net income for the tax year, and

(b) has not already been taken into account for the purposes of any relief for any other tax year or any year of assessment (whether under ITA 2007, this section or otherwise).

261B(4) When the relevant amount can no longer be varied–

(a) by the tribunal on appeal, or

(b) on the order of a court,

it is treated for the purposes of capital gains tax as an allowable loss accruing to the person in the year of assessment corresponding to the tax year.

261B(5) But so much of the relevant amount as exceeds the maximum amount (see section 261C) is not to be treated for the purposes of capital gains tax as an allowable loss.

261B(6) The excess may, however, be used in giving effect to any other loss relief under Part 4 of ITA 2007 (depending on the terms of the relief).

261B(7) The amount treated as an allowable loss under this section–

(a) is no longer to be regarded as an amount available for income tax relief, and

(b) is not to be deductible from chargeable gains accruing to a person in any year of assessment that begins after the person has permanently ceased to carry on the trade, profession, vocation, employment or office in which the loss was made.

261B(8) A claim under this section must be made on or before the first anniversary of the normal self-assessment filing date for the tax year in which the loss was made in the trade, profession, vocation, employment or office.

261B(9) In this section **"normal self-assessment filing date"**, **"tax year"** and **"total income"** have the same meaning as in the Income Tax Acts (see section 989 of ITA 2007).

History – In s. 261B(4)(a) the word "tribunal" substituted for the word "Commissioners" by SI 2009/56, art. 3(1) and Sch. 1, para. 182, operative from 1 April 2009, subject to transitional and saving provisions in SI 2009/56, Sch. 3.
S. 261B inserted by ITA 2007, s. 1027 and Sch. 1, para. 329 with effect from 6 April 2007.

Cross references – FA 2014, s. 253(5) (promoters of tax avoidance schemes: duty of persons to notify Commissioners): circumstances under which a report under FA 2014, s. 253 must be made in a claim made under s. 261B.

261C Meaning of "the maximum amount" for purposes of section 261B

261C(1) For the purposes of section 261B **"the maximum amount"** is the amount on which the person would be chargeable to capital gains tax for the year of assessment if–

(a) the provisions mentioned below were ignored, and

(b) no account were taken of the event mentioned below.

261C(2) The provisions are–

(a) [omitted by FA 2008, s. 8 and Sch. 2, para. 39.]

(b) section 3(1) (annual exempt amount), and

(c) section 261B.

261C(3) The event is any event–

(a) which occurs after the date on which the relevant amount (see section 261B(3)) can no longer be varied by the tribunal on appeal or on the order of a court, and

(b) in consequence of which the amount chargeable to capital gains tax is reduced as a result of an enactment relating to capital gains tax.

History – S. 261C(2)(a) omitted by FA 2008, s. 8 and Sch. 2, para. 39 with effect in relation to chargeable gains accruing or treated as accruing in the tax year 2008–09 or any subsequent tax year (FA 2008, Sch. 2, para. 56(3)).
In s. 261C(3)(a) the word "tribunal" substituted for the word "Commissioners" by SI 2009/56, art. 3(1) and Sch. 1, para. 183, operative from 1 April 2009, subject to transitional and saving provisions in SI 2009/56, Sch. 3.
S. 261C inserted by ITA 2007, s. 1027 and Sch. 1, para. 329, with effect from 6 April 2007.

261D Treating excess post-cessation trade or property relief as CGT loss

261D(1) A person may make a claim under this section if–

(a) relief is available to the person under section 96 or 125 of ITA 2007 (post-cessation trade or property relief) for a tax year in relation to an amount, and

(b) the person makes a claim under that section to deduct the amount in calculating the person's net income for the tax year.

261D(2) A person may also make a claim under this section if–

(a) relief is available to the person as mentioned in subsection (1)(a) for a tax year in relation to an amount, but

(b) the person's total income for the tax year is nil.

261D(3) A claim under this section is for treating for the purposes of capital gains tax so much of the amount as is not deducted in calculating the person's net income for the tax year ("the relevant amount") as an allowable loss accruing to the person in the year of assessment corresponding to the tax year.

261D(4) But so much of the relevant amount as exceeds the maximum amount (see section 261E) is not to be treated for the purposes of capital gains tax as an allowable loss.

261D(5) The relevant amount is no longer to be regarded as an amount available for income tax relief.

261D(6) A claim under this section must be made on or before the first anniversary of the normal self-assessment filing date for the tax year mentioned in subsection (1) or (2) (as the case may be).

261D(7) In this section **"normal self-assessment filing date"**, **"tax year"** and **"total income"** have the same meaning as in the Income Tax Acts (see section 989 of ITA 2007).

History – S. 261D inserted by ITA 2007, s. 1027 and Sch. 1, para. 329, with effect from 6 April 2007.

261E Meaning of "the maximum amount" for purposes of section 261D

261E(1) For the purposes of section 261D **"the maximum amount"** is the amount on which the person would be chargeable to capital gains tax for the year of assessment if the following were ignored.

261E(2) The matters to be ignored are–

(a) any allowable losses falling to be carried forward to that year from a previous year for the purposes of section 2(2),

(b) section 3(1) (annual exempt amount), and

(c) any relief under section 261B or 261D.

History – S. 261E inserted by ITA 2007, s. 1027 and Sch. 1, para. 329, with effect from 6 April 2007.

REPURCHASE PRICE UNDER REPOS

261F Deemed manufactured payments: effect on repurchase price

261F(1) This section applies if–

(a) the repurchase price of UK shares, UK securities or overseas securities is treated by section 604(2), (4) or (5) of ITA 2007 (deemed increase in repurchase price: repos and options) as increased for the purposes of section 607 of that Act (treatment of price differences under repos),

(b) condition A or B is met, and

(c) section 263A does not apply.

261F(2) Condition A is that, as a result of the increase, there is no difference for the purposes of section 607 of that Act between the sale price and the repurchase price.

261F(3) Condition B is that, as a result of an exception in section 608 of that Act, section 607 of that Act does not apply.

261F(4) The deemed increase of the repurchase price also has effect for capital gains tax purposes.

261F(5) Expressions used in this section and in section 605 of ITA 2007 (deemed increase in repurchase price: other income tax purposes) have the same meanings in this section as in that section.

History – S. 261F inserted by ITA 2007, s. 1027 and Sch. 1, para. 330, with effect from 6 April 2007.

261G Price differences under repos: effect on repurchase price

261G(1) Subsections (2) and (3) apply if–

(a) section 607 of ITA 2007 (treatment of price differences under repos) applies,

(b) an amount is treated under that section as a payment of interest, and

(c) section 263A does not apply.

261G(2) If the repurchase price is more than the sale price, the repurchase price is treated for capital gains tax purposes as reduced by the amount of the payment of interest.

261G(3) If the sale price is more than the repurchase price, the repurchase price is treated for capital gains tax purposes as increased by the amount of the payment of interest.

261G(4) Expressions used in this section and in section 609 of ITA 2007 (additional income tax consequences of price differences under repos) have the same meanings in this section as in that section.

History – S. 261G inserted by ITA 2007, s. 1027 and Sch. 1, para. 331, with effect from 6 April 2007.

261H Power to modify section 261G in non-arm's length case

261H(1) The Treasury may by regulations provide for section 261G to apply with modifications if the exception in section 608(2) of ITA 2007 (agreement not at arm's length) would otherwise prevent it from applying.

261H(2) Regulations under this section may make different provision for different cases.

261H(3) Regulations under this section may contain incidental, supplemental, consequential and transitional provision and savings.

261H(4) The incidental, supplemental, and consequential provision may include modifications of section 261F (deemed manufactured payments: effect on repurchase price).

261H(5) In this section **"modifications"** includes exceptions and omissions.

261H(6) Accordingly, the power in subsection (1) includes power to provide for any provision of section 261G not to apply in relation to the case mentioned in that subsection.

History – S. 261H inserted by ITA 2007, s. 1027 and Sch. 1, para. 332, with effect from 6 April 2007.

MISCELLANEOUS RELIEFS AND EXEMPTIONS

262 Chattel exemption

262(1) Subject to this section a gain accruing on a disposal of an asset which is tangible movable property shall not be a chargeable gain if the amount or value of the consideration for the disposal does not exceed £6,000.

262(2) Where the amount or value of the consideration for the disposal of an asset which is tangible movable property exceeds £6,000, there shall be excluded from any chargeable gain accruing on the disposal so much of it as exceeds five-thirds of the difference between–

(a) the amount or value of the consideration, and

(b) £6,000.

262(3) Subsections (1) and (2) above shall not affect the amount of an allowable loss accruing on the disposal of an asset, but for the purposes of computing under this Act the amount of a loss accruing on the disposal of tangible movable property the consideration for the disposal shall, if less than £6,000, be deemed to be £6,000 and the losses which are allowable losses shall be restricted accordingly.

262(4) If 2 or more assets which have formed part of a set of articles of any description all owned at one time by one person are disposed of by that person, and–

(a) to the same person, or

(b) to persons who are acting in concert or who are connected persons,

whether on the same or different occasions, the 2 or more transactions shall be treated as a single transaction disposing of a single asset, but with any necessary apportionments of the reductions in chargeable gains, and in allowable losses, under subsections (2) and (3) above.

262(5) If the disposal is of a right or interest in or over tangible movable property–

(a) in the first instance subsections (1), (2) and (3) above shall be applied in relation to the asset as a whole, taking the consideration as including the market value of what remains undisposed of, in addition to the actual consideration,

(b) where the sum of the actual consideration and that market value exceeds £6,000, the part of any chargeable gain that is excluded from it under subsection (2) above shall be so much of the gain as exceeds five-thirds of the difference between that sum and £6,000 multiplied by the fraction equal to the actual consideration divided by the said sum, and

(c) where that sum is less than £6,000 any loss shall be restricted under subsection (3) above by deeming the consideration to be the actual consideration plus the said fraction of the difference between the said sum and £6,000.

262(6) This section shall not apply–

(a) in relation to a disposal of commodities of any description by a person dealing on a terminal market or dealing with or through a person ordinarily engaged in dealing on a terminal market, or

(b) in relation to a disposal of currency of any description.

Derivations – CGTA 1979, s. 128, as amended by FA 1989, s. 123.

Cross references – TMA 1970, s. 12(2): unless the consideration for their acquisition exceeded the given limit, chattels are excluded from requirements to divulge information about assets for capital gains tax purposes unless they fall within s. 262(6).
FA 1998, Sch. 18, para. 13(2): exemption from requirements to provide details of assets (for corporation tax purposes), upon service of appropriate notice, does not apply to assets within s. 262(6).

HMRC interpretations – IRInt. 200: capital gains tax treatment of wines and spirits.
IRInt. 206: capital gains tax treatment of shotguns: valuation of single shotguns within a pair for which overall consideration is £12,000 or less.

Notes – S. 15: meaning of "chargeable gain".
S. 16: meaning of "allowable loss".
S. 21–34: general meaning of "disposal".
For disposals before 6 April 1989 the exemption limit was £3,000.

263 Passenger vehicles

263 A mechanically propelled road vehicle constructed or adapted for the carriage of passengers, except for a vehicle of a type not commonly used as a private vehicle and unsuitable to be so used, shall not be a chargeable asset; and accordingly no chargeable gain or allowable loss shall accrue on its disposal.

Derivations – CGTA 1979, s. 130.

Cross references – TMA 1970, s. 12(2): assets within s. 263 excluded from requirements to divulge information about assets for capital gains tax purposes.
FA 1998, Sch. 18, para. 13(2): exemption from requirements to provide details of assets (for corporation tax purposes), upon service of appropriate notice, applies to vehicles within s. 263.

HMRC interpretations – IRInt. 86: vehicles of a type not commonly used as private vehicles and unsuitable to be so used may be treated as wasting assets and thus not giving rise to a chargeable gain on disposal.

Notes – S. 15: meaning of "chargeable gain".
S. 16: meaning of "allowable loss".

263AZA Renewables obligation certificates for domestic microgeneration

263AZA(1) A gain accruing to an individual on a disposal of a renewables obligation certificate is not a chargeable gain if–

(a) the individual acquired the certificate in connection with the generation of electricity by a microgeneration system,

(b) the system is installed at or near domestic premises occupied by the individual, and

(c) the individual intends that the amount of electricity generated by it will not significantly exceed the amount of electricity consumed in those premises.

263AZA(2) In subsection (1)–

"domestic premises" means premises used wholly or mainly as a separate private dwelling,

"microgeneration system" means any plant (including any equipment, apparatus or appliance) or system of plant for generating electricity or producing heat–

(a) which, in generating electricity or (as the case may be) producing heat, relies wholly or mainly on a source of energy or a technology mentioned in subsection (7) of section 82 of the Energy Act 2004, and

(b) whose capacity to generate electricity or (as the case may be) to produce heat does not exceed the capacity mentioned in subsection (8) of that section,

"renewables obligation certificate" means a certificate issued under section 32B of the Electricity Act 1989 or Article 54 of the Energy (Northern Ireland) Order 2003.

History – In s. 263AZA(2), definition of "microgeneration system" substituted by Deregulation Act 2015, s. 57(3)(a), with effect from the end of the period of 2 months beginning with 26 March 2015.

S. 263AZA inserted by FA 2007, s. 21(2), with effect in relation to disposals made on or after 6 April 2007 (FA 2007, s. 21(4)).

Cross references – ITTOIA 2005, s. 782A: income tax exemption for the sale of electricity produced by domestic microgeneration, for 2007–08 onwards.

ITTOIA 2005, s. 782B: income tax exemption for the receipt of renewables obligation certificates for domestic microgeneration, for 2007–08 onwards.

Notes – In s. 262AZA(2) the term "microgeneration system" is defined by reference to s. 4(9) of the *Climate Change and Sustainable Energy Act* 2006, where it means: any plant or system of plant for generating electricity or producing heat which, in generating electricity or (as the case may be) producing heat, relies wholly or mainly on a source of energy or a technology mentioned in s. 82(7) of the *Energy Act* 2004, and whose capacity to generate electricity energy or (as the case may be) to produce heat does not exceed the capacity mentioned in s. 82(8) of the *Energy Act* 2004.

263ZA Former employees: employment-related liabilities

263ZA(1) This section applies if–

(a) a deduction of the amount of one or more deductible payments may be made under section 555 of ITEPA 2003 (former employee entitled to deduction in calculating net income in respect of liabilities related to the former employment) in calculating a former employee's net income for a tax year, and

(b) the total amount which may be deducted exceeds the remaining total income for that year.

263ZA(2) In this section **"excess relief"** means the amount of the difference between–

(a) the total amount which may be deducted, and

(b) the remaining total income.

263ZA(2A) In this section **"the remaining total income"**, in relation to a tax year, means the former employee's total income for the tax year less reliefs already deducted for the tax year at Step 2 of the calculation in section 23 of ITA 2007 for the purpose of calculating the former employee's income tax liability.

263ZA(3) The amount of the excess relief may be treated as an allowable loss accruing to the former employee for that tax year.

This subsection applies only if the former employee makes a claim for the purpose.

263ZA(4) But no relief is available under subsection (3) in respect of any amount of the excess relief that exceeds the maximum amount.

263ZA(5) For the purposes of this section the **"maximum amount,"** in relation to the excess relief for a tax year, means the amount on which the former employee would be chargeable to capital gains tax for that year if the following were disregarded–

(a) any relief available under this section,

(b) any allowable losses falling to be carried forward to that year from a previous year for the purposes of section 2(2),

(c) section 3(1) (the annual exempt amount),

(d) any relief under section 261B (deduction of trading losses), and

(e) any relief under section 261D (relief for post-cessation expenditure).

263ZA(6) A former employee may make a claim under subsection (3) and a claim under section 555(3) of ITEPA 2003 in the same notice.

History – In s. 263ZA(1)(a), the words "in calculating net income" substituted for "from total income" and the words "in calculating a former employee's net income" substituted for "when computing a former employee's total income" by ITA 2007, s. 1027 and Sch. 1, para. 333(2)(a) and (b), with effect from 6 April 2007.
In s. 263ZA(1)(b), the words "the remaining total income" substituted for "the total income" by ITA 2007, s. 1027 and Sch. 1, para. 333(3), with effect from 6 April 2007.
In s. 263ZA(2)(b), the words "the remaining total income" substituted for "the total income" by ITA 2007, s. 1027 and Sch. 1, para. 333(4), with effect from 6 April 2007.
S. 263ZA(2A) inserted by ITA 2007, s. 1027 and Sch. 1, para. 333(5), with effect from 6 April 2007.
In s. 263ZA(5)(d), the words "under section 261B" substituted for "against capital gains tax under section 72 of the Finance Act 1991" by ITA 2007, s. 1027 and Sch. 1, para. 333(6)(a), with effect from 6 April 2007.
In s. 263ZA(5)(e), the words "under section 261D" substituted for "against capital gains tax under section 90(4) of the Finance Act 1995" by ITA 2007, s. 1027 and Sch. 1, para. 333(6)(b), with effect from 6 April 2007.
S. 263ZA inserted by ITEPA 2003, Sch. 6, para. 217 with effect for 2003–04 and subsequent tax years.

Cross references – ITEPA 2003, s. 555: supplementary provisions about employee benefit trusts – former employee entitled to deduction from total income.

263A Agreements for sale and repurchase of securities: capital gains tax

263A(A1) For the purposes of this section there is a repo in respect of securities if–

(a) a person ("the original owner") has agreed to sell the securities to another person ("the interim holder"), and

(b) the original owner or a person connected with the original owner–

(i) is required to buy back the securities by the agreement or a related agreement,

(ii) is required to buy back the securities as a result of the exercise of an option acquired under the agreement or a related agreement, or

(iii) exercises an option to buy back the securities which was acquired under the agreement or a related agreement.

263A(1) Subject to subsections (3) and (4) below, in any case where under a repo in respect of securities the original owner has transferred the securities to the interim holder–

(a) the acquisition of the securities in question by the interim holder and the disposal of those securities by him to the repurchaser; and

(b) except where the repurchaser is or may be different from the original owner, the disposal of those securities by the original owner and any acquisition of those securities by the original owner as the repurchaser,

shall be disregarded for the purposes of capital gains tax.

263A(1A) If, at any time after the acquisition mentioned in subsection (1)(a) above, it becomes apparent that the interim holder will not dispose of the securities to the repurchaser, the interim holder shall be treated for the purposes of capital gains tax as acquiring them at that time for a consideration equal to their market value at that time.

263A(1B) If, at any time after the disposal mentioned in subsection (1)(b) above, it becomes apparent that the original owner will not acquire the securities as the repurchaser, the original owner shall be treated for the purposes of capital gains tax as disposing of them at that time for a consideration equal to their market value at that time.

263A(2) [Omitted by FA 2007, s. 47(2) and Sch. 14, para. 12(4); repealed by FA 2007, s. 114 and Sch 27, Pt. 2(14).]

263A(3) Subsection (1) above does not apply if–

(a) the agreement or agreements under which provision is made for the sale and repurchase are not such as would be entered into by persons dealing with each other at arm's length; or

(b) any of the benefits or risks arising from fluctuations, before the repurchase takes place, in the market value of the securities sold accrues to, or falls on, the interim holder.

263A(4) Subsection (1) above does not apply in relation to any disposal or acquisition of qualifying corporate bonds in a case where the securities disposed of by the original owner or those acquired by him, or by any other person, as the repurchaser are not such bonds.

263A(5) [Omitted by FA 2013, s. 28 and Sch. 12, para. 9(4).]

263A(6) This section does not apply for the purposes of corporation tax in respect of chargeable gains.

History – The heading of s. 263A substituted by FA 2007, s. 47(2) and Sch. 14, para. 12(6), with effect in relation to arrangements coming into force on or after 1 October 2007, by virtue of SI 2007/2483, art. 3. The heading read as follows: "Agreements for sale and repurchase of securities".
S. 263A(A1) inserted by FA 2013, s. 28 and Sch. 12, para. 9(2), with effect for the tax year 2013–14 and subsequent tax years, subject to FA 2013, Sch. 12, para. 18.
In s. 263A(1) the words "where under a repo in respect of securities the original owner has transferred the securities to the interim holder" substituted for the words "falling within section 607(1) of ITA 2007 (treatment of price differences under repos)" by FA 2013, s. 28 and Sch. 12, para. 9(3), with effect for the tax year 2013–14 and subsequent tax years, subject to FA 2013, Sch. 12, para. 18.
In s. 263A(1) the words "Subject to subsections (3) and (4) below, in any case falling within section 607(1) of ITA 2007 (treatment of price differences under repos)" substituted for the former wording, "Subject to subsections (2) to (4) below, in any case falling within subsection (1) of section 730A of the Taxes Act or section 607(1) of ITA 2007 (treatment of price differential on sale and repurchase of securities) and in any case which would fall within section 730A(1) of the Taxes Act if the sale price and the repurchase price were different", by FA 2007, s. 47(2) and Sch. 14, para. 12(2), with effect in relation to arrangements coming into force on or after 1 October 2007, by virtue of SI 2007/2483, art. 3.
In s. 263A(1), the words "or section 607(1) of ITA 2007" inserted and the words "section 703A(1) of the Taxes Act" substituted for "that subsection" by ITA 2007, s. 1027 and Sch. 1, para. 334(2)(a) and (b) with effect from 6 April 2007.
S. 263A(1A) and (1B) inserted by FA 2007, s. 47(2) and Sch. 14, para. 12(3), with effect in relation to arrangements coming into force on or after 1 October 2007, by virtue of SI 2007/2483, art. 3.
S. 263A(2) omitted by FA 2007, s. 47(2) and Sch. 14, para. 12(4) and repealed by FA 2007, s. 114 and Sch 27, Pt. 2(14), with effect in relation to arrangements coming into force on or after 1 October 2007, by virtue of SI 2007/2483, art. 3.
S. 263A(5) omitted by FA 2013, s. 28 and Sch. 12, para. 9(4), with effect for the tax year 2013–14 and subsequent tax years, subject to FA 2013, Sch. 12, para. 18.
Formers. 263A(5) and s. 263A(6) substituted by FA 2007, s. 47(2) and Sch. 14, para. 12(5), with effect in relation to arrangements coming into force on or after 1 October 2007, by virtue of SI 2007/2483, art. 3.
In former s. 263A(5), the words "For corporation tax purposes" inserted by ITA 2007, s. 1027 and Sch. 1, para. 334(3) with effect from 6 April 2007.
S. 263A(6) inserted by ITA 2007, s. 1027 and Sch. 1, para. 334(4) with effect from 6 April 2007.
S. 263A inserted by FA 1995, s. 80(4) where the agreement to sell the securities is entered into on or after 1 May 1995.

Cross references – Sch. 7AC, para. 12: relief for disposal of substantial shareholding: effect where shares transferred under a repurchase agreement.
ICTA 1988, s. 730A: treatment of price differential on sale and repurchase of securities.
ICTA 1988, s. 730BB: exchange gains and losses on sale and repurchase of securities.
ICTA 1988, s. 737C: provisions relating to deemed manufactured payments.
ICTA 1988, s. 737E(4) and (6)(b): power to modify s. 263A.
SI 1995/3220, reg. 5: modifications of s. 263A in cases where securities are redeemed instead of being repurchased, and where other securities are substituted for those originally transferred.

263AA Section 263A: interpretation

263AA(1) Subsections (2) to (7) apply for the purposes of section 263A.

263AA(2) References to buying back securities include references to–

(a) buying similar securities, and

(b) in the case of a person connected with the person who is the original owner under the repo, buying the securities sold by the original owner or similar securities.

263AA(3) Subsection (2) applies even if the person buying the securities has not held them before.

263AA(4) References to repurchase or a repurchaser are to be read accordingly.

263AA(5) For the purposes of subsection (2) securities are similar if they give their holders–

(a) the same rights against the same persons as to capital and distributions, interest and dividends, and

(b) the same remedies to enforce those rights.

263AA(6) Subsection (5) applies even if there is a difference in–

(a) the total nominal amounts of the securities,

(b) the form in which they are held, or

(c) the manner in which they can be transferred.

263AA(7) Agreements are related if they are entered into in pursuance of the same arrangement (regardless of the date on which either agreement is entered into).

263AA(8) In section 263A and this section **"securities"** means–

(a) shares in a company wherever resident,

(b) loan stock or other securities of–

 (i) the government of the United Kingdom,

 (ii) a local authority in the United Kingdom,

 (iii) another public authority in the United Kingdom,

 (iv) a company resident in the United Kingdom or other body resident in the United Kingdom, or

(c) *shares, loan stock, stock* or other securities issued by–

 (i) a government, local authority or other public authority of a territory outside the United Kingdom, or

 (ii) another body of persons not resident in the United Kingdom.

History – S. 263AA inserted by FA 2013, s. 28 and Sch. 12, para. 10, with effect for the tax year 2013–14 and subsequent tax years, subject to FA 2013, Sch. 12, para. 18.

263B Stock lending arrangements

263B(1) In this section **"stock lending arrangement"** means so much of any arrangements between two persons (**"the borrower"** and **"the lender"**) as are arrangements under which–

(a) the lender transfers securities to the borrower otherwise than by way of sale; and

(b) a requirement is imposed on the borrower to transfer those securities back to the lender otherwise than by way of sale.

263B(2) Subject to the following provisions of this section and sections 263C(2) and 263CA(3) and (5), the disposals and acquisitions made in pursuance of any stock lending arrangement shall be disregarded for the purposes of capital gains tax.

263B(3) Where–

(a) the borrower under any stock lending arrangement disposes of any securities transferred to him under the arrangement,

(b) that disposal is made otherwise than in the discharge of the requirement for the transfer of securities back to the lender, and

(c) that requirement, so far as it relates to the securities disposed of, has been or will be discharged by the transfer of securities other than those transferred to the borrower,

any question relating to the acquisition of the securities disposed of shall be determined (without prejudice to the provisions of Chapter I of Part IV) as if the securities disposed of were the securities with which that requirement (so far as relating to the securities disposed of) has been or will be discharged.

263B(4) Where, in the case of any stock lending arrangement, it becomes apparent, at any time after the making of the transfer by the lender, that the requirement for the borrower to make a transfer back to the lender will not be complied with–

(a) the lender shall be deemed for the purposes of this Act to have made a disposal at that time of the securities transferred to the borrower for a consideration equal to their market value at that time;

(b) the borrower shall be deemed to have acquired them at that time for that consideration; and

(c) subsection (3) above shall have effect in relation to any disposal before that time by the borrower of securities transferred to him by the lender as if the securities deemed to have been acquired by the borrower in accordance with paragraph (b) above were to be used for discharging a requirement to transfer securities back to the lender.

This subsection does not apply where section 263CA (insolvency of borrower) applies.

263B(5) References in this section, in relation to a person to whom securities are transferred, to the transfer of those securities back to another person shall be construed as if the cases where those securities are taken to be transferred back to that other person included any case where securities of the same description as those securities are transferred to that other person either–

(a) in accordance with a requirement to transfer securities of the same description; or

(b) in exercise of a power to substitute securities of the same description for the securities that are required to be transferred back.

263B(6) For the purposes of this section securities shall not be taken to be of the same description as other securities unless they are in the same quantities, give the same rights against the same persons and are of the same type and nominal value as the other securities.

263B(7) In this section **"securities"** has the meaning given by section 263AA.

History – In s. 263B(2), the words "sections 263C(2) and 263CA(3) and (5)" substituted for the words "section 263C(2)" by FA 2009, s. 32 and Sch. 13, para. 2(2), with effect (a) for any case where the borrower (B) becomes insolvent on or after 24 November 2008; and (b) where the lender (L) makes an election under FA 2009, Sch. 13, para. 4, in any case where B becomes insolvent in the period beginning on 1 September 2008 and ending on 23 November 2008.

In s. 263B(4)(a), the words "for a consideration equal to their market value at that time" inserted and in para. (b) the words "for that consideration" inserted by FA 2009, s. 32 and Sch. 13, para. 2(3)(a) and (b), with effect from 21 July 2009 (Royal Assent).

In s. 263B(4), the words "This subsection does not apply where section 263CA (insolvency of borrower) applies." substituted for the words "section 263C(2)" by FA 2009, s. 32 and Sch. 13, para. 2(3)(c), with effect (a) for any case where the borrower (B) becomes insolvent on or after 24 November 2008; and (b) where the lender (L) makes an election under FA 2009, Sch. 13, para. 4, in any case where B becomes insolvent in the period beginning on 1 September 2008 and ending on 23 November 2008.

S. 263B(7) substituted by FA 2013, s. 77 and Sch. 29, para. 5 with effect from 1 January 2014.

In s. 263B(7), in the definition of "securities", the words "means UK shares or overseas securities (within the meaning of Part 17 of CTA 2010: see section 814 of that Act) or UK securities within the meaning of section 805 of CTA 2010 (see section 806 of that Act)" substituted for the words "means United Kingdom equities, United Kingdom securities or overseas securities (within the meaning, in each case, of Schedule 23A to the Taxes Act)" by CTA 2010, s. 1177 and Sch. 1, para. 259, with effect for corporation tax purposes for accounting periods ending on or after 1 April 2010, and for income tax and capital gains tax purposes for the tax year 2010–11 and subsequent tax years.

In s. 263B(7), the definition of "interest" omitted by FA 2009, s. 32 and Sch. 13, para. 2(4), with effect from 21 July 2009 (Royal Assent).

S. 263B inserted by FA 1997, s. 76 and Sch. 10, para. 5 with effect in relation to any to, and to transfers under, any arrangement made on or after 1 July 1997 (the appointed day for the purposes of FA 1997, Sch. 10, para. 7(1) by virtue of SI 1997/991 (C. 33)).

Cross references – Sch. 7AC, para. 13: relief for disposal of substantial shareholding: effect where shares transferred under a stock lending arrangement.
SI 2007/2486: modification of s. 263A in relation to arrangements where the transfer of securities within ITA 2007, s. 607(1)(b).

Other material – IR/Customs press release, 29 July 1998: proposed tax treatment of redenominations of debt securities into euros for repo/stock lending and related purposes; cases where continuity of asset treatment will apply; and treatment of representative payments on "cashing out".

Notes – S. 263B rewritten for income tax as ITA 2007, s. 568(1), (2), (3), (4), 592(1).

263C Stock lending involving redemption

263C(1) In section 263B references to the transfer back to a person of securities transferred by him shall be taken to include references to the payment to him, in pursuance of an obligation arising on any person's becoming entitled to receive an amount in respect of the redemption of those securities, of an amount equal to the amount of the entitlement.

263C(2) Where, in pursuance of any such obligation, the lender under any stock lending arrangement is paid any amount in respect of the redemption of any securities to which the arrangement relates–

(a) that lender shall be deemed for the purposes of this Act to have disposed, for that amount, of the securities in respect of whose redemption it is paid (**"the relevant lent securities"**);

(b) the borrower shall not, in respect of the redemption, be taken for the purposes of this Act to have made any disposal of the relevant lent securities; and

(c) section 263B(3) shall have effect in relation to disposals of any of the relevant lent securities made by the borrower before the redemption as if–

 (i) the amount paid to the lender were an amount paid for the acquisition of securities, and

 (ii) the securities acquired were to be used by the borrower for discharging a requirement under the arrangement to transfer the relevant lent securities back to the lender.

263C(3) Expressions used in this section and section 263B have the same meanings in this section as in that section.

History – S. 263C inserted by FA 1997, s. 76 and Sch. 10, para. 5(1) with effect in relation to, and to transfers under, any arrangement made on or after 1 July 1997 (the appointed day for the purposes of FA 1997, Sch. 10, para. 7(1) by virtue of SI 1997/991 (C. 33)).

Notes – S. 263C(1) rewritten for income tax as ITA 2007, s. 568(2), (5), (6).

263CA Stock lending: insolvency etc of borrower

263CA(1) This section applies where, in the case of any stock lending arrangement–

(a) the borrower (B) becomes insolvent after the lender (L) has transferred the securities,

(b) as a result of the insolvency, the requirement for B to make a transfer back to L will not be complied with as regards some or all of the securities,

(c) collateral is used (whether directly or indirectly) to enable L to acquire securities ("replacement securities") of the same description as the securities which will not be transferred back, and

(d) the replacement securities are acquired before the end of the period of 30 days beginning with the day on which B becomes insolvent ("the insolvency date").

263CA(2) In accordance with section 263B(2), the transfer of the securities under the arrangement is not to be regarded as a disposal by L for the purposes of this Act (but this is subject to subsection (5)).

263CA(3) B is to be treated for the purposes of this Act as having acquired the securities which will not be transferred back to L; and that acquisition is to be treated–

(a) as being made on the insolvency date, and

(b) as being for a consideration equal to their market value on that date.

263CA(4) The acquisition of the replacement securities is to be treated, as regards L, as if it were a transfer back of securities in accordance with the arrangement (so that, in accordance with section 263B(2), that acquisition is not regarded as an acquisition by L for the purposes of this Act).

263CA(5) If the number of replacement securities is less than the number of securities which B is treated as having acquired, L is to be treated for the purposes of this Act as having made a disposal, at the insolvency date, of the difference ("the deemed disposal").

263CA(6) The consideration for the deemed disposal is–

(a) where all the collateral is used to enable L to acquire replacement securities, nil, and

(b) where not all the collateral is so used, the difference between–

 (i) the market value (at the insolvency date) of the number of securities which could have been acquired using the collateral, and

 (ii) the market value (at that date) of the number of securities which were in fact so acquired.

263CA(7) But if L at any time receives any amount (whether arising out of B's insolvency or otherwise) in respect of B's liability to L in respect of the securities which are treated under subsection (5) as having been disposed of by L, that amount is to be treated as a chargeable gain accruing at that time to L.

263CA(8) The liability mentioned in subsection (7) is not be treated as giving rise to a relevant non-lending relationship for the purposes of Part 6 of CTA 2009 (relationships treated as loan relationships etc).

263CA(9) For the purposes of this section, B becomes insolvent–

(a) if a company voluntary arrangement takes effect under Part 1 of the Insolvency Act 1986,

(b) if an administration application (within the meaning of Schedule B1 to that Act) is made or a receiver or manager, or an administrative receiver, is appointed,

(c) on the commencement of a creditor's voluntary winding up (within the meaning of Part 4 of that Act) or a winding up by the court under Chapter 6 of that Part,

(d) if an individual voluntary arrangement takes effect under Part 8 of that Act,

(e) on bankruptcy application made or the presentation of a bankruptcy petition (within the meaning of Part 9 of that Act),

(f) if a compromise or arrangement takes effect under Part 26 of the Companies Act 2006,

(g) if a bank insolvency order takes effect under Part 2 of the Banking Act 2009,

(h) if a bank administration order takes effect under Part 3 of that Act, or

(i) on the occurrence of any corresponding event which has effect under or as a result of the law of Scotland or Northern Ireland or a country or territory outside the United Kingdom.

263CA(10) In this section–

(a) **"collateral"** means an amount of money or other property which–

  (i) is provided under the arrangement (or under arrangements of which the arrangement forms part), and

  (ii) is payable to or made available for the benefit of L for the purpose of securing the discharge of the requirement to transfer any or all of the securities back to L, and

(b) any expression used in this section and in section 263B has the same meaning as in that section.

History – In s. 263CA(9)(e), the words "the presentation of a bankruptcy petition" insert "bankruptcy application made or" inserted by SI 2016/481, reg. 2(1) and Sch. 1, para. 10, with effect from 6 April 2016.

S. 263CA inserted by FA 2009, s. 32 and Sch. 13, para. 3, with effect (a) for any case where the borrower (B) becomes insolvent on or after 24 November 2008; and (b) where the lender (L) makes an election under FA 2009, Sch. 13, para. 4, in any case where B becomes insolvent in the period beginning on 1 September 2008 and ending on 23 November 2008.

Cross references – FA 2009, Sch. 13, para. 4(3): modification of s. 263CA in respect of periods before CTA 2009 has effect.

263D Gains accruing to persons paying manufactured dividends

263D [Omitted by FA 2013, s. 77 and Sch. 29, para. 6.]

History – S. 263D omitted by FA 2013, s. 77 and Sch. 29, para. 6 with effect from 1 January 2014.

263E Structured finance arrangements

263E(1) This section applies if–

(a) section 809BZB or 809BZC of ITA 2007 or section 759 or 760 of CTA 2010 (disregard of intended effects of arrangement involving disposals of assets) applies in relation to a structured finance arrangement,

(b) the borrower or a person connected with the borrower makes a disposal of any security at any time under the arrangement to or for the benefit of the lender or a person connected with the lender, and

(c) condition A or B is met.

263E(2) Condition A is that the person making the disposal (and no-one else) has the right or obligation under the arrangement to acquire the asset disposed of by that disposal at any subsequent time (whether or not the right or obligation is subject to any conditions).

263E(3) Condition B is that–

(a) the asset disposed of by that disposal will subsequently cease to exist at any time, and

(b) it is intended that that asset will be held by the lender, or a person connected with the lender, from the time of the disposal until that time.

263E(4) The disposal of the security by the borrower or a person connected with the borrower is to be disregarded for the purposes of this Act.

263E(4A) If, at any time after that disposal, it becomes apparent that–

(a) the person making the disposal will not subsequently acquire under the arrangement the asset disposed of by that disposal, or

(b) that asset will not be held as mentioned in subsection (3)(b),

that person is to be treated for the purposes of this Act as disposing of that asset at that time for a consideration equal to its market value at that time.

263E(5) Except in a case falling within subsection (4A), any subsequent acquisition by the person making the disposal of the asset disposed of by that disposal is to be disregarded for the purposes of this Act.

263E(6) In this section–

"the borrower", in relation to a structured finance arrangement, means the person who is the borrower under the arrangement for the purposes of the defining section,

"the defining section" in relation to a structured finance arrangement–

(a) means section 809BZA of ITA 2007 if it is section 809BZB or 809BZC of ITA 2007 that applies in relation to the arrangement, and

(b) means section 758 of CTA 2010 if it is section 759 or 760 of CTA 2010 that applies in relation to the arrangement,

"the lender", in relation to a structured finance arrangement, means the person who is the lender under the arrangement for the purposes of the defining section,

"security" means any such asset as is mentioned in subsection (2)(b) and (c) of the defining section.

263E(7) For the purposes of this section.

(a) references to a person connected with the borrower do not include the lender, and

(b) references to a person connected with the lender do not include the borrower.

History – In s. 263E(1)(a), the words "or section 759 or 760 of CTA 2010" inserted by CTA 2010, s. 1177 and Sch. 1, para. 260, with effect for corporation tax purposes for accounting periods ending on or after 1 April 2010, and for income tax and capital gains tax purposes for the tax year 2010–11 and subsequent tax years.

In s. 263E(1)(a), the words "section 809BZB or 809BZC of ITA 2007" substituted for "section 774B of the Taxes Act" by TIOPA 2010, s. 374 and Sch. 8, para. 268(2), with effect for corporation tax purposes for accounting periods ending on or after 1 April 2010, for income tax and capital gains tax purposes for the tax year 2010–11 and subsequent tax years, and for petroleum revenue tax purposes for chargeable periods beginning on or after 1 July 2010.

In s. 263E(2) the words "(and no-one else) has the right or obligation under the arrangement to acquire the asset disposed of by that disposal at any subsequent time (whether or not the right or obligation is subject to any conditions)" substituted for the words "subsequently acquires under the arrangement the asset disposed of by that disposal" by FA 2007, s. 30 and Sch. 5 para. 8(2), with effect in relation to disposals made on or after 6 March 2007, except where, in relation to a disposal made before that date, the person making the disposal makes a claim to apply the amended provisions to that disposal (FA 2007, Sch. 5, para. 8(6) and (7) for the claim).

In s. 263E(3)(a) the words "will subsequently cease" substituted for the words "subsequently ceases" by FA 2007, s. 30 and Sch. 5 para. 8(3)(a), with effect in relation to disposals made on or after 6 March 2007, except where, in relation to a disposal made before that date, the person making the disposal makes a claim to apply the amended provisions to that disposal (FA 2007, Sch. 5, para. 8(6) and (7) for the claim).

In s. 263E(3)(a) the words "it is intended that that asset will be held" substituted for the words "that asset was held" by FA 2007, s. 30 and Sch. 5 para. 8(3)(b), with effect in relation to disposals made on or after 6 March 2007, except where, in relation to a disposal made before that date, the person making the disposal makes a claim to apply the amended provisions to that disposal (FA 2007, Sch. 5, para. 8(6) and (7) for the claim).

S. 263E(4A) inserted by FA 2007, s. 30 and Sch. 5 para.8(4), with effect in relation to disposals made on or after 6 March 2007, except where, in relation to a disposal made before that date, the person making the disposal makes a claim to apply the amended provisions to that disposal (FA 2007, Sch. 5, para.8(6) and (7) for the claim).

In s. 263E(5) the words "Except in a case falling within subsection (4A), any" substituted for the words "Any" by FA 2007, s. 30 and Sch. 5 para. 8(5), with effect in relation to disposals made on or after 6 March 2007, except where, in relation to a disposal made before that date, the person making the disposal makes a claim to apply the amended provisions to that disposal (FA 2007, Sch. 5, para. 8(6) and (7) for the claim).

In s. 263E(6), in the definition of "the borrower", the words "the defining section" substituted for "section 774A of the Taxes Act" by TIOPA 2010, s. 374 and Sch. 8, para. 268(3), with effect for corporation tax purposes for accounting periods ending on or after 1 April 2010, for income tax and capital gains tax purposes for the tax year 2010–11 and subsequent tax years, and for petroleum revenue tax purposes for chargeable periods beginning on or after 1 July 2010.

In s. 263E(6), after the definition of "the borrower", the definition of "the defining section" inserted by TIOPA 2010, s. 374 and Sch. 8, para. 268(4), with effect for corporation tax purposes for accounting periods ending on or after 1 April 2010, for income tax and capital gains tax purposes for the tax year 2010–11 and subsequent tax years, and for petroleum revenue tax purposes for chargeable periods beginning on or after 1 July 2010.

In s. 263E(6), in the definition of "the lender", the words "the defining section" substituted for "that section" by TIOPA 2010, s. 374 and Sch. 8, para. 268(5), with effect for corporation tax purposes for accounting periods ending on or after 1 April 2010, for income tax and capital gains tax purposes for the tax year 2010–11 and subsequent tax years, and for petroleum revenue tax purposes for chargeable periods beginning on or after 1 July 2010.

In s. 263E(6), in the definition of "security", the words "subsection (2)(b) and (c) of the defining section" substituted for "subsection (2)(c) and (d) of that section" by TIOPA 2010, s. 374 and Sch. 8, para. 268(6), with effect for corporation tax purposes for accounting periods ending on or after 1 April 2010, for income tax and capital gains tax purposes for the tax year 2010–11 and subsequent tax years, and for petroleum revenue tax purposes for chargeable periods beginning on or after 1 July 2010.

S. 263E inserted by FA 2006, s. 81 and Sch. 6, para. 9(1) with effect in relation to disposals made on or after 6 June 2006 and also effective in relation to any disposal made before 6 June 2006 if the person making the disposal makes a claim under Sch. 6, para. 9(3).

263F Power to modify repo provisions: non-standard repo cases

263F(1) The Treasury may by regulations provide for–

(a) section 261F (deemed manufactured payments: effect on repurchase price),

(b) section 261G (price differences under repos: effect on repurchase price),

(c) section 263A (agreements for sale and repurchase of securities), or

(d) [omitted by FA 2013, s. 77 and Sch. 29, para. 7(a)(ii),]

(e) any of those sections,

to apply with modifications in relation to non-standard repo cases.

263F(2) The power in subsection (1) to make provision for section 263A to apply with modifications is exercisable only so far as the section applies to any case mentioned in section 263A(1).

263F(3) A case is a non-standard repo case if–

(a) there is a repo in respect of securities,

(b) under the repo there has been a sale (**"the original sale"**) of the securities by the original owner to the interim holder, and

(c) any of conditions A to E is met in relation to the repo.

263F(4) Condition A is that–

(a) the obligation to buy back the securities is not performed, or

(b) the option to buy them back is not exercised.

263F(5) Condition B is that provision is made by or under an agreement for different or additional UK shares, UK securities or overseas securities to be treated as (or as included with) representative securities.

263F(6) Condition C is that provision is made by or under an agreement for any UK shares, UK securities or overseas securities to be treated as not included with representative securities.

263F(7) Condition D is that provision is made by or under an agreement for the sale price or repurchase price to be decided or varied wholly or partly by reference to post-agreement fluctuations.

263F(8) Condition E is that provision is made by or under an agreement for a person to be required, in a case where there are post-agreement fluctuations, to make a payment in the period–

(a) beginning immediately after the making of the agreement for the original sale, and

(b) ending when the repurchase price becomes due.

263F(9) "Post-agreement fluctuations" are fluctuations in the value of–

(a) securities transferred in pursuance of the original sale, or

(b) representative securities,

which occur in the period after the making of the agreement for the original sale.

263F(10) **"Representative securities"** are securities which, for the purposes of the repurchase, are to represent securities transferred in pursuance of the original sale.

History – S. 263F(1)(d) (and the "or" at the end of it) omitted (and the "or" after (c) inserted) by FA 2013, s. 77 and Sch. 29, para. 7(a), with effect from 1 January 2014.

In s. 263F(2), the words "or 263D" omitted by FA 2013, s. 77 and Sch. 29, para. 7(b) with effect from 1 January 2014.

In s. 263F(2) the words "any case mentioned in section 263A(1)" substituted for the words "cases falling within section 607 of ITA 2007 (treatment of price differences under repos)" by FA 2013, s. 28 and Sch. 12, para. 11(2), with effect for the tax year 2013–14 and subsequent tax years, subject to FA 2013, Sch. 12, para. 18.

S. 263F(9) and (10) substituted for (9) by FA 2013, s. 28 and Sch. 12, para. 11(3), with effect for the tax year 2013–14 and subsequent tax years, subject to FA 2013, Sch. 12, para. 18.

S. 263F inserted by ITA 2007, s. 1027 and Sch. 1, para. 336, with effect from 6 April 2007.

Statutory instruments – SI 2007/2486: made partly under s. 263F.

263G Power to modify repo provisions: redemption arrangements

263G(1) The Treasury may by regulations provide for–

(a) section 261F (deemed manufactured payments: effect on repurchase price),

(b) section 261G (price differences under repos: effect on repurchase price),

(c) section 263A (agreements for sale and repurchase of securities),

(d) [omitted by FA 2013, s. 77 and Sch. 29, para. 8(a), or]

(e) any of those sections,

to apply with modifications in relation to cases involving redemption arrangements.

263G(2) The power in subsection (1) to make provision for section 263A to apply with modifications is exercisable only so far as the section applies to any case mentioned in section 263A(1).

263G(3) A case involves redemption arrangements if–

(a) arrangements, corresponding to those made in cases where there is a repo, are made by an agreement, or one or more related agreements, in relation to securities that are to be redeemed in the period after their sale,

(b) the securities are UK shares, UK securities or overseas securities, and

(c) the arrangements are such that the seller or a person connected with the seller (instead of being required to repurchase the securities or acquiring an option to do so) is granted rights in respect of the benefits that will result from the redemption.

263G(4) [Omitted by FA 2013, s. 28 and Sch. 12, para. 12(b).]

History – S. 263G(1)(d) (but not the word "or" at the end of it) omitted by FA 2013, s. 77 and Sch. 29, para. 8(a), with effect from 1 January 2014.

In s. 263G(2), the words "or 263D" omitted by FA 2013, s. 77 and Sch. 29, para. 8(b), with effect from 1 January 2014.

In s. 263G(2) the words "any case mentioned in section 263A(1)" substituted for the words "cases falling within section 607 of ITA 2007 (treatment of price differences under repos)" by FA 2013, s. 28 and Sch. 12, para. 12(a), with effect for the tax year 2013–14 and subsequent tax years, subject to FA 2013, Sch. 12, para. 18.

S. 263G(4) omitted by FA 2013, s. 28 and Sch. 12, para. 12(b), with effect for the tax year 2013–14 and subsequent tax years, subject to FA 2013, Sch. 12, para. 18.

S. 263G inserted by ITA 2007, s. 1027 and Sch. 1, para. 337, with effect from 6 April 2007.

Statutory instruments – SI 2007/2486: made partly under s. 263G.

263H Sections 263F and 263G: supplementary provisions

263H(1) Regulations under section 263F or 263G may make different provision for different cases.

263H(2) Regulations under either section may contain incidental, supplemental, consequential and transitional provision and savings.

263H(3) The incidental, supplemental and consequential provision may include–

(a) in the case of regulations about section 261G, modifications of section 261F, and

(b) in the case of regulations about section 263A, modifications of the operation of this Act in relation to cases where, by virtue of the regulations, any acquisition or disposal is excluded from those which are to be ignored for the purposes of capital gains tax.

263H(4) In this section and sections 263F and 263G **"modifications"** includes exceptions and omissions.

263H(5) Accordingly, a power in sections 263F and 263G to provide for a provision to apply with modifications in relation to a particular case includes power to provide for the provision not to apply in relation to that case.

History – In s. 263H(3)(b), the words "or 263D" omitted by FA 2013, s. 77 and Sch. 29, para. 9, with effect from 1 January 2014.

S. 263H inserted by ITA 2007, s. 1027 and Sch. 1, para. 338, with effect from 6 April 2007.

Statutory instruments – SI 2007/2486: made partly under s. 263H.

263I Powers about manufactured overseas dividends

263I(1) The Treasury may by regulations make provision as mentioned in subsection (2) about prescribed cases where a person–

(a) pays or receives an amount (a "manufactured overseas dividend") which is representative of an overseas dividend on overseas securities where the payment or receipt is required to be made under an arrangement for the transfer of the securities, or

(b) is treated as doing so for any purposes of the Tax Acts.

263I(2) The regulations may provide for adjusting a relevant amount by reference to a provision which has effect under the law of a territory outside the United Kingdom.

263I(3) A **"relevant amount"** is an amount which is treated for prescribed capital gains tax purposes as the amount paid or payable to a person in respect of a relevant transaction.

263I(4) A **"relevant transaction"** is a sale, repurchase or other transfer of the overseas securities to which the manufactured overseas dividend relates.

263I(5) In this section **"prescribed"** means prescribed in regulations under this section.

263I(6) In this section–

(a) **"overseas securities"** means shares, stock or other securities issued by–

(i) a government, local authority or other public authority of a territory outside the United Kingdom, or

(ii) another body of persons not resident in the United Kingdom,

(b) **"overseas securities"** includes shares in a company which is not resident in the United Kingdom,

(c) **"overseas dividend"** means any interest, dividend or other annual payment payable in respect of overseas securities, and

(d) **"securities"** includes loan stock or any similar security.

History – S. 263I(1)(a) and (b) substituted by FA 2013, s. 77 and Sch. 29, para. 10(2), with effect from 1 January 2014.
S. 263I(6) substituted by FA 2013, s. 77 and Sch. 29, para. 10(3), with effect from 1 January 2014.
S. 263I inserted by ITA 2007, s. 1027 and Sch. 1, para. 339, with effect from 6 April 2007.

264 Relief for local constituency associations of political parties on reorganisation of constituencies

264(1) In this section **"relevant date"** means the date of coming into operation of an Order in Council under the Parliamentary Constituencies Act 1986 (orders specifying new parliamentary constituencies) and, in relation to any relevant date–

(a) **"former parliamentary constituency"** means an area which, for the purposes of parliamentary elections, was a constituency immediately before that date but is no longer such a constituency after that date; and

(b) **"new parliamentary constituency"** means an area which, for the purposes of parliamentary elections, is a constituency immediately after that date but was not such a constituency before that date.

264(2) In this section **"local constituency association"** means an unincorporated association (whether described as an association, a branch or otherwise) whose primary purpose is to further the aims of a political party in an area which at any time is or was the same or substantially the same as the area of a parliamentary constituency or 2 or more parliamentary constituencies and, in relation to any relevant date–

(a) **"existing association"** means a local constituency association whose area was the same, or substantially the same, as the area of a former parliamentary constituency or 2 or more such constituencies; and

(b) **"new association"** means a local constituency association whose area is the same, or substantially the same, as the area of a new parliamentary constituency or 2 or more such constituencies.

264(3) For the purposes of this section, a new association is a successor to an existing association if any part of the existing association's area is comprised in the new association's area.

264(4) In any case where, before, on or after a relevant date–

(a) an existing association disposes of land to a new association which is a successor to the existing association, or

(b) an existing association disposes of land to a body (whether corporate or unincorporated) which is an organ of the political party concerned and, as soon as practicable thereafter, that body disposes of the land to a new association which is a successor to the existing association,

the parties to the disposal or, where paragraph (b) above applies, to each of the disposals, shall be treated for the purposes of tax on chargeable gains as if the land disposed of were acquired from the existing association or the body making the disposal for a consideration of such an amount as would secure that on the disposal neither a gain nor a loss accrued to that association or body.

264(5) In a case falling within subsection (4) above, the new association shall be treated for the purposes of Schedule 2 as if the acquisition by the existing association of the land disposed of as mentioned in that subsection had been the new association's acquisition of it.

264(6) In any case where–

(a) before, on or after a relevant date, an existing association disposes of any land which was used and occupied by it for the purposes of its functions, and

(b) the existing association transfers the whole or part of the proceeds of the disposal to a new association which is a successor to the existing association,

then, subject to subsection (7) below, this Act (and, in particular, the provisions of sections 152 to 158) shall have effect as if, since the time it was acquired by the existing association, the land disposed of had been the property of the new association and, accordingly, as if the disposal of it had been by the new association.

264(7) If, in a case falling within subsection (6) above, only part of the proceeds of the disposal is transferred to the new association, that subsection shall apply–

(a) as if there existed in the land disposed of as mentioned in paragraph (a) of that subsection a separate asset in the form of a corresponding undivided share in that land, and subject to any necessary apportionments of consideration for an acquisition or disposal of, or of an interest in, that land; and

(b) as if the references in that subsection (other than paragraph (a) thereof) to the land disposed of and the disposal of it were references respectively to the corresponding undivided share referred to in paragraph (a) above and the disposal of that share;

and for this purpose a corresponding undivided share in the land disposed of is a share which bears to the whole of that land the same proportion as the part of the proceeds transferred bears to the whole of those proceeds.

264(8) In this section **"political party"** means a political party which qualifies for exemption under section 24 of the Inheritance Tax Act 1984 (gifts to political parties).

Derivations – F(No. 2)A 1983, s. 7, as amended by Parliamentary Constituencies Act 1986, Sch. 3, para. 6.

Cross references – S. 35(3)(d), (5): re-basing not to apply to disposal under these provisions unless an election exists for the simplified scheme (re-basing of all assets held at 31 March 1982 irrespective of matters in s. 35(3)).
S. 152–158: roll-over relief for replacement of business assets.
Sch. 2: assets held on 6 April 1965.
Sch. 3, para. 1: person disposing of asset acquired through disposal under these provisions after 31 March 1982 treated as holding asset at 31 March 1982 for purposes of re-basing.

Notes – S. 56(2): no gain, no loss calculated after applying indexation allowance.
S. 288: interpretation, including "land" as embracing messuages, tenements, and hereditaments, houses and buildings of any tenure.

265 Designated international organisations

265(1) Where–

(a) the United Kingdom or any of the Communities is a member of an international organisation; and

(b) the agreement under which it became a member provides for exemption from tax, in relation to the organisation, of the kind for which provision is made by this section;

the Treasury may by order designate that organisation for the purposes of this section.

265(2) The Treasury may by order designate any of the Communities or the European Investment Bank for the purposes of this section.

265(3) Where an organisation has been designated for the purposes of this section, then any security issued by the organisation shall be taken, for the purposes of this Act, to be situated outside the United Kingdom.

History – In s. 265(3), words "this Act" substituted for words "capital gains tax" by F(No. 2)A 2005, s. 34 and Sch. 4, para. 3(2), with effect, in accordance with F(No. 2)A 2005, Sch. 4, para. 10(1), at any time on or after 16 March 2005 (irrespective of when asset was acquired by person holding it), for determining (for purposes of TCGA 1992) situation of any asset or whether situation of any asset is in UK.

Derivations – FA 1984, s. 126, as amended by FA 1985, s. 96(1).

Cross references – S. 275(4): operation of S. 275(1), in determining situation of assets for purposes of TCGA 1992, subject to s. 265(3).
FA 1985, s. 96(2): orders within s. 265(2) may revoke or vary the European Communities (Loan Stock) (Stamp Duties) Order 1972.

Statutory instruments – SI 1984/1215, SI 1984/1634; SI 1985/1172; SI 1991/1202: designated bodies are The Asian Development Bank, The African Development Bank, The European Economic Community, The European Coal and Steel Community, The European Atomic Energy Community, The European Investment Bank and The European Bank for Reconstruction and Development.

Notes – S. 10: charge on non-residents only in relation to assets situated in the UK.
S. 287: power of Treasury exercisable by statutory instrument, but negative resolution procedure does not apply.

266 Inter-American Development Bank

266 A security issued by the Inter-American Development Bank shall be taken for the purposes of this Act to be situated outside the United Kingdom.

Derivations – FA 1976, s. 131.

Cross references – S. 275(4): operation of S. 275(1), in determining situation of assets for purposes of TCGA 1992, subject to s. 266.

Notes – S. 10: charge on non-residents only in relation to assets situated in the UK.

267 Sharing of transmission facilities

267(1) This section applies to any agreement relating to the sharing of transmission facilities–

(a) to which the parties are national broadcasting companies,

(b) which is entered into on or after 25th July 1991 (the day on which the Finance Act 1991 was passed) and before 1st January 1992 or such later date as may be specified for the purposes of this paragraph by the Secretary of State, and

(c) in relation to which the Secretary of State has certified that it is expedient that this section should apply.

267(2) Where under an agreement to which this section applies one party to the agreement disposes of an asset to another party to the agreement, both parties shall be treated for the purposes of corporation tax on chargeable gains as if the asset acquired by the party to whom the disposal is made were acquired for a consideration of such amount as would secure that on the other's disposal neither a gain nor a loss would accrue to that other.

267(3) Where under an agreement to which this section applies one party to the agreement disposes of an asset to another party to the agreement and the asset is one which the party making the disposal acquired on a part disposal by the party to whom the disposal under the agreement is made, then in applying subsection (2) above–

(a) section 42 shall be deemed to have had effect in relation to the part disposal with the omission of subsection (4),

(b) the amount or value of the consideration for the part disposal shall be taken to have been nil, and

(c) if the disposal under the agreement is one to which section 35(2) applies, the market value of the asset on 31st March 1982 shall be taken to have been nil.

267(4) In this section **"national broadcasting company"** means a body corporate engaged in the broadcasting for general reception by means of wireless telegraphy of radio or television services or both on a national basis.

Derivations – FA 1991, s. 78(1)–(3), (8).

Cross references – S. 35(2), (3)(d), (5): re-basing but not to apply to disposal under s. 267(2) unless an election exists for the simplified scheme (re-basing of all assets held at 31 March 1982 irrespective of matters in s. 35(3)).
S. 42: apportionment of allowable expenditure on a part disposal other than (s. 42(4)) expenditure wholly attributable to the part disposed of or the part retained.
Sch. 3, para. 1: person disposing of asset acquired through disposal under s. 267(2) after 31 March 1982 treated as holding asset at 31 March 1982 for purposes of re-basing.

Notes – S. 21–34: general meaning of "disposal" and "asset".
S. 56(2): no gain, no loss calculated after applying indexation allowance.

268 Decorations for valour or gallant conduct

268 A gain shall not be a chargeable gain if accruing on the disposal by any person of a decoration awarded for valour or gallant conduct which he acquired otherwise than for consideration in money or money's worth.

Derivations – CGTA 1979, s. 131.

Cross references – TMA 1970, s. 12(2): assets within s. 268 excluded from requirements to divulge information about assets for capital gains tax purposes.

Notes – S. 15: meaning of "chargeable gain".
S. 21–34: general meaning of "disposal".

268A Victims of National-Socialist persecution

268A(1) A gain accruing on a disposal is not a chargeable gain if it accrues on–

(a) a disposal of the right to receive the whole or any part of a qualifying payment in respect of National-Socialist persecution, or

(b) a disposal of an interest in any such right.

268A(2) A payment is a qualifying payment in respect of National-Socialist persecution if it is payable as mentioned in paragraphs (a) to (c) of section 756A(1) of ITTOIA 2005 (income tax exemption for payments to or in respect of victims of National-Socialist persecution).

268A(3) In this section **"interest"**, in relation to any right, means an interest as a co-owner of the right.

268A(4) It does not matter–

(a) whether the right is owned jointly or in common, or

(b) whether or not the interests of the co-owners are equal.

History – S. 268A inserted by FA 2006, s. 64(4) as if it had effect in relation to disposals on or after 6 April 1996, with the proviso that no loss arising before 6 April 2006 is to cease to be an allowable loss as result of s. 64(4).

Cross references – FA 2006, s. 64(10)–(12): giving effect to adjustments in relation to 2005–06 or earlier years. Any adjustments to tax liability as a result of the exemption as are necessary (which may be by way of discharge or repayment of tax or by making an assessment etc.) are subject to a claim being made before 31 January 2012 by the person entitled to the exemption.

268B Compensation for deprivation of foreign assets

268B(1) A gain is not a chargeable gain if–

(a) it accrues to a person on receipt of a capital sum paid by way of compensation for the deprivation of a foreign asset,

(b) no legal redress was available when the deprivation occurred, and

(c) the sum is paid as the result of a relevant compensation award.

268B(2) A relevant compensation award is an award or distribution made–

(a) under–

(i) an Order in Council made under the Foreign Compensation Act 1950, or

(ii) arrangements established by the government of a territory outside the United Kingdom that are equivalent in effect to such an Order,

(b) as a result of a recommendation of–

(i) the Spoliation Advisory Panel, or

(ii) a body outside the United Kingdom whose purposes and functions are equivalent to those of the Panel, or

(c) in settlement of a legal claim to the effect that the deprivation was unlawful or in accordance with an order to that effect made by a court, tribunal or other competent authority with jurisdiction to decide such a claim.

268B(3) Reference in this section to the payment of a capital sum by way of compensation for the deprivation of a foreign asset includes–

(a) payment as a result of the abandonment or extinguishment of rights in respect of the deprivation;

(b) return of the asset itself.

268B(4) In the case of a gain accruing to a person other than the original owner–

(a) subsection (1) does not apply if consideration had been given at any time (whether by that person or someone else) for the right to receive the compensation, but

(b) consideration given on an acquisition falling within section 58(1) or 171(1) is to be ignored for these purposes.

268B(5) If the capital sum is paid (or the foreign asset returned) to a person to whom an allowable loss has accrued as a result of–

(a) the deprivation of the foreign asset, or

(b) the abandonment or extinguishment of rights in respect of the deprivation,

subsection (1) applies only to so much of any gain as exceeds that loss.

268B(6) For a person to obtain relief under this section, the person must make a claim.

268B(7) If the capital sum is paid by means of the transfer of an asset (or the foreign asset is returned), that asset is to be treated for the purposes of computing a gain or a loss on its subsequent disposal as if it were acquired for a consideration equal to its market value at the time of the transfer.

268B(8) In this section–

"capital sum" means money or money's worth;

"deprivation", in relation to a foreign asset, includes deprivation resulting from–

(a) the seizure, confiscation, forfeiture, destruction or expropriation of the asset,

(b) the disposal of the asset by a sale under duress for less than market value;

"foreign asset" means an asset which was situated outside the United Kingdom at the time of the deprivation;

"legal redress", in relation to the deprivation of a foreign asset, means a right to recover the asset or to receive compensation for the deprivation;

"original owner" means the person who owned the foreign asset at the time of the deprivation;

"Spoliation Advisory Panel" includes any successor to that Panel.

268B(9) This section does not apply in relation to a gain to which section 268A applies.

History – S. 268B inserted by SI 2010/157, art. 9(1), with effect in relation to capital sums received on or after 1 April 2010 (for corporation tax purposes) or 6 April 2010 (for capital gains tax purposes).

269 Foreign currency for personal expenditure

269 A gain shall not be a chargeable gain if accruing on the disposal by an individual of currency of any description acquired by him for the personal expenditure outside the United Kingdom of himself or his family or dependants (including expenditure on the provision or maintenance of any residence outside the United Kingdom).

Derivations – CGTA 1979, s. 133.

Cross references – TMA 1970, s. 12(2): assets within s. 269 excluded from requirements to divulge information about assets for capital gains tax purposes.

Notes – S. 15: meaning of "chargeable gain".
S. 21–34: general meaning of "disposal".
S. 276: UK territorial sea is part of the UK.

270 Chevening Estate

270 The enactments relating to capital gains tax (apart from this section) shall not apply in respect of property held on the trusts of the trust instrument set out in the Schedule to the Chevening Estate Act 1959.

Derivations – FA 1981, s. 135.

Notes – S. 2: charge to capital gains tax.

271 Other miscellaneous exemptions

271(1) The following gains shall not be chargeable gains–

(a) gains accruing on the disposal of stock–

(i) transferred, in pursuance of any Act of Parliament, to accounts in the books of the Bank of England in the name of the Treasury or the National Debt Commissioners;

(ia) transferred, in pursuance of any Act of Parliament, to the Treasury or the National Debt Commissioners and in respect of which the Treasury or those Commissioners are entered as holder in the registers kept by the Registrar of Government Stock; or

(ii) belonging to the Crown, in whatever name it may stand in the books of the Bank of England or in the registers kept by the Registrar of Government Stock;

(b) any gain accruing to a person from his acquisition and disposal of assets held by him as part of the Fund mentioned in section 613(4) of the Taxes Act (House of Commons Members' Fund);

(c) any gain accruing to a person from his acquisition and disposal of assets held by him as part of a fund–

(i) mentioned in section 614(2) of the Taxes Act,

(ii) to which section 615(3) of the Taxes Act applies, or

(iii) mentioned in section 648, 649, 650, 651 or 653 of ITEPA 2003;.

(d) [Omitted by FA 2004, s. 187(3); and repealed by FA 2004, s. 326 and Sch. 42, Pt. 3.]

(e) any gain accruing on the disposal by the trustees of any settled property held on trusts in accordance with directions which are valid and effective under section 9 of the Superannuation and Trust Funds (Validation) Act 1927 (trust funds for the reduction of the National Debt);

(ea) any gain accruing on the disposal by the trustees of an asbestos compensation settlement of any property comprised in the settlement;

(f) any gain accruing to a consular officer or employee, within the meaning of section 771 of ITTOIA 2005, of any foreign state to which that section applies on the disposal of assets which at the time of the disposal were situated outside the United Kingdom;

(g) [Omitted by FA 2004, s. 187(3); and repealed by FA 2004, s. 326 and Sch. 42, Pt. 3.]

(h) [Omitted by FA 2004, s. 187(3); and repealed by FA 2004, s. 326 and Sch. 42, Pt. 3.]

(j) [Omitted by FA 2004, s. 187(3); and repealed by FA 2004, s. 326 and Sch. 42, Pt. 3.]

271(1ZA) In subsection (1)(ea) above **"asbestos compensation settlement"** means a settlement–

(a) the sole or main purpose of which is making compensation payments to or in respect of individuals who have, or had before their death, an asbestos-related condition, and

(b) which is made before 24 March 2010 in pursuance of an arrangement within subsection (1ZB) below.

271(1ZB) An arrangement is within this subsection if it is–

(a) a voluntary arrangement that has taken effect under Part 1 of the Insolvency Act 1986 or Part 2 of the Insolvency (Northern Ireland) Order 1989,

(b) a compromise or arrangement that has taken effect under section 425 of the Companies Act 1985, Article 418 of the Companies (Northern Ireland) Order 1986 or Part 26 of the Companies Act 2006, or

(c) an arrangement or compromise of a kind corresponding to any of those mentioned in paragraph (a) or (b) above that has taken effect under, or as a result of, the law of a country or territory outside the United Kingdom.

271(1A) A gain accruing to a person on a disposal of investments held for the purposes of a registered pension scheme or an overseas pension scheme is not a chargeable gain.

271(1B) But subsection (1A) does not prevent such a gain from being treated as a chargeable gain for the purposes of sections 185F to 185I of the Finance Act 2004 (scheme chargeable payments: gains from taxable property).

271(2) [Omitted by FA 2004, s. 187(5) and repealed by FA 2004, s. 326 and Sch. 42, Pt. 3.]

271(3) A local authority, a local authority association and a health service body shall be exempt from capital gains tax.

In this subsection–

"health service body" has the meaning given by section 986 of CTA 2010, and

"local authority association" has the meaning given by section 1000 of ITA 2007.

271(4) Any interest to which section 702 of ITTOIA 2005 (certified SAYE savings arrangements) applies shall be disregarded for all purposes of the enactments relating to capital gains tax.

In any case where there is a transfer to which section 216 applies, this subsection shall have effect in relation to any interest payable after the transfer under a savings arrangement which immediately before the transfer was a certified SAYE savings arrangement notwithstanding that it ceased to be such a arrangement by reason of the transfer.

In this subsection **"certified SAYE savings arrangement"** has the meaning given by section 703 of ITTOIA 2005.

271(5) A signatory to the Operating Agreement made pursuant to the Convention on the International Maritime Satellite Organisation which came into force on 16th July 1979, other than a signatory designated for the purposes of the Agreement by the United Kingdom in accordance with the Convention, shall be exempt from capital gains tax in respect of any payment received by that signatory from the Organisation in accordance with the Agreement.

271(6) The following shall, on a claim made in that behalf to the Board, be exempt from tax in respect of all chargeable gains–

(a) the Trustees of the British Museum and the Trustees of the Natural History Museum; and

(b) an association (in the sense that word has in section 469(1)(a) of CTA 2010) which meets conditions A and B in that section (conditions for qualifying as a scientific research association).

271(7) The Historic Buildings and Monuments Commission for England, the Trustees of the National Heritage Memorial Fund and the National Endowment for Science, Technology and the Arts shall be exempt from tax in respect of chargeable gains.

271(7A) Chargeable gains are exempt from tax if they accrue to a bank, or issue department of a bank, to which this subsection applies for the time being.

271(7B) Her Majesty may by Order in Council direct that subsection (7A) applies to a bank or its issue department if it appears to Her Majesty that the bank–

(a) is not resident in the United Kingdom, and

(b) is entrusted by the government of a territory outside the United Kingdom with the custody of the territory's principal foreign exchange reserves.

271(7C) No recommendation may be made to Her Majesty in Council to make an order under subsection (7B) unless a draft of the order has been laid before and approved by a resolution of the House of Commons.

271(8) There shall be exempt from tax any chargeable gains accruing to the issue department of the Reserve Bank of India constituted under an Act of the Indian legislature called the Reserve Bank of India Act 1934, or to the issue department of the State Bank of Pakistan constituted under certain orders made under section 9 of the Indian Independence Act 1947.

271(9) [Repealed by FA 1997, s. 76 and Sch. 10, para. 5(2) and s. 113 and Sch. 18, Pt. VI(10).]

271(10) In subsection (1A) above–

"investments" includes futures contracts and options contracts;

"overseas pension scheme" has the same meaning as in Part 4 of the Finance Act 2004 (see section 150(7) of that Act).

271(11) For the purposes of subsection (10) above a contract is not prevented from being a futures contract or an options contract by the fact that any party is or may be entitled to receive or liable to make, or entitled to receive and liable to make, only a payment of a sum (as opposed to a transfer of assets other than money) in full settlement of all obligations.

271(12) Subsections (1)(b) and (c) and (1A) above do not apply to gains accruing to a person from the acquisition and disposal by him of assets held as a member of a property investment LLP.

History – S. 271(1)(a)(i) and s. 271(1)(a)(ia) substituted for former s. 271(1)(a)(i) by SI 2004/2744, Schedule, para. 3(2)(a), with effect from 15 November 2004.

In s. 271(1)(a)(ii) the words "or in the registers kept by the Registrar of Government Stock" inserted by SI 2004/2744, Schedule, para. 3(2)(b), with effect from 15 November 2004.

In s. 271(1)(b), the words "the Fund mentioned in section 613(4) of the Taxes Act (House of Commons Members' Fund);" substituted for the words "a fund mentioned in section 613(4) of the Taxes Act (Parliamentary pension funds) or of which income is exempt from income tax under section 614(1) of that Act (social security supplementary schemes);" by FA 2004, s. 187(2) with effect from 6 April 2006 by virtue of FA 2004, s. 284(1).

S. 271(1)(c) substituted by ITEPA 2003, Sch. 6, para. 218 with effect for 2003–04 and subsequent tax years.

S. 271(1)(d), (g), (h), (j) and the second sentence of that subsection which read "In this subsection **"exempt approved scheme"** and **"approved personal pension scheme"** have the same meanings as in Part XIV of the Taxes Act." omitted by FA 2004, s. 187(3); and repealed by FA 2004, s. 326 and Sch. 42, Pt. 3 with effect from 6 April 2006 by virtue of FA 2004, s. 284(1).

S. 271(1)(ea) inserted by F(No. 3)A 2010, s. 31 and Sch. 14, para. 2(2) and treated as having come into force on 6 April 2006.

In s. 271(1)(f), "section 771 of ITTOIA 2005" substituted for "section 322 of the Taxes Act" by virtue of ITTOIA 2005, s. 882 and Sch. 1, para. 445(2) which, in accordance with ITTOIA 2005, s. 883, have effect, for income tax purposes, for tax year 2005–06 and subsequent tax years, and, for corporation tax purposes, for accounting periods ending after 5 April 2005.

In s. 271(1)(g) and (2) the words "the extent" substituted for "such extent as the Board are satisfied" and in s. 271(2) the words "the Board are satisfied that" (occurring after "unless") omitted by FA 1996, s. 134 and Sch. 20, para. 63 and repealed by FA 1996, s. 205 and Sch. 41, Pt. V(10), with effect as respects years after 1995–96 and, for corporation tax purposes, as respects accounting periods ending on or after 1 July 1999, the day appointed for corporation tax self-assessment under FA 1994, s. 199 by virtue of SI 1998/3173 (C. 78).

S. 271(1ZA) inserted by F(No. 3)A 2010, s. 31 and Sch. 14, para. 2(3) and treated as having come into force on 6 April 2006.

S. 271(1ZB) inserted by F(No. 3)A 2010, s. 31 and Sch. 14, para. 2(3) and treated as having come into force on 6 April 2006.

In s. 271(1A), the words "or an overseas pension scheme" inserted by FA 2013, s. 65 and Sch. 25, para. 14(a), with effect in relation to disposals occurring on or after 6 April 2013.

S. 271(1A) inserted by FA 2004, s. 187(4) witheffect from 6 April 2006 by virtue of FA 2004, s. 284(1).
S. 271(1B) inserted by FA 2006, s. 158 and Sch. 21, para. 1, with effect from 6 April 2006 (FA 2006, s. 158(2).
S. 271(2) omitted by FA 2004, s. 187(5) and repealed by FA 2004, s. 326 and Sch. 42, Pt. 3 with effect on 6 April 2006 by virtue of FA 2004, s. 284(1) (subject to Sch. 36).
In s. 271(3), the words "section 986 of CTA 2010" substituted for "section 519A of the Taxes Act" by CTA 2010, s. 1177 and Sch. 1, para. 261(2), with effect for corporation tax purposes for accounting periods ending on or after 1 April 2010, and for income tax and capital gains tax purposes for the tax year 2010–11 and subsequent tax years.
In s. 271(3), the definitions of "health service body" and "local authority association" substituted by ITA 2007, s. 1027 and Sch. 1, para. 340(2), with effect from 6 April 2007.
In s. 271(4), word "interest" substituted for "bonus" twice, by virtue of ITTOIA 2005, s. 882 and Sch. 1, para. 445(3)(a) which, in accordance with ITTOIA 2005, s. 883, have effect, for income tax purposes, for tax year 2005–06 and subsequent tax years, and, for corporation tax purposes, for accounting periods ending after 5 April 2005.
In s. 271(4), words "section 702 of ITTOIA 2005 (certified SAYE savings arrangements)" substituted for "section 326 or 326A of the Taxes Act (certified contractual savings schemes and tax-exempt special savings accounts)" by virtue of ITTOIA 2005, s. 882 and Sch. 1, para. 445(3)(b) which, in accordance with ITTOIA 2005, s. 883, have effect, for income tax purposes, for tax year 2005–06 and subsequent tax years, and, for corporation tax purposes, for accounting periods ending after 5 April 2005.
In s. 271(4) after words "after the transfer under a", words "savings arrangement" substituted for "savings scheme" by virtue of ITTOIA 2005, s. 882 and Sch. 1, para. 445(3)(c) which, in accordance with ITTOIA 2005, s. 883, have effect, for income tax purposes, for tax year 2005–06 and subsequent tax years, and, for corporation tax purposes, for accounting periods ending after 5 April 2005.
In s. 271(4), words "certified SAYE savings arrangement" substituted for "certified contractual savings scheme" by virtue of ITTOIA 2005, s. 882 and Sch. 1, para. 445(3)(d) which, in accordance with ITTOIA 2005, s. 883, have effect, for income tax purposes, for tax year 2005–06 and subsequent tax years, and, for corporation tax purposes, for accounting periods ending after 5 April 2005.
In s. 271(4) after words "it ceased to be such a", word "arrangement" substituted for "scheme" by virtue of ITTOIA 2005, s. 882 and Sch. 1, para. 445(3)(e) which, in accordance with ITTOIA 2005, s. 883, have effect, for income tax purposes, for tax year 2005–06 and subsequenttax years, and, for corporation tax purposes, for accounting periods ending after 5 April 2005 [CCH Note: ITTOIA 2005, Sch. 1, para. 445(3) does not amend indefinite article "a" which immediately preceded former word "scheme".].
In s. 271(4), words "In this subsection "certified SAYE savings arrangement" has the meaning given by section 703 of ITTOIA 2005." inserted by ITTOIA 2005, s. 882 and Sch. 1, para. 445(3)(f) which, in accordance with ITTOIA 2005, s. 883, have effect, for income tax purposes, for tax year 2005–06 and subsequent tax years, and, for corporation tax purposes, for accounting periods ending after 5 April 2005.
In s. 271(6)(a) the words "Natural History Museum" substituted by the Museums and Galleries Act 1992, s. 11(2) and Sch. 8, para. 1(9), with effect from 1 September 1992 by virtue of SI 1992/1847.
In s. 271(6)(b), the words "association (in the sense that word has in section 469(1)(a) of CTA 2010) which meets conditions A and B in that section (conditions for qualifying as a scientific research association)." substituted for the words "Association within the meaning of section 508 of the Taxes Act (scientific research organisations)" by CTA 2010, s. 1177 and Sch. 1, para. 261(3), with effect for corporation tax purposes for accounting periods ending on or after 1 April 2010, and for income tax and capital gains tax purposes for the tax year 2010–11 and subsequent tax years.
In s. 271(7), words "the National Endowment for Science, Technology and the Arts," inserted by National Lottery Act 1998, s. 24(2), with effect from 2 July 1998.
In s. 271(7), words "Memorial Fund and the" substituted for words "Memorial Fund, the" by F(No. 2)A 2005, s. 46(3)(a) which has effect in relation to gains accruing after 1 April 2005.
In s. 271(7), words ", the United Kingdom Atomic Energy Authority" omitted by F(No. 2)A 2005, s. 46(3)(b) and repealed by F(No. 2)A 2005, s. 70 and Sch. 11, Pt. 2(12), with effect in relation to gains accruing on or after 1 April 2005, and without affecting, in accordance with F(No. 2)A 2005, s. 46(7)(a), any accounting period of the United Kingdom Atomic Energy Authority ending before 1 April 2005.
In s. 271(7), words "and the National Radiological Protection Board" omitted by F(No. 2)A 2005, s. 46(3)(c) and repealed by F(No. 2)A 2005, s. 70 and Sch. 11, Pt. 2(12), with effect in relation to gains accruing after 1 April 2005, and without affecting, in accordance with F(No. 2)A 2005, s. 46(7)(b), any accounting period of the National Radiological Protection Board ending on or before 1 April 2005.
In s. 271(7), the words "; and for the purposes of this subsection gains accruing from investments or deposits held forthe purposes of any pension scheme provided and maintained by the United Kingdom Atomic Energy Authority shall be treated as if these gains and investments and deposits belonged to the Authority" omitted by F(No. 2)A 2005, s. 46(3)(d) and repealed by F(No. 2)A 2005, s. 70 and Sch. 11, Pt. 2(12), with effect in relation to gains accruing on or after 1 April 2005.
S. 271(7A) inserted by ITA 2007, s. 1027 and Sch. 1, para. 340(3) with effect from 6 April 2007.
S. 271(7B) inserted by ITA 2007, s. 1027 and Sch. 1, para. 340(3) with effect from 6 April 2007.
S. 271(7C) inserted by ITA 2007, s. 1027 and Sch. 1, para. 340(3) with effect from 6 April 2007.
S. 271(9) ceased to have effect by virtue of FA 1997, s. 76 and Sch. 10, para. 5(2) and was repealed by s. 113 and Sch. 18, Pt. VI(10) with effect in relation to, and to transfers under, any arrangement made on or after 1 July 1997 (the appointed day for the purposes of FA 1997, Sch. 10, para. 7(1) by virtue of SI 1997/991 (C. 33)).
In s. 271(10), the definition of "investments" substituted (and the "–" before it inserted) and definition of "overseas pension scheme" inserted by FA 2013, s. 65 and Sch. 25, para. 14(b), with effect in relation to disposals occurring on or after 6 April 2013
In s. 271(10), "subsection (1A)" substituted for "subsections (1)(g) and (h) and (2)" by FA 2004, s. 187(6)(a) with effect from 6 April 2006 by virtue of FA 2004, s. 284(1).
In s. 271(10), the words "; and paragraph 7(3)(d) of Schedule 22 to the Taxes Act shall be construed accordingly" which appeared after "options contracts" omitted by FA 2004, s. 187(6)(b) and repealed by FA 2004, s. 326 and Sch. 42, Pt. 3 with effect on 6 April 2006 by virtue of FA 2004, s. 284(1).
In s. 271(12), the words "Subsections (1)(b) and (c) and (1A)" are substituted for the words "Subsection (1)(b), (c), (d), (g) and (h) and subsection (2)" by FA 2004, s. 187(7) with effect from 6 April 2006 by virtue of FA 2004, s. 284(1).
S. 271(12) inserted by FA 2001, Sch. 25, para. 4 with effect from 6 April 2001.

Derivations – S. 271(1)–(2): CGTA 1979, s. 149B, as inserted by ICTA 1988, s. 844 and Sch. 29, para. 26, and amended (subs. (1)(c)) by FA 1988, s. 146 and Sch. 13, para. 17.
S. 271(3): CGTA 1979, s. 149B(3), (3A), as substituted by FA 1990, s. 127 and Sch. 18, para. 3.
S. 271(4): CGTA 1979, s. 149B(4), as inserted by FA 1990, s. 28(3); FA 1988, Sch. 12, para. 7(b).
S. 271(5)–(9): CGTA 1979, s. 149B(5)–(9), as inserted by ICTA 1988, s. 844 and Sch. 29, para. 26, and as amended (subs. (9)) by FA 1991, s. 57(4).
S. 271(10), (11): CGTA 1979, s. 149B(10), (11), as inserted by FA 1990, s. 81(3).

Cross references – S. 13(10B): exemption from chargeable gain accruing to a person under s. 13(2).
S. 99A: authorised unit trusts: treatment of umbrella schemes.
S. 207(4): securities continue to form part of Lloyd's underwriter's premiums trust fund where they have been disposed of within s. 271(9) but securities have not yet been returned.
S. 216: incorporation of a building society.
ICTA 1988, s. 438(8): exemption under s. 271(1)(h) does not prevent exempt pension business gains from being taken into account as receipts in computing profits or losses for other purposes.
ICTA 1988, s. 592(10): an authorised unit trust which is an exempt approved scheme used as a top-up scheme to which the employer is not a contributor.
ICTA 1988, s. 608: superannuation funds approved before 6 April 1980.

ICTA 1988, s. 620(5)(b), 621(5): funds to provide retirement annuities to groups of individuals engaged in or connected with a particular occupation or their spouses or dependants.
ICTA 1988, s. 727(2): certain exemptions from the accrued income scheme for stock lending.
ICTA 1988, Sch. 5A, para. 1(1): interest on cash collateral given in the course of arrangements to which s. 271(9) applies treated as income of the borrower of the stock for which collateral is given.
ICTA 1988, Sch. 22, para. 7(3)(d): application of s. 271(1)(g) to a reduced percentage of any gain in certain cases involving pension funds with surpluses.
ICTA 1988, Sch. 23A, para. 1(1): approved and unapproved stock lending arrangements by reference to s. 271(9) for purposes of provisions dealing with manufactured dividends and interest.
FA 1995, s. 85 and Sch. 19, para. 1: "approved stock lending arrangements" for the purpose of the provisions on stock lending: interest on collateral are arrangements to which s. 271(9) apply.
SI 1989/1299, as amended: stock lending regulations made under ICTA 1988, s. 129.

Extra-statutory concessions – C31: temporary concession governing eligibility for SRA scientific research association (SRA) status (s. 271(6)) for accounting periods beginning before 1 September 1999 pending introduction of updated approval criteria by DTI.

HMRC interpretations – IRInt. 253: swaps held by non-corporates such as approved pension schemes.

Notes – S. 2: charge to capital gains tax.
S. 15: meaning of "chargeable gain".
S. 21–34: general meaning of "disposal" and "assets".
S. 265: security issued by designated international organisations taken to be situated outside the UK.
S. 266: security issued by the Inter-American Development Bank taken as situated outside the UK.
S. 275: location of assets (see also s. 265, 266, 276).
S. 276: territorial sea of the UK deemed to be part of the UK and certain exploration or exploitation rights effectively deemed to be UK assets.
S. 288: interpretation, including the "Taxes Act" as ICTA 1988 and reference to other sections as being those of this Act.
TMA 1970, s. 42–43B: procedures and time limits for making claims.
Greater London Authority Act 1999, s. 419 : Greater London Authority to be treated as a local authority for the purposes of s. 271 but see s. 154 of that Act (withdrawal of tax exemption from Greater London Authority in certain circumstances if it fails to comply with a direction of the Secretary of State under s. 157(3) of that Act.
FA 2004, s. 326 and Sch. 42, Pt. 3 repeal the words after "chargeable gains" in s. 271(7) with effect on 6 April 2006. However, following other amendments to that section there are no such words left to repeal.

PART 7A – UK REPRESENTATIVES OF NON-UK RESIDENTS

History – Pt. 7A inserted by TIOPA 2010, s. 370 and Sch. 6, para. 24–33, with effect for corporation tax purposes for accounting periods ending on or after 1 April 2010, for income tax and capital gains tax purposes for the tax year 2010–11 and subsequent tax years, and for petroleum revenue tax purposes for chargeable periods beginning on or after 1 July 2010.

Chapter 1 – Treatment of Branch or Agency as UK Representative of Non-UK Resident

INTRODUCTION

271A Overview of Chapter

271A(1) This Chapter provides for a branch or agency to be treated as the UK representative of a non-UK resident in respect of certain amounts chargeable to capital gains tax.

271A(2) For obligations and liabilities in relation to capital gains tax imposed on a branch or agency which under this Chapter is treated as the UK representative of a non-UK resident, see Chapter 2.

History – S. 271A inserted by TIOPA 2010, s. 370 and Sch. 6, para. 24, with effect for corporation tax purposes for accounting periods ending on or after 1 April 2010, for income tax and capital gains tax purposes for the tax year 2010–11 and subsequent tax years, and for petroleum revenue tax purposes for chargeable periods beginning on or after 1 July 2010.

BRANCHES AND AGENCIES

271B Branch or agency treated as UK representative

271B(1) This section applies if–

(a) a non-UK resident carries on (alone or in partnership) any trade, profession or vocation through a branch or agency in the United Kingdom, and

(b) the branch or agency is to be treated under Chapter 2B of Part 14 of ITA 2007 as the UK representative of the non-UK resident in relation to amounts within section 835E(2) of that Act.

271B(2) The branch or agency is the UK representative of the non-UK resident in relation to amounts which, by reference to the branch or agency, are chargeable to capital gains tax under section 10 above.

271B(3) The following rules are to be applied for the purposes of subsection (2) and Chapter 2 in relation to an amount within that subsection.

Rule 1

The UK representative continues to be the UK representative of the non-UK resident in relation to the amount even after ceasing to be a branch or agency through which the non-UK resident carries on the trade, profession or vocation concerned.

Rule 2

The UK representative is treated in relation to the amount as a distinct and separate person from the non-UK resident (if the representative would not otherwise be so treated).

Rule 3

If the branch or agency is carried on by persons in partnership, the partnership, as such, is treated in relation to the amount as the UK representative of the non-UK resident.

271B(4) For further rules that apply where a trade or profession carried on by a non-UK resident in the United Kingdom is carried on in partnership, see section 271C.

History – S. 271B inserted by TIOPA 2010, s. 370 and Sch. 6, para. 25, with effect for corporation tax purposes for accounting periods ending on or after 1 April 2010, for income tax and capital gains tax purposes for the tax year 2010–11 and subsequent tax years, and for petroleum revenue tax purposes for chargeable periods beginning on or after 1 July 2010.

271C Trade or profession carried on in partnership

271C(1) Subsection (2) applies if a trade or profession carried on by a non-UK resident through a branch or agency in the United Kingdom is carried on by the non-UK resident in partnership.

271C(2) The trade or profession carried on through the branch or agency is, for the purposes of section 271B and Chapter 2, to be treated as including the notional trade or profession.

271C(3) Subsection (4) applies (in addition to subsection (2) if that subsection also applies) if–

(a) a trade or profession carried on by a non-UK resident in the United Kingdom is carried on by the non-UK resident in partnership, and

(b) any member of the partnership is resident in the United Kingdom.

271C(4) The notional trade or profession is, for the purposes of section 271B and Chapter 2, to be treated as being a trade carried on in the United Kingdom through the partnership as such.

271C(5) In this section **"the notional trade or profession"** means the notional trade from which the non-UK resident's share in the partnership's profits or losses is treated for the purposes of section 852 of ITTOIA 2005 as deriving.

History – S. 271C inserted by TIOPA 2010, s. 370 and Sch. 6, para. 26, with effect for corporation tax purposes for accounting periods ending on or after 1 April 2010, for income tax and capital gains tax purposes for the tax year 2010–11 and subsequent tax years, and for petroleum revenue tax purposes for chargeable periods beginning on or after 1 July 2010.

271D Interpretation of Chapter

271D In this Chapter–

"branch or agency" means any factorship, agency, receivership, branch or management, and

"non-UK resident" means a person who is not resident in the United Kingdom.

History – S. 271D inserted by TIOPA 2010, s. 370 and Sch. 6, para. 27, with effect for corporation tax purposes for accounting periods ending on or after 1 April 2010, for income tax and capital gains tax purposes for the tax year 2010–11 and subsequent tax years, and for petroleum revenue tax purposes for chargeable periods beginning on or after 1 July 2010.

Chapter 2 – Capital Gains Tax Obligations and Liabilities Imposed on UK Representatives

271E Introduction to Chapter

271E(1) This Chapter applies to the enactments contained in–

(a) this Act,

(b) the Tax Acts, and

(c) subordinate legislation made under this Act or the Tax Acts,

so far as they make provision for or in connection with the assessment, collection and recovery of tax, or of interest on tax.

271E(2) Those enactments have effect in accordance with section 271F in relation to amounts in respect of which a branch or agency is to be treated as the UK representative of a non-UK resident under Chapter 1.

271E(3) In this section **"subordinate legislation"** has the same meaning as in the Interpretation Act 1978.

History – S. 271E inserted by TIOPA 2010, s. 370 and Sch. 6, para. 28, with effect for corporation tax purposes for accounting periods ending on or after 1 April 2010, for income tax and capital gains tax purposes for the tax year 2010–11 and subsequent tax years, and for petroleum revenue tax purposes for chargeable periods beginning on or after 1 July 2010.

271F Obligations and liabilities of UK representative

271F(1) The obligations and liabilities of a non-UK resident are to be treated, for the purposes of the enactments to which this Chapter applies, as if they were also the obligations and liabilities of the UK representative of the non-UK resident.

271F(2) Subsection (3) applies if–

(a) the UK representative of a non-UK resident discharges an obligation or liability imposed by this section that corresponds to one to which the non-UK resident is subject, or

(b) a non-UK resident discharges an obligation or liability that corresponds to one to which the non-UK resident's UK representative is subject by virtue of this section.

271F(3) The corresponding obligation or liability–

(a) of the non-UK resident (in a case within subsection (2)(a)), or

(b) of the UK representative (in a case within subsection (2)(b)),

is discharged.

271F(4) A non-UK resident is bound, as if they were the non-UK resident's own, by acts or omissions of the non-UK resident's UK representative in the discharge of the obligations and liabilities imposed on the representative by this section.

271F(5) This section is subject to sections 271G and 271H.

History – S. 271F inserted by TIOPA 2010, s. 370 and Sch. 6, para. 29, with effect for corporation tax purposes for accounting periods ending on or after 1 April 2010, for income tax and capital gains tax purposes for the tax year 2010–11 and subsequent tax years, and for petroleum revenue tax purposes for chargeable periods beginning on or after 1 July 2010.

271G Exceptions: notices and information

271G(1) An obligation or liability attaching to a non-UK resident ("X") by reason of a notice or other document having been given or served on X does not also attach to the UK representative of X by virtue of section 271F unless the notice or other document (or a copy of it) has been given to or served on the representative.

271G(2) An obligation or liability attaching to X by reason of a request or demand having been received by X does not also attach to the UK representative of X by virtue of section 271F unless the representative has been notified of the request or demand.

271G(3) Subsection (4) applies to obligations relating to the provision of information that are imposed on the UK representative of X by section 271F in a case where the representative is X's independent agent.

271G(4) The obligations do not require the UK representative to do anything except so far as it is practicable for the representative to do so.

271G(5) For this purpose, the representative must act to the best of the representative's knowledge and belief after taking all reasonable steps to obtain the necessary information.

271G(6) An obligation of X to provide information is not discharged by virtue of section 271F in a case where the UK representative of X has discharged the obligation only so far as required by subsection (4) of this section.

271G(7) X is not bound by virtue of section 271F by mistakes in information provided by the UK representative of X in discharging, so far as required under subsection (4) of this section, an obligation imposed on the representative by section 271F unless–

(a) the mistake is the result of an act or omission of X, or

(b) the mistake is one to which X consented or in which X connived.

271G(8) In this section **"information"** includes anything contained in a return, self-assessment, account, statement or report required to be provided to the Commissioners for Her Majesty's Revenue and Customs or to any officer of Revenue and Customs.

History – S. 271G inserted by TIOPA 2010, s. 370 and Sch. 6, para. 30, with effect for corporation tax purposes for accounting periods ending on or after 1 April 2010, for income tax and capital gains tax purposes for the tax year 2010–11 and subsequent tax years, and for petroleum revenue tax purposes for chargeable periods beginning on or after 1 July 2010.

271H Exceptions: criminal offences and penalties etc

271H(1) A person is not by virtue of section 271F liable to be proceeded against for a criminal offence unless the person–

(a) committed the offence, or

(b) consented to or connived in its commission.

271H(2) An independent agent of a non-UK resident is not by virtue of section 271F liable to any civil penalty or surcharge in respect of an act or omission if conditions A and B are met.

271H(3) Condition A is that the act or omission is not–

(a) an act or omission of the independent agent, or

(b) an act or omission to which the agent consented or in which the agent connived.

271H(4) Condition B is that the independent agent is able to show that the amount of the penalty or surcharge will not be recoverable out of the sums mentioned in section 271I(3) (after being indemnified for any other liabilities under section 271I).

History – S. 271H inserted by TIOPA 2010, s. 370 and Sch. 6, para. 31, with effect for corporation tax purposes for accounting periods ending on or after 1 April 2010, for income tax and capital gains tax purposes for the tax year 2010–11 and subsequent tax years, and for petroleum revenue tax purposes for chargeable periods beginning on or after 1 July 2010.

271I Indemnities

271I(1) An independent agent of a non-UK resident is entitled to be indemnified for the amount of any liability of the non-UK resident which the agent has discharged by virtue of section 271F.

271I(2) An independent agent of a non-UK resident is entitled to retain, from the sums mentioned in subsection (3), amounts sufficient to meet any liabilities which by virtue of section 271F the agent has discharged or to which the agent is subject.

271I(3) The sums are those which–

(a) (ignoring subsection (2)) are due from the independent agent to the non-UK resident, or

(b) are received by the independent agent on behalf of the non-UK resident.

History – S. 271I inserted by TIOPA 2010, s. 370 and Sch. 6, para. 32, with effect for corporation tax purposes for accounting periods ending on or after 1 April 2010, for income tax and capital gains tax purposes for the tax year 2010–11 and subsequent tax years, and for petroleum revenue tax purposes for chargeable periods beginning on or after 1 July 2010.

271J Meaning of 'non-UK resident' and 'independent agent'

271J(1) In this Chapter **"non-UK resident"** means a person who is not resident in the United Kingdom.

271J(2) In this Chapter **"independent agent"**, in relation to a non-UK resident ("X"), means a person who is the UK representative of X in respect of any agency in which the person is acting on behalf of X in an independent capacity.

271J(3) For this purpose a person does not act in an independent capacity on behalf of X unless the relationship between them, having regard to its legal, financial and commercial characteristics, is a relationship between persons carrying on independent businesses dealing with each other at arm's length.

History – S. 271J inserted by TIOPA 2010, s. 370 and Sch. 6, para. 33, with effect for corporation tax purposes for accounting periods ending on or after 1 April 2010, for income tax and capital gains tax purposes for the tax year 2010–11 and subsequent tax years, and for petroleum revenue tax purposes for chargeable periods beginning on or after 1 July 2010.

PART VIII – SUPPLEMENTAL

272 Valuation: general

272(1) In this Act **"market value"** in relation to any assets means the price which those assets might reasonably be expected to fetch on a sale in the open market.

272(2) In estimating the market value of any assets no reduction shall be made in the estimate on account of the estimate being made on the assumption that the whole of the assets is to be placed on the market at one and the same time.

272(3) The Treasury may make regulations as to the manner for determining for the purposes of this Act–

(a) the market value at any time of shares or securities which are included in the official UK list, and

(b) the market value at any time of shares or securities which are listed on a recognised stock exchange outside the United Kingdom.

272(4) The regulations may–

(a) make different provision for different cases, and

(b) contain incidental, supplemental, consequential and transitional provision and savings.

272(5) In this Act **"market value"** in relation to any rights of unit holders in any unit trust scheme the buying and selling prices of which are published regularly by the managers of the scheme shall mean an amount equal to the buying price (that is the lower price) so published on the relevant date, or if none were published on that date, on the latest date before.

272(6) The provisions of this section, with sections 273 and 274, have effect subject to sections 25A and 41A and Part I of Schedule 11.

History – S. 272(3) and (4) substituted by FA 2007, s. 109 and Sch. 26, para. 4(1), with effect where the date of valuation falls on or after 6 April 2015 (SI 2015/635, art. 2).
In s. 272(3) the word "quoted" substituted for "listed" by FA 1996, s. 199 and Sch. 38, para. 12 where the relevant date falls on or after 1 April 1996.
In s. 272(6), the words "sections 25A and 41A and" inserted by FA 2006, s. 81 and Sch. 9, para. 6(2) with effect from 19 July 2006.

Derivations – CGTA 1979, s. 150(1)–(4), (6).

Cross references – S. 147(1): application of s. 272(3) to determine the market value of a quoted option which is treated as part of a new holding following a reorganisation etc.
Sch. 11, para. 1–9 (Pt. I): transitional provisions and savings in respect of valuation of gifts and transactions between connected persons before 20 March 1985, of assets held on 6 April 1965 or before 6 July 1973, of quotation before 25 March 1973 or exchange control restrictions, of depreciated values referable to death before 31 March 1973 and of estate duty.
ITA 2007, s. 438 and CTA 2010, s. 210: s. 272 applies to determine market value of the interest in an offshore fund for purposes of relief on gifts of shares and securities to charities.
ITEPA 2003, s. 421: application of market value to income tax charges on certain gains from shares or options acquired by directors and employees.
ITTOIA 2005, s. 412(5): application of s. 272(3) to determine market value of shares given by way of stock dividend.
ITEPA 2003, s. 397: certain lump sums – calculation of amount taxed by virtue of section 394 and the use of "market value".
FA 2003, s.118: application of market value for purposes of stamp duty land tax in FA 2003, Pt. 4.
FA 2003, Sch. 23, para. 30: corporation tax relief for employee share acquisition.
FA 2004, s. 278(1): application of s. 272 for the purposes of FA 2004, Pt. 4 (pension schemes etc.).
SI 2006/964, reg. 108: modification of s. 272 for the purposes of authorised investment funds.

Statutory instruments – SI 2015/616: partly made under s. 272(3) and (4).

Extra-statutory concessions – D44: where individual or company disposes of shares, acquired by way of no gain/no loss transaction from spouse or group company which held the shares of 31 March 1982, a more favourable basis of valuation may be adopted.
SI 1997/1154, reg. 5(3)(k), 7(4)(f), 22: modifications of s. 272 in relation to open-ended investment companies, holdings in and assets of such companies, and transactions involving such companies.

Notes – S. 18(6) to (8): determination of market value on a transaction between connected persons where the asset is subject to a particular right or restriction.
S. 21–34: general meaning of "asset".
S. 29: where value shifting in point, actual consideration plus other consideration obtainable treated as market value of the interest deemed acquired.
TMA 1970, s. 111: power of inspector or other officer of the Board to inspect assets to ascertain their value.
For provisions for which market value is to be determined, see list in annotations to s. 38.
FA 1994, Sch. 24, para. 18(5): application of market value in relation to securities issued under the Railways Act 1993, s. 98 or 106.

273 Unquoted shares and securities

273(1) The provisions of subsection (3) below shall have effect in any case where, in relation to an asset to which this section applies, there falls to be determined by virtue of section 272(1) the price which the asset might reasonably be expected to fetch on a sale in the open market.

273(2) The assets to which this section applies are shares and securities which are not listed on a recognised stock exchange at the time as at which their market value for the purposes of tax on chargeable gains falls to be determined.

273(3) For the purposes of a determination falling within subsection (1) above, it shall be assumed that, in the open market which is postulated for the purposes of that determination, there is available to any prospective purchaser of the asset in question all the information which a prudent prospective purchaser of the asset might reasonably require if he were proposing to purchase it from a willing vendor by private treaty and at arm's length.

History – In s. 273(2) the word "listed " substituted for the word ("quoted") by FA 2007, s. 109 and Sch. 26, para. 8(5), with effect from 19 July 2007 (Royal Assent).

Derivations – CGTA 1979, s. 152.

Cross references – ICTA 1988, s. 251(6): application to determination of market value of shares given by way of stock dividend.
ITEPA 2003, s. 397: certain lump sums – calculation of amount taxed by virtue of section 394 and the use of "market value".
FA 2003, s.118: application of market value for purposes of stamp duty land tax in FA 2003, Pt. 4.
FA 2003, Sch. 23, para. 30: corporation tax relief for employee share acquisition.

Other material – HMRC press release, 18 November 1991 (not reproduced): where 31 March 1982 values are needed and shareholders with similar holdings agree, Shares Valuation Division will begin valuation negotiations in advance of a formal request to do so from the tax office.

Notes – ICTA 1988, s. 440(5): application of market value to deemed disposal and reacquisition on transfer of asset between different categories of insurance business.

274 Value determined for inheritance tax

274 Where on the death of any person inheritance tax is chargeable on the value of his estate immediately before his death and the value of an asset forming part of that estate has been ascertained (whether in any proceedings or otherwise) for the purposes of the application of that tax to the estate, the value so ascertained shall be taken for the purposes of this Act to be the market value of that asset at the date of the death.

History – In s. 274, the words "the application of that tax to the estate" substituted for "that tax" by FA 2008, s. 10 and Sch. 4, para. 8 with effect in relation to any ascertainment of value made on or after 6 April 2008.

Derivations – CGTA 1979, s. 153.

Cross references – IHTA 1984, s. 187: attribution of values to specific investments.

ITEPA 2003, s. 397: certain lump sums – calculation of amount taxed by virtue of section 394 and the use of "market value".
FA 2003, s.118: application of market value for purposes of stamp duty land tax in FA 2003, Pt. 4.

Notes – IHTA 1984, s. 4: deemed transfers occasioned by death.
IHTA 1984, s. 160–198: valuation for inheritance tax.

275 Location of assets

275(1) For the purposes of this Act –

(a) the situation of rights or interests (otherwise than by way of security) in or over immovable property is that of the immovable property,

(b) subject to the following provisions of this subsection, the situation of rights or interests (otherwise than by way of security) in or over tangible movable property is that of the tangible movable property,

(c) subject to the following provisions of this subsection, a debt, secured or unsecured, is situated in the United Kingdom if and only if the creditor is resident in the United Kingdom,

(d) shares or debentures issued by any municipal or governmental authority, or by any body created by such an authority, are situated in the country of that authority,

(da) subject to paragraph (d) above, shares in or debentures of a company incorporated in any part of the United Kingdom are situated in the United Kingdom,

(e) subject to paragraphs (d) and (da) above, registered shares or debentures are situated where they are registered and, if registered in more than one register, where the principal register is situated,

(f) a ship or aircraft is situated in the United Kingdom if and only if the owner is then resident in the United Kingdom, and an interest or right in or over a ship or aircraft is situated in the United Kingdom if and only if the person entitled to the interest or right is resident in the United Kingdom,

(g) the situation of good-will as a trade, business or professional asset is at the place where the trade, business or profession is carried on,

(h) patents, trade marks, registered designs and corresponding rights are situated where they are registered, and if registered in more than one register, where each register is situated, and licences or other rights in respect of any such rights are situated in the United Kingdom if they or any right derived from them are exercisable in the United Kingdom,

(j) copyright, design right, franchises and corresponding rights, and licences or other rights in respect of any such rights, are situated in the United Kingdom if they or any right derived from them are exercisable in the United Kingdom,

(k) a judgment debt is situated where the judgment is recorded,

(l) a debt which–

  (i) is owed by a bank, and

  (ii) is not in sterling, and

  (iii) is represented by a sum standing to the credit of an account in the bank of an individual who is not domiciled in the United Kingdom,

is situated in the United Kingdom if and only if that individual is resident in the United Kingdom and the branch or other place of business of the bank at which the account is maintained is itself situated in the United Kingdom.

275(2) In subsection (1) above–

(a) in paragraphs (d), (da) and (e), the references to shares or debentures, in relation to a company that has no share capital, include any interests in the company possessed by members of the company, and

(b) in paragraphs (d) and (e), the references to debentures, in relation to a person other than a company, include securities.

275(3) In subsection (1) above, in each of paragraphs (h) and (j), **"corresponding rights"** means any rights under the law of a country or territory outside the United Kingdom that correspond or are similar to those within that paragraph.

275(4) Subsection (1) above is subject to–

section 265(3) (securities issued by designated international organisations to be taken to be situated outside UK),

section 266 (securities issued by Inter-American Development Bank to be taken to be situated outside UK), and

section 275C (location of assets: interests of co-owners).

History – S. 275 renumbered as s. 275(1) by F(No. 2)A 2005, s. 34 and Sch. 4, para. 4(2) with effect, in accordance with Sch. 4, para. 10(1), at any time on or after 16 March 2005 (irrespective of when asset was acquired by person holding it), for determining (for purposes of TCGA 1992) situation of any asset or whether situation of any asset is in UK.
In s. 275(1)(d), word "debentures" substituted for word "securities" by F(No. 2)A 2005, s. 34 and Sch. 4, para. 4(3) with effect, in accordance with Sch. 4, para. 10(1), at any time on or after 16 March 2005 (irrespective of when asset was acquired by person holding it), for determining (for purposes of TCGA 1992) situation of any asset or whether situation of any asset is in UK.
S. 275(1)(da) inserted by F(No. 2)A 2005, s. 34 and Sch. 4, para. 4(4) with effect, in accordance with Sch. 4, para. 10(1), at any time on or after 16 March 2005 (irrespective of when asset was acquired by person holding it), for determining (for purposes of TCGA 1992) situation of any asset or whether situation of any asset is in UK.
In s. 275(1)(e), words "subject to paragraphs (d) and (da)" substituted for words "subject to paragraph (d)" and word "debentures" substituted for word "securities" by F(No. 2)A 2005, s. 34 and Sch. 4, para. 4(5) with effect, in accordance with Sch. 4, para. 10(1), at any time on or after 16 March 2005 (irrespective of when asset was acquired by person holding it), for determining (for purposes of TCGA 1992) situation of any asset or whether situation of any asset is in UK.
S. 275(1)(h) substituted by F(No. 2)A 2005, s. 34 and Sch. 4, para. 4(6) with effect, in accordance with Sch. 4, para. 10(1), at any time on or after 16 March 2005 (irrespective of when asset was acquired by person holding it), for determining (for purposes of TCGA 1992) situation of any asset or whether situation of any asset is in UK.
S. 275(1)(j) substituted by F(No. 2)A 2005, s. 34 and Sch. 4, para. 4(7) with effect, in accordance with Sch. 4, para. 10(1), at any time on or after 16 March 2005 (irrespective of when asset was acquired by person holding it), for determining (for purposes of TCGA 1992) situation of any asset or whether situation of any asset is in UK.
S. 275(2) inserted by F(No. 2)A 2005, s. 34 and Sch. 4, para. 4(8) with effect, in accordance with Sch. 4, para. 10(1), at any time on or after16 March 2005 (irrespective of when asset was acquired by person holding it), for determining (for purposes of TCGA 1992) situation of any asset or whether situation of any asset is in UK.
S. 275(3) inserted by F(No. 2)A 2005, s. 34 and Sch. 4, para. 4(8) with effect, in accordance with Sch. 4, para. 10(1), at any time on or after 16 March 2005 (irrespective of when asset was acquired by person holding it), for determining (for purposes of TCGA 1992) situation of any asset or whether situation of any asset is in UK.
S. 275(4) inserted by F(No. 2)A 2005, s. 34 and Sch. 4, para. 4(8) with effect, in accordance with Sch. 4, para. 10(1), at any time on or after 16 March 2005 (irrespective of when asset was acquired by person holding it), for determining (for purposes of TCGA 1992) situation of any asset or whether situation of any asset is in UK.

Derivations – CGTA 1979, s. 18(4), as amended by Copyright, Designs and Patents Act 1988, s. 303(1) and Sch. 7, para. 26, and by FA 1984, s. 69(1).

Cross references – ICTA 1988, s. 715(8): certain exemptions and reliefs from the accrued income scheme, by reference to location of securities within s. 275.
ICTA 1988, s. 723(8): certain exemptions and reliefs from the accrued income scheme, by reference to location of securities within s. 275.

Notes – S. 9: meaning of "resident".
S. 10: extent of charge on non-residents by reference to assets in the UK.
S. 12: remittance basis in respect of foreign assets of person with foreign domicile.
S. 16: losses accruing on foreign assets to an individual resident or ordinarily resident but not domiciled in the UK are not allowable losses.
S. 25(1): deemed disposal on non-residents where certain assets become situated outside the UK.
S. 185: exception of certain UK assets from deemed disposal where company ceases to be UK resident.
S. 187: postponement of charge in respect of certain foreign assets on deemed disposal where company ceases to be UK resident.
S. 271(1)(f): exemption for certain consular officials from gains in respect of foreign assets.
Trade Marks Act 1994, Sch. 4: construction of references in s. 275(h) to trade marks and registered trade marks.

275A Location of certain intangible assets

275A(1) This section applies for the purpose of determining whether the situation of an intangible asset ("asset A") is in the United Kingdom if the situation of asset A is not otherwise determined (see section 275B(1)).

275A(2) In this section **"intangible asset"** means–

(a) intangible or incorporeal property and includes a thing in action, or

(b) anything that under the law of a country or territory outside the United Kingdom corresponds or is similar to intangible or incorporeal property or a thing in action.

275A(3) If asset A is subject to UK law (see section 275B(2)) at the time it is created, it shall be taken for the purposes of this Act to be situated in the United Kingdom at all times.

275A(4) Subsections (5) to (9) below have effect if asset A–

(a) is a future or option (see section 275B(3)), and

(b) is not subject to UK law at the time it is created.

275A(5) If, as a result of the application of the rule in subsection (6) below in relation to asset A or any other asset or assets, asset A falls to be treated as being subject to UK law at the time it is created, it shall be taken for the purposes of this Act to be situated in the United Kingdom at all times.

275A(6) That rule is that where, in the case of any intangible asset,–

(a) the asset is a future or option,

(b) the underlying subject matter (see section 275B(4)) of the asset consists of or includes an asset which is an intangible asset, and

(c) either–

(i) that intangible asset is subject to UK law at the time it is created and, on the assumption that there were no rights or interests in or over that asset, the situation of that asset would not be otherwise determined, or

(ii) that intangible asset is treated by this subsection as being so subject at that time, the intangible asset mentioned in paragraph (a) above is to be treated for the purposes of subsection (5) above and this subsection as being so subject at the time it is created.

275A(7) If–

(a) asset A is not taken to be situated in the United Kingdom by virtue of subsection (5) above, and

(b) as a result of the application of the rule in subsection (8) below in relation to asset A or any other asset or assets, asset A falls to be treated as being situated in the United Kingdom at any time,

it shall be taken for the purposes of this Act to be situated in the United Kingdom at that time.

275A(8) That rule is that where, in the case of any intangible asset,–

(a) the asset is a future or option, and

(b) the underlying subject matter of the asset consists of or includes an asset–

(i) which is, by virtue of subsection (9) below or of any provision of this Act apart from this section, situated in the United Kingdom at any time, or

(ii) which is treated by this subsection as being so situated at any time,

the intangible asset mentioned in paragraph (a) above is to be treated for the purposes of subsection (7) above and this subsection as being so situated at that time.

275A(9) Where–

(a) the underlying subject matter of a future or option consists of or includes shares or debentures issued by a company incorporated in any part of the United Kingdom, but

(b) at the time the future or option is created, those shares or debentures have not been issued,

the underlying subject matter of the future or option, so far as consisting of or including those shares or debentures, is to be taken, for the purposes of subsection (8) above, to consist of or include an asset which is situated in the United Kingdom at all times.

History – S. 275A inserted by F(No. 2)A 2005, s. 34 and Sch. 4, para. 5 with effect, in accordance with Sch. 4, para. 10(1), at any time on or after 16 March 2005 (irrespective of when asset was acquired by person holding it), for determining (for purposes of TCGA 1992) situation of any asset or whether situation of any asset is in UK.

275B Section 275A: supplementary provisions

275B(1) For the purposes of section 275A, the situation of an asset is not otherwise determined if, apart from that section, this Act does not make any provision for determining–

(a) the situation of the asset, or

(b) whether the situation of the asset is in the United Kingdom.

275B(2) For the purposes of section 275A, an intangible asset is subject to UK law at a particular time if any right or interest which comprises or forms part of the asset is, at that time,–

(a) governed by, or otherwise subject to, or

(b) enforceable under,

the law of any part of the United Kingdom.

275B(3) In section 275A–

"future" has the meaning given by section 581 of CTA 2009, and

"option" has the meaning given by section 580 of that Act.

275B(4) For the purposes of section 275A–

(a) the underlying subject matter of a future is the property which, if the future were to run to delivery, would fall to be delivered at the date and price agreed when the contract is made, and

(b) the underlying subject matter of an option is the property which would fall to be delivered if the option were exercised.

275B(5) Section 275A is subject to section 275C (location of assets: interests of co-owners).

275B(6) This section is to be construed as one with section 275A.

History – S. 275B(3) substituted by CTA 2009, s. 1322 and Sch. 1, para. 383, with effect for corporation tax purposes for accounting periods ending on or after 1 April 2009, and for income tax and capital gains tax purposes for the tax year 2009–10 and subsequent tax years.

S. 275B inserted by F(No. 2)A 2005, s. 34 and Sch. 4, para. 5 with effect, in accordance with Sch. 4, para. 10(1), at any time on or after 16 March 2005 (irrespective of when asset was acquired by person holding it), for determining (for purposes of TCGA 1992) situation of any asset or whether situation of any asset is in UK.

275C Location of assets: interests of co-owners

275C(1) This section applies for determining for the purposes of this Act–

(a) the situation of an interest (see subsection (4)) in an asset, or

(b) whether the situation of an interest in an asset is in the United Kingdom.

275C(2) The situation of the interest in the asset shall be taken to be the same as the situation of the asset, as determined in accordance with subsection (3) below.

275C(3) The situation of the asset for the purposes of subsection (2) above shall be determined on the assumption that the asset is wholly-owned by the person holding the interest in the asset.

275C(4) In this section **"interest"**, in relation to an asset, means an interest as a co-owner of the asset (whether the asset is owned jointly or in common and whether or not the interests of the co-owners are equal).

History – S. 275C inserted by F(No. 2)A 2005, s. 34 and Sch. 4, para. 6 with effect, in accordance with Sch. 4, para. 10(1), at any time on or after 16 March 2005 (irrespective of when asset was acquired by person holding it), for determining (for purposes of TCGA 1992) situation of any asset or whether situation of any asset is in UK.

Cross references – S. 275(4): operation of s. 275(1), in determining situation of assets for TCGA 1992 purposes, subject to s. 275C.

276 The territorial sea and the continental shelf

Notes – In s. 276(7); the reference to a "branch or agency" shall be read, in relation to a company, as if it were a reference to a "permanent establishment" (FA 2003, s. 153(2)(b); with effect in relation to accounting periods beginning on or after 1 January 2003).

276(1) The territorial sea of the United Kingdom shall for all purposes of the taxation of chargeable gains (including the following provisions of this section) be deemed to be part of the United Kingdom.

276(2) In this section–

(a) **"exploration or exploitation activities"** means activities carried on in connection with the exploration or exploitation of so much of the seabed and subsoil and their natural resources as is situated in the United Kingdom or a designated area; and

(b) **"exploration or exploitation rights"** means rights to assets to be produced by exploration or exploitation activities or to interests in or to the benefit of such assets; and

(c) references to the disposal of exploration or exploitation rights include references to the disposal of shares deriving their value or the greater part of their value directly or indirectly from such rights, other than shares listed on a recognised stock exchange; and

(d) **"shares"** includes stock and any security as defined in section 1117(1) of CTA 2010; and

(e) **"designated area"** means an area designated by Order in Council under section 1(7) of the Continental Shelf Act 1964.

276(3) Any gains accruing on the disposal of exploration or exploitation rights shall be treated for the purposes of this Act as gains accruing on the disposal of assets situated in the United Kingdom.

276(4) Gains accruing on the disposal of–

(a) exploration or exploitation assets which are situated in a designated area, or

(b) unquoted shares deriving their value or the greater part of their value directly or indirectly from exploration or exploitation assets situated in the United Kingdom or a designated area or from such assets and exploration or exploitation rights taken together,

shall be treated for the purposes of this Act as gains accruing on the disposal of assets situated in the United Kingdom.

276(5) For the purposes of this section, an asset disposed of is an exploration or exploitation asset if either–

(a) it is not a mobile asset and it is being or has at some time been used in connection with exploration or exploitation activities carried on in the United Kingdom or a designated area; or

(b) it is a mobile asset which has at some time been used in connection with exploration or exploitation activities so carried on and is dedicated to an oil field in which the person making the disposal, or a person connected with him, is or has been a participator;

and expressions used in paragraphs (a) and (b) above have the same meaning as if those paragraphs were included in Part I of the Oil Taxation Act 1975.

276(6) In subsection (4)(b) above **"unquoted shares"** means shares other than those which are listed on a recognised stock exchange; and references in subsections (7) and (8) below to exploration or exploitation assets include references to unquoted shares falling within subsection (4)(b).

276(7) Gains accruing to a person not resident in the United Kingdom on the disposal of exploration or exploitation rights or of exploration or exploitation assets shall, for the purposes of capital gains tax or corporation tax on chargeable gains, be treated as gains accruing on the disposal of assets used for the purposes of a trade carried on by that person in the United Kingdom through a branch or agency.

276(8) Subsection (9) below shall apply in relation to a disposal of exploration or exploitation rights or exploration or exploitation assets if (and only if) the disposal is–

(a) by a company resident in a territory outside the United Kingdom to a company resident in the same territory,

(b) by a company resident in the United Kingdom to another company which is also resident, or

(c) by a company which is not resident in the United Kingdom to another company which is resident there.

276(9) Those provisions are–

(a) section 41(8),

(b) section 171 (except subsections (1)(b) and (1A)),

(c) section 173 (with the omission of the words "to which this section applies" in subsections (1)(a) and (2)(a) and "such" in subsections (1)(c) and (2)(c) and with the omission of subsection (3)),

(d) section 174(4) (with the substitution of "at a time when both were members of the group" for "in a transfer to which section 171(1) applied"),

(e) section 179 (except subsections (1)(b) and (1A)), and

(f) section 181.

276(10) The provisions specified in subsection (9) above shall apply in accordance with subsection (8) above with the following modifications–

(a) for the purposes of paragraph (a) of subsection (9) above, section 41(8) applies as if section 170 applied, for the purposes of section 171, with the omission of subsection (9), and

(b) for the purposes of paragraphs (b) to (f) of subsection (9) above, the provisions specified in those paragraphs apply as if in section 170 subsection (9) were omitted.

History – In s. 276(2)(c) and (6) the word "listed" substituted for "quoted" by FA 1996, s. 199 and Sch. 38, para. 10 for disposals on or after 1 April 1996.
In s. 276(2)(d), the words "section 1117(1) of CTA 2010" substituted for "section 254(1) of the Taxes Act" by CTA 2010, s. 1177 and Sch. 1, para. 262, with effect for corporation tax purposes for accounting periods ending on or after 1 April 2010, and for income tax and capital gains tax purposes for the tax year 2010–11 and subsequent tax years.
S. 276(8) substituted and s. 276(9)and (10) inserted by FA 2000, Sch. 29, para. 35(1) with effect in accordance with FA 2000, Sch. 29, para. 35(2) (broadly, disposals, acquisitions, etc., on or after 1 April 2000).

Derivations – S. 276(1): FA 1973, s. 38(1) (see also ICTA 1988, s. 830(1)).
S. 276(2), (3): FA 1973, s. 38(2), (3).
S. 276(4)–(6): FA 1973, s. 38(3A)–(3C), as inserted by FA 1984, s. 81(2), and amended (subs. (3B)) by FA 1989, s. 130(1).
S. 276(7): FA 1973, s. 38(4), as substituted by ICTA 1988, s. 844 and Sch. 29, para. 12.
S. 276(8): FA 1973, s. 38(5), as amended by FA 1984, s. 81(4).

Cross references – S. 2(1): persons and gains chargeable to capital gains tax.
S. 25(2), (6): disapplication of deemed market value disposal provisions where exploration or exploitation asset becomes situated outside the UK.
S. 171–174, 178–181: within a group, as defined by s. 170 with references to companies being restricted to those established within the Companies Acts etc. (s. 170(9)) and which are UK-resident (s. 170(2)(a)), deemed no gain, no loss on transfers of capital assets or on domestication of UK branch (and subsequent effects), deemed appropriations where transfers are stock for one company but not for the other.
TMA 1970, s. 31(3)(c): appeal under s. 276 is specifically to the special commissioners.
ICTA 1988, s. 254(1): "security" includes securities not creating or evidencing a charge on assets.
FA 1973, s. 38 and Sch. 15, para. 2, 4: power of Board to demand information for purposes of s. 276 and certain provisions for collecting tax.
FA 2003, s. 153(2)(b): when dealing with a company; requirement to read any reference to a "branch or agency" (in s. 276(7)), as if it were a reference to a "permanent establishment" (effective for accounting periods beginning on or after 1 January 2003).

Statements of practice – 6/84: HMRC do not tax profits or gains of non-resident lessors leasing rigs, vessels etc. used for exploration or exploitation activities, subject to certain conditions.

Notes – S. 10: extent of charge on non-residents by reference to assets used or held for a UK branch or agency.
S. 21–34: general meaning of "asset".
S. 199: deemed disposal of exploration or exploitation assets in certain circumstances.
TMA 1970, S. 46B: questions as to the application of s. 276 determined by the Special Commissioners.
Territorial Sea Act 1987, s. 1: breadth of territorial sea is 12 nautical miles from coastline.

276A No gain/no loss: foreign permanent establishment exemption

276A(1) On a no gain/no loss disposal by a company in relation to which an election under section 18A of CTA 2009 (exemption for profits or losses of foreign permanent establishments) has effect, the amount of the consideration which would secure that neither a gain nor a loss would accrue to the company on the disposal is to be arrived at after taking account of the operation of the provisions of Chapter 3A of Part 2 of that Act (with the result that that amount includes the amount which for the purposes of that Chapter would in the case of the company be the foreign permanent establishments amount attributable to the disposal for the accounting period in which it was made if the disposal were not a no gain/no loss disposal).

276A(2) For the purposes of this section a no gain/no loss disposal is one on which by virtue of section 152 or any of the no gain/no loss provisions neither a gain nor a loss accrues to the company making the disposal.

History – S. 276A inserted by FA 2011, s. 48 and Sch. 13, para. 13, with effect from 19 July 2011, subject to the transitional provisions in FA 2011, Sch. 13, Pt 3.

277 Double taxation relief

277 [Omitted by TIOPA 2010, s. 374 and Sch. 8, para. 45 and repealed by TIOPA 2010, s. 378 and Sch. 10, Pt. 1.]

History – S. 277 omitted by TIOPA 2010, s. 374 and Sch. 8, para. 12 and repealed by TIOPA 2010, s. 378 and Sch. 10, Pt. 1, with effect for corporation tax purposes for accounting periods ending on or after 1 April 2010, for income tax and capital gains tax purposes for the tax year 2010–11 and subsequent tax years, and for petroleum revenue tax purposes for chargeable periods beginning on or after 1 July 2010.

Notes – S. 277 rewritten as follows:
S. 277(1): TIOPA 2010, s. 2(1), (2), (3), 3(1), (2), 6(3), (7), 8(2), (3) (2), (5), 9(2), (5), (6), 18(1), 19(2), 26(1), (3), (4), 27, 28(5), (6), 30(2), (4), (5), (6), (7), 31(1), (2), (4), 32(1), (2), (5), 35(3), (4), (5), 40(1), (2), (3), (4), (5), 41(1), (2), (4), 57(1), 79(1), (2), 80(6), 81(5), 82(2), (7), 84(1), 85(5), 87(5), (6), 88(2), 95(2), 105, 106(4), 124(1), 125(1), 129(3), (4), 134(1), (2), (3), (4), (5) and Sch.9, para. 16.
S. 277(1A): TIOPA 2010, s. 32(3).
S. 277(1B): TIOPA 2010, s. 32(2), (4).
S. 277(1C): TIOPA 2010, s. 32(6).
S. 277(2): TIOPA 2010, Sch. 9, para. 12.
S. 277(3): TIOPA 2010, s. 106(1), (2), (3), (5).
S. 277(4): TIOPA 2010, s. 129(1), (2), (3), (4).

278 Allowance for foreign tax

278 [Omitted by TIOPA 2010, s. 374 and Sch. 8, para. 46 and repealed by TIOPA 2010, s. 378 and Sch. 10, Pt. 1.]

History – S. 278 omitted by TIOPA 2010, s. 374 and Sch. 8, para. 46 and repealed by TIOPA 2010, s. 378 and Sch. 10, Pt. 1, with effect for corporation tax purposes for accounting periods ending on or after 1 April 2010, for income tax and capital gains tax purposes for the tax year 2010–11 and subsequent tax years, and for petroleum revenue tax purposes for chargeable periods beginning on or after 1 July 2010.

Notes – S. 278 rewritten as follows:
S. 278(1): TIOPA 2010, s. 113(1), (2), (3).
S. 278(2): TIOPA 2010, s. 114(1), (2), (3), (4).
S. 278(3): TIOPA 2010, s. 115(2), (3), (4).
S. 278(4): TIOPA 2010, s. 115(4).
S. 278(5): TIOPA 2010, s. 115(5).
S. 278(6): TIOPA 2010, s. 115(5).
S. 278(7): TIOPA 2010, s. 115(6).

279 Foreign assets: delayed remittances

279(1) Subsection (2) below applies where–

(a) chargeable gains accrue from the disposal of assets situated outside the United Kingdom, and

(b) the person charged or chargeable makes a claim, and

(c) the conditions set out in subsection (3) below are, so far as applicable, satisfied as respects those gains ("the qualifying gains");

and subsection (2)(b) also applies where a claim has been made under section 13 of the 1979 Act.

279(2) For the purposes of capital gains tax–

(a) the amount of the qualifying gains shall be deducted from the amounts on which the claimant is assessed to capital gains tax for the year in which the qualifying gains accrued to the claimant, but

(b) the amount so deducted shall be assessed to capital gains tax on the claimant (or his personal representatives) as if it were an amount of chargeable gains accruing in the year of assessment in which the conditions set out in subsection (3) below cease to be satisfied.

279(3) The conditions are–

(a) that the claimant was unable to transfer the qualifying gains to the United Kingdom, and

(b) that that inability was due to the laws of the territory where the assets were situated at the time of the disposal, or to the executive action of its government, or to the impossibility of obtaining foreign currency in that territory, and

(c) that the inability was not due to any want of reasonable endeavours on the part of the claimant.

279(4) Where under an agreement entered into under arrangements made by the Secretary of State in pursuance of section 1 of the Overseas Investment and Export Guarantees Act 1972 or section 11 of the Export Guarantees and Overseas Investment Act 1978 any payment is made by the Exports Credits Guarantee Department in respect of any gains which cannot be transferred to the United Kingdom, then, to the extent of the payment, the gains shall be treated as gains with respect to which the conditions mentioned in subsection (3) above are not satisfied (and accordingly cannot cease to be satisfied).

279(5) No claim under this section in respect of a chargeable gain shall be made–

(a) in the case of a claim for the purposes of capital gains tax, more than 4 years after the end of the year of assessment in which the gain accrues; or

(b) *in the case of a claim* for the purposes of corporation tax, more than 4 years after the end of the accounting period in which the gain accrues.

279(6) The personal representatives of a deceased person may make any claim which he might have made under this section if he had not died.

279(7) Where–

(a) a claim under this section is made (or has been made under section 13 of the 1979 Act) by a man in respect of chargeable gains accruing to his wife before 6th April 1990, and

(b) by virtue of this section the amount of the gains falls to be assessed to capital gains tax as if it were an amount of gains accruing in the year 1992–93 or a subsequent year of assessment,

it shall be assessed not on the claimant (or his personal representatives) but on the person to whom the gains accrued (or her personal representatives).

279(8) In relation to disposals before 19th March 1991 subsection (3)(b) above shall have effect with the substitution of the words "income arose" for the words "assets were situated at the time of the disposal".

History – S. 279(1)(b) and (c) substituted for former para. (b) by FA 1996, s. 134 and Sch. 20, para. 64 for 1996–97 and later years of assessment and accounting periods ending on or after 1 July 1999, the appointed day for self-assessment to corporation tax (FA 1994, s. 199 and SI 1998/3173 (C. 78)).

In s. 279(2)(a), the words "(before the application of any taper relief)" omitted by FA 2008, s. 8 and Sch. 2, para. 40 with effect in relation to chargeable gains accruing or treated as accruing in the tax year 2008–09 or any subsequent tax year (FA 2008, Sch. 2, para. 56(3)).

In s. 279(2)(a), words "(before the application of any taper relief)" inserted by FA 1998, s. 121 and Sch. 21, para. 9 with effect for 1998–99 and subsequent years.

In s. 279(5), the words "more than 4 years after the end of" and "4 years" substituted for the words "at any time after the fifth anniversary of the 31st January next following" and "6 years" (respectively) by FA 2008, s. 118(1) and Sch. 39, para. 31, with effect from 1 April 2010 (SI 2009/403, art. 2(2) subject to SI 2009/403, art. 3–10 – in particular art. 10).

S. 279(5) substituted by FA 1996, s. 135 and Sch. 21, para. 41 for 1996–97 and later years of assessment and accounting periods ending on or after 1 July 1999, the appointed day for self-assessment to corporation tax (see note above).

Derivations – S. 279(1)–(6): CGTA 1979, s. 13, as amended (subs. (3)(b)) by FA 1991, s. 97.

S. 279(7): FA 1988, s. 104(3).

S. 279(8): CGTA 1979, s. 13(3)(b) before amendment by FA 1991, s. 97.

Notes – S. 15: meaning of "chargeable gains".

S. 21–34: general meaning of "disposal" and "asset".

TMA 1970, s. 29: assessing procedure.

TMA 1970, s. 42–43B: procedures for making claims.

279A Deferred unascertainable consideration: election for treatment of loss

279A(1) Where–

(a) a person (**"the taxpayer"**) makes a disposal of a right to which this section applies (see subsection (2) below),

(b) on that disposal an allowable loss (**"the relevant loss"**) would, apart from section 279C, accrue to him in any year (**"the year of the loss"**), and

(c) the year of the loss is a year in which the taxpayer is within the charge to capital gains tax (see section 279B(1)),

the taxpayer may make an election under this section for the relevant loss to be treated as accruing in an earlier year in accordance with section 279C if condition 1 in subsection (3) below and condition 2 in subsection (5) below are satisfied.

279A(2) This section applies to a right if each of the following conditions is satisfied–

(a) the right was, in whole or in part, acquired by the taxpayer as the whole or part of the consideration for a disposal (the **"original disposal"**) by him of another asset (the **"original asset"**),

(b) the original disposal was made in a year (**"the year of the original disposal"**) earlier than the year in which the disposal mentioned in subsection (1)(a) above is made (**"the year of the right's disposal"**),

(c) where the right was acquired by the taxpayer as the whole or part of the consideration for two or more disposals (each of which is accordingly an **"original disposal"**), the condition in paragraph (b) above is satisfied with respect to each of those disposals (the **"original disposals"**),

(d) on the taxpayer's acquisition of the right, there was no corresponding disposal of it,

(e) the right is a right to unascertainable consideration (see section 279B(2) to (6)).

279A(3) Condition 1 for making an election in relation to the relevant loss is that a chargeable gain accrued to the taxpayer on any one or more of the following events–

(a) the original disposal,

(b) an earlier disposal of the original asset by the taxpayer in the year of the original disposal,

(c) a later disposal of the original asset by the taxpayer in a year earlier than the year of the right's disposal,

or would have so accrued but for paragraph 2(2)(a) of Schedule 5B or 5C (postponement of original gain). This subsection is subject to subsection (4) below.

279A(4) If the right to which this section applies was acquired by the taxpayer as the whole or part of the consideration for two or more original disposals (including cases where there are two or more original assets (the **"original assets"**))–

(a) any reference in subsection (3) above to the original disposal is a reference to any of the original disposals,

(b) any reference in that subsection to the original asset is a reference to the asset which is the original asset in relation to that original disposal, and

(c) any reference in that subsection to the year of the original disposal shall be construed accordingly.

279A(5) Condition 2 for making an election in relation to the relevant loss is that there is a year (an **"eligible year"**)–

(a) which is earlier than the year of the loss but not earlier than the year 1992–93,

(b) in which a chargeable gain falling within subsection (3) above or subsection (6) below accrued to the taxpayer, and

(c) for which, immediately before the election, there remains a relevant amount on which capital gains tax is chargeable (see subsection (7) below).

279A(6) A chargeable gain falling within this subsection accrues to the taxpayer in a year if–

(a) in that year a chargeable gain (the "revived gain") is treated as accruing to the taxpayer in accordance with paragraphs 4 and 5 of Schedule 5B or 5C (chargeable gain accruing to person on chargeable event), and

(b) the gain which, in determining the amount of the revived gain in accordance with those paragraphs, is the original gain consists of or represents the whole or some part of a gain that would have accrued as mentioned in subsection (3) above but for paragraph 2(2)(a) of Schedule 5B or 5C.

279A(7) For the purposes of subsection (5)(c) above, a year is one for which, immediately before an election, there remains a relevant amount on which capital gains tax is chargeable if, immediately before the making of that election, there remains an amount in respect of which the taxpayer is chargeable to capital gains tax for the year–

(a) after taking account of any previous elections made by the taxpayer under this section,

(b) after excluding the total amount of chargeable gains treated as accruing in that year by virtue of section 87 or 89(2) (read, where appropriate, with section 10A), and

(c) on the assumption that no part of the relevant loss (or of any other loss in respect of which an election under this section may be, but has not been, made) falls to be deducted in consequence of an election under this section from the chargeable gains accruing to the taxpayer in that year.

279A(8) In this section **"year"** means year of assessment.

279A(9) This section and sections 279B to 279D are to be construed as one.

History – In s. 279A(7)(b), the words "the total amount of chargeable gains treated as accruing in that year by virtue of section 87 or 89(2) (read, where appropriate, with section 10A)," substituted for the words "any amounts that fall to be brought into account for that year under section 2(4)(b) by virtue of section 2(5)(b)," by FA 2008, s. 8 and Sch. 2, para. 41 where the eligible year is 2008–09 or later (FA 2008, Sch. 2, para. 56(2)).

S. 279A inserted by FA 2003, s. 162(1) which has effect in relation to allowable losses that would, apart from the insertion of s. 279A by s. 162(1), accrue on or after 10 April 2003; for this purpose, losses that would, apart from the insertion of s. 279A, be treated by virtue of TCGA 1992, s. 10A (temporary non-residents), as accruing in the tax year 2003–04 shall be treated as so accruing on or after 10 April 2003.

Cross references – S. 138A: use of earn-out rights for exchange of securities.

S. 162(2): deferred unascertainable consideration – restrictions on the s. 138A election for treatment of earn-out rights as security.

279B Provisions supplementary to section 279A

279B(1) For the purposes of section 279A(1)(c) a person is within the charge to capital gains tax in any year if–

(a) he is chargeable to capital gains tax in respect of chargeable gains accruing to him in that year, or

(b) the person would be so chargeable if–

(i) chargeable gains accrued to the person in the year, and

(ii) the amount calculated under section 2(2) for the year in relation to the person exceeded the exempt amount for the year (within the meaning of section 3).

279B(2) Subsections (3) to (6) below have effect for the purposes of section 279A(2)(e) (right to *unascertainable consideration*).

279B(3) A right is a right to unascertainable consideration if, and only if,–

(a) it is a right to consideration the amount or value of which is unascertainable at the time when the right is conferred, and

(b) that amount or value is unascertainable at that time on account of its being referable, in whole or in part, to matters which are uncertain at that time because they have not yet occurred.

This subsection is subject to subsections (4) to (6) below.

279B(4) The amount or value of any consideration is not to be regarded as being unascertainable by reason only–

(a) that the right to receive the whole or any part of the consideration is postponed or contingent, if the consideration or, as the case may be, that part of it is, in accordance with section 48, brought into account in the computation of the gain accruing to the taxpayer on the disposal of an asset, or

(b) in a case where the right to receive the whole or any part of the consideration is postponed and is to be, or may be, to any extent satisfied by the receipt of property of one description or property of some other description, that some person has a right to select the property, or the description of property, that is to be received.

279B(5) A right is not to be taken to be a right to unascertainable consideration by reason only that either the amount or the value of the consideration has not been fixed, if–

(a) the amount will be fixed by reference to the value, and the value is ascertainable, or

(b) the value will be fixed by reference to the amount, and the amount is ascertainable.

279B(6) A right which is by virtue of subsection (2) or (4) of section 138A (use of earn-out rights for exchange of securities) assumed in accordance with subsection (3)(a) of that section to be a security, within the definition in section 132, is not to be regarded as a right to unascertainable consideration.

279B(7) For the purposes of section 279A, any question as to–

(a) whether a chargeable gain or a loss is one that accrues (or would, apart from any particular provision, accrue) on a particular disposal or a disposal of any particular description, or

(b) the time at which, or year in which, any particular disposal takes place,

is to be determined without regard to section 10A(2) (chargeable gains and losses accruing during temporary non-residence to be treated as accruing in period of return).

This subsection is subject to subsection (8) below.

279B(8) Subsection (7) above does not affect the determination of any question–

(a) as to the period in which the chargeable gain or loss is, by virtue of section 10A(2), to be treated as accruing (apart from section 279C), or

(b) where (apart from section 279C) a loss is to be treated by virtue of section 10A(2) as accruing in a particular period, whether the loss is an allowable loss.

History – S. 279B(1)(b) substituted by FA 2008, s. 8 and Sch. 2, para. 42 with effect in relation to chargeable gains accruing or treated as accruing in the tax year 2008–09 or any subsequent tax year (FA 2008, Sch. 2, para. 56(3)).

In s. 279B(7), the words "period of return" substituted for the words "year of return" by FA 2013, s. 218 and Sch. 45, para. 122(2), with effect if the year of departure (as defined in FA 2013, Sch. 45, Pt. 4) is the tax year 2013–14 or a subsequent tax year, subject to the transitional and saving provision in FA 2013, Sch. 45, para. 154–159.

In s. 279B(8)(a) and (b), the word "period" substituted for the word "year" by FA 2013, s. 218 and Sch. 45, para. 122(3), with effect if the year of departure (as defined in FA 2013, Sch. 45, Pt. 4) is the tax year 2013–14 or a subsequent tax year, subject to the transitional and saving provision in FA 2013, Sch. 45, para. 154–159.

S. 279B inserted by FA 2003, s. 162(1) which has effect in relation to allowable losses that would, apart from the insertion of s. 279A by s. 162(1), accrue on or after 10 April 2003; for this purpose, losses that would, apart from the insertion of s. 279A , be treated by virtue of TCGA 1992, s. 10A (temporary non-residents), as accruing in the tax year 2003–04 shall be treated as so accruing on or after 10 April 2003.

279C Effect of election under section 279A

279C(1) This section applies where an election is made under section 279A by the taxpayer for the relevant loss to be treated as accruing in an earlier year in accordance with this section.

279C(2) Where this section applies, the relevant loss shall be treated for the purposes of capital gains tax as if it were a loss accruing to the taxpayer in the earliest year which is an eligible year (the **"first eligible year"**), instead of in the year of the loss (but subject to, and in accordance with, the following provisions of this section).

279C(3) The amount of the relevant loss that falls to be deducted (in accordance with section 2(2)(a)) from the chargeable gains of the first eligible year is limited to the first year limit.

279C(4) The first year limit is the amount calculated under section 2(2) (read, where appropriate, with section 2(4)(a)) for the first eligible year.

279C(4A) For the purpose of making that calculation–

(a) no account is to be taken of the relevant loss, but

(b) the effect of any previous election under section 279A is to be taken into account.

279C(5) As respects any later year before the year of the loss, the relevant loss (so far as not previously allowed as a deduction from chargeable gains accruing in any previous year) falls to be deducted in accordance with section 2(2)(b) only if that later year is an eligible year.

279C(6) The amount of the relevant loss that falls to be deducted from chargeable gains of that later eligible year in accordance with section 2(2)(b) is limited to the amount (the **"later year limit"**) in respect of which the taxpayer would be chargeable to capital gains tax for that later year–

(a) on the assumption in subsection (7) below,

(b) taking account of any previous elections under section 279A, and

(c) apart from amounts of chargeable gains treated as accruing in that later year by virtue of section 87 or 89(2) (read, where appropriate, with section 10A).

279C(7) The assumption is that no part of–

(a) the relevant loss, or

(b) any loss in respect of which an election under section 279A may be, but has not been, made,

falls to be deducted, in consequence of an election under section 279A, from any chargeable gains accruing to the taxpayer in that later eligible year.

The assumption falls to be made immediately after the making of the election in respect of the relevant loss.

279C(8) [Omitted by FA 2008, s. 8 and Sch. 2, para. 43(4).]

279C(9) All such adjustments shall be made, whether by discharge or repayment of tax, the making of assessments or otherwise, as are required to give effect to the election under section 279A made by the taxpayer for the relevant loss to be treated as accruing in an earlier year in accordance with this section.

279C(10) [Omitted by FA 2008, s. 8 and Sch. 2, para. 43(5).]

History – S. 279C(3) substituted for s. 279C(3)–(4) by FA 2008, s. 8 and Sch. 2, para. 43(2) where the eligible year is 2008–09 or later (FA 2008, Sch. 2, para. 56(2)).
S. 279C(4) substituted for s. 279C(3)–(4) by FA 2008, s. 8 and Sch. 2, para. 43(2) where the eligible year is 2008–09 or later (FA 2008, Sch. 2, para. 56(2)).
S. 279C(4A) substituted for s. 279C(3)–(4) by FA 2008, s. 8 and Sch. 2, para. 43(2) where the eligible year is 2008–09 or later (FA 2008, Sch. 2, para. 56(2)).
In s. 279C(6)(c), the words "amounts of chargeable gains treated as accruing in that later year by virtue of section 87 or 89(2) (read, where appropriate, with section 10A)" substituted for the words "the provisions specified in subsection (8) below" by FA 2008, s. 8 and Sch. 2, para. 43(3) where the eligible year is 2008–09 or later (FA 2008, Sch. 2, para. 56(2)).
S. 279C(8) omitted by FA 2008, s. 8 and Sch. 2, para. 43(4) where the eligible year is 2008–09 or later (FA 2008, Sch. 2, para. 56(2)).
S. 279C(10) omitted by FA 2008, s. 8 and Sch. 2, para. 43(5) where the eligible year is 2008–09 or later (FA 2008, Sch. 2, para. 56(2)).
S. 279C inserted by FA 2003, s. 162(1) which has effect in relation to allowable losses that would, apart from the insertion of s. 279A by s. 162(1), accrue on or after 10 April 2003; for this purpose, losses that would, apart from the insertion of s. 279A , be treated by virtue of TCGA 1992, s. 10A (temporary non-residents), as accruing in the tax year 2003–04 shall be treated as so accruing on or after 10 April 2003.

Cross references – TCGA 1992, s. 138A: use of earn-out rights for exchange of securities.
S. 162(2): deferred unascertainable consideration – restrictions on the s. 138A election for treatment of earn-out rights as security.

279D Elections under section 279A

279D(1) An election under section 279A is irrevocable.

279D(2) Any election under that section must be made by giving a notice in accordance with this section.

279D(3) The notice must be given to an officer of the Board.

279D(4) Subsections (5) to (8) below have effect in relation to the notice given by the taxpayer in respect of the relevant loss.

279D(5) The notice must specify each of the following–

(a) the amount of the relevant loss;

(b) the right disposed of;

(c) the year of the right's disposal;

(d) the year of the loss (if different from the year of the right's disposal);

(e) the year in which the right was acquired;

(f) the original asset or assets.

279D(6) The notice must also specify each of the following–

(a) the eligible year in which the relevant loss is to be treated in accordance with section 279C(2) as accruing to the taxpayer;

(b) the first year limit (see section 279C(3) and (4));

(c) how much of the relevant loss falls to be deducted in accordance with section 2(2)(a) from chargeable gains accruing to the taxpayer in that year.

279D(7) If, in accordance with section 279C, any part of the relevant loss falls to be deducted in accordance with section 2(2)(b) from chargeable gains accruing to the taxpayer in any later eligible year, the notice must also specify–

(a) each such year;

(b) in the case of each such year, the later year limit (see section 279C(6));

(c) how much of the relevant loss falls to be deducted in accordance with section 2(2)(b) in each such year from chargeable gains accruing to the taxpayer in that year.

279D(8) The notice must be given on or before the first anniversary of the 31st January next following the year of the loss.

279D(9) An election under section 279A is made on the date on which the notice of the election is given.

279D(10) Different notices must be given in respect of different losses.

279D(11) Where a person makes two or more elections under section 279A on the same day, the notices must specify the order in which the elections are made.

279D(12) For the purposes of any provisions of sections 279A to 279C whose operation is affected by the order in which any elections under section 279A are made, elections made by a person on the same day shall be treated as made at different times and in the order specified in accordance with subsection (11) above.

History – S. 279D inserted by FA 2003, s. 162(1) which has effect in relation to allowable losses that would, apart from the insertion of s. 279A by s. 162(1), accrue on or after 10 April 2003; for this purpose, losses that would, apart from the insertion of s. 279A, be treated by virtue of TCGA 1992, s. 10A (temporary non-residents), as accruing in the tax year 2003–04 shall be treated as so accruing on or after 10 April 2003.

280 Consideration payable by instalments

280 If the consideration, or part of the consideration, taken into account in the computation of the gain is payable by instalments over a period beginning not earlier than the time when the disposal is made, being a period exceeding 18 months, then, at the option of the person making the disposal, the tax on a chargeable gain accruing on the disposal may be paid by such instalments as the Board may allow over a period not exceeding 8 years and ending not later than the time at which the last of the first-mentioned instalments is payable.

History – In s. 280 words "at the option of the person making the disposal, the tax on a chargeable gain accruing on the disposal may" substituted for "if the person making the disposal satisfies the Board that he would otherwise suffer undue hardship, the tax on a chargeable gain accruing on the disposal may, at his option," by FA 1996, s. 134 and Sch. 20, para. 65 for 1996–97 and later years of assessment and accounting periods ending on or after 1 July 1999, the appointed day for self-assessment to corporation tax under FA 1994, s. 199 by virtue of SI 1998/3173 (C. 78).

Derivations – CGTA 1979, s. 40(1).

Notes – S. 7: time for payment of capital gains tax.
S. 15, 37: importance of consideration in that every gain is a chargeable gain, subject to specific provisions such as the exclusion for amounts chargeable to tax as income.
ICTA 1988, s. 12: time for payment of corporation tax.

281 Payment by instalments of tax on gifts

281(1) Subsection (2) below applies where–

(a) the whole or any part of any assets to which this section applies is disposed of by way of gift or is deemed to be disposed of under section 71(1) or 72(1), and

(b) the disposal is one–

(i) to which neither section 165(4) nor section 260(3) applies (or would apply if a claim were duly made), or

(ii) to which either of those sections does apply but on which the held-over gain (within the meaning of the section applying) is less than the chargeable gain which would have accrued on that disposal apart from that section.

281(2) Where this subsection applies, the capital gains tax chargeable on a gain accruing on the disposal may, if the person paying it by notice to an officer of the Board so elects, be paid by 10 equal yearly instalments.

281(3) The assets to which this section applies are–

(a) land or an estate or interest in land,

(b) any shares or securities of a company which, immediately before the disposal, gave control of the company to the person by whom the disposal was made or deemed to be made, and

(c) any shares or securities of a company not falling under paragraph (b) above and not listed on a recognised stock exchange.

281(4) Where tax is payable by instalments by virtue of this section, the first instalment shall be due on the day on which the tax would be payable apart from this section.

281(5) Subject to the following provisions of this section–

(a) tax payable by instalments by virtue of this section carries interest in accordance with Part IX of the Management Act as that Part applies where no election is made under subsection (2) above, and

(b) the interest on the unpaid portion of the tax shall be added to each instalment and paid accordingly.

281(6) Tax payable by instalments by virtue of this section which is for the time being unpaid, with interest (determined in accordance with subsection (5)(a) above) to the date of payment, may be paid at any time.

281(7) Tax which apart from this subsection would be payable by instalments by virtue of this section and which is for the time being unpaid, with interest (determined in accordance with subsection (5)(a) above as if the tax were tax payable by instalments by virtue of this section) to the date of payment, shall become due and payable immediately if–

(a) the disposal was by way of gift to a person connected with the donor or was deemed to be made under section 71(1) or 72(1), and

(b) the assets are disposed of for valuable consideration under a subsequent disposal (whether or not the subsequent disposal is made by the person who acquired them under the first disposal).

281(8) Subsection (2) above applies in relation to a chargeable gain accruing to a transferor under section 169C(7) (clawback of relief under section 165 or 260 if settlement becomes settlor-interested etc) as it applies in relation to a gain accruing to a person on a disposal if–

(a) the relevant disposal (within the meaning of section 169C) in question was a disposal of the whole or any part of any assets to which this section applies, and

(b) at the material time (within the meaning of that section), no part of the subject-matter of that relevant disposal has been disposed of for valuable consideration under a subsequent disposal (whether made by the trustees to whom that relevant disposal was made or by some other person).

281(9) Where subsection (2) above so applies, subsections (4) to (7) above apply accordingly but as if for paragraphs (a) and (b) of subsection (7) there were substituted "any part of the subject-matter of the relevant disposal in question is disposed of for valuable consideration under a subsequent disposal (whether made by the trustees to whom that relevant disposal was made or by some other person)."

History – In s. 281(2), the words "the inspector" were substituted by the words "an officer of the Board" by FA 2004, s. 116 and Sch. 21, para. 6(2) with effect, by virtue of FA 2004, Sch. 21, para. 10(3), in relation to any notice given in respect of the year 2004–05 or any subsequent year of assessment.

In s. 281(3)(c), the words "nor dealt in on the Unlisted Securities Market" repealed by FA 2004, s. 326 and Sch. 42, Pt. 2(14) with effect in relation to disposals on or after 22 July 2004.

In s. 281(3)(c) the word "listed" substituted for "quoted" by FA 1996, s. 199 and Sch. 38, para. 10 for disposals on or after 1 April 1996.

S. 281(5)(a) substituted by FA 1996, s. 132 and Sch. 18, para. 15 with effect as provided by para. 17(3).

In s. 281(6) the words "(determined in accordance with subsection (5)(a) above)" inserted by FA 1996, s. 132 and Sch. 18, para. 15 with effect as provided by para. 17(3).

In s. 281(7) the words "(determined in accordance with subsection (5)(a) above as if the tax were tax payable by instalments by virtue of this section)" inserted by FA 1996, s. 132 and Sch. 18, para. 15 with effect as provided by para. 17(3).

S. 281(8) inserted by FA 2004, s. 116 and Sch. 21, para. 6(3) with effect, by virtue of FA 2003, Sch. 21, para. 10(4)], in relation to disposals on or after 10 December 2003 (whenever any earlier disposal as mentioned in section 169B(3)(b) or 169C(3)(b) was made).

S. 281(9) inserted by FA 2004, s. 116 and Sch. 21, para. 6(3) with effect, by virtue of FA 2003, Sch. 21, para. 10(4), in relation to disposals on or after 10 December 2003 (whenever any earlier disposal as mentioned in section 169B(3)(b) or 169C(3)(b) was made).

Derivations – CGTA 1979, s. 7A, as inserted by FA 1989, s. 124 and Sch. 14, para. 5.

Cross references – S. 71(1): person becoming absolutely entitled to settled property.
S. 72(1): termination of life interest on death of person entitled.
S. 165(4): hold-over relief for gifts of business assets.
S. 260(3): hold-over relief for gifts in respect of which inheritance tax is chargeable.
TMA 1970, s. 86–92 (Pt. IX): interest on overdue tax.

282 Recovery of tax from donee

282(1) If in any year of assessment a chargeable gain accrues to any person on the disposal of an asset by way of gift and any amount of capital gains tax assessed on that person for that year of assessment is not paid within 12 months from the date when the tax becomes payable, the donee may, by an assessment made not later than 2 years from the date when the tax became payable, be assessed and charged (in the name of the donor) to capital gains tax on an amount not exceeding the amount of the chargeable gain so accruing, and not exceeding the grossed up amount of that capital gains tax unpaid at the time when he is so assessed, grossing up at the marginal rate of tax, that is to say, taking capital gains tax on a chargeable gain at the amount which would not have been chargeable but for that chargeable gain.

282(2) A person paying any amount of tax in pursuance of this section shall be entitled to recover a sum of that amount from the donor.

282(3) References in this section to a **donor** include, in the case of an individual who has died, references to his personal representatives.

282(4) In this section references to a **gift** include references to any transaction otherwise than by way of a bargain made at arm's length so far as money or money's worth passes under the transaction without full consideration in money or money's worth, and **"donor"** and **"donee"** shall be construed accordingly; and this section shall apply in relation to a gift made by 2 or more donors with the necessary modifications and subject to any necessary apportionments.

282(5) This section applies in relation to a chargeable gain accruing to a transferor under section 169C(7) (clawback of relief under section 165 or 260 if settlement becomes settlor-interested etc) as it applies in relation to a chargeable gain accruing to a person on the disposal of an asset by way of gift.

282(6) For the purposes of this section as applied by subsection (5) above–

(a) the transferor shall be taken to be the donor, and

(b) the trustees to whom the relevant disposal (within the meaning of section 169C) in question was made shall be taken to be the donee.

History – S. 282(5) inserted by FA 2004, s. 116 and Sch. 21, para. 7(2) with effect, by virtue of FA 2003, Sch. 21, para. 10(4), in relation to disposals on or after 10 December 2003 (whenever any earlier disposal as mentioned in section 169B(3)(b) or 169C(3)(b) was made).

S. 282(6) inserted by FA 2004, s. 116 and Sch. 21, para. 7(2) with effect, by virtue of FA 2003, Sch. 21, para. 10(4), in relation to disposals on or after 10 December 2003 (whenever any earlier disposal as mentioned in section 169B(3)(b) or 169C(3)(b) was made).

Derivations – CGTA 1979, s. 59.

Cross references – IHTA 1984, s. 165: in some cases, where a chargeable transfer includes a disposal, capital gains tax borne by the donee, as defined in s. 282, is treated as reducing the value transferred.

Notes – S. 2: charges to capital gains tax.
S. 7: time for payment of capital gains tax.
S. 15: meaning of "chargeable gains".
S. 21–34: general meaning of "disposal" and "asset".
TMA 1970, s. 29: assessing procedure.

283 Repayment supplements

283(1) Subject to the provisions of this section, where in the case of capital gains tax paid by or on behalf of an individual for a year of assessment a repayment of that tax is made by the Board or an officer of the Board, the repayment shall be increased under this section by an amount (**"a repayment supplement"**) equal to interest on the amount repaid at the rate applicable under section 178 of the Finance Act 1989 for the period (if any) between the relevant time and the date on which the order for the repayment is issued.

283(2) For the purposes of subsection (1) above, the relevant time is the date on which the tax was paid.

283(3) A repayment supplement shall not be payable under this section in respect of a repayment or payment made in consequence of an order or judgment of a court having power to allow interest on the repayment or payment.

283(4) Subsections (1) to (3) above shall apply in relation to the trustees of a settlement or the personal representatives of a deceased person as they apply in relation to an individual.

283(5) [Repealed by FA 1994, Sch. 19, para. 46(4).]

History – In s. 283(1) the words "a repayment … of the Board" substituted for "for which he was resident in the United Kingdom, a repayment of that tax is made by the Board or an inspector after the end of the 12 months following that year of assessment", and "the date on which" substituted for "the end of the tax month in which", by FA 1994, Sch. 19, para. 46(1), with effect for years after 1995–96.

In s. 283(1) the words "of not less than £25" which appeared after "tax" repealed by FA 1989, s. 158(2) with effect in relation to repayments of tax made on or after 6 April 1993 by virtue of SI 1993/753.

In s. 283(2) words "the relevant time … tax was paid" substituted by FA 1997, s. 92(5) with effect for 1997–98 and subsequent years of assessment and with deemed effect for 1996–97.

S. 283(2) substituted by FA 1994, s. 196 and Sch. 19, para. 46(2), with effect for years after 1995–96.

In s. 283(4), the words "the trustees of a settlement or" substituted for "a trust or," by FA 2006, s. 88 and Sch. 12, para 24(1)(a) with effect in relation to a repayment made on or after 6 April 2006.

In s. 283(4), the words "as such (within the meaning of section 701(4) of that Act)" omitted by FA 2006, s. 88 and Sch. 12, para. 24(1)(b) and repealed by FA 2006, s. 178 and Sch. 26, Pt. 3(15) with effect in relation to a repayment made on or after 6 April 2006 (irrespective of when the deceased died).

In s. 283(4) the words "trust or" substituted for "partnership or a United Kingdom trust (as defined in section 231(5) of the Taxes Act) or, in the case of a United Kingdom estate (as defined by section 701(9) of that Act)" by FA 1994, Sch. 19, para. 46(3), with effect for years after 1995–96.

S. 283(5) repealed by FA 1994, s. 196 and Sch. 19, para. 46(4), with effect for years after 1995–96.

Derivations – S. 283(1) (as originally enacted): F(No. 2)A 1975, s. 47(1), as amended by FA 1989, s. 179(1)(a)(vi).
S. 283(2)–(5) (as originally enacted): F(No. 2)A 1975, s. 47(4), (8), (11), (12).

Cross references – ICTA 1988, s. 231(5): definition of UK trust, largely repealed by FA 1989, s. 110 and Sch. 17 on introduction of provisions for determining the residence of trustees, by reference to a trust administered under UK law unless it is generally administered outside the UK by trustees a majority of whom are not resident or not ordinarily resident.

ICTA 1988, s. 701(4), (9): personal representatives defined by reference to the Administration of Estates Act 1925 (or similar under overseas law) and UK estate defined by reference to income which has borne UK income tax at source or on which the personal representatives are directly assessable unless they could claim any exemption by virtue of being not resident or not ordinarily resident.
ICTA 1988, s. 824(8): repayment supplement is not chargeable to tax as income.
TMA 1970, s. 30: recovery of repayment supplement overpaid.
TMA 1970, s. 70A: deemed date of payment of a cheque for the purposes of s. 283, where it is received after 5 April 1996.
FA 1989, s. 178: power of Treasury to set rates of interest for certain purposes by regulations.
FA 1990, s. 25(13): donations to charity by individuals.
FA 2004, s. 83(5): meaning of "tax repayment" for the purposes of charitable-giving through the individual's self-assessment return.
FA 2004, s. 109: capital gains tax credit etc. for special withholding tax.
SI 2011/701, art. 5: s. 283 does not apply to any self-assessment amount (as defined in SI 2011/701, art. 2) which becomes payable or repayable on or after 31 October 2011 (the date of the coming into force of FA 2009, s. 101–103).

Statutory instruments – SI 1989/1297, reg. 3AB: applicable rate of interest for the purposes of s. 283.

Hansard – 2 July 1975, col. 746 (not reproduced): where a taxpayer simultaneously has tax due under one assessment and has overpaid on another and he draws this fact to the Revenue's attention and asks for a set-off, interest will not be charged on the tax due as of the date that the set-off request is made (to the extent that it can be met from the overpayment).

Other material – ICAEW Technical Release TR 798: confirmation of Hansard statement (see Hansard note).

Notes – S. 9: meaning of "resident".

284 Income tax decisions

284 Any assessment to income tax or decision on a claim under the Income Tax Acts, and any decision on an appeal under the Income Tax Acts against such an assessment or decision, shall be conclusive so far as, under any provision of this Act, liability to tax depends on the provisions of the Income Tax Acts.

Derivations – CGTA 1979, s. 154.

Notes – Interpretation Act 1978, s. 5 and Sch. 1: the Income Tax Acts mean the enactments relating to income tax.

284A Concessions that defer a charge

284A(1) This section applies where–

(a) a person ("the original taxpayer") has at any time obtained for any chargeable period ("the first chargeable period") the benefit of any capital gains relief to which he had no statutory entitlement;

(b) the benefit of the relief was obtained in reliance on any concession;

(c) the concession was first published by the Board before 9th March 1999 or (having been published on or after that date) replaced a concession satisfying the requirements of this paragraph with a concession to the same or substantially the same effect; and

(d) the concession involved the application (with or without modifications), to a case to which they would not otherwise have applied, of the provisions of any enactment ("the relevant statutory provisions").

284A(2) This section applies only if, at the time when the original taxpayer obtained the benefit of the relief, the concession was one available generally to any person falling within its terms.

284A(3) If the benefit obtained for the first chargeable period by the original taxpayer is repudiated for any later chargeable period (whether by the original taxpayer or by another person), the enactments relating to the taxation of chargeable gains shall have effect as if a chargeable gain equal to the amount of that benefit accrued in the later chargeable period to the person repudiating the benefit.

284A(4) For the purposes of this section–

(a) a capital gains relief for any chargeable period is a relief (of whatever description) the effect of which is that the amount of the chargeable gains taken to have accrued to that person in that period is less than it otherwise would have been; and

(b) the amount of the benefit of any such relief is the amount by which, as a consequence of that relief, those gains are less than they otherwise would have been.

284A(5) Where, without applying a specific enactment, any concession has the effect that–

(a) any asset is treated as the same as another asset and as acquired as the other asset was acquired,

(b) any two or more assets are treated as a single asset, or

(c) any disposal is treated as having been a disposal on which neither a gain nor a loss accrued,

that concession shall be assumed for the purposes of this section to have involved the application, to a case to which it would not otherwise have applied, of the provisions of an enactment to the corresponding effect.

284A(6) For the purposes of this section the benefit of any relief obtained by the original taxpayer for the first chargeable period is repudiated by a person for a later chargeable period if–

(a) circumstances arise such that, had the equivalent circumstances arisen in the case of the corresponding relief under the relevant statutory provisions, the whole or a part of the benefit of that relief would have fallen to be recouped from that person in the later chargeable period;

(b) apart from this section, the recoupment in the actual circumstances of the whole or a part of the benefit obtained by the original taxpayer is prevented by the fact that the original taxpayer relied on a concession (rather than on the relevant statutory provisions) to obtain that benefit; and

(c) the person from whom, in the equivalent circumstances, the amount of the benefit or any part of it would have fallen to be recouped is not precluded by subsection (8) below from relying on that fact in relation to that amount or part.

284A(7) For the purposes of this section an amount of the benefit of a capital gains relief is recouped from any person in a chargeable period to the extent that an amount is so brought into account in his case for that period as to secure that–

(a) the amount of his chargeable gains for that period is taken to be more than it otherwise would have been by an amount directly or indirectly representing the whole or a part of the amount of the benefit; or

(b) the amount of his allowable losses for that period is taken to be less than it otherwise would have been by an amount directly or indirectly representing the whole or a part of the amount of the benefit.

284A(8) Where–

(a) any such circumstances as are mentioned in subsection (6)(a) above have arisen in relation to the relief the benefit of which has been obtained by the original taxpayer,

(b) the person from whom, in the equivalent circumstances, the whole or any part of the amount of the benefit would have fallen to be recouped has accepted that, in the actual circumstances, the whole or a part of the benefit obtained by the original taxpayer may be recouped from him, and

(c) that acceptance is indicated in writing to the Board (whether by the making or amendment of a self-assessment or otherwise),

that person's rights subsequently to amend, appeal against or otherwise challenge any assessment shall not be exercised in any manner inconsistent with his acceptance of that matter (which shall be irrevocable).

284A(9) In this section **"concession"** includes any practice, interpretation or other statement in the nature of a concession.

History – S. 284A inserted by FA 1999, s. 76(1), with effect in relation to any case in which the circumstances arising as mentioned in s. 284A(6)(a) are circumstances arising on or after 9th March 1999, whether the benefit mentioned in s. 284A(1) was obtained as so mentioned before or after 27th July 1999 (the passing of Finance Act 1999).

284B Provisions supplementary to section 284A

284B(1) [Omitted by FA 2008, s. 8 and Sch. 2, para. 44.]

284B(2) The total amount of chargeable gains that are treated as accruing to any person under subsection (3) of section 284A in respect of any such benefit as is referred to in that subsection shall not exceed the amount of that benefit.

284B(3) Where, after any assessment to tax has been made on the basis that any chargeable gain is treated as having accrued to any person under section 284A(3)–

(a) the person assessed, within any of the periods allowed by subsection (4) below, gives an indication for the purposes of section 284A(8), or

(b) a final determination of the original taxpayer's liability to tax for the first chargeable period is made on the basis that the original taxpayer did not, or was not entitled to, rely on the concession in question,

all such adjustments shall be made (whether by way of assessment, amendment of an assessment, repayment of tax or otherwise) as are necessary to secure that no person is subjected to any greater liability by virtue of section 284A(3) than he would have been had the indication been given, or the final determination made, before the making of the assessment.

284B(4) The periods allowed by this subsection are–

(a) the period of twelve months beginning with the making of the assessment;

(b) the period within which the person is entitled to amend his self-assessment or company tax return for the chargeable period in which the chargeable gain under section 284A(3) is treated as having accrued to him;

(c) where the person makes a claim for any further relief against the amount that may be recouped from him by virtue of his indication under section 284A(8), the period allowed for making that claim.

284B(5) Subsection (3) above has effect notwithstanding any time limits relating to the making or amendment of an assessment for any chargeable period.

History – S. 284B(1) omitted by FA 2008, s. 8 and Sch. 2, para. 44 with effect in relation to chargeable gains accruing or treated as accruing in the tax year 2008–09 or any subsequent tax year (FA 2008, Sch. 2, para. 56(3)).

S. 284B inserted by FA 1999, s. 76(1), with effect in relation to any case in which the circumstances arising as mentioned in s. 284A(6)(a) are circumstances arising on or after 9th March 1999, whether the benefit mentioned in s. 284A(1) was obtained as so mentioned before or after 27 July 1999 (the passing of Finance Act 1999).

285 Recognised investment exchanges

285 [Omitted by FA 2007, s. 109 and Sch. 26, para. 8(6), and repealed by FA 2007, s. 114 and Sch. 27, Pt. 6(5).]

History – S. 285 omitted by FA 2007, s. 109 and Sch. 26, para. 8(6), and repealed by FA 2007, s. 114 and Sch. 27, Part 6(5), with effect from 19 July 2007 (Royal Assent).

285A European Economic Interest Groupings

285A(1) The following rules about European Economic Interest Groupings apply for the purposes of charging tax in respect of chargeable gains–

Rule 1

A grouping is treated as acting as the agent of its members.

Rule 2

The activities of a grouping are treated as those of its members acting jointly.

Rule 3

Each member of a grouping is treated as having a share of the grouping's property, rights and liabilities.

Rule 4

Any trade or profession carried on by the grouping is treated as carried on in partnership by members of the grouping.

Rule 5

A person is to be regarded as acquiring or disposing of a share of the assets of the grouping not only where there is an acquisition or disposal of assets by the grouping while he is a member of it, but also where he becomes or ceases to be a member of a grouping or there is a change in his share of the property of the grouping.

285A(2) For the purposes of Rule 3, a member's share of any property, rights or liabilities of a grouping is determined according to the contract under which the grouping is established.

285A(3) If the contract does not provide for this, the member's share is determined by reference to the share of the profits of the grouping to which the member is entitled under the contract.

285A(4) If the contract does not provide for this either, the members are treated as having equal shares of the property, rights and liabilities of the grouping.

285A(5) **"European Economic Interest Grouping"** means a European Economic Interest Grouping formed under Council Regulation (EEC) No 2137/85 of 25th July 1985, whether registered in Great Britain, Northern Ireland or elsewhere.

History – S. 285A inserted by ITA 2007, s. 1027 and Sch. 1, para. 341, with effect from 6 April 2007.

286 Connected persons: interpretation

286(1) Any question whether a person is connected with another shall for the purposes of this Act be determined in accordance with the following subsections of this section (any provision that one person is connected with another being taken to mean that they are **connected** with one another).

286(2) A person is **connected** with an individual if that person is the individual's spouse or civil partner, or is a relative, or the spouse or civil partner of a relative, of the individual or of the individual's spouse or civil partner.

286(3) A person, in his capacity as trustee of a settlement, is connected with–

(a) any individual who in relation to the settlement is a settlor,

(b) any person who is connected with such an individual,

(c) any body corporate which is connected with that settlement

(d) if the settlement is the principal settlement in relation to one or more sub-fund settlements, the trustees of the sub-fund settlements, and

(e) if the settlement is a sub-fund settlement in relation to a principal settlement, the trustees of any other sub-fund settlements in relation to the principal settlement.

286(3ZA) For the purpose of subsection (3) above–

(a) **"settlement"** has the same meaning as in section 620 of ITTOIA 2005, and

(b) **"trustee"**, in relation to a settlement in relation to which there would be no trustees apart from this paragraph, means any person in whom the settled property or its management is for the time being vested.

286(3A) For the purpose of subsection (3) above a body corporate is connected with a settlement if–

(a) it is a close company (or only not a close company because it is not resident in the United Kingdom) and the participators include the trustees of the settlement; or

(b) it is controlled (within the meaning of section 1124 of CTA 2010) by a company falling within paragraph (a) above.

286(4) Except in relation to acquisitions or disposals of partnership assets pursuant to bona fide commercial arrangements, a person is connected with any person with whom he is in partnership, and with the spouse or civil partner or a relative of any individual with whom he is in partnership.

286(5) A company is connected with another company–

(a) if the same person has control of both, or a person has control of one and persons connected with him, or he and persons connected with him, have control of the other, or

(b) if a group of 2 or more persons has control of each company, and the groups either consist of the same persons or could be regarded as consisting of the same persons by treating (in one or more cases) a member of either group as replaced by a person with whom he is connected.

286(6) A company is connected with another person, if that person has control of it or if that person and persons connected with him together have control of it.

286(7) Any 2 or more persons acting together to secure or exercise control of a company shall be treated in relation to that company as connected with one another and with any person acting on the directions of any of them to secure or exercise control of the company.

286(8) In this section **"relative"** means brother, sister, ancestor or lineal descendant.

History – In s. 286(2) the words "spouse or civil partner" substituted for the words "husband or wife" three times by SI 2005/3229, reg. 121, with effect from 5 December 2005.

In s. 286(3)(b), the word "and" at the end omitted by FA 2006, s. 88 and Sch. 12, para. 43(a) and repealed by FA 2006, s. 178, Sch. 26, Pt. 3(15) with effect for years of assessment beginning on or after 6 April 2006.

In s. 286(3), the words following para. (c) (then the last para.) omitted by FA 2006, s. 88 and Sch. 12, para. 25(1) and repealed by FA 2006, s. 178 and Sch. 26, Pt. 3(15) with effect from 6 April 2006 (in relation to settlements whenever created).

S. 286(3)(d)–(e) inserted by FA 2006, s. 88 and Sch. 12, para. 43(b), with effect for years of assessment beginning on or after 6 April 2006.

In s. 286(3), words "Chapter 5 of Part 5 of ITTOIA 2005 (see section 620 of that Act)" substituted for the words "Chapter 1A of Part XV of the Taxes Act (see section 660G(1) and (2) of that Act)" substituted by words by ITTOIA 2005, s. 882 and Sch. 1, para. 446 which, in accordance with ITTOIA 2005, s. 883, have effect, for income tax purposes, for tax year 2005–06 and subsequent tax years, and, for corporation tax purposes, for accounting periods ending after 5 April 2005.

S. 286(3) substituted by FA 1995, s. 74 and Sch. 17, para. 31, with effect for 1995–96 and subsequent years of assessment and applying in relation to every settlement wherever and whenever it was made or entered into.

S. 286(3ZA) inserted by FA 2006, s. 88 and Sch. 12, para. 25(2), with effect from 6 April 2006 (in relation to settlements whenever created).

In s. 286(3A), the words "section 1124 of CTA 2010" substituted for "section 840 of the Taxes Act" by CTA 2010, s. 1177 and Sch. 1, para. 263, with effect for corporation tax purposes for accounting periods ending on or after 1 April 2010, and for income tax and capital gains tax purposes for the tax year 2010–11 and subsequent tax years.

S. 286(3A) inserted by FA 1995, s. 74 and Sch. 17, para. 31, with effect for 1995–96 and subsequent years of assessment and applying in relation to every settlement wherever and whenever it was made or entered into.

In s. 286(4) the words "spouse or civil partner" substituted for the words "husband or wife" by SI 2005/3229, reg. 121, with effect from 5 December 2005.

Derivations – CGTA 1979, s. 63.

Cross references – S. 177(7): in relation to loss restriction by reference to dividend stripping, s. 286(7) also refers to actions to acquire holdings of shares or securities.

ICTA 1988, Pt. XV, Ch. IA: settlements and the liability of the settlor.

ICTA 1988, s. 660G: "settlement" includes any disposition, trust, covenant, agreement, arrangement or transfer of assets and "settlor" means any person by whom the settlement was made.

IHTA 1984, s. 270: application to inheritance tax.

FA 1986, s. 90(9)(a): application as regards exceptions to the charge to stamp duty reserve tax.

HMRC interpretations – IRInt. 38: settlements – connected persons.

Notes – FA 1985, s. 81: in relation to stamp duty on certain renounceable letters of allotment where there are arrangements between connected persons, that term is defined by reference to its use for the purposes of this Act.

286A Residence of companies

286A Chapter 3 of Part 2 of CTA 2009 (rules for determining residence of companies) applies for the purposes of–

(a) this Act (so far as relating to capital gains tax), and

(b) any other enactment relating to capital gains tax,

as it applies for the purposes of the Corporation Tax Acts.

History – S. 286A inserted by CTA 2009, s. 1322 and Sch. 1, para. 384, with effect for corporation tax purposes for accounting periods ending on or after 1 April 2009, and for income tax and capital gains tax purposes for the tax year 2009–10 and subsequent tax years.

287 Orders and regulations made by the Treasury or the Board

287(1) Subject to subsections (2) and (2A) below, any power of the Treasury or the Board to make any order or regulations under this Act or any other or enactment relating to the taxation of chargeable gains passed after this Act shall be exercisable by statutory instrument.

287(2) Subsection (1) above shall not apply in relation to any power conferred by section 288(6).

287(2A) Subsection (1) above shall not apply in relation to any power conferred by TIOPA 2010 (see instead section 372 of that Act).

287(3) Subject to subsection (4) below and to any other provision to the contrary, any statutory instrument to which subsection (1) above applies shall be subject to annulment in pursuance of a resolution of the House of Commons.

287(4) Subsection (3) above shall not apply in relation to an order or regulations made under section 3(4) or 265 or paragraph 1 of Schedule 9, or–

(a) if any other Parliamentary procedure is expressly provided; or

(b) if the order or regulations provide for any provision of an enactment relating to the taxation of chargeable gains to come into force or have effect in accordance with the order or regulations.

History – In s. 287(1), the words "subsections (2) and (2A)" substituted for "subsection (2)" by TIOPA 2010, s. 374 and Sch. 8, para. 318(2), with effect from 18 March 2010.
S. 287(2A) inserted by TIOPA 2010, s. 374 and Sch. 8, para. 318(3), with effect from 18 March 2010.
S. 287(4)(b) substituted by FA 2015, s. 125(1), with effect in relation to powers conferred after 26 March 2015.

Derivations – CGTA 1979, s. 5(1C) as inserted by FA 1982, s. 80(2); CGTA 1979, s. 92(3), as inserted by FA 1987, s. 40(4); CGTA 1979, s. 102(5), (7), as substituted by FA 1991, s. 94; CGTA 1979, s. 137(10) as substituted by F(No. 2)A 1987, s. 81(5); CGTA 1979, s. 142A(5), 149D(3) as inserted by ICTA 1988, s. 844 and Sch. 29, para. 24, 26; CGTA 1979, Sch. 2, para. 1; FA 1984, s. 64(3F), (12) as inserted by FA 1991, s. 51 and Sch. 10, para. 1; FA 1984, s. 126(1), (4) as inserted (subs. (4)) by FA 1985, s. 96(1); FA 1985, Sch. 19, para. 21(4); F(No. 2)A 1987, s. 73, 95(2); ICTA 1988, s. 828; FA 1991, Sch. 17, para. 4(8).

Cross references – S. 3(4): annual exempt amount.
S. 265: designated international organisations.
Sch. 9, para. 1: gilt-edged securities.

288 Interpretation

288(1) In this Act, unless the context otherwise requires–

"the 1979 Act" means the Capital Gains Tax Act 1979;

"allowable loss" shall be construed in accordance with sections 8(2), 16, 16A, 261B, 261D and 263ZA;

"ATED-related", in relation to a gain or loss, is to be construed in accordance with section 57A and Schedule 4ZZA;

"the Board" means the Commissioners of Inland Revenue;

"building society" has the same meaning as in the Building Societies Act 1986;

"the Capital Allowances Act" means the Capital Allowances Act 2001;

"chargeable period" means a year of assessment or an accounting period of a company for purposes of corporation tax;

"class", in relation to shares or securities, means a class of shares or securities of any one company;

"close company" shall be construed in accordance with Chapter 2 of Part 10 of CTA 2010 (see in particular section 439);

"collective investment scheme" has the meaning given by section 235 of the Financial Services and Markets Act 2000 (subject to section 99A);

"company" includes any body corporate or unincorporated association but does not include a partnership, and shall be construed in accordance with sections 99 and 103A;

"control" shall be construed in accordance with sections 450 and 451 of CTA 2010;

"CTA 2009" means the Corporation Tax Act 2009;

"CTA 2010" means the Corporation Tax Act 2010;

"disposal of a UK residential property interest" has the meaning given by Schedule B1;

"double taxation relief arrangements"

(a) in relation to a company means arrangements that have effect under section 2(1) of TIOPA 2010 except so far as they have effect in relation to petroleum revenue tax, and

(b) in relation to any other person means arrangements that have effect under section 2(1) of TIOPA 2010 but only so far as they have effect in relation to capital gains tax;

"dual resident investing company" has the meaning given by section 404 of the Taxes Act;

"inspector" means any inspector of taxes;

"investment trust" has the meaning given by section 1158 of CTA 2010;

"ITEPA 2003" means the Income Tax (Earnings and Pensions) Act 2003;

"ITTOIA 2005" means the Income Tax (Trading and Other Income) Act 2005;

"ITA 2007" means the Income Tax Act 2007;

"land" includes messuages, tenements, and hereditaments, houses and buildings of any tenure;

"local authority" has the meaning given by section 999 of ITA 2007 of the Taxes Act;

"the Management Act" means the Taxes Management Act 1970;

"net income" has the same meaning as in the Income Tax Acts (see section 989 of ITA 2007);

"non-resident CGT disposal" has the meaning given by section 14B;

"notice" means notice in writing;

"NRCGT gain" is to be interpreted in accordance with section 57B and Schedule 4ZZB;

"NRCGT group" is to be interpreted in accordance with section 188B (read with sections 188F and 188G);

"NRCGT loss" is to be interpreted in accordance with section 57B and Schedule 4ZZB;

"NRCGT return" has the meaning given by section 12ZB(2) of the Management Act;

"offshore fund" has the meaning given in section 355 of TIOPA 2010 (but where two or more offshore funds make up a collective investment scheme they are to be treated as a single offshore fund subject to section 99A of this Act));

"participant", in relation to a collective investment scheme, has the meaning given by section 103C(10)

"period of account" has the meaning given by section 989 of ITA 2007;

"permanent establishment", in relation to a company, is to be read in accordance with Chapter 2 of Part 24 of CTA 2010;

"personal representatives" has the same meaning as in the Corporation Tax Acts (see section 1119 of CTA 2010);

"property investment LLP" has the meaning given by section 1004 of ITA 2007;

"recognised stock exchange" has the meaning given by section 1005 of ITA 2007;

"registered pension scheme" has the meaning given by section 150(2) of the Finance Act 2004;

"Registrar of Government Stock" means the person or persons appointed in accordance with regulations under section 47(1)(b) of the Finance Act 1942 (see regulation 3 of the Government Stock Regulations 2004);

"relevant high value disposal" has the meaning given by section 2C;

"resident" means resident in accordance with the statutory residence test in Part 1 of Schedule 45 to the Finance Act 2013;

"shares" includes stock;

"split year", as respects an individual, means a tax year that, as respects that individual, is a split year within the meaning of Part 3 of Schedule 45 to the Finance Act 2013 (statutory residence test: split year treatment);

"stepchild", in relation to a civil partner, shall be construed in accordance with section 246 of the Civil Partnership Act 2004;

"the Taxes Act" means the Income and Corporation Taxes Act 1988;

"TIOPA 2010" means the Taxation (International and Other Provisions) Act 2010;

"trade" has the same meaning as in the Income Tax Acts;

"trading stock" has the meaning given by section 163 of CTA 2009;

"the tribunal" means the First-tier Tribunal or, where determined by or under Tribunal Procedure Rules, the Upper Tribunal;

"UK property business" means–

(a) a UK property business within the meaning of the Income Tax Acts (see section 989 of ITA 2007), or

(b) a UK property business within the meaning of the Corporation Tax Acts (see section 1119 of CTA 2010);

"venture capital trust" has the same meaning as in Part 6 of ITA 2007;

"wasting asset" has the meaning given by section 44 and paragraph 1 of Schedule 8;

"year of assessment" means tax year;

and any reference to a particular section, Part or Schedule is a reference to that section or Part of, or that Schedule to, this Act.

288(1ZA) In this Act and other enactments relating to capital gains tax **"tax year"** means a year beginning on 6 April and ending on the following 5 April; and **"the tax year 2008–09"** means the tax year beginning on 6 April 2008 (and any corresponding expression in which two years are similarly mentioned is to be read in the same way).

288(1ZB) A reference in this Act to **"the overseas part"** or **"the UK part"** of a split year is to be read in accordance with Part 3 of Schedule 45 to the Finance Act 2013 (statutory residence test: split year treatment).

288(1A) If any employment-related securities option would not otherwise be regarded as an option for the purposes of this Act, it shall be so regarded; and the acquisition of securities by an associated person pursuant to an employment-related securities option is to be treated for the purposes of this Act as the exercise of the option.

In this subsection **"employment-related securities option"** means a securities option within the meaning of Chapter 5 of Part 7 of ITEPA 2003 (see section 420(8) of that Act) to which that Chapter applies (see section 471 of that Act); and other expressions used in this subsection and that Chapter have the same meaning in this subsection as in that Chapter.

288(2) In this Act **"retail prices index"** has the same meaning as in the Income Tax Acts and, accordingly, any reference in this Act to the retail prices index shall be construed in accordance with section 989 of ITA 2007.

288(2A) In this Act **"consumer prices index"** means the all items consumer prices index published by the Statistics Board.

288(3) References in this Act to an individual living with his spouse or civil partner shall be construed in accordance with section 1011 of ITA 2007.

288(3A) For the purposes of this Act, the following are **"the no gain/no loss provisions"**–

(a) sections 58, 73, 139, 140A, 140E, 171, 211, 211B, 215, 216, 217A, 217D, 218 to 220, 257(3), 258(4), 264 and 267(2) of this Act;

(b) section 148 of the 1979 Act;

(c) section 148 of the Finance Act 1982;

(d) section 130(3) of the Transport Act 1985;

(e) [Omitted by CTA 2010, s. 1177 and Sch. 1, para. 264(3)(b) and repealed by CTA 2010, s. 1181 and Sch. 3, Pt. 1.]

(f) paragraph 2(1) of Schedule 7 to the Broadcasting Act 1996;

(g) paragraphs 3 and 9 of Schedule 26 to the Transport Act 2000;

(h) paragraphs 3, 18, 29 and 32 of Schedule 9 to the Energy Act 2004;

(i) paragraph 9 of Schedule 4 to the Consumers, Estate Agents and Redress Act 2007.

(j) Schedule 7 to the Housing and Regeneration Act 2008.

(k) paragraph 4 of Schedule 4 to the Budget Responsibility and National Audit Act 2011.

(l) paragraph 1(2) or 4 of Schedule 2 to the Postal Services Act 2011.

(m) paragraph 6(1) of Schedule 24 to the Localism Act 2011.

288(4) [Repealed by FA 1996, s. 205 and Sch. 41, Pt. VIII(3) in relation to times falling after 31 March 1996.]

288(5) For the purposes of this Act, shares or debentures comprised in any letter of allotment or similar instrument shall be treated as **issued** unless the right to the shares or debentures thereby conferred remains provisional until accepted and there has been no acceptance.

288(5A) References in this Act to shares or securities which are listed on a recognised stock exchange shall be construed in accordance with subsections (3) and (4) of section 1005 of ITA 2007.

288(5B) References in this Act to shares or securities which are included in the official UK list shall be construed in accordance with subsection (5) of that section.

288(6) In this Act **"recognised futures exchange"** means the London International Financial Futures Exchange and any other futures exchange which is for the time being designated for the purposes of this Act by order made by the Board.

288(7) An order made by the Board under subsection (6) above–

(a) may designate a futures exchange by name or by reference to any class or description of futures exchanges, including, in the case of futures exchanges in a country outside the United Kingdom, a class or description framed by reference to any authority or approval given in that country; and

(b) may contain such transitional and other supplemental provisions as appear to the Board to be necessary or expedient.

288(7A) In the application of this Act to Scotland "surrender" includes renunciation.

288(7B) For the purposes of this Act, a person is Treaty non-resident at any time if, at that time, he falls to be regarded as resident in a territory outside the United Kingdom for the purposes of double taxation relief arrangements having effect at that time.

288(8) The Table below indexes other general definitions in this Act.

Expression defined	*Reference*
"Absolutely entitled as against the trustee"	S. 60(2)
"Authorised contractual scheme"	s 103D(5)
"Authorised unit trust"	S. 99 and 99A
"Branch or agency"	S. 10(6)
"Chargeable gain"	S. 15(2)
"Connected", in references to persons being connected with one another	S. 286
"Co-ownership scheme"	s 103D(5)
"Court investment fund"	S. 100
"Gilt-edged securities"	Sch. 9
"Indexation allowance"	S. 53
"Lease" and cognate expressions	Sch. 8 para. 10(1)
"Legatee"	S. 64(2), (3)
"Market value"	S. 272 to 274 and Sch. 11
"Part disposal"	S. 21(2)
"Principal settlement"	Sch. 4ZA para. 1
"Qualifying corporate bond"	S. 117
"Relevant allowable expenditure"	S. 53
"Settled property"	S. 68
"Settlor"	S. 68A
"Settlor of property"	S. 68A
"Sub-fund"	Sch. 4ZA para. 1
"Sub-fund election"	Sch. 4ZA para. 2
"Sub-fund settlement"	Sch. 4ZA para. 1
"Unit trust scheme" and "unit holder"	Ss. 99, 99A and 151W(a)

History – In s. 288(1):

- in the definition of "allowable loss", the words ", 16A" inserted by FA 2007, s. 27(4), with effect in relation to losses accruing on disposals made on or after 6 December 2006 (FA 2007, s. 27(6)).
- in the definition of "allowable loss", the words ", 261B, 261D" inserted by ITA 2007, s. 1027 and Sch. 1, para. 342(2)(a), with effect from 6 April 2007.
- in the definition of "allowable loss", the words ", 16 and 263ZA" substituted for "and 16" by ITEPA 2003, Sch. 6, para. 219(2), with effect for 2003–04 and subsequent tax years.
- definition of "ATED-related" inserted by FA 2013, s. 65 and Sch. 25, para. 15, with effect in relation to disposals occurring on or after 6 April 2013.
- definition of "the Capital Allowances Act" inserted by CAA 2001, s. 578 and Sch. 2, para. 80, with effect as respects allowances and charges falling to be made for chargeable periods ending, for income tax purposes, on or after 6 April 2001, and for corporation tax purposes, on or after 1 April 2001.
- in the definition of "close company", the words "shall be construed in accordance with Chapter 2 of Part 10 of CTA 2010 (see in particular section 439)" substituted for "has the meaning given by sections 414 and 415 of the Taxes Act" by CTA 2010, s. 1177 and Sch. 1, para. 264(2)(a), with effect for corporation tax purposes for accounting periods ending on or after 1 April 2010, and for income tax and capital gains tax purposes for the tax year 2010–11 and subsequent tax years
- in the definition of "control", the words "sections 450 and 451 of CTA 2010" substituted for "section 416 of the Taxes Act" by CTA 2010, s. 1177 and Sch. 1, para. 264(2)(b), with effect for corporation tax purposes for accounting periods ending on or after 1 April 2010, and for income tax and capital gains tax purposes for the tax year 2010–11 and subsequent tax years.
- definition of "CTA 2009" inserted by CTA 2009, s. 1322 and Sch. 1, para. 385(a), with effect for corporation tax purposes for accounting periods ending on or after 1 April 2009, and for income tax and capital gains tax purposes for the tax year 2009–10 and subsequent tax years.
- definition of "CTA 2010" inserted by CTA 2010, s. 1177 and Sch. 1, para. 264(2)(g), with effect for corporation tax purposes for accounting periods ending on or after 1 April 2010, and for income tax and capital gains tax purposes for the tax year 2010–11 and subsequent tax years.
- at end of the definition of "collective investment scheme", the words "(subject to section 99A)" inserted by FA 2004, s. 118(4)(a), with effect, by virtue of FA 2004, s. 118(5), in relation to years of assessment and accounting periods beginning on or after 1 April 2004.
- in the definition of "collective investment scheme", the words "meaning given by section 235 of the Financial Services and Markets Act 2000" substituted for the words "same meaning as in the Financial Services Act 1986" by SI 2001/3629, art. 70 operative from 1 December 2001.
- in the definition of "company" the words "sections 99 and 103A" substituted for the words "section 99" by FA 2009, s. 44 and Sch. 22, para. 10, with effect in relation to the acquisition, holding and disposal of rights in a relevant offshore fund on or after 1 December 2009 (capital gains tax) or 1 April 2010 (corporation tax, by virtue of SI 2010/670) and subject to FA 2009, Sch. 22, para. 13 and 15.

- definition of "disposal of a UK residential property interest" inserted by FA 2015, s. 37 and Sch. 7, para. 34, with effect in relation to disposals made on or after 6 April 2015.
- definition of "double taxation relief arrangements" substituted by TIOPA 2010, s. 374 and Sch. 8, para. 47, with effect for corporation tax purposes for accounting periods ending on or after 1 April 2010, for income tax and capital gains tax purposes for the tax year 2010–11 and subsequent tax years, and for petroleum revenue tax purposes for chargeable periods beginning on or after 1 July 2010.
- in the definition of "investment trust", the words "section 1158 of CTA 2010" substituted for "section 842 of the Taxes Act" by CTA 2010, s. 1177 and Sch. 1, para. 264(2)(c), with effect for corporation tax purposes for accounting periods ending on or after 1 April 2010, and for income tax and capital gains tax purposes for the tax year 2010–11 and subsequent tax years.
- definition of "ITEPA 2003" inserted by ITEPA 2003, Sch. 6, para. 219(3) with effect for 2003–04 and subsequent tax years.
- definition of "ITTOIA 2005" inserted by ITTOIA 2005, s. 882 and Sch. 1, para. 447(2) which, in accordance with ITTOIA 2005, s. 883, have effect, for income tax purposes, for tax year 2005–06 and subsequent tax years, and, for corporation tax purposes, for accounting periods ending after 5 April 2005.
- definition of "ITA 2007" inserted by ITA 2007, s. 1027 and Sch. 1, para. 342(2)(b), with effect from 6 April 2007.
- in the definition of "local authority", the words "section 999 of ITA 2007" substituted for the words "section 842A of the Taxes Act" by ITA 2007, s. 1027 and Sch. 1, para. 342(2)(c), with effect from 6 April 2007.
- definition of "net income" inserted by ITA 2007, s. 1027 and Sch. 1, para. 342(2)(d), with effect from 6 April 2007.
- definition of "non-resident CGT disposal" inserted by FA 2015, s. 37 and Sch. 7, para. 34, with effect in relation to disposals made on or after 6 April 2015.
- definition of "NRCGT gain" inserted by FA 2015, s. 37 and Sch. 7, para. 34, with effect in relation to disposals made on or after 6 April 2015.
- definition of "NRCGT group" inserted by FA 2015, s. 37 and Sch. 7, para. 34, with effect in relation to disposals made on or after 6 April 2015.
- definition of "NRCGT loss" inserted by FA 2015, s. 37 and Sch. 7, para. 34, with effect in relation to disposals made on or after 6 April 2015.
- definition of "NRCGT return" inserted by FA 2015, s. 37 and Sch. 7, para. 34, with effect in relation to disposals made on or after 6 April 2015.
- definition of "offshore fund" inserted by SI 2013/1400, reg. 12, with effect in relation to disposals on or after 8 June 2013.
- definition of "participant" inserted by SI 2013/1400, reg. 7(a), with effect in relation to disposals on or after 8 June 2013.
- in the definition of "period of account", the words "section 989 of ITA 2007" substituted for the words "section 832(1) of the Taxes Act" by ITA 2007, s. 1027 and Sch. 1, para. 342(2)(e), with effect from 6 April 2007.
- definition of "period of account" inserted by FA 2002, s. 103(3).
- definition of "permanent establishment" substituted by CTA 2010, s. 1177 and Sch. 1, para. 264(2)(d), with effect for corporation tax purposes for accounting periods ending on or after 1 April 2010, and for income tax and capital gains tax purposes for the tax year 2010–11 and subsequent tax years.
- in the definition of "personal representatives", the words "the Corporation Tax Acts (see section 1119 of CTA 2010)" substituted for "Chapter 3 of Part 10 of CTA 2009 (see section 968 of that Act)" by CTA 2010, s. 1177 and Sch. 1, para. 264(2)(e), with effect for corporation tax purposes for accounting periods ending on or after 1 April 2010, and for income tax and capital gains tax purposes for the tax year 2010–11 and subsequent tax years.
- definition of "personal representatives" substituted by CTA 2009, s. 1322 and Sch. 1, para. 385(b), with effect for corporation tax purposes for accounting periods ending on or after 1 April 2009, and for income tax and capital gains tax purposes for the tax year 2009–10 and subsequent tax years.
- former definition of "permanent establishment" inserted by FA 2003, s. 148(6) with effect (apparently) from 10 July 2003 (date of Royal Assent for FA 2003).
- in the definition of "property investment LLP", the words "section 1004 of ITA 2007" substituted for the words "section 842B of the Taxes Act" by ITA 2007, s. 1027 and Sch. 1, para. 342(2)(f) with effect from 6 April 2007.
- definition of "property investment LLP" inserted by FA 2001, Sch. 25, para. 1(3) with effect from 6 April 2001.
- in the definition of "recognised stock exchange", the words "section 1005 of ITA 2007" substituted for the words "section 841 of the Taxes Act" by ITA 2007, s. 1027 and Sch. 1, para. 342(2)(g), with effect from 6 April 2007.
- definition of "Registrar of Government Stock" inserted by SI 2004/2744, Schedule, para. 3(3), with effect from 15 November 2004.
- definition of "registered pension scheme" inserted by FA 2004, s. 281 and Sch. 35, para. 41 with effect from 6 April 2006 by virtue of FA 2004, s. 284(1).
- definition of "relevant high value disposal" inserted by FA 2013, s. 65 and Sch. 25, para. 15, with effect in relation to disposals occurring on or after 6 April 2013.
- definition of "resident" inserted by FA 2013, s. 218 and Sch. 45, para 148(3)(a), with effect from 17 July 2013.
- definition of "split year" inserted by FA 2013, s. 218 and Sch. 45, para. 104(2), with effect in calculating an individual's liability to income tax or capital gains tax for the tax year 2013–14 or any subsequent tax year, subject to the transitional and saving provision in FA 2013, Sch. 45, para. 154 to 159
- definition of "stepchild" inserted by SI 2005/3229, reg. 122(a), with effect from 5 December 2005.
- the definition of "TIOPA 2010" inserted by TIOPA 2010, s. 374 and Sch. 8, para. 319, with effect from 18 March 2010.
- in the definition of "trading stock" the words "section 163 of CTA 2009" substituted for the words "section 100(2) of the Taxes Act" by CTA 2009, s. 1322 and Sch. 1, para. 385(c), with effect for corporation tax purposes for accounting periods ending on or after 1 April 2009, and for income tax and capital gains tax purposes for the tax year 2009–10 and subsequent tax years.
- definition of "tribunal" inserted by SI 2009/56, art. 3(1) and Sch. 1, para. 184, operative from 1 April 2009, subject to transitional and saving provisions in SI 2009/56, Sch. 3.
- in the definition of "UK property business", para. (b) , the words "Corporation Tax Acts (see section 1119 of CTA 2010)" substituted for the words from "enactments" to the end by CTA 2010, s. 1177 and Sch. 1, para. 264(2)(f), with effect for corporation tax purposes for accounting periods ending on or after 1 April 2010, and for income tax and capital gains tax purposes for the tax year 2010–11 and subsequent tax years.
- definition of "UK property business" inserted by CTA 2009, s. 1322 and Sch. 1, para. 385(d), with effect for corporation tax purposes for accounting periods ending on or after 1 April 2009, and for income tax and capital gains tax purposes for the tax year 2009–10 and subsequent tax years.
- in the definition of "venture capital trust", the words "the same meaning as in Part 6 of ITA 2007" substituted for "the meaning given by section 842AA of the Taxes Act" by ITA 2007, s. 1027 and Sch. 1, para. 342(2)(h), with effect from 6 April 2007.
- definition of "venture capital trust" inserted by FA 1995, s. 72(7) with effect for 1995–96 and subsequent years of assessment.
- definition of "year of assessment" substituted by FA 2008, s. 8 and Sch. 2, para. 101(2) with effect from Royal Assent (21 July 2008).
- in the former definition of "year of assessment", the words ""year of assessment 1992–93" means the year of assessment beginning on 6th April 1992 (and any corresponding expression in which two years are similarly mentioned is to be read in the same way) " substituted for ""1992–93" and so on indicate years of assessment as in the Income Tax Acts " by ITA 2007, s. 1027 and Sch. 1, para. 342(2)(i), with effect from 6 April 2007.

S. 288(1ZA) inserted by FA 2008, s. 8 and Sch. 2, para. 101(2) with effect from Royal Assent (21 July 2008).
S. 288(1ZB) inserted by FA 2013, s. 218 and Sch. 45, para. 104(3), with effect in calculating an individual's liability to income tax or capital gains tax for the tax year 2013–14 or any subsequent tax year, subject to the transitional and saving provision in FA 2013, Sch. 45, para. 154–159.
In s. 288(1A), the words "or would, apart from section 474 of that Act, apply" omitted by FA 2014, s. 52 and Sch. 9, para. 28, with effect from 6 April 2015 in relation to employment-related securities and employment-related securities options irrespective of the date of the acquisition.
In s. 288(1A), second sentence substituted by F(No. 2)A 2005, s. 35 and Sch. 5, para. 5(2) with effect, in accordance with F(No. 2)A 2005, Sch. 5, para. 6(2), in relation to options granted on or after 2 December 2004. Former second sentence of s. 288(1A) read: "Expressions used in this subsection and Chapter 5 of Part 7 of ITEPA 2003 have the same meaning in this subsection as in that Chapter.".
S. 288(1A) inserted by FA 2003, s. 140 and Sch. 22, para. 54(1) which, by virtue of Sch. 22, para. 10(2) and Sch. 22, para. 54(2), have effect: (a) on and after 16 April 2003 in relation to employment-related securities options that are not share options, and (b) on and after such day appointed by the Treasury, by order made by statutory instrument, in relation to employment-related securities options that are share options; for the purpose of determining the effective date, "share options" means rights to acquire shares in a company, or securities as defined in ICTA 1988, s. 254(1), issued by a company (Sch. 22, para. 10(2)).
In s. 288(2), the words "section 989 of ITA 2007" substituted for the words "section 832(1) of the Taxes Act" by ITA 2007, s. 1027 and Sch. 1, para. 342(3), with effect from 6 April 2007.
S. 288(2A) inserted by FA 2012, s. 34(4), with effect for the tax year 2013–14 and subsequent tax years.
In s. 288(3), the words "section 1011 of ITA 2007" substituted for the words "section 282 of the Taxes Act" by ITA 2007, s. 1027, Sch. 1, para. 342(4), with effect from 6 April 2007.
In s. 288(3) the words "an individual living with his spouse or civil partner" substituted for the words "a married woman living with her husband" by SI 2005/3229, reg. 122(b), with effect from 5 December 2005.
S. 288(3A)(m) inserted by Localism Act 2011, s. 233 and Sch. 24, para. 6(3) with effect from 30 March 2012 in relation to England and Wales (SI 2012/628, art. 3).
S. 288(3A)(l) inserted by PSA 2011, s. 10 and Sch. 12, para. 145, with effect from 1 October 2011 (SI 2011/2329).
In s. 288(3A)(a), "211B," inserted by SI 2013/1400, reg. 7(b), with effect in relation to disposals on or after 8 June 2013.
In s. 288(3A)(a), "220" substituted for "221" by FA 2012, s. 227 and Sch. 39, para. 17(a), with effect in relation to any transfer occurring on or after 1 April 2013.
In s. 288(3A)(a), "217D," inserted after "217A," by CTA 2010, s. 1177 and Sch. 1, para. 264(3)(a), with effect for corporation tax purposes for accounting periods ending on or after 1 April 2010, and for income tax and capital gains tax purposes for the tax year 2010–11 and subsequent tax years.
S. 288(3A)(e), omitted by CTA 2010, s. 1177 and Sch. 1, para. 264(3)(b) and repealed by CTA 2010, s. 1181 and Sch. 3, Pt. 1, with effect for corporation tax purposes for accounting periods ending on or after 1 April 2010, and for income tax and capital gains tax purposes for the tax year 2010–11 and subsequent tax years.
S. 288(3A)(j) inserted by SI 2008/3002, art. 4 and Sch. 1, para. 43, with effect from 1 December 2008.
S. 288(3A)(k) inserted by the Budget Responsibility and National Audit Act 2011, s. 26 and Sch. 5, para. 16, with effect from 1 April 2012 (SI 2011/2576, art. 5).
S. 288(3A) inserted by FA 2008, s. 8 and Sch. 2, para. 63 with effect in relation to disposals on or after 6 April 2008 (FA 2008, Sch. 2, para. 71).
S. 288(4) repealed by FA 1996, s. 205 and Sch. 41, Pt. VIII(3) in relation to times falling after 31 March 1996.
S. 288(5A) inserted by FA 2007, s. 109 and Sch. 26, para. 3, with effect from 19 July 2007 (Royal Assent).
S. 288(5B) inserted by FA 2007, s. 109 and Sch. 26, para. 3, with effect from 19 July 2007 (Royal Assent).
S. 288(7A) inserted by ITTOIA 2005, s. 882 and Sch. 1, para. 447(3) which, in accordance with ITTOIA 2005, s. 883, have effect, for income tax purposes, for tax year 2005–06 and subsequent tax years, and, for corporation tax purposes, for accounting periods ending after 5 April 2005.
S. 288(7B) inserted by FA 2006, s. 74(3) with effect in relation to any time on or after 22 March 2006.
In s. 288(8), entries for "Authorised contractual scheme" and "Co-ownership scheme" inserted by SI 2013/1400, reg. 7(c), with effect in relation to disposals on or after 8 June 2013.
In s. 288(8), entries for "resident" and "ordinarily resident" omitted by FA 2013, s. 218 and Sch. 45, para. 148(3)(b) with effect from 17 July 2013.
In s. 288(8), in the entries for "unit trust scheme" and "unit holder", the words ", 99A and 151W(a)" substituted for "and 99A" by TIOPA 2010, s. 374 and Sch. 8, para. 202, with effect for corporation tax purposes for accounting periods ending on or after 1 April 2010, for income tax and capital gains tax purposes for the tax year 2010-11 and subsequent tax years, and for petroleum revenue taxpurposes for chargeable periods beginning on or after 1 July 2010.
In s. 288(8), definitions of "principal settlement", "settlor", "settlor of property", "sub-fund", "sub-fund election" and "sub-fund settlement" inserted by FA 2006, s. 88 and Sch. 12, para. 26(1) with effect from 6 April 2006 (in relation to settlements whenever created).
In s. 288(8), in the first column of the Table after ""Unit trust scheme"", the words "and "unit holder"" were inserted by FA 2004, s. 118(4)(b)(i) with effect, by virtue of FA 2004, s. 118(5), in relation to years of assessment and accounting periods beginning on or after 1 April 2004.
In s. 288(8), in the second column of the Table, "ss 99 and 99A" substituted for "s 99" by FA 2004, s. 118(4)(b)(ii) with effect, by virtue of FA 2004, s. 118(5), in relation to years of assessment and accounting periods beginning on or after 1 April 2004.

Derivations – CGTA 1979, s. 155, as amended by FA 1990, s. 127(2), FA 1989, s. 124 and Sch. 14, para. 6(2), ICTA 1988, s. 844 and Sch. 29, para. 27, and FA 1985, s. 72(6); CGTA 1979, s. 64, 92(1)(c), and 149A(1); ICTA 1970, s. 267(4) ("trading stock").

Cross references – Sch. 5C, para. 6(3): for the purpose of deferring a charge on reinvestment in a venture capital trust shares are not treated as issued by reason only of being comprised in a letter of allotment or similar instrument.
SI 1997/1154, reg. 23: modifications of s. 288 in relation to open-ended investment companies, holdings in and assets of such companies, and transactions involving such companies.
SI 2006/964, reg. 109: modification of s. 288 for the purposes of authorised investment funds.
SI 2012/1709, art. 5: a disposal constituted by a relevant transfer by British Waterways Board to Canal & River Trust or Canal & River Trading CIC is to be treated as one of the no gain/no loss provisions in s. 288(3A).
SI 2013/2242, art. 3(a): a disposal constituted by a relevant transfer from BRB (Residuary) Limited ("BRB Residuary") to London & Continental Railways Limited ("LCR") or the Secretary of State for Transport is to be treated in relation to BRB Residuary and LCR as made for a consideration such that no gain or loss accrues to BRB Residuary and for the purposes of any tax provision is to be treated as one of the no gain/no loss provisions in s. 288(3A).
SI 2015/1540, reg. 6: a disposal constituted by a transfer in accordance with transfer schemes under section 333DA of the Greater London Authority Act 1999 and under section 53A of the Housing and Regeneration Act 2008 is to be taken in relation to the transferor and transferee to be for a consideration such that no gain or loss accrues to the transferor.

HMRC interpretations – IRInt. 42: HMRC review of depreciating assets regarding roll over relief in respect of land and buildings.

Notes – Interpretation Act 1978, s. 5 and Sch. 1: the Income Tax Acts mean the enactments relating to income tax.
A list of currently recognised futures exchanges is given in Hardman's Tax Rates and Tables, ¶15-050.

289 Commencement

289(1) Except where the context otherwise requires, this Act has effect in relation to tax for the year 1992–93 and subsequent years of assessment, and tax for other chargeable periods beginning on or after 6th April 1992, and references to the coming into force of this Act or any provision in this Act shall be construed accordingly.

289(2) The following provisions of this Act, that is–

(a) so much of any provision of this Act as authorises the making of any order or other instrument, and

(b) except where the tax concerned is all tax for chargeable periods to which this Act does not apply, so much of any provision of this Act as confers any power or imposes any duty the exercise or performance of which operates or may operate in relation to tax for more than one chargeable period,

shall come into force for all purposes on 6th April 1992 to the exclusion of the corresponding enactments repealed by this Act.

290 Savings, transitionals, consequential amendments and repeals

290(1) Schedules 10 (consequential amendments) and 11 (transitory provisions and savings) shall have effect.

290(2) No letters patent granted or to be granted by the Crown to any person, city, borough or town corporate of any liberty, privilege, or exemption from subsidies, tolls, taxes, assessments or aids, and no statute which grants any salary, annuity or pension to any person free of any taxes, deductions or assessments, shall be construed or taken to exempt any person, city, borough or town corporate, or any inhabitant of the same, from tax chargeable in pursuance of this Act.

290(3) Subject to Schedule 11, the enactments and instruments mentioned in Schedule 12 to this Act are hereby repealed to the extent specified in the third column of that Schedule (but Schedule 12 shall not have effect in relation to any enactment in so far as it has previously been repealed subject to a saving which still has effect on the coming into force of this section).

290(4) The provisions of this Part of this Act are without prejudice to the provisions of the Interpretation Act 1978 as respects the effect of repeals.

291 Short title

291 This Act may be cited as the Taxation of Chargeable Gains Act 1992.

SCHEDULES

SCHEDULE A1 – APPLICATION OF TAPER RELIEF

Section 2A

History – Sch. A1 omitted by FA 2008, s. 8 and Sch. 2, para. 45 with effect in relation to chargeable gains accruing or treated as accruing in the tax year 2008–09 or any subsequent tax year (FA 2008, Sch. 2, para. 56(3)).

[Omitted by FA 2008, s. 8 and Sch. 2, para. 45.]

SCHEDULE B1 – DISPOSALS OF UK RESIDENTIAL PROPERTY INTERESTS

History – Sch. B1 inserted by FA 2015, s. 37 and Sch. 7, para. 36, with effect in relation to disposals made on or after 6 April 2015.

MEANING OF "DISPOSAL OF A UK RESIDENTIAL PROPERTY INTEREST"

1(1) For the purposes of this Act, the disposal by a person ("P") of an interest in UK land (whether made before or after this Schedule comes into force) is a "disposal of a UK residential property interest" if the first or second condition is met.

1(2) The first condition is that–

(a) the land has at any time in the relevant ownership period consisted of or included a dwelling, or

(b) the interest in UK land subsists for the benefit of land that has at any time in the relevant ownership period consisted of or included a dwelling.

1(3) The second condition is that the interest in UK land subsists under a contract for an off-plan purchase.

1(4) In sub-paragraph (2) **"relevant ownership period"** means the period–

(a) beginning with the day on which P acquired the interest in UK land or the relevant date (whichever is later), and

(b) ending with the day before the day on which the disposal occurs.

1(4A) In sub-paragraph (4) **"the relevant date"** means–

(a) for the purpose of determining whether a disposal is a non-resident CGT disposal, 6 April 2015;

(b) for any other purpose, 31 March 1982.

1(5) If the interest in UK land disposed of by P as mentioned in sub-paragraph (1) results from interests in UK land which P has acquired at different times ("the acquired interests"), P is regarded for the purposes of sub-paragraph (4)(a) as having acquired the interest when P first acquired any of the acquired interests.

1(6) In this paragraph–

"contract for an off-plan purchase" means a contract for the acquisition of land consisting of, or including, a building or part of a building that is to be constructed or adapted for use as a dwelling;

"dwelling" has the meaning given by paragraph 4.

1(7) Paragraphs 10 and 21 of Schedule 4ZZB and paragraphs 6 and 20 of Schedule 4ZZC contain further provision about interests under contracts for off-plan purchases.

History – In para. 1(4) the words "the relevant date" substituted for the words "6 April 2015" by FA 2016, s. 83 and Sch. 11, para. 4(a), with effect in relation to gains accruing on or after 6 April 2016.
Para. 1(4A) inserted by FA 2016, s. 83 and Sch. 11, para. 4(b), with effect in relation to gains accruing on or after 6 April 2016.
In para. 1(7) the words "and paragraphs 6 and 20 of Schedule 4ZZC" inserted by FA 2016, s. 83 and Sch. 12, para. 4, with effect in relation to gains accruing on or after 6 April 2016.

"INTEREST IN UK LAND"

2(1) In this Schedule, **"interest in UK land"** means–

(a) an estate, interest, right or power in or over land in the United Kingdom, or

(b) the benefit of an obligation, restriction or condition affecting the value of any such estate, interest, right or power,

other than an excluded interest.

2(2) The following are excluded interests–

(a) any security interest;

(b) a licence to use or occupy land;

(c) in England and Wales or Northern Ireland–

 (i) a tenancy at will;

 (ii) a manor.

2(3) In sub-paragraph (2) **"security interest"** means an interest or right (other than a rentcharge) held for the purpose of securing the payment of money or the performance of any other obligation.

2(4) In relation to land in Scotland the reference in sub-paragraph (3) to a rentcharge is to be read as a reference to a feu duty or a payment mentioned in section 56(1) of the Abolition of Feudal Tenure etc (Scotland) Act 2000 (asp 5).

2(5) The Treasury may by regulations provide that any other description of interest or right in relation to land in the United Kingdom is an excluded interest.

2(6) Regulations under sub-paragraph (5) may make incidental, consequential, supplementary or transitional provision or savings.

GRANTS OF OPTIONS

3(1) Sub-paragraph (2) applies where–

(a) a person ("P") grants at any time an option binding P to sell an interest in UK land, and

(b) a disposal by P of that interest in UK land at that time would be a disposal of a UK residential property interest by virtue of paragraph 1.

3(2) The grant of the option is regarded for the purposes of this Schedule as the disposal of an interest in the land in question (if it would not be so regarded apart from this paragraph).
References in Schedule 4ZZB (non-resident CGT disposals: gains and losses) to the interest in land disposed of by a non-resident CGT disposal are to be construed accordingly.

3(3) Nothing in this paragraph affects the operation of section 144 in relation to the grant of the option (or otherwise).

3(4) Subsection (6) of section 144 (interpretation of references to "sale" etc) applies for the purposes of this paragraph as it applies for the purposes of that section.

MEANING OF "DWELLING"

4(1) For the purposes of this Schedule, a building counts as a dwelling at any time when–

(a) it is used or suitable for use as a dwelling, or

(b) it is in the process of being constructed or adapted for such use.

4(2) Land that at any time is, or is intended to be, occupied or enjoyed with a dwelling as a garden or grounds (including any building or structure on such land) is taken to be part of that dwelling at that time.

4(3) For the purposes of sub-paragraph (1) a building is not used (or suitable for use) as a dwelling if it is used as–

(a) residential accommodation for school pupils;

(b) residential accommodation for members of the armed forces;

(c) a home or other institution providing residential accommodation for children;

(d) a home or other institution providing residential accommodation with personal care for persons in need of personal care by reason of old age, disability, past or present dependence on alcohol or drugs or past or present mental disorder;

(e) a hospital or hospice;

(f) a prison or similar establishment;

(g) a hotel or inn or similar establishment.

4(4) For the purposes of sub-paragraph (1) a building is not used (or suitable for use) as a dwelling if it is used, or suitable for use, as an institution (not falling within any of paragraphs (c) to (f) of sub-paragraph (3)) that is the sole or main residence of its residents.

4(5) For the purposes of sub-paragraph (1) a building is not used (or suitable for use) as a dwelling if it falls within–

(a) paragraph 4 of Schedule 14 to the Housing Act 2004 (certain buildings occupied by students and managed or controlled by their educational establishment etc),

(b) any corresponding provision having effect in Scotland, or

(c) any corresponding provision having effect in Northern Ireland.

4(6) In sub-paragraph (5) **"corresponding provision"** means provision designated by regulations made by the Treasury as corresponding to the provision mentioned in sub-paragraph (5)(a).

4(7) If the accommodation provided by a building meets the conditions in sub-paragraph (8) in a tax year, the building is not to be regarded for the purposes of sub-paragraph (1) as used or suitable for use as a dwelling at any time in that tax year.

4(8) The conditions are that the accommodation–

(a) includes at least 15 bedrooms,

(b) is purpose-built for occupation by students, and

(c) is occupied by students on at least 165 days in the tax year. In the expression **"purpose-built"** the reference to building includes conversion.

4(9) For the purposes of sub-paragraph (8), accommodation is occupied by students if it is occupied exclusively or mainly by persons who occupy it for the purpose of undertaking a course of education (otherwise than as school pupils).

4(10) A building which (for any reason) becomes temporarily unsuitable for use as a dwelling is treated for the purposes of sub-paragraph (1) as continuing to be suitable for use as a dwelling; but see also the special rules in–

(a) paragraph 6 (damage to a dwelling), and

(b) paragraph 8(7) (periods before or during certain works).

4(11) In this paragraph **"building"** includes a part of a building.

POWER TO MODIFY MEANING OF "USE AS A DWELLING"

5(1) The Treasury may by regulations amend paragraph 4 for the purpose of clarifying or changing the cases where a building is or is not to be regarded as being used as a dwelling (or suitable for use as a dwelling).

5(2) The provision that may be made under sub-paragraph (1) includes, in particular, provision omitting or adding cases where a building is or is not to be regarded as being used (or as suitable for use) as a dwelling.

5(3) Regulations under this paragraph may make incidental, consequential, supplementary or transitional provision or savings.

5(4) In this paragraph **"building"** includes a part of a building.

DAMAGE TO A DWELLING

6(1) Sub-paragraph (2) applies where a person disposes of an interest in UK land and a building that forms, or has formed, part of the land has at any time in the relevant ownership period been temporarily unsuitable for use as a dwelling.

6(2) Paragraph 4(10) (disregard of temporary unsuitability) does not apply in relation to the building's temporary unsuitability for use as a dwelling if–

(a) the temporary unsuitability resulted from damage to the building, and

(b) the first and second conditions are met.

6(3) The first condition is that the damage was–

(a) accidental, or

(b) otherwise caused by events beyond the control of the person disposing of the interest in UK land.

6(4) The second condition is that, as a result of the damage, the building was unsuitable for use as a dwelling for a period of at least 90 consecutive days.

6(5) Where the first and second conditions are met, work done in the 90-day period to restore the building to suitability for use as a dwelling does not count, for the purposes of paragraph 4(1), as construction or adaptation of the building for use as a dwelling.

6(6) The first condition is regarded as not being met if the damage occurred in the course of work that–

(a) was being done for the purpose of altering the building, and

(b) itself involved, or could be expected to involve, making the building unsuitable for use as a dwelling for 30 days or more.

6(7) The 90-day period mentioned in sub-paragraph (4) must end at or before the end of the relevant ownership period but may begin at any time (whether or not within the ownership period).

6(8) In this paragraph–

(a) references to alteration include partial demolition;

(b) **"building"** includes a part of a building;

(c) **"relevant ownership period"** has the meaning given by paragraph 1(4).

DEMOLITION OF A BUILDING

7 A building is regarded as ceasing to exist from the time when it has either–

(a) been demolished completely to ground level, or

(b) been demolished to ground level except for a single facade (or, in the case of a building on a corner site, a double facade) the retention of which is a condition or requirement of planning permission or development consent.

DISPOSAL OF A BUILDING THAT HAS UNDERGONE WORKS

8(1) This paragraph applies where a person disposes of an interest in UK land, and a building which is (or was formerly) on the land and has at any time in the relevant ownership period been suitable for use as a dwelling–

(a) has undergone complete or partial demolition or any other works during the relevant ownership period, and

(b) as a result of the works, has, at or at any time before the completion of the disposal, either ceased to exist or become unsuitable for use as a dwelling.

8(2) If the conditions in sub-paragraph (4) are met at, or at any time before, the completion of the disposal, the building is taken to have been unsuitable for use as a dwelling throughout the part of the relevant ownership period when the works were in progress.

8(3) If the conditions in sub-paragraph (4) are met at, or at any time before, the completion of the disposal, the building is also taken to have been unsuitable for use as a dwelling throughout any period which–

(a) ends immediately before the commencement of the works, and

(b) is a period throughout which the building was, for reasons connected with the works, not used as a dwelling.

8(4) The conditions are that–

(a) as a result of the works the building has (at any time before the completion of the disposal) either ceased to exist or become suitable for use otherwise than as a dwelling,

(b) any planning permission or development consent required for the works, or for any change of use with which they are associated, has been granted, and

(c) the works have been carried out in accordance with any such permission or consent.

8(5) If at the completion of the disposal the conditions in sub-paragraph (4) have not been met, the works are taken not to have affected the building's suitability for use as a dwelling (at any time before the disposal).

8(6) Sub-paragraph (2) does not apply in relation to any time when–

(a) the building was undergoing any work, or put to a use, in relation to which planning permission or development consent was required but had not been granted, or

(b) anything was being done in contravention of a condition or requirement attached to a planning permission or development consent relating to the building.

8(7) Where a building is treated under sub-paragraph (2) or (3) as unsuitable for use as a dwelling, the unsuitability is not regarded as temporary for the purposes of paragraph 4(10).

8(8) In this paragraph–

"building" includes a part of a building;

"relevant ownership period" has the meaning given by paragraph 1(4).

RETROSPECTIVE PLANNING PERMISSION OR DEVELOPMENT CONSENT

9(1) The condition in paragraph 8(4)(b) is taken to have been met at the time of the completion of the disposal if the required planning permission or development consent is given subsequently.

9(2) For the purposes of paragraph 8(6)(a), the fact that planning permission or development consent had not been given at any time in relation to any work or use of a building is ignored if the required planning permission or development consent is given subsequently.

INTERPRETATION

10(1) For the purposes of this Schedule, the **"completion"** of the disposal of an interest in UK land is taken to occur–

(a) at the time of the disposal, or

(b) if the disposal is under a contract which is completed by a conveyance, at the time when the interest is conveyed.

10(2) In this Schedule–

"conveyance" includes any instrument (and "conveyed" is to be construed accordingly);

"development consent" means development consent under the Planning Act 2008;

"interest in UK land" has the meaning given by paragraph 2;

"land" includes a building;

"planning permission" has the meaning given by the relevant planning enactment.

10(3) In sub-paragraph (2) **"the relevant planning enactment"** means–

(a) in relation to land in England and Wales, section 336(1) of the Town and Country Planning Act 1990;

(b) in relation to land in Scotland, section 227(1) of the Town and Country Planning (Scotland) Act 1997;

(c) in relation to land in Northern Ireland, Article 2(2) of the Planning (Northern Ireland) Order 1991 (S.I. 1991/1220 (N.I. 11)).

SCHEDULE BA1 – DISPOSALS OF NON-UK RESIDENTIAL PROPERTY INTERESTS

Section 4BB.

History – Sch. BA1 inserted by FA 2016, s. 83 and Sch. 11, para. 5, with effect in relation to gains accruing on or after 6 April 2016.

MEANING OF "DISPOSAL OF A NON-UK RESIDENTIAL PROPERTY INTEREST"

1(1) For the purposes of this Act, the disposal by a person ("P") of an interest in non-UK land (whether made before or after this Schedule comes into force) is a **"disposal of a non-UK residential property interest"** if the first or second condition is met.

1(2) The first condition is that–

(a) the land has at any time in the relevant ownership period consisted of or included a dwelling, or

(b) the interest in non-UK land subsists for the benefit of land that has at any time in the relevant ownership period consisted of or included a dwelling.

1(3) The second condition is that the interest in non-UK land subsists under a contract for an off-plan purchase.

1(4) In sub-paragraph (2) **"relevant ownership period"** means the period–

(a) beginning with the day on which P acquired the interest in non-UK land or 31 March 1982 (whichever is later), and

(b) ending with the day before the day on which the disposal occurs.

1(5) If the interest in non-UK land disposed of by P as mentioned in sub-paragraph (1) results from interests in non-UK land which P has acquired at different times ("the acquired interests"), P is regarded for the purposes of sub-paragraph (4)(a) as having acquired the interest when P first acquired any of the acquired interests.

1(6) In this paragraph–

"contract for an off-plan purchase" means a contract for the acquisition of land consisting of, or including, a building or part of a building that is to be constructed or adapted for use as a dwelling;

"dwelling" is to be read in accordance with paragraph 4.

1(7) Paragraphs 6 and 20 of Schedule 4ZZC contain further provision about interests under contracts for off-plan purchases.

"INTEREST IN NON-UK LAND"

2(1) In this Schedule **"interest in non-UK land"** means–

(a) an estate, interest, right or power in or over land outside the United Kingdom, or

(b) the benefit of an obligation, restriction or condition affecting the value of any such estate, interest, right or power,

other than an excluded interest.

2(2) The following are excluded interests–

(a) any security interest;

(b) a licence to use or occupy land.

2(3) In sub-paragraph (2) **"security interest"** means an interest or right held for the purpose of securing the payment of money or the performance of any other obligation.

2(4) The Treasury may by regulations–

(a) provide that any other description of interest or right in relation to land outside the United Kingdom is an excluded interest;

(b) exclude from sub-paragraph (2) such interests or rights as may be prescribed in the regulations.

2(5) Regulations under sub-paragraph (4) may make incidental, consequential, supplementary or transitional provision or savings.

GRANTS OF OPTIONS

3(1) Sub-paragraph (2) applies where–

(a) a person ("P") grants at any time an option binding P to sell an interest in non-UK land, and

(b) a disposal by P of that interest in non-UK land at that time would be a disposal of a non-UK residential property interest by virtue of paragraph 1.

3(2) The grant of the option is regarded for the purposes of this Schedule as the disposal of an interest in the land in question (if it would not be so regarded apart from this paragraph).

3(3) Nothing in this paragraph affects the operation of section 144 in relation to the grant of the option (or otherwise).

3(4) Subsection (6) of section 144 (interpretation of references to "sale" etc) applies for the purposes of this paragraph as it applies for the purposes of that section.

MEANING OF "DWELLING"

4(1) Paragraph 4 of Schedule B1 (meaning of "dwelling"), read with paragraphs 6 to 10 of that Schedule, applies for the purposes of this Schedule as it applies for the purposes of Schedule B1, but as if–

(a) in paragraph 4, sub-paragraphs (5) and (6) were omitted,

(b) in paragraphs 6 and 8–

(i) any reference to an interest in UK land were to an interest in non-UK land within the meaning of this Schedule, and

(ii) any reference to paragraph 1(4) of that Schedule were a reference to paragraph 1(4) of this Schedule, and

(c) in paragraphs 7 to 9 any reference to planning permission or development consent were to any permission or consent corresponding to planning permission or development consent within the meaning of that Schedule.

4(2) In paragraph 5 of Schedule B1 (power to amend), the reference to paragraph 4 includes paragraph 4 as applied by this paragraph.

4(3) The Treasury may by regulations under this sub-paragraph make provision changing or clarifying the cases where a building outside the United Kingdom counts as a dwelling for the purposes of this Schedule (and sub-paragraph (1) has effect subject to any such regulations).

4(4) Provision made under sub-paragraph (3) may include provision corresponding to paragraph 4(5) of Schedule B1.

INTERPRETATION

5 In this Schedule **"land"** includes a building.

SCHEDULE C1 – SECTION 14F: MEANING OF 'CLOSELY-HELD COMPANY' AND 'WIDELY-MARKETED SCHEME'

History – Sch. C1 inserted by FA 2015, s. 37 and Sch. 7, para. 37, with effect in relation to disposals made on or after 6 April 2015.

Part 1 – Meaning of "Closely-Held Company"

INTRODUCTION

1 This Part of this Schedule sets out the rules for determining, for the purposes of sections 14F and 14G, whether or not a company is a closely-held company.

MAIN DEFINITION

2(1) **"Closely-held company"** means a company in relation to which condition A or B is met. See also paragraphs 5 and 6.

2(2) Condition A is that the company is under the control of 5 or fewer participators.

2(3) Condition B is that 5 or fewer participators together possess or are entitled to acquire–

(a) such rights as would, in the event of the winding up of the company ("the relevant company") on the basis set out in paragraph 3, entitle them to receive the greater part of the assets of the relevant company which would then be available for distribution among the participators, or

(b) such rights as would, in that event, so entitle them if there were disregarded any rights which any of them or any other person has as a loan creditor (in relation to the relevant company or any other company).

3(1) This paragraph applies for the purposes of paragraph 2(3).

3(2) In the notional winding up of the relevant company, the part of the assets available for distribution among the participators which any person is entitled to receive is the aggregate of–

(a) any part of those assets which the person would be entitled to receive in the event of the winding up of the relevant company, and

(b) any part of those assets which the person would be entitled to receive if–

(i) any other company which is a participator in the relevant company and is entitled to receive any assets in the notional winding up were also wound up on the basis set out in this paragraph, and

(ii) the part of the assets of the relevant company to which the other company is entitled were distributed among the participators in the other company in proportion to their respective entitlement to the assets of the other company available for distribution among the participators.

3(3) In the application of sub-paragraph (2)–

(a) to the notional winding up of the other company mentioned in paragraph (b) of that sub-paragraph, and

(b) to any further notional winding up required by that paragraph (or by any further application of that paragraph),

references to **"the relevant company"** are to be read as references to the company concerned.

4(1) This paragraph applies for the purpose of determining whether, under sub-paragraph (3) of paragraph 2, 5 or fewer participators together possess or are entitled to acquire rights such as are mentioned in paragraph (a) or (b) of that sub-paragraph.

4(2) A person is to be treated as a participator in the relevant company if the person is a participator in any other company which would be entitled to receive assets in the notional winding up of the relevant company on the basis set out in paragraph 3.

4(3) No account is to be taken of a participator which is a company unless the company possesses or is entitled to acquire the rights in a fiduciary or representative capacity.

4(4) But sub-paragraph (3) does not apply for the purposes of paragraph 3.

5(1) A company is not to be treated as a closely-held company if condition A or B is met.

5(2) Condition A is that the company cannot be treated as a closely-held company except by taking, as one of the 5 or fewer participators requisite for its being so treated, a person which is a diversely-held company.

5(3) Condition B is that the company–

(a) would not be a closely-held company were it not for paragraph (a) of paragraph 2(3) or paragraph (d) of paragraph 7(2), and

(b) would not be a closely-held company if the references in paragraphs 2(3)(a) and 7(2)(d) to participators did not include loan creditors which are diversely-held companies or qualifying institutional investors.

5(4) In this paragraph **"qualifying institutional investor"** means any of the following persons–

(a) a scheme (as defined in section 14F(7)) which is a widely-marketed scheme;

(b) the trustee or manager of a qualifying pension scheme;

(c) a company carrying on life assurance business (as defined in section 56 of the Finance Act 2012);

(d) a person who cannot be liable for corporation tax or income tax (as relevant) on the ground of sovereign immunity.

5(5) In sub-paragraph (4)(b) **"qualifying pension scheme"** means a pension scheme (as defined in section 150(1) of the Finance Act 2004) other than–

(a) an investment-regulated pension scheme within the meaning of Part 1 of Schedule 29A to that Act, or

(b) a pension scheme that would be an investment-regulated pension scheme if it were a registered pension scheme.

5(6) The Treasury may by regulations amend sub-paragraphs (4) and (5).

5(7) Regulations under sub-paragraph (6) may make incidental, consequential, supplementary or transitional provision or savings.

6(1) Sub-paragraph (2) applies where a participator in a company is a qualifying institutional investor.

6(2) For the purpose of determining whether or not the company is a closely-held company, any share or interest which the qualifying institutional investor has as a participator in the company (in any of the ways set out in section 454(2) of CTA 2010 or otherwise) is treated as a share or interest held by more than 5 participators.

6(3) Sub-paragraph (4) applies where a participator in a company is a general partner of a limited partnership which is a collective investment scheme (as defined in section 235 of the Financial Services and Markets Act 2000).

6(4) For the purpose of determining whether or not the company is a closely-held company, any share or interest which the general partner has as a participator in the company (in any of the ways set out in section 454(2) of CTA 2010 or otherwise) is treated as a share or interest held by more than 5 participators.

6(5) Sub-paragraph (4) does not apply to–

(a) any rights which would, in the event of the winding up of the company ("the relevant company") on the basis set out in paragraph 3, or in any other circumstances, entitle the general partner (or a participator in the general partner) to receive assets of the company which would then be available for distribution among the participators, or

(b) any rights which would, in that event, so entitle the general partner (or a participator in the general partner) if there were disregarded any rights which a person has as a loan creditor (in relation to the relevant company or another company).

6(6) In this paragraph **"limited partnership"** means–

(a) a limited partnership registered under the Limited Partnerships Act 1907, or

(b) a firm or entity of a similar character formed under the law of a territory outside the United Kingdom.

6(7) In this paragraph, **"general partner"**, in relation to a limited partnership, means a partner other than a limited partner.

6(8) In this paragraph, **"limited partner"** means a person carrying on business as a partner in a limited partnership who–

(a) is not entitled to take part in the management of that business, and

(b) is entitled to have any liabilities of that business (or those beyond a certain limit) for debts or obligations incurred for the purposes of that business met or reimbursed by some other person.

6(9) In this paragraph **"qualifying institutional investor"** has the same meaning as in paragraph 5.

MEANING OF "CONTROL"

7(1) For the purposes of this Schedule, a person ("P") is treated as having control of a company ("C") if P–

(a) exercises,

(b) is able to exercise, or

(c) is entitled to acquire,

direct or indirect control over C's affairs.

7(2) In particular, P is treated as having control of C if P possesses or is entitled to acquire–

(a) the greater part of the share capital or issued share capital of C,

(b) the greater part of the voting power in C,

(c) so much of the issued share capital of C as would, on the assumption that the whole of the income of C were distributed among the participators, entitle P to receive the greater part of the amount so distributed, or

(d) such rights as would entitle P, in the event of the winding up of C or in any other circumstances, to receive the greater part of the assets of C which would then be available for distribution among the participators.

7(3) Any rights that P or any other person has as a loan creditor are to be disregarded for the purposes of the assumption in sub-paragraph (2)(c).

7(4) If two or more persons together satisfy any of the conditions in sub-paragraphs (1) and (2), they are treated as having control of C.

8(1) This paragraph applies for the purposes of paragraph 7.

8(2) If a person–

(a) possesses any rights or powers on behalf of another person ("A"), or

(b) may be required to exercise any rights or powers on A's direction or on A's behalf,

those rights or powers are to be attributed to A.

8(3) There are also to be attributed to P all the rights and powers of any associate of P (including rights and powers exercisable jointly by any two or more associates of P).

8(4) In this paragraph **"associate"**, in relation to P, means–

(a) any relative of P,

(b) the trustees of any settlement in relation to which P is a settlor, and

(c) the trustees of any settlement in relation to which any relative of P (living or dead) is or was a settlor.

8(5) In this paragraph **"relative"** means–

(a) a spouse or civil partner,

(b) a parent or remoter forebear,

(c) a child or remoter issue, or

(d) a brother or sister.

INTERPRETATION

9 In this Part of this Schedule–

"diversely-held company" means a company which is not a closely-held company;

"loan creditor" has the meaning given by section 453 of CTA 2010;

"open-ended investment company" has the same meaning as in Part 17 of the Financial Services and Markets Act 2000 (see section 236 of that Act);

"participator", in relation to a company, has the meaning given by section 454 of CTA 2010.

Part 2 – Unit Trust Schemes and OEICs: Widely-Marketed Schemes

INTRODUCTION

10(1) This Part of this Schedule sets out the rules for determining, for the purposes of this Schedule and section 14F, whether or not a scheme is a widely-marketed scheme at any time.

10(2) In this Part of this Schedule **"scheme"** has the same meaning as in section 14F.

WIDELY-MARKETED SCHEMES

11(1) A scheme is a widely-marketed scheme at any time when the scheme meets conditions A to C.

11(2) Condition A is that the scheme produces documents, available to investors and to Her Majesty's Revenue and Customs, which contain–

(a) a statement specifying the intended categories of investor,

(b) an undertaking that units in the scheme will be widely available, and

(c) an undertaking that units in the scheme will be marketed and made available in accordance with the requirements of sub-paragraph (5)(a).

11(3) Condition B is that–

(a) the specification of the intended categories of investor does not have a limiting or deterrent effect, and

(b) any other terms or conditions governing participation in the scheme do not have a limiting or deterrent effect.

11(4) In sub-paragraph (3) **"limiting or deterrent effect"** means an effect which–

(a) limits investors to a limited number of specific persons or specific groups of connected persons, or

(b) deters a reasonable investor falling within one of (what are specified as) the intended categories of investor from investing in the scheme.

11(5) Condition C is that–

(a) units in the scheme are marketed and made available–

   (i) sufficiently widely to reach the intended categories of investors, and

   (ii) in a manner appropriate to attract those categories of investors, and

(b) a person who falls within one of the intended categories of investors can, upon request to the manager of the scheme, obtain information about the scheme and acquire units in it.

11(6) A scheme is not regarded as failing to meet condition C at any time by reason of the scheme's having, at that time, no capacity to receive additional investments, unless–

(a) the capacity of the scheme to receive investments in it is fixed by the scheme documents (or otherwise), and

(b) a pre-determined number of specific persons or specific groups of connected persons make investments in the scheme which collectively exhaust all, or substantially all, of that capacity.

INTERPRETATION

12 In this Part of this Schedule–

"open-ended investment company" has the same meaning as in Part 17 of the Financial Services and Markets Act 2000 (see section 236 of that Act);

"units" means the rights or interests (however described) of the participants in a unit trust scheme or open-ended investment company.

SCHEDULE 1 – APPLICATION OF EXEMPT AMOUNT AND REPORTING LIMITS IN CASES INVOLVING SETTLED PROPERTY

Section 3

History – In the heading to Sch. 1, the words "and reporting limits" inserted by FA 2003, s. 159 and Sch. 28, para. 2(1) which apply, by virtue of FA 2003, Sch. 28, para. 7, in relation to any notice given under s. 8 or 8A of the Taxes Management Act in relation to the year 2003–04 or any subsequent year of assessment.

A1(1) In determining the exempt amount available to the trustees of a settlement in relation to a year of assessment–

(a) a principal settlement and its sub-fund settlements shall be treated, for the purposes of paragraphs 1 and 2 below, as if no sub-fund elections had been made, and

(b) paragraph 3 below shall apply for the purposes of determining the exempt amount available to each member of the class consisting of a principal settlement and its sub-fund settlements.

A1(2) The reference in sub-paragraph (1) above to a principal settlement and its sub-fund settlements means a principal settlement in respect of which one or more sub-fund elections are treated as having taken effect.

History – Sch. 1, para. A1 inserted by FA 2006, s. 88 and Sch. 12, para. 44(1) with effect for years of assessment beginning on or after 6 April 2006.

1(1) For any year of assessment during the whole or part of which settled property is held on trusts which secure that, during the lifetime of a disabled person–

(a) if any of the property is applied for the benefit of a beneficiary, it is applied for the disabled person's benefit, and

(b) either–

(i) the disabled person is entitled to all of the income (if there is any) arising from any of the property, or

(ii) if any such income is applied for the benefit of a beneficiary, it is applied for the disabled person's benefit,

sections 3(1) to (5D) and 3A shall apply to the trustees of the settlement as they apply to an individual, but with the modifications specified in this paragraph.

1(1A) The trusts on which settled property is held are not to be treated as falling outside sub-paragraph (1) by reason only of–

(a) the trustees' having powers that enable them to apply in any tax year otherwise than for the benefit of the disabled person amounts (whether consisting of income or capital, or both) not exceeding the annual limit,

(b) the trustees' having the powers conferred by section 32 of the Trustee Act 1925 (powers of advancement),

(c) the trustees' having those powers but free from, or subject to a less restrictive limitation than, the limitation imposed by proviso (a) of subsection (1) of that section,

(d) the trustees' having the powers conferred by section 33 of the Trustee Act (Northern Ireland) 1958 (corresponding provision for Northern Ireland),

(e) the trustees' having those powers but free from, or subject to a less restrictive limitation than, the limitation imposed by subsection (1)(a) of that section, or

(f) the trustees' having powers to the like effect as the powers mentioned in any of paragraphs (b) to (e).

1(1B) For the purposes of this paragraph, the **"annual limit"** for a tax year is whichever is the lower of the following amounts–

(a) £3,000, and

(b) 3% of the amount that is the maximum value of the settled property during the tax year in question.

1(1C) The Treasury may by order–

(a) specify circumstances in which sub-paragraph (1A)(a) is, or is not, to apply in relation to a trust, and

(b) amend the definition of "the annual limit" in sub-paragraph (1B).

1(1D) An order under sub-paragraph (1C) may–

(a) make different provision for different cases, and

(b) contain transitional and saving provision.

1(1E) A statutory instrument containing an order under sub-paragraph (1C) may not be made unless a draft of the instrument has been laid before, and approved by a resolution of, the House of Commons.

1(2) The reference in sub-paragraph (1) to the lifetime of a person shall, where the income from the settled property is held for his benefit on trusts of the kind described in section 33 of the Trustee Act 1925 (protective trusts), be construed as a reference to the period during which the income is held on trust for him.

1(2A) As they apply by virtue of sub-paragraph (1) above–

(a) section 3(5A) has effect with the omission of paragraph (b), and

(b) section 3(5B) has effect with the omission of the words "or (b)".

1(3) In relation to a settlement which is one of 2 or more qualifying settlements comprised in a group, this paragraph shall have effect as if for the references in sections 3 and 3A(1)(a) to the exempt amount for the year (except the one in section 3(2)) there were substituted references to one-tenth of that exempt amount or, if it is more, to such amount as results from dividing the exempt amount for the year by the number of settlements in the group.

1(4) For the purposes of sub-paragraph (3) above–

(a) a qualifying settlement is any settlement (other than an excluded settlement) which is made on or after 10th March 1981 and to the trustees of which this paragraph applies for the year of assessment; and

(b) all qualifying settlements in relation to which the same person is the settlor constitute a group.

1(5) If, in consequence of 2 or more persons being settlors in relation to it, a settlement is comprised in 2 or more groups comprising different numbers of settlements, sub-paragraph (3) above shall apply to it as if the number by which the exempt amount for the year is to be divided were the number of settlements in the largest group.

1(5A) In its application to the trustees of a settlement, section 3A(1) has effect with the substitution for the reference to section 8 of the Management Act of a reference to section 8A of that Act.

1(6) In this paragraph–

"disabled person" has the meaning given by Schedule 1A to the Finance Act 2005; and

"excluded settlement" has the same meaning as in paragraph 2 below.

1(7) [Omitted by SI 2009/2035, art. 2 and Schedule, para. 33.]

History – In para. 1(1) the words "(5D)" substituted for the words "(5C)" by FA 2015, s. 37 and Sch. 7, para. 35(2) with effect in relation to disposals made on or after 6 April 2015.

In para. 1(1) the words "disabled person" substituted for the words "mentally disabled person or a person in receipt of attendance allowance or of a disability living allowance by virtue of entitlement to the care component at the highest or middle rate" by FA 2013, s. 216 and Sch. 44, para. 13(2)(a), with effect in relation to the tax year 2013–14 and subsequent tax years, subject to the provisions of FA 2013, Sch. 44, para. 13(7).

Para. 1(1)(a) and (b) substituted by FA 2013, s. 216 and Sch. 44, para. 13(2)(b), with effect in relation to the tax year 2013–14 and subsequent tax years, subject to the provisions of FA 2013, Sch. 44, para. 13(7).

In para. 1(1), the words "sections 3(1) to (5C) and 3A" substituted for the words "section 3(1) to (6)" by FA 2003, s. 159 and Sch. 28, para. 4(2)(a) which apply, by virtue of FA 2003, Sch. Sch. 28, para. 7, in relation to any notice given under section 8 or 8A of the Taxes Management Act 1970 in relation to the year 2003–04 or any subsequent year of assessment.

At the end of para. 1(1), the words ", but with the modifications specified in this paragraph" inserted by Sch. 28, para. 4(2)(b) which, by virtue of Sch. 28, para. 8, shall be deemed always to have had effect.

Para. 1(1A)–(1E) inserted by FA 2013, s. 216 and Sch. 44, para. 13(3), with effect in relation to the tax year 2013–14 and subsequent tax years, subject to the provisions of FA 2013, Sch. 44, para. 13(7).

In para. 1(2), the words "The reference in sub-paragraph (1)" substituted for the words "The trusts on which settled property is held shall not be treated as falling outside sub-paragraph (1) above by reason only of the powers conferred on the trustees by section 32 of the Trustee Act 1925 or section 33 of the Trustee Act (Northern Ireland) 1958 (powers of advancement); and the reference in that sub-paragraph" by FA 2013, s. 216 and Sch. 44, para. 13(4), with effect in relation to the tax year 2013–14 and subsequent tax years, subject to the provisions of FA 2013, Sch. 44, para. 13(7).

Para. 1(2A) inserted by Sch. 28, para. 4(3) which, by virtue of Sch. 28, para. 8, shall be deemed always to have had effect.

In para. 1(3), the words "sections 3 and 3A(1)(a)" substituted for the words "section 3" by Sch. 28, para. 4(4)(a) which applies, by virtue of FA 2003, Sch. 28, para. 7, in relation to any notice given under section 8 or 8A of the Taxes Management Act in relation to the year 2003–04 or any subsequent year of assessment.

In para. 1(3), the words "(except the one in section 3(2))" inserted by Sch. 28, para. 4(4)(b) which, by virtue of Sch. 28, para. 8, shall be deemed always to have had effect.

Para. 1(5A) inserted by FA 2003, s. 159 and Sch. 28, para. 2(2) which apply, by virtue of FA 2003, Sch. 28 para. 7, in relation to any notice given under section 8 or 8A of the Taxes Management Act in relation to the year 2003–04 or any subsequent year of assessment.

In para. 1(6), definition of "disabled person" substituted for definitions of "mentally disabled person", "attendance allowance" and "disability living allowance" by FA 2013, s. 216 and Sch. 44, para. 13(5), with effect in relation to the tax year 2013–14 and subsequent tax years, subject to the provisions of FA 2013, Sch. 44, para. 13(7).

In para. 1(6), the words "**"excluded settlement"** has the same meaning" substituted for "**"settlor"** and **"excluded settlement"** have the same meanings" by FA 2006, s. 88 and Sch. 12, para. 28(1) with effect for the purpose of determining on or after 6 April 2006 whether a person is a settlor in relation to a settlement (whenever created) for the purposes of Sch. 1.

Para. 1(7) omitted by SI 2009/2035, art. 2 and Schedule, para. 33, with effect from 13 August 2009.

In former para. 1(7), the words "An officer of the Board" substituted for the words "An inspector" by Sch. 28, para. 4(5) which, by virtue of Sch. 28, para. 9, has effect in relation to any notice given, whether or not after the passing of the FA 2003, in respect of the year 2002–03 or any subsequent year of assessment.

Derivations – Para. 1(1): CGTA 1979, Sch. 1, para. 5(1), as amended by FA 1982, s. 89(2) and by FA 1980, s. 77(4)(c); Disability Living Allowance and Disability Working Allowance Act 1991, Sch. 2, para. 9 and Disability Living Allowance and Disability Working Allowance (Northern Ireland Consequential Amendments) Order 1991, art. 2.

Para. 1(2): CGTA 1979, Sch. 1, para. 5(1A), as inserted by FA 1981, s. 89(3).

Para. 1(3): CGTA 1979, Sch. 1(1B), as inserted by FA 1981, s. 89(3), and amended by FA 1982, s. 80(3)(c).

Para. 1(4): CGTA 1979, Sch. 1(1C), as inserted by FA 1981, s. 89(3).

Para. 1(5): CGTA 1979, Sch. 1, para. 5(1D), as inserted by FA 1981, s. 89(3) and amended by FA 1982, s. 80(3)(b).
Para. 1(6): CGTA 1979, Sch. 1, para. 5(2), as amended by FA 1981, s. 89(4); Mental Health Act 1983, Sch. 4, para. 49; Disability Living Allowance and Disability Working Allowance Act, Sch. 2, para. 9 and Disability Living Allowance and Disability Working Allowance (Northern Ireland Consequential Amendments) Order 1991, art. 2; SS(CP)A 1992 and Social Security (Consequential Provisions) Act (Northern Ireland) 1992.
Para. 1(7): CGTA 1979, Sch. 1, para. 5(3), as inserted by FA 1981, s. 89(5).

Cross references – TMA 1970, s. 98 (first column of the Table): penalty for failure to furnish particulars etc.
ICTA 1988, s. 715(8): certain exemptions from the accrued income scheme, by reference to securities held in disabled persons' trusts.

Notes – S. 68: meaning of "settled property".
S. 288: interpretation, including "notice" as being in writing.

2(1) For any year of assessment during the whole or part of which any property is settled property, not being a year of assessment for which paragraph 1(1) above applies, sections 3(1) to (5D) and 3A shall apply to the trustees of a settlement as they apply to an individual but with the following modifications.

2(2) In section 3(1), (5A), (5B) and (5C) and section 3A(1)(a) for "the exempt amount for the year" there shall be substituted "one-half of the exempt amount for the year".

2(2A) As they apply by virtue of sub-paragraph (1) above–

(a) section 3(5A) has effect with the omission of paragraph (b), and

(b) section 3(5B) has effect with the omission of the words "or (b)".

2(3) [Omitted by FA 2003, s. 159 and Sch. 28, para. 5(5) and repealed by FA 2003, s. 216 and Sch. 43, Pt. 3(7).]

2(4) In relation to a settlement which is one of 2 or more qualifying settlements comprised in a group, sub-paragraph (2) above shall have effect as if for the reference to one-half of the exempt amount for the year there were substituted a reference to one-tenth of that exempt amount or, if it is more, to such amount as results from dividing one-half of the exempt amount for the year by the number of settlements in the group.

2(5) For the purposes of sub-paragraph (4) above–

(a) a qualifying settlement is any settlement (other than an excluded settlement) which is made after 6th June 1978 and to the trustees of which this paragraph applies for the year of assessment; and

(b) all qualifying settlements in relation to which the same person is the settlor constitute a group.

2(6) If, in consequence of 2 or more persons being settlors in relation to it, a settlement is comprised in 2 or more groups comprising different numbers of settlements, sub-paragraph (4) above shall apply to it as if the number by which one-half of the exempt amount for the year is to be divided were the number of settlements in the largest group.

2(6A) In its application to the trustees of a settlement, section 3A(1) has effect with the substitution for the reference to section 8 of the Management Act of a reference to section 8A of that Act.

2(7) In this paragraph **"excluded settlement"** means–

(a) any settlement the trustees of which are not for the whole or any part of the year of assessment resident in the United Kingdom; and

(b) any settlement the property comprised in which–

(i) is held for charitable purposes only and cannot become applicable for other purposes; or

(ii) is held for the purposes of a registered pension scheme, a superannuation fund to which section 615(3) of the Taxes Act applies or an occupational pension scheme (within the meaning of section 150(5) of the Finance Act 2004) that is not a registered pension scheme.

2(8) [Omitted by FA 2004, s. 281 and Sch. 35, para. 42(3); and repealed by FA 2004, s. 326 and Sch. 42, Pt. 3.]

2(9) [Omitted by SI 2009/2035, art. 2 and Schedule, para. 33.]

History – In para. 2(1) the words "(5D)" substituted for the words "(5C)" by FA 2015, s. 37 and Sch. 7, para. 35(3) with effect in relation to disposals made on or after 6 April 2015.
In para. 2(1), words "sections 3(1) to (5C) and 3A" substituted for words "section 3(1) to (6)" by FA 2003, Sch. 28, para. 5(2) which applies, by virtue of Sch. 28, para. 7, in relation to any notice given under section 8 or 8A of the Taxes Management Act 1970 in relation to the year 2003–04 or any subsequent year of assessment.
In para. 2(2), words "section 3(1), (5A), (5B) and (5C)" substituted for words "subsections (1) and (5)" by FA 2003, Sch. 28, para. 5(3)(a) which, by virtue of Sch. 28, para. 8, shall be deemed always to have effect.
In para. 2(2), words "and section 3A(1)(a)" inserted by FA 2003, Sch. 28, para. 5(3)(b) which applies, by virtue of Sch. 28, para. 7, in relation to any notice given under section 8 or 8A of the Taxes Management Act 1970 in relation to the year 2003–04 or any subsequent year of assessment.
Para. 2(2A) inserted by FA 2003, Sch. 28, para. 5(4) which, by virtue of Sch. 28, para. 8, shall be deemed always to have effect.
Para. 2(3) omitted by FA 2003, s. 159 and Sch. 28, para. 5(5), and repealed by FA 2003, s. 216 and Sch. 43, Pt. 3(7) which apply, by virtue of FA 2003, Sch. 28, para. 7, in relation to any notice given under section 8 or 8A of the Taxes Management Act 1970 in relation to the year 2003–04 or any subsequent year of assessment.
Para. 2(6A) inserted by FA 2003, s. 159 and Sch. 28, para. 2(3) which apply, by virtue of FA 2003, Sch. 28, para. 7, in relation to any notice given under section 8 or 8A of the Taxes Management Act in relation to the year 2003–04 or any subsequent year of assessment.
In para. 2(7), the meaning of "settlor" omitted by FA 2006, s. 88 and Sch. 12, para. 28(2) and repealed by FA 2006, s. 178 and Sch. 26, Pt. 3(15) with effect for the purpose of determining on or after 6 April 2006 whether a personis a settlor in relation to a settlement (whenever created) for the purposes of Sch. 1.

In para. 2(7)(a), the words "and ordinarily resident" omitted by FA 2013, s. 219 and Sch. 46, para. 105, with effect in relation to a person's liability to capital gains tax for the tax year 2013–14 or any subsequent tax year, without prejudice to any provision in FA 2013, Sch. 46, Pt. 3 about the application of a particular amendment.
In para. 2(7)(a), at the end of the paragraph the words "treated under section 69(1) as" omitted by FA 2006, s. 88 and Sch. 12, para. 38 and repealed by FA 2006, s. 178 and Sch. 26, Pt. 3(15), with effect from 6 April 2007 (in relation to settlements whenever created) (FA 2006, s. 88 and Sch. 12, para. 41).
In para. 2(7)(b)(ii), the words "a registered pension scheme, a superannuation fund to which section 615(3) of the Taxes Act applies or an occupational pension scheme (within the meaning of section 150(5) of the Finance Act 2004) that is not a registered pension scheme" substituted for the words "any such scheme or fund as is mentioned in sub-paragraph (8) below" by FA 2004, s. 281 and Sch. 35, para. 42(2) which, by virtue of FA 2004, s. 284(1), come into force on 6 April 2006.
In para. 2(7), words "section 620 of ITTOIA 2005" substituted for "section 660G(1) and (2) of the Taxes Act" by virtue of ITTOIA 2005, s. 882 and Sch. 1, para. 449 which, in accordance with ITTOIA 2005, s. 883, have effect, for income tax purposes, for tax year 2005–06 and subsequent tax years, and, for corporation tax purposes, for accounting periods ending after 5 April 2005.
In para. 2(7), words "section 660G(1) and (2)" substituted for "section 681(4)" by FA 1995, s. 74 and Sch. 17, para. 32, with effect for 1995–96 and subsequent years of assessment.
Para. 2(8) omitted by FA 2004, s. 281 and Sch. 35, para. 42(3); and repealed by FA 2004, s. 326 and Sch. 42, Pt. 3 which, by virtue of FA 2004, s. 284(1), come into force on 6 April 2006.
Para. 2(9) omitted by SI 2009/2035, art. 2 and Schedule, para. 33, with effect from 13 August 2009.
In former para. 2(9), words "An officer of the Board" substituted for words "An inspector" by Sch. 28, para. 5(6) which, by virtue of FA 2003, Sch. 28, para. 9, has effect in relation to any notice given, whether or not after the passing of the FA 2003, in respect of the year 2002–03 or any subsequent year of assessment.

Derivations – Para. 2(1): CGTA 1979, Sch. 1, para. 6(1), as amended by FA 1980, s. 78(2).
Para. 2(2)–(4): CGTA 1979, Sch. 1, para. 6(2)–(4), as substituted by FA 1980, s. 78(3), and amended by FA 1982, s. 80(3)(b)–(e).
Para. 2(5): CGTA 1979, Sch. 1, para. 6(5), as substituted by FA 1980, s. 78(3).
Para. 2(6): CGTA 1979, Sch. 1, para. 6(6), as substituted by FA 1980, s. 78(3) and amended by FA 1982, s. 80(3)(d).
Para. 2(7)–(9) (as originally enacted): CGTA 1979, Sch. 1, para. 6(7)–(9), as substituted by FA 1978, s. 78(3).

Cross references – S. 69(1): trustees treated as resident and ordinarily resident unless the general administration of the trusts is ordinarily carried on outside the UK and a majority of the trustees are not resident or not ordinarily resident.
ICTA 1988, s. 590–612 (Pt. XIV, Ch. I), 615(3), 620, 621, 624: exemptions etc. in relation to various pension arrangements.
ICTA 1988, s. 660G(1), (2): "settlement" includes any disposition, trust, covenant, agreement, arrangement or transfer of assets and "settlor" means any person by whom the settlement was made.

Notes – S. 68: meaning of "settled property".
S. 288: interpretation, including "notice" as being in writing.

3(1) The exempt amount available in relation to a year of assessment to the trustees of each settlement in the class consisting of a principal settlement and its sub-fund settlements shall be the exempt amount available to the trustees of the principal settlement in relation to the year, determined in accordance with paragraph 1 or 2 above as if no sub-fund elections had been made.

3(2) But if there are two or more non-excluded settlements in the class consisting of a principal settlement and its sub-fund settlements, the exempt amount available to the trustees of each settlement in the class in relation to the year shall be the amount specified in sub-paragraph (1) above divided by the number of non-excluded settlements in the class.

3(3) In this paragraph–

"excluded settlement" has the meaning given by paragraph 2(7) above, and

references to a settlement having sub-fund settlements, and similar expressions, are references to a settlement being the principal settlement in respect of which one or more sub-fund elections are treated as having taken effect.

History – Para. 3 inserted by FA 2006, s. 88 and Sch.12, para. 44(2) with effect for years of assessment beginning on or after 6 April 2006.

SCHEDULE 2 – ASSETS HELD ON 6TH APRIL 1965

Section 35

Cross references – S. 139(1): on reconstruction or amalgamation involving the transfer of business, transferee steps into the shoes of the transferor as regards Sch. 2.
S. 221: on certified harbour reorganisation scheme, harbour authority steps into the shoes of the transferor as regards Sch. 2.
S. 264(5): on reorganisation of parliamentary constituencies, new association steps into the shoes of the old association as regards Sch. 2.
FA 1990, Sch. 12, para. 2: on transfer of any asset from the Independent Broadcasting Authority to the Independent Television Commission and Radio Authority, transferee steps into the shoes of the transferor as regards Sch. 2.
FA 1994, Sch. 24, para. 10: in connection with relevant transfers under railways privatisation transferee steps into predecessor's shoes for the purposes of Sch. 2.
British Telecommunications Act 1981, s. 82(1): on transfer of assets to effect privatisation of telecommunications, transferee steps into the shoes of the transferee as regards Sch. 2.
TSBA 1985, Sch. 2, para. 2(2): successor to the Trustee Savings Banks steps into the shoes of those companies as regards Sch. 2.
Transport Act 1985, s. 130(3): on reorganisation of transport authorities, successors step into the shoes of the predecessors as regards Sch. 2.
Broadcasting Act 1996, Sch. 7, para. 5: Sch. 2 has effect in relation to any assets which are transferred to a successor company under a preparatory scheme, within the meaning of that Act, as if the BBC and the successor company were the same person, and as if those assets, to the extent that they were acquired or provided by the BBC, were acquired or, as the case may be, provided by the successor company.

Part I – Quoted Securities

DEEMED ACQUISITION AT 6TH APRIL 1965 VALUE

1(1) This paragraph applies–

(a) to shares and securities which on 6th April 1965 had quoted market values on a recognised stock exchange, or which had such quoted market values at any time in the period of 6 years ending on 6th April 1965, and

(b) to rights of unit holders in any unit trust scheme the prices of which are published regularly by the managers of the scheme.

1(2) For the purposes of this Act it shall be assumed, wherever relevant, that any assets to which this paragraph applies were sold by the owner, and immediately reacquired by him, at their market value on 6th April 1965.

1(3) [Omitted by FA 2008, s. 8 and Sch. 2, para. 64(2).]

History – Para. 1(3) omitted by FA 2008, s. 8 and Sch. 2, para. 64(2) with effect in relation to disposals on or after 6 April 2008 (FA 2008, Sch. 2, para. 71).

Derivations – Para. 1: CGTA 1979, Sch. 5, para. 1.

Cross references – S. 272–274 and Sch. 11: meaning of "market value" with specific provision (para. 6) for ascertaining market value in accordance with para. 1(2).

Notes – S. 21–34: general meaning of "disposal".
S. 99: meaning of "unit trust scheme".
S. 288: interpretation, including the meaning of "company", "recognised stock exchange" and "shares" as embracing stock.

RESTRICTION OF GAIN OR LOSS BY REFERENCE TO ACTUAL COST

2(1) Subject to paragraph 4 below and section 109(4), paragraph 1(2) above shall not apply in relation to a disposal of assets–

(a) if on the assumption in paragraph 1(2) a gain would accrue on that disposal to the person making the disposal and either a smaller gain or a loss would so accrue if paragraph 1(2) did not apply, or

(b) if on the assumption in paragraph 1(2) a loss would so accrue and either a smaller loss or a gain would accrue if paragraph 1(2) did not apply,

and accordingly the amount of the gain or loss accruing on the disposal shall be computed without regard to the preceding provisions of this Schedule except that in a case where this sub-paragraph would otherwise substitute a loss for a gain or a gain for a loss it shall be assumed, in relation to the disposal, that the relevant assets were sold by the owner, and immediately reacquired by him, for a consideration such that, on the disposal, neither a gain nor a loss accrued to the person making the disposal.

2(2) For the purpose of–

(a) identifying shares or securities held on 6th April 1965 with shares or securities previously acquired, and

(b) identifying the shares or securities held on that date with shares or securities subsequently disposed of, and distinguishing them from shares or securities acquired subsequently,

so far as that identification is needed for the purposes of sub-paragraph (1) above, and so far as the shares or securities are of the same class, shares or securities acquired at a later time shall be deemed to be disposed of before shares or securities acquired at an earlier time.

2(3) Sub-paragraph (2) above has effect subject to section 105.

Derivations – Para. 2: CGTA 1979, Sch. 5, para. 2, as amended by FA 1982, s. 86, 88 and Sch. 13, para. 11; see also FA 1985, Sch. 19, para. 6(3).

Cross references – S. 105: identification with securities acquired on the same day and any excess is matched with subsequent acquisitions on a FIFO basis (so far as not otherwise matched with prior acquisitions).
S. 109(4): election for shares to form part of a "1982 holding" for pooling.

Notes – S. 21–34: general meaning of "disposal" and "asset".

3(1) Where–

(a) a disposal was made out of quoted securities before 20th March 1968, and

(b) by virtue of paragraph 2 of Schedule 7 to the Finance Act 1965 some of the quoted securities out of which the disposal was made were acquired before 6th April 1965 and some later,

then in computing the gain accruing on any disposal of quoted securities the question of what remained *undisposed of on the earlier* disposal shall be decided on the footing that paragraph 2 of that Schedule did not apply as respects that earlier disposal.

3(2) The rules of identification in paragraph 2(2) above shall apply for the purposes of this paragraph as they apply for the purposes of that paragraph.

Derivations – Para. 3: CGTA 1979, Sch. 5, para. 3.

ELECTION FOR POOLING

4(1) This paragraph applies in relation to quoted securities as respects which an election under paragraphs 4 to 7 of Schedule 5 to the 1979 Act had not been made before the operative date, within the meaning of Part II of Schedule 13 to the Finance Act 1982, (so that they do not constitute a 1982 holding within the meaning of section 109), but does not apply in relation to relevant securities within the meaning of section 108.

4(2) If a person so elects, quoted securities covered by the election shall be excluded from paragraph 2 above, so that paragraph 1(2) above is not excluded by that paragraph as respects those securities, and sub-paragraphs (3) to (7) (which re-enact section 65 of the 1979 Act) apply.

4(3) Subject to section 105, any number of quoted securities of the same class held by one person in one capacity shall for the purposes of this Act be regarded as indistinguishable parts of a single asset (in this paragraph referred to as a holding) growing or diminishing on the occasions on which additional securities of the class in question are acquired, or some of the securities of the class in question are disposed of.

4(4) Without prejudice to the generality of sub-paragraph (3) above, a disposal of quoted securities in a holding, other than the disposal outright of the entire holding, is a disposal of part of an asset and the provisions of this Act relating to the computation of a gain accruing on a disposal of part of an asset shall apply accordingly.

4(5) Securities shall not be treated for the purposes of this paragraph as being of the same class unless they are so treated by the practice of a recognised stock exchange or would be so treated if dealt with on such a stock exchange, but shall be treated in accordance with this paragraph notwithstanding that they are identified in some other way by the disposal or by the transfer or delivery giving effect to it.

4(6) [Omitted by FA 2008, s. 8 and Sch. 2, para. 64(3)(a).]

4(7) Nothing in this paragraph shall be taken as affecting the manner inwhich the market value of any asset is to be ascertained.

4(8) An election made by any person under this paragraph shall be as respects all disposals made by the person at any time, including disposals made before the election but after 19th March 1968–

(a) of quoted securities of kinds other than fixed-interest securities and preference shares, or

(b) of fixed-interest securities and preference shares,

and references to the quoted securities covered by an election shall be construed accordingly.

Any person may make both of the elections.

4(9) An election under this paragraph shall not cover quoted securities which the holder acquired on a disposal after 19th March 1968 in relation to which section 171(1) applies, but this paragraph shall apply to the quoted securities so held if the person who made the original disposal (that is to say the other member of the group of companies) makes an election covering quoted securities of the kind in question.

For the purpose of identifying quoted securities disposed of by the holder with quoted securities acquired by the holder on a disposal in relation to which section 171(1) applies, so far as they are of the same class quoted securities acquired at an earlier time shall be deemed to be disposed of before quoted securities acquired at a later time.

4(10) For the avoidance of doubt it is hereby declared–

(a) that where a person makes an election under this paragraph as respects quoted securities which the person holds in one capacity, that election does not cover quoted securities which the person holds in another capacity, and

(b) that an election under this paragraph is irrevocable.

4(11) An election under this paragraph shall be made by notice to an officer of the Board given–

(a) [omitted by FA 2008, s. 8 and Sch. 2, para. 64(3)(e)(i);]

(b) not later than the expiration of 2 years from the end of the accounting period in which the first relevant disposal is made; or

(c) within such further time as the Board may allow.

4(12) Subject to paragraph 5 below, in this paragraph the **"first relevant disposal"**, in relation to each of the elections referred to in sub-paragraph (8) of this paragraph, means the first disposal after 19th March 1968 by the person making the election of quoted securities of the kind covered by that election.

4(13) All such adjustments shall be made, whether by way of discharge or repayment of tax, or the making of assessments or otherwise, as are required to give effect to an election under this paragraph.

History – Para. 4(6) omitted by FA 2008, s. 8 and Sch. 2, para. 64(3)(a) with effect in relation to disposals on or after 6 April 2008 (FA 2008, Sch. 2, para. 71).

In para. 4(8), the words "the person" substituted for "him" by FA 2008, s. 8 and Sch. 2, para. 64(3)(b) with effect in relation to disposals on or after 6 April 2008 (FA 2008, Sch. 2, para. 71).
In para. 4(9), the word "section" substituted for the words "either section 58 or" twice and the words "the spouse or civil partner of the holder, or" omitted by FA 2008, s. 8 and Sch. 2, para. 64(3)(c)(i), (ii) with effect in relation to disposals on or after 6 April 2008 (FA 2008, Sch. 2, para. 71).
In para. 4(9), the words "the holder" substituted for "him" by FA 2008, s. 8 and Sch. 2, para. 64(3)(c)(iii) with effect in relation to disposals on or after 6 April 2008 (FA 2008, Sch. 2, para. 71).
In para. 4(9) the words "spouse or civil partner" substituted for the words "wife or husband" by SI 2005/3229, reg. 124(a), with effect from 5 December 2005.
In para. 4(10)(a), the words "the person" twice substituted for "he" by FA 2008, s. 8 and Sch. 2, para. 64(3)(d) with effect in relation to disposals on or after 6 April 2008 (FA 2008, Sch. 2, para. 71).
Para. 4(11)(a) omitted by FA 2008, s. 8 and Sch. 2, para. 64(3)(e)(i) with effect in relation to disposals on or after 6 April 2008 (FA 2008, Sch. 2, para. 71).
In para. 4(11)(b), the words "in the case of an election for the purposes of corporation tax," omitted by FA 2008, s. 8 and Sch. 2, para. 64(3)(e)(ii) with effect in relation to disposals on or after 6 April 2008 (FA 2008, Sch. 2, para. 71).
In para. 4(11)(c), the words "in either case," omitted by FA 2008, s. 8 and Sch. 2, para. 64(3)(e)(iii) with effect in relation to disposals on or after 6 April 2008 (FA 2008, Sch. 2, para. 71).
In para. 4(11), the words following "notice to" were substituted by FA 1996, s. 135 and Sch. 21, para. 42(2), with effect for the year 1996–97 and subsequent years (capital gains tax) and for corporation tax accounting periods ending on or after 1 July 1999, the appointed day for corporation tax self-assessment (FA 1994, s. 199 and SI 1998/3173 (C. 78)).

Derivations – Para. 4(2): CGTA 1979, Sch. 5, para. 4(1).
Para. 4(3)–(7): CGTA 1979, s. 65.
Para. 4(8)–(13): CGTA 1979, Sch. 5, para. 4(2)–(7).

Cross references – S. 58: deemed no gain, no loss on transfers between spouses.
S. 108(8): special identification rules for relevant securities (accrued income scheme securities or material interests in non-qualifying offshore funds) do not apply to quoted securities held at 6 April 1965 unless an election has been made under para. 4 (or s. 109(4)).
S. 109(5): application to election for quoted securities to form part of any "1982 holding" of para. 4(8)–(13).
S. 171(1): deemed no gain, no loss on transfers of capital assets within a group.
CGTA 1979, Sch. 5, para. 4–7: see derivations of para. 4–7 of this Schedule.
FA 1982, Sch. 13, para. 8–11 (Pt. II): the operative date was 6 April 1982 or, for companies, 1 April 1982.

Other material – CCAB press release, 1967 (not reproduced): rights of election under para. 4 (and hence s. 109(4), as above) can be exercised, where appropriate, by the taxpayer's legal representative.

Notes – S. 21–34: general meaning of "disposal".
S. 288: interpretation, including the meaning of "recognised stock exchange", "inspector" as being any inspector of taxes and reference to sections being those of this Act.
TMA 1970, s. 29: assessing procedure.

ELECTION BY PRINCIPAL COMPANY OF GROUP

5(1) In the case of companies which at the relevant time are members of a group of companies–

(a) an election under paragraph 4 above by the company which at that time is the principal company of the group shall have effect also as an election by any other company which at that time is a member of the group, and

(b) no election under that paragraph may be made by any other company which at that time is a member of the group.

5(2) In this paragraph **"the relevant time"**, in relation to a group of companies, and in relation to each of the elections referred to in paragraph 4(8) above, is the first occasion after 19th March 1968 when any company which is then a member of a group disposes of quoted securities of a kind covered by that election, and for the purposes of paragraph 4(11) above that occasion is, in relation to the group, **"the first relevant disposal"**.

5(3) This paragraph shall not apply in relation to quoted securities of either kind referred to in paragraph 4(8) above which are owned by a company which, in some period after 19th March 1968 and before the relevant time, was not a member of the group if in that period it had made an election under paragraph 4 above in relation to securities of that kind (or was treated by virtue of this paragraph, in relation to another group, as having done so), or had made a disposal of quoted securities of that kind and did not make an election within the time limited by paragraph 4(11) above.

5(4) This paragraph shall apply notwithstanding that a company ceases to be a member of the group at any time after the relevant time.

5(5) In this paragraph **"company"** and **"group"** shall be construed in accordance with section 170(2) to (9).

Derivations – CGTA 1979, Sch. 5, para. 5.

Cross references – S. 109(5): application to election for quoted securities to form part of any "1982 holding".
S. 170(2)–(9) with (2)(a) and (9)(b) omitted: definition of company by reference to those within the Companies Acts etc. and meaning of group by reference to 75 per cent subsidiary relationships (and see FA 2000, Sch. 29, para. 37 for determination of a member, or principal company, of a group on or after 1 April 2000).

POOLING AT VALUE ON 6TH APRIL 1965: EXCHANGE OF SECURITIES ETC.

6(1) Where a person who has made only one of the elections under paragraph 4 above disposes of quoted securities which, in accordance with Chapter II of Part IV, are to be regarded as being or forming part of a new holding, the election shall apply according to the nature of the quoted securities disposed of, notwithstanding that under that Chapter the new holding is to be regarded as the same asset as the original holding and that the election would apply differently to the original holding.

6(2) Where the election does not cover the disposal out of the new holding but does cover quoted securities of the kind comprised in the original holding, then in computing the gain accruing on the disposal out of the new holding (in accordance with paragraph 3 above) the question of what remained undisposed of on any disposal out of the original holding shall be decided on the footing that paragraph 3 above applied to that earlier disposal.

6(3) In the converse case (that is to say, where the election covers the disposal out of the new holding, but does not cover quoted securities of the kind comprised in the original holding) the question of how much of the new holding derives from quoted securities held on 6th April 1965 and how much derives from other quoted securities, shall be decided as it is decided for the purposes of paragraph 3 above.

Derivations – CGTA 1979, Sch. 5, para. 6.

Cross references – S. 109(5): application to election for quoted securities to form part of any "1982 holding'.

UNDERWRITERS

7 No election under paragraph 4 above shall cover quoted securities comprised in any underwriter's premiums trust fund, or premiums trust fund deposits, or personal reserves, being securities comprised in funds to which section 206 applies.

Derivations – CGTA 1979, Sch. 5, para. 7.

Cross references – S. 109(5): application to election for quoted securities to form part of any "1982 holding'.
S. 206: a member is treated as absolutely entitled to investments of a premiums trust fund, a special reserve fund or other trust fund required or authorised by the rules of Lloyd's or required by the underwriting agent.

INTERPRETATION OF PARAGRAPHS 3 TO 7

8(1) In paragraphs 3 to 7 above–

"quoted securities" means assets to which paragraph 1 above applies,

"fixed interest security" means any security as defined by section 132,

"preference share" means any share the holder whereof has a right to a dividend at a fixed rate, but has no other right to share in the profits of the company.

8(2) If and so far as the question whether at any particular time a share was a preference share depends on the rate of dividends payable on or before 5th April 1973, the reference in the definition of **"preference share"** in sub-paragraph (1) above to a dividend at a fixed rate includes a dividend at a rate fluctuating in accordance with the standard rate of income tax.

Derivations – CGTA 1979, Sch. 5, para. 8.

Cross references – S. 109(5): application to election for quoted securities to form part of any "1982 holding".
S. 132: definition of security by reference to any loan stock or similar security.

Part II – Land Reflecting Development Value

9(1) Subject to paragraph 17(2) of Schedule 11, this Part of this Schedule shall apply in relation to a disposal of an asset which is an interest in land situated in the United Kingdom–

(a) if, but for this paragraph, the expenditure allowable as a deduction in computing the gain accruing on the disposal would include any expenditure incurred before 6th April 1965, and

(b) if the consideration for the asset acquired on the disposal exceeds the current use value of the asset at the time of the disposal, or if any material development of the land has been carried out after 17th December 1973 since the person making the disposal acquired the asset.

9(2) For the purposes of this Act, it shall be assumed that, in relation to the disposal and, if it is a part disposal, in relation to any subsequent disposal of the asset which is an interest in land situated in the United Kingdom, that asset was sold by the person making the disposal, and immediately reacquired by him, at its market value on 6th April 1965.

9(3) Sub-paragraph (2) above shall apply also in relation to any prior part disposal of the asset and, if tax has been charged, or relief allowed, by reference to that part disposal on a different footing, all such adjustments shall be made, whether by way of assessment or discharge or repayment of tax, as are required to give effect to the provisions of this sub-paragraph.

9(4) Sub-paragraph (2) above shall not apply in relation to a disposal of assets–

(a) on the assumption in that sub-paragraph a gain would accrue on that disposal to the person making the disposal and either a smaller gain or a loss would so accrue (computed in accordance with the provisions of this Act) if it did not apply, or

(b) if on the assumption in sub-paragraph (2) a loss would so accrue and either a smaller loss or a gain would accrue if that sub-paragraph did not apply,

and accordingly the amount of the gain or loss accruing on the disposal shall be computed without regard to the provisions of this Schedule except that in a case where this sub-paragraph would otherwise substitute a loss for a gain or a gain for a loss it shall be assumed, in relation to the disposal, that the relevant assets were sold by the owner, and immediately reacquired by him, for a consideration such that, on the disposal, neither a gain nor a loss accrued to the person making the disposal.

9(5) For the purposes of this Part of this Schedule–

(a) **"interest in land"** means any estate or interest in land, any right in or over land or affecting the use or disposition of land, and any right to obtain such an estate, interest or right from another which is conditional on that other's ability to grant the estate, interest or right in question, except that it does not include the interest of a creditor (other than a creditor in respect of a rentcharge) whose debt is secured by way of a mortgage, an agreement for a mortgage or a charge of any kind over land, or, in Scotland, the interest of a creditor in a charge or security of any kind over land; and

(b) **"land"** includes buildings.

Derivations – CGTA 1979, Sch. 5, para. 9, 10; FA 1974, s. 44(1).

Cross references – Sch. 11, para. 17(2): claim by person having paid betterment levy for application of para. 9 notwithstanding that para. 9(1)(b) is not satisfied.

Notes – S. 21–34: general meaning of "disposal" and "asset", including a part disposal as a disposal.
S. 275: location of assets.
S. 272–274 and Sch. 11: meaning of "market value".

10(1) For the purposes of this Part of this Schedule, the current use value of an interest in land shall be ascertained in accordance with the following provisions of this Part, and in this Part the time as at which current use value is to be ascertained is referred to as **"the relevant time"**.

10(2) Subject to the following provisions of this Part of this Schedule, the **current use value** of an interest in land at the relevant time is the market value of that interest at that time calculated on the assumption that it was at that time, and would continue to be, unlawful to carry out any material development of the land other than any material development thereof which, being authorised by planning permission in force at that time, was begun before that time.

In relation to any material development which was begun before 18th December 1973 this sub-paragraph shall have effect with the omission of the words from "other than" to "before that time".

10(3) In this paragraph **"planning permission"** has the same meaning as in the Town and Country Planning Act 1990 or, in Scotland, the Town and Country Planning (Scotland) Act 1972, or, in Northern Ireland, the Planning (Northern Ireland) Order 1991, and in determining for the purposes of this paragraph what material development of any land was authorised by planning permission at a time when there was in force in respect of the land planning permission granted on an outline application (that is to say, an application for planning permission subject to subsequent approval on any matters), any such development of the land which at that time–

(a) was authorised by that permission without any requirement as to subsequent approval; or

(b) not being so authorised, had been approved in the manner applicable to that planning permission,

but no other material development, shall for those purposes be taken to have been authorised by that permission at that time.

10(4) Where the value to be ascertained is the current use value of an interest in land which has been disposed of by way of a part disposal of an asset (**"the relevant asset"**) consisting of an interest in land, the current use value at the relevant time of the interest disposed of shall be the relevant fraction of the current use value of the relevant asset at that time, calculated on the same assumptions as to the lawfulness or otherwise of any material development as fall to be made under this Part in calculating the current use value at that time of the interest disposed of.

10(5) For the purposes of sub-paragraph (4) above **"the relevant fraction"** means that fraction of the sums mentioned in paragraph (6) below which under subsection (2) of section 42 is, or would but for subsection (4) of that section be, allowable as a deduction in computing the amount of the gain accruing on the part disposal.

10(6) The sums referred to in sub-paragraph (5) above are the sums which, if the entire relevant asset had been disposed of at the time of the part disposal, would be allowable by virtue of section 38(1)(a) and (b) as a deduction in computing the gain accruing on that disposal of the relevant asset.

10(7) Sub-paragraphs (4) to (6) above shall not apply–

(a) in the case of a disposal interest in land by way of a part disposal if, on making the disposal, the person doing so no longer has any in the land which is subject to that interest; or

(b) in a case to which the following provisions of this paragraph apply.

10(8) In computing any gain accruing to a person on a part disposal of an interest in land resulting under subsection (1) of section 22 from the receipt as mentioned in paragraph (a), (c) or (d) of that subsection of a capital sum, the current use value at the relevant time of the interest out of which the part disposal was made shall be taken to be what it would have been at that time if the circumstances which caused the capital sum to be received had not arisen.

Derivations – CGTA 1979, Sch. 5, para. 9(5); FA 1974, Sch. 3, para. 1–3.

Cross references – S. 22(1)(a), (c), (d): there is a disposal where a capital sum is derived from an asset, in particular by way of compensation for risk or damage, of forfeiture etc. of rights or of use or exploitation.
S. 38(1)(a), (b): acquisition, enhancement or title expenditure and incidental costs.
S. 42(2), (4): apportionment of base cost to a part disposal on the basis of the fraction the consideration represents of the aggregate of that consideration and the market value of the remainder, except in relation to expenditure wholly attributable to either part.

Notes – S. 288: interpretation, including reference to sections being those of this Act.

11(1) The current use value of an interest in land which is either–

(a) a freehold interest which is subject to a lease or an agreement for a lease, or

(b) an interest under a lease or agreement for a lease,

shall be ascertained without regard to any premium required under the lease or agreement for a lease or any sublease, or otherwise under the terms subject to which the lease or sublease was or is to be granted, but with regard to all other rights under the lease or prospective lease (and, for the current use value of an interest under a lease subject to a sublease, under the sublease).

11(2) If under sub-paragraph (1) above an interest under a lease or agreement for a lease would have a negative value, the current use value of the interest shall be nil.

11(3) If a lease is granted out of any interest in land after 17th December 1973, then, in computing any gain accruing on any disposal of the reversion on the lease made while the lease subsists, the current use value of the reversion at any time after the grant of the lease shall not exceed what would have been at that time the current use value of the interest in the land of the person then owning the reversion if that interest had not been subject to the lease.

11(4) In the application of this paragraph to Scotland, **"freehold"** means the estate or interest of the proprietor of the dominium utile or, in the case of property other than feudal property, of the owner, and **"reversion"** means the interest of the landlord in property subject to a lease.

Derivations – CGTA 1979, Sch. 5, para. 9(5); FA 1974, Sch. 3, para. 4.

Notes – Sch. 8, para. 10: meaning of lease and cognate expressions.

12 In computing any gain accruing to a person on a disposal of a lease which is a wasting asset, the current use value of the lease at the time of its acquisition by the person making the disposal shall be the fraction–

$$\frac{A}{B}$$

of what its current use value at that time would be apart from this paragraph, where–

A is equal to so much of the expenditure attributable to the lease under section 38(1)(a) and (b) as is not under paragraph 1 of Schedule 8 excluded therefrom for the purposes of the computation of the gain accruing on the disposal, and

B is equal to the whole of the expenditure which would be so attributable to the lease for those purposes apart from the said paragraph 1.

Derivations – CGTA 1979, Sch. 5, para. 9(5); FA 1974, Sch. 3, para. 5.

Cross references – S. 38(1)(a), (b): acquisition, enhancement or title expenditure and incidental costs.
Sch. 8, para. 1: curved line restriction of allowable expenditure on a short lease.

Notes – S. 21–34: general meaning of "disposal".
S. 288: meaning of "wasting asset" and reference to sections and schedules as being those of this Act.

13(1) In this Part of this Schedule, **"material development"**, in relation to any land, means the making of any change in the state, nature or use of the land, but the doing of any of the following things in the case of any land shall not be taken to involve material development of the land, that is to say–

(a) the carrying out of works for the maintenance, improvement, enlargement or other alteration of any building, so long as the cubic content of the original building is not exceeded by more than one-tenth;

(b) the carrying out of works for the rebuilding, as often as occasion may require, of any building which was in existence at the relevant time, or of any building which was in existence in the period of 10 years immediately preceding the day on which that time falls but was destroyed or demolished before the relevant time, so long as (in either case) the cubic content of the original building is not exceeded by more than one-tenth;

(c) the use of any land for the purposes of agriculture or forestry, the use for any of those purposes of any building occupied together with land so used, and the carrying out on any land so used of any building or other operations required for the purposes of that use;

(d) the carrying out of operations on land for, or the use of land for, the display of an advertisement, announcement or direction of any kind;

(e) the carrying out of operations for, or the use of the land for, car parking, provided that such use shall not exceed 3 years;

(f) in the case of a building or other land which at the relevant time was used for a purpose falling within any class specified in sub-paragraph (4) below or which, being unoccupied at that time, was last used for any such purpose, the use of that building or land for any other purpose falling within the same class;

(g) in the case of a building or other land which at the relevant time was in the occupation of a person by whom it was used as to part only for a particular purpose, the use for that purpose of any additional part of the building or land not exceeding one-tenth of the cubic content of the part of the building used for that purpose at the relevant time or, as the case may be, one-tenth of the area of the land so used at that time;

(h) in the case of land which at the relevant time was being temporarily used for a purpose other than the purpose for which it was normally used, the resumption of the use of the land for the last-mentioned purpose;

(i) in the case of land which was unoccupied at the relevant time, the use of the land for the purpose for which it was last used before that time.

References in this paragraph to the cubic content of a building are references to that content as ascertained by external measurement.

13(2) For the purposes of sub-paragraph (1)(a) and (b)–

(a) where 2 or more buildings are included in a single development the whole of that development may be regarded as a single building, and where 2 or more buildings result from the redevelopment of a single building the new buildings may together be regarded as a single building, but 2 or more buildings shall not be treated as included in a single development unless they are or were comprised in the same curtilage; and

(b) in determining whether or not the cubic content of the original building has been exceeded by more than one-tenth, the cubic content of the building after the carrying out of the works in question shall be treated as reduced by the amount (if any) by which so much of that cubic content as is attributable to one or more of the matters mentioned in sub-paragraph (3) below exceeds so much of the cubic content of the original building as was attributable to one or more of the matters so mentioned.

13(3) The matters referred to in sub-paragraph (2)(b) are the following, that is to say–

(a) means of escape in case of fire;

(b) car-parking or garage space;

(c) accommodation for plant providing heating, air-conditioning or similar facilities.

13(4) The classes of purposes mentioned in sub-paragraph (1)(f) are the following–

Class A – Use as a dwelling-house or for the purpose of any activities which are wholly or mainly carried on otherwise than for profit, except use for a purpose falling within Class B, C or E.

Class B – Use as an office or retail shop.

Class C – Use as a hotel, boarding-house or guest-house, or as premises licensed for the sale of intoxicating liquors for consumption on the premises.

Class D – Use for the purpose of any activities wholly or mainly carried on for profit, except–

(a) use as a dwelling-house or for the purposes of agriculture or forestry; and

(b) use for a purpose falling within Class B, C or E.

Class E – Use for any of the following purposes, namely–

(a) the carrying on of any process for or incidental to any of the following purposes, namely–

(i) the making of any article or of any part of any article, or the production of any substance;

(ii) the altering, repairing, ornamenting, finishing, cleaning, washing, packing or canning, or adapting for sale, or breaking up or demolishing of any article; or

(iii) without prejudice to (i) or (ii) above, the getting, dressing or treatment of minerals,

being a process carried on in the course of a trade or business other than agriculture or forestry, but excluding any process carried on at a dwelling-house or retail shop;

(b) storage purposes (whether or not involving use as a warehouse or repository) other than storage purposes ancillary to a purpose falling within Class B or C.

Derivations – Para. 13(1): CGTA 1979, Sch. 5, para. 9(5); FA 1974, Sch. 3, para. 6, 7(1), 10(2).
Para. 13(2): CGTA 1979, Sch. 5, para. 9(5); FA 1974, Sch. 3, para. 10(3), 7(2).
Para. 13(3): CGTA 1979, Sch. 5, para. 9(5); FA 1974, Sch. 3, para. 7(3).
Para. 13(4): CGTA 1979, Sch. 5, para. 9(5); FA 1974, Sch. 3, para. 8.

14(1) For the purposes of this Part, material development shall be taken to be begun on the earliest date on which any specified operation comprised in the material development is begun.

14(2) In this paragraph **"specified operation"** means any of the following, that is to say–

(a) any work of construction in the course of the erection of a building;

(b) the digging of a trench which is to contain the foundations, or part of the foundations, of a building;

(c) the laying of any underground main or pipe to the foundations, or part of the foundations, of a building or to any such trench as is mentioned in (b) above;

(d) any operation in the course of laying out or constructing a road or part of a road;

(e) any change in the use of any land.

14(3) Subject to sub-paragraph (4) below, material development shall for the purposes of this Part of this Schedule not be treated as carried out after a particular date if it was begun on or before that date.

14(4) If, in the case of any land–

(a) material development thereof was begun on or before 17th December 1973 but was not completed on or before that date, and

(b) the development was on that date to any extent not authorised by planning permission (within the meaning of paragraph 10(3) above) then in force

then, for the purposes of this Part of this Schedule, so much of the development carried out after that date as was not so authorised on that date shall be treated as begun on the earliest date after 17th December 1973 on which any specified operation comprised therein is begun, and shall accordingly be treated as material development of the land carried out after 17th December 1973.

Derivations – Para. 14(1), (2): CGTA 1979, Sch. 5, para. 9(5); FA 1974, Sch. 3, para. 9.
Para. 14(3), (4): CGTA 1979, Sch. 5, para. 9(5); FA 1974, Sch. 3, para. 14(1), (2).

15 In this Part of this Schedule, unless the context otherwise requires–

"agriculture" includes horticulture, fruit growing, seed growing, dairy farming, the keeping and breeding of livestock (including any creature kept for the production of food, wool, skins or fur or for the purpose of its use in the farming of land), the use of land as grazing land, meadow land, osier land, market gardens and nursery grounds, and the use of land for woodlands where that use is ancillary to the farming of land for other agricultural purposes, and

"agricultural" shall be construed accordingly;

"article" means an article of any description;

"building" includes part of a building and references to a building may include references to land occupied therewith and used for the same purposes;

"forestry" includes afforestation;

"minerals" includes all minerals and substances in or under land of a kind ordinarily worked for removal by underground or surface working;

"retail shop" includes any premises of a similar character where retail trade or business (including repair work) is carried on;

"substance" means any natural or artificial substance or material, whether in solid or liquid form or in the form of a gas or vapour.

Derivations – CGTA 1979, Sch. 5, para. 9(5); FA 1974, Sch. 3, para. 10(1).

Part III – Other Assets

APPORTIONMENT BY REFERENCE TO STRAIGHTLINE GROWTH OF GAIN OR LOSS OVER PERIOD OF OWNERSHIP

16(1) This paragraph applies subject to Parts I and II of this Schedule.

16(2) On the disposal of assets by a person whose period of ownership began before 6th April 1965 only so much of any gain accruing on the disposal as is under this paragraph to be apportioned to the period beginning with 6th April 1965 shall be a chargeable gain.

16(3) Subject to the following provisions of this Schedule, the gain shall be assumed to have grown at a uniform rate from nothing at the beginning of the period of ownership to its full amount at the time of the disposal so that, calling the part of that period before 6th April 1965, P, and the time beginning with

6th April 1965 and ending with the time of the disposal T, the fraction of the gain which is a chargeable gain is–

$$\frac{T}{P+T}$$

16(4) If any of the expenditure which is allowable as a deduction in the computation of the gain is within section 38(1)(b)–

(a) the gain shall be attributed to the expenditure, if any, allowable under section 38(1)(a) as one item of expenditure, and to the respective items of expenditure under section 38(1)(b) in proportion to the respective amounts of those items of expenditure,

(b) sub-paragraph (3) of this paragraph shall apply to the part of the gain attributed to the expenditure under section 38(1)(a),

(c) each part of the gain attributed to the items of expenditure under section 38(1)(b) shall be assumed to have grown at a uniform rate from nothing at the time when the relevant item of expenditure was first reflected in the value of the asset to the full amount of that part of the gain at the time of the disposal,

so that, calling the respective proportions of the gain E(0), E(1), E(2) and so on (so that they add up to unity) and calling the respective periods from the times when the items under section 38(1)(b) were reflected in the value of the asset to 5th April 1965 P(1), P(2) and so on, and employing also the abbreviations in sub-paragraph (3) above, the fraction of the gain which is a chargeable gain is–

$$E(0)\frac{T}{P+T} + E(1)\frac{T}{P(1)+T} + E(2)\frac{T}{P(2)+T} \text{ and so on.}$$

16(5) In a case within sub-paragraph (4) above where there is no initial expenditure (that is no expenditure under section 38(1)(a)) or that initial expenditure is, compared with any item of expenditure under section 38(1)(b), disproportionately small having regard to the value of the asset immediately before the subsequent item of expenditure was incurred, the part of the gain which is not attributable to the enhancement of the value of the asset due to any item of expenditure under section 38(1)(b) shall be deemed to be attributed to expenditure incurred at the beginning of the period of ownership and allowable under section 38(1)(a), and the part or parts of the gain attributable to expenditure under section 38(1)(b) shall be reduced accordingly.

16(6) The beginning of the period over which a gain, or part of a gain, is under sub-paragraphs (3) and (4) above to be treated as growing shall not be earlier than 6th April 1945, and this sub-paragraph shall have effect notwithstanding any provision in this Schedule or elsewhere in this Act.

16(7) If in pursuance of section 42 an asset's market value at a date before 6th April 1965 is to be ascertained, sub-paragraphs (3) to (5) above shall have effect as if that asset had been on that date sold by the owner, and immediately reacquired by him, at that market value.

16(8) If in pursuance of section 42 an asset's market value at a date on or after 6th April 1965 is to be ascertained sub-paragraphs (3) to (5) above shall have effect as if–

(a) the asset on that date had been sold by the owner, and immediately reacquired by him, at that market value, and

(b) accordingly, the computation of any gain on a subsequent disposal of that asset shall be computed–

  (i) by apportioning in accordance with this paragraph the gain or loss over a period ending on that date (the date of the part disposal), and

  (ii) by bringing into account the entire gain or loss over the period from the date of the part disposal to the date of subsequent disposal.

16(9) For the purposes of this paragraph the period of ownership of an asset shall, where under section 43 account is to be taken of expenditure in respect of an asset from which the asset disposed of was derived, or where it would so apply if there were any relevant expenditure in respect of that other asset, include the period of ownership of that other asset.

16(10) If under this paragraph part only of a gain is a chargeable gain, the fraction in section 223(2) shall be applied to that part instead of to the whole of the gain.

Derivations – CGTA 1979, Sch. 5, para. 11.

Cross references – S. 38(1): acquisition expenditure, including incidental costs (s. 38(1)(a)) and enhancement or title expenditure (s. 38(1)(b)).
S. 42: apportionment of base cost on a part disposal.
S. 43: apportionment of base cost where the values of assets have been derived from other assets on merger, division etc.
S. 223(2): private residence relief where the dwelling-house has not been the only or main residence throughout the period of ownership.
Sch. 3, para. 6: certain re-basing exclusions apply by reference to the gain or loss as reduced under para. 16.
TSBA 1985, Sch. 2, para. 3: formula for valuing shares in successors to the Trustee Savings Banks.

Other material – ICAEW Technical Release TR 500 (not reproduced): period of tenancy prior to ownership may be included as part of time apportionment denominator.

Notes – S. 15: meaning of "chargeable gain".
S. 21–34: general meaning of "disposal" and "asset".

ELECTION FOR VALUATION AT 6TH APRIL 1965

17(1) If the person making a disposal so elects, paragraph 16 above shall not apply in relation to that disposal and it shall be assumed, both for the purposes of computing the gain accruing to that person on the disposal, and for all other purposes both in relation to that person and other persons, that the assets disposed of, and any assets of which account is to be taken in relation to the disposal under section 43, being assets which were in the ownership of that person on 6th April 1965, were on that date sold, and immediately reacquired, by him at their market value on 6th April 1965.

17(2) Sub-paragraph (1) above shall not apply in relation to a disposal of assets if on the assumption in that sub-paragraph a loss would accrue on that disposal to the person making the disposal and either a smaller loss or a gain would accrue if sub-paragraph (1) did not apply, but in a case where this sub-paragraph would otherwise substitute a gain for a loss it shall be assumed, in relation to the disposal, that the relevant assets were sold by the owner and immediately reacquired by him, for a consideration such that, on the disposal, neither a gain nor a loss accrued to the person making the disposal.

The displacement of sub-paragraph (1) above by this sub-paragraph shall not be taken as bringing paragraph 16 above into operation.

17(3) An election under this paragraph shall be made by notice to an officer of the Board given–

(a) [omitted by FA 2008, s. 8 and Sch. 2, para. 64(3)(f)(i);]

(b) within 2 years from the end of the accounting period in which the disposal is made; or

(c) within such further time as the Board may by notice allow.

17(4) For the avoidance of doubt it is hereby declared that an election under this paragraph is irrevocable.

17(5) An election may not be made under this paragraph as respects, or in relation to, an asset the market value of which at a date on or after 6th April 1965, and before the date of the disposal to which the election relates, is to be ascertained in pursuance of section 42.

History – Para. 17(3)(a) omitted by FA 2008, s. 8 and Sch. 2, para. 64(3)(f)(i) with effect in relation to disposals on or after 6 April 2008 (FA 2008, Sch. 2, para. 71).
In para. 17(3)(b), the words "in the case of an election for the purposes of corporation tax," omitted by FA 2008, s. 8 and Sch. 2, para. 64(3)(f)(ii) with effect in relation to disposals on or after 6 April 2008 (FA 2008, Sch. 2, para. 71).
In para. 17(3)(c), the opening words (reference to elections) omitted by FA 2008, s. 8 and Sch. 2, para. 64(3)(f)(iii) with effect in relation to disposals on or after 6 April 2008 (FA 2008, Sch. 2, para. 71).
In para. 17(3), the words following "by notice to" substituted by FA 1996, s. 135 and Sch. 21, para. 42(3), with effect for the year 1996–97 and subsequent years (capital gains tax) and for corporation tax accounting periods ending on or after 1 July 1999, the appointed day for corporation tax self-assessment (FA 1994, s. 199 and SI 1998/3173 (C. 78)).

Derivations – CGTA 1979, Sch. 5, para. 12.

Cross references – S. 42: apportionment of base cost on a part disposal.
S. 43: apportionment of base cost where the values of assets have been derived from other assets on merger, division etc.
S. 108(8): special identification rules for relevant securities do not apply to securities to which para. 17 applies.

Statements of practice – D21: HMRC has discretion to extend time limit in para. 17(3) as appropriate where a company leaving a group triggers a charge under s. 178, 179.

Notes – S. 272–274 and Sch. 11: meaning of "market value".
S. 288: interpretation, including "inspector" as being any inspector of taxes, "notice" as being in writing and reference to sections being those of this Act.

UNQUOTED SHARES, COMMODITIES ETC.

18(1) This paragraph has effect as respects shares held by any person on 6th April 1965 other than quoted securities within the meaning of paragraph 8 above and shares as respects which an election is made under paragraph 17 above.

18(2) For the purpose of–

(a) identifying the shares so held on 6th April 1965 with shares previously acquired, and

(b) identifying the shares so held on that date with shares subsequently disposed of, and distinguishing them from shares acquired subsequently,

so far as the shares are of the same class, shares bought at a later time shall be deemed to have been disposed of before shares bought at an earlier time.

18(3) Sub-paragraph (2) above has effect subject to section 105.

18(4) Shares shall not be treated for the purposes of this paragraph as being of the same class unless if dealt with on a recognised stock exchange they would be so treated, but shall be treated in accordance with this paragraph notwithstanding that they are identified in a different way by disposal or by the transfer or delivery giving effect to it.

18(5) This paragraph, without sub-paragraph (4), shall apply in relation to any assets, other than shares, which are of a nature to be dealt with without identifying the particular assets disposed of or acquired.

Derivations – CGTA 1979, Sch. 5, para. 18, as amended by FA 1982, s. 86, 88 and Sch. 13, para. 11.

Cross references – S. 105: identification with securities acquired on the same day and any excess is matched with subsequent acquisitions on a FIFO basis (so far as not otherwise matched with prior acquisitions).
S. 108(8): special identification rules for relevant securities do not apply to securities to which para. 18 applies.

Notes – S. 288: interpretation, including "shares" as embracing stock, reference to shares of the same class being in the same company and reference to sections being those of this Act.

REORGANISATION OF SHARE CAPITAL, CONVERSION OF SECURITIES ETC.

19(1) For the purposes of this Act, it shall be assumed that any shares or securities held by a person on 6th April 1965 (identified in accordance with paragraph 18 above) which, in accordance with Chapter II of Part IV, are to be regarded as being or forming part of a new holding were sold and immediately reacquired by him on 6th April 1965 at their market value on that date.

19(2) If, at any time after 5th April 1965, a person comes to have, in accordance with Chapter II of Part IV, a new holding, paragraph 16(3) to (5) above shall have effect as if–

(a) the new holding had at that time been sold by the owner, and immediately reacquired by him, at its market value at that time, and

(b) accordingly, the amount of any gain on a disposal of the new holding or any part of it shall be computed–

  (i) by apportioning in accordance with paragraph 16 above the gain or loss over a period ending at that time, and

  (ii) by bringing into account the entire gain or loss over the period from that time to the date of the disposal.

19(3) This paragraph shall not apply in relation to a reorganisation of a company's share capital if the new holding differs only from the original shares in being a different number, whether greater or less, of shares of the same class as the original shares.

Derivations – CGTA 1979, Sch. 5, para. 14.

Cross references – S. 126–140 (Pt. IV, Ch. II): equation of original and new holdings on a reorganisation, conversion, exchange, reconstruction etc.

Extra-statutory concessions – D10: on a disposal of the entire new holding, tax is not charged on more than the actual gain realised.

Statements of practice – SP 14/79: application of para. 19 to unquoted shares or securities.

Notes – S. 272–274 and Sch. 11: meaning of "market value".

Part IV – Miscellaneous

CAPITAL ALLOWANCES

20 If under any provision in this Schedule it is to be assumed that any asset was on 6th April 1965 sold by the owner, and immediately reacquired by him, sections 41 and 47 shall apply in relation to any capital allowance or renewals allowance made in respect of the expenditure actually incurred by the owner in providing the asset, and so made for the year 1965–66 or for any subsequent year of assessment, as if it were made in respect of the expenditure which, on that assumption, was incurred by him in reacquiring the asset on 7th April 1965.

Derivations – CGTA 1979, Sch. 5, para. 15.

Cross references – S. 41: restriction of losses by reference to the availability of capital allowances etc.
S. 47: special rules for wasting assets qualifying for capital allowances etc.

Notes – S. 288: reference to sections and schedules as being those of this Act.

ASSETS TRANSFERRED TO CLOSE COMPANIES

21(1) This paragraph has effect where–

(a) at any time, including a time before 7th April 1965, any of the persons having control of a close company, or any person who is connected with a person having control of a close company, has transferred assets to the company, and

(b) paragraph 16 above applies in relation to a disposal by one of the persons having control of the company of shares or securities in the company, or in relation to a disposal by a person having, up to the time of disposal, a substantial holding of shares or securities in the company, being in either case a disposal after the transfer of the assets.

21(2) So far as the gain accruing to the said person on the disposal of the shares is attributable to a profit on the assets so transferred, the period over which the gain is to be treated under paragraph 16 above as growing at a uniform rate shall begin with the time when the assets were transferred to the company, and accordingly a part of a gain attributable to a profit on assets transferred on or after 6th April 1965 shall all be a chargeable gain.

21(3) This paragraph shall not apply where a loss, and not a gain, accrues on the disposal.

Derivations – CGTA 1979, Sch. 5, para. 16.

Notes – S. 286: "connected" in references to persons being connected with one another.
S. 288: meaning of "close company", "control" and reference to sections and schedules as being those of this Act.

SPOUSES AND CIVIL PARTNERS

History – The wording of the cross-heading substituted for "HUSBANDS AND WIVES" by SI 2005/3229, reg. 124(c), with effect from 5 December 2005.

22 [Omitted by FA 2008, s. 8 and Sch. 2, para. 65.]

History – Para. 22 omitted by FA 2008, s. 8 and Sch. 2, para. 65 with effect in relation to disposals on or after 6 April 2008 (FA 2008, Sch. 2, para. 71).
In para. 22 the words "an individual to his spouse or civil partner" substituted for the words "a man to his wife, or by a man's wife to him" by SI 2005/3229, reg. 124(b), with effect from 5 December 2005.

Derivations – CGTA 1979, Sch. 5, para. 17.

Cross references – S. 58: deemed no gain, no loss on transfers between spouses.

Notes – S. 288: interpretation, including reference to sections being those of this Act.

COMPENSATION AND INSURANCE MONEY

23 Where section 23(4)(a) applies to exclude a gain which, in consequence of this Schedule, is not all chargeable gain, the amount of the reduction to be made under section 23(4)(b) shall be the amount of the chargeable gain and not the whole amount of the gain; and in section 23(5)(b) for the reference to the amount by which the gain is reduced under section 23(5)(a) there shall be substituted a reference to the amount by which the chargeable gain is proportionately reduced under section 23(5)(a).

Derivations – CGTA 1979, Sch. 5, para. 18.

Cross references – S. 23(4), (5): deferral of tax on reinvestment of compensation moneys etc. in a replacement asset by exclusion of the gain and reduction of the new acquisition consideration (s. 23(4)(a), (b)) and, where only part of the sum is reinvested, as if the gain were reinvested last so that a reduced gain may be excluded (with a proportionate reduction in chargeable gain) and the new acquisition consideration is reduced by the amount by which the gain is reduced (s. 23(5)(a), (b)).

Notes – S. 288: interpretation, including reference to sections being those of this Act.

SCHEDULE 3 – ASSETS HELD ON 31ST MARCH 1982

Section 35

Cross references – SI 1992/58, Sch. 2, para. 13: disapplication of Sch. 3 in relation to reorganisation of port authorities.

PREVIOUS NO GAIN/NO LOSS DISPOSALS

1(1) For the purposes of corporation tax, where–

(a) a person makes a disposal, not being a no gain/no loss disposal, of an asset which the person acquired after 31st March 1982, and

(b) the disposal by which the person acquired the asset and any previous disposal of the asset after 31st March 1982 was a no gain/no loss disposal,

the person shall be treated for the purposes of section 35 as having held the asset on 31st March 1982.

1(2) For the purposes of this paragraph a no gain/no loss disposal is one on which by virtue of any of the no gain/no loss provisions or any of sections 195B, 195C or 195E neither a gain nor a loss accrues to the person making the disposal.

History – In para. 1(1), the opening words (reference to corporation tax) substituted by FA 2008, s. 8 and Sch. 2, para. 65(2)(a)(i) with effect in relation to disposals on or after 6 April 2008 (Sch. 2, para. 71).
In para. 1(1), the words "the person" substituted three times for "he" by FA 2008, s. 8 and Sch. 2, para. 65(2)(a)(ii) with effect in relation to disposals on or after 6 April 2008 (Sch. 2, para. 71).
In para. 1(2), the words "or any of sections 195B, 195C or 195E" inserted by FA 2009, s. 86 and Sch. 40, para. 7, with effect in relation to disposals made on or after 22 April 2009.
In para. 1(2), the words "no gain/no loss provisions" substituted for the words "enactments specified in section 35(3)(d)" by FA 2008, s. 8 and Sch. 2, para. 65(2)(b) with effect in relation to disposals on or after 6 April 2008 (Sch. 2, para. 71).

Derivations – FA 1988, Sch. 8, para. 1, as amended by FA 1991, s. 78(7), by FA 1990, s. 70(7)(b), 80 and Sch. 12, para. 2(2), and by FA 1989, s. 141 and Sch. 15, para. 4(2).

Cross references – S. 164FF: reinvestment relief reductions under s. 164A(2)(b) or s. 164F(10A)(b) are not defeated by anything in Sch. 3, para. 1 as regards disposals between husband and wife on or after 20 June 1994.

Statements of practice – 1/89: change in partnership sharing ratios where no adjustment made through the accounts may be treated as a no gain, no loss disposal within para. 1.
5/89: shares or securities acquired on a relevant no gain, no loss disposal added to any existing holding before 1982 valuation, the proportion taken on the basis of the number of shares or securities.

HMRC interpretations – IRInt. 26: person deemed to have held an asset at 31 March 1982 for indexation or rebasing purposes can be treated as having incurred expenditure incurred after that date by a previous holder of the asset.

Notes – S. 21–34: general meaning of "disposal" and "asset", including timing of certain disposals.

1A(1) This paragraph applies where–

(a) paragraph 1(1) applies to a disposal of shares in or securities of a company that are of a class,

(b) accordingly, the shares or securities constitute or form part of a holding which the person making the disposal ("P") is treated as having held on 31st March 1982 ("the deemed 1982 holding"),

(c) the disposal by which P acquired the shares or securities, and any previous disposal of them after 31st March 1982, was a disposal to which section 171(1) (transfers within a group) applied,

(d) some or all of the shares or securities constituting the deemed 1982 holding were in fact held on 31st March 1982 by a person other than P, and

(e) in the hands of that person on that date they formed part of a holding which–

(i) consisted of shares or securities of the same class as the shares or securities disposed of, and

(ii) was larger than the deemed 1982 holding.

1A(2) If P makes a claim, then for the purposes of section 35(2) the market value on 31st March 1982 of the shares or securities disposed of is to be treated as being–

$$VLH \times \frac{NDO}{NLH}$$

where–

VLH is the market value on 31st March 1982 of the larger holding mentioned in sub-paragraph (1)(e) (in the hands of the person who in fact held it on that date),

NDO is the number of shares or securities disposed of, and

NLH is the number of shares or securities comprised in the larger holding on that date.

1A(3) Sub-paragraph (4) applies where sub-paragraph (1)(d) and (e) are met by two or more persons holding the shares or securities as two or more holdings or parts of holdings ("the original holdings").

1A(4) Sub-paragraph (2) applies for the purpose of calculating the market value on 31st March 1982 of the shares or securities disposed of, except that–

(a) VLH is the market value on 31st March 1982 of the largest of the original holdings, and

(b) NLH is the number of shares or securities comprised in that holding.

1A(5) A claim under sub-paragraph (2) must be made on or before the second anniversary of the end of the accounting period of P in which the disposal takes place.

1A(6) Shares in or securities of a company shall not be treated as being of the same class unless they are so treated by the practice of a recognised stock exchange or would be so treated if dealt with on a recognised stock exchange.

History – Para. 1A inserted by SI 2010/157, art. 7(3), with effect in relation to disposals made on or after 1 April 2010.

2(1) Sub-paragraph (2) below applies where a person makes a disposal of an asset acquired by him on or after 6th April 1988 in circumstances in which section 171 applied.

2(2) Where this sub-paragraph applies–

(a) an election under section 35(5) by the person making the disposal shall not cover the disposal, but

(b) the making of such an election by the person from whom the asset was acquired shall cause the disposal to fall outside subsection (3) of that section (so that subsection (2) of that section is not excluded by it) whether or not the person making the disposal makes such an election.

2(3) Where the person from whom the asset was acquired by the person making the disposal himself acquired it on or after 6th April 1988 in circumstances in which section 171 applied, an election made by him shall not have the effect described in sub-paragraph (2)(b) above but an election made by–

(a) the last person by whom the asset was acquired after 5th April 1988 otherwise than in such circumstances, or

(b) if there is no such person, the person who held the asset on 5th April 1988,

shall have that effect.

History – In para. 2(1), the reference to s. 58 omitted by FA 2008, s. 8 and Sch. 2, para. 65(3) with effect in relation to disposals on or after 6 April 2008 (Sch. 2, para. 71).

In para. 2(3), the reference to s. 58 omitted by FA 2008, s. 8 and Sch. 2, para. 65(3) with effect in relation to disposals on or after 6 April 2008 (Sch. 2, para. 71).

Derivations – FA 1988, Sch. 8, para. 2(1)–(3).

Cross references – S. 58: deemed no gain, no loss on transfers between spouses.
S. 171: deemed no gain, no loss on transfers of capital assets within a group.

Notes – S. 288: interpretation, including reference to sections being those of this Act.

CAPITAL ALLOWANCES

3 If under section 35 it is to be assumed that any asset was on 31st March 1982 sold by the person making the disposal and immediately reacquired by him, sections 41 and 47 shall apply in relation to any capital allowance or renewals allowance made in respect of the expenditure actually incurred by him in providing the asset as if it were made in respect of expenditure which, on that assumption, was incurred by him in reacquiring the asset on 31st March 1982.

Derivations – FA 1988, Sch. 8, para. 3.

Cross references – S. 41: restriction of losses by reference to the availability of capital allowances etc.
S. 47: special rules for wasting assets qualifying for capital allowances etc.

Notes – S. 288: interpretation, including reference to sections as being those of this Act.

PART DISPOSALS ETC.

4(1) Where, in relation to a disposal to which section 35(2) applies, section 42 has effect by reason of an earlier disposal made after 31st March 1982 and before 6th April 1988, the sums to be apportioned under section 42 shall for the purposes of the later disposal be ascertained on the assumption stated in section 35(2).

4(2) In any case where–

(a) subsection (2) of section 35 applies in relation to the disposal of an asset,

(b) if that subsection did not apply, section 23(2), 122(4), 133(4) or 244 would operate to disallow expenditure as a deduction in computing a gain accruing on the disposal, and

(c) the disallowance would be attributable to the reduction of the amount of the consideration for a disposal made after 31st March 1982 but before 6th April 1988,

the amount allowable as a deduction on the disposal shall be reduced by the amount which would be disallowed if section 35(2) did not apply.

Derivations – FA 1988, Sch. 8, para. 4; FA 1989, Sch. 15, para. 3.

Cross references – S. 23(2): election for allowable expenditure to be wholly deductible from proceeds where part disposal on receipt of compensation or insurance (so that none is carried forward).
S. 42: apportionment of base cost on a part disposal.
S. 122(4): election for allowable expenditure to be wholly deductible from proceeds where part disposal on receipt of a capital distribution (so that none is carried forward).
S. 133(4): election for allowable expenditure to be wholly deductible from proceeds where part disposal on receipt of a premium on conversion of securities (so that none is carried forward).
S. 244: election for allowable expenditure to be wholly deductible from proceeds where small part disposal of land (so that none is carried forward).

Notes – S. 288: interpretation, including reference to sections as being those of this Act.

ASSETS DERIVED FROM OTHER ASSETS

5 Section 35 shall have effect with the necessary modifications in relation to a disposal of an asset which on 31st March 1982 was not itself held by the person making the disposal, if its value is derived from another asset of which account is to be taken in relation to the disposal under section 43.

Derivations – FA 1988, Sch. 8, para. 5.

Cross references – S. 43: apportionment of base cost where the values of assets have been derived from other assets on merger, division, etc.

Notes – S. 21–34: general meaning of "disposal" and "asset", including timing of certain disposals.
S. 288: interpretation, including reference to sections as being those of this Act.

APPORTIONMENT OF PRE-1965 GAINS AND LOSSES

6 In a case where because of paragraph 16 of Schedule 2 only part of a gain or loss is a chargeable gain or allowable loss, section 35(3)(a) and (b) shall have effect as if the amount of the gain or loss that would accrue if subsection (2) did not apply were equal to that part.

Derivations – FA 1988, Sch. 8, para. 10.

Cross references – Sch. 2, para. 16: time apportionment of gains on assets held at 6 April 1965.

Notes – S. 288: interpretation, including reference to sections and schedules as being those of this Act.

ELECTIONS UNDER SECTION 35(5): EXCLUDED DISPOSALS

7(1) An election under section 35(5) shall not cover disposals such as are specified in sub-paragraph (2) below.

7(2) The disposals mentioned in sub-paragraph (1) above are disposals of, or of an interest in–

(a) plant or machinery,

(b) an asset which the person making the disposal has at any time held for the purposes of or in connection with–

(i) a trade consisting of the working of a source of mineral deposits, or

(ii) where a trade involves (but does not consist of) such working, the part of the trade which involves such working, or

(c) a licence under the Petroleum (Production) Act 1934 or the Petroleum (Production) Act (Northern Ireland) 1964; or

(d) shares which, on 31st March 1982, were unquoted and derived their value, or the greater part of their value, directly or indirectly from oil exploration or exploitation assets situated in the United Kingdom or a designated area or from such assets and oil exploration or exploitation rights taken together;

but a disposal does not fall within paragraph (a) or (b) above unless a capital allowance in respect of any expenditure attributable to the asset has been made to the person making the disposal or would have been made to him had he made a claim.

7(3) For the purposes of sub-paragraph (2)(d) above,–

(a) **"shares"** includes stock and any security, as defined in section 1117(1) of CTA 2010; and

(b) shares (as so defined) were **unquoted** on 31st March 1982 if, on that date, they were neither quoted on a recognised stock exchange nor dealt in on the Unlisted Securities Market;

but nothing in this paragraph affects the operation, in relation to such unquoted shares, of sections 126 to 130.

7(4) In sub-paragraph (2)(d) above–

"designated area" means an area designated by Order in Council under section 1(7) of the Continental Shelf Act 1964;

"oil exploration or exploitation assets" shall be construed in accordance with sub-paragraphs (5) and (6) below; and

"oil exploration or exploitation rights" means rights to assets to be produced by oil exploration or exploitation activities (as defined in sub-paragraph (6) below) or to interests in or to the benefit of such assets.

7(5) For the purposes of sub-paragraph (2)(d) above an asset is an oil exploration or exploitation asset if either–

(a) it is not a mobile asset and is being or has at some time been used in connection with oil exploration or exploitation activities carried on in the United Kingdom or a designated area; or

(b) it is a mobile asset which has at some time been used in connection with oil exploration or exploitation activities so carried on and is dedicated to an oil field in which the company whose shares are disposed of by the disposal, or a person connected with that company, is or has been a participator;

and, subject to sub-paragraph (6) below, expressions used in paragraphs (a) and (b) above have the same meaning as if those paragraphs were included in Part I of the Oil Taxation Act 1975.

7(6) In the preceding provisions of this paragraph **"oil exploration or exploitation activities"** means activities carried on in connection with–

(a) the exploration of land (including the seabed and subsoil) in the United Kingdom or a designated area, as defined in sub-paragraph (4) above, with a view to searching for or winning oil; or

(b) the exploitation of oil found in any such land;

and in this sub-paragraph **"oil"** has the same meaning as in Part I of the Oil Taxation Act 1975.

7(7) Where the person making the disposal acquired the asset on a no gain/no loss disposal, the references in sub-paragraph (2) above to that person are references to the person making the disposal, the person who last acquired the asset otherwise than on a no gain/no loss disposal or any person who subsequently acquired the asset on such a disposal.

7(8) In this paragraph–

(a) **"source of mineral deposits"** shall be construed in accordance with section 394 of the Capital Allowances Act, and

(b) references to a **no gain/no loss disposal** shall be construed in accordance with paragraph 1 above.

History – *In para. 7(3)(a), the words* "section 1117(1) of CTA 2010" substituted for "section 254(1) of the Taxes Act" by CTA 2010, s. 1177 and Sch. 1, para. 265, with effect for corporation tax purposes for accounting periods ending on or after 1 April 2010, and for income tax and capital gains tax purposes for the tax year 2010–11 and subsequent tax years.

In para. 7(8), words "section 394 of the Capital Allowances Act" substituted for words "section 121 of the 1990 Act" by CAA 2001, s. 578 and Sch. 2, para. 81, with effect as respects allowances and charges falling to be made for chargeable periods ending, for income tax purposes, on or after 6 April 2001, and for corporation tax purposes, on or after 1 April 2001.

Derivations – FA 1988, Sch. 8, para. 12, as amended by FA 1990, s. 63(1)–(3).

Cross references – S. 126–130: equation of original and new holdings and treatment of other consideration on a reorganisation.
ICTA 1988, s. 254(1): "security" includes securities not creating or evidencing a charge on assets.
CAA 1990, s. 121: reference to mineral deposits is a reference to mineral deposits of a wasting nature and "source of mineral deposits" includes a mine, an oil well and a source of geothermal energy.

Statements of practice – SP 1/89: change in partnership sharing ratios where no adjustment made through the accounts may be treated as a no gain, no loss disposal.

Notes – S. 288: interpretation, including "the Taxes Act" as ICTA 1988 and reference to sections and schedules as being those of this Act.

ELECTIONS UNDER SECTION 35(5): GROUP OF COMPANIES

8(1) A company may not make an election under section 35(5) at a time when it is a member but not the principal company of a group unless the company did not become a member of the group until after the relevant time.

8(2) Subject to sub-paragraph (3) below, an election under section 35(5) by a company which is the principal company of a group shall have effect also as an election by any other company which at the relevant time is a member of the group.

8(3) Sub-paragraph (2) above shall not apply in relation to a company which, in some period after 5th April 1988 and before the relevant time, is not a member of the group if–

(a) during that period the company makes a disposal to which section 35 applies, and

(b) the period during which an election under subsection (5) of that section could be made expires without such an election having been made.

8(4) Sub-paragraph (2) above shall apply in relation to a company notwithstanding that the company ceases to be a member of the group at any time after the relevant time except where–

(a) the company is an outgoing company in relation to the group, and

(b) the election relating to the group is made after the company ceases to be a member of the group.

8(5) In relation to a company which is the principal company of a group the reference in section 35(6) to the first relevant disposal is a reference to the first disposal to which that section applies by a company which is–

(a) a member of the group but not an outgoing company in relation to the group, or

(b) an incoming company in relation to the group.

Derivations – FA 1988, Sch. 8, para. 13, as amended by FA 1989, s. 141 and Sch. 15, para. 5.

Cross references – S. 170(2)–(9) with (2)(a) and (9)(b) omitted: meaning of group by reference to 75 per cent subsidiary relationships (and see FA 2000, Sch. 29, para. 38 for determining whether a company is a member, or principal company, of a group on or after 1 April 2000).

9(1) In paragraph 8 above **"the relevant time"**, in relation to a group of companies, is–

(a) the first time when any company which is then a member of the group, and is not an outgoing company in relation to the group, makes a disposal to which section 35 applies,

(b) the time immediately following the first occasion when a company which is an incoming company in relation to the group becomes a member of the group,

(c) the time when an election is made by the principal company,

whichever is earliest.

9(2) In paragraph 8 above and this paragraph–

"incoming company", in relation to a group of companies, means a company which–

(a) makes its first disposal to which section 35 applies at a time when it is not a member of the group, and

(b) becomes a member of the group before the end of the period during which an election under section 35(5) could be made in relation to it and at a time when no such election has been made, and

"outgoing company", in relation to a group of companies, means a company which ceases to be a member of the group before the end of the period during which an election under section 35(5) could be made in relation to it and at a time when no such election has been made.

9(3) Section 170 shall have effect for the purposes of paragraph 8 above and this paragraph as for those of sections 170 to 181.

Derivations – FA 1988, Sch. 8, para. 14.

Cross references – S. 170 with (2)(a) and (9)(b) omitted: definition of group, in relation to special charges and reliefs in respect of chargeable gains of groups, by reference to a principal company and its 75 per cent subsidiaries (and see FA 2000, Sch. 29, para. 38 for determining whether a company is a member, or principal company, of a group on or after 1 April 2000).

SCHEDULE 4 – DEFERRED CHARGES ON GAINS BEFORE 31ST MARCH 1982

Section 36

Cross references – SI 1992/58, Sch. 2, para. 13: disapplication of Sch. 4 in relation to reorganisation of port authorities.
Statements of practice – SP 8/92: Revenue's practice for dealing with valuation of assets where a claim to gifts hold-over relief has been made.

APPLICATION OF SCHEDULE

A1 This Schedule applies only for the purposes of corporation tax.

History – Para. A1 inserted by FA 2008, s. 8 and Sch. 2, para. 74(2) with effect in relation to disposals on or after 6 April 2008 and to which Sch. 4 would otherwise apply (FA 2008, Sch. 2, para. 76).

REDUCTION OF DEDUCTION OR GAIN

1 Where this Schedule applies–

(a) in a case within paragraph 2 below, the amount of the deduction referred to in that paragraph, and

(b) in a case within paragraph 3 or 4 below, the amount of the gain referred to in that paragraph,

shall be one half of what it would be apart from this Schedule.

Derivations – FA 1988, Sch. 9, para. 1, as amended by FA 1991, s. 101(2).

Statements of practice – SP 1/89: change in partnership sharing ratios where no adjustment made through the accounts may be treated as a no gain, no loss disposal within para. 1.

CHARGES ROLLED-OVER OR HELD-OVER

2(1) Subject to sub-paragraphs (2) to (4) below, this Schedule applies on a disposal, not being a no gain/no loss disposal, of an asset if–

(a) the person making the disposal acquired the asset after 31st March 1982,

(b) a deduction falls to be made by virtue of any of the enactments specified in sub-paragraph (5) below from the expenditure which is allowable in computing the amount of any gain accruing on the disposal, and

(c) the deduction is attributable (whether directly or indirectly and whether in whole or in part) to a chargeable gain accruing on the disposal before 6th April 1988 of an asset acquired before 31st March 1982 by the person making that disposal.

2(2) This Schedule does not apply where, by reason of the previous operation of this Schedule, the amount of the deduction is less than it otherwise would be.

2(3) This Schedule does not apply if the amount of the deduction would have been less had relief by virtue of a previous application of this Schedule been duly claimed.

2(4) Where–

(a) the asset was acquired on or after 19th March 1991,

(b) the deduction is partly attributable to a claim by virtue of section 154(4), and

(c) the claim applies to the asset,

this Schedule does not apply by virtue of this paragraph.

2(5) The enactments referred to in sub-paragraph (1) above are sections 23(4) and (5), 152 and 247.

History – In para. 2(5), the words ", 162, 165" and "of this Act and section 79 of the Finance Act 1980" omitted by FA 2008, s. 8 and Sch. 2, para. 74(3) with effect in relation to disposals on or after 6 April 2008 and to which Sch. 4 would otherwise apply (FA 2008, Sch. 2, para. 76).

Derivations – FA 1988, Sch. 9, para. 2, as amended by FA 1991, s. 101(3), (4).

Cross references – S. 23(4), (5): deferral of tax on reinvestment of compensation moneys etc. in a replacement asset.
S. 152: roll-over relief on replacement of business assets.
S. 154(4): substitution of roll-over relief for hold-over relief on replacement of business assets where non-depreciating asset subsequently acquired.
S. 162: roll-over relief on incorporation of a business.
S. 165: deferral of tax on gifts of business assets.
S. 247: roll-over relief on compulsory acquisition of land.
FA 1980, s. 79: for disposals before 14 March 1989, deferral of tax on gifts generally, subject to relief in respect of inheritance tax where the transfer proves to be chargeable (see s. 67). The text of FA 1980, s. 79(1)–(3) is reproduced earlier in this volume.

Notes – S. 21–34: general meaning of "disposal" and "asset", including timing of certain disposals.
S. 288: interpretation, including reference to sections as being those of this Act.

3(1) This paragraph applies where this Schedule would have applied on a disposal but for paragraph 2(4) above.

3(2) This Schedule applies on the disposal if paragraph 4 below would have applied had–

(a) section 154(2) continued to apply to the gain carried forward as a result of the claim by virtue of section 154(4), and

(b) the time of the disposal been the time when that gain was treated as accruing by virtue of section 154(2).

Derivations – FA 1988, Sch. 9, para. 2A, as inserted by FA 1991, s. 101(5).

Cross references – S. 154(2), (4): crystallisation of held-over gain on replacement of business assets by a depreciating asset, but substituted by a subsequent roll-over claim where a non-depreciating asset later acquired.

POSTPONED CHARGES

4(1) Subject to sub-paragraphs (3) to (5) below, this Schedule applies where–

(a) a gain is treated as accruing by virtue of any of the enactments specified in sub-paragraph (2) below, and

(b) that gain is attributable (whether directly or indirectly and whether in whole or in part) to the disposal before 6th April 1988 of an asset acquired before 31st March 1982 by the person making that disposal.

4(2) The enactments referred to in sub-paragraph (1) above are sections 116(10) and (11), 134, 140, 154(2), and 248(3).

4(3) [Repealed by FA 2000, s. 156 and Sch. 40, Pt. II(12).]

4(4) Where a gain is treated as accruing in consequence of an event, this Schedule does not apply if–

(a) the gain is attributable (whether directly or indirectly and whether in whole or part) to the disposal of an asset on or after 6th April 1988, or

(b) the amount of the gain would have been less had relief by virtue of a previous application of this Schedule been duly claimed.

4(5) None of sections 134, 140(4), 154(2) and 248(3) shall apply in consequence of an event occurring on or after 6th April 1988 if its application would be directly attributable to the disposal of an asset on or before 31st March 1982.

History – In para. 4(2), the reference to s. 168 omitted by FA 2008, s. 8 and Sch. 2, para. 74(4) with effect in relation to disposals on or after 6 April 2008 and to which Sch. 4 would otherwise apply (FA 2008, Sch. 2, para. 76).
In para. 4(2) words "178(3), 179(3)" and para. 4(3) repealed by FA 2000, s. 156 and Sch. 40, Pt. II(12) with effect in relation to assets acquired on or after 1 April 2000.

Derivations – Para. 4(1)–(4): FA 1988, Sch. 9, para. 3, as amended by FA 1989, s. 141 and Sch. 15, para. 2, and by FA 1991, s. 101(6)–(8). Para. 4(5): FA 1989, Sch. 15, para. 1.

Cross references – S. 116(10), (11): crystallisation of charge which was deferred on a reorganisation etc. involving acquisition of qualifying corporate bonds.
S. 134: crystallisation of charge deferred where gilts were acquired on compulsory acquisition of shares.
S. 140: crystallisation of charge deferred where securities were acquired in exchange for the transfer of business on domestication of a foreign branch.
S. 154(2): crystallisation of charge deferred on replacement of business assets with depreciating assets.
S. 168: crystallisation by emigration of donee in respect of charge deferred on a gift of business assets or for which inheritance tax chargeable, as modified to apply to gifts of assets generally (s. 67(6)).
S. 178(3), 179(3): crystallisation by company leaving a group holding an asset of notional market value gain or loss on transfer of that asset to it by a fellow group company.
S. 248(3): crystallisation of charge deferred on replacement of land compulsorily acquired with depreciating assets.

PREVIOUS NO GAIN/NO LOSS DISPOSALS

5 Where–

(a) a person makes a disposal of an asset which he acquired on or after 31st March 1982, and

(b) the disposal by which he acquired the asset and any previous disposal of the asset on or after 31st March 1982 was a no gain/no loss disposal,

he shall be treated for the purposes of paragraphs 2(1)(c) and 4(1)(b) above as having acquired the asset before 31st March 1982.

Derivations – FA 1988, Sch. 9, para. 4.

Notes – S. 21–34: general meaning of "disposal" and "asset", including timing of certain disposals.

6(1) Sub-paragraph (2) below applies where–

(a) a person makes a disposal of an asset which he acquired on or after 31st March 1982,

(b) the disposal by which he acquired the asset was a no gain/no loss disposal, and

(c) a deduction falling to be made as mentioned in paragraph (b) of sub-paragraph (1) of paragraph 2 above which was attributable as mentioned in paragraph (c) of that sub-paragraph was made–

(i) on that disposal, or

(ii) where one or more earlier no gain/no loss disposals of the asset have been made on or after 31st March 1982 and since the last disposal of the asset which was not a no gain/no loss disposal, on any such earlier disposal.

6(2) Where this sub-paragraph applies the deduction shall be treated for the purposes of paragraph 2 above as falling to be made on the disposal mentioned in sub-paragraph (1)(a) above and not on the no gain/no loss disposal.

Derivations – FA 1988, Sch. 9, para. 5.

Notes – S. 21–34: general meaning of "disposal" and "asset", including timing of certain disposals.

7 For the purposes of this Schedule a **no gain/no loss disposal** is one on which by virtue of any of the no gain/no loss provisions neither a gain nor a loss accrues to the person making the disposal.

History – In para. 7, the words "no gain/no loss provisions" substituted for the words "enactments specified in section 35(3)(d)" by FA 2008, s. 8 and Sch. 2, para. 66 with effect in relation to disposals on or after 6 April 2008 (Sch. 2, para. 71).

Derivations – FA 1988, Sch. 9, para. 6.

Statements of practice – SP 1/89: change in partnership sharing ratios where no adjustment is made through the accounts may be treated as a no gain, no loss disposal.

ASSETS DERIVED FROM OTHER ASSETS

8 The references in paragraphs 2(1)(c) and 4(1)(b) above to the disposal of an asset acquired by a person before 31st March 1982 include references to the disposal of an asset which was not acquired by the person before that date if its value is derived from another asset which was so acquired and of which account is to be taken in relation to the disposal under section 43.

Derivations – FA 1988, Sch. 9, para. 7.

Cross references – S. 43: apportionment of base cost where the values of assets have been derived from other assets on merger, division, etc.

CLAIMS

9(1) No relief shall be given under this Schedule unless a claim is made–

(a) [repealed by FA 2000, s. 156 and Sch. 40, Pt. II(12),]

(b) within the period of 2 years beginning at the end of the accounting period in which the disposal in question is made, or the gain in question is treated as accruing,

(c) [omitted by FA 2008, s. 8 and Sch. 2, para. 74(5)(b),]

or within such longer period as the Board may by notice allow.

9(2) A claim under sub-paragraph (1) above shall be supported by such particulars as the inspector may require for the purpose of establishing entitlement to relief under this Schedule and the amount of relief due.

History – Para. 9(1)(a) repealed by FA 2000, s. 156 and Sch. 40, Pt. II(12) with effect in relation to assets acquired on or after 1 April 2000.

In para. 9(1)(b), the words "in the case of a disposal made by, or a gain treated as accruing to, a person chargeable to corporation tax," omitted by FA 2008, s. 8 and Sch. 2, para. 74(5)(a) with effect in relation to disposals on or after 6 April 2008 and to which Sch. 4 would otherwise apply (FA 2008, Sch. 2, para. 76).

In para. 9(1)(b) words "the case…corporation tax" substituted for "any other case" and words "year of assessment or" (occurring before "accounting period") omitted by FA 1996, s. 135 and Sch. 21, para. 43(a) (and as regards the latter amendment by FA 1996, Sch. 41, Pt. V(11)) with effect for 1996–97 and subsequent years of assessment and for corporation tax accounting periods ending on or after 1 July 1999, the appointed day for corporation tax self-assessment (FA 1994, s. 199 and SI 1998/3173 (C. 78)).

Para. 9(1)(c) omitted by FA 2008, s. 8 and Sch. 2, para. 74(5)(b) with effect in relation to disposals on or after 6 April 2008 and to which Sch. 4 would otherwise apply (FA 2008, Sch. 2, para. 76).

Former para. 9(1)(c) inserted by FA 1996, s. 135 and Sch. 21, para. 43(b) with effect for 1996–97 and subsequent years of assessment and for corporation tax accounting periods ending on or after 1 July 1999; the appointed day (FA 1994, s. 199, announced by IR press releases of 25 November 1997 and 17 March 1998).

In para. 9(1), in the closing words, the words "or (as the case may be) on or before such later date" omitted by FA 2008, s. 8 and Sch. 2, para. 74(5)(c) with effect in relation to disposals on or after 6 April 2008 and to which Sch. 4 would otherwise apply (FA 2008, Sch. 2, para. 76).

In para. 9(1) at the end, words "or (as the case may be) … later date" inserted by FA 1996, s. 135 and Sch. 21, para. 43(c) with effect for 1996–97 and subsequent years of assessment and for corporation tax accounting periods ending on or after 1 July 1999; the appointed day for corporation tax self-assessment (see above).

Derivations – FA 1988, Sch. 9, para. 8, as amended by FA 1991, s. 101(9).

Cross references – S. 178(3), 179(3): crystallisation by company leaving a group holding an asset of notional market value gain or loss on transfer of that asset to it by a fellow group company.

Other material – HMRC press release, 19 March 1991 (not reproduced): the Board's discretion referred to in para. 9(1) will be exercised to extend the time limit in relation to changes made to the provisions in this Schedule by FA 1991, s. 101, to 5 April 1992 where the normal time limit expired before 25 July 1991.

Notes – S. 288: interpretation, including "notice" as being in writing and "inspector" as being any inspector of taxes.
TMA 1970, s. 42–43B: procedure for making claims.

SCHEDULE 4ZZA – RELEVANT HIGH VALUE DISPOSALS: GAINS AND LOSSES

History – Sch. 4ZZA inserted by FA 2013, s. 65 and Sch. 25, para. 16, with effect in relation to disposals occurring on or after 6 April 2013.

INTRODUCTORY

1(1) This Schedule applies for the purposes of determining in relation to a relevant high value disposal made by a person ("P")–

(a) whether a gain or loss which is ATED-related accrues to P on the disposal, and

(b) whether a gain or loss which is not ATED-related accrues to P on the disposal.

1(2) See also Part 4 of Schedule 4ZZB, which–

(a) makes provision about non-resident CGT disposals which are, or involve, relevant high value disposals, and

(b) includes provision about the computation of gains or losses on such disposals which are neither NRCGT gains or losses (as defined in section 57B and Schedule 4ZZB) nor ATED-related.

History – Para. 1(2) inserted and existing text renumbered as para. 1(1) by FA 2015, s. 37 and Sch. 7, para. 38(2) and (3), with effect in relation to disposals made on or after 6 April 2015.

ASSETS HELD ON 5 APRIL 2013, 5 APRIL 2015 OR 5 APRIL 2016: NO PARAGRAPH 5 ELECTION

History – Heading to para. 2 substituted by FA 2015, s. 38 and Sch. 8, para. 7, with effect from 26 March 2015.

2(1) In Cases 1 to 3 below–

(a) paragraph 3 applies for the purposes of computing the gain or loss accruing to P which is ATED-related, and

(b) paragraph 4 applies for the purposes of computing the gain or loss accruing to P which is not ATED-related.

See also the special rule in paragraph 6A (which takes precedence over paragraphs 3 and 4 where it applies).

2(2) Case 1 is that–

(a) the interest disposed of was held by P on 5 April 2013, and

(b) neither Case 2 nor Case 3 applies.

2(3) Case 2 is that–

(a) the interest disposed of was held by P on 5 April 2015,

(b) Case 3 does not apply, and

(c) no relevant single dwelling interest was subject to ATED on one or more days in the period ending with 31 March 2015 during which P held the interest disposed of.

2(4) Case 3 is that–

(a) the interest disposed of was held by P on 5 April 2016, and

(b) no relevant single dwelling interest was subject to ATED on one or more days in the period ending with 31 March 2016 during which P held the interest disposed of.

2(5) For the purposes of this paragraph–

(a) **"relevant single-dwelling interest"** means the single-dwelling interest by reference to which Condition B in section 2C is met in relation to the relevant high value disposal, or, if Condition B is met by reference to more than one such interest, each of them;

(b) a relevant single dwelling interest is **"subject to ATED"** on a day if P–

  (i) was within the charge to annual tax on enveloped dwellings with respect to that interest on that day, or

  (ii) would have been within that charge but for the day being "relievable" by virtue of any of the provisions mentioned in section 132 of the Finance Act 2013 (ATED: effect of reliefs).

2(6) In paragraphs 3 and 4, **"the relevant year"** means–

(a) in relation to Case 1, 2013;

(b) in relation to Case 2, 2015;

(c) in relation to Case 3, 2016.

History – Para. 2 substituted by FA 2015, s. 38 and Sch. 8, para. 8, with effect from 26 March 2015.
In para. 2(1) the words "paragraph 6A" substituted for the words "paragraph 6" by FA 2016, s. 90(1), with effect in relation to disposals made on or after 6 April 2015.

In para. 2(1), the words "See also the special rule in paragraph 6 (which takes precedence over paragraphs 3 and 4 where it applies)." inserted by FA 2015, s. 37 and Sch. 7, para. 38(4), with effect in relation to disposals made on or after 6 April 2015.

3(1) An amount equal to the relevant fraction of the notional post-commencement gain or loss is the ATED-related gain or loss (as the case may be).

3(2) **"Notional post-commencement gain or loss"** means the gain or loss which (in the absence of section 2B and this Schedule) would have accrued on the relevant high value disposal had P acquired the interest on 5 April in the relevant year for a consideration equal to its market value on that date.

3(3) For the purposes of sub-paragraph (2), the amount of the gain or loss accruing to P is to be computed (whether or not that would otherwise be the case) as if P were within the charge to capital gains tax (but not within the charge to corporation tax on chargeable gains).

3(4) **"The relevant fraction"** is–

$$\frac{CD}{TD}$$

where–

"CD" is the number of days in the relevant ownership period which are ATED chargeable days;

"TD" is the total number of days in the relevant ownership period.

3(5) **"The relevant ownership period"** means the period beginning with 6 April in the relevant year and ending with the day before the day on which the relevant high value disposal occurs.

3(6) **"ATED chargeable day"** means any day by virtue of which condition C in section 2C(4) is met in relation to the relevant high value disposal.

History – In para. 3(1), the words "post-commencement" substituted for the words "post-April 2013" by FA 2015, s. 38 and Sch. 8, para. 9(2), with effect from 26 March 2015.

In para. 3(2), the words "post-commencement" substituted for the words "post-April 2013" by FA 2015, s. 38 and Sch. 8, para. 9(3)(a), with effect from 26 March 2015.

In para. 3(2), the words "5 April in the relevant year" substituted for the words "5 April 2013" by FA 2015, s. 38 and Sch. 8, para. 9(3)(b), with effect from 26 March 2015.

In para. 3(5), "6 April in the relevant year" substituted for "6 April 2013" by FA 2015, s. 38 and Sch. 8, para. 9(4), with effect from 26 March 2015.

4(1) The gain or loss accruing on the relevant high value disposal which is not ATED-related is computed as follows.

Step 1

Determine the amount of the notional pre-commencement gain or loss.

Step 2

In a case where there is a notional post-commencement gain–

(a) determine the amount of that gain remaining after the deduction of the ATED-related gain determined under paragraph 3, and

(b) adjust that remaining gain by reducing it by the notional indexation allowance.

Step 3

In a case where there is a notional post-commencement loss, determine the amount of that loss remaining after deduction of the ATED-related loss determined under paragraph 3.

Step 4

Add–

(a) the amount of any gain or loss determined under Step 1, and

(b) the amount of any adjusted gain determined under Step 2 or (as the case may be) any loss determined under Step 3,

(treating any amount which is a loss as a negative amount).

If the result is a positive amount, that amount is the gain on the relevant high value disposal which is not ATED-related.

If the result is a negative amount, that amount (expressed as a positive number) is the loss on the relevant high value disposal which is not ATED-related.

4(2) **"The notional pre-commencement gain or loss"** means the gain or loss which would have accrued on 5 April in the relevant year had the interest been disposed of for a consideration equal to its market value on that date.

4(3) For the purposes of sub-paragraph (2), the amount of the gain or loss accruing to P is to be computed (whether or not that would otherwise be the case) as if P were within the charge to corporation tax on chargeable gains (but not within the charge to capital gains tax).

4(4) Paragraph 3(2) and (3) (meaning of "notional post-commencement gain or loss") also applies for the purposes of this paragraph.

4(5) **"Notional indexation allowance"** means the relevant fraction of an amount equal to the difference between–

(a) the indexation allowance which (in the absence of section 2B and this Schedule) would be made under Chapter 4 of Part 2 in determining the gain accruing on the relevant high value disposal were that gain being computed for corporation tax purposes, and

(b) the indexation allowance which is made under Chapter 4 of Part 2 in determining the notional pre-commencement gain.

4(6) "The relevant fraction" is–

$$\frac{TD - CD}{TD}$$

where **"CD"** and **"TD"** have the same meaning as in paragraph 3(4).

History – In para. 4(1), the words "pre-commencement" substituted for the words "pre-April 2013" by FA 2015, s. 38 and Sch. 8, para. 10(2)(a), with effect from 26 March 2015.
In para. 4(1), the words "post-commencement" substituted for the words "post-April 2013" in both places, by FA 2015, s. 38 and Sch. 8, para. 10(2)(b), with effect from 26 March 2015.
In para. 4(2), the words "pre-commencement" substituted for the words "pre-April 2013" by FA 2015, s. 38 and Sch. 8, para. 10(3)(a), with effect from 26 March 2015.
In para. 4(2), the words "5 April in the relevant year" substituted for the words "5 April 2013" by FA 2015, s. 38 and Sch. 8 para. 10(3)(b), with effect from 26 March 2015.
In para. 4(4), the words "post-commencement" substituted for the words "post-April 2013" by FA 2015, s. 38 and Sch. 8, para. 10(4), with effect from 26 March 2015.
In para. 4(5), the words "pre-commencement" substituted for the words "pre-April 2013" by FA 2015, s. 38 and Sch. 8, para. 10(5), with effect from 26 March 2015.

ELECTION FOR PARAGRAPH 2 TO 4 NOT TO APPLY TO A CHARGEABLE INTEREST

5(1) A person may make an election under this paragraph for paragraphs 2 to 4 not to apply in relation to a chargeable interest held by (or any part of which is held by) the person on 5 April in the relevant year.

5(2) An election is irrevocable.

5(3) An election must be made by being included in a tax return under the Management Act for the tax year in which the first relevant high value disposal by the person of the chargeable interest (or any part of it) on or after 6 April in the relevant year occurs.

5(3A) An election made in relation to an asset under paragraph 2(1)(b) of Schedule 4ZZB (disposals by non-residents etc of UK residential property interests: gains and losses) also has effect as an election made under this paragraph in relation to the asset.

5(4) The reference in sub-paragraph (3) to an election being included in a return includes an election being included by virtue of an amendment of the return.

5(5) All such adjustments are to be made, whether by way of discharge or repayment of tax, the making of assessments or otherwise, as are required to give effect to an election.

5(6) In this paragraph–

"chargeable interest" has the same meaning as in Part 3 of the Finance Act 2013 (annual tax on enveloped dwellings) (see section 107 of that Act);

"relevant year" has the meaning given by paragraph 2.

History – In para. 5(1), the words "5 April in the relevant year" substituted for the words "5 April 2013" by FA 2015, s. 38 and Sch. 8, para. 11(2), with effect from 26 March 2015.
In para. 5(3), the words "6 April in the relevant year" substituted for the words "6 April 2013" by FA 2015, s. 38 and Sch. 8, para. 11(3), with effect from 26 March 2015.
Para. 5(3A) inserted by FA 2015, s. 37 and Sch. 7, para. 38(5), with effect in relation to disposals made on or after 6 April 2015.
Para. 5(6) substituted by FA 2015, s. 38 and Sch. 8, para. 11(4), with effect from 26 March 2015.

CASES WHERE ELECTION MADE OR NONE OF CASES 1 TO 3 APPLY

History – In the heading before para. 6, the words "or none of Cases 1 to 3 apply" substituted for the words "assets acquired after 5 April 2013" by FA 2015, s. 38 and Sch. 8, para. 12, with effect from 26 March 2015.

6(1) This paragraph applies if–

(a) an election is made by P under paragraph 5 in respect of the chargeable interest which (or a part of which) is the subject of the relevant high value disposal, or

(b) none of Cases 1, 2 and 3 in paragraph 2 applies to the disposal.

6(2) The ATED-related gain or loss accruing on the relevant high value disposal is computed as follows.

Step 1

Determine the amount of the gain or loss which would accrue to P, ignoring section 2B and this Schedule (but not the remainder of this Step).

For this purpose, the amount of the gain or loss is to be computed (whether or not that would otherwise be the case) as if P were within the charge to capital gains tax (but not within the charge to corporation tax on chargeable gains).

Step 2

An amount equal to the relevant fraction of that gain or loss is the ATED-related gain or loss accruing on the relevant high value disposal.

6(3) The gain or loss accruing on the relevant high value disposal which is not ATED-related is to be computed as follows.

Step 1

In a case where there is a gain under Step 1 of sub-paragraph (2)–

(a) determine the amount of the gain remaining after the deduction of the ATED-related gain, and

(b) adjust the remaining gain by reducing it by an amount equal to the notional indexation allowance.

That adjusted gain is the gain accruing on the relevant high value disposal which is not ATED-related.

Step 2

In a case where there is a loss under Step 1 of sub-paragraph (2), determine the amount of the loss remaining after deduction of the ATED-related loss.

That remaining loss is the loss accruing on the relevant high value disposal which is not ATED-related.

6(4) **"Notional indexation allowance"** means the relevant fraction of the indexation allowance which would be made under Chapter 4 of Part 2 in determining the gain under Step 1 in sub-paragraph (2) were that gain being computed for corporation tax purposes.

6(5) Subject to sub-paragraph (6), **"the relevant fraction"**–

(a) in sub-paragraph (2) has the same meaning as in paragraph 3(4), and

(b) in sub-paragraph (4) has the same meaning as in paragraph 4(6).

6(6) For the purpose of determining the relevant fraction under sub-paragraph (5), paragraph 3(5) has effect as if the relevant ownership period began on the day on which P acquired the interest or, if later, 31 March 1982.

History – Para. 6(1)(b) substituted by FA 2015, s. 38 and Sch. 8, para. 13, with effect from 26 March 2015.

SPECIAL RULE FOR CERTAIN DISPOSALS TO WHICH BOTH THIS SCHEDULE AND SCHEDULE 4ZZB RELATE

6A(1) This paragraph applies where conditions A and B are met.

6A(2) Condition A is that the relevant high value disposal is–

(a) a non-resident CGT disposal (see section 14B), or

(b) one of two or more disposals which are (by virtue of section 2C and this Schedule) treated as comprised in a non-resident CGT disposal.

6A(3) Condition B is that–

(a) the interest disposed of by the relevant high value disposal was held by P on 5 April 2015,

(b) neither Case 2 nor Case 3 in paragraph 2 applies, and

(c) no election under paragraph 5 of this Schedule (or paragraph 2(1)(b) of Schedule 4ZZB) is or has been made in relation to the chargeable interest which (or a part of which) is the subject of the relevant high value disposal.

6A(4) The ATED-related gain or loss accruing on the relevant high value disposal is computed as follows.

Step 1

Determine the amount of the post-April 2015 ATED-related gain or loss.

Step 2

Determine the amount of the pre-April 2015 ATED-related gain or loss.

Step 3

Add–

(a) the amount of any gain or loss determined under Step 1, and

(b) the amount of any gain or loss determined under Step 2,

(treating any amount which is a loss as a negative amount).

If the result is a positive amount, that amount is the ATED-related gain on the relevant high value disposal. If the result is a negative amount, that amount (expressed as a positive number) is the ATED-related loss on the relevant high value disposal.

6A(5) The post-April 2015 ATED-related gain or loss is equal to the amount that would be given by paragraph 3(1) as the amount of the ATED-related gain or loss if the relevant year for the purposes of that paragraph were 2015.

6A(6) The **"pre-April 2015 ATED-related gain or loss"** means the relevant fraction of the notional pre-April 2015 gain or loss.

6A(7) **"The relevant fraction"** is–

$$\frac{CD}{TD}$$

where–

"**CD**" is the number of days in the relevant ownership period which are ATED chargeable days;

"**TD**" is the total number of days in the relevant ownership period.

6A(8) If the interest disposed of was not held by P on 5 April 2013, the **"notional pre-April 2015 gain or loss"** is the gain or loss which would have accrued on 5 April 2015 had the interest been disposed of on that date for a consideration equal to its market value on that date.

6A(9) If the interest disposed of was held by P on 5 April 2013, the **"notional pre-April 2015 gain or loss"** is the gain or loss which would have accrued on 5 April 2015 if P had–

(a) acquired the interest on 5 April 2013 for a consideration equal to its market value on that date, and

(b) disposed of it on 5 April 2015 for a consideration equal to its market value on that date.

6A(10) Paragraph 3(3) applies for the purposes of sub-paragraphs (8) and (9) as for the purposes of paragraph 3(2).

6A(11) In sub-paragraph (7) **"relevant ownership period"** means the period–

(a) beginning with the day on which P acquired the chargeable interest or, if later, 6 April 2013, and

(b) ending with 5 April 2015.

6A(12) For how to compute the amount of the gain or loss on the relevant high value disposal that is neither ATED-related nor an NRCGT gain or loss (as defined in section 57B and Schedule 4ZZB) see paragraphs 16 to 19 of Schedule 4ZZB.

History – Para. 6A inserted by FA 2015, s. 37 and Sch. 7, para. 38(6), with effect in relation to disposals made on or after 6 April 2015.

ADJUSTMENTS OF ATED CHARGEABLE DAYS

7(1) This paragraph applies where, as a result of a claim under section 106(3) of the Finance Act 2013 (adjustment of chargeable amount), or an amendment of or adjustment to such a claim, there is an alteration in the number of ATED chargeable days.

7(2) All such adjustments are to be made, whether by way of discharge or repayment of tax, the making of assessments or otherwise, as are required to give effect to any change in liability to tax as a result of that alteration.

WASTING ASSETS

8(1) Sub-paragraph (2) applies where it is necessary, in computing in accordance with paragraph 3(2) the notional post-commencement gain or loss accruing to a person on a relevant high value disposal, to determine whether or not the interest which is the subject of the disposal is a wasting asset.

8(2) The assumption in paragraph 3(2) that the interest was acquired on a particular 5 April is to be ignored in determining that question.

8(3) Sub-paragraph (4) applies where it is necessary, in computing in accordance with paragraph 6A(9) the notional pre-April 2015 gain or loss accruing to a person on a disposal, to determine whether or not the interest which is the subject of the disposal is a wasting asset.

8(4) The assumption in paragraph 6A(9) that the interest was acquired on 5 April 2013 is to be ignored in determining that question.

8(5) In this paragraph references to a **"wasting asset"** are to a wasting asset as defined for the purposes of Chapter 2 of Part 2 of this Act.

History – Para. 8 inserted by FA 2015, s. 37 and Sch. 7, para. 38(7), with effect in relation to disposals made on or after 6 April 2015.

CAPITAL ALLOWANCES

9(1) Sub-paragraph (2) applies where it is to be assumed for the purpose of computing–

(a) the notional post-commencement gain or loss accruing to a person on a relevant high value disposal in accordance with paragraph 3(2), or

(b) the notional pre-April 2015 gain or loss accruing to a person on a disposal in accordance with paragraph 6A(9), that an asset was acquired by a person on 5 April 2013 for a consideration equal to its market value on that date.

9(2) For the purposes of that computation, sections 41 (restriction of losses by reference to capital allowances etc) and 47 (wasting assets qualifying for capital allowances) are to apply in relation to any capital allowance or renewals allowance made in respect of the expenditure actually incurred by the person in acquiring or providing the asset as if that allowance were made in respect of the expenditure treated as incurred by the person on 5 April 2013 as mentioned in sub-paragraph (1).

History – Para. 9 inserted by FA 2015, s. 37 and Sch. 7, para. 38(7), with effect in relation to disposals made on or after 6 April 2015.

SCHEDULE 4ZZB – NON-RESIDENT CGT DISPOSALS: GAINS AND LOSSES

Part 1 – Introduction

History – Sch. 4ZZB inserted by FA 2015, s. 37 and Sch. 7, para. 39, with effect in relation to disposals made on or after 6 April 2015.

1(1) This Schedule applies for the purpose of determining, in relation to a non-resident CGT disposal made by a person ("P")–

(a) whether an NRCGT gain or loss accrues to P on the disposal, and the amount of any such gain or loss, and

(b) whether a gain or loss other than an NRCGT gain or loss accrues to P on the disposal, and the amount of any such gain or loss;

(and see also sub-paragraph (2)(c)).

1(2) In this Schedule–

(a) Part 2 is about elections to vary the method of computation of gains and losses;

(b) Part 3 contains the main rules for computing the gains and losses;

(c) Part 4 contains separate rules for computing, in a case where the non-resident CGT disposal is, or involves, a relevant high value disposal (as defined in section 2C)–

  (i) the amount of any NRCGT gains or losses accruing on the disposal, and

  (ii) the amount of any gains or losses accruing on the disposal that are neither ATED-related nor NRCGT gains or losses;

(d) Part 5 contains special rules about non-resident CGT disposals made by companies;

(e) Part 6 (miscellaneous provisions) contains special rules relating to wasting assets and capital allowances;

(f) Part 7 contains definitions for the purposes of this Schedule.

1(3) See section 14B for the meaning of **"non-resident CGT disposal"**.

Part 2 – Elections for Alternative Methods of Computation

2(1) A person ("P") making a non-resident CGT disposal of (or of a part of) an interest in UK land which P held on 5 April 2015 may–

(a) make an election for straight-line time apportionment in relation to the interest in UK land;

(b) make an election for the retrospective basis of computation to apply in relation to that interest,

(but may not do both).

2(2) P may not make an election under sub-paragraph (1)(a) if the disposal is one to which Part 4 of this Schedule applies (cases involving relevant high value disposals).

2(3) For the effect of making an election under sub-paragraph (1)(a), see paragraph 8.

2(4) For the effect of making (or not making) an election under sub-paragraph (1)(b), see paragraphs 5(1)(b), 9(1)(b), 13(1)(b), 14(1)(a) and 15(1)(c) (and paragraph 6A(3)(c) of Schedule 4ZZA).

2(5) An election made under paragraph 5 of Schedule 4ZZA (including any such election made before the coming into force of this paragraph) has effect as if it were also an election under sub-paragraph (1)(b). (But references in paragraph 3 to an election under paragraph 2(1) do not include an election under paragraph 5 of Schedule 4ZZA.)

3(1) An election under paragraph 2(1) is irrevocable (and where an election has been made under paragraph 2(1) or paragraph 5 of Schedule 4ZZA in relation to an asset, no election may subsequently be made under either of those provisions in relation to the asset).

3(2) An election under paragraph 2(1) may (regardless of section 42(2) of the Management Act) be made by being included in–

(a) a tax return under the Management Act for the tax year in which the first non-resident CGT disposal by P of the interest in UK land (or any part of it) is made, or

(b) the NRCGT return relating to the disposal,

(but not by any other method).

3(3) References in sub-paragraph (2) to an election being included in a return include an election being included by virtue of an amendment of the return.

3(4) All such adjustments are to be made, whether by way of discharge or repayment of tax, the making of assessments or otherwise, as are required to give effect to an election under paragraph 2(1)

Part 3 – Main Computation Rules

DISPOSALS TO WHICH THIS PART APPLIES

4(1) This Part of this Schedule applies where a person ("P") makes a non-resident CGT disposal of (or of a part of) an interest in UK land.

4(2) But this Part of this Schedule does not apply if the disposal is–

(a) a relevant high value disposal, or

(b) a disposal in which a relevant high value disposal is comprised (see paragraph 12(3)).

4(3) In this Part of this Schedule **"the disposed of interest"** means–

(a) the interest in UK land, or

(b) if the disposal is of part of that interest, the part disposed of.

INTRODUCTION TO PARAGRAPHS 6 TO 8

5(1) Paragraphs 6 to 8 apply where–

(a) the disposed of interest was held by P on 5 April 2015, and

(b) P has not made an election under paragraph 2(1)(b) in relation to the interest in UK land.

5(2) In paragraphs 6 and 7–

(a) **"notional post-April 2015 gain or loss"** means the gain or loss which would have accrued on the disposal had P acquired the disposed of interest on 5 April 2015 for a consideration equal to its market value on that date;

(b) **"notional pre-April 2015 gain or loss"** means the gain or loss which would have accrued on 5 April 2015 had the disposed of interest been disposed of for a consideration equal to its market value on that date;

but see also paragraph 8(1).

5(3) For the purpose of determining the amount of the hypothetical gain or loss mentioned in sub-paragraph (2)(a), no account is taken of section 57B or this Schedule (apart from paragraph 23).

ASSETS HELD AT 5 APRIL 2015: DEFAULT METHOD

6(1) The NRCGT gain or loss accruing on the disposal is equal to the relevant fraction of the notional post-April 2015 gain or loss (as the case may be).

But see also sub-paragraph (3).

6(2) **"The relevant fraction"** is–

$$\frac{RD}{TD}$$

where–

"RD" is the number of days in the post-commencement ownership period on which the subject matter of the disposed of interest consists wholly or partly of a dwelling;

"TD" is the total number of days in the post-commencement ownership period.

6(3) If there has been mixed use of the subject matter of the disposed of interest on one or more days in the post-commencement ownership period, the NRCGT gain or loss accruing on the disposal is the fraction of the amount that would (apart from this sub-paragraph) be given by sub-paragraphs (1) and (2) that is, on a just and reasonable apportionment, attributable to the dwelling or dwellings.

6(4) For the purposes of this paragraph there is **"mixed use"** of land on any day on which the land consists partly, but not exclusively, of one or more dwellings.

6(5) **"Post-commencement ownership period"** means the period beginning with 6 April 2015 and ending with the day before the day on which the disposal occurs.

7 The gain or loss accruing on the disposal which is not an NRCGT gain or (as the case may be) loss is computed as follows.

Step 1

Determine the amount of the notional pre-April 2015 gain or loss.

Step 2

In a case where there is a notional post-April 2015 gain, determine the amount of that gain remaining after the deduction of the NRCGT gain determined under paragraph 6.

Step 3

In a case where there is a notional post-April 2015 loss, determine the amount of that loss remaining after the deduction of the NRCGT loss determined under paragraph 6.

Step 4

Add–

(a) the amount of any gain or loss determined under Step 1, and

(b) the amount of any gain determined under Step 2 or (as the case may be) any loss determined under Step 3,

(treating any amount which is a loss as a negative amount).

If the result is a positive amount, that amount is the gain on the disposal which is not an NRCGT gain.

If the result is a negative amount, that amount (expressed as a positive number) is the loss on the disposal which is not an NRCGT loss.

MODIFIED APPLICATION OF PARAGRAPHS 5 TO 7 WHERE ELECTION MADE FOR STRAIGHT-LINE TIME APPORTIONMENT

8(1) Where the non-resident CGT disposal is of (or of a part of) an interest in UK land in respect of which P makes, or has made, an election for straight-line time apportionment under paragraph 2(1)(a)–

(a) paragraphs (a) and (b) of paragraph 5(2) do not apply in relation to the disposal, and

(b) for the purposes of paragraphs 6 and 7, the **"notional pre-April 2015 gain or loss"** and the **"notional post-April 2015 gain or loss"** are to be determined in accordance with the following steps.

Step 1

Determine the amount of the gain or loss which accrues to P on the disposal.

For the purpose of determining that amount, no account is taken of section 57B or this Schedule (apart from paragraph 23).

Step 2

An amount equal to the post-commencement fraction of that gain or loss is the notional post-April 2015 gain or (as the case may be) loss.

Step 3

An amount equal to the pre-commencement fraction of that gain or loss is the notional pre-April 2015 gain or (as the case may be) loss.

8(2) The **"post-commencement fraction"** is–

$$\frac{\text{PCD}}{\text{TD}}$$

where–

"PCD" is the number of days in the post-commencement ownership period;

"TD" is the total number of days in the ownership period.

8(3) The **"pre-commencement fraction"** is–

$$\frac{\text{TD} - \text{PCD}}{\text{TD}}$$

where **"PCD"** and **"TD"** have the same meanings as in sub-paragraph (2).

8(4) *In this paragraph–*

"ownership period" means the period beginning with the day on which P acquired the disposed of interest or, if later, 31 March 1982 and ending with the day before the day on which the disposal occurs;

"post-commencement ownership period" has the meaning given by paragraph 6(5).

CASES WHERE ASSET ACQUIRED AFTER 5 APRIL 2015 OR ELECTION MADE UNDER PARAGRAPH 2(1)(B)

9(1) This paragraph applies if–

(a) the disposed of interest was not held by P throughout the period beginning with 5 April 2015 and ending with the disposal, or

(b) the non-resident CGT disposal is of (or of part of) an interest in UK land in respect of which P makes, or has made, an election under paragraph 2(1)(b).

9(2) The NRCGT gain or loss accruing on the disposal is computed as follows.

Step 1

Determine the amount of the gain or loss which accrues to P.

For the purpose of determining the amount of that gain or loss, no account is taken of section 57B or this Schedule (apart from paragraph 23).

Step 2

The NRCGT gain or (as the case may be) loss accruing on the disposal is an amount equal to the relevant fraction of that gain or loss (but see Step 3).

Step 3

If there has been mixed use of the subject matter of the disposed of interest on one or more days in the relevant ownership period, the NRCGT gain or loss accruing on the disposal is equal to the appropriate fraction of the amount given by Step 2.

9(3) For the purposes of this paragraph there is **"mixed use"** of land on any day on which the land consists partly, but not exclusively, of one or more dwellings.

9(4) In Step 3 **"the appropriate fraction"** means the fraction that is, on a just and reasonable apportionment, attributable to the dwelling or dwellings.

9(5) The gain or loss accruing on the disposal which is not an NRCGT gain or (as the case may be) loss is to be computed as follows.

Step 1

In a case where there is a gain under Step 1 of sub-paragraph (2), determine the amount of that gain remaining after the deduction of the NRCGT gain determined under that sub-paragraph.

That remaining gain is the gain accruing on the disposal which is not an NRCGT gain.

Step 2

In a case where there is a loss under Step 1 of sub-paragraph (2), determine the amount of that loss remaining after deduction of the NRCGT loss determined under that sub-paragraph.

That remaining loss is the loss accruing on the disposal which is not an NRCGT loss.

9(6) For the purposes of sub-paragraph (2), **"the relevant fraction"** is–

$$\frac{RD}{TD}$$

where–

"RD" is the number of days in the relevant ownership period on which the subject matter of the disposed of interest consists wholly or partly of a dwelling;

"TD" is the total number of days in the relevant ownership period.

9(7) **"The relevant ownership period"** means the period–

(a) beginning with the day on which P acquired the disposed of interest or, if later, 31 March 1982, and

(b) ending with the day before the day on which the disposal mentioned in paragraph 4(1) occurs.

INTEREST SUBSISTING UNDER CONTRACT FOR OFF-PLAN PURCHASE

10(1) Sub-paragraph (2) applies where the non-resident CGT disposal referred to in paragraph 4(1) is a disposal of a UK residential property interest only because of the second condition in paragraph 1 of Schedule B1 (interest subsisting under a contract for the acquisition of land that consists of, or includes, a building that is to be constructed for use as a dwelling etc).

10(2) The land that is the subject of the contract concerned is treated for the purposes of this Part of this Schedule as consisting of (or, as the case requires, including) a dwelling throughout P's period of ownership of the disposed of interest.

Part 4 – Cases Involving Relevant High Value Disposals

OVERVIEW

11(1) This Part is about non-resident CGT disposals which are, or involve, relevant high value disposals (see section 2B, which charges capital gains tax on ATED-related gains on relevant high value disposals).

11(2) Paragraphs 12 to 15 contain provision about how any NRCGT gains and losses on such a disposal are computed, including provision–

(a) for the NRCGT gains or losses to be computed for each relevant high value disposal comprised in the non-resident CGT disposal (paragraphs 13 to 15), and

(b) for the results to be added (where necessary) to find the NRCGT gain or loss on the non-resident CGT disposal (see paragraph 12).

11(3) For provision about how to compute any ATED-related gains or losses accruing on the relevant high value disposals, see Schedule 4ZZA.

11(4) Paragraphs 16 to 19 contain provisions for computing any gains or losses accruing on the disposals mentioned in sub-paragraph (1) which are neither ATED-related nor NRCGT gains or losses, including provision–

(a) for such balancing gains or losses to be computed for each relevant high value disposal comprised in the non-resident CGT disposal, and

(b) for the results to be added together (where necessary) to find the balancing gain or loss on the non-resident CGT disposal (see paragraph 16).

11(5) Paragraph 20 is about cases where a disposal which is not a relevant high value disposal is also comprised in the non-resident CGT disposal.

DISPOSAL INVOLVING ONE OR MORE RELEVANT HIGH VALUE DISPOSALS

12(1) This Part of this Schedule applies where–

(a) a person (other than an excluded person) ("P") makes a non-resident CGT disposal of (or of part of) an interest in UK land, and

(b) that disposal ("the disposal of land") is a relevant high value disposal or a relevant high value disposal is comprised in it.

In this sub-paragraph **"excluded person"** has the meaning given by section 2B(2).

12(2) The NRCGT gain or loss accruing on the disposal of land is computed as follows.

Step 1

Determine in accordance with paragraphs 13 to 15 the amount of the NRCGT gain or loss accruing on each relevant high value disposal.

Step 2

Add together the amounts of any gains or losses determined under Step 1 (treating any amount which is a loss as a negative amount).

If the result is a positive amount, that amount is the NRCGT gain on the disposal of land.

If the result is a negative amount, that amount (expressed as a positive number) is the NRCGT loss on the disposal of land.

See paragraphs 16 to 19 for how to compute the gain or loss on the disposal of land which is neither ATED-related nor an NRCGT gain or loss.

12(3) For the purposes of this Schedule, a relevant high value disposal is **"comprised in"** a non-resident CGT disposal if–

(a) the non-resident CGT disposal is treated for the purposes of section 2C and Schedule 4ZZA as two or more disposals, and

(b) the relevant high value disposal is one of those.

12(4) In this Part of this Schedule–

(a) **"the asset"**, in relation to a relevant high value disposal, means the chargeable interest which (or a part of which) is the subject of that disposal, and

(b) **"the disposed of interest"**, in relation to a relevant high value disposal, means the asset or, if only part of the asset is the subject of the relevant high value disposal, that part of the asset.

12(5) For the purposes of this Part of this Schedule a day is a **"section 14D chargeable day"** in relation to a relevant high value disposal if–

(a) it is a day on which the subject matter of the disposed of interest consists wholly or partly of a dwelling, but

(b) it is not an ATED chargeable day (as defined in paragraph 3 of Schedule 4ZZA).

ASSETS HELD AT 5 APRIL 2015 (WHERE NO ELECTION MADE AND NO REBASING IN 2016 REQUIRED)

13(1) This paragraph applies where–

(a) the disposed of interest was held by P on 5 April 2015,

(b) P has not made an election under paragraph 2(1)(b) (or paragraph 5 of Schedule 4ZZA) in respect of the asset, and

(c) paragraph 15 does not apply.

13(2) The NRCGT gain or loss accruing on the relevant high value disposal is equal to the special fraction of the notional post-April 2015 gain or loss (as the case may be) on that disposal.

13(3) **"Notional post-April 2015 gain or loss"** means the gain or loss which would have accrued on the relevant high value disposal had P acquired the disposed of interest on 5 April 2015 for a consideration equal to the market value of that interest on that date.

13(4) **"The special fraction"** is–

$$\frac{SD}{TD}$$

where–

"SD" is the number of section 14D chargeable days (see paragraph 12(5)) in the post-commencement ownership period;

"TD" is the total number of days in the post-commencement ownership period.

13(5) **"The post-commencement ownership period"** means the period beginning with 6 April 2015 and ending with the day before the day on which the relevant high value disposal occurs.

ASSET ACQUIRED AFTER 5 APRIL 2015 OR ELECTION MADE UNDER PARAGRAPH 2(1)(B) (BUT NO REBASING IN 2016 REQUIRED)

14(1) This paragraph applies where–

(a) P makes, or has made, an election under paragraph 2(1)(b) (or paragraph 5 of Schedule 4ZZA) in respect of the asset, or

(b) the disposed of interest was not held by P throughout the period beginning with 5 April 2015 and ending with the disposal.

14(2) But this paragraph does not apply if paragraph 15 applies.

14(3) The NRCGT gain or loss accruing on the relevant high value disposal is computed as follows.

Step 1

Determine the amount of the gain or loss which accrues to P.

(For the purpose of determining the amount of that gain or loss, no account need be taken of section 57B or this Schedule (apart from paragraph 23).)

Step 2

The NRCGT gain or loss accruing on the relevant high value disposal is equal to the special fraction of that gain or loss.

14(4) For this purpose **"the special fraction"** is–

$$\frac{SD}{TD}$$

where–

"SD" is the number of section 14D chargeable days (see paragraph 12(5)) in the relevant ownership period;

"TD" is the total number of days in the relevant ownership period.

14(5) **"Relevant ownership period"** means the period–

(a) beginning with the day on which P acquired the disposed of interest or, if later, 31 March 1982, and

(b) ending with the day before the day on which the relevant high value disposal occurs.

CERTAIN DISPOSALS AFTER 5 APRIL 2016 (COMPUTATION INVOLVING ADDITIONAL REBASING IN 2016)

15(1) This paragraph applies where–

(a) the disposed of interest was held by P on 5 April 2016,

(b) the relevant high value disposal falls within Case 3 for the purposes of Schedule 4ZZA (see paragraph 2(4) of that Schedule), and

(c) no election is or has been made (or treated as made) by P under paragraph 2(1)(b) in respect of the asset.

15(2) The NRCGT gain or loss accruing on the relevant high value disposal is computed as follows.

Step 1

Determine the amount equal to the special fraction of the notional post-April 2016 gain or loss (as the case may be).

Step 2

Determine the amount equal to the special fraction of the notional pre-April 2016 gain or loss (as the case may be).

Step 3

Add–

(a) the amount of any gain or loss determined under Step 1, and

(b) the amount of any gain or loss determined under Step 2,

(treating any amount which is a loss as a negative amount).

If the result is a positive amount, that amount is the NRCGT gain on the relevant high value disposal.

If the result is a negative amount, that amount (expressed as a positive number) is the NRCGT loss on the relevant high value disposal.

15(3) **"The special fraction"** is–

$$\frac{SD}{TD}$$

where–

"SD" is the number of section 14D chargeable days (see paragraph 12(5)) in the relevant ownership period;

"TD" is the total number of days in the relevant ownership period.

15(4) The **"relevant ownership period"** is–

(a) for the purpose of computing under Step 1 of sub-paragraph (2) the special fraction of the notional post-April 2016 gain or loss, the period beginning with 6 April 2016 and ending with the day before the day on which the relevant high value disposal occurs;

(b) for the purpose of computing under Step 2 of sub-paragraph (2) the special fraction of the notional pre-April 2016 gain or loss, the period beginning with the day on which P acquired the disposed of interest or, if later, 6 April 2015 and ending with 5 April 2016.

15(5) **"Notional post-April 2016 gain or loss"** means the gain or loss which would have accrued on the relevant high value disposal had P acquired the disposed of interest on 5 April 2016 for a consideration equal to its market value on that date.

15(6) If the disposed of interest was not held by P on 5 April 2015, **"notional pre-April 2016 gain or loss"** means the gain or loss which would have accrued on 5 April 2016 had the disposed of interest been disposed of for a consideration equal to the market value of the interest on that date.

15(7) If the disposed of interest was held by P on 5 April 2015, **"notional pre-April 2016 gain or loss"** means the gain or loss which would have accrued to P on the disposal mentioned in paragraph (b), had P–

(a) acquired the disposed of interest on 5 April 2015 for a consideration equal to the market value of that interest on that date, and

(b) disposed of that interest on 5 April 2016 for a consideration equal to the market value of that interest on that date.

AMOUNT OF GAIN OR LOSS THAT IS NEITHER ATED-RELATED NOR AN NRCGT GAIN OR LOSS

16(1) The gain or loss on the disposal of land (see paragraph 12(1)(b)) which is neither ATED-related nor an NRCGT gain or loss ("the balancing gain or loss") is computed as follows.

Step 1

Determine in accordance with paragraphs 17 to 19 the amount of the gain or loss accruing on each relevant high value disposal which is neither ATED-related nor an NRCGT gain or loss.

This is the "balancing" gain or loss for each such disposal.

Step 2

Add together the amounts of any balancing gains or losses determined under Step 1 (treating any amount which is a loss as a negative amount).

If the result is a positive amount, that amount is the balancing gain on the disposal of land.

If the result is a negative amount, that amount (expressed as a positive number) is the balancing loss on the disposal of land.

16(2) In relation to a relevant high value disposal, **"balancing day"** means a day which is neither–

(a) a section 14D chargeable day (see paragraph 12(5)), nor

(b) an ATED chargeable day.

16(3) In relation to a relevant high value disposal, **"non-ATED chargeable day"** means a day which is not an ATED chargeable day.

16(4) The references in sub-paragraphs (2) and (3) to an **"ATED chargeable day"** are to be interpreted in accordance with paragraph 3(6) of Schedule 4ZZA.

17(1) This paragraph applies in relation to a relevant high value disposal to which paragraph 13 applies.

17(2) [Omitted by FA 2016, s. 90(2)(a).]

17(3) The amount of the balancing gain or loss on the relevant high value disposal is found by adding–

(a) the amount of the balancing gain or loss belonging to the notional post-April 2015 gain or loss,

(b) the amount of the balancing gain or loss belonging to the notional pre-April 2015 gain or loss, and

(c) if P held the disposed of interest on 5 April 2013, the amount of the notional pre-April 2013 gain or loss,

(treating any amount which is a loss as a negative amount).

If the result is a positive amount, that amount is the balancing gain on the relevant high value disposal.

If the result is a negative amount, that amount (expressed as a positive number) is the balancing loss on the relevant high value disposal.

17(4) The balancing gain or loss belonging to the notional post-April 2015 gain or loss is equal to the balancing fraction of the notional post-April 2015 gain or loss.

17(5) The balancing gain or loss belonging to the notional pre-April 2015 gain or loss is equal to the non-ATED related fraction of the notional pre-April 2015 gain or loss.

17(6) **"The balancing fraction"** is–

$$\frac{BD}{TD}$$

where–

"BD" is the number of balancing days (see paragraph 16(2)) in the appropriate ownership period;

"TD" is the total number of days in the appropriate ownership period.

17(7) **"The non-ATED related fraction"** is–

$$\frac{NAD}{TD}$$

where–

"NAD" is the number of non-ATED chargeable days (see paragraph 16(3)) in the appropriate ownership period;

"TD" is the total number of days in the appropriate ownership period.

17(8) **"Appropriate ownership period"** means–

(a) for the purpose of computing the balancing gain or loss belonging to the notional post-April 2015 gain or loss, the post-commencement ownership period defined in paragraph 13(5);

(b) for the purpose of computing the balancing gain or loss belonging to the notional pre-April 2015 gain or loss, the relevant ownership period defined in paragraph 6A(11) of Schedule 4ZZA.

17(9) In this paragraph–

(a) **"notional post-April 2015 gain or loss"** has the same meaning as in paragraph 13;

(b) **"notional pre-April 2015 gain or loss"** has the same meaning as in paragraph 6A of Schedule 4ZZA;

(c) **"notional pre-April 2013 gain or loss"** means the gain or loss which would have accrued on 5 April 2013 had the disposed of interest been disposed of for a consideration equal to the market value of that interest at that date.

History – Para. 17(2) omitted by FA 2016, s. 90(2)(a), with effect in relation to disposals made on or after 26 November 2015. Former para. 17(2) read as follows:

"If paragraph 6A of Schedule 4ZZA does not apply, the amount of the balancing gain or loss on the relevant high value disposal is found by adding–

(a) the amount of the balancing gain or loss belonging to the notional post-April 2015 gain or loss, and

(b) the amount of the balancing gain or loss belonging to the notional pre-April 2015 gain or loss,

(treating any amount which is a loss as a negative amount).

If the result is a positive amount, that amount is the balancing gain on the relevant high value disposal.
If the result is a negative amount, that amount (expressed as a positive number) is the balancing loss on the relevant high value disposal.".
In para. 17(3), the words "If paragraph 6A of Schedule 4ZZA applies," omitted (the amending provision does not require the removal of the comma but this has been done by CCH) by FA 2016, s. 90(2)(b), with effect in relation to disposals made on or after 26 November 2015.

18(1) In the case of a relevant high value disposal to which paragraph 14 applies, the amount of the balancing gain or loss is determined as follows.

18(2) Determine the number of balancing days (see paragraph 16(2)) in the relevant ownership period.

18(3) The balancing gain or loss on the disposal is equal to the balancing fraction of the amount of the gain or (as the case may be) loss determined under Step 1 of paragraph 14(3).

18(4) **"The balancing fraction"** is–

$$\frac{BD}{TD}$$

where–

"**BD**" is the number of balancing days in the relevant ownership period;

"**TD**" is the total number of days in the relevant ownership period.

18(5) In this paragraph **"relevant ownership period"** has the same meaning as in paragraph 14.

19(1) The amount of the balancing gain or loss on a relevant high value disposal to which paragraph 15 applies is found by adding–

(a) the amount of the balancing gain or loss belonging to the notional post-April 2016 gain or loss,

(b) the amount of the balancing gain or loss belonging to the notional pre-April 2016 gain or loss, and

(c) if P held the disposed of interest on 5 April 2015, the amount of the notional pre-April 2015 gain or loss,

(treating any amount which is a loss as a negative amount).
If the result is a positive amount, that amount is the balancing gain on the relevant high value disposal.
If the result is a negative amount, that amount (expressed as a positive number) is the balancing loss on the relevant high value disposal.

19(2) The balancing gain or loss belonging to the notional post-April 2016 gain or loss is equal to the balancing fraction of the notional post-April 2016 gain or loss.

19(3) The balancing gain or loss belonging to the notional pre-April 2016 gain or loss is equal to the balancing fraction of the notional pre-April 2016 gain or loss.

19(4) **"The balancing fraction"** is–

$$\frac{BD}{TD}$$

where–

"**BD**" is the number of balancing days (see paragraph 16(2)) in the appropriate ownership period;

"**TD**" is the total number of days in the appropriate ownership period.

19(5) The appropriate ownership period is–

(a) for the purpose of computing the balancing gain or loss belonging to the notional post-April 2016 gain or loss, the relevant ownership period mentioned in paragraph 15(4)(a);

(b) for the purpose of computing the balancing gain or loss belonging to the notional pre-April 2016 gain or loss, the relevant ownership period mentioned in paragraph 15(4)(b).

19(6) In this paragraph–

(a) **"notional post-April 2016 gain or loss"** and **"notional pre-April 2016 gain or loss"** mean the same as in paragraph 15;

(b) **"notional pre-April 2015 gain or loss"** means the gain or loss which would have accrued on 5 April 2015 if the disposed of interest had been disposed of for a consideration equal to the market value of that interest on that date.

WHERE RELEVANT HIGH VALUE DISPOSAL AND "OTHER" DISPOSAL ARE COMPRISED IN THE DISPOSAL OF LAND

20(1) This paragraph applies where the disposals comprised in the disposal of land (see paragraph 12(3)) include a disposal (the "non-ATED related disposal") which is not a relevant high value disposal.

20(2) This Part of this Schedule (apart from this paragraph) applies in relation to the non-ATED related disposal as if it were a relevant high value disposal.

20(3) Sub-paragraph (4) applies if there has, at any time in the relevant ownership period, been mixed use of the subject matter of the disposed of interest.

For this purpose there is **"mixed use"** of land on any day on which the land consists partly, but not exclusively, of one or more dwellings.

20(4) The amount of any NRCGT gain or loss on the non-ATED related disposal computed under this Part of this Schedule is taken to be the appropriate fraction of the amount that it would otherwise be.

20(5) In sub-paragraph (4) **"the appropriate fraction"** means the fraction that is, on a just and reasonable apportionment, attributable to the dwelling or dwellings.

20(6) In this paragraph **"the relevant ownership period"** means, as applicable–

(a) the post-commencement ownership period, as defined in paragraph 13(5),

(b) the relevant ownership period, as defined in paragraph 14(5), or

(c) the relevant ownership period as defined in paragraph 15(4).

INTEREST SUBSISTING UNDER CONTRACT FOR OFF-PLAN PURCHASE

21(1) Sub-paragraph (2) applies where the non-resident CGT disposal made by P as mentioned in paragraph 12(1) is a disposal of a UK residential property interest only because of the second condition in paragraph 1 of Schedule B1 (interest subsisting under a contract for the acquisition of land that consists of, or includes, a building that is to be constructed for use as a dwelling etc).

21(2) The land that is the subject of the contract concerned is treated for the purposes of this Part of this Schedule as consisting of (or, as the case requires, including) a dwelling throughout P's period of ownership of the interest in UK land.

Part 5 – Special Rules for Companies

22 This Part of this Schedule applies where the person making the non-resident CGT disposal is a company.

INDEXATION

23 The following amounts are computed as if the computation were for corporation tax purposes–

(a) the notional post-April 2015 gain or loss for the purposes of paragraphs 6 and 7;

(b) the notional pre-April 2015 gain or loss for the purposes of paragraphs 6 and 7;

(c) the gain or loss determined under Step 1 of paragraph 9(2);

(d) the notional post-April 2015 gain or loss for the purposes of paragraph 13;

(e) the gain or loss determined under Step 1 of paragraph 14(3);

(f) the notional post-April 2016 gain or loss for the purposes of paragraph 15;

(g) the notional pre-April 2016 gain or loss for the purposes of paragraph 15;

(h) the notional post-April 2015 gain or loss, the notional pre-April 2015 gain or loss and the notional pre-April 2013 gain or loss for the purposes of paragraph 17;

(i) the notional post-April 2016 gain or loss, the notional pre-April 2016 gain or loss and the notional pre-April 2015 gain or loss for the purposes of paragraph 19.

Part 6 – Miscellaneous Provisions

WASTING ASSETS

24(1) Sub-paragraph (2) applies where it is necessary, for the purposes of a relevant computation, to determine whether or not the asset which is the subject of the disposal in question is a wasting asset (as defined for the purposes of Chapter 2 of Part 2).

24(2) The assumption (which operates for the purposes of that computation) that the asset was acquired on 5 April 2015 or, as the case may be, 5 April 2016 is to be ignored in determining that question.

24(3) In sub-paragraph (1) **"relevant computation"** means a computation of–

(a) the notional post-April 2015 gain or loss accruing to a person on a non-resident CGT disposal in accordance with paragraph 5(2)(a),

(b) the notional post-April 2015 gain or loss accruing to a person on a relevant high value disposal in accordance with paragraph 13(3),

(c) the notional post-April 2016 gain or loss accruing to a person on a relevant high value disposal in accordance with paragraph 15(5), or

(d) the notional pre-April 2016 gain or loss accruing to a person on a disposal in accordance with paragraph 15(7).

CAPITAL ALLOWANCES

25(1) Sub-paragraph (2) applies where it is to be assumed for the purpose of computing–

(a) the notional post-April 2015 gain or loss accruing to a person on a non-resident CGT disposal in accordance with paragraph 5(2)(a),

(b) the notional post-April 2015 gain or loss accruing to a person on a relevant high value disposal in accordance with paragraph 13(3),

(c) the notional post-April 2016 gain or loss accruing to a person on a relevant high value disposal in accordance with paragraph 15(5), or

(d) the notional pre-April 2016 gain or loss accruing to a person on a disposal in accordance with paragraph 15(7),

that an asset was acquired by a person on 5 April 2015 or (as the case may be) 5 April 2016 ("the deemed acquisition date") for a consideration equal to its market value on that date.

25(2) For the purposes of that computation, sections 41 (restriction of losses by reference to capital allowances and renewals allowances) and 47 (wasting assets qualifying for capital allowances) are to apply in relation to any capital allowance or renewals allowance made in respect of the expenditure actually incurred by the person in acquiring or providing the asset as if that allowance were made in respect of the expenditure treated as incurred by the person on the deemed acquisition date as mentioned in sub-paragraph (1).

Part 7 – Interpretation

26 In this Schedule–

"chargeable interest" has the same meaning as in Part 3 of the Finance Act 2013 (annual tax on enveloped dwellings) (see section 107 of that Act);

"dwelling" has the meaning given by paragraph 4 of Schedule B1;

"subject matter", in relation to an interest in UK land (or a chargeable interest) means the land to which the interest relates.

SCHEDULE 4ZZC – DISPOSALS OF RESIDENTIAL PROPERTY INTERESTS: GAINS AND LOSSES

Section 57C

History – Sch. 4ZZC inserted by FA 2016, s. 83 and Sch. 12, para. 5, with effect in relation to gains accruing on or after 6 April 2016.

Part 1 – Introduction and Interpretation

INTRODUCTION

1(1) In this Schedule **"RPI disposal"** means a disposal of a residential property interest which is not a non-resident CGT disposal.

1(2) This Schedule applies for the purpose of determining, in relation to an RPI disposal–

(a) whether a residential property gain or loss accrues on the disposal, and the amount of any such gain or loss, and

(b) whether a gain or loss other than a residential property gain or loss accrues on the disposal, and the amount of any such gain or loss.

1(3) In this Schedule–

(a) Part 2 contains the main rules for computing the gains and losses;

(b) Part 3 contains the rules for computing the gains and losses in a case where the RPI disposal is, or involves, a relevant high value disposal (as defined in section 2C).

INTERPRETATION

2(1) For the purposes of this Schedule, a relevant high value disposal is **"comprised in"** an RPI disposal if–

(a) the RPI disposal is treated for the purposes of section 2C and Schedule 4ZZA as two or more disposals, and

(b) the relevant high value disposal is one of those.

2(2) In this Schedule–

"chargeable interest" has the same meaning as in Part 3 of the Finance Act 2013 (annual tax on enveloped dwellings) (see section 107 of that Act);

"dwelling" has the meaning given by–

(a) paragraph 4 of Schedule B1, in relation to a disposal of a UK residential property interest;

(b) paragraph 4 of Schedule BA1, in relation to a disposal of a non-UK residential property interest;

"subject-matter", in relation to an interest in land (or a chargeable interest) means the land to which the interest relates.

Part 2 – RPI Disposals not Involving Relevant High Value Disposals

APPLICATION OF PART

3(1) This Part of this Schedule applies where a person ("P") makes an RPI disposal of (or of part of) an interest in land.

3(2) But this Part of this Schedule does not apply if the disposal is–

(a) a relevant high value disposal, or

(b) a disposal in which a relevant high value disposal is comprised.

3(3) In this Part of this Schedule **"the disposed of interest"** means–

(a) the interest in land, or

(b) if the disposal is of part of that interest, the part disposed of.

COMPUTATION OF RESIDENTIAL PROPERTY GAINS AND LOSSES

4(1) The residential property gain or loss accruing on the disposal is computed as follows.

Step 1

Determine the amount of the gain or loss that accrues to P.

(For the purpose of determining the amount of that gain or loss, no account is taken of section 57C or this Schedule.)

Step 2

The residential property gain or loss accruing on the disposal is an amount equal to the relevant fraction of that gain or loss (but see Step 3).

Step 3

If there has been mixed use of the subject matter of the disposed of interest on one or more days in the relevant ownership period, the residential property gain or loss accruing on the disposal is equal to the appropriate fraction of the amount given by Step 2.

4(2) In Step 2 **"the relevant fraction"** means–

$$\frac{RD}{TD}$$

where–

"RD" is the number of days in the relevant ownership period on which the subject matter of the disposed of interest consists wholly or partly of a dwelling;

"TD" is the total number of days in the relevant ownership period.

4(3) For the purposes of Step 3 there is **"mixed use"** of land on any day on which the land consists partly, but not exclusively, of one or more dwellings.

4(4) In Step 3 **"the appropriate fraction"** means the fraction that is, on a just and reasonable apportionment, attributable to the dwelling or dwellings.

4(5) In this paragraph the **"relevant ownership period"** means the period–

(a) beginning with the day on which P acquired the disposed of interest or, if later, 31 March 1982, and

(b) ending with the day before the day on which the disposal occurs.

COMPUTATION OF BALANCING GAINS AND LOS[S]ES

5 The gain or loss accruing on the disposal which is not a residential property gain or loss is computed as follows.

Step 1

In a case where there is a gain under Step 1 of paragraph 4(1), determine the amount of that gain remaining after the deduction of the residential property gain determined under that paragraph. That remaining gain is the gain accruing on the disposal which is not a residential property gain.

Step 2

In a case where there is a loss under Step 1 of paragraph 4(1), determine the amount of that loss remaining after the deduction of the residential property loss determined under that paragraph. That remaining loss is the loss accruing on the disposal which is not a residential property loss.

INTEREST SUBSISTING UNDER CONTRACT FOR OFF-PLAN PURCHASE

6(1) This paragraph applies where the disposal referred to in paragraph 3(1) is a disposal of a residential property interest only because of–

(a) the second condition in paragraph 1 of Schedule B1, or

(b) the second condition in paragraph 1 of Schedule BA1,

(interest subsisting under a contract for the acquisition of land that consists of, or includes, a building that is to be constructed for use as a dwelling).

6(2) The land that is the subject of the contract concerned is treated for the purposes of this Part of this Schedule as consisting of (or, as the case requires, including) a dwelling throughout P's period of ownership of the disposed of interest.

Part 3 – RPI Disposals Involving Relevant High Value Disposals

APPLICATION OF PART

7(1) This Part of this Schedule applies where–

(a) a person (other than an excluded person) ("P") makes an RPI disposal of (or of part of) an interest in land, and

(b) that disposal ("the disposal of land") is a relevant high value disposal or a relevant high value disposal is comprised in it.

7(2) **"Excluded person"** has the meaning given by section 2B(2).

INTERPRETATION OF PART

8(1) This paragraph applies for the interpretation of this Part of this Schedule.

8(2) **"The asset"**, in relation to a relevant high value disposal, means the chargeable interest which (or a part of which) is the subject of that disposal.

8(3) **"The disposed of interest"**, in relation to a relevant high value disposal, means the asset or, if only part of the asset is the subject of the relevant high value disposal, that part of the asset.

8(4) A day is a **"residential property chargeable day"** in relation to a relevant high value disposal if–

(a) it is a day on which the subject matter of the disposed of interest consists wholly or partly of a dwelling, but

(b) it is not an ATED chargeable day (as defined in paragraph 3 of Schedule 4ZZA).

COMPUTATION OF RESIDENTIAL PROPERTY GAINS OR LOSSES ON THE RPI DISPOSAL

9(1) The residential property gain or loss accruing on the disposal of land is computed as follows.

Step 1

Determine in accordance with paragraphs 10 to 15 the amount of the residential property gain or loss accruing on each relevant high value disposal.

Step 2
Add together the amounts of any gains or losses determined under Step 1 (treating any amount which is a loss as a negative amount).

9(2) If the result is a positive amount, that amount is the residential property gain on the disposal of land.

9(3) If the result is a negative amount, that amount (expressed as a positive number) is the residential property loss on the disposal of land.

COMPUTATION OF RESIDENTIAL PROPERTY GAINS OR LOSSES ON RELEVANT HIGH VALUE DISPOSAL NOT WITHIN CASE 1, 2 OR 3 (OR WHERE AN ELECTION IS MADE)

10(1) This paragraph applies to a relevant high value disposal where–

(a) the disposal does not fall within any of Cases 1, 2 or 3 in paragraph 2 of Schedule 4ZZA, or

(b) P has made an election under paragraph 5 of that Schedule in respect of the asset.

10(2) The residential property gain or loss accruing on the relevant high value disposal is computed as follows–
Step 1
Determine the amount of gain or loss which accrues to P.
(For the purpose of determining the amount of that gain or loss, no account is taken of section 57C or this Schedule.)
Step 2
The residential property gain or loss accruing on the relevant high value disposal is equal to the special fraction of that gain or loss.

10(3) The **"special fraction"** is–

$$\frac{SD}{TD}$$

where–

"SD" is the number of residential property chargeable days in the relevant ownership period;

"TD" is the total number of days in the relevant ownership period.

10(4) **"Relevant ownership period"** means the period–

(a) beginning with the day on which P acquired the disposed of interest or, if later, 31 March 1982, and

(b) ending with the day before the day on which the relevant high value disposal occurs.

COMPUTATION OF RESIDENTIAL PROPERTY GAINS AND LOSSES ON RELEVANT HIGH VALUE DISPOSAL WITHIN CASE 1, 2 OR 3 (AND NO ELECTION MADE)

11(1) This paragraph applies to a relevant high value disposal where–

(a) the disposal falls within Case 1, 2 or 3 in paragraph 2 of Schedule 4ZZA, and

(b) P has not made an election under paragraph 5 of that Schedule in respect of the asset.

11(2) The residential property gain or loss accruing on the relevant high value disposal is computed in accordance with paragraphs 12 to 15.

11(3) In those paragraphs **"the relevant year"** means–

(a) where the relevant high value disposal falls within Case 1 in paragraph 2 of Schedule 4ZZA, 2013,

(b) where it falls within Case 2 in that paragraph, 2015, and

(c) where it falls within Case 3 in that paragraph, 2016.

12(1) Take the following steps–
Step 1
Determine the amount equal to the special fraction of the notional pre-ATED gain or loss (as the case may be) (see paragraph 13).
Step 2
Determine the amount equal to the special fraction of the notional post-ATED gain or loss (as the case may be) (see paragraph 14).
Step 3
Add (treating any amount which is a loss as a negative amount)–

(a) the amount of any gain or loss determined under Step 1, and

(b) the amount of any gain or loss determined under Step 2.

12(2) If the result is a positive amount, that amount is the residential property gain on the relevant high value disposal.

12(3) If the result is a negative amount, that amount (expressed as a positive number) is the residential property loss on the relevant high value disposal.

13(1) This paragraph applies for the purposes of Step 1 in paragraph 12.

13(2) **"Notional pre-ATED gain or loss"** means the gain or loss which would have accrued on 5 April of the relevant year had the disposed of interest been disposed of for a consideration equal to the market value of the interest on that date.

13(3) The **"special fraction"** is–

$$\frac{SD}{TD}$$

where–

"SD" is the number of residential property chargeable days in the relevant ownership period;

"TD" is the total number of days in the relevant ownership period.

13(4) The **"relevant ownership period"** is the period–

(a) beginning with the day on which P acquired the disposed of interest or, if later, 31 March 1982, and

(b) ending with 5 April of the relevant year.

14(1) This paragraph applies for the purposes of Step 2 in paragraph 12.

14(2) **"Notional post-ATED gain or loss"** means the gain or loss which would have accrued on the relevant high value disposal had P acquired the disposed of interest on 5 April of the relevant year for a consideration equal to its market value on that date (and see paragraph 15).

14(3) The **"special fraction"** is–

$$\frac{SD}{TD}$$

where–

"SD" is the number of residential property chargeable days in the relevant ownership period;

"TD" is the total number of days in the relevant ownership period.

14(4) The **"relevant ownership period"** is the period beginning with 6 April of the relevant year and ending with the day before the day on which the relevant high value disposal occurs.

15(1) This paragraph applies for the purposes of computing the notional post-ATED gain or loss for the purposes of Step 2 in paragraph 12.

15(2) In determining whether the asset which is the subject of the relevant high value disposal is a wasting asset (as defined for the purposes of Chapter 2 of Part 2), ignore the assumption that the asset was acquired on 5 April of the relevant year.

15(3) Sections 41 (restriction of losses by reference to capital allowances and renewals allowances) and 47 (wasting assets subject to capital allowances) apply in relation to any capital allowance or renewals allowance made in respect of the expenditure actually incurred by P in acquiring or providing the asset as if that allowance were made in respect of the expenditure treated as incurred by P on 5 April of the relevant year.

COMPUTATION OF BALANCING GAINS OR LOSSES ON THE RPI DISPOSAL

16(1) The gain or loss on the disposal of land which is neither ATED-related nor a residential property gain or loss ("the balancing gain or loss") is computed as follows.

Step 1

Determine in accordance with paragraphs 17 and 18 the amount of the gain or loss accruing on each relevant high value disposal which is neither ATED-related nor a residential property gain or loss.

This is the **"balancing"** gain or loss for each disposal.

Step 2

Add together the amounts of any balancing gains or losses determined under Step 1 (treating any amount which is a loss as a negative amount).

16(2) If the result is a positive amount, that amount is the balancing gain on the disposal of land.

16(3) If the result is a negative amount, that amount (expressed as a positive number) is the balancing loss on the disposal of land.

COMPUTATION OF BALANCING GAINS OR LOSSES ON RELEVANT HIGH VALUE DISPOSAL NOT WITHIN CASE 1, 2 OR 3 (OR WHERE AN ELECTION IS MADE)

17(1) In the case of a relevant high value disposal to which paragraph 10 applies, the amount of the balancing gain or loss is determined as follows.

17(2) Determine the number of balancing days in the relevant ownership period.

17(3) **"Balancing day"** means a day which is neither–

(a) a residential property chargeable day, nor

(b) an ATED chargeable day (as defined in paragraph 3 of Schedule 4ZZA).

17(4) The balancing gain or loss on the disposal is equal to the balancing fraction of the amount of the gain or (as the case may be) loss determined under Step 1 of paragraph 10(2).

17(5) The **"balancing fraction"** is–

$$\frac{BD}{TD}$$

where–

"BD" is the number of balancing days in the relevant ownership period;

"TD" is the total number of days in the relevant ownership period.

17(6) In this paragraph **"relevant ownership period"** has the same meaning as in paragraph 10.

COMPUTATION OF BALANCING GAINS OR LOSSES ON RELEVANT HIGH VALUE DISPOSAL WITHIN CASE 1, 2 OR 3 (AND NO ELECTION MADE)

18(1) The amount of the balancing gain or loss on a relevant high value disposal to which paragraph 11 applies is found by adding–

(a) the amount of the balancing gain or loss belonging to the notional pre-ATED gain or loss, and

(b) the amount of the balancing gain or loss belonging to the notional post-ATED gain or loss,

(treating any amount which is a loss as a negative amount).

18(2) If the result is a positive amount, that amount is the balancing gain on the relevant high value disposal.

18(3) If the result is a negative amount, that amount (expressed as a positive number) is the balancing loss on the relevant high value disposal.

18(4) The balancing gain or loss belonging to the notional pre-ATED gain or loss is equal to the balancing fraction of the notional pre-ATED gain or loss.

18(5) The balancing gain or loss belonging to the notional post-ATED gain or loss is equal to the balancing fraction of the notional post-ATED gain or loss.

18(6) The balancing fraction is–

$$\frac{BD}{TD}$$

where–

"BD" is the number of balancing days in the appropriate ownership period;

"TD" is the total number of days in the appropriate ownership period.

18(7) **"Balancing day"** means a day which is neither–

(a) a residential property chargeable day, nor

(b) an ATED chargeable day (as defined in paragraph 3 of Schedule 4ZZA).

18(8) The appropriate ownership period is–

(a) for the purpose of computing the balancing gain or loss belonging to the notional pre-ATED gain or loss, the relevant ownership period mentioned in paragraph 13(4);

(b) for the purpose of computing the balancing gain or loss belonging to the notional post-ATED gain or loss, the relevant ownership period mentioned in paragraph 14(4).

18(9) In this paragraph–

"notional pre-ATED gain or loss" means the same as in paragraph 13(2);

"notional post-ATED gain or loss" means the same as in paragraph 14(2).

RELEVANT HIGH VALUE DISPOSAL AND "OTHER" DISPOSAL ARE COMPRISED IN THE DISPOSAL OF LAND

19(1) This paragraph applies where the disposals comprised in the disposal of land include a disposal (the "non-ATED related disposal") which is not a relevant high value disposal.

19(2) This Part of this Schedule (apart from this paragraph) applies in relation to the non-ATED related disposal as if it were a relevant high value disposal.

19(3) Sub-paragraph (4) applies if there has, at any time in the relevant ownership period, been mixed use of the subject matter of the disposed of interest.

19(4) The amount of any residential property gain or loss on the non-ATED related disposal computed under this Part of this Schedule is taken to be the appropriate fraction of the amount that it would otherwise be.

19(5) In sub-paragraph (4) **"the appropriate fraction"** means the fraction that is, on a just and reasonable apportionment, attributable to the dwelling or dwellings.

19(6) In this paragraph the **"relevant ownership period"** means–

(a) where paragraph 10 applies, the relevant ownership period as defined in paragraph 10(4), or

(b) where paragraph 11 applies, the relevant ownership period as defined in paragraphs 13(4) and 14(4).

INTEREST SUBSISTING UNDER CONTRACT FOR OFF-PLAN PURCHASE

20(1) This paragraph applies where the RPI disposal made by P is a disposal of a residential property interest only because of–

(a) the second condition in paragraph 1 of Schedule B1, or

(b) the second condition in paragraph 1 of Schedule BA1,

(interest subsisting under a contract for the acquisition of land that consists of, or includes, a building that is to be constructed for use as a dwelling).

20(2) The land that is the subject of the contract concerned is treated for the purposes of this Part of this Schedule as consisting of (or, as the case requires, including) a dwelling throughout P's period of ownership of the interest in land.

SCHEDULE 4ZA – SUB-FUND SETTLEMENTS

History – Sch. 4ZA inserted by FA 2006, s. 88 and Sch. 12, para. 6(2), with effect in relation to years of assessment beginning on or after 6 April 2006.

Cross references – FA 2006, s. 88 and Sch.12, para. 6(3): a sub-fund election may not be treated as having taken place before 6 April 2006.

MAKING A SUB-FUND ELECTION

1 The trustees of a settlement (the "principal settlement") may elect that a fund or other specified portion of the settled property (the "sub-fund") be treated, unless the context otherwise requires, as a separate settlement (the "sub-fund settlement") for the purposes of this Act, and the election shall have effect.

2(1) An election under paragraph 1 (a "sub-fund election") must specify the date on which it is to be treated as having taken effect, which must not be later than the date on which it is made.

2(2) The election shall be treated as having taken effect–

(a) at the beginning of the specified date, or

(b) if there is a deemed disposal of an asset by the trustees of the principal settlement under section 71(1) (by virtue of paragraph 19) or section 80(2) (by virtue of paragraph 18(2)), on the specified date immediately after the deemed disposal.

3 Trustees may make a sub-fund election only if–

(a) Conditions 1 to 4 are satisfied when the election is made, and

(b) Conditions 2 to 4 were satisfied throughout the period beginning with the time when the election is to be treated as having taken effect and ending immediately before the election is made.

4 Condition 1 is that the principal settlement is not itself a sub-fund settlement.

5 Condition 2 is that the sub-fund is not the whole of the property comprised in the principal settlement.

6 Condition 3 is that, if the sub-fund election had taken effect, the sub-fund settlement would not consist of or include an interest in an asset any other interest in which would be comprised in the principal settlement.

7 For the purpose of Condition 3–

(a) section 104(1) shall not have effect, and

(b) **"interest"**, in relation to any asset, means an interest as a co-owner of the asset (whether the asset is owned jointly or in common and whether or not the interests of the co-owners are equal).

History – In para. 7, the words "section 104(1)" substituted for the words "sections 104(1) and 109(2)(a)" by FA 2008, s. 8 and Sch. 2, para. 67 with effect in relation to disposals on or after 6 April 2008 (Sch. 2, para. 71).

8 Condition 4 is that, if the sub-fund election had taken effect, no person would be a beneficiary under both the sub-fund settlement and the principal settlement.

9(1) For the purpose of Condition 4 a person is a beneficiary under a settlement–

(a) if–

(i) any property which is or may at any time be comprised in the settlement, or

(ii) any derived property,

is, or will or may become, payable to him or applicable for his benefit in any circumstances whatsoever, or

(b) if he enjoys a benefit deriving directly or indirectly from–

(i) any property which is comprised in the settlement, or

(ii) any derived property.

9(2) But for the purpose of Condition 4 a person is not to be regarded as a beneficiary under a settlement if property comprised in the settlement, or any derived property, will or may become payable to him or applicable for his benefit by reason only of–

(a) his marrying, or entering into a civil partnership with, a beneficiary under the settlement,

(b) the death of a beneficiary under the settlement,

(c) the exercise by the trustees of the settlement of–

(i) a power conferred by section 32 of the Trustee Act 1925 (c. 19) or section 33 of the Trustee Act (Northern Ireland) 1958 (c. 23 (N.I.)) (powers of advancement),

(ii) a power conferred by the law of a jurisdiction other than England and Wales or Northern Ireland which makes provision similar to the provisions specified in sub-paragraph (i), or

(iii) a power of advancement which is conferred by the instrument creating the principal settlement, or by another instrument made in accordance with the terms of the principal settlement, and which is subject to the same restrictions as those specified in section 32(1)(a) and (c) of the Trustee Act 1925, or

(d) the failure or determination of trusts of the kind described in section 33 of the Trustee Act 1925 (protective trusts).

9(3) In this paragraph **"derived property"**, in relation to any property, means–

(a) income from that property,

(b) property directly or indirectly representing–

(i) proceeds of that property, or

(ii) proceeds of income from that property, or

(c) income from property which is derived property by virtue of paragraph (b).

SUB-FUND ELECTIONS: PROCEDURE

10 A sub-fund election must be made–

(a) by notice to an officer of Revenue and Customs, and

(b) in such form as the Commissioners for Her Majesty's Revenue and Customs may require.

11 A sub-fund election may not be made after the second 31st January after the year of assessment in which the date on which the election is to be treated as having taken effect falls.

12 A sub-fund election must contain–

(a) a declaration by each trustee of the principal settlement that he consents to the election,

(b) a statement by the trustees of the principal settlement that the requirement in paragraph 3 is satisfied,

(c) such information as the Commissioners for Her Majesty's Revenue and Customs may require in relation to the principal settlement (which may, in particular, include information relating to the trustees, the trusts, property which is or has been comprised in the settlement, the settlors or the beneficiaries),

(d) a declaration by the trustees of the principal settlement that the information given in the election is correct, to the best of their knowledge and belief, and

(e) such other declarations as the Commissioners for Her Majesty's Revenue and Customs may require.

13 A sub-fund election may not be revoked.

POWER TO MAKE ENQUIRIES

14 [Omitted by SI 2009/2035, art. 2 and Schedule, para. 34.]

History – Para. 14 omitted by SI 2009/2035, art. 2 and Schedule, para. 34, with effect from 13 August 2009.

15 [Omitted by SI 2009/2035, art. 2 and Schedule, para. 34.]

History – Para. 15 omitted by SI 2009/2035, art. 2 and Schedule, para. 34, with effect from 13 August 2009.

16 [Omitted by SI 2009/2035, art. 2 and Schedule, para. 34.]

History – Para. 16 omitted by SI 2009/2035, art. 2 and Schedule, para. 34, with effect from 13 August 2009.

CONSEQUENCES OF A SUB-FUND ELECTION

17 The sub-fund settlement shall be treated, for the purposes of this Act, as having been created at the time when the sub-fund election is treated as having taken effect.

18(1) Each trustee of the trusts on which the property comprised in the sub-fund settlement is held shall be treated as a trustee of the sub-fund settlement for the purposes of this Act.

18(2) A person who is a trustee of the sub-fund settlement shall be treated for the purposes of this Act, from the time when the election is treated as having taken effect, as having ceased to be a trustee of the principal settlement unless he is also a trustee of trusts on which property comprised in the principal settlement is held.

18(3) A person who is a trustee of the principal settlement shall not be treated for the purposes of this Act as a trustee of the sub-fund settlement unless he is also a trustee of trusts on which property comprised in the sub-fund settlement is held.

19 The trustees of the sub-fund settlement shall be treated for the purposes of this Act as having become absolutely entitled, at the time when the sub-fund election is treated as having taken effect, to the property comprised in that settlement as against the trustees of the principal settlement.

20(1) A deemed disposal by the trustees of the principal settlement of an asset under section 71(1) (by virtue of paragraph 19) or section 80(2) (by virtue of paragraph 18(2)) shall be treated as having been made at the beginning of the date on which the sub-fund election is treated as having taken effect.

20(2) If the trustees of the sub-fund settlement have acquired an asset of which the trustees of the principal settlement are deemed to have disposed under section 71(1) (by virtue of paragraph 19), they shall be deemed to have acquired it at the time when the election is treated as having taken effect.

20(3) The trustees of the principal settlement shall not be treated as having disposed of an asset under section 80(2) by virtue of paragraph 18(2) if they are treated as having disposed of the same asset under section 71(1) by virtue of paragraph 19.

21 If the trustees of the sub-fund settlement are treated by virtue of paragraph 19 as having become absolutely entitled to money expressed in sterling, for the purposes of this Act–

(a) the trustees of the principal settlement shall be treated as having disposed of the money at the beginning of the day on which the sub-fund election is treated as having taken effect, and

(b) the trustees of the sub-fund settlement shall be treated as having acquired the money at the time when the election is treated as having taken effect.

22(1) If the trustees of the principal settlement are deemed to have disposed of an asset under section 71(1) (by virtue of paragraph 19), the trustees of the principal settlement shall be treated for the purposes of sections 90 and 94 as having transferred the asset to the trustees of the sub-fund settlement.

22(2) Sub-paragraph (1) also applies where the trustees of the principal settlement would be deemed to have disposed of money expressed in sterling under subsection (1) of section 71 if in that subsection–

(a) the reference to "assets" were a reference to "property", and

(b) for "their" there were substituted "its".

SCHEDULE 4A – DISPOSAL OF INTEREST IN SETTLED PROPERTY: DEEMED DISPOSAL OF UNDERLYING ASSETS

Section 76A

History – Sch. 4A inserted by FA 2000, s. 91(2) and Sch. 24 with effect in relation to any disposal of an interest in settled property made, or the effective completion of which falls, on or after 21 March 2000.

HMRC interpretations – IRInt. 249: taxation of chargeable gains: sale of trust interests and transfers linked to trustee borrowing: HMRC views.

CIRCUMSTANCES IN WHICH THIS SCHEDULE APPLIES

1 This Schedule applies where there is a disposal of an interest in settled property for consideration.

MEANING OF "INTEREST IN SETTLED PROPERTY"

2(1) For the purposes of this Schedule an **"interest in settled property"** means any interest created by or arising under a settlement.

2(2) This includes any right to, or in connection with, the enjoyment of a benefit–

(a) created by or arising directly under a settlement, or

(b) arising as a result of the exercise of a discretion or power–

  (i) by the trustees of a settlement, or

  (ii) by any person in relation to settled property.

MEANING OF "FOR CONSIDERATION"

3(1) For the purposes of this Schedule a disposal is **"for consideration"** if consideration is given or received by any person for, or otherwise in connection with, any transaction by virtue of which the disposal is effected.

3(2) In determining for the purposes of this Schedule whether a disposal is for consideration there shall be disregarded any consideration consisting of another interest under the same settlement that has not previously been disposed of by any person for consideration.

3(3) In this Schedule **"consideration"** means actual consideration, as opposed to consideration deemed to be given by any provision of this Act.

HMRC interpretations – IRInt. 249: taxation of chargeable gains: sale of trust interests and transfers linked to trustee borrowing: HMRC view that "consideration" not extended to incidental costs of transaction, in particular reasonable fees charged by professional advisers for giving guidance as to legal and fiscal effects of transaction or for drafting and executing relevant paperwork.

DEEMED DISPOSAL OF UNDERLYING ASSETS

4(1) Where this Schedule applies and the following conditions are met–

(a) the condition as to UK residence of the trustees (see paragraph 5),

(b) the condition as to UK residence of the settlor (see paragraph 6), and

(c) the condition as to settlor interest in the settlement (see paragraph 7),

the trustees of the settlement are treated for all purposes of this Act as disposing of and immediately reacquiring the relevant underlying assets.

This is referred to below in this Schedule as the "deemed disposal".

4(2) In paragraphs 5, 6 and 7 **"the relevant year of assessment"** means the year of assessment in which the disposal of the interest in settled property is made.

4(3) The deemed disposal is treated as taking place when the disposal of the interest in settled property is made.

This is subject to paragraph 13(3)(a) where the beginning of the disposal and its effective completion fall in different years of assessment.

CONDITION AS TO UK RESIDENCE OF TRUSTEES

5(1) The condition as to UK residence of the trustees is that the trustees of the settlement were either resident in the United Kingdom during any part of the year.

5(2) For this purpose the trustees shall not be regarded as resident in the United Kingdom at any time when they fall to be regarded for the purposes of any double taxation relief arrangements as resident in a territory outside the United Kingdom.

5(3) This paragraph has effect subject to paragraph 13(3)(b) where the beginning of the disposal and its effective completion fall in different years of assessment.

History – In para. 5(1), the words "and ordinarily resident" omitted by FA 2013, s. 219 and Sch. 46, para. 106(2), with effect in relation to a person's liability to capital gains tax for the tax year 2013–14 or any subsequent tax year, without prejudice to any provision in FA 2013, Sch. 46, Pt. 3 about the application of a particular amendment.
In para. 5(1), the words "resident and ordinarily resident in the United Kingdom during any part of the year" substituted for the words from "either" by FA 2006, s. 88 and Sch. 12, para. 39, with effect from 6 April 2007 (in relation to settlements whenever created) (FA 2006, s. 88 and Sch. 12, para. 41).
In para. 5(2), the words "and ordinarily resident" omitted by FA 2013, s. 219 and Sch. 46, para. 106(2), with effect in relation to a person's liability to capital gains tax for the tax year 2013–14 or any subsequent tax year, without prejudice to any provision in FA 2013, Sch. 46, Pt. 3 about the application of a particular amendment.
In para. 5(2), the words "resident and ordinarily resident in the United Kingdom" substituted for "resident or ordinarily resident in the United Kingdom" by FA 2006, s. 88 and Sch. 12, para. 34(1), (2)(e), with effect from 6 April 2007 (in relation to settlements whenever created).

CONDITION AS TO UK RESIDENCE OF SETTLOR

6(1) The condition as to UK residence of the settlor is that as respects the relevant year of assessment, or any of the previous five years of assessment, a person who is a settlor in relation to the settlement met the residence condition set out in section 2(1A).

6(2) Sub-paragraph (1) has effect subject to paragraph 13(3)(c) where the beginning of the disposal and its effective completion fall in different years of assessment.

6(3) No account shall be taken for the purposes of this paragraph of any year of assessment before the year 1999–00.

History – In para. 6(1), the words "as respects the relevant" substituted for the words "in the relevant" by FA 2013, s. 219 and Sch. 46, para. 106(3)(a), with effect in relation to a person's liability to capital gains tax for the tax year 2013–14 or any subsequent tax year, without prejudice to any provision in FA 2013, Sch. 46, Pt. 3 about the application of a particular amendment, but if any of the previous 5 years of assessment mentioned in para. 6(1) ends before 6 April 2013, the test in that paragraph is to be applied, as respects any such year ending before that date, as if that paragraph had not been amended by FA 2013, Sch. 46, para. 106(3).
In para. 6(1), the words "met the residence condition set out in section 2(1A)" substituted for the words "either– (a) was resident in the United Kingdom during the whole or part of the year, or (b) was ordinarily resident in the United Kingdom during the year." by FA 2013, s. 219 and Sch. 46, para. 106(3)(b), with effect in relation to a person's liability to capital gains tax for the tax year 2013–14 or any subsequent tax year, without prejudice to any provision in FA 2013, Sch. 46, Pt. 3 about the application of a particular amendment, but if any of the previous 5 years of assessment mentioned in para. 6(1) ends before 6 April 2013, the test in that paragraph is to be applied, as respects any such year ending before that date, as if that paragraph had not been amended by FA 2013, Sch. 46, para. 106(3).

CONDITION AS TO SETTLOR INTEREST IN THE SETTLEMENT

7(1) The condition as to settlor interest in the settlement is that at any time in the relevant period the settlement–

(a) was a settlor-interested settlement, or

(b) comprised property derived, directly or indirectly, from a settlement that at any time in that period was a settlor-interested settlement.

7(2) The relevant period for this purpose is the period–

(a) beginning two years before the beginning of the relevant year of assessment, and

(b) ending with the date of the disposal of the interest in settled property.

This is subject to paragraph 13(3)(d) where the beginning of the disposal and its effective completion fall in different years of assessment.

7(3) The relevant period shall not be treated as beginning before 6th April 1999.
If the rule in sub-paragraph (2) (or, where relevant, that in paragraph 13(3)(d)) would produce that result, the relevant period shall be treated as beginning on that date.

7(4) For the purposes of this paragraph a **"settlor-interested settlement"** means a settlement in which a person who is a settlor in relation to the settlement has an interest or had an interest at any time in the relevant period.
The provisions of section 169F(2) to (6) apply to determine for the purposes of this paragraph whether a settlor has (or had) an interest in the settlement.

7(5) The condition as to settlor interest in the settlement is treated as not met in a year of assessment–

(a) where the settlor dies during the year,

(b) in a case where the settlor is regarded as having an interest in the settlement by reason only of–

(i) *the fact that property* is, or will or may become, payable to or applicable for the benefit of his spouse or civil partner, or

(ii) the fact that a benefit is enjoyed by his spouse or civil partner,

where the spouse or civil partner dies, or the settlor and the spouse or civil partners cease to be married or to be civil partners of each other, during the year, or

(c) in a case where the settlor is regarded as having an interest in a settlement by reason only of–

(i) the fact that property is, or will or may become, payable to or applicable for the benefit of a dependent child of his, or

(ii) the fact that a benefit is enjoyed by such a child,

where the settlor ceases during the year to have (and does not in that year subsequently come to have) any dependent child in relation to whom section 169F(3A)(a) or (b) applies.

History – In para. 7(4), reference to s. 169F(2)–(6) substituted for reference to s. 77(2)–(5), (8) by FA 2008, s. 8 and Sch. 2, para. 7(2)(a) with effect from 2008–09 (FA 2008, Sch. 2, para. 22).

In para. 7(5)(c), reference to s. 169F(3A)(a) and (b) substituted for reference to s. 77(2A)(a) and (b) by FA 2008, s. 8 and Sch. 2, para. 7(2)(b) with effect from 2008–09 (FA 2008, Sch. 2, para. 22).

In para. 7(5)(a), the word "or" at the end left out by FA 2006, s. 88 and Sch, 12, para. 5(1)(a) and repealed by FA 2006, s. 178 and Sch. 26, Pt. 3(15), with effect for the purpose of determining whether a settlor is regarded as having an interest in a settlement (whenever created) on or after 6 April 2006.

Para. 7(5)(c) and the preceding word "; or" inserted by FA 2006, s. 88 and Sch. 12, para. 5(1)(b), with effect for the purpose of determining whether a settlor is regarded as having an interest in a settlement (whenever created) on or after 6 April 2006.

In para. 7(5), the words "or civil partner" inserted four times and the words "or to be civil partners of each other" inserted by SI 2005/3229, reg. 125, with effect from 5 December 2005.

THE RELEVANT UNDERLYING ASSETS

8(1) Where the interest disposed of is a right in relation to a specific fund or other defined part of the settled property, the deemed disposal is of the whole or part of each of the assets comprised in that fund or part.

In any other case the deemed disposal is of the whole or part of each of the assets comprised in the settled property.

8(2) Where the interest disposed of is an interest in a specific fraction or amount of the income or capital of–

(a) the settled property, or

(b) a specific fund or other defined part of the settled property,

the deemed disposal is of a corresponding part of each of the assets comprised in the settled property or, as the case may be, each of the assets comprised in that fund or part.

In any other case the deemed disposal is of the whole of each of the assets so comprised.

8(3) Sub-paragraphs (1) and (2) have effect subject to paragraph 13(4)(a) where the identity of the underlying assets changes during the period between the beginning of the disposal and its effective completion.

8(4) Where part only of an asset is comprised in a specific fund or other defined part of the settled property, that part of the asset shall be treated for the purposes of this Schedule as if it were a separate asset.

CHARACTER OF DEEMED DISPOSAL

9(1) The deemed disposal shall be taken–

(a) to be for a consideration equal to the whole or, as the case may be, a corresponding part of the market value of each of the assets concerned, and

(b) to be a disposal under a bargain at arm's length.

9(2) Sub-paragraph (1)(a) shall be read with paragraph 13(4)(b) where the value of the assets changes during the period between the beginning of the disposal and its effective completion.

AVOIDANCE OF DOUBLE-COUNTING

10(1) The provisions of this paragraph have effect to prevent there being both a deemed disposal under this Schedule in relation to the disposal of an interest in settled property and a chargeable disposal of the interest itself.

A **"chargeable disposal"** means one in relation to which section 76(1) does not apply.

10(2) If there would be a chargeable gain on the disposal of the interest in the settlement, then–

(a) if–

(i) the chargeable gain on the disposal of the interest would be greater than the net chargeable gain on the deemed disposal, or

(ii) there would be no net chargeable gain on the deemed disposal,

the provisions of this Schedule as to a deemed disposal do not apply; and

(b) in any other case, the provisions of this Schedule as to a deemed disposal apply and no chargeable gain is treated as accruing on the disposal of the interest in the settlement.

10(3) If there would be an allowable loss on the disposal of the interest in the settlement, then–

(a) if there would be a greater net allowable loss on the deemed disposal, the provisions of this Schedule as to a deemed disposal do not apply; and

(b) in any other case, the provisions of this Schedule as to a deemed disposal apply and no allowable loss is treated as accruing on the disposal of the interest in the settlement.

10(4) If there would be neither a chargeable gain nor an allowable loss on the disposal of the interest in the settlement, then–

(a) if there would be a net allowable loss on the deemed disposal, the provisions of this Schedule as to a deemed disposal do not apply; and

(b) in any other case, the provisions of this Schedule as to a deemed disposal apply.

10(5) For the purposes of this paragraph–

(a) there is a net chargeable gain on a deemed disposal if the aggregate of the chargeable gains accruing to the trustees in respect of the assets involved exceeds the aggregate of the allowable losses so accruing; and

(b) there is a net allowable loss on a deemed disposal if the aggregate of the allowable losses accruing to the trustees in respect of the assets involved exceeds the aggregate of the chargeable gains so accruing.

RECOVERY OF TAX FROM PERSON DISPOSING OF INTEREST

11(1) This paragraph applies where chargeable gains accrue to the trustees on the deemed disposal and–

(a) tax becomes chargeable on and is paid by the trustees in respect of those gains, or

(b) a person who is a settlor in relation to the settlement recovers from the trustees under section 78 an amount of tax in respect of those gains.

11(2) The trustees are entitled to recover the amount of the tax referred to in sub-paragraph (1)(a) or (b) from the person who disposed of the interest in the settlement.

11(3) For this purpose the trustees may require an inspector to give that person a certificate specifying–

(a) the amount of the gains in question, and

(b) the amount of tax that has been paid.

Any such certificate shall be conclusive evidence of the facts stated in it.

MEANING OF "SETTLOR"

12 The provisions of paragraphs 7 and 8(1), (3), (6) and (7) of Schedule 5 (meaning of "settlor") apply for the purposes of this Schedule as they apply for the purposes of section 86.

History – In para. 12, reference to Sch. 5, para. 7, 8(1), (3), (6) and (7) substituted for reference to s. 79(1) and (3)–(5A) by FA 2008, s. 8 and Sch. 2, para. 7(3)(a) with effect from 2008–09 (FA 2008, Sch. 2, para. 22).

In para. 12, reference to s. 86 substituted for reference to s. 77, 78 by FA 2008, s. 8 and Sch. 2, para. 7(3)(b) with effect from 2008–09 (FA 2008, Sch. 2, para. 22).

In para. 12, the words "(3) to (5A)" substituted for "(3) to (5)" by FA 2006, s. 88 and Sch. 12, para. 29(1) with effect to determine any question arising or after 6 April 2006 whether a person is a settlor in relation to a settlement (whenever created) for the purposes of Sch. 4A.

CASES WHERE THERE IS A PERIOD BETWEEN THE BEGINNING OF THE DISPOSAL AND ITS EFFECTIVE COMPLETION

13(1) This paragraph applies in a case where there is a period between the beginning of the disposal of an interest in settled property and the effective completion of the disposal.

13(2) For the purposes of this Schedule–

(a) the beginning of the disposal is–

(i) in the case of a disposal involving the exercise of an option, when the option is granted, and

(ii) in any other case of a disposal under a contract, when the contract is entered into; and

(b) the effective completion of the disposal means the point at which the person acquiring the interest becomes for practical purposes unconditionally entitled to the whole of the intended subject matter of the disposal.

13(3) Where this paragraph applies and the beginning of the disposal and its effective completion fall in different years of assessment–

(a) the deemed disposal is treated as taking place in the year of assessment in which the disposal is effectively completed;

(b) the condition in paragraph 5 (condition as to residence of trustees) is treated as met if it is met in relation to either of those years of assessment or any intervening year;

(c) the condition in paragraph 6 (condition as to residence of settlor) is treated as met if it is met in relation to either or both of those years of assessment or any intervening year; and

(d) the relevant period for the purposes of paragraph 7 (condition as to settlor interest) is the period–

(i) beginning two years before the beginning of the first of those years of assessment, and

(ii) ending with the effective completion of the disposal.

13(4) If the identity or value of the underlying assets changes during the period between the beginning of the disposal and its effective completion, the following provisions apply–

(a) an asset is treated as comprised in the settled property and, where relevant, in any specific fund or other defined part of the settled property to which the deemed disposal relates if it is so comprised at any time in that period;

(b) the market value of any asset for the purposes of the deemed disposal is taken to be its highest market value at any time during that period.

13(5) The provisions in sub-paragraph (4) do not apply to an asset if during that period it is disposed of by the trustees under a bargain at arm's length and is not reacquired.

HMRC interpretations – IRInt. 249: taxation of chargeable gains: sale of trust interests and transfers linked to trustee borrowing: HMRC view that main purpose of words "for practical purposes" is to cover cases where buyer has power to compel trustees to transfer property to him or her on giving due notice: another example would be where buyer has right to enjoy property now but he or she is not entitled to property until a particular contingency is fulfilled, and there is no likelihood of the contingency not being fulfilled.

EXCEPTION: MAINTENANCE FUNDS FOR HISTORIC BUILDINGS

14 If the trustees of a settlement have elected that section 508 of ITA 2007 (trustees' election in respect of income arising from heritage maintenance property) shall have effect in the case of a settlement or part of a settlement in relation to a year of assessment, this Schedule does not apply in relation to the settlement or part for that year.

History – In para. 14, the words "508 of ITA 2007 (trustees' election in respect of income arising from heritage maintenance property)" substituted for the words "691(2) of the Taxes Act (certain income of maintenance funds for historic buildings not to be income of settlor etc)" by ITA 2007, s. 1027 and Sch. 1, para. 344, with effect from 6 April 2007.

SCHEDULE 4B – TRANSFERS OF VALUE BY TRUSTEES LINKED WITH TRUSTEE BORROWING

Section 76B

History – Sch. 4B inserted by FA 2000, s. 92(2) and Sch. 25 with effect in relation to any transfer of value in relation to which the material time is on or after 21 March 2000.

HMRC interpretations – IRInt. 249: taxation of chargeable gains: sale of trust interests and transfers linked to trustee borrowing: HMRC views.

GENERAL SCHEME OF THIS SCHEDULE

1(1) This Schedule applies where trustees of a settlement–

(a) make a transfer of value (see paragraph 2) in a year of assessment in which the settlement is within section 86 or 87 (see paragraph 3), and

(b) in accordance with this Schedule the transfer of value is treated as linked with trustee borrowing (see paragraphs 4 to 9).

1(2) Where this Schedule applies the trustees are treated as disposing of and immediately reacquiring the whole or a proportion of each of the chargeable assets that continue to form part of the settled property (see paragraphs 10 to 13).

History – In para. 1(1), reference to s. 77 omitted by FA 2008, s. 8 and Sch. 2, para. 8(2) with effect from 2008–09 (FA 2008, Sch. 2, para. 22).

TRANSFERS OF VALUE

2(1) For the purposes of this Schedule trustees of a settlement make a transfer of value if they–

(a) lend money or any other asset to any person,

(b) transfer an asset to any person and receive either no consideration or a consideration whose amount or value is less than the market value of the asset transferred, or

(c) issue a security of any description to any person and receiver either no consideration or a consideration whose amount or value is less than the value of the security.

2(2) References in this Schedule to "the material time", in relation to a transfer of value, are to the time when the loan is made, the transfer is effectively completed or the security is issued.
The effective completion of a transfer means the point at which the person acquiring the asset becomes for practical purposes unconditionally entitled to the whole of the intended subject matter of the transfer.

2(3) In the case of a loan, the amount of value transferred is taken to be the market value of the asset.

2(4) In the case of a transfer, the amount of value transferred is taken to be–

(a) if any part of the value of the asset is attributable to trustee borrowing, the market value of the asset;

(b) if no part of the value of the asset is attributable to trustee borrowing, the market value of the asset reduced by the amount or value of any consideration received for it.

Paragraph 12 below explains what is meant by the value of an asset being attributable to trustee borrowing.

2(5) In the case of the issue of a security, the amount of value transferred shall be taken to be the value of the security reduced by the amount or value of any consideration received by the trustees for it.

2(6) References in this paragraph to the value of an asset are to its value immediately before the material time, unless the asset does not exist before that time in which case its value immediately after that time shall be taken.

HMRC interpretations – IRInt. 249: taxation of chargeable gains: sale of trust interests and transfers linked to trustee borrowing: HMRC view on whether there is "transfer of value" in respect of "cash distributions which are income" and "beneficiary exercising rights of occupation under Trustee etc. Act 1996, s. 12": meaning of "issue a security".

SETTLEMENTS WITHIN SECTION 86 OR 87

History – In para. 3, in the heading, reference to s. 77 omitted by FA 2008, s. 8 and Sch. 2, para. 8(3) with effect from 2008–09 (FA 2008, Sch. 2, para. 22).

3(1) This paragraph explains what is meant in this Schedule by a settlement being "within section 86 or 87" in a year of assessment.

3(2) [Omitted by FA 2008, s. 8 and Sch. 2, para. 8(3)(b).]

3(3) A settlement is "within section 86" in a year of assessment if, assuming–

(a) that there were chargeable gains accruing to the trustees by virtue of disposals of any of the settled property originating from the settlor, and

(b) that the other elements of the condition in subsection (1)(e) of that section were met,

chargeable gains would, under that section, be treated as accruing to the settlor in that year.
Expressions used in this sub-paragraph have the same meaning as in section 86.

3(4) A settlement is "within section 87" for a tax year if–

(a) section 87 applies to the settlement for that year, or

(b) chargeable gains would be treated under section 89(2) as accruing in that year to a beneficiary who received a capital payment from the trustees of the settlement in that year.

3(5) The reference in subsection (4)(b) to chargeable gains treated as accruing includes offshore income gains treated as arising.

History – In para. 3(1), reference to s. 77 omitted by FA 2008, s. 8 and Sch. 2, para. 8(3)(a) with effect from 2008–09 (FA 2008, Sch. 2, para. 22).
Para. 3(2) omitted by FA 2008, s. 8 and Sch. 2, para. 8(3)(b) with effect from 2008–09 (FA 2008, Sch. 2, para. 22).
In former para. 3(2), words "(otherwise than by virtue of section 31 of the Finance Act 2005)" inserted by FA 2005, s. 44(2) with effect for the tax year beginning on 6 April 2004 and subsequent tax years.
Para. 3(4) (together with para. 3(5)) substituted for former para. 3(4) by FA 2008, s. 25 and Sch. 7, para. 130 with effect in relation to transfers of value to which Sch. 4B applies that are made on or after 6 April 2008 (FA 2008, Sch. 7, para. 147).
Para. 3(5) (together with para. 3(4)) substituted for former para. 3(4) by FA 2008, s. 25 and Sch. 7, para. 130 with effect in relation to transfers of value to which Sch. 4B applies that are made on or after 6 April 2008 (FA 2008, FA 2008, Sch. 7, para. 147).

TRUSTEE BORROWING

4(1) For the purposes of this Schedule trustees of a settlement are treated as borrowing if–

(a) money or any other asset is lent to them, or

(b) an asset is transferred to them and in connection with the transfer the trustees assume a contractual obligation (whether absolute or conditional) to restore or transfer to any person that or any other asset.

In the following provisions of this Schedule **"loan obligation"** includes any such obligation as is mentioned in paragraph (b).

4(2) The amount borrowed (the "proceeds" of the borrowing) is taken to be–

(a) in the case of a loan, the market value of the asset;

(b) in the case of a transfer, the market value of the asset reduced by the amount or value of any consideration received for it.

4(3) References in this paragraph to the market value of an asset are to its market value immediately before the loan is made, or the transfer is effectively completed, unless the asset does not exist before that time in which case its market value immediately after that time shall be taken.

The effective completion of a transfer means the point at which the person acquiring the asset becomes for practical purposes unconditionally entitled to the whole of the intended subject matter of the transfer.

HMRC interpretations – IRInt. 249: taxation of chargeable gains: sale of trust interests and transfers linked to trustee borrowing: HMRC view that trustees borrowing from non-resident company that they control is still borrowing and is not trustees borrowing from themselves: it does not matter whether the borrowing is from a company controlled by the trustees or their associates, or from an entirely unconnected company, but what matters is the use to which the borrowing is put.

TRANSFER OF VALUE LINKED WITH TRUSTEE BORROWING

5(1) For the purposes of this Schedule a transfer of value by trustees is treated as linked with trustee borrowing if at the material time there is outstanding trustee borrowing.

5(2) For the purposes of this Schedule there is outstanding trustee borrowing at any time to the extent that–

(a) any loan obligation is outstanding, and

(b) there are proceeds of trustee borrowing that have not been either–

  (i) applied for normal trust purposes, or

  (ii) taken into account under this Schedule in relation to an earlier transfer of value.

5(3) An amount of trustee borrowing is "taken into account" under this Schedule in relation to a transfer of value if the transfer of value is in accordance with this Schedule treated as linked with trustee borrowing. The amount so taken into account is–

(a) the amount of the value transferred by that transfer of value, or

(b) if less, the amount of outstanding trustee borrowing at the material time in relation to that transfer of value.

APPLICATION OF PROCEEDS OF BORROWING FOR NORMAL TRUST PURPOSES

6(1) For the purposes of this Schedule the proceeds of trustee borrowing are applied for normal trust purposes in the following circumstances, and not otherwise.

6(2) They are applied for normal trust purposes if they are applied by the trustees in making a payment in respect of an ordinary trust asset and the following conditions are met–

(a) the payment is made under a transaction at arm's length or is not more than the payment that would be made if the transaction were at arm's length;

(b) the asset forms part of the settled property immediately after the material time or, if it does not do so, the alternative condition in paragraph 8 below is met; and

(c) the sum paid is (or but for section 17 or 39 would be) allowable under section 38 as a deduction in computing a gain accruing to the trustees on a disposal of the asset.

6(3) They are applied for normal trust purposes if–

(a) they are applied by the trustees in wholly or partly discharging a loan obligation of the trustees, and

(b) the whole of the proceeds of the borrowing connected with that obligation (or all but an insignificant amount) have been applied by the trustees for normal trust purposes.

6(4) They are applied for normal trust purposes if they are applied by the trustees in making payments to meet bona fide current expenses incurred by them in administering the settlement or any of the settled property.

HMRC interpretations – IRInt. 249: taxation of chargeable gains: sale of trust interests and transfers linked to trustee borrowing: HMRC do not regard "current" as restricting qualification to expenditure which for accounting purposes must fall in the year of borrowing, but they do regard "current" as excluding borrowing to make a provision for future expenditure or to meet expenditure that was incurred long before but left unpaid: Revenue view that the expression "administering the settlement or any of the settled property" should be construed widely to cover not only those expenses properly chargeable to income, or which would be so chargeable but for express provisions of the trust deed, but also capital expenditure such as capital taxes in the UK or elsewhere, or legal costs of a reorganisation, in particular the costs of an application under the Variation of Trusts Act.

ORDINARY TRUST ASSETS

7(1) The following are **"ordinary trust assets"** for the purposes of this Schedule–

(a) shares or securities;

(b) tangible property, whether movable or immovable, or a lease of such property;

(c) property not within paragraph (a) or (b) which is used for the purposes of a trade, profession or vocation carried on–

(i) by the trustees, or

(ii) by a beneficiary who has an interest in possession in the settled property;

(d) any right in or over, or any interest in, property of a description within paragraph (b) or (c).

7(2) In sub-paragraph (1)(a) **"securities"** has the same meaning as in section 132.

HMRC interpretations – IRInt. 249: taxation of chargeable gains: sale of trust interests and transfers linked to trustee borrowing: HMRC view that a futures contract relating to commodities is not an "ordinary trust asset".

THE ALTERNATIVE CONDITION FOR ASSETS NO LONGER PART OF THE SETTLED PROPERTY

8(1) The alternative condition referred to in paragraph 6(2)(b) in relation to an asset which no longer forms part of the settled property is that–

(a) the asset is treated as having been disposed of by virtue of section 24(1), or

(b) one or more ordinary trust assets which taken together directly or indirectly represent the asset–

(i) form part of the settled property immediately after the material time, or

(ii) are treated as having been disposed of by virtue of section 24(1).

8(2) Where there has been a part disposal of the asset, the condition in paragraph 6(2)(b) and the provisions of sub-paragraph (1) above may be applied in any combination in relation to the subject matter of the part disposal and what remains.

8(3) References in this paragraph to an asset include part of an asset.

NORMAL TRUST PURPOSES: POWER TO MAKE PROVISION BY REGULATIONS

9(1) The Treasury may make provision by regulations as to the circumstances in which the proceeds of trustee borrowing are to be treated for the purposes of this Schedule as applied for normal trust purposes.

9(2) The regulations may–

(a) add to, amend or repeal any of the provisions of paragraphs 6 to 8 above,

(b) make different provision for different cases, and

(c) contain such supplementary, incidental, consequential and transitional provision as the Treasury may think fit.

DEEMED DISPOSAL OF REMAINING CHARGEABLE ASSETS

10(1) Where in accordance with this Schedule a transfer of value by trustees is treated as linked with trustee borrowing, the trustees are treated for all purposes of this Act–

(a) as having at the material time disposed of, and

(b) as having immediately reacquired,

the whole or a proportion (see paragraph 11) of each of the chargeable assets that form part of the settled property immediately after the material time ("the remaining chargeable assets").

10(2) The deemed disposal and reacquisition shall be taken–

(a) to be for a consideration equal to the whole or, as the case may be, a proportion of the market value of each of those assets, and

(b) to be under a bargain at arm's length.

10(3) For the purposes of sub-paragraph (1) an asset is a chargeable asset if a gain on a disposal of the asset by the trustees at the material time would be a chargeable gain.

WHETHER DEEMED DISPOSAL IS OF WHOLE OR A PROPORTION OF THE ASSETS

11(1) This paragraph provides for determining whether the deemed disposal and reacquisition is of the whole or a proportion of each of the remaining chargeable assets.

11(2) If the amount of value transferred–

(a) *is less than the amount* of outstanding trustee borrowing, and

(b) is also less than the effective value of the remaining chargeable assets, the deemed disposal and reacquisition is of the proportion of each of the remaining chargeable assets given by:

$$\frac{VT}{EV}$$

where–

VT is the amount of value transferred, and

EV is the effective value of the remaining chargeable assets.

11(3) If the amount of value transferred–

(a) is not less than the amount of outstanding trustee borrowing, but

(b) is less than the effective value of the remaining chargeable assets,

the deemed disposal and reacquisition is of the proportion of each of the remaining chargeable assets given by:

$$\frac{TB}{EV}$$

where–

TB is the amount of outstanding trustee borrowing, and

EV is the effective value of the remaining chargeable assets.

11(4) In any other case the deemed disposal and reacquisition is of the whole of each of the remaining chargeable assets.

11(5) For the purposes of this paragraph the effective value of the remaining chargeable assets means the aggregate market value of those assets reduced by so much of that value as is attributable to trustee borrowing.

11(6) References in this paragraph to amounts or values, except in relation to the amount of value transferred, are to amounts or values immediately after the material time.

VALUE ATTRIBUTABLE TO TRUSTEE BORROWING

12(1) For the purposes of this Schedule the value of an asset is attributable to trustee borrowing to the extent determined in accordance with the following rules.

12(2) Where the asset itself has been borrowed by trustees, the value of the asset is attributable to trustee borrowing to the extent that the proceeds of that borrowing have not been applied for normal trust purposes. This is in addition to any extent to which the value of the asset may be attributable to trustee borrowing by virtue of sub-paragraph (3).

12(3) The value of any asset is attributable to trustee borrowing to the extent that–

(a) the trustees have applied the proceeds of trustee borrowing in acquiring or enhancing the value of the asset, or

(b) the asset represents directly or indirectly an asset whose value was attributable to the trustees having so applied the proceeds of trustee borrowing.

12(4) For the purposes of this paragraph an amount is applied by the trustees in acquiring or enhancing the value of an asset if it is applied wholly and exclusively by them–

(a) as consideration in money or money's worth for the acquisition of the asset,

(b) for the purpose of enhancing the value of the asset in a way that is reflected in the state or nature of the asset,

(c) in establishing, preserving or defending their title to, or to a right over, the asset, or

(d) where the asset is a holding of shares or securities that is treated as a single asset, by way of consideration in money or money's worth for additional shares or securities forming part of the same holding.

12(5) Trustees are treated as applying the proceeds of borrowing as mentioned in sub-paragraph (4) if and to the extent that at the time the expenditure is incurred there is outstanding trustee borrowing.

12(6) In sub-paragraph (4)(d) **"securities"** has the same meaning as in section 132.

ASSETS AND TRANSFERS

13(1) In this Schedule any reference to an asset includes money expressed in sterling.
References to the value or market value of such an asset are to its amount.

13(2) Subject to sub-paragraph (3), references in this Schedule to the transfer of an asset include anything that is or is treated as a disposal of the asset for the purposes of this Act, or would be if sub-paragraph (1) above applied generally for the purposes of this Act.

13(3) References in this Schedule to a transfer of an asset do not include a transfer of an asset that is created by the part disposal of another asset.

SCHEDULE 4C – TRANSFERS OF VALUE: ATTRIBUTION OF GAINS TO BENEFICIARIES

Section 85A

History – Sch. 4C inserted by FA 2000, s. 92(4) and Sch. 26, para. 1 with effect in relation to any transfer of value in relation to which the material time is on or after 21 March 2000.

Cross references – FA 2008, Sch. 7, para. 152: disapplication of para. 7B, 9(2) in relation to Sch. 4C pools created before 6 April 2008. SI 2009/3001, reg. 20: offshore income gains of non-resident settlements: modified application of Sch. 4C.

Notes – In FA 2008, Sch. 7, para. 153–155, there are transitional measures relating to the application of Sch. 4C following the changes to the remittance rules. However, these transitional measures appear to contain errors and to some extent are meaningless.

Amendments to some paragraphs of Sch. 4C have been made by FA 2003, s. 163(2) and Sch. 29, para. 2 which came into force in accordance with FA 2003, s. 163(4). Hence, for the purposes of those paragraphs (see History annotation for a paragraph, for identification of those paragraphs), FA 2003, s. 163(4) reads as follows:

"**163(4)** The following provisions have effect with respect to the coming into force of the amendments made by this section and Schedule 29–

(a) the amendments apply where the trustees of a settlement have made a transfer to which Schedule 4B applies at any time on or after 21st March 2000;

(b) where there has been a transfer of value to which Schedule 4B applies before 9th April 2003, the transferor settlement shall be treated as having a Schedule 4C pool as from that date containing such Schedule 4C gains as would fall to be included in the pool if–
  (i) a year of assessment had ended with 8th April 2003, and
  (ii) the reference in paragraph 1(2)(b) of Schedule 4C as amended to the end of the year of assessment in which the transfer of value was made were to that date;

(c) where a transferor settlement ceased to exist on or after 21st March 2000 and before 9th April 2003, Schedule 4C as amended applies as if it had ceased to exist on 8th April 2003 (so that paragraph (b) above applies);

(d) so much of Schedule 4C as amended as provides–
  (i) that gains treated as accruing to beneficiaries who are not chargeable to tax are treated as outstanding section 87/89 gains, or
  (ii) that gains in a settlement's Schedule 4C pool are not to be treated as accruing to such beneficiaries,
 applies only in relation to capital payments made on or after 9th April 2003;

(e) gains included in a settlement's Schedule 4C pool by virtue of paragraph 1(2)(b) of that Schedule as amended shall only be attributed in accordance with the provisions of that Schedule to beneficiaries who receive capital payments on or after 9th April 2003.".

By virtue of FA 2003, s. 163(6), expressions used in FA 2003, s. 163(4) have the same meaning as those in Sch. 4C as amended by FA 2003, Sch. 29.

INTRODUCTION

1(1) This Schedule applies where the trustees of a settlement (**"the transferor settlement"**) make a transfer of value to which Schedule 4B applies (**"the original transfer"**).

1(2) The transferor settlement is regarded for the purposes of this Schedule as having a "Schedule 4C pool".

1(3) The Schedule 4C pool contains the section 2(2) amounts for the settlement that are outstanding at the end of the tax year in which the original transfer is made (see paragraph 1A).

1(3A) The section 2(2) amount for that tax year is increased by–

(a) the amount of Schedule 4B trust gains accruing by virtue of the original transfer (see paragraphs 3 to 7), and

(b) the total amount of any further Schedule 4B trust gains accruing by virtue of any further transfers of value to which that Schedule applies that are made by the trustees in that tax year.

1(4) Paragraphs 8 to 9 provide for the attribution of gains in a settlement's Schedule 4C pool.

1(5) References in this Schedule to a transfer to which Schedule 4B applies include any such transfer, whether or not any chargeable gain or allowable loss accrues under that Schedule by virtue of the transfer.

History – Para. 1(2) (together with para. 1(3), (3A)) substituted for former para. 1(2), (3) by FA 2008, s. 25 and Sch. 7, para. 132 with effect in relation to transfers of value to which Sch. 4B applies that are made on or after 6 April 2008 (FA 2008, Sch. 7, para. 147).

Para. 1(3) (together with para. 1(2), (3A)) substituted for former para. 1(2), (3) by FA 2008, s. 25 and Sch. 7, para. 132 with effect in relation to transfers of value to which Sch. 4B applies that are made on or after 6 April 2008 (FA 2008, Sch. 7, para. 147).

Para. 1(3A) (together with para. 1(2), (3)) substituted for former para. 1(2), (3) by FA 2008, s. 25 and Sch. 7, para. 132 with effect in relation to transfers of value to which Sch. 4B applies that are made on or after 6 April 2008 (FA 2008, Sch. 7, para. 147).

Para. 1 substituted for paragraphs 1 and 2 (introduction and general scheme of Schedule) by FA 2003, s. 163(2) and Sch. 29, para. 2 which came into force in accordance with FA 2003, s. 163(4).

Former para. 1 inserted by FA 2000, s. 92(4) and Sch. 26, para. 1 with effect in relation to any transfer of value in relation to which the material time is on or after 21 March 2000.

OUTSTANDING SECTION 2(2) AMOUNTS

1A(1) The following steps are to be taken for the purpose of calculating the section 2(2) amounts for a settlement that are outstanding at the end of a tax year ("the relevant tax year").

Step 1

Find the section 2(2) amount for the settlement for the relevant tax year and earlier tax years, as reduced under section 87A as it applies for the relevant tax year and earlier tax years.

Step 2

This Step applies if, by virtue of the matching of the section 2(2) amount for the settlement for a tax year ("the applicable year") with a capital payment, chargeable gains are treated under section 87 or section 89(2) as accruing in the relevant tax year to a beneficiary who is not chargeable to tax for that year. Increase the section 2(2) amount for the applicable year (found under Step 1) by the amount of the chargeable gains.

1A(2) For the purposes of Step 1 of sub-paragraph (1) take into account the effect of section 90 in relation to any transfer of settled property from or to the trustees of the settlement made in or before the relevant tax year.

1A(3) For the purposes of this Schedule a beneficiary is "chargeable to tax" for a tax year if, as respects that year, the beneficiary meets the residence condition set out in section 2(1A).

History – In para. 1A(3), the words ", as respects that year, the beneficiary meets the residence condition set out in section 2(1A)" substituted for the words "the beneficiary is resident or ordinarily resident in the United Kingdom in that year" by FA 2013, s. 219 and Sch. 46, para. 107(2), with effect in relation to a person's liability to capital gains tax for the tax year 2013–14 or any subsequent tax year, without prejudice to any provision in FA 2013, Sch. 46, Pt. 3 about the application of a particular amendment.
Para. 1A inserted by FA 2008, s. 25 and Sch. 7, para. 133 with effect in relation to transfers of value to which Sch. 4B applies that are made on or after 6 April 2008 (FA 2008, Sch. 7, para. 147).

GENERAL SCHEME OF THIS SCHEDULE

2 [Para. 1 above substituted for paragraph 2.]

History – Para. 1 above substituted for paragraph 2 by FA 2003, s. 163(2) and Sch. 29, para. 2 which came into force in accordance with FA 2003, s. 163(4).

COMPUTATION OF SCHEDULE 4B TRUST GAINS

3(1) This paragraph explains what is meant for the purposes of this Schedule by "Schedule 4B trust gains".

3(2) The Schedule 4B trust gains are computed in relation to each transfer of value to which that Schedule applies.

3(3) In relation to a transfer of value the amount of the Schedule 4B trust gains for the purposes of this Schedule is given by–

$$CA - SG - AL$$

where–

CA is the chargeable amount computed under paragraph 4 or 5 below,

SG is the amount of any gains attributed to the settlor that fall to be deducted under paragraph 6 below, and

AL is the amount of any allowable losses that may be deducted under paragraph 7 below.

History – Para. 3 inserted by FA 2000, s. 92(4) and Sch. 26, para. 1 with effect in relation to any transfer of value in relation to which the material time is on or after 21 March 2000.

CHARGEABLE AMOUNT: NON-RESIDENT SETTLEMENT

4(1) If the transfer of value is made in a year of assessment during which the trustees of the transferor settlement are at no time resident in the United Kingdom the chargeable amount is computed under this paragraph.

4(2) Where this paragraph applies the chargeable amount is the amount on which the trustees would have been chargeable to tax under section 2(2) by virtue of Schedule 4B if they had been resident in the United Kingdom in the year (and had made the disposals which Schedule 4B treats them as having made).

4(3) Where any of the disposals which the trustees are treated as having made as mentioned in sub-paragraph (2) is a non-resident CGT disposal–

(a) any chargeable gain or allowable loss accruing on that disposal, other than an NRCGT gain chargeable to, or an NRCGT loss allowable for the purposes of, capital gains tax by virtue of section 14D, is to be treated for the purposes of sub-paragraph (2) as if it were a chargeable gain or (as the case requires) allowable loss falling to be taken into account in calculating the chargeable amount, and

(b) that disposal is otherwise to be disregarded for the purpose of calculating the chargeable amount.

History – In para. 4(1), the words "and ordinarily resident" omitted by FA 2013, s. 219 and Sch. 46, para. 107(3)(a), with effect in relation to a person's liability to capital gains tax for the tax year 2013–14 or any subsequent tax year, without prejudice to any provision in FA 2013, Sch. 46, Pt. 3 about the application of a particular amendment.
In para. 4(1), the words "at no time resident and ordinarily resident in the United Kingdom" substituted for "at no time resident or ordinarily resident in the United Kingdom" by FA 2006, s. 88 and Sch. 12, para. 36(1), (2)(b)) with effect in relation to a transfer of value made on or after 6 April 2007 (in relation to settlements whenever created).
In para. 4(2), the words "and ordinarily resident" omitted by FA 2013, s. 219 and Sch. 46, para. 107(3)(b), with effect in relation to a person's liability to capital gains tax for the tax year 2013–14 or any subsequent tax year, without prejudice to any provision in FA 2013, Sch. 46, Pt. 3 about the application of a particular amendment.
In para. 4(2), the words "(and had made the disposals which Schedule 4B treats them as having made)" inserted by FA 2008, s. 25 and Sch. 7, para. 134 with effect in relation to transfers of value to which Sch. 4B applies that are made on or after 6 April 2008 (FA 2008, Sch. 7, para. 147).
In para. 4(2), the words "resident and ordinarily resident in the United Kingdom" substituted for "resident or ordinarily resident in the United Kingdom" by FA 2006, s. 88 and Sch. 12, para. 34(1), (2)(f) with effect from 6 April 2007 (in relation to settlements whenever created).
Para. 4(3) inserted by FA 2015, s. 37 and Sch. 7, para. 40, with effect in relation to disposals made on or after 6 April 2015.
Para. 4 inserted by FA 2000, s. 92(4) and Sch. 26, para. 1 with effect in relation to any transfer of value in relation to which the material time is on or after 21 March 2000.

CHARGEABLE AMOUNT: DUAL RESIDENT SETTLEMENT

5(1) If the transfer of value is made in a year of assessment where–

(a) the trustees of the transferor settlement are resident in the United Kingdom during any part of the year, and

(b) at any time of such residence they fall to be regarded for the purposes of any double taxation relief arrangements as resident in a territory outside the United Kingdom,

the chargeable amount is computed under this paragraph.

5(2) Where this paragraph applies the chargeable amount is the lesser of–

(a) the amount on which the trustees would be chargeable to tax under section 2(2) by virtue of Schedule 4B on the assumption that the double taxation relief arrangements did not apply (and the disposals which Schedule 4B treats them as having made were made), and

(b) the amount on which the trustees would be so chargeable to tax by virtue of disposals of protected assets.

5(3) For this purpose assets **"protected assets"** has the meaning given by section 88(4).

History – In para. 5(1)(a), the words "and ordinarily resident" omitted by FA 2013, s. 219 and Sch. 46, para. 107(4)(a), with effect in relation to a person's liability to capital gains tax for the tax year 2013–14 or any subsequent tax year, without prejudice to any provision in FA 2013, Sch. 46, Pt. 3 about the application of a particular amendment.
In para. 5(1)(b), the words "and ordinary residence" omitted by FA 2013, s. 219 and Sch. 46, para. 107(4)(b), with effect in relation to a person's liability to capital gains tax for the tax year 2013–14 or any subsequent tax year, without prejudice to any provision in FA 2013, Sch. 46, Pt. 3 about the application of a particular amendment.
In para. 5(1), the words "resident and ordinarily resident in the United Kingdom during any part of the year" substituted for "resident in the United Kingdom during any part of the year or ordinarily resident in the United Kingdom during the year" and the words "such residence and ordinary residence" substituted for "such residence or ordinary residence" by FA 2006, s. 88 and Sch. 12, para. 35(1), (2)(c) with effect in relation to a transfer of value made on or after 6 April 2007 (in relation to settlements whenever created).
In para. 5(2)(a), the words "(and the disposals which Schedule 4B treats them as having made were made)" inserted by FA 2008, s. 25 and Sch. 7, para. 135 with effect in relation to transfers of value to which Sch. 4B applies that are made on or after 6 April 2008 (FA 2008, Sch. 7, para. 147).
Para. 5 inserted by FA 2000, s. 92(4) and Sch. 26, para. 1 with effect in relation to any transfer of value in relation to which the material time is on or after 21 March 2000.

GAINS ATTRIBUTED TO SETTLOR

6(1) For the purposes of this Schedule the chargeable amount in relation to a transfer of value shall be reduced by the amount of any chargeable gains arising by virtue of that transfer of value that–

(a) are by virtue of section 86(4) treated as accruing to the settlor, or

(b) where section 10A applies, are treated by virtue of that section (as it has effect subject to paragraph 12 below) as accruing to the settlor in the period of return.

6(1A) [Omitted by FA 2008, s. 8 and Sch. 2, para. 47(3).]

6(2) In determining for the purposes of sub-paragraph (1)(a) the amount of chargeable gains arising by virtue of a transfer of value that are treated as accruing to the settlor, there shall be disregarded any losses which arise otherwise than by virtue of Schedule 4B.

6(3) [Omitted by FA 2008, s. 8 and Sch. 2, para. 9.]

History – In para. 6(1)(b), the words "period of return" substituted for the words "year of return" by FA 2013, s. 218 and Sch. 45, para. 123(2), with effect if the year of departure (as defined in FA 2013, Sch. 45, Pt. 4) is the tax year 2013–14 or a subsequent tax year, subject to the transitional and saving provision in FA 2013, Sch. 45, para. 154–159.

In para. 6(1), the words "the amount of any chargeable gains" substituted for the words "the tapered amount of any chargeable gains" by FA 2008, s. 8 and Sch. 2, para. 47(2) with effect in relation to chargeable gains accruing or treated as accruing in the tax year 2008–09 or any subsequent tax year (FA 2008, Sch. 2, para. 56(3)).
In para. 6(1), the words "the tapered amount of any chargeable gains" substituted for the words "the amount of any chargeable gains" by FA 2003, s. 163(2) and Sch. 29, para. 5(2) which came into force in accordance with FA 2003, s.163(4).
Para. 6(1A) omitted by FA 2008, s. 8 and Sch. 2, para. 47(3) with effect in relation to chargeable gains accruing or treated as accruing in the tax year 2008–09 or any subsequent tax year (FA 2008, Sch. 2, para. 56(3)).
Former para. 6(1A) inserted by FA 2003, s. 163(2) and Sch. 29, para. 5(3) which came into force in accordance with FA 2003, s.163(4).
Para. 6(3) omitted by FA 2008, s. 8 and Sch. 2, para. 9 with effect from 2008–09 (FA 2008, Sch. 2, para. 22).
Para. 6 inserted by FA 2000, s. 92(4) and Sch. 26, para. 1 with effect in relation to any transfer of value in relation to which the material time is on or after 21 March 2000.

REDUCTION FOR ALLOWABLE LOSSES

7(1) An allowable loss arising under Schedule 4B in relation to a transfer of value by the trustees of a settlement may be taken into account in accordance with this paragraph to reduce for the purposes of this Schedule the chargeable amount in relation to another transfer of value by those trustees.

7(2) Any such allowable loss goes first to reduce chargeable amounts arising from other transfers of value made in the same year of assessment.
If there is more than one chargeable amount and the aggregate amount of the allowable losses is less than the aggregate of the chargeable amounts, each of the chargeable amounts is reduced proportionately.

7(3) If in any year of assessment the aggregate amount of the allowable losses exceeds the aggregate of the chargeable amounts, the excess shall be carried forward to the next year of assessment and treated for the purposes of this paragraph as if it were an allowable loss arising in relation to a transfer of value made in that year.

7(4) Any reduction of a chargeable amount under this paragraph is made after any deduction under paragraph 6.

History – Para. 7 inserted by FA 2000, s. 92(4) and Sch. 26, para. 1 with effect in relation to any transfer of value in relation to which the material time is on or after 21 March 2000.

OUTSTANDING SECTION 87/89 GAINS

7A [Omitted by FA 2008, s. 25 and Sch. 7, para. 136.]

History – Para. 7A omitted by FA 2008, s. 25 and Sch. 7, para. 136 with effect in relation to transfers of value to which Sch. 4B applies that are made on or after 6 April 2008 (FA 2008, Sch. 7, para. 147).

GAINS TO BE BROUGHT INTO POOL ON SUBSEQUENT TRANSFER OF VALUE

7B(1) This paragraph applies if the trustees of the transferor settlement make a further transfer of value to which Schedule 4B applies in a tax year ("the year of the transfer") after the tax year mentioned in paragraph 1(3).

7B(2) If the settlement has a Schedule 4C pool at the beginning of the year of the transfer–

(a) the section 2(2) amounts in the Schedule 4C pool are increased by the section 2(2) amounts for the settlement that are outstanding at the end of the year of the transfer, and

(b) the section 2(2) amount in the pool for the year of transfer is increased (or further increased) by the amount of Schedule 4B trust gains accruing by virtue of the further transfer.

7B(3) If the settlement does not have a Schedule 4C pool at the beginning of the year of the transfer, this Schedule applies in relation to the further transfer as it applied in relation to the original transfer.

7B(4) For the purposes of this paragraph a settlement has a Schedule 4C pool until the end of the tax year in which all section 2(2) amounts in the pool have been reduced to nil.

History – Para. 7B substituted by FA 2008, s. 25 and Sch. 7, para. 137 with effect in relation to transfers of value to which Sch. 4B applies that are made on or after 6 April 2008 (FA 2008, Sch. 7, para. 147).
Para. 7B inserted by FA 2003, s. 163(2) and Sch. 29, para. 3 which came into force in accordance with FA 2003, s. 163(4).

Cross references – FA 2008, Sch. 7, para. 152: disapplication of para. 7B, 9(2) in relation to Sch. 4C pools created before 6 April 2008.

ATTRIBUTION OF SCHEDULE 4C GAINS TO BENEFICIARIES

8(1) Chargeable gains are treated as accruing in a tax year ("the relevant tax year") to a beneficiary who has received a capital payment from the trustees of a relevant settlement in the relevant tax year or any earlier tax year if all or part of the capital payment is matched (under section 87A as it applies for the relevant tax year) with the section 2(2) amount in the Schedule 4C pool for the relevant tax year or any earlier tax year.

8(2) The amount of chargeable gains treated as accruing is equal to–

(a) the amount of the capital payment, or

(b) if only part of the capital payment is matched, the amount of that part.

8(3) Section 87A applies for a tax year for the purposes of matching capital payments received from the trustees of a relevant settlement with section 2(2) amounts in the Schedule 4C pool as if–

(a) references to section 2(2) amounts were to section 2(2) amounts in the Schedule 4C pool,

(b) references to a capital payment received from the trustees by a beneficiary were to a capital payment received from the trustees of a relevant settlement by a beneficiary who is chargeable to tax for that year,

(d) for section 87A(3)(b) there were substituted–

"(b) all section 2(2) amounts in the Schedule 4C pool have been reduced to nil.", and

8(4) Section 87A applies for a tax year by virtue of this paragraph before it applies for that year otherwise than by virtue of this paragraph; but this is subject to sub-paragraph (5).

8(5) If section 87A applies for a tax year by virtue of section 762(3) of the Taxes Act (offshore income gains), it applies for that year by virtue of that provision before it applies for that year by virtue of this paragraph.

History – Para. 8 substituted by FA 2008, s. 25 and Sch. 7, para. 138 with effect in relation to transfers of value to which Sch. 4B applies that are made on or after 6 April 2008 (FA 2008, Sch. 7, para. 147).
Para. 8, 8A, 8B, 8C and 9 substituted for former paragraphs 8 and 9 by FA 2003, s. 163(2) and Sch. 29, para. 4(1) which came into force in accordance with FA 2003, s. 163(4).
Former para. 8 inserted by FA 2000, s. 92(4) and Sch. 26, para. 1 with effect in relation to any transfer of value in relation to which the material time is on or after 21 March 2000.

Cross references – FA 2008, Sch. 7, para. 148: no account to be taken of any capital payment received before 21 March 2000.
FA 2008, Sch. 7, para. 150: FA 2008, Sch. 7, para. 124 to apply in relation to para. 8 as it applies in relation to s. 87: where individual not domiciled in the UK, individual not to be charged in respect of certain amounts arising before 6 April 2008.
FA 2008, Sch. 7, para. 151: no account to be taken of any capital payment received between 12 March and 5 April 2008 (inclusive) where individual not domiciled in the UK in 2007–08 or in the tax year in question.

RELEVANT SETTLEMENTS

8A(1) This paragraph specifies what settlements are relevant settlements in relation to a Schedule 4C pool.

8A(2) The transferor and transferee settlements in relation to the original transfer of value are relevant settlements.

8A(3) If the trustees of any settlement that is a relevant settlement in relation to a Schedule 4C pool–

(a) make a transfer of value to which Schedule 4B applies, or

(b) make a transfer of settled property to which section 90 applies,

any settlement that is a transferee settlement in relation to that transfer is also a relevant settlement in relation to that pool.

8A(4) If the trustees of a settlement that is a relevant settlement in relation to a Schedule 4C pool make a transfer of value to which Schedule 4B applies, any other settlement that is a relevant settlement in relation to that pool is also a relevant settlement in relation to the Schedule 4C pool arising from the further transfer.

History – Para. 8, 8A, 8B, 8C and 9 substituted for former paragraphs 8 and 9 by FA 2003, s. 163(2) and Sch. 29, para. 4(1) which came into force in accordance with FA 2003, s. 163(4); furthermore, by virtue of FA 2003, s. 163(5), para. 8A(3) and (4) applies only where the transfer, referred to therein, occurs on or after 9 April 2003.

ATTRIBUTION OF GAINS: REMITTANCE BASIS

8AA Section 87B (remittance basis) applies in relation to chargeable gains treated under paragraph 8 as accruing as it applies in relation to chargeable gains treated under section 87 as accruing.

History – Para. 8AA inserted by FA 2008, s. 25 and Sch. 7, para. 139 with effect in relation to transfers of value to which Sch. 4B applies that are made on or after 6 April 2008 (FA 2008, Sch. 7, para. 147).

ATTRIBUTION OF GAINS IN SCHEDULE 4C POOL

8B [Omitted by FA 2008, s. 25 and Sch. 7, para. 140.]

History – Para. 8B omitted by FA 2008, s. 25 and Sch. 7, para. 140 with effect in relation to transfers of value to which Sch. 4B applies that are made on or after 6 April 2008 (FA 2008, Sch. 7, para. 147).

ATTRIBUTION OF GAINS: SCHEDULE 4C POOL GAINS AND OTHER GAINS

8C [Omitted by FA 2008, s. 25 and Sch. 7, para. 140.]

History – Para. 8C omitted by FA 2008, s. 25 and Sch. 7, para. 140 with effect in relation to transfers of value to which TCGA 1992, Sch. 4B applies that are made on or after 6 April 2008 (FA 2008, Sch. 7, para. 147).

ATTRIBUTION OF GAINS: DISREGARD OF CERTAIN CAPITAL PAYMENTS

9(1) For the purposes of paragraph 8 (and section 87A as it applies for the purposes of that paragraph), no account is to be taken of a capital payment to which any of sub-paragraphs (2) to (4) applies (or a part of a capital payment to which sub-paragraph (4) applies).

9(2) This sub-paragraph applies to a capital payment received before the tax year preceding the tax year in which the original transfer is made.

9(3) This sub-paragraph applies to a capital payment that–

(a) is received by a beneficiary of a settlement from the trustees in a tax year during the whole of which the trustees–

 (i) are resident in the United Kingdom, and

 (ii) are not Treaty non-resident,

(b) was made before any transfer of value to which Schedule 4B applies was made, and

(c) was not made in anticipation of the making of any such transfer of value or of chargeable gains accruing under that Schedule.

9(4) This sub-paragraph applies to a capital payment if (and to the extent that) it is received (or treated as received) in a tax year from the trustees by a company that–

(a) is not resident in the United Kingdom in that year, and

(b) would be a close company if it were resident in the United Kingdom,

(and is not treated under any of subsections (3) to (5) of section 96 as received by another person).

History – In para. 9(3)(a)(i), the words "and ordinarily resident" omitted by FA 2013, s. 219 and Sch. 46, para. 107(5), with effect in relation to a person's liability to capital gains tax for the tax year 2013–14 or any subsequent tax year, without prejudice to any provision in FA 2013, Sch. 46, Pt. 3 about the application of a particular amendment.

Para. 9 substituted by FA 2008, s. 25 and Sch. 7, para. 141 with effect in relation to transfers of value to which Sch. 4B applies that are made on or after 6 April 2008 (FA 2008, Sch. 7, para. 147).

RESIDENCE OF TRUSTEES FROM WHOM CAPITAL PAYMENT RECEIVED

10(1) Subject to paragraph 9(3), it is immaterial for the purposes of paragraph 8 that the trustees of any relevant settlement are or have at any time been resident in the United Kingdom.

10(2) [Omitted by FA 2008, s. 25 and Sch. 7, para. 142(b).]

10(3) [Omitted by FA 2008, s. 25 and Sch. 7, para. 142(b).]

History – In para. 10(1), the words "and ordinarily resident" omitted by FA 2013, s. 219 and Sch. 46, para. 107(6), with effect in relation to a person's liability to capital gains tax for the tax year 2013–14 or any subsequent tax year, without prejudice to any provision in FA 2013, Sch. 46, Pt. 3 about the application of a particular amendment.

In para. 10(1), the words "paragraph 9(3)" substituted for "sub-paragraph (2) below" by FA 2008, s. 25 and Sch. 7, para. 142(a) with effect in relation to transfers of value to which Sch. 4B applies that are made on or after 6 April 2008 (FA 2008, Sch. 7, para. 147).

In para. 10(1), the words "resident and ordinarily resident in the United Kingdom" substituted for "resident or ordinarily resident in the United Kingdom" by FA 2006, s. 88 and Sch. 12, para. 34(1), (2)(f) with effect from 6 April 2007 (in relation to settlements whenever created).

In para. 10(1), the words "of any relevant settlement" substituted for the words "of the transferor settlement, or any transferee settlement," by FA 2003, s. 163(2) and Sch. 29, para. 6(1), which came into force in accordance with FA 2003, s. 163(4).

Para. 10(2) omitted by FA 2008, s. 25 and Sch. 7, para. 142(b) with effect in relation to transfers of value to which Sch. 4B applies that are made on or after 6 April 2008 (FA 2008, Sch. 7, para. 147).

In former para. 10(2), the words "during the whole of which the trustees are resident and ordinarily resident in the United Kingdom" substituted for para. (a)–(b) by FA 2006, s. 88 and Sch. 12, para. 40 with effect from 6 April 2007 (in relation to settlements whenever created).

Para. 10(3) omitted by FA 2008, s. 25 and Sch. 7, para. 142(b) with effect in relation to transfers of value to which Sch. 4B applies that are made on or after 6 April 2008 (FA 2008, Sch. 7, para. 147).

In former para. 10(3), the words "resident and ordinarily resident in the United Kingdom" substituted for "resident or ordinarily resident in the United Kingdom" by FA 2006, s. 88 and Sch. 12, para. 34(1), (2)(f) with effect from 6 April 2007 (in relation to settlements whenever created).

Para. 10 inserted by FA 2000, s. 92(4) and Sch. 26, para. 1, with effect in relation to any transfer of value in relation to which the material time is on or after 21 March 2000.

TAPER RELIEF

11 [Omitted by FA 2008, s. 8 and Sch. 2, para. 48.]

History – Para. 11 omitted by FA 2008, s. 8 and Sch. 2, para. 48 with effect in relation to chargeable gains accruing or treated as accruing in the tax year 2008–09 or any subsequent tax year (FA 2008, Sch. 2, para. 56(3)).

ATTRIBUTION OF GAINS TO SETTLOR IN SECTION 10A CASES

12(1) This paragraph applies if–

(a) by virtue of section 10A, an amount of chargeable gains within section 86(1)(e) that accrued in a tax year ("year A") to the trustees of a settlement would be treated as accruing to a person ("the settlor") in the period of return, and

(b) after paragraph 8 has applied for the year of return, the section 2(2) amount for year A that is in the Schedule 4C pool for the settlement is less than the amount mentioned in paragraph (a).

12(2) The amount of chargeable gains treated as mentioned in sub-paragraph (1)(a) as accruing to the settlor in the period of return is limited to the section 2(2) amount referred to in sub-paragraph (1)(b).

12(3) [Effectively omitted by FA 2008, s. 25 and Sch. 7, para. 143.]

12(4) Where the property comprised in the transferor settlement has at any time included property not originating from the settlor, only so much (if any) of any capital payment taken into account for the purposes of paragraph 8 above as, on a just and reasonable apportionment, is properly referable to property originating from the settlor shall be taken into account in computing the amount charged to beneficiaries.

12(5) Expressions used in this paragraph and section 10A have the same meanings in this paragraph as in that section; and paragraph 8 of Schedule 5 shall apply for the construction of the references in sub-paragraph (4) above to property originating from the settlor as it applies for the purposes of that Schedule.

History – Para. 12(1)(a) substituted by FA 2013, s. 218 and Sch. 45, para. 123(3)(a), with effect if the year of departure (as defined in FA 2013, Sch. 45, Pt. 4) is the tax year 2013–14 or a subsequent tax year, subject to the transitional and saving provision in FA 2013, Sch. 45, para. 154–159.
In para. 12(1)(b), the words "year A" substituted for the words "the intervening year" by FA 2013, s. 218 and Sch. 45, para. 123(3)(b), with effect if the year of departure (as defined in FA 2013, Sch. 45, Pt. 4) is the tax year 2013–14 or a subsequent tax year, subject to the transitional and saving provision in FA 2013, Sch. 45, para. 154–159.
Para. 12(1) (together with para. 12(2) and (3)) substituted for former para. 12(1)–(3) by FA 2008, s. 25 and Sch. 7, para. 143 with effect in relation to transfers of value to which Sch. 4B applies that are made on or after 6 April 2008 (FA 2008, Sch. 7, para. 147).
In former para. 12(1)(a), the words "included in a settlement's Schedule 4C pool" substituted for the words "arising under Schedule 4B" by FA 2003, s. 163(2) and Sch. 29, para. 6(2)(a) which came into force in accordance with FA 2003, s. 163(4).
In para. 12(2), the words "period of return" substituted for the words "year of return" by FA 2013, s. 218 and Sch. 45, para. 123(4), with effect if the year of departure (as defined in FA 2013, Sch. 45, Pt. 4) is the tax year 2013–14 or a subsequent tax year, subject to the transitional and saving provision in FA 2013, Sch. 45, para. 154–159.
Para. 12(2) (together with para. 12(1) and (3)) substituted for former para. 12(1)–(3) by FA 2008, s. 25 and Sch. 7, para. 143 with effect in relation to transfers of value to which Sch. 4B applies that are made on or after 6 April 2008 (FA 2008, Sch. 7, para. 147).
In former para. 12(2), the words "the settlement's Schedule 4C gains" substituted for the words "the Schedule 4B trust gains" by FA 2003, s. 163(2) and Sch. 29, para. 6(2)(b) which came into force in accordance with FA 2003, s. 163(4).
Para. 12(3) (together with para. 12(1), (2)) substituted for former para. 12(1)–(3) by FA 2008, s. 25 and Sch. 7, para. 143 with effect in relation to transfers of value to which Sch. 4B applies that are made on or after 6 April 2008 (FA 2008, Sch. 7, para. 147).
In former para. 12(3), the words "any relevant settlement" substituted for the words "the transferor or transferee settlements" by FA 2003, s. 163(2) and Sch. 29, para. 6(2)(c) which came into force in accordance with FA 2003, s. 163(4).
Para. 12 inserted by FA 2000, s. 92(4) and Sch. 26, para. 1 with effect in relation to any transfer of value in relation to which the material time is on or after 21 March 2000.

ATTRIBUTION OF GAINS TO BENEFICIARIES IN SECTION 10A CASES

12A(1) This paragraph applies where by virtue of section 10A an amount of gains would (apart from this Schedule) be treated under section 87 as accruing to a person (**"the beneficiary"**) in the period of return by virtue of a capital payment made to him in the temporary period of non-residence.

12A(2) Where this paragraph applies, a capital payment equal to so much of that capital payment as exceeds the amount otherwise charged shall be deemed for the purposes of this Schedule to be made to the beneficiary in the year of return.

12A(3) The **"amount otherwise charged"** means the total of any chargeable gains attributed to the beneficiary under section 87(2) or 89(2) by virtue of the capital payment.

12A(4) For the purposes of paragraph 13(5)(b) a deemed capital payment under this paragraph shall be treated as made when the actual capital payment mentioned in sub-paragraph (1) above was made.

12A(5) Expressions used in this paragraph and section 10A have the same meanings in this paragraph as in that section.

History – In para. 12A(1), the words "period of return" substituted for the words "year of return" by FA 2013, s. 218 and Sch. 45, para. 123(5)(a), with effect if the year of departure (as defined in FA 2013, Sch. 45, Pt. 4) is the tax year 2013–14 or a subsequent tax year, subject to the transitional and saving provision in FA 2013, Sch. 45, para. 154–159.
In para. 12A(1), the words "the temporary period of non-residence" substituted for the words "an intervening year" by FA 2013, s. 218 and Sch. 45, para. 123(5)(b), with effect if the year of departure (as defined in FA 2013, Sch. 45, Pt. 4) is the tax year 2013–14 or a subsequent tax year, subject to the transitional and saving provision in FA 2013, Sch. 45, para. 154–159.
In para. 12A(3), the words "87(2)" substituted for "87(4)" by FA 2008, s. 25 and Sch. 7, para. 144 with effect in relation to transfers of value to which Sch. 4B applies that are made on or after 6 April 2008 (FA 2008, Sch. 7, para. 147).
Para. 12A inserted by FA 2003, s. 163(2) and Sch. 29, para. 4(2) which came into force in accordance with FA 2003, s. 163(4).

INCREASE IN TAX PAYABLE UNDER THIS SCHEDULE

13(1) This paragraph applies if–

(a) chargeable gains are treated under paragraph 8 as accruing to a beneficiary by virtue of the matching (under section 87A) of all or part of a capital payment with the section 2(2) amount for a tax year ("the relevant tax year"), and

(b) the beneficiary is charged to tax by virtue of the matching.

13(1A) Where part of a capital payment is matched, references in sub-paragraphs (2) and (3) to the capital payment are to the part matched.

13(2) The tax payable by the beneficiary in respect of the payment shall be increased by the amount found under sub-paragraph (3) below, except that it shall not be increased beyond the amount of the payment; and an assessment may charge tax accordingly.

13(3) The amount is one equal to the interest that would be yielded if an amount equal to the tax which would be payable by the beneficiary in respect of the payment (apart from this paragraph) carried interest for the chargeable period at the specified rate.

The **"specified rate"** means the rate for the time being specified in section 91(3).

13(4) The chargeable period is the period which–

(a) begins with the later of the 2 days specified in sub-paragraph (5) below, and

(b) ends with 30th November in the year of assessment following that in which the capital payment is made.

13(5) The 2 days are–

(a) 1st December in the tax year immediately after the relevant tax year, and

(b) 1st December falling 6 years before 1st December in the year of assessment following that in which the capital payment is made.

History – Para. 13(1) (together with para. 13(1A)) substituted for former para. 13(1) by FA 2008, s. 25 and Sch. 7, para. 145(2) with effect in relation to transfers of value to which Sch. 4B applies that are made on or after 6 April 2008 (FA 2008, Sch. 7, para. 147).
Para. 13(1A) (together with para. 13(1)) substituted for former para. 13(1) by FA 2008, s. 25 and Sch. 7, para. 145(2) with effect in relation to transfers of value to which Sch. 4B applies that are made on or after 6 April 2008 (FA 2008, Sch. 7, para. 147).
In para. 13(5)(a), the words "tax year immediately after the relevant tax year," substituted for "year of assessment following the year of the gain (determined in accordance with paragraph 8B(3))," by FA 2008, s. 25 and Sch. 7, para. 145(3) with effect in relation to transfers of value to which Sch. 4B applies that are made on or after 6 April 2008 (FA 2008, Sch. 7, para. 147).
In para. 13(5)(a), the words "the year of the gain (determined in accordance with paragraph 8B(3))" substituted for the words "that in which the transfer of value was made" by FA 2003, s. 163(2) and Sch. 29, para. 6(3) which came into force in accordance with FA 2003, s. 163(4).
Para. 13 inserted by FA 2000, s. 92(4) and Sch. 26, para. 1 with effect in relation to any transfer of value in relation to which the material time is on or after 21 March 2000.

EFFECT OF SETTLEMENT CEASING TO EXIST AFTER TRANSFER OF VALUE

13A Where a settlement ceases to exist after the trustees have made a transfer of value to which Schedule 4B applies, this Schedule has effect as if a year of assessment had ended immediately before the settlement ceased to exist.

History – Para. 13A inserted by FA 2003, s. 163(2) and Sch. 29, para. 6(4) which came into force in accordance with FA 2003, s. 163(4).

INTERPRETATION

14(1) In this Schedule–

(a) **"transfer of value"** has the same meaning as in Schedule 4B; and

(b) references to the time at which a transfer of value was made are to the time which is the material time for the purposes of that Schedule.

14(2) In this Schedule, in relation to a transfer of value–

(a) references to the transferor settlement are to the settlement the trustees of which made the transfer of value; and

(b) references to a transferee settlement are to any settlement of which the settled property includes property representing, directly or indirectly, the proceeds of the transfer of value.

14(3) References in this Schedule to beneficiaries of a settlement include–

(a) persons who have ceased to be beneficiaries by the time the chargeable gains accrue, and

(b) persons who were beneficiaries of the settlement before it ceased to exist,

but who were beneficiaries of the settlement at a time in a previous year of assessment when a capital payment was made to them.

History – Para. 14 inserted by FA 2000, s. 92(4) and Sch. 26, para. 1 with effect in relation to any transfer of value in relation to which the material time is on or after 21 March 2000.

SCHEDULE 5 – ATTRIBUTION OF GAINS TO SETTLORS WITH INTEREST IN NON-RESIDENT OR DUAL RESIDENT SETTLEMENT

Section 86

CONSTRUCTION OF SECTION 86(1)(e)

1(1) In construing section 86(1)(e) as regards a particular year of assessment, the effect of section 3 shall be ignored.

1(2) In construing section 86(1)(e) as regards a particular year of assessment–

(a) any deductions provided for by section 2(2) shall be made in respect of disposals of any of the settled property originating from the settlor, and

(b) section 16(3) shall be assumed not to prevent losses accruing to trustees in one year of assessment from being allowed as a deduction from chargeable gains accruing in a later year of assessment (so far as not previously set against gains).

1(3) In a case where–

(a) the trustees are participators in a company in respect of property which originates from the settlor, and

(b) under section 13 gains or losses would be treated as accruing to the trustees in a particular year of assessment by virtue of so much of their interest as participators as arises from that property if the assumption as to residence specified in section 86(3) were made,

the gains or losses shall be taken into account in construing section 86(1)(e) as regards that year as if they had accrued by virtue of disposals of settled property originating from the settlor. Subsections (12) and (13) of section 13 shall apply for the purposes of this sub-paragraph as they apply for the purposes of that section.

1(4) Where, as regards a particular year of assessment, there would be an amount under section 86(1)(e) (apart from this sub-paragraph) and the trustees fall within section 86(2)(b), the following rules shall apply–

(a) assume that the references in section 86(1)(e) and sub-paragraphs (2)(a) and (3) above to settled property originating from the settlor were to such of it as constitutes protected assets;

(b) assume that the reference in sub-paragraph (3)(a) above to shares originating from the settlor were to such of them as constitute protected assets;

(c) find the amount (if any) which would be arrived at under section 86(1)(e) on those assumptions;

(d) if no amount is so found there shall be deemed to be no amount for the purposes of section 86(1)(e);

(e) if an amount is found under paragraph (c) above it must be compared with the amount arrived at under section 86(1)(e) apart from this sub-paragraph and the smaller of the 2 shall be taken to be the amount arrived at under section 86(1)(e).

1(5) Sub-paragraphs (2) to (4) above shall have effect subject to sub-paragraphs (6) and (7) below.

1(6) The following rules shall apply in construing section 86(1)(e) as regards a particular year of assessment ("the year concerned") in a case where the trustees fall within section 86(2)(a)–

(a) if the conditions mentioned in section 86(1) are not fulfilled as regards the settlement in any year of assessment falling before the year concerned, no deductions shall be made in respect of losses accruing before the year concerned;

(b) if the conditions mentioned in section 86(1) are fulfilled as regards the settlement in any year or years of assessment falling before the year concerned, no deductions shall be made in respect of losses accruing before that year (or the first of those years) so falling,

but nothing in the preceding provisions of this sub-paragraph shall prevent deductions being made in respect of losses accruing in a year of assessment in which the conditions mentioned in section 86(1)(a) to (d) and (f) are fulfilled as regards the settlement.

1(7) In construing section 86(1)(e) as regards a particular year of assessment and in relation to a settlement created before 19th March 1991, no account shall be taken of disposals made before 19th March 1991 (whether for the purpose of arriving at gains or for the purpose of arriving at losses).

1(8) For the purposes of sub-paragraph (4) above assets are **protected assets** if–

(a) they are of a description specified in the arrangements mentioned in section 86(2)(b), and

(b) were the trustees to dispose of them at any relevant time, the trustees would fall to be regarded for the purposes of the arrangements as not liable in the United Kingdom to tax on gains accruing to them on the disposal.

1(9) For the purposes of sub-paragraph (8) above–

(a) the assumption as to residence specified in section 86(3) shall be ignored;

(b) a **relevant time** is any time, in the year of assessment concerned, when the trustees fall to be regarded for the purposes of the arrangements as resident in a territory outside the United Kingdom;

(c) if different assets are identified by reference to different relevant times, all of them are protected assets.

History – In para. 1(1), reference to s. 77–79 omitted by FA 2008, s. 8 and Sch. 2, para. 10 with effect from 2008–09 (FA 2008, Sch. 2, para. 22).

In para. 1(3)(a), the words "are participators in…property which originates" were substituted by FA 1996, s 174(10)(a), in relation to gains accruing on or after 28 November 1995.

In para. 1(3)(b), the words "so much of their…from that property " were substituted by FA 1996, s. 174(10)(b), in relation to gains accruing on or after 28 November 1995.

In para. 1(3), at the end, the words "Subsections (12) and (13)…of that section." were inserted by FA 1996, s. 174(10)(c), in relation to gains accruing on or after 28 November 1995.

Derivations – FA 1991, Sch. 16, para. 3.

Cross references – S. 2(2): deduction for current year and brought forward losses.
S. 3: annual exempt amount.
S. 13: attribution of gains or losses to members of non-resident companies.
S. 16(3): losses of persons not resident or ordinarily resident are not allowable except to the extent that any gain would be charged as attributable to UK assets of a UK branch etc.
S. 77–79: charge on settlor with an interest in possession.

TEST WHETHER SETTLOR HAS INTEREST

2(1) For the purposes of section 86(1)(d) a settlor has an interest in a settlement if–

(a) any relevant property which is or may at any time be comprised in the settlement is, or will or may become, applicable for the benefit of or payable to a defined person in any circumstances whatever,

(b) any relevant income which arises or may arise under the settlement is, or will or may become, applicable for the benefit of or payable to a defined person in any circumstances whatever, or

(c) any defined person enjoys a benefit directly or indirectly from any relevant property which is comprised in the settlement or any relevant income arising under the settlement;

but this sub-paragraph is subject to sub-paragraphs (4) to (6) and paragraph 2A below.

2(2) For the purposes of sub-paragraph (1) above–

(a) relevant property is property originating from the settlor,

(b) relevant income is income originating from the settlor.

2(3) For the purposes of sub-paragraph (1) above each of the following is a defined person–

(a) the settlor,

(b) the settlor's spouse or civil partner;

(c) any child of the settlor or of the settlor's spouse or civil partner;

(d) the spouse or civil partner of any such child;

(da) any grandchild of the settlor or of the settlor's spouse or civil partner;

(db) the spouse or civil partner of any such grandchild;

(e) a company controlled by a person or persons falling within paragraphs (a) to (db) above;

(f) a company associated with a company falling within paragraph (e) above.

2(4) A settlor does not have an interest in a settlement by virtue of paragraph (a) of sub-paragraph (1) above at any time when none of the property concerned can become applicable or payable as mentioned in that paragraph except in the event of–

(a) the bankruptcy of some person who is or may become beneficially entitled to the property.

(b) any assignment of or charge on the property being made or given by some such person,

(c) in the case of a marriage settlement or civil partnership settlement, the death of both parties to the marriage or civil partnership and of all or any of the children of the family of the parties to the marriage or civil partnership, or

(d) the death under the age of 25 or some lower age of some person who would be beneficially entitled to the property on attaining that age.

2(4A) In sub-paragraph (4) **"child of the family"**, in relation to parties to a marriage or civil partner, means a child of one or both of them.

2(5) A settlor does not have an interest in a settlement by virtue of paragraph (a) of sub-paragraph (1) above at any time when some person is alive and under the age of 25 if during that person's life none of the property concerned can become applicable or payable as mentioned in that paragraph except in the event of that person becoming bankrupt or assigning or charging his interest in the property concerned.

2(6) Sub-paragraphs (4) and (5) above apply for the purposes of paragraph (b) of sub-paragraph (1) above as they apply for the purposes of paragraph (a), reading "income" for "property".

2(7) In this paragraph–

"child" includes a stepchild; and

"grandchild" means a child of a child.

2(8) For the purposes of sub-paragraph (3) above the question whether a company is controlled by a person or persons shall be construed in accordance with sections 450 and 451 of CTA 2010; but in deciding that question for those purposes no rights or powers of (or attributed to) an associate or associates of a person shall be attributed to him under section 451(4) to (6) of CTA 2010 if he is not a participator in the company.

2(9) For the purposes of sub-paragraph (3) above the question whether a company is associated with another shall be construed in accordance with section 449 of CTA 2010; but where in deciding that question for those purposes it falls to be decided whether a company is controlled by a person or persons, no rights or powers of (or attributed to) an associate or associates of a person shall be attributed to him under section 451(4) to (6) of CTA 2010 if he is not a participator in the company.

2(10) In sub-paragraphs (8) and (9) **"participator"** has the meaning given by section 454 of CTA 2010.

History – In para. 2(1) words "and paragraph 2A" inserted by FA 1998, s. 131 and Sch. 22, para. 2(1) with effect for 1998–99 and subsequent years, and with deemed effect for 1997–98.
In para. 2(3) the words "or civil partner" inserted five times by SI 2005/3229, reg. 126(2)(a), with effect from 5 December 2005.
Para. 2(3)(da) and (db) inserted, and para. 2(7) substituted, by FA 1998, s. 131 with effect for 1998–99 and subsequent years, and with deemed effect for 1997–98.
Para. 2(4)(c) substituted by SI 2005/3229, reg. 126(2)(b), with effect from 5 December 2005.
Para. 2(4A) inserted by SI 2005/3229, reg. 126(2)(c), with effect from 5 December 2005.
In para. 2(8), the words "sections 450 and 451 of CTA 2010" substituted for "section 416 of the Taxes Act" by CTA 2010, s. 1177 and Sch. 1, para. 266(2)(a)(i), with effect for corporation tax purposes for accounting periods ending on or after 1 April 2010, and for income tax and capital gains tax purposes for the tax year 2010–11 and subsequent tax years.
In para. 2(8), the words "section 451(4) to (6) of CTA 2010" substituted for "section 416(6)" by CTA 2010, s. 1177 and Sch. 1, para. 266(2)(a)(ii), with effect for corporation tax purposes for accounting periods ending on or after 1 April 2010, and for income tax and capital gains tax purposes for the tax year 2010–11 and subsequent tax years.
In para. 2(9), the words "section 449 of CTA 2010" substituted for "section 416 of the Taxes Act" by CTA 2010, s. 1177 and Sch. 1, para. 266(2)(b)(i), with effect for corporation tax purposes for accounting periods ending on or after 1 April 2010, and for income tax and capital gains tax purposes for the tax year 2010–11 and subsequent tax years.
In para. 2(9), the words "section 451(4) to (6) of CTA 2010" substituted for "section 416(6)" by CTA 2010, s. 1177 and Sch. 1, para. 266(2)(b)(ii), with effect for corporation tax purposes for accounting periods ending on or after 1 April 2010, and for income tax and capital gains tax purposes for the tax year 2010–11 and subsequent tax years.
In para. 2(10), the words "section 454 of CTA 2010" substituted for "section 417(1) of the Taxes Act" by CTA 2010, s. 1177 and Sch. 1, para. 266(2)(c), with effect for corporation tax purposes for accounting periods ending on or after 1 April 2010, and for income tax and capital gains tax purposes for the tax year 2010–11 and subsequent tax years.

Derivations – FA 1991, Sch. 16, para. 4.

Cross references – ICTA 1988, s. 416, 417: control by reference to the company's affairs but, in particular, entitlement etc. to the majority of share capital, issued share capital, voting power, income or assets; participator as a person having a share or interest in the capital or income of the company etc.
Civil Partnership Act 2004, Sch. 21, para. 54: references to an individual's stepchildren to include references to children of that individual's civil partner; in force from 5 December 2005.

Other material – ICAEW Tax Faculty, Guidance Note TAX 20/92 (not reproduced): Revenue view that where there is no prima facie possibility of a defined person (para. 2(3)) benefiting, the settlor will not be treated as having an interest unless circumstances etc. indicate intention to benefit someone who may become a defined person in the future.

Notes – S. 288: interpretation, including "the Taxes Act" as ICTA 1988.

SETTLEMENTS CREATED BEFORE 17TH MARCH 1998

2A(1) In determining for the purposes of section 86(1)(d) whether the settlor has an interest at any time during any year of assessment in a settlement created before 17th March 1998, paragraphs (da) and (db) of paragraph 2(3) above, and the reference to those paragraphs in paragraph 2(3)(e), shall be disregarded unless–

(a) that year is a year in which one of the four conditions set out in the following provisions of this paragraph becomes fulfilled as regards the settlement; or

(b) one of those conditions became fulfilled as regards that settlement in any previous year of assessment ending on or after 5th April 1998.

2A(2) The first condition is (subject to sub-paragraph (3) below) that on or after 17th March 1998 property or income is provided directly or indirectly for the purposes of the settlement–

(a) otherwise than under a transaction entered into at arm's length, and

(b) otherwise than in pursuance of a liability incurred by any person before that date.

2A(3) For the purposes of the first condition, where the settlement's expenses relating to administration and taxation for a year of assessment exceed its income for the year, property or income provided towards meeting those expenses shall be ignored if the value of the property or income so provided does not exceed the difference between the amount of those expenses and the amount of the settlement's income for the year.

2A(4) The second condition is that–

(a) the trustees cease on or after 17 March 1998 to be resident in the United Kingdom, or

(b) the trustees, while continuing to be resident in the United Kingdom, become on or after 17th March 1998 trustees who fall to be regarded for the purposes of any double taxation relief arrangements as resident in a territory outside the United Kingdom.

2A(5) The third condition is that on or after 17th March 1998 the terms of the settlement are varied so that any person falling within sub-paragraph (7) below becomes for the first time a person who will or might benefit from the settlement.

2A(6) The fourth condition is that–

(a) on or after 17th March 1998 a person falling within sub-paragraph (7) below enjoys a benefit from the settlement for the first time, and

(b) the person concerned is not one who (looking only at the terms of the settlement immediately before 17th March 1998) would be capable of enjoying a benefit from the settlement on or after that date.

2A(7) Each of the following persons falls within this sub-paragraph–

(a) any grandchild of the settlor or of the settlor's spouse or civil partner;

(b) the spouse or civil partner of any such grandchild;

(c) a company controlled by a person or persons falling within paragraph (a) or (b) above;

(d) a company controlled by any such person or persons together with any person or persons (not so falling) each of whom is for the purposes of paragraph 2(1) above a defined person in relation to the settlement;

(e) a company associated with a company falling within paragraph (c) or (d) above.

2A(8) For the purposes of sub-paragraph (7) above the question whether a company is controlled by a person or persons shall be construed in accordance with sections 450 and 451 of CTA 2010; but in deciding that question for those purposes no rights or powers of (or attributed to) an associate or associates of a person shall be attributed to him under section 451(4) to (6) of CTA 2010 if he is not a participator in the company.

2A(9) For the purposes of sub-paragraph (7) above the question whether one company is associated with another shall be construed in accordance with section 449 of CTA 2010; but where in deciding that question for those purposes it falls to be decided whether a company is controlled by a person or persons, no rights or powers of (or attributed to) an associate or associates of a person shall be attributed to him under section 451(4) to (6) of CTA 2010 if he is not a participator in the company.

2A(10) In this paragraph–

"child" includes a step-child;

"grandchild" means a child of a child;

"participator" has the meaning given by section 454 of CTA 2010.

History – In para. 2A(4)(a), the words "cease on or after 17 March 1998 to be resident" substituted for the words "become on or after 17th March 1998 neither resident nor ordinarily resident" by FA 2013, s. 219 and Sch. 46, para. 108(2)(a), with effect in relation to a person's liability to capital gains tax for the tax year 2013–14 or any subsequent tax year, without prejudice to any provision in FA 2013, Sch. 46, Pt. 3 about the application of a particular amendment.

In para. 2A(4)(b), the words "and ordinarily resident" by FA 2013, s. 219 and Sch. 46, para. 108(2)(b), with effect in relation to a person's liability to capital gains tax for the tax year 2013–14 or any subsequent tax year, without prejudice to any provision in FA 2013, Sch. 46, Pt. 3 about the application of a particular amendment.

In para. 2A(7)(a) and (b) the words "or civil partner" inserted by SI 2005/3229, reg. 126(3), with effect from 5 December 2005.

Para. 2A inserted by FA 1998, s. 131 and Sch. 22, para. 2(2) with effect for 1998–99 and subsequent years, and with deemed effect for 1997–98.

In para. 2A(8), the words "sections 450 and 451 of CTA 2010" substituted for "section 416 of the Taxes Act" by CTA 2010, s. 1177 and Sch. 1, para. 266(3)(a)(i), with effect for corporation tax purposes for accounting periods ending on or after 1 April 2010, and for income tax and capital gains tax purposes for the tax year 2010–11 and subsequent tax years.

In para. 2A(8), the words "section 451(4) to (6) of CTA 2010" substituted for "section 416(6)" by CTA 2010, s. 1177 and Sch. 1, para. 266(3)(a)(ii), with effect for corporation tax purposes for accounting periods ending on or after 1 April 2010, and for income tax and capital gains tax purposes for the tax year 2010–11 and subsequent tax years.

In para. 2A(9), the words "section 449 of CTA 2010" substituted for "section 416 of the Taxes Act" by CTA 2010, s. 1177 and Sch. 1, para. 266(3)(b)(i), with effect for corporation tax purposes for accounting periods ending on or after 1 April 2010, and for income tax and capital gains tax purposes for the tax year 2010-11 and subsequent tax years.

In para. 2A(9), the words "section 451(4) to (6) of CTA 2010" substituted for "section 416(6)" by CTA 2010, s. 1177 and Sch. 1, para. 266(3)(b)(ii), with effect for corporation tax purposes for accounting periods ending on or after 1 April 2010, and for income tax and capital gains tax purposes for the tax year 2010–11 and subsequent tax years.

In para. 2A(10), in the definition of "participator", the words "section 454 of CTA 2010" substituted for "section 417(1) of the Taxes Act" by CTA 2010, s. 1177 and Sch. 1, para. 266(3)(c),with effect for corporation tax purposes for accounting periods ending on or after 1 April 2010, and for income tax and capital gains tax purposes for the tax year 2010–11 and subsequent tax years.

Cross references – Civil Partnership Act 2004, Sch. 21, para. 54: references to an individual's stepchildren to include references to children of that individual's civil partner; in force from 5 December 2005.

EXCEPTIONS FROM SECTION 86

3 Section 86 does not apply if the settlor dies in the year.

Derivations – FA 1991, Sch. 16, para. 5.

4(1) This paragraph applies where for the purposes of section 86(1)(d) the settlor has no interest in the settlement at any time in the year except for one of the following reasons, namely, that–

(a) property is, or will or may become, applicable for the benefit of or payable to one of the persons falling within paragraph 2(3)(b) to (db) above,

(b) income is, or will or may become, applicable for the benefit of or payable to one of those persons, or

(c) one of those persons enjoys a benefit from property or income.

4(2) This paragraph also applies where sub-paragraph (1) above is fulfilled by virtue of 2 or all of paragraphs (a) to (c) being satisfied by reference to the same person.

4(3) Where this paragraph applies, section 86 does not apply if the person concerned dies in the year.

4(4) In a case where–

(a) this paragraph applies, and

(b) the person concerned falls within paragraph 2(3)(b), (d) or (db) above,

section 86 does not apply if during the year the person concerned ceases to be married to, or a civil partner of the settlor, child or grandchild concerned (as the case may be).

History – In para. 4(1)(a), "(db)" substituted for "(d)"; and in para. 4(4), "(d) or (db)" substituted for "or (d)", and "child or grandchild" substituted for "or child" by FA 1998, s. 131 and Sch. 22, para. 3 with effect for 1998–99 and subsequent years, and with deemed effect for 1997–98.

In para. 4(4) the words ", or a civil partner of" inserted by SI 2005/3229, reg. 126(4), with effect from 5 December 2005.

Derivations – FA 1991, Sch. 16, para. 6.

5(1) This paragraph applies where for the purposes of section 86(1)(d) the settlor has no interest in the settlement at any time in the year except for the reason that there are 2 or more persons, each of whom–

(a) falls within paragraph 2(3)(b) to (db) above, and

(b) stands to gain for the reason stated in sub-paragraph (2) below.

5(2) The reason is that–

(a) property is, or will or may become, applicable for his benefit or payable to him,

(b) income is, or will or may become, applicable for his benefit or payable to him,

(c) he enjoys a benefit from property or income, or

(d) 2 or all of paragraphs (a) to (c) above apply in his case.

5(3) Where this paragraph applies, section 86 does not apply if each of the persons concerned dies in the year.

History – In para. 5(1)(a), "(db)" substituted for "(d)" by FA 1998, s. 131 and Sch. 22, para. 3(1) with effect for 1998–99 and subsequent years, and with deemed effect for 1997–98.

Derivations – FA 1991, Sch. 16, para. 7.

RIGHT OF RECOVERY

6(1) This paragraph applies where any tax becomes chargeable on, and is paid by, a person in respect of gains treated as accruing to him in a year under section 86(4).

6(2) The person shall be entitled to recover the amount of the tax from any person who is a trustee of the settlement.

6(3) For the purposes of recovering that amount, the person shall also be entitled to require an inspector to give him a certificate specifying–

(a) the amount of the gains concerned, and

(b) the amount of tax paid,

and any such certificate shall be conclusive evidence of the facts stated in it.

Derivations – FA 1991, Sch. 16, para. 8.

Cross references – FA 2002, Sch. 11, para. 8: election for deduction of personal losses from gains accruing to settlors to apply for years before 2003–04.

Statements of practice – SP 5/92: settlor's right of reimbursement under para. 6 is not regarded as creating an interest in a trust for the settlor under ICTA 1988, Pt. XV, subject to conditions; nor is the settlor brought within ICTA 1988, s. 677, 739 and 740; nor does a capital payment under s. 97 arise.

MEANING OF "SETTLOR"

7 For the purposes of section 86 and this Schedule, a person is a **settlor** in relation to a settlement if the settled property consists of or includes property originating from him.

Derivations – FA 1991, Sch. 16, para. 9.

MEANING OF "ORIGINATING"

8(1) References in section 86 and this Schedule to property **originating** from a person are references to–

(a) property provided by that person;

(b) property representing property falling within paragraph (a) above;

(c) so much of any property representing both property falling within paragraph (a) above and other property as, on a just apportionment, can be taken to represent property so falling.

8(2) References in this Schedule to income **originating** from a person are references to–

(a) income from property originating from that person;

(b) income provided by that person.

8(3) Where a person who is a settlor in relation to a settlement makes reciprocal arrangements with another person for the provision of property or income, for the purposes of this paragraph–

(a) property or income provided by the other person in pursuance of the arrangements shall be treated as provided by the settlor, but

(b) property or income provided by the settlor in pursuance of the arrangements shall be treated as provided by the other person (and not by the settlor).

8(4) For the purposes of this paragraph–

(a) where property is provided by a qualifying company controlled by one person alone at the time it is provided, that person shall be taken to provide it;

(b) where property is provided by a qualifying company controlled by 2 or more persons (taking each one separately) at the time it is provided, those persons shall be taken to provide the property and each one shall be taken to provide an equal share of it;

(c) where property is provided by a qualifying company controlled by 2 or more persons (taking them together) at the time it is provided, the persons who are participators in the company at the time it is provided shall be taken to provide it and each one shall be taken to provide so much of it as is attributed to him on the basis of a just apportionment;

but where a person would be taken to provide less than one-twentieth of any property by virtue of paragraph (c) above and apart from this provision, he shall not be taken to provide any of it by virtue of that paragraph.

8(5) For the purposes of sub-paragraph (4) above a qualifying company is a close company or a company which would be a close company if it were resident in the United Kingdom.

8(6) For the purposes of this paragraph references to property representing other property include references to property representing accumulated income from that other property.

8(7) For the purposes of this paragraph property or income is provided by a person if it is provided directly or indirectly by the person.

8(8) For the purposes of this paragraph the question whether a company is controlled by a person or persons shall be construed in accordance with sections 450 and 451 of CTA 2010; but in deciding that question for those purposes no rights or powers of (or attributed to) an associate or associates of a person shall be attributed to him under section 451(4) to (6) of CTA 2010 if he is not a participator in the company.

8(9) In this paragraph **"participator"** has the meaning given by section 454 of CTA 2010.

8(10) [Repealed by FA 1996, s. 205 and Sch. 41, Pt. V(30).]

History – In para. 8(8), the words "sections 450 and 451 of CTA 2010" substituted for "section 416 of the Taxes Act" by CTA 2010, s. 1177 and Sch. 1, para. 266(4)(a)(i), with effect for corporation tax purposes for accounting periods ending on or after 1 April 2010, and for income tax and capital gains tax purposes for the tax year 2010–11 and subsequent tax years.

In para. 8(8), the words "section 451(4) to (6) of CTA 2010" substituted for "section 416(6)" by CTA 2010, s. 1177 and Sch. 1, para. 266(4)(b)(ii), with effect for corporation tax purposes for accounting periods ending on or after 1 April 2010, and for income tax and capital gains tax purposes for the tax year 2010–11 and subsequent tax years.

In para. 8(9), the words "section 454 of CTA 2010" substituted for "section 417(1) of the Taxes Act" by CTA 2010, s. 1177 and Sch. 1, para. 266(4)(b), with effect for corporation tax purposes for accounting periods ending on or after 1 April 2010, and for income tax and capital gains tax purposes for the tax year 2010–11 and subsequent tax years.

Para. 8(10) repealed by FA 1996, s. 205 and Sch. 41, Pt. V(30), with effect in relation to gains accruing after 27 November 1995.

Derivations – FA 1991, Sch. 16, para. 10.

Cross references – ICTA 1988, s. 416, 417: control by reference to the company's affairs but, in particular, entitlement etc. to the majority of share capital, issued share capital, voting power, income or assets; participator as a person having a share or interest in the capital or income of the company etc.

FA 1998, Sch 23, para. 6(6): application of para. 8 to transitional rules relating to charge on settlors of pre-19 March 1991 settlements.

Extra-statutory concessions – D40: in applying s. 96 and Sch. 5, para. 8, a trust beneficiary not regarded as a participator in a company solely because of his beneficiary status.

Notes – S. 288: interpretation, including "the Taxes Act" as ICTA 1988.

QUALIFYING SETTLEMENTS, AND COMMENCEMENT

9(1) A settlement created on or after 19th March 1991 is a **qualifying settlement** for the purposes of section 86 and this Schedule in–

(a) the year of assessment in which it is created, and

(b) subsequent years of assessment.

9(1A) Subject to sub-paragraph (1B) below, a settlement created before 19th March 1991 is a qualifying settlement for the purposes of section 86 and this Schedule in–

(a) the year 1999–00, and

(b) subsequent years of assessment.

9(1B) Where a settlement created before 19th March 1991 is a protected settlement immediately after the beginning of 6th April 1999, that settlement shall be treated as a qualifying settlement for the purposes of section 86 and this Schedule in a year of assessment mentioned in sub-paragraph (1A)(a) or (b) above only if–

(a) any of the five conditions set out in subsections (3) to (6A) below becomes fulfilled as regards the settlement in that year; or

(b) any of those five conditions became so fulfilled in any previous year of assessment ending after 19th March 1991.

9(2) [Repealed by FA 1998, s. 132(2), s. 165 and Sch. 27, Pt. III(30).]

9(3) The first condition is that on or after 19th March 1991 property or income is provided directly or indirectly for the purposes of the settlement–

(a) otherwise than under a transaction entered into at arm's length, and

(b) otherwise than in pursuance of a liability incurred by any person before that date;

but if the settlement's expenses relating to administration and taxation for a year of assessment exceed its income for the year, property or income provided towards meeting those expenses shall be ignored for the purposes of this condition if the value of the property or income so provided does not exceed the difference between the amount of those expenses and the amount of the settlement's income for the year.

9(4) The second condition is that–

(a) the trustees cease on or after 19 March 1991 to be resident in the United Kingdom, or

(b) the trustees, while continuing to be resident in the United Kingdom, become on or after 19th March 1991 trustees who fall to be regarded for the purposes of any double taxation relief arrangements as resident in a territory outside the United Kingdom.

9(5) The third condition is that on or after 19th March 1991 the terms of the settlement are varied so that any person falling within sub-paragraph (7) below becomes for the first time a person who will or might benefit from the settlement.

9(6) The fourth condition is that–

(a) on or after 19th March 1991 a person falling within sub-paragraph (7) below enjoys a benefit from the settlement for the first time, and

(b) the person concerned is not one who (looking only at the terms of the settlement immediately before 19th March 1991) would be capable of enjoying a benefit from the settlement on or after that date.

9(6A) The fifth condition is that the settlement ceases to be a protected settlement at any time on or after 6th April 1999.

9(7) Each of the following persons falls within this sub-paragraph–

(a) a settlor;

(b) the spouse or civil partner of a settlor;

(c) any child of a settlor or of a settlor's spouse or civil partner;

(d) the spouse or civil partner of any such child;

(da) any grandchild of a settlor or of a settlor's spouse or civil partner;

(db) the spouse or civil partner of any such grandchild;

(e) a company controlled by a person or persons falling within paragraphs (a) to (db) above;

(f) a company associated with a company falling within paragraph (e) above.

9(8) [Repealed by FA 1998, s. 165 and Sch. 27, Pt. III(30).]

9(9) For the purposes of sub-paragraph (7) above the question whether a company is controlled by a person or persons shall be construed in accordance with sections 450 and 451 of CTA 2010; but in deciding that question for those purposes no rights or powers of (or attributed to) an associate or associates of a person shall be attributed to him under section 451(4) to (6) of CTA 2010 if he is not a participator in the company.

9(10) For the purposes of sub-paragraph (7) above the question whether one company is associated with another shall be construed in accordance with section 449 of CTA 2010; but where in deciding that question for those purposes it falls to be decided whether a company is controlled by a person or persons, no rights or powers of (or attributed to) an associate or associates of a person shall be attributed to him under section 451(4) to (6) of CTA 2010 if he is not a participator in the company.

9(10A) Subject to sub-paragraph (10B) below, a settlement is a protected settlement at any time in a year of assessment if at that time the beneficiaries of that settlement are confined to persons falling within some or all of the following descriptions, that is to say–

(a) children of a settlor or of a spouse or civil partner of a settlor who are under the age of eighteen at that time or who were under that age at the end of the immediately preceding year of assessment;

(b) unborn children of a settlor, of a spouse or civil partner of a settlor, or of a future spouse or civil partner of a settlor;

(c) future spouses or civil partners of any children or future children of a settlor, a spouse or civil partner of a settlor or any future spouse or civil partner of a settlor;

(d) a future spouse or civil partner of a settlor;

(e) persons outside the defined categories.

9(10B) For the purposes of sub-paragraph (10A) above a person is outside the defined categories at any time if, and only if, there is no settlor by reference to whom he is at that time a defined person in relation to the settlement for the purposes of paragraph 2(1) above.

9(10C) For the purposes of sub-paragraph (10A) above a person is a beneficiary of a settlement if–

(a) there are any circumstances whatever in which relevant property which is or may become comprised in the settlement is or will or may become applicable for his benefit or payable to him;

(b) there are any circumstances whatever in which relevant income which arises or may arise under the settlement is or will or may become applicable for his benefit or payable to him;

(c) he enjoys a benefit directly or indirectly from any relevant property comprised in the settlement or any relevant income arising under the settlement.

9(10D) In sub-paragraph (10C) above–

"relevant property" means property originating from a settlor; and

"relevant income" means income originating from a settlor.

9(11) In this paragraph–

"child" includes a step-child;

"grandchild" means a child of a child;

"participator" has the meaning given by section 454 of CTA 2010.

History – Para. 9(1A), (1B), (6A), (10A), (10B), (10C), (10D) inserted by FA 1998, s. 132.
Para. 9(2) repealed by FA 1998, s. 132(2) s. 165 and Sch. 27, Pt. III(30), with effect for the purpose of determining whether any settlement is a qualifying settlement in the year 1999–00 or any subsequent year of assessment.
In para. 9(4)(a), the words "cease on or after 19 March 1991 to be resident" substituted for the words "become on or after 19th March 1991 neither resident nor ordinarily resident" by FA 2013, s. 219 and Sch. 46, para. 108(3)(a), with effect in relation to changes in the residence status of trustees on or after 6 April 2013.
In para. 9(4)(b), the words "and ordinarily resident" omitted by FA 2013, s. 219 and Sch. 46, para. 108(3)(b), with effect in relation to changes in the residence status of trustees on or after 6 April 2013.
In para. 9(7) the words "or civil partner" inserted four times by SI 2005/3229, reg. 126(5)(a), with effect from 5 December 2005.
In para. 9(7), subpara. (da) and (db) inserted, and in subpara. (e) "(db)" substituted for "(d)" by FA 1998, s. 131 and Sch. 22, para. 4(1) with effect for 1998–99 and subsequent years of assessment, and with deemed effect for 1997–98 – but with the proviso that the changes are disregarded for the purpose of determining whether either of the conditions in para. 9(5) and (6) became fulfilled at any time before 17 March 1998.
In para. 9(9), the words "sections 450 and 451 of CTA 2010" substituted for "section 416 of the Taxes Act" by CTA 2010, s. 1177 and Sch. 1, para. 266(5)(a)(i), with effect for corporation tax purposes for accounting periods ending on or after 1 April 2010, and for income tax and capital gains tax purposes for the tax year 2010–11 and subsequent tax years.
In para. 9(9), the words "section 451(4) to (6) of CTA 2010" substituted for "section 416(6)" by CTA 2010, s. 1177 and Sch. 1, para. 266(5)(a)(ii), with effect for corporation tax purposes for accounting periods ending on or after 1 April 2010, and for income tax and capital gains tax purposes for the tax year 2010–11 and subsequent tax years.
In para. 9(10), the words "section 449 of CTA 2010" substituted for "section 416 of the Taxes Act" by CTA 2010, s. 1177 and Sch. 1, para. 266(5)(b)(i), with effect for corporation tax purposes for accounting periods ending on or after 1 April 2010, and for income tax and capital gains tax purposes for the tax year 2010–11 and subsequent tax years.
In para. 9(10), the words "section 451(4) to (6) of CTA 2010" substituted for "section 416(6)" by CTA 2010, s. 1177 and Sch. 1, para. 266(5)(b)(ii), with effect for corporation tax purposes for accounting periods ending on or after 1 April 2010, and for income tax and capital gains tax purposes for the tax year 2010–11 and subsequent tax years.
Para.9(8) repealed by FA 1998, s. 131(4), s. 165 and Sch. 27, Pt. III(30) with effect for 1998–99 and subsequent years, and with deemed effect for 1997–98.

In para. 9(10A) the words "or civil partner" inserted six times and the words "or civil partners" inserted by SI 2005/3229, reg. 126(5)(b), with effect from 5 December 2005.
In para. 9(11), in the definition of "participator", the words "section 454 of CTA 2010" substituted for "section 417(1) of the Taxes Act" by CTA 2010, s. 1177 and Sch. 1, para. 266(5)(c), with effect for corporation tax purposes for accounting periods ending on or after 1 April 2010, and for income tax and capital gains tax purposes for the tax year 2010–11 and subsequent tax years.
Para. 9(11) substituted by FA 1998, s. 131 and Sch. 22, para. 4(2) with effect for 1998–99 and subsequent years, and with deemed effect for 1997–98.

Derivations – FA 1991, Sch. 16, para. 11.

Cross references – ICTA 1988, s. 416, 417: control by reference to the company's affairs but, in particular, entitlement etc. to the majority of share capital, issued share capital, voting power, income or assets; participator as a person having a share or interest in the capital or income of the company etc.
FA 1998, Sch 23, para. 6(3): modified application of para. 9(10A)(a) to transitional rules relating to charge on settlors of pre-19 March 1991 settlements.
Civil Partnership Act 2004, Sch. 21, para. 54: references to an individual's stepchildren to include references to children of that individual's civil partner; in force from 5 December 2005.

Extra-statutory concessions – D40: a beneficiary of a trust is not regarded as a participator in the company solely because of his status as a beneficiary.

Statements of practice – SP 5/92: trustees who became not resident and not ordinarily resident in the UK between 6 April 1990 and 18 March 1991 and remain so until after 5 April 1992 are not liable to a s. 80 charge, and are not regarded as having met the condition in para. 9(4); further clarification, including guidance on when a transaction is generally regarded as being at arm's length under, and examples of transactions outside the scope of, para. 9(3).

HMRC interpretations – IRInt. 189: HMRC do not regard the existence of the settlor's (or the settlor's spouse's) grandchildren of whatever age as beneficiaries of a pre-1991 trust as causing the settlement to fall outside the definition of a "protected settlement" for the purposes of para. 9(10A)–(10D).

Other material – ICAEW Tax Faculty Guidance Note TAX 20/92 (not reproduced): correspondence on application of SP 5/92.
Taxline 1992/96 (not reproduced): in a case where a trust had no income but a CGT liability arose under FA 1981, s. 79, Revenue confirmed that payment of this tax by the settlor was not an addition to the funds, by virtue of para. 9(3); this exemption also extends to interest and penalties on such liabilities.

Notes – S. 69: residence and ordinary residence of trustees.
S. 288: interpretation, including "the Taxes Act" as ICTA 1988.

INFORMATION

10 [Omitted by SI 2009/2035, art. 2 and Schedule, para. 35.]

History – Para. 10 omitted by SI 2009/2035, art. 2 and Schedule, para. 35, with effect from 13 August 2009.

Derivations – FA 1991, Sch. 16, para. 12.

11-14 [Repealed by FA 1994, s. 97(4) and s. 258 and Sch. 26, Pt. V(10).]

History – Para. 11–14 repealed by FA 1994, s. 97(4) and s. 258 and Sch. 26, Pt. V(10) with effect from 3 May 1994 (the date of Royal Assent to FA 1994).

SCHEDULE 5A – SETTLEMENTS WITH FOREIGN ELEMENT: INFORMATION

Section 98A

History – Sch. 5A inserted by FA 1994, s. 97(3) with effect from 3 May 1994 (the date of Royal Assent to FA 1994).

1 In this Schedule **"the commencement day"** means the day on which the Finance Act 1994 was passed.

Notes – FA 1994 was passed on 3 May 1994.

2(1) This paragraph applies if–

(a) a settlement was created before 17th March 1998,

(b) on or after the commencement day a person transfers property to the trustees otherwise than under a transaction entered into at arm's length and otherwise than in pursuance of a liability incurred by any person before that day,

(c) the trustees are not resident in the United Kingdom at the time the property is transferred, and

(d) the transferor knows, or has reason to believe, that the trustees are not so resident.

2(2) Before the expiry of the period of twelve months beginning with the relevant day, the transferor shall deliver to the Board a return which–

(a) identifies the settlement, and

(b) specifies the property transferred, the day on which the transfer was made, and the consideration (if any) for the transfer.

2(3) For the purposes of sub-paragraph (2) above the **relevant day** is the day on which the transfer is made.

History – In para. 2(1)(a), "17th March 1998" substituted for "19th March 1991" by FA 1998, Sch. 22, para. 5, with effect in relation to transfers on or after 17 March 1998.
In para. 2(1)(c), the words "not resident" substituted for the words "neither resident nor ordinarily resident" by FA 2013, s. 219 and Sch. 46, para. 109(2)(a), with effect in relation to transfers of property made on or after 6 April 2013.
In para. 2(1)(c), the words "neither resident nor ordinarily resident in the United Kingdom" substituted for "not resident or ordinarily resident in the United Kingdom" by FA 2006, s. 88 and Sch.12, para. 30(1), (2)(c) with effect in relation to transfers of property made on or after 6 April 2007 (in relation to settlements whenever created).

In para. 2(1)(d), the words "and ordinarily resident" omitted by FA 2013, s. 219 and Sch. 46, para. 109(2)(b), with effect in relation to transfers of property made on or after 6 April 2013.
In para. 2(1)(d), the words "resident and ordinarily resident" substituted for "resident or ordinarily resident" by FA 2006, s. 88 and Sch. 12, para. 30(3), with effect in relation to transfers of property made on or after 6 April 2007 (in relation to settlements whenever created).

Cross references – TMA 1970, s. 98: penalties relating to special returns.

3(1) This paragraph applies if a settlement is created on or after the commencement day, and at the time it is created–

(a) the trustees are not resident in the United Kingdom, or

(b) the trustees are resident in the United Kingdom but fall to be regarded for the purposes of any double taxation relief arrangements as resident in a territory outside the United Kingdom.

3(2) Any person who–

(a) is a settlor in relation to the settlement at the time it is created, and

(b) at that time fulfils the condition mentioned in sub-paragraph (3) below,

shall, before the expiry of the period of three months beginning with the relevant day, deliver to the Board a return specifying the particulars mentioned in sub-paragraph (4) below.

3(3) The condition is that the person concerned is domiciled in the United Kingdom and is resident in the United Kingdom.

3(4) The particulars are–

(a) the day on which the settlement was created;

(b) the name and address of the person delivering the return;

(c) the names and addresses of the persons who are the trustees immediately before the delivery of the return.

3(5) For the purposes of sub-paragraph (2) above the **relevant day** is the day on which the settlement is created.

History – In para. 3(1)(a), the words "not resident" substituted for the words "neither resident nor ordinarily resident" by FA 2013, s. 219 and Sch. 46, para. 109(3)(a)(i), with effect in relation to settlements created on or after 6 April 2013.
In para. 3(1)(a), the words "neither resident nor ordinarily resident in the United Kingdom" substituted for "not resident or ordinarily resident in the United Kingdom" by FA 2006, s. 88 and Sch. 12, para. 30(1), (2)(c) with effect in relation to settlements created on or after 6 April 2007.
In para. 3(1)(b), the words "resident and ordinarily resident in the United Kingdom" substituted for "resident or ordinarily resident in the United Kingdom" by FA 2006, s. 88 and Sch. 12, para. 34(1), (2)(g) with effect in relation to settlements created on or after 6 April 2007.
In para. 3(1)(c), the words "and ordinarily resident" omitted by FA 2013, s. 219 and Sch. 46, para. 109(3)(a)(ii), with effect in relation to settlements created on or after 6 April 2013.
In para. 3(3), the word "resident" substituted for the words "either resident or ordinarily resident" by FA 2013, s. 219 and Sch. 46, para. 109(3)(b), with effect in relation to settlements created on or after 6 April 2013.

Cross references – TMA 1970, s. 98: penalties relating to special returns.

4(1) This paragraph applies if a settlement is created on or after 19th March 1991, and at the time it is created–

(a) the trustees are not resident in the United Kingdom, or

(b) the trustees are resident in the United Kingdom in the United Kingdom but fall to be regarded for the purposes of any double taxation relief arrangements as resident in a territory outside the United Kingdom.

4(2) Any person who–

(a) is a settlor in relation to the settlement at the time it is created,

(b) at that time does not fulfil the condition mentioned in sub-paragraph (3) below, and

(c) first fulfils that condition at a time falling on or after the commencement day,

shall, before the expiry of the period of twelve months beginning with the relevant day, deliver to the Board a return specifying the particulars mentioned in sub-paragraph (4) below.

4(3) The condition is that the person concerned is domiciled in the United Kingdom and is resident in the United Kingdom.

4(4) The particulars are–

(a) the day on which the settlement was created;

(b) the name and address of the person delivering the return;

(c) the names and addresses of the persons who are the trustees immediately before the delivery of the return.

4(5) For the purposes of sub-paragraph (2) above the **relevant day** is the day on which the person first fulfils the condition as mentioned in paragraph (c) of that sub-paragraph.

History – In para. 4(1)(a), the words "not resident" substituted for the words "neither resident nor ordinarily resident" by FA 2013, s. 219 and Sch. 46, para. 109(4)(a)(i), with effect in relation to settlements created on or after 6 April 2013.

In para. 4(1)(a), the words "neither resident nor ordinarily resident in the United Kingdom" substituted for "not resident or ordinarily resident in the United Kingdom" by FA 2006, s. 88 and Sch. 12, para. 30(1), (2)(c) with effect in relation to settlements created on or after 6 April 2007.
In para. 4(1)(b), the words "and ordinarily resident" omitted by FA 2013, s. 219 and Sch. 46, para. 109(4)(a)(ii), with effect in relation to settlements created on or after 6 April 2013.
In para. 4(1)(b), the words "resident and ordinarily resident in the United Kingdom" substituted for "resident or ordinarily resident in the United Kingdom" by FA 2006, s. 88 and Sch. 12, para. 34(1), (2)(g) with effect in relation to settlements created on or after 6 April 2007.
In para. 4(3), the word "resident" substituted for the words "either resident or ordinarily resident" by FA 2013, s. 219 and Sch. 46, para. 109(4)(b), with effect in relation to settlements created on or after 6 April 2013.

Cross references – TMA 1970, s. 98: penalties relating to special returns.

5(1) This paragraph applies if–

(a) the trustees of a settlement cease at any time (the relevant time) on or after the commencement day to be resident in the United Kingdom, or

(b) the trustees of a settlement, while continuing to be resident in the United Kingdom, become at any time (the relevant time) on or after the commencement day trustees who fall to be regarded for the purposes of any double taxation relief arrangements as resident in a territory outside the United Kingdom.

5(2) Any person who was a trustee of the settlement immediately before the relevant time shall, before the expiry of the period of twelve months beginning with the relevant day, deliver to the Board a return specifying–

(a) the day on which the settlement was created,

(b) the name and address of each person who is a settlor in relation to the settlement immediately before the delivery of the return, and

(c) the names and addresses of the persons who are the trustees immediately before the delivery of the return.

5(3) For the purposes of sub-paragraph (2) above the **relevant day** is the day when the relevant time falls.

History – In para. 5(1)(a), the words "cease at any time (the relevant time) on or after the commencement day to be resident" substituted for the words "become at any time (the relevant time) on or after the commencement day neither resident nor ordinarily resident" by FA 2013, s. 219 and Sch. 46, para. 109(5)(a), with effect in relation to changes in the residence status of trustees on or after 6 April 2013.
In para. 5(1)(b), the words "and ordinarily resident" omitted by FA 2013, s. 219 and Sch. 46, para. 109(5)(b), with effect in relation to changes in the residence status of trustees on or after 6 April 2013.

Cross references – TMA 1970, s. 98: penalties relating to special returns.

6(1) Nothing in paragraph 2, 3, 4 or 5 above shall require information to be contained in the return concerned to the extent that–

(a) before the expiry of the period concerned the information has been provided to the Board by any person in pursuance of the paragraph concerned or of any other provision, or

(b) after the expiry of the period concerned the information falls to be provided to the Board by any person in pursuance of any provision other than the paragraph concerned.

6(2) Nothing in paragraph 2, 3, 4 or 5 above shall require a return to be delivered if–

(a) before the expiry of the period concerned all the information concerned has been provided to the Board by any person in pursuance of the paragraph concerned or of any other provision, or

(b) after the expiry of the period concerned all the information concerned falls to be provided to the Board by any person in pursuance of any provision other than the paragraph concerned.

Cross references – TMA 1970, s. 98: penalties relating to special returns.

SCHEDULE 5AZA – MEANING OF "SCHEME OF RECONSTRUCTION"

Section 103J

History – Sch. 5AZA inserted by SI 2013/1400, reg. 13, with effect in relation to disposals on or after 8 June 2013.

INTRODUCTORY

1 In sections 103H and 103I, **"scheme of reconstruction"** means a scheme within paragraph 2 which meets the conditions in paragraphs 3 and 4.

FORM OF SCHEME

2(1) A scheme ("the relevant scheme") is within this paragraph if under the relevant scheme some or all of the property subject to one or more collective investment schemes becomes subject to one or more other collective investment schemes.

2(2) In this Schedule **"original collective investment scheme"** means a collective investment scheme property subject to which becomes subject to another collective investment scheme; and **"successor collective investment scheme"** is to be read accordingly.

FIRST CONDITION: ISSUE OF UNITS

3(1) The first condition is that the relevant scheme involves the issue of units in a successor collective investment scheme or schemes or a feeder fund–

(a) where there is one original collective investment scheme, to holders of units in that scheme or, if there are different classes of units in that scheme, to holders of one or more classes of units in that scheme (the classes "involved in the scheme of reconstruction"), or

(b) where there is more than one original collective investment scheme, to holders of units in any of those schemes or, if there are different classes of units in one or more of those schemes, to holders of units in any of those schemes or of one or more classes of units in any of those schemes (the classes "involved in the scheme of reconstruction"),

and does not involve the issue of units in any successor collective investment scheme or feeder fund to anyone else.

3(2) In this Schedule, **"feeder fund"** means a collective investment scheme, 85% or more of the property subject to which is constituted by units in a successor collective investment scheme or schemes.

SECOND CONDITION: EQUAL ENTITLEMENT TO NEW UNITS

4(1) The second condition is that under the relevant scheme the entitlement of any participant to acquire units in a successor collective investment scheme or schemes or a feeder fund by virtue of holding relevant units, or relevant units of any class, is the same as that of any other participant holding such units or units of that class.

4(2) For this purpose **"relevant units"** means units comprised–

(a) where there is one original collective investment scheme, in the units of that scheme or, as the case may be, in the units of that scheme of a class involved in the scheme of reconstruction;

(b) where there is more than one original collective investment scheme, in the units of any of those schemes or, as the case may be, in the units of any of those schemes of a class involved in the scheme of reconstruction.

PRELIMINARY REORGANISATION OF UNITS TO BE DISREGARDED

5 Where a reorganisation of the units in an original collective investment scheme or schemes within case 2 of section 103F(1) is carried out for the purposes of the relevant scheme, the provisions of the first and second conditions apply in relation to the position after the reorganisation.

SUBSEQUENT ISSUE OF UNITS TO BE DISREGARDED

6 An issue of units in any successor collective investment scheme or schemes or feeder fund after the latest date on which any units in any successor collective investment scheme or schemes or feeder fund are issued in consideration of property becoming subject to any successor collective investment scheme or schemes under the relevant scheme shall be disregarded for the purposes of the first and second conditions.

SCHEDULE 5AA – MEANING OF "SCHEME OF RECONSTRUCTION"

History – Sch. 5AA inserted by FA 2002, s. 45 and Sch. 9, para. 3 with effect in relation to shares or debentures issued on or after 17 April 2002.

INTRODUCTORY

1 In section 136 **"scheme of reconstruction"** means a scheme of merger, division or other restructuring that meets the first and second, and either the third or the fourth, of the following conditions.

FIRST CONDITION: ISSUE OF ORDINARY SHARE CAPITAL

2 The first condition is that the scheme involves the issue of ordinary share capital of a company ("the successor company") or of more than one company ("the successor companies")–

(a) to holders of ordinary share capital of another company ("the original company") or, where there are different classes of ordinary share capital of that company, to holders of one or more classes of ordinary share capital of that company (the classes "involved in the scheme of reconstruction"), or

(b) to holders of ordinary share capital of more than one other company ("the original companies") or, where there are different classes of ordinary share capital of one or more of the original company or companies, to holders of ordinary share capital of any of those companies or of one or more classes of ordinary share capital of any of those companies (the classes "involved in the scheme of reconstruction"),

and does not involve the issue of ordinary share capital of the successor company, or (as the case may be) any of the successor companies, to anyone else.

SECOND CONDITION: EQUAL ENTITLEMENT TO NEW SHARES

3(1) The second condition is that under the scheme the entitlement of any person to acquire ordinary share capital of the successor company or companies by virtue of holding relevant shares, or relevant shares of any class, is the same as that of any other person holding such shares or shares of that class.

3(2) For this purpose **"relevant shares"** means shares comprised–

(a) where there is one original company, in the ordinary share capital of that company or, as the case may be, in the ordinary share capital of that company of a class involved in the scheme of reconstruction;

(b) where there is more than one original company, in the ordinary share capital of any of those companies or, as the case may be, in the ordinary share capital of any of those companies of a class involved in the scheme of reconstruction.

THIRD CONDITION: CONTINUITY OF BUSINESS

4(1) The third condition is that the effect of the restructuring is–

(a) where there is one original company, that the business or substantially the whole of the business carried on by the company is carried on–

(i) by a successor company which is not the original company, or

(ii) by two or more successor companies (which may include the original company);

(b) where there is more than one original company, that all or part of the business or businesses carried on by one or more of the original companies is carried on by a different company, and the whole or substantially the whole of the businesses carried on by the original companies are carried on–

(i) where there is one successor company, by that company (which may be one of the original companies), or

(ii) where there are two or more successor companies, by those companies (which may be the same as the original companies or include any of those companies).

4(2) The reference in sub-paragraph (1)(a)(ii) or (b)(ii) to the whole or substantially the whole of a business, or businesses, being carried on by two or more companies includes the case where the activities of those companies taken together embrace the whole or substantially the whole of the business, or businesses, in question.

4(3) For the purposes of this paragraph a business carried on by a company that is under the control of another company is treated as carried on by the controlling company as well as by the controlled company. Section 1124 of CTA 2010 (meaning of **"control"**) applies for the purposes of this sub-paragraph.

4(4) For the purposes of this paragraph the holding and management of assets that are retained by the original company, or any of the original companies, for the purpose of making a capital distribution in respect of shares in the company shall be disregarded.

In this sub-paragraph **"capital distribution"** has the same meaning as in section 122.

History – In para. 4(3), the words "Section 1124 of CTA 2010" substituted for "Section 840 of the Taxes Act" by CTA 2010, s. 1177 and Sch. 1, para. 267(2), with effect for corporation tax purposes for accounting periods ending on or after 1 April 2010, and for income tax and capital gains tax purposes for the tax year 2010–11 and subsequent tax years.

FOURTH CONDITION: COMPROMISE OR ARRANGEMENT WITH MEMBERS

5 The fourth condition is that–

(a) the scheme is carried out in pursuance of a compromise or arrangement–

(i) to which Part 26 of the Companies Act 2006 (arrangements and reconstructions) applies,

(ii) under any corresponding provision of the law of a country or territory outside the United Kingdom, and

(b) no part of the business of the original company, or of any of the original companies, is transferred under the scheme to any other person.

History – Para. 5(a)(i) substituted by SI 2008/954, art. 17, with effect from 6 April 2008.

PRELIMINARY REORGANISATION OF SHARE CAPITAL TO BE DISREGARDED

6 Where a reorganisation of the share capital of the original company, or of any of the original companies, is carried out for the purposes of the scheme of reconstruction, the provisions of the first and second conditions apply in relation to the position after the reorganisation.

SUBSEQUENT ISSUE OF SHARES OR DEBENTURES TO BE DISREGARDED

7 An issue of shares in or debentures of the successor company, or any of the successor companies, after the latest date on which any ordinary share capital of the successor company, or any of them, is issued–

(a) in consideration of the transfer of any business, or part of a business, under the scheme, or

(b) in pursuance of the compromise or arrangement mentioned in paragraph 5(a),

shall be disregarded for the purposes of the first and second conditions.

INTERPRETATION

8(1) In this Schedule **"ordinary share capital"** has the meaning given by section 1119 of CTA 2010 and also includes–

(a) in relation to a unit trust scheme, any rights that are treated by section 99(1)(b) of this Act (application of Act to unit trust schemes) as shares in a company, and

(b) in relation to a company that has no share capital, any interests in the company possessed by members of the company.

8(2) Any reference in this Schedule to a reorganisation of a company's share capital is to a reorganisation within the meaning of section 126.

History – In para. 8(1), the words "section 1119 of CTA 2010" substituted for "section 832(1) of the Taxes Act" by CTA 2010, s. 1177 and Sch. 1, para. 267(3), with effect for corporation tax purposes for accounting periods ending on or after 1 April 2010, and for income tax and capital gains tax purposes for the tax year 2010–11 and subsequent tax years.

SCHEDULE 5B – ENTERPRISE INVESTMENT SCHEME: RE-INVESTMENT

Section 150C

History – Sch. 5B inserted by FA 1995, s. 67 and Sch. 13, para. 4(3) in relation to gains accruing and events occurring on or after 29 November 1994.

Cross references – S. 105A: shares acquired on the same day – election for alternative treatment.
FA 2008, Sch. 3, para. 8: interaction of Pt. 5, Ch. 3 (entrepreneurs' relief) rules in cases where the original gain would have accrued before 6 April 2008, but for the provisions of Sch. 5B (enterprise investment scheme) or 5C (venture capital trusts).
SI 2004/712, Reg. 1(3)(c): the operation of Sch. 5B unaffected by the Research and Development (Prescribed Activities) Regulations 2004 (2004/712), in relation to shares issued before 6 April 2004.

Notes – FA 2004, s. 146 and Sch. 27, para. 4(6): offshore installation: nothing in FA 2004, Sch. 27, para. 4 affects the operation of the provisions of TCGA 1992, Sch. 5B in relation to shares issued before 6 April 2004.

APPLICATION OF SCHEDULE

1(1) This Schedule applies where–

(a) there would (apart from paragraph 2(2)(a) below) be a chargeable gain (**"the original gain"**) accruing to an individual (**"the investor"**) at any time (**"the accrual time"**) on or after 29th November 1994;

(b) the gain is one accruing either on the disposal by the investor of any asset or in accordance with section 164F or 164FA, section 169N, paragraphs 4 and 5 below or paragraphs 4 and 5 of Schedule 5C;

(c) the investor makes a qualifying investment; and

(d) the investor is resident in the United Kingdom at the accrual time and the time when he makes the qualifying investment and is not, in relation to the qualifying investment, a person to whom sub-paragraph (4) below applies.

1(2) The investor makes a qualifying investment for the purposes of this Schedule if–

(a) eligible shares in a company for which he has subscribed are issued to him at a qualifying time and, where that time is before the accrual time, the shares are still held by the investor at the accrual time,

(aza) he subscribed for the shares (other than any of them which are bonus shares) wholly in cash,

(b) the company is a qualifying company in relation to the shares,

(c) at the time when they are issued the shares (other than any of them which are bonus shares) are fully paid up,

(d) the shares are subscribed for, and issued, for bona fide commercial purposes and not as part of arrangements the main purpose or one of the main purposes of which is the avoidance of tax,

(da) the total amount of relevant investments made in the company in the year ending with the date the shares are issued does not exceed £5 million,

(e) the requirements of section 289(1A) of the Taxes Act (read with section 289(1B) to (1E) of that Act) or the requirements of section 183 of ITA 2007 are satisfied in relation to the company,

(f) the shares (other than any of them which are bonus shares) are issued in order to raise money for the purpose of a qualifying business activity, and

(g) all of the money raised by the issue of the shares (other than any of them which are bonus shares) is, no later than the time mentioned in section 175(3) of ITA 2007, employed wholly for the purpose of that activity,

(h) [effectively omitted by FA 2009, s. 27 and Sch. 8, para. 2(2),]

and for the purposes of this Schedule, the condition in paragraph (g) above does not fail to be satisfied by reason only of the fact that an amount of money which is not significant is employed for another purpose.

1(3) In sub-paragraph (2) above **"a qualifying time"**, in relation to any shares subscribed for by the investor, means–

(a) any time in the period beginning one year before and ending three years after the accrual time, or

(b) any such time before the beginning of that period or after it ends as the Board may by notice allow.

1(4) This sub-paragraph applies to the investor in relation to a qualifying investment if–

(a) though resident in the United Kingdom at the time when he makes the investment, he is regarded for the purposes of any double taxation relief arrangements as resident in a territory outside the United Kingdom, and

(b) were section 150A to be disregarded, the arrangements would have the effect that he would not be liable in the United Kingdom to tax on a gain arising on a disposal, immediately after their acquisition, of the shares acquired in making that investment.

1(5) Shares are not fully paid up for the purposes of sub-paragraph (2)(c) above if there is any undertaking to pay cash to any person at a future date in respect of the acquisition of the shares.

1(5A) The reference in sub-paragraph (1)(b) to a gain accruing in accordance with section 169N does not include such a gain so far as it is chargeable to capital gains tax at the rate in section 169N(3).

1(6) Section 173A(3) and (4) of ITA 2007 (meaning of **"relevant investment"**) apply for the purposes of sub-paragraph (2)(da).

1(7) In sub-paragraph (2)(da), the reference to relevant investments made in the company includes relevant investments made in a company that is, or has at any time in the year mentioned there been, a subsidiary of the company (whether or not it was such a subsidiary when the investment was made).

History – In para. 1(1)(b), the words "section 169N," inserted by FA 2008, s. 9 and Sch. 3, para. 4, with effect in relation to disposals, reorganisations (within the meaning of s. 169Q) and relevant transactions (within the meaning of s. 116) taking place on or after 6 April 2008 (FA 2008, Sch. 3, para. 5).

In para. 1(1)(b), words "section 164F or 164FA," inserted by FA 1998, s. 74 and Sch. 13, para. 27(1) with effect in relation to shares issued on or after 6 April 1998.

In para. 1(1)(d), the words "or ordinarily resident" omitted by FA 2013, s. 219 and Sch. 46, para. 110(2)(a), with effect in relation to cases where the accrual time is on or after 6 April 2013 (even if the qualifying investment was made before that date).

In para. 1(2)(a), the words "wholly in cash" omitted by FA 2004, s. 93 and Sch. 18, para. 13(1)(a) and repealed by FA 2004, s. 326 and Sch. 42, Pt. 2(13) in relation to shares issued on or after 17 March 2004, by virtue of FA 2004, Sch. 18, para. 21.

Para. 1(2)(aza) inserted by FA 2004, s. 93 and Sch. 18, para. 13(1)(b) which have effect, by virtue of FA 2004, Sch. 18, para. 21, in relation to shares issued on or after 17 March 2004.

In para. 1(2)(c), the words "(other than any of them which are bonus shares) are fully paid up" substituted for the words "are fully paid up (disregarding for this purpose any undertaking to pay cash to the company at a future date)" by FA 2004, s. 93 and Sch. 18, para. 13(1)(c) which have effect, by virtue of FA 2004, Sch. 18, para. 21, in relation to shares issued on or after 17 March 2004.

In para. (1)(2)(da), "£5 million" substituted for "£2 million" by FA 2012, s. 39 and Sch. 7, para. 29, with effect from 19 July 2012 (SI 2012/1896). The amendment will have effect in relation to shares issued on or after 6 April 2012.

Para. 1(2)(da) inserted by FA 2007, s. 51 and Sch. 16, para. 7(2)(a), with effect from 19 July 2007 (Royal Assent).

In para. 1(2)(e), the words "or the requirements of section 183 of ITA 2007" inserted by ITA 2007, s. 1027 and Sch. 1, para. 345(2)(a), with effect from 6 April 2007.

In para. 1(2)(e), the words "(read with section 289(1B) to (1E) of that Act)" inserted by FA 2004, s. 93 and Sch. 18, para. 13(1)(d) which have effect, by virtue of FA 2004, Sch. 18, para. 21, in relation to shares issued on or after 17 March 2004.

In para. 1(2)(f), the words "the shares (other than any of them which are bonus shares)" substituted for the words "all the shares comprised in the issue" by FA 2004, s. 93 and Sch. 18, para. 13(1)(e) which have effect, by virtue of FA 2004, Sch. 18, para. 21, in relation to shares issued on or after 17 March 2004.

In para.1(2)(f), word "and" deleted by FA 2001, Sch. 33, Pt. 2(3) in respect of shares issued under EIS on or after 7 March 2001 or before that date for which income tax or deferral relief was due immediately before 7 March 2001.

Para. 1(2)(g) substituted for former para. 1(2)(g) and (h) by FA 2009, s. 27 and Sch. 8, para. 2(2), with effect in relation to shares issued on or after 22 April 2009.

In former para. 1(2)(g), the words "or section 175(3) of ITA 2007" inserted by ITA 2007, s. 1027, Sch. 1, para. 345(2)(b), with effect from 6 April 2007.
Former para. 1(2)(g) substituted by FA 2004, s. 93 and Sch. 18, para. 13(1)(f) which have effect, by virtue of FA 2004, Sch. 18, para. 21, in relation to shares issued on or after 17 March 2004.
Former para. 1(2)(g) and (h), substituted for para. 1(2)(g), and words "conditions in paragraphs (g) and (h) above do" substituted for "condition in paragraph (g) above does" by FA 2001, Sch. 15, para. 26 in respect of shares issued under EIS on or after 7 March 2001 or before that date for which income tax or deferral relief was due immediately before 7 March 2001.
In para. 1(2), in the words following the paragraphs, the words "condition in paragraph (g) above does" substituted for the words "conditions in paragraphs (g) and (h) above do" by FA 2009, s. 27 and Sch. 8, para. 2(3), with effect in relation to shares issued on or after 22 April 2009.
Para. 1(2), (3), substituted by FA 1998, s. 74 and Sch. 13, para. 27(2) with effect in relation to shares issued on or after 6 April 1998.
In para. 1(4)(a), the words "or ordinarily resident" omitted by FA 2013, s. 219 and Sch. 46, para. 110(2)(b), with effect in relation to cases where the accrual time is on or after 6 April 2013 (even if the qualifying investment was made before that date).
Para. 1(5) inserted by FA 2004, s. 93 and Sch. 18, para. 13(2) which have effect, by virtue of FA 2004, Sch. 18, para. 21, in relation to shares issued on or after 17 March 2004.
Para. 1(5A) inserted by F(No. 2)A 2010, s. 2 and Sch. 1, para. 9(2), with effect in relation to qualifying business disposals occurring on or after 23 June 2010, subject to transitional provisions in F(No. 2)A 2010, Sch. 1, para. 18–22.
Para. 1(6) inserted by FA 2007, s. 51 and Sch. 16, para. 7(2)(b), with effect from 19 July 2007 (Royal Assent).
Para. 1(7) inserted by FA 2007, s. 51 and Sch. 16, para. 7(2)(b), with effect from 19 July 2007 (Royal Assent).

Cross references – S. 150A: capital gains tax relief on disposal of EIS shares.
Sch. 5C: postponement of gains on disposal of shares in a venture capital trust following the making of a qualifying investment.
ICTA 1988, Pt. VII, Ch. III: income tax relief under the EIS.
Sch. 15, para. 55(4): persons connected with an investing company can not receive EIS relief for shares included in a return of value transaction.

FAILURE OF CONDITIONS OF APPLICATION

1A(1) If the condition in sub-paragraph (2)(b) or (2)(da) of paragraph 1 above is not satisfied in consequence of an event occurring after the issue of eligible shares, the shares mentioned in sub-paragraph (2)(a) of that paragraph shall be treated for the purposes of this Schedule as ceasing to be eligible shares on the date of the event.

1A(2) If the condition in sub-paragraph (2)(e) of that paragraph is not satisfied in consequence of an event occurring after the issue of eligible shares, the shares mentioned in sub-paragraph (2)(a) of that paragraph shall be treated for the purposes of this Schedule as ceasing to be eligible shares on the date of the event.

1A(3) If the condition in sub-paragraph (2)(f) of that paragraph is not satisfied in relation to the shares mentioned in sub-paragraph (2)(a) of that paragraph, the shares shall be treated for the purposes of this Schedule as never having been eligible shares.

1A(4) If the condition in sub-paragraph (2)(g) of that paragraph is not satisfied in relation to the issue of eligible shares, the shares mentioned in sub-paragraph (2)(a) of that paragraph shall be treated for the purposes of this Schedule–

(a) if the claim under this Schedule is made after the time mentioned in section 175(3) of ITA 2007, as never having been eligible shares; and

(b) if that claim is made before that time, as ceasing to be eligible shares at that time.

1A(4A) [Omitted by FA 2009, s. 27 and Sch. 8, para. 3(3).]

1A(5) None of the preceding sub-paragraphs applies unless–

(a) the company has given notice under paragraph 16(2) or (4) below, section 310(2) of the Taxes Act or section 241(3) of ITA 2007; or

(b) an inspector has given notice to the company stating that, by reason of the matter mentioned in that sub-paragraph, the shares mentioned in paragraph 1(2)(a) above should, in his opinion, be treated for the purposes of this Schedule as never having been or, as the case may be, as ceasing to be eligible shares.

1A(6) The giving of notice by an inspector under sub-paragraph (5) above shall be taken, for the purposes of the provisions of the Management Act relating to appeals against decisions on claims, to be a decision refusing a claim made by the company.

1A(7) Where any issue has been determined on an appeal brought by virtue of section 307(1B) of the Taxes Act or section 236(1) of ITA 2007 (appeal against notice that relief was not due), the determination shall be conclusive for the purposes of any appeal brought by virtue of sub-paragraph (6) above on which that issue arises.

History – In para. 1A(1) the words "or (2)(da)" inserted by FA 2007, s. 51 and Sch. 16, para. 7(3), with effect from 19 July 2007 (Royal Assent).
In para. 1A(1), the words "mentioned in sub-paragraph (2)(a) of that paragraph" inserted by FA 2004, s. 93 and Sch. 18, para. 14(a) which have effect, by virtue of FA 2004, Sch. 18, para. 21, in relation to shares issued on or after 17 March 2004.
In para. 1A(2), the words "mentioned in sub-paragraph (2)(a) of that paragraph" inserted by FA 2004, s. 93 and Sch. 18, para. 14(b) which have effect, by virtue of FA 2004, Sch. 18, para. 21, in relation to shares issued on or after 17 March 2004.
In para. 1A(3), the words "the shares mentioned in sub-paragraph (2)(a) of that paragraph" substituted for the words "an issue of eligible shares" by FA 2004, s. 93 and Sch. 18, para. 14(c) which have effect, by virtue of FA 2004, Sch. 18, para. 21, in relation to shares issued on or after 17 March 2004.

In para. 1A(4), the words "or (h)" omitted and the words "section 175(3) of ITA 2007" substituted for the words "sub-paragraph (4A) below" by FA 2009, s. 27 and Sch. 8, para. 3(2), with effect in relation to shares issued on or after 22 April 2009.
In para. 1A(4), the words "the issue of eligible shares, the shares mentioned in sub-paragraph (2)(a) of that paragraph" substituted for the words "an issue of eligible shares, the shares" by FA 2004, s. 93 and Sch. 18, para. 14(d) which have effect, by virtue of FA 2004, Sch. 18, para. 21, in relation to shares issued on or after 17 March 2004.
In the opening words of para. 1A(4), the words "or (h)" inserted by FA 2001, Sch. 15, para. 27(1) in respect of shares issued under EIS on or after 7 March 2001 or before that date for which income tax or deferral relief was due immediately before 7 March 2001.
In para. 1A(4)(a), the words "sub-paragraph (4A) below" substituted for "section 289(3) of the Taxes Act" by FA 2001, Sch. 15, para. 27(1) in respect of shares issued under EIS on or after 7 March 2001 or before that date for which income tax or deferral relief was due immediately before 7 March 2001.
Para. 1A(4A) omitted by FA 2009, s. 27 and Sch. 8, para. 3(3), with effect in relation to shares issued on or after 22 April 2009.
In former para. 1A(4A), the words "or section 175(3) of ITA 2007" inserted by ITA 2007, s. 1027 and Sch. 1, para. 345(3)(a), with effect from 6 April 2007.
Former para. 1A(4A) inserted by FA 2001, Sch. 15, para. 27(2) in respect of shares issued under EIS on or after 7 March 2001 or before that date for which income tax or deferral relief was due immediately before 7 March 2001.
In para. 1A(5)(a), the words ", section 310(2) of the Taxes Act or section 241(3) of ITA 2007" substituted for "or section 310(2) of the Taxes Act" by ITA 2007, s. 1027 and Sch. 1, para. 345(3)(b), with effect from 6 April2007.
In para. 1A(5)(b), the words "mentioned in paragraph 1(2)(a) above" inserted by FA 2004, s. 93 and Sch. 18, para. 14(e) which have effect, by virtue of FA 2004, Sch. 18, para. 21, in relation to shares issued on or after 17 March 2004.
In para. 1A(7), the words "or section 236(1) of ITA 2007" inserted by ITA 2007, s. 1027 and Sch. 1, para. 345(3)(c), with effect from 6 April 2007.
Para. 1A inserted by FA 1998, s. 74 and Sch. 13, para. 28 with effect in relation to shares issued on or after 6 April 1998.

POSTPONEMENT OF ORIGINAL GAIN

2(1) On the making of a claim by the investor for the purposes of this Schedule, so much of the investor's unused qualifying expenditure on the relevant shares as–

(a) is specified in the claim, and

(b) does not exceed so much of the original gain as is unmatched,

shall be set against a corresponding amount of the original gain.

2(2) Where an amount of qualifying expenditure on the relevant shares is set under this Schedule against the whole or part of the original gain–

(a) so much of that gain as is equal to that amount shall be treated as not having accrued at the accrual time; but

(b) paragraphs 4 and 5 below shall apply for determining the gain that is to be treated as accruing on the occurrence of any chargeable event in relation to any of the relevant shares.

2(3) For the purposes of this Schedule–

(a) the investor's qualifying expenditure on the relevant shares is the amount subscribed by him for the shares; and

(b) that expenditure is unused to the extent that it has not already been set under this Schedule or paragraph 1(5) of Schedule 5BB against the whole or any part of a chargeable gain.

2(4) For the purposes of this paragraph the original gain is unmatched, in relation to any qualifying expenditure on the relevant shares, to the extent that it has not had any other expenditure set against it under this Schedule or paragraph 1(5) of Schedule 5BB.

History – In para. 2(1), the words "the relevant shares" substituted for the words "relevant shares" by FA 1999, s. 73 and Sch. 8, para. 4(a)–(c), with effect in relation to shares issued on or after 6 April 1999.
In para. 2(2), the words "the relevant shares" substituted for the words "any relevant shares" by FA 1999, s. 73 and Sch. 8, para. 4(a)–(c), with effect in relation to shares issued on or after 6 April 1999.
In para. 2(2)(b), the words "the relevant shares" substituted for the words "those relevant shares" by FA 1999, s. 73 and Sch. 8, para. 4(a)–(c), with effect in relation to shares issued on or after 6 April 1999.
In para. 2(3)(b), the words "or paragraph 1(5) of Schedule 5BB" inserted by FA 2012, s. 38 and Sch. 6, para. 22(a) with effect from 17 July 2012.
In para. 2(3), the words "the relevant shares" substituted for the words "any relevant shares" by FA 1999, s. 73 and Sch. 8, para. 4(a)–(c), with effect in relation to shares issued on or after 6 April 1999.
Para. 2(3)(a) substituted by FA 1998, s. 74 and Sch. 13, para. 29 with effect in relation to shares issued on or after 6 April 1998.
In para. 2(4), the words "or paragraph 1(5) of Schedule 5BB" inserted by FA 2012, s. 38 and Sch. 6, para. 22(b) with effect from 17 July 2012.
In para. 2(4), the words "or Schedule 5C" omitted by FA 2004, s. 94 and Sch. 19, para. 6(2) which have effect, by virtue of FA 2004, Sch. 19, para. 7(1), in relation to shares issued on or after 6 April 2004 that are shares by reference to which an individual is given relief under ICTA 1988, Sch. 15B, Pt. 1. However, in accordance with FA 2004, Sch. 19, para. 7(2), nothing in FA 2004 affects the continuing operation of TCGA 1992, Sch. 5C for the purposes of TCGA 1992, s. 151B(8)(b)(ii).
In para. 2(4), the words "the relevant shares" substituted for the words "relevant shares" by FA 1999, s. 73 and Sch. 8, para. 4(a)–(c), with effect in relation to shares issued on or after 6 April 1999.

Cross references – Sch. 5BA: application of taper relief to gain postponed under para. 2.
Sch. 5C: postponement of gains on disposal of shares in a venture capital trust following the making of a qualifying investment.
ICTA 1988, s. 289A: amount of relief is lower of (a) income tax at the lower rate on the amount subscribed for eligible shares in the year *in which the individual is eligible for relief and (b) the amount which reduces the individual's income tax liability for the year to nil.*

CHARGEABLE EVENTS

3(1) Subject to the following provisions of this paragraph, there is for the purposes of this Schedule a chargeable event in relation to any of the relevant shares if, after the making of the qualifying investment–

(a) the investor disposes of those shares otherwise than by way of a disposal within marriage or civil partnership;

(b) those shares are disposed of, otherwise than by way of a disposal to the investor, by a person who acquired them on a disposal made by the investor within marriage or civil partnership;

(c) the investor becomes a non-resident while holding those shares and before the termination date relating to those shares;

(d) a person who acquired those shares on a disposal within marriage or civil partnership becomes a non-resident while holding those shares and before the termination date relating to those shares; or

(e) those shares cease (or are treated for the purposes of this Schedule as ceasing) to be eligible shares.

3(2) [Repealed by FA 1998, s. 74 and Sch. 13, para. 30(2); s. 165 and Sch. 27, Pt. III(14).]

3(3) For the purposes of this Schedule there shall not be a chargeable event by virtue of sub-paragraph (1)(c) or (d) above in relation to any shares if–

(a) the reason why the person in question becomes a non-resident is that he works in an employment or office all the duties of which are performed outside the United Kingdom, and

(b) he again becomes resident in the United Kingdom within the period of three years from the time when he became a non-resident, without having meanwhile disposed of any of those shares;

and accordingly no assessment shall be made by virtue of sub-paragraph (1)(c) or (d) above before the end of that period in a case where the condition in paragraph (a) above is satisfied and the condition in paragraph (b) above may be satisfied.

3(4) For the purposes of sub-paragraph (3) above a person shall be taken to have disposed of any shares if and only if there has been such a disposal as would have been a chargeable event in relation to those shares if the person making the disposal had been resident in the United Kingdom.

3(5) Where in any case–

(a) the investor or a person who has acquired any of the relevant shares on a disposal within marriage or civil partnership dies, and

(b) an event occurs at or after the time of the death which (apart from this sub-paragraph) would be a chargeable event in relation to any of the relevant shares held by the deceased immediately before his death,

that event shall not be chargeable event in relation to the shares so held.

3(6) Any reference in the following provisions of this Schedule to a chargeable event falling within a particular paragraph of sub-paragraph (1) above is a reference to a chargeable event arising for the purposes of this Schedule by virtue of that paragraph.

History – In para. 3 the words "or civil partnership" inserted four times by SI 2005/3229, reg. 127, with effect from 5 December 2005.
In para. 3(1), "any of the relevant shares" substituted for "any relevant shares" by FA 1999, s. 73 and Sch. 8, para. 4(d), with effect in relation to shares issued on or after 6 April 1999.
In para. 3(1)(c), (d), words "before the termination date relating to those shares" substituted for "within the designated period" by FA 2001, Sch. 15, para. 29 with effect for shares issued on or after 7 March 2001 or for shares issued before that date where income tax relief or deferral relief was due immediately before that date. Previously the word "designated" substituted for "five year" by FA 2000, s. 64 and Sch. 17, para. 7(3) with effect in relation to shares issued on or after 6 April 2000.
In para. 3(1)(c), (d), "the five year period" substituted for "the first relevant period", and para. 3(1)(e) substituted for para. 3(1)(e), (f) by FA 1998, s. 74 and Sch. 13, para. 30(1) in relation to shares issued on or after 6 April 1998.
Para. 3(2) repealed by FA 1998, s. 74 and Sch. 13, para. 30(2); s. 165 and Sch. 27, Pt. III(14) in relation to shares issued on or after 6 April 1998.
In para. 3(3)(b), the words "or ordinarily resident" omitted by FA 2013, s. 219 and Sch. 46, para. 110(3), with effect in relation to cases where the accrual time is on or after 6 April 2013 (even if the qualifying investment was made before that date).
In para. 3(5)(a), (b), "any of the relevant shares" substituted for "any relevant shares" by FA 1999, s. 73 and Sch. 8, para. 4(d), with effect in relation to shares issued on or after 6 April 1999.
Para. 3(6) inserted by FA 1998, s. 74 and Sch. 13, para. 30(3) in relation to shares issued on or after 6 April 1998.

Cross references – ICTA 1988, s. 289A: relief is lower of (a) income tax at the lower rate on the amount subscribed for eligible shares in the year in which the individual is eligible for relief and (b) the amount which reduces the individual's income tax liability for the year to nil.
ICTA 1988, s. 293: definition of a qualifying company.
ICTA 1988, s. 312(1A)(a): "relevant period" is the period ending five years after the later of the company's incorporation and the date which falls two years before the issue of the shares.
ICTA 1988, s. 312(1A)(b): "relevant period" is the period beginning with date on which the shares are issued and ending (a) three years afterwards or (b) three years after the company or subsidiary begins to trade if it was not trading when the shares were issued.

GAIN ACCRUING ON CHARGEABLE EVENT

4(1) On the occurrence of a chargeable event in relation to any of the relevant shares in relation to which there has not been a previous chargeable event–

(a) a chargeable gain shall be treated as accruing at the time of the event; and

(b) the amount of the gain shall be equal to so much of the deferred gain as is attributable to the shares in relation to which the chargeable event occurs.

4(2) Any question for the purposes of capital gains tax as to whether any shares to which a disposal (including a disposal within marriage or civil partnership) relates are shares to which deferral relief is attributable shall be determined in accordance with sub-paragraphs (3) and (4) below.

4(3) Where shares of any class in a company have been acquired by an individual on different days, any disposal by him of shares of that class shall be treated as relating to those acquired on an earlier day rather than to those acquired on a later day.

4(4) Where shares of any class in a company have been acquired by an individual on the same day, any of those shares disposed of by him shall be treated as disposed of in the following order, namely–

(a) first any to which neither deferral relief nor relief under Chapter III of Part VII of the Taxes Act or Part 5 of ITA 2007 is attributable;

(b) next any to which deferral relief, but not relief under that Chapter or that Part, is attributable;

(c) next any to which relief under that Chapter or that Part, but not deferral relief, is attributable; and

(d) finally any to which both deferral relief and relief under that Chapter or that Part are attributable.

(4A) The following, namely–

(a) any shares to which deferral relief, but not relief under Chapter III of Part VII of the Taxes Act or Part 5 of ITA 2007, is attributable and which were disposed of to an individual by a disposal within marriage or civil partnership; and

(b) any shares to which relief under that Chapter or that Part is attributable and which were transferred to an individual as mentioned in section 304 of the Taxes Act or section 245 of ITA 2007,

shall be treated for the purposes of sub-paragraphs (3) and (4) above as acquired by him on the day on which they were issued.

4(4B) Chapter I of Part IV of this Act has effect subject to sub-paragraphs (2) to (4A) above.

4(4C) Sections 104, 105 and 106A shall not apply to shares to which deferral relief, but not relief under Chapter III of Part VII of the Taxes Act or Part 5 of ITA 2007, is attributable.

4(5) Where at the time of a chargeable event any of the relevant shares are treated for the purposes of this Act as represented by assets which consist of or include assets other than those shares–

(a) so much of the deferred gain as is attributable to those shares shall be treated, in determining for the purposes of this paragraph the amount of the deferred gain to be treated as attributable to each of those assets, as apportioned in such manner as may be just and reasonable between those assets; and

(b) as between different assets treated as representing the same shares, sub-paragraphs (3) to (4A) above shall apply with the necessary modifications in relation to those assets as they would apply in relation to the shares.

4(6) In order to determine, for the purposes of this paragraph, the amount of the deferred gain attributable to any shares, a proportionate part of the amount of the gain shall be attributed to each of the relevant shares held, immediately before the occurrence of the chargeable event in question, by the investor or a person who has acquired any of the relevant shares from the investor on a disposal within marriage or civil partnership.

4(7) In this paragraph **"the deferred gain"** means–

(a) the amount of the original gain against which expenditure has been set under this Schedule, less

(b) the amount of any gain treated as accruing under this paragraph previously as a result of a disposal of any of the relevant shares.

History – In para. 4 the words "or civil partnership" inserted three times by SI 2005/3229, reg. 127, with effect from 5 December 2005.
In para. 4(1), "any of the relevant shares" substituted for "any relevant shares" by FA 1999, s. 73 and Sch. 8, para. 4(e), with effect in relation to shares issued on or after 6 April 1999.
Para. 4(1)(b) substituted by FA 1999, s. 73 and Sch. 8, para. 2(1), with effect in relation to shares issued on or after 6 April 1999.
Para. 4(2)–(4C) substituted for para. 4(2)–(4) by FA 1998, s. 74 and Sch. 13, para. 31(1) in relation to disposals made on or after 6 April 1998.
In para. 4(4), the reference to ITA 2007, Pt. 5 inserted in clause (a) and the words "or that Part" inserted in clauses (b), (c) and (d) by ITA 2007, s. 1027 and Sch. 1, para. 345(4)(a), with effect from 6 April 2007.
In para. 4(4A), the words "or Part 5 of ITA 2007" inserted in clause (a) and the words "or that Part" inserted in clause (b), and the words "the Taxes Act or section 245 of ITA 2007" substituted for "that Act" in clause (b) by ITA 2007, s. 1027 and Sch. 1, para. 345(4)(b), with effect from 6 April 2007.
In para. 4(4C), the words "or Part 5 of ITA 2007" inserted by ITA 2007, s. 1027 and Sch. 1, para. 345(4)(c), with effect from 6 April 2007.
In para. 4(5), "any of the relevant shares" substituted for "any relevant shares" by FA 1999, s. 73 and Sch. 8, para. 4(e), with effect in relation to shares issued on or after 6 April 1999.
Para. 4(5)(a) substituted by FA 1999, s. 73 and Sch. 8, para. 2(2), with effect in relation to shares issued on or after 6 April 1999.
In para. 4(5)(b), "the same shares" substituted for "the same relevant shares" by FA 1999, s. 73 and Sch. 8, para. 4(f), with effect in relation to shares issued on or after 6 April 1999.
In para. 4(5)(b), words "sub-paragraphs (3) to (4A) above" substituted for "the assumptions for which sub-paragraph (3) above provides" by FA 1998, s. 74 and Sch. 13, para. 31(2) in relation to disposals made on or after 6 April 1998.
Para. 4(6), (7) inserted by FA 1999, s. 73 and Sch. 8, para. 2(3), with effect in relation to shares issued on or after 6 April 1999.

Cross references – S. 260(6A) (hold-over relief): s. 260(3) disapplied, so far as any gain under para. 4 is concerned, to the disposal which is the chargeable event on which the gain accrues.
Sch. 5BA: application of taper relief to gain accruing under para. 4.
Sch. 5C: deferred charge on re-investment in venture capital trusts.
ICTA 1988, Pt. VII, Ch. III: income tax relief under the EIS.
ICTA 1988, s. 289A: relief from income tax for EIS shares.
ICTA 1988, s. 304: EIS relief for income tax not withdrawn when shares which attracted the relief are disposed by one spouse to another at a time whilst they are living together.

PERSON TO WHOM GAIN ACCRUES

5(1) The chargeable gain which accrues, in accordance with paragraph 4 above, on the occurrence in relation to any of the relevant shares of a chargeable event shall be treated as accruing, as the case may be–

(a) to the person who makes the disposal,

(b) to the person who becomes a non-resident, or

(c) to the person who holds the shares in question when they cease (or are treated for the purposes of this Schedule as ceasing) to be eligible shares.

5(2) Where–

(a) sub-paragraph (1) above provides for the holding of shares at a particular time to be what identifies the person to whom any chargeable gain accrues, and

(b) at that time, some of those shares are held by the investor and others are held by a person to whom the investor has transferred them by a disposal within marriage or civil partnership,

the amount of the chargeable gain accruing by virtue of paragraph 4 above shall be computed separately in relation to the investor and that person without reference to the shares held by the other.

History – In para. 5 the words "or civil partnership" inserted by SI 2005/3229, reg. 127, with effect from 5 December 2005.
In para. 5(1), "any of the relevant shares" substituted for "any relevant shares" by FA 1999, s. 73 and Sch. 8, para. 4(g), with effect in relation to shares issued on or after 6 April 1999.
Para. 5(1)(c) substituted for para. 5(1)(c), (d) by FA 1998, s. 74 and Sch. 13, para. 31(1) in relation to disposals made on or after 6 April 1998.

Cross references – Sch. 5C: deferred charge on re-investment in venture capital trusts.

CLAIMS

6(1) Subject to sub-paragraph (2) below, section 306 of the Taxes Act or sections 202(1), 203(1) and 204 to 207 of ITA 2007 shall apply in relation to a claim under this Schedule in respect of the relevant shares as it applies in relation to a claim for relief under Chapter III of Part VII of the Taxes Act or Part 5 of ITA 2007 in respect of eligible or relevant shares.

6(2) Section 306, as it so applies, shall have effect as if–

(a) any reference to the conditions for the relief were a reference to the conditions for the application of this Schedule;

(b) in subsection (1), the words "(or treated by section 289B(5) as so issued)" were omitted; and

(c) subsections (7) to (9) were omitted.

6(3) sections 202(1), 203(1) and 204 to 207 of ITA 2007, as they so apply, shall have effect as if any reference to the requirements for the relief were a reference to the conditions for the application of this Schedule.

History – In para. 6(1), the words "or sections 202(1), 203(1) and 204 to 207 of ITA 2007" inserted and the words "the Taxes Act or Part 5 of ITA 2007 in respect of eligible or relevant shares" substituted for "that Act in respect of eligible shares" by ITA 2007, s. 1027 and Sch. 1, para. 345(5)(a), with effect from 6 April 2007.
In para. 6(1), "the relevant shares" substituted for "relevant shares" by FA 1999, s. 73 and Sch. 8, para. 4(h), with effect in relation to shares issued on or after 6 April 1999.
In para. 6(2), the words "Section 306" substituted for "That section", by ITA 2007, s. 1027, Sch. 1, para. 345(5)(b), with effect from 6 April 2007.
Para. 6(3) inserted by ITA 2007, s. 1027 and Sch. 1, para. 345(5)(c), with effect from 6 April 2007.
Para. 6 substituted by FA 1998, s. 74 and Sch. 13, para. 33 with effect in relation to shares issued on or after 6 April 1998.

Cross references – S. 58: disposals between husband and wife living together treated as no gain/no loss transactions.
S. 288(5): shares or debentures comprised in a letter of allotment or similar instrument treated as issued unless the right to the share or debentures remains provisional until accepted and there is no acceptance.
ICTA 1988, Pt. VII, Ch. III: income tax relief under the EIS.

REORGANISATIONS

7(1) Where an individual holds shares which form part of the ordinary share capital of a company and include shares of more than one of the following kinds, namely–

(a) shares to which deferral relief and relief under Chapter III of Part VII of the Taxes Act or Part 5 of ITA 2007 are attributable;

(b) shares to which deferral relief but not relief under that Chapter or that Part is attributable; and

(c) shares to which deferral relief is not attributable,

then, if there is within the meaning of section 126 a reorganisation affecting those shares, section 127 shall apply (subject to the following provisions of this paragraph) separately to shares falling within paragraph (a), (b) or (c) above (so that shares of each kind are treated as a separate holding of original shares and identified with a separate new holding).

7(2) Where–

(a) an individual holds shares (the existing holding) which form part of the ordinary share capital of a company,

(b) there is, by virtue of any such allotment for payment as is mentioned in section 126(2)(a), a reorganisation affecting the existing holding, and

(c) immediately following the reorganisation, the existing holding or the allotted shares are shares to which deferral relief is attributable,

sections 127 to 130 shall not apply in relation to the existing holding.

History – In para. 7(1), the words "or Part 5 of ITA 2007" in clause (a) and the words "or that Part" in clause (b), inserted by ITA 2007, s. 1027 and Sch. 1, para. 345(6)(a) and (b), with effect from 6 April 2007.
Para. 7 inserted by FA 1998, s. 74 and Sch. 13, para. 34 with effect in relation to shares issued on or after 6 April 1998.

Cross references – ICTA 1988, Pt. VII, Ch. III: income tax relief under the EIS.

ACQUISITION OF SHARE CAPITAL BY NEW COMPANY

8(1) This paragraph applies where–

(a) a company ("the new company") in which the only issued shares are subscriber shares acquires all the shares ("old shares") in another company ("the old company");

(b) the consideration for the old shares consists wholly of the issue of shares ("new shares") in the new company;

(c) the consideration for new shares of each description consists wholly of old shares of the corresponding description;

(d) new shares of each description are issued to the holders of old shares of the corresponding description in respect of and in proportion to their holdings;

(e) at some time before the issue of the new shares–

 (i) the old company issued eligible shares; and

 (ii) a certificate in relation to those eligible shares was issued by that company for the purposes of section 306(2) of the Taxes Act or section 203(1) of ITA 2007 (as applied by paragraph 6 above) and in accordance with section 306 of the Taxes Act or sections 204 and 205 of ITA 2007 (as so applied); and

(f) by virtue of section 127 as applied by section 135(3), the exchange of shares is not treated as involving a disposal of the old shares or an acquisition of the new shares.

8(2) For the purposes of this Schedule, deferral relief attributable to any old shares shall be attributable instead to the new shares for which they are exchanged.

8(3) Where, in the case of any new shares held by an individual to which deferral relief becomes so attributable, the old shares for which they were exchanged were subscribed for by and issued to the individual, this Schedule shall have effect as if–

(a) the new shares had been subscribed for by him at the time when, and for the amount for which, the old shares were subscribed for by him;

(b) the new shares had been issued to him by the new company at the time when the old shares were issued to him by the old company; and

(c) the claim under this Schedule made in respect of the old shares had been made in respect of the new shares.

8(4) Where, in the case of any new shares held by an individual to which deferral relief becomes so attributable, the old shares for which they are exchanged were acquired by the individual on a disposal within marriage or civil partnership, this Schedule shall have effect as if–

(a) the new shares had been subscribed for at the time when, and for the amount for which, the old shares were subscribed for;

(b) the new shares had been issued by the new company at the time when the old shares were issued by the old company; and

(c) the claim under this Schedule made in respect of the old shares had been made in respect of the new shares.

8(5) Where deferral relief becomes so attributable to any new shares–

(a) this Schedule shall have effect as if anything which, under paragraph 1A(5) above, paragraph 16 below or section 306(2) of the Taxes Act or section 203(1) of ITA 2007 as applied by paragraph 6 above has been done, or is required to be done, by or in relation to the old company had been done, or were required to be done, by or in relation to the new company: and

(b) any appeal brought by the old company against a notice under paragraph 1A(5)(b) may be prosecuted by the new company as if it had been brought by that company.

8(6) For the purposes of this paragraph old shares and new shares are of a corresponding description if, on the assumption that they were shares in the same company, they would be of the same class and carry the same rights; and in sub-paragraph (1) above references to shares, except in the expressions **"eligible shares"** and **"subscriber shares"**, include references to securities.

8(7) Nothing in section 293(8) of the Taxes Act or section 185 of ITA 2007, as applied by the definition of qualifying company in paragraph 19(1) below, shall apply in relation to such an exchange of shares, or shares and securities, as is mentioned in sub-paragraph (1) above or arrangements with a view to such an exchange.

History – In para. 8(1)(e)(ii), the words "section 306(2) of the Taxes Act or section 203(1) of ITA 2007" substituted for "subsection (2) of section 306 of the Taxes Act" and the words "section 306 of the Taxes Act or sections 204 and 205 of ITA 2007" substituted for "that section", by ITA 2007, s. 1027 and Sch. 1, para. 345((7)(a), with effect from 6 April 2007.
In para. 8(4) the words "or civil partnership" inserted by SI 2005/3229, reg. 127, with effect from 5 December 2005.
In para. 8(5)(a), the words "or section 203(1) of ITA 2007" inserted by ITA 2007, s. 1027 and Sch. 1, para. 345(7)(b), with effect from 6 April 2007.
In para. 8(7), the words "or section 185 of ITA 2007" inserted by ITA 2007, s. 1027 and Sch. 1, para. 345(7)(c), with effect from 6 April 2007.
Para. 8 inserted by FA 1998, s. 74 and Sch. 13, para. 34 with effect in relation to shares issued on or after 6 April 1998.

Cross references – ICTA 1988, s. 306: rules, procedures and time limits for verifying entitlement to and claiming EIS income tax relief.

OTHER RECONSTRUCTIONS AND AMALGAMATIONS

9(1) This paragraph applies if section 135 or 136 (company reconstructions) applies in relation to shares to which deferral relief, but not relief under Part 5 of ITA 2007 (or Chapter 3 of Part 7 of the Taxes Act), is attributable.

9(1A) Paragraphs 3 and 4 of this Schedule have effect as if section 135 or 136 did not apply in relation to the shares.

9(2) Sub-paragraph (1A) does not apply if–

(a) the new holding consists of new ordinary shares ("the new shares") carrying no present or future preferential right to dividends or to a company's assets on its winding up and no present or future right to be redeemed,

(b) the new shares are issued after the end of the relevant period, and

(c) the condition in sub-paragraph (4) below is satisfied.

9(3) Sub-paragraph (1A) does not apply if paragraph 8 applies in relation to the shares.

9(4) The condition is that at some time before the issue of the new shares–

(a) the company issuing them issued eligible shares, and

(b) a certificate in relation to those eligible shares was issued by the company for the purposes of section 306(2) of the Taxes Act or section 203(1) of ITA 2007 (as applied by paragraph 6 above) and in accordance with section 306 of the Taxes Act or sections 204 and 205 of ITA 2007 (as so applied).

9(5) In sub-paragraph (2) above **"new holding"** shall be construed in accordance with sections 126, 127, 135 and 136.

History – Para. 9(1) and (1A) substituted for former para. 9(1) by FA 2009, s. 27 and Sch. 8, para. 4(2), with effect in relation (a) to any exchange of shares to which TCGA 1992, s. 135 applies, where the new holding is issued on or after 22 April 2009 and (b) any arrangement within TCGA 1992, s. 136(1) entered into on or after 22 April 2009.
In para. 9(1), the words "or Part 5 of ITA 2007" inserted by ITA 2007, s. 1027 and Sch. 1, para. 345(8)(a), with effect from 6 April 2007.
In para. 9(2), the words "Sub-paragraph (1A) does not apply if" substituted for the words "Sub-paragraph (1) above shall not have effect to disapply section 135 or 136 where" by FA 2009, s. 27 and Sch. 8, para. 4(3), with effect in relation (a) to any exchange of shares to which TCGA 1992, s. 135 applies, where the new holding is issued on or after 22 April 2009 and (b) any arrangement within TCGA 1992, s. 136(1) entered into on or after 22 April 2009.
Para. 9(3) substituted by FA 2009, s. 27 and Sch. 8, para. 4(4), with effect in relation (a) to any exchange of shares to which TCGA 1992, s. 135 applies, where the new holding is issued on or after 22 April 2009 and (b) any arrangement within TCGA 1992, s. 136(1) entered into on or after 22 April 2009.
In former para. 9(3), the words "or Part 5 of ITA 2007" inserted by ITA 2007, s. 1027 and Sch. 1, para. 345(8)(b), with effect from 6 April 2007.
In para. 9(4)(b), the words "section 306(2) of the Taxes Act or section 203(1) of ITA 2007 " substituted for "subsection (2) of section 306 of the Taxes Act" and the words "section 306 of the Taxes Act or sections 204 and 205 of ITA 2007 " substituted for "that section" by ITA 2007, s. 1027, Sch. 1, para. 345(8)(c), with effect from 6 April 2007.
Para. 9 inserted by FA 1998, s. 74 and Sch. 13, para. 34 with effect in relation to shares issued on or after 6 April 1998.

Cross references – ICTA 1988, Pt. VII, Ch. III: income tax relief under the EIS.
ICTA 1988, s. 306: rules, procedures and time limits for verifying entitlement to and claiming EIS income tax relief.

RE-INVESTMENT IN SAME COMPANY ETC.

10(1) An individual to whom any eligible shares in a qualifying company are issued shall not be regarded for the purposes of this Schedule as making a qualifying investment if, where the asset disposed of consisted of shares in or securities of any company ("the initial holding"), the qualifying company–

(a) is the company in which the initial holding subsisted; or

(b) is a company that was, at the time of the disposal of the initial holding, or is, at the time of the issue of the eligible shares, a member of the same group of companies as the company in which the initial holding subsisted.

10(2) Where–

(a) any eligible shares in a qualifying company ("the acquired holding") are issued to an individual;

(b) an amount of qualifying expenditure on those shares has been set under this Schedule against the whole or part of any chargeable gain (the "postponed gain"); and

(c) after the issue of those shares, eligible shares in a relevant company are issued to him,

he shall not be regarded in relation to the issue to him of the shares in the relevant company as making a qualifying investment for the purposes of this Schedule.

10(3) For the purposes of sub-paragraph (2) above a company is a relevant company if–

(a) where that individual has disposed of any of the acquired holding, it is the company in which the acquired holding has subsisted or a company which was a member of the same group of companies as that company at any time since the acquisition of the acquired holding;

(b) it is a company in relation to the disposal of any shares in which there has been a claim under this Schedule such that, without that claim, there would have been no postponed gain in relation to the acquired holding; or

(c) it is a company which, at the time of the disposal or acquisition to which the claim relates, was a member of the same group of companies as a company falling within paragraph (b) above.

10(4) In this paragraph **"group of companies"** means a company which has one or more 51 per cent. subsidiaries, together with those subsidiaries.

History – In para. 10(1), "securities" substituted for "other securities" by FA 2004, s. 93 and Sch. 18, para. 15(1)(a) which have effect, by virtue of FA 2004, Sch. 18, para. 15(2), in relation to holdings of shares or securities disposed of on or after 17 March 2004.
Para. 10(4) inserted by FA 2004, s. 93 and Sch. 18, para. 15(1)(b) which have effect: (a) by virtue of FA 2004, Sch. 18, para. 15(2), for the purposes of TCGA 1992, Sch. 5B, para. 10(1), in relation to holdings of shares or securities disposed of on or after 17 March 2004, and (b) by virtue of FA 2004, Sch. 18, para. 15(3), for the purposes of TCGA 1992, Sch. 5B, para. 10(2), in relation to eligible shares in a relevant company issued on or after 17 March 2004.
Para. 10 inserted by FA 1998, s. 74 and Sch. 13, para. 35 with effect in relation to shares issued on or after 6 April 1998.

PRE-ARRANGED EXITS

11(1) Where an individual subscribes for eligible shares ("the shares") in a company, the shares shall be treated as not being eligible shares for the purposes of this Schedule if the relevant arrangements include–

(a) arrangements with a view to the subsequent repurchase, exchange or other disposal of the shares or of other shares in or securities of the same company;

(b) arrangements for or with a view to the cessation of any trade which is being or is to be or may be carried on by the company or a person connected with the company;

(c) arrangements for the disposal of, or of a substantial amount of, the assets of the company or of a person connected with the company;

(d) arrangements the main purpose of which, or one of the main purposes of which, is (by means of any insurance, indemnity or guarantee or otherwise) to provide partial or complete protection for persons investing in shares in that company against what would otherwise be the risks attached to making the investment.

11(2) The arrangements referred to in sub-paragraph (1)(a) above do not include any arrangements with a view to such an exchange of shares, or shares and securities, as is mentioned in paragraph 8(1) above.

11(3) The arrangements referred to in sub-paragraph (1)(b) and (c) above do not include any arrangements applicable only on the winding up of a company except in a case where–

(a) the relevant arrangements include arrangements for the company to be wound up; or

(b) the company is wound up otherwise than for bona fide commercial reasons.

11(4) The arrangements referred to in sub-paragraph (1)(d) above do not include any arrangements which are confined to the provision–

(a) for the company itself, or

(b) in the case of a company which is a parent company of a trading group, for the company itself, for the company itself and one or more of its subsidiaries or for one or more of its subsidiaries, of any such protection against the risks arising in the course of carrying on its business as it might reasonably be expected so to provide in normal commercial circumstances.

11(5) The reference in sub-paragraph (4) above to the parent company of a trading group

(a) shall be construed in accordance with the provision contained for the purposes of section 293 of the Taxes Act in that section, or

(b) is a reference to a company that meets the trading requirement in section 181(2)(b) of ITA 2007.

11(6) In this paragraph **"the relevant arrangements"** means–

(a) the arrangements under which the shares are issued to the individual; and

(b) any arrangements made before the issue of the shares to him in relation to or in connection with that issue.

History – In para. 11(5), the words from "shall be construed" to "that section" converted into clause (a) by ITA 2007, s. 1027 and Sch. 1, para. 345(9)(a) and clause (b) (and the preceding word "or") inserted by ITA 2007, s. 1027 and Sch. 1, para. 345(9)(b), both with effect from 6 April 2007.

Para. 11 inserted by FA 1998, s. 74 and Sch. 13, para. 35; with effect in relation to shares issued on or after 6 April 1998.

DISQUALIFYING ARRANGEMENTS

11A(1) Where an individual subscribes for eligible shares ("the shares") in a company ("the company"), the shares are to be treated as not being eligible shares for the purposes of this Schedule if the shares are issued, nor any money raised by the issue employed, in consequence or anticipation of, or otherwise in connection with, disqualifying arrangements.

11A(2) Arrangements are **"disqualifying arrangements"** if–

(a) the main purpose, or one of the main purposes, of the arrangements is to secure–

  (i) that a qualifying business activity is or will be carried on by the company or a qualifying 90% subsidiary of the company, and

  (ii) that one or more persons (whether or not including any party to the arrangements) may obtain relevant tax relief in respect of shares issued by the company which raise money for the purposes of that activity or that such shares may comprise part of the qualifying holdings of a venture capital trust,

(b) that activity is the relevant qualifying business activity, and

(c) one or both of conditions A and B are met.

11A(3) Condition A is that, as a (direct or indirect) result of the money raised by the issue of the shares being employed as required by paragraph 1(2)(g), an amount representing the whole or the majority of the amount raised is, in the course of the arrangements, paid to or for the benefit of a relevant person or relevant persons.

11A(4) Condition B is that, in the absence of the arrangements, it would have been reasonable to expect that the whole or greater part of the component activities of the relevant qualifying business activity would have been carried on as part of another business by a relevant person or relevant persons.

11A(5) For the purposes of this paragraph, it is immaterial whether the company is a party to the arrangements.

11A(6) In this paragraph–

"component activities" means–

(a) if the relevant qualifying business activity is activity A (see section 179(2) of ITA 2007), the carrying on of a qualifying trade, or preparing to carry on such a trade, which constitutes that activity, and

(b) if the relevant qualifying business activity is activity B (see section 179(4) of that Act), the carrying on of research and development which constitutes that activity;

"qualifying holdings", in relation to the issuing company, is to be construed in accordance with section 286 of ITA 2007 (VCTs: qualifying holdings);

"qualifying 90% subsidiary" has the meaning given by section 190 of ITA 2007;

"relevant person" means a person who is a party to the arrangements or a person connected with such a party;

"relevant qualifying business activity" means the activity for the purposes of which the issue of the shares raised money;

"relevant tax relief", in respect of shares, means one or more of the following–

(a) relief under this Schedule in consequence of which deferral relief is attributable to the shares;

(b) relief under section 150A or 150E (enterprise investment scheme or seed enterprise investment scheme) in respect of the shares;

(c) relief under Schedule 5BB (seed enterprise investment scheme: re-investment) in consequence of which SEIS re-investment relief is attributable to the shares (see paragraph 4 of that Schedule);

(d) relief under Chapter 6 of Part 4 of ITA 2007 (losses on disposal of shares) in respect of the shares;

(e) EIS relief (within the meaning of Part 5 of that Act) in respect of the shares, and

(f) SEIS relief (within the meaning of Part 5A of that Act) in respect of the shares.

History – Para. 11A inserted by FA 2012, s. 39 and Sch. 7, para. 30 with effect in relation to shares issued on or after 6 April 2012, regardless of whether the disqualifying arrangements were entered into before or on or after that date.

PUT OPTIONS AND CALL OPTIONS

12(1) Sub-paragraph (2) below applies where an individual subscribes for eligible shares ("the shares") in a company and–

(a) an option, the exercise of which would bind the grantor to purchase such shares, is granted to the individual during the relevant period; or

(b) an option, the exercise of which would bind the individual to sell such shares, is granted by the individual during the relevant period.

12(2) The shares to which the option relates shall be treated for the purposes of this Schedule–

(a) if the option is granted on or before the date of the issue of the shares, as never having been eligible shares; and

(b) if the option is granted after that date, as ceasing to be eligible shares on the date when the option is granted.

12(3) The shares to which the option relates shall be taken to be those which, if–

(a) the option were exercised immediately after the grant; and

(b) any shares in the company acquired by the individual after the grant were disposed of immediately after being acquired,

would be treated for the purposes of this Schedule as disposed of in pursuance of the option.

12(4) Nothing in this paragraph shall prejudice the operation of paragraph 11 above.

12(5) An individual who acquires any eligible shares on a disposal within marriage or civil partnership shall be treated for the purposes of this paragraph and paragraphs 13 to 15 below as if he subscribed for those shares.

History – In para. 12 the words "or civil partnership" inserted by SI 2005/3229, reg. 127, with effect from 5 December 2005. Para. 12 inserted by FA 1998, s. 74 and Sch. 13, para. 35 with effect in relation to shares issued on or after 6 April 1998.

VALUE RECEIVED BY INVESTOR

13(1) Where an individual who subscribes for eligible shares ("the shares") in a company receives any value (other than insignificant value) from the company at any time in the period of restriction, the shares shall be treated as follows for the purposes of this Schedule–

(a) if the individual receives the value on or before the date of the issue of the shares, as never having been eligible shares; and

(b) if the individual receives the value after that date, as ceasing to be eligible shares on the date when the value is received.

13(1A) This paragraph is subject to paragraph 13B below.

13(1B) Where–

(a) the individual who subscribes for the shares receives value (**"the relevant receipt"**) from the company during the period of restriction,

(b) the individual has received from the company one or more receipts of insignificant value at a time or times–

 (i) during that period, but

 (ii) not later than the time of the relevant receipt, and

(c) the aggregate amount of the value of the receipts within paragraphs (a) and (b) above is not an *amount of insignificant value*,

the individual shall be treated for the purposes of this Schedule as if the relevant receipt had been a receipt of an amount of value equal to the aggregate amount.

For this purpose a receipt does not fall within paragraph (b) above if it has previously been aggregated under this sub-paragraph.

13(2) For the purposes of this paragraph an individual receives value from the company if the company–

(a) repays, redeems or repurchases any of its share capital or securities which belong to the individual or makes any payment to him for giving up his right to any of the company's share capital or any security on its cancellation or extinguishment;

(b) repays, in pursuance of any arrangements for or in connection with the acquisition of the shares, any debt owed to the individual other than a debt which was incurred by the company–

  (i) on or after the date of issue of the shares; and

  (ii) otherwise than in consideration of the extinguishment of a debt incurred before that date;

(c) makes to the individual any payment for giving up his right to any debt on its extinguishment;

(d) releases or waives any liability of the individual to the company or discharges, or undertakes to discharge, any liability of his to a third person;

(e) makes a loan or advance to the individual which has not been repaid in full before the issue of the shares;

(f) provides a benefit or facility for the individual;

(g) disposes of an asset to the individual for no consideration or for a consideration which is or the value of which is less than the market value of the asset;

(h) acquires an asset from the individual for a consideration which is or the value of which is more than the market value of the asset; or

(i) makes any payment to the individual other than a qualifying payment.

13(3) For the purposes of sub-paragraph (2)(e) above there shall be treated as if it were a loan made by the company to the individual–

(a) the amount of any debt (other than an ordinary trade debt) incurred by the individual to the company; and

(b) the amount of any debt due from the individual to a third person which has been assigned to the company.

13(4) [Repealed by FA 2001, Sch. 33, Pt. 2(3) in respect of shares issued under EIS on or after 7 March 2001 or before that date for which value is received on or after 7 March 2001.]

13(5) For the purposes of this paragraph an individual also receives value from the company if any person who would, for the purposes of section 291 of the Taxes Act or Chapter 2 of Part 5 of ITA 2007, be treated as connected with the company–

(a) purchases any of its share capital or securities which belong to the individual; or

(b) makes any payment to him for giving up any right in relation to any of the company's share capital or securities.

13(6) Where an individual's disposal of shares in a company gives rise to a chargeable event falling within paragraph 3(1)(a) or (b) above, the individual shall not be treated for the purposes of this paragraph as receiving value from the company in respect of the disposal.

13(7) In this paragraph **"qualifying payment"** means–

(a) the payment by any company of such remuneration for service as an officer or employee of that company as may be reasonable in relation to the duties of that office or employment;

(b) any payment or reimbursement by any company of travelling or other expenses wholly, exclusively and necessarily incurred by the individual to whom the payment is made in the performance of duties as an officer or employee of that company;

(c) the payment by any company of any interest which represents no more than a reasonable commercial return on money lent to that company;

(d) the payment by any company of any dividend or other distribution which does not exceed a normal return on any investment in shares in or other securities of that company;

(e) any payment for the supply of goods which does not exceed their market value;

(f) any payment for the acquisition of an asset which does not exceed its market value;

(g) the payment by any company, as rent for any property occupied by the company, of an amount not exceeding a reasonable and commercial rent for the property;

(h) any reasonable and necessary remuneration which–

  (i) is paid by any company for services rendered to that company in the course of a trade or profession carried on wholly or partly in the United Kingdom; and

  (ii) is taken into account in calculating for tax purposes the profits of that trade or profession;

(i) a payment in discharge of an ordinary trade debt.

13(8) For the purposes of this paragraph a company shall be treated as having released or waived a liability if the liability is not discharged within 12 months of the time when it ought to have been discharged.

13(9) In this paragraph–

(a) references to a debt or liability do not, in relation to a company, include references to any debt or liability which would be discharged by the making by that company of a qualifying payment; and

(b) references to a benefit or facility do not include references to any benefit or facility provided in circumstances such that, if a payment had been made of an amount equal to its value, that payment would be a qualifying payment.

13(10) In this paragraph and paragraph 13A(1) below –

(a) any reference to a payment or disposal to an individual includes a reference to a payment or disposal made to him indirectly or to his order or for his benefit;

(b) any reference to an individual includes a reference to an associate of his; and

(c) any reference to a company includes a reference to a person who at any time in the relevant period is connected with the company, whether or not he is so connected at the material time.

13(11) In this paragraph **"ordinary trade debt"** means any debt for goods or services supplied in the ordinary course of a trade or business where any credit given–

(a) does not exceed six months; and

(b) is not longer than that normally given to customers of the person carrying on the trade or business.

13(12) In paragraphs 13A to 13C below (except paragraph 13C(4))–

(a) references to **"the shares"** shall be construed in accordance with sub-paragraph (1) above, and

(b) references to **"the period of restriction"** shall be construed as references to the period of restriction relating to the shares.

History – In para. 13(1), word "designated" substituted for "seven year" by FA 2000, s. 64 and Sch. 17, para. 7(4) with effect in relation to shares issued on or after 6 April 2000.

In para. 13(1), words "period of restriction" substituted for "designated period" and words "(other than insignificant value)" and sub-paragraphs 13(1A), (1B) and 13(12) inserted by FA 2001, Sch. 15, para. 30, with effect for all EIS shares issued on or after 7 March 2001 and EIS shares issued before that date in relation to value received on or after 7 March 2001.

In para. 13(2)(b)(i), words "of issue of the shares" substituted for words "on which he subscribed for the shares" by FA 2004, s. 93 and Sch. 18, para. 18, para. 16(1) which have effect, by virtue of FA 2004, Sch. 18, para. 16(2), in relation to shares issued on or after 17 March 2004. However, by virtue of FA 2004, Sch. 18, para. 16(3), the substitution by FA 2004, s. 93 and Sch. 18, para. 18, para. 16(1) does not take effect in relation to the repayment of a debt incurred before 17 March 2004 if: (a) the shares were subscribed for before 17 March 2004, and (b) the debt was incurred on or after the date on which the shares were subscribed for.

Para. 13(4) omitted by FA 2001, s. 63 and Sch. 15, para. 30(4) and repealed by FA 2001, s. 110 and Sch. 33, Pt. 2(3) in respect of shares issued under EIS on or after 7 March 2001 or before that date for which value is received on or after 7 March 2001.

In para. 13(5), the words "or Chapter 2 of Part 5 of ITA 2007" inserted by ITA 2007, s. 1027, Sch. 1, para. 345(10), with effect from 6 April 2007.

In para. 13(7), words "carried on wholly or partly in the United Kingdom" inserted by ITTOIA 2005, s. 882 and Sch. 1, para. 450(a) which, in accordance with ITTOIA 2005, s. 883, have effect, for income tax purposes, for tax year 2005–06 and subsequent tax years, and, for corporation tax purposes, for accounting periods ending after 5 April 2005.

In para. 13(7), words "in calculating for tax purposes the profits of that trade or profession" substituted for "in computing the profits of the trade or profession under Case I or II of Schedule D or would be so taken into account if it fell in a period on the basis of which those profits are assessed under that Schedule" by virtue of ITTOIA 2005, s. 882 and Sch. 1, para. 450(b) which, in accordance with ITTOIA 2005, s. 883, have effect, for income tax purposes, for tax year 2005–06 and subsequent tax years, and, for corporation tax purposes, for accounting periods ending after 5 April 2005.

In para. 13(10), words "and paragraph 13A(1) below" inserted by FA 2001, Sch. 15, para. 30(5) with effect for all EIS shares issued on or after 7 March 2001 and for EIS shares issued before that date in relation to value received on or after 7 March 2001.

Para. 13 inserted by FA 1998, s. 74 and Sch. 13, para. 35; witheffect in relation to shares issued on or after 6 April 1998.

Cross references – ICTA 1988, s. 303: repayment of share capital.

FA 2000, Sch. 15B, para. 56: value received by other persons.

Other material – Taxline 2000/2 (not reproduced): the Revenue will not treat a debt repayment that is not a return of value under 13(2)(b) as a return of value under 13(2)(b)(i).

PROVISION SUPPLEMENTAL TO PARAGRAPH 13

13A(1) For the purposes of paragraph 13 above, the value received by the individual in question is–

(a) in a case within sub-paragraph (2)(a), (b) or (c) of that paragraph, the amount received by the individual or, if greater, the market value of the share capital, securities or debt in question;

(b) in a case within sub-paragraph (2)(d) of that paragraph, the amount of the liability;

(c) in a case within sub-paragraph (2)(e) of that paragraph, the amount of the loan or advance reduced by the amount of any repayment made before the issue of the shares;

(d) in a case within sub-paragraph (2)(f) of that paragraph, the cost to the company of providing the benefit or facility less any consideration given for it by the individual;

(e) in a case within sub-paragraph (2)(g) or (h) of that paragraph, the difference between the market value of the asset and the consideration (if any) given for it;

(f) in a case within sub-paragraph (2)(i) of that paragraph, the amount of the payment;

(g) in a case within sub-paragraph (5) of that paragraph, the amount received by the individual or, if greater, the market value of the share capital or securities in question.

13A(2) In this paragraph and paragraph 13 above references to a receipt of insignificant value (however expressed) are references to a receipt of an amount of insignificant value.
This is subject to sub-paragraph (4) below.

13A(3) For the purposes of this paragraph and paragraph 13 above **"an amount of insignificant value"** means an amount of value which–

(a) does not exceed £1,000, or

(b) if it exceeds that amount, is insignificant in relation to the total amount of expenditure on the shares which is set under this Schedule against a corresponding total amount of the whole or any part of any chargeable gains.

13A(4) For the purposes of paragraph 13 above, if, at any time in the period–

(a) beginning one year before the shares are issued, and

(b) expiring at the end of the issue date,

arrangements are in existence which provide for the individual who subscribes for the shares to receive or to be entitled to receive, at any time in the period of restriction, any value from the company that issued the shares, no amount of value received by the individual shall be treated as a receipt of insignificant value.

13A(5) In sub-paragraph (4) above–

(a) any reference to the individual includes a reference to any person who, at any time in the period of restriction, is an associate of his (whether or not he is such an associate at the material time), and

(b) the reference to the company includes a reference to any person who, at any time in the period of restriction, is connected with the company (whether or not that person is so connected at the material time).

History – Para. 13A inserted by FA 2001, Sch. 15, para. 31 with effect for shares issued on or after 7 March 2001 and for EIS shares issued before that date in relation to value received on or after 7 March 2001.

RECEIPT OF REPLACEMENT VALUE

13B(1) Where–

(a) by reason of a receipt of value within sub-paragraph (2) (other than paragraph (b)) or sub-paragraph (5) of paragraph 13 above (**"the original value"**), the shares would, in the absence of this paragraph, be treated as never having been eligible shares or as ceasing to be eligible shares on the date when the value is received,

(b) the original supplier receives value (**"the replacement value"**) from the original recipient by reason of a qualifying receipt, and

(c) the amount of the replacement value is not less than the amount of the original value,

the receipt of the original value shall be disregarded for the purposes of paragraph 13 above.

13B(2) This paragraph is subject to paragraph 13C below.

13B(3) For the purposes of this paragraph and paragraph 13C below–

"the original recipient" means the person who receives the original value, and

"the original supplier" means the person from whom that value was received.

13B(4) A receipt of the replacement value is a qualifying receipt for the purposes of sub-paragraph (1) above if it arises–

(a) by reason of the original recipient doing one or more of the following–

(i) making a payment to the original supplier, other than a payment which falls within paragraph (c) below or to which sub-paragraph (5) below applies;

(ii) acquiring any asset from the original supplier for a consideration the amount or value of which is more than the market value of the asset;

(iii) disposing of any asset to the original supplier for no consideration or for a consideration the amount or value of which is less than the market value of the asset;

(b) where the receipt of the original value was within paragraph 13(2)(d) above, by reason of an event the effect of which is to reverse the event which constituted the receipt of the original value; or

(c) where the receipt of the original value was within paragraph 13(5) above, by reason of the original recipient repurchasing the share capital or securities in question, or (as the case may be) reacquiring the right in question, for a consideration the amount or value of which is not less than the amount of the original value.

13B(5) This sub-paragraph applies to–

(a) any payment for any goods, services or facilities, provided (whether in the course of a trade or otherwise) by–

(i) the original supplier, or

(ii) any other person who, at any time in the period of restriction, is an associate of, or connected with, that supplier (whether or not that person is such an associate, or so connected, at the material time),

which is reasonable in relation to the market value of those goods, services or facilities;

(b) any payment of any interest which represents no more than a reasonable commercial return on money lent to–

(i) the original recipient, or

(ii) any person who, at any time in the period of restriction, is an associate of his (whether or not he is such an associate at the material time);

(c) any payment for the acquisition of an asset which does not exceed its market value;

(d) any payment, as rent for any property occupied by–

(i) the original recipient, or

(ii) any person who, at any time in the period of restriction, is an associate of his (whether or not he is such an associate at the material time),

of an amount not exceeding a reasonable and commercial rent for the property;

(e) any payment in discharge of an ordinary trade debt (within the meaning of paragraph 13(11) above); and

(f) any payment for shares in or securities of any company in circumstances that do not fall within sub-paragraph (4)(a)(ii) above.

13B(6) For the purposes of this paragraph, the amount of the replacement value is–

(a) in a case within paragraph (a) of sub-paragraph (4) above, the aggregate of–

(i) the amount of any payment within sub-paragraph (i) of that paragraph, and

(ii) the difference between the market value of any asset within sub-paragraph (ii) or (iii) of that paragraph and the amount or value of the consideration (if any) received for it,

(b) in a case within sub-paragraph (4)(b) above, the same as the amount of the original value, and

(c) in a case within sub-paragraph (4)(c) above, the amount or value of the consideration received by the original supplier,

and paragraph 13A(1) above applies for the purposes of determining the amount of the original value.

13B(7) In this paragraph any reference to a payment to a person (however expressed) includes a reference to a payment made to him indirectly or to his order or for his benefit.

History – Para. 13B inserted by FA 2001, Sch. 15, para. 31 with effect for shares issued on or after 7 March 2001 and for EIS shares issued before that date in relation to value received on or after 7 March 2001.

PROVISION SUPPLEMENTAL TO PARAGRAPH 13B

13C(1) The receipt of the replacement value by the original supplier shall be disregarded for the purposes of paragraph 13B above, as it applies in relation to the shares, to the extent to which that receipt has previously been set (under that paragraph) against any receipts of value which are, in consequence, disregarded for the purposes of paragraph 13 above as that paragraph applies in relation to those shares or any other shares subscribed for by the individual in question (**"the individual"**).

13C(2) The receipt of the replacement value by the original supplier (**"the event"**) shall also be disregarded for the purposes of paragraph 13B above if–

(a) the event occurs before the start of the period of restriction, or

(b) in a case where the event occurs after the time the original recipient receives the original value, it does not occur as soon after that time as is reasonably practicable in the circumstances, or

(c) where an appeal has been brought by the individual against an assessment made by virtue of paragraph 3(1)(e) above by reason of that receipt, the event occurs more than 60 days after the appeal has been finally determined.

But nothing in paragraph 13B above or this paragraph requires the replacement value to be received after the original value.

13C(3) This sub-paragraph applies where–

(a) the receipt of the replacement value by the original supplier is a qualifying receipt for the purposes of paragraph 13B(1) above, and

(b) the event which gives rise to the receipt is (or includes) a subscription for shares by–
  (i) the individual, or
  (ii) any person who, at any time in the period of restriction, is an associate of the individual, whether or not he is such an associate at the material time.

13C(4) Where either of the following applies–

(a) sub-paragraph (3) above, and

(b) section 223(3) of ITA 2007 (which makes corresponding provision in relation to EIS relief under Part 5 of that Act),

the person who subscribes for the shares shall not by virtue of his subscription for those shares or any other shares in the same issue be treated as making a qualifying investment for the purposes of this Schedule.

13C(5) In this paragraph **"the original value"** and **"the replacement value"** shall be construed in accordance with paragraph 13B above.

History – In para. 13C(3), the words "This sub-paragraph" substituted for "Sub-paragraph (4) below", by ITA 2007, s. 1027, Sch. 1, para. 345(11)(a), with effect from 6 April 2007.
Para. 13C(4) substituted by ITA 2007, s. 1027 and Sch. 1, para. 345(11)(b), with effect from 6 April 2007.
Para. 13C inserted by FA 2001, Sch. 15, para. 31 with effect for shares issued on or after 7 March 2001 and for EIS shares issued before that date in relation to value received on or after 7 March 2001.

Notes – Para. 13C(4) rewritten for income tax as ITA 2007, s. 223(4).

VALUE RECEIVED BY OTHER PERSONS

14(1) Sub-paragraph (2) below applies where an individual subscribes for eligible shares ("the shares") in a company and at any time in the period of restriction the company or any subsidiary–

(a) repays, redeems or repurchases any of its share capital which belongs to any member other than the individual or a person falling within sub-paragraph (3) below, or

(b) makes any payment (directly or indirectly) to any such member, or to his order or for his benefit, for the giving up of his right to any of the share capital of the company or subsidiary on its cancellation or extinguishment.

This is subject to paragraphs 14AA and 14A below.

14(2) The shares shall be treated for the purposes of this Schedule–

(a) if the repayment, redemption, repurchase or payment in question is made or effected on or before the date of the issue of the shares, as never having been eligible shares; and

(b) if it is made or effected after that date, as ceasing to be eligible shares on the date when it is made or effected.

14(3) A person falls within this sub-paragraph if the repayment, redemption, repurchase or payment in question–

(a) gives rise to a qualifying chargeable event in respect of him, or

(b) causes any relief under Chapter III of Part VII of the Taxes Act or Part 5 of ITA 2007 attributable to his shares in the company to be withdrawn or reduced by virtue of section 299 or 300(2)(a) of the Taxes Act or section 209 or 216(2)(a) of ITA 2007, or

(c) causes any investment relief attributable to shares held by that person (within the meaning of Schedule 15 to the Finance Act 2000) to be withdrawn or reduced by virtue of paragraph 46 (disposal of shares) or 49(1)(a) (repayment etc. of share capital or securities) of that Schedule.

or it would have the effect mentioned in paragraph (a), (b) or (c) above were it not a receipt of insignificant value for the purposes of paragraph 13 above, section 300 of the Taxes Act or 214 of ITA 2007 or paragraph 47 of Schedule 15 to the Finance Act 2000, as the case may be.

14(4) In sub-paragraph (3) above **"qualifying chargeable event"** means–

(a) a chargeable event falling within paragraph 3(1)(a) or (b) above; or

(b) a chargeable event falling within paragraph 3(1)(e) above by virtue of sub-paragraph (1)(b) of paragraph 13 above (as it applies by virtue of sub-paragraph (2)(a) of that paragraph).

14(5) Where–

(a) a company issues share capital ("the original shares") of nominal value equal to the authorised minimum (within the meaning of the Companies Act 2006) for the purposes of complying with the requirements of section 761 of that Act (public company: requirement as to minimum share capital); and

(b) after the registrar of companies has issued the company with a certificate under section 761, it issues eligible shares, the preceding provisions of this paragraph shall not apply in relation to any redemption of any of the original shares within 12 months of the date on which those shares were issued.

14(6) [Omitted by SI 2008/954, art. 18, and art. 3 and Schedule.]

14(7) References in this paragraph and paragraphs 14AA and 14A below to a subsidiary of a company are references to a company which at any time in the relevant period is a 51 per cent subsidiary of the first mentioned company, whether or not it is such a subsidiary at the time of the repayment, redemption, repurchase or payment in question.

History – In para. 14(1), "period of restriction", substituted for "designated period" by FA 2001, Sch. 15, para. 32 with effect for all EIS shares issued on or after 7 March 2001 and for receipts of value received after that date made in respect of EIS shares issued before that date. Previously "designated" substituted for "seven year" by FA 2000, s. 64 and Sch. 17, para. 7(4), with effect in relation to shares issued on or after 6 April 2000.

In para. 14(1)(a), "a person" substituted for "an individual", and second sentence of para. 4(1) inserted, by FA 2000, s. 63(2) and Sch. 16, para. 4(2)(a), (b), with effect in relation to shares issued on or after 1 April 2000 but before 1 April 2010.

In para. 14(1)(b), "paragraphs 14AA and 14A" substituted for "paragraph 14A" by FA 2001, Sch. 15, para. 32 with effect for all EIS shares issued on or after 7 March 2001 and for receipts of value received after that date made in respect of EIS shares issued before that date.

In para. 14(3)(b), the words "or Part 5 of ITA 2007" inserted and the words "the Taxes Act or section 209 or 216(2)(a) of ITA 2007" substituted for "that Act" by ITA 2007, s. 1027 and Sch. 1, para. 345(12)(a) and (b), with effect from 6 April 2007.

In para. 14(3), the words "or 214 of ITA 2007" inserted by ITA 2007, s. 1027 and Sch. 1, para. 345(12)(c), with effect from 6 April 2007.

In para. 14(3), "A person" substituted for "An individual", and para. (c) and word "or" at end of para. (b) inserted, by FA 2000, s. 63(2) and Sch. 16, para. 4(2)(c), (d), with effect in relation to shares issued on or after 1 April 2000 but before 1 April 2010.

In para. 14(3), words "attributable to shares held by that person" and at the end of the sub-paragraph words from "or it would" to "as the case may be" inserted by FA 2001, Sch. 15, para. 32 with effect for all EIS shares issued on or after 7 March 2001 and for receipts of value received after that date made in respect of EIS shares issued before that date.

In para. 14(5)(a) the words "(within the meaning of the Companies Act 2006) for the purposes of complying with the requirements of section 761 of that Act (public company: requirement as to minimum share capital);" substituted for "(within the meaning of the Companies Act 1985) for the purposes of complying with the requirements of section 117 of that Act (public company not to do business unless requirements as to share capital complied with);" by SI 2008/954, art. 18, with effect from 6 April 2008.

Para. 14(6) omitted by SI 2008/954, art. 18, and art. 3 and Schedule, with effect from 6 April 2008.

In para. 14(7), words "paragraphs 14AA and 14A" substituted for words "paragraph 14AA" by FA 2004, s. 93 and Sch. 18, para. 18(1) which have effect, by virtue of FA 2004, Sch. 18,para. 18(2), in relation to any repayment (within the meaning of TCGA 1992, Sch. 5B, para. 14A) made on or after 17 March 2004.

In para. 14(7), words "and paragraph 14AA below" inserted by FA 2001, Sch. 15, para. 32 with effect for all EIS shares issued on or after 7 March 2001 and for receipts of value received after that date made in respect of EIS shares issued before that date.

Para. 14 inserted by FA 1998, s. 74 and Sch. 13, para. 35 with effect in relation to shares issued on or after 6 April 1998.

Cross references – ICTA 1988, Pt. VII, Ch. III: income tax relief under the EIS.

INSIGNIFICANT REPAYMENTS DISREGARDED FOR PURPOSES OF PARAGRAPH 14

14AA(1) Any repayment shall be disregarded for the purposes of paragraph 14 above if whichever is the greater of–

(a) the market value of the shares to which it relates (**"the target shares"**) immediately before the event occurs, and

(b) the amount received by the member in question,

is insignificant in relation to the market value of the remaining issued share capital of the company in question (or, as the case may be, subsidiary in question) immediately after the event occurs.

This is subject to sub-paragraph (4) below.

14AA(2) For the purposes of this paragraph **"repayment"** means a repayment, redemption, repurchase or payment mentioned in paragraph 14(1) above.

14AA(3) For the purposes of sub-paragraph (1) above it shall be assumed that the target shares are cancelled at the time the repayment is made.

14AA(4) Where an individual subscribes for eligible shares in a company, sub-paragraph (1) above does not apply to prevent paragraph 14(2) above having effect in relation to the shares if, at a relevant time, arrangements are in existence that provide–

(a) for a repayment by the company or any subsidiary of the company (whether or not it is such a subsidiary at the time the arrangements are made), or

(b) for anyone to be entitled to such a repayment,

at any time in the period of restriction.

14AA(5) For the purposes of sub-paragraph (4) above **"a relevant time"** means any time in the period–

(a) beginning one year before the eligible shares were issued, and

(b) expiring at the end of the issue date.

History – Para. 14AA inserted by FA 2001, Sch. 13, para. 33 with effect in relation to shares issued on or after 7 March 2001 and for receipts of value made after that date in respect of EIS shares issued before that date.

CERTAIN RECEIPTS TO BE DISREGARDED FOR PURPOSES OF PARAGRAPH 14

14A(1) Sub-paragraph (4) below applies where, by reason of a repayment, any investment relief which is attributable under Schedule 15 to the Finance Act 2000 to any shares is withdrawn under paragraph 56(2) of that Schedule.

14A(2) For the purposes of this paragraph **"repayment"** has the meaning given in paragraph 14AA(2) above.

14A(3) For the purposes of sub-paragraph (4) below **"the relevant amount"** is the amount determined by the formula–

$$X - 5Y$$

where–

X is the amount of the repayment, and

Y is the aggregate amount of the investment relief withdrawn by reason of the repayment.

14A(4) Where the relevant amount does not exceed £1,000, the repayment shall be disregarded for the purposes of paragraph 14 above, unless repayment arrangements are in existence at any time in the period–

(a) beginning one year before the shares mentioned in sub-paragraph (1) above are issued, and

(b) expiring at the end of the issue date of those shares.

14A(5) For this purpose **"repayment arrangements"** means arrangements which provide–

(a) for a repayment by the company that issued the shares ("the issuing company") or any subsidiary of that company, or

(b) for anyone to be entitled to such a repayment,

at any time.

14A(6) Sub-paragraph (5)(a) above applies in relation to a subsidiary of the issuing company whether or not it was such a subsidiary–

(a) [omitted by FA 2004, s. 93 and Sch. 18, para. 18(1) and repealed by FA 2004, s. 326 and Sch. 42, Pt. 2(13).]

(b) when the arrangements were made.

14A(7) [Repealed by FA 2001, Sch. 33, Pt. 2(3) in respect of shares issued under EIS on or after 7 March 2001, or before that date for which a value was received after that date.]

14A(8) In this paragraph–

(a) **"investment relief"** has the same meaning as in Schedule 15 to the Finance Act 2000 (corporate venturing scheme); and

(b) references to the withdrawal of investment relief include its reduction.

History – Para. 14A(2) substituted by FA 2001, Sch. 15, para. 34 in respect of EIS shares issued on or after 7 March 2001 and for receipts of value made on or after that date in respect of EIS shares issued before that date.

Para. 14A(6)(a) omitted by FA 2004, s. 93 and Sch. 18, para. 18(1) and repealed by FA 2004, s. 326 and Sch. 42, Pt. 2(13), which have effect, in accordance with FA 2004, Sch. 18, para. 18(2), in relation to any repayment (within the meaning of TCGA 1992, Sch. 5B, para. 14A) made on or after 17 March 2004.

Para. 14A(7) repealed by FA 2001, Sch. 33, Pt. 2(3) in respect of shares issued under EIS on or after 7 March 2001, or before that date for which a value was received after that date.

In para. 14A(8), words "Schedule 15 to the Finance Act 2000 (corporate venturing scheme)" inserted by FA 2001, Sch. 15, para. 34 in respect of EIS shares issued on or after 7 March 2001 and for receipts of value made on or after that date in respect of EIS shares issued before that date.

Para. 14A inserted by FA 2000, s. 63(2) and Sch. 16, para. 4(3), with effect in relation to shares issued on or after 1 April 2000 but before 1 April 2010.

INVESTMENT-LINKED LOANS

15(1) Where at any time in the relevant period an investment-linked loan is made by any person to an individual who subscribes for eligible shares ("the shares") in a company, the shares shall be treated for the purposes of this Schedule–

(a) if the loan is made on or before the date of the issue of the shares, as never having been eligible shares; and

(b) if the loan is made after that date, as ceasing to eligible shares on the date when the loan is made.

15(2) A loan made by any person to an individual is an investment-linked loan for the purposes of this paragraph if the loan is one which would not have been made, or would not have been made on the same terms, if the individual had not subscribed for the shares or had not been proposing to do so.

15(3) References in this paragraph to the making by any person of a loan to an individual include references–

(a) to the giving by that person of any credit to that individual; and

(b) to the assignment or assignation to that person of any debt due from that individual.

15(4) In this paragraph any reference to an individual includes a reference to an associate of his.

History – Para. 15 inserted by FA 1998, s. 74 and Sch. 13, para. 35 with effect in relation to shares issued on or after 6 April 1998.

Statements of practice – SP 6/98: HMRC understanding of way in which loan linked investments rules operate.

INFORMATION

16(1) Where, in relation to any of the relevant shares held by an individual–

(a) a chargeable event falling within paragraph 3(1)(a) or (b) above occurs at any time before the termination date relating to those shares,

(b) a chargeable event falling within paragraph 3(1)(c) or (d) above occurs, or

(c) a chargeable event falling within paragraph 3(1)(e) above occurs by virtue of paragraph 12(2)(b), 13(1)(b) or 15(1)(b) above,

the individual shall within 60 days of his coming to know of the event give a notice to the inspector containing particulars of the circumstances giving rise to the event.

16(2) Where, in relation to any of the relevant shares in a company, a chargeable event falling within paragraph 3(1)(e) above occurs by virtue of paragraph 1A(1) or (2), 13(1)(b) or 14(2)(b) above–

(a) the company, and

(b) any person connected with the company who has knowledge of that matter,

shall within 60 days of the event or, in the case of a person within paragraph (b) above, of his coming to know of it, give a notice to the inspector containing particulars of the circumstances giving rise to the event.

16(2A) In determining, for the purposes of sub-paragraph (1) or (2) above, whether a chargeable event falling within paragraph 3(1)(e) above has occurred by virtue of paragraph 13(1)(b) above, the effect of paragraph 13B above shall be disregarded.

16(3) A chargeable event falling within paragraph 3(1)(e) above which, but for paragraph 1A(5) above, would occur at any time by virtue of paragraph 1A(1) or (2) above shall be treated for the purposes of sub-paragraph (2) above as occurring at that time.

16(3A) Where–

(a) a person is required to give a notice under sub-paragraph (1) or (2) above in respect of a chargeable event which occurs by virtue of paragraph 13(1)(b) above or would occur by virtue of that paragraph but for the operation of paragraph 13B above, and

(b) that person has knowledge of the replacement value received (or expected to be received) from the original recipient by the original supplier by reason of a qualifying receipt,

the notice shall include particulars of that receipt of the replacement value (or expected receipt).

In this sub-paragraph **"the replacement value"**, **"the original recipient"**, **"the original supplier"** and **"qualifying receipt"** shall be construed in accordance with paragraph 13B above.

16(4) Where a company has issued a certificate under section 306(2) of the Taxes Act or section 203(1) of ITA 2007 (as applied by paragraph 6 above) in respect of any eligible shares in the company, and the condition in paragraph 1(2)(g) above is not satisfied in relation to the shares–

(a) the company, and

(b) any person connected with the company who has knowledge of that matter,

shall within 60 days of the time mentioned in section 289(3) of the Taxes Act or section 175(3) of ITA 2007 or, in the case of a person within paragraph (b) above, of his coming to know that the condition is not satisfied, give notice to the inspector setting out the particulars of the case.

16(4A) [Omitted by FA 2009, s. 27 and Sch. 8, para. 5.]

16(5) If the inspector has reason to believe–

(a) that a person has not given a notice which he is required to give–

(i) under sub-paragraph (1) or (2) above in respect of any chargeable event, or

(ii) under sub-paragraph (4) above in respect of any particular case, or

(b) that a person has given or received value (within the meaning of paragraph 13(2) or (5) above) which, but for the fact that the amount given or received was an amount of insignificant value (within the meaning of paragraph 13A(3) above), would have triggered a requirement to give a notice under sub-paragraph (1) or (2) above, or

(c) that a person has made or received any repayment (within the meaning of paragraph 14AA(2) above) which, but for the fact that it falls to be disregarded for the purposes of paragraph 14 above by virtue of paragraph 14AA(1) above, would have triggered a requirement to give a notice under sub-paragraph (2) above, the inspector may by notice require that person to furnish him within such time (not being less than 60 days) as may be specified in the notice with such information relating to the event or case as the inspector may reasonably require for the purposes of this Schedule.

16(6) Where a claim is made under this Schedule in respect of shares in a company and the inspector has reason to believe that it may not be well founded by reason of any such arrangements as are mentioned in paragraphs 1(2)(d) or , 11(1) or 11A above, or 289(1D) or (9)(e), 289A(8)(b) or (8A), 293(4B), (6) or (8) or 308(2)(e), (3), (3A) or (4) of the Taxes Act, or section 176(4)(b) or (5)(b), 182(2) or (4), 183(6), 185(1), 190(1)(e) or 191(2)(c), (3), (4) or (5) of ITA 2007 he may by notice require any person concernedto furnish him within such time (not being less than 60 days) as may be specified in the notice with–

(a) a declaration in writing stating whether or not, according to the information which that person has or can reasonably obtain, any such arrangements exist or have existed;

(b) such other information as the inspector may reasonably require for the purposes of the provision in question and as that person has or can reasonably obtain.

16(7) For the purposes of sub-paragraph (6) above, the persons who are persons concerned are–

(a) in relation to paragraph 1(2)(d) above or section 293(4B) or (6) of the Taxes Act or section 182(2) or (4) of ITA 2007, the claimant, the company and any person controlling the company;

(aa) in relation to section 289(1D), 289A(8)(b) or (8A) or 308(3), (3A) or (4) of the Taxes Act or section 176(4)(b) or (5)(b), 183(6), or 191(3), (4) or (5) of ITA 2007, the claimant, the company, any other company in question and any person controlling the company or any other company in question;

(b) in relation to paragraph 11(1) above, the claimant, the company and any person connected with the company;

(ba) in relation to paragraph 11A, the claimant, the company, any person controlling the company and any person whom an officer of Revenue and Customs has reason to believe may be a party to the arrangements in question; and

(c) in relation to section 289(3), 293(8) or 308(2)(e) of the Taxes Act or section 185(1), 190(1)(e) or 191(2)(c) of ITA 2007, the company and any person controlling the company;

and for those purposes the references in paragraphs (a), (aa), (b) and (ba) above to the claimant include references to any person to whom the claimant appears to have made a disposal within marriage or civil partnership of any of the shares in question.

16(7A) The references in sub-paragraphs (6) and (7) above to subsections (3), (3A) and (4) of section 308 of the Taxes Act and subsections (3), (4) and (5) of section 191 of ITA 2007 are to be read as including those provisions as applied by section 289(10) and (11) of the Taxes Act or section 190(2) of ITA 2007.

16(8) Where deferral relief is attributable to shares in a company–

(a) any person who receives from the company any payment or asset which may constitute value received (by him or another) for the purposes of paragraph 13 above; and

(b) any person on whose behalf such a payment or asset is received,

shall, if so required by the inspector, state whether the payment or asset received by him or on his behalf is received on behalf of any person other than himself and, if so, the name and address of that person.

16(9) Where a claim has been made under this Schedule in relation to shares in a company, any person who holds or has held shares in the company and any person on whose behalf any such shares are or were held shall, if so required by the inspector, state–

(a) whether the shares which are or were held by him or on his behalf are or were held on behalf of any person other than himself; and

(b) if so, the name and address of that person.

16(10) No obligation as to secrecy imposed by statute or otherwise shall preclude the inspector from disclosing to a company that relief has been given or claimed in respect of a particular number or proportion of its shares.

History – In para. 16 the words "or civil partnership" inserted by SI 2005/3229, reg. 127, with effect from 5 December 2005.

In para. 16(1), "any of the relevant shares" substituted for "any relevant shares" by FA 1999, s. 73 and Sch. 8, para. 4(i), with effect in relation to shares issued on or after 6 April 1999.

In para. 16(1), "designated" substituted for "five year" by FA 2000, s. 63(2) and Sch. 17, para. 7(3) with effect in relation to shares issued on or after 6 April 2000.

In para. 16(1)(a), words "before the termination date relating to those shares" substituted and in para. 16(5) words from "If the inspector has reason to believe" to the end of subpara. 16(5)(c) substituted for words from "If" to "particular case," by FA 2001, Sch. 15, para. 35 with effect in relation to events occurring on or after 7 March 2001.

In para. 16(2), "any of the relevant shares" substituted for "any relevant shares" by FA 1999, s. 73 and Sch 8, para. 4(i), with effect in relation to shares issued on or after 6 April 1999.

Para. 16(2A) inserted by FA 2001, Sch. 15, para. 35 with effect in relation to events occurring on or after 7 March 2001.

Para. 16(3A) inserted by FA 2001, Sch. 15, para. 35 with effect in relation to events occurring on or after 7 March 2001.

In para. 16(4), the words "or section 203(1) of ITA 2007" and "or section 175(3) of ITA 2007" inserted by ITA 2007, s. 1027 and Sch. 1, para. 345(13)(a)(i) and (ii), both with effect from 6 April 2007.

Para. 16(4A) omitted by FA 2009, s. 27 and Sch. 8, para. 5, with effect in relation to shares issued on or after 22 April 2009.
In former para. 16(4A), the words "or section 175(3) of ITA 2007" inserted by ITA 2007, s. 1027 and Sch. 1, para. 345(13)(b), with effect from 6 April 2007.
Former para. 16(4A) inserted by FA 2001, Sch. 15, para. 28 with effect for EIS shares issued on or after 7 March 2001 and for EIS shares issued before that date where income tax relief or deferral relief was attributable immediately before 7 March 2001.
In para. 16(6), ", 11(1) or 11A" substituted for "or 11(1)" by FA 2012, s. 39 and Sch. 7, para. 31(a) with effect in relation to shares issued on or after 6 April 2012, regardless of whether the disqualifying arrangements were entered into before or on or after that date.
In para. 16(6), the words "or section 176(4)(b) or (5)(b), 182(2) or (4), 183(6), 185(1), 190(1)(e) or 191(2)(c), (3), (4) or (5) of ITA 2007" inserted by ITA 2007, s. 1027 and Sch. 1, para. 345(13)(c), with effect from 6 April 2007.
In para. 16(6), words "289(1D) or (9)(e), 289A(8)(b) or (8A), 293(4B), (6) or (8) or 308(2)(e), (3), (3A) or (4)" substituted for words "293(8) or 308(2)(e)" by FA 2004, s. 93 and Sch. 18, para. 19(1)(a) which have effect, by virtue of FA 2004, Sch. 18, para. 19(2), in relation to any notice givenafter the passing of FA 2004, which occurred on 22 July 2004, in respect of shares issued on or after 17 March 2004.
In para. 16(7)(a), the words "or section 182(2) or (4) of ITA 2007" inserted by ITA 2007, s. 1027 and Sch. 1, para. 345(13)(d)(i), with effect from 6 April 2007.
In para. 16(7)(a), words "or section 293(4B) or (6) of the Taxes Act" inserted by FA 2004, s. 93 and Sch. 18, para. 19(1)(b)(i) which have effect, by virtue of FA 2004, Sch. 18, para. 19(2), in relation to any notice given after the passing of FA 2004 (passing of FA 2004 occurred on 22 July 2004) in respect of shares issued on or after 17 March 2004.
In para. 16(7)(aa), the words "or section 176(4)(b) or (5)(b), 183(6), or 191(3), (4) or (5) of ITA 2007" inserted by ITA 2007, s. 1027 and Sch. 1, para. 345(13)(d)(ii), with effect from 6 April 2007.
Para. 16(7)(aa) inserted by FA 2004, s. 93 and Sch. 18, para. 19(1)(b)(ii) which have effect, by virtue of FA 2004, Sch. 18, para. 19(2), in relation to any notice given after the passing of FA 2004 (passing of FA 2004 occurred on 22 July 2004) in respect of shares issued on or after 17 March 2004.
In para. 16(7), the word "and" omitted from the end of para. 16(7)(b) and para. 16(7)(ba) inserted by FA 2012, s. 39 and Sch. 7, para. 31(b) with effect in relation to shares issued on or after 6 April 2012, regardless of whether the disqualifying arrangements were entered into before or on or after that date.
In para. 16(7), ", (b) and (ba)" substituted for "and (b)" by FA 2012, s. 39 and Sch. 7, para. 31(c) with effect in relation to shares issued on or after 6 April 2012, regardless of whether the disqualifying arrangements were entered into before or on or after that date.
In para. 16(7)(c), the words "or section 185(1), 190(1)(e) or 191(2)(c) of ITA 2007" inserted by ITA 2007, s. 1027 and Sch. 1, para. 345(13)(d)(iii), with effect from 6 April 2007.
In para. 16(7)(c), "289(9)(e)," inserted by FA 2004, s. 93 and Sch. 18, para. 19(1)(b)(iii) which have effect, by virtue of FA 2004, Sch. 18, para. 19(2), in relation to any notice given after the passing of FA 2004 (passing of FA 2004 occurred on 22 July 2004) in respect of shares issued on or after 17 March 2004.
In para. 16(7), at the end of the full-out words, "(a), (aa)" substituted for "(a)" by FA 2004, s. 93 and Sch. 18, para. 19(1)(b)(iv) which have effect, by virtue of FA 2004, Sch. 18, para. 19(2), in relation to any notice given after the passing of FA 2004 (passing of FA 2004 occurred on 22 July 2004) in respect of shares issued on or after 17 March 2004.
In para. 16(7A), the words "and subsections (3), (4) and (5) of section 191 of ITA 2007" inserted and the words "the Taxes Act or section 190(2) of ITA 2007" substituted for "that Act" by ITA 2007, s. 1027 and Sch. 1, para. 345(13)(e)(i) and (ii), with effect from 6 April 2007.
Para. 16(7A)inserted by FA 2004, s. 93 and Sch. 18, para. 19(1)(c) which have effect, by virtue of FA 2004, Sch. 18, para. 19(2), in relation to any notice given after the passing of FA 2004 (passing of FA 2004 occurred on 22 July 2004) in respect of shares issued on or after 17 March 2004.
Para. 16 inserted by FA 1998, s. 74 and Sch. 13, para. 36 with effect in relation to shares issued on or after 6 April 1998.

TRUSTEES

17(1) Subject to the following provisions of this paragraph, this Schedule shall apply as if–

(a) any reference to an individual included a reference to the trustees of a settlement, and

(b) in relation to any such trustees, the reference in paragraph 1(1) above to any asset were a reference to any asset comprised in any settled property to which this paragraph applies (a "trust asset").

17(2) This paragraph applies–

(a) to any settled property in which the interests of the beneficiaries are not interests in possession, if all the beneficiaries are individuals, and

(b) to any settled property in which the interests of the beneficiaries are interests in possession, if any of the beneficiaries are individuals.

17(3) If, at the time of the disposal of the trust asset in a case where this Schedule applies by virtue of this paragraph–

(a) the settled property comprising that asset is property to which this paragraph applies by virtue of sub-paragraph (2)(b) above, but

(b) not all the beneficiaries are individuals,

only the relevant proportion of the gain which would accrue to the trustees on the disposal shall be taken into account for the purposes of this Schedule as it so applies.

17(4) This Schedule shall not apply by virtue of this paragraph in a case where, at the time of the disposal of the trust asset, the settled property which comprises that asset is property to which this paragraph applies by virtue of sub-paragraph (2)(a) above unless, immediately after the acquisition of the relevant shares, the settled property comprising the shares is also property to which this paragraph applies by virtue of sub-paragraph (2)(a) above.

17(5) This Schedule shall not apply by virtue of this paragraph in a case where, at the time of the disposal of the trust asset, the settled property which comprises that asset is property to which this paragraph applies by virtue of sub-paragraph (2)(b) above unless, immediately after the acquisition of the relevant shares–

(a) the settled property comprising the shares is also property to which this paragraph applies by virtue of sub-paragraph (2)(b) above, and

(b) if not all the beneficiaries are individuals, the relevant proportion is not less than the proportion which was the relevant proportion at the time of the disposal of the trust asset.

17(6) If, at any time, in the case of settled property to which this paragraph applies by virtue of sub-paragraph (2)(b) above, both individuals and others have interests in possession, "the relevant proportion" at that time is the proportion which the amount specified in paragraph (a) below bears to the amount specified in paragraph (b) below, that is–

(a) the total amount of the income of the settled property, being income the interests in which are held by beneficiaries who are individuals, and

(b) the total amount of all the income of the settled property.

17(7) Where, in the case of any settled property in which any beneficiary holds an interest in possession, one or more beneficiaries ("the relevant beneficiaries") hold interests not in possession, this paragraph shall apply as if–

(a) the interests of the relevant beneficiaries were a single interest in possession, and

(b) that interest were held, where all the relevant beneficiaries are individuals, by an individual and, in any other case, by a person who is not an individual.

17(8) In this paragraph references to interests in possession do not include interests for a fixed term and, except in sub-paragraph (1), references to individuals include any charity.

History – Para. 17 inserted by FA 1998, s. 74 and Sch. 13, para. 36 with effect in relation to shares issued on or after 6 April 1998.

TRUSTEES: ANTI-AVOIDANCE

18(1) Paragraphs 13 to 13C and 15 above shall have effect in relation to the subscription for shares by the trustees of a settlement as if references to the individual subscribing for the shares were references to–

(a) those trustees;

(b) any individual or charity by virtue of whose interest, at a relevant time, paragraph 17 above applies to the settled property; or

(c) any associate of such an individual, or any person connected with such a charity.

18(2) The relevant times for the purposes of sub-paragraph (1)(b) above are the time when the shares are issued and–

(a) in a case where sub-paragraph (1) of paragraph 13 above applies, or that sub-paragraph would apply were it not for the fact that the amount of value is an amount of insignificant value for the purposes of that sub-paragraph, the time when the value is received;

(ab) in a case where paragraph 13(1) above would apply were it not for the operation of paragraph 13B above, the time when the original value (within the meaning of paragraph 13B above) in question is received;

(b) in a case where paragraph 15 above applies, the time when the loan is made.

History – In para. 18(1), reference to para. 13C inserted by FA 2001, Sch. 15, para. 36 with effect for all EIS shares issued on or after 7 March 2001 and for value receive on or after that date in respect of EIS shares issued before that date.
In para. 18(2), words from "sub-paragraph (1) of paragraph 13" to "purposes of that sub-paragraph" and para. 18(2)(ab) inserted by FA 2001, Sch. 15, para. 36 with effect for all EIS shares issued on or after 7 March 2001 and for value receive on or after that date in respect of EIS shares issued before that date.
Para. 18 inserted by FA 1998, s. 74 and Sch. 13, para. 36 with effect in relation to shares issued on or after 6 April 1998.

INTERPRETATION

19(1) For the purposes of this Schedule–

"51 per cent. subsidiary" has the meaning given by Chapter 3 of Part 24 of CTA 2010;

"arrangements" includes any scheme, agreement, understanding, transaction or series of transactions (whether or not legally enforceable);

"associate" has the meaning that would be given by section 448 of CTA 2010 if in that section "relative" did not include a brother or sister;

"bonus shares" means shares which are issued otherwise than for payment (whether in cash or otherwise);

"eligible shares" has the meaning given by section 289(7) of the Taxes Act or means shares that meet the requirement in section 173(2) of ITA 2007;

"non-resident" means a person who is not resident in the United Kingdom;

"ordinary share capital" has the meaning given by section 989 of ITA 2007;

"ordinary shares", in relation to a company, means shares forming part of its ordinary share capital;

"the period of restriction", in relation to any shares, means the period–

(a) beginning one year before the shares are issued, and

(b) ending immediately before the termination date relating to the shares;

"qualifying business activity" has the meaning given by section 289(2) of the Taxes Act or section 179 of ITA 2007;

"qualifying company", in relation to any eligible shares, means a company which, in relation to those shares, is–

(a) a qualifying company for the purposes of Chapter 3 of Part 7 of the Taxes Act (except that for the purposes of this Schedule the reference in section 293(1B)(b)(i) of that Act to section 304A of that Act shall be read as a reference to paragraph 8 above), or

(b) a qualifying company for the purposes of Part 5 of ITA 2007 (except that for the purposes of this Schedule the reference in section 184(1)(c)(i) of that Act to section 247 of that Act shall be read as a reference to paragraph 8 above).

"the relevant period", in the case of any shares, means the period found by applying section 312(1A)(a) of the Taxes Act or section 159(2) of ITA 2007 by reference to the company that issued the shares and by reference to the shares;

"termination date", in relation to any shares, means the date found by applying the definition of **"termination date"** in section 312(1) of the Taxes Act or section 256 of ITA 2007 by reference to the company that issued the shares and by reference to the shares.

19(1A) For the purposes of this Schedule, **"the relevant shares"**, in relation to a case to which this Schedule applies, means the shares which–

(a) are acquired by the investor in making the qualifying investment, and

(b) where the qualifying investment is made before the time at which the original gain accrues, are still held by the investor at that time.

This is subject to sub-paragraphs (1b) and (1d) below.

19(1B) If any corresponding bonus shares in the same company are issued to the investor or any person who has acquired any of the relevant shares from the investor on a disposal within marriage or civil partnership, this Schedule shall apply as if references to the relevant shares were to all the shares comprising the relevant shares and the bonus shares so issued.

19(1C) In sub-paragraph (1B) above **"corresponding bonus shares"** means bonus shares which–

(a) are issued in respect of the relevant shares; and

(b) are of the same class, and carry the same rights, as those shares.

19(1D) If, in circumstances in which paragraph 8 above applies, new shares are issued in exchange for old shares, references in this Schedule to the relevant shares, so far as they relate to the old shares, shall be construed as references to the new shares and not to the old shares.

19(1E) In sub-paragraph (1D) above **"new shares"** and **"old shares"** have the same meaning as in paragraph 8 above.

19(2) For the purposes of this Schedule, "deferral relief" is attributable to any shares if–

(a) expenditure on the shares has been set under this Schedule against the whole or part of any gain; and

(b) in relation to the shares there has been no chargeable event for the purposes of this Schedule.

19(3) In this Schedule–

(a) references (however expressed) to an issue of eligible shares in any company are to any eligible shares in the company that are of the same class and are issued on the same day;

(b) references to a disposal within marriage or civil partnership are references to any disposal to which section 58 applies;

(c) references to Chapter III of Part VII of the Taxes Act or any provision of that Chapter are to that Chapter or provision as it applies in relation to shares issued on or after 1st January 1994; and

(d) references to Part 5 of ITA 2007 or any provision of that Part are to a Part or provision that applies only in relation to shares issued on or after 6th April 2007.

19(4) For the purposes of this Schedule shares in a company shall not be treated as being of the same class unless they would be so treated if dealt with on the Stock Exchange.

19(5) Notwithstanding anything in section 288(5), shares shall not for the purposes of this Schedule be treated as issued by reason only of being comprised in a letter of allotment or similar instrument.

History – In para. 19(1):

- In the definition of "51 per cent. subsidiary", the words "Chapter 3 of Part 24 of CTA 2010" substituted for "section 838 of the Taxes Act" by CTA 2010, s. 1177 and Sch. 1, para. 268(a), with effect for corporation tax purposes for accounting periods ending on or after 1 April 2010, and for income tax and capital gains tax purposes for the tax year 2010-11 and subsequent tax years.
- definition of "51 per cent. subsidiary" inserted by FA 2004, s. 93 and Sch. 18, para. 20(1)(a) which has effect in relation to shares issued on or after 17 March 2004. However, for the purposes of the TCGA 1992, Sch. 5B, para. 10(4) (definition of "group of companies"), this definition takes effect, for the purposes of TCGA 1992, Sch. 5B, para. 10(1) (reinvestment in same company) in relation to holdings of shares or securities disposed of on or after 17 March 2004 and, for the purposes of TCGA 1992, Sch. 5B, para. 10(2) (reinvestment in a relevant company), in relation to eligible shares in a relevant company issued on or after 17 March 2004 (FA 2004, Sch. 18, para. 20(2)).
- definition of "arrangements" substituted by FA 2012, s. 39 and Sch. 7, para. 32. The amendment is treated as having come into force on 6 April 2012.
- In the definition of "associate", the words "section 448 of CTA 2010 if in that section" substituted for "subsections (3) and (4) of section 417 of the Taxes Act if in those subsections" by CTA 2010, s. 1177 and Sch. 1, para. 268(b), with effect for corporation tax purposes for accounting periods ending on or after 1 April 2010, and for income tax and capital gains tax purposes for the tax year 2010–11 and subsequent tax years.
- definition of "bonus shares" inserted by FA 2004, s. 93 and Sch. 18, para. 20(1)(b) which have effect, by virtue of FA 2004, Sch. 18, para. 21, in relation to shares issued on or after 17 March 2004.
- definition of "the designated period" (inserted by FA 2000, s. 64 and Sch. 17, para. 7(2) with effect in relation to shares issued on or after 6 April 2000) repealed by FA 2001, s. 110 and Sch. 33, Pt. 2(3) in respect of shares issued on or after 7 March 2001 or shares issued after 31 December 1993 but before 7 March 2001 for which income tax relief or deferral relief was due immediately before 7 March 2001.
- definition of "eligible shares", the words "the Taxes Act or means shares that meet the requirement in section 173(2) of ITA 2007" substituted for "that Act", by ITA 2007, s. 1027 and Sch. 1, para. 345(14)(a), with effect from 6 April 2007.
- definition of "the five year period" repealed by FA 2000, s. 56 and Sch. 40, Pt. II(5) with effect in relation to shares issued on or after 6 April 2000.
- in the definition of "non-resident", the words "not resident" substituted for the words "neither resident nor ordinarily resident" by FA 2013, s. 219 and Sch. 46, para. 110(4), with effect in relation to cases where the accrual time is on or after 6 April 2013 (even if the qualifying investment was made before that date).
- in the definition of "ordinary share capital", the words "the meaning given by section 923 of ITA 2007" substituted for "the same meaning as in the Taxes Act", by ITA 2007, s. 1027 and Sch. 1, para. 345(14)(b), with effect from 6 April 2007.
- definition of "the period of restriction" inserted by FA 2001, s. 63 and Sch. 15, para. 37(a) in respect of shares issued on or after 7 March 2001 or shares issued after 31 December 1993 but before 7 March 2001 for which income tax relief or deferral relief was due immediately before 7 March 2001 (FA 2001, s. 40(2)).
- in the definition of "qualifying business activity", the words "or section 179 of ITA 2007" inserted by ITA 2007, s. 1027 and Sch. 1, para. 345(14)(c), with effect from 6 April 2007.
- definition of "qualifying company" substituted by ITA 2007, s. 1027 and Sch. 1, para. 345(14)(d), with effect from 6 April 2007. That former definition was amended by FA 2001, s. 63 and Sch. 15, para. 37(b) by the insertion of the words "(except that for the purposes of this Schedule the reference in section 293(1B)(b)(i) of that Act to section 304A of that Act shall be read as a reference to paragraph 8 above)" in respect of shares issued on or after 7 March 2001 or shares issued after 31 December 1993 but before 7 March 2001 for which income tax relief or deferral relief was due immediately before 7 March 2001 (FA 2001, s. 40(2)).
- in the definition of "the relevant period", the words "the Taxes Act or section 159(2) of ITA 2007" substituted for the words "that Act" by ITA 2007, s. 1027 and Sch. 1, para. 345(14)(e), with effect from 6 April 2007.
- definition of "relevant shares" omitted by FA 1999, s. 73 and Sch. 8, para. 3(1) and repealed by s. 139 and Sch. 20, Pt. III(17), with effect in relation to shares issued on or after 6 April 1999.
- definition of "the seven year period" repealed by FA 2000, s. 56 and Sch. 40, Pt. II(5) with effect in relation to shares issued on or after 6 April 2000.
- in the definition of "termination date" the words "or section 256 of ITA 2007" inserted by ITA 2007, s. 1027 and Sch. 1, para. 345(14)(f), with effect from 6 April 2007.
- definition of "termination date" inserted by FA 2001, s. 63 and Sch. 15, para. 37(a) in respect of shares issued on or after 7 March 2001 or shares issued after 31 December 1993 but before 7 March 2001 for which income tax relief or deferral relief was due immediately before 7 March 2001 (FA 2001, s. 40(2)).

In para. 19(1B) the words "or civil partnership" inserted twice by SI 2005/3229, reg. 127, with effect from 5 December 2005.
Para. 19(1A)–(1E) inserted by FA 1999, s. 73 and Sch. 8, para. 3(2), with effect in relation to shares issued on or after 6 April 1999.
In para. 19(3), the word "and" immediately before clause (c) omitted by ITA 2007, s. 1027 and Sch. 1, para. 345(15), and repealed by s. 1031 and Sch. 3, Pt. 1, and clause (d) inserted by ITA 2007, s. 1027 and Sch. 1, para. 345(15), all with effect from 6 April 2007.
Para. 19 inserted by FA 1998, s. 74 and Sch. 13, para. 36 with effect in relation to shares issued on or after 6 April 1998.

Cross references – S. 105B: any shares to which deferral relief (within the meaning of this Schedule), but not relief under ICTA 1988, Pt. 7, Ch. 3, is attributable, and if acquired by an individual on a disposal to which s. 58 of this Act applies, shall be treated as acquired by the individual on the day on which they were issued.

SCHEDULE 5BB – SEED ENTERPRISE INVESTMENT SCHEME: RE-INVESTMENT

SEIS RE-INVESTMENT RELIEF

Other material – HMRC guidance on SEIS capital gains tax re-investment relief is available at http://www.hmrc.gov.uk/seedeis/background.htm#2.

1(1) Sub-paragraph (5) applies where conditions A to C are met in relation to an individual ("the investor").

1(2) Condition A is that–

(a) there would (ignoring sub-paragraphs (5) and (6)) be a chargeable gain ("the original gain") accruing to the investor at any time in the tax year 2012–13 or any subsequent tax year (the year in question being referred to in this Schedule as "the relevant year"), and

(b) the original gain is one accruing on the disposal of an asset by the investor at any time ("the disposal time") in the relevant year.

1(3) Condition B is that–

(a) the investor is eligible for SEIS relief for the relevant year in respect of an amount subscribed for an issue of shares in a company made to the investor in that year,

(b) the investor makes a claim for and obtains SEIS relief for that year in respect of all or some of those shares ("the relevant SEIS shares"), and

(c) if the relevant SEIS shares, or any corresponding bonus shares in relation to those shares, were issued before the disposal time, they are still held by the investor at the disposal time.

1(4) Condition C is that–

(a) the investor has made a claim under this paragraph for relief in relation to the original gain, and

(b) the claim is in respect of the amount on which SEIS relief is claimed by the investor in respect of the relevant SEIS shares ("the SEIS expenditure") or part of that amount.

1(5) The relevant percentage of the available SEIS expenditure is to be set against a corresponding amount of the original gain.

1(5A) In sub-paragraph (5)–

"the available SEIS expenditure" means so much of the SEIS expenditure as–

(a) is specified in the claim,

(b) is unused, and

(c) does not exceed so much of the original gain as is unmatched;

"the relevant percentage" means–

(a) if the relevant year is the tax year 2012–13, 100%, and

(b) if the relevant year is any subsequent tax year, 50%.

1(6) Where an amount of the SEIS expenditure is set against the whole or part of the original gain under sub-paragraph (5), so much of that gain as is equal to that amount is to be treated as not being a chargeable gain.

1(7) For the purposes of this paragraph–

(a) the SEIS expenditure is unused to the extent that it has not already been set under sub-paragraph (5) or paragraph 2(1) of Schedule 5B against the whole or any part of a chargeable gain, and

(b) the original gain is unmatched, in relation to the SEIS expenditure, to the extent that it has not had any other expenditure set against it under sub-paragraph (5) or paragraph 2(1) of Schedule 5B.

History – In para. 1(2)(a), the words "or any subsequent tax year" substituted for the words "or the tax year 2013–14" by FA 2014, s. 55(1)(a), with effect from 17 July 2014.

In para. 1(2)(a), the words "or the tax year 2013–14 (the year in question being referred to in this Schedule as "the relevant year")" inserted by FA 2013, s. 57(2)(a)(i), with effect from 17 July 2013.

In para. 1(2)(b), the words "the relevant year" substituted for the words "that year" by FA 2013, s. 57(2)(a)(ii), with effect from 17 July 2013.

In para. 1(3)(a), the words "relevant year" substituted for the words "tax year 2012–13" by FA 2013, s. 57(2)(b), with effect from 17 July 2013.

In para. 1(5A), in the definition of "the relevant percentage", in para. (b), the words "any subsequent tax year" substituted for the words "the tax year 2013–14" by FA 2014, s. 55(1)(b), with effect from 17 July 2014.

Para. 1(5) and (5A) substituted for (5), by FA 2013, s. 57(2)(c), with effect from 17 July 2013.

RESTRICTIONS ON RELIEF UNDER PARAGRAPH 1

2(1) Sub-paragraph (2) applies if the investor's tax reduction under section 257AB of ITA 2007 for the relevant year is limited by subsection (2)(b) of that section (calculation of tax reduction where claim made for amounts subscribed for shares which exceed £100,000).

2(2) Paragraph 1(5) to (7) has effect as if references to the SEIS expenditure were references to so much of that expenditure as is given by the formula–

$$\frac{SA}{TSA} \times £100{,}000$$

where–

SA means the SEIS expenditure (ignoring this paragraph);

TSA means the total of the amounts subscribed for shares issued in the relevant year in respect of which the investor is eligible for and claims SEIS relief for that year.

2(3) Sub-paragraph (4) applies if the amount of SEIS relief attributable to any of the relevant SEIS shares has been reduced under Chapter 6 of Part 5A of ITA 2007 before the SEIS relief was obtained (otherwise than by virtue of corresponding bonus shares being issued in respect of those shares).

2(4) Paragraph 1(5) to (7) has effect as if the SEIS expenditure were the amount found by multiplying that expenditure by the fraction–

$$\frac{R1}{R2}$$

where–

"R1" means the amount of SEIS relief attributable to the relevant SEIS shares when the relief is obtained;

"R2" means the amount of SEIS relief which would have been so attributable in the absence of the reduction.

2(5) In a case where sub-paragraphs (2) and (4) both apply, sub-paragraph (2) is to be applied before sub-paragraph (4).

History – In para. 2(1), the words "relevant year" substituted for the words "tax year 2012–13" by FA 2013, s. 57(3)(a), with effect from 17 July 2013.

In para. 2(2), the words "relevant year" substituted for the words "tax year 2012–13" and the words "that year" substituted for the words "that tax year" by FA 2013, s. 57(3)(b), with effect from 17 July 2013.

CLAIMS

3(1) Section 257EA of ITA 2007 (time for making claims for SEIS relief) applies in relation to a claim made by the investor for the purposes of paragraph 1 in relation to the SEIS expenditure as it applies in relation to a claim for SEIS relief in respect of that expenditure.

3(2) Nothing in paragraph 1(3) prevents a claim being made by the investor under paragraph 1 before SEIS relief has actually been obtained by the investor in relation to the SEIS relief.

ATTRIBUTION OF SEIS RE-INVESTMENT RELIEF TO RELEVANT SEIS SHARES

4(1) References in this Schedule to the SEIS re-investment relief attributable to any shares are to be read as references to the total amount attributed to those shares in accordance with this paragraph.

4(2) Sub-paragraph (3) applies where the whole or part of the SEIS expenditure is set off against a chargeable gain under paragraph 1(5).

4(3) A proportionate part of the expenditure which is so set off is attributed to each of the relevant SEIS shares.

4(4) Sub-paragraph (5) applies if corresponding bonus shares are issued in respect of all or some of the relevant SEIS shares ("the original shares") to which relief is attributed under this paragraph.

4(5) A proportionate part of the total amount attributed to the original shares immediately before those bonus shares are issued is attributed to each of the shares in the holding comprising the original shares and those bonus shares.

REMOVAL OR REDUCTION OF THE RELIEF

5(1) This paragraph applies where in respect of shares issued to an individual–

(a) SEIS relief is attributable to the shares,

(b) SEIS re-investment relief is also attributable to the shares, and

(c) the SEIS relief which is attributable to the shares is withdrawn or reduced under Chapters 6 and 7 of Part 5A of ITA 2007.

5(2) A chargeable gain accrues to the individual in the tax year in which the shares were issued on a disposal made in that tax year.

5(3) The amount of that gain is–

(a) in a case where the SEIS relief is withdrawn, the amount of SEIS re-investment relief which is attributable to the shares immediately before the withdrawal, and

(b) in a case where the SEIS relief is reduced, the appropriate fraction of that amount.

5(4) In a case where the SEIS re-investment relief is withdrawn, the SEIS re-investment relief ceases to be attributable to the shares.

5(5) In a case where the SEIS relief is reduced, the appropriate fraction of the SEIS re-investment relief ceases to be attributable to the shares.

5(6) **"The appropriate fraction"** is–

$$\frac{R1 - R2}{R1}$$

where–

"**R1**" is the total amount of the SEIS relief attributable to those shares immediately before the reduction, and

"**R2**" is the total amount of the SEIS relief attributable to those shares immediately after the reduction.

History – In para. 5(2), the words "in which the shares were issued" substituted for the words "2012–13" by FA 2013, s. 57(4), with effect from 17 July 2013.

TRANSFERS OF SHARES TO SPOUSES AND CIVIL PARTNERS

6(1) This paragraph applies if–

(a) shares to which an amount of SEIS relief is attributable were issued to an individual ("A"),

(b) A transferred the shares to another individual ("B") during their lives,

(c) A was married to, or was the civil partner of, B at the time of the transfer, and

(d) subsection (4) of section 257FA of ITA 2007 (provision about disposals of shares disapplied where disposal between spouses or civil partners) prevented that section applying to the transfer.

6(2) Any chargeable gain which accrues by virtue of paragraph 5(2), as a result of SEIS relief attributable to the shares being withdrawn or reduced after the shares are transferred, is to accrue to B (instead of to A).

ADJUSTMENT OF CAPITAL GAINS TAX LIABILITY

7(1) All such adjustments of capital gains tax are to be made, whether by way of assessment or by way of discharge or repayment of tax, as may be required in consequence of relief being obtained, or a gain accruing, under this Schedule.

7(2) In its application to an assessment made by virtue of this paragraph, section 86 of TMA 1970 (interest on overdue capital gains tax) has effect as if the relevant date were 31 January next following the tax year in which the assessment is made.

INTERPRETATION ETC

8(1) In this Schedule–

"**bonus shares**" means shares which are issued otherwise than for payment (whether in cash or otherwise);

"**corresponding bonus shares**", in relation to any shares ("the original shares"), means bonus shares which are in the same company, of the same class, and carry the same rights as the original shares;

"**SEIS relief**" has the same meaning as in Part 5A of ITA 2007.

8(2) In this Schedule, references (however expressed) to an issue of shares in any company to an individual are to such of the shares in the company as are of the same class and are issued to the individual in one capacity and on the same day. This is subject to sub-paragraph (3).

8(3) If section 257AB(1) and (2) of ITA 2007 applies, in the case of any issue of shares made to an individual, as if part of the issue had been issued in a previous tax year, this Schedule has effect as if that part and the remainder were separate issues of shares (and that part had been issued on a day in the previous tax year).

8(4) Part 5A of ITA 2007 applies, for the purposes of this Schedule, to determine whether SEIS relief is attributable to any shares and, if so, the amount of relief so attributable.

History – Sch. 5BB inserted by FA 2012, s. 38 and Sch. 6, para. 5 with effect from 17 July 2012.

SCHEDULE 5BA – ENTERPRISE INVESTMENT SCHEME: APPLICATION OF TAPER RELIEF

Section 150D

History – Sch. 5BA omitted by FA 2008, s. 8 and Sch. 2, para. 49 with effect in relation to chargeable gains accruing or treated as accruing in the tax year 2008–09 or any subsequent tax year (FA 2008, Sch. 2, para. 56(3)).

[Omitted by FA 2008, s. 8 and Sch. 2, para. 49.]

SCHEDULE 5C – VENTURE CAPITAL TRUSTS: DEFERRED CHARGE ON RE-INVESTMENT

Section 151A

[Repealed by FA 2004, s. 326 and Sch. 42, Pt. 2(13); and ceases to have effect by FA 2004, s. 94 and Sch. 19, para. 5.]

History – Sch. 5C ceases to have effect by virtue of FA 2004, s. 94 and Sch. 19, para. 5; and FA 2004, s. 326 and Sch. 42, Pt. 2(13); which have effect, by virtue of FA 2004, Sch. 19, para. 7(1), in relation to shares issued on or after 6 April 2004; that are shares by reference to which an individual is given relief under ICTA 1988, Sch. 15B, Pt. 1 (venture capital trust: relief on investment). However, by virtue of FA 2004, Sch. 19, para. 7(2), nothing in FA 2004 affects the continuing operation of TCGA 1992, Sch. 5C for the purposes of TCGA 1992, s. 151B(8)(b)(ii). Former Sch. 5C read as follows:

"APPLICATION OF SCHEDULE

Cross references – SI 2004/2199: VCTs (winding up and mergers): modified application of Sch. 5C.

1(1) This Schedule applies where–

(a) there would (apart from paragraph 2(2)(a) below) be a chargeable gain (**"the original gain"**) accruing to an individual (**"the investor"**) at any time (**"the accrual time"**) on or after 6th April 1995;

(b) that gain is one accruing on the disposal by the investor of any asset or in accordance with paragraphs 4 and 5 of Schedule 5B or paragraphs 4 and 5 below;

(c) the investor makes a qualifying investment; and

(d) the investor is resident or ordinarily resident in the United Kingdom at the accrual time and the time when he makes the qualifying investment and is not, in relation to the qualifying investment, a person to whom sub-paragraph (4) below applies.

1(2) The investor makes a qualifying investment for the purposes of this Schedule if–

(a) he subscribes for any shares by reference to which he is given relief under Part I of Schedule 15B to the Taxes Act on any amount;

(b) those shares are issued at a qualifying time; and

(c) where that time is before the accrual time, those shares are still held by the investor at the accrual time;

and in this Schedule **"relevant shares"**, in relation to a case to which this Schedule applies, means any of the shares in a venture capital trust which are acquired by the investor in making the qualifying investment.

1(3) In this Schedule **"a qualifying time"**, in relation to any shares subscribed for by the investor, means–

(a) any time in the period beginning twelve months before the accrual time and ending twelve months after the accrual time, or

(b) any such time before the beginning of that period or after it ends as the Board may by notice allow.

1(4) This sub-paragraph applies to an individual in relation to a qualifying investment if–

(a) though resident or ordinarily resident in the United Kingdom at the time when he makes the investment, he is regarded for the purposes of any double taxation relief arrangements as resident in a territory outside the United Kingdom; and

(b) were section 151A(1) to be disregarded, the arrangements would have the effect that he would not be liable in the United Kingdom to tax on a gain arising on a disposal, immediately after their acquisition, of the shares acquired in making that investment.

Cross references – S. 151A(1): an individual's gain or loss on qualifying disposal of ordinary shares in a company not chargeable or allowable if it was a venture capital trust both when the individual acquired and disposed of the shares.

Sch. 5B: postponement of gains on disposal of enterprise investment scheme shares following the making of a qualifying investment.

ICTA 1988, Sch. 15B, Pt. I: income tax relief for individuals subscribing for eligible shares in venture capital trusts.

THE POSTPONEMENT OF THE ORIGINAL GAIN

2(1) On the making of a claim by the investor for the purposes of this Schedule, so much of the investor's unused qualifying expenditure on relevant shares as–

(a) is specified in the claim, and

(b) does not exceed so much of the original gain as is unmatched,

shall be set against a corresponding amount of the original gain.

2(2) Where the amount of any qualifying expenditure on any relevant shares is set under this Schedule against the whole or any part of the original gain–

(a) so much of that gain as is equal to that amount shall be treated as not having accrued at the accrual time; but

(b) paragraphs 4 and 5 below shall apply for determining the gain that is to be treated as accruing on the occurrence of any chargeable event in relation to any of those relevant shares.

2(3) For the purposes of this Schedule, but subject to the following provisions of this paragraph–

(a) the investor's qualifying expenditure on any relevant shares is the sum equal to the amount on which he is given relief under Part I of Schedule 15B to the Taxes Act by reference to those shares; and

(b) that expenditure is unused to the extent that it has not already been set under this Schedule against the whole or any part of a chargeable gain.

2(4) For the purposes of this paragraph the original gain is unmatched, in relation to any qualifying expenditure on relevant shares, to the extent that it has not had any other amount set against it under this Schedule or Schedule 5B.

Cross references – Sch. 5B: postponement of gains on disposal of enterprise investment scheme shares following the making of a qualifying investment.

ICTA 1988, Sch. 15B, Pt. I: income tax relief for individuals subscribing for eligible shares in venture capital trusts.

CHARGEABLE EVENTS

3(1) Subject to the following provisions of this paragraph, there is for the purposes of this Schedule a chargeable event in relation to any relevant shares if, after the making of the qualifying investment–

(a) the investor disposes of those shares otherwise than by way of a disposal within marriage or civil partnership;

(b) those shares are disposed of, otherwise than by way of a disposal to the investor, by a person who acquired them on a disposal made by the investor within marriage or civil partnership;

(c) there is, in a case where those shares fall within section 151B(3)(c), such an actual or deemed exchange of those shares for any non-qualifying holdings as, under section 135 or 136, requires, or but for section 116 would require, those holdings to be treated for the purposes of this Act as the same assets as those shares;

(d) the investor becomes a non-resident while holding those shares and within the relevant period;

(e) a person who acquired those shares on a disposal within marriage or civil partnership becomes a non-resident while holding those shares and within the relevant period;

(f) the company in which those shares are shares has its approval as a venture capital trust withdrawn in a case to which section 281(3) of ITA 2007 does not apply; or

(g) the relief given under Part I of Schedule 15B to the Taxes Act by reference to those shares is withdrawn or reduced in circumstances not falling within any of paragraphs (a) to (f) above.

3(2) In sub-paragraph (1) above–

"non-qualifying holdings" means any shares or securities other than any ordinary shares (within the meaning of section 151A) in a venture capital trust; and

"the relevant period", in relation to any relevant shares, means the period of three years beginning with the time when the investor made the qualifying investment by virtue of which he acquired those shares.

3(3) For the purposes of sub-paragraph (1) above there shall not be a chargeable event by virtue of sub-paragraph (1)(d) or (e) above in relation to any shares if–

(a) the reason why the person in question becomes a non-resident is that he works in an employment or office all the duties of which are performed outside the United Kingdom, and

(b) he again becomes resident or ordinarily resident in the United Kingdom within the period of three years from the time when he became a non-resident, without having meanwhile disposed of any of those shares;

and, accordingly, no assessment shall be made by virtue of sub-paragraph (1)(d) or (e) above before the end of that period in any case where the condition in paragraph (a) above is satisfied and the condition in paragraph (b) above may be satisfied.

3(4) For the purposes of sub-paragraph (3) above a person shall be taken to have disposed of any shares if and only if there has been such a disposal as would, if the person making the disposal had been resident in the United Kingdom, have been a chargeable event in relation to those shares.

3(5) Where in any case–

(a) the investor or a person who has acquired any relevant shares on a disposal within marriage or civil partnership dies, and

(b) an event occurs at or after the time of the death which (apart from this sub-paragraph) would be a chargeable event in relation to any relevant shares held by the deceased immediately before his death,

that event shall not be a chargeable event in relation to the shares so held.

3(6) Without prejudice to the operation of paragraphs 4 and 5 below in a case falling within sub-paragraph (1)(f) above, the references in this paragraph to a disposal shall not include references to the disposal which by virtue of section 151B(6) is deemed to take place in such a case.

History – In para. 3(1)(f), the words "section 281(3) of ITA 2007" substituted for the words "section 842AA(8) of the Taxes Act" by ITA 2007, s. 1027 and Sch. 1, para. 347, with effect from 6 April 2007.
In para. 3 the words "or civil partnership" inserted four times by SI 2005/3229, reg. 128, with effect from 5 December 2005.
In para. 3(2) in the definition of "the relevant period" "three" substituted for "five" by FA 2000, s. 65 and Sch. 18, para 2 with effect in relation to shares issued on or after 6 April 2000.

Cross references – S. 116: application of provisions on reorganisation, conversions and reconstructions to situations in which either the original shares or the new holding consist of qualifying corporate bonds.
S. 135, 136: equation of original and new holdings on an exchange or a company reconstruction involving the issue of securities.
S. 151A: ordinary shares in a venture capital trust are shares forming part of the company's ordinary share capital, i.e. its issued share capital (by whatever name called) except for capital with a right to a fixed-rate dividend but with no other right to share in the company's profits.
S. 151B(3)(c): shares in a venture capital trust on which income tax relief has or may be given, but which are not eligible for capital gains tax relief under s. 151A(1).
S. 151B(6): deemed disposal and immediate reacquisition at market value of shares in a venture capital trust upon withdrawal of the trust's approval (other than approval deemed never to have been given).
ICTA 1988, s. 842AA(8): if approval given in expectation that conditions for approval would be fulfilled within specified times is withdrawn, approval is deemed never to have been given.
ICTA 1988, Sch. 15B, Pt. I: income tax relief for individuals subscribing for eligible shares in venture capital trusts.

GAIN ACCRUING ON CHARGEABLE EVENT

4(1) On the occurrence of a chargeable event in relation to any relevant shares in relation to which there has not been a previous chargeable event–

(a) a chargeable gain shall be treated as accruing at the time of the event; and

(b) the amount of the gain shall be equal to so much of the original gain as is an amount against which there has under this Schedule been set any expenditure on those shares.

4(2) In determining for the purposes of this Schedule any question whether any shares to which a chargeable event relates are shares the expenditure on which has under this Schedule been set against the whole or any part of any gain, the assumptions in sub-paragraph (3) below shall apply and, in a case where the shares are not (within the meaning of section 151B) eligible for relief under section 151A(1), shall apply notwithstanding anything in any of sections 104, 105 and 106A.

4(3) Those assumptions are that–

(a) as between shares acquired by the same person on different days, those acquired on an earlier day are disposed of by that person before those acquired on a later day; and

(b) as between shares in a company that were acquired on the same day, those the expenditure on which has been set under this Schedule against the whole or any part of any gain are disposed of by that person only after he has disposed of any other shares in that company that were acquired by him on that day.

4(4) Where at the time of a chargeable event any relevant shares are treated for the purposes of this Act as represented by assets which consist of or include assets other than the relevant shares–

(a) the expenditure on those shares which was set against the gain in question shall be treated, in determining for the purposes of this paragraph the amount of expenditure on each of those assets which is to be treated as having been set against that gain, as apportioned in such manner as may be just and reasonable between those assets; and

(b) as between different assets treated as representing the same relevant shares, the assumptions mentioned in sub-paragraph (3) above shall apply with the necessary modifications in relation to those assets as they would apply in relation to the shares.

History – In para. 4(2), reference to TCGA 1992, s. 106A substituted for reference to TCGA 1992, s. 107 by FA 1998, s. 124(6) with effect in relation to disposals on or after 6 April 1998, and in circumstances described in FA 1998, s. 124(8) to disposals on or after 17 March 1998.

Cross references – S. 104: all securities of same class acquired by same person in same capacity to be regarded as indistinguishable parts of a single asset.
S. 105: matching of disposals of securities of same class acquired by same person in same capacity with same-day acquisitions.
S. 107: matching of disposals of securities of same class acquired by same person in same capacity with acquisitions in the preceding ten days.
S. 151A(1): an individual's gain or loss on qualifying disposal of ordinary shares in a company not chargeable or allowable if it was a venture capital trust both when the individual acquired and disposed of the shares.
S. 151B: shares are eligible for relief under s. 151A(1) at any time if they are held by an individual whose disposal of them then would be one to which s. 151A(1) would apply.
S. 260(6B) (hold-over relief): s. 260(3) disapplied, so far as any gain under para. 4 is concerned, as regards the disposal which is the chargeable event on which the gain accrues.

PERSONS TO WHOM GAIN ACCRUES

5(1) The chargeable gain which accrues in accordance with paragraph 4 above on the occurrence in relation to any relevant shares of a chargeable event shall be treated as accruing, as the case may be–

(a) to the person who makes the disposal,

(b) to the person who holds the shares in question at the time of the exchange or deemed exchange,

(c) to the person who becomes a non-resident,

(d) to the person who holds the shares in question when the withdrawal of the approval takes effect, or

(e) to the person who holds the shares in question when the circumstances arise in respect of which the relief is withdrawn or reduced.

5(2) Where–

(a) sub-paragraph (1) above provides for the holding of shares at a particular time to be what identifies the person to whom any chargeable gain accrues, and

(b) at that time, some of those shares are held by the investor and others are held by a person to whom the investor has transferred them by a disposal within marriage or civil partnership,

the amount of the chargeable gain accruing by virtue of paragraph 4 above shall be computed separately in relation to the investor and that person without reference to the shares held by the other.

History – In para. 5(2) the words "or civil partnership" inserted by SI 2005/3229, reg. 128, with effect from 5 December 2005.

Cross references – S. 260(6B) (hold-over relief): s. 260(3) disapplied, so far as any gain under para. 4 is concerned, as regards the disposal which is the chargeable event on which the gain accrues.

INTERPRETATION

6(1) In this Schedule **"non-resident"** means a person who is neither resident nor ordinarily resident in the United Kingdom.

6(2) In this Schedule references to a disposal within marriage or civil partnership are references to any disposal to which section 58 applies.

6(3) Notwithstanding anything in section 288(5), shares shall not for the purposes of this Schedule be treated as issued by reason only of being comprised in a letter of allotment or similar instrument.

History – In para. 6(2) the words "or civil partnership" inserted by SI 2005/3229, reg. 128, with effect from 5 December 2005.

Cross references – S. 58: disposals between husband and wife living together treated as no gain/no loss transactions.
S. 288(5): shares or debentures comprised in a letter of allotment or similar instrument treated as issued unless the right to the share or debentures remains provisional until accepted and there is no acceptance.
ICTA 1988, Pt. VII, Ch. III: income tax relief under the EIS."
Former Sch. 5C inserted by FA 1995, s. 72(4) and Sch. 16 with effect for 1995–96 and subsequent years of assessment.

Cross references – FA 2002, Sch. 33: winding up of venture capital trusts.
FA 2008, Sch. 3, para. 8: interaction of Pt. 5, Ch. 3 (entrepreneurs' relief) rules in cases where the original gain would have accrued before 6 April 2008, but for the provisions of Sch. 5B (enterprise investment scheme) or 5C (venture capital trusts).

SCHEDULE 6 – RETIREMENT RELIEF ETC.

Sections 163, 164

[Repealed by FA 1998, s. 140(2)(c), s. 165 and Sch. 27, Pt. III(31).]

History – Sch. 6 repealed by FA 1998, s. 140(2)(c), s. 165 and Sch. 27, Pt. III(31) which have effect in relation to disposals in the year 2003–04 and subsequent years.

SCHEDULE 7 – RELIEF FOR GIFTS OF BUSINESS ASSETS

Section 165

Part I – Agricultural Property and Settled Property

AGRICULTURAL PROPERTY

1(1) This paragraph applies where–

(a) there is a disposal of an asset which is, or is an interest in, agricultural property within the meaning of Chapter II of Part V of the Inheritance Tax Act 1984 (inheritance tax relief for agricultural property), and

(b) apart from this paragraph, the disposal would not fall within section 165(1) by reason only that the agricultural property is not used for the purposes of a trade carried on as mentioned in section 165(2)(a).

1(2) Where this paragraph applies, section 165(1) shall apply in relation to the disposal if the circumstances are such that a reduction in respect of the asset–

(a) is made under Chapter II of Part V of the Inheritance Tax Act 1984 in relation to a chargeable transfer taking place on the occasion of the disposal, or

(b) would be so made if there were a chargeable transfer on that occasion, or

(c) would be so made but for section 124A of that Act (assuming, where there is no chargeable transfer on that occasion, that there were).

Derivations – CGTA 1979, Sch. 4, para. 1, as amended by FA 1989, s. 124 and Sch. 14, para. 3(2).

Statements of practice – SP 8/92: HMRC's practice for dealing with valuation of assets where a claim to gifts hold-over relief has been made.

HMRC interpretations – IRInt. 8: the fact that agricultural property transferred has "hope" or "development" value does not preclude or restrict relief under s. 165 as extended by Sch. 7, para. 1.

Notes – IHTA 1984, s. 2: meaning of "chargeable transfer".
IHTA 1984, s. 124A: transfers of agricultural property within seven years before death.

SETTLED PROPERTY

2(1) If–

(a) the trustees of a settlement make a disposal otherwise than under a bargain at arm's length of an asset within sub-paragraph (2) below, and

(b) a claim for relief under section 165 is made by the trustees and the person who acquires the asset (**"the transferee"**) or, where the trustees of a settlement are also the transferee, by the trustees making the disposal alone,

then, subject to sections 165(3), 166, 167, 169, 169B and 169C, section 165(4) shall apply in relation to the disposal.

2(2) An asset is within this sub-paragraph if–

(a) it is, or is an interest in, an asset used for the purposes of a trade, profession or vocation carried on by–

(i) the trustees making the disposal, or

(ii) a beneficiary who had an interest in possession in the settled property immediately before the disposal, or

(b) it consists of shares or securities of a trading company, or of the holding company of a trading group, where–

(i) the shares or securities are not listed on a recognised stock exchange, or

(ii) not less than 25 per cent of the voting rights exercisable by shareholders of the company in general meeting are exercisable by the trustees at the time of the disposal.

2(3) Where section 165(4) applies by virtue of this paragraph, references to the trustees shall be substituted for the references in section 165(4)(a) to the transferor; and where it applies in relation to a disposal which is deemed to occur by virtue of section 71(1) or 72(1) section 165(7) shall not apply.

History – In para. 2(1), the words ", 169, 169B and 169C" substituted for "and 169" by FA 2004, s. 116 and Sch. 21, para. 9(2) with effect, by virtue of FA 2004, Sch. 21, para. 10(4), in relation to disposals on or after 10 December 2003 (whenever any earlier disposal as mentioned in section 169B(3)(b) or 169C(3)(b) was made).
In para. 2(2)(b)(i), the word "listed" was substituted by FA 1996, s. 199 and Sch. 38, para. 10(2)(f), with effect in relation to disposals on or after 1 April 1996. Words "not listed on a recognised stock exchange" substituted for "neither listed on a recognised stock exchange nor dealt in on the Unlisted Securities Market" by FA 2000, s. 90(3) with effect in relation to disposals made on or after 9 November 1999.

Derivations – CGTA 1979, Sch. 4, para. 2, as substituted by FA 1989, s. 124 and Sch. 14, para. 3(3).

Cross references – S. 71(1): person becoming absolutely entitled to settled property.
S. 72(1): death of life tenant.

Statements of practice – SP 8/92: HMRC's practice for dealing with valuation of assets where a claims to gifts hold-over relief has been made.

Notes – S. 68: meaning of "settled property".

3(1) This paragraph applies where–

(a) there is a disposal of an asset which is, or is an interest in, agricultural property within the meaning of Chapter II of Part V of the Inheritance Tax Act 1984, and

(b) apart from this paragraph, the disposal would not fall within paragraph 2(1)(a) above by reason only that the agricultural property is not used for the purposes of a trade as mentioned in paragraph 2(2)(a) above.

3(2) Where this paragraph applies paragraph 2(1) above shall apply in relation to the disposal if the circumstances are such that a reduction in respect of the asset–

(a) is made under Chapter II of Part V of the Inheritance Tax Act 1984 in relation to a chargeable transfer taking place on the occasion of the disposal, or

(b) would be so made if there were a chargeable transfer on that occasion, or

(c) would be so made but for section 124A of that Act (assuming, where there is no chargeable transfer on that occasion, that there were).

Derivations – CGTA 1979, Sch. 4, para. 3, as amended by FA 1989, s. 124 and Sch. 14, para. 3(4).

Statements of practice – SP 8/92: HMRC's practice for dealing with valuation of assets where a claim to gifts hold-over relief has been made.

Notes – IHTA 1984, s. 2: meaning of "chargeable transfer".
IHTA 1984, s. 124A: transfers of agricultural property within seven years before death.

Part II – Reductions in Held-Over Gain

APPLICATION AND INTERPRETATION

4(1) The provisions of this Part of this Schedule apply in cases where a claim for relief is made under section 165.

4(2) In this Part of this Schedule–

(a) **"the principal provision"** means section 165(2), or, as the case may require, sub-paragraph (2) of paragraph 2 above,

(b) **"shares"** includes securities,

(c) **"the transferor"** has the same meaning as in section 165 except that, in a case where paragraph 2 above applies, it refers to the trustees mentioned in that paragraph, and

(d) **"unrelieved gain"**, in relation to a disposal, has the same meaning as in section 165(7).

4(3) In this Part of this Schedule–

(a) any reference to a disposal of an asset is a reference to a disposal which falls within subsection (1) of section 165 by virtue of subsection (2)(a) of that section or, as the case may be, falls within sub-paragraph (1) of paragraph 2 above by virtue of sub-paragraph (2)(a) of that paragraph, and

(b) any reference to a disposal of shares is a reference to a disposal which falls within subsection (1) of section 165 by virtue of subsection (2)(b) of that section or, as the case may be, falls within sub-paragraph (1) of paragraph 2 above by virtue of sub-paragraph (2)(b) of that paragraph.

4(4) In relation to a disposal of an asset or of shares, any reference in the following provisions of this Part of this Schedule to the held-over gain is a reference to the held-over gain on that disposal as determined under subsection (6) or, where it applies, subsection (7) of section 165.

Derivations – CGTA 1979, Sch. 4, para. 4, as amended by FA 1989, s. 124 and Sch. 14, para. 3(5).

REDUCTIONS PECULIAR TO DISPOSALS OF ASSETS

5(1) If, in the case of a disposal of an asset, the asset was not used for the purposes of the trade, profession or vocation referred to in paragraph (a) of the principal provision throughout the period of its ownership by the transferor, the amount of the held-over gain shall be reduced by multiplying it by the fraction–

$$\frac{A}{B}$$

where–

A is the number of days in that period of ownership during which the asset was so used, and

B is the number of days in that period.

5(2) This paragraph shall not apply where the circumstances are such that a reduction in respect of the asset–

(a) is made under Chapter II of Part V of the Inheritance Tax Act 1984 in relation to a chargeable transfer taking place on the occasion of the disposal, or

(b) would be so made if there were a chargeable transfer on that occasion, or

(c) would be so made but for section 124A of that Act (assuming, where there is no chargeable transfer on that occasion, that there were).

Derivations – CGTA 1979, Sch. 4, para. 5, as amended by FA 1989, s. 124 and Sch. 14, para. 3(6).

Notes – IHTA 1984, s. 2: meaning of "chargeable transfer".
IHTA 1984, s. 124A: transfers of agricultural property within seven years before death.

6(1) If, in the case of a disposal of an asset, the asset is a building or structure and, over the period of its ownership by the transferor or any substantial part of that period, part of the building or structure was, and part was not, used for the purposes of the trade, profession or vocation referred to in paragraph (a) of the principal provision, there shall be determined the fraction of the unrelieved gain on the disposal which it is just and reasonable to apportion to the part of the asset which was so used, and the amount of the held-over gain (as reduced, if appropriate, under paragraph 5 above) shall be reduced by multiplying it by that fraction.

6(2) This paragraph shall not apply where the circumstances are such that a reduction in respect of the asset–

(a) is made under Chapter II of Part V of the Inheritance Tax Act 1984 in relation to a chargeable transfer taking place on the occasion of the disposal, or

(b) would be so made if there were a chargeable transfer on that occasion, or

(c) would be so made but for section 124A of that Act (assuming, where there is no chargeable transfer on that occasion, that there were).

Derivations – CGTA 1979, Sch. 4, para. 6, as amended by FA 1989, s. 124 and Sch. 14, para. 3(6).

Notes – IHTA 1984, s. 2: meaning of "chargeable transfer".
IHTA 1984, s. 124A: transfers of agricultural property within seven years before death.

REDUCTION PECULIAR TO DISPOSAL OF SHARES

7(1) If in the case of a disposal of shares assets which are not business assets are included in the chargeable assets of the company whose shares are disposed of, or, where that company is the holding company of a trading group, in the group's chargeable assets, and either–

(a) at any time within the period of 12 months before the disposal not less than 25 per cent of the voting rights exercisable by shareholders of the company in general meeting are exercisable by the transferor, or

(b) the transferor is an individual and, at any time within that period, the company is his personal company,

the amount of the held-over gain shall be reduced by multiplying it by the fraction–

$$\frac{A}{B}$$

where–

A is the market value on the date of the disposal of those chargeable assets of the company or of the group which are business assets, and

B is the market value on that date of all the chargeable assets of the company, or as the case may be of the group.

7(2) For the purposes of this paragraph–

(a) an asset is a business asset in relation to a company or a group if it is or is an interest in an asset used for the purposes of a trade, profession or vocation carried on by the company, or as the case may be by a member of the group; and

(b) an asset is a chargeable asset in relation to a company or a group at any time if, on a disposal at that time, a gain accruing to the company, or as the case may be to a member of the group, would be a chargeable gain.

7(3) Where the shares disposed of are shares of the holding company of a trading group, then for the purposes of this paragraph–

(a) the holding by one member of the group of the ordinary share capital of another member shall not count as a chargeable asset, and

(b) if the whole of the ordinary share capital of a 51 per cent subsidiary of the holding company is not owned directly or indirectly by that company, the value of the chargeable assets of the subsidiary shall be taken to be reduced by multiplying it by the fraction–

$$\frac{A}{B}$$

where–

A is the amount of the ordinary share capital of the subsidiary owned directly or indirectly by the holding company, and

B is the whole of that share capital.

7(4) Expressions used in sub-paragraph (3) above have the same meanings as in section 838 of the Taxes Act.

History – In para. 7(1), the words "personal company" substituted for "family company" by FA 1993, s. 87 and Sch. 7, para. 1 in relation to disposals on or after 16 March 1993.

Derivations – (as originally enacted) – CGTA 1979, Sch. 4, para. 7, as substituted by FA 1989, s. 124 and Sch. 14, para. 3(7).

Cross references – ICTA 1988, s. 838: determination of 51 per cent subsidiary by reference to beneficial ownership directly or indirectly of more than 50 per cent of ordinary share capital.

Notes – S. 15: meaning of "chargeable gain".

REDUCTION WHERE GAIN PARTLY RELIEVED BY RETIREMENT RELIEF

8 [Repealed by FA 1998, s. 165 and Sch. 27, Pt. III(31) which have effect in relation to disposals in the year 2003–04 and subsequent years of assessment.]

SCHEDULE 7ZA – ENTREPRENEURS' RELIEF: "TRADING COMPANY" AND "TRADING GROUP"

Section 169SA

History – Sch. 7ZA inserted by FA 2016, s. 86 and Sch. 13, para. 5, with effect in relation to disposals made on or after 18 March 2015, but only for the purposes of determining what is a trading company or trading group at times on or after that date.

Part 1 – Meaning of "Trading Company" and "Trading Group"

1(1) This paragraph gives the meaning of **"trading company"** and **"trading group"** where used in the following provisions of Chapter 3 of Part 5 (entrepreneurs' relief)–

(a) in section 169I (material disposal of business assets)–

(i) paragraphs (a) and (b) of subsection (6) (which apply for the purposes of conditions A and B in that section), and

(ii) sub-paragraphs (i) and (ii) of subsection (7A)(c) (which apply for the purposes of conditions C and D in that section), and

(b) section 169J(4) (disposal of trust business assets).

1(2) **"Trading company"** and **"trading group"** have the same meaning as in section 165 (see section 165A), but as modified by Part 2 of this Schedule.

1(3) **"Trading activities"** (see section 165A(4) and (9)) is to be read in accordance with Part 3 of this Schedule.

2 In provisions of Chapter 3 of Part 5 not mentioned in paragraph 1(1), **"trading company"** and **"trading group"** have the same meaning as in section 165 (see section 165A), except that subsections (7) and (12) of section 165A are to be disregarded.

Part 2 – Joint Venture Companies

ATTRIBUTION OF ACTIVITIES OF A JOINT VENTURE COMPANY

3 In relation to a disposal of assets consisting of (or of interests in) shares in or securities of a company ("company A"), activities of a joint venture company are to be attributed to a company under subsections (7) and (12) of section 165A only if P–

(a) passes the shareholding test in relation to the joint venture company (see paragraphs 5 to 8), and

(b) passes the voting rights test in relation to the joint venture company (see paragraphs 9 to 12).

MEANING OF "INVESTING COMPANY"

4(1) For the purposes of this Part, a company is an **"investing company"** in relation to P and a joint venture company if it meets conditions 1 and 2.

4(2) Condition 1 is that–

(a) the company is company A (see paragraph 3), or

(b) P directly owns some portion of the ordinary share capital of the company.

4(3) Condition 2 is that the company owns some portion of the ordinary share capital of the joint venture company (whether it is owned directly, indirectly, or partly directly and partly indirectly).

4(4) In sub-paragraph (3) the reference to a company owning share capital indirectly is to be read in accordance with section 1155 of CTA 2010.

SHAREHOLDING TEST

5 P passes the shareholding test in relation to a joint venture company if, throughout the relevant period, the sum of the percentages given by paragraphs (a) and (b) is at least 5%–

(a) the percentage of the ordinary share capital of the joint venture company that is owned directly by P, and

(b) P's indirect shareholding percentage (see paragraph 6).

6 P's **"indirect shareholding percentage"** is found by–

(a) calculating the percentage of the ordinary share capital of the joint venture company that is owned indirectly by P through a particular investing company (see paragraph 7), and

(b) where there are two or more investing companies, adding those percentages together.

7 The percentage of the ordinary share capital of a joint venture company that is owned indirectly by P through a particular investing company ("company IC") at a particular time is given by–

$$R \times S \times 100$$

where–

R is the fraction of company IC's ordinary share capital that is owned by P at that time, and

S is the fraction of the joint venture company's ordinary share capital that is owned by company IC at that time (whether it is owned directly, indirectly, or partly directly and partly indirectly) (see paragraph 8).

8(1) The fraction of the joint venture company's ordinary share capital that is owned indirectly by company IC is calculated–

(a) by applying sections 1156 and 1157 of CTA 2010, as read with section 1155 of that Act, and

(b) on the assumptions specified in sub-paragraph (2).

8(2) The assumptions are–

(a) where company IC directly owns more than 50% of the ordinary share capital of a company, company IC is taken to own the whole of the ordinary share capital of that company;

(b) where a company other than company IC ("company B") directly owns more than 50% of the ordinary share capital of another company ("company C") which is a member of a group of companies of which company IC is a member, company B is taken to own the whole of the ordinary share capital of company C.

VOTING RIGHTS TEST

9 P passes the voting rights test in relation to a joint venture company if, throughout the relevant period, the sum of the percentages given by paragraphs (a) and (b) is at least 5%–

(a) the percentage of the voting rights that P holds directly in the joint venture company, and

(b) P's indirect voting rights percentage (see paragraph 10).

10 P's **"indirect voting rights percentage"** is found by–

(a) calculating the percentage of the voting rights in the joint venture company that P holds indirectly through a particular investing company (see paragraph 11), and

(b) where there are two or more investing companies, adding those percentages together.

11 The percentage of the voting rights in a joint venture company that P holds indirectly through a particular investing company ("company IC") at a particular time is given by–

$$T \times U \times 100$$

where–

T is the fraction of the voting rights in company IC that is held by P at that time, and

U is the fraction of the voting rights in the joint venture company that is held by company IC at that time (whether the voting rights are held directly, indirectly, or partly directly and partly indirectly) (see paragraph 12).

12(1) The fraction of the voting rights in the joint venture company that is held indirectly by company IC is calculated–

(a) by applying sections 1156 and 1157 of CTA 2010, as read with section 1155 of that Act, as if references in those sections to owning the ordinary share capital of a company were references to holding voting rights in a company, and

(b) on the assumptions specified in sub-paragraph (2).

12(2) The assumptions are–

(a) where company IC directly holds more than 50% of the voting rights in a company, company IC is taken to hold all the voting rights in that company;

(b) where a company other than company IC ("company B") directly holds more than 50% of the voting rights in another company ("company C") which is a member of a group of companies of which company IC is a member, company B is taken to hold all the voting rights in company C.

Part 3 – Partnerships

ACTIVITIES OF A COMPANY AS A MEMBER OF A PARTNERSHIP

13(1) In relation to a disposal of assets consisting of (or of interests in) shares in or securities of a company ("company A"), activities carried on by a company as a member of a partnership are to be treated as not being trading activities of the company (see section 165A(4) and (9)) if P fails either or both of the following–

(a) the profits and assets test in relation to the partnership (see paragraphs 15 to 20);

(b) the voting rights test in relation to the partnership (see paragraphs 21 to 23).

13(2) In relation to such a disposal, activities carried on by a company as a member of a partnership are also to be treated as not being trading activities of the company if the company is not a member of the partnership throughout the relevant period.

MEANING OF "DIRECT INTEREST COMPANY" AND "RELEVANT CORPORATE PARTNER"

14(1) This paragraph applies for the purposes of this Part.

14(2) A company is a **"direct interest company"** in relation to P if–

(a) it is company A (see paragraph 13(1)), or

(b) P directly owns some portion of the ordinary share capital of the company.

14(3) A company is a **"relevant corporate partner"** in relation to P and a partnership if–

(a) a direct interest company in relation to P ("company DIC") owns some portion of the ordinary share capital of the company (whether it is owned directly, indirectly or partly directly and partly indirectly),

(b) the company is a member of a group of companies of which company DIC is a member, and

(c) the company is a member of the partnership.

14(4) In sub-paragraph (3) the reference to a company owning share capital indirectly is to be read in accordance with section 1155 of CTA 2010.

PROFITS AND ASSETS TEST

15 P passes the profits and assets test in relation to a partnership if, throughout the relevant period, the sum of the percentages given by paragraphs (a), (b) and (c) is at least 5%–

(a) the percentage which is P's direct interest in the assets of the partnership,

(b) the percentage which is P's share of the partnership through direct interest companies that are members of the partnership (see paragraph 16), and

(c) the percentage which is P's share of the partnership through direct interest companies and relevant corporate partners in the partnership (see paragraph 18).

16 P's **"share of the partnership through direct interest companies that are members of the partnership"** is found by–

(a) calculating the percentage which is P's indirect share of the partnership through each direct interest company that is a member of the partnership (see paragraph 17), and

(b) where there are two or more direct interest companies that are members of the partnership, adding those percentages together.

17 The percentage which is P's indirect share of the partnership through a particular direct interest company that is a member of the partnership ("company DICP") at a particular time is given by–

$$R \times V \times 100$$

where–

R is the fraction of company DICP's ordinary share capital that is owned by P at that time, and

V is the lower of–

(a) the fraction of the profits of the partnership in which company DICP has an interest at that time, and

(b) the fraction of the assets of the partnership in which company DICP has an interest at that time.

TCGA 1992

18 P's **"share of the partnership through direct interest companies and relevant corporate partners in the partnership"** is found by–

(a) calculating the percentage which is P's indirect share of the partnership through each direct interest company and each relevant corporate partner in the partnership (see paragraph 19), and

(b) where there are two or more direct interest companies or two or more relevant corporate partners, or both, adding those percentages together.

19 The percentage which is P's indirect share of the partnership through a particular direct interest company ("company DIC") and a particular relevant corporate partner in the partnership ("company CP") at a particular time is given by–

$$R \times V \times W \times 100$$

where–

R is the fraction of company DIC's ordinary share capital that is owned by P at that time,

V is the lower of–

(a) the fraction of the profits of the partnership in which company CP has an interest at that time, and

(b) the fraction of the assets of the partnership in which company CP has an interest at that time, and

W is the fraction of company CP's ordinary share capital that is owned by company DIC at that time (whether it is owned directly, indirectly, or partly directly and partly indirectly) (see paragraph 20).

20(1) The fraction of a company's ordinary share capital that is owned indirectly by company DIC is calculated–

(a) by applying sections 1156 and 1157 of CTA 2010, as read with section 1155 of that Act, and

(b) on the assumptions specified in sub-paragraph (2).

20(2) The assumptions are–

(a) where company DIC directly owns more than 50% of the ordinary share capital of a company, company DIC is taken to own the whole of the ordinary share capital of that company;

(b) where a company other than company DIC ("company B") directly owns more than 50% of the ordinary share capital of another company ("company C") which is a member of a group of companies of which company DIC is a member, company B is taken to own the whole of the ordinary share capital of company C.

VOTING RIGHTS TEST

21(1) P passes the voting rights test in relation to a partnership if, throughout the relevant period, the sum of P's direct voting rights percentage and P's indirect voting rights percentage is at least 5%.

21(2) P's **"direct voting rights percentage"** is found by–

(a) taking the percentage of the voting rights that P holds directly in each direct interest company that is a member of the partnership, and

(b) where P directly holds voting rights in two or more direct interest companies that are members of the partnership, adding those percentages together.

21(3) P's **"indirect voting rights percentage"** is found by–

(a) calculating the percentage which is P's indirect holding of voting rights in each relevant corporate partner in the partnership through each direct interest company (see paragraph 22), and

(b) where there are two or more relevant corporate partners or two or more direct interest companies, or both, adding those percentages together.

22 The percentage which is P's indirect holding of voting rights in a particular relevant corporate partner in the partnership ("company CP") through a particular direct interest company ("company DIC") at a particular time is given by–

$$T \times X \times 100$$

where–

T is the fraction of the voting rights in company DIC that is held by P at that time, and

X is the fraction of the voting rights in company CP that is held by company DIC at that time (whether the voting rights are held directly, indirectly, or partly directly and partly indirectly) (see paragraph 23).

23(1) The fraction of the voting rights in a company that is held indirectly by company DIC is calculated–

(a) by applying sections 1156 and 1157 of CTA 2010, as read with section 1155 of that Act, as if references in those sections to owning the ordinary share capital of a company were references to holding voting rights in a company, and

(b) on the assumptions specified in sub-paragraph (2).

23(2) The assumptions are–

(a) where company DIC directly holds more than 50% of the voting rights in a company, company DIC is taken to hold all the voting rights in that company;

(b) where a company other than company DIC ("company B") directly holds more than 50% of the voting rights in another company ("company C") which is a member of a group of companies of which company DIC is a member, company B is taken to hold all the voting rights in company C.

Part 4 – Interpretation of this Schedule

MEANING OF "P"

24(1) In the case of a material disposal of business assets, **"P"** means the individual making the disposal.

24(2) In the case of a disposal of trust business assets–

(a) **"P"** means any relevant beneficiary, but

(b) in any reference to P passing or failing the tests mentioned in paragraphs 3 and 13(1), P is to be read as being a single body consisting of all the relevant beneficiaries (so that, for the purposes of determining if those tests are met, percentages are to be calculated in respect of each relevant beneficiary and then aggregated).

24(3) The following are **"relevant beneficiaries"**–

(a) the qualifying beneficiary in relation to the disposal (see section 169J(3)), and

(b) any other beneficiary who is, in relation to the disposal, a beneficiary mentioned in section 169O(1).

MEANING OF "RELEVANT PERIOD"

25 **"The relevant period"** means–

(a) for the purposes of conditions A and C in section 169I, the period of 1 year ending with the date of the disposal,

(b) for the purposes of conditions B and D in section 169I, the period of 1 year ending with the date mentioned in subsection (7)(a) or (b) or (7O)(a) or (b) of that section, and

(c) for the purposes of section 169J(4), a period of 1 year ending not earlier than 3 years before the date of the disposal.

OTHER INTERPRETATION PROVISIONS

26(1) Terms used in this Schedule which are defined in subsection (14) of section 165A have the same meaning as they have in that subsection.

26(2) References to a person holding voting rights include references to a person who has the ability to control the exercise of voting rights by another person.

26(3) For the purposes of Part 3 of this Schedule, the assets of–

(a) a Scottish partnership, or

(b) a partnership under the law of any other country or territory under which assets of a partnership are regarded as held by or on behalf of the partnership as such,

are to be treated as held by the members of the partnership in the proportions in which they are entitled to share in the capital profits of the partnership.

References in Part 3 to a person's interest in the assets of a partnership are to be construed accordingly.

SCHEDULE 7ZB – INVESTORS' RELIEF: DISQUALIFICATION OF SHARES

Section 169VB

History – Sch. 7ZB inserted by FA 2016, s. 87 and Sch. 14, para. 3, with effect from 15 September 2016 (Royal Assent).

DISQUALIFICATION OF SHARES WHERE VALUE RECEIVED IN PERIOD OF RESTRICTION

1(1) Sub-paragraph (2) applies where–

(a) shares in a company are issued to a qualifying person ("the investor") on a particular date,

(b) any of those shares would, apart from this Schedule, be or be treated as being qualifying shares or potentially qualifying shares at a particular time ("the relevant time"), and

(c) the investor receives any value, other than insignificant value, from the company at any time in the period of restriction.

1(2) The shares in question are to be treated for the purposes of this Chapter as being excluded shares at the relevant time.

1(3) Where–

(a) the investor receives value ("the relevant receipt") from the company during the period of restriction,

(b) the investor has received from the company one or more receipts of insignificant value at a time or times–

(i) during that period, but

(ii) not later than the time of the relevant receipt, and

(c) the aggregate amount of the value of the receipts within paragraphs (a) and (b) is not an amount of insignificant value,

the investor is to be treated for the purposes of this Schedule as if the relevant receipt had been a receipt of an amount equal to that aggregate amount.

For this purpose a receipt does not fall within paragraph (b) in relation to the shares if it has previously been aggregated under this sub-paragraph in relation to them.

1(4) In this Schedule **"the period of restriction"** means the period–

(a) beginning one year before the date the shares are issued, and

(b) ending immediately before the third anniversary of the date the shares are issued.

1(5) In sub-paragraphs (3) and (4) and in the following provisions of this Schedule references to **"the shares"** are to the shares referred to in sub-paragraph (1)(a).

1(6) This paragraph is subject to paragraph 4.

"RECEIVES VALUE"

2(1) For the purposes of this Schedule the investor receives value from the company if the company–

(a) repays, redeems or repurchases any of its share capital or securities which belong to the investor or makes any payment to the investor for giving up a right to any of the company's share capital or any security on its cancellation or extinguishment,

(b) repays, in pursuance of any arrangements for or in connection with the acquisition of the shares, any debt owed to the investor other than a debt which was incurred by the company–

(i) on or after the date of issue of the shares, and

(ii) otherwise than in consideration of the extinguishment of a debt incurred before that date,

(c) makes to the investor any payment for giving up the investor's right to any debt on its extinguishment,

(d) releases or waives any liability of the investor to the company or discharges, or undertakes to discharge, any liability of the investor to a third person,

(e) makes a loan or advance to the investor which has not been repaid in full before the issue of the shares,

(f) provides a benefit or facility for the investor,

(g) disposes of an asset to the investor for no consideration or for a consideration which is or the value of which is less than the market value of the asset,

(h) acquires an asset from the investor for a consideration which is or the value of which is more than the market value of the asset, or

(i) makes any payment to the investor other than a qualifying payment.

2(2) For the purposes of sub-paragraph (1)(e) there is to be treated as if it were a loan made by the company to the investor–

(a) the amount of any debt (other than an ordinary trade debt) incurred by the investor to the company, and

(b) the amount of any debt due from the investor to a third person which has been assigned to the company.

2(3) For the purposes of this paragraph the investor also receives value from the company if any person connected with the company–

(a) purchases any of its share capital or securities which belong to the investor, or

(b) makes any payment to the investor for giving up any right in relation to any of the company's share capital or securities.

2(4) In this paragraph **"qualifying payment"** means–

(a) the payment by any company of such remuneration for service as an officer or employee of that company as may be reasonable in relation to the duties of that office or employment,

(b) any payment or reimbursement by any company of travelling or other expenses wholly, exclusively and necessarily incurred by the investor to whom the payment is made in the performance of duties as an officer or employee of that company,

(c) the payment by any company of any interest which represents no more than a reasonable commercial return on money lent to that company,

(d) the payment by any company of any dividend or other distribution which does not exceed a normal return on any investment in shares in or other securities of that company,

(e) any payment for the supply of goods which does not exceed their market value,

(f) any payment for the acquisition of an asset which does not exceed its market value,

(g) the payment by any company, as rent for any property occupied by the company, of an amount not exceeding a reasonable and commercial rent for the property,

(h) any reasonable and necessary remuneration which–

  (i) is paid by any company for services rendered to that company in the course of a trade or profession carried on wholly or partly in the United Kingdom; and

  (ii) is taken into account in calculating for tax purposes the profits of that trade or profession, or

(i) a payment in discharge of an ordinary trade debt.

2(5) For the purposes of this paragraph a company is to be treated as having released or waived a liability if the liability is not discharged within 12 months of the time when it ought to have been discharged.

2(6) In this paragraph–

(a) references to a debt or liability do not, in relation to a company, include references to any debt or liability which would be discharged by the making by that company of a qualifying payment, and

(b) references to a benefit or facility do not include references to any benefit or facility provided in circumstances such that, if a payment had been made of an amount equal to its value, that payment would be a qualifying payment.

2(7) In this paragraph and paragraph 3–

(a) any reference to a payment or disposal to the investor includes a reference to a payment or disposal made to the investor indirectly or to the investor's order or for the investor's benefit;

(b) any reference to the investor includes an associate of the investor;

(c) any reference to a company includes a person who at any time in the period of restriction is connected with the company, whether or not that person is connected at the material time.

2(8) In this paragraph **"ordinary trade debt"** means any debt for goods or services supplied in the ordinary course of a trade or business where any credit given–

(a) does not exceed six months, and

(b) is not longer than that normally given to customers of the person carrying on the trade or business.

AMOUNT OF VALUE

3(1) For the purposes of paragraph 1, the value received by the investor is–

(a) in a case within paragraph 2(1)(a), (b) or (c), the amount received by the investor or, if greater, the market value of the share capital, securities or debt in question;

(b) in a case within paragraph 2(1)(d), the amount of the liability;

(c) in a case within paragraph 2(1)(e), the amount of the loan or advance reduced by the amount of any repayment made before the issue of the shares;

(d) in a case within paragraph 2(1)(f), the cost to the company of providing the benefit or facility less any consideration given for it by the investor;

(e) in a case within paragraph 2(1)(g) or (h), the difference between the market value of the asset and the consideration (if any) given for it;

(f) in a case within paragraph 2(1)(i), the amount of the payment;

(g) in a case within paragraph 2(3), the amount received by the investor or, if greater, the market value of the share capital or securities in question.

3(2) In this Schedule references to a receipt of insignificant value (however expressed) are references to a receipt of an amount of insignificant value.
This is subject to sub-paragraph (4).

3(3) For the purposes of this Schedule **"an amount of insignificant value"** means an amount of value which does not exceed £1,000.

3(4) For the purposes of this Schedule, if at any time in the period–

(a) beginning one year before the shares are issued, and

(b) expiring at the end of the issue date,

arrangements are in existence which provide for the investor to receive or to be entitled to receive, at any time in the period of restriction, any value from the company that issued the shares, no amount of value received by the investor is to be treated as a receipt of insignificant value.

3(5) In sub-paragraph (4)–

(a) any reference to the investor includes a reference to any person who, at any time in the period of restriction, is an associate of the investor (whether or not that person is such an associate at the material time), and

(b) the reference to the company includes a reference to any person who, at any time in the period of restriction, is connected with the company (whether or not that person is so connected at the material time).

RECEIPT OF REPLACEMENT VALUE

4(1) Where–

(a) by reason of a receipt of value within sub-paragraph (1) (other than paragraph (b)) or sub-paragraph (3) of paragraph 2 ("the original value"), any shares would, in the absence of this paragraph, be treated under this Schedule as excluded shares at a particular time,

(b) at or before that time the original supplier receives value ("the replacement value") from the original recipient by reason of a qualifying receipt, and

(c) the amount of the replacement value is not less than the amount of the original value,

the receipt of the original value is to be disregarded for the purposes of this Schedule.

4(2) This paragraph is subject to paragraph 5.

4(3) For the purposes of this paragraph and paragraph 5–

(a) **"the original recipient"** means the person who receives the original value, and

(b) **"the original supplier"** means the person from whom that value was received.

4(4) A receipt of the replacement value is a qualifying receipt for the purposes of sub-paragraph (1) if it arises–

(a) by reason of the original recipient doing one or more of the following–

(i) making a payment to the original supplier, other than a payment which falls within paragraph (c) or to which sub-paragraph (5) applies,

(ii) acquiring any asset from the original supplier for a consideration the amount or value of which is more than the market value of the asset,

(iii) disposing of any asset to the original supplier for no consideration or for a consideration the amount or value of which is less than the market value of the asset,

(b) where the receipt of the original value was within paragraph 2(1)(d), by reason of an event the effect of which is to reverse the event which constituted the receipt of the original value, or

(c) where the receipt of the original value was within paragraph 2(3), by reason of the original recipient repurchasing the share capital or securities in question, or (as the case may be) reacquiring the right in question, for a consideration the amount or value of which is not less than the amount of the original value.

4(5) This sub-paragraph applies to–

(a) any payment for any goods, services or facilities, provided (whether in the course of a trade or otherwise) by–

(i) the original supplier, or

(ii) any other person who, at any time in the period of restriction, is an associate of, or connected with, that supplier (whether or not that person is such an associate, or so connected, at the material time),

which is reasonable in relation to the market value of those goods, services or facilities,

(b) any payment of any interest which represents no more than a reasonable commercial return on money lent to–

(i) the original recipient, or

(ii) any person who, at any time in the period of restriction, is an associate of the original recipient (whether or not such an associate at the material time),

(c) any payment for the acquisition of an asset which does not exceed its market value,

(d) any payment, as rent for any property occupied by–

(i) the original recipient, or

(ii) any person who, at any time in the period of restriction, is an associate of the original recipient (whether or not such an associate at the material time),

of an amount not exceeding a reasonable and commercial rent for the property,

(e) any payment in discharge of an ordinary trade debt (within the meaning of paragraph 2(8)), and

(f) any payment for shares in or securities of any company in circumstances that do not fall within sub-paragraph (4)(a)(ii).

4(6) For the purposes of this paragraph, the amount of the replacement value is–

(a) in a case within paragraph (a) of sub-paragraph (4), the aggregate of–

(i) the amount of any payment within sub-paragraph (i) of that paragraph, and

(ii) the difference between the market value of any asset within sub-paragraph (ii) or (iii) of that paragraph and the amount or value of the consideration (if any) received for it,

(b) in a case within sub-paragraph (4)(b), the same as the amount of the original value, and

(c) in a case within sub-paragraph (4)(c), the amount or value of the consideration received by the original supplier,

and paragraph 3(1) applies for the purposes of determining the amount of the original value.

4(7) In this paragraph any reference to a payment to a person (however expressed) includes a reference to a payment made to the person indirectly or to the person's order or for the person's benefit.

5(1) The receipt of the replacement value by the original supplier is to be disregarded for the purposes of paragraph 4, as it applies in relation to the shares, to the extent to which that receipt has previously been set (under that paragraph) against any receipts of value which are, in consequence, disregarded for the purposes of paragraph 4 as that paragraph applies in relation to those shares or any other shares subscribed for by the investor.

5(2) The receipt of the replacement value by the original supplier ("the event") is also be disregarded for the purposes of paragraph 4 if–

(a) the event occurs before the start of the period of restriction, or

(b) in a case where the event occurs after the time the original recipient receives the original value, it does not occur as soon after that time as is reasonably practicable in the circumstances.

But nothing in paragraph 4 or this paragraph requires the replacement value to be received after the original value.

5(3) In this paragraph **"the original value"** and **"the replacement value"** are to be construed in accordance with paragraph 4.

INTERPRETATION

6 In this Schedule–

"arrangements" includes any scheme, agreement, understanding, transaction or series of transactions (whether or not legally enforceable);

"associate" has the meaning that would be given by section 448 of CTA 2010 if in that section **"relative"** did not include a brother or sister;

"period of restriction" has the meaning given by paragraph 1(4);

"the shares" has the meaning given by paragraph 1(5).

SCHEDULE 7A – RESTRICTION ON SET-OFF OF PRE-ENTRY LOSSES

Section 177A

History – Sch. 7A inserted by FA 1993, s. 88 and Sch. 8 in respect of chargeable gains in a company's total profits for any accounting period ending on or after 16 March 1993 but to apply only in respect of carried forward pre-entry losses accruing to a company which joined a group on or after 1 April 1987. (In relation to accounting periods beginning before 6 April 1992, Sch. 7A takes effect as if inserted by and referring to the predecessor Act.)

Cross references – ICTA 1988, Sch. 28A: deductions on change of ownership of investment company.
FA 1996, Sch. 15, para. 8(7): loan relationships transitional provisions for relevant gains disregard Sch. 7A losses.

Notes – Sch. 7A not to apply where s. 184A (restrictions on buying losses) has effect in respect of any loss (see Sch. 7A, para. 1(1)).

APPLICATION AND CONSTRUCTION OF SCHEDULE

1(1) This Schedule shall have effect, in the case of a company which becomes a member of a group of companies (**"the relevant group"**), in relation to any pre-entry losses of that company, but this Schedule shall have no effect in any case where section 184A (restrictions on buying losses: tax avoidance schemes) has effect in relation to those losses.

1(2) In this Schedule **"pre-entry loss"**, in relation to any company, means any allowable loss that accrued to that company at a time before it became a member of the relevant group.

1(3) [Omitted by FA 2011, s. 46 and Sch. 11, para. 3(4).]

1(3A) [Omitted by FA 2011, s. 46 and Sch. 11, para. 3(4).]

1(4) [Omitted by FA 2011, s. 46 and Sch. 11, para. 3(4).]

1(5) [Omitted by FA 2011, s. 46 and Sch. 11, para. 3(4).]

1(6) If–

(a) the principal company of a group of companies (**"the first group"**) has at any time become a member of another group (**"the second group"**) so that the two groups are treated as the same by virtue of subsection (10) or (10A) of section 170 or (10A) of section 170, and

(b) the second group, together in pursuance of that subsection with the first group, is the relevant group,

then, except where sub-paragraph (7) below applies, the members of the first group shall be treated for the purposes of this Schedule as having become members of the relevant group at that time, and not by virtue of that subsection at the times when they became members of the first group.

1(7) This sub-paragraph applies where–

(a) the persons who immediately before the time when the principal company of the first group became a member of the second group owned the shares comprised in the issued share capital of the principal company of the first group are the same as the persons who, immediately after that time, owned the shares comprised in the issued share capital of the principal company of the relevant group; and

(b) the company which is the principal company of the relevant group immediately after that time–

(i) was not the principal company of any group immediately before that time; and

(ii) immediately after that time had assets consisting entirely, or almost entirely, of shares comprised in the issued share capital of the principal company of the first group.

1(8) [Omitted by FA 2011, s. 46 and Sch. 11, para. 3(6).]

1(9) In determining for the purposes of this Schedule whether any allowable loss accruing to a company under section 116(10)(b) is a loss that accrued before the company became a member of the relevant group, any loss so accruing shall be deemed to have accrued at the time of the relevant transaction within the meaning of section 116(2).

1(10) In determining for the purposes of this Schedule whether any allowable loss accruing to a company on a disposal under section 212 is a loss that accrued before the company became a member of the relevant group, the provisions of section 213 shall be disregarded.

History – In para. 1(1), the word "becomes" substituted for the words "is or has been" by FA 2011, s. 46 and Sch. 11 para. 3(2), with effect on and after 19 July 2011 in relation to the deduction of any allowable loss that has accrued to a company at a time before it became a member of the relevant group (FA 2011, Sch. 11, para. 11), subject to a transitional provision concerning the pre-entry proportion of an allowable loss accruing to a company on the disposal of a pre-entry asset (FA 2011, Sch. 11, para. 12).
In para. 1(1), the words ", but this Schedule shall have no effect in any case where section 184A (restrictions on buying losses: tax avoidance schemes) has effect in relation to those losses" inserted by FA 2006, s. 70(3) in respect of any accounting period ending on or after *5 December 2005 (but not in relation to the deduction of a loss arising before that date from a chargeable gain accruing before* that date).
Para. 1(2) substituted by FA 2011, s. 46 and Sch. 111, para. 3(3), with effect on and after 19 July 2011 in relation to the deduction of any allowable loss that has accrued to a company at a time before it became a member of the relevant group (FA 2011, Sch. 11, para. 11), subject to a transitional provision concerning the pre-entry proportion of an allowable loss accruing to a company on the disposal of a pre-entry asset (FA 2011, Sch. 11, para. 12). Former para. 1(2) read as follows:

"**1(2)** In this Schedule **"pre-entry loss"**, in relation to any company, means–
(a) any allowable loss that accrued to that company at a time before it became a member of the relevant group; or
(b) the pre-entry proportion of any allowable loss accruing to that company on the disposal of any pre-entry asset
and for the purposes of this Schedule the pre-entry proportion of any loss shall be calculated in accordance with paragraphs 2 to 5 below.".

Para. 1(3) omitted by FA 2011, s. 46 and Sch. 11, para 3(4), with effect on and after 19 July 2011 in relation to the deduction of any allowable loss that has accrued to a company at a time before it became a member of the relevant group (FA 2011, Sch. 11, para. 11), subject to a transitional provision concerning the pre-entry proportion of an allowable loss accruing to a company on the disposal of a pre-entry asset (FA 2011, Sch. 11, para. 12). Former para. 1(3) read as follows:

"**1(3)** In this Schedule **"pre-entry asset"**, in relation to any disposal, means (subject to sub-paragraph (4) below) any asset which was held, at the time immediately before the relevant event occurred in relation to it, by any company (whether or not the one which makes the disposal) which is or has at any time been a member of the relevant group.".

In former para. 1(3)(a) and (4)(a) words "the relevant event occurred in relation to it" substituted for "it became a member of the relevant group" and in para. 1(3)(b) words "the relevant group" substituted for "that group", by FA 2000, s. 102 and Sch. 29, para. 7(2), (4) with effect in relation to the amount to be included in respect of chargeable gains in a company's total profits for any accounting period ending on or after 21 March 2000.

Para. 1(3A) omitted by FA 2011, s. 46 and Sch. 11, para 3(4), with effect on and after 19 July 2011 in relation to the deduction of any allowable loss that has accrued to a company at a time before it became a member of the relevant group (FA 2011, Sch. 11, para. 11), subject to a transitional provision concerning the pre-entry proportion of an allowable loss accruing to a company on the disposal of a pre-entry asset (FA 2011, Sch. 11, para. 12). Former para. 1(3A) read as follows:

"**1(3A)** In this paragraph references to the relevant event occurring in relation to a company–
(a) in a case in which–
 (i) the company was resident in the United Kingdom at the time when it became a member of the relevant group, or
 (ii) the asset was a chargeable asset in relation to the company at that time,
are references to the company becoming a member of that group;
(aa) in a case in which (whether or not paragraph (a)(i) also applies)–
 (i) the company is an SE resident in the United Kingdom, and
 (ii) the asset was transferred to the SE as part of the process of its formation by the merger by acquisition of two or more companies in accordance with Articles 2(1) and 17(2)(a) or (b) of Council Regulation (EC) 2157/2001 on the Statute for a European Company (Societas Europaea),
are references to the asset becoming a chargeable asset in relation to the SE or, if at the time of the formation of the SE the asset was a chargeable asset in relation to a company which ceased to exist as part of the process of the formation of the SE, to the asset becoming a chargeable asset in relation to that company;
(b) in any other case, are references to whichever is the first of–
 (i) the company becoming resident in the United Kingdom, or
 (ii) the asset becoming a chargeable asset in relation to the company.
For this purpose an asset is a chargeable asset in relation to a company at any time if, were the asset to be disposed of by the company at that time, any gain accruing to the company would be a chargeable gain and would by virtue of section 10B (or, if the company is an SE, by reason of the asset having been transferred to the SE on its formation) form part of its chargeable profits for corporation tax purposes.".

Former para. 1(3A) inserted by FA 2000, s. 102 and Sch. 29, para. 7(3) with effect in relation to the amount to be included in respect of chargeable gains in a company's total profits for any accounting period ending on or after 21 March 2000.

In former para. 1(3A), reference "10B" substituted for reference "10(3)" by FA 2003, s. 154 and Sch. 27, para. 2(3) which have effect in relation to accounting periods beginning on or after 1 January 2003.

Former para. 1(3A)(aa) inserted by F(No. 2)A 2005, s. 65(2) with effect in relation to formation of an SE (Societas Europaea or, in other words, European Company) which occurs on or after 1 April 2005.

In former para. 1(3A), in definition of "chargeable asset", words "(or, if the company is an SE, by reason of the asset having been transferred to the SE on its formation)" inserted by F(No. 2)A 2005, s. 65(3) with effect in relation to formation of an SE (Societas Europaea or, in other words, European Company) which occurs on or after 1 April 2005.

Para. 1(4) omitted by FA 2011, s. 46 and Sch. 11, para 3(4), with effect on and after 19 July 2011 in relation to the deduction of any allowable loss that has accrued to a company at a time before it became a member of the relevant group (FA 2011, Sch. 11, para. 11), subject to a transitional provision concerning the pre-entry proportion of an allowable loss accruing to a company on the disposal of a pre-entry asset (FA 2011, Sch. 11, para. 12). Former para. 1(4) read as follows:

"**1(4)** Subject to paragraph 3 below, an asset is not a pre-entry asset if–
(a) the company which held the asset at the time the relevant event occurred in relation to it is not the company which makes the disposal; and
(b) since that time that asset has been disposed of otherwise than by a disposal to which section 171 applies;
but (without prejudice to sub-paragraph (8) below) where, on a disposal to which section 171 does not apply, any asset would cease to be a pre-entry asset by virtue of this sub-paragraph but the company making the disposal retains any interest in or over the asset in question, that interest shall be a pre-entry asset for the purposes of this Schedule.".

Para. 1(5) omitted by FA 2011, s. 46 and Sch. 11, para 3(4), with effect on and after 19 July 2011 in relation to the deduction of any allowable loss that has accrued to a company at a time before it became a member of the relevant group (FA 2011, Sch. 11, para. 11), subject to a transitional provision concerning the pre-entry proportion of an allowable loss accruing to a company on the disposal of a pre-entry asset (FA 2011, Sch. 11, para. 12). Former para. 1(5) read as follows:

"**1(5)** References in this Schedule, in relation to a pre-entry asset, to **the relevant time** are references to the time when the relevant event occurred in relation to the company by reference to which that asset is a pre-entry asset; and for the purposes of this Schedule–
(a) where a relevant event has occurred in relation to a company on more than one occasion, an asset is a pre-entry asset by reference to that company if it would be a pre-entry asset by reference to that company in respect of any one of those occasions; but
(b) references in the following provisions of this Schedule to the time when a relevant event occurred in relation to a company, in relation to assets held on more than one such occasion as is mentioned in paragraph (a) above, are references to the later or latest of those occasions.".

In former para. 1(5) in the opening words "the relevant event occurred in relation to the company by reference to which that asset is a pre-entry asset" substituted for the words from "the company by reference to which that asset is a pre-entry asset became a member of the relevant group", and in para. 1(5)(a) words "a relevant event has occurred in relation to a company" substituted for "a company has become a member of the relevant group", and in para. 1(5)(b) words "a relevant event occurred in relation to a company" substituted for "a company became a member of the relevant group" by FA 2000, s. 102 and Sch. 29, para. 7(5) with effect in relation to the amount to be included in respect of chargeable gains in a company's total profits for any accounting period ending on or after 21 March 2000.

In para. 1(6), the words "If" substituted for the words "Subject to so much of sub-paragraph (6) of paragraph 9 below as requires groups of companies to be treated as separate groups for the purposes of that paragraph, if" by FA 2011, s. 46 and Sch. 11, para. 3(5), with effect on and after 19 July 2011 in relation to the deduction of any allowable loss that has accrued to a company at a time before it became a member of the relevant group (FA 2011, Sch. 11, para. 11), subject to a transitional provision concerning the pre-entry proportion of an allowable loss accruing to a company on the disposal of a pre-entry asset (FA 2011, Sch. 11, para. 12).

Para. 1(8) omitted by FA 2011, s. 46 and Sch. 11, para 3(6), with effect on and after 19 July 2011 in relation to the deduction of any allowable loss that has accrued to a company at a time before it became a member of the relevant group (FA 2011, Sch. 11, para. 11), subject to a transitional provision concerning the pre-entry proportion of an allowable loss accruing to a company on the disposal of a pre-entry asset (FA 2011, Sch. 11, para. 12). Former para. 1(8) read as follows:

"**1(8)** For the purposes of this Schedule, but subject to paragraph 3 below–

(a) an asset acquired or held by a company at any time and an asset held at a later time by that company, or by any company which is or has been a member of the same group of companies as that company, shall be treated as the same asset if the value of the second asset is derived in whole or in part from the first asset; and

(b) if –

(i) any asset is treated (whether by virtue of paragraph (a) above or otherwise) as the same as an asset held by a company at a later time, and

(ii) the first asset would have been a pre-entry asset in relation to that company,

the second asset shall also be treated as a pre-entry asset in relation to that company;

and paragraph (a) above shall apply, in particular, where the second asset is a freehold and the first asset is a leasehold the lessee of which acquires the reversion.".

In para. 1(6)(a), words "or (10A)" inserted by F(No. 2)A 2005, s. 65(4) with effect in relation to formation of an SE (Societas Europaea or, in other words, European Company) which occurs on or after 1 April 2005.

Cross references – S. 116: reorganisations, conversions and reconstructions involving qualifying corporate bonds.
S. 171: general provisions relating to transfers within groups.
S. 212: annual deemed disposal of holdings of unit trusts etc.
S. 213: spreading of gains and losses under s. 212.
Sch. 7B, para. 15: modification in respect of overseas life insurance companies.
FA 2000, Sch. 29, para. 7(6)–(9): determination of whether a company was a member of a group at various times in relation to s. 170 as amended by FA 2000, s. 102 and Sch 29, para 1, and as not so amended.
SI 2006/3271, reg. 32: modification of Sch. 7A, para. 1(4) with effect from 31 December 2006 in relation to periods of account ending on or after that day.

PRE-ENTRY PROPORTION OF LOSSES ON PRE-ENTRY ASSETS

2 [Omitted by FA 2011, s. 46 and Sch. 11, para. 4.]

History – Para. 2 omitted by FA 2011, s. 46 and Sch. 11, para. 4, with effect on and after 19 July 2011 in relation to the deduction of any allowable loss that has accrued to a company at a time before it became a member of the relevant group (FA 2011, Sch. 11, para. 11), subject to a transitional provision concerning the pre-entry proportion of an allowable loss accruing to a company on the disposal of a pre-entry asset (FA 2011, Sch. 11, para. 12). Former para. 2 read as follows:

"**2(1)** Subject to paragraphs 3 to 5 below, the pre-entry proportion of an allowable loss accruing on the disposal of a pre-entry asset shall be whatever would be the allowable loss accruing on that disposal if that loss were the sum of the amounts determined, for every item of relevant allowable expenditure, according to the following formula–

$$A \times \frac{B}{C} \times \frac{D}{E}$$

2(2) In sub-paragraph (1) above, in relation to any disposal of a pre-entry asset–

A is the total amount of the allowable loss;

B is the amount of the item of relevant allowable expenditure for which an amount falls to be determined under this paragraph;

C is the total amount of all the relevant allowable expenditure;

D is the length of the period beginning with the relevant pre-entry date and ending with the relevant time or, if that date is after that time, nil; and

E is the length of the period beginning with the relevant pre-entry date and ending with the day of the disposal.

2(3) In sub-paragraph (2) above **"the relevant pre-entry date"**, in relation to any item of relevant allowable expenditure, means whichever is the later of–

(a) the date on which that item of expenditure is, or (on the assumptions applying by virtue of sub-paragraphs (4) to (6B) below) would be, treated for the purposes of section 54 as having been incurred; and

(b) 1st April 1982.

2(4) Where any asset (**"the second asset"**) is treated by virtue of section 127 as the same as another asset (**"the first asset"**) previously held by any company, this paragraph and (so far as applicable) paragraph 3 below shall have effect–

(a) as if any item of relevant allowable expenditure consisting in consideration given for the acquisition of the second asset had been incurred at the same time as the expenditure consisting in the consideration for the acquisition of the first asset; and

(b) where there is more than one such time as if that item were incurred at those different times in the same proportions as the consideration for the acquisition of the first asset.

2(5) Without prejudice to sub-paragraph (4) above, this paragraph shall have effect in relation to any asset which–

(a) was held by a company at the time when it became a member of the relevant group, and

(b) is treated as having been acquired by that company for such a consideration as secured that on the disposal in pursuance of which it was acquired neither a gain nor a loss accrued,

as if that company and every person who acquired that asset or the equivalent asset at a material time had been the same person and, accordingly, as if the asset had been acquired by that company when it or the equivalent asset was acquired by the first of those persons to have acquired it at a material time and the time at which any expenditure had been incurred were to be determined accordingly.

2(6) In sub-paragraph (5) above, the reference, in relation to any asset, to a material time is a reference to any time which–

(a) is before the occasion on which the company in question is treated as having acquired the asset for such a consideration as is mentioned in that sub-paragraph; and

(b) *is or is after the last occasion* before that occasion on which any person acquired that asset or the equivalent asset otherwise than by virtue of an acquisition which–

(i) is treated as an acquisition for such a consideration; or

(ii) is the acquisition by virtue of which any asset is treated as the equivalent asset;

and this paragraph shall have effect in relation to any asset to which that sub-paragraph applies without regard to the provisions of section 56(2).

2(6A) Notwithstanding anything in section 56(2), where in the case of the disposal of any pre-entry asset–

(a) any company has at any time between the relevant time and the time of the disposal acquired that asset or the equivalent asset, and
(b) the acquisition was either an acquisition in pursuance of a disposal on which there is treated by virtue of section 171 as having been neither a gain nor a loss accruing or an acquisition by virtue of which an asset is treated as the equivalent asset,

the items of relevant allowable expenditure and the times when those items shall be treated as having been incurred shall be determined for the purposes of this paragraph on the assumptions specified in sub-paragraph (6B) below.

2(6B) Those assumptions are that–
(a) the company by reference to which the asset in question is a pre-entry asset, and
(b) the company mentioned in sub-paragraph (6A) above and every other company which has made an acquisition which, in relation to the disposal of that asset, falls within that sub-paragraph,

were the same person and, accordingly, that the pre-entry asset had been acquired by the company disposing of it at the time when it or the equivalent asset would have been treated for the purposes of this paragraph as acquired by the company mentioned in paragraph (a) above.

2(7) In sub-paragraphs (5) to (6B) above the references to the equivalent asset, in relation to another asset acquired or disposed of by any company, are references to any asset which falls in relation to that company to be treated (whether by virtue of paragraph 1(8) above or otherwise) as the same as the other asset or which would fall to be so treated after applying, as respects other assets, the assumptions for which those sub-paragraphs provide.

2(8) The preceding provisions of this paragraph and (so far as applicable) paragraph 3 below shall have effect where–
(a) a loss accrues to any company under section 116(10)(b), and
(b) the old asset consists in or is treated for the purposes of that paragraph as including pre-entry assets,

as if the disposal on which the loss accrues were that disposal of the old asset which is assumed to have been made for the purposes of the calculation required by section 116(10)(a).

2(8A) Where by virtue of section 55(8) the allowable loss accruing on the disposal of a pre-entry asset, or any part of the loss, is attributable to an amount ("the rolled-up amount") of rolled-up indexation (as defined in section 55(9) to (11)), then, for the purposes of this paragraph–
(a) the total amount of all the relevant allowable expenditure shall be treated as increased by the rolled-up amount, and
(b) the amount of each item of relevant allowable expenditure shall be treated as increased by so much (if any) of the rolled-up amount as is attributable to that item.

2(8B) Where–
(a) section 56(3) applies on the disposal of a pre-entry asset on which an allowable loss accrues, and
(b) in accordance with that subsection, the total amount of all the relevant allowable expenditure is reduced by any amount ("the global reduction"),

the amount of each item of relevant allowable expenditure shall be treated for the purposes of this paragraph as reduced by so much (if any) of the global reduction as is attributable to that item.

2(9) In this paragraph–

"relevant allowable expenditure", in relation to any allowable loss, means the expenditure which falls by virtue of section 38(1)(a) or (b) to be taken into account in the computation of that loss.".

In former para. 2(2), the definitions of "A" and "B" substituted by FA 1994, s. 93(8)(a) in relation to disposals made on or after 30 November 1993.

In former para. 2(3)(a), the words "assumptions applying … to (6B)" substituted by FA 1994, s. 94(2) in relation to the making, in respect of any loss, of any deduction from a chargeable gain where either the gain or the loss is one accruing on or after 11 March 1994.

In former para. 2(4), the words "except in relation to the calculation of any indexed rise" which appeared immediately before para. (a) repealed, in relation to disposals made on or after 30 November 1993, by FA 1994, s. 93(8)(b), s. 258 and Sch. 26, Pt. V(8).

Former para. 2(6A) and (6B) inserted and para. 2(7) substituted by FA 1994, s. 94(2) in relation to the making, in respect of any loss, of any deduction from a chargeable gain where either the gain or the loss is one accruing on or after 11 March 1994.

Former para. 2(8A) and (8B) inserted by FA 1994, s. 93(8)(c) in relation to disposals made on or after 30 November 1993.

In former para. 2(9), the definition of "indexed rise" repealed by FA 1994, s. 93(8)(d), s. 258 and Sch. 26, Pt. V(8) in relation to disposals made on or after 30 November 1993.

Cross references – S. 38(1)(a), (b): allowable acquisition expenditure and incidental costs thereof plus enhancement or title expenditure.
S. 54: calculation of indexation allowance generally.
S. 56: part disposals and disposals on a no gain/no loss basis.
S. 110: calculation of indexation allowance on a new holding of shares.
S. 116: reorganisations, conversions and reconstructions involving qualifying corporate bonds.
S. 127: equation of original shares and new holding on a reorganisation (as also applied to exchanges, reconstructions and amalgamations).

DISPOSALS OF POOLED ASSETS

3 [Omitted by FA 2011, s. 46 and Sch. 11, para. 4]

History – Para. 3 omitted by FA 2011, s. 46 and Sch. 11, para. 4, with effect on and after 19 July 2011 in relation to the deduction of any allowable loss that has accrued to a company at a time before it became a member of the relevant group (FA 2011, Sch. 11, para. 11), subject to a transitional provision concerning the pre-entry proportion of an allowable loss accruing to a company on the disposal of a pre-entry asset (FA 2011, Sch. 11, para. 12). Former para. 3 read as follows:

"**3(1)** This paragraph shall apply (subject to paragraphs 4 and 5 below) where any assets acquired by any company fall to be treated with other assets as indistinguishable parts of the same asset (**"a pooled asset"**) and the whole or any part of that asset is referable to pre-entry assets.

3(2) For the purposes of this Schedule, where a pooled asset has at any time contained a pre-entry asset–
(a) the pooled asset shall be treated, until all the pre-entry assets included in that asset have (on the assumptions for which this paragraph provides) been disposed of, as incorporating a part which is referable to pre-entry assets; and
(b) the size of that part shall be determined in accordance with the following provisions of this paragraph.

3(3) Where there is a disposal of any part of a pooled asset and the proportion of the asset which is disposed of does not exceed the proportion of that asset which is represented by any part of it which is not, at the time of the disposal, referable to pre-entry assets, that disposal shall be deemed for the purposes of this Schedule to be confined to assets which are not pre-entry assets so that–
(a) except where paragraph 4(2) below applies, no part of any loss accruing on that disposal shall be deemed to be a pre-entry loss, and
(b) the part of the pooled asset which after the disposal is to be treated as referable to pre-entry assets shall be correspondingly increased.

3(4) Where there is a disposal of any part of a pooled asset and the proportion of the asset which is disposed of does exceed the proportion of that asset mentioned in sub-paragraph (3) above, that disposal shall be deemed for the purposes of this Schedule to relate to pre-entry assets only so far as required for the purposes of the excess, so that–
(a) any loss accruing on that disposal shall be deemed for the purposes of this Schedule to be an allowable loss on the disposal of a pre-entry asset;

(b) the pre-entry proportion of that loss shall be deemed (except where paragraph 4(3) below applies) to be the amount (so far as it does not exceed the amount of the loss actually accruing) which would have been the pre-entry proportion under paragraph 2 above of any loss accruing on the disposal of the excess if the excess were a separate asset; and
(c) the pooled asset shall be treated after the disposal as referable entirely to pre-entry assets.

3(5) Where there is a disposal of the whole of a pooled asset or of any part of a pooled asset which, at the time of the disposal, is referable entirely to pre-entry assets, paragraphs (a) and (b) of sub-paragraph (4) above shall apply to the disposal of the asset or the part as they apply in relation to the assumed disposal of the excess mentioned in that sub-paragraph but, in the case of the disposal of the whole of a pooled asset only a part of which is referable to pre-entry assets, as if the reference in paragraph (b) of that sub-paragraph to the excess were a reference to that part.

3(6) For the purpose of determining, under sub-paragraph (4) or (5) above, what would have been the pre-entry proportion of any loss accruing on the disposal of any assets as a separate asset it shall be assumed that none of the assets treated as comprised in that asset has ever been comprised in a pooled asset with any assets other than those which are taken to constitute that separate asset for the purposes of the determination.

3(7) The assets which are comprised in any asset which is treated for any of the purposes of this paragraph as a separate asset shall be identified on the following assumptions, that is to say–
(a) that assets are disposed of in the order of the dates which for the purposes of paragraph 2 above are the relevant pre-entry dates in relation to the consideration for their acquisition;
(b) subject to that, that assets with earlier relevant times are disposed of before those with later relevant times;
(c) that disposals made when a company was not a member of the relevant group are made in accordance with the preceding provisions of this paragraph, as they have effect in relation to the group of companies of which the company was a member at the time of the disposal or, as the case may be, of which it had most recently been a member before that time; and
(d) subject to paragraphs (a) to (c) above, that a company disposes of assets in the order in which it acquired them.

3(8) Where in the case of any asset there is more than one date which is the relevant pre-entry date in relation to the consideration for its acquisition, the date taken into account for the purposes of sub-paragraph (7)(a) above shall be the date which is the earlier or earliest of those dates if any date which is the relevant pre-entry date in relation to the acquisition of an option to acquire that asset is disregarded.

3(9) In applying the formula set out in paragraph 2(1) above in relation to the disposal of an asset which is treated for any of the purposes of this paragraph as comprised in a separate asset–
(a) the amount or value of any consideration for the acquisition or disposal of that asset; and
(b) the incidental costs of the acquisition or disposal of that asset,

shall be determined (to the exclusion of any apportionment under section 129 or 130) by apportioning any consideration or costs relating to both that asset and other assets acquired or disposed of at the same time according to the proportion that is borne by that asset to all the assets to which the consideration or costs related.

3(10) Where–
(a) any asset (**"the latest asset"**) falls (whether by virtue of paragraph 1(8) above or otherwise) to be treated as acquired at the same time as another asset (**"the original asset"**) which was acquired before the latest asset, and
(b) the latest asset is either comprised in a pooled asset a part of which is referable to pre-entry assets or is or includes an asset which is to be treated as so comprised,

sub-paragraph (7) above shall apply not only in relation to the latest asset as if it were the original asset but also, in the first place, for identifying the asset which is to be treated as the original asset for the purposes of this paragraph.

3(11) Sub-paragraphs (3)(b) and (4)(c) above shall have effect in relation to any disposal without prejudice to the effect of any subsequent acquisition of assets falling to be treated as part of a pooled asset on the determination of whether, and to what extent, any part of that pooled asset is to be treated as referable to pre-entry assets.".

Cross references – S. 129: part disposal of new holding.
S. 130: apportionment of acquisition costs in relation to composite new holdings.

RULE TO PREVENT PRE-ENTRY LOSSES ON POOLED ASSETS BEING TREATED AS POST-ENTRY LOSSES

4 [Omitted by FA 2011, s. 46 and Sch. 11, para. 4]

History – Para. 4 omitted by FA 2011, s. 46 and Sch. 11, para. 4, with effect on and after 19 July 2011 in relation to the deduction of any allowable loss that has accrued to a company at a time before it became a member of the relevant group (FA 2011, Sch. 11, para. 11), subject to a transitional provision concerning the pre-entry proportion of an allowable loss accruing to a company on the disposal of a pre-entry asset (FA 2011, Sch. 11, para. 12). Former para. 4 read as follows:

"**4(1)** This paragraph shall apply if–
(a) there is a disposal of any part of a pooled asset which for the purposes of paragraph 3 above is treated as incorporating a part which is referable to pre-entry assets;
(b) the assets disposed of are or include assets (**"the post-entry element of the disposal"**) which for the purposes of that paragraph are treated as having been incorporated in the part of the pooled asset which is not referable to pre-entry assets;
(c) an allowable loss (**"the actual loss"**) accrues on the disposal; and
(d) the amount which in computing the allowable loss is allowed as a deduction of relevant allowable expenditure (**"the expenditure actually allowed"**) exceeds the relevant allowable expenditure attributable to the post-entry element of the disposal.

4(2) Subject to sub-paragraph (6) below, where the post-entry element of the disposal comprises all of the assets disposed of–
(a) the actual loss shall be treated for the purposes of this Schedule as a loss accruing on the disposal of a pre-entry asset; and
(b) the pre-entry proportion of that loss shall be treated as being the amount (so far as it does not exceed the amount of the actual loss) by which the expenditure actually allowed exceeds the relevant allowable expenditure attributable to the post-entry element of the disposal.

4(3) Subject to sub-paragraph (6) below, where–
(a) the actual loss is treated by virtue of paragraph 3 above as a loss accruing on the disposal of a pre-entry asset, and
(b) the expenditure actually allowed exceeds the actual cost of the assets to which the disposal is treated as relating,

the pre-entry proportion of the loss shall be treated as being the amount which (so far as it does not exceed the amount of the actual loss) is equal to the sum of that excess and what would, apart from this paragraph and paragraph 5 below, be the pre-entry proportion of the loss accruing on the disposal.

4(4) For the purposes of sub-paragraph (3) above the actual cost of the assets to which the disposal is treated as relating shall be taken to be the sum of–
(a) the relevant allowable expenditure attributable to the post-entry element of the disposal; and
(b) the amount which, in computing the pre-entry proportion of the loss in accordance with paragraph 3(4)(b) and (6) above, would be treated for the purposes of C in the formula in paragraph 2(1) above as the total amount allowable as a deduction of relevant allowable expenditure in respect of such of the assets disposed of as are treated as having been incorporated in the part of the pooled asset which is referable to pre-entry assets.

4(5) Without prejudice to sub-paragraph (6) below, where sub-paragraph (2) or (3) above applies for the purpose of determining the pre-entry proportion of any loss, no election shall be capable of being made under paragraph 5 below for the purpose of enabling a different amount to be taken as the pre-entry proportion of that loss.

4(6) Where–
(a) the pre-entry proportion of the loss accruing to any company on the disposal of any part of a pooled asset falls to be determined under sub-paragraph (2) or (3) above,
(b) the amount determined under that sub-paragraph exceeds the amount determined under sub-paragraph (7) below (**"the alternative pre-entry loss"**), and
(c) the company makes an election for the purposes of this sub-paragraph,

the pre-entry proportion of the loss determined under sub-paragraph (2) or (3) above shall be reduced to the amount of the alternative pre-entry loss.

4(7) For the purposes of sub-paragraph (6) above the alternative pre-entry loss is whatever apart from this paragraph would have been the pre-entry proportion of the loss on the disposal in question, if for the purposes of this Schedule the identification of the assets disposed of were to be made disregarding the part of the pooled asset which was not referable to pre-entry assets, except to the extent (if any) by which the part referable to pre-entry assets fell short of what was disposed of.

4(8) An election for the purposes of sub-paragraph (6) above with respect to any loss shall be made by the company to which the loss accrued by notice to the inspector given within–
(a) the period of two years beginning with the end of the accounting period of that company in which the disposal is made on which the loss accrues; or
(b) such longer period as the Board may by notice allow;

and paragraph 5 below may be taken into account under sub-paragraph (7) above in determining the amount of the alternative pre-entry loss as if an election had been made under that paragraph but shall be so taken into account only if the election for the purposes of sub-paragraph (6) above contains an election corresponding to the election that, apart from this paragraph, might have been made under that paragraph.

4(9) For the purposes of this paragraph the relevant allowable expenditure attributable to the post-entry element of the disposal shall be the amount which, in computing any allowable loss accruing on a disposal of that element as a separate asset, would have been allowed as a deduction of relevant allowable expenditure if none of the assets comprised in that element had ever been comprised in a pooled asset with any assets other than those which are taken to constitute that separate asset for the purposes of this sub-paragraph.

4(10) For the purpose of identifying the assets which are to be treated for the purposes of sub-paragraph (9) above as comprised in the post-entry element of the disposal, a company shall be taken to dispose of assets in the order in which it acquired them.

4(11) Paragraph 3(9) above shall apply for the purposes of sub-paragraph (9) above as it applies for the purposes of the application as mentioned in paragraph 3(9) above of the formula so mentioned; and paragraph 3(10) above shall apply for the purposes of this paragraph in relation to sub-paragraph (10) above as it applies for the purposes of paragraph 3 above in relation to sub-paragraph (7) of that paragraph.

4(12) In this paragraph references to an amount allowed as a deduction of relevant allowable expenditure are references to the amount falling to be so allowed in accordance with section 38(1)(a) and (b) and (so far as applicable) section 42.

4(13) [Repealed by FA 1994, s. 93(9), s.258 and Sch. 26, Pt. V(8).]

4(14) Nothing in this paragraph shall affect the operation of the rules contained in paragraph 3 above for determining, for any purposes other than those of sub-paragraph (7) above, how much of any pooled asset at any time consists of a part which is referable to pre-entry assets.".

In former para. 4(12), the words "together with the indexed rises in the items comprised in that expenditure or, as the case may be, in the appropriate portions of those items" which appeared at the end repealed by FA 1994, s. 93(9)(a), s. 258 and Sch. 26, Pt. V(8) in relation to disposals made on or after 30 November 1993.

Former para. 4(13) repealed by FA 1994, s. 93(9)(b), s. 258 and Sch. 26, Pt. V(8) in relation to disposals made on or after 30 November 1993.

Cross references – S. 38(1)(a), (b): sums allowable as deductions from consideration in respect of acquisition expenditure and incidental costs thereof plus enhancement or title expenditure.

S. 42: apportionment of allowable expenditure (s. 38(1)(a), (b)) where part disposal of asset.

ALTERNATIVE CALCULATION BY REFERENCE TO MARKET VALUE

5 [Omitted by FA 2011, s. 46 and Sch. 11, para. 4]

History – Para. 5 omitted by FA 2011, s. 46 and Sch. 11, para. 4, with effect on and after 19 July 2011 in relation to the deduction of any allowable loss that has accrued to a company at a time before it became a member of the relevant group (FA 2011, Sch. 11, para. 11), subject to a transitional provision concerning the pre-entry proportion of an allowable loss accruing to a company on the disposal of a pre-entry asset (FA 2011, Sch. 11, para. 12). Former para. 5 read as follows:

"5(1) Subject to paragraph 4(5) above and the following provisions of this paragraph, if–
(a) an allowable loss accrues on the disposal by any company of any pre-entry asset; and
(b) that company makes an election for the purposes of this paragraph in relation to that loss,

the pre-entry proportion of that loss (instead of being the amount determined under the preceding provisions of this Schedule) shall be whichever is the smaller of the amounts mentioned in sub-paragraph (2) below.

5(2) Those amounts are–
(a) the amount of any loss which would have accrued if that asset had been disposed of at the relevant time at its market value at that time; and
(b) the amount of the loss accruing on the disposal mentioned in sub-paragraph (1)(a) above.

5(2A) In determining for the purposes of sub-paragraph (2)(a) above the amount of any loss which would have accrued if the asset had been disposed of at the relevant time at its market value at that time–
(a) it shall be assumed that the amendments of this Act made by section 93(1) to (5) of the Finance Act 1994 (indexation losses) had effect in relation to that disposal and, accordingly,
(b) references in those amendments and in subsection (11) of that section to 30th November 1993 shall be read as references to the day on which the relevant time falls.

5(3) Where no loss would have accrued on the disposal assumed for the purposes of sub-paragraph (2)(a) above, the loss accruing on the disposal mentioned in sub-paragraph (1)(a) above shall be deemed not to have a pre-entry proportion.

5(4) Sub-paragraph (5) below shall apply where–
(a) an election is made for the purposes of this paragraph in relation to any loss accruing on the disposal (**"the real disposal"**) of the whole or any part of a pooled asset; and
(b) the case is one in which (but for the election) paragraph 3 above would apply for determining the pre-entry proportion of a loss accruing on the real disposal.

5(5) In a case falling within sub-paragraph (4) above, this paragraph shall have effect as if the amount specified in sub-paragraph (2)(a) above were to be calculated–
(a) on the basis that the disposal which is assumed to have taken place was a disposal of all the assets falling within sub-paragraph (6) below; and
(b) by apportioning any loss that would have accrued on that disposal between–
 (i) such of the assets falling within paragraph (6) below as are assets to which the real disposal is treated as relating, and
 (ii) the remainder of the assets so falling,

according to the proportions of any pooled asset whose disposal is assumed which would have been, respectively, represented by assets mentioned in sub-paragraph (i) above and by assets mentioned in sub-paragraph (ii) above,

and where assets falling within sub-paragraph (6) below have different relevant times there shall be assumed to have been a different disposal at each of those times.

5(6) Assets fall within this sub-paragraph if–

(a) immediately before the time which is the relevant time in relation to those assets, they were comprised in a pooled asset which consisted of or included assets which fall to be treated for the purposes of paragraph 3 above as–

(i) comprised in the part of the pooled asset referable to pre-entry assets; and

(ii) disposed of on the real disposal;

(b) they were also comprised in such a pooled asset immediately after that time; and

(c) the pooled asset in which they were so comprised immediately after that time was held by a member of the relevant group.

5(7) Where–

(a) an election is made under paragraph 4(6) above requiring the determination by reference to this paragraph of the alternative pre-entry loss accruing on the disposal of any assets comprised in a pooled asset, and

(b) in pursuance of that election any amount of the loss that would have accrued on an assumed disposal is apportioned in accordance with sub-paragraph (5) above to assets (**"the relevant assets"**) which–

(i) are treated for the purposes of that determination as assets to which the disposal related, but

(ii) otherwise continue after the disposal to be treated as incorporated in the part of that pooled asset which is referable to pre-entry assets,

then, on any further application of this paragraph for the purpose of determining the pre-entry proportion of the loss accruing on a subsequent disposal of assets comprised in that pooled asset, that amount (without being apportioned elsewhere) shall be deducted from so much of the loss accruing on the same assumed disposal as, apart from the deduction, would be apportioned to the relevant assets on that further application of this paragraph.

5(8) An election under this paragraph with respect to any loss shall be made by the company in question by notice to the inspector given within–

(a) the period of two years beginning with the end of the accounting period of that company in which the disposal is made on which the loss accrues; or

(b) such longer period as the Board may by notice allow.".

Former para. 5(2A) inserted by FA 1994, s. 93(10) in relation to disposals made on or after 30 November 1993.

Notes – The reference in para. 5(5) to "paragraph (6)" follows the Queen's printer's copy.

RESTRICTIONS ON THE DEDUCTION OF PRE-ENTRY LOSSES

6(1) In the calculation of the amount to be included in respect of chargeable gains in any company's total profits for any accounting period–

(a) if in that period there is any chargeable gain from which the whole or any part of any pre-entry loss accruing in that period is deductible in accordance with paragraph 7 below, the loss or, as the case may be, that part of it shall be deducted from that gain;

(b) if, after all such deductions as may be made under paragraph (a) above have been made, there is in that period any chargeable gain from which the whole or any part of any pre-entry loss carried forward from a previous accounting period is deductible in accordance with paragraph 7 below, the loss or, as the case may be, that part of it shall be deducted from that gain;

(c) the total chargeable gains (if any) remaining after the making of all such deductions as may be made under paragraph (a) or (b) above shall be subject to deductions in accordance with section 8(1) in respect of any allowable losses that are not pre-entry losses; and

(d) any pre-entry loss which has not been the subject of a deduction under paragraph (a) or (b) above (as well as any other losses falling to be carried forward under section 8(1)) shall be carried forward to the following accounting period of that company.

6(2) Subject to sub-paragraph (1) above, any question as to which or what part of any pre-entry loss has been deducted from any particular chargeable gain shall be decided–

(a) [omitted by FA 2011, s. 46 and Sch. 11, para. 5(2)(a)]

(b) in accordance with such elections as may be made by the company to which the loss accrued;

and any question as to which or what part of any pre-entry loss has been carried forward from one accounting period to another shall be decided accordingly.

6(3) An election by any company under this paragraph shall be made by notice to the inspector given–

(a) [omitted by FA 2011, s. 46 and Sch. 11, para. 5(3)(a)]

(b) before the end of the period of two years beginning with the end of the accounting period of that company in which the gain in question accrued.

6(4) For the purposes of this Schedule where any matter falls to be determined under this paragraph by reference to an election but no election is made, it shall be assumed, so far as consistent with any elections that have been made–

(a) that losses are set against gains in the order in which the losses accrued; and

(b) that the gains against which they are set are also determined according to the order in which they accrued with losses being set against earlier gains before they are set against later ones.

History – Para. 6(2)(a) and the word "and" after it omitted by FA 2011, s. 46 and Sch. 11, para. 5(2)(a), with effect on and after 19 July 2011 in relation to the deduction of any allowable loss that has accrued to a company at a time before it became a member of the relevant group (FA 2011, Sch. 11, para. 11), subject to a transitional provision concerning the pre-entry proportion of an allowable loss accruing to a company on the disposal of a pre-entry asset (FA 2011, Sch. 11, para. 12). Former para. 6(2)(a) read as follows:

"(a) where it falls to be decided in respect of the setting of losses against gains in any accounting period ending before 16th March 1993 as if–
(i) pre-entry losses accruing in any such period had been set against chargeable gains before any other allowable losses accruing in that period were set against those gains;
(ii) pre-entry losses carried forward to any such period had been set against chargeable gains before any other allowable losses carried forward to that period were set against those gains; and
(iii) subject to sub-paragraphs (i) and (ii) above, the pre-entry losses carried forward to any accounting period ending on or after 16th March 1993 were identified with such losses as may be determined in accordance with such elections as may be made by the company to which they accrued; and".

In para. 6(2)(b), the words "in any other case" omitted by FA 2011, s. 46 and Sch. 11, para. 5(2)(b), with effect on and after 19 July 2011 in relation to the deduction of any allowable loss that has accrued to a company at a time before it became a member of the relevant group (FA 2011, Sch. 11, para. 11), subject to a transitional provision concerning the pre-entry proportion of an allowable loss accruing to a company on the disposal of a pre-entry asset (FA 2011, Sch. 11, para. 12).

Para. 6(3)(a) and the word "and" after it omitted by FA 2011, s. 46 and Sch. 11, para. 5(3)(a), with effect on and after 19 July 2011 in relation to the deduction of any allowable loss that has accrued to a company at a time before it became a member of the relevant group (FA 2011, Sch. 11, para. 11), subject to a transitional provision concerning the pre-entry proportion of an allowable loss accruing to a company on the disposal of a pre-entry asset (FA 2011, Sch. 11, para. 12). Former para. 6(3)(a) read as follows:

"(a) in the case of an election under sub-paragraph (2)(a)(iii) above, before the end of the period of two years beginning with the end of the accounting period of that company which was current on 16th March 1993; and".

In para. 6(3)(b), the words "in the case of an election under sub-paragraph (2)(b) above," omitted by FA 2011, s. 46 and Sch. 11, para. 5(3)(b), with effect on and after 19 July 2011 in relation to the deduction of any allowable loss that has accrued to a company at a time before it became a member of the relevant group (FA 2011, Sch. 11, para. 11), subject to a transitional provision concerning the pre-entry proportion of an allowable loss accruing to a company on the disposal of a pre-entry asset (FA 2011, Sch. 11, para. 12).

Cross references – S. 8(1): amounts to be included in respect of chargeable gains in a company's total profits.

ICTA 1988, s. 786C: restriction to set-off of management expenses and charges defrayed and paid by an investment company before a change in ownership against chargeable gains on disposal of assets acquired intra-group in three years following the change.

SI 1994/3226, reg. 9(3): treatment of assets held by a company on its commencement day (for the purposes of FA 1993, Pt. II, Ch. II) where the company was non-resident at any time before its commencement day.

SI 1994/3226, reg. 16(4): a company's pre-commencement day (for the purposes of FA 1993, Pt. II, Ch. II) losses are not available for set-off against exchange gains if deductible under s. 8(1).

SI 1994/3226, reg. 16(6): computation of available losses on assets held by a company on its commencement day (for the purposes of FA 1993, Pt. II, Ch. II) where the company was non-resident at any time before its commencement day.

SI 1994/3226, reg. 16(12): losses specified in an election to set available losses against exchange gains not deductible under s. 8(1).

GAINS FROM WHICH PRE-ENTRY LOSSES ARE TO BE DEDUCTIBLE

7(1) A pre-entry loss that accrued to a company before it became a member of the relevant group shall be deductible from a chargeable gain accruing to that company if the gain is one accruing–

(a) on a disposal made by that company before the date on which it became a member of the relevant group (**"the entry date"**);

(b) on the disposal of an asset which was held by that company immediately before the entry date; or

(c) on the disposal of any asset in respect of which the conditions in sub-paragraph (1A) are met.

7(1A) The conditions referred to in sub-paragraph (1)(c) are–

(a) that the asset was acquired, on or after the entry date, by–
(i) the company to which the pre-entry loss accrued ("company A"), or
(ii) a company which, at the time of the acquisition, was a group company of company A,

from a person who at the time of the acquisition was not a group company of company A, and

(b) that the asset has not, since its acquisition from that person, been used or held for any purposes other than those of a trade or business which–
(i) was being carried on by company A immediately before the entry date, and
(ii) continued until the disposal to be carried on by company A or a company which, when it carried on the trade or business, was a group company of company A.

7(1B) For the purposes of sub-paragraph (1A), a company is a "group company of company A" at any time when it is a member of a group of companies of which company A is also a member.

7(1C) Where a company, having become a member of the relevant group, subsequently becomes a member of another group ("the new group")–

(a) sub-paragraph (1) continues to have effect, in relation to any loss which accrued to the company before it became a member of the relevant group, by reference to the date on which it became such a member, and

(b) accordingly, that sub-paragraph does not apply separately in relation to the loss by reason of it also having accrued to the company before it became a member of the new group.

7(2) [Omitted by FA 2011, s. 46 and Sch. 11, para. 6(4).]

7(3) Where two or more companies become members of the relevant group at the same time and those companies were all members of the same group of companies immediately before they became members of the relevant group, then,

(a) an asset shall be treated for the purposes of sub-paragraph (1)(b) above as held, immediately before it became a member of the relevant group, by the company to which the pre-entry loss in question accrued if that company is one of those companies and the asset was in fact so held by another of those companies; and

(b) [omitted by FA 2011, s. 46 and Sch. 11, para. 6(5).]

(c) the acquisition of an asset shall be treated for the purposes of sub-paragraph (1A) above as an acquisition by the company to which the pre-entry loss in question accrued if that company is one of those companies and the asset was in fact acquired (whether before or after they became members of the relevant group) by another of those companies.

7(4) Sub-paragraphs (4A) and (4B) apply for determining for the purposes of this paragraph whether an asset on the disposal of which a chargeable gain accrues was an asset held by a company immediately before the entry date (a "pre-entry asset").

7(4A) Except as provided by sub-paragraph (4B), an asset is not a pre-entry asset if–

(a) the company which held the asset at the entry date is not the company which makes the disposal, and

(b) since the entry date that asset has been disposed of otherwise than by a disposal to which section 171 applies.

7(4B) Without prejudice to sub-paragraph (4C), where, on a disposal to which section 171 does not apply–

(a) an asset would cease to be a pre-entry asset by virtue of sub-paragraph (4A), but

(b) the company making the disposal retains an interest in or over the asset in question,

that interest is a pre-entry asset.

7(4C) For the purposes of this paragraph–

(a) an asset acquired or held by a company at any time and an asset held at a later time by that company, or by any company which is or has been a member of the same group of companies as that company, is to be treated as the same asset if the value of the second asset is derived in whole or in part from the first asset, and

(b) if–

(i) any asset is treated (whether by virtue of paragraph (a) or otherwise) as the same as an asset held by a company at a later time, and

(ii) the first asset would have been a pre-entry asset in relation to that company,

the second asset is also to be treated as a pre-entry asset in relation to that company;

and paragraph (a) applies, in particular, where the second asset is a freehold and the first asset is a leasehold the lessee of which acquires the reversion.

7(5) Subject to sub-paragraph (6) below, where a gain accrues on the disposal of the whole or any part of–

(a) any asset treated as a single asset but comprising assets only some of which were held at the time mentioned in paragraph (b) of sub-paragraph (1) above, or

(b) an asset which is treated as held at that time by virtue of a provision requiring an asset which was not held at that time to be treated as the same as an asset which was so held,

a pre-entry loss shall be deductible by virtue of paragraph (b) of sub-paragraph (1) above from the amount of that gain to the extent only of such proportion of that gain as is attributable to assets held at that time or, as the case may be, represents the gain that would have accrued on the asset so held.

7(6) Where–

(a) a chargeable gain accrues by virtue of subsection (10) of section 116 on the disposal of a qualifying corporate bond,

(b) that bond was not held as required by paragraph (b) of sub-paragraph (1) above at the time mentioned in that paragraph, and

(c) the whole or any part of the asset which is the old asset for the purposes of that section was so held,

the question whether that gain is one accruing on the disposal of an asset the whole or any part of which was held by a particular company at that time shall be determined for the purposes of this paragraph as if the bond were deemed to have been so held to the same extent as the old asset.

History – Para. 7(1)(c) substituted by FA 2011, s. 46 and Sch. 11, para. 6(2), with effect on and after 19 July 2011 in relation to the deduction of any allowable loss that has accrued to a company at a time before it became a member of the relevant group (FA 2011, Sch. 11, para. 11), subject to a transitional provision concerning the pre-entry proportion of an allowable loss accruing to a company on the disposal of a pre-entry asset (FA 2011, Sch. 11, para. 12). Former para. 7(1)(c) read as follows:

"(c) on the disposal of any asset which–

(i) was acquired by that company on or after the entry date from a person who was not a member of the relevant group at the time of the acquisition; and

(ii) since its acquisition from that person has not been used or held for any purposes other than those of a trade which was being carried on by that company at the time immediately before the entry date and which continued to be carried on by that company until the disposal.".

Para. 7(1A)–(1C) inserted by FA 2011, s. 46 and Sch. 11, para. 6(3), with effect on and after 19 July 2011 in relation to the deduction of any allowable loss that has accrued to a company at a time before it became a member of the relevant group (FA 2011, Sch. 11,

para. 11), subject to a transitional provision concerning the pre-entry proportion of an allowable loss accruing to a company on the disposal of a pre-entry asset (FA 2011, Sch. 11, para. 12).
Para. 7(2) omitted by FA 2011, s. 46 and Sch. 11, para. 6(4). Former para. 7(2) read as follows:
"7(2) The pre-entry proportion of an allowable loss accruing to any company on the disposal of a pre-entry asset shall be deductible from a chargeable gain accruing to that company if–
(a) the gain is one accruing on a disposal made, before the date on which it became a member of the relevant group, by that company and that company is the one (**"the initial company"**) by reference to which the asset on the disposal of which the loss accrues is a pre-entry asset;
(b) the pre-entry asset and the asset on the disposal of which the gain accrues were each held by the same company at a time immediately before it became a member of the relevant group; or
(c) the gain is one accruing on the disposal of an asset which–
(i) was acquired by the initial company (whether before or after it became a member of the relevant group) from a person who, at the time of the acquisition, was not a member of that group; and
(ii) since its acquisition from that person has not been used or held for any purposes other than those of a trade which was being carried on, immediately before it became a member of the relevant group, by the initial company and which continued to be carried on by the initial company until the disposal.".
In para. 7(3), the words " , without prejudice to paragraph 9 below" (which immediately preceded sub-paragraph (a)) omitted, sub-paragraph (b) omitted and, in sub-paragraph (c), the words "sub-paragraph (1A)" substituted for the words "sub-paragraphs (1)(c) and (2)(c)" by FA 2006, s. 46 and Sch. 11, para. 6(5), with effect on and after 19 July 2011 in relation to the deduction of any allowable loss that has accrued to a company at a time before it became a member of the relevant group (FA 2011, Sch. 11, para. 11), subject to a transitional provision concerning the pre-entry proportion of an allowable loss accruing to a company on the disposal of a pre-entry asset (FA 2011, Sch. 11, para. 12). Former para. 7(3)(b) read as follows:
"(b) two or more assets shall be treated for the purposes of sub-paragraph (2)(b) above as assets held by the same company immediately before it became a member of the relevant group wherever they would be so treated if all those companies were treated as a single company;"
Para. 7(4)–(4C) substituted for former para. 7(4) by Fa 2011, s. 46 and Sch. 11, para. 6(6), with effect on and after 19 July 2011 in relation to the deduction of any allowable loss that has accrued to a company at a time before it became a member of the relevant group (FA 2011, Sch. 11, para. 11), subject to a transitional provision concerning the pre-entry proportion of an allowable loss accruing to a company on the disposal of a pre-entry asset (FA 2011, Sch. 11, para. 12). Former para. 7(4) reads as follows:
"7(4) Paragraph 1(4) above shall apply for determining for the purposes of this paragraph whether an asset on the disposal of which a chargeable gain accrues was held at the time when a company became a member of the relevant group as it applies for determining whether that asset is a pre-entry asset in relation to that group by reference to that company.".
In para. 7(5), the words "or 2" omitted in both places where they followed the words "sub-paragraph (1)" by FA 2011, s. 46 and Sch. 11, para. 6(7), with effect on and after 19 July 2011 in relation to the deduction of any allowable loss that has accrued to a company at a time before it became a member of the relevant group (FA 2011, Sch. 11, para. 11), subject to a transitional provision concerning the pre-entry proportion of an allowable loss accruing to a company on the disposal of a pre-entry asset (FA 2011, Sch 11, para. 12).
In para. 7(6)(b), the words "or 2" omitted by FA 2011, s. 46 and Sch. 11, para. 6(8), with effect on and after 19 July 2011 in relation to the deduction of any allowable loss that has accrued to a company at a time before it became a member of the relevant group (FA 2011, Sch. 11, para. 11), subject to a transitional provision concerning the pre-entry proportion of an allowable loss accruing to a company on the disposal of a pre-entry asset (FA 2011, Sch. 11, para. 12).

Cross references – S. 116(10): crystallisation of notional market value gain which was held over on reorganisation where new holding included a qualifying corporate bond.
ICTA 1988, s. 786C: restriction to set-off of management expenses and charges defrayed and paid by an investment company before a change in ownership against chargeable gains on disposal of assets acquired intra-group in three years following the change.
SI 1994/3226, reg. 9(3): treatment of assets held by a company on its commencement day (for the purposes of FA 1993, Pt. II, Ch. II) where the company was non-resident at any time before its commencement day.
SI 1994/3226, reg. 16(4): a company's pre-commencement day (for the purposes of FA 1993, Pt. II, Ch. II) losses are not available for set-off against exchange gains if deductible under s. 8(1).
SI 1994/3226, reg. 16(6): computation of available losses on assets held by a company on its commencement day (for the purposes of FA 1993, Pt. II, Ch. II) where the company was non-resident at any time before its commencement day.
SI 1994/3226, reg. 16(12): losses specified in an election to set available losses against exchange gains not deductible under s. 8(1).

Statements of practice – SP 10/91: Revenue interpretation of "major change in the nature or conduct of a trade (or business)".

CHANGE OF A COMPANY'S NATURE

8(1) If–
(a) within any period of three years, a company becomes a member of a group of companies and there is (either earlier or later in that period, or at the same time) a major change in the nature or conduct of a trade or business which was carried on by that company immediately before it became a member of that group, or
(b) at any time after the scale of the activities in a trade or business carried on by a company has become small or negligible, and before any considerable revival of the trade or business, that company becomes a member of a group of companies,

the trade or business carried on before that change, or which has become small or negligible, shall be disregarded for the purposes of paragraph 7(1A) above in relation to any time before the company became a member of the group in question.

8(2) In sub-paragraph (1) **"a major change in the nature or conduct of a trade or business"** includes–
(a) a major change in the type of property dealt in, or services or facilities provided, in the trade or business,
(b) a major change in customers, markets or outlets of the trade or business, or
(c) in the case of a company with investment business (within the meaning of section 1218B of CTA 2009), a major change in the nature of the investments held;

and this paragraph applies even if the change is the result of a gradual process which began outside the period of three years mentioned in sub-paragraph (1)(a).

8(3) Where the operation of this paragraph depends on circumstances or events at a time after the company becomes a member of any group of companies (but not more than three years after), an assessment to give effect to this paragraph shall not be out of time if made within six years from that time or the latest such time.

History – In para. 8(1), the words "or business" inserted after the word "trade" (in the four places where it occurs), the words "which was carried on by that company immediately before it became a member of that group" substituted for the words "carried on by that company" and the words "paragraph 7(1A)" substituted for the words "paragraph 7(1)(c) and (2)(c)" by FA 2011, s. 46 and Sch. 11, para. 7(2), with effect on and after 19 July 2011 in relation to the deduction of any allowable loss that has accrued to a company at a time before it became a member of the relevant group (FA 2011, Sch. 11, para. 11), subject to a transitional provision concerning the pre-entry proportion of an allowable loss accruing to a company on the disposal of a pre-entry asset (FA 2011, Sch. 11, para. 12). In para. 8(2)(c), the words "section 1218B" substituted for the words "section 1218" by FA 2016, s. 55(a), with effect from 15 September 2016 (Royal Assent).

Para. 8(2) substituted by FA 2011, s. 46 and Sch. 11, para. 7(3), with effect on and after 19 July 2011 in relation to the deduction of any allowable loss that has accrued to a company at a time before it became a member of the relevant group (FA 2011, Sch. 11, para. 11), subject to a transitional provision concerning the pre-entry proportion of an allowable loss accruing to a company on the disposal of a pre-entry asset (FA 2011, Sch. 11, para. 12). Former para. 8(2) read as follows:

"**8(2)** In sub-paragraph (1) above the reference to a major change in the nature or conduct of a trade includes a reference to–

(a) a major change in the type of property dealt in, or services or facilities provided, in the trade; or

(b) a major change in customers, markets or outlets of the trade;

and this paragraph shall apply even if the change is the result of a gradual process which began outside the period of three years mentioned in sub-paragraph (1)(a) above.".

Statements of practice – SP 10/91: HMRC interpretation of "major change in the nature or conduct of a trade (or business)".

IDENTIFICATION OF "THE RELEVANT GROUP" AND APPLICATION OF SCHEDULE TO EVERY CONNECTED GROUP

9 [Omitted by FA 2011, s. 46 and Sch. 11, para. 8.]

History – Omitted by FA 2011, s. 46 and Sch. 11, para. 8, with effect on and after 19 July 2011 in relation to the deduction of any allowable loss that has accrued to a company at a time before it became a member of the relevant group (FA 2011, Sch. 11, para. 11), subject to a transitional provision concerning the pre-entry proportion of an allowable loss accruing to a company on the disposal of a pre-entry asset (FA 2011, Sch. 11, para. 12). Former para. 9 read as follows:

"**9(1)** This paragraph shall apply where there is more than one group of companies which would be the relevant group in relation to any company.

9(2) Where any loss has accrued on the disposal by any company of any asset, this Schedule shall not apply by reference to any group of companies in relation to any loss accruing on that disposal unless–

(a) that group is a group in relation to which that loss is a pre-entry loss by virtue of paragraph 1(2)(a) above or, if there is more than one such group, the one of which that company most recently became a member;

(b) that group, in a case where there is no group falling within paragraph (a) above, is either–

(i) the group of which that company is a member at the time of the disposal, or

(ii) if it is not a member of a group of companies at that time, the group of which that company was last a member before that time;

(c) that group, in a case where there is a group falling within paragraph (a) or (b) above, is a group of which that company was a member at any time in the accounting period of that company in which it became a member of the group falling within that paragraph;

(d) that group is a group the principal company of which is or has been, or has been under the control of–

(i) the company by which the disposal is made, or

(ii) another company which is or has been a member of a group by reference to which this Schedule applies in relation to the loss in question by virtue of paragraph (a), (b) or (c) above; or

(e) that group is a group of which either–

(i) the principal company of a group by reference to which this Schedule so applies, or

(ii) a company which has had that principal company under its control,

is or has been a member;

and sub-paragraphs (3) to (5) below shall apply in the case of any loss accruing on the disposal of any asset where, by virtue of this sub-paragraph, there are two or more groups (**"connected groups"**) by reference to which this Schedule applies.

9(3) This Schedule shall apply separately in relation to each of the connected groups (so far as they are not groups in relation to which the loss is a pre-entry loss by virtue of paragraph 1(2)(a) above) for the purpose of–

(a) determining whether the loss on the disposal of any asset is a loss on the disposal of a pre-entry asset; and

(b) calculating the pre-entry proportion of that loss.

9(4) Subject to sub-paragraph (5) below, paragraph 6 above shall have effect–

(a) as if the pre-entry proportion of any loss accruing on the disposal of an asset which is a pre-entry asset in the case of more than one of the connected groups were the largest pre-entry proportion of that loss calculated in accordance with sub-paragraph (3) above; and

(b) so that, where the loss accruing on the disposal of any asset is a pre-entry loss by virtue of paragraph 1(2)(a) above in the case of any of the connected groups, that loss shall be the pre-entry loss for the purposes of paragraph 6 above, and not any amount which is the pre-entry proportion of that loss in relation to any of the other groups.

9(5) Where, on the separate application of this Schedule in the case of each of the groups by reference to which this Schedule applies, there is, in the case of the disposal of any asset, a pre-entry loss by reference to each of two or more of the connected groups, no amount in respect of the loss accruing on the disposal shall be deductible under paragraph 7 above from any chargeable gain if any of the connected groups is a group in the case of which, on separate applications of that paragraph in relation to each group, the amount deductible from that gain in respect of that loss is nil.

9(6) Notwithstanding that the principal company of one group (**"the first group"**) has become a member of another (**"the second group"**), those two groups shall not by virtue of section 170(10) or (10A) be treated in relation to any company that is or has become a member of the second group ("the relevant company") as the same group for the purposes of this paragraph if–

(a) the time at which the relevant company became a member of the first group is a time in the same accounting period as that in which the principal company of the first group became a member of the second group; or

(b) the principal company of the first group was under the control, immediately before it became a member of the second group, of a company which at that time was already a member of the second group.

9(7) Where, in the case of the disposal of any asset–

(a) two or more groups which but for sub-paragraph (6) above would be treated as the same group are treated as separate groups by virtue of that sub-paragraph; and

(b) one of those groups is a group of which either–

(i) the principal company of a group by reference to which this Schedule applies by virtue of sub-paragraph (2)(a), (b) or (c) above in relation to any loss accruing on the disposal, or

(ii) a company which has had that principal company under its control,

is or has been a member,

this paragraph shall have effect as if that principal company had been a member of each of the groups mentioned in paragraph (a) above.".

In former para. 9(2)(c), the words "or (b)" inserted by FA 1994, s. 94(3) with effect in relation to the making, in respect of any loss, of any deduction from a chargeable gain where either the gain or the loss is one accruing on or after 11 March 1994.

In former para. 9(6), words "or (10A)" inserted by F(No. 2)A 2005, s. 65(5) with effect, in accordance with F(No. 2)A 2005, s. 65(6), in relation to formation of an SE (Societas Europaea or, in other words, European Company) which occurs on or after 1 April 2005.

In former para. 9(6), the words:

"in relation to any company that is or has become a member of the second group ("the relevant company") as the same group for the purposes of this paragraph if–

(a) the time at which the relevant company became a member of the first group is a time in the same accounting period as that in which the principal company of the first group became a member of the second group; or

(b) "

substituted for "for the purposes of this paragraph as the same group if" by FA 1998, s. 138 in relation to accounting periods ending on or after 17 March 1998.

Cross references – S. 170: interpretation of terms in relation to groups of companies – definition of group (s. 170(10)).

APPROPRIATIONS TO STOCK IN TRADE

10 Where, but for an election under subsection (3) of section 161, there would be deemed to have been a disposal at any time by any company of any asset–

(a) the amount by which the market value of the asset may be treated as increased in pursuance of that election shall not include the amount of any pre-entry loss that would have accrued on that disposal; and

(b) this Schedule shall have effect as if the pre-entry loss of the last mentioned amount had accrued to that company at that time.

Cross references – S. 161(3): election to reduce for income tax the acquisition cost and for capital gains tax the disposal consideration by the notional gain where asset appropriated from trading stock.

10A Section 161(3ZB)(a) and (b) does not apply to a loss if, in the absence of an election under section 161(3ZA), the loss would have been a pre-entry loss.

History – Para. 10A inserted by FA 2013, s. 65 and Sch. 25, para. 17, with effect in relation to disposals occurring on or after 6 April 2013.

CONTINUITY PROVISIONS

11(1) This paragraph applies where provision has been made by or under any enactment (**"the transfer legislation"**) for the transfer of property, rights and liabilities to any person from–

(a) a body established by or under any enactment for the purpose, in the exercise of statutory functions, of carrying on any undertaking or industrial or other activity in the public sector or of exercising any other statutory functions;

(b) a subsidiary of such a body; or

(c) a company wholly owned by the Crown.

11(2) A loss shall not be a pre-entry loss for the purposes of this Schedule in relation to any company to whom a transfer has been made by or under the transfer legislation if that loss–

(a) accrued to the person from whom the transfer has been made; and

(b) falls to be treated, in accordance with any enactment made in relation to transfers by or under that legislation, as a loss accruing to that company.

11(3) For the purposes of this Schedule where a company became a member of the relevant group by virtue of the transfer by or under the transfer legislation of any shares in or other securities of that company or any other company–

(a) a loss that accrued to that company before it so became a member of that group shall not be a pre-entry loss in relation to that group;

(b) [omitted by FA 2011, s. 46 and Sch. 11, para. 9.]

11(4) For the purposes of this paragraph a company shall be regarded as wholly owned by the Crown if it is–

(a) a company limited by shares in which there are no issued shares held otherwise than by, or by a nominee of, the Treasury, a Minister of the Crown, a Northern Ireland department or another company wholly owned by the Crown; or

(b) a company limited by guarantee of which no person other than the Treasury, a Minister of the Crown or a Northern Ireland department, or a nominee of the Treasury, a Minister of the Crown or a Northern Ireland department, is a member.

11(5) In this paragraph–

"enactment" includes any provision of any Northern Ireland legislation, within the meaning of section 24 of the Interpretation Act 1978; and

"statutory functions" means functions under any enactment, under any subordinate legislation, within the meaning of the Interpretation Act 1978, or under any statutory rules, within the meaning of the Statutory Rules (Northern Ireland) Order 1979.

History – Para. 11(3)(b) and the word "and" before it omitted by FA 2011, s. 46 and Sch. 11, para. 9, with effect on and after 19 July 2011 in relation to the deduction of any allowable loss that has accrued to a company at a time before it became a member of the relevant group (FA 2011, Sch. 11, para. 11), subject to a transitional provision concerning the pre-entry proportion of an allowable loss accruing to a company on the disposal of a pre-entry asset (FA 2011, Sch. 11, para. 12). Former para. 11(3)(b) read as follows:
"(b) no asset held by that company when it so became a member of that group shall by virtue of that fact be a pre-entry asset.".

COMPANIES CHANGING GROUPS ON CERTAIN TRANSFERS OF SHARES ETC.

12 For the purposes of this Schedule, and without prejudice to paragraph 11 above, where–

(a) a company which is a member of a group of companies becomes at any time a member of another group of companies as the result of a disposal of shares in or other securities of that company or any other company; and

(b) that disposal is one on which, by virtue of any of the no gain/no loss provisions, neither a gain nor a loss would accrue,

this Schedule shall have effect in relation to the losses that accrued to that company before that time and the assets held by that company at that time as if any time when it was a member of the first group were included in the period during which it is treated as having been a member of the second group.

History – In para. 12(b), the words "no gain/no loss provisions" substituted for the words "enactment specified in section 35(3)(d)" by FA 2008, s. 8 and Sch. 2, para. 68 with effect in relation to disposals on or after 6 April 2008 (Sch. 2, para. 71).

Cross references – S. 35(3)(d): list of enactments to which rebasing does not apply unless application for simplified rebasing scheme (rebasing of all assets held at 31 March 1982) is in force.

SCHEDULE 7AA – RESTRICTIONS ON SETTING LOSSES AGAINST PRE-ENTRY GAINS

Section 177B

[Sch. 7AA ceases to have effect by virtue of FA 2006, s. 70(4) and repealed by FA 2006, s. 178 and Sch. 26, Pt. 3(9)]

History – Sch. 7AA ceases to have effect by virtue of FA 2006, s. 70(4) and repealed by FA 2006, s. 178 and Sch. 26, Pt. 3(9) in respect of any accounting period ending on or after 5 December 2005 (but not in relation to the deduction of a loss arising before that date from a chargeable gain accruing before that date).

SCHEDULE 7AB – ROLL-OVER OF DEGROUPING CHARGE: MODIFICATION OF ENACTMENTS

[Repealed by FA 2011, s. 45 and Sch. 10, para. 5(c).]

History – Sch. 7AB repealed by FA 2011, s. 45 and Sch. 10, para. 5(c), with effect in relation to any disposal of an asset by one company (B) to another company (A) made at a time when B is a member of a group if either A ceases to be a member of the group on or after 19 July 2011 or ceased to be so before 19 July 2011 in circumstances where TCGA 1992, s. 179(6)–(8) applied and ceases to satisfy the conditions in TCGA 1992, s. 179(7) on or after 19 July 2011 (see FA 2011, Sch. 10, para. 9(1)). But references to 19 July 2011 may be replaced by references to 1 April 2011 if an "early commencement election" is made (see FA 2011, Sch. 10, para. 9(4)–(8)).

SCHEDULE 7AC – EXEMPTIONS FOR DISPOSALS BY COMPANIES WITH SUBSTANTIAL SHAREHOLDING

History – Sch. 7AC inserted by FA 2002, s. 44 and Sch. 8 with effect in relation to disposal on or after 1 April 2002.

Other material – HMRC Brief 41/07: COP10 facility has been reinstated for substantial shareholdings exemption.
HMRC Brief 29/11: corporation tax and the substantial shareholding exemption: joint ventures and entities without ordinary share capital.

Part 1 – The Exemptions

THE MAIN EXEMPTION

1(1) A gain accruing to a company (**"the investing company"**) on a disposal of shares or an interest in shares in another company (**"the company invested in"**) is not a chargeable gain if the requirements of this Schedule are met.

1(2) The requirements are set out in–

Part 2 (the substantial shareholding requirement), and

Part 3 (requirements to be met in relation to the investing company and the company invested in).

1(3) The exemption conferred by this paragraph does not apply in the circumstances specified in paragraph 5 or the cases specified in paragraph 6.

SUBSIDIARY EXEMPTION: DISPOSAL OF ASSET RELATED TO SHARES WHERE MAIN EXEMPTION CONDITIONS MET

2(1) A gain accruing to a company ("company A") on a disposal of an asset related to shares in another company ("company B") is not a chargeable gain if either of the following conditions is met.

2(2) The first condition is that–

(a) immediately before the disposal company A holds shares or an interest in shares in company B, and

(b) any gain accruing to company A on a disposal at that time of the shares or interest would, by virtue of paragraph 1, not be a chargeable gain.

2(3) The second condition is that–

(a) immediately before the disposal company A does not hold shares or an interest in shares in company B but is a member of a group and another member of that group does hold shares or an interest in shares in company B, and

(b) if company A, rather than that other company, held the shares or interest, any gain accruing to company A on a disposal at that time of the shares or interest would, by virtue of paragraph 1, not be a chargeable gain.

2(4) Where assets of a company are vested in a liquidator under section 145 of the Insolvency Act 1986 (c. 45) or Article 123 of the Insolvency (Northern Ireland) Order 1989 or otherwise, this paragraph applies as if the assets were vested in, and the acts of the liquidator in relation to the assets were the acts of, the company (acquisitions from or disposals to him by the company being disregarded accordingly).

2(5) The exemption conferred by this paragraph does not apply in the circumstances specified in paragraph 5 or the cases specified in paragraph 6.

SUBSIDIARY EXEMPTION: DISPOSAL OF SHARES OR RELATED ASSET WHERE MAIN EXEMPTION CONDITIONS PREVIOUSLY MET

3(1) A gain accruing to a company ("company A") on a disposal of shares, or an interest in shares or an asset related to shares, in another company ("company B") is not a chargeable gain if the following conditions are met.

3(2) The conditions are–

(a) that at the time of the disposal company A meets the requirement in paragraph 7 (the substantial shareholding requirement) in relation to company B;

(b) that a chargeable gain or allowable loss would, apart from this paragraph, accrue to company A on the disposal (but see sub-paragraph (3) below);

(c) that at the time of the disposal–

  (i) company A is resident in the United Kingdom, or

  (ii) any chargeable gain accruing to company A on the disposal would, by virtue of section 10B, form part of that company's chargeable profits for corporation tax purposes;

(d) that there was a time within the period of two years ending with the disposal (**"the relevant period"**) when, if–

  (i) company A, or

  (ii) a company that at any time in the relevant period was a member of the same group as company A,

had disposed of shares or an interest in shares in company B that it then held, a gain accruing would, by virtue of paragraph 1, not have been a chargeable gain; and

(e) that, if at the time of the disposal the requirements of paragraph 19 (requirements relating to company invested in) are not met in relation to company B, there was a time within the relevant period when company B was controlled by–

  (i) company A, or

  (ii) company A together with any persons connected with it, or

  (iii) a company that at any time in the relevant period was a member of the same group as company A, or

  (iv) any such company together with any persons connected with it.

3(3) Sub-paragraph (1) does not apply if–

(a) the condition in sub-paragraph (2)(b) is met but would not be met but for a failure to meet the requirement in pararaph 18(1)(b) (requirement as to investing company to be met immediately after the disposal), and

(b) the failure to meet that requirement is not due to–

(i) the fact that company A has been wound up or dissolved, or

(ii) where the winding up or dissolution takes place as soon as is reasonably practicable in the circumstances, the fact that company A is about to be wound up or dissolved.

3(4) In determining for the purpose of sub-paragraph (2)(d) whether a gain accruing on the hypothetical disposal referred to would have been a chargeable gain, the requirements of paragraph 18(1)(b) and of paragraph 19(1)(b) (requirement as to company invested in to be met immediately after the disposal) shall be assumed to be met.

3(5) Where–

(a) immediately before the disposal company B holds an asset,

(b) the expenditure allowable in computing any gain or loss on that asset, were it to be disposed of by company B immediately before that disposal, would fall to be reduced because of a claim to relief under section 165 (gifts relief) in relation to an earlier disposal, and

(c) that earlier disposal took place within the relevant period,

sub-paragraph (1) does not prevent a gain accruing to company A on the disposal from being a chargeable gain but any loss so accruing is not an allowable loss.

3(6) Where assets of company B are vested in a liquidator under section 145 of the Insolvency Act 1986 (c. 45) or Article 123 of the Insolvency (Northern Ireland) Order 1989 or otherwise, sub-paragraph (5)(a) applies as if the assets were vested in the company.

3(7) In determining **"the relevant period"** for the purposes of sub-paragraph (2)(d) or (e) or sub-paragraph (5)(c), section 28 (time of disposal under contract) applies with the omission of subsection (2) (postponement of time of disposal in case of conditional contract).

3(8) The exemption conferred by this paragraph does not apply in the circumstances specified in paragraph 5 or the cases specified in paragraph 6.

History – In para. 3(2)(c)(ii), reference "section 10B" substituted for reference "section 10(3)" by F(No. 2)A 2005, s. 34 and Sch. 4, para. 9(2) with effect, in accordance with F(No. 2)A 2005, Sch. 4, para. 10(4), in relation to disposals on or after 16 March 2005.

APPLICATION OF EXEMPTIONS IN PRIORITY TO PROVISIONS DEEMING THERE TO BE NO DISPOSAL ETC

4(1) For the purposes of determining whether an exemption conferred by this Schedule applies, the question whether there is a disposal shall be determined without regard to–

(a) section 116(10) (reorganisation, conversion of securities, etc treated as not involving disposal),

(b) section 127 (share reorganisations etc treated as not involving disposal), or

(c) section 192(2)(a) (distribution not treated as capital distribution).

4(2) Sub-paragraph (1) does not apply to a disposal of shares if the effect of its applying would be that relief attributable to the shares under Schedule 15 to the Finance Act 2000 (c. 17) (corporate venturing scheme) would be withdrawn or reduced under paragraph 46 of that Schedule (withdrawal or reduction of investment relief on disposal of shares).

4(3) Where or to the extent that an exemption conferred by this Schedule does apply–

(a) the provisions mentioned in sub-paragraph (1)(a) and (b) do not apply in relation to the disposal, and

(b) the provision mentioned in sub-paragraph (1)(c) does not apply in relation to the subject matter of the disposal.

4(4) Where section 127 is disapplied by sub-paragraph (3)(a) in a case in which that section would otherwise have applied in relation to the disposal by virtue of paragraph 84 of Schedule 15 to the Finance Act 2000 (corporate venturing scheme: share exchanges), paragraph 85 of that Schedule (attribution of relief to new shares) does not apply.

4(5) In this paragraph any reference to section 127 includes a reference to that provision as applied by any enactment relating to corporation tax.

CIRCUMSTANCES IN WHICH EXEMPTIONS DO NOT APPLY

5(1) Where in pursuance of arrangements to which this paragraph applies–

(a) an untaxed gain accrues to a company ("company A") on a disposal of shares, or an interest in shares or an asset related to shares, in another company ("company B"), and

(b) before the accrual of that gain–

(i) company A acquired control of company B, or the same person or persons acquired control of both companies, or

(ii) there was a significant change of trading activities affecting company B at a time when it was controlled by company A, or when both companies were controlled by the same person or persons,

none of the exemptions in this Schedule applies to the disposal.

5(2) This paragraph applies to arrangements from which the sole or main benefit that (but for this paragraph) could be expected to arise is that the gain on the disposal would, by virtue of this Schedule, not be a chargeable gain.

5(3) For the purposes of sub-paragraph (1)(a) a gain is "untaxed" if the gain, or all of it but a part that is not substantial, represents profits that have not been brought into account (in the United Kingdom or elsewhere) for the purposes of tax on profits for a period ending on or before the date of the disposal.

5(4) The reference in sub-paragraph (3) to profits being brought into account for the purposes of tax on profits includes a reference to the case where–

(a) an amount in respect of those profits is apportioned to a company resident in the United Kingdom by virtue of subsection (3) of section 747 of the Taxes Act 1988 (imputation of chargeable profits etc of controlled foreign companies), and

(b) a sum is chargeable on that company in respect of that amount by virtue of subsection (4) of that section for an accounting period of that company ending on or before the date of the disposal.

5(5) For the purposes of sub-paragraph (1)(b)(ii) there is a "significant change of trading activities affecting company B" if–

(a) there is a major change in the nature or conduct of a trade carried on by company B or a 51% subsidiary of company B, or

(b) there is a major change in the scale of the activities of a trade carried on by company B or a 51% subsidiary of company B, or

(c) company B or a 51% subsidiary of company B begins to carry on a trade.

5(6) In this paragraph–

"arrangements" includes any scheme, agreement or understanding, whether or not legally enforceable;

"major change in the nature or conduct of a trade" has the same meaning as in section 673 of CTA 2010 (change of ownership of company: disallowance of trading losses);

"profits" means income or gains (including unrealised income or gains).

History – In para. 5(6), the words "section 673 of CTA 2010" substituted for "section 768 of the Taxes Act" by CTA 2010, s. 1177 and Sch. 1, para. 269(2), with effect for corporation tax purposes for accounting periods ending on or after 1 April 2010, and for income tax and capital gains tax purposes for the tax year 2010–11 and subsequent tax years.

Statements of practice – SP 5/02: HMRC practice in applying anti-avoidance rule in para. 5.

OTHER CASES EXCLUDED FROM EXEMPTIONS

6(1) The exemptions conferred by this Schedule do not apply–

(a) to a disposal that by virtue of any enactment relating to chargeable gains is deemed to be for a consideration such that no gain or loss accrues to the person making the disposal,

(b) to a disposal a gain on which would, by virtue of any enactment not contained in this Schedule, not be a chargeable gain, or

(c) to a deemed disposal under any of sections 116 to 118 of the Finance Act 2012 (deemed disposal on transfer of asset of insurance company from one category to another).

6(2) The hypothetical disposal referred to in paragraph 2(2)(b) or (3)(b) or paragraph 3(2)(d) shall be assumed not to be a disposal within sub-paragraph (1)(a), (b) or (c) above.

History – In para. 6(1)(c), the words "any of sections 116 to 118 of the Finance Act 2012" substituted for "section 440(1) or (2) of the Taxes Act" by FA 2012, s. 146 and Sch. 16, para. 88(2) in relation to accounting periods beginning on or after 1 January 2013 (FA 2012, s. 148) but subject to transitional provisions in FA 2012, Sch. 17. Where an accounting period would otherwise straddle 1 January 2013, it is deemed to end on 31 December 2012 (FA 2012, s. 149).

Part 2 – The Substantial Shareholding Requirement

THE REQUIREMENT

7 The investing company must have held a substantial shareholding in the company invested in throughout a twelve-month period beginning not more than two years before the day on which the disposal takes place.

MEANING OF "SUBSTANTIAL SHAREHOLDING"

8(1) For the purposes of this Schedule a company holds a **"substantial shareholding"** in another company if it holds shares or interests in shares in that company by virtue of which–

(a) it holds not less than 10% of the company's ordinary share capital,

(b) it is beneficially entitled to not less than 10% of the profits available for distribution to equity holders of the company, and

(c) it would be beneficially entitled on a winding up to not less than 10% of the assets of the company available for distribution to equity holders.

This is without prejudice to what is meant by "substantial" where the word appears in other contexts.

8(2) Chapter 6 of Part 5 of CTA 2010 (group relief: equity holders and profits or assets available for distribution) applies for the purposes of sub-paragraph (1) as it applies for the purposes of the provisions mentioned in section 157(1) of that Act, but as if–

(a) in section 158 of that Act after subsection (2) there were inserted–

> **"158(2A)** But for those purposes a person carrying on a business of banking is not treated as a loan creditor of a company in respect of any loan capital or debt issued or incurred by the company for money lent by the person to the company in the ordinary course of that business.", and

(b) sections 171(1)(b) and (3), 173, 174 and 176 to 181 of that Act were omitted.

History – In para. 8(2), the words "but as if–" to the end substituted for the former words by SI 2010/2902, art. 2(3) (effective from 1 January 2011 but with deemed effect from 1 April 2010). This amendment is deemed to have come into force for corporation tax purposes for accounting periods ending on or after 1 April 2010, and for income tax and capital gains tax purposes for the tax year 2010–11 and subsequent tax years.

Para. 8(2) substituted for former para. 8(2) and (3) by CTA 2010, s. 1177 and Sch. 1, para. 269(3), with effect for corporation tax purposes for accounting periods ending on or after 1 April 2010, and for income tax and capital gains tax purposes for the tax year 2010–11 and subsequent tax years.

AGGREGATION OF HOLDINGS OF GROUP COMPANIES

9(1) For the purposes of paragraph 7 (the substantial shareholding requirement) a company that is a member of a group is treated–

(a) as holding any shares or interest in shares held by any other company in the group, and

(b) as having the same entitlement as any such company to any rights enjoyed by virtue of holding shares or an interest in shares.

9(2) Sub-paragraph (1) is subject to paragraph 17(4) (exclusion of aggregation in case of assets of long-term insurance fund of insurance company).

EFFECT OF EARLIER NO-GAIN/NO-LOSS TRANSFER

10(1) For the purposes of this Part the period for which a company has held shares is treated as extended by any earlier period during which the shares concerned, or shares from which they are derived, were held–

(a) by a company from which the shares concerned were transferred to the first-mentioned company on a no-gain/no-loss transfer, or

(b) by a company from which the shares concerned, or shares from which they are derived, were transferred on a previous no-gain/no-loss transfer–

  (i) to a company within paragraph (a), or

  (ii) to another company within this paragraph.

10(2) For the purposes of sub-paragraph (1)–

(a) a **"no-gain/no-loss transfer"** means a disposal and corresponding acquisition that by virtue of any enactment relating to chargeable gains are deemed to be for a consideration such that no gain or loss accrues to the person making the disposal;

(b) a transfer shall be treated as if it had been a no-gain/no-loss transfer if it is a transfer to which subsection (1) of section 171 (transfers within a group) would apply but for subsection (3) of that section.

10(3) Where sub-paragraph (1) applies to extend the period for which a company ("company A") is treated as having held any shares, that company shall be treated for the purposes of this Part as having had at any time the same entitlement–

(a) to shares, and

(b) to any rights enjoyed by virtue of holding shares,

as the company ("company B") that at that time held the shares concerned or, as the case may be, the shares from which they are derived.

10(4) The shares and rights to be so attributed to company A include any holding or entitlement attributed at that time to company B under paragraph 9 (aggregation of holdings of group companies).

10(5) In this paragraph, except in paragraphs (a) to (c) of sub-paragraph (6), **"shares"** includes an interest in shares.

10(6) For the purposes of this paragraph shares are **"derived"** from other shares only where–

(a) a company becomes a co-owner of shares previously owned by it alone, or vice versa,

(b) a company's interest in shares as co-owner changes (without the company ceasing to be a co-owner),

(c) one holding of shares is treated by virtue of section 127 as the same asset as another, or

(d) there is a sequence of two or more of the occurrences mentioned in paragraphs (a) to (c).

The reference in paragraph (c) to section 127 includes a reference to that provision as applied by any enactment relating to corporation tax.

EFFECT OF DEEMED DISPOSAL AND REACQUISITION

11(1) For the purposes of this Part a company is not regarded as having held shares throughout a period if, at any time during that period, there is a deemed disposal and reacquisition of–

(a) the shares concerned, or

(b) shares, or an interest in shares, from which those shares are derived.

11(2) For the purposes of this Part a company is not regarded as having held an interest in shares throughout a period if, at any time during that period, there is a deemed disposal and reacquisition of–

(a) the interest concerned, or

(b) shares, or an interest in shares, from which that interest is derived.

11(3) In this paragraph–

"deemed disposal and reacquisition" means a disposal and immediate reacquisition treated as taking place under any enactment relating to corporation tax;

"derived" has the same meaning as in paragraph 10.

EFFECT OF REPURCHASE AGREEMENT

12(1) This paragraph applies where–

(a) a company ("the borrower") which holds shares in another company sells the shares under an arrangement by reference to which the borrower has a debtor repo, and

(b) by virtue of paragraph 6 of Schedule 13 to the Finance Act 2007 (sale and repurchase of securities) the sale is ignored for the purposes of corporation tax in respect of chargeable gains.

12(2) For the period for which the arrangement is in force–

(a) the borrower shall be treated for the purposes of this Part as continuing to hold the shares and accordingly as retaining its entitlement to any rights attaching to them, and

(b) the lender shall be treated for those purposes as not holding the shares and as not becoming entitled to any such rights.

This is subject to the following qualification.

12(3) If at any time before the end of that period the borrower, or another member of the same group as the borrower, becomes the holder–

(a) of any of the shares, or

(b) of any shares directly or indirectly representing any of them,

sub-paragraph (2) does not apply after that time in relation to those shares or, as the case may be, the shares represented by them.

12(4) Expressions used in this paragraph and in Schedule 13 to the Finance Act 2007 have the same meaning in this paragraph as in that Schedule.

History – Para. 12 substituted by FA 2007, s. 47 and Sch. 14, para. 13(1), with effect in relation to arrangements coming into force on or after 1 October 2007, by virtue of SI 2007/2483, art. 3.

Para. 12(4)(b) originally substituted by FA 2003, s. 181 and Sch. 38, para. 9 which, by virtue of Sch. 38, para. 21(2), have effect in relation to agreements, to sell securities, made on or after 9 April 2003.

EFFECT OF STOCK LENDING ARRANGEMENTS

13(1) This paragraph applies where–

(a) a company that holds shares in another company transfers the shares under a stock lending arrangement, and

(b) by virtue of section 263B(2) (stock lending arrangements) the disposal is disregarded for the purposes of the enactments relating to chargeable gains.

13(2) During the period of the stock lending arrangement–

(a) the lender shall be treated for the purposes of this Part as continuing to hold the shares transferred and accordingly as retaining his entitlement to any rights attached to them, and

(b) the borrower shall be treated for those purposes as not holding the shares transferred and as not becoming entitled to any such rights.

This is subject to the following qualification.

13(3) If at any time before the end of the period of the stock lending arrangement the lender, or another member of the same group as the lender, becomes the holder–

(a) of any of the shares transferred, or

(b) of any shares directly or indirectly representing any of the shares transferred,

sub-paragraph (2) does not apply after that time in relation to those shares or, as the case may be, in relation to the shares represented by those shares.

13(4) In this paragraph a **"stock lending arrangement"** means arrangements between two persons (**"the borrower"** and **"the lender"**) under which–

(a) the lender transfers shares to the borrower otherwise than by way of sale, and

(b) a requirement is imposed on the borrower to transfer those shares back to the lender otherwise than by way of sale.

13(5) Any reference in this paragraph to the period of a stock lending arrangement is to the period beginning with the transfer of the shares by the lender to the borrower and ending–

(a) with the transfer of the shares back to the lender in pursuance of the arrangement, or

(b) when it becomes apparent that the requirement for the borrower to make a transfer back to the lender will not be complied with.

13(6) The following provisions apply for the purposes of this paragraph as they apply for the purposes of section 263B–

(a) subsections (5) and (6) of that section (references to transfer back of securities to include transfer of other securities of the same description);

(b) section 263C (references to transfer back of securities to include payment in respect of redemption).

EFFECT IN RELATION TO COMPANY INVESTED IN OF EARLIER COMPANY RECONSTRUCTION ETC

14(1) This paragraph applies where shares in one company ("company X")–

(a) are exchanged (or deemed to be exchanged) for shares in another company ("company Y"), or

(b) are deemed to be exchanged by virtue of section 136 for shares in company X and shares in another company ("company Y"),

in circumstances such that, under section 127 as that section applies by virtue of section 135 or 136, the original shares and the new holding are treated as the same asset.

14(2) Where company Y–

(a) is the company invested in, and is accordingly the company by reference to which the requirement of paragraph 7 (the substantial shareholding requirement) falls to be met, or

(b) is a company by reference to which, by virtue of this paragraph, that requirement may be met, or

(c) is a company by reference to which, by virtue of paragraph 15 (effect of earlier demerger) that requirement may be met,

that requirement may instead be met, in relation to times before the exchange (or deemed exchange), by reference to company X.

14(3) If in any case that requirement can be met by virtue of this paragraph (or by virtue of this paragraph together with paragraph 15), it shall be treated as met.

14(4) In sub-paragraph 1 **"original shares"** and **"new holding"** shall be construed in accordance with sections 126, 127, 135 and 136.

EFFECT IN RELATION TO COMPANY INVESTED IN OF EARLIER DEMERGER

15(1) This paragraph applies where shares in one company (**"the subsidiary"**) are transferred by another company (**"the parent company"**) on a demerger.

15(2) Where the subsidiary–

(a) is the company invested in, and is accordingly the company by reference to which the requirement of paragraph 7 (the substantial shareholding requirement) falls to be met, or

(b) is a company by reference to which, by virtue of this paragraph, that requirement may be met, or

(c) is a company by reference to which, by virtue of paragraph 14 (effect of earlier company reconstruction etc), that requirement may be met,

that requirement may instead be met, in relation to times before the transfer, by reference to the parent company.

15(3) If in any case that requirement can be met by virtue of this paragraph (or by virtue of this paragraph together with paragraph 14), it shall be treated as met.

15(4) In this paragraph a **"transfer of shares on a demerger"** means a transfer such that, by virtue of section 192(2)(b), sections 126 to 130 apply as if the parent company and the subsidiary were the same company and the transfer were a reorganisation of that company's share capital not involving a disposal or acquisition.

EFFECT OF TRANSFER OF TRADING ASSETS WITHIN A GROUP

15A(1) For the purposes of this Part, the period for which the investing company is treated as holding a substantial shareholding in the company invested in is extended in accordance with sub-paragraph (3) if the following conditions are met.

15A(2) The conditions are–

(a) that, immediately before the disposal, the investing company holds a substantial shareholding in the company invested in,

(b) that an asset which, at the time of the disposal, is being used for the purposes of a trade carried on by the company invested in was transferred to it by the investing company or another company,

(c) that, at the time of the transfer of the asset, the company invested in, the investing company and, if different, the company which transferred the asset were all members of the same group, and

(d) that the asset was previously used by a member of the group (other than the company invested in) for the purposes of a trade carried on by that member at a time when it was such a member.

15A(2A) For the purposes of sub-paragraph (2)(b) and (d), **"trade"** includes oil and gas exploration and appraisal.

15A(3) The investing company is to be treated as having held the substantial shareholding at any time during the final 12 month period when the asset was used as mentioned in sub-paragraph (2)(d) (if it did not hold a substantial shareholding at that time).

15A(4) **"The final 12 month period"** means the period of 12 months ending with the time of the disposal.

History – Para. 15A(2A) inserted by FA 2014, s. 72(1), with effect in relation to disposals made on or after 1 April 2014.
Para. 15A inserted by FA 2011, s. 45 and Sch. 10, para. 6(2), with effect in relation to disposals of shares made on or after 19 July 2011 (see FA 2011, Sch. 10, para. 9(2)). But the reference to 19 July 2011 may be replaced by a reference to 1 April 2011 if an "early commencement election" is made (see FA 2011, Sch. 10, para. 9(4)–(8)).

EFFECT OF INVESTING COMPANY'S LIQUIDATION

16 Where assets of the investing company, or of a company that is a member of the same group as the investing company, are vested in a liquidator under section 145 of the Insolvency Act 1986 (c. 45) or Article 123 of the Insolvency (Northern Ireland) Order 1989 or otherwise, this Part applies as if the assets were vested in, and the acts of the liquidator in relation to the assets were the acts of, the company (acquisitions from or disposals to him by the company being disregarded accordingly).

SPECIAL RULES FOR ASSETS OF INSURANCE COMPANY HELD FOR THE PURPOSES OF ITS LONG-TERM BUSINESS

17(1) In the following two cases paragraph 8(1) (meaning of substantial shareholding) has effect as if, in paragraphs (a), (b) and (c), "30%" were substituted for "10%".

17(2) The first case is where the investing company is an insurance company and the disposal is of an asset held by it for the purposes of its long-term business.

17(3) The second case is where–

(a) the investing company is a 51% subsidiary of an insurance company, and

(b) the insurance company holds as an asset for the purposes of its long-term business shares or an interest in shares–

(i) in the investing company, or

(ii) in another company through which it owns shares in the investing company.

The reference in paragraph (b)(ii) to owning shares through another company has the same meaning as in Chapter 3 of Part 24 of CTA 2010 (subsidiaries).

17(4) Where the investing company is a member of a group that includes an insurance company, paragraph 9 (aggregation of holdings of group companies) does not apply in relation to shares or an interest in shares held by the insurance company for the purposes of its long-term business.

17(4A) The reference in sub-paragraph (2) to an asset held by the investing company for the purposes of its long-term business, and the references in sub-paragraphs (3) and (4) to shares or an interest in shares held for the purposes of its long-term business, do not include an asset or assets which formed part of the long-term business fixed capital of the company in question.

17(5) [Omitted by FA 2007, s. 41 and Sch. 10, para. 14(5), and repealed by FA 2007, s. 114 and Sch. 27, Pt. 2(10).]

History – In the heading before para. 17, "insurance company held for the purposes of its long-term business" substituted for "insurance company's long-term insurance fund" by FA 2012, s. 146 and Sch. 16, para. 88(8) in relation to accounting periods beginning on or after 1 January 2013 (FA 2012, s. 148) but subject to transitional provisions in FA 2012, Sch. 17. Where an accounting period would otherwise straddle 1 January 2013, it is deemed to end on 31 December 2012 (FA 2012, s. 149).

In para. 17(2) the words "held by it for the purposes of its long-term business" substituted for the words "of its long-term insurance fund" by FA 2012, s. 146 and Sch. 16, para. 88(4) in relation to accounting periods beginning on or after 1 January 2013 (FA 2012, s. 148) but subject to transitional provisions in FA 2012, Sch. 17. Where an accounting period would otherwise straddle 1 January 2013, it is deemed to end on 31 December 2012 (FA 2012, s. 149).

In para. 17(3)(b) the words "for the purposes of its long-term business" substituted for the words "of its long-term insurance fund" by FA 2012, s. 146 and Sch. 16, para. 88(5) in relation to accounting periods beginning on or after 1 January 2013 (FA 2012, s. 148) but subject to transitional provisions in FA 2012, Sch. 17. Where an accounting period would otherwise straddle 1 January 2013, it is deemed to end on 31 December 2012 (FA 2012, s. 149).

In para. 17(3), the words "Chapter 3 of Part 24 of CTA 2010" substituted for "section 838 of the Taxes Act" by CTA 2010, s. 1177 and Sch. 1, para. 269(4), with effect for corporation tax purposes for accounting periods ending on or after 1 April 2010, and for income tax and capital gains tax purposes for the tax year 2010–11 and subsequent tax years.

In para. 17(4) the words "for the purposes of its long-term business" substituted for the words "as assets of its long-term insurance fund" by FA 2012, s. 146 and Sch. 16, para. 88(6) in relation to accounting periods beginning on or after 1 January 2013 (FA 2012, s. 148) but subject to transitional provisions in FA 2012, Sch. 17. Where an accounting period would otherwise straddle 1 January 2013, it is deemed to end on 31 December 2012 (FA 2012, s. 149).

In para. 17(4A) the words "held by the investing company for the purposes of its long-term business" substituted for the words "of the investing company's long-term insurance fund" by FA 2012, s. 146 and Sch. 16, para. 88(7)(a) in relation to accounting periods beginning on or after 1 January 2013 (FA 2012, s. 148) but subject to transitional provisions in FA 2012, Sch. 17. Where an accounting period would otherwise straddle 1 January 2013, it is deemed to end on 31 December 2012 (FA 2012, s. 149).

In para. 17(4A) the words "an asset or assets which formed part of the long-term business fixed capital of the company in question" substituted for the words "a structural asset, or structural assets, within the meaning of section 83XA of the Finance Act 1989" by FA 2012, s. 146 and Sch. 16, para. 88(7)(c) in relation to accounting periods beginning on or after 1 January 2013 (FA 2012, s. 148) but subject to transitional provisions in FA 2012, Sch. 17. Where an accounting period would otherwise straddle 1 January 2013, it is deemed to end on 31 December 2012 (FA 2012, s. 149).

In para. 17(4A) the words "for the purposes of its long-term business" substituted for the words "as assets of its long-term insurance fund" by FA 2012, s. 146 and Sch. 16, para. 88(7)(b) in relation to accounting periods beginning on or after 1 January 2013 (FA 2012, s. 148) but subject to transitional provisions in FA 2012, Sch. 17. Where an accounting period would otherwise straddle 1 January 2013, it is deemed to end on 31 December 2012 (FA 2012, s. 149).

Former para. 17(4A) inserted by FA 2007, s. 41 and Sch. 10, para. 2(5) with effect in relation to periods of account beginning on or after 1 January 2007 (FA 2007, Sch. 10, para. 17(2)).

Para. 17(5) omitted by FA 2007, s. 41 and Sch. 10, para. 14(5), and repealed by FA 2007, s. 114 and Sch. 27, Pt. 2(10) with effect in relation to periods of account beginning on or after 1 January 2007 (FA 2007, Sch. 10, para. 17(2)).

Part 3 – Requirements to be Met in Relation to Investing Company and Company Invested In

REQUIREMENTS RELATING TO THE INVESTING COMPANY

18(1) The investing company must–

(a) have been a sole trading company or a member of a qualifying group throughout the period (**"the *qualifying period*"**)–

(i) beginning with the start of the latest twelve-month period by reference to which the requirement of paragraph 7 (the substantial shareholding requirement) is met, and

(ii) ending with the time of the disposal, and

(b) be a sole trading company or a member of a qualifying group immediately after the time of the disposal.

18(2) For this purpose a **"qualifying group"** means–

(a) a trading group, or

(b) a group that would be a trading group if the activities of any group member that is not established for profit were disregarded to the extent that they are carried on otherwise than for profit.

In determining whether a company is established for profit, no account shall be taken of any object or power of the company that is only incidental to its main objects.

18(3) The requirement in sub-paragraph (1)(a) is met if the investing company was a sole trading company for some of the qualifying period and a member of a qualifying group for the remainder of that period.

18(4) The requirement in sub-paragraph (1)(a) is treated as met if at the time of the disposal–

(a) the investing company is a member of a group, and

(b) there is another member of the group in relation to which that requirement would have been met if–

(i) the subject matter of the disposal had been transferred to it immediately before the disposal in circumstances in which section 171(1) (transfers within a group) applied, and

(ii) it had made the disposal.

18(5) If the disposal is by virtue of section 28(1) or (2) (asset disposed of under contract) treated as made at a time before the asset is conveyed or transferred, the requirements in sub-paragraph (1)(a) and (b) must also be complied with as they would have effect if the references in those provisions and sub-paragraph (4) to the time of the disposal were to the time of the conveyance or transfer.

18(6) In this paragraph a **"sole trading company"** means a trading company that is not a member of a group.

REQUIREMENTS RELATING TO THE COMPANY INVESTED IN

19(1) The company invested in must–

(a) have been a qualifying company throughout the period–

(i) beginning with the start of the latest twelve-month period by reference to which the requirement of paragraph 7 (the substantial shareholding requirement) is met, and

(ii) ending with the time of the disposal, and

(b) be a qualifying company immediately after the time of the disposal.

19(2) For this purpose a **"qualifying company"** means a trading company or the holding company of a trading group or a trading subgroup.

19(2A) If the conditions in paragraph 15A(2)(b) to (d) are met, sub-paragraph (2B) applies for the purpose of determining whether the requirement of sub-paragraph (1)(a) is satisfied.

19(2B) The company invested in is to be treated as having been a trading company at any time during the final 12 month period when the asset was used as mentioned in paragraph 15A(2)(d) (if it was not a trading company at that time).

19(2C) **"The final 12 month period"** has the meaning given in paragraph 15A(4).

19(3) If the disposal is by virtue of section 28(1) or (2) (asset disposed of under contract) treated as made at a time before the asset is conveyed or transferred, the requirements in sub-paragraph (1)(a) and (b) must also be complied with as they would have effect if the references there to the time of the disposal were to the time of the conveyance or transfer.

History – Para. 19(2A)–(2C) inserted by FA 2011, s. 45 and Sch. 10, para. 6(3), with effect in relation to disposals of shares made on or after 19 July 2011 (see FA 2011, Sch. 10, para. 9(2)). But the reference to 19 July 2011 may be replaced by a reference to 1 April 2011 if an "early commencement election" is made (see FA 2011, Sch. 10, para. 9(4)–(8)).

MEANING OF "TRADING COMPANY"

20(1) In this Schedule **"trading company"** means a company carrying on trading activities whose activities do not include to a substantial extent activities other than trading activities.

20(2) For the purposes of sub-paragraph (1) **"trading activities"** means activities carried on by the company–

(a) in the course of, or for the purposes of, a trade being carried on by it,

(b) for the purposes of a trade that it is preparing to carry on,

(c) with a view to its acquiring or starting to carry on a trade, or

(d) with a view to its acquiring a significant interest in the share capital of another company that–

(i) is a trading company or the holding company of a trading group or trading subgroup, and

(ii) if the acquiring company is a member of a group, is not a member of that group.

20(3) Activities do not qualify as trading activities under sub-paragraph (c) or (d) unless the acquisition is made, or (as the case may be) the company starts to carry on the trade, as soon as is reasonably practicable in the circumstances.

20(4) The reference in sub-paragraph (2)(d) to the acquisition of a significant interest in the share capital of another company is to an acquisition of ordinary share capital in the other company–

(a) such as would make that company a 51% subsidiary of the acquiring company, or

(b) such as would give the acquiring company a qualifying shareholding in a joint venture company without making the two companies members of the same group.

HMRC Manuals – CG17953I to CG17953R and CG53113 to CG53120: taxation of chargeable gains – taper relief and exemption for disposals by companies with substantial shareholdings (meaning of "trading company", "trading group", "trading sub-group", "holding group" and related issues).

MEANING OF "TRADING GROUP"

21(1) In this Schedule **"trading group"** means a group–

(a) one or more of whose members carry on trading activities, and

(b) the activities of whose members, taken together, do not include to a substantial extent activities other than trading activities.

21(2) For the purposes of sub-paragraph (1) **"trading activities"** means activities carried on by a member of the group–

(a) in the course of, or for the purposes of, a trade being carried on by any member of the group,

(b) for the purposes of a trade that any member of the group is preparing to carry on,

(c) with a view to any member of the group acquiring or starting to carry on a trade, or

(d) with a view to any member of the group acquiring a significant interest in the share capital of another company that–

(i) is a trading company or the holding company of a trading group or trading subgroup, and

(ii) is not a member of the same group as the acquiring company.

21(3) Activities do not qualify as trading activities under sub-paragraph (2)(c) or (d) unless the acquisition is made, or (as the case may be) the group member in question starts to carry on the trade, as soon as is reasonably practicable in the circumstances.

21(4) The reference in sub-paragraph (2)(d) to the acquisition of a significant interest in the share capital of another company is to an acquisition of ordinary share capital in the other company–

(a) such as would make that company a member of the same group as the acquiring company, or

(b) such as would give the acquiring company a qualifying shareholding in a joint venture company without making the joint venture company a member of the same group as the acquiring company.

21(5) For the purposes of this paragraph the activities of the members of the group shall be treated as one business (with the result that activities are disregarded to the extent that they are intra-group activities).

HMRC interpretations – IRInt. 239: taxation of chargeable gains – taper relief and exemption for disposals by companies with substantial shareholdings (meaning of "trading company", "trading group", "trading sub-group", "holding group" and related issues).

MEANING OF "TRADING SUBGROUP"

22(1) In this Schedule **"trading subgroup"** means a subgroup–

(a) one or more of whose members carry on trading activities, and

(b) the activities of whose members, taken together, do not include to a substantial extent activities other than trading activities.

22(2) For the purposes of sub-paragraph (1) **"trading activities"** means activities carried on by a member of the subgroup–

(a) in the course of, or for the purposes of, a trade being carried on by any member of the subgroup,

(b) for the purposes of a trade that any member of the subgroup is preparing to carry on,

(c) with a view to any member of the subgroup acquiring or starting to carry on a trade, or

(d) with a view to any member of the subgroup acquiring a significant interest in the share capital of another company that–

(i) is a trading company or the holding company of a trading group or trading subgroup, and

(ii) is not a member of the same group as the acquiring company.

22(3) Activities do not qualify as trading activities under sub-paragraph (2)(c) or (d) unless the acquisition is made, or (as the case may be) the subgroup member in question starts to carry on the trade, as soon as is reasonably practicable in the circumstances.

22(4) The reference in sub-paragraph (2)(d) to the acquisition of a significant interest in the share capital of another company is to an acquisition of ordinary share capital in the other company–

(a) such as would make that company a member of the same subgroup as the acquiring company, or

(b) such as would give the acquiring company a qualifying shareholding in a joint venture company without making the two companies members of the same group.

22(5) For the purposes of this paragraph the activities of the members of the subgroup shall be treated as one business (with the result that activities are disregarded to the extent that they are intra-subgroup activities).

HMRC interpretations – IRInt. 239: taxation of chargeable gains – taper relief and exemption for disposals by companies with substantial shareholdings (meaning of "trading company", "trading group", "trading sub-group", "holding group" and related issues).

TREATMENT OF HOLDINGS IN JOINT VENTURE COMPANIES

23(1) This paragraph applies where a company (**"the company"**) has a qualifying shareholding in a joint venture company.

23(2) In determining whether the company is a trading company–

(a) its holding of shares in the joint venture company shall be disregarded, and

(b) it shall be treated as carrying on an appropriate proportion–

(i) of the activities of the joint venture company, or

(ii) where the joint venture company is a holding company, of the activities of that company and its 51% subsidiaries.

This sub-paragraph does not apply if the company is a member of a group and the joint venture company is a member of the same group.

23(3) In determining whether the company is a member of a trading group or the holding company of a trading group–

(a) every holding of shares in the joint venture company by a member of the group having a qualifying shareholding in that company shall be disregarded, and

(b) each member of the group having a qualifying shareholding in the joint venture company shall be treated as carrying on an appropriate proportion–

(i) of the activities of the joint venture company, or

(ii) where the joint venture company is a holding company, of the activities of that company and its 51% subsidiaries.

This sub-paragraph does not apply if the joint venture company is a member of the group.

23(4) In determining whether the company is the holding company of a trading subgroup–

(a) every holding of shares in the joint venture company by the company and any of its 51% subsidiaries having a qualifying shareholding in the joint venture company shall be disregarded, and

(b) the company and each of its 51% subsidiaries having a qualifying shareholding in the joint venture company shall be treated as carrying on an appropriate proportion–

(i) of the activities of the joint venture company, or

(ii) where the joint venture company is a holding company, of the activities of that company and its 51% subsidiaries.

This sub-paragraph does not apply if the joint venture company is a member of the same group as the company.

23(5) In sub-paragraphs (2)(b), 3(b) and 4(b) **"an appropriate proportion"** means a proportion corresponding to the percentage of the ordinary share capital of the joint venture company held by the company concerned.

23(6) In this paragraph **"shares"**, in relation to a joint venture company, includes securities of that company or an interest in shares in or securities of that company.

23(7) For the purposes of this paragraph the activities of a joint venture company that is a holding company and its 51% subsidiaries shall be treated as a single business (so that activities are disregarded to the extent that they are intra-group activities or, as the case may be, intra-subgroup, activities).

MEANING OF 'JOINT VENTURE COMPANY' AND 'QUALIFYING SHAREHOLDING'

24(1) For the purposes of this Schedule a company is a **"joint venture company"** if, and only if–

(a) it is a trading company or the holding company of a trading group or trading subgroup, and
(b) there are five or fewer persons who between them hold 75% or more of its ordinary share capital.

In determining whether there are five or fewer such persons as are mentioned in paragraph (b), the members of a group are treated as if they were a single company.

24(2) For the purposes of this Schedule–

(a) a company that is not a member of a group has a **"qualifying shareholding"** in a joint venture company if, and only if, it holds shares or an interest in shares in the joint venture company by virtue of which it holds 10% or more of that company's ordinary share capital;
(b) a company that is a member of a group has a **"qualifying shareholding"** in a joint venture company if, and only if–
    (i) it holds ordinary share capital of the joint venture company, and
    (ii) the members of the group between them hold 10% or more of the ordinary share capital of that company.

Other material – HMRC Brief 29/11: corporation tax and the substantial shareholding exemption: joint ventures and entities without ordinary share capital.

EFFECT IN RELATION TO COMPANY INVESTED IN OF EARLIER COMPANY RECONSTRUCTION, DEMERGER ETC

25 The provisions of–

(a) paragraph 14 (effect of earlier company reconstruction etc), and
(b) paragraph 15 (effect of earlier demerger),

have effect in relation to the requirements of paragraph 19 (requirements in relation to company invested in) as they have effect in relation to the requirement of paragraph 7 (the substantial shareholding requirement).

Part 4 – Interpretation

MEANING OF "COMPANY", "GROUP" AND RELATED EXPRESSIONS

26(1) In this Schedule–

(a) **"company"** has the meaning given by section 170(9); and
(b) references to a group, or to membership of a group, shall be construed in accordance with the provisions of section 170 read as if "51 per cent" were substituted for "75 per cent".

26(2) References in this Schedule to a **"subgroup"** are to companies that would form a group but for the fact that one of them is a 51% subsidiary of another company.

26(3) In this Schedule **"holding company"**–

(a) in relation to a group, means the company described in section 170 as the principal company of the group;
(b) in relation to a subgroup, means a company that would be the holding company of a group but for being a 51% subsidiary of another company.

26(4) In this Schedule **"51% subsidiary"** has the meaning given by Chapter 3 of Part 24 of CTA 2010. In applying that Chapter for the purposes of this Schedule, any share capital of a registered society (see section 1119 of that Act shall be treated as ordinary share capital.

26(5) References in this Schedule to a **"group"** or **"subsidiary"** shall be construed with any necessary modifications where applied to a company incorporated under the law of a country or territory outside the United Kingdom.

History – In para. 26(4) the words "registered society (see section 1119 of that Act)" substituted for the words "registered industrial and provident society" by Co-operative and Community Benefit Societies Act 2014, s. 151 and Sch. 4, para. 53, with effect from 1 August 2014.

In para. 26(4), the words "Chapter 3 of Part 24 of CTA 2010" substituted for "section 838 of the Taxes Act" by CTA 2010, s. 1177 and Sch. 1, para. 269(5)(a), with effect for corporation tax purposes for accounting periods ending on or after 1 April 2010, and for income tax and capital gains tax purposes for the tax year 2010–11 and subsequent tax years.

In para. 26(4), the words "that Chapter" substituted for "that section" by CTA 2010, s. 1177 and Sch. 1, para. 269(5)(b), with effect for corporation tax purposes for accounting periods ending on or after 1 April 2010, and for income tax and capital gains tax purposes for the tax year 2010–11 and subsequent tax years.

HMRC interpretations – IRInt. 239: taxation of chargeable gains – taper relief and exemption for disposals by companies with substantial shareholdings (meaning of "trading company", "trading group", "trading sub-group", "holding group" and related issues).

MEANING OF "TRADE"

27 In this Schedule **"trade"** means anything that–

(a) is a trade, profession or vocation, within the meaning of the Income Tax Acts, and

(b) is conducted on a commercial basis with a view to the realisation of profits.

MEANING OF "TWELVE-MONTH PERIOD"

28 For the purposes of this Schedule a **"twelve-month period"** means a period ending with the day before the first anniversary of the day with which, or in the course of which, the period began.

MEANING OF "INTEREST IN SHARES"

29(1) References in this Schedule to an interest in shares are to an interest as a co-owner of shares.

29(2) It does not matter whether the shares are owned jointly or in common, or whether the interests of the co-owners are equal.

MEANING OF "ASSET RELATED TO SHARES"

30(1) This paragraph explains what is meant by an **"asset related to shares"** in a company.

30(2) An asset is related to shares in a company if it is–

(a) an option to acquire or dispose of shares or an interest in shares in that company, or

(b) a security to which are attached rights by virtue of which the holder is or may become entitled to acquire or dispose of (whether by conversion or exchange or otherwise)–

  (i) shares or an interest in shares in that company, or

  (ii) an option to acquire or dispose of shares or an interest in shares in that company, or

  (iii) another security falling within this paragraph, or

(c) an option to acquire or dispose of any security within paragraph (b) or an interest in any such security, or

(d) an interest in, or option over, any such option or security as is mentioned in paragraph (a), (b) or (c), or

(e) any interest in, or option over, any such interest or option as is mentioned in paragraph (d) or this paragraph.

30(3) In determining whether a security is within sub-paragraph (2)(b), no account shall be taken–

(a) of any rights attached to the security other than rights relating, directly or indirectly, to shares of the company in question, or

(b) of rights as regards which, at the time the security came into existence, there was no more than a negligible likelihood that they would in due course be exercised to a significant extent.

30(4) The references in this paragraph to an interest in a security or option have a meaning corresponding to that given by paragraph 29 in relation to an interest in shares.

INDEX OF DEFINED EXPRESSIONS

31 In this Schedule the expressions listed below are defined or otherwise explained by the provisions indicated:

asset related to shares	paragraph 30
company	paragraph 26(1)(a)
company invested in	paragraph 1
51% subsidiary	paragraph 26(4) and (5)
group (and member of group)	paragraph 26(1)(b) and (5)
holding company	paragraph 26(3)
interest in shares	paragraph 29
investing company	paragraph 1
joint venture company	paragraph 24(1)
qualifying shareholding (in joint venture company)	paragraph 24(2)

subgroup	paragraph 26(2)
trade	paragraph 27
trading company	paragraph 20
trading group	paragraph 21
trading subgroup	paragraph 22
twelve-month period	paragraph 28

Part 5 – Consequential Provisions

MEANING OF 'CHARGEABLE SHARES' OR 'CHARGEABLE ASSET'

32 Any exemption conferred by this Schedule shall be disregarded in determining whether shares are **"chargeable shares"**, or an asset is a **"chargeable asset"**, for the purposes of any enactment relating to corporation tax or capital gains tax.

NEGLIGIBLE VALUE CLAIMS

33(1) This paragraph applies where–

(a) a company makes a claim under section 24(2) (assets of negligible value) in relation to shares held by it, and

(b) by virtue of this Schedule any loss accruing to the company on a disposal of the shares at the time of the claim would not be an allowable loss.

33(2) Where this paragraph applies the company may not exercise the option under section 24(2) to specify a time earlier than the time of the claim as the time when the shares are treated as sold and reacquired by virtue of that subsection.

33(3) This paragraph applies to–

(a) an interest in shares in a company, or

(b) an asset related to shares in a company,

as it applies to shares in that company.

REORGANISATIONS ETC: DEEMED ACCRUAL OF CHARGEABLE GAIN OR ALLOWABLE LOSS HELD OVER ON EARLIER TRANSACTION

34(1) The exemptions conferred by this Schedule do not apply to or affect a chargeable gain or allowable loss deemed to accrue on a disposal by virtue of section 116(10)(b) (reorganisations, conversions and reconstructions: deemed accrual of gain or loss held over on earlier transaction).

34(2) Sub-paragraph (1) does not apply where the relevant earlier transaction is a disposal and reacquisition deemed to have occurred (in a period of account beginning before 1 January 2005) under section 92(7) of the Finance Act 1996 (convertible securities etc: creditor relationships).

History – Para. 34(2) inserted by SI 2010/614, art. 2, with effect for accounting periods ending on or after 1 April 2009.
Former para. 34(2) omitted by CTA 2009, s. 1322 and Sch. 1, para. 386 and repealed by CTA 2009, s. 1326 and Sch. 3, Pt. 1, with effect for corporation tax purposes for accounting periods ending on or after 1 April 2009, and for income tax and capital gains tax purposes for the tax year 2009–10 and subsequent tax years.

RECOVERY OF CHARGE POSTPONED ON TRANSFER OF ASSETS TO NON-RESIDENT COMPANY

35 [Omitted by FA 2010, s. 37(2).]

History – Para. 35 omitted by FA 2010, s. 37(2), with effect in relation to disposals of securities on or after 6 January 2010.

APPROPRIATION OF ASSET TO TRADING STOCK

36(1) Where–

(a) an asset acquired by a company otherwise than as trading stock of a trade carried on by it is appropriated by the company for the purposes of the trade as trading stock (whether on the commencement of the trade or otherwise), and

(b) if the company had then sold the asset for its market value, a chargeable gain or allowable loss would have accrued to the company but for an exemption conferred by this Schedule, the company is treated for the purposes of the enactments relating to chargeable gains as if it had thereby disposed of the asset for its market value.

36(2) Section 173 (transfers within a group: trading stock) applies in relation to this paragraph as it applies in relation to section 161 (appropriations to and from stock).

RECOVERY OF HELD-OVER GAIN ON CLAIM FOR GIFTS RELIEF

37(1) This paragraph applies where–

(a) a company disposes of an asset,

(b) the expenditure allowable in computing a gain or loss on that disposal falls to be reduced because of a claim for relief under section 165 (gifts relief) in relation to an earlier disposal, and

(c) by virtue of this Schedule any gain accruing to the company on the disposal mentioned in paragraph (a) would not be a chargeable gain.

37(2) Where this paragraph applies the amount of the held-over gain, or an appropriate proportion of it, shall be treated as accruing to the company, at the time of the disposal mentioned in sub-paragraph (1)(a), as a chargeable gain to which this Schedule does not apply.

37(3) An **"appropriate proportion"** means a proportion determined on a just and reasonable basis having regard to the subject matter of the disposal mentioned in sub-paragraph (1)(a) and the subject matter of the earlier disposal that was the subject of the claim for relief under section 165.

37(4) In this paragraph **"held-over gain"** has the same meaning as in section 165.

DEGROUPING: TIME WHEN DEEMED SALE AND REACQUISITION TREATED AS TAKING PLACE

38(1) Where–

(a) a company, as a result of ceasing at any time (**"the time of degrouping"**) to be a member of a group, is treated by section 179(3) as having sold and immediately reacquired an asset, and

(b) if the company owning the asset at the time of degrouping had disposed of it immediately before that time, any gain accruing on the disposal would by virtue of this Schedule not have been a chargeable gain,

section 179(3) shall have effect as if it provided for the deemed sale and reacquisition to be treated as taking place immediately before the time of degrouping.

38(2) Where–

(a) a company, as a result of ceasing at any time (**"the relevant time"**) to satisfy the conditions in section 179(7), is treated by section 179(6) as having sold and immediately reacquired an asset, and

(b) if the company owning the asset at the relevant time had disposed of it immediately before that time, any gain accruing on the disposal would by virtue of this Schedule not have been a chargeable gain,

section 179(6) shall have effect as if it provided for the deemed sale and reacquisition to be treated as taking place immediately before the relevant time.

38(3) Any reference in this paragraph to a disposal or other event taking place immediately before the time of degrouping or the relevant time is to its taking place immediately before that time but on the same day.

EFFECT OF FOREX MATCHING REGULATIONS

39(1) No gain or loss shall be treated as arising under the FOREX matching regulations on a disposal on which by virtue of this Schedule any gain would not be a chargeable gain.

39(2) The **"FOREX matching regulations"** means any regulations made under Schedule 15 to the Finance Act 1993 (c. 34) (exchange gains and losses: alternative method of calculation).

SCHEDULE 7AD – GAINS OF INSURANCE COMPANY FROM VENTURE CAPITAL INVESTMENT PARTNERSHIP

History – Sch. 7AD inserted by FA 2002, s. 85 and Sch. 31 with effect from 24 July 2002.

INTRODUCTION

1 This Schedule applies where the assets held by an insurance company ("the company") for the purposes of its long-term business include assets held by the company as a limited partner in a venture capital investment partnership (**"the partnership"**).

History – In para. 1 the words "the assets held by an insurance company ("the company") for the purposes of its long-term business" substituted for the words "the assets of the long-term insurance fund of an insurance company ("the company")" by FA 2012, s. 146 and Sch. 16, para. 89 in relation to accounting periods beginning on or after 1 January 2013 (FA 2012, s. 148) but subject to transitional provisions in FA 2012, Sch. 17. Where an accounting period would otherwise straddle 1 January 2013, it is deemed to end on 31 December 2012 (FA 2012, s. 149).

MEANING OF "VENTURE CAPITAL INVESTMENT PARTNERSHIP"

2(1) A **"venture capital investment partnership"** means a partnership in relation to which the following conditions are met.

2(2) The first condition is that the sole or main purpose of the partnership is to invest in unquoted shares or securities.

This condition shall not be regarded as met unless it appears from–

(a) the agreement constituting the partnership, or

(b) any prospectus issued to prospective partners,

that that is the sole or main purpose of the partnership.

2(3) The second condition is that the partnership does not carry on a trade.

2(4) The third condition is that not less than 90% of the book value of the partnership's investments is attributable to investments that are either–

(a) shares or securities that were unquoted at the time of their acquisition by the partnership, or

(b) shares that were quoted at the time of their acquisition by the partnership but which it was reasonable to believe would cease to be quoted within the next twelve months.

2(5) For the purposes of the third condition–

(a) the following shall be disregarded–

(i) any holding of cash, including cash deposited in a bank account or similar account but not cash acquired wholly or partly for the purpose of realising a gain on its disposal;

(ii) any holding of quoted shares or securities acquired by the partnership in exchange for unquoted shares or securities;

(b) whether the 90% test is met shall be determined by reference to the values shown in the partnership's accounts at the end of a period of account of the partnership.

2(6) Where a partnership ceases to meet the above conditions, the company shall be treated as if the partnership had continued to be a venture capital investment partnership until the end of the period of account of the partnership during which it ceased to meet the conditions.

2(7) A partnership that ceases to meet those conditions cannot qualify again as a venture capital investment partnership.

For this purpose a partnership is treated as the same partnership notwithstanding a change in membership if any person who was a member before the change remains a member.

INTEREST IN RELEVANT ASSETS OF PARTNERSHIP TREATED AS SINGLE ASSET

3(1) Where this Schedule applies section 59 (partnerships) does not have effect to make the company chargeable on its share of gains accruing on each disposal of relevant assets of the partnership.

3(2) Instead–

(a) the company's interest in relevant assets of the partnership is treated as a single asset (**"the single asset"**) acquired by the company when it became a member of the partnership, and

(b) the following provisions of this Schedule have effect.

3(3) For the purposes of this Schedule the **"relevant assets"** of the partnership are the shares and securities held by the partnership, other than qualifying corporate bonds.

3(4) Nothing in this Schedule shall be read–

(a) as affecting the operation of section 59 in relation to partners who are not insurance companies carrying on long-term business or are not limited partners, or

(b) as imposing any liability on the partnership as such.

THE COST OF THE SINGLE ASSET

4(1) The company is treated as having given, wholly and exclusively for the acquisition of the single asset, consideration equal to the amount of capital contributed by it on becoming a member of the partnership.

4(2) Any further amounts of capital contributed by it to the partnership are treated on a disposal of the single asset as expenditure incurred wholly and exclusively on the asset for the purpose of enhancing its value and reflected in its state or nature at the time of the disposal.

4(3) Where the investments of the partnership include qualifying corporate bonds, the amount to be taken into account under sub-paragraph (1) or (2) is proportionately reduced.

4(4) The reduction is made by applying to that amount the fraction:

$$\frac{A - B}{A}$$

where–

A is the book value of all shares and securities held by the partnership at the end of the period of account of the partnership in which the amount of capital in question is fully invested by the partnership, and

B is the book value of all qualifying corporate bonds held by the partnership at the end of that period of account,

4(5) For the purposes of sub-paragraph (5) the **"book value"** means the value shown in the partnership's accounts at the end of the period of account.

DEEMED DISPOSAL OF SINGLE ASSET IN CASE OF DISTRIBUTION

5(1) There is a disposal of the single asset on each occasion on which the company receives a distribution from the partnership that does not consist entirely of income or the proceeds of sale or redemption of assets that are not relevant assets.

5(2) The disposal is taken to be for a consideration equal to the amount of the distribution or of so much of it as does not consist of income or the proceeds of sale or redemption of assets that are not relevant assets.

5(3) Where–

(a) the partnership disposes of relevant assets on which a chargeable gain or allowable loss would accrue if they were held by the company alone, and

(b) no distribution of the proceeds of the disposal is made within twelve months of the disposal,

the company is treated as having received its share of the proceeds as a distribution at the end of the period of account of the partnership following that in which the disposal took place, or at the end of the period of six months after the date of the disposal, whichever is the later.

5(4) The operation of sub-paragraph (3) is not affected by the partnership having ceased to be a venture capital investment partnership before the time at which the distribution is treated as received by the company.

5(5) Where sub-paragraph (3) applies, any subsequent actual distribution of the proceeds is disregarded.

APPORTIONMENT IN CASE OF PART DISPOSAL

6(1) For the purposes of section 42 (apportionment of cost etc in case of part disposal) the market value of the property remaining undisposed of on a part disposal of the single asset shall be determined as follows.

6(2) If there is no further disposal of that asset in the period of account in which the part disposal in question takes place, the market value of the property remaining undisposed of shall be taken to be equal to the company's share of the book value of the relevant assets of the partnership as shown in the partnership's accounts at the end of that period of account.

6(3) If there is a further disposal of that asset in the period of account in which the part disposal in question takes place, or more than one, the market value of the property remaining undisposed of shall be taken to be equal to the sum of–

(a) the amount or value of the consideration on the further disposal or, as the case may be, the total amount or value of the consideration on the further disposals, and

(b) the amount (if any) of the company's share of the book value of the relevant assets of the partnership as shown in the partnership's accounts at the end of that period of account.

DISPOSAL OF PARTNERSHIP ASSET GIVING RISE TO OFFSHORE INCOME GAIN

7(1) Nothing in this Schedule shall be read as affecting the operation of regulations under section 354(1) of TIOPA 2010 (see the Offshore Funds (Tax) Regulations 2009 (S.I. 2009/3001)).

7(2) Where an offshore income gain accrues to the company under such regulations from the disposal of any relevant asset of the partnership, the amount of any distribution received or treated as received by the company from the partnership that represents the whole or part of the proceeds of disposal of that asset is treated for the purposes of this Schedule as reduced by the amount of the whole or a corresponding part of the offshore income gain.

History – In para. 7(1), the words "under section 354(1) of TIOPA 2010" substituted for "made under section 41(1) of the Finance Act 2008" by TIOPA 2010, s. 374 and Sch. 8, para. 166, with effect for corporation tax purposes for accounting periods ending on or after 1 April 2010, for income tax and capital gains tax purposes for the tax year 2010–11 and subsequent tax years, and for petroleum revenue tax purposes for chargeable periods beginning on or after 1 July 2010.

In para. 7(1), the words "regulations made under section 41(1) of the Finance Act 2008 (see the Offshore Funds (Tax) Regulations 2009 (S.I. 2009/3001))" substituted for the words "Chapter 5 of Part 17 of the Taxes Act (offshore funds)" by SI 2009/3001, reg. 127(4)(a), with effect from 1 December 2009 for various purposes (in accordance with the provisions of SI 2009/3001, reg. 1), subject to transitional and savings provisions in SI 2009/3001, Sch. 1.

In para. 7(2), the words "such regulations" substituted for the words "that Chapter" by SI 2009/3001, reg. 127(4)(b), with effect from 1 December 2009 for various purposes (in accordance with the provisions of SI 2009/3001, reg. 1), subject to transitional and savings provisions in SI 2009/3001, Sch. 1.

EXCLUSION OF NEGLIGIBLE VALUE CLAIM

8 No claim may be made in respect of the single asset under section 24(2) (assets that have become of negligible value).

INVESTMENT IN OTHER VENTURE CAPITAL INVESTMENT PARTNERSHIPS

9(1) For the purposes of paragraph 2 (meaning of "venture capital investment partnership") an investment by way of capital contribution to another venture capital investment partnership shall be treated as an investment in unquoted shares or securities.

9(2) The Treasury may by regulations make provision, in place of but corresponding to that made by paragraphs 3 to 8, in relation to gains accruing on a disposal of relevant assets by such a partnership.

9(3) The regulations may make provision for any period of account to which, in accordance with paragraphs 11 to 13, this Schedule applies.

INTERPRETATION

10(1) In this Schedule–

"limited partner" means–

(a) a person carrying on a business as a limited partner in a partnership registered under the Limited Partnership Act 1907, or

(b) a person carrying on a business jointly with others who, under the law of a country or territory outside the United Kingdom, is not entitled to take part in the management of the business and is not liable beyond a certain limit for debts or obligations incurred for the purposes of the business;

"relevant assets" has the meaning given by paragraph 3(3);

"securities" has the same meaning as in section 132 and also includes any debentures;

"unquoted" and **"quoted"**, in relation to shares or securities, refer to listing on a recognised stock exchange.

10(2) References in this Schedule to the partnership's accounts are to accounts drawn up in accordance with generally accepted accounting practice.

If no such accounts are drawn up, the references to the treatment of any matter, or the amounts shown, in the accounts of the partnership are to what would have appeared if accounts had been drawn up in accordance with generally accepted accounting practice.

10(3) References in this Schedule to capital contributed to a limited partnership include amounts purporting to be provided by way of loan if–

(a) the loan carries no interest

(b) all the limited partners are required to make such loans, and

(c) the loans are accounted for as partners' capital, or partners' equity, in the accounts of the partnership.

10(4) For the purposes of this Schedule the assets of–

(a) a Scottish partnership, or

(b) a partnership under the law of any other country or territory under which assets of a partnership are regarded as held by or on behalf of the partnership as such,

shall be treated as held by the members of the partnership in the proportions in which they are entitled to share in the profits of the partnership.

References in this Schedule to the company's interest in, or share of, the partnership's assets shall be construed accordingly.

History – In para. 10(1), the definitions of "insurance company", "long-term business" and "long-term insurance fund" repealed by FA 2003, s. 216 and Sch. 43, Pt. 3(12) which, by virtue of FA 2003, s. 216(2), came into force on 10 July 2003 (i.e. date of passing of FA 2003).

GENERAL COMMENCEMENT AND TRANSITIONAL PROVISIONS

11(1) Subject to paragraph 11 (election to remain outside Schedule), this Schedule applies–

(a) to periods of account of the partnership beginning on or after 1st January 2002, and

(b) to a period of account of the partnership beginning before that date and ending on or after it, unless the company elects that it shall not do so.

11(2) Where the company became a member of the partnership before the beginning of the first period of account of the partnership to which this Schedule applies, the cost of the single asset at the beginning of that period of account shall be taken to be equal to the total of the relevant indexed base costs.

11(3) For the purposes of sub-paragraph (2)–

(a) the **"indexed base cost"** means–

(i) in relation to a holding that by virtue of section 104 is to be treated as a single asset, what would be the indexed pool of expenditure within the meaning of section 110 if the holding were disposed of, and

(ii) in relation to any other asset, the amount of expenditure together with the indexation allowance that would be fall to be deducted if the asset were disposed of; and

(b) the **"relevant indexed base costs"** means the indexed base costs that would be taken into account in computing in accordance with section 59 the gain or loss of the company if all the shares and securities (other than qualifying corporate bonds) held by the partnership were disposed of on the last day of the company's accounting period immediately preceding its first accounting period beginning on or after 1st January 2002.

11(4) No account shall be taken under this Schedule of a distribution by the partnership in a period of account to which this Schedule applies to the extent that it represents a chargeable gain accruing in an earlier period to which this Schedule does not apply.

ELECTION TO REMAIN OUTSIDE SCHEDULE

12 If the company–

(a) became a member of the partnership before the beginning of the first period of account of the partnership to which this Schedule would otherwise apply, or

(b) made its first contribution of capital to the partnership before 17th April 2002,

it may elect that the provisions of this Schedule shall not apply to it in relation to that partnership.

HOW AND WHEN ELECTION TO BE MADE

13 Any election under paragraph 11 or 12 must be made–

(a) by notice to an officer of the Board,

(b) not later than the end of the period of two years after the end of the company's first accounting period beginning on or after 1st January 2002.

SCHEDULE 7B – MODIFICATION OF ACT IN RELATION TO OVERSEAS LIFE INSURANCE COMPANIES

Section 214B

[Repealed by SI 2006/3271, reg. 43 and Schedule, Pt. 2 with effect from 31 December 2006 in relation to accounting periods ending on or after that day.]

History – Sch. 7B repealed by SI 2006/3271, reg. 43 and Schedule, Pt. 2 with effect from 31 December 2006 in relation to accounting periods ending on or after that day.

SCHEDULE 7C – RELIEF FOR TRANSFERS TO SCHEDULE 2 SHARE PLANS

Section 236A

History – In the title to Sch. 7C, the words "SCHEDULE 2" substituted for the word "APPROVED" by FA 2014, s. 51 and Sch. 8, para. 37, which is treated as having come into force on 6 April 2014, subject to the transitional provisions in FA 2014, Sch. 8, para. 90–96. Sch. 7C inserted by FA 2000, s. 48 and Sch. 9.

Cross references – FA 2000, Sch. 29, para. 41: TCGA 1992, s. 170 as amended by FA 2000, s. 102 and Sch. 29, para.1 has effect for this schedule.

INTRODUCTORY

1(1) A person ("the claimant") who makes a disposal of shares ("the disposal") to the trustees of the plan trust of a share incentive plan ("the plan") is entitled to claim relief under paragraph 5 if–

(a) the conditions in paragraph 2 are fulfilled, and

(b) paragraph 3(1) or (2) applies.

1(2) Sub-paragraph (1) does not apply to a company that makes a disposal of shares.

1(3) In this paragraph the references to a disposal of shares include a disposal of an interest in shares.

History – In para. 1(1), the words "a share incentive" substituted for the words "an employee share ownership" by ITEPA 2003, Sch. 6, para. 220(2) with effect for 2003–04 and subsequent tax years.

CONDITIONS RELATING TO THE DISPOSAL

2(1) The first condition is that, at the time of the disposal, the plan is a Schedule 2 SIP under Schedule 2 to ITEPA 2003.

2(2) The second condition is that the relevant shares meet the requirements in Part 4 of that Schedule (types of shares that may be awarded) in relation to the plan.

For this purpose that Part applies as if 27(1)(a) and (c) and (2) (listed shares and shares in a company under the control of a company whose shares are listed) were omitted.

2(3) The third condition is that, at any time in the entitlement period, the trustees hold, for the beneficiaries of the plan trust, shares in the relevant company that–

(a) constitute not less than 10% of the ordinary share capital of the company, and

(b) carry rights to not less than 10% of–

(i) any profits available for distribution to shareholders of the company, and

(ii) any assets of that company available for distribution to its shareholders in the event of a winding up.

2(4) For the purposes of sub-paragraph (3), shares that have been appropriated to, or acquired on behalf of, an individual under the plan shall continue to be treated as held by the trustees of the plan trust for the beneficiaries of that trust until such time as they cease to be subject to the plan (within the meaning given by paragraph 97 of Schedule 2 to ITEPA 2003).

2(5) The fourth condition is that, at all times in the proscribed period, there are no unauthorised arrangements under which the claimant or a person connected with him may be entitled to acquire (directly or indirectly) from the trustees of the plan trust any shares, or an interest in or right deriving from any shares.

2(6) For the purposes of this paragraph–

"ordinary share capital" has the meaning given in section 989 of ITA 2007;

"the relevant company" means the company of whose share capital the relevant shares form part; and

"the relevant shares" means the shares that are, or an interest in which is, the subject of the disposal.

History – In para. 2(1), the words "a Schedule 2 SIP" substituted for the word "approved" by FA 2014, s. 51 and Sch. 8, para. 38, which is treated as having come into force on 6 April 2014, subject to the transitional provisions in FA 2014, Sch. 8, para. 90 to 96.
In para. 2(1), the words "ITEPA 2003, Sch. 2" substituted for the words "Schedule 8 to the Finance Act 2000" by ITEPA 2003, Sch. 6, para. 220(3)(a) with effect for 2003–04 and subsequent tax years.
In para. 2(2), the words "Part 4" substituted for the words "Part VIII" by ITEPA 2003, Sch. 6, para. 220(3)(b)(i) with effect for 2003–04 and subsequent tax years.
In para. 2(2), the word "awarded" substituted for the words "used in plan" by ITEPA 2003, Sch. 6, para. 220(3)(b)(ii) with effect for 2003–04 and subsequent tax years.
In para. 2(2), the words "27(1)(a) and (c) and (2)" substituted for the words "61(a) and (c)" by ITEPA 2003, Sch. 6, para. 220(3)(b)(iii) with effect for 2003–04 and subsequent tax years.
In para. 2(4), the words "given by paragraph 97 of Schedule 2 to ITEPA 2003" substituted for the words "of Schedule 8 to the Finance Act 2000" by ITEPA 2003, Sch. 6, para. 220(3)(c) with effect for 2003–04 and subsequent tax years.
In para. 2(6), the definition of "ordinary share capital", the words "section 989 of ITA 2007" substituted for the words "section 832(1) of the Taxes Act" by ITA 2007, s. 1027 and Sch. 1, para. 348(2), with effect from 6 April 2007.
Cross references – ITEPA 2003, Sch. 3: approved share incentive plans.

REINVESTMENT OF DISPOSAL PROCEEDS

3(1) This sub-paragraph applies if the claimant obtains consideration for the disposal and, at any time in the acquisition period, all of the amount or value of the consideration is applied by him in making an acquisition of assets or an interest in assets ("replacement assets") which–

(a) are, immediately after the time of the acquisition, chargeable assets in relation to the claimant, and

(b) are not shares in, or debentures issued by, the relevant company or a company which is (at the time of the acquisition) in the same group as the relevant company;

but the preceding provisions of this sub-paragraph shall have effect without the words, "at any time in the acquisition period," if the acquisition is made pursuant to an unconditional contract entered into in the acquisition period.

3(2) This sub-paragraph applies if–

(a) sub-paragraph (1) would have applied but for the fact that part only of the amount or value mentioned in that sub-paragraph is applied as there mentioned, and

(b) all the amount or value so mentioned except for a part which is less than the amount of the gain (whether all chargeable gain or not) accruing on the disposal is so applied.

3(3) In sub-paragraph (1)(b)–

"relevant company" has the meaning given in paragraph 2(6); and

"group" shall be construed in accordance with section 170.

PROVISION SUPPLEMENTARY TO PARAGRAPHS 2 AND 3

4(1) This paragraph applies for the purposes of paragraphs 2 and 3.

4(2) The entitlement period is the period beginning with the disposal and ending on the expiry of 12 months beginning with the date of the disposal.

4(3) The acquisition period is the period beginning with the disposal and ending on the expiry of six months beginning with–

(a) the date of the disposal, or

(b) if later, the date on which the third condition (set out in paragraph 2(3)) is first fulfilled.

4(4) The proscribed period is the period beginning with the disposal and ending on–

(a) the date of the acquisition, or

(b) if later, the date on which the third condition (set out in paragraph 2(3)) is first fulfilled.

4(5) All arrangements are unauthorised unless they only allow shares to be appropriated to or acquired on behalf of an individual under the plan.

THE RELIEF

5(1) Where the claimant is entitled to claim relief under this paragraph and paragraph 3(1) applies, he shall, on making a claim in the period of 2 years beginning with the acquisition, be treated for the purposes of this Act–

(a) as if the consideration for the disposal were (if otherwise of a greater amount or value) of such amount as would secure that on the disposal neither a gain nor a loss accrues to him, and

(b) as if the amount or value of the consideration for the acquisition were reduced by the excess of the amount or value of the actual consideration for the disposal over the amount of the consideration which the claimant is treated as receiving under paragraph (a).

5(2) Where the claimant is entitled to claim relief under this paragraph and paragraph 3(2) applies, he shall, on making a claim in the period of 2 years beginning with the acquisition, be treated for the purposes of this Act–

(a) as if the amount of the gain accruing on the disposal were reduced to the amount of the part mentioned in paragraph 3(2)(b), and

(b) as if the amount or value of the consideration for the acquisition were reduced by the amount by which the gain is reduced under paragraph (a) above.

5(3) Nothing in sub-paragraph (1) or (2) shall affect the treatment for the purposes of this Act of the other party to the disposal or of the other party to the acquisition.

5(4) The provisions of this Act fixing the amount of the consideration deemed to be given for a disposal or acquisition shall be applied before the preceding provisions of this paragraph are applied.

DWELLING-HOUSES: SPECIAL PROVISION

6(1) Sub-paragraph (2) applies where–

(a) a claim is made under paragraph 5,

(b) immediately after the time of the acquisition mentioned in paragraph 3 and apart from this paragraph, any replacement asset was a chargeable asset in relation to the claimant,

(c) the asset is a dwelling-house or part of a dwelling-house or land, and

(d) there was a time in the period beginning with the acquisition and ending with the time when paragraph 5(1) or (2) falls to be applied such that, if the asset (or an interest in it) were disposed of at that time, it would be within section 222(1) and the individual there mentioned would be the claimant or the claimant's spouse or civil partner.

6(2) In such a case the asset shall be treated as if, immediately after the time of the acquisition mentioned in paragraph 3, it was not a chargeable asset in relation to the claimant.

6(3) Sub-paragraph (4) applies where–

(a) the provisions of paragraph 5(1) or (2) have been applied,

(b) any replacement asset which, immediately after the time of the acquisition mentioned in paragraph 3 and apart from this paragraph, was a chargeable asset in relation to the claimant consists of a dwelling-house or part of a dwelling-house or land, and

(c) there is a time after paragraph 5(1) or (2) has been applied such that, if the asset (or an interest in it) were disposed of at that time, it would be within section 222(1) and the individual there mentioned would be the claimant or the claimant's spouse or civil partner.

6(4) In such a case–

(a) the asset shall be treated as if, immediately after the time of the acquisition mentioned in paragraph 3, it was not a chargeable asset in relation to the claimant and adjustments shall be made accordingly, but

(b) any gain treated as accruing in consequence of the application of paragraph (a) shall be treated as accruing at the time mentioned in sub-paragraph (3)(c) or, if there is more than one such time, at the earliest of them.

6(5) Sub-paragraph (6) applies where–

(a) a claim is made under paragraph 5,

(b) immediately after the time of the acquisition mentioned in paragraph 3 and apart from this paragraph, any replacement asset was a chargeable asset in relation to the claimant,

(c) the asset was an option to acquire (or to acquire an interest in) a dwelling-house or part of a dwelling-house or land,

(d) the option has been exercised, and

(e) there was a time in the period beginning with the exercise of the option and ending with the time when paragraph 5(1) or (2) falls to be applied such that, if the asset acquired on exercise of the option were disposed of at that time, it would be within section 222(1) and the individual there mentioned would be the claimant or the claimant's spouse or civil partner.

6(6) In such a case the option shall be treated as if, immediately after the time of the acquisition mentioned in paragraph 3, it was not a chargeable asset in relation to the claimant.

6(7) Sub-paragraph (8) applies where–

(a) the provisions of paragraph 5(1) or (2) have been applied,

(b) any replacement asset which, immediately after the time of the acquisition mentioned in paragraph 3 and apart from this paragraph, was a chargeable asset in relation to the claimant consisted of an option to acquire (or to acquire an interest in) a dwelling-house or part of a dwelling-house or land,

(c) the option has been exercised, and

(d) there is a time after paragraph 5(1) or (2) has been applied such that, if the asset acquired on exercise of the option were disposed of at that time, it would be within section 222(1) and the individual there mentioned would be the claimant or the claimant's spouse or civil partner.

6(8) In such a case–

(a) the option shall be treated as if, immediately after the time of the acquisition mentioned in paragraph 3, it was not a chargeable asset in relation to the claimant and adjustments shall be made accordingly, but

(b) any gain treated as accruing in consequence of the application of paragraph (a) shall be treated as accruing at the time mentioned in sub-paragraph (7)(d) or, if there is more than one such time, at the earliest of them.

6(9) References in this paragraph to an individual include a person entitled to occupy under the terms of a settlement.

History – In para. 6(1)(d), (3)(c), (5)(e) and (7)(d) the words "or civil partner" inserted by SI 2005/3229, reg. 129, with effect from 5 December 2005.

SHARES: SPECIAL PROVISION

7(1) Sub-paragraph (2) applies where–

(a) a claim is made under paragraph 5,

(b) immediately after the time of the acquisition mentioned in paragraph 3 and apart from this paragraph, any replacement asset was a chargeable asset in relation to the claimant,

(c) the asset consists of shares, and

(d) relief is claimed under Chapter III of Part VII of the Taxes Act or Part 5 of ITA 2007 (enterprise investment scheme) at any time in the period beginning with the acquisition and ending when paragraph 5(1) or (2) falls to be applied.

7(2) In such a case the asset shall be treated as if, immediately after the time of the acquisition mentioned in paragraph 3, it was not a chargeable asset in relation to the claimant.

7(3) Sub-paragraph (4) applies where–

(a) the provisions of paragraph 5(1) or (2) have been applied,

(b) any replacement asset which, immediately after the time of the acquisition mentioned in paragraph 3 and apart from this paragraph, was a chargeable asset in relation to the claimant consists of shares, and

(c) at any time after paragraph 5(1) or (2) has been applied relief is claimed in respect of the asset under Chapter III of Part VII of the Taxes Act or Part 5 of ITA 2007 (enterprise investment scheme).

7(4) In such a case the asset shall be treated as if, immediately after the time of the acquisition mentioned in paragraph 3, it was not a chargeable asset in relation to the claimant and adjustments shall be made accordingly.

History – In para. 7(1), the words "or Part 5 of ITA 2007" inserted by ITA 2007, s. 1027 and Sch. 1, para. 348(3), with effect from 6 April 2007.

In para. 7(3), the words "or Part 5 of ITA 2007" inserted by ITA 2007, s. 1027 and Sch. 1, para. 348(3), with effect from 6 April 2007.

MEANING OF "CHARGEABLE ASSET"

8 For the purposes of this Schedule an asset is a chargeable asset in relation to the claimant at a particular time if, were the asset to be disposed of at that time, any gain accruing to him on the disposal would be a chargeable gain, and either–

(a) the claimant would be chargeable to capital gains tax under section 2(1) (persons and gains chargeable to capital gains tax) in respect of the gain, or

(b) he would be chargeable to capital gains tax under section 10(1) (non-resident with United Kingdom branch or agency) in respect of the gain,

unless (were he to dispose of the asset at that time) the claimant would fall to be regarded for the purposes of any double taxation relief arrangements as not liable in the United Kingdom to tax on any gains accruing to him on the disposal.

History – Para. 8(a) substituted by FA 2013, s. 219 and Sch. 46, para. 111, with effect in relation to a person's liability to capital gains tax for the tax year 2013–14 or any subsequent year, without prejudice to any provision in FA 2013, Sch. 46, Pt. 3 about the application of a particular amendment.

SCHEDULE 7D – SHARE SCHEMES AND SHARE INCENTIVES

Section 238A

History – In the title to Sch. 7D, the word "APPROVED" omitted from the beginning by FA 2014, s. 51 and Sch. 8, para. 40, which is treated as having come into force on 6 April 2014, subject to the transitional provisions in FA 2014, Sch. 8, para. 90–96.
Sch. 7D inserted by ITEPA 2003, Sch. 6, para. 221 with effect for 2003–04 and subsequent tax years.

Part 1 – Schedule 2 Share Incentive Plans

History – In the title to Pt. 1, the words "Schedule 2" substituted for the word "Approved" by FA 2014, s. 51 and Sch. 8, para. 41, which is treated as having come into force on 6 April 2014, subject to the transitional provisions in FA 2014, Sch. 8, para. 90–96.

Cross references – ITEPA 2003, s. 515: approved share incentive plans – tax advantages and charges under other Acts.
ITEPA 2003, Sch. 2, para. 87: approved share incentive plans – consequences of company reconstructions.

INTRODUCTORY

1(1) The provisions of this Part of this Schedule apply for capital gains tax purposes in relation to a Schedule 2 share incentive plan (**"the plan"**).

1(2) This Part of this Schedule forms part of the SIP code (see section 488 of ITEPA 2003 (share incentive plans)).

1(3) Accordingly, expressions used in this Part of this Schedule and contained in the index at the end of Schedule 2 to that Act (share incentive plans) have the meaning indicated by the index.

1(4) In particular, for the purposes of paragraphs 5 and 7 of this Schedule **"market value"** has the meaning given by paragraph 92 of Schedule 2 to that Act (determination of market value); and Part 8 of this Act has effect subject to this paragraph.

History – In para. 1(1), the words "a Schedule 2" substituted for the words "an approved" by FA 2014, s. 51 and Sch. 8, para. 42(2), which is treated as having come into force on 6 April 2014, subject to the transitional provisions in FA 2014, Sch. 8, para. 90–96.
In para. 1(2), the word "approved" (which appeared before the words "share incentive plans") omitted by FA 2014, s. 51 and Sch. 8, para. 42(3), which is treated as having come into force on 6 April 2014, subject to the transitional provisions in FA 2014, Sch. 8, para. 90–96.
In para. 1(3), the word "approved" (which appeared before the words "share incentive plans") omitted by FA 2014, s. 51 and Sch. 8, para. 42(3), which is treated as having come into force on 6 April 2014, subject to the transitional provisions in FA 2014, Sch. 8, para. 90–96.

GAINS ACCRUING TO TRUSTEES

2(1) Any gain accruing to the trustees is not a chargeable gain if the shares–

(a) are shares in relation to which the requirements of Part 4 of Schedule 2 to ITEPA 2003 (share incentive plans: types of shares that may be awarded) are met, and

(b) are awarded to employees, or acquired on their behalf as dividend shares, in accordance with the plan within the relevant period.

2(2) If any of the shares in the company in question are readily convertible assets at the time the shares are acquired by the trustees, the relevant period is the period of two years beginning with the date on which the shares were acquired by the trustees.

This is subject to sub-paragraph (4).

2(3) If at the time of the acquisition of the shares by the trustees none of the shares in the company in question are readily convertible assets, the relevant period is–

(a) the period of five years beginning with the date on which the shares were acquired by the trustees, or

(b) if within that period any of the shares in that company become readily convertible assets, the period of two years beginning with the date on which they did so,

whichever ends first.

This is subject to sub-paragraph (4).

2(4) If the shares are acquired by the trustees by virtue of a payment in respect of which a deduction is allowed under section 989 of CTA 2009 (deduction for contribution to plan trust), the relevant period is the period of ten years beginning with the date of acquisition.

2(5) For the purposes of determining whether shares are awarded to a participant within the relevant period, shares acquired by the trustees at an earlier time are taken to be awarded to a participant before shares of the same class acquired by the trustees at a later time.

2(6) Sub-paragraph (5) is subject to paragraph 78(1) of Schedule 2 to ITEPA 2003 (acquisition by trustees of shares from employee share ownership trust).

2(7) For the purposes of this paragraph **"readily convertible assets"** has the meaning given by sections 701 and 702 of that Act (readily convertible assets).

This is subject to sub-paragraph (8).

2(8) In determining for the purposes of this paragraph whether shares are readily convertible assets any market for the shares that–

(a) is created by virtue of the trustees acquiring shares for the purposes of the plan, and

(b) exists solely for the purposes of the plan,

shall be disregarded.

2(9) In relation to shares acquired by the trustees before 11 May 2001 this paragraph has effect with the substitution–

(a) in sub-paragraph (2), of "If the shares are readily convertible assets at the time they" for the words before "are acquired", and

(b) in sub-paragraph (3)–

(i) of "If at the time of their acquisition by the trustees the shares are not readily convertible assets" for the words before "the relevant period", and

(ii) in paragraph (b), of "the shares in question" for "any of the shares in that company".

History – In para. 2(1)(a), the word "approved" (which appeared before the words "share incentive plans") omitted by FA 2014, s. 51 and Sch. 8, para. 43, which is treated as having come into force on 6 April 2014, subject to the transitional provisions in FA 2014, Sch. 8, para. 90–96.

In para. 2(4) the words "section 989 of CTA 2009" substituted for the words "paragraph 9 of Schedule 4AA to the Taxes Act" by CTA 2009, s. 1322 and Sch. 1, para. 387, with effect for corporation tax purposes for accounting periods ending on or after 1 April 2009, and for income tax and capital gains tax purposes for the tax year 2009–10 and subsequent tax years.

Cross references – ITEPA 2003, Sch. 7, para. 86 (Sch. 7: transitionals and savings): relevant period when trustees of an approved share incentive plan acquire shares from trustees of an approved profit sharing scheme.

PARTICIPANT ABSOLUTELY ENTITLED AS AGAINST TRUSTEES

3(1) Sub-paragraph (2) applies to any shares awarded to a participant under the plan.

3(2) The participant is treated for capital gains tax purposes as absolutely entitled to those shares as against the trustees.

3(3) Sub-paragraph (2) applies notwithstanding anything in the plan or the trust instrument.

DIFFERENT CLASSES OF SHARES

4(1) For the purposes of Chapter 1 of Part 4 of this Act (shares, securities, options etc: general) a participant's plan shares are treated, so long as they are subject to the plan, as of a different class from any shares (which would otherwise be treated as of the same class) that are not plan shares.

4(2) For the purposes of that Chapter, any shares to which sub-paragraph (3) applies shall be treated as of a different class from any shares to which sub-paragraph (4) applies, even if they would otherwise fall to be treated as of the same class.

4(3) This sub-paragraph applies to any shares transferred to the trustees of the plan trust by a qualifying transfer that have not been awarded to participants under the plan.

4(4) This sub-paragraph applies to any shares held by the trustees that were not transferred to them by a qualifying transfer.

4(5) In this paragraph **"qualifying transfer"** has the meaning given in paragraph 78(2) of Schedule 2 to ITEPA 2003 (acquisition by trustees of shares from employee share ownership trust)

4(6) For the purposes of Chapter 1 of Part 4 of this Act any shares which–

(a) were acquired by the trustees by virtue of a payment in respect of which a deduction is allowed under paragraph 9 of Schedule 4AA to the Taxes Act (deduction for contribution to plan trust), and

(b) have not been awarded under the plan,

shall be treated as of a different class from any shares held by the trustees that were not so acquired by them, even if they would otherwise fall to be treated as of the same class.

NO CHARGEABLE GAIN ON SHARES CEASING TO BE SUBJECT TO THE PLAN

5(1) Shares which cease to be subject to the plan are treated as having been disposed of and immediately reacquired by the participant at market value.

5(2) Any gain accruing on that disposal is not a chargeable gain.

DEEMED DISPOSAL BY TRUSTEES ON DISPOSAL OF BENEFICIAL INTEREST

6(1) If at any time the participant's beneficial interest in any of his shares is disposed of, the shares in question shall be treated for the purposes of the SIP code as having been disposed of at that time by the trustees for the like consideration as was obtained for the disposal of the beneficial interest.

6(2) For this purpose there is no disposal of the participant's beneficial interest if and at the time when–

(a) in England and Wales or Northern Ireland, that interest becomes vested in any person on the insolvency of the participant or otherwise by operation of law, or

(b) in Scotland, that interest becomes vested in a judicial factor, in a trustee of the participant's sequestrated estate or in a trustee for the benefit of the participant's creditors.

6(3) If a disposal of shares falling within this paragraph is not at arm's length, the proceeds of the disposal shall be taken for the purposes of the SIP code to be equal to the market value of the shares at the time of the disposal.

Cross references – ITEPA 2003, s. 512: approved share incentive plans – disposal of beneficial interest by participant.

TREATMENT OF FORFEITED SHARES

7(1) If any of the participant's plan shares are forfeited, they are treated as having been disposed of by the participant and acquired by the trustees at market value at the date of forfeiture.

7(2) Any gain accruing on that disposal is not a chargeable gain.

DISPOSAL OF RIGHTS UNDER RIGHTS ISSUE

8(1) Any gain accruing on the disposal of rights under paragraph 77 of Schedule 2 to ITEPA 2003 (power of trustees to raise funds to subscribe for rights issue) is not a chargeable gain.

8(2) Sub-paragraph (1) does not apply to a disposal of rights unless similar rights are conferred in respect of all ordinary shares in the company.

Part 2 – Schedule 3 SAYE Option Schemes

History – In the title to Pt. 2, the words "Schedule 3" substituted for the word "Approved" by FA 2014, s. 51 and Sch. 8, para. 126, which is treated as having come into force on 6 April 2014, subject to the transitional provisions in FA 2014, Sch. 8, para. 147–157.

INTRODUCTORY

9(1) This Part of this Schedule forms part of the SAYE code (see section 516 of ITEPA 2003 SAYE option schemes)).

9(2) Accordingly, expressions used in this Part of this Schedule and contained in the index at the end of Schedule 3 to that Act (SAYE option schemes) have the meaning indicated by the index.

History – In para. 9(1), the word "approved", which appeared before the words "SAYE option schemes", omitted by FA 2014, s. 51 and Sch. 8, para. 127, which is treated as having come into force on 6 April 2014, subject to the transitional provisions in FA 2014, Sch. 8, para. 147–157.

In para. 9(2), the word "approved", which appeared before the words "SAYE option schemes", omitted by FA 2014, s. 51 and Sch. 8, para. 127, which is treated as having come into force on 6 April 2014, subject to the transitional provisions in FA 2014, Sch. 8, para. 147–157.

MARKET VALUE RULE NOT TO APPLY

10(1) This paragraph applies where–

(a) a share option (**"the option"**) has been granted to an individual–

(i) in accordance with the provisions of a Schedule 3 SAYE option scheme, and

(ii) by reason of the individual's office or employment as a director or employee of a company,

(b) the individual exercises the option in accordance with the provisions of the SAYE option scheme at a time when the scheme is a Schedule 3 SAYE option scheme, and

(c) Condition A or Condition B in section 519(2) or (3) of ITEPA 2003 (no charge in respect of exercise of option) is met.

10(2) The company mentioned in sub-paragraph (1)(a)(ii) may be–

(a) the company whose shares are the subject of the option, or

(b) some other company.

10(3) Sub-paragraph (3A) applies for the purposes of sub-paragraph (1)(b) if–

(a) the SAYE option scheme is not to be a Schedule 3 SAYE option scheme by virtue of paragraph 40H or 40I of Schedule 3 to ITEPA 2003, and

(b) the option was granted before, but exercised at or after, the time mentioned in paragraph 40H(2)(a)(i) or (ii) or 40I(7)(a)(i) or (ii) of that Schedule (as the case may be).

10(3A) The scheme is to be taken still to be a Schedule 3 SAYE option scheme when the option is exercised.

10(4) Section 17(1) (disposals and acquisitions treated as made at market value) shall not apply in calculating the consideration for–

(a) the individual's acquisition of shares by the exercise of the option, or

(b) any corresponding disposal of those shares to the individual.

10(5) References in sub-paragraphs (1)(b) and (4) above to the individual include references to a person exercising the option in accordance with provision included in the scheme by virtue of paragraph 32 of Schedule 3 to ITEPA 2003 (exercise of options: death); and sub-paragraph (1)(c) above does not apply in relation to a person so exercising the option.

History – In para. 10(1)(a)(i), the words "a Schedule 3" substituted for the words "an approved" by FA 2014, s. 51 and Sch. 8, para. 128(2)(a), which is treated as having come into force on 6 April 2014, subject to the transitional provisions in FA 2014, Sch. 8, para. 147–157.

In para. 10(1)(b), the words "a Schedule 3 SAYE option scheme" substituted for the word "approved" by FA 2014, s. 51 and Sch. 8, para. 128(2)(b), which is treated as having come into force on 6 April 2014, subject to the transitional provisions in FA 2014, Sch. 8, para. 147–157.

Para. 10(3) and (3A) substituted for former para. 10(3) by FA 2014, s. 51 and Sch. 8, para. 128(3), which is treated as having come into force on 6 April 2014, subject to the transitional provisions in FA 2014, Sch. 8, para. 147–157.

Part 3 – Schedule 4 CSOP Schemes

History – In the title to Pt. 3, the words "Schedule 4" substituted for the word "Approved" by FA 2014, s. 51 and Sch. 8, para. 186, which is treated as having come into force on 6 April 2014, subject to the transitional provisions in FA 2014, Sch. 8, para. 205–215.

INTRODUCTORY

11(1) This Part of this Schedule forms part of the CSOP code (see section 521 of ITEPA 2003 (CSOP schemes)).

11(2) Accordingly, expressions used in this Part of this Schedule and contained in the index at the end of Schedule 4 to that Act (CSOP schemes) have the meaning indicated by the index.

11(3) This Part of this Schedule applies where–

(a) a share option (**"the option"**) has been granted to an individual–

  (i) in accordance with the provisions of a Schedule 4 CSOP scheme, and

  (ii) by reason of the individual's office or employment as a director or employee of a company, and

(b) shares (**"the relevant shares"**) are acquired by the exercise of the option.

11(4) The company mentioned in sub-paragraph (3)(a)(ii) may be–

(a) the company whose shares are the subject of the option, or

(b) some other company.

History – In para. 11(1), the word "approved", which appeared before the words "CSOP schemes", omitted by FA 2014, s. 51 and Sch. 8, para. 187(2), which is treated as having come into force on 6 April 2014, subject to the transitional provisions in FA 2014, Sch. 8, para. 205–215.

In para. 11(2), the word "approved", which appeared before the words "CSOP schemes", omitted by FA 2014, s. 51 and Sch. 8, para. 187(2), which is treated as having come into force on 6 April 2014, subject to the transitional provisions in FA 2014, Sch. 8, para. 205–215.

In para. 11(3)(a)(i), the words "a Schedule 4" substituted for the words "an approved" by FA 2014, s. 51 and Sch. 8, para. 187(3), which is treated as having come into force on 6 April 2014, subject to the transitional provisions in FA 2014, Sch. 8, para. 205–215.

RELIEF WHERE INCOME TAX CHARGED IN RESPECT OF GRANT OF OPTION

12(1) This paragraph applies where an amount (the **"employment income amount"**) counted as employment income of the individual under section 526 of ITEPA 2003 (charge where option granted at a discount) in respect of the option.

12(2) For the purposes of section 38(1)(a) (acquisition and disposal costs etc.), that part of the employment income amount which is attributable to the relevant shares shall be treated as consideration given for the acquisition of the relevant shares.

12(3) This paragraph also applies where the individual was chargeable to income tax on an amount in respect of the option under–

(a) subsection (6) of section 185 of ICTA (as it had effect before 1st January 1992),

(b) subsection (6A) of that section (as it had effect in relation to options obtained on or after 1st January 1992 but before 29 April 1996), or

(c) subsection (6) of that section (as it had effect in relation to options obtained on or after 29 April 1996);

and in such a case the **"employment income amount"** means the amount on which the individual was so chargeable.

12(4) This paragraph applies whether or not–

(a) the exercise of the option is in accordance with the provisions of the CSOP scheme, or

(b) the CSOP scheme is a Schedule 4 CSOP scheme at the time of the exercise.

History – In para. 12(4)(b), the words "a Schedule 4 CSOP scheme" substituted for the word "approved" by FA 2014, s. 51 and Sch. 8, para. 188, which is treated as having come into force on 6 April 2014, subject to the transitional provisions in FA 2014, Sch. 8, para. 205–215.

MARKET VALUE RULE NOT TO APPLY

13(1) This paragraph applies where–

(a) the individual exercises the option in accordance with the provisions of the CSOP scheme at a time when the scheme is a Schedule 4 CSOP scheme, and

(b) the condition in section 524(2) of ITEPA 2003 (no charge in respect of exercise of option) is met.

13(2) Section 17(1) (disposals and acquisitions treated as made at market value) shall not apply in calculating the consideration for–

(a) the individual's acquisition of the relevant shares by the exercise of the option, or

(b) any corresponding disposal of the relevant shares to the individual.

13(3) Sub-paragraph (2) also applies where the option is exercised at a time when the scheme is a Schedule 4 CSOP scheme in accordance with provision included in the scheme by virtue of paragraph 25 of Schedule 4 to ITEPA 2003 (exercise of options: death); and references in that sub-paragraph to the individual are to be read accordingly.

History – In para. 13(1)(a), the words "a Schedule 4 CSOP scheme" substituted for the word "approved" by FA 2014, s. 51 and Sch. 8, para. 189, which is treated as having come into force on 6 April 2014, subject to the transitional provisions in FA 2014, Sch. 8, para. 205 to 215.
In para. 13(3), the words "a Schedule 4 CSOP scheme" substituted for the word "approved" by FA 2014, s. 51 and Sch. 8, para. 189, which is treated as having come into force on 6 April 2014, subject to the transitional provisions in FA 2014, Sch. 8, para. 205 to 215.

Part 4 – Enterprise Management Incentives

[Omitted by FA 2016, s. 16 and Sch. 3, para. 9(2).]

History – Pt. 4 omitted by FA 2016, s. 16 and Sch. 3, para. 9(2), with effect from 15 September 2016 (Royal Assent), subject to the savings provisions in FA 2016, Sch. 3, para. 9(4). Former Pt. 4 read as follows:

"Part 4 – Enterprise Management Incentives

Cross references – SI 2004/712, reg. 1(8): the Research and Development (Prescribed Activities) Regulations 2004 (2004/712) is effective, for the purposes of Part 4, in relation to share options granted on or after 6 April 2004 (but not share options granted before that date (reg. 1(9)).

INTRODUCTORY

14(1) This Part of this Schedule forms part of the EMI code(see section 527 of ITEPA 2003 (enterprise management incentives: qualifying options)).

14(2) Accordingly, expressions used in this Part of this Schedule and contained in the index at the end of Schedule 5 to that Act (enterprise management incentives) have the meaning indicated by the index.

14(3) In this Part of this Schedule, **"qualifying shares"**–
(a) means shares acquired by the exercise of a qualifying option, subject to sub-paragraphs (4) and (5), and
(b) includes shares (**"replacement shares"**) which–
(i) are treated under section 127 (equation of original shares and new holding) as the same asset as a holding of qualifying shares, and
(ii) meet the requirements of paragraph 35 of Schedule 5 to ITEPA 2003 (type of shares that may be acquired).

14(4) If a disqualifying event occurs in relation to a qualifying option (whether the original option or a replacement option), shares acquired by the exercise of that option are qualifying shares only if the option is exercised within 40 days of that event.

14(5) References in this Part of this Schedule to **"the original option"**, where there has been one or more replacement options, are to the option that the replacement option (or, if there has been more than one, the first of them) replaced.

TAPER RELIEF ON DISPOSAL OF QUALIFYING SHARES

15 [Omitted by FA 2008, s. 8 and Sch. 2, para. 50.]

History – Para. 15 omitted by FA 2008, s. 8 and Sch. 2, para. 50 with effect in relation to chargeable gains accruing or treated as accruing in the tax year 2008–09 or any subsequent tax year (FA 2008, Sch. 2, para. 56(3)).

RIGHTS ISSUES IN RESPECT OF QUALIFYING SHARES

16 Where–
(a) an individual holds qualifying shares, and
(b) there is, by virtue of any such allotment for payment as is mentioned in section 126(2)(a) (allotment in proportion to shareholdings), a reorganisation affecting that holding,

sections 127 to 130 (which relate to reorganisation or reduction of share capital) shall not apply in relation to that holding."

SCHEDULE 8 – LEASES

Section 240

Cross references – ICTA 1988, s. 508B(1)(f): investment trusts investing in housing and meaning of "premium".

LEASES OF LAND AS WASTING ASSETS: CURVED LINE RESTRICTION OF ALLOWABLE EXPENDITURE

1(1) A lease of land shall not be a wasting asset until the time when its duration does not exceed 50 years.

1(2) If at the beginning of the period of ownership of a lease of land it is subject to a sublease not at a rackrent and the value of the lease at the end of the duration of the sublease, estimated as at the beginning of the period of ownership, exceeds the expenditure allowable under section 38(1)(a) in computing the gain accruing on a disposal of the lease, the lease shall not be a wasting asset until the end of the duration of the sublease.

1(3) In the case of a wasting asset which is a lease of land the rate at which expenditure is assumed to be written off shall, instead of being a uniform rate as provided by section 46, be a rate fixed in accordance with the Table below.

1(4) Accordingly, for the purposes of the computation of the gain accruing on a disposal of a lease, and given that–

(a) the percentage derived from the Table for the duration of the lease at the beginning of the period of ownership is P(1),

(b) the percentage so derived for the duration of the lease at the time when any item of expenditure attributable to the lease under section 38(1)(b) is first reflected in the nature of the lease is P(2), and

(c) the percentage so derived for the duration of the lease at the time of the disposal is P(3), then–

(i) there shall be excluded from the expenditure attributable to the lease under section 38(1)(a) a fraction equal to–

$$\frac{P(1) - P(3)}{P(1)}$$

(ii) there shall be excluded from any item of expenditure attributable to the lease under section 38(1)(b) a fraction equal to–

$$\frac{P(2) - P(3)}{P(2)}$$

1(5) This paragraph applies notwithstanding that the period of ownership of the lease is a period exceeding 50 years and, accordingly, no expenditure shall be written off under this paragraph in respect of any period earlier than the time when the lease becomes a wasting asset.

1(6) Section 47 shall apply in relation to this paragraph as it applies in relation to section 46.

Years	Percentage	Years	Percentage
50 (or more)	100	25	81.100
49	99.657	24	79.622
48	99.289	23	78.055
47	98.902	22	76.399
46	98.490	21	74.635
45	98.059	20	72.770
44	97.595	19	70.791
43	97.107	18	68.697
42	96.593	17	66.470
41	96.041	16	64.116
40	95.457	15	61.617
39	94.842	14	58.971
38	94.189	13	56.167
37	93.497	12	53.191

36	92.761	11	50.038
35	91.981	10	46.695
34	91.156	9	43.154
33	90.280	8	39.399
32	89.354	7	35.414
31	88.371	6	31.195
30	87.330	5	26.722
29	86.226	4	21.983
28	85.053	3	16.959
27	83.816	2	11.629
26	82.496	1	5.983
		0	0

If the duration of the lease is not an exact number of years the percentage to be derived from the Table above shall be the percentage for the whole number of years plus one-twelfth of the difference between that and the percentage for the next higher number of years for each odd month counting an odd 14 days or more as one month.

Derivations – CGTA 1979, Sch. 3, para. 1.

Cross references – S. 38: allowable acquisition expenditure including incidental costs (s. 38(1)(a)) and enhancement or title expenditure (s. 38(1)(b)).
S. 46: straightline write-off of wasting assets generally.
S. 47: special rules for wasting assets qualifying for capital allowances.
Sch. 2, para. 12: in relation to land held at 6 April 1965, current use value of a lease is reduced in parallel with the curved line restriction.
IHTA 1984, s. 138: similar write-off by reference to the Table in relation to the loss in value of transfers within seven years before death.
IHTA 1984, s. 194: in valuing a leasehold interest on death by reference to the actual sale subsequently, an addition must be made to reflect the Table reduction during that time.

Extra-statutory concessions – D42: allowable expenditure and indexation allowance on a disposal following mergers of leases within s. 43.

Notes – S. 23: insurance recoveries in respect of short leases, etc. not to be treated as disposals.

PREMIUMS FOR LEASES

2(1) Subject to this Schedule where the payment of a premium is required under a lease of land, or otherwise under the terms subject to which a lease of land is granted, there is a part disposal of the freehold or other asset out of which the lease is granted.

2(2) In applying section 42 to such a part disposal, the property which remains undisposed of includes a right to any rent or other payments, other than a premium, payable under the lease, and that right shall be valued as at the time of the part disposal.

Derivations – CGTA 1979, Sch. 3, para. 2.

Cross references – S. 42: apportionment of base cost on a part disposal.

3(1) This paragraph applies in relation to a lease of land.

3(2) Where under the terms subject to which a lease is granted, a sum becomes payable by the tenant in lieu of the whole or part of the rent for any period, or as consideration for the surrender of the lease, the lease shall be deemed for the purposes of this Schedule to have required the payment of a premium to the landlord (in addition to any other premium) of the amount of that sum, being a premium which–

(a) is due when the sum is payable by the tenant; and

(b) where the sum is payable in lieu of rent, is in respect of the period in relation to which the sum is payable.

3(3) Where, as consideration for the variation or waiver of any of the terms of a lease, a sum becomes payable by the tenant otherwise than by way of rent, the lease shall be deemed for the purposes of this Schedule to have required the payment of a premium to the landlord (in addition to any other premium) of the amount of that sum, being a premium which–

(a) is due when the sum is payable by the tenant; and

(b) is in respect of the period from the time when the variation or waiver takes effect to the time when it ceases to have effect.

3(4) Where under sub-paragraph (2) or (3) above a premium is deemed to have been received by the landlord, that shall not be the occasion of any recomputation of the gain accruing on the receipt of any other premium, and the premium shall be regarded–

(a) in the case of a premium deemed to have been received for the surrender of a lease, as consideration for a separate transaction which is effected when the premium is deemed to be due and consists of the disposal by the landlord of his interest in the lease; and

(b) in any other case, as consideration for a separate transaction which is effected when the premium is deemed to be due and consists of a further part disposal of the freehold or other asset out of which the lease is granted.

3(5) If under sub-paragraph (2) or (3) above a premium is deemed to have been received by the landlord, otherwise than as consideration for the surrender of the lease, and the landlord is a tenant under a lease the duration of which does not exceed 50 years, this Schedule shall apply–

(a) as if an amount equal to the amount of that premium deemed to have been received had been given by way of consideration for the grant of the part of the sublease covered by the period in respect of which the premium is deemed to have been paid; and

(b) as if that consideration were expenditure incurred by the sublessee and attributable to that part of the sublease under section 38(1)(b).

3(6) [Effectively omitted by FA 1996, s. 142(4).]

3(7) Sub-paragraph (3) above shall apply in relation to a transaction not at arm's length, and in particular in relation to a transaction entered into gratuitously, as if such sum had become payable by the tenant otherwise than by way of rent as might have been required of him if the transaction had been at arm's length.

History – In para. 3(2), the words ", being a premium which–... respect of the period in relation to which the sum is payable." were substituted by FA 1996, s. 142(2), as respects sums payable on or after 6 April 1996.
In para. 3(3), the words ", being a premium which–...takes effect to the time when it ceases to have effect." were substituted by FA 1996, s. 142(3), as respects sums payable on or after 6 April 1996.
Para. 3(4) and (5) were substituted for former para. 3(4)–(6) by FA 1996, s. 142(4), as respects sums payable on or after 6 April 1996.

Derivations – CGTA 1979, Sch. 3, para. 3.

Cross references – S. 38(1)(b): allowable enhancement or title expenditure.

Extra-statutory concessions – D39: extension of a lease by surrender of the old lease and grant of a new lease will not be regarded as a disposal.

Notes – S. 288: interpretation, including meaning of "land" and reference to sections being those of this Act.
TMA 1970, s. 29: assessing procedure.

SUBLEASES OUT OF SHORT LEASES

4(1) In the computation of the gain accruing on the part disposal of a lease which is a wasting asset by way of the grant of a sublease for a premium the expenditure attributable to the lease under paragraphs (a) and (b) of section 38(1) shall be apportioned in accordance with this paragraph, and section 42 shall not apply.

4(2) Out of each item of the expenditure attributable to the lease under paragraphs (a) and (b) of section 38 there shall be apportioned to what is disposed of–

(a) if the amount of the premium is not less than what would be obtainable by way of premium for the said sublease if the rent payable under that sublease were the same as the rent payable under the lease, the fraction which, under paragraph 1(3) of this Schedule, is to be written off over the period which is the duration of the sublease, and

(b) if the amount of the premium is less than the said amount so obtainable, the said fraction multiplied by a fraction equal to the amount of the said premium divided by the said amount so obtainable.

4(3) If the sublease is a sublease of part only of the land comprised in the lease this paragraph shall apply only in relation to a proportion of the expenditure attributable to the lease under paragraphs (a) and (b) of section 38(1) which is the same as the proportion which the value of the land comprised in the sublease bears to the value of that and the other land comprised in the lease; and the remainder of that expenditure shall be apportioned to what remains undisposed of.

Derivations – CGTA 1979, Sch. 3, para. 4.

Cross references – S. 38(1)(a) and (b): allowable acquisition expenditure including incidental costs and enhancement or title expenditure.
S. 42: normal rules for apportionment of base cost on a part disposal.

EXCLUSION OF PREMIUMS TAXED AS RECEIPTS OF A PROPERTY BUSINESS ETC.

History – In the above cross heading the words "AS RECEIPTS OF A PROPERTY BUSINESS" substituted for the words "UNDER SCHEDULE A" by CTA 2009, s. 1322 and Sch. 1, para. 388(3), with effect for corporation tax purposes for accounting periods ending on or after 1 April 2009, and for income tax and capital gains tax purposes for the tax year 2009–10 and subsequent tax years.

5(1) Where by reference to any premium any amount is brought into account by virtue of any of sections 277 to 281 of ITTOIA 2005 or sections 217 to 221 of CTA 2009 as a receipt of a UK property business (within the meaning of that Act), that amount out of the premium shall be excluded from the consideration brought into account in the computation of the gain accruing on the disposal for which the premium is consideration except where the consideration is taken into account in the denominator of the fraction by reference to which an apportionment is made under section 42.

5(2) Where by reference to any premium in respect of a sublease granted out of a lease the duration of which (that is of the lease) does not, at the time of granting the lease, exceed 50 years, any amount is brought into account by virtue of any of sections 277 to 281 of ITTOIA 2005 or sections 217 to 221 of CTA 2009 as a receipt of a UK property business (within the meaning of that Act) that amount shall be deducted from any gain accruing on the disposal for which the premium is consideration as computed in accordance with the provisions of this Act apart from this sub-paragraph, but not so as to convert the gain into a loss, or to increase any loss.

5(3) Subject to subsection (4) below, where any amount is brought into account by virtue of section 284 or 285 of ITTOIA 2005 or section 224 or 225 of CTA 2009 (sale of land with right to reconveyance or leaseback) as a receipt of a UK property business, a sum of that amount shall be excluded from the consideration brought into account in the computation of the gain accruing on the disposal of the estate or interest in respect of which income tax becomes so chargeable, except where the consideration is taken into account in the denominator of the fraction by reference to which an apportionment is made under section 42.

5(4) If what is disposed of is the remainder of a lease or a sublease out of a lease the duration of which does not exceed 50 years, sub-paragraph (3) shall not apply but the amount there referred to shall be deductedfrom any gain accruing on the disposal as computed in accordance with the provisions of this Act apart from this sub-paragraph and sub-paragraph (3), but not so as to convert the gain into a loss, or to increase any loss.

5(5) References in sub-paragraphs (1) and (2) above to a premium include references to–

(a) [Omitted by CTA 2009, s. 1322 and Sch. 1, para. 388(2)(d) and repealed by CTA 2009, s. 1326 and Sch. 3, Pt. 1.]

(b) a sum that becomes payable by the tenant under the terms subject to which a lease is granted in lieu of the whole or a part of the rent for any period,

(c) a sum that becomes payable by the tenant under the terms subject to which a lease is granted as consideration for the surrender of the lease, and

(d) a sum that becomes payable by the tenant (otherwise than by way of rent) as consideration for the variation or waiver of any of the terms of a lease.

5(6) Section 37 shall not be taken as authorising the exclusion of any amount from the consideration for a disposal of assets taken into account in the computation of the gain by reference to any amount from which a sum representing income tax is required to be deducted under Part 15 of ITA 2007.

History – In para. 5(1) the words "any of sections 277 to 281 of ITTOIA 2005 or sections 217 to 221 of CTA 2009 as a receipt of a UK property business" substituted for the words "section 34 of the Taxes Act as a receipt of a Schedule A business (within the meaning of that Act) or by virtue of any of sections 277 to 281 of ITTOIA 2005 as a receipt of a UK property business" by CTA 2009, s. 1322 and Sch. 1, para. 388(2)(a), with effect for corporation tax purposes for accounting periods ending on or after 1 April 2009, and for income tax and capital gains tax purposes for the tax year 2009–10 and subsequent tax years.

In para. 5(1), words "or by virtue of any of sections 277 to 281 of ITTOIA 2005 as a receipt of a UK property business (within the meaning of that Act)" inserted by ITTOIA 2005, s. 882 and Sch. 1, para. 451(2)(a) which, in accordance with ITTOIA 2005, s. 883, have effect, for income tax purposes, for tax year 2005–06 and subsequent tax years, and, for corporation tax purposes, for accounting periods ending after 5 April 2005.

In para. 5(1), (2) words "any amount is brought into account ... (within the meaning of that Act)" substituted for "income tax has become chargeable under section 34 of the Taxes Act on any amount" by FA 1998, s. 38 and Sch. 5, para. 63(2); with effect for 1998–99 and subsequent years, and for corporation tax from 1 April 1998, subject to transitional provisions in FA 1998, Sch. 5, paras. 65–76. The same amendment was deemed effective for capital gains tax purposes for 1995–96 and subsequent years of assessment by FA 1995, s. 39 and Sch. 6, para. 37(2)(a), subject to FA 1995, s. 39(5).

In para. 5(2) the words "any of sections 277 to 281 of ITTOIA 2005 or sections 217 to 221 of CTA 2009 as a receipt of a UK property business" substituted for the words "section 34 of the Taxes Act as a receipt of a Schedule A business (within the meaning of that Act) or by virtue of any of sections 277 to 281 of ITTOIA 2005 as a receipt of a UK property business" by CTA 2009, s. 1322 and Sch. 1, para. 388(2)(b), with effect for corporation tax purposes for accounting periods ending on or after 1 April 2009, and for income tax and capital gains tax purposes for the tax year 2009–10 and subsequent tax years.

In para. 5(2), words "or by virtue of any of sections 277 to 281 of ITTOIA 2005 as a receipt of a UK property business (within the meaning of that Act)" inserted by ITTOIA 2005, s. 882 and Sch. 1, para. 451(2)(b) which, in accordance with ITTOIA 2005, s. 883, have effect, for income tax purposes, for tax year 2005–06 and subsequent tax years, and, for corporation tax purposes, for accounting periods ending after 5 April 2005.

In para. 5(3) the words "section 284 or 285 of ITTOIA 2005 or section 224 or 225 of CTA 2009 (sale of land with right to reconveyance or leaseback) as a receipt of a UK property business" substitutedfor the words "section 36 of the Taxes Act (sale of land with right of re-conveyance) as a receipt of a Schedule A business (within the meaning of that Act) or by virtue of section 284 or 285 of ITTOIA 2005 (sale of land with right to reconveyance or leaseback) as a receipt of a UK property business (within the meaning of that Act)" by CTA 2009, s. 1322 and Sch. 1, para. 388(2)(c), with effect for corporation tax purposes for accounting periods ending on or after 1 April 2009, and for income tax and capital gains tax purposes for the tax year 2009–10 and subsequent tax years.

In para. 5(3), words "or by virtue of section 284 or 285 of ITTOIA 2005 (sale of land with right to reconveyance or leaseback) as a receipt of a UK property business (within the meaning of that Act)," inserted by ITTOIA 2005, s. 882 and Sch. 1, para. 451(2)(c)

which, in accordance with ITTOIA 2005, s. 883, have effect, for income tax purposes, for tax year 2005–06 and subsequent tax years, and, for corporation tax purposes, for accounting periods ending after 5 April 2005.
In para. 5(3), words "any amount is brought into account ... (within the meaning of that Act)" substituted for "income tax has become chargeable under section 36 of the Taxes Act (sale of land with right of re-conveyance) on any amount" by FA 1998, s. 38 and Sch. 5, para. 63(2) with effect for 1998–99 and subsequent years, and for corporation tax from 1 April 1998, subject to transitional provisions in FA 1998, Sch. 5, paras. 65–76. The same amendment was deemed effective for capital gains tax purposes for 1995–96 and subsequent years of assessment by FA 1995, s. 39 and Sch. 6, para. 37(2)(b), subject to FA 1995, s. 39(5).
Para. 5(5)(a) omitted by CTA 2009, s. 1322 and Sch. 1, para. 388(2)(d) and repealed by CTA 2009, s. 1326 and Sch. 3, Pt. 1, with effect for corporation tax purposes for accounting periods ending on or after 1 April 2009, and for income tax and capital gains tax purposes for the tax year 2009–10 and subsequent tax years.
Para. 5(5) substituted by ITTOIA 2005, s. 882 and Sch. 1, para. 451(2)(d) which, in accordance with ITTOIA 2005, s. 883, have effect, for income tax purposes, for tax year 2005–06 and subsequent tax years, and, for corporation tax purposes, for accounting periods ending after 5 April 2005.
In para. 5(6), the words "any amount from which a sum representing income tax is required to be deducted under Part 15 of ITA 2007" substituted for "any amount chargeable to tax under section 348 or 349 of the Taxes Act" by ITA 2007, s. 1027 and Sch. 1, para. 349, with effect from 6 April 2007.

Derivations – (as originally enacted) – CGTA 1979, Sch. 3, para. 5.

Cross references – S. 37: general exclusion in computing a gain of consideration chargeable to tax as income.
S. 42: normal rules for apportionment of base cost on a part disposal.
ICTA 1988, s. 34: treatment of part of premiums on short leases as rent (or Sch. D, Case VI profits for anyone other than the landlord).
ICTA 1988, s. 36: charge under Sch. D, Case VI where there is a right to reconveyance, by reference to the excess of the sale proceeds over the expected reconveyance price etc.
ICTA 1988, s. 348, 349: deduction of tax at source from certain payments.
FA 1995, s. 39 and Sch. 6, para. 37(2): modification of para. 5(1)–(3) for capital gains tax purposes for, subject to FA 1995, s. 39(5), 1995–96 and subsequent years of assessment.

Notes – ICTA 1988, s. 348, 349: reference to these provisions was substituted, apparently by mistake, into the predecessor provision to para. 5(6) for the previous reference to ICTA 1970, Pt. III (Sch. A and associated charges under Sch. D) on consolidation by ICTA 1988; the provisions comparable to the former Pt. III are ICTA 1988, Pt. II (s. 21–43).

6(1) If under section 292 of ITTOIA 2005 or section 232 of CTA 2009 (allowance where, by the grant of a sublease, a lessee has converted a capital amount into a right to income) a person is to be treated as incurring expenses in consequence of having granted a sublease, the amount of any loss accruing to the person on the disposal by way of the grant of the sublease shall be reduced by the total amount of rent which the person is thereby treated as paying, or the total amount of expenses which the person is thereby treated as incurring, over the term of the sublease (and without regard to whether relief is thereby effectively given over the term of the sublease), but not so as to convert the loss into a gain, or to increase any gain.

6(2) Nothing in section 37 of this Act shall be taken as applying in relation to any amount brought into account by virtue of section 282 of ITTOIA 2005 or section 222 of CTA 2009 (assignments for profit of lease granted at undervalue) as a receipt of a UK property business.

6(3) If any adjustment is made–

(a) under section 301 or 302 of ITTOIA 2005, or

(b) under section 238 or 239 of CTA 2009,

on a claim made under that section, any necessary adjustment shall be made to give effect to the consequences of the claim on the operation of this paragraph or paragraph 5 above.

History – In para. 6(1), the words "If under section 292 of ITTOIA 2005 or section 232 of CTA 2009 (allowance where, by the grant of a sublease, a lessee has converted a capital amount into a right to income) a person is to be treated as incurring expenses in consequence of having granted a sublease," substituted by CTA 2009, s. 1322 and Sch. 1, para. 388(4)(a), with effect for corporation tax purposes for accounting periods ending on or after 1 April 2009, and for income tax and capital gains tax purposes for the tax year 2009–10 and subsequent tax years.
Para. 6(1) substituted by ITTOIA 2005, s. 882 and Sch. 1, para. 451(3)(a) which, in accordance with ITTOIA 2005, s. 883, have effect, for income tax purposes, for tax year 2005–06 and subsequent tax years, and, for corporation tax purposes, for accounting periods ending after 5 April 2005.
In para. 6(2), the words "by virtue of section 282 of ITTOIA 2005 or section 222 of CTA 2009 (assignments for profit of lease granted at undervalue) as a receipt of a UK property business." substituted for the words "by virtue of section 35 of the Taxes Act (charge on assignment of a lease granted at an undervalue) as a receipt of a Schedule A business (within the meaning of that Act) or by virtue of section 282 of ITTOIA 2005 (assignments for profit of lease granted at undervalue) as a receipt of a UK property business (within the meaning of that Act)" by CTA 2009, s. 1322 and Sch. 1, para. 388(4)(b), with effect for corporation tax purposes for accounting periods ending on or after 1 April 2009, and for income tax and capital gains tax purposes for the tax year 2009–10 and subsequent tax years.
In para. 6(2), words "or by virtue of section 282 of ITTOIA 2005 (assignments for profit of lease granted at undervalue) as a receipt of a UK property business (within the meaning of that Act)" inserted by ITTOIA 2005, s. 882 and Sch. 1, para. 451(3)(b) which, in accordance with ITTOIA 2005, s. 883, have effect, for income tax purposes, for tax year 2005–06 and subsequent tax years, and, for corporation tax purposes, for accounting periods ending after 5 April 2005.
In para. 6(2), words "brought into account ... (within the meaning of that Act)" substituted for "on which tax is paid under section 35 of the Taxes Act (charge on assignment of lease granted at undervalue)" by FA 1998, s. 38 and Sch. 5, para. 63(3) with effect for 1998–99 and subsequent years, and for corporation tax from 1 April 1998, subject to transitional provisions in FA 1998, Sch. 5, paras. 65–76. The same amendment was deemed effective for capital gains tax purposes for 1995–96 and subsequentyears of assessment by FA 1995, s. 39 and Sch. 6, para. 37(3), subject to FA 1995, s. 39(5).
Para. 6(3) substituted by CTA 2009, s. 1322 and Sch. 1, para. 388(4)(c), with effect for corporation tax purposes for accounting periods ending on or after 1 April 2009, and for income tax and capital gains tax purposes for the tax year 2009–10 and subsequent tax years.
In former para. 6(3), words "or under section 301 or 302 of ITTOIA 2005 on a claim under that section," inserted by ITTOIA 2005, s. 882 and Sch. 1, para. 451(3)(c) which, in accordance with ITTOIA 2005, s. 883, have effect, for income tax purposes, for tax year 2005–06 and subsequent tax years, and, for corporation tax purposes, for accounting periods ending after 5 April 2005.

Derivations – (as originally enacted) – CGTA 1979, Sch. 3, para. 6.

Cross references – S. 37: general exclusion in computing a gain of consideration chargeable to tax as income.
S. 42: normal rules for apportionment of base cost on a part disposal.

ICTA 1988, s. 35: charge under Sch. D, Case VI on the amount foregone where a lease is granted at an undervalue and subsequently assigned, essentially, at a profit.
ICTA 1988, s. 36(2)(b): claim for repayment of any excess charge under Sch. D, Case VI where a right to reconveyance is exercised at any time and the charge was made on sale by reference to the excess of the sale proceeds over the lowest possible reconveyance price because the date of reconveyance was not fixed.
FA 1995, s. 39 and Sch. 6, para. 37(3): modification of para. 6(2) for capital gains tax purposes for, subject to FA 1995, s. 39(5), 1995–96 and subsequent years of assessment.

Notes – S. 288: interpretation, including "the Taxes Act" as ICTA 1988.

7 If–

(a) under section 277 of ITTOIA 2005 any amount is brought into account by virtue of section 278 of that Act as a receipt of a UK property business which is carried on by any person, or

(b) under section 217 of CTA 2009 any amount is brought into account by virtue of section 218 of that Act as a receipt of a UK property business which is carried on by any company,

that person shall be treated for the purposes of the computation of any gain accruing to him as having incurred at the time the lease was granted expenditure of that amount (in addition to any other expenditure) attributable to the asset under section 38(1)(b).

History – Para. 7(a) and (b) substituted by CTA 2009, s. 1322 and Sch. 1, para. 388(5), with effect for corporation tax purposes for accounting periods ending on or after 1 April 2009, and for income tax and capital gains tax purposes for the tax year 2009–10 and subsequent tax years.
Para. 7 substituted by ITTOIA 2005, s. 882 and Sch. 1, para. 451(4) which, in accordance with ITTOIA 2005, s. 883, have effect, for income tax purposes, for tax year 2005–06 and subsequent tax years, and, for corporation tax purposes, for accounting periods ending after 5 April 2005.
In former para. 7, words "any amount is brought into account … carried on by any person, that person" substituted for "income tax is chargeable on any amount, as being a premium the payment of which is deemed to be required by the lease, the person so chargeable" by FA 1998, s. 38 and Sch. 5, para. 63(4) with effect for 1998–99 and subsequent years, and for corporation tax from 1 April 1998, subject to transitional provisions in FA 1998, Sch. 5, paras. 65–76. The same amendment was deemed effective for capital gains tax purposes for 1995–96 and subsequent years of assessment by FA 1995, s. 39 and Sch. 6, para. 37(4), subject to FA 1995, s. 39(5).

Derivations – (as originally enacted) – CGTA 1979, Sch. 3, para. 7.

Cross references – S. 38(1)(b): allowable enhancement or title expenditure.
ICTA 1988, s. 34(2), (3): charge as rent (or Sch. D, Case VI profits) for the value of any obligation on a tenant under a lease to carry out work to the extent that a deduction would not have been available to the landlord had he carried out the work.
FA 1995, s. 39 and Sch. 6, para. 37(4): modification of para. 7 for capital gains tax purposes for, subject to FA 1995, s. 39(5), 1995–96 and subsequent years of assessment.

Notes – S. 288: interpretation, including "the Taxes Act" as ICTA 1988.

7A References in paragraphs 5 to 7 above to an amount brought into account as a receipt of a UK property business include references to an amount brought into account as a receipt of an overseas property business.

History – In para. 7A, the words "Schedule A business or" omitted by CTA 2009, s. 1322 and Sch. 1, para. 388(6) and repealed by CTA 2009, s. 1326 and Sch. 3, Pt. 1, with effect for corporation tax purposes for accounting periods ending on or after 1 April 2009, and for income tax and capital gains tax purposes for the tax year 2009–10 and subsequent tax years.
In para. 7A, words "or UK property business" inserted by ITTOIA 2005, s. 882 and Sch. 1, para. 451(5) which, in accordance with ITTOIA 2005, s. 883, have effect, for income tax purposes, for tax year 2005–06 and subsequent tax years, and, for corporation tax purposes, for accounting periods ending after 5 April 2005.
Para. 7A substituted by FA 1998, s. 38 and Sch. 5, para. 63(5) with effect for income tax for the year 1998–99 and subsequent years, and for corporation tax from 1 April 1998 subject to transitional provisions in FA 1998, Sch. 5, para. 65–76.
Para. 7A inserted by FA 1995, s. 41(4) for 1995–96 and subsequent years of assessment, subject to transitional provisions in FA 1995, s. 41(5)–(9).

Cross references – ICTA 1988, s. 65(2A): rules for computing profits or gains of a Schedule A business applied to non-trading income from land chargeable to income tax under Sch. D, Case V.

DURATION OF LEASES

8(1) In ascertaining for the purposes of this Act the duration of a lease of land the following provisions shall have effect.

8(2) Where the terms of the lease include provision for the determination of the lease by notice given by the landlord, the lease shall not be treated as granted for a term longer than one ending at the earliest date on which it could be determined by notice given by the landlord.

8(3) Where any of the terms of the lease (whether relating to forfeiture or to any other matter) or any other circumstances render it unlikely that the lease will continue beyond a date falling before the expiration of the term of the lease, the lease shall not be treated as having been granted for a term longer than one ending on that date.

8(4) Sub-paragraph (3) applies in particular where the lease provides for the rent to go up after a given date, or for the tenant's obligations to become in any other respect more onerous after a given date, but includes provision for the determination of the lease on that date, by notice given by the tenant, and those provisions render it unlikely that the lease will continue beyond that date.

8(5) Where the terms of the lease include provision for the extension of the lease beyond a given date by notice given by the tenant this paragraph shall apply as if the term of the lease extended for as long as it could be extended by the tenant, but subject to any right of the landlord by notice to determine the lease.

8(6) It is hereby declared that the question what is the duration of a lease is to be decided, in relation to the grant or any disposal of the lease, by reference to the facts which were known or ascertainable at the time when the lease was acquired or created.

Derivations – CGTA 1979, Sch. 3, para. 8.

Extra-statutory concessions – D39: extension of a lease by surrender of the old lease and grant of a new lease will not be regarded as a disposal.

Notes – S. 288: interpretation, including "land" as embracing messuages, tenements, and hereditaments, houses and buildings of any tenure.

LEASES OF PROPERTY OTHER THAN LAND

9(1) Paragraphs 2, 3, 4 and 8 of this Schedule shall apply in relation to leases of property other than land as they apply to leases of land, but subject to any necessary modifications.

9(2) Where by reference to any capital sum within the meaning of section 681DM of ITA 2007 (leases of assets other than land) any person has been charged to income tax on any amount, that amount out of the capital sum shall be deducted from any gain accruing on the disposal for which that capital sum is consideration, as computed in accordance with the provisions of this Act apart from this sub-paragraph, but not so as to convert the gain into a loss, or increase any loss.

9(3) In the case of a lease of a wasting asset which is movable property the lease shall be assumed to terminate not later than the end of the life of the wasting asset.

History – In para. 9(2), the words "section 681DM of ITA 2007" substituted for "section 785 of the Taxes Act" by TIOPA 2010, s. 374 and Sch. 8, para. 244, with effect for corporation tax purposes for accounting periods ending on or after 1 April 2010, for income tax and capital gains tax purposes for the tax year 2010–11 and subsequent tax years, and for petroleum revenue tax purposes for chargeable periods beginning on or after 1 July 2010.

Derivations – CGTA 1979, Sch. 3, para. 9.

Cross references – ICTA 1988, s. 785: "capital sum" by reference to a sum of money, or any money's worth, not taken into account in taxing a trade, etc. and, except by way of clawback of deductions in respect of leased assets, not charged under Sch. D, Case VI.

Notes – S. 288: interpretation, including "land" as embracing messuages, tenements, and hereditaments, houses and buildings of any tenure and "the Taxes Act" as ICTA 1988.

INTERPRETATION

10(1) In this Act, unless the context otherwise requires **"lease"**–

(a) in relation to land, includes an underlease, sublease or any tenancy or licence, and any agreement for a lease, underlease, sublease or tenancy or licence and, in the case of land outside the United Kingdom, any interest corresponding to a lease as so defined,

(b) in relation to any description of property other than land, means any kind of agreement or arrangement under which payments are made for the use of, or otherwise in respect of, property,

and **"lessor"**, **"lessee"** and **"rent"** shall be construed accordingly.

10(2) In this Schedule **"premium"** includes any like sum, whether payable to the intermediate or a superior landlord, and for the purposes of this Schedule any sum (other than rent) paid on or in connection with the granting of a tenancy shall be presumed to have been paid by way of premium except in so far as other sufficient consideration for the payment can be shown to have been given.

10(3) In the application of this Schedule to Scotland **"premium"** includes in particular a grassum payable to any landlord or intermediate landlord on the creation of a sublease.

History – In para. 10(2), the words "other sufficient consideration...have been given" were substituted for the words " the other sufficient consideration for the payment is shown to have been given", by FA 1996, s. 134 and Sch. 20, para. 67, with effect for the year 1996–97 and subsequent years (capital gains tax) and for accounting periods ending on or after 1 July 1999, the appointed day for corporation tax self-assessment (FA 1994, s. 199 and SI 1998/3173 (C. 78)).

Derivations – CGTA 1979, Sch. 3, para. 10.

Cross references – FA 1988, s. 50(4): tenancy granted at a premium within para 10 excluded from being a qualifying tenancy as regards the application of the Business Expansion Scheme to private rented housing.

SCHEDULE 8A – FOREIGN CURRENCY BANK ACCOUNTS

[Omitted by FA 2012, s. 35(5).]

History – Sch. 8A omitted by FA 2012, s. 35(5) with effect in relation to disposals occurring on or after 6 April 2012.

SCHEDULE 8B – HOLD-OVER RELIEF FOR GAINS RE-INVESTED IN SOCIAL ENTERPRISES

Section 255A

History – Sch. 8B inserted by FA 2014, s. 57 and Sch. 12, para. 3, with effect from 17 July 2014.

Other material – Misc. 22/2014: Social Investment Tax Relief (Sitr): Guide For Social Enterprises.
Misc. 23/2014: Social Investment Tax Relief (Sitr) – Investors.
Misc. 24/2014: Social Investment Tax Relief (Sitr): Guidance For Social Enterprises – Process To Follow.
Misc. 25/2014: Social Investment Tax Relief (Sitr): Guidance For Investors – How To Claim Tax Relief.
Misc. 26/2014: Social Investment Tax Relief Compliance Statement Sitr(2014).

WHEN DOES THE SCHEDULE APPLY?

1(1) This Schedule applies if–

(a) a chargeable gain accrues to an individual ("the investor"),

(b) the investor acquires one or more assets ("the social holding"),

(c) the investor is eligible for SI relief under Part 5B of ITA 2007 in respect of the consideration given for the social holding, and

(d) conditions A, B, C, D and E are met.

1(2) Condition A is that the gain is one that accrues–

(a) on the disposal by the investor of an asset,

(b) in accordance with section 169N (but see sub-paragraph (7)), or

(c) as a result of the operation of paragraph 5 in connection with a chargeable event within paragraph 6(1)(c) or (d).

1(3) Condition B is that the gain is one that accrues–

(a) on or after 6 April 2014, and

(b) before 6 April 2019 (but see sub-paragraph (8)).

1(4) Condition C is that the investor is resident in the United Kingdom–

(a) when the gain accrues, and

(b) when the social holding is acquired.

1(5) Condition D is that the social holding is acquired by the investor on the investor's own behalf.

1(6) Condition E is that the social holding is acquired–

(a) in the 3 years beginning with the day when the gain accrues, or

(b) in the year that ends at the beginning of that day.

1(7) The reference in sub-paragraph (2)(b) to a gain accruing in accordance with section 169N does not include such a gain so far as it is chargeable to capital gains tax at the rate in section 169N(3) (rate where entrepreneurs' relief is available).

1(8) The Treasury may by order substitute a later date for the date for the time being specified in sub-paragraph (3)(b).

2(1) This Schedule also applies if–

(a) a chargeable gain accrues to an individual ("the investor"),

(b) the gain accrues as a result of the operation of paragraph 5 in connection with a chargeable event within paragraph 6(1)(a), (b) or (c),

(c) the chargeable event is either–

(i) a disposal to a social enterprise of shares in or debentures of the social enterprise, or

(ii) the cancellation, extinguishment, redemption or repayment by a social enterprise of shares in or debentures of the social enterprise,

(d) as part of the chargeable event or in connection with it, and in place of the shares or debentures, the investor acquires one or more assets ("the social holding") from the social enterprise,

(e) other than the investor's ceasing to hold the shares or debentures, no detriment is suffered in return for the acquisition of the social holding,

(f) the asset acquired, or each of the assets acquired, is a share in or debenture of the social enterprise,

(g) but for section 257LA of ITA 2007 (consideration for acquisition must be wholly in cash and fully paid) the investor would be eligible for SI relief under Part 5B of ITA 2007 in respect of the consideration given for the social holding, and

(h) conditions F, G, H and J are met.

2(2) Condition F is that the gain is one that accrues–

(a) on or after 6 April 2014, and

(b) before 6 April 2019 (but see sub-paragraph (6)).

2(3) Condition G is that the investor is resident in the United Kingdom–

(a) when the gain accrues, and

(b) when the social holding is acquired.

2(4) Condition H is that the social holding is acquired by the investor on the investor's own behalf.

2(5) Condition J is that the social holding is acquired–

(a) in the 3 years beginning with the day when the gain accrues, or

(b) in the year that ends at the beginning of that day.

2(6) The Treasury may by order substitute a later date for the date for the time being specified in sub-paragraph (2)(b).

2(7) In this paragraph **"debenture"** includes any instrument creating or acknowledging indebtedness.

2(8) A reference in this paragraph to a social enterprise is a reference to a body that is a social enterprise for the purposes of Part 5B of ITA 2007 (see section 257J of that Act).

INTERPRETATION OF SCHEDULE

3(1) In the following provisions of this Schedule–

"the amount invested" means, in a case where this Schedule applies because of paragraph 1, the consideration mentioned in paragraph 1(1)(c),

"the investor" means the individual mentioned in paragraph 1(1)(a) or, as the case may be, paragraph 2(1)(a),

"the original gain" means the chargeable gain mentioned in paragraph 1(1)(a) or, as the case may be, paragraph 2(1)(a), and

"the social holding" means the asset or assets mentioned in paragraph 1(1)(b) or, as the case may be, paragraph 2(1)(d).

3(2) In this Schedule, a **"disposal within marriage or civil partnership"** is a disposal to which section 58 (certain disposals between spouses or civil partners) applies.

CLAIM TO HOLD GAIN OVER WHILE INVESTED IN A SOCIAL ENTERPRISE

4(1) The investor may make a claim for the original gain to be reduced–

(a) in a case within paragraph 1, by the amount invested, or by a part of that amount specified in the claim, or

(b) in a case within paragraph 2, to the extent specified in the claim,

but, in either case, subject as follows.

4(2) The reduction may not be more than the original gain or, if the original gain has already been reduced under one or more of the listed provisions, the reduction may not be more than the reduced gain.

4(3) In a case within paragraph 1, the claim may not relate to any part of the amount invested that under any of the listed provisions has already been set against a chargeable gain.

4(4) The **"listed provisions"** are–

(a) sub-paragraph (1),

(b) Schedule 5B, and

(c) paragraph 1(5) of Schedule 5BB.

4(5) The total of all reductions claimed by the investor under sub-paragraph (1) in any tax year must not be more than £1,000,000.

4(6) If there is relief by way of a reduction under sub-paragraph (1) then, for the purposes of this Schedule, that relief–

(a) is attributable to the asset or assets that form the social holding, but

(b) ceases to be attributable to any particular asset, or to any particular part of a particular asset, when–

(i) a chargeable event occurs in relation to that asset or part, or

(ii) the person holding the asset or part dies.

HELD-OVER GAIN TREATED AS ACCRUING ON DISPOSAL ETC OF THE QUALIFYING INVESTMENT

5(1) This paragraph applies if there has been a reduction under paragraph 4(1).

5(2) A chargeable gain equal to the amount of the reduction is treated as accruing when a chargeable event occurs in relation to the social holding without any chargeable event having previously occurred in relation to any of the holding.

5(3) When a chargeable event occurs in relation to part only of the social holding without any chargeable event having previously occurred in relation to any of that part, a chargeable gain calculated in accordance with sub-paragraph (4) is treated as accruing.

5(4) The calculation is–

Step 1

Subtract from the amount of the reduction any chargeable gains previously treated as accruing as a result of the operation of sub-paragraph (3).

Step 2

Attribute a proportionate part of the amount calculated at Step 1 to each part of the social holding held, immediately before the occurrence of the chargeable event in question, by the investor or a person who has acquired any part of the holding from the investor on a disposal within marriage or civil partnership.

Step 3

The amount attributed at Step 2 to the part of the social holding in relation to which that chargeable event occurs is the chargeable gain treated as accruing as a result of the operation of sub-paragraph (3) on the occurrence of that event.

CHARGEABLE EVENTS

6(1) A chargeable event occurs in relation to an asset that forms the whole or any part of the social holding if (after the acquisition of the holding)–

(a) the investor disposes of the asset otherwise than by way of a disposal within marriage or civil partnership,

(b) the asset is disposed of, otherwise than by way of a disposal to the investor, by a person who acquired the asset on a disposal made within marriage or civil partnership,

(c) the asset is cancelled, extinguished, redeemed or repaid, or

(d) any of the conditions in Chapters 3 and 4 of Part 5B of ITA 2007 for the investor's eligibility for SI relief under that Part in respect of the amount invested fails to be met.

In this sub-paragraph **"asset"** includes part of an asset.

6(2) In the event of the death of–

(a) the investor, or

(b) a person who, on a disposal within marriage or civil partnership, has acquired the whole or any part of the social holding,

nothing which occurs at or after the time of death is a chargeable event in relation to any part of the holding held by the deceased person immediately before the time of death.

6(3) If a person makes a disposal of assets of a particular class while retaining other assets of that class–

(a) assets of that class acquired by the person on an earlier day are treated for the purposes of this Schedule as disposed of before assets of that class acquired by the person on a later day, and

(b) assets of that class acquired by the person on the same day are treated for the purposes of this Schedule as disposed of in the following order–

(i) first, any to which neither relief under this Schedule, nor SI relief under Part 5B of ITA 2007, is attributable,

(ii) next, any to which relief under this Schedule, but not SI relief under that Part, is attributable,

(iii) next, any to which SI relief under that Part, but not relief under this Schedule, is attributable, and

(iv) finally, any to which both SI relief under that Part, and relief under this Schedule, are attributable.

6(4) For the purposes of sub-paragraph (3), assets–

(a) to which relief under this Schedule is attributable, and

(b) which have not been held continuously by the investor since the social holding was acquired,

are treated as having been acquired when the social holding was acquired if SI relief under Part 5B of ITA 2007 is not also attributable to them.

6(5) For the purposes of sub-paragraph (3), assets–

(a) to which SI relief under Part 5B of ITA 2007 is attributable, and

(b) which were transferred to an individual as mentioned in section 257T of ITA 2007 (transfers between spouses or civil partners),

are treated as having been acquired when the social holding was acquired.

6(6) Chapter 1 of Part 4 of this Act has effect subject to sub-paragraphs (3) to (5).

6(7) Sections 104, 105 and 106A do not apply to assets to which relief under this Schedule is attributable if SI relief under Part 5B of ITA 2007 is not also attributable to them.

6(8) Where, at the time of a chargeable event, an asset that formed the whole or any part of the social holding is treated for the purposes of this Act as represented by assets which consist of or include assets other than that asset–

(a) so much of the original gain as is attributable to the asset is treated, in determining for the purposes of this paragraph the amount of the original gain to be treated as attributable to each of those assets, as apportioned in such manner as may be just and reasonable between those assets, and

(b) as between different assets treated as representing the same asset, sub-paragraphs (3) to (5) apply with the necessary modifications in relation to those assets as they would apply in relation to the asset.

6(9) In order to determine, for the purposes of sub-paragraph (8), the amount of the original gain attributable to any asset, a proportionate part of the amount of the original gain is to be attributed to each asset that forms the whole or any part of so much of the social holding as is held, immediately before the occurrence of the chargeable event in question, by the investor or a person who has acquired any part of the social holding from the investor on a disposal within marriage or civil partnership

6(10) In subsections (8) and (9) references to the original gain are to so much of the original gain as remains after deduction from it of the amount of any chargeable gain treated as accruing as a result of the previous operation of paragraph 5.

PERSON TO WHOM HELD-OVER GAIN IS TREATED AS ACCRUING

7(1) This paragraph applies where a chargeable gain is treated as accruing as a result of the operation of paragraph 5.

7(2) If the chargeable event is a disposal, that chargeable gain is treated as accruing to the person who makes the disposal.

7(3) If the chargeable event occurs–

(a) when an asset, or part of an asset, is cancelled, extinguished, redeemed or repaid, or

(b) when a condition, for eligibility for relief in respect of the consideration given for the acquisition of an asset, fails to be met,

that chargeable gain is treated as accruing to the person who holds the asset, or part, when the chargeable event occurs.

CLAIMS: PROCEDURE

8(1) Sections 257P(1), 257PA(1) and 257PB to 257PD of ITA 2007–

(a) apply in relation to a claim under this Schedule in respect of the social holding as they apply in relation to a claim under Part 5B to ITA 2007 in respect of an investment, and

(b) as they so apply, have effect as if any reference to the requirements for relief under that Part were a reference to the conditions for the application of this Schedule.

8(2) In section 257PE(2) of ITA 2007 (power to make consequential amendments etc when amending provision about claims for SI relief) **"enactment"** includes (in particular) sub-paragraph (1).

SCHEDULE 9 – GILT-EDGED SECURITIES

Section 288

Part I – General

1 For the purposes of this Act **"gilt-edged securities"** means the securities specified in Part II of this Schedule, and such stocks and bonds issued under section 12 of the National Loans Act 1968, denominated in sterling and issued after 15th April 1969, as may be specified by order made by the Treasury.

Derivations – CGTA 1979, Sch. 2, para. 1.

Cross references – S. 287(4): power of the Treasury exercisable by statutory instrument but not subject to the negative resolution procedure.
Sch. 11, para. 15: inclusion of certain securities redeemed before 1 January 1992.
ICTA 1988, s. 50: interest on gilt-edged securities paid without deduction of income tax.
ICTA 1988, s. 722A: deemed transfers of gilt strips.
ICTA 1988, Sch. 23A, para. 3A: manufactured interest on gilt-edged securities, etc.
FA 1996, s. 103(1): application of definition of gilt-edged securities to legislation on loan relationships.
FA 1998, s. 161: Non-FOTRA securities.

Statutory instruments – See history note to Pt. II to this Schedule for orders within para. 1.

Notes – S. 287: power of the Treasury is exercisable by statutory instrument but not subject to the negative resolution procedure.

1A(1) Any security which is a strip of a security which is a gilt-edged security for the purposes of this Act is also itself a gilt-edged security for those purposes.

1A(2) In this paragraph **"strip"** has the same meaning as in section 47 of the Finance Act 1942.

History – Para. 1A inserted by FA 1996, s. 202 and Sch. 40, para. 8.

2 The Treasury shall cause particulars of any order made under paragraph 1 above to be published in the London and Edinburgh Gazettes as soon as may be after the order is made.

Derivations – CGTA 1979, Sch. 2, para. 2.

3 Section 14(b) of the Interpretation Act 1978 (implied power to amend orders made by statutory instrument) shall not apply to the power of making orders under paragraph 1 above.

Derivations – CGTA 1979, Sch. 2, para. 3.

Part II – Existing Gilt-Edged Securities

STOCKS AND BONDS CHARGED ON THE NATIONAL LOANS FUND

21/2% Annuities 1905 or after
23/4% Annuities 1905 or after
21/2% Consolidated Stock 1923 or after
31/2% War Loan 1952 or after
4% Consolidated Loan 1957 or after
31/2% Conversion Loan 1961 or after
3% Treasury Stock 1966 or after
21/2% Treasury Stock 1975 or after
123/4% Treasury Loan 1992
8% Treasury Loan 1992
10% Treasury Stock 1992
3% Treasury Stock 1992
121/4% Exchequer Stock 1992
131/2% Exchequer Stock 1992
101/2% Treasury Convertible Stock 1992
2% Index-Linked Treasury Stock 1992
121/2% Treasury Loan 1993
6% Funding Loan 1993
133/4% Treasury Loan 1993
10% Treasury Loan 1993
81/4% Treasury Stock 1993

141/2%	Treasury Loan 1994
121/2%	Exchequer Stock 1994
9%	Treasury Loan 1994
10%	Treasury Loan 1994
131/2%	Exchequer Stock 1994
81/2%	Treasury Stock 1994
81/2%	Treasury Stock 1994 ‘‘A’’
2%	Index-Linked Treasury Stock 1994
3%	Exchequer Gas Stock 1990–95
12%	Treasury Stock 1995
101/4%	Exchequer Stock 1995
123/4%	Treasury Loan 1995
9%	Treasury Loan 1992–96
151/4%	Treasury Loan 1996
131/4%	Exchequer Loan 1996
14%	Treasury Stock 1996
2%	Index-Linked Treasury Stock 1996
10%	Conversion Stock 1996
10%	Conversion Stock 1996 ‘‘A’’
10%	Conversion Stock 1996 ‘‘B’’
131/4%	Treasury Loan 1997
101/2%	Exchequer Stock 1997
83/4%	Treasury Loan 1997
83/4%	Treasury Loan 1997 ‘‘B’’
83/4%	Treasury Loan 1997 ‘‘C’’
83/4%	Treasury Loan 1997 ‘‘D’’
83/4%	Treasury Loan 1997 ‘‘E’’
15%	Exchequer Stock 1997
7%	Treasury Convertible Stock 1997
63/4%	Treasury Loan 1995–98
151/2%	Treasury Loan 1998
12%	Exchequer Stock 1998
12%	Exchequer Stock 1998 ‘‘A’’
93/4%	Exchequer Stock 1998
93/4%	Exchequer Stock 1998 ‘‘A’’
71/4%	Treasury Stock 1998 ‘‘A’’
71/4%	Treasury Stock 1998 ‘‘B’’
12%	Exchequer Stock 1998 ‘‘B’’
45/8%	Index-Linked Treasury Stock 1998
71/4%	Treasury Stock 1998
91/2%	Treasury Loan 1999
101/2%	Treasury Stock 1999
121/4%	Exchequer Stock 1999
121/4%	Exchequer Stock 1999 ‘‘A’’
121/4%	Exchequer Stock 1999 ‘‘B’’
21/2%	Index-Linked Treasury Convertible Stock 1999

101/4%	Conversion Stock 1999
6%	Treasury Stock 1999
	Floating Rate Treasury Stock 1999
9%	Conversion Stock 2000
9%	Conversion Stock 2000 "A"
9%	Conversion Stock 2000 "B"
9%	Conversion Stock 2000 "C"
81/2%	Treasury Loan 2000
8%	Treasury Stock 2000
8%	Treasury Stock 2000 "A"
13%	Treasury Stock 2000
13%	Treasury Stock 2000 "A"
7%	Treasury Stock 2001
7%	Treasury Stock 2001 "A"
14%	Treasury Stock 1998–2001
21/2%	Index-Linked Treasury Stock 2001
93/4%	Conversion Stock 2001
10%	Treasury Stock 2001
91/2%	Conversion Loan 2001
10%	Treasury Stock 2001 "A"
10%	Treasury Stock 2001 "B"
	Floating Rate Treasury Stock 2001
12%	Exchequer Stock 1999–2002
12%	Exchequer Stock 1999–2002 "A"
91/2%	Conversion Stock 2002
10%	Conversion Stock 2002
9%	Exchequer Stock 2002
7%	Treasury Stock 2002
93/4%	Treasury Stock 2002
93/4%	Treasury Stock 2002 "A"
93/4%	Treasury Stock 2002 "B"
93/4%	Treasury Stock 2002 "C"
133/4%	Treasury Stock 2000–2003
133/4%	Treasury Stock 2000–2003 "A"
21/2%	Index-Linked Treasury Stock 2003
93/4%	Conversion Loan 2003
61/2%	Treasury Stock 2003
8%	Treasury Stock 2003
8%	Treasury Stock 2003 "A"
10%	Treasury Stock 2003
10%	Treasury Stock 2003 "A"
10%	Treasury Stock 2003 "B"
31/2%	Funding Stock 1999–2004
111/2%	Treasury Stock 2001–2004
91/2%	Conversion Stock 2004
10%	Treasury Stock 2004

63/4%	Treasury Stock 2004
5%	Treasury Stock 2004
63/4%	Treasury Stock 2004 ‘‘A’’
43/8%	Index-Linked Treasury Stock 2004
91/2%	Conversion Stock 2004 ‘‘A’’
121/2%	Treasury Stock 2003–2005
121/2%	Treasury Stock 2003–2005 ‘‘A’’
101/2%	Exchequer Stock 2005
91/2%	Conversion Stock 2005
91/2%	Conversion Stock 2005 ‘‘A’’
81/2%	Treasury Stock 2005
8%	Treasury Loan 2002–2006
8%	Treasury Loan 2002–2006 ‘‘A’’
2%	Index-Linked Treasury Stock 2006
93/4%	Conversion Stock 2006
71/2%	Treasury Stock 2006
73/4%	Treasury Stock 2006
113/4%	Treasury Stock 2003–2007
113/4%	Treasury Stock 2003–2007 ‘‘A’’
71/4%	Treasury Stock 2007
41/2%	Treasury Stock 2007
81/2%	Treasury Loan 2007
81/2%	Treasury Loan 2007 ‘‘A’’
81/2%	Treasury Loan 2007 ‘‘B’’
81/2%	Treasury Loan 2007 ‘‘C’’
131/2%	Treasury Stock 2004–2008
9%	Treasury Loan 2008
9%	Treasury Loan 2008 ‘‘A’’
9%	Treasury Loan 2008 ‘‘B’’
9%	Treasury Loan 2008 ‘‘C’’
9%	Treasury Loan 2008 ‘‘D’’
5%	Treasury Stock 2008
21/2%	Index-Linked Treasury Stock 2009
53/4%	Treasury Stock 2009
8%	Treasury Stock 2009
4%	Treasury Stock 2009
8%	Treasury Stock 2009 ‘‘A’’
43/4%	Treasury Stock 2010
61/4%	Treasury Stock 2010
21/2%	Index-Linked Treasury Stock 2011
9%	Conversion Loan 2011
9%	Conversion Loan 2011 ‘‘A’’
9%	Conversion Loan 2011 ‘‘B’’
9%	Conversion Loan 2011 ‘‘C’’
9%	Conversion Loan 2011 ‘‘D’’
31/4%	Treasury Gilt 2011

41/4%	Treasury Gilt 2011
51/2%	Treasury Stock 2008–2012
9%	Treasury Stock 2012
9%	Treasury Stock 2012 "A"
5%	Treasury Stock 2012
51/4%	Treasury Gilt 2012
21/2%	Index-Linked Treasury Stock 2013
41/2%	Treasury Gilt 2013
8%	Treasury Stock 2013
21/4%	Treasury Gilt 2014
5%	Treasury Stock 2014
73/4%	Treasury Loan 2012–2015
23/4%	Treasury Gilt 2015
43/4%	Treasury Stock 2015
8%	Treasury Stock 2015
8%	Treasury Stock 2015 "A"
2%	Treasury Gilt 2016
21/2%	Treasury Stock 1986–2016
21/2%	Index-Linked Treasury Stock 2016
21/2%	Index-Linked Treasury Stock 2016 "A"
4%	Treasury Gilt 2016
12%	Exchequer Stock 2013–2017
1%	Treasury Gilt 2017
11/4%	Index-Linked Treasury Gilt 2017
13/4%	Treasury Gilt 2017
83/4%	Treasury Stock 2017
83/4%	Treasury Stock 2017 "A"
5%	Treasury Gilt 2018
11/4	Treasury Gilt 2018
01/8%	Index-linked Treasury Gilt 2019
33/4%	Treasury Gilt 2019
13/4	Treasury Gilt 2019
41/2%	Treasury Gilt 2019
21/2%	Index-Linked Treasury Stock 2020
2%	Treasury Gilt 2020
33/4%	Treasury Gilt 2020
43/4%	Treasury Stock 2020
11/2%	Treasury Gilt 2021
33/4%	Treasury Gilt 2021
8%	Treasury Stock 2021
13/4%	Treasury Gilt 2022
4%	Treasury Gilt 2022
17/8%	Index-Linked Treasury Gilt 2022
21/4	Treasury Gilt 2023
21/2%	Index-Linked Treasury Stock 2024
23/4	Treasury Gilt 2024
01/8%	Index-linked Treasury Gilt 2024

2%	Treasury Gilt 2025
5%	Treasury Stock 2025
01/8%	Index-linked Treasury Gilt 2026
11/4%	Index-Linked Treasury Gilt 2027
41/4%	Treasury Gilt 2027
6%	Treasury Stock 2028
01/8%	Index-linked Treasury Gilt 2029
41/8%	Index-Linked Treasury Stock 2030
43/4%	Treasury Gilt 2030
41/4%	Treasury Stock 2032
11/4%	Index-Linked Treasury Gilt 2032
03/4%	Index-linked Treasury Gilt 2034
41/2%	Treasury Gilt 2034
2%	Index-linked Treasury Stock 2035
41/4%	Treasury Stock 2036
11/8%	Index-Linked Treasury Gilt 2037
43/4%	Treasury Stock 2038
41/4%	Treasury Gilt 2039
05/8%	Index-Linked Treasury Gilt 2040
41/4%	Treasury Gilt 2040
41/2%	Treasury Gilt 2042
05/8%	Index-Linked Treasury Gilt 2042
31/4%	Treasury Gilt 2044
01/8%	Index-linked Treasury Gilt 2044
31/2%	Treasury Gilt 2045
41/4%	Treasury Gilt 2046
01/8%	Index-linked Treasury Gilt 2046
03/4%	Index-Linked Treasury Gilt 2047
41/4%	Treasury Gilt 2049
01/2%	Index-Linked Treasury Gilt 2050
33/4%	Treasury Gilt 2052
01/4%	Index-linked Treasury Gilt 2052
11/4%	Index-linked Treasury Gilt 2055
41/4%	Treasury Gilt 2055
01/8%	Index-linked Treasury Gilt 2058
4%	Treasury Gilt 2060
01/2%	Index-Linked Treasury Gilt 2060
03/8%	Index-linked Treasury Gilt 2062
01/8	Index-linked Treasury Gilt 2068
31/2	Treasury Gilt 2068

SECURITIES ISSUED BY CERTAIN PUBLIC CORPORATIONS AND GUARANTEED BY THE TREASURY

3%	North of Scotland Electricity Stock 1989–92

History – The list of securities in Sch. 9, Pt. II includes securities added by SI 1993/950, SI 1994/2656, SI 1996/1031, SI 2001/1122, SI 2002/2849, SI 2004/438, SI 2005/276, SI 2006/184, SI 2006/3170, SI 2008/1588, SI 2010/416, SI 2011/1295, SI 2012/1843, SI 2013/13, 2013/2983, SI 2014/1120 and SI 2015/1790.

Derivations – CGTA 1979, Sch. 2, Pt. II, including securities added by SI 1979/1231 and 1979/1676, SI 1980/507, 1980/922 and 1980/1910, SI 1981/615 and 1981/1879, SI 1982/413 and 1982/1774, SI 1983/1774, SI 1984/1966, SI 1986/12, SI 1987/259, SI 1988/360, SI 1989/944, SI 1991/2678.

SCHEDULE 10 – CONSEQUENTIAL AMENDMENTS

Section 290

POST OFFICE ACT 1969 c. 48

1 [Amends Post Office Act 1969, s. 74.]

TAXES MANAGEMENT ACT 1970 c. 9

2(1) The Taxes Management Act 1970 shall have effect subject to the following amendments.

2(2) [Amends TMA 1970 s. 11(1)(b), 27(1), 47(1), 57(1)(a), 111 and 119(4).]

2(3) [Amends TMA 1970, s. 12(2).]

2(4) [Amends TMA 1970, s. 25(9).]

2(5) [Omitted by SI 2009/2035, art. 2 and Schedule, para. 60(f)(i).]

2(6) [Amends TMA 1970, s. 30(2)(a), (3)(a).]

2(7) [Amends TMA 1970, s. 31(3)(c).]

2(8) [Amends TMA 1970, s. 86(4).]

2(9) [Amends TMA 1970, s. 87A(3).]

2(10) [Amends TMA 1970, s. 98; partially omitted by SI 2009/2035, art. 2 and Schedule, para. 60(f)(ii).]

2(11) [Amends TMA 1970, s. 118(1).]

History – In para. 2(2) words "78(3)(b)" repealed by FA 1995, s. 162 and Sch. 29, Pt. VIII(16) with effect for years after 1995–96 and, for corporation tax purposes, for accounting periods beginning after 31 March 1996.
Para. 2(5) omitted by SI 2009/2035, art. 2 and Schedule, para. 60(f)(i), with effect from 13 August 2009.
Para. 2(10)(a)(iv) and (v) omitted by SI 2009/2035, art. 2 and Schedule, para. 60(f)(ii), with effect from 13 August 2009.

Notes – The appointed day (para. 2(9)) is 30 September 1993 (the appointed day for Pay and File) by virtue of SI 1992/3066.

FINANCE ACT 1973 c. 51

3 [Repealed by TIOPA 2010, s. 378 and Sch. 10, Pt. 12.]

History – Para. 3 repealed by TIOPA 2010, s. 378 and Sch. 10, Pt. 12, with effect for corporation tax purposes for accounting periods ending on or after 1 April 2010, for income tax and capital gains tax purposes for the tax year 2010–11 and subsequent tax years, and for petroleum revenue tax purposes for chargeable periods beginning on or after 1 July 2010.

BRITISH AEROSPACE ACT 1980 c. 26

4 [Amends British Aerospace Act 1980, s. 12(2).]

BRITISH TELECOMMUNICATIONS ACT 1981 c. 38

5 [Amends British Telecommunications Act 1981, s. 82(1).]

VALUE ADDED TAX ACT 1983 c. 55

6 [Amends VATA 1983, Sch. 6, Grp. 11; subsequently repealed by VATA 1994, Sch. 15, with effect from 1 September 1994.]

TELECOMMUNICATIONS ACT 1984 c. 12

7 [Amends Telecommunications Act 1984, s. 72(2).]

INHERITANCE TAX ACT 1984 c. 51

8(1) The Inheritance Tax Act shall have effect subject to the following amendments.

8(2) [Amends IHTA 1984, s. 31(4G)(b).]

8(3) [Amends IHTA 1984, s. 79(2).]

8(4) [Amends IHTA 1984, s. 97.]

8(5) [Amends IHTA 1984, s. 107(4), 113A(6) and 124A(6).]

8(6) [Amends IHTA 1984, s. 135.]

8(7) [Amends IHTA 1984, s. 138.]

8(8) [Amends IHTA 1984, s. 165.]

8(9) [Amends IHTA 1984, s. 183.]

8(10) [Amends IHTA 1984, s. 187.]

8(11) [Amends IHTA 1984, s. 194.]

8(12) [Amends IHTA 1984, s. 270.]

8(13) [Amends IHTA 1984, s. 272.]

FINANCE ACT 1985 c. 54

9 [Amends FA 1985, s. 81.]

TRUSTEE SAVINGS BANK ACT 1985 c. 58

10(1) [Amends Trustee Savings Bank Act 1985, Sch. 2, para. 2.]

10(2) [Amends Trustee Savings Bank Act 1985, Sch. 2, para. 3.]

10(3) [Amends Trustee Savings Bank Act 1985, Sch. 2, para. 4.]

10(4) [Amends Trustee Savings Bank Act 1985, Sch. 2, para. 9.]

TRANSPORT ACT 1985 c. 67

11 [Amends Transport Act 1985, s. 130.]

AIRPORTS ACT 1986 c. 31

12 [Amends Airports Act 1986, s. 77(2).]

GAS ACT 1986 c. 44

13 [Amends Gas Act 1986, s. 60(2).]

INCOME AND CORPORATION TAXES ACT 1988 c. 1

14(1) The Income and Corporation Taxes Act 1988 shall have effect subject to the following amendments.

14(2) [Substitutes ICTA 1988, s. 11(2)(b).]

14(3) [Amends ICTA 1988, s. 56(5).]

14(4) [Amends ICTA 1988, s. 119(1).]

14(5) [Repealed by ITTOIA 2005, s. 884 and Sch. 3 with effect, for income tax purposes, for tax year 2005–06 and subsequent tax years, and, for corporation tax purposes, for accounting periods ending after 5 April 2005.]

14(6) [Repealed by FA 1996, s. 205 and Sch. 41, Pt. V(3) as respects accounting periods ending after 31 March 1996.]

14(7) [Repealed by CTA 2009, s. 1326 and Sch. 3, Pt. 1.]

History – Para. 14(7) repealed by CTA 2009, s. 1326 and Sch. 3, Pt. 1, with effect for corporation tax purposes for accounting periods ending on or after 1 April 2009, and for income tax and capital gains tax purposes for the tax year 2009–10 and subsequent tax years.

14(8) [Repealed by FA 1997, s. 113 and Sch. 18, Pt. VI(10), with effect in relation to, and transfers under, any arrangement made on or after 1 July 1997 (the appointed day for the purposes of FA 1997, Sch. 10 by virtue of SI 1997/991 (C. 33)); previously amended ICTA 1988, s. 129(4).]

14(9)–(12) [Repealed by ITEPA 2003, Sch. 8, Pt. 1 with effect for 2003–04 and subsequent tax years.]

14(13) [Amends ICTA 1988, s. 187(2).]

14(14) [Repealed by CTA 2010, s. 1181 and Sch. 3, Pt. 1.]

History – Para. 14(14) repealed by CTA 2010, s. 1181 and Sch. 3, Pt. 1, with effect for corporation tax purposes for accounting periods ending on or after 1 April 2010, and for income tax and capital gains tax purposes for the tax year 2010–11 and subsequent tax years.

14(15) [Repealed by FA 1998, s. 165 and Sch. 27, Pt. III(2) with effect in relation to disposals on or after 6 April 1999.]

14(16) [Repealed by ITTOIA 2005, s. 884 and Sch. 3 with effect, for income tax purposes, for tax year 2005–06 and subsequent tax years, and, for corporation tax purposes, for accounting periods ending after 5 April 2005.]

Notes – Para. 14(6) has been rewritten into the provisions of ITTOIA 2005, s. 412(5).

14(17) [Amends ICTA 1988, s. 299, 305.]

14(18) [Amends ICTA 1988, s. 312.]

14(19) [Repealed by CTA 2010, s. 1181 and Sch. 3, Pt. 1.]

History – Para. 14(19) repealed by CTA 2010, s. 1181 and Sch. 3, Pt. 1, with effect for corporation tax purposes for accounting periods ending on or after 1 April 2010, and for income tax and capital gains tax purposes for the tax year 2010–11 and subsequent tax years. Para. 14(19) previously repealed in part by ITTOIA 2005, s. 884 and Sch. 3 with effect, for income tax purposes, for tax year 2005–06 and subsequent tax years, and, for corporation tax purposes, for accounting periods ending after 5 April 2005

14(20) [Repealed by CTA 2010, s. 1181 and Sch. 3, Pt. 1.]

History – Para. 14(20) repealed by CTA 2010, s. 1181 and Sch. 3, Pt. 1, with effect for corporation tax purposes for accounting periods ending on or after 1 April 2010, and for income tax and capital gains tax purposes for the tax year 2010–11 and subsequent tax years.

14(21) [Repealed by FA 2004, s. 326 and Sch. 42, Pt. 3 with effect on 6 April 2006.]

14(22) [Omitted by FA 2012, s. 146 and Sch. 16, para. 247(d).]

History – Para. 14(22) omitted by FA 2012, s. 146 and Sch. 16, para. 247(d) in relation to accounting periods beginning on or after 1 January 2013 (FA 2012, s. 148) but subject to transitional provisions in FA 2012, Sch. 17. Where an accounting period would otherwise straddle 1 January 2013, it is deemed to end on 31 December 2012 (FA 2012, s. 149).
Former para. 14(22)(b) repealed by FA 2007, s. 114 and Sch. 27, Part 2(10), with effect in relation to periods of account beginning on or after 1 January 2007 (the same date from which ICTA 1988, s. 440(5) is omitted by FA 2007, s. 41 and Sch. 10, para. 10(2)(b)).

14(23) [Omitted by FA 2012, s. 146 and Sch. 16, para. 247(d).]

History – Para. 14(23) omitted by FA 2012, s. 146 and Sch. 16, para. 247(d) in relation to accounting periods beginning on or after 1 January 2013 (FA 2012, s. 148) but subject to transitional provisions in FA 2012, Sch. 17. Where an accounting period would otherwise straddle 1 January 2013, it is deemed to end on 31 December 2012 (FA 2012, s. 149).

14(24) [Omitted by FA 2012, s. 146 and Sch. 16, para. 247(d).]

History – Para. 14(24) omitted by FA 2012, s. 146 and Sch. 16, para. 247(d) in relation to accounting periods beginning on or after 1 January 2013 (FA 2012, s. 148) but subject to transitional provisions in FA 2012, Sch. 17. Where an accounting period would otherwise straddle 1 January 2013, it is deemed to end on 31 December 2012 (FA 2012, s. 149).

14(25) [Repealed by FA 2007, s. 114 and Sch. 27, Part 2(10).]

History – Para. 14(25) (which amended the repealed ICTA 1988, s. 444A(8)) repealed by FA 2007, s. 114 and Sch. 27, Part 2(9), with effect in relation to periods of account beginning on or after 1 January 2007 (the same date from which ICTA 1988, s. 444A(8) is omitted by FA 2007, s. 40 and Sch. 9, para. 2(3)(b)).

14(26) [Amends ICTA 1988, s. 450(6).]

14(27) [Repealed by CTA 2009, s. 1326 and Sch. 3, Pt. 1.]

History – Para. 14(27) repealed by CTA 2009, s. 1326 and Sch. 3, Pt. 1, with effect for corporation tax purposes for accounting periods ending on or after 1 April 2009, and for income tax and capital gains tax purposes for the tax year 2009–10 and subsequent tax years.

14(28) [Repealed by CTA 2009, s. 1326 and Sch. 3, Pt. 1.]

History – Para. 14(28) repealed by CTA 2009, s. 1326 and Sch. 3, Pt. 1, with effect for corporation tax purposes for accounting periods ending on or after 1 April 2009, and for income tax and capital gains tax purposes for the tax year 2009–10 and subsequent tax years.

14(29) [Repealed by FA 1996, s. 205 and Sch. 41, Pt. V(3) as respects accounting periods ending after 31 March 1996.]

14(30) [Amends ICTA 1988, s. 502(1); inserts s. 502(1A).]

14(31) [Amends ICTA 1988, s. 505(3), (5)(b) and (6).]

14(32) [Repealed by CTA 2010, s. 1181 and Sch. 3, Pt. 1.]

History – Para. 14(32) repealed by CTA 2010, s. 1181 and Sch. 3, Pt. 1, with effect for corporation tax purposes for accounting periods ending on or after 1 April 2010, and for income tax and capital gains tax purposes for the tax year 2010–11 and subsequent tax years.

14(33) [Amends ICTA 1988, s. 574(1).]

14(34) [Amends provisions as below.]

(a) [Amends ICTA 1988, s. 575(1)(c).]

(b) [Amends ICTA 1988, s. 575(2).]

(c) [Amends ICTA 1988, s. 575(3).]

14(35) [Repealed by ITA 2007, s. 1031 and Sch. 3, Pt. 1.]

History – Para. 14(35) repealed by ITA 2007, s. 1031 and Sch. 3, Pt. 1, with effect from 6 April 2007.

Notes – Para. 14(35) rewritten for income tax as ITA 2007, s. 148(8).

14(36) [Repealed by ITA 2007, s. 1031 and Sch. 3, Pt. 1.]

History – Para. 14(36) repealed by ITA 2007, s. 1031 and Sch. 3, Pt. 1, with effect from 6 April 2007.

Notes – Para. 14(36) rewritten for income tax as ITA 2007, s. 619(1), 620(7).

14(37) [Repealed by ITA 2007, s. 1031 and Sch. 3, Pt. 1.]

History – Para. 14(37) repealed by ITA 2007, s. 1031 and Sch. 3, Pt. 1, with effect from 6 April 2007.

Notes – Para. 14(37) rewritten for income tax as ITA 2007, s. 643(6).

14(38) [Repealed by ITA 2007, s. 1031 and Sch. 3, Pt. 1.]

History – Para. 14(38) repealed by ITA 2007, s. 1031 and Sch. 3, Pt. 1, with effect from 6 April 2007.

Notes – Para. 14(38) rewritten for income tax as ITA 2007, s. 668(6).

14(39) [Repealed by FA 1997, s. 113 and Sch. 18, Pt. VI(10), with effect in relation to, and transfers under, any arrangement made on or after 1 July 1997 (the appointed day for the purposes of FA 1997, Sch. 10 by virtue of SI 1997/991 (C. 33)); previously amended ICTA 1988, s. 727(2).]

14(40) [Omitted by FA 2008, s. 66(4)(d).]

History – Para. 14(40) omitted by FA 2008, s. 66(4)(d) with effect in relation to cases where the purchase by the first buyer (within the meaning of ICTA 1988, s. 731(2)) is made on or after 1 April 2008.

14(41) [Omitted by FA 2008, s. 66(4)(d).]

History – Para. 14(41) omitted by FA 2008, s. 66(4)(d) with effect in relation to cases where the purchase by the first buyer (within the meaning of ICTA 1988, s. 731(2)) is made on or after 1 April 2008.

14(42) [Repealed by FA 2000, s. 156 and Sch. 40, Pt. II(10) with effect in relation to any transfer of value to which the material time is on or after 21 March 2000.]

14(43) [Repealed by SI 2009/3001, reg. 13(2) and Sch. 2.]

History – Para. 14(43) repealed by SI 2009/3001, reg. 13(2) and Sch. 2, with effect from 1 December 2009 for various purposes (in accordance with the provisions of SI 2009/3001, reg. 1), subject to transitional and savings provisions in SI 2009/3001, Sch. 1.
At the time of its repeal by SI 2009/3001, para. 14(43) was to have been omitted prospectively by FA 2008, s. 41(7)(c), with effect from a day which was to have been appointed (FA 2008, s. 41(8)).

14(44) [Repealed by SI 2009/3001, reg. 13(2) and Sch. 2.]

History – Para. 14(44) repealed by SI 2009/3001, reg. 13(2) and Sch. 2, with effect from 1 December 2009 for various purposes (in accordance with the provisions of SI 2009/3001, reg. 1), subject to transitional and savings provisions in SI 2009/3001, Sch. 1.
At the time of its repeal by SI 2009/3001, para. 14(44) was to have been omitted prospectively by FA 2008, s. 41(7)(c), with effect from a day which was to have been appointed (FA 2008, s. 41(8)).

14(45) [Repealed by SI 2009/3001, reg. 13(2) and Sch. 2.]

History – Para. 14(45) repealed by SI 2009/3001, reg. 13(2) and Sch. 2, with effect from 1 December 2009 for various purposes (in accordance with the provisions of SI 2009/3001, reg. 1), subject to transitional and savings provisions in SI 2009/3001, Sch. 1.
At the time of its repeal by SI 2009/3001, para. 14(45) was to have been omitted prospectively by FA 2008, s. 41(7)(c), with effect from a day which was to have been appointed (FA 2008, s. 41(8)).

14(46) [Repealed by FA 2004, s. 326 and Sch. 42, Pt. 2(18) with effect for account periods (within the meaning of ICTA 1988, Pt. 17, Ch. 5) ending on or after 22 July 2004.]

14(47) [Repealed by SI 2009/3001, reg. 13(2) and Sch. 2.]

(a) [Repealed by SI 2009/3001, reg. 13(2) and Sch. 2.]

(b) [Repealed by SI 2009/3001, reg. 13(2) and Sch. 2.]

(c) [Omitted by FA 2008, s. 25 and Sch. 7, para. 95.]

(d) [Repealed by SI 2009/3001, reg. 13(2) and Sch. 2.]

History – Para. 14(47) repealed by SI 2009/3001, reg. 13(2) and Sch. 2, with effect from 1 December 2009 for various purposes (in accordance with the provisions of SI 2009/3001, reg. 1), subject to transitional and savings provisions in SI 2009/3001, Sch. 1.
At the time of its repeal by SI 2009/3001, para. 14(47) was to have been omitted prospectively by FA 2008, s. 41(7)(c), with effect from a day which was to have been appointed (FA 2008, s. 41(8)).
Para. 14(47)(c) omitted by FA 2008, s. 25 and Sch. 7, para. 95 with effect from 2008–09 (FA 2008, Sch. 7, para. 98).

14(48) [Repealed by SI 2009/3001, reg. 13(2) and Sch. 2.]

(a) [Repealed by SI 2009/3001, reg. 13(2) and Sch. 2.]

(b) [Omitted by FA 2008, s. 25 and Sch. 7, para. 95.]

(c) [Omitted by FA 2008, s. 25 and Sch. 7, para. 95.]

(d) [Omitted by FA 2008, s. 25 and Sch. 7, para. 95.]

History – Para. 14(48) repealed by SI 2009/3001, reg. 13(2) and Sch. 2, with effect from 1 December 2009 for various purposes (in accordance with the provisions of SI 2009/3001, reg. 1), subject to transitional and savings provisions in SI 2009/3001, Sch. 1.
At the time of its repeal by SI 2009/3001, para. 14(48) was to have been omitted prospectively by FA 2008, s. 41(7)(c), with effect from a day which was to have been appointed (FA 2008, s. 41(8)).
Para. 14(48)(b)–(d) omitted by FA 2008, s. 25 and Sch. 7, para. 95 with effect from 2008–09 (FA 2008, s. 41(8)). Former para. 14(48)(b)–(d) amended ICTA 1988, s. 762.

14(49) [Repealed by SI 2009/3001, reg. 13(2) and Sch. 2.]

History – Para. 14(49) repealed by SI 2009/3001, reg. 13(2) and Sch. 2, with effect from 1 December 2009 for various purposes (in accordance with the provisions of SI 2009/3001, reg. 1), subject to transitional and savings provisions in SI 2009/3001, Sch. 1.
At the time of its repeal by SI 2009/3001, para. 14(49) was to have been omitted prospectively by FA 2008, s. 41(7)(c), with effect from a day which was to have been appointed (FA 2008, s. 41(8)).

14(50) [Repealed by ITA 2007, s. 1031 and Sch. 3, Pt. 1.]

History – Para. 14(50) repealed by ITA 2007, s. 1031 and Sch. 3, Pt. 1, with effect from 6 April 2007.

14(51) [Repealed by CTA 2010, s. 1181 and Sch. 3, Pt. 1.]

History – Para. 14(51) repealed by CTA 2010, s. 1181 and Sch. 3, Pt. 1, with effect for corporation tax purposes for accounting periods ending on or after 1 April 2010, and for income tax and capital gains tax purposes for the tax year 2010–11 and subsequent tax years.

14(52) [Repealed by ITTOIA 2005, s. 884 and Sch. 3 with effect, for income tax purposes, for tax year 2005–06 and subsequent tax years, and, for corporation tax purposes, for accounting periods ending after 5 April 2005.]

Notes – Para. 14(52) has been rewritten into the provisions of ITTOIA 2005, s. 749.

14(53) [Amends provisions as below.]

(a) [Amends ICTA 1988, s. 831(3).]

(b) [Amends ICTA 1988, s. 831(5).]

14(54) [Repealed by CTA 2010, s. 1181 and Sch. 3, Pt. 1.]

History – Para. 14(54) repealed by CTA 2010, s. 1181 and Sch. 3, Pt. 1, with effect for corporation tax purposes for accounting periods ending on or after 1 April 2010, and for income tax and capital gains tax purposes for the tax year 2010–11 and subsequent tax years.

14(55) [Repealed by CTA 2010, s. 1181 and Sch. 3, Pt. 1.]

History – Para. 14(55) repealed by CTA 2010, s. 1181 and Sch. 3, Pt. 1, with effect for corporation tax purposes for accounting periods ending on or after 1 April 2010, and for income tax and capital gains tax purposes for the tax year 2010–11 and subsequent tax years.

14(56) [Amends ICTA 1988, s. 843(2).]

14(57) [Repealed by FA 1996, s. 205 and Sch. 41, Pt. V(3) as respects accounting periods ending after 31 March 1996.]

14(58) [Amends ICTA 1988, Sch. 10, para. 5(7).]

14(59) [Amends ICTA 1988, Sch. 20, para. 12(2).]

14(60) [Amends ICTA 1988, Sch. 22, para. 7.]

14(61) [Repealed by FA 1997, s. 113 and Sch. 18, Pt. VI(10), with effect in relation to, and transfers under, any arrangement made on or after 1 July 1997 (the appointed day for the purposes of FA 1997, Sch. 10 by virtue of SI 1997/991 (C. 33)); previously amended ICTA 1988, Sch. 23A.]

14(62) [Amends ICTA 1988, Sch. 26, para. 3.]

14(63) [Repealed by SI 2009/3001, reg. 13(2) and Sch. 2.]

History – Para. 14(63) repealed by SI 2009/3001, reg. 13(2) and Sch. 2, with effect from 1 December 2009 for various purposes (in accordance with the provisions of SI 2009/3001, reg. 1), subject to transitional and savings provisions in SI 2009/3001, Sch. 1.

At the time of its repeal by SI 2009/3001, para. 14(63) was to have been omitted prospectively by FA 2008, s. 41(7)(c), with effect from a day which was to have been appointed (FA 2008, s. 41(8)).

Para. 14(63)(b)(iv) repealed by FA 1995, s. 162 and Sch. 29, Pt. VIII(5) in relation to accounting periods beginning on or after 1 November 1994, subject to the provisions of FA 1995, s. 51 and Sch. 8, para. 55(2).

BRITISH STEEL ACT c. 35

15 [Amends British Steel Act 1988 s. 11(2).]

FINANCE ACT 1988 c. 39

16(1) The Finance Act 1988 shall have effect subject to the following amendments.

16(2) [Amends FA 1988, s. 50(4).]

16(3)–(5) [Repealed by ITEPA 2003, Sch. 8, Pt. 1 with effect for 2003–04 and subsequent tax years.]

16(6) [Repealed by TIOPA 2010, s. 378 and Sch. 10, Pt. 12.]

16(7) [Amends FA 1988, Sch. 12, para. 6(2).]

History – Para. 16(6) repealed by TIOPA 2010, s. 378 and Sch. 10, Pt. 12, with effect for corporation tax purposes for accounting periods ending on or after 1 April 2010, for income tax and capital gains tax purposes for the tax year 2010–11 and subsequent tax years, and for petroleum revenue tax purposes for chargeable periods beginning on or after 1 July 2010.

HEALTH AND MEDICINES ACT 1988 c. 49

17 [Amends Health and Medicines Act 1988, s. 6(2).]

WATER ACT 1989 c. 15

18 [Amends provisions as below.]

(a) [Amends Water Act 1989, s. 95(4).]

(b) [Amends Water Act 1989, s. 95(5).]

(c) [Amends Water Act 1989, s. 95(6).]

FINANCE ACT 1989 c. 26

19(1) [Amends FA 1989, s. 69(9).]

19(2) *[Amends FA 1989, s. 70(2).]*

19(3) [Amends FA 1989, s. 158(2).]

19(4) [Substitutes FA 1989, s. 178(2)(i).]

19(5) [Amends FA 1989, Sch. 5, para. 8, 11.]

19(6) [Repealed by FA 1996, Sch. 41, Pt. V(3) as respects accounting periods ending after 31 March 1996.]

ELECTRICITY ACT 1989 c. 29

20(1) [Amends Electricity Act 1989, Sch. 11, para. 2; inserts para. 2A.]

20(2) [Amends Electricity Act 1989, Sch. 11, para. 3.]

20(3) [Amends Electricity Act 1989, Sch. 11, para. 4, 5.]

CAPITAL ALLOWANCES ACT 1990 c. 1

21(1) [Repealed by CAA 2001, s. 580 and Sch. 4.]

History – Para. 21, repealed by CAA 2001, s. 580 and Sch. 4, with effect as respects allowances and charges falling to be made for chargeable periods ending, for income tax purposes, on or after 6 April 2001, and for corporation tax purposes, on or after 1 April 2001; para. 21(1) previously inserted CAA 1990, s. 118A, para. 21(2) inserted CAA 1990, s. 138(7A)

FINANCE ACT 1990 c. 29

22(1) The Finance Act 1990 shall have effect subject to the following amendments.

22(2) [Amends FA 1990, s. 116(5).]

22(3) [Amends FA 1990, s. 120.]

22(4) [Repealed by FA 1996, Sch. 41, Pt. V(3) as respects accounting periods ending after 31 March 1996.]

22(5) [Amends provisions as below.]

(a) [Amends FA 1990, Sch. 12, para. 2.]

(b) [Amends FA 1990, Sch. 12, para. 4–6.]

(c) [Amends FA 1990, Sch. 12, para. 7.]

(d) [Amends FA 1990, Sch. 12, para. 10.]

FINANCE ACT 1991 c. 31

23 [Amends FA 1991, s. 72(4).]

PORTS ACT 1991 c. 52

24(1) [Amends Ports Act 1991, s. 16.]

24(2) [Amends provisions as below.]

(a) [Amends Ports Act 1991, s. 17.]

(b) [Amends Ports Act 1991, s. 17(6).]

(c) [Amends Ports Act 1991, s. 17(7) as below.]

  (i) [Substitutes Ports Act 1991, s. 17(7)(a).]

  (ii) [Amends Ports Act 1991, s. 17(7)(b).]

(d) [Amends Ports Act 1991, s. 17(13).]

24(3) [Amends provisions as below.]

(a) [Amends Ports Act 1991 s. 18(2), (8).]

(b) [Amends Ports Act 1991, s. 18(4).]

24(4) [Amends Ports Act 1991, s. 20.]

24(5) [Amends provisions as below.]

(a) [Amends Ports Act 1991, s. 35(3).]

(b) [Amends Ports Act 1991, s. 35(6).]

24(6) [Amends Ports Act 1991, s. 40(1).]

BRITISH TECHNOLOGY GROUP ACT 1991 c. 66

25 [Amends British Technology Group Act 1991, s. 12(2).]

SCHEDULE 11 – TRANSITIONAL PROVISIONS AND SAVINGS

Section 290

Part I – Valuation

PRELIMINARY

1(1) This Part of this Schedule has effect in cases where the market value of an asset at a time before the commencement of this Act is material to the computation of a gain under this Act; and in this Part any reference to an asset includes a reference to any part of an asset.

1(2) Where sub-paragraph (1) above applies, the market value of an asset (or part of an asset) at any time before the commencement of this Act shall be determined in accordance with sections 272 to 274 but subject to the following provisions of this Part.

1(3) In any case where section 274 applies in accordance with sub-paragraph (2) above the reference in that section to inheritance tax shall be construed as a reference to capital transfer tax.

Derivations – CGTA 1979, Sch. 6, para. 1.

Cross references – S. 272(6): priority of Pt. I over provisions generally determining market value.

GIFTS AND TRANSACTIONS BETWEEN CONNECTED PERSONS BEFORE 20TH MARCH 1985

2(1) Where sub-paragraph (1) above applies for the purpose of determining the market value of any asset at any time before 20th March 1985 (the date when section 71 of the Finance Act 1985, now section 19, replaced section 151 of the 1979 Act, which is reproduced below) sub-paragraphs (2) to (4) below shall apply.

2(2) Except as provided by sub-paragraph (4) below section 19 shall not apply in relation to transactions occurring before 20th March 1985.

2(3) If a person is given, or acquires from one or more persons with whom he is connected, by way of 2 or more gifts or other transactions, assets of which the aggregate market value, when considered separately, in relation to the separate gifts or other transactions, is less than their aggregate market value when considered together, then for the purposes of this Act their market value shall be taken to be the larger market value, to be apportioned rateably to the respective disposals.

2(4) Where–

(a) one or more transactions occurred on or before 19th March 1985 and one or more after that date, and

(b) had all the transactions occurred before that date sub-paragraph (3) above would apply, and had all the transactions occurred after that date section 19 would have applied,

then those transactions which occurred on or before that date and not more than 2 years before the first of those which occurred after that date shall be treated as material transactions for the purposes of section 19.

Derivations – CGTA 1979, s. 151; FA 1985, s. 71(8).

VALUATION OF ASSETS BEFORE 6TH JULY 1973

3 Section 273 shall apply for the purposes of determining the market value of any asset at any time before 6th July 1973 (the date when the provisions of section 51(1) to (3) of the Finance Act 1973, which are now contained in section 273, came into force) notwithstanding that the asset was acquired before that date or that the market value of the asset may have been fixed for the purposes of a contemporaneous disposal, and in paragraphs 4 and 5 below a **"section 273 asset"** is an asset to which section 273 applies.

Derivations – CGTA 1979, Sch. 6, para. 3.

4(1) This paragraph applies if, in a case where the market value of a section 273 asset at the time of its acquisition is material to the computation of any chargeable gain under this Act–

(a) the acquisition took place on the occasion of a death occurring after 30th March 1971 and before 6th July 1973, and

(b) by virtue of paragraph 9 below, the principal value of the asset for the purposes of estate duty on that death would, apart from this paragraph, be taken to be the market value of the asset at the date of the death for the purposes of this Act.

4(2) If the principal value referred to in sub-paragraph (1)(b) above falls to be determined as mentioned in section 55 of the Finance Act 1940 or section 15 of the Finance (No. 2) Act (Northern Ireland) 1946 (certain controlling shareholdings to be valued on an assets basis), nothing in section 273 shall affect the operation of paragraph 9 below for the purpose of determining the market value of the asset at the date of the death.

4(3) If sub-paragraph (2) above does not apply, paragraph 9 below shall not apply as mentioned in sub-paragraph (1)(b) above and the market value of the asset on its acquisition at the date of the death shall be determined in accordance with sections 272 (but with the same modifications as are made by paragraphs 7 and 8 below) and 273.

Derivations – CGTA 1979, Sch. 6, para. 7.

5(1) In any case where–

(a) before 6th July 1973 there has been a part disposal of a section 273 asset (**"the earlier disposal"**), and

(b) by virtue of any enactment, the acquisition of the asset or any part of it was deemed to be for a consideration equal to its market value, and

(c) on or after 6th July 1973 there is a disposal (including a part disposal) of the property which remained undisposed of immediately before that date (**"the later disposal"**),

sub-paragraph (2) below shall apply in computing any chargeable gain accruing on the later disposal.

5(2) Where this sub-paragraph applies, the apportionment made by virtue of paragraph 7 of Schedule 6 of the Finance Act 1965 (corresponding to section 42 of this Act) on the occasion of the earlier disposal shall be recalculated on the basis that section 273(3) of this Act was in force at the time, and applied for the purposes of the determination of–

(a) the market value referred to in sub-paragraph (1)(b) above, and

(b) the market value of the property which remained undisposed of after the earlier disposal, and

(c) if the consideration for the earlier disposal was, by virtue of any enactment, deemed to be equal to the market value of the property disposed of, that market value.

Derivations – CGTA 1979, Sch. 6, para. 8.

VALUATION OF ASSETS ON 6TH APRIL 1965

6(1) For the purpose of ascertaining the market value of any shares or securities in accordance with paragraph 1(2) of Schedule 2, section 272 shall have effect subject to the provisions of this paragraph.

6(2) Subsection (3)(a) shall have effect as if for the words, "one-quarter" there were substituted the words "one-half", and as between the amount under paragraph (a) and the amount under paragraph (b) of that subsection the higher, and not the lower, amount shall be chosen.

6(3) Subsection (5) shall have effect as if for the reference to an amount equal to the buying price there were substituted a reference to an amount halfway between the buying and selling prices.

6(4) Where the market value of any shares or securities not within section 272(3) falls to be ascertained by reference to a pair of prices quoted on a stock exchange, an adjustment shall be made so as to increase the market value by an amount corresponding to that by which any market value is increased under sub-paragraph (2) above.

Derivations – CGTA 1979, Sch. 6, para. 3.

REFERENCES TO THE LONDON STOCK EXCHANGE BEFORE 25TH MARCH 1973 AND EXCHANGE CONTROL RESTRICTIONS BEFORE 13TH DECEMBER 1979

7(1) For the purposes of ascertaining the market value of an asset before 25th March 1973 section 272(3) and (4) shall have effect subject to the following modifications–

(a) for "quoted in The Stock Exchange Daily Official List" and "quoted in that List" there shall be substituted respectively "quoted on the London Stock Exchange" and "so quoted";

(b) for "The Stock Exchange Daily Official List" there shall be substituted "the Stock Exchange Official Daily List";

(c) for "The Stock Exchange provides a more active market elsewhere than on the London trading floor" there shall be substituted "some other stock exchange in the United Kingdom affords a more active market"; and

(d) for "if the London trading floor is closed" there shall be substituted "if the London Stock Exchange is closed".

7(2) For the purposes of ascertaining the market value of an asset before 13th December 1979 section 272 shall have effect as if the following subsection were inserted after subsection (5)–

> "**272(5)** In any case where the market value of an asset is to be determined at a time before 13th December 1979 and the asset is of a kind the sale of which was (at the time the market value

is to be determined) subject to restrictions imposed under the Exchange Control Act 1947 such that part of what was paid by the purchaser was not retainable by the seller, the market value, as arrived at under subsection (1), (3), (4) or (5) above, shall be subject to such adjustment as is appropriate having regard to the difference between the amount payable by a purchaser and the amount receivable by a seller."

History – In para. 7(1)(a), the word "quoted" was substituted before the words "in The Stock Exchange" by FA 1996, s. 199 and Sch. 38, para. 12(2), with effect where the relevant date falls on or after 1 April 1996.

Derivations – Para. 7(1): CGTA 1979, Sch. 6, para. 4.
Para. 7(2): CGTA 1979, s. 150(5), Sch. 6, para. 2(5); FA 1987, s. 68(3).

DEPRECIATED VALUATIONS REFERABLE TO DEATHS BEFORE 31ST MARCH 1973

8 In any case where this Part applies, section 272(2) shall have effect as if the following proviso were inserted at the end–

"Provided that where capital gains tax is chargeable, or an allowable loss accrues, in consequence of a death before 31st March 1973 and the market value of any property on the date of death taken into account for the purposes of that tax or loss has been depreciated by reason of the death the estimate of the market value shall take that depreciation into account."

Derivations – CGTA 1979, Sch. 6, para. 2(2), proviso.

ESTATE DUTY

9(1) Where estate duty (including estate duty leviable under the law of Northern Ireland) is chargeable in respect of any property passing on a death after 30th March 1971 and the principal value of an asset forming part of that property has been ascertained (whether in any proceedings or otherwise) for the purposes of that duty, the principal value so ascertained shall, subject to paragraph 4(3) above, be taken for the purposes of this Act to be the market value of that asset at the date of the death.

9(2) Where the principal value has been reduced under section 35 of the Finance Act 1968 or section 1 of the Finance Act (Northern Ireland) 1968 (tapering relief for gifts inter vivos etc.), the reference in sub-paragraph (1) above to the principal value as ascertained for the purposes of estate duty is a reference to that value as so ascertained before the reduction.

Derivations – CGTA 1979, Sch. 6, para. 9.

Part II – Other Transitory Provisions

VALUE-SHIFTING

10(1) Section 30 applies only where the reduction in value mentioned in subsection (1) of that section (or, in a case within subsection (9) of that section, the reduction or increase in value) is after 29th March 1977.

10(2) No account shall be taken by virtue of section 31 of any reduction in the value of an asset attributable to the payment of a dividend before 14th March 1989.

10(3) No account shall be taken by virtue of section 32 of any reduction in the value of an asset attributable to the disposal of another asset before 14th March 1989.

10(4) Section 34 shall not apply where the reduction in value, by reason of which the amount referred to in subsection (1)(b) of that section falls to be calculated, occurred before 14th March 1989.

Derivations – Para. 10(1): CGTA 1979, Sch. 6, para. 11.
Para. 10(2), (3): FA 1989, s. 136(2).
Para. 10(4): FA 1989, s. 137(2).

ASSETS ACQUIRED ON DISPOSAL CHARGEABLE UNDER CASE VII OF SCHEDULE D

11(1) In this paragraph references to a disposal chargeable under Case VII are references to cases where the acquisition and disposal was in circumstances that the gain accruing on it was chargeable under Case VII of Schedule D, or where it would have been so chargeable if there were a gain so accruing.

11(2) The amount or value of the consideration for the acquisition of an asset by the person acquiring it on a disposal chargeable under Case VII shall not under any provision of this Act be deemed to be an amount greater than the amount taken into account as consideration on that disposal for the purposes of Case VII.

11(3) Any apportionment of consideration or expenditure falling to be made in relation to a disposal chargeable under Case VII in accordance with section 164(4) of the Income and Corporation Taxes

Act 1970, and in particular in a case where section 164(6) of that Act (enhancement of value of land by acquisition of adjoining land) applied, shall be followed for the purposes of this Act both in relation to a disposal of the assets acquired on the disposal chargeable under Case VII and, where the disposal chargeable under Case VII was a part disposal, in relation to a disposal of what remains undisposed of.

11(4) Sub-paragraph (3) above has effect notwithstanding section 52(4).

Derivations – CGTA 1979, Sch. 6, para. 12.

UNRELIEVED CASE VII LOSSES

12 Where no relief from income tax (for a year earlier than 1971–72) has been given in respect of a loss or part of a loss allowable under Case VII of Schedule D, the loss or part shall, notwithstanding that the loss accrued before that year, be an allowable loss for the purposes of capital gains tax, but subject to any restrictions imposed by section 18.

Derivations – CGTA 1979, Sch. 6, para. 13.

DEVALUATION OF STERLING: SECURITIES ACQUIRED WITH BORROWED FOREIGN CURRENCY

13(1) This paragraph applies where, in pursuance of permission granted under the Exchange Control Act 1947, currency other than Sterling was borrowed before 19th November 1967 for the purpose of investing in foreign securities (and had not been repaid before that date), and it was a condition of the permission–

(a) that repayment of the borrowed currency should be made from the proceeds of the sale in foreign currency of the foreign securities so acquired or out of investment currency, and

(b) that the foreign securities so acquired should be kept in separate accounts to distinguish them from others in the same ownership,

and securities held in such a separate account on 19th November 1967 are in this paragraph referred to as **"designated securities"**.

13(2) In computing the gain accruing to the borrower on the disposal of any designated securities or on the disposal of any currency or amount standing in a bank account on 19th November 1967 and representing the loan, the sums allowable as a deduction under section 38(1)(a) shall, subject to sub-paragraph (3) below, be increased by multiplying them by seven-sixths.

13(3) The total amount of the increases so made in computing all gains (and losses) which are referable to any one loan (made before 19th November 1967) shall not exceed one-sixth of the sterling parity value of that loan at the time it was made.

13(4) Designated securities which on the commencement of this paragraph constitute a separate 1982 holding (within the meaning of section 109), shall continue to constitute a separate 1982 holding until such time as a disposal takes place on the occurrence of which sub-paragraph (3) above operates to limit the increases which would otherwise be made under sub-paragraph (2) in allowable deductions.

13(5) In this paragraph and paragraph 14 below, **"foreign securities"** means securities expressed in a currency other than sterling, or shares having a nominal value expressed in a currency other than sterling, or the dividends on which are payable in a currency other than sterling.

Derivations – CGTA 1979, Sch. 6, para. 17.

DEVALUATION OF STERLING: FOREIGN INSURANCE FUNDS

14(1) The sums allowable as a deduction under section 38(1)(a) in computing any gains to which this paragraph applies shall be increased by multiplying by seven-sixths.

14(2) This paragraph applies to gains accruing–

(a) to any underwriting member of Lloyd's, or

(b) to any company engaged in the business of marine protection and indemnity insurance on a mutual basis,

on the disposal by that person after 18th November 1967 of any foreign securities which on that date formed part of a trust fund–

(i) established by that person in any country or territory outside the United Kingdom, and

(ii) representing premiums received in the course of that person's business, and

(iii) wholly or mainly used for the purpose of meeting liabilities arising in that country or territory in respect of that business.

Derivations – CGTA 1979, Sch. 6, para. 18.

GILT-EDGED SECURITIES PAST REDEMPTION DATE

15 So far as material for the purposes of this or any other Act, the definition of **"gilt-edged securities"** in Schedule 9 to this Act shall include any securities which were gilt-edged securities for the purposes of the 1979 Act, and the redemption date of which fell before 1st January 1992.

Derivations – CGTA 1979, Sch. 6, para. 19.

QUALIFYING CORPORATE BONDS, COMPANY REORGANISATIONS, SHARE CONVERSIONS ETC.

16(1) Part IV of this Act has effect subject to the provisions of this paragraph.

16(2) The substitution of Chapter II of that Part for the enactments repealed by this Act shall not alter the law applicable to any reorganisation or reduction of share capital, conversion of securities or company amalgamation taking place before the coming into force of this Act.

16(3) Sub-paragraph (2) above applies in particular to the law determining whether or not any assets arising on an event mentioned in that sub-paragraph are to be treated as the same asset as the original holding of shares, securities or other assets.

16(4) In relation to a disposal or exchange on or after 6th April 1992, the following amendments shall be regarded as always having had effect, that is to say, the amendments to section 64 of, or Schedule 13 to, the Finance Act 1984 made by section 139 of, or paragraph 6 of Schedule 14 to, the Finance Act 1989, paragraph 28 of Schedule 10 to the Finance Act 1990 or section 98 of, or paragraph 1 of Schedule 10 to, the Finance Act 1991 or by virtue of the amendments to paragraph 1 of Schedule 18 to the Taxes Act made by section 77 of the Finance Act 1991.

Derivations – CGTA 1979, Sch. 6, para. 20; and see (para. 16(4)) FA 1989, s. 139(1), FA 1990, Sch. 10, para. 29, FA 1991, s. 98(4)(b), 77(2)(b).

LAND: ALLOWANCE FOR BETTERMENT LEVY

17(1) Where betterment levy charged in the case of any land in respect of an act or event which fell within Case B or Case C or, if it was the renewal, extension or variation of a tenancy, Case F–

(a) has been paid, and

(b) has not been allowed as a deduction in computing the profits or gains or losses of a trade for the purposes of Case I of Schedule D;

then, if the person by whom the levy was paid disposes of the land or any part of it and so claims, the following provisions of this paragraph shall have effect.

17(2) Paragraph 9 of Schedule 2 shall apply where the condition stated in sub-paragraph (1)(a) of that paragraph is satisfied, notwithstanding that the condition in sub-paragraph (1)(b) of that paragraph is not satisfied.

17(3) Subject to the following provisions of this paragraph, there shall be ascertained the excess, if any, of–

(a) the net development value ascertained for the purposes of the levy, over

(b) the increment specified in sub-paragraph (6) below;

and the amount of the excess shall be treated as an amount allowable under section 38(1)(b).

17(4) Where the act or event in respect of which the levy was charged was a part disposal of the land, section 38 shall apply as if the part disposal had not taken place and sub-paragraph (5) below shall apply in lieu of sub-paragraph (3) above.

17(5) The amount or value of the consideration for the disposal shall be treated as increased by the amount of any premium or like sum paid in respect of the part disposal, and there shall be ascertained the excess, if any, of–

(a) the aggregate specified in sub-paragraph (7) below, over

(b) the increment specified in sub-paragraph (6) below;

and the amount of the excess shall be treated as an amount allowable under section 38(1)(b).

17(6) The increment referred to in sub-paragraphs (3)(b) and (5)(b) above is the excess, if any, of–

(a) the amount or value of the consideration brought into account under section 38(1)(a), over

(b) the base value ascertained for the purposes of the levy.

17(7) The aggregate referred to in sub-paragraph (5)(a) above is the aggregate of–

(a) the net development value ascertained for the purposes of the levy, and

(b) the amount of any premium or like sum paid in respect of the part disposal, in so far as charged to tax under Schedule A (or, as the case may be, Case VIII of Schedule D), and

(c) the chargeable gain accruing on the part disposal.

17(8) Where betterment levy in respect of more than one act or event has been charged and paid as mentioned in sub-paragraph (1) above, sub-paragraphs (2) to (7) above shall apply without modifications in relation to the betterment levy in respect of the first of them; but in relation to the other or others sub-paragraph (3) or, as the case may be, (5) above shall have effect as if the amounts to be treated thereunder as allowable under section 38(1)(b) were the net development value specified in sub-paragraph (3)(a) or, as the case may be, the aggregate referred to in subparagraph (5)(a) of this paragraph.

17(9) Where the disposal is of part only of the land sub-paragraphs (2) to (8) above shall have effect subject to the appropriate apportionments.

17(10) References in this paragraph to a premium include any sum payable as mentioned in section 34(4) or (5) of the Taxes Act (sums payable in lieu of rent or as consideration for the surrender of lease or for variation or waiver of term) and, in relation to Scotland, a grassum.

Derivations – CGTA 1979, Sch. 6, para. 21.

NON-RESIDENT TRUSTS

18 Without prejudice to section 289 or Part III of this Schedule–

(a) any tax chargeable on a person which is postponed under subsection (4)(b) of section 17 of the 1979 Act, shall continue to be postponed until that person becomes absolutely entitled to the part of the settled property concerned or disposes of the whole or part of his interest, as mentioned in that subsection; and

(b) section 70 of and Schedule 14 to the Finance Act 1984 shall continue to have effect in relation to amounts of tax which are postponed under that Schedule, and accordingly in paragraph 12 of that Schedule the references to section 80 of the Finance Act 1981 and to subsections (3) and (4) of that section include references to section 87 of this Act and subsections (4) and (5) of that section respectively.

Derivations – See CGTA 1979, s. 17; FA 1984, s. 70 and Sch. 14.

PRIVATE RESIDENCES

19 The reference in section 222(5)(a) to a notice given by any person within 2 years from the beginning of the period mentioned in section 222(5) includes a notice given before the end of the year 1966–67, if that was later.

WORKS OF ART ETC.

20 The repeals made by this Act do not affect the continued operation of sections 31 and 32 of the Finance Act 1965, in the form in which they were before 13th March 1975, in relation to estate duty in respect of deaths occurring before that date.

Derivations – CGTA 1979, Sch. 6, para. 24.

DISPOSAL BEFORE ACQUISITION

21 The substitution of this Act for the corresponding enactments repealed by this Act shall not alter the effect of any provision enacted before this Act (whether or not there is a corresponding provision in this Act) so far as it relates to an asset which–

(a) was disposed of before being acquired, and

(b) was disposed of before the commencement of this Act.

Derivations – CGTA 1979, Sch. 6, para. 25.

ESTATE DUTY

22 Nothing in the repeals made by this Act shall affect any enactment as it applies to the determination of any principal value for the purposes of estate duty.

Derivations – CGTA 1979, Sch. 6, para. 26.

VALIDITY OF SUBORDINATE LEGISLATION

23 So far as this Act re-enacts any provision contained in a statutory instrument made in exercise of powers conferred by any Act, it shall be without prejudice to the validity of that provision, and any question as to its validity shall be determined as if the re-enacted provision were contained in a statutory instrument made under those powers.

Derivations – CGTA 1979, Sch. 6, para. 28.

AMENDMENTS IN OTHER ACTS

24(1) The repeal by this Act of the Income and Corporation Taxes Act 1970 does not affect–

(a) the amendment made by paragraph 3 of Schedule 15 of that Act to section 26 of the Finance Act 1956, or

(b) paragraph 10 of that Schedule so far it applies in relation to the Management Act.

24(2) The repeal by this Act of Schedule 7 to the 1979 Act does not affect the amendments made by that Schedule to any enactment not repealed by this Act.

SAVING FOR PART III OF THIS SCHEDULE

25 The provisions of this Part of this Schedule are without prejudice to the generality of Part III of this Schedule.

Derivations – CGTA 1979, Sch. 6, para. 29.

Part III – Assets Acquired Before Commencement

26(1) The substitution of this Act for the enactments repealed by this Act shall not alter the effect of any provision enacted before this Act (whether or not there is a corresponding provision in this Act) so far as it determines–

(a) what amount the consideration is to be taken to be for the purpose of the computation under this Act of any chargeable gain; or

(b) whether and to what extent events in, or expenditure incurred in, or other amounts referable to, a period earlier than the chargeable periods to which this Act applies may be taken into account for any tax purposes in a chargeable period to which this Act applies.

26(2) Without prejudice to sub-paragraph (1) above, the repeals made by this Act shall not affect–

(a) the enactments specified in Part V of Schedule 14 to the Finance Act 1971 (charge on death) so far as their operation before repeal falls to be taken into account in chargeable periods to which this Act applies,

(b) the application of the enactments repealed by the 1979 Act to events before 6th April 1965 in accordance with paragraph 31 of Schedule 6 to the Finance Act 1965.

26(3) This paragraph has no application to the law relating to the determination of the market value of assets.

Derivations – CGTA 1979, Sch. 6, para. 10.

27 Where the acquisition or provision of any asset by one person was, immediately before the commencement of this paragraph and by virtue of any enactment, to be taken for the purposes of Schedule 5 to the 1979 Act to be the acquisition or disposal of it by another person, then, notwithstanding the repeal by this Act of that enactment, Schedule 2 to this Act shall also have effect as if the acquisition or provision of the asset by the first-mentioned person had been the acquisition or provision of it by that other person.

Part IV – Other General Savings

28 Where under any Act passed before this Act and relating to a country or territory outside the United Kingdom there is a power to affect Acts passed or in force before a particular time, or instruments made or having effect under such Acts, and the power would, but for the passing of this Act, have included power to change the law which is reproduced in, or is made or has effect under, this Act, then that power shall include power to make such provision as will secure the like change in the law reproduced in, or made or having effect under, this Act notwithstanding that this Act is not an Act passed or in force before that time.

29(1) The continuity of the law relating to the taxation of chargeable gains shall not be affected by the substitution of this Act for the enactments repealed by this Act and earlier enactments repealed by and corresponding to any of those enactments (**"the repealed enactments"**).

29(2) Any reference, whether express or implied, in any enactment, instrument or document (including this Act or any Act amended by this Act) to, or to things done or falling to be done under or for the purposes of, any provision of this Act shall, if and so far as the nature of the reference permits, be construed as including, in relation to the times, years or periods, circumstances or purposes in relation to which the corresponding provision in the repealed enactments has or had effect, a reference to, or as the case may be, to things done or falling to be done under or for the purposes of, that corresponding provision.

29(3) Any reference, whether express or implied, in any enactment, instrument or document (including the repealed enactments and enactments, instruments and documents passed or made after the passing of this Act) to, or to things done or falling to be done under or for the purposes of, any of the repealed enactments shall, if and so far as the nature of the reference permits, be construed as including, in relation to the times, years or periods, circumstances or purposes in relation to which the corresponding provision of this Act has effect, a reference to, or as the case may be to things done or falling to be done under or for the purposes of, that corresponding provision.

SCHEDULE 12 – REPEALS

Section 290

[Not reproduced here.]

FINANCE ACT 1992

(1992 Chapter 20)

[*16th March 1992*]

ARRANGEMENT OF SECTIONS

INCOME TAX

9 Lower rate

9 [Repealed by ITA 2007, s. 1031 and Sch. 3, Pt. 1.]

History – S. 9 repealed by ITA 2007, s. 1031 and Sch. 3, Pt. 1, with effect from 6 April 2007.

Notes – S. 9 rewritten as follows:
S. 9(3): ITA 2007, s. 10(2), 11(1).
S. 9(6): ITA 2007, s. 21(2), (3).
S. 9(7): ITA 2007, s. 21(5).
S. 9(8): ITA 2007, s. 17(1), (2).

GENERAL

11 Short title and interpretation

11(1) This Act may be cited as the Finance Act 1992.

11(2) In this Act **"the Taxes Act 1988"** means the Income and Corporation Taxes Act 1988.

FINANCE (NO. 2) ACT 1992

(1992 Chapter 48)

[*16th July 1992*]

ARRANGEMENT OF SECTIONS

PART II – INCOME TAX, CORPORATION TAX AND CAPITAL GAINS TAX

CHAPTER I – GENERAL

PART II – INCOME TAX, CORPORATION TAX AND CAPITAL GAINS TAX

Chapter I – General

LOWER RATE

19 Lower rate: further provisions

19(1) [Amends TMA 1970, s. 7(4).]

19(2) [Amends TMA 1970, s. 91(3)(c) and ICTA 1988, s. 599(7) and amended ICTA 1988, s. 550(3).]

19(3) [Repealed by ITA 2007, s. 1031 and Sch. 1, Pt. 1.]

19(4) [Repealed by FA 1996, Sch. 41, Pt. V(1), for years after 1995–96.]

19(5) [Repealed by FA 1994, s. 258 and Sch. 26, Pt. V(2).]

19(6) [Repealed by ITTOIA 2005, s. 884 and Sch. 3.]

19(7) This section shall apply for the year 1992–93 and subsequent years of assessment.

History – In s. 19(2) the reference to ICTA 1988, s. 550(3) repealed by ITTOIA 2005, s. 884 and Sch. 3; effective for income tax purposes for 2005–06 onwards and for corporation tax purposes for accounting periods ending after 5 April 2005 (ITTOIA 2005, s. 883(1)).
S. 19(3) repealed by ITA 2007, s. 1031 and Sch. 1, Pt. 1, with effect from 6 April 2007.
In former s. 19(3) the references to s. 549(2) and 699(2) repealed by ITTOIA 2005, s. 884 and Sch. 3; effective for income tax purposes for 2005–06 onwards and for corporation tax purposes for accounting periods ending after 5 April 2005 (ITTOIA 2005, s. 883(1)). ICTA 1988, s. 549(2) and 699(2) are principally rewritten at ITTOIA 2005, s. 669.
S. 19(3) partially repealed by omitting references to ICTA 1988, s. 683(2), 684(2) and 689(2) by FA 1995, s. 162 and Sch. 29, Pt. VIII(8) with effect for 1995–96 and subsequent years of assessment.
S. 19(3) partially repealed by omitting references to ICTA 1988, s. 353(5) and 369(3B) by FA 1994, s. 258 and Sch. 26, Pt. V(2) in relation to payments of loan interest made on or after 6 April 1994 and in relation to relevant loan interest, as regards payments of interest due on or after 6 April 1994 and made during the period 30 November 1993 to 6 April 1994.
S. 19(3) partially repealed by FA 1993, s. 213 and Sch. 23, Pt. III(6) by omitting references to ICTA 1988, s. 233(2) and 233(1)(c) respectively with effect for 1993–94 and subsequent years of assessment.
S. 19(4) repealed by FA 1996, Sch. 41, Pt. V(1), for years after 1995–96.
S. 19(4) partially repealed by FA 1993, s. 213 and Sch. 23, Pt. III(6) by omitting references to ICTA 1988, s. 233(2) and 233(1)(c) respectively with effect for 1993–94 and subsequent years of assessment.
S. 19(5) repealed by FA 1994, s. 258 and Sch. 26, Pt. V(2) in relation to payments of loan interest made on or after 6 April 1994 and in relation to relevant loan interest, as regards payments of interest due on or after 6 April 1994 and made during the period 30 November 1993 to 6 April 1994.
S. 19(6) repealed by ITTOIA 2005, s. 884 and Sch. 3; effective for income tax purposes for 2005–06 onwards and for corporation tax purposes for accounting periods ending after 5 April 2005 (ITTOIA 2005, s. 883(1)).

MARRIED COUPLE'S ALLOWANCE ETC.

20 Married couple's allowance etc.

20 Schedule 5 to this Act (which makes provision in relation to the married couple's allowance) shall have effect.

GROUPS ETC.

24 Amendments relating to group relief etc.

24 Schedule 6 to this Act (which contains amendments relating to group relief etc.) shall have effect.

25 Companies ceasing to be members of groups

25(1) [Repealed by FA 2000, Sch. 40, Pt. II(12).]

25(2) Subject to the repeals made by the Taxation of Chargeable Gains Act 1992, in relation to a company which ceases to be a member of a group of companies on or after 15th November 1991 section 278 of the Income and Corporation Taxes Act 1970 (deemed sale etc. where company ceases to be member of a group) shall have effect, and be deemed to have had effect, with the substitution in subsection (1) of the words "in consequence of another member of the group ceasing to exist" for the words from "by being wound up" to the end of the subsection.

History – S. 25(1) repealed by FA 2000, Sch. 40, Pt. II(12) with effect for assets acquired on or after 1 April 2000 (the footnotes to Pt. II(12) specify FA 2000, Sch. 29, para. 4(6) as providing the effective date). The original text of s. 25(1) is set out below:
"**25(1)** Sections 178 and 179 of the Taxation of Chargeable Gains Act 1992 (deemed sale etc. where company ceases to be member of a group) shall have effect, and be deemed always to have had effect, with the substitution in subsection (1) of each of those sections of the words "in consequence of another member of the group ceasing to exist" for the words from "by being wound up" to the end of the subsection."

CHARITIES ETC.

28 Powers of inspection

28(1) [Omitted by FA 2008, s. 113 and Sch. 36, para. 86.]

28(2) [Omitted by FA 2008, s. 113 and Sch. 36, para. 86.]

28(3) [Omitted by FA 2008, s. 113 and Sch. 36, para. 86.]

28(4) [Amends TMA 1970, s. 98.]

28(5) [Repeals FA 1990, s. 94.]

28(6) This section shall apply in relation to claims made after the day on which this Act is passed.

History – S. 28(1)–(3) omitted by FA 2008, s. 113 and Sch. 36, para. 86, with effect from 1 April 2009 (SI 2009/404, art. 2, subject to savings at SI 2009/404, art. 3).
In former s. 28(1)(a) the words "or under Part 10 of the Income Tax Act 2007" inserted by ITA 2007, s. 1027 and Sch. 1, para. 350, with effect from 6 April 2007.

Cross references – ICTA 1988, s. 505(1): general claim for exemption from income tax by charity.
TCGA 1992, s. 256(1): capital gains tax exemptions for charities.

INTEREST, DIVIDENDS AND DISTRIBUTIONS

29 Returns of interest

29(1) [Amends TMA 1970, s. 17(4), inserts TMA 1970, s. 17(4A)–(4C).]

29(2) This section shall apply to interest paid or credited after the day on which this Act is passed.

31 Equity notes

31 [Repealed by CTA 2010, s. 1181 and Sch. 3, Pt. 1.]

History – S. 31 repealed by CTA 2010, s. 1181 and Sch. 3, Pt. 1, with effect for corporation tax purposes for accounting periods ending on or after 1 April 2010, and for income tax and capital gains tax purposes for the tax year 2010–11 and subsequent tax years.

32 Information relating to distributions

32(1) [Repealed by CTA 2010, s. 1181 and Sch. 3, Pt. 1.]

32(2) [Amends provisions as below.]

(a) [Repealed by CTA 2010, s. 1181 and Sch. 3, Pt. 1.]

(b) [Omits ICTA 1988, s. 234(3), (4).]

32(3) [Repealed by CTA 2010, s. 1181 and Sch. 3, Pt. 1.]

32(4) This section shall apply in relation to distributions begun after the day on which this Act is passed.

History – S. 32(1) repealed by CTA 2010, s. 1181 and Sch. 3, Pt. 1, with effect for corporation tax purposes for accounting periods ending on or after 1 April 2010, and for income tax and capital gains tax purposes for the tax year 2010–11 and subsequent tax years.
S. 32(2)(a) repealed by CTA 2010, s. 1181 and Sch. 3, Pt. 1, with effect for corporation tax purposes for accounting periods ending on or after 1 April 2010, and for income tax and capital gains tax purposes for the tax year 2010–11 and subsequent tax years.
S. 32(3) repealed by CTA 2010, s. 1181 and Sch. 3, Pt. 1, with effect for corporation tax purposes for accounting periods ending on or after 1 April 2010, and for income tax and capital gains tax purposes for the tax year 2010–11 and subsequent tax years.

SECURITIES AND DEPOSITS

34 Rights in pursuance of deposits

34 Schedule 8 to this Act (which contains provisions about arrangements relating to rights in pursuance of deposits) shall have effect.

35 Exchange of securities

35(1) [Repealed by FA 2002, s. 141 and Sch. 40, Pt. 3(2).]

35(2) [Inserts CGTA 1979, s. 85(1)(c).]

EMPLOYEE SHARES

36 Employee share ownership trusts

36(1) [Inserts FA 1989, s. 69(3A).]

36(2) This section applies in relation to exchanges made on or after 1st January 1992.

37 Employee share schemes: special benefits

37 [Repealed by ITEPA 2003, Sch. 8, Pt. 1.]

History – S. 37 repealed by ITEPA 2003, Sch. 8, Pt. 1 which has effect, for income tax purposes, for the tax year 2003–04 and subsequent tax years and, for corporation tax purposes, for accounting periods ending after 5 April 2003.

FILMS

40A Revenue nature of expenditure on master versions of films

40A [Does not apply by virtue of FA 2006, s. 46(1) and is repealed by FA 2006, s. 178 and Sch. 26, Pt. 3(4).]

History – S. 40A does not apply by virtue of FA 2006, s. 46(1) and is repealed by FA 2006, s. 178 and Sch. 26, Pt. 3(4), with effect from 1 January 2007 (see FA 2006, s. 52 and 53).

40B Allocation of expenditure to periods

40B [Does not apply by virtue of FA 2006, s. 46(1) and is repealed by FA 2006, s. 178 and Sch. 26, Pt. 3(4).]

History – S. 40B does not apply by virtue of FA 2006, s. 46(1) and is repealed by FA 2006, s. 178 and Sch. 26, Pt. 3(4), with effect from 1 January 2007 (see FA 2006, s. 52 and 53).

40C Cases where section 40B does not apply

40C [Does not apply by virtue of FA 2006, s. 46(1) and is repealed by FA 2006, s. 178 and Sch. 26, Pt. 3(4).]

History – S. 40C does not apply by virtue of FA 2006, s. 46(1) and is repealed by FA 2006, s. 178 and Sch. 26, Pt. 3(4), with effect from 1 January 2007 (see FA 2006, s. 52 and 53).

40D Election for sections 40A and 40B not to apply

40D [Does not apply by virtue of FA 2006, s. 46(1) and is repealed by FA 2006, s. 178 and Sch. 26, Pt. 3(4).]

History – S. 40D does not apply by virtue of FA 2006, s. 46(1) and is repealed by FA 2006, s. 178 and Sch. 26, Pt. 3(4), with effect from 1 January 2007 (see FA 2006, s. 52 and 53).

41 Relief for preliminary expenditure

41 [Does not apply by virtue of FA 2006, s. 46(2) and repealed by FA 2006, s. 178 and Sch. 26, Pt. 3(4).]

History – S. 41 does not apply to expenditure incurred on or after 19 July 2006 by virtue of FA 2006, s. 46(2) and is repealed from that date by FA 2006, s. 178 and Sch. 26, Pt. 3(4).

42 Relief for production or acquisition expenditure

42 [Does not apply by virtue of FA 2006, s. 46(3) and is repealed by FA 2006, s. 178 and Sch. 26, Pt. 3(4).]

History – S. 42 does not apply by virtue of FA 2006, s. 46(3) and is repealed by FA 2006, s. 178 and Sch. 26, Pt. 3(4), with effect from 1 January 2007 (see FA 2006, s. 52 and 53).

43 Interpretation of sections 41 and 42

43 [Repealed by FA 2006, s. 178 and Sch. 26, Pt. 3(4).]

History – S. 43 repealed by FA 2006, s. 178 and Sch. 26, Pt. 3(4), with effect from 1 January 2007 (FA 2006, s. 52 and 53).

TRANSFERS OF TRADE

Notes – For a list of UK tax provisions, introduced by F(No. 2)A 1992 which implement EC direct tax legislation, see the direct tax "European material".

44 Transfer of a UK trade: amendment of 1992 Act

44 [Inserts TCGA 1992, s. 140A, 140B.]

45 Transfer of a non-UK trade: amendment of 1992 Act

45 [Inserts TCGA 1992, s. 140C, 140D.]

46 Transfer of a trade: supplementary (1)

46(1) The Taxation of Chargeable Gains Act 1992 shall have effect, and be deemed always to have had effect, with the following amendments.

46(2) [Omitted by FA 2008, s. 8 and Sch. 2, para. 70(a)(i).]

46(3) [Amends TCGA 1992, s. 116(11).]

46(4) [Inserts TCGA 1992, s. 140(6A).]

46(5) [Amends provisions as below.]

(a) [Amends TCGA 1992, s. 174(2).]

(b) [Amends TCGA 1992, s. 174(3).]

46(6) [Amends TCGA 1992, s. 177(2).]

46(7) [Amends TCGA 1992, s. 184(2).]

History – S. 46(2) omitted by FA 2008, s. 8 and Sch. 2, para. 70(a)(i), with effect in relation to disposals on or after 6 April 2008.

47 Transfer of a UK trade: amendment of 1970 Act

47 [Repealed by Statute Law (Repeals) Act 2013, s. 1 and Sch. 1, Pt. 10.]

History – S. 47 repealed by Statute Law (Repeals) Act 2013, s. 1 and Sch. 1, Pt. 10, with effect from 31 January 2013.

48 Transfer of a non-UK trade: amendment of 1970 Act

48 [Repealed by Statute Law (Repeals) Act 2013, s. 1 and Sch. 1, Pt. 10.]

History – S. 48 repealed by Statute Law (Repeals) Act 2013, s. 1 and Sch. 1, Pt. 10, with effect from 31 January 2013.

49 Transfer of a trade: supplementary (2)

49 [Repealed by Statute Law (Repeals) Act 2013, s. 1 and Sch. 1, Pt. 10.]

History – S. 49 repealed by Statute Law (Repeals) Act 2013, s. 1 and Sch. 1, Pt. 10, with effect from 31 January 2013.

DOUBLE TAXATION RELIEF

50 Transfer of a non-UK trade

50 [Repealed by TIOPA 2010, s. 378 and Sch. 10, Pt. 1.]

History – S. 50 repealed by TIOPA 2010, s. 378 and Sch. 10, Pt. 1, with effect for corporation tax purposes for accounting periods ending on or after 1 April 2010, for income tax and capital gains tax purposes for the tax year 2010–11 and subsequent tax years, and for petroleum revenue tax purposes for chargeable periods beginning on or after 1 July 2010.

51 The Arbitration Convention

51(1) [Repealed by TIOPA 2010, s. 378 and Sch. 10, Pt. 1.]

51(2) [Repealed by TIOPA 2010, s. 378 and Sch. 10, Pt. 1.]

51(3) [Inserts FA 1989, s. 182A.]

History – S. 51(1) repealed by TIOPA 2010, s. 378 and Sch. 10, Pt. 1, with effect for corporation tax purposes for accounting periods ending on or after 1 April 2010, for income tax and capital gains tax purposes for the tax year 2010–11 and subsequent tax years, and for petroleum revenue tax purposes for chargeable periods beginning on or after 1 July 2010.
S. 51(2) repealed by TIOPA 2010, s. 378 and Sch. 10, Pt. 1, with effect for corporation tax purposes for accounting periods ending on or after 1 April 2010, for income tax and capital gains tax purposes for the tax year 2010–11 and subsequent tax years, and for petroleum revenue tax purposes for chargeable periods beginning on or after 1 July 2010.

52 Interest

52 [Repealed by TIOPA 2010, s. 378 and Sch. 10, Pt. 1.]

History – S. 52 repealed by TIOPA 2010, s. 378 and Sch. 10, Pt. 1, with effect for corporation tax purposes for accounting periods ending on or after 1 April 2010, for income tax and capital gains tax purposes for the tax year 2010–11 and subsequent tax years, and for petroleum revenue tax purposes for chargeable periods beginning on or after 1 July 2010.

MISCELLANEOUS

53 Car fuel: cash equivalents

53(1) [Amends ICTA 1988, s. 158 as follows.]

53(2) [Substitutes ICTA 1988, s. 158(2)–(2B).]

53(3) [Amends ICTA 1988, s. 158(4).]

53(4) This section shall have effect for the year 1992–93 and subsequent years of assessment.

54 Foreign earnings

54 [Repealed by ITEPA 2003, Sch. 8, Pt. 1.]

History – S. 54 repealed by ITEPA 2003, Sch. 8, Pt. 1 which has effect, for income tax purposes, for the tax year 2003–04 and subsequent tax years and, for corporation tax purposes, for accounting periods ending after 5 April 2003.

55 Oil extraction activities: extended transportation

55 [Repealed by CTA 2010, s. 1181 and Sch. 3, Pt. 2; also repealed by TIOPA 2010, s. 378 and Sch. 10, Pt. 6.]

History – S. 55 repealed by CTA 2010, s. 1181 and Sch. 3, Pt. 2, with effect for corporation tax purposes only for accounting periods ending on or after 1 April 2010. S. 55 also repealed by TIOPA 2010, s. 378 and Sch. 10, Pt. 6, with effect for corporation tax purposes for accounting periods ending on or after 1 April 2010, for income tax and capital gains tax purposes for the tax year 2010–11 and subsequent tax years, and for petroleum revenue tax purposes for chargeable periods beginning on or after 1 July 2010.

56 Friendly societies

56 Schedule 9 to this Act (which makes provision in relation to friendly societies) shall have effect.

Notes – Sch. 9 came into force with effect from 19 February 1993 by virtue of SI 1993/236.

57 Rents or receipts between connected persons

57 [Repealed by FA 1998, s. 165 and Sch. 27, Pt. III(4).]

History – S. 57 repealed by FA 1998, s. 165 and Sch. 27, Pt. III(4), with effect, so far as relating to income tax, for the year 1998–99 and subsequent years of assessment and, so far as relating to corporation tax, from 1 April 1998, subject to the transitional provisions in FA 1998, Sch. 5, Pt. IV.

58 Rents etc. chargeable under Case VI

58 [Repealed by FA 1998, s. 165 and Sch. 27, Pt. III(4).]

History – S. 57 repealed by FA 1998, s. 165 and Sch. 27, Pt. III(4), with effect, so far as relating to income tax, for the year 1998–99 and subsequent years of assessment and, so far as relating to corporation tax, from 1 April 1998, subject to the transitional provisions in FA 1998, Sch. 5, Pt. IV.

59 Furnished accommodation

59 [Omitted by ITTOIA 2005, s. 882(1) and Sch. 1, para. 460 and repealed by ITTOIA 2005, s. 884 and Sch. 3.]

History – S. 59 omitted by ITTOIA 2005, s. 882(1) and Sch. 1, para. 460; and repealed by ITTOIA 2005, s. 884 and Sch. 3 effective for income tax purposes for 2005–06 onwards and for corporation tax purposes for accounting periods ending after 5 April 2005 (ITTOIA 2005, s. 883(1)).

60 Deduction on account of certain payments

60(1) [Repealed by ITTOIA 2005, s. 884 and Sch. 3.]

60(2) [Repealed by ITTOIA 2005, s. 884 and Sch. 3.]

History – S. 60 repealed by ITTOIA 2005, s. 884 and Sch. 3 effective for income tax purposes for 2005–06 onwards and for corporation tax purposes for accounting periods ending after 5 April 2005 (ITTOIA 2005, s. 883(1)).

61 Qualifying maintenance payments: extension to member States

61 [Repealed by ITA 2007, s. 1031 and Sch. 1, Pt. 1.]

History – S. 61 repealed by ITA 2007, s. 1031 and Sch. 1, Pt. 1, with effect from 6 April 2007.
Notes – S. 61 rewritten as ITA 2007, s. 454(4).

62 Qualifying maintenance payments: maintenance assessments etc.

62 [Repealed by ITA 2007, s. 1031 and Sch. 1, Pt. 1.]

History – S. 62 repealed by ITA 2007, s. 1031 and Sch. 1, Pt. 1, with effect from 6 April 2007.
S. 62 originally came into force on 6 April 1993 by virtue of SI 1992/2642, art. 2.
Notes – S. 62 rewritten as ITA 2007, s. 454(7), (8), 455(1), (2), (3), 456(1), (2).

63 Paying and collecting agents etc.

63 [Repealed by Statute Law (Repeals) Act 2013, s. 1 and Sch. 1, Pt. 10.]

History – S. 63 repealed by Statute Law (Repeals) Act 2013, s. 1 and Sch. 1, Pt. 10, with effect from 31 January 2013.

64 Reduced and composite rate

64 [Repealed by ITA 2007, s. 1031 and Sch. 1, Pt. 1.]

History – S. 64 repealed by ITA 2007, s. 1031 and Sch. 1, Pt. 1, with effect from 6 April 2007.

65 Life assurance business: I minus E basis

65 [Omitted by FA 2007, s. 39(1) and Sch. 8, para. 19 and repealed by FA 2007, s. 114 and Sch. 27, Pt. 2(8).]

History – S. 65 omitted by FA 2007, s. 39(1) and Sch. 89, para. 199 and repealed by FA 2007, s. 114 and Sch. 27, Pt. 2(8) with effect for the purposes of corporation tax, for periods of insurance companies beginning on or after 1 January 2007 (subject to any transitional provisions contained in FA 2007, Sch. 8, para. 28 and 29 (FA 2007, s. 39(2))). Former s. 65 read:

"Life assurance business: I minus E basis

65(1) For the purposes of this section a claim is a relevant claim if it is made under or by virtue of any of the following provisions–
(a) section 393(1) of the Taxes Act 1988 (claim for carry forward of trading losses);
(b) section 393A(1) of the Taxes Act 1988 (claim for carry sideways and backwards of trading losses);
(c) section 402(2) of the Taxes Act 1988 (surrender of relief between members of groups and consortia: group claim);
(d) section 402(3) of the Taxes Act 1988 (surrender of relief between members of groups and consortia: consortium claim);
(e) any provision reproduced in any of the provisions mentioned in paragraphs (a) to (d) above (whether directly or indirectly and whether with or without modification).

65(2) For the purposes of this section the following are relevant provisions–
(aa) section 434(1) and (1A) of the Taxes Act 1988 (section 208 not to apply in relation to life assurance profits computed in accordance with Case I of Schedule D etc.);
(ab) [omitted by SI 2004/2200, reg. 8(2).]
(a) section 434A(1) of the Taxes Act 1988 (profits derived from investments held for purposes of life assurance business treated as profits of that business in ascertaining loss);
(b) [repealed by FA 1996, s. 205 and Sch. 41, Pt. V(3).]
(c) [repealed by FA 1996, s.205 and Sch. 41, Pt. V(3).]
(d) section 83(2) of the Finance Act 1989 (amounts to be taken into account as receipts or expenses);
(e) section 37(1) of the Taxation of Chargeable Gains Act 1992 (exclusion from consideration for disposal of asset of any money or moneys worth taken into account in computing profits or losses etc.);
(f) any provision reproduced in any of the provisions mentioned in paragraphs (a) and (e) above (whether directly or indirectly and whether with or without modification).

65(3) For the purposes of this section–
(a) the **"I minus E basis"** is the basis commonly so called (under which a company carrying on life assurance business is charged to tax in respect of that business otherwise that under Case I of Schedule D);
(b) **"life assurance business"** includes annuity business.

65(4) Neither the making of a relevant claim in respect of a trading loss incurred by a company in an accounting period nor the application of any commercial or accounting principal or practice in computing that loss–

(a) shall prevent the I minus E basis being applied for that or any other accounting period in respect of the company's life assurance business;

(b) shall affect the calculation of the income or gains of that business for that or any other accounting period in applying that basis.

65(5) The application of a relevant provision as regards a company for an accounting period shall not–

(a) prevent the I minus E basis being applied for that or any other accounting period in respect of its life assurance business;

(b) affect the calculation of the income or gains of that business for that or any other accounting period in applying that basis.

65(6) This section–

(a) shall apply in relation to accounting periods beginning on or after the day on which this Act is passed;

(b) shall apply and be deemed always to have applied in relation to accounting periods beginning before that day but, in relation to any case in which by virtue of section 99 of the Finance Act 1990 losses may be set off under subsection (1) of section 393 of the Taxes Act 1988 without the making of a claim, this section shall have effect as if references to the making of a claim under that subsection were references to the setting off of any loss under that subsection."

Former s. 65(2)(ab) omitted by SI 2004/2200, reg. 8(2) with effect, in relation to overseas life insurance companies, for accounting periods beginning on or after 1 January 2003 (reg. 1(1)).

Former s. 65(2)(aa) and (ab) inserted by F(No. 2)A 1997, s. 23 and Sch. 3, para. 15.

Former s. 65(2)(b), (c), and in former s. 65(2)(f) references to para. (b) and (c), repealed by FA 1996, s. 205 and Sch. 41, Pt. V(3), in relation to accounting periods ending after 31 March 1996.

Former s. 65(2)(a) substituted by FA 1995, s. 51 and Sch. 8, para. 20(2) in relation to accounting periods beginning on or after 1 January 1995.

Former s. 65(2)(d) substituted by FA 1995, s. 51 and Sch. 8, para. 16(6) in relation to accounting periods beginning on or after 1 January 1995.

In former s. 65(6), the words "but, in relation … that subsection" inserted by FA 1993, s. 120 and Sch. 14, para. 9 in connection with the introduction of Pay and File.

Cross references – SI 1999/498, reg. 13: modification of s. 65 so far as it relates to capital redemption business carried on by insurance companies.

SI 2006/3271, reg. 33: modification of s. 65 in relation to overseas life insurance companies with effect from 31 December 2006 for accounting periods ending on or after that date.

66 Banks etc. in compulsory liquidation

66 [Omitted by CTA 2010, s. 1177 and Sch. 1, para. 270(2) and repealed by CTA 2010, s 1181 and Sch. 3, Pt. 2; also omitted by TIOPA 2010, s. 371 and Sch. 7, para. 64 and repealed by TIOPA 2010, s. 378 and Sch. 10, Pt. 12.]

History – S. 66 omitted by CTA 2010, s. 1177 and Sch. 1, para. 270(2) and repealed by CTA 2010, s. 1181 and Sch. 3, Pt. 2, with effect for corporation tax purposes only for accounting periods ending on or after 1 April 2010. S. 66 also omitted by TIOPA 2010, s. 371 and Sch. 7, para. 64 and repealed by TIOPA 2010, s. 378 and Sch. 10, Pt. 12, with effect for corporation tax purposes for accounting periods ending on or after 1 April 2010, for income tax and capital gains tax purposes for the tax year 2010–11 and subsequent tax years, and for petroleum revenue tax purposes for chargeable periods beginning on or after 1 July 2010.

Notes – S. 66 not rewritten, as introductory.

Chapter II – Capital Allowances

67 Transfer of a UK trade

67 [Repealed by CAA 2001, s. 580 and Sch. 4.]

History – S. 67, repealed by CAA 2001, s. 580 and Sch. 4, with effect as respects allowances and charges falling to be made for chargeable periods ending, for income tax purposes, on or after 6 April 2001, and for corporation tax purposes, on or after 1 April 2001.

68 Computer software

68 [Repealed by CAA 2001, s. 580 and Sch. 4.]

History – S. 68, repealed by CAA 2001, s. 580 and Sch. 4, with effect as respects allowances and charges falling to be made for chargeable periods ending, for income tax purposes, on or after 6 April 2001, and for corporation tax purposes, on or after 1 April 2001.

69 Films etc.

69 [Repealed by CAA 2001, s. 580 and Sch. 4.]

History – S. 69, repealed by CAA 2001, s. 580 and Sch. 4, with effect as respects allowances and charges falling to be made for chargeable periods ending, for income tax purposes, on or after 6 April 2001, and for corporation tax purposes, on or after 1 April 2001.

70 Enterprise zones

70 [Repealed by CAA 2001, s. 580 and Sch. 4.]

History – S. 70, repealed by CAA 2001, s. 580 and Sch. 4, with effect as respects allowances and charges falling to be made for chargeable periods ending, for income tax purposes, on or after 6 April 2001, and for corporation tax purposes, on or after 1 April 2001.

71 Expensive motor cars

71 [Repealed by CAA 2001, s. 580 and Sch. 4.]

History – S. 71, repealed by CAA 2001, s. 580 and Sch. 4, with effect as respects allowances and charges falling to be made for chargeable periods ending, for income tax purposes, on or after 6 April 2001, and for corporation tax purposes, on or after 1 April 2001.

PART III – MISCELLANEOUS AND GENERAL

GENERAL AND SPECIAL COMMISSIONERS

75 Change of name

75 [S. 75 and the heading which preceded it omitted by SI 2009/56, art. 3 and Sch. 1, para. 186.]

History – S. 75 and the heading which preceded it omitted by SI 2009/56, art. 3 and Sch. 1, para. 186, with effect from 1 April 2009, subject to transitional and saving provisions in SI 2009/56, Sch. 3. Former s. 75 read as follows:

"*Change of name*

75(1) The Lord Chancellor may, with the consent of the Secretary of State, make regulations providing for–

(a) [Repealed by TCEA 2007, s. 146 and Sch. 23, Pt. 1.]

(b) Commissioners for the special purposes of the Income Tax Acts to hold office by a different name (and to be referred to otherwise than as "Special Commissioners").

75(2) The regulations may make such consequential amendments of any Act or instrument made under any Act as the Lord Chancellor thinks appropriate.

75(3) Regulations under this section shall be made by statutory instrument subject to annulment in pursuance of a resolution of either House of Parliament.

History – S. 75(1)(a) repealed by TCEA 2007, s. 146 and Sch. 23, Pt. 1, with effect from 1 April 2009 (SI 2008/2696, art. 6(c)(v) – subject to transitional provisions at art. 3). Former para. (a) read as follows:

"(a) Commissioners for the general purposes of the income tax to hold office by a different name (and to be referred to otherwise than as "General Commissioners"), and"

In s. 75(1) the reference to Secretary of State substituted for a reference to the Lord Advocate by SI 1999/678, with effect from 19 May 1999."

76 Miscellaneous

76 [Omitted by SI 2009/56, art. 3 and Sch. 1, para. 186.]

History – S. 76 omitted by SI 2009/56, art. 3 and Sch. 1, para. 186, with effect from 1 April 2009, subject to transitional and saving provisions in SI 2009/56, Sch. 3. Former s. 76 read as follows:

"*Miscellaneous*

76 Schedule 16 to this Act (which makes provision in relation to the remuneration, jurisdiction, practice and procedure of the General and Special Commissioners etc.) shall have effect."

GENERAL

81 Interpretation

81 In this Act **"the Taxes Act 1988"** means the Income and Corporation Taxes Act 1988.

83 Short title

83 This Act may be cited as the Finance (No. 2) Act 1992.

SCHEDULES

SCHEDULE 5 – MARRIED COUPLE'S ALLOWANCE ETC.

Section 20

1 The Taxes Act 1988 shall be amended in accordance with paragraphs 2 to 8 below.

2 [Omitted by FA 2009, s. 5 and Sch. 1, para. 6(d).]

History – Para. 2 omitted by FA 2009, s. 5 and Sch. 1, para. 6(d), with effect from the tax year 2010–11 and subsequent tax years.

3 [Repealed by FA 1999, s. 139 and Sch. 20, Pt. III(3).]

History – Para. 3 repealed by FA 1999, s. 139 and Sch. 20, Pt. III(3), with effect for the year 2000–01 and subsequent years of assessment.

4 [Repealed by FA 1999, s. 139 and Sch. 20, Pt. III(3).]

History – Para. 4 repealed by FA 1999, s. 139 and Sch. 20, Pt. III(3), with effect for the year 2000–01 and subsequent years of assessment.

5 [Repealed by FA 1999, s. 139 and Sch. 20, Pt. III(4); and ITA 2007, s. 1031 and Sch. 1, Pt. 1.]

History – Para. 5 repealed by ITA 2007, s. 1031 and Sch. 1, Pt. 1, with effect from 6 April 2007.

Para. 5 previously repealed by FA 1999, s. 139 and Sch. 20, Pt. III(4), with effect for the year 2000–01 and subsequent years of assessment.

6 [Repealed by FA 1999, s. 139 and Sch. 20, Pt. III(4); and ITA 2007, s. 1031 and Sch. 1, Pt. 1.]

History – Para. 6 repealed by ITA 2007, s. 1031 and Sch. 1, Pt. 1, with effect from 6 April 2007.

Para. 6 previously repealed by FA 1999, s. 139 and Sch. 20, Pt. III(4), with effect for the year 2000–01 and subsequent years of assessment.

7 [Repealed by FA 1999, s. 139 and Sch. 20, Pt. 111(5); and ITA 2007, s. 1031 and Sch. 1, Pt. 1.]

History – Para. 7 repealed by ITA 2007, s. 1031 and Sch. 1, Pt. 1, with effect from 6 April 2007.

Para. 7 previously repealed by FA 1999, s. 139 and Sch. 20, Pt. 111(5), with effect for the year 2001–02 and subsequent years of assessment.

8(1) [Amends ICTA 1988, s. 265 (as follows).]

8(2) [Repealed by FA 1994, s. 258 and Sch. 26, Pt. V(1).]

8(3) [Amends ICTA 1988, s. 265(4).]

8(4) [Omitted by FA 2009, s. 5 and Sch. 1, para. 6(d).]

History – The repeal of para. 8(2) has effect for 1994–95 and subsequent years of assessment.
Para. 8(4) omitted by FA 2009, s. 5 and Sch. 1, para. 6(d), with effect from the tax year 2010–11 and subsequent tax years.

9(1) The Taxes Management Act 1970 shall be amended as follows.

9(2) [Inserts TMA 1970, s. 36(3A).]

9(3) [Omitted by FA 2009, s. 5 and Sch. 1, para. 6(d).]

9(4) [Inserts TMA 1970, s. 43A(2A).]

History – Para. 9(3) omitted by FA 2009, s. 5 and Sch. 1, para. 6(d), with effect from the tax year 2010–11 and subsequent tax years.

10 This Schedule shall apply in relation to tax for the year 1993–94 and subsequent years of assessment.

SCHEDULE 6 – GROUP RELIEF ETC.: AMENDMENTS

Section 24

MAIN AMENDMENTS

1 [Repealed by CTA 2010, s. 1181 and Sch. 3, Pt. 1.]

History – Para. 1 repealed by CTA 2010, s. 1181 and Sch. 3, Pt. 1, with effect for corporation tax purposes for accounting periods ending on or after 1 April 2010, and for income tax and capital gains tax purposes for the tax year 2010–11 and subsequent tax years.

2 [Repealed by CTA 2010, s. 1181 and Sch. 3, Pt. 1.]

History – Para. 2 repealed by CTA 2010, s. 1181 and Sch. 3, Pt. 1, with effect for corporation tax purposes for accounting periods ending on or after 1 April 2010, and for income tax and capital gains tax purposes for the tax year 2010–11 and subsequent tax years.

OTHER AMENDMENTS

3 [Repealed by CTA 2010, s. 1181 and Sch. 3, Pt. 1.]

History – Para. 3 repealed by CTA 2010, s. 1181 and Sch. 3, Pt. 1, with effect for corporation tax purposes for accounting periods ending on or after 1 April 2010, and for income tax and capital gains tax purposes for the tax year 2010–11 and subsequent tax years.

4 [Amended ICTA 1970, s. 272(1F) (since repealed).]

5 [Amends TCGA 1992, s. 170(8).]

APPLICATION OF AMENDMENTS

6(1) Sub-paragraph (2) below shall apply where either of the following events occurs on or after 15th November 1991–

(a) any shares or securities of the relevant company are issued in circumstances where they carry both rights referred to in paragraph 4(1) of Schedule 18 and rights referred to in paragraph 5(1) of Schedule 18;

(b) any shares or securities of the relevant company issued before 15th November 1991 begin to carry both rights referred to in paragraph 4(1) of Schedule 18 and rights referred to in paragraph 5(1) of Schedule 18 (whether or not they previously carried rights referred to in one of those paragraphs).

6(2) In such a case paragraph 1 above shall apply in relation to the accounting period in which the event occurs and subsequent accounting periods.

6(3) In this paragraph–

(a) references to the **"relevant company"** are to the second company referred to in paragraphs 2(1) and 3(1) of Schedule 18;

(b) references to **"accounting periods"** are to accounting periods of that company.

7 Paragraph 2 above shall apply where the option arrangements are made on or after 15th November 1991.

8 Paragraph 3 above shall apply in accordance with paragraphs 6 and 7 above.

9 Subject to the repeals made by the Taxation of Chargeable Gains Act 1992, paragraph 4 above shall apply in accordance with paragraph 7 above.

10 The Taxation of Chargeable Gains Act 1992 shall have effect, and be deemed always to have had effect, with the amendment made by paragraph 5 above.

SCHEDULE 8 – RIGHTS IN PURSUANCE OF DEPOSITS

Section 34

DISPOSAL OR EXERCISE OF RIGHTS

1 [Inserts ICTA 1988, s. 56A.]

BUILDING SOCIETIES

2 [Repealed by ITA 2007, s. 1031 and Sch. 1, Pt. 1.]

History – Para. 2 repealed by ITA 2007, s. 1031 and Sch. 1, Pt. 1, with effect from 6 April 2007.

3 [Repealed by ITA 2007, s. 1031 and Sch. 1, Pt. 1.]

History – Para. 3 repealed by ITA 2007, s. 1031 and Sch. 1, Pt. 1, with effect from 6 April 2007.
Notes – Para. 3 rewritten as ITA 2007, s. 872(5).

DEPOSIT-TAKERS

4 [Repealed by ITA 2007, s. 1031 and Sch. 1, Pt. 1.]

History – Para. 4 repealed by ITA 2007, s. 1031 and Sch. 1, Pt. 1, with effect from 6 April 2007.

ACCRUED INCOME SCHEME

5 [Repealed by ITA 2007, s. 1031 and Sch. 1, Pt. 1.]

History – Para. 5 repealed by ITA 2007, s. 1031 and Sch. 1, Pt. 1, with effect from 6 April 2007.
Notes – Para. 5 rewritten as ITA 2007, s. 619(3).

GENERAL

6 This Schedule shall apply in relation to arrangements made after the day on which this Act is passed.

SCHEDULE 9 – FRIENDLY SOCIETIES

Section 56

Notes – Sch. 9 came into force with effect from 19 February 1993 by virtue of SI 1993/236.

AMENDMENTS OF THE TAXES ACT 1988

1 The Taxes Act 1988 shall be amended in accordance with paragraphs 2 to 19 below.

2(1) [Amends ICTA 1988, s. 266 as follows.]

2(2) [Amends ICTA 1988, s. 266(2)(a)(iii).]

2(3) [Inserts ICTA 1988, s. 266(13).]

History – In para. 2(2) the reference to ICTA 1988, s. 266(6)(a) repealed by ITA 2007, s. 1031 and Sch. 1, Pt. 1, with effect from 6 April 2007.

3(1) [Amends ICTA 1988, s. 376 as follows.]

3(2) [Substitutes ICTA 1988, s. 376(4)(g).]

3(3) [Inserts ICTA 1988, s. 376(4A).]

4 [Amends ICTA 1988, s. 459.]

5(1) [Amends ICTA 1988 s. 460 as follows.]

5(2) [Amends ICTA 1988, s. 460(1).]

5(3) [Amends provisions as below.]

(a) [amends ICTA 1988, s. 460(2)(a);]

(b) [inserts ICTA 1988, s. 460(2)(aa).]

5(4) [Amends ICTA 1988, s. 460(5)–(10).]

5(5) [Amends ICTA 1988, s. 460(11).]

6 [Amends ICTA 1988, s. 461(4)(a).]

7 [Inserts ICTA 1988, s. 461A–461C.]

8(1) [Amends ICTA 1988, s. 462 as follows.]

8(2) [Amends ICTA 1988, s. 462(2).]

8(3) [Repealed by FA 2007, s. 114 and Sch. 27, Pt. 2(12).]

History – Para. 8(3) repealed by FA 2007, s. 114 and Sch. 27, Pt. 2(12) with effect in accordance with the provisions of FA 2007, Sch. 12, para. 6.

9 [Omitted by FA 2008, s. 44 and Sch. 18, para. 5(3)(b).]

History – Para. 9 omitted by FA 2008, s. 44 and Sch. 18, para. 5(3)(b), with effect from 21 July 2008.

10 [Amends ICTA 1988, s. 463(1).]

11(1) [Amends ICTA 1988, s. 464 as follows.]

11(2) [Repealed by FA 2007, s. 114 and Sch. 27, Pt. 2(12).]

11(3) [Amends ICTA 1988, s. 464(5)(d)(ii).]

11(4) [Amends ICTA 1988, s. 464(7).]

History – Para. 11(2) repealed by FA 2007, s. 114 and Sch. 27, Pt. 2(12) with effect in accordance with the provisions of FA 2007, Sch. 12, para. 6.

12 [Inserts ICTA 1988, s. 465(6).]

13 [Inserts ICTA 1988, s. 465A.]

14(1) [Amends ICTA 1988, s. 466 as follows.]

14(2) [Repealed by FA 1996, s. 205 and Sch. 41, Pt. V(28), with effect in accordance with FA 1996, s. 171.]

14(3-7) [Amends ICTA 1988, s. 466(2).]

14(8) [Amends ICTA 1988, s. 466(3).]

14(9) [Inserts ICTA 1988, s. 466(5).]

15 [Omitted by FA 2008, s. 36 and Sch. 14, para. 17(c).]

History – Para. 15 omitted by FA 2008, s. 36 and Sch. 14, para. 17(c), with effect for accounting periods beginning on or after 1 April 2008 (so far as relating to corporation tax) and for the tax year 2008–09 (so far as relating to income tax).

16 [Substitutes ICTA 1988, s. 599(8)(b).]

17 [Substitutes ICTA 1988, s. 630(b).]

18(1) [Amends ICTA 1988, Sch. 14 as follows.]

18(2) [Amends ICTA 1988, Sch. 14 para. (2)(1)(b), 3(1).]

18(3) [Amends ICTA 1988, Sch. 14, para. 3(3)(a).]

19(1) [Amends ICTA 1988, Sch. 15 as follows.]

19(2) [Amends ICTA 1988, Sch. 15, para. 3(1).]

19(3) [Repealed by FA 1995, s. 162 and Sch. 29, Pt. VIII(6).]

19(4) [Amends ICTA 1988, Sch. 15, para. 3(4)(c).]

19(5) [Inserts ICTA 1988, Sch. 15, para. 3(4A).]

19(6) [Substitutes ICTA 1988, Sch. 15, para. 4(3)(b)(i).]

19(7) [Amends ICTA 1988, Sch. 15, para. 6(1).]

History – Para. 19(3) repealed by FA 1995, s. 162 and Sch. 29, Pt. VIII(6) with effect from 1 May 1995.

AMENDMENTS OF ENACTMENTS RELATING TO CHARGEABLE GAINS

20(1) Subject to the repeals made by the Taxation of Chargeable Gains Act 1992, after section 143 of the Capital Gains Tax Act 1979 there shall be inserted–

[Inserted CGTA 1979, s. 143A, 143B (since repealed).]

20(2) Subject to the repeals made by the Taxation of Chargeable Gains Act 1992–

(a) [Amended FA 1985, s. 68 (since repealed).]

(b) [Amended FA 1988, Sch. 8, para. 1(3)(a) (since repealed).]

21(1) The Taxation of Chargeable Gains Act 1992 shall be amended as follows.

21(2) [Omitted by FA 2008, s. 8 and Sch. 2, para. 70(a)(ii).]

21(3) [Inserts TCGA 1992, s. 217A–217C.]

History – Para. 21(2) omitted by FA 2008, s. 8 and Sch. 2, para. 70(a)(ii), with effect in relation to disposals on or after 6 April 2008.

COMMENCEMENT

22(1) This Schedule shall come into force on such day as the Treasury may by order made by statutory instrument appoint, and different days may be appointed for different provisions or different purposes.

22(2) An order under this paragraph may contain such transitional provisions and savings (whether or not involving the modification of any statutory provision) as appear to the Treasury necessary or expedient in connection with the provisions brought into force.

Statutory instruments – SI 1993/236 (made under Sch. 9, para. 22): the appointed day for the coming into force of Sch. 9 was 19 February 1993.

SCHEDULE 10 – FURNISHED ACCOMMODATION

Section 59

1-13 [Omitted by ITTOIA 2005, s. 882(1) and Sch. 1, para. 461; and repealed by ITTOIA 2005, s. 884 and Sch. 3.]

History – Sch. 10 omitted by ITTOIA 2005, s. 882(1) and Sch. 1, para. 461; and repealed by ITTOIA 2005, s. 884 and Sch. 3 effective for income tax purposes for 2005–06 onwards and for corporation tax purposes for accounting periods ending after 5 April 2005 (ITTOIA 2005, s. 883(1)).

Notes – The repealed income tax material relating to the "rent-a-room relief" is principally rewritten at ITTOIA 2005, s. 789–802.

SCHEDULE 11 – PAYING AND COLLECTING AGENTS ETC.

Section 63

[Repealed by Statute Law (Repeals) Act 2013, s. 1 and Sch. 1, Pt. 10.]

History – Sch. 11 repealed by Statute Law (Repeals) Act 2013, s. 1 and Sch. 1, Pt. 10, with effect from 31 January 2013.

SCHEDULE 12 – BANKS ETC. IN COMPULSORY LIQUIDATION

Section 66

[Repealed by CTA 2010, s. 1177 and Sch. 1, para. 270(3) and also repealed by CTA 2010, s. 1181 and Sch. 3, Pt. 2; also omitted by TIOPA 2010, s. 371 and Sch. 7, para. 65 and repealed by TIOPA 2010, s. 378 and Sch. 10, Pt. 12.]

History – Sch. 12 repealed by CTA 2010, s. 1177 and Sch. 1, para. 270(3) and also repealed by CTA 2010, s. 1181 and Sch. 3, Pt. 2, with effect for corporation tax purposes only for accounting periods ending on or after 1 April 2010. Sch. 12 also omitted by TIOPA 2010, s. 371 and Sch. 7, para. 65 and repealed by TIOPA 2010, s. 378 and Sch. 10, Pt. 12, with effect for corporation tax purposes for accounting periods ending on or after 1 April 2010, for income tax and capital gains tax purposes for the tax year 2010–11 and subsequent tax years, and for petroleum revenue tax purposes for chargeable periods beginning on or after 1 July 2010.

Notes – Sch. 12 rewritten for corporation purposes as follows:
Para. 1(1): CTA 2010, s. 635(1), (2), (3), (4), (6).
Para. 1(2): CTA 2010, s. 635(5).
Para. 2(1): CTA 2010, s. 641(1).
Para. 2(2): CTA 2010, s. 641(5).
Para. 2(3): CTA 2010, s. 641(2).
Para. 2(4): CTA 2010, s. 641(3).
Para. 2(5): CTA 2010, s. 641(4).
Para. 3(1): CTA 2010, s. 636(1), (3).
Para. 3(1A): CTA 2010, s. 636(1); TIOPA 2010, Sch. 7, para. 71.
Para. 3(2): CTA 2010, s. 636(1), (2).
Para. 3(3): CTA 2010, s. 636(4).
Para. 3(4): CTA 2010, s. 640(1).
Para. 3(5): CTA 2010, s. 640(2).
Para. 4(1): CTA 2010, s. 638(1), (2), (6).
Para. 4(2): CTA 2010, s. 638(3), (4), (5).
Para. 5: CTA 2010, s. 637(1), (2), (3).
Para. 6(1): CTA 2010, s. 639(1).
Para. 6(2): CTA 2010, s. 639(4), (2), (3).
Para. 7: not rewritten, as spent.
Sch. 12 rewritten for income tax purposes as follows:
Para. 1–6: TIOPA 2010, Sch. 7, para. 71.
Para. 7: not rewritten, as spent.

SCHEDULE 13 – CAPITAL ALLOWANCES: ENTERPRISE ZONES

Section 70

[Repealed by CAA 2001, s. 580 and Sch. 4.]

History – Sch. 13 repealed by CAA 2001, s. 580 and Sch. 4, with effect as respects allowances and charges falling to be made for chargeable periods ending, for income tax purposes, on or after 6 April 2001, and for corporation tax purposes, on or after 1 April 2001.

SCHEDULE 16 – GENERAL AND SPECIAL COMMISSIONERS

Section 76

[Omitted by SI 2009/56, art. 3 and Sch. 1, para. 186.]

History – Sch. 16 omitted by SI 2009/56, art. 3 and Sch. 1, para. 186, with effect from 1 April 2009, subject to transitional and saving provisions in SI 2009/56, Sch. 3.

"REMUNERATION OF GENERAL COMMISSIONERS ETC.

2 [Repealed by TCEA 2007, s. 146 and Sch. 23, Pt. 1.]

History – Para. 2 repealed by TCEA 2007, s. 146 and Sch. 23, Pt. 1, with effect from 1 April 2009 (SI 2008/2696, art. 6(c)(v) – subject to transitional provisions at art. 3).

JURISDICTION

3 [Inserts TMA 1970, s. 46A.]

PRACTICE AND PROCEDURE

4 [Inserts TMA 1970, s. 56B–56D.]
5 [Omits TMA 1970, s. 57B.]"

FINANCE ACT 1993

(1993 Chapter 34)

[*27th July 1993*]

ARRANGEMENT OF SECTIONS

PART II – INCOME TAX, CORPORATION TAX AND CAPITAL GAINS TAX

CHAPTER I – GENERAL

CORPORATION TAX: CURRENCY

OVERSEAS LIFE INSURANCE COMPANIES

APPROVED SHARE OPTION SCHEMES

INDEXATION: MISCELLANEOUS

MISCELLANEOUS PROVISIONS ABOUT RELIEFS

CAPITAL ALLOWANCES

MISCELLANEOUS

CHAPTER II – EXCHANGE GAINS AND LOSSES

ACCRUAL OF GAINS AND LOSSES

TRADING GAINS AND LOSSES

NON-TRADING GAINS AND LOSSES

ALTERNATIVE CALCULATION

MAIN BENEFIT TEST

ARM'S LENGTH TEST

DEFERRAL OF UNREALISED GAINS

IRRECOVERABLE DEBTS

CURRENCY CONTRACTS: SPECIAL CASES

EXCESS GAINS OR LOSSES

LOCAL CURRENCY TO BE USED

EXCHANGE RATE TO BE USED

INTERPRETATION: COMPANIES

PART II – INCOME TAX, CORPORATION TAX AND CAPITAL GAINS TAX

Chapter I – General

INCOME TAX: CHARGE, RATES AND ALLOWANCES

51 Charge and rates of income tax for 1993–94

51 [Repealed by ITA 2007, s. 1031 and Sch. 3, Pt. 1.]

History – S. 51 repealed by ITA 2007, s. 1031 and Sch. 3, Pt. 1, with effect from 6 April 2007.

52 Personal and married couple's allowances

52 [Repealed by ITA 2007, s. 1031 and Sch. 3, Pt. 1.]

History – S. 52 repealed by ITA 2007, s. 1031 and Sch. 3, Pt. 1, with effect from 6 April 2007.

CORPORATION TAX CHARGE AND RATE

53 Charge and rate of corporation tax for 1993

53 [Spent; set rate of corporation tax for the financial year 1993]

54 Small companies

54 [Repealed by CTA 2010, s. 1181 and Sch. 3, Pt. 1.]

History – S. 54 repealed by CTA 2010, s. 1181 and Sch. 3, Pt. 1, with effect for corporation tax purposes for accounting periods ending on or after 1 April 2010, and for income tax and capital gains tax purposes for the tax year 2010–11 and subsequent tax years.

Notes – S. 54 not rewritten for corporation tax purposes as spent.

INTEREST: GENERAL

55 Relief for interest

55 [Spent; set qualifying maximum for purposes of ICTA 1988, s. 367(5) for 1993–94.]

56 Interest relief: substitution of security

56 [Repealed by FA 1999, s. 139 and Sch. 20, Pt. III(7).]

History – S. 56 repealed by FA 1999, s. 139 and Sch. 20, Pt. III(7), with effect in relation to any payment of interest falling within FA 1999, s. 38(3) or (4) (broadly, any payment made on or after 6 April 2000, or made on or after 9 March 1999 and before 6 April 2000 but not falling due until on or after 6 April 2000).

57 Temporary relief for interest payments

57(1) [Repealed by FA 1999, s. 139 and Sch. 20, Pt. III(7).]

57(2) [Repealed by FA 1999, s. 139 and Sch. 20, Pt. III(7).]

57(3) [Inserts ICTA 1988, s. 365(1A) and (1B).]

57(4) [Repealed by FA 1999, s. 139 and Sch. 20, Pt. III(7).]

57(5) This section shall have effect in relation to payments of interest made on or after 16th March 1993 (whenever falling due).

57(6) [Repealed by FA 1999, s. 139 and Sch. 20, Pt. III(7).]

57(7) [Repealed by FA 1994, s. 81 and Sch. 9, para. 12 and s. 258 and Sch. 26, Pt. V(2).]

History – S. 57(1), (2), (4), (6) repealed by FA 1999, s. 139 and Sch. 20, Pt. III(7), with effect in relation to any payment of interest falling within FA 1999, s. 38(3) or (4) (broadly, any payment made on or after 6 April 2000, or made on or after 9 March 1999 and before 6 April 2000 but not falling due until on or after 6 April 2000).
S. 57(7) repealed by FA 1994, s. 81 and Sch. 9, para. 12 and s. 258 and Sch. 26, Pt. V(2), in relation to payments of interest made on or after 6 April 1994 (whenever falling due) and also so far as they relate to relevant loan interest, in relation to any payments of interest becoming due on or after 6 April 1994 which have been made at any time before that date but on or after 30 November 1993.

58 Overclaims in respect of deductions of mortgage interest

58(1) [Inserts ICTA 1988, s. 369(7).]

58(2) This section shall not apply in relation to any payment if the payment, or the claim on which it is made, was made before the day on which this Act is passed.

59 Interest payments to persons not ordinarily resident in UK

59 [Repealed by ITA 2007, s. 1031 and Sch. 3, Pt. 1.]

History – S. 59 repealed by ITA 2007, s. 1031 and Sch. 3, Pt. 1, with effect from 6 April 2007.

60 Certain interest not allowed as a deduction

60 [Repealed by FA 2002, s. 141 and Sch. 40, Pt. 3(10).]

History – S. 60 repealed by FA 2002, s. 141 and Sch. 40, Pt. 3(10) with effect in relation to accounting periods beginning on or after 1 October 2002.

INTEREST ETC. ON DEBTS BETWEEN ASSOCIATED COMPANIES

61 Qualifying debts for purposes of sections 63 to 66

61 [Repealed by FA 1996, s. 205 and Sch. 41, Pt. V(3).]

History – S. 61 repealed by FA 1996, s. 205 and Sch. 41, Pt. V(3) with effect in relation to accounting periods ending after 31 March 1996, subject to FA 1996, Sch. 15.
S. 61(3) repealed by FA 1994, s. 251(12) and s. 258 and Sch. 26, Pt. VIII(1), with effect from 30 November 1993.

62 Exempted debts for those purposes

62 [Repealed by FA 1996, s. 205 and Sch. 41, Pt. V(3).]

History – S. 62 repealed by FA 1996, s. 205 and Sch. 41, Pt. V(3) with effect in relation to accounting periods ending after 31 March 1996, subject to FA 1996, Sch. 15.

62A Application of sections 63 to 66: supplementary

62A [Repealed by FA 1996, s. 205 and Sch. 41, Pt. V(3).]

History – S. 62A repealed by FA 1996, s. 205 and Sch. 41, Pt. V(3) with effect in relation to accounting periods ending after 31 March 1996, subject to FA 1996, Sch. 15.
S. 62A inserted by FA 1995, s. 88(2) and deemed always to have had effect.

63 Accrued income securities

63 [Repealed by FA 1996, s. 205 and Sch. 41, Pt. V(3).]

History – S. 63 is repealed by FA 1996, s. 205 and Sch. 41, Pt. V(3) with effect in relation to accounting periods ending after 31 March 1996, subject to FA 1996, Sch. 15.
Former s. 63(12) repealed by FA 1995, s. 88(3), s. 162 and Sch. 29, Pt. VIII(13).

64 Deep discount securities

64 [Repealed by FA 1996, s. 205 and Sch. 41, Pt. V(3).]

History – S. 64 repealed by FA 1996, s. 205 and Sch. 41, Pt. V(3) with effect in relation to accounting periods ending after 31 March 1996, subject to FA 1996, Sch. 15.

65 Deep gain securities

65 [Repealed by FA 1996, s. 205 and Sch. 41, Pt. V(3).]

History – S. 65 repealed by FA 1996, s. 205 and Sch. 41, Pt. V(3) with effect in relation to accounting periods ending after 31 March 1996, subject to FA 1996, Sch. 15.

66 Avoidance of double charging

66 [Repealed by FA 1996, s. 205 and Sch. 41, Pt. V(3).]

History – S. 66 repealed by FA 1996, s. 205 and Sch. 41, Pt. V(3) with effect in relation to accounting periods ending after 31 March 1996, subject to FA 1996, Sch. 15.

CHARITABLE DONATIONS

67 Donations from companies and individuals

67 [Repealed by Statute Law (Repeals) Act 2013, s. 1 and Sch. 1, Pt. 10.]

History – S. 67 repealed by Statute Law (Repeals) Act 2013, s. 1 and Sch. 1, Pt. 10, with effect from 31 January 2013.
Former s. 67(1) repealed by CTA 2010, s. 1181 and Sch. 3, Pt. 1, with effect for corporation tax purposes for accounting periods ending on or after 1 April 2010, and for income tax and capital gains tax purposes for the tax year 2010–11 and subsequent tax years.

68 Payroll deduction schemes

68 [Repealed by ITEPA 2003, Sch. 8, Pt. 1 which has effect for the tax year 2003–04 and subsequent tax years.]

69 Contributions to agent's expenses

69 [Repealed by CTA 2009, s. 1326 and Sch. 3, Pt. 1.]

History – S. 69 repealed by CTA 2009, s. 1326 and Sch. 3, Pt. 1, with effect for corporation tax purposes for accounting periods ending on or after 1 April 2009, and for income tax and capital gains tax purposes for the tax year 2009–10 and subsequent tax years.

BENEFITS IN KIND

70 Car benefits: 1993–94

70(1) [Substitutes ICTA 1988, Sch. 6, Pt. I.]

70(2) This section shall have effect for the year 1993–94.

71 Car fuel: 1993–94

71(1) [Substitutes ICTA 1988, s. 158, Tables A, AB and B.]

71(2) [Amends ICTA 1988, s. 158(5).]

71(3) This section shall have effect for the year 1993–94.

72 Car and car fuel benefits: 1994–95 onwards

72 [Repealed by TIOPA 2010, s. 378 and Sch. 10, Pt. 13.]

History – S. 72 repealed by TIOPA 2010, s. 378 and Sch. 10, Pt. 13, with effect for corporation tax purposes for accounting periods ending on or after 1 April 2010, for income tax and capital gains tax purposes for the tax year 2010–11 and subsequent tax years, and for petroleum revenue tax purposes for chargeable periods beginning on or after 1 July 2010.

Notes – S. 72 not rewritten, as introductory.

73 Vans

73 [Repealed by ITEPA 2003, Sch. 8, Pt. 1 which has effect for the tax year 2003–04 and subsequent tax years.]

74 Heavier commercial vehicles

74 [Repealed by ITEPA 2003, Sch. 8, Pt. 1 which has effect for the tax year 2003–04 and subsequent tax years.]

75 Sporting and recreational facilities

75 [Repealed by ITEPA 2003, Sch. 8, Pt. 1 which has effect for the tax year 2003–04 and subsequent tax years.]

76 Removal expenses and benefits

76 [Repealed by ITEPA 2003, Sch. 8, Pt. 1 which has effect for the tax year 2003–04 and subsequent tax years.]

TAXATION OF DISTRIBUTIONS ETC.

77 Application of lower rate

77(1,2) [Repealed by FA 1996, Sch. 41, Pt. V(1).]

77(3) [Repealed by ITTOIA 2005, s. 884 and Sch. 3.]

77(4) [Repealed by CTA 2010, s. 1181 and Sch. 3, Pt. 1.]

77(5) This section shall apply in relation to the year 1993–94 and subsequent years of assessment.

History – S. 77(1) and (2) repealed by FA 1996, Sch. 41, Pt. V(1) with effect in relation to years after 1995–96.
S. 77(3) repealed by ITTOIA 2005, s. 884 and Sch. 3 effective for income tax purposes for 2005–06 onwards and for corporation tax purposes for accounting periods ending after 5 April 2005 (ITTOIA 2005, s. 883(1)).
S. 77(4) repealed by CTA 2010, s. 1181 and Sch. 3, Pt. 1, with effect for corporation tax purposes for accounting periods ending on or after 1 April 2010, and for income tax and capital gains tax purposes for the tax year 2010–11 and subsequent tax years.

78 Rate of advance corporation tax and tax credits

78 [Repealed by FA 1998, s. 165 and Sch. 27, Pt. III(2).]

History – S. 78 repealed by FA 1998, s. 165 and Sch. 27, Pt. III(2), with effect in relation to distributions made on or after 6 April 1999.

79 Provisions supplemental to sections 77 and 78

79(1) Schedule 6 to this Act (which makes further provision for the purposes of and in connection with the provisions of sections 77 and 78 above) shall have effect.

79(2) [Repealed by Statute Law (Repeals) Act 2013, s. 1 and Sch. 1, Pt. 10.]

79(3) [Repealed by FA 1996, Sch. 41, Pt. V(1) with effect in relation to years after 1995–96.]

History – S. 79(2) repealed by Statute Law (Repeals) Act 2013, s. 1 and Sch. 1, Pt. 10, with effect from 31 January 2013.
Former s. 79(2)(b) and the word "and " immediately before it, repealed by ITA 2007, s. 1031 and Sch. 3, Pt. 1, with effect from 6 April 2007.

Notes – Former s. 79(2)(b) rewritten as ITA 2007, s. 498(1), (2).

80 Transitional relief for charities etc.

80 [Omitted by ITA 2007, s. 1027 and Sch. 1, para. 355, and repealed by s. 1031 and Sch. 3, Pt. 1.]

History – S. 80 omitted by ITA 2007, s. 1027 and Sch. 1, para. 355, and repealed by s. 1031 and Sch. 3, Pt. 1, with effect from 6 April 2007.

81 Restriction of set-off of ACT

81 [Repealed by FA 1998, s. 165 and Sch. 27, Pt. III(2).]

History – S. 81 repealed by FA 1998, s. 165 and Sch. 27, Pt. III(2) with effect in relation to changes of ownership (within the meaning of ICTA 1988, s. 245) occurring on or after 6 April 1999.

CHARGEABLE GAINS

82 Annual exempt amount for 1993–94

82 [Spent; set exempt amount for purposes of TCGA 1992, s. 3 for 1993–94.]

83 Annual exempt amount: indexation for 1994–95 onwards

83(1) [Amends TCGA 1992, s. 3(3).]

83(2) This section shall have effect for the year 1994–95 and subsequent years of assessment.

84 Re-organisations etc. involving debentures

84(1) [Inserts TCGA 1992, s. 117(6A).]

84(2) [Inserts TCGA 1992, s. 251(6).]

84(3) This section shall have effect in relation to any chargeable period ending on or after 16th March 1993 but, in relation to any accounting period of a company which began before 6th April 1992, this section shall have effect as if the references in this section, and in the amendments made by this section, to provisions of the Taxation of Chargeable Gains Act 1992 were references to such of the provisions of the Capital Gains Tax Act 1979 and the Finance Act 1984 as correspond to those provisions and have effect in relation to that accounting period.

85 Personal equity plans

85 [Inserts TCGA 1992, s. 151(4).]

86 Roll-over relief

86(1) [Inserts TCGA 1992, s. 155, Class 6.]

86(2) The Treasury may by order made by statutory instrument amend section 155 of the Taxation of Chargeable Gains Act 1992 (roll-over relief: relevant classes of assets) so as to add to or amend the classes of assets specified in that section.

86(2A) But an order under subsection (2) may not restrict the assets which fall within a class listed in that section (whether by virtue of subsection (2) or otherwise).

86(2B) An order under subsection (2) may make such consequential amendments of section 156ZB of, or Schedule 7AB to, the Taxation of Chargeable Gains Act 1992 as appear to the Treasury to be appropriate.

86(3) A statutory instrument containing an order under subsection (2) above shall be subject to annulment in pursuance of a resolution of the House of Commons.

86(4) Subsection (1) above shall apply where the disposal of the old assets (or an interest in them) or the acquisition of the new assets (or an interest in them) is on or after 1st January 1993; but, in relation to any accounting period of a company which began before 6th April 1992, subsection (1) above shall have effect as if the inserted class were numbered 5 and were inserted after Class 4 in section 118 of the Capital Gains Tax Act 1979.

History – S. 86(2)–(2B) substituted for former s. 86(2) by FA 2012, s. 37(2) with effect from 17 July 2012.

Former s. 86(2)(a) and (b) substituted for the words "Schedule 7AB" by F(No. 2)A 2005, s. 41(5), with effect from 20 July 2005 (Royal Assent).

In former s. 86(2), the words "Any such order" to the end of that subsection inserted by FA 2002, s. 43(3) with effect in relation to a case where a company is treated by virtue of TCGA 1992, s. 179(3) as having sold and immediately reacquired an asset, where the company's ceasing to be a member of the group in question happens on or after 1 April 2002, and in relation to a case where a company is so treated by virtue of TCGA 1992, s. 179(6) where the relevant time (within the meaning of that subsection) is on or after 1 April 2002.

Statutory instruments – SI 1999/564: fish quota added as a new class of assets which qualify for relief under TCGA 1992, s. 152, 153, 155.

87 Relief on retirement or re-investment

87(1) Schedule 7 to this Act (which amends the provisions of the Taxation of Chargeable Gains Act 1992 with respect to retirement relief and makes new provision in relation to relief on the re-investment of certain gains) shall have effect.

87(2) This section and that Schedule shall have effect in relation to any disposal made on or after 16th March 1993.

88 Restriction on set-off of pre-entry losses

88(1) [Inserts TCGA 1992, s. 177A.]

88(2) The Schedule set out in Schedule 8 to this Act shall be inserted after Schedule 7 to that Act.

88(3) This section and that Schedule–

(a) shall apply for the calculation of the amount to be included in respect of chargeable gains in a company's total profits for any accounting period ending on or after 16th March 1993; but

(b) shall so apply only in relation to the deduction from chargeable gains accruing on or after 16th March 1993 of amounts in respect of, or of amounts carried forward in respect of–

(i) pre-entry losses accruing before it became a member of the relevant group to a company whose membership of that group began or begins at a time on or after 1st April 1987; and

(ii) losses accruing on the disposal of any assets so far as it is by reference to such a company that the assets fall to be treated as being or having been pre-entry assets or assets incorporating a part referable to pre-entry assets.

88(4) In relation to accounting periods beginning before 6th April 1992 this section and that Schedule shall have effect as if–

(a) the section and Schedule inserted by subsections (1) and (2) above were inserted in the Capital Gains Tax Act 1979; and

(b) references in the Schedule so inserted to provisions of the Taxation of Chargeable Gains Act 1992 were references to such of the provisions of that Act of 1979 or of any other enactment as correspond to the provisions referred to and have effect in relation to that accounting period.

89 De-grouping charges

89(1) [Amends TCGA 1992, s. 179(4).]

89(2) This section shall have effect in relation to accounting periods ending after the day appointed for the purposes of section 180(1)(b) of that Act.

Notes – The appointed day for the purposes of TCGA 1992, s. 180(1)(b) is 30 September 1993.

90 Insurance: transfers of business

90 [Repealed by FA 2000, Sch. 40, Pt. II(12).]

History – Repealed by FA 2000, Sch. 40, Pt. II(12) in accordance with Sch. 29, para. 5(4).

91 Deemed disposals of unit trusts by insurance companies

91(1) Section 212 of the Taxation of Chargeable Gains Act 1992 (annual deemed disposal by insurance companies of unit trusts) shall have effect in relation to accounting periods beginning on or after 1st January 1993; and neither that section nor section 46 of the Finance Act 1990 (which is consolidated in that section) shall have effect in relation to any earlier accounting period in relation to which either of them would have applied apart from this subsection.

91(2) [Omitted by FA 2012, s. 146 and Sch. 16, para. 91.]

91(3) [Amends TCGA 1992, s. 212(7).]

91(4) [Inserts TCGA 1992, s. 213(1A).]

91(5) [Repealed by FA 2007, s. 114 and Sch. 27, Pt. 2(10).]

91(6) [Repealed by FA 2007, s. 114 and Sch. 27, Pt. 2(10).]

History – S. 91(2) omitted by FA 2012, s. 146 and Sch. 16, para. 91 in relation to accounting periods beginning on or after 1 January 2013 (FA 2012, s. 148) but subject to transitional provisions in FA 2012, Sch. 17. Where an accounting period would otherwise straddle 1 January 2013, it is deemed to end on 31 December 2012 (FA 2012, s. 149).
S. 91(5) and (6) repealed by FA 2007, s. 114 and Sch. 27, Pt. 2(10) with effect in relation to periods of account beginning on or after 1 January 2007.

CORPORATION TAX: CURRENCY

Notes – The legislative history of s. 92–96 is complex. There have been multiple substitutions, effective repeals and numerous amendments since the original sections were set out in Finance Act 1993. In outline the principal changes are as follows:

- New s. 92–92E substituted for former s. 92–94AB by FA 2004, s. 52 and Sch. 10, para. 77, with effect in relation to periods of account beginning on or after 1 January 2005 or earlier in the case of companies required or permitted to prepare accounts in accordance with international accounting standards.
- S. 92 and 93 are amended; a new s. 93A is inserted; s. 94 (as inserted by FA 2000, s. 105) is substituted by s. 94AA; and s. 94AB is inserted after the newly substituted s. 94AA, by FA 2002, s. 80 and Sch. 24, para. 2–6; this effectively omits s. 94.
- Original s. 92–95 are substituted with new s. 92, 93 and 94, by FA 2000, s. 105; this substitution effectively omits the original s. 95.
- The effective operation of s. 96 (which inserted an amendment into ICTA 1988, Sch. 24, para. 4A) disabled by FA 1995, s. 133 and Sch. 25, para. 6(3); which deemed the insertion of the para. 4A never to have occurred; this leaves s. 96 effectively redundant.
- S. 94A inserted after s. 94, and amendments made to s. 95(6), by FA 1994, s. 136.
- Original s. 92–96 set out in Finance Act 1993.

92 The basic rule: sterling to be used

92 [Omitted by CTA 2010, s. 1177 and Sch. 1, para. 277 and repealed by CTA 2010, s. 1181 and Sch. 3, Pt. 1.]

History – S. 92 omitted by CTA 2010, s. 1177 and Sch. 1, para. 277 and repealed by CTA 2010, s. 1181 and Sch. 3, Pt. 1, with effect for corporation tax purposes for accounting periods ending on or after 1 April 2010, and for income tax and capital gains tax purposes for the tax year 2010–11 and subsequent tax years.

Notes – S. 92 rewritten for corporation tax purposes as follows:
S. 92(1): CTA 2010, s. 5(1).
S. 92(2): not rewritten as unnecessary.

92A Company operating in sterling and preparing accounts in another currency

92A [Omitted by CTA 2010, s. 1177 and Sch. 1, para. 277 and repealed by CTA 2010, s. 1181 and Sch. 3, Pt. 1.]

History – S. 92A omitted by CTA 2010, s. 1177 and Sch. 1, para. 277 and repealed by CTA 2010, s. 1181 and Sch. 3, Pt. 1, with effect for corporation tax purposes for accounting periods ending on or after 1 April 2010, and for income tax and capital gains tax purposes for the tax year 2010–11 and subsequent tax years.

92B Company operating in currency other than sterling and preparing accounts in another currency

92B [Omitted by CTA 2010, s. 1177 and Sch. 1, para. 277 and repealed by CTA 2010, s. 1181 and Sch. 3, Pt. 1.]

History – S. 92B omitted by CTA 2010, s. 1177 and Sch. 1, para. 277 and repealed by CTA 2010, s. 1181 and Sch. 3, Pt. 1, with effect for corporation tax purposes for accounting periods ending on or after 1 April 2010, and for income tax and capital gains tax purposes for the tax year 2010–11 and subsequent tax years.

Notes – S. 92B rewritten for corporation tax purposes as follows:
S. 92B(1): CTA 2010, s. 7(1).
S. 92B(2): CTA 2010, s. 7(2).
S. 92B(3): CTA 2010, s. 7(3).
S. 92B(4): CTA 2010, s. 10(1), (2).

92C Company preparing accounts in currency other than sterling

92C [Omitted by CTA 2010, s. 1177 and Sch. 1, para. 277 and repealed by CTA 2010, s. 1181 and Sch. 3, Pt. 1.]

History – S. 92C omitted by CTA 2010, s. 1177 and Sch. 1, para. 277 and repealed by CTA 2010, s. 1181 and Sch. 3, Pt. 1, with effect for corporation tax purposes for accounting periods ending on or after 1 April 2010, and for income tax and capital gains tax purposes for the tax year 2010–11 and subsequent tax years.

Notes – S. 92C rewritten for corporation tax purposes as follows:
S. 92C(1): CTA 2010, s. 8(1).
S. 92C(2): CTA 2010, s. 9(1).
S. 92C(3): CTA 2010, s. 8(2), 9(2).
S. 92C(4): CTA 2010, s. 8(3), 9(3).
S. 92C(5): CTA 2010, s. 10(1), (2).

92D Sterling equivalents: the basic rule

92D [Omitted by CTA 2010, s. 1177 and Sch. 1, para. 277 and repealed by CTA 2010, s. 1181 and Sch. 3, Pt. 1.]

History – S. 92D omitted by CTA 2010, s. 1177 and Sch. 1, para. 277 and repealed by CTA 2010, s. 1181 and Sch. 3, Pt. 1, with effect for corporation tax purposes for accounting periods ending on or after 1 April 2010, and for income tax and capital gains tax purposes for the tax year 2010–11 and subsequent tax years.

Notes – S. 92D rewritten for corporation tax purposes as follows:
S. 92D(1): CTA 2010, s. 11(1).
S. 92D(2): CTA 2010, s. 11(2).
S. 92D(3): CTA 2010, s. 11(4).

92DA Sterling equivalents: carried-back amounts

92DA [Omitted by CTA 2010, s. 1177 and Sch. 1, para. 277 and repealed by CTA 2010, s. 1181 and Sch. 3, Pt. 1.]

History – S. 92DA omitted by CTA 2010, s. 1177 and Sch. 1, para. 277 and repealed by CTA 2010, s. 1181 and Sch. 3, Pt. 1, with effect for corporation tax purposes for accounting periods ending on or after 1 April 2010, and for income tax and capital gains tax purposes for the tax year 2010–11 and subsequent tax years.

Notes – S. 92DA rewritten for corporation tax purposes as follows:
S. 92DA(1): CTA 2010, s. 12(1).
S. 92DA(2): CTA 2010, s. 12(2).
S. 92DA(3): CTA 2010, s. 12(2), (3).
S. 92DA(4): CTA 2010, s. 12(2).
S. 92DA(5): CTA 2010, s. 12(2).
S. 92DA(6): CTA 2010, s. 12(2).
S. 92DA(7): CTA 2010, s. 12(2).
S. 92DA(8): CTA 2010, s. 12(2).
S. 92DA(9): CTA 2010, s. 12(3).

92DB Sterling equivalents: carried-forward amounts

92DB [Omitted by CTA 2010, s. 1177 and Sch. 1, para. 277 and repealed by CTA 2010, s. 1181 and Sch. 3, Pt. 1.]

History – S. 92DB omitted by CTA 2010, s. 1177 and Sch. 1, para. 277 and repealed by CTA 2010, s. 1181 and Sch. 3, Pt. 1, with effect for corporation tax purposes for accounting periods ending on or after 1 April 2010, and for income tax and capital gains tax purposes for the tax year 2010–11 and subsequent tax years.

Notes – S. 92DB rewritten for corporation tax purposes as follows:
S. 92DB(1): CTA 2010, s. 13(1).
S. 92DB(2): CTA 2010, s. 13(2).
S. 92DB(3): CTA 2010, s. 13(2), (3).
S. 92DB(4): CTA 2010, s. 13(2).
S. 92DB(5): CTA 2010, s. 13(2).
S. 92DB(6): CTA 2010, s. 13(2).
S. 92DB(7): CTA 2010, s. 13(2).
S. 92DB(8): CTA 2010, s. 13(2).
S. 92DB(9): CTA 2010, s. 13(3).

92DC Adjustment of sterling losses: carried-back amounts

92DC [Omitted by CTA 2010, s. 1177 and Sch. 1, para. 277 and repealed by CTA 2010, s. 1181 and Sch. 3, Pt. 1.]

History – S. 92DC omitted by CTA 2010, s. 1177 and Sch. 1, para. 277 and repealed by CTA 2010, s. 1181 and Sch. 3, Pt. 1, with effect for corporation tax purposes for accounting periods ending on or after 1 April 2010, and for income tax and capital gains tax purposes for the tax year 2010–11 and subsequent tax years.

Notes – S. 92DC rewritten for corporation tax purposes as follows:
S. 92DC(1): CTA 2010, s. 14(1).
S. 92DC(2): CTA 2010, s. 14(2).
S. 92DC(3): CTA 2010, s. 14(3).
S. 92DC(4): CTA 2010, s. 14(4).
S. 92DC(5): CTA 2010, s. 14(5).
S. 92DC(6): CTA 2010, s. 14(6).

92DD Adjustment of sterling losses: carried-forward amounts

92DD [Omitted by CTA 2010, s. 1177 and Sch. 1, para. 277 and repealed by CTA 2010, s. 1181 and Sch. 3, Pt. 1.]

History – S. 92DD omitted by CTA 2010, s. 1177 and Sch. 1, para. 277 and repealed by CTA 2010, s. 1181 and Sch. 3, Pt. 1, with effect for corporation tax purposes for accounting periods ending on or after 1 April 2010, and for income tax and capital gains tax purposes for the tax year 2010–11 and subsequent tax years.

Notes – S. 92DD rewritten for corporation tax purposes as follows:
S. 92DD(1): CTA 2010, s. 15(1).
S. 92DD(2): CTA 2010, s. 15(2).
S. 92DD(3): CTA 2010, s. 15(3).
S. 92DD(4): CTA 2010, s. 15(4).
S. 92DD(5): CTA 2010, s. 15(5).
S. 92DD(6): CTA 2010, s. 15(6).

92DE Meaning of 'carried-back amount' and 'carried-forward amount'

92DE [Omitted by CTA 2010, s. 1177 and Sch. 1, para. 277 and repealed by CTA 2010, s. 1181 and Sch. 3, Pt. 1.]

History – S. 92DE omitted by CTA 2010, s. 1177 and Sch. 1, para. 277 and repealed by CTA 2010, s. 1181 and Sch. 3, Pt. 1, with effect for corporation tax purposes for accounting periods ending on or after 1 April 2010, and for income tax and capital gains tax purposes for the tax year 2010–11 and subsequent tax years.

Notes – S. 92DE rewritten for corporation tax purposes as follows:
S. 92DE(1): CTA 2010, s. 17(2).
S. 92DE(2): CTA 2010, s. 17(3).
S. 92DE(3): CTA 2010, s. 16(2).
S. 92DE(4): CTA 2010, s. 16(1).

92E Interpretation of sections 92A to 92DD

92E [Omitted by CTA 2010, s. 1177 and Sch. 1, para. 277 and repealed by CTA 2010, s. 1181 and Sch. 3, Pt. 1.]

History – S. 92E omitted by CTA 2010, s. 1177 and Sch. 1, para. 277 and repealed by CTA 2010, s. 1181 and Sch. 3, Pt. 1, with effect for corporation tax purposes for accounting periods ending on or after 1 April 2010, and for income tax and capital gains tax purposes for the tax year 2010–11 and subsequent tax years.

Notes – S. 92E rewritten for corporation tax purposes as follows:
S. 92E(A1): CTA 2010, s. 9(1), (4), 10(2), (3), 11(2), 17(1), (4), (5).
S. 92E(1): CTA 2010, s. 17(1).
S. 92E(2): CTA 2010, s. 9(1), (4).
S. 92E(3): CTA 2010, s. 17(4).
S. 92E(4): CTA 2010, s. 10(2), (3), 11(2), (3).
S. 92E(5): CTA 2010, s. 17(5).

94A Parts of trades: petroleum extraction companies

94A [Effectively omitted by FA 2000, s. 105(1), which substituted new s. 92, 93 and 94 in place of the old s. 92–95]

History – S. 92–95 substituted by s. 92–94, by FA 2000, s. 105(1), with effect for accounting periods beginning on or after 1 January 2000 and ending on or after 21 March 2000, or with effect in relation to the first accounting period beginning on or after 1 July 2000 where the conditions in s. 105(5) are fulfilled (this has the effect of omitting s. 94A).
Former s. 94A inserted by FA 1994, s. 136.

95 Currency to be used: supplementary

[S. 92–95 substituted by s. 92–94 by FA 2000, s. 105(1).]

History – S. 92–95 substituted by s. 92–94 by FA 2000, s. 105(1), with effect for accounting periods beginning on or after 1 January 2000 and ending on or after 21 March 2000, or with effect in relation to the first accounting period beginning on or after 1 July 2000 where the conditions in s. 105(5) are fulfilled.

96 Foreign companies: trading currency

96 [Effectively omitted by FA 1995, s. 133 and Sch. 25, para. 6(3), that deemed the amendment made by s. 96 (the insertion of ICTA 1988, Sch. 24, para 4A) to never have been made.]

OVERSEAS LIFE INSURANCE COMPANIES

97 Modification of Taxes Act 1988

97 [Repealed by SI 2006/3271, reg. 43(1) and Schedule, Pt. 1.]

History – S. 97 repealed by SI 2006/3271, reg. 43(1) and Schedule, Pt. 1 with effect from 31 December 2006, in relation to accounting periods ending on or after that date.

98 Modification of section 440 of Taxes Act 1988

98 [Repealed by SI 2006/3271, reg. 43(1) and Schedule, Pt. 1.]

History – S. 98 repealed by SI 2006/3271, reg. 43(1) and Schedule, Pt. 1 with effect from 31 December 2006, in relation to accounting periods ending on or after that date.

100 Income from investments attributable to BLAGAB, etc.

100(1) [Repealed by FA 1995, s. 162 and Sch. 29, Pt. VIII(5).]

100(2) [Amends ICTA 1988, s. 475(6); s. 100(2)(a) repealed in part by FA 1995, s. 162 and Sch. 29, Pt. VIII(5), for accounting periods beginning on or after 1 January 1995.]

100(3) This section shall apply in relation to accounting periods beginning after 31st December 1992.

History – S. 100(1) repealed by FA 1995, s. 162 and Sch. 29, Pt. VIII(5), for accounting periods beginning on or after 1 January 1995.

101 Modification of Finance Act 1989

101 [Repealed by SI 2006/3271, reg. 43(1) and Schedule, Pt. 1.]

History – S. 101 repealed by SI 2006/3271, reg. 43(1) and Schedule, Pt. 1 with effect from 31 December 2006, in relation to accounting periods ending on or after that date.

102 Modification of Taxation of Chargeable Gains Act 1992

102 [Repealed by SI 2006/3271, reg. 43(1) and Schedule, Pt. 1.]

History – S. 102 repealed by SI 2006/3271, reg. 43(1) and Schedule, Pt. 1 with effect from 31 December 2006, in relation to accounting periods ending on or after that date.

103 Amendment of definition and repeals

103(1) [Omitted by FA 2012, s. 146 and Sch. 16, para. 247.]

103(2) [Repeals ICTA 1988, s. 445, 446(1), 447(1), (2) and (4), 448, 449, 724(5)–(8), 811(2)(c) and Sch. 19AB para. 1(9).]

103(3) [Omitted by FA 2012, s. 146 and Sch. 16, para. 247.]

103(4) [Repealed by FA 1996, Sch. 41, Pt. V(3) with effect in relation to accounting periods ending after 31 March 1996 subject to FA 1996, Sch. 15.]

History – S. 103(1) omitted by FA 2012, s. 146 and Sch. 16, para. 247 in relation to accounting periods beginning on or after 1 January 2013 (FA 2012, s. 148) but subject to transitional provisions in FA 2012, Sch. 17. Where an accounting period would otherwise straddle 1 January 2013, it is deemed to end on 31 December 2012 (FA 2012, s. 149).
S. 103(3) omitted by FA 2012, s. 146 and Sch. 16, para. 247 in relation to accounting periods beginning on or after 1 January 2013 (FA 2012, s. 148) but subject to transitional provisions in FA 2012, Sch. 17. Where an accounting period would otherwise straddle 1 January 2013, it is deemed to end on 31 December 2012 (FA 2012, s. 149).
S. 103(4) repealed by FA 1996, Sch. 41, Pt. V(3) with effect in relation to accounting periods ending after 31 March 1996 subject to FA 1996, Sch. 15, para. 18(3).

Cross references – FA 1995, s. 55(8): effect of amendments to ICTA 1988, s. 553 restricted for accounting periods prior to the entry into force of FA 1993, s. 103.
FA 1996, Sch. 15, para. 18(3): transitional provision for accrued income scheme.

APPROVED SHARE OPTION SCHEMES

104 Calculation of consideration

104 [Inserts TCGA 1992, s. 149A.]

105 Expenditure on shares

105(1) [Repealed by ITEPA 2003, Sch. 8, Pt. 1 which has effect for the tax year 2003–04 and subsequent tax years.]

105(2) [Repealed by ITEPA 2003, Sch. 8, Pt. 1 which has effect for the tax year 2003–04 and subsequent tax years.]

105(3) [Amends CGTA 1979, s. 32A(5).]

105(4) The amendments made by subsection (3) above shall be deemed to have come into force on 1st January 1992 (but shall have effect subject to the repeals made by the Taxation of Chargeable Gains Act 1992).

INDEXATION: MISCELLANEOUS

106 Earnings cap etc.: no indexation in 1993–94

106 [Repealed by FA 2004, s. 326 and Sch. 42, Pt. 3.]

History – S. 106 repealed by FA 2004, s. 326 and Sch. 42, Pt. 3 with effect from 6 April 2006 subject to Sch. 36.

107 Indexation of allowances etc. for 1994–95 onwards

107(1) The Taxes Act 1988 shall be amended as mentioned in subsections (2) to (6) below.

107(2) [Repealed by Statute Law (Repeals) Act 2013, s. 1 and Sch. 1, Pt. 10.]

107(3) In section 257C–

(a) [repealed by FA 2009, s. 5 and Sch. 1, para. 6(e),]

(b) [omits ICTA 1988, s. 257C(2).]

107(4-7) [Repealed by FA 2004, s. 326 and Sch. 42, Pt. 3.]

107(8) This section shall have effect for the year 1994–95 and subsequent years of assessment.

History – S. 107(2) repealed by Statute Law (Repeals) Act 2013, s. 1 and Sch. 1, Pt. 10, with effect from 31 January 2013. Former s. 107(2)(a) had previously been repealed (see below) and former s. 107(2)(b) omitted ICTA 1988, s. 1(5).
Former s. 107(2)(a) repealed by TIOPA 2010, s. 378 and Sch. 10, Pt. 13, with effect for corporation tax purposes for accounting periods ending on or after 1 April 2010, for income tax and capital gains tax purposes for the tax year 2010–11 and subsequent tax years, and for petroleum revenue tax purposes for chargeable periods beginning on or after 1 July 2010.
S. 107(3)(a) omitted by FA 2009, s. 5 and Sch. 1, para. 6(e), with effect from the tax year 2010–11 and subsequent tax years.
S. 107(4)–(7) repealed by FA 2004, s. 326 and Sch. 42, Pt. 3 with effect from 6 April 2006 subject to Sch. 36.

MISCELLANEOUS PROVISIONS ABOUT RELIEFS

108 Counselling services for employees

108 [Repealed by CTA 2009, s. 1326 and Sch. 3, Pt. 1.]

History – S. 108 repealed by CTA 2009, s. 1326 and Sch. 3, Pt. 1, with effect for corporation tax purposes for accounting periods ending on or after 1 April 2009, and for income tax and capital gains tax purposes for the tax year 2009–10 and subsequent tax years.

109 Pre-trading expenditure

109(1) [Repealed by CTA 2009, s. 1326 and Sch. 3, Pt. 1.]

109(2) [Repealed by CTA 2009, s. 1326 and Sch. 3, Pt. 1.]

109(3) [Repealed by CTA 2010, s. 1181 and Sch. 3, Pt. 1.]

109(4) [Repealed by CTA 2009, s. 1326 and Sch. 3, Pt. 1.]

History – S. 109(1) repealed by CTA 2009, s. 1326 and Sch. 3, Pt. 1, with effect for corporation tax purposes for accounting periods ending on or after 1 April 2009, and for income tax and capital gains tax purposes for the tax year 2009–10 and subsequent tax years.
S. 109(2) repealed by CTA 2009, s. 1326 and Sch. 3, Pt. 1, with effect for corporation tax purposes for accounting periods ending on or after 1 April 2009, and for income tax and capital gains tax purposes for the tax year 2009–10 and subsequent tax years.
S. 109(3) repealed by CTA 2010, s. 1181 and Sch. 3, Pt. 1, with effect for corporation tax purposes for accounting periods ending on or after 1 April 2010, and for income tax and capital gains tax purposes for the tax year 2010–11 and subsequent tax years.
S. 109(4) repealed by CTA 2009, s. 1326 and Sch. 3, Pt. 1, with effect for corporation tax purposes for accounting periods ending on or after 1 April 2009, and for income tax and capital gains tax purposes for the tax year 2009–10 and subsequent tax years.

110 Waste disposal expenditure

110 [Repealed by CTA 2009, s. 1326 and Sch. 3, Pt. 1.]

History – S. 110 repealed by CTA 2009, s. 1326 and Sch. 3, Pt. 1, with effect for corporation tax purposes for accounting periods ending on or after 1 April 2009, and for income tax and capital gains tax purposes for the tax year 2009–10 and subsequent tax years.

Notes – S. 100(3): rewritten at CTA 2009, Sch. 2, para. 31, 32.

111 Business expansion scheme: loan linked investments

111 [Repealed by ITA 2007, s. 1031 and Sch. 3, Pt. 2.]

History – S. 111 repealed by ITA 2007, s. 1031 and Sch. 3, Pt. 2, with effect in relation to shares issued after 5 April 2007. Former s. 111(1) inserted ICTA 1988, s. 299A; former s. 111(2) amended ICTA 1988, s. 289(12)(a), 310(1) and (10)(a) and s. 111(3) inserted ICTA 1988, s. 307(6)(ca) all in relation to any case in which the claim for relief is made on or after 16 March 1993.

Notes – S. 111 rewritten as ITA 2007, s. 164(1), (2), (3), 239(1), (2), 240(1), (2).

112 Employers' pension contributions

112 [Repealed by FA 2004, s. 326 and Sch. 42, Pt. 3.]

History – S. 112 repealed by FA 2004, s. 326 and Sch. 42, Pt. 3, with effect from 6 April 2006 subject to Sch. 36. Former s. 112 read as follows:

"Employers' pension contributions

112(1) [Amends ICTA 1988, s. 592(4).]

112(2) Subsection (1) above shall have effect in the case of any employer in relation to, as the case may be–

(a) any accounting period of that employer ending with a day after 5th April 1993; or

(b) any year of assessment the employer's basis period for which ends with a day after that date.

112(3) Where–

(a) there is after 5th April 1993 an actual payment by an employer of a contribution under an exempt approved scheme,

(b) that payment would, apart from this subsection, be allowed to be deducted as an expense, or expense of management, of the employer in relation to any chargeable period in relation to which subsection (1) above has effect, and

(c) the total of previously allowed deductions exceeds the relevant maximum,

the amount allowed to be so deducted in respect of the payment mentioned in paragraph (a) above and of any other actual payments of contributions under the scheme which, having been made after 5th April 1993, fall within paragraph (b) above in relation to the same chargeable period shall be reduced by whichever is the smaller of the excess and the amount which reduces the deduction to nil.

112(4) In relation to any such actual payment by an employer of a contribution under an exempt approved scheme as would be allowed to be deducted as mentioned in subsection (3) above in relation to any chargeable period–

(a) the reference in that subsection to the total of previously allowed deductions is a reference to the aggregate of every amount in respect of the making, or any provision for the making, of that or any other contributions under the scheme, which has been allowed to be deducted as an expense, or expense of management, of that person in relation to a previous chargeable period; and

(b) the reference to the relevant maximum is a reference to the amount which would have been that aggregate if the restriction on deductions imposed by virtue of subsection (1) above had been applied in relation to every previous chargeable period;

and for the purposes of this subsection an amount the deduction of the whole or any part of which falls to be taken into account as allowed in relation to more than one chargeable period shall be treated as if the amount allowed were a different amount in the case of each of those periods.

112(5) For the purposes of this section any payment which is treated under subsection (6) of section 592 of the Taxes Act 1988 as spread over a period of years shall be treated as actually paid at the time when it is treated as paid in accordance with that subsection.

112(6) [Inserts ICTA 1988, s. 592(6A) in relation to any payment made after 26 July 1993.]

112(7) In this section–

"basis period", in relation to any person, means a period on the profits or gains of which income tax for any year of assessment falls to be finally computed under Case I or II of Schedule D or under Part 2 of the Income Tax (Trading and Other Income) Act 2005 in respect of the trade, profession or vocation of that person (being the later period in any case where the profits and gains of an earlier period are taken to be the profits and gains of a later period); and

"exempt approved scheme" has the meaning given by section 592(1) of the Taxes Act 1988.".

In former s. 112(7), in the definition of "basis period ", the phrase "or under Part 2 of the Income Tax (Trading and Other Income) Act 2005" inserted by ITTOIA 2005, s. 882(1) and Sch. 1, para. 463 effective for income tax purposes for 2005–06 onwards and for corporation tax purposes for accounting periods ending after 5 April 2005 (ITTOIA 2005, s. 883(1)).

CAPITAL ALLOWANCES

113 Initial allowances: industrial buildings and structures

113 [Repealed by CAA 2001, s. 580 and Sch. 4.]

History – S. 113 repealed by CAA 2001, s. 580 and Sch. 4, with effect for income tax purposes, as respects allowances and charges falling to be made for chargeable periods ending on or after 6 April 2001, and for corporation tax purposes, as respects allowances and charges falling to be made for chargeable periods ending on or after 1 April 2001.

114 Initial allowances: agricultural buildings etc.

114 [Repealed by CAA 2001, s. 580 and Sch. 4.]

History – S. 114 repealed by CAA 2001, s. 580 and Sch. 4, with effect for income tax purposes, as respects allowances and charges falling to be made for chargeable periods ending on or after 6 April 2001, and for corporation tax purposes, as respects allowances and charges falling to be made for chargeable periods ending on or after 1 April 2001.

115 First year allowances: machinery and plant

115 [Repealed by CAA 2001, s. 580 and Sch. 4.]

History – S. 115 repealed by CAA 2001, s. 580 and Sch. 4, with effect for income tax purposes, as respects allowances and charges falling to be made for chargeable periods ending on or after 6 April 2001, and for corporation tax purposes, as respects allowances and charges falling to be made for chargeable periods ending on or after 1 April 2001.

116 Leasing

116 [Repealed by CAA 2001, s. 580 and Sch. 4.]

History – S. 116 repealed by CAA 2001, s. 580 and Sch. 4, with effect for income tax purposes, as respects allowances and charges falling to be made for chargeable periods ending on or after 6 April 2001, and for corporation tax purposes, as respects allowances and charges falling to be made for chargeable periods ending on or after 1 April 2001.

117 Transactions between connected persons etc.

117 [Repealed by CAA 2001, s. 580 and Sch. 4.]

History – S. 117 repealed by CAA 2001, s. 580 and Sch. 4, with effect for income tax purposes, as respects allowances and charges falling to be made for chargeable periods ending on or after 6 April 2001, and for corporation tax purposes, as respects allowances and charges falling to be made for chargeable periods ending on or after 1 April 2001.

MISCELLANEOUS

118 Scottish trusts

118 [Omitted by ITA 2007, s. 1027 and Sch. 1, para. 356, and repealed by s. 1031 and Sch. 3, Pt. 1.]

History – S. 118 omitted by ITA 2007, s. 1027 and Sch. 1, para. 356 and repealed by s. 1031 and Sch. 3, Pt. 1, with effect from 6 April 2007.

Notes – S. 118(1) rewritten as ITA 2007, s. 464(1), (2).

119 Controlled foreign companies

119(1) [Amends ICTA 1988, s. 750(1).]

119(2) Subsection (1) above shall apply in relation to accounting periods beginning on or after 16th March 1993.

119(3) Where a company is by virtue of section 749(1) or (2) of the Taxes Act 1988 regarded as resident in a territory outside the United Kingdom and (apart from this section)–

(a) an accounting period of the company would begin before 16th March 1993 and end on or after that date, and

(b) the company would not be considered to be subject, by virtue of section 750(1) of that Act, to a lower level of taxation in that accounting period in the territory in which it is regarded as resident,

for the purposes of Chapter IV of Part XVII of that Act that accounting period shall be treated as ending on 15th March 1993.

Cross references – ICTA 1988, s. 749: residence in relation to controlled foreign companies.

120 Pay and file: miscellaneous amendments

120 Schedule 14 to this Act (which makes various amendments of the Taxes Management Act 1970, the Taxes Act 1988 and the Finance Act 1989 with a view to, or in connection with, the introduction of "pay and file") shall have effect.

Notes – Pay and File applies in relation to accounting periods ending after 30 September 1993 (SI 1992/3066).
Some of the provisions of Sch. 14 continue to apply under CTSA which applies in respect of accounting periods ending on or after 1 July 1999.

121 Repayments and payments to friendly societies

121 [Repealed by FA 2001, s. 110 and Sch. 33, Pt. 2(12).]

History – S. 121 repealed by FA 2001, s. 110 and Sch. 33, Pt. 2(12) in respect of distributions made on or after 6 April 2004.

122 Application of Income Tax Acts etc. to public departments

122(1) [Amends ICTA 1988, s. 829(2).]

122(2) The provisions of Parts IX and X of the Taxes Management Act 1970 (interest and penalties) shall apply in relation to public offices and departments of the Crown for the purposes, so far as they so apply, of the other provisions of that Act and of the provisions of the Income Tax Acts mentioned in section 829(1) of the Taxes Act 1988.

122(3) This section shall have effect in relation to the year 1993–94 and subsequent years of assessment.

123 Expenditure involving crime

123 [Repealed by CTA 2009, s. 1326 and Sch. 3, Pt. 1.]

History – S. 123 repealed by CTA 2009, s. 1326 and Sch. 3, Pt. 1, with effect for corporation tax purposes for accounting periods ending on or after 1 April 2009, and for income tax and capital gains tax purposes for the tax year 2009–10 and subsequent tax years.

124 Expenses of Members of Parliament

124 [Repealed by ITEPA 2003, Sch. 8, Pt. 1 which has effect for the tax year 2003–04 and subsequent tax years.]

Chapter II – Exchange Gains and Losses

ACCRUAL OF GAINS AND LOSSES

Cross references – ICTA 1988, s. 15: Profits of a Sch. A business shall be computed without regard to items giving rise to exchange gains or losses within FA 1993, Ch. II, Pt. II.
ICTA 1988, s. 434A(1) as amended: no relief under FA 1993, Pt. II, Ch. II (as it affects losses treated as non-trading losses for the purposes of FA 1994, s. 160) for a company carrying on life assurance business against the policy holders' share of the relevant profits for any accounting period.
ICTA 1988, s. 798B: application of provisions in FA 1993, Pt. II, Ch. II to qualifying losses in calculations of credit for foreign tax.
ICTA 1988, Sch. 24, para. 13–19: application of provisions in FA 1993, Pt. II, Ch. II to assumptions for calculating chargeable profits, creditable tax and corresponding UK tax of controlled foreign companies.
ICTA 1988, Sch. 27, para. 5(2A) as substituted: provisions in FA 1993, s. 125–133 on exchange gains and losses ignored in applying para. 5(1) and non-qualifying offshore funds.
ICTA 1988, Sch. 28AA: application of arm's length test not to apply to amounts brought into account by virtue of provisions in FA 1993, Pt. II, Ch. II.
FA 1994, s. 226(2): no asset forming part of or liability attaching to a premiums trust fund of a corporate member shall be a qualifying asset or liability for the purposes of FA 1993, Pt. II, Ch. II.

Statements of practice – SP 9/94: application of foreign exchange and financial instruments legislation to partnerships which include companies.

Notes – The provisions of this chapter are supplemented by regulations contained in the following statutory instruments:

- Finance Act 1993, s. 165, (Appointed Day) Order 1994 (SI 1994/3224 (C. 79))
- Exchange Gains and Losses (Transitional Provisions) Regulations 1994 (SI 1994/3226)
- Exchange Gains and Losses (Alternative Method of Calculation of Gain or Loss) Regulations 1994 (SI 1994/3227)
- Exchange Gains and Losses (Deferral of Gains and Losses) Regulations 1994 (SI 1994/3228)
- Exchange Gains and Losses (Excess Gains and Losses) Regulations 1994 (SI 1994/3229)
- Exchange Gains and Losses (Insurance Companies) Regulations 1994 (SI 1994/3231)
- Exchange Gains and Losses (Debts of Varying Amounts) Regulations 1994 (SI 1994/3232).

125 Accrual on qualifying assets and liabilities

125 [Repealed by FA 2002, s. 79(1), s. 141 and Sch. 40, Pt. 3(10).]

History – S. 125 repealed by FA 2002, s. 79(1), s. 141 and Sch. 40, Pt. 3(10) with effect for accounting periods beginning on or after 1 October 2002, subject to the transitional provisions in FA 2002, s. 79 and Sch. 23, Pt. 3.

126 Accrual on currency contracts

126 [Repealed by FA 2002, s. 79(1), s. 141 and Sch. 40, Pt. 3(10).]

History – S. 126 repealed by FA 2002, s. 79(1)), s. 141 and Sch. 40, Pt. 3(10) with effect in relation to accounting periods ending on or after 1 October 2002, subject to the transitional provisions in FA 2002, s. 79 and Sch. 23, Pt. 3.

127 Accrual on debts whose amounts vary

127 [Repealed by FA 2002, s. 79(1), s. 141 and Sch. 40, Pt.3(10).]

History – S. 127 repealed by FA 2002, s.79(1), s. 141 and Sch. 40, Pt. 3(10) with effect in relation to accounting periods beginning on or after 1 October 2002, subject to the transitional provisions in FA 2002, s. 79 and Sch. 23, Pt. 3.

TRADING GAINS AND LOSSES

128 Trading gains and losses

128 [Repealed by FA 2002, s. 79(1), s. 141 and Sch. 40, Pt. 3(10).]

History – S. 128 repealed by FA 2002, s. 79(1), s. 141 and Sch. 40, Pt. 3(10) with effect in relation to accounting periods beginning on or after 1 October 2002, subject to the transitional provisions in FA 2002, s. 79 and Sch. 23, Pt. 3.

NON-TRADING GAINS AND LOSSES

129 Non-trading gains and losses: general

129 [Repealed by FA 2002, s. 79(1), s. 141 and Sch. 40, Pt. 3(10).]

History – S. 129 repealed by FA 2002, s. 79(1), s. 141 and Sch. 40, Pt. 3(10) with effect in relation to accounting periods beginning on or after 1 October 2002, subject to the transitional provisions in FA 2002, s. 79 and Sch. 23, Pt. 3.

130 Non-trading gains and losses

130 [Repealed by FA 2002, s. 79(1), s. 141 and Sch. 40, Pt. 3(10).]

History – S. 130 repealed by FA 2002, s. 79(1), s. 141 and Sch. 40, Pt. 3(10) with effect in relation to accounting periods beginning on or after 1 October 2002, subject to the transitional provisions in FA 2002, s. 79 and Sch. 23, Pt. 3.

131 Non-trading gains and losses: relief

131 [Substituted by FA 1996, s. 104 and Sch. 14, para. 69.]

History – Former s. 130 substituted for s. 130–133 by FA 1996, Sch. 14, para. 69 with effect in relation to accounting periods ending after 31 March 1996, subject to the transitional provisions and savings FA 1996, Sch. 15.

132 Modifications where loss carried forward

132 [Substituted by FA 1996, s. 104 and Sch. 14, para. 69.]

History – Former s. 130 substituted for s. 130–133 by FA 1996, Sch. 14, para. 69 with effect in relation to accounting periods ending after 31 March 1996, subject to the transitional provisions and savings FA 1996, Sch. 15.

133 Interaction with ICTA

133 [Substituted by FA 1996, s. 104 and Sch. 14, para. 69.]

History – Former s. 130 substituted for s. 130–133 by FA 1996, Sch. 14, para. 69 with effect in relation to accounting periods ending after 31 March 1996, subject to the transitional provisions and savings FA 1996, Sch. 15.

ALTERNATIVE CALCULATION

134 Alternative calculation

134 [Repealed by FA 2002, s. 79(1), s. 141 and Sch. 40, Pt. 3(10).]

History – S. 134 repealed by FA 2002, s. 79 and s. 141 and Sch. 40, Pt. 3(10) with effect in relation to accounting periods beginning on or after 1 October 2002, subject to the transitional provisions in FA 2002, s. 79 and Sch. 23, Pt. 3.

MAIN BENEFIT TEST

135 Loss disregarded if the main benefit

135 [Repealed by FA 2002, s. 79(1), s. 141 and Sch. 40, Pt. 3(10).]

History – S. 135 repealed by FA 2002, s. 79(1), s. 141 and Sch. 40, Pt. 3(10) with effect in relation to accounting periods ending on or after 1 October 2002, subject to the transitional provisions in FA 2002, s. 79 and Sch. 23, Pt. 3.

135A Sterling used if avoidance of gain is the main benefit

135A [Repealed by FA 2002, s. 79(1), s. 141 and Sch. 40, Pt. 3(10).]

History – S. 135A repealed by FA 2002, s. 79(1), s. 141 and Sch. 40, Pt. 3(10) with effect in relation to accounting periods beginning on or after 1 October 2002, subject to the transitional provisions in FA 2002, s. 79 and Sch. 23, Pt. 3.

ARM'S LENGTH TEST

136 Arm's length test: assets and liabilities

136 [Repealed by FA 2002, s. 79(1), s. 141 and Sch. 40, Pt. 3(10).]

History – s. 136 repealed by FA 2002, s. 79(1), s. 141 and Sch. 40, Pt. 3(10) with effect in relation to accounting periods beginning on or after 1 October 2002, subject to the transitional provisions in FA 2002, s. 79 and Sch. 23, Pt. 3.

136A Arm's length test: debts of varying amounts

136A [Repealed by FA 2002, s. 79(1), s. 141 and Sch. 40, Pt. 3(10).]

History – S. 136A repealed by FA 2002, s. 79(1), s. 141 and Sch. 40, Pt. 3(10) with effect in relation to accounting periods beginning on or after 1 October 2002, subject to the transitional provisions in FA 2002, s. 79 and Sch. 23, Pt. 3.

137 Arm's length test: currency contracts

137 [Repealed by FA 2002, s. 79(1), s. 141 and Sch. 40, Pt. 3(10).]

History – S. 137 repealed by FA 2002, s. 79(1), s. 141 and Sch. 40, Pt. 3(10) with effect in relation to accounting periods beginning on or after 1 October 2002, subject to the transitional provisions in FA 2002, s. 79 and Sch. 23, Pt. 3.

138 Arm's length test: non-sterling trades

138 [Repealed by FA 2002, s. 79(1), s. 141 and Sch. 40, Pt. 3(10).]

History – S. 138 repealed by FA 2002, s. 79(1), s. 141 and Sch. 40, Pt. 3(10) with effect in relation to accounting periods beginning on or after 1 October 2002, subject to the transitional provisions in FA 2002, s. 79 and Sch. 40, Pt. 3.

DEFERRAL OF UNREALISED GAINS

139 Claim to defer unrealised gains

139 [Repealed by FA 2002, s. 79(1), s. 141 and Sch. 40, Pt. 3(10).]

History – S. 139 repealed by FA 2002, s. 79(1), s. 141 and Sch. 40, Pt. 3(10) with effect in relation to accounting periods ending on or after 1 October 2002, subject to the transitional provisions in FA 2002, s. 79 and Sch. 23, Pt. 3.

140 Deferral of unrealised gains

140 [Repealed by FA 2002, s. 79(1), s. 141 and Sch. 40, Pt. 3(10).]

History – S. 140 repealed by FA 2002, s. 79(1), s. 141 and Sch. 40, Pt. 3(10) with effect in relation to accounting periods beginning on or after 1 October 2002, subject to the transitional provisions in FA 2002, s. 79 and Sch. 23, Pt. 3.

141 Deferral: amount available for relief

141 [Repealed by FA 2002, s. 79(1), s. 141 and Sch. 40, Pt. 3(10).]

History – S. 141 repealed by FA 2002, s. 79(1), s. 141 and Sch. 40, Pt. 3(10) with effect in relation to accounting periods beginning on or after 1 October 2002, subject to the transitional provisions in FA 2002, s. 79 and Sch. 23, Pt. 3.

142 Deferral: non-sterling trades

142 [Repealed by FA 2002, s. 79(1), s. 141 and Sch. 40, Pt. 3(10).]

History – S. 142 repealed by FA 2002, s. 79(1), s. 141 and Sch. 40, Pt. 3(10) with effect in relation to accounting periods beginning on or after 1 October 2002, subject to the transitional provisions in FA 2002, s. 79, and Sch. 23, Pt. 3.

143 Deferral: supplementary

143 [Repealed by FA 2002, s. 79(1), s. 141 and Sch. 40, Pt. 3(10).]

History – S. 143 repealed by FA 2002, s. 79(1), s. 141 and Sch. 40, Pt. 3(10) with effect in relation to accounting periods beginning on or after 1 October 2002, subject to the transitional provisions in FA 2002, s. 79 and Sch. 23, Pt. 3.

IRRECOVERABLE DEBTS

144 Irrecoverable debts

144 [Repealed by FA 2002, s. 79(1), s. 141 and Sch. 40, Pt. 3(10).]

History – S. 144 repealed by FA 2002, s. 79(1), s. 141 and Sch. 40, Pt. 3(10) with effect in relation to accounting periods beginning on or after 1 October 2002, subject to the transitional provisions in FA 2002, s. 79 and Sch. 23, Pt. 3.

145 Irrecoverable debts that become recoverable

145 [Repealed by FA 2002, s. 79(1), s. 141 and Sch. 40, Pt. 3(10).]

History – S. 145 repealed by FA 2002, s. 79(1), s. 141 and Sch. 40, Pt. 3(10) with effect for accounting periods beginning on or after 1 October 2002, subject to the transitional provisions in FA 2002, s. 79 and Sch. 23, Pt. 3.

CURRENCY CONTRACTS: SPECIAL CASES

146 Early termination of currency contract

146 [Repealed by FA 2002, s. 79(1) and Sch. 40, Pt. 3(10).]

History – S. 146 repealed by FA 2002, s. 79(1) and Sch. 40, Pt. 3(10) with effect for accounting periods ending on or after I October 2002, subject to the transitional provisions in FA 2002, s. 79 and Sch. 23, Pt. 3.

147 Reciprocal currency contracts

147 [Repealed by FA 2002, s. 79(1), s. 141 and Sch. 40, Pt. 3(10).]

History – S. 147 repealed by FA 2002, s. 79(1), s. 141 and Sch. 40, Pt. 3(10) with effect in relation to accounting periods beginning on or after 1 October 2002, subject to the transitional provisions in FA 2002, s. 79 and Sch. 23, Pt. 3.

EXCESS GAINS OR LOSSES

148 Excess gains or losses

148 [Repealed by FA 2002, s. 79(1), s. 141 and Sch. 40, Pt. 3(10).]

History – S. 148 repealed by FA 2002, s. 79(1), s. 141 and Sch. 40, Pt. 3(10) with effect in relation to accounting periods beginning on or after 1 October 2002, subject to the transitional provisions in FA 2002, s. 79 and Sch. 23, Pt. 3.

LOCAL CURRENCY TO BE USED

149 Local currency to be used

149 [Repealed by FA 2002, s. 79(1), s. 141 and Sch. 40, Pt. 3(10).]

History – S. 149 repealed by FA 2002, s. 79(1), s. 141 and Sch. 40, Pt. 3(10) with effect in relation to accounting periods beginning on or after 1 October 2002, subject to the transitional provisions in FA 2002, s. 79 and Sch. 23, Pt. 3.

EXCHANGE RATE TO BE USED

150 Exchange rate at translation times

150 [Repealed by FA 2002, s. 79(1), s. 141 and Sch. 40, Pt. 3(10).]

History – S. 150 repealed by FA 2002, s. 79(1), s. 141 and Sch. 40, Pt. 3(10) with effect in relation to accounting periods beginning on or after 1 October 2002, subject to the transitional provisions in FA 2002, s. 79, s. 141 and Sch. 23, Pt. 3.

151 Exchange rate for debts whose amounts vary

151 [Repealed by FA 2002, s. 79(1), s. 141 and Sch. 40, Pt. 3(10).]

History – S. 151 repealed by FA 2002, s. 79(1), s. 141 and Sch. 40, Pt. 3(10) with effect in relation to accounting periods beginning on or after 1 October 2002, subject to the transitional provisions in FA 2002, s. 79 and Sch. 23, Pt. 3.

INTERPRETATION: COMPANIES

152 Qualifying companies

152 [Repealed by FA 2002, s. 79(1), s. 141 and Sch. 40, Pt. 3(10).]

History – S. 152 repealed by FA 2002, s. 79(1), s. 141 and Sch. 40, Pt. 3(10) with effect for accounting periods beginning on or after 1 October 2002, subject to the transitional provisions in FA 2002, s. 79 and Sch. 23, Pt. 3.

INTERPRETATION: ASSETS, LIABILITIES AND CONTRACTS

153 Qualifying assets and liabilities

153 [Repealed by FA 2002, s. 79(1), s. 141 and Sch. 40, Pt. 3(10).]

History – S. 153 repealed by FA 2002, s. 79(1), s. 141 and Sch. 40, Pt. 3(10) with effect in relation to accounting periods beginning on or after 1 October 2002, subject to the transitional provisions in FA 2002, s. 79 and Sch. 23, Pt. 3.

154 Definitions connected with assets

154 [Repealed by FA 2002, s. 79(1), s. 141 and Sch. 40, Pt. 3(10).]

History – S. 154 repealed by FA 2002, s. 79(1), s. 141 and Sch. 40, Pt. 3(10) with effect in relation to accounting periods beginning on or after 1 October 2002, subject to the transitional provisions in FA 2002, s. 79 and Sch. 23, Pt. 3.

155 Definitions connected with liabilities

155 [Repealed by FA 2002, s. 79(1), s. 141 and Sch. 40, Pt. 3(10).]

History – S. 155 repealed by FA 2002, s. 79(1), s. 141 and Sch. 40, Pt. 3(10) with effect in relation to accounting periods beginning on or after 1 October 2002, subject to the transitional provision in FA 2002, s. 79 and Sch. 23, Pt. 3.

156 Assets and liabilities: other matters

156 [Repealed by FA 2002, s. 79(1), s. 141 and Sch. 40, Pt. 3(10).]

History – S. 156 repealed by FA 2002, s. 79(1), s. 141 and Sch. 40, Pt. 3(10) with effect in relation to accounting periods beginning on or after 1 October 2002, subject to the transitional provisions in FA 2002, s. 79 and Sch. 23, Pt. 3.

157 Definitions connected with currency contracts

157 [Repealed by FA 2002, s. 79(1), s. 141 and Sch. 40, Pt. 3(10).]

History – S. 157 repealed by FA 2002, s. 79(1), s. 141 and Sch. 40, Pt. 3(10) with effect in relation to accounting periods ending on or after 1 October 2002, subject to the transitional provisions in FA 2002, s. 79 and Sch. 23, Pt. 3.

INTERPRETATION: OTHER PROVISIONS

158 Translation times and accrual periods

158 [Repealed by FA 2002, s. 79(1), s. 141 and Sch. 40, Pt. 3(10).]

History – S. 158 repealed by FA 2002, s. 79(1), s. 141 and Sch. 40, Pt. 3(10) with effect in relation to accounting periods ending on or after 1 October 2002, subject to the transitional provisions in FA 2002, s. 79 and Sch. 23, Pt. 3.

159 Basic valuation

159 [Repealed by FA 2002, s. 79(1), s. 141 and Sch. 40, Pt. 3(10).]

History – S. 159 repealed by FA 2002, s. 79(1), s. 141 and Sch. 40, Pt. 3(10) with effect in relation to accounting periods beginning on or after 1 October 2002, subject to the transitional provisions in FA 2002, s. 79 and Sch. 23, Pt. 3.

160 Nominal currency of assets and liabilities

160 [Repealed by FA 2002, s. 79(1), s. 141 and Sch. 40, Pt. 3(10).]

History – S. 160 repealed by FA 2002, s. 79(1), s. 141 and Sch. 40, Pt. 3(10) with effect in relation to accounting periods begiuning on or after 1 October 2002, subject to the transitional provisions in FA 2002, s. 79 and Sch. 23, Pt. 3.

161 Settlement currency of a debt

161 [Repealed by FA 2002, s. 79(1), s. 141 and Sch. 40, Pt. 3(10).]

History – S. 161 repealed by FA 2002, s. 79(1), s. 141 and Sch. 40, Pt. 3(10) with effect in relation to accounting periods beginning on or after 1 October 2002, subject to the transitional provisions in FA 2002, s. 79 and Sch. 23, Pt. 3.

162 Nominal amount of a debt

162 [Repealed by FA 2002, s. 79(1), s. 141 and Sch. 40, Pt. 3(10).]

History – S. 162 repealed by FA 2002, s. 79(1), s. 141 and Sch. 40, Pt. 3(10) with effect in relation to accounting periods ending on or after 1 October 2002, subject to the transitional provisions in FA 2002, s. 79 and Sch. 23, Pt. 3.

163 Local currency of a trade

163 [Repealed by FA 2002, s. 79(1), s. 141 and Sch. 40, Pt. 3(10).]

History – S. 163 repealed by FA 2002, s. 79(1), s. 141 and Sch. 40, Pt. 3(10) with effect in relation to accounting periods beginning on or after 1 October 2002, subject to the transitional provisions in FA 2002, s. 79 and Sch. 23, Pt. 3.

164 Interpretation: miscellaneous

164 [Repealed by FA 2002, s. 79(1), s. 141 and Sch. 40, Pt. 3(10).]

History – S. 164 repealed by FA 2002, s. 79(1), s. 141 and Sch. 40, Pt. 3(10) with effect in relation to accounting periods ending on or after 1 October 2002, subject to the transitional provisions in FA 2002, s. 79 and Sch. 23, Pt. 3.

MISCELLANEOUS

165 Commencement and transitionals

165 [Repealed by FA 2002, s. 79(1), s. 141 and Sch. 40, Pt. 3(10).]

History – S. 165 repealed by FA 2002, s. 79(1), s. 141 and Sch. 40, Pt. 3(10) with effect in relation to accounting periods beginning on or after 1 October 2002, subject to the transitional provisions in FA 2002, s. 79 and Sch. 23, Pt. 3.

166 Anti-avoidance: change of accounting period

166 [Repealed by FA 2002, s. 79(1), s. 141 and Sch. 40, Pt. 3(10).]

History – S. 166 repealed by FA 2002, s. 79(1), s. 141 and Sch. 40, Pt. 3(10) with effect in relation to accounting periods beginning on after 1 October 2002, subject to the transitional provisions in FA 2002, s. 79 and Sch. 23, Pt. 3.

167 Orders and regulations

167 [Repealed by FA 2002, s. 79(1), s. 141 and Sch. 40, Pt. 3(10).]

History – S. 167 repealed by FA 2002, s. 79(1), s. 141 and Sch. 40, Pt. 3(10) with effect in relation to accounting periods beginning on or after 1 October 2002, subject to the transitional provisions in FA 2002, s. 79 and Sch. 23, Pt. 3.

168 Insurance companies

168 [Repealed by FA 2002, s. 79(1), s. 141 and Sch. 40, Pt. 3(10).]

History – S. 168 repealed by FA 2002, s. 79(1), s. 141 and Sch. 40, Pt. 3(10) with effect in relation to accounting periods beginning on or after 1 October 2002, subject to the transitional provisions in FA 2002, s. 79 and Sch. 23, Pt. 3.

168A Application of Chapter to certain companies becoming resident in the United Kingdom

168A *[Repealed by FA 2002, s. 79(1), s. 141 and Sch. 40, Pt. 3(10).]*

History – S. 168A repealed by FA 2002, s. 79(1), s. 141 and Sch. 40, Pt. 3(10) with effect in relation to accounting periods beginning on or after 1 October 2002, subject to the transitional provisions in FA 2002, s. 79 and Sch. 23, Pt. 3.

169 Chargeable gains

169 [Repealed by FA 2002, s. 79(1), s. 141 and Sch. 40, Pt. 3(10).]

History – S. 169 repealed by FA 2002, s. 79(1), s. 141 and Sch. 40, Pt. 3(10) with effect in relation to accounting periods beginning on or after 1 October 2002, subject to the transitional provisions in FA 2002, s. 79 and Sch. 23, Pt. 3.

170 Amendments

170 Schedule 18 to this Act (which contains amendments) shall have effect.

Chapter III – Lloyd's Underwriters etc.

Cross references – SI 1995/351: Lloyd's Underwriters (Tax) Regulations 1995 supplement the provisions of Ch. III.
SI 1997/2681, reg. 3: application of provisions of Pt. II, Ch. III to Lloyd's Scottish limited partnership as though partnership were an individual, where ICTA 1988, s. 111(2) applies.

MAIN PROVISIONS

171 Taxation of profits and allowance of losses

171(1) Income tax for any year of assessment on the profits arising from a member's underwriting business shall be computed on the profits of that year of assessment.

171(2) As respects the profits arising to a member from his underwriting business for any year of assessment–

(a) the aggregate of those profits shall be chargeable to tax under Chapter 2 of Part 2 of the Income Tax (Trading and Other Income) Act 2005 as the profits of a trade carried on in the United Kingdom; and

(b) accordingly, no part of those profits shall be treated as relevant foreign income, or be charged to tax under any other Part of that Act or any Part of the Income Tax (Earnings and Pensions) Act 2003;

but nothing in this subsection shall affect the manner in which the amount of any profits arising from assets forming part of an ancillary trust fund is to be computed.

171(2A) [Repealed by F(No. 2)A 1997, s. 36 and Sch. 6, para. 20(2), and s. 52 and Sch. 8, Pt. II(11).]

171(2B) [Omitted by FA 2016, s. 5 and Sch. 1, para. 55.]

171(3) [Repealed by FA 1994, and Sch. 21, para. 1(2).]

171(4) Subsection (2) above does not apply in relation to any profits arising before 6th April 1993 from assets forming part of an ancillary trust fund.

History – S. 171(2) para. (a) and (b) substituted by ITTOIA 2005, s. 882(1) and Sch. 1, para. 464(2); effective for income tax purposes for 2005–06 onwards and for corporation tax purposes for accounting periods ending after 5 April 2005 (ITTOIA 2005, s. 883(1)).
S. 171(2A), which was inserted by FA 1994, s. 228(1) and Sch. 21, para. 1(1), repealed by F(No. 2)A 1997, s. 36 and Sch. 6, para. 20(2), and s. 52 and Sch. 8, Pt. II(11) with effect in relation to distributions made on or after 6 April 1999.
S. 171(2B) omitted by FA 2016, s. 5 and Sch. 1, para. 55, with effect in relation to dividends paid or arising (or treated as paid), and other distributions made (or treated as made), in the tax year 2016–17 or at any later time. Former s. 171(2B) read as follows:
"**171(2B)** Sections 397(1) and 397A(1) of the Income Tax (Trading and Other Income) Act 2005 (entitlement to tax credit) shall not apply where the distribution there mentioned is a distribution in respect of any asset of a member's premium trust fund.".
In former s. 171(2B), the reference to "397A(1)" substituted for "397A(2)" by FA 2009, s. 40 and Sch. 19, para. 11, with effect for:
- qualifying distributions arising on or after 22 April 2009;
- cash dividends paid over to a person under ITEPA 2003, Sch. 2, para. 68(4) on or after 22 April 2009;
- dividends treated under ITTOIA 2005, s. 407 as paid to a person on or after 22 April 2009; and
- manufactured overseas dividends that are representative of any of the above distributions (FA 2009, Sch. 19, para. 14(1)).

In former s. 171(2B), the words "Sections 397(1) and 397A(2)" substituted for the words "Section 397(1)" by FA 2008, s. 34 and Sch. 12, para. 16, with effect for the tax year 2008–09 and subsequent tax years.
In former s. 171(2B) the words "section 397(1) of the Income Tax (Trading and Other Income) Act 2005" substituted for the words "section 231(1) of the Taxes Act 1988" by ITTOIA 2005, s. 882(1) and Sch. 1, para. 464(3); effective for income tax purposes for 2005–06 onwards and for corporation tax purposes for accounting periods ending after 5 April 2005 (ITTOIA 2005, s. 883(1)).
In former s. 171(2B), the word "premium" substituted for the word "premiums" by SI 2001/3629, art. 82(a) operative from 1 December 2001.
Former s. 171(2B) inserted by F(No. 2)A 1997, s. 22(1) with effect in relation to distributions made on or after 2 July 1997.
S. 171(3) repealed by FA 1994, s. 228(1) and Sch. 21, para. 1(2) and s. 258 and Sch. 26, Pt. V(25), with effect for years after 1995–96.
Cross references – FA 1995, s. 128(3)(d): income arising from brokers or investment managers is not part of a non-resident's excluded income if chargeable under s. 171(2).
SI 1995/351, reg. 4; SI 1995/352, reg. 4: application of provisions of TMA 1970 etc. relating to assessment and collection of tax charged under s. 171.
SI 1995/352, reg. 13: allocation of profits or losses of Lloyd's underwriting business where accounts of a syndicate remain open beyond the end of a closing year (underwriting years 1994 and 1995).

172 Year of assessment in which profits or losses arise

172(1) Subject to the provisions of this Chapter, for the purposes of section 171 above and all other purposes of the Income Tax Acts the profits or losses in any year of assessment of a member's underwriting business shall be taken to be–

(a) in the case of profits or losses arising directly from his membership of one or more syndicates, those of any previous year or years which are declared in the corresponding underwriting year;

(b) in the case of profits or losses arising from assets forming part of a premium trust fund, those allocated under the rules or practice of Lloyd's to any previous year or years the profits or losses of which are declared in the corresponding underwriting year; and

(c) in the case of other profits or losses, those derived from payments received or made in the corresponding underwriting year.

172(2) Subsection (1)(c) above does not apply in relation to payments received or made before 6th April 1993.

History – In s. 172(1)(b), the word "premium" substituted for the word "premiums" by SI 2001/3629, art. 82(b) operative from 1 December 2001.
S. 172(1)(a) and (b) substituted by FA 1994, s. 228(1) and Sch. 21, para. 2(1), with effect for 1997–98 and subsequent years of assessment.

Cross references – FA 2000, s. 107(9)(b): (general insurance reserves): an amount which is treated as a receipt of an underwriting trade under FA 2000, s. 107(2)) may be regarded as arising directly from his membership of one or more syndicates for the purposes of s. 172(1)(a).
SI 1997/2681, reg. 6(1)(b), (2): modified application of s. 172 in relation to a Lloyd's Scottish limited partnership treated as an individual member by virtue of reg. 3(1) of those regulations.

173 Assessment and collection of tax

173 [Omitted by F(No. 2)A 2005, s. 45(1) and repealed by F(No. 2)A 2005, s. 70 and Sch. 11, Pt. 2(11).]

History – S. 173 omitted by F(No. 2)A 2005, s. 45(1) and repealed by F(No. 2)A 2005, s. 70 and Sch. 11, Pt. 2(11) with effect from 6 April 2006, although for the purposes of enabling regulations to be made under FA 1993, s. 182(1)(a) or under FA 1994, s. 229(1)(a), the omission and repeal took effect from 20 July 2005 (Royal Assent) (F(No. 2)A 2005, s. 45(8)).

MEMBERS' TRUST FUNDS

174 Premium trust funds

History – In the sidenote to s. 174, the word "premium" substituted for the word "premiums" by SI 2001/3629, art. 82(c) operative from 1 December 2001.

174(1) For the purposes of the Income Tax Acts and the Gains Tax Acts–

(a) a member shall be treated as absolutely entitled as against the trustees to the assets forming part of a premium trust fund of his; and

(b) where a deposit required by a regulatory authority in a country or territory outside the United Kingdom is paid out of such a fund, the money so paid shall be treated as still forming part of that fund.

174(2) Where an asset forms part of a premium trust fund at the beginning of any underwriting year, for the purposes of the Income Tax Acts–

(a) the trustees of the fund shall be treated as acquiring it on that day, and

(b) they shall be treated as paying in respect of the acquisition an amount equal to the value of the asset at the time of the acquisition.

174(3) Where an asset forms part of a premium trust fund at the end of any underwriting year, for the purposes of the Income Tax Acts–

(a) the trustees of the fund shall be treated as disposing of it on that day, and

(b) they shall be treated as obtaining in respect of the disposal an amount equal to the value of the asset at the time of the disposal.

174(4) [Repealed by FA 1997, s. 76 and Sch. 10, para. 6 and s. 113 and Sch. 18, Pt, VI(10).]

174(5) [Repealed by FA 1997, s. 76 and Sch. 10, para. 6 and s. 113 and Sch. 18, Pt. VI(10).]

174(6) [Repealed by FA 1996, Sch. 41, Pt. V(18).]

174(7) In this section–

"underwriting year" does not include the year 1993 or any earlier underwriting year.

History – S. 174(1) substituted by FA 1994, s. 228(1) and Sch. 21, para. 3, with effect for the year 1994–95 and subsequent years of assessment.
In s. 174(1)(a), the word "premium" substituted for the word "premiums" by SI 2001/3629, art. 82(c) operative from 1 December 2001.
In s. 174(2), the word "premium" substituted for the word "premiums" by SI 2001/3629, art. 82(c) operative from 1 December 2001.
In s. 174(3), the word "premium" substituted for the word "premiums" by SI 2001/3629, art. 82(c) operative from 1 December 2001.
S. 174(4) and (5) repealed by FA 1997, s. 76 and Sch. 10, para. 6, and s. 113 and Sch. 18, Pt. VI(10), with effect in relation to, and to transfers under, any arrangement made on or after 1 July 1997 (the appointed day for the purposes of FA 1997, Sch. 10, para. 7(1) by virtue of SI 1997/991 (C. 33)).
S. 174(6), and in s. 174(7) definitions of "FOTRA securities" and "non-resident United Kingdom trader" repealed by FA 1996, Sch. 41, Pt. V(18), with effect for years after 1995–96.

175 Special reserve funds

175(1) If arrangements are made by the Council of Lloyd's which–

(a) enable such a special reserve fund as is referred to in Part I of Schedule 20 to this Act to be set up in relation to each member; and

(b) comply with the requirements of that Part and are approved by the Board,

the provisions of that Part relating to taxation shall have effect in relation to any special reserve fund of a member set up under the arrangements.

175(2) The arrangements may from time to time be varied with the consent of the Board.

175(3) If, after giving notice of their intention to do so to the Council of Lloyd's, the Board cancel the approval which they have given with respect to the arrangements, paragraph 3 of Schedule 20 to this Act shall not apply, in the case of any member, to any year of assessment after the year of assessment in which the approval is cancelled.

175(4) The provisions of Part II of Schedule 20 to this Act shall have effect as respects the winding up of any special reserve fund which–

(a) was set up under the arrangements mentioned in section 452(1) of the Taxes Act 1988; and

(b) belongs to a member for whom a special reserve fund may be set up under the arrangements mentioned in subsection (1) above.

Cross references – Sch. 20, para. 3: the amount which may be paid into a member's special reserve fund where he has made a syndicate profit for an underwriting year.
Sch. 20, Pt. II: winding-up of special reserve funds set up under ICTA 1988, s. 452(1) ("old-style" funds).
SI 1995/351, reg. 15: omission of s. 175(4)(b) where member dies, and no new-style fund has been set up in relation to him during his lifetime.
SI 1997/2681, reg. 7: s. 175 does not apply in relation to a Lloyd's Scottish limited partnership treated as an individual member by virtue of reg. 3(1) of those regulations.
SI 1999/3308, reg. 3: sch 20 para. 6(2) amended in consequence of a variation to the arrangements referred to in s. 175(1).

176 Ancillary trust funds

176(1) A member shall be treated for the purposes of the Income Tax Acts and the Gains Tax Acts as absolutely entitled as against the trustees to the assets forming part of an ancillary trust fund of his.

176(2) The cost of acquisition and the consideration for the disposal of assets forming part of an ancillary trust fund–

(a) shall be left out of account in computing for the purposes of income tax the profits or losses of the member's underwriting business; and

(b) accordingly, shall not be excluded for the purposes of capital gains tax under section 37 or 39 of the Gains Tax Act.

176(3) None of the following provisions (which apply where an individual entitled to securities dies), namely–

(a) section 636 of ITA 2007 (exception where there is a transfer to a legatee);

(b)–(d) [Repealed by FA 1996, Sch. 41, Pt. V(3).]

shall apply where the individual concerned is a member and the security concerned forms part of an ancillary trust fund of his.

176(4) In a case where subsection (3)(a) above applies, the deceased's personal representatives shall be treated for the purposes of Part 12 of ITA 2007 and section 728 of the Taxes Act 1988 as the transferor or transferee in relation to transfers of securities as to which the deceased was the transferor or transferee (as the case may be) in the interest period in which he died.

History – S. 176(3)(a) substituted by ITA 2007, s. 1027 and Sch. 1, para. 357(2), with effect from 6 April 2007.
S. 176(3)(b)–(d) repealed by FA 1996, Sch. 41, Pt. V(3) with effect in relation to years after 1995–96.
In s. 176(4) the words "Part 12 of ITA 2007 and section" substituted for the words "sections 710 to" by ITA 2007, s. 1027 and Sch. 1, para. 357(3), with effect from 6 April 2007.

Cross references – ICTA 1988, s. 710–728: the accrued income scheme.
TCGA 1992, s. 37: consideration chargeable to income tax as income excluded from consideration for the purpose of computing chargeable gains.
TCGA 1992, s. 39: expenditure allowed as a deduction in computing income for income tax purposes excluded from deductions for the purpose of computing chargeable gains.
SI 1997/2681, reg. 5: for purposes of s. 176(2) an ancillary trust fund set up in relation to a Lloyd's Scottish limited partnership is regarded as an ancillary trust fund of that partnership, and s. 176(3) and (4) treated as omitted.

OTHER SPECIAL CASES

177 Reinsurance to close

177 [Repealed by FA 2000, s. 107(11) and Sch. 40, Pt. II(16).]

History – S. 177 superseded by FA 2000, s. 107(11) with effect in relation to profits of underwriting members' trades which are declared in periods of account beginning on or after 1 January 2000.

178 Stop-loss and quota share insurance

178(1) In computing for the purposes of income tax the profits of a member's underwriting business, each of the following shall be deductible as an expense, namely–

(a) any premium payable by him under a stop-loss insurance, and any repayment of insurance money paid to him under such an insurance;

(b) any amount payable by him into the High Level Stop Loss Fund, and any repayment of an amount paid to him out of that Fund; and

(c) where an amount is payable by him under a quota share contract–

(i) so much of that amount as exceeds the amount of transferred losses that are declared on or before the date the contract takes effect (**"the declared amount"**), or

(ii) if the contract does not take effect, the amount so payable under the contract.

178(2) Subject to subsection (3) below, each of the following, namely–

(a) any insurance money payable to a member under a stop-loss insurance in respect of a loss in his underwriting business; and

(b) any amount payable to a member out of the High Level Stop Loss Fund in respect of such a loss,

shall be treated as a trading receipt in computing the profits arising from that business for the year of assessment which corresponds to the underwriting year in which the loss was declared.

178(3) Where, as respects the payment of any such insurance money or amount as is mentioned in subsection (2) above–

(a) the inspector is not notified of the payment at least 30 days before the time after which any assessment or further assessment of profits for the year of assessment is precluded by section 34 of the Management Act (ordinary time limit of 4 years), and

(b) the inspector is not entitled, after that time, to make any such assessment or further assessment by virtue of section 36 (loss of tax brought about carelessly or deliberately) or 40(2) (assessment on personal representatives) of that Act,

that subsection shall have effect in relation to that insurance money or amount as if it referred instead to the year of assessment which corresponds to the underwriting year in which the payment is made.

178(3A) Where the amount payable by a member under a quota share contract is less than the declared amount, the difference between the two amounts shall be treated as a trading receipt in computing the profits arising from the member's underwriting business in the year of assessment which corresponds to the underwriting year in which the contract takes effect.

178(3B) Where a member has entered a quota share contract, any amount paid by him to cover a cash call in respect of transferred losses that are not declared at the time the contract takes effect shall be treated–

(a) for the purposes of subsections (1)(c)(i) and (3A) above, as an amount payable under the contract, and

(b) for the purposes of section 172, as a payment made at the time the contract takes effect.

178(4) For the purposes of this section–

"cash call" has the same meaning as in Part 1 of Schedule 20 to this Act;

"quota share contract" means any contract between a member and another person which–

(a) is made in accordance with the rules or practice of Lloyd's, and

(b) provides for that other person to take over any rights and liabilities of the member under any of the syndicates of which he is a member;

and where the taking over of a member's rights and liabilities is conditional upon the occurrence of any event, the contract does not take effect until that event occurs; and

"transferred loss", in relation to such a contract, means a loss for which that other person takes over liability under the contract (disregarding, in the case of a loss that has been declared at the time it is taken over, any part of it in respect of which the member has paid a cash call before that time).

History – S. 178(1)(c) substituted by FA 2002, s. 86 and Sch. 32, para. 2 with effect in relation to quota share contracts entered into on or after 17 April 2002.

In s. 178(2), the words "a member" and "was declared" substituted by FA 1994, s. 228(1) and Sch. 21, para. 5(1), with effect as respects insurance money and other amounts payable in respect of losses declared in the underwriting year 1997 or subsequent underwriting years.

In s. 178(3)(a) the words "4 years" substituted for "six years" by FA 2008, s. 118 and Sch. 39, para. 63(a), with effect from 1 April 2010 (SI 2009/403, art. 2(2) subject to SI 2009/403, art. 3–10 – in particular art. 10).

In s. 178(3)(b), the words "loss of tax brought about carelessly or deliberately" substituted for the words "fraudulent or negligent conduct" by FA 2008, s. 118 and Sch. 39, para. 63(b), with effect from 1 April 2010 (SI 2009/403, art. 2(2) subject to SI 2009/403, art. 3–10 – in particular art. 10).

S. 178(3A), (3B) inserted by FA 2002, s. 86 and Sch. 32, para. 3 with effect in relation to quota share contracts entered into on or after 17 April 2002.
S. 178(4)substituted by FA 2002, s. 86 and Sch. 32, para. 4 with effect in relation to quota share contracts entered into on or after 17 April 2002.

Cross references – SI 1995/351, reg. 5: assessment in respect of amount payable under stop-loss insurance to an individual member of Lloyd's is not out of time if made before end of underwriting year following the underwriting year in which amount received.

MISCELLANEOUS

179 Cessation: final year of assessment

179(1) Subject to subsection (5) below, this section applies where a member ceases to carry on his underwriting business, whether by reason of death or otherwise.

179(2) Subject to the provisions of any regulations made by the Board, the member's final year of assessment shall be that which corresponds to the underwriting year in which his deposit at Lloyd's is paid over to him or his personal representatives or assigns.

179(3) [Repealed by FA 1994, s. 228(1) and Sch. 21, para. 6(1), and s. 258 and Sch. 26, Pt. V(25).]

179(4) For the purposes of section 171 above and all other purposes of the Income Tax Acts any profits or losses arising to the member from his underwriting business which are not taken (by virtue of the provisions of this Chapter) to be profits or losses of an earlier year of assessment shall be taken to be profits or losses of his final year of assessment.

179(5) This section does not apply in any case where the member's deposit at Lloyd's is paid over to him or his personal representatives or assigns before 1st January 1993.

History – In s. 179(2), the words "to subsection (3) below and" repealed by FA 1994, s. 228(1) and Sch. 21, para. 6(1) and s. 258 and Sch. 26, Pt. V(25), with effect in any case where the member dies after the end of the year 1993–94.
S. 179(3) repealed by FA 1994, s. 228(1) and Sch. 21, para. 6(1), and s. 258 and Sch. 26, Pt. V(25), with effect in any case where the member dies after the end of the year 1993–94.

Cross references – SI 1995/351, reg. 14: notwithstanding anything in s. 179, date on which a member's underwriting business is permanently discontinued for purposes of terminal loss relief is 5 April in last tax year in which profits or losses arise directly from membership of syndicates, or from assets forming part of a premium trust fund.
SI 1997/2681, reg. 4(1): s. 179 does not apply in relation to a Lloyd's Scottish limited partnership which is treated as an individual member by virtue of reg. 3(1) of those regulations.

Statutory instruments – SI 1995/351.

179A Death of member

179A(1) This section applies where a member ceases to carry on his underwriting business by reason of death.

179A(2) For the purposes of assessing the profits of the member's underwriting business, the member shall be treated as having died at the end of the year of assessment which corresponds to the underwriting year immediately preceding that in which he actually died.

179A(3) For the purposes of the Income Tax Acts–

(a) the carrying on of the member's underwriting business by his personal representatives shall not be treated as a change in the persons engaged in the carrying on of that business; and

(b) subject to the provisions of any regulations made by the Board, the business shall be treated as continuing until the member's deposit at Lloyd's is paid over to his personal representatives.

History – S. 179A inserted by FA 1994, s. 228(1) and Sch. 21, para. 6(2), with effect in any case where the member dies after the end of the year 1993–94.

Cross references – FA 1993, Sch. 20, para. 11(5): meaning of "the relevant year of assessment" in the case of a member who dies.
SI 1993/351, reg. 14: notwithstanding anything in s. 179, date on which a member's underwriting business is permanently discontinued for purposes of terminal loss relief is 5 April in last tax year in which profits or losses arise directly from membership of syndicates, or from assets forming part of a premium trust fund.
SI 1997/2681, reg. 4(1): s. 179A does not apply in relation to a Lloyd's Scottish limited partnership which is treated as an individual member by virtue of reg. 3(1) of those regulations.

Statutory instruments – SI 1995/351.

179B Conversion to underwriting through partnership or company

History – In s. 179B heading, the words "underwriting through partnership or company" substituted for "limited liability underwriting" by SI 2014/3133, reg. 3(b), with effect from 19 December 2014.

Schedule 20A to this Act (which makes provision for certain reliefs to be available where a member converts to limited liability underwriting or a Lloyd's partnership converts to underwriting through a company) shall have effect.

History – In s. 179B, the words " or a Lloyd's partnership converts to underwriting through a company" inserted by SI 2014/3133, reg. 3(a), with effect from 19 December 2014.
S. 179B inserted by FA 2004, s. 144 and Sch. 25, para. 2, with effect from 22 July 2004.

180 Underwriting profits to be relevant UK earnings etc

History – In the heading to s. 180 the words "relevant UK earnings etc" substituted for the words "earned income" by ITA 2007, s. 1027 and Sch. 1, para. 358(3), with effect from 6 April 2007.

180(1) In relation to any member, all profits arising to him from his underwriting business–

(a) shall be treated for the purposes of the Income Tax Acts as immediately derived from the carrying on by him of that business, and

(b) accordingly, shall constitute–

(i) for the purposes of Part 4 of the Finance Act 2004, relevant UK earnings within section 189(2)(b) of that Act, and

(ii) income in relation to which the treatment in section 836(2) of ITA 2007 does not apply.

180(2) This section does not apply in relation to profits of the year 1992–93 or earlier years of assessment.

History – S. 180(1)(b) substituted by ITA 2007, s. 1027 and Sch. 1, para. 358(2), with effect from 6 April 2007.

Cross references – SI 1997/2681, reg. 8: s. 180 does not apply in relation to the profits arising to an individual as a partner in a Lloyd's Scottish limited partnership.

Other material – Taxline 1993/138 (not reproduced): the Contributions Agency have confirmed that Class 2/Class 4 National Insurance contributions will not be payable by non-working Names as they are not gainfully employed.

181 Lloyd's underwriting agents

181 In section 43 of the Finance Act 1989 (Schedule D: computation), subsections (6) and (7) (which extend certain time limits for persons permitted by the Council of Lloyd's to act as underwriting agents at Lloyd's) shall cease to have effect in relation to periods of account ending on or after 30th June 1993.

SUPPLEMENTAL

182 Regulations

182(1) The Board may by regulations provide–

(a) for the assessment and collection of tax charged in accordance with section 171 above;

(b) for making, in the event of any changes in the rules or practice of Lloyd's, such amendments of this Chapter as appear to the Board to be expedient having regard to those changes;

(c) for modifying the application of this Chapter in cases where a syndicate continues after the end of its closing year or a member dies or otherwise ceases to carry on his underwriting business;

(ca) [Repealed by Statute Law (Repeals) Act 2013, s. 1 and Sch. 1, Pt. 10.]

(d) for giving credit for foreign tax.

182(2)–(4) [Repealed by FA 1994, s. 228(1) and Sch. 21, para. 7(1), and s. 258 and Sch. 26, Pt. V(25).]

182(5) Regulations made, or deemed to have been made, under any of the following enactments (regulations about Lloyd's underwriters), namely–

(a) section 451(1) or (1A) of the Taxes Act 1988,

(b) section 92(5) of the Finance Act 1989, or

(c) section 209(4) of the Gains Tax Act,

which were in force immediately before 6th April 1992 shall continue in force for the year 1992–93 and subsequent years of assessment notwithstanding the repeal of that enactment by this Act, and shall be deemed to have been made under this section.

182(6) Any power to make regulations conferred by this section includes power to make–

(a) different provision for different cases or different purposes, and

(b) incidental, supplemental or transitional provision and savings.

History – In s. 182(1)(a), the words "(so far as not provided for by Schedule 19 to this Act)", which followed the words "section 171 above", omitted by F(No. 2)A 2005, s. 45(2) and repealed by F(No. 2)A 2005, s. 70 and Sch. 11, Pt. 2(11) with effect from 6 April 2006, although for the purposes of enabling regulations to be made under this section or under FA 1994, s. 229(1)(a), the omission and repeal took effect from 20 July 2005 (Royal Assent) (F(No. 2)A 2005, s. 45(8)).

S. 182(1)(ca) repealed by Statute Law (Repeals) Act 2013, s. 1 and Sch. 1, Pt. 10, with effect from 31 January 2013.

Former s. 182(1)(ca)(ii) the words "section 569 (repos) or 613 (redemption arrangements) of ITA 2007;" substituted for "section 737E(2) and (8) of the Taxes Act 1988 (sale and repurchase of securities etc.);" by ITA 2007, s. 1027 and Sch. 1, para. 359, with effect from 6 April 2007.

In former s. 182(1)(ca), the word "premium" substituted for the word "premiums" by SI 2001/3629, art. 82(d) operative from 1 December 2001.

Former s. *182(1)(ca)(i) repealed by FA 1997,* s. 76 and Sch. 10, para. 6, and s. 113 and Sch. 18, Pt. VI (10), with effect in relation to, and to transfers under, any arrangement made on or after 1 July 1997 (the day appointed for the purposes of FA 1997, Sch. 10, para. 7(1) by virtue of SI 1997/991 (C. 33)).

Former s. 182(1)(ca) inserted by FA 1995, s. 83(2).

S. 182(2)–(4) repealed by FA 1994, s. 228(1) and Sch. 21, para. 7(1), and s. 258 and Sch. 26, Pt. V(25), with effect for the year 1997–98 and subsequent years of assessment.

S. 182(6) inserted by F(No. 2)A 2005, s. 45(3) with effect from 6 April 2006, although for the purposes of enabling regulations to be made under this section or under FA 1994, s. 229(1)(a), the insertion took effect from 20 July 2005 (Royal Assent) (F(No. 2)A 2005, s. 45(8)).

Cross references – Sch. 19: assessment and collection of tax in respect of Lloyd's underwriters.
ICTA 1988, s. 806(5): disapplication of notice requirements under ICTA 1988, s. 806(3) (adjustment of excessive double tax credit) in respect of Lloyds underwriters.
ICTA 1988, s. 811(7)(a): disapplication of notice requirements under s. 811(5), (6) where adjustment is one whose consequences in relation to the reduction are given effect in accordance with regulations made under s. 182(1) (regulations relating to individual members of Lloyd's).
FA 2007, Sch. 11, para. 3(14): application (by regulations) of FA 2007, Sch. 11, para. 2 with modifications.

Statutory instruments – SI 1995/351 as amended by SI 1996/781, SI 1995/352 as amended by SI 1996/782, SI 1995/353, SI 1995/1185, SI 1997/405, SI 1997/2681 as amended by SI 2006/111.
SI 1999/3308 (made under s. 182(1)(b), (c)).
SI 2005/3338 (made under s. 182(1)(a) and (6), (c)).
SI 2006/112 (made under s. 182(1)(b)).

183 Consequential amendments

183(1) [Repealed by ITTOIA 2005, s. 884 and Sch. 3.]

183(2) [Repealed by ITA 2007, s. 1031 and Sch. 3, Pt. 1.]

183(3) [Repealed by FA 1994, s. 228(2)(c), and s. 258 and Sch. 26, Pt. V(25).]

183(4-6) [Repealed by FA 1993, s. 213 and Sch. 23, Pt. III(12).]

183(7,8) [Repealed by FA 1993, s. 213 and Sch. 23, Pt. III(12).]

History – S. 183(1) repealed by ITTOIA 2005, s. 884 and Sch. 3; effective for income tax purposes for 2005–06 onwards and for corporation tax purposes for accounting periods ending after 5 April 2005 (ITTOIA 2005, s. 883(1)).
S. 183(2) repealed by ITA 2007, s. 1031 and Sch. 3, Pt. 1, with effect from 6 April 2007.
S. 183(3) repealed by FA 1994, s. 228(2)(c), and s. 258 and Sch. 26, Pt. V(25), with effect for 1997–98 and subsequent years of assessment.
S. 183(4)–(6) repealed by FA 1993, s. 213 and Sch. 23, Pt. III(12), with effect for 1994 and subsequent underwriting years.
S. 183(7) and (8) repealed by FA 1993, s. 213 and Sch. 23, Pt. III(12), with effect for 1994–95 and subsequent years of assessment.

Notes – S. 183(2) rewritten as ITA 2007, s. 867(1), (2).

184 Interpretation and commencement

184(1) In this Chapter, unless the context otherwise requires–

"ancillary trust fund", in relation to a member, does not include a premium trust fund of his or his special reserve fund (if any) but, subject to that, means any trust fund required or authorised by the rules of Lloyd's, or required by a members' agent of his;

"closing year" –

(a) in relation to a year of assessment, means the year of assessment next but one following that year;

(b) in relation to an underwriting year, means the underwriting year next but one following that year; and

(c) in relation to a syndicate, means the closing year of the underwriting year for which it was formed;

"the Gains Tax Act" means the Taxation of Chargeable Gains Act 1992 and

"the Gains Tax Acts" means that Act and any other enactments relating to capital gains tax;

"the High Level Stop Loss Fund" means the fund of that name which, under the rules of Lloyd's, has been established for the year 1993 and subsequent underwriting years;

"inspector" includes any officer of the Board;

"Lloyd's partnership" means–

(a) a limited partnership formed under the law of Scotland which is a member of Lloyd's and is or has been an underwriting member, or

(b) a limited liability partnership formed under the law of any part of the United Kingdom which is a member of Lloyd's and is or has been an underwriting member;

"the Management Act" means the Taxes Management Act 1970;

"managing agent", in relation to a syndicate and a year of assessment, means–

(a) the person registered as a managing agent at Lloyd's who was acting as such an agent for the syndicate at the end of the corresponding underwriting year, or

(b) such other person as may be determined in accordance with regulations made by the Board;

"member" (except in Part 1A of Schedule 20A) means an individual who is a member of Lloyd's and is or has been an underwriting member;

"members' agent", in relation to a member of a syndicate and a year of assessment, means–

(a) the person registered as a members' agent at Lloyd's who was acting as such an agent for the member at the end of the corresponding underwriting year, or

(b) if two or more such persons were so acting and one of them was appointed by the member to be responsible for complying with the requirements of the Lloyd's Underwriters (Tax) Regulations 2005 in relation to all of the syndicates of which he is a member, that person, or

(c) if two or more such persons were so acting and none of them was so appointed, the person who was so acting for the member in his capacity as a member of the syndicate, or

(d) such other person as may be determined in accordance with regulations made by the Board;

"premiums trust fund" means a trust fund into which premiums receivable by members are paid in compliance with a trust deed under Rule 8.2.19 of the Insurance Prudential Sourcebook made by the Financial Services Authority under the Financial Services and Markets Act 2000;

"prescribed" means prescribed by regulations made by the Board;

"profits" includes gains;

"special reserve fund", unless the contrary intention appears, means a special reserve fund set up under the arrangements mentioned in section 175(1) above;

"stop-loss insurance" means any insurance taken out by a member against losses in his underwriting business, except insurance taken out by entering a quota share contract (within the meaning of section 178 above);

"syndicate" means a syndicate of underwriting members of Lloyd's formed for an underwriting year;

"underwriting business", in relation to a member, means his underwriting business as a member of Lloyd's, whether carried on personally or through an underwriting agent, and does not include any other business carried on by him, and in particular, where he is himself an underwriting agent, does not include his business as such an agent;

"underwriting year" means the calendar year.

184(2) For the purposes of this Chapter–

(a) an underwriting year and a year of assessment shall be deemed to correspond to each other if the underwriting year ends in the year of assessment;

(b) the profits or losses of a member's underwriting business include profits or losses arising to him from assets forming part of a premiums trust fund or an ancillary trust fund; and

(c) any charge made on a member by the managing agent of a syndicate of which he is a member, and any expense incurred on his behalf by the managing agent of such a syndicate, shall be treated as expenses arising directly from his membership of that syndicate.

184(3) Subject to any provision to the contrary, the provisions of this Chapter have effect for the year 1992–93 and subsequent years of assessment.

History – In s. 184(1), in the definition of "ancillary trust fund", the word "premium" substituted for the word "premiums" by SI 2001/3629, art. 82(e) operative from 1 December 2001.
In s. 184(1), in the definition of "ancillary trust fund", the words "or the managing …is a member" repealed by FA 1994, s. 228(1), and Sch. 21, para. 8(1), and s. 258 and Sch. 26, Pt. V(25), with effect for the year 1994–95 and subsequent years of assessment.
In s. 184(1), the definition of "Lloyd's partnership" inserted by SI 2014/3133, reg. 4(a), with effect from 19 December 2014.
In s. 184(1), in the definition of "member", the words "(except in Part 1A of Schedule 20A)" inserted by SI 2014/3133, reg. 4(b), with effect from 19 December 2014.
In s. 184(1), in the definition of "member", the words "an individual … Lloyd's and" substituted by FA 1994, s. 228(1) and Sch. 21, para. 8(1), with effect for the year 1994–95 and subsequent years of assessment.
In s. 184(1), in the definition of "member's agent", "the Lloyd's Underwriters (Tax) Regulations 2005" substituted for "Part II of Schedule 19 to this Act" by SI 2005/3338, reg. 16, with effect for 2006–07 and subsequent years of assessment (individuals) and for accounting periods ending after 31 December 2005 (corporate members).
In s. 184(1), in the definition of "premiums trust fund", the words "Rule 8.2.19 of the Insurance Prudential Sourcebook" substituted for the words "section 17.7 of the Lloyd's Sourcebook" by SI 2006/3273, reg. 2, with effect from 31 December 2006.
In s. 184(1), in the definition of "premium trust fund", "section 17.7" substituted for "section 10.3" by SI 2005/1538, art. 2, with effect from 1 July 2005.
In s. 184(1), in the definition of "stop-loss insurance", the words ", except insurance taken out by entering a quota share contract (within the meaning of section 178 above)" inserted by FA 2002, s. 86 and Sch. 32, para. 5 with effect in relation to quota share contracts taken out 17 April 2002.
In s. 184(2)(c), in two places, the words "managing agent" substituted for former word "agent" by FA 1994, s. 228(1) and Sch. 21, para. 8(2), with effect for the year 1994–95 and subsequent years of assessment.

Statutory instruments – SI 1995/351, SI 1995/352 as amended by SI 1996/782, SI 1995/353.
SI 2005/3338.

Notes – S. 184(1) rewritten as ITA 2007, s. 867(2).

PART VI – MISCELLANEOUS AND GENERAL

STATUTORY EFFECT OF RESOLUTIONS ETC.

205 The 1968 Act

205(1) The Provisional Collection of Taxes Act 1968 shall be amended as follows.

205(2) [Amends PCTA 1968, s. 1(1).]

205(3) [Repealed by Statute Law (Repeals) Act 2013, s. 1 and Sch. 1, Pt. 10.]

205(4) [Repealed by FA 2011, s. 88(8)(a).]

205(5) [Amends PCTA 1968, s. 1(4).]

205(6) [Amends PCTA 1968, s. 5(1) and (2).]

205(7) This section shall apply in relation to resolutions passed after the day on which this Act is passed.

History – S. 205(3) repealed by Statute Law (Repeals) Act 2013, s. 1 and Sch. 1, Pt. 10, with effect from 31 January 2013.
S. 205(4) repealed by FA 2011, s. 88(8)(a), with effect from 30 December 2011 (SI 2011/2934).

206 Corporation tax

206(1) [Repeals ICTA 1988, s. 8(4)–(6).]

206(2) [Repealed by FA 1996, s. 205 and Sch. 41, Pt. V(13).]

206(3) [Repealed by F(No. 2)A 1997, s. 52 and Sch. 8, Pt. III.]

MISCELLANEOUS

208 Residence: available accommodation

208(1) [Repealed by ITA 2007, s. 1031 and Sch. 3, Pt. 1.]

208(2) [Inserts TCGA 1992, s. 9(4).]

208(3) [Inheritance tax.]

208(4) Subsections (1) and (2) above shall have effect for the year 1993–94 and subsequent years of assessment.

208(5) [Inheritance tax.]

History – S. 208(1) repealed by ITA 2007, s. 1031 and Sch. 3, Pt. 1, with effect from 6 April 2007.

Notes – S. 208(1) rewritten as ITA 2007, s. 831(1), 832(1).

GENERAL

212 Interpretation

212 In this Act **"the Taxes Act 1988"** means the Income and Corporation Taxes Act 1988, and **"ITA 2007"** means the Income Tax Act 2007.

History – In s. 212 the words ", and **"ITA 2007"** means the Income Tax Act 2007" inserted by ITA 2007, s. 1027 and Sch. 1, para. 360, with effect from 6 April 2007.

213 Repeals

213 The enactments specified in Schedule 23 to this Act (which include provisions which are already spent) are hereby repealed to the extent specified in the third column of that Schedule, but subject to any provision of that Schedule.

214 Short title

214 This Act may be cited as the Finance Act 1993.

SCHEDULES

SCHEDULE 3 – CAR AND CAR FUEL BENEFITS: 1994–95 ONWARDS

Section 72

[Repealed by ITEPA 2003, Sch. 8, Pt. 1 which has effect for the tax year 2003–04 and subsequent tax years.]

SCHEDULE 4 – VANS

Section 73

[Repealed by ITEPA 2003, Sch. 8, Pt. 1 which has effect for the tax year 2003–04 and subsequent tax years.]

SCHEDULE 5 – REMOVAL EXPENSES AND BENEFITS

Section 76

[Repealed by ITEPA 2003, Sch. 8, Pt. 1 which has effect for the tax year 2003–04 and subsequent tax years.]

SCHEDULE 6 – TAXATION OF DISTRIBUTIONS SUPPLEMENTAL PROVISIONS

Section 79

THE TAXES ACT 1988

1 [Amends ICTA 1988, s. 167(2A) and 819(2) and Sch. 7, para. 19(1). Former entries relating to ICTA 1988, s. 353(5) and 369(3B) repealed by FA 1994, s. 258 and Sch. 26, Pt. V(2), in relation to payments of interest made on or after 6 April 1994 and former entry relating to ICTA 1988, s. 683(2) and 684(2) repealed by FA 1995, s. 162 and Sch. 29, Pt. VIII(8) with effect for 1995–96 and subsequent years of assessment.]

2 [Repealed by ITTOIA 2005, s. 884 and Sch. 3.]

History – Para. 2 repealed by ITTOIA 2005, s. 884 and Sch. 3 effective for income tax purposes for 2005–06 onwards and for corporation tax purposes for accounting periods ending after 5 April 2005 (ITTOIA 2005, s. 883(1)).

3 [Repealed by F(No. 2)A 1997, s. 52 and Sch. 8, Pt. II(9), with effect in relation to distributions made on or after 6 April 1999.]

4 [Repealed by FA 1994, s. 258 and Sch. 26, Pt. V(13), in relation to distribution periods beginning on or after 1 April 1994.]

5 [Repealed by FA 1994, s. 258 and Sch. 26, Pt. V(13), in relation to distribution periods beginning on or after 1 April 1994.]

6 [Repealed by ITTOIA 2005, s. 884 and Sch. 3.]

History – Para. 6 repealed by ITTOIA 2005, s. 884 and Sch. 3 effective for income tax purposes for 2005–06 onwards and for corporation tax purposes for accounting periods ending after 5 April 2005 (ITTOIA 2005, s. 883(1)).

7 [Repealed by ITTOIA 2005, s. 884 and Sch. 3]

History – Para. 7 repealed by ITTOIA 2005, s. 884 and Sch. 3 effective for income tax purposes for 2005–06 onwards and for corporation tax purposes for accounting periods ending after 5 April 2005 (ITTOIA 2005, s. 883(1)).

8 [Repealed by ITA 2007, s. 1031 and Sch. 3, Pt. 1.]

History – Para. 8 repealed by ITA 2007, s. 1031 and Sch. 3, Pt. 1, with effect from 6 April 2007.

Notes – Para. 8 rewritten as follows:
Para. 8(1): ITA 2007, s. 479(1), (2), 481(2).
Para. 8(2): ITA 2007, s. 9(1), (2).
Para. 8(3): ITA 2007, s. 487(1), (2), (3), (4), 1023.
Para. 8(4): ITA 2007, s. 483(2).
Para. 9(1): ITA 2007, s. 494(2).
Para. 9(2): ITA 2007, s. 498(1), (2).
Para. 15: ITA 2007, s. 989.

9 [Repealed by ITA 2007, s. 1031 and Sch. 3, Pt. 1.]

History – Para. 9 repealed by ITA 2007, s. 1031 and Sch. 3, Pt. 1, with effect from 6 April 2007.

10 *[Repealed by TIOPA 2010*, s. 378 and Sch. 10, Pt. 13 and Statute Law (Repeals) Act 2013, s. 1 and Sch. 1, Pt. 10.]

History – Para. 10 repealed by Statute Law (Repeals) Act 2013, s. 1 and Sch. 1, Pt. 10, with effect from 31 January 2013. Fomer para. 10 had previously been repealed (see note below).
Para. 10 repealed by TIOPA 2010, s. 378 and Sch. 10, Pt. 13, with effect for corporation tax purposes for accounting periods ending on or after 1 April 2010, for income tax and capital gains tax purposes for the tax year 2010–11 and subsequent tax years, and for petroleum revenue tax purposes for chargeable periods beginning on or after 1 July 2010.

11 [Repealed by CTA 2009, s. 1326 and Sch. 3, Pt. 1.]

History – Para. 11 repealed by CTA 2009, s. 1326 and Sch. 3, Pt. 1, with effect for corporation tax purposes for accounting periods ending on or after 1 April 2009, and for income tax and capital gains tax purposes for the tax year 2009–10 and subsequent tax years.

12 [Repealed by FA 1998, Sch. 27, Part. III(2) with effect for the year 1999–2000 and subsequent years of assessment.]

13 [Repealed by ITA 2007, s. 1031 and Sch. 3, Pt. 1.]

History – Para. 13 repealed by ITA 2007, s. 1031 and Sch. 3, Pt. 1, with effect from 6 April 2007.

14 [Repealed by FA 1996, Sch. 41, Pt. V(1) with effect in relation to years after 1995–96.]

15 [Repealed by ITA 2007, s. 1031 and Sch. 3, Pt. 1.]

History – Para. 15 repealed by ITA 2007, s. 1031 and Sch. 3, Pt. 1, with effect from 6 April 2007.

16 [Repealed by FA 1998, Sch. 27, Part. III(2), with effect in relation to distributions made on or after 6 April 1999.]

17 [Repealed by FA 1996, Sch. 41, Pt. V(2) with effect, for income tax purposes, in relation to years after 1995–96 and for corporation tax purposes, in relation to accounting periods ending after 31 March 1996 without prejudice to FA 1996, Sch. 6, para. 25.]

18 [Repealed by FA 1996, Sch. 41, Pt. V(3) with effect, for corporation tax purposes, in relation to accounting periods ending after 31 March 1996 and, for income tax purposes, in relation to years after 1995–96.]

19 [Repealed by FA 1997, s. 113 and Sch. 18, Pt. VI(10), with effect in relation to, and to transfers under, any arrangement made on or after 1 July 1997 (the day appointed for the purposes of FA 1997, Sch. 10, para. 7(1) by virtue of SI 1997/991 (C. 33)); previously inserted ICTA 1988, Sch. 23A, para. 2(5).]

THE FINANCE ACT 1989 (c. 26)

20 [Amends FA 1989, s. 68(2)(c) and 71(4)(c).]

THE FINANCE ACT 1990 (c. 29)

21 [Repealed by FA 1996, Sch. 41, Pt. V(3) with effect in relation to years after 1995–96.]

THE TAXATION OF CHARGEABLE GAINS ACT 1992 (c. 12)

22 [Repealed by FA 1999, s. 139 and Sch. 20, Pt. III(1), with effect for the year 1999–2000 and subsequent years of assessment.]

23 [Repealed by FA 1998, Sch. 27, Part. III(29) with effect for the year 1998–99 and subsequent years of assessment.]

24 [Repealed by FA 1995, s. 162 and Sch. 29, Pt. VIII(8) with effect for 1995–96 and subsequent years of assessment.]

COMMENCEMENT

25(1) This Schedule, except the provisions to which sub-paragraphs (2) to (5) below apply, shall have effect for the year 1993–94 and subsequent years of assessment.

25(2) [Repealed by FA 1994, s. 258 and Sch. 26, Pt. V(13), in relation to distribution periods beginning on or after 1 April 1994.]

25(3) [Repealed by FA 1997, s. 113 and Sch. 18, Pt. VI(10).]

25(4) [Repealed by FA 1997, s. 113 and Sch. 18, Pt. VI(10).]

25(5) [Repealed by FA 1996, Sch. 41, Pt. V(2) with effect, for income tax purposes, in relation to years after 1995–96 and, for corporation tax purposes, in relation to accounting periods ending after 31 March 1996 (without prejudice to FA 1996, Sch. 6, para. 25).]

History – Para. 25(3) and (4) repealed by FA 1997, s. 113 and Sch. 18, Pt. VI(10), with effect in relation to, and to transfers under, any arrangement made on or after 1 July 1997 (the day appointed for the purposes of FA 1997, Sch. 10, para. 7(1) by virtue of SI 1997/991 (C. 33)).

SCHEDULE 7 – RELIEF ON RETIREMENT OR RE-INVESTMENT

Section 87

Part I – Retirement Relief etc.

EXTENSION OF REFERENCES TO "FAMILY COMPANY"

1(1) [Amends TCGA 1992, s. 157 and 163–165 and Sch. 6, para. 12(2) and Sch. 7, para. 7(1).]

1(2) [Repealed by FA 1998, Sch. 27, Part. III(31) with effect in relation to disposals in the year 2003–04 and subsequent years of assessment.]

History – Para. 1(2) repealed by FA 1998, Sch. 27, Part. III(31) with effect in relation to disposals in the year 2003–04 and subsequent years of assessment.

EXTENSION OF REFERENCES TO FULL-TIME WORKING DIRECTORS ETC.

2 [Repealed by FA 1998, Sch. 27, Part. III(31).]

History – Para. 2 repealed by FA 1998, Sch. 27, Part. III(31) with effect in relation to disposals in the year 2003–04 and subsequent years of assessment.

Part II – Roll-Over Relief on Re-investment

3 [Inserts TCGA 1992, Pt. V, Ch. IA.]

SCHEDULE 8 – RESTRICTION ON SET-OFF OF PRE-ENTRY LOSSES

Section 88

[Inserts TCGA 1992, Sch. 7A.]

SCHEDULE 9 – OVERSEAS LIFE INSURANCE COMPANIES: AMENDMENT OF TAXES ACT 1988ETC.

Section 97

INSERTION OF SCHEDULE 19AC INTO THE TAXES ACT 1988

1 [Repealed by SI 2006/3271, reg. 43(1) and Schedule, Pt. 1.]

DEEMED DISPOSAL AND REACQUISITION

2 [Repealed by SI 2006/3271, reg. 43(1) and Schedule, Pt. 1.]

History – Sch. 9 repealed by SI 2006/3271, reg. 43(1) and Schedule, Pt. 1 with effect from 31 December 2006, in relation to accounting periods ending on or after that date.

SCHEDULE 10 – OVERSEAS LIFE INSURANCE COMPANIES: AMENDMENT OF FINANCE ACT 1989

Section 101

[Repealed by SI 2006/3271, reg. 43(1) and Schedule, Pt. 1.]

History – Sch. 10 repealed by SI 2006/3271, reg. 43(1) and Schedule, Pt. 1 with effect from 31 December 2006, in relation to accounting periods ending on or after that date.

SCHEDULE 11 – OVERSEAS LIFE INSURANCE COMPANIES: AMENDMENT OF TAXATION OF CHARGEABLE GAINS ACT 1992

Section 102

[Repealed by SI 2006/3271, reg. 43(1) and Schedule, Pt. 1.]

History – Sch. 11 repealed by SI 2006/3271, reg. 43(1) and Schedule, Pt. 1 with effect from 31 December 2006, in relation to accounting periods ending on or after that date.

SCHEDULE 12 – INITIAL ALLOWANCES FOR AGRICULTURAL BUILDINGS

Section 114

[Repealed by CAA 2001, s. 580 and Sch. 4.]

History – Sch. 12, repealed by CAA 2001, s. 580 and Sch. 4, with effect as respects allowances and charges falling to be made for chargeable periods ending, for income tax purposes, on or after 6 April 2001, and for corporation tax purposes, on or after 1 April 2001.

SCHEDULE 13 – FIRST-YEAR ALLOWANCES FOR MACHINERY AND PLANT

Section 115

[Repealed by CAA 2001, s. 580 and Sch. 4.]

History – Sch. 13, repealed by CAA 2001, s. 580 and Sch. 4, with effect as respects allowances and charges falling to be made for chargeable periods ending, for income tax purposes, on or after 6 April 2001, and for corporation tax purposes, on or after 1 April 2001.

SCHEDULE 14 – PAY AND FILE: MISCELLANEOUS AMENDMENTS

Section 120

FAILURE TO GIVE NOTICE OF LIABILITY FOR CORPORATION TAX

1 [Repealed by FA 1998, Sch. 27, Pt. III(28).]

History – Para. 1 repealed by FA 1998, Sch. 27, Pt. III(28) with effect from 1 July 1999 (the appointed day for the purposes of corporation tax self assessment under FA 1994, s. 199 by virtue of SI 1998/3173 (C. 78)).

FURTHER CLAIMS ETC. WHERE ASSESSMENT MADE

2 [Repealed by FA 1998, Sch. 27, Pt. III(28).]

History – Para. 2 repealed by FA 1998, Sch. 27, Pt. III(28) with effect from 1 July 1999 (the appointed day for the purposes of corporation tax self assessment under FA 1994, s. 199 by virtue of SI 1998/3173 (C. 78)).

INTEREST ON OVERDUE CORPORATION TAX: TRANSITIONAL CASES

3(1) Section 86 of that Act of 1970 (interest on overdue tax) shall be amended as follows.

3(2) [Amends TMA 1970, s. 86(3)(b).]

3(3) [Amends TMA 1970, s. 86(3A).]

3(4) [Inserts TMA 1970, s. 86(4A) and (4B).]

INTEREST ON OVERDUE CORPORATION TAX: PAY AND FILE CASES

4 [Repealed by FA 1998, Sch. 27, Pt. III(2) where the later period mentioned in TMA 1970, s. 87A(4) begins on or after 6 April 1999.]

EFFECT ON INTEREST OF RELIEFS

5 [Amends TMA 1970, s. 91(1B).]

FAILURE TO MAKE RETURN FOR CORPORATION TAX

6 [Repealed by FA 1998, Sch. 27, Pt. III(28).]

History – Para. 6 repealed by FA 1998, Sch. 27, Pt. III(28) with effect from 1 July 1999 (the appointed day for the purposes of corporation tax self assessment under FA 1994, s. 199 by virtue of SI 1998/3173 (C. 78)).

THINGS TO BE DONE BY COMPANIES

7 [Amends TMA 1970, s. 108(1).]

RELIEF UNDER SECTION 393 OF THE TAXES ACT 1988

8(1) In relation to any case in which by virtue of section 99 of the Finance Act 1990 losses may be set off under subsection (1) of section 393 or of section 396 of the Taxes Act 1988 without the making of a claim, the Taxes Act 1988 shall have effect with the following amendments.

8(2) [Repealed by CTA 2010, s. 1181 and Sch. 3, Pt. 1.]

8(3) [Repealed by CTA 2010, s. 1181 and Sch. 3, Pt. 1.]

8(4) [Amends ICTA 1988, s. 398.]

8(5) [Repealed by CTA 2010, s. 1181 and Sch. 3, Pt. 1.]

History – Para. 8(2) repealed by CTA 2010, s. 1181 and Sch. 3, Pt. 1, with effect for corporation tax purposes for accounting periods ending on or after 1 April 2010, and for income tax and capital gains tax purposes for the tax year 2010–11 and subsequent tax years.
Para. 8(3) repealed by CTA 2010, s. 1181 and Sch. 3, Pt. 1, with effect for corporation tax purposes for accounting periods ending on or after 1 April 2010, and for income tax and capital gains tax purposes for the tax year 2010–11 and subsequent tax years.
Para. 8(5) repealed by CTA 2010, s. 1181 and Sch. 3, Pt. 1, with effect for corporation tax purposes for accounting periods ending on or after 1 April 2010, and for income tax and capital gains tax purposes for the tax year 2010–11 and subsequent tax years.

9 [Repealed by FA 2007, s. 114 and Sch. 27, Pt. 2(8).]

History – Para. 9 repealed by FA 2007, s. 114 and Sch. 27, Pt. 2(8) with effect for the purposes of corporation tax, for periods of insurance companies beginning on or after 1 January 2007 (subject to any transitional provisions contained in FA 2007, Sch. 8, para. 28 and 29 (FA 2007, s. 39(2))).

INTEREST ON TAX OVERPAID

10(1) [Repealed by FA 1998, Sch. 27, Pt. III(2).]

10(2) [Amends ICTA 1988, s. 826(7A).]

10(3) [Repealed by FA 1998, Sch. 27, Pt. III(2).]

10(4) [Amends ICTA 1988, s. 826(7B).]

10(5) [Repealed by FA 1998, Sch. 27, Pt. III(2).]

10(6) [Repealed by FA 1998, Sch. 27, Pt. III(2).]

History – Sch. 14, para. 10(1), (3), (5), and (6) repealed by FA 1998, Sch. 27, Pt. III(2) with effect from:

- subpara. (1) – where the later period mentioned in ICTA 1988, s. 826(7) begins on or after 6 April 1999; and
- subpara. (3), (5) and (6) – where the earlier period mentioned in ICTA 1988, s. 826(7AA) begins on or after 6 April 1999.

SURRENDER OF REFUNDS

11 [Repealed by CTA 2010, s. 1181 and Sch. 3, Pt. 1.]

History – Para. 11 repealed by CTA 2010, s. 1181 and Sch. 3, Pt. 1, with effect for corporation tax purposes for accounting periods ending on or after 1 April 2010, and for income tax and capital gains tax purposes for the tax year 2010–11 and subsequent tax years.

SCHEDULE 15 – EXCHANGE GAINS AND LOSSES: ALTERNATIVE CALCULATION

Section 134

[Repealed by FA 2002. s. 141 and Sch. 40, Pt. 3(10).]

History – Sch. 15 repealed by FA 2002. s. 141 and Sch. 40, Pt. 3(10) with effect in relation to accounting periods beginning on or after 1 October 2002, subject to the transitional provisions in FA 2002, s. 79 and Sch. 23, Pt. 3.

SCHEDULE 16 – EXCHANGE GAINS AND LOSSES: TRANSITIONALS

Section 165

[Repealed by FA 2002, s. 141 and Sch. 40, Pt. 3(10).]

History – Sch. 16 repealed by FA 2002, s. 141 and Sch. 40, Pt. 3(10) with effect in relation to accounting periods beginning on or after 1 October 2002, subject to the transitional provisions in FA 2002, s. 79 and Sch. 23, Pt. 3.

Statutory instruments – SI 1994/3226: regulations made under Sch. 16.

SCHEDULE 17 – EXCHANGE GAINS AND LOSSES: CHARGEABLE GAINS

Section 169

[Repealed by FA 2002, s. 141 and Sch. 40, Pt. 3(10).]

History – Sch. 17 repealed by FA 2002, s. 141 and Sch. 40, Pt. 3(10) with effect in relation to accounting periods beginning on after 1 October 2002, subject to the transitional provisions in FA 2002, s. 79 and Sch. 23, Pt. 3.

SCHEDULE 18 – EXCHANGE GAINS AND LOSSES: AMENDMENTS

Section 170

TAXES MANAGEMENT ACT 1970 (c. 9)

1 [Inserts TMA 1970, s. 87A(4A).]

INCOME AND CORPORATION TAXES ACT 1988 (c. 1)

2 [Repealed by FA 2002, s. 141 and Sch. 40, Pt. 3(10) with effect in relation to accounting periods beginning on or after 1 October 2002.]

3 [Repealed by FA 1996, Sch. 41, Pt. V(3).]

4 [Inserts ICTA 1988, s. 407(2)(c).]

5 [Inserts ICTA 1988, s. 826(7C).]

6 [Repealed by Statute Law (Repeals) Act 2013, s. 1 and Sch. 1, Pt. 10.]

History – Para. 6 repealed by Statute Law (Repeals) Act 2013, s. 1 and Sch. 1, Pt. 10, with effect from 31 January 2013.

FINANCE ACT 1989(c. 26)

7 [Repealed by FA 1996, Sch. 41, Pt. V(3).]

SCHEDULE 19 – LLOYD'S UNDERWRITERS: ASSESSMENT AND COLLECTION OF TAX

Section 173

[Omitted by F(No. 2)A 2005, s. 45(1) and repealed by F(No. 2)A 2005, s. 70 and Sch. 11, Pt. 2(11).]

History – Sch. 19 omitted by F(No. 2)A 2005, s. 45(1) and repealed by F(No. 2)A 2005, s. 70 and Sch. 11, Pt. 2(11) with effect from 6 April 2006 (F(No. 2)A 2005, s. 45(9)), although for the purposes of enabling regulations to be made under this section or under FA 1994, s. 229(1)(a), the omission and repeal took effect from 20 July 2005 (Royal Assent) (F(No. 2)A 2005, s. 45(8)).

SCHEDULE 20 – LLOYD'S UNDERWRITERS: SPECIAL RESERVE FUNDS

Section 175

Cross references – SI 1997/2681, reg. 7: Sch. 20 does not apply in relation to a Lloyd's Scottish limited partnership treated as an individual member by virtue of reg. 3(1) of those regulations.

Part I – Requirements for and Tax Consequences of New-Style Funds

PRELIMINARY

1(1) In this Part of this Schedule–

"the arrangements" means the arrangements mentioned in section 175(1) of this Act;

"cash call" means a request for funds which, in pursuance of a contract made in accordance with the rules and practices of Lloyd's, is made to a member by the agent of a syndicate of which he is a member;

"overall premium limit", in relation to a member and an underwriting year, means the maximum amount which, under the rules of Lloyd's, the member may accept by way of premiums in that year;

"payment", unless the contrary intention appears, means a payment in money;

"stop-loss payment" means a payment of insurance money under a stop-loss insurance or a payment out of the High Level Stop Loss Fund;

"syndicate profit", in relation to a member and an underwriting year, means the amount by which the aggregate of his profits exceeds the aggregate of his losses for the year, and

"syndicate loss" shall be construed accordingly.

1(2) For the purposes of the definitions of "syndicate profit" and "syndicate loss" in sub-paragraph (1) above–

(a) any reference to **profits or losses of a member** is a reference to profits or losses which, in the accounts of the syndicates of which he is a member, are shown as arising to him, and

(b) any payments under paragraph 3(1), 4(1), (2), (3) or (6), 5(1), (4) or (7) or 6(2) below shall be disregarded.

History – In para. 1(1), definition of "payment" inserted by FA 1994, s. 228(1) and Sch. 21, para. 12(1), with effect for the year 1992–93 and subsequent years of assessment.

Cross references – SI 1995/353, reg. 3: modification of para. 1(2) as applied to running-off syndicates.
SI 1995/353, reg. 7: circumstances in which references to a member (other than relating to a member's special reserve fund) construed as including references to the member's personal representatives.

GENERAL REQUIREMENTS

2(1) The arrangements must provide–

(a) for the setting up, in relation to any member, of a special reserve fund vested in one or more trustees who have control over it, and

(b) for the appointment of an authorised fund manager (who may be the trustees or one of the trustees) to invest the capital of the fund and to vary the investments;

and in this sub-paragraph **"authorised"** means authorised under the rules of Lloyd's.

2(2) The arrangements must be such as to secure that–

(a) any income arising to the trustee or trustees of the special reserve fund shall be added to the capital of the fund and held on the same trusts as the fund; and

(b) except as required or permitted by this Schedule, no payments shall be made into or out of the special reserve fund.

History – Para. 2 deemed to have been enacted with the substitution of para. 2(2) for para. 2(2) and (3) by FA 1995, s. 143(2).

PAYMENTS INTO FUND OUT OF SYNDICATE PROFITS

3(1) The arrangements must be such as to secure that, if the member has made a syndicate profit for an underwriting year, he has the right to make, into his special reserve fund, payments the amount of which is not in the aggregate greater than whichever of the following is the less, namely–

(a) 50 per cent of that profit; and

(b) the amount (if any) by which 50 per cent of the member's overall premium limit for the closing year exceeds the value of the fund as at the end of that year.

3(2) Any payments which a member is entitled to make by virtue of sub-paragraph (1) above must be made before the end of such period as may be prescribed.

3(3) Where the member did not accept premiums in the closing year, the reference in sub-paragraph (1)(b) above to the member's overall premium limit for that year shall be construed as a reference to that limit for the latest underwriting year in which he did so.

Cross references – SI 1995/353, reg. 5(1): period prescribed under para. 3(1) for any payments into or out of special reserve fund.
SI 1995/353, reg. 6(3), (4): fund manager must state, in report to member on value of fund for 1994 and subsequent underwriting years, the amount of any payment made under para. 3(1).
SI 1995/353, reg. 7: circumstances in which references to a member (other than relating to a member's special reserve fund) construed as including references to the member's personal representatives.

Statutory instruments – SI 1995/353.

PAYMENTS OUT OF FUND TO COVER CASH CALLS

4(1) The arrangements must be such as to secure that, if a cash call is made on the member in respect of an underwriting year, there shall be made into a premium trust fund of his, out of his special reserve fund, payments the amount of which is equal in the aggregate to the amount of the call, or the amount of his special reserve fund, whichever is the less.

4(2) Where the aggregate amount of any payments made under sub-paragraph (1) above in respect of any year is found to exceed the amount of the member's syndicate loss for the year, there shall be made into his special reserve fund, out of a premium trust fund or ancillary trust fund of his, payments the amount of which is equal in the aggregate to the amount of the excess.

4(3) Where a stop-loss payment is made to the member in respect of his syndicate loss for any year, so much of the stop-loss payment as does not exceed the requisite amount shall be paid into his special reserve fund.

4(4) In sub-paragraph (3) above **"the requisite amount"** means so much of the amount (if any) given by sub-paragraph (5) below as does not exceed the aggregate amount mentioned in paragraph (b) of that sub-paragraph.

4(5) The amount given by this sub-paragraph is the amount by which–

(a) the amount of the stop-loss payment, and

(b) the aggregate amount of the payments under sub-paragraph (1) above as reduced by the aggregate amount of any payments under sub-paragraph (2) above,

exceeds in the aggregate the amount of the member's syndicate loss.

4(6) Where the whole or any part of a stop-loss payment made to a member is repaid, there shall be made to the member or his personal representatives or assigns, out of his special reserve fund, payments the amount of which is equal in the aggregate to the amount (if any) to which sub-paragraph (7) below applies or the amount of his special reserve fund, whichever is the less.

4(7) This sub-paragraph applies to any amount which –

(a) has been paid into the member's special reserve fund under sub-paragraph (2) or (3) above, but

(b) would not have been so paid but for the stop-loss payment or (as the case may be) the part repaid.

4(8) Any payments required by sub-paragraph (1), (2), (3) or (6) above shall be made before the end of such period as may be prescribed.

History – In para. 4(1), the word "premium" substituted for the word "premiums" by SI 2001/3629, art. 82(g)(i) operative from 1 December 2001.

In para. 4(2), the word "premium" substituted for the word "premiums" by SI 2001/3629, art. 82(g)(i) operative from 1 December 2001.

Cross references – SI 1995/353, reg. 4: modification of para. 4 as applied to running-off syndicates.

SI 1995/353, reg. 5(2)–(5): periods prescribed under para. 4(1)–(3), (6) for any payments into or out of special reserve fund.

SI 1995/353, reg. 6(3), (4): fund manager must state, in report to member on value of fund for 1994 and subsequent underwriting years, the amount of any payment made under para. 4(1)–(3), (6).

SI 1995/353, reg. 7: circumstances in which references to a member (other than relating to a member's special reserve fund) construed as including references to the member's personal representatives.

Statutory instruments – SI 1995/353.

PAYMENTS OUT OF FUND TO COVER SYNDICATE LOSSES

5(1) The arrangements must be such as to secure that, if the member has sustained a syndicate loss for an underwriting year, there shall be made into a premium trust fund of his, out of his special reserve fund, payments the amount of which is equal in the aggregate to the net amount of the loss or the amount of his special reserve fund, whichever is the less.

5(2) Sub-paragraphs (3) and (4) below apply where a stop-loss payment is made to the member in respect of his syndicate loss for any year.

5(3) If any payments are subsequently made for the year under sub-paragraph (1) above, the aggregate amount of those payments shall be determined as if the net amount of the syndicate loss were reduced by the amount of the stop-loss payment.

5(4) If any payments have previously been made for the year under sub-paragraph (1) above, so much of the stop-loss payment as does not exceed the requisite amount shall be paid into his special reserve fund.

5(5) In sub-paragraph (4) above **"the requisite amount"** means so much of the amount (if any) given by sub-paragraph (6) below as does not exceed the amount mentioned in paragraph (b) of that sub-paragraph.

5(6) The amount given by this sub-paragraph is the amount by which–

(a) the amount of the stop-loss payment, and

(b) the aggregate amount of the payments made under sub-paragraph (1) above,

exceeds in the aggregate the net amount of the member's syndicate loss.

5(7) Where the whole or any part of a stop-loss payment made to a member is repaid, there shall be made to the member or his personal representatives or assigns, out of his special reserve fund, payments theamount of which is equal in the aggregate to the aggregate of the amounts (if any) to which sub-paragraphs (8) and (9) below apply or the amount of his special reserve fund, whichever is the less.

5(8) This sub-paragraph applies to any amount which–

(a) has not been paid out of the member's special reserve fund under sub-paragraph (1) above, but

(b) would have been so paid but for the stop-loss payment or (as the case may be) the part repaid.

5(9) This sub-paragraph applies to any amount which–

(a) has been paid into the member's special reserve fund under sub-paragraph (4) above, but

(b) would not have been so paid but for the stop-loss payment or (as the case may be) the part repaid.

5(10) Any payments required by sub-paragraph (1), (4) or (7) above shall be made before the end of such period as may be prescribed.

5(11) In this paragraph **"net amount"**, in relation to a member's syndicate loss for any year, means the amount of the loss as reduced by the amount of any payments made under paragraph 4(1) above for the year.

History – In para. 5(1), the word "premium" substituted for the word "premiums" by SI 2001/3629, art. 82(g)(ii) operative from 1 December 2001.

Cross references – SI 1995/353, reg. 5(6)–(8): periods prescribed under para. 5(1), (4), (7) for any payments into or out of special reserve fund.
SI 1995/353, reg. 6(3), (4): fund manager must state, in report to member on value of fund for 1994 and subsequent underwriting years, the amount of any payment made under para. 5(1), (4), (7).
SI 1995/353, reg. 7: circumstances in which references to a member (other than relating to a member's special reserve fund) construed as including references to the member's personal representatives.

Statutory instruments – SI 1995/353.

VALUATION AND PAYMENTS OUT OF FUND OF EXCESS AMOUNTS

6(1) The arrangements must be such as to secure that the fund manager of a member's special reserve fund–

(a) shall determine in the prescribed manner the value of the fund as at the end of the year 1994 and each subsequent underwriting year; and

(b) shall report the value so determined to the member;

and the report shall also state such other matters as may be prescribed.

6(2) If the value (determined under sub-paragraph (1) above) of the fund as at the end of any underwriting year exceeds 50 per cent of–

(a) the higher of–

(i) the member's overall premium limit for that year, and

(ii) his overall premium limit for the immediately preceding year; or

(b) where he did not accept premiums in either of those years, his overall premium limit for the last underwriting year in which he did so,

there shall be made to the member or his personal representatives or assigns, out of his special reserve fund, payments the amount of which is equal in the aggregate to the excess.

6(3) The payments required by sub-paragraph (2) above shall be made before the end of such period as may be prescribed.

History – In para. 6(2) words "(determined under sub-paragraph (1) above) of the fund as at the end" substituted for "of the fund as so determined in respect" by SI 1999/3308, reg. 3(a), with effect from 31st December 1999.
Para. 6(2)(a) substituted by SI 1999/3308, reg. 3(b), with effect from 31st December 1999.
In para. 6(2)(b) words "either of those years" substituted for "that year" by SI 1999/3308, reg. 3(c), with effect from 31 December 1999.

Cross references – SI 1995/353, reg. 5(9): periods prescribed under para. 6(2) for any payments into or out of special reserve fund.
SI 1995/353, reg. 6(3), (4): fund manager must state, in report to member on value of fund for 1994 and subsequent underwriting years, the amount of any payment made under para. 6(2).
SI 1995/353, reg. 7: circumstances in which references to a member (other than relating to a member's special reserve fund) construed as including references to the member's personal representatives.

Statutory instruments – SI 1995/353.

PAYMENTS OUT OF FUND ON CESSATION

7(1) The arrangements must provide that, on the member ceasing to carry on his underwriting business, whether by reason of death or otherwise, the amount of his special reserve fund, so far as not required for giving effect to the requirements of paragraph 4 or 5 above, shall be paid over to the member or his personal representatives or assigns.

7(2) For the purposes of sub-paragraph (1) above, a payment of an amount shall be in money or in assets forming part of the fund or both, as the member or his personal representatives or assigns may direct.

History – In para. 7(2), the words "in assets forming part of the fund" substituted by FA 1994, s. 228(1) and Sch. 21, para. 12(2), with effect for the year 1992–93 and subsequent years of assessment.

Cross references – SI 1995/353, reg. 6(3), (4): fund manager must state, in report to member on value of fund for 1994 and subsequent underwriting years, the amount of any payment made under para. 7(1).

ENTITLEMENT OF MEMBER FOR TAX PURPOSES

8(1) Subject to sub-paragraph (2) and paragraph 11(2) to (4) below, a member shall be treated for the purposes of the Income Tax Acts and the Gains Tax Acts as absolutely entitled as against the trustees to the assets forming part of his special reserve fund.

8(2) Where an asset is disposed of by a member to the trustees of his special reserve fund, nothing in sub-paragraph (1) above shall affect the operation of the Gains Tax Acts in relation to that disposal.

History – Para. 8 substituted by FA 1994, s. 228(1) and Sch. 21, para. 13(1), with effect for the year 1994–95 and subsequent years of assessment.
In para. 8(1) after "(2)" the words "and paragraph 11(2) to (4)" inserted by SI 1999/3308, reg. 4, with effect for the year 2000–2001 and subsequent years of assessment, and in relation to payments and transfers of assets made on or after 1 January 2000.

Cross references – SI 1995/353, reg. 7: circumstances in which references to a member (other than relating to a member's special reserve fund) construed as including references to the member's personal representatives.

TAX EXEMPTION FOR PROFITS ARISING FROM ASSETS OF FUND

9(1) Profits or losses arising from assets forming part of a special reserve fund shall be excluded for the purposes of income tax under the Income Tax Acts, and for the purposes of capital gains tax under the Gains Tax Acts.

9(2) Where for any underwriting year income tax has been deducted from any profits arising from assets forming part of a special reserve fund, the fund manager may, at any time after the end of that year, claim repayment of that tax.

9(3) [Repealed by F(No. 2)A 1997, s. 34 and Sch. 4, para. 30(1)(a), and s. 52 and Sch. 8, Pt II(10).]

History – Para. 9(3) repealed by F(No. 2)A 1997, s. 34 and Sch. 4, para. 30(1)(a), and s. 52 and Sch. 8, Pt. II(10) with effect in relation to distributions made on or after 6 April 1999.

Cross references – SI 1995/353, reg. 7A: modifications of para. 9 relating to profits or losses arising after the death of a member from the investment of income retained by the trustees.

TAX CONSEQUENCES OF PAYMENTS INTO AND OUT OF FUND

Notes – Para. 10 deemed omitted, with effect for the years 1994–95 to 1996–97.

10(1) In computing for the purposes of income tax the profits of a member's underwriting business for any year of assessment, the aggregate amount of any payments which, in respect of the relevant underwriting year, are made into his special reserve fund under paragraph 3(1) above shall be deducted as an expense.

10(2) In computing for the purposes of income tax the profits of a member's underwriting business for any year of assessment–

(a) the aggregate amount of any payments which, in respect of the relevant underwriting year, are made out of his special reserve fund under paragraph 4(1) or 5(1) above shall be treated as a trading receipt; and

(b) the aggregate amount of any payments which, in respect of that year, are made into that fund under paragraph 4(2) or (3) or 5(4) above shall be deducted as an expense.

10(3) In computing for the purposes of income tax the profits of a member's underwriting business for any year of assessment, the aggregate amount of any payments which, as a result of the repayment of stop-loss payments in the relevant underwriting year, are made out of his special reserve fund under paragraph 4(6) or 5(7) above shall be treated as a trading receipt.

10(4) In computing for the purposes of income tax the profits of a member's underwriting business for any year of assessment, the aggregate amount of any payments which, in respect of the relevant underwriting year's closing year, are made out of his special reserve fund under paragraph 6(2) above (including where they are also made under paragraph 7(1) above) shall be treated as a trading receipt.

10(5) In this paragraph **"the relevant underwriting year"**, in relation to a year of assessment, means the underwriting year next but two before its corresponding underwriting year.

History – Para. 10(5) inserted, and in para. 10(1)–(4) the word "relevant" substituted by FA 1994, s. 228(1) and Sch. 21, para. 14(2) and 14(3) respectively, in relation to 1997–98 and subsequent years of assessment.
In para. 10(4) after "above" the words "(including where they are also made under paragraph 7(1) above)" inserted by SI 1999/3308, reg. 5, with effect for the year 2000–2001 and subsequent years of assessment, and in relation to payments and transfers of assets made on or after 1 January 2000.

Cross references – SI 1995/353, reg. 7: circumstances in which references to a member (other than relating to a member's special reserve fund) construed as including references to the member's personal representatives.

TAX CONSEQUENCES OF CESSATION

11(1) This paragraph applies where a member ceases to carry on his underwriting business, whether by reason of death or otherwise.

11(2) In computing for the purposes of income tax the profits of the member's underwriting business for the relevant year of assessment, any payment under paragraph 7(1) above which is made to him or his personal representatives or assigns out of his special reserve fund shall be treated–

(a) as made immediately after the end of the relevant underwriting year; and

(b) as being a trading receipt of an amount equal to that mentioned in sub-paragraph (3) below.

11(3) The amount referred to in sub-paragraph (2) above is the value of the fund, as determined under paragraph 6(1) above for the penultimate underwriting year and–

(a) as reduced by the aggregate amount of any payments under paragraph 4(1) or (6) or 5(1) or (7) above made after the end of that year;

(b) as increased by the aggregate amount of any payments under paragraph 4(2) or (3) or 5(4) above so made; and

(c) as increased by the amount of any tax repayment under paragraph 9(2) above after the end of that year.

11(4) Where an asset is transferred to the member or his personal representatives or assigns under paragraph 7(1) above, the transfer shall be treated, for the purposes of the Gains Tax Acts, to be an acquisition of the asset by the member or his personal representatives or assigns for a consideration equal to its market value as at the end of the penultimate underwriting year.

11(5) In this paragraph, subject to the provisions of any regulations made by the Board–

"the penultimate underwriting year" means the underwriting year immediately preceding that in which the member's deposit at Lloyd's is paid over to him or his personal representatives or assigns;

"the relevant underwriting year" means–

(a) in the case of a member who dies before his deposit at Lloyd's is paid over to him or his assigns, the underwriting year immediately preceding that corresponding to the relevant year of assessment; and

(b) in any other case, the underwriting year immediately preceding that in which his deposit at Lloyd's is paid over to him or his assigns;

"the relevant year of assessment" means–

(a) in the case of a member who dies before his deposit at Lloyd's is paid over to him or his assigns, the year of assessment at the end of which he is treated, by virtue of section 179A(2) of this Act, as having died; and

(b) in any other case, his final year of assessment.

History – In para. 11(2), the words "the relevant year of assessment" and "the relevant underwriting year" substituted by FA 1994, s. 228(1) and Sch. 21, para. 15(1), with effect for the year 1994–95 and subsequent years of assessment.
In para. 11(3)(c), words "or tax credit received" after "tax repayment" and "or (3)" after "paragraph 9(2)" repealed by F(No. 2)A 1997, s. 34 and Sch. 4, para. 30(1)(b), and s. 52 and Sch. 8, Pt. II(10), with effect in relation to distributions made on or after 6 April 1999.
In para. 11(3), the words "the penultimate underwriting year" substituted by FA 1994, s. 228(1) and Sch. 21, para. 15(2), with effect for the year 1994–95 and subsequent years of assessment.
In para. 11(4), the words "the penultimate underwriting year" substituted by FA 1994, s. 228(1) and Sch. 21, para. 15(2), with effect for the year 1994–95 and subsequent years of assessment.
Para. 11(5) substituted by FA 1994, s. 228(1) and Sch. 21, para. 15(3), with effect for the year 1994–95 and subsequent years of assessment.

Cross references – SI 1995/353, reg. 8: modifications of para. 11 where cessation of underwriting business.
SI 1999/3308, reg. 6: modifications of para. 11 where a syndicate continues after the end of its closing year or a member dies or otherwise ceases to carry on his underwriting business.

Part II – Winding up of Old-style Funds

PRELIMINARY

12(1) In this Part of this Schedule–

"new-style fund" means a special reserve fund set up under the arrangements mentioned in section 175(1) of this Act;

"old-style fund" means a special reserve fund set up under the arrangements mentioned in section 452(1) of the Taxes Act 1988;

"the relevant period", in relation to an old-style fund, means the period of three months beginning with the closing date.

12(2) For the purposes of sub-paragraph (1) above, the closing date for an old-style fund shall be the earliest date on which each of the following has occurred as respects the year 1991–92 and earlier years of assessments, namely–

(a) the time for making any payments into the fund under section 452(5) of the Taxes Act 1988 has expired, or the member has given notice to the inspector that he will not be making any (or any further) such payments; and

(b) any payments required by section 453(1) of that Act to be made out of the fund have been so made.

WINDING UP OF OLD-STYLE FUNDS

13(1) A member may, at any time before the end of the relevant period, direct that so much of the capital of any old-style fund of his as represents sums paid into it under section 452(5) of the Taxes Act 1988 shall be transferred, at the end of that period, into his new-style fund.

13(2) Where an amount of capital is transferred into a member's new-style fund under sub-paragraph (1) above, there shall be paid into that fund by the Board an amount equal to the amount of tax which, if the amount transferred were a net amount corresponding to a gross amount from which income tax had been duly deducted at the basic rate for the year 1992–93, would have been so deducted.

13(3) If a member does not give a direction under sub-paragraph (1) above in relation to any old-style fund of his, so much of the capital of that fund as represents sums paid into it under section 452(5) of the Taxes Act 1988 shall be paid over, at the end of the relevant period, to the member or his personal representatives or assigns.

13(4) In either event, the remaining capital of any old-style fund of a member shall be paid over, at the end of the relevant period, to the member or his personal representatives or assigns.

13(5) For the purposes of sub-paragraphs (1) and (3) above, any payments made out of an old-style fund under section 453(1) of the Taxes Act 1988 shall be treated as having been met, so far as possible, out of payments made into the fund under section 452(5) of that Act.

13(6) A transfer or payment under this paragraph of an amount of capital shall be in money or in assets forming part of the fund or both, as the member may direct.

History – In para. 13(1), the closing words "and a transfer ... member may direct" omitted by FA 1994, s. 228(1) and Sch. 21, para. 16(1), and s. 258 and Sch. 26 Pt. V(25), with effect for the year 1992–93 and subsequent years of assessment.
Para. 13(6) inserted by FA 1994, s. 228(1) and Sch. 21, para. 16(2), with effect for 1992–93 and subsequent years of assessment.

TAX CONSEQUENCES OF WINDING UP

14(1) Where an asset is transferred into a member's new-style fund under paragraph 13(1) above, the transfer shall be treated, for the purposes of the Gains Tax Acts, to be a disposal of the asset by the member for a consideration equal to its market value.

14(2) Sub-paragraph (3) below applies where an amount is paid over to the member or his personal representatives or assigns under paragraph 13(3) above.

14(3) In computing for the purposes of income tax the profits of the member's underwriting business for the year 1992–93, it shall be assumed–

(a) that the amount paid were a net amount corresponding to a gross amount from which income tax had been duly deducted at the basic rate for that year; and

(b) that the corresponding gross amount were a trading receipt for that year.

SCHEDULE 20A – LLOYD'S UNDERWRITERS: CONVERSION TO LIMITED LIABILITY UNDERWRITING

Section 179B

History – In the heading, the words "Lloyd's underwriters:" inserted (at the beginning) by SI 2016/597, reg. 9, with effect from 16 June 2016. [Note: this amendment appears to be a drafting error as the heading inserted by FA 2004, Sch. 25, para. 3 already included these words.]
Sch. 20A inserted by FA 2004, s. 144 and Sch. 25, para. 3 effectively from 6 April 2004. Detailed commencement provisions are contained within para. 11.

Part 1 – Conversion to Underwriting Through Successor Companies

INTRODUCTION

1(1) This Part of this Schedule applies if the following conditions are satisfied.

1(2) Condition 1 is that–

(a) a member gives notice of his resignation from membership of Lloyd's in accordance with the rules or practice of Lloyd's,

(b) in accordance with such rules or practice, the member does not undertake any new insurance business at Lloyd's after the end of the member's last underwriting year, and

(c) the member does not withdraw that notice.

1(3) Condition 2 is that all of the member's outstanding syndicate capacity is disposed of by the member under a conversion arrangement to a successor company (**"the syndicate capacity disposal"**) with effect from the beginning of the underwriting year next following the member's last underwriting year.

1(4) Condition 3 is that, immediately before the syndicate capacity disposal,–

(a) the member controls the successor company, and

(b) more than 50% of the ordinary share capital of the successor company is beneficially owned by the member.

1(5) Condition 4 is that the syndicate capacity disposal is made in consideration solely of the issue to the member of shares in the successor company.

1(6) Condition 5 is that the successor company starts to carry on its underwriting business in the underwriting year next following the member's last underwriting year.

1(7) In this paragraph **"the member's last underwriting year"**, in relation to a member who gives notice of his resignation from membership of Lloyd's, means the underwriting year during which, or at the end of which, he ceases to be an underwriting member and becomes a non-underwriting member in accordance with the rules or practice of Lloyd's.

1(8) In this paragraph **"outstanding syndicate capacity"**, in relation to a member, means the syndicate capacity of the member other than any which–

(a) the member disposes of to a person other than a successor member at or before the end of the member's last underwriting year, or

(b) ceases to exist with effect from the end of that year.

History – In para. 1(6), the words "(**"the successor company's first underwriting year"**)" (which appeared after the words "in the underwriting year") omitted by SI 2016/597, reg. 3, with effect from 16 June 2016.

INCOME TAX: CARRY FORWARD OF LOSS RELIEF FOLLOWING CONVERSION

2(1) This paragraph applies if–

(a) the member's total income for a year of assessment includes any income derived by the member from the successor company (whether by way of dividends on the shares issued to the member or otherwise), and

(b) throughout the period beginning with the time of the syndicate capacity disposal and ending with the end of that year of assessment,–

  (i) the member controls the successor company, and

  (ii) more than 50% of the ordinary share capital of the successor company is beneficially owned by the member.

2(2) Section 83 of ITA 2007 shall apply as if the income so derived were profits on which the member was assessed under Part 2 of the Income Tax (Trading and Other Income) Act 2005 in respect of the member's underwriting business for that year.

2(3) [Omitted by ITA 2007, s. 1027 and Sch. 1, para. 361(2)(b), and repealed by s. 1031 and Sch. 3, Pt. 1.]

2(4) [Omitted by ITA 2007, s. 1027 and Sch. 1, para. 361(2)(b), and repealed by s. 1031 and Sch. 3, Pt. 1.]

History – In para. 2(2) the words "Section 83 of ITA 2007" substituted for the words "The carry-forward provision" by ITA 2007, s. 1027 and Sch. 1, para. 361(2)(a), with effect from 6 April 2007.

In para. 2(2) the words "Part 2 of the Income Tax (Trading and Other Income) Act 2005" substituted for the words "Schedule D" by ITTOIA 2005, s. 882(1) and Sch. 1, para. 466(2); effective for income tax purposes for 2005–06 onwards and for corporation tax purposes for accounting periods ending after 5 April 2005 (ITTOIA 2005, s. 883(1)).

Para. 2(3) omitted by ITA 2007, s. 1027 and Sch. 1, para. 361(2)(b), and repealed by s. 1031 and Sch. 3, Pt. 1, with effect from 6 April 2007.

Para. 2(4) omitted by ITA 2007, s. 1027 and Sch. 1, para. 361(2)(b), and repealed by s. 1031 and Sch. 3, Pt. 1, with effect from 6 April 2007.

CAPITAL GAINS TAX: ROLL-OVER RELIEF ON DISPOSAL OF SYNDICATE CAPACITY

3(1) This paragraph applies if–

(a) the aggregate of any chargeable gains accruing to the member on the syndicate capacity disposal exceeds the aggregate of any allowable losses accruing to him on that disposal, and

(b) the member makes a claim under this paragraph to an officer of the Board.

3(2) The amount of the excess mentioned in sub-paragraph (1)(a) above ("the amount of the syndicate capacity gain") shall for the purposes of capital gains tax be reduced by the amount of the rolled-over gain.

3(3) For the purpose of computing any chargeable gain accruing to the member on a disposal by him of any issued share or any asset directly or indirectly derived from any issued share–

(a) the amount of the rolled-over gain shall be apportioned between the issued shares as a whole, and

(b) the sums allowable as a deduction under section 38(1)(a) of the Gains Tax Act shall be reduced by the amount apportioned to the issued share under paragraph (a) above; but, in the case of a derived asset, the reduction shall be by an appropriate proportion of that amount;

and if the issued shares are not all of the same class, the apportionment between the shares under paragraph (a) above shall be in accordance with their market values at the time they were acquired by the member.

3(4) In this paragraph **"the amount of the rolled-over gain"** means the lesser of–

(a) the amount of the syndicate capacity gain, and

(b) the aggregate amount of any sums which would be allowable as a deduction under section 38(1)(a) of the Gains Tax Act if the issued shares were disposed of as a whole by the member in circumstances giving rise to a chargeable gain.

3(5) In this paragraph the **"issued shares"** means the shares in the successor company issued to the member in consideration for the syndicate capacity disposal.

CAPITAL GAINS TAX: ROLL-OVER RELIEF ON DISPOSAL OF ASSETS OF ANCILLARY TRUST FUND

4(1) This paragraph applies if–

(a) at the time of, or after, the syndicate capacity disposal, assets forming some or all of the member's ancillary trust fund are–

  (i) withdrawn from the fund, and

  (ii) without unreasonable delay, disposed of by him to the successor company (the "ATF disposal"),

(b) the aggregate of any chargeable gains accruing to the member on the ATF disposal exceeds the aggregate of any allowable losses accruing to him on that disposal,

(c) throughout the period beginning with the time of the syndicate capacity disposal and ending with the time of the ATF disposal,–

  (i) the member controls the successor company, and

  (ii) more than 50% of the ordinary share capital of the successor company is beneficially owned by the member,

(d) the ATF disposal is made in consideration solely of the issue to the member of shares (the "issued shares") in the successor company, and

(e) the member makes a claim under this paragraph to an officer of the Board.

4(2) But this paragraph does not apply if–

(a) the member could have made a claim under paragraph 3 above, and

(b) at the time the member makes a claim under this paragraph, no claim under paragraph 3 above is or has been made by him.

4(3) The amount of the excess mentioned in sub-paragraph (1)(b) above ("the amount of the ATF assets gain") shall for the purposes of capital gains tax be reduced by the amount of the rolled-over gain.

4(4) For the purpose of computing any chargeable gain accruing to the member on a disposal by him of any issued share or any asset directly or indirectly derived from any issued share–

(a) the amount of the rolled-over gain shall be apportioned between the issued shares as a whole, and

(b) the sums allowable as a deduction under section 38(1)(a) of the Gains Tax Act shall be reduced by the amount apportioned to the issued share under paragraph (a) above; but, in the case of a derived asset, the reduction shall be by an appropriate proportion of that amount;

and if the issued shares are not all of the same class, the apportionment between the shares under paragraph (a) above shall be in accordance with their market values at the time they were acquired by the member.

4(5) In this paragraph **"the amount of the rolled-over gain"** means the lesser of–

(a) subject to sub-paragraph (6) below, the amount of the ATF assets gain, and

(b) the aggregate amount of any sums which would be allowable as a deduction under section 38(1)(a) of the Gains Tax Act if the issued shares were disposed of as a whole by the member in circumstances giving rise to a chargeable gain.

4(6) If the market value, immediately before the ATF disposal, of the assets disposed of under that disposal exceeds 120% of the amount of the ATF assets required, the amount of the ATF assets gain shall for the purposes of sub-paragraph (5)(a) above be reduced by multiplying it by–

$$\frac{R}{T}$$

where–

R is the amount of the ATF assets required, and

T is the market value, immediately before the ATF disposal, of the assets disposed of under that disposal.

4(7) In sub-paragraph (6) above **"the amount of the ATF assets required"** means the appropriate percentage of the amount of security required to be provided by the successor company in respect of its underwriting business in the underwriting year in which the ATF disposal is made.

4(7A) In sub-paragraph (7) above "the appropriate percentage" means the percentage that equates to the percentage of the ordinary share capital of the successor company that is beneficially owned by the member immediately before the ATF disposal.

4(8) This paragraph applies only on the first occasion on or after 6th April 2004 on which the member makes an ATF disposal.

4(9) If a claim made by the member under paragraph 3 above is revoked, this paragraph shall apply as if the claim had never been made.

History – In para. 4(6), the words "120% of" inserted by SI 2016/597, reg. 4(a), with effect in relation to ATF disposals (within the meaning of FA 1993, Sch. 20A, para. 4) made on or after 16 June 2016 (even if the corresponding syndicate capacity disposal was made before that date).

In para. 4(7), the words "appropriate percentage of the amount of security required to be provided by the successor company in respect of its underwriting business in the underwriting year in which the ATF disposal is made." substituted for the words below by SI 2016/597, reg. 4(b), with effect in relation to ATF disposals (within the meaning of FA 1993, Sch. 20A, para. 4) made on or after 16 June 2016 (even if the corresponding syndicate capacity disposal was made before that date). Former words read as follows:

"lesser of–

(a) the amount of security required to be provided by the member in respect of his underwriting business in the member's last underwriting year, and

(b) the amount of security required to be provided by the successor company in respect of its underwriting business in the successor company's first underwriting year.".

Para. 4(7A) inserted by SI 2016/597, reg. 4(c), with effect in relation to ATF disposals (within the meaning of FA 1993, Sch. 20A, para. 4) made on or after 16 June 2016 (even if the corresponding syndicate capacity disposal was made before that date).

INTERPRETATION OF THIS PART OF THIS SCHEDULE

5(1) In this Part of this Schedule–

"control" shall be construed in accordance with sections 450 and 451 of the Corporation Tax Act 2010;

"ordinary share capital" has the meaning given by section 989 of ITA 2007;

"successor company" means a corporate member (within the meaning of Chapter 5 of Part 4 of the Finance Act 1994) which is a successor member;

"the syndicate capacity disposal" has the meaning given by paragraph 1(3) above;

"underwriting business", in relation to a successor company, has the same meaning as in Chapter 5 of Part 4 of the Finance Act 1994.

5(2) For the purposes of this Part of this Schedule, shares comprised in any letter of allotment or similar instrument shall be treated as issued unless–

(a) the right to the shares conferred by it remains provisional until accepted, and

(b) there has been no acceptance.

5(3) Paragraphs 3 and 4 above (and paragraph 1 above so far as relating to those paragraphs) are to be construed as one with the Gains Tax Act.

History – In para. 5(1), in the definition of "control", the words "sections 450 and 451 of CTA 2010" substituted for "section 416 of the Taxes Act 1988" by CTA 2010, s. 1177 and Sch. 1, para. 279, with effect for corporation tax purposes for accounting periods ending on or after 1 April 2010, and for income tax and capital gains tax purposes for the tax year 2010–11 and subsequent tax years.

In para. 5(1), definition of "the member's last underwriting year" and "the successor company's first underwriting year" omitted by SI 2016/597, reg. 5, with effect from 16 June 2016. Former definitions read as follows:

""**the member's last underwriting year**" has the meaning given by paragraph 1(7) above;

"**the successor company's first underwriting year**" has the meaning given by paragraph 1(6) above;".

In para. 5(1) the words "section 989 of ITA 2007" substituted for the words "section 832(1) of the Taxes Act 1988" by ITA 2007, s. 1027 and Sch. 1, para. 361(3), with effect from 6 April 2007.

PART 1A – CONVERSION OF PARTNERSHIPS TO UNDERWRITING THROUGH SUCCESSOR COMPANIES

History – Pt. 1A inserted by SI 2014/3133, reg. 5(2), with effect from 19 December 2014.

INTRODUCTION

5A(1) This Part of this Schedule applies if the following conditions are satisfied.

5A(2) Condition 1 is that–

(a) a Lloyd's partnership gives notice of its resignation from membership of Lloyd's in accordance with the rules or practice of Lloyd's,

(b) in accordance with the rules or practice, the partnership does not undertake any new insurance business at Lloyd's after the end of the partnership's last underwriting year, and

(c) the partnership does not withdraw that notice.

5A(3) Condition 2 is that all of the partnership's outstanding syndicate capacity is disposed of by the partnership under a conversion arrangement to a successor company (the "syndicate capacity disposal") with effect from the beginning of the underwriting year next following the partnership's last underwriting year.

5A(4) Condition 3 is that, immediately before the syndicate capacity disposal,–

(a) the converting partners together control the successor company, and

(b) the ordinary share capital of the successor company is beneficially owned by the converting partners in the same, or as nearly as may be the same, proportions as those in which pursuant to the partnership agreement the converting partners are at that time treated as having interests in the partnership's syndicate capacity.

5A(5) For the purposes of sub-paragraph (4)(b), ignore any interest of a person other than a converting partner in the partnership's syndicate capacity.

5A(6) Condition 4 is that the syndicate capacity disposal is made in consideration solely of the issue to the converting partners of shares in the successor company.

5A(7) Condition 5 is that the successor company starts to carry on its underwriting business in the underwriting year next following the partnership's last underwriting year.

5A(8) In this paragraph **"the partnership's last underwriting year"**, in relation to a partnership which gives notice of its resignation from Lloyd's, means the underwriting year during which, or at the end of which, the partnership ceases to be an underwriting member and becomes a non-underwriting member in accordance with the rules or practice of Lloyd's.

5A(9) In this paragraph **"outstanding syndicate capacity"**, in relation to a partnership, means the syndicate capacity of the partnership other than any which–

(a) the partnership disposes of to a person other than a successor member at or before the end of the partnership's last underwriting year, or

(b) ceases to exist with effect from the end of that year.

History – In para. 5A(7), the words "("the successor company's first underwriting year")" (which appeared after the words "in the underwriting year") omitted by SI 2016/597, reg. 6, with effect from 16 June 2016.

CAPITAL GAINS TAX: ROLL-OVER RELIEF ON DISPOSAL OF SYNDICATE CAPACITY

5B(1) This paragraph applies if–

(a) the aggregate of any chargeable gains accruing to a converting partner on the syndicate capacity disposal exceeds the aggregate of any allowable losses accruing to the partner on that disposal, and

(b) the partner makes a claim under this paragraph to an officer of Revenue and Customs.

5B(2) The amount of the excess mentioned in sub-paragraph (1)(a) above ("the amount of the syndicate capacity gain") shall for the purposes of capital gains tax be reduced by the amount of the rolled-over gain.

5B(3) For the purpose of computing any chargeable gain accruing to the partner on a disposal by the partner of any issued share or any asset directly or indirectly derived from any issued share–

(a) the amount of the rolled-over gain shall be apportioned between the issued shares as a whole, and

(b) the sums allowable as a deduction under section 38(1)(a) of the Gains Tax Act shall be reduced by the amount apportioned to the issued share under paragraph (a) above; but, in the case of a derived asset, the reduction shall be by an appropriate proportion of that amount;

and if the issued shares are not all of the same class, the apportionment between the shares under paragraph (a) above shall be in accordance with their market values at the time they were acquired by the partner.

5B(4) In this paragraph **"the amount of the rolled-over gain"** means the lesser of–

(a) the amount of the syndicate capacity gain, and

(b) the aggregate of any sums which would be allowable as a deduction under section 38(1)(a) of the Gains Tax Act if the issued shares were disposed of as a whole by the partner in circumstances giving rise to a chargeable gain.

5B(5) In this paragraph the **"issued shares"** means the shares in the successor company issued to the partner in consideration for the syndicate capacity disposal.

CAPITAL GAINS TAX: ROLL-OVER RELIEF ON DISPOSAL OF ASSETS OF ANCILLARY TRUST FUND

5C(1) This paragraph applies if–

(a) at the time of, or after, the syndicate capacity disposal, assets forming some or all of the ancillary trust fund of the Lloyd's partnership or of a converting partner are–
   (i) withdrawn from the fund, and
   (ii) without unreasonable delay, disposed of by the partnership or partner to the successor company (the "ATF disposal"),

(b) the aggregate of any chargeable gains accruing to a converting partner (the "relevant partner") on the ATF disposal exceeds the aggregate of any allowable losses available to the relevant partner on that disposal,

(c) throughout the period beginning with the time of the syndicate capacity disposal and ending with the time of the ATF disposal–
   (i) the converting partners together control the successor company, and
   (ii) the proportion of the successor company's ordinary share capital beneficially owned by the relevant partner is more than 50% of the proportion of that share capital that was beneficially owned by the relevant partner at the time of the syndicate capacity disposal,

(d) the consideration received by the relevant partner on the ATF disposal consists solely of the issue to the relevant partner of shares (the "issued shares") in the successor company, and

(e) the relevant partner makes a claim under this paragraph to an officer of Revenue and Customs.

5C(2) But this paragraph does not apply if–

(a) the relevant partner could have made a claim under paragraph 5B above, and

(b) at the time the relevant partner makes a claim under this paragraph, no claim under paragraph 5B above is or has been made by the relevant partner.

5C(3) The amount of the excess mentioned in sub-paragraph (1)(b) above ("the amount of the ATF assets gain") shall for the purposes of capital gains tax be reduced by the amount of the rolled-over gain.

5C(4) For the purpose of computing any chargeable gain accruing to the relevant partner on a disposal by the relevant partner of any issued share or any asset directly or indirectly derived from any issued share–

(a) the amount of the rolled-over gain shall be apportioned between the issued shares as a whole, and

(b) the sums allowable as a deduction under section 38(1)(a) of the Gains Tax Act are reduced by the amount apportioned to the issued share under paragraph (a) above; but, in the case of a derived asset, the reduction shall be by an appropriate proportion of that amount;

and if the issued shares are not all of the same class, the apportionment between the shares under paragraph (a) above shall be in accordance with their market values at the time they were acquired by the relevant partner.

5C(5) In this paragraph **"the amount of the rolled-over gain"** means the lesser of–

(a) subject to sub-paragraph (6), the amount of the ATF assets gain, and

(b) the aggregate amount of any sums which would be allowable as a deduction under section 38(1)(a) of the Gains Tax Act if the issued shares were disposed of as a whole by the relevant partner in circumstances giving rise to a chargeable gain.

5C(6) If the market value, immediately before the ATF disposal, of the assets disposed of under that disposal exceeds 120% of the amount of the ATF assets required, the amount of the ATF assets gain shall for the purposes of sub-paragraph (5)(a) be reduced by multiplying it by–

$$\frac{R}{T}$$

where–

R is the amount of the ATF assets required, and

T is the market value, immediately before the ATF disposal, of the assets disposed of under that disposal.

5C(7) In sub-paragraph (6) above **"the amount of the ATF assets required"** means the appropriate percentage of the amount of security required to be provided by the successor company in respect of its underwriting business in the underwriting year in which the ATF disposal is made.

5C(7A) In sub-paragraph (7) above "the appropriate percentage" means the percentage that equates to the percentage of the ordinary share capital of the successor company that is beneficially owned by the relevant partner immediately before the ATF disposal.

5C(8) This paragraph applies–

(a) in relation to assets forming some or all of the Lloyd's partnership's ancillary trust fund, only on the first occasion on or after 19th December 2014 on which the partnership makes an ATF disposal, and

(b) in relation to assets forming some or all of a converting partner's ancillary trust fund, only on the first occasion on or after 19th December 2014 on which the partner makes an ATF disposal.

5C(9) If a claim made under paragraph 5B is revoked, this paragraph applies as if the claim had never been made.

History – In para. 5C(6), the words "120% of" inserted by SI 2016/597, reg. 7(a), with effect in relation to ATF disposals (within the meaning of FA 1993, Sch. 20A, para. 5C) made on or after 16 June 2016 (even if the corresponding syndicate capacity disposal was made before that date).

In para. 5C(7), the words "appropriate percentage of the amount of security required to be provided by the successor company in respect of its underwriting business in the underwriting year in which the ATF disposal is made." substituted for the words below by SI 2016/597, reg. 7(b), with effect in relation to ATF disposals (within the meaning of FA 1993, Sch. 20A, para. 5C) made on or after 16 June 2016 (even if the corresponding syndicate capacity disposal was made before that date). Former words read as follows:

"lesser of–

(a) the amount of security required to be provided by the relevant partner in respect of the Lloyd's partnership's underwriting business in the partnership's last underwriting year, and

(b) the amount of security required to be provided by the relevant partner in respect of the successor company's underwriting business in its first underwriting year.".

Para. 5C(7A) inserted by SI 2016/597, reg. 7(c), with effect in relation to ATF disposals (within the meaning of FA 1993, Sch. 20A, para. 5C) made on or after 16 June 2016 (even if the corresponding syndicate capacity disposal was made before that date).

INTERPRETATION OF THIS PART OF THIS SCHEDULE

5D(1) In this Part of this Schedule–

"ancillary trust fund"–

(a) in relation to a Lloyd's partnership, does not include a premium trust fund but, subject to that, means any trust fund required or authorised by the rules of Lloyd's, or required by a member's agent, and

(b) in relation to a converting partner, means any trust fund required or authorised by the rules of Lloyd's in connection with being a partner in, or member of, the partnership, or required by a member's agent in that connection;

"control" is to be construed in accordance with sections 450 and 451 of the Corporation Tax Act 2010;

"converting partner", in relation to a syndicate capacity disposal by a Lloyd's partnership,–

(a) means any person who, immediately before the disposal, is a partner in, or member of, the partnership and pursuant to the partnership agreement is treated at that time as having an interest in the partnership's syndicate capacity, but

(b) does not include any partner or member whose resignation from the partnership takes effect on the day of the disposal;

"ordinary share capital" has the meaning given by section 989 of ITA 2007;

"successor company" means a corporate member (within the meaning of Chapter 5 of Part 4 of the Finance Act 1994) which is a successor member;

"syndicate capacity disposal" has the meaning given by paragraph 5A(3);

"underwriting business"–

(a) in relation to a Lloyd's partnership, means the partnership's underwriting business as a member of Lloyd's, and

(b) in relation to a successor company, has the same meaning as in Chapter 5 of Part 4 of the Finance Act 1994.

5D(2) For the purposes of this Part of this Schedule, shares comprised in any letter of allotment or similar instrument shall be treated as issued unless–

(a) the right to the shares conferred by it remains provisional until accepted, and

(b) there has been no acceptance.

5D(3) Paragraphs 5B and 5C above (and paragraph 5A above so far as relating to those paragraphs) are to be construed as one with the Gains Tax Act.

History – In para. 5D(1), definitions of "the partnership's last underwriting year" and "the successor company's first underwriting year" omitted by SI 2016/597, reg. 8, with effect from 16 June 2016. Former definitions read as follows:

"**"the partnership's last underwriting year"** has the meaning given by paragraph 5A(8);

"the successor company's first underwriting year" has the meaning given by paragraph 5A(7);"

Part 2 – Conversion to Underwriting Through Successor Partnerships

INTRODUCTION

6(1) This Part of this Schedule applies if the following conditions are satisfied.

6(2) Condition 1 is that–

(a) a member gives notice of his resignation from membership of Lloyd's in accordance with the rules or practice of Lloyd's,

(b) in accordance with such rules or practice, the member does not undertake any new insurance business at Lloyd's after the end of the member's last underwriting year, and

(c) the member does not withdraw that notice.

6(3) Condition 2 is that all of the member's outstanding syndicate capacity is disposed of by the member under a conversion arrangement to a successor partnership ("the syndicate capacity disposal") with effect from the beginning of the underwriting year next following the member's last underwriting year.

6(4) Condition 3 is that the member is the only person who disposes of syndicate capacity under a conversion arrangement to the successor partnership.

6(5) Condition 4 is that the successor partnership starts to carry on its underwriting business in the underwriting year next following the member's last underwriting year.

6(6) In this paragraph **"the member's last underwriting year"**, in relation to a member who gives notice of his resignation from membership of Lloyd's, means the underwriting year during which, or at the end of which, he ceases to be an underwriting member and becomes a non-underwriting member in accordance with the rules or practice of Lloyd's.

6(7) In this paragraph **"outstanding syndicate capacity"**, in relation to a member, means the syndicate capacity of the member other than any which–

(a) the member disposes of to a person other than a successor member at or before the end of the member's last underwriting year, or

(b) ceases to exist with effect from the end of that year.

INCOME TAX: CARRY FORWARD OF LOSS RELIEF FOLLOWING CONVERSION

7(1) This paragraph applies if–

(a) the member's total income for a year of assessment includes profits of the successor partnership's underwriting business, and

(b) throughout the period beginning with the time of the syndicate capacity disposal and ending with the end of that year of assessment, the member is beneficially entitled to more than 50% of the profits of that business.

7(2) Section 83 of ITA 2007 (carry-forward of trading losses against subsequent profits) shall have effect, in its application in relation to the losses of the old underwriting business, as if the profits of the successor partnership's underwriting business to which the member is beneficially entitled for that year were profits on which the member was assessed under Part 2 of the Income Tax (Trading and Other Income) Act 2005 in respect of the old underwriting business for that year.

7(3) In sub-paragraph (2) above **"the old underwriting business"** means the member's underwriting business carried on otherwise than through the successor partnership.

History – In para. 7(2) the words "Section 83 of ITA 2007" substituted for the words "Section 385 of the Taxes Act 1988" by ITA 2007, s. 1027 and Sch. 1, para. 361(4), with effect from 6 April 2007.

In para. 7(2) the words "Part 2 of the Income Tax (Trading and Other Income) Act 2005" substituted for the former wording ("Schedule D") by ITTOIA 2005, s. 882(1) and Sch. 1, para. 466(3); effective for income tax purposes for 2005–06 onwards and for corporation tax purposes for accounting periods ending after 5 April 2005 (ITTOIA 2005, s. 883(1)).

INTERPRETATION OF THIS PART OF THIS SCHEDULE

8 In this Part of this Schedule–

"successor partnership" means–

(a) a *limited partnership* formed under the law of Scotland which is a successor member, or

(b) a limited liability partnership formed under the law of any part of the United Kingdom which is a successor member.

"the syndicate capacity disposal" has the meaning given by paragraph 6(3) above.

History – In para. 8 the definition of "successor partnership" substituted by SI 2006/112, reg. 2 with effect from 14 February 2006.

Part 3 – Supplementary Provisions

WITHDRAWAL OF RESIGNATION NOTICE

9(1) This paragraph applies if a member–

(a) makes a claim for relief under or by virtue of Part 1 or 2 of this Schedule, and

(b) subsequently withdraws the notice of his resignation from membership of Lloyd's.

9(2) The member must give written notice of such withdrawal to an officer of the Board.

9(3) Such a notice must be given no later than six months from the date of the withdrawal of the notice of resignation.

9(4) All such adjustments shall be made, whether by discharge or repayment of tax, the making of assessments or otherwise, as are required as a result of the withdrawal of the notice of resignation (notwithstanding any limitation on the time within which any adjustment may be made).

9(5) If a member fails, fraudulently or negligently, to comply with sub-paragraphs (2) and (3) above, section 95 of the Taxes Management Act 1970 shall apply to him as if he had fraudulently or negligently made an incorrect return, statement or declaration in connection with the claim for relief made by him under or by virtue of this Schedule.

9(6) In this paragraph **"tax"** means income tax, capital gains tax or inheritance tax.

History – In para. 9(1)(a), the words "Part 1 or 2 of" inserted by SI 2014/3133, reg. 5(3), with effect from 19 December 2014.

9A(1) This paragraph applies if–

(a) a person makes a claim for relief under or by virtue of Part 1A of this Schedule, and

(b) the Lloyd's partnership in respect of which the claim is made withdraws the notice of its resignation from Lloyd's.

9A(2) The person must give written notice of such withdrawal to an officer of Revenue and Customs.

9A(3) Such a notice must be given no later than 6 months from the date on which the person first became aware of the withdrawal of the notice of resignation.

9A(4) Unless the person proves otherwise, it shall be assumed that the person became aware of the withdrawal of the notice on the day on which it was withdrawn.

9A(5) All such adjustments shall be made, whether by discharge or repayment of tax, the making of assessments or otherwise, as are required as a result of the withdrawal of the notice of resignation (notwithstanding any limitation on the time within which any adjustment may be made).

9A(6) If a person fails, carelessly or deliberately, to comply with sub-paragraph (2) or (3) above, Schedule 24 to the Finance Act 2007 shall apply as if–

(a) the person had given HMRC a document of a kind listed in the Table in paragraph 1 of that Schedule, and

(b) the document contained an inaccuracy which was careless or deliberate on the person's part and amounted to an understatement of a liability to tax equivalent to the amount of the adjustments required by sub-paragraph (5) to be made.

9A(7) In this paragraph **"tax"** means income tax, capital gains tax or inheritance tax.

History – Para. 9A inserted by SI 2014/3133, reg. 5(4), with effect from 19 December 2014.

INTERPRETATION OF THIS SCHEDULE

10 In this Schedule–

"conversion arrangement" means a conversion arrangement made under the rules or practice of Lloyd's;

"successor member" has the meaning given by the rules or practice of Lloyd's;

"syndicate capacity", in relation to a member or Lloyd's partnership, means an asset comprising the rights of the member or partnership under a syndicate in which the member or partnership participates.

History – In para. 10, the definition of "syndicate capacity" substituted by SI 2014/3133, reg. 5(5), with effect from 19 December 2014.

CONVERSION TO UNDERWRITING THROUGH PARTNERSHIP OR COMPANY

History – The heading substituted by SI 2014/3133, reg. 5(7), with effect from 19 December 2014.

11(1) Paragraphs 2 and 3 above (and the other provisions of this Schedule so far as relating to those paragraphs) have effect in relation to syndicate capacity disposals (within the meaning of Part 1 of this Schedule) made on or after 6th April 2004.

11(2) Paragraph 4 above (and the other provisions of this Schedule so far as relating to that paragraph) have effect in relation to ATF disposals (within the meaning of that paragraph above) made on or after 6th April 2004 (even if the syndicate capacity disposal mentioned in that paragraph was made before that date).

11(2A) Paragraph 5B above (and the other provisions of this Schedule so far as relating to that paragraph) have effect in relation to syndicate capacity disposals (within the meaning of Part 1A of this Schedule) made on or after 19th December 2014.

11(2B) Paragraph 5C above (and the other provisions of this Schedule so far as relating to that paragraph) have effect in relation to ATF disposals (within the meaning of that paragraph) made on or after 19th December 2014 (even if the syndicate capacity disposal was made before that date).

11(3) Paragraph 7 above (and the other provisions of this Schedule so far as relating to that paragraph) have effect in relation to syndicate capacity disposals (within the meaning of Part 2 of this Schedule) made on or after 6th April 2004.

History – Para. 11(2A) and (2B) inserted by SI 2014/3133, reg. 5(6), with effect from 19 December 2014.

FINANCE ACT 1994

(1994 Chapter 9)

[*3rd May 1994*]

ARRANGEMENT OF SECTIONS

PART IV – INCOME TAX, CORPORATION TAX AND CAPITAL GAINS TAX

CHAPTER I – GENERAL

INCOME TAX: CHARGE, RATES AND RELIEFS

CHAPTER IV – CHANGES FOR FACILITATING SELF-ASSESSMENT

CHAPTER V – LLOYD'S UNDERWRITERS: CORPORATIONS ETC.

TRUST FUNDS

OTHER SPECIAL CASES

MISCELLANEOUS

SUPPLEMENTAL

PART VIII – MISCELLANEOUS AND GENERAL

COMPANIES TREATED AS NON-RESIDENT

MANAGEMENT

GENERAL

SCHEDULES

PART IV – INCOME TAX, CORPORATION TAX AND CAPITAL GAINS TAX

Chapter I – General

INCOME TAX: CHARGE, RATES AND RELIEFS

75 Charge and rates of income tax for 1994–95

75 [Repealed by ITA 2007, s. 1031 and Sch. 3, Pt. 1.]

History – S. 75 repealed by ITA 2007, s. 1031 and Sch. 3, Pt. 1, with effect from 6 April 2007.

76 Personal allowance

76 [Repealed by ITA 2007, s. 1031 and Sch. 3, Pt. 1.]

History – S. 76 repealed by ITA 2007, s. 1031 and Sch. 3, Pt. 1, with effect from 6 April 2007.

77 Rate of relief to married couples etc.

77(1) [Inserts ICTA 1988, s. 256(2) and (3).]

77(2) [Omitted by FA 2009, s. 5 and Sch. 1, para. 6(f).]

77(3) [Repealed by FA 1999, s. 139 and Sch. 20, Pt. III(4).]

77(4) [Repealed by FA 1999, s. 139 and Sch. 20, Pt. III(4).]

77(5) [Repealed by FA 1999, s. 139 and Sch. 20, Pt. III(3).]

77(6) The Taxes Act 1988 and the Taxes Management Act 1970 shall have effect with the amendments specified in Schedule 8 to this Act (which supplements the provisions of this section).

77(7) This section and Schedule 8 to this Act shall have effect for the year 1994–95 and, subject to the following provisions of this section, for subsequent years of assessment.

77(8) [Repealed by ITA 2007, s. 1031 and Sch. 3, Pt. 1.]

77(9) [Repealed by ITA 2007, s. 1031 and Sch. 3, Pt. 1.]

77(10) [Repealed by ITA 2007, s. 1031 and Sch. 3, Pt. 1.]

History – S. 77(1) and (2) omitted by FA 2009, s. 5 and Sch. 1, para. 6(f), with effect for the tax year 2010–11 and subsequent tax years.
Former s. 77(2)(a) repealed by FA 1999, s. 139 and Sch. 20, Pt. III(3), with effect for the year 2000–01 and subsequent years of assessment.
S. 77(3), (4) repealed by FA 1999, s. 139 and Sch. 20, Pt. III(4), with effect for the year 2000–01 and subsequent years of assessment.
S. 77(5) repealed by FA 1999, s. 139 and Sch. 20, Pt. III(3) with effect for 2001–02 and subsequent tax years.
S. 77(8) repealed by ITA 2007, s. 1031 and Sch. 3, Pt. 1, with effect from 6 April 2007.
S. 77(9) repealed by ITA 2007, s. 1031 and Sch. 3, Pt. 1, with effect from 6 April 2007.
S. 77(10) repealed by ITA 2007, s. 1031 and Sch. 3, Pt. 1, with effect from 6 April 2007.

78 Amount by reference to which MCA is reduced

78 [Repealed by ITA 2007, s. 1031 and Sch. 3, Pt. 1.]

History – S. 78 repealed by ITA 2007, s. 1031 and Sch. 3, Pt. 1, with effect from 6 April 2007.

79 Relief for maintenance payments

79(1) Sections 347A and 347B of the Taxes Act 1988 (which contain provision with respect to the deductions from income allowed on account of maintenance payments) shall have effect in relation to payments becoming due on or after 6th April 1994 with the following modifications.

79(2) [Repealed by FA 1999, s. 139 and Sch. 20, Pt. III(6).]

79(3-6) [Repealed by ITA 2007, s. 1031 and Sch. 3, Pt. 1.]

79(7) [Repealed by FA 1999, s. 139 and Sch. 20, Pt. III(6).]

79(8) [Repealed by FA 1999, s. 139 and Sch. 20, Pt. III(6).]

History – In s. 79(1) the words "and section 38 of the Finance Act 1988" repealed by FA 1999, s. 139 and Sch. 20, Pt. III(6), with effect in relation to any payment falling due on or after 6 April 2000.
S. 79(2) repealed by FA 1999, s. 139 and Sch. 20, Pt. III(6), with effect in relation to any payment falling due on or after 6 April 2000.
S. 79(3) repealed by ITA 2007, s. 1031 and Sch. 3, Pt. 1, with effect from 6 April 2007.
S. 79(4) repealed by ITA 2007, s. 1031 and Sch. 3, Pt. 1, with effect from 6 April 2007.
S. 79(5) repealed by ITA 2007, s. 1031 and Sch. 3, Pt. 1, with effect from 6 April 2007. S. 79(5) already repealed by FA 1999, s. 139 and Sch. 20, Pt. III(6), with effect in relation to any payment falling due on or after 6 April 2000.
S. 79(6) repealed by ITA 2007, s. 1031 and Sch. 3, Pt. 1, with effect from 6 April 2007.
S. 79(7) repealed by FA 1999, s. 139 and Sch. 20, Pt. III(6), with effect in relation to any payment falling due on or after 6 April 2000.
S. 79(8) repealed by FA 1999, s. 139 and Sch. 20, Pt. III(6), with effect in relation to any payment falling due on or after 6 April 2000.

Notes – S. 79 rewritten as ITA 2007, s. 453(2).

80 Limit on relief for interest

80 [Spent: specified mortgage interest relief threshold for 1994–95 and 1995–96.]

81 Mortgage interest relief etc.

81(1) [Substitutes ICTA 1988, s. 353(1).]

81(2) [Inserts ICTA 1988, s. 353(1A)–(1H).]

81(3) [Repealed by FA 1999, s. 139 and Sch. 20, Pt. III(7).]

81(4) [Substitutes ICTA 1988, s. 369(3) and s. (5B).]

81(5) Schedule 9 to this Act (which for the purposes of or in connection with the provisions of this section makes further modifications of certain enactments in relation to tax relief on interest payments) shall have effect.

81(6) The preceding provisions of this section and that Schedule–

(a) shall have effect in relation to payments of interest made on or after 6th April 1994 (whenever falling due); and

(b) shall also have effect, so far as they relate to relevant loan interest, in relation to any payments of interest becoming due on or after 6th April 1994 which have been made at any time before that date but on or after 30th November 1993.

81(7) Any provision made before the passing of this Act by reference to the basic rate of income tax and contained in any instrument or agreement under or in accordance with which payments of relevant loan interest have been or are to be made shall be taken, in relation to any such payment as is mentioned in subsection (6)(a) or (b) above, to have been made, instead, by reference to a rate which, in the case of that payment, is the applicable percentage for the purposes of subsection (1) of section 369 of the Taxes Act 1988.

81(8) [Repealed by FA 1999, s. 139 and Sch. 20, Pt. III(7).]

81(9) In this section **"relevant loan interest"** has the same meaning as in Part IX of the Taxes Act 1988.

History – S. 81(3) and (8) repealed by FA 1999, s. 139 and Sch. 20, Pt. III(7), with effect in relation to any payment of interest falling within FA 1999, s. 38(3) or (4) (broadly, payments made on or after 6 April 2000, or on or after 9 March 1999 and before 6 April 2000 but not falling due until on or after 6 April 2000).

82 Relief for blind persons

82(1) [Amends ICTA 1988, s. 265(1).]

82(2) This section shall apply for the year 1994–95 and subsequent years of assessment.

83 Medical insurance

83 [Repealed by F(No. 2)A 1997, s. 52 and Sch. 8, Pt. II(2), with effect for the year 1997–98 and subsequent years of asessment.]

84 Relief for vocational training

84 [Repealed by FA 1999, s. 139 and Sch. 20, Pt. III(14).]

History – S. 84 repealed by FA 1999, s. 139 and Sch. 20, Pt. III(14), with effect in relation to payments made on or after 1 September 2000 (SI 2000/2004 (C. 53))

CORPORATION TAX CHARGE AND RATE

85 Charge and rate of corporation tax for 1994

85 [Spent: specified rate of corporation tax for financial year 1994.]

86 Small companies

86 [Repealed by CTA 2010, s. 1181 and Sch. 3, Pt. 1.]

History – S. 86 repealed by CTA 2010, s. 1181 and Sch. 3, Pt. 1, with effect for accounting periods ending on or after 1 April 2010.

BENEFITS IN KIND

87 Car fuel

87(1) [Amends ICTA 1988, s. 158(2).]

87(2) This section shall have effect for the year 1994–95 and subsequent years of assessment.

88 Beneficial loan arrangements

88 [Repealed by ITEPA 2003, Sch. 8, Pt. 1.]

History – S. 88 repealed by ITEPA 2003, Sch. 8, Pt. 1 which has effect for the tax year 2003–04 and subsequent tax years. S. 88(5) repealed by FA 2000, Sch. 40, Pt. II(2) with effect for the tax year 2000–01 and subsequent tax years.

89 Vouchers and credit-tokens

89 [Repealed by ITEPA 2003, Sch. 8, Pt. 1.]

History – S. 89 repealed by ITEPA 2003, Sch. 8, Pt. 1 which has effect for the tax year 2003–04 and subsequent tax years.

CHARGEABLE GAINS

90 Annual exempt amount for 1994–95

90 [Spent: specified annual exempt amount for 1994–95.]

91 Relief on re-investment

91(1) Schedule 11 to this Act (which extends the relief on re-investment for individuals and trustees provided by Chapter IA of Part V of the Taxation of Chargeable Gains Act 1992) shall have effect.

91(2) That Schedule shall have effect in relation to disposals made on or after 30th November 1993.

91(3) [Amends TCGA 1992, s. 164H(1).]

91(4) Subsection (3) above shall apply to determine whether a company is a qualifying company on or after 30th November 1993.

92 Relief on retirement

92 [Repealed by FA 1998, s. 165 and Sch. 27, Pt. III(31).]

History – S. 92 repealed by FA 1998, s. 165 and Sch. 27, Pt. III(31), with effect in relation to disposals in the year 2003–04 and subsequent years.

93 Indexation losses

93(1) [Amends TCGA 1992, s. 53(1).]

93(2) [Amends TCGA 1992, s. 53(2).]

93(3) [Inserts TCGA 1992, s. 53(2A).]

93(4) [Inserts TCGA 1992, s. 55(7)–(11).]

93(5) [Amends TCGA 1992, s. 56(2) and inserts TCGA 1992, s. 56(3) and (4).]

93(6) [Inserts TCGA 1992, s. 110(6A).]

93(7) [Repeals TCGA 1992, s. 103, s. 111, s. 182–184, and s. 200.]

93(8) [Omitted by FA 2011, s. 46 and Sch. 11, para. 10(a).]

93(9) [Omitted by FA 2011, s. 46 and Sch. 11, para. 10(a).]

93(10) [Omitted by FA 2011, s. 46 and Sch. 11, para. 10(a).]

93(11) This section shall have effect in relation to disposals made on or after 30th November 1993.

History – S. 93(8) to (10) omitted by FA 2011, s. 46 and Sch. 11, para. 10(a), with effect from 19 July 2011 in relation to the deduction of any pre-entry loss within TCGA 1992, Sch. 7A, para. 1(2), subject to the provisions of FA 2011, Sch. 11, para. 11(2) and 12.

Cross references – TCGA 1992, s. 24(2)(c): application of indexation provisions to certain negligible value claims.

94 Set-off of pre-entry losses

94 [Omitted by FA 2011, s. 46 and Sch. 11, para. 10(a).]

History – S. 94 omitted by FA 2011, s. 46 and Sch. 11, para. 10(a) with effect from 19 July 2011 in relation to the deduction of any pre-entry loss within FA 2011, Sch. 11, para. 11(2) and 12, subject to the provisions of FA 2011, Sch. 11, para. 11(2) and 12.

95 Commodity and financial futures

95(1) [Repeals TCGA 1992, s. 143(4), substitutes TCGA 1992, s. 143(6) and inserts TCGA 1992, s. 143(7), (8).]

95(2) This section shall apply in relation to contracts entered into on or after 30th November 1993.

96 Cash-settled options

96(1) [Inserts TCGA 1992, s. 144A.]

96(2) This section shall apply in relation to options granted on or after 30th November 1993.

97 Settlements with foreign element: information

97(1) The Taxation of Chargeable Gains Act 1992 shall be amended as mentioned in subsections (2) to (4) below.

97(2) [Inserts TCGA 1992, s. 98A.]

97(3) [Inserts TCGA 1992, Sch. 5A.]

97(4) [Repeals TCGA 1992, Sch. 5, para. 11–14.]

97(5) Subsection (4) above shall have effect where the relevant day falls on or after the day on which this Act is passed.

97(6) [Amends TMA 1970, s. 98.]

PROFIT-RELATED PAY

98 The distributable pool

98 [Repealed by FA 1997, s. 113 and Sch. 18, Pt. VI(3).]

History – S. 98 repealed by FA 1997, s. 113 and Sch. 18, Pt. VI(3), in accordance with s. 61(2), (3) of that Act, but not so as to affect the operation of s. 98, or prevent the exercise of any power under it, in relation to profit periods beginning before 1 January 2000 or for purposes connected with, or with the doing or not doing of anything in or in relation to, any such periods (FA 1997, Sch. 18, Pt. VI(3), note 2).

99 Parts of undertakings

99 [Repealed by FA 1997, s. 113 and Sch. 18, Pt. VI(3).]

History – S. 99 repealed by FA 1997, s. 113 and Sch. 18, Pt. VI(3), in accordance with s. 61(2), (3) of that Act, but not so as to affect the operation of s. 99, or prevent the exercise of any power under it, in relation to profit periods beginning before 1 January 2000 or for purposes connected with, or with the doing or not doing of anything in or in relation to, any such periods (FA 1997, Sch. 18, Pt. VI(3), note 2).

PROFIT SHARING SCHEMES

100 Relevant age for purpose of appropriate percentage

100(1) Schedule 10 to the Taxes Act 1988 (profit sharing schemes) shall be amended as follows.

100(2) [Amends ICTA 1988, Sch. 10, para. 3.]

100(3) [Inserts ICTA 1988, Sch. 10, para. 3A.]

101 Acceptance of qualifying corporate bonds for shares

101(1) Schedule 10 to the Taxes Act 1988 (profit sharing schemes) shall be amended as mentioned in subsections (2) to (4) below.

101(2) [Inserts ICTA 1988, Sch. 10, para. 1(1)(cc).]

101(3) [Inserts ICTA 1988, Sch. 10, para. 1(4).]

101(4) [Inserts ICTA 1988, Sch. 10, para. 5A.]

101(5) [Amends ICTA 1988, Sch. 9, para. 32(1).]

101(6) In paragraph 33(a) of Schedule 9 to the Taxes Act 1988 (which provides that the trust instrument must contain certain provision by reference to new shares within the meaning of paragraph 5 of Schedule 10) the reference to paragraph 5 of Schedule 10 shall be construed as including a reference to that paragraph as applied by paragraph 5A.

101(7) Subsections (2) and (3) above shall have effect where a direction is made on or after the day on which this Act is passed.

101(8) Subsection (4) above shall have effect where what would be the new holding comes into being on or after the day on which this Act is passed; but this is subject to subsection (13) below.

101(9) Subsection (5) above shall have effect in relation to any scheme not approved before the day on which this Act is passed.

101(10) In a case where–

(a) a scheme is approved before the day on which this Act is passed, and

(b) on or after that day the trust instrument is altered in such a way that paragraph 32(1) of Schedule 9 to the Taxes Act 1988 would be fulfilled if subsection (5) above applied in relation to the scheme,

subsection (5) above shall apply in relation to the scheme with effect from the time the alteration is made.

101(11) Subsection (6) above shall have effect in relation to any scheme not approved before the day on which this Act is passed.

101(12) In a case where–

(a) a scheme is approved before the day on which this Act is passed, and

(b) on or after that day the trust instrument is altered in such a way that paragraph 33(a) of Schedule 9 to the Taxes Act 1988 would be fulfilled if subsection (6) above applied in relation to the scheme,

subsection (6) above shall apply in relation to the scheme with effect from the time the alteration is made.

101(13) In a case where–

(a) a scheme is approved before the day on which this Act is passed,

(b) subsection (4) above would apply in relation to the scheme by virtue of subsection (8) above and apart from this subsection, and

(c) the trust instrument is not altered as mentioned in subsection (12)(b) above before what would be the new holding comes into being,

subsection (4) above shall not apply in relation to the scheme.

101(14) Subsection (6) above shall not imply a contrary intention for the purposes of section 20(2) of the Interpretation Act 1978 in its application to other references to paragraph 5 of Schedule 10 to the Taxes Act 1988.

Notes – S. 101(8)–(13): FA 1994 was passed on 3 May 1994.

EMPLOYEE SHARE OWNERSHIP TRUSTS

102 Employee share ownership trusts

102 Schedule 13 to this Act (which contains provisions about employee share ownership trusts) shall have effect.

RETIREMENT BENEFITS SCHEMES

103 The administrator

103 [Repealed by FA 2004, s. 326 and Sch. 42, Pt. 3.]

History – S. 103 repealed by FA 2004, s. 326 and Sch. 42, Pt. 3 with effect from 6 April 2006 subject to FA 2004, Sch. 36. Former s. 103 read as follows:

"The administrator

103(1) [Inserts ICTA 1988, s. 611AA.]

103(2) [Repeals definition of "administrator" in ICTA 1988, s. 612(1).]

103(3) This section–

(a) so far as it relates to section 591B(1) of the Taxes Act 1988, shall apply in relation to notices given on or after the day on which this Act is passed;

(b) so far as it relates to section 593(3) of that Act, shall apply in relation to contributions paid on or after that day;

(c) so far as it relates to section 596A(3) of that Act, shall apply in relation to benefits received on or after that day;

(d) so far as it relates to sections 598(2) and (4), 599(3) and 599A(2) of that Act, shall apply in relation to payments made on or after that day;

(e) so far as it relates to section 602(1) and (2) of that Act and regulations made under section 602, shall apply in relation to amounts becoming recoverable on or after that day;

(f) so far as it relates to section 604(1) of that Act, shall apply in relation to applications made on or after that day;

(g) so far as it relates to section 605(1) and (4) of that Act, shall apply in relation to notices given on or after that day.".

104 Default of administrator etc.

104 [Repealed by FA 2004, s. 326 and Sch. 42, Pt. 3.]

History – S. 104 repealed by FA 2004, s. 326 and Sch. 42, Pt. 3 with effect from 6 April 2006 subject to FA 2004, Sch. 36. Former s. 104 substituted ICTA 1988, s. 606 and amended ICTA 1988, s. 607(3)(b)(iii).

Notes – FA 1994 was passed on 3 May 1994.

105 Information

105 [Repealed by FA 2004, s. 326 and Sch. 42, Pt. 3.]

History – S. 105 repealed by FA 2004, s. 326 and Sch. 42, Pt. 3 with effect from 6 April 2006 subject to FA 2004, Sch. 36. Former s. 105 inserted ICTA 1988, s. 605(1A)–(1E), repealed ICTA 1988, s. 605(1) and (2) and amends TMA 1970, s. 98.

Notes – The appointed day for the coming into force of s. 105(3) and (4)(b) was 1 January 1996 (SI 1995/3125 (C. 72)).

106 False statements etc.

106 *[Repealed by FA 2004, s. 326 and Sch. 42, Pt. 3.]*

History – S. 106 repealed by FA 2004, s. 326 and Sch. 42, Pt. 3 with effect from 6 April 2006 subject to FA 2004, Sch. 36. Former s. 106 inserted ICTA 1988, s. 605A.

Notes – FA 1994 was passed on 3 May 1994.

107 Discretionary approval

107 [Repealed by FA 2004, s. 326 and Sch. 42, Pt. 3.]

History – S. 107 repealed by FA 2004, s. 326 and Sch. 42, Pt. 3 with effect from 6 April 2006 subject to FA 2004, Sch. 36. Former s. 107 amended ICTA 1988, s. 591(2)(g) and inserted ICTA 1988, s. 591(2A).

108 Taxation of benefits of non-approved schemes

108(1)–(6) [Repealed by ITEPA 2003, Sch. 8, Pt. 1.]

108(7) Subject to subsection (8) below, in the Taxes Act 1988–

(a) in section 188(1), paragraph (c), and

(b) [repealed by ITEPA 2003, Sch. 8, Pt. 1]

(exemption from tax where recipient of benefit or lump sum chargeable to tax in respect of sums paid or treated as paid with a view to the provision of the benefit or lump sum) shall cease to have effect in relation to any benefit provided or lump sum paid on or after 1st December 1993.

108(8) The repeals made by subsection (7) above shall not have effect in relation to any benefit provided or lump sum paid on or after 1st December 1993 in pursuance of a scheme or arrangement entered into before that day unless the scheme or arrangement is varied on or after that day with a view to the provision of the benefit or lump sum.

History – S. 108(1) to (6) repealed by ITEPA 2003, Sch. 8, Pt. 1 which has effect for the tax year 2003–04 and subsequent tax years. S. 108(7)(b) repealed by ITEPA 2003, Sch. 8, Pt. 1 which has effect for the tax year 2003–04 and subsequent tax years.

Notes – S. 108(6) has been rewritten into the provision of ITEPA 2003, Sch. 7, para. 41 (Sch. 7: Transitionals and savings).

ANNUITIES

109 Annuities derived from personal pension schemes

109 [Repealed by ITEPA 2003, Sch. 8, Pt. 1.]

History – S. 109 repealed by ITEPA 2003, Sch. 8, Pt. 1 which has effect for the tax year 2003–04 and subsequent tax years

110 Annuities derived from retirement benefits schemes

110 [Repealed by ITEPA 2003, Sch. 8, Pt. 1.]

History – S. 110 repealed by ITEPA 2003, Sch. 8, Pt. 1 which has effect for the tax year 2003–04 and subsequent tax years

AUTHORISED UNIT TRUSTS

112 Distributions of authorised unit trusts

112 Schedule 14 to this Act (distributions of authorised unit trusts) shall have effect.

113 Umbrella schemes

113 [Repealed by CTA 2010, s. 1181 and Sch. 3, Pt. 1.]

History – S. 113 repealed by CTA 2010, s. 1181 and Sch. 3, Pt. 1, with effect for corporation tax purposes for accounting periods ending on or after 1 April 2010, and for income tax and capital gains tax purposes for the tax year 2010–11 and subsequent tax years.

EXCHANGE GAINS AND LOSSES

114 Assets and liabilities

114 [Repealed by FA 2002, s. 141 and Sch. 40, Pt. 3(10).]

History – S. 114 repealed by FA 2002, s. 141 and Sch. 40, Pt. 3(10) with effect in relation to accounting periods beginning on or after 1 October 2002.

115 Currency contracts: net payments

115 [Repealed by FA 2002, s. 141 and Sch. 40, Pt. 3(10).]

History – S. 115 repealed by FA 2002, s. 141 and Sch. 40, Pt. 3(10) with effect in relation to accounting periods beginning on or after 1 October 2002.

116 Currency contracts: matching

116 [Repealed by FA 2002, s. 141 and Sch. 40, Pt. 3(10).]

History – S. 116 repealed by FA 2002, s. 141 and Sch. 40, Pt. 3(10) with effect in relation to accounting periods beginning on or after 1 October 2002.

CAPITAL ALLOWANCES

117 Expenditure on machinery or plant

117(1) [Repealed by CAA 2001, s. 580 and Sch. 4.]

117(2) [Repealed by CAA 2001, s. 580 and Sch. 4.]

History – S. 117 repealed by CAA 2001, s. 580 and Sch. 4, with effect as respects allowances and charges falling to be made for chargeable periods ending, for income tax purposes, on or after 6 April 2001, and for corporation tax purposes, on or after 1 April 2001.

118 Expenditure on machinery or plant: notification

118(1) [Repealed by FA 2000, s. 73(1)(a) and Sch. 40, Pt. II(8).]

118(2) [Repealed by FA 2000, s. 73(1)(a) and Sch. 40, Pt. II(8).]

118(3) [Repealed by FA 2000, s. 73(1)(a) and Sch. 40, Pt. II(8).]

118(3A) [Repealed by FA 2000, s. 73(1)(a) and Sch. 40, Pt. II(8).]

118(4) [Repealed by FA 2000, s. 73(1)(a) and Sch. 40, Pt. II(8).]

118(5) [Repealed by FA 2000, s. 73(1)(a) and Sch. 40, Pt. II(8).]

118(6) For the purposes of

(a) [Repealed by CAA 2001, s. 580 and Sch. 4.]

(b) section 44(4) of the Finance Act 1971 (provision corresponding to section 25(1) applicable to earlier chargeable periods), expenditure which has not formed part of a person's qualifying expenditure for a previous chargeable period may not form part of his qualifying expenditure for a subsequent chargeable period unless the machinery or plant on which the expenditure was incurred belongs to that person at some time in that subsequent period or its basis period.

118(7) [Repealed by FA 2000, s. 73(1)(a) and Sch. 40, Pt. II(8).]

118(8) [Repealed by FA 2000, s. 73(1)(a) and Sch. 40, Pt. II(8).]

118(9) [Repealed by FA 2000, s. 73(1)(a) and Sch. 40, Pt. II(8).]

History – S. 118(1) repealed by FA 2000, s. 73(1)(a) and Sch. 40, Pt. II(8) with effect for chargeable periods as respects which the notification period specified in former s. 118(3A) ends on or after 1 April 2000.
S. 118(2) repealed by FA 2000, s. 73(1)(a) and Sch. 40, Pt. II(8) with effect for chargeable periods as respects which the notification period specified in former s. 118(3A) ends on or after 1 April 2000.
S. 118(3) repealed by FA 2000, s. 73(1)(a) and Sch. 40, Pt. II(8) with effect for chargeable periods as respects which the notification period specified in former s. 118(3A) ends on or after 1 April 2000.
In s. 118(3), the words "an officer of the Board … subsection (3A) below" substituted by FA 1996, Sch. 21, para. 48(2), with effect for 1996–97 and subsequent years of assessment for income tax and for accounting periods ending after 31 March 1996 for corporation tax (subject to the exception noted below).
S. 118(3) has effect, as amended by FA 1996, s. 135(5), for 1996–97 in relation to trades, professions or vocations (income tax only) set up and commenced before 6 April 1994.
From 1997–98, s. 118(3) as amended by FA 1996, Sch. 21, para 48(2) (see above) applies.
S. 118(3A) repealed by FA 2000, s. 73(1)(a) and Sch. 40, Pt. II(8) with effect for chargeable periods as respects which the notification period specified in former s. 118(3A) ends on or after 1 April 2000.
S. 118(3A) inserted by FA 1996, Sch. 21, para. 48(3), with effect for 1996–97 and subsequent years of assessment for income tax and for accounting periods ending after 31 March 1996 for corporation tax. It does not apply for 1996–97 in relation to trades, professions or vocations (income tax only) set up and commenced before 6 April 1994.
S. 118(4) repealed by FA 2000, s. 73(1)(a) and Sch. 40, Pt. II(8) with effect for chargeable periods as respects which the notification period specified in former s. 118(3A) ends on or after 1 April 2000.
S. 118(5) repealed by FA 2000, s. 73(1)(a) and Sch. 40, Pt. II(8) with effect for chargeable periods as respects which the notification period specified in former s. 118(3A) ends on or after 1 April 2000.
S. 118(6)(a), repealed by CAA 2001, s. 580 and Sch. 4, with effect as respects allowances and charges falling to be made for chargeable periods ending, for income tax purposes, on or after 6 April 2001, and for corporation tax purposes, on or after 1 April 2001.
S. 118(6)(a), (b) substituted for the words "the provisions mentioned in subsection (2) above" by FA 2000, s. 73(1)(b) with effect for chargeable periods as respects which the period specified in s. 118(3A) ends on or after 1 April 2000.
S. 118(7) repealed by FA 2000, s. 73(1)(a) and Sch. 40, Pt. II(8) with effect for chargeable periods as respects which the notification period specified in former s. 118(3A) ends on or after 1 April 2000.
S.118(7) substituted by FA 1999, s. 93 and Sch. 11, para. 8, with effect in relation to accounting periods ending on or after 1 July 1999.
S. 118(8) repealed by FA 2000, s. 73(1)(a) and Sch. 40, Pt. II(8) with effect for chargeable periods as respects which the notification period specified in former s. 118(3A) ends on or after 1 April 2000.
S. 118(9) repealed by FA 2000, s. 73(1)(a) and Sch. 40, Pt. II(8) with effect for chargeable periods as respects which the notification period specified in former s. 118(3A) ends on or after 1 April 2000.

Statements of practice – SP 6/94: capital allowances – notification of expenditure on machinery and plant made outside the normal time limit.

HMRC interpretations – IRInt. 174: Revenue accept that for income tax, a claim for capital allowances incorporated in a self-assessment return (or amended return) will give satisfactory notification of the expenditure on machinery and plant included in the underlying computation of the claim, provided that the return has been made within the time limit of s. 118.

HMRC Manuals – Capital Allowances, CA 2099d: Board's power to extend time limits.

Other material – Exchange of letters between the Institute of Taxation and the Revenue released December 1994: Revenue do not require immense detail when notifying expenditure on machinery and plant; on the other hand, they will not accept "a single enormous figure of expenditure on "machinery and plant" without further explanation; inspectors instructed to agree arrangements which meet the particular circumstances of individual cases".
Letter to Chartered Institute of Taxation from Inland Revenue's Company Tax Division, 10 October 1995 (not reproduced): extent to which individual items need to be identified for the effective notification of capital expenditure.

Taxline 1997/14 (not reproduced): capital allowances on the plant and machinery element of a building, not claimed at the time of purchase, can be claimed in a later chargeable period to the extent that plant and machinery is still owned by the claimant in that later chargeable period.

119 Transactions between connected persons

119(1) [Repealed by CAA 2001, s. 580 and Sch. 4.]

119(2) Paragraph 4(2) of Schedule 7 to the Capital Allowances Act 1968 (provision corresponding to section 158(2)) shall be assumed always to have had effect subject to amendments corresponding to those made to section 158(2) of the 1990 Act by section 117(2) and (3) of the Finance Act 1993.

History – S. 119(1) repealed by CAA 2001, s. 580 and Sch. 4, with effect as respects allowances and charges falling to be made for chargeable periods ending, for income tax purposes, on or after 6 April 2001, and for corporation tax purposes, on or after 1 April 2001.

120 Balancing charge on realisation of capital value

120 [Repealed by CAA 2001, s. 580 and Sch. 4.]

History – S. 120 repealed by CAA 2001, s. 580 and Sch. 4, with effect as respects allowances and charges falling to be made for chargeable periods ending, for income tax purposes, on or after 6 April 2001, and for corporation tax purposes, on or after 1 April 2001.

121 Used buildings etc. in enterprise zones

121 [Repealed by CAA 2001, s. 580 and Sch. 4.]

History – S. 121 repealed by CAA 2001, s. 580 and Sch. 4, with effect as respects allowances and charges falling to be made for chargeable periods ending, for income tax purposes, on or after 6 April 2001, and for corporation tax purposes, on or after 1 April 2001.

SECURITIES

122 Sale and repurchase of securities: deemed manufactured payments

122 [Repealed by FA 2007, s. 114 and Sch. 27, Pt. 2(14).]

History – S. 122 repealed by FA 2007, s. 114 and Sch. 27, Pt. 2(14), with effect in relation to arrangements that come into force on or after 1 October 2007 (SI 2007/2484).

123 Manufactured payments

123(1) [Repealed by ITA 2007, s. 1031 and Sch. 3, Pt. 1.]

123(2-5) [Repealed by FA 1997, s. 113 and Sch. 18, Pt. VI(10).]

123(6) [Repealed by ITA 2007, s. 1031 and Sch. 3, Pt. 1.]

123(7) [Repealed by FA 1997, s. 113 and Sch. 18, Pt. VI(10).]

History – S. 123(1) repealed by ITA 2007, s. 1031 and Sch. 3, Pt. 1, with effect from 6 April 2007.
S. 123(2)–(5) repealed by FA 1997, s. 113 and Sch. 18, Pt. VI(10), with effect in relation to, and to transfers under, any arrangement made on or after 1 July 1997.
S. 123(6) repealed by ITA 2007, s. 1031 and Sch. 3, Pt. 1, with effect from 6 April 2007.
S. 123(7) repealed by FA 1997, s. 113 and Sch. 18, Pt. VI(10), with effect in relation to, and to transfers under, any arrangement made on or after 1 July 1997.

Notes – S. 123(1) rewritten as ITA 2007, s. 647(2), (4).

PAYE

125 Payment by intermediary

125 [Repealed by ITEPA 2003, Sch. 8, Pt. 1.]

History – S. 125 repealed by ITEPA 2003, Sch. 8, Pt. 1 which has effect for the tax year 2003–04 and subsequent tax years.

126 Employees working for persons other than their employers, etc.

126 [Repealed by ITEPA 2003, Sch. 8, Pt. 1.]

History – S. 126 repealed by ITEPA 2003, Sch. 8, Pt. 1 which has effect for the tax year 2003–04 and subsequent tax years.

127 Tradeable assets

127 [Repealed by ITEPA 2003, Sch. 8, Pt. 1.]

History – S. 127 repealed by ITEPA 2003, Sch. 8, Pt. 1 which has effect for the tax year 2003–04 and subsequent tax years.

128 Non-cash vouchers

128 [Repealed by ITEPA 2003, Sch. 8, Pt. 1.]

History – S. 128 repealed by ITEPA 2003, Sch. 8, Pt. 1 which has effect for the tax year 2003–04 and subsequent tax years.

129 Credit-tokens

129 [Repealed by ITEPA 2003, Sch. 8, Pt. 1.]

History – S. 129 repealed by ITEPA 2003, Sch. 8, Pt. 1 which has effect for the tax year 2003–04 and subsequent tax years.

130 Cash vouchers

130 [Repealed by ITEPA 2003, Sch. 8, Pt. 1.]

History – S. 130 repealed by ITEPA 2003, Sch. 8, Pt. 1 which has effect for the tax year 2003–04 and subsequent tax years.

131 Supplementary

131 [Repealed by ITEPA 2003, Sch. 8, Pt. 1.]

History – S. 131 repealed by ITEPA 2003, Sch. 8, Pt. 1 which has effect for the tax year 2003–04 and subsequent tax years.

132 Payments etc. received free of tax

132 [Repealed by ITEPA 2003, Sch. 8, Pt. 1.]

History – S. 132 repealed by ITEPA 2003, Sch. 8, Pt. 1 which has effect for the tax year 2003–04 and subsequent tax years.

133 PAYE regulations: past cases

133(1) Regulation 4 of the 1993 Regulations (intermediate employers) is hereby revoked; but in relation to any time before its revocation it shall be deemed to have been validly made.

133(2) Regulation 3 of the 1973 Regulations (intermediate employers) shall, in relation to any time before its revocation, be deemed to have been validly made.

133(3) Where, at any time before the passing of this Act–

(a) a payment has been made of, or on account of, any income of an employee not resident or, if resident, not ordinarily resident in the United Kingdom,

(b) at the time when the payment was made it appeared that some of the income would be assessable to income tax under Case II of Schedule E, but that some of the income might prove not to be assessable to income tax under that Schedule, and

(c) the payment or any proportion of it was treated for the purposes of the 1993 Regulations or the 1973 Regulations as a payment to which the regulations applied,

then the treatment of that payment or that proportion of the payment as being a payment to which the regulations applied shall be deemed to have been lawful.

133(4) In this section–

(a) **"employee"** means a person holding an office or employment under or with any other person;

(b) **"the 1993 Regulations"** means the Income Tax (Employments) Regulations 1993; and

(c) **"the 1973 Regulations"** means the Income Tax (Employments) Regulations 1973.

MISCELLANEOUS PROVISIONS ABOUT COMPANIES

134 Controlled foreign companies

134 [Omitted by FA 2009, s. 36 and Sch. 16, para. 5(b).]

History – S. 134 omitted by FA 2009, s. 36 and Sch. 16, para. 5(b), with effect in relation to accounting periods of controlled foreign companies beginning on or after 1 July 2009, subject to transitional provisions in FA 2009, Sch. 16, para. 8.

135 Prevention of avoidance of corporation tax

135 [Repealed by CTA 2010, s. 1181 and Sch. 3, Pt. 1.]

History – S. 135 repealed by CTA 2010, s. 1181 and Sch. 3, Pt. 1, with effect for accounting periods ending on or after 1 April 2010.

136 Parts of trades: computations in different currencies

136(1) [Inserts FA 1993, s. 94A.]

136(2) [Amends FA 1993, s. 95(6).]

MISCELLANEOUS

137 Enterprise investment scheme

137(1) [Repealed by ITA 2007, s. 1031 and Sch. 3, Pt. 2.]

137(2) [Repealed by ITA 2007, s. 1031 and Sch. 3, Pt. 2.]

137(3) The Taxation of Chargeable Gains Act 1992 shall have effect with the amendments made by that Schedule.

History – S. 137(1) repealed by ITA 2007, s. 1031 and Sch. 3, Pt. 2, with effect in relation to shares issued after 5 April 2007.
S. 137(2) repealed by ITA 2007, s. 1031 and Sch. 3, Pt. 2, with effect in relation to shares issued after 5 April 2007.

138 Foreign income dividends

138 Schedule 16 to this Act (which contains provisions about foreign income dividends) shall have effect.

139 Taxation of incapacity benefit

139 [Repealed by ITEPA 2003, Sch. 8, Pt. 1.]

History – S. 139 repealed by ITEPA 2003, Sch. 8, Pt. 1 which has effect for the tax year 2003–04 and subsequent tax years.

Notes – S. 139 rewritten as follows:
S. 139(1): ITEPA 2003, s. 660, s. 664(1) and s. 676.
S. 139(2): ITEPA 2003, s. 663.
S. 139(3): ITEPA 2003, s. 661.
S. 139(4) is omitted from ITEPA 2003 because the subsection is unnecessary in enabling the PAYE regulations to have effect on incapacity benefit.
S. 139(5): ITEPA 2003, s. 660, s. 663 and s. 664(1).
S. 139(6): ITEPA 2003, s. 664(2).

140 Restriction on deduction from income

140 [Repealed by CTA 2010, s. 1181 and Sch. 3, Pt. 1.]

History – S. 140 repealed by CTA 2010, s. 1181 and Sch. 3, Pt. 1, with effect for corporation tax purposes for accounting periods ending on or after 1 April 2010, and for income tax and capital gains tax purposes for the tax year 2010–11 and subsequent tax years.

141 Expenditure involving crime

141 [Repealed by CTA 2009, s. 1326 and Sch. 3, Pt. 1.]

History – S. 141 repealed by CTA 2009, s. 1326 and Sch. 3, Pt. 1, with effect for corporation tax purposes for accounting periods ending on or after 1 April 2009, and for income tax and capital gains tax purposes for the tax year 2009–10 and subsequent tax years.

142 Mortgage interest payable under deduction of tax: qualifying lenders

142(1) [Amends ICTA 1988, s. 376(4)(p) and repeals ICTA 1988, s. 376(5).]

142(2) [Inserts ICTA 1988, s. 376A.]

142(3) Any body which is, immediately before the date on which this Act is passed, a prescribed body for the purposes of section 376 of the Taxes Act 1988 (by virtue of an order made under subsection (5) of that section) shall be entitled to be entered in the register maintained under section 376A of that Act as a qualifying lender except that if it was, immediately before that date, a qualifying lender only in relation to such description of loan as was specified in the order, it shall be entitled to be entered in the register as a qualifying lender only in relation to that description of loan.

142(4) Until such time as the Board enter any such body in the register, that body shall be deemed to have been registered in accordance with its entitlement.

144 Debts released in voluntary arrangement: relief from tax

144 [Repealed by CTA 2009, s. 1326 and Sch. 3. Pt. 1.]

History – S. 144 repealed by CTA 2009, s. 1326 and Sch. 3. Pt. 1, with effect for corporation tax purposes for accounting periods ending on or after 1 April 2009, and for income tax and capital gains tax purposes for the tax year 2009–10 and subsequent tax years.
Former s. 144(1) repealed by FA 2005, s. 104 and Sch. 11, Pt. 2(5), with effect for periods of account beginning on or after 1 January 2005.
Former s. 144(5) repealed by FA 2005, s. 104 and Sch. 11, Pt. 2(5), with effect for periods of account beginning on or after 1 January 2005.
Former s. 144(6) repealed by FA 2005, s. 104 and Sch. 11, Pt. 2(5), with effect for periods of account beginning on or after 1 January 2005.

Notes – The equivalent rewritten income tax provisions are at ITTOIA 2005, s. 35.

145 Relief for business donations

145 [Repealed by CTA 2009, s. 1326 and Sch. 3. Pt. 1.]

History – S. 145 repealed by CTA 2009, s. 1326 and Sch. 3. Pt. 1, with effect for corporation tax purposes for accounting periods ending on or after 1 April 2009, and for income tax and capital gains tax purposes for the tax year 2009–10 and subsequent tax years.
Former s. 145(1) repealed by FA 2000, Sch. 40, Pt. II(9)).

146 Minor corrections

146 Schedule 17 to this Act (which corrects various mistakes made in or introduced into the Taxes Act 1988) shall have effect.

Chapter II – Interest Rate and Currency Contracts

QUALIFYING CONTRACTS

Statements of practice – SP 9/94: application of foreign exchange and financial instruments legislation to partnerships which include companies.

147 Qualifying contracts

147 [Repealed by FA 2002, s. 83(2), s. 141 and Sch. 40, Pt. 3(13).]

History – S. 147 repealed by FA 2002, s. 83(2), s. 141 and Sch. 40, Pt. 3(13) with effect for accounting periods beginning on or after 1 October 2002.

147A Debt contracts and options to be qualifying contracts

147A [Repealed by FA 2002, s. 83(2), s. 141 and Sch. 40, Pt. 3(13).]

History – S. 147A repealed by FA 2002, s. 83(2), s. 141 and Sch. 40, Pt. 3(13) with effect in relation to accounting periods beginning on or after 1 October 2002.

148 Contracts which may become qualifying contracts

148 [Repealed by FA 2002, s. 83(2), s. 141 and Sch. 40, Pt. 3(13).]

History – S. 148 repealed by FA 2002, s. 83(2), s. 141 and Sch. 40, Pt. 3(13) with effect in relation to accounting periods beginning on or after 1 October 2002.

INTEREST RATE AND CURRENCY CONTRACTS AND OPTIONS

149 Interest rate contracts and options

149 [Repealed by FA 2002, s. 83(2), s. 141 and Sch. 40, Pt. 3(13).]

History – S. 149 repealed by FA 2002, s. 83(2), s. 141 and Sch. 40, Pt. 3(13) with effect in relation to accounting periods beginning on or after 1 October 2002.

150 Currency contracts and options

150 [Repealed by FA 2002, s. 83(2), s. 141 and Sch. 40, Pt. 3(13).]

History – S. 150 repealed by FA 2002, s. 83(2), s. 141 and Sch. 40, Pt. 3(13) with effect in relation to accounting periods beginning on or after 1 October 2002.

150A Debt contracts and options

150A [Repealed by FA 2002, s. 83(2), s. 141 and Sch. 40, Pt. 3(13).]

History – S. 150A repealed by FA 2002, s. 83(2), s. 141 and Sch. 40, Pt. 3(13) with effect in relation to accounting periods beginning on or after 1 October 2002.

151 Provisions which may be included

151 [Repealed by FA 2002, s. 83(2), s. 141 and Sch. 40, Pt. 3(13).]

History – S. 151 repealed by FA 2002, s. 83(2), s. 141 and Sch. 40, Pt. 3(13) with effect in relation to accounting periods beginning on or after 1 October 2002.

152 Provisions which may be disregarded

152 [Repealed by FA 2002, s. 83(2), s. 141 and Sch. 40, Pt. 3(13).]

History – S. 152 repealed by FA 2002, s. 83(2), s. 141 and Sch. 40, Pt. 3(13) with effect in relation to accounting periods beginning on or after 1 October 2002.

OTHER BASIC DEFINITIONS

153 Qualifying payments

153 [Repealed by FA 2002, s. 83(2), s. 141 and Sch. 40, Pt. 3(13).]

History – S. 153 repealed by FA 2002, s. 83(2), s. 141 and Sch. 40, Pt. 3(13) with effect in relation to accounting periods beginning on or after 1 October 2002.

154 Qualifying companies

154 [Repealed by FA 2002, s. 83(2), s. 141 and Sch. 40, Pt. 3(13).]

History – S. 154 repealed by FA 2002, s. 83(2), s. 141 and Sch. 40, Pt. 3(13) with effect in relation to accounting periods ending on or after 1 October 2002.

ACCRUAL OF PROFITS AND LOSSES

155 Accrual of profits and losses

155 [Repealed by FA 2002, s. 83(2), s. 141 and Sch. 40, Pt. 3(13).]

History – S. 155 repealed by FA 2002, s. 83(2), s. 141 and Sch. 40, Pt. 3(13) with effect in relation to accounting periods beginning on or after 1 October 2002.

156 Basis of accounting: general

156 [Repealed by FA 2002, s. 83(2), s. 141 and Sch. 40, Pt. 3(13).]

History – S. 156 repealed by FA 2002, s. 83(2), s. 141 and Sch. 40, Pt. 3(13) with effect in relation to accounting periods beginning on or after 1 October 2002.

157 Basis of accounting for linked currency options

157 [Repealed by FA 2002, s. 83(2), s. 141 and Sch. 40, Pt. 3(13).]

History – S. 157 repealed by FA 2002, s. 83(2), s. 141 and Sch. 40, Pt. 3(13) with effect in relation to accounting periods beginning on or after 1 October 2002.

158 Adjustments for changes in basis of accounting

158 [Repealed by FA 2002, s. 83(2), s. 141 and Sch. 40, Pt. 3(13).]

History – S. 158 repealed by FA 2002, s. 83(2), s. 141 and Sch. 40, Pt. 3(13) with effect in relation to accounting periods beginning on or after 1 October 2002.

TREATMENT OF PROFITS AND LOSSES

159 Trading profits and losses

159 [Repealed by FA 2002, s. 83(2), s. 141 and Sch. 40, Pt. 3(13).]

History – S. 159 repealed by FA 2002, s. 83(2), s. 141 and Sch. 40, Pt. 3(13) with effect in relation to accounting periods beginning on or after 1 October 2002.

160 Non-trading profits and losses

160 [Repealed by FA 2002, s. 83(2), s. 141 and Sch. 40, Pt. 3(13).]

History – S. 160 repealed by FA 2002, s. 83(2), s. 141 and Sch. 40, Pt. 3(13) with effect in relation to accounting periods beginning on or after 1 October 2002.

SPECIAL CASES

161 Termination etc. of qualifying contracts

161 [Repealed by FA 2002, s. 83(2), s. 141 and Sch. 40, Pt. 3(13).]

History – S. 161 repealed by FA 2002, s. 83(2), s. 141 and Sch. 40, Pt. 3(13) with effect in relation to accounting periods beginning on or after 1 October 2002.

162 Exchange gains and losses on currency contracts

162 [Repealed by FA 2002, s. 83(2), s. 141 and Sch. 40, Pt. 3(13).]

History – S. 162 repealed by FA 2002, s. 83(2), s. 141 and Sch. 40, Pt. 3(13) with effect in relation to accounting periods beginning on or after 1 October 2002.

163 Irrecoverable payments

163 [Repealed by FA 2002, s. 83(2), s. 141 and Sch. 40, Pt. 3(13).]

History – S. 163 repealed by FA 2002, s. 83(2), s. 141 and Sch. 40, Pt. 3(13) with effect in relation to accounting periods beginning on or after 1 October 2002.

164 Released payments

164 [Repealed by FA 2002, s. 83(2), s. 141 and Sch. 40, Pt. 3(13).]

History – S. 164 repealed by FA 2002, s. 83(2), s. 141 and Sch. 40, Pt. 3(13) with effect in relation to accounting periods beginning on or after 1 October 2002.

ANTI-AVOIDANCE AND RELATED PROVISIONS

165 Transfers of value by qualifying companies

165 [Repealed by FA 2002, s. 83(2), s. 141 and Sch. 40, Pt. 3(13).]

History – S. 165 repealed by FA 2002, s. 83(2), s. 141 and Sch. 40, Pt. 3(12) with effect in relation to accounting periods beginning on or after 1 October 2002.

166 Transfers of value to associated companies

166 [Repealed by FA 2002, s. 83(2), s. 141 and Sch. 40, Pt. 3(13).]

History – S. 166 repealed by FA 2002, s. 83(2), s. 141 and Sch. 40, Pt. 3(13) with effect in relation to accounting periods beginning on or after 1 October 2002.

167 Transactions not at arm's length

167 [Repealed by FA 2002, s. 83(2), s. 141 and Sch. 40, Pt. 3(13).]

History – S. 167 repealed by FA 2002, s. 83(2), s. 141 and Sch. 40, Pt. 3(13) with effect in relation to accounting periods beginning on or after 1 October 2002.

168 Qualifying contracts with non-residents

168 [Repealed by FA 2002, s. 83(2), s. 141 and Sch. 40, Pt. 3(13).]

History – S. 168 repealed by FA 2002, s. 83(2), s. 141 and Sch. 40, Pt. 3(13) with effect in relation to accounting periods beginning on or after 1 October 2002.

168A Qualifying contracts for unallowable purposes

168A [Repealed by FA 2002, s. 83(2), s. 141 and Sch. 40, Pt. 3(13).]

History – S. 168A repealed by FA 2002, s. 83(2), s. 141 and Sch. 40, Pt. 3(13) with effect in relation to accounting periods beginning on or after 1 October 2002.

MISCELLANEOUS

169 Insurance and mutual trading companies

169 [Repealed by FA 2002, s. 83(2), s. 141 and Sch. 40, Pt. 3(13).]

History – S. 169 repealed by FA 2002, s. 83(2), s. 141 and Sch. 40, Pt. 3(13) with effect in relation to accounting periods beginning on or after 1 October 2002.

170 Investment trusts

170 [Repealed by FA 2002, s. 83(2), s. 141 and Sch. 40, Pt. 3(13).]

History – S. 170 repealed by FA 2002, s. 83(2), s. 141 and Sch. 40, Pt. 3(13) with effect in relation to accounting periods beginning on or after 1 October 2002.

171 Charities

171 [Repealed by FA 1996, Sch. 41, Pt. V(3) with effect for accounting periods ending after 31 March 1996.]

172 Partnerships involving qualifying companies

172 [Repealed by FA 2002, s. 83(2), s. 141 and Sch. 40, Pt. 3(13).]

History – S. 172 repealed by FA 2002, s. 83(2), s. 141 and Sch. 40, Pt. 3(13) with effect in relation to accounting periods ending on or after 1 October 2002.

SUPPLEMENTAL

173 Prevention of double charging etc.

173 [Repealed by FA 2002, s. 83(2), s. 141 and Sch. 40, Pt. 3(13).]

History – S. 173 repealed by FA 2002, s. 83(2), s. 141 and Sch. 40, Pt. 3(13) with effect in relation to accounting periods beginning on or after 1 October 2002.

174 Prevention of deduction of tax

174 [Repealed by FA 2002, s. 83(2), s. 141 and Sch. 40, Pt. 3(13).]

History – S. 174 repealed by FA 2002, s. 83(2), s. 141 and Sch. 40, Pt. 3(13) with effect in relation to accounting periods beginning on or after 1 October 2002.

175 Transitional provisions

175 [Repealed by FA 2002, s. 83(2), s. 141 and Sch. 40,Pt. 3(13).]

History – S. 175 repealed by FA 2002, s. 83(2), s. 141 and Sch. 40, Pt. 3(13) with effect in relation to accounting periods beginning on or after 1 October 2002.

176 Minor and consequential amendments

176(1) [Repealed by FA 1995, s. 162 and Sch. 29, Pt. VIII(5).]

176(2) [Repealed by Statute Law (Repeals) Act 2013, s. 1 and Sch. 1, Pt. 10.]

History – S. 176(1) repealed by FA 1995, s. 162 and Sch. 29, Pt. VIII(5) with effect in relation to accounting periods beginning on or after 1 January 1995.
S. 176(2) repealed by Statute Law (Repeals) Act 2013, s. 1 and Sch. 1, Pt. 10, with effect from 31 January 2013.

177 Interpretation of Chapter II

177 [Repealed by FA 2002, s. 83(2), s. 141 and Sch. 40, Pt. 3(13).]

History – S. 177 repealed by FA 2002, s. 83(2), s. 141 and Sch. 40, Pt. 3(13) with effect in relation to accounting periods ending on or after 1 October 2002.

Chapter III – Management: Self-Assessment etc.

Cross references – FA 1996, s. 121(8), 124(1), 130(1), 134(2), 135(2), 137(2), 140(2), 168(6), 169(3), 170(2): appointed day for this Chapter applied to other provisions.
FA 1996, Sch. 18, para. 17(1) and (9), Sch. 19, para. 1, Sch. 22, para. 12, Sch. 24, para. 8(1), Sch. 25, para. 3, Sch. 33, para. 4, Sch. 34, para. 4(6): appointed day for this Chapter applied to other provisions.

INCOME TAX AND CAPITAL GAINS TAX

178 Personal and trustee's returns

178(1) [Substitutes TMA 1970, s. 8(1)–(1C) for former s. 8(1).]

178(2) [Substitutes TMA 1970, s. 8A(1) and (1A) for former s. 8A(1).]

179 Returns to include self-assessment

179 [Substitutes TMA 1970, s. 9.]

180 Power to enquire into returns

180 [Repealed by FA 2001, s. 110 and Sch. 33, Pt. II(13).]

History – S. 180 repealed by FA 2001, s. 110 and Sch. 33, Pt. 2(13) with effect from 11 May 2001 in relation to returns made before or after that date, and whether relating to periods before or after that date; previously inserted TMA 1970, s. 9A.

CORPORATION TAX

181 Return of profits

181 [Repealed by FA 1998, s. 165 and Sch. 27, Pt. III(28).]

182 Return of profits to include self-assessment

182 [Repealed by FA 1998, s. 165 and Sch. 27, Pt. III(28).]

183 Power to enquire into return of profits

183 [Repealed by FA 1998, s. 165 and Sch. 27, Pt. III(28).]

PARTNERSHIPS

184 Partnership return

184 [Inserts TMA 1970, s. 12AA.]

185 Partnership return to include partnership statement

185 [Inserts TMA 1970, s. 12AB.]

186 Power to enquire into partnership return

186 [Repealed by FA 2001, s. 110 and Sch. 33, Pt. 2(13).]

History – S. 186 repealed by FA 2001, s. 110 and Sch. 33, Pt. II(13) with effect from 11 May 2001 in relation to returns made before or after that date, and whether relating to periods before or after that date; previously inserted TMA 1970, s. 12AC.

ENQUIRIES: PROCEDURE

187 Power to call for documents

187 [Omitted by FA 2008, s. 113 and Sch. 36, para. 92(c).]

History – S. 187 omitted by FA 2008, s. 113 and Sch. 36, para. 92(c), with effect from 1 April 2009 (SI 2009/404, art. 2, subject to savings at SI 2009/404, art. 3).

188 Amendment of self-assessment

188 [Repealed by FA 2001, s. 110 and Sch. 33, Pt. II(13).]

History – S. 188 repealed by FA 2001, s. 110 and Sch. 33, Pt. 2(13) with effect from 11 May 2001 in relation to returns made before or after that date, and whether relating to periods before or after that date; previously inserted TMA 1970, s. 28A.

189 Amendment of partnership statement

189 [Repealed by FA 2001, s. 110 and Sch. 33, Pt. II(13).]

History – S. 189 repealed by FA 2001, s. 110 and Sch. 33, Pt. 2(13) with effect from 11 May 2001 in relation to returns made before or after that date, and whether relating to periods before or after that date; previously inserted TMA 1970, s. 28B.

DETERMINATIONS AND ASSESSMENTS TO PROTECT REVENUE

190 Determination of tax where no return delivered

190 [Inserts TMA 1970, s. 28C.]

191 Assessment where loss of tax discovered

191(1) [Substitutes TMA 1970, s. 29.]

191(2) This section, so far as it relates to partnerships whose trades, professions or businesses are set up and commenced before 6th April 1994, has effect as respects the year 1997–98 and subsequent years of assessment.

Cross references – FA 1995, Sch. 22, para. 11: normal fetters on assessing may not apply where assessment is made for the purposes of the current-year basis transitional anti-avoidance rules.

PAYMENT OF TAX

192 Payments on account of income tax

192 [Inserts TMA 1970, s. 59A.]

193 Payment of income tax and capital gains tax

193 [Inserts TMA 1970, s. 59B.]

194 Surcharges on unpaid income tax and capital gains tax

194 [Inserts TMA 1970, s. 59C.]

195 Payment of corporation tax

195 [Repealed by FA 1998, s. 165 and Sch. 27, Pt. III(28).]

MISCELLANEOUS AND SUPPLEMENTAL

196 Management: other amendments

196 Schedule 19 to this Act (which makes other amendments relating to the management of tax) shall have effect.

197 Construction of certain references

Notes – S. 197 applies only for income tax and capital gains tax purposes – for corporation tax, see history note.

197(1) In the Tax Acts and the Gains Tax Acts, any reference (however expressed) to a person being **"assessed to tax"**, or being **"charged to tax by an assessment"**, shall be construed as including a reference to his being so assessed, or being so charged–

(a) by a self-assessment under section 9 or 11AA of the Management Act, or

(b) by a determination under section 28C, 28D or 28E of that Act (which, until superseded by such a self-assessment, has effect as if it were one).

197(2) In this section **"the Gains Tax Acts"** means the Taxation of Chargeable Gains Tax Act 1992 and all other enactments relating to capital gains tax.

History – S. 197 repealed for corporation tax purposes by FA 1998, s. 165 and Sch. 27, Pt. III(28), with effect in relation to accounting periods ending on or after 1 July 1999, the appointed day for company self-assessment under FA 1994, s. 199(2) by virtue of SI 1998/3173 (C. 78).
The words ", 28D or 28E" inserted by FA 1996, s. 138 and Sch. 24, para. 13, with effect from 29 April 1996.

198 Transitional provisions

198 [Repealed by FA 1995, s. 116(2) and 162 and Sch. 29, Pt. VIII(14) with effect from 1 May 1995.]

Notes – The transitional provisions are now given by FA 1995, s. 116(1) and Sch. 21.

199 Interpretation and commencement of Chapter III

Notes – The appointed day for the purposes of FA 1994, Pt. IV, Ch. III is 1 July 1999 (SI 1998/3173).

199(1) In this Chapter **"the Management Act"** means the Taxes Management Act 1970.

199(2) Unless the contrary intention appears, this Chapter–

(a) so far as it relates to income tax and capital gains tax, has effect as respects the year 1996–97 and subsequent years of assessment, and

(b) so far as it relates to corporation tax, has effect as respects accounting periods ending on or after the appointed day.

199(3) For the purposes of this Chapter the appointed day is such day, not earlier than 1st April 1996, as the Treasury may by order appoint.

Cross references – FA 1996, s. 124(1): amendment of record-keeping provisions in TMA 1970 effective from s. 199 appointed day.
FA 1996, s. 130(1): amendment of procedure for giving notice provisions in TMA 1970 effective from s. 199 appointed day.
FA 1996, s. 134(2): amendment of provisions in TMA 1970 regarding discretions exerciseable by the Revenue, effective from s. 199 appointed day.
FA 1996, s. 135(2): amendment of time limits for claims in TMA 1970 effective from s. 199 appointed day.
FA 1996, s. 140(2): transfer of company's assets to investment trust provision effective from s. 199 appointed day.
FA 1996, s. 168(6): capital redemption business provisions effective from s. 199 appointed day.
FA 1996, s. 169(3): provisions covering provisional repayments in connection with pension business effective from s. 199 appointed day.
FA 1996, Sch. 19, para. 1: amendments to TMA 1970 provisions on claims and enquiries effective from s. 199 appointed day.
FA 1996, Sch. 22, para. 12: amendments to TMA 1970 provisions on appeals effective from s. 199 appointed day.
FA 1996, Sch. 33, para. 4: provisions concerning management expenses of capital redemption business effective from s. 199 appointed day.
FA 1996, Sch. 34, para. 4(4): certain provisions concerning provisional repayments in connection with pension business effective from s. 199 appointed day.

Chapter IV – Changes for Facilitating Self-Assessment

ASSESSMENT UNDER CASES I AND II OF SCHEDULE D

200 Assessment on current year basis

200 [Repealed by ITTOIA 2005, s. 884 and Sch. 3.]

History – S. 200 repealed by ITTOIA 2005, s. 884 and Sch. 3 effective for income tax purposes for 2005–06 onwards (ITTOIA 2005, s. 883(1)).

201 Basis of assessment at commencement

201 [Repealed by ITTOIA 2005, s. 884 and Sch. 3.]

History – S. 201 repealed by ITTOIA 2005, s. 884 and Sch. 3 effective for income tax purposes for 2005–06 onwards (ITTOIA 2005, s. 883(1)).

202 Change of basis period

202 [Repealed by ITTOIA 2005, s. 884 and Sch. 3.]

History – S. 202 repealed by ITTOIA 2005, s. 884 and Sch. 3 effective for income tax purposes for 2005–06 onwards (ITTOIA 2005, s. 883(1)).

203 Conditions for such a change

203 [Repealed by ITTOIA 2005, s. 884 and Sch. 3.]

History – S. 203 repealed by ITTOIA 2005, s. 884 and Sch. 3 effective for income tax purposes for 2005–06 onwards (ITTOIA 2005, s. 883(1)).

204 Basis of assessment on discontinuance

204 [Repealed by ITTOIA 2005, s. 884 and Sch. 3.]

History – S. 204 repealed by ITTOIA 2005, s. 884 and Sch. 3 effective for income tax purposes for 2005–06 onwards (ITTOIA 2005, s. 883(1)).

205 Overlap profits and overlap losses

205 [Repealed by ITTOIA 2005, s. 884 and Sch. 3.]

History – S. 205 repealed by ITTOIA 2005, s. 884 and Sch. 3 effective for income tax purposes for 2005–06 onwards (ITTOIA 2005, s. 883(1)).

ASSESSMENT UNDER CASES III TO VI OF SCHEDULE D

206 Basis of assessment under Case III

206 [Repealed by ITTOIA 2005, s. 884 and Sch. 3.]

History – S. 206 repealed by ITTOIA 2005, s. 884 and Sch. 3 effective for income tax purposes for 2005–06 onwards (ITTOIA 2005, s. 883(1)).

207 Basis of assessment under Cases IV and V

207 [Repealed by ITTOIA 2005, s. 884 and Sch. 3.]

History – S. 207 repealed by ITTOIA 2005, s. 884 and Sch. 3 effective for income tax purposes for 2005–06 onwards (ITTOIA 2005, s. 883(1)).

208 Basis of assessment under Case VI

208 [Repealed by ITTOIA 2005, s. 884 and Sch. 3.]

History – S. 208 repealed by ITTOIA 2005, s. 884 and Sch. 3 effective for income tax purposes for 2005–06 onwards (ITTOIA 2005, s. 883(1)).

LOSS RELIEF

209 Loss relief: general

209 [Repealed by ITA 2007, s. 1031 and Sch. 3, Pt. 1.]

History – S. 209 repealed by ITA 2007, s. 1031 and Sch. 3, Pt. 1, with effect from 6 April 2007.

Notes – S. 209 rewritten as follows:
S. 209(1): ITA 2007, s. 63, 64(1), (2), (5), 65(1), (2), (3), 128(1), (2), (5), 129(1), (2), (3).
S. 209(2): ITA 2007, s. 72(2), 73.
S. 209(3): ITA 2007, s. 61(2), 62(2).
S. 209(4): ITA 2007, s. 61(2), 62(2), 83(1), (2), (3), (4), 84.

210 Relief for losses on unquoted shares

210 [Repealed by ITA 2007, s. 1031 and Sch. 3, Pt. 1.]

History – S. 210 repealed by ITA 2007, s. 1031 and Sch. 3, Pt. 1, with effect from 6 April 2007.

Notes – S. 210 rewritten as ITA 2007, s. 131(1), 132(1), (3), (4), 133(1), (3), (4).

CAPITAL ALLOWANCES

211 Income tax allowances and charges in taxing a trade etc.

211(1) [Repealed by CAA 2001, s. 580 and Sch. 4.]

211(2) Subject to section 214(7) below, this section and sections 212 to 214 below, in their application to trades, professions or vocations set up and commenced before 6th April 1994 or employments or offices entered into before that date, have effect as respects the year 1997–98 and subsequent years of assessment.

212 Chargeable periods for income tax purposes

212(1) [Repealed by CAA 2001, s. 580 and Sch. 4.]

212(2) [Repealed by CAA 2001, s. 580 and Sch. 4.]

History – S. 112, repealed by CAA 2001, s. 580 and Sch. 4, with effect as respects allowances and charges falling to be made for chargeable periods ending, for income tax purposes, on or after 6 April 2001, and for corporation tax purposes, on or after 1 April 2001.

213 Other amendments of Capital Allowances Act 1990

213 [Repealed by CAA 2001, s. 580 and Sch. 4.]

History – S. 213, repealed by CAA 2001, s. 580 and Sch. 4, with effect as respects allowances and charges falling to be made for chargeable periods ending, for income tax purposes, on or after 6 April 2001, and for corporation tax purposes, on or after 1 April 2001.

214 Amendments of other enactments

214(1) [Amends provisions as below.]

(a) [Repeals ICTA 1988, s. 96(7)(b).]

(b) [Repeals ICTA 1988, s. 383.]

(c) [Amends ICTA 1988, s. 384(1), (2).]

(d) [Amends ICTA 1988, s. 388(6), (7).]

(e) [Repeals ICTA 1988, s. 389(5)–(7).]

214(2) [Repealed by ITA 2007, s. 1031 and Sch. 3, Pt. 1.]

214(3) [Repealed by CTA 2010, s. 1181 and Sch. 3, Pt. 1.]

214(4–6) [Repealed by CAA 2001, s. 580 and Sch. 4.]

214(7) Subsection (1)(a) above–

(a) except in its application to a trade set up and commenced on or after 6th April 1994, has effect where the first of the two years of assessment to which the claim relates is the year 1996–97 or any subsequent year, and

(b) in its application to a trade so set up and commenced, has effect where the first of those two years of assessment is the year 1995–96 or any subsequent year.

History – S. 214(2) repealed by ITA 2007, s. 1031 and Sch. 3, Pt. 1, with effect from 6 April 2007.
S. 214(3) repealed by CTA 2010, s. 1181 and Sch. 3, Pt. 1, with effect for corporation tax purposes for accounting periods ending on or after 1 April 2010, and for income tax and capital gains tax purposes for the tax year 2010–11 and subsequent tax years.
S. 214(3)(a) previously repealed by ITA 2007, s. 1031 and Sch. 3, Pt. 1, with effect from 6 April 2007.
S. 214(4)–(6), repealed by CAA 2001, s. 580 and Sch. 4, with effect as respects allowances and charges falling to be made for chargeable periods ending, for income tax purposes, on or after 6 April 2001, and for corporation tax purposes, on or after 1 April 2001.

Notes – S. 214 rewritten as follows:
S. 214(2): ITA 2007, s. 75(1), (2), (5), (6).
S. 214(3): ITA 2007, s. 67(2).

MISCELLANEOUS AND SUPPLEMENTAL

215 Treatment of partnerships

215 [Repealed by CTA 2009, s. 1326 and Sch. 3, Pt. 1.]

History – S. 215 repealed by CTA 2009, s. 1326 and Sch. 3, Pt. 1, with effect for corporation tax purposes for accounting periods ending on or after 1 April 2009, and for income tax and capital gains tax purposes for the tax year 2009–10 and subsequent tax years.
Former s. 215(1) substituted, s. 215(1A) inserted, and s. 215(2), (3) amended by FA 1995, s. 117. These changes are deemed always to have had effect.
Former s. 215(5)(b) repealed by FA 1995, s. 125, 162 and Sch. 29, Pt. VIII(16), as respects the year 1995–96 and subsequent years of assessment.

216 Effect of change in ownership of trade, profession or vocation

216(1) [Repealed by ITTOIA 2005, s. 884 and Sch. 3.]

216(2) [Repeals ICTA 1988, s. 113(3)–(5) and amends ICTA 1988, s. 113(6).]

216(3) [Amends provisions as below.]

(a) [Amends ICTA 1988, s. 96(6).]

(b)–(g) [Repeals ICTA 1988, s. 380(3), 381(6), 384(5), 385(2), (5), 386(4), 389(3).]

216(4) [Repealed by ITTOIA 2005, s. 884 and Sch. 3.]

216(5) Subsection (3)(a) above–

(a) except in its application to a trade set up and commenced on or after 6th April 1994, has effect where the first of the two years of assessment to which the claim relates is the year 1996–97 or any subsequent year, and

(b) in its application to a trade so set up and commenced, has effect where the first of those two years of assessment is the year 1995–96 or any subsequent year.

History – S. 216(1) repealed by ITTOIA 2005, s. 884 and Sch. 3 effective for income tax purposes for 2005–06 onwards (ITTOIA 2005, s. 883(1)).
S. 216(4) repealed by ITTOIA 2005, s. 884 and Sch. 3 effective for income tax purposes for 2005–06 onwards (ITTOIA 2005, s. 883(1)).
Cross references – S. 215(4): commencement provisions.

217 Double taxation relief in respect of overlap profits

217 [Repealed by TIOPA 2010, s. 378 and Sch. 10, Pt. 1.]

History – S. 217 repealed by TIOPA 2010, s. 378 and Sch. 10, Pt. 1, with effect for corporation tax purposes for accounting periods ending on or after 1 April 2010, for income tax and capital gains tax purposes for the tax year 2010–11 and subsequent tax years, and for petroleum revenue tax purposes for chargeable periods beginning on or after 1 July 2010.

218 Commencement, transitional provisions and savings

218(1) Unless the contrary intention appears, this Chapter–

(a) except in its application to a trade set up and commenced on or after 6th April 1994 or income from a source arising to a person on or after that date, has effect as respects the year 1996–97 and subsequent years of assessment, and

(b) in its application to a trade so set up and commenced or income from a source so arising, has effect as respects the year 1994–95 and subsequent years of assessment.

218(1A) In a case where–

(a) a trade is set up and commenced by a company, and

(b) it is not set up and commenced before 6th April 1994,

sections 213(4) and (8) and 214(4) and (6) have effect only if it is set up and commenced on or after 6th April 1995.

218(2) Any reference in subsection (1) above to a trade includes a reference to a profession, vocation, employment or office.

218(3) Where the first underwriting year of the underwriting business of a member of Lloyd's is the year 1994, subsection (1) above shall have effect in relation to that business as if it had been set up and commenced on 6th April 1994.

218(4) Where, as respects income from any source, income tax is to be charged under Case IV or V of Schedule D by reference to the amounts of income received in the United Kingdom, the source shall be treated for the purposes of subsection (1) above as arising on the date on which the first amount of income is so received.

218(5) This Chapter shall have effect subject to the transitional provisions and savings contained in Schedule 20 to this Act.

History – S. 218(1A) inserted, and FA 1994, Pt. IV, Ch. IV deemed to have been enacted with that modification, by FA 1995, s. 102.

Chapter V – Lloyd's Underwriters: Corporations etc.

MAIN PROVISIONS

Cross references – FA 1995, s. 129(4): limit on income chargeable on non UK-resident companies disapplied in relation to corporate Lloyd's underwriters.

FA 2002, Sch. 29, para. 129: application of FA 2002, Sch. 29 (gains and losses of a company from intangible fixed assets) to an asset consisting of the rights of a member of Lloyds under a syndicate.

FA 2003, Sch. 27, para. 6(2)(a): non-resident underwriting companies and independent agents.

SI 1997/2681, reg. 3(2)(a): application of provisions of Pt. IV, Ch. V to Lloyd's Scottish limited partnership, where ICTA 1988, s. 114(1) applies, as if partnership were a corporate member.

HMRC Manuals – Lloyd's Manual LM4.110ff.: general guidance on the taxation of corporate members of Lloyd's.

219 Taxation of profits

219(1) Corporation tax for any accounting period on the profits arising from a corporate member's underwriting business shall be computed on the profits of that accounting period.

219(2) As respects the profits arising to a corporate member for any accounting period directly from its membership of one or more syndicates, or from assets forming part of a premium trust fund–

(a) the aggregate of those profits shall be computed for tax purposes under Part 3 of the Corporation Tax Act 2009; and

(b) accordingly, no part of those profits shall be computed for those purposes otherwise than under Part 3 of the Corporation Tax Act 2009.

219(3) The profits arising to a corporate member for any accounting period–

(a) from assets forming part of an ancillary trust fund; or

(b) from assets employed by it in, or in connection with, its underwriting business,

shall be computed for tax purposes under Part 3 of the Corporation Tax Act 2009 if, and to the extent that, they do not fall to be computed for those purposes otherwise than under Part 3 of that Act.

219(4) [Omitted by FA 2009, s. 34 and Sch. 14, para. 18(b).]

219(4A) [Omitted by FA 2009, s. 34 and Sch. 14, para. 18(b).]

219(4B) [Omitted by FA 2016, s. 5 and Sch. 1, para. 56.]

219(4C) [Omitted by FA 2009, s. 34 and Sch. 14, para. 18(b).]

219(5) [Repealed by ITTOIA 2005, s. 884 and Sch. 3.]

History – In s. 219(2)(a), the words "Part 3 of the Corporation Tax Act 2009" substituted for the words "Case I of Schedule D" by CTA 2009, s. 1322 and Sch. 1, para. 392(2)(a), with effect for corporation tax purposes for accounting periods ending on or after 1 April 2009, and for income tax and capital gains tax purposes for the tax year 2009–10 and subsequent tax years.

In s. 219(2)(b), the words "otherwise than under Part 3 of the Corporation Tax Act 2009" substituted for the words "under any other Schedule or any other Case of Schedule D" by CTA 2009, s. 1322 and Sch. 1, para. 392(2)(b), with effect for corporation tax

purposes for accounting periods ending on or after 1 April 2009, and for income tax and capital gains tax purposes for the tax year 2009–10 and subsequent tax years.
In s. 219(2), the word "premium" substituted for the word "premiums" by SI 2001/3629, art. 87(a) operative from 1 December 2001.
In s. 219(3), the words "Subject to subsection (4A) below," omitted by FA 2009, s. 34 and Sch. 14, para. 18(a), with effect in relation to distributions paid on or after 1 July 2009, subject to transitional provisions in FA 2009, Sch. 14, para. 32.
In s. 219(3), the words "Part 3 of the Corporation Tax Act 2009" substituted for the words "Case I of Schedule D" and the words "otherwise than under Part 3 of that Act" substituted for the words "under any other Schedule or any other Case of Schedule D" by CTA 2009, s. 1322 and Sch. 1, para. 392(3), with effect for corporation tax purposes for accounting periods ending on or after 1 April 2009, and for income tax and capital gains tax purposes for the tax year 2009–10 and subsequent tax years.
In s. 219(3) opening words "Subject to subsection (4A) below" inserted by F(No. 2)A 1997, s. 22(2) with effect in relation to distributions made on or after 2 July 1997.
S. 219(4) omitted by FA 2009, s. 34 and Sch. 14, para. 18(b), with effect in relation to distributions paid on or after 1 July 2009, subject to transitional provisions in FA 2009, Sch. 14, para. 32.
In s. 219(4), the words "section 1285 of the Corporation Tax Act 2009 (exemption for UK company distributions" substituted for the words "section 11(2)(a) or 208 of the Taxes Act 1988" by CTA 2009, s. 1322 and Sch. 1, para. 392(4), with effect for corporation tax purposes for accounting periods ending on or after 1 April 2009, and for income tax and capital gains tax purposes for the tax year 2009–10 and subsequent tax years.
In s. 219(4), the word "premium" substituted for the word "premiums" by SI 2001/3629, art. 87(a) operative from 1 December 2001.
In s. 219(4) the words "UK distributions" substituted for the words "dividendsor other distributions of a company resident in the United Kingdom", the words "(and any associated tax credits)" which followed "those distributions" repealed by F(No. 2)A 1997, s. 22(3) and (4) and s. 52 and Sch. 8, Pt. II(5) with effect in relation to distributions made on or after 2 July 1997.
S. 219(4A) omitted by FA 2009, s. 34 and Sch. 14, para. 18(b), with effect in relation to distributions paid on or after 1 July 2009, subject to transitional provisions in FA 2009, Sch. 14, para. 32.
In former s. 219(4A), the words "1285 of the Corporation Tax Act 2009" substituted for the words "208 of the Taxes Act 1988" and, in para. (b), the words "Part 3 of the Corporation Tax Act 2009" substituted for the words "Case I of Schedule D" and the words "(and not under any other provision of the Corporation Tax Acts)" substituted for the words "(and not under any other Schedule or any other Case of Schedule D)" by CTA 2009, s. 1322 and Sch. 1, para. 392(5), with effect for corporation tax purposes for accounting periods ending on or after 1 April 2009, and for income tax and capital gains tax purposes for the tax year 2009–10 and subsequent tax years.
In former s. 219(4A), the reference to ICTA 1988, s. 11(2)(a) repealed by FA 2003, s. 216 and Sch. 43, Pt.3(6) in relation to accounting periods beginning on or after 1 January 2003.
Former s. 219(4A) inserted by F(No. 2)A 1997, s. 22(3) and (4) and s. 52 and Sch. 8, Pt. II(5) with effect in relation to distributions made on or after 2 July 1997.
S. 219(4B) omitted by FA 2016, s. 5 and Sch. 1, para. 56, with effect in relation to dividends paid or arising (or treated as paid), and other distributions made (or treated as made), in the tax year 2016–17 or at any later time. Former s. 219(4B) read as follows:
"**219(4B)** Section 1109 of the Corporation Tax Act 2010 (entitlement to tax credit) shall not apply where the distribution there mentioned is a distribution in respect of any asset of a corporate member's premium trust fund.".
In former s. 219(4B), the words "Section 1109 of the Corporation Tax Act 2010" substituted for the words "Section 231(1) of the Taxes Act 1988" by CTA 2010, s. 1177 and Sch. 1, para. 282, with effect for corporation tax purposes for accounting periods ending on or after 1 April 2010, and for income tax and capital gains tax purposes for the tax year 2010–11 and subsequent tax years.
In former s. 219(4B), the word "premium" substituted for the word "premiums" by SI 2001/3629, art. 87(a) operative from 1 December 2001.
Former s. 219(4B) inserted by F(No. 2)A 1997, s. 22(3) and (4) and s. 52 and Sch. 8, Pt. II(5) with effect in relation to distributions made on or after 2 July 1997.
S. 219(4C) omitted by FA 2009, s. 34 and Sch. 14, para. 18(b), with effect in relation to distributions paid on or after 1 July 2009, subject to transitional provisions in FA 2009, Sch. 14, para. 32.
Former s. 219(4C) inserted by F(No. 2)A 1997, s. 22(3) and (4) and s. 52 and Sch. 8, Pt. II(5) with effect in relation to distributions made on or after 2 July 1997.
S. 219(5) repealed by ITTOIA 2005, s. 884 and Sch. 3 effective for income tax purposes for 2005–06 onwards (ITTOIA 2005, s. 883(1)).

Cross references – ICTA 1988, s. 208: UK company distributions not generally chargeable to corporation tax.
SI 1995/351, reg. 4: application of provisions of TMA 1970 etc. relating to assessment and collection of tax to tax charged under s. 219.

220 Accounting period in which certain profits or losses arise

220(1) For the purposes of section 219 above and all other purposes of the Corporation Tax Acts, the profits or losses arising to a corporate member in any accounting period directly from its membership of one or more syndicates, or from assets forming part of a premium trust fund, shall be taken to be–

(a) if two underwriting years each fall partly within that period, the aggregate of the apportioned parts of those profits or losses in those years; and

(b) if a single underwriting year falls wholly or partly within that period, those profits or losses or (as the case may be) the apportioned part of those profits or losses in that year.

220(2) Subject to the provisions of this Chapter, for the purposes of subsection (1) above and all other purposes of the Corporation Tax Acts–

(a) the profits or losses arising to a corporate member in any underwriting year directly from its membership of one or more syndicates shall be taken to be those of any previous year or years which are declared in that year; and

(b) the profits or losses arising to a corporate member from assets forming part of a premium trust fund which shall be taken to be profits or losses of any underwriting year are–

  (i) those allocated under the rules or practice of Lloyd's to any previous year or years the profits or losses of which are declared in that year, and

  (ii) those arising in that year and not so allocated to any previous year or years.

220(3) In this section **"apportioned part"**, in relation to the profits or losses of an underwriting year, means a part apportioned under section 52 of the Corporation Tax Act 2009.

History – In s. 220(1), the word "premium" substituted for the word "premiums" by SI 2001/3629, art. 87(b) operative from 1 December 2001.

S. 220(2)(b), substituted by SI 2007/1616, reg. 2, with effect for accounting periods ending on or after 1 July 2007.
In s. 220(2)(b), the word "premium" substituted for the word "premiums" by SI 2001/3629, art. 87(b) operative from 1 December 2001.
In s. 220(3), the words "section 52 of the Corporation Tax Act 2009" substituted for the words "section 72 of the Taxes Act 1988" by CTA 2009, s. 1322 and Sch. 1, para. 393, with effect for corporation tax purposes for accounting periods ending on or after 1 April 2009, and for income tax and capital gains tax purposes for the tax year 2009–10 and subsequent tax years.

Cross references – FA 2000, s. 107(9)(b) (general insurance reserves): an amount which is treated as a receipt of an underwriting trade under FA 2000, s. 107(2) may be regarded as arising directly from his membership of one or more syndicates for the purposes of s. 220(2)(a).

221 Assessment and collection of tax

221 [Repealed by F(No. 2)A 2005, s. 45(4).]

History – S. 221 omitted by F(No. 2)A 2005, s. 45(4) and repealed by F(No. 2)A 2005, s. 70 and Sch. 11, Pt. 2(11) with effect from 1 January 2006, although for the purposes of enabling regulations to be made under this section or under FA 1993, s. 182(1)(a), the omission and repeal took effect from 20 July 2005 (Royal Assent) (F(No. 2)A 2005, s. 45(8)).

TRUST FUNDS

222 Premium trust funds

222(1) For the purposes of the Corporation Tax Acts–

(a) a corporate member shall be treated as absolutely entitled as against the trustees to the assets forming part of a premium trust fund belonging to it; and

(b) where a deposit required by a regulatory authority in a country or territory outside the United Kingdom is paid out of such a fund, the money so paid shall be treated as still forming part of that fund.

222(2) Where an asset forms part of a corporate member's premium trust fund at the beginning of any underwriting year, for the purposes of the Corporation Tax Acts–

(a) the trustees of the fund shall be treated as acquiring it on that day, and

(b) they shall be treated as paying in respect of the acquisition an amount equal to the value of the asset at the time of the acquisition.

222(3) Where an asset forms part of a corporate member's premium trust fund at the end of any underwriting year, for the purposes of the Corporation Tax Acts–

(a) the trustees of the fund shall be treated as disposing of it on that day, and

(b) they shall be treated as obtaining in respect of the disposal an amount equal to the value of the asset at the time of the disposal.

222(4-5) [Repealed by FA 1997, s. 76 and Sch. 10, para. 6(b), and s. 113 and Sch. 18, Pt. VI(10).]

222(6) [Repealed by FA 1996, Sch. 41, Pt. V(18).]

222(7) [Repealed by FA 1996, Sch. 41, Pt. V(18).]

History – In the sidenote to s. 222, the word "premium" substituted for the word "premiums" by SI 2001/3629, art. 87(c) operative from 1 December 2001.
In s. 222(1)(a), the word "premium" substituted for the word "premiums" by SI 2001/3629, art. 87(c) operative from 1 December 2001.
In s. 222(2), the word "premium" substituted for the word "premiums" by SI 2001/3629, art. 87(c) operative from 1 December 2001.
In s. 222(3), the word "premium" substituted for the word "premiums" by SI 2001/3629, art. 87(c) operative from 1 December 2001.
S. 222(4) and (5) repealed by FA 1997, s. 76 and Sch. 10, para. 6(b), and s. 113 and Sch. 18, Pt. VI(10), with effect in relation to, and to transfers under, any arrangement made on or after 1 July 1997.
S. 222(6) and (7) repealed by FA 1996, s. 205 and Sch. 41, Pt. V(18), with effect for 1996–97 and subsequent years of assessment for income tax and for accounting periods ending after 31 March 1996 for corporation tax.

223 Ancillary trust funds

223 A corporate member shall be treated for the purposes of the Corporation Tax Acts as absolutely entitled as against the trustees to the assets forming part of an ancillary trust fund belonging to it.

Cross references – SI 1997/2681, reg. 5: for purposes of s. 223 an ancillary trust fund set up in relation to a Lloyd's Scottish limited partnership is regarded as an ancillary trust fund of that partnership.

OTHER SPECIAL CASES

224 Reinsurance to close

224 [Repealed by FA 2000, Sch. 40, Pt. II(16) (see history note).]

History – S. 224 superseded by FA 2000, s. 107(11) with effect in relation to profits of underwriting members' trades which are declared in periods of account beginning on or after 1 January 2000.

225 Stop-loss and quota share insurance

225(1) In computing for the purposes of corporation tax the profits of a corporate member's underwriting business, each of the following shall be deductible as an expense, namely–

(a) any premium payable by it under a stop-loss insurance, and any repayment of insurance money paid to it under such an insurance; and

(b) where an amount is payable by it under a quota share contract–

(i) so much of that amount as exceeds the amount of transferred losses that are declared on or before the date the contract takes effect (**"the declared amount"**), or

(ii) if the contract does not take effect, the amount so payable under the contract.

225(2) Subject to subsection (3) below, the following provisions apply where any insurance money is payable to a corporate member under a stop-loss insurance in respect of a loss in its underwriting business–

(a) if the underwriting year in which the loss is declared falls within two or more accounting periods, the apportioned part of the insurance money shall be treated as a trading receipt in computing the profits arising from the business for each of those periods; and

(b) if the underwriting year in which the loss is declared falls within a single accounting period, the insurance money shall be treated as a trading receipt in computing the profits arising from the business for that period.

225(3) Where, as respects the payment of any such insurance money as is mentioned in subsection (2) above–

(a) the inspector is not notified of the payment at least 30 days before the time after which any assessment or further assessment of profits for any of the accounting periods or (as the case may be) the accounting period is precluded by section 34 of the Management Act (ordinary time limit), and

(b) the inspector is not entitled, after that time, to make any such assessment or further assessment by virtue of section 36 (loss of tax brought about carelessly or deliberately) of that Act,

that subsection shall have effect in relation to the apportioned part of that insurance money or (as the case may be) that insurance money as if, instead of that accounting period, it referred to the accounting period in which the payment is made.

225(3A) Where the amount payable by a corporate member under a quota share contract is less than the declared amount–

(a) if the underwriting year in which the contract takes effect falls within a single accounting period, the difference between the two amounts (**"the surplus"**) shall be treated as a trading receipt in computing the profits arising from the member's underwriting business for that period, and

(b) if that underwriting year falls within two or more accounting periods, the apportioned part of the surplus shall be treated as a trading receipt in computing the profits arising from the member's underwriting business for each of those periods.

225(3B) Where a corporate member has entered a quota share contract, any amount paid by it to cover a cash call in respect of transferred losses that are not declared at the time the contract takes effect shall be treated, for the purposes of subsections (1)(b)(i) and (3A) above, as an amount payable under the contract at that time.

225(3C) Subsection (3D) applies to any premium which is payable by a corporate member under a stop-loss insurance taken out in respect of its underwriting business and in relation to which section 220(2)(a) does not apply.

225(3D) The premium is to be treated for the purposes of the Corporation Tax Acts–

(a) as an amount that arises to the member directly from its membership of the syndicate or syndicates in relation to the activities of which the stop-loss insurance was taken out, and

(b) as if it were payable in the underwriting year in which the profits or losses arising to the member directly from its membership of the syndicate or syndicates concerned are declared.

225(3E) If a premium is payable under a stop-loss insurance in respect of two or more underwriting years, the amount of the premium treated, as a result of subsection (3D)(b), as payable in each of those years is to be determined on a just and reasonable basis.

225(3F) If–

(a) a corporate member enters into a quota share contract, and

(b) the main purpose, or one of the main purposes, of entering into it was to secure that amounts payable by the member under the contract were not dealt with on the basis set out in subsection (3G),

the contract is treated for the purposes of subsections (3C) to (3E) as if it were a stop-loss insurance (and, accordingly, the amounts payable under it are treated for those purposes as premiums).

225(3G) Amounts are dealt with on the basis set out in this subsection if they are treated as payable in the underwriting year in which the profits or losses arising to a corporate member directly from its membership of one or more syndicates are declared.

225(4) In this section–

"apportioned part", in relation to any insurance money or other amount, means a part apportioned under section 52 of the Corporation Tax Act 2009;

"cash call" means a request for funds which, in pursuance of a contract made in accordance with the rules and practices of Lloyd's, is made to a corporate member by the agent of a syndicate of which it is a member;

"quota share contract" means any contract between a corporate member and another person which–

(a) is made in accordance with the rules or practice of Lloyd's; and

(b) provides for that other person to take over any rights and liabilities of the member under any of the syndicates of which it is a member;

and where the taking over of a member's rights and liabilities is conditional upon the occurrence of any event, the contract does not take effect until that event occurs; and

"transferred loss", in relation to such a contract, means a loss for which that other person takes over liability under the contract (disregarding, in the case of a loss that has been declared at the time it is taken over, any part of it in respect of which the member has paid a cash call before that time).

History – In s. 225(1), para. (b) substituted by FA 2002, s. 86 and Sch. 32, para. 7 in relation to quota share contracts entered into on or after 17 April 2002.
In s. 225(3)(b), the words "loss of tax brought about carelessly or deliberately" substituted for the words "fraudulent or negligent conduct" by FA 2008, s. 118 and Sch. 39, para. 64, with effect from 1 April 2010 (SI 2009/403, art. 2(2) subject to SI 2009/403, art. 3–10 – in particular art. 10).
S. 225(3A), (3B) inserted by FA 2002, s. 86 and Sch. 32, para. 8 in relation to quota share contracts entered into on or after 17 April 2002.
S. 225(3C)-(3G) inserted by FA 2012, s. 25 in relation to any stop-loss insurance (as defined by FA 1994, s. 230(1)) taken out on or after 6 December 2011 or any quota share contract entered into on or after that date, subject to transitional provisions in FA 2012, s. 25(3) to (5).
In s. 225(4), in the definition of "apportioned part", the words "section 52 of the Corporation Tax Act 2009" substituted for the words "section 72 of the Taxes Act 1988" by CTA 2009, s. 1322 and Sch. 1. para. 394, with effect for corporation tax purposes for accounting periods ending on or after 1 April 2009, and for income tax and capital gains tax purposes for the tax year 2009–10 and subsequent tax years.
S. 225(4) substituted by FA 2002, s. 86 and Sch. 32, para. 9 in relation to quota share contracts entered into on or after 17 April 2002.
Cross references – SI 1995/351, reg. 6: assessment in respect of amount payable under stop-loss insurance to a corporate member of Lloyd's is not out of time if made before end of underwriting year following the underwriting year in which amount received.

MISCELLANEOUS

226 Provisions which are not to apply

226(1) [Repealed by FA 2002, s. 141 and Sch. 40, Pt. 3(11).]

226(2) [Repealed by FA 2002, s. 141 and Sch. 40, Pt. 3(10).]

226(3) No relevant contract (within the meaning of Part 7 of the Corporation Tax Act 2009) forming part of a premium trust fund of a corporate member shall be a derivative contract.

History – S. 226(1) repealed by FA 2002, s. 80 and Sch. 24, para. 7 and s. 141 and Sch. 40, Pt. 3(11) with effect in relation to accounting periods beginning on or after 1 October 2002.
S. 226(2) repealed by FA 2002, s. 141 and Sch. 40, Pt. 3(10) with effect in relation to accounting periods beginning on or after 1 October 2002.
In s. 226(3), the words "Part 7 of the Corporation Tax Act 2009" substituted for the words "Schedule 26 to the Finance Act 2002" by CTA 2009, s. 1322 and Sch. 1, para. 395, with effect for corporation tax purposes for accounting periods ending on or after 1 April 2009, and for income tax and capital gains tax purposes for the tax year 2009–10 and subsequent tax years.
S. 226(3) substituted by FA 2002, s. 83 and Sch. 27, para. 16 with effect in relation to accounting periods beginning on or after 1 October 2002.

227 Cessation: final underwriting year

227(1) This section applies where a corporate member ceases to carry on its underwriting business, whether by reason of being wound up or otherwise.

227(2) Subject to the provisions of any regulations made by the Board–

(a) the member's final underwriting year shall be that in which its deposit at Lloyd's is paid over to it or its liquidator, and

(b) the member's underwriting business shall be treated as continuing until the end of that year.

Cross references – SI 1997/2681, reg. 4(2): s. 227 does not apply in relation to a Lloyd's Scottish limited partnership which is treated as a corporate member by virtue of reg. 3(2) of those regulations.
Statutory instruments – SI 1995/351.

227A Restriction of group relief

227A(1) Losses of the last active underwriting year of a corporate member are not eligible for surrender by the corporate member as group relief to another company unless the group-relief continuity condition is satisfied.

227A(2) In this section **"last active underwriting year"**, in relation to a corporate member, means–

(a) if the corporate member writes insurance business in only one underwriting year, that underwriting year, and

(b) otherwise, the last underwriting year in which the corporate member writes insurance business.

227A(3) Where in an underwriting year–

(a) the corporate member writes an amount of insurance business which is insignificant when compared with that written by it in the preceding underwriting year, or

(b) the only insurance business written by the corporate member consists of the acceptance of reinsurance to close premiums,

the underwriting year is not to be regarded for the purposes of subsection (2)(b) above as an underwriting year in which the corporate member writes insurance business.

227A(4) In subsection (3)(b) above **"reinsurance to close premium"** means a premium or other consideration under a contract in pursuance of which, in accordance with the rules or practice of Lloyd's, one underwriting member agrees with another to meet liabilities arising from the latter's underwriting business in an underwriting year so that the accounts of the business for that year may be closed.

227A(5) The group-relief continuity condition is satisfied if the corporate member (as the surrendering company) and the other company (as the claimant company) meet the conditions in section 131 (the group condition), section 132 (consortium condition 1) or section 133 (consortium conditions 2 and 3) of the Corporation Tax Act 2010 throughout the period–

(a) beginning with the last day of the last active underwriting year of the corporate member, and

(b) ending with the first day of the first underwriting year in which losses of the last active underwriting year are declared.

History – In s. 227A(5), the words "section 131 (the group condition), section 132 (consortium condition 1) or section 133 (consortium conditions 2 and 3) of the Corporation Tax Act 2010" substituted for the words "section 402(2) or (3) of the Taxes Act 1988" by CTA 2010, s. 1177 and Sch. 1, para. 283, with effect for corporation tax purposes for accounting periods ending on or after 1 April 2010, and for income tax and capital gains tax purposes for the tax year 2010–11 and subsequent tax years.

S. 227A inserted by FA 2007, s. 33(1) with effect in relation to any case where the corporate member (as the surrendering company) and the other company (as the claimant company) first meet the conditions in ICTA 1988, s. 402(2) or (3) on or after 21 March 2007.

227B Transfer of underwriting business without change of ownership

227B(1) This section applies where, in accordance with the rules or practice of Lloyd's, a corporate member ("the successor") has taken up the syndicate capacity of another corporate member ("the predecessor").

227B(2) Chapter 1 of Part 22 of the Corporation Tax Act 2010 (transfers of trade without a change of ownership) applies as if–

(a) the transferred trade referred to in that Chapter were the underwriting business of the predecessor,

(b) the predecessor ceases to carry it on, and the successor begins to carry it on, at the end of the first underwriting year in which profits or losses of the predecessor's last active underwriting year are declared, and

(c) sections 951 and 952 were omitted.

227B(3) For the purposes of subsection (1) above the successor has taken up the predecessor's syndicate capacity if it has taken up the rights to participate in syndicates which were (or otherwise would be) offered to the predecessor.

227B(4) In subsection (2)(b) above **"last active underwriting year"** has the same meaning as in section 227A above (see subsections (2) to (4) of that section).

History – In s. 227B(2), the words "Chapter 1 of Part 22 of the Corporation Tax Act 2010 (transfers of trade without a change of ownership)" substituted for the words "Section 343 of the Taxes Act 1988 (company reconstructions without a change of ownership)" by SI 2013/463, art. 7(2)(a), with effect from 1 April 2013.

In s. 227B(2)(a), the words "the transferred trade referred to in that Chapter" substituted for the words "the trade mentioned in that section" by SI 2013/463, art. 7(2)(b), with effect from 1 April 2013.

In s. 227B(2)(c), the words "sections 951 and 952" substituted for the words "subsections (8) to (10) and (12)" by SI 2013/463, art. 7(2)(c), with effect from 1 April 2013.

S. 227B inserted by FA 2007, s. 43(1) with effect in relation to any case where the first underwriting year in which profits or losses of the predecessor's final underwriting year are declared is 2007 or a later underwriting year.

227C Exemption for profits or losses of foreign permanent establishments

227C(1) This section applies for the purposes of section 18A(6) and (7) of the Corporation Tax Act 2009 (exemption for profits or losses of foreign permanent establishments: "relevant profits amount" and "relevant losses amount").

227C(2) Any regulations made under section 229(1)(d) below are to be ignored.

227C(3) Profits or losses which are taken to arise to a corporate member in an underwriting year from its membership of one or more syndicates are to be left out of account in relation to any relevant accounting period so far as they are profits or losses of a previous underwriting year which began before the relevant day (as defined in section 18F of the 2009 Act (effect of election under section 18A)).

227C(4) Profits or losses arising to a corporate member from assets forming part of a premium trust fund which are taken to be profits or losses of an underwriting year are to be left out of account in relation to any relevant accounting period so far as they are allocated under the rules or practice of Lloyds to a previous underwriting year which began before the relevant day (as defined in section 18F of the 2009 Act).

History – S. 227C inserted by FA 2012, s. 180 and Sch. 20, para. 8 with effect for relevant accounting periods beginning on or after 1 January 2013.

228 Lloyd's underwriters: individuals

228(1) Chapter III of Part II of the 1993 Act (Lloyd's underwriters: individuals) shall have effect subject to the amendments specified in Schedule 21 to this Act.

228(2) The following provisions shall cease to have effect, namely–

(a) section 627 of the Taxes Act 1988 (elections by Lloyd's underwriters with respect to retirement annuities);

(b) in section 641 of that Act, subsection (2) (elections by Lloyd's underwriters with respect to carry-back of contributions); and

(c) in section 183 of the 1993 Act, subsection (3) (amendments of sections 627(5) and 641(2) of the Taxes Act 1988).

228(3) Subject to any provision to the contrary, the provisions of Schedule 21 to this Act have effect for the year 1994–95 and subsequent years of assessment.

228(4) Subsection (2) above has effect for the year 1997–98 and subsequent years of assessment.

SUPPLEMENTAL

229 Regulations

229(1) The Board may by regulations provide–

(a) for the assessment and collection of tax charged in accordance with section 219 above;

(b) for making, in the event of any changes in the rules or practice of Lloyd's, such amendments of this Chapter as appear to the Board to be expedient having regard to those changes;

(c) for modifying the application of this Chapter in cases where a syndicate continues after the end of its closing year or a corporate member becomes insolvent or otherwise ceases to carry on its underwriting business;

(ca) for modifying the application of this Chapter in relation to cases where assets forming part of a premium trust fund are the subject of–

(i) [Repealed by FA 1997, s. 76 and Sch. 10, para. 6(b), and s. 113 and Sch. 18, Pt. VI(10).]

(ii) arrangements involving repos (within the meaning given by section 554(4) of the Corporation Tax Act 2009); or

(iii) arrangements meeting the conditions in section 554(2) of that Act (redemption arrangements);

(d) for giving credit for foreign tax.

229(2) Any power to make regulations conferred by this section includes power to make–

(a) different provision for different cases or different purposes, and

(b) incidental, supplemental or transitional provision and savings.

History – *S. 229 renumbered as subs. (1) of that section by F(No. 2)A 2005, s. 45(5) with effect from 1 January 2006, although for the purposes of enabling regulations to be made under FA 1993, s. 182(1)(a) or under FA 1994, s. 229(1)(a), the amendment took effect from 20 July 2005 (Royal Assent) (F(No. 2)A 2005, s. 45(8)).*

The words "(so far as not provided for by Schedule 19 to the 1993 Act as applied by section 221 above)" omitted by F(No. 2)A 2005, s. 45(6) and repealed by F(No. 2)A 2005, s. 70 and Sch. 11, Pt. 2(11) with effect from 1 January 2006, although for the purposes of enabling regulations to be made under FA 1993, s. 182(1)(a) or under FA 1994, s. 229(1)(a), the omission and repeal took effect from 20 July 2005 (Royal Assent) (F(No. 2)A 2005, s. 45(8)).

In s. 229(1)(ca), the word "premium" substituted for the word "premiums" by SI 2001/3629, art. 87(e) operative from 1 December 2001.
S. 229(1)(ca)(i) repealed by FA 1997, s. 76 and Sch. 10, para. 6(b), and s. 113 and Sch. 18, Pt. VI(10), with effect in relation to, and to transfers under, any arrangement made on or after 1 July 1997.
S. 229(1)(ca) inserted by FA 1995, s. 83(2).
S. 229(1)(ca)(ii) and (iii) substituted for former s. 229(1)(ca)(ii) by CTA 2009, s. 1322 and Sch. 1, para. 396, with effect for corporation tax purposes for accounting periods ending on or after 1 April 2009, and for income tax and capital gains tax purposes for the tax year 2009–10 and subsequent tax years.
S. 229(1)(ca)(ii) substituted by FA 2007, s. 47(2) and Sch. 14, para. 19 with effect in relation to arrangements coming into force on or after 1 October 2007, by virtue of SI 2007/2483, art. 3.
S. 229(2) inserted by F(No. 2)A 2005, s. 45(7) with effect from 1 January 2006, although for the purposes of enabling regulations to be made under FA 1993, s. 182(1)(a) or under FA 1994, s. 229(1)(a), the omission and repeal took effect from 20 July 2005 (Royal Assent) (F(No. 2)A 2005, s. 45(8)).

Cross references – ICTA 1988, s. 806(5): disapplication of the notification requirements where foreign tax credit adjustment given under s. 229.
ICTA 1988, s. 811(7)(a): disapplication of notice requirements under s. 811(5), (6) where adjustment is one whose consequences in relation to the reduction are given effect in accordance with regulations made under s. 229 (regulations relating to corporate members of Lloyd's).
FA 1993, Sch. 19: Lloyd's underwriters – assessment and collection of tax.
FA 2007, Sch. 11, para. 3(14): application (by regulations) of FA 2007, Sch. 11, para. 2 with modifications.
Statutory instruments – SI 1995/351, SI 1997/2681 (amended by SI 2006/111), SI 2005/3338, and SI 2006/3262.

230 Interpretation and commencement

230(1) In this Chapter, unless the context otherwise requires–

"the 1993 Act" means the Finance Act 1993;

"ancillary trust fund", in relation to a corporate member, does not include a premium trust fund but, subject to that, means any trust fund required or authorised by the rules of Lloyd's, or required by a members' agent or regulating trustee of the corporate member;

"closing year"–

(a) in relation to an underwriting year, means the underwriting year next but one following that year; and

(b) in relation to a syndicate, means the closing year of the underwriting year for which it was formed;

"corporate member" means a body corporate which is a member of Lloyd's and is or has been an underwriting member;

"inspector" includes any officer of the Board;

"the Management Act" means the Taxes Management Act 1970;

"managing agent", in relation to a syndicate and an underwriting year, means–

(a) the person registered as a managing agent at Lloyd's who was acting as such an agent for the syndicate at the end of that year, or

(b) such other person as may be determined in accordance with regulations made by the Board;

"member" means a member of Lloyd's who is or has been an underwriting member;

"members' agent", in relation to a corporate member, means a person registered as a members' agent at Lloyd's who has been appointed by the corporate member to act as its members' agent in respect of all or any part of its underwriting business;

"premium trust fund" means a trust fund into which premiums receivable by members are paid in compliance with a trust deed under Rule 8.2.19 of the Insurance Prudential Sourcebook made by the Financial Services Authority under the Financial Services and Markets Act 2000;

"prescribed" means prescribed by regulations made by the Board;

"profits" includes gains;

"regulating trustee", in relation to a corporate member, means a person designated as such by the terms of any trust deed by which a premiums trust fund of the corporate member is constituted;

"stop-loss insurance" means any insurance taken out by a corporate member against losses in its underwriting business, except insurance taken out by entering a quota share contract (within the meaning of section 225 above);

"syndicate" means a syndicate of underwriting members of Lloyd's formed for an underwriting year;

"underwriting business", in relation to a corporate member, means its underwriting business as a member of Lloyd's;

"underwriting year" means the calendar year.

230(2) For the purposes of this Chapter, unless the contrary intention appears–

(a) the profits or losses of a corporate member's underwriting business include profits or losses arising to it–

(i) from assets forming part of a premium trust fund or an ancillary trust fund; or
(ii) from assets employed by it in, or in connection with, its underwriting business; and

(b) any charge made on a corporate member by the managing agent of a syndicate of which it is a member, and any expense incurred on its behalf by the managing agent of such a syndicate, shall be treated as expenses arising directly from its membership of that syndicate.

230(3) Subject to any provision to the contrary, the provisions of this Chapter have effect for accounting periods ending on or after 1st January 1994 or, as the case may require, for the underwriting year 1994 and subsequent underwriting years.

History – In s. 230(1), in the definition of "premium trust fund", the words "Rule 8.2.19 of the Insurance Prudential Sourcebook" substituted for the words "section 17.7 of the Lloyd's Sourcebook" by SI 2006/3273, art. 3, with effect from 31 December 2006.
In s. 230(1), in the definition of "premium trust fund", "section 17.7" substituted for "section 10.3" by SI 2005/1538, art. 3, with effect from 1 July 2005.
In s. 230(1), in definition of "stop loss insurance", the words ", except insurance taken out by entering a quota share contract (within the meaning of section 225 above)" inserted by FA 2002, s. 86 and Sch. 32, para. 10 with effect in relation to quota share contracts entered into on or after 17 April 2002.
In s. 230(1), in the definition of "ancillary trust fund", the word "premium" substituted for the word "premiums" by SI 2001/3629, art. 87(f) operative from 1 December 2001.
In s. 230(1), the definition of "premium trust fund" substituted by SI 2001/3629, art. 85 operative from 1 December 2001.
In s. 230(2)(a)(i), the word "premium" substituted for the word "premiums" by SI 2001/3629, art. 87(f) operative from 1 December 2001.

Cross references – FA 1996, Sch. 11, para. 7(2): application of s. 230 to loan relationships legislation affecting Lloyd's underwriters.
FA 2002, s. 65(5): postponement of change to mark to market in certain cases.
FA 2003, Sch. 26, para. 6(2)(b): non-resident underwriting companies and independent agents.

Statutory instruments – SI 1995/351 and SI 2005/3338.

PART VIII – MISCELLANEOUS AND GENERAL

COMPANIES TREATED AS NON-RESIDENT

249 Certain companies treated as non-resident

249 [Omitted by CTA 2009, s. 1322 and Sch. 1, para. 397 and repealed by CTA 2009, s. 1326 and Sch. 3, Pt. 1.]

History – S. 249 omitted by CTA 2009, s. 1322 and Sch. 1, para. 397 and repealed by CTA 2009, s. 1326 and Sch. 3, Pt. 1, with effect for corporation tax purposes for accounting periods ending on or after 1 April 2009, and for income tax and capital gains tax purposes for the tax year 2009–10 and subsequent tax years.
In former s. 249(3), the words ", by virtue of section 66A of that Act (residence of SE)" inserted by F(No. 2)A 2005, s. 60(2), with effect from 20 July 2005 (Royal Assent).

Cross references – TMA 1970, s. 118(1): meaning of "the Taxes Acts".
ICTA 1988, s. 747(1B): s. 249 disregarded in determining whether a company is UK resident for the purposes of ICTA 1988, Pt. XVI, Ch. IV (controlled foreign companies).
ICTA 1988, s. 788: double taxation relief by agreement with other countries.

HMRC Manuals – Company Tax Manual CTM3394ff.: general guidance on the application of s. 249 and 250.
International Tax Handbook ITH367: general guidance on the application of s. 249 and 250

Other material – Tax Bulletin Special Edition 6: UK/US dual resident company will only cease to be resident for UK tax purposes under s. 249(1) if the company has made a claim under the new treaty and the competent authorities have awarded residence to the US.
Tax Bulletin 14, December 1994: extended article on the Revenue's views on; and policies regarding the operation of s. 249 and 250.
Taxline 1994/46 (not reproduced): exemption for gains from alienation of certain property under relevant double tax treaty applies to TCGA 1992, s. 185 exit charge where company ceased to be resident at 30 November 1993 by virtue of s. 249.

Notes – S. 249 rewritten as follows:
S. 249(1): CTA 2009, s. 18(1), (2), Sch. 1, para. 307, 383, 705.
S. 249(2): CTA 2009, s. 18(4).
S. 249 (3): CTA 2009, s. 18(3), Sch. 1, para. 307, 383, 705.
S. 249(4): CTA 2009, Sch. 1, para. 307, 383, 705.

250 Companies treated as non-resident: supplementary

250 [Omitted by CTA 2009, s. 1322 and Sch. 1, para. 397 and repealed by CTA 2009, s. 1326 and Sch. 3, Pt. 1.]

History – S. 250 omitted by CTA 2009, s. 1322 and Sch. 1, para. 397 and repealed by CTA 2009, s. 1326 and Sch. 3, Pt. 1, with effect for corporation tax purposes for accounting periods ending on or after 1 April 2009, and for income tax and capital gains tax purposes for the tax year 2009–10 and subsequent tax years.

Cross references – TCGA 1992, s. 179: companies ceasing to be group numbers under Pay and File.
TCGA 1992, s. 185(2): deemed disposal of assets on company ceasing to be UK-resident.

251 Companies treated as non-resident: repeals

251(1) For the purposes of this section–

(a) the relevant date is 30th November 1993;

(b) the 1992 Act is the Taxation of Chargeable Gains Act 1992.

251(2) [Amends ICTA 1988, s. 468F(1), (8).]

251(3) [Repealed by ITA 2007, s. 1031 and Sch. 3, Pt. 1.]

251(4) [Repeals ICTA 1988, s. 749(4A), 751(2)(bb).]

251(5) [Repeals TCGA 1992, s. 139(3).]

251(6) [Repeals TCGA 1992, s. 160.]

251(7) [Amends TCGA 1992, s. 166(2), 171(2), 172(3).]

251(8) [Amends TCGA 1992, s. 175(2).]

251(9) [Repeals TCGA 1992, s. 186 and amends TCGA 1992, s. 187(1), (6).]

251(10) [Repeals TCGA 1992, s. 188.]

251(11) [Amends TCGA 1992, s. 211(3).]

251(12) [Repealed by FA 1996, Sch. 41, Pt. V(3).]

History – S. 251(3) repealed by ITA 2007, s. 1031 and Sch. 3, Pt. 1, with effect from 6 April 2007.
S. 251(12) repealed by FA 1996, s. 205 and Sch. 41, Pt. V(3), with effect for 1996–97 and subsequent years of assessment for income tax and for accounting periods ending after 31 March 1996 for corporation tax.

Notes – S. 251 rewritten as follows:
S. 251(1): ITA 2007, Sch. 2, para. 138, 139(1), (2).
S. 251(3): ITA 2007, Sch. 2, para. 138, 139(1), (2).

MANAGEMENT

254 Practice and procedure in connection with appeals

254(1) Section 56B of the Taxes Management Act 1970 (regulations about practice and procedure in connection with appeals) shall be amended as follows.

254(2) [Amends TMA 1970, s. 56B(2)(b).]

254(3) [Inserts TMA 1970, s. 56B(2A).]

255 Calling for documents of taxpayers and others

255 [Omitted by FA 2008, s. 113 and Sch. 36, para. 92(c).]

History – S. 255 omitted by FA 2008, s. 113 and Sch. 36, para. 92(c), with effect from 1 April 2009 (SI 2009/404, art. 2, subject to savings at SI 2009/404, art. 3).

GENERAL

257 Interpretation and construction

257(1) In this Act **"the Taxes Act 1988"** means the Income and Corporation Taxes Act 1988.

257(2) Part V of this Act shall be construed as one with Part I of the Oil Taxation Act 1975, and in Part V that Act is referred to as "the principal Act".

257(3) Part VI of this Act shall be construed as one with the Stamp Act 1891.

258 Repeals

258 The enactments specified in Schedule 26 to this Act (which include provisions which are already spent) are hereby repealed to the extent specified in the third column of that Schedule, but subject to any provision of that Schedule.

259 Short title

259 This Act may be cited as the Finance Act 1994.

SCHEDULES

SCHEDULE 8 – SUPPLEMENTAL PROVISIONS RELATING TO PERSONAL RELIEFS

Section 77

THE TAXES ACT 1988

1 [Amends ICTA 1988, s. 257A(6).]

2(1) [Amends ICTA 1988, s. 257BA(1), (2).]

2(2) [Amends ICTA 1988, s. 257BA(3).]

2(3) Any election made for the purposes of section 257BA of the Taxes Act 1988 which–

(a) has been made before the coming into force of this paragraph, and

(b) apart from this paragraph, would have effect in accordance with that section for the year 1994–95 or any subsequent year,

shall so have effect as if it were an election for the purposes of that section as amended by this paragraph.

Notes – Para. 2(3) came into force on 6 April 1994 (s. 77(7)).

3(1) [Amends ICTA 1988, s. 257BB(1).]

3(2) [Amends ICTA 1988, s. 257BB(3).]

3(3) [Repealed by ITA 2007, s. 1031 and Sch. 3, Pt. 1.]

3(4) [Repeals ICTA 1988, s. 257BB(6).]

History – Para. 3(3) repealed by ITA 2007, s. 1031 and Sch. 3, Pt. 1, with effect from 6 April 2007.

4 [Repealed by FA 1999, s. 139 and Sch. 20, Pt. III(3).]

History – Para. 4 repealed by FA 1999, s. 139 and Sch. 20, Pt. III(3), with effect for the year 2000–01 and subsequent years of assessment.

5 [Repealed by FA 1999, s. 139 and Sch. 20, Pt. III(3).]

History – Para. 5 repealed by FA 1999, s. 139 and Sch. 20, Pt. III(3), with effect for the year 2000–01 and subsequent years of assessment.

6 [Repealed by FA 1999, s. 139 and Sch. 20, Pt. III(4).]

History – Para. 6 repealed by FA 1999, s. 139 and Sch. 20, Pt. III(4), with effect for the year 2000–01 and subsequent years of assessment.

7 [Repealed by FA 1999, s. 139 and Sch. 20, Pt. III(4).]

History – Para. 7 repealed by FA 1999, s. 139 and Sch. 20, Pt. III(4), with effect for the year 2000–01 and subsequent years of assessment.

8(1) [Repealed by FA 1999, s. 139 and Sch. 20, Pt. III(4).]

History – Para. 8 repealed by FA 1999, s. 139 and Sch. 20, Pt. III(4), with effect for the year 2000–01 and subsequent years of assessment.

9 [Repealed by FA 1999, s. 139 and Sch. 20, Pt. III(5).]

History – Para. 9 repealed by FA 1999, s. 139 and Sch. 20, Pt. III(5), with effect for the year 2001–02 and subsequent years of assessment.

10 [Repealed by ITA 2007, s. 1031 and Sch. 3, Pt. 1.]

History – Para. 10 repealed by ITA 2007, s. 1031 and Sch. 3, Pt. 1, with effect from 6 April 2007.

11 [Repealed by ITA 2007, s. 1031 and Sch. 3, Pt. 1.]

History – Para. 11 repealed by ITA 2007, s. 1031 and Sch. 3, Pt. 1, with effect from 6 April 2007.

12 [Repealed by TIOPA 2010, s. 378 and Sch. 10, Pt. 1.]

History – Para. 12 repealed by TIOPA 2010, s. 378 and Sch. 10, Pt. 1, with effect for corporation tax purposes for accounting periods ending on or after 1 April 2010, for income tax and capital gains tax purposes for the tax year 2010–11 and subsequent tax years, and for petroleum revenue tax purposes for chargeable periods beginning on or after 1 July 2010.

THE TAXES MANAGEMENT ACT 1970 (C.9)

13 [Amends TMA 1970, s. 37A.]

SCHEDULE 9 – MORTGAGE INTEREST RELIEF ETC.

Section 81

THE TAXES ACT 1988

1 [Repealed by ITTOIA 2005, s. 884 and Sch. 3.]

History – Sch. 9, para. 1 repealed by ITTOIA 2005, s. 884 and Sch. 3 effective for income tax purposes for 2005–06 onwards (ITTOIA 2005, s. 883(1)).

2 [Repealed by F(No. 2)A 1997, s. 52 and Sch. 8, Pt. II(9) with effect in relation to distributions made on or after 6 April 1999.]

3 [Repeals ICTA 1988, s. 353(4), (5).]

4–6 [Repealed by FA 1995, s. 162 and Sch. 29, Pt. VIII(2), with effect in relation to interest paid on or after 6 April 1995, subject to FA 1995, s. 42(3)–(5).]

7(1) [Repealed by FA 1999, s. 139 and Sch. 20, Pt. III(7).]

7(2)–(4) [Repealed by FA 1995, s. 162 and Sch. 29, Pt. VIII(2).]

History – Para. 7(1) repealed by FA 1999, s. 139 and Sch. 20, Pt. III(7), with effect in relation to any payment of interest falling within FA 1999, s. 38(3) or (4) (broadly, payments made on or after 6 April 2000, or on or after 9 March 1999 and before 6 April 2000 but not falling due until on or after 6 April 2000).
Para 7(2)–(4) repealed by FA 1995, s. 162 and Sch. 29, Pt. VIII(2), with effect in relation to interest paid on or after 6 April 1995, subject to FA 1995, s. 42(3)–(5).

8 [Repealed by FA 1995, s. 162 and Sch. 29, Pt. VIII(2) with effect in relation to interest paid on or after 6 April 1995, subject to FA 1995, s. 42(3)–(5).]

9 [Repealed by ITA 2007, s. 1031 and Sch. 3, Pt. 1.]

History – Para. 9 repealed by ITA 2007, s. 1031 and Sch. 3, Pt. 1, with effect from 6 April 2007.

10(1) [Amends ICTA 1988, s. 370(2).]

10(2) [Repealed by FA 1999, s. 139 and Sch. 20, Pt. III(7).]

History – Para. 10(2) repealed by FA 1999, s. 139 and Sch. 20, Pt. III(7), with effect in relation to any payment of interest falling within FA 1999, s. 35(3) or (4) (broadly, payments made on or after 6 April 2000, or on or after 9 March 1999 and before 6 April 2000 but not falling due until on or after 6 April 2000).

11 [Amends ICTA 1988, s. 375(3).]

THE FINANCE ACT 1993 (c. 34)

12 [Repeals FA 1993, s. 57(7).]

SCHEDULE 10 – MEDICAL INSURANCE

Section 83

[Repealed by F(No. 2)A 1997, s. 52 and Sch. 8, Pt. II(2) with effect for the year 1997–98 and subsequent years of assessment.]

SCHEDULE 11 – EXTENSION OF ROLL-OVER RELIEF ON RE-INVESTMENT

Section 91

1 Chapter IA of Part V of the Taxation of Chargeable Gains Act 1992 shall be amended as follows.

DISPOSALS ON WHICH RELIEF AVAILABLE

2 [Amends TCGA 1992, s. 164A(1)(a), (2), (9), repeals TCGA 1992, s. 164A(3)–(7), and substitutes TCGA 1992, s. 164A(12).]

3 [Substitutes TCGA 1992, s. 164B.]

4 [Repeals TCGA 1992, s. 164C–164E.]

5 [Amends TCGA 1992, s. 164H(1).]

6 [Amends TCGA 1992, s. 164L(10).]

ACQUISITIONS ON WHICH RELIEF AVAILABLE

7 [Substitutes TCGA 1992, s. 164A(8).]

RETIREMENT RELIEF

8 [Repeals TCGA 1992, s. 164A(11) and inserts TCGA 1992, s. 164BA.]

CLAWBACK

9(1) [Substitutes TCGA 1992, s. 164F(1), (4), amends TCGA 1992, s. 164F(3), (5), (10) and inserts TCGA 1992, s. 164F(4A), (10A), (10B).]

9(2) Section 164F as amended by this section shall have effect as follows–

(a) the reference in subsection (1) to consideration treated as reduced under section 164A includes consideration treated as reduced under section 164D,

(b) the reference in subsection (3) to a gain having been charged on any disposal includes any gain having been carried forward from any disposal of shares, and

(c) the amounts referred to in subsection (4A)(a) and (b)(i) shall be treated as reduced by any amounts carried forward from any disposal of shares.

9(3) References in sub-paragraph (2) above to an amount being carried forward from a disposal of shares are references to the reduction by that amount, in accordance with section 164D(3)(a), of the amount of the consideration for the disposal of those shares.

ANTI-AVOIDANCE

10 [Inserts TCGA 1992, s. 164L(10A), (10B) and substitutes definition of "chargeable business asset" in TCGA 1992, s. 164L(11).]

MISCELLANEOUS

11 [Inserts TCGA 1992, s. 164N(1A).]

SCHEDULE 12 – INDEXATION LOSSES: TRANSITIONAL RELIEF

Section 93

[Spent]

SCHEDULE 13 – EMPLOYEE SHARE OWNERSHIP TRUSTS

Section 102

INTRODUCTION

1 The Finance Act 1989 shall be amended as provided in this Schedule.

TRUSTEES

2 [Inserts FA 1989, Sch. 5, para. 3(5).]

3 [Inserts FA 1989, Sch. 5, para. 3A–3C.]

4 [Amends FA 1989, Sch. 5, para. 12.]

5 [Inserts FA 1989, Sch. 5, para. 12A.]

SECURITIES

6(1) Section 69 (chargeable events) shall be amended as follows.

6(2) [Amends FA 1989, s. 69(1)(c).]

6(3) [Inserts FA 1989, s. 69(4A).]

7(1) *Paragraph 9 of Schedule 5* (transfer of securities) shall be amended as follows.

7(2) [Amends FA 1989, Sch. 5, para. 9(1)(b).]

7(3) [Inserts FA 1989, Sch. 5, para. 9(2A).]

INTERPRETATION

8 [Inserts FA 1989, Sch. 5, para. 17.]

SCHEDULE 14 – DISTRIBUTIONS OF AUTHORISED UNIT TRUSTS

Section 112

1 Chapter III of Part XII of the Taxes Act 1988 shall be amended in accordance with paragraphs 2 to 5 of this Schedule.

THE NEW SECTIONS

2 [Repealed by Statute Law (Repeals) Act 2013, s. 1 and Sch. 1, Pt. 10.]

History – Para. 2 repealed by Statute Law (Repeals) Act 2013, s. 1 and Sch. 1, Pt. 10, with effect from 31 January 2013.

OTHER AMENDMENTS

3 [Repealed by CTA 2010, s. 1181 and Sch. 3, Pt. 1.]

History – Para. 3 repealed by CTA 2010, s. 1181 and Sch. 3, Pt. 1, with effect for corporation tax purposes for accounting periods ending on or after 1 April 2010, and for income tax and capital gains tax purposes for the tax year 2010–11 and subsequent tax years.

4 [Repealed by Statute Law (Repeals) Act 2013, s. 1 and Sch. 1, Pt. 10.]

History – Para. 4 repealed by Statute Law (Repeals) Act 2013, s. 1 and Sch. 1, Pt. 10, with effect from 31 January 2013.

5 [Repealed by CTA 2009, s. 1326 and Sch. 3, Pt. 1.]

History – Para. 5 repealed by CTA 2009, s. 1326 and Sch. 3, Pt. 1, with effect for corporation tax purposes for accounting periods ending on or after 1 April 2009, and for income tax and capital gains tax purposes for the tax year 2009–10 and subsequent tax years.

6 [Repealed by CTA 2010, s. 1181 and Sch. 3, Pt. 1.]

History – Para. 6 repealed by CTA 2010, s. 1181 and Sch. 3, Pt. 1, with effect for corporation tax purposes for accounting periods ending on or after 1 April 2010, and for income tax and capital gains tax purposes for the tax year 2010–11 and subsequent tax years.

COMMENCEMENT

7(1) Subject to sub-paragraph (2) below, this Schedule shall have effect in relation to distribution periods beginning on or after 1st April 1994.

7(2) Nothing in the amendments made by this Schedule shall be taken to permit–

(a) the total amount shown in the distribution accounts for a distribution period of an authorised unit trust, or

(b) a part of that total amount, to be shown as available for distribution as foreign income dividends unless the distribution date for that distribution period is 1st July 1994 or a subsequent date.

SCHEDULE 15 – ENTERPRISE INVESTMENT SCHEME

Section 137

AMENDMENTS OF THE TAXES ACT 1988

1 [Repealed by ITA 2007, s. 1031 and Sch. 3, Pt. 2.]

History – Para. 1 repealed by ITA 2007, s. 1031 and Sch. 3, Pt. 2, with effect in relation to shares issued after 5 April 2007.

2 [Repealed by ITA 2007, s. 1031 and Sch. 3, Pt. 2.]

History – Para. 2 repealed by ITA 2007, s. 1031 and Sch. 3, Pt. 2, with effect in relation to shares issued after 5 April 2007.

Notes – Para. 2 rewritten as ITA 2007, s. 157(1), 158(1), (2), (4), (5), 165, 173(1), (2), (3), 174, 175(1), (2), (3), 176(1), (2), (3), (4), 178, 179(1), (2), (3), (4), (5), 201(1), (2), (3), (4), (5), (6), (7), 202(2), 210(2), 219(1), (2), 228(1), (2).

3 [Repealed by ITA 2007, s. 1031 and Sch. 3, Pt. 2.]

History – Para. 3 repealed by ITA 2007, s. 1031 and Sch. 3, Pt. 2, with effect in relation to shares issued after 5 April 2007.

Notes – Para. 3(1) rewritten as ITA 2007, s. 158(2).

4 [Repealed by ITA 2007, s. 1031 and Sch. 3, Pt. 2.]

History – Para. 4 repealed by ITA 2007, s. 1031 and Sch. 3, Pt. 2, with effect in relation to shares issued after 5 April 2007.

5 [Repealed by ITA 2007, s. 1031 and Sch. 3, Pt. 2.]

History – Para. 5 repealed by ITA 2007, s. 1031 and Sch. 3, Pt. 2, with effect in relation to shares issued after 5 April 2007.

Notes – Para. 5 rewritten as ITA 2007, s. 157(1), 163(1), (2), 166(1), 167(1), (2), (3), 168(1), (2), (3), (4), (5), 169(1), (2), (3), (4), (5), (6), 170(1), (2), (3), (4), (6), (7), (8), (9), (10), 171(1), (2), 1021(2).

6 [Repealed by ITA 2007, s. 1031 and Sch. 3, Pt. 2.]

History – Para. 6 repealed by ITA 2007, s. 1031 and Sch. 3, Pt. 2, with effect in relation to shares issued after 5 April 2007.

7 [Repealed by ITA 2007, s. 1031 and Sch. 3, Pt. 2.]

History – Para. 7 repealed by ITA 2007, s. 1031 and Sch. 3, Pt. 2, with effect in relation to shares issued after 5 April 2007.

Notes – Para. 7 rewritten as ITA 2007, s. 137(1), (7), 139(1), (2), (3), 181(1), (2), (8), 185(1), (2), (3), Sch. 1, para. 122, 124.

8 [Repealed by ITA 2007, s. 1031 and Sch. 3, Pt. 2.]

History – Para. 8 repealed by ITA 2007, s. 1031 and Sch. 3, Pt. 2, with effect in relation to shares issued after 5 April 2007.

9 [Repealed by ITA 2007, s. 1031 and Sch. 3, Pt. 2.]

History – Para. 9 repealed by ITA 2007, s. 1031 and Sch. 3, Pt. 2, with effect in relation to shares issued after 5 April 2007.

10 [Repealed by ITA 2007, s. 1031 and Sch. 3, Pt. 2.]

History – Para. 10 repealed by ITA 2007, s. 1031 and Sch. 3, Pt. 2, with effect in relation to shares issued after 5 April 2007. Para. 10(d) repealed by FA 2001, Sch. 33, Pt. 2(3) and s. 110 with effect in accordance with FA 2001, Sch. 15, para. 40(2). Para. 10(c) repealed by FA 2000, Sch. 40, Pt. II(5) with effect in relation to shares issued on or after 6 April 2000.

Notes – Para. 10 rewritten as ITA 2007, s. 192(1), 199(1).

11 [Repealed by ITA 2007, s. 1031 and Sch. 3, Pt. 2.]

History – Para. 11 repealed by ITA 2007, s. 1031 and Sch. 3, Pt. 2, with effect in relation to shares issued after 5 April 2007.

Notes – Para. 11 rewritten as ITA 2007, s. 144, 189(1), 200, Sch. 1, para. 129.

12 [Repealed by ITA 2007, s. 1031 and Sch. 3, Pt. 2.]

History – Para. 12 repealed by ITA 2007, s. 1031 and Sch. 3, Pt. 2, with effect in relation to shares issued after 5 April 2007.

Notes – Para. 12 rewritten as ITA 2007, s. 209(1), (2), (3), (4), 210(1), (2), 211(1), (2), 212(1), (2), 219(1), (2), 220(1), 228(1), (2), 229(1), (2).

13 [Repealed by ITA 2007, s. 1031 and Sch. 3, Pt. 2.]

History – Para. 13 repealed by ITA 2007, s. 1031 and Sch. 3, Pt. 2, with effect in relation to shares issued after 5 April 2007.

Notes – Para. 13 rewritten as ITA 2007, s. 164(1).

14 [Repealed by ITA 2007, s. 1031 and Sch. 3, Pt. 2.]

History – Para. 14 repealed by ITA 2007, s. 1031 and Sch. 3, Pt. 2, with effect in relation to shares issued after 5 April 2007.

Notes – Para. 14 rewritten as ITA 2007, s. 213(2), (4), 214(1), 216(2), (8), (9), 219(1), (2), 220(1), 221.

15 [Repealed by ITA 2007, s. 1031 and Sch. 3, Pt. 2.]

History – Para. 15 repealed by ITA 2007, s. 1031 and Sch. 3, Pt. 2, with effect in relation to shares issued after 5 April 2007.

Notes – Para. 15 rewritten as ITA 2007, s. 216(3), (4), (10), 221, 222(7).

16 [Repealed by ITA 2007, s. 1031 and Sch. 3, Pt. 2.]

History – Para. 16 repealed by ITA 2007, s. 1031 and Sch. 3, Pt. 2, with effect in relation to shares issued after 5 April 2007.

Notes – Para. 16 rewritten as ITA 2007, s. 232(1), (2), (3), (5), (6), 233(1), (2), (3), (4).

17(a) [Repealed by ITA 2007, s. 1031 and Sch. 3, Pt. 2.]

17(b) [Repealed by FA 2001, Sch. 33 Pt. 2(3) and s. 110 with effect in accordance with Sch. 15, para. 40(3); previously amended ICTA 1988, s. 303(3).]

17(c) [Repealed by FA 2001, Sch. 33 Pt. 2(3) and s. 110 with effect in accordance with Sch. 15, para. 40(3); previously inserted ICTA 1988, s. 303(6A).]

17(d,e,f) [Repealed by ITA 2007, s. 1031 and Sch. 3, Pt. 2.]

History – Para. 17(a) and (d)–(f) repealed by ITA 2007, s. 1031 and Sch. 3, Pt. 2, with effect in relation to shares issued after 5 April 2007. Para. 17(b), (c) repealed by FA 2001, Sch. 33, Pt. 2(3) and s. 110 with effect in accordance with Sch. 15, para. 40(3).

Notes – Para. 17 rewritten as ITA 2007, s. 224(7).

18 [Repealed by ITA 2007, s. 1031 and Sch. 3, Pt. 2.]

History – Para. 18 repealed by ITA 2007, s. 1031 and Sch. 3, Pt. 2, with effect in relation to shares issued after 5 April 2007.

Notes – Para. 18 rewritten as ITA 2007, s. 209(4), 245(1), (2), (3), (4).

19 [Repealed by ITA 2007, s. 1031 and Sch. 3, Pt. 2.]

History – Para. 19 repealed by ITA 2007, s. 1031 and Sch. 3, Pt. 1, with effect from 6 April 2007.

20 [Repealed by ITA 2007, s. 1031 and Sch. 3, Pt. 1.]

History – Para. 20 repealed by ITA 2007, s. 1031 and Sch. 3, Pt. 1, with effect from 6 April 2007.

Notes – Para. 20 rewritten as ITA 2007, s. 131(1), (2), 136(1).

21(a)

(i) [Repealed by FA 2001, Sch. 33, Pt. 2(3) and s. 110 with effect in relation to shares issued on or after 6 April 2001.]

(ii) [Repealed by FA 1996, s. 205 and Sch. 41, Pt. V(11).]

21(b) [Repealed by ITA 2007, s. 1031 and Sch. 3, Pt. 2.]

21(c) [Repealed by ITA 2007, s. 1031 and Sch. 3, Pt. 2.]

21(d) [Repealed by ITA 2007, s. 1031 and Sch. 3, Pt. 2.]

21(e) [Repealed by ITA 2007, s. 1031 and Sch. 3, Pt. 2.]

History – Para. 21(b)–(e) repealed by ITA 2007, s. 1031 and Sch. 3, Pt. 2, with effect in relation to shares issued after 5 April 2007. Para. 21(a)(i) repealed by FA 2001, Sch. 33, Pt. 2(3) and s. 110 with effect, in accordance with FA 2001 Sch. 15, para. 22(2), in relation to shares issued on or after 6 April 2001.

Para. 21(a)(ii) repealed by FA 1996, s. 205 and Sch. 41, Pt. V(11), with effect, so far as relating to income tax and capital gains tax, as respects the year 1996–97 and subsequent years of assessment, and so far as relating to corporation tax, as respects accounting periods ending on or after 1 July 1999, the appointed day for corporation tax self-assessment under FA 1994, s. 199 by virtue of SI 1998/3173 (C. 78).

Notes – Para. 21 rewritten as ITA 2007, s. 202(1), 203(3), 205(1), (4), 206.

22 [Repealed by ITA 2007, s. 1031 and Sch. 3, Pt. 2.]

History – Para. 22 repealed by ITA 2007, s. 1031 and Sch. 3, Pt. 2, with effect in relation to shares issued after 5 April 2007.

Notes – Para. 22 rewritten as ITA 2007, s. 234(1), (2), (3), 235, 236(1), 237(1), (2), 238(1), (2), (3), 239(1).

23 [Repealed by ITA 2007, s. 1031 and Sch. 3, Pt. 2.]

History – Para. 23 repealed by ITA 2007, s. 1031 and Sch. 3, Pt. 2, with effect in relation to shares issued after 5 April 2007.

Notes – Para. 23 rewritten as ITA 2007, s. 187.

24 [Repealed by ITA 2007, s. 1031 and Sch. 3, Pt. 2.]

History – Para. 24 repealed by ITA 2007, s. 1031 and Sch. 3, Pt. 2, with effect in relation to shares issued after 5 April 2007.

25 [Repealed by ITA 2007, s. 1031 and Sch. 3, Pt. 2.]

History – Para. 25 repealed by ITA 2007, s. 1031 and Sch. 3, Pt. 2, with effect in relation to shares issued after 5 April 2007.
Para. 25(d) repealed by FA 1998, s. 165 and Sch. 27, Pt. III(13), with effect in relation to shares issued on or after 2 July 1997.

Notes – Para. 25 rewritten as ITA 2007, s. 240(1), (2), 241(1), (2), (3), (4), (5), 243(1), (2), (3).

26 [Repealed by ITA 2007, s. 1031 and Sch. 3, Pt. 2.]

History – Para. 26 repealed by ITA 2007, s. 1031 and Sch. 3, Pt. 2, with effect in relation to shares issued after 5 April 2007.

Notes – Para. 26 rewritten as ITA 2007, s. 250(2), (3), 251(2).

27 [Repealed by ITA 2007, s. 1031 and Sch. 3, Pt. 2.]

History – Para. 27 repealed by ITA 2007, s. 1031 and Sch. 3, Pt. 2, with effect in relation to shares issued after 5 April 2007.

Notes – Para. 27 rewritten as ITA 2007, s. 143(3), 184(2), (3), (4), (5), (6), 257(2), (3), (4), (6), 1014(2), Sch. 1, para. 128.

AMENDMENTS OF THE TAXATION OF CHARGEABLE GAINS ACT 1992

28 The Taxation of Chargeable Gains Act 1992 shall be amended as follows:

29 [Amends TCGA 1992, s. 150.]

30 [Inserts TCGA 1992, s. 150A.]

31 [Amends TCGA 1992, s. 164M.]

32(1) [Inserts TCGA 1992, s. 164MA.]

32(2) This paragraph has effect in relation to shares issued on or after 1st January 1994.

33 [Amends TCGA 1992, s. 164N(1).]

34 [Amends TCGA 1992, s. 231(1)(d).]

SCHEDULE 16 – FOREIGN INCOME DIVIDENDS

Section 138

Part I – The New Chapter

1 [Repealed by F(No. 2)A 1997, s. 52 and Sch. 8, Pt. II(11), with effect in relation to distributions made on or after 6 April 1999.]

Part II – Liability for and Collection of Advance Corporation Tax

2 [Repealed by FA 1998, s. 165 and Sch. 27, Pt. III(2), with effect in relation to distributions made on or after 6 April 1999.]

3(1) Schedule 13 to the Taxes Act 1988 (collection of advance corporation tax) shall be amended as follows.

3(2) [Repealed by FA 1998, s. 165 and Sch. 27, Pt. III(2), with effect in relation to return periods and accounting periods ending on or after 6 April 1999; previously substituted ICTA 1988, Sch. 13, para. 1(1).]

3(3) [Repealed by FA 1998, s. 165 and Sch. 27, Pt. III(2), with effect in relation to return periods and accounting periods ending on or after 6 April 1999; previously substituted ICTA 1988, Sch. 13, para. 1(4).]

3(4) [Repealed by FA 1998, s. 165 and Sch. 27, Pt. III(2), with effect in relation to return periods and accounting periods ending on or after 6 April 1999; previously substituted ICTA 1988, Sch. 13, para. 2(1).]

3(5)–(10) [Repealed by F(No. 2)A 1997, s. 52 and Sch. 8, Pt. II(11), with effect in relation to distributions made on or after 6 April 1999.]

3(11) [Repealed by FA 1998, s. 165 and Sch. 27, Pt. III(2), with effect in relation to return periods and accounting periods ending on or after 6 April 1999; previously amended ICTA 1988, Sch. 13, para. 7(3).]

3(12) [Repealed by F(No. 2)A 1997, s. 52 and Sch. 8, Pt. II(11) with effect in relation to distributions made on or after 6 April 1999.]

3(13) [Repealed by FA 1998, s. 165 and Sch. 27, Pt. III(2), with effect in relation to return periods and accounting periods ending on or after 6 April 1999; previously provided for para. 3 to have effect in relation to any return period ending after 30th June 1994.]

Part III – Insurance Companies etc.

4 [Repealed by F(No. 2)A 1997, s. 52 and Sch. 8, Pt. II(11), with effect in relation to distributions made on or after 6 April 1999.]

5(1) [Repealed by Statute Law (Repeals) Act 2013, s. 1 and Sch. 1, Pt. 10, with effect from 31 January 2013.]

5(2)–(3) [Repealed by FA 1995, s. 162 and Sch. 29, Pt. VIII(5), with effect in relation to accounting periods beginning on or after 1 January 1995.]

5(4)–(5) [Repealed by F(No. 2)A 1997, s. 52 and Sch. 8, Pt. II(11), with effect in relation to distributions made on or after 6 April 1999.]

6 [Repealed by F(No. 2)A 1997, s. 52 and Sch. 8, Pt. II(6) with effect in relation to distributions made on or after 2 July 1997.]

7–9 [Repealed by F(No. 2)A 1997, s. 52 and Sch. 8, Pt. II(11) with effect in relation to distributions made on or after 6 April 1999.]

Part IV – Other Provisions

PENALTIES

10 [Omitted by SI 2009/2035, art. 2 and Schedule, para. 60(g).]

History – Para. 10 omitted by SI 2009/2035, art. 2 and Schedule, para. 60(g), with effect from 13 August 2009.

SMALL COMPANIES' RELIEF

11-16 [Repealed by F(No. 2)A 1997, s. 52 and Sch. 8, Pt. II(11) with effect in relation to distributions made on or after 6 April 1999.]

PURCHASE AND SALE OF SECURITIES

17 [Omitted by FA 2008, s. 66(4)(e).]

History – Para. 17 omitted by FA 2008, s. 66(4)(e), with effect in relation to cases where the purchase by the first buyer (within the meaning of ICTA 1988, s. 731(2)) is made on or after 1 April 2008.

MANUFACTURED DIVIDENDS

18 [Repealed by FA 1997, s. 113 and Sch. 18, Pt. VI(10) with effect in relation to, and to transfers under, any arrangement made on or after 1 July 1997.]

19 [Repealed by FA 1997, s. 113 and Sch. 18, Pt. VI(10) with effect in relation to payments made on or after 1 July 1997.]

INTEREST ON TAX OVERPAID

20(1) Section 826 of the Taxes Act 1988 shall be amended as follows.

20(2) [Inserts ICTA 1988, s. 826(1)(aa).]

20(3) [Repealed by FA 1998, s. 165 and Sch. 27. Pt. III(2) with effect in relation to accounting periods beginning on or after 6 April 1999.]

SCHEDULE 17 – MINOR CORRECTIONS

Section 146

1 *[Repealed by Statute Law (Repeals) Act 2013, s. 1 and Sch. 1, Pt. 10.]*

History – Para. 1 repealed by Statute Law (Repeals) Act 2013, s. 1 and Sch. 1, Pt. 10, with effect from 31 January 2013.

2(1) [Amends ICTA 1988, s. 271(1).]

2(2) [Amends ICTA 1988, s. 271(2).]

3 [Repealed by FA 1999, s. 139 and Sch. 20, Pt. III(7).]

History – Para. 3 repealed by FA 1999, s. 139 and Sch. 20, Pt. III(7), with effect in relation to any payment of interest falling within FA 1999, s. 38(3) or (4) (broadly, payments made on or after 6 April 2000, or on or after 9 March 1999 and before 6 April 2000 but not falling due until on or after 6 April 2000).

4 [Repealed by FA 1995, s. 162 and Sch. 29, Pt. VIII(5) with effect in relation to accounting periods beginning on or after 1 January 1995.]

5 [Repealed by FA 2004, s. 326 and Sch. 42, Pt. 2(7).]

History – Para. 5 repealed by FA 2004, s. 326 and Sch. 42, Pt. 2(7) in relation to payments made on or after 6 April 2007 by virtue of notice given in pursuance of SI 2005/2045, reg. 1.

6 [Repealed by ITA 2007, s. 1031 and Sch. 3, Pt. 1.]

History – Para. 6 repealed by ITA 2007, s. 1031 and Sch. 3, Pt. 1, with effect from 6 April 2007.

7 [Repealed by CTA 2010, s. 1181 and Sch. 3, Pt. 1.]

History – Para. 7 repealed by CTA 2010, s. 1181 and Sch. 3, Pt. 1, with effect for corporation tax purposes for accounting periods ending on or after 1 April 2010, and for income tax and capital gains tax purposes for the tax year 2010–11 and subsequent tax years.

8 [Amends ICTA 1988, 843(2).]

History – In para. 8, the words "842(4) and" repealed by CTA 2010, s. 1181 and Sch. 3, Pt. 1, with effect for corporation tax purposes for accounting periods ending on or after 1 April 2010, and for income tax and capital gains tax purposes for the tax year 2010–11 and subsequent tax years. In the summary of this paragraph the words "ICTA 1988, s. 842(4)" therefore deleted.

9 [Amends ICTA 1988, Sch. 11, para. 8(b).]

SCHEDULE 18 – INTEREST RATE AND CURRENCY CONTRACTS: INSURANCE AND MUTUAL TRADING COMPANIES

Section 169

[Repealed by FA 2002, s. 141 and Sch. 40, Pt. 3(13).]

History – Sch. 18 repealed by FA 2002, s. 141 and Sch. 40, Pt. 3(13) with effect in relation to accounting periods beginning on or after 1 October 2002.

SCHEDULE 19 – MANAGEMENT: OTHER AMENDMENTS

Section 196

Notes – S. 199 and SI 1998/3173 (C. 78): unless the contrary intention appears, Sch. 19, so far as it relates to income tax and capital gains tax, has effect for 1996–97 and subsequent tax years and, so far as it relates to corporation tax, has effect for accounting periods ending on or after 1 July 1999, the appointed day for corporation tax self-assessment (CTSA).

Part I – Amendments of Management Act

NOTICE OF LIABILITY TO INCOME TAX AND CAPITAL GAINS TAX

1(1) [Substitutes TMA 1970, s. 7.]

1(2) This paragraph has effect as respects the year 1995–96 and subsequent years of assessment.

EUROPEAN ECONOMIC INTEREST GROUPINGS

2 [Amends TMA 1970, s. 12A(2).]

RECORDS FOR PURPOSES OF RETURNS

3 [Inserts TMA 1970, s. 12B.]

RECOVERY OF OVERPAYMENT OF TAX ETC.

4(1) [Inserts TMA 1970, s. 30(1B).]

4(2) [Substitutes TMA 1970, s. 30(5).]

ASSESSING PROCEDURE

5(1) [Inserts TMA 1970, s. 30A.]

5(2) This paragraph, so far as it relates to partnerships whose trades, professions or businesses are set up and commenced before 6th April 1994, has effect as respects the year 1997–98 and subsequent years of assessment.

AMENDMENT OF PARTNERSHIP STATEMENT WHERE LOSS OF TAX DISCOVERED

6 [Inserts TMA 1970, s. 30B.]

RIGHT OF APPEAL

7 [Repealed by FA 2001, s. 110 and Sch. 33, Pt. II(13).]

History – Para. 7 repealed by FA 2001, s. 110 and Sch. 33, Pt. 2(13) with effect from 11 May 2001 in relation to returns made before or after that date, and whether relating to periods before or after that date.

ERROR OR MISTAKE

8(1) [Repealed by FA 1998, s. 165 and Sch. 27, Pt. III(28).]

8(2) [Amends TMA 1970, s. 33(2) and inserts TMA 1970, s. 33(2A).]

History – Para. 8(1) repealed by FA 1998, s. 165 and Sch. 27, Pt. III(28), with effect in relation to accounting periods ending on or after 1 July 1999, the appointed day for company self-assessment, and superseded by the CTSA provisions in FA 1998, Sch. 18.

9 [Inserts TMA 1970, s. 33A.]

TIME LIMITS FOR ASSESSMENTS

10 [Amends TMA 1970, s. 34(1).]

History – Para. 10 repealed by FA 1998, s. 165 and Sch. 27, Pt. III(28), with effect in relation to accounting periods ending on or after 1 July 1999, the appointed day for company self-assessment, and superseded by the CTSA provisions in FA 1998, Sch. 18.

11(1) [Amends TMA 1970, s. 36(1).]

11(2) [Substitutes TMA 1970, s. 36(2).]

12 [Amends TMA 1970, s. 40(1) and (2).]

CLAIMS ETC.

13 [Substitutes TMA 1970, s. 42.]

14 [Repealed by FA 1998, s. 165 and Sch. 27, Pt. III(28).]

History – Para. 14 repealed by FA 1998, s. 165 and Sch. 27, Pt. III(28), with effect in relation to accounting periods ending on or after 1 July 1999, the appointed day for company self-assessment, and superseded by the CTSA provisions in FA 1998, Sch. 18.

15 [Repealed by FA 1998, s. 165 and Sch. 27, Pt. III(28).]

History – Para. 15 repealed by FA 1998, s. 165 and Sch. 27, Pt. III(28), with effect in relation to accounting periods ending on or after 1 July 1999, the appointed day for company self-assessment, and superseded by the CTSA provisions in FA 1998, Sch. 18.

DETERMINATION OF COMMISSIONERS

16 [Repealed by FA 1998, s. 165 and Sch. 27, Pt. III(28).]

History – Para. 16 repealed by FA 1998, s. 165 and Sch. 27, Pt. III(28), with effect in relation to accounting periods ending on or after 1 July 1999, the appointed day for company self-assessment, and superseded by the CTSA provisions in FA 1998, Sch. 18.

PROCEDURE ON APPEAL

17(1) [Substitutes TMA 1970, s. 50(6) and (7).]

17(2) [Amends TMA 1970, s. 50(8).]

17(3) [Repealed by FA 1998, s. 165 and Sch. 27, Pt. III(28).]

History – Para. 17(3) repealed by FA 1998, s. 165 and Sch. 27, Pt. III(28), with effect in relation to accounting periods ending on or after 1 July 1999, the appointed day for company self-assessment, and superseded by the CTSA provisions in FA 1998, Sch. 18.

POSTPONEMENT OF TAX PENDING APPEAL

18(1) [Substitutes TMA 1970, s. 55(1).]

18(2) [Amends TMA 1970, s. 50(2)–(11).]

COLLECTION AND RECOVERY

19 [Repealed by FA 1998, s. 165 and Sch. 27, Pt. III(28).]

History – Para. 19 repealed by FA 1998, s. 165 and Sch. 27, Pt. III(28), with effect in relation to accounting periods ending on or after 1 July 1999, the appointed day for company self-assessment, and superseded by the CTSA provisions in FA 1998, Sch. 18.

20 [Repealed by FA 2001, Sch. 33, Pt. 2(14) and s. 110.]

History – Sch. 19, para. 20 repealed by FA 2001, Sch. 33, Pt. 2(14) and s. 110 with effect from 11 May 2001 in relation to proceedings begun (or a counterclaim made) after that date, and a set-off first claimed after that date.

21 [Omitted by FA 2008, s. 138 and Sch. 44, para. 11(a).]

History – Para. 21 omitted by FA 2008, s. 138 and Sch. 44, para. 11(a), with effect from 21 July 2008.

22 [Inserts TMA 1970, s. 70A.]

22(2) This paragraph has effect as respects cheques received on or after 6th April 1996.

INTEREST ON OVERDUE TAX OR TAX RECOVERED

23 [Repealed by FA 1996, s. 131(3) and s. 205 and Sch. 41, Pt. V(6), with effect as respects the year 1996–97 and subsequent years of assessment.]

24 [Amends TMA 1970, s. 87A(1).]

PENALTIES

25 [Substitutes TMA 1970, s. 93.]

26 [Inserts TMA 1970, s. 93A.]

27(1) [Repealed by FA 2007, s. 114 and Sch. 27, Pt. 5(5).]

27(2) [Amends TMA 1970, s. 95(3).]

History – Para. 27(1) repealed by FA 2007, s. 114 and Sch. 27, Pt. 5(5), with effect from 1 April 2008 in relation to incorrect returns or accounts for income tax or capital gains tax relating to tax periods commencing on or after that date, except for any period for which a return is required to be made before 1 April 2009 (SI 2008/568 bringing into force FA 2007, Sch. 24, para. 29, which omits TMA 1970, s. 95).

28 [Repealed by FA 2007, s. 114 and Sch. 27, Pt. 5(5).]

History – Para. 28 repealed by FA 2007, s. 114 and Sch. 27, Pt. 5(5), with effect from 1 April 2008 in relation to incorrect partnership returns or accounts relating to tax periods commencing on or after that date, except for any period for which a return is required to be made before 1 April 2009 (SI 2008/568 bringing into force FA 2007, Sch. 24, para. 29, which omits TMA 1970, s. 95A).

29 [Omitted by FA 2008, s. 113 and Sch. 36, para. 92(c).]

History – Para. 29 omitted by FA 2008, s. 113 and Sch. 36, para. 92(c), with effect from 1 April 2009 (SI 2009/404, art. 2, subject to savings at SI 2009/404, art. 3).

30(1) [Substitutes TMA 1970, s. 98B(2), and inserts TMA 1970, s. 98B(2A), (2B).]

30(2) [Amends TMA 1970, s. 98B(3).]

30(3) [Amends TMA 1970, s. 98B(4).]

31(1) [Amends TMA 1970, s. 100B(1).]

31(2) [Amends TMA 1970, s. 100B(2).]

History – Insertion into TMA 1970, s. 100B(1) provided by para. 31(1) amended to include the word "and" following "95A of this Act" by FA 1995, s. 115(7).

32 [Repealed by FA 2007, s. 114 and Sch. 27, Pt. 5(5).]

History – Para. 32 repealed by FA 2007, s. 114 and Sch. 27, Pt. 5(5), with effect from 1 April 2008 in relation to assessments for tax periods commencing on or after that date, except for any period for which a return is required to be made before 1 April 2009 (SI 2008/568 bringing into force FA 2007, Sch. 24, para. 29, which omits TMA 1970, s. 103(2)).

33 [Inserts TMA 1970, s. 103A.]

History – TMA 1970, s. 103A, as inserted prospectively by para. 33, amended by FA 1995, s. 115(8).

INTERPRETATION

34(1) [Amends TMA 1970, s. 118(1).]

34(2) [Repeals TMA 1970, s. 118(3).]

34(3) Sub-paragraph (2) above, so far as it relates to partnerships whose trades, professions or businesses are set up and commenced before 6th April 1994, has effect as respects the year 1997–98 and subsequent years of assessment.

History – In para. 34(1) the words "the Special Commissioners Regulations" substituted for the word "return" by SI 1994/1813, Sch. 1, para. 25(c), with effect from 1 September 1994.

CLAIMS ETC. NOT INCLUDED IN RETURNS

35 [Inserts TMA 1970, Sch. 1A.]

36 [Repealed by FA 1996, s. 205 and Sch. 41, Pt. V(12).]

History – Para. 36 repealed by FA 1996, s. 205 and Sch. 41, Pt. V(12), with effect in relation to any proceedings relating to the year 1996–97 or any subsequent year of assessment, and any proceedings relating to an accounting period ending on or after 1 July 1999, the day appointed under FA 1994, s. 199 by virtue of SI 1998/3173 (C. 78).

Part II – Amendments of Taxes Act 1988

TIME LIMITS FOR CLAIMS UNDER SECTION 96

37 [Repealed by TIOPA 2010, s. 378 and Sch. 10, Pt. 13.]

History – Para. 27 repealed by TIOPA 2010, s. 378 and Sch. 10, Pt. 13, with effect for corporation tax purposes for accounting periods ending on or after 1 April 2010, for income tax and capital gains tax purposes for the tax year 2010–11 and subsequent tax years, and for petroleum revenue tax purposes for chargeable periods beginning on or after 1 July 2010.

INTEREST ON SCHEDULE E TAX

38 [Repealed by Statute Law (Repeals) Act 2013, s. 1 and Sch. 1, Pt. 10.]

History – Para. 38 repealed by Statute Law (Repeals) Act 2013, s. 1 and Sch. 1, Pt. 10, with effect from 31 January 2013.

TIME LIMITS FOR CLAIMS UNDER SECTIONS 534 AND 537A

39 [Repealed by Statute Law (Repeals) Act 2013, s. 1 and Sch. 1, Pt. 10.]

History – Para. 39 repealed by Statute Law (Repeals) Act 2013, s. 1 and Sch. 1, Pt. 10, with effect from 31 January 2013.

40 [Repealed by Statute Law (Repeals) Act 2013, s. 1 and Sch. 1, Pt. 10.]

History – Para. 40 repealed by Statute Law (Repeals) Act 2013, s. 1 and Sch. 1, Pt. 10, with effect from 31 January 2013.

REPAYMENT SUPPLEMENTS: INCOME TAX

41(1) [Substitutes ICTA 1988, s. 824(1).]

41(2) [Substitutes ICTA 1988, s. 824(3).]

41(3) [Repeals ICTA 1988, s. 824(5), (9) (partially), and (10).]

41(4) This paragraph, so far as it relates to partnerships whose trades, professions or businesses are set up and commenced before 6th April 1994, has effect as respects the year 1997–98 and subsequent years of assessment.

INTEREST ON TAX OVERPAID

42 [Amends ICTA 1988, s. 826(2).]

TIME LIMITS FOR ELECTIONS UNDER SCHEDULE 5

43(1) [Amends ICTA 1988, Sch. 5, para. 2(3).]

43(2) [Amends ICTA 1988, Sch. 5, para. 2(4).]

43(3) [Inserts ICTA 1988, Sch. 5, para. 2(5), (6).]

43(4) [Substitutes ICTA 1988, Sch .5, para. 6(2)–(4).]

Part III – Amendments of Other Enactments

SETTING OF RATES OF INTEREST

44 [Amends FA 1989, s. 178(2)(f).]

CLASS 4 CONTRIBUTIONS

45 [Substitutes SSCBA 1992, s. 16(1)(b).]

REPAYMENT SUPPLEMENTS: CAPITAL GAINS TAX

46(1) [Amends TCGA 1992, s. 283(1).]

46(2) [Substitutes TCGA 1992, s. 283(2).]

46(3) [Amends TCGA 1992, s. 283(4).]

46(4) [*Repeals TCGA* 1992, s. 283(5).]

SCHEDULE 20 – CHANGES FOR FACILITATING SELF-ASSESSMENT: TRANSITIONAL PROVISIONS AND SAVINGS

Section 218

Notes – ITTOIA 2005 makes a number of changes to Sch. 20. See the History notes for details. The legislation in Sch. 20 that is not spent is rewritten and can be principally found at ITTOIA 2005, Sch. 2, para. 52 and 53.

ASSESSMENT UNDER CASES I AND II OF SCHEDULE D

1 [Omitted by ITTOIA 2005, s. 882(1) and Sch. 1, para. 472(2); and repealed by ITTOIA 2005, s. 884 and Sch. 3.]

History – Para. 1 omitted by ITTOIA 2005, s. 882(1) and Sch. 1, para. 472(2); and repealed by ITTOIA 2005, s. 884 and Sch. 3; effective for income tax purposes for 2005–06 onwards (ITTOIA 2005, s. 883(1)).

Cross references – ITTOIA 2005, Sch. 1, para. 52(5): continuance rules in para. 1, despite repeal, for purposes of para. 52.

2 [Omitted by ITTOIA 2005, s. 882(1) and Sch. 1, para. 472(2); and repealed by ITTOIA 2005, s. 884 and Sch. 3.]

History – Para. 2 omitted by ITTOIA 2005, s. 882(1) and Sch. 1, para. 472(2); and repealed by ITTOIA 2005, s. 884 and Sch. 3; effective for income tax purposes for 2005–06 onwards (ITTOIA 2005, s. 883(1)).

3 [Omitted by ITTOIA 2005, s. 882(1) and Sch. 1, para. 472(2); and repealed by ITTOIA 2005, s. 884 and Sch. 3.]

History – Para. 3 omitted by ITTOIA 2005, s. 882(1) and Sch. 1, para. 472(2); and repealed by ITTOIA 2005, s. 884 and Sch. 3; effective for income tax purposes for 2005–06 onwards (ITTOIA 2005, s. 883(1)).

ASSESSMENT UNDER CASE III OF SCHEDULE D

4 [Omitted by ITTOIA 2005, s. 882(1) and Sch. 1, para. 472(2); and repealed by ITTOIA 2005, s. 884 and Sch. 3.]

History – Para. 4. omitted by ITTOIA 2005, s. 882(1) and Sch. 1, para. 472(2); and repealed by ITTOIA 2005, s. 884 and Sch. 3 effective for income tax purposes for 2005–06 onwards (ITTOIA 2005, s. 883(1)).

5 [Omitted by ITTOIA 2005, s. 882(1) and Sch. 1, para. 472(2); and repealed by ITTOIA 2005, s. 884 and Sch. 3.]

History – Para. 5 omitted by ITTOIA 2005, s. 882(1) and Sch. 1, para. 472(2); and repealed by ITTOIA 2005, s. 884 and Sch. 3 effective for income tax purposes for 2005–06 onwards (ITTOIA 2005, s. 883(1)).

ASSESSMENT UNDER CASES IV AND V OF SCHEDULE D

6 [Omitted by ITTOIA 2005, s. 882(1) and Sch. 1, para. 472(2); and repealed by ITTOIA 2005, s. 884 and Sch. 3.]

History – Para. 6 omitted by ITTOIA 2005, s. 882(1) and Sch. 1, para. 472(2); and repealed by ITTOIA 2005, s. 884 and Sch. 3 effective for income tax purposes for 2005–06 onwards (ITTOIA 2005, s. 883(1)).

7 [Omitted by ITTOIA 2005, s. 882(1) and Sch. 1, para. 472(2); and repealed by ITTOIA 2005, s. 884 and Sch. 3.]

History – Para. 7 omitted by ITTOIA 2005, s. 882(1) and Sch. 1, para. 472(2); and repealed by ITTOIA 2005, s. 884 and Sch. 3 effective for income tax purposes for 2005–06 onwards (ITTOIA 2005, s. 883(1)).

LOSS RELIEF

8 [Omitted by ITTOIA 2005, s. 882(1) and Sch. 1, para. 472(2); and repealed by ITTOIA 2005, s. 884 and Sch. 3 effective for income tax purposes for 2005–06 onwards (ITTOIA 2005, s. 883(1)).]

History – Para. 8 omitted by ITTOIA 2005, s. 882(1) and Sch. 1, para. 472(2); and repealed by ITTOIA 2005, s. 884 and Sch. 3 effective for income tax purposes for 2005–06 onwards (ITTOIA 2005, s. 883(1)).

CAPITAL ALLOWANCES

9 [Omitted by ITTOIA 2005, s. 882(1) and Sch. 1, para. 472(2); and repealed by ITTOIA 2005, s. 884 and Sch. 3.]

History – Para. 9 omitted by ITTOIA 2005, s. 882(1) and Sch. 1, para. 472(2); and repealed by ITTOIA 2005, s. 884 and Sch. 3 effective for income tax purposes for 2005–06 onwards (ITTOIA 2005, s. 883(1)).

DOUBLE TAXATION RELIEF

10 [Omitted by ITTOIA 2005, s. 882(1) and Sch. 1, para. 472(2); and repealed by ITTOIA 2005, s. 884 and Sch. 3.]

History – Para. 10 omitted by ITTOIA 2005, s. 882(1) and Sch. 1, para. 472(2); and repealed by ITTOIA 2005, s. 884 and Sch. 3 effective for income tax purposes for 2005–06 onwards (ITTOIA 2005, s. 883(1)).

11(1) This paragraph applies in the case of–

(a) a trade, profession or vocation set up and commenced before 6th April 1994 and continuing after 5th April 1998; or

(b) income from a source arising before the former date and continuing after the latter date.

11(2) Sub-paragraph (3) below applies where–

(a) credit against income tax for the year 1995–96 or any earlier year of assessment is or has been allowed by virtue of subsection (1) of section 804 of the Taxes Act 1988 in respect of any income (**"the original income"**), and

(b) the source of that income ceases in a subsequent year of assessment (**"the subsequent year"**).

11(3) The following shall be set off one against the other, namely–

(a) the amount of the credit which, under Part XVIII of the Taxes Act 1988 (including section 804), has been allowed against income tax in respect of the original income, and

(b) the aggregate of–

(i) the amount of the credit which, apart from that section, would have been so allowed, and

(ii) the difference between the amount of the credit which, on the assumptions mentioned in sub-paragraph (4) below, would have been allowable under Part XVIII of that Act for the year 1996–97 and the amount of credit which has been so allowed;

and if the amount given by paragraph (a) exceeds that given by paragraph (b) above, the person chargeable in respect of income (if any) arising in the subsequent year from the same source as the original income shall be chargeable for that year to an amount of income tax equal to the excess, and the person shall be liable for any tax so chargeable.

11(4) The assumptions are–

(a) that the words "the appropriate percentage of" were omitted from paragraph 2(2) above;

(b) that the words "50 per cent of" were omitted from paragraphs (a), (b) and (c) of paragraph 6(2) above; and

(c) that paragraph 10 above had not been enacted.

11(5) Where the period on the income of which income tax is chargeable for the year 1996–97 is that year, sub-paragraph (3) above shall have effect as if for paragraph (b) there were substituted the following paragraph–

"(b) the amount of the credit which, apart from that section, would have been so allowed;".

11(6) Any reference in sub-paragraph (2) or (3) above to section 804 or Part XVIII of the Taxes Act 1988 includes a reference to the corresponding provisions of any earlier enactments.

11(7) [Omitted by ITA 2007, s. 1027 and Sch. 1, para. 363(3), and repealed by s. 1031 and Sch. 3, Pt. 1.]

History – In para. 11(1) the words at the beginning, "Subject to paragraph 12(2) below,", omitted by ITTOIA 2005, s. 882(1) and Sch. 1, para. 472(3)(a); and repealed by ITTOIA 2005, s. 884 and Sch. 3; effective for income tax purposes for 2005–06 onwards (ITTOIA 2005, s. 883(1). The initial letter "T" of the first word of the para. ("This") amended by CCH.

In para. 11(3) the words "to income tax" substituted for the words "under Case VI of Schedule D" by ITTOIA 2005, s. 882(1) and Sch. 1, para. 472(3)(b) effective for income tax purposes for 2005–06 onwards (ITTOIA 2005, s. 883(1)).

In para. 11(3) the words "be chargeable for that year to an amount of income tax equal to the excess" substituted for the words "be treated as having received in that year a payment chargeable to income tax of an amount such that income tax on it at the basic rate is equal to the excess", by ITA 2007, s. 1027 and Sch. 1, para. 363(2), with effect from 6 April 2007.

In para. 11(3) the words at the end ", and the person shall be liable for any tax so chargeable" inserted by ITTOIA 2005, s. 882(1) and Sch. 1, para. 472(3)(c) effective for income tax purposes for 2005–06 onwards (ITTOIA 2005, s. 883(1)).

Para. 11(7) omitted by ITA 2007, s. 1027 and Sch. 1, para. 363(3), and repealed by s. 1031 and Sch. 3, Pt. 1, with effect from 6 April 2007.

Cross references – ICTA 1988, s. 348: right to deduct income tax from certain annual payments etc. made out of profits chargeable to income tax.

ICTA 1988, Pt. XVIII: (s. 788–816): double taxation relief.

ICTA 1988, s. 804: double taxation relief in respect of income arising in years of commencement.

12 [Omitted by ITTOIA 2005, s. 882(1) and Sch. 1, para. 472(4); and repealed by ITTOIA 2005, s. 884 and Sch. 3.]

History – Para. 12 omitted by ITTOIA 2005, s. 882(1) and Sch. 1, para. 472(4); and repealed by ITTOIA 2005, s. 884 and Sch. 3 effective for income tax purposes for 2005–06 onwards (ITTOIA 2005, s. 883(1)).

13 [Omitted by ITTOIA 2005, s. 882(1) and Sch. 1, para. 472(4); and repealed by ITTOIA 2005, s. 884 *and Sch. 3.]*

History – Para. 13 omitted by ITTOIA 2005, s. 882(1) and Sch. 1, para. 472(4); and repealed by ITTOIA 2005, s. 884 and Sch. 3 effective for income tax purposes for 2005–06 onwards (ITTOIA 2005, s. 883(1)).

SUPPLEMENTAL

14(1) In this Schedule–

(a) any reference to a source of income arising before any date (**"the earlier date"**) and continuing after or ceasing before some other date (**"the later date"**) is a reference to a source of income arising to any person before the earlier date and continuing to be possessed by that person after, or (as the case may be) ceasing to be possessed by that person before, the later date; and

(b) any reference to a source of income includes a reference to a part of such a source.

14(2) Where, as respects income from any source, income tax is to be charged under Case IV or V of Schedule D by reference to the amounts of income received in the United Kingdom, the source shall be treated for the purposes of this Schedule as arising on the date on which the first amount of income is so received.

SCHEDULE 21 – LLOYD'S UNDERWRITERS: INDIVIDUALS

Section 228

YEAR OF ASSESSMENT IN WHICH PROFITS OR LOSSES ARISE

1(1) [Repealed by F(No. 2)A 1997, s. 52 and Sch. 8, Pt. II(11).]

1(2) [Repeals FA 1993, s. 171(3).]

1(3) In this paragraph–

(a) [repealed by F(No. 2)A 1997, s. 52 and Sch. 8, Pt. II(11)]

(b) sub-paragraph (2) has effect for the year 1996–97 and subsequent years of assessment.

History – Para. 1(1) and (3)(a) repealed by F(No. 2)A 1997, s. 52 and Sch. 8, Pt. II(11) with effect in relation to distributions made on or after 6 April 1999.

2(1) [Substitutes FA 1993, s. 172(1).]

2(2) [Spent.]

PREMIUMS TRUST FUNDS

3 [Substitutes FA 1993, s. 174(1).]

REINSURANCE TO CLOSE

4(1) [Inserts FA 1993, s. 177(5).]

4(2) This paragraph has effect for the underwriting year 1993 and subsequent underwriting years.

STOP-LOSS AND QUOTA SHARE INSURANCE

5(1) [Amends FA 1993, s. 178(2).]

5(2) This paragraph has effect as respects insurance money and other amounts payable in respect of losses declared in the underwriting year 1997 or subsequent underwriting years.

CESSATION ETC.

6(1) [Amends FA 1993, s. 179(2) and repeals FA 1993, s. 179(3).]

6(2) [Inserts FA 1993, s. 179A.]

6(3) This paragraph has effect in any case where the member dies after the end of the year 1993–94.

REGULATIONS

7(1) [Repeals FA 1993, s. 182(2)–(4).]

7(2) This paragraph has effect for the year 1997–98 and subsequent years of assessment.

INTERPRETATION

8(1) [Amends FA 1993, s. 184(1).]

8(2) [Amends FA 1993, s. 184(2)(c).]

ASSESSMENT AND COLLECTION OF TAX

9 [Omitted by F(No. 2)A 2005, s. 45(4) and repealed by F(No. 2)A 2005, s. 70 and Sch. 11, Pt. 2(11).]

History – Para. 9 omitted by F(No. 2)A 2005, s. 45(4) and repealed by F(No. 2)A 2005, s. 70 and Sch. 11, Pt. 2(11) with effect from 1 January 2006, although for the purposes of enabling regulations to be made under this section or under FA 1993, s. 182(1)(a), the omission and repeal took effect from 20 July 2005 (Royal Assent) (F(No. 2)A 2005, s. 45(8)).

10 [Omitted by F(No. 2)A 2005, s. 45(4) and repealed by F(No. 2)A 2005, s. 70 and Sch. 11, Pt. 2(11).]

History – Para. 10 omitted by F(No. 2)A 2005, s. 45(4) and repealed by F(No. 2)A 2005, s. 70 and Sch. 11, Pt. 2(11) with effect from 1 January 2006, although for the purposes of enabling regulations to be made under this section or under FA 1993, s. 182(1)(a), the omission and repeal took effect from 20 July 2005 (Royal Assent) (F(No. 2)A 2005, s. 45(8)).

11 [Repealed by F(No. 2)A 1997, s. 52 and Sch. 8, Pt. II(5) with effect in relation to distributions made on or after 2 July 1997.]

SPECIAL RESERVE FUNDS

12(1) [Inserts definition of "payment" in FA 1993, Sch. 20, para. 1(1).]

12(2) [Amends FA 1993, Sch. 20, para. 7(2).]

12(3) This paragraph has effect for the year 1992–93 and subsequent years of assessment.

13(1) [Substitutes FA 1993, Sch. 20, para. 8.]

13(2) This paragraph has effect for the year 1994–95 and subsequent years of assessment.

14(1) [Amends FA 1993, Sch. 20, para. 10(1)–(4).]

14(2) [Inserts FA 1993, Sch. 20, para. 10(5).]

14(3) [Spent.]

15(1) [Amends FA 1993, Sch. 20, para. 11(2).]

15(2) [Amends FA 1993, Sch. 20, para. 11(3), (4).]

15(3) [Substitutes FA 1993, Sch. 20, para. 11(5).]

16(1) [Amends FA 1993, Sch. 20, para. 13(1).]

16(2) [Inserts FA 1993, Sch. 20, para. 13(6).]

16(3) This paragraph has effect for the year 1992–93 and subsequent years of assessment.

FINANCE ACT 1995

(1995 Chapter 4)

[*1st May 1995*]

ARRANGEMENT OF SECTIONS

PART III – INCOME TAX, CORPORATION TAX AND CAPITAL GAINS TAX

PART III – INCOME TAX, CORPORATION TAX AND CAPITAL GAINS TAX

INCOME TAX: CHARGE, RATES AND RELIEFS

35 Charge and rates of income tax for 1995–96

35(1)–(2) [Repealed by ITA 2007, s. 1031 and Sch. 3, Pt. 1.]

History – S. 35 repealed by ITA 2007, Sch. 3, Pt. 1, with effect from 6 April 2007.

36 Personal allowance

36 [Repealed by ITA 2007, Sch. 3, Pt. 1.]

History – S. 36 repealed by ITA 2007, s. 1031 and Sch. 3, Pt. 1, with effect from 6 April 2007.

CORPORATION TAX: CHARGE AND RATE

37 Charge and rate of corporation tax for 1995

37 [Spent: specified rate of corporation tax for financial year 1995.]

38 Small companies

38 [Repealed by CTA 2010, s. 1181 and Sch. 3, Pt. 1.]

History – S. 38 repealed by CTA 2010, s. 1181 and Sch. 3, Pt. 1, with effect for accounting periods ending on or after 1 April 2010.

TAXATION OF INCOME FROM LAND

40 Non-residents and their representatives

40(1) [Repealed by ITA 2007, s. 1031 and Sch. 3, Pt. 1.]

40(2) [Repealed by ITA 2007, s. 1031 and Sch. 3, Pt. 1.]

40(3) [Repeals ICTA 1988, s. 43.]

History – S. 40(1) repealed by ITA 2007, s. 1031 and Sch. 3, Pt. 1, with effect from 6 April 2007.
S. 40(2) repealed by ITA 2007, s. 1031 and Sch. 3, Pt. 1, with effect from 6 April 2007.

42 Abolition of interest relief for commercially let property

42(1) [Repealed by FA 1999, s. 139 and Sch. 20, Pt. III(7).]

(a) [repealed by ITA 2007, s. 1031 and Sch. 3, Pt. 1,]

(b)–(e) [Amends 355, 356(1), 356B(5), 357A(7), 357B(1)(c), (6), and 357C(1)(e), (2).]

42(3)–(5) [Repealed by Statute Law (Repeals) Act 2013, s. 1 and Sch. 1, Pt. 10.]

42(6) [Repealed by FA 1996, Sch. 41, Pt. V(3).]

History – S. 42(1) and (2)(b)–(e) repealed by FA 1999, s. 139 and Sch. 20, Pt. III(7), with effect in relation to any payment of interest falling within FA 1999, s. 38(3) or (4) (broadly, payments made on or after 6 April 2000, or on or after 9 March 1999 and before 6 April 2000 but not falling due until on or after 6 April 2000).
S. 42(2)(a) repealed by ITA 2007, s. 1031 and Sch. 3, Pt. 1, with effect from 6 April 2007.
S. 42(3)–(5) repealed by Statute Law (Repeals) Act 2013, s. 1 and Sch. 1, Pt. 10, with effect from 31 January 2013.
S. 42(6) repealed by FA 1996, Sch. 41, Pt. V(3) with effect for accounting periods ending after 31 March 1996.

BENEFITS IN KIND

43 Cars available for private use

43 [Repealed by ITEPA 2003, Sch. 8, Pt. 1.]

History – S. 43 repealed by ITEPA 2003, Sch. 8, Pt. 1 which has effect for the tax year 2003–04 and subsequent tax years.

44 Cars: accessories for the disabled

44 [Repealed by ITEPA 2003, Sch. 8, Pt. 1.]

History – S. 44 repealed by ITEPA 2003, Sch. 8, Pt. 1 which has effect for the tax year 2003–04 and subsequent tax years.

45 Beneficial loan arrangements: replacement loans

45 [Repealed by ITEPA 2003, Sch. 8, Pt. 1.]

History – S. 45 repealed by ITEPA 2003, Sch. 8, Pt. 1 which has effect for the tax year 2003–04 and subsequent tax years.

CHARGEABLE GAINS

46 Relief on re-investment: property companies etc.

46(1) Chapter IA of Part V of the Taxation of Chargeable Gains Act 1992 (roll-over relief on re-investment) shall be amended as follows.

46(2) [Inserts TCGA 1992, s. 164A(13).]

46(3) [Inserts TCGA 1992, s. 164F(2A).]

46(4) [Inserts TCGA 1992, s. 164I(4A).]

47 Relief on re-investment: amount of relief, etc.

47(1) Chapter IA of Part V of the Taxation of Chargeable Gains Act 1992 (roll-over relief on re-investment) shall be amended as follows.

47(2) [Inserts TCGA 1992, s. 164A(14).]

47(3) [Inserts TCGA 1992, s. 164F(10C).]

47(4) [Inserts TCGA 1992, s. 164FF.]

47(5) [Inserts TCGA 1992, s. 164FG.]

47(6) Subsection (4) above (and subsections (1) to (3) above so far as relating to subsection (4) above) shall apply to a claim as respects a qualifying investment if–

(a) the qualifying investment is acquired on or after 20th June 1994; or

(b) the claim is under section 164A(2) and relates to a disposal on or after that day; or

(c) the claim is under subsection (10A) of section 164F and relates to a gain which (apart from that subsection) would accrue on or after that day.

47(7) Subsection (5) above (and subsections (1) to (3) above so far as relating to subsection (5) above) shall apply to a claim as respects a qualifying investment if–

(a) the qualifying investment is acquired on or after 20th June 1994; or

(b) the claim is under section 164A(2) and relates to a disposal on or after that day; or

(c) the claim is under subsection (10A) of section 164F and relates to a gain which (apart from that subsection) would accrue on or after that day; or

(d) there is another claim as respects that qualifying investment which is under section 164A(2) and which relates to a disposal on or after that day; or

(e) there is another claim as respects that qualifying investment which is under subsection (10A) of section 164F and which relates to a gain which (apart from that subsection) would accrue on or after that day.

47(8) Any such adjustment as is appropriate in consequence of this section may be made (whether by discharge or repayment of tax, the making of an assessment or otherwise).

48 Roll-over relief and groups of companies

48(1) [Inserts TCGA 1992, s. 175(2A)–(2C).]

48(2) [Inserts TCGA 1992, s. 247(5A).]

48(3) Subject to subsection (4) below–

(a) the subsection inserted into section 175 of the Taxation of Chargeable Gains Act 1992 by subsection (1) above as subsection (2A) shall be deemed always to have had effect; and

(b) the earlier enactments corresponding to that section shall be deemed to have contained provision to the same effect as that subsection (2A).

48(4) Paragraph (c) of that subsection (2A) shall not apply unless the claim is made on or after 29th November 1994.

48(5) The subsection inserted into section 175 of the Taxation of Chargeable Gains Act 1992 by subsection (1) above as subsection (2B) shall apply where the disposal or the acquisition is on or after 29th November 1994; and the subsection so inserted as subsection (2C) shall apply where the acquisition is on or after that date.

48(6) The subsection inserted into section 247 of the Taxation of Chargeable Gains Act 1992 by subsection (2) above shall apply–

(a) so far as it relates to section 175(2A), where the disposal or the acquisition is on or after 29th November 1994; and

(b) so far as it relates to section 175(2C), where the acquisition is on or after that date.

49 De-grouping charges

49(1) [Inserts TCGA 1992, s. 179(2A) and (2B).]

49(2) [Inserts TCGA 1992, s. 179(9A).]

49(3) This section has effect in relation to a company in any case in which the time of the company's ceasing to be a member of the second group is on or after 29th November 1994.

INSURANCE COMPANIES AND FRIENDLY SOCIETIES

51 Companies carrying on life assurance business

51 [Omitted by FA 2012, s. 146 and Sch. 16, para. 247.]

History – S. 51 omitted by FA 2012, s. 146 and Sch. 16, para. 247 in relation to accounting periods beginning on or after 1 January 2013 (FA 2012, s. 148) but subject to transitional provisions in FA 2012, Sch. 17. Where an accounting period would otherwise straddle 1 January 2013, it is deemed to end on 31 December 2012 (FA 2012, s. 149).

52 Meaning of "insurance company"

52(1) [Amends ICTA 1988, s. 431(2).]

52(2) [Repealed by FA 2002, s. 141 and Sch. 40, Pt. 3(10).]

52(3) [Repealed by FA 2002, s. 141 and Sch. 40, Pt. 3(13).]

52(4) [Amends IHTA 1984, s. 59(3)(b).]

52(5) Subsections (1) to (3) above shall have effect in relation to any accounting period ending after 30th June 1994; and subsection (4) above shall have effect for the purposes of the making, on an anniversary or other occasion after that date, of any charge to tax under section 64 or 65 of the Inheritance Tax Act 1984.

History – S. 52(2) repealed by FA 2002, s. 141 and Sch. 40, Pt. 3(10) with effect in relation to accounting periods beginning on or after 1 October 2002.
S. 52(3) repealed by FA 2002, s. 141 and Sch. 40, Pt. 3(13) with effect in relation to accounting periods beginning on or after 1 October 2002.

53 Transfer of life insurance business

53(1) The amendments specified in Schedule 9 to this Act (which relate to enactments referring to the transfer of the whole or part of the long term business of an insurance company) shall have effect.

53(2) This section and that Schedule shall have effect in relation to any transfers sanctioned or authorised after 30th June 1994.

54 Friendly societies

54 Schedule 10 to this Act (which makes provision about friendly societies) shall have effect.

INSURANCE POLICIES

55 Qualifying life insurance policies

55(1) Subject to subsections (2) and (3) below–

(a) paragraph 21 of Schedule 15 to the Taxes Act 1988 (certification of policies and of standard forms etc.) shall not apply, in relation to any time on or after the appointed date, for determining whether a policy is or would be a qualifying policy at that time; and

(b) no certificate may be issued under that paragraph at any time on or after that date except, in the case of a certificate under subparagraph (1)(a) of that paragraph, in relation to a time before that date.

55(2) Subsection (1) above shall not affect the right of any person to bring or continue with an appeal under paragraph 21(3) of that Schedule against either a refusal before the appointed date to certify any policy or a refusal on or after that date to certify any policy in relation to times before that date.

55(3) A certificate issued–

(a) before the appointed date in pursuance of paragraph 21(1)(a) of that Schedule, or

(b) in pursuance of a determination on an appeal determined after that date by virtue of subsection (2) above,

shall, in relation to any time on or after that date or, as the case may be, the date on which it is issued, be conclusive evidence that the policy to which it relates is (subject to paragraphs A1(2), B2(2) and B3(3) of that Schedule and to any variation of the policy) a qualifying policy.

55(4) Paragraph 22 of that Schedule (certificates from body issuing policy) shall cease to have effect in relation to any time on or after the appointed date.

55(5) Paragraph 24 of that Schedule (policies issued by non-resident companies) shall have effect in relation to times on or after the appointed date–

(a) [substitutes ICTA 1988, Sch. 15, para. 24(2) and (2A),]

(b) [amends ICTA 1988, Sch. 15, para. 24(3) and omits (4).]

55(6) [Substitutes ICTA 1988, Sch. 15, para. 25(2).]

55(7) [Substitutes ICTA 1988, Sch. 15, para. 27(1).]

55(8) [Omitted by FA 2008, s. 36 and Sch. 14, para. 17(d); s. 55(8)(b) previously omitted by ITTOIA 2005, s. 884.]

55(9) In this section **"the appointed date"** means such date as may be specified for the purpose in an order made by the Board.

Commencement Date – The appointed date for the purpose of s. 55 is 6 April 2013 (SI 2013/759, art. 2).

History – In s. 55(3), the words "to paragraphs A1(2), B2(2) and B3(3) of that Schedule and" inserted by FA 2013, s. 25 and Sch. 9, para. 6(1), with effect from 6 April 2013 ("the appointed date" under s. 55(9)).
S. 55(8) omitted by FA 2008, s. 36 and Sch. 14, para. 17(d), with effect for accounting periods beginning on or after 1 April 2008 (so far as relating to corporation tax) and for the tax year 2008–09 (so far as relating to income tax). S. 55(8)(b) previously repealed by ITTOIA 2005, s. 884 and Sch. 3; effective for income tax purposes for 2005–06 onwards and for corporation tax purposes for accounting periods ending after 5 April 2005.
S. 55(9) inserted by FA 1996, s. 162(1).
The words "the appointed date" substituted for the words "5th May 1996" wherever they occurred inserted by FA 1996, s. 162(1).

Cross references – ICTA 1988, Sch. 15, para. 24(2A) (as inserted by s. 55(5)) and 25(2): qualifying life insurance policies.

56 Foreign life policies etc.

56 [Omitted by ITTOIA 2005, s. 882(1) and Sch. 1, para. 476; and repealed by ITTOIA 2005, s. 884 and Sch. 3.]

History – S. 56 omitted by ITTOIA 2005, s. 882(1) and Sch. 1, para. 476; and repealed by ITTOIA 2005, s. 884 and Sch. 3 effective for income tax purposes for 2005–06 onwards and for corporation tax purposes for accounting periods ending after 5 April 2005 (ITTOIA 2005, s. 883(1)).

Notes – S. 56 is mainly rewritten at ITTOIA 2005, s. 531–534.

57 Duties of insurers in relation to life policies etc.

57 [Repealed by Statute Law (Repeals) Act 2013, s. 1 and Sch. 1, Pt. 10.]

History – S. 57 repealed by Statute Law (Repeals) Act 2013, s. 1 and Sch. 1, Pt. 10, with effect from 31 January 2013.

PENSIONS

58 Personal pensions: income withdrawals

58 [Repealed by FA 2004, s. 326 and Sch. 42, Pt. 3.]

History – S. 58 repealed by FA 2004, s. 326 and Sch. 42, Pt. 3, with effect from 6 April 2006 subject to FA 2004, Sch. 36.

59 Pensions: meaning of insurance company etc.

59 [Repealed by FA 2004, s. 326 and Sch. 42, Pt. 3.]

History – S. 59 repealed by FA 2004, s. 326 and Sch. 42, Pt. 3, with effect from 6 April 2006 subject to FA 2004, Sch. 36. Former s. 59 substituted ICTA 1988, s. 591(3) and s. 599(8), amended ICTA 1988, s. 630 and inserted ICTA 1988, s. 659B and 659C.

60 Application of section 59

60 [Repealed by FA 2004, s. 326 and Sch. 42, Pt. 3.]

History – S. 60 repealed by FA 2004, s. 326 and Sch. 42, Pt. 3, with effect from 6 April 2006 subject to FA 2004, Sch. 36. Former s. 60 read as follows:

"Application of section 59

60(1) Section 59(2) above and the new section 659B, so far as relating to section 591(2)(g), shall apply in relation to a scheme not approved by virtue of section 591 before the day on which this Act is passed.
60(2) Section 59(3) above and the new section 659B, so far as relating to section 599(7), shall apply where tax is charged under section 599 on or after the day on which this Act is passed.
60(3) Section 59(4) above and the new section 659B, so far as relating to Chapter IV of Part XIV, shall apply in relation to a scheme not approved under that Chapter before the day on which this Act is passed.
60(4) Subsection (5) below applies where–
(a) a scheme is approved under Chapter IV of Part XIV before the day on which this Act is passed,
(b) on or after that day the person who established the scheme proposes to amend it, and
(c) the scheme as proposed to be amended would make provision such that, if the scheme had not been approved before that day, section 59(4) above and the new section 659B (so far as relating to that Chapter) would allow the Board to approve it.
60(5) The Board may at their discretion approve the amendment notwithstanding anything in Chapter IV of Part XIV, and if the amendment is made–
(a) section 59(4) above and the new section 659B, so far as relating to that Chapter, shall apply in relation to the scheme, and
(b) any question as to the validity of the Board's approval of the scheme shall be determined accordingly.".

61 Cessation of approval of certain retirement benefits schemes

61 [Repealed by FA 2004, s. 326 and Sch. 42, Pt. 3.]

History – S. 61 repealed by FA 2004, s. 326 and Sch. 42, Pt. 3, with effect from 6 April 2006 subject to FA 2004, Sch. 36. Former s. 61 inserted ICTA 1988, s. 591C and 591D and TCGA 1992, s. 239A.

Cross references – ICTA 1988, s. 591B: withdrawal of Board's approval from an approved scheme to have effect from date specified by the Board.

SAVING AND INVESTMENT: GENERAL

62 Follow-up TESSAs

62 [Repealed by ITTOIA 2005, s. 884 and Sch. 3.]

History – S. 62 repealed by ITTOIA 2005, s. 884 and Sch. 3 effective for income tax purposes for 2005–06 onwards and for corporation tax purposes for accounting periods ending after 5 April 2005 (ITTOIA 2005, s. 883(1)).

63 TESSAs: European institutions

63 [Repealed by ITTOIA 2005, s. 884 and Sch. 3.]

History – S. 63 repealed by ITTOIA 2005, s. 884 and Sch. 3 effective for income tax purposes for 2005–06 onwards and for corporation tax purposes for accounting periods ending after 5 April 2005 (ITTOIA 2005, s. 883(1)).

64 Personal equity plans: tax representatives

64 [Repealed by ITTOIA 2005, s. 884 and Sch. 3.]

History – S. 64 repealed by ITTOIA 2005, s. 884 and Sch. 3 effective for income tax purposes for 2005–06 onwards and for corporation tax purposes for accounting periods ending after 5 April 2005 (ITTOIA 2005, s. 883(1)).

Notes – The repealed material is mainly rewritten at ITTOIA 2005, s. 697 and 698.

65 Contractual savings schemes

65 [Repealed by ITTOIA 2005, s. 884 and Sch. 3.]

History – S. 65 repealed by ITTOIA 2005, s. 884 and Sch. 3 effective for income tax purposes for 2005–06 onwards and for corporation tax purposes for accounting periods ending after 5 April 2005 (ITTOIA 2005, s. 883(1)).

66 Enterprise investment scheme: ICTA amendments

66 [Repealed by ITA 2007, s. 1031 and Sch. 3, Pt. 2.]

History – S. 66 repealed by ITA 2007, s. 1031 and Sch. 3, Pt. 2, with effect in relation to shares issued after 5 April 2007.

67 Enterprise investment scheme: TCGA amendments

67 Schedule 13 to this Act (which contains amendments relating to chargeable gains as regards the enterprise investment scheme) shall have effect.

68 Business expansion scheme: ICTA amendments

68(1) Chapter III of Part VII of the Taxes Act 1988 as it has effect in relation to shares issued before 1st January 1994 (the business expansion scheme) shall be amended as follows.

68(2) [Inserts ICTA 1988, s. 289(12A).]

68(3) [Inserts ICTA 1988, s. 305(5) and (6).]

69 Business expansion scheme: TCGA amendments

69 [Inserts TCGA 1992, s. 150(8A)–(8C).]

VENTURE CAPITAL TRUSTS

70 Approval of companies as trusts

70 [Repealed by ITA 2007, s. 1031 and Sch. 3, Pt. 1.]

History – S. 70 repealed by ITA 2007, s. 1031 and Sch. 3, Pt. 1, with effect from 6 April 2007.

71 Income tax relief

71 [Repealed by ITA 2007, s. 1031 and Sch. 3, Pt. 1.]

History – S. 71 repealed by ITA 2007, s. 1031 and Sch. 3, Pt. 1, with effect from 6 April 2007.

72 Capital gains

72(1) The Taxation of Chargeable Gains Act 1992 shall be amended as follows.

72(2) [Amends TCGA 1992, s. 100(1).]

72(3) [Inserts TCGA 1992, s. 151A and 151B.]

72(4) [Repealed by FA 2004, s. 326 and Sch. 42, Pt. 2(13).]

72(5) [Amends TCGA 1992, s. 257(1).]

72(6) [Repealed by FA 2004, s. 326 and Sch. 42, Pt. 2(14).]

72(7) [Amends TCGA 1992, s. 288(1).]

72(8) Subsection (2) above shall have effect in relation to gains accruing on or after 6th April 1995 and the other provisions of this section have effect for the year 1995–96 and subsequent years of assessment.

History – S. 72(4) repealed by FA 2004, s. 326 and Sch. 42, Pt. 2(13), with effect in relation to shares issued on or after 6 April 2004. S. 72(4) introduced FA 1995, Sch. 16 which became TCGA 1992, Sch. 5C. However, the repeal does not affect the continuing operation of TCGA 1992, Sch. 5C for the purposes of TCGA 1992, s. 151B(8)(b)(ii) (FA 2004, s. 94 and Sch. 19, para. 7).
S. 72(6) repealed by FA 2004, s. 326 and Sch. 42, Pt. 2(14) with effect in relation to gains accruing on or after 6 April 2004 (FA 2004, s. 116 and Sch. 21, para. 10(8)).

73 Regulations

73 [Omitted by ITA 2007, s. 1027 and Sch. 1, para. 365 and repealed by s. 1031 and Sch. 3, Pt. 1.]

History – S. 73 omitted by ITA 2007, s. 1027 and Sch. 1, para. 365 and repealed by s. 1031 and Sch. 3, Pt. 1, with effect from 6 April 2007.

Notes – S. 73 rewritten as follows:
S. 73(1): ITA 2007, s. 272(1), (2).
S. 73(2): ITA 2007, s. 272(3), 284.

SETTLEMENTS AND ESTATES

74 Settlements: liability of settlor

74(1) Schedule 17 to this Act has effect with respect to settlements and the liability of the settlor, as follows–

Part I inserts new provisions in place of sections 660 to 676 and 683 to 685 of the Taxes Act 1988,

Part II makes minor and consequential amendments of that Act, and

Part III contains consequential amendments of other enactments.

74(2) The amendments made by Schedule 17 have effect for the year 1995–96 and subsequent years of assessment and apply to every settlement, wherever and whenever it was made or entered into.

75 Deceased persons' estates: taxation of beneficiaries

75 Part XVI of the Taxes Act 1988 (deceased persons' estates) shall have effect with the amendments specified in Schedule 18 to this Act.

76 Untaxed income of a deceased person's estate

76(1) [Repealed by F(No. 2)A 1997, s. 52 and Sch. 8, Pt. II(11), with effect in relation to distributions made on or after 6 April 1999.]

76(2) [Repealed by ITTOIA 2005, s. 884 and Sch. 3.]

76(3) [Repealed by ITTOIA 2005, s. 884 and Sch. 3.]

76(4) [Repealed by CTA 2009, s. 1326 and Sch. 3, Pt. 1.]

76(5) [Repealed by CTA 2009, s. 1326 and Sch. 3. Pt. 1.]

76(6) [Repealed by CTA 2009, s. 1326 and Sch. 3. Pt. 1.]

History – S. 76(2) repealed by ITTOIA 2005, s. 884 and Sch. 3 effective for income tax purposes for 2005–06 onwards and for corporation tax purposes for accounting periods ending after 5 April 2005 (ITTOIA 2005, s. 883(1)).
S. 76(3) repealed by ITTOIA 2005, s. 884 and Sch. 3 effective for income tax purposes for 2005–06 onwards and for corporation tax purposes for accounting periods ending after 5 April 2005 (ITTOIA 2005, s. 883(1)).
S. 76(4) repealed by CTA 2009, s. 1326 and Sch. 3, Pt. 1, with effect for corporation tax purposes for accounting periods ending on or after 1 April 2009, and for income tax and capital gains tax purposes for the tax year 2009–10 and subsequent tax years.
S. 76(5) repealed by CTA 2009, s. 1326 and Sch. 3, Pt. 1, with effect for corporation tax purposes for accounting periods ending on or after 1 April 2009, and for income tax and capital gains tax purposes for the tax year 2009–10 and subsequent tax years.
S. 76(6) repealed by CTA 2009, s. 1326 and Sch. 3, Pt. 1, with effect for corporation tax purposes for accounting periods ending on or after 1 April 2009, and for income tax and capital gains tax purposes for the tax year 2009–10 and subsequent tax years.

SECURITIES

79 Sale and repurchase of securities: exclusion from accrued income scheme

79 [Repealed by ITA 2007, s. 1031 and Sch. 3, Pt. 1.]

History – S. 79 repealed by ITA 2007, s. 1031 and Sch. 3, Pt. 1, with effect from 6 April 2007.

Notes – S. 79 rewritten as follows:
S. 79(1): ITA 2007, s. 654(2), (3), (4), (5), (7), (8), 655(1), (2), 1021(1).
S. 79(3): ITA 2007, Sch. 2, para. 125.
S. 79(4): ITA 2007, Sch. 2, para. 125.

80 Treatment of price differential on sale and repurchase of securities

80(1) [Repealed by FA 2007, s. 114 and Sch. 27, Pt. 2(14).]

80(2) [Repealed by FA 1996, s. 205 and Sch. 41, Pt. V(21).]

80(3) [Repealed by FA 2007, s. 114 and Sch. 27, Pt. 2(14).]

80(4) [Inserts TCGA 1992, s. 263A.]

80(5) This section shall have effect where the agreement to sell the securities is entered into on or after the date on which this Act is passed.

History – S. 80(1) repealed by FA 2007, s. 114 and Sch. 27, Pt. 2(14), with effect in relation to arrangements that comes into force on or after 1 October 2007 (SI 2007/2483).
S. 80(2) repealed by FA 1996, s. 205 and Sch. 41, Pt. V(21), for sales or transfers of securities or other property where the initial agreement to sell or transfer was made after 6 November 1996 (SI 1996/2646).
S. 80(3) repealed by FA 2007, s. 114 and Sch. 27, Pt. 2(14), with effect in relation to arrangements that comes into force on or after 1 October 2007 (SI 2007/2483).

81 Manufactured interest payments: exclusion from bond-washing provisions

81 [Omitted by FA 2008, s. 66(4)(f).]

History – S. 81 omitted by FA 2008, s. 66(4)(f), with effect in relation to cases where the purchase by the first buyer (within the meaning of ICTA 1988, s. 731(2)) is made on or after 1 April 2008.

83 Power to make special provisions for special cases

83(1) [Omitted by FA 2008, s. 43 and Sch. 17, para. 35(2)(a).]

83(2) [Inserts FA 1993, s. 182(1)(ca) and FA 1994, s. 229(ca).]

History – S. 83(1) omitted by FA 2008, s. 43 and Sch. 17, para. 35(2)(a), with effect from 21 July 2008.

INTEREST

86 Deduction of tax from interest on deposits

86 [Repealed by ITA 2007, s. 1031 and Sch. 3, Pt. 1.]

History – S. 86 repealed by ITA 2007, s. 1031 and Sch. 3, Pt. 1, with effect from 6 April 2007.

Notes – S. 86 rewritten as follows:
S. 86(1): ITA 2007, s. 856(2), (6).
S. 86(2): ITA 2007, s. 873(1), (2).
S. 86(3): ITA 2007, s. 858(2), (3), 859(2), (3), 860(2), (3), 861(2), (3).
S. 86(4): ITA 2007, Sch. 2, para. 154(1), (2), (3).
S. 86(5): ITA 2007, s. 858(4), 859(4), 861(4).
S. 86(6): ITA 2007, s. 873(3), (4), (5), (6).
S. 86(7): ITA 2007, s. 860(4), 861(5).
S. 86(12): ITA 2007, Sch. 2, para. 155(5).

87 Interest payments deemed to be distributions

87 [Repealed by CTA 2010, s. 1181 and Sch. 3, Pt. 1.]

History – S. 87 repealed by CTA 2010, s. 1181 and Sch. 3, Pt. 1, with effect for corporation tax purposes for accounting periods ending on or after 1 April 2010, and for income tax and capital gains tax purposes for the tax year 2010–11 and subsequent tax years.
S. 87(1) previously repealed by FA 2004, s. 326 and Sch. 42, Pt. 2(2), in relation to chargeable periods beginning on or after 1 April 2004 (FA 2004, s. 37(2)).
S. 87(3) previously repealed by FA 2004, s. 326 and Sch. 42(2), in relation to chargeable periods beginning on or after 1 April 2004 (FA 2004, s. 37(2)).
S. 87(4) previously repealed by FA 2004, s. 326 and Sch. 42, Pt. 2(2), in relation to chargeable periods beginning on or after 1 April 2004 (FA 2004, s. 37(2)).
S. 87(5) previously repealed by ITA 2007, s. 1031 and Sch. 3, Pt. 1, with effect from 6 April 2007. See ITA 2007, Sch. 2, for transitional and saving provisions.
S. 87(5) previously repealed by FA 2004, s. 326 and Sch. 42, Pt. 2(2), in relation to chargeable periods beginning on or after 1 April 2004 (FA 2004, s. 37(2)). .
S. 87(6) previously repealed by FA 1996, Sch. 41, Pt. V(3), with effect for 1996–97 and subsequent years of assessment (income tax) and for accounting periods ending after 31 March 1996 (corporation tax).

RELIEFS

90 Relief for post-cessation expenditure

90 [Omitted by ITA 2007, s. 1027 and Sch. 1, para. 366 and repealed by s. 1031 and Sch. 3, Pt. 1.]

History – S. 90 repealed by ITA 2007, s. 1027 and Sch. 1, para. 366 and s. 1031 and Sch. 1, Pt. 1, with effect from 6 April 2007.

Notes – S. 90 rewritten as follows:
S. 90(1): ITA 2007, s. 96(1), (2), (3), (4), 97(1), (2), (3), (4), (5), 98(2), (3), (5), (6), (7), (8), 99(1), (2), (3), (4), (5), 100(1), (2), 125(1), (2), (3), (4).
S. 90(4): ITA 2007, Sch. 1, para. 329.
S. 90(5): ITA 2007, Sch. 1, para. 329.

91 Employee liabilities and indemnity insurance

91 [Repealed by ITEPA 2003, Sch. 8, Pt. 1.]

History – S. 91 repealed by ITEPA 2003, Sch. 8, Pt. 1 which has effect for the tax year 2003–04 and subsequent tax years.

92 Post-employment deductions

92 [Repealed by ITEPA 2003, Sch. 8, Pt. 1.]

History – S. 92 repealed by ITEPA 2003, Sch. 8, Pt. 1 which has effect for the tax year 2003–04 and subsequent tax years.

Notes – S. 92 rewritten as follows:
S. 92(1): ITEPA 2003, s. 555(1), (2), (3) and ITEPA 2003, s. 564(1).
S. 92(2): ITEPA 2003, s. 556(1), s. 558, s. 559, s. 560(2), (3), (4), (5), s. 561(1), (2), (3), (4), (5) and (6).
S. 92(3) is unnecessary and so it has not been rewritten.
S. 92(4): s. 557(1), (2), s. 563 and s. 718.
S. 92(5): s. 555(1), s. 557(3) and (4).
S. 92(6), (7) and (8): TCGA 1992, s. 263ZA by virtue of ITEPA 2003, Sch. 6, para. 217.
S. 92(9): ITEPA 2003, s. 563.
S. 92(10): s. 409(1), (3), (4), (5), s. 410(1), (3), (4) and (5).

93 Incidental overnight expenses etc.

93 [Repealed by ITEPA 2003, Sch. 8, Pt. 1.]

History – S. 93 has been repealed by ITEPA 2003, Sch. 8, Pt. 1 which has effect for the tax year 2003–04 and subsequent tax years.

CAPITAL ALLOWANCES: SHIPS

94 Deferment of balancing charges in respect of ships

94 [Repealed by CAA 2001, s. 580 and Sch. 4.]

History – S. 94 repealed by CAA 2001, s. 580 and Sch. 4, with effect as respects allowances and charges falling to be made for chargeable periods ending, for income tax purposes, on or after 6 April 2001, and for corporation tax purposes, on or after 1 April 2001.

95 Reimposition of deferred charge

95 [Repealed by CAA 2001, s. 580 and Sch. 4.]

History – S. 95 repealed by CAA 2001, s. 580 and Sch. 4, with effect as respects allowances and charges falling to be made for chargeable periods ending, for income tax purposes, on or after 6 April 2001, and for corporation tax purposes, on or after 1 April 2001.

96 Ships in respect of which charge may be deferred

96 [Repealed by CAA 2001, s. 580 and Sch. 4.]

History – S. 96 repealed by CAA 2001, s. 580 and Sch. 4, with effect as respects allowances and charges falling to be made for chargeable periods ending, for income tax purposes, on or after 6 April 2001, and for corporation tax purposes, on or after 1 April 2001.

97 Procedural provisions relating to deferred charges

97(1) [Repealed by CAA 2001, s. 580 and Sch. 4.]

97(2) [Repealed by CAA 2001, s. 580 and Sch. 4.]

97(3) [Repealed by CAA 2001, s. 580 and Sch. 4.]

History – S. 97 repealed by CAA 2001, s. 580 and Sch. 4, with effect as respects allowances and charges falling to be made for chargeable periods ending, for income tax purposes, on or after 6 April 2001, and for corporation tax purposes, on or after 1 April 2001.

98 Deferred charges: commencement and transitional provisions

98 [Repealed by CAA 2001, s. 580 and Sch. 4.]

History – S. 98 repealed by CAA 2001, s. 580 and Sch. 4, with effect as respects allowances and charges falling to be made for chargeable periods ending, for income tax purposes, on or after 6 April 2001, and for corporation tax purposes, on or after 1 April 2001.

CAPITAL ALLOWANCES: OTHER PROVISIONS

99 Highway concessions

99 [Repealed by CAA 2001, s. 580 and Sch. 4.]

History – S. 99 repealed by CAA 2001, s. 580 and Sch. 4, with effect as respects allowances and charges falling to be made for chargeable periods ending, for income tax purposes, on or after 6 April 2001, and for corporation tax purposes, on or after 1 April 2001.

100 Arrangements affecting the value of a relevant interest

100 [Repealed by CAA 2001, s. 580 and Sch. 4.]

History – S. 100 repealed by CAA 2001, s. 580 and Sch. 4, with effect as respects allowances and charges falling to be made for chargeable periods ending, for income tax purposes, on or after 6 April 2001, and for corporation tax purposes, on or after 1 April 2001.

101 Import warehouses etc.

101 [Repealed by CAA 2001, s. 580 and Sch. 4.]

History – S. 101 repealed by CAA 2001, s. 580 and Sch. 4, with effect as respects allowances and charges falling to be made for chargeable periods ending, for income tax purposes, on or after 6 April 2001, and for corporation tax purposes, on or after 1 April 2001.

102 Capital allowances: commencement of certain provisions

102(1) Chapter IV of Part IV of the Finance Act 1994 (changes for facilitating self-assessment) shall be deemed to have been enacted with the following modification.

102(2) [Inserts FA 1994, s. 218(1A).]

MANAGEMENT: SELF-ASSESSMENT ETC.

103 Liability of trustees

103(1) [Amends TMA 1970, s. 7(2).]

103(2) [Inserts TMA 1970, s. 7(9).]

103(3) [Amends TMA 1970, s. 8A(1).]

103(4) [Inserts TMA 1970, s. 8A(5).]

103(5) [Inserts TMA 1970, s. 107A.]

103(6) [Amends TMA 1970, s. 118.]

103(7) Unless the contrary intention appears, this section, sections 104 to 115 below and Schedule 20 to this Act–

(a) so far as they relate to income tax and capital gains tax, have effect as respects the year 1996–97 and subsequent years of assessment, and

(b) so far as they relate to corporation tax, have effect as respects accounting periods ending on or after the appointed day for the purposes of Chapter III of Part IV of the Finance Act 1994.

Notes – The appointed day for the purposes of FA 1994, Pt. IV, Ch. III is 1 July 1999 (SI 1998/3173 C. 78)).

104 Returns and self-assessments

104(1) [Amends TMA 1970, s. 8(1A) and s. 8A(1A).]

104(2) [Amends TMA 1970, s, 8(1B).]

104(3) [Inserts TMA 1970, s. 8(5).]

104(4) [Amends TMA 1970, s. 9(1).]

104(5) [Repealed by FA 1998, s. 165 and Sch. 27, Pt. III(28).]

104(6) [Substitutes TMA 1970, s. 12AA(1).]

104(7) [Substitutes TMA 1970, s. 12AB(1).]

104(8) [Amends TMA 1970, s. 12AB(5).]

History – S. 104(5) repealed by FA 1998, s. 165 and Sch. 27, Pt. III(28) with effect in relation to accounting periods ending on or after 1 July 1999, the appointed day for corporation tax self-assessment under FA 1994, s. 199 by virtue of SI 1998/3173 (C. 78).

105 Records for purposes of returns

105(1) [Substitutes TMA 1970, s. 12B(1)(b).]

105(2) [Amends TMA 1970, s. 12B(2).]

105(3) [Inserts TMA 1970, s. 12B(2A).]

105(4) [Amends TMA 1970, s. 12B(3). Partially omitted by FA 2008, s. 115 and Sch. 37, para. 11(a).]

105(5) [Amends TMA 1970, s. 12B(4).]

105(6) [Amends TMA 1970, s. 12B(5).]

105(7) [Inserts TMA 1970, s. 12B(5A).]

History – S. 105(4)(b) omitted by FA 2008, s. 115 and Sch. 37, para. 11(a), with effect from 1 April 2009 (SI 2009/402, art. 2).

106 Return of employees' emoluments etc.

106(1) [Substitutes TMA 1970, s. 15.]

106(2) This section has effect as respects payments made or benefits provided on or after 6th April 1996.

107 Procedure for making claims etc.

107(1) [Inserts TMA 1970, s. 42(1A).]

107(2) [Amends TMA 1970, s. 42(2).]

107(3) [Amends TMA 1970, s. 42(3).]

107(4) [Inserts TMA 1970, s. 42(3A), 42(3B).]

107(5)–(6) [Repealed by F(No. 2)A 1997, s. 52 and Sch. 8, Pt. II(9) and by FA 1998, s. 165 and Sch. 27, Pt. III(28).]

107(8) [Amends TMA 1970, s. 42(7)(a).]

107(9) [Amends TMA 1970, s. 42(10).]

107(10) [Repeals TMA 1970, s. 42(11)(b).]

107(11) Schedule 1A to that Act (claims etc. not included in returns) shall have effect subject to the amendments specified in Schedule 20 to this Act.

History – S. 107(5) and (6) repealed by FA 1998, s. 165 and Sch. 27, Pt. III(28) with effect in relation to accounting periods ending on or after 1 July 1999, the appointed day for corporation tax self-assessment under FA 1994, s. 199 by virtue of SI 1998/3173 (C. 78). S. 107(5) and (6) also repealed by F(No. 2)A 1997, s. 52 and Sch. 8, Pt. II(9), with effect in relation to tax credits in respect of distributions made on or after 6 April 1999.

108 Payments on account of income tax

108(1) [Amends TMA 1970, s. 59A(1).]

108(2) [Amends TMA 1970, s. 59A(2).]

108(3) [Inserts TMA 1970, s. 59A(4A).]

108(4) [Amends TMA 1970, s. 59A(5).]

108(5) [Substitutes TMA 1970, s. 59A(8) and inserts TMA 1970, s. 59A(9).]

History – The repeal of s. 108 by ITEPA 2003, Sch. 8, Pt. 1 deemed retrospectively not to have been effected by FA 2004, s. 92 and Sch. 17, para. 6. However, the repeal is to be treated as effective in relation to anything done on or after 6 April 2003 and before the date FA 2004 was passed (22 July 2004) in reliance on the view that the repeal had in fact been effective.
S. 108 was repealed by ITEPA 2003, Sch. 8, Pt. 1 which has effect for the tax year 2003–04 and subsequent tax years.

109 Surcharges on unpaid tax

109(1) [Amends TMA 1970, s. 59C(4).]

109(2) That section of that Act shall apply in relation to any income tax or capital gains tax which–

(a) is charged by an assessment made on or after 6th April 1998; and

(b) is for the year 1995–96 or an earlier year of assessment,

as it applies in relation to any income tax or capital gains tax which becomes payable in accordance with section 55 or 59B of that Act and is for the year 1996–97 or a subsequent year of assessment.

Cross references – TMA 1970, s. 55 (as substituted and amended by FA 1994, s. 196 and Sch. 19, para. 18): payment of tax charged in an assessment and postponement of some or all of it pending an appeal.
TMA 1970, s. 59B (inserted by FA 1994, s. 193): payment or repayment of difference between tax charged in a self-assessment and tax deducted at source for the same year.

110 Interest on overdue tax

110(1) [Substitutes TMA 1970, s. 86.]

110(2) That section of that Act shall apply in relation to any income tax or capital gains tax which–

(a) is charged by an assessment made on or after 6th April 1998; and

(b) is for the year 1995–96 or an earlier year of assessment,

as it applies in relation to any income tax or capital gains tax which becomes due and payable in accordance with section 55 or 59B of that Act and is for the year 1996–97 or a subsequent year of assessment.

110(3) In that section of that Act as it so applies, **"the relevant date"** means the 31st January next following the year of assessment.

110(4) So far as it relates to partnerships whose trades, professions or businesses were set up and commenced before 6th April 1994, subsection (1) above has effect as respects the year 1997–98 and subsequent years of assessment.

History – S. 110 is deemed to have been enacted with the insertion of s. 110(4) (FA 1996, s. 131(1)).

111 Assessments in respect of income taken into account under PAYE

111 [Repealed by ITEPA 2003, Sch. 8, Pt. 1.]

History – S. 111 has been repealed by ITEPA 2003, Sch. 8, Pt. 1 which has effect for the tax year 2003–04 and subsequent tax years.

112 Recovery of certain amounts deducted or paid under MIRAS

112(1) [Inserts ICTA 1988, s. 374A.]

112(2) [Inserts ICTA 1988, s. 375(2)(aa).]

112(3) [Substitutes ICTA 1988, s. 375(4) and inserts s. 375(4A).]

112(4) [Inserts ICTA 1988, s. 375(8A).]

112(5) This section applies in relation to deductions made by borrowers, and payments made by the Board, after the passing of this Act.

Notes – The Finance Act 1995 was passed on 1 May 1995.

113 Allowable losses: capital gains tax

113(1) [Inserts TCGA 1992, s. 16(2A).]

113(2) Deductions under that Act in respect of allowable losses shall be given preference as follows–

(a) a deduction in respect of a loss accruing to a person in the year 1996–97 or a subsequent year of assessment shall be preferred to a deduction in respect of a loss accruing to him in an earlier year of assessment; and

(b) a deduction in respect of a loss accruing to a company in an accounting period ending on or after the appointed day for the purposes of Chapter III of Part IV of the Finance Act 1994 shall be preferred to a deduction in respect of a loss accruing to the company in an accounting period ending before that day.

Cross references – TCGA 1992, s. 71(2C), (2D): order of set off of losses where a beneficiary becomes absolutely entitled to trust property in circumstances where an asset comprised in that property shows a loss.

114 Liability of trustees and personal representatives: capital gains tax

114(1) [Substitutes TCGA 1992, s. 65(1).]

114(2) [Inserts TCGA 1992, s. 65(3) and (4).]

115 Minor amendments and repeals

115(1) [Amends TMA 1970, s. 7(7).]
115(2) [Amends TMA 1970, s. 9(3).]
115(3) [Repeals TMA 1970, s. 11A.]
115(4) [Amends TMA 1970, s. 12AA(2).]
115(5) [Amends TMA 1970, s. 30B(1)(c).]
115(6) [Amends TMA 1970, s. 59B(6).]
115(7) [Amends TMA 1970, s. 100B(1).]
115(8) [Amends TMA 1970, s. 103A.]
115(9) [Repeals ICTA 1988, s. 73.]
115(10) [Amends ICTA 1988, s. 536 and 537B.]
115(11) [Repeals ICTA 1988, Sch. 3, para. 6E(1) and (3).]
115(12) [Repeals TCGA 1992, s. 7.]
115(13) Subsection (3) above has effect as respects the year 1995–96 and subsequent years of assessment.

116 Transitional provisions

116(1) The provisions of the Management Act specified in Schedule 21 to this Act shall have effect subject to the transitional provisions contained in that Schedule.
116(2) [Repeals FA 1994, s. 198.]

CHANGES FOR FACILITATING SELF-ASSESSMENT

117 Treatment of partnerships

117 [Repealed by CTA 2009, s. 1326 and Sch. 3, Pt. 1.]

History – S. 117 repealed by CTA 2009, s. 1326 and Sch. 3, Pt. 1, with effect for corporation tax purposes for accounting periods ending on or after 1 April 2009, and for income tax and capital gains tax purposes for the tax year 2009–10 and subsequent tax years.
Cross references – FA 1994, s. 215: substitutes ICTA 1988, s. 111 and amends related provisions for facilitation of self-assessment.

118 Loss relief: general

118 [Repealed by ITA 2007, s. 1031 and Sch. 3, Pt. 1.]

History – S. 118 repealed by ITA 2007, s. 1031 and Sch. 3, Pt. 1, with effect from 6 April 2007.

119 Relief for losses on unquoted shares

119 [Repealed by ITA 2007, s. 1031 and Sch. 3, Pt. 1.]

History – S. 119 repealed by ITA 2007, s. 1031 and Sch. 3, Pt. 1, with effect from 6 April 2007.

120 Relief for pre-trading expenditure

120 [Repealed by CTA 2009, s. 1326 and Sch. 3, Pt. 1.]

History – S. 120 repealed by CTA 2009, s. 1326 and Sch. 3, Pt. 1, with effect for corporation tax purposes for accounting periods ending on or after 1 April 2009, and for income tax and capital gains tax purposes for the tax year 2009–10 and subsequent tax years.

121 Basis of apportionment for Cases I, II and VI of Schedule D

121 [Repealed by CTA 2009, s. 1326 and Sch. 3, Pt. 1.]

History – S. 121 repealed by CTA 2009, s. 1326 and Sch. 3, Pt. 1, with effect for corporation tax purposes for accounting periods ending on or after 1 April 2009, and for income tax and capital gains tax purposes for the tax year 2009–10 and subsequent tax years.

122 Amendments of transitional provisions

122 [Repealed by ITTOIA 2005, s. 884 and Sch. 3.]

History – S. 122 repealed by ITTOIA 2005, s. 884 and Sch. 3; effective for income tax purposes for 2005–06 onwards and for corporation tax purposes for accounting periods ending after 5 April 2005 (ITTOIA 2005, s. 883(1)).

123 Prevention of exploitation of transitional provisions

123 Schedule 22 to this Act shall have effect for preventing the exploitation of, and (in certain cases) penalising attempts to exploit, the transitional provisions set out in paragraphs 52 and 53 of

Schedule 2 to the Income Tax (Trading and Other Income) Act 2005 (changes for facilitating self-assessment: transitional provisions and savings).

History – In s. 123 the words "52 and 53 of Schedule 2 to the Income Tax (Trading and Other Income) Act 2005" substituted for the words ("paragraphs 2(2) and (4), 4(2) and 6(2)(a) and (4) of Schedule 20 to the Finance Act 1994") by ITTOIA 2005, s. 882(1) and Sch. 1, para. 478, effective for income tax purposes for 2005–06 onwards and for corporation tax purposes for accounting periods ending after 5 April 2005 (ITTOIA 2005, s. 883(1)).

Cross references – FA 1994, Sch. 20, para. 2: transitional provisions for opening and closing year rules for assessment under Sch. D, Case I of trades etc. set up and commenced before 6 April 1994 and continuing after 5 April 1997.

CHANGE OF RESIDENCE AND NON-RESIDENTS

124 Change of residence

124 [Repealed by ITTOIA 2005, s. 884 and Sch. 3.]

History – S. 124 repealed by ITTOIA 2005, s. 884 and Sch. 3; effective for income tax purposes for 2005–06 onwards and for corporation tax purposes for accounting periods ending after 5 April 2005 (ITTOIA 2005, s. 883(1)).

125 Non-resident partners

125 [Repealed by CTA 2009, s. 1326 and Sch. 3, Pt. 1.]

History – S. 125 repealed by CTA 2009, s. 1326 and Sch. 3, Pt. 1, with effect for corporation tax purposes for accounting periods ending on or after 1 April 2009, and for income tax and capital gains tax purposes for the tax year 2009–10 and subsequent tax years.
Former s. 125(2) repealed by ITTOIA 2005, s. 884 and Sch. 3; effective for income tax purposes for 2005–06 onwards and for corporation tax purposes for accounting periods ending after 5 April 2005 (ITTOIA 2005, s. 883(1)).
Former s. 125(3) repealed by ITTOIA 2005, s. 884 and Sch. 3; effective for income tax purposes for 2005–06 onwards and for corporation tax purposes for accounting periods ending after 5 April 2005 (ITTOIA 2005, s. 883(1)).

126 UK representatives of non-residents

126 [Omitted by TIOPA 2010, s. 374 and Sch. 8, para. 277 and repealed by TIOPA 2010, s. 378 and Sch. 10, Pt. 11.]

History – S. 126 omitted by TIOPA 2010, s. 374 and Sch. 8, para. 277 and repealed by TIOPA 2010, s. 378 and Sch. 10, Pt. 11, with effect for corporation tax purposes for accounting periods ending on or after 1 April 2010, for income tax and capital gains tax purposes for the tax year 2010–11 and subsequent tax years, and for petroleum revenue tax purposes for chargeable periods beginning on or after 1 July 2010.

Notes – S. 126 rewritten in TIOPA 2010 as follows:
S. 126(1): TIOPA 2010, Sch. 6, para. 27, 33.
S. 126(2): TIOPA 2010, Sch. 6, para. 3, 25.
S. 126(3): TIOPA 2010, Sch. 6, para, 3, 25.
S. 126(4): TIOPA 2010, Sch. 6, para. 3, 25.
S. 126(5): TIOPA 2010, Sch. 6, para. 3, 25.
S. 126(6): TIOPA 2010, Sch. 6, para. 4, 26.
S. 126(7): TIOPA 2010, Sch. 6, para. 4, 26.
S. 126(7A): TIOPA 2010, Sch. 6, para. 4, 26.
S. 126(8): TIOPA 2010, Sch. 6, para. 17, 27.
S. 126(10): TIOPA 2010, Sch. 6, para. 2.

127 Persons not treated as UK representatives

127 [Omitted by TIOPA 2010, s. 374 and Sch. 8, para. 278 and repealed by TIOPA 2010, s. 378 and Sch. 10, Pt. 11.]

History – S. 127 omitted by TIOPA 2010, s. 374 and Sch. 8, para. 278 and repealed by TIOPA 2010, s. 378 and Sch. 10, Pt. 11, with effect for corporation tax purposes for accounting periods ending on or after 1 April 2010, for income tax and capital gains tax purposes for the tax year 2010–11 and subsequent tax years, and for petroleum revenue tax purposes for chargeable periods beginning on or after 1 July 2010.

Notes – S. 127 rewritten in ITA 2007 as follows:
S. 127(1): ITA 2007, s. 814(1), (2), (3), (4), 817(1), 818(1).
S. 127(2): ITA 2007, s. 814(5), 817(1), (2), (3), (4), (5).
S. 127(3): ITA 2007, s. 814(5), 818(1), (2), (3), (4), (5), (6), (7).
S. 127(4): ITA 2007, s. 819(1), (2), (3).
S. 127(5): ITA 2007, s. 821(2), (4).
S. 127(6): ITA 2007, s. 822(2), (3).
S. 127(7): ITA 2007, s. 820(2).
S. 127(8): ITA 2007, s. 823(1), (2), (3).
S. 127(9): ITA 2007, s. 824(1), (2), (4).
S. 127(10): ITA 2007, s. 824(3), (4), (7).
S. 127(11): ITA 2007, s. 824(5), (6), (7).
S. 127(12): ITA 2007, s. 827(2).
S. 127(13): ITA 2007, s. 827(3).
S. 127(14): ITA 2007, s. 828(2).
S. 127(15): ITA 2007, s. 814(1), (2), (3), (4), (5), 828(1).
S. 127(17): ITA 2007, s. 824(7), 1021(1).
S. 127(18): ITA 2007, s. 818(4).
S. 127 rewritten in TIOPA 2010 as follows:
S. 127(1): TIOPA 2010, Sch. 6, para. 5, 6, 7, 8, 9.
S. 127(2): TIOPA 2010, Sch. 6, para. 6, 10.
S. 127(3): TIOPA 2010, Sch. 6, para. 7, 11.

S. 127(4): TIOPA 2010, Sch. 6, para. 12.
S. 127(5): TIOPA 2010, Sch. 6, para .13.
S. 127(6): TIOPA 2010, Sch. 6, para .13.
S. 127(7): TIOPA 2010, Sch. 6, para .13.
S. 127(8): TIOPA 2010, Sch. 6, para. 14.
S. 127(9): TIOPA 2010, Sch. 6, para. 15.
S. 127(10): TIOPA 2010, Sch. 6, para. 15.
S. 127(11): TIOPA 2010, Sch. 6, para. 15.
S. 127(12): TIOPA 2010, Sch. 6, para. 17.
S. 127(13): TIOPA 2010, Sch. 6, para. 17.
S. 127(14): TIOPA 2010, Sch. 6, para. 16.
S. 127(15): TIOPA 2010, Sch. 6, para. 5, 6, 7, 16.
S. 127(16): TIOPA 2010, Sch. 6, para. 9.
S. 127(17): TIOPA 2010, Sch. 6, para. 15.
S. 127(18): TIOPA 2010, Sch. 6, para. 11.

128 Limit on income chargeable on non-residents: income tax

128 [Omitted by ITA 2007, s. 1027 and Sch. 1, para. 368 and repealed by s. 1031 and Sch. 3, Pt. 1.]

History – S. 128 omitted by ITA 2007, s. 1027 and Sch. 1, para. 368 and repealed by s. 1031 and Sch. 3, Pt. 1, with effect from 6 April 2007.

Notes – S. 128 rewritten as follows:
S. 128(1): ITA 2007, s. 811(1), (3), (4), (5), (6), 1023.
S. 128(2): ITA 2007, s. 811(4), 813(1), (2).
S. 128(3): ITA 2007, s. 813(1), (3), (4), (5), 814(1), (2), 825(1), (2), (3), (4), (6), 817(1), 818(1), 826.
S. 128(4): ITA 2007, s. 811(4).
S. 128(5): ITA 2007, s. 812(1).
S. 128(6): ITA 2007, s. 812(2), (3), (4), (5).

129 Limit on income chargeable on non-residents: corporation tax

129 [Omitted by FA 2003, s. 155 and Sch. 27, para. 7 and repealed by FA 2003, s. 216 and Sch. 43, Pt. 3(6).]

History – S. 129 omitted by FA 2003, s. 155 and Sch. 27, para. 7 and repealed by FA 2003, s. 216 and Sch. 43, Pt. 3(6) in relation to accounting periods beginning on or after 1 January 2003.

EXCHANGE GAINS AND LOSSES AND CURRENCY CONTRACTS

130 Exchange gains and losses: general

130 Schedule 24 to this Act (which amends the provisions of the Finance Act 1993 relating to exchange gains and losses and other provisions connected with exchange gains and losses) shall have effect.

131 Exchange gains and losses: transitional provision

131 [Repealed by FA 2002, s. 79 and Sch. 23, para. 22(2) and s. 141 and Sch. 40, Pt. 3(10).]

History – S. 131 repealed by FA 2002, s. 79 and Sch. 23, para. 22(2) and s. 141 and Sch. 40, Pt. 3(10) with effect in relation to accounting periods beginning on or after 1 October 2002.

132 Currency contracts: transitional provisions

132 [Repealed by FA 2002, s. 141 and Sch. 40, Pt. 3(13).]

History – S. 132 repealed by FA 2002, s. 141 and Sch. 40, Pt. 3(13) with effect for accounting periods beginning on or after 1 October 2002.

PROVISIONS WITH A FOREIGN ELEMENT

133 Controlled foreign companies

133 Schedule 25 to this Act (which contains amendments of Chapter IV of Part XVII of the Taxes Act 1988 and connected amendments) shall have effect.

134 Offshore funds

134 [Repealed by SI 2009/3001, reg. 13(2) and Sch. 2.]

History – S. 134 repealed by SI 2009/3001, reg. 13(2) and Sch. 2, with effect from 1 December 2009 for various purposes (in accordance with the provisions of SI 2009/3001, reg. 1), subject to transitional and savings provisions in SI 2009/3001, Sch. 1.
At the time of the repeal of s. 134 by SI 2009/3001, s. 134(4) was to have been omitted prospectively by FA 2008. s. 41(7)(d), with effect from a day which was to have been appointed (FA 2008, s. 41(8)).
S. 134(1) repealed by FA 2004, s. 326 and Sch. 42, Pt. 2(1) for account periods ending on or after 22 July 2004.
S. 134(2) repealed by FA 2004, s. 326 and Sch. 42, Pt. 2(18) for account periods ending on or after 22 July 2004.
S. 134(3) repealed by FA 2004, s. 326 and Sch. 42, Pt. 2(18) for account periods ending on or after 22 July 2004.
S. 134(8) repealed by FA 2004, s. 326 and Sch. 42, Pt. 2(18) for account periods ending on or after 22 July 2004.

MISCELLANEOUS

135 Change in ownership of investment company: deductions

135 [Repealed by CTA 2010, s. 1181 and Sch. 3, Pt. 1.]

History – S. 135 repealed by CTA 2010, s. 1181 and Sch. 3, Pt. 1, with effect for accounting periods ending on or after 1 April 2010.

136 Profit-related pay

136 [Repealed by FA 1997, s. 113 and Sch. 18, Pt. VI(3).]

History – S. 136 repealed by FA 1997, s. 113 and Sch. 18, Pt. VI(3), with effect in relation to payments made by reference to a profit period beginning on or after 1 January 2000 but not so as to affect the operation of s. 136, or prevent the exercise of any power under s. 136, in relation to profit periods beginning before 1 January 2000 or for purposes connected with, or with the doing or not doing of anything in relation to, any such periods.

137 Part-time workers: miscellaneous provisions

137(1) [Repealed by FA 1997, s. 113 and Sch. 18, Pt. VI(3).]

137(2) [Repealed by ITEPA 2003, Sch. 8, Pt. 1.]

137(3) [Repealed by ITEPA 2003, Sch. 8, Pt. 1.]

137(4) [Amends ICTA 1988, Sch. 9, para. 36(1)(a).]

137(5) [Amends FA 1989, Sch. 5, para. 4(2)(c).]

137(6) [Repealed by FA 1997, s. 113 and Sch. 18, Pt. VI(3).]

137(7) Subsection (4) above shall apply in relation to any scheme not approved before the date on which this Act is passed.

137(8) [Repealed by ITEPA 2003, Sch. 8, Pt. 1.]

137(9) Subsection (5) above shall apply in relation to trusts established on or after the day on which this Act is passed; and for this purpose a trust is established when the deed under which it is established is executed.

History – S. 137(1) repealed by FA 1997, s. 113 and Sch. 18, Pt. VI(3), with effect in relation to payments made by reference to a profit period beginning on or after 1 January 2000 but not so as to affect the operation of s. 137, or prevent the exercise of any power under s. 137, in relation to profit periods beginning before 1 January 2000 or for purposes connected with, or with the doing or not doing of anything in relation to, any such periods.
S. 137(2) repealed by ITEPA 2003, Sch. 8, Pt. 1 which has effect for the tax year 2003–04 and subsequent tax years.
S. 137(3) repealed by ITEPA 2003, Sch. 8, Pt. 1 which has effect for the tax year 2003–04 and subsequent tax years.
S. 137(6) repealed by FA 1997, s. 113 and Sch. 18, Pt. VI(3), with effect in relation to payments made by reference to a profit period beginning on or after 1 January 2000 but not so as to affect the operation of s. 137, or prevent the exercise of any power under s. 137, in relation to profit periods beginning before 1 January 2000 or for purposes connected with, or with the doing or not doing of anything in relation to, any such periods.
In s. 137(7), the word "Subsection" substituted for the words "Subsections (2) to" by ITEPA 2003, Sch. 6, para. 227 which has effect for the tax year 2003–04 and subsequent tax years.
S. 137(8) repealed by ITEPA 2003, Sch. 8, Pt. 1 which has effect for the tax year 2003–04 and subsequent tax years.

138 Charities, etc: lotteries

138 [Repealed by CTA 2010, s. 1181 and Sch. 3, Pt. 1.]

History – S. 138 repealed by CTA 2010, s. 1181 and Sch. 3, Pt. 1, with effect for corporation tax purposes for accounting periods ending on or after 1 April 2010, and for income tax and capital gains tax purposes for the tax year 2010–11 and subsequent tax years.

139 Sub-contractors in the construction industry

139 [Repealed by FA 2004, s. 326 and Sch. 42, Pt. 2(7).]

History – S. 139 repealed by FA 2004, s. 326 and Sch. 42, Pt. 2(7), in relation to payments made on or after 6 April 2007 under contracts relating to construction payments, by virtue of notice given pursuant to SI 2005/2045.

140 Valuation of trading stock on discontinuance of trade

140 [Repealed by CTA 2009, s. 1326 and Sch. 3, Pt. 1.]

History – S. 140 repealed by CTA 2009, s. 1326 and Sch. 3, Pt. 1, with effect for corporation tax purposes for accounting periods ending on or after 1 April 2009, and for income tax and capital gains tax purposes for the tax year 2009–10 and subsequent tax years.

141 Incapacity benefit

141 [Repealed by ITEPA 2003, Sch. 8, Pt. 1.]

History – S. 141 repealed by ITEPA 2003, Sch. 8, Pt. 1 which has effect for the tax year 2003–04 and subsequent tax years.

142 Annuities purchased where certain claims or actions are settled

142 [Repealed by FA 1996, Sch. 41, Pt. V(16).]

143 Lloyd's underwriters: new-style special reserve funds

143(1) In Schedule 20 to the Finance Act 1993 (Lloyd's underwriters: special reserve funds) paragraph 2 (general requirements about special reserve funds) shall be deemed to have been enacted with the modification in subsection (2) below.

143(2) [Substitutes FA 1993, Sch. 20, para. 2(2) and omits para. 2(3).]

144 Local government residuary body

144 [Repealed by CTA 2010, s. 1181 and Sch. 3, Pt. 1.]

History – S. 144 repealed by CTA 2010, s. 1181 and Sch. 3, Pt. 1, with effect for corporation tax purposes for accounting periods ending on or after 1 April 2010, and for income tax and capital gains tax purposes for the tax year 2010–11 and subsequent tax years.

145 Payment of rent, etc., under deduction of tax

145(1) [Amends ICTA 1988, s. 119(1).]

145(2) [Repealed by ITTOIA 2005, s. 884 and Sch. 3.]

145(3) The provisions of this section have effect in relation to payments made after the passing of this Act.

History – S. 145(2) repealed by ITTOIA 2005, s. 884 and Sch. 3 effective for income tax purposes for 2005–06 onwards and for corporation tax purposes for accounting periods ending after 5 April 2005 (ITTOIA 2005, s. 883(1)).

Notes – The Finance Act 1995 was passed on 1 May 1995.

PART VI – MISCELLANEOUS AND GENERAL

MISCELLANEOUS

152 Open-ended investment companies

152(1) The Treasury may, by regulations, make such provision as they consider appropriate for securing that the enactments specified in subsection (2) below have effect in relation to–

(a) open-ended investment companies of any such description as may be specified in the regulations,

(b) holdings in, and the assets of, such companies, and

(c) transactions involving such companies,

in a manner corresponding, subject to such modifications as the Treasury consider appropriate, to the manner in which they have effect in relation to unit trusts, to rights under, and the assets subject to, such trusts and to transactions for purposes connected with such trusts.

152(2) The enactments referred to in subsection (1) above are–

(a) the Tax Acts and the Taxation of Chargeable Gains Act 1992; and

(b) the enactments relating to stamp duty and stamp duty reserve tax).

152(3) The power of the Treasury to make regulations under this section in relation to any such enactments shall include power to make provision which does any one or more of the following, that is to say–

(a) identifies the payments which are or are not to be treated, for the purposes of any prescribed enactment, as the distributions of open-ended investment companies;

(b) modifies the operation in relation to open-ended investment companies, or in relation to payments falling to be treated as the distributions of such companies, of any of the following provisions of Part 23 of the Corporation Tax Act 2010–;

  (i) any provision of Chapter 2, except section 1000(2),

  (ii) sections 1030 to 1048,

  (iii) section 1049(1) and (3),

  (iv) sections 1059 to 1063, and

  (v) Chapter 5;

(c) applies and adapts any of the provisions of the enactments relating to stamp duty or stamp duty reserve tax for the purpose of making in relation to transactions involving open-ended investment companies any provision corresponding (with or without modifications) to that which applies under those enactments in the case of equivalent transactions involving unit trusts;

(d) provides for any or all of the provisions of sections 75 to 77 of the Finance Act 1986 to have effect or not to have effect in relation to open-ended investment companies or the undertakings of, or any shares in, such companies;

(e) so modifies the operation of any prescribed enactment in relation to any such companies as to secure that arrangements for treating the assets of an open-ended investment company as assets comprised in separate pools are given an effect corresponding, in prescribed respects, to that of equivalent arrangements constituting the separate parts of an umbrella scheme;

(f) requires prescribed enactments to have effect in relation to an open-ended investment company as if it were, or were not, a member of the same group of companies as one or more other companies;

(g) identifies the holdings in open-ended investment companies which are, or are not, to be treated for the purposes of any prescribed enactment as comprised in the same class of holdings;

(h) preserves a continuity of tax treatment where, in connection with any scheme of re-organisation, assets of one or more unit trusts become assets of one or more open-ended investment companies, or vice versa;

(i) treats the separate parts of the undertaking of an open-ended investment company in relation to which provision is made by virtue of paragraph (e) above as distinct companies for the purposes of any regulations under this section;

(j) amends, adapts or applies the provisions of any subordinate legislation made under or by reference to any enactment modified by the regulations.

152(4) The power to make regulations under this section shall be exercisable by statutory instrument and shall include power–

(a) to make different provision for different cases; and

(b) to make such incidental, supplemental, consequential and transitional provision as the Treasury may think fit.

152(5) A statutory instrument containing regulations under this section shall be subject to annulment in pursuance of a resolution of the House of Commons.

152(6) In this section–

"the enactments relating to stamp duty" means the Stamp Act 1891, and any enactment (including any Northern Ireland legislation) which amends or is required to be construed together with that Act;

"the enactments relating to stamp duty reserve tax" means Part IV of the Finance Act 1986 and any enactment which amends or is required to be construed as one with that Part;

"Northern Ireland legislation" shall have the meaning given by section 24(5) of the Interpretation Act 1978;

"open-ended investment company" shall have the meaning given by section 236 of the Financial Services and Markets Act 2000;

"prescribed" means prescribed by regulations under this section;

"subordinate legislation" means any subordinate legislation within the meaning of the Interpretation Act 1978 or any order or regulations made by statutory instrument under Northern Ireland legislation; and

"umbrella scheme" shall have the meaning given by section 619 of the Corporation Tax Act 2010; and references in this section to the enactments relating to stamp duty, or to any of them, or to Part IV of the Finance Act 1986 shall have effect as including references to enactments repealed by sections 107 to 110 of the Finance Act 1990.

152(7) Any reference in this section to unit trusts has effect–

(a) for the purposes of so much of this section as confers power in relation to the enactments specified in paragraph (a) of subsection (2) above, as a reference to authorised unit trusts (within the meaning of sections 616 and 619(3) of the Corporation Tax Act 2010), and

(b) for the purposes of so much of this section as confers power in relation to the enactments specified in paragraph (b) of that subsection, as a reference to any unit trust scheme (within the meaning given by section 57 of the Finance Act 1946).

152(8) For the purposes of this section the enactments which shall be taken to make provision in relation to companies that are members of the same group of companies shall include any enactments which make provision in relation to a case–

(a) where one company has, or in relation to another company is, a subsidiary, or a subsidiary of a particular description, or

(b) where one company controls another or two or more companies are under the same control.

History – In s. 152(2)(b), references to the enactments relating to stamp duty reserve tax substituted for references to FA 1986, Pt. IV by FA 1999, s. 123(4) and Sch. 19, para. 13, with effect from 6 February 2000.

In s. 152(3)(b), the words "in relation to open-ended investment companies, or in relation to payments falling to be treated as the distributions of such companies, of any of the following provisions of Part 23 of the Corporation Tax Act 2010–" and the list (i)–(v) that

follows these words substituted for the words "of Chapters II, III and VA of Part VI of the Taxes Act 1988 in relation to open-ended investment companies or in relation to payments falling to be treated as the distributions of such companies" by CTA 2010, s. 1177 and Sch. 1, para. 288(2), with effect for corporation tax purposes for accounting periods ending on or after 1 April 2010, and for income tax and capital gains tax purposes for the tax year 2010–11 and subsequent tax years.
In s. 152(3)(c), references to the enactments relating to stamp duty reserve tax substituted for references to FA 1986, Pt. IV, and in s. 152(6), definition of "the enactments relating to stamp duty reserve tax" inserted, by FA 1999, s. 123(4) and Sch. 19, para. 13, with effect from 6 February 2000.
In s. 152(6), in the definition of "umbrella scheme", the words "section 619 of the Corporation Tax Act 2010" substituted for the words "section 468 of the Taxes Act 1988" by CTA 2010, s. 1177 and Sch. 1, para. 288(3), with effect for corporation tax purposes for accounting periods ending on or after 1 April 2010, and for income tax and capital gains tax purposes for the tax year 2010–11 and subsequent tax years.
In s. 152(6), the definition of "open-ended investment company" substituted by SI 2001/3629, art. 90 operative from 1 December 2001.
In s. 152(6), definition of "the enactments relating to stamp duty reserve tax" inserted, by FA 1999, s. 123(4) and Sch. 19, para. 13, with effect from 6 February 2000.
In s. 152(7)(a), the words "sections 616 and 619(3) of the Corporation Tax Act 2010)" substituted for the words "section 468 of the Taxes Act 1988)" by CTA 2010, s. 1177 and Sch. 1, para. 288(4), with effect for corporation tax purposes for accounting periods ending on or after 1 April 2010, and for income tax and capital gains tax purposes for the tax year 2010–11 and subsequent tax years.

Cross references – ITTOIA 2005, Sch. 2, para. 78: continuation of powers to make regulations under s. 152.
ICTA 1988, Pt. VI, Ch. II: matters which are distributions for the purposes of corporation tax.
ICTA 1988, Pt. VI, Ch. III: matters which are not distributions for the purposes of corporation tax.
ICTA 1988, Pt. VI, Ch. VA: foreign income dividends.
ICTA 1988, s. 468: definitions and other provisions relating to authorised unit trusts.
FA 1946, s. 57: exemption from stamp duty for transfers of stock guaranteed by the Treasury.
FA 1986, s. 75–77: exemption from stamp duty for transfers in the course of specified company reconstructions.
FA 1990, s. 107–110: abolitions of stamp duty on bearer instruments, transfers or vestings of securities by instrument (with certain consequential repeals) and of stamp duty reserve tax from a day to be appointed by the Treasury.

Statutory instruments – SI 2006/964: made under s. 152.
SI 1997/1154: Open-Ended Investment Companies (Tax) Regulations 1997.

153 Electronic lodgement of tax returns, etc.

153 Schedule 28 to this Act (which makes provision with respect to the electronic lodgement of certain tax returns and documents required in connection with tax returns) shall have effect.

Prospective amendments – S. 153 repealed by FA 1999, s. 139 and Sch. 20, Pt. VII, with effect from a day to be appointed.

Statements of practice – SP 1/97: the Electronic Lodgement Service.

154 Short rotation coppice

154(1) The cultivation of short rotation coppice shall be regarded for the purposes of the Taxation of Chargeable Gains Act 1992 as farming (and, where relevant, as husbandry or agriculture) and not as forestry; and land in the United Kingdom on which the activity is carried on shall accordingly be regarded for those purposes as farm land or agricultural land, as the case may be, and not as woodlands.

154(1A) [Omitted by ITA 2007, s. 1027 and Sch. 1, para. 369(3) and repealed by s. 1031 and Sch. 3, Pt. 1.]

154(2) For the purposes of the Inheritance Tax Act 1984 the cultivation of short rotation coppice shall be regarded as agriculture; and accordingly for those purposes–

(a) land on which short rotation coppice is cultivated shall be regarded as agricultural land, and

(b) buildings used in connection with the cultivation of short rotation coppice shall be regarded as farm buildings.

154(3) In subsections (1) and (2) **"short rotation coppice"** means a perennial crop of tree species planted at high density, the stems of which are harvested above ground level at intervals of less than ten years.

154(4) Subsection (1) and subsection (3) so far as relating to subsection (1) shall be deemed to have come into force on 29th November 1994.

154(5) Subsection (2) and subsection (3) so far as relating to subsection (2) shall have effect in relation to transfers of value or other events occurring on or after 6th April 1995.

History – In s. 154(1), the words "the Corporation Tax Acts and" (which followed immediately after the words "for the purposes of") omitted by CTA 2010, s. 1177 and Sch. 1, para. 289 and repealed by CTA 2010, s. 1181 and Sch. 3, Pt. 1, with effect for corporation tax purposes for accounting periods ending on or after 1 April 2010, and for income tax and capital gains tax purposes for the tax year 2010–11 and subsequent tax years.
At the beginning of s. 154(1) the words "Subject to subsection (1A)," omitted by ITA 2007, s. 1027 and Sch. 1, para. 369(2)(a) and repealed by s. 1031 and Sch. 3, Pt. 1, with effect from 6 April 2007.
In s. 154(1) the words "Corporation Tax Acts" substituted for the words "Tax Acts" by ITA 2007, s. 1027 and Sch. 1, para. 369(2)(b), with effect from 6 April 2007.
At the beginning of s. 154(1) the words "Subject to subsection (1A)," originally inserted by ITTOIA 2005, s. 882(1) and Sch. 1, para. 481(2); effective for income tax purposes for 2005–06 onwards and for corporation tax purposes for accounting periods ending after 5 April 2005 (ITTOIA 2005, s. 883(1)).
S. 154(1A) omitted by ITA 2007, s. 1027 and Sch. 1, para. 369(3) and repealed by s. 1031 and Sch. 3, Pt. 1, with effect from 6 April 2007.
Former s. 154(1A) inserted by ITTOIA 2005, s. 882(1) and Sch. 1, para. 481(3); effective for income tax purposes for 2005–06 onwards and for corporation tax purposes for accounting periods ending after 5 April 2005 (ITTOIA 2005, s. 883(1)).

HMRC Manuals – Business Income Manual BIM55205: explanatory comments regarding the meaning of "short rotation coppice".

Other material – TB10/95–3: HMRC clarify their views on the taxation of "short rotation coppice", in particular the treatment of initial planting and cultivation of the cuttings or "stools" as a capital expense, with cultivation and other costs consequent to the first cropping being revenue, the application of the renewals treatment as used in orchards for the replacement of old "stools" will generally be acceptable.

Notes – S. 154 rewritten for income tax purposes as follows:
S. 154(1): ITA 2007, s. 996(3), (4).
S. 154(3): ITA 2007, s. 996(6).
The income tax material omitted by ITTOIA 2005 is principally rewritten at ITTOIA 2005, s. 876.
S. 154(1) rewritten for corporation tax purposes as CTA 2010, s. 1125(3), (4)

156 Proceedings for tax in sheriff court

156(1) Section 67 of the Taxes Management Act 1970 (proceedings for tax in sheriff court) shall be amended as follows.

156(2) [Amends TMA 1970, s. 67(1).]

156(3) [Inserts TMA 1970, s. 67(1A).]

156(4) This section shall apply in relation to proceedings commenced after the day on which this Act is passed.

Notes – The Finance Act 1995 was passed on 1 May 1995.

157 Certificates of tax deposit

157(1) If, whether before or after the passing of this Act–

(a) any person (**"the depositor"**) has received any sum on the making, on or after 6th April 1990, of a withdrawal for cash of a tax deposit made before that date,

(b) the whole or any part of any qualifying tax liability has been discharged by any payment made otherwise than by the application of a tax deposit, and

(c) that payment was made in the period beginning one month before the withdrawal and ending one month afterwards,

the depositor shall be entitled to receive compensation under this section from the Board.

157(2) In this section **"qualifying tax liability"**, in relation to a tax deposit, means so much of any liability as is–

(a) a liability of any person for any tax for the year 1990–91 or any subsequent year of assessment, or for interest on such tax;

(b) a liability that relates to tax for a year of assessment during the whole or any part of which that person was married to the depositor; and

(c) a liability of such a description that, if it had been a liability of the depositor (and the withdrawal were to be disregarded), the whole or any part of it could have been discharged, immediately before the time of the payment mentioned in subsection (1)(b) above, by the application of that deposit and of accrued interest thereon.

157(3) Subject to the following provisions of this section, the amount of the compensation to which the depositor is entitled under this section in the case of any deposit withdrawn for cash shall be equal to the difference between–

(a) the sum received as mentioned in subsection (1)(a) above on the withdrawal; and

(b) the sum that would have been received if interest had accrued on the relevant part of the sum received at the rate applicable under the relevant terms to sums applied in the payment of tax, instead of at the rate applicable to a withdrawal for cash.

157(4) In subsection (3) above, the reference to the relevant part of the sum received on the withdrawal of a deposit is a reference to the following amount, that is to say–

(a) in a case where the sum received on the withdrawal is equal to or smaller than the amount of the liability discharged by the payment mentioned in subsection (1)(b) above, the amount equal to such part of the sum actually received as does not represent interest that has accrued under the relevant terms; and

(b) in any other case, to the amount which would have been the amount specified in paragraph (a) above if the sum actually received on the withdrawal had been equal to the amount of qualifying tax liability so discharged.

157(5) The amount of compensation to which any person is entitled under this section shall also include an amount equal to interest, for the period from the withdrawal mentioned in subsection (1)(a) above until the payment of the compensation, on the amount determined in accordance with subsection (3) above; and a liability to compensation under this section shall not bear interest apart from in accordance with this subsection.

157(6) Section 178 of the Finance Act 1989 (interest rates) shall apply to subsection (5) above for determining the rate of the interest treated, by virtue of that subsection, as included in any compensation under this section; and any regulations under that section which are in force at the passing of this Act shall be deemed, subject to the powers of the Treasury under that section, to have effect in relation to this section as they have effect in relation to the enactments specified in subsection (2)(f) of that section (interest on overdue tax).

157(7) The part of any compensation under this section that represents interest under subsection (5) above shall not be treated as included in the income of the depositor for the purposes of income tax; but the remainder shall be chargeable to income tax under Chapter 2 of Part 4 of the Income Tax (Trading and Other Income) Act 2005 (interest).

157(8) No compensation shall be paid under this section unless a claim for it has been made to the Board.

157(9) Where any claim is made under this section with respect to any withdrawal for cash of a tax deposit–

(a) this section shall have effect if there is, in the period mentioned in subsection (1)(c) above, more than one such payment as is mentioned in subsection (1)(b) above as if (subject to paragraph (b) below) all the payments in that period were, for the purposes of that claim, to be aggregated and treated as one such payment; and

(b) the amount of compensation payable under this section on that claim shall be computed without regard to so much of any payment discharging a qualifying tax liability as, in pursuance of any claim under this section, has been or is to be so taken into account as to affect the amount of compensation payable in the case of any other withdrawal.

157(10) Sums required by the Board for paying compensation under this section shall be issued to the Board by the Treasury out of the National Loans Fund.

157(11) A withdrawal for cash of a tax deposit shall be taken for the purposes of this section to occur at the same time as, under the relevant terms, it is deemed to occur for the purposes of the calculation of interest on the amount withdrawn.

157(12) This section shall be construed as one with the Tax Acts, and in this section–

(a) references to a **"tax deposit"** are references to the whole or any part of any deposit in respect of which a certificate of tax deposit has been issued by the Treasury under section 12 of the National Loans Act 1968; and

(b) references to the **"relevant terms"**, in relation to a tax deposit, are references to the terms applicable to that deposit and to the certificate issued in respect of it.

History – In s. 157(7) the words "Chapter 2 of Part 4 of the Income Tax (Trading and Other Income) Act 2005 (interest)" substituted for the words ("Case III of Schedule D") by ITTOIA 2005, s. 882(1) and Sch. 1, para. 482); effective for income tax purposes for 2005–06 onwards and for corporation tax purposes for accounting periods ending after 5 April 2005 (ITTOIA 2005, s 883(1)).

Cross references – FA 1989, s. 178: power of Treasury to set interest rates.

158 Amendment of the Exchequer and Audit Departments Act 1866

158 [Ceased to have effect by virtue of CRCA 2005, s. 50(6) and repealed by Sch. 4, para. 60 and s. 52(2) and Sch. 5.]

History – S. 158 ceased to have effect by virtue of CRCA 2005, s. 50(6) and Sch. 4, para. 60 and repealed by s. 52(2) and Sch. 5, from 18 April 2005 (SI 2005/1126 (C. 51), art. 2(2)).

GENERAL

161 Interpretation etc.

161(1) In this Act **"the Taxes Act 1988"** means the Income and Corporation Taxes Act 1988.

161(2) In Part III of this Act **"the Management Act"** means the Taxes Management Act 1970.

161(3) Part V of this Act shall be construed as one with the Stamp Act 1891.

162 Repeals

162 The provisions specified in Schedule 29 to this Act (which include provisions which are already spent) are hereby repealed to the extent specified in the third column of that Schedule, but subject to any provision of that Schedule.

163 Short title

163 This Act may be cited as the Finance Act 1995.

SCHEDULES

SCHEDULE 6 – AMENDMENTS IN CONNECTION WITH CHARGE UNDER SCHEDULE A

Section 39

THE TAXES ACT 1988

1 [Repealed by FA 1998, s. 165 and Sch. 27, Pt. III(4) with effect, so far as relating to income tax, for the year 1998–99 and subsequent years of assessment, and, so far as relating to corporation tax, from 1 April 1998, subject to the transitional provisions in FA 1998, Sch. 5, Pt. IV.]

2 [Repealed by CTA 2009, s. 1326 and Sch. 3, Pt. 1.]

History – Para. 2 repealed by CTA 2009, s. 1326 and Sch. 3, Pt. 1, with effect for corporation tax purposes for accounting periods ending on or after 1 April 2009, and for income tax and capital gains tax purposes for the tax year 2009–10 and subsequent tax years.

3 [Repeals ICTA 1988, s. 22 and 23.]

4–7 [Repealed by FA 1998, s. 165 and Sch. 27, Pt. III(4) with effect, so far as relating to income tax, for the year 1998–99 and subsequent years of assessment, and, so far as relating to corporation tax, from 1 April 1998, subject to the transitional provisions in FA 1998, Sch. 5, Pt. IV.]

9–16 [Repealed by FA 1998, s. 165 and Sch. 27, Pt. III(4) with effect, so far as relating to income tax, for the year 1998–99 and subsequent years of assessment, and, so far as relating to corporation tax, from 1 April 1998, subject to the transitional provisions in FA 1998, Sch. 5, Pt. IV.]

17 [Repealed by ITTOIA 2005, s. 884 and Sch. 3; effective for income tax purposes for 2005–06 onwards and for corporation tax purposes for accounting periods ending after 5 April 2005 (ITTOIA 2005, s. 883(1)).]

History – Para. 17 repealed by ITA 2007, s. 1031 and Sch. 3, Pt. 1, with effect from 6 April 2007. See ITA 2007, Sch. 2 for transitional and saving provisions.

18 [Repealed by FA 1999, s. 139 and Sch. 20, Pt. III(7).]

History – Para. 18 repealed by FA 1999, s. 139 and Sch. 20, Pt. III(7), with effect in relation to any payment of interest falling within FA 1999, s. 38(3) or (4) (broadly, payments made on or after 6 April 2000, or on or after 9 March 1999 and before 6 April 2000 but not falling due until on or after 6 April 2000).

19 [Repealed by ITA 2007, s. 1031 and Sch. 3, Pt. 1.]

History – Para. 19 repealed by ITA 2007, s. 1031 and Sch. 3, Pt. 1, with effect from 6 April 2007.

Notes – Para. 19 rewritten as ITA 2007, s. 118(1), (2), (3), (4), (5), 119, 120(1), (2), (4), 121(1), (2), (3), 122(2), (3), (4), (5), 123(2), (3), (4), (5), (6), (7), 124(1), (2).

20–25 [Repealed by FA 1998, s. 165 and Sch. 27, Pt. III(4) with effect, so far as relating to income tax, for the year 1998–99 and subsequent years of assessment, and, so far as relating to corporation tax, from 1 April 1998, subject to the transitional provisions in FA 1998, Sch. 5, Pt. IV.]

26 [Amends ICTA 1988, s. 692(1).]

27 [Repealed by Statute Law (Repeals) Act 2013, s. 1 and Sch. 1, Pt. 10.]

History – Para. 27 repealed by Statute Law (Repeals) Act 2013, s. 1 and Sch. 1, Pt. 10, with effect from 31 January 2013.

28 [Repealed by CTA 2010, s. 1181 and Sch. 3, Pt. 1.]

History – Para. 28 repealed by CTA 2010, s. 1181 and Sch. 3, Pt. 1, with effect for corporation tax purposes for accounting periods ending on or after 1 April 2010, and for income tax and capital gains tax purposes for the tax year 2010–11 and subsequent tax years.

THE CAPITAL ALLOWANCES ACT 1990

29–30 [Repealed by FA 1998, s. 165 and Sch. 27, Pt. III(4) with effect, so far as relating to income tax, for the year 1998–99 and subsequent years of assessment, and, so far as relating to corporation tax, from 1 April 1998, subject to the transitional provisions in FA 1998, Sch. 5, Pt. IV.]

31 [Repealed by FA 1997, s. 113 and Sch. 18, Pt. VI(11) in relation to 1997–98 and subsequent years of assessment (income tax) and in relation to accounting periods ending on or after 1 April 1997 (corporation tax).]

32 [Repealed by FA 1998, s. 165 and Sch. 27, Pt. III(4) with effect, so far as relating to income tax, for the year 1998–99 and subsequent years of assessment, and, so far as relating to corporation tax, from *1 April 1998*, subject to the transitional provisions in FA 1998, Sch. 5, Pt. IV.]

33 [Repealed by FA 1997, s. 113 and Sch. 18, Pt. VI(11) in relation to 1997–98 and subsequent years of assessment (income tax) and in relation to accounting periods ending on or after 1 April 1997 (corporation tax).]

34–35 [Repealed by FA 1998, s. 165 and Sch. 27, Pt. III(4) with effect, so far as relating to income tax, for the year 1998–99 and subsequent years of assessment, and, so far as relating to corporation tax, from 1 April 1998, subject to the transitional provisions in FA 1998, Sch. 5, Pt. IV.]

THE TAXATION OF CHARGEABLE GAINS ACT 1992

36–37 [Repealed by FA 1998, s. 165 and Sch. 27, Pt. III(4) with effect, so far as relating to income tax, for the year 1998–99 and subsequent years of assessment, and, so far as relating to corporation tax, from 1 April 1998, subject to the transitional provisions in FA 1998, Sch. 5, Pt. IV.]

THE FINANCE (NO. 2) ACT 1992

38 [Repealed by ITTOIA 2005, s. 884 and Sch. 3; effective for income tax purposes for 2005–06 onwards and for corporation tax purposes for accounting periods ending after 5 April 2005 (ITTOIA 2005, s. 883(1)).]

SCHEDULE 7 – COMMERCIALLY LET PROPERTY: CORPORATION TAX

Section 42

1–2 [Repealed by FA 1996, Sch. 41, Pt. V(3) with effect for 1996–97 and subsequent years of assessment (income tax) and for accounting periods ending after 31 March 1996 (corporation tax).]

SCHEDULE 8 – LIFE ASSURANCE BUSINESS

Section 51

[Omitted by FA 2012, s. 146 and Sch. 16, para. 247.]

History – Schedule 8 omitted by FA 2012, s. 146 and Sch. 16, para. 247 in relation to accounting periods beginning on or after 1 January 2013 (FA 2012, s. 148) but subject to transitional provisions in FA 2012, Sch. 17. Where an accounting period would otherwise straddle 1 January 2013, it is deemed to end on 31 December 2012 (FA 2012, s. 149).

SCHEDULE 9 – TRANSFER OF LIFE INSURANCE BUSINESS

Section 53

CONSEQUENTIAL AMENDMENT OF REFERENCES TO SANCTIONED TRANSFERS

1 [Omitted by FA 2012, s. 146 and Sch. 16, para. 247.]

History – Para. 1(1) omitted by FA 2012, s. 146 and Sch. 16, para. 247 in relation to accounting periods beginning on or after 1 January 2013 (FA 2012, s. 148) but subject to transitional provisions in FA 2012, Sch. 17. Where an accounting period would otherwise straddle 1 January 2013, it is deemed to end on 31 December 2012 (FA 2012, s. 149).

Para. 1(2) omitted by FA 2012, s. 146 and Sch. 16, para. 247 in relation to accounting periods beginning on or after 1 January 2013 (FA 2012, s. 148) but subject to transitional provisions in FA 2012, Sch. 17. Where an accounting period would otherwise straddle 1 January 2013, it is deemed to end on 31 December 2012 (FA 2012, s. 149).

In para. 1(2)(d), the references to s. 214(11) and 214A(7) repealed by FA 2007, s. 114 and Sch. 27, Pt. 2(10) with effect in relation to periods of account beginning on or after 1 January 2007.

Para. 1(3) omitted by FA 2012, s. 146 and Sch. 16, para. 247 in relation to accounting periods beginning on or after 1 January 2013 (FA 2012, s. 148) but subject to transitional provisions in FA 2012, Sch. 17. Where an accounting period would otherwise straddle 1 January 2013, it is deemed to end on 31 December 2012 (FA 2012, s. 149).

Para. 1(3) repealed by FA 2007, s. 114 and Sch. 27, Pt. 2(7) with effect (FA 2007, s. 38):

- for the purposes of corporation tax, for periods of account of insurance companies beginning on or after 1 January 2007; and
- for the purposes of income tax, for the 2007-08 tax year and subsequent tax years.

MODIFICATION OF THE TAXES ACT 1988IN RELATION TO OVERSEAS LIFE INSURANCE COMPANIES

2 [Repealed by SI 2006/3271, reg. 43 and Schedule, Pt. 1]

History – Para. 2 repealed by SI 2006/3271, reg. 43 and Schedule, Pt. 1, with effect from 31 December 2006 for accounting periods ending on or after that date.

MODIFICATION OF THE CAPITAL ALLOWANCES ACT 1990

3 [Repealed by CAA 2001, s. 580 and Sch. 4.]

History – Sch. 9, para. 3 repealed by CAA 2001, s. 580 and Sch. 4, with effect as respects allowances and charges falling to be made for chargeable periods ending, for income tax purposes, on or after 6 April 2001, and for corporation tax purposes, on or after 1 April 2001.

MODIFICATION OF THE TAXATION OF CHARGEABLE GAINS ACT 1992

4 [Amends TCGA 1992, s. 213(5) and inserts s. 213(5A).]

5 [Repealed by FA 2007, s. 114 and Sch. 27, Pt. 2(10).]

History – Para. 5 repealed by FA 2007, s. 114 and Sch. 27, Pt. 2(10) with effect in relation to periods of account beginning on or after 1 January 2007.

6 [Repealed by SI 2006/3271, reg. 43 and Schedule, Pt. 1.]

History – Para. 6 repealed by SI 2006/3271, reg. 43 and Schedule, Pt. 1, with effect from 31 December 2006 for accounting periods ending on or after that date.

SCHEDULE 10 – FRIENDLY SOCIETIES

Section 54

TAX EXEMPT LIFE OR ENDOWMENT BUSINESS

1 [Omitted by FA 2012, s. 176 and Sch. 18, para. 23.]

History – Para. 1 omitted by FA 2012, s. 176 and Sch. 18, para. 23 in relation to accounting periods of companies beginning on or after 1 January 2013.

MAXIMUM BENEFITS PAYABLE TO MEMBERS

2 [Omitted by FA 2012, s. 176 and Sch. 18, para. 23.]

History – Para. 2 omitted by FA 2012, s. 176 and Sch. 18, para. 23 in relation to accounting periods of companies beginning on or after 1 January 2013 .

QUALIFYING POLICIES

3 [Repeals ICTA 1988, Sch. 15, para. 3(2)(c).]

4(1) This paragraph applies to any policy which–

(a) was issued by a friendly society, or a branch of a friendly society, in the course of tax exempt life or endowment business (as defined in section 466 of the Taxes Act 1988); and

(b) was effected by a contract made after 31st August 1987 and before the day on which this Act is passed.

4(2) Where–

(a) the amount payable by way of premium under a policy to which this paragraph applies is increased by virtue of a variation made in the period beginning with the day on which this Act is passed and ending with 31st March 1996, and

(b) the variation is not such as to cause a person to become in breach of the limits in section 464 of the Taxes Act 1988,

Schedule 15 to that Act, in its application to the policy, shall have effect, in relation to that variation, with the omission of paragraph 4(3)(a) and the insertion at the end of paragraph 18(2) of the words set out in sub-paragraph (3) below.

4(3) Those words are as follows, that is to say, "and as if for paragraph 3(2)(b) above there were substituted–

"(b) subject to sub-paragraph (4) below, the premiums payable under the policy shall be premiums of equal or rateable amounts payable at yearly or shorter intervals–

(i) over the whole of the term of the policy as from the variation, or

(ii) where premiums are not payable for any period after the person liable to pay them or whose life is insured has attained a specified age, being an age attained at a time not less than ten years after the beginning of the term of the policy, over the whole of the remainder of the period for which premiums are payable."."

Cross references – ICTA 1988, s. 464: maximum benefits payable to members of friendly societies.
ICTA 1988, Sch. 15, para. 3–6: friendly society policies which are qualifying policies for life assurance premium relief.

SCHEDULE 11 – PERSONAL PENSIONS: INCOME WITHDRAWALS

Section 58

[Repealed by FA 2004, s. 326 and Sch. 42, Pt. 3.]

History – Sch. 11 repealed by FA 2004, s. 326 and Sch. 42, Pt. 3, with effect from 6 April 2006 subject to FA 2004, Sch. 36. Former Sch. 11 read as follows:

"SCHEDULE 11 – PERSONAL PENSIONS: INCOME WITHDRAWALS

Section 58

INTRODUCTORY

1(1) Chapter IV of Part XIV of the Taxes Act 1988 (personal pension schemes) is amended as follows.
1(2) The amendments have effect in relation to approvals, of schemes or amendments, given under that Chapter after the passing of this Act.
1(3) They do not affect any approval previously given.

INTERPRETATION

2(1) Section 630 (interpretation) is amended as follows.
2(2) [Amends ICTA 1988, s. 630(1).]
2(3) [Inserts ICTA 1988, s. 630(2)–(4).]

CONDITIONS OF APPROVAL: BENEFITS THAT MAY BE PROVIDED

3(1) Section 633(1) (conditions of approval: benefits that may be provided) is amended as follows.
3(2) [Amends ICTA 1988, s. 633(1)(a).]
3(3) [Amends ICTA 1988, s. 633(1)(c).]
3(4) [Amends ICTA 1988, s. 633(1)(d).]
3(5) [Inserts ICTA 1988, s. 633(1)(e).]

INCOME WITHDRAWALS

4 [Inserts ICTA 1988, s. 634A.]

LUMP SUM TO MEMBER

5(1) Section 635 (lump sum to member) is amended as follows.
5(2) [Amends ICTA 1988, s. 635(1).]
5(3) [Amends ICTA 1988, s. 635(2).]
5(4) [Amends ICTA 1988, s. 635(3)(a) and (b).]

ANNUITY AFTER DEATH OF MEMBER

6 [Amends ICTA 1988, s. 636(3).]

INCOME WITHDRAWALS AFTER DEATH OF MEMBER

7 [Inserts ICTA 1988, s. 636A.]

LUMP SUM ON DEATH OF MEMBER

8 [Substitutes ICTA 1988, s. 637 and 637A for former s. 637.]

OTHER RESTRICTIONS ON APPROVAL

9 [Inserts ICTA 1988, s. 638(7A).]

MAXIMUM AMOUNT OF DEDUCTIONS

10 [Amends ICTA 1988, s. 640(3).]

TREATMENT OF PERSONAL PENSION INCOME

11 [Inserts ICTA 1988, s. 643(5).]

TAX CHARGE ON RETURN OF CONTRIBUTIONS AFTER PENSION DATE

12 [Omits the heading before ICTA 1988, s. 648A and inserts s. 648B.]".

SCHEDULE 12 – CONTRACTUAL SAVINGS SCHEMES

Section 65

1-8 [Repealed by ITTOIA 2005, s. 884 and Sch. 3.]

History – Repealed by ITTOIA 2005, s. 884 and Sch. 3, effective for income tax purposes for 2005–06 onwards and for corporation tax purposes for accounting periods ending after 5 April 2005 (ITTOIA 2005, s. 883(1)).

Notes – The repealed legislation is principally rewritten at ITTOIA 2005, s. 702 to s. 708, with some transitional rules at ITTOIA 2005, Sch. 2 para. 139–141.

SCHEDULE 13 – ENTERPRISE INVESTMENT SCHEME

Section 67

INTRODUCTION

1 The Taxation of Chargeable Gains Act 1992 shall be amended as mentioned in this Schedule.

AMENDMENTS OF SECTION 150A

2(1) Section 150A (enterprise investment scheme) shall be amended as mentioned in sub-paragraphs (2) to (4) below; and the amendments made by sub-paragraphs (2) and (3) below shall apply in relation to shares issued on or after 1st January 1994.

2(2) [Inserts TCGA 1992, s. 150A(2A).]

2(3) [Inserts TCGA 1992, s. 150A(3)(aa).]

2(4) [Inserts TCGA 1992, s. 150A(8A)–(8C).]

REDUCTION OF RELIEF

3 [Inserts TCGA 1992, s. 150B.]

RE-INVESTMENT

4(1) [Inserts TCGA 1992, s. 150C.]

4(2) [Repealed by FA 2004, s. 326 and Sch. 42, Pt. 2(14).]

4(3) [Inserts TCGA 1992, Sch. 5B.]

4(4) This paragraph has effect in relation to gains accruing and events occurring on or after 29th November 1994.

History – Para. 4(2) repealed by FA 2004, s. 326 and Sch. 42, Pt. 2(14), with effect in relation to gains accruing on or after 6 April 2004 (FA 2004, s. 116 and Sch. 21, para. 10(8)).

SCHEDULE 14 – VENTURE CAPITAL TRUSTS: MEANING OF "QUALIFYING HOLDINGS"

Section 70

[Repealed by ITA 2007, s. 1031 and Sch. 3, Pt. 1.]

History – Sch. 14 repealed by ITA 2007, s. 1031 and Sch. 3, Pt. 1, with effect from 6 April 2007.

Notes – Sch. 14 rewritten as ITA 2007, s. 1014(2), 1022(1).

SCHEDULE 15 – VENTURE CAPITAL TRUSTS: RELIEF FROM INCOME TAX

Section 71

[Repealed by ITA 2007, s. 1031 and Sch. 3, Pt. 1.]

History – Sch. 15 repealed by ITA 2007, s. 1031 and Sch. 3, Pt. 1, with effect from 6 April 2007.

SCHEDULE 16 – VENTURE CAPITAL TRUSTS: DEFERRED CHARGE ON RE-INVESTMENT

Section 72

[Repealed by FA 2004, s. 326 and Sch. 42, Pt. 2(13).]

History – Sch. 16 repealed by FA 2004, s. 326 and Sch. 42, Pt. 2(13), with effect in relation to shares issued on or after 6 April 2004. Sch. 16 contained what became TCGA 1992, Sch. 5C. However, the repeal does not affect the continuing operation of TCGA 1992, Sch. 5C for the purposes of TCGA 1992, s. 151B(8)(b)(ii) (FA 2004, s. 94 and Sch. 19, para. 7).

SCHEDULE 17 – SETTLEMENTS: LIABILITY OF SETTLOR

Section 74

Part I – The New Provisions

1 [Inserts ICTA 1988, s. 660A–660G.]

Part II – Minor and Consequential Amendments of the Taxes Act 1988

2 [Repealed by ITTOIA 2005, s. 884 and Sch. 3; with effect for income tax purposes for 2005–06 onwards and for corporation tax purposes for accounting periods ending after 5 April 2005 (ITTOIA 2005, s. 883(1)).]

3 [Repealed by CTA 2010, s. 1181 and Sch. 3, Pt. 1.]

History – Para. 3 repealed by CTA 2010, s. 1181 and Sch. 3, Pt. 1, with effect for corporation tax purposes for accounting periods ending on or after 1 April 2010, and for income tax and capital gains tax purposes for the tax year 2010–11 and subsequent tax years.

4(1) [Repealed by FA 1999, s. 139 and Sch. 20, Pt. III(6).]

4(2) [Inserts ICTA 1988, s. 347A(7) and (8).]

History – Para. 4(1) repealed by FA 1999, s. 139 and Sch. 20, Pt. III(6), with effect in relation to any payment falling due on or after 6 April 2000.

5 [Repealed by ITTOIA 2005, s. 884 and Sch. 3; with effect for income tax purposes for 2005–06 onwards and for corporation tax purposes for accounting periods ending after 5 April 2005 (ITTOIA 2005, s. 883(1)).]

6 [Repealed by ITTOIA 2005, s. 884 and Sch. 3; with effect for income tax purposes for 2005–06 onwards and for corporation tax purposes for accounting periods ending after 5 April 2005 (ITTOIA 2005, s. 883(1)).]

7 [Amends ICTA 1988, s. 505(6).]

8 [Repealed by ITTOIA 2005, s. 884 and Sch. 3; with effect for income tax purposes for 2005–06 onwards and for corporation tax purposes for accounting periods ending after 5 April 2005 (ITTOIA 2005, s. 883(1)).]

9 [Repealed by ITTOIA 2005, s. 884 and Sch. 3; with effect for income tax purposes for 2005–06 onwards and for corporation tax purposes for accounting periods ending after 5 April 2005 (ITTOIA 2005, s. 883(1)).]

10 [Omits ICTA 1988, s. 678(7).]

11 [Repealed by ITTOIA 2005, s. 884 and Sch. 3; with effect for income tax purposes for 2005–06 onwards and for corporation tax purposes for accounting periods ending after 5 April 2005 (ITTOIA 2005, s. 883(1)).]

12 [Substitutes the heading before ICTA 1988, s. 686.]

13 [Repealed by ITA 2007, s. 1031 and Sch. 3, Pt. 1.]

History – Para. 13 repealed by ITA 2007, s. 1031 and Sch. 3, Pt. 1, with effect from 6 April 2007.

Notes – Para. 13 rewritten as ITA 2007, s. 480(3).

14 [Repealed by ITA 2007, s. 1031 and Sch. 3, Pt. 1.]

History – Para. 14 repealed by ITA 2007, s. 1031 and Sch. 3, Pt. 1, with effect from 6 April 2007.

Notes – Para. 14 rewritten as follows:
Para. 14(2): ITA 2007, s. 493(1), (2), (3).
Para. 14(3): ITA 2007, s. 494(4).
Para. 14(4): ITA 2007, s. 493(5).

15 [Omits ICTA 1988, s. 689.]

16 [Repealed by ITTOIA 2005, s. 884 and Sch. 3; with effect for income tax purposes for 2005–06 onwards and for corporation tax purposes for accounting periods ending after 5 April 2005 (ITTOIA 2005, s. 883(1)).]

17 [Repealed by ITA 2007, s. 1031 and Sch. 3, Pt. 1.]

History – Para. 17 repealed by ITA 2007, s. 1031 and Sch. 3, Pt. 1, with effect from 6 April 2007.

18 [Repealed by ITTOIA 2005, s. 884 and Sch. 3; with effect for income tax purposes for 2005–06 onwards and for corporation tax purposes for accounting periods ending after 5 April 2005 (ITTOIA 2005, s. 883(1)).]

19 [Repealed by ITTOIA 2005, s. 884 and Sch. 3; with effect for income tax purposes for 2005–06 onwards and for corporation tax purposes for accounting periods ending after 5 April 2005 (ITTOIA 2005, s. 883(1)).]

20 [Repealed by CTA 2010, s. 1181 and Sch. 3, Pt. 1.]

History – Para. 20 repealed by CTA 2010, s. 1181 and Sch. 3, Pt. 1, with effect for corporation tax purposes for accounting periods ending on or after 1 April 2010, and for income tax and capital gains tax purposes for the tax year 2010–11 and subsequent tax years.

Part III – Consequential Amendments of Other Enactments

TAXES MANAGEMENT ACT 1970 (c. 9)

21 [Repealed by ITTOIA 2005, s. 884 and Sch. 3; with effect for income tax purposes for 2005–06 onwards and for corporation tax purposes for accounting periods ending after 5 April 2005 (ITTOIA 2005, s. 883(1)).]

22 [Amends TMA 1970, s. 31(3).]

23 [Repealed by ITTOIA 2005, s. 884 and Sch. 3; with effect for income tax purposes for 2005–06 onwards and for corporation tax purposes for accounting periods ending after 5 April 2005 (ITTOIA 2005, s. 883(1)).]

FINANCE ACT 1989 (C. 26)

24 [Repealed by Statute Law (Repeals) Act 2013, s. 1 and Sch. 1, Pt. 10.]

History – Para. 24 repealed by Statute Law (Repeals) Act 2013, s. 1 and Sch. 1, Pt. 10, with effect from 31 January 2013.

25 [Omits FA 1989, s. 60(3) and amends s. 60(4).]

FINANCE ACT 1990 (C. 29)

26 [Repealed by Statute Law (Repeals) Act 2013, s. 1 and Sch. 1, Pt. 10.]

History – Para. 26 repealed by Statute Law (Repeals) Act 2013, s. 1 and Sch. 1, Pt. 10, with effect from 31 January 2013.

TAXATION OF CHARGEABLE GAINS ACT 1992 (C. 12)

27 [Omitted by FA 2008, s. 8 and Sch. 2, para. 21(a).]

History – Para. 27 omitted by FA 2008, s. 8 and Sch. 2, para. 21(a), with effect for the tax year 2008–09 and subsequent tax years.

28 [Omitted by FA 2008, s. 8 and Sch. 2, para. 21(a).]

History – Para. 28 omitted by FA 2008, s. 8 and Sch. 2, para. 21(a), with effect for the tax year 2008–09 and subsequent tax years.

29 [Omitted by FA 2008, s. 8 and Sch. 2, para. 21(a).]

History – Para. 29 omitted by FA 2008, s. 8 and Sch. 2, para. 21(a), with effect for the tax year 2008–09 and subsequent tax years.

30 [Repealed by ITTOIA 2005, s. 884 and Sch. 3; with effect for income tax purposes for 2005–06 onwards and for corporation tax purposes for accounting periods ending after 5 April 2005 (ITTOIA 2005, s. 883(1)).]

31 [Substitutes TCGA 1992, s. 286(3) and (3A) for former s. 286(3).]

32 [Repealed by ITTOIA 2005, s. 884 and Sch. 3; with effect for income tax purposes for 2005–06 onwards and for corporation tax purposes for accounting periods ending after 5 April 2005 (ITTOIA 2005, s. 883(1)).]

SCHEDULE 18 – DECEASED PERSONS' ESTATES

Section 75

INTRODUCTORY

1 Part XVI of the Taxes Act 1988 shall be amended as follows.

LIMITED INTERESTS IN RESIDUE

2 [Repealed by CTA 2009, s. 1326 and Sch. 3, Pt. 1.]

History – Para. 2 repealed by CTA 2009, s. 1326 and Sch. 3, Pt. 1, with effect for corporation tax purposes for accounting periods ending on or after 1 April 2009, and for income tax and capital gains tax purposes for the tax year 2009–10 and subsequent tax years.

ABSOLUTE INTERESTS IN RESIDUE

3(1) [Substitutes ICTA 1988, s. 696(3)–(3B) for former s. 696(3).]

3(2) [Substitutes ICTA 1988, s. 696(5).]

3(3) Sub-paragraph (1) above has effect, subject to sub-paragraph (4) below, in relation to any payment made on or after 6th April 1995; and sub-paragraph (2) above shall have effect in relation to any estate the administration of which is completed on or after 6th April 1995.

3(4) Where any sum is deemed by virtue of subsection (3) of section 696 of the Taxes Act 1988 (as it has effect apart from this Schedule) and sections 652, 660 and 665 of the Income Tax (Trading and Other Income) Act 2005) to have been paid to any person as income for the year 1994–95 or any previous year of assessment, that sum shall be treated for the purposes of subsections (3A) and (5) of that section (as they have effect by virtue of this Schedule) as a sum actually paid in respect of that person's absolute interest in that year of assessment.

History – In para. 3(4) the words "and sections 652, 660 and 665 of the Income Tax (Trading and Other Income) Act 2005" inserted by ITTOIA 2005, s. 882(1) and Sch. 1, para. 483, effective for income tax purposes for 2005–06 onwards and for corporation tax purposes for accounting periods ending after 5 April 2005 (ITTOIA 2005, s. 883(1)).

SUPPLEMENTAL PROVISIONS RELATING TO SECTION 696

4(1) [Inserts ICTA 1988, s. 697(1A).]

4(2) [Amends ICTA 1988, s. 697(2).]

4(3) Sub-paragraph (1) above has effect for ascertaining the residuary income of an estate for the year 1995–96 or any subsequent year of assessment; and sub-paragraph (2) above has effect in relation to any estate the administration of which is completed on or after 6th April 1995.

SPECIAL PROVISIONS AS TO SUCCESSIVE INTERESTS IN RESIDUE

5(1) [Substitutes ICTA 1988, s. 698(1A)–(2) for former s. 698(2).]

5(2) This paragraph has effect in relation to any payment made on or after 6th April 1995 and, so far as it relates to the operation of section 695(3) or 696(5) of the Taxes Act 1988, in relation to any estate the administration of which is completed on or after that date.

ADJUSTMENTS AND INFORMATION

6 [Repealed by TIOPA 2010, s. 378 and Sch. 10, Pt. 12.]

History – Para. 6 repealed by TIOPA 2010, s. 378 and Sch. 10, Pt. 12, with effect for corporation tax purposes for accounting periods ending on or after 1 April 2010, for income tax and capital gains tax purposes for the tax year 2010–11 and subsequent tax years, and for petroleum revenue tax purposes for chargeable periods beginning on or after 1 July 2010.

INTERPRETATION

7 [Repeals ICTA 1988, s. 701(14).]

SCHEDULE 19 – STOCK LENDING: INTEREST ON CASH COLLATERAL

INTRODUCTORY

1 [Repealed by FA 1997, s. 113 and Sch. 18, Pt. VI(10), with effect in relation to, and to transfers under, any arrangement made on or after 1 July 1997, the day appointed under FA 1997, Sch. 10, para. 7(1) by virtue of SI 1997/991 (C. 33).]

TREATMENT OF INTEREST EARNED ON CASH COLLATERAL

2 [Repealed by FA 1997, s. 113 and Sch. 18, Pt. VI(10), with effect in relation to, and to transfers under, any arrangement made on or after 1 July 1997, the day appointed under FA 1997, Sch. 10, para. 7(1) by virtue of SI 1997/991 (C. 33).]

APPLICATION OF PARAGRAPH 2 IN CASE OF CHAIN OF ARRANGEMENTS

3 [Repealed by FA 1997, s. 113 and Sch. 18, Pt. VI(10), with effect in relation to, and to transfers under, any arrangement made on or after 1 July 1997, the day appointed under FA 1997, Sch. 10, para. 7(1) by virtue of SI 1997/991 (C. 33).]

INTERPRETATION

4 [Repealed by FA 1997, s. 113 and Sch. 18, Pt. VI(10), with effect in relation to, and to transfers under, any arrangement made on or after 1 July 1997, the day appointed under FA 1997, Sch. 10, para. 7(1) by virtue of SI 1997/991 (C. 33).]

SCHEDULE 20 – CLAIMS ETC. NOT INCLUDED IN RETURNS

Section 107(11)

MAKING OF CLAIMS

1 [Substitutes TMA 1970, Sch. 1A, para. 2(5)(b).]

KEEPING AND PRESERVING OF RECORDS

2 [Inserts TMA 1970, Sch. 1A, para. 2A.]

AMENDMENTS OF CLAIMS

3(1) [Amends TMA 1970, Sch. 1A, para. 3(1)(a).]

GIVING EFFECT TO CLAIMS AND AMENDMENTS

4(1) [Amends TMA 1970, Sch. 1A, para. 4(1).]

4(2) [Inserts TMA 1970, Sch. 1A, para. 4(1A).]

4(3) [Amends TMA 1970, Sch. 1A, para. 4(2).]

4(4) [Inserts TMA 1970, Sch. 1A, para. 4(3).]

POWER TO ENQUIRE INTO CLAIMS

5 [Substitutes TMA 1970, Sch. 1A, para. 5(2) and (3).]

SCHEDULE 21 – SELF-ASSESSMENT ETC.: TRANSITIONAL PROVISIONS

Section 116(1)

Other material – Taxline 1997/12 (not reproduced): when looking to reduce a payment on account because the source no longer exists in 1996–97, it is necessary to consider the aggregate liability for 1996–97.

NOTICE OF LIABILITY

1 Section 7 of the Management Act (notice of liability) shall have effect as respects the year 1995–96 as if the reference in subsection (7) to a self-assessment made under section 9 of that Act in respect of that year were a reference to assessments made more than six months after the end of that year.

Cross references – TMA 1970, s. 7(7): income excluded from requirement to give notice of chargeability.
TMA 1970, s. 9 (as amended by FA 1994, s. 179): returns to include self-assessments unless filed on or before 30 September following the year assessment for which they are made.

PAYMENTS ON ACCOUNT OF INCOME TAX

2(1) Section 59A of that Act (payments on account of income tax) shall have effect as respects the year 1996–97 with the modifications made by sub-paragraphs (2) to (7) below.

2(2) The references in subsections (1)(a) and (4A) to a person being assessed to income tax under section 9 of that Act shall be construed as references to his being assessed to income tax under section 29 of that Act.

2(3) The reference in subsection (1)(b) to the assessed amount shall be construed as a reference to the difference between that amount and the aggregate of the following, namely–

(a) so much of any income tax charged at a higher rate on any income–

(i) from which tax has been deducted otherwise than under section 203 of the Taxes Act 1988, or

(ii) from or on which income tax is treated as having been deducted or paid,

as is attributable to the difference between that rate and the basic rate; and

(b) so much of any income tax charged at a higher rate on any income chargeable under Schedule F as is attributable to the difference between that rate and the lower rate.

2(4) The reference in subsection (1)(c) to the relevant amount shall be construed as a reference to the difference between that amount and the amount of any income tax charged under Schedule E which–

(a) has not been deducted under section 203 of the Taxes Act 1988; and

(b) is not charged by an assessment made under regulation 103 of the Income Tax (Employments) Regulations 1993.

2(5) Subsection (2) shall have effect as if it required–

(a) the first payment on account to be of an amount equal to the aggregate of–

(i) such part of the relevant amount as represents tax charged under Schedule A or any of Cases III to VI of Schedule D; and

(ii) 50 per cent of the remaining part of the relevant amount, and

(b) the second payment on account to be of an amount equal to 50 per cent of that remaining part.

2(6) Subsection (4) shall have effect as if it provided that, in the circumstances there mentioned–

(a) the amount of the first payment on account should be, and should be deemed always to have been, equal to the aggregate of–

(i) such part of the stated amount as represents tax charged under Schedule A or any of Cases III to VI of Schedule D; and

(ii) 50 per cent of the remaining part of the stated amount, and

(b) the amount of the second payment on account should be, and should be deemed always to have been, equal to 50 per cent of that remaining part.

2(7) Subsection (4A) shall have effect as if it provided that, in the circumstances and subject as there mentioned–

(a) the amount of the first payment on account should be, and should be deemed always to have been, equal to the aggregate of–

(i) such part of the relevant amount (as determined on the basis of the assessment or, as the case may be, the assessment as amended) as represents tax charged under Schedule A or any of Cases III to VI of Schedule D; and

(ii) 50 per cent of the remaining part of the relevant amount, as so determined, and

(b) the amount of the second payment on account should be, and should be deemed always to have been, equal to 50 per cent of that remaining part.

2(8) In this paragraph **"higher rate"** means a rate other than the basic rate or the lower rate.

Cross references – TMA 1970, s. 9 (as amended by FA 1994, s. 179): returns to include self-assessments unless filed on or before 30 September following the year of assessment for which they are made.
TMA 1970, s. 29 (as substituted by FA 1994, s. 191): an assessment made when an inspector discovers that an existing assessment has become insufficient.

PARTNERSHIPS

3(1) This paragraph applies in the case of a partnership whose trade, profession or business is set up and commenced before 6th April 1994.

3(2) Section 32 of the Management Act (relief for double assessments to tax) shall have effect, as respects each partner and the year 1996–97, as if the partnership had not been assessed to income tax for that year.

3(3) Section 59B of that Act (payment of income tax and capital gains tax) shall have effect, as respects each partner and that year, as if his share of any income tax to which the partnership is assessed for that year were income tax which in respect of that year had been deducted at source.

SCHEDULE 22 – PREVENTION OF EXPLOITATION OF SCHEDULE 2 TO ITTOIA 2005 (SO FAR AS RELATING TO OVERLAP PROFIT)

Section 123

History – In the heading to Sch. 22 the words "SCHEDULE 2 TO ITTOIA 2005 (SO FAR AS RELATING TO OVERLAP PROFIT)" substituted for the words "SCHEDULE 20 TO FINANCE ACT 1994" by ITTOIA 2005, s. 882(1) and Sch. 1, para. 484(12), with effect for income tax purposes for 2005–06 onwards and for corporation tax purposes for accounting periods ending after 5 April 2005 (ITTOIA 2005, s. 883(1)).

Part I – Cases I and II of Schedule D

INCREASE OF PROFITS OR GAINS OF TRANSITIONAL PERIOD

1(1) This paragraph applies where, in the case of a trade, profession or vocation carried on by any person–

(a) paragraph 2(2) of Schedule 20 to the Finance Act 1994 applies without the modification made by paragraph 2(3) of that Schedule; and

(b) any amount which is included in the profits or gains of the transitional period would not have been so included if–

(i) any relevant change made by that person had not been made; or

(ii) any relevant transaction entered into by that person had not been entered into.

1(2) Subject to sub-paragraph (3) below, the said paragraph 2(2) shall have effect as if the reference to the appropriate percentage of the aggregate of the amounts there mentioned were a reference to the aggregate of–

(a) that percentage of each of those amounts; and

(b) 1.25 times the complementary percentage of each of the amounts falling within sub-paragraph (1)(b) above.

1(3) Sub-paragraph (2) above does not apply where–

(a) the aggregate of the amounts falling within sub-paragraph (1)(b) above is less than such amount as may be prescribed by regulations made by the Board;

(b) the proportion which the aggregate of those amounts bears to the aggregate of the amounts mentioned in the said paragraph 2(2) is less than such proportion as may be so prescribed; or

(c) the appropriate percentage of the turnover for the transitional period is less than such amount as may be so prescribed;

and regulations under this sub-paragraph may make as respects trades or professions carried on by persons in partnership provision different from that made as respects trades, professions or vocations carried on by individuals.

1(4) In this paragraph–

"the appropriate percentage" means the following expressed as a percentage, that is, 365 divided by the number of days in the transitional period;

"the complementary percentage" means the difference between 100 per cent and the appropriate percentage;

"the transitional period" means the basis period for the year 1996–97 and the relevant period (within the meaning of paragraph 2 of Schedule 20 to the Finance Act 1994) taken together.

Cross references – FA 1994, Sch. 20, para. 2: transitional provisions for opening and closing year rules for assessment under Sch. D, Case I of trades etc. set up and commenced before 6 April 1994 and continuing after 5 April 1997.
SI 1997/1158, reg. 3: amounts prescribed under para. 1(3) – persons other than partners.
SI 1997/1158, reg. 4: amount prescribed under para. 1(3)(a) – persons in partnership.
SI 1997/1158, reg. 5: amount prescribed under para. 1(3)(c) – persons in partnership.

Statutory instruments – SI 1997/1158.

2 [Omitted by ITTOIA 2005, s. 882(1) and Sch. 1, para. 484(2); and repealed by ITTOIA 2005, s. 884 and Sch. 3; with effect for income tax purposes for 2005–06 onwards and for corporation tax purposes for accounting periods ending after 5 April 2005 (ITTOIA 2005, s. 883(1)).]

INCREASE OF PROFITS OR GAINS OF TRANSITIONAL OVERLAP PERIOD

3(1) This paragraph applies where, in the case of a trade, profession or vocation carried on by any person–

(a) paragraph 52 of Schedule 2 to the Income Tax (Trading and Other Income) Act 2005 ("ITTOIA 2005") applies; and

(b) any amount which is included in the transitional overlap profit would not have been so included if–

(i) any relevant change made by that person had not been made; or

(ii) any relevant transaction entered into by that person had not been entered into.

3(2) Subject to sub-paragraph (3) below, paragraph 52 of that Schedule shall have effect as if the reference to the transitional overlap profit were a reference to the amount (if any) by which that profit exceeds 1.25 times the aggregate of the amounts falling within sub-paragraph (1)(b) above.

3(3) Sub-paragraph (3) of paragraph 1 above shall apply for the purposes of this paragraph as it applies for the purposes of that paragraph but subject to the following modifications, namely–

(a) the reference to the aggregate of the amounts mentioned in the said paragraph 2(2) shall have effect as a reference to the transitional overlap profit; and

(b) the reference to the appropriate percentage of the turnover for the transitional period shall have effect as a reference to the appropriate percentage of the turnover for the transitional overlap period.

3(4) In this paragraph–

"the appropriate percentage" means the following expressed as a percentage, that is, 365 divided by the number of days in the transitional overlap period;

"the transitional overlap period" means the period beginning immediately after the end of–

(a) the basis period for the year 1996–97 (determined in accordance with paragraph 1 of Schedule 20 to the Finance Act 1994 despite the repeal by ITTOIA 2005 of that paragraph; or

(b) in the case of a trade or profession carried on by any person in partnership with other persons, the basis period of the partnership for that year (as so determined),

and (in either case) ending with 5th April 1997;

"the transitional overlap profit" means the amount mentioned in paragraph 52(2) of Schedule 2 to ITTOIA 2005.

History – In para. 3(1)(a) the words "paragraph 52 of Schedule 2 to the Income Tax (Trading and Other Income) Act 2005 ("ITTOIA 2005")" substituted for the former wording by ITTOIA 2005, s. 882(1) and Sch. 1, para. 484(3)(a); effective for income tax purposes for 2005–06 onwards and for corporation tax purposes for accounting periods ending after 5 April 2005 (ITTOIA 2005, s. 883(1)).

In para. 3(2) the words "paragraph 52 of that Schedule" substituted for the former wording by ITTOIA 2005, s. 882(1) and Sch. 1, para. 484(3)(b); effective for income tax purposes for 2005–06 onwards and for corporation tax purposes for accounting periods ending after 5 April 2005 (ITTOIA 2005, s. 883(1)).

In para. 3(4), in the definition of "the transitional overlap period", the words "(determined in accordance with paragraph 1 of Schedule 20 to the Finance Act 1994 despite the repeal by ITTOIA 2005 of that paragraph" inserted; and the words "(as so determined)" also inserted by ITTOIA 2005, s. 882(1) and Sch. 1, para. 484(3)(c); effective for income tax purposes for 2005–06 onwards and for corporation tax purposes for accounting periods ending after 5 April 2005 (ITTOIA 2005, s. 883(1)).

In para. 3(4), in the definition of "the transitional overlap profit", the words "paragraph 52(2) of Schedule 2 to ITTOIA 2005" substituted for the former wording by ITTOIA 2005, s. 882(1) and Sch. 1, para. 484(3)(d); effective for income tax purposes for 2005–06 onwards and for corporation tax purposes for accounting periods ending after 5 April 2005 (ITTOIA 2005, s. 883(1)).

Cross references – FA 1994, Sch. 20, para. 2: transitional provisions for opening and closing year rules for assessment under Sch. D, Case I of trades etc. set up and commenced before 6 April 1994 and continuing after 5 April 1997

Statutory instruments – SI 1997/1158.

4 [Omitted by ITTOIA 2005, s. 882(1) and Sch. 1, para. 484(4); and repealed by ITTOIA 2005, s. 884 and Sch. 3; with effect for income tax purposes for 2005–06 onwards and for corporation tax purposes for accounting periods ending after 5 April 2005 (ITTOIA 2005, s. 883(1)).]

5(1) This paragraph applies where, in the case of a trade or profession carried on by any person in partnership with other persons–

(a) paragraph 52 of Schedule 2 to ITTOIA 2005 applies with or without the modification made by paragraph 3(2) above;

(b) a claim is made under section 383 of the Income Tax Act 2007 (relief for interest payments) in respect of interest on a loan to defray money contributed or advanced by him (**"the partner"**) to the partnership; and

(c) sub-paragraph (2) below applies to any of the money so contributed or advanced.

5(2) This sub-paragraph applies to money so contributed or advanced unless it was contributed or advanced wholly or mainly–

(a) for bona fide commercial reasons; or

(b) for a purpose other than the reduction of the partnership's borrowings for a relevant period.

5(3) Subject to sub-paragraph (4) below, paragraph 52 of Schedule 2 to ITTOIA 2005 shall have effect as if the reference to the transitional overlap profit were a reference to the difference between that profit and the amount of interest paid by the partner in respect of the transitional overlap period on money to which sub-paragraph (2) above applies.

5(4) Sub-paragraph (3) above does not apply where–

(a) the loan was made before 1st April 1994; or

(b) the aggregate amount of interest paid as mentioned in that sub-paragraph is less than such amount as may be prescribed by regulations made by the Board.

5(5) In this paragraph–

"relevant period" means a period the whole or part of which falls within the transitional overlap period;

"the transitional overlap period" has the same meaning as in paragraph 3 above;

"the transitional overlap profit" means the amount mentioned in paragraph 52(2) of Schedule 2 to ITTOIA 2005 (whether having effect with or without the modification made by paragraph 3(2) above).

History – In para. 5(1)(a) the words "paragraph 52 of Schedule 2 to ITTOIA 2005" substituted for the former wording by ITTOIA 2005, s. 882(1) and Sch. 1, para. 484(5)(a); effective for income tax purposes for 2005–06 onwards and for corporation tax purposes for accounting periods ending after 5 April 2005 (ITTOIA 2005, s. 883(1)).

In para. 5(1)(b) the words "section 383 of the Income Tax Act 2007 (relief for interest payments)" substituted for "section 353 of the Taxes Act 1988 (relief for interest: general provision)" by ITA 2007, s. 1027 and Sch. 1, para. 370(2), with effect from 6 April 2007.

In para. 5(3) the words "paragraph 52 of Schedule 2 to ITTOIA 2005" substituted for the former wording by ITTOIA 2005, s. 882(1) and Sch. 1, para. 484(5)(b); effective for income tax purposes for 2005–06 onwards and for corporation tax purposes for accounting periods ending after 5 April 2005 (ITTOIA 2005, s. 883(1)).
In para. 5(5), in the definition of "the transitional overlap profit", the words "paragraph 52(2) of Schedule 2 to ITTOIA 2005" substituted for the former wording by ITTOIA 2005, s. 882(1) and Sch. 1, para. 484(5)(c); effective for income tax purposes for 2005–06 onwards and for corporation tax purposes for accounting periods ending after 5 April 2005 (ITTOIA 2005, s. 883(1)).

Cross references – ICTA 1988, s. 353: claim for relief in respect of payments of interest eligible for relief by virtue of ICTA 1988, s. 354–365.
SI 1997/1158, reg. 7: £7,500 is prescribed for the purposes of para. 5(4)(b).

Statutory instruments – SI 1997/1158)

Part II – Cases III, IV and V of Schedule D

INCREASE OF TRADE ETC. PROFITS OR GAINS ARISING IN 1995–96 AND 1996–97

6 [Omitted by ITTOIA 2005, s. 882(1) and Sch. 1, para. 484(6); and repealed by ITTOIA 2005, s. 884 and Sch. 3; with effect for income tax purposes for 2005–06 onwards and for corporation tax purposes for accounting periods ending after 5 April 2005 (ITTOIA 2005, s. 883(1)).]

INCREASE OF TRADE ETC. PROFITS OR GAINS ARISING IN TRANSITIONAL OVERLAP PERIOD

7(1) This paragraph applies where, in the case of any income derived by any person from the carrying on by him of a trade, profession or vocation–

(a) paragraph 53 of Schedule 2 to ITTOIA 2005 applies; and

(b) any amount which is included in the transitional overlap profit would not have been so included if–

  (i) any relevant change made by that person had not been made; or

  (ii) any relevant transaction entered into by that person had not been entered into.

7(2) Subject to sub-paragraph (3) below, paragraph 53 of that Schedule shall have effect as if the reference to the transitional overlap profit were a reference to the amount (if any) by which that profit exceeds 1.25 times the aggregate of the amounts falling within sub-paragraph (1)(b) above.

7(3) Sub-paragraph (3) of paragraph 1 above shall apply for the purposes of this paragraph as it applies for the purposes of that paragraph but subject to the following modifications, namely–

(a) the reference to the aggregate of the amounts mentioned in the said paragraph 2(2) shall have effect as a reference to the transitional overlap profit; and

(b) the reference to the appropriate percentage of the turnover for the transitional period shall have effect as a reference to the appropriate percentage of the turnover for the transitional overlap period.

7(4) In this paragraph–

"the appropriate percentage" means the following expressed as a percentage, that is, 365 divided by the number of days in the transitional overlap period;

"the transitional overlap period" means the period beginning immediately after the end of–

(a) the basis period for the year 1996–97 (determined in accordance with paragraph 1 of Schedule 20 to the Finance Act 1994 despite the repeal by ITTOIA 2005 of that paragraph); or

(b) in the case of any income derived by any person from the carrying on by him of a trade or profession in partnership with other persons, the basis period of the partnership for that year (as so determined),

and (in either case) ending with 5th April 1997;

"the transitional overlap profit" means the amount mentioned in paragraph 53(3) of Schedule 2 to ITTOIA 2005.

History – In para. 7(1) the words "paragraph 53 of Schedule 2 to ITTOIA 2005" substituted for the former wording by ITTOIA 2005, s. 882(1) and Sch. 1, para. 484(7)(a); effective for income tax purposes for 2005–06 onwards and for corporation tax purposes for accounting periods ending after 5 April 2005 (ITTOIA 2005, s. 883(1)).
In para. 7(2) the words "paragraph 53 of that Schedule" substituted for the former wording by ITTOIA 2005, s. 882(1) and Sch. 1, para. 484(7)(b); effective for income tax purposes for 2005–06 onwards and for corporation tax purposes for accounting periods ending after 5 April 2005 (ITTOIA 2005, s. 883(1)).
In para. 7(4), in the definition of "the transitional overlap period", the words "(determined in accordance with paragraph 1 of Schedule 20 to the Finance Act 1994 despite the repeal by ITTOIA 2005 of that paragraph)" inserted; and the words "(as so determined)" also inserted by ITTOIA 2005, s. 882(1) and Sch. 1, para. 484(7)(c); effective for income tax purposes for 2005–06 onwards and for corporation tax purposes for accounting periods ending after 5 April 2005 (ITTOIA 2005, s. 883(1)).
In para. 7(4), in the definition of "the transitional overlap profit", the words "paragraph 53(3) of Schedule 2 to ITTOIA 2005" substituted for the former wording by ITTOIA 2005, s. 882(1) and Sch. 1, para. 484(7)(d); effective for income tax purposes for 2005–06 onwards and for corporation tax purposes for accounting periods ending after 5 April 2005 (ITTOIA 2005, s. 883(1)).

Cross references – FA 1994, Sch. 20, para. 6: provisions for changing the basis of assessment under Sch. D, Cases IV and V from preceding to current year.

Statutory instruments – SI 1997/1158.

8 [Omitted by ITTOIA 2005, s. 882(1) and Sch. 1, para. 484(8); and repealed by ITTOIA 2005, s. 884 and Sch. 3; with effect for income tax purposes for 2005–06 onwards and for corporation tax purposes for accounting periods ending after 5 April 2005 (ITTOIA 2005, s. 883(1)).]

INCREASE OF INTEREST ARISING IN 1995–96 AND 1996–97

9 [Omitted by ITTOIA 2005, s. 882(1) and Sch. 1, para. 484(8); and repealed by ITTOIA 2005, s. 884 and Sch. 3; with effect for income tax purposes for 2005–06 onwards and for corporation tax purposes for accounting periods ending after 5 April 2005 (ITTOIA 2005, s. 883(1)).]

INCREASE OF OTHER INCOME ARISING IN 1995–96 AND 1996–97

10 [Omitted by ITTOIA 2005, s. 882(1) and Sch. 1, para. 484(8); and repealed by ITTOIA 2005, s. 884 and Sch. 3; with effect for income tax purposes for 2005–06 onwards and for corporation tax purposes for accounting periods ending after 5 April 2005 (ITTOIA 2005, s. 883(1)).]

Part III – Procedural Provisions

TIME LIMITS FOR PURPOSES OF PARAGRAPHS 1, 2, 4, 6 AND 8 TO 10

11(1) Nothing in subsection (2) or (3) of section 29 of the Management Act (as substituted by section 191 of the Finance Act 1994) shall prevent an assessment being made under subsection (1) of that section in any case where–

(a) the loss of tax there mentioned is attributable to any failure to give effect to any of paragraphs 1, 2, 4, 6 and 8 to 10 above; and

(b) at the time when the assessment is made, the condition mentioned in sub-paragraph (3) below is fulfilled.

11(2) Nothing in subsection (3) or (4) of section 30B of the Management Act (amendment of partnership return where loss of tax discovered) shall prevent an amendment being made under subsection (1) of that section in any case where–

(a) the omission, deficiency or excess there mentioned is attributable to any failure to give effect to any of paragraphs 1, 2, 4, 6 and 8 to 10 above; and

(b) at the time when the amendment is made, the condition mentioned in sub-paragraph (3) below is fulfilled.

11(3) The condition referred to in sub-paragraphs (1) and (2) above is that either–

(a) a return under section 8 or 8A of the Management Act (personal or trustee return) or, as the case may require, a partnership return has been made for the year 1997–98 and that return is still capable of being amended; or

(b) no such return has been so made.

History – In para. 11(2), the words "partnership return" substituted for "partnership statement" by FA 2001, s. 88 and Sch. 29, para. 37(2) with effect from 11 May 2001 in relation to returns made before or after that date, and whether relating to periods before or after that date.

Para. 11(3)(a) amended by FA 2001, s. 88 and Sch. 29, para. 37(3)(a) with effect from 11 May 2001 in relation to returns made before or after that date, and whether relating to periods before or after that date.

Para. 11(3)(b), substituted by FA 2001, s. 88 and Sch. 29, para. 37(3)(b) with effect from 11 May 2001 in relation to returns made before or after that date, and whether relating to periods before or after that date.

Cross references – TMA 1970, s. 9ZA: the taxpayer may amend his return (which include all references to self-assessments) during the 12 months following the filing date.

TMA 1970, s. 12AB (as inserted by FA 1994, s. 185): partnership returns may be amended during the 12 months following the filing date.

TMA 1970, s. 29(2) (as substituted by FA 1994, s. 191): discovery assessment prevented where returns prepared under generally prevailing practice at the time the return is made.

TMA 1970, s. 29(3) (as substituted by FA 1994, s. 191): discovery assessment prevented unless taxpayer's conduct is fraudulent or negligent or officer could not have been expected to have known of the situation representing the discovery when making enquiries.

TMA 1970, s. 30B(3) (as inserted by FA 1994, Sch. 19, para. 6): amendment of partnership return on "discovery" assessment prevented where prepared under generally prevailing practice at the time the return is made.

TMA 1970, s. 30B(4) (as inserted by FA 1994, Sch. 19, para. 6): discovery assessment prevented unless representative's partner's conduct is fraudulent or negligent or officer could not have been expected to have known of the situation representing the discovery when making enquiries.

ADVANCE NOTICE FOR PURPOSES OF PARAGRAPHS 3, 5 AND 7

12(1) An officer of the Board shall not so amend a return under section 8 or 8A of the Management Act (personal or trustee return) as to give effect to paragraph 3, 5 or 7 above unless a notice stating–

(a) in the case of paragraph 3 or 7 above, the aggregate of the amounts falling within sub-paragraph (1)(b) of that paragraph; and

(b) in the case of paragraph 5 above, the aggregate amount of interest paid as mentioned in sub-paragraph (3) of that paragraph,

is given by such an officer at a time when the condition mentioned in sub-paragraph (2) below is fulfilled.

12(2) The condition referred to in sub-paragraph (1) above is that either–

(a) a return under section 8 or 8A of the Management Act (personal or trustee return) has been made for the year 1998–99 and that return is still capable of being amended; or

(b) no such return has been so made.

12(3) Subject to sub-paragraph (4) below, a notice under sub-paragraph (1) above shall be conclusive of the matters stated in it.

12(4) An appeal may be brought against a notice under sub-paragraph (1) above at any time within the period of 30 days beginning with the date on which the notice is given.

12(5) Subject to sub-paragraph (6) below, the provisions of the Management Act relating to appeals shall have effect in relation to an appeal under sub-paragraph (4) above as they have effect in relation to an appeal against an assessment to tax.

12(6) On an appeal under sub-paragraph (4) above, section 50(6) to (8) of the Management Act (procedure on appeals) shall not apply but the Commissioners may–

(a) if it appears to them that the matters stated in the notice under sub-paragraph (1) above are correct, confirm the notice; or

(b) if it does not so appear to them, set aside or modify the notice accordingly.

History – In para. 12(1), the words "a return under section 8 or 8A of the Management Act (personal or trustee return)" substituted for "an assessment made under section 9 of the Management Act (returns to include self-assessment)" by FA 2001, s. 88 and Sch. 29, para. 37(4) with effect from 11 May 2001 in relation to returns made before or after that date, and whether relating to periods before or after that date.

Para. 12(2)(a) amended by, and para. 12(2)(b) substituted by FA 2001, s. 88 and Sch. 29, para. 37(5) with effect from 11 May 2001 in relation to returns made before or after that date, and whether relating to periods before or after that date.

Cross references – TMA 1970, s. 9ZA: the taxpayer may amend his return during the 12 months following the filing date.

TMA 1970, s. 50(6)–(8): commissioners powers to reduce or increase assessments on appeal.

PENALTIES NOT TO APPLY IN CERTAIN CASES

13(1) Where a **relevant return** (as originally made) states–

(a) that paragraph 1, 3 or 4 above applies in the case of a trade, profession or vocation carried on by any person; or

(b) that paragraph 7 or 8 above applies in the case of any income derived by any person from the carrying on by him of a trade, profession or vocation,

sub-paragraph (2) of that paragraph shall have effect, in its application to any amounts stated in the return (as so made) to fall within sub-paragraph (1)(b) of that paragraph or, in the case of paragraph 4 or 8 above, to be amounts which would have fallen within paragraph (1)(b) of the preceding paragraph, as if the words "1.25 times" were omitted.

13(2) Where a relevant return (as originally made) states–

(a) that paragraph 6 above applies in the case of any income derived by any person from the carrying on by him of a trade, profession or vocation; or

(b) that paragraph 9 or 10 above applies in the case of any income arising to any person from any source,

sub-paragraph (2) of that paragraph shall have effect, in its application to any amounts stated in the return (as so made) to fall within sub-paragraph (1)(b) of that paragraph, as if for the words "62.5 per cent" there were substituted the words "50 per cent".

13(3) In this paragraph–

"relevant return" means a return which, for the **relevant year**, is made under section 8, 8A or 12AA of the Management Act in respect of the trade, profession or vocation or, as the case may be, the source of the income;

"the relevant year" means–

(a) in relation to paragraph 1, 6, 9 or 10 above, the year 1996–97;

(b) in relation to paragraph 3, 4, 7 or 8 above, the year 1997–98.

Part IV – Interpretation

RELEVANT CHANGES FOR PURPOSES OF PARAGRAPHS 1, 3, 6 AND 7

History – In the heading to para. 14 any reference to para. 6 is redundant, for income tax purposes for 2005–06 onwards and for corporation tax purposes for accounting periods ending after 5 April 2005, since para. 6 is repealed by ITTOIA 2005, see the History note for para. 6 for details.

14(1) Any accounting change or change of business practice is a **relevant change** for the purposes of paragraphs 1, 3 and 7 above unless–

(a) the change is made exclusively for bona fide commercial reasons; or

(b) the obtaining of a tax advantage is not the main benefit that could reasonably be expected to arise from the making of the change.

14(2) In this paragraph **"accounting change"**–

(a) does not include any change of accounting date which brings the end of the basis period for the year 1996–97 closer to 5th April 1997; but

(b) subject to that, means any change of accounting date or other modification of an accounting policy or any substitution of one such policy for another.

14(3) In this paragraph **"change of business practice"** means any change in an established practice of trade, profession or vocation carried on by any person–

(a) as to the timing of any of the following, namely–

(i) the supply of goods or services, the invoicing of customers or clients and the collection of outstanding debts; and

(ii) the obtaining of goods or services, the incurring of business expenses and the settlement of outstanding debts; or

(b) as to the obtaining or making of payments in advance or payments on account.

History – In para. 14(1) the words "paragraphs 1, 3 and 7" substituted for the former wording by ITTOIA 2005, s. 882(1) and Sch. 1, para. 484(9); effective for income tax purposes for 2005–06 onwards and for corporation tax purposes for accounting periods ending after 5 April 2005 (ITTOIA 2005, s. 883(1)).

RELEVANT TRANSACTIONS FOR PURPOSES OF PARAGRAPHS 1, 3, 6 AND 7

History – In the heading to para. 15 any reference to para. 6 is redundant, for income tax purposes for 2005–06 onwards and for corporation tax purposes for accounting periods ending after 5 April 2005, since para. 6 is repealed by ITTOIA 2005, see the History note for para. 6 for details.

15 Any **"self-cancelling transaction"** or transaction with a connected person is a **"relevant transaction"** for the purposes of paragraphs 1, 3 and 7 above unless–

(a) the transaction is entered into exclusively for bona fide commercial reasons; or

(b) the obtaining of a tax advantage is not the main benefit that could reasonably be expected to arise from the entering into of the transaction.

History – In para. 15 the words "paragraphs 1, 3 and 7" substituted for the former wording by ITTOIA 2005, s. 882(1) and Sch. 1, para. 484(10); effective for income tax purposes for 2005–06 onwards and for corporation tax purposes for accounting periods ending after 5 April 2005 (ITTOIA 2005, s. 883(1)).

16(1) An agreement by which the person by whom a trade, profession or vocation is carried on agrees to sell or transfer trading stock or work in progress is a **self-cancelling transaction** for the purposes of paragraph 15 above if by the same or any collateral agreement that person–

(a) agrees to buy back or re-acquire the trading stock or work in progress; or

(b) acquires or grants an option, which is subsequently exercised, for him to buy back or re-acquire the trading stock or work in progress.

16(2) In sub-paragraph (1) above–

"trading stock" has the same meaning as in section 100 of the Taxes Act 1988;

"work in progress", in relation to a profession or vocation, means–

(a) any services performed in the ordinary course of the profession or vocation, the performance of which is wholly or partly completed at the time of the sale or transfer and for which it would be reasonable to expect that a charge would have been made on their completion if the sale or transfer had not been effected; and

(b) any article produced, and any such material as is used, in the performance of any such services,

and references in that sub-paragraph to the **"sale or transfer of work in progress"** shall include references to the sale or transfer of any benefits and rights which accrue, or might reasonably be expected to accrue, from the carrying out of the work.

17(1) For the purposes of paragraph 15 above, any question whether the person by whom a trade, profession or vocation is carried on is connected with another person shall be determined in accordance with sub-paragraphs (2) to (5) below.

17(2) An individual carrying on a trade, profession or vocation is connected with another person if they are connected with each other within the meaning of section 993 of the Income Tax Act 2007 (but as if, in subsection (4) of that section, the words from "But this subsection" to the end were omitted).

17(3) Persons carrying on a trade or profession in partnership are connected with an individual if he controls the partnership.

17(4) Persons carrying on a trade or profession in partnership are connected with a company if the company controls the partnership or the same person controls both the company and the partnership.

17(5) Persons carrying on a trade or profession in partnership are connected with persons carrying on another trade or profession in partnership if the same person controls both partnerships.

17(6) In this paragraph–

(a) **"control"** shall be construed–

  (i) in relation to a company, in accordance with sections 450 and 451 of the Corporation Tax Act 2010;

  (ii) in relation to a partnership, in accordance with section 995 of the Income Tax Act 2007; and

(b) any reference to a person controlling a company or partnership is a reference to his doing so either alone or with one or more persons connected with him.

History – In para. 17(2) the words "section 993 of the Income Tax Act 2007 (but as if, in subsection (4) of that section, the words from "But this subsection" to the end were omitted)." substituted for "section 839 of the Taxes Act 1988 (disregarding for this purpose the exception in subsection (4) of that section)." by ITA 2007, s. 1027 and Sch. 1, para. 370(3)(a), with effect from 6 April 2007.
In para. 17(6)(a), the words "sections 450 and 451 of the Corporation Tax Act 2010" substituted for the words "section 416 of the Taxes Act 1988" by CTA 2010, s. 1177 and Sch. 1, para. 290, with effect for corporation tax purposes for accounting periods ending on or after 1 April 2010, and for income tax and capital gains tax purposes for the tax year 2010–11 and subsequent tax years.
In para. 17(6)(a)(ii) of the definition of "control" the words "section 995 of the Income Tax Act 2007" substituted for "section 840 of that Act" by ITA 2007, s. 1027 and Sch. 1, para. 370(3)(b), with effect from 6 April 2007.

RELEVANT ARRANGEMENTS FOR PURPOSES OF PARAGRAPH 9

18 [Omitted by ITTOIA 2005, s. 882(1) and Sch. 1, para. 484(11); and repealed by ITTOIA 2005, s. 884 and Sch. 3; with effect for income tax purposes for 2005–06 onwards and for corporation tax purposes for accounting periods ending after 5 April 2005 (ITTOIA 2005, s. 883(1)).]

RELEVANT ARRANGEMENTS FOR PURPOSES OF PARAGRAPH 10

19 [Omitted by ITTOIA 2005, s. 882(1) and Sch. 1, para. 484(11); and repealed by ITTOIA 2005, s. 884 and Sch. 3; with effect for income tax purposes for 2005–06 onwards and for corporation tax purposes for accounting periods ending after 5 April 2005 (ITTOIA 2005, s. 883(1)).]

RELEVANT TRANSACTIONS FOR PURPOSES OF PARAGRAPH 10

20 [Omitted by ITTOIA 2005, s. 882(1) and Sch. 1, para. 484(11); and repealed by ITTOIA 2005, s. 884 and Sch. 3; with effect for income tax purposes for 2005–06 onwards and for corporation tax purposes for accounting periods ending after 5 April 2005 (ITTOIA 2005, s. 883(1)).]

GENERAL

21(1) In this Schedule **"turnover"**, in relation to a trade, profession or vocation, means the amounts derived from the provision of goods or services falling within its ordinary activities, after deduction of trade discounts and value added tax.

21(2) Obtaining a tax advantage shall not be regarded as a bona fide commercial reason for the purposes of this Schedule.

SCHEDULE 23 – OBLIGATIONS ETC. IMPOSED ON UK REPRESENTATIVES

Section 126

[Omitted by TIOPA 2010, s. 374 and Sch. 8, para. 279 and repealed by TIOPA 2010, s. 378 and Sch. 10, Pt. 11.]

History – Sch. 23 omitted by TIOPA 2010, s. 374 and Sch. 8, para. 279 and repealed by TIOPA 2010, s. 378 and Sch. 10, Pt. 11, with effect for corporation tax purposes for accounting periods ending on or after 1 April 2010, for income tax and capital gains tax purposes for the tax year 2010–11 and subsequent tax years, and for petroleum revenue tax purposes for chargeable periods beginning on or after 1 July 2010.

Notes – Sch. 23 rewritten in TIOPA 2010 as follows:
Para. 1(1): TIOPA 2010, Sch. 6, para. 18, 19, 28, 29.
Para. 1(2): TIOPA 2010, Sch. 6, para. 18, 28.
Para. 2: TIOPA 2010, Sch. 6, para. 19, 29.
Para. 3: TIOPA 2010, Sch. 6, para. 20, 30.
Para. 4(1): TIOPA 2010, Sch. 6, para. 20, 30.
Para. 4(2): TIOPA 2010, Sch. 6, para. 20, 30.
Para. 4(3): TIOPA 2010, Sch. 6, para. 20, 30.
Para. 5(1): TIOPA 2010, Sch. 6, para. 21, 31.
Para. 5(2): TIOPA 2010, Sch. 6, para. 21, 31.
Para. 6: TIOPA 2010, Sch. 6, para. 22, 32.
Para. 7(1): TIOPA 2010, Sch. 6, para. 23, 33.
Para. 7(2): TIOPA 2010, Sch. 6, para. 23, 33.

SCHEDULE 24 – EXCHANGE GAINS AND LOSSES

Section 130

Part I – Amendments of Finance Act 1993

INTRODUCTION

1 [Repealed by FA 2002, s. 141 and Sch. 40, Pt. 3(10).]

History – Para. 1 repealed by FA 2002, s. 141 and Sch. 40, Pt. 3(10) with effect in relation to accounting periods beginning on or after 1 October 2002.

TRADING GAINS AND LOSSES

2 [Repealed by FA 2002, s. 141 and Sch. 40, Pt. 3(10).]

History – Para. 2 repealed by FA 2002, s. 141 and Sch. 40, Pt. 3(10) with effect in relation to accounting periods beginning on or after 1 October 2002.

NON-TRADING GAINS AND LOSSES

3 [Repealed by FA 2002, s. 141 and Sch. 40, Pt. 3(10).]

History – Para. 3 repealed by FA 2002, s. 141 and Sch. 40. Pt. 3(10) with effect in relation to accounting periods beginning on or after 1 October 2002.

ASSETS AND LIABILITIES

4 [Repealed by FA 1996, s. 205, Sch. 41, Pt. V(3), with effect for 1996–97 and subsequent years of assessment (income tax) and for accounting periods ending after 31 March 1996 (corporation tax).]

CHARGEABLE GAINS

5-6 [Repealed by FA 1996, s. 205, Sch. 41, Pt. V(3), with effect for 1996–97 and subsequent years of assessment (income tax) and for accounting periods ending after 31 March 1996 (corporation tax).]

Part II – Amendments of Other Provisions

INTRODUCTION

7 Paragraphs 8 to 12 below shall be deemed to have come into force on 23rd March 1995.

History – In para. 7, the words "23rd March 1995" substituted for the words"the day appointed under section 165(7)(b) of the Finance Act 1993 (which relates to exchange gains and losses)" by FA 2002, s. 79 and Sch. 23, para. 22(3).

INTEREST ON OVERDUE TAX

8 [Amends TMA 1970, s. 87A(4A).]

9(1) [Repealed by FA 1998, s. 165 and Sch. 27, Pt. III(2).]

9(2) [Repealed by FA 1998, s. 165 and Sch. 27, Pt. III(2).]

History – Para. 9 repealed by FA 1998, s. 165 and Sch. 27, Pt. III(2) with effect in relation to periods beginning on or after 6 April 1999 (Sch. 3, para. 4).

10 [Amends TMA 1970, s. 91(1B).]

INTEREST ON TAX OVERPAID

11 [Amends ICTA 1988, s. 826(7C).]

12(1) [Repealed by FA 1998, s. 165, Sch. 27, Pt. III(2); amended ICTA 1988, s. 826(7).]

12(2) [Repealed by FA 1998, s. 165, Sch. 27, Pt. III(2).]

12(3) [Repealed by CTA 2010, s. 1181 and Sch. 3, Pt. 1.]

12(4)–(5) [Repealed by FA 1998, s. 165, Sch. 27, Pt. III(2).]

History – Para. 12(1), (2), (4) and (5) repealed by FA 1998, s. 165, Sch. 27, Pt. III(2) with effect in relation to periods beginning on or after 6 April 1999 (Sch. 3, para. 38).

Para. 12(3) repealed by CTA 2010, s. 1181 and Sch. 3, Pt. 1, with effect for corporation tax purposes for accounting periods ending on or after 1 April 2010, and for income tax and capital gains tax purposes for the tax year 2010–11 and subsequent tax years.

SCHEDULE 25 – CONTROLLED FOREIGN COMPANIES

Section 133

INTRODUCTION

1 In this Schedule–

(a) paragraph 2 contains an amendment designed to secure that in certain cases the chargeable profits of a company resident outside the United Kingdom are to be computed and expressed in the currency used in its accounts;

(b) the other paragraphs contain amendments connected with that amendment.

THE PRINCIPAL AMENDMENT

2 [Repealed by FA 2005, s. 104 and Sch. 11, Pt. 2(6).]

History – Para. 2 repealed by FA 2005, s. 104 and Sch. 11, Pt. 2(6), with effect for periods of account beginning on or after 16 March 2005.

CONNECTED AMENDMENTS

3 [Repealed by FA 2005, s. 104 and Sch. 11, Pt. 2(6).]

History – Para. 3 repealed by FA 2005, s. 104 and Sch. 11, Pt. 2(6), with effect for periods of account beginning on or after 16 March 2005.

4 [Repealed by FA 2005, s. 104 and Sch. 11, Pt. 2(6).]

History – Para. 4 repealed by FA 2005, s. 104 and Sch. 11, Pt. 2(6), with effect for periods of account beginning on or after 16 March 2005.

5 [Repealed by FA 2005, s. 104 and Sch. 11, Pt. 2(6).]

History – Para. 5 repealed by FA 2005, s. 104 and Sch. 11, Pt. 2(6), with effect for periods of account beginning on or after 16 March 2005.

6(1) Schedule 24 to the Taxes Act 1988 (assumptions for calculating chargeable profits etc.) shall be amended as mentioned in sub-paragraphs (2) to (5) below; and–

(a) the amendment made by sub-paragraph (2) below shall be deemed always to have had effect, and

(b) paragraph 1(4) of Schedule 16 to the Finance Act 1984 shall be deemed always to have had effect subject to the same amendment.

6(2) [Amends ICTA 1988, Sch. 24, para. 1(4).]

6(3) [Repeals ICTA 1988, Sch. 24, para. 4A.]

6(4) [Repealed by FA 2005, s. 104 and Sch. 11, Pt. 2(6).]

6(5) [Repealed by FA 2002, s. 141 and Sch. 40, Pt. 3(10).]

History – Para. 6(4) repealed by FA 2005, s. 104 and Sch. 11, Pt. 2(6), with effect for periods of account beginning on or after 16 March 2005.

Para. 6(5) repealed by FA 2002, s. 141 and Sch. 40, Pt. 3(10) with effect in relation to accounting periods beginning on or after 1 October 2002.

7 [Repealed by FA 2002, s. 141 and Sch. 40, Pt. 3(10).]

History – Para. 7 repealed by FA 2002, s. 141 and Sch. 40, Pt. 3(10) with effect in relation to accounting periods beginning on or after 1 October 2002.

SCHEDULE 26 – CHANGE IN OWNERSHIP OF INVESTMENT COMPANY: DEDUCTIONS

Section 135

[Repealed by CTA 2010, s. 1181 and Sch. 3, Pt. 1.]

History – Sch. 26 repealed by CTA 2010, s. 1181 and Sch. 3, Pt. 1, with effect for corporation tax purposes for accounting periods ending on or after 1 April 2010, and for income tax and capital gains tax purposes for the tax year 2010–11 and subsequent tax years.

SCHEDULE 27 – SUB-CONTRACTORS IN THE CONSTRUCTION INDUSTRY

Section 139

1–9 [Repealed by FA 2004, s. 326 and Sch. 42, Pt. 2(7).]

History – Sch. 27 repealed by FA 2004, s. 326 and Sch. 42, Pt. 2(7), in relation to payments made on or after 6 April 2007, under contracts relating to construction payments subject to FA 2004, s. 77, by virtue of notice given pursuant to SI 2005/2045.

SCHEDULE 28 – ELECTRONIC LODGEMENT OF TAX RETURNS, ETC.

Section 153

Prospective amendments – Repealed by FA 1999, s. 139 and Sch. 20, Pt. VII, with effect from a day to be appointed.

1 [Inserts TMA 1970, s. 115A.]

2 [Inserts TMA 1970, Sch. 3A.]

EMPLOYMENT RIGHTS ACT 1996

(1996 Chapter 18)

[*22nd May 1996*]

ARRANGEMENT OF SECTIONS

PART V – PROTECTION FROM SUFFERING DETRIMENT IN EMPLOYMENT

RIGHTS NOT TO SUFFER DETRIMENT

47G Employee shareholder status

47G(1) An employee has the right not to be subjected to a detriment by any act, or any deliberate failure to act, by the employee's employer done on the ground that the employee refused to accept an offer by the employer for the employee to become an employee shareholder (within the meaning of section 205A).

47G(2) This section does not apply if the detriment in question amounts to dismissal within the meaning of Part 10.

History – S. 47G inserted by Growth and Infrastructure Act 2013, s. 31(2), with effect from 1 September 2013 (SI 2013/1766, art. 2).

ENFORCEMENT

48 Complaints to employment tribunals

History – In the heading to s. 48, the words "employment tribunal" substituted by the Employment Rights (Dispute Resolution) Act 1986, s. 1(2)(b), with effect from 1 August 1998 (SI 1998/1658, art. 2 and Sch. 1).

48(1) An employee may present a complaint to an employment tribunal that he has been subjected to a detriment in contravention of section 43M, 44, 45, 46, 47, 47A, 47C(1) 47E, 47F or 47G.

48(1ZA) A worker may present a complaint to an employment tribunal that he has been subjected to a detriment in contravention of section 45A.

48(1A) A worker may present a complaint to an employment tribunal that he has been subjected to a detriment in contravention of section 47B.

48(1AA) An agency worker may present a complaint to an employment tribunal that the agency worker has been subjected to a detriment in contravention of section 47C(5) by the temporary work agency or the hirer.

48(1B) A person may present a complaint to an employment tribunal that he has been subjected to a detriment in contravention of section 47D.

48(2) On a complaint under subsection (1), (1ZA), (1A), or (1B) it is for the employer to show the ground on which any act, or deliberate failure to act, was done.

48(2A) On a complaint under subsection (1AA) it is for the temporary work agency or (as the case may be) the hirer to show the ground on which any act, or deliberate failure to act, was done.

48(3) An employment tribunal shall not consider a complaint under this section unless it is presented–

(a) before the end of the period of three months beginning with the date of the act or failure to act to which the complaint relates or, where that act or failure is part of a series of similar acts or failures, the last of them, or

(b) within such further period as the tribunal considers reasonable in a case where it is satisfied that it was not reasonably practicable for the complaint to be presented before the end of that period of three months.

48(4) For the purposes of subsection (3)–

(a) where an act extends over a period, the **"date of the act"** means the last day of that period, and

(b) a deliberate failure to act shall be treated as done when it was decided on;

and, in the absence of evidence establishing the contrary, an employer, a temporary work agency or a hirer shall be taken to decide on a failure to act when he does an act inconsistent with doing the failed act or, if he has done no such inconsistent act, when the period expires within which he might reasonably have been expected to do the failed act if it was to be done.

48(4A) Section 207A(3) (extension because of mediation in certain European cross-border disputes) and section 207B (extension of time limits to facilitate conciliation before institution of proceedings) apply for the purposes of subsection (3)(a).

48(5) In this section and section 49 any reference to the employer includes, where a person complains that he has been subjected to a detriment in contravention of section 47A, the principal (within the meaning of section 63A(3)).

48(6) In this section and section 49 the following have the same meaning as in the Agency Workers Regulations 2010 (S.I. 2010/93)–

"agency worker";

"hirer";

"temporary work agency"

History – In s. 48(1), "47C(1)" substituted for "47C" by Children and Families Act 2014, s. 129(2), with effect from 1 October 2014 (SI 2014/1640, art. 4(b)).
In s. 48(1), the words ", 47F or 47G" substituted for the words "or 47F" by Growth and Infrastructure Act 2013, s. 31(3), with effect from 1 September 2013 (SI 2013/1766, art. 2).
In s. 48(1), the words "or 47E" omitted and words ", 47E or 47F" inserted by the Apprenticeships, Skills, Children and Learning Act 2009, s. 40(5) and Sch. 1, with effect (except for small employers and their employees) from 6 April 2010 (SI 2010/303, art. 4 and Sch. 3.
In s. 48(1), the words "or 47E" inserted by the Employment Relations Act 2004, s. 41(3), with effect from 6 April 2005 (SI 2005/872, art. 4 and Sch. 1).
In s. 48(1), the words "43M" inserted by the Employment Relations Act 2004, s. 40(2), with effect from 6 April 2005 (SI 2005/872, art. 4 and Sch. 1).
In s. 48(1), the words ", 47C or" substituted by the Employment Act 2002, s. 53 and Sch. 7, with effect from 6 April 2003 (SI 2002/2866, art. 2 and Sch. 1).
In s. 48(1), the words "47A" inserted by the Employment Relations Act 1999, s. 9 and Sch. 24, with effect from 15 December 1999 (SI 1999/2830, art. 2 and Sch. 1).
In s. 48(1), the words "46, 47" substituted by the Teaching and Higher Education Act 1998, s. 44(1) and Sch. 3, para. 11, with effect from 1 September 1999 (SI 1999/987, art. 2)
In s. 48(1), the words "employment tribunal" substituted by the Employment Rights (Dispute Resolution) Act 1986, s. 1(2)(b), with effect from 1 August 1998 (SI 1998/1658, art. 2 and Sch. 1).
S. 48(1ZA) inserted by SI 1998/1833, reg. 31(2), with effect from 1 October 1998.
S. 48(1A) inserted by the Public Interest Disclosure Act 1998, s. 3, with effect from 2 July 1999 (SI 1999/1547, art. 2)
S. 48(1AA) inserted by Children and Families Act 2014, s. 129(2), with effect from 1 October 2014 (SI 2014/1640, art. 4(b)).
S. 48(1B) inserted by the Tax Credits Act 2002, s. 27 and Sch. 1, para. 1, with effect from 1 September 2002 (SI 2002/1727, art. 2).
In s. 48(2), the words "a complaint under subsection (1), (1ZA), (1A), or (1B)" substituted for the words "such a complaint" by Children and Families Act 2014, s. 129(2), with effect from 1 October 2014 (SI 2014/1640, art. 4(b)).
S. 48(2A) inserted by Children and Families Act 2014, s. 129(2), with effect from 1 October 2014 (SI 2014/1640, art. 4(b)).
In s. 48(3), the words "employment tribunal" substituted by the Employment Rights (Dispute Resolution) Act 1986, s. 1(2)(a), with effect from 1 August 1998 (SI 1998/1658, art. 2 and Sch. 1).
In s. 48(4), the words ", a temporary work agency or a hirer" inserted by Children and Families Act 2014, s. 129(2), with effect from 1 October 2014 (SI 2014/1640, art. 4(b)).
In s. 48(4A), the words "andsection 207B (extension of time limits to facilitate conciliation before institution of proceedings) apply" substituted for the word "applies" by Enterprise and Regulatory Reform Act 2013, s. 8 and Sch. 2, para. 19, with effect from 6 April 2014 (SI 2014/253, art. 3).
S. 48(4A) inserted by SI 2011/1133, reg 34, with effect from 20 May 2011.

S. 48(5) inserted by the Teaching and Higher Education Act 1998, s. 44(1) and Sch. 3, para. 11, with effect from 1 September 1999 (SI 1999/987, art. 2).
S. 48(6) inserted by Children and Families Act 2014, s. 129(2), with effect from 1 October 2014 (SI 2014/1640, art. 4(b)).

PART X – UNFAIR DISMISSAL

Chapter I – Right not to be Unfairly Dismissed

EXCLUSION OF RIGHT

104G Employee shareholder status

104G An employee who is dismissed is to be regarded for the purposes of this Part as unfairly dismissed if the reason (or, if more than one, the principal reason) for the dismissal is that the employee refused to accept an offer by the employer for the employee to become an employee shareholder (within the meaning of section 205A).

History – S. 104G inserted by Growth and Infrastructure Act 2013, s. 31(4), with effect from 1 September 2013 (SI 2013/1766, art. 2).

PART XIII – MISCELLANEOUS

Chapter II – Other Miscellaneous Matters

EMPLOYEE SHAREHOLDER STATUS

205A Employee shareholders

205A(1) An individual who is or becomes an employee of a company is an **"employee shareholder"** if–

(a) the company and the individual agree that the individual is to be an employee shareholder,

(b) in consideration of that agreement, the company issues or allots to the individual fully paid up shares in the company, or procures the issue or allotment to the individual of fully paid up shares in its parent undertaking, which have a value, on the day of issue or allotment, of no less than £2,000,

(c) the company gives the individual a written statement of the particulars of the status of employee shareholder and of the rights which attach to the shares referred to in paragraph (b) ("the employee shares") (see subsection (5)), and

(d) the individual gives no consideration other than by entering into the agreement.

205A(2) An employee who is an employee shareholder does not have–

(a) the right to make an application under section 63D (request to undertake study or training),

(b) the right to make an application under section 80F (request for flexible working),

(c) the right under section 94 not to be unfairly dismissed, or

(d) the right under section 135 to a redundancy payment.

205A(3) The following provisions are to be read in the case of an employee who is an employee shareholder as if for "8 weeks' notice", in each place it appears, there were substituted "16 weeks' notice"–

(a) regulation 11 of the Maternity and Parental Leave etc. Regulations 1999 (S.I. 1999/3312) (requirement for employee to notify employer of intention to return to work during maternity leave period), and

(b) regulation 25 of the Paternity and Adoption Leave Regulations 2002 (S.I. 2002/2788) (corresponding provision for adoption leave).

205A(4) Regulation 30 of the Additional Paternity Leave Regulations 2010 (S.I. 2010/1055) (requirement for employee to notify employer of intention to return to work during additional paternity leave period) is to be read in the case of an employee who is an employee shareholder as if for "six weeks' notice", in each place it appears, there were substituted "16 weeks' notice".

205A(5) The statement referred to in subsection (1)(c) must–

(a) state that, as an employee shareholder, the individual would not have the rights specified in subsection (2),

(b) specify the notice periods that would apply in the individual's case as a result of subsections (3) and (4),

(c) state whether any voting rights attach to the employee shares,

(d) state whether the employee shares carry any rights to dividends,

(e) state whether the employee shares would, if the company were wound up, confer any rights to participate in the distribution of any surplus assets,

(f) if the company has more than one class of shares and any of the rights referred to in paragraphs (c) to (e) attach to the employee shares, explain how those rights differ from the equivalent rights that attach to the shares in the largest class (or next largest class if the class which includes the employee shares is the largest),

(g) state whether the employee shares are redeemable and, if they are, at whose option,

(h) state whether there are any restrictions on the transferability of the employee shares and, if there are, what those restrictions are,

(i) state whether any of the requirements of sections 561 and 562 of the Companies Act 2006 are excluded in the case of the employee shares (existing shareholders' right of pre-emption), and

(j) state whether the employee shares are subject to drag-along rights or tag-along rights and, if they are, explain the effect of the shares being so subject.

205A(6) Agreement between a company and an individual that the individual is to become an employee shareholder is of no effect unless, before the agreement is made–

(a) the individual, having been given the statement referred to in subsection (1)(c), receives advice from a relevant independent adviser as to the terms and effect of the proposed agreement, and

(b) seven days have passed since the day on which the individual receives the advice.

205A(7) Any reasonable costs incurred by the individual in obtaining the advice (whether or not the individual becomes an employee shareholder) which would, but for this subsection, have to be met by the individual are instead to be met by the company.

205A(8) The reference in subsection (2)(b) to making an application under section 80F does not include a reference to making an application within the period of 14 days beginning with the day on which the employee shareholder returns to work from a period of parental leave under regulations under section 76.

205A(9) The reference in subsection (2)(c) to unfair dismissal does not include a reference to a dismissal–

(a) which is required to be regarded as unfair for the purposes of Part 10 by a provision (whenever made) contained in or made under this or any other Act, or

(b) which amounts to a contravention of the Equality Act 2010.

205A(10) The reference in subsection (2)(c) to the right not to be unfairly dismissed does not include a reference to that right in a case where section 108(2) (health and safety cases) applies.

205A(11) The Secretary of State may by order amend subsection (1) so as to increase the sum for the time being specified there.

205A(12) The Secretary of State may by regulations provide that any agreement for a company to buy back from an individual the shares referred to in subsection (1)(b) in the event that the individual ceases to be an employee shareholder or ceases to be an employee must be on terms which meet the specified requirements.

205A(13) In this section–

"company" means–

(a) a company or overseas company (within the meaning, in each case, of the Companies Act 2006) which has a share capital, or

(b) a European Public Limited-Liability Company (or Societas Europaea) within the meaning of Council Regulation 2157/2001/EC of 8 October 2001 on the Statute for a European company;

"drag-along rights", in relation to shares in a company, means the right of the holders of a majority of the shares, where they are selling their shares, to require the holders of the minority to sell theirs;

"parent undertaking" has the same meaning as in the Companies Act 2006;

"relevant independent adviser" has the meaning that it has for the purposes of section 203(3)(c);

"tag-along rights", in relation to shares in a company, means the right of the holders of a minority of the shares to sell their shares, where the holders of the majority are selling theirs, on the same terms as those on which the holders of the majority are doing so.

205A(14) The reference in this section to the value of shares in a company is a reference to their market value within the meaning of the Taxation of Chargeable Gains Act 1992 (see sections 272 and 273 of that Act).

History – S. 205A inserted by Growth and Infrastructure Act 2013, s. 31(1), with effect from 1 September 2013 (SI 2013/1766, art. 2).

PART XV – GENERAL AND SUPPLEMENTARY

GENERAL

236 Orders and regulations

236(1) Any power conferred by any provision of this Act to make any order (other than an Order in Council) or regulations is exercisable by statutory instrument.

236(2) A statutory instrument made under any power conferred by this Act to make an Order in Council or other order or regulations, except–

(a) an Order in Council or other order or regulations to which subsection (3) applies,

(b) an order under section 35 or Part II of Schedule 2, or

(c) an order made in accordance with section 208,

is subject to annulment in pursuance of a resolution of either House of Parliament.

236(3) No recommendation shall be made to Her Majesty to make an Order in Council under section 192(3), and no order or regulations shall be made under section 27B, 43FA (but see subsection (3A)), 43K(4), 47C, 49B, 63D, 63F(7), 71, 72, 73, 75A, 75B, 75E, 75F(16), 75G, 75H(16), (17) or (18)[,] 76, 80A, 80B, 80G, 99, 120(2), 124(2), 125(7) or 205A(11) or (12) or (subject to subsection (4)) section 209, unless a draft of the Order in Council, order or regulations has been laid before Parliament and approved by a resolution of each House of Parliament.

236(3A) Subsection (3) does not apply to regulations under section 43FA that contain only the provision mentioned in section 43FA(2), (3) or (4).

236(4) Subsection (3) does not apply to an order under section 209(1)(b) which specifies only provisions contained in Part XI.

236(5) Any power conferred by this Act which is exercisable by statutory instrument includes power to make such incidental, supplementary or transitional provisions as appear to the authority exercising the power to be necessary or expedient.

Prospective amendments – S. 236(2)(c) omitted by the Employment Relations Act 1999, s. 44 and Sch. 9, with effect from a day to be appointed.

In s. 236(3), words "120(2), 124(2)" omitted by the Employment Relations Act 1999, s. 44 and Sch. 9, with effect from a day to be appointed.

History – In s. 236(2)(a) the words "or regulations" inserted by the Employment Relations Act 1999, s. 9 and Sch. 4, with effect from 15 December 1999 (SI 1999/2830, art. 2).

In s. 236(3), the words "43FA (but see subsection (3A))," inserted by Small Business, Enterprise and Employment Act 2015, s. 148(3)(a), with effect from 1 January 2016 (SI 2015/2029, reg. 2(a)).

In s. 236(3), "49B," inserted by Small Business, Enterprise and Employment Act 2015, s. 149(4), with effect from 26 May 2015 (SI 2015/1329, reg. 2(e)).

In s. 236(3), "27B" inserted by Small Business, Enterprise and Employment Act 2015, s. 153(3), with effect from 26 May 2015 (SI 2015/1329, reg. 2(g)).

In s. 236(3), the words "75E, 75F(16), 75G, 75H(16), (17) or (18)" inserted by Children and Families Act 2014, s. 117(2), with effect from 30 June 2014 (SI 2014/1640, art. 3(a)).

In s. 236(3), the words "80AA," and "80BB," (which appeared after the words "80A," and "80B," respectively) repealed by Children and Families Act 2014, s. 126(1) and Sch. 7, para. 43, with effect from 30 June 2014 (SI 2014/1640, art. 3(a)).

In s. 236(3), the words ", 125(7) or 205A(11) or (12)" substituted for the words "or 125(7)" by Growth and Infrastructure Act 2013, s. 31(6), with effect from 1 September 2013 (SI 2013/1766, art. 2).

In s. 236(3), the words "43K(4)," inserted by Enterprise and Regulatory Reform Act 2013, s. 20(8), with effect the end of the period of 2 months beginning with 25 April 2013.

In s. 236(3) the words "63D, 63F(7)" inserted by Apprenticeships, Skills, Children and Learning Act 2009, s. 40 and Sch. 1, para. 11, with effect from 6 April 2010 (except for small businesses and their employees) (SI 2020/303).

In s. 236(3) the words "80A. 80AA, 80B, 80BB, 80G" substituted by the Work and Families Act 2006, s. 11 and Sch. 1, para. 44, with effect from 3 March 2010 (SI 2010/495).

In s. 236(3) the words "75A, 75B" and "80A, 80B, 80G" inserted by the Employment Act 2002, s. 53 and Sch. 7, with effect from 8 December 2002 (except as relatesd to "80G") and 6 April 2003 (for "80G") (SI 2002/2866, art. 2 and Sch. 1).

In s. 236(3) words inserted and words substituted by the Employment Relations Act 1999, s. 9 and Sch. 4, with effect from 15 December 1999 (SI 1999/2830, art. 2).

S. 236(3A) inserted by Small Business, Enterprise and Employment Act 2015, s. 148(3)(a), with effect from 1 January 2016 (SI 2015/2029, reg. 2(a)).

FINANCE ACT 1996

1996 Chapter 8

[*29th April 1996*]

ARRANGEMENT OF SECTIONS

PART IV – INCOME TAX, CORPORATION TAX AND CAPITAL GAINS TAX

CHAPTER I – PRINCIPAL PROVISIONS

INCOME TAX CHARGE, RATES AND RELIEFS

CORPORATION TAX CHARGE AND RATE

ABOLITION OF SCHEDULE C CHARGE ETC.

CHAPTER II – LOAN RELATIONSHIPS

INTRODUCTORY PROVISIONS

TAXATION OF PROFITS AND GAINS AND RELIEF FOR DEFICITS

COMPUTATIONAL PROVISIONS ETC.

SHARES TREATED AS LOAN RELATIONSHIPS

CHAPTER V – SELF ASSESSMENT, GENERAL MANAGEMENT ETC.

CHAPTER VI – MISCELLANEOUS PROVISIONS

	Part I – Corporation Tax
	Part II – Income Tax and Capital Gains Tax
16.	SHARE OPTION SCHEMES APPROVED BEFORE PASSING OF THIS ACT
17.	CLAIMS FOR RELIEF INVOLVING TWO OR MORE YEARS
18.	OVERDUE TAX AND EXCESSIVE PAYMENTS BY THE BOARD
19.	SELF-ASSESSMENT: CLAIMS AND ENQUIRIES
20.	SELF-ASSESSMENT: DISCRETIONS EXERCISABLE BY THE BOARD ETC.
21.	SELF-ASSESSMENT: TIME LIMITS
22.	SELF-ASSESSMENT: APPEALS
23.	SELF-ASSESSMENT: SCHEDULES 13 AND 16 TO THE TAXES ACT 1988
	Part I – Schedule 13 to the Taxes Act 1988
	Part II – Schedule 16 to the Taxes Act 1988
24.	SELF-ASSESSMENT: ACCOUNTING PERIODS ETC.
	Part I – Amendments of the Taxes Management Act 1970
	Part II – Other Amendments
25.	SELF-ASSESSMENT: SURRENDERS OF ADVANCE CORPORATION TAX
26.	DAMAGES AND COMPENSATION FOR PERSONAL INJURY
27.	FOREIGN INCOME DIVIDENDS
28.	FOTRA SECURITIES: CONSEQUENTIAL AMENDMENTS
29.	PAYING AND COLLECTING AGENTS ETC.
	Part 1 – The New Chapter
	Part II – Other Provisions
30.	INVESTMENTS IN HOUSING
31.	LIFE ASSURANCE BUSINESS LOSSES
32.	EQUALISATION RESERVES
33.	MANAGEMENT EXPENSES OF CAPITAL REDEMPTION BUSINESS
34.	PROVISIONAL REPAYMENTS IN CONNECTION WITH PENSION BUSINESS
35.	ROLL-OVER RELIEF IN RESPECT OF SHIPS
36.	CONTROLLED FOREIGN COMPANIES
37.	BANKS
	Part I – "Bank" Re-defined for Certain Purposes
	Part II – Amendments of the Taxes Act 1988
	Part III – Other Amendments
38.	QUOTATION OR LISTING OF SECURITIES
39.	ENACTMENT OF CERTAIN INLAND REVENUE EXTRA-STATUTORY CONCESSIONS
	Part I – Income Tax and Corporation Tax
	Part II – Chargeable Gains
	Part III – Stamp Duty
40.	GILT STRIPPING: TAXATION PROVISIONS

PART IV – INCOME TAX, CORPORATION TAX AND CAPITAL GAINS TAX

Chapter I – Principal Provisions

INCOME TAX CHARGE, RATES AND RELIEFS

72 Charge and rates of income tax for 1996–97

72(1) [Repealed by ITA 2007, s. 1031 and Sch. 3, Pt. 1.]

72(2) [Repealed by ITA 2007, s. 1031 and Sch. 3, Pt. 1.]

72(3) [Repealed by FA 2004, s. 326 and Sch. 42, Pt. 2(7).]

History – S. 72(1) and (2) repealed by ITA 2007, s. 1031 and Sch. 3, Pt. 1, with effect from 6 April 2007.
S. 72(3) repealed by FA 2004, s. 326 and Sch. 42, Pt. 2(7) from 6 April 2007, in relation to construction operations (FA 2004, s. 77), by virtue of notice given pursuant to SI 2005/2045.

Cross references – FA 1995, s. 139(3): meaning of "the appointed day".

73 Application of lower rate to income from savings

73(1) [Repealed by ITA 2007, s. 1031 and Sch. 3, Pt. 1.]

73(2) [Repealed by ITA 2007, s. 1031 and Sch. 3, Pt. 1.]

73(3) [Repealed by ITA 2007, s. 1031 and Sch. 3, Pt. 1.]

73(4) Schedule 6 to this Act (which makes further amendments in connection with the charge at the lower rate on income from savings etc.) shall have effect.

73(5) [Repealed by ITA 2007, s. 1031 and Sch. 3, Pt. 1.]

History – S. 73(1)–(3) repealed by ITA 2007, s. 1031 and Sch. 3, Pt. 1, with effect from 6 April 2007.
S. 73(5) repealed by ITA 2007, s. 1031 and Sch. 3, Pt. 1, with effect from 6 April 2007.

Notes – S. 73 rewritten as follows:
S. 73(1): ITA 2007, s. 7, 12(1), (2), 13(1), 14(1), (2), 16(1), (2), (3), (4), (5), (7), 18(1), (2), (3), (4), 19(1), (2), (3), 1012(2), (3), (4), (5).
S. 73(2): ITA 2007, s. 874(2), 902(3), (4).

74 Personal allowances for 1996–97

74(1,2) [Repealed by ITA 2007, s. 1031 and Sch. 3, Pt. 1.]

History – S. 74 repealed by ITA 2007, s. 1031 and Sch. 3, Pt. 1, with effect from 6 April 2007.

75 Blind person's allowance

75 [Repealed by ITA 2007, s. 1031 and Sch. 3, Pt. 1.]

History – S. 75 repealed by ITA 2007, s. 1031 and Sch. 3, Pt. 1, with effect from 6 April 2007.

76 Limit on relief for interest

76 [Repealed by ITA 2007, s. 1031 and Sch. 3, Pt. 1.]

History – S. 76 repealed by ITA 2007, s. 1031 and Sch. 3, Pt. 1, with effect from 6 April 2007.

CORPORATION TAX CHARGE AND RATE

77 Charge and rate of corporation tax for 1996

77 [Spent: set the corporation tax rate for the financial year 1996.]

78 Small companies

78 [Repealed by CTA 2010, s. 1181 and Sch. 3, Pt. 1.]

History – S. 78 repealed by CTA 2010, s. 1181 and Sch. 3, Pt. 1, with effect for accounting periods ending on or after 1 April 2010.

ABOLITION OF SCHEDULE C CHARGE ETC.

79 Abolition of Schedule C charge etc.

79(1) The charge to tax under Schedule C is abolished–

(a) for the purposes of income tax, for the year 1996–97 and subsequent years of assessment;

(b) for the purposes of corporation tax, for accounting periods ending after 31st March 1996.

79(2) Schedule 7 to this Act (which, together with Chapter II of this Part of this Act, makes provision for imposing a charge under Schedule D on descriptions of income previously charged under Schedule C, and makes connected amendments) shall have effect.

Chapter II – Loan Relationships

INTRODUCTORY PROVISIONS

80 Taxation of loan relationships

80 [Omitted by CTA 2009, s. 1322 and Sch. 1, para. 403 and repealed by CTA 2009, s. 1326 and Sch. 3, Pt. 1.]

History – S. 80 omitted by CTA 2009, s. 1322 and Sch. 1, para. 403 and repealed by CTA 2009, s. 1326 and Sch. 3, Pt. 1, with effect *for corporation tax purposes for accounting periods* ending on or after 1 April 2009, and for income tax and capital gains tax purposes for the tax year 2009–10 and subsequent tax years.

Notes – S. 80 rewritten as follows:
S. 80(1): CTA 2009, s. 295(1), 299(1)
S. 80(2): CTA 2009, s. 297(1), (2), (3)
S. 80(3): CTA 2009, s. 299(1)
S. 80(4): CTA 2009, s. 300(1), (3)
S. 80(5): CTA 2009, s. 464(1), (2)

81 Meaning of "loan relationship" etc.

81 [Omitted by CTA 2009, s. 1322 and Sch. 1, para. 404 and repealed by CTA 2009, s. 1326 and Sch. 3, Pt. 1.]

History – S. 81 omitted by CTA 2009, s. 1322 and Sch. 1, para. 404 and repealed by CTA 2009, s. 1326 and Sch. 3, Pt. 1, with effect for corporation tax purposes for accounting periods ending on or after 1 April 2009, and for income tax and capital gains tax purposes for the tax year 2009–10 and subsequent tax years.

Notes – S. 81(2) rewritten as ITA 2007, Sch. 2, para. 140.
S. 81 rewritten for corporation tax as follows:
S. 81(1): CTA 2009, s. 302(1), (2)
S. 81(2): CTA 2009, s. 303(1), (2)
S. 81(3): CTA 2009, s. 303(3)
S. 81(4): CTA 2009, s. 303(4)
S. 81(5): CTA 2009, s. 305(1), (2), (3)

TAXATION OF PROFITS AND GAINS AND RELIEF FOR DEFICITS

82 Method of bringing amounts into account

82 [Omitted by CTA 2009, s. 1322 and Sch. 1, para. 405 and repealed by CTA 2009, s. 1326 and Sch. 3, Pt. 1.]

History – S. 82 omitted by CTA 2009, s. 1322 and Sch. 1, para. 405 and repealed by CTA 2009, s. 1326 and Sch. 3, Pt. 1, with effect for corporation tax purposes for accounting periods ending on or after 1 April 2009, and for income tax and capital gains tax purposes for the tax year 2009–10 and subsequent tax years.

Notes – S. 82 rewritten as follows:
S. 82(1): CTA 2009, s. 296, 301(1)
S. 82(2): CTA 2009, s. 297(1), (2), (3)
S. 82(3): CTA 2009, s. 301(2), (4), (6)
S. 82(4): CTA 2009, s. 301(4), (5), (6), (7)
S. 82(5): CTA 2009, s. 301(4), (5)
S. 82(6): CTA 2009, s. 301(6), (7)
S. 82(7): CTA 2009, s. 297(4)

83 Non-trading deficit on loan relationships

83 [Omitted by CTA 2009, s. 1322 and Sch. 1, para. 406 and repealed by CTA 2009, s. 1326 and Sch. 3, Pt. 1.]

History – S. 83 omitted by CTA 2009, s. 1322 and Sch. 1, para. 406 and repealed by CTA 2009, s. 1326 and Sch. 3, Pt. 1, with effect for corporation tax purposes for accounting periods ending on or after 1 April 2009, and for income tax and capital gains tax purposes for the tax year 2009–10 and subsequent tax years.

Notes – S. 83 rewritten as follows:
S. 83(1): CTA 2009, s. 456(1), (2).
S. 83(2): CTA 2009, s. 459(1), (2).
S. 83(3A): CTA 2009, s. 457(1), (2).
S. 83(5): CTA 2009, s. 459(3).
S. 83(6): CTA 2009, s. 460(1).
S. 83(7): CTA 2009, s. 460(1).
S. 83(8): CTA 2009, s. 460(2), (3).

COMPUTATIONAL PROVISIONS ETC.

84 Debits and credits brought into account

84 [Omitted by CTA 2009, s. 1322 and Sch. 1, para. 407 and repealed by CTA 2009, s. 1326 and Sch. 3, Pt. 1.]

History – S. 84 omitted by CTA 2009, s. 1322 and Sch. 1, para. 407 and repealed by CTA 2009, s. 1326 and Sch. 3, Pt. 1, with effect for corporation tax purposes for accounting periods ending on or after 1 April 2009, and for income tax and capital gains tax purposes for the tax year 2009–10 and subsequent tax years.

Notes – S. 84 rewritten as follows:
S. 84(1): CTA 2009, s. 293(1), (3), 307(3).
S. 84(3): CTA 2009, s. 307(4).
S. 84(4): CTA 2009, s. 329(1), (2).
S. 84(5): CTA 2009, s. 304(1).
S. 84(6): CTA 2009, s. 304(2).

84A Exchange gains and losses from loan relationships

84A [Omitted by CTA 2009, s. 1322 and Sch. 1, para. 408 and repealed by CTA 2009, s. 1326 and Sch. 3, Pt. 1.]

History – S. 84A omitted by CTA 2009, s. 1322 and Sch. 1, para. 408 and repealed by CTA 2009, s. 1326 and Sch. 3, Pt. 1, with effect for corporation tax purposes for accounting periods ending on or after 1 April 2009, and for income tax and capital gains tax purposes for the tax year 2009–10 and subsequent tax years.

Notes – S. 84A rewritten as follows:
S. 84A(1): CTA 2009, s. 328(1).
S. 84A(2): CTA 2009, s. 328(2).

S. 84A(3): CTA 2009, s. 328(3).
S. 84A(3A): CTA 2009, s. 328(4).
S. 84A(8): CTA 2009, s. 328(5) and Sch. 1, para. 369.
S. 84A(9): CTA 2009, s. 328(6) and Sch. 1, para. 369.
S. 84A(10): CTA 2009, s. 328(7) and Sch. 1, para. 369.
Former s. 84A was to have ceased to have effect by virtue of F(No. 2)A 2005, Sch. 6, para. 9 and to have been repealed by F(No. 2)A 2005, s. 70 and Sch. 11, Pt. 2(6) from a date to be appointed by Treasury order, but no such order was ever made.

85 Authorised accounting methods

85 [Former s. 85A and 85B substituted for former s. 85 by FA 2004, s. 52 and Sch. 10, para. 3.]

History – Former s. 85A and 85B substituted for former s. 85 by FA 2004, s. 52 and Sch. 10, para. 3 with effect in relation to periods of account beginning on or after 1 January 2005, or for earlier periods of account in the case of companies required or permitted to prepare accounts in accordance with international accounting standards.

85A Computation in accordance with generally accepted accounting practice

85A [Omitted by CTA 2009, s. 1322 and Sch. 1, para. 409 and repealed by CTA 2009, s. 1326 and Sch. 3, Pt. 1.]

History – S. 85A omitted by CTA 2009, s. 1322 and Sch. 1, para. 409 and repealed by CTA 2009, s. 1326 and Sch. 3, Pt. 1, with effect for corporation tax purposes for accounting periods ending on or after 1 April 2009, and for income tax and capital gains tax purposes for the tax year 2009–10 and subsequent tax years.
Notes – S. 85A rewritten as follows:
S. 85A(1): CTA 2009, s. 307(2), (6), 313(1).
S. 85A(2): CTA 2009, s. 309(1), (2), (4).
S. 85A(3): CTA 2009, s. 309(2), (3).
S. 85A(4): CTA 2009, s. 309(1).

85B Amounts recognised in determining company's profit or loss

85B [Omitted by CTA 2009, s. 1322 and Sch. 1, para. 410 and repealed by CTA 2009, s. 1326 and Sch. 3, Pt. 1.]

History – S. 85B omitted by CTA 2009, s. 1322 and Sch. 1, para. 410 and repealed by CTA 2009, s. 1326 and Sch. 3, Pt. 1, with effect for corporation tax purposes for accounting periods ending on or after 1 April 2009, and for income tax and capital gains tax purposes for the tax year 2009–10 and subsequent tax years.
Notes – S. 85B rewritten as follows:
S. 85B(1): CTA 2009, s. 308(1).
S. 85B(2): CTA 2009, s. 308(2) and (3).
S. 85B(3): CTA 2009, s. 310(1).
S. 85B(4): CTA 2009, s. 310(2).
S. 85B(5): CTA 2009, s. 310(3).
S. 85B(6): CTA 2009, s. 310(5).
The reference in former s. 85B(3)(b) to "that subsection" appears to have referred to s. 85B(1) and (2) as excluded by regulations under s. 85B(3)(a).
S. 85B(6) was to have been repealed by F(No. 2)A 2005, s. 70 and Sch. 11, Pt. 2(6) from a date to be appointed by Treasury order (per F(No. 2)A 2005, Sch. 6, para. 9(2)), but no such order was ever made.

85C Amounts not fully recognised for accounting purposes

85C [Omitted by CTA 2009, s. 1322 and Sch. 1, para. 411 and repealed by CTA 2009, s. 1326 and Sch. 3, Pt. 1.]

History – S. 85C omitted by CTA 2009, s. 1322 and Sch. 1, para. 411 and repealed by CTA 2009, s. 1326 and Sch. 3, Pt. 1, with effect for corporation tax purposes for accounting periods ending on or after 1 April 2009, and for income tax and capital gains tax purposes for the tax year 2009–10 and subsequent tax years.
Notes – S. 85C rewritten as follows:
S. 85C(1): CTA 2009, s. 311(1), (2), (3), (4), (5).
S. 85C(2): CTA 2009, s. 311(6).
S. 85C(3): CTA 2009, s. 311(1), 312(1).
S. 85C(4): CTA 2009, s. 311(1), 312(1).
S. 85C(5): CTA 2009, s. 312(3).
S. 85C(6): CTA 2009, s. 312(2).
S. 85C(7): CTA 2009, s. 312(4), (5).
S. 85C(8): CTA 2009, s. 312(6).

86 Application of accounting methods

86 [Former s. 85A and 85B substituted for former s. 85 and 86 by FA 2004, s. 52 and Sch. 10, para. 3.]

History – Former s. 85A and 85B substituted for former s. 85 and 86 by FA 2004, s. 52 and Sch. 10, para. 3 with effect in relation to periods of account beginning on or after 1 January 2005, or for earlier periods of account in the case of companies required or permitted to prepare accounts in accordance with international accounting standards.

87 Accounting method where parties have a connection

87 [Omitted by CTA 2009, s. 1322 and Sch. 1, para. 412 and repealed by CTA 2009, s. 1326 and Sch. 3, Pt. 1.]

History – S. 87 omitted by CTA 2009, s. 1322 and Sch. 1, para. 412 and repealed by CTA 2009, s. 1326 and Sch. 3, Pt 1, with effect for corporation tax purposes for accounting periods ending on or after 1 April 2009, and for income tax and capital gains tax purposes for the tax year 2009–10 and subsequent tax years.

Notes – S. 87 rewritten as follows:
S. 87(1): CTA 2009, s. 348(2), (4), 349(1).
S. 87(2): CTA 2009, s. 349(2).
S. 87(2A): CTA 2009, s. 350(1), 351(1).
S. 87(2B): CTA 2009, s. 350(2), (3), (4), (5).
S. 87(2C): CTA 2009, s. 351(2), (3), (4), (5).
S. 87(3): CTA 2009, s. 348(6), (8), 353(4), 466(2), (4).
S. 87(4): CTA 2009, s. 466(3).
S. 87(5): CTA 2009, s. 348(3), (5), (7).
S. 87(5A): CTA 2009, s. 467(1), (2), (3), (5), 476(1).
S. 87(5B): CTA 2009, s. 467(4), 476(1).

87A Meaning of "control" in section 87

87A [Omitted by CTA 2009, s. 1322 and Sch. 1, para. 413 and repealed by CTA 2009, s. 1326 and Sch. 3, Pt. 1.]

History – S. 87A omitted by CTA 2009, s. 1322 and Sch. 1, para. 413 and repealed by CTA 2009, s. 1326 and Sch. 3, Pt. 1, with effect for corporation tax purposes for accounting periods ending on or after 1 April 2009, and for income tax and capital gains tax purposes for the tax year 2009–10 and subsequent tax years.

Notes – S. 87A is rewritten as follows:
S. 87A(1): CTA 2009, s. 466(6), 472(1), (2).
S. 87A(2): CTA 2009, s. 472(3), (4).
S. 87A(3): CTA 2009, s. 472(5), (6), (7), 476(1).

88 Exemption from section 87 in certain cases

88 [Omitted by CTA 2009, s. 1322 and Sch. 1, para. 414 and repealed by CTA 2009, s. 1326 and Sch. 3, Pt. 1.]

History – S. 88 omitted by CTA 2009, s. 1322 and Sch. 1, para. 414 and repealed by CTA 2009, s. 1326 and Sch. 3, Pt. 1, with effect for corporation tax purposes for accounting periods ending on or after 1 April 2009, and for income tax and capital gains tax purposes for the tax year 2009–10 and subsequent tax years.

Notes – S. 88 rewritten as follows:
S. 88(1); CTA 2009, s. 468(1).
S. 88(2); CTA 2009, s. 469(2), (3), (4), (6).
S. 88(3); CTA 2009, s. 469(5), 471(2), (3), (4).
S. 88(4); CTA 2009, s. 470(1), (2), (3).
S. 88(5); CTA 2009, s. 468(3), (4).
S. 88(6); CTA 2009, s. 468(5), (6).

88A Accounting method where rate of interest is reset

88A [Omitted by CTA 2009, s. 1322 and Sch. 1, para. 415 and repealed by CTA 2009, s. 1326 and Sch. 3, Pt. 1.]

History – S. 88A omitted by CTA 2009, s. 1322 and Sch. 1, para. 415 and repealed by CTA 2009, s. 1326 and Sch. 3, Pt. 1, with effect for corporation tax purposes for accounting periods ending on or after 1 April 2009, and for income tax and capital gains tax purposes for the tax year 2009–10 and subsequent tax years.

Notes – S. 88A rewritten as follows:
S. 88A(1): CTA 2009, s. 454(1), (6), 476(1).
S. 88A(2): CTA 2009, s. 454(2).
S. 88A(3): CTA 2009, s. 454(3).
S. 88A(4): CTA 2009, s. 454(4).
S. 88A(6): CTA 2009, s. 454(5).

89 Inconsistent application of accounting methods

89 [Repealed by FA 2002, s. 82, Sch. 25, para. 9, s. 141 and Sch. 40, Pt. 3(12).]

History – S. 89 repealed (following the introduction of "generally accepted accounting practice" to s. 84) by FA 2002, s. 82, Sch. 25, para. 9, s. 141 and Sch. 40, Pt. 3(12) with effect in relation to accounting periods beginning on or after 1 October 2002.

90 Changes of accounting method

90 [Omitted by FA 2004, s. 52 and Sch. 10, para. 7 and repealed by FA 2004, s. 326 and Sch. 42, Pt. 2(6).]

History – S. 90 omitted by FA 2004, s. 52 and Sch. 10, para. 7 and repealed by FA 2004, s. 326 and Sch. 42, Pt. 2(6) with effect in relation to periods of account beginning on or after 1 January 2005, or for earlier periods of account in the case of companies required or permitted to prepare accounts in accordance with international accounting standards.

90A Change of accounting basis applicable to assets or liabilities

90A [Omitted by CTA 2009, s. 1322 and Sch. 1, para. 416 and repealed by CTA 2009, s. 1326 and Sch. 3, Pt. 1.]

History – S. 90A omitted by CTA 2009, s. 1322 and Sch. 1, para. 416 and repealed by CTA 2009, s. 1326 and Sch. 3, Pt. 1, with effect for corporation tax purposes for accounting periods ending on or after 1 April 2009, and for income tax and capital gains tax purposes for the tax year 2009–10 and subsequent tax years.

Notes – S. 90A rewritten as follows:
S. 90A(1): CTA 2009, s. 314(1), (2).
S. 90A(2): CTA 2009, s. 314(3).

91 Payments subject to deduction of tax

91 [Repealed by FA 2002, s. 82, Sch. 25, para. 11, s. 141 and Sch. 40, Pt. 3(12).]

History – S. 91 repealed by FA 2002, s. 82, Sch. 25, para. 11, s. 141 and Sch. 40, Pt. 3(12) with effect in relation to accounting periods beginning on or after 1 October 2002.

Cross references – ICTA 1988, s. 7(2): provisions allowing set-off of income tax against corporation tax liability (UK companies).
ICTA 1988, s. 11(3): provisions allowing set-off of income tax against corporation tax liability (non-UK companies).
ICTA 1988, Sch. 16, para. 5: set-off of income tax borne against income tax payable.

SHARES TREATED AS LOAN RELATIONSHIPS

History – Heading inserted by F(No. 2)A 2005, Sch. 7, para. 10(1) in relation to shares held by a company on or after 16 March 2005 (F(No. 2)A 2005, Sch. 7, para. 10(7)).

91A Shares subject to outstanding third party obligations

91A [Omitted by CTA 2009, s. 1322 and Sch. 1, para. 417 and repealed by CTA 2009, s. 1326 and Sch. 3, Pt. 1.]

History – S. 91A omitted by CTA 2009, s. 1322 and Sch. 1, para. 417 and repealed by CTA 2009, s. 1326 and Sch. 3, Pt. 1, with effect for corporation tax purposes for accounting periods ending on or after 1 April 2009, and for income tax and capital gains tax purposes for the tax year 2009–10 and subsequent tax years.

Notes – S. 91A rewritten as follows:
S. 91A(1): CTA 2009, s. 522(1), (3), 523(1), 524(1).
S. 91A(2): CTA 2009, s. 523(2).
S. 91A(2A): CTA 2009, s. 523(3).
S. 91A(3): CTA 2009, s. 534(1).
S. 91A(4): CTA 2009, s. 534(4).
S. 91A(5): CTA 2009, s. 524(2), (3).
S. 91A(5A): CTA 2009, s. 524(5).
S. 91A(6): CTA 2009, s. 524(4).
S. 91A(7): CTA 2009, s. 525(1), (2).
S. 91A(8): CTA 2009, s. 525(4).
S. 91A(9): CTA 2009, s. 525(3), 534(3).
S. 91A(10): CTA 2009, s. 522(4).
S. 91A(11): CTA 2009, s. 522(6).

91B Non-qualifying shares

91B [Omitted by CTA 2009, s. 1322 and Sch. 1, para. 418 and repealed by CTA 2009, s. 1326 and Sch. 3, Pt. 1.]

History – S. 91B omitted by CTA 2009, s. 1322 and Sch. 1, para. 418 and repealed by CTA 2009, s. 1326 and Sch. 3, Pt. 1, with effect for corporation tax purposes for accounting periods ending on or after 1 April 2009, and for income tax and capital gains tax purposes for the tax year 2009–10 and subsequent tax years.

Notes – S. 91B rewritten as follows:
S. 91B(1): CTA 2009, s. 522(1), (3), 523(1), 526(1).
S. 91B(2): CTA 2009, s. 523(2).
S. 91B(2A): CTA 2009, s. 523(3).
S. 91B(3): CTA 2009, s. 534(1).
S. 91B(4): CTA 2009, s. 534(5).
S. 91B(5): CTA 2009, s. 588(3), (4), 603(3), (4).
S. 91B(6): CTA 2009, s. 526(1), (2).
S. 91B(6A): CTA 2009, s. 523(3), 534(6), (7).
S. 91B(7): CTA 2009, s. 522(4).
S. 91B(8): CTA 2009, s. 522(6).

91C Condition 1 for section 91B(6)(b)

91C [Omitted by CTA 2009, s. 1322 and Sch. 1, para. 419 and repealed by CTA 2009, s. 1326 and Sch. 3, Pt. 1.]

History – S. 91C omitted by CTA 2009, s. 1322 and Sch. 1, para. 419 and repealed by CTA 2009, s. 1326 and Sch. 3, Pt. 1, with effect for corporation tax purposes for accounting periods ending on or after 1 April 2009, and for income tax and capital gains tax purposes for the tax year 2009–10 and subsequent tax years.

Notes – S. 91C rewritten as follows:
S. 91C(1): CTA 2009, s. 527(1), (2)
S. 91C(2): CTA 2009, s. 527(3).
S. 91C(3): CTA 2009, s. 527(4).
S. 91C(4): CTA 2009, s. 528(1).
S. 91C(5): CTA 2009, s. 528(2).
S. 91C(6): CTA 2009, s. 527(5).
S. 91C(7): CTA 2009, s. 522(6).

91D Condition 2 for section 91B(6)(b)

91D [Omitted by CTA 2009, s. 1322 and Sch. 1, para. 420 and repealed by CTA 2009, s. 1326 and Sch. 3, Pt. 1.]

History – S. 91D omitted by CTA 2009, s. 1322 and Sch. 1, para. 420 and repealed by CTA 2009, s. 1326 and Sch. 3, Pt. 1, with effect for corporation tax purposes for accounting periods ending on or after 1 April 2009, and for income tax and capital gains tax purposes for the tax year 2009–10 and subsequent tax years.

Notes – S. 91D rewritten as follows:
S. 91D(1): CTA 2009, s. 529(1).
S. 91D(2): CTA 2009, s. 529(2), (3), (4), (6).
S. 91D(2A): CTA 2009, s. 529(5), (7).
S. 91D(3): CTA 2009, s. 530(1).
S. 91D(4): CTA 2009, s. 530(2).
S. 91D(5): CTA 2009, s. 530(3).
S. 91D(6): CTA 2009, s. 530(4), (5).
S. 91D(7): CTA 2009, s. 530(4).
S. 91D(8): CTA 2009, s. 530(5).
S. 91D(9): CTA 2009, s. 531(1).
S. 91D(10): CTA 2009, s. 531(2), (3).
S. 91D(11): CTA 2009, s. 476(1), 530(2), (4), (6), 531(4), (5).
S. 91D(12): CTA 2009, s. 1316(1).
S. 91D(13): CTA 2009, s. 522(6).

91E Condition 3 for section 91B(6)(b)

91E [Omitted by CTA 2009, s. 1322 and Sch. 1, para. 421 and repealed by CTA 2009, s. 1326 and Sch. 3, Pt. 1.]

History – S. 91E omitted by CTA 2009, s. 1322 and Sch. 1, para. 421 and repealed by CTA 2009, s. 1326 and Sch. 3, Pt. 1, with effect for corporation tax purposes for accounting periods ending on or after 1 April 2009, and for income tax and capital gains tax purposes for the tax year 2009–10 and subsequent tax years.

Notes – S. 91E rewritten as follows:
S. 91E(1): CTA 2009, s. 532(1).
S. 91E(2): CTA 2009, s. 532(2).
S. 91E(3): CTA 2009, s. 532(3), (4).
S. 91E(4): CTA 2009, s. 522(6).

91F Power to add, vary or remove Conditions for section 91B(6)(b)

91F [Omitted by CTA 2009, s. 1322 and Sch. 1, para. 422 and repealed by CTA 2009, s. 1326 and Sch. 3, Pt. 1.]

History – S. 91F omitted by CTA 2009, s. 1322 and Sch. 1, para. 422 and repealed by CTA 2009, s. 1326 and Sch. 3, Pt. 1, with effect for corporation tax purposes for accounting periods ending on or after 1 April 2009, and for income tax and capital gains tax purposes for the tax year 2009–10 and subsequent tax years.

Notes – S. 91F rewritten as follows:
S. 91F(1): CTA 2009, s. 533(1), Sch. 1, para. 369.
S. 91F(2): CTA 2009, s. 533(2), (3), Sch. 1, para. 369.
S. 91F(3): CTA 2009, s. 533(4), (5), Sch. 1, para. 369.

91G Shares beginning or ceasing to be subject to section 91A or 91B

91G [Omitted by CTA 2009, s. 1322 and Sch. 1, para. 423 and repealed by CTA 2009, s. 1326 and Sch. 3, Pt. 1.]

History – S. 91G omitted by CTA 2009, s. 1322 and Sch. 1, para. 423 and repealed by CTA 2009, s. 1326 and Sch. 3, Pt. 1, with effect for corporation tax purposes for accounting periods ending on or after 1 April 2009, and for income tax and capital gains tax purposes for the tax year 2009–10 and subsequent tax years.

Notes – S. 91G rewritten as follows:
S. 91G(1): CTA 2009, Sch. 1, para. 366.
S. 91G(2): CTA 2009, s. 535(1), (2), Sch. 1, para. 366.

PARTNERSHIPS

91H Payments in return for capital contribution

91H [Omitted by CTA 2009, s. 1322 and Sch. 1, para. 424 and repealed by CTA 2009, s. 1326 and Sch. 3, Pt. 1.]

History – S. 91H omitted by CTA 2009, s. 1322 and Sch. 1, para. 424 and repealed by CTA 2009, s. 1326 and Sch. 3, Pt. 1, with effect for corporation tax purposes for accounting periods ending on or after 1 April 2009, and for income tax and capital gains tax purposes for the tax year 2009–10 and subsequent tax years.

Notes – S. 91H rewritten as follows:
S. 91H(1): CTA 2009, s. 536(1), 537(1).
S. 91H(2): CTA 2009, s. 536(2), 537(2).
S. 91H(3): CTA 2009, s. 537(3), (4).
S. 91H(4): CTA 2009, s. 537(5), (6).
S. 91H(5): CTA 2009, s. 1316(1).
S. 91H(6): CTA 2009, s. 476(1), 536(3).

91I Change of partnership shares

91I [Omitted by CTA 2009, s. 1322 and Sch. 1, para. 425 and repealed by CTA 2009, s. 1326 and Sch. 3, Pt. 1.]

History – S. 91I omitted by CTA 2009, s. 1322 and Sch. 1, para. 425 and repealed by CTA 2009, s. 1326 and Sch. 3, Pt. 1, with effect for corporation tax purposes for accounting periods ending on or after 1 April 2009, and for income tax and capital gains tax purposes for the tax year 2009–10 and subsequent tax years.

Notes – S. 91I rewritten as follows:
S. 91I(1): CTA 2009, s. 536(1), 538(1).
S. 91I(2): CTA 2009, s. 536(2), 538(2).
S. 91I(3): CTA 2009, s. 538(3), (4).
S. 91I(4): CTA 2009, s. 538(5), (6).
S. 91I(5): CTA 2009, s. 538(7).
S. 91I(6): CTA 2009, s. 1316(1).
S. 91I(7): CTA 2009, s. 476(1), 536(3).

SPECIAL CASES

92 Convertible securities etc.: creditor relationships

92 [Omitted by FA 2004, s. 52 and Sch. 10, para. 9(1) and repealed by FA 2004, s. 326 and Sch. 42, Pt. 2(6).]

History – S. 92 omitted by FA 2004, s. 52 and Sch. 10, para. 9(1) and repealed by FA 2004, s. 326 and Sch. 42, Pt. 2(6) with effect in relation to periods of account beginning on or after 1 January 2005, or for earlier periods of account in the case of companies required or permitted to prepare accounts in accordance with international accounting standards.

92A Convertible securities etc: debtor relationships

92A [Omitted by FA 2004, s. 52 and Sch. 10, para. 9(1) and repealed by FA 2004, s. 326 and Sch. 42, Pt. 2(6).]

History – S. 92A omitted by FA 2004, s. 52 and Sch 10, para. 10 and repealed by FA 2004, s. 326 and Sch. 42, Pt. 2(6) with effect in relation to periods of account beginning on or after 1 January 2005, or for earlier periods of account in the case of companies required or permitted to prepare accounts in accordance with international accounting standards.

93 Relationships linked to the value of chargeable assets

93 [Omitted by FA 2004, s. 52 and Sch. 10, para. 9(1) and repealed by FA 2004, s. 326 and Sch. 42, Pt. 2(6).]

History – S. 93 omitted by FA 2004, s. 52 and Sch. 10, para. 11(1)) and repealed by FA 2004, s. 326 and Sch. 42, Pt. 2(6) with effect in relation to periods of account beginning on or after 1 January 2005, or for earlier periods of account in the case of companies required or permitted to prepare accounts in accordance with international accounting standards.

93A Relationships linked to the value of chargeable assets: guaranteed returns

93A [Omitted by FA 2004, s. 52 and Sch. 10, para. 9(1) and repealed by FA 2004, s. 326 and Sch. 42, Pt. 2(6).]

History – S. 93A omitted by FA 2004, s. 52 and Sch. 10, para. 11(1)) and repealed by FA 2004, s. 326 and Sch. 42, Pt. 2(6) with effect in relation to periods of account beginning on or after 1 January 2005, or for earlier periods of account in the case of companies required or permitted to prepare accounts in accordance with international accounting standards.

93B Loan relationships ceasing to be within section 93

93B [Omitted by FA 2004, s. 52 and Sch. 10, para. 9(1) and repealed by FA 2004, s. 326 and Sch. 42, Pt. 2(6).]

History – S. 93B omitted by FA 2004, s. 52 and Sch. 10, para. 11(1) and repealed by FA 2004, s. 326 and Sch. 42, Pt. 2(6) with effect in relation to periods of account beginning on or after 1 January 2005, or for earlier periods of account in the case of companies required or permitted to prepare accounts in accordance with international accounting standards.

93C Creditor relationships and benefit derived by connected persons

93C [Omitted by CTA 2009, s. 1322 and Sch. 1, para. 426 and repealed by CTA 2009, s. 1326 and Sch. 3, Pt. 1.]

History – S. 93C omitted by CTA 2009, s. 1322 and Sch. 1, para. 426 and repealed by CTA 2009, s. 1326 and Sch. 3, Pt. 1, with effect for corporation tax purposes for accounting periods ending on or after 1 April 2009, and for income tax and capital gains tax purposes for the tax year 2009–10 and subsequent tax years.

Notes – S. 93C rewritten as follows:
S. 93C(1): CTA 2009, s. 453(1), (5).
S. 93C(2): CTA 2009, s. 453(2).
S. 93C(3): CTA 2009, s. 453(3).
S. 93C(4): CTA 2009, s. 1316(1).
S. 93C(5): CTA 2009, s. 453(5).
S. 93C(6): CTA 2009, s. 453(4).

94 Indexed gilt-edged securities

94 [Omitted by CTA 2009, s. 1322 and Sch. 1, para. 427 and repealed by CTA 2009, s. 1326 and Sch. 3, Pt. 1.]

History – S. 94 omitted by CTA 2009, s. 1322 and Sch. 1, para. 427 and repealed by CTA 2009, s. 1326 and Sch. 3, Pt. 1, with effect for corporation tax purposes for accounting periods ending on or after 1 April 2009, and for income tax and capital gains tax purposes for the tax year 2009–10 and subsequent tax years.

Notes – S. 94 rewritten as follows:
S. 94(1): CTA 2009, s. 399(1), (2), (3).
S. 94(2): CTA 2009, s. 399(3), 400(1).
S. 94(3): CTA 2009, s. 400(2), (3).
S. 94(4): CTA 2009, s. 400(4).
S. 94(5): CTA 2009, s. 400(5).
S. 94(6): CTA 2009, s. 400(6), (7).
S. 94(7): CTA 2009, s. 399(4).

94A Loan relationships with embedded derivatives

94A [Omitted by CTA 2009, s. 1322 and Sch. 1, para. 428 and repealed by CTA 2009, s. 1326 and Sch. 3, Pt. 1.]

History – S. 94A omitted by CTA 2009, s. 1322 and Sch. 1, para. 428 and repealed by CTA 2009, s. 1326 and Sch. 3, Pt. 1, with effect for corporation tax purposes for accounting periods ending on or after 1 April 2009, and for income tax and capital gains tax purposes for the tax year 2009–10 and subsequent tax years.

Notes – S. 94A rewritten as follows:
S. 94A(1): CTA 2009, s. 415(1), 585(1).
S. 94A(2): CTA 2009, s. 415(2), 585(2).
S. 94A(3): CTA 2009, s. 585(3).

94B Loan relationships treated differently by connected debtor and creditor

94B [Omitted by CTA 2009, s. 1322 and Sch. 1, para. 429 and repealed by CTA 2009, s. 1326 and Sch. 3, Pt. 1.]

History – S. 94B omitted by CTA 2009, s. 1322 and Sch. 1, para. 429 and repealed by CTA 2009, s. 1326 and Sch. 3, Pt. 1, with effect for corporation tax purposes for accounting periods ending on or after 1 April 2009, and for income tax and capital gains tax purposes for the tax year 2009–10 and subsequent tax years.

Notes – S. 94B rewritten as follows:
S. 94B(1): CTA 2009, s. 418(1).
S. 94B(2): CTA 2009, s. 418(2).
S. 94B(3): CTA 2009, s. 418(3).
S. 94B(4): CTA 2009, s. 418(4).
S. 94B(5): CTA 2009, s. 418(5).
S. 94B(6): CTA 2009, s. 418(6).
S. 94B(7): CTA 2009, s. 419(1), (2).
S. 94B(8): CTA 2009, s. 419(3).
S. 94B(9): CTA 2009, s. 419(4).
S. 94B(10): CTA 2009, s. 419(5), (6), 1316(1).

95 Gilt strips

95 [Omitted by CTA 2009, s. 1322 and Sch. 1, para. 430 and repealed by CTA 2009, s. 1326 and Sch. 3, Pt. 1.]

History – S. 95 omitted by CTA 2009, s. 1322 and Sch. 1, para. 430 and repealed by CTA 2009, s. 1326 and Sch. 3, Pt. 1, with effect for corporation tax purposes for accounting periods ending on or after 1 April 2009, and for income tax and capital gains tax purposes for the tax year 2009–10 and subsequent tax years.

Notes – S. 95 rewritten as follows:
S. 95(1): CTA 2009, s. 401(1).
S. 95(2): CTA 2009, s. 401(2), (3), (4).
S. 95(3): CTA 2009, s. 401(5), (6), (7).
S. 95(4): CTA 2009, s. 402(1).
S. 95(5): CTA 2009, s. 402(2).
S. 95(6): CTA 2009, s. 402(3).
S. 95(7): CTA 2009, s. 403(1), (2), (3), (4), (5).

96 Special rules for certain other gilts

96 [Omitted by CTA 2009, s. 1322 and Sch. 1, para. 431 and repealed by CTA 2009, s. 1326 and Sch. 3, Pt. 1.]

History – S. 96 omitted by CTA 2009, s. 1322 and Sch. 1, para. 431 and repealed by CTA 2009, s. 1326 and Sch. 3, Pt. 1, with effect for corporation tax purposes for accounting periods ending on or after 1 April 2009, and for income tax and capital gains tax purposes for the tax year 2009–10 and subsequent tax years.

Notes – S. 96 rewritten as follows:
S. 96(1): CTA 2009, Sch. 2, para. 69(1).
S. 96(2): CTA 2009, Sch .2, para. 69(2).

97 Manufactured interest

97 [Omitted by CTA 2009, s. 1322 and Sch. 1, para. 432 and repealed by CTA 2009, s. 1326 and Sch. 3, Pt. 1.]

History – S. 97 omitted by CTA 2009, s. 1322 and Sch. 1, para. 432 and repealed by CTA 2009, s. 1326 and Sch. 3, Pt. 1, with effect for corporation tax purposes for accounting periods ending on or after 1 April 2009, and for income tax and capital gains tax purposes for the tax year 2009–10 and subsequent tax years.

Notes – S. 97 rewritten as follows:
S. 97(1): CTA 2009, s. 539(2), (3), (4), (5), (6).
S. 97(2): CTA 2009, s. 540(1), (2), (3).
S. 97(2A): CTA 2009, s. 540(4), (5).
S. 97(4): CTA 2009, s. 539(7).
S. 97(4A): CTA 2009, s. 541(1), (2).
S. 97(4B): CTA 2009, s. 540(6).

98 Collective investment schemes

98 [Omitted by CTA 2009, s. 1322 and Sch. 1, para. 433 and repealed by CTA 2009, s. 1326 and Sch. 3, Pt. 1.]

History – S. 98 omitted by CTA 2009, s. 1322 and Sch. 1, para. 433 and repealed by CTA 2009, s. 1326 and Sch. 3, Pt. 1, with effect for corporation tax purposes for accounting periods ending on or after 1 April 2009, and for income tax and capital gains tax purposes for the tax year 2009–10 and subsequent tax years.

99 Insurance companies

99 [Omitted by CTA 2009, s. 1322 and Sch. 1, para. 434 and repealed by CTA 2009, s. 1326 and Sch. 3, Pt. 1.]

History – S. 99 omitted by CTA 2009, s. 1322 and Sch. 1, para. 434 and repealed by CTA 2009, s. 1326 and Sch. 3, Pt. 1, with effect for corporation tax purposes for accounting periods ending on or after 1 April 2009, and for income tax and capital gains tax purposes for the tax year 2009–10 and subsequent tax years.

MISCELLANEOUS OTHER PROVISIONS

100 Money debts etc. not arising from the lending of money

History – Heading to s. 100 substituted by FA 2005, s. 80(1) and Sch. 4, para. 9(2) with effect for periods of account beginning on or after 1 January 2005 (s. 80(4)). Heading previously read "*Interest, and exchange gains and losses, on debts etc not arising from the lending of money*".
Heading to s. 100 substituted by FA 2002, s. 79(2) and Sch. 23, para. 6.

100 [Omitted by CTA 2009, s. 1322 and Sch. 1, para. 435 and repealed by CTA 2009, s. 1326 and Sch. 3, Pt. 1.]

History – S. 100 omitted by CTA 2009, s. 1322 and Sch. 1, para. 435 and repealed by CTA 2009, s. 1326 and Sch. 3, Pt. 1, with effect for corporation tax purposes for accounting periods ending on or after 1 April 2009, and for income tax and capital gains tax purposes for the tax year 2009–10 and subsequent tax years.

Notes – S. 100 rewritten as follows:
S. 100(1): CTA 2009, s. 479(1), (2), (3), 480(1), 481(4).
S. 100(1A): CTA 2009, s. 480(1), (2), (4), (6).
S. 100(1B): CTA 2009, s. 480(3).
S. 100(2): CTA 2009, s. 481(1), (2), (3).
S. 100(2ZA): CTA 2009, s. 481(3), (5).
S. 100(2ZB): CTA 2009, s. 481(6), (7).
S. 100(3): CTA 2009, s. 484(1), (2).
S. 100(3A): CTA 2009, s. 480(5), 481(8).
S. 100(3B): CTA 2009, s. 482(2).
S. 100(7): CTA 2009, s. 482(1).
S. 100(9): CTA 2009, s. 486(1), (2), (3), (4)
S. 100(10): CTA 2009, s. 483(1), (2), (6), (7).
S.100(11): CTA 2009, s. 483(1), (3), (6), (7).
S. 100(12): CTA 2009, s. 483(3), (4), (5).
S. 100(14): CTA 2009, s. 485.

101 Financial instruments

101 [Omitted by CTA 2009, s. 1322 and Sch. 1, para. 436 and repealed by CTA 2009, s. 1326 and Sch. 3, Pt. 1.]

History – S. 101 omitted by CTA 2009, s. 1322 and Sch. 1, para. 436 and repealed by CTA 2009, s. 1326 and Sch. 3, Pt. 1, with effect for corporation tax purposes for accounting periods ending on or after 1 April 2009, and for income tax and capital gains tax purposes for the tax year 2009–10 and subsequent tax years.

Notes – S. 101 rewritten as follows:
S. 101(1): CTA 2009, s. 700(1), (2).
S. 101(1A): CTA 2009, s. 700(3).

102 Discounted securities: income tax provisions

102 [Omitted by ITTOIA 2005, s. 882(1) and Sch. 1, para. 487; and repealed by ITTOIA 2005, s. 884 and Sch. 3.]

History – S. 102 omitted by ITTOIA 2005, s. 882(1) and Sch. 1, para. 487; and repealed by ITTOIA 2005, s. 884 and Sch. 3; effective for income tax purposes for 2005–06 onwards (ITTOIA 2005, s. 883(1)).

SUPPLEMENTAL

103 Interpretation of Chapter

103 [Omitted by CTA 2009, s. 1322 and Sch. 1, para. 437 and repealed by CTA 2009, s. 1326 and Sch. 3, Pt. 1.]

History – S. 103 omitted by CTA 2009, s. 1322 and Sch. 1, para. 437 and repealed by CTA 2009, s. 1326 and Sch. 3, Pt. 1, with effect for corporation tax purposes for accounting periods ending on or after 1 April 2009, and for income tax and capital gains tax purposes for the tax year 2009–10 and subsequent tax years.

Notes – S. 103 rewritten as follows:
S. 103(1): CTA 2009, s. 302(5), (6), 313(4), (5), (6), 444(2), 476(1), (2).
S. 103(1A): CTA 2009, s. 475(1), (2).
S. 103(1AA): CTA 2009, s. 475(3), (4).
S. 103(1B): CTA 2009, s. 475(5).
S. 103(2): CTA 2009, s. 298(1).
S. 103(3): CTA 2009, s. 298(3), (4), (5).
S. 103(4): CTA 2009, s. 476(3).
S. 103(6): CTA 2009, s. 331(1), (2).
S. 103(7): CTA 2009, s. 331(3), (4).
S. 103(8): CTA 2009, s. 331(5), (6).

104 Minor and consequential amendments

104 Schedule 14 to this Act (which, for the purposes of both corporation tax and income tax, makes certain minor and consequential amendments in connection with the provisions of this Chapter) shall have effect.

105 Commencement and transitional provisions

105(1) Subject to Schedule 15 to this Act, this Chapter has effect–

(a) for the purposes of corporation tax, in relation to accounting periods ending after 31st March 1996; and

(b) so far as it makes provision for the purposes of income tax, in relation to the year 1996–97 and subsequent years of assessment.

105(2) Schedule 15 to this Act (which contains transitional provisions and savings in connection with the coming into force of this Chapter) shall have effect.

Chapter III – Provisions Relating to the Schedule E Charge

106 Living accommodation provided for employees

106 [Repealed by ITEPA 2003, Sch. 8, Pt. 1.]

History – S. 106 repealed by ITEPA 2003, Sch. 8, Pt. 1 which has effect for the tax year 2003–04 and subsequent tax years.

107 Beneficial loans

107 [Repealed by ITEPA 2003, Sch. 8, Pt. 1.]

History – S. 107 repealed by ITEPA 2003, Sch. 8, Pt. 1 which has effect for the tax year 2003–04 and subsequent tax years.

108 Incidental benefits for holders of certain offices etc.

108 [Repealed by ITEPA 2003, Sch. 8, Pt. 1.]

History – S. 108 repealed by ITEPA 2003, Sch. 8, Pt. 1 which has effect for the tax year 2003–04 and subsequent tax years.

109 Charitable donations: payroll deduction schemes

109 [Repealed by ITEPA 2003, Sch. 8, Pt. 1.]

History – S. 109 repealed by ITEPA 2003, Sch. 8, Pt. 1 which has effect for the tax year 2003–04 and subsequent tax years.

110 PAYE settlement agreements

110 [Repealed by ITEPA 2003, Sch. 8, Pt. 1.]

History – S. 110 repealed by ITEPA 2003, Sch. 8, Pt. 1 which has effect for the tax year 2003–04 and subsequent tax years.

Chapter IV – Share Options, Profit Sharing and Employee Share Ownership

SHARE OPTIONS

111 Amount or value of consideration for option

111(1) Section 149A of the Taxation of Chargeable Gains Act 1992 (consideration for grant of option under approved share option schemes not to be deemed to be equal to market value of option) shall be amended as follows.

111(2) [Repealed by F(No. 2)A 2005, s. 70 and Sch. 11, Pt. 2(5).]

111(3) [Amends TCGA 1992, s. 149A(2).]

111(4) [Repeals TCGA 1992, s. 149A(4).]

111(5) [Repealed by F(No. 2)A 2005, s. 70 and Sch. 11, Pt. 2(5).]

111(6) This section has effect in relation to any right to acquire shares in a body corporate obtained on or after 28th November 1995 by an individual by reason of his office or employment as a director or employee of a body corporate.

History – S. 111(2) and 111(5) repealed by F(No. 2)A 2005, s. 70 and Sch. 11, Pt. 2(5) in relation to options granted on or after 2 December 2004 (F(No. 2)A 2005, Sch. 5, para. 6(2)).

112 Release and replacement

112(1) [Inserts TCGA 1992, s. 237A.]

112(2) [Repeals TCGA 1992, s. 238(4).]

112(3) This section has effect in relation to transactions effected on or after 28th November 1995.

SAVINGS-RELATED SHARE OPTION SCHEMES

113 Exercise of rights by employees of non-participating companies

113 [Repealed by ITEPA 2003, Sch. 8, Pt. 1.]

History – S. 113 repealed by ITEPA 2003, Sch. 8, Pt. 1 which has effect for the tax year 2003–04 and subsequent tax years.

OTHER SHARE OPTION SCHEMES

114 Requirements to be satisfied by approved schemes

114 [Repealed by ITEPA 2003, Sch. 8, Pt. 1.]

History – S. 114 repealed by ITEPA 2003, Sch. 8, Pt. 1 which has effect for the tax year 2003–04 and subsequent tax years.

115 Transitional provisions

115 [Repealed by ITEPA 2003, Sch. 8, Pt. 1.]

History – S. 115 repealed by ITEPA 2003, Sch. 8, Pt. 1 which has effect for the tax year 2003–04 and subsequent tax years.

Cross references – ITEPA 2003, Sch. 7, para. 76 (Transitionals and savings): if right treated as granted otherwise than in accordance with approved discretionary share option scheme then also right treated as granted otherwise than in accordance with approved CSOP scheme for purposes of CSOP code.

PROFIT SHARING SCHEMES

116 The release date

116(1) [Amends ICTA 1988, s. 187(2).]

116(2) The amendment made by subsection (1) above shall have effect in relation to shares of a participant in a profit sharing scheme if the third anniversary of the appropriation of the shares to the participant occurs on or after the day on which this Act is passed.

116(3) If the third anniversary of the appropriation of any shares to a participant in a profit sharing scheme has occurred, but the fifth anniversary of their appropriation to him has not occurred, before the passing of this Act, then, in the application of sections 186 and 187 of, and Schedules 9 and 10 to, the Taxes Act 1988 in relation to those shares, the release date shall be the day on which this Act is passed.

117 The appropriate percentage

117(1) [Substitutes ICTA 1988, Sch. 10, para. 3.]

117(2) [Repeals ICTA 1988, s.187(8)(b).]

117(3) Subsections (1) and (2) above have effect in relation to the occurrence, on or after the day on which this Act is passed, of events by reason of whose occurrence any provision of section 186 or 187 of, or Schedule 9 or 10 to, the Taxes Act 1988 charges an individual to income tax under Schedule E.

Cross references – ICTA 1988, s. 186: approved profit sharing schemes.
ICTA 1988, s. 187: interpretation of ICTA 1988, s. 185, 186, Sch. 9 and 10.
ICTA 1988, Sch. 9: approved share option schemes.
ICTA 1988, Sch. 10: profit sharing schemes.

118 The appropriate allowance

118(1) [Amends ICTA 1988, s. 186(12).]

118(2) Subsection (1) above has effect for the year 1997–98 and subsequent years of assessment.

EMPLOYEE SHARE OWNERSHIP TRUSTS

119 Removal of requirement for at least one year's service

119(1) [Amends FA 1989, Sch. 5, para. 4(5)(a).]

119(2) This section applies to trusts established on or after the day on which this Act is passed.

120 Grant and exercise of share options

120(1) [Inserts FA 1989, Sch. 5, para. 4(2A) and (2B).]

120(2) In consequence of the amendment made by subsection (1) above, section 69 of, and Schedule 5 to, the Finance Act 1989 (which respectively make provision about chargeable events in relation to the trustees of qualifying employee share ownership trusts and the requirements to be satisfied by such trusts) shall be amended in accordance with the following provisions of this section.

120(3) [Amends FA 1989, s. 69(4).]

120(4) [Inserts FA 1989, s. 69(4ZA).]

120(5) [Amends FA 1989, Sch. 5, para. 4(4).]

120(6) [Amends FA 1989, Sch. 5, para. 4(7).]

120(7) [Amends FA 1989, Sch. 5, para. 4(8).]

120(8) [Inserts FA 1989, Sch. 5, para. 5(2)(cc).]

120(9) [Amends FA 1989, Sch. 5, para. 9.]

120(10) [Inserts FA 1989, Sch. 5, para. 9(2ZA).]

(a) [Amends FA 1989, Sch. 5, para. 10; and]

(b) [repealed by ITEPA 2003, Sch. 8, Pt. 1.]

120(12) This section has effect in relation to trusts established on or after the day on which this Act is passed.

History – S. 120(11)(b) repealed by ITEPA 2003, Sch. 8, Pt. 1 which has effect for the tax year 2003–04 and subsequent tax years.

Chapter V – Self Assessment, General Management etc.

GENERAL

121 Returns and self assessment

121(1) [Amends TMA 1970, s. 8(1) and 8A(1).]

121(2) [Amends TMA 1970, s. 8(1A) and 8A(1A).]

121(3) [Inserts TMA 1970, s. 8(1AA) and s. 8A(1AA).]

121(4) [Substitutes TMA 1970, s. 9(1).]

121(5) [Repealed by FA 1998, s. 165 and Sch. 27, Pt. III(28).]

121(6) [Amends TMA 1970, s. 12AA(1)(a).]

121(7) [Substitutes TMA 1970, s. 12AA(1A).]

121(8) This section and sections 122, 123, 125 to 127 and 141 below–

(a) so far as they relate to income tax and capital gains tax, have effect as respects the year 1996–97 and subsequent years of assessment, and

(b) so far as they relate to corporation tax, have effect as respects accounting periods ending on or after the appointed day for the purposes of Chapter III of Part IV of the Finance Act 1994.

History – S. 121(5) repealed by FA 1998, s. 165 and Sch. 27, Pt. III(28), with effect in relation to accounting periods ending on or after 1 July 1999, the corporation tax self-assessment appointed day by virtue of FA 1994, s. 199 and SI 1998/3173 (C. 78).

122 Notional tax deductions and payments

122(1) [Amends TMA 1970, s. 9(1).]

122(2) [Amends TMA 1970, s. 59B(1).]

122(3) [Repealed by ITTOIA 2005, s. 884 and Sch. 3.]

122(4) [Repealed by ITTOIA 2005, s. 884 and Sch. 3.]

(a) [Repealed by F(No. 2)A 1997, s. 52 and Sch. 8, Pt. II(11).]

(b) [Repealed by ITTOIA 2005, s. 884 and Sch. 3.]

122(6) [Amends ICTA 1988, s. 421(1)(b).]

(a) [Repealed by ITTOIA 2005, s. 884 and Sch. 3.]

(b) [Amends ICTA 1988, s. 599A(6).]

(c) [Repeals ICTA 1988, s. 599A(7).]

History – S. 122(3) to (5) repealed by ITTOIA 2005, s. 884 and Sch. 3 effective for income tax purposes for 2005–06 onwards (ITTOIA 2005, s. 883(1)).
S. 122(5)(a) repealed by F(No. 2)A 1997, s. 52 and Sch. 8, Pt. II(11) (in accordance with s. 36 and Sch. 6, para. 3(1) and (2)), with effect in relation to distributions made on or after 6 April 1999.
S. 122(7)(a) repealed by ITTOIA 2005, s. 884 and Sch. 3 effective for income tax purposes for 2005–06 onwards (ITTOIA 2005, s. 883(1)).

123 Liability of partners

123(1) [Amends TMA 1970, s. 12AA(2).]

123(2) [Amends TMA 1970, s. 12AA(3).]

123(3) [Amends TMA 1970, s. 12AA(7)(a).]

123(4) [Inserts TMA 1970, s. 12AA(11)–(13).]

123(5) [Amends TMA 1970, s. 12AB(1).]

123(6) [Repealed by FA 2001, s. 110 and Sch. 33, Pt. 2(13).]

123(7) [Repealed by FA 2001, s. 110 and Sch. 33, Pt. 2(13).]

123(8) [Amends TMA 1970, s. 93A(1)(b).]

123(9) [Amends TMA 1970, s. 93A(3),(4).]

123(10) [Amends TMA 1970, s. 93A(6).]

123(11) [Amends TMA 1970, s. 93A(7).]

123(12) [Repealed by FA 2007, s. 114 and Sch. 27, Pt. 5(5).]

123(13) [Repealed by FA 2007, s. 114 and Sch. 27, Pt. 5(5).]

123(14) [Amends TMA 1970, s. 118.]

History – S. 123(6) and (7) repealed by FA 2001, s. 110 and Sch. 33, Pt. 2(13) with effect from 11 May 2001 in relation to returns made before or after that date, and whether relating to periods before or after that date.
S. 123(12) and (13) repealed by FA 2007, s. 114 and Sch. 27, Pt. 5(5), with effect from a variety of dates, but the latest being 1 April 2009, by virtue of SI 2008/568, art. 2.

Other material – Taxline 1997/43 (not reproduced): Revenue confirmation that there is no formal procedure to follow in the appointment of a successor to a partner nominated to handle the partnership's tax affairs.

124 Retention of original records

124(1) The Taxes Management Act 1970, as it has effect–

(a) for the purposes of income tax and capital gains tax, as respects the year 1996–97 and subsequent years of assessment, and

(b) for the purposes of corporation tax, as respects accounting periods ending on or after the day appointed under section 199 of the Finance Act 1994 for the purposes of Chapter III of Part IV of that Act (self-assessment management provisions),

shall be amended in accordance with the following provisions of this section.

124(2) [Omitted by FA 2008, s. 115 and Sch. 37, para. 11(b).]

124(3) [Inserts TMA 1970, s. 12B(4A).]

124(4) [Amends TMA 1970, s. 12B(5).]

124(5) [Inserts TMA 1970, s. 12B(5B).]

124(6) [Omitted by FA 2008, s. 115 and Sch. 37, para. 11(b).]

124(7) [Amends TMA 1970, Sch, 1A, para.2A(4).]

124(8) [Inserts TMA 1970, Sch. 1A, para. 2A(5).]

124(9) The amendments made by this section shall not have effect in relation to–

(a) any time before this Act is passed, or

(b) any records which a person fails to preserve before this Act is passed.

History – S. 124(2) omitted by FA 2008, s. 115 and Sch. 37, para. 11(b), with effect from 1 April 2009 (SI 2009/402, art. 2).
S. 124(6) omitted by FA 2008, s. 115 and Sch. 37, para. 11(b), with effect from 1 April 2009 (SI 2009/402, art. 2).

125 Determination of tax where no return delivered

125(1) [Substitutes TMA 1970, s. 28C(1).]

125(2) [Amends TMA 1970, s. 11AA(3).]

125(3) [Repealed by FA 2007, s. 114 and Sch. 27, Pt. 5(3).]

125(4) [Inserts TMA 1970, s. 59B(5A).]

History – S. 125(3) repealed by FA 2007, s. 114 and Sch. 27, Pt. 5(3) with effect (FA 2007, s. 92):

- in relation to personal and trustee returns, in respect of a return for a year of assessment beginning on or after 6 April 2007; and
- in relation to a partnership return where the partnership includes one or more companies, in respect of a return for a relevant period beginning on or after 6 April 2007.

126 PAYE regulations

126(1) [Inserts TMA 1970, s. 59A(10).]

126(2) [Amends TMA 1970, s. 59B(8).]

127 Repayment postponed pending completion of enquiries

127 [Inserts TMA 1970, s. 59B(4A).]

128 Claims for reliefs involving two or more years

(a) [Repeals TMA 1970, s. 42(3A) and (3B).]

(b) [Amends TMA 1970, s. 42(7)(a).]

(c) [Inserts TMA 1970, s. 42(11A).]

128(2) [Inserts TMA 1970, Sch. 1B.]

128(3) [Repealed by ITTOIA 2005, s. 884 and Sch. 3.]

128(4) [Repealed by ITTOIA 2005, s. 884 and Sch. 3.]

128(5) [Repealed by FA 2001, s. 110 and Sch. 33, Pt. 2(6).]

128(6) [Repealed by FA 2001, s. 110 and Sch. 33, Pt. 2(6).]

128(7) [Repealed by FA 2001, s. 110 and Sch. 33, Pt. 2(6).]

128(8) [Repealed by FA 2001, s. 110 and Sch. 33, Pt. 2(6).]

128(9) [Repealed by FA 2001, s. 110 and Sch. 33, Pt. 2(6).]

128(10) [Repealed by FA 2001, s. 110 and Sch. 33, Pt. 2(6).]

128(11) This section (except subsections (1)(b) and (6) above) and Schedule 17 to this Act have effect as respects claims made (or deemed to be made) in relation to the year 1996–97 or later years of assessment.

128(12) Subsection (1)(b) above has effect as respects claims made in relation to the year 1997–98 or later years of assessment.

History – S. 128(3), (4) repealed by ITTOIA 2005, s. 884 and Sch. 3 effective for income tax purposes for 2005–06 onwards (ITTOIA 2005, s. 883(1)).
S. 128(5)–(10) repealed by FA 2001, s. 110 and Sch. 33, Pt. 2(6) with effect in relation to payments actually receivable on or after 6 April 2001.

129 Claims for medical insurance and vocational training relief

129(1) Nothing in section 42 of the Taxes Management Act 1970 (procedure for making claims etc.), or Schedule 1A to that Act (claims etc. not included in returns), shall apply in relation to–

(a) [Repealed by F(No. 2)A 1997, s. 52 and Sch. 8, Pt. II(2).]

(b) [Repealed by FA 1999, s. 139 and Sch. 20, Pt. III(15).]

129(2) [Amends FA 1991, s. 32(5)(b); partially repealed by FA 1999, s. 139 and Sch. 20, Pt. III(15).]

129(3) [Repealed by F(No. 2)A 1997, s. 52 and Sch. 8, Pt. II(2).]

129(4) [Repealed by FA 1999, s. 139 and Sch. 20, Pt. III(15).]

129(5) [Repealed by F(No. 2)A 1997, s. 52 and Sch. 8, Pt. II(2).]

129(6) [Repealed by FA 1999, s. 139 and Sch. 20, Pt. III(15).]

History – S. 129(1)(b), s. 129(2) (partially), and s. 129(4) and (6), repealed by FA 1999, s. 139, Sch. 20, Pt. III(15), with effect in relation to payments made on or after 1 September 2000 (SI 2000/2004 (C. 53)).
S. 129(1)(a), in subsection (2) the reference to FA 1989, s. 54(6)(b), and subsections (3) and (5), repealed by F(No. 2)A 1997, s. 52 and Sch. 8, Pt. II(2) with effect for the year 1997–98 and subsequent years of assessment except where relief given under FA 1989, s. 54 (in respect of any payment) is unaffected by the provisions of F(No. 2)A 1997, s. 17(1).

Cross references – TMA 1970, s. 42: procedure for making claims.
TMA 1970, Sch. 1A: claims not included in returns.

130 Procedure for giving notices

130(1) Section 42 of, and Schedule 1A to, the Taxes Management Act 1970, as they have effect–

(a) for the purposes of income tax and capital gains tax, as respects the year 1996–97 and subsequent years of assessment, and

(b) for the purposes of corporation tax, as respects accounting periods ending on or after the day appointed under section 199 of the Finance Act 1994 for the purposes of Chapter III of Part IV of that Act (self-assessment management provisions),

shall be amended in accordance with the following provisions of this section.

130(2) In subsection (7) of section 42 (which contains a list of provisions, claims under which must be made in accordance with subsection (6)) the following words shall cease to have effect, that is to say–

(a) in paragraph (a), "62A," and "401,"; and

(b) in paragraph (c), "30,", "33,", "48, 49," and "124A,".

130(3) In subsection (10) of that section (section 42 to apply in relation to elections and notices as it applies in relation to claims) the words "and notices" shall cease to have effect.

130(4) In subsection (11) of that section (Schedule 1A to apply as respects any claim, election or notice made otherwise than in a return under section 8 etc.) for the words ", election or notice" there shall be substituted "or election".

130(5) In paragraph 1 of Schedule 1A (claims etc. not included in returns), in the definition of "claim", for the words "means a claim, election or notice" there shall be substituted "means a claim or election".

131 Interest on overdue tax

131(1) [Inserts FA 1995, s. 110(4).]

131(2) [Amends TMA 1970, s. 86(3).]

131(3) [Repeals FA 1994, Sch. 19, para. 23.]

132 Overdue tax and excessive payments by the Board

132 Schedule 18 to this Act (which amends enactments relating to overdue tax or excessive payments by the Board) shall have effect.

133 Claims and enquiries

133 Schedule 19 to this Act (which, for purposes connected with self-assessment, further amends provisions relating to claims and enquiries) shall have effect.

134 Discretions exercisable by the Board etc.

134(1) Schedule 20 to this Act (which in connection with self-assessment modifies enactments by virtue of which a decision or other action affecting an assessment may be or is required to be taken by the Board, or one of their officers, before the making of the assessment) shall have effect.

134(2) Subject to subsection (3) below, the amendments made by that Schedule shall have effect–

(a) for the purposes of income tax and capital gains tax, as respects the year 1996–97 and subsequent years of assessment; and

(b) for the purposes of corporation tax, as respects accounting periods ending on or after the day appointed under section 199 of the Finance Act 1994 for the purposes of Chapter III of Part IV of that Act (self-assessment management provisions).

134(3) Paragraphs 22 and 23 of that Schedule shall have effect in relation to shares issued on or after 6th April 1996.

Notes – *The appointed day for the purposes of FA 1994, s. 199 is 1 July 1999 (SI 1998/3173 (C. 78)).*

135 Time limits for claims etc.

135(1) Schedule 21 to this Act (which in connection with self-assessment modifies enactments which impose time limits on the making of claims, elections, adjustments and assessments and the giving of notices, and enactments which provide for the giving of notice to the inspector) shall have effect.

135(2) Subject to subsections (3) to (5) below, the amendments made by that Schedule shall have effect–

(a) for the purposes of income tax and capital gains tax, as respects the year 1996–97 and subsequent years of assessment; and

(b) for the purposes of corporation tax, as respects accounting periods ending on or after the day appointed under section 199 of the Finance Act 1994 for the purposes of Chapter III of Part IV of that Act (self-assessment management provisions).

135(3-5) [Repealed by CA 2001, s. 580 and Sch. 4.]

History – S. 135(3)–(5) repealed by CAA 2001, s. 580 and Sch. 4 with effect as respects allowances and charges falling to be made for chargeable periods ending, for income tax purposes, on or after 6 April 2001, and, for corporation tax purposes, on or after 1 April 2001.

136 Appeals

136 Schedule 22 to this Act (which makes provision, in connection with self-assessment, about appeals) shall have effect.

COMPANIES

137 Schedules 13 and 16 to the Taxes Act 1988

137 [Repealed by ITA 2007, s. 1031 and Sch. 3, Pt. 1.]

History – S. 137 repealed by ITA 2007, s. 1031 and Sch. 3, Pt. 1, with effect from 6 April 2007.

138 Accounting periods

138 Schedule 24 to this Act (which makes provision, in connection with self-assessment, in relation to accounting periods) shall have effect.

139 Surrenders of advance corporation tax

139 [Repealed by FA 1998, s. 165 and Sch. 27, Pt. III(2).]

History – S. 139 repealed with effect for any accounting period of a "surrendering company" (ICTA 1988 s. [illegible]1)) beginning on or after 6 April 1999, by FA 1998, s. 165 and Sch. 27, Pt. III(2).

CHARGEABLE GAINS

140 Transfer of company's assets to investment trust

140(1) [Inserts TCGA 1992, s. 101(1A).]

140(2) This section shall have effect as respects accounting periods ending on or after the day appointed under section 199 of the Finance Act 1994 for the purposes of Chapter III of Part IV of that Act (self-assessment management provisions).

Notes – The day appointed under FA 1994, s. 199 for the purposes of corporation tax self-assessment is 1 July 1999 by virtue of SI 1998/3173 (C. 78).

141 Roll-over relief

141(1) [Amends TCGA 1992, s. 152(4).]

141(2) [Inserts TCGA 1992, s. 153A.]

141(3) [Amends TCGA 1992, s. 175.]

141(4) [Amends TCGA 1992, s. 246.]

141(5) [Amends TCGA 1992, s. 247(5)(b).]

141(6) [Inserts TCGA 1992, s. 247A.]

142 Premiums for leases

142(1) Paragraph 3 of Schedule 8 to the Taxation of Chargeable Gains Act 1992 (premiums for leases) shall be amended as follows.

142(2) [Amends TCGA 1992, Sch. 8, para. 3(2).]

142(3) [Amends TCGA 1992, Sch. 8, para. 3(3).]

142(4) [Substitutes TCGA 1992, Sch. 8, para. 3(4) and (5).]

142(5) This section has effect as respects sums payable on or after 6th April 1996.

Chapter VI – Miscellaneous provisions

RELIEFS

143 Annual payments under certain insurance policies

143 [Repealed by ITTOIA 2005, s. 884 and Sch. 3.]

History – S. 143 repealed by ITTOIA 2005, s. 884 and Sch. 3 effective for income tax purposes for 2005–06 onwards (ITTOIA 2005, s. 883(1)).

Notes – These repealed income tax rules are principally rewritten at ITTOIA 2005, s. 735–743.

144 Vocational training

144 [Repealed by FA 1999, s. 139 and Sch. 20, Pt. III(15).]

History – S. 144 repealed by FA 1999, s. 139, Sch. 20, Pt. III(15), with effect in relation to payments made on or after 1 September 2000 (SI 2000/2004 (C. 53)).

145 Personal reliefs for non-resident EEA nationals

145 [Omitted by FA 2008, s. 70(3).]

History – S. 145 omitted by FA 2008, s. 70(3) with effect for the tax year 2008–09 and subsequent tax years.

146 Exemptions for charities

146 [Repealed by CTA 2010, s. 1181 and Sch. 3, Pt. 1.]

History – S. 146 repealed by CTA 2010, s. 1181 and Sch. 3, Pt. 1, with effect for corporation tax purposes for accounting periods ending on or after 1 April 2010, and for income tax and capital gains tax purposes for the tax year 2010–11 and subsequent tax years.

147 Withdrawal of relief for Class 4 contributions

147(1) [Repealed by CTA 2009, s. 1326 and Sch. 3, Pt. 1.]

147(2) [Amends SSCBA 1992 and SSCB(Northern Ireland)A 1992, Sch. 2, para. 3(2).]

147(3) This section shall have effect in relation to the year 1996–97 and subsequent years of assessment.

History – S. 147(1) repealed by CTA 2009, s. 1326 and Sch. 3, Pt. 1, with effect for corporation tax purposes for accounting periods ending on or after 1 April 2009, and for income tax and capital gains tax purposes for the tax year 2009–10 and subsequent tax years.

148 Mis-sold personal pensions etc.

148(1) Income tax shall not be chargeable on any payment falling within subsection (3) or (5) below.

148(2) Receipt of a payment falling within subsection (3) below shall not be regarded for the purposes of capital gains tax as the disposal of an asset.

148(3) A payment falls within this subsection if it is a capital sum by way of compensation for loss suffered, or reasonably likely to be suffered, by a person in a case where that person, or some other person, acting in reliance on bad investment advice at least some of which was given during the period beginning with 29th April 1988 and ending with 30th June 1994,–

(a) has, while eligible, or reasonably likely to become eligible, to be a member of an occupational pension scheme, instead become a member of a personal pension scheme or entered into a retirement annuity contract;

(b) has ceased to be a member of, or to pay contributions to, an occupational pension scheme and has instead become a member of a personal pension scheme or entered into a retirement annuity contract;

(c) has transferred to a personal pension scheme accrued rights of his under an occupational pension scheme; or

(d) has ceased to be a member of an occupational pension scheme and has instead (by virtue of such a provision as is mentioned in section 591(2)(g) of the Taxes Act 1988) entered into arrangements for securing relevant benefits by means of an annuity contract.

148(4) A payment chargeable to income tax apart from subsection (1) above may nevertheless be regarded as a capital sum for the purpose of determining whether it falls within subsection (3) above.

148(5) A payment falls within this subsection if and to the extent that it is a payment of interest, on the whole or any part of a capital sum such as is mentioned in subsection (3) above, for a period ending on or before the earliest date on which a determination (whether or not subsequently varied on an appeal or in any other proceedings) of the amount of the particular capital sum in question is made, whether by agreement or by a decision of–

(a) a court, tribunal or commissioner,

(b) an arbitrator or (in Scotland) arbiter, or

(c) any other person appointed for the purpose.

148(6) In this section–

"bad investment advice" means investment advice in respect of which an action against the person who gave it has been, or may be, brought–

(a) in or for negligence;

(b) for breach of contract;

(c) by reason of a breach of a fiduciary obligation; or

(d) by reason of a contravention which is actionable–

(i) under section 62 of the Financial Services Act 1986; or

(ii) under section 150 of the Financial Services and Markets Act 2000;

"investment advice"–

(a) in relation to a time before 1st December 2001, means advice such as is mentioned in paragraph 15 of Schedule 1 to the Financial Services Act 1986; and

(b) in relation to a time on or after that date, means advice such as is mentioned in Article 53 of the Financial Services and Markets Act 2000 (Regulated Activities) Order 2001;

"occupational pension scheme" means–

(a) a scheme approved, or being considered for approval, under Chapter I of Part XIV of the Taxes Act 1988 (retirement benefit schemes);

(b) a relevant statutory scheme, as defined in section 611A(1) of that Act; or

(c) a fund to which section 608 of that Act applies (superannuation funds approved before 6th April 1980 etc.);

"personal pension scheme" has the meaning given by section 630(1) of the Taxes Act 1988;

"relevant benefits" has the meaning given by section 612(1) of the Taxes Act 1988;

"retirement annuity contract" means a contract made before 1st July 1988 and approved by the Board under or by virtue of any provision of Chapter III of Part XIV of the Taxes Act 1988.

148(6A) References in subsections (3)(d) and (6) to provisions of Part 14 of the Taxes Act 1988 are to those provisions as they had effect at the time in question.

148(7) This section shall have effect, and be taken always to have had effect, in relation to any payment falling within subsection (3) or (5) above, whether made before or after the passing of this Act.

History – In s. 148(6), in the definition of "bad investment advice", para. (d) substituted by SI 2001/3629, art. 93(2) operative from 1 December 2001.

In s. 148(6), the definition of "investment advice", substituted by SI 2001/3629, art. 93(3) operative from 1 December 2001.

S. 148(6A) inserted by FA 2004, s. 281 and Sch. 35, para. 44 with effect from 6 April 2006.

Cross references – ICTA 1988, s. 591(2)(g): approval of schemes to secure relevant benefits under a retirement benefit scheme by entering into an annuity contract.

ICTA 1988, s. 608: superannuation funds approved before 6 April 1980.

ICTA 1988, s. 612(1): pension funds – interpretative provisions.

ICTA 1988, s. 611A(1): definition of relevant statutory scheme.

ICTA 1988, s. 630(1): personal pension schemes – interpretative provisions.

ICTA 1988, Pt. XIV, Ch. I: retirement benefit schemes.

ICTA 1988, Pt. XIV, Ch. III: personal pension schemes.

FSA 1986, s. 62: actions for damages.

FSA 1986, Sch. 1, para. 15: investment advice.

HMRC Manuals – Inspectors' Manual IM1527: guidance on the IT and CGT exemption for compensation; and interest on compensation for mis-sold personal pensions, including confirmation that the tax exemption does not extend to compensation and interest on compensation for mis-sold endowment policies and other financial products (but see ESC A99, which extends the exemption to mis-sold Free Standing Additional Voluntary Contributions that were mis-sold in the period 28 April 1998 to 15 August 1999).

Other material – Extra Statutory Concession ESC A99: a payment (being either compensation for capital loss or interest on the capital loss) made as a result of a Financial Services Authority/Personal Investment Authority review of a FSAVC sold between 28 April 1998 to 15 August 1999 will not be chargeable to income tax or capital gains tax.

Tax Bulletin, August 2004: review of exemption for interest paid with compensation, including comments on the restricted scope of the relief afforded by s. 148.

149 Annual payments in residuary cases

149 [Repealed by FA 1999, s. 139 and Sch. 20, Pt. III(6).]

History – S. 149 repealed by FA 1999, s. 139 and Sch. 20, Pt. III(6), with effect in relation to any payment falling due on or after 6 April 2000.

150 Income tax exemption for periodical payments of damages and compensation for personal injury

150 [Repealed by ITTOIA 2005, s. 884 and Sch. 3.]

History – S. 150 repealed by ITTOIA 2005, s. 884 and Sch. 3 effective for income tax purposes for 2005–06 onwards (ITTOIA 2005, s. 883(1)).

TAXATION OF BENEFITS

151 Benefits under pilot schemes

151(1) The Treasury may by order make provision for the Income Tax Acts to have effect in relation to any amount of benefit payable by virtue of a Government pilot scheme as if it was, as they think fit, either–

(a) wholly or partly exempt from income tax and, accordingly, to be disregarded in computing the amount of any receipts brought into account for income tax purposes; or

(b) to the extent specified in the order, to be brought into account for the purposes of income tax as income of a description so specified or as a receipt of a description so specified.

151(2) The Treasury may by order provide for any amount of benefit payable by virtue of a Government pilot scheme to be left out of account, to the extent specified in the order, in the determination for the purposes of section 532 of the Capital Allowances Act (exclusion of expenditure met by contributions) of how far any expenditure has been or is to be met directly or indirectly by the Crown or by an authority or person other than the person actually incurring it.

151(3) In this section **"Government pilot scheme"** means any arrangements (whether or not contained in a scheme) which–

(a) are made, under any enactment or otherwise, by the Secretary of State or any Northern Ireland department;

(b) make provision for or about the payment of amounts of benefit either–

  (i) for purposes that are similar to those for which any social security or comparable benefit is payable; or

  (ii) for purposes connected with the carrying out of any functions of the Secretary of State or any such department in relation to employment or training for employment;

(c) are arrangements relating to a temporary experimental period; and

(d) are made wholly or partly for the purpose of facilitating a decision as to whether, or to what extent, it is desirable for provision to be made on a permanent basis for or in relation to any benefit.

151(4) In subsection (3)(b) above the reference to making provision for or about the payment of amounts of benefit for purposes that are similar to those for which any social security or comparable benefit is payable shall include a reference to making provision by virtue of which there is a modification of the conditions of entitlement to, or the conditions for the payment of, an existing social security or comparable benefit.

151(5) An order under this section may–

(a) make different provision for different cases, and

(b) contain such incidental, supplemental, consequential and transitional provision (including provision modifying provision made by or under the Income Tax Acts) as the Treasury may think fit.

151(6) In this section **"benefit"** includes any allowance, grant or other amount the whole or any part of which is payable directly or indirectly out of public funds.

151(7) The power to make an order under this section–

(a) shall be exercisable for the year 1996–97 and subsequent years of assessment; and

(b) so far as exercisable for the year 1996–97, shall be exercisable in relation to benefits, allowances and other amounts paid at times on or after 6th April 1996 but before the making of the order.

151(8) The Treasury shall not make an order under this section containing any such provision as is mentioned in subsection (1)(b) above unless a draft of the order has been laid before, and approved by a resolution of, the House of Commons.

History – In s. 151(2), reference to CAA 2001, s. 532 substituted for former reference to CAA 1990, s. 153 by CAA 2001, s. 578 and Sch. 2, para. 95, with effect as respects allowances and charges falling to be made for chargeable periods ending, for income tax purposes, on or after 6 April 2001, and, for corporation tax purposes, on or after 1 April 2001.

Cross references – CAA 1990, s. 153: treatment of expenditure met directly or indirectly by the Crown.
ITEPA 2003, s. 655(2): structure of ITEPA 2003, Pt. 10 and references to provisions in other Acts about the taxation of social security benefits.

Statutory instruments – SI 1996/2396: Taxation of Benefits under Pilot Schemes (Earnings Top-up) Order 1996.
SI 2003/2339: Taxation of Benefits under Government Pilot Schemes (Return to Work Credit and Employment Retention and Advancement Schemes) Order 2003.
SI 2004/575: Taxation of Benefits under Government Pilot Schemes (Working Neighbourhoods Pilot and In Work Credit) Order 2004.
SI 2008/1464: Taxation of Benefits under Government Pilot Schemes (Up-Front Childcare Fund) Order 2008.
SI 2008/2603: Taxation of Benefits under Government Pilot Schemes (Better Off in Work Credit) Order 2008.

152 Jobfinder's grant

152 [Repealed by ITEPA 2003, Sch. 8, Pt. 1.]

History – S. 152 repealed by ITEPA 2003, Sch. 8, Pt. 1 which has effect for the tax year 2003–04 and subsequent tax years.

INVESTMENTS

153 Foreign income dividends

153 [Repealed by Statute Law (Repeals) Act 2013, s. 1 and Sch. 1, Pt. 10.]

History – S. 153 repealed by Statute Law (Repeals) Act 2013, s. 1 and Sch. 1, Pt. 10, with effect from 31 January 2013.

154 FOTRA securities

154(1) The modifications which, under section 60 of the Finance Act 1940, may be made for the purposes of any issue of securities to the conditions about tax exemption specified in section 22 of the Finance (No. 2) Act 1931 shall include a modification by virtue of which the tax exemption contained in any condition of the issue applies, as respects capital, irrespective of where the person with the beneficial ownership of the securities is domiciled.

154(2) [Omitted by CTA 2009, s. 1322 and Sch. 1, para. 438 and repealed by CTA 2009, s. 1326 and Sch. 3, Pt. 1.]

154(3) [Omitted by CTA 2009, s. 1322 and Sch. 1, para. 438 and repealed by CTA 2009, s. 1326 and Sch. 3, Pt. 1.]

154(4) [Omitted by ITTOIA 2005, s. 882(1) and Sch. 1, para. 488(3); and repealed by ITTOIA 2005, s. 884 and Sch. 3.]

154(5) [Omitted by CTA 2009, s. 1322 and Sch. 1, para. 438 and repealed by CTA 2009, s. 1326 and Sch. 3, Pt. 1.]

154(6) [Omitted by CTA 2009, s. 1322 and Sch. 1, para. 438 and repealed by CTA 2009, s. 1326 and Sch. 3, Pt. 1.]

154(7) Schedule 28 to this Act (which contains amendments consequential on the provisions of this section) shall have effect.

154(8) [Omitted by CTA 2009, s. 1322 and Sch. 1, para. 438 and repealed by CTA 2009, s. 1326 and Sch. 3, Pt. 1.]

154(9) This section and Schedule 28 to this Act shall have effect–

(a) for the purposes of income tax, for the year 1996–97 and subsequent years of assessment; and

(b) for the purposes of corporation tax, for accounting periods ending after 31st March 1996.

History – S. 154(2) omitted by CTA 2009, s. 1322 and Sch. 1, para. 438 and repealed by CTA 2009, s. 1326 and Sch. 3, Pt. 1, with effect for corporation tax purposes for accounting periods ending on or after 1 April 2009, and for income tax and capital gains tax purposes for the tax year 2009–10 and subsequent tax years.
In former s. 154(2) the words "(3) and" substituted for the former wording by ITTOIA 2005, s. 882(1) and Sch. 1, para. 488(2)(a) effective for income tax purposes for 2005–06 onwards and for corporation tax purposes for accounting periods ending after 5 April 2005 (ITTOIA 2005, s. 883(1)).
In s. 154(2) the final sentence (from "This does not" to "income tax charges).") inserted by ITTOIA 2005, s. 882(1) and Sch. 1, para. 488(2)(b) effective for income tax purposes for 2005–06 onwards and for corporation tax purposes for accounting periods ending after 5 April 2005 (ITTOIA 2005, s. 883(1)).
S. 154(3) omitted by CTA 2009, s. 1322 and Sch. 1, para. 438 and repealed by CTA 2009, s. 1326 and Sch. 3, Pt. 1, with effect for corporation tax purposes for accounting periods ending on or after 1 April 2009, and for income tax and capital gains tax purposes for the tax year 2009–10 and subsequent tax years.
S. 154(4) omitted by ITTOIA 2005, s. 882(1) and Sch. 1, para. 488(3); and repealed by ITTOIA 2005, s. 884 and Sch. 3 effective for income tax purposes for 2005–06 onwards and for corporation tax purposes for accounting periods ending after 5 April 2005 (ITTOIA 2005, s. 883(1)).
S. 154(5) omitted by CTA 2009, s. 1322 and Sch. 1, para. 438 and repealed by CTA 2009, s. 1326 and Sch. 3, Pt. 1, with effect for corporation tax purposes for accounting periods ending on or after 1 April 2009, and for income tax and capital gains tax purposes for the tax year 2009–10 and subsequent tax years.
S. 154(6) omitted by CTA 2009, s. 1322 and Sch. 1, para. 438 and repealed by CTA 2009, s. 1326 and Sch. 3, Pt. 1, with effect for corporation tax purposes for accounting periods ending on or after 1 April 2009, and for income tax and capital gains tax purposes for the tax year 2009–10 and subsequent tax years.
In former s. 154(6) the words "income tax or" that immediately followed the words "entitled for the purposes of" omitted by ITTOIA 2005, s. 882(1) and Sch. 1, para. 488(4); and repealed by ITTOIA 2005, s. 884 and Sch. 3 effective for income tax purposes for 2005–06 onwards and for corporation tax purposes for accounting periods ending after 5 April 2005 (ITTOIA 2005, s. 883(1)).
S. 154(8) omitted by CTA 2009,s. 1322 and Sch. 1, para. 438 and repealed by CTA 2009, s. 1326 and Sch. 3, Pt. 1, with effect for corporation tax purposes for accounting periods ending on or after 1 April 2009, and for income tax and capital gains tax purposes for the tax year 2009–10 and subsequent tax years.

Cross references – Sch. 9, para. 19A(4B): adjustment on change of accounting policy.
ICTA 1988, Pt. XV, Ch. IA: settlements; liability of settlor.
ICTA 1988, Pt. XVII, Ch. III: tax avoidance; transfer of assets abroad.
F(No. 2)A 1931, s. 22: provisions in cases where Treasury has power to borrow money.
FA 1940, s. 60: power of the Treasury to attach exemptions from taxation to securities.

FA 1998, s. 161: any gilt-edged security issued before 6 April 1998 without FOTRA conditions is to be treated in relation to payments of interest falling due on or after that date as if it were a security issued with the post-1996 Act conditions, and those conditions had been authorised in relation to the issue of the security by virtue of F(No. 2)A 1931, s. 22.

Extra-statutory concessions – A14: circumstances in which beneficiaries may claim to have tax liability on residuary income received during administration of estate adjusted to enable them to claim exemption in respect of FOTRA securities issued under s. 154, if they would have been so entitled had they received income directly.
B18: circumstances in which beneficiaries may claim exemption in respect of FOTRA securities issued under s. 154 where payment received from certain discretionary trustees, and beneficiaries would have been so entitled if they had received the income directly.

HMRC Manuals – Advanced Instruction Manual G.52, G.53: lists of securities issued on FOTRA terms.

Notes – The omitted income tax material is principally rewritten at ITTOIA 2005, s. 713–716.
S. 154 rewritten for corporation tax purposes as follows:
S. 154(2): CTA 2009, s. 1279(1), (3).
S. 154(3): CTA 2009, s. 1279(4).
S. 154(5): CTA 2009, s. 1279(5).
S. 154(6): CTA 2009, s. 404(1), (2), (3).
S. 154(8): CTA 2009, s. 404(4), 1280(1), (3), (4), (5).

155 Directions for payment without deduction of tax

155 [Repealed by ITA 2007, s. 1031 and Sch. 3, Pt. 1.]

History – S. 155 repealed by ITA 2007, s. 1031 and Sch. 3, Pt. 1, with effect from 6 April 2007.

Notes – S. 155 rewritten as ITA 2007, 636(1), (2), (3).

156 Paying and collecting agents etc.

156 [Repealed by Statute Law (Repeals) Act 2013, s. 1 and Sch. 1, Pt. 10.]

History – S. 156 repealed by Statute Law (Repeals) Act 2013, s. 1 and Sch. 1, Pt. 10, with effect from 31 January 2013.

157 Stock lending fees

157(1) [Inserts ICTA 1988, s. 129B.]

157(2) This section has effect in relation to any arrangements entered into on or after 2nd January 1996.

158 Transfers on death under the accrued income scheme

158 [Repealed by ITA 2007, s. 1031 and Sch. 3, Pt. 1.]

History – S. 158 repealed by ITA 2007, s. 1031 and Sch. 3, Pt. 1, with effect from 6 April 2007.

Notes – S. 158 rewritten as follows:
S. 158(1): ITA 2007, s. 620(2).
S. 158(3): ITA 2007, s. 636(1), (2), (3).

159 Manufactured payments, repos, etc.

159(1) [Repeals ICTA 1988, s. 729, 737A(2)(b) and 786(4) except in relation to cases where the initial agreement to sell or transfer the securities or other property was made before the appointed day.]

159(2) [Repealed by FA 1997, s. 113 and Sch. 18, Pt. VI(10).]

159(3) [Repealed by FA 1997, s. 113 and Sch. 18, Pt. VI(10).]

159(4)–(6) [Repealed by ITA 2007, s. 1031 and Sch. 3, Pt. 1.]

(a) [Repealed by CTA 2010, s. 1181 and Sch. 3, Pt. 1.]

(b) [Repealed by FA 1997, s. 113 and Sch. 18, Pt. VI(10).]

159(8) [Repealed by CTA 2010, s. 1181 and Sch. 3, Pt. 1.]

159(9) Subsections (2), (4) and (5) above have effect–

(a) for the purposes of corporation tax, in relation to accounting periods ending after 31st March 1996; and

(b) for the purposes of income tax, in relation to the year 1996–97 and subsequent years of assessment.

159(10) In this section **"the appointed day"** means such day as the Treasury may by order appoint, and different days may be appointed under this subsection for different purposes.

History – S. 159(2) and (3) repealed by FA 1997, s. 113 and Sch. 18, Pt. VI(10), with effect in relation to, and to transfers under, any arrangements made on or after 1 July 1997 (SI 1997/991 (C. 33)).
S. 159(4)–(6) repealed by ITA 2007, s. 1031 and Sch. 3, Pt. 1, with effect from 6 April 2007.
S. 159(7)(a) repealed by CTA 2010, s. 1181 and Sch. 3, Pt. 1, with effect for corporation tax purposes for accounting periods ending on or after 1 April 2010, and for income tax and capital gains tax purposes for the tax year 2010–11 and subsequent tax years.
S. 159(7)(b) (and the word "and" which immediately preceded it) repealed by FA 1997, s. 113 and Sch. 18, Pt. VI(10), with effect in relation to, and to transfers under, any arrangements made on or after 1 July 1997 (SI 1997/991 (C. 33)).
S. 159(8) repealed by CTA 2010, s. 1181 and Sch. 3, Pt. 1, with effect for corporation tax purposes for accounting periods ending on or after 1 April 2010, and for income tax and capital gains tax purposes for the tax year 2010–11 and subsequent tax years.

Notes – S. 159 rewritten as follows:
S. 159(4): ITA 2007, s. 581(1), 922(1), 923(1), (2), (3).
S. 159(6): ITA 2007, s. 925(1), (2), (3), (4), (5).
The day appointed for the purposes of s. 159(1), (3) was 6 November 1996 (SI 1996/2646).

160 Investments in housing

160 [Ceases to have effect by virtue of FA 2006, s. 143.]

History – S. 160 ceases to have effect by virtue of FA 2006, s. 143 with effect in relation to accounting periods beginning on or after 19 July 2006.

161 Venture capital trusts: control of companies etc.

161 [Repealed by ITA 2007, s. 1031 and Sch. 3, Pt. 1.]

History – S. 161 repealed by ITA 2007, s. 1031 and Sch. 3, Pt. 1, with effect from 6 April 2007.

Notes – S. 161(3) rewritten as ITA 2007, s. 313(4), (5), (6).

INSURANCE POLICIES

162 Qualifying life insurance policies: certification

162(1)

(a) [Amends FA 1995, s. 55.]

(b) [Inserts FA 1995, s. 55(9).]

162(2) [Amends ICTA 1988, Sch. 15, para. 24(2A) and 25(2).]

INSURANCE COMPANIES

163 Life assurance business losses

163 [Omitted by FA 2012, s. 146 and Sch. 16, para. 247(g)(i).]

History – S. 163 omitted by FA 2012, s. 146 and Sch. 16, para. 247(g)(i), with effect in relation to accounting periods beginning on or after 1 January 2013 (FA 2012, s. 148) but subject to transitional provisions in FA 2012, Sch. 17. Where an accounting period would otherwise straddle 1 January 2013, it is deemed to end on 31 December 2012 (FA 2012, s. 149).

164 Limits on relief for expenses

164(1) [Repealed by FA 2004, s. 326 and Sch. 42, Pt. 2(3).]

164(2) [Repealed by FA 2004, s. 326 and Sch. 42, Pt. 2(3).]

164(3) [Repealed by SI 2006/3271, reg. 43 and Schedule, Pt. 1.]

164(4) [Omitted by FA 2008, s. 43 and Sch. 17, para. 24(2).]

164(5) Subject to subsection (6) below, this section has effect in relation to accounting periods beginning on or after 1st January 1996.

164(6) [Repealed by FA 2004, s. 326 and Sch. 42, Pt. 2(3).]

History – S. 164(1) repealed by FA 2004, s. 326 and Sch. 42, Pt. 2(3) with effect for accounting periods beginning on or after 1 April 2004.

S. 164(2) repealed by FA 2004, s. 326 and Sch. 42, Pt. 2(3) with effect for accounting periods beginning on or after 1 April 2004.

S. 164(3) repealed by SI 2006/3271, reg. 43 and Schedule, Pt. 1, with effect from 31 December 2006 in relation to periods of account ending on or after that date.

S. 164(3)(a) repealed by F(No. 2)A 1997, s. 52 and Sch. 8, Pt. II(6) (in accordance with s. 23 and Sch. 3, para. 13(3) and (14)) with effect for accounting periods beginning on or after 2 July 1997.

S. 164(4) omitted by FA 2008, s. 43 and Sch. 17, para. 24(2), with effect from 21 July 2008.

S. 164(6) repealed by FA 2004, s. 326 and Sch. 42, Pt. 2(3) with effect for accounting periods beginning on or after 1 April 2004.

165 Annual payments under insurance policies: deductions

165(1) [Inserts ICTA 1988, s. 337(2A) and (2B).]

165(2) [Repealed by CTA 2010, s. 1181 and Sch. 3, Pt. 1.]

165(3) [Repealed by FA 1997, s. 113 and Sch. 18, Pt. VI(6).]

165(4) Subject to subsection (5) below, this section has effect in relation to accounting periods beginning on or after 1st January 1996.

165(5) In relation to any accounting period beginning on or after 1st January 1996 but ending before 1st April 1996, this section shall have effect as if any reference in provisions inserted by this section to an annuity payable or paid by an insurance company included a reference to any such interest as was mentioned in section 434B(1) of the Taxes Act 1988 before its repeal by virtue of this section.

History – S. 165(2) repealed by CTA 2010, s. 1181 and Sch. 3, Pt. 1, with effect for corporation tax purposes for accounting periods ending on or after 1 April 2010, and for income tax and capital gains tax purposes for the tax year 2010–11 and subsequent tax years.

S. 165(3) repealed by FA 1997, s. 113 and Sch. 18, Pt. VI(6), with effect in relation to accounting periods beginning after 5 March 1997.

166 Equalisation reserves

166 [Omitted by FA 2012, s. 26(2)(b).]

History – S. 166 omitted by FA 2012, s. 26(2)(b), with effect in relation to accounting periods ending on or after 1 January 2016 (SI 2015/1999, art. 2). Former s. 166 read as follows:

"Equalisation reserves

166 Schedule 32 to this Act (which makes provision about the tax treatment of equalisation reserves maintained by insurance companies) shall have effect.".

167 Industrial assurance business

167(1) [Repeals ICTA 1988, s. 432(2).]

167(2) [Repealed by FA 2007, s. 114 and Sch. 27, Pt. 2(7)]

167(3) [Omitted by FA 2012, s. 146 and Sch. 16, para. 247(g)(ii).]

167(4) [Repealed by ITA 2007, s. 1031 and Sch. 3, Pt. 1.]

167(5) [Amends ICTA 1988, Sch. 14, para. 8(4).]

167(6) [Inserts ICTA 1988, Sch. 14, para 8(8).]

167(7) In Schedule 15 to the Taxes Act 1988 (qualifying policies)–

(a) in paragraph 1(6) (calculation of amount included in premiums of whole life and term insurances in respect of their payment otherwise than annually), for "and if the policy is issued in the course of an industrial assurance business," there shall be substituted "and if the policy provides for payment otherwise than annually without providing for the amount of the premiums if they are paid annually,"; and

(b) in paragraph 2(2) (the equivalent calculation for endowment assurances), for "issued in the course of an industrial assurance business," there shall be substituted "that provides for the payment of premiums otherwise than annually without providing for the amount of the premiums if they are paid annually,".

167(8) [Inserts ICTA 1988, Sch. 15, para 8A.]

167(9) [Inserts ICTA 1988, Sch. 15, para. 18(3)(c).]

167(10) [Omitted by FA 2012, s. 146 and Sch. 16, para. 247(g)(ii).]

167(11) Subsection (4) above shall come into force on such day as the Board may by order appoint.

167(12) Subsection (7) above shall have effect in relation to policies issued on or after such day as the Board may by order appoint.

Prospective amendments – S. 167(5) and (6) repealed by FA 2012, s. 227 and Sch. 39, para. 28(1), with effect from a date to be appointed by Treasury order.

History – S. 167(2) repealed by FA 2007, s. 114 and Sch. 27, Pt. 2(7) with effect (FA 2007, s. 38):

- for the purposes of corporation tax, for periods of account of insurance companies beginning on or after 1 January 2007; and
- for the purposes of income tax, for the 2007–08 tax year and subsequent tax years.

S. 167(3) omitted by FA 2012, s. 146 and Sch. 16, para. 247(g)(ii), with effect in relation to accounting periods beginning on or after 1 January 2013 (FA 2012, s. 148) but subject to transitional provisions in FA 2012, Sch. 17. Where an accounting period would otherwise straddle 1 January 2013, it is deemed to end on 31 December 2012 (FA 2012, s. 149).
S. 167(4) repealed by ITA 2007, s. 1031 and Sch. 3, Pt. 1, with effect from 6 April 2007.
S. 167(10) omitted by FA 2012, s. 146 and Sch. 16, para. 247(g)(ii), with effect in relation to accounting periods beginning on or after 1 January 2013 (FA 2012, s. 148) but subject to transitional provisions in FA 2012, Sch. 17. Where an accounting period would otherwise straddle 1 January 2013, it is deemed to end on 31 December 2012 (FA 2012, s. 149).

Statutory instruments – SI 2001/3643 (C. 118), art. 2(a): the appointed day for the purposes of s. 167(11), (12) is 1 December 2001.

Notes – S. 167(4) rewritten as ITA 2007, s. 989, Sch. 1, para. 83, 232(2), (4), 233.

168 Capital redemption business

168(1) [Repealed by FA 2007, s. 114 and Sch. 27, Pt. 2(7).]

168(2) [Omitted by FA 2012, s. 146 and Sch. 16, para. 247(g)(iii).]

168(3) [Repealed by FA 2007, s. 114 and Sch. 27, Pt. 2(7).]

168(4) [Omitted by FA 2008, s. 36 and Sch. 14, para. 17.]

168(5) [Omitted by FA 2008, s. 36 and Sch. 14, para. 17.]

168(6) [Omitted by FA 2008, s. 36 and Sch. 14, para. 17.]

History – S. 168(1) and (3) repealed by FA 2007, s. 114 and Sch. 27, Pt. 2(7) with effect:

- for the purposes of corporation tax, for periods of account of insurance companies beginning on or after 1 January 2007; and
- for the purposes of income tax, for the 2007–08 tax year and subsequent tax years.

S. 168(2) omitted by FA 2012, s. 146 and Sch. 16, para. 247(g)(iii), with effect in relation to accounting periods beginning on or after 1 January 2013 (FA 2012, s. 148) but subject to transitional provisions in FA 2012, Sch. 17. Where an accounting period would otherwise straddle 1 January 2013, it is deemed to end on 31 December 2012 (FA 2012, s. 149).
S. 168(4)–(6) omitted by FA 2008, s. 36 and Sch. 14, para. 17, with effect:

- for the purposes of corporation tax, for accounting periods beginning on or after 1 April 2008; and
- for the purposes of income tax, for the tax year 2008–09 and subsequent tax years.

169 Provisional repayments in connection with pension business

Notes – S. 169 repealed by FA 2001, s. 110 and Sch. 33 Pt. 2(12) in accordance with s. 87, (i.e. broadly in relation to income tax borne by deduction from payments received after 30 September 2001 but not in relation to tax credits referable to the tax exempt business of friendly societies and the ISA business of insurance companies and friendly societies, in respect of distributions made before 6 April 2004).

169(1) Schedule 19AB to the Taxes Act 1988 (pension business: payments on account of tax credits and deducted tax) shall be amended in accordance with the provisions of Part I of Schedule 34 to this Act.

169(2) Schedule 19AC to the Taxes Act 1988 (modification of that Act in relation to overseas life insurance companies) shall be amended in accordance with the provisions of Part II of Schedule 34 to this Act.

169(3) The amendments made by Schedule 34 to this Act shall have effect in relation to provisional repayment periods, within the meaning of Schedule 19AB to the Taxes Act 1988, falling in accounting periods ending on or after the day appointed under section 199 of the Finance Act 1994 for the purposes of Chapter III of Part IV of that Act (self-assessment management provisions).

Notes – The day appointed under FA 1994, s. 199 for the purposes of corporation tax self-assessment is 1 July 1999 by virtue of SI 1998/3173 (C. 78).

170 Time for amending and enquiring into returns

170 [Repealed by FA 1998, s. 165 and ch. 27, Pt. III(28) with effect in relation to accounting periods ending on or after 1 July 1999, the corporation tax self-assessment appointed day under FA 1994 s. 199 by virtue of SI 3173 (C. 78).]

FRIENDLY SOCIETIES

171 Life or endowment business

171 [Omitted by FA 2012, s. 176 and Sch. 18, para. 23(d).]

History – S. 171 omitted by FA 2012, s. 176 and Sch. 18, para. 23(d), with effect in relation to accounting periods beginning on or after 1 January 2013 (FA 2012, s. 178) but subject to transitional provisions in FA 2012, Sch. 19. Where an accounting period would otherwise straddle 1 January 2013, it is deemed to end on 31 December 2012 (FA 2012, s. 179). Note that s. 171(3) and (4) had already been repealed (see below).

Former s. 171(3) and (4) repealed by ITA 2007, s. 1031 and Sch. 3, Pt. 1, with effect from 6 April 2007.

PERSONAL PENSION SCHEMES

172 Return of contributions on or after death of member

172 [Repealed by FA 2004, s. 326 and Sch. 42, Pt. 3.]

History – S. 172 repealed by FA 2004, s. 326 and Sch. 42, Pt. 3, with effect from 6 April 2006 subject to FA 2004, Sch. 36.

PARTICIPATORS IN CLOSE COMPANIES

173 Loans to participators etc.

173(1)–(4) [Repealed by CTA 2010, s. 1181 and Sch. 3, Pt. 1.]

173(5) [Substitutes ICTA 1988, s. 826(4)(a).]

173(6) This section has effect in relation to any loan or advance made in an accounting period ending on or after 31st March 1996.

History – S. 173(1)–(4) repealed by CTA 2010, s. 1181 and Sch. 3, Pt. 1, with effect for corporation tax purposes for accounting periods ending on or after 1 April 2010, and for income tax and capital gains tax purposes for the tax year 2010–11 and subsequent tax years.

174 Attribution of gains to participators in non-resident companies

174(1) Section 13 of the Taxation of Chargeable Gains Act 1992 (attribution of gains to members of non-resident companies) shall be amended in accordance with subsections (2) to (9) below.

174(2) [Amends TCGA 1992, s. 13(2).]

174(3) [Substitutes TCGA 1992, s. 13(3) and (4).]

174(4) [Omits TCGA 1992, s. 13(5)(a) and inserts s. 13(5A).]

174(5) [Amends TCGA 1992, s. 13(7).]

174(6) [Inserts TCGA 1992, s. 13(7A).]

174(7) [Amends TCGA 1992, s. 13(9).]

174(8) [Amends TCGA 1992, s. 13(10).]

174(9) [Inserts TCGA 1992, s. 13(12)–(15).]

(a) [Amends TCGA 1992, Sch. 5, para. 1(3)(a).]

(b) [Amends TCGA 1992, Sch. 5, para. 1(3)(b).]

(c) [Amends TCGA 1992, Sch. 5, para. 1(3).]

174(11) This section applies to gains accruing on or after 28th November 1995.

CANCELLATION OF TAX ADVANTAGES

175 Transactions in certain securities

175 [Omitted by CTA 2010, s. 1177 and Sch. 1, para. 292 and repealed by CTA 2010, s. 1181 and Sch. 3, Pt. 1.]

History – S. 175 omitted by CTA 2010, s. 1177 and Sch. 1, para. 292 and repealed by CTA 2010, s. 1181 and Sch. 3, Pt. 1, with effect for corporation tax purposes for accounting periods ending on or after 1 April 2010, and for income tax and capital gains tax purposes for the tax year 2010–11 and subsequent tax years.
S. 175(2) and (3) previously repealed by FA 1996, s. 205 and Sch. 41, Pt. V(31), from the date on which the Unlisted Securities Market closed (31 December 1996).

CHARGEABLE GAINS: RELIEFS

176 Retirement relief: age limits

176 [Repealed by FA 1998, s. 165 and Sch. 27, Pt. III(31).]

History – S. 176 repealed with effect in relation to disposals in 2003–04 and subsequent years of assessment, by FA 1998, s. 165 and Sch. 27, Pt. III(31).

177 Reinvestment relief on disposal of qualifying corporate bond

177 [Inserts TCGA 1992, s. 164A(2A) and (2B).]

SPECIAL CASES

178 Sub-contractors in the construction industry

178 [Repealed by FA 2004, s. 326 and Sch. 42, Pt. 2(7).]

History – S. 178 repealed by FA 2004, s. 326 and Sch. 42, Pt. 2(7) from 6 April 2007, in relation to construction operations (FA 2004, s. 77), by virtue of notice given pursuant to SI 2005/2045.

179 Roll-over relief in respect of ships

179 [Repealed by CAA 2001, s. 580 and Sch. 4.]

History – S. 179 repealed by CAA 2001, Sch. 4 with effect as respects allowances and charges falling to be made for chargeable periods ending, for income tax purposes, on or after 6 April 2001, and, for corporation tax purposes, on or after 1 April 2001.

180 Scientific research expenditure: oil licences

180 [Repealed by CAA 2001, s. 580 and Sch. 4.]

History – S. 180 repealed by CAA 2001, Sch 4 with effect as respects allowances and charges falling to be made for chargeable periods ending, for income tax purposes, on or after 6 April 2001, and, for corporation tax purposes, on or after 1 April 2001.

181 Overseas petroleum

181(1) [Amends TCGA 1992, s. 196(1).]

181(2) [Inserts TCGA 1992, s. 196(1A) and amends s. 196(2).]

181(3) [Substitutes TCGA 1992, s. 196(5) and (5A).]

181(4) Subsections (1) to (3) above shall have effect in relation to any disposal on or after 13th September 1995 and subsection (3) shall also have effect, and be deemed always to have had effect, for the construction of section 195 of the Taxation of Chargeable Gains Act 1992 in its application to disposals before that date.

181(5) Where enactments re-enacted in the Taxation of Chargeable Gains Act 1992 apply, instead of that Act, in the case of any disposal before 13th September 1995, this section shall have effect as if it required amendments equivalent to those made by subsection (3) above to have effect, and be deemed always to have had effect, for the construction of any enactment corresponding to section 195 of that Act.

182 Controlled foreign companies

182 Schedule 36 to this Act (which contains amendments of Chapter IV of Part XVII of the Taxes Act 1988) shall have effect in relation to accounting periods of a controlled foreign company, within the meaning of that Chapter, beginning on or after 28th November 1995.

PART VII – MISCELLANEOUS AND SUPPLEMENTAL

MISCELLANEOUS: DIRECT TAXATION

198 Banks

198 Schedule 37 to this Act (which re-defines "bank" for certain purposes, and makes related amendments) shall have effect.

199 Quotation or listing of securities

199 Schedule 38 to this Act (which contains amendments of enactments referring to the quotation or listing of securities) shall have effect.

200 Domicile for tax purposes of overseas electors

200(1) In determining–

(a) for the purposes of inheritance tax or capital gains tax where a person is domiciled at any time on or after 6th April 1996, or

(b) for the purposes of section 267(1)(a) of the Inheritance Tax Act 1984 (deemed UK domicile for three years after ceasing to be so domiciled) where a person was domiciled at any time on or after 6th April 1993,

there shall be disregarded any relevant action taken by that person (whether before, on or after that date) in connection with electoral rights.

200(2) Relevant action is taken by a person in connection with electoral rights where–

(a) he does anything with a view to, or in connection with, being registered as an overseas elector; or

(b) when registered as an overseas elector, he votes in any election at which he is entitled to vote by virtue of being so registered.

200(3) For the purposes of this section, a person is registered as an overseas elector if he is–

(a) registered in any register of parliamentary electors in pursuance of such a declaration as is mentioned in section 1(1)(a) of the Representation of the People Act 1985 (extension of parliamentary franchise to certain non-resident British citizens); or

(b) registered under section 3 of that Act of 1985 (certain non-resident peers entitled to vote at European Parliamentary elections).

200(4) Nothing in subsection (1) above prevents regard being had, in determining the domicile of a person at any time, to any relevant action taken by him in connection with electoral rights if–

(a) his domicile at that time falls to be determined for the purpose of ascertaining his or any other person's liability to either of the taxes mentioned in subsection (1)(a) above; and

(b) the person whose liability is being ascertained wishes regard to be had to that action;

and a person's domicile determined in accordance with any such wishes shall be taken to have been so determined for the purpose only of ascertaining the liability in question.

History – In s. 200(1)(a), the words ", income tax" omitted by TIOPA 2010, s. 371 and Sch. 7, para. 74(2) and repealed by TIOPA 2010, s. 378 and Sch. 10, Pt. 12, with effect for income tax and capital gains tax purposes for the tax year 2010–11 and subsequent tax years.
In s. 200(3)(a) the words "of parliamentary electors in pursuance of such a declaration as is mentioned in section 1(1)(a)" substituted for the words "mentioned in section 12(10) of the Representation of the People Act 1993 (right to be registered of persons entitled to vote at parliamentary elections) on account of any entitlement to vote conferred on him by section 1" by the Representation of the People Act 2000, s. 15 and Sch. 6 para. 19 with effect from 16 February 2001.
In s. 200(4)(a), the word "either" substituted for the word "any" by TIOPA 2010, s. 371 and Sch. 7, para. 74(3), with effect for income tax and capital gains tax purposes for the tax year 2010–11 and subsequent tax years.

Cross references – IHTA 1984, s. 267(1)(a): deemed UK domicile for three years after ceasing to be so domiciled.

Notes – S. 200(1) rewritten as TIOPA 2010, Sch. 7, para. 77.

201 Enactment of Inland Revenue concessions

201 Schedule 39 to this Act has effect for the purpose of enacting certain extra-statutory concessions relating to income tax, corporation tax, capital gains tax, and stamp duty.

Notes – ESCs B19, B28, D1, D19, D28, D36, D43, D48, G1 and G2 enacted.

MISCELLANEOUS: OTHER MATTERS

202 Gilt stripping

202(1) [Inserts FA 1942, s. 47(1)(bc) and (bd).]

202(2) [Inserts FA 1942, s. 47(1B)–(1F).]

202(3) [Inserts National Debt (Stockholders) Relief Act 1892, s. 2A.]

202(4) [Inserts National Loan Act 1968, s. 16(4A).]

202(5) The Treasury may by regulations make provision for securing that enactments and subordinate legislation which–

(a) apply in relation to government securities or to any description of such securities, or

(b) for any other purpose refer (in whatever terms) to such securities or to any description of them,

have effect with such modifications as the Treasury may think appropriate in consequence of the making of any provision or arrangements for, or in connection with, the issue or transfer of strips of government securities or the consolidation of such strips into other securities.

202(6) Regulations under subsection (5) above may–

(a) impose a charge to income tax, corporation tax, capital gains tax, inheritance tax, stamp duty or stamp duty reserve tax;

(b) include provision applying generally to, or to any description of, enactments or subordinate legislation;

(c) make different provision for different cases; and

(d) contain such incidental, supplemental, consequential and transitional provision as the Treasury think appropriate.

202(7) The power to make regulations under subsection (5) above shall be exercisable by statutory instrument subject to annulment in pursuance of a resolution of the House of Commons.

202(8) Schedule 40 to this Act (which makes provision in relation to strips for taxation purposes) shall have effect.

202(9) The enactments that may be modified by regulations under this section shall include section 95 above and the enactments contained in Schedule 40 to this Act.

202(10) In this section–

"government securities" means any securities included in Part I of Schedule 11 to the Finance Act 1942;

"modifications" includes amendments, additions and omissions; and

"subordinate legislation" has the same meaning as in the Interpretation Act 1978;

and expressions used in this section and in section 47 of the Finance Act 1942 have the same meanings in this section as in that section.

SUPPLEMENTAL

204 Interpretation

204 In this Act **"the Taxes Act 1988"** means the Income and Corporation Taxes Act 1988.

206 Short title

206 This Act may be cited as the Finance Act 1996.

SCHEDULES

SCHEDULE 6 – TAXATION OF SAVINGS AT THE LOWER RATE

Section 73

THE TAXES MANAGEMENT ACT 1970 (C. 9)

1 [Repealed by ITA 2007, s. 1031 and Sch. 3, Pt. 1.]

History – Para. 1 repealed by ITA 2007, s. 1031 and Sch. 3, Pt. 1, with effect from 6 April 2007.

THE TAXES ACT 1988

2 [Repealed by ITA 2007, s. 1031 and Sch. 3, Pt. 1.]

History – Para. 2 repealed by ITA 2007, s. 1031 and Sch. 3, Pt. 1, with effect from 6 April 2007.

Notes – Para. 2 rewritten as ITA 2007, s. 874(2), 900(2), 901(3), 902(2), (3), 903(5), (6), (7), 906(5), 910(2), 928(2).

3 [Repealed by ITA 2007, s. 1031 and Sch. 3, Pt. 1.]

History – Para. 3 repealed by ITA 2007, s. 1031 and Sch. 3, Pt. 1, with effect from 6 April 2007.

6 [Repealed by ITTOIA 2005, s. 884 and Sch. 3 effective for income tax purposes for 2005–06 onwards (ITTOIA 2005, s. 883(1).]

7 [Repealed by ITTOIA 2005, s. 884 and Sch. 3 effective for income tax purposes for 2005–06 onwards (ITTOIA 2005, s. 883(1).]

8 [Repealed by ITA 2007, s. 1031 and Sch. 3, Pt. 1.]

History – Para. 8 repealed by ITA 2007, s. 1031 and Sch. 3, Pt. 1, with effect from 6 April 2007.

9 [Repealed by ITTOIA 2005, s. 884 and Sch. 3 effective for income tax purposes for 2005–06 onwards (ITTOIA 2005, s. 883(1).]

10(1-2) [Repealed by CTA 2010, s. 1181 and Sch. 3, Pt. 1.]

10(3) [Repeals ICTA 1988, s. 468E and 468EE.]

History – Para. 10(1)–(2) repealed by CTA 2010, s. 1181 and Sch. 3, Pt. 1, with effect for corporation tax purposes for accounting periods ending on or after 1 April 2010, and for income tax and capital gains tax purposes for the tax year 2010–11 and subsequent tax years.

11 [Repealed by Statute Law (Repeals) Act 2013, s. 1 and Sch. 1, Pt. 10.]

History – Para. 11 repealed by Statute Law (Repeals) Act 2013, s. 1 and Sch. 1, Pt. 10, with effect from 31 January 2013.

12–15 [Repealed by ITA 2007, s. 1031 and Sch. 3, Pt. 1.]

History – Para. 12–15 repealed by ITA 2007, s. 1031 and Sch. 3, Pt. 1, with effect from 6 April 2007.

Notes – Para. 12 rewritten as ITA 2007, s. 504(3).
Para. 13 rewritten as ITA 2007, s. 479(2), 481(2).
Para. 14 rewritten as ITA 2007, s. 939(2).
Para. 15 rewritten as ITA 2007, s. 487(5), (6).

16 [Repealed by CTA 2010, s. 1181 and Sch. 3, Pt. 1.]

History – Para. 16 repealed by CTA 2010, s. 1181 and Sch. 3, Pt. 1, with effect for corporation tax purposes for accounting periods ending on or after 1 April 2010, and for income tax and capital gains tax purposes for the tax year 2010–11 and subsequent tax years.

17 [Repealed by ITA 2007, s. 1031 and Sch. 3, Pt. 1.]

History – Para. 17 repealed by ITA 2007, s. 1031 and Sch. 3, Pt. 1, with effect from 6 April 2007.

Notes – Para. 20 rewritten as ITA 2007, s. 745(1).

20–21 [Repealed by ITA 2007, s. 1031 and Sch. 3, Pt. 1.]

History – Para. 20 and 21 repealed by ITA 2007, s. 1031 and Sch. 3, Pt. 1, with effect from 6 April 2007.
Para. 21 also omitted by FA 2008, s. 5 and Sch. 1 para. 49, with effect for the tax year 2008–09 and subsequent tax years.

22 [Repealed by CTA 2009, s. 1326 and Sch. 3, Pt. 1.]

History – Para. 22 repealed by CTA 2009, s. 1326 and Sch. 3, Pt. 1, with effect for corporation tax purposes for accounting periods ending on or after 1 April 2009, and for income tax and capital gains tax purposes for the tax year 2009–10 and subsequent tax years.

23 [Amends ICTA 1988, s. 822(1).]

24–25 [Repealed by ITA 2007, s. 1031 and Sch. 3, Pt. 1.]

History – Para. 24 and 25 repealed by ITA 2007, s. 1031 and Sch. 3, Pt. 1, with effect from 6 April 2007.

THE FINANCE ACT 1989 (C. 26)

26 [Repealed by FA 2003, s. 216 and Sch. 43, Pt. 3(12).]

History – Para. 26 repealed by FA 2003, s. 216 and Sch. 43, Pt. 3(12) in relation to the financial year 2003 and subsequent financial years.

COMMENCEMENT OF SCHEDULE

28 Subject to any express provisions as to commencement that are contained in the preceding provisions of this Schedule, this Schedule has effect for the year 1996–97 and subsequent years of assessment.

SCHEDULE 7 – TRANSFER OF CHARGE UNDER SCHEDULE C TO SCHEDULE D

Section 79

AMENDMENTS OF THE TAXES ACT 1988

1 The Taxes Act 1988 shall be amended in accordance with paragraphs 2 to 28 below.

2 [Repealed by ITA 2007, s. 1031 and Sch. 3, Pt. 1.]

History – Para. 2 repealed by ITA 2007, s. 1031 and Sch. 3, Pt. 1, with effect from 6 April 2007.

3 [Omits ICTA 1988, s. 17.]

4(1) [Repealed by CTA 2009, s. 1326 and Sch. 3, Pt. 1.]

4(2) [Subpara. (a) and (c) repealed by CTA 2009, s. 1326 and Sch. 3, Pt. 1.]

4(3) [Repealed by CTA 2009, s. 1326 and Sch. 3, Pt. 1.]

4(4) [Repealed by CTA 2009, s. 1326 and Sch. 3, Pt. 1.]

History – Para. 4(1), (2)(a) and (c), (3) and (4) repealed by CTA 2009, s. 1326 and Sch. 3, Pt. 1, with effect for corporation tax purposes for accounting periods ending on or after 1 April 2009, and for income tax and capital gains tax purposes for the tax year 2009–10 and subsequent tax years.

5 [Repealed by ITEPA 2003, Sch. 8, Pt. 1.]

History – Para. 5 repealed by ITEPA 2003, Sch. 8, Pt. 1 which has effect for the tax year 2003–04 and subsequent tax years.

6 [Substitutes the heading to ICTA 1988, Pt. III.]

7 [Omits ICTA 1988, s. 44.]

8 [Omits ICTA 1988, s. 45.]

9 [Omits ICTA 1988, s. 48.]

10 [Inserts ICTA 1988, s. 49(3).]

11 [Amends ICTA 1988, s. 50(1) and 51A(1).]

12 [Omits ICTA 1988, s. 52.]

13 [Omits ICTA 1988, s. 123.]

14

(a) [Amends ICTA 1988, s. 124(6).]

(b) [Omits ICTA 1988, s. 124(7).]

15 [Repealed by ITTOIA 2005, s. 884 and Sch. 3 effective for income tax purposes for 2005–06 onwards (ITTOIA 2005, s. 883(1).]

16 [Amends ICTA 1988, s. 398(b).]

17 [Repealed by FA 2003, s. 216 and Sch. 43, Pt. 5(3).]

History – Para. 17 repealed by FA 2003, s. 216 and Sch. 43, Pt. 5(3) in relation to interest distributions made on or after 16 October 2002.

18 [Omits ICTA 1988, s. 474(1) and (3).]

19 [Repealed by CTA 2010, s. 1181 and Sch. 3, Pt. 1.]

History – Para. 19 repealed by CTA 2010, s. 1181 and Sch. 3, Pt. 1, with effect for corporation tax purposes for accounting periods ending on or after 1 April 2010, and for income tax and capital gains tax purposes for the tax year 2010–11 and subsequent tax years.

20 [Repealed by Statute Law (Repeals) Act 2013, s. 1 and Sch. 1, Pt. 10.]

History – Para. 20 repealed by Statute Law (Repeals) Act 2013, s. 1 and Sch. 1, Pt. 10, with effect from 31 January 2013.

21(1) [Amends ICTA 1988, s. 516(1).]

21(2) [Amends ICTA 1988, s. 516(2).]

22 [Omits ICTA 1988, s. 582A(3).]

23 [Omitted by FA 2009, s. 49 and Sch. 25, para. 9(3)(c).]

History – Para. 23 omitted by FA 2009, s. 49 and Sch. 25, para. 9(3)(c), with effect in relation to transfers on or after 22 April 2009.

24 [Repealed by CTA 2010, s. 1181 and Sch. 3, Pt. 1.]

History – Para. 24 repealed by CTA 2010, s. 1181 and Sch. 3, Pt. 1, with effect for corporation tax purposes for accounting periods ending on or after 1 April 2010, and for income tax and capital gains tax purposes for the tax year 2010–11 and subsequent tax years.

25 [Amends ICTA 1988, s. 832(1).]

26 [Repealed by Statute Law (Repeals) Act 2013, s. 1 and Sch. 1, Pt. 10.]

History – Para. 26 repealed by Statute Law (Repeals) Act 2013, s. 1 and Sch. 1, Pt. 10, with effect from 31 January 2013.

27 [Omits ICTA 1988, Sch. 3.]

28 [Repealed by FA 2000, Sch. 40, Pt. II(17).]

History – Para. 28 repealed by FA 2000, Sch. 40, Pt. II(17) with effect in accordance with FA 2000, s. 111(6)(a) and (b) on and after 1 April 2001.

OTHER AMENDMENTS

29 [Amends the Table in TMA 1970, s. 98.]

30 [Amends FA 1989, s. 178(2)(m).]

31 [Amends FA 1995, s. 128(3)(a).]

COMMENCEMENT, ETC.

32 Subject to paragraphs 33 and 34 below, this Schedule has effect–

(a) for the purposes of income tax, for the year 1996–97 and subsequent years of assessment;

(b) for the purposes of corporation tax, for accounting periods ending after 31st March 1996.

POSITION OF PAYING AND COLLECTING AGENTS

33(1) Subject to the following provisions of this paragraph and paragraph 34 below–

(a) nothing in section 79 of this Act or this Schedule shall affect the obligations of any person under Schedule 3, in relation to times to which this paragraph applies, to set apart, retain or pay any amount of tax; and

(b) Schedule 3 shall have effect accordingly in relation to amounts set apart, retained or paid in pursuance of those obligations.

33(2) The repeal of Schedule 3 shall not affect the operation of paragraph 6B of that Schedule in relation to any amount–

(a) which became due and payable in relation to a transaction occurring before the day on which this Act was passed; but

(b) which remains unpaid at any time on or after that day.

33(3) The Board may by regulations make provision with respect to returns to be made for the quarter which includes both times before the day on which this Act was passed and times on and after that day.

33(4) Regulations under sub-paragraph (3) above may, in particular, provide that section 98 of the Taxes Management Act 1970 shall have effect as if it included a reference in the second column of the Table to any specified provision of the regulations.

33(5) In this paragraph **"Schedule 3"** means Schedule 3 to the Taxes Act 1988.

Cross references – ICTA 1988, Sch. 3 (repealed by FA 1996): machinery for assessment, charge and payment of income tax under Sch. C.

POSITION OF TAXPAYERS

34(1) Transitional payments of tax made on a person's behalf in relation to times to which this paragraph applies shall be treated as made only for the purpose of being applied in the discharge of that person's liability to tax charged under Schedule D.

34(2) If a transitional payment of tax has been made on a person's behalf, but it appears to the Board that–

(a) that person was not liable to tax, or

(b) the sum paid exceeded his liability,

the Board shall make or allow such repayments, adjustments or set-offs against unpaid tax as they think appropriate.

34(3) In this paragraph **"transitional payment of tax"** means a payment to which paragraph 33 above applies.

TIMES TO WHICH PARAGRAPHS 33 AND 34 APPLY

35 Paragraphs 33 and 34 above apply in relation to times falling–

(a) within a year of assessment or an accounting period mentioned in paragraph 32 above, but

(b) before the day on which this Act was passed.

SCHEDULE 8 – LOAN RELATIONSHIPS: CLAIMS ETC RELATING TO DEFICITS

[Omitted by CTA 2009, s. 1322 and Sch. 1, para. 440 and repealed by CTA 2009, s. 1326 and Sch. 3, Pt. 1.]

History – Sch. 8 omitted by CTA 2009, s. 1322 and Sch. 1, para. 440 and repealed by CTA 2009, s. 1326 and Sch. 3, Pt. 1, with effect for corporation tax purposes for accounting periods ending on or after 1 April 2009, and for income tax and capital gains tax purposes for the tax year 2009–10 and subsequent tax years, subject to the transitional and savings provisions in CTA 2009, Sch. 2, Pt. 8 and 9.

Notes – Sch. 8 rewritten as follows:
Para. 1(1): CTA 2009, s. 461(1).
Para. 1(2): CTA 2009, s. 461(2), (3).
Para. 1(3): CTA 2009, s. 461(5), (6).
Para. 1(4): CTA 2009, s. 461(7).
Para. 3(1): CTA 2009, s. 462(1).
Para. 3(2): CTA 2009, s. 462(2).
Para. 3(3): CTA 2009, s. 462(4), (5).
Para. 3(4): CTA 2009, s. 463(1), (2), (3).
Para. 3(5): CTA 2009, s. 463(3), (4).
Para. 3(6): CTA 2009, s. 463(5).
Para. 3(7): CTA 2009, s. 463(2).
Para. 4(1): CTA 2009, s. 457(1), (3).
Para. 4(2): CTA 2009, s. 457(1), (3), (4).
Para. 4(3): CTA 2009, s. 457(3), 458(1).
Para. 4(4): CTA 2009, s. 458(2).
Para. 4(5): CTA 2009, s. 458(3), (4), (5).
Para. 4(6): CTA 2009, s. 457(5).
Para. 5: CTA 2009, s. 456(2).

SCHEDULE 9 – LOAN RELATIONSHIPS: SPECIAL COMPUTATIONAL PROVISIONS

[Omitted by CTA 2009, s. 1322 and Sch. 1, para. 441 and repealed by CTA 2009, s. 1326 and Sch. 3, Pt. 1.]

History – Sch. 9 omitted by CTA 2009, s. 1322 and Sch. 1, para. 441 and repealed by CTA 2009, s. 1326 and Sch. 3, Pt. 1, with effect for corporation tax purposes for accounting periods ending on or after 1 April 2009, and for income tax and capital gains tax purposes for the tax year 2009–10 and subsequent tax years, subject to the transitional and savings provisions in CTA 2009, Sch. 2, Pt. 8 and 9.

Notes – Sch. 9 rewritten as follows:
Para. 1(1): CTA 2009, s. 465(1).
Para. 1(1A): CTA 2009, s. 465(1), (4), (5), 476(1).
Para. 1(2): CTA 2009, s. 464(2), 465(2).
Para. 2(1): CTA 2009, s. 372(1), 373(1).
Para. 2(1A): CTA 2009, s. 374(1), (2).
Para. 2(1B): CTA 2009, s. 375(1), (2).
Para. 2(1C): CTA 2009, s. 377.
Para. 2(1D): CTA 2009, s. 378(1), (2), (3), (4), (5), (6).
Para. 2(1E): CTA 2009, s. 375(1).
Para. 2(1F): CTA 2009, s. 375(1), (3).
Para. 2(1G): CTA 2009, s. 375(1), (4).
Para. 2(2): CTA 2009, s. 372(1), 373(1), (2), (3).
Para. 2(3): CTA 2009, s. 379(1), (3).
Para. 2(4): CTA 2009, s. 379(2).
Para. 2(5): CTA 2009, s. 376(1).
Para. 2(5A): CTA 2009, s. 376(2).
Para. 2(6): CTA 2009, s. 373(5), 376(3), (4), (5), 472(1), 476(1).
Para. 2(7): CTA 2009, s. 473(1).
Para. 3(1): CTA 2009, s. 420(1), (2), (3).
Para. 3(2): CTA 2009, s. 420(3), (4), (5).
Para. 3(3): CTA 2009, s. 476(1).
Para. 4A(1): CTA 2009, s. 361(1), 362(1).
Para. 4A(2): CTA 2009, s. 361(1), (5).
Para. 4A(3): CTA 2009, s. 361(2).
Para. 4A(4): CTA 2009, s. 362(1), (4).
Para. 4A(5): CTA 2009, s. 361(3), 362(2).
Para. 4A(6): CTA 2009, s. 361(3), (4).
Para. 4A(7): CTA 2009, s. 362(2), (3).
Para. 4A(8): CTA 2009, s. 353(5), 363(1), (2), (3), (4), (5), 472(1).
Para. 4A(9): CTA 2009, s. 363(6), (7).
Para. 4A(10): CTA 2009, s. 361(6), 362(5).
Para. 5(3): CTA 2009, s. 322(1), (2), 358(1), (2), 359(1), (2).
Para. 5(4): CTA 2009, s. 322(3).
Para. 5(5): CTA 2009, s. 358(1), (2), (3).
Para. 5(6): CTA 2009, s. 359(1).
Para. 5(7): CTA 2009, s. 322(5), (6), 323(1), (2), (3), (4), (5).
Para. 5(8): CTA 2009, s. 322(4).
Para. 5ZA: CTA 2009, s. 353(3), 364(1), (4), 365(2), (4).
Para. 5A(1): CTA 2009, s. 364(1).
Para. 5A(2): CTA 2009, s. 364(1), (2), 371(1).
Para. 5A(3): CTA 2009, s. 364(2), 371(1).
Para. 5A(4): CTA 2009, s. 364(2), 371(1).
Para. 5A(5): CTA 2009, s. 365(2), (3), 371(1).
Para. 5A(6): CTA 2009, s. 365(1), (4), (5).
Para. 5A(7): CTA 2009, s. 365(4), (5).
Para. 5A(8): CTA 2009, s. 367(1).
Para. 5A(9): CTA 2009, s. 367(2), (3).
Para. 5A(10): CTA 2009, s. 367(3).
Para. 5A(11): CTA 2009, s. 368(1).
Para. 5A(12): CTA 2009, s. 368(3), (4), (5).
Para. 5A(13): CTA 2009, s. 368(1).
Para. 5A(14): CTA 2009, s. 369(1), (2).
Para. 5A(15): CTA 2009, s. 366(1), (2).
Para. 5A(16): CTA 2009, s. 364(5).
Para. 5A(17): CTA 2009, s. 370(1), (2).
Para. 5A(18): CTA 2009, s. 370(3), (4), (5), (6).
Para. 5A(19): CTA 2009, s. 365(2), 371(1).
Para. 5A(20): CTA 2009, s. 371(3).
Para. 5A(21): CTA 2009, s. 371(2).
Para. 6(1): CTA 2009, s. 352(1), 354(1).
Para. 6(2): CTA 2009, s. 352(1), 354(1).
Para. 6(3): CTA 2009, s. 354(2).
Para. 6(3A): CTA 2009, s. 360(1).
Para. 6(4): CTA 2009, s. 356(1), (2), (3).
Para. 6(5): CTA 2009, s. 356(4).
Para. 6(6): CTA 2009, s. 352(1), (2), (3).
Para. 6(7): CTA 2009, s. 352(2), (3).
Para. 6(8): CTA 2009, s. 352(4), 354(3), 360(2).
Para. 6A(1): CTA 2009, s. 357(1), (2), (3), (4), (5), (6).
Para. 6A(2): CTA 2009, s. 357(1), (2), (3), (4), (5), (6).
Para. 6A(3): CTA 2009, s. 323(1), (2).
Para. 6A(4): CTA 2009, s. 323(3).
Para. 6A(5): CTA 2009, s. 323(4), (5).
Para. 6C(1): CTA 2009, s. 353(4), 355(1).

Para. 6C(3): CTA 2009, s. 355(2).
Para. 6D(1): CTA 2009, s. 324(1).
Para. 6D(2): CTA 2009, s. 325(1), Sch. 2, para. 61(1).
Para. 6D(3): CTA 2009, s. 324(3).
Para. 6D(4): CTA 2009, s. 324(4).
Para. 6D(5): CTA 2009, s. 324(5), 325(2), Sch. 2, para. 61(2).
Para. 7(1): CTA 2009, s. 326(1), (2).
Para. 7(2): CTA 2009, s. 326(3).
Para. 10(1): CTA 2009, s. 327(1), (7).
Para. 10(2): CTA 2009, s. 327(2).
Para. 10(3): CTA 2009, s. 327(3).
Para. 10(4): CTA 2009, s. 327(4).
Para. 10(5): CTA 2009, s. 327(5), (6).
Para. 10A(1): CTA 2009, s. 333(1), 334(1).
Para. 10A(1A): CTA 2009, s. 333(3), (4), 334(3), (4).
Para. 10A(2): CTA 2009, s. 333(1).
Para. 10A(3): CTA 2009, s. 333(2).
Para. 10A(4): CTA 2009, s. 334(2).
Para. 11(1): CTA 2009, s. 444(1), (2), (3).
Para. 11(1A): CTA 2009, s. 445(1), (2).
Para. 11(1B): CTA 2009, s. 445(3).
Para. 11(2): CTA 2009, s. 444(4).
Para. 11(3): CTA 2009, s. 444(5).
Para. 11(3A): CTA 2009, s. 444(6).
Para. 11A(1): CTA 2009, s. 447(1), (2), 448(1), (2).
Para. 11A(2): CTA 2009, s. 447(1), (3).
Para. 11A(3): CTA 2009, s. 447(4).
Para. 11A(4): CTA 2009, s. 449(1), (2), (3), (4), 450(1), (2), (3), (4), (5), (6).
Para. 11A(5): CTA 2009, s. 449(6), 451(1), (2), (3), (5).
Para. 11A(6): CTA 2009, s. 451(4).
Para. 11A(7): CTA 2009, s. 452(1), (2).
Para. 11A(8): CTA 2009, s. 452(6).
Para. 11A(9): CTA 2009, s. 452(3), (4), (5).
Para. 11A(10): CTA 2009, s. 452(4), (5).
Para. 11B(1): CTA 2009, s. 455(1).
Para. 11B(2): CTA 2009, s. 455(2).
Para. 11B(3): CTA 2009, s. 455(3).
Para. 11B(4): CTA 2009, s. 455(4).
Para. 11B(5): CTA 2009, s. 455(5).
Para. 12(1): CTA 2009, s. 335(1), (2), 336(1), (2), (3), (5), 337(1), (2), (3), (7), 340(1), (8), 341(8).
Para. 12(2): CTA 2009, s. 340(2), (3), (4), (6).
Para. 12(2ZA): CTA 2009, s. 340(7).
Para. 12(2A): CTA 2009, s. 340(8), 341(1), (2), (3), (4).
Para. 12(2B): CTA 2009, s. 341(5), (6).
Para. 12(2C): CTA 2009, s. 340(5), (6), 341(4), (7).
Para. 12(2D): CTA 2009, s.347(1), (2), (3).
Para. 12(2E): CTA 2009, s. 347(5), 476(1), 1316(1).
Para. 12(2F): CTA 2009, s. 347(4).
Para. 12(3): CTA 2009, s. 336(4).
Para. 12(4): CTA 2009, s. 337(2), (4).
Para. 12(5): CTA 2009, s. 337(5), (6).
Para. 12(6): CTA 2009, s. 338(1), (2).
Para. 12(7): CTA 2009, s. 338(3), (4).
Para. 12(7A): CTA 2009, s. 338(5), (6).
Para. 12(8): CTA 2009, s. 335(6).
Para. 12(9): CTA 2009, s. 340(6).
Para. 12A(1): CTA 2009, s. 344(1), 345(1).
Para. 12A(2): CTA 2009, s. 345(1), (2).
Para. 12A(3): CTA 2009, s. 345(3), 346(3).
Para. 12A(4): CTA 2009, s. 345(4), 346(4).
Para. 12A(5): CTA 2009, s. 344(1), 345(1), 346(1).
Para. 12A(5A): CTA 2009, s. 344(2), (3).
Para. 12A(6): CTA 2009, s. 346(2).
Para. 12A(7): CTA 2009, s. 346(3), (4).
Para. 12A(8): CTA 2009, s. 344(4), 345(1), 346(1).
Para. 12A(9): CTA 2009, s. 345(5), 346(5).
Para. 12B(1): CTA 2009, s. 431(1), (3), (4), (5), (6), (7).
Para. 12B(2): CTA 2009, s. 431(1), (3), (4), (5), (6), (7), (8).
Para. 12B(3): CTA 2009, s. 433(1), (2), (3).
Para. 12B(4): CTA 2009, s. 434(1), (2), (3), (4), (5).
Para. 12B(6): CTA 2009, s. 437(1).
Para. 12B(7): CTA 2009, s. 437(2).
Para. 12B(8): CTA 2009, s. 437(3).
Para. 12B(9): CTA 2009, s. 432(1), (2), 439(1).
Para. 12C(1): CTA 2009, Sch. 1, para. 258.
Para. 12C(2): CTA 2009, s. 431(9), Sch. 1, para. 258.
Para. 12C(3): CTA 2009, Sch. 1, para. 259.
Para. 12C(4): CTA 2009, Sch. 1, para. 259.
Para. 12C(5): CTA 2009, Sch. 1, para. 258, 259.
Para. 12D(1): CTA 2009, s. 421(1), (3), 422(1).
Para. 12D(2): CTA 2009, s. 421(1), (4), 422(1).
Para. 12D(3): CTA 2009, s. 421(4).
Para. 12D(4): CTA 2009, s. 421(4).
Para. 12D(6): CTA 2009, s. 422(1), (2), (3).

Para. 12D(7): CTA 2009, s. 423(1), (2), (3), (4), (5).
Para. 12E(1): CTA 2009, Sch.1, para. 256.
Para. 12E(2): CTA 2009, s. 421(5), Sch. 1, para. 256.
Para. 12E(3): CTA 2009, Sch. 1, para. 256.
Para. 12E(4): CTA 2009, Sch. 1, para. 256.
Para. 12E(5): CTA 2009, Sch. 1, para. 256, 257.
Para. 12E(6): CTA 2009, Sch. 1, para. 257.
Para. 12F(1): CTA 2009, s. 426(1), Sch. 1, para. 257.
Para. 12F(2): CTA 2009, s. 426(2), Sch. 1, para. 257.
Para. 12F(3): CTA 2009, s. 427(1), (2), (3), (4), (5), 428(1), (2), (3), (4), Sch. 1, para. 257 (see also Sch. 2, para. 148).
Para. 12G(1): CTA 2009, s. 335(1), 339(1), (2), (3), (6), 342(1), 421(1), (2), 424(1), 431(2), 435(1).
Para. 12G(2): CTA 2009, s. 339(6), 421(1), (2), 424(1), 431(2), 435(1).
Para. 12G(3): CTA 2009, s. 339(1), (2), (4), 342(1).
Para. 12G(4): CTA 2009, s. 335(1), 342(2), (3), (4), 424(2),(3), (4), 435(2), (3), (4).
Para. 12G(5): CTA 2009, s. 342(5), 343(1), (2), (3), (4), 425(1), (2), (3), (4), 436(1), (2), (3), (4).
Para. 12G(6): CTA 2009, s. 339(7), 424(4), 435(4).
Para. 12H(1): CTA 2009, s. 421(1), 429(1), (2), Sch. 1, para. 260.
Para. 12H(2): CTA 2009, s. 429(1), (2).
Para. 12H(3): CTA 2009, Sch. 1, paras. 260, 261.
Para. 12H(4): CTA 2009, Sch. 1, para. 260.
Para. 12H(5): CTA 2009, Sch. 1, para. 261.
Para. 12I(1): CTA 2009, s. 431(1), 438(1), Sch. 1, para. 260.
Para. 12I(2): CTA 2009, s. 438(2), (3).
Para. 12I(3): CTA 2009, Sch.1, para. 260, 261.
Para. 12I(4): CTA 2009, Sch. 1, para. 260.
Para. 12I(5): CTA 2009, Sch. 1, para. 261.
Para. 12J(1): CTA 2009, s. 421(6), 429(3), 430(1), 438(4), 439(1), Sch. 1, para. 256, 258, 260.
Para. 12J(2): CTA 2009, s. 339(5), 430(2), 439(2), Sch. 1, para. 256, 258.
Para. 13(1): CTA 2009, s. 441(1), (2), (3).
Para. 13(1A): CTA 2009, s. 441(4), (5).
Para. 13(2): CTA 2009, s. 442(1).
Para. 13(3): CTA 2009, s. 442(2).
Para. 13(4): CTA 2009, s. 442(3), (4).
Para. 13(5): CTA 2009, s. 442(5).
Para. 13(6): CTA 2009, s. 476(1).
Para. 14(1): CTA 2009, s. 320(1).
Para. 14(2): CTA 2009, s. 320(2).
Para. 14(3): CTA 2009, s. 320(3).
Para. 14(4): CTA 2009, s. 320(4), (5), (6).
Para. 14A: CTA 2009, s. 321(1), (2).
Para. 15(1): CTA 2009, s. 332(1).
Para. 15(2): CTA 2009, s. 332(2), (3).
Para. 15(3): CTA 2009, s. 332(5).
Para. 15(4): CTA 2009, s. 332(4).
Para. 16(1): CTA 2009, s. 446(2), (4), (6).
Para. 16(2): CTA 2009, s. 446(3), (5), (7).
Para. 17(1): CTA 2009, s. 407(1).
Para. 17(2): CTA 2009, s. 407(2).
Para. 17(3): CTA 2009, s. 406(3), 407(3).
Para. 17(4): CTA 2009, s. 406(2), (4).
Para. 17(5): CTA 2009, s. 407(5), 408(1), (2), (3).
Para. 17(8): CTA 2009, s. 412(1), (4).
Para. 17(8A): CTA 2009, s. 412(2).
Para. 17(9): CTA 2009, s. 408(4), 472(1).
Para. 17(10): CTA 2009, s. 473(1).
Para. 18(1): CTA 2009, s. 409(1), 410(5).
Para. 18(1ZA): CTA 2009, s. 409(1), 410(1).
Para. 18(1A): CTA 2009, s. 410(2).
Para. 18(1B): CTA 2009, s. 410(3).
Para. 18(1C): CTA 2009, s. 410(4).
Para. 18(2): CTA 2009, s. 409(1), (2).
Para. 18(2A): CTA 2009, s. 409(3), (4).
Para. 18(2B): CTA 2009, s. 406(3), 409(5).
Para. 18(2C): CTA 2009, s. 412(1), (4).
Para. 18(2D): CTA 2009, s. 412(3).
Para. 18(3): CTA 2009, s. 406(2), (4).
Para. 18(3B): CTA 2009, s. 411(1), 472(1).
Para. 18(3C): CTA 2009, s. 411(2).
Para. 18(4): CTA 2009, s. 410(5), 411(3), 476(1).
Para. 18(5): CTA 2009, s. 411(4).
Para. 19(1): CTA 2009, s. 380(1).
Para. 19(2): CTA 2009, s. 380(2), (3), 476(1).
Para. 19(3): CTA 2009, s. 381(1).
Para. 19(4): CTA 2009, s. 381(2), (3), (4).
Para. 19(5): CTA 2009, s. 381(5).
Para. 19(6): CTA 2009, s. 381(6), (7).
Para. 19(7): CTA 2009, s. 383(1), (2), (3), (4).
Para. 19(8): CTA 2009, s. 383(5).
Para. 19(9): CTA 2009, s. 383(7).
Para. 19(11): CTA 2009, s. 382(1), (2).
Para. 19(12): CTA 2009, s. 384(1), (2), (3).
Para. 19(13): CTA 2009, s. 385(1), (2), (3), (4).
Para. 19(14): CTA 2009, s. 383(8), 472(1).
Para. 19A(1): CTA 2009, s. 315(1), (2).

Para. 19A(2): CTA 2009, s. 315(3).
Para. 19A(3): CTA 2009, s. 316(1), (2), (3), (4).
Para. 19A(4): CTA 2009, s. 317(1).
Para. 19A(4A): CTA 2009, s. 317(2).
Para. 19A(4B): CTA 2009, s. 317(4), (5).
Para. 19A(4BA): CTA 2009, Sch. 2, para. 62(1), (2).
Para. 19A(4C): CTA 2009, s.318(1), (2), (3).
Para. 19A(4D): CTA 2009, s. 318(5), (6).
Para. 19A(5): CTA 2009, s. 316(5), 318(4).
Para. 19B(1): CTA 2009, s. 319(1).
Para. 19B(2): CTA 2009, s. 319(2).
Para. 19B(3): CTA 2009, s. 319(3).
Para. 19B(4): CTA 2009, s. 319(4).
Para. 20(1): CTA 2009, s. 473(2).
Para. 20(3): CTA 2009, s. 473(3).
Para. 20(4): CTA 2009, s. 474(1).
Para. 20(5): CTA 2009, s. 474(2), (3), (7), 476(1).
Para. 20(6): CTA 2009, s. 474(4), (5), (6), (7), 476(1).
Para. 20(7): CTA 2009, s. 474(8).
Para. 20(8): CTA 2009, s. 473(5).
Para. 20(9): CTA 2009, s. 472(1), 473(6).
Para. 20(10): CTA 2009, s. 473(7).

SCHEDULE 10 – LOAN RELATIONSHIPS: COLLECTIVE INVESTMENT SCHEMES

[Omitted by CTA 2009, s. 1322 and Sch. 1, para. 442 and repealed by CTA 2009, s. 1326 and Sch. 3, Pt. 1.]

History – Sch. 10 omitted by CTA 2009, s. 1322 and Sch. 1, para. 442 and repealed by CTA 2009, s. 1326 and Sch. 3, Pt. 1, with effect for corporation tax purposes for accounting periods ending on or after 1 April 2009, and for income tax and capital gains tax purposes for the tax year 2009–10 and subsequent tax years, subject to the transitional and savings provisions in CTA 2009, Sch. 2, Pt. 8 and 9.

Notes – Sch. 10 rewritten as follows:
Para. 1A(1): CTA 2009, s. 395(1).
Para. 1A(2): CTA 2009, s. 395(2), (4).
Para. 1A(3): CTA 2009, s. 395(2).
Para. 1A(4): CTA 2009, s. 395(3).
Para. 1B(1): CTA 2009, s. 396(1).
Para. 1B(2): CTA 2009, s. 396(2), (4).
Para. 1B(3): CTA 2009, s. 396(2).
Para. 1B(4): CTA 2009, s. 396(3).
Para. 4(1): CTA 2009, s. 490(1), (6).
Para. 4(2): CTA 2009, s. 490(2).
Para. 4(3): CTA 2009, s. 490(3).
Para. 4(4): CTA 2009, s. 490(4), (5).
Para. 4(5): CTA 2009, s. 492(1).
Para. 4(6): CTA 2009, s. 492(2).
Para. 5(1): CTA 2009, s. 491(1), Sch. 1, para. 366.
Para. 5(2): CTA 2009, Sch. 1, para. 366.
Para. 5(3): CTA 2009, Sch. 1, para. 366.
Para. 5(4): CTA 2009, Sch. 1, para. 366.
Para. 5(5): CTA 2009, Sch. 1, para. 366.
Para. 6: CTA 2009, s. 491(1), (2).
Para. 7(1): CTA 2009, s.489(1), (2), (3), 490(1).
Para. 7(2): CTA 2009, s. 489(1), (2).
Para. 8(1): CTA 2009, s. 493(1).
Para. 8(2): CTA 2009, s. 494(1).
Para. 8(3): CTA 2009, s. 495(1), (4).
Para. 8(3A): CTA 2009, s. 493(1), 495(1).
Para. 8(4): CTA 2009, s. 495(2).
Para. 8(5): CTA 2009, s. 493(3), (4).
Para. 8(5A): CTA 2009, s. 493(2).
Para. 8(6): CTA 2009, s. 495(3).
Para. 8(7): CTA 2009, s. 494(2).
Para. 8(7A): CTA 2009, s. 476(1), 488(1), 493(2), (5).
Para. 8(7B): CTA 2009, s. 488(1).
Para. 8(7C): CTA 2009, s. 493(2), (6), 495(3).
Para. 8(7D): CTA 2009, s. 488(2).
Para. 8(7E): CTA 2009, s. 494(2).
Para. 8(7F): CTA 2009, s. 489(1), (2).
Para. 8(7G): CTA 2009, s. 496(1), (2), (3).
Para. 8(7H): CTA 2009, s. 496(4).
Para. 8(7I): CTA 2009, s. 501(2), (3).
Para. 8(8): CTA 2009, s. 497(1).
Para. 9(1): CTA 2009, s. 395(5), 396(5), 497(2).
Para. 9(2): CTA 2009, s. 497(3).

SCHEDULE 11 – LOAN RELATIONSHIPS: SPECIAL PROVISIONS FOR INSURERS

[Omitted by CTA 2009, s. 1322 and Sch. 1, para. 443 and repealed by CTA 2009, s. 1326 and Sch. 3, Pt. 1.]

History – Sch. 11 omitted by CTA 2009, s. 1322 and Sch. 1, para. 443 and repealed by CTA 2009, s. 1326 and Sch. 3, Pt. 1, with effect for corporation tax purposes for accounting periods ending on or after 1 April 2009, and for income tax and capital gains tax purposes for the tax year 2009–10 and subsequent tax years, subject to the transitional and savings provisions in CTA 2009, Sch. 2, Pt. 8 and 9.

Notes – Sch. 11 rewritten as follows:
Para. 3A(1): CTA 2009, s. 393(1), (2), 394(1).
Para. 3A(2): CTA 2009, s. 394(7).
Para. 3A(2A): CTA 2009, s. 394(4), (5), (6).
Para. 3A(2B): CTA 2009, s. 394(5), (6).
Para. 3A(3): CTA 2009, s. 394(2), (3).
Para. 3A(4): CTA 2009, s. 393(3), (4).
Para. 3A(5): CTA 2009, s. 393(5).
Para. 4(1): CTA 2009, s. 387(1).
Para. 4(2): CTA 2009, s. 388(1), (2), (3).
Para. 4(3): CTA 2009, s. 389(1), (4).
Para. 4(4): CTA 2009, s. 391(1), (2), (3).
Para. 4(5): CTA 2009, s. 389(1), (2), (4).
Para. 4(7): CTA 2009, s. 390(1), (4).
Para. 4(8): CTA 2009, s. 390(1).
Para. 4(9): CTA 2009, s.390(1).
Para. 4(9A): CTA 2009, s. 390(2), (3).
Para. 4(10): CTA 2009, s. 390(5).
Para. 4(11): CTA 2009, s. 390(6), (7), (8).
Para. 4(15): CTA 2009, s. 389(5).
Para. 7(1): CTA 2009, s. 392(1), (2).
Para. 7(2): CTA 2009, s. 392(3).

SCHEDULE 12 – MEANING OF DEBT CONTRACT OR OPTION

Section 101

[Repealed by FA 2002, s. 83(1), Sch. 27, para. 21, s. 141 and Sch. 40, Pt. 3(13).]

History – Sch. 12 omitted and repealed by FA 2002, s. 83(1), Sch. 27, para. 21, s. 141 and Sch. 40, Pt. 3(13) with effect in relation to accounting periods beginning on or after 1 October 2002, subject to the transitional provisions in FA 2002, Sch. 28.

SCHEDULE 13 – DISCOUNTED SECURITIES: INCOME TAX PROVISIONS

Section 102

1–16 [Omitted by ITTOIA 2005, s. 882(1) and Sch. 1, para. 490; and repealed by ITTOIA 2005, s. 884 and Sch. 3.]

History – Omitted by ITTOIA 2005, s. 882(1) and Sch. 1, para. 490; and repealed by ITTOIA 2005, s. 884 and Sch. 3, effective for income tax purposes for 2005–06 onwards and for corporation tax purposes for accounting periods ending after 5 April 2005 (ITTOIA 2005, s. 883(1)).

Notes – The repealed income tax material is principally rewritten at ITTOIA 2005, s. 427–460.

SCHEDULE 14 – LOAN RELATIONSHIPS: MINOR AND CONSEQUENTIAL AMENDMENTS

Section 104

THE TAXES MANAGEMENT ACT 1970 (c. 9)

1(1) [Amends TMA 1970, s. 87A(4A).]

1(2) [Repealed by FA 1998, s. 165 and Sch. 27, Pt. III(2).]

History – Para. 1(2) repealed with effect for any "earlier period" (TMA 1970s. 87A(4B)) beginning on or after 6 April 1999, by FA 1998, s. 165 and Sch. 27, Pt. III(2).

THE TAXES ACT 1988

5 [Repealed by CTA 2009, s. 1326 and Sch. 3, Pt. 1.]

History – Para. 5 repealed by CTA 2009, s. 1326 and Sch. 3, Pt. 1, with effect for corporation tax purposes for accounting periods ending on or after 1 April 2009, and for income tax and capital gains tax purposes for the tax year 2009–10 and subsequent tax years.

6 [Inserts ICTA 1988, s. 56(4A) and (4B).]

7 [Repealed by CTA 2009, s. 1326 and Sch. 3, Pt. 1.]

History – Para. 7 repealed by CTA 2009, s. 1326 and Sch. 3, Pt. 1, with effect for corporation tax purposes for accounting periods ending on or after 1 April 2009, and for income tax and capital gains tax purposes for the tax year 2009–10 and subsequent tax years.

8 [Repealed by FA 2004, s. 326 and Sch. 42, Pt. 2(3).]

History – Para. 8 repealed by FA 2004, s. 326 and Sch. 42, Pt. 2(3) with effect for accounting periods beginning on or after 1 April 2004.

9 [Repealed by ITTOIA 2005, s. 884 and Sch. 3 effective for income tax purposes for 2005–06 onwards (ITTOIA 2005, s. 883(1)).]

10(1) [Repeals ICTA 1988, s. 78 except in relation to bills of exchange drawn before 1 April 1996.]

10(2) Where any bill so drawn is paid on or after 1st April 1996–

(a) the amount which subsection (2) of that section provides to be treated as a deduction against total profits and as a charge on income shall (instead of being so treated) be brought into account for the purposes of this Chapter as a non-trading debit; and

(b) that amount shall be the only amount brought into account for the purposes of this Chapter in respect of the discount in question.

11 [Repealed by CTA 2010, s. 1181 and Sch. 3, Pt. 1.]

History – Para. 11 repealed by CTA 2010, s. 1181 and Sch. 3, Pt. 1, with effect for corporation tax purposes for accounting periods ending on or after 1 April 2010, and for income tax and capital gains tax purposes for the tax year 2010–11 and subsequent tax years.

12(1)–(2) [Repealed by F(No. 2)A 1997, s. 52 and Sch. 8, Pt. II(4).]

History – Para. 12 repealed by F(No. 2)A 1997, s. 52 and Sch. 8, Pt. II(4) with effect for any accounting period beginning on or after 2 July 1997.

13(1) [Repealed by FA 2001, s. 110 and Sch. 33, Pt. 2(10).]

13(2) [Repealed by FA 2001, s. 110 and Sch. 33, Pt. 2(10).]

History – Para. 13(1) repealed by FA 2001, s. 110 and Sch. 33, Pt. 2(10) with effect in relation to payments made after 11 May 2001. Para. 13(2) repealed by FA 2001, s. 110 and Sch. 33, Pt. 2(10) with effect in relation to payments made after 11 May 2001.

14(1) [Amends ICTA 1988, s. 337(2)(b).]

14(2) [Repeals ICTA 1988, s. 337(3).]

15 [Inserts ICTA 1988, s. 337A.]

16 [Repealed by CTA 2010, s. 1181 and Sch. 3, Pt. 1.]

History – Para. 16 repealed by CTA 2010, s. 1181 and Sch. 3, Pt. 1, with effect for corporation tax purposes for accounting periods ending on or after 1 April 2010, and for income tax and capital gains tax purposes for the tax year 2010–11 and subsequent tax years.

17 [Repeals ICTA 1988, s. 338A, 340 and 341.]

18 [Repealed by ITA 2007, s. 1031 and Sch. 3, Pt. 1.]

History – Para. 18 repealed by ITA 2007, s. 1031 and Sch. 3, Pt. 1, with effect from 6 April 2007.

19 [Repealed by CTA 2010, s. 1181 and Sch. 3, Pt. 1.]

History – Para. 19 repealed by CTA 2010, s. 1181 and Sch. 3, Pt. 1, with effect for corporation tax purposes for accounting periods ending on or after 1 April 2010, and for income tax and capital gains tax purposes for the tax year 2010–11 and subsequent tax years.

20 [Repealed by CTA 2009, s. 1326 and Sch. 3, Pt. 1.]

History – Para. 20 repealed by CTA 2009, s. 1326 and Sch. 3, Pt. 1, with effect for corporation tax purposes for accounting periods ending on or after 1 April 2009, and for income tax and capital gains tax purposes for the tax year 2009–10 and subsequent tax years.

21 [Repealed by CTA 2010, s. 1181 and Sch. 3, Pt. 1.]

History – Para. 21 repealed by CTA 2010, s. 1181 and Sch. 3, Pt. 1, with effect for corporation tax purposes for accounting periods ending on or after 1 April 2010, and for income tax and capital gains tax purposes for the tax year 2010–11 and subsequent tax years.

22 [Repealed by CTA 2010, s. 1181 and Sch. 3, Pt. 1.]

History – Para. 22 repealed by CTA 2010, s. 1181 and Sch. 3, Pt. 1, with effect for corporation tax purposes for accounting periods ending on or after 1 April 2010, and for income tax and capital gains tax purposes for the tax year 2010–11 and subsequent tax years.

23 [Omitted by FA 2012, s. 146 and Sch. 16, para. 247(g)(iv).]

History – Para. 23 omitted by FA 2012, s. 146 and Sch. 16, para. 247(g)(iv), with effect in relation to accounting periods beginning on or after 1 January 2013 (FA 2012, s. 148) but subject to transitional provisions in FA 2012, Sch. 17. Where an accounting period would otherwise straddle 1 January 2013, it is deemed to end on 31 December 2012 (FA 2012, s. 149).

24 Where this Chapter has effect in relation to any accounting period in relation to which section 434B of that Act (treatment of interest and annuities in the case of insurance companies) has effect without the amendments made by section 165 of this Act, that section of that Act shall have effect in relation to that period as if the words "interest or", in each place where they occur, were omitted.

25 [Repealed by FA 2007, s. 114 and Sch. 27, Pt. 2(10).]

History – Para. 25 repealed by FA 2007, s. 114 and Sch. 27, Pt. 2(10) with effect from Royal Assent 19 July 2007.

26 [Repealed by Statute Law (Repeals) Act 2013, s. 1 and Sch. 1, Pt. 10.]

History – Para. 26 repealed by Statute Law (Repeals) Act 2013, s. 1 and Sch. 1, Pt. 10, with effect from 31 January 2013.

27 [Repealed by TIOPA 2010, s. 378 and Sch. 10, Pt. 12.]

History – Para. 27 repealed by TIOPA 2010, s. 378 and Sch. 10, Pt. 12, with effect for corporation tax purposes for accounting periods ending on or after 1 April 2010, for income tax and capital gains tax purposes for the tax year 2010–11 and subsequent tax years, and for petroleum revenue tax purposes for chargeable periods beginning on or after 1 July 2010.

28(1) [Substitutes ICTA 1988, s. 477A(3)(a) and (aa).]

28(2) [Repeals ICTA 1988, s. 477A(3A)–(3C).]

29 [Repeals ICTA 1988, s. 484 and 485.]

30

(a) [Amends ICTA 1988, s. 486(1).]

(b) [Amends ICTA 1988, s. 486(7).]

31 [Repealed by CTA 2009, s. 1326 and Sch. 3, Pt. 1.]

History – Para. 31 repealed by CTA 2009, s. 1326 and Sch. 3, Pt. 1, with effect for corporation tax purposes for accounting periods ending on or after 1 April 2009, and for income tax and capital gains tax purposes for the tax year 2009–10 and subsequent tax years.

32(1-3) [Repealed by CTA 2010, s. 1181 and Sch. 3, Pt. 1.]

32(4) [Repealed by FA 1998, s. 165 and Sch. 27, Pt. III(4).]

History – Para. 32(1)–(3) repealed by CTA 2010, s. 1181 and Sch. 3, Pt. 1, with effect for corporation tax purposes for accounting periods ending on or after 1 April 2010, and for income tax and capital gains tax purposes for the tax year 2010–11 and subsequent tax years.

Para. 32(4) repealed by FA 1998, s. 165 and Sch. 27, Pt. III(4) with effect, so far as relating to income tax, for the year 1998–99 and subsequent years of assessment, and so far as relating to corporation tax from 1 April 1998.

33 [Repealed by ITA 2007, s. 1031 and Sch. 3, Pt. 1.]

History – Para. 33 repealed by ITA 2007, s. 1031 and Sch. 3, Pt. 1, with effect from 6 April 2007.

34 [Inserts ICTA 1988, s. 614(2A).]

35-36 [Repealed by ITA 2007, s. 1031 and Sch. 3, Pt. 1.]

History – Para. 35 and 36 repealed by ITA 2007, s. 1031 and Sch. 3, Pt. 1, with effect from 6 April 2007.

Notes – Para. 35 rewritten as ITA 2007, s. 498(1).

37 [Repealed by FA 2007, s. 114 and Sch. 27, Pt. 2(14).]

History – Repealed by FA 2007, s. 114 and Sch. 27, Pt. 2(14), with effect in relation to arrangements coming into force on or after 1 October 2007, by virtue of SI 2007/2483, art. 3.

38 [Repealed by FA 1997, s. 113 and Sch. 18, Pt. VI(10) with effect in relation to, and to transfers under, any arrangement made on or after 1 July 1997 (SI 1997/991 (C. 33)).]

39 [Repealed by CTA 2010, s. 1181 and Sch. 3, Pt. 1.]

History – Para. 39 repealed by CTA 2010, s. 1181 and Sch. 3, Pt. 1, with effect for corporation tax purposes for accounting periods ending on or after 1 April 2010, and for income tax and capital gains tax purposes for the tax year 2010–11 and subsequent tax years.

40 [Repealed by CTA 2010, s. 1181 and Sch. 3, Pt. 1.]

History – Para. 40 repealed by CTA 2010, s. 1181 and Sch. 3, Pt. 1, with effect for corporation tax purposes for accounting periods ending on or after 1 April 2010, and for income tax and capital gains tax purposes for the tax year 2010–11 and subsequent tax years.

41 [Repealed by TIOPA 2010, s. 378 and Sch. 10, Pt. 1.]

History – Para. 41 repealed by TIOPA 2010, s. 378 and Sch. 10, Pt. 1, with effect for corporation tax purposes for accounting periods ending on or after 1 April 2010, for income tax and capital gains tax purposes for the tax year 2010–11 and subsequent tax years, and for petroleum revenue tax purposes for chargeable periods beginning on or after 1 July 2010.

42 [Repealed by TIOPA 2010, s. 378 and Sch. 10, Pt. 1.]

History – Para. 42 repealed by TIOPA 2010, s. 378 and Sch. 10, Pt. 1, with effect for corporation tax purposes for accounting periods ending on or after 1 April 2010, for income tax and capital gains tax purposes for the tax year 2010–11 and subsequent tax years, and for petroleum revenue tax purposes for chargeable periods beginning on or after 1 July 2010.

43 [Repealed by TIOPA 2010, s. 378 and Sch. 10, Pt. 1.]

History – Para. 43 repealed by TIOPA 2010, s. 378 and Sch. 10, Pt. 1, with effect for corporation tax purposes for accounting periods ending on or after 1 April 2010, for income tax and capital gains tax purposes for the tax year 2010–11 and subsequent tax years, and for petroleum revenue tax purposes for chargeable periods beginning on or after 1 July 2010.

44 [Repealed by TIOPA 2010, s. 378 and Sch. 10, Pt. 1.]

History – Para. 44 repealed by TIOPA 2010, s. 378 and Sch. 10, Pt. 1, with effect for corporation tax purposes for accounting periods ending on or after 1 April 2010, for income tax and capital gains tax purposes for the tax year 2010–11 and subsequent tax years, and for petroleum revenue tax purposes for chargeable periods beginning on or after 1 July 2010.

45 [Repealed by TIOPA 2010, s. 378 and Sch. 10, Pt. 1.]

History – Para. 45 repealed by TIOPA 2010, s. 378 and Sch. 10, Pt. 1, with effect for corporation tax purposes for accounting periods ending on or after 1 April 2010, for income tax and capital gains tax purposes for the tax year 2010–11 and subsequent tax years, and for petroleum revenue tax purposes for chargeable periods beginning on or after 1 July 2010.

46 [Repealed by TIOPA 2010, s. 378 and Sch. 10, Pt. 1.]

History – Para. 46 repealed by TIOPA 2010, s. 378 and Sch. 10, Pt. 1, with effect for corporation tax purposes for accounting periods ending on or after 1 April 2010, for income tax and capital gains tax purposes for the tax year 2010–11 and subsequent tax years, and for petroleum revenue tax purposes for chargeable periods beginning on or after 1 July 2010.

47 [Repealed by TIOPA 2010, s. 378 and Sch. 10, Pt. 1.]

History – Para. 47 repealed by TIOPA 2010, s. 378 and Sch. 10, Pt. 1, with effect for corporation tax purposes for accounting periods ending on or after 1 April 2010, for income tax and capital gains tax purposes for the tax year 2010–11 and subsequent tax years, and for petroleum revenue tax purposes for chargeable periods beginning on or after 1 July 2010.

48(1)

(a) [Amends ICTA 1988, s. 826(7C)(a).]

(b) [Amends ICTA 1988, s. 826(7C)(b).]

(c) [Amends ICTA 1988, s. 826(7C).]

48(2) [Repealed by FA 1998, s. 165 and Sch. 27, Pt. III(2).]

History – Para. 48(2) repealed with effect for any "earlier period" (ICTA 1988, s. 826(7AA)) beginning on or after 6 April 1999, by FA 1998, s. 165 and Sch. 27, Pt. III(2).

49 [Amends ICTA 1988, s. 834(1).]

50 [Repeals ICTA 1988, Sch. 4.]

51 [Repealed by F(No. 2)A 1997, s. 52 and Sch. 8, Pt. II(6).]

History – Para. 51 repealed by F(No. 2)A 1997, s. 52 and Sch. 8, Pt. II(6) (in accordance with s. 23 and Sch. 3, para. 13(5) and (14)) with effect for accounting periods beginning on or after 2 July 1997.

52 [Repealed by CTA 2010, s. 1181 and Sch. 3, Pt. 1.]

History – Para. 52 repealed by CTA 2010, s. 1181 and Sch. 3, Pt. 1, with effect for corporation tax purposes for accounting periods ending on or after 1 April 2010, and for income tax and capital gains tax purposes for the tax year 2010–11 and subsequent tax years. Para. 52(2), (3), (5) and (6) previously repealed by FA 1997, Sch. 18, Pt. VI(10).

53 [Inserts ICTA 1988, Sch. 26, para. 1(3)(f).]

54 [Repealed by CTA 2010, s. 1181 and Sch. 3, Pt. 1.]

History – Para. 54 repealed by CTA 2010, s. 1181 and Sch. 3, Pt. 1, with effect for corporation tax purposes for accounting periods ending on or after 1 April 2010, and for income tax and capital gains tax purposes for the tax year 2010–11 and subsequent tax years.

THE FINANCE ACT 1989 (c. 26)

56 [Omitted by FA 2008, s. 43 and Sch. 17, para. 18(5)(d).]

History – Para. 56 omitted by FA 2008, s. 43 and Sch. 17, para. 18(5)(d), with effect in relation to accounting periods beginning on or after 1 January 2008.

57 [Repeals FA 1989, Sch. 11.]

THE FINANCE ACT 1990 (c. 29)

58 [Repeals FA 1990, Sch. 10.]

THE TAXATION OF CHARGEABLE GAINS ACT 1992 (c. 12)

59 [Inserts TCGA 1992, s. 108(1)(aa).]

60(1) Section 116 of that Act (reorganisations, conversions and reconstructions) shall be amended as follows.

60(2) [Inserts TCGA 1992, s. 116(4A).]

60(3) [Inserts TCGA 1992, s. 116(8A).]

60(4) [Inserts TCGA 1992, s. 116(16).]

61(1) [Inserts TCGA 1992, s. 117(A1).]

61(2) [Inserts TCGA 1992, s. 117(2AA).]

61(3) [Inserts TCGA 1992, s. 117(6B) and (6C).]

61(4) [Inserts TCGA 1992, s. 117(8A).]

62 [Inserts TCGA 1992, s. 117A and 117B.]

63 [Repealed by FA 2007, s. 114 and Sch. 27, Pt. 2(10).]

History – Para. 63 repealed by FA 2007, s. 114 and Sch. 27, Pt. 2(10) with effect in relation to periods of account beginning on or after 1 January 2007.

64 [Inserts TCGA 1992, s. 251(7) and (8).]

65 [Amends TCGA 1992, s. 253(3).]

66(1) [Amends TCGA 1992, s. 254(1)(c).]

66(2) [Inserts TCGA 1992, s. 254(13).]

THE FINANCE ACT 1993 (c. 34)

67 [Repealed by FA 2002, s. 141 and Sch. 40, Pt. 3(10).]

History – Para. 67 repealed by FA 2002, s. 141 and Sch. 40, Pt. 3(10) with effect in relation to accounting periods beginning on or after 1 October 2002.

68 [Repealed by FA 2002, s. 141 and Sch. 40, Pt. 3(10).]

History – Para. 68 repealed by FA 2002, s. 141 and Sch. 40, Pt. 3(10) with effect in relation to accounting periods beginning on or after 1 October 2002.

69 [Repealed by FA 2002, s. 141 and Sch. 40, Pt. 3(10).]

History – Para. 69 repealed by FA 2002, s. 141 and Sch. 40, Pt. 3(10) with effect in relation to accounting periods beginning on or after 1 October 2002.

70 [Repealed by FA 2002, s. 141 and Sch. 40, Pt. 3(10).]

History – Para. 70 repealed by FA 2002, s. 141 and Sch. 40, Pt. 3(10) with effect in relation to accounting periods beginning on or after 1 October 2002.

71 [Repealed by FA 2002, s. 141 and Sch. 40, Pt. 3(10).]

History – Para. 71 repealed by FA 2002, s. 141 and Sch. 40, Pt. 3(10) with effect in relation to accounting periods beginning on or after 1 October 2002.

72 [Repealed by FA 2002, s. 141 and Sch. 40, Pt. 3(10).]

History – Para. 72 repealed by FA 2002, s. 141 and Sch. 40, Pt. 3(10) with effect in relation to accounting periods beginning on or after 1 October 2002.

73 [Repealed by FA 2002, s. 141 and Sch. 40, Pt. 3(10).]

History – Para. 73 repealed by FA 2002, s. 141 and Sch. 40, Pt. 3(10) with effect in relation to accounting periods beginning on or after 1 October 2002.

74 [Repealed by FA 2002, s. 141 and Sch. 40, Pt. 3(10).]

History – Para. 74 repealed by FA 2002, s. 141 and Sch. 40, Pt. 3(10) with effect in relation to accounting periods beginning on or after 1 October 2002.

THE FINANCE ACT 1994 (c. 9)

75 [Repealed by FA 2002, s. 141 and Sch. 40, Pt. 3(13).]

History – Para. 75 repealed by FA 2002, s. 141 and Sch. 40, Pt. 3(13) with effect in relation to accounting periods beginning on or after 1 October 2002.

76 [Repealed by FA 2002, s. 141 and Sch. 40, Pt. 3(13).]

History – Para. 76 repealed by FA 2002, s. 141 and Sch. 40, Pt. 3(13) with effect in relation to accounting periods beginning on or after 1 October 2002.

77 [Repealed by FA 2002, s. 141 and Sch. 40, Pt. 3(13).]

History – Para. 77 repealed by FA 2002, s. 141 and Sch. 40, Pt. 3(13) with effect in relation to accounting periods beginning on or after 1 October 2002.

78 [Repealed by FA 2002, s. 141 and Sch. 40, Pt. 3(13).]

History – Para. 78 repealed by FA 2002, s. 141 and Sch. 40, Pt. 3(13) with effect in relation to accounting periods beginning on or after 1 October 2002.

79 [Repealed by FA 2002, s. 141 and Sch. 40, Pt. 3(13).]

History – Para. 79 repealed by FA 2002, s. 141 and Sch. 40, Pt. 3(13) with effect in relation to accounting periods beginning on or after 1 October 2002.

SCHEDULE 15 – LOAN RELATIONSHIPS: SAVINGS AND TRANSITIONAL PROVISIONS

Section 105

Part I – Corporation Tax

APPLICATION AND INTERPRETATION OF PART I

1(1) This Part of this Schedule has effect for the purposes of corporation tax.

1(2) In this Part of this Schedule–

"the 1992 Act" means the Taxation of Chargeable Gains Act 1992;

"continuing loan relationship", in relation to any company, means any loan relationship to which the company was a party both immediately before and on 1st April 1996;

"first relevant accounting period", in relation to a company, means the first accounting period of the company to end after 31st March 1996; and

"transitional accounting period", in relation to a company, means any accounting period of the company beginning before and ending on or after 1st April 1996.

1(3) [Omitted by FA 2007, s. 41 and Sch. 10, para. 16(5)(d) and repealed by FA 2007, s. 114 and Sch. 27, Pt. 2(10).]

1(4) In this Part of this Schedule references to this Chapter include references to any repeals having effect for the purposes of this Chapter.

History – Para. 1(3) omitted by FA 2007, s. 41 and Sch. 10, para. 16(5)(d) and repealed by FA 2007, s. 114 and Sch. 27, Pt. 2(10) with effect from 19 July 2007.

In para. 1(3), the words "long-term" substituted for the words "long term" by SI 2001/3629, art. 96(1)(c) operative from 1 December 2001.

LOAN RELATIONSHIPS TERMINATED BEFORE 1ST APRIL 1996

2 [Omitted by CTA 2009, s. 1322 and Sch. 1, para. 444(2)(a) and repealed by CTA 2009, s. 1326 and Sch. 3, Pt. 1.]

History – Para. 2 omitted by CTA 2009, s. 1322 and Sch. 1, para. 444(2)(a) and repealed by CTA 2009, s. 1326 and Sch. 3, Pt. 1, with effect for corporation tax purposes for accounting periods ending on or after 1 April 2009, and for income tax and capital gains tax purposes for the tax year 2009–10 and subsequent tax years, subject to the provisions of CTA 2009, Sch. 2, Pt. 8 and Pt. 9.

BASIC RULES FOR TRANSITIONAL ACCOUNTING PERIODS

3 [Omitted by CTA 2009, s. 1322 and Sch. 1, para. 444(2)(b) and repealed by CTA 2009, s. 1326 and Sch. 3, Pt. 1.]

History – Para. 3 omitted by CTA 2009, s. 1322 and Sch. 1, para. 444(2)(b) and repealed by CTA 2009, s. 1326 and Sch. 3, Pt. 1, with effect for corporation tax purposes for accounting periods ending on or after 1 April 2009, and for income tax and capital gains tax purposes for the tax year 2009–10 and subsequent tax years, subject to the provisions of CTA 2009, Sch. 2, Pt. 8 and Pt. 9.
Former para. 3(5A) inserted by FA 1997, s. 83 and Sch. 13, para. 2, with effect for the purposes of determining the credits and debits to be brought into account in any accounting period ending on or after 14 November 1996.

ADJUSTMENT OF OPENING VALUE WHERE NEW ACCOUNTING BASIS ADOPTED AS FROM AN ACCOUNTING PERIOD BEGINNING ON 1ST APRIL 1996

3A [Omitted by CTA 2009, s. 1322 and Sch. 1, para. 444(2)(c) and repealed by CTA 2009, s. 1326 and Sch. 3, Pt. 1.]

History – Para. 3A omitted by CTA 2009, s. 1322 and Sch. 1, para. 444(2)(c) and repealed by CTA 2009, s. 1326 and Sch. 3, Pt. 1, with effect for corporation tax purposes for accounting periods ending on or after 1 April 2009, and for income tax and capital gains tax purposes for the tax year 2009–10 and subsequent tax years, subject to the provisions of CTA 2009, Sch. 2, Pt. 8 and Pt. 9.

APPLICATION OF ACCRUALS BASIS TO PRE-COMMENCEMENT RELATIONSHIPS

4 [Omitted by CTA 2009, s. 1322 and Sch. 1, para. 444(2)(d) and repealed by CTA 2009, s. 1326 and Sch. 3, Pt. 1.]

History – Para. 4 omitted by CTA 2009, s. 1322 and Sch. 1, para. 444(2)(d) and repealed by CTA 2009, s. 1326 and Sch. 3, Pt. 1, with effect for corporation tax purposes for accounting periods ending on or after 1 April 2009, and for income tax and capital gains tax purposes for the tax year 2009–10 and subsequent tax years, subject to the provisions of CTA 2009, Sch. 2, Pt. 8 and Pt. 9.

ADJUSTMENTS IN RESPECT OF PRE-COMMENCEMENT TRADING RELATIONSHIPS

5(1) This paragraph applies in the case of any continuing loan relationship of a company as respects which any amounts would have been brought into account for the purposes of corporation tax in computing the profits or losses of the company from any trade carried on by it if–

(a) the company had ceased to be a party to the relationship on 31st March 1996; and

(b) where it is not otherwise the case, an accounting period of the company had ended on that date.

5(2) Where there is a difference between–

(a) the notional closing value of the relationship as at 31st March 1996, and

(b) the adjusted closing value of that relationship as at that date,

that difference shall be brought into account as provided for in paragraph 6 below.

5(3) Except where sub-paragraph (4) or (6) below applies, the notional closing value as at 31st March 1996 of a loan relationship of a company shall be taken for the purposes of this paragraph to be the amount which, for the purposes of computing the profits or losses of the company from any trade carried on by it–

(a) was as at that date, or

(b) had an accounting period of the company ended on that date, would have been,

the amount falling to be brought into account as representing the value of the company's rights or liabilities under the relationship.

5(4) Except where sub-paragraph (6) below applies, if no amount is given by sub-paragraph (3) above, the notional closing value as at 31st March 1996 of a loan relationship of a company shall be taken for the purposes of this paragraph to be the amount which, for the purposes of computing the profits or losses of the company from any trade carried on by it, would have been deductible as representing the cost of becoming a party to the relationship if the company had ceased to be a party to the relationship on 31st March 1996.

5(4A) In sub-paragraph (4) above the reference, in relation to a creditor relationship, to the amount deductible as representing the cost of a company's becoming a party to the relationship shall not, except where sub-paragraph (4B) or (4C) below applies, include a reference to so much of that amount as would represent the cost of acquiring any right to accrued interest under the loan relationship.

5(4B) This sub-paragraph applies where–

(a) the company became a party to the relationship before the beginning of its first relevant accounting period,

(b) interest accruing under the relationship before the company became a party to it was paid to the company after it became a party to it but before the beginning of the company's first relevant accounting period, and

(c) the interest under the relationship which, in the case of that company, has been brought into account for the purposes of corporation tax has included interest accruing under the relationship before the company became a party to it but paid afterwards.

5(4C) This sub-paragraph applies where–

(a) the company became a party to the loan relationship in a transitional accounting period, and

(b) in the case of that company, interest under the relationship which–

(i) accrued before the company became a party to the relationship, but

(ii) became due and payable afterwards,

is brought into account for the purposes of this Chapter in accordance with an authorised mark to market basis of accounting.

5(5) Except where sub-paragraph (6) below applies, the adjusted closing value of that relationship as at that date shall be taken for the purposes of this paragraph to be the amount which for the purposes of this Chapter (as it had effect immediately before 1st April 2009) was the opening value as at 1st April 1996 of the company's rights and liabilities under the relationship.

5(6) For the purposes of this paragraph where the asset representing a loan relationship of a company is a relevant qualifying asset of the company, or the liabilities of the company under the relationship are relevant liabilities–

(a) the notional closing value of the relationship as at 31st March 1996 shall be taken for the purposes of this paragraph to be the value given by paragraph 12 below as the notional closing value as at 31st March 1996 of that asset or, as the case may be, of those liabilities; and

(b) the adjusted closing value of the relationship as at 31st March 1996 shall be taken for those purposes to be the amount which was as at 1st April 1996 the opening value of the asset or liabilities for the purposes of this Chapter (as it had effect immediately before 1st April 2009).

5(7) For the purposes of this paragraph, where an accruals basis of accounting is used as respects a loan relationship for the first relevant accounting period of the company, the opening value as at 1st April 1996 of the company's rights and liabilities under the relationship shall be taken to have been the value which (disregarding interest) was treated in accordance with paragraph 4 above (as it had effect immediately before 1st April 2009) as having accrued to the company before that date.

5(8) In this paragraph–

"attributed amount" means any attributed gain or loss falling to be calculated in accordance with any regulations made under Schedule 16 to the Finance Act 1993 (transitional provisions for exchange gains and losses) which contain any such provision as is mentioned in paragraph 3(1) of that Schedule;

"commencement day", in relation to a company, means its commencement day for the purposes of Chapter II of Part II of the Finance Act 1993;

"market value" has the same meaning as in the 1992 Act;

"relevant liability", in relation to a company, means any liability under a loan relationship the value of which has been determined as at the company's commencement day for the purpose of calculating any attributed amount;

"relevant qualifying asset", in relation to a company, means any qualifying asset for the purposes of Chapter II of Part II of the Finance Act 1993 the value of which has been determined as at the company's commencement day for the purpose of calculating any attributed amount.

History – Para. 5(4A)–(4C) inserted by FA 1997, s. 83 and Sch. 13, para. 4, with effect for the purposes of determining the credits and debits to be brought into account in any accounting period ending on or after 14 November 1996, subject to the provisions in Sch. 13, para. 7(2).

In para. 5(5), the words "this Chapter (as it had effect immediately before 1st April 2009) was" substituted for the words "this Chapter is" by CTA 2009, s. 1322 and Sch. 1, para. 444(3)(a), with effect for corporation tax purposes for accounting periods ending on or after 1 April 2009, and for income tax and capital gains tax purposes for the tax year 2009–10 and subsequent tax years.

In para. 5(6)(b), the words "which was" substituted for the words "which is" and the words "(as it had effect immediately before 1st April 2009)" inserted by CTA 2009, s. 1322 and Sch. 1, para. 444(3)(b), with effect for corporation tax purposes for accounting periods ending on or after 1 April 2009, and for income tax and capital gains tax purposes for the tax year 2009–10 and subsequent tax years.

In para. 5(7), the words "taken to have been" substituted for the words "taken to be", the words "was treated" substituted for the words "is treated" and the words "(as it had effect immediately before 1st April 2009)" inserted by CTA 2009, s. 1322 and Sch. 1, para. 444(3)(c), with effect for corporation tax purposes for accounting periods ending on or after 1 April 2009, and for income tax and capital gains tax purposes for the tax year 2009–10 and subsequent tax years.

Cross references – FA 1993, Sch. 16, para. 3(1) (repealed by FA 2002): regulations for attributing exchange gains and losses to an existing asset or liability.
FA 1993, Pt. II, Ch. II: exchange gains and losses.

METHOD OF GIVING EFFECT TO PARAGRAPH 5 ADJUSTMENTS

6(1) Subject to sub-paragraph (4) below, the difference mentioned in paragraph 5(2) above shall be brought into account in accordance with sub-paragraph (2) or (3) below in the accounting period in which the company ceases to be a party to the relationship.

6(2) If–

(a) the relationship is a creditor relationship and the difference consists in an excess of the amount mentioned in paragraph 5(2)(b) above over the amount mentioned in paragraph 5(2)(a) above, or

(b) the relationship is a debtor relationship and the difference consists in an excess of the amount mentioned in paragraph 5(2)(a) above over the amount mentioned in paragraph 5(2)(b) above,

the difference shall be brought into account as a credit given for the purposes of this Chapter for the period mentioned in sub-paragraph (1) above.

6(3) In any other case, the difference shall be brought into account as a debit given for the purposes of Part 5 of the Corporation Tax Act 2009 for the period so mentioned.

6(4) Sub-paragraphs (1) to (3) above do not apply if the company duly made an election for the purposes of this sub-paragraph as it had effect on 30th September 1996.

6(5) [Effectively omitted by CTA 2009, s. 1322 and Sch. 1, para. 444(4)(b).]

6(6) [Effectively omitted by CTA 2009, s. 1322 and Sch. 1, para. 444(4)(b).]

6(7) [Effectively omitted by CTA 2009, s. 1322 and Sch. 1, para. 444(4)(b).]

6(8) Where any credit or debit falls to be brought into account under this paragraph for any accounting period for the whole or any part of which the company carries on the trade in question, the credit or debit shall be brought into account under section 297 of the Corporation Tax Act 2009 in relation to that trade; and, in any other case, it shall be brought into account as a non-trading credit or non-trading debit under Part 5 of that Act.

History – In para. 6(3), the words "Part 5 of the Corporation Tax Act 2009" substituted for the words "this Chapter" by CTA 2009, s. 1322 and Sch. 1, para. 444(4)(a), with effect for corporation tax purposes for accounting periods ending on or after 1 April 2009, and for income tax and capital gains tax purposes for the tax year 2009–10 and subsequent tax years.
Para. 6(4) substituted for former para. 6(4)–(7) by CTA 2009, s. 1322 and Sch. 1, para. 444(4)(b), with effect for corporation tax purposes for accounting periods ending on or after 1 April 2009, and for income tax and capital gains tax purposes for the tax year 2009–10 and subsequent tax years.
In para. 6(8), the words "section 297 of the Corporation Tax Act 2009" substituted for the words "section 82(2) of this Act" and the words "under Part 5 of that Act" inserted by CTA 2009, s. 1322 and Sch. 1, para. 444(4)(c), with effect for corporation tax purposes for accounting periods ending on or after 1 April 2009, and for income tax and capital gains tax purposes for the tax year 2009–10 and subsequent tax years.

Cross references – FA 1997, Sch. 13, para. 7(3): relevant assumption, in respect of transactions where continuity of treatment applicable (e.g. groups, transfers of insurance business), when determining a credit or debit a fraction of which falls to be brought into account under para. 6(4) in an accounting period ending on or after 14 November 1996.
FA 1999, s. 81(3): amounts to be brought into account where an asset representing a creditor relationship is disposed of by an insurance company and special arrangements with the Revenue applied when asset was previously transferred intra-group.

GENERAL SAVINGS FOR THE TAXATION OF CHARGEABLE GAINS

7 The amendments of the 1992 Act contained in Schedule 14 to this Act and the related repeals made by this Act–

(a) so far as they relate to section 253 of the 1992 Act, do not apply to any loan the outstanding amount of principal on which became irrecoverable before 1st April 1996;

(b) so far as they relate to section 254 of the 1992 Act, do not apply to any security whose value became negligible before 1st April 1996;

(c) so far as they relate to anything else, do not apply in relation to any disposal made, or deemed to be made, before 1st April 1996.

Cross references – TCGA 1992, s. 8(1): calculation of chargeable gain to be included in a company's taxable profits.
TCGA 1992, s. 253: relief in respect of qualifying loans to traders.
TCGA 1992, s. 254: relief for debts on qualifying corporate bonds.

TRANSITIONAL PROVISION FOR CHARGEABLE ASSETS HELD AFTER COMMENCEMENT

8(1) This paragraph applies where–

(a) on 31st March 1996 any company (**"the relevant company"**) held any asset representing, in whole or in part, any loan relationship to which it was a party on that date;

(b) the company did not dispose of that asset on that date and does not fall (apart from by virtue of this paragraph) to be treated for the purposes of the 1992 Act as having made a disposal of it on that date;

(c) the asset is not one to which section 92 of this Act or paragraph 15 below applies;

(d) that asset is not an asset representing a loan relationship to which section 93 of this Act applies;

(e) that asset is not a relevant qualifying asset; and

(f) a relevant event occurs.

8(2) For the purposes of this paragraph a relevant event occurs on the first occasion after 31st March 1996 when the relevant company or any other company falls to be treated for the purposes of the 1992 Act as making a disposal, other than one to which section 139, 140A, or 171(1) of that Act (disposals on which neither a gain nor a loss accrues) applies, of–

(a) the asset in question, so far as it has not come to be represented by an asset falling within paragraph (b) below, or

(b) any such asset as falls to be treated for the purposes of that Act as the same as that asset.

8(3) The amount of any chargeable gain or allowable loss which would have been treated as accruing to the relevant company on the assumption–

(a) that it had made a disposal of the asset on 31st March 1996, and

(b) (so far as relevant for the purpose of computing the amount of that gain or loss) that the disposal had been for a consideration equal to the market value of the asset,

shall be brought into account (subject to the following provisions of this paragraph and to paragraph 9 below) as one accruing to the company (**"the chargeable company"**) which makes the disposal constituting the relevant event, and shall be so brought into account in the accounting period in which that event occurs.

8(4) The amount of the deemed chargeable gain or deemed allowable loss falling to be brought into account in accordance with sub-paragraph (3) above shall be treated as reduced by the extent (if any) to which it is, in relation to the company, an amount that already has been, or falls to be, taken into account for the purposes of corporation tax by virtue of the use of any accruals or mark to market basis of accounting–

(a) for those purposes;

(b) as respects times before 1st April 1996; and

(c) in relation to the asset in question.

8(5) To the extent that any deemed chargeable gain or deemed allowable loss falling to be brought into account under sub-paragraph (3) above includes any gain or loss deemed to accrue under section 116(10)(b) of the 1992 Act (qualifying corporate bonds acquired in a reorganisation etc.), that gain or loss shall be deemed to have accrued for the purposes of that sub-paragraph and (without prejudice to its being brought into account in accordance with that sub-paragraph) shall not be taken to accrue again on the occurrence of the relevant event or any subsequent disposal of any asset.

8(5A) In any case where the relevant event has not occurred before 14th November 1996, the deemed chargeable gain or deemed allowable loss falling to be brought into account in accordance with sub-paragraph (3) above shall be computed without any account being taken of the provisions of section 119(6) and (7) of the 1992 Act (transfer of securities with or without accrued interest).

8(6) In any case where–

(a) the relevant company is one which at any time before 1st April 1996 was not resident in the United Kingdom,

(b) the asset was held by the relevant company at such a time, and

(c) if the asset had been disposed of at that time and a gain had accrued to the relevant company on that disposal, it would not have been included in the company's chargeable profits by virtue of section 10B of the 1992 Act (gain attributable to a permanent establishment of a non-resident company),

the relevant company shall be deemed for the purposes of sub-paragraph (3) above to have acquired the asset, at market value, on the first day on which any relevant gain would have been included in the company's chargeable profits for the purposes of corporation tax (whether because it is a day on which the company became resident, or the asset became situated, in the United Kingdom or for any other reason).

8(7) In sub-paragraph (6) above the reference, in relation to a company, to a relevant gain is a reference to any gain which would have accrued to the company on the following assumptions, that is to say–

(a) that the relevant company disposed of the asset on the day in question;

(b) that that disposal gave rise to a gain; and

(c) that any allowable losses which might have been available for deduction under section 8(1) of, or Schedule 7A to, the 1992 Act were to be disregarded.

8(8) In any case where the company acquired the asset on a disposal on which, by virtue of any enactment specified in section 35(3)(d) of the 1992 Act, neither a gain nor a loss accrued to the person making the disposal, the reference in sub-paragraph (6) or (7) above to the relevant company includes–

(a) a reference to the company from which it acquired the asset; and

(b) if that company also acquired the asset on such a disposal, a reference to the company from which the asset was acquired by that company, and so on through any number of such disposals.

8(9) In any case where section 176 of the 1992 Act (depreciatory transactions within a group) would have applied in relation to the disposal referred to in sub-paragraph (3) above if that disposal had actually taken place, that section shall apply for the calculation of any deemed allowable loss to be brought into account by virtue of that sub-paragraph.

8(10) For the purposes of this paragraph a company that ceases to be within the charge to corporation tax shall be deemed to make a disposal of all its assets at their market value immediately before ceasing to be within that charge.

8(11) In this section–

"market value" has the same meaning as in the 1992 Act; and

"relevant qualifying asset" has the same meaning as in paragraph 5 above.

History – In para. 8(2) the words "or 171(1)" substituted for "171(1) or 172" by FA 2000, Sch. 29, para. 45(1) with effect in relation to disposals on or after 1 April 2000.

Para. 8(5A) inserted by FA 1997, s. 83 and Sch. 13, para. 5, with effect for the purposes of determining the credits and debits to be brought into account in any accounting period ending on or after 14 November 1996, subject to the provisions in Sch. 13, para. 7(2).

In para. 8(6)(c) the words "10B" and "attributable to a permanent establishment" substituted for "10(3)" and "on a disposal by a branch or agency" respectively by FA 2003, s.155 and Sch. 27, para. 8 in relation to accounting periods beginning on or after 1 January 2003.

Cross references – TCGA 1992, s. 35(3)(d): provisions deeming that transactions to be at no gain no loss.
TCGA 1992, s. 116: reorganisations, conversions and reconstructions involving qualifying corporate bonds.
TCGA 1992, s. 139: reconstruction or amalgamation involving the transfer of business.
TCGA 1992, s. 140A: transfer of a UK trade.
TCGA 1992, s. 171(1): transfer within a group to be at no gain no loss.
TCGA 1992, s. 172: transfer of a UK branch or agency.
TCGA 1992, s. 176: depreciatory transactions within a group.
TCGA 1992, Sch. 7A: restriction on the set off of pre-entry losses.

ELECTION FOR ALTERNATIVE TREATMENT OF AMOUNTS SPECIFIED IN PARAGRAPH 8

9(1) Subject to the following provisions of this paragraph, where (apart from this paragraph) any amount representing a deemed allowable loss would fall in the case of any company to be brought into account for any accounting period in accordance with sub-paragraph (3) of paragraph 8 above, the chargeable company may elect for that amount to be brought into account for that period for the purposes of this Chapter or Part 5 of the Corporation Tax Act 2009, instead of in accordance with that sub-paragraph.

9(2) An amount brought into account for the purposes of this Chapter or that Part by virtue of an election under this paragraph shall be so brought into account as a debit given for that period for the purposes of this Chapter or, as the case may be, that Part.

9(3) The question whether or not any debit brought into account for any accounting period in accordance with sub-paragraph (2) above is to be brought into account for that period as a non-trading debit shall be determined according to how other credits or debits relating to the loan relationship in question are, or (if there were any) would be, brought into account for that period.

9(4) No election shall be made under this paragraph in respect of any deemed allowable loss in any case where the asset in respect of which that loss is deemed to have accrued was one which, as at 1st April 1996, either–

(a) fell in accordance with section 127 or 214(9) of the 1992 Act (equation of new holding with previous holding) to be treated as the same as an asset which was not an asset representing a loan relationship; or

(b) would have so fallen but for section 116(5) of that Act.

9(5) An election shall not be made under this paragraph at any time more than two years after the occurrence of the relevant event by virtue of which the amount to which the election relates would fall to be brought into account in accordance with paragraph 8(3) above.

History – In para. 9(1), the words "or Part 5 of the Corporation Tax Act 2009" inserted by CTA 2009, s. 1322 and Sch. 1, para. 444(5)(a), with effect for corporation tax purposes for accounting periods ending on or after 1 April 2009, and for income tax and capital gains tax purposes for the tax year 2009–10 and subsequent tax years, subject to the provisions of CTA 2009.
In para. 9(2), the words "or that Part" and "or, as the case may be, that Part" inserted by CTA 2009, s. 1322 and Sch. 1, para. 444(5)(b), with effect for corporation tax purposes for accounting periods ending on or after 1 April 2009, and for income tax and capital gains tax purposes for the tax year 2009–10 and subsequent tax years.

Cross references – TCGA 1992, s. 116: reorganisation, conversion or reconstruction involving qualifying corporate bonds.
TCGA 1992, s. 127: equation of original shares and new holding where reorganisation or conversion.
TCGA 1992, s. 214(9): equation of original shares and new holding to exchanges involving certain assets of an insurance company.

ADJUSTMENTS OF OPENING VALUE FOR MARK TO MARKET ACCOUNTING IN THE CASE OF CHARGEABLE ASSETS

10 [Omitted by CTA 2009, s. 1322 and Sch. 1, para. 444(6) and repealed by CTA 2009, s. 1326 and Sch. 3, Pt. 1.]

History – Para. 10 omitted by CTA 2009, s. 1322 and Sch. 1, para. 444(6) and repealed by CTA 2009, s. 1326 and Sch. 3, Pt. 1, with effect for corporation tax purposes for accounting periods ending on or after 1 April 2009, and for income tax and capital gains tax purposes for the tax year 2009–10 and subsequent tax years, subject to the provisions of CTA 2009, Sch. 2, Pt. 8 and Pt. 9.

OTHER ADJUSTMENTS IN THE CASE OF CHARGEABLE ASSETS ETC.

11(1) Where–

(a) an authorised accruals basis of accounting is applied as respects any continuing loan relationship of a company for the company's first relevant accounting period,

(b) an asset representing that relationship is a relevant asset or any liability under it is a relevant liability, and

(c) the relationship is not one as respects which, if the company had ceased to be a party to the relationship on 31st March 1996, any amounts would have been brought into account in computing, for an accounting period ending on or after that date, the profits or losses of the company from any trade carried on by it,

that accounting method shall be taken for the purposes of Part 5 of the Corporation Tax Act 2009 to require the asset or liability to be given a notional closing value as at 31st March 1996 in accordance with paragraph 12 below and the following provisions of this paragraph shall apply if there is any difference in the case of that relationship between the amounts mentioned in sub-paragraph (2) below.

11(2) Those amounts are–

(a) the notional closing value of the relationship as at 31st March 1996; and

(b) the amount which would be taken on a computation made–

 (i) in accordance with an authorised accruals basis of accounting, and

 (ii) on the assumption that such a basis of accounting had always been used as respects that relationship,

to represent the accrued value of the loan relationship in question on 1st April 1996.

11(2A) If, in a case where the continuing loan relationship is a creditor relationship,–

(a) the company acquired its rights under the relationship on or before 31st March 1996 by virtue of an arm's length transaction,

(b) for the accounting period in which it acquired those rights–

 (i) there was no connection (as defined in sub-paragraph (2C) below) between the company and the person from whom the company acquired the asset, but

 (ii) there was such a connection between the company and a company standing in the position of a debtor as respects the money debt, and

(c) there had been no such connection between the companies mentioned in paragraph (b)(ii) above at any time in the period which–

 (i) begins 4 years before the date on which the company acquired those rights, and

 (ii) ends twelve months before that date,

this paragraph shall have effect as if the amount mentioned in sub-paragraph (2)(b) above were an amount equal to the greater of the amounts mentioned in sub-paragraph (2B) below.

11(2B) Those amounts are–

(a) the fair value of the rights at the time when the company ceases to be a party to the loan relationship; and

(b) the fair value of the rights on 1st April 1996.

11(2C) For the purposes of sub-paragraph (2A) above there is a connection between a company and another person at any time if at that time–

(a) the other person is a company and one of the companies has control of the other,

(b) the other person is a company and both companies are under the control of the same person, or

(c) the company is a close company and the other person is a participator in that company or the associate of a person who is such a participator,

and there is a connection between a company and another person for an accounting period if there is a connection (within paragraphs (a) to (c) above) between the company and the person at any time in that accounting period.

11(2D) For the purposes of sub-paragraph (2C) above–

(a) sections 450 and 451 of the Corporation Tax Act 2010 (meaning of control) apply as they apply for the purposes of Part 10 of that Act;

(b) subject to paragraph (c) below, **"associate"** and **"participator"** have the same meaning as in that Part (see sections 448 and 454 of that Act);

(c) a person shall not be regarded as a participator in relation to a company by reason only that he is a loan creditor of the company.

11(3) Where there is a difference between the amounts mentioned in sub-paragraph (2) above, that difference shall be brought into account–

(a) where the amount mentioned in paragraph (a) of that sub-paragraph is the smaller, as a credit given for the purposes of Part 5 of the Corporation Tax Act 2009 for the accounting period in which the company ceases to be a party to the relationship; and

(b) in any other case, as a debit so given.

11(4) [Substituted by para. 11(2) and (3): see History note.]

11(5) Where the company ceases to be within the charge to corporation tax, it shall be deemed for the purposes of this paragraph to have ceased to be a party to the relationship in question immediately before ceasing to be within that charge.

11(6) A credit or debit brought into account under this paragraph shall be brought into account as a non-trading credit or non-trading debit under Part 5 of the Corporation Tax Act 2009.

11(7) In this paragraph–

"chargeable asset", in relation to a company, means (subject to sub-paragraph (8) below) any asset held by the company on 31st March 1996 in the case of which one of the following conditions is satisfied, that is to say–

(a) a gain accruing to the company on a disposal of that asset on that date would have fallen to be treated in relation to the company as a chargeable gain; or

(b) a chargeable gain or allowable loss would be deemed to have accrued to the company on any disposal of that asset on that date; and

"relevant asset" means a chargeable asset or a relevant qualifying asset.

11(8) An asset is not a chargeable asset for the purposes of this paragraph if (disregarding the provisions of this Chapter and Part 5 of the Corporation Tax Act 2009) it is an asset any disposal of which on 31st March 1996 would have fallen to be regarded for the purposes of the 1992 Act as a disposal of a qualifying corporate bond.

11(9) Expressions used in this paragraph and paragraph 5 above have the same meanings in this paragraph as in that paragraph.

History – In para. 11(1), the words "Part 5 of the Corporation Tax Act 2009" substituted for the words "this Chapter" by CTA 2009, s. 1322 and Sch. 1, para. 444(7)(a), with effect for corporation tax purposes for accounting periods ending on or after 1 April 2009, and for income tax and capital gains tax purposes for the tax year 2009–10 and subsequent tax years.

Para. 11(2D)(a) and (b) substituted for former para. 11(2D)(a) and (b) by CTA 2010, s. 1177 and Sch. 1 para. 293, with effect for corporation tax purposes for accounting periods ending on or after 1 April 2010, and for income tax and capital gains tax purposes for the tax year 2010–11 and subsequent tax years.

Para. 11(2A)–(2D) inserted by FA 2002, s. 82 and Sch. 25, para. 41 with effect in relation to accounting periods beginning on or after 1 October 2002.

In para. 11(3)(a), the words "Part 5 of the Corporation Tax Act 2009" substituted for the words "this Chapter" by CTA 2009, s. 1322 and Sch. 1, para. 444(7)(a), with effect for corporation tax purposes for accounting periods ending on or after 1 April 2009, and for income tax and capital gains tax purposes for the tax year 2009–10 and subsequent tax years.

Para. 11(2) and (3) substituted for former para. 11(2)–(4) by FA 1997, s. 83 and Sch. 13, para. 6, with effect for the purposes of determining the credits and debits to be brought into account in any accounting period ending on or after 14 November 1996, subject to the provisions in Sch. 13, para. 7(2).

In para. 11(6), the words "under Part 5 of the Corporation Tax Act 2009" inserted by CTA 2009, s. 1322 and Sch. 1, para. 444(7)(b), with effect for corporation tax purposes for accounting periods ending on or after 1 April 2009, and for income tax and capital gains tax purposes for the tax year 2009–10 and subsequent tax years.

In para. 11(8), the words "and Part 5 of the Corporation Tax Act 2009" inserted by CTA 2009, s. 1322 and Sch. 1, para. 444(7)(c), with effect for corporation tax purposes for accounting periods ending on or after 1 April 2009, and for income tax and capital gains tax purposes for the tax year 2009–10 and subsequent tax years.

REDUCTION OF PARA. 11 CREDIT WHERE S. 251(4) OF 1992 ACT PREVENTS PARA. 8 LOSS

11A(1) This paragraph applies where, in the case of any asset representing in whole or in part a loan relationship of a company, an amount representing a deemed allowable loss would (apart from this paragraph) fall or have fallen to be brought into account in accordance with paragraph 8(3) above for an accounting period (whenever beginning or ending), but for section 251(4) of the 1992 Act (no allowable loss on disposal of debt acquired from connected person).

11A(2) Where this paragraph applies, the amount of any credit falling within sub-paragraph (3) below shall be treated for the purposes of Part 5 of the Corporation Tax Act 2009 as reduced (but not below nil) by the amount described in sub-paragraph (1) above.

11A(3) A credit falls within this sub-paragraph if (apart from this paragraph)–

(a) the credit falls to be given by virtue of paragraph 11(3)(a) above for an accounting period beginning on or after 1st October 2002; and

(b) the loan relationship mentioned in paragraph 11(1)(a) above in the case of the credit is the same loan relationship as the one mentioned in sub-paragraph (1) above.

History – In para. 11A(2), the words "Part 5 of the Corporation Tax Act 2009" substituted for the words "this Chapter" by CTA 2009, s. 1322 and Sch. 1, para. 444(8), with effect for corporation tax purposes for accounting periods ending on or after 1 April 2009, and for income tax and capital gains tax purposes for the tax year 2009–10 and subsequent tax years.
Para. 11A inserted by FA 2002, s. 82 and Sch. 25, para. 42 with effect in relation to accounting periods beginning on or after 1 October 2002.

NOTIONAL CLOSING VALUES OF RELEVANT ASSETS

12(1) Subject to sub-paragraph (2) below, the notional closing value as at 31st March 1996 of any relevant asset representing a loan relationship of a company, or of any relevant liability, shall be taken for the purposes of paragraphs 5 and 11 above, to be an amount equal to the following amount, that is to say–

(a) in the case of a chargeable asset, its market value on that date;

(b) in the case of a relevant qualifying asset or relevant liability, the value given to it as at the company's commencement day for the purpose of computing any attributed amount.

12(2) Sub-paragraph (3) below applies where a company, by notice in writing given on or before 30th September 1996 to an officer of the Board, made an election for the purposes of that sub-paragraph in relation to all of its relevant qualifying assets which–

(a) apart from the election, would be given a notional closing value as at 31st March 1996 by sub-paragraph (1) above; and

(b) but for Chapter II of Part II of the Finance Act 1993 (exchange gains and losses), would be chargeable assets.

12(3) Where such an election was made as respects those assets–

(a) sub-paragraph (1) above shall not apply as respects those assets; but

(b) the value of each of those assets as at 1st April 1996 shall be taken for the purposes of this Chapter and Part 5 of the Corporation Tax Act 2009 to be its market value on that date.

12(4) In this paragraph **"chargeable asset"** and **"relevant asset"** have the same meanings as in paragraph 11 above; and expressions used in this paragraph and paragraph 5 above have the same meanings in this paragraph as in that paragraph.

History – In para. 12(2), the word "made" substituted for the word "makes" by CTA 2009, s. 1322 and Sch. 1, para. 444(9)(a), with effect for corporation tax purposes for accounting periods ending on or after 1 April 2009, and for income tax and capital gains tax purposes for the tax year 2009–10 and subsequent tax years.
In para. 12(3), the words "was made" substituted for the words "is made" and the words "and Part 5 of the Corporation Tax Act 2009" inserted by CTA 2009, s. 1322 and Sch. 1, para. 444(9)(b), with effect for corporation tax purposes for accounting periods ending on or after 1 April 2009, and for income tax and capital gains tax purposes for the tax year 2009–10 and subsequent tax years.

Cross references – FA 1993, Pt. II, Ch. II: exchange gains and losses.

FURTHER TRANSITIONAL RULES FOR INTEREST UNDER LOAN RELATIONSHIPS

13 [Omitted by CTA 2009, s. 1322 and Sch. 1, para. 444(10)(a) and repealed by CTA 2009, s. 1326 and Sch. 3, Pt. 1.]

History – *Para. 13 omitted by CTA 2009, s. 1322 and Sch. 1, para. 444(10)(a) and repealed by CTA 2009, s. 1326 and Sch. 3, Pt. 1,* with effect for corporation tax purposes for accounting periods ending on or after 1 April 2009, and for income tax and capital gains tax purposes for the tax year 2009–10 and subsequent tax years, subject to the provisions of CTA 2009, Sch. 2, Pt. 8 and Pt. 9.

TRANSITIONAL IN RESPECT OF INCIDENTAL EXPENSES ALREADY ALLOWED

14 [Omitted by CTA 2009, s. 1322 and Sch. 1, para. 444(10)(b) and repealed by CTA 2009, s. 1326 and Sch. 3, Pt. 1.]

History – Para. 14 omitted by CTA 2009, s. 1322 and Sch. 1, para. 444(10)(b) and repealed by CTA 2009, s. 1326 and Sch. 3, Pt. 1, with effect for corporation tax purposes for accounting periods ending on or after 1 April 2009, and for income tax and capital gains tax purposes for the tax year 2009–10 and subsequent tax years, subject to the provisions of CTA 2009, Sch. 2, Pt. 8 and Pt. 9.

HOLDINGS OF UNIT TRUSTS ETC

15 [Omitted by CTA 2009, s. 1322 and Sch. 1, para. 444(10)(c) and repealed by CTA 2009, s. 1326 and Sch. 3, Pt. 1.]

History – Para. 15 omitted by CTA 2009, s. 1322 and Sch. 1, para. 444(10)(c) and repealed by CTA 2009, s. 1326 and Sch. 3, Pt. 1, with effect for corporation tax purposes for accounting periods ending on or after 1 April 2009, and for income tax and capital gains tax purposes for the tax year 2009–10 and subsequent tax years, subject to the provisions of CTA 2009, Sch. 2, Pt. 8 and Pt. 9.

BAD DEBT RELIEVED BEFORE COMMENCEMENT

16(1) This paragraph applies where–

(a) an amount becomes, or is to become, due and payable under a creditor relationship of a company in an accounting period ending on or after 1st April 1996, but

(b) by virtue of any of sub-paragraphs (i) to (iii) of section 74(1)(j) of the Taxes Act 1988 (or any enactment re-enacted in those sub-paragraphs), a deduction of an amount representing the whole or any part of the amount payable was authorised to be made, and was made, in computing for the purposes of corporation tax the profits of the company for any accounting period ending before that date.

16(2) Subject to sub-paragraph (3) below, nothing in this Chapter or Part 5 of the Corporation Tax Act 2009 shall require it to be assumed for the purposes of this Chapter or that Part that any part of the amount to which the deduction relates will be paid in full as it becomes due.

16(3) Subject to sub-paragraph (4) below, where–

(a) the deduction relates to an amount payable under a creditor relationship of a company which has been proved or estimated to be a bad debt, but

(b) in an accounting period ending on or after 1st April 1996 the whole or any part of the liability under that relationship to pay that amount is discharged by payment,

this Chapter and Part 5 of the Corporation Tax Act 2009 shall have effect, in the case of that company, as if there were a credit equal to the amount of the payment to be brought into account for the purposes of this Chapter and that Part for that period.

16(4) Sub-paragraph (3) above does not apply to so much of any payment as is an amount in relation to which a credit fell to be brought into account for the purposes of this Chapter in accordance with paragraph 13(4) above.

History – In para. 16(2), the words "or Part 5 of the Corporation Tax Act 2009" and "or that Part" inserted by CTA 2009, s. 1322 and Sch. 1, para. 444(11)(a), with effect for corporation tax purposes for accounting periods ending on or after 1 April 2009, and for income tax and capital gains tax purposes for the tax year 2009–10 and subsequent tax years.

In para. 16(3), the words "and Part 5 of the Corporation Tax Act 2009" and "and that Part" inserted by CTA 2009, s. 1322 and Sch. 1, para. 444(11)(b), with effect for corporation tax purposes for accounting periods ending on or after 1 April 2009, and for income tax and capital gains tax purposes for the tax year 2009–10 and subsequent tax years.

In para. 16(4), the word "fell" substituted for the word "falls" by CTA 2009, s. 1322 and Sch. 1, para. 444(11)(c), with effect for corporation tax purposes for accounting periods ending on or after 1 April 2009, and for income tax and capital gains tax purposes for the tax year 2009–10 and subsequent tax years.

Cross references – ICTA 1988, s. 74(1)(j): bad debt relief for Sch. D purposes.

TRANSITIONAL FOR OVERSEAS SOVEREIGN DEBT ETC.

17(1) Subject to any regulations under sub-paragraph (4) below and notwithstanding anything in the preceding provisions of this Schedule, the value which for the purposes of this Chapter and Part 5 of the Corporation Tax Act 2009 is to be taken to be the value as at 1st April 1996 of a company's rights under any creditor relationship relating to a relevant overseas debt any part of which falls to be estimated as bad, is the following amount–

(a) where the company was not entitled to the debt before the end of its last period of account to end before 1st April 1996, the amount for which the company acquired those rights; and

(b) in any other case, the amount of so much of that debt as did not fall, in accordance with section 88B of the Taxes Act 1988, to be estimated as at the end of that period to be bad.

17(2) Subject to any regulations under sub-paragraph (4) below, sub-paragraph (3) below shall apply where there is a loss incurred before 1st April 1996 to which section 88C of the Taxes Act 1988 has applied or applies by virtue of paragraph 2 above.

17(3) Where, apart from this Chapter and Part 5 of the Corporation Tax Act 2009, any amount would have been allowed in respect of the loss as a deduction for any accounting period ending after 31st March 1996, that amount shall not be so allowed but shall, instead, be brought into account for the purposes of this Chapter and that Part as if it were a debit given for that accounting period by paragraph 9 of Schedule 9 to this Act in respect of a loss incurred on or after 1st April 1996.

17(4) The Treasury may by regulations–

(a) make such transitional provision as they consider appropriate for purposes connected with the coming into force of paragraphs 8 and 9 of Schedule 9 to this Act and the repeal of sections 88A to 88C of the Taxes Act 1988 (which contained corresponding provisions); and

(b) in connection with any such provision, make such modifications of this Schedule (including sub-paragraphs (1) to (3) above) as they consider appropriate;

and regulations made by virtue of this sub-paragraph may have retrospective effect in relation to any accounting periods ending on or after 1st April 1996.

17(5) The Treasury shall not make any regulations under sub-paragraph (4) above unless a draft of them has been laid before and approved by a resolution of the House of Commons.

17(6) In this paragraph **"relevant overseas debt"** has the same meaning as in paragraphs 8 and 9 of Schedule 9 to this Act.

History – In para. 17(1), the words "and Part 5 of the Corporation Tax Act 2009" inserted by CTA 2009, s. 1322 and Sch. 1, para. 444(12)(a), with effect for corporation tax purposes for accounting periods ending on or after 1 April 2009, and for income tax and capital gains tax purposes for the tax year 2009–10 and subsequent tax years.

In para. 17(3), the words "and Part 5 of the Corporation Tax Act 2009" and "and that Part" inserted by CTA 2009, s. 1322 and Sch. 1, para. 444(12)(b), with effect for corporation tax purposes for accounting periods ending on or after 1 April 2009, and for income tax and capital gains tax purposes for the tax year 2009–10 and subsequent tax years.

Cross references – ICTA 1988, s. 88B (repealed by FA 1996): restrictions on bad debt relief in respect of debts of overseas governments. ICTA 1988, s. 88C (repealed by FA 1996): restriction on the deduction for debts of overseas governments.

TRANSITIONAL FOR ACCRUED INCOME SCHEME

18 [Omitted by CTA 2009, s. 1322 and Sch. 1, para. 444(13) and repealed by CTA 2009, s. 1326 and Sch. 3, Pt. 1.]

History – Para. 18 omitted by CTA 2009, s. 1322 and Sch. 1, para. 444(13) and repealed by CTA 2009, s. 1326 and Sch. 3, Pt. 1, with effect for corporation tax purposes for accounting periods ending on or after 1 April 2009, and for income tax and capital gains tax purposes for the tax year 2009–10 and subsequent tax years, subject to the provisions of CTA 2009, Sch. 2, Pt. 8 and Pt. 9.

DEEP DISCOUNT SECURITIES

19(1) [Omitted by CTA 2009, s. 1322 and Sch. 1, para. 444(14)(a) and repealed by CTA 2009, s. 1326 and Sch. 3, Pt. 1.]

19(2) [Omitted by CTA 2009, s. 1322 and Sch. 1, para. 444(14)(a) and repealed by CTA 2009, s. 1326 and Sch. 3, Pt. 1.]

19(3) The repeal by this Act of section 64 of the Finance Act 1993 (deemed transfers in the case of deep discount securities) and of enactments relating to that section shall not apply in relation to relevant times falling before 1st April 1996; but for the purposes of that section and this sub-paragraph 31st March 1996 shall be deemed (where it would not otherwise be so) to be the last day of an accounting period.

19(3A) Any income that is treated as arising at the time mentioned in subsection (5) of that section, as it applies by virtue of sub-paragraph (3) above, shall be brought into account as a non-trading credit given for the purposes of Part 5 of the Corporation Tax Act 2009 for the accounting period in which that time falls.

19(4) Where–

(a) a company issued a deep discount security before 1st April 1996 which was not redeemed before that date, and

(b) there is a difference between the adjusted issue price of the security as at 31st March 1996 and the adjusted closing value of that security as at that date,

the amount of that difference shall, in the case of that company, be brought into account for the purposes of Part 5 of the Corporation Tax Act 2009 in accordance with sub-paragraph (5) below.

19(5) An amount falling to be brought into account for the purposes of Part 5 of the Corporation Tax Act 2009 in accordance with this sub-paragraph shall be brought into account for those purposes for the accounting period in which the security is redeemed–

(a) if the adjusted issue price of the security as at 31st March 1996 is greater than the adjusted closing value of the security as at that date, as a non-trading credit; and

(b) if the adjusted closing value of the security as at that date is the greater, as a non-trading debit.

19(6) Where–

(a) a company held a deep discount security on 31st March 1996,

(b) the company did not make any disposal of that security on that date,

(c) the security is not one in relation to which there is, or is deemed to be, a relevant time on that date for the purposes of section 64 of the Finance Act 1993, and

(d) there is an amount which, if the company had made a disposal of that security on that date, would have been treated under paragraph 4 of Schedule 4 to the Taxes Act 1988 as income chargeable to tax under Case III or IV of Schedule D,

that amount shall be brought into account as a non-trading credit given for the purposes of Part 5 of the Corporation Tax Act 2009 for the accounting period mentioned in sub-paragraph (9) below.

19(7) Where–

(a) a company held a deep discount security on 31st March 1996,

(b) the company did not make any disposal of that security on that date,

(c) the security is not an asset falling to be treated as a relevant asset of the company for the purposes of paragraph 11 above, and

(d) there is a difference between the adjusted issue price of the security as at 31st March 1996 and the adjusted closing value of that security as at that date,

the amount of that difference (in addition to any amount given by sub-paragraph (6) above) shall, in the case of that company, be brought into account for the purposes of Part 5 of the Corporation Tax Act 2009 in accordance with sub-paragraph (8) below.

19(8) An amount falling to be brought into account for the purposes of Part 5 of the Corporation Tax Act 2009 in accordance with this sub-paragraph shall be brought into account for those purposes for the accounting period mentioned in sub-paragraph (9) below–

(a) if the adjusted issue price of the security as at 31st March 1996 is greater than the adjusted closing value of the security as at that date, as a non-trading debit; and

(b) if the adjusted closing value of the security as at that date is the greater, as a non-trading credit.

19(9) That period is the accounting period in which falls whichever is the earliest of the following, that is to say–

(a) the earliest day after 31st March 1996 on which, under the terms on which the security was issued, the company holding the security is entitled to require it to be redeemed;

(b) the day on which the security is redeemed; and

(c) the day on which the company makes a disposal of that security.

19(10) [Omitted by CTA 2009, s. 1322 and Sch. 1, para. 444(14)(c) and repealed by CTA 2009, s. 1326 and Sch. 3, Pt. 1.]

19(11) For the purposes of this paragraph, in relation to any company–

(a) the adjusted issue price of a deep discount security as at 31st March 1996 is whatever for the purposes of Schedule 4 to the Taxes Act 1988 would have been the adjusted issue price for that security for an income period beginning with 1st April 1996; and

(b) the adjusted closing value of a security as at 31st March 1996 is the amount which for the purposes of this Chapter was the opening value as at 1st April 1996 of the company's rights and liabilities under the loan relationship of the company that is represented by that security;

and sub-paragraph (7) of paragraph 5 above shall apply for the purposes of this sub-paragraph as it applies for the purposes of that paragraph.

19(12) In this paragraph **"deep discount security"**, **"disposal"** and **"income period"** have the same meanings as in Schedule 4 to the Taxes Act 1988.

History – Para. 19(1) omitted by CTA 2009, s. 1322 and Sch. 1, para. 444(14)(a) and repealed by CTA 2009, s. 1326 and Sch. 3, Pt. 1, with effect for corporation tax purposes for accounting periods ending on or after 1 April 2009, and for income tax and capital gains tax purposes for the tax year 2009–10 and subsequent tax years, subject to the provisions of CTA 2009, Sch. 2, Pt. 8 and Pt. 9.

Para. 19(2) omitted by CTA 2009, s. 1322 and Sch. 1, para. 444(14)(a) and repealed by CTA 2009, s. 1326 and Sch. 3, Pt. 1, with effect for corporation tax purposes for accounting periods ending on or after 1 April 2009, and for income tax and capital gains tax purposes for the tax year 2009–10 and subsequent tax years, subject to the provisions of CTA 2009, Sch. 2, Pt. 8 and Pt. 9.

In para. 19(3A), the words "Part 5 of the Corporation Tax Act 2009" substituted for the words "this Chapter" by CTA 2009, s. 1322 and Sch. 1, para. 444(14)(b), with effect for corporation tax purposes for accounting periods ending on or after 1 April 2009, and for income tax and capital gains tax purposes for the tax year 2009–10 and subsequent tax years.

Para. 19(3A) inserted by FA 1999, s. 67(1) with effect in relation to income treated as arising on or after 15 February 1999.

In para. 19(4), (5), (6) and (7), the words "Part 5 of the Corporation Tax Act 2009" substituted for the words "this Chapter" by CTA 2009, s. 1322 and Sch. 1, para. 444(14)(b), with effect for corporation tax purposes for accounting periods ending on or after 1 April 2009, and for income tax and capital gains tax purposes for the tax year 2009–10 and subsequent tax years.

Para. 19(7)(b) substituted by FA 1999, s. 67(3), with effect in any case where the day mentioned in para. 19(9) falls on or after 15 February 1999.

In para. 19(8), the words "Part 5 of the Corporation Tax Act 2009" substituted for the words "this Chapter" by CTA 2009, s. 1322 and Sch. 1, para. 444(14)(b), with effect for corporation tax purposes for accounting periods ending on or after 1 April 2009, and for income tax and capital gains tax purposes for the tax year 2009–10 and subsequent tax years.
Para. 19(10) omitted by CTA 2009, s. 1322 and Sch. 1, para. 444(14)(c) and repealed by CTA 2009, s. 1326 and Sch. 3, Pt. 1, with effect for corporation tax purposes for accounting periods ending on or after 1 April 2009, and for income tax and capital gains tax purposes for the tax year 2009–10 and subsequent tax years, subject to the provisions of CTA 2009, Sch. 2, Pt. 8 and Pt. 9.
In para. 19(11)(b), the words "this Chapter was" substituted for the words "this Chapter is" by CTA 2009, s. 1322 and Sch. 1, para. 444(14)(d), with effect for corporation tax purposes for accounting periods ending on or after 1 April 2009, and for income tax and capital gains tax purposes for the tax year 2009–10 and subsequent tax years.

Cross references – ICTA 1988, Sch. 4, para. 3 (repealed by FA 1996): charge to tax after acquisition of deep discount securities.
ICTA 1988, Sch. 4, para. 4 (repealed by FA 1996): charge to tax on disposal of deep discount securities.
ICTA 1988, Sch. 4, para. 5 (repealed by FA 1996): relief in respect of income element of deep discount securities.
FA 1993, s. 64 (repealed by FA 1996): deemed transfers for the purposes of deep discount securities.

DEEP GAIN SECURITIES

20(1) [Omitted by CTA 2009, s. 1322 and Sch. 1, para. 444(15)(a) and repealed by CTA 2009, s. 1326 and Sch. 3, Pt. 1.]

20(2) The repeal by this Act of section 65 of the Finance Act 1993 (deemed transfers in the case of deep gain securities) and of enactments relating to that section shall not apply in relation to relevant days falling before 1st April 1996; but for the purposes of that section and this sub-paragraph 31st March 1996 shall be deemed (where it would not otherwise be so) to be the last day of an accounting period.

20(2A) Any income that is treated as arising on the day mentioned in subsection (5) of that section, as it applies by virtue of sub-paragraph (2) above, shall be brought into account as a non-trading credit given for the purposes of Part 5 of the Corporation Tax Act 2009 for the accounting period in which that day falls.

20(3) Where–

(a) a company held a deep gain security on 31st March 1996,

(b) the security was not transferred or redeemed by that company on that date,

(c) the security is not one in relation to which that date is, or is deemed to be, a relevant day for the purposes of section 65 of the Finance Act 1993, and

(d) there is an amount which, if the company had made a transfer of that security on that date by selling it for its adjusted closing value, would have been treated under paragraph 5 of Schedule 11 to the Finance Act 1989 as income chargeable to tax under Case III or IV of Schedule D,

that amount shall be brought into account as a non-trading credit given for the purposes of Part 5 of the Corporation Tax Act 2009 for the accounting period mentioned in sub-paragraph (4) below.

20(4) That period is the accounting period in which falls whichever is the earliest of the following, that is to say–

(a) the earliest day after 31st March 1996 on which, under the terms on which the security was issued, the company holding the security is entitled to require it to be redeemed;

(b) the day on which the security is redeemed; and

(c) the day on which the company makes a disposal of that security.

20(5) For the purposes of this paragraph the adjusted closing value of a deep gain security held by a company on 31st March 1996 shall be the amount which for the purposes of this Chapter (as it had effect immediately before 1st April 2009) was the opening value as at 1st April 1996 of the company's rights and liabilities under the relationship represented by that security; and sub-paragraph (7) of paragraph 5 above shall apply for the purposes of this sub-paragraph as it applies for the purposes of that paragraph.

20(6) In this paragraph **"deep gain security"** and **"transfer"** have the same meanings as in Schedule 11 to the Finance Act 1989.

History – Para. 20(1) omitted by CTA 2009, s. 1322 and Sch. 1, para. 444(15)(a) and repealed by CTA 2009, s. 1326 and Sch. 3, Pt. 1, with effect for corporation tax purposes for accounting periods ending on or after 1 April 2009, and for income tax and capital gains tax purposes for the tax year 2009–10 and subsequent tax years, subject to the provisions of CTA 2009, Sch. 2, Pt. 8 and Pt. 9.
In para. 20(2A), the words "Part 5 of the Corporation Tax Act 2009" substituted for the words "this Chapter" by CTA 2009, s. 1322 and Sch. 1, para. 444(15)(b), with effect for corporation tax purposes for accounting periods ending on or after 1 April 2009, and for income tax and capital gains tax purposes for the tax year 2009–10 and subsequent tax years.
Para. 20(2A) inserted by FA 1999, s. 67(2) with effect in relation to income treated as arising on or after 15 February 1999.
In para. 20(3), the words "Part 5 of the Corporation Tax Act 2009" substituted for the words "this Chapter" by CTA 2009, s. 1322 and Sch. 1, para. 444(15)(b), with effect for corporation tax purposes for accounting periods ending on or after 1 April 2009, and for income tax and capital gains tax purposes for the tax year 2009–10 and subsequent tax years.
In para. 20(5), the words "this Chapter (as it had effect immediately before 1st April 2009) was" substituted for the words "this Chapter is" by CTA 2009, s. 1322 and Sch. 1, para. 444(15)(c), with effect for corporation tax purposes for accounting periods ending on or after 1 April 2009, and for income tax and capital gains tax purposes for the tax year 2009–10 and subsequent tax years.

Cross references – FA 1989, Sch. 11, para. 5 (repealed by FA 1996): charge to tax on the transfer of deep gain securities.
FA 1993, s. 65 (repealed by FA 1996): deemed transfers of deep gain securities.

CONVERTIBLE SECURITIES

21(1) [Omitted by CTA 2009, s. 1322 and Sch. 1, para. 444(16)(a) and repealed by CTA 2009, s. 1326 and Sch. 3, Pt. 1.]

21(2) Where–

(a) a company held a qualifying convertible security on 31st March 1996,

(b) that date was not a date on which any chargeable event occurred in relation to that security, and

(c) there is an amount which, if there had been a chargeable event on that date, would have been treated under paragraph 12 of Schedule 10 to the Finance Act 1990 as income chargeable to tax under Case III or IV of Schedule D,

that amount shall be brought into account, in the case of that company, as a non-trading credit given for the purposes of Part 5 of the Corporation Tax Act 2009 for the accounting period mentioned in sub-paragraph (3) below.

21(3) That period is the accounting period in which falls whichever is the earliest of the following, that is to say–

(a) the earliest day after 31st March 1996 on which, under the terms on which the security was issued, the company holding the security is entitled to require it to be redeemed;

(b) the day on which the security is redeemed; and

(c) the day on which the company makes a disposal of that security.

21(4) Where–

(a) any qualifying convertible security is redeemed, and

(b) that security is one in the case of which any amount falls to be brought into account under sub-paragraph (2) above,

an amount equal to that amount shall be brought into account, in the case of the company that issued the security, as a non-trading debit given for the purposes of Part 5 of the Corporation Tax Act 2009 for the accounting period in which the redemption occurs.

21(5) In this paragraph **"chargeable event"** and **"qualifying convertible security"** have the same meanings as in Schedule 10 to the Finance Act 1990.

History – Para. 21(1) omitted by CTA 2009, s. 1322 and Sch. 1, para. 444(16)(a) and repealed by CTA 2009, s. 1326 and Sch. 3, Pt. 1, with effect for corporation tax purposes for accounting periods ending on or after 1 April 2009, and for income tax and capital gains tax purposes for the tax year 2009–10 and subsequent tax years, subject to the provisions of CTA 2009, Sch. 2, Pt. 8 and Pt. 9.
In para. 21(2), the words "Part 5 of the Corporation Tax Act 2009" substituted for the words "this Chapter" by CTA 2009, s. 1322 and Sch. 1, para. 444(16)(b), with effect for corporation tax purposes for accounting periods ending on or after 1 April 2009, and for income tax and capital gains tax purposes for the tax year 2009–10 and subsequent tax years.
In para. 21(4), the words "Part 5 of the Corporation Tax Act 2009" substituted for the words "this Chapter" by CTA 2009, s. 1322 and Sch. 1, para. 444(16)(b), with effect for corporation tax purposes for accounting periods ending on or after 1 April 2009, and for income tax and capital gains tax purposes for the tax year 2009–10 and subsequent tax years.

Cross references – FA 1990, Sch. 10, para 12: charge to tax in respect of convertible securities.
FA 1990, Sch. 10, para 25: relief for the issuing company for amount paid on redemption of a convertible security.

TRANSITIONAL AND SAVINGS FOR CHAPTER II OF PART II OF THE FINANCE ACT 1993

22 [Repealed by FA 2002, s. 79(2), Sch. 23, para. 16, s. 141 and Sch. 40, Pt. 3(10).]

History – Para. 22 repealed by FA 2002, s. 79(2), Sch. 23, para. 16, s. 141 and Sch. 40, Pt. 3(10) with effect in relation to accounting periods beginning on or after 1 October 2002.

CARRYING BACK NON-TRADING LOSSES AGAINST EXCHANGE PROFITS ETC

23 [Repealed by FA 2002, s. 79(2), Sch. 23, para. 16, s. 141 and Sch. 40, Pt. 3(10).]

History – Para. 23 repealed by FA 2002, s. 79(2), Sch. 23, para. 16, s. 141 and Sch. 40, Pt. 3(10) with effect in relation to accounting periods beginning on or after 1 October 2002.

EXCHANGE LOSSES ETC. CARRIED FORWARD FROM BEFORE 1ST APRIL 1996

24 [Repealed by FA 2002, s. 79(2), Sch. 23, para. 16, s. 141 and Sch. 40, Pt. 3(10).]

History – Para. 24 repealed by FA 2002, s. 79(2), Sch. 23, para. 16, s. 141 and Sch. 40, Pt. 3(10) with effect in relation to accounting periods beginning on or after 1 October 2002.

TRANSITIONAL FOR DEBT CONTRACTS AND OPTIONS TO WHICH CHAPTER II OF PART IV OF THE FINANCE ACT 1994IS APPLIED

25 [Repealed by FA 2002, s. 141 and Sch. 40, Pt. 3(13).]

History – Para. 25 repealed by FA 2002, s. 141 and Sch. 40, Pt. 3(13) with effect in relation to accounting periods beginning on or after 1 October 2002.

Part II – Income Tax and Capital Gains Tax

APPLICATION AND INTERPRETATION OF PART II

26(1) This Part of this Schedule (except paragraph 29) has effect for the purposes of income tax and capital gains tax but not for the purposes of corporation tax.

26(2) In this Part of this Schedule–

"the 1992 Act" means the Taxation of Chargeable Gains Act 1992;

"market value" has the same meaning as in the 1992 Act;

"qualifying indexed security" has the meaning given by paragraph 2 of Schedule 11 to the Finance Act 1989; and

"deeply discounted security" has the same meaning as in Chapter 8 of Part 4 of the Income Tax (Trading and Other Income) Act 2005 (see section 430).

26(3) References in this Part of this Schedule to a disposal within marriage or civil partnership are references to any disposal to which section 58 of the 1992 Act applies.

History – In para. 26(2) the definition of "deeply discounted security" substituted for the definition of "relevant discounted security" by ITTOIA 2005, s. 882(1) and Sch. 1, para. 491(2); effective for income tax purposes for 2005–06 onwards and for corporation tax purposes for accounting periods ending after 5 April 2005 (ITTOIA 2005, s. 883(1)).
In para. 26(3) the words "or civil partnership" inserted by SI 2005/3229, reg. 130, with effect from 5 December 2005.

Cross references – TCGA 1992, s. 58: transfers of assets between spouses.

QUALIFYING INDEXED SECURITIES

27(1) This paragraph applies where–

(a) on 5th April 1996 any person ("the relevant person") held a qualifying indexed security;

(b) that person did not dispose of that security on that date and does not fall (apart from by virtue of this paragraph) to be treated for the purposes of the 1992 Act as having made a disposal of it on that date; and

(c) a relevant event occurs.

27(2) For the purposes of this paragraph a relevant event occurs on the first occasion after 5th April 1996 when the relevant person, or a person to whom that person has made a disposal of the security within marriage, falls to be treated for the purposes of the 1992 Act as making a disposal (otherwise than within marriage) which is–

(a) a disposal of the security in question; or

(b) a disposal of any such asset as falls to be treated for the purposes of that Act as the same as that security.

27(3) The amount of any chargeable gain or allowable loss which would have been treated as accruing to the relevant person if–

(a) he had made a disposal of the asset on 5th April 1996, and

(b) that disposal had been for a consideration equal to the market value of the asset,

shall be brought into account as one accruing to the person who makes the disposal constituting the relevant event in the year of assessment in which that event occurs.

28 For the purposes of Chapter 8 of Part 4 of the Income Tax (Trading and Other Income) Act 2005 where–

(a) a person held a qualifying indexed security both on and immediately after 5th April 1996, and

(b) that security is a deeply discounted security,

the amount which that person shall be taken to have paid in respect of his acquisition of that security on or before 5th April 1996 shall be an amount equal to its market value on that date.

History – In para. 28 the words "Chapter 8 of Part 4 of the Income Tax (Trading and Other Income) Act 2005" substituted for the words "Schedule 13 to this Act"; and the word "deeply" in para. 28(b) substituted for the former word ("relevant") by ITTOIA 2005, s. 882(1) and Sch. 1, para. 491(3); effective for income tax purposes for 2005–06 onwards and for corporation tax purposes for accounting periods ending after 5 April 2005 (ITTOIA 2005, s. 883(1)).

29 For the purposes of paragraph 2 of Schedule 10 to this Act paragraphs 27 and 28 above shall have effect in relation to an authorised unit trust for the first of its accounting periods to end after 31st March 1996 as if references in those paragraphs to 5th April 1996 were references to 31st March 1996.

TRANSITIONAL IN RELATION TO QUALIFYING CORPORATE BONDS

30(1) This paragraph applies where–

(a) any person holds any asset on and immediately after 5th April 1996;

(b) that asset is one which came to be held by that person as a result of a transaction to which section 127 of the 1992 Act applies; and

(c) that asset falls from 5th April 1996 to be treated as a deeply discounted security but is neither a qualifying indexed security nor such that it would have fallen to be treated as a qualifying corporate bond in relation to any disposal of it on that date.

30(2) Section 116 of the 1992 Act (reorganisations etc. involving qualifying corporate bonds) shall have effect as if–

(a) there had been a transaction on 5th April 1996 by which the person holding the asset had disposed of it and immediately re-acquired it;

(b) the asset re-acquired had been a qualifying corporate bond; and

(c) the transaction had been a transaction to which section 127 of the 1992 Act would have applied but for section 116(5) of that Act.

History – In para. 30(1)(c) the word "deeply" substituted for the word "relevant" by ITTOIA 2005, s. 882(1) and Sch. 1, para. 491(4); effective for income tax purposes for 2005–06 onwards and for corporation tax purposes for accounting periods ending after 5 April 2005 (ITTOIA 2005, s. 883(1)).

Cross references – TCGA 1992, s. 116: reorganisations, conversions and reconstructions involving qualifying corporate bonds. TCGA 1992, s. 127: equation of original shares and new holding on a reorganisation or conversion.

SCHEDULE 16 – SHARE OPTION SCHEMES APPROVED BEFORE PASSING OF THIS ACT

Section 114

[Repealed by ITEPA 2003, Sch. 8, Pt. 1.]

History – Sch. 16 repealed by ITEPA 2003, Sch. 8, Pt. 1 which has effect, for income tax purposes, for the tax year 2003–04 and subsequent tax years and, for corporation tax purposes, for accounting periods ending after 5 April 2003.

Cross references – ITEPA 2003, Sch. 7, para. 75 (Schedule 7: Transitionals and savings): continued effect, under the CSOP code, of a discretionary share option scheme which was approved (under ICTA 1988, Sch. 9) before 29th April 1996 and which was subject to the modifications made by FA 1996, Sch. 16, para. 2 and 3.

SCHEDULE 17 – CLAIMS FOR RELIEF INVOLVING TWO OR MORE YEARS

Section 128

[Inserts TMA 1970, Sch. 1B.]

SCHEDULE 18 – OVERDUE TAX AND EXCESSIVE PAYMENTS BY THE BOARD

Section 132.

THE TAXES MANAGEMENT ACT 1970

1 [Substitutes TMA 1970, s. 55(1)(b).]

2(1) Section 59A of the Taxes Management Act 1970 (payments on account of income tax) shall be amended in accordance with the following provisions of this paragraph.

2(2) [Amends TMA 1970, s. 59A(2).]

2(3) [Amends TMA 1970, s. 59A(4A).]

2(4) [Inserts TMA 1970 s. 59A(4B).]

2(5) [Amends TMA 1970, s. 59A(5).]

3(1) Section 86 of the Taxes Management Act 1970 (interest on overdue income tax and capital gains tax) shall be amended in accordance with the following provisions of this paragraph.

3(2) [Amends TMA 1970, s. 86(4)(b) and inserts s. 86(4)(b)(ii).]

3(3) [Amends TMA 1970, s. 86(6).]

4(1) [Repeals TMA 1970, s. 88.]

4(2)

(a) [Repeals TMA 1970, s. 88A.]

(b) [Amends TMA 1970, s. 91(1).]

(c) [Repeals TMA 1970, s. 113(1C).]

THE TAXES ACT 1988

5 [Amends ICTA 1988, s. 307(6).]

6(1) Section 369 of the Taxes Act 1988 (MIRAS) shall be amended in accordance with the following provisions of this paragraph.

6(2)

(a) [Substitutes ICTA 1988, s. 369(7)(a)]

(b) [Amends ICTA 1988, s. 369(7)(b).]

(c) [Amends ICTA 1988, s. 369(7)(c).]

(d) [Amends ICTA 1988, s. 369(7).]

6(3) [Inserts ICTA 1988, s. 369(8) and (9).]

7 [Amends ICTA 1988, s. 374A(4).]

8 [Amends ICTA 1988, s. 375(4).]

9 [Amends ICTA 1988 s. 412(4).]

10 [Repealed by ITTOIA 2005, s. 884 and Sch. 3 effective for income tax purposes for 2005–06 onwards and for corporation tax purposes for accounting periods ending after 5 April 2005 (ITTOIA 2005, s. 883(1)).]

11(1) Schedule 14 to the Taxes Act 1988 (life assurance premium relief: provisions ancillary to section 266) shall be amended in accordance with the following provisions of this paragraph.

11(2) [Amends ICTA 1988, Sch. 14, para. 6(2).]

11(3) [AmendsICTA 1988 Sch. 14, para. 7(3).]

11(4) [Inserts ICTA 1988, Sch. 14, para. 7(4) and (5).]

Prospective amendments – Para. 11 repealed by FA 2012, s. 227 and Sch. 39, para. 28(1), with effect from a date to be appointed by Treasury order.

THE FINANCE ACT 1989

12 [Repealed by F(No. 2)A 1997, s. 52 and Sch. 8, Pt. II(2).]

History – Para. 12 repealed by F(No. 2)A 1997, s. 52 and Sch. 8, Pt. II(2), with effect for the year 1997–98 and subsequent years of assessment except where relief given under FA 1989, s. 54 (in respect of any payment) is unaffected by the provisions of F(No. 2)A 1997, s. 17(1).

13 [Amends FA 1989, s. 178(2)(f).]

THE FINANCE ACT 1991

14 [Repealed by FA 1999, s. 139 and Sch. 20, Pt. III(15).]

History – Para. 14 repealed by FA 1999, s. 139 and Sch. 20, Pt. III(15), with effect in relation to payments made on or after such date after 1 September 2000 (SI 2000/2004 (C. 53)).

THE TAXATION OF CHARGEABLE GAINS ACT 1992

15(1) Section 281 of the Taxation of Chargeable Gains Act 1992 (payment by instalments of tax on gifts) shall be amended in accordance with the following provisions of this paragraph.

15(2) [Substitutes TCGA 1992, s. 281(5)(a).]

15(3) [Amends TCGA 1992, s. 281(6).]

15(4) [Amends TCGA 1992, s. 281(7).]

THE FINANCE ACT 1995

16 In section 73(4) of the Finance Act 1995 (power to apply certain provisions of the Taxes Management Act 1970 in relation to certain sums payable in connection with venture capital trusts)–

(a) for "section 29(3)(c)" there shall be substituted "section 29(1)(c)";

(b) [Amends FA 1995, s. 73(4).]

(c) [Amends FA 1995, s. 73(4).]

COMMENCEMENT

17(1) Paragraphs 1 to 3, 6(2)(a) and (b), 8, 11(3)(a) and (b), 14(2)(a) and (b) and 16(a) above have effect, subject to sub-paragraph (2) below–

(a) for the purposes of income tax and capital gains tax, as respects the year 1996–97 and subsequent years of assessment; and

(b) for the purposes of corporation tax, as respects accounting periods ending on or after the day appointed under section 199 of the Finance Act 1994 for the purposes of Chapter III of Part IV of that Act (self-assessment management provisions).

17(2) Paragraphs 1, 3, 6(2)(a) and (b), 11(3)(a) and (b), and 14(2)(a) and (b) above, so far as relating to partnerships whose trades, professions or businesses were set up and commenced before 6th April 1994, has effect as respects the year 1997–98 and subsequent years of assessment.

17(3) Paragraphs 4, 5, 6(2)(c) and (3), 11(3)(c) and (4), 13, 14(2)(c) and (3), 15 and 16(b) and (c) above have effect, subject to sub-paragraph (4) below–

(a) as respects the year 1996–97 and subsequent years of assessment; and

(b) in relation to any income tax or capital gains tax which–

(i) is charged by an assessment made on or after 6th April 1998; and

(ii) is for the year 1995–96 or any earlier year of assessment;

and where sub-paragraph (4) of paragraph 11, sub-paragraph (3) of paragraph 12, or sub-paragraph (3) of paragraph 14 has effect by virtue of paragraph (b) of this sub-paragraph it shall have effect with the substitution, in the provision inserted by that sub-paragraph, for "section 29(1)(c)" of "section 29(3)(c)".

17(4) Paragraphs 4, 6(2)(c) and (3), 11(3)(c) and (4), 12(2)(c) and (3), 13 and 14(2)(c) and (3) above, so far as relating to partnerships whose trades, professions or businesses were set up and commenced before 6th April 1994 have effect–

(a) as respects the year 1997–98 and subsequent years of assessment; and

(b) in relation to any income tax which–

(i) is charged by an assessment made on or after 6th April 1998; and

(ii) is for the year 1995–96 or any earlier year of assessment.

17(5) Paragraphs 7 and 11(2) above have effect–

(a) as respects the year 1996–97 and subsequent years of assessment; and

(b) subject to sub-paragraphs (6) and (7) below, in relation to any income tax or capital gains tax which–

(i) is charged by an assessment made on or after 6th April 1998; and

(ii) is for the year 1995–96 or any earlier year of assessment.

17(6) Sub-paragraph (5)(b) above does not apply to paragraph 7 above so far as paragraph 7 provides for the omission of–

(a) paragraph (a) of subsection (4) of section 374A of the Taxes Act 1988, and

(b) the words "and as if" so far as they relate to paragraph (a) of that subsection.

17(7) Sub-paragraph (5)(b) above does not apply to paragraph 11(2) above so far as paragraph 11(2) provides for the omission of–

(a) the words "sections 55(1) (recovery of tax not postponed) and", and

(b) the words "and as if–

(a) the assessment were among those specified in"

so far as those words relate to the words mentioned in paragraph (a) of this sub-paragraph.

17(8) Paragraphs 6(2)(d), 11(3)(d), and 14(2)(d) above shall not apply in relation to any payment if the payment, or the claim on which it is made, was made before the day on which this Act is passed.

17(9) Paragraph 9 above has effect as respects accounting periods ending on or after the day appointed under section 199 of the Finance Act 1994 for the purposes of Chapter III of Part IV (self-assessment management provisions).

17(10) Any power to make regulations exercisable by virtue of an amendment made by any of the preceding provisions of this Schedule may he exercised so as to make provision having effect in relation to any year of assessment in relation to which that provision has effect in accordance with sub-paragraphs (1) to (9) above.

History – In both para. 17(1) and (2) references to FA 1996, Sch. 18, para. 10 repealed by ITTOIA 2005, s. 884 and Sch. 3 effective for income tax purposes for 2005–06 onwards and for corporation tax purposes for accounting periods ending after 5 April 2005 (ITTOIA 2005, s. 883(1)).

In para. 17(1) and (2), references to "12(2)(a) and (b)" , the words "12(2)(c) and (3)" in para. 17(3) and (4), and the reference to "12(2)(d)" in para. 17(8), repealed by F(No. 2)A 1997, s. 52 and Sch. 8, Pt. II(2) with effect for the year 1997–98 and subsequent years of assessment, except where relief given under FA 1989, s. 54 (in respect of any payment) is unaffected by the provisions of F(No. 2)A 1997, s. 17(1).

Notes – The day appointed for the purposes of FA 1994, s. 199 (corporation tax self-assessment) is 1 July 1999 (SI 1998/3173 (C. 78)).

SCHEDULE 19 – SELF-ASSESSMENT: CLAIMS AND ENQUIRIES

Section 133

INTRODUCTORY

1 The Taxes Management Act 1970, as it has effect–

(a) for the purposes of income tax and capital gains tax, as respects the year 1996–97 and subsequent years of assessment, and

(b) for the purposes of corporation tax, as respects accounting periods ending on or after the day appointed under section 199 of the Finance Act 1994 for the purposes of Chapter III of Part IV of that Act (self-assessment management provisions),

shall be amended in accordance with the following provisions of this Schedule.

Notes – The day appointed for the purposes of FA 1994, s. 199 (corporation tax self-assessment) is 1 July 1999 (SI 1998/3173 (C. 78)).

MATTERS SUBJECT TO ENQUIRY

2 [Spent.]

POWER TO CALL FOR DOCUMENTS

3 [Omitted by FA 2008, s. 113 and Sch. 36, para. 92(e).]

History – Para. 3 omitted by FA 2008, s. 113 and Sch. 36, para. 92(e), with effect from 1 April 2009 (SI 2009/404, art. 2, subject to savings at SI 2009/404, art. 3).

FURTHER AMENDMENTS OF SECTION 28A

4(1) [Repealed by FA 2001, s. 110 and Sch. 33, Pt. 2(13).]

History – Para. 4 repealed by FA 2001, s. 110 and Sch. 33, Pt. 2(13), with effect from 11 May 2001 in relation to returns made before or after that date, and whether relating to periods before or after that date.

FURTHER AMENDMENTS OF SECTION 28B

5(1) [Repealed by FA 2001, s. 110 and Sch. 33, Pt. 2(13).]

History – Para. 5 repealed by FA 2001, s. 110 and Sch. 33, Pt. 213), with effect from 11 May 2001 in relation to returns made before or after that date, and whether relating to periods before or after that date.

RIGHT OF APPEAL AGAINST NOTICE DISALLOWING CLAIM IN RETURN

6(1) [Repealed by FA 2001, s. 110 and Sch. 33, Pt. 2(13).]

History – Para. 6 repealed by FA 2001, s. 110 and Sch. 33, Pt. 2(13), with effect from 11 May 2001 in relation to returns made before or after that date, and whether relating to periods before or after that date.

7 [Inserts TMA 1970, s. 50(7A).]

CLAIMS NOT INCLUDED IN RETURNS

8(1) [Amends TMA 1970, Sch. 1A, para. 4(1).]

8(2) [Amends TMA 1970, Sch. 1A, para. 4(2).]

8(3) [Inserts TMA 1970, Sch. 1A, para. 4.]

9 [Repealed by FA 2001, s. 110 and Sch. 33, Pt. 2(13).]

History – Para. 9 repealed by FA 2001, s. 110 and Sch. 33, Pt. 2(13), with effect from 11 May 2001 in relation to returns made before or after that date, and whether relating to periods before or after that date.

RIGHT OF APPEAL AGAINST NOTICE DISALLOWING CLAIM NOT IN RETURN

10(1) [Repealed by FA 2001, s. 110 and Sch. 33, Pt. 2(13).]

10(2) [Amends TMA 1970, Sch. 1A, para. 9(2).]

10(3) [Amends TMA 1970, Sch. 1A, para. 9(3).]

10(4) [Inserts TMA 1970, Sch. 1A, para. 9(5).]

History – Para. 10(1) repealed by FA 2001, s. 110 and Sch. 33, Pt. 2(13), with effect from 11 May 2001 in relation to returns made before or after that date, and whether relating to periods before or after that date.

SCHEDULE 20 – SELF-ASSESSMENT: DISCRETIONS EXERCISABLE BY THE BOARD ETC.

Section 134

THE TAXES ACT 1988

1 [Amends ICTA 1988, s. 24(2).]

2 [Repealed by CTA 2009, s. 1326 and Sch. 3, Pt. 1.]

History – Para. 2 repealed by CTA 2009, s. 1326 and Sch. 3, Pt. 1, with effect for corporation tax purposes for accounting periods ending on or after 1 April 2009, and for income tax and capital gains tax purposes for the tax year 2009–10 and subsequent tax years.

3 [Repealed by ITTOIA 2005, s. 884 and Sch. 3 effective for income tax purposes for 2005–06 onwards and for corporation tax purposes for accounting periods ending after 5 April 2005 (ITTOIA 2005, s. 883(1)).]

4 [Amends ICTA 1988, s. 74(1)(j).]

5 [Repealed by ITA 2007, s. 1031 and Sch. 3, Pt. 1.]

History – Para. 5 repealed by ITA 2007, s. 1031 and Sch. 3, Pt. 1, with effect from 6 April 2007.

Notes – Para. 5 rewritten as follows:
Para. 5(1): ITA 2007, s. 98(2), (3).
Para. 5(2): ITA 2007, s. 98(5), (6), (7), (8)

6 [Repealed by ITEPA 2003, Sch. 8, Pt. 1.]

History – Para. 6 repealed by ITEPA 2003, Sch. 8, Pt. 1 which has effect for the tax year 2003–04 and subsequent tax years.

7 [Repealed by ITEPA 2003, Sch. 8, Pt. 1.]

History – Para. 7 repealed by ITEPA 2003, Sch. 8, Pt. 1 which has effect for the tax year 2003–04 and subsequent tax years.

8 [Repealed by ITEPA 2003, Sch. 8, Pt. 1.]

History – Para. 8 repealed by ITEPA 2003, Sch. 8, Pt. 1 which has effect for the tax year 2003–04 and subsequent tax years.

9 [Repealed by ITEPA 2003, Sch. 8, Pt. 1.]

History – Para. 9 repealed by ITEPA 2003, Sch. 8, Pt. 1 which has effect for the tax year 2003–04 and subsequent tax years.

10 [Repealed by ITEPA 2003, Sch. 8, Pt. 1.]

History – Para. 10 repealed by ITEPA 2003, Sch. 8, Pt. 1 which has effect for the tax year 2003–04 and subsequent tax years.

11

(a) [Substitutes ICTA 1988, s. 186(10)(b).]

(b) [Amends ICTA 1988, s. 186(10)(c).]

12 [Repealed by ITTOIA 2005, s. 884 and Sch. 3 effective for income tax purposes for 2005–06 onwards and for corporation tax purposes for accounting periods ending after 5 April 2005 (ITTOIA 2005, s. 883(1)).]

13

(a) [Amends ICTA 1988, s. 257(2).]

(b) [Amends ICTA 1988, s. 257(3).]

14(1) Section 257A of the Taxes Act 1988 (married couple's allowance) shall be amended in accordance with the following provisions of this paragraph.

14(2) [Repealed by FA 1999, s. 139 and Sch. 20, Pt. III(3).]

14(3) [Omitted by FA 2009, s. 5 and Sch. 1, para. 6(g).]

History – Para. 14(2) repealed by FA 1999, s. 139 and Sch. 20, Pt. III(3), with effect for the year 2000–01 and subsequent years of assessment.
Para. 14(3) omitted by FA 2009, s. 5 and Sch. 1, para. 6(g), with effect from the tax year 2010–11 and subsequent tax years.

15 [Repealed by FA 1999, s. 139 and Sch. 20, Pt. III(3).]

History – Para. 15 repealed by FA 1999, s. 139 and Sch. 20, Pt. III(3), with effect for the year 2000–01 and subsequent years of assessment.

16 [Repealed by FA 1999, s. 139 and Sch. 20, Pt. III(3).]

History – Para. 16 repealed by FA 1999, s. 139 and Sch. 20, Pt. III(3), with effect for the year 2000–01 and subsequent years of assessment.

17 [Repealed by FA 1999, s. 139 and Sch. 20, Pt. III(4).]

History – Para. 17 repealed by FA 1999, s. 139 and Sch. 20, Pt. III(4), with effect for the year 2000–01 and subsequent years of assessment.

18 [Repealed by FA 1999, s. 139 and Sch. 20, Pt. III(4).]

History – Para. 18 repealed by FA 1999, s. 139 and Sch. 20, Pt. III(4), with effect for the year 2000–01 and subsequent years of assessment.

19 [Amends ICTA 1988, s. 265(1).]

20 [Amends ICTA 1988, s. 274(4).]

Prospective amendments – Para. 20 repealed by FA 2012, s. 227 and Sch. 39, para. 28(1), with effect from a date to be appointed by Treasury order.

21 [Amends ICTA 1988, s. 278(2).]

22 [Repealed by ITA 2007, s. 1031 and Sch. 3, Pt. 2.]

History – Para. 22 repealed by ITA 2007, s. 1031 and Sch. 3, Pt. 2, with effect in relation to shares issued after 5 April 2007.

Notes – Para. 22 rewritten as ITA 2007, s. 203(1), 204(1).

23 [Repealed by ITA 2007, s. 1031 and Sch. 3, Pt. 2.]

History – Para. 23 repealed by ITA 2007, s. 1031 and Sch. 3, Pt. 2, with effect from 6 April 2007, in relation to shares issued after 5 April 2007.

Notes – Para. 23 rewritten as ITA 2007, s. 251(4), (5).

24 [Amends ICTA 1988, s. 381(4).]

25(1) [Amends ICTA 1988, s. 384(1).]

25(2) [Repealed by ITA 2007, s. 1031 and Sch. 3, Pt. 1.]

History – Para. 25(2) repealed by ITA 2007, s. 1031 and Sch. 3, Pt. 1, with effect from 6 April 2007.

Notes – Para. 25(2) rewritten as ITA 2007, s. 66(3).

26 [Repealed by CTA 2010, s. 1181 and Sch. 3, Pt. 1.]

History – Para. 26 repealed by CTA 2010, s. 1181 and Sch. 3, Pt. 1, with effect for corporation tax purposes for accounting periods ending on or after 1 April 2010, and for income tax and capital gains tax purposes for the tax year 2010–11 and subsequent tax years.

27 [Repealed by CTA 2010, s. 1181 and Sch. 3, Pt. 1.]

History – Para. 27 repealed by CTA 2010, s. 1181 and Sch. 3, Pt. 1, with effect for corporation tax purposes for accounting periods ending on or after 1 April 2010, and for income tax and capital gains tax purposes for the tax year 2010–11 and subsequent tax years.

28 [Repealed by CTA 2010, s. 1181 and Sch. 3, Pt. 1.]

History – Para. 28 repealed by CTA 2010, s. 1181 and Sch. 3, Pt. 1, with effect for corporation tax purposes for accounting periods ending on or after 1 April 2010, and for income tax and capital gains tax purposes for the tax year 2010–11 and subsequent tax years.
Para. 28(5) also previously repealed by FA 1999, s. 128 and Sch. 20, Pt. III(7) with effect in relation to any payment of interest falling within FA 1999, s. 38(3) or (4) (broadly, payments made on or after 6 April 2000, or on or after 9 March 1999 and before 6 April 2000 but not falling due until on or after 6 April 2000).
Para. 28(5) previously repealed by FA 1998, s. 165 and Sch. 27, Pt. III(28) with effect in relation to accounting periods ending on or after 1 July 1999, the corporation tax self-assessment appointed day under FA 1994 s. 199 by virtue of SI 1998/3173 (C. 78).

29 [Repealed by CTA 2010, s. 1181 and Sch. 3, Pt. 1.]

History – Para. 29 repealed by CTA 2010, s. 1181 and Sch. 3, Pt. 1, with effect for corporation tax purposes for accounting periods ending on or after 1 April 2010, and for income tax and capital gains tax purposes for the tax year 2010–11 and subsequent tax years.

30 [Repealed by FA 1998, s. 165 and Sch. 27, Pt. III(4), with effect, so far as relating to income tax, for 1998–99 and subsequent years of assessment and so far as relating to corporation tax from 1 April 1998.]

31 [Amends ICTA 1988, s. 570(2).]

32(a) [Amends ICTA 1988, s. 582(2)(b).]

32(b) [Repealed by ITA 2007, s. 1031 and Sch. 3, Pt. 1.]

History – Para. 32(b) repealed by ITA 2007, s. 1031 and Sch. 3, Pt. 1, with effect from 6 April 2007.

Notes – Para. 32 rewritten as ITA 2007, s. 940(1), (3).

33 [Repealed by CTA 2009, s. 1326 and Sch. 3, Pt. 1.]

History – Para. 33 repealed by CTA 2009, s. 1326 and Sch. 3, Pt. 1, with effect for corporation tax purposes for accounting periods ending on or after 1 April 2009, and for income tax and capital gains tax purposes for the tax year 2009–10 and subsequent tax years.

34 [Repealed by ITTOIA 2005, s. 884 and Sch. 3 effective for income tax purposes for 2005–06 onwards and for corporation tax purposes for accounting periods ending after 5 April 2005 (ITTOIA 2005, s. 883(1)).]

35 [Repealed by ITA 2007, s. 1031 and Sch. 3, Pt. 1.]

History – Para. 35 repealed by ITA 2007, s. 1031 and Sch. 3, Pt. 1, with effect from 6 April 2007.

Notes – Para. 35 rewritten as ITA 2007, s. 631(3), 635(2).

36 [Omitted by FA 2008, s. 66(4)(g)(i).]

History – Para. 36 omitted by FA 2008, s. 66(4)(g)(i), with effect in relation to cases where the purchase by the first buyer (within the meaning of section 731(2) of ICTA) is made on or after 1 April 2008.

37 [Repealed by CTA 2010, s. 1181 and Sch. 3, Pt. 1.]

History – Para. 37 repealed by CTA 2010, s. 1181 and Sch. 3, Pt. 1, with effect for corporation tax purposes for accounting periods ending on or after 1 April 2010, and for income tax and capital gains tax purposes for the tax year 2010–11 and subsequent tax years.

38 [Repealed by Statute Law (Repeals) Act 2013, s. 1 and Sch. 1, Pt. 10.]

History – Para. 38 repealed by Statute Law (Repeals) Act 2013, s. 1 and Sch. 1, Pt. 10, with effect from 31 January 2013.

39 [Repealed by TIOPA 2010, s. 378 and Sch. 10, Pt. 1.]

History – Para. 39 repealed by TIOPA 2010, s. 378 and Sch. 10, Pt. 1, with effect for corporation tax purposes for accounting periods ending on or after 1 April 2010, for income tax and capital gains tax purposes for the tax year 2010–11 and subsequent tax years, and for petroleum revenue tax purposes for chargeable periods beginning on or after 1 July 2010.

40 [Repealed by FA 2000, Sch. 40, Pt II(3).]

History – Para. 40 repealed by FA 2000, Sch. 40, Pt II(3) with effect for the year 2002–03 and subsequent years of assessment.

41 [Repealed by ITEPA 2003, Sch. 8, Pt. 1.]

History – Para. 41 repealed by ITEPA 2003, Sch. 8, Pt. 1 which has effect for the tax year 2003–04 and subsequent tax years.

42 [Repealed by ITEPA 2003, Sch. 8, Pt. 1.]

History – Para. 42 repealed by ITEPA 2003, Sch. 8, Pt. 1 which has effect for the tax year 2003–04 and subsequent tax years.

43 [Repeals ICTA 1988, Sch. 21, para. 3.]

THE CAPITAL ALLOWANCES ACT 1990

44 [Repealed by CAA 2001, s. 580 and Sch. 4.]

History – FA 1996, Sch. 20, para. 44 repealed by CAA 2001, Sch. 4, with effect as respects allowances and charges falling to be made for chargeable periods ending, for income tax purposes, on or after 6 April 2001, and, for corporation tax purposes, on or after 1 April 2001.

THE TAXATION OF CHARGEABLE GAINS ACT 1992

45 In the following provisions of this Schedule **"the Gains Act"** means the Taxation of Chargeable Gains Act 1992.

46 [Amends TCGA 1992, s. 30(4).]

47 [Partially repealed. Amends TCGA 1992, s. 30(5) and (6).]

History – Para. 47(b) and (c) repealed by FA 2011, s. 44 and Sch. 9, para. 5(a), with effect in relation to disposals of shares and securities by companies made on or after 19 July 2011, subject to the transitional provision in FA 2011, Sch. 9, para. 6(2).

48 [Amends TCGA 1992, s. 48.]

49 [Substitutes TCGA 1992, s. 49(2).]

50 [Amends TCGA 1992, s. 52(4).]

51 [Amends TCGA 1992, s. 116(13).]

52(1) [Amends TCGA 1992, s. 122.]

52(2) [Repeals TCGA 1992, s. 122(3).]

52(3) [Amends TCGA 1992, s. 122(4)(a).]

53(1) [Amends TCGA 1992, s. 133.]

53(2) [Repeals TCGA 1992, s. 133(3).]

53(3) [Amends TCGA 1992, s. 133(4)(a).]

54 [Amends TCGA 1992, s. 150(10)(a) and 150A(9)(a).]

55 [Amends TCGA 1992, s. 164F(8)(a).]

56 [Amends TCGA 1992, s. 164FG(2).]

57(1) [Amends TCGA 1992, s. 176(4) and s. 176(6).]

57(2) [Amends TCGA 1992, s. 176(5).]

58 [Amends TCGA 1992, s. 181(1)(b).]

59(1) Section 222 of the Gains Act (relief on disposal of residence and land up to the permitted area, which is 0.5 of a hectare) shall be amended in accordance with the following provisions of this paragraph.

59(2) [Substitutes TCGA 1992, s. 222(3).]

59(3) [Amends TCGA 1992, s. 222(5).]

59(4) [Amends TCGA 1992, s. 222(6) and repeals s. 222(6)(b).]

60 [Amends TCGA 1992, s. 224(2).]

61 [Repeals TCGA 1992, s. 226(5).]

62 [Amends TCGA 1992, s. 241(7).]

63(1) [Amends TCGA 1992, s. 271(1)(g) and s. 271(2).]

63(2) [Amends TCGA 1992, s. 271(2).]

64 [Substitutes s. 279(1)(b), (c).]

65 [Amends TCGA 1992, s. 280.]

66 [Repealed by FA 1998, s. 165 and Sch. 27, Pt. III(31).]

History – Para. 66 repealed by FA 1998, s. 165 and Sch. 27, Pt. III(31), with effect in relation to disposals in 2003–04 and subsequent years of assessment.

67 [Amends TCGA 1992, Sch. 8 para 10(2).]

THE FINANCE ACT 1993

68 [Repealed by FA 2002, s. 141 and Sch. 40, Pt. 3(10).]

History – Para. 68 repealed by FA 2002, s. 141 and Sch. 40, Pt. 3(10) in relation to accounting periods beginning on or after 1 October 2002.

69 [Repealed by FA 2002, s. 141 and Sch. 40, Pt. 3(10).]

History – Para. 69 repealed by FA 2002, s. 141 and Sch. 40, Pt. 3(10) with effect in relation to accounting periods beginning on or after 1 October 2002.

70 [Repealed by FA 2002, s. 141 and Sch. 40, Pt. 3(10).]

History – Para. 70 repealed by FA 2002, s. 141 and Sch. 40, Pt. 3(10) with effect in relation to accounting periods beginning on or after 1 October 2002.

THE FINANCE ACT 1994

71 [Repealed by FA 2002, s. 141 and Sch. 40, Pt. 3(13).]

History – Para. 71 repealed by FA 2002, s. 141 and Sch. 40, Pt. 3(13) in relation to accounting periods beginning on or after 1 October 2002.

SCHEDULE 21 – SELF-ASSESSMENT: TIME LIMITS

Section 135

THE TAXES ACT 1988

1 [Repealed by ITTOIA 2005, s. 884 and Sch. 3 effective for income tax purposes for 2005–06 onwards and for corporation tax purposes for accounting periods ending after 5 April 2005 (ITTOIA 2005, s. 883(1)).]

2 [Repealed by CTA 2009, s. 1326 and Sch. 3, Pt. 1.]

History – Para. 2 repealed by CTA 2009, s. 1326 and Sch. 3, Pt. 1, with effect for corporation tax purposes for accounting periods ending on or after 1 April 2009, and for income tax and capital gains tax purposes for the tax year 2009–10 and subsequent tax years.

3 [Repealed by CTA 2009, s. 1326 and Sch. 3, Pt. 1.]

History – Para. 3 repealed by CTA 2009, s. 1326 and Sch. 3, Pt. 1, with effect for corporation tax purposes for accounting periods ending on or after 1 April 2009, and for income tax and capital gains tax purposes for the tax year 2009–10 and subsequent tax years.

4 [Omitted by FA 2008, s. 118 and Sch. 39, para. 65(b) and by FA 2009, s. 5 and Sch. 1, para. 6(g).]

History – Para. 4 omitted by FA 2009, s. 5 and Sch. 1, para. 6(g), with effect from the tax year 2010–11 and subsequent tax years. This provision was made despite the fact that para. 4 was omitted by FA 2008, s. 118 and Sch. 39, para. 65(b) as indicated below.
Para. 4 omitted by FA 2008, s. 118 and Sch. 39, para. 65(b), with effect from 1 April 2010 (SI 2009/403, art. 2(2) subject to SI 2009/403, art. 3–10 – in particular art. 10).

5 [Repealed by FA 1999, s. 139 and Sch. 20, Pt. III(3).]

History – Para. 5 omitted by FA 2009, s. 5 and Sch. 1, para. 6(g), with effect from the tax year 2010–11 and subsequent tax years. This provision was made despite the earlier repeal of para. 5 by FA 1999 (see below).
Para. 5 repealed by FA 1999, s. 139 and Sch. 20, Pt. III(3), with effect for the year 2000–01 and subsequent years of assessment.

6 [Omitted by FA 2008, s. 118 and Sch. 39, para. 65(b) and by FA 2009, s. 5 and Sch. 1, para. 6(g).]

History – Para. 6 omitted by FA 2009, s. 5 and Sch. 1, para. 6(g), with effect from the tax year 2010–11 and subsequent tax years. This provision was made despite the fact that para. 4 was omitted by FA 2008, s. 118 and Sch. 39, para. 65(b) as indicated below.
Para. 6 omitted by FA 2008, s. 118 and Sch. 39, para. 65(b), with effect from 1 April 2010 (SI 2009/403, art. 2(2) subject to SI 2009/403, art. 3–10 – in particular art. 10). Former para. 4 amended ICTA 1988, s. 257BB(5)(a).

7 [Repealed by ITA 2007, s. 1031 and Sch. 3, Pt. 2.]

History – Para. 7 repealed by ITA 2007, s. 1031 and Sch. 3, Pt. 2, with effect from 6 April 2007, in relation to shares issued after 5 April 2007. Former para. 7 substituted ICTA 1988, s. 306(1)(b).

Notes – Para. 7 rewritten as ITA 2007, s. 202(1).

8 [Repealed by FA 1999, s. 139 and Sch. 20, Pt. III(7).]

History – Para. 8 repealed by FA 1999, s. 139 and Sch. 20, Pt. III(7) with effect in relation to any payment of interest falling within FA 1999, s. 3835(3) or (4) (broadly, payments made on or after 6 April 2000, or on or after 9 March 1999 and before 6 April 2000 but not falling due until on or after 6 April 2000).

9 [Repealed by FA 1999, s. 139 and Sch. 20, Pt. III(7).]

History – Para. 9 repealed by FA 1999, s. 139 and Sch. 20, Pt. III(7) with effect in relation to any payment of interest falling within FA 1999, s. 38(3) or (4) (broadly, payments made on or after 6 April 2000, or on or after 9 March 1999 and before 6 April 2000 but not falling due until on or after 6 April 2000).

10 [Repealed by ITA 2007, s. 1031 and Sch. 3, Pt. 1.]

History – Para. 10 repealed by ITA 2007, s. 1031 and Sch. 3, Pt. 1, with effect from 6 April 2007.

Notes – Para. 10 rewritten as ITA 2007, s. 72(3).

11 [Repealed by ITTOIA 2005, s. 884 and Sch. 3 effective for income tax purposes for 2005–06 onwards and for corporation tax purposes for accounting periods ending after 5 April 2005 (ITTOIA 2005, s. 883(1)).]

12 [Repealed by FA 1998, s. 165 and Sch. 27, Pt. III(23).]

History – Para. 12 repealed by FA 1998, s. 165 and Sch. 27, Pt. III(23) with effect in relation to exchanges made after 31 July 1998.

13 [Repealed by FA 1998, s. 165 and Sch. 27, Pt. III(23).]

History – Para. 13 repealed by FA 1998, s. 165 and Sch. 27, Pt. III(23) with effect in relation to issues of securities occurring after 31 July 1998.

14(1) Section 504 of the Taxes Act 1988 shall be amended in accordance with the following provisions of this paragraph.

14(2) [Amends ICTA 1988, s. 504(6).]

14(3) [Inserts ICTA 1988, s. 540(6a).]

15 [Repealed by CTA 2009, s. 1326 and Sch. 3, Pt. 1.]

History – Para. 15 repealed by CTA 2009, s. 1326 and Sch. 3, Pt. 1, with effect for corporation tax purposes for accounting periods ending on or after 1 April 2009, and for income tax and capital gains tax purposes for the tax year 2009–10 and subsequent tax years.

16 [Repealed by ITTOIA 2005, s. 884 and Sch. 3 effective for income tax purposes for 2005–06 onwards and for corporation tax purposes for accounting periods ending after 5 April 2005 (ITTOIA 2005, s. 883(1)).]

17 [Repealed by FA 2004, s. 326 and Sch. 42, Pt. 3.]

History – Para. 17 repealed by FA 2004, s. 326 and Sch. 42, Pt. 3 with effect from 6 April 2006.

18 [Repealed by FA 2000, Sch. 40, Pt. II(4).]

History – Para. 18 repealed by FA 2000, Sch. 40, Pt. II(4) with effect for the year 2001–02.

19 [Repealed by Statute Law (Repeals) Act 2013, s. 1 and Sch. 1, Pt. 10.]

History – Para. 19 repealed by Statute Law (Repeals) Act 2013, s. 1 and Sch. 1, Pt. 10, with effect from 31 January 2013.

20 [Repealed by CTA 2009, s. 1326 and Sch. 3, Pt. 1.]

History – Para. 20 repealed by CTA 2009, s. 1326 and Sch. 3, Pt. 1, with effect for corporation tax purposes for accounting periods ending on or after 1 April 2009, and for income tax and capital gains tax purposes for the tax year 2009–10 and subsequent tax years.

21 [Repealed by CTA 2010, s. 1181 and Sch. 3, Pt. 2 and TIOPA 2010, s. 378 and Sch. 10, Pt. 9.]

History – Para. 21 repealed by CTA 2010, s. 1181 and Sch. 3, Pt. 2, with effect for accounting periods ending on or after 1 April 2010 and TIOPA 2010, s. 378 and Sch. 10, Pt. 9, with effect for corporation tax purposes for accounting periods ending on or after 1 April 2010, for income tax and capital gains tax purposes for the tax year 2010–11 and subsequent tax years, and for petroleum revenue tax purposes for chargeable periods beginning on or after 1 July 2010.

22 [Repealed by TIOPA 2010, s. 378 and Sch. 10, Pt. 1.]

History – Para. 22 repealed by TIOPA 2010, s. 378 and Sch. 10, Pt. 1, with effect for corporation tax purposes for accounting periods ending on or after 1 April 2010, for income tax and capital gains tax purposes for the tax year 2010–11 and subsequent tax years, and for petroleum revenue tax purposes for chargeable periods beginning on or after 1 July 2010.

23 [Repealed by TIOPA 2010, s. 378 and Sch. 10, Pt. 1.]

History – Para. 23 repealed by TIOPA 2010, s. 378 and Sch. 10, Pt. 1, with effect for corporation tax purposes for accounting periods ending on or after 1 April 2010, for income tax and capital gains tax purposes for the tax year 2010–11 and subsequent tax years, and for petroleum revenue tax purposes for chargeable periods beginning on or after 1 July 2010.

24 [Repealed by FA 1998, s. 165 and Sch. 27, Pt. III(9).]

History – Para. 24 repealed by FA 1998, s. 165 and Sch. 27, Pt. III(9), with effect as respects payments or benefits received on or after 6 April 1998 (except where the payment or benefit or the right to receive it has been brought into charge to tax before that date).

THE FINANCE ACT 1988 (c. 39)

25 [Repealed by FA 1999, s. 139 and Sch. 20, Pt. III(6).]

History – Para. 25 repealed by FA 1999, s. 139 and Sch. 20, Pt. III(6), with effect in relation to any payment falling due on or after 6 April 2000.

THE CAPITAL ALLOWANCES ACT 1990 (c. 1)

26–33 [Repealed by CAA 2001, s. 580 and Sch. 4, with effect as respects allowances and charges falling to be made for chargeable periods ending, for income tax purposes, on or after 6 April 2001, and, for corporation tax purposes, on or after 1 April 2001.]

34 [Repealed by FA 1997, s. 113 and Sch. 18, Pt. VI(11), in relation to 1997–98 and subsequent years.]

THE TAXATION OF CHARGEABLE GAINS ACT 1992 (c. 12)

35 [Amends TCGA 1992, s. 35(6) and substitutes TCGA 1992, s. 35(6)(a) to (b).]

36 [Inserts TCGA 1992, s. 161(3A).]

37 [Inserts TCGA 1992, s. 242(2A).]

38 [Inserts TCGA 1992, s. 243(2A).]

39 [Inserts TCGA 1992, s. 244(3).]

40 [Inserts TCGA 1992, s. 253(4A).]

41 [Inserts TCGA 1992, s. 279(5).]

42(1) Schedule 2 to the Taxation of Chargeable Gains Act 1992 shall be amended in accordance with the following provisions of this paragraph.

42(2) [Amends TCGA 1992, Sch. 2 para. 4(11) and inserts TCGA 1992, Sch. 2 para. 4(11)(a)–(c).]

42(3) [Amends TCGA 1992, Sch. 2 para. 17(3) and inserts TCGA 1992, Sch. 2 para. 17(3)(a)–(c).]

43 [Omitted by FA 2008, s. 8 and Sch. 2, para. 75.]

History – Para. 43 omitted by FA 2008, s. 8 and Sch. 2, para. 75, with effect in relation to disposals which occur on or after 6 April 2008 and to which Schedule 4 to TCGA 1992 would otherwise apply. Former para. 43 amended TCGA 1992, Sch. 4, para. 9(1).

44 [Repealed by FA 1998, s. 165 and Sch. 27, Pt. III(31).]

History – Para. 44 repealed by FA 1998, s. 165 and Sch. 27, Pt. III(31) with effect in relation to disposals in 2003–04 and subsequent years of assessment.

THE FINANCE (NO. 2) ACT 1992 (c. 48)

45 [Repealed by Statute Law (Repeals) Act 2013, s. 1 and Sch. 1, Pt. 10.]

History – Para. 45 repealed by Statute Law (Repeals) Act 2013, s. 1 and Sch. 1, Pt. 10, with effect from 31 January 2013.

46 [Repealed by Statute Law (Repeals) Act 2013, s. 1 and Sch. 1, Pt. 10.]

History – Para. 46 repealed by Statute Law (Repeals) Act 2013, s. 1 and Sch. 1, Pt. 10, with effect from 31 January 2013.

47 [Repealed by ITTOIA 2005, s. 884 and Sch. 3 effective for income tax purposes for 2005–06 onwards and for corporation tax purposes for accounting periods ending after 5 April 2005 (ITTOIA 2005, s. 883(1)).]

THE FINANCE ACT 1994 (c. 9)

48 [Repealed by Statute Law (Repeals) Act 2013, s. 1 and Sch. 1, Pt. 10.]

History – Para. 48 repealed by Statute Law (Repeals) Act 2013, s. 1 and Sch. 1, Pt. 10, with effect from 31 January 2013.

SCHEDULE 22 – SELF-ASSESSMENT: APPEALS

Section 136

THE TAXES MANAGEMENT ACT 1970

1 The Taxes Management Act 1970 shall be amended in accordance with paragraphs 2 to 10 below.

2 [Omitted by FA 2008, s. 113 and Sch. 36, para. 92(e).]

History – Para. 2 omitted by FA 2008, s. 113 and Sch. 36, para. 92(e), with effect from 1 April 2009 (SI 2009/404, art. 2, subject to savings at SI 2009/404, art. 3). Former para. 2 substituted TMA 1970, s. 19A(11).

3 [Repealed by FA 2001, s. 110 and Sch. 33, Pt. 2(13).]

History – Para. 3 repealed by FA 2001, s. 110 and Sch. 33, Pt. II(13), with effect from 11 May 2001 in relation to returns made before or after that date, and whether relating to periods before or after that date.

4 [Repealed by FA 2001, s. 110 and Sch. 33, Pt. 2(13).]

History – Para. 4 repealed by FA 2001, s. 110 and Sch. 33, Pt. II(13), with effect from 11 May 2001 in relation to returns made before or after that date, and whether relating to periods before or after that date.

5 [Substitutes TMA 1970, s. 33A(8) and s. 33A(8A).]

6 [Repeals TMA 1970, s. 42(12) and Sch. 2.]

7 [Inserts TMA 1970, s. 46B–46D and repeals TMA 1970, s. 47.]

8 [Amends TMA 1970, s. 57(3)(c).]

9 [Inserts TMA 1970, Sch. 1A para. 10–11.]

10 [Substitutes TMA 1970, Sch. 3.]

SECTION 102 OF THE TAXES ACT 1988

11 [Amends ICTA 1988, s. 102(1)(a).]

COMMENCEMENT OF SCHEDULE

12 This Schedule has effect in relation to–

(a) any proceedings relating to the year 1996–97 or any subsequent year of assessment, and

(b) any proceedings relating to an accounting period ending on or after the day appointed under section 199 of the Finance Act 1994 for the purposes of Chapter III of Part IV of that Act (self-assessment).

Notes – The appointed day for the purposes of FA 1994, s. 199 is 1 July 1999 (SI 1998/3173 (C.78)).

SCHEDULE 23 – SELF-ASSESSMENT: SCHEDULES 13 AND 16 TO THE TAXES ACT 1988

Section 137

Part I – Schedule 13 to the Taxes Act 1988

1 [Repealed by FA 1998, s. 165 and Sch. 27, Pt. III(2); ITA 2007, s. 1031 and Sch. 3, Pt. 1.]

History – Sch. 23 repealed by ITA 2007, s. 1031 and Sch. 3, Pt. 1, with effect from 6 April 2007. See ITA 2007, Sch. 2 for transitional and saving provisions.

Para. 1 previously repealed by FA 1998, s. 165 and Sch. 27, Pt. III(2) with effect in relation to return periods beginning and accounting periods beginning on or after 6 April 1999.

2 [Repealed by FA 1998, s. 165 and Sch. 27, Pt. III(2); ITA 2007, s. 1031 and Sch. 3, Pt. 1.]

History – Sch. 23 repealed by ITA 2007, s. 1031 and Sch. 3, Pt. 1, with effect from 6 April 2007. See ITA 2007, Sch. 2 for transitional and saving provisions.

Para. 2 previously repealed by FA 1998, s. 165 and Sch. 27, Pt. III(2) with effect in relation to return periods beginning and accounting periods beginning on or after 6 April 1999.

3 [Repealed by FA 1998, s. 165 and Sch. 27, Pt. III(2); ITA 2007, s. 1031 and Sch. 3, Pt. 1.]

History – Sch. 23 repealed by ITA 2007, s. 1031 and Sch. 3, Pt. 1, with effect from 6 April 2007. See ITA 2007, Sch. 2 for transitional and saving provisions.

Para. 3 previously repealed by FA 1998, s. 165 and Sch. 27, Pt. III(2), with effect in relation to return periods beginning and accounting periods beginning on or after 6 April 1999.

4(1) [Repealed by F(No. 2)A 1997, s. 52 and Sch. 8, Pt. II(11); ITA 2007, s. 1031 and Sch. 3, Pt. 1.]

History – Sch. 23 repealed by ITA 2007, s. 1031 and Sch. 3, Pt. 1, with effect from 6 April 2007. See ITA 2007, Sch. 2 for transitional and saving provisions.

Para. 4 previously repealed by F(No. 2)A 1997, s. 52 and Sch. 8, Pt. II(11) (in accordance with s. 36 and Sch. 6, para. 16(6) and (13)), with effect for return periods beginning on or after 6 April 1999.

5 [Repealed by FA 1998, s. 165 and Sch. 27, Pt. III(2); ITA 2007, s. 1031 and Sch. 3, Pt. 1.]

History – Sch. 23 repealed by ITA 2007, s. 1031 and Sch. 3, Pt. 1, with effect from 6 April 2007. See ITA 2007, Sch. 2 for transitional and saving provisions.

Para. 5 previously repealed by FA 1998, s. 165 and Sch. 27, Pt. III(2), with effect in relation to return periods beginning and accounting periods beginning on or after 6 April 1999.

6 [Repealed by F(No. 2)A 1997, s. 52 and Sch. 8, Pt. II(11); ITA 2007, s. 1031 and Sch. 3, Pt. 1.]

History – Sch. 23 repealed by ITA 2007, s. 1031 and Sch. 3, Pt. 1, with effect from 6 April 2007. See ITA 2007, Sch. 2 for transitional and saving provisions.

Para. 6 previously repealed by F(No. 2)A 1997, s. 52 and Sch. 8, Pt. II(11) (in accordance with s. 36 and Sch. 6, para.16(9) and (13)), with effect for return periods beginning on or after 6 April 1999.

7 [Repealed by FA 1998, s. 165 and Sch. 27, Pt. III(2); ITA 2007, s. 1031 and Sch. 3, Pt. 1.]

History – Sch. 23 repealed by ITA 2007, s. 1031 and Sch. 3, Pt. 1, with effect from 6 April 2007. See ITA 2007, Sch. 2 for transitional and saving provisions.

Para. 7 previously repealed by FA 1998, s. 165 and Sch. 27, Pt. III(2), with effect in relation to return periods beginning and accounting periods beginning on or after 6 April 1999.

8 [Repealed by FA 1998, s. 165 and Sch. 27, Pt. III(2); ITA 2007, s. 1031 and Sch. 3, Pt. 1.]

History – Sch. 23 repealed by ITA 2007, s. 1031 and Sch. 3, Pt. 1, with effect from 6 April 2007. See ITA 2007, Sch. 2 for transitional and saving provisions.

Para. 8 previously repealed by FA 1998, s. 165 and Sch. 27, Pt. III(2), with effect in relation to return periods beginning and accounting periods beginning on or after 6 April 1999.

9 [Repealed by FA 1998, s. 165 and Sch. 27, Pt. III(2); ITA 2007, s. 1031 and Sch. 3, Pt. 1.]

History – Sch. 23 repealed by ITA 2007, s. 1031 and Sch. 3, Pt. 1, with effect from 6 April 2007. See ITA 2007, Sch. 2 for transitional and saving provisions.

Para. 9 previously repealed by FA 1998, s. 165 and Sch. 27, Pt. III(2), with effect in relation to return periods beginning and accounting periods beginning on or after 6 April 1999.

Part II – Schedule 16 to the Taxes Act 1988

10-13 [Repealed by ITA 2007, s. 1031 and Sch. 3, Pt. 1.]

History – Sch. 23 repealed by ITA 2007, s. 1031 and Sch. 3, Pt. 1, with effect from 6 April 2007. See ITA 2007, Sch. 2 for transitional and saving provisions.

Notes – Para. 11 rewritten as ITA 2007, s. 957(1), (2).
Para. 12 rewritten as ITA 2007, s. 958(1), (2), (3), (4).

SCHEDULE 24 – SELF-ASSESSMENT: ACCOUNTING PERIODS ETC.

Section 138

Part I – Amendments of the Taxes Management Act 1970

INTRODUCTORY

1 The Taxes Management Act 1970 shall be amended in accordance with this Part of this Schedule.

2 [Repealed by FA 1998, s. 165 and Sch. 27, Pt. III(28).]

History – Para. 2 repealed by FA 1998, s. 165 and Sch. 27, Pt. III(28), with effect in relation to accounting periods ending on or after 1 July 1999, the corporation tax self-assessment appointed day under FA 1994 s. 199 by virtue of SI 1998/3173 (C. 78).

POWER TO ENQUIRE INTO RETURN FOR WRONG PERIOD, ETC.

3 [Repealed by FA 1998, s. 165 and Sch. 27, Pt. III(28).]

History – Para. 3 repealed by FA 1998, s. 165 and Sch. 27, Pt. III(28), with effect in relation to accounting periods ending on or after 1 July 1999, the corporation tax self-assessment appointed day under FA 1994 s. 199 by virtue of SI 1998/3173 (C. 78).

4 [Repealed by FA 1998, s. 165 and Sch. 27, Pt. III(28).]

History – Para. 4 repealed by FA 1998, s. 165 and Sch. 27, Pt. III(28), with effect in relation to accounting periods ending on or after 1 July 1999, the corporation tax self-assessment appointed day under FA 1994 s. 199 by virtue of SI 1998/3173 (C. 78).

5 [Repealed by FA 2001, s. 110 and Sch. 33, Pt. 2(13).]

History – Para. 5 repealed by FA 2001, s. 110 and Sch. 33, Pt. 2(13), with effect from 11 May 2001 in relation to returns made before or after that date, and whether relating to periods before or after that date

AMENDMENT OF RETURN FOR WRONG PERIOD

6 [Repealed by FA 1998, s. 165 and Sch. 27, Pt. III(28).]

History – Para. 6 repealed by FA 1998, s. 165 and Sch. 27, Pt. III(28), with effect in relation to accounting periods ending on or after 1 July 1999, the corporation tax self-assessment appointed day under FA 1994 s. 199 by virtue of SI 1998/3173 (C. 78).

FAILURE TO DELIVER RETURN: DETERMINATIONS

7 [Repealed by FA 1998, s. 165 and Sch. 27, Pt. III(28).]

History – Para. 7 repealed by FA 1998, s. 165 and Sch. 27, Pt. III(28), with effect in relation to accounting periods ending on or after 1 July 1999, the corporation tax self-assessment appointed day under FA 1994 s. 199 by virtue of SI 1998/3173 (C. 78).

COMMENCEMENT

8(1) Paragraphs 3 to 6 above have effect in relation to returns made for periods ending on or after the day appointed under section 199 of the Finance Act 1994 for the purposes of Chapter III of Part IV of that Act (self-assessment).

8(2) [Repealed by FA 1998, s. 165 and Sch. 27, Pt. III(28).]

History – Para. 8(2) repealed by FA 1998, s. 165 and Sch. 27, Pt. III(28), with effect in relation to accounting periods ending on or after the corporation tax self-assessment appointed day (see note below).
The day appointed for the purposes of FA 1994, s. 199 (corporation tax self-assessment) is 1 July 1999 (SI 1998/3173 (C. 78)).

Part II – Other Amendments

GENERAL

9 In this Part of this Schedule **"the appointed day"** means the day appointed as mentioned in paragraph 8(1) above.

REPEAL OF SECTION 8A OF THE TAXES ACT 1988

10 [Repeals ICTA 1988, s. 8A.]

DETERMINATION OF ACCOUNTING DATE

11 [Repealed by CTA 2009, s. 1326 and Sch. 3, Pt. 1.]

History – Para. 11 repealed by CTA 2009, s. 1326 and Sch. 3, Pt. 1, with effect for corporation tax purposes for accounting periods ending on or after 1 April 2009, and for income tax and capital gains tax purposes for the tax year 2009–10 and subsequent tax years.

COMPANIES IN LIQUIDATION

12 [Repealed by CTA 2010, s. 1181 and Sch. 3, Pt. 1.]

History – Para. 12 repealed by CTA 2010, s. 1181 and Sch. 3, Pt. 1, with effect for corporation tax purposes for accounting periods ending on or after 1 April 2010, and for income tax and capital gains tax purposes for the tax year 2010–11 and subsequent tax years.

CONSTRUCTION OF REFERENCES TO ASSESSMENTS

13 [Repealed by FA 1998, s. 165 and Sch. 27, Pt. III(28).]

History – Para. 13 repealed by FA 1998, s. 165 and Sch. 27, Pt. III(28), with effect in relation to accounting periods ending on or after 1 July 1999, the corporation tax self-assessment appointed day under FA 1994 s. 199 by virtue of SI 1998/3173 (C. 78).

SCHEDULE 25 – SELF-ASSESSMENT: SURRENDERS OF ADVANCE CORPORATION TAX

Section 139

[Repealed by FA 1998, s. 165 and Sch. 27, Pt. III(2).]

History – Sch. 25 repealed by FA 1998, s. 165 and Sch. 27, Pt. III(2), with effect in relation to accounting periods of the "surrendering company" (ICTA 1988 s. (1)) beginning on or after 6 April 1999.

SCHEDULE 26 – DAMAGES AND COMPENSATION FOR PERSONAL INJURY

Section 150

[Repealed by ITTOIA 2005, s. 884 and Sch. 3.]

History – Sch. 26 repealed by ITTOIA 2005, s. 884 and Sch. 3 effective for income tax purposes for 2005–06 onwards (ITTOIA 2005, s. 883(1)).

SCHEDULE 27 – FOREIGN INCOME DIVIDENDS

Section 153

CALCULATION OF THE DISTRIBUTABLE FOREIGN PROFIT AND THE NOTIONAL FOREIGN SOURCE ACT

3 [Repealed by F(No. 2)A 1997, s. 52 and Sch. 8, Pt. II(11).]

History – Para. 3 repealed by F(No. 2)A 1997, s. 52 and Sch. 8, Pt. II(11) (in accordance with s. 36 and Sch. 6, para. 3(3)) with effect for accounting periods beginning on or after 6 April 1999.

INTERNATIONAL HEADQUARTERS COMPANY

4 [Repealed by F(No. 2)A 1997, s. 52 and Sch. 8, Pt. II(11).]

History – Para. 4 repealed by F(No. 2)A 1997, s. 52 and Sch. 8, Pt. II(11) (in accordance with s. 36 and Sch. 6, para. 3(3)) with effect for accounting periods beginning on or after 6 April 1999.

LIFE ASSURANCE BUSINESS CHARGED UNDER CASE I OF SCHEDULE D

5(1-2) [Repealed by F(No. 2)A 1997, s. 52 and Sch. 8, Pt. II(6).]

History – Para. 5 repealed by F(No. 2)A 1997, s. 52 and Sch. 8, Pt. II(6) (in accordance with s. 23 and Sch. 3, para. 8) with effect in relation to distributions made on or after 2 July 1997.

SCHEDULE 28 – FOTRA SECURITIES: CONSEQUENTIAL AMENDMENTS

Section 154

THE TAXES ACT 1988

1 [Repeals ICTA 1988, s. 47.]

2 [Repeals ICTA 1988, s. 474(2).]

3(1) [Repealed by TIOPA 2010, s. 378 and Sch. 10, Pt. 12.]

3(2) [Repealed by TIOPA 2010, s. 378 and Sch. 10, Pt. 12.]

3(3) [Repeals ICTA 1988, s. 475(6) and (7).]

History – Para. 3(1) repealed by TIOPA 2010, s. 378 and Sch. 10, Pt. 12, with effect for corporation tax purposes for accounting periods ending on or after 1 April 2010, for income tax and capital gains tax purposes for the tax year 2010–11 and subsequent tax years, and for petroleum revenue tax purposes for chargeable periods beginning on or after 1 July 2010.
Para. 3(2) repealed by TIOPA 2010, s. 378 and Sch. 10, Pt. 12, with effect for corporation tax purposes for accounting periods ending on or after 1 April 2010, for income tax and capital gains tax purposes for the tax year 2010–11 and subsequent tax years, and for petroleum revenue tax purposes for chargeable periods beginning on or after 1 July 2010.

4 [Repealed by SI 2000/2188.]

History – Para. 4 repealed by SI 2000/2188, reg. 6, operative from 1 September 2000, with effect in relation to accounting periods of a company beginning on or after 1 January 2000 and ending on or after 1 September 2000.

5 [Repealed by SI 2006/3271, reg. 43 and Schedule, Pt. 1.]

History – Para. 5 repealed by SI 2006/3271, reg. 43 and Schedule, Pt. 1, with effect from 31 December 2006 in relation to periods of account ending on or after that date.

6 [Amends ICTA 1988, Sch. 24, para. 1(3) and Sch. 27, para. 5(5).]

History – In para. 6, the reference to ICTA 1988, Sch. 27, para. 5(5) repealed by SI 2009/3001, reg. 13(2) and Sch. 2, with effect from 1 December 2009 for various purposes (in accordance with the provisions of SI 2009/3001, reg. 1), subject to transitional and savings provisions in SI 2009/3001, Sch. 1. At the time of this repeal, the reference was to have been omitted prospectively by FA 2008, s. 41(7), with effect from a day which was to have been appointed.

SCHEDULE 29 – PAYING AND COLLECTING AGENTS ETC.

Section 156

Part 1 – The New Chapter

1 [Repealed by FA 2000, s. 156 and Sch. 40, Pt. II(17).]

History – Para. 1 repealed by FA 2000, s. 156 and Sch. 40, Pt. II(17) with effect for relevant payments or receipts in relation to which the chargeable date for the purposes of ICTA 1988, Pt. IV, Ch. VIIA is on or after 1 April 2001.

Part II – Other Provisions

PENALTIES

2 [Repealed by FA 2000, s. 156 and Sch. 40, Pt. II(17).]

History – Para. 2 repealed by FA 2000, s. 156 and Sch. 40, Pt. II(17) with effect for relevant payments or receipts in relation to which the chargeable date for the purposes of ICTA 1988, Pt. IV, Ch. VIIA is on or after 1 April 2001.

AMENDMENTS OF THE TAXES ACT 1988

3 [Repealed by FA 2000, s. 156 and Sch. 40, Pt. II(17).]

History – Para. 3 repealed by FA 2000, s. 156 and Sch. 40, Pt. II(17) with effect for relevant payments or receipts in relation to which the chargeable date for the purposes of ICTA 1988, Pt. IV, Ch. VIIA is on or after 1 April 2001.

4 [Repealed by FA 2000, s. 156 and Sch. 40, Pt. II(17).]

History – Para. 4 repealed by FA 2000, s. 156 and Sch. 40, Pt. II(17) with effect for relevant payments or receipts in relation to which the chargeable date for the purposes of ICTA 1988, Pt. IV, Ch. VIIA is on or after 1 April 2001.

5(1) [Repealed by FA 2000, s. 156 and Sch. 40, Pt. II(17).]

5(2) [Repealed by FA 2000, s. 156 and Sch. 40, Pt. II(17).]

History – Para. 5 repealed by FA 2000, s. 156 and Sch. 40, Pt. II(17) with effect for relevant payments or receipts in relation to which the chargeable date for the purposes of ICTA 1988, Pt. IV, Ch. VIIA is on or after 1 April 2001.

6 [Repealed by FA 2000, s. 156 and Sch. 40, Pt. II(17).]

History – Para. 6 repealed by FA 2000, s. 156 and Sch. 40, Pt. II(17) with effect for relevant payments or receipts in relation to which the chargeable date for the purposes of ICTA 1988, Pt. IV, Ch. VIIA is on or after 1 April 2001.

7 [Repealed by FA 2000, s. 156 and Sch. 40, Pt. II(17).]

History – Para. 7 repealed by FA 2000, s. 156 and Sch. 40, Pt. II(17) with effect for relevant payments or receipts in relation to which the chargeable date for the purposes of ICTA 1988, Pt. IV, Ch. VIIA is on or after 1 April 2001.

AMENDMENT OF THE FINANCE ACT 1989

8 [Repealed by FA 2000, s. 156 and Sch. 40, Pt. II(17).]

History – Para. 8 repealed by FA 2000, s. 156 and Sch. 40, Pt. II(17) with effect for relevant payments or receipts in relation to which the chargeable date for the purposes of ICTA 1988, Pt. IV, Ch. VIIA is on or after 1 April 2001.

SCHEDULE 30 – INVESTMENTS IN HOUSING

Section 160

1-3 [Ceases to have effect by virtue of FA 2006, s. 143 and repealed by FA 2006, s. 178 and Sch. 26, Pt. 4.]

History – Sch. 30 ceases to have effect by virtue of FA 2006, s. 143 and is repealed by FA 2006, s. 178 and Sch. 26, Pt. 4 with effect in relation to accounting periods beginning on or after 19 July 2006.

SCHEDULE 31 – LIFE ASSURANCE BUSINESS LOSSES

Section 163

[Omitted by FA 2012, s. 146 and Sch. 16, para. 247(g)(v).]

History – Sch. 31 omitted by FA 2012, s. 146 and Sch. 16, para. 247(g)(v), with effect in relation to accounting periods beginning on or after 1 January 2013 (FA 2012, s. 148) but subject to transitional provisions in FA 2012, Sch. 17. Where an accounting period would otherwise straddle 1 January 2013, it is deemed to end on 31 December 2012 (FA 2012, s. 149).

SCHEDULE 32 – EQUALISATION RESERVES

Section 166

[Omitted by FA 2012, s. 26(2)(b).]

History – Sch. 32 omitted by FA 2012, s. 26(2)(b), with effect in relation to accounting periods ending on or after 1 January 2016 (SI 2015/1999, art. 2). Former Sch. 32 inserted ICTA 1988, s. 444BA-444BD and amended the Table in TMA 1970, s. 98.

SCHEDULE 33 – MANAGEMENT EXPENSES OF CAPITAL REDEMPTION BUSINESS

Section 168

[Omitted by FA 2012, s. 146 and Sch. 16, para. 247(g)(vi).]

History – Sch. 33 omitted by FA 2012, s. 146 and Sch. 16, para. 247(g)(v), with effect in relation to accounting periods beginning on or after 1 January 2013 (FA 2012, s. 148) but subject to transitional provisions in FA 2012, Sch. 17. Where an accounting period would otherwise straddle 1 January 2013, it is deemed to end on 31 December 2012 (FA 2012, s. 149).

SCHEDULE 34 – PROVISIONAL REPAYMENTS IN CONNECTION WITH PENSION BUSINESS

Section 169

[Repealed by FA 2001, s. 110 and Sch. 33 Pt. 2(12).]

History – Repealed by FA 2001, s. 110 and Sch. 33 Pt. 2(12) in accordance with s. 87, (i.e. broadly in relation to income tax borne by deduction from payments received after 30 September 2001 but not in relation to tax credits referable to the tax exempt business of friendly societies and the ISA business of insurance companies and friendly societies, in respect of distributions made before 6 April 2004).

SCHEDULE 35 – ROLL-OVER RELIEF IN RESPECT OF SHIPS

Section 179

[Repealed by CAA 2001, s. 580 and Sch. 4, with effect as respects allowances and charges falling to be made for chargeable periods ending, for income tax purposes, on or after 6 April 2001, and, for corporation tax purposes, on or after 1 April 2001.]

SCHEDULE 36 – CONTROLLED FOREIGN COMPANIES

Section 182

1 [Repealed by Statute Law (Repeals) Act 2013, s. 1 and Sch. 1, Pt. 10.]

History – Para. 1 repealed by Statute Law (Repeals) Act 2013, s. 1 and Sch. 1, Pt. 10, with effect from 31 January 2013.
Former para. 1(3)(b) and (c) repealed by FA 2005, s. 104 and Sch. 11, Pt. 2(6), with effect in relation to accounting periods beginning on or after 16 March 2005.

2 [Amends ICTA 1988, s. 748(3)(a).]

3(1) Schedule 24 to the Taxes Act 1988 (assumptions for calculating chargeable profits etc.) shall be amended in accordance with the following provisions of this paragraph.

3(2) [Inserts ICTA 1988, Sch. 24, para. 1(3A).]

3(3) [Omitted by FA 2009, s. 36 and Sch. 16, para. 5(c).]

3(4) [Amends ICTA 1988, Sch. 24, para. 2(1).]

3(5) [Inserts ICTA 1988, Sch. 24, para. 4(1A).]

3(6)

(a) [Amends ICTA 1988, Sch. 24, para. 4(2).]

(b) [Repealed by FA 1998, s. 165 and Sch. 27, Pt. III(27).]

3(7) [Repealed by FA 1998, s. 165 and Sch. 27, Pt. III(27).]

3(8) [Omitted by FA 2009, s. 36 and Sch. 16, para. 5(c).]

3(9) [Omitted by FA 2009, s. 36 and Sch. 16, para. 5(c).]

3(10) [Amends ICTA 1988, Sch. 24, para. 10.]

3(11) [Repealed by Statute Law (Repeals) Act 2013, s. 1 and Sch. 1, Pt. 10.]

History – Para. 3(3) omitted by FA 2009, s. 36 and Sch. 16, para. 5(c), with effect in relation to accounting periods of controlled foreign companies beginning on or after 1 July 2009, subject to transitional provisions in FA 2009, Sch. 16, para. 8.
Para. 3(6)(b) and word "and" immediately preceding it, and para. 3(7), repealed by FA 1998, s. 165 and Sch. 27, Pt. III(27), with effect as respects accounting periods of companies resident in the UK which end on or after 1 July 1999, the corporation tax self-assessment appointed day by virtue of SI 1998/3173 (C. 78).
Para. 3(8) omitted by FA 2009, s. 36 and Sch. 16, para. 5(c), with effect in relation to accounting periods of controlled foreign companies beginning on or after 1 July 2009, subject to transitional provisions in FA 2009, Sch. 16, para. 8.
Para. 3(9) omitted by FA 2009, s. 36 and Sch. 16, para. 5(c), with effect in relation to accounting periods of controlled foreign companies beginning on or after 1 July 2009, subject to transitional provisions in FA 2009, Sch. 16, para. 8.
Para. 3(11) repealed by Statute Law (Repeals) Act 2013, s. 1 and Sch. 1, Pt. 10, with effect from 31 January 2013.

4(1) Schedule 25 to the Taxes Act 1988 (cases excluded from direction-making powers) shall be amended as follows.

4(2) [Omitted by FA 2009, s. 36 and Sch. 16, para. 5(c).]

4(3)

(a) [Amends ICTA 1988, Sch. 25, para. 2A(1).]

(b) [Omitted by FA 2009, s. 36 and Sch. 16, para. 5(c).]

(c) [Omits ICTA 1988, Sch. 25, para. 2A(6) and (7).]

4(4)

(a) [Omits ICTA 1988, Sch. 25, para. 3(1)–(4).]

(b) [Amends ICTA 1988, Sch. 25, para. 3(5).]

4(5) [Amends ICTA 1988, Sch. 25, para. 6(2)(b).]

4(6)

(a) [Amends ICTA 1988, Sch. 25, para. 16(2)(a).]

(b) [Amends ICTA 1988, Sch. 25, para. 16(2)(b).]

History – Para. 4(2) omitted by FA 2009, s. 36 and Sch. 16, para. 5(c), with effect in relation to accounting periods of controlled foreign companies beginning on or after 1 July 2009, subject to transitional provisions in FA 2009, Sch. 16, para. 8.
Para. 4(3)(b) omitted by FA 2009, s. 36 and Sch. 16, para. 5(c), with effect in relation to accounting periods of controlled foreign companies beginning on or after 1 July 2009, subject to transitional provisions in FA 2009, Sch. 16, para. 8. .

SCHEDULE 37 – BANKS

Section 198

Part I – "Bank" Re-defined for Certain Purposes

1(1) [Repealed by CTA 2010, s. 1181 and Sch. 3, Pt. 1.]

1(2) [Amends ICTA 1988, s. 828(4).]

History – Para. 1(1) repealed by CTA 2010, s. 1181 and Sch. 3, Pt. 1, with effect for corporation tax purposes for accounting periods ending on or after 1 April 2010, and for income tax and capital gains tax purposes for the tax year 2010–11 and subsequent tax years.

Part II – Amendments of the Taxes Act 1988

PROVISIONS IN WHICH NEW MEANING OF "BANK" APPLIES

2(1) [Provides the text variously inserted by para. 2(2).]

2(2)

(a) [Repealed by CTA 2010, s. 1181 and Sch. 3, Pt. 1.]

(b) [Repealed by ITA 2007, s. 1031 and Sch. 3, Pt. 1.]

(c) [Repealed by ITA 2007, s. 1031 and Sch. 3, Pt. 1.]

(d) [Inserts ICTA 1988, s. 816(3A).]

2(3) [Repealed by ITA 2007, s. 1031 and Sch. 3, Pt. 1 and CTA 2010, s. 1181 and Sch. 3, Pt. 1.]

2(4) [Repealed by CTA 2010, s. 1181 and Sch. 3, Pt. 1.]

History – Para. 2(2)(a) repealed by CTA 2010, s. 1181 and Sch. 3, Pt. 1, with effect for corporation tax purposes for accounting periods ending on or after 1 April 2010, and for income tax and capital gains tax purposes for the tax year 2010–11 and subsequent tax years. Para. 2(2)(b), (c) and (d) repealed by ITA 2007, s. 1031 and Sch. 3, Pt. 1, with effect from 6 April 2007.

Para. 2(3) repealed by CTA 2010, s. 1181 and Sch. 3, Pt. 1, with effect for corporation tax purposes for accounting periods ending on or after 1 April 2010, and for income tax and capital gains tax purposes for the tax year 2010–11 and subsequent tax years. Para. 2(3) also previously repealed by ITA 2007, s. 1031 and Sch. 3, Pt. 1.

Para. 2(4) repealed by CTA 2010, s. 1181 and Sch. 3, Pt. 1, with effect for corporation tax purposes for accounting periods ending on or after 1 April 2010, and for income tax and capital gains tax purposes for the tax year 2010–11 and subsequent tax years.

Notes – Para. 2(2) rewritten as ITA 2007, s. 750(4), 878(2), 879(2).

RELATED AMENDMENTS

3 [Repealed by ITA 2007, s. 1031 and Sch. 3, Pt. 1.]

History – Para. 3 repealed by ITA 2007, s. 1031 and Sch. 3, Pt. 1, with effect from 6 April 2007.

Notes – Para. 3 rewritten as ITA 2007, s. 878(1), 879(1).

4 [Repealed by ITA 2007, s. 1031 and Sch. 3, Pt. 1.]

History – Para. 4 repealed by ITA 2007, s. 1031 and Sch. 3, Pt. 1, with effect from 6 April 2007.

Notes – Para. 4 rewritten as ITA 2007, s. 879(4).

5 [Repealed by CTA 2010, s. 1181 and Sch. 3, Pt. 1.]

History – Para. 5 repealed by CTA 2010, s. 1181 and Sch. 3, Pt. 1, with effect for corporation tax purposes for accounting periods ending on or after 1 April 2010, and for income tax and capital gains tax purposes for the tax year 2010–11 and subsequent tax years.

APPLICATION

6 The amendments of the Taxes Act 1988 made by paragraphs 2 to 5 above apply as mentioned in paragraphs 7 to 10 below.

7 [Repealed by CTA 2010, s. 1181 and Sch. 3, Pt. 1.]

History – Para. 7 repealed by CTA 2010, s. 1181 and Sch. 3, Pt. 1, with effect for corporation tax purposes for accounting periods ending on or after 1 April 2010, and for income tax and capital gains tax purposes for the tax year 2010–11 and subsequent tax years.

8 [Repealed by ITA 2007, s. 1031 and Sch. 3, Pt. 1.]

History – Para. 8 repealed by ITA 2007, s. 1031 and Sch. 3, Pt. 1, with effect from 6 April 2007.

9 The amendments of sections 816 apply in relation to requirements imposed on or after the day on which this Act is passed.

History – In para. 9 the words "745 and" repealed by ITA 2007, s. 1031 and Sch. 3, Pt. 1, with effect from 6 April 2007. Amendment follows Sch. 3, Pt. 1 exactly so does not alter the words "sections" or "apply".

10 The amendments of paragraphs 7 and 10 of Schedule 20 apply in relation to deposits made or, as the case may be, money placed on or after the day on which this Act is passed.

Part III – Other Amendments

AMENDMENTS OF THE MANAGEMENT ACT

11(1) [Provides the text variously inserted by para. 11(2).]

11(2)

(a) [Inserts TMA 1970, s. 17(1A).]

(b) [Repealed by Statute Law (Repeals) Act 2013, s. 1 and Sch. 1, Pt. 10.]

(c) [Inserts TMA 1970, s. 24(3A).]

11(3) [Amends TMA 1970, s. 17(1).]

11(4) [Amends TMA 1970, s. 18(3).]

11(5) This paragraph applies as follows–

(a) the amendments of section 17 apply in relation to interest paid on or after the day on which this Act is passed; and

(b) the amendments of sections 18 and 24 apply in relation to requirements imposed on or after the day on which this Act is passed.

History – Para. 11(2)(b) repealed by Statute Law (Repeals) Act 2013, s. 1 and Sch. 1, Pt. 10, with effect from 31 January 2013.

SCHEDULE 38 – QUOTATION OR LISTING OF SECURITIES

Section 199

THE FINANCE ACT 1973

1 [Repealed by TIOPA 2010, s. 378 and Sch. 10, Pt. 12 .]

History – Para. 1 repealed by TIOPA 2010, s. 378 and Sch. 10, Pt. 12, with effect for corporation tax purposes for accounting periods ending on or after 1 April 2010, for income tax and capital gains tax purposes for the tax year 2010–11 and subsequent tax years, and for petroleum revenue tax purposes for chargeable periods beginning on or after 1 July 2010.

THE TAXES ACT 1988

6(1) [Provides for the amendment of provisions listed in para. 6(2).]

6(2)

(a) [Repealed by FA 2000, Sch. 40, Pt. II(17).]

(b) [Repealed by CTA 2010, s. 1181 and Sch. 3, Pt. 1.]

(c) [Repealed by F(No. 2)A 1997, s. 52 and Sch. 8, Pt. II(11).]

(d) [Repealed by CTA 2010, s. 1181 and Sch. 3, Pt. 1.]

(e) [Repealed by ITA 2007, s. 1031 and Sch. 3, Pt. 1.]

(f) [Repealed by CTA 2010, s. 1181 and Sch. 3, Pt. 1.]

(g) [Repealed by ITA 2007, s. 1031 and Sch. 3, Pt. 1.]

(h) [Repealed by ITA 2007, s. 1031 and Sch. 3, Pt. 1.]

(j) [Amends ICTA 1988, Sch. 9, para. 11(a) and (c).]

(k) [Amends ICTA 1988, Sch. 18, para. 1(5C)(c).]

(l) [Amends ICTA 1988, Sch. 20, para. 5.]

(m) [Repealed by FA 2007, s. 114 and Sch. 27, Pt. 2(15).]

6(3) [Repealed by FA 2000, Sch. 40, Pt. II(17).]

6(4) [Repealed by CTA 2010, s. 1181 and Sch. 3, Pt. 1.]

6(5) [See note below] So far as relating to the provisions mentioned in above, sub-paragraph (1) above has effect in relation to accounting periods ending on or after 1st April 1996.

6(6) [Repealed by CTA 2010, s. 1181 and Sch. 3, Pt. 1.]

6(7) [Repealed by ITA 2007, s. 1031 and Sch. 3, Pt. 1.]

6(8) [Repealed by CTA 2010, s. 1181 and Sch. 3, Pt. 1.]

6(9) So far as relating to the provision mentioned in sub-paragraph (2)(h) above, sub-paragraph (1) above has effect in relation to relevant periods ending on or after 1st April 1996.

6(10) So far as relating to the provisions mentioned in sub-paragraph (2)(j) and (k) above, sub-paragraph (1) above has effect in relation to any time falling on or after 1st April 1996.

6(11) So far as relating to the provision mentioned in sub-paragraph (2)(l) above, sub-paragraph (1) above has effect in relation to chargeable periods ending on or after 1st April 1996.

History – Para. 6(2)(a) repealed by FA 2000, Sch. 40, Pt. II(17) with effect for payments of interest made on or after 1 April 2001.
Para. 6(2)(b) repealed by CTA 2010, s. 1181 and Sch. 3, Pt. 1, with effect for corporation tax purposes for accounting periods ending on or after 1 April 2010, and for income tax and capital gains tax purposes for the tax year 2010–11 and subsequent tax years.
Para. 6(2)(c) repealed by F(No. 2)A 1997, s. 52 and Sch. 8, Pt. II(11) (in accordance with s. 36 and Sch. 6, para. 3(3)) with effect for accounting periods beginning on or after 6 April 1999.
Para. 6(2)(d) repealed by CTA 2010, s. 1181 and Sch. 3, Pt. 1, with effect for corporation tax purposes for accounting periods ending on or after 1 April 2010, and for income tax and capital gains tax purposes for the tax year 2010–11 and subsequent tax years.
Para. 6(2)(e) repealed by ITA 2007, s. 1031 and Sch. 3, Pt. 1, with effect from 6 April 2007.
Para. 6(2)(f) repealed by CTA 2010, s. 1181 and Sch. 3, Pt. 1, with effect for corporation tax purposes for accounting periods ending on or after 1 April 2010, and for income tax and capital gains tax purposes for the tax year 2010–11 and subsequent tax years.
Para. 6(2)(g) repealed by ITA 2007, s. 1031 and Sch. 3, Pt. 1, with effect from 6 April 2007.
Para. 6(2)(h) repealed by ITA 2007, s. 1031 and Sch. 3, Pt. 1, with effect from 6 April 2007.
Para. 6(2)(m) (and the word "and" before it repealed by FA 2007, s. 114 and Sch. 27, Pt. 2(15) with effect in relation to accounting periods of controlled foreign companies beginning on or after 6 December 2006 (subject to the transitional provisions in FA 2007, Sch. 15, para. 10). Former para. 6(2)(m) amended ICTA 1988, Sch. 25, para. 13(2)(c).
Para. 6(3) repealed by FA 2000, Sch. 40, Pt. II(17) with effect for payments of interest made on or after 1 April 2001.
Para. 6(4) repealed by CTA 2010, s. 1181 and Sch. 3, Pt. 1, with effect for corporation tax purposes for accounting periods ending on or after 1 April 2010, and for income tax and capital gains tax purposes for the tax year 2010–11 and subsequent tax years.
In para. 6(5), the reference to para. 6(2)(m) repealed by FA 2007, s. 114 and Sch. 27, Pt. 2(15) with effect in relation to accounting periods of controlled foreign companies beginning on or after 6 December 2006 (subject to the transitional provisions in FA 2007, Sch. 15, para. 10). See also Note below.
In para. 6(5), the reference to para.6(2)(c) repealed by F(No. 2)A 1997, s. 52 and Sch. 8, Pt. II(11) (in accordance with s. 36 and Sch. 6, para. 3(3)) with effect for accounting periods beginning on or after 6 April 1999.

Para. 6(6) repealed by CTA 2010, s. 1181 and Sch. 3, Pt. 1, with effect for corporation tax purposes for accounting periods ending on or after 1 April 2010, and for income tax and capital gains tax purposes for the tax year 2010–11 and subsequent tax years. Former para. 6(6) provided that the amendments made by para. 6(2)(d) should have effect in relation to securities issued on or after 1 April 1996.

Para. 6(7) repealed by ITA 2007, s. 1031 and Sch. 3, Pt. 1, with effect from 6 April 2007.

Para. 6(8) repealed by CTA 2010, s. 1181 and Sch. 3, Pt. 1, with effect for corporation tax purposes for accounting periods ending on or after 1 April 2010, and for income tax and capital gains tax purposes for the tax year 2010–11 and subsequent tax years.

Notes – Para. 6(2) rewritten as ITA 2007, s. 559(1), 872(5), 889(2).

In para. 6(5), the repeal of the reference to para. 6(2)(m) was worded apparently without regard to the amendment made by F(No. 2)A 1997. The text above is the best attempt to reflect the words effecting the changes in FA 2007 although it would appear that the whole subparagraph should now be ignored as redundant.

7 [Repealed by FA 2007, s. 114 and Sch. 27, Pt. 6(5).]

History – Para. 7 repealed by FA 2007, s. 114 and Sch. 27, Pt. 6(5) with effect from 19 July 2007.

Notes – Para. 7(2) rewritten as ITA 2007, s. 274(2).

8 [Repealed by ITTOIA 2005, s. 884 and Sch. 3 effective for income tax purposes for 2005–06 onwards (ITTOIA 2005, s. 883(1)).]

9 [Omitted by FA 2008, s. 66(4)(g)(ii).]

History – Para. 9 omitted by FA 2008, s. 66(4)(g)(ii), with effect in relation to cases where the purchase by the first buyer (within the meaning of section 731(2) of ICTA) is made on or after 1 April 2008.

THE TAXATION OF CHARGEABLE GAINS ACT 1992

10(1) [Provides for the amendment of provisions listed in para. 10(2).]

10(2)

(a) [Amends TCGA 1992, s. 144(8)(b).]

(b) [Amends TCGA 1992, s. 164N(1).]

(c) [Repealed by FA 2000, Sch. 40, Pt. II(10).]

(d) [Amends TCGA 1992, s. 276(2)(c) and (6).]

(e) [Amends TCGA 1992, s. 281(3)(c).]

(f) [Repealed by FA 2000, Sch. 40, Pt. II(10).]

10(3) So far as relating to the provisions mentioned in sub-paragraph (2)(a) and (c) to (f) above, sub-paragraph (1) above has effect in relation to disposals on or after 1st April 1996.

10(4) So far as relating to the provision mentioned in sub-paragraph (2)(b) above, sub-paragraph (1) above has effect in relation to acquisitions of qualifying investments (within the meaning of section 164A of that Act) on or after 1st April 1996.

History – Para. 10(2)(c), (f) repealed by FA 2000, Sch. 40, Pt. II(10) with effect in relation to disposals made on or after 9 November 1999.

11(1) [Amends TCGA 1992, s. 146(4)(b).]

11(2) This paragraph has effect in relation to disposals of options on or after 1st April 1996.

12(1) [Repealed by FA 2007, s. 114 and Sch. 27, Pt. 6(5).]

12(2) [Amends TCGA 1992, Sch. 11, para. 7(1)(a).]

12(3) This paragraph has effect where the relevant date falls on or after 1st April 1996.

History – Para. 12(1) repealed by FA 2007, s. 114 and Sch. 27, Pt. 6(5) with effect from Royal Assent 19 July 2007.

SCHEDULE 39 – ENACTMENT OF CERTAIN INLAND REVENUE EXTRA-STATUTORY CONCESSIONS

Section 201

Part I – Income Tax and Corporation Tax

CAPITAL ALLOWANCES

1 [Repealed by CAA 2001, s. 580 and Sch. 4.]

History – Para. 1 repealed by CAA 2001, s. 580 and Sch. 4, with effect as respects allowances and charges falling to be made for chargeable periods ending, for income tax purposes, on or after 6 April 2001, and, for corporation tax purposes, on or after 1 April 2001.

CONTRIBUTIONS TO OVERSEAS PENSION SCHEMES

2 [Repealed by FA 2004, s. 326 and Sch. 42, Pt. 3.]

History – Para. 2 repealed by FA 2004, s. 326 and Sch. 42, Pt. 3 with effect from 6 April 2006.

Part II – Chargeable Gains

TREATMENT OF COMPENSATION AND INSURANCE MONEY

3(1) Section 23 of the Taxation of Chargeable Gains Act 1992 (receipt of compensation and insurance money not treated as a disposal) shall be amended as follows.

3(2) [Substitutes TCGA 1992, s. 23(6)–(8).]

3(3) The amendments made by this paragraph shall have effect in relation to capital sums received on or after 6th April 1996.

Notes – Para. 3: enactment of ESC D1 and ESC D19.

ASSETS OF NEGLIGIBLE VALUE

4(1) [Substitutes TCGA 1992, s. 24(2).]

4(2) The amendment made by this paragraph shall have effect in relation to claims made on or after 6th April 1996.

Notes – Para. 4: enactment of ESC D28.

SETTLED PROPERTY

5(1) Section 72 of the Taxation of Chargeable Gains Act 1992 (termination of life interest on death of person entitled) shall be amended as follows.

5(2) [Amends TCGA 1992, s. 72(1), (2) and (5).]

5(3) [Substitutes TCGA 1992, s. 72(3) and (4).]

5(4) The amendments made by this paragraph shall have effect in relation to deaths occurring on or after 6th April 1996.

Notes – Para. 5: partial enactment of ESC D43.

6(1) Section 73 of the Taxation of Chargeable Gains Act 1992 (death of life tenant: exclusion of chargeable gain) shall be amended as follows.

6(2) [Amends TCGA 1992, s. 73(1).]

6(3) [Amends TCGA 1992, s. 73(2).]

6(4) [Amends TCGA 1992, s. 73(3).]

6(5) The amendments made by this paragraph shall have effect in relation to deaths occurring on or after 6th April 1996.

Notes – Para. 6: partial enactment of ESC A43.

RETIREMENT RELIEF

7 [Repealed by FA 1998, s. 165 and Sch. 27, Pt. III(31).]

History – Para. 7 repealed by FA 1998, s. 165 and Sch. 27, Pt. III(31), with effect in relation to disposals in 2003–04 and subsequent years of assessment.

Notes – Para. 7: enactment of ESC D48.

RELIEF FOR LOANS TO TRADERS

8(1) Section 253 of the Taxation of Chargeable Gains Act 1992 (relief for loans to traders) shall be amended as follows.

8(2) [Amends TCGA 1992, s. 253(3).]

8(3) [Inserts TCGA 1992, s. 253(3A)].

8(4) [Amends TCGA 1992, s. 253(4).]

8(5) The amendments made by this paragraph shall have effect in relation to claims made on or after 6th April 1996.

Notes – Para. 8: partial enactment of ESC D36.

RELIEF FOR DEBTS ON QUALIFYING CORPORATE BONDS

9(1) Section 254 of the Taxation of Chargeable Gains Act 1992 (relief for debts on qualifying corporate bonds) shall be amended as follows.

9(2) [Amends TCGA 1992, s. 254(2).]

9(3) [Amends TCGA 1992, s. 254(6) and (7).]

9(4) [Amends TCGA 1992, s. 254(8).]

9(5) [Inserts TCGA 1992, s. 254(8A).]

9(6) [Amends TCGA 1992, s. 254(11).]

9(7) The amendments made by this paragraph shall have effect in relation to claims made on or after 6th April 1996.

Notes – Para. 9: partial enactment of ESC D36.

Part III – Stamp Duty

LOST OR SPOILED INSTRUMENTS

10 [Not reproduced here.]

SCHEDULE 40 – GILT STRIPPING: TAXATION PROVISIONS

Section 202

THE TAXES ACT 1988

3-6 [Repealed by ITA 2007, s. 1031 and Sch. 3, Pt. 1.]

History – Para. 3–6 repealed by ITA 2007, s. 1031 and Sch. 3, Pt. 1, with effect from 6 April 2007.

Notes – Para. 3(1) rewritten as ITA 2007, s. 648(7).
Para. 3(2) rewritten as ITA 2007, s. 673(4), (5).
Para. 4 rewritten as ITA 2007, s. 648(5), (6).
Para. 5 rewritten as ITA 2007, s. 674(5).
Para. 6 rewritten as ITA 2007, s. 648(1), (2), (3), (4), (8), 673(6).

7 [Repealed by ITTOIA 2005, s. 884 and Sch. 3 effective for income tax purposes for 2005–06 onwards (ITTOIA 2005, s. 883(1)).]

THE TAXATION OF CHARGEABLE GAINS ACT 1992(c. 12)

8 [Inserts TCGA 1992, Sch. 9, para. 1A.]

FINANCE ACT 1997

(1997 Chapter 16)

[19th March 1997]

ARRANGEMENT OF SECTIONS

PART V – INCOME TAX, CORPORATION TAX AND CAPITAL GAINS TAX

PART V – INCOME TAX, CORPORATION TAX AND CAPITAL GAINS TAX

INCOME TAX CHARGE, RATES AND RELIEFS

54 Charge and rates of income tax for 1997–98

54(1) [Repealed by ITA 2007, s. 1031 and Sch. 3, Pt. 1.]

54(2) [Repealed by ITA 2007, s. 1031 and Sch. 3, Pt. 1.]

54(3) [Repealed by ITA 2007, s. 1031 and Sch. 3, Pt. 1.]

54(4) [Repealed by ITA 2007, s. 1031 and Sch. 3, Pt. 1.]

54(5) [Repealed by FA 2004, s. 326 and Sch. 42, Pt. 2(7).]

History – S. 54(1)–(4) repealed by ITA 2007, s. 1031 and Sch. 3, Pt. 1, with effect from 6 April 2007.
S. 54(5) repealed by FA 2004, s. 326 and Sch. 42, Pt. 2(7), with effect in relation to payments made under contracts relating to construction operations on or after 6 April 2007, by virtue of notice given pursuant to SI 2005/2045, reg. 1. S. 54(5).

Cross references – FA 1995, s. 139(3): definition of "appointed day" for the purposes of ICTA 1988, s. 559(4), (1 August 1999).

55 Modification of indexed allowances

55 [Repealed by ITA 2007, s. 1031 and Sch. 3, Pt. 1.]

History – S. 55 repealed by ITA 2007, s. 1031 and Sch. 3, Pt. 1, with effect from 6 April 2007.

Post-TCGA 1992

56 Blind person's allowance

56(1) [Spent: amends ICTA 1988, s. 265(1).]

56(2) [Omitted by FA 2009, s. 5 and Sch. 1, para. 6(h).]

56(3) Subsection (1) above shall apply for the year 1997–98 and, subject to subsection (2) above, for subsequent years of assessment.

History – S. 56(2) omitted by FA 2009, s. 5 and Sch. 1, para. 6(h), with effect from the tax year 2010–11 and subsequent tax years.

57 Limit on relief for interest

57 [Repealed by ITA 2007, s. 1031 and Sch. 3, Pt. 1.]

History – S. 57 repealed by ITA 2007, s. 1031 and Sch. 3, Pt. 1, with effect from 6 April 2007.

CORPORATION TAX CHARGE AND RATE

58 Charge and rate of corporation tax for 1997

58 [Repealed by F(No. 2)A 1997, s. 52 and Sch. 8, Pt. II(3).]

59 Small companies

59 [Repealed by CTA 2010, s. 1181 and Sch. 3, Pt. 1.]

History – S. 59 repealed by CTA 2010, s. 1181 and Sch. 3, Pt. 1, with effect for accounting periods ending on or after 1 April 2010. S. 59(a) previously repealed by F(No. 2)A 1997, s. 52 and Sch. 8, Pt. II(3).

PAYMENTS FOR WAYLEAVES

60 Wayleaves for electricity cables, telephone lines, etc.

60(1) Section 120 of the Taxes Act 1988 (payments for wayleaves for electricity cables, telephone lines, etc.) shall be amended as follows.

60(2) [Amends ICTA 1988, s. 120(1).]

60(3) [Inserts ICTA 1988, s. 120(1A).]

60(4) [Repeals ICTA 1988, s. 120(2)–(4) and (5)(c).]

60(5) This section has effect in relation to payments made on or after 6th April 1997.

SCHEDULE E

61 Phasing out of relief for profit-related pay

61 [Repealed by Statute Law (Repeals) Act 2013, s. 1 and Sch. 1, Pt. 10, with effect from 31 January 2013.]

62 Travelling expenses etc.

62 [Repealed by ITEPA 2003, Sch. 8, Pt. 1.]

History – S. 62 repealed by ITEPA 2003, Sch. 8, Pt. 1 which has effect for the tax year 2003–04 and subsequent tax years.

63 Work-related training

63 [Repealed by ITEPA 2003, Sch. 8, Pt. 1.]

History – S. 63 repealed by ITEPA 2003, Sch. 8, Pt. 1 which has effect for the tax year 2003–04 and subsequent tax years.

RELIEVED EXPENDITURE, LOSSES ETC.

64 Postponed company donations to charity

64 [Repealed by CTA 2010, s. 1181 and Sch. 3, Pt. 1.]

History – S. 64 repealed by CTA 2010, s. 1181 and Sch. 3, Pt. 1, with effect for corporation tax purposes for accounting periods ending on or after 1 April 2010, and for income tax and capital gains tax purposes for the tax year 2010–11 and subsequent tax years.

65 National Insurance contributions

65 [Repealed by CTA 2009, s. 1326 and Sch. 3, Pt. 1.]

History – S. 65 repealed by CTA 2009, s. 1326 and Sch. 3, Pt. 1, with effect for corporation tax purposes for accounting periods ending on or after 1 April 2009, and for income tax and capital gains tax purposes for the tax year 2009–10 and subsequent tax years.

66 Expenditure on production wells etc.

66 [Repealed by CTA 2009, s. 1326 and Sch. 3, Pt. 1.]

History – S. 66 repealed by CTA 2009, s. 1326 and Sch. 3, Pt. 1, with effect for corporation tax purposes for accounting periods ending on or after 1 April 2009, and for income tax and capital gains tax purposes for the tax year 2009–10 and subsequent tax years. Former s. 66(2) and (5) repealed by CAA 2001, s. 580 and Sch. 4 in respect of allowances and charges falling to be made for chargeable periods ending on or after 6 April 2001 for income tax purposes and 1 April 2001 for corporation tax.

67 Annuity business of insurance companies

67 [Omitted by FA 2012, s. 146 and Sch. 16, para. 247(h).]

History – S. 67 omitted by FA 2012, s. 146 and Sch. 16, para. 247(h) in relation to accounting periods beginning on or after 1 January 2013 (FA 2012, s. 148) but subject to transitional provisions in FA 2012, Sch. 17. Where an accounting period would otherwise straddle 1 January 2013, it is deemed to end on 31 December 2012 (FA 2012, s. 149).

68 Consortium claims for group relief

68 [Repealed by CTA 2010, s. 1181 and Sch. 3, Pt. 1.]

History – S. 68 repealed by CTA 2010, s. 1181 and Sch. 3, Pt. 1, with effect for accounting periods ending on or after 1 April 2010.

DISTRIBUTIONS ETC.

69 Special treatment for certain distributions

69 Schedule 7 to this Act (which makes provision for the treatment of distributions arising on the purchase etc. by a company of its own shares and for cases where a distribution has a connection with a transaction in securities) shall have effect.

70 Distributions of exempt funds

70 [Repealed by F(No. 2)A 1997, s. 52 and Sch. 8, Pt. II(9).]

History – S. 70 repealed by F(No. 2)A 1997, s. 52 and Sch. 8, Pt. II(9), with effect in relation to distributions made on or after 6 April 1999.

71 Set-off against franked investment income

71 [Repealed by F(No. 2)A 1997, s. 52 and Sch. 8, Pt. II(4).]

History – S. 71 repealed by F(No. 2)A 1997, s. 52 and Sch. 8, Pt. II(4), consequentially upon the repeal by that Schedule of ICTA 1988, s. 242 with effect in accordance with F(No. 2)A 1997, s. 20.

72 FIDs paid to unauthorised unit trusts

72 [Repealed by F(No. 2)A 1997, s. 52 and Sch. 8, Pt. II(11).]

History – S. 72 repealed by F(No. 2)A 1997, s. 52 and Sch. 8, Pt. II(11), with effect in accordance with F(No. 2)A 1997, s. 36 and Sch. 6 (i.e. broadly in relation to distributions made on or after 6 April 1999).

73 Tax advantages to include tax credits

73 [Omitted by FA 2008, s. 66(3)(a).]

History – S. 73 omitted by FA 2008, s. 66(3)(a), with effect in relation to transactions in securities entered into on or after 1 April 2008.

INVESTMENTS ETC.

74 Enterprise investment scheme

74 [Repealed by ITA 2007, s. 1031 and Sch. 3, Pt. 2.]

History – S. 74 repealed by ITA 2007, s. 1031 and Sch. 3, Pt. 2, with effect in relation to shares issued after 6 April 2007.

75 Venture capital trusts

75 [Repealed by ITA 2007, s. 1031 and Sch. 3, Pt. 1.]

History – S. 75 repealed by ITA 2007, s. 1031 and Sch. 3, Pt. 1, with effect from 6 April 2007.

Notes – S. 78(1) rewritten as ITA 2007, s. 881.

76 Stock lending and manufactured payments

76 Schedule 10 to this Act (which makes provision for the treatment for the purposes of income tax, corporation tax and capital gains tax of stock lending arrangements and manufactured payments) shall have effect.

77 Bond washing and repos

77 [Omitted by FA 2008, s. 66(4)(h).]

History – S. 77 omitted by FA 2008, s. 66(4)(h), with effect in relation to cases where the purchase by the first buyer (within the meaning of section 731(2) of ICTA) is made on or after 1 April 2008.

78 National Savings Bank interest

78 [Repealed by ITA 2007, s. 1031 and Sch. 3, Pt. 1.]

History – S. 78 repealed by ITA 2007, s. 1031 and Sch. 3, Pt. 1, with effect from 6 April 2007.

Notes – S. 78 rewritten as follows:
S. 78(1): ITA 2007, s. 280(1), (2).
S. 78(2): ITA 2007, s. 281(1).

79 Payments under certain life insurance policies

79 [Omitted by FA 2008, s. 36 and Sch. 14, para. 17(f).]

History – S. 79 omitted by FA 2008, s. 36 and Sch. 14, para. 17(f), with effect–
- so far as relating to corporation tax, for accounting periods beginning on or after 1 April 2008, and
- so far as relating to income tax, for the tax year 2008–09 and subsequent tax years.

Notes – The omitted income tax material is principally rewritten at ITTOIA 2005, s. 490–493, 500 and 504.

80 Futures and options: transactions with guaranteed returns

80(1)–(4) [Repealed by ITTOIA 2005, s. 884 and Sch. 3; effective for income tax purposes for 2005–06 onwards and for corporation tax purposes for accounting periods ending after 5 April 2005 (ITTOIA 2005, s. 883(1)).]

80(5) [Repealed by ITA 2007, s. 1031 and Sch. 3, Pt. 1.]

80(6) [Repealed by ITA 2007, s. 1031 and Sch. 3, Pt. 1.]

80(7) [Repealed by ITTOIA 2005, s. 884 and Sch. 3.]

History – S. 80(5) and (6) repealed by ITA 2007, s. 1031 and Sch. 3, Pt. 1, with effect from 6 April 2007.
S. 80(1)–(4) and (7) repealed by ITTOIA 2005, s. 884 and Sch. 3; effective for income tax purposes for 2005–06 onwards and for corporation tax purposes for accounting periods ending after 5 April 2005 (ITTOIA 2005, s. 883(1)).

Notes – S. 80(5) rewritten as ITA 2007, s. 504(4).

TRANSFER OF ASSETS ABROAD

81 Transfer of assets abroad

81 [Repealed by ITA 2007, s. 1031 and Sch. 3, Pt. 1.]

History – S. 81 repealed by ITA 2007, s. 1031 and Sch. 3, Pt. 1, with effect from 6 April 2007.

Notes – S. 81 rewritten as ITA 2007, s. 721(5), 728(3).

LEASING AND LOAN ARRANGEMENTS

82 Finance leases and loans

82 [Omitted by TIOPA 2010, s. 374 and Sch. 8, para. 232(2) and repealed by TIOPA 2010, s. 378 and Sch. 10, Pt. 8.]

History – S. 82 omitted by TIOPA 2010, s. 374 and Sch. 8, para. 232(2) and repealed by TIOPA 2010, s. 378 and Sch. 10, Pt. 8, with effect for corporation tax purposes for accounting periods ending on or after 1 April 2010, for income tax and capital gains tax purposes for the tax year 2010–11 and subsequent tax years, and for petroleum revenue tax purposes for chargeable periods beginning on or after 1 July 2010.

83 Loan relationships: transitions

83(1)–(5) [Repealed by FA 2004, s. 326 and Sch. 42, Pt. 2(6).]

83(6) Schedule 13 to this Act (which contains amendments of the transitional provisions in Schedule 15 to the Finance Act 1996) shall have effect.

History – S. 83(1)–(5) repealed by FA 2004, s. 326 and Sch. 42, Pt. 2(6) with effect in relation to:
(a) periods of account beginning on or after 1 January 2005, and
(b) in the case of a company required to prepare accounts under the Companies Act 1985 or the Companies (Northern Ireland) Order 1986, any period of account beginning before that date for which the company is required or permitted to prepare such accounts in accordance with international accounting standards.

CAPITAL ALLOWANCES

84 Writing-down allowances on long-life assets

84 Repealed by CAA 2001, s. 580 and Sch. 4.

History – S. 84 repealed by CAA 2001, s. 580 and Sch. 4 in respect of allowances and charges falling to be made for chargeable periods ending on or after 6 April 2001 for income tax purposes and 1 April 2001 for corporation tax.

85 Schedule A cases etc.

85 Schedule 15 to this Act (which makes provision in relation to capital allowances for cases where persons have income chargeable to tax under Schedule A or make lettings of furnished holiday accommodation in the United Kingdom) shall have effect.

86 Capital allowances on fixtures

86 [Repealed by CAA 2001, s. 580 and Sch. 4.]

History – S. 86 repealed by CAA 2001, s. 580 and Sch. 4 in respect of allowances and charges falling to be made for chargeable periods ending on or after 6 April 2001 for income tax purposes and 1 April 2001 for corporation tax.

CHARGEABLE GAINS

87 Re-investment relief

87 Schedule 17 to this Act (which amends Chapter IA of Part V of the Taxation of Chargeable Gains Act 1992) shall have effect.

88 Conversion of securities: QCBs and debentures

88(1) The Taxation of Chargeable Gains Act 1992 shall be amended as follows.

88(2) [Amends TCGA 1992, s. 132(3)(a).]

88(3) [Inserts TCGA 1992, s. 132(4) and (5).]

88(4) [Amends TCGA 1992, s. 116(2).]

88(5) [Amends TCGA 1992, s. 251(6).]

88(6) This section has effect for the purposes of the application of the Taxation of Chargeable Gains Act 1992 in relation to any disposal on or after 26th November 1996 and shall so have effect, where a conversion took place at a time before that date, as if it had come into force before that time.

89 Earn-out rights

89(1) [Inserts TCGA 1992, s. 138A.]

89(2) Subject to subsections (3) to (8) below–

(a) the section 138A inserted by subsection (1) above shall be deemed always to have been a section of the Taxation of Chargeable Gains Act 1992; and

(b) the enactments applying to chargeable periods beginning before 6th April 1992 shall be deemed always to have included a corresponding section.

89(3) Subject to subsections (4) to (6) below, an election under section 138A of the Taxation of Chargeable Gains Act 1992 in respect of a right conferred on any person before 26th November 1996 may be made at any time before the end of the period for the making of such an election in respect of a right conferred on that person on that date.

89(4) An election in respect of a right conferred on any person shall not be made by virtue of subsection (3) above at any time after the final determination of his liability to corporation tax or capital gains tax for the chargeable period in which the right was in fact conferred on him.

89(5) A notice given to an officer of the Board before the day on which this Act is passed shall not have effect as an election under section 138A of the Taxation of Chargeable Gains Act 1992, or the corresponding provision applying to chargeable periods beginning before 6th April 1992, except in accordance with subsection (6) below.

89(6) Where–

(a) any person has given a notification to an officer of the Board before the day on which this Act is passed, and

(b) that notification was given either–

  (i) in anticipation of the right to make an election under section 138A of the Taxation of Chargeable Gains Act 1992, or

  (ii) for the purposes of an extra-statutory concession available to be used by that person for purposes similar to those of that section,

that notification shall, unless the Board otherwise direct, be treated as if it were a valid and irrevocable election made by that person for the purposes of that section or, as the case may be, the corresponding provision.

89(7) Where any notification given as mentioned in subsection (6)(b)(ii) above is treated as an election for the purposes of section 138A of the Taxation of Chargeable Gains Act 1992 or any corresponding provision, that section or, as the case may be, the corresponding provision shall be taken to have no effect by virtue of that election in relation to any disposal before 26th November 1996 of any asset which–

(a) was issued to any person in pursuance of an earn-out right;

(b) was issued to any person in pursuance of any such right as is mentioned in subsection (4) of that section; or

(c) falls for the purposes of that Act to be treated as the same as an asset issued at any time to any person in pursuance of such a right as is mentioned in paragraph (a) or (b) above but is not an asset first held by that person before that time.

89(8) Subsection (7) above shall not prevent section 138A of the Taxation of Chargeable Gains Act 1992 from being taken, for the purposes of applying that Act to any disposal on or after 26th November 1996, to have had effect in relation to–

(a) any disposal before that date on which, by virtue of any of the no gain/no loss provisions (within the meaning of that Act: see section 288(3A) of that Act), neither a gain nor a loss accrued,

(b) any deemed disposal before that date by reference to which a gain or loss falls to be calculated in accordance with section 116(10)(a) of that Act, or

(c) any transaction before that date that would have fallen to be treated as a disposal but for section 127 of that Act.

History – In s. 89(8)(a), the words "no gain/no loss provisions (within the meaning of that Act: see section 288(3A) of that Act)" substituted for the words "enactments specified in section 35(3)(d) of that Act" by FA 2008, s. 8 and Sch. 2, para. 69(2), with effect in relation to disposals on or after 6 April 2008.

Cross references – TCGA 1992, s. 116(10)(a): situation in which the gain or loss is calculated even though the transaction is treated as not involving a disposal of the old asset.
TCGA 1992, s. 127: where reorganisation is not treated as involving a disposal of the original shares.

DOUBLE TAXATION RELIEF

90 Restriction of relief for underlying tax

90 [Repealed by TIOPA 2010, s. 378 and Sch. 10, Pt. 1.]

History – S. 90 repealed by TIOPA 2010, s. 378 and Sch. 10, Pt. 1, with effect for corporation tax purposes for accounting periods ending on or after 1 April 2010, for income tax and capital gains tax purposes for the tax year 2010–11 and subsequent tax years, and for petroleum revenue tax purposes for chargeable periods beginning on or after 1 July 2010.

91 Disposals of loan relationships with or without interest

91 [Repealed by TIOPA 2010, s. 378 and Sch. 10, Pt. 1.]

History – S. 91 repealed by TIOPA 2010, s. 378 and Sch. 10, Pt. 1, with effect for corporation tax purposes for accounting periods ending on or after 1 April 2010, for income tax and capital gains tax purposes for the tax year 2010–11 and subsequent tax years, and for petroleum revenue tax purposes for chargeable periods beginning on or after 1 July 2010.
S. 91(4) previously omitted by FA 2008, s. 62 and Sch. 22, para. 2(2)(b), with effect in relation to related transactions on or after 12 March 2008.
S. 91(5) previously repealed by FA 2007, s. 114 and Sch. 27, Pt. 2(14), with effect on or after 1 October 2007 in relation to those arrangements detailed in the provisions of SI 2007/2483, art. 4(2), (3).

REPAYMENT SUPPLEMENT

92 Time from which entitlement runs

92(1) Section 824 of the Taxes Act 1988 (repayment supplements), where it has effect as amended by paragraph 41 of Schedule 19 to the Finance Act 1994, shall be amended in accordance with subsections (2) to (4) below.

92(2) [Substitutes ICTA 1988, s. 824(3)(a) and (b).]

92(3) [Amends ICTA 1988, s. 824(3)(c).]

92(4) [Substitutes ICTA 1988, s. 824(4).]

92(5) [Amends TCGA 1992, s. 283(2).]

92(6) This section has effect as respects the year 1997–98 and subsequent years of assessment and shall be deemed to have had effect as respects the year 1996–97.

PART VIII – MISCELLANEOUS AND SUPPLEMENTAL

MISCELLANEOUS

110 Obtaining information from social security authorities

110(1) This section applies to–

(a) any information held by the Secretary of State or the Department of Health and Social Services for Northern Ireland for the purposes of any of his or its functions relating to social security; and

(b) any information held by a person in connection with the provision by him to the Secretary of State or that Department of any services which that person is providing for purposes connected with any of those functions.

110(2) Subject to the following provisions of this section, the person holding any information to which this section applies shall be entitled to supply it to–

(a) the Commissioners of Customs and Excise or any person by whom services are being provided to those Commissioners for purposes connected with any of their functions; or

(b) the Commissioners of Inland Revenue or any person by whom services are being provided to those Commissioners for purposes connected with any of their functions.

110(3) Information shall not be supplied to any person under this section except for one or more of the following uses–

(a) use in the prevention, detection, investigation or prosecution of criminal offences which it is a function of the Commissioners of Customs and Excise, or of the Commissioners of Inland Revenue, to prevent, detect, investigate or prosecute;

(b) use in the prevention, detection or investigation of conduct in respect of which penalties which are not criminal penalties are provided for by or under any enactment;

(c) use in connection with the assessment or determination of penalties which are not criminal penalties;

(d) use in checking the accuracy of information relating to, or provided for purposes connected with, any matter under the care and management of the Commissioners of Customs and Excise or the Commissioners of Inland Revenue;

(e) use (where appropriate) for amending or supplementing any such information; and

(f) use in connection with any legal or other proceedings relating to anything mentioned in paragraphs (a) to (e) above.

110(4) An enactment authorising the disclosure of information by a person mentioned in subsection (2)(a) or (b) above shall not authorise the disclosure by such a person of information supplied to him under this section except to the extent that the disclosure is also authorised by a general or specific permission granted by the Secretary of State or by the Department of Health and Social Services for Northern Ireland.

110(5) In this section references to functions relating to social security include references to–

(a) functions in relation to social security benefits (whether contributory or not) or national insurance numbers; and

(b) functions under the Jobseekers Act 1995 or the Jobseekers (Northern Ireland) Order 1995.

110(5AA) [Repealed by TCA 2002, s. 60 and Sch. 6.]

110(5A) Nothing in this section affects any disclosure authorised by section 121F of the Social Security Administration Act 1992 (supply to Inland Revenue of information for purposes of contributions, statutory sick pay or statutory maternity pay of information held by Secretary of State), paragraph 3 of Schedule 5 to the Tax Credits Act 1999 (supply to Inland Revenue for purposes of tax credit of information so held) or section 14 of the Employment Act 2002 (supply to Inland Revenue for purposes of ordinary statutory paternity pay, additional statutory paternity pay or statutory adoption pay of information so held).

110(6) In this section **"conduct"** includes acts, omissions and statements.

110(7) This section shall come into force on such day as the Treasury may by order made by statutory instrument appoint, and different days may be appointed under this subsection for different purposes.

History – In s. 110(5), former reference to social security contributions repealed by Social Security Contributions (Transfer of Functions, etc.) Act 1999, s. 6 and Sch. 6, para. 10(2) and s. 26(3) and Sch. 10, with effect from 1 April 1999 by SI 1999/527 (C. 11), art. 2(b).

In s. 110(5A), the words "ordinary statutory paternity pay, additional statutory paternity pay" substituted for the words "statutory paternity pay" by the Work and Families Act 2006, s. 11 and Sch. 1, para. 45, with effect from 6 April 2010 (SI 2010/495).

In s. 110(5A) the words ", paragraph 3 of Schedule 5 to the Tax Credits Act 1999 (supply to Inland Revenue for purposes of tax credit of information so held) or section 14 of the Employment Act 2002 (supply to Inland Revenue for purposes of statutory paternity pay or statutory adoption pay of information so held)" substituted for former wording by Employment Act 2002, s. 53 and Sch. 7, para. 50, with effect from 26 February 2003 for the purpose of making subordinate legislation in relation to child benefit and guardian's allowance (SI 2003/392); 1 April 2003 for certain other purposes (SI 2003/392); and 1 August 2002 for other purposes (SI 2002/1727).

In s. 110(5A), words from "or paragraph 3" to the end inserted by Tax Credits Act, s. 12(6) and Sch. 5, para. 7(3), with effect from 5 October 1999.
S. 110(5A) inserted by Social Security Contributions (Transfer of Functions, etc.) Act 1999, s. 6 and Sch. 6, para. 10(3), with effect from 1 April 1999 by virtue of SI 1999/527 (C. 11), art. 2(b).
S. 110(5AA) repealed by TCA 2002, s. 60 and Sch. 6, with effect from 8 April 2003 (SI 2003/962).
Former s. 110(5AA) inserted by Tax Credits Act 1999, s. 12(6) and Sch. 5, para. 7(2), with effect from 5 October 1999.

SUPPLEMENTAL

112 Interpretation

112 In this Act **"the Taxes Act 1988"** means the Income and Corporation Taxes Act 1988.

113 Repeals

113(1) The enactments mentioned in Schedule 18 to this Act (which include spent provisions) are hereby repealed to the extent specified in the third column of that Schedule.

113(2) The repeals specified in that Schedule have effect subject to the commencement provisions and savings contained or referred to in the notes set out in that Schedule.

114 Short title

114 This Act may be cited as the Finance Act 1997.

SCHEDULES

SCHEDULE 7 – SPECIAL TREATMENT FOR CERTAIN DISTRIBUTIONS

Section 69

DISTRIBUTIONS TO WHICH SCHEDULE APPLIES

1 [Repealed by F(No. 2)A 1997, s. 52 and Sch. 8, Pt. II(12).]

History – Para. 1 repealed by F(No. 2)A 1997, s. 52 and Sch. 8, Pt. II(12), with effect in relation to distributions made on or after 6 April 1999.

DISTRIBUTIONS TREATED AS FIDs

2 [Repealed by F(No. 2)A 1997, s. 36 and Sch. 6, para. 21(2), s. 52 and Sch. 8, Pt. II(11).]

History – Para. 2 repealed by F(No. 2)A 1997, s. 36 and Sch. 6, para. 21(2), s. 52 and Sch. 8, Pt. II(11), with effect in relation to distributions made on or after 6 April 1999.

Cross references – F(No. 2)A 1997, s. 36(3): no distribution made on or after 6 April 1999 to be treated as a foreign income dividend by virtue of former para. 2(1).

DISTRIBUTIONS TREATED AS SECTION 686 INCOME OF TRUSTEES

3 [Repealed by F(No. 2)A 1997, s. 52 and Sch. 8, Pt. II(9).]

History – Para. 3 repealed by F(No. 2)A 1997, s. 52 and Sch. 8, Pt. II(9), with effect in relation to distributions made on or after 6 April 1999.

STOCK OPTIONS

4 [Repealed by F(No. 2)A 1997, s. 36 and Sch. 6, para. 21(3), s. 52 and Sch. 8, Pt. II(11).]

History – Para. 4 repealed by F(No. 2)A 1997, s. 36 and Sch. 6, para. 21(3), s. 52 and Sch. 8, Pt. II(11), with effect in relation to distributions made on or after 6 April 1999.

DIVIDENDS ON FIXED RATE PREFERENCE SHARES

5 [Repealed by F(No. 2)A 1997, s. 36 and Sch. 6, para. 21(3), s. 52 and Sch. 8, Pt. II(11).]

History – Para. 5 repealed by F(No. 2)A 1997, s. 36 and Sch. 6, para. 21(3), s. 52 and Sch. 8, Pt. II(11), with effect in relation to distributions made on or after 6 April 1999.

PRE-SALE DISTRIBUTIONS

6 [Repealed by F(No. 2)A 1997, s. 36 and Sch. 6, para. 21(3), s. 52 and Sch. 8, Pt. II(11).]

History – Para. 6 repealed by F(No. 2)A 1997, s. 36 and Sch. 6, para. 21(3), s. 52 and Sch. 8, Pt. II(11), with effect in relation to distributions made on or after 6 April 1999.

MANUFACTURED PAYMENTS

7 [Repealed by F(No. 2)A 1997, s. 52 and Sch. 8, Pt. II(12).]

History – Para. 7 repealed by F(No. 2)A 1997, s. 52 and Sch. 8, Pt. II(12), with effect in relation to payments which are representative of distributions made on or after 6 April 1999.

AMENDMENT OF SECTION 95 OF THE TAXES ACT 1988

8(1) [Repealed by CTA 2009, s. 1326 and Sch. 3, Pt. 1.]

8(2) [Partially repealed by ITTOIA 2005, s. 884 and Sch. 3; effective for income tax purposes for 2005–06 onwards and for corporation tax purposes for accounting periods ending after 5 April 2005 (ITTOIA 2005, s. 883(1)).]

8(3) This paragraph has effect in relation to distributions made on or after 26th November 1996.

History – Para. 8(1) repealed by CTA 2009, s. 1326 and Sch. 3, Pt. 1, with effect for corporation tax purposes for accounting periods ending on or after 1 April 2009, and for income tax and capital gains tax purposes for the tax year 2009–10 and subsequent tax years.

INFORMATION TO BE PROVIDED ABOUT DEEMED FID

9 [Repealed by F(No. 2)A 1997, s. 52 and Sch. 8, Pt. II(11).]

History – Para. 9 repealed by F(No. 2)A 1997, s. 52 and Sch. 8, Pt. II(11), with effect in accordance with F(No. 2)A 1997, s. 36 and Sch. 6 (i.e., broadly in relation to distributions made on or after 6 April 1999).

GROUP INCOME

10 [Repealed by F(No. 2)A 1997, s. 52 and Sch. 8, Pt. II(11).]

History – Para. 10 repealed by F(No. 2)A 1997, s. 52 and Sch. 8, Pt. II(11), with effect in accordance with F(No. 2)A 1997, s. 36 and Sch. 6 (i.e., broadly in relation to distributions made on or after 6 April 1999).

DISTRIBUTION ACCOUNTS

11 [Repealed by F(No. 2)A 1997, s. 52 and Sch. 8, Pt. II(11).]

History – Para. 11 repealed by F(No. 2)A 1997, s. 52 and Sch. 8, Pt. II(11), with effect in accordance with F(No. 2)A 1997, s. 36 and Sch. 6 (i.e., broadly in relation to distribution accounts for any distribution period the distribution date for which falls on or after 6 April 1999).

AMENDMENTS CONSEQUENTIAL ON PARAGRAPH 3 ABOVE

12(1) [Repeals ICTA 1988, s. 686(2)(d) and inserts s. 686(2AA). Partially repealed by ITA 2007, s. 1031 and Sch. 3, Pt. 1.]

12(2) [Repealed by ITA 2007, s. 1031 and Sch. 3, Pt. 1.]

12(3) [Repealed by ITTOIA 2005, s. 884 and Sch. 3; effective for income tax purposes for 2005–06 onwards and for corporation tax purposes for accounting periods ending after 5 April 2005 (ITTOIA 2005, s. 883(1)).]

12(4) This paragraph has effect for the year 1997–98 and subsequent years of assessment and shall be deemed to have had effect for the year 1996–97.

History – In para. 12(1) words repealed by ITA 2007, s. 1031 and Sch. 3, Pt. 1, with effect from 6 April 2007.
Para. 12(2) repealed by ITA 2007, s. 1031 and Sch. 3, Pt. 1, with effect from 6 April 2007.

Notes – Para. 12(1) rewritten as ITA 2007, s. 484(1), (2), (4), (5), Sch. 2, para. 102.
Para. 12(2) rewritten as ITA 2007, s. 487(1), (2), (3), (4).

SCHEDULE 8 – ENTERPRISE INVESTMENT SCHEME: QUALIFYING COMPANIES

Section 74

1–6 [Repealed by ITA 2007, s. 1031 and Sch. 3, Pt. 2.]

History – Sch. 8 repealed by ITA 2007, s. 1031 and Sch. 3, Pt. 2, with effect in relation to shares issued after 5 April 2007.

Notes – Para. 2 rewritten as ITA 2007, s. 180.
Para. 4(1) rewritten as ITA 2007, s. 137(1), 181(2), (8).
Para. 4(2) rewritten as ITA 2007, s. 137(1), (3), (4), (5), (7), 140(1), 181(2), (4), (5), (6), (8), 187, Sch. 1, para. 122, 125.
Para. 5 rewritten as ITA 2007, s. 193(5), 194(7).

SCHEDULE 9 – VENTURE CAPITAL TRUSTS: QUALIFYING HOLDINGS

Section 75

1–6 [Repealed by ITA 2007, s. 1031 and Sch. 3, Pt. 1.]

History – Sch. 9 repealed by ITA 2007, s. 1031 and Sch. 3, Pt. 1, with effect from 6 April 2007.

Notes – Para. 2(1) rewritten as ITA 2007, s. 290(1).
Para. 2(2) rewritten as ITA 2007, s. 290(1), (3), (4), (5), (7).
Para. 3 rewritten as ITA 2007, s. 305(7).
Para. 5(1) rewritten as ITA 2007, s. 302(1).
Para. 5(3) rewritten as ITA 2007, s. 302(3), (5).
Para. 5(4) rewritten as ITA 2007, s. 302(3).

SCHEDULE 10 – STOCK LENDING ARRANGEMENTS AND MANUFACTURED PAYMENTS

Section 76

Part I – Stock Lending

APPROVED STOCK LENDING ARRANGEMENTS: TRADERS

1(1) Section 129 of the Taxes Act 1988 (treatment of approved stock lending arrangements when computing the profits of a trade) shall cease to have effect.

1(2) Section 129A of, and Schedule 5A to, that Act (interest on cash collateral for approved stock lending arrangements) shall also cease to have effect.

STOCK LENDING FEES

2(1) [Amends ICTA 1988, s. 129B(3).]

2(2) [Substitutes ICTA 1988, s. 129B(4).]

STOCK LENDING AGREEMENTS UNDER WHICH MANUFACTURED PAYMENTS ARE NOT MADE

3 [Repealed by CTA 2010, s. 1181 and Sch. 3, Pt. 1.]

History – Para. 3 repealed by CTA 2010, s. 1181 and Sch. 3, Pt. 1, with effect for corporation tax purposes for accounting periods ending on or after 1 April 2010, and for income tax and capital gains tax purposes for the tax year 2010–11 and subsequent tax years.

MANUFACTURED PAYMENTS IN STOCK LENDING CASES ETC.

(a) [Repeals ICTA 1988, Sch. 23A, para. 6.]

(b) [Para. 4(b)(iii) repealed by CTA 2010, s. 1181 and Sch. 3, Pt. 1. Remainder of para. 4(b) amends ICTA 1988, Sch. 23A, para. 7(3)(a) and omits Sch. 23A, para. 7(3(b)).]

History – Para. 4(b)(iii) repealed by CTA 2010, s. 1181 and Sch. 3, Pt. 1, with effect for corporation tax purposes for accounting periods ending on or after 1 April 2010, and for income tax and capital gains tax purposes for the tax year 2010–11 and subsequent tax years.

STOCK LENDING ARRANGEMENTS: CAPITAL GAINS

5(1) [Inserts TCGA 1992, s. 263B and s. 263C.]

5(2) [Repeals TCGA 1992, s. 271(9).]

5(3) [Repealed by ITA 2007, s. 1031 and Sch. 3, Pt. 1.]

History – Para. 5(3) repealed by ITA 2007, s. 1031 and Sch. 3, Pt. 1, with effect from 6 April 2007.

Notes – Para. 5(3) rewritten as ITA 2007, s. 653.

PREMIUMS TRUST FUNDS OF LLOYD'S MEMBERS

6 *[Repeals FA 1993, s. 174(4) and (5) and s. 182(1)(ca)(i) and FA 1994, s. 222(4) and (5) and s. 229(ca)(i).]*

COMMENCEMENT

7(1) This Part of this Schedule (except paragraph 4 above) has effect in relation to, and to transfers under, any arrangement made on or after such day as the Treasury may by order made by statutory instrument appoint.

7(2) Paragraph 4 above has effect in relation to any manufactured payment made on or after the day appointed under sub-paragraph (1) above.

Notes – Para. 7(1) rewritten as ITA 2007, Sch. 2, para. 111.
SI 1997/991: the appointed day for the purposes of para. 7(1) is 1 July 1997.

Part II – Manufactured Payments

REPEAL OF SECTION 737 OF THE TAXES ACT 1988

8 [Repeals ICTA 1988, s. 737.]

MEANING OF "FOREIGN INCOME DIVIDEND"

9 [Repealed by F(No. 2)A 1997, s. 52 and Sch. 8, Pt. II(11).]

History – Para. 9 repealed by F(No. 2)A 1997, s. 52 and Sch. 8, Pt. II(11), with effect in accordance with F(No. 2)A 1997, s. 36 and Sch. 6 (i.e. broadly in relation to distributions made on or after 6 April 1999).

MANUFACTURED DIVIDENDS ON UK EQUITIES

10 [Repealed by CTA 2010, s. 1181 and Sch. 3, Pt. 1.]

History – Para. 10 repealed by CTA 2010, s. 1181 and Sch. 3, Pt. 1, with effect for corporation tax purposes for accounting periods ending on or after 1 April 2010, and for income tax and capital gains tax purposes for the tax year 2010–11 and subsequent tax years. Para. 10(2), (3) previously repealed by F(No. 2)A 1997, s. 52 and Sch. 8, Pt. II(11), with effect in accordance with F(No. 2)A 1997, s. 36 and Sch. 6 (i.e. broadly in relation to distributions made on or after 6 April 1999).

MANUFACTURED INTEREST ON UK SECURITIES

11 [Repealed by ITA 2007, s. 1031 and Sch. 3, Pt. 1.]

History – Para. 11 repealed by ITA 2007, s. 1031 and Sch. 3, Pt. 1, with effect from 6 April 2007.

Notes – Para. 11(1) rewritten as ITA 2007, s. 578(1), (2), (3), 579(1), (2), (3), (4), (5), (6), (7), (10), 580(1), (2), (3), 589(1), (2), 591(1), 919(1), (2), (3), 920(1), (2), (3), (4), 921(1), (2), 926(1), 946, 975(1), (2), (5), (6), 1024.
Para. 11(2) rewritten as ITA 2007, s. 602(2), 603(3), 604(4), 606(1), (9).
Para. 11(3) rewritten as ITA 2007, s. 586(2).

REPEAL OF PARAGRAPH 5 OF SCHEDULE 23A

12 [Repeals ICTA 1988, Sch. 23A, para. 5.]

CONSEQUENTIAL AMENDMENTS IN SCHEDULE 23A

13 [Repealed by CTA 2010, s. 1181 and Sch. 3, Pt. 1.]

History – Para. 13 repealed by CTA 2010, s. 1181 and Sch. 3, Pt. 1, with effect for corporation tax purposes for accounting periods ending on or after 1 April 2010, and for income tax and capital gains tax purposes for the tax year 2010–11 and subsequent tax years. Para. 13(3) previously repealed by ITA 2007, s. 1031 and Sch. 3, Pt. 1, with effect from 6 April 2007.

AMENDMENTS OF TAXES MANAGEMENT ACT 1970

14(1) Section 21 of the Taxes Management Act 1970 (information about a market maker's business) shall be amended as follows.

14(2) [Substitutes TMA 1970, s. 21(1).]

14(3) [Amends TMA 1970, s. 21(2).]

14(4) [Amends TMA 1970, s. 21(3).]

14(5) [Substitutes TMA 1970, s. 21(4) and (4A).]

14(6) [Amends TMA 1970, s. 21(5).]

14(7) [Inserts TMA 1970, s. 21(5A).]

14(8) [Substitutes TMA 1970, s. 21(7).]

REPEAL OF POWERS TO MODIFY INFORMATION PROVISIONS

15 [Repeals FA 1986, Sch. 18, para. 7 and 9.]

COMMENCEMENT

16(1) Subject to the following provisions of this paragraph, this Part of this Schedule has effect in relation to any payment of a manufactured dividend or manufactured interest which is a payment made on or after such day as the Treasury may by order made by statutory instrument appoint.

16(2) Paragraph 14 above has effect (instead of in accordance with sub-paragraph (1) above but subject to sub-paragraph (3) below) for the purpose of conferring powers for obtaining information about–

(a) transactions entered into on or after such day as the Treasury may by order made by statutory instrument appoint; and

(b) payments made on or after that day (whether under such transactions or under transactions entered into before that day).

16(3) Nothing in this Part of this Schedule shall affect the exercise, at any time on or after the day appointed under sub-paragraph (2) above, of the powers conferred apart from this Schedule by–

(a) section 21 of the Taxes Management Act 1970, or by any regulations modifying that section, or

(b) section 737(8) of the Taxes Act 1988,

for obtaining information about transactions entered into, or payments made, before that day.

Notes – SI 1997/991: the appointed day for the purposes of para. 16(1), (2) is 1 July 1997.

SCHEDULE 11 – FUTURES AND OPTIONS: TAXATION OF GUARANTEED RETURNS

Section 80

[Repealed by ITTOIA 2005, s. 884 and Sch. 3.]

History – Sch. 11 repealed by ITTOIA 2005, s. 884 and Sch. 3; effective for income tax purposes for 2005–06 onwards and for corporation tax purposes for accounting periods ending after 5 April 2005 (ITTOIA 2005, s. 883(1)).

Notes – The rewritten income tax material is principally at ITTOIA 2005, s. 555 to s. 569.

SCHEDULE 12 – LEASING ARRANGEMENTS: FINANCE LEASES AND LOANS

[All paragraphs of Sch. 12 have been repealed. Para. 1–7, 9–11, 13–17 and 20–30 omitted by CTA 2010, s. 1177 and Sch. 1, para. 296 and repealed by CTA 2010, s. 1181 and Sch. 3, Pt. 2 and also omitted by TIOPA 2010, s. 374 and Sch. 8, para. 232(3) and repealed by TIOPA 2010, s. 378 and Sch. 10, Pt. 8. Para. 12 omitted by TIOPA 2010, s. 374 and Sch. 8, para. 232(3) and repealed by TIOPA 2010, s. 378 and Sch. 10, Pt. 8. Para. 8, 18 and 19 previously repealed as indicated in the History notes attached to those paragraphs (see below).]

History – Para. 1–7, 9–11, 13–17 and 20–30 omitted by CTA 2010, s. 1177 and Sch. 1, para. 296 and repealed by CTA 2010, s. 1181 and Sch. 3, Pt. 2, with effect for accounting periods ending on or after 1 April 2010. Para. 1–7, 9–11, 12, 13–17 and 20–30 omitted by TIOPA 2010, s. 374 and Sch. 8, para. 232(3) and repealed by TIOPA 2010, s. 378 and Sch. 10, Pt. 8, with effect for corporation tax purposes for accounting periods ending on or after 1 April 2010, for income tax and capital gains tax purposes for the tax year 2010–11 and subsequent tax years, and for petroleum revenue tax purposes for chargeable periods beginning on or after 1 July 2010. Para. 8, 18 and 19 previously repealed (see History notes for those paragraphs).

Notes – Sch. 12 rewritten in CTA 2010 as follows:
Para. 1(1): CTA 2010, s. 899(1), (2), (3), (4).
Para. 1(2): CTA 2010, s. 900(1), (2), (3), (4), (5), (6).
Para. 2(1): CTA 2010, s. 899(4), 901(1).
Para. 2(1A): CTA 2010, s. 901(2).
Para. 2(2): CTA 2010, s. 901(3), (4), (6).
Para. 2(3): CTA 2010, s. 901(5).
Para. 2(4): CTA 2010, s. 901(7).
Para. 3(1): CTA 2010, s. 902(2), (3), (4).
Para. 3(2): CTA 2010, s. 902(5).
Para. 3(3): CTA 2010, s. 902(6).
Para. 3(4): CTA 2010, s. 902(7).
Para. 3(5): CTA 2010, s. 902(8).
Para. 3(7): CTA 2010, s. 903(3), (4), (5).
Para. 3(8): CTA 2010, s. 903(1).
Para. 4(1): CTA 2010, s. 904(1).
Para. 4(2): CTA 2010, s. 904(3).
Para. 4(3): CTA 2010, s. 904(4).
Para. 4(4): CTA 2010, s. 904(5), (6).
Para. 4(5): CTA 2010, s. 904(2).
Para. 5(1): CTA 2010, s. 905(1), (2).
Para. 5(2): CTA 2010, s. 905(3).
Para. 6(1): CTA 2010, s. 909(1), (2).
Para. 6(2): CTA 2010, s. 909(5).
Para. 6(3): CTA 2010, s. 907(1), (2).
Para. 6(4): CTA 2010, s. 907(5).
Para. 6(5): CTA 2010, s. 906(3), 908(1).
Para. 6(6): CTA 2010, s. 906(1), 908(2), 909(3), (4).

Para. 6(7): CTA 2010, s. 906(3), 910(1).
Para. 6(8): CTA 2010, s. 906(1), 907(3), (4), 910(2).
Para. 6(9): CTA 2010, s. 906(2).
Para. 7(1): CTA 2010, s. 916(1), (6).
Para.7(2): CTA 2010, s. 916(2).
Para. 7(3): CTA 2010, s. 916(3), (4).
Para. 7(4): CTA 2010, s. 916(3), (4).
Para. 9(1): CTA 2010, s. 911(1), (2).
Para. 9(2): CTA 2010, s. 911(1), (3).
Para. 9(3): CTA 2010, s. 911(4).
Para. 9(4): CTA 2010, s. 911(3), (5).
Para. 9(5): CTA 2010, s. 912(1), (2).
Para. 9(6): CTA 2010, s. 912(3).
Para. 9(7): CTA 2010, s. 911(6), 912(5), Sch. 2, para. 98.
Para. 10(1): CTA 2010, s. 913(1), (2).
Para. 10(2): CTA 2010, s. 913(1), (3).
Para. 10(3): CTA 2010, s. 913(4).
Para. 10(4): CTA 2010, s. 913(3), (5).
Para. 10(5): CTA 2010, s. 914(1), (2), (3).
Para. 10(6): CTA 2010, s. 914(4).
Para. 10(7): CTA 2010, s. 913(6), 914(5).
Para. 11(1): CTA 2010, s. 917(1).
Para. 11(2): CTA 2010, s. 917(1).
Para. 11(3): CTA 2010, s. 918(1), (2).
Para. 11(4): CTA 2010, s. 918(3).
Para. 11(5): CTA 2010, s. 918(4).
Para. 11(6): CTA 2010, s. 918(5).
Para. 11(7): CTA 2010, s. 918(6).
Para. 11(8): CTA 2010, s. 919(1), (2), (3).
Para. 11(9): CTA 2010, s. 921(1), (2).
Para. 11(10): CTA 2010, s. 921(1), (3), (4).
Para. 11(11): CTA 2010, s. 920(1).
Para. 11(12): CTA 2010, s. 920(2), (3).
Para. 11(13): CTA 2010, s. 922(1), (2).
Para. 11(14): CTA 2010, s. 919(4).
Para. 13(1): CTA 2010, s. 923(1).
Para. 13(2): CTA 2010, s. 923(3).
Para. 13(3): CTA 2010, s. 923(4), (5), (9).
Para. 13(4): CTA 2010, s. 923(8), (9).
Para. 13(5): CTA 2010, s. 923(6).
Para. 13(6): CTA 2010, s. 923(7).
Para. 14: CTA 2010, s. 924(1), (2), (3).
Para. 15(1): CTA 2010, s. 925(1), (2).
Para. 15(2): CTA 2010, s. 926(1), (2), (3).
Para. 16(1): CTA 2010, s. 927(1).
Para. 16(1A): CTA 2010, s. 927(3).
Para. 16(2): CTA 2010, s. 927(4), (5), (7).
Para. 16(3): CTA 2010, s. 927(6).
Para. 16(4): CTA 2010, s. 927(8).
Para. 17: CTA 2010, s. 928(1), (2), (3), 929.
Para. 20: CTA 2010, s. 896(1), (2).
Para. 21(1): CTA 2010, s. 897(1).
Para. 21(2): CTA 2010, s. 897(2).
Para. 21(3): CTA 2010, s. 897(2).
Para. 22: CTA 2010, s. 898(1), (2).
Para.23: CTA 2010, s. 932(3).
Para. 24(1): CTA 2010, s. 931(1), (3).
Para. 24(2): CTA 2010, s. 931(2), (4).
Para. 24(3): CTA 2010, s. 931(5).
Para. 25(1): CTA 2010, s. 933(1), (2).
Para. 25(2): CTA 2010, s. 1176(1).
Para. 26: CTA 2010, s. 934(1), (2).
Para. 27(1): CTA 2010, s. 930(1).
Para. 27(2): CTA 2010, s. 930(2).
Para. 27(3): CTA 2010, s. 930(3).
Para. 27(4): CTA 2010, s. 930(4).
Para. 28(5): CTA 2010, s. 935(1), (2).
Para. 28(6): CTA 2010, s. 935(3).
Para. 29: CTA 2010, s. 936.
Para. 30(1): CTA 2010, s. 932(1), (2), 937, 1166(1).
Para. 30(2): CTA 2010, s. 932(4), (5).
Sch. 12 rewritten in TIOPA 2010 as follows:
Para. 1(1): TIOPA 2010, Sch. 3, para. 3.
Para. 1(2): TIOPA 2010, Sch. 3, para. 3.
Para. 2(1): TIOPA 2010, Sch. 3, para. 3.
Para. 2(1A):TIOPA 2010, Sch. 3, para. 3.
Para. 2(2): TIOPA 2010, Sch. 3, para. 3.
Para. 2(3): TIOPA 2010, Sch. 3, para. 3.
Para. 2(4): TIOPA 2010, Sch. 3, para. 3.
Para. 3(1): TIOPA 2010, Sch. 3, para. 3.
Para. 3(2): TIOPA 2010, Sch. 3, para. 3.
Para. 3(3): TIOPA 2010, Sch. 3, para. 3.
Para. 3(4): TIOPA 2010, Sch. 3, para. 3.
Para. 3(5): TIOPA 2010, Sch. 3, para. 3.

Para. 3(7): TIOPA 2010, Sch. 3, para. 3.
Para. 3(8): TIOPA 2010, Sch. 3, para. 3.
Para. 4(1): TIOPA 2010, Sch. 3, para. 3.
Para. 4(2): TIOPA 2010, Sch. 3, para. 3.
Para. 4(3): TIOPA 2010, Sch. 3, para. 3.
Para. 4(4): TIOPA 2010, Sch. 3, para. 3.
Para. 4(5): TIOPA 2010, Sch. 3, para. 3.
Para. 5(1): TIOPA 2010, Sch. 3, para. 3.
Para. 5(2): TIOPA 2010, Sch. 3, para. 3.
Para. 6(1): TIOPA 2010, Sch. 3, para. 3.
Para. 6(2): TIOPA 2010, Sch. 3, para. 3.
Para. 6(3): TIOPA 2010, Sch. 3, para. 3.
Para. 6(4): TIOPA 2010, Sch. 3, para. 3.
Para. 6(5): TIOPA 2010, Sch. 3, para. 3.
Para. 6(6): TIOPA 2010, Sch. 3, para. 3.
Para.6(7): TIOPA 2010, Sch. 3, para. 3.
Para. 6(8): TIOPA 2010, Sch. 3, para. 3.
Para. 6(9): TIOPA 2010, Sch. 3, para. 3.
Para. 7(1): TIOPA 2010, Sch. 3, para. 3.
Para. 7(2): TIOPA 2010, Sch. 3, para. 3.
Para. 7(3): TIOPA 2010, Sch. 3, para. 3.
Para. 7(4): TIOPA 2010, Sch. 3, para. 3.
Para. 9(1): TIOPA 2010, Sch. 3, para. 3.
Para. 9(2): TIOPA 2010, Sch. 3, para. 3.
Para. 9(3): TIOPA 2010, Sch. 3, para. 3.
Para. 9(4): TIOPA 2010, Sch. 3, para. 3.
Para. 9(5): TIOPA 2010, Sch. 3, para. 3.
Para. 9(6): TIOPA 2010, Sch. 3, para. 3.
Para. 9(7): TIOPA 2010, Sch. 3, para. 3.
Para. 10(1): TIOPA 2010, Sch. 3, para. 3.
Para. 10(2): TIOPA 2010, Sch. 3, para. 3.
Para. 10(3): TIOPA 2010, Sch. 3, para. 3.
Para. 10(4): TIOPA 2010, Sch. 3, para. 3.
Para. 10(5): TIOPA 2010, Sch. 3, para. 3.
Para. 10(6): TIOPA 2010, Sch. 3, para. 3.
Para. 10(7): TIOPA 2010, Sch. 3, para. 3.
Para. 11(1): TIOPA 2010, Sch. 3, para. 3.
Para. 11(2): TIOPA 2010, Sch. 3, para. 3.
Para. 11(3): TIOPA 2010, Sch. 3, para. 3.
Para. 11(4): TIOPA 2010, Sch. 3, para. 3.
Para. 11(5): TIOPA 2010, Sch. 3, para. 3.
Para. 11(6): TIOPA 2010, Sch. 3, para. 3.
Para. 11(7): TIOPA 2010, Sch. 3, para. 3.
Para. 11(8): TIOPA 2010, Sch. 3, para. 3.
Para. 11(9): TIOPA 2010, Sch. 3, para. 3.
Para. 11(10): TIOPA 2010, Sch. 3, para. 3.
Para. 11(11): TIOPA 2010, Sch. 3, para. 3.
Para. 11(12): TIOPA 2010, Sch. 3, para. 3.
Para. 11(13): TIOPA 2010, Sch. 3, para. 3.
Para. 11(14): TIOPA 2010, Sch. 3, para. 3.
Para. 12(1): TIOPA 2010, Sch. 3, para. 7.
Para. 12(2): TIOPA 2010, Sch. 3, para. 7.
Para. 12(3): TIOPA 2010, Sch. 3, para. 7.
Para. 12(4): TIOPA 2010, Sch. 3, para. 7.
Para. 12(5): TIOPA 2010, Sch. 3, para. 3.
Para. 12(6): TIOPA 2010, Sch. 3, para. 3, 7.
Para. 12(7): TIOPA 2010, Sch. 3, para. 3.
Para. 13(1): TIOPA 2010, Sch. 3, para. 3.
Para. 13(2): TIOPA 2010, Sch. 3, para. 3.
Para. 13(3): TIOPA 2010, Sch. 3, para. 3.
Para. 13(4): TIOPA 2010, Sch. 3, para. 3.
Para. 13(5): TIOPA 2010, Sch. 3, para. 3.
Para. 13(6):TIOPA 2010, Sch. 3, para. 3.
Para. 14: TIOPA 2010, Sch. 3, para. 3.
Para. 15(1): TIOPA 2010, Sch. 3, para. 4.
Para. 15(2): TIOPA 2010, Sch. 3, para. 4.
Para. 16(1): TIOPA 2010, Sch. 3, para. 4.
Para. 16(1A): TIOPA 2010, Sch. 3, para. 4.
Para. 16(2): TIOPA 2010, Sch. 3, para. 4.
Para. 16(3): TIOPA 2010, Sch. 3, para. 4.
Para. 16(4): TIOPA 2010, Sch. 3, para. 4.
Para. 17: TIOPA 2010, Sch. 3, para. 4.
Para. 20: TIOPA 2010, Sch. 3, para. 2.
Para. 21(1): TIOPA 2010, Sch. 3, para. 2.
Para. 21(2): TIOPA 2010, Sch. 3, para. 2.
Para. 21(3): TIOPA 2010, Sch. 3, para. 2.
Para. 22: TIOPA 2010, Sch. 3, para. 2.
Para. 23: TIOPA 2010, Sch. 3, para. 5.
Para. 24(1): TIOPA 2010, Sch. 3, para. 5.
Para. 24(2): TIOPA 2010, Sch. 3, para. 5.
Para. 24(3): TIOPA 2010, Sch. 3, para. 5.
Para. 25(1): TIOPA 2010, Sch. 3, para. 5.
Para. 25(2): Unnecessary for income tax purposes as ITA 2007, s. 993 will apply: see ITA 2007, s. 1021(1).
Para. 26: TIOPA 2010, Sch. 3, para. 5.

Para. 27(1): TIOPA 2010, Sch. 3, para. 5.
Para.27(2): TIOPA 2010, Sch. 3, para. 5.
Para. 27(3): TIOPA 2010, Sch. 3, para. 5.
Para. 27(4): TIOPA 2010, Sch. 3, para. 5.
Para. 28(5): TIOPA 2010, Sch. 3, para. 5.
Para. 28(6): TIOPA 2010, Sch. 3, para. 5.
Para. 29: TIOPA 2010, Sch. 3, para. 5.
Para. 30(1): TIOPA 2010, Sch. 3, para. 5.
Para. 30(2): TIOPA 2010, Sch. 3, para. 5.

SCHEDULE 13 – LOAN RELATIONSHIPS: AMENDMENT OF TRANSITIONAL PROVISIONS

Section 83

INTRODUCTORY

1 Schedule 15 to the Finance Act 1996 (transitional provisions and savings for loan relationships) shall be amended as follows.

TRANSITIONAL RULES FOR TRANSITIONAL ACCOUNTING PERIODS

2 [Repealed by CTA 2009, s. 1326 and Sch. 3, Pt. 1.]

History – Para. 2 repealed by CTA 2009, s. 1326 and Sch. 3, Pt. 1, with effect for corporation tax purposes for accounting periods ending on or after 1 April 2009, and for income tax and capital gains tax purposes for the tax year 2009–10 and subsequent tax years.

OPENING VALUATIONS AS AT 1ST APRIL 1996

3 [Repealed by CTA 2009, s. 1326 and Sch. 3, Pt. 1.]

History – Para. 3 repealed by CTA 2009, s. 1326 and Sch. 3, Pt. 1, with effect for corporation tax purposes for accounting periods ending on or after 1 April 2009, and for income tax and capital gains tax purposes for the tax year 2009–10 and subsequent tax years.

ADJUSTMENTS IN THE CASE OF PRE-COMMENCEMENT TRADING RELATIONSHIPS

4 [Inserts FA 1996, Sch. 15, para. 5(4A)–(4C).]

CHARGEABLE ASSETS HELD AFTER COMMENCEMENT

5 [Inserts FA 1996, Sch. 15, para. 8(5A).]

ADJUSTMENTS IN THE CASE OF CHARGEABLE ASSETS

6 [Substitutes FA 1996, Sch. 15, para. 11(2) and para. 11(3).]

COMMENCEMENT OF SCHEDULE

7(1) Subject to sub-paragraph (2) below, this Schedule has effect for the purpose of determining the credits and debits to be brought into account in any accounting period ending on or after 14th November 1996.

7(2) Paragraphs 4 and 6 above do not apply in the case of a loan relationship to which the company in question has ceased to be a party before 14th November 1996 unless–

(a) that company ceased to be a party to the relationship as a result of being directly or indirectly replaced as a party to that relationship by another company, and

(b) the transaction, or series of transactions, by virtue of which the replacement took place fell within any of paragraphs (a) to (d) of paragraph 12(1) of Schedule 9 to the Finance Act 1996 (continuity of treatment in the case of groups and certain transfers of insurance business).

7(3) A credit or debit a fraction of which falls to be brought into account under paragraph 6(4) of Schedule 15 to the Finance Act 1996 (election as to adjustments) in an accounting period ending on or after 14th November 1996 shall be determined, for the purposes mentioned in sub-paragraph (1) above, without applying sub-paragraph (2) above in relation to the relevant assumption.

SCHEDULE 14 – CAPITAL ALLOWANCES ON LONG-LIFE ASSETS

Section 84

1 [Repealed by CAA 2001, s. 580 and Sch. 4.]

History – Sch. 14 repealed by CAA 2001, s. 580 and Sch. 4 in respect of allowances and charges falling to be made for chargeable periods ending on or after 6 April 2001 for income tax purposes and 1 April 2001 for corporation tax.

SCHEDULE 15 – CAPITAL ALLOWANCES: SCHEDULE A CASES ETC

Section 85

REPEAL OF EXISTING RULES

1 [Repeals ICTA 1988, s. 32.]

REMOVAL OF RESTRICTION ON SET-OFF OF LOSSES

2(1) [Amends ICTA 1988, s. 379A(2).]

2(2) [Repealed by FA 1998, s. 165 and Sch. 27, Pt. III(4).]

History – Para. 2(2) repealed by FA 1998, s. 165 and Sch. 27, Pt. III(4), with effect, so far as relating to income tax for the year 1998–99 and subsequent years of assessment and, so far as relating to corporation tax, from 1 April 1998 (subject to transitional provisions in FA 1998, Sch. 5, Pt. IV).

NEW GENERAL PROVISION

3 [Repealed by CAA 2001, s. 580 and Sch. 4.]

History – Para. 3 repealed by CAA 2001, s. 580 and Sch. 4 in respect of allowances and charges falling to be made for chargeable periods ending on or after 6 April 2001 for income tax purposes and 1 April 2001 for corporation tax.

4 [Repealed by CAA 2001, s. 580 and Sch. 4.]

History – Para. 34 repealed by CAA 2001, s. 580 and Sch. 4 in respect of allowances and charges falling to be made for chargeable periods ending on or after 6 April 2001 for income tax purposes and 1 April 2001 for corporation tax.

MANNER OF MAKING ALLOWANCES AND CHARGES

5(1) [Repealed by FA 1998, s. 165 and Sch. 27, Pt. III(4).]

5(2) [Repealed by FA 1998, s. 165 and Sch. 27, Pt. III(4).]

5(3) [Repealed by CAA 2001, s. 580 and Sch. 4.]

History – Para. 5(1) and (2) repealed by FA 1998, s. 165 and Sch. 27, Pt. III(4), with effect, so far as relating to income tax for the year 1998–99 and subsequent years of assessment and, so far as relating to corporation tax, from 1 April 1998 (subject to transitional provisions in FA 1998, Sch. 5, Pt. IV).

Para. 5(3) repealed by CAA 2001, s. 580 and Sch. 4 in respect of allowances and charges falling to be made for chargeable periods ending on or after 6 April 2001 for income tax purposes and 1 April 2001 for corporation tax.

6 [Repealed by FA 1998, s. 165 and Sch. 27, Pt. III(4).]

History – Para. 6 repealed by FA 1998, s. 165 and Sch. 27, Pt. III(4), with effect, so far as relating to income tax, for the year 1998–99 and subsequent years of assessment and, so far as relating to corporation tax, from 1 April 1998 (subject to transitional provisions in FA 1998, Sch. 5, Pt. IV).

MEANING OF CAPITAL EXPENDITURE

7 [Repealed by CAA 2001, s. 580 and Sch. 4.]

History – Para. 7 repealed by CAA 2001, s. 580 and Sch. 4 in respect of allowances and charges falling to be made for chargeable periods ending on or after 6 April 2001 for income tax purposes and 1 April 2001 for corporation tax.

CONSEQUENTIAL AMENDMENT OF SECTION 434E OF THE TAXES ACT 1988

8 [Repealed by CAA 2001, s. 580 and Sch. 4.]

History – Para. 8 repealed by CAA 2001, s. 580 and Sch. 4 in respect of allowances and charges falling to be made for chargeable periods ending on or after 6 April 2001 for income tax purposes and 1 April 2001 for corporation tax.

COMMENCEMENT

9(1) Subject to sub-paragraph (2) below, this Schedule has effect–

(a) for the purposes of income tax, in relation to the year 1997–98 and subsequent years of assessment; and

(b) for the purposes of corporation tax, in relation to accounting periods ending on or after 1st April 1997.

9(2) [Repealed by CAA 2001, s. 580 and Sch. 4.]

History – Para. 9(2) repealed by CAA 2001, s. 580 and Sch. 4 in respect of allowances and charges falling to be made for chargeable periods ending on or after 6 April 2001 for income tax purposes and 1 April 2001 for corporation tax.

SCHEDULE 16 – CAPITAL ALLOWANCES ON FIXTURES

Section 86

1 [Repealed by CAA 2001, s. 580 and Sch. 4.]

History – Sch. 16 repealed by CAA 2001, s. 580 and Sch. 4 in respect of allowances and charges falling to be made for chargeable periods ending on or after 6 April 2001 for income tax purposes and 1 April 2001 for corporation tax.

SCHEDULE 17 – CHARGEABLE GAINS: RE-INVESTMENT RELIEF

Section 87

INTRODUCTORY

1 The Taxation of Chargeable Gains Act 1992 shall be amended in accordance with the provisions of this Schedule.

QUALIFYING INVESTMENTS

2(1) [Amends TCGA 1992, s. 164A(8).]

2(2) [Inserts TCGA 1992, s. 164A(8A) and s. 164A(8B).]

LOSS OF RELIEF

3(1) [Amends TCGA 1992, s. 164F(1).]

3(2) [Inserts TCGA 1992, s. 164FA.]

MEANING OF "QUALIFYING COMPANY"

4(1) [Substitutes TCGA 1992, s. 164G(2)(aa).]

4(2) [Substitutes TCGA 1992, s. 164G(4)–(4F).]

MEANING OF "QUALIFYING TRADE"

5(1) [Amends TCGA 1992, s. 164I(1)(a).]

5(2) [Amends TCGA 1992, s. 164I(1)(b).]

INTERPRETATION OF CHAPTER IA OF PART V

6(1) [Substitutes TCGA 1992, s. 164N(2).]

6(2) [Inserts TCGA 1992, s. 164N(5).]

COMMENCEMENT

7(1) This Schedule–

(a) applies in relation to shares acquired after 26th November 1996; and

(b) subject to sub-paragraph (3) below, applies after 26th November 1996 in relation to shares that fall within sub-paragraph (2) below.

7(2) Shares fall within this sub-paragraph if–

(a) they were acquired by a person at any time on or before 26th November 1996;

(b) they were held by him throughout the period beginning with that time and ending with 26th November 1996; and

(c) at all times in that period they were, for the purposes of Chapter IA of Part V of the Taxation of Chargeable Gains Act 1992, eligible shares in a qualifying company.

7(3) The application of the preceding provisions of this Schedule in relation to any shares falling within sub-paragraph (2) above shall not prevent those shares from being (or having been) shares in a qualifying company at any relevant time when those shares would have been shares in such a company if this Schedule had not been enacted.

7(4) For the purposes of sub-paragraph (3) above a time is a relevant time in relation to any shares falling within sub-paragraph (2) above if it is a time after 26th November 1996 and within the period of 3 years after the acquisition of the shares.

FINANCE (NO. 2) ACT 1997

(1997 Chapter 58)

[*31st July 1997*]

ARRANGEMENT OF SECTIONS

PART III – INCOME TAX AND CORPORATION TAX

RELIEFS FOR INTEREST AND PRIVATE MEDICAL INSURANCE

15 Mortgage interest payments

15(1) [Repealed by FA 1999, s. 139 and Sch. 20, Pt. III(7); ITA 2007, s. 1031 and Sch. 3, Pt. 1.]

15(2) [Repealed by FA 1999, s. 139 and Sch. 20, Pt. III(7).]

15(3) [Repealed by FA 1999, s. 139 and Sch. 20, Pt. III(7).]

History – S. 15(1) repealed by ITA 2007, s. 1031 and Sch. 3, Pt. 1, with effect from 6 April 2007. Transitional and saving provisions contained in ITA 2007, Sch. 2.

S. 15 repealed by FA 1999, s. 139 and Sch. 20, Pt. III(7) with effect in relation to any payment of interest falling within FA 1999, s. 38(3) or (4) (broadly, payments made on or after 6 April 2000, or on or after 9 March 1999 and before 6 April 2000 but not falling due until on or after 6 April 2000).

16 Limit on relief for interest for 1998–99

16 [Repealed by ITA 2007, s. 1031 and Sch. 3, Pt. 1.]

History – S. 16 repealed by ITA 2007, s. 1031 and Sch. 3, Pt. 1, with effect from 6 April 2007.

17 Withdrawal of relief on medical insurance premiums

17 [Repealed by Statute Law (Repeals) Act 2013, s. 1 and Sch. 1, Pt. 10.]

History – S. 17 repealed by Statute Law (Repeals) Act 2013, s. 1 and Sch. 1, Pt. 10, with effect from 31 January 2013.

CORPORATION TAX

18 Rates for financial year 1997

18 [Spent: set the rate of corporation tax and the small companies' rate of corporation tax for the financial year 1997.]

DISTRIBUTIONS, TAX CREDITS ETC ON AND AFTER 2ND JULY 1997

20 Losses etc. not to be set against surplus franked investment income

20(1) No claim shall be made under section 242 or 243 of the Taxes Act 1988 (set off of losses etc. against surplus of franked investment income) for any accounting period beginning on or after 2nd July 1997; and section 244(1) of that Act shall cease to have effect accordingly.

20(2) Sections 242(5) and (6) and 243(4) of the Taxes Act 1988 (restoration of loss etc. in later accounting period for which there is a surplus of franked payments) shall not have effect where the later accounting period mentioned in section 242(5)(b) begins on or after 2nd July 1997.

20(3) No amount shall be deducted under paragraph (a), or carried forward and deducted under paragraph (b), of section 244(2) (deduction of tax credit paid from ACT subsequently available for set off or surrender) for any accounting period beginning on or after 2nd July 1997.

20(4) For the purposes of sections 242 and 243 of the Taxes Act 1988, if–

(a) a company has a surplus of franked investment income for an accounting period beginning before 2nd July 1997 and ending on or after that date, and

(b) that surplus exceeds the surplus of franked investment income which the company would have had for that accounting period had it ended on 1st July 1997,

the surplus shall be treated as reduced by the excess.

20(5) Sections 242 to 244 of the Taxes Act 1988 cease to have effect in consequence of, and in accordance with, the foregoing provisions of this section.

20(6) [Amends ICTA 1988, s. 237(4).]

20(7) Subsection (6) above has effect in accordance with subsection (5) above.

21 Estates in administration: distributions to which s. 233(1) applies

21 [Repealed by CTA 2009, s. 1326 and Sch. 3, Pt. 1.]

History – S. 21 repealed by CTA 2009, s. 1326 and Sch. 3, Pt. 1, with effect for corporation tax purposes for accounting periods ending on or after 1 April 2009, and for income tax and capital gains tax purposes for the tax year 2009–10 and subsequent tax years.

22 Lloyd's underwriters

22(1) [Omitted by FA 2016, s. 5 and Sch. 1, para. 57(2).]

22(2) [Omitted by FA 2009, s. 34 and Sch. 14, para. 30(a).]

22(3) In subsection (4) of that section (subsection (2) applies in relation to distributions and associated tax credits notwithstanding section 11(2)(a) or 208 of the Taxes Act 1988)–

(a) [omitted by FA 2009, s. 34 and Sch. 14, para. 30(a).]

(b) [amends FA 1994, s. 219(4)]

22(4) [Inserts FA 1994, s. 219(4A), (4B) and (4C).]

22(5) [Repealed by ITTOIA 2005, s. 884 and Sch. 3 effective for income tax purposes for 2005–06 onwards (ITTOIA 2005, s. 883(1)).]

22(6) [Amends ICTA 1988, s. 231(1).]

22(7) This section has effect in relation to distributions made on or after 2nd July 1997.

History – S. 22(1) omitted by FA 2016, s. 5 and Sch. 1, para. 57(2), with effect in relation to dividends paid or arising (or treated as paid), and other distributions made (or treated as made), in the tax year 2016–17 or at any later time. Former s. 22(1) inserted FA 1993, s. 171(2B).

S. 22(2) omitted by FA 2009, s. 34 and Sch. 14, para. 30(a), with effect in relation to distributions paid on or after 1 July 2009, subject to transitional provisions in FA 2009, Sch. 14, para. 32. Former s. 22(2) amended FA 1994, s. 219(3).

S. 22(3)(a) omitted by FA 2009, s. 34 and Sch. 14, para. 30(a), with effect in relation to distributions paid on or after 1 July 2009, subject to transitional provisions in FA 2009, Sch. 14, para. 32.

23 Insurance companies and friendly societies

23 Schedule 3 to this Act (which makes provision in relation to insurance companies and friendly societies) shall have effect.

DISTRIBUTIONS, TAX CREDITS ETC.: AVOIDANCE

24 Taxation of dealers in respect of distributions etc.

24(1)–(9) [Repealed by CTA 2009, s. 1326 and Sch. 3, Pt. 1.]

24(10) [Repealed by ITTOIA 2005, s. 884 and Sch. 3 effective for income tax purposes for 2005–06 onwards (ITTOIA 2005, s. 883(1)).]

24(11) [Amends ICTA 1988, s. 234.]

24(12) [Amends ICTA 1988, s. 246D(1).]

24(13) [Repeals ICTA 1988, Sch. 23A, para. 2A(2).]

24(14) [Amends FA 1997, Sch. 7, para. 2(3).]

24(15) This section has effect in relation to–

(a) any distribution made on or after 2nd July 1997; and

(b) any payment which is representative of such a distribution.

History – S. 24(1)–(9) repealed by CTA 2009, s. 1326 and Sch. 3, Pt. 1, with effect for corporation tax purposes for accounting periods ending on or after 1 April 2009, and for income tax and capital gains tax purposes for the tax year 2009–10 and subsequent tax years.

25 Repeal of s. 95(5) of the Taxes Act 1988: consequential amendments

25(1) [Repealed by Statute Law (Repeals) Act 2013, s. 1 and Sch. 1, Pt. 10.]

25(2)–(4) [Repealed by ITA 2007, s. 1031 and Sch. 3, Pt. 1.]

25(5)–(7) [Repealed by Statute Law (Repeals) Act 2013, s. 1 and Sch. 1, Pt. 10.]

25(8) This section has effect on and after 2nd July 1997.

History – S. 25(1), (5), (6) and (7) repealed by Statute Law (Repeals) Act 2013, s. 1 and Sch. 1, Pt. 10, with effect from 31 January 2013. S. 25(2) to (4) repealed by ITA 2007, s. 1031 and Sch. 3, Pt. 1, with effect from 6 April 2007.

Notes – S. 25(4) rewritten as ITA 2007, s. 313(7).

26 Purchase and sale of securities

26 [Omitted by FA 2008, s. 66(4)(i)(i).]

History – S. 26 omitted by FA 2008, s. 66(4)(i)(i), with effect in relation to cases where the purchase by the first buyer (within the meaning of ICTA 1988, s. 731(2)) is made on or after 1 April 2008.

27 Payments to companies under section 687 of the Taxes Act 1988

27 [Repealed by CTA 2010, s. 1181 and Sch. 3, Pt. 1.]

History – S. 27 repealed by CTA 2010, s. 1181 and Sch. 3, Pt. 1, with effect for corporation tax purposes for accounting periods ending on or after 1 April 2010, and for income tax and capital gains tax purposes for the tax year 2010–11 and subsequent tax years.

28 Arrangements to pass on value of tax credit

28 [Omitted by FA 2016, s. 5 and Sch. 1, para. 57(3).]

History – S. 28 omitted by FA 2016, s. 5 and Sch. 1, para. 57(3), with effect in relation to dividends paid or arising (or treated as paid), and other distributions made (or treated as made), in the tax year 2016–17 or at any later time. Former s. 28 read as follows:

"*Arrangements to pass on value of tax credit*

28(1) [Inserts ICTA 1988, s. 231B.]

28(2) This section has effect in relation to distributions made on or after 2nd July 1997.".

29 Unauthorised unit trusts

29 [Omitted by ITA 2007, s. 1027 and Sch. 1, para. 378 and repealed by s. 1031 and Sch. 3, Pt. 1.]

History – S. 29 omitted by ITA 2007, s. 1027 and Sch. 1, para. 378 and repealed by s. 1031 and Sch. 3, Pt. 1, with effect from 6 April 2007.

DISTRIBUTIONS, TAX CREDITS ETC. IN AND AFTER 1999–00

30 Tax credits

30(1) Section 231 of the Taxes Act 1988 (tax credits for certain recipients of qualifying distributions) shall be amended in accordance with subsections (2) to (7) below.

30(2) [Partially repealed by ITTOIA 2005, s. 884 and Sch. 3 and repealed by CTA 2010, s. 1181 and Sch. 3, Pt. 1.]

30(3) [Repealed by CTA 2010, s. 1181 and Sch. 3, Pt. 1.]

30(4) [Repeals ICTA 1988, s. 231(2).]

30(5) [Partially repealed by ITTOIA 2005, s. 884 and Sch. 3 effective for income tax purposes for 2005–06 onwards (ITTOIA 2005, s. 883(1)).]

30(6) [Repealed by ITTOIA 2005, s. 884 and Sch. 3 effective for income tax purposes for 2005–06 onwards (ITTOIA 2005, s. 883(1)).]

30(7) [Repeals ICTA 1988, s. 231(3A)–(3D).]

30(8) [Repeals ICTA 1988, s. 231A.]

30(9) [Omitted by FA 2016, s. 5 and Sch. 1, para. 57(4).]

30(10) [Omitted by FA 2016, s. 5 and Sch. 1, para. 57(4).]

30(11) This section has effect in relation to distributions made on or after 6th April 1999.

History – S. 30(2) repealed by CTA 2010, s. 1181 and Sch. 3, Pt. 1, with effect for corporation tax purposes for accounting periods ending on or after 1 April 2010, and for income tax and capital gains tax purposes for the tax year 2010–11 and subsequent tax years. S. 30(2)(a) previously repealed by ITTOIA 2005, s. 884 and Sch. 3 effective for income tax purposes for 2005–06 onwards (ITTOIA 2005, s. 883(1)).

S. 30(3) repealed by CTA 2010, s. 1181 and Sch. 3, Pt. 1, with effect for corporation tax purposes for accounting periods ending on or after 1 April 2010, and for income tax and capital gains tax purposes for the tax year 2010–11 and subsequent tax years.

S. 30(5)(a) and (6) repealed by ITTOIA 2005, s. 884 and Sch. 3 effective for income tax purposes for 2005–06 onwards and for corporation tax purposes for accounting periods ending after 5 April 2005 (ITTOIA 2005, s. 883(1)).

S. 30(9) omitted by FA 2016, s. 5 and Sch. 1, para. 57(4), with effect in relation to dividends paid or arising (or treated as paid), and other distributions made (or treated as made), in the tax year 2016–17 or at any later time. Former s. 30(9) read as follows:

"**30(9)** The amendments made by subsections (5) and (6) above and rewritten in section 397(3) of the Income Tax (Trading and Other Income) Act 2005 do not affect the entitlement of a person who is not resident in the United Kingdom to payment in respect of a tax credit by virtue of arrangements having effect under section 2(1) of the Taxation (International and Other Provisions) Act 2010 of the Taxes Act 1988 (relief by agreement with other countries).".

In former s. 30(9), the words "section 2(1) of the Taxation (International and Other Provisions) Act 2010" substituted for the words "section 788 of the Taxes Act 1988" by TIOPA 2010, s. 374 and Sch. 8, para. 52(2), with effect for corporation tax purposes for accounting periods ending on or after 1 April 2010, for income tax and capital gains tax purposes for the tax year 2010–11 and subsequent tax years, and for petroleum revenue tax purposes for chargeable periods beginning on or after 1 July 2010.
In former s. 30(9) the words "and rewritten in section 397(3) of the Income Tax (Trading and Other Income) Act 2005" inserted by ITTOIA 2005, s. 882(1) and Sch. 1, para. 496(a); effective for income tax purposes for 2005–06 onwards (ITTOIA 2005, s. 883(1)).
S. 30(10) omitted by FA 2016, s. 5 and Sch. 1, para. 57(4), with effect in relation to dividends paid or arising (or treated as paid), and other distributions made (or treated as made), in the tax year 2016–17 or at any later time. Former s. 30(10) read as follows:
"**30(10)** Where–
(a) arrangements having effect under section 2(1) of the Taxation (International and Other Provisions) Act 2010 confer on a person not resident in the United Kingdom the right to a tax credit under section 397 of the Income Tax (Trading and Other Income) Act 2005 in respect of a dividend of a company resident in the United Kingdom, and
(b) the arrangements contain provision for permitting–
(i) tax to be charged or deducted, or
(ii) a reduction in the amount of the tax credit that is paid to be made,
by reference to the aggregate of the dividend and the tax credit, and
(c) the amount of that tax or that reduction exceeds the amount of the tax credit,
that provision shall only have the effect of reducing to nil the amount of the payment to which the person is entitled in respect of the tax credit.".
In former s. 30(10)(a), the words "under section 2(1) of the Taxation (International and Other Provisions) Act 2010" substituted for the words "by virtue of section 788 of the Taxes Act 1988" by TIOPA 2010, s. 374 and Sch. 8, para. 52(3), with effect for corporation tax purposes for accounting periods ending on or after 1 April 2010, for income tax and capital gains tax purposes for the tax year 2010–11 and subsequent tax years, and for petroleum revenue tax purposes for chargeable periods beginning on or after 1 July 2010.
In former s. 30(10)(a) the words "section 397 of the Income Tax (Trading and Other Income) Act 2005" substituted for the former wording by ITTOIA 2005, s. 882(1) and Sch. 1, para. 496(b); effective for income tax purposes for 2005–06 onwards (ITTOIA 2005, s. 883(1)).

Cross references – ICTA 1988, s. 333B(2): power of Treasury to modify effect of s. 30(4) in relation to distributions received before 6 April 2004 by an insurance company in respect of investments of so much of its long term business fund as is referable to section 333 business.
FA 1998, s. 76(1), (2): modification of s. 30 in relation to distributions made before 6 April 2004 in respect of investments held in ISAs and PEPs.
FA 1998, s. 90(1), (2): modification of s. 30(4) in relation to distributions made to friendly societies before 6 April 2004.

31 Rates of tax applicable to Schedule F income etc.

31 [Repealed by ITA 2007, s. 1031 and Sch. 3, Pt. 1.]

History – S. 31 repealed by ITA 2007, s. 1031 and Sch. 3, Pt. 1, with effect from 6 April 2007.

Notes – S. 31 rewritten as follows:
S. 31(2): ITA 2007, s. 13(1), 14(1).
S. 31(3): ITA 2007, s. 12(1), 13(1), 14(1).
S. 31(4): ITA 2007, s. 16(1), (2), (3), (4), (5), (7).
S. 31(5): ITA 2007, s. 8(1), (2), 13(2), 19(1), (2), (3).

32 Trusts

32 [Repealed by ITA 2007, s. 1031 and Sch. 3, Pt. 1.]

History – S. 32 repealed by ITA 2007, s. 1031 and Sch. 3, Pt. 1, with effect from 6 April 2007.

Notes – S. 32 rewritten as follows:
S. 32(2): ITA 2007, s. 479(1), (2), 481(2).
S. 32(3): ITA 2007, s. 479(3), (4), 481(3), (4).
S. 32(4): ITA 2007, s. 9(1), (2).
S. 32(6): ITA 2007, s. 484(2), (4).
S. 32(7): ITA 2007, s. 479(3), 481(3).
S. 32(9): ITA 2007, s. 481(3), 483(1), (2), (3).

33 Estates of deceased persons in administration.

33(1) [Repealed by ITA 2007, s. 1031 and Sch. 3, Pt. 1.]

33(2)–(11) [Repealed by CTA 2009, s. 1326 and Sch. 3, Pt. 1.]

History – S. 33(1) repealed by ITA 2007, s. 1031 and Sch. 3, Pt. 1, with effect from 6 April 2007.
S. 33(2)–(11) repealed by CTA 2009, s. 1326 and Sch. 3, Pt. 1, with effect for corporation tax purposes for accounting periods ending on or after 1 April 2009, and for income tax and capital gains tax purposes for the tax year 2009–10 and subsequent tax years.

Notes – S. 33(1) rewritten as ITA 2007, Sch. 1, para. 566.

34 Tax credits and taxation of distributions: miscellaneous provisions

34 Schedule 4 to this Act (which contains provisions relating to tax credits and the taxation of distributions) shall have effect.

35 Transitional relief for charities etc.

35 [Repealed by FA 2011, s. 91 and Sch. 26, para. 1(1).]

History – S. 35 repealed by FA 2011, s. 91 and Sch. 26, para. 1(1) with effect from 19 July 2011.

36 Foreign income dividends

36(1) No election shall be made under section 246A of the Taxes Act 1988 (election for dividend to be treated as foreign income dividend) in respect of any distributions made on or after 6th April 1999.

36(2) No amount shall be shown as available for distribution as foreign income dividends in the distribution accounts of an authorised unit trust for a distribution period the distribution date for which falls on or after 6th April 1999.

36(3) No distribution made on or after 6th April 1999 shall be treated as a foreign income dividend by virtue of paragraph 2(1) of Schedule 7 to the Finance Act 1997 (Tax Acts to have effect as if qualifying distributions to which Schedule 7 applies were foreign income dividends).

36(4) Schedule 6 to this Act (which makes provision for and in connection with the repeal of provisions relating to foreign income dividends) shall have effect.

36(5) In subsection (2) above, **"distribution accounts"**, **"distribution date"** and **"distribution period"** shall be construed in accordance with section 468H of the Taxes Act 1988 (interpretation of sections 468I to 468R of that Act).

GILT-EDGED SECURITIES

37 Interest to be paid gross

37(1) The Taxes Act 1988 shall be amended as follows.

37(2)–(4) [Repealed by ITA 2007, s. 1031 and Sch. 3, Pt. 1.]

37(5) [Repeals ICTA 1988, s. 51A.]

37(6) [Repealed by FA 1998, s. 165 and Sch. 27, Pt. III(3).]

37(7) [Repealed by ITA 2007, s. 1031 and Sch. 3, Pt. 1.]

37(8) This section has effect in relation to payments of interest falling due on or after 6th April 1998.

37(9)–(13) [Repealed by ITA 2007, s. 1031 and Sch. 3, Pt. 1.]

History – S. 37(2) to (4) repealed by ITA 2007, s. 1031 and Sch. 3, Pt. 1, with effect from 6 April 2007.
S. 37(6), and in s. 37(11) the word "51B", repealed by FA 1998, s. 165 and Sch. 27, Pt. III(3), with effect in relation only to payments of interest falling due on or after 1 April 1999, the day appointed by virtue of SI 1999/619.
S. 37(7) repealed by ITA 2007, s. 1031 and Sch. 3, Pt. 1, with effect from 6 April 2007.
In former s. 37(7) the words "section 722A(5), and in paragraph 3A(2)(a) of Schedule 23A, (which" substituted for the former wording by ITTOIA 2005, s. 882(1) and Sch. 1, para. 497; effective for income tax purposes for 2005–06 onwards and for corporation tax purposes for accounting periods ending after 5 April 2005 (ITTOIA 2005, s. 883(1)).
In s. 37(8) the words "Subject to subsections (9) to (13) below," repealed by ITA 2007, s. 1031 and Sch. 3, Pt. 1, with effect from 6 April 2007.
S. 37(9) to (13) repealed by ITA 2007, s. 1031 and Sch. 3, Pt. 1, with effect from 6 April 2007.
In former s. 37(11) the words "Section 50" substituted for "Sections 50 and 118D(4)" by FA 2000, s. 111(5) with effect for relevant payments or receipts in relation to which the chargeable date for the purposes of ICTA 1988, Pt. IV, Ch. VIIA is on or after 1 April 2001.

Notes – S. 37 rewritten as follows:
S. 37(2): ITA 2007, s. 892(1), 893(1), (2).
S. 37(3): ITA 2007, s. 892(1), 893(1), (2), 894(2), 895(2), (3), 896(3).
S. 37(4): ITA 2007, s. 1024.
S. 37(7): ITA 2007, s. 1024.
S. 37(10): ITA 2007, Sch. 2, para. 165.
S. 37(11): ITA 2007, Sch. 2, para. 166(2).
S. 37(12): ITA 2007, Sch. 2, para. 166(3).

38 Paying and collecting agents

38 [Repealed by FA 2000, s. 156 and Sch. 40, Pt. II(17).]

History – S. 38 repealed by FA 2000, s. 156 and Sch. 40, Pt. II(17) with effect for relevant payments or receipts in relation to which the chargeable date for the purposes of ICTA 1988, Pt. IV, Ch. VIIA is on or after 1 April 2001.

RELIEF FOR LOSSES ETC.

39 Carry-back of trading losses

39 [Repealed by CTA 2010, s. 1181 and Sch. 3, Pt. 1.]

History – S. 39 repealed by CTA 2010, s. 1181 and Sch. 3, Pt. 1, with effect for accounting periods ending on or after 1 April 2010.

40 Carry-back of loan relationship deficits

40 [Omitted by CTA 2009, s. 1322 and Sch. 1, para. 450 and repealed by CTA 2009, s. 1326 and Sch. 3, Pt. 1.]

History – S. 40 omitted by CTA 2009, s. 1322 and Sch. 1, para. 450 and repealed by CTA 2009, s. 1326 and Sch. 3, Pt. 1, with effect for corporation tax purposes for accounting periods ending on or after 1 April 2009, and for income tax and capital gains tax purposes for the tax year 2009–10 and subsequent tax years.

41 Restrictions on group relief

41 [Repealed by CTA 2010, s. 1181 and Sch. 3, Pt. 1.]

History – S. 41 repealed by CTA 2010, s. 1181 and Sch. 3, Pt. 1, with effect for accounting periods ending on or after 1 April 2010.

CAPITAL ALLOWANCES FOR SMALL AND MEDIUM-SIZED BUSINESSES

42 Temporary first-year allowances

42 [Repealed by CAA 2001, s. 580 and Sch. 4.]

History – S. 42 repealed by CAA 2001, s. 580 and Sch. 4 in respect of allowances and charges falling to be made for chargeable periods ending on or after 6 April 2001 for income tax purposes and 1 April 2001 for corporation tax.
S. 42(6), (7) previously repealed by FA 1998, s. 165 and Sch. 27, Pt. III(18) and replaced with FA 1998, s 85(4), (5) with effect in relation to every chargeable period ending on or after 2 July 1998.

43 Expenditure of a small company or small business

43 [Repealed by CAA 2001, s. 580 and Sch. 4.]

History – S. 43 repealed by CAA 2001, s. 580 and Sch. 4 in respect of allowances and charges falling to be made for chargeable periods ending on or after 6 April 2001 for income tax purposes and 1 April 2001 for corporation tax.

CAPITAL ALLOWANCES AND FINANCE LEASES

44 Writing-down allowances for finance lessors

44 [Repealed by CAA 2001, s. 580 and Sch. 4.]

History – S. 44 repealed by CAA 2001, s. 580 and Sch. 4 in respect of allowances and charges falling to be made for chargeable periods ending on or after 6 April 2001 for income tax purposes and 1 April 2001 for corporation tax.

45 Hire-purchase by finance lessors

45 [Repealed by CAA 2001, s. 580 and Sch. 4.]

History – S. 45 repealed by CAA 2001, s. 580 and Sch. 4 in respect of allowances and charges falling to be made for chargeable periods ending on or after 6 April 2001 for income tax purposes and 1 April 2001 for corporation tax.

46 Sale and leaseback etc. using finance leases

46 [Repealed by CAA 2001, s. 580 and Sch. 4.]

History – S. 46 repealed by CAA 2001, s. 580 and Sch. 4 in respect of allowances and charges falling to be made for chargeable periods ending on or after 6 April 2001 for income tax purposes and 1 April 2001 for corporation tax.

47 Meaning of "finance lease"

47 [Repealed by CAA 2001, s. 580 and Sch. 4.]

History – S. 47 repealed by CAA 2001, s. 580 and Sch. 4 in respect of allowances and charges falling to be made for chargeable periods ending on or after 6 April 2001 for income tax purposes and 1 April 2001 for corporation tax.

FILMS

48 Relief for expenditure on production and acquisition

48 [Does not apply by virtue of FA 2006, s. 46(3) and is repealed by FA 2006, s. 178 and Sch. 26, Pt. 3(4).]

History – S. 48 does not apply by virtue of FA 2006, s. 46(3) and is repealed by FA 2006, s. 178 and Sch. 26, Pt. 3(4), with effect from 1 January 2007 (see FA 2006, s. 52 and 53).

PART IV – MISCELLANEOUS AND SUPPLEMENTAL

PROVISIONAL COLLECTION OF TAXES

50 Statutory effect of resolutions etc.

50(1) [Repealed by FA 2011, s. 88(8)(b).]

50(2) [Repealed by FA 1998, s. 165 and Sch. 27, Pt. III(2).]

50(3) [Repealed by FA 2011, s. 88(8)(b).]

History – S. 50(1) and (3) repealed by FA 2011, s. 88(8)(b), with effect from 30 December 2011 (SI 2011/2934).
S. 50(2) repealed by FA 1998, s. 165 and Sch. 27, Pt. III(2), with effect in relation to distributions made on or after 6 April 1999.

SUPPLEMENTAL

51 Interpretation

51 In this Act **"the Taxes Act 1988"** means the Income and Corporation Taxes Act 1988.

52 Repeals

52(1) The enactments mentioned in Schedule 8 to this Act (which include spent provisions) are hereby repealed to the extent specified in the third column of that Schedule.

52(2) The repeals specified in that Schedule have effect subject to the commencement provisions and savings contained or referred to in the notes set out in that Schedule.

53 Short title

53 This Act may be cited as the Finance (No. 2) Act 1997.

SCHEDULES

SCHEDULE 3 – INSURANCE COMPANIES AND FRIENDLY SOCIETIES

Section 23

SECTION 76 OF THE TAXES ACT 1988

1 [Repealed by FA 2004, s. 326 and Sch. 42, Pt. 2(3).]

History – Para. 1 repealed by FA 2004, s. 326 and Sch. 42, Pt. 2(3), with effect, subject to the transitional provisions at s. 43 and 44, for accounting periods beginning on or after 1 April 2004.

SECTION 432E OF THE TAXES ACT 1988

2(1) [Repeals ICTA 1988, s. 432E(6)(b).]

2(2) This paragraph has effect in relation to distributions made on or after 2nd July 1997.

SECTION 434 OF THE TAXES ACT 1988

3 [Repealed by FA 2007, s. 114 and Sch. 27, Pt. 2(7).]

History – Para. 3 repealed by FA 2007, s. 114 and Sch. 27, Pt. 2(7) with effect (FA 2007, s. 38):

- for the purposes of corporation tax, for periods of account of insurance companies beginning on or after 1 January 2007; and
- for the purposes of income tax, for the 2007–08 tax year and subsequent tax years.

Former para. 3(3), (6) repealed by FA 1998, s. 165 and Sch. 27, Pt. III(2), with effect in relation to franked investment income which is attributable to distributions made on or after 6 April 1999.

Former para. 3(4), (7) repealed by FA 1998, s. 165 and Sch. 27, Pt. III(2), with effect in relation to accounting periods beginning on or after 6 April 1999.

SECTION 434A OF THE TAXES ACT 1988

4(1) [Repeals ICTA 1988, s. 434A(1).]

4(2) This paragraph has effect for accounting periods beginning on or after 2nd July 1997.

SECTION 436 OF THE TAXES ACT 1988

5(1) [Repeals ICTA 1988, s. 436(3)(d), (e).]

5(2) This paragraph has effect in relation to distributions made on or after 2nd July 1997.

SECTION 438 OF THE TAXES ACT 1988

6(1) Section 438 of the Taxes Act 1988 (pension business: exemption from tax) shall be amended as follows.

6(2) [Repeals ICTA 1988, s. 438(3), (3AA).]

6(3) [Repealed by FA 2007, s. 114 and Sch. 27, Pt. 2(7).]

6(4) [Repeals ICTA 1988, s. 438(5).]

6(5) [Repeals ICTA 1988, s. 438(6), (7).]

6(6) [Repeals ICTA 1988, s. 438(9).]

6(7) Sub-paragraphs (2) to (4) above have effect in relation to distributions made on or after 2nd July 1997.

6(8) Sub-paragraphs (5) and (6) above have effect for accounting periods beginning on or after 2nd July 1997.

6(9) In determining, for the purposes of subsections (6) to (7) of section 438 of the Taxes Act 1988, the franked investment income of, or foreign income dividends arising to, an insurance company for an accounting period beginning before 2nd July 1997 and ending on or after that date, there shall be left out of account any distributions which are made on or after 2nd July 1997.

History – Para. 6(3) repealed by FA 2007, s. 114 and Sch. 27, Pt. 2(7) with effect (FA 2007, s. 38):

- for the purposes of corporation tax, for periods of account of insurance companies beginning on or after 1 January 2007; and
- for the purposes of income tax, for the 2007–08 tax year and subsequent tax years.

SECTION 439B OF THE TAXES ACT 1988

7(1) [Repeals ICTA 1988, s. 439B(7).]

7(2) This paragraph has effect in relation to distributions made on or after 2nd July 1997.

SECTION 440B OF THE TAXES ACT 1988

8(1) Section 440B of the Taxes Act 1988 (modifications where tax charged under Case I of Schedule D) shall be amended as follows.

8(2) [Repeals ICTA 1988, s. 440B(1A).]

8(3) [Repeals ICTA 1988, s. 440B(2).]

8(4) Sub-paragraph (2) above has effect in relation to distributions made on or after 2nd July 1997.

8(5) Sub-paragraph (3) above has effect for accounting periods beginning on or after 2nd July 1997.

SECTION 441A OF THE TAXES ACT 1988

9 [Repealed by Statute Law (Repeals) Act 2013, s. 1 and Sch. 1, Pt. 10.]

History – Para. 9 repealed by Statute Law (Repeals) Act 2013, s. 1 and Sch. 1, Pt. 10, with effect from 31 January 2013.

SCHEDULE 19AB TO THE TAXES ACT 1988

10 [Repealed by FA 2001, s. 87 and Sch. 33, Pt. 2(12).]

History – Para. 10 repealed by FA 2001, s. 87 and Sch. 33, Pt. 2(12) in relation to tax credits in respect of distributions made on or after 6 April 2004, and in relation to income tax borne by deduction from payments received on or after 30 September 2001.

11 [Repealed by FA 2001, s. 87 and Sch. 33, Pt. 2(12).]

History – Para. 11 repealed by FA 2001, s. 87 and Sch. 33, Pt. 2(12) in relation to tax credits in respect of distributions made on or after 6 April 2004, and in relation to income tax borne by deduction from payments received on or after 30 September 2001.

12 [Repealed by FA 2001, s. 87 and Sch. 33, Pt. 2(12).]

History – Para. 12 repealed by FA 2001, s. 87 and Sch. 33, Pt. 2(12) in relation to tax credits in respect of distributions made on or after 6 April 2004, and in relation to income tax borne by deduction from payments received on or after 30 September 2001. Para. 12(2) was repealed from 11 May 2001.

Cross references – FA 1998, s. 90(3): modification of para. 12(2) with regard to exempt distributions to friendly societies falling within FA 1998, s. 90(1)(b).

SCHEDULE 19AC TO THE TAXES ACT 1988

13 [Repealed by SI 2006/3271, reg. 43 and Schedule, Pt. 1.]

History – Para. 13 repealed by SI 2006/3271, reg. 43 and Schedule, Pt. 1 with effect from 31 December 2006 in relation to accounting periods ending on or after that date.
Former para. 13(13) repealed by FA 2001, s. 87 and Sch. 33, Pt. 2(12) in relation to tax credits in respect of distributions made on or after 6 April 2004, and in relation to income tax borne by deduction from payments received on or after 30 September 2001.

SECTION 89 OF THE FINANCE ACT 1989

14(1) Section 89 of the Finance Act 1989 (policy holders' share of profits) shall be amended as follows.

14(2)

(a) [Repeals FA 1989, s. 89(2)(a).]

(b) [Amends FA 1989, s. 89(2)(b).]

(c) [Amends FA 1989, s. 89(2)(c).]

14(3) [Repeals FA 1989, s. 89(8).]

14(4) This paragraph has effect in relation to distributions made on or after 2nd July 1997.

SECTION 65 OF THE FINANCE (NO. 2) ACT 1992

15 [Repealed by FA 2007, s. 114 and Sch. 27, Pt. 2(7).]

History – Para. 15 repealed by FA 2007, s. 114 and Sch. 27, Pt. 2(7) with effect for periods of account of insurance companies beginning on or after 1 January 2007 (subject to the transitional provisions at FA 2007, Sch. 8, para. 28 and 29) (FA 2007, s. 39).

SCHEDULE 4 – TAX CREDITS, TAXATION OF DISTRIBUTIONS ETC.

Section 34

Part I – General

THE TAXES MANAGEMENT ACT 1970

Section 7

1(1) [Amends TMA 1970, s. 7(6).]

1(2) This paragraph has effect for the year 1999–00 and subsequent years of assessment.

SECTION 42 (PRE-CORPORATION TAX SELF-ASSESSMENT VERSION)

2(1) [Repeals pre-self assessment versions of TMA 1970, s. 42(5) (part), (5A) and (10A).]

2(2) This paragraph has effect in relation to tax credits in respect of distributions made on or after 6th April 1999.

Cross references – FA 1998, s. 90(2)(b): disapplication of para. 2 in respect of any exempt distribution to a friendly society falling within FA 1998, s. 90(1).

SI 1998/1871, reg. 4(2)(a): para. 2 deemed to be omitted in relation to any distribution made to an insurance company on or after 6 April 1999 but before 6 April 2004 which is a distribution received by the insurance company in respect of investments of so much of its long term business fund as is referable to its individual savings account business.

SECTION 42 (CORPORATION TAX SELF-ASSESSMENT VERSION)

3 [Repealed by FA 1998, s. 165 and Sch. 27, Pt. III(28).]

History – Para. 3 repealed by FA 1998, s. 165 and Sch. 27, Pt. III(28) with effect in relation to accounting periods ending on or after 1 July 1999, the self-assessment appointed day (FA 1999, s. 199 and SI 1998/3173 (C. 78).

THE TAXES ACT 1988

SECTION 231

4 [Repealed by ITTOIA 2005, s. 884 and Sch. 3 effective for income tax purposes for 2005–06 onwards and for corporation tax purposes for accounting periods ending after 5 April 2005 (ITTOIA 2005, s. 883(1)).]

SECTION 232

5 [Repealed by ITTOIA 2005, s. 884 and Sch. 3 effective for income tax purposes for 2005–06 onwards and for corporation tax purposes for accounting periods ending after 5 April 2005 (ITTOIA 2005, s. 883(1)).]

SECTION 233

6 [Repealed by ITTOIA 2005, s. 884 and Sch. 3 effective for income tax purposes for 2005–06 onwards and for corporation tax purposes for accounting periods ending after 5 April 2005 (ITTOIA 2005, s. 883(1)).]

SECTIONS 235 TO 237

7(1) [Repeals ICTA 1988, s. 235–237.]

7(2) This paragraph has effect in relation to distributions made on or after 6th April 1999.

SECTION 238

8 [Repealed by FA 1998, s. 31 and Sch. 3, para. 45, s. 165 and Sch. 27, Pt. III(2) with the effect that the prospective amendment of ICTA 1988, s. 238(1) does not take effect.]

SECTION 241

9 [Repealed by FA 1998, s. 31 and Sch. 3, para. 46, s. 165 and Sch. 27, Pt. III(2) with the effect that the prospective substitution of ICTA 1988, s. 241(2) does not take effect.]

SECTION 249

10 [Repealed by ITTOIA 2005, s. 884 and Sch. 3 effective for income tax purposes for 2005–06 onwards and for corporation tax purposes for accounting periods ending after 5 April 2005 (ITTOIA 2005, s. 883(1)).]

SECTION 421

11 [Partially repealed by ITTOIA 2005, s. 884 and Sch. 3 and repealed by CTA 2010, s. 1181 and Sch. 3, Pt. 1.]

History – Para. 11 repealed by CTA 2010, s. 1181 and Sch. 3, Pt. 1, with effect for corporation tax purposes for accounting periods ending on or after 1 April 2010, and for income tax and capital gains tax purposes for the tax year 2010–11 and subsequent tax years. Para. 11(1) previously repealed (in part) by ITTOIA 2005, s. 884 and Sch. 3 effective for income tax purposes for 2005–06 onwards and for corporation tax purposes for accounting periods ending after 5 April 2005 (ITTOIA 2005, s. 883(1)).

SECTION 469

12 [Repealed by ITA 2007, s. 1031 and Sch. 3, Pt. 1.]

History – Para. 12 repealed by ITA 2007, s. 1031 and Sch. 3, Pt. 1, with effect from 6 April 2007.

Notes – Para. 12 rewritten as follows:
Para. 12(2): ITA 2007, s. 504(3).
Para. 12(3): ITA 2007, s. 504(4).

SECTION 549

13 [Repealed by ITTOIA 2005, s. 884 and Sch. 3 effective for income tax purposes for 2005–06 onwards and for corporation tax purposes for accounting periods ending after 5 April 2005 (ITTOIA 2005, s. 883(1)).]

SECTION 660C

14 [Repealed by ITTOIA 2005, s. 884 and Sch. 3 effective for income tax purposes for 2005–06 onwards and for corporation tax purposes for accounting periods ending after 5 April 2005 (ITTOIA 2005, s. 883(1)).]

SECTION 687

15 [Repealed by ITA 2007, s. 1031 and Sch. 3, Pt. 1.]

History – Para. 15 repealed by ITA 2007, s. 1031 and Sch. 3, Pt. 1, with effect from 6 April 2007.

Notes – Para. 15 rewritten as ITA 2007, s. 498(1), (2).

SECTION 689B

16 [Partially repealed by ITTOIA 2005, s. 884 and Sch. 3 and repealed by CTA 2010, s. 1181 and Sch. 3, Pt. 1.]

History – Para. 16 repealed by CTA 2010, s. 1181 and Sch. 3, Pt. 1, with effect for corporation tax purposes for accounting periods ending on or after 1 April 2010, and for income tax and capital gains tax purposes for the tax year 2010–11 and subsequent tax years. Para. 16(3) previously repealed by ITTOIA 2005, s. 884 and Sch. 3 effective for income tax purposes for 2005–06 onwards and for corporation tax purposes for accounting periods ending after 5 April 2005 (ITTOIA 2005, s. 883(1)).

SECTION 699

17 [Repealed by ITTOIA 2005, s. 884 and Sch. 3 effective for income tax purposes for 2005–06 onwards and for corporation tax purposes for accounting periods ending after 5 April 2005 (ITTOIA 2005, s. 883(1)).]

SECTION 703

18 [Repealed by FA 1998, s. 31 and Sch. 3, para. 47, s. 165 and Sch. 27, Pt. III(2) with the effect that the prospective amendment of ICTA 1988, s. 703 does not take effect.]

SECTION 709

19(1) [Amends ICTA 1988, s. 709(2A).]

19(2) This paragraph has effect for the year 1999–00 and subsequent years of assessment.

SECTION 743

20 [Repealed by ITA 2007, s. 1031 and Sch. 3, Pt. 1.]

History – Para. 20 repealed by ITA 2007, s. 1031 and Sch. 3, Pt. 1, with effect from 6 April 2007.

Notes – Para. 20 rewritten as ITA 2007, s. 745(1), (3), (4).

SECTION 819

21 [Repealed by TIOPA 2010, s. 378 and Sch. 10, Pt. 13.]

History – Para. 21 repealed by TIOPA 2010, s. 378 and Sch. 10, Pt. 13, with effect for corporation tax purposes for accounting periods ending on or after 1 April 2010, for income tax and capital gains tax purposes for the tax year 2010–11 and subsequent tax years, and for petroleum revenue tax purposes for chargeable periods beginning on or after 1 July 2010.

SECTION 832

22 [Repealed by ITA 2007, s. 1031 and Sch. 3, Pt. 1.]

History – Para. 22 repealed by ITA 2007, s. 1031 and Sch. 3, Pt. 1, with effect from 6 April 2007.

Notes – Para. 22 rewritten as ITA 2007, s. 989.

SCHEDULE 13

23 [Repealed by FA 1998, s. 31 and Sch. 3, para. 48, s. 165 and Sch. 27, Pt. III(2) with the effect that the prospective amendment of ICTA 1988, Sch. 13 does not take effect.]

THE TAXATION OF CHARGEABLE GAINS ACT 1992

SECTION 4

24 [Omitted by FA 2008, s. 8 and Sch. 2, para. 21(b).]

History – Para. 24 omitted by FA 2008, s. 8 and Sch. 2, para. 21(b), with effect for the tax year 2008–09 and subsequent tax years.

SECTION 6

25 [Omitted by FA 2008, s. 8 and Sch. 2, para. 21(b).]

History – Para. 25 omitted by FA 2008, s. 8 and Sch. 2, para. 21(b), with effect for the tax year 2008–09 and subsequent tax years.

Part II – Insurance Companies and Lloyd's Underwriters

THE TAXES ACT 1988

SECTION 231B

26(1) [Amends ICTA 1988, s. 231B(4)(b).]

26(2) This paragraph has effect in relation to distributions made on or after 6th April 1999.

SECTION 434

27 [Repealed by ITTOIA 2005, s. 884 and Sch. 3 effective for income tax purposes for 2005–06 onwards and for corporation tax purposes for accounting periods ending after 5 April 2005 (ITTOIA 2005, s. 883(1)).]

SECTION 441A

28(1) [Repeals ICTA 1988, s. 441A(2)–(8).]

28(2) This paragraph has effect in relation to distributions made on or after 6th April 1999.

SCHEDULE 19AC

29 [Repealed by Statute Law (Repeals) Act 2013, s. 1 and Sch. 1, Pt. 10.]

History – Para. 29 repealed by Statute Law (Repeals) Act 2013, s. 1 and Sch. 1, Pt. 10, with effect from 31 January 2013.

THE FINANCE ACT 1993

SCHEDULE 20

30(1) [Repeals FA 1993, Sch. 20, para. 9(3) and amends para. 11(3)(c).]

30(2) Sub-paragraph (1) above has effect in relation to distributions made on or after 6th April 1999.

SCHEDULE 5 – LIMITATION OF ENTITLEMENT TO RELIEF UNDER SECTION 35

Section 35

[Repealed by FA 2011, s. 91 and Sch. 26, para. 1(1).]

History – Sch. 5 repealed by FA 2011, s. 91 and Sch. 26, para. 1(1) with effect from 19 July 2011.

SCHEDULE 6 – FOREIGN INCOME DIVIDENDS

Section 36

SECTION 13 OF THE TAXES ACT 1988

1(1) Section 13 of the Taxes Act 1988 (small companies' relief) shall be amended as follows.

1(2) [Amends ICTA 1988, s. 13(7).]

1(3) [Repeals ICTA 1988, s. 13(8A).]

1(4) This paragraph has effect for accounting periods beginning on or after 6th April 1999.

SECTION 75 OF THE TAXES ACT 1988

2 [Repealed by FA 2004, s. 326 and Sch. 42, Pt. 2(3).]

History – Para. 2 repealed by FA 2004, s. 326 and Sch. 42, Pt. 2(3), with effect, subject to the transitional provisions at s. 43 and 44, for accounting periods beginning on or after 1 April 2004.

CHAPTER VA OF PART VI OF THE TAXES ACT 1988

3(1) [Repeals ICTA 1988, s. 246A–246Y.]

3(2) The repeal of sections 246A to 246E and 246G of the Taxes Act 1988 has effect in relation to distributions made on or after 6th April 1999.

3(3) The repeal of sections 246F, 246H to 246J and 246N to 246Y of the Taxes Act 1988 has effect for accounting periods beginning on or after 6th April 1999.

3(4) The repeal of sections 246K to 246M of the Taxes Act 1988 has effect for accounting periods of the parent (within the meaning of those sections) beginning on or after 6th April 1999.

SECTION 247 OF THE TAXES ACT 1988

4(1) [Repeals ICTA 1988, s. 247(5A)–(5D).]

4(2) This paragraph has effect in relation to distributions made on or after 6th April 1999.

SECTION 431 OF THE TAXES ACT 1988

5(1) [Amends ICTA 1988, s. 431(2).]

5(2) This paragraph has effect for accounting periods beginning on or after 6th April 1999.

SECTION 434 OF THE TAXES ACT 1988

6(1) Section 434 of the Taxes Act 1988 (franked investment income etc.) shall be amended as follows.

6(2) [Repeals ICTA 1988, s. 434(3B)–(3D).]

6(3) [Repeals ICTA 1988, s. 434(6A)(aa)–(ac).]

6(4) This paragraph has effect for accounting periods beginning on or after 6th April 1999.

SECTION 458 OF THE TAXES ACT 1988

7(1) [Amends ICTA 1988, s. 458(2).]

7(2) This paragraph has effect in relation to distributions made on or after 6th April 1999.

CHAPTER III OF PART XII OF THE TAXES ACT 1988

8(1) [Amends ICTA 1988, s. 468H.]

8(2) [Amends ICTA 1988, s. 468I.]

8(3) [Amends ICTA 1988, s. 468J.]

8(4) [Repeals ICTA 1988, s. 468K.]

8(5) [Repeals ICTA 1988, s. 468M(5)(c).]

8(6) In section 468Q of the Taxes Act 1988 (dividend distribution to corporate unit holder)–

(a) [repeals words in ICTA 1988, s. 468Q(2)(a);]

(b) [amends ICTA 1988, s. 468Q(3);]

(c) [repeals ICTA 1988, s. 468Q(4).]

8(7) [Repeals ICTA 1988, s. 468R.]

8(8) Sub-paragraphs (1)(a), (5) and (6) above have effect for distribution periods beginning on or after 6th April 1999.

8(9) Sub-paragraphs (1)(b), (2) to (4) and (7) above have effect for distribution periods the distribution date for which falls on or after 6th April 1999.

Cross references – ICTA 1988, s. 468Q, as amended by F(No. 2)A 1997, Sch. 6, para. 8(6), also amended by FA 1998, s. 31 and Sch. 3, para. 27(2)–(4)].

SECTION 490 OF THE TAXES ACT 1988

9(1) Section 490 of the Taxes Act 1988 (companies carrying on a mutual business or not carrying on a business) shall be amended as follows.

9(2) [Amends ICTA 1988, s. 490(1).]

9(3) [Amends ICTA 1988, s. 490(4).]

9(4) [Repeals ICTA 1988, s. 490(5).]

9(5) This paragraph has effect in relation to distributions made on or after 6th April 1999.

SECTION 687 OF THE TAXES ACT 1988

10(1) [Repeals ICTA 1988, s. 687(3)(aaa).]

10(2) This paragraph has effect in relation to distributions made on or after 6th April 1999.

SECTION 689B OF THE TAXES ACT 1988

11(1) [Amends ICTA 1988, s. 689B(2)(b).]

11(2) This paragraph has effect in relation to distributions made on or after 6th April 1999.

SECTION 699A OF THE TAXES ACT 1988

12 [Repealed by CTA 2009, s. 1326 and Sch. 3, Pt. 1.]

History – Para. 12 repealed by CTA 2009, s. 1326 and Sch. 3, Pt. 1, with effect for corporation tax purposes for accounting periods ending on or after 1 April 2009, and for income tax and capital gains tax purposes for the tax year 2009–10 and subsequent tax years.

SECTION 701 OF THE TAXES ACT 1988

13 [Repealed by CTA 2009, s. 1326 and Sch. 3, Pt. 1.]

History – Para. 13 repealed by CTA 2009, s. 1326 and Sch. 3, Pt. 1, with effect for corporation tax purposes for accounting periods ending on or after 1 April 2009, and for income tax and capital gains tax purposes for the tax year 2009–10 and subsequent tax years.

SECTION 731 OF THE TAXES ACT 1988

14 [Omitted by FA 2008, s. 66(4)(i)(ii).]

History – Para. 14 omitted by FA 2008, s. 66(4)(i)(ii), with effect in relation to cases where the purchase by the first buyer (within the meaning of section 731(2) of ICTA) is made on or after that date.

SECTION 802 OF THE TAXES ACT 1988

15(1) Section 802 of the Taxes Act 1988 (UK insurance companies trading overseas) shall be amended as follows.

15(2) [Amends ICTA 1988, s. 802(2).]

15(3) [Repeals ICTA 1988, s. 802(4).]

15(4) This paragraph has effect in relation to distributions made on or after 6th April 1999.

SCHEDULE 13 TO THE TAXES ACT 1988

16(1) Schedule 13 to the Taxes Act 1988 shall be amended as follows.

16(2) [Repeals ICTA 1988, Sch. 13, para. 1(b) and amends (c).]

16(3) [Amends ICTA 1988, Sch. 13, para. 1(4).]

16(4) [Amends ICTA 1988, Sch. 13, para. 2(1) and repeals para. 2(5) and (6).]

16(5) [Amends ICTA 1988, Sch. 13, para. 3(1), (3).]

16(6) [Repeals ICTA 1988, Sch. 13, para. 3A and 3B.]

16(7) [Amends ICTA 1988, Sch. 13, para. 4(2).]

16(8) [Repeals ICTA 1988, Sch. 13, para. 4A.]

16(9) [Repeals ICTA 1988, Sch. 13, para. 6A.]

16(10) [Amends ICTA 1988, Sch. 13, para. 7(3).]

16(11) [Repeals ICTA 1988, Sch. 13, para. 9A.]

16(12) Sub-paragraph (2) above has effect for accounting periods beginning on or after 6th April 1999.

16(13) Sub-paragraphs (3) to (10) above have effect for return periods beginning on or after 6th April 1999.

16(14) Sub-paragraph (11) above has effect in relation to manufactured dividends which are representative of dividends paid on or after 6th April 1999.

SCHEDULE 23A TO THE TAXES ACT 1988

17(1) Schedule 23A to the Taxes Act 1988 (manufactured dividends and interest) shall be amended as follows.

17(2) [Amends ICTA 1988, Sch. 23A, para. 1(1).]

17(3) [Amends ICTA 1988, Sch. 23A, para. 2(6).]

17(4) [Repeals ICTA 1988, Sch. 23A, para. 2B.]

17(5) This paragraph has effect in relation to manufactured dividends which are representative of dividends paid on or after 6th April 1999.

SECTION 88A OF THE FINANCE ACT 1989

18(1) [Amends FA 1989, s. 88A(3).]

18(2) This paragraph has effect in relation to distributions made on or after 6th April 1999.

SECTION 89 OF THE FINANCE ACT 1989

19(1) Section 89 of the Finance Act 1989 (policy holders' share of profits) shall be amended as follows.

19(2) [Repeals FA 1989, s. 89(2)(c).]

19(3) [Repeals FA 1989, s. 89(2A).]

19(4) This paragraph has effect in relation to distributions made on or after 6th April 1999.

SECTION 171 OF THE FINANCE ACT 1993

20(1) Section 171 of the Finance Act 1993 (taxation of profits and allowance of losses of Lloyd's underwriters) shall be amended as follows.

20(2) [Repeals FA 1993, s. 171(2A).]

20(3) This paragraph has effect in relation to distributions made on or after 6th April 1999.

SCHEDULE 7 TO THE FINANCE ACT 1997

21(1) Schedule 7 to the Finance Act 1997 shall be amended as follows.

21(2) [Repeals FA 1997, Sch. 7, para. 2.]

21(3) [Repeals FA 1997, Sch. 7, para. 4–6.]

21(4) Sub-paragraphs (2) and (3) above have effect in relation to distributions made on or after 6th April 1999.

TRANSITIONAL PROVISIONS

22(1) Where, in the case of an accounting period of a company beginning before 6th April 1999 and ending on or after 5th April 1999 ("a transitional period"), there would (apart from this sub-paragraph) be such an excess as is mentioned in section 246F(3) of the Taxes Act 1988, no such excess shall be deemed to have arisen.

22(2) In their application in relation to foreign income dividends paid in an accounting period of a company beginning before 6th April 1999, sections 246J(5) and 246K(10) of the Taxes Act 1988 shall have effect as if the reference to any subsequent accounting period–

(a) included an accounting period which immediately follows a transitional period, but

(b) did not include any later accounting period.

23 Where a foreign income dividend paid by a company before 6th April 1999–

(a) is received by a person on or after that date, and

(b) is not one in relation to which section 246D of the Taxes Act 1988 applies,

the recipient shall be treated, for all purposes of the Tax Acts, as receiving instead a distribution made by a company resident in the United Kingdom of an amount equal to the amount of the foreign income dividend.

History – In para. 23, the words "qualifying" (which appeared before the word "distribution") and the words "nine tenths of " (which appeared before the words " the amount") omitted by FA 2016, s. 5 and Sch. 1, para. 57(5) in relation to foreign income dividends received on or after 6 April 2016.

SCHEDULE 7 – RESTRICTIONS ON GROUP RELIEF

Section 41

[Repealed by CTA 2010, s. 1181 and Sch. 3, Pt. 1.]

History – Sch. 7 repealed by CTA 2010, s. 1181 and Sch. 3, Pt. 1, with effect for accounting periods ending on or after 1 April 2010.

DATA PROTECTION ACT 1998

(1998 Chapter 29)

[*16th July 1998*]

ARRANGEMENT OF SECTIONS

PART I – PRELIMINARY

PART II – RIGHTS OF DATA SUBJECTS AND OTHERS

PART IV – EXEMPTIONS

PART VI – MISCELLANEOUS AND GENERAL

GENERAL

SCHEDULES

PART I – PRELIMINARY

1 Basic interpretative provisions

1(1) In this Act, unless the context otherwise requires–

"data" means information which–

(a) is being processed by means of equipment operating automatically in response to instructions given for that purpose,

(b) is recorded with the intention that it should be processed by means of such equipment,

(c) is recorded as part of a relevant filing system or with the intention that it should form part of a relevant filing system,

(d) does not fall within paragraph (a), (b) or (c) but forms part of an accessible record as defined by section 68; or

(e) is recorded information held by a public authority and does not fall within any of paragraphs (a) to (d);

"data controller" means, subject to subsection (4), a person who (either alone or jointly or in common with other persons) determines the purposes for which and the manner in which any personal data are, or are to be, processed;

"data processor", in relation to personal data, means any person (other than an employee of the data controller) who processes the data on behalf of the data controller;

"data subject" means an individual who is the subject of personal data;

"personal data" means data which relate to a living individual who can be identified–

(a) from those data, or

(b) from those data and other information which is in the possession of, or is likely to come into the possession of, the data controller,

and includes any expression of opinion about the individual and any indication of the intentions of the data controller or any other person in respect of the individual;

"processing", in relation to information or data, means obtaining, recording or holding the information or data or carrying out any operation or set of operations on the information or data, including–

(a) organisation, adaptation or alteration of the information or data,

(b) retrieval, consultation or use of the information or data,

(c) disclosure of the information or data by transmission, dissemination or otherwise making available, or

(d) alignment, combination, blocking, erasure or destruction of the information or data;

"public authority" means a public authority as defined by the Freedom of Information Act 2000 or a Scottish public authority as defined by the Freedom of Information (Scotland) Act 2002;

"relevant filing system" means any set of information relating to individuals to the extent that, although the information is not processed by means of equipment operating automatically in response to instructions given for that purpose, the set is structured, either by reference to individuals or by reference to criteria relating to individuals, in such a way that specific information relating to a particular individual is readily accessible.

1(2) In this Act, unless the context otherwise requires–

(a) **"obtaining"** or **"recording"**, in relation to personal data, includes obtaining or recording the information to be contained in the data, and

(b) **"using"** or **"disclosing"**, in relation to personal data, includes using or disclosing the information contained in the data.

1(3) In determining for the purposes of this Act whether any information is recorded with the intention–

(a) that it should be processed by means of equipment operating automatically in response to instructions given for that purpose, or

(b) that it should form part of a relevant filing system,

it is immaterial that it is intended to be so processed or to form part of such a system only after being transferred to a country or territory outside the European Economic Area.

1(4) Where personal data are processed only for purposes for which they are required by or under any enactment to be processed, the person on whom the obligation to process the data is imposed by or under that enactment is for the purposes of this Act the data controller.

1(5) In paragraph (e) of the definition of "data" in subsection (1), the reference to information "held" by a public authority shall be construed in accordance with section 3(2) of the Freedom of Information Act 2000 or section 3(2), (4) and (5) of the Freedom of Information (Scotland) Act 2002.

1(6) Where

(a) section 7 of the Freedom of Information Act 2000 prevents Parts I to V of that Act or

(b) section 7(1) of the Freedom of Information (Scotland) Act 2002 prevents that Act,

from applying to certain information held by a public authority, that information is not to be treated for the purposes of paragraph (e) of the definition of "data" in subsection (1) as held by a public authority.

History – In s. 1(1), in the definition of "data", the word "or" at the end of para. (c) omitted by FOIA 2000, s. 68(2)(a) and repealed by FOIA 2000, s. 86 and Sch. 8, Pt. III with effect from 1 January 2005 (by virtue of SI 2004/3122, art. 2).

In s. 1(1), in the definition of "data", para. (e) (and the preceding word "or") inserted by FOIA 2000, s. 68(2)(a) with effect from 1 January 2005 (by virtue of SI 2004/1909, art. 2(2)(f)).

In s. 1(1), the definition of "public authority" substituted by the Freedom of Information (Scotland) Act 2002 (Consequential Modifications) Order 2004 (SI 2004/3089), art. 2(2)(a) with effect 1 January 2005.

In s. 1(1), the definition of "public authority" inserted by FOIA 2000, s. 68(2)(b) with effect from 1 January 2005 (by virtue of SI 2004/1909, art. 2(2)(f)).

In s. 1(5), the reference to the FOI(S)A inserted by the Freedom of Information (Scotland) Act 2002 (Consequential Modifications) Order 2004 (SI 2004/3089), art. 2(2)(b) with effect 1 January 2005.

S. 1(5) inserted by FOIA 2000, s. 68(3) with effect from 1 January 2005 (by virtue of SI 2004/1909, art. 2(2)(f)).

In s. 1(6), the reference to the FOI(S)A inserted (and the subsection reparagraphed) by the Freedom of Information (Scotland) Act 2002 (Consequential Modifications) Order 2004 (SI 2004/3089), art. 2(2)(c) with effect 1 January 2005.

S. 1(6) inserted by FOIA 2000, s. 68(3) with effect from 1 January 2005 (by virtue of SI 2004/1909, art. 2(2)(f)).

4 The data protection principles

4(1) References in this Act to the data protection principles are to the principles set out in Part I of Schedule 1.

4(2) Those principles are to be interpreted in accordance with Part II of Schedule 1.

4(3) Schedule 2 (which applies to all personal data) and Schedule 3 (which applies only to sensitive personal data) set out conditions applying for the purposes of the first principle; and Schedule 4 sets out cases in which the eighth principle does not apply.

4(4) Subject to section 27(1), it shall be the duty of a data controller to comply with the data protection principles in relation to all personal data with respect to which he is the data controller.

Commencement Date – S. 4 brought into force on 1 March 2000 by SI 2000/183, art. 2(1).

PART II – RIGHTS OF DATA SUBJECTS AND OTHERS

7 Right of access to personal data

7(1) Subject to the following provisions of this section and to sections 8, 9 and 9A, an individual is entitled–

(a) to be informed by any data controller whether personal data of which that individual is the data subject are being processed by or on behalf of that data controller,

(b) if that is the case, to be given by the data controller a description of–

  (i) the personal data of which that individual is the data subject,

  (ii) the purposes for which they are being or are to be processed, and

  (iii) the recipients or classes of recipients to whom they are or may be disclosed,

(c) to have communicated to him in an intelligible form–

  (i) the information constituting any personal data of which that individual is the data subject, and

  (ii) any information available to the data controller as to the source of those data, and

(d) where the processing by automatic means of personal data of which that individual is the data subject for the purpose of evaluating matters relating to him such as, for example, his performance at work, his creditworthiness, his reliability or his conduct, has constituted or is likely to constitute the sole basis for any decision significantly affecting him, to be informed by the data controller of the logic involved in that decision-taking.

7(2) A data controller is not obliged to supply any information under subsection (1) unless he has received–

(a) a request in writing, and

(b) except in prescribed cases, such fee (not exceeding the prescribed maximum) as he may require.

7(3) Where a data controller–

(a) reasonably requires further information in order to satisfy himself as to the identity of the person making a request under this section and to locate the information which that person seeks, and

(b) has informed him of that requirement,

the data controller is not obliged to comply with the request unless he is supplied with that further information.

7(4) Where a data controller cannot comply with the request without disclosing information relating to another individual who can be identified from that information, he is not obliged to comply with the request unless–

(a) the other individual has consented to the disclosure of the information to the person making the request, or

(b) it is reasonable in all the circumstances to comply with the request without the consent of the other individual.

7(5) In subsection (4) the reference to information relating to another individual includes a reference to information identifying that individual as the source of the information sought by the request; and that subsection is not to be construed as excusing a data controller from communicating so much of the information sought by the request as can be communicated without disclosing the identity of the other individual concerned, whether by the omission of names or other identifying particulars or otherwise.

7(6) In determining for the purposes of subsection (4)(b) whether it is reasonable in all the circumstances to comply with the request without the consent of the other individual concerned, regard shall be had, in particular, to–

(a) any duty of confidentiality owed to the other individual,

(b) any steps taken by the data controller with a view to seeking the consent of the other individual,

(c) whether the other individual is capable of giving consent, and

(d) any express refusal of consent by the other individual.

7(7) An individual making a request under this section may, in such cases as may be prescribed, specify that his request is limited to personal data of any prescribed description.

7(8) Subject to subsection (4), a data controller shall comply with a request under this section promptly and in any event before the end of the prescribed period beginning with the relevant day.

7(9) If a court is satisfied on the application of any person who has made a request under the foregoing provisions of this section that the data controller in question has failed to comply with the request in contravention of those provisions, the court may order him to comply with the request.

7(10) In this section–

"prescribed" means prescribed by the Secretary of State by regulations;

"the prescribed maximum" means such amount as may be prescribed;

"the prescribed period" means forty days or such other period as may be prescribed;

"the relevant day", in relation to a request under this section, means the day on which the data controller receives the request or, if later, the first day on which the data controller has both the required fee and the information referred to in subsection (3).

7(11) Different amounts or periods may be prescribed under this section in relation to different cases.

History – In s. 7(1), the reference to s. 9A substituted by FOIA 2000, s. 69(1) with effect from 1 January 2005 (by virtue of SI 2004/1909, art. 2(2)(f)).
S. 7(3) substituted by FOIA 2000, s. 73 and Sch. 6. para. 1 with effect from 1 January 2005 (by virtue of SI 2004/1909, art. 2(2)(f)).
In s. 7(10), the reference to "Secretary of State" substituted for "Lord Chancellor" by SI 2003/1887, art. 9 and Sch. 2, para. 9(1) with effect from 19 August 2003.
In s. 7(10), the reference to "Lord Chancellor" substituted for "Secretary of State" by SI 2001/3500, art. 8 and Sch. 2, para. 6(1) with effect from 26 November 2001.

8 Provisions supplementary to section 7

8(1) The Secretary of State may by regulations provide that, in such cases as may be prescribed, a request for information under any provision of subsection (1) of section 7 is to be treated as extending also to information under other provisions of that subsection.

8(2) The obligation imposed by section 7(1)(c)(i) must be complied with by supplying the data subject with a copy of the information in permanent form unless–

(a) the supply of such a copy is not possible or would involve disproportionate effort, or

(b) the data subject agrees otherwise;

and where any of the information referred to in section 7(1)(c)(i) is expressed in terms which are not intelligible without explanation the copy must be accompanied by an explanation of those terms.

8(3) Where a data controller has previously complied with a request made under section 7 by an individual, the data controller is not obliged to comply with a subsequent identical or similar request under that section by that individual unless a reasonable interval has elapsed between compliance with the previous request and the making of the current request.

8(4) In determining for the purposes of subsection (3) whether requests under section 7 are made at reasonable intervals, regard shall be had to the nature of the data, the purpose for which the data are processed and the frequency with which the data are altered.

8(5) Section 7(1)(d) is not to be regarded as requiring the provision of information as to the logic involved in any decision-taking if, and to the extent that, the information constitutes a trade secret.

8(6) The information to be supplied pursuant to a request under section 7 must be supplied by reference to the data in question at the time when the request is received, except that it may take account of any amendment or deletion made between that time and the time when the information is supplied, being an amendment or deletion that would have been made regardless of the receipt of the request.

8(7) *For the purposes of section* 7(4) and (5) another individual can be identified from the information being disclosed if he can be identified from that information, or from that and any other information which, in the reasonable belief of the data controller, is likely to be in, or to come into, the possession of the data subject making the request.

Commencement Date – S. 8 brought into force on 1 March 2000 by SI 2000/183, art. 2(1).

History – In s. 8(1), the reference to "Secretary of State" substituted for "Lord Chancellor" by SI 2003/1887, art. 9 and Sch. 2, para. 9(1) with effect from 19 August 2003.
In s. 8(1), the reference to "Lord Chancellor" substituted for "Secretary of State" by SI 2001/3500, art. 8 and Sch. 2, para. 6(1) with effect from 26 November 2001.

9A Unstructured personal data held by public authorities

9A(1) In this section **"unstructured personal data"** means any personal data falling within paragraph (e) of the definition of "data" in section 1(1), other than information which is recorded as part of, or with the intention that it should form part of, any set of information relating to individuals to the extent that the set is structured by reference to individuals or by reference to criteria relating to individuals.

9A(2) A public authority is not obliged to comply with subsection (1) of section 7 in relation to any unstructured personal data unless the request under that section contains a description of the data.

9A(3) Even if the data are described by the data subject in his request, a public authority is not obliged to comply with subsection (1) of section 7 in relation to unstructured personal data if the authority estimates that the cost of complying with the request so far as relating to those data would exceed the appropriate limit.

9A(4) Subsection (3) does not exempt the public authority from its obligation to comply with paragraph (a) of section 7(1) in relation to the unstructured personal data unless the estimated cost of complying with that paragraph alone in relation to those data would exceed the appropriate limit.

9A(5) In subsections (3) and (4) **"the appropriate limit"** means such amount as may be prescribed by the Secretary of State by regulations, and different amounts may be prescribed in relation to different cases.

9A(6) Any estimate for the purposes of this section must be made in accordance with regulations under section 12(5) of the Freedom of Information Act 2000.

History – In s. 9A(5), the reference to "Secretary of State" substituted for "Lord Chancellor" by SI 2003/1887, art. 9 and Sch. 2, para. 9(1) with effect from 19 August 2003.
In s. 9A(5), the reference to "Lord Chancellor" substituted for "Secretary of State" by SI 2001/3500, art. 8 and Sch. 2, para. 6(1) with effect from 26 November 2001.
S. 9A inserted by FOI 2000, s. 69(2) with effect from 1 January 2005 (by virtue of SI 2004/1909, art. 2(2)(f)).

10 Right to prevent processing likely to cause damage or distress

10(1) Subject to subsection (2), an individual is entitled at any time by notice in writing to a data controller to require the data controller at the end of such period as is reasonable in the circumstances to cease, or not to begin, processing, or processing for a specified purpose or in a specified manner, any personal data in respect of which he is the data subject, on the ground that, for specified reasons–

(a) the processing of those data or their processing for that purpose or in that manner is causing or is likely to cause substantial damage or substantial distress to him or to another, and

(b) that damage or distress is or would be unwarranted.

10(2) Subsection (1) does not apply–

(a) in a case where any of the conditions in paragraphs 1 to 4 of Schedule 2 is met, or

(b) in such other cases as may be prescribed by the Secretary of State by order.

10(3) The data controller must within twenty-one days of receiving a notice under subsection (1) ("the data subject notice") give the individual who gave it a written notice–

(a) stating that he has complied or intends to comply with the data subject notice, or

(b) stating his reasons for regarding the data subject notice as to any extent unjustified and the extent (if any) to which he has complied or intends to comply with it.

10(4) If a court is satisfied, on the application of any person who has given a notice under subsection (1) which appears to the court to be justified (or to be justified to any extent), that the data controller in question has failed to comply with the notice, the court may order him to take such steps for complying with the notice (or for complying with it to that extent) as the court thinks fit.

10(5) The failure by a data subject to exercise the right conferred by subsection (1) or section 11(1) does not affect any other right conferred on him by this Part.

Commencement Date – S. 10 brought into force on 1 March 2000 by SI 2000/183, art. 2(1).

History – In s. 10(2), the reference to "Secretary of State" substituted for "Lord Chancellor" by SI 2003/1887, art. 9 and Sch. 2, para. 9(1) with effect from 19 August 2003.
In s. 10(2), the reference to "Lord Chancellor" substituted for "Secretary of State" by SI 2001/3500, art. 8 and Sch. 2, para. 6(1) with effect from 26 November 2001.

12 Rights in relation to automated decision-taking

12(1) An individual is entitled at any time, by notice in writing to any data controller, to require the data controller to ensure that no decision taken by or on behalf of the data controller which significantly affects that individual is based solely on the processing by automatic means of personal data in respect of which that individual is the data subject for the purpose of evaluating matters relating to him such as, for example, his performance at work, his creditworthiness, his reliability or his conduct.

12(2) Where, in a case where no notice under subsection (1) has effect, a decision which significantly affects an individual is based solely on such processing as is mentioned in subsection (1)–

(a) the data controller must as soon as reasonably practicable notify the individual that the decision was taken on that basis, and

(b) the individual is entitled, within twenty-one days of receiving that notification from the data controller, by notice in writing to require the data controller to reconsider the decision or to take a new decision otherwise than on that basis.

12(3) The data controller must, within twenty-one days of receiving a notice under subsection (2)(b) ("the data subject notice") give the individual a written notice specifying the steps that he intends to take to comply with the data subject notice.

12(4) A notice under subsection (1) does not have effect in relation to an exempt decision; and nothing in subsection (2) applies to an exempt decision.

12(5) In subsection (4) **"exempt decision"** means any decision–

(a) in respect of which the condition in subsection (6) and the condition in subsection (7) are met, or

(b) which is made in such other circumstances as may be prescribed by the Secretary of State by order.

12(6) The condition in this subsection is that the decision–

(a) is taken in the course of steps taken–

(i) for the purpose of considering whether to enter into a contract with the data subject,

(ii) with a view to entering into such a contract, or

(iii) in the course of performing such a contract, or

(b) is authorised or required by or under any enactment.

12(7) The condition in this subsection is that either–

(a) the effect of the decision is to grant a request of the data subject, or

(b) steps have been taken to safeguard the legitimate interests of the data subject (for example, by allowing him to make representations).

12(8) If a court is satisfied on the application of a data subject that a person taking a decision in respect of him ("the responsible person") has failed to comply with subsection (1) or (2)(b), the court may order the responsible person to reconsider the decision, or to take a new decision which is not based solely on such processing as is mentioned in subsection (1).

12(9) An order under subsection (8) shall not affect the rights of any person other than the data subject and the responsible person.

Commencement Date – S. 12 brought into force on 1 March 2000 by SI 2000/183, art. 2(1).

History – In s. 12(5), the reference to "Secretary of State" substituted for "Lord Chancellor" by SI 2003/1887, art. 9 and Sch. 2, para. 9(1) with effect from 19 August 2003.

In s. 12(5), the reference to "Lord Chancellor" substituted for "Secretary of State" by SI 2001/3500, art. 8 and Sch. 2, para. 6(1) with effect from 26 November 2001.

12A Rights of data subjects in relation to exempt manual data

12A [No longer in force.]

History – S. 12A temporarily inserted until 23 October 2007 by DPA 1998, Sch. 13, para. 1.

15 Jurisdiction and procedure

15(1) The jurisdiction conferred by sections 7 to 14 is exercisable in England and Wales by the High Court or the county court or, in Northern Ireland, by the High Court or a county court or, in Scotland, by the Court of Session or the sheriff.

15(2) For the purpose of determining any question whether an applicant under subsection (9) of section 7 is entitled to the information which he seeks (including any question whether any relevant data are exempt from that section by virtue of Part IV) a court may require the information constituting any data processed by or on behalf of the data controller and any information as to the logic involved in any decision-taking as mentioned in section 7(1)(d) to be made available for its own inspection but shall not, pending the determination of that question in the applicant's favour, require the information sought by the applicant to be disclosed to him or his representatives whether by discovery (or, in Scotland, recovery) or otherwise.

Commencement Date – S. 15 brought into force on 1 March 2000 by SI 2000/183, art. 2(1).

History – In s. 15(1), the words "in England and Wales by the High Court or the county court or, in Northern Ireland," inserted by Crime and Courts Act 2013, s. 17 and Sch. 9, para. 77, with effect from 22 April 2014 (SI 2014/954, art. 2).

PART IV – EXEMPTIONS

27 Preliminary

27(1) References in any of the data protection principles or any provision of Parts II and III to personal data or to the processing of personal data do not include references to data or processing which by virtue of this Part are exempt from that principle or other provision.

27(2) In this Part **"the subject information provisions"** means–

(a) the first data protection principle to the extent to which it requires compliance with paragraph 2 of Part II of Schedule 1, and

(b) section 7.

27(3) In this Part **"the non-disclosure provisions"** means the provisions specified in subsection (4) to the extent to which they are inconsistent with the disclosure in question.

27(4) The provisions referred to in subsection (3) are–

(a) the first data protection principle, except to the extent to which it requires compliance with the conditions in Schedules 2 and 3,

(b) the second, third, fourth and fifth data protection principles, and

(c) sections 10 and 14(1) to (3).

27(5) Except as provided by this Part, the subject information provisions shall have effect notwithstanding any enactment or rule of law prohibiting or restricting the disclosure, or authorising the withholding, of information.

Commencement Date – S. 27 brought into force on 1 March 2000 by SI 2000/183, art. 2(1).

29 Crime and taxation

29(1) Personal data processed for any of the following purposes–

(a) the prevention or detection of crime,

(b) the apprehension or prosecution of offenders, or

(c) the assessment or collection of any tax or duty or of any imposition of a similar nature,

are exempt from the first data protection principle (except to the extent to which it requires compliance with the conditions in Schedules 2 and 3) and section 7 in any case to the extent to which the application of those provisions to the data would be likely to prejudice any of the matters mentioned in this subsection.

29(2) Personal data which–

(a) are processed for the purpose of discharging statutory functions, and

(b) consist of information obtained for such a purpose from a person who had it in his possession for any of the purposes mentioned in subsection (1),

are exempt from the subject information provisions to the same extent as personal data processed for any of the purposes mentioned in that subsection.

29(3) Personal data are exempt from the non-disclosure provisions in any case in which–

(a) the disclosure is for any of the purposes mentioned in subsection (1), and

(b) the application of those provisions in relation to the disclosure would be likely to prejudice any of the matters mentioned in that subsection.

29(4) Personal data in respect of which the data controller is a relevant authority and which–

(a) consist of a classification applied to the data subject as part of a system of risk assessment which is operated by that authority for either of the following purposes–

  (i) the assessment or collection of any tax or duty or any imposition of a similar nature, or

  (ii) the prevention or detection of crime, or apprehension or prosecution of offenders, where the offence concerned involves any unlawful claim for any payment out of, or any unlawful application of, public funds, and

(b) are processed for either of those purposes,

are exempt from section 7 to the extent to which the exemption is required in the interests of the operation of the system.

29(5) In subsection (4)–

"public funds" includes funds provided by any Community institution;

"relevant authority" means–

(a) a government department,

(b) a local authority, or

(c) any other authority administering housing benefit or council tax benefit.

Commencement Date – S. 29 brought into force on 1 March 2000 by SI 2000/183, art. 2(1).

PART VI – MISCELLANEOUS AND GENERAL

GENERAL

75 Short title, commencement and extent

75(1) This Act may be cited as the Data Protection Act 1998.

75(2) The following provisions of this Act–

(a) sections 1 to 3,

(b)–(d) [Not relevant to tax.]

(e) this section,

((f)–(i)) [Not relevant to tax.]

shall come into force on the day on which this Act is passed.

75(3) The remaining provisions of this Act shall come into force on such day as the Secretary of State may by order appoint; and different days may be appointed for different purposes.

75(4) [Not relevant to tax.]

75(4A) Subsection (4) does not apply to section 56 so far as that section relates to a record containing information relating to–

(a) the Secretary of State's functions under the Safeguarding Vulnerable Groups Act 2006 or the Safeguarding of Vulnerable Groups (Northern Ireland) Order 2007,

(b) the Independent Safeguarding Authority's functions under that Act or that Order, or

(c) the Scottish Ministers' functions under Parts 1 and 2 of the Protection of Vulnerable Groups (Scotland) Act 2007.

75(5) Subject to subsections (5A) and (6), this Act extends to Northern Ireland.

75(5A) In section 56(6) (prohibition of requirement as to production of certain records), paragraph (2)(e) of the Table in that section, insofar as it relates to Part 1 of the Welfare Reform Act 2007 and Part 1 of the Welfare Reform Act 2012, extends to England and Wales and Scotland only.

75(6) Any amendment, repeal or revocation made by Schedule 15 or 16 has the same extent as that of the enactment or instrument to which it relates.

History – In s. 75(4A)(a) the words "or the Safeguarding of Vulnerable Groups (Northern Ireland) Order 2007" inserted and in s. 75(4A)(b) the words "or that Order" inserted by SI 2007/1351, art. 60(1) and Sch. 7, para. 4(2), with effect from 29 May 2008 (SI 2008/233, art. 3).

In s. 75(4A)(b), the words "Independent Safeguarding Authority's" substituted for the words "Independent Barring Board's" by Policing and Crime Act 2009, s. 81(2) and (3)(i), with effect from 12 November 2009.

In s. 75(4A)(c) inserted (and the "or" after (a) omitted) by SI 2011/565, art. 3 with effect from 31 October 2011.

S. 75(4A) inserted by Safeguarding Vulnerable Groups Act 2006, Sch. 9, para. 15(1), (3), with effect from 19 May 2008 (SI 2008/1320, art. 3).

In s. 75(5), the words "subsections (5A) and (6)" substituted for the words "subsection (6)" by SI 2011/2545, reg. 4(b)(i), with effect from 31 October 2011.

In s. 75(5A), the words "and Part 1 of the Welfare Reform Act 2012" inserted by SI 2013/630, reg. 14(3), with effect from 29 April 2013.

S. 75(5A) inserted by SI 2011/2425, reg. 4(b)(ii), with effect from 31 October 2011.

Statutory instruments – SI 2000/183: The Data Protection Act 1998 (Commencement) Order 2000.

SCHEDULES

SCHEDULE 1 – THE DATA PROTECTION PRINCIPLES

Part I – The Principles

1 Personal data shall be processed fairly and lawfully and, in particular, shall not be processed unless–

(a) at least one of the conditions in Schedule 2 is met, and

(b) in the case of sensitive personal data, at least one of the conditions in Schedule 3 is also met.

2 Personal data shall be obtained only for one or more specified and lawful purposes, and shall not be further processed in any manner incompatible with that purpose or those purposes.

3 Personal data shall be adequate, relevant and not excessive in relation to the purpose or purposes for which they are processed.

4 Personal data shall be accurate and, where necessary, kept up to date.

5 Personal data processed for any purpose or purposes shall not be kept for longer than is necessary for that purpose or those purposes.

6 Personal data shall be processed in accordance with the rights of data subjects under this Act.

7 Appropriate technical and organisational measures shall be taken against unauthorised or unlawful processing of personal data and against accidental loss or destruction of, or damage to, personal data.

8 Personal data shall not be transferred to a country or territory outside the European Economic Area unless that country or territory ensures an adequate level of protection for the rights and freedoms of data subjects in relation to the processing of personal data.

Part II – Interpretation of the Principles in Part I

THE FIRST PRINCIPLE

1(1) In determining for the purposes of the first principle whether personal data are processed fairly, regard is to be had to the method by which they are obtained, including in particular whether any person from whom they are obtained is deceived or misled as to the purpose or purposes for which they are to be processed.

1(2) Subject to paragraph 2, for the purposes of the first principle data are to be treated as obtained fairly if they consist of information obtained from a person who–

(a) is authorised by or under any enactment to supply it, or

(b) is required to supply it by or under any enactment or by any convention or other instrument imposing an international obligation on the United Kingdom.

2(1) Subject to paragraph 3, for the purposes of the first principle personal data are not to be treated as processed fairly unless–

(a) in the case of data obtained from the data subject, the data controller ensures so far as practicable that the data subject has, is provided with, or has made readily available to him, the information specified in sub-paragraph (3), and

(b) in any other case, the data controller ensures so far as practicable that, before the relevant time or as soon as practicable after that time, the data subject has, is provided with, or has made readily available to him, the information specified in sub-paragraph (3).

2(2) In sub-paragraph (1)(b) **"the relevant time"** means–

(a) the time when the data controller first processes the data, or

(b) in a case where at that time disclosure to a third party within a reasonable period is envisaged–

(i) if the data are in fact disclosed to such a person within that period, the time when the data are first disclosed,

(ii) if within that period the data controller becomes, or ought to become, aware that the data are unlikely to be disclosed to such a person within that period, the time when the data controller does become, or ought to become, so aware, or

(iii) in any other case, the end of that period.

2(3) The information referred to in sub-paragraph (1) is as follows, namely–

(a) the identity of the data controller,

(b) if he has nominated a representative for the purposes of this Act, the identity of that representative,

(c) the purpose or purposes for which the data are intended to be processed, and

(d) any further information which is necessary, having regard to the specific circumstances in which the data are or are to be processed, to enable processing in respect of the data subject to be fair.

3(1) Paragraph 2(1)(b) does not apply where either of the primary conditions in sub-paragraph (2), together with such further conditions as may be prescribed by the Secretary of State by order, are met.

3(2) The primary conditions referred to in sub-paragraph (1) are–

(a) that the provision of that information would involve a disproportionate effort, or

(b) that the recording of the information to be contained in the data by, or the disclosure of the data by, the data controller is necessary for compliance with any legal obligation to which the data controller is subject, other than an obligation imposed by contract.

History – In para. 3, the reference to "Secretary of State" substituted for "Lord Chancellor" by SI 2003/1887, art. 9 and Sch. 2, para. 9(1) with effect from 19 August 2003.
In para. 3, the reference to "Lord Chancellor" substituted for "Secretary of State" by SI 2001/3500, art. 8 and Sch. 2, para. 6(1) with effect from 26 November 2001.

Statutory instruments – SI 2000/185: made under para. 3(1).

4(1) Personal data which contain a general identifier falling within a description prescribed by the Secretary of State by order are not to be treated as processed fairly and lawfully unless they are processed in compliance with any conditions so prescribed in relation to general identifiers of that description.

4(2) In sub-paragraph (1) **"a general identifier"** means any identifier (such as, for example, a number or code used for identification purposes) which–

(a) relates to an individual, and

(b) forms part of a set of similar identifiers which is of general application.

History – In para. 4, the reference to "Secretary of State" substituted for "Lord Chancellor" by SI 2003/1887, art. 9 and Sch. 2, para. 9(1) with effect from 19 August 2003.
In para. 4, the reference to "Lord Chancellor" substituted for "Secretary of State" by SI 2001/3500, art. 8 and Sch. 2, para. 6(1) with effect from 26 November 2001.

THE SECOND PRINCIPLE

5 The purpose or purposes for which personal data are obtained may in particular be specified–

(a) in a notice given for the purposes of paragraph 2 by the data controller to the data subject, or

(b) in a notification given to the Commissioner under Part III of this Act.

6 In determining whether any disclosure of personal data is compatible with the purpose or purposes for which the data were obtained, regard is to be had to the purpose or purposes for which the personal data are intended to be processed by any person to whom they are disclosed.

THE FOURTH PRINCIPLE

7 The fourth principle is not to be regarded as being contravened by reason of any inaccuracy in personal data which accurately record information obtained by the data controller from the data subject or a third party in a case where–

(a) having regard to the purpose or purposes for which the data were obtained and further processed, the data controller has taken reasonable steps to ensure the accuracy of the data, and

(b) if the data subject has notified the data controller of the data subject's view that the data are inaccurate, the data indicate that fact.

THE SIXTH PRINCIPLE

8 A person is to be regarded as contravening the sixth principle if, but only if–

(a) he contravenes section 7 by failing to supply information in accordance with that section,

(b) he contravenes section 10 by failing to comply with a notice given under subsection (1) of that section to the extent that the notice is justified or by failing to give a notice under subsection (3) of that section,

(c) he contravenes section 11 by failing to comply with a notice given under subsection (1) of that section, or

(d) he contravenes section 12 by failing to comply with a notice given under subsection (1) or (2)(b) of that section or by failing to give a notification under subsection (2)(a) of that section or a notice under subsection (3) of that section.

(e) [No longer in force.]

History – Para. 8(e) and the preceding word "or" temporarily inserted until 23 October 2007 by Sch. 13, para. 5.

THE SEVENTH PRINCIPLE

9 Having regard to the state of technological development and the cost of implementing any measures, the measures must ensure a level of security appropriate to–

(a) the harm that might result from such unauthorised or unlawful processing or accidental loss, destruction or damage as are mentioned in the seventh principle, and

(b) the nature of the data to be protected.

10 The data controller must take reasonable steps to ensure the reliability of any employees of his who have access to the personal data.

11 Where processing of personal data is carried out by a data processor on behalf of a data controller, the data controller must in order to comply with the seventh principle–

(a) choose a data processor providing sufficient guarantees in respect of the technical and organisational security measures governing the processing to be carried out, and

(b) take reasonable steps to ensure compliance with those measures.

12 Where processing of personal data is carried out by a data processor on behalf of a data controller, the data controller is not to be regarded as complying with the seventh principle unless–

(a) the processing is carried out under a contract–

(i) which is made or evidenced in writing, and

(ii) under which the data processor is to act only on instructions from the data controller, and

(b) the contract requires the data processor to comply with obligations equivalent to those imposed on a data controller by the seventh principle.

THE EIGHTH PRINCIPLE

13 An adequate level of protection is one which is adequate in all the circumstances of the case, having regard in particular to–

(a) the nature of the personal data,

(b) the country or territory of origin of the information contained in the data,

(c) the country or territory of final destination of that information,

(d) the purposes for which and period during which the data are intended to be processed,

(e) the law in force in the country or territory in question,

(f) the international obligations of that country or territory,

(g) any relevant codes of conduct or other rules which are enforceable in that country or territory (whether generally or by arrangement in particular cases), and

(h) any security measures taken in respect of the data in that country or territory.

14 The eighth principle does not apply to a transfer falling within any paragraph of Schedule 4, except in such circumstances and to such extent as the Secretary of State may by order provide.

History – In para. 14, the reference to "Secretary of State" substituted for "Lord Chancellor" by SI 2003/1887, art. 9 and Sch. 2, para. 9(1) with effect from 19 August 2003.

In para. 14, the reference to "Lord Chancellor" substituted for "Secretary of State" by SI 2001/3500, art. 8 and Sch. 2, para. 6(1) with effect from 26 November 2001.

15(1) Where–

(a) in any proceedings under this Act any question arises as to whether the requirement of the eighth principle as to an adequate level of protection is met in relation to the transfer of any personal data to a country or territory outside the European Economic Area, and

(b) a Community finding has been made in relation to transfers of the kind in question,

that question is to be determined in accordance with that finding.

15(2) In sub-paragraph (1) **"Community finding"** means a finding of the European Commission, under the procedure provided for in Article 31(2) of the Data Protection Directive, that a country or territory outside the European Economic Area does, or does not, ensure an adequate level of protection within the meaning of Article 25(2) of the Directive.

SCHEDULE 2 – CONDITIONS RELEVANT FOR PURPOSES OF THE FIRST PRINCIPLE: PROCESSING OF ANY PERSONAL DATA

1 The data subject has given his consent to the processing.

2 The processing is necessary–

(a) for the performance of a contract to which the data subject is a party, or

(b) for the taking of steps at the request of the data subject with a view to entering into a contract.

3 The processing is necessary for compliance with any legal obligation to which the data controller is subject, other than an obligation imposed by contract.

4 The processing is necessary in order to protect the vital interests of the data subject.

5 The processing is necessary–

(a) for the administration of justice,

(aa) for the exercise of any functions of either House of Parliament,

(b) for the exercise of any functions conferred on any person by or under any enactment,

(c) for the exercise of any functions of the Crown, a Minister of the Crown or a government department, or

(d) for the exercise of any other functions of a public nature exercised in the public interest by any person.

History – Para. 5(aa) inserted by FOIA 2000, s. 73 and Sch. 6. para. 4 with effect from 1 January 2005 (by virtue of SI 2004/1909, art. 2(2)(f)).

6(1) The processing is necessary for the purposes of legitimate interests pursued by the data controller or by the third party or parties to whom the data are disclosed, except where the processing is unwarranted in any particular case by reason of prejudice to the rights and freedoms or legitimate interests of the data subject.

6(2) The Secretary of State may by order specify particular circumstances in which this condition is, or is not, to be taken to be satisfied.

History – In para. 6, the reference to "Secretary of State" substituted for "Lord Chancellor" by SI 2003/1887, art. 9 and Sch. 2, para. 9(1) with effect from 19 August 2003.
In para. 6, the reference to "Lord Chancellor" substituted for "Secretary of State" by SI 2001/3500, art. 8 and Sch. 2, para. 6(1) with effect from 26 November 2001.

SCHEDULE 3 – CONDITIONS RELEVANT FOR PURPOSES OF THE FIRST PRINCIPLE: PROCESSING OF SENSITIVE PERSONAL DATA

1 The data subject has given his explicit consent to the processing of the personal data.

2(1) The processing is necessary for the purposes of exercising or performing any right or obligation which is conferred or imposed by law on the data controller in connection with employment.

2(2) The Secretary of State may by order–

(a) exclude the application of sub-paragraph (1) in such cases as may be specified, or

(b) provide that, in such cases as may be specified, the condition in sub-paragraph (1) is not to be regarded as satisfied unless such further conditions as may be specified in the order are also satisfied.

History – In para. 2, the reference to "Secretary of State" substituted for "Lord Chancellor" by SI 2003/1887, art. 9 and Sch. 2, para. 9(1) with effect from 19 August 2003.
In para. 2, the reference to "Lord Chancellor" substituted for "Secretary of State" by SI 2001/3500, art. 8 and Sch. 2, para. 6(1) with effect from 26 November 2001.

3 The processing is necessary–

(a) in order to protect the vital interests of the data subject or another person, in a case where–

(i) consent cannot be given by or on behalf of the data subject, or

(ii) the data controller cannot reasonably be expected to obtain the consent of the data subject, or

(b) in order to protect the vital interests of another person, in a case where consent by or on behalf of the data subject has been unreasonably withheld.

4 The processing–

(a) is carried out in the course of its legitimate activities by any body or association which–

(i) is not established or conducted for profit, and

(ii) exists for political, philosophical, religious or trade-union purposes,

(b) is carried out with appropriate safeguards for the rights and freedoms of data subjects,

(c) relates only to individuals who either are members of the body or association or have regular contact with it in connection with its purposes, and

(d) does not involve disclosure of the personal data to a third party without the consent of the data subject.

5 The information contained in the personal data has been made public as a result of steps deliberately taken by the data subject.

6 The processing–

(a) is necessary for the purpose of, or in connection with, any legal proceedings (including prospective legal proceedings),

(b) is necessary for the purpose of obtaining legal advice, or

(c) is otherwise necessary for the purposes of establishing, exercising or defending legal rights.

7(1) The processing is necessary–

(a) for the administration of justice,

(aa) for the exercise of any functions of either House of Parliament,

(b) for the exercise of any functions conferred on any person by or under an enactment, or

(c) for the exercise of any functions of the Crown, a Minister of the Crown or a government department.

7(2) The Secretary of State may by order–

(a) exclude the application of sub-paragraph (1) in such cases as may be specified, or

(b) provide that, in such cases as may be specified, the condition in sub-paragraph (1) is not to be regarded as satisfied unless such further conditions as may be specified in the order are also satisfied.

History – Para. 7(1)(aa) inserted by FOIA 2000, s. 73 and Sch. 6, para. 5 (although the Queen's Printer copy does not specify which subparagraph of para. 7 is to be amended) with effect from 1 January 2005 (by virtue of SI 2004/1909, art. 2(2)(f)).

In para. 7(2), the reference to "Secretary of State" substituted for "Lord Chancellor" by SI 2003/1887, art. 9 and Sch. 2, para. 9(1) with effect from 19 August 2003.

In para. 7(2), the reference to "Lord Chancellor" substituted for "Secretary of State" by SI 2001/3500, art. 8 and Sch. 2, para. 6(1) with effect from 26 November 2001.

7A(1) The processing–

(a) is either–

(i) the disclosure of sensitive personal data by a person as a member of an anti-fraud organisation or otherwise in accordance with any arrangements made by such an organisation; or

(ii) any other processing by that person or another person of sensitive personal data so disclosed; and

(b) is necessary for the purposes of preventing fraud or a particular kind of fraud.

7A(2) In this paragraph **"an anti-fraud organisation"** means any unincorporated association, body corporate or other person which enables or facilitates any sharing of information to prevent fraud or a particular kind of fraud or which has any of these functions as its purpose or one of its purposes.

History – Para 7A inserted by the Serious Crime Act 2007, s. 72, with effect from 1 October 2008 (SI 2008/2504, art. 2).

8(1) The processing is necessary for medical purposes and is undertaken by–

(a) a health professional, or

(b) a person who in the circumstances owes a duty of confidentiality which is equivalent to that which would arise if that person were a health professional.

8(2) In this paragraph **"medical purposes"** includes the purposes of preventative medicine, medical diagnosis, medical research, the provision of care and treatment and the management of healthcare services.

9(1) The processing–

(a) is of sensitive personal data consisting of information as to racial or ethnic origin,

(b) is necessary for the purpose of identifying or keeping under review the existence or absence of equality of opportunity or treatment between persons of different racial or ethnic origins, with a view to enabling such equality to be promoted or maintained, and

(c) is carried out with appropriate safeguards for the rights and freedoms of data subjects.

9(2) The Secretary of State may by order specify circumstances in which processing falling within sub-paragraph (1)(a) and (b) is, or is not, to be taken for the purposes of sub-paragraph (1)(c) to be carried out with appropriate safeguards for the rights and freedoms of data subjects.

History – In para. 9, the reference to "Secretary of State" substituted for "Lord Chancellor" by SI 2003/1887, art. 9 and Sch. 2, para. 9(1) with effect from 19 August 2003.

In para. 9, the reference to "Lord Chancellor" substituted for "Secretary of State" by SI 2001/3500, art. 8 and Sch. 2, para. 6(1) with effect from 26 November 2001.

10 The personal data are processed in circumstances specified in an order made by the Secretary of State for the purposes of this paragraph.

History – In para. 10, the reference to "Secretary of State" substituted for "Lord Chancellor" by SI 2003/1887, art. 9 and Sch. 2, para. 9(1) with effect from 19 August 2003.

In para. 10, the reference to "Lord Chancellor" substituted for "Secretary of State" by SI 2001/3500, art. 8 and Sch. 2, para. 6(1) with effect from 26 November 2001.

FINANCE ACT 1998

(1998 Chapter 36) [*31st July 1998*]

ARRANGEMENT OF SECTIONS

PART III – INCOME TAX, CORPORATION TAX AND CAPITAL GAINS TAX

CHAPTER I – INCOME TAX AND CORPORATION TAX

PART III – INCOME TAX, CORPORATION TAX AND CAPITAL GAINS TAX

Chapter I – INCOME TAX AND CORPORATION TAX

INCOME TAX CHARGE, RATES AND RELIEFS

25 Charge and rates for 1998–99

25 [Repealed by ITA 2007, s. 1031 and Sch. 3, Pt. 1.]

History – S. 25 repealed by ITA 2007, s. 1031 and Sch. 3, Pt. 1, with effect from 6 April 2007.

26 Relief for a woman with a child and an incapacitated husband

26 [Repealed by FA 1999, s. 139 and Sch. 20, Pt. III(4).]

History – S. 26 repealed by FA 1999, s. 139 and Sch. 20, Pt. III(4), with effect for the year 2000–01 and subsequent years of assessment.

27 Married couple's allowance etc. in and after 1999–00

27(1) The Taxes Act 1988 shall have effect for the year 1999–00 and subsequent years of assessment with the following amendments–

(a) [omitted by FA 2009, s. 5 and Sch. 1, para. 6(i);]

(b) [repealed by TIOPA 2010, s. 378 and Sch. 10, Pt. 13.]

27(2) For the purposes only of applying section 257C of the Taxes Act 1988 (indexation) for the year 1999–00, the amounts specified for the year 1998–99 in subsections (2) and (3) of section 257A of that Act (married couple's allowance for persons of 65 or more) shall be taken to have been £4,965 and £5,025, respectively.

History – S. 27(1)(a) omitted by FA 2009, s. 5 and Sch. 1, para. 6(i), with effect for the tax year 2010–11 and subsequent tax years. S. 27(1)(b) repealed by TIOPA 2010, s. 378 and Sch. 10, Pt. 13, with effect for corporation tax purposes for accounting periods ending on or after 1 April 2010, for income tax and capital gains tax purposes for the tax year 2010–11 and subsequent tax years, and for petroleum revenue tax purposes for chargeable periods beginning on or after 1 July 2010.

CORPORATION TAX CHARGE AND RATES

28 Charge and rates for financial year 1998

28(1) [Spent; set rate of corporation tax for the financial year 1998.]

28(2) [Repealed by CTA 2010, s. 1181 and Sch. 3, Pt. 1.]

History – S. 28(2) repealed by CTA 2010, s. 1181 and Sch. 3, Pt. 1, with effect for corporation tax purposes for accounting periods ending on or after 1 April 2010, and for income tax and capital gains tax purposes for the tax year 2010–11 and subsequent tax years.

Notes – S. 28(2) not rewritten, as spent.

29 Charge and rates for financial year 1999

29(1) [Spent; set rate of corporation tax for the financial year 1999.]

29(2) [Repealed by CTA 2010, s. 1181 and Sch. 3, Pt. 1.]

History – S. 29(2) repealed by CTA 2010, s. 1181 and Sch. 3, Pt. 1, with effect for corporation tax purposes for accounting periods ending on or after 1 April 2010, and for income tax and capital gains tax purposes for the tax year 2010–11 and subsequent tax years.

Notes – S. 29(2) not rewritten, as spent.

CORPORATION TAX: PERIODIC PAYMENTS ETC.

30 Corporation tax: due and payable date

30(1) [Inserts TMA 1970, s. 59E.]

30((2)–(6)) [Repealed by Statute Law (Repeals) Act 2013, s. 1 and Sch. 1, Pt. 10.]

History – S. 30(2)–(6) repealed by Statute Law (Repeals) Act 2013, s. 1 and Sch. 1, Pt. 10, with effect from 31 January 2013.

Cross references – SI 2003/282: electronic delivery of information and payments required to be delivered under s. 30.

31 Abolition of advance corporation tax

31(1) No company resident in the United Kingdom shall be liable to pay advance corporation tax in respect of any qualifying distribution made on or after 6th April 1999.

31(2) For the purposes of the Tax Acts, no distribution made on or after 6th April 1999 shall be treated as giving rise to the making of a franked payment.

31(3) No franked investment income which is attributable to a distribution made on or after 6th April 1999 shall be used to frank any distributions of a company.

31(4) Section 238(3) of the Taxes Act 1988 shall apply for the purposes of subsection (3) above as it applies for the purposes of Chapter V of Part VI of that Act.

31(5) Schedule 3 to this Act (which makes provision for and in connection with the abolition of advance corporation tax) shall have effect.

32 Unrelieved surplus advance corporation tax

32(1) The Treasury may by regulations make provision for or in connection with enabling unrelieved surplus advance corporation tax to be set against liability to corporation tax on profits charged to corporation tax for accounting periods ending on or after 6th April 1999 (and thus to discharge a corresponding amount of any such liability).

32(2) Without prejudice to the generality of subsection (1) above, regulations under this section may make provision–

(a) for or in connection with imposing a limit or limits on the amount of unrelieved surplus advance corporation tax which may be set against liability to corporation tax on profits charged to corporation tax for an accounting period;

(b) for or in connection with the carrying forward of unrelieved surplus advance corporation tax from earlier accounting periods to later accounting periods;

(c) for or in connection with the recovery of corporation tax from companies in prescribed circumstances where any such liability as is mentioned in paragraph (a) above is or has been discharged by the set-off of unrelieved surplus advance corporation tax;

(d) for or in connection with the reduction or extinguishment of unrelieved surplus advance corporation tax;

(e) for or in connection with treating notional amounts of advance corporation tax ("shadow ACT") as paid by companies in respect of distributions made on or after 6th April 1999;

(f) for or in connection with the determination of amounts of shadow ACT which are treated as paid by companies in respect of distributions made on or after 6th April 1999;

(g) in relation to the treatment of shadow ACT;

(h) in relation to the treatment of companies which have prescribed relationships or connections with each other;

(i) in relation to the treatment of prescribed events, arrangements or transactions involving companies with unrelieved surplus advance corporation tax.

32(3) The provision which may be made by regulations under this section includes provision–

(a) for or in connection with treating shadow ACT as reducing any limit or limits on the amount of unrelieved surplus advance corporation tax which may be set against any such liability as is mentioned in subsection (2)(a) above;

(b) for or in connection with the carrying forward of shadow ACT from earlier accounting periods to later accounting periods;

(c) for or in connection with the carrying back of shadow ACT from later accounting periods to earlier accounting periods;

(d) for or in connection with the transfer of shadow ACT between companies;

(e) for or in connection with the reduction or extinguishment of shadow ACT.

32(4) The provision which may be made by virtue of subsection (2)(c) above includes provision for or in connection with the recovery of corporation tax from a company which has a prescribed relationship or connection with a company whose liability to corporation tax is or has been discharged by the set-off of unrelieved surplus advance corporation tax.

32(5) The provision which may be made by regulations under this section includes provision for or in connection with enabling unrelieved surplus advance corporation tax to be set against liability to a sum charged at step 5 in section 371BC(1) of the Taxation (International and Other Provisions) Act 2010 (controlled foreign companies) as if it were an amount of corporation tax for an accounting period.

32(6) In this section **"unrelieved surplus advance corporation tax"** means the advance corporation tax (if any) which, apart from sub-paragraph (3) of paragraph 12 of Schedule 3 to this Act but otherwise in accordance with that paragraph, would be treated by virtue of section 239(4) of the Taxes Act 1988 as paid in respect of distributions made by a company in the first accounting period of the company to begin on or after 6th April 1999.

32(7) The reference in subsection (6) above to an accounting period beginning on or after 6th April 1999 includes a reference to a separate accounting period mentioned in section 245(2) of the Taxes Act 1988 which begins on 6th April 1999.

32(8) Regulations under this section–

(a) may make such modifications of any provisions of the Tax Acts, or

(b) may apply such provisions of the Tax Acts,

as the Treasury think necessary or expedient for or in connection with giving effect to the provisions of this section.

32(9) Regulations under this section which apply any provisions of the Tax Acts may apply those provisions either without modifications or with such modifications as the Treasury think necessary or expedient for or in connection with giving effect to the provisions of this section.

32(10) Regulations under this section–

(a) may make different provision for different purposes, cases or circumstances;

(b) may make different provision in relation to companies or accounting periods of different descriptions;

(c) may make such supplementary, incidental, consequential or transitional provision as appears to the Treasury to be necessary or expedient.

32(11) Regulations under this section may make provision in relation to accounting periods beginning before (as well as accounting periods beginning on or after) the date on which the regulations are made.

32(12) In this section–

"modifications" includes amendments, additions and omissions;

"prescribed" means prescribed by regulations made under this section.

History – S. 32(5) substituted by FA 2012, s. 180 and Sch. 20, para. 16, with effect in relation to accounting periods of controlled foreign companies beginning on or after 1 January 2013 (subject to the transitional provisions at FA 2012, Sch. 20, para. 50).
In s. 32(6), "paragraph 12" substituted by FA 1999, s. 91(4), and deemed always to have had effect.

Cross references – ICTA 1988, s. 501B: assessment recovery and postponement of supplementary charge.

Statutory instruments – SI 1999/358: made under s. 32.

33 Relief for interest payable under the Tax Acts

33(1) *Section 90 of the* Taxes Management Act 1970 (interest on overdue tax to be paid without deduction of income tax and not to be allowed as a deduction in computing income, profits or losses) shall be amended as follows.

33(2) [Amends TMA 1970, s. 90(1)]

(a) [amends TMA 1970, s. 90(1)]

(b) [repealed by CTA 2009, s. 1326 and Sch. 3, Pt. 1.]

33(3) [Repealed by CTA 2009, s. 1326 and Sch. 3, Pt. 1.]

33(4) [Repealed by CTA 2009, s. 1326 and Sch. 3, Pt. 1.]

33(5) [Repealed by CTA 2009, s. 1326 and Sch. 3, Pt. 1.]

History – S. 33(2)(b), and the word "and" immediately before it, repealed by CTA 2009, s. 1326 and Sch. 3, Pt. 1, with effect for corporation tax purposes for accounting periods ending on or after 1 April 2009, and for income tax and capital gains tax purposes for the tax year 2009–10 and subsequent tax years.

S. 33(3) repealed by CTA 2009, s. 1326 and Sch. 3, Pt. 1, with effect for corporation tax purposes for accounting periods ending on or after 1 April 2009, and for income tax and capital gains tax purposes for the tax year 2009–10 and subsequent tax years.

S. 33(4) repealed by CTA 2009, s. 1326 and Sch. 3, Pt. 1, with effect for corporation tax purposes for accounting periods ending on or after 1 April 2009, and for income tax and capital gains tax purposes for the tax year 2009–10 and subsequent tax years.

S. 33(5) repealed by CTA 2009, s. 1326 and Sch. 3, Pt. 1, with effect for corporation tax purposes for accounting periods ending on or after 1 April 2009, and for income tax and capital gains tax purposes for the tax year 2009–10 and subsequent tax years.

Notes – The day appointed under FA 1994, s. 199 is 1 July 1999 (SI 1998/3173 (C. 78)).

34 Charge to tax on interest payable under the Tax Acts

34(1) Section 826 of the Taxes Act 1988 (interest on tax overpaid) shall be amended as follows.

34(2) [Amends ICTA 1988, s. 826(5).]

34(3) [Amends ICTA 1988, s. 826(5)(b).]

34(4) [Inserts ICTA 1988, s. 826(5A).]

34(5) The amendments made by subsections (3) and (4) above have effect in relation to interest payable by virtue of any paragraph of section 826(1) of the Taxes Act 1988 if the accounting period mentioned in that paragraph is one which ends on or after the day appointed under section 199 of the Finance Act 1994 for the purposes of Chapter III of Part IV of that Act (corporation tax self-assessment).

Notes – The day appointed under FA 1994, s. 199 is 1 July 1999 (SI 1998/3173 (C. 78)).

35 Further provision about interest payable under the Tax Acts

35 Schedule 4 to this Act (which makes further amendments relating to interest payable under the Tax Acts by or to companies) shall have effect.

36 Arrangements with respect to payment of corporation tax

36 [Omitted by TIOPA 2010, s. 371 and Sch. 7, para. 82 and repealed by TIOPA 2010, s. 378 and Sch. 10, Pt. 12.]

History – S. 36 omitted by TIOPA 2010, s. 371 and Sch. 7, para. 82 and repealed by TIOPA 2010, s. 378 and Sch. 10, Pt. 12, with effect for corporation tax purposes for accounting periods ending on or after 1 April 2010, for income tax and capital gains tax purposes for the tax year 2010–11 and subsequent tax years, and for petroleum revenue tax purposes for chargeable periods beginning on or after 1 July 2010.

Notes – S. 36 rewritten in TIOPA 2010, Sch. 7, para. 79.

GILT-EDGED SECURITIES

37 Abolition of periodic accounting

37(1) [Repeals ICTA 1988, s. 51B.]

37(2) [Repealed by FA 2001, s. 110 and Sch. 33, Pt. 2(12).]

37(3) The preceding provisions of this section have effect in relation only to payments of interest falling due on or after such day as the Treasury may by order appoint.

History – S. 37(2) repealed by FA 2001, s. 110 and Sch. 33, Pt. 2(12) in relation to tax credits in respect of distributions made on or after 6 April 2004, and in relation to income tax borne by deduction from payments received after 30 September 2001.

Notes – The day appointed under s. 37 is 1 April 1999 by virtue of SI 1999/619 (C. 16).

RENTS AND OTHER RECEIPTS FROM LAND

38 Taxation of rents and other receipts from land

38(1) The provisions of Schedule 5 to this Act have effect with respect to tax on rents and other receipts from land.

Part I contains amendments relating to the charge to tax under Schedule A or Case V of Schedule D on rents and other receipts from land.

Part II contains amendments about relief for losses incurred in a Schedule A business or overseas property business, and the relationship between such relief and other reliefs.

Part III contains minor and consequential amendments.

38(2) So far as relating to income tax, the provisions of Parts I to III of that Schedule have effect for the year 1998–99 and subsequent years of assessment.

38(3) So far as relating to corporation tax, the provisions of Parts I to III of that Schedule come into force on 1st April 1998, subject to the transitional provisions in Part IV of the Schedule.

39 Land managed as one estate and maintenance funds for historic buildings

39 Sections 26 and 27 of the Taxes Act 1988 (deductions from rent: land managed as one estate and maintenance funds for historic buildings) shall cease to have effect–

(a) for income tax purposes, on and after 6th April 2001;

(b) for corporation tax purposes, for accounting periods beginning on or after 1st April 2001.

40 Treatment of premiums as rent

40 [Repealed by CTA 2009, s. 1326 and Sch. 3, Pt. 1.]

History – S. 40 repealed by CTA 2009, s. 1326 and Sch. 3, Pt. 1, with effect for corporation tax purposes for accounting periods ending on or after 1 April 2009, and for income tax and capital gains tax purposes for the tax year 2009–10 and subsequent tax years.

41 Tied premises: receipts and expenses treated as those of trade

41(1) [Repealed by CTA 2009, s. 1326 and Sch. 3, Pt. 1.]

41(2) [Substitutes TCGA 1992, s. 156(4).]

41(3) The above amendments have effect on and after 17th March 1998, subject to the following transitional provisions. In those provisions–

"before commencement" and **"after commencement"** mean, respectively, before 17th March 1998 and on or after that date; and

"the new section 98" means the section as substituted by subsection (1) above.

41(4) [Repealed by CTA 2009, s. 1326 and Sch. 3, Pt. 1.]

41(5) [Repealed by CTA 2009, s. 1326 and Sch. 3, Pt. 1.]

41(6) [Repealed by CTA 2009, s. 1326 and Sch. 3, Pt. 1.]

41(7) [Repealed by CTA 2009, s. 1326 and Sch. 3, Pt. 1.]

History – S. 41(1) repealed by CTA 2009, s. 1326 and Sch. 3, Pt. 1, with effect for corporation tax purposes for accounting periods ending on or after 1 April 2009, and for income tax and capital gains tax purposes for the tax year 2009–10 and subsequent tax years.
S. 41(4) repealed by CTA 2009, s. 1326 and Sch. 3, Pt. 1, with effect for corporation tax purposes for accounting periods ending on or after 1 April 2009, and for income tax and capital gains tax purposes for the tax year 2009–10 and subsequent tax years.
S. 41(5) repealed by CTA 2009, s. 1326 and Sch. 3, Pt. 1, with effect for corporation tax purposes for accounting periods ending on or after 1 April 2009, and for income tax and capital gains tax purposes for the tax year 2009–10 and subsequent tax years.
S. 41(6) repealed by CTA 2009, s. 1326 and Sch. 3, Pt. 1, with effect for corporation tax purposes for accounting periods ending on or after 1 April 2009, and for income tax and capital gains tax purposes for the tax year 2009–10 and subsequent tax years.
S. 41(7) repealed by CTA 2009, s. 1326 and Sch. 3, Pt. 1, with effect for corporation tax purposes for accounting periods ending on or after 1 April 2009, and for income tax and capital gains tax purposes for the tax year 2009–10 and subsequent tax years.

COMPUTATION OF PROFITS OF TRADE, PROFESSION OR VOCATION

42 Computation of profits of trade, profession or vocation

42 [Omitted by CTA 2009, s. 1322 and Sch. 1, para. 452 and repealed by CTA 2009, s. 1326 and Sch. 3, Pt. 1.]

History – S. 42 omitted by CTA 2009, s. 1322 and Sch. 1, para. 452 and repealed by CTA 2009, s. 1326 and Sch. 3, Pt. 1, with effect for corporation tax purposes for accounting periods ending on or after 1 April 2009, and for income tax and capital gains tax purposes for the tax year 2009–10 and subsequent tax years.

Notes – S. 42 rewritten for corporation tax purposes as follows:
S. 42(1): CTA 2009, s. 46(1).
S. 42(2): CTA 2009, s. 46(2).
S. 42(5): CTA 2009, s. 46(3).

43 Barristers and advocates in early years of practice

43 [Omitted by ITTOIA 2005, s. 882(1) and Sch. 1, para. 501; and repealed by ITTOIA 2005, s. 884 and Sch. 3.]

History – S. 43 omitted by ITTOIA 2005, s. 882(1) and Sch. 1, para. 501; and repealed by ITTOIA 2005, s. 884 and Sch. 3 effective for income tax purposes for 2005–06 onwards and for corporation tax purposes for accounting periods ending after 5 April 2005 (ITTOIA 2005, s. 883(1)).

Notes – The repealed income tax material is principally rewritten at ITTOIA 2005, s. 160.

44 Change of accounting basis

44 [Repealed by FA 2002, s. 64(6), s. 141 and Sch. 40, Pt. 3(8).]

History – S. 44 repealed by FA 2002, s. 64(6) and s. 141 and Sch. 40, Pt. 3(8) with effect for a change of basis taking effect in an accounting period ending on or after 1 August 2001.

Notes – FA 2002, s. 64 and Sch. 22 have effect in place of s. 44 and Sch. 6, where a change of basis takes effect in a period of account ending on or after 1 August 2001, subject to transitional rules where certain changes of basis take effect in a period of account ending prior to 1 August 2001 if the relevant return is delivered or amended on or after that date (FA 2002, Sch. 22, para. 16 and 17).

45 Meaning of "period of account"

45 [Repealed by FA 2002, s. 141 and Sch. 40, Pt. 3(16).]

History – S. 45 repealed by FA 2002, s. 141 and Sch. 40, Pt. 3(16) with effect from 24 July 2002.

46 Minor and consequential provisions about computations

46(1) [Omitted by CTA 2009, s. 1322 and Sch. 1, para. 453 and repealed by CTA 2009, s. 1326 and Sch. 3, Pt. 1.]

46(2) [Omitted by CTA 2009, s. 1322 and Sch. 1, para. 453 and repealed by CTA 2009, s. 1326 and Sch. 3, Pt. 1.]

46(3) In the provisions of the Tax Acts which refer to the subject of the charge under Case I or II of Schedule D as "profits or gains" or "profits and gains" of a trade, profession or vocation–

(a) for "profits or gains" or "profits and gains", wherever occurring, substitute "profits", and

(b) for "arising or accruing", in reference to such profits or gains, substitute "arising".

The provisions affected are listed in Schedule 7 to this Act.

History – S. 46(1) omitted by CTA 2009, s. 1322 and Sch. 1, para. 453 and repealed by CTA 2009, s. 1326 and Sch. 3, Pt. 1, with effect for corporation tax purposes for accounting periods ending on or after 1 April 2009, and for income tax and capital gains tax purposes for the tax year 2009–10 and subsequent tax years.
In former s. 46(1) the words "Corporation Tax Acts" substituted for the words "Tax Acts" by ITTOIA 2005, s. 882(1) and Sch. 1, para. 502(2) effective for income tax purposes for 2005–06 onwards and for corporation tax purposes for accounting periods ending after 5 April 2005 (ITTOIA 2005, s. 883(1)).
S. 46(2) omitted by CTA 2009, s. 1322 and Sch. 1, para. 453 and repealed by CTA 2009, s. 1326 and Sch. 3, Pt. 1, with effect for corporation tax purposes for accounting periods ending on or after 1 April 2009, and for income tax and capital gains tax purposes for the tax year 2009–10 and subsequent tax years.
In former s. 46(2) the words "corporation tax purposes" substituted for the words "any purpose of the Tax Acts" by ITTOIA 2005, s. 882(1) and Sch. 1, para. 502(3) effective for income tax purposes for 2005–06 onwards and for corporation tax purposes for accounting periods ending after 5 April 2005 (ITTOIA 2005, s. 883(1)).

Notes – S. 46 rewritten for corporation tax purposes as follows:
S. 46(1): CTA 2009, s. 48(1), (2) and (3).
S. 46(2): CTA 2009, s. 47(1) and (2).
The income tax rules are principally rewritten at ITTOIA 2005, s. 26 and s. 27.

GIFTS TO CHARITIES

47 Gifts in kind for relief in poor countries

47 [Repealed by FA 1999, s. 55(2), s. 139 and Sch. 20, Pt. III(12).]

History – S. 47 repealed by FA 1999, s. 55(2), 139 and Sch. 20, Pt. III(12), with effect in relation to gifts made on or after 27 July 1999.

48 Gifts of money for relief in poor countries

48 [Repealed by FA 2011, s. 91 and Sch. 26, para. 2(1).]

History – S. 48 repealed by FA 2011, s. 91 and Sch. 26, para. 2(1) with effect from 19 July 2011.

EMPLOYEE SHARE INCENTIVES

49 Employee Share Options

49 [Repealed by ITEPA 2003, Sch. 8, Pt. 1.]

History – S. 49 repealed by ITEPA 2003, Sch. 8, Pt. 1 which has effect for the tax year 2003–04 and subsequent tax years.

Notes – S. 49(2) has been rewritten into the provision of ITEPA 2003, Sch. 7, para. 62.

50 Conditional acquisition of shares

50 [Repealed by ITEPA 2003, Sch. 8, Pt. 1.]

History – S. 50 repealed by ITEPA 2003, Sch. 8, Pt. 1 which has effect for the tax year 2003–04 and subsequent tax years.

Notes – S. 50(4) has been rewritten into the provision of ITEPA 2003, Sch. 7, para. 44.

51 Convertible shares provided to directors and employees

51 [Repealed by ITEPA 2003, Sch. 8, Pt. 1.]

History – S. 51 repealed by ITEPA 2003, Sch. 8, Pt. 1 which has effect for the tax year 2003–04 and subsequent tax years.
Notes – S. 51(3) has been rewritten into the provision of ITEPA 2003, Sch. 7, para. 49.

52 Information powers

52 [Repealed by ITEPA 2003, Sch. 8, Pt. 1.]

History – S. 52 repealed by ITEPA 2003, Sch. 8, Pt. 1 which has effect for the tax year 2003–04 and subsequent tax years.

53 Provision supplemental to sections 50 to 52

53 [Repealed by ITEPA 2003, Sch. 8, Pt. 1.]

History – S. 53 repealed by ITEPA 2003, Sch. 8, Pt. 1 which has effect for the tax year 2003–04 and subsequent tax years.

54 Amendments consequential on sections 50 to 53

54(1) The Taxation of Chargeable Gains Act 1992 shall be amended as follows.

54(2) [Inserts TCGA 1992, s. 120(5A), (5B).]

54(3) [Amends TCGA 1992, s. 120(7).]

54(4) [Inserts TCGA 1992, s. 120(8).]

54(5) [Inserts TCGA 1992, s. 149B.]

54(6) This section has effect in relation to disposals on or after 17th March 1998 of interests and shares acquired on or after that date.

CONSTRUCTION INDUSTRY WORKERS

55 Construction workers supplied by agencies

55(1) [Repealed by ITEPA 2003, Sch. 8, Pt. 1.]

55(2) [Repealed by FA 2004, s. 326 and Sch. 40, Pt. 2(7).]

55(3) Subsections (1) and (2) above have effect in relation to–

(a) any payments made on or after 6th April 1998 other than any made in respect of services rendered before that date; and

(b) any payments made before 6th April 1998 in respect of services to be rendered on or after that date.

History – S. 55(1) repealed by ITEPA 2003, Sch. 8, Pt. 1 which has effect for the tax year 2003–04 and subsequent tax years.
S. 55(2) repealed by FA 2004, s. 326 and Sch. 40, Pt. 2(7), with effect in relation to payments made under contracts relating to construction operations, on or after 6 April 2007, by virtue of notice given pursuant to SI 2005/2045, reg. 1.

56 Transitional provisions in connection with section 55

56(1) Subject to subsection (6) below, subsection (2) below applies if–

(a) a construction trade is being carried on by a person ("the sub-contractor") at the end of the year 1997–98; and

(b) there are receipts of that trade which, but for section 134(5)(c) of the Taxes Act 1988, would have fallen to be treated for the year 1997–98 as the emoluments of an office or employment.

56(2) Where this subsection applies, then, subject to subsections (4) and (5) below–

(a) the trade shall be deemed to have been permanently discontinued at the end of the year 1997–98; and

(b) to the extent (if any) that the trade includes activities in addition to the rendering of services falling by virtue of section 55 to be treated as the duties of an office or employment, a new trade shall be deemed to have been set up and commenced on 6th April 1998.

56(3) Subsection (4) below applies if –

(a) a construction trade ("the old trade") is deemed by virtue of subsection (2)(a) above to have been permanently discontinued; and

(b) a construction trade ("the new trade")–

   (i) is deemed by virtue of subsection (2)(b) above to have been set up and commenced; or

   (ii) (where sub-paragraph (i) above does not apply) is actually set up and commenced in the year 1998–99.

56(4) Where this subsection applies then, notwithstanding the deemed discontinuance, the old trade and the new trade shall be treated as the same for the purposes of section 83 of the Income Tax Act 2007 (carry-forward of losses against subsequent profits).

56(5) An officer of the Board shall not become entitled by virtue of anything in this section to give a direction under paragraph 3(2) of Schedule 20 to the Finance Act 1994 (power to revise assessment so that made on the actual basis) in the case of a person whose trade is deemed under subsection (2) above to cease on 5th April 1998.

56(6) Subsection (2) above does not apply if the sub-contractor by notice to an officer of the Board otherwise elects.

56(7) An election under subsection (6) above–

(a) if it relates to a trade carried on by an individual, must be included in a return under section 8 of the Taxes Management Act 1970 which is made and delivered in that individual's case on or before the day on which it is required to be made and delivered under that section; and

(b) if it relates to a trade carried on by persons in partnership, must be included in a return under section 12AA of that Act which is made and delivered in the partners' case, or in the case of any one or more of them, on or before the day specified in relation to that return under subsection (2) or (3) of that section.

56(8) In this section **"construction trade"** means a trade consisting in or including the rendering of services under contracts relating to construction operations (within the meaning of section 74 of the Finance Act 2004).

56(9) Where at any time on or after 17th March 1998 and before the day on which this Act is passed any election corresponding to an election under subsection (6) above has been made under a resolution of the House of Commons having effect in accordance with the provisions of the Provisional Collection of Taxes Act 1968, this section has effect, on and after the day on which this Act is passed, as if that election were an election under subsection (6) above.

History – In s. 56(4) the words "section 83 of the Income Tax Act 2007" substituted for "section 385 of the Taxes Act 1988" by ITA 2007, s. 1027 and Sch. 1, para. 381, with effect from 6 April 2007.
In s. 56(8) the words "section 74 of the Finance Act 2004 " substituted by the words "Chapter IV of Part XIII of the Taxes Act 1988" by FA 2004, s. 76 and Sch. 12, para. 15(2), with effect, in relation to payments made under contracts relating to construction operations, on or after 6 April 2007, by virtue of notice given pursuant to SI 2005/2045, reg. 1.

57 Sub-contractors in the construction industry

57 [Repealed by FA 2004, s. 326 and Sch. 40, Pt. 2(7).]

History – S. 57 repealed by FA 2004, s. 326 and Sch. 40, Pt. 2(7), with effect in relation to payments made under contracts relating to construction operations, on or after 6 April 2007, by virtue of notice given pursuant to SI 2005/2045, reg. 1.

PAYMENTS AND OTHER BENEFITS IN CONNECTION WITH TERMINATION OF EMPLOYMENT ETC.

58 Payments and other benefits in connection with termination of employment etc.

58 [Repealed by ITEPA 2003, Sch. 8, Pt. 1.]

History – S. 58 repealed by ITEPA 2003, Sch. 8, Pt. 1 which has effect for the tax year 2003–04 and subsequent tax years.

BENEFITS IN KIND

59 Car fuel

59(1) [Substitutes Table in ICTA 1988, s. 158(2).]

59(2) This section shall have effect for the year 1998–99 and subsequent years of assessment.

60 Reductions for road fuel gas cars

60 [Repealed by ITEPA 2003, Sch. 8, Pt. 1.]

History – S. 60 repealed by ITEPA 2003, Sch. 8, Pt. 1 which has effect for the tax year 2003–04 and subsequent tax years.

61 Travelling expenses

61 [Repealed by ITEPA 2003, Sch. 8, Pt. 1.]

History – S. 61 repealed by ITEPA 2003, Sch. 8, Pt. 1 which has effect for the tax year 2003–04 and subsequent tax years.

PROFIT-RELATED PAY

62 Provision preventing manipulation of profit periods

62 [Repealed by Statute Law (Repeals) Act 2013, s. 1 and Sch. 1, Pt. 10.]

History – S. 62 repealed by Statute Law (Repeals) Act 2013, s. 1 and Sch. 1, Pt. 10, with effect from 31 January 2013.

FOREIGN EARNINGS DEDUCTION

63 Withdrawal except in relation to seafarers

63 [Repealed by ITEPA 2003, Sch. 8, Pt. 1.]

History – S. 63 repealed by ITEPA 2003, Sch. 8, Pt. 1 which has effect for the tax year 2003–04 and subsequent tax years.

PAYE: NON-CASH BENEFITS ETC.

64 Transitory provision relating to tradeable assets

64 [Repealed by ITEPA 2003, Sch. 8, Pt. 1.]

History – S. 64 repealed by ITEPA 2003, Sch. 8, Pt. 1 which has effect for the tax year 2003–04 and subsequent tax years.

65 Payment in the form of a readily convertible asset

65 [Repealed by ITEPA 2003, Sch. 8, Pt. 1.]

History – S. 65 repealed by ITEPA 2003, Sch. 8, Pt. 1 which has effect, for income tax purposes, for the tax year 2003–04 and subsequent tax years and, for corporation tax purposes, for accounting periods ending after 5 April 2003.

66 Enhancing the value of an asset

66 [Repealed by ITEPA 2003, Sch. 8, Pt. 1.]

History – S. 66 repealed by ITEPA 2003, Sch. 8, Pt. 1 which has effect, for income tax purposes, for the tax year 2003–04 and subsequent tax years and, for corporation tax purposes, for accounting periods ending after 5 April 2003.

67 Gains from share options etc.

67 [Repealed by ITEPA 2003, Sch. 8, Pt. 1.]

History – S. 67 repealed by ITEPA 2003, Sch. 8, Pt. 1 which has effect, for income tax purposes, for the tax year 2003–04 and subsequent tax years and, for corporation tax purposes, for accounting periods ending after 5 April 2003.

68 Vouchers and credit-tokens

68 [Repealed by ITEPA 2003, Sch. 8, Pt. 1.]

History – S. 68 repealed by ITEPA 2003, Sch. 8, Pt. 1 which has effect, for income tax purposes, for the tax year 2003–04 and subsequent tax years and, for corporation tax purposes, for accounting periods ending after 5 April 2003.

69 Intermediaries, non-UK employers, agencies etc.

69 [Repealed by ITEPA 2003, Sch. 8, Pt. 1.]

History – S. 69 repealed by ITEPA 2003, Sch. 8, Pt. 1 which has effect, for income tax purposes, for the tax year 2003–04 and subsequent tax years and, for corporation tax purposes, for accounting periods ending after 5 April 2003.

THE ENTERPRISE INVESTMENT SCHEME AND VENTURE CAPITAL TRUSTS

70 Qualifying trades for EIS and VCTs

70(1) [Repealed by ITA 2007, s. 1031 and Sch. 3, Pt. 2.]

70(2) [Repealed by ITA 2007, s. 1031 and Sch. 3, Pt. 2.]

70(3) [Repealed by ITA 2007, s. 1031 and Sch. 3, Pt. 1.]

70(4) [Repealed by ITA 2007, s. 1031 and Sch. 3, Pt. 2.]

History – S. 70(1) and (2) repealed by ITA 2007, s. 1031 and Sch. 3, Pt. 2, with effect in relation to shares issued after 5 April 2007.
S. 70(3) repealed by ITA 2007, s. 1031 and Sch. 3, Pt. 1, with effect from 6 April 2007.
S. 70(4) repealed by ITA 2007, s. 1031 and Sch. 3, Pt. 2, with effect in relation to shares issued after 5 April 2007.

Notes – S. 70 rewritten as follows:
S. 70(2): ITA 2007, s. 144, 200, Sch. 1, para. 129.
S. 70(3): ITA 2007, s. 311.

71 Pre-arranged exits from EIS

71 [Repealed by ITA 2007, s. 1031 and Sch. 3, Pt. 2.]

History – S. 71 repealed by ITA 2007, s. 1031 and Sch. 3, Pt. 2, with effect in relation to shares issued after 5 April 2007.

Notes – S. 71 rewritten as follows:
S. 71(1): ITA 2007, s. 177(1), (2), (3), (4), (5).
S. 71(2): ITA 2007, s. 239(1).
S. 71(3): ITA 2007, s. 243(1), (2), (3).
S. 71(4): ITA 2007, s. 243(4).

72 Qualifying holdings for VCTs after 2nd July 1997

72 [Repealed by ITA 2007, s. 1031 and Sch. 3, Pt. 1.]

History – S. 72 repealed by ITA 2007, s. 1031 and Sch. 3, Pt. 1, with effect from 6 April 2007.

Notes – S. 72 rewritten as follows:
S. 72(1): ITA 2007, s. 288(1), (2), (3), (4).
S. 72(2): ITA 2007, s. 289(1), (2), (3), (4), (5).
S. 72(4): ITA 2007, Sch. 2, para. 69.
S. 72(5): ITA 2007, Sch. 2, para. 70(1).
S. 72(6): ITA 2007, Sch. 2, para. 70(2).

73 Other changes to requirements for VCTs

73 [Repealed by ITA 2007, s. 1031 and Sch. 3, Pt. 1.]

History – S. 73 repealed by ITA 2007, s. 1031 and Sch. 3, Pt. 1, with effect from 6 April 2007. Transitional and savings provisions contained in ITA 2007, Sch. 2.
S. 73(2) previously repealed by FA 2004, s. 326 and Sch. 42, Pt. 2(13), with effect for the purpose of determining whether shares or securities issued on or after 17 March 2004 are, for the purposes of ICTA 1988, s. 842AA, to be regarded as comprised in a company's qualifying holdings.
S. 73(3) and (4) partly repealed by FA 2004, s. 326 and Sch. 42, Pt. 2(13), with effect for the purpose of determining whether shares or securities issued on or after 17 March 2004 are, for the purposes of ICTA 1988, s. 842AA, to be regarded as comprised in a company's qualifying holdings.
S. 73(5) repealed by FA 2006, s. 178 and Sch. 26, Pt. 3(16), with effect in relation to relevant holdings issued on or after 6 April 2006, subject to FA 2006, Sch. 14, para. 2(3) and (4). Former s. 73(5) amended ICTA 1988, Sch. 28B, para. 8(1).

Notes – S. 73 rewritten as follows:
S. 73(1): ITA 2007, s. 273(1), 285(3).
S. 73(3): ITA 2007, s. 291(7).
S. 73(4): ITA 2007, s. 293(8), 294(7).
S. 73(5): ITA 2007, s. 297(1) and (2), Sch. 2, para. 76(3).
S. 73(6): ITA 2007, Sch. 2, para. 76(3).

74 Other changes to EIS etc.

74(1) Schedule 13 to this Act, which amends the provisions mentioned in subsection (2) below, shall have effect.

74(2) The provisions are–

(a) [repealed by ITA 2007, s. 1031 and Sch. 3, Pt. 2.]

(b) sections 150A and 150B of the Taxation of Chargeable Gains Act 1992 (EIS relief in respect of chargeable gains);

(c) Schedule 5B to that Act (EIS deferral of chargeable gains); and

(d) that Chapter as it has effect in relation to shares issued before 1st January 1994 (BES income tax relief) and section 150 of that Act (BES relief in respect of chargeable gains).

74(3) Unless the contrary intention appears, the amendments made by that Schedule have effect in relation to shares issued on or after 6th April 1998.

History – S. 74(2)(a) repealed by ITA 2007, s. 1031 and Sch. 3, Pt. 2, with effect in relation to shares issued after 5 April 2007.

INDIVIDUAL SAVINGS ACCOUNTS ETC.

75 Use of PEPs powers to provide for accounts

75 [Repealed by ITTOIA 2005, s. 884 and Sch. 3 effective for income tax purposes for 2005–06 onwards and for corporation tax purposes for accounting periods ending after 5 April 2005 (ITTOIA 2005, s. 883(1)).]

76 Tax credits for accounts and for PEPs

76(1) [Repealed by ITTOIA 2005, s. 884 and Sch. 3.]

76(2) [Repealed by ITTOIA 2005, s. 884 and Sch. 3.]

76(3) [Omitted by FA 2016, s. 5 and Sch. 1, para. 58(2).]

76(4) [Repealed by ITTOIA 2005, s. 884 and Sch. 3.]

76(5) [Repealed by ITTOIA 2005, s. 884 and Sch. 3.]

History – S. 76(1), (2), (4) and (5) repealed by ITTOIA 2005, s. 884 and Sch. 3 effective for income tax purposes for 2005–06 onwards and for corporation tax purposes for accounting periods ending after 5 April 2005 (ITTOIA 2005, s. 883(1)).
S. 76(3) omitted by FA 2016, s. 5 and Sch. 1, para. 58(2), with effect in relation to dividends paid or arising (or treated as paid), and any other distributions made (or treated as made), in the tax year 2016–17 or at any later time. Former s. 76(3) read as follows:

"**76(3)** The Treasury may by regulations make provision for individuals who–

(a) are not resident in the United Kingdom, but

(b) have made investments under plans for which provision is made by regulations under Chapter 3 of Part 6 of the Income Tax (Trading and Other Income) Act 2005,

to be treated in relation to any such investments as if they were so resident for the purposes of any enactment conferring an entitlement to, or to the payment of, tax credits.".

In former s. 76(3) the words "Chapter 3 of Part 6 of the Income Tax (Trading and Other Income) Act 2005" substituted for the words "section 333 of the Taxes Act 1988" by ITTOIA 2005, s. 882(1) and Sch. 1, para. 503 effective for income tax purposes for 2005–06 onwards and for corporation tax purposes for accounting periods ending after 5 April 2005 (ITTOIA 2005, s. 883(1)).

Statutory instruments – SI 1998/1870: made under s. 76(3).

77 The insurance element etc.

77 [Repealed by FA 2007, s. 114 and Sch. 27, Pt. 2(7).]

History – S. 77 repealed by FA 2007, s. 114 and Sch. 27, Pt. 2(7) with effect (FA 2007, s. 38):

- for the purposes of corporation tax, for periods of account of insurance companies beginning on or after 1 January 2007; and
- for the purposes of income tax, for the 2007/08 tax year and subsequent tax years.

78 Phasing out of TESSAs

78 [Repealed by ITTOIA 2005, s. 884 and Sch. 3 effective for income tax purposes for 2005–06 onwards and for corporation tax purposes for accounting periods ending after 5 April 2005 (ITTOIA 2005, s. 883(1)).]

RELIEF FOR INTEREST AND LOSSES ETC.

79 Relief for loan to acquire interest in a close company

79(1) [Repealed by ITA 2007, s. 1031 and Sch. 3, Pt. 1.]

79(2) [Repealed by TIOPA 2010, s. 378 and Sch. 10, Pt. 13.]

History – S. 79(1) repealed by ITA 2007, s. 1031 and Sch. 3, Pt. 1, with effect from 6 April 2007.
S. 79(2) repealed by TIOPA 2010, s. 378 and Sch. 10, Pt. 13, with effect for corporation tax purposes for accounting periods ending on or after 1 April 2010, for income tax and capital gains tax purposes for the tax year 2010–11 and subsequent tax years, and for petroleum revenue tax purposes for chargeable periods beginning on or after 1 July 2010.

Notes – S. 79 rewritten as ITA 2007, Sch. 2, para. 92.

80 Relief for losses on unlisted shares in trading companies

80 [Repealed by CTA 2010, s. 1181 and Sch. 3, Pt. 1.]

History – S. 80 repealed by CTA 2010, s. 1181 and Sch. 3, Pt. 1, with effect for corporation tax purposes for accounting periods ending on or after 1 April 2010, and for income tax and capital gains tax purposes for the tax year 2010–11 and subsequent tax years.
S. 80(2)–(4) previously repealed by ITA 2007, s. 1031 and Sch. 3, Pt. 1, with effect from 6 April 2007.
S. 80(5)(b) previously repealed by ITA 2007, s. 1031 and Sch. 3, Pt. 1, with effect from 6 April 2007.

Notes – S. 80 rewritten as follows:
S. 80(2): ITA 2007, s. 148(3), (6).
S. 80(3): ITA 2007, s. 134(1), (2), (3), (4), (5), 137(1), (3), (4), (5), (7), 139(1), (2), (3), 140(1), 142(1), (2), (3), 143(3), 145(1), (2), (3), (4), 146(1), (2), Sch. 1, para. 121, 122, 124, 125, 127, 128, 130, 131, Sch.2, para. 38(2).
S. 80(4): ITA 2007, s. 134(5), 151(1), (3), (4), (6), (7), Sch. 1, para. 121, 132, Sch. 2, para. 40(3), 41(5), 42(4), 43(1), 45(3), 46(4), 47(1), 48(2), 49(1), 50(1).
S. 80(5): ITA 2007, s. Sch. 2 para. 38(2), 40(3), 41(5), 42(4), 43(1), 45(3), 46(4), 47(1), 48(2), 49(1), 50(1).

81 Group relief: special rules for consortium cases

81 [Repealed by FA 2000, Sch. 40, Pt. II(11)).]

History – Repealed by FA 2000, Sch. 40, Pt. II(11)) and deemed always to have effect in accordance with s. 100(5).

82 Carry forward of non-trading deficit on loan relationships

82(1) [Repealed by FA 2002, s. 141 and Sch. 40, Pt. 3(12).]

82(2) [Repealed by TIOPA 2010, s. 378 and Sch. 10, Pt. 1.]

82(3) [Repealed by CTA 2010, s. 1181 and Sch. 3, Pt. 1.]

82(4) The amendments made by this section shall be deemed always to have had effect.

History – S. 82(1) repealed by FA 2002, s. 141 and Sch. 40, Pt. 3(12) with effect in relation to accounting periods beginning on or after 1 October 2002.
S. 82(2) repealed by TIOPA 2010, s. 378 and Sch. 10, Pt. 1, with effect for corporation tax purposes for accounting periods ending on or after 1 April 2010, for income tax and capital gains tax purposes for the tax year 2010–11 and subsequent tax years, and for petroleum revenue tax purposes for chargeable periods beginning on or after 1 July 2010.
S. 82(2)(c) previously repealed by FA 2002, s. 141 and Sch. 40, Pt. 3(12) with effect in relation to accounting periods beginning on or after 1 October 2002.
S. 82(2)(e) previously repealed by FA 2002, s. 141 and Sch. 40, Pt. 3(12) with effect in relation to accounting periods beginning on or after 1 October 2002.
S. 82(3) repealed by CTA 2010, s. 1181 and Sch. 3, Pt. 1, with effect for corporation tax purposes for accounting periods ending on or after 1 April 2010, and for income tax and capital gains tax purposes for the tax year 2010–11 and subsequent tax years.

CAPITAL ALLOWANCES

83 First-year allowances for investment in Northern Ireland

83 [Repealed by CAA 2001, s. 580 and Sch. 4.]

History – S. 83 repealed by CAA 2001, s. 580 and Sch. 4 in respect of allowances and charges falling to be made for chargeable periods ending on or after 6 April 2001 for income tax purposes and 1 April 2001 for corporation tax.

84 First-year allowances for small businesses etc.

84 [Repealed by CAA 2001, s. 580 and Sch. 4.]

History – S. 84 repealed by CAA 2001, s. 580 and Sch. 4 in respect of allowances and charges falling to be made for chargeable periods ending on or after 6 April 2001 for income tax purposes and 1 April 2001 for corporation tax.

85 First-year allowances: consequential amendments etc.

85 [Repealed by CAA 2001, s. 580 and Sch. 4.]

History – S. 85 repealed by CAA 2001, s. 580 and Sch. 4 in respect of allowances and charges falling to be made for chargeable periods ending on or after 6 April 2001 for income tax purposes and 1 April 2001 for corporation tax.

INSURANCE, INSURANCE COMPANIES AND FRIENDLY SOCIETIES

86 Life policies etc.

86 Schedule 14 to this Act (which makes provision in relation to the taxation of life policies etc. under Chapter II of Part XIII of the Taxes Act 1988) shall have effect.

87 Non-resident insurance companies: tax representatives

87 [Inserts ICTA 1988, s. 552A, 552B.]

88 Overseas life assurance business

88 [Omitted by FA 2008, s. 36 and Sch. 14, para. 17(g).]

History – S. 88 omitted by FA 2008, s. 36 and Sch. 14, para. 17(g), with effect–

- so far as relating to corporation tax, for accounting periods beginning on or after 1 April 2008, and
- so far as relating to income tax, for the tax year 2008–09 and subsequent tax years.

89 Personal portfolio bonds

89 [Omitted by FA 2008, s. 36 and Sch. 14, para. 17(g).]

History – S. 89 omitted by FA 2008, s. 36 and Sch. 14, para. 17(g), with effect–

- so far as relating to corporation tax, for accounting periods beginning on or after 1 April 2008, and
- so far as relating to income tax, for the tax year 2008–09 and subsequent tax years.

90 Distributions to friendly societies

90(1) The repeal by section 30(4) of the Finance (No. 2) Act 1997 of section 231(2) of the Taxes Act 1988 (payment of tax credit to a company resident in the UK) shall not have effect in relation to any distribution made to a friendly society before 6th April 2004 which is–

(a) a distribution to a friendly society all of whose profits are exempt from corporation tax by virtue of section 460(1) of the Taxes Act 1988 (life or endowment business of friendly society); or

(b) a distribution not falling within paragraph (a) above in relation to which exemption is given under section 460(1) of that Act.

90(2) In relation to any distribution falling within paragraph (a) or (b) of subsection (1) above–

(a) paragraph 3 of Schedule 4 to the Finance (No. 2) Act 1997 (which, from 6th April 1999, repeals certain provisions about claims for tax credits for accounting periods to which self-assessment applies) shall have effect as if the reference in sub-paragraph (2) of that paragraph to 6th April 1999 were a reference to 6th April 2004; and

(b) paragraph 2 of that Schedule (which repeals certain provisions about claims for tax credits for earlier periods) shall have no effect.

90(3) [Repealed by FA 2001, s. 110 and Sch. 33, Pt. 2(12).]

90(4) Schedule 8 to the Finance (No. 2) Act 1997 (repeals), so far as it relates to any repeal referred to in the preceding provisions of this section, shall have effect subject to those provisions.

History – S. 90(3) repealed by FA 2001, s. 110 and Sch. 33, Pt. 2(12), with effect from 11 May 2001.

91 Provisional repayments in connection with pension business

91 [Repealed by FA 2001, s. 110 and Sch. 33, Pt. 2(12).]

History – S. 91 repealed by FA 2001, s. 110 and Sch. 33, Pt. 2(12) in relation to tax credits in respect of distributions made on or after 6 April 2004, and in relation to income tax borne by deduction from payments received after 30 September 2001

PENSIONS

92 Approved retirement benefit schemes etc.

92 [Repealed by FA 2004, s. 326 and Sch. 42, Pt. 3.]

History – S. 92 repealed by FA 2004, s. 326 and Sch. 42, Pt. 3, with effect, subject to FA 2004, Sch. 36, from 6 April 2006.

93 Benefits received under non-approved retirement benefits scheme

93 [Repealed by ITEPA 2003, Sch. 8, Pt. 1.]

History – S. 93 repealed by ITEPA 2003, Sch. 8, Pt. 1 which has effect for the tax year 2003–04 and subsequent tax years.

94 Approval of personal pension schemes

94 [Repealed by FA 2004, s. 326 and Sch. 42, Pt. 3.]

History – S. 94 repealed by FA 2004, s. 326 and Sch. 42, Pt. 3, with effect, subject to FA 2004, Sch. 36, from 6 April 2006.

95 Personal pensions: charge on withdrawal of approval

95 [Repealed by FA 2004, s. 326 and Sch. 42, Pt. 3.]

History – S. 95 repealed by FA 2004, s. 326 and Sch. 42, Pt. 3, with effect, subject to FA 2004, Sch. 36, from 6 April 2006.

96 Information relating to personal pension schemes etc.

96 [Repealed by FA 2004, s. 326 and Sch. 42, Pt. 3.]

History – S. 96 repealed by FA 2004, s. 326 and Sch. 42, Pt. 3, with effect, subject to FA 2004, Sch. 36, from 6 April 2006.

97 Notices to be given to scheme administrator

97 [Repealed by FA 2004, s. 326 and Sch. 42, Pt. 3.]

History – S. 97 repealed by FA 2004, s. 326 and Sch. 42, Pt. 3, with effect, subject to FA 2004, Sch. 36, from 6 April 2006.

98 Assessments on scheme administrators

98(1) [Repealed by FA 2004, s. 326 and Sch. 42, Pt. 3.]

98(2) [Amends TMA 1970, s. 9(1); inserts s. 9(1A).]

98(3) Subsection (2) above shall have effect for the year 1998–99 and subsequent years of assessment and shall be deemed to have had effect for the years 1996–97 and 1997–98.

History – S. 98(1) repealed by FA 2004, s. 326 and Sch. 42, Pt. 3, with effect, subject to FA 2004, Sch. 36, from 6 April 2006.

FUTURES AND OPTIONS

99 Extension of provisions relating to guaranteed returns

99(1) [Repealed by ITTOIA 2005, s. 884 and Sch. 3.]

99(2) [Repealed by FA 2002, s. 141 and Sch. 40, Pt. 3(13).]

99(3) [Repealed by FA 2002, s. 141 and Sch. 40, Pt. 3(13).]

99(4) [Repealed by ITTOIA 2005, s. 884 and Sch. 3.]

99(5) [Repealed by ITTOIA 2005, s. 884 and Sch. 3.]

History – S. 99(1) repealed by ITTOIA 2005, s. 884 and Sch. 3 effective for income tax purposes for 2005–06 onwards and for corporation tax purposes for accounting periods ending after 5 April 2005 (ITTOIA 2005, s. 883(1)).
S. 99(2) repealed by FA 2002, s. 141 and Sch. 40, Pt. 3(13) with effect in relation to accounting periods beginning on or after 1 October 2002.
S. 99(3) repealed by FA 2002, s. 141 and Sch. 40, Pt. 3(13) with effect in relation to accounting periods beginning on or after 1 October 2002.
S. 99(4) repealed by ITTOIA 2005, s. 884 and Sch. 3 effective for income tax purposes for 2005–06 onwards and for corporation tax purposes for accounting periods ending after 5 April 2005 (ITTOIA 2005, s. 883(1)).
S. 99(5) repealed by ITTOIA 2005, s. 884 and Sch. 3 effective for income tax purposes for 2005–06 onwards and for corporation tax purposes for accounting periods ending after 5 April 2005 (ITTOIA 2005, s. 883(1)).

SECURITIES

100 Accrued income scheme

100 [Repealed by ITA 2007, s. 1031 and Sch. 3, Pt. 1.]

History – S. 100 repealed by ITA 2007, s. 1031 and Sch. 3, Pt. 1, with effect from 6 April 2007.

Notes – S. 100 rewritten as follows:
S. 100(1): ITA 2007, s. 12(2), 14(2).
S. 100(2): ITA 2007, s. 18(3).

101 Dealers in securities etc.

101(1) [Repeals ICTA 1988, s. 471.]

101(2) [Repeals ICTA 1988, s. 472.]

101(3) Subsection (1) above applies in relation to exchanges made after the day on which this Act is passed.

101(4) Subsection (2) above applies in relation to issues of securities occurring after that day.

102 Manufactured dividends

102(1) [Repealed by CTA 2010, s. 1181 and Sch. 3, Pt. 1.]

102(2) [Repealed by CTA 2010, s. 1181 and Sch. 3, Pt. 1.]

102(3) [Amends ICTA 1988, s. 737D(2).]

102(4) Schedule 23A to the Taxes Act 1988 (manufactured dividends and interest) shall be amended in accordance with subsections (5) to (8) below.

102(5) [Repealed by CTA 2010, s. 1181 and Sch. 3, Pt. 1.]

102(6) [Repeals ICTA 1988, Sch. 23A, para. 2(3)(a).]

102(7) [Repealed by ITA 2007, s. 1031 and Sch. 3, Pt. 1.]

102(8) [Repeals ICTA 1988, Sch. 23A, para. 2(4), (5), (6)(b) and amends para. 2A(1).]

102(9) [Repealed by CTA 2010, s. 1181 and Sch. 3, Pt. 1.]

102(10) Subsections (2) to (8) above have-effect in relation to manufactured dividends paid (or treated for the purposes of Schedule 23A to the Taxes Act 1988 as paid) on or after 6th April 1999.

History – S. 102(1) repealed by CTA 2010, s. 1181 and Sch. 3, Pt. 1, with effect for corporation tax purposes for accounting periods ending on or after 1 April 2010, and for income tax and capital gains tax purposes for the tax year 2010–11 and subsequent tax years.
S. 102(2) repealed by CTA 2010, s. 1181 and Sch. 3, Pt. 1, with effect for corporation tax purposes for accounting periods ending on or after 1 April 2010, and for income tax and capital gains tax purposes for the tax year 2010–11 and subsequent tax years.
S. 102(5) repealed by CTA 2010, s. 1181 and Sch. 3, Pt. 1, with effect for corporation tax purposes for accounting periods ending on or after 1 April 2010, and for income tax and capital gains tax purposes for the tax year 2010–11 and subsequent tax years.
S. 102(7) repealed by ITA 2007, s. 1031 and Sch. 3, Pt. 1, with effect from 6 April 2007.
S. 102(9) repealed by CTA 2010, s. 1181 and Sch. 3, Pt. 1, with effect for corporation tax purposes for accounting periods ending on or after 1 April 2010, and for income tax and capital gains tax purposes for the tax year 2010–11 and subsequent tax years.

Notes – S. 102(7) rewritten as ITA 2007, s. 577(1), (3), (5).

DOUBLE TAXATION RELIEF

103 Restriction of relief on certain interest and dividends

103 [Repealed by Statute Law (Repeals) Act 2013, s. 1 and Sch. 1, Pt. 10.]

History – S. 103 repealed by Statute Law (Repeals) Act 2013, s. 1 and Sch. 1, Pt. 10, with effect from 31 January 2013.

104 Adjustments of interest and dividends for spared tax etc.

104 [Repealed by Statute Law (Repeals) Act 2013, s. 1 and Sch. 1, Pt. 10.]

History – S. 104 repealed by Statute Law (Repeals) Act 2013, s. 1 and Sch. 1, Pt. 10, with effect from 31 January 2013.

105 Meaning of "financial expenditure"

105 [Repealed by Statute Law (Repeals) Act 2013, s. 1 and Sch. 1, Pt. 10.]

History – S. 105 repealed by Statute Law (Repeals) Act 2013, s. 1 and Sch. 1, Pt. 10, with effect from 31 January 2013.

106 Underlying tax reflecting interest or dividends

106 [Repealed by TIOPA 2010, s. 378 and Sch. 10, Pt. 1 and Statute Law (Repeals) Act 2013, s. 1 and Sch. 1, Pt. 10.]

History – S. 106(4)–(9) repealed by Statute Law (Repeals) Act 2013, s. 1 and Sch. 1, Pt. 10, with effect from 31 January 2013. Note that s. 106 had previously been repealed (see note below).
S. 106 repealed by TIOPA 2010, s. 378 and Sch. 10, Pt. 1, with effect for corporation tax purposes for accounting periods ending on or after 1 April 2010, for income tax and capital gains tax purposes for the tax year 2010–11 and subsequent tax years, and for petroleum revenue tax purposes for chargeable periods beginning on or after 1 July 2010.

107 Notification of foreign tax adjustment

107 [Repealed by TIOPA 2010, s. 378 and Sch. 10, Pt. 1.]

History – S. 107 repealed by TIOPA 2010, s. 378 and Sch. 10 , Pt. 1, with effect for corporation tax purposes for accounting periods ending on or after 1 April 2010, for income tax and capital gains tax purposes for the tax year 2010–11 and subsequent tax years, and for petroleum revenue tax purposes for chargeable periods beginning on or after 1 July 2010.

TRANSFER PRICING, FOREX AND FINANCIAL INSTRUMENTS

108 New regime for transfer pricing etc.

108(1) [Repealed by TIOPA 2010, s. 378 and Sch. 10, Pt. 2.]

108(2) [Repealed by TIOPA 2010, s. 378 and Sch. 10, Pt. 2.]

108(3) [Repealed by FA 2002, s. 141 and Sch. 40, Pt. 3(10).]

(a) [Repealed by FA 2002, s. 141 and Sch. 40, Pt. 3(10).]

(b) [Amends ICTA 1988, Sch. 9, para. 16.]

108(5) Subject to subsection (6) below, this section and Schedule 16 to this Act have effect (in relation to provision made or imposed at any time) –

(a) for the purposes of corporation tax, as respects accounting periods ending on or after the day appointed under section 199 of the Finance Act 1994 for the purposes of Chapter III of Part IV of that Act (self-assessment management provisions); and

(b) for the purposes of income tax, as respects any year of assessment ending on or after that day.

108(6) The Schedule 28AA to the Taxes Act 1988 that is inserted by subsection (2) above shall not, in the case of any potentially advantaged person, apply as respects the consequences at any time of the difference between the actual provision and the arm's length provision if–

(a) that time falls before 17th March 2001;

(b) the actual provision is a provision made or imposed by means of contractual arrangements entered into by that person before 17th March 1998;

(c) the requirements of paragraph 1(1)(b) of Schedule 28AA to that Act (control requirements) are satisfied in the case of the actual provision and that person by reference only to paragraph 4(2)(b) of that Schedule (joint ventures etc.);

(d) the rights and obligations of that person by virtue of the actual provision are not ones that have been varied or continued in pursuance of any transaction entered into by that person in the period between 17th March 1998 and that time; and

(e) that person is not a party, and has not been a party, to any transaction by virtue of which he could during that period have secured the variation or termination of those rights and obligations.

108(7) Expressions used in subsection (6) above and in Schedule 28AA to the Taxes Act 1988 have the same meanings in that subsection as in that Schedule.

History – S. 108(1) repealed by TIOPA 2010, s. 378 and Sch. 10, Pt. 2, with effect for corporation tax purposes for accounting periods ending on or after 1 April 2010, for income tax and capital gains tax purposes for the tax year 2010–11 and subsequent tax years, and for petroleum revenue tax purposes for chargeable periods beginning on or after 1 July 2010.
S. 108(2) repealed by TIOPA 2010, s. 378 and Sch. 10, Pt. 2, with effect for corporation tax purposes for accounting periods ending on or after 1 April 2010, for income tax and capital gains tax purposes for the tax year 2010–11 and subsequent tax years, and for petroleum revenue tax purposes for chargeable periods beginning on or after 1 July 2010.
S. 108(3) repealed by FA 2002, s. 141 and Sch. 40, Pt. 3(10) with effect in relation to accounting periods beginning on or after 1 October 2002.
S. 108(4)(a) repealed by FA 2002, s.141 and Sch. 40, Pt. 3(10) with effect in relation to accounting periods beginning on or after 1 October 2002.

Notes – The day appointed under FA 1994, s. 199 is 1 July 1999 (SI 1998/3173 (C. 78)).

109 Abolition of requirements for direction

109(1) [Repealed by FA 2002, s. 141 and Sch. 40, Pt. 3(10).]

109(2) [Repealed by FA 2002, s. 141 and Sch. 40, Pt. 3(10).]

109(3) [Repealed by FA 2002, s. 141 and Sch. 40, Pt. 3(13).]

109(4) [Repealed by FA 2002, s. 141 and Sch. 40, Pt. 3(10), and Sch. 40, Pt. 3(13).]

109(5) [Repealed by FA 2002, s. 141 and Sch. 40, Pt. 3(10), and Sch. 40, Pt. 3(13).]

History – S. 109(1) and (2) repealed by FA 2002, s. 141 and Sch. 40, Pt. 3(10) with effect in relation to accounting periods beginning on or after 1 October 2002.
S. 109(3) repealed by FA 2002, s. 141 and Sch. 40, Pt. 3(13) with effect in relation to accounting periods beginning on or after 1 October 2002.
S. 109(4) repealed in so far as it relates to former s. 109(1), (2) by FA 2002, s. 141 and Sch. 40, Pt. 3(10) and in relation to former s. 109(3) by FA 2002, s. 141 and Sch. 40, Pt. 3(13) with effect in relation to accounting periods beginning on or after 1 October 2002.
S. 109(5) repealed in so far as it relates to FA 1993, s. 135(1)(d), 136(1)(d), (5) or (9), 136A(3) or (7) or 137(1)(d), by FA 2002, s. 141 and Sch. 40, Pt. 3(10) and in so far as it relates to FA 1994, s. 167(2)(b) by FA 2002, s. 141 and Sch. 40, Pt. 3(13) with effect in relation to accounting periods beginning on or after 1 October 2002.

110 Determinations requiring the sanction of the Board

110 [Omitted by TIOPA 2010, s. 374 and Sch. 8, para. 113 and repealed by TIOPA 2010, s. 378 and Sch. 10, Pt. 2.]

History – S. 110 omitted by TIOPA 2010, s. 374 and Sch. 8, para. 113, and repealed by TIOPA 2010, s. 378 and Sch. 10, Pt. 2, with effect for corporation tax purposes for accounting periods ending on or after 1 April 2010, for income tax and capital gains tax purposes for the tax year 2010–11 and subsequent tax years, and for petroleum revenue tax purposes for chargeable periods beginning on or after 1 July 2010.

Notes – S. 110 rewritten as follows:
S. 110(1): TIOPA 2010, s. 208(3), 210(1), (3), (6).
S. 110(2): TIOPA 2010, s. 210(2), (4).
S. 110(3): TIOPA 2010, s. 210(5), (6).
S. 110(4): TIOPA 2010, s. 208(1), (2), (4).
S. 110(5): TIOPA 2010, s. 209(1), (2), (6).
S. 110(6): TIOPA 2010, s. 209(3), (4).
S. 110(7): TIOPA 2010, s. 209(5).
S. 110(8): TIOPA 2010, s. 211(1), (2), (3), (4).
S. 110(9): TIOPA 2010, s. 208(3).
S. 110(10): not rewritten, as spent.

111 Notice to potential claimants

111 [Omitted by TIOPA 2010, s. 374 and Sch. 8, para. 114 and repealed by TIOPA 2010, s. 378 and Sch. 10, Pt. 2.]

History – S. 111 omitted by TIOPA 2010, s. 374 and Sch. 8, para. 114, and repealed by TIOPA 2010, s. 378 and Sch. 10, Pt. 2, with effect for corporation tax purposes for accounting periods ending on or after 1 April 2010, for income tax and capital gains tax purposes for the tax year 2010–11 and subsequent tax years, and for petroleum revenue tax purposes for chargeable periods beginning on or after 1 July 2010.

Notes – S. 111 rewritten as follows:
S. 111(1): TIOPA 2010. s. 185(1), (2), (5).
S. 111(2): TIOPA 2010. s. 185(2).
S. 111(3): TIOPA 2010. s. 186(1), (2), (3), (4).
S. 111(4): TIOPA 2010. s. 185(3).
S. 111(5): TIOPA 2010. s. 185(4).
S. 111(6): TIOPA 2010, s. 190.
S. 111(7): not rewritten, as spent.

CONTROLLED FOREIGN COMPANIES

112 Exempt activities

112(1) Part II of Schedule 25 to the Taxes Act 1988 (exempt activities) shall be amended as follows.

112(2) [Substitutes ICTA 1988, Sch. 25, para. 9(1A).]

112(3) [Substitutes ICTA 1988, Sch. 25, para. 11(1)(c).]

112(4) [Amends ICTA 1988, Sch. 25, para. 9(3), 11(3).]

112(5) This section has effect in relation to accounting periods of a controlled foreign company, within the meaning of Chapter IV of Part XVII of the Taxes Act 1988, beginning on or after 17th March 1998.

113 Miscellaneous amendments

113 Schedule 17 to this Act (which makes provision in relation to controlled foreign companies) shall have effect.

CHANGES IN COMPANY OWNERSHIP

114 Postponed corporation tax

114 [Repealed by CTA 2010, s. 1181 and Sch. 3, Pt. 1.]

History – S. 114 repealed by CTA 2010, s. 1181 and Sch. 3, Pt. 1, with effect for corporation tax purposes for accounting periods ending on or after 1 April 2010, and for income tax and capital gains tax purposes for the tax year 2010–11 and subsequent tax years.

115 Information powers where ownership changes

115 [Repealed by CTA 2010, s. 1181 and Sch. 3, Pt. 1.]

History – S. 115 repealed by CTA 2010, s. 1181 and Sch. 3, Pt. 1, with effect for corporation tax purposes for accounting periods ending on or after 1 April 2010, and for income tax and capital gains tax purposes for the tax year 2010-11 and subsequent tax years. S. 115 previously omitted by FA 2008, s. 113 and Sch. 36, para. 92(f), with effect from 1 April 2009 (SI 2009/404, art. 2, subject to savings at SI 2009/404, art. 3).

116 Provisions supplemental to sections 114 and 115

116 [Repealed by CTA 2010, s. 1181 and Sch. 3, Pt. 1.]

History – S. 116 repealed by CTA 2010, s. 1181 and Sch. 3, Pt. 1, with effect for corporation tax purposes for accounting periods ending on or after 1 April 2010, and for income tax and capital gains tax purposes for the tax year 2010–11 and subsequent tax years.

CORPORATION TAX SELF ASSESSMENT

117 Company tax returns, assessments and related matters

117(1) The provisions of Schedule 18 to this Act have effect in place of–

(a) the provisions of Parts II and IV of the Taxes Management Act 1970 (returns, assessment and claims), so far as they relate to corporation tax,

(b) certain related provisions of Part X of that Act (penalties), and

(c) Schedule 17A to the Taxes Act 1988 (group relief: claims), and also make provision in relation to claims for allowances under the Capital Allowances Act.

117(2) Schedule 18 to this Act, the Taxes Management Act 1970 and the Tax Acts shall be construed and have effect as if that Schedule were contained in that Act.

117(3) The enactments mentioned in Schedule 19 to this Act have effect with the amendments specified there, which are minor amendments and amendments consequential on Schedule 18.

117(4) Except as otherwise provided, the provisions of Schedules 18 and 19 to this Act have effect in relation to accounting periods ending on or after the self-assessment appointed day.

117(5) In this section **"the self-assessment appointed day"** means the day appointed by the Treasury under section 199 of the Finance Act 1994 for the purposes of Chapter III of Part IV of that Act (corporation tax self-assessment).

History – In s. 117(1), the word "and" substituted at the end of para. (b) and for para. (d) and the word "and" before it the words "and also make provision in relation to claims for allowances under the Capital Allowances Act." substituted by CAA 2001, s. 578 and Sch. 2, para. 100.

Notes – The day appointed under FA 1994, s. 199 is 1 July 1999 (SI 1998/3173 (C. 78)).

TELEPHONE CLAIMS ETC.

118 Claims for income tax purposes

118 [Omitted by TIOPA 2010, s. 371 and Sch. 7, para. 88, and repealed by TIOPA 2010, s. 378 and Sch. 10, Pt. 12.]

History – S. 118 omitted by TIOPA 2010, s. 371 and Sch. 7, para. 88, and repealed by TIOPA 2010, s. 378 and Sch. 10, Pt. 12, with effect for corporation tax purposes for accounting periods ending on or after 1 April 2010, for income tax and capital gains tax purposes for the tax year 2010–11 and subsequent tax years, and for petroleum revenue tax purposes for chargeable periods beginning on or after 1 July 2010.

Notes – S. 118(1)–(9) rewritten in TIOPA 2010, Sch. 7, para. 86.
S. 118(10) rewritten as ITA 2007, s. 989.

119 Evidential provisions in PAYE regulations

119 [Repealed by TIOPA 2010, s. 378 and Sch. 10, Pt. 13.]

History – S. 119 repealed by TIOPA 2010, s. 378 and Sch. 10, Pt. 13, with effect for corporation tax purposes for accounting periods ending on or after 1 April 2010, for income tax and capital gains tax purposes for the tax year 2010–11 and subsequent tax years, and for petroleum revenue tax purposes for chargeable periods beginning on or after 1 July 2010.

Chapter II – Taxation of Chargeable Gains

RATE FOR TRUSTEES

120 Rate of CGT for trustees etc.

120 [Omitted by FA 2008, s. 8 and Sch. 2, para. 21(c)(i).]

History – S. 120 omitted by FA 2008, s. 8 and Sch. 2, para. 21(c)(i), with effect for the tax year 2008–09 and subsequent tax years.

TAPER RELIEF AND INDEXATION ALLOWANCE

121 Taper relief for CGT

121(1) [Omitted by FA 2008, s. 8 and Sch. 2, para. 55(a)(i).]

121(2) [Omitted by FA 2008, s. 8 and Sch. 2, para. 55(a)(i).]

121(3) *Schedule 21 to this Act* (which makes incidental and consequential provision in connection with the introduction of taper relief) shall have effect.

121(4) This section and those two Schedules have effect for the year 1998–99 and subsequent years of assessment.

History – S. 121(1) omitted by FA 2008, s. 8 and Sch. 2, para. 55(a)(i), with effect in relation to chargeable gains accruing or treated as accruing in the tax year 2008–09 or any subsequent tax year.

S. 121(2) omitted by FA 2008, s. 8 and Sch. 2, para. 55(a)(i), with effect in relation to chargeable gains accruing or treated as accruing in the tax year 2008–09 or any subsequent tax year.

122 Freezing of indexation allowance for CGT

122(1) [Omitted by FA 2008, s. 8 and Sch. 2, para. 82.]

122(2) [Omitted by FA 2008, s. 8 and Sch. 2, para. 82.]

122(3) [Omitted by FA 2008, s. 8 and Sch. 2, para. 82.]

122(4) [Inserts TCGA 1992, s. 13(11A).]

122(5) [Omitted by FA 2008, s. 8 and Sch. 2, para. 82.]

122(6) Subject to subsection (7) below, the preceding provisions of this section have effect in relation to disposals on or after 6th April 1998.

122(7) This section does not affect the computation of the amount of so much of any gain as–

(a) is treated for the purposes of the taxation of chargeable gains as having accrued on a disposal on or after 6th April 1998; but

(b) is taken for those purposes to be equal to the whole or any part of a gain that–

(i) would (but for any enactment relating to the taxation of chargeable gains) have accrued on an actual disposal made before that date, or

(ii) would have accrued on a disposal assumed under any such enactment to have been made before that date.

History – S. 122(1) omitted by FA 2008, s. 8 and Sch. 2, para. 82, with effect in computing gains on disposals made on or after 6 April 2008.
S. 122(2) omitted by FA 2008, s. 8 and Sch. 2, para. 82, with effect in computing gains on disposals made on or after 6 April 2008.
S. 122(3) omitted by FA 2008, s. 8 and Sch. 2, para. 82, with effect in computing gains on disposals made on or after 6 April 2008.
S. 122(5) omitted by FA 2008, s. 8 and Sch. 2, para. 82, with effect in computing gains on disposals made on or after 6 April 2008.

POOLING AND IDENTIFICATION OF SHARES ETC.

123 Abolition of pooling for CGT

123(1) [Omitted by FA 2008, s. 8 and Sch. 2, para. 96(a).]

123(2) [Omitted by FA 2008, s. 8 and Sch. 2, para. 96(a).]

123(3) [Amends TCGA 1992, s. 104(3).]

123(4) [Substitutes TCGA 1992, s. 104(4).]

123(5) [Amends TCGA 1992, s. 104(6), 107 and 110.]

123(6) The preceding provisions of this section have effect in relation to any disposal on or after 6th April 1998 of any securities (whenever acquired).

123(7) The powers of the Treasury to make provision by regulations under one or more of–

(a) section 333 of the Taxes Act 1988 (investment plan regulations)

(b) section 151 of the Taxation of Chargeable Gains Act 1992 (capital gains tax and investment plans), and

(c) Chapter 3 of Part 6 of the Income Tax (Trading and Other Income) Act 2005 (income from individual investment plans),

shall include power to provide, to such extent as appears to them to be appropriate for purposes connected with the enactment of this section and section 124 below, for any provision contained in any such regulations to have effect retrospectively in relation to such times falling on or after 17th March 1998 as may be specified in the regulations.

History – S. 123(1) omitted by FA 2008, s. 8 and Sch. 2, para. 96(a), with effect in relation to disposals on or after 6 April 2008.
S. 123(2) omitted by FA 2008, s. 8 and Sch. 2, para. 96(a), with effect in relation to disposals on or after 6 April 2008.
S. 123(5)(a) omitted by FA 2012, s. 146 and Sch. 16, para. 247(i)(i), with effect in relation to accounting periods beginning on or after 1 January 2013 (FA 2012, s. 148) but subject to transitional provisions in FA 2012, Sch. 17. Where an accounting period would otherwise straddle 1 January 2013, it is deemed to end on 31 December 2012 (FA 2012, s. 149).
In s. 123(7) the word "more" substituted for the word "both" by ITTOIA 2005, s. 882(1) and Sch. 1, para. 504(a); effective for income tax purposes for 2005–06 onwards and for corporation tax purposes for accounting periods ending after 5 April 2005 (ITTOIA 2005, s. 883(1)).
In s. 123(7)(a) the words "(investment plan regulations)" substituted for the former wording by ITTOIA 2005, s. 882(1) and Sch. 1, para. 504(b); effective for income tax purposes for 2005–06 onwards and for corporation tax purposes for accounting periods ending after 5 April 2005 (ITTOIA 2005, s. 883(1)).
S. 123(7)(c) and the word "and" preceding it inserted by ITTOIA 2005, s. 882(1) and Sch. 1, para. 504(c); effective for income tax purposes for 2005–06 onwards and for corporation tax purposes for accounting periods ending after 5 April 2005 (ITTOIA 2005, s. 883(1)).

124 New identification rules for CGT

124(1) [Inserts TCGA 1992, s. 106A.]

124(2) [Amends TCGA 1992, s. 105(1) and inserts s. 105(2).]

124(3) [Substitutes TCGA 1992, s. 107(1)–(2).]

124(4) [Inserts TCGA 1992, s. 108(A1).]

124(5) [Amends TCGA 1992, s. 108(2), (7).]

124(6) [Amends TCGA 1992, s. 151B(1), (7) and Sch. 5C, para. 4(2).]

124(7) Subject to subsection (8) below, the preceding provisions of this section have effect in relation to any disposal on or after 6th April 1998.

124(8) For the purposes of capital gains tax for the year 1997–98 (but not for the purposes of corporation tax), the following provisions have effect in relation to any disposal of securities made on or after 17th March 1998 and before 6th April 1998, that is to say–

(a) the identification rule in subsection (5) of the section 106A of the Taxation of Chargeable Gains Act 1992 set out in subsection (1) above shall apply in accordance with subsections (3) and (4) of that section;

(b) that rule shall have priority over any other rule, except the one in section 105(1) of that Act; and

(c) section 104(1) of that Act shall not apply to any securities identified by virtue of this subsection with the securities disposed of.

124(9) In subsection (8) above **"securities"** means any securities within the meaning of section 104 of the Taxation of Chargeable Gains Act 1992 or any relevant securities within the meaning of section 108 of that Act.

125 Indexation and share pooling etc.

125(1) [Amends TCGA 1992, s. 110(1).]

125(2) [Omitted by FA 2008, s. 8 and Sch. 2, para. 96(b).]

125(3) [Omitted by FA 2008, s. 8 and Sch. 2, para. 96(b).]

125(4) Subject to subsection (5) below, the preceding provisions of this section have effect in relation to disposals on or after 6th April 1998.

125(5) This section does not affect the computation of the amount of so much of any gain as–

(a) is treated for the purposes of the taxation of chargeable gains as having accrued on a disposal on or after 6th April 1998; but

(b) is taken for those purposes to be equal to the whole or any part of a gain that–

(i) would (but for any enactment relating to the taxation of chargeable gains) have accrued on an actual disposal made before that date, or

(ii) would have accrued on a disposal assumed under any such enactment to have been made before that date.

History – S. 125(2) omitted by FA 2008, s. 8 and Sch. 2, para. 96(b), with effect in relation to disposals on or after 6 April 2008.
S. 125(3) omitted by FA 2008, s. 8 and Sch. 2, para. 96(b), with effect in relation to disposals on or after 6 April 2008.

STOCK DIVIDENDS

126 Capital gains on stock dividends

126(1) [Substitutes TCGA 1992, s. 141, 142.]

126(2) This section applies to any share capital issued on or after 6th April 1998.

NON-RESIDENTS ETC.

127 Charge to CGT on temporary non-residents

127(1) [Inserts TCGA 1992, s. 10A.]

127(2) [Amends TCGA 1992, s. 9(3).]

127(3) [Inserts TCGA 1992, s. 96(9A), (9B).]

127(4) This section has effect–

(a) in any case in which the year of departure is the year 1998–99 or a subsequent year of assessment; and

(b) in any case in which the year of departure is the year 1997–98 and the taxpayer was resident or ordinarily resident in the United Kingdom at a time in that year on or after 17th March 1998.

128 Disposal of interests in a settlement

128(1) [Amends TCGA 1992, s. 76.]

128(2) [Inserts TCGA 1992, s. 76(1A), (1B).]

128(3) [Inserts TCGA 1992, s. 76(3).]

128(4) This section has effect in relation to any disposal on or after 6th March 1998.

129 Attribution of gains to settlor in section 10A cases

129(1) [Inserts TCGA 1992, s. 86A.]

129(2) [Amends TCGA 1992, s. 97(1)–(5), (7), (8).]

129(3) This section has effect where the year of departure is the year 1997–98 or any subsequent year of assessment.

130 Charge on beneficiaries of settlements with non-resident settlors

130(1) [Omitted by FA 2008, s. 25 and Sch. 7, para. 114(a).]

130(2) [Amends TCGA 1992, s. 88(1).]

130(3) Subject to subsection (4) below, the preceding provisions of this section apply for the year 1998–99 and subsequent years of assessment and shall be deemed to have applied for the year 1997–98.

130(4) [Omitted by FA 2008, s. 25 and Sch. 7, para. 114(a).]

History – S. 130(1) omitted by FA 2008, s. 25 and Sch. 7, para. 114(a), with effect for the tax year 2008–09 and subsequent tax years. S. 130(4) omitted by FA 2008, s. 25 and Sch. 7, para. 114(a), with effect for the tax year 2008–09 and subsequent tax years.

131 Charge on settlors of settlements for grandchildren

131(1) [Inserts TCGA 1992, Sch. 5, para. 2(3)(da), (db) and amends para. 2(3)(e).]

131(2) [Substitutes TCGA 1992, Sch. 5, para. 2(7).]

131(3) Schedule 22 to this Act (which makes transitional provision and consequential amendments in connection with the provisions of this section) shall have effect.

131(4) The preceding provisions of this section and Schedule 22 to this Act apply for the year 1998–99 and subsequent years of assessment and shall be deemed to have applied for the year 1997–98.

132 Charge on settlors of pre-19th March 1991 settlements

132(1) [Inserts TCGA 1992, Sch. 5, para. 9(1A), (1B).]

132(2) Sub-paragraph (2) of that paragraph shall not have effect for the purpose of determining whether any settlement is a qualifying settlement in the year 1999–00 or any subsequent year of assessment.

132(3) [Inserts TCGA 1992, Sch. 5, para. 9(6A).]

132(4) [Inserts TCGA 1992, Sch. 5, para. 9(10A)–(10D).]

132(5) In construing section 86(1)(e) of the Taxation of Chargeable Gains Act 1992 (which specifies the amount by reference to which a charge arises under that section) as regards a particular year of assessment and in relation to a settlement created before 19th March 1991 which–

(a) is a qualifying settlement in the year 1999–00, but

(b) was not a qualifying settlement in any earlier year of assessment,

no account shall be taken of disposals made before 6th April 1999 (whether for the purpose of arriving at gains or for the purpose of arriving at losses).

132(6) Schedule 23 (which makes transitional provision in connection with the coming into force of this section) shall have effect.

GROUPS OF COMPANIES ETC.

133 Transfer within group to investment trust

133(1) [Inserts TCGA 1992, s. 101A.]

133(2) [Inserts TCGA 1992, s. 179(2C).]

133(3) Subsections (1) and (2) above apply to any company which becomes an investment trust for an accounting period beginning on or after 17th March 1998.

134 Transfer of company's assets to venture capital trust

134(1) [Amends TCGA 1992, s. 139(4).]

134(2) [Inserts TCGA 1992, s. 101B.]

134(3) [Inserts TCGA 1992, s. 101(1B).]

134(4) Subsection (1) above applies to transfers made on or after 17th March 1998.

134(5) Subsections (2) and (3) above apply to a company in respect of which an approval for the purposes of Part 6 of the Income Tax Act 2007 (venture capital trusts) has effect as from a time falling on or after 17th March 1998.

History – In s. 134(5) the words "Part 6 of the Income Tax Act 2007" substituted for the words "section 842AA of the Taxes Act 1988" by ITA 2007, s. 1027 and Sch. 1, para. 382, with effect from 6 April 2007.

135 Transfer within group to venture capital trust

135(1) [Inserts TCGA 1992, s. 171(2)(cc).]

135(2) [Inserts TCGA 1992, s. 101C.]

135(3) [Inserts TCGA 1992, s. 179(2D).]

135(4) Subsection (1) above applies to disposals made on or after 17th March 1998.

135(5) Subsections (2) and (3) above apply to a company in respect of which an approval for the purposes of Part 6 of the Income Tax Act 2007 (venture capital trusts) has effect as from a time falling on or after 17th March 1998.

History – In s. 135(5) the words "Part 6 of the Income Tax Act 2007" substituted for "section 842AA of the Taxes Act 1988" by ITA 2007, s. 1027 and Sch. 1, para. 383, with effect from 6 April 2007.

136 Incorporated friendly societies

136(1) [Inserts TCGA 1992, s. 170(9)(cc).]

136(2) [Inserts TCGA 1992, s. 171(2)(cd).]

136(3) [Inserts TCGA 1992, s. 171(5).]

136(4) Subsection (1) above applies for the purpose of determining, in relation to times on and after 17th March 1998, whether a friendly society is a company within the meaning of the provisions of sections 170 to 181 of the Taxation of Chargeable Gains Act 1992.

136(5) Subsections (2) and (3) above apply in relation to disposals made on or after 17th March 1998.

137 Pre-entry gains

137(1) [Repealed by FA 2006, s. 178 and Sch. 26, Pt. 3(9).]

137(2) [Repealed by FA 2006, s. 178 and Sch. 26, Pt. 3(9).]

137(3) [Amends TCGA 1992, s. 213(3).]

137(4) [Repealed by FA 2003, s. 216(1) and Sch. 43, Pt. 3(12).]

137(5) [Repealed by FA 2006, s. 178 and Sch. 26, Pt. 3(9).]

137(6) Subsection (3) above has effect in relation to any intervening period ending on or after 17th March 1998.

137(7) [Repealed by FA 2003, s. 216(1) and Sch. 43, Pt. 3(12).]

History – S. 137(1), (2) and (5) repealed by FA 2006, s. 178 and Sch. 26, Pt. 3(9), with effect for calculating the amount to be included in respect of chargeable gains in a company's total profits for any accounting period ending on or after 5 December 2005, subject to the provisions of FA 2006, s. 70(7)–(11).

S. 137(4) and (7) repealed by FA 2003, s. 216(1) and Sch. 43, Pt. 3(12), with effect where the accounting period for which the net amount represents an excess of losses over gains is an accounting period beginning on or after 1 January 2003.

138 Pre-entry losses

138 [Omitted by FA 2011, s. 46 and Sch. 11, para. 10(b).]

History – S. 138 omitted by FA 2011, s. 46 and Sch. 11, para. 10(b) with effect from 19 July 2011 in relation to the deduction of any pre-entry loss within TCGA 1992, Sch. 7A, para. 1(2), subject to the provisions of FA 2011, Sch. 11, para. 11(2) and 12.

139 De-grouping charges

139(1) [Amends TCGA 1992, s. 179(2B).]

139(2) Subsection (1) above has effect in relation to a company in any case in which the time of the company's ceasing to be a member of the second group is on or after 17th March 1998.

ABOLITION OF RELIEFS

140 Phasing out of retirement relief

140(1) In Schedule 6 to the Taxation of Chargeable Gains Act 1992 (retirement relief etc.), paragraph 13(1) (amount available for relief: basic rule) shall have effect, in relation to qualifying disposals in a year of assessment specified in the first column of the following Table, as if–

(a) for the references to £250,000 there were substituted references to the amount specified in the second column of that Table; and

(b) for the reference to £1 million there were substituted a reference to the amount specified in the third column of that Table.

TABLE

Year	*£250,000*	*£1 million*
1999–00	£200,000	£800,000
2000–01	£150,000	£600,000
2001–02	£100,000	£400,000
2002–03	£50,000	£200,000

140(2) The following provisions, namely–

(a) section 163 of that Act (relief for disposals by individuals on retirement from family business);

(b) section 164 of that Act (other retirement relief); and

(c) Schedule 6 to that Act,

shall cease to have effect in relation to disposals in the year 2003–04 and subsequent years of assessment.

140(3) [Amends TCGA 1992, s. 157.]

140(4) [Substitutes TCGA 1992, s. 165(8)(a)–(aa) for (a).]

140(5) [Omitted by FA 2008, s. 8 and Sch. 2, para. 55(a)(ii).]

140(6) Subsections (3) to (5) above have effect in relation to the year 2003–04 and subsequent years of assessment.

History – S. 140(5) omitted by FA 2008, s. 8 and Sch. 2, para. 55(a)(ii), with effect in relation to chargeable gains accruing or treated as accruing in the tax year 2008–09 or any subsequent tax year.

141 Abolition of certain other CGT reliefs

141(1) The following provisions of the Taxation of Chargeable Gains Act 1992 shall cease to have effect, namely–

(a) Chapter IA of Part V (roll-over relief on re-investment); and

(b) sections 254 and 255 (relief for debts on qualifying corporate bonds).

141(2) In subsection (1) above–

(a) paragraph (a) has effect in relation to acquisitions made on or after 6th April 1998; and

(b) paragraph (b) has effect in relation to loans made on or after 17th March 1998.

PART VI – MISCELLANEOUS AND SUPPLEMENTAL

GOVERNMENT BORROWING

161 Non-FOTRA securities

161(1) Subject to the following provisions of this section, any gilt-edged security issued before 6th April 1998 without FOTRA conditions shall be treated in relation to times on or after that date as if–

(a) it were a security issued with the post-1996 Act conditions; and

(b) those conditions had been authorised in relation to the issue of that security by virtue of section 22 of the Finance (No. 2) Act 1931.

161(2) Where a gilt-edged security falls to be treated as mentioned in subsection (1) above that treatment shall have effect–

(a) for the purposes of Chapter 2 of Part 12 of the Income Tax Act 2007 (accrued income profits) in relation only to accrued income profits which a person is treated as making under section 628(5) or 630(2) of that Act on or after 6th April 1998;

(b) for the other purposes of the Tax Acts, in relation only to payments of interest falling due on or after that date; and

(c) for the purposes of the Inheritance Tax Act 1984, in relation only to a determination of whether property is excluded property at a time falling on or after that date.

161(3) No charge to tax shall be treated as arising under section 65 of the Inheritance Tax Act 1984 (property becoming excluded property) by reason only of the coming into force of this section.

161(4) In this section **"FOTRA conditions"** means any such conditions about exemption from taxation as are authorised in relation to the issue of a gilt-edged security by virtue of section 22 of the Finance (No. 2) Act 1931.

161(5) In this section **"the post-1996 Act conditions"** means the FOTRA conditions with which 7.25% Treasury Stock 2007 was first issued by virtue of section 22 of the Finance (No. 2) Act 1931.

161(6) In this section **"gilt-edged securities"** means any securities which are gilt-edged securities for the purposes of the Taxation of Chargeable Gains Act 1992.

161(7) This section does not apply to any 31/2% War Loan 1952 Or After which was issued with a condition authorised by virtue of section 47 of the Finance (No. 2) Act 1915.

History – In s. 161(2)(a) the words "Chapter 2 of Part 12 … of that Act" substituted for "sections 711 to 728 of the Taxes Act 1988 (accrued income scheme), in relation only to amounts which a person is treated under those sections as receiving" by ITA 2007, s. 1027 and Sch. 1, para. 384, with effect from 6 April 2007.

THE EUROPEAN SINGLE CURRENCY

163 Adoption of single currency by other member States

163(1) The Treasury may, to such extent as appears to them appropriate in connection with any of the matters falling within subsection (2) below, by regulations modify the application and effect as respects–

(a) transactions in a currency other than sterling,

(b) instruments denominated in such a currency, and

(c) the bringing into account of amounts expressed in, or by reference to, such a currency,

of any enactment or subordinate legislation relating to any matter for which the Commissioners for Her Majesty's Revenue and Customs are responsible and to which section 7 of the Commissioners for Revenue and Customs Act 2005 (former Inland Revenue matters) applies.

163(2) The matters falling within this subsection are–

(a) the adoption or proposed adoption by other member States of the single currency; and

(b) any transitional measures or other arrangements applying or likely to apply in relation to the adoption of the single currency by other member States.

163(3) Without prejudice to the generality of subsection (1) above, the power conferred by that subsection includes power by regulations to provide–

(a) for liabilities to pay amounts to the Commissioners of Inland Revenue under any enactment or subordinate legislation relating to taxation to be capable of being discharged, in accordance with the regulations, by payments in the single currency;

(b) [repealed by FA 2002, s. 141 and Sch. 40, Pt. 3(11);]

(c) [repealed by FA 2002, s. 141 and Sch. 40, Pt. 3(11);]

163(4) The power to make regulations under this section includes–

(a) power to impose charges to taxation;

(b) power to amend or repeal any enactment; and

(c) power to make such incidental, supplemental, consequential and transitional provision as appears to the Treasury to be appropriate.

163(5) The power to make regulations under this section shall be exercisable by statutory instrument subject to annulment in pursuance of a resolution of the House of Commons.

163(6) In this section–

"enactment" includes any enactment contained in this Act (other than this section) and any enactment passed after this Act;

"other member State" means a member State other than the United Kingdom;

"subordinate legislation" has the same meaning as in the Interpretation Act 1978.

163(7) References in this section to the adoption of the single currency are references to the adoption of the single currency in accordance with the Treaty establishing the European Community, and the reference in subsection (3)(a) above to that currency shall be construed accordingly.

History – In s. 163(1) the words "any matter for which the Commissioners for Her Majesty's Revenue and Customs are responsible and to which section 7 of the Commissioners for Revenue and Customs Act 2005 (former Inland Revenue matters) applies." substituted for the words "*any matter under the care and management of the Commissioners of Inland Revenue.*" by CRCA 2005, s. 16 and 17 and Sch. 2, para. 10, with effect from 18 April 2005 (by virtue of SI 2005/1126, art. 2).

S. 163(3)(b) and (c) repealed by FA 2002, s. 141 and Sch. 40, Pt. 3(11) with effect in relation to accounting periods beginning on or after 1 October 2002.

Notes – See also SI 1998/3177 European Single Currency (Taxes) Regulations 1998.

SUPPLEMENTAL

164 Interpretation

164 In this Act **"the Taxes Act 1988"** means the Income and Corporation Taxes Act 1988.

166 Short title

166 This Act may be cited as the Finance Act 1998.

SCHEDULES

SCHEDULE 3 – ADVANCE CORPORATION TAX

Section 31

SECTION 1 OF THE PROVISIONAL COLLECTION OF TAXES ACT 1968

1 [Repealed by Statute Law (Repeals) Act 2013, s. 1 and Sch. 1, Pt. 10.]

History – Para. 1 repealed by Statute Law (Repeals) Act 2013, s. 1 and Sch. 1, Pt. 10, with effect from 31 January 2013.

SECTION 10 OF THE TAXES MANAGEMENT ACT 1970

2 [Repealed by Statute Law (Repeals) Act 2013, s. 1 and Sch. 1, Pt. 10.]

History – Para. 2 repealed by Statute Law (Repeals) Act 2013, s. 1 and Sch. 1, Pt. 10, with effect from 31 January 2013.

SECTION 87 OF THE TAXES MANAGEMENT ACT 1970

3 [Repealed by Statute Law (Repeals) Act 2013, s. 1 and Sch. 1, Pt. 10.]

History – Para. 3 repealed by Statute Law (Repeals) Act 2013, s. 1 and Sch. 1, Pt. 10, with effect from 31 January 2013.

SECTION 87A OF THE TAXES MANAGEMENT ACT 1970

4 [Repealed by Statute Law (Repeals) Act 2013, s. 1 and Sch. 1, Pt. 10.]

History – Para. 4 repealed by Statute Law (Repeals) Act 2013, s. 1 and Sch. 1, Pt. 10, with effect from 31 January 2013.

SECTION 94 OF THE TAXES MANAGEMENT ACT 1970

5(1) Section 94 of the Taxes Management Act 1970 (failure to make return for corporation tax) shall be amended as follows.

5(2) [Repeals TMA 1970, s. 94(8).]

5(3) This paragraph has effect in relation to accounting periods beginning on or after 6th April 1999.

SECTION 109 OF THE TAXES MANAGEMENT ACT 1970

6(1) Section 109 of the Taxes Management Act 1970 (corporation tax on close company in connection with loans to participators etc) shall be amended as follows.

6(2) [Amends TMA 1970, s. 109(3A).]

6(3) This paragraph has effect in relation to the release or writing off of the whole or part of a debt on or after 6th April 1999.

SECTION 13 OF THE TAXES ACT 1988

7 [Repealed by CTA 2010, s. 1181 and Sch. 3, Pt. 1.]

History – Para. 7 repealed by CTA 2010, s. 1181 and Sch. 3, Pt. 1, with effect for corporation tax purposes for accounting periods ending on or after 1 April 2010, and for income tax and capital gains tax purposes for the tax year 2010–11 and subsequent tax years.

SECTION 14 OF THE TAXES ACT 1988

8 [Repealed by Statute Law (Repeals) Act 2013, s. 1 and Sch. 1, Pt. 10.]

History – Para. 8 repealed by Statute Law (Repeals) Act 2013, s. 1 and Sch. 1, Pt. 10, with effect from 31 January 2013.

SECTION 75 OF THE TAXES ACT 1988

9 [Repealed by FA 2004, s. 326, Sch. 42, Pt. 2(3).]

History – Para. 9 repealed by FA 2004, s. 326, Sch. 42, Pt. 2(3), with effect, subject to the transitional provisions at s. 43, 44 and Sch. 6, for accounting periods beginning on or after 1 April 2004.

SECTION 116 OF THE TAXES ACT 1988

10 [Repealed by CTA 2010, s. 1181 and Sch. 3, Pt. 1.]

History – Para. 10 repealed by CTA 2010, s. 1181 and Sch. 3, Pt. 1, with effect for corporation tax purposes for accounting periods ending on or after 1 April 2010, and for income tax and capital gains tax purposes for the tax year 2010–11 and subsequent tax years. Para. 10 also omitted by FA 2009, s. 5 and Sch. 1, para. 6(i), with effect for the tax year 2010–11 and subsequent tax years.

SECTION 238 OF THE TAXES ACT 1988

11 [Repealed by Statute Law (Repeals) Act 2013, s. 1 and Sch. 1, Pt. 10.]

History – Para. 11 repealed by Statute Law (Repeals) Act 2013, s. 1 and Sch. 1, Pt. 10, with effect from 31 January 2013.

SECTION 239 OF THE TAXES ACT 1988

12 [Repealed by Statute Law (Repeals) Act 2013, s. 1 and Sch. 1, Pt. 10.]

History – Para. 12 repealed by Statute Law (Repeals) Act 2013, s. 1 and Sch. 1, Pt. 10, with effect from 31 January 2013. .

SECTION 240 OF THE TAXES ACT 1988

13 [Repealed by Statute Law (Repeals) Act 2013, s. 1 and Sch. 1, Pt. 10.]

History – Para. 13 repealed by Statute Law (Repeals) Act 2013, s. 1 and Sch. 1, Pt. 10, with effect from 31 January 2013.

SECTION 241 OF THE TAXES ACT 1988

14 [Repealed by Statute Law (Repeals) Act 2013, s. 1 and Sch. 1, Pt. 10.]

History – Para. 14 repealed by Statute Law (Repeals) Act 2013, s. 1 and Sch. 1, Pt. 10, with effect from 31 January 2013.

SECTION 245 OF THE TAXES ACT 1988

15 [Repealed by Statute Law (Repeals) Act 2013, s. 1 and Sch. 1, Pt. 10.]

History – Para. 15 repealed by Statute Law (Repeals) Act 2013, s. 1 and Sch. 1, Pt. 10, with effect from 31 January 2013.

SECTION 245A OF THE TAXES ACT 1988

16 [Repealed by Statute Law (Repeals) Act 2013, s. 1 and Sch. 1, Pt. 10.]

History – Para. 16 repealed by Statute Law (Repeals) Act 2013, s. 1 and Sch. 1, Pt. 10, with effect from 31 January 2013.

SECTION 245B OF THE TAXES ACT 1988

17 [Repealed by Statute Law (Repeals) Act 2013, s. 1 and Sch. 1, Pt. 10.]

History – Para. 17 repealed by Statute Law (Repeals) Act 2013, s. 1 and Sch. 1, Pt. 10, with effect from 31 January 2013.

SECTION 246 OF THE TAXES ACT 1988

18 [Repealed by Statute Law (Repeals) Act 2013, s. 1 and Sch. 1, Pt. 10.]

History – Para. 18 repealed by Statute Law (Repeals) Act 2013, s. 1 and Sch. 1, Pt. 10, with effect from 31 January 2013.

SECTION 247 OF THE TAXES ACT 1988

19 [Repealed by Statute Law (Repeals) Act 2013, s. 1 and Sch. 1, Pt. 10.]

History – Para. 19 repealed by Statute Law (Repeals) Act 2013, s. 1 and Sch. 1, Pt. 10, with effect from 31 January 2013. Note that former para. 19(3) and (4)(a) had previously been repealed (see note below) and former para. 19(2) and (5)–(7) repealed ICTA 1988, s. 247(1), (2) and (3), and amended ICTA 1988, s. 247(6), (7) and (10).

Former para. 19(3) and (4)(a) repealed by FA 2001, s. 110 and Sch. 33, Pt. 2(10), with effect for payments made after 11 May 2001.

SECTION 248 OF THE TAXES ACT 1988

20 [Repealed by Statute Law (Repeals) Act 2013, s. 1 and Sch. 1, Pt. 10.]

History – Para. 20 repealed by Statute Law (Repeals) Act 2013, s. 1 and Sch. 1, Pt. 10, with effect from 31 January 2013.

SECTION 252 OF THE TAXES ACT 1988

21 [Repealed by Statute Law (Repeals) Act 2013, s. 1 and Sch. 1, Pt. 10.]

History – Para. 21 repealed by Statute Law (Repeals) Act 2013, s. 1 and Sch. 1, Pt. 10, with effect from 31 January 2013.

SECTION 253 OF THE TAXES ACT 1988

22 [Repealed by Statute Law (Repeals) Act 2013, s. 1 and Sch. 1, Pt. 10.]

History – Para. 22 repealed by Statute Law (Repeals) Act 2013, s. 1 and Sch. 1, Pt. 10, with effect from 31 January 2013.

SECTION 255 OF THE TAXES ACT 1988

23 [Repealed by Statute Law (Repeals) Act 2013, s. 1 and Sch. 1, Pt. 10.]

History – Para. 23 repealed by Statute Law (Repeals) Act 2013, s. 1 and Sch. 1, Pt. 10, with effect from 31 January 2013.

SECTION 419 OF THE TAXES ACT 1988

24 [Repealed by CTA 2010, s. 1181 and Sch. 3, Pt. 1.]

History – Para. 24 repealed by CTA 2010, s. 1181 and Sch. 3, Pt. 1, with effect for corporation tax purposes for accounting periods ending on or after 1 April 2010, and for income tax and capital gains tax purposes for the tax year 2010–11 and subsequent tax years.

SECTION 434 OF THE TAXES ACT 1988

25 [Repealed by Statute Law (Repeals) Act 2013, s. 1 and Sch. 1, Pt. 10.]

History – Para. 25 repealed by Statute Law (Repeals) Act 2013, s. 1 and Sch. 1, Pt. 10, with effect from 31 January 2013.

SECTION 434C OF THE TAXES ACT 1988

26 [Repealed by Statute Law (Repeals) Act 2013, s. 1 and Sch. 1, Pt. 10.]

History – Para. 26 repealed by Statute Law (Repeals) Act 2013, s. 1 and Sch. 1, Pt. 10, with effect from 31 January 2013.

SECTION 468Q OF THE TAXES ACT 1988

27 [Repealed by Statute Law (Repeals) Act 2013, s. 1 and Sch. 1, Pt. 10.]

History – Para. 27 repealed by Statute Law (Repeals) Act 2013, s. 1 and Sch. 1, Pt. 10, with effect from 31 January 2013.

SECTION 490 OF THE TAXES ACT 1988

28 [Repealed by Statute Law (Repeals) Act 2013, s. 1 and Sch. 1, Pt. 10.]

History – Para. 28 repealed by Statute Law (Repeals) Act 2013, s. 1 and Sch. 1, Pt. 10, with effect from 31 January 2013.

SECTION 497 OF THE TAXES ACT 1988

29 [Repealed by Statute Law (Repeals) Act 2013, s. 1 and Sch. 1, Pt. 10.]

History – Para. 29 repealed by Statute Law (Repeals) Act 2013, s. 1 and Sch. 1, Pt. 10, with effect from 31 January 2013.

SECTION 498 OF THE TAXES ACT 1988

30 [Repealed by Statute Law (Repeals) Act 2013, s. 1 and Sch. 1, Pt. 10.]

History – Para. 30 repealed by Statute Law (Repeals) Act 2013, s. 1 and Sch. 1, Pt. 10, with effect from 31 January 2013.

SECTION 499 OF THE TAXES ACT 1988

31 [Repealed by Statute Law (Repeals) Act 2013, s. 1 and Sch. 1, Pt. 10.]

History – Para. 31 repealed by Statute Law (Repeals) Act 2013, s. 1 and Sch. 1, Pt. 10, with effect from 31 January 2013.

SECTION 703 OF THE TAXES ACT 1988

32 [Repealed by Statute Law (Repeals) Act 2013, s. 1 and Sch. 1, Pt. 10.]

History – Para. 32 repealed by Statute Law (Repeals) Act 2013, s. 1 and Sch. 1, Pt. 10, with effect from 31 January 2013. Note that former para. 32(2) and (4) had previously been repealed (see notes below)
Former para. 32(2) repealed by ITA 2007, s. 1031 and Sch. 3, Pt. 1, with effect from 6 April 2007.
Former para. 32(4) repealed by ITA 2007, s. 1031 and Sch. 3, Pt. 1, with effect from 6 April 2007.

SECTION 704 OF THE TAXES ACT 1988

33 [Repealed by Statute Law (Repeals) Act 2013, s. 1 and Sch. 1, Pt. 10.]

History – Para. 33 repealed by Statute Law (Repeals) Act 2013, s. 1 and Sch. 1, Pt. 10, with effect from 31 January 2013.

SECTION 705 OF THE TAXES ACT 1988

34 [Repealed by Statute Law (Repeals) Act 2013, s. 1 and Sch. 1, Pt. 10.]

History – Para. 34 repealed by Statute Law (Repeals) Act 2013, s. 1 and Sch. 1, Pt. 10, with effect from 31 January 2013.

SECTION 797 OF THE TAXES ACT 1988

35 [Repealed by Statute Law (Repeals) Act 2013, s. 1 and Sch. 1, Pt. 10.]

History – Para. 35 repealed by Statute Law (Repeals) Act 2013, s. 1 and Sch. 1, Pt. 10, with effect from 31 January 2013.

SECTION 802 OF THE TAXES ACT 1988

36 [Repealed by Statute Law (Repeals) Act 2013, s. 1 and Sch. 1, Pt. 10.]

History – Para. 36 repealed by Statute Law (Repeals) Act 2013, s. 1 and Sch. 1, Pt. 10, with effect from 31 January 2013.

SECTION 813 OF THE TAXES ACT 1988

37 [Repealed by Statute Law (Repeals) Act 2013, s. 1 and Sch. 1, Pt. 10.]

History – Para. 37 repealed by Statute Law (Repeals) Act 2013, s. 1 and Sch. 1, Pt. 10, with effect from 31 January 2013.

SECTION 826 OF THE TAXES ACT 1988

38 [Repealed by Statute Law (Repeals) Act 2013, s. 1 and Sch. 1, Pt. 10.]

History – Para. 38 repealed by Statute Law (Repeals) Act 2013, s. 1 and Sch. 1, Pt. 10, with effect from 31 January 2013.

SECTION 832 OF THE TAXES ACT 1988

39 [Repealed by Statute Law (Repeals) Act 2013, s. 1 and Sch. 1, Pt. 10.]

History – Para. 39 repealed by Statute Law (Repeals) Act 2013, s. 1 and Sch. 1, Pt. 10, with effect from 31 January 2013. Note that former para. 39(2) and (7) had previously been repealed (see notes below)

Former para. 39(2) repealed by CTA 2010, s. 1181 and Sch. 3, Pt. 1, with effect for corporation tax purposes for accounting periods ending on or after 1 April 2010, and for income tax and capital gains tax purposes for the tax year 2010–11 and subsequent tax years.

Former para. 39(7) repealed by CTA 2010, s. 1181 and Sch. 3, Pt. 1, with effect for corporation tax purposes for accounting periods ending on or after 1 April 2010, and for income tax and capital gains tax purposes for the tax year 2010–11 and subsequent tax years.

SECTION 835 OF THE TAXES ACT 1988

40 [Repealed by ITA 2007, s. 1031 and Sch. 3, Pt. 1.]

History – Para. 40 repealed by ITA 2007, s. 1031 and Sch. 3, Pt. 1, with effect from 6 April 2007.

SCHEDULE 13 TO THE TAXES ACT 1988

41 [Repealed by Statute Law (Repeals) Act 2013, s. 1 and Sch. 1, Pt. 10.]

History – Para. 41 repealed by Statute Law (Repeals) Act 2013, s. 1 and Sch. 1, Pt. 10, with effect from 31 January 2013.

SCHEDULE 13A TO THE TAXES ACT 1988

42 [Repealed by Statute Law (Repeals) Act 2013, s. 1 and Sch. 1, Pt. 10.]

History – Para. 42 repealed by Statute Law (Repeals) Act 2013, s. 1 and Sch. 1, Pt. 10, with effect from 31 January 2013.

SCHEDULE 24 TO THE TAXES ACT 1988

43 [Repealed by Statute Law (Repeals) Act 2013, s. 1 and Sch. 1, Pt. 10.]

History – Para. 43 repealed by Statute Law (Repeals) Act 2013, s. 1 and Sch. 1, Pt. 10, with effect from 31 January 2013.

SCHEDULE 26 TO THE TAXES ACT 1988

44 [Repealed by Statute Law (Repeals) Act 2013, s. 1 and Sch. 1, Pt. 10.]

History – Para. 44 repealed by Statute Law (Repeals) Act 2013, s. 1 and Sch. 1, Pt. 10, with effect from 31 January 2013.

PARAGRAPH 8 OF SCHEDULE 4 TO THE FINANCE (NO. 2) ACT 1997

45 [Repealed by Statute Law (Repeals) Act 2013, s. 1 and Sch. 1, Pt. 10.]

History – Para. 45 repealed by Statute Law (Repeals) Act 2013, s. 1 and Sch. 1, Pt. 10, with effect from 31 January 2013.

PARAGRAPH 9 OF SCHEDULE 4 TO THE FINANCE (NO. 2) ACT 1997

46 [Repealed by Statute Law (Repeals) Act 2013, s. 1 and Sch. 1, Pt. 10.]

History – Para. 46 repealed by Statute Law (Repeals) Act 2013, s. 1 and Sch. 1, Pt. 10, with effect from 31 January 2013.

PARAGRAPH 18 OF SCHEDULE 4 TO THE FINANCE (NO. 2) ACT 1997

47 [Repealed by Statute Law (Repeals) Act 2013, s. 1 and Sch. 1, Pt. 10.]

History – Para. 47 repealed by Statute Law (Repeals) Act 2013, s. 1 and Sch. 1, Pt. 10, with effect from 31 January 2013.

PARAGRAPH 23 OF SCHEDULE 4 TO THE FINANCE (NO. 2) ACT 1997

48 [Repealed by Statute Law (Repeals) Act 2013, s. 1 and Sch. 1, Pt. 10.]

History – Para. 48 repealed by Statute Law (Repeals) Act 2013, s. 1 and Sch. 1, Pt. 10, with effect from 31 January 2013.

SCHEDULE 4 – INTEREST PAYABLE UNDER THE TAX ACTS BY OR TO COMPANIES

Section 35

INTEREST ON OVERPAID OR EARLY PAID CORPORATION TAX

1(1) [Amends ICTA 1988, s. 826(2).]

1(2) [Inserts ICTA 1988, s. 826A.]

1(3) [Amends FA 1989, s. 178(2)(m).]

THE "MATERIAL DATE" FOR INTEREST ON A REPAYMENT OF INCOME TAX

2(1) [Amends ICTA 1988, s. 826(3).]

2(2) This paragraph has effect in relation to accounting periods ending on or after the day appointed under section 199 of the Finance Act 1994 for the purposes of Chapter III of Part IV of that Act (corporation tax self-assessment).

Notes – The day appointed under FA 1994, s. 199 is 1 July 1999 (SI 1998/3173 (C. 78)).

RECOVERY OF INTEREST OVERPAID UNDER SECTION 826(1)(a)

3(1) [Inserts ICTA 1988, s. 826(8A), (8B) and (8C).]

3(2) [Repealed by FA 2001, s. 110 and Sch. 33, Pt. 2(14).]

3(3) The amendments made by this paragraph have effect in relation to interest on repayments of corporation tax paid for accounting periods ending on or after the day appointed under section 199 of the Finance Act 1994 for the purposes of Chapter III of Part IV of that Act (corporation tax self-assessment).

History – Para. 3(2) repealed by FA 2001, s. 110 and Sch. 33, Pt. 2(14) with effect in relation to proceedings begun, (or a counterclaim made), and a set-off first claimed, after 11 May 2001.

Notes – The day appointed under FA 1994, s. 199 is 1 July 1999 (SI 1998/3173 (C. 78)).

INTEREST ON UNDERPAID TAX WHERE RELIEFS ARE CARRIED BACK

4(1) Section 87A of the Taxes Management Act 1970 (interest on overdue corporation tax etc.) shall be amended as follows.

4(2) [Amends TMA 1970, s. 87A(4), (4A) and (6).]

4(3) [Inserts TMA 1970, s. 87A(8).]

4(4) [Inserts TMA 1970, s. 87A(9).]

4(5) The amendments made by this paragraph have effect where the accounting period whose due and payable date falls to be determined is an accounting period ending on or after the day appointed under section 199 of the Finance Act 1994 for the purposes of Chapter III of Part IV of that Act (corporation tax self-assessment).

4(6) In sub-paragraph (5) above **"due and payable date"**, in relation to an accounting period, means the date on which corporation tax for that period becomes, or (as the case may be) would become, due and payable.

Notes – The day appointed under FA 1994, s. 199 is 1 July 1999 (SI 1998/3173 (C. 78)).

INTEREST ON OVERPAID TAX WHERE RELIEFS ARE CARRIED BACK

5(1) Section 826 of the Taxes Act 1988 (interest on tax overpaid) shall be amended as follows.

5(2) [Amends ICTA 1988,s. 826(7), (7A), (7B) and (7C).]

5(3) [Inserts ICTA 1988,s. 826(7D).]

5(4) [Inserts ICTA 1988,s. 826(7E).]

5(5) The amendments made by this paragraph have effect where the accounting period whose due and payable date falls to be determined is an accounting period ending on or after the day appointed under section 199 of the Finance Act 1994 for the purposes of Chapter III of Part IV of that Act (corporation tax self-assessment).

5(6) In sub-paragraph (5) above **"due and payable date"**, in relation to an accounting period, means the date on which corporation tax for that period becomes, or (as the case may be) would become, due and payable.

Notes – The day appointed under FA 1994, s. 199 is 1 July 1999 (SI 1998/3173 (C. 78)).

COMPANY LIQUIDATIONS

6 [Repealed by CTA 2010, s. 1181 and Sch. 3, Pt. 1.]

History – Para. 6 repealed by CTA 2010, s. 1181 and Sch. 3, Pt. 1, with effect for corporation tax purposes for accounting periods ending on or after 1 April 2010, and for income tax and capital gains tax purposes for the tax year 2010–11 and subsequent tax years. F

LOAN RELATIONSHIPS

7 [Repealed by FA 2002, s. 141 and Sch. 40, Pt. 3(10).]

History – Para. 7 repealed by FA 2002, s. 141 and Sch. 40, Pt. 3(10) with effect in relation to accounting periods beginning on or after 1 October 2002.

SCHEDULE 5 – RENT AND OTHER RECEIPTS FROM LAND

Section 38(1)

Part I – Main Charging Provisions

1 [Substitutes ICTA 1988, s. 15(1).]

2 [Inserts ICTA 1988, s. 15(1A).]

3 [Substitutes heading to ICTA 1988, Pt. II.]

4 [Substitutes ICTA 1988, s. 21–21B.]

5 [Inserts ICTA 1988, s. 21C.]

6 [Repeals ICTA 1988, s. 25.]

7(1) Section 26 of the Taxes Act 1988 (land managed as one estate) is amended as follows.

7(2) [Amends ICTA 1988, s. 26(1).]

7(3) [Repeals ICTA 1988, s. 26(2)(a).]

7(4) [Inserts ICTA 1988, s. 26(2A).]

8 [Substitutes ICTA 1988, s. 27(3).]

9 [Repeals ICTA 1988, s. 28.]

10 [Repeals ICTA 1988, s. 29.]

11 [Amends ICTA 1988, s. 30(1).]

12 [Repeals ICTA 1988, s. 31.]

13 [Repeals ICTA 1988, s. 33.]

14 [Repeals ICTA 1988, s. 33A, 33B.]

15 [Repealed by CTA 2009, s. 1326 and Sch. 3, Pt. 1.]

History – Para. 15 repealed by CTA 2009, s. 1326 and Sch. 3, Pt. 1, with effect for corporation tax purposes for accounting periods ending on or after 1 April 2009, and for income tax and capital gains tax purposes for the tax year 2009–10 and subsequent tax years.

16 [Repealed by CTA 2009, s. 1326 and Sch. 3, Pt. 1.]

History – Para. 16 repealed by CTA 2009, s. 1326 and Sch. 3, Pt. 1, with effect for corporation tax purposes for accounting periods ending on or after 1 April 2009, and for income tax and capital gains tax purposes for the tax year 2009–10 and subsequent tax years.

17 [Repealed by CTA 2009, s. 1326 and Sch. 3, Pt. 1.]

History – Para. 17 repealed by CTA 2009, s. 1326 and Sch. 3, Pt. 1, with effect for corporation tax purposes for accounting periods ending on or after 1 April 2009, and for income tax and capital gains tax purposes for the tax year 2009–10 and subsequent tax years.

18 [Repealed by CTA 2009, s. 1326 and Sch. 3, Pt. 1.]

History – Para. 18 repealed by CTA 2009, s. 1326 and Sch. 3, Pt. 1, with effect for corporation tax purposes for accounting periods ending on or after 1 April 2009, and for income tax and capital gains tax purposes for the tax year 2009–10 and subsequent tax years.

19 [Substitutes heading before ICTA 1988, s. 40.]

20(1) Section 40 of the Taxes Act 1988 (tax treatment of receipts and outgoings on sale of land) is amended as follows.

20(2) [Amends ICTA 1988, s. 40(1).]

20(3) [Amends ICTA 1988, s. 40(3)(b).]

20(4) [Inserts ICTA 1988, s. 40(4A).]

20(5) [Repeals ICTA 1988, s. 40(5).]

21 [Repeals ICTA 1988, s. 41.]

22 [Repeals ICTA 1988, s. 42A(8).]

23 [Repealed by ITTOIA 2005, s. 884 and Sch. 3 effective for income tax purposes for 2005–06 onwards and for corporation tax purposes for accounting periods ending after 5 April 2005 (ITTOIA 2005, s. 883(1)).]

24 [Repealed by ITTOIA 2005, s. 884 and Sch. 3 effective for income tax purposes for 2005–06 onwards and for corporation tax purposes for accounting periods ending after 5 April 2005 (ITTOIA 2005, s. 883(1)).]

25 [Inserts ICTA 1988, s. 70A.]

Part II – Treatment of Losses

26 [Repealed by ITA 2007, s. 1031 and Sch. 3, Pt. 1.]

History – Para. 26 repealed by ITA 2007, s. 1031 and Sch. 3, Pt. 1, with effect from 6 April 2007.

27 [Repealed by ITA 2007, s. 1031 and Sch. 3, Pt. 1.]

History – Para. 27 repealed by ITA 2007, s. 1031 and Sch. 3, Pt. 1, with effect from 6 April 2007.

Notes – Para. 27 rewritten as ITA 2007, s. 118(1), (2), (3), (4), (5), 119, 120(1), (2), (4), 121(1), (2), (3), 122(2), (3), (4), (5), 123(2), (3), (4), (5), (6), (7), 124(1), (2).

28 [Repealed by CTA 2010, s. 1181 and Sch. 3, Pt. 1.]

History – Para. 28 repealed by CTA 2010, s. 1181 and Sch. 3, Pt. 1, with effect for corporation tax purposes for accounting periods ending on or after 1 April 2010, and for income tax and capital gains tax purposes for the tax year 2010–11 and subsequent tax years.

29 [Repealed by CTA 2010, s. 1181 and Sch. 3, Pt. 1.]

History – Para. 29 repealed by CTA 2010, s. 1181 and Sch. 3, Pt. 1, with effect for corporation tax purposes for accounting periods ending on or after 1 April 2010, and for income tax and capital gains tax purposes for the tax year 2010–11 and subsequent tax years.

30 [Repealed by CTA 2010, s. 1181 and Sch. 3, Pt. 1.]

History – Para. 30 repealed by CTA 2010, s. 1181 and Sch. 3, Pt. 1, with effect for corporation tax purposes for accounting periods ending on or after 1 April 2010, and for income tax and capital gains tax purposes for the tax year 2010–11 and subsequent tax years.

31 [Repealed by CTA 2010, s. 1181 and Sch. 3, Pt. 1.]

History – Para. 31 repealed by CTA 2010, s. 1181 and Sch. 3, Pt. 1, with effect for corporation tax purposes for accounting periods ending on or after 1 April 2010, and for income tax and capital gains tax purposes for the tax year 2010–11 and subsequent tax years.

32 [Repealed by CTA 2010, s. 1181 and Sch. 3, Pt. 1.]

History – Para. 32 repealed by CTA 2010, s. 1181 and Sch. 3, Pt. 1, with effect for corporation tax purposes for accounting periods ending on or after 1 April 2010, and for income tax and capital gains tax purposes for the tax year 2010–11 and subsequent tax years.

Part III – Minor and Consequential Amendments

TAXES MANAGEMENT ACT 1970 (C. 9)

33 [Substitutes TMA 1970, s. 41A(9)(b).]

INCOME AND CORPORATION TAXES ACT 1988 (C. 1)

34 [Repealed by CTA 2009, s. 1326 and Sch. 3, Pt. 1.]

History – Para. 34 repealed by CTA 2009, s. 1326 and Sch. 3, Pt. 1, with effect for corporation tax purposes for accounting periods ending on or after 1 April 2009, and for income tax and capital gains tax purposes for the tax year 2009–10 and subsequent tax years.

35 [Repealed by CTA 2010, s. 1181 and Sch. 3, Pt. 1.]

History – Para. 35 repealed by CTA 2010, s. 1181 and Sch. 3, Pt. 1, with effect for corporation tax purposes for accounting periods ending on or after 1 April 2010, and for income tax and capital gains tax purposes for the tax year 2010–11 and subsequent tax years.

36 [Repealed by CTA 2010, s. 1181 and Sch. 3, Pt. 1.]

History – Para. 36 repealed by CTA 2010, s. 1181 and Sch. 3, Pt. 1, with effect for corporation tax purposes for accounting periods ending on or after 1 April 2010, and for income tax and capital gains tax purposes for the tax year 2010–11 and subsequent tax years.

37 [Repealed by CTA 2010, s. 1181 and Sch. 3, Pt. 1.]

History – Para. 37 repealed by CTA 2010, s. 1181 and Sch. 3, Pt. 1, with effect for corporation tax purposes for accounting periods ending on or after 1 April 2010, and for income tax and capital gains tax purposes for the tax year 2010–11 and subsequent tax years.

38 [Repealed by CTA 2010, s. 1181 and Sch. 3, Pt. 1.]

History – Para. 38 repealed by CTA 2010, s. 1181 and Sch. 3, Pt. 1, with effect for corporation tax purposes for accounting periods ending on or after 1 April 2010, and for income tax and capital gains tax purposes for the tax year 2010–11 and subsequent tax years.

39 [Omitted by FA 2012, s. 146 and Sch. 16, para. 247(i)(ii).]

History – Para. 39 omitted by FA 2012, s. 146 and Sch. 16, para. 247(i)(ii), with effect in relation to accounting periods beginning on or after 1 January 2013 (FA 2012, s. 148) but subject to transitional provisions in FA 2012, Sch. 17. Where an accounting period would otherwise straddle 1 January 2013, it is deemed to end on 31 December 2012 (FA 2012, s. 149).

40 [Repealed by CAA 2001, s. 580 and Sch. 4.]

History – Para. 40 repealed by CAA 2001, s. 580 and Sch. 4 in respect of allowances and charges falling to be made for chargeable periods ending on or after 6 April 2001 for income tax purposes and 1 April 2001 for corporation tax.

41 [Repealed by SI 2007/2086, reg. 6(2)(c).]

History – Para. 41 repealed by SI 2007/2086, reg. 6(2)(c), with effect for accounting periods beginning on or after 13 August 2007.

42 [Repealed by CTA 2010, s. 1181 and Sch. 3, Pt. 1.]

History – Para. 42 repealed by CTA 2010, s. 1181 and Sch. 3, Pt. 1, with effect for corporation tax purposes for accounting periods ending on or after 1 April 2010, and for income tax and capital gains tax purposes for the tax year 2010–11 and subsequent tax years.

43 [Repealed by CTA 2009, s. 1326 and Sch. 3, Pt. 1.]

History – Para. 43 repealed by CTA 2009, s. 1326 and Sch. 3, Pt. 1, with effect for corporation tax purposes for accounting periods ending on or after 1 April 2009, and for income tax and capital gains tax purposes for the tax year 2009–10 and subsequent tax years.

44 [Amends ICTA 1988, s. 787(3).]

45 [Repealed by ITTOIA 2005, s. 884 and Sch. 3 effective for income tax purposes for 2005–06 onwards and for corporation tax purposes for accounting periods ending after 5 April 2005 (ITTOIA 2005, s. 883(1)).]

46 [Repealed by CTA 2010, s. 1181 and Sch. 3, Pt. 1.]

History – Para. 46 repealed by CTA 2010, s. 1181 and Sch. 3, Pt. 1, with effect for corporation tax purposes for accounting periods ending on or after 1 April 2010, and for income tax and capital gains tax purposes for the tax year 2010–11 and subsequent tax years.

CAPITAL ALLOWANCES ACT 1990 (C. 1)

47–61 [Repealed by CAA 2001, s. 580 and Sch. 4.]

History – Para. 47 to 61 repealed by CAA 2001, s. 580 and Sch. 4 in respect of allowances and charges falling to be made for chargeable periods ending on or after 6 April 2001 for income tax purposes and 1 April 2001 for corporation tax.

TAXATION OF CHARGEABLE GAINS ACT 1992 (C. 12)

62 [Substitutes TCGA 1992, s. 241(3)(a).]

63(1) Schedule 8 to the Taxation of Chargeable Gains Act 1992 (leases) is amended as follows.

63(2) [Amends TCGA 1992, Sch. 8, para. 5.]

63(3) [Amends TCGA 1992, Sch, 8, para. 6(2).]

63(4) [Repealed by ITTOIA 2005, s. 884 and Sch. 3 effective for income tax purposes for 2005–06 onwards and for corporation tax purposes for accounting periods ending after 5 April 2005 (ITTOIA 2005, s. 883(1)).]

63(5) [Substitutes TCGA 1992, Sch. 8, para. 7A.]

FINANCE ACT 1996 (C. 8)

64 [Repealed by CTA 2009, s. 1326 and Sch. 3, Pt. 1.]

History – Para. 64 repealed by CTA 2009, s. 1326 and Sch. 3, Pt. 1, with effect for corporation tax purposes for accounting periods ending on or after 1 April 2009, and for income tax and capital gains tax purposes for the tax year 2009–10 and subsequent tax years.

Part IV – Transitional Provisions for Corporation Tax

INTRODUCTION

65(1) This Part of this Schedule makes provision with respect to the application of the provisions of Parts I to III of this Schedule for corporation tax purposes.

65(2) In this Part of this Schedule–

"before commencement" and **"after commencement"** mean, respectively, before 1st April 1998 and on or after that date; and

"the new rules" means the provisions of the Tax Acts relating to Schedule A taxation or, as the case may be, to the taxation under Case V of Schedule D of income from land outside the United Kingdom, as they have effect after commencement.

RECEIPTS AND EXPENSES NOT TO BE COUNTED TWICE

66(1) To the extent that receipts or expenses have been taken into account before commencement, they shall not be taken into account again under the new rules after commencement.

66(2) Nothing in section 43 of the Finance Act 1989 (computation of profits: effect of delayed payment of emoluments) shall be construed as affecting the rule in sub-paragraph (1) above.

RECEIPTS AND EXPENSES NOT TO BE LEFT OUT OF ACCOUNT

67 To the extent that receipts or expenses would under the new rules have been brought into account before commencement, and were not so brought into account, they shall be brought into account immediately after commencement.

EXPENSES NOT TO BE CARRIED BACK TO BEFORE COMMENCEMENT

68 Expenses which were incurred before commencement but were not taken into account before commencement shall not, by virtue of section 25(3) or 31(3) of the Taxes Act 1988, be carried back and taken into account before commencement.

EFFECT OF TRANSFER OF UNDERLYING RIGHTS

69 If any estate, interest or rights in or over land is or are transferred from one person to another, the references in paragraphs 66 to 68 to receipts or expenses being taken into account shall be construed as references to their being taken into account in relation to either of those persons.

BAD DEBT RELIEF

70(1) Where relief under section 41 of the Taxes Act 1988 (relief for rent, etc. not paid) has been given in respect of an amount before commencement, any receipt after commencement shall be taken into account under the new rules.

70(2) Any writing off of an amount after commencement shall be taken into account under the new rules, even where it relates to a receipt brought into account before commencement.

MEANING OF "TAKEN INTO ACCOUNT"

71 For the purposes of paragraphs 66 to 70 an amount is **"taken into account"** if–

(a) it is brought into account for tax purposes, or

(b) it would have been so brought into account if the person concerned were chargeable to tax

UNRELIEVED CASE VI LOSSES

72(1) A loss to which this paragraph applies which a company would, apart from this Schedule, have been entitled to carry forward under section 396 of the Taxes Act 1988 (Case VI losses) shall be treated after commencement as a loss of an earlier period within section 392A or 392B of that Act and accordingly available to be set off under those provisions.

72(2) This paragraph applies to a loss sustained in a business or transaction of a kind that after commencement would be treated as carried on or entered into in the course of a Schedule A business or overseas property business carried on by the company.

SOURCE CEASING IN TRANSITIONAL ACCOUNTING PERIOD

73(1) The provisions of Parts I to III of this Schedule do not apply in relation to a source which ceases in the course of a company's transitional accounting period to be a source within the charge to tax under Schedule A or Case V or VI of Schedule D in relation to that company and any other person.

73(2) This paragraph does not apply if the company acquired the source in that accounting period or in the preceding twelve months.

SUPERSEDED PROVISIONS RELATING TO FINANCE LEASING

74(1) In Schedule 12 to the Finance Act 1997 (leasing arrangements: finance leases and loans), the following provisions (which apply concepts from Case I of Schedule D in relation to rent taxed under Schedule A) shall cease to have effect in accordance with this paragraph.

74(2) Paragraphs 3(6), 6(9)(b), 8(1) to (7) and 20(b) do not apply in relation to periods of account beginning on or after 1st April 1998.

A **"period of account"** means a period for which accounts are made up.

74(3) Paragraph 8(8) does not apply if the time mentioned in that provision is on or after 1st April 1998.

74(4) Paragraph 8(9) does not apply if the time mentioned in paragraph (a) of that provision is on or after 1st April 1998.

COMPUTATION OF AMOUNTS AVAILABLE FOR SURRENDER AS GROUP RELIEF

75 In computing under section 403 of the Taxes Act the amounts available for surrender as group relief in a company's transitional accounting period, the amounts referable to the period before commencement shall be computed separately from the amounts referable to the period after commencement.

MEANING OF "TRANSITIONAL ACCOUNTING PERIOD"

76 For the purposes of paragraphs 73 and 75 a **"transitional accounting period"** means an accounting period beginning before, and ending on or after, 1st April 1998.

SCHEDULE 6 – ADJUSTMENT ON CHANGE OF ACCOUNTING BASIS

Section 44

[Repealed by FA 2002, s. 64(6) and FA 2002, s. 141 and Sch. 40, Pt. 3(8).]

History – Sch. 6 repealed by FA 2002, s. 64(6) and FA 2002, s. 141 and Sch. 40, Pt. 3(8) with effect in relation to a change of basis taking effect in an accounting period ending on or after 1 August 2001.

Notes – FA 2002, s. 64(6) and Sch. 22 have effect in place of s. 44 and Sch. 6, where a change of basis takes effect in a period of account ending on or after 1 August 2001, subject to transitional rules where certain changes of basis take effect in a period of account ending prior to 1 August 2001 if the relevant return is delivered or amended on or after that date (FA 2002, Sch. 22, para. 16 and 17).

SCHEDULE 7 – REMOVAL OF UNNECESSARY REFERENCES TO GAINS

Section 46(3)

The following are the provisions of the Taxes Acts in which the amendments specified in section 46(3) are to be made.

1 In the Taxes Act 1988: sections 568(1), 570(1), Schedule 21, paragraph 6(1)(b) and (3) (twice).

History – In para. 1, the words "375A(1)(b)," and the words "770(2)(a)(iii) and (b)(iii)" repealed by Statute Law (Repeals) Act 2013, s. 1 and Sch. 1, Pt. 10, with effect from 31 January 2013.

In para. 1, "84A(2)(a)," repealed by TIOPA 2010, s. 378 and Sch. 10, Pt. 12, with effect for corporation tax purposes for accounting periods ending on or after 1 April 2010, for income tax and capital gains tax purposes for the tax year 2010–11 and subsequent tax years, and for petroleum revenue tax purposes for chargeable periods beginning on or after 1 July 2010.

In para. 1, the following words repealed by TIOPA 2010, s. 378 and Sch. 10, Pt. 13, with effect for corporation tax purposes for accounting periods ending on or after 1 April 2010, for income tax and capital gains tax purposes for the tax year 2010–11 and subsequent tax years, and for petroleum revenue tax purposes for chargeable periods beginning on or after 1 July 2010.

- "109A(2)(d), (4) and (4A),"
- "117(1), (3)(b) and (4),"
- "160(1C)(b),"
- "368(3),"
- "526(1)(b),"
- "830(4) in the second place,"

In para. 1, the words "779(13)(b), 780(3)(a), 781(4)(a) and (5)(b), 782(1)(a), (2) and (3), 785 definition of "capital sum" where the words first occur," repealed by CTA 2010, s. 1181 and Sch. 3, Pt. 2, for corporation tax purposes only, with effect for accounting periods ending on or after 1 April 2010. The same entries also repealed by TIOPA 2010, s. 378 and Sch. 10, Pt. 9, with effect for corporation tax purposes for accounting periods ending on or after 1 April 2010, for income tax and capital gains tax purposes for the tax year 2010–11 and subsequent tax years, and for petroleum revenue tax purposes for chargeable periods beginning on or after 1 July 2010.

In para. 1 the following words repealed by CTA 2010, s. 1181 and Sch. 3, Pt. 1, with effect for corporation tax purposes for accounting periods ending on or after 1 April 2010, and for income tax and capital gains tax purposes for the tax year 2010–11 and subsequent tax years.

- "118(1)"
- "400(6)"
- "776(6)(a) and (b)"

In para. 1 the following words repealed by CTA 2009, s. 1326 and Sch. 3, Pt. 1, with effect for corporation tax purposes for accounting periods ending on or after 1 April 2009, and for income tax and capital gains tax purposes for the tax year 2009–10 and subsequent tax years.

- "53(1) and (3), 55(1),"
- "74(1) opening words and paragraph (m),"
- "79(1), 79A(1),"
- "83,"
- "85(1)(a), 85A(2)(a),"

- "86A(2)(a), 87(2) and (6), 88(a), 89 (twice), 90(1)(a), 91(1) and (4)(a)(i), 91A(2) and (3)(a), 91B(2), (5)(a) and (6)(a), 91C(b), 94(1),"
- "97, 99(1) and (2), 100(1), (1D) and (1E) (twice each), 101(1) (twice) and (2)(a), 102(1), 103(1), (2)(a) (twice), (2)(b) (twice), (4)(a) and (5), 104(1) (twice), (2), (4), (5) and (7), 105(1)(a) (twice) and (4), 106(2),"
- "110(3) (twice), (4) and (5) (three times),"
- "401(1)(b), 486(10) (twice), 491(3) (twice), (4), (6), (8)(b) (twice) and (11), 509(1) (twice),"
- "577(1)(a) and (9), 577A(1) and (1A), 579(2), 588(3), 589A(8),"
- "Schedule 5, paragraphs 1(1), 2(6) meaning of "qualifying year of assessment", 3(1) and (4)(b), 5(1), 6(5) and 8(7) (three times), "

In para. 1 the words "379A(1)(a), (1)(b) (twice) and (7), 382(3), 385(4) (three times), 386(1), 388(1), (4) (four times), (5) (in the first two places) and (7)," repealed by ITA 2007, s. 1031 and Sch. 3, Pt. 1, with effect from 6 April 2007.
In para. 1 the words "291A(3)(f)(ii) (twice)" repealed by ITA 2007, s. 1031 and Sch. 3, Pt. 2, with effect in relation to shares issued after 5 April 2007.
In para. 1 (which specifies the references that are to be amended under FA 1998, s. 46(3)) the following references to sections and Schedules in ICTA 1988 are repealed by ITTOIA 2005, s. 884 and Sch. 3 effective for income tax purposes for 2005–06 onwards and for corporation tax purposes for accounting periods ending after 5 April 2005 (ITTOIA 2005, s. 883(1)):
s. 60(1) and (2), 61(1), 63A(1), (3) and (5), 65(2A) and (5)(b), 65A(2), 68(1), 77(1) and (2)(a)(i), 80(10), 82(1) and (5), 96(7), 107, 109(1)(b), 110A(1), 111(2), (3), (4), (7), (8)(a) and (11), 112(1A) and (1B), 113(1), 369(4)(a), 491(5), 556(3)(a), 557 side note and (1), (2)(a), (b) and (c) and 730C(1) and Sch. 5, para. 6(4) (meaning of "qualifying year of assessment").
In para. 1 the words "86(2) definition of deductible," repealed by FA 2004, s. 326, Sch. 42, Pt. 2(3), with effect, subject to the transitional provisions at FA 2004, s. 43, 44 and Sch. 6, for accounting periods beginning on or after 1 April 2004.
In para. 1 the word "528(1)(a)" and para. 4 repealed by CAA 2001, s. 580 and Sch. 4 in respect of allowances and charges falling to be made for chargeable periods ending on or after 6 April 2001 for income tax purposes and 1 April 2001 for corporation tax.
In para. 1, the words " 559(4)(b) and (5) (twice)" repealed by FA 2002, s. 141 and Sch. 40, Pt. 3(1) with effect in relation to deductions made under ICTA 1988, s. 559 on or after 6 April 2002.

Notes – Para. 1 rewritten as ITA 2007, s. 89(2), (3), 119, 168(3) .

2 [Repealed by Statute Law (Repeals) Act 2013, s. 1 and Sch. 1, Pt. 10.]

History – Para. 2 repealed by Statute Law (Repeals) Act 2013, s. 1 and Sch. 1, Pt. 10, with effect from 31 January 2013.

3 In the Finance Act 1989: sections 67(2)(a).

History – In para. 3, the words ", 76(1) and (4)(a) and 112(1)" repealed by Statute Law (Repeals) Act 2013, s. 1 and Sch. 1, Pt. 10, with effect from 31 January 2013.
In para. 3, the words "and 112(1)", which appeared at the end, repealed by TIOPA 2010, s. 378 and Sch. 10, Pt. 13, with effect for corporation tax purposes for accounting periods ending on or after 1 April 2010, for income tax and capital gains tax purposes for the tax year 2010–11 and subsequent tax years, and for petroleum revenue tax purposes for chargeable periods beginning on or after 1 July 2010.

4 [Repealed by CAA 2001, s. 580 and Sch. 4.]

5 [Repealed by CTA 2009, s. 1326 and Sch. 3, Pt. 1.]

History – Para. 5 repealed by CTA 2009, s. 1326 and Sch. 3, Pt. 1, with effect for corporation tax purposes for accounting periods ending on or after 1 April 2009, and for income tax and capital gains tax purposes for the tax year 2009–10 and subsequent tax years.

6 [Repealed by CTA 2009, s. 1326 and Sch. 3, Pt. 1.]

History – Para. 6 repealed by CTA 2009, s. 1326 and Sch. 3, Pt. 1, with effect for corporation tax purposes for accounting periods ending on or after 1 April 2009, and for income tax and capital gains tax purposes for the tax year 2009–10 and subsequent tax years.

7 In the Taxation of Chargeable Gains Act 1992: sections 39(1) (in the first place) and (2) (in both places), 41(4) and (5) and 164L(8) (twice).

8 [Repealed by Statute Law (Repeals) Act 2013, s. 1 and Sch. 1, Pt. 10.]

History – Para. 8 repealed by Statute Law (Repeals) Act 2013, s. 1 and Sch. 1, Pt. 10, with effect from 31 January 2013.

9 In the Finance Act 1994: Schedule 24, paragraph 12(2).

10 [Repealed by TIOPA 2010, s. 378 and Sch. 10, Pt. 11.]

History – Para. 10 repealed by TIOPA 2010, s. 378 and Sch. 10 , Pt. 11, with effect for corporation tax purposes for accounting periods ending on or after 1 April 2010, for income tax and capital gains tax purposes for the tax year 2010–11 and subsequent tax years, and for petroleum revenue tax purposes for chargeable periods beginning on or after 1 July 2010.

11 [Repealed by CTA 2009, s. 1326 and Sch. 3, Pt. 1.]

History – Para. 11 repealed by CTA 2009, s. 1326 and Sch. 3, Pt. 1, with effect for corporation tax purposes for accounting periods ending on or after 1 April 2009, and for income tax and capital gains tax purposes for the tax year 2009–10 and subsequent tax years.

12 [Repealed by CTA 2010, s. 1181 and Sch. 3, Pt. 2; also repealed by TIOPA 2010, s. 378 and Sch. 10, Pt. 8 and Statute Law (Repeals) Act 2013, s. 1 and Sch. 1, Pt. 10.]

History – Para. 12 repealed by Statute Law (Repeals) Act 2013, s. 1 and Sch. 1, Pt. 10, with effect from 31 January 2013. Note that former para. 12 had previously been repealed (see note below).
Para. 12 repealed by CTA 2010, s. 1181 and Sch. 3, Pt. 2, for corporation tax purposes only, with effect for accounting periods ending on or after 1 April 2010. Para. 12 also repealed by TIOPA 2010, s. 378 and Sch. 10, Pt. 8, with effect for corporation tax purposes for accounting periods ending on or after 1 April 2010, for income tax and capital gains tax purposes for the tax year 2010–11 and subsequent tax years, and for petroleum revenue tax purposes for chargeable periods beginning on or after 1 July 2010.

SCHEDULE 8 – SUB-CONTRACTORS IN THE CONSTRUCTION INDUSTRY

Section 57

1-7 [Repealed by FA 2004, s. 326 and Sch. 40, Pt. 2(7).]

History – Sch. 8 repealed by FA 2004, s. 326 and Sch. 40, Pt. 2(7), with effect in relation to payments made under contracts relating to construction operations, on or after 6 April 2007, by virtue of notice given pursuant to SI 2005/2045, reg. 1.

SCHEDULE 9 – PAYMENTS AND OTHER BENEFITS IN CONNECTION WITH TERMINATION OF EMPLOYMENT ETC.

Section 58(2)

[Sch. 9 repealed by ITEPA 2003, Sch. 8, Pt. 1.]

History – Sch. 9 repealed by ITEPA 2003, Sch. 8, Pt. 1 which has effect for the tax year 2003–04 and subsequent tax years.

SCHEDULE 10 – ORDINARY COMMUTING AND PRIVATE TRAVEL

Section 61(2)

[Repealed by ITEPA 2003, Sch. 8, Pt. 1.]

History – Sch. 10 repealed by ITEPA 2003, Sch. 8, Pt. 1 which has effect for the tax year 2003–04 and subsequent tax years.

SCHEDULE 11 – TRANSITIONAL PROVISIONS FOR PROFIT-RELATED PAY

Section 62

[Repealed by Statute Law (Repeals) Act 2013, s. 1 and Sch. 1, Pt. 10.]

History – Sch. 11 repealed by Statute Law (Repeals) Act 2013, s. 1 and Sch. 1, Pt. 10, with effect from 31 January 2013.

SCHEDULE 12 – EIS AND VCTs: MEANING OF QUALIFYING TRADE

Section 70

NEW EXCLUSIONS FOR THE ENTERPRISE INVESTMENT SCHEME

1 [Repealed by ITA 2007, s. 1031 and Sch. 3, Pt. 2.]

History – Para. 1 repealed by ITA 2007, s. 1031 and Sch. 3, Pt. 2, with effect in relation to shares issued after 5 April 2007.

Notes – Para. 1(1) rewritten as ITA 2007, s. 192(1).
Para. 1(2) rewritten as ITA 2007, s. 199(1).
Para. 1(3) rewritten as ITA 2007, s. 197(3), 198(4).

DEFINITION OF EXCLUDED ACTIVITIES FOR THE ENTERPRISE INVESTMENT SCHEME

2 [Repealed by ITA 2007, s. 1031 and Sch. 3, Pt. 2.]

History – Para. 2 repealed by ITA 2007, s. 1031 and Sch. 3, Pt. 2, with effect in relation to shares issued after 5 April 2007.

Notes – Para. 2(1) rewritten as ITA 2007, s. 198(2).
Para. 2(2) rewritten as ITA 2007, s. 196(2), 198(3).
Para. 2(3) rewritten as ITA 2007, s. 196(3), (4), 197(2).

NEW EXCLUSIONS FOR VCTs

3 [Repealed by ITA 2007, s. 1031 and Sch. 3, Pt. 1.]

History – Para. 3 repealed by ITA 2007, s. 1031 and Sch. 3, Pt. 1, with effect from 6 April 2007.

Notes – Para. 3(1) rewritten as ITA 2007, s. 303(1), Sch. 2, para. 81.
Para. 3(2) rewritten as ITA 2007, s. 310(1), Sch. 2, para. 85(2).
Para. 3(3) rewritten as ITA 2007, s. 308(3), 309(4), Sch. 2, para. 81, 85(2).

DEFINITION OF EXCLUDED ACTIVITIES FOR VCTs

4 [Repealed by ITA 2007, s. 1031 and Sch. 3, Pt. 1.]

History – Para. 4 repealed by ITA 2007, s. 1031 and Sch. 3, Pt. 1, with effect from 6 April 2007.

Notes – Para. 4(1) rewritten as ITA 2007, s. 309(2).
Para. 4(2) rewritten as ITA 2007, s. 307(2).
Para. 4(3) rewritten as ITA 2007, s. 309(3).
Para. 4(4) rewritten as ITA 2007, s. 307(3).
Para. 4(5) rewritten as ITA 2007, s. 307(4), 308(2).

COMMENCEMENT

5(1) [Repealed by ITA 2007, s. 1031 and Sch. 3, Pt. 2.]

5(2) [Repealed by ITA 2007, s. 1031 and Sch. 3, Pt. 1.]

5(3) [Repealed by ITA 2007, s. 1031 and Sch. 3, Pt. 1.]

History – Para. 5(1) repealed by ITA 2007, s. 1031 and Sch. 3, Pt. 2, with effect in relation to shares issued after 5 April 2007. Para. 5(2) and (3) repealed by ITA 2007, s. 1031 and Sch. 3, Pt. 1, with effect from 6 April 2007.

Notes – Para. 5(2) rewritten as ITA 2007, Sch. 2, para. 81, 85(2).

SCHEDULE 13 – CHANGES TO EIS ETC.

Section 74(1)

Part I – EIS Income Tax Relief

[Pt. I repealed by ITA 2007, s. 1031 and Sch. 3, Pt. 2, with effect in relation to shares issued after 5 April 2007.]

History – Pt. I repealed by ITA 2007, s. 1031 and Sch. 3, Pt. 2, with effect in relation to shares issued after 5 April 2007.

Notes – Para. 1(1) rewritten as ITA 2007, s. 173(3), (4), 175(1).
Para. 1(3) rewritten as ITA 2007, s. 165.
Para. 1(4) rewritten as ITA 2007, s. 173(2).
Para. 3(1) rewritten as ITA 2007, s. 201(3), (4).
Para. 3(2) rewritten as ITA 2007, s. 201(5).
Para. 3(3) rewritten as ITA 2007, s. 255(1), (2).
Para. 3(4) rewritten as ITA 2007, s. 201(6), 202(2), 219(1), (2), 228(1), (2).
Para. 6(2) rewritten as ITA 2007, s. 166(1).
Para. 6(3) rewritten as ITA 2007, s. 167(2).
Para. 8(1) rewritten as ITA 2007, s. 170(5).
Para. 8(2) rewritten as ITA 2007, s. 170(7).
Para. 9(1) rewritten as ITA 2007, s. 181(8).
Para. 9(2) rewritten as ITA 2007, s. 138(4), 182(4).
Para. 9(3) rewritten as ITA 2007, s. 142(1), (2), (3), 186(1), (2), (3), Sch. 1, para. 127.
Para. 9(5) rewritten as ITA 2007, s. 139(1), (2), (3), 185(1), (2), Sch. 1, para. 124.
Para. 12(1) rewritten as ITA 2007, s. 209(1), (2), (3), (4).
Para. 12(3) rewritten as ITA 2007, s. 210(1), (2), 219(1), (2), 220(1), 228(1), (2), 229(1), (2).
Para. 12(4) rewritten as ITA 2007, s. 212(3).
Para. 12(5) rewritten as ITA 2007, s. 246(2), (3), (4), (5), (6), (7).
Para. 13(1) rewritten as ITA 2007, s. 213(1).
Para. 13(3) rewritten as ITA 2007, s. 216(7).
Para. 14(1) rewritten as ITA 2007, s. 213(5).
Para. 14(2) rewritten as ITA 2007, s. 216(10), 222(7).
Para. 15(1) rewritten as ITA 2007, s. 224(1), (2), (4), (5), 228(1), (2), 229(1), (2).
Para. 15(3) rewritten as ITA 2007, s. 224(7).
Para. 16(1) rewritten as ITA 2007, s. 246(2), (3), (4), (5), (6), (7).
Para. 17(1) rewritten as ITA 2007, s. 247(1), (2), (3), (4), (5), 248(1), (2), (3), 249(1), (2), (3), (4).
Para. 19(1) rewritten as ITA 2007, s. 202(1).
Para. 19(2) rewritten as ITA 2007, s. 203(1), 204(1).
Para. 19(3) rewritten as ITA2007, s. 204(2), 205(1), (2).
Para. 19(5) rewritten as ITA 2007, s. 204(3), (4), 205(3).
Para. 20(1) rewritten as ITA 2007, s. 234(2), (3).
Para. 20(2) rewritten as ITA 2007, s. 236(2).
Para. 20(3) rewritten as ITA 2007, s. 238(2), (3).
Para. 20(4) rewritten as ITA 2007, s. 239(1).
Para. 22(1) rewritten as ITA 2007, s. 240(1), (2).
Para. 22(2) rewritten as ITA 2007, s. 240(1), (2).
Para. 22(3) rewritten as ITA 2007, s. 243(5).
Para. 22(4) rewritten as ITA 2007, s. 240(1), 241(1).
Para. 23(1) rewritten as ITA 2007, s. 156(1), 257(1).
Para. 23(3) rewritten as ITA 2007, s. 184(3).
Para. 23(4) rewritten as ITA 2007, s. 257(2).
Para. 23(5) rewritten as ITA 2007, s. 255(1), 257(5).

Part II – EIS Relief Against Chargeable Gains

24(1) [Amends TCGA 1992, s. 150A(1), (2).]

24(2) [Amends TCGA 1992, s. 150A(4)(a).]

24(3) [Amends TCGA 1992, s. 150A(5).]

24(4) [Substitutes TCGA 1992, s. 150A(6), (6A).]

24(5) [Amends TCGA 1992, s. 150A(8A)(a).]

24(6) [Inserts TCGA 1992, s. 150A(8D).]

24(7) [Inserts TCGA 1992, s. 150A(10A).]

24(8) In this paragraph–

(a) sub-paragraphs (1) to (3) have effect in relation to disposals made on or after 6th April 1998;

(b) sub-paragraph (4) has effect in relation to reorganisations taking effect on or after that date;

(c) sub-paragraph (5) has effect in relation to new shares (within the meaning of section 150A(8A) of the Taxation of Chargeable Gains Act 1992) issued on or after that date;

(d) sub-paragraph (6) has effect in relation to new shares (within the meaning of section 304A of the Taxes Act 1988) issued on or after that date; and

(e) sub-paragraph (7) has effect in relation to events occurring on or after that date.

25(1) [Amends TCGA 1992, s. 150B(1).]

25(2) This paragraph has effect in relation to disposals made on or after 6th April 1998.

Part III – EIS Deferral of Chargeable Gains

PRELIMINARY

26 Schedule 5B to the Taxation of Chargeable Gains Act 1992 (enterprise investment scheme: re-investment) shall be amended in accordance with the following provisions of this Part.

APPLICATION OF SCHEDULE

27(1) [Amends TCGA 1992, Sch. 5B, para. 1(1)(b).]

27(2) [Substitutes TCGA 1992, Sch. 5B, para. 1(2), (3).]

FAILURE OF CONDITIONS OF APPLICATION

28 [Inserts TCGA 1992, Sch. 5B, para. 1A.]

POSTPONEMENT OF ORIGINAL GAIN

29 [Substitutes TCGA 1992, Sch. 5B, para. 2(3)(a).]

CHARGEABLE EVENTS

30(1) [Amends TCGA 1992, Sch. 5B, para. 3(1), partially repealed by FA 2001, s. 110 and Sch. 33, Pt. 2(3).]

30(2) [Repeals TCGA 1992, Sch. 5B, para. 3(2).]

30(3) [Inserts TCGA 1992, Sch. 5B, para. 3(6).]

History – Para. 30(1)(a) repealed by FA 2001, s. 110 and Sch. 33, Pt. 2(3), with effect for EIS shares issued on or after 7 March 2001 and for EIS shares issued before that date which have income tax relief or deferral relief attributable to them immediately before that date.

GAINS ACCRUING ON CHARGEABLE EVENT

31(1) [Substitutes TCGA 1992, Sch. 5B, para. 4(2)–4(C).]

31(2) [Amends TCGA 1992, Sch. 5B, para. 4(5)(b).]

31(3) This paragraph has effect in relation to disposals made on or after 6th April 1998.

PERSONS TO WHOM GAIN ACCRUES

32 [Substitutes TCGA 1992, Sch. 5B, para. 5(1)(c).]

CLAIMS

33 [Substitutes TCGA 1992, Sch. 5B, para. 6.]

REORGANISATIONS AND RECONSTRUCTIONS

34 [Inserts TCGA 1992, Sch. 5B, para. 7–9.]

ANTI-AVOIDANCE PROVISIONS

35 [Inserts TCGA 1992, Sch. 5B, para. 10–15.]

SUPPLEMENTARY PROVISIONS

36 [Inserts TCGA 1992, Sch. 5B, para. 16–19.]

Part IV – BES Income Tax Relief and Relief Against Chargeable Gains

37 Any reference in this Part to a provision of Chapter III of Part VII of the Taxes Act 1988 is a reference to that provision as it has effect in relation to shares issued before 1st January 1994.

38(1) [Amends ICTA 1988, s. 293(8).]

38(2) This paragraph has effect in relation to new shares (within the meaning of section 304A of the Taxes Act 1988) issued on or after 6th April 1998.

39(1) [Amends ICTA 1988, s. 299(1).]

39(2) [Substitutes ICTA 1988, s. 299(4)–(4C).]

39(3) This paragraph has effect in relation to disposals made on or after 6th April 1998.

40(1) [Inserts ICTA 1988, s. 304(7).]

40(2) This paragraph has effect in relation to disposals made on or after 6th April 1998.

41(1) [Inserts ICTA 1988, s. 304A.]

41(2) This paragraph has effect in relation to new shares (within the meaning of section 304A of the Taxes Act 1988) issued on or after 6th April 1998.

42(1) [Amends TCGA 1992, s. 150(4)(a).]

42(2) [Amends TCGA 1992, s. 150(5).]

42(3) [Amends TCGA 1992, s. 150(7).]

42(4) [Amends TCGA 1992, s. 150(8).]

42(5) [Amends TCGA 1992, s. 150(8A)(a).]

42(6) [Inserts TCGA 1992, s. 150(8D).]

42(7) [Inserts TCGA 1992, s. 150(12).]

42(8) In this paragraph–

(a) sub-paragraphs (1) and (2) have effect in relation to disposals made on or after 6th April 1998;

(b) sub-paragraph (3) has effect in relation to subsequent disposals made on or after that date;

(c) sub-paragraph (4) has effect in relation to events occurring on or after that date;

(d) sub-paragraph (5) has effect in relation to new shares (within the meaning of section 150(8A) of the Taxation of Chargeable Gains Act 1992) issued on or after that date;

(e) sub-paragraph (6) has effect in relation to new shares (within the meaning of section 304A of the Taxes Act 1988) issued on or after that date; and

(f) sub-paragraph (7) has effect in relation to events occurring on or after that date.

SCHEDULE 14 – LIFE POLICIES, LIFE ANNUITIES AND CAPITAL REDEMPTION POLICIES

Section 86

SECTION 547

1 [Omitted by FA 2008, s. 36 and Sch. 14, para. 17(g).]

History – Para. 1 omitted by FA 2008, s. 36 and Sch. 14, para. 17(g), with effect–
- so far as relating to corporation tax, for accounting periods beginning on or after 1 April 2008, and
- so far as relating to income tax, for the tax year 2008–09 and subsequent tax years.

MULTIPLE INTERESTS

2 [Omitted by FA 2008, s. 36 and Sch. 14, para. 17(g).]

History – Para. 2 omitted by FA 2008, s. 36 and Sch. 14, para. 17(g), with effect–
- so far as relating to corporation tax, for accounting periods beginning on or after 1 April 2008, and
- so far as relating to income tax, for the tax year 2008–09 and subsequent tax years.

RIGHT OF COMPANY TO RECOVER TAX FROM TRUSTEES

3 [Omitted by FA 2008, s. 36 and Sch. 14, para. 17(g).]

History – Para. 3 omitted by FA 2008, s. 36 and Sch. 14, para. 17(g), with effect–

- so far as relating to corporation tax, for accounting periods beginning on or after 1 April 2008, and
- so far as relating to income tax, for the tax year 2008–09 and subsequent tax years.

FOREIGN INSTITUTION POLICIES: NO REDUCTION UNDER SECTION 553

4 [Omitted by FA 2008, s. 36 and Sch. 14, para. 17(g).]

History – Para. 4 omitted by FA 2008, s. 36 and Sch. 14, para. 17(g), with effect–

- so far as relating to corporation tax, for accounting periods beginning on or after 1 April 2008, and
- so far as relating to income tax, for the tax year 2008–09 and subsequent tax years.

CONSEQUENTIAL AMENDMENTS

5 [Amends TMA 1970, s. 7(9).]

6 [Repealed by TIOPA 2010, s. 378 and Sch. 10, Pt. 12.]

History – Para. 6 repealed by TIOPA 2010, s. 378 and Sch. 10, Pt. 12, with effect for corporation tax purposes for accounting periods ending on or after 1 April 2010, for income tax and capital gains tax purposes for the tax year 2010–11 and subsequent tax years, and for petroleum revenue tax purposes for chargeable periods beginning on or after 1 July 2010.

COMMENCEMENT

7(1,2) [Repealed by ITTOIA 2005, s. 884 and Sch. 3]

7(3) [Repealed by TIOPA 2010, s. 378 and Sch. 10, Pt. 12.]

7(4) [Repealed by ITTOIA 2005, s. 884 and Sch. 3.]

7(5) This Schedule has effect in relation to chargeable events happening on or after 6th April 1998.

History – Para. 7(1), (2) and (4) repealed by ITTOIA 2005, s. 884 and Sch. 3 effective for income tax purposes for 2005–06 onwards and for corporation tax purposes for accounting periods ending after 5 April 2005 (ITTOIA 2005, s. 883(1)).
Para. 7(3) repealed by TIOPA 2010, s. 378 and Sch. 10, Pt. 12, with effect for corporation tax purposes for accounting periods ending on or after 1 April 2010, for income tax and capital gains tax purposes for the tax year 2010–11 and subsequent tax years, and for petroleum revenue tax purposes for chargeable periods beginning on or after 1 July 2010.
In para. 7(5), the words "Except as provided by the preceding provisions of this paragraph,", which appeared at the beginning, repealed by TIOPA 2010, s. 378 and Sch. 10, Pt. 12, with effect for corporation tax purposes for accounting periods ending on or after 1 April 2010, for income tax and capital gains tax purposes for the tax year 2010–11 and subsequent tax years, and for petroleum revenue tax purposes for chargeable periods beginning on or after 1 July 2010.

Cross references – FA 2003, Sch. 34, para. 12(1): with effect from 9 April 2003, para. 7(1) has effect in relation to ICTA 1988, s. 547(1)(cc) as it has in relation to s. 547(1)(d) of that Act.

SCHEDULE 15 – APPROVED RETIREMENT BENEFITS SCHEMES

Section 92

1-7 [Sch. 15 repealed by FA 2004, s. 326 and Sch. 42, Pt. 3.]

History – Sch. 15 repealed by FA 2004, s. 326 and Sch. 42, Pt. 3, with effect from 6 April 2006 subject to FA 2004, Sch. 36. Former Sch. 15, para. 1 to 6 amended ICTA 1988, s. 591C, 591D, 604, 605 and 606 and former para. 7 read as follows:

"MODIFICATION OF CERTAIN EXISTING APPROVED SCHEMES

7(1) This paragraph applies in relation to any retirement benefits scheme which–

(a) was approved by the Board on or before 17th March 1998; and
(b) contains provision requiring one of the trustees of the scheme to be an approved independent trustee.

7(2) Notwithstanding anything to the contrary in the scheme or its rules, the appointment (whenever made) of any person to be a trustee of the scheme, and any requirement on him or entitlement of his to act as such, shall be (and be treated as having been) incapable of termination at any time on or after 17th March 1998 except–

(a) by the death of that person;
(b) by an order of the court;
(c) by virtue of section 3, 4 or 29 of the Pensions Act 1995 or Article 3, 4 or 29 of the Pensions (Northern Ireland) Order 1995 (prohibition, suspension or disqualification); or
(d) in circumstances mentioned in sub-paragraph (3)(a), (b) or (c) below, in accordance with the rules of the scheme.

7(3) Those circumstances are–

(a) where the trustee is not the trustee by reference to whom the requirement mentioned in sub-paragraph (1)(b) above was satisfied immediately before the termination;
(b) where immediately after the termination that requirement is satisfied by reference to a trustee whose appointment takes effect at that time;
(c) where the trustee whose appointment is terminated has committed a fraudulent breach of trust in relation to the scheme and that is the reason for the termination.

7(4) Any provisions of the scheme or of any instrument by which the administration of the scheme is governed which require a successor to an approved independent trustee of the scheme to be appointed in specified circumstances shall have effect, in relation to any case in which those circumstances arise at a time on or after the day on which this Act is passed, as if they required the appointment to be made no more than 30 days after that time.

7(5) Subsection (5) of section 591D of the Taxes Act 1988 (meaning of "approved independent trustee") shall apply for the purposes of this paragraph as it applies for the purposes of that section.

7(6) In this paragraph "retirement benefits scheme" has the same meaning as in Chapter I of Part XIV of the Taxes Act 1988, and "approved" means approved for the purposes of that Chapter or any enactment re-enacted in that Chapter.".

SCHEDULE 16 – TRANSFER PRICING ETC.: NEW REGIME

Section 108

[Repealed by TIOPA 2010, s. 378 and Sch. 10, Pt. 2.]

History – Sch. 16 repealed by TIOPA 2010, s. 378 and Sch. 10, Pt. 2, with effect for corporation tax purposes for accounting periods ending on or after 1 April 2010, for income tax and capital gains tax purposes for the tax year 2010–11 and subsequent tax years, and for petroleum revenue tax purposes for chargeable periods beginning on or after 1 July 2010.

SCHEDULE 17 – CONTROLLED FOREIGN COMPANIES

Section 113

SECTION 747

1(1) Section 747 of the Taxes Act 1988 (imputation of chargeable profits and creditable tax of controlled foreign companies) shall be amended as follows.

1(2) [Amends ICTA 1988, s. 747(1).]

1(3) [Amends ICTA 1988, s. 747(3).]

1(4) [Amends ICTA 1988, s. 747(4).]

1(5) [Amends ICTA 1988, s. 747(5).]

SECTION 747A

2 [Repealed by FA 2005, s. 104 and Sch. 11, Pt. 2(6).]

History – Para. 2 repealed by FA 2005, s. 104 and Sch. 11, Pt. 2(7), with effect for periods of account beginning on or after 16 March 2005.

SECTION 748

3(1) Section 748 of the Taxes Act 1988 (limitations on direction-making power) shall be amended as follows.

3(2) [Amends ICTA 1988, s. 748(1).]

3(3) [Amends ICTA 1988, s. 748(1)(d).]

3(4) [Inserts ICTA 1988, s. 748(1)(e).]

3(5) [Inserts ICTA 1988, s. 748(1A).]

3(6) [Repeals ICTA 1988, s. 748(2).]

3(7) [Omitted by FA 2011, s. 47 and Sch. 12, para. 13(a).]

3(8) [Amends ICTA 1988, s. 748(3).]

3(9) [Substitutes the sidenote to ICTA 1988, s. 748.]

History – Sch. 17, para. 3(7) omitted by FA 2011, s. 47 and Sch. 12, para. 13(a), with effect in relation to accounting periods of controlled foreign companies beginning on or after 1 January 2011.

SECTION 749

4 [Substitutes ICTA 1988, s. 749.]

SECTION 750

5(1) Section 750 of the Taxes Act 1988 (territories with a lower level of taxation) shall be amended as follows.

5(2) [Amends ICTA 1988, s. 750(1).]

5(3) [Amends ICTA 1988, s. 750(3).]

SECTION 751

6(1) Section 751 of the Taxes Act 1988 (accounting periods and creditable tax) shall be amended as follows.

6(2) [Amends ICTA 1988, s. 751(1).]

6(3) [Amends ICTA 1988, s. 751(5).]

6(4) [Amends ICTA 1988, s. 751(5).]

6(5) [Inserts ICTA 1988, s. 751(5A).]

6(6) [Amends ICTA 1988, s. 751(6).]

SECTION 752

7 [Substitutes ICTA 1988, s. 752.]

SECTION 753

8 [Repeals ICTA 1988, s. 753.]

SECTION 754

9(1) Section 754 of the Taxes Act 1988 (assessment, recovery and postponement of tax) shall be amended as follows.

9(2) [Amends ICTA 1988, s. 754(1).]

9(3) [Inserts ICTA 1988, s. 754(1A).]

9(4) [Substitutes ICTA 1988, s. 754(2).]

9(5) [Inserts ICTA 1988, s. 754(2A)–(2E).]

9(6) [Substitutes ICTA 1988, s. 754(3).]

9(7) [Repeals ICTA 1988, s. 754(4).]

9(8) [Amends ICTA 1988, s. 754(6).]

9(9) [Amends ICTA 1988, s. 754(7).]

9(10) [Amends ICTA 1988, s. 754(8).]

RETURNS WHERE IT IS NOT ESTABLISHED WHETHER ACCEPTABLE DISTRIBUTION POLICY APPLIES

10 [Omitted by FA 2009, s. 36 and Sch. 16, para. 5(d).]

History – Para. 10 omitted by FA 2009, s. 36 and Sch. 16, para. 5(d), with effect in relation to accounting periods of controlled foreign companies beginning on or after 1 July 2009.

DETERMINATIONS REQUIRING THE SANCTION OF THE BOARD

11 [Inserts ICTA 1988, s. 754B.]

SECTION 755

12 [Repeals ICTA 1988, s. 755.]

TREATMENT OF CHARGEABLE PROFITS AND CREDITABLE TAX APPORTIONED TO COMPANY CARRYING ON LIFE ASSURANCE BUSINESS

13 [Inserts ICTA 1988, s. 755A.]

AMENDMENT OF RETURN WHERE GENERAL INSURANCE BUSINESS OF FOREIGN COMPANY ACCOUNTED FOR ON NON-ANNUAL BASIS

14 [Inserts ICTA 1988, s. 755B.]

APPLICATION OF CHAPTER WHERE GENERAL INSURANCE BUSINESS OF FOREIGN COMPANY ACCOUNTED FOR ON NON-ANNUAL BASIS

15 [Inserts ICTA 1988, s. 755C.]

SECTION 756

16(1) Section 756 of the Taxes Act 1988 (interpretation and construction of Chapter IV) shall be amended as follows.

16(2) [Amends ICTA 1988, s. 756(1).]

PARAGRAPH 1 OF SCHEDULE 24

17(1) In Schedule 24 to the Taxes Act 1988 (assumptions for calculating chargeable profits, creditable tax and corresponding United Kingdom tax of foreign companies) paragraph 1 shall be amended as follows.

17((2)–(5)) [Omitted by FA 2009, s. 36 and Sch. 16, para. 5(d).]

17(6) [Amends ICTA 1988, Sch. 24, para. 1(4).]

17(7) [Amends ICTA 1988, Sch. 24, para. 1(4).]

17(8) [Amends ICTA 1988, Sch. 24, para. 1(4).]

17(9) [Amends ICTA 1988, Sch. 24, para. 1(4).]

History – Para. 17(2)–(5) omitted by FA 2009, s. 36 and Sch. 16, para. 5(d), with effect in relation to accounting periods of controlled foreign companies beginning on or after 1 July 2009.

PARAGRAPH 2 OF SCHEDULE 24

18 [Amends ICTA 1988, Sch. 24, para. 2(1).]

PARAGRAPH 4 OF SCHEDULE 24

19(1) Paragraph 4 of Schedule 24 to the Taxes Act 1988 (assumption that claims or elections giving maximum relief have been made, subject to notice to the contrary) shall be amended as follows.

19(2) [Amends ICTA 1988, Sch. 24, para. 4(1A).]

19(3) [Amends ICTA 1988, Sch. 24, para. 4(2).]

19(4) [Repeals ICTA 1988, Sch. 24, para. 4(2A).]

19(5) [Amends ICTA 1988, Sch. 24, para. 4(3).]

19(6) [Amends ICTA 1988, Sch. 24, para. 4(3A).]

PARAGRAPH 9 OF SCHEDULE 24

20(1) Paragraph 9 of Schedule 24 to the Taxes Act 1988 (losses in pre-direction accounting periods) shall be amended as follows.

20(2) [Amends ICTA 1988, Sch. 24, para. 9.]

20(3) [Amends ICTA 1988, Sch. 24, para. 9(1).]

20(4) [Amends ICTA 1988, Sch. 24, para. 9(2).]

20(5) [Amends ICTA 1988, Sch. 24, para. 9(3).]

20(6) [Substitutes ICTA 1988, Sch. 24, para. 9(4).]

20(7) [Repeals ICTA 1988, Sch. 24, para. 9(5).]

20(8) [Repeals ICTA 1988, Sch. 24, para. 9(6).]

20(9) [Inserts ICTA 1988, Sch. 24, para. 9(7).]

PARAGRAPH 10 OF SCHEDULE 24

21 [Amends ICTA 1988, Sch. 24, para. 10(1).]

PARAGRAPH 11 OF SCHEDULE 24

22 [Repeals ICTA 1988, Sch. 24, para. 11.]

PARAGRAPH 11A OF SCHEDULE 24

23 [Repeals ICTA 1988, Sch. 24, para. 11A(3) and (6).]

TRANSFER PRICING

24 [Repealed by FA 2004, s. 326 and Sch. 42, Pt. 2(1), with effect, subject to the transitional provisions at s. 37, in relation to chargeable periods beginning on or after 1 April 2004 (whenever the actual provision, within the meaning of ICTA 1988, Sch. 28AA is or was made or imposed.]

SCHEDULE 25

25 [Substitutes the heading to ICTA 1988, Sch. 25.]

PARAGRAPH 1 OF SCHEDULE 25

26 [Omitted by FA 2009, s. 36 and Sch. 16, para. 5(d).]

History – Para. 26 omitted by FA 2009, s. 36 and Sch. 16, para. 5(d), with effect in relation to accounting periods of controlled foreign companies beginning on or after 1 July 2009.

PARAGRAPH 2A OF SCHEDULE 25

27 [Omitted by FA 2009, s. 36 and Sch. 16, para. 5(d).]

History – Para. 27 omitted by FA 2009, s. 36 and Sch. 16, para. 5(d), with effect in relation to accounting periods of controlled foreign companies beginning on or after 1 July 2009.

PARAGRAPH 3 OF SCHEDULE 25

28 [Omitted by FA 2009, s. 36 and Sch. 16, para. 5(d).]

History – Para. 28 omitted by FA 2009, s. 36 and Sch. 16, para. 5(d), with effect in relation to accounting periods of controlled foreign companies beginning on or after 1 July 2009.

PARAGRAPH 5 OF SCHEDULE 25

29 [Amends ICTA 1988, Sch. 25, para. 5.]

PARAGRAPH 6 OF SCHEDULE 25

30(1) Paragraph 6 of Schedule 25 to the Taxes Act 1988 (exemption for controlled foreign companies engaged in exempt activities) shall be amended as follows.

30(2) [Amends ICTA 1988, Sch. 25, para. 6(1)(c).]

30(3) [Amends ICTA 1988, Sch. 25, para. 6(2)(b).]

30(4) [Partly omitted by FA 2009, s. 36. and Sch. 16, para. 11(a).]

30(5) [Omitted by FA 2009, s. 36. and Sch. 16, para. 11(a).]

30(6) [Omitted by FA 2009, s. 36. and Sch. 16, para. 11(a).]

30(7) [Amends ICTA 1988, Sch. 25, para. 6(4C).]

30(8) [Omitted by FA 2009, s. 36. and Sch. 16, para. 11(a).]

30(9) [Inserts ICTA 1988, Sch. 25, para. 6(5).]

History – Para. 30(4)(a), (5), (6) and (8) omitted by FA 2009, s. 36 and Sch. 16, para. 11(a), with effect in relation to accounting periods of controlled foreign companies beginning on or after 1 July 2011 (a qualifying holding company).
Para. 30(4)(a), (5), (6) and (8) omitted by FA 2009, s. 36 and Sch. 16, para. 11(a), with effect in relation to accounting periods of controlled foreign companies beginning on or after 1 July 2009 (a controlled foreign company other than a qualifying holding company).

PARAGRAPH 8 OF SCHEDULE 25

31(1) Paragraph 8 of Schedule 25 to the Taxes Act 1988 (which relates to the condition in paragraph 6(1)(b) of that Schedule) shall be amended as follows.

31(2) [Amends ICTA 1988, Sch. 25, para. 8(3).]

PARAGRAPH 12 OF SCHEDULE 25

32(1) Paragraph 12 of Schedule 25 to the Taxes Act 1988 (meaning of "holding company" in paragraphs 6 and 8(3)) shall be amended as follows.

32(2) [Amends ICTA 1988, Sch. 25, para. 12(1).]

32(3) [Amends ICTA 1988, Sch. 25, para. 12(5).]

SUPERIOR HOLDING COMPANIES: SUPPLEMENTARY PROVISIONS

33 [Inserts ICTA 1988, Sch. 25, para. 12A.]

PARAGRAPH 1 OF SCHEDULE 26

34(1) *In Schedule 26* to the Taxes Act 1988 (reliefs against liability for tax in respect of chargeable profits apportioned to UK resident company) paragraph 1 (trading losses and group relief etc.) shall be amended as follows.

34(2) [Amends ICTA 1988, Sch. 26, para. 1(1).]

34(3) [Amends ICTA 1988, Sch. 26, para. 1(2)(a).]

SCHEDULE 18 – COMPANY TAX RETURNS, ASSESSMENTS AND RELATED MATTERS

Section 117(1)

Cross references – SI 2003/282: electronic delivery of information and payments required to be delivered under Sch. 18.
Other material – COP14: Revenue Code of Practice for enquiries into self-assessment company tax returns.

Part I – Introduction

MEANING OF "TAX"

1 In this Schedule "**tax**" means corporation tax including, except as otherwise indicated, any amount assessable or chargeable as if it was corporation tax.

Amounts are assessable or chargeable as if they were corporation tax under–

section 269DA of the Corporation Tax Act 2010 (surcharge on banking companies),

section 455 of that Act (tax on loan or advance made by close company to a participator),

section 464A of that Act (tax on other benefit conferred on participator),

section 330(1) of that Act (supplementary charge in respect of ring fence trades), and

step 5 in section 371BC(1) of the Taxation (International and Other Provisions) Act 2010 (controlled foreign companies).

paragraphs 50 and 51 of Schedule 19 to the Finance Act 2011 (the bank levy).

History – In para. 1, the words "section 269DA of the Corporation Tax Act 2010 (surcharge on banking companies)," inserted by F(No. 2)A 2015, s. 17 and Sch. 3, para. 3(2)(a), with effect for accounting periods ending on or after 1 January 2016.
In para. 1, in the entry relating to CTA 2010, s. 455, the words "that Act" substituted for the words "the Corporation Tax Act 2010" by F(No. 2)A 2015, s. 17 and Sch. 3, para. 3(2)(b), with effect for accounting periods ending on or after 1 January 2016.
In para. 1, the words "section 464A of that Act (tax on other benefit conferred on participator)," inserted by FA 2013, s. 79 and Sch. 30, para. 13(2), with effect from 20 March 2013.
In para. 1, the words "step 5 in section 371BC(1) of the Taxation (International and Other Provisions) Act 2010 (controlled foreign companies)" substituted for the words "section 747(4)(a) of the Taxes Act 1988 (tax on profits of controlled foreign company)" by FA 2012, s. 180 and Sch. 20, para. 17(2), with effect in relation to accounting periods of controlled foreign companies beginning on or after 1 January 2013 (subject to the transitional provisions at FA 2012, Sch. 20, para. 50).
In para. 1, the words "paragraphs 50 and 51 of Schedule 19 to the Finance Act 2011 (the bank levy)" inserted by FA 2011, s. 73 and Sch. 19, para. 61, with effect from 19 July 2011.
In para. 1, the words "section 455 of the Corporation Tax Act 2010" substituted for the words "section 419(1) of the Taxes Act 1988" by CTA 2010, s. 1177 and Sch. 1, para. 297(2)(a), with effect for corporation tax purposes for accounting periods ending on or after 1 April 2010, and for income tax and capital gains tax purposes for the tax year 2010–11 and subsequent tax years.
In para. 1, the words "section 330(1)" substituted for the words "section 501A(1)" by CTA 2010, s. 1177 and Sch. 1, para. 297(2)(b), with effect for corporation tax purposes for accounting periods ending on or after 1 April 2010, and for income tax and capital gains tax purposes for the tax year 2010–11 and subsequent tax years.
In para. 1, the words "of the Taxes Act 1988" substituted for the words "of that Act" by CTA 2010, s. 1177 and Sch. 1, para. 297(2)(c), with effect for corporation tax purposes for accounting periods ending on or after 1 April 2010, and for income tax and capital gains tax purposes for the tax year 2010–11 and subsequent tax years.
In para. 1, the para. beginning "section 501A(1)" substituted for the word "and" that formerly appeared at the end of the preceding para. by FA 2002, s. 92(3) with effect from 24 July 2002.

Cross references – SI 2005/3454, reg. 13: modification of para. 1 to exclude the operation of Sch. 18 in respect of a charge under ITEPA 2003, s. 394(2).

DUTY TO GIVE NOTICE OF CHARGEABILITY

2(1) A company which–

(a) is chargeable to tax for an accounting period, and

(b) has not received a notice requiring a company tax return,

must give notice to an officer of Revenue and Customs that it is so chargeable.

2(2) The notice must be given within twelve months from the end of the accounting period.

2(3) [Omitted by FA 2008, s. 123 and Sch. 41, para. 25(j).]

2(4) [Omitted by FA 2008, s. 123 and Sch. 41, para. 25(j).]

History – In para. 2(1) the words "an officer of Revenue and Customs" substituted for the words "the Inland Revenue" by CRCA 2005, s. 50 and Sch. 4, para. 68(a), with effect from 18 April 2005 by virtue of SI 2005/1126, art. 2(2).
Para. 2(3) omitted by FA 2008, s. 123 and Sch. 41, para. 25(j), with effect from 1 April 2010 (SI 2009/511, art. 2 and 3 (subject to transitional provisions at SI 2009/511, art. 4).
Para. 2(4) omitted by FA 2008, s. 123 and Sch. 41, para. 25(j), with effect from 1 April 2010 (SI 2009/511, art. 2 and 3 (subject to transitional provisions at SI 2009/511, art. 4).
In para. 2(4), the words "section 458 of the Corporation Tax Act 2010" substituted for the words "section 419(4) of the Taxes Act 1988" by CTA 2010, s. 1177 and Sch. 1, para. 297(3)(a), with effect for corporation tax purposes for accounting periods ending on or after 1 April 2010, and for income tax and capital gains tax purposes for the tax year 2010–11 and subsequent tax years.
In para. 2(4), the words "subsection (5)" substituted for the words "subsection (4A)" by CTA 2010, s. 1177 and Sch. 1, para. 297(3)(b), with effect for corporation tax purposes for accounting periods ending on or after 1 April 2010, and for income tax and capital gains tax purposes for the tax year 2010–11 and subsequent tax years.

34(4) [Repeals ICTA 1988, Sch. 26, para. 1(4).]

34(5) [Repeals ICTA 1988, Sch. 26, para. 1(6).]

PARAGRAPH 3 OF SCHEDULE 26

35(1) Paragraph 3 of Schedule 26 to the Taxes Act 1988 (gains on disposal of shares in controlled foreign companies) shall be amended as follows.

35(2) [Amends ICTA 1988, Sch. 26, para. 3(1).]

35(3) [Amends ICTA 1988, Sch. 26, para. 3(1).]

35(4) [Amends ICTA 1988, Sch. 26, para. 3(1).]

35(5) [Amends ICTA 1988, Sch. 26, para. 3(3).]

35(6) [Amends ICTA 1988, Sch. 26, para. 3(4).]

35(7) [Inserts ICTA 1988, Sch. 26, para. 3(6A).]

PARAGRAPH 4 OF SCHEDULE 26

36(1) Paragraph 4 of Schedule 26 to the Taxes Act 1988 (dividends from the controlled foreign company) shall be amended as follows.

36(2) [Amends ICTA 1988, Sch. 26, para. 4(1).]

36(3) [Amends ICTA 1988, Sch. 26, para. 4(1).]

36(4) [Amends ICTA 1988, Sch. 26, para. 4(2).]

36(5) [Amends ICTA 1988, Sch. 26, para. 4(5).]

COMMENCEMENT AND TRANSITIONAL PROVISION

37(1) The preceding provisions of this Schedule have effect as respects accounting periods of companies resident in the United Kingdom which end on or after the corporation tax self-assessment appointed day.

37(2) Where by virtue of sub-paragraph (1) above any question as to liability (if any) to tax by virtue of Chapter IV of Part XVII of the Taxes Act 1988 as respects any particular accounting period of a non-resident company which ends before the corporation tax self-assessment appointed day falls to be determined–

(a) in the case of at least one company resident in the United Kingdom, for an accounting period of its which ends on or after that day, and

(b) in the case of at least one other such company, for an accounting period of its which ends before that day,

such separate determinations and computations shall be made as are necessary for determining the liability of the companies which fall within paragraph (a) above and the liability of the companies which fall within paragraph (b) above.

37(3) For the purposes of sub-paragraph (2) above–

(a) any question as to the liability (if any) of a company falling within paragraph (a) shall be determined as if, in the case of every company resident in the United Kingdom, the accounting period of the non-resident company ended in an accounting period of the company ending on or after the corporation tax self-assessment appointed day; and

(b) any question as to the liability (if any) of a company falling within paragraph (b) shall be determined as if, in the case of every company resident in the United Kingdom, the accounting period of the non-resident company ended in an accounting period of the company ending before the corporation tax self-assessment appointed day.

37(4) In this paragraph–

"accounting period", in relation to a non-resident company, has the same meaning as it has in Chapter IV of Part XVII of the Taxes Act 1988;

"the corporation tax self-assessment appointed day" means the day which is the appointed day for the purposes of section 199 of the Finance Act 1994 (corporation tax self-assessment);

"non-resident company" means a company resident outside the United Kingdom.

Notes – The appointed day under FA 1994, s. 199 is 1 July 1999.

Part II – Company Tax Return

COMPANY TAX RETURN

3(1) An officer of Revenue and Customs may by notice require a company to deliver a return (a "company tax return") of such information, accounts, statements and reports–

(a) relevant to the tax liability of the company, or

(b) otherwise relevant to the application of the Corporation Tax Acts to the company,

as may reasonably be required by the notice.

3(2) Different information, accounts, statements and reports may be required from different descriptions of company.

3(3) A company tax return must include a declaration by the person making the return that the return is to the best of his knowledge correct and complete.

3(4) The return must be delivered to the officer of the Board by whom the notice was issued not later than the filing date.

3(5) Sub-paragraph (1)(b) has effect as if the reference to the Corporation Tax Acts included a reference to sections 911, 912, 914 and 915 of the Income Tax Act 2007.

History – In para. 3(1) the words "an officer of Revenue and Customs" substituted for the words "the Inland Revenue" by CRCA 2005, s. 50 and Sch. 4, para. 68(a), with effect from 18 April 2005 by virtue of SI 2005/1126, art. 2(2).
Para. 3(5) inserted by ITA 2007, s. 1027 and Sch. 1, para. 385(2), with effect from 6 April 2007.

Cross references – CAA 2001, s. 3(3): the claim for capital allowances must be made in a tax return.
FA 2004, s. 101(6): modification of para. 3(1) in respect of payment of royalties without deduction at source.
FA 2009, Sch. 55, para. 1–6: penalty for failure to make returns etc under para. 3.

Other material – HMRC Direction 4/3/03: use of the Internet for returns under para. 3.
HMRC Direction 6/01/10: electronic delivery of returns under para. 3.

3A(1) Her Majesty's Revenue and Customs may from time to time publish requirements as to the information, accounts, statements and reports which a company must deliver as part of its company tax return where the company has a tax liability by virtue of paragraph 50 or 51 of Schedule 19 to the Finance Act 2011 (the bank levy); and such information, accounts, statements and reports must be delivered as if the notice to the company under paragraph 3(1) had required them to be delivered (and paragraph 4 is to be read accordingly).

3A(2) The publication of any requirements under sub-paragraph (1) does not stop a notice under paragraph 3(1) requiring the delivery of any additional information, accounts, statements and reports as part of a company tax return.

History – Para. 3A inserted by FA 2011, s. 73 and Sch. 19, para. 62, with effect from 19 July 2011.

MEANING OF DELIVERY OF RETURN

4 References in this Schedule to the delivery of a company tax return are to the delivery of all the information, accounts, statements and reports required to comply with the notice requiring the return.

PERIOD FOR WHICH RETURN REQUIRED

5(1) A notice requiring a company tax return must specify the period to which the notice relates.

5(2) If an accounting period of the company ended during (or at the end of) the specified period, a return is required for that accounting period.

If there is more than one, a separate company tax return is required for each of them.

5(3) If sub-paragraph (2) does not apply but an accounting period of the company began during the specified period, a company tax return is required for the part of the specified period before the accounting period began.

5(4) If the company was outside the charge to corporation tax for the whole of the specified period, a company tax return is required for the whole of the specified period.

5(5) If none of the above provisions applies, no company tax return is required in response to the notice.

NOTICE RELATING TO PERIOD BEGINNING BEFORE APPOINTED DAY

6(1) A notice requiring a company tax return may be given on or after the self-assessment appointed day in relation to a period beginning before that day.

6(2) Where the effect of such a notice is to require a return for an accounting period ending before that day, the provisions of the Tax Acts apply as if it were a notice under section 11 of the Taxes Management Act 1970.

6(3) The provisions of this Act relating to company tax returns, or amending other provisions of the Tax Acts so as to refer to such returns, do not affect the operation of those Acts in relation to such a notice.

RETURN TO INCLUDE SELF-ASSESSMENT

7(1) Every company tax return for an accounting period must include an assessment (a "self-assessment") of the amount of tax which is payable by the company for that period–

(a) on the basis of the information contained in the return, and

(b) taking into account any relief or allowance for which a claim is included in the return or which is required to be given in relation to that accounting period.

7(2) For this purpose a company tax return is regarded as a return for an accounting period if the period is treated in the return as an accounting period and is not longer than twelve months, even though it is not, or may not be, an accounting period.

CALCULATION OF TAX PAYABLE

8(1) The amount of tax payable for an accounting period is calculated as follows.

First step

Calculate the corporation tax chargeable on the company's profits:

1. Take the amount of the company's profits for that period on which corporation tax is chargeable (see section 4(1) and (2) of the Corporation Tax Act 2010).
2. Apply the rate or rates of corporation tax applicable to the company (other than the restitution payments rate).

Second step

Then give effect to any reliefs or set-offs available against corporation tax chargeable on profits:

1. Any reduction under Chapter 3A of Part 8 of the Corporation Tax Act 2010 (marginal relief for companies with small ring fence profits etc).

1A. Any relief under Part V of Schedule 15 to the Finance Act 2000 (corporate venturing scheme: investment relief).

1B. Any relief under Part 7 of the Corporation Tax Act 2010 (community investment tax relief).

2. Any double taxation relief under under sections 2 and 6 of TIOPA 2010 or under section 18(1)(b) and (2) of that Act.

3. Any set off for advance corporation tax under section 239 of the Taxes Act 1988 or under regulations made under section 32 of this Act.

Third step

Then add any amounts assessable or chargeable as if they were corporation tax (reduced by any reliefs specific to those amounts):

1. Any amount due under section 455 or 464A of the Corporation Tax Act 2010 (tax on a loan, advance or benefit to a participator).

1ZA. Any sum chargeable under section 269DA of that Act (surcharge on banking companies).

1A. Any sum chargeable under section 330(1) of that Act (supplementary charge in respect of ring fence trades).

2. Any sum charged at step 5 in section 371BC(1) of the Taxation (International and Other Provisions) Act 2010 (controlled foreign companies).

3. Any amount of the bank levy chargeable by virtue of paragraph 50 or 51 of Schedule 19 to the Finance Act 2011 (the bank levy).

Fourth step

Then deduct any amounts to be set off against the company's overall tax liability for that period:

1. Any amount to be set off under section 967 or 968 of the Corporation Tax Act 2010 (income tax borne by deduction).

2. Any amount to be set off under section 246N or 246Q of the Taxes Act 1988 (advance corporation tax paid in respect of foreign income dividend).

Fifth step

Calculate the corporation tax chargeable on any profits of the company that are charged as restitution interest.

1. Find the amount in respect of which the company is chargeable for the period under the charge to corporation tax on income under Part 8C of CTA 2010.
2. Apply the restitution payments rate in accordance with section 357YK(1) of that Act.

The amount of tax payable for the accounting period is the sum of the amounts resulting from the first to fourth steps and this step.

8(1A) Sub-paragraph (1B) applies if an amount of the bank levy chargeable by virtue of paragraph 50 or 51 of Schedule 19 to the Finance Act 2011 (the bank levy) is added at the third step.

8(1B) Any deductions made at the fourth step are to be treated as made from all other amounts before being made from the amount of the bank levy.

8(2) Except as otherwise provided, references in this Schedule to the amount of tax payable by a company for an accounting period are to the amount shown in the company's self-assessment as the amount payable.

History – In para. 8(1), in item 1 in the first step, the words "(see section 4(1) and (2) of the Corporation Tax Act 2010)" inserted by CTA 2010, s. 1177 and Sch. 1, para. 297(4)(a), with effect for corporation tax purposes for accounting periods ending on or after 1 April 2010, and for income tax and capital gains tax purposes for the tax year 2010–11 and subsequent tax years.
In para. 8(1), item 2 of the first step the words "(other than the restitution payments rate)" inserted by F(No. 2)A 2015, s. 38(4)(a), with effect in relation to interest (whether arising before or on or after 21 October 2015) which falls within F(No. 2)A 2015, s. 38(11).
In para. 8(1), in item 1 of the second step, the words "Chapter 3A of Part 8 of the Corporation Tax Act 2010 (marginal relief for companies with small ring fence profits etc)" substituted for the words "section 19, 20 or 21 of the Corporation Tax Act 2010 (marginal relief for companies with small profits)" by FA 2014, s. 7 and Sch. 1, para. 6, with effect for the financial year 2015 and subsequent financial years.
In para. 8(1), in item 1 of the second step, the words "section 19, 20 or 21 of the Corporation Tax Act 2010 (marginal relief for companies with small profits)" substituted for the words "section 13(2) of the Taxes Act 1988 (marginal small companies' relief)" by CTA 2010, s. 1177 and Sch. 1, para. 297(4)(b), with effect for corporation tax purposes for accounting periods ending on or after 1 April 2010, and for income tax and capital gains tax purposes for the tax year 2010–11 and subsequent tax years.
In para. 8(1) the words "or 13AA(2)" in item 1 of the second step omitted by FA 2006, s. 26(7) and repealed by FA 2006, s. 178 and Sch. 26, Pt. 3(1), with effect for the financial year 2006 and subsequent financial years, subject to the provisions of FA 2006, s. 26(9)–(11). Those words previously inserted by FA 1999, s. 28(5), with effect, subject to FA 1999, s. 28(7), in relation to corporation tax for the financial year 2000 or any subsequent financial year.
In para. 8(1), item 1A inserted in the second step by FA 2000, Sch. 16, para. 5(2) with effect for relief given on or after 1 April 2000.
In para. 8(1), in item 1B of the second step, the words "Part 7 of the Corporation Tax Act 2010" substituted for the words "Part 5 of Schedule 16 to the Finance Act 2002" by CTA 2010, s. 1177 and Sch. 1, para. 297(4)(c), with effect for corporation tax purposes for accounting periods ending on or after 1 April 2010, and for income tax and capital gains tax purposes for the tax year 2010–11 and subsequent tax years.
In para. 8(1), item 1B inserted in the second stepby FA 2002, s. 57 and Sch. 17, para. 5 with effect for accounting periods ending on or after 17 April 2002 in relation to investments made on or after 17 April 2002 and claims made on or after 23 January 2003, by virtue of SI 2003/88 (C.5).
In para. 8(1), in item 2 of the second step, the words "under sections 2 and 6 of TIOPA 2010 or under section 18(1)(b) and (2) of that Act" substituted for the words "section 788 or 790 of that Act" by TIOPA 2010, s. 374 and Sch. 8, Pt. 1, para. 54(2)(a), with effect for corporation tax purposes for accounting periods ending on or after 1 April 2010, for income tax and capital gains tax purposes for the tax year 2010–11 and subsequent tax years, and for petroleum revenue tax purposes for chargeable periods beginning on or after 1 July 2010.
In para. 8(1), in item 3 of the second step, the words "the Taxes Act 1988" substituted for the words "that Act" by TIOPA 2010, s. 374 and Sch. 8, Pt. 1, para. 54(2)(b), with effect for corporation tax purposes for accounting periods ending on or after 1 April 2010, for income tax and capital gains tax purposes for the tax year 2010–11 and subsequent tax years, and for petroleum revenue tax purposes for chargeable periods beginning on or after 1 July 2010.
In para. 8(1), in item 1 in the third step, the words "or 464A" inserted and the words ", advance or benefit" substituted for the words "or advance made by close company" by FA 2013, s. 79 and Sch. 30, para. 13(3), with effect from 20 March 2013.
In para. 8(1), in item 2 in the third step, the words "Any sum charged at step 5 in section 371BC(1) of the Taxation (International and Other Provisions) Act 2010 (controlled foreign companies)." substituted for the words "Any sum chargeable under section 747(4)(a) of the Taxes Act 1988 (tax on profits of a controlled foreign company)." by FA 2012, s. 180 and Sch. 20, para. 17(3), with effect from in relation to accounting periods of controlled foreign companies beginning on or after 1 January 2013 (subject to the transitional provisions at FA 2012, Sch. 20, para. 50).
In para. 8(1), in item 1 of the third step, the words "section 455 of the Corporation Tax Act 2010" substituted for the words "section 419(1) of the Taxes Act 1988" by CTA 2010, s. 1177 and Sch. 1, para. 297(4)(d), with effect for corporation tax purposes for accounting periods ending on or after 1 April 2010, and for income tax and capital gains tax purposes for the tax year 2010–11 and subsequent tax years.
In para. 8(1), item 1ZA of the third step inserted by F(No. 2)A 2015, s. 17 and Sch. 3, para. 3(3), with effect for accounting periods ending on or after 1 January 2016.
In para. 8(1), in item 1A of the third step, the words "section 330(1)" substituted for the words "section 501A(1)" by CTA 2010, s. 1177 and Sch. 1, para. 297(4)(e), with effect for corporation tax purposes for accounting periods ending on or after 1 April 2010, and for income tax and capital gains tax purposes for the tax year 2010–11 and subsequent tax years.
In para. 8(1), item 1A inserted in the third step by FA 2002, s. 92(4).
In para. 8(1), in item 2 of the third step, the words "the Taxes Act 1988" substituted for the words "that Act" by CTA 2010, s. 1177 and Sch. 1, para. 297(4)(f), with effect for corporation tax purposes for accounting periods ending on or after 1 April 2010, and for income tax and capital gains tax purposes for the tax year 2010–11 and subsequent tax years.
In para.8(1), item 3 of the third step inserted by FA 2011, s. 73 and Sch. 19, para. 63(2), with effect from 19 July 2011.
In para. 8(1), in item 1 of the fourth step, the words "section 967 or 968 of the Corporation Tax Act 2010" substituted for the words "section 7(2) or 11(3) of the Taxes Act 1988" by CTA 2010, s. 1177 and Sch. 1, para. 297(4)(g), with effect for corporation tax purposes for accounting periods ending on or after 1 April 2010, and for income tax and capital gains tax purposes for the tax year 2010–11 and subsequent tax years.
In para. 8(1), in item 2 of the fourth step, the words "the Taxes Act 1988" substituted for the words "that Act" by CTA 2010, s. 1177 and Sch. 1, para. 297(4)(h), with effect for corporation tax purposes for accounting periods ending on or after 1 April 2010, and for income tax and capital gains tax purposes for the tax year 2010–11 and subsequent tax years.
In para. 8(1), the fifth step inserted by F(No. 2)A 2015, s. 38(4)(b) with effect in relation to interest (whether arising before or on or after 21 October 2015) which falls within F(No. 2)A 2015, s. 38(11).
Para. 8(1A) and (1B) inserted by FA 2011, s. 73 and Sch. 19, para. 63(3), with effect from 19 July 2011.

CLAIMS THAT CANNOT BE MADE WITHOUT A RETURN

9(1) No claim to which this paragraph applies may be made by a company before it delivers a company tax return for the period to which the claim relates.

9(2) This paragraph applies to a claim by a company for any repayment of income tax called for by virtue of–

(a) section 3 of the Corporation Tax Act 2009 (exclusion of income tax charge in case of UK resident company or income within chargeable profits for corporation tax), or

(b) exemptions from income tax conferred by the Corporation Tax Acts.

This is subject to sub-paragraphs (2A) and (2B).

9(2A) This paragraph does not apply to a claim by a company for repayment of income tax treated as having been paid by virtue of–

(a) section 471 of the Corporation Tax Act 2010 (gifts qualifying for gift aid relief: charitable companies),

(b) section 475 of that Act (gifts qualifying for gift aid relief: eligible bodies), or

(c) section 661D of that Act (gifts qualifying for gift aid relief: community amateur sports clubs).

9(2B) This paragraph also does not apply to a claim by a company for repayment of income tax deducted at source from income which is exempt from tax by virtue of–

(a) section 486 of the Corporation Tax Act 2010 (investment income and non-trading profits from loan relationships),

(b) section 487 of that Act (public revenue dividends),

(c) section 488 of that Act (certain miscellaneous income),

(d) section 489 of that Act (income from estates in administration), or

(e) section 664 of that Act (interest and gift aid income: community amateur sports clubs).

9(3) [Omitted by FA 2016, s. 5 and Sch. 1, para. 58(3)(a).]

9(4) This paragraph applies to a claim by a company for relief under Part V of Schedule 15 to the Finance Act 2000 (corporate venturing scheme: investment relief).

History – In para. 9(2), the words "This is subject to sub-paragraphs (2A) and (2B)." inserted by FA 2012, s. 51 and Sch. 15, para. 14(2), with effect in relation to claims whenever made.

In para. 9(2) the words "section 3 of the Corporation Tax Act 2009" substituted for the words "section 6(2) of the Taxes Act 1988" by CTA 2009, s. 1322 and Sch. 1, para. 454(2), with effect for corporation tax purposes for accounting periods ending on or after 1 April 2009, and for income tax and capital gains tax purposes for the tax year 2009–10 and subsequent tax years.

Para. 9(2A) and (2B) substituted for former para. 9(2A) by FA 2012, s. 51 and Sch. 15, para. 14(3), with effect in relation to claims whenever made.

Former para. 9(2A) inserted by FA 2010, s. 32 and Sch. 8, para. 6(2), with effect in relation to claims whenever made.

Para. 9(3) omitted by FA 2016, s. 5 and Sch. 1, para. 58(3)(a), with effect in relation to dividends paid or arising (or treated as paid), and any other distributions made (or treated as made), in the tax year 2016–17 or at any later time. Former para. 9(3) read as follows:

"**9(3)** This paragraph applies to a claim by a company for payment of a tax credit, unless–

(a) the company is wholly exempt from corporation tax or is only not so exempt in respect of trading income, and

(b) [repealed by FA 2001, s. 110 and Sch. 33, Pt. 2(12).]".

Former para. 9(3)(b) repealed by FA 2001, s. 110 and Sch. 33, Pt. 2(12) in relation to tax credits in respect of distributions made on or after 6 April 2004 and to income tax borne by deduction from payments received after 30 September 2001.

Para. 9(4) inserted by FA 2000, Sch. 16, para. 5(3) with effect for claims made on or after 1 April 2000.

OTHER CLAIMS AND ELECTIONS TO BE INCLUDED IN RETURN

10(1) In Part VII of this Schedule (general provisions as to claims and elections) paragraphs 57 to 59 contain provisions as to the circumstances in which a claim or election may or must be made, or is to be treated as having been made, in a company tax return.

10(2) A claim to which Part VIII, IX or IXA of this Schedule applies (claims for group relief, capital allowances, first-year tax credits, R&D expenditure credits or R&D tax relief) can only be made by being included in a company tax return (see paragraphs 67, 79, 83ZA and 83B).

10(2A) A claim to which Part 9B of this Schedule applies (claims for land remediation tax credit and life assurance company tax credit) can only be made by being included in a company tax return (see paragraph 83H).

10(2B) [Omitted by CTA 2009, s. 1322 and Sch. 1, para. 454(3)(a).]

10(3) [Omitted by CTA 2009, s. 1322 and Sch. 1, para. 454(3)(a).]

10(4) A claim to which Part 9D of this Schedule applies (certain claims for tax relief under Part 15, 15A, 15B, 15C or 15D of the Corporation Tax Act 2009) can only be made by being included in a company tax return (see paragraph 83T).

10(5) An election under section 1182(7) of the Corporation Tax Act 2009 (election not to be a film production company) can only be made by being included in a company tax return (see section 1182(8)(a) of that Act).

10(6) An election under section 1216AE(7) of the Corporation Tax Act 2009 (election not to be a television production company) can only be made by being included in a company tax return (see section 1216AE(8)(a) of that Act).

10(7) An election under section 1217AB(6) of the Corporation Tax Act 2009 (election not to be a video games development company) can only be made by being included in a company tax return (see section 1217AB(7)(a) of that Act).

History – In para. 10(2), the words ", R&D expenditure credits" inserted by FA 2013, s. 35 and Sch. 15, para. 5, with effect in relation to expenditure incurred on or after 1 April 2013.
In para. 10(2), the words ", first-year tax credits" and ", 83ZA" inserted by FA 2008, s. 79 and Sch. 25, para. 8(2), with effect in relation to expenditure incurred on or after 1 April 2008.
In para. 10(2) the words "R&D tax relief" substituted for the words "R&D tax credit" by FA 2006, s. 29 and Sch. 3, para. 2(2), with effect in relation to accounting periods ending on or after 31 March 2006, subject to the provisions of FA 2006, Sch. 3, para. 11.
Para. 10(2) substituted by FA 2000, Sch. 21, para. 2, with effect for accounting periods ending on or after 1 April 2000.
Para. 10(2A) inserted by FA 2001, s. 70 and Sch. 23, para. 4, with effect for accounting periods ending on or after 1 April 2001.
Para. 10(2B) omitted by CTA 2009, s. 1322 and Sch. 1, para. 454(3)(a) and repealed by CTA 2009, s. 1326 and Sch. 3, Pt. 1, with effect for corporation tax purposes for accounting periods ending on or after 1 April 2009, and for income tax and capital gains tax purposes for the tax year 2009–10 and subsequent tax years.
Para. 10(2B) inserted by FA 2006, s. 29 and Sch. 3, para. (2(3), with effect in relation to accounting periods ending on or after 31 March 2006, subject to the provisions of FA 2006, Sch. 3, para. 11.
Para. 10(3) omitted by CTA 2009, s. 1322 and Sch. 1, para. 454(3)(a) and repealed by CTA 2009, s. 1326 and Sch. 3, Pt. 1, with effect for corporation tax purposes for accounting periods ending on or after 1 April 2009, and for income tax and capital gains tax purposes for the tax year 2009–10 and subsequent tax years.
In former para. 10(3) the words "tax relief under Schedule 13 to the Finance Act 2002" substituted for the words "tax credits under Schedule 13 to the Finance Act 2002" by FA 2006, s. 29 and Sch. 3, para. 2(4), with effect in relation to accounting periods ending on or after 31 March 2006, subject to the provisions of FA 2006, Sch. 3, para. 11.
Former para. 10(3) inserted by FA 2002, s. 54 and Sch. 14, para. 2, with effect in relation to tax credits payable under FA 2002, Sch. 13 in respect of expenditure incurred on or after 22 April 2003 by virtue of SI 2003/1472 (C. 64) (the day appointed by the Treasury under FA 2002, Sch. 13, para. 28).
In para. 10(4), the words ", 15C or 15D" substituted for the words "or 15C" by FA 2016 s. 54 and Sch. 8, para. 4, with effect in relation to accounting periods beginning on or after 1 April 2016 (subject to provisions of Sch. 8, para. 17(2) and (3))
In para. 10(4) the word "certain" inserted before the word "claims" by FA 2014, s. 36 and Sch. 4, para 4(a), with effect from 22 August 2014, in relation to accounting periods beginning on or after 1 September 2014, subject to the transitional provisions in FA 2014, Sch. 4, para. 17.
In para. 10(4) ", 15B or 15C" substituted for "or 15B" by FA 2014, s. 36 and Sch. 4, para. 4(b), with effect from 22 August 2014, in relation to accounting periods beginning on or after 1 September 2014, subject to the transitional provisions in FA 2014, Sch. 4, para. 17.
In para. 10(4), the words "or 15B" inserted after the words "15A" by FA 2013, s. 36 and Sch. 18, para. 3(2), with effect from 1 April 2014 (SI 2014/1962) in relation to accounting periods beginning on or after "the relevant day" (as defined in FA 2013, Sch. 18, para. 23).
In para. 10(4), the words "tax relief under Part 15, 15A of the Corporation Tax Act 2009" substituted for the words "film tax relief" by FA 2013, s. 36 and Sch. 18, para. 3(2), with effect from 19 July 2013 (SI 2013/1817) in relation to accounting periods beginning on or after "the relevant day" (as defined in FA 2013, Sch. 18, para. 23).
Para. 10(4) inserted by FA 2006, s. 42 and Sch. 5, para. 27, with effect from 1 January 2007 (FA 2006, s. 53).
In para. 10(5) the words "section 1182(7) of the Corporation Tax Act 2009" substituted for the words "section 32(7) of the Finance Act 2006" and the words "section 1182(8)(a)" substituted for the words "section 32(8)(a)" by CTA 2009, s. 1322 and Sch. 1, para. 454(3)(b), with effect for corporation tax purposes for accounting periods ending on or after 1 April 2009, and for income tax and capital gains tax purposes for the tax year 2009–10 and subsequent tax years.
Para. 10(5) inserted by FA 2007, s. 58(2) with effect from Royal Assent (19 July 2007).
As regards video games relief, para. 10(6) and (7) inserted by FA 2013, s. 36 and Sch. 18, para. 3(3), with effect from 1 April 2014 (SI 2014/1962) in relation to accounting periods beginning on or after "the relevant day" (as defined in FA 2013, Sch. 18, para. 23).
Para. 10(6) and (7) inserted by FA 2013, s. 36 and Sch. 18, para. 3(3), with effect from 19 July 2013 (SI 2013/1817) in relation to accounting periods beginning on or after "the relevant day" (as defined in FA 2013, Sch. 18, para. 23).

ACCOUNTS REQUIRED IN CASE OF COMPANIES ACT COMPANY

11(1) In the case of a company which–

(a) is required to deliver a company tax return for a period,

(b) is resident in the United Kingdom throughout that period, and

(c) is required under the Companies Act 2006 to prepare accounts for a period consisting of or including the whole of that period,

the power to require the delivery of accounts as part of the return is limited to such accounts, containing such information and having annexed to them such documents, as are required to be prepared under that Act.

11(2) Sub-paragraph (1) does not affect–

(a) the power to require the delivery of accounts, information or documents in relation to a company's tax liability by virtue of paragraph 50 or 51 of Schedule 19 to the Finance Act 2011 (the bank levy), or

(b) the requirements which may be imposed under paragraph 3A.

History – Para. 11 renumbered as para. 11(1) by FA 2011, s. 73 and Sch. 19, para. 64(2), with effect from 19 July 2011.
Para. 11(2) inserted by FA 2011, s. 73 and Sch. 19, para. 64(3), with effect from 19 July 2011.
Para. 11 substituted by SI 2008/954, art. 25, with effect from 6 April 2008.

INFORMATION ABOUT BUSINESS CARRIED ON IN PARTNERSHIP

12(1) A company tax return of a company which carries on a trade, profession or business in partnership must include any amount which in a relevant partnership statement is stated to be its share of any income, loss, consideration, tax, credit or charge.

12(2) A **"relevant partnership statement"** means a statement under section 12AB of the Taxes Management Act 1970 for the period for which the return is made or a period which includes that period or any part of it.

INFORMATION ABOUT CHARGEABLE GAINS

13 [Omitted by SI 2009/2035, art. 2 and Sch., para. 37.]

History – Para. 13 omitted by SI 2009/2035, art. 2 and Sch., para. 37, with effect from 13 August 2009.

FILING DATE

14(1) The filing date for a company tax return is the last day of whichever of the following periods is the last to end–

(a) twelve months from the end of the period for which the return is made;

(b) if the company's relevant period of account is not longer than 18 months, twelve months from the end of that period;

(c) if the company's relevant period of account is longer than 18 months, 30 months from the beginning of that period;

(d) three months from the date on which the notice requiring the return was served.

14(2) In sub-paragraph (1) **"relevant period of account"** means, in relation to a return for an accounting period, the period of account of the company in which the last day of that accounting period falls.

History – In para. 14(2), the second sentence repealed by FA 2002, s. 141 and Sch. 40, Pt. 3(16), with effect from 24 July 2002.

Cross references – ICTA 1988 s. 826(3B) filing date in relation to land remediation tax credit.
FA 2009, Sch. 56, para. 1 and 4: penalty for failure to make payments on time by reference to para. 14.

AMENDMENT OF RETURN BY COMPANY

15(1) A company may amend its company tax return by notice to an officer of Revenue and Customs.

15(2) The notice must be in such form as an officer of Revenue and Customs may require.

15(3) The notice must contain such information and be accompanied by such statements as an officer of Revenue and Customs may reasonably require.

15(4) Except as otherwise provided, an amendment may not be made more than twelve months after–

(a) the filing date, or

(b) in the case of a return for the wrong period, what would be the filing date if the period for which the return was made were an accounting period.

History – In para. 15(1), (2) and (3) the words "an officer of Revenue and Customs" substituted for the words "the Inland Revenue" by CRCA 2005, s. 50 and Sch. 4, para. 68(a), with effect from 18 April 2005 by virtue of SI 2005/1126, art. 2(2).

Cross references – SI 2005/3338, reg. 5: modification of para. 15 for the purposes of Lloyd's underwriters.

CORRECTION OF RETURN BY REVENUE

16(1) An officer of Revenue and Customs may amend a company tax return so as to correct–

(a) obvious errors or omissions in the return (whether errors of principle, arithmetical mistakes or otherwise), and

(b) anything else in the return that the officer has reason to believe is incorrect in the light of information available to the officer.

16(2) A correction under this paragraph is made by notice to the company concerned.

16(3) No such correction may be made more than nine months after–

(a) the day on which the return was delivered, or

(b) if the correction is required in consequence of an amendment by the company under paragraph 15, the day on which that amendment was made.

16(4) A correction under this paragraph is of no effect if the company–

(a) amends its return so as to reject the correction, or

(b) after the end of the period within which it may amend its return, but within three months from the date of issue of the notice of correction, gives notice rejecting the correction.

16(5) Notice under sub-paragraph (4)(b) must be given–

(a) in writing,

(b) to the officer of the Board by whom notice of the correction was given.

History – In para. 16(1), "– (a)" inserted by FA 2008, s. 119(4)(a), with effect from 1 April 2010 (SI 2009/405).
In para. 16(1) the words "an officer of Revenue and Customs" substituted for the words "the Inland Revenue" by CRCA 2005, s. 50 and Sch. 4, para. 68(a), with effect from 18 April 2005 by virtue of SI 2005/1126, art. 2(2).
Para. 16(1)(b) and the "and" before it inserted by FA 2008, s. 119(4)(b), with effect from 1 April 2010 (SI 2009/405).

Cross references – SI 2005/3338, reg. 5: modification of para. 16 for the purposes of Lloyd's underwriters.

FAILURE TO DELIVER RETURN: FLAT-RATE PENALTY

17(1) A company which is required to deliver a company tax return and fails to do so by the filing date is liable to a flat-rate penalty under this paragraph.
It may also be liable to a tax-related penalty under paragraph 18.

17(2) The penalty is–

(a) £100, if the return is delivered within three months after the filing date, and

(b) £200, in any other case.

17(3) The amounts are increased to £500 and £1,000 for a third successive failure, that is, where–

(a) the company is within the charge to corporation tax for three consecutive accounting periods (and at no time between the beginning of the first of those periods and the end of the last is it outside the charge to corporation tax),

(b) a company tax return is required for each of those accounting periods,

(c) the company was liable to a penalty under this paragraph in respect of each of the first two of those periods, and

(d) the company is again liable to a penalty under this paragraph in respect of the third period.

17(4) The first or second period mentioned in sub-paragraph (3) may be a period ending before the self-assessment appointed day, in relation to which–

(a) the reference in paragraph (b) to a company tax return shall be construed as a reference to a return under section 11 of the Taxes Management Act 1970, and

(b) the references in paragraphs (c) and (d) to a penalty under this paragraph shall be construed as a reference to a penalty under section 94 of that Act.

FAILURE TO DELIVER RETURN: TAX-RELATED PENALTY

18(1) A company which is required to deliver a company tax return for an accounting period and fails to do so–

(a) within 18 months after the end of that period, or

(b) if the filing date is later than that, by the filing date,

is liable to a tax-related penalty under this paragraph.
This is in addition to any flat-rate penalty under paragraph 17.

18(2) The penalty is–

(a) 10 per cent of the unpaid tax, if the return is delivered within two years after the end of the period for which the return is required, and

(b) 20 per cent of the unpaid tax, in any other case.

18(3) The **"unpaid tax"** means the amount of tax payable by the company for the accounting period for which the return was required which remains unpaid on the date when the liability to the penalty arises under sub-paragraph (1).

18(4) In determining that amount no account is to be taken of–

(a) any relief under section 458 of the Corporation Tax Act 2010 (relief in respect of repayment, etc of loan) which is deferred under subsection (5) of that section, or

(b) any relief under section 464B of that Act (relief in respect of return payment) which is deferred under subsection (5) of that section.

History – Para. 18(4) substituted by FA 2013, s. 79 and Sch. 30, para. 13(4), with effect from 20 March 2013.
In para. 18(4), the words "section 458 of the Corporation Tax Act 2010" substituted for the words "section 419(4) of the Taxes Act 1988" by CTA 2010, s. 1177 and Sch. 1, para. 297(5)(a), with effect for corporation tax purposes for accounting periods ending on or after 1 April 2010, and for income tax and capital gains tax purposes for the tax year 2010–11 and subsequent tax years.
In para. 18(4), the words "subsection (5)" substituted for the words "subsection (4A)" by CTA 2010, s. 1177 and Sch. 1, para. 297(5)(b), with effect for corporation tax purposes for accounting periods ending on or after 1 April 2010, and for income tax and capital gains tax purposes for the tax year 2010–11 and subsequent tax years.

Cross references – FA 1989, s. 102(6): surrender of company tax refund, etc., within group: any penalty to which recipient company liable is calculated on amount of refund as though it were paid on the day the companies notify the inspector.

EXCUSE FOR LATE DELIVERY OF RETURN

19 A company is not liable to a penalty under paragraph 17 (flat rate penalty) if–

(a) the period for which the return is required is one for which the company is required to deliver accounts under the Companies Act 2006, and

(b) the return is delivered no later than the last day for the delivery of those accounts to the registrar of companies.

History – Para. 19 substituted by SI 2008/954, art. 25, with effect from 6 April 2008.

Other material – Taxline 2000/9 (not reproduced): Taxline gives two examples of the type of allowable excuse ever actually likely to arise in practice.

PENALTY FOR INCORRECT OR UNCORRECTED RETURN

20 [Omitted by FA 2007, s. 97 and Sch. 24, para. 29(c) and repealed by FA 2007, s. 114 and Sch. 27, Pt. 5(5).]

History – Para. 20 omitted by FA 2007, s. 97 and Sch. 24, para. 29(c) and repealed by FA 2007, s. 114 and Sch. 27, Pt. 5(5), with effect as follows by virtue of SI 2008/568, art. 2:

- 1 April 2008 in relation to relevant documents relating to tax periods commencing on or after that date;
- 1 April 2008 in relation to assessments falling within paragraph 2 for tax periods commencing on or after that date;
- 1 July 2008 in relation to relevant documents relating to claims under the Thirteenth Council Directive (arrangements for the refund of value added tax to persons not established in Community territory) for years commencing on or after that date;
- 1 January 2009 in relation to relevant documents relating to claims under the Eighth Council Directive (arrangements for the refund of value added tax to taxable persons not established in the territory of the country) for years commencing on or after that date;
- 1 April 2009 in relation to documents relating to all other claims for repayments of relevant tax made on or after 1 April 2009 which are not related to a tax period; and
- in any other case, 1 April 2009 in relation to documents given where a person's liability to pay relevant tax arises on or after that date.

However, no person will be liable to a penalty under Sch. 24 in respect of any tax period for which a return is required to be made before 1 April 2009.

Part III – Duty to Keep and Preserve Records

DUTY TO KEEP AND PRESERVE RECORDS

21(1) A company which may be required to deliver a company tax return for any period must–

(a) keep such records as may be needed to enable it to deliver a correct and complete return for the period, and

(b) preserve those records in accordance with this paragraph.

21(2) The records must be preserved until the end of the relevant day.

21(2A) In this paragraph **"relevant day"** means–

(a) the sixth anniversary of the end of the period for which the company may be required to deliver a company tax return, or

(b) such earlier day as may be specified in writing by the Commissioners for Her Majesty's Revenue and Customs (and different days may be specified for different cases).

21(3) If the company is required to deliver a company tax return by notice given before the end of the relevant day, the records must be preserved until any later date on which–

(a) any enquiry into the return is completed, or

(b) if there is no enquiry, an officer of Revenue and Customs no longer have power to enquire into the return.

21(4) If the company is required to deliver a company tax return by notice given after the end of the relevant day and has in its possession at that time any records that may be needed to enable it to deliver a correct and complete return, it is under a duty to preserve those records until the date on which–

(a) any enquiry into the return is completed, or

(b) if there is no enquiry, an officer of Revenue and Customs no longer have power to enquire into the return.

21(5) The records required to be kept and preserved under this paragraph include records of–

(a) all receipts and expenses in the course of the company's activities, and the matters in respect of which the receipts and expenses arise, and

(b) in the case of a trade involving dealing in goods, all sales and purchases made in the course of the trade.

21(5A) The Commissioners for Her Majesty's Revenue and Customs may by regulations–

(a) provide that the records required to be kept and preserved under this paragraph include, or do not include, records specified in the regulations, and

(b) provide that those records include supporting documents so specified.

21(5B) Regulations under this paragraph may–

(a) make different provision for different cases, and

(b) make provision by reference to things specified in a notice published by the Commissioners for Her Majesty's Revenue and Customs in accordance with the regulations (and not withdrawn by a subsequent notice).

21(6) **"Supporting documents"** includes accounts, books, deeds, contracts, vouchers and receipts.

History – In para. 21(2), the words "until the end of the relevant day." substituted for the words from "for six years from the end of the period for which the company may be required to deliver a company tax return." by FA 2008, s. 115 and Sch. 37, para. 8(2), with effect from 1 April 2009 (SI 2009/402, art. 2).
Para. 21(2A) inserted by FA 2008, s. 115 and Sch. 37, para. 8(3), with effect from 1 April 2009 (SI 2009/402, art. 2).
In para. 21(3), the words "the relevant day" substituted for the words "that six year period" by FA 2008, s. 115 and Sch. 37, para. 8(4), with effect from 1 April 2009 (SI 2009/402, art. 2).
In para. 21(3)(b) the words "an officer of Revenue and Customs" substituted for the words "the Inland Revenue" by CRCA 2005, s. 50 and Sch. 4, para. 68(a), with effect from 18 April 2005 by virtue of SI 2005/1126, art. 2(2).
In para. 21(4), the words "the relevant day" substituted for the words "that six year period" by FA 2008, s. 115 and Sch. 37, para. 8(5), with effect from 1 April 2009 (SI 2009/402, art. 2).
In para. 21(4)(b) the words "an officer of Revenue and Customs" substituted for the words "the Inland Revenue" by CRCA 2005, s. 50 and Sch. 4, para. 68(a), with effect from 18 April 2005 by virtue of SI 2005/1126, art. 2(2).
Para. 21(5A) and (5B) inserted after para. 21(5) by FA 2008, s. 115 and Sch. 37, para. 8(6), with effect from 1 April 2009 (SI 2009/402, art. 2).
In para. 21(6), the words "The duty to preserve records under this paragraph includes a duty to preserve all supporting documents relating to the items mentioned in sub-paragraph (5)(a) and (b)." omitted by FA 2008, s. 115 and Sch. 37, para. 8(7), with effect from 1 April 2009 (SI 2009/402, art. 2).

Other material – Tax Bulletin TB10/98-1: guidance notes on record keeping under 1998 transfer pricing legislation.
Tax Bulletin TB10/98-3: record keeping requirements under self-assessment for companies and other concerns within the charge to corporation tax.

PRESERVATION OF INFORMATION ETC

History – In the heading before para. 22, the word "etc" substituted for the words "instead of original records" by FA 2008, s. 115 and Sch. 37, para. 9(5), with effect from 1 April 2009 (SI 2009/402, art. 2).

22(1) The duty under paragraph 21 to preserve records may be discharged–

(a) by preserving them in any form and by any means, or

(b) by preserving the information contained in them in any form and by any means,

subject to sub-paragraph (3) and any conditions or exceptions specified in writing by the Commissioners for Her Majesty's Revenue and Customs.

22(2) [Omitted by FA 2008, s. 115 and Sch. 37, para. 9(3).]

22(3) Sub-paragraph (1)(b) does not apply in the case of the following kinds of record–

(a) any statement in writing such as is mentioned in–

(i) section 1100(1) of the Corporation Tax Act 2010 (amount of distribution, but formerly amount of qualifying distribution and tax credit), or

(ii) section 495(1) or 975(2) or (4) of the Income Tax Act 2007 (statements about deduction of income tax),

provided by the company or person there mentioned whether after the making of a request or otherwise;

(b) any record (however described) which is required by regulations under section 70(1)(c) of the Finance Act 2004 to be given to a sub-contractor (within the meaning of section 58 of that Act) on the making of a payment to which section 61 of that Act (deductions on account of tax) applies;

(c) any record relating to an amount of tax–

(i) paid under the law of a territory outside the United Kingdom, or

(ii) which would have been payable under the law of a territory outside the United Kingdom ("territory F") but for a development relief.

22(4) In sub-paragraph (3)(c) **"development relief"** means a relief–

(a) given under the law of territory F with a view to promoting industrial, commercial, scientific, educational or other development in a territory outside the United Kingdom, and

(b) about which provision is made in arrangements which have effect under section 2(1) of TIOPA 2010 (double taxation relief by agreement with territories outside the United Kingdom).

History – Para. 22(1) substituted by FA 2008, s. 115 and Sch. 37, para. 9(2), with effect from 1 April 2009 (SI 2009/402, art. 2).
Para. 22(2) omitted by FA 2008, s. 115 and Sch. 37, para. 9(3), with effect from 1 April 2009 (SI 2009/402, art. 2).
In para. 22(3), the words "Sub-paragraph (1)(b) does not apply in the case of the following kinds of records" substituted for the words "The records excluded from sub-paragraph (1) are" by FA 2008, s. 115 and Sch. 37, para. 9(4), with effect from 1 April 2009 (SI 2009/402, art. 2).

In para. 22(3)(a)(i), the words "of distribution, but formerly amount" inserted by FA 2016, s. 5 and Sch. 1, para. 58(3)(b), with effect in relation to dividends paid or arising (or treated as paid), and any other distributions made (or treated as made), in the tax year 2016–17 or at any later time.
In para. 22(3)(a)(i), the words "section 1100(1) of the Corporation Tax Act 2010" substituted for the words "section 234(1) of the Taxes Act 1988" by CTA 2010, s. 1177 and Sch. 1, para. 297(6), with effect for corporation tax purposes for accounting periods ending on or after 1 April 2010, and for income tax and capital gains tax purposes for the tax year 2010–11 and subsequent tax years.
Para. 22(3)(a)(ii) substituted by ITA 2007, s. 1027 and Sch. 1, para. 385(4), with effect from 6 April 2007.
Para. 22(3)(b) substituted by FA 2004, s. 76 and Sch. 12, para. 16(2), with effect, in relation to payments made under contracts relating to construction operations, on or after 6 April 2007, by virtue of notice given pursuant to SI 2005/2045, reg. 1.
Para. 22(3)(c)(ii) substituted by TIOPA 2010, s. 374 and Sch. 8, para. 54(3), with effect for corporation tax purposes for accounting periods ending on or after 1 April 2010, for income tax and capital gains tax purposes for the tax year 2010–11 and subsequent tax years, and for petroleum revenue tax purposes for chargeable periods beginning on or after 1 July 2010.
Para. 22(4) inserted by TIOPA 2010, s. 374 and Sch. 8, para. 54(4), with effect for corporation tax purposes for accounting periods ending on or after 1 April 2010, for income tax and capital gains tax purposes for the tax year 2010–11 and subsequent tax years, and for petroleum revenue tax purposes for chargeable periods beginning on or after 1 July 2010.
Other material – Tax Bulletin TB10/98-3: record keeping requirements under self-assessment for companies and other concerns within the charge to corporation tax.

PENALTY FOR FAILURE TO KEEP AND PRESERVE RECORDS

23(1) A company which fails to comply with paragraph 21 in relation to an accounting period is liable to a penalty not exceeding £3,000, subject to the following exceptions.

23(2) No penalty is incurred if the records which the company fails to keep or preserve are records which might have been needed only for the purposes of claims, elections or notices not included in the return.

23(3) No penalty is incurred if–

(a) the records which the company fails to keep or preserve are statements in writing such as are mentioned in–

(i) section 1100(1) of the Corporation Tax Act 2010 (amount of distribution, but formerly amount of qualifying distribution and tax credit), or

(ii) section 495(1) or 975(2) or (4) of the Income Tax Act 2007 (statements about deduction of income tax),

provided by the company or person there mentioned whether after the making of a request or otherwise, and

(b) an officer of Revenue and Customs is satisfied that any facts which they reasonably require to be proved, and which would have been proved by the records, are proved by other documentary evidence furnished to them.

History – In para. 23(3)(a)(i), the words "of distribution, but formerly amount" inserted by FA 2016, s. 5 and Sch. 1, para. 58(3)(b), with effect in relation to dividends paid or arising (or treated as paid), and any other distributions made (or treated as made), in the tax year 2016–17 or at any later time.
In para. 23(3)(a)(i), the words "section 1100(1) of the Corporation Tax Act 2010" substituted for the words "section 234(1) of the Taxes Act 1988" by CTA 2010, s. 1177 and Sch. 1, para. 297(7), with effect for corporation tax purposes for accounting periods ending on or after 1 April 2010, and for income tax and capital gains tax purposes for the tax year 2010–11 and subsequent tax years.
Para. 23(3)(a)(ii) substituted by ITA 2007, s. 1027 and Sch. 1, para. 385(4), with effect from 6 April 2007.
In para. 23(3)(b) the words "an officer of Revenue and Customs" substituted for the words "the Inland Revenue" by CRCA 2005, s. 50 and Sch. 4, para. 68(a) and the word "is" substituted for the word "are" by virtue of para. 68(c), with effect from 18 April 2005 by virtue of SI 2005/1126, art. 2(2).
Cross references – FA 2004, s. 33(3)(b) and (4): temporary relaxation of penalty provisions in respect of provisions not at arm's length.
Other material – Tax Bulletin TB10/98-3: record keeping requirements under self-assessment for companies and other concerns within the charge to corporation tax.

Part IV – Enquiry into Company Tax Return

NOTICE OF ENQUIRY

24(1) An officer of Revenue and Customs may enquire into a company tax return if the officer gives notice to the company of the officer's intention to do so ("notice of enquiry") within the time allowed.

24(2) If the return was delivered on or before the filing date, notice of enquiry may be given at any time up to twelve months from the day on which the return was delivered (subject to sub-paragraph (6)).

24(3) If the return was delivered after the filing date, notice of enquiry may be given at any time up to and including the 31st January, 30th April, 31st July or 31st October next following the first anniversary of the day on which the return was delivered.

24(4) If the company amends its return, notice of enquiry may be given at any time up to and including the 31st January, 30th April, 31st July or 31st October next following the first anniversary of the day on which the amendment was made.

24(5) A return which has been the subject of one notice of enquiry may not be the subject of another, except one given in consequence of an amendment (or another amendment) by the company of its return.

24(6) In the case of a company which is a member of a group other than a small group, the 12-month period in sub-paragraph (2) shall start not from the day on which the return was delivered but from the filing date.

24(7) In sub-paragraph (6) "group" and "small group" have the same meaning as in sections 474(1) and 383 of the Companies Act 2006.

History – In para. 24(1) the words "An officer of Revenue and Customs" substituted for the words "The Inland Revenue" by CRCA 2005, s. 50 and Sch. 4, para. 68(a) and the words "the officer gives" substituted for the words "they give", and the words "the officer's" substituted for the word "their" by virtue of para. 68(c), with effect from 18 April 2005 by virtue of SI 2005/1126, art. 2(2). In para. 24(2), the words "from the day on which the return was delivered (subject to sub-paragraph (6))" substituted for "from the filing date" by FA 2007, s. 96(3) with effect in relation to returns relating to accounting periods ending after 31 March 2008.
Para. 24(6) inserted by FA 2007, s. 96(4) with effect in relation to returns relating to accounting periods ending after 31 March 2008.
Para. 24(7) substituted by SI 2008/954, art. 25, with effect from 6 April 2008.
Former para. 24(7) inserted by FA 2007, s. 96(4) with effect in relation to returns relating to accounting periods ending after 31 March 2008.

Cross references – TMA 1970, s. 12AC: enquiry into partnership return.
SI 2005/3338, reg. 5: modification of para. 24 for the purposes of Lloyd's underwriters.

Other material – HMRC practice relating to large and medium-sized groups following FA 2007 enquiry window changes, reproduced at M06/2008.

SCOPE OF ENQUIRY

25(1) An enquiry into a company tax return extends to anything contained in the return, or required to be contained in the return, including–

(a) any claim or election included in the return,

(b) any amount that affects or may affect–

  (i) the tax payable by that company for another accounting period, or

  (ii) the tax liability of another company for any accounting period,

and also extends to consideration of whether to give the company a notice within sub-paragraph (3). But this is subject to the following limitation.

25(2) If the notice of enquiry is given–

(a) as a result of an amendment by the company of its return, and

(b) at a time when it is no longer possible to give notice of enquiry under paragraph 24(2) or (3),

the enquiry into the return is limited to matters to which the amendment relates or which are affected by the amendment.

25(3) A notice is within this sub-paragraph if it is–

(a) a notice under section 184G or 184H of the Taxation of Chargeable Gains Act 1992 (avoidance involving capital losses),

(b) a notice under section 81(2) of TIOPA 2010 (schemes and arrangements designed to increase relief), or

(c) a transfer pricing notice under section 168(1) of TIOPA 2010 (provision not at arm's length: medium-sized enterprise).

(d) [omitted by FA 2016, s. 66 and Sch. 10, para. 3.]

History – In para. 25(1), the words "a notice within sub-paragraph (3)" substituted for the words "a transfer pricing notice under paragraph 5C of Schedule 28AA to the Taxes Act 1988 (provision not at arm's length: medium-sized enterprise) or a notice under section 804ZA of the Taxes Act 1988 (schemes and arrangements designed to increase relief) or a notice under section 184G or 184H of the Taxation of Chargeable Gains Act 1992 (avoidance involving capital losses) or a notice under section 24 or 26 of the Finance (No. 2) Act 2005 (avoidance involving tax arbitrage)" by TIOPA 2010, s. 374 and Sch. 8, para. 321(2), with effect for corporation tax purposes for accounting periods ending on or after 1 April 2010, for income tax and capital gains tax purposes for the tax year 2010–11 and subsequent tax years, and for petroleum revenue tax purposes for chargeable periods beginning on or after 1 July 2010.
In para. 25(1) the words "or a notice under section 184G or 184H of the Taxation of Chargeable Gains Act 1992 (avoidance involving capital losses)" inserted by FA 2006, s. 71(2), with effect in relation to chargeable gains accruing on any disposal that is made on or after 5 December 2005.
In para. 25(1) the words "or a notice under section 24 or 26 of the Finance (No. 2) Act 2005 (avoidance involving tax arbitrage)" inserted by F(No. 2)A 2005, s. 29(1) with effect:

- in relation to accounting periods of a company beginning on or after 16 March 2005 (but subject to transitional provisions in F(No. 2)A 2005, s. 31(2) and 31(3)), in respect of notices under F(No. 2)A 2005, s. 24;
- in relation to any contribution to the capital of a UK-resident company made on or after 16 March 2005.

In para. 25(1) the words "or a notice under section 804ZA of the Taxes Act 1988 (schemes and arrangements designed to increase relief)" inserted by FA 2005, s. 88(3) with effect from 10 February 2005 (where foreign tax credit is affected by a scheme or arrangement to which ICTA 1988, Sch. 28AB, para. 5 applies) or 16 March 2005 (where the credit is affected by any other scheme or arrangement prescribed by ICTA 1988, Sch. 28AB.)
In para. 25(1)(b), the end words substituted by FA 2004, s. 30 and Sch. 5, para. 10(1), with effect in relation to chargeable periods beginning on or after 1 April 2004 (whenever the actual provision, within the meaning of ICTA 1988, Sch. 28AA, is or was made or imposed).
Para. 25(3)(d) (and the word "or" at the end of para. (c)) omitted and the word "or" inserted at end of para. (b)) by FA 2016, s. 66 and Sch. 10, para. 3, with effect in relation to accounting periods beginning on or after 1 January 2017. Former para. 25(3)(d) read as follows:
  "(d) a notice under section 232 or 249 of TIOPA 2010 (avoidance involving tax arbitrage).".

Para. 25(3) inserted by TIOPA 2010, s. 374 and Sch. 8, para. 321(3), with effect for corporation tax purposes for accounting periods ending on or after 1 April 2010, for income tax and capital gains tax purposes for the tax year 2010–11 and subsequent tax years, and for petroleum revenue tax purposes for chargeable periods beginning on or after 1 July 2010.

Cross references – SI 2005/3338, reg. 5: modification of para. 25 for the purposes of Lloyd's underwriters.

ENQUIRY INTO RETURN FOR WRONG PERIOD

26(1) In the case of a company tax return which appears to an officer of Revenue and Customs–

(a) is or may be a return for the wrong period, or

(b) has become a return for the wrong period as a result of a direction under section 11(3) of the Corporation Tax Act 2009 (power of officer of Revenue and Customs to direct which accounting date to be used where company carries on several trades),

the power to enquire into the return includes power to enquire into the period for which the return ought to have been made.

26(2) A return is a **"return for the wrong period"** in the following cases.

26(3) The first case is where the return is made for a period which is treated in the return as an accounting period, but which is not an accounting period of the company.

26(4) The second case is where the return is made on the basis that there is no accounting period ending in or at the end of the specified period, but there is such an accounting period.

26(5) In relation to a return for the wrong period the references to the filing date in paragraph 24(2) and (3) (period within which notice of enquiry may be given) are to the date that would be the filing date if the period for which the return was made were a period of the kind it is treated as in the return.

26(6) In this paragraph **"the specified period"** means the period specified in the notice requiring a company tax return.

History – In para. 26(1)(b), the words "section 11(3) of the Corporation Tax Act 2009 (power of officer of Revenue and Customs" substituted for the words "section 12(5A) of the Taxes Act 1988 (power of Board" by CTA 2009, s. 1322 and Sch. 1, para. 454(5), with effect for corporation tax purposes for accounting periods ending on or after 1 April 2009, and for income tax and capital gains tax purposes for the tax year 2009–10 and subsequent tax years.

In para. 26(1) the words "an officer of Revenue and Customs" substituted for the words "the Inland Revenue" by CRCA 2005, s. 50 and Sch. 4, para. 68(a), with effect from 18 April 2005 by virtue of SI 2005/1126, art. 2(2).

NOTICE TO PRODUCE DOCUMENTS, ETC. FOR PURPOSES OF ENQUIRY

27 [Omitted by FA 2008, s. 113 and Sch. 36, para. 88.]

History – Para. 27 omitted by FA 2008, s. 113 and Sch. 36, para. 88, with effect from 1 April 2009 (SI 2009/404, art. 2, subject to savings at SI 2009/404, art. 3).

APPEAL AGAINST NOTICE TO PRODUCE DOCUMENTS, ETC.

28 [Omitted by FA 2008, s. 113 and Sch. 36, para. 88.]

History – Para. 28 omitted by FA 2008, s. 113 and Sch. 36, para. 88, with effect from 1 April 2009 (SI 2009/404, art. 2, subject to savings at SI 2009/404, art. 3).

PENALTY FOR FAILURE TO PRODUCE DOCUMENTS, ETC.

29 [Omitted by FA 2008, s. 113 and Sch. 36, para. 88.]

History – Para. 29 omitted by FA 2008, s. 113 and Sch. 36, para. 88, with effect from 1 April 2009 (SI 2009/404, art. 2, subject to savings at SI 2009/404, art. 3).

AMENDMENT OF SELF-ASSESSMENT DURING ENQUIRY TO PREVENT LOSS OF TAX

30(1) If after notice of enquiry has been given and before the enquiry is completed an officer of Revenue and Customs forms the opinion–

(a) that the amount stated in the company's self-assessment as the amount of tax payable is insufficient, and

(b) that unless the assessment is immediately amended there is likely to be a loss of tax to the Crown,

the officer may by notice to the company amend its self-assessment to make good the deficiency.

30(2) *In the case of an enquiry which under paragraph 25(2) is limited to matters arising from an amendment of the return, sub-paragraph (1) above only applies so far as the deficiency is attributable to the amendment.*

30(3) An appeal may be brought against an amendment of a company's self-assessment by an officer of Revenue and Customs under this paragraph.

30(4) Notice of appeal must be given–

(a) in writing,

(b) within 30 days after the amendment was notified to the company,

(c) to the officer of the Board by whom the notice of amendment was given.

30(5) None of the steps mentioned in section 49A(2)(a) to (c) of the Taxes Management Act 1970 may be taken in relation to the appeal before the completion of the enquiry.

History – In para. 30(1) and (3) the words "an officer of Revenue and Customs" substituted for the words "the Inland Revenue" by CRCA 2005, s. 50 and Sch. 4, para. 68(a) and in para. 30(1) the word "forms" substituted for the word "form" and the words "the officer" substituted for the word "they" by virtue of para. 68(c), with effect from 18 April 2005 by virtue of SI 2005/1126, art. 2(2). Para. 30(5) substituted by SI 2009/56, art. 3(1) and Sch. 1, para. 257, operative from 1 April 2009, subject to transitional and saving provisions in SI 2009/56, Sch. 3.

Cross references – TMA 1970, s. 46B(2): questions to be determined by the Special Commissioners.
TMA 1970, s. 46C(2): jurisdiction of the Special Commissioners.
TMA 1970, s. 46D(2): questions to be determined by the Lands Tribunal.
TMA 1970, s. 55(1): recovery of tax.

AMENDMENT OF RETURN BY COMPANY DURING ENQUIRY

31(1) This paragraph applies if a company amends its company tax return at a time when an enquiry is in progress into the return.

31(2) The amendment does not restrict the scope of the enquiry but may be taken into account (together with any matters arising) in the enquiry.

31(3) So far as the amendment affects–

(a) the amount stated in the company's self-assessment as the amount of tax payable, or

(b) any amount that affects or may affect–

(i) the tax payable by the company for another accounting period, or

(ii) the tax liability of another company for any accounting period,

it does not take effect until after the enquiry is completed.

This does not affect any claim by the company under section 59DA of the Taxes Management Act 1970 (claim for repayment in advance of liability being established).

31(4) An amendment whose effect is deferred under sub-paragraph (3) takes effect as follows–

(a) if the conclusions in the closure notice state either–

(i) that the amendment was not taken into account in the enquiry, or

(ii) that no amendment of the return is required arising from the enquiry,

the amendment takes effect on the completion of the enquiry;

(b) in any other case, the amendment takes effect as part of the amendments made by the closure notice.

31(5) For the purposes of this paragraph the period during which an enquiry is in progress is the whole of the period–

(a) beginning with the day on which an officer of Revenue and Customs gives notice of enquiry into the return, and

(b) ending with the day on which the enquiry is completed.

History – Para. 31(4)(b) substituted by FA 2008, s. 119(5), with effect from 1 April 2010 (SI 2009/405).
In para. 31(5)(a) the words "an officer of Revenue and Customs" substituted for the words "the Inland Revenue" by CRCA 2005, s. 50 and Sch. 4, para. 68(a) and the word "gives" substituted for the word "give" by virtue of para. 68(c), with effect from 18 April 2005 by virtue of SI 2005/1126, art. 2(2).

Cross references – SI 2005/3338, reg. 5: modification of para. 31 for the purposes of Lloyd's underwriters.

REFERRAL OF QUESTIONS TO THE TRIBUNAL DURING ENQUIRY

History – In the above heading the words "THE TRIBUNAL" substituted for the words "SPECIAL COMMISSIONERS" by SI 2009/56, art. 3(1) and Sch. 1, para. 258(2), operative from 1 April 2009, subject to transitional and saving provisions in SI 2009/56, Sch. 3.

31A(1) At any time when an enquiry is in progress into a company's tax return any question arising in connection with the subject-matter of the enquiry may be referred to the tribunal for determination.

31A(2) Notice of referral must be given–

(a) jointly by the company and an officer of Revenue and Customs,

(b) [omitted by SI 2009/56, art. 3(1) and Sch. 1, para. 258(4),]

(c) to the tribunal.

31A(3) [Omitted by SI 2009/56, art. 3(1) and Sch. 1, para. 258(5).]

31A(4) More than one notice of referral may be given under this paragraph in relation to an enquiry.

31A(5) For the purposes of this paragraph the period during which an enquiry is in progress is the whole of the period–

(a) beginning with the day on which an officer of Revenue and Customs gives notice of enquiry into the return, and

(b) ending with the day on which the enquiry is completed.

History – In para. 31A(1), the word "tribunal" substituted for the words "Special Commissioners" and the word "their" omitted by SI 2009/56, art. 3(1) and Sch. 1, para. 258(3), operative from 1 April 2009, subject to transitional and saving provisions in SI 2009/56, Sch. 3.
In para. 31A(2)(a) the words "an officer of Revenue and Customs" substituted for the words "the Inland Revenue" by CRCA 2005, s. 50 and Sch. 4, para. 68(a) and the word "gives" substituted for the word "give" by virtue of para. 68(c), with effect from 18 April 2005 by virtue of SI 2005/1126, art. 2(2).
Para. 31A(2)(b) omitted and in para. (c) the word "tribunal" substituted for the words "Special Commissioners" by SI 2009/56, art. 3(1) and Sch. 1, para. 258(4), operative from 1 April 2009, subject to transitional and saving provisions in SI 2009/56, Sch. 3.
Para. 31A(3) omitted by SI 2009/56, art. 3(1) and Sch. 1, para. 258(5), operative from 1 April 2009, subject to transitional and saving provisions in SI 2009/56, Sch. 3.
In para. 31A(5)(a) the words "an officer of Revenue and Customs" substituted for the words "the Inland Revenue" by CRCA 2005, s. 50 and Sch. 4, para. 68(a) and the word "gives" substituted for the word "give" by virtue of para. 68(c), with effect from 18 April 2005 by virtue of SI 2005/1126, art. 2(2).
Para. 31A inserted by FA 2001, s. 88 and Sch. 29, para. 7 with effect for any enquiry in progress under Pt. 4 of Sch. 18 to FA 1998 on 11 May 2001 or where notice is given on or after that date for an enquiry under that Part.

Cross references – TMA 1970, s. 28ZC: regulations with respect to referrals to the Special Commissioners.
SI 2005/3338, reg. 5: modification of para. 31A for the purposes of Lloyd's underwriters.

WITHDRAWAL OF NOTICE OF REFERRAL

31B(1) An officer of Revenue and Customs or the company may withdraw a notice of referral under paragraph 31A.

31B(2) [Omitted by SI 2009/56, art. 3(1) and Sch. 1, para. 259(2).]

History – In para. 31B(1), the words "by notice in accordance with this paragraph" omitted by SI 2009/56, art. 3(1) and Sch. 1, para. 259(2), operative from 1 April 2009, subject to transitional and saving provisions in SI 2009/56, Sch. 3.
In para. 31B(1) the words "an officer of Revenue and Customs" substituted for the words "the Inland Revenue" by CRCA 2005, s. 50 and Sch. 4, para. 68(a), with effect from 18 April 2005 by virtue of SI 2005/1126, art. 2(2).
Para. 31B(2) omitted by SI 2009/56, art. 3(1) and Sch. 1, para. 259(2), operative from 1 April 2009, subject to transitional and saving provisions in SI 2009/56, Sch. 3.
Para. 31B inserted by FA 2001, s. 88 and Sch. 29, para. 7 with effect for any enquiry in progress under Pt. 4 of Sch. 18 to FA 1998 on 11 May 2001 or where notice is given on or after that date for an enquiry under that Part.

Cross references – SI 2005/3338, reg. 5: modification of para. 31B for the purposes of Lloyd's underwriters.

EFFECT OF REFERRAL ON ENQUIRY

31C(1) While proceedings on a referral under paragraph 31A are in progress in relation to an enquiry–

(a) no closure notice shall be given in relation to the enquiry, and

(b) no application may be made for a direction to give such a notice.

31C(2) For the purposes of this paragraph proceedings on a referral are in progress where–

(a) notice of referral has been given,

(b) the notice has not been withdrawn, and

(c) the questions referred have not been finally determined.

31C(3) For the purposes of sub-paragraph (2)(c) a question referred is finally determined when–

(a) it has been determined by the tribunal, and

(b) there is no further possibility of that determination being varied or set aside (disregarding any power to grant permission to appeal out of time).

History – In para. 31C(3)(a), the word "tribunal" substituted for the words "Special Commissioners" by SI 2009/56, art. 3(1) and Sch. 1, para. 260, operative from 1 April 2009, subject to transitional and saving provisions in SI 2009/56, Sch. 3.
Para. 31C inserted by FA 2001, s. 88 and Sch. 29, para. 7 with effect for any enquiry in progress under Pt. 4 of Sch. 18 to FA 1998 on 11 May 2001 or where notice is given on or after that date for an enquiry under that Part.

Cross references – SI 2005/3338, reg. 5: modification of para. 31C for the purposes of Lloyd's underwriters.

EFFECT OF DETERMINATION

31D(1) The determination of a question referred to the tribunal under paragraph 31A is binding on the parties to the referral in the same way, and to the same extent, as a decision on a preliminary issue in an appeal.

31D(2) The determination shall be taken into account by an officer of Revenue and Customs in reaching the officer's conclusions on the enquiry.

31D(3) Any right of appeal under paragraph 30 or 34(3) may not be exercised so as to reopen the question determined except to the extent (if any) that it could be reopened if it had been determined as a preliminary issue in that appeal.

History – In para. 31D(1), the word "tribunal" substituted for the words "Special Commissioners" by SI 2009/56, art. 3(1) and Sch. 1, para. 261, operative from 1 April 2009, subject to transitional and saving provisions in SI 2009/56, Sch. 3.

In para. 31D(2) the words "an officer of Revenue and Customs" substituted for the words "the Inland Revenue" by CRCA 2005, s. 50 and Sch. 4, para. 68(a) and the words "the officer's" substituted for the word "their" by virtue of para. 68(c), with effect from 18 April 2005 by virtue of SI 2005/1126, art. 2(2).
Para. 31D inserted by FA 2001, s. 88 and Sch. 29, para. 7 with effect for any enquiry in progress under Pt. 4 of Sch. 18 to the FA 1998 on 11 May 2001 or where notice is given on or after that date for an enquiry under that Part.

Cross references – SI 2005/3338, reg. 5: modification of para. 31D for the purposes of Lloyd's underwriters.

COMPLETION OF ENQUIRY

32(1) An enquiry is completed when an officer of Revenue and Customs by notice (a "closure notice") informs the company the officer has completed the officer's enquiry and states the officer's conclusions.
The notice takes effect when it is issued.

32(2) If an officer of Revenue and Customs concludes that the return was a return for the wrong period, the closure notice must designate the accounting period for which a return should have been made (specifying the dates on which the period begins and ends).

32(3) If there is more than one accounting period ending in or at the end of the period specified in the notice requiring a return, the closure notice shall only designate the first of those accounting periods for which no return has been delivered.
Paragraph 35 provides for a return to be delivered for any other outstanding accounting period.

History – In para. 32(1) and (2) the words "an officer of Revenue and Customs" substituted for the words "the Inland Revenue" by CRCA 2005, s. 50 and Sch. 4, para. 68(a) and in para. 32(1) the words "informs", "the officer has", "the officer's" (twice) and "states" substituted for the words "inform", "they have", "their" (twice) and "state" and in para. 32(2) the word "concludes" substituted for the word "conclude" by virtue of para. 68(c), with effect from 18 April 2005 by virtue of SI 2005/1126, art. 2(2).

Cross references – FA 2001, Sch. 22, para. 16(3): payment in respect of land remediation tax credit.
FA 2002, s. 54 and Sch. 13, para. 16: tax relief for expenditure on vaccine research – payments in respect of tax credits.
SI 2005/3338, reg. 5: modification of para. 32 for the purposes of Lloyd's underwriters.

DIRECTION TO COMPLETE ENQUIRY

33(1) The company may apply to the tribunal for a direction that an officer of Revenue and Customs gives a closure notice within a specified period.

33(2) Any such application is to be subject to the relevant provisions of Part 5 of the Taxes Management Act 1970 (see, in particular, section 48(2)(b) of that Act).

33(3) The tribunal shall give a direction unless satisfied that an officer of Revenue and Customs has reasonable grounds for not giving a closure notice within a specified period.

History – In para. 33(1), the word "tribunal" substituted for the word "Commissioners" by SI 2009/56, art. 3(1) and Sch. 1, para. 262(2), operative from 1 April 2009, subject to transitional and saving provisions in SI 2009/56, Sch. 3.
In para. 33(1) the words "an officer of Revenue and Customs" substituted for the words "the Inland Revenue" by CRCA 2005, s. 50 and Sch. 4, para. 68(a) and the word "gives" substituted for the word "give" by virtue of para. 68(c), with effect from 18 April 2005 by virtue of SI 2005/1126, art. 2(2).
Para. 33(2) substituted by SI 2009/56, art. 3(1) and Sch. 1, para. 262(3), operative from 1 April 2009, subject to transitional and saving provisions in SI 2009/56, Sch. 3.
In para. 33(3), the word "tribunal" substituted for the words "Commissioners hearing the application" and the words "they are" omitted by SI 2009/56, art. 3(1) and Sch. 1, para. 262(4), operative from 1 April 2009, subject to transitional and saving provisions in SI 2009/56, Sch. 3.
In para. 33(3) the words "an officer of Revenue and Customs" substituted for the words "the Inland Revenue" by CRCA 2005, s. 50 and Sch. 4, para. 68(a) and the word "has" substituted for the word "have" by virtue of para. 68(c), with effect from 18 April 2005 by virtue of SI 2005/1126, art. 2(2).

Cross references – SI 2005/3338, reg. 5: modification of para. 33 for the purposes of Lloyd's underwriters.

AMENDMENT OF RETURN AFTER ENQUIRY

34(1) This paragraph applies where a closure notice is given to a company by an officer.

34(2) The closure notice must–

(a) state that, in the officer's opinion, no amendment is required of the return that was the subject of the enquiry, or

(b) make the amendments of that return that are required–

  (i) to give effect to the conclusions stated in the notice, and

  (ii) in the case of a return for the wrong period, to make it a return appropriate to the designated period.

34(2A) The officer may by further notice to the company make any amendments of other company tax returns delivered by the company that are required to give effect to the conclusions stated in the closure notice.

34(3) An appeal may be brought against an amendment of a company's return under sub-paragraph (2) or (2A).

34(4) Notice of appeal must be given–

(a) in writing,

(b) within 30 days after the amendment was notified to the company,

(c) to the officer of the Board by whom the closure notice was given.

34(5) In this paragraph **"the designated period"** means the period designated in the closure notice.

History – Para. 34(1), (2) and (2A) substituted for former para. 34(1) and (2) by FA 2008, s. 119(6), with effect from 1 April 2010 (SI 2009/405).

In former para. 34(2) the words "an officer of Revenue and Customs" substituted for the words "the Inland Revenue" by CRCA 2005, s. 50 and Sch. 4, para. 68(a) and the words "is", "the officer" and "the officer considers" substituted for the words "are", "they" and "they consider" by virtue of para. 68(c), with effect from 18 April 2005 by virtue of SI 2005/1126, art. 2(2).

In para. 34(3), the words "an amendment of a company's return under sub-paragraph (2) or (2A)" substituted for the words "any such amendment of a company's return" by FA 2008, s. 119(7), with effect from 1 April 2010 (SI 2009/405).

In para. 34(4)(c), the words "closure notice" substituted for "notice of amendment" by FA 2008, s. 119(8), with effect from 1 April 2010 (SI 2009/405).

Cross references – TMA 1970, s. 46B(2): questions to be determined by the Special Commissioners.
TMA 1970, s. 46C(2): jurisdiction of the Special Commissioners.
TMA 1970, s. 46D(2): questions to be determined by the Lands Tribunal.
TMA 1970, s. 55(1): recovery of tax.
FA 1998, Sch. 18, para. 93: general jurisdiction of Special Commissioners.
SI 2005/3338, reg. 5: modification of para. 34 for the purposes of Lloyd's underwriters.

Statements of practice – SP 5/01: Board's approach to extending time limits for making claims for loss relief, capital allowances and group relief.

FURTHER RETURN FOR OUTSTANDING PERIOD

35(1) Where, following an enquiry into a company tax return–

(a) it is finally determined–

(i) that the return is a return for the wrong period, and

(ii) what the period is for which the return should have been made, and

(b) the effect of the determination is that there is a further period ("the outstanding period") for which a company tax return should have been made under the original notice requiring a return,

then, if there is no such return delivered by the company which can be amended so as to become a return for the outstanding period, the original notice shall be taken to require the company to deliver a return in respect of that period.

35(2) The filing date for such a return for an outstanding period is whichever is the later of–

(a) the original filing date, and

(b) the last day of the period of 30 days beginning with the day on which the matters mentioned in sub-paragraph (1)(a) are finally determined.

Part V – Revenue Determinations and Assessments

DETERMINATION OF TAX PAYABLE IF NO RETURN DELIVERED IN RESPONSE TO NOTICE

36(1) If no return is delivered in response to a notice requiring a company tax return, an officer of Revenue and Customs may determine to the best of the officer's information and belief the amount of tax payable by the company.

36(2) The power to make a determination under this paragraph becomes exercisable if no return is delivered on or before the following date–

(a) if the filing date for any return required by the notice can be ascertained, that date;

(b) if no such date can be ascertained, the later of–

(i) 18 months from the end of the period specified in the notice, or

(ii) three months from the day on which the notice was served.

36(3) The accounting period or periods for which a determination may be made are–

(a) if there is only one accounting period ending in or at the end of the period specified in the notice, that period;

(b) if there is more than one accounting period ending in or at the end of the period specified in the notice, each of those periods;

(c) if an officer of Revenue and Customs has insufficient information to identify the accounting periods of the company, such period or periods ending in or at the end of the period specified in the notice as the officer may determine.

36(4) Notice of a determination under this paragraph must be served on the company, stating the date on which the determination is issued.

36(5) No determination under this paragraph may be made more than 3 years after the day on which the power becomes exercisable.

36(6) If the company shows–

(a) that there is no accounting period of the company ending in or at the end of the period specified in the notice, or

(b) that it has delivered a return for the accounting period, or each accounting period, ending in or at the end of the period specified in the notice, or

(c) that no return is yet due for any such period,

any determination under this paragraph is of no effect.

History – In para. 36(1) and (3)(c) the words "an officer of Revenue and Customs" substituted for the words "the Inland Revenue" by CRCA 2005, s. 50 and Sch. 4, para. 68(a) and in para. 36(1) the words "the officer's" substituted for the words "their" and in para. 36(3)(c) the words "has" and "the officer" substituted for the words "have" and "they" by virtue of para. 68(c), with effect from 18 April 2005 by virtue of SI 2005/1126, art. 2(2).

In para. 36(5), "3 years" substituted for "five years" by FA 2008, s. 118 and Sch. 39, para. 38, with effect from 1 April 2010 (SI 2009/403, art. 2(2) subject to SI 2009/403, art. 3–10 – in particular art. 10).

Cross references – FA 2002, s. 84(1) and Sch. 29, para. 70: time limit for recovery of a degrouping charge from another group company or controlling director.

SI 2005/3338, reg. 6: modification of para. 36 for the purposes of Lloyd's underwriters.

DETERMINATION OF TAX PAYABLE IF NOTICE COMPLIED WITH IN PART

37(1) If a notice requiring a company tax return is served on a company and–

(a) a return is delivered for an accounting period ending in or at the end of the period specified in the notice, but

(b) there is another period so ending (the "outstanding period") which appears to an officer of Revenue and Customs is or may be an accounting period,

an officer of Revenue and Customs may determine to the best of their information and belief the amount of corporation tax payable by the company for the outstanding period.

37(2) The power to make a determination under this paragraph becomes exercisable–

(a) if the filing date for the outstanding period can be ascertained and no return is delivered on or before that date;

(b) if no such date can be ascertained and no return for that period is delivered by the later of–

  (i) 30 months from the end of the period specified in the notice, or

  (ii) three months from the day on which the notice was served.

37(3) Notice of a determination under this paragraph must be served on the company, stating the date on which the determination is issued.

37(4) No determination under this paragraph may be made more than 3 years after the day on which the power first became exercisable.

37(5) If the company shows–

(a) that the outstanding period is not an accounting period, or

(b) that it has delivered a return for that period,

any determination under this paragraph is of no effect.

History – In para. 37(1) the words "an officer of Revenue and Customs" substituted for the words "the Inland Revenue" twice by CRCA 2005, s. 50 and Sch. 4, para. 68(a), with effect from 18 April 2005 by virtue of SI 2005/1126, art. 2(2).

In para. 37(4), "3 years" substituted for "five years" by FA 2008, s. 118 and Sch. 39, para. 39, with effect from 1 April 2010 (SI 2009/403, art. 2(2) subject to SI 2009/403, art. 3–10 – in particular art. 10).

Cross references – FA 2002, s. 84(1) and Sch. 29, para. 70: time limit for recovery of a degrouping charge from another group company or controlling director.

EXTENT OF POWER TO MAKE DETERMINATION

38(1) The power to make a determination under paragraph 36 or 37 includes power to determine–

(a) any of the amounts mentioned in paragraph 8(1) (calculation of amount of tax payable), and

(b) any amount forming part of the calculation of any of those amounts.

38(2) Notice of a determination under either of those paragraphs may be accompanied by notice of any determination by an officer of Revenue and Customs relating to the dates on which amounts of tax become due and payable under section 59D or 59E of the Taxes Management Act 1970.

History – In para. 38(2) the words "an officer of Revenue and Customs" substituted for the words "the Inland Revenue" by CRCA 2005, s. 50 and Sch. 4, para. 68(a), with effect from 18 April 2005 by virtue of SI 2005/1126, art. 2(2).

DETERMINATION TO HAVE EFFECT AS SELF-ASSESSMENT

39(1) A determination under paragraph 36 or 37 has effect for enforcement purposes as if it were a self-assessment by the company.

39(2) In sub-paragraph (1) **"or enforcement purposes"** means for the purposes of–

(a) the following Parts of the Taxes Management Act 1970–
Part VA (payment),
Part VI (collection and recovery),
Part IX (interest on overdue tax), and
Part XI (miscellaneous and supplementary provisions);

(b) the provisions of this Schedule imposing tax-related penalties; and

(c) the provisions of the Corporation Tax Acts enabling unpaid tax assessed on a company to be assessed on other persons.

39(3) For those purposes the period for which the determination is made shall be treated as an accounting period of the company, even though–

(a) in the case of a determination under paragraph 36, an officer of Revenue and Customs has insufficient information to determine the accounting periods of the company and exercise the officer's power under sub-paragraph (3)(c) of that paragraph, or

(b) in the case of a determination under paragraph 37, an officer of Revenue and Customs has insufficient information to determine whether the outstanding period is an accounting period.

History – In para. 39(3)(a) and (b) the words "an officer of Revenue and Customs" substituted for the words "the Inland Revenue" by CRCA 2005, s. 50 and Sch. 4, para. 68(a) and the words "has" (twice) and "the officer's" substituted for the words "have" (twice) and "their" by virtue of para. 68(c), with effect from 18 April 2005 by virtue of SI 2005/1126, art. 2(2).

DETERMINATION SUPERSEDED BY ACTUAL SELF-ASSESSMENT

40(1) If after a determination has been made under paragraph 36–

(a) the company delivers a company tax return for a period ending in or at the end of the period specified in the notice requiring a company tax return, and

(b) the period is, or is treated in the return as, an accounting period,

the self-assessment included in that return supersedes the determination or, if there is more than one, the determination for the period which is, or most closely approximates to, the period for which the return is made.

40(2) If after a determination has been made under paragraph 37–

(a) the company delivers a further company tax return for a period ending in or at the end of the period specified in the notice requiring a company tax return, and

(b) the period is, or is treated in the return as, an accounting period,

the self-assessment included in that return supersedes the determination.

40(3) Sub-paragraphs (1) and (2) do not apply to a return made–

(a) more than 3 years after the day on which the power to make the determination first became exercisable (see paragraph 36(2) or 37(2)), or

(b) more than twelve months after the date of the determination,

whichever is the later.

40(4) Where–

(a) proceedings have been begun for the recovery of any tax charged by a determination under paragraph 36 or 37, and

(b) before the proceedings are concluded the determination is superseded by a self-assessment,

the proceedings may be continued as if they were proceedings for the recovery of so much of the tax charged by the self-assessment as is due and payable and has not been paid.

40(5) Where–

(a) action is being taken under Part 1 of Schedule 8 to the Finance (No. 2) Act 2015 (enforcement of deduction from accounts) for the recovery of an amount (**"the original amount"**) of any tax charged by a determination under paragraph 36 or 37, and

(b) before that action is concluded, the determination is superseded by a self-assessment,

that action may be continued as if it were action for the purposes of the recovery of so much of the tax charged by the self-assessment as is due and payable, has not been paid and does not exceed the original amount.

History – In para. 40(3), "3 years" substituted for "five years" by FA 2008, s. 118 and Sch. 39, para. 40, with effect from 1 April 2010 (SI 2009/403, art. 2(2) subject to SI 2009/403, art. 3–10 – in particular art. 10).

In para. 40(4) words "proceedings have been begun" substituted for "the Inland Revenue have begun proceedings" by FA 2001, s. 88 and Sch. 29, para. 17(2), in relation to proceedings begun after 11 May 2001.
Para. 40(5) inserted by F(No. 2)A 2015, s. 51 and Sch. 8, para. 40, with effect from 18 November 2015 (Royal Assent).

Cross references – FA 2002, s. 84(1) and Sch. 29, para. 70: time limit for recovery of a degrouping charge from another group company or controlling director.
SI 2005/3338, reg. 6: modification of para. 40 for the purposes of Lloyd's underwriters.

ASSESSMENT WHERE LOSS OF TAX DISCOVERED OR DETERMINATION OF AMOUNT DISCOVERED TO BE INCORRECT

41(1) If an officer of Revenue and Customs discovers as regards an accounting period of a company that–

(a) an amount which ought to have been assessed to tax has not been assessed, or

(b) an assessment to tax is or has become insufficient, or

(c) relief has been given which is or has become excessive,

the officer may make an assessment (a "discovery assessment") in the amount or further amount which ought in their opinion to be charged in order to make good to the Crown the loss of tax.

41(2) If an officer of Revenue and Customs discovers that a company tax return delivered by a company for an accounting period incorrectly states–

(a) an amount that affects, or may affect, the tax payable by that company for another accounting period, or

(b) an amount that affects, or may affect, the tax liability of another company,

the officer may make a determination (a "discovery determination") of the amount which in their opinion ought to have been stated in the return.

History – In para. 41(1) and (2) the words "an officer of Revenue and Customs" substituted for the words "the Inland Revenue" by CRCA 2005, s. 50 and Sch. 4, para. 68(a) and the words "discovers" and "the officer" substituted for the words "discover" and "they" by virtue of para. 68(c), with effect from 18 April 2005 by virtue of SI 2005/1126, art. 2(2).

Cross references – ICTA 1988, s. 588(5): time limit for discovery assessment or determination for employers incurring training costs in respect of employees.
SI 2005/3338, reg. 7: modification of para. 41(2) for the purposes of Lloyd's underwriters.

Statements of practice – SP 5/01: HMRC's approach to extending time limits for making claims for loss relief, capital allowances and group relief.
SP 01/06: HMRC approach to finality and discovery.

Other material – Tax Bulletin TB08/01-6: guidance on when Revenue will find it more convenient to raise a "discovery" assessment than to open an enquiry.

RESTRICTIONS ON POWER TO MAKE DISCOVERY ASSESSMENT OR DETERMINATION

42(1) The power to make–

(a) a discovery assessment for an accounting period for which the company has delivered a company tax return, or

(b) a discovery determination,

is only exercisable in the circumstances specified in paragraph 43 or 44 and subject to paragraph 45 below.

42(2) Those restrictions do not apply to an assessment or determination which only gives effect to a discovery determination duly made with respect to an amount stated in another company's company tax return.

42(2A) Those restrictions, other than the restriction in paragraph 45, do not apply so far as regards any income or chargeable gains of the company in relation to which the company has been given, after any enquiries have been completed into the return, a notice within sub-paragraph (4).

42(3) Any objection to a discovery assessment or determination on the ground that those paragraphs have not been complied with can only be made on an appeal against the assessment or determination.

42(4) A notice is within this sub-paragraph if it is–

(a) a notice under section 184G or 184H of the Taxation of Chargeable Gains Act 1992 (avoidance involving capital losses), or

(b) a notice under section 81(2) of TIOPA 2010 (schemes and arrangements designed to increase relief),

(c) [omitted by FA 2016, s. 66 and Sch. 10, para. 4.]

History – In para. 42(2A), the words "within sub-paragraph (4)." substituted for the words "under section 804ZA of the Taxes Act 1988 or section 184G or 184H of the Taxation of Chargeable Gains Act 1992 or section 24 or 26 of the Finance (No. 2) Act 2005." by TIOPA 2010, s. 374 and Sch. 8, para. 321(4), with effect for corporation tax purposes for accounting periods ending on or after 1 April 2010, for income tax and capital gains tax purposes for the tax year 2010–11 and subsequent tax years, and for petroleum revenue tax purposes for chargeable periods beginning on or after 1 July 2010.
In para. 42(2A) the words "or section 184G or 184H of the Taxation of Chargeable Gains Act 1992" inserted by FA 2006, s. 71(3), with effect in relation to chargeable gains accruing on any disposal that is made on or after 5 December 2005.
In para. 42(2A) the words "or section 24 or 26 of the Finance (No. 2) Act 2005" inserted by F(No. 2)A 2005, s. 29(2) with effect:

- in relation to accounting periods of a company beginning on or after 16 March 2005 (but subject to transitional provisions in F(No. 2)A 2005, s. 31(2) and 31(3)), in respect of notices under F(No. 2)A 2005, s. 24;
- in relation to any contribution to the capital of a UK resident company made on or after 16 March 2005.

Para. 42(2A) inserted by FA 2005, s. 88(4) with effect from 10 February 2005 (where foreign tax credit is affected by a scheme or arrangement to which ICTA 1988, Sch. 28AB, para 5, applies) or 16 March 2005 (where the credit is affected by any other scheme or arrangement prescribed by ICTA 1988, Sch. 28AB).

Para. 42(4)(c) (and the word "or" at the end of para. (b)) omitted and the word "or" inserted at end of para. (a)) by FA 2016, s. 66 and Sch. 10, para. 4, with effect in relation to accounting periods beginning on or after 1 January 2017. Former para. 42(4)(c) read as follows:

"(c) a notice under section 232 or 249 of TIOPA 2010 (avoidance involving tax arbitrage).".

Para. 42(4) inserted by TIOPA 2010, s. 374 and Sch. 8, para. 321(5), with effect for corporation tax purposes for accounting periods ending on or after 1 April 2010, for income tax and capital gains tax purposes for the tax year 2010–11 and subsequent tax years, and for petroleum revenue tax purposes for chargeable periods beginning on or after 1 July 2010.

Cross references – SI 2005/3338, reg. 7: modification of para. 42 for the purposes of Lloyd's underwriters.

Other material – Tax Bulletin TB08/01-6: guidance on when HMRC will find it more convenient to raise a "discovery" assessment than to open an enquiry.

LOSS OF TAX BROUGHT ABOUT CARELESSLY OR DELIBERATELY

History – The wording of the heading before para. 43 substituted by FA 2008, s. 118 and Sch. 39, para. 41(3), with effect from 1 April 2010 (SI 2009/403, art. 2(2) subject to SI 2009/403, art. 3–10 – in particular art. 10). The former wording was "Fraudulent or negligent conduct".

43 A discovery assessment for an accounting period for which the company has delivered a company tax return, or a discovery determination, may be made if the situation mentioned in paragraph 41(1) or (2) was brought about carelessly or deliberately by–

(a) the company, or

(b) a person acting on behalf of the company, or

(c) a person who was a partner of the company at the relevant time.

History – In para. 43, the words "was brought about carelessly or deliberately by" substituted for the words "is attributable to fraudulent or negligent conduct on the part of" by FA 2008, s. 118 and Sch. 39, para. 41(2), with effect from 1 April 2010 (SI 2009/403, art. 2(2) subject to SI 2009/403, art. 3–10 – in particular art. 10).

Cross references – SI 2005/3338, reg. 7: modification of para. 43 for the purposes of Lloyd's underwriters.

Other material – Tax Bulletin TB08/01-6: guidance on when HMRC will find it more convenient to raise a "discovery" assessment than to open an enquiry.

SITUATION NOT DISCLOSED BY RETURN OR RELATED DOCUMENTS ETC.

44(1) A discovery assessment for an accounting period for which the company has delivered a company tax return, or a discovery determination, may be made if at the time when an officer of Revenue and Customs–

(a) ceased to be entitled to give a notice of enquiry into the return, or

(b) completed the officer's enquiries into the return,

the officer could not have been reasonably expected, on the basis of the information made available to them before that time, to be aware of the situation mentioned in paragraph 41(1) or (2).

44(2) For this purpose information is regarded as made available to an officer of Revenue and Customs if–

(a) it is contained in a relevant return by the company or in documents accompanying any such return, or

(b) it is contained in a relevant claim made by the company or in any accounts, statements or documents accompanying any such claim, or

(c) it is contained in any documents, accounts or information produced or provided by the company to an officer of Revenue and Customs for the purposes of an enquiry into any such return or claim, or

(d) it is information the existence of which, and the relevance of which as regards the situation mentioned in paragraph 41(1) or (2)–

  (i) could reasonably be expected to be inferred by an officer of Revenue and Customs from information falling within paragraphs (a) to (c) above, or

  (ii) are notified in writing to an officer of Revenue and Customs by the company or a person acting on its behalf.

44(3) In sub-paragraph (2)–

"relevant return" means the company's company tax return for the period in question or either of the two immediately preceding accounting periods, and

"relevant claim" means a claim made by or on behalf of the company as regards the period in question or an application under section 751A of the Taxes Act 1988 made by or on behalf of the company which affects the company's tax return for the period in question.

History – In para. 44(1) the words "an officer of Revenue and Customs" substituted for the words "the Inland Revenue" by CRCA 2005, s. 50 and Sch. 4, para. 68(a) and the words "the officer's" and "the officer" substituted for the words "their" and "they" by virtue of para. 68(c), with effect from 18 April 2005 by virtue of SI 2005/1126, art. 2(2).
In para. 44(2) the words "an officer of Revenue and Customs" substituted for the words "the Inland Revenue" four times by CRCA 2005, s. 50 and Sch. 4, para. 68(a), with effect from 18 April 2005 by virtue of SI 2005/1126, art. 2(2).
In para. 44(3), in the definition of "relevant claim", the words "or an application under section 751A of the Taxes Act 1988 made by or on behalf of the company which affects the company's tax return for the period in question" inserted by FA 2007, s. 48 and Sch. 15, para. 9 with effect in relation to accounting periods of controlled foreign companies beginning on or after 6 December 2006 (subject to the transitional provisions in FA 2007, Sch. 15, para. 10(2)).

Cross references – ICTA 1988, s. 804ZC(6): Para. 44(2) and (3) apply for the purposes of s. 804
F(No. 2)A 2005, s. 28(6): para. 44(2) and 44(3) to apply for the purposes of s. 28(5).
ICTA 1988, s. 184I (6): para 44(2) and 44(3) to apply for the purposes of requirement A of that section.
SI 2005/3338, reg. 7: modification of para. 44 for the purposes of Lloyd's underwriters.

Statements of practice – SP 01/06: HMRC approach to finality and discovery.

Other material – Tax Bulletin TB08/01-6: guidance on when HMRC will find it more convenient to raise a "discovery" assessment than to open an enquiry.

RETURN MADE IN ACCORDANCE WITH PREVAILING PRACTICE

45 No discovery assessment for an accounting period for which the company has delivered a company tax return, or discovery determination, may be made if–

(a) the situation mentioned in paragraph 41(1) or (2) is attributable to a mistake in the return as to the basis on which the company's liability ought to have been computed, and

(b) the return was in fact made on the basis or in accordance with the practice generally prevailing at the time when it was made.

Other material – Tax Bulletin TB08/01-6: guidance on when HMRC will find it more convenient to raise a "discovery" assessment than to open an enquiry.

GENERAL TIME LIMITS FOR ASSESSMENTS

46(1) Subject to any provision of the Taxes Acts allowing a longer period in any particular class of case no assessment may be made more than 4 years after the end of the accounting period to which it relates.

46(2) An assessment in a case involving a loss of tax brought about carelessly by the company (or a related person) may be made at any time not more than 6 years after the end of the accounting period to which it relates (subject to sub-paragraph (2A) and to any other provision of the Taxes Acts allowing a longer period).

46(2A) An assessment in a case involving a loss of tax–

(a) brought about deliberately by the company (or a related person),

(b) attributable to a failure by the company to comply with an obligation under paragraph 2,

(c) attributable to arrangements in respect of which the company has failed to comply with an obligation under section 309, 310 or 313 of the Finance Act 2004 (obligation of parties to tax avoidance schemes to provide information to Her Majesty's Revenue and Customs), or

(d) attributable to arrangements which were expected to give rise to a tax advantage in respect of which the company was under an obligation to notify the Commissioners for Her Majesty's Revenue and Customs under section 253 of the Finance Act 2014 (duty to notify Commissioners of promoter reference number) but failed to do so.

may be made at any time not more than 20 years after the end of the accounting period to which it relates (subject to any provision of the Taxes Acts allowing a longer period).

46(2B) In this paragraph, **"related person"**, in relation to a company, means–

(a) a person acting on behalf of the company, or

(b) a person who was a partner of the company at the relevant time.

46(3) Any objection to the making of an assessment on the ground that the time limit for making it has expired can only be made on an appeal against the assessment.

History – In para. 46(1), "4 years" substituted for "six years" by FA 2008, s. 118 and Sch. 39, para. 42(2), with effect from 1 April 2010 (SI 2009/403, art. 2(2) subject to SI 2009/403, art. 3–10 – in particular art. 10).
Para. 46(2A)(d) inserted (and the "or" at the end of para. 46(2A)(b) omitted, and the ", or" at the end of para. 46(2A)(c) inserted) by FA 2014, s. 277(4), with effect from 17 July 2014. It is assumed that the full stop at the end of para. 46(2A)(d) is included due to a parliamentary drafting error.
Para. 46(2), (2A) and (2B) substituted for former para. 46(2) by FA 2008, s. 118 and Sch. 39, para. 42(3), with effect from 1 April 2010 (SI 2009/403, art. 2(2) subject to SI 2009/403, art. 3–10 – in particular art. 10).

Cross references – SI 2005/3338, reg. 7: modification of para. 46 for the purposes of Lloyd's underwriters.

ASSESSMENT PROCEDURE

47(1) Notice of an assessment to tax on a company must be served on the company stating–

(a) the date on which the notice is issued, and

(b) the time within which any appeal against the assessment may be made.

47(2) After that notice has been served on the company, the assessment may not be altered except in accordance with the express provisions of the Taxes Acts.

Cross references – SI 2005/3338, reg. 7: modification of para. 47 for the purposes of Lloyd's underwriters.

APPEAL AGAINST ASSESSMENT

48(1) An appeal may be brought against any assessment to tax on a company which is not a self-assessment.

48(2) Notice of appeal must be given–

(a) in writing,

(b) within 30 days after notice of the assessment was issued,

(c) to the officer of the Board by whom the notice of the assessment was given.

Cross references – SI 2005/3338, reg. 7: modification of para. 48 for the purposes of Lloyd's underwriters.

APPLICATION OF PROVISIONS TO DISCOVERY DETERMINATIONS

49 The provisions of paragraphs 46 to 48 (assessments: general provisions as to time limits, procedure and appeals) apply to a discovery determination as they apply to an assessment.

Cross references – SI 2005/3338, reg. 7: modification of para. 49 for the purposes of Lloyd's underwriters.

Part VI – Overpaid Tax, Excessive Assessments or Repayments, etc.

History – In the heading of Pt. VI, the words "Overpaid Tax," inserted by FA 2009, s. 100 and Sch. 52, para. 14, with effect in relation to claims made on or after 1 April 2010.

RELIEF IN CASE OF DOUBLE ASSESSMENT

50(1) A company which believes it has been assessed to tax more than once for the same cause and for the same accounting period may make a claim for relief–

(a) by notice in writing,

(b) given to the Board.

50(2) If on a claim being made the Board are satisfied that the company has been assessed to tax more than once for the same cause and for the same accounting period, they shall amend the assessment or assessments concerned, or give relief by way of discharge or repayment of tax or otherwise, so as to eliminate the double charge.

50(3) An appeal may be brought against the Board's decision on a claim for relief under this paragraph.

History – Para. 50(3) substituted by SI 2009/56, art. 3(1) and Sch. 1, para. 263, operative from 1 April 2009, subject to transitional and saving provisions in SI 2009/56, Sch. 3.

CLAIM FOR RELIEF FOR OVERPAID TAX ETC

51(1) This paragraph applies where–

(a) a person has paid an amount by way of tax but believes that the tax was not due, or

(b) a person has been assessed as liable to pay an amount by way of tax, or there has been a determination or direction to that effect, but the person believes that the tax is not due.

51(2) The person may make a claim to the Commissioners for Her Majesty's Revenue and Customs for repayment or discharge of the amount.

51(3) Paragraph 51A makes provision about cases in which the Commissioners for Her Majesty's Revenue and Customs are not liable to give effect to a claim under this paragraph.

51(4) The following make further provision about making and giving effect to claims under this paragraph–

(a) paragraphs 51B to 51F and Part 7 of this Schedule, and

(b) Schedule 1A to the Taxes Management Act 1970 (which is applied by that Part).

51(5) Paragraph 51G makes provision about the application of this paragraph and paragraphs 51A to 51F to amounts paid under contract settlements.

51(6) The Commissioners for Her Majesty's Revenue and Customs are not liable to give relief in respect of a case described in sub-paragraph (1)(a) or (b) except as provided–

(a) by this Schedule and Schedule 1A to the Taxes Management Act 1970 (following a claim under this paragraph), or

(b) by or under another provision of the Corporation Tax Acts.

51(7) For the purposes of this paragraph and paragraphs 51A to 51G, an amount paid by one person on behalf of another is treated as paid by the other person.

History – Para. 51 substituted (with para. 51A–51G) for current para. 51 by FA 2009, s. 100 and Sch. 52, para. 13, with effect in relation to claims made on or after 1 April 2010.
In former para. 51(1)(c) , "4 years" substituted for "six years" by FA 2008, s. 118 and Sch. 39, para. 43, with effect from 1 April 2010 (SI 2009/403, art. 2(2) subject to SI 2009/403, art. 3–10 – in particular art. 10).
In former para. 51(5), the words "tribunal shall" substituted for the words "Special Commissioners shall hear and" by SI 2009/56, art. 3(1) and Sch. 1, para. 264(2), operative from 1 April 2009, subject to transitional and saving provisions in SI 2009/56, Sch. 3.
In former para. 51(6), the words "under section 56A of the Taxes Management Act 1970" omitted and the word "tribunal" substituted for the words "Special Commissioners" by SI 2009/56, art. 3(1) and Sch. 1, para. 264(3), operative from 1 April 2009, subject to transitional and saving provisions in SI 2009/56, Sch. 3.

CASES IN WHICH COMMISSIONERS NOT LIABLE TO GIVE EFFECT TO A CLAIM

51A(1) The Commissioners for Her Majesty's Revenue and Customs are not liable to give effect to a claim under paragraph 51 if or to the extent that the claim falls within a case described in this paragraph (see also paragraphs 51BA and 51C(5)).

51A(2) Case A is where the amount paid, or liable to be paid, is excessive by reason of–

(a) a mistake in a claim, election or a notice,

(b) a mistake consisting of making or giving, or failing to make or give, a claim, election or notice,

(c) a mistake in allocating expenditure to a pool for the purposes of the Capital Allowances Act or a mistake consisting of making, or failing to make, such an allocation, or

(d) a mistake in bringing a disposal value into account for the purposes of that Act or a mistake consisting of bringing, or failing to bring, such a value into account.

51A(3) Case B is where the claimant is or will be able to seek relief by taking other steps under the Corporation Tax Acts.

51A(4) Case C is where the claimant–

(a) could have sought relief by taking such steps within a period that has now expired, and

(b) knew, or ought reasonably to have known, before the end of that period that such relief was available.

51A(5) Case D is where the claim is made on grounds that–

(a) have been put to a court or tribunal in the course of an appeal by the claimant relating to the amount paid or liable to be paid, or

(b) have been put to Her Majesty's Revenue and Customs in the course of an appeal by the claimant relating to that amount that is treated as having been determined by a tribunal (by virtue of section 54 of the Taxes Management Act 1970 (settling of appeals by agreement)).

51A(6) Case E is where the claimant knew, or ought reasonably to have known, of the grounds for the claim before the latest of the following–

(a) the date on which an appeal by the claimant relating to the amount paid, or liable to be paid, in the course of which the ground could have been put forward (a "relevant appeal") was determined by a court or tribunal (or is treated as having been so determined),

(b) the date on which the claimant withdrew a relevant appeal to a court or tribunal, and

(c) the end of the period in which the claimant was entitled to make a relevant appeal to a court or tribunal.

51A(7) Case F is where the amount in question was paid or is liable to be paid–

(a) in consequence of proceedings enforcing the payment of that amount brought against the claimant by Her Majesty's Revenue and Customs, or

(b) in accordance with an agreement between the claimant and Her Majesty's Revenue and Customs settling such proceedings.

51A(8) Case G is where–

(a) the amount paid, or liable to be paid, is excessive by reason of a mistake in calculating the claimant's liability to corporation tax, and

(b) liability was calculated in accordance with the practice generally prevailing at the time.

51A(9) Case G does not apply where the amount paid, or liable to be paid, is tax which has been charged contrary to EU law.

51A(10) For the purposes of sub-paragraph (9), an amount of tax is charged contrary to EU law if, in the circumstances in question, the charge to tax is contrary to–

(a) the provisions relating to the free movement of goods, persons, services and capital in Titles II and IV of Part 3 of the Treaty on the Functioning of the European Union, or

(b) the provisions of any subsequent treaty replacing the provisions mentioned in paragraph (a).

History – In para. 51A(1), "paragraphs 51BA and 51C(5)" substituted for "paragraph 51C(5)" by SI 2011/1037, art. 3(2), with effect from 1 April 2011, and in relation to determinations (within the meaning of para. 36 or 37) made before 1 April 2011 (as in relation to determinations made on or after that date). But the substitution does not apply in relation to a determination made before that date if a claim for relief in respect of it has already been refused before that date.
Para. 51A(9) inserted by FA 2013, s. 231(3), with effect in relation to any claim (in respect of overpaid tax, excessive assessment etc) made after the end of the six month period beginning with 17 July 2013.
Para. 51A(10) inserted by FA 2013, s. 231(3), with effect in relation to any claim (in respect of overpaid tax, excessive assessment etc) made after the end of the six month period beginning with 17 July 2013.
Para. 51A effectively inserted by FA 2009, s. 100 and Sch. 52, para. 13, with effect in relation to claims made on or after 1 April 2010.

MAKING A CLAIM

51B(1) A claim under paragraph 51 may not be made more than 4 years after the end of the relevant accounting period.

51B(2) In relation to a claim made in reliance on paragraph 51(1)(a), the relevant accounting period is–

(a) where the amount paid, or liable to be paid, is excessive by reason of a mistake in a company tax return or returns, the accounting period to which the return (or, if more than one, the first return) relates, and

(b) otherwise, the accounting period in respect of which the amount was paid.

51B(3) In relation to a claim made in reliance on paragraph 51(1)(b), the relevant accounting period is–

(a) where the amount liable to be paid is excessive by reason of a mistake in a company tax return or returns, the accounting period to which the return (or, if more than one, the first return) relates, and

(b) otherwise, the accounting period to which the assessment, determination or direction relates.

51B(4) A claim under paragraph 51 may not be made by being included in a company tax return.

51B(5) Sub-paragraph (1) is subject to paragraph 51BA.

History – Para. 51B(3)(a) and (b) (and the "–" before) inserted by FA 2013, s. 232 with effect in relation to any claim (in respect of overpaid tax, excessive assessment etc) made after the end of the six month period beginning with 17 July 2013.
Para. 51B(5) inserted by SI 2011/1037, art. 3(3), with effect from 1 April 2011, and in relation to determinations (within the meaning of para. 36 or 37) made before 1 April 2011 (as in relation to determinations made on or after that date). But the insertion does not apply in relation to a determination made before that date if a claim for relief in respect of it has already been refused before that date.
Para. 51B effectively inserted by FA 2009, s. 100 and Sch. 52, para. 13, with effect in relation to claims made on or after 1 April 2010.

DETERMINATIONS UNDER PARAGRAPHS 36 AND 37: SPECIAL RULES

51BA(1) This paragraph applies where–

(a) a determination has been made under paragraph 36 or 37 of an amount that a person is liable to pay by way of tax, but the person believes the tax is not due or, if it has been paid, was not due,

(b) relief would be available under paragraph 51 but for the fact that–

(i) the claim falls within Case C (see paragraph 51A(4)),

(ii) the claim falls within Case F(a) (see paragraph 51A(7)(a)), or

(iii) more than 4 years have elapsed since the end of the relevant accounting period (see paragraph 51B(1)), and

(c) if the claim falls within Case F(a), the person was neither present nor legally represented during the enforcement proceedings in question.

51BA(2) A claim under paragraph 51 for repayment or discharge of the amount may be made, and effect given to it, despite paragraph 51A(4), paragraph 51A(7)(a) or paragraph 51B(1), as the case may be.

51BA(3) But the Commissioners for Her Majesty's Revenue and Customs are not liable to give effect to a claim made in reliance on this paragraph unless conditions A, B and C are met.

51BA(4) Condition A is that in the opinion of the Commissioners for Her Majesty's Revenue and Customs it would be unconscionable for the Commissioners for Her Majesty's Revenue and Customs to seek to recover the amount (or to withhold repayment of it, if it has already been paid).

51BA(5) *Condition* B is that the person's affairs (as respects matters concerning the Commissioners for Her Majesty's Revenue and Customs) are otherwise up to date or arrangements have been put in place, to the satisfaction of the Commissioners for Her Majesty's Revenue and Customs, to bring them up to date so far as possible.

51BA(6) Condition C is that either–

(a) the person has not relied on this paragraph on a previous occasion (whether or not in respect of the same determination), or

(b) the person has done so, but in the exceptional circumstances of the case should be allowed to do so again on the present occasion.

51BA(7) For the purposes of sub-paragraph (6)–

(a) a person has relied on this paragraph on a previous occasion if the person has made a claim (or a composite set of claims involving one or more determinations and accounting periods) in reliance on this paragraph on a previous occasion, and

(b) it does not matter whether that claim (or set of claims) succeeded.

51BA(8) A claim made in reliance on this paragraph must include (in addition to anything required by Schedule 1A to the Taxes Management Act 1970) such information and documentation as is reasonably required for the purpose of determining whether conditions A, B and C are met.

History – Para. 51BA inserted by SI 2011/1037, art. 3(4), with effect from 1 April 2011, and in relation to determinations (within the meaning of para. 36 or 37) made before 1 April 2011 (as in relation to determinations made on or after that date). But the insertion does not apply in relation to a determination made before that date if a claim for relief in respect of it has already been refused before that date.

Notes – By virtue of SI 2011/1037, art. 4 (not reproduced), in para. 51BA(6) and (7) references to reliance "on this paragraph" include reliance before 1 April 2011 on the concession which para. 51BA replaces (the "equitable liability" concession, described in TB 08/95-7).

THE CLAIMANT: ONE PERSON ACCOUNTABLE FOR AMOUNTS PAYABLE BY ANOTHER

51C(1) Sub-paragraph (2) applies where a person ("P") is accountable to the Commissioners for Her Majesty's Revenue and Customs under a relevant enactment for an amount that has been or is to be set off against a liability of another person ("T") under a relevant enactment.

51C(2) A claim under paragraph 51 in respect of the amount may be made only by T.

51C(3) Sub-paragraph (4) applies where–

(a) a person ("P") has paid an amount described in sub-paragraph (1) in the belief that P was accountable to the Commissioners for the amount under a relevant enactment, but

(b) P was not so accountable.

51C(4) A claim under paragraph 51 in respect of the amount may be made only by P.

51C(5) The Commissioners for her Majesty's Revenue and Customs are not liable to give effect to a claim under sub-paragraph (4) if or to the extent that the amount has been repaid to T or set against amounts payable to the Commissioners by T.

51C(6) **"Relevant enactment"** means–

(a) Chapter 3 of Part 3 of the Finance Act 2004 or regulations under that Chapter (construction industry scheme), or

(b) any other provision of or made under the Taxes Acts.

History – Para. 51C effectively inserted by FA 2009, s. 100 and Sch. 52, para. 13, with effect in relation to claims made on or after 1 April 2010.

THE CLAIMANT: PARTNERSHIPS

51D(1) This paragraph applies where–

(a) a trade, profession or business is carried on by two or more persons in partnership,

(b) an amount is paid, or liable to be paid, by one or more of those persons in accordance with a self-assessment, and

(c) the amount is excessive by reason of a mistake in a partnership return.

51D(2) A claim under paragraph 51 in respect of the amount–

(a) may be made by the relevant partner nominated to make the claim by all of the relevant partners, and

(b) may not be made by any other person.

51D(3) In relation to such a claim, references in paragraphs 51A to 51F to the claimant are to any of the relevant partners.

51D(4) **"Relevant partner"** means–

(a) a person who was a partner in the partnership at any time during the period in respect of which the partnership return was made, or

(b) the personal representative of such a person.

History – Para. 51D effectively inserted by FA 2009, s. 100 and Sch. 52, para. 13, with effect in relation to claims made on or after 1 April 2010.

ASSESSMENT OF CLAIMANT IN CONNECTION WITH CLAIM

51E(1) This paragraph applies where–

(a) a claim is made under paragraph 51,

(b) the grounds for giving effect to the claim also provide grounds for a discovery assessment or discovery determination on the claimant in respect of any accounting period, and

(c) such an assessment or determination could be made but for a relevant restriction.

51E(2) The following are relevant restrictions–

(a) the restrictions in paragraphs 42 to 45, and

(b) the expiry of a time limit for making a discovery assessment or discovery determination.

51E(3) Where this paragraph applies–

(a) the relevant restrictions are to be disregarded, and

(b) the discovery assessment or discovery determination is not out of time if it is made before the final determination of the claim.

51E(4) A claim is not finally determined until it, or the amount to which it relates, can no longer be varied (whether on appeal or otherwise).

History – Para. 51E effectively inserted by FA 2009, s. 100 and Sch. 52, para. 13, with effect in relation to claims made on or after 1 April 2010.

AMENDMENT OF PARTNERSHIP RETURN ETC IN CONNECTION WITH CLAIM

51F(1) This paragraph applies where–

(a) a claim is made under paragraph 51,

(b) the claimant is one of two or more persons carrying on a trade, profession or business in partnership,

(c) the grounds for giving effect to the claim also provide grounds for amending, under section 30B(1) of the Taxes Management Act 1970 (discovery of loss of tax from partnership), a return made by the partnership or any of the partners in respect of any period, and

(d) such an amendment could be made but for a relevant restriction.

51F(2) The following are relevant restrictions–

(a) the conditions in section 30B(4) to (6) of the Taxes Management Act 1970, and

(b) the expiry of a time limit for making an assessment under that section.

51F(3) Where this paragraph applies–

(a) the relevant conditions are to be disregarded, and

(b) the amendment is not out of time if it is made before the final determination of the claim.

51F(4) A claim is not finally determined until it, or the amount to which it relates, can no longer be varied (whether on appeal or otherwise).

History – Para. 51F effectively inserted by FA 2009, s. 100 and Sch. 52, para. 13, with effect in relation to claims made on or after 1 April 2010.

CONTRACT SETTLEMENTS

51G(1) In paragraph 51(1)(a), the reference to an amount paid by a company by way of tax includes an amount paid by a person under a contract settlement in connection with tax believed to be due.

51G(2) Sub-paragraphs (3) to (6) apply if the person who paid the amount under the contract settlement ("the payer") and the person from whom the tax was due ("the taxpayer") are not the same person.

51G(3) In relation to a claim under paragraph 51 in respect of that amount–

(a) the references to the claimant in paragraph 51A(5) to (7) (Cases D, E and F) have effect as if they included the taxpayer,

(b) the reference to the claimant in paragraph 51A(8) (Case G) has effect as if it were a reference to the taxpayer,

(c) the references to the claimant in paragraphs 51E(1)(b) and 51F(1)(b) have effect as if they were references to the taxpayer, and

(d) references to tax in Schedule 1A to the Taxes Management Act 1970 (as it applies to a claim under this Part of this Schedule) include such an amount.

51G(4) Sub-paragraph (5) applies where the grounds for giving effect to a claim by the payer in respect of the amount also provide grounds for a discovery assessment or discovery determination on the taxpayer in respect of any chargeable period.

51G(5) The Commissioners for Her Majesty's Revenue and Customs may set any amount repayable to the payer by virtue of the claim against any amount payable by the taxpayer by virtue of the assessment or determination.

51G(6) The obligations of the Commissioners for Her Majesty's Revenue and Customs and the taxpayer are discharged to the extent of any set-off under sub-paragraph (5).

51G(7) **"Contract settlement"** means an agreement made in connection with any person's liability to make a payment to the Commissioners for Her Majesty's Revenue and Customs under or by virtue of an enactment.

History – Para. 51G effectively inserted by FA 2009, s. 100 and Sch. 52, para. 13, with effect in relation to claims made on or after 1 April 2010.

RECOVERY OF EXCESSIVE REPAYMENTS ETC.

52(1) The provisions of paragraphs 41 to 48 relating to discovery assessments apply to an amount to which this paragraph applies as if it were unpaid tax, unless–

(a) it is assessable under those provisions apart from this paragraph, or

(b) it is recoverable under section 826(8A) of the Taxes Act 1988 (interest overpaid which is recoverable in same way as interest charged).

52(2) This paragraph applies to an amount paid to a company by way of–

(a) repayment of tax (or income tax),

(b) repayment supplement under section 825 of the Taxes Act 1988,

(bza) R&D expenditure credit under Chapter 6A of Part 3 of the Corporation Tax Act 2009,

(ba) R&D tax credit under Chapter 2 or 7 of Part 13 of the Corporation Tax Act 2009,

(bb) land remediation tax credit or life assurance company tax credit under Part 14 of the Corporation Tax Act 2009, or

(bc) [Omitted by CTA 2009, s. 1322 and Sch. 1, para. 454(6)(a) and repealed by CTA 2009, s. 1326 and Sch. 3, Pt. 1,]

(bd) film tax credit under Part 15 of the Corporation Tax Act 2009,

(be) television tax credit under Part 15A of that Act,

(bf) video game credit under Part 15B of that Act,

(bg) theatre tax credit under Part 15C of that Act,

(bh) orchestra tax credit under Part 15D of that Act,

(c) interest paid under section 826 of the Taxes Act 1988,

to the extent that it ought not to have been paid.

52(2A) The provisions of paragraphs 41 and 45 to 48 relating to discovery assessments apply to an amount paid to a company by way of first-year tax credit under Schedule A1 to the Capital Allowances Act as if it were unpaid tax, but only to the extent that the company was not, or is no longer, entitled to it.

52(3) For the purposes of this paragraph–

(a) an amount is regarded as paid if it is allowed by way of set-off, and

(b) an amount is regarded as a repayment if it was intended as repayment but exceeds the amount paid by the company.

52(4) [Omitted by CTA 2009, s. 1322 and Sch. 1, para. 454(6)(b) and repealed by CTA 2009, s. 1326 and Sch. 3, Pt. 1.]

52(5) An assessment to recover–

(a) an amount of tax repaid to a company in respect of an accounting period, or interest on any such repayment,

(aa) an amount of R&D expenditure credit paid to a company for an accounting period,

(ab) an amount of R&D tax credit paid to a company for an accounting period,

(ac) an amount of land remediation tax credit or life assurance company tax credit paid to a company for an accounting period, or

(ad) [omitted by CTA 2009, s. 1322 and Sch. 1, para. 454(6)(c) and repealed by CTA 2009, s. 1326 and Sch. 3, Pt. 1,]

(ae) an amount of film tax credit paid to a company for an accounting period,

(af) an amount of first-year tax credit under Schedule A1 to the Capital Allowances Act paid to a company for an accounting period,

(ag) an amount of television tax credit paid to a company for an accounting period, (ah) an amount of video game tax credit paid to a company for an accounting period,

(ai) an amount of theatre tax credit paid to a company for an accounting period,

(aj) an amount of orchestra tax credit paid to a company for an accounting period,

(b) an amount of income tax repaid to a company in respect of a payment received by the company in an accounting period, or interest on any such repayment,

shall be treated as an assessment to tax for the accounting period referred to in paragraph (a), (aa), (ab), (ac), (ae), (ag), (ah), (ai), (aj) or (b).

52(6) The sum assessed shall carry interest at the prescribed rate for the purposes of section 87A of the Taxes Management Act 1970 (interest on overdue corporation tax, etc.) from the date when the payment being recovered was made until payment.

History – In para. 52(2)(a) the words "or payment of a tax credit" (which appeared after "(or income tax)") omitted by FA 2016, s. 5 and Sch. 1, para. 58(3)(c), with effect in relation to dividends paid or arising (or treated as paid), and any other distributions made (or treated as made), in the tax year 2016–17 or at any later time.

Para. 52(2)(bza) inserted by FA 2013, s. 35 and Sch. 15, para. 6(2), with effect in relation to expenditure incurred on or after 1 April 2013.

In para. 52(2)(ba), the words "Chapter 2 or 7 of Part 13 of the Corporation Tax Act 2009" substituted for the words "Schedule 20 to the Finance Act 2000"; in para. (bb) the words "Part 14 of the Corporation Tax Act 2009" substituted for the words "Schedule 22 to the Finance Act 2001"; para. (bc) omitted and repealed by CTA 2009, s. 1326 and Sch. 3, Pt. 1; and in para. (bd) the words "under Part 15 of the Corporation Tax Act 2009" inserted by CTA 2009, s. 1322 and Sch. 1, para. 454(6)(a), with effect for corporation tax purposes for accounting periods ending on or after 1 April 2009, and for income tax and capital gains tax purposes for the tax year 2009–10 and subsequent tax years.

Para. 52(2)(ba) inserted by FA 2000, Sch. 21, para. 3(a) and 3(b) respectively with effect for accounting periods ending on or after 1 April 2000.

Para. 52(2)(bb) and (5)(ac) inserted by FA 2001, s. 70 and Sch. 23, para. 5 with effect for accounting periods ending on or after 1 April 2001.

Para. 52(2)(bc) inserted by FA 2002, s. 54 and Sch. 14, para. 3 with effect in relation to tax credits payable under FA 2002, Sch. 13 in respect of expenditure incurred on or after 22 April 2003 by virtue of SI 2003/1472 (C. 64) (the day appointed by the Treasury under FA 2002, Sch. 13, para. 28).

Para. 52(2)(bd) inserted by FA 2006, s. 42 and Sch. 5, para. 28(a), with effect from 1 January 2007 (FA 2006, s. 53).

Para. 52(2)(be) inserted by FA 2013, s. 36 and Sch. 18, para. 4(2), with effect from 19 July 2013 (SI 2013/1817) in relation to accounting periods beginning on or after "the relevant day" (as defined in FA 2013, Sch. 18, para. 23).

Para. 52(2)(bf) inserted by FA 2013, s. 36 and Sch. 18, para. 4(2), with effect from 1 April 2014 (SI 2014/1962) in relation to accounting periods beginning on or after "the relevant day" (as defined in FA 2013, Sch. 18, para. 23).

Para. 52(2)(bg) inserted by FA 2014, s. 36 and Sch. 4, para. 5(2), with effect from 22 August 2014, in relation to accounting periods beginning on or after 1 September 2014, subject to the transitionalprovisions in FA 2014, Sch. 4, para. 17.

Para. 52(2)(bh) inserted by FA 2016 s. 54 and Sch. 8, para. 5(2), with effect in relation to accounting periods beginning on or after 1 April 2016 (subject to provisions of Sch. 8, para. 17(2) and (3)).

In para. 52(2)(c) reference to "the Taxes Act 1988" substituted for "that Act" by FA 2001, s. 70 and Sch. 23, para. 5(b) with effect for accounting periods ending on or after 1 April 2001.

Para. 52(2A) inserted by FA 2008, s. 79 and Sch. 25, para. 8(3), with effect in relation to expenditure incurred on or after 1 April 2008.

Para. 52(4) omitted by CTA 2009, s. 1322 and Sch. 1, para. 454(6)(b) and repealed by CTA 2009, s. 1326 and Sch. 3, Pt. 1, with effect for corporation tax purposes for accounting periods ending on or after 1 April 2009, and for income tax and capital gains tax purposes for the tax year 2009–10 and subsequent tax years.

Para. 52(5)(aa) (and in (5), "(aa),") inserted by FA 2013, s. 35 and Sch. 15, para. 6(3), with effect in relation to expenditure incurred on or after 1 April 2013.

Para. 52(5)(ab) inserted by FA 2000, Sch. 21, para. 3(a) and 3(b) respectively with effect for accounting periods ending on or after 1 April 2000.

Para. 52(5)(ad) omitted by CTA 2009, s. 1322 and Sch. 1, para. 454(6)(c) and repealed by CTA 2009, s. 1326 and Sch. 3, Pt. 1, with effect for corporation tax purposes for accounting periods ending on or after 1 April 2009, and for income tax and capital gains tax purposes for the tax year 2009–10 and subsequent tax years.

Former para. 52(5)(ad) inserted by FA 2002, s. 54 and Sch. 14, para. 3 with effect in relation to tax credits payable under FA 2002, Sch. 13 in respect of expenditure incurred on or after 22 April 2003 by virtue of SI 2003/1472 (C. 64) (the day appointed by the Treasury under FA 2002, Sch. 13, para. 28).

Para. 52(5)(ae) inserted by FA 2006, s. 42 and Sch. 5, para. 28(b), with effect from 1 January 2007 (FA 2006, s. 53).

Para. 52(5)(af) inserted by FA 2008, s. 79 and Sch. 25, para. 8(4), with effect in relation to expenditure incurred on or after 1 April 2008.

Para. 52(5)(ag) inserted (and ", (ag)" inserted after "(ae)") by FA 2013, s. 36 and Sch. 18, para. 4(3), with effect from 19 July 2013 (SI 2013/1817) in relation to accounting periods beginning on or after "the relevant day" (as defined in FA 2013, Sch. 18, para. 23).

Para. 52(5)(ah) inserted (and ", (ah)" inserted after "(ag)") by FA 2013, s. 36 and Sch.18, para. 4(3), with effect from 1 April 2014 (SI 2014/1962) in relation to accounting periods beginning on or after "the relevant day" (as defined in FA 2013, Sch. 18, para. 23).

Para. 52(5)(ai) inserted by FA 2014, s. 36 and Sch. 4, para. 5(3)(a), with effect from 22 August 2014, in relation to accounting periods beginning on or after 1 September 2014, subject to the transitional provisions in FA 2014, Sch. 4, para. 17.

Para. 52(5)(aj) and in the words after para. 52(5)(b) the words ", (aj)" inserted by FA 2016 s. 54 and Sch. 8, para. 5(3), with effect in relation to accounting periods beginning on or after 1 April 2016 (subject to provisions of Sch. 8, para. 17(2) and (3)).

In para. 52(5), in the words after para. (b), ", (ai)" inserted after "(ah)" by FA 2014, s. 36 and Sch. 4, para. 5(3)(b), with effect from 22 August 2014, in relation to accounting periods beginning on or after 1 September 2014, subject to the transitional provisions in FA 2014, Sch. 4, para. 17.

In para. 52(5) reference to "(5)(ab)" inserted by FA 2000, Sch. 21, para. 3(c) with effect for accounting periods ending on or after 1 April 2000.

In para. 52(5) reference to "(5)(ac)" inserted by FA 2001, s. 70 and Sch. 23, para. 5 with effect for accounting periods ending on or after 1 April 2001.

In para. 52(5) reference to "(5)(ad)" omitted by CTA 2009, s. 1322 and Sch. 1, para. 454(6)(c), with effect for corporation tax purposes for accounting periods ending on or after 1 April 2009, and for income tax and capital gains tax purposes for the tax year 2009–10 and subsequent tax years. Formerly inserted by FA 2002, s. 54 and Sch. 14, para. 3 with effect in relation to tax credits payable under FA 2002, Sch. 13 in respect of expenditure incurred on or after 22 April 2003 by virtue of SI 2003/1472 (C. 64) (the day appointed by the Treasury under FA 2002, Sch. 13, para. 28).

In para. 52(5) reference to ", (ae)" inserted by FA 2006, s. 42 and Sch. 5, para. 28(c), with effect from 1 January 2007 (FA 2006, s. 53).

Cross references – FA 2000, s. 46(2)(d): exemption under that section (small charitable trades) denied in respect of income which is chargeable to tax by virtue of para. 52(4).

TIME LIMIT FOR RECOVERY OF EXCESSIVE REPAYMENTS, ETC.

53(1) An assessment made by virtue of paragraph 52 is not out of time under paragraph 46(1) (general 4 year time limit for assessments) if it is made–

(a) before the end of the accounting period following that in which the amount assessed was paid, or

(b) if later, before the end of the period of three months beginning with the day on which an officer of Revenue and Customs completes an enquiry into a relevant company tax return by the company concerned.

53(2) Sub-paragraph (1) above is without prejudice to paragraph 46(2) and (2A) (time limit for assessment in case of loss of tax brought about carelessly or deliberately).

History – In para. 53(1), "4 year" substituted for "six year" by FA 2008, s. 118 and Sch. 39, para. 44(2), with effect from 1 April 2010 (SI 2009/403, art. 2(2) subject to SI 2009/403, art. 3–10 – in particular art. 10).

In para. 53(1)(b) the words "an officer of Revenue and Customs" substituted for the words "the Inland Revenue" by CRCA 2005, s. 50 and Sch. 4, para. 68(a) and the word "completes" substituted for the word "complete" by virtue of para. 68(c), with effect from 18 April 2005 by virtue of SI 2005/1126, art. 2(2).

In para. 53(2), the words "paragraph 46(2) and (2A) (time limit for assessment in case of loss of tax brought about carelessly or deliberately)" substituted for the words "paragraph 46(2) (time limit for assessment in case of fraud or negligence)" by FA 2008, s. 118 and Sch. 39, para. 44(3), with effect from 1 April 2010 (SI 2009/403, art. 2(2) subject to SI 2009/403, art. 3–10 – in particular art. 10).

Part VII – General Provisions as to Claims and Elections

CLAIMS MUST BE QUANTIFIED

54 A claim under any provision of the Corporation Tax Acts for a relief, an allowance or a repayment of tax must be for an amount which is quantified at the time when the claim is made.

Cross references – ICTA 1988, s. 444AD(3): nothing in para. 54–60 applies to an election under ICTA 1988, s. 444AD(2) (transfers of business: modification of s. 83(2B) FA 1989).

CAA 2001, s. 3(5): para. 54–60 apply for corporation tax purposes to a claim for an allowance under CAA 2001, s. 260(3)(b) or CAA 2001, s. 355.

CAA 2001, s. 201(5): nothing in para. 54–60 applies to an election under CAA 2001, s. 201(5) (election to apportion sale price of fixture).

CAA 2001, s. 227(5)(b): nothing in para. 54–60 applies to an election under CAA 2001, s. 227(5)(b) (special provision for sale and leaseback cases).

TCGA, s. 213(8G): nothing in para. 54–60 applies to an election under TCGA, s. 213(8A)(e) (spreading of gains and losses under section 212).

GENERAL TIME LIMIT FOR MAKING CLAIMS

55 Subject to any provision prescribing a longer or shorter period, a claim for relief under any provision of the Corporation Tax Acts must be made within 4 years from the end of the accounting period to which it relates.

History – In para. 55, "4 years" substituted for "six years" by FA 2008, s. 118 and Sch. 39, para. 45, with effect from 1 April 2010 (SI 2009/403, art. 2(2) subject to SI 2009/403, art. 3–10 – in particular art. 10).

Cross references – ICTA 1988, s. 444AD(3): nothing in para. 54–60 applies to an election under ICTA 1988, s. 444AD(2) (transfers of business: modification of s. 83(2B) FA 1989).

CAA 2001, s. 3(5): para. 54–60 apply for corporation tax purposes to a claim for an allowance under CAA 2001, s. 260(3)(b) or CAA 2001, s. 355.

CAA 2001, s. 201(5): nothing in para. 54–60 applies to an election under CAA 2001, s. 201(5) (election to apportion sale price of fixture).

CAA 2001, s. 227(5)(b): nothing in para. 54–60 applies to an election under CAA 2001, s. 227(5)(b) (special provision for sale and leaseback cases).

TCGA, s. 213(8G): nothing in para. 54–60 applies to an election under TCGA, s. 213(8A)(e) (spreading of gains and losses under section 212).

SUPPLEMENTARY CLAIM OR ELECTION

56 A company which has made a claim or election under any provision of the Corporation Tax Acts (by including it in a return or otherwise) and subsequently discovers that a mistake has been made in it may make a supplementary claim or election within the time allowed for making the original claim or election.

Cross references – ICTA 1988, s. 444AD(3): nothing in para. 54–60 applies to an election under ICTA 1988, s. 444AD(2) (transfers of business: modification of s. 83(2B) FA 1989).

CAA 2001, s. 3(5): para. 54–60 apply for corporation tax purposes to a claim for an allowance under CAA 2001, s. 260(3)(b) or CAA 2001, s. 355.

CAA 2001, s. 201(5): nothing in para. 54–60 applies to an election under CAA 2001, s. 201(5) (election to apportion sale price of fixture).

CAA 2001, s. 227(5)(b): nothing in para. 54–60 applies to an election under CAA 2001, s. 227(5)(b) (special provision for sale and leaseback cases).

TCGA, s. 213(8G): nothing in para. 54–60 applies to an election under TCGA, s. 213(8A)(e) (spreading of gains and losses under section 212).

CLAIMS OR ELECTIONS AFFECTING A SINGLE ACCOUNTING PERIOD

57(1) This paragraph applies to a claim or election for tax purposes which affects only one accounting period ("the relevant accounting period"). This is subject to sub-paragraphs (1A) to (1C).

57(1A) This paragraph does not apply to a claim by a company for repayment of income tax treated as having been paid by virtue of–

(a) section 471 of the Corporation Tax Act 2010 (gifts qualifying for gift aid relief: charitable companies),

(b) section 475 of that Act (gifts qualifying for gift aid relief: eligible bodies), or

(c) section 661D of that Act (gifts qualifying for gift aid relief: community amateur sports clubs).

57(1B) This paragraph also does not apply to a claim by a company for repayment of income tax deducted at source from income which is exempt from tax by virtue of–

(a) section 486 of the Corporation Tax Act 2010 (investment income and non-trading profits from loan relationships),

(b) section 487 of that Act (public revenue dividends),

(c) section 488 of that Act (certain miscellaneous income),

(d) section 489 of that Act (income from estates in administration), or

(e) section 664 of that Act (interest and gift aid income: community amateur sports clubs).

57(1C) This paragraph also does not apply to a claim by a company for an amount to be exempt from tax by virtue of–

(a) section 472 of the Corporation Tax Act 2010 (gifts qualifying for gift aid relief: charitable companies),

(b) section 475 of that Act (gifts qualifying for gift aid relief: eligible bodies), or

(c) any of the provisions mentioned in sub-paragraph (1B).

57(2) If notice has been given under paragraph 3 requiring a company to deliver a company tax return for the relevant accounting period, a claim or election by the company which can be made by being included in the return (as originally made or by amendment) must be so made.

57(3) If a company has delivered a company tax return for the relevant accounting period, a claim or election made by the company which could be made by amending the return is treated as an amendment of the return.

The provisions of paragraph 15 (amendment of return by company) apply.

57(4) Schedule 1A to the Taxes Management Act 1970 (claims and elections not included in returns) applies to a claim or election made by a company which cannot be included in a company tax return for the relevant accounting period.

This applies in particular to a claim or election made–

(a) before any notice is given under paragraph 3 requiring a company tax return for the relevant accounting period, or

(b) at a time when its return for the relevant accounting period cannot be amended.

History – In para. 57(1), the words "This is subject to sub-paragraphs (1A) to (1C)." inserted by FA 2012, s. 51 and Sch. 15, para. 15(2), with effect in relation to claims whenever made.

Para. 57(1A), (1B) and (1C) substituted for former para. 57(1A) by FA 2012, s. 51 and Sch. 15, para. 15(3), with effect in relation to claims whenever made.

Former para. 57(1A) inserted by FA 2010, s. 32 and Sch. 8, para. 6(3), with effect in relation to claims whenever made.

Cross references – ICTA 1988, s. 444AD(3): nothing in para. 54–60 applies to an election under ICTA 1988, s. 444AD(2) (transfers of business: modification of s. 83(2B) FA 1989).

ICTA 1988, Sch. 28AA, para. 6C(6): para. 57 does not apply to a claim under that paragraph.

TCGA 1992, s. 213(8G): nothing in para. 54–60 applies to an election under TCGA 1992, s. 213(8A)(e) (spreading of gains and losses under section 212).

CAA 2001, s. 3(5): para. 54–60 apply for corporation tax purposes to a claim for an allowance under CAA 2001, s. 260(3)(b) or CAA 2001, s. 355.

CAA 2001, s. 201(5): nothing in para. 54–60 applies to an election under CAA 2001, s. 201(5) (election to apportion sale price of fixture).

CAA 2001, s. 227(5)(b): nothing in para. 54–60 applies to an election under CAA 2001, s. 227(5)(b) (special provision for sale and leaseback cases).

SI 1999/623: disapplication of para. 57 in relation to claims made by insurance companies carrying on pension business in respect of notional repayments of tax on excess gilt interest.

CLAIMS OR ELECTIONS INVOLVING MORE THAN ONE ACCOUNTING PERIOD

58(1) This paragraph applies to a claim or election for tax purposes if–

(a) the event or occasion giving rise to it occurs in one accounting period (the period to which it "relates"), and

(b) it affects one or more other accounting periods (whether or not it also affects the period to which it relates).

58(2) If a company makes a claim or election which–

(a) relates to an accounting period for which the company has delivered a company tax return and could be made by amendment of the return, or

(b) affects an accounting period for which the company has delivered a company tax return and could be given effect by amendment of the return,

the claim or election is treated as an amendment of the return.

The provisions of paragraph 15 (amendment of return by company) apply.

58(3) Schedule 1A to the Taxes Management Act 1970 (claims and elections not included in returns) applies to a claim or election made by a company if or to the extent that it is not–

(a) made by being included (by amendment or otherwise) in the company tax return for the accounting period to which it relates, and

(b) given effect by being included (by amendment or otherwise) in company tax returns for the accounting periods affected by it.

Cross references – ICTA 1988, s. 444AD(3): nothing in para. 54–60 applies to an election under ICTA 1988, s. 444AD(2) (transfers of business: modification of s. 83(2B) FA 1989).
ICTA 1988, Sch. 28AA, para. 6C(6): para. 58 does not apply to a claim under that paragraph.
TCGA 1992, s. 213(8G): nothing in para. 54–60 applies to an election under TCGA 1992, s. 213(8A)(e) (spreading of gains and losses under section 212).
CAA 2001, s. 3(5): para. 54–60 apply for corporation tax purposes to a claim for an allowance under CAA 2001, s. 260(3)(b) or CAA 2001, s. 355.
CAA 2001, s. 201(5): nothing in para. 54–60 applies to an election under CAA 2001, s. 201(5) (election to apportion sale price of fixture).
CAA 2001, s. 227(5)(b): nothing in para. 54–60 applies to an election under CAA 2001, s. 227(5)(b) (special provision for sale and leaseback cases).
SI 1999/623: disapplication of para. 58 in relation to claims made by insurance companies carrying on pension business in respect of notional repayments of tax on excess gilt interest.

OTHER CLAIMS AND ELECTIONS

59(1) Schedule 1A to the Taxes Management Act 1970 applies to a claim or election for tax purposes which is not within paragraph 57 or 58, whether or not it is included (by amendment or otherwise) in a company tax return.

59(2) The provisions of this Schedule do not apply where or to the extent that the provisions of Schedule 1A apply.

Cross references – ICTA 1988, s. 444AD(3): nothing in para. 54–60 applies to an election under ICTA 1988, s. 444AD(2) (transfers of business: modification of s. 83(2B) FA 1989).
ICTA 1988, Sch. 28AA, para. 6C(6): para. 598 does applies to a claim under that paragraph.
CAA 2001, s. 3(5): para. 54–60 apply for corporation tax purposes to a claim for an allowance under CAA 2001, s. 250(3)(b) or CAA 2001, s. 355.
CAA 2001, s. 201(5): nothing in para. 54–60 applies to an election under CAA 2001, s. 201(5) (election to apportion sale price of fixture).
CAA 2001, s. 227(5)(b): nothing in para. 54–60 applies to an election under CAA 2001, s. 227(5)(b) (special provision for sale and leaseback cases).
TCGA, s. 213(8G): nothing in para. 54–60 applies to an election under TCGA, s. 213(8A)(e) (spreading of gains and losses under section 212).
SI 1999/623: disapplication of para. 59 in relation to claims made by insurance companies carrying on pension business in respect of notional repayments of tax on excess gilt interest.

PROVISIONS SUPPLEMENTARY TO PARAGRAPHS 57 TO 59

60(1) Paragraphs 57 to 59 have effect subject to any express provision to the contrary.

60(2) Nothing in those paragraphs affects the time limit or any other conditions for making a claim or election.

60(3) Where Schedule 1A to the Taxes Management Act 1970 applies by virtue of any of those paragraphs and the claim or election results in an increase in the amount of tax payable, all such adjustments by way of assessment or otherwise shall be made as are necessary to give effect to it.

Cross references – ICTA 1988, s. 444AD(3): nothing in para. 54–60 applies to an election under ICTA 1988, s. 444AD(2) (transfers of business: modification of s. 83(2B) FA 1989).
CAA 2001, s. 3(5): para. 54–60 apply for corporation tax purposes to a claim for an allowance under CAA 2001, s. 260(3)(b) or CAA 2001, s. 355.
CAA 2001, s. 201(5): nothing in para. 54–60 applies to an election under CAA 2001, s. 201(5) (election to apportion sale price of fixture).
CAA 2001, s. 227(5)(b): nothing in para. 54–60 applies to an election under CAA 2001, s. 227(5)(b) (special provision for sale and leaseback cases).
TCGA, s. 213(8G): nothing in para. 54–60 applies to an election under TCGA, s. 213(8A)(e) (spreading of gains and losses under section 212).
SI 1999/623: disapplication of para. 60 in relation to claims made by insurance companies carrying on pension business in respect of notional repayments of tax on excess gilt interest.

CONSEQUENTIAL CLAIMS, ETC. ARISING OUT OF CERTAIN REVENUE AMENDMENTS OR ASSESSMENTS

61(1) Paragraphs 62 to 64 have effect to allow certain claims, elections, applications and notices to be made or given, or if previously given to be revoked or varied, where–

(a) an amendment of a company tax return is made under paragraph 34(2A) (amendments of other returns required in consequence of closure notice) which has the effect of increasing the amount of tax payable by a company,

(b) a discovery assessment is made, or

(c) an assessment is made under paragraph 76 (recovery of excessive group relief).

61(2) Paragraphs 62 to 64 do not apply in relation to an assessment made in a case involving a loss of tax brought about carelessly or deliberately by–

(a) the company, or

(b) a person acting on behalf of the company, or

(c) a person who was a partner of the company at the relevant time.

In such a case more limited provision is made by paragraph 65.

61(3) In paragraphs 62 to 64 **"the relevant accounting period"**, in relation to the time limit for making a consequential claim, election, application or notice, means–

(a) in relation to an amendment of a company tax return under paragraph 34(2A), the accounting period in which the closure notice was issued;

(b) in relation to an assessment, the accounting period in which the assessment was made.

History – In para. 61(1)(a), "34(2A)" substituted for "34(2)(b)" by FA 2008, s. 119(9), with effect from 1 April 2010 (SI 2009/405).
In para. 61(2), the words "a loss of tax brought about carelessly or deliberately by" substituted for "fraudulent or negligent conduct on the part of" by FA 2008, s. 118 and Sch. 39, para. 46, with effect from 1 April 2010 (SI 2009/403, art. 2(2) subject to SI 2009/403, art. 3–10 – in particular art. 10).
In para. 61(3)(a), "34(2A)" substituted for "34(2)(b)" by FA 2008, a. 119(9), with effect from 1 April 2010 (SI 2009/405).

Statements of practice – SP 5/01: Board's approach to extending time limits for making claims for loss relief, capital allowances and group relief.

CONSEQUENTIAL CLAIMS ETC. THAT MAY BE MADE

62(1) A claim, election, application or notice to which this paragraph applies–

(a) may be made or given at any time within one year from the end of the relevant accounting period, or

(b) if previously made or given may at any such time be revoked or varied–

(i) in the same manner as it was made or given, and

(ii) by or with the consent of the same person or persons who made, gave or consented to it (or, if a person has died, by or with the consent of his personal representatives),

unless, by virtue of any enactment, it is irrevocable.

62(1A) This paragraph applies to a claim under paragraph 51 relating to the accounting period in respect of which the amendment or assessment is made.

62(2) This paragraph applies to any other claim, election, application or notice–

(a) relating to the accounting period in respect of which the amendment or assessment is made, or

(b) made or given by reference to an event occurring in that period,

whose making, giving, revocation or variation has or could have the effect of reducing a relevant liability of the company.

62(3) The following are relevant liabilities of the company for this purpose–

(a) the increased liability to tax resulting from the amendment or assessment;

(b) any other liability to tax of the company–

(i) for the accounting period to which the amendment or assessment relates, or

(ii) for any subsequent accounting period ending not later than one year after the end of the relevant accounting period.

62(4) Where a claim, election, application or notice is made, given, revoked or varied by virtue of this paragraph, all such adjustments shall be made, whether by way of discharge or repayment of tax or the making of amendments, assessments or otherwise, as are required to take account of the effect of the taking of that action on any person's liability to tax for any chargeable period.

62(5) The provisions of the Taxes Management Act 1970 relating to appeals against decisions on claims apply with any necessary modifications to a decision on the revocation or variation of a claim by virtue of this paragraph.

62(6) This paragraph has effect subject to–

paragraph 63 (consequential claims etc. affecting tax liability of another person), and

paragraph 64 (consequential claims etc. not to give rise to reduction in liability).

History – Para. 62(1A) inserted by FA 2009, s. 100 and Sch. 52, para. 15(2), with effect in relation to claims made on or after 1 April 2010.

In para. 62(2), the words "any other claim" substituted for the words "a claim" by FA 2009, s. 100 and Sch. 52, para. 15(3), with effect in relation to claims made on or after 1 April 2010.

CONSEQUENTIAL CLAIMS ETC. AFFECTING TAX LIABILITY OF ANOTHER PERSON

63(1) If the effect of the exercise by any person of a power conferred by paragraph 62 would be to alter the liability to tax of another person, the power may not be exercised except with the consent in writing of that other person or, if he has died, of his personal representatives.

63(2) Where such a power is exercised so as to increase the liability to tax of another person, neither paragraph 61 above nor section 43A of the Taxes Management Act 1970 (which makes corresponding provision in relation to income tax or capital gains tax) applies in relation to any amendment or assessment made because of that increased liability.

63(3) In this paragraph "tax" includes income tax or capital gains tax.

CONSEQUENTIAL CLAIMS ETC. NOT TO GIVE RISE TO REDUCTION IN LIABILITY

64(1) If in any case–

(a) one or more claims, elections, applications or notices are made, given, revoked or varied under paragraph 62 in consequence of an amendment or assessment, and

(b) the total of the reductions in liability to tax resulting from that action would exceed the additional liability to tax resulting from the amendment or assessment,

the excess is not available to reduce any liability to tax.

64(2) Where sub-paragraph (1) has the effect of limiting either–

(a) the reduction in a person's liability to tax for more than one period, or

(b) the reduction in the liability to tax of more than one person,

the limited amount shall be apportioned between the periods or persons concerned.

64(3) The apportionment shall be made in such manner as an officer of Revenue and Customs may specify by notice in writing to the person or persons concerned, unless notice is given under the following provision.

64(4) If the person concerned gives (or the persons concerned jointly give) notice in writing to an officer of Revenue and Customs within the period of 30 days beginning with–

(a) the day on which notice under sub-paragraph (3) is given to the person concerned, or

(b) where more than one person is concerned, the latest date on which such notice is given to any of them,

the apportionment shall be made in such manner as may be specified in the notice given by the person or persons concerned.

64(5) In this paragraph "tax" includes income tax or capital gains tax.

History – In para. 64(3) and (4) the words "an officer of Revenue and Customs" substituted for the words "the Inland Revenue" by CRCA 2005, s. 50 and Sch. 4, para. 68(a), with effect from 18 April 2005 by virtue of SI 2005/1126, art. 2(2).

CONSEQUENTIAL CLAIMS IN CASE OF LOSS OF TAX BROUGHT ABOUT CARELESSLY OR DELIBERATELY

History – In the heading before para. 65, the words "loss of tax brought about carelessly or deliberately" substituted for the words "fraud or negligence" by FA 2008, s. 118 and Sch. 39, para. 47(3), with effect from 1 April 2010 (SI 2009/403, art. 2(2) subject to SI 2009/403, art. 3–10 – in particular art. 10).

65(1) This paragraph applies where an assessment is made on a company in a case involving a loss of tax brought about carelessly or deliberately by–

(a) the company, or

(b) a person acting on behalf of the company, or

(c) a person who was a partner of the company at the relevant time.

65(2) If the company so requires, effect shall be given in determining the amount of the tax charged by the assessment to any relief or allowance to which the company would have been entitled for that accounting period on a claim or application made within the time allowed by the Taxes Acts.

History – In para. 65(1), the words "a loss of tax brought about carelessly or deliberately by" substituted for the words "fraudulent or negligent conduct on the part of" by FA 2008, s. 118 and Sch. 39, para. 47(2), with effect from 1 April 2010 (SI 2009/403, art. 2(2) subject to SI 2009/403, art. 3–10 – in particular art. 10).

Statements of practice – SP 5/01: HMRC's approach to extending time limits for making claims for loss relief, capital allowances and group relief.

Part VIII – Claims for Group Relief

Cross references – FA 2000, Sch. 22, para. 81(3): application of Pt. VIII with the exception of para. 77, to surrender of unrelieved qualifying expenditure by a tonnage tax company.

INTRODUCTION

66 This Part of this Schedule applies to claims for relief under Part 5 of the Corporation Tax Act 2010 (group relief).

History – In para. 66, the words "Part 5 of the Corporation Tax Act 2010" substituted for the words "Chapter IV of Part X of the Taxes Act 1988" by CTA 2010, s. 1177 and Sch. 1, para. 297(8), with effect for corporation tax purposes for accounting periods ending on or after 1 April 2010, and for income tax and capital gains tax purposes for the tax year 2010–11 and subsequent tax years.

CLAIM TO BE INCLUDED IN COMPANY TAX RETURN

67(1) A claim for group relief must be made by being included in the claimant company's company tax return for the accounting period for which the claim is made.

67(2) It may be included in the return originally made or by amendment.

CONTENT OF CLAIMS

68(1) A claim for group relief must specify–

(a) the amount of relief claimed, and

(b) the name of the surrendering company.

68(2) The amount specified must be an amount which is quantified at the time the claim is made.

68(3) A claim for group relief must also state whether or not there is a company mentioned in sub-paragraph (4) that was not resident in the United Kingdom in either or both of the following periods–

(a) the accounting period of the surrendering company to which the surrender relates,

(b) the corresponding accounting period of the claimant company.

68(4) Those companies are the claimant company, the surrendering company and any other company by reference to which–

(a) the claimant company and the surrendering company are members of the same group, or

(b) consortium condition 1, 2 or 3 in sections 132 and 133 of the Corporation Tax Act 2010 is satisfied in the case of the claimant company and the surrendering company.

History – Para. 68(4)(b) substituted by CTA 2010, s. 1177 and Sch. 1, para. 297(9), with effect for corporation tax purposes for accounting periods ending on or after 1 April 2010, and for income tax and capital gains tax purposes for the tax year 2010–11 and subsequent tax years.

Para. 68(3) and (4) inserted by FA 2000, Sch. 27, para. 11, with effect in relation to accounting periods ending on or after 1 April 2000.

CLAIMS FOR MORE OR LESS THAN THE AMOUNT AVAILABLE FOR SURRENDER

69(1) A claim for group relief may be made for less than the amount available for surrender at the time the claim is made.

69(2) A claim is ineffective if the amount claimed exceeds the amount available for surrender at the time the claim is made.

69(3) For these purposes the amount available for surrender at any time is calculated as follows.

First step

Determine the total amount available for surrender under Part 5 of the Corporation Tax Act 2010–

(a) on the basis of the information in company's company tax return, and

(b) disregarding any amendments whose effect is deferred under paragraph 31(3).

Second step

Then deduct the total of all amounts for which notices of consent have been given by the company and not withdrawn.

69(4) Where one or more claims are withdrawn on the same day as one or more claims are made, the withdrawals are given effect first.

69(5) Where more than one claim is made on the same day, and the claims together take the amount claimed over the limit of what is available for surrender, an officer of Revenue and Customs may determine which of the claims is to be ineffective.

69(6) The power under sub-paragraph (5) shall not be exercised to any greater extent than is necessary to bring the total amount claimed within the amount available for surrender.

History – In para. 69(3), the words "Part 5 of the Corporation Tax Act 2010" substituted for the words "section 403 of the Taxes Act 1988" by CTA 2010, s. 1177 and Sch. 1, para. 297(10), with effect for corporation tax purposes for accounting periods ending on or after 1 April 2010, and for income tax and capital gains tax purposes for the tax year 2010–11 and subsequent tax years.
In para. 69(5) the words "an officer of Revenue and Customs" substituted for the words "the Inland Revenue" by CRCA 2005, s. 50 and Sch. 4, para. 68(a), with effect from 18 April 2005 by virtue of SI 2005/1126, art. 2(2).

CONSENT TO SURRENDER

70(1) In accordance with Requirement 1 in section 130(2) of the Corporation Tax Act 2010 or Requirement 1 in section 135(2) of that Act (as the case may be), a claim for group relief requires the consent of the surrendering company.

70(2) A consortium claim also requires the consent of each member of the consortium.

70(3) The necessary consent or consents must be given–

(a) by notice in writing,

(b) to the officer of the Board to whom the surrendering company makes its company tax returns,

(c) at or before the time the claim is made.

Otherwise the claim is ineffective.

70(4) A claim for group relief is ineffective unless it is accompanied by a copy of the notice of consent to surrender given by the surrendering company.

70(5) A consortium claim is ineffective unless it is also accompanied by a copy of the notice of consent to surrender given by each member of the consortium.

70(6) In this paragraph **"consortium claim"** means a claim for group relief under Part 5 of the Corporation Tax Act 2010 based on consortium condition 1, 2 or 3 (see Requirement 3 in section 130(2) of that Act).

History – In para. 70(1), the words "In accordance with Requirement 1 in section 130(2) of the Corporation Tax Act 2010 or Requirement 1 in section 135(2) of that Act (as the case may be), a" substituted for the word "A" by CTA 2010, s. 1177 and Sch. 1, para. 297(11)(a), with effect for corporation tax purposes for accounting periods ending on or after 1 April 2010, and for income tax and capital gains tax purposes for the tax year 2010–11 and subsequent tax years.
Para. 70(6) inserted by CTA 2010, s. 1177 and Sch. 1, para. 297(11)(b), with effect for corporation tax purposes for accounting periods ending on or after 1 April 2010, and for income tax and capital gains tax purposes for the tax year 2010–11 and subsequent tax years.

NOTICE OF CONSENT

71(1) Notice of consent by the surrendering company must contain all the following details–

(a) the name of the surrendering company;

(b) the name of the company to which relief is being surrendered;

(c) the amount of relief being surrendered;

(d) the accounting period of the surrendering company to which the surrender relates;

(e) the tax district references of the surrendering company and the company to which relief is being surrendered.

Otherwise the notice is ineffective.

71(2) Notice of consent may not be amended, but it may be withdrawn and replaced by another notice of consent.

71(3) Notice of consent may be withdrawn by notice to the officer of the Board to which the notice of consent was given.

71(4) Except where the consent is withdrawn under paragraph 75 (withdrawal in consequence of reduction of amount available for surrender), the notice of withdrawal must be accompanied by a notice signifying the consent of the claimant company to the withdrawal.
Otherwise the notice is ineffective.

71(5) The claimant company must, so far as it may do so, amend its company tax return for the accounting period for which the claim was made so as to reflect the withdrawal of consent.

NOTICE OF CONSENT REQUIRING AMENDMENT OF RETURN

72(1) Where notice of consent by the surrendering company is given after the company has made a company tax return for the period to which the surrender relates, the surrendering company must at the same time amend its return so as to reflect the notice of consent.

72(2) Where notice of consent by the surrendering company relates to a loss in respect of which relief has been given under section 45 of the Corporation Tax Act 2010 (carry forward of trading losses), the surrendering company must at the same time amend its company tax return for the period or, if more than one, each of the periods in which relief for that loss has been given under section 45 so as to reflect the new notice of consent.

For this purpose relief under section 45 is treated as given for losses incurred in earlier accounting periods before losses incurred in later accounting periods.

72(3) The time limits otherwise applicable to amendment of a company tax return do not prevent an amendment being made under sub-paragraph (1) or (2).

72(4) If the surrendering company fails to comply with sub-paragraph (1) or (2), the notice of consent is ineffective.

History – In para. 72(2) the words "section 45 of the Corporation Tax Act 2010" substituted for the words "section 393(1) of the Taxes Act 1988" by CTA 2010, s. 1177 and Sch. 1, para. 297(12)(a), with effect for corporation tax purposes for accounting periods ending on or after 1 April 2010, and for income tax and capital gains tax purposes for the tax year 2010–11 and subsequent tax years.
In para. 72(2) the words "section 45" substituted for the words "section 393(1)" in both places by CTA 2010, s. 1177 and Sch. 1, para. 297(12)(b), with effect for corporation tax purposes for accounting periods ending on or after 1 April 2010, and for income tax and capital gains tax purposes for the tax year 2010–11 and subsequent tax years.

WITHDRAWAL OR AMENDMENT OF CLAIM

73(1) A claim for group relief may be withdrawn by the claimant company only by amending its company tax return.

73(2) A claim for group relief may not be amended, but must be withdrawn and replaced by another claim.

TIME LIMIT FOR CLAIMS

74(1) A claim for group relief may be made or withdrawn at any time up to whichever is the last of the following dates–

(a) the first anniversary of the filing date for the company tax return of the claimant company for the accounting period for which the claim is made;

(b) if notice of enquiry is given into that return, 30 days after the enquiry is completed;

(c) if after such an enquiry an officer of Revenue and Customs amends the return under paragraph 34(2), 30 days after notice of the amendment is issued;

(d) if an appeal is brought against such an amendment, 30 days after the date on which the appeal is finally determined.

74(2) A claim for group relief may be made or withdrawn at a later time if an officer of Revenue and Customs allows it.

74(3) The time limits otherwise applicable to amendment of a company tax return do not apply to an amendment to the extent that it makes or withdraws a claim for group relief within the time allowed by or under this paragraph.

74(4) The references in sub-paragraph (1) to an enquiry into a company tax return do not include an enquiry restricted to a previous amendment making or withdrawing a claim for group relief.

An enquiry is so restricted if–

(a) the scope of the enquiry is limited as mentioned in paragraph 25(2), and

(b) the amendment giving rise to the enquiry consisted of the making or withdrawing of a claim for group relief.

History – In para. 74(1)(c) and (2) the words "an officer of Revenue and Customs" substituted for the words "the Inland Revenue" by CRCA 2005, s. 50 and Sch. 4, para. 68(a) and the words "amends" and "allows" substituted for the words "amend" and "allow" by virtue of para. 68(c), with effect from 18 April 2005 by virtue of SI 2005/1126, art. 2(2).

Cross references – ICTA 1988, Sch. 19B, para. 15(3): para. 74 shall apply in relation to a claim for post-commencement supplement as it applies in relation to group relief.
ICTA 1988, Sch. 19C, para. 14(2): para. 74 shall apply in relation to a claim for pre-commencement supplement as it applies in relation to group relief.
ICTA 1988, Sch. 19C, para. 15(3): para. 74 shall apply in relation to a claim for post-commencement supplement as it applies in relation to group relief.

Statements of practice – SP 5/01: HMRC's approach to extending time limits for making claims for loss relief, capital allowances and group relief.

REDUCTION IN AMOUNT AVAILABLE FOR SURRENDER

75(1) This paragraph applies if, after the surrendering company has given one or more notices of consent to surrender, the total amount available for surrender is reduced to less than the amount stated in the notice, or the total of the amounts stated in the notices, as being surrendered.

75(2) The company must within 30 days withdraw the notice of consent, or as many of the notices as is necessary to bring the total amount surrendered within the new total amount available for surrender, and may give one or more new notices of consent.

75(3) The company must give notice in writing of the withdrawal of consent, and send a copy of any new notice of consent–

(a) to each of the companies affected, and

(b) to an officer of Revenue and Customs.

75(4) If the surrendering company fails to act in accordance with sub-paragraph (2), an officer of Revenue and Customs may by notice to the surrendering company give such directions as the officer thinks fit as to which notice or notices are to be ineffective or are to have effect in a lesser amount.

This power shall not be exercised to any greater extent than is necessary to secure that the total amount stated in the notice or notices is consistent with the total amount available for surrender.

75(5) An officer of Revenue and Customs must at the same time send a copy of the notice to the claimant company, or each claimant company, affected by their action.

75(6) A claimant company which receives–

(a) notice of the withdrawal of consent, or a copy of a new notice of consent, under sub-paragraph (3), or

(b) a copy of a notice containing directions by an officer of Revenue and Customs under sub-paragraph (4),

must, so far as it may do so, amend its company tax return for the accounting period for which the claim is made so that it is consistent with the new position with regard to consent to surrender.

75(7) An appeal may be brought by the surrendering company against any directions given by an officer of Revenue and Customs under sub-paragraph (4).

75(8) Notice of appeal must be given–

(a) in writing,

(b) within 30 days after the notice containing the directions was issued,

(c) to the officer of the Board by whom the notice was given.

History – In para. 75(1), words "total amount available for surrender" substituted, and in para. 75(2), (4) word "total" inserted before "amount available for surrender", by FA 1999, s. 95(2), with effect in relation to accounting periods ending on or after 1 July 1999.
In para. 75(3)(b), (4), (5), (6)(b) and (7) the words "an officer of Revenue and Customs" substituted for the words "the Inland Revenue" by CRCA 2005, s. 50 and Sch. 4, para. 68(a) and in para. 75(4) the words "the officer thinks" substituted for the words "they think" by virtue of para. 68(c), with effect from 18 April 2005 by virtue of SI 2005/1126, art. 2(2).

ASSESSMENT ON OTHER CLAIMANT COMPANIES

75A(1) This paragraph applies where, after the surrendering company has given notice of consent to surrender, a claimant company ("the chargeable company") has become liable to tax in consequence of receiving–

(a) notice of the withdrawal of consent, or a copy of a new notice of consent, under paragraph 75(3), or

(b) a copy of a notice containing directions by an officer of Revenue and Customs under paragraph 75(4).

75A(2) If any of the tax is unpaid six months after the chargeable company's time limit for claims, an officer of Revenue and Customs may make an assessment to tax in the name of the chargeable company on any other company that has obtained group relief as a result of the surrender.

75A(3) The assessment may not be made more than two years after that time limit.

75A(4) The amount of the assessment must not exceed–

(a) the amount of the unpaid tax, or

(b) if less, the amount of tax which the other company saves by virtue of the surrender.

75A(5) A company assessed to an amount of tax under sub-paragraph (2) is entitled to recover from the chargeable company–

(a) a sum equal to that amount, and

(b) any interest on that amount which it has paid under section 87A of the Taxes Management Act 1970 (interest on unpaid corporation tax).

75A(6) For the purposes of this paragraph the chargeable company's time limit for claims is the last of the dates mentioned in paragraph 74(1) on which the chargeable company could make or withdraw a claim for group relief for the accounting period for which the claim in question is made.

History – In para. 75A(1)(b) and (2) the words "an officer of Revenue and Customs" substituted for the words "the Inland Revenue" by CRCA 2005, s. 50 and Sch. 4, para. 68(a), with effect from 18 April 2005 by virtue of SI 2005/1126, art. 2(2).
Para. 75A inserted by FA 1999, s. 92(3), with effect in relation to accounting periods ending on or after 1 July 1999.

ASSESSMENT TO RECOVER EXCESSIVE GROUP RELIEF

76(1) If an officer of Revenue and Customs discovers that any group relief which has been given is or has become excessive, the officer may make an assessment to tax in the amount which in the officer's opinion ought to be charged.

76(2) This power is without prejudice to–

(a) the power to make a discovery assessment under paragraph 41(1);

(b) the making of all such adjustments by way of discharge or repayment of tax or otherwise as may be required where a claimant company has obtained too much relief, or a surrendering company has forgone relief in respect of a corresponding amount.

76(3) If an assessment under this paragraph is made because a claimant company fails, or is unable, to amend its company tax return under paragraph 75(6), the assessment is not out of time if it is made within one year from–

(a) the date on which the surrendering company gives notice of the withdrawal of consent, or (if later) sends a copy of a new notice of consent, to the claimant company under paragraph 75(3), or

(b) the date on which an officer of Revenue and Customs sends the claimant company a copy of a notice containing their directions under paragraph 75(4).

History – In para. 76(1) and (3)(b) the words "an officer of Revenue and Customs" substituted for the words "the Inland Revenue" by CRCA 2005, s. 50 and Sch. 4, para. 68(a) and in para. 76(1) the words "discovers", "the officer" and "the officer's" substituted for the words "discover", "they" and "their" and in para. 76(3)(b) the word "sends" substituted for the word "send" by virtue of para. 68(c), with effect from 18 April 2005 by virtue of SI 2005/1126, art. 2(2).

Para. 76(3) added by FA 1999, s. 92(4), with effect in relation to accounting periods ending on or after 1 July 1999.

Statements of practice – SP 5/01:HMRC's approach to extending time limits for making claims for loss relief, capital allowances and group relief.

JOINT AMENDED RETURNS

77(1) The Treasury may by regulations make provision for arrangements under which–

(a) a claim for group relief may be made without being accompanied by a copy of the notice of consent to surrender given by the surrendering company, provided authority for the claim being so made is given by a company which is authorised in relation to the claimant company as mentioned in paragraph (b), and

(b) one company may be authorised to act on behalf of two or more companies in the same group in amending their company tax returns for the purpose of claiming or surrendering group relief or revising the amounts of group relief claimed or surrendered by them.

77(2) Regulations under this paragraph may add to, exclude or modify the operation of any provisions of this Part of this Schedule to such extent as the Treasury think necessary or expedient for the purpose of, or in connection with, such arrangements.

77(3) Provision may in particular be made–

(a) altering the conditions for making and withdrawing claims for group relief, and

(b) giving an officer of Revenue and Customs power to recover from the authorised company or another company in the group any amount which might be recovered from the claimant company by an assessment under paragraph 76.

History – In para. 77(1)(a) the words ", provided authority for the claim being so made is given by a company which is authorised in relation to the claimant company as mentioned in paragraph (b)" inserted by FA 2000, s. 99.

In para. 77(3)(b) the words "an officer of Revenue and Customs" substituted for the words "the Inland Revenue" by CRCA 2005, s. 50 and Sch. 4, para. 68(a), with effect from 18 April 2005 by virtue of SI 2005/1126, art. 2(2).

Statutory instruments – SI 1999/2975: made under para. 77.

CLAIMS IN RESPECT OF OVERSEAS LOSSES OF NON-RESIDENT COMPANIES

77A(1) This paragraph applies if a claim for group relief is made in respect of any loss or other amount as a result of the condition in section 136 of the Corporation Tax Act 2010 being met (claims for group relief based on the EEA group condition).

77A(2) In relation to the surrendering company, this Part of this Schedule applies as if–

(a) references to the relief being surrendered were to the EEA amount and to the relief being claimed, and

(b) references to its accounting period were to the accounting period that the company is assumed to have under section 125 of the Corporation Tax Act 2010 for the purpose of recalculating the EEA amount at Step 3 in section 113 of that Act.

77A(3) Notice of consent of the surrendering company–

(a) is to be given to the officer of the Board under paragraph 70(3)(b) by the claimant company (and not by the surrendering company), and

(b) is to be given to the officer to whom the claimant company makes its company tax returns.

77A(4) If the surrendering company is not within the charge to income or corporation tax, the requirement under paragraph 71(1)(e) for notice of consent by the surrendering company to contain details of its tax district reference is not to apply.

77A(5) If notice of consent is withdrawn under paragraph 71, the notice of the withdrawal is to be given to the officer of the Board by the claimant company (and not by the surrendering company).

77A(6) If notice of consent is withdrawn under paragraph 75–

(a) the notice of withdrawal, and any copy of any new notice of consent, is to be sent to an officer of Revenue and Customs by the claimant company (and not by the surrendering company), and

(b) any notice containing directions by an officer of Revenue and Customs under sub-paragraph (4) of that paragraph is to be given to the claimant company (and not to the surrendering company).

77A(7) The remaining provisions of that paragraph, and the rest of this Part of this Schedule, are, accordingly, to be read with the appropriate modifications (so that, in particular, it is the claimant company (and not the surrendering company) which can bring an appeal under paragraph 75(7)).

77A(8) A notice under paragraph 1 of Schedule 36 to the Finance Act 2008 (notice to taxpayer to produce documents etc) given to the claimant company may require the claimant company–

(a) to explain why the EEA amount meets the conditions mentioned in Step 2 in section 113(2) of the Corporation Tax Act 2010 and is not prevented from being surrendered by section 127 of that Act, and

(b) to provide details of the recalculation required under Step 3 in section 113(2) of that Act in relation to the EEA amount.

77A(9) Except where expressly indicated, requirements imposed under this paragraph are in addition to those imposed apart from this paragraph.

77A(10) In this paragraph **"the EEA amount"** has the same meaning as in Chapter 3 of Part 5 of the Corporation Tax Act 2010.

History – In para. 77A(1), the words "section 136 of the Corporation Tax Act 2010 being met (claims for group relief based on the EEA group condition)." substituted for the words "section 402(2A) of the Taxes Act 1988 being satisfied (relief in respect of overseas losses of non-resident companies)." by CTA 2010, s. 1177 and Sch. 1, para. 297(13)(a), with effect for corporation tax purposes for accounting periods ending on or after 1 April 2010, and for income tax and capital gains tax purposes for the tax year 2010–11 and subsequent tax years.
In para. 77A(8), the words "paragraph 1 of Schedule 36 to the Finance Act 2008 (notice to taxpayer to produce documents etc)" substituted for the words "paragraph 27 (notice to produce documents etc for purposes of an enquiry)" by SI 2009/2035, art. 2 and Sch., para. 38, with effect from 13 August 2009.
In para. 77A(8)(a), the words "Step 2 in section 113(2) of the Corporation Tax Act 2010 and is not prevented from being surrendered by section 127" substituted for the words "subsection (2)(a) to (d) of section 403F of the Taxes Act 1988 and is not prevented from being surrendered by section 403G" by CTA 2010, s. 1177 and Sch. 1, para. 297(13)(c), with effect for corporation tax purposes for accounting periods ending on or after 1 April 2010, and for income tax and capital gains tax purposes for the tax year 2010–11 and subsequent tax years.
In para. 77A(8)(b), the words "Step 3 in section 113(2) of that Act" substituted for the words "Part 2 of Schedule 18A to that Act" by CTA 2010, s. 1177 and Sch. 1, para. 297(13)(d), with effect for corporation tax purposes for accounting periods ending on or after 1 April 2010, and for income tax and capital gains tax purposes for the tax year 2010–11 and subsequent tax years.
In para. 77A(9B), the words "the accounting period that the company is assumed to have under section 125 of the Corporation Tax Act 2010 for the purpose of recalculating the EEA amount at Step 3 in section 113 of that Act." substituted for the words "its deemed accounting period under Part 2 of Schedule 18A to the Taxes Act 1988." by CTA 2010, s. 1177 and Sch. 1, para. 297(13)(b), with effect for corporation tax purposes for accounting periods ending on or after 1 April 2010, and for income tax and capital gains tax purposes for the tax year 2010–11 and subsequent tax years.
In para. 77A(10), the words "Chapter 3 of Part 5 of the Corporation Tax Act 2010" substituted for the words "Part 2 of Schedule 18A to the Taxes Act 1988" by CTA 2010, s. 1177 and Sch. 1, para. 297(13)(e), with effect for corporation tax purposes for accounting periods ending on or after 1 April 2010, and for income tax and capital gains tax purposes for the tax year 2010–11 and subsequent tax years.
S. 77A inserted by FA 2006, s. 27 and Sch. 1, para. 8, with effect in relation to any accountingperiod of a claimant company beginning on or after 1 April 2006, and in relation to any period beginning on or after 1 April 2006 in which any loss or other amount arises to a non-resident company. Transitional provisions are at FA 2006, Sch. 1, para. 9(2)–(6).

Part IX – Claims for Capital Allowances

Cross references – CAA 2001, s. 135: application of Pt. IX to claims under CAA 2001, s. 135 (deferment of balancing charges on ship disposals, etc.).

INTRODUCTION

78 This Part of this Schedule applies to claims for allowances under the Capital Allowances Act which–

(a) are made for corporation tax purposes, and

(b) are required under section 3 of that Act to be included in a tax return.

History – Para. 78 substituted by CA 2001, s. 578 and Sch. 2, para. 103.

CLAIM TO BE INCLUDED IN COMPANY TAX RETURN

79(1) A claim for capital allowances must be included in the claimant company's company tax return for the accounting period for which the claim is made.

79(2) It may be included in the return originally made or by amendment.

History – Para. 79(1) substituted by CA 2001, s. 578 and Sch. 2, para. 103.

CONTENT OF CLAIMS

80 A claim for capital allowances must specify the amount claimed, which must be an amount which is quantified at the time the claim is made.

AMENDMENT OR WITHDRAWAL OF CLAIM

81 A claim for capital allowances may be amended or withdrawn by the claimant company only by amending its company tax return.

TIME LIMIT FOR CLAIMS

82(1) A claim for capital allowances may be made, amended or withdrawn at any time up to whichever is the last of the following dates–

(a) the first anniversary of the filing date for the company tax return of the claimant company for the accounting period for which the claim is made;

(b) if notice of enquiry is given into that return, 30 days after the enquiry is completed;

(c) if after such an enquiry an officer of Revenue and Customs amends the return under paragraph 34(2), 30 days after notice of the amendment is issued;

(d) if an appeal is brought against such an amendment, 30 days after the date on which the appeal is finally determined.

82(2) A claim for capital allowances may be made, amended or withdrawn at a later time if an officer of Revenue and Customs allows it.

82(3) The time limits otherwise applicable to amendment of a company tax return do not apply to an amendment to the extent that it makes, amends or withdraws a claim for capital allowances within the time allowed by or under this paragraph.

82(4) The references in sub-paragraph (1) to an enquiry into a company tax return do not include an enquiry restricted to a previous amendment making, amending or withdrawing a claim for capital allowances.

An enquiry is so restricted if–

(a) the scope of the enquiry is limited as mentioned in paragraph 25(2), and

(b) the amendment giving rise to the enquiry consisted of the making, amending or withdrawing of a claim for capital allowances.

History – In para. 82(1)(c) and (2) the words "an officer of Revenue and Customs" substituted for the words "the Inland Revenue" by CRCA 2005, s. 50 and Sch. 4, para. 68(a) and the words "amends" and "allows" substituted for the words "amend" and "allow" by virtue of para. 68(c), with effect from 18 April 2005 by virtue of SI 2005/1126, art. 2(2).

Statements of practice – SP 5/01: HMRC's approach to extending time limits for making claims for loss relief, capital allowances and group relief.

CONSEQUENTIAL AMENDMENT OF RETURN FOR ANOTHER ACCOUNTING PERIOD

83(1) This paragraph applies if the effect of a claim for capital allowances is to reduce the amount available by way of capital allowances for another accounting period of the company for which a company tax return has been delivered.

83(2) The company has 30 days within which to make any necessary amendments of the company tax return for that other period.

83(3) If it does not do so, an officer of Revenue and Customs may by notice in writing to the company amend the return to make it consistent with the amount available by way of capital allowances.

83(4) The time limits otherwise applicable to amendment of a company tax return do not prevent an amendment being made under sub-paragraph (2) or (3).

83(5) An appeal may be brought by the company against any such amendment.

83(6) Notice of appeal must be given–

(a) in writing,

(b) within 30 days after notice of the amendment was issued,

(c) to the officer of the Board by whom the notice of amendment was issued.

History – In para. 83(3) the words "an officer of Revenue and Customs" substituted for the words "the Inland Revenue" by CRCA 2005, s. 50 and Sch. 4, para. 68(a), with effect from 18 April 2005 by virtue of SI 2005/1126, art. 2(2).

83ZA(1) Subject as follows, this Part of this Schedule applies to claims for a first-year tax credit under Schedule A1 to the Capital Allowances Act as it applies to claims for allowances under that Act.

83ZA(2) A company tax return in which a claim to a first-year tax credit is made must specify–

(a) the plant or machinery to which the relevant first-year expenditure relates,

(b) the amount of the relevant first-year expenditure incurred in respect of that plant or machinery, and

(c) the date on which that expenditure was incurred.

83ZA(3) Where an order under section 45B or 45I of that Act (first-year allowance available only if relevant certificate in force) applies in relation to the plant or machinery, the company tax return must be accompanied by the relevant certificate.

83ZA(4) [Omitted by FA 2008, s. 122 and Sch. 40, para. 21(f).]

83ZA(5) [Omitted by FA 2008, s. 122 and Sch. 40, para. 21(f).]

History – Para. 83ZA(4) omitted by FA 2008, s. 122 and Sch. 40, para. 21(f), with effect from 1 April 2009 (SI 2009/571, art. 2 but subject to transitional provisions at SI 2009/571, art. 6 and 7).
Para. 83ZA(5) omitted by FA 2008, s. 122 and Sch. 40, para. 21(f), with effect from 1 April 2009 (SI 2009/571, art. 2 but subject to transitional provisions at SI 2009/571, art. 6 and 7).
Para. 83ZA inserted by FA 2008, s. 79 and Sch. 25, para. 8(5), with effect in relation to expenditure incurred on or after 1 April 2008.

Part IXA – Claims for R&D Expenditure Credits or R&D Tax Relief

History – Heading to Pt. IXA substituted by FA 2013, s. 35 and Sch. 15, para. 7(4), with effect in relation to expenditure incurred on or after 1 April 2013.
In the heading to Pt. IXA the words "R&D tax relief" substituted for the words "R&D tax credit" by FA 2006, s. 29 and Sch. 3, para. 5, with effect in relation to accounting periods ending on or after 31 March 2006, subject to the provisions of FA 2006, Sch. 3, para. 11.

INTRODUCTION

83A This Part of this Schedule applies to–

(a) claims for R&D expenditure credits under Chapter 6A of Part 3 of the Corporation Tax Act 2009, and

(b) claims for R&D tax relief under Part 13 of that Act.

History – Para. 83A(a) and (b) (and the word "to–" before) substituted for the words "to claims for R&D tax relief under Part 13 of the Corporation Tax Act 2009." by FA 2013, s. 35 and Sch. 15, para. 7(2), with effect in relation to expenditure incurred on or after 1 April 2013.
In para. 83A, the words "Part 13 of the Corporation Tax Act 2009" substituted for the words "Schedule 20 to the Finance Act 2000" by CTA 2009, s. 1322 and Sch. 1, para. 454(7), with effect for corporation tax purposes for accounting periods ending on or after 1 April 2009, and for income tax and capital gains tax purposes for the tax year 2009–10 and subsequent tax years.
In para. 83A the words "claims for R&D tax relief" substituted for the words "claims for R&D tax credits" by FA 2006, s. 29 and Sch. 3, para. 3, with effect in relation to accounting periods ending on or after 31 March 2006, subject to the provisions of FA 2006, Sch. 3, para. 11.
Para. 83A inserted by FA 2000, Sch. 21, para. 4, with effect in relation to accounting periods ending on or after 1 April 2000.

CLAIM TO BE INCLUDED IN COMPANY TAX RETURN

83B(1) A claim to which this Part of this Schedule applies must be made by being included in the claimant company's company tax return for the accounting period for which the claim is made.

83B(2) It may be included in the return originally made or by amendment.

History – In para. 83B(1) the words "claim to which this Part of this Schedule applies" substituted for the words "claim for an R&D tax credit" by FA 2006, s. 29 and Sch. 3, para. 4, with effect in relation to accounting periods ending on or after 31 March 2006, subject to the provisions of FA 2006, Sch. 3, para. 11.
Para. 83B inserted by FA 2000, Sch. 21, para. 4, with effect in relation to accounting periods ending on or after 1 April 2000.

CONTENT OF CLAIM

83C A claim to which this Part of this Schedule applies must specify the amount of the credit or relief claimed, which must be an amount quantified at the time the claim is made.

History – In para. 83C, the words "credit or" inserted by FA 2013, s. 35 and Sch. 15, para. 7(3), with effect in relation to expenditure incurred on or after 1 April 2013.
In para. 83C the words "claim to which this Part of this Schedule applies" substituted for the words "claim for an R&D tax credit" by FA 2006, s. 29 and Sch. 3, para. 4, with effect in relation to accounting periods ending on or after 31 March 2006, subject to the provisions of FA 2006, Sch. 3, para. 11.
Para. 83C inserted by FA 2000, Sch. 21, para. 4, with effect in relation to accounting periods ending on or after 1 April 2000.

AMENDMENT OR WITHDRAWAL OF CLAIM

83D A claim to which this Part of this Schedule applies may be amended or withdrawn by the claimant company only by amending its company tax return.

History – In para. 83D the words "claim to which this Part of this Schedule applies" substituted for the words "claim for an R&D tax credit" by FA 2006, s. 29 and Sch. 3, para. 4, with effect in relation to accounting periods ending on or after 31 March 2006, subject to the provisions of FA 2006, Sch. 3, para. 11.
Para. 83D inserted by FA 2000, Sch. 21, para. 4, with effect in relation to accounting periods ending on or after 1 April 2000.

TIME LIMIT FOR CLAIMS

83E(1) A claim to which this Part of this Schedule applies may be made, amended or withdrawn at any time up to the first anniversary of the filing date for the company tax return of the claimant company for the accounting period for which the claim is made.

83E(2) The claim may be made, amended or withdrawn at a later date if an officer of Revenue and Customs allows it.

History – In para. 83E(1) the words "claim to which this Part of this Schedule applies" substituted for the words "claim for an R&D tax credit" by FA 2006, s. 29 and Sch. 3, para. 4, with effect in relation to accounting periods ending on or after 31 March 2006, subject to the provisions of FA 2006, Sch. 3, para. 11.
In para. 83E(2) the words "an officer of Revenue and Customs" substituted for the words "the Inland Revenue" by CRCA 2005, s. 50 and Sch. 4, para. 68(a) and the word "allows" substituted for the word "allow" by virtue of para. 68(c), with effect from 18 April 2005 by virtue of SI 2005/1126, art. 2(2).
Para. 83E inserted by FA 2000, Sch. 21, para. 4, with effect in relation to accounting periods ending on or after 1 April 2000.

PENALTY

83F [Omitted by FA 2008, s. 122 and Sch. 40, para. 21(f).]

History – Para. 83F omitted by FA 2008, s. 122 and Sch. 40, para. 21(f), with effect from 1 April 2009 (SI 2009/571, art. 2 but subject to transitional provisions at SI 2009/571, art. 6 and 7).

Part 9B – Claims Relating to Remediation of Contaminated or Derelict Land

History – In the heading to Part 9B, the words "or Derelict" inserted by FA 2009, s. 26 and Sch. 7, para. 25, with effect in relation to expenditure incurred on or after 1 April 2009.

INTRODUCTION

83G This Part of this Schedule applies to claims for–

(a) land remediation tax credits under section 1151 of the Corporation Tax Act 2009 (**"land remediation tax credits"**), and

(b) life assurance company tax credits under section 1164 of that Act (**"life assurance company tax credits"**).

History – In para. 83G(a) the words "section 1151 of the Corporation Tax Act 2009" substituted for the words "paragraph 14 of Schedule 22 to the Finance Act 2001" and in para. (b) the words "section 1164 of that Act" substituted for the words "paragraph 24 of that Schedule" by CTA 2009, s. 1322 and Sch. 1, para. 454(9), with effect for corporation tax purposes for accounting periods ending on or after 1 April 2009, and for income tax and capital gains tax purposes for the tax year 2009–10 and subsequent tax years.
Para. 83G inserted by FA 2001, s. 70 and Sch. 23, para. 6, with effect for accounting periods ending on or after 1 April 2001.

CLAIM TO BE INCLUDED IN COMPANY TAX RETURN

83H(1) A claim for a land remediation tax credit or a life assurance company tax credit must be made by being included in the claimant company's company tax return for the accounting period for which the claim is made.

83H(2) It may be included in the return originally made or by amendment.

History – Para. 83H inserted by FA 2001, s. 70 and Sch. 23, para. 6, with effect for accounting periods ending on or after 1 April 2001.

CONTENT OF CLAIM

83I A claim for a land remediation tax credit or a life assurance company tax credit must specify the amount of the tax credit claimed, which must be an amount quantified at the time the claim is made.

History – Para. 83I inserted by FA 2001, s. 70 and Sch. 23, para. 6, with effect for accounting periods ending on or after 1 April 2001.

AMENDMENT OR WITHDRAWAL OF CLAIM

83J A claim for a land remediation tax credit or a life assurance company tax credit may be amended or withdrawn by the claimant company only by amending its company tax return.

History – Para. 83J inserted by FA 2001, s. 70 and Sch. 23, para. 6, with effect for accounting periods ending on or after 1 April 2001.

TIME LIMIT FOR CLAIMS

83K(1) A claim for a land remediation tax credit or a life assurance company tax credit may be made, amended or withdrawn at any time up to the first anniversary of the filing date for the company tax return of the claimant company for the accounting period for which the claim is made.

83K(2) The claim may be made, amended or withdrawn at a later date if an officer of Revenue and Customs allows it.

History – In para. 83K(2) the words "an officer of Revenue and Customs" substituted for the words "the Inland Revenue" by CRCA 2005, s. 50 and Sch. 4, para. 68(a) and the word "allows" substituted for the word "allow" by virtue of para. 68(c), with effect from 18 April 2005 by virtue of SI 2005/1126, art. 2(2).

Para. 83K inserted by FA 2001, s. 70 and Sch. 23, para. 6, with effect for accounting periods ending on or after 1 April 2001

PENALTY

83L [Omitted by FA 2008, s. 122 and Sch. 40, para. 21(f).]

History – Para. 83L omitted by FA 2008, s. 122 and Sch. 40, para. 21(f), with effect from 1 April 2009 (SI 2009/571, art. 2 but subject to transitional provisions at SI 2009/571, art. 6 and 7).

Part 9BA – Claims for Relief under Schedule 12 to the Finance Act 2002

[Omitted by CTA 2009, s. 1322 and Sch. 1, para. 454(10) and repealed by CTA 2009, s. 1326 and Sch. 3, Pt. 1.]

History – Pt. 9BA (para. 83LA–para. 83LE) omitted by CTA 2009, s. 1322 and Sch. 1, para. 454(10) and repealed by CTA 2009, s. 1326 and Sch. 3, Pt. 1, with effect for corporation tax purposes for accounting periods ending on or after 1 April 2009, and for income tax and capital gains tax purposes for the tax year 2009–10 and subsequent tax years.

Part 9C – Claims For Tax Relief Under Schedule 13 to the Finance Act 2002

[Omitted by CTA 2009, s. 1322 and Sch. 1, para. 454(11) and repealed by CTA 2009, s. 1326 and Sch. 3, Pt. 1.]

History – Pt. 9C (para. 83M–para. 83R) omitted by CTA 2009, s. 1322 and Sch. 1, para. 454(11) and repealed by CTA 2009, s. 1326 and Sch. 3, Pt. 1, with effect for corporation tax purposes for accounting periods ending on or after 1 April 2009, and for income tax and capital gains tax purposes for the tax year 2009–10 and subsequent tax years.

Part 9D – Claims for Tax Relief Under Part 15, 15A, 15B, 15C or 15D of the Corporation Tax Act 2009

History – In the heading to Pt. 9D ", 15C or 15D" substituted for "or 15C" by FA 2016 s. 54 and Sch. 8, para. 6(a), with effect in relation to accounting periods beginning on or after 1 April 2016 (subject to provisions of Sch. 8, para. 17(2) and (3)).

Heading to Pt. 9D substituted by FA 2014, s. 36 and Sch. 4, para. 6(3), with effect from 22 August 2014, in relation to accounting periods beginning on or after 1 September 2014, subject to the transitional provisions in FA 2014, Sch. 4, para. 17.

In the former Heading to Pt. 9D "or 15B" inserted after "15A" by FA 2013, s. 36 and Sch. 18, para. 5(3), with effect from 1 April 2014 (SI 2014/1962) in relation to accounting periods beginning on or after "the relevant day" (as defined in FA 2013, Sch. 18, para. 23).

Heading to Pt. 9D substituted by FA 2013, s. 36 and Sch. 18, para. 5(3), with effect from 19 July 2013 (SI 2013/1817) in relation to accounting periods beginning on or after "the relevant day" (as defined in FA 2013, Sch. 18, para. 23). Former heading read "Claims for Film Tax Relief".

INTRODUCTION

83S This Part of this Schedule applies to claims for the following reliefs–

(a) film tax relief,

(b) television tax relief,

(c) video games tax relief[,]

(d) an additional deduction under Part 15C of CTA 2009,

(e) a theatre tax credit under that Part of that Act[,]

(f) orchestra tax relief.

History – Para. 83S(a)–(b) (and the words "the following reliefs–" before) substituted for the words "film tax relief" by FA 2013, s. 36 and Sch. 18, para. 5(2), with effect from 19 July 2013 (SI 2013/1817) in relation to accounting periods beginning on or after "the relevant day" (as defined in FA 2013, Sch. 18, para. 23).
Para. 83S(c) inserted by FA 2013, s. 36 and Sch. 18, para. 5(2), with effect from 1 April 2014 (SI 2014/1962) in relation to accounting periods beginning on or after "the relevant day" (as defined in FA 2013, Sch. 18, para. 23).
Para. 83S(d) and (e) inserted by FA 2014, s. 36 and Sch. 4, para. 6(2), with effect from 22 August 2014, in relation to accounting periods beginning on or after 1 September 2014, subject to the transitional provisions in FA 2014, Sch. 4, para. 17.
Para. 83S(f) inserted by FA 2016 s. 54 and Sch. 8, para. 6(b), with effect in relation to accounting periods beginning on or after 1 April 2016 (subject to provisions of Sch. 8, para. 17(2) and (3)).
Para. 83S inserted by FA 2006, s. 42 and Sch. 5, para. 29, with effect from 1 January 2007 (FA 1996, s. 53(1)).

CLAIM TO BE INCLUDED IN COMPANY TAX RETURN

83T(1) A claim to which this Part of this Schedule applies must be made by being included in the claimant company's tax return for the accounting period for which the claim is made.

83T(2) It may be included in the return originally made or by amendment.

History – Para. 83T inserted by FA 2006, s. 42 and Sch. 5, para. 29, with effect from 1 January 2007 (FA 1996, s. 53(1)).

CONTENT OF CLAIM

83U A claim to which this Part of this Schedule applies must specify the amount of the relief claimed, which must be an amount quantified at the time the claim is made.

History – Para. 83U inserted by FA 2006, s. 42 and Sch. 5, para. 29, with effect from 1 January 2007 (FA 1996, s. 53(1)).

AMENDMENT OR WITHDRAWAL OF CLAIM

83V A claim to which this Part of this Schedule applies may be amended or withdrawn by the claimant company only by amending its company tax return.

History – Para. 83V inserted by FA 2006, s. 42 and Sch. 5, para. 29, with effect from 1 January 2007 (FA 1996, s. 53(1)).

TIME LIMITS FOR CLAIM

83W(1) A claim to which this part of this Schedule applies may be made, amended or withdrawn at any time up to the first anniversary of the filing date for the company tax return of the claimant company for the accounting period for which the claim is made.

83W(2) The claim may be made, amended or withdrawn at a later date if an officer of Revenue and Customs allows it.

History – Para. 83W inserted by FA 2006, s. 42 and Sch. 5, para. 29, with effect from 1 January 2007 (FA 1996, s. 53(1)).

PENALTY

83X [Omitted by FA 2008, s. 122 and Sch. 40, para. 21(f).]

History – Para. 83X omitted by FA 2008, s. 122 and Sch. 40, para. 21(f), with effect from 1 April 2009 (SI 2009/571, art. 2 but subject to transitional provisions at SI 2009/571, art. 6 and 7).

Part 9E – Designation of Losses as Unrestricted Losses for the Purposes of Chapter 3 of Part 7A of the Corporation Tax Act 2010

History – Part 9E inserted by FA 2015, s. 32 and Sch. 2, para. 2, with effect for the purposes of calculating the taxable profits of companies for accounting periods beginning on or after 1 April 2015 (subject to the provisions of FA 2015, Sch. 2, para. 7(2)–(4)).

INTRODUCTION

83Y(1) This Part of this Schedule applies to the designation of losses within sub-paragraph (2) as unrestricted losses by a banking company under section 269CH of the Corporation Tax Act 2010 (losses covered by carried-forward loss allowance).

83Y(2) The losses mentioned in sub-paragraph (1) are losses which, in relation to any accounting period, would (in the absence of that section) be relevant carried-forward losses.

83Y(3) *Expressions used in* this Part of this Schedule and in Chapter 3 of Part 7A of the Corporation Tax Act 2010 have the same meaning in this Part of this Schedule as they have in that Chapter.

History – Para. 83Y inserted by FA 2015, s. 32 and Sch. 2, para. 2, with effect for the purposes of calculating the taxable profits of companies for accounting periods beginning on or after 1 April 2015 (subject to the provisions of FA 2015, Sch. 2, para. 7(2)–(4)).

DESIGNATION TO BE MADE IN COMPANY TAX RETURN

83YA(1) A designation to which this Part of this Schedule applies must be made by being included in the company's tax return for the accounting period for which the company makes a deduction in respect of the losses.

83YA(2) It may be included in the return originally made or by amendment.

History – Para. 83YA inserted by FA 2015, s. 32 and Sch. 2, para. 2, with effect for the purposes of calculating the taxable profits of companies for accounting periods beginning on or after 1 April 2015 (subject to the provisions of FA 2015, Sch. 2, para. 7(2)–(4)).

IDENTIFICATION OF LOSSES

83YB Where a company designates any relevant carried-forward loss in a company tax return, the return must specify–

(a) the amount of the loss, and

(b) whether the loss is–

(i) a pre-2015 carried-forward trading loss,

(ii) a pre-2015 carried-forward non-trading deficit, or

(iii) pre-2015 carried-forward management expenses.

History – Para. 83YB inserted by FA 2015, s. 32 and Sch. 2, para. 2, with effect for the purposes of calculating the taxable profits of companies for accounting periods beginning on or after 1 April 2015 (subject to the provisions of FA 2015, Sch. 2, para. 7(2)–(4)).

AMENDMENT OR WITHDRAWAL OF DESIGNATION

83YC A designation to which this Part of this Schedule applies may be amended or withdrawn by the company only by amending its company tax return.

History – Para. 83YC inserted by FA 2015, s. 32 and Sch. 2, para. 2, with effect for the purposes of calculating the taxable profits of companies for accounting periods beginning on or after 1 April 2015 (subject to the provisions of FA 2015, Sch. 2, para. 7(2)–(4)).

Part X – Special Provisions

84 [Omitted by CTA 2009, s. 1322 and Sch. 1, para. 454(12) and repealed by CTA 2009, s. 1326 and Sch. 3, Pt. 1.]

History – Para. 84 and the cross-heading which preceded it omitted by CTA 2009, s. 1322 and Sch. 1, para. 454(12) and repealed by CTA 2009, s. 1326 and Sch. 3, Pt. 1, with effect for corporation tax purposes for accounting periods ending on or after 1 April 2009, and for income tax and capital gains tax purposes for the tax year 2009–10 and subsequent tax years.

NON-ANNUAL ACCOUNTING OF GENERAL INSURANCE BUSINESS

85(1) This paragraph applies where a company carrying on insurance business delivers a company tax return based wholly or partly on accounts drawn up using the method described in paragraph 58 in Section E of Part 2 of Schedule 3 to the Large and Medium-sized Companies and Groups (Accounts and Reports) Regulations 2008.

That paragraph provides for a technical provision to be made in the accounts which is later replaced by a provision for estimated claims outstanding.

85(2) Where this paragraph applies–

(a) the company may make any amendments of its return arising from the replacement of the technical provision at any time within twelve months from the date on which the provision was replaced, and

(b) an officer of Revenue and Customs may give notice of enquiry into the return at any time up to two years from that date.

85(3) Nothing in this paragraph prevents notice of enquiry being given at any later time in accordance with the general rule in paragraph 24(3).

History – In para. 85(1), the words "paragraph 58 in Section E of Part 2 of Schedule 3 to the Large and Medium-sized Companies and Groups (Accounts and Reports) Regulations 2008" substituted for the words "paragraph 52 of Schedule 9A to the Companies Act 1985" by SI 2009/1890, art. 5(2)(b), with effect from 1 October 2009.

In para. 85(2)(b) the words "an officer of Revenue and Customs" substituted for the words "the Inland Revenue" by CRCA 2005, s. 50 and Sch. 4, para. 68(a), with effect from 18 April 2005 by virtue of SI 2005/1126, art. 2(2).

Cross references – SI 2008/410: Large and Medium-sized Companies and Groups (Accounts and Reports) Regulations 2008.

INSURANCE COMPANIES WITH NON-ANNUAL ACTUARIAL INVESTIGATIONS

86 [Omitted by FA 2007, s. 41 and Sch. 10, para. 16(7) and repealed by FA 2007, s. 114 and Sch. 27, Pt. 2(10).]

History – Para. 86 omitted by FA 2007, s. 41 and Sch. 10, para. 16(7) and repealed by FA 2007, s. 114 and Sch. 27, Pt. 2(10) with effect from 19 July 2007.

FRIENDLY SOCIETIES WITH NON-ANNUAL ACTUARIAL INVESTIGATIONS

87(1) This paragraph applies where a company tax return is delivered by a friendly society which is required by section 5.2 of the Prudential Sourcebook (Friendly Societies) to cause an investigation to be made into its financial condition at least once in every period of three years.

87(2) Where this paragraph applies–

(a) the society may make any amendments of its return arising from the relevant investigation at any time within 15 months from the date as at which that investigation is carried out, and

(b) an officer of Revenue and Customs may give notice of enquiry into the return at any time up to 27 months from that date.

87(3) **"The relevant investigation"** means–

(a) if the return is for a period as at the end of which there is carried out an investigation under section 5.2 of the Prudential Sourcebook (Friendly Societies) into the financial condition of the society, that investigation;

(b) if the return is not for such a period, the first such investigation to be made into the financial condition of the company as at the end of a subsequent period.

87(4) In this paragraph **"the Prudential Sourcebook (Friendly Societies)"** means the Interim Prudential Sourcebook for Friendly Societies made by the Financial Services Authority under the Financial Services and Markets Act 2000.

History – In para. 87 (1) and (3), the words "47 of the Friendly Societies Act 1992" substituted by the words "5.2 of the Prudential Sourcebook (Friendly Societies)", by virtue of SI 2001/3629, art. 103(4)(a) which has effect in relation to periods of account ending on or after 1 December 2001.

In para. 87(2)(b) the words "an officer of Revenue and Customs" substituted for the words "the Inland Revenue" by CRCA 2005, s. 50 and Sch. 4, para. 68(a), with effect from 18 April 2005 by virtue of SI 2005/1126, art. 2(2).

Para. 87(4) inserted by SI 2001/3629, art. 103(4)(b) which has effect in relation to periods of account ending on or after 1 December 2001.

PART 10A – SES

History – Pt. 10A inserted by TIOPA 2010, s. 371 and Sch. 7, para. 108(2), with effect for corporation tax purposes for accounting periods ending on or after 1 April 2010, for income tax and capital gains tax purposes for the tax year 2010–11 and subsequent tax years, and for petroleum revenue tax purposes for chargeable periods beginning on or after 1 July 2010.

COMPANY CEASING TO BE UK RESIDENT ON FORMATION OF SE BY MERGER

87A(1) Sub-paragraph (2) applies if at any time a company ceases to be resident in the United Kingdom in the course of the formation of an SE by merger, whether or not the company continues to exist after the formation of the SE.

87A(2) The other Parts of this Schedule apply after that time, but in relation to liabilities accruing and matters arising before that time–

(a) as if the company were still resident in the United Kingdom, and

(b) if the company has ceased to exist, as if the SE were the company.

History – Para. 87A inserted by TIOPA 2010, s. 371 and Sch. 7, para. 108(2), with effect for corporation tax purposes for accounting periods ending on or after 1 April 2010, for income tax and capital gains tax purposes for the tax year 2010–11 and subsequent tax years, and for petroleum revenue tax purposes for chargeable periods beginning on or after 1 July 2010.

SE CEASING TO BE UK RESIDENT

87B(1) Sub-paragraph (2) applies if at any time an SE–

(a) transfers its registered office from the United Kingdom, and

(b) ceases to be resident in the United Kingdom.

87B(2) The other Parts of this Schedule apply after that time, but in relation to liabilities accruing and matters arising before that time, as if the SE were still resident in the United Kingdom.

History – Para. 87B inserted by TIOPA 2010, s. 371 and Sch. 7, para. 108(2), with effect for corporation tax purposes for accounting periods ending on or after 1 April 2010, for income tax and capital gains tax purposes for the tax year 2010–11 and subsequent tax years, and for petroleum revenue tax purposes for chargeable periods beginning on or after 1 July 2010.

MEANING OF SE

87C In this Part **"SE"** means a European public limited-liability company (or Societas Europaea) within the meaning of Council Regulation (EC) No. 2157/2001 on the Statute for a European company.

History – Para. 87C inserted by TIOPA 2010, s. 371 and Sch. 7, para. 108(2), with effect for corporation tax purposes for accounting periods ending on or after 1 April 2010, for income tax and capital gains tax purposes for the tax year 2010–11 and subsequent tax years, and for petroleum revenue tax purposes for chargeable periods beginning on or after 1 July 2010.

Part XI – Supplementary Provisions

CONCLUSIVENESS OF AMOUNTS STATED IN RETURNS

88(1) This paragraph applies to an amount stated in a company tax return for an accounting period which is required to be included in the return and which affects or may affect–

(a) the tax payable by the company making the return for another accounting period, or

(b) the tax liability of another company for any accounting period.

88(2) If such an amount can no longer be altered it is taken to be conclusively determined for the purposes of the Corporation Tax Acts in relation to that other period or other company.
Sub-paragraphs (3) to (5) explain what is meant by "can no longer be altered".

88(3) An amount is regarded as one that can no longer be altered if–

(a) the period specified in paragraph 15(4) (general period for amendment by company) has ended,

(b) any enquiry into the return has been completed,

(c) if an officer of Revenue and Customs amends the return under paragraph 34, the period within which an appeal may be brought against that amendment has ended, and

(d) if an appeal is brought, the appeal has been finally determined.

88(4) If the return is amended by the company under a provision that allows an amendment after the end of the period specified in paragraph 15(4), an amount affected by the amendment ceases to be regarded as one that can no longer be altered until after whichever is the last of the following–

(a) the end of the period within which notice of enquiry into the return may be given in consequence of the amendment;

(b) if such a notice is given, the completion of the enquiry;

(c) if an officer of Revenue and Customs amends the return under paragraph 34, the end of the period within which an appeal against that amendment may be brought;

(d) if an appeal is brought, the date on which the appeal is finally determined.

88(5) If the return is amended by an officer of Revenue and Customs under paragraph 83(3) (consequential amendment or return where amount available by way of capital allowances is reduced), an amount affected by the amendment ceases to be regarded as one that can no longer be altered until after–

(a) the end of the period within which an appeal against that amendment may be brought, or

(b) if an appeal is brought, the date on which the appeal is finally determined.

88(6) For the purposes of this paragraph an amount carried forward from a period for which a return was made under section 11 of the Taxes Management Act 1970 is not regarded as one required to be included in a company tax return for a later period.

88(7) Nothing in this paragraph affects any power to make an assessment other than a self-assessment or the power to make a discovery determination.

88(8) Nothing in this paragraph affects a power of the company making the return to make a claim under paragraph 51 (claim for relief for overpaid tax).

History – In para. 88(3)(b), the words "and the period specified in paragraph 34(1) (period for amendment by company after enquiry) has ended", which appeared at the end, omitted by FA 2008, s. 119(10)(a), with effect from 1 April 2010 (SI 2009/405).
In para. 88(3)(c), "34" substituted for "34(2)" by FA 2008, s. 119(10)(b), with effect from 1 April 2010 (SI 2009/405).
In para. 88(3)(c), (4)(c) and (5) the words "an officer of Revenue and Customs" substituted for the words "the Inland Revenue" by CRCA 2005, s. 50 and Sch. 4, para. 68(a) and in para. 83(3)(c) and (4)(c) the word "amends" substituted for the word "amend" by virtue of para. 68(c), with effect from 18 April 2005 by virtue of SI 2005/1126, art. 2(2).
In para. 88(4)(b), the words "the completion of the enquiry" substituted for the words "the end of the period specified in paragraph 34(1)" by FA 2008, s. 119(10)(c), with effect from 1 April 2010 (SI 2009/405).
In para. 88(4)(c), "34" substituted for "34(2)" by FA 2008, s. 119(10)(d), with effect from 1 April 2010 (SI 2009/405).
Para. 88(8) inserted by FA 2009, s. 100 and Sch. 52, para. 16, with effect in relation to claims made on or after 1 April 2010.

Cross references – FA 1993, s. 94(10): disapplication of para. 88 in ascertaining currency equivalents under s. 94.
FA 1993, s. 94AA: general rules for ascertaining currency equivalents.
FA 1993, s. 94AB: rules for ascertaining sterling equivalents.

PENALTY FOR FRAUD OR NEGLIGENCE

89 [Omitted by FA 2007, s. 97 and Sch. 24, para. 29(c) and repealed by FA 2007, s. 114 and Sch. 27, Pt. 5(5).]

History – Para. 89 omitted by FA 2007, s. 97 and Sch. 24, para. 29(c) and repealed by FA 2007, s. 114 and Sch. 27, Pt. 5(5), with effect as follows by virtue of SI 2008/568, art. 2:

- 1 April 2008 in relation to relevant documents relating to tax periods commencing on or after that date;
- 1 April 2008 in relation to assessments falling within paragraph 2 for tax periods commencing on or after that date;
- 1 July 2008 in relation to relevant documents relating to claims under the Thirteenth Council Directive (arrangements for the refund of value added tax to persons not established in Community territory) for years commencing on or after that date;

- 1 January 2009 in relation to relevant documents relating to claims under the Eighth Council Directive (arrangements for the refund of value added tax to taxable persons not established in the territory of the country) for years commencing on or after that date;
- 1 April 2009 in relation to documents relating to all other claims for repayments of relevant tax made on or after 1 April 2009 which are not related to a tax period; and
- in any other case, 1 April 2009 in relation to documents given where a person's liability to pay relevant tax arises on or after that date.

However, no person will be liable to a penalty under Sch. 24 in respect of any tax period for which a return is required to be made before 1 April 2009.

MULTIPLE TAX-RELATED PENALTIES IN RESPECT OF SAME ACCOUNTING PERIOD

90(1) This paragraph applies where a company incurs more than one penalty whose amount falls to be determined by reference to the tax payable by it for an accounting period.

90(2) Each penalty after the first shall be reduced so that the total amount of the penalties, so far as determined by reference to any particular part of the tax, does not exceed whichever is, or but for this paragraph would be, the greater or greatest of them, so far as so determined.

EUROPEAN ECONOMIC INTEREST GROUPINGS

91 An act or omission such as is mentioned in section 98B of the Taxes Management Act 1970 (European Economic Interest Groupings: acts or omissions attracting penalties) on the part of a grouping, or a member of a grouping, is treated as the act or omission of each member of the grouping for the purposes of–

paragraphs 43 and 46(2) (assessment in case of fraud or negligence), and

paragraphs 61(2) and 65(1) (consequential claims in case of such an assessment).

NOTICES OF APPEAL

92(1) This paragraph applies in relation to any appeal under this Schedule.

92(2) The notice of appeal shall specify the grounds of appeal.

92(3) [Omitted by SI 2009/56, art. 3(1) and Sch. 1, para. 266.]

History – Para. 92(3) omitted by SI 2009/56, art. 3(1) and Sch. 1, para. 266, operative from 1 April 2009, subject to transitional and saving provisions in SI 2009/56, Sch. 3.

GENERAL JURISDICTION OF SPECIAL OR GENERAL COMMISSIONERS

93 [Omitted by SI 2009/56, art. 3(1) and Sch. 1, para. 267.]

History – Para. 93 omitted by SI 2009/56, art. 3(1) and Sch. 1, para. 267, operative from 1 April 2009, subject to transitional and saving provisions in SI 2009/56, Sch. 3.

ELECTION TO TAKE APPEAL TO SPECIAL COMMISSIONERS

94 [Omitted by SI 2009/56, art. 3(1) and Sch. 1, para. 267.]

History – Para. 94 omitted by SI 2009/56, art. 3(1) and Sch. 1, para. 267, operative from 1 April 2009, subject to transitional and saving provisions in SI 2009/56, Sch. 3.

MEANING OF "THE INLAND REVENUE"

95 [Omitted by CRCA 2005, s. 50 and Sch. 4, para. 68(b) and repealed by CRCA 2005, s. 52 and Sch. 5.]

History – Para. 95 omitted by CRCA 2005, s. 50 and Sch. 4, para. 68(b) and repealed by CRCA 2005, s. 52 and Sch. 5, with effect from 18 April 2005 by virtue of SI 2005/1126, art. 2(2).

THE SELF-ASSESSMENT APPOINTED DAY

96 In this Schedule **"the self-assessment appointed day"** means the day appointed by the Treasury under section 199 of the Finance Act 1994 for the purposes of Chapter III of Part IV of that Act (corporation tax self-assessment).

Notes – The day appointed under FA 1994, s. 199 (the self-assessment appointed day) is 1 July 1999 (SI 1998/3173 (C. 78)).

CONSTRUCTION OF REFERENCES TO ASSESSMENT

97 Any reference in the Tax Acts (however expressed) to a person being assessed to tax, or being charged to tax by an assessment, include a reference to his being so assessed, or being so charged–

(a) by a self-assessment under this Schedule, or an amendment of such a self-assessment, or

(b) by a determination under paragraph 36 or 37 of this Schedule (which, until superseded by a self-assessment, has effect as if it were one).

MEANING OF TIOPA 2010

97A In this Schedule **"TIOPA 2010"** means the Taxation (International and Other Provisions) Act 2010.

History – Para. 97A inserted by TIOPA 2010, s. 374 and Sch. 8, para. 321(6), with effect for corporation tax purposes for accounting periods ending on or after 1 April 2010, for income tax and capital gains tax purposes for the tax year 2010–11 and subsequent tax years, and for petroleum revenue tax purposes for chargeable periods beginning on or after 1 July 2010.

INDEX OF DEFINED EXPRESSIONS

98 In this Schedule the expressions listed below are defined or otherwise explained by the provisions indicated–

the Board	paragraph 95(6)
closure notice	paragraph 32(1)
company tax return	paragraph 3(1)
delivery (in relation to company tax return)	paragraph 4
discovery assessment	paragraph 41(1)
discovery determination	paragraph 41(2)
filing date	paragraph 14
Inland Revenue	paragraph 95
notice of enquiry	paragraph 24(1)
notice requiring company tax return	paragraph 3(1)
SE (in Part 10A)	paragraph 87C
self-assessment	paragraph 7
self-assessment appointed day	paragraph 96
tax	paragraph 1 (and see paragraphs 63(3) and 64(5))
tax payable	paragraph 8
TIOPA 2010	paragraph 97A
wrong period (return for)	paragraph 26(2) to (4)

History – In para. 98, in the table, the entry for "SE (in Part 10A)" inserted by TIOPA 2010, s. 371 and Sch. 7, para. 108(3), with effect for corporation tax purposes for accounting periods ending on or after 1 April 2010, for income tax and capital gains tax purposes for the tax year 2010–11 and subsequent tax years, and for petroleum revenue tax purposes for chargeable periods beginning on or after 1 July 2010.

In para. 98, in the table, the entry for "TIOPA 2010" inserted by TIOPA 2010, s. 374 and Sch. 8, para. 321(7), with effect for corporation tax purposes for accounting periods ending on or after 1 April 2010, for income tax and capital gains tax purposes for the tax year 2010–11 and subsequent tax years, and for petroleum revenue tax purposes for chargeable periods beginning on or after 1 July 2010.

SCHEDULE 19 – COMPANY TAX RETURNS, ETC.: MINOR AND CONSEQUENTIAL AMENDMENTS

Section 117(3)

TAXES MANAGEMENT ACT 1970 (C. 9)

1 [Repeals TMA 1970, s. 10, 11, 11AA, 11AB and 11AC to 11AE.]

2 [Amends TMA 1970, s. 12(2).]

3 [Amends TMA 1970, s. 12AA(7).]

4 [Repealed by FA 2001, s. 110 and Sch. 33, Pt. 2(13).]

History – Para. 4 repealed by FA 2001, s. 110 and Sch. 33, Pt. 2(13), with effect from 11 May 2001 in relation to returns made at any time in respect of any period.

5 [Repealed by FA 2001, s. 110 and Sch. 33, Pt. 2(13).]

History – Para. 5 repealed by FA 2001, s. 110 and Sch. 33, Pt. 2(13), with effect from 11 May 2001 in relation to returns made at any time in respect of any period.

6 [Amends TMA 1970, s. 12B(1).]

7 [Amends TMA 1970, s. 19A(1).]

8 [Repealed by FA 2001, s. 110 and Sch. 33, Pt. 2(13).]

History – Para. 8 repealed by FA 2001, s. 110 and Sch. 33, Pt. 2(13), with effect from 11 May 2001 in relation to returns made at any time in respect of any period.

9 [Repeals TMA 1970, s. 28AA and 28AB.]

10 [Repealed by FA 2001, s. 110 and Sch. 33, Pt. 2(13).]

History – Para. 10 repealed by FA 2001, s. 110 and Sch. 33, Pt. 2(13), with effect from 11 May 2001 in relation to returns made at any time in respect of any period.

11 [Repeals TMA 1970, s. 28D, 28E and 28F.]

12(1) Section 29 of the Taxes Management Act 1970 (assessment where loss of tax discovered) is amended as follows.

12(2) [Amends TMA 1970, s. 29(1).]

12(3) [Amends TMA 1970, s. 29.]

12(4) [Amends TMA 1970, s. 29(2), (3), (5)(a), (6)(a) and (7)(a).]

12(5) [Amends TMA 1970, s. 29(3).]

12(6) [Omits TMA 1970, s. 29(10).]

13(1) Section 30 of the Taxes Management Act 1970 (recovery of overpayment of tax, etc.) is amended as follows.

13(2) [Amends TMA 1970, s. 30(1).]

13(3) [Amends TMA 1970, s. 30(2)(a).]

13(4) [Omits TMA 1970, s. 30(2A).]

13(5) [Amends TMA 1970, s. 30(3).]

13(6) [Omits TMA 1970, s. 30(3A).]

13(7) [Repealed by ITTOIA 2005, s. 884 and Sch. 3.]

13(8) [Omits TMA 1970, s. 30(4A).]

History – Para. 13(7) repealed by ITTOIA 2005, s. 884 and Sch. 3 effective for income tax purposes for 2005–06 onwards and for corporation tax purposes for accounting periods ending after 5 April 2005 (ITTOIA 2005, s. 883(1)).

14(1) Section 30B of the Taxes Management Act 1970 (amendment of partnership statement where loss of tax discovered) is amended as follows.

14(2) [Repealed by FA 2001, s. 110 and Sch. 33, Pt. 2(13).]

14(3) [Amends TMA 1970, s. 30B(7)(b).]

14(4) [Amends TMA 1970, s. 30B(9).]

History – Para. 14(2) repealed by FA 2001, s. 110 and Sch. 33, Pt. 2(13), with effect from 11 May 2001 in relation to returns made at any time in respect of any period.

15(1) Section 33 of the Taxes Management Act 1970 (error or mistake) is amended as follows.

15(2) [Substitutes TMA 1970, s. 33(1).]

15(3) [Amends TMA 1970, s. 33(5).]

16(1) Section 33A of the Taxes Management Act 1970 (error or mistake in partnership statement) is amended as follows.

16(2) [Amends TMA 1970, s. 33A(1).]

16(3) [Repealed by FA 2001, s. 110 and Sch. 33, Pt. 2(13).]

History – Para. 16(3) repealed by FA 2001, s. 110 and Sch. 33, Pt. 2(13)2(13), with effect from 11 May 2001 in relation to returns made at any time in respect of any period.

17 [Amends TMA 1970, s. 34(1).]

18 [Omitted by FA 2008, s. 118 and Sch. 39, para. 65(d).]

History – Para. 18 omitted by FA 2008, s. 118 and Sch. 39, para. 65(d), with effect from 1 April 2010 (SI 2009/403, art. 2(2) subject to SI 2009/403, art. 3–10 – in particular art. 10). Former para. 18 amended TMA 1970, s. 36(1).

19 [Repeals TMA 1970, s. 41A, 41B and 41C.]

20(1) Section 42 of the Taxes Management Act 1970 (procedure for making claims, etc.) is amended as follows.

20(2) [Amends TMA 1970, s. 42(2), (9) and (11)(a).]

20(3) [Omits TMA 1970, s. 42(4) and (4A).]

20(4) [Omits TMA 1970, s. 42(13(c)).]

21 [Substitutes TMA 1970, s. 43(1).]

22(1) Section 43A of the Taxes Management Act 1970 (further assessments: claims etc.) is amended as follows.

22(2) [Substitutes TMA 1970, s. 43A(1)(a).]

22(3) [Amends TMA 1970, s. 43A(2), (3), (4) and (5).]

23 [Amends TMA 1970, s. 46(2).]

24 [Repealed by FA 2001, s. 110 and Sch. 33, Pt. 2(13).]

History – Para. 24 repealed by FA 2001, s. 110 and Sch. 33, Pt. 2(13), with effect from 11 May 2001 in relation to returns made at any time in respect of any period.

25 [Repealed by FA 2001, s. 110 and Sch. 33, Pt. 2(13).]

History – Para. 25 repealed by FA 2001, s. 110 and Sch. 33, Pt. 2(13), with effect from 11 May 2001 in relation to returns made at any time in respect of any period.

26 [Repealed by FA 2001, s. 110 and Sch. 33, Pt. 2(13).]

History – Para. 26 repealed by FA 2001, s. 110 and Sch. 33, Pt. 2(13), with effect from 11 May 2001 in relation to returns made at any time in respect of any period.

27(1) Section 50 of the Taxes Management Act 1970 (procedure) is amended as follows.

27(2) [Repealed by FA 2001, s. 110 and Sch. 33, Pt. 2(13).]

27(3) [Repealed by FA 2001, s. 110 and Sch. 33, Pt. 2(13).]

27(4) [Substitutes TMA 1970, s. 50(9).]

History – Para. 27(2) and (3) repealed by FA 2001, s. 88 and Sch. 33, Pt. 2(13), with effect from 11 May 2001 in relation to returns made at any time in respect of any period.

28 [Amends TMA 1970, s. 55(1).]

29(1) [Inserts the heading before TMA 1970, s. 59A.]

29(2) [Substitutes TMA 1970, s. 59D.]

30(1) Section 65 of the Taxes Management Act 1970 (recovery of small amounts of tax by civil proceedings in the magistrates' court) is amended as follows.

30(2) [Amends TMA 1970, s. 65(1).]

30(3) [Amends TMA 1970, s. 65(3).]

30(4) [Amends TMA 1970, s. 65(5).]

31 [Repealed by FA 2001, s. 110 and Sch. 33, Pt. 2(14).]

History – Para. 31 repealed by FA 2001, s. 110 and Sch. 33, Pt. 2(14), in relation to proceedings begun or a counterclaim made after 11 May 2001 and in relation to a set-off first claimed after that date.

32 [Omitted by FA 2008, s. 138 and Sch. 44, para. 11(c).]

History – Para. 32 omitted by FA 2008, s. 138 and Sch. 44, para. 11(c), with effect from 21 July 2008.

33 [Repeals TMA 1970, s. 94.]

34 [Repeals TMA 1970, s. 96.]

35 [Amends TMA 1970, s. 97.]

36 [Omitted by FA 2008, s. 113 and Sch. 36, para. 92(f).]

History – Para. 36 omitted by FA 2008, s. 113 and Sch. 36, para. 92(f), with effect from 1 April 2009 (SI 2009/404, art. 2, subject to the savings at SI 2009/404, art. 3-12). Former para. 36 amended TMA 1970, s. 97AA(1).

37 [Amends TMA 1970, s. 97A.]

38 [Amends TMA 1970, s. 100(6)(a).]

39 [Substitutes TMA 1970, s. 101.]

40 [Amends TMA 1970, s. 103A.]

41 [Amends TMA 1970, s. 113(1B).]

42(1) Schedule 1A to the Taxes Management Act 1970 (claims, etc. not included in returns) is amended as follows.

42(2) [Amends TMA 1970, Sch. 1A, para. 1.]

42(3) [Amends TMA 1970, Sch. 1A, para. 2(5)(c).]

42(4) [Amends TMA 1970, Sch. 1A, para. 2A.]

42(5) [Amends TMA 1970, Sch. 1A, para. 5.]

42(6) [Omitted by FA 2008, s. 113 and Sch. 36, para. 92(f).]

42(7) [Omitted by FA 2008, s. 113 and Sch. 36, para. 92(f).]

History – Para. 42(6) and (7) omitted by FA 2008, s. 113 and Sch. 36, para. 92(f), with effect from 1 April 2009 (SI 2009/404, art. 2, subject to the savings at SI 2009/404, art. 3-12). Former para. 42(6) and (7) substituted TMA 1970, Sch. 1A, para. 6(3) and inserted TMA 1970, Sch. 1A, para. 6A.

43(1) Schedule 3A to the Taxes Management Act 1970 (electronic lodgement of tax returns) is amended as follows.

43(2) [Amends TMA 1970, Sch. 3A, para. 1(4)(a).]

43(3) [Amends TMA 1970, Sch. 3A, para. 8(2)(a).]

Prospective amendments – Para. 43 repealed by FA 1999, s. 139 and Sch. 20, Pt. VII, with effect from a day to be appointed.

INCOME AND CORPORATION TAXES ACT 1988 (c.1)

44(1) Section 246Q of the Taxes Act 1988 (repayment or set-off of ACT in respect of foreign income dividend) is amended as follows.

44(2) [Amends ICTA 1988, s. 246Q(6).]

44(3) [Amends ICTA 1988, s. 246Q(7).]

45(1) Section 246U of the Taxes Act 1988 (repayments treated as repayments of ACT in case of international headquarters company) is amended as follows.

45(2) [Substitutes ICTA 1988, s. 246U(7)(a).]

45(3) [Amends ICTA 1988, s. 246U(8).]

46 [Repealed by CTA 2010, s. 1181 and Sch. 3, Pt. 1.]

History – Para. 46 repealed by CTA 2010, s. 1181 and Sch. 3, Pt. 1, with effect for corporation tax purposes for accounting periods ending on or after 1 April 2010, and for income tax and capital gains tax purposes for the tax year 2010–11 and subsequent tax years.

47 [Repealed by CTA 2010, s. 1181 and Sch. 3, Pt. 1.]

History – Para. 47 repealed by CTA 2010, s. 1181 and Sch. 3, Pt. 1, with effect for corporation tax purposes for accounting periods ending on or after 1 April 2010, and for income tax and capital gains tax purposes for the tax year 2010-11 and subsequent tax years.

48(1) Section 488 of the Taxes Act 1988 (co-operative housing associations) is amended as follows.

48(2) [Repealed by CTA 2010, s. 1181 and Sch. 3, Pt. 1.]

48(3) [Inserts ICTA 1988, s. 488(12).]

History – Para. 48(2) repealed by CTA 2010, s. 1181 and Sch. 3, Pt. 1, with effect for corporation tax purposes for accounting periods ending on or after 1 April 2010, and for income tax and capital gains tax purposes for the tax year 2010–11 and subsequent tax years.

49 [Repealed by CTA 2010, s. 1181 and Sch. 3, Pt. 1.]

History – Para. 49 repealed by CTA 2010, s. 1181 and Sch. 3, Pt. 1, with effect for corporation tax purposes for accounting periods ending on or after 1 April 2010, and for income tax and capital gains tax purposes for the tax year 2010–11 and subsequent tax years.

50(1) Schedule 13A to the Taxes Act 1988 (surrenders of advance corporation tax) is amended as follows.

50(2) [Amends ICTA 1988, Sch. 13A, para. 5(1).]

50(3) [Substitutes ICTA 1988, Sch. 13A, para. 5(2).]

50(4) [Amends ICTA 1988, Sch. 13A, para. 14(1).]

50(5) [Amends ICTA 1988, Sch. 13A, para. 14(6).]

50(6) [Amends ICTA 1988, Sch. 13A, para. 14(8).]

51 [Repealed by FA 2001, s. 110, Sch. 33, Pt. 2(12).]

History – Para. 51 repealed by FA 2001, s. 110, Sch. 33, Pt. 2(12) in relation to tax credits in respect of distributions made on or after 6 April 2004, and in relation to income tax borne by deduction from payments received after 30 September 2001.

SCHEDULE 20 – APPLICATION OF TAPER RELIEF

Section 121

[Omitted by FA 2008, s. 8 and Sch. 2, para. 55(a)(iii).]

History – Sch. 20 omitted by FA 2008, s. 8 and Sch. 2, para. 55(a)(iii), with effect in relation to chargeable gains accruing or treated as accruing in the tax year 2008–09 or any subsequent tax year.

SCHEDULE 21 – AMENDMENTS IN CONNECTION WITH TAPER RELIEF

Section 121

INTRODUCTORY

1 The Taxation of Chargeable Gains Act 1992 shall be amended in accordance with the following provisions of this Schedule.

GAINS OF TRUSTEES ATTRIBUTED TO SETTLOR

2 [Omitted by FA 2008, s. 8 and Sch. 2, para. 55(a)(iv).]

History – Para. 2 omitted by FA 2008, s. 8 and Sch. 2, para. 55(a)(iv), with effect in relation to chargeable gains accruing or treated as accruing in the tax year 2008–09 or any subsequent tax year.

ANNUAL EXEMPT AMOUNT

3 [Substitutes TCGA 1992, s. 3(5)–(5C).]

GAINS ATTRIBUTED TO MEMBERS OF NON-RESIDENT COMPANIES

4 [Omitted by FA 2008, s. 8 and Sch. 2, para. 55(a)(iv).]

History – Para. 4 omitted by FA 2008, s. 8 and Sch. 2, para. 55(a)(iv), with effect in relation to chargeable gains accruing or treated as accruing in the tax year 2008–09 or any subsequent tax year.

CARRY BACK OF LOSSES ON DEATH

5 [Inserts TCGA 1992, s. 62(2A), (2B).]

GAINS ATTRIBUTED TO SETTLORS AND BENEFICIARIES

6(1) [Repealed by FA 2002, s. 141 and Sch. 40, Pt. 3(4) and omitted by FA 2008, s. 8 and Sch. 2, para, 21(c)(ii).]

6(2) [Repealed by FA 2002, s. 141 and Sch. 40, Pt. 3(4).]

6(3) [Omitted by FA 2008, s. 8 and Sch. 2, para. 55(a)(iv) and FA 2008, s. 25 and Sch. 7, para. 114(a).]

6(4) [Omitted by FA 2008, s. 8 and Sch. 2, para. 55(a)(iv) and FA 2008, s. 25 and Sch. 7, para. 114(a).]

History – Para. 6(1) omitted by FA 2008, s. 8 and Sch. 2, para. 21(c)(ii), with effect for the tax year 2008–09 and subsequent tax years. This omission supersedes the repeal, subject to election, made by FA 2002, s. 141 and Sch. 40, Pt. 3(4).
Para. 6(1) and (2) repealed by FA 2002, s. 141 and Sch. 40, Pt. 3(4) with effect in relation to 2003–04 and subsequent tax years, but subject to an election for earlier application in accordance with FA 2002, s. 51 and Sch. 11, para. 8.
Para. 6(3) omitted by FA 2008, s. 8 and Sch. 2, para. 55(a)(iv), with effect in relation to chargeable gains accruing or treated as accruing in the tax year 2008–09 or any subsequent tax years. Para. 6(3) also omitted by FA 2008, s. 25 and Sch. 7, para. 114(a), with effect for the tax year 2008–09 and subsequent tax years.
Para. 6(4) omitted by FA 2008, s. 8 and Sch. 2, para. 55(a)(iv), with effect in relation to chargeable gains accruing or treated as accruing in the tax year 2008–09 or any subsequent tax year. Para. 6(4) also omitted by FA 2008, s. 25 and Sch. 7, para. 114(a), with effect for the tax year 2008–09 and subsequent tax years.

GAINS ON ASSETS DERIVING FROM REORGANISATION OF BODY CARRYING ON A MUTUAL BUSINESS ETC.

7 [Omitted by FA 2008, s. 8 and Sch. 2, para. 55(a)(iv).]

History – Para. 7 omitted by FA 2008, s. 8 and Sch. 2, para. 55(a)(iv), with effect in relation to chargeable gains accruing or treated as accruing in the tax year 2008–09 or any subsequent tax year.

COMMERCIAL LETTING OF FURNISHED HOLIDAY DWELLINGS

8 [Amends TCGA 1992, s. 241(3).]

DELAYED REMITTANCES IN RESPECT OF FOREIGN ASSETS

9 [Omitted by FA 2008, s. 8 and Sch. 2, para. 55(a)(iv).]

History – Para. 9 omitted by FA 2008, s. 8 and Sch. 2, para. 55(a)(iv), with effect in relation to chargeable gains accruing or treated as accruing in the tax year 2008–09 or any subsequent tax year.

SCHEDULE 22 – TRANSITIONAL PROVISION AND CONSEQUENTIAL AMENDMENTS FOR SECTION 131

Section 131

INTRODUCTORY

1 The Taxation of Chargeable Gains Act 1992 shall be amended as follows.

TRANSITIONAL FOR SETTLEMENTS CREATED BEFORE 17TH MARCH 1998

2(1) [Amends TCGA 1992, Sch. 5, para. 2(1).]

2(2) [Inserts TCGA 1992, Sch. 5, para. 2A.]

2(3) In construing section 86(1)(e) as regards any year of assessment and in relation to a settlement which–

(a) was created before 17th March 1998, and

(b) is a settlement in which the settlor has an interest during that year by virtue only of the fulfilment for the purposes of the paragraph inserted by sub-paragraph (2) above of one of the conditions set out in that paragraph, no account shall be taken of disposals made before the relevant day (whether for the purpose of arriving at gains or for the purpose of arriving at losses).

2(4) In sub-paragraph (3) above **"the relevant day"** means–

(a) for the year 1997–98, 17th March 1998; and

(b) for any other year of assessment, the 6th April which is the first day of that year.

CONSEQUENTIAL AMENDMENTS OF PARAGRAPHS 4 AND 5 OF SCHEDULE 5 TO THE 1992 ACT

3(1) [Amends TCGA 1992, Sch. 5, para. 4(1)(a)) and 5(1)(a).]

3(2) [Amends TCGA 1992, Sch. 5, para. 4(4).]

CONSEQUENTIAL AMENDMENT OF PARAGRAPH 9 OF SCHEDULE 5 TO THE 1992 ACT

4(1) [Amends TCGA 1992, Sch. 5, para. 9(7).]

4(2) [Substitutes TCGA 1992, Sch. 5, para. 9(11).]

4(3) Sub-paragraph (1) above shall be disregarded for the purpose of determining whether either of the conditions set out in sub-paragraphs (5) and (6) of that paragraph became fulfilled at any time before 17th March 1998.

CONSEQUENTIAL AMENDMENT OF SCHEDULE 5A

5(1) [Amends TCGA 1992, Sch. 5A, para. 2(1).]

5(2) This paragraph has effect in relation to transfers on or after 17th March 1998.

SCHEDULE 23 – TRANSITIONAL PROVISION IN CONNECTION WITH SECTION 132

Section 132

PRE-6TH APRIL 1999 GAINS AND LOSSES OF SETTLEMENTS THAT BECOME QUALIFYING

1(1) This paragraph applies to a settlement in the case of any person who is a settlor in relation to that settlement if that settlement–

(a) is one created before 19th March 1991;

(b) is not a qualifying settlement in the year 1998–99; and

(c) is a qualifying settlement in the year 1999–00 without having been a protected settlement in relation to that settlor immediately after the beginning of 6th April 1999.

1(2) Subject to sub-paragraph (3) below, section 86 of the 1992 Act (attribution of gains to settlor of non-resident or dual resident trusts) shall have effect in relation to any settlement to which this paragraph applies–

(a) as if any relevant gains or relevant losses accruing to the trustees of the settlement on or after 17th March 1998 and before 6th April 1999 were gains or losses accruing to those trustees on 6th April 1999; and

(b) where it is not the case, as if the trustees fulfilled the condition as to residence in the year 1999–00.

1(3) Where (apart from sub-paragraph (2)(b) above) the trustees of a settlement to which this paragraph applies do not fulfil the condition as to residence in the year 1999–00, section 86 of the 1992 Act shall have effect (without prejudice to any charge imposed otherwise than by virtue of that section) as if the only gains and losses accruing to the trustees of that settlement in that year were those which are treated as accruing to those trustees on 6th April 1999 by virtue of sub-paragraph (2)(a) above.

1(4) The gains and losses that are relevant gains or relevant losses for the purposes of this paragraph are those which (apart from this paragraph) accrue to the trustees of a settlement to which this paragraph applies in any year of assessment in which those trustees fulfil the condition as to residence.

PRE-6TH APRIL 1999 GAINS AND LOSSES WHERE THERE IS A TRANSFER TO ANOTHER SETTLEMENT

2(1) This paragraph applies, subject to sub-paragraph (5) below, to any chargeable gain or loss accruing on the disposal of any asset by the trustees of a settlement ("the transferor settlement") if–

(a) that settlement was created before 19th March 1991;

(b) the disposal on which the gain or loss accrues is one made–

(i) on or after 17th March 1998 and before 6th April 1999; and

(ii) in a year of assessment in which the trustees of the transferor settlement fulfil the condition as to residence but the settlement is not a qualifying settlement;

(c) a person who is a settlor in relation to the transferor settlement ("the chargeable settlor")–

(i) is domiciled in the United Kingdom at some time in the year 1999–00 and in the year of assessment in which the disposal is made;

(ii) is either resident in the United Kingdom during any part of each of those years or ordinarily resident in the United Kingdom during each of those years; and

(iii) is alive at the end of the year 1999–00;

(d) the asset disposed of is property originating from the chargeable settlor;

(e) the property comprised in another settlement ("the transferee settlement") at any time after the disposal and before 6th April 1999 is or includes (whether in consequence of the disposal or otherwise) the asset disposed of or any relevant property;

(f) the transferor settlement has a relevant connection with the transferee settlement; and

(g) the gain or loss in question is not one treated under paragraph 1 above as accruing on 6th April 1999 to the trustees of the transferor settlement.

2(2) If, in the case of the chargeable settlor, section 86 of the 1992 Act applies (apart from this paragraph) for the year 1999–00 in relation to the transferee settlement, that section shall apply for that year in relation to that settlement as if any chargeable gain or loss to which this paragraph applies–

(a) were a gain or loss accruing on 6th April 1999 to the trustees of the transferee settlement; and

(b) so accrued on the disposal by those trustees of any asset that was property originating from the chargeable settlor.

2(3) Where sub-paragraph (2) above does not apply, section 86 of the 1992 Act shall have effect in relation to the chargeable settlor as if–

(a) in the year 1999–00 the conditions specified in paragraphs (a) to (d) and (f) of subsection (1) of that section were fulfilled in his case in relation to the transferee settlement;

(b) any gain or loss to which this paragraph applies–

(i) were a gain or loss accruing on 6th April 1999 to the trustees of the transferee settlement; and

(ii) so accrued on the disposal by them of an asset that was property originating from the chargeable settlor;

and

(c) any chargeable gains and losses accruing to the trustees of the transferee settlement which are not gains or losses to which this paragraph applies were to be disregarded for the purposes of that section.

2(4) Where (but for this sub-paragraph) the same gain or loss would fall to be treated by virtue of sub-paragraph (2) or (3) above as a gain or loss accruing to the trustees of more than one settlement–

(a) that gain or loss shall be apportioned between those settlements in such manner as may be just and reasonable; and

(b) only such part of the gain or loss as on that apportionment is attributable to a particular settlement shall be treated in accordance with that sub-paragraph as accruing to that settlement.

2(5) This paragraph does not apply to any chargeable gain or loss accruing on any disposal if, for the year of assessment in which that disposal is made, section 86 of the 1992 Act would, on the relevant assumption, have been prevented by virtue of paragraph 3, 4 or 5 of Schedule 5 to that Act–

(a) from applying in the case of the chargeable settlor in relation to the transferor settlement; or

(b) from applying in his case in relation to the transferee settlement.

2(6) The relevant assumption for the purposes of sub-paragraph (5) above is that section 86 of the 1992 Act would have applied in the case of the chargeable settlor apart from paragraphs 3 to 5 of Schedule 5 to that Act.

2(7) In this paragraph **"relevant property"**, in relation to any disposal made by the trustees of the transferor settlement, means any property (not being the asset disposed of) which–

(a) is or represents property or income originating from the chargeable settlor;

(b) has been comprised in, or has arisen to, the transferor settlement at any time after the time of that disposal; and

(c) is property or income of the trustees of the transferee settlement acquired or otherwise deriving, directly or indirectly, from the trustees of the transferor settlement.

2(8) For the purposes of this paragraph the transferor settlement has, in relation to a disposal by its trustees, a relevant connection with the transferee settlement if–

(a) immediately before the time of the disposal, the beneficiaries of the transferor settlement are or include persons who are defined persons in relation to that settlement at that time;

(b) the transferor settlement is not a protected settlement at that time in relation to the chargeable settlor;

(c) at the beginning of 6th April 1999, the beneficiaries of the transferee settlement are or include persons who–

(i) have attained the age of eighteen; and

(ii) have been defined persons in relation to the transferor settlement;

and

(d) the property comprised in the transferee settlement in respect of which some or all of the persons mentioned in paragraph (c) above are beneficiaries of that settlement at the beginning of 6th April 1999 is or includes anything which, in relation to either that settlement or the transferor settlement, is property or income originating from the chargeable settlor.

2(9) For the purposes of this paragraph a person is a defined person in relation to a settlement at a time if he would fall at that time to be treated, by reference to the chargeable settlor, as a defined person in relation to that settlement for the purposes of paragraph 2 of Schedule 5 to the 1992 Act.

2(10) Sub-paragraph (3)(c) above is without prejudice to any charge imposed otherwise than by virtue of this paragraph.

PRE-6TH APRIL 1999 GAINS AND LOSSES WHERE THERE IS A TRANSFER TO A FOREIGN INSTITUTION

3(1) This paragraph applies, subject to sub-paragraphs (4) and (6) below, to a chargeable gain or loss accruing on the disposal of any asset by the trustees of a settlement ("the transferor settlement") if–

(a) that settlement was created before 19th March 1991;

(b) the disposal on which the gain or loss accrues is one made–

(i) on or after 17th March 1998 and before 6th April 1999; and

(ii) in a year of assessment in which the trustees of the transferor settlement fulfil the condition as to residence but the settlement is not a qualifying settlement;

(c) a person who is a settlor in relation to the transferor settlement ("the chargeable settlor")–

(i) is domiciled in the United Kingdom at some time in the year 1999–00 and in the year of assessment in which the disposal is made;

(ii) is either resident in the United Kingdom during any part of each of those years or ordinarily resident in the United Kingdom during each of those years; and

(iii) is alive at the end of the year 1999–00;

(d) the asset disposed of is property originating from the chargeable settlor;

(e) the property comprised in a foreign institution ("the transferee institution") at any time after the disposal and before 6th April 1999 is or includes (whether in consequence of the disposal or otherwise) the asset disposed of or any relevant property;

(f) the transferor settlement has a relevant connection with the transferee institution; and

(g) the gain or loss in question is neither–

(i) a gain or loss treated under paragraph 1 above as accruing on 6th April 1999 to the trustees of any settlement; nor

(ii) a gain or loss to which paragraph 2 above applies.

3(2) If, in the case of the chargeable settlor, section 86 of the 1992 Act applies (apart from this paragraph) for the year 1999–00 in relation to the transferor settlement, that section shall apply for that year in relation to that settlement as if any chargeable gain or loss to which this paragraph applies–

(a) were a gain or loss accruing on 6th April 1999 to the trustees of the transferor settlement; and

(b) so accrued on the disposal by them of an asset that was property originating from the chargeable settlor.

3(3) Where sub-paragraph (2) above does not apply, section 86 of the 1992 Act shall have effect in relation to the chargeable settlor as if–

(a) (where it is not the case) the transferor settlement existed in the year 1999–00;

(b) that settlement were a settlement in relation to which all the conditions specified in paragraphs (a) to (d) and (f) of subsection (1) of that section were fulfilled in the case of the chargeable settlor in that year;

(c) any gain or loss to which this paragraph applies–

(i) were a gain or loss accruing on 6th April 1999 to the trustees of the transferor settlement; and

(ii) so accrued on the disposal by them of an asset that was property originating from the chargeable settlor;

and

(d) any chargeable gains and losses which are not gains or losses to which this paragraph applies were to be disregarded for the purposes of that section.

3(4) This paragraph does not apply to any chargeable gain or loss accruing on any disposal if, for the year of assessment in which that disposal is made, section 86 of the 1992 Act would, on the relevant assumption, have been prevented by virtue of paragraph 3, 4 or 5 of Schedule 5 to that Act from applying in the case of the chargeable settlor in relation to the transferor settlement.

3(5) The relevant assumption for the purposes of sub-paragraph (4) above is that section 86 of the 1992 Act would have applied in the case of the chargeable settlor apart from paragraphs 3 to 5 of Schedule 5 to that Act.

3(6) This paragraph does not apply to any chargeable gain or loss accruing on any disposal if the chargeable settlor stands in such a relationship to the foreign institution that if–

(a) that institution were a settlement,

(b) property of the institution were property comprised in the settlement, and

(c) income arising to the institution were income arising under the settlement,

paragraph 4 or 5 of Schedule 5 to the 1992 Act would (assuming that nothing else did) prevent section 86 of that Act from applying in the case of the chargeable settlor in relation to that settlement for the year of assessment in which that disposal is made.

3(7) In this paragraph **"relevant property"**, in relation to any disposal made by the trustees of the transferor settlement, means any property which–

(a) is or represents property or income originating from the chargeable settlor;

(b) has been comprised in, or has arisen to, the transferor settlement at any time after the time of that disposal; and

(c) is property or income of the transferee institution acquired or otherwise deriving, directly or indirectly, from the trustees of the transferor settlement.

3(8) For the purposes of this paragraph the transferor settlement has, in relation to a disposal by its trustees, a relevant connection with the transferee institution if–

(a) immediately before the time of the disposal, the beneficiaries of the transferor settlement are or include persons who are defined persons in relation to that settlement at that time;

(b) the transferor settlement is not a protected settlement at that time in relation to the chargeable settlor; and

(c) the transferee institution is–

(i) one in which a relevant defined person is a participator at the beginning of 6th April 1999;

(ii) one which is under the control of a company in which, or two or more companies in any of which, a relevant defined person is a participator at that time; or

(iii) one whose relevant property or relevant income includes property or income in which a relevant defined person has an interest at that time.

3(9) For the purposes of this paragraph a person is a relevant defined person at any time if he–

(a) has attained the age of eighteen; and

(b) has been, by reference to the chargeable settlor, a defined person in relation to the transferor settlement.

3(10) For the purposes of this paragraph a person has an interest in any property or income of a foreign institution at any time if–

(a) there are any circumstances whatever in which that property or income is or will or may become applicable for his benefit or payable to him;

(b) there are any circumstances whatever in which income which is or may arise from that property or income is or will or may become applicable for his benefit or payable to him;

(c) he enjoys a benefit directly or indirectly from that property or income or from any income arising from that property or income.

3(11) For the purposes of this paragraph a person is a defined person in relation to a settlement at a time if he would fall at that time to be treated, by reference to the chargeable settlor, as a defined person in relation to that settlement for the purposes of paragraph 2 of Schedule 5 to the 1992 Act.

3(12) In this paragraph–

"foreign institution" means any company or other institution resident outside the United Kingdom;

"participator" has the meaning given (for the purposes of Part XI of the Taxes Act 1988 (close companies)) by section 417(1) of that Act;

"relevant income", in relation to a foreign institution, means any income of that institution which, if that institution were a settlement, would be treated for the purposes of Schedule 5 to the 1992 Act as originating from the chargeable settlor;

"relevant property", in relation to a foreign institution, means any property of that institution which, if that institution were a settlement, would be treated for the purposes of Schedule 5 to the 1992 Act as originating from the chargeable settlor.

3(13) Sub-paragraph (3)(d) above is without prejudice to any charge imposed otherwise than by virtue of this paragraph.

RULE TO PREVENT A DOUBLE CHARGE

4(1) This paragraph applies, in the case of a person who is a settlor in relation to any settlement ("the relevant settlement"), to so much (if any) of the amount falling in his case within section 86(1)(e) of the 1992 Act for the year 1999–00 as (apart from this paragraph) would be treated by virtue only of the preceding provisions of this Schedule, as gains accruing to him in that year.

4(2) Where there is an excess of the relevant chargeable amounts for the transitional period over the amount of the section 87 pool on 17th March 1998, only so much (if any) of the amount to which this paragraph applies as exceeds that excess shall fall in accordance with this Schedule to be, or (as the case may be) to be included in, the amount treated as accruing to the settlor in the year 1999–00.

4(3) In sub-paragraph (2) above, the reference to the relevant chargeable amounts for the transitional period is (subject to sub-paragraph (5) below) a reference to the aggregate of the amounts on which beneficiaries of the relevant settlement are charged to tax under section 87 or 89(2) of the 1992 Act for any year of assessment ending after 17th March 1998 and before 6th April 1999 in respect of capital payments received by them.

4(4) In sub-paragraph (2) above, the reference to the section 87 pool on 17th March 1998 is (subject to sub-paragraph (5) below) a reference to the amount (if any) which, in accordance with subsection (2) of section 87 of the 1992 Act, would have fallen in relation to the relevant settlement to be carried forward from the year 1997–98 to be included in the amount of the trust gains for the year 1998–99 if–

(a) the year 1997–98 had ended with 16th March 1998; and

(b) the year 1998–99 had begun with 17th March 1998.

4(5) Where the property comprised in the relevant settlement has at any time included property not originating from the settlor, only so much (if any) of any capital payment or of any amount that would have been carried forward in accordance with section 87(2) of the 1992 Act as, on a just and reasonable apportionment, is properly referable to property originating from the settlor shall be taken into account for the purposes of sub-paragraphs (3) and (4) above.

4(6) Where any reduction falls to be made by virtue of sub-paragraph (2) above in the amount to be attributed in accordance with this Schedule to any settlor for the year 1999–00, the reduction to be treated as made for that year in accordance with section 87(3) of the 1992 Act in the case of the settlement in question shall not be made until–

(a) the reduction (if any) falling to be made by virtue of that sub-paragraph has been made in the case of every settlor to whom any amount is so attributed; and

(b) effect has been given to any reduction required to be made under paragraph 5(1) below.

4(7) In this paragraph **"the transitional period"** means the period beginning with 17th March 1998 and ending with 5th April 1999.

5(1) Where in the case of any settlement there is (after the making of any reduction or reductions in accordance with paragraph 4(2) above) any amount or amounts falling in accordance with this Schedule to be attributed for the year 1999–00 to settlors of the settlement, the amount or (as the case may be) aggregate amount falling in accordance with this Schedule to be so attributed shall be applied in reducing the amount which (after any reductions in accordance with section 86A(6A) of that Act) is carried forward to that year in accordance with section 87(2) of that Act.

5(2) Where an amount or aggregate amount has been applied, in accordance with sub-paragraph (1) above, in reducing the amount which in the case of any settlement is carried forward to the year 1999–00 in accordance with section 87(2) of the 1992 Act, that amount (or, as the case may be, so much of it as does not exceed the amount which it is applied in reducing) shall be deducted from the amount used for that year in the case of that settlement for making the reduction under section 87(3) of that Act.

INTERPRETATION OF SCHEDULE

6(1) In this Schedule–

"the 1992 Act" means the Taxation of Chargeable Gains Act 1992;

"qualifying settlement", in relation to any year of assessment, means a settlement that is a qualifying settlement in that year for the purposes of section 86 of and Schedule 5 to the 1992 Act;

"settlor", in relation to a settlement, has the same meaning as in Schedule 5 to the 1992 Act.

6(2) In this Schedule **"protected settlement"**, in relation to any time and any settlor, means (subject to sub-paragraph (3) below) –

(a) a settlement that is a protected settlement at that time, within the meaning given by sub-paragraph (10A) of paragraph 9 of Schedule 5 to the 1992 Act, or

(b) a settlement that would be such a settlement at that time if that settlor were the only settlor of the settlement.

6(3) For the purposes of construing, in accordance with sub-paragraph (2) above, the references in paragraphs 2(8) and 3(8) above to a protected settlement, paragraph 9(10A)(a) of Schedule 5 to the 1992 Act shall be deemed to have effect with the omission of the words "or who were under that age at the end of the immediately preceding year of assessment".

6(4) References in this Schedule to the condition as to residence are references to the condition set out in section 86(2) of the 1992 Act.

6(5) For the purposes of this Schedule a person is a beneficiary of a settlement if–

(a) there are any circumstances whatever in which property which is or may become comprised in the settlement is or will or may become applicable for his benefit or payable to him;

(b) there are any circumstances whatever in which income which arises or may arise from property comprised in the settlement is or will or may become applicable for his benefit or payable to him;

(c) he enjoys a benefit directly or indirectly from any property comprised in the settlement or any income arising from any such property;

and references in this paragraph to the property comprised in the settlement in respect of which a person is a beneficiary shall be construed accordingly.

6(6) For the purposes of this paragraph, paragraph 8 of Schedule 5 to the 1992 Act shall apply for determining if property is property originating from any person as it applies for the purposes of that Schedule.

6(7) Expressions used in this Schedule and in the 1992 Act have the same meanings in this Schedule as in that Act.

SCHEDULE 24 – RESTRICTIONS ON SETTING LOSSES AGAINST PRE-ENTRY GAINS

Section 137

[Repealed by FA 2006, s. 178 and Sch. 26, Pt. 3(9).]

History – Sch. 24 repealed by FA 2006, s. 178 and Sch. 26, Pt. 3(9), with effect for calculating the amount to be included in respect of chargeable gains in a company's total profits for any accounting period ending on or after 5 December 2005, subject to the provisions of FA 2006, s. 70(7)–(11).

HUMAN RIGHTS ACT 1998

(1998 Chapter 42) [*9th November 1998*]

ARRANGEMENT OF SECTIONS

Notes – Commencement:
S. 19 (statements of compatibility) was brought into force on 24 November 1998 by the Human Rights Act 1998 (Commencement No. 1) Order 1998 (SI 1998/2882).
The remaining provisions of the Act were brought into force on 2 October 2000 by the Human Rights Act 1998 (Commencement No. 2) Order 2000 (SI 2000/1851).

INTRODUCTION

1 The Convention Rights

1(1) In this Act **"the Convention rights"** means the rights and fundamental freedoms set out in–

(a) Articles 2 to 12 and 14 of the Convention,

(b) Articles 1 to 3 of the First Protocol, and

(c) Article 1 of the Thirteenth Protocol,

as read with Articles 16 to 18 of the Convention.

1(2) Those Articles are to have effect for the purposes of this Act subject to any designated derogation or reservation (as to which see sections 14 and 15).

1(3) The Articles are set out in Schedule 1.

1(4) The Secretary of State may by order make such amendments to this Act as he considers appropriate to reflect the effect, in relation to the United Kingdom, of a protocol.

1(5) In subsection (4) **"protocol"** means a protocol to the Convention–

(a) which the United Kingdom has ratified; or

(b) which the United Kingdom has signed with a view to ratification.

1(6) No amendment may be made by an order under subsection (4) so as to come into force before the protocol concerned is in force in relation to the United Kingdom.

History – S. 1(1)(c) substituted by SI 2004/1574, art. 2(1), operative from 22 June 2004.
In s. 1(4), the words "Secretary of State" substituted for the words "Lord Chancellor" by SI 2003/1887, art. 9 and Sch. 2, para. 10(1) with effect from 19 August 2003.
In s. 1(4), the words "Lord Chancellor" previously substituted by SI 2001/3500, Sch. 2, with effect from 26 November 2001.

Notes – S. 1 was brought into force on 2 October 2000 by the Human Rights Act 1998 (Commencement No. 2) Order 2000 (SI 2000/1851).

2 Interpretation of Convention rights

2(1) A court or tribunal determining a question which has arisen in connection with a Convention right must take into account any–

(a) judgment, decision, declaration or advisory opinion of the European Court of Human Rights,

(b) opinion of the Commission given in a report adopted under Article 31 of the Convention,

(c) decision of the Commission in connection with Article 26 or 27(2) of the Convention, or

(d) decision of the Committee of Ministers taken under Article 46 of the Convention,

whenever made or given, so far as, in the opinion of the court or tribunal, it is relevant to the proceedings in which that question has arisen.

2(2) Evidence of any judgement, decision, declaration or opinion of which account may have to be taken under this section is to be given in proceedings before any court or tribunal in such manner as may be provided by rules.

2(3) In this section **"rules"** means rules of court or, in the case of proceedings before a tribunal, rules made for the purposes of this section–

(a) by the Lord Chancellor or the Secretary of State, in relation to any proceedings outside Scotland;

(b) by the Secretary of State, in relation to proceedings in Scotland; or

(c) by a Northern Ireland department, in relation to proceedings before a tribunal in Northern Ireland–

(i) which deals with transferred matters; and

(ii) for which no rules made under paragraph (a) are in force.

History – In s. 2(3)(a), the words "the Lord Chancellor or" inserted by SI 2005/3429, art. 8 and Schedule, para. 3, with effect from 12 January 2006 (SI 2005/3429, art. 1(2)).
In s. 2(3)(a), the words "the Lord Chancellor or", which preceded the words "Secretary of State", repealed by SI 2003/1887 art. 9 and Sch. 2, para. 10(2) with effect from 19 August 2003.

Notes – S. 2 was brought into force on 2 October 2000 by the Human Rights Act 1998 (Commencement No. 2) Order 2000 (SI 2000/1851).

LEGISLATION

3 Interpretation of legislation

3(1) So far as it is possible to do so, primary legislation and subordinate legislation must be read and given effect in a way which is compatible with the Convention rights.

3(2) This section–

(a) applies to primary legislation and subordinate legislation whenever enacted;

(b) does not affect the validity, continuing operation or enforcement of any incompatible primary legislation; and

(c) does not affect the validity, continuing operation or enforcement of any incompatible subordinate legislation if (disregarding any possibility of revocation) primary legislation prevents removal of the incompatibility.

Notes – S. 3 was brought into force on 2 October 2000 by the Human Rights Act 1998 (Commencement No. 2) Order 2000 (SI 2000/1851).

4 Declaration of incompatibility

4(1) Subsection (2) applies in any proceedings in which a court determines whether a provision of primary legislation is compatible with a Convention right.

4(2) If the court is satisfied that the provision is incompatible with a Convention right, it may make a declaration of that incompatibility.

4(3) Subsection (4) applies in any proceedings in which a court determines whether a provision of subordinate legislation, made in the exercise of a power conferred by primary legislation, is compatible with a Convention right.

4(4) If the court is satisfied–

(a) that the provision is incompatible with a Convention right, and

(b) that (disregarding any possibility of revocation) the primary legislation concerned prevents removal of the incompatibility,

it may make a declaration of that incompatibility.

4(5) In this section **"court"** means–

(a) the Supreme Court;

(b) the Judicial Committee of the Privy Council;

(c) the Court Martial Appeal Court;

(d) in Scotland, the High Court of Justiciary sitting otherwise than as a trial court or the Court of Session;

(e) in England and Wales or Northern Ireland, the High Court or the Court of Appeal.

(f) the Court of Protection, in any matter being dealt with by the President of the Family Division, the Chancellor of the High Court or a puisne judge of the High Court.

4(6) A declaration under this section ("a declaration of incompatibility")–

(a) does not affect the validity, continuing operation or enforcement of the provision in respect of which it is given; and

(b) is not binding on the parties to the proceedings in which it is made.

History – S. 4(5)(a) substituted by Constitutional Reform Act 2005, s. 40 and Sch. 9, para. 66(2), with effect from 1 October 2009 (SI 2009/1604).

In s. 4(5)(c), the words "Court Martial Appeal Court" substituted for the words "Courts-Martial Appeal Court" by the Armed Forces Act 2006, s. 378(1), Sch. 16, para. 156, with effect from 28 March 2009 (SI 2009/812, art. 3) for certain purposes, and from 31 October for other purposes (SI 2009/1167).

In s. 4(5)(f), the words "Chancellor of the High Court" substituted for the words "Vice-Chancellor" by Crime and Courts Act 2013, s. 21 and Sch. 14, para. 5(5), with effect from 1 October 2013 (SI 2013/2200, art. 3).

S. 4(5)(f) inserted by Mental Capacity Act 2005, s. 67(1) and Sch. 6, para. 43, with effect from 1 October 2007 (SI 2007/1897, art. 2(1)(d)).

Notes – S. 4 was brought into force on 2 October 2000 by the Human Rights Act 1998 (Commencement No. 2) Order 2000 (SI 2000/1851).

5 Right of Crown to intervene

5(1) Where a court is considering whether to make a declaration of incompatibility, the Crown is entitled to notice in accordance with rules of court.

5(2) In any case to which subsection (1) applies–

(a) a Minister of the Crown (or a person nominated by him),

(b) a member of the Scottish Executive,

(c) a Northern Ireland Minister,

(d) a Northern Ireland department,

is entitled, on giving notice in accordance with rules of court, to be joined as a party to the proceedings.

5(3) Notice under subsection (2) may be given at any time during the proceedings.

5(4) A person who has been made a party to criminal proceedings (other than in Scotland) as the result of a notice under subsection (2) may, with leave, appeal to the Supreme Court against any declaration of incompatibility made in the proceedings.

5(5) In subsection (4)–

"criminal proceedings" includes all proceedings before the Court Martial Appeal Court; and

"leave" means leave granted by the court making the declaration of incompatibility or by the Supreme Court.

History – In s. 5(4), the words "Supreme Court" substituted for the words "House of Lords" by Constitutional Reform Act 2005, s. 40 and Sch. 9, para. 66(3), with effect from 1 October 2009 (SI 2009/1604).

In s. 5(5), the words "Supreme Court" substituted for the words "House of Lords" by Constitutional Reform Act 2005, s. 40 and Sch. 9, para. 66(3), with effect from 1 October 2009 (SI 2009/1604).

In s. 5(5), in the definition of "criminal proceedings", the words "Court Martial Appeal Court" substituted for the words "Courts-Martial Appeal Court" by the Armed Forces Act 2006, s. 378(1), Sch. 16, para. 157, with effect from 28 March 2009 (for certain purposes) (SI 2009/812) and from 31 October 2009 (otherwise) (SI 2009/1167).

Notes – S. 5 was brought into force on 2 October 2000 by the Human Rights Act 1998 (Commencement No. 2) Order 2000 (SI 2000/1851).

PUBLIC AUTHORITIES

6 Acts of public authorities

6(1) It is unlawful for a public authority to act in a way which is incompatible with a Convention right.

6(2) Subsection (1) does not apply to an act if–

(a) as the result of one or more provisions of primary legislation, the authority could not have acted differently; or

(b) in the case of one or more provisions of, or made under, primary legislation which cannot be read or given effect in a way which is compatible with the Convention rights, the authority was acting so as to give effect to or enforce those provisions.

6(3) In this section **"public authority"** includes–

(a) a court or tribunal, and

(b) any person certain of whose functions are functions of a public nature,

but does not include either House of Parliament or a person exercising functions in connection with proceedings in Parliament.

6(4) [Repealed by Constitutional Reform Act 2005, s. 40 and Sch. 9, para. 66(4).]

6(5) In relation to a particular act, a person is not a public authority by virtue only of subsection (3)(b) if the nature of the act is private.

6(6) **"An act"** includes a failure to act but does not include a failure to–

(a) introduce in, or lay before, Parliament a proposal for legislation; or

(b) make any primary legislation or remedial order.

History – S. 6(4) repealed by Constitutional Reform Act 2005, s. 40 and Sch. 9, para. 66(4), with effect from 1 October 2009 (SI 2009/1604).

Notes – S. 6 was brought into force on 2 October 2000 by the Human Rights Act 1998 (Commencement No. 2) Order 2000 (SI 2000/1851).

7 Proceedings

7(1) A person who claims that a public authority has acted (or proposes to act) in a way which is made unlawful by section 6(1) may–

(a) bring proceedings against the authority under this Act in the appropriate court or tribunal, or

(b) rely on the Convention right or rights concerned in any legal proceedings,

but only if he is (or would be) a victim of the unlawful act.

7(2) In subsection (1)(a) **"appropriate court or tribunal"** means such court or tribunal as may be determined in accordance with rules; and proceedings against an authority include a counterclaim or similar proceeding.

7(3) If the proceedings are brought on an application for judicial review, the applicant is to be taken to have a sufficient interest in relation to the unlawful act only if he is, or would be, a victim of that act.

7(4) If the proceedings are made by way of a petition for judicial review in Scotland, the applicant shall be taken to have title and interest to sue in relation to the unlawful act only if he is, or would be, a victim of that act.

7(5) Proceedings under subsection (1)(a) must be brought before the end of–

(a) the period of one year beginning with the date on which the act complained of took place; or

(b) such longer period as the court or tribunal considers equitable having regard to all the circumstances,

but that is subject to any rule imposing a stricter time limit in relation to the procedure in question.

7(6) In subsection (l)(b) **"legal proceedings"** includes–

(a) proceedings brought by or at the instigation of a public authority; and

(b) an appeal against the decision of a court or tribunal.

7(7) For the purposes of this section, a person is a victim of an unlawful act only if he would be a victim for the purposes of Article 34 of the Convention if proceedings were brought in the European Court of Human Rights in respect of that act.

7(8) Nothing in this Act creates a criminal offence.

7(9) In this section **"rules"** means–

(a) in relation to proceedings before a court or tribunal outside Scotland, rules made by the Lord Chancellor or the Secretary of State for the purposes of this section or rules of court,

(b) in relation to proceedings before a court or tribunal in Scotland, rules made by the Secretary of State for those purposes,

(c) in relation to proceedings before a tribunal in Northern Ireland–

(i) which deals with transferred matters; and

(ii) for which no rules made under paragraph (a) are in force,

rules made by a Northern Ireland department for those purposes,

and includes provision made by order under section I of the Courts and Legal Services Act 1990.

7(10) In making rules, regard must be had for section 9.

7(11) The Minister who has power to make rules in relation to a particular tribunal may, to the extent he considers it necessary to ensure that the tribunal can provide an appropriate remedy in relation to an act (or proposed act) of a public authority which is (or would be) unlawful as a result of section 6(1), by order add to–

(a) the relief or remedies which the tribunal may grant; or

(b) the grounds on which it may grant any of them.

7(12) An order made under subsection (11) may contain such incidental, supplemental, consequential or transitional provision as the Minister making it considers appropriate.

7(13) **"The Minister"** includes the Northern Ireland department concerned.

History – In s. 7(9)(a), the words "the Lord Chancellor or" inserted by SI 2005/3429, art. 8 and Sch., para. 3, with effect from 12 January 2006 (SI 2005/3429, art. 1(2)).

In s. 7(9)(a), the words "the Lord Chancellor or", which preceded the words "Secretary of State", repealed by SI 2003/1887, art. 9 and Sch. 2, para. 10(2) with effect from 19 August 2003.

Notes – S. 7 was brought into force on 2 October 2000 by the Human Rights Act 1998 (Commencement No. 2) Order 2000 (SI 2000/1851).

8 Judicial remedies

8(1) In relation to any act (or proposed act) of a public authority which the court finds is (or would be) unlawful, it may grant such relief or remedy, or make such order, within its powers as it considers just and appropriate.

8(2) But damages may be awarded only by a court which has power to award damages, or to order the payment of compensation, in civil proceedings.

8(3) No award of damages is to be made unless, taking account of all the circumstances of the case, including–

(a) any other relief or remedy granted, or order made, in relation to the act in question (by that or any other court), and

(b) the consequences of any decision (of that or any other court) in respect of that act,

the court is satisfied that the award is necessary to afford just satisfaction to the person in whose favour it is made.

8(4) In determining–

(a) whether to award damages, or

(b) the amount of an award,

the court must take into account the principles applied by the European Court of Human Rights in relation to the award of compensation under Article 41 of the Convention.

8(5) A public authority against which damages are awarded is to be treated–

(a) in Scotland, for the purposes of section 3 of the Law Reform (Miscellaneous Provisions) (Scotland) Act 1940 as if the award were made in an action of damages in which the authority has been found liable in respect of loss or damage to the person to whom the award is made;

(b) for the purposes of the Civil Liability (Contribution) Act 1978 as liable in respect of damage suffered by the person to whom the award is made.

8(6) In this section–

"court" includes a tribunal;

"damages" means damages for an unlawful act of a public authority; and

"unlawful" means unlawful under section 6(1).

Notes – S. 8 was brought into force on 2 October 2000 by the Human Rights Act 1998 (Commencement No. 2) Order 2000 (SI 2000/1851).

9 Judicial acts

9(1) Proceedings under section 7(1)(a) in respect of a judicial act may be brought only–

(a) by exercising a right of appeal;

(b) on an application (in Scotland a petition) for judicial review; or

(c) in such other forum as may be prescribed by rules.

9(2) That does not affect any rule of law which prevents a court from being the subject of judicial review.

9(3) In proceedings under this Act in respect of a judicial act done in good faith, damages may not be awarded otherwise than to compensate a person to the extent required by Article 5(5) of the Convention.

9(4) An award of damages permitted by subsection (3) is to be made against the Crown; but no award may be made unless the appropriate person, if not a party to the proceedings, is joined.

9(5) In this section–

"appropriate person" means the Minister responsible for the court concerned, or a person or government department nominated by him;

"court" includes a tribunal;

"judge" includes a member of a tribunal, a justice of the peace (or, in Northern Ireland, a lay magistrate) and a clerk or other officer entitled to exercise the jurisdiction of a court;

"judicial act" means a judicial act of a court and includes an act done on the instructions, or on behalf, of a judge; and

"rules" has the same meaning as in section 7(9).

History – In s. 9(5), in the definition of "judge" the words "(or, in Northern Ireland, a lay magistrate)" inserted by the Justice (Northern Ireland) Act 2002, s. 10 and Sch. 4, para. 39, with effect from 1 April 2005 (SR 2005/109, art. 2 and Sch.).

Notes – S. 9 was brought into force on 2 October 2000 by the Human Rights Act 1998 (Commencement No. 2) Order 2000 (SI 2000/1851).

REMEDIAL ACTION

10 Power to take remedial action

10(1) This section applies if–

(a) a provision of legislation has been declared under section 4 to be incompatible with a Convention right and, if an appeal lies–

(i) all persons who may appeal have stated in writing that they do not intend to do so;

(ii) the time for bringing an appeal has expired and no appeal has been brought within that time; or

(iii) an appeal brought within that time has been determined or abandoned; or

(b) it appears to a Minister of the Crown or Her Majesty in Council that, having regard to a finding of the European Court of Human Rights made after the coming into force of this section in proceedings against the United Kingdom, a provision of legislation is incompatible with an obligation of the United Kingdom arising from the Convention.

10(2) If a Minister of the Crown considers that there are compelling reasons for proceeding under this section, he may by order make such amendments to the legislation as he considers necessary to remove the incompatibility.

10(3) If, in the case of subordinate legislation, a Minister of the Crown considers–

(a) that it is necessary to amend the primary legislation under which the subordinate legislation in question was made, in order to enable the incompatibility to be removed, and

(b) that there are compelling reasons for proceeding under this section,

he may by order make such amendments to the primary legislation as he considers necessary.

10(4) This section also applies where the provision in question is in subordinate legislation and has been quashed, or declared invalid, by reason of incompatibility with a Convention right and the Minister proposes to proceed under paragraph 2(b) of Schedule 2.

10(5) If the legislation is an Order in Council, the power conferred by subsection (2) or (3) is exercisable by Her Majesty in Council.

10(6) In this section **"legislation"** does not include a Measure of the Church Assembly or of the General Synod of the Church of England.

10(7) Schedule 2 makes further provision about remedial orders.

Notes – S. 10 was brought into force on 2 October 2000 by the Human Rights Act 1998 (Commencement No. 2) Order 2000 (SI 2000/1851).

OTHER RIGHTS AND PROCEEDINGS

11 Safeguard for existing human rights

11 A person's reliance on a Convention right does not restrict–

(a) any other right or freedom conferred on him by or under any law having effect in any part of the United Kingdom; or

(b) his right to make any claim or bring any proceedings which he could make or bring apart from sections 7 to 9.

Notes – S. 11 was brought into force on 2 October 2000 by the Human Rights Act 1998 (Commencement No. 2) Order 2000 (SI 2000/1851).

12 Freedom of expression

12(1) This section applies if a court is considering whether to grant any relief which, if granted, might affect the exercise of the Convention right to freedom of expression.

12(2) If the person against whom the application for relief is made (**"the respondent"**) is neither present nor represented, no such relief is to be granted unless the court is satisfied–

(a) that the applicant has taken all practicable steps to notify the respondent; or

(b) that there are compelling reasons why the respondent should not be notified.

12(3) No such relief is to be granted so as to restrain publication before trial unless the court is satisfied that the applicant is likely to establish that publication should not be allowed.

12(4) The court must have particular regard to the importance of the Convention right to freedom of expression and, where the proceedings relate to material which the respondent claims, or which appears to the court, to be journalistic, literary or artistic material (or to conduct connected with such material), to–

(a) the extent to which–

(i) the material has, or is about to, become available to the public; or

(ii) it is, or would be, in the public interest for the material to be published;

(b) any relevant privacy code.

12(5) In this section–

"court" includes a tribunal; and

"relief" includes any remedy or order (other than in criminal proceedings).

Notes – S. 12 was brought into force on 2 October 2000 by the Human Rights Act 1998 (Commencement No. 2) Order 2000 (SI 2000/1851).

13 Freedom of thought, conscience and religion

13(1) If a court's determination of any question arising under this Act might affect the exercise by a religious organisation (itself or its members collectively) of the Convention right to freedom of thought, conscience and religion, it must have particular regard to the importance of that right.

13(2) In this section **"court"** includes a tribunal.

Notes – S. 13 was brought into force on 2 October 2000 by the Human Rights Act 1998 (Commencement No. 2) Order 2000 (SI 2000/1851).

DERogations AND RESERVATIONS

14 Derogations

14(1) In this act **"designated derogation"** means any derogation by the United Kingdom from an Article of the Convention, or of any protocol to the Convention, which is designated for the purposes of this Act in an order made by the Secretary of State.

14(2) [Repealed by SI 2001/1216, art. 2(b).]

14(3) If a designated derogation is amended or replaced it ceases to be a designated derogation.

14(4) But subsection (3) does not prevent the Secretary of State from exercising his power under subsection (1) to make a fresh designation order in respect of the Article concerned.

14(5) The Secretary of State must by order make such amendments to Schedule 3 as he considers appropriate to reflect–

(a) any designation order; or

(b) the effect of subsection (3).

14(6) A designation order may be made in anticipation of the making by the United Kingdom of a proposed derogation.

History – In s. 14(1) the words "Secretary of State" substituted for the words "Lord Chancellor" by SI 2003/1887, art. 9 and Sch. 2, para. 10(1), with effect from 19 August 2003.

In s. 14(1), the words "(a) the United Kingdom's derogation from article 5(3) of the Convention; and (b)" repealed by SI 2001/1216, art. 2(a) with effect from 1 April 2001.

S. 14(2) repealed by SI 2001/1216, art. 2(b) with effect from 1 April 2001.

In s. 14(4), the word "b", repealed by SI 2001/1216, art. 2(c) with effect from 1 April 2001.

In s. 14(4) the words "Secretary of State" substituted for the words "Lord Chancellor" by SI 2003/1887, art. 9 and Sch. 2, para 10(1), with effect from 19 August 2003.

In s. 14(5) the words "Secretary of State" substituted for the words "Lord Chancellor" by SI 2003/1887, art. 9 and Sch. 2, para 10(1), with effect from 19 August 2003.

In s. 14(1), (4), (5), the words, "Lord Chancellor" previously substituted by SI 2001/3500, Sch. 2, with effect from 26 November 2001.

Notes – S. 14 was brought into force on 2 October 2000 by the Human Rights Act 1998 (Commencement No. 2) Order 2000 (SI 2000/1851).

15 Reservations

15(1) In this Act **"designated reservation"** means–

(a) the United Kingdom's reservation to Article 2 of the First Protocol to the Convention; and

(b) any other reservation by the United Kingdom to an Article of the Convention, or of any protocol to the Convention, which is designated for the purposes of this Act in an order made by the Secretary of State.

15(2) The text of the reservation referred to in subsection (l)(a) is set out in Part II of Schedule 3.

15(3) If a designated reservation is withdrawn wholly or in part it ceases to be a designated reservation.

15(4) But subsection (3) does not prevent the Secretary of State from exercising his power under subsection (1) to make a fresh designation order in respect of the Article concerned.

15(5) The Secretary of State must by order make such amendments to this Act as he considers appropriate to reflect–

(a) any designation order; or

(b) the effect of subsection (3).

History – In s. 15(1)(b), s. 15(4) and s. 15(5), the words "Secretary of State" substituted for the words "Lord Chancellor" by SI 2003/1887, art. 9 and Sch. 2, para. 10(1), with effect from 19 August 2003.

In s. 15(1)(b), (4), (5), the words "Lord Chancellor" previously substituted by SI 2001/3500, Sch. 2, with effect from 26 November 2001.

Notes – S. 15 was brought into force on 2 October 2000 by the Human Rights Act 1998 (Commencement No. 2) Order 2000 (SI 2000/1851).

16 Period for which designated derogations have effect

16(1) If it has not already been withdrawn by the United Kingdom, a designated derogation ceases to have effect for the purposes of this Act–

(a) [Repealed by SI 2001/1216, art. 3.]

(b) at the end of the period of five years beginning with the date on which the order designating it was made.

16(2) At any time before the period–

(a) fixed by subsection (1), or

(b) extended by an order under this subsection,

comes to an end, the Secretary of State may by order extend it by a further period of five years.

16(3) An order under section 14(1) ceases to have effect at the end of the period for consideration, unless a resolution has been passed by each House approving the order.

16(4) Subsection (3) does not affect–

(a) anything done in reliance on the order; or

(b) the power to make a fresh order under section 14(1).

16(5) In subsection (3) **"period for consideration"** means the period of forty days beginning with the day on which the order was made.

16(6) In calculating the period for consideration, no account is to be taken of any time during which–

(a) Parliament is dissolved or prorogued; or

(b) both Houses are adjourned for more than four days.

16(7) If a designated derogation is withdrawn by the United Kingdom, the Secretary of State must by order make such amendments to this Act as he considers are required to reflect that withdrawal.

History – In s. 16(1), former para. (a) and the words at the beginning of para. (b), "any other derogation" repealed by SI 2001/1216, art. 3 with effect from 1 April 2001.
In s. 16(2) and s. 16(7), the words "Secretary of State" substituted for the words "Lord Chancellor" by SI 2003/1887, art. 9 and Sch. 2, para. 10(1), with effect from 19 August 2003.
In s. 16(2), the words "(a) or (b)" that formerly appeared after "(1)" repealed by SI 2001/1216, art. 3 with effect from 1 April 2001.
In s. 16(2), (7) the words "Lord Chancellor" substituted by SI 2001/3500, Sch. 2, with effect from 26 November 2001.
In s. 16(3), the word "(b)" which appeared after "14(1)" repealed by SI 2001/1216, art. 3 with effect from 1 April 2001.
In s. 16(4), the word "(b)" which appeared after "14(1)" repealed by SI 2001/1216, art. 3 with effect from 1 April 2001.

Notes – S. 16 was brought into force on 2 October 2000 by the Human Rights Act 1998 (Commencement No. 2) Order 2000 (SI 2000/1851).

17 Periodic review of designated reservations

17(1) The appropriate Minister must review the designated reservation referred to in section 15(1)(a)–

(a) before the end of the period of five years beginning with the date on which section 1(2) came into force; and

(b) if that designation is still in force, before the end of the period of five years beginning with the date on which the last report relating to it was laid under subsection (3).

17(2) The appropriate Minister must review each of the other designated reservations (if any)–

(a) before the end of the period of five years beginning with the date on which the order designating the reservation first came into force; and

(b) if the designation is still in force, before the end of the period of five years beginning with the date on which the last report relating to it was laid under subsection (3).

17(3) The Minister conducting a review under this section must prepare a report on the result of the review and lay a copy of it before each House of Parliament.

Notes – S. 17 was brought into force on 2 October 2000 by the Human Rights Act 1998 (Commencement No. 2) Order 2000 (SI 2000/1851).

JUDGES OF THE EUROPEAN COURT OF HUMAN RIGHTS

18 Appointment to European Court of Human Rights

18(1) In this section **"judicial office"** means the office of–

(a) Lord Justice of Appeal, Justice of the High Court or Circuit judge, in England and Wales;

(b) judge of the Court of Session or sheriff, in Scotland;

(c) Lord Justice of Appeal, judge of the High Court or county court judge, in Northern Ireland.

18(2) The holder of a judicial office may become a judge of the European Court of Human Rights ("the Court") without being required to relinquish his office.

18(3) But he is not required to perform the duties of his judicial office while he is a judge of the Court.

18(4) In respect of any period during which he is a judge of the Court–

(a) a Lord Justice of Appeal or Justice of the High Court is not to count as a judge of the relevant court for the purposes of section 2(1) or 4(1) of the Senior Courts Act 1981 (maximum number of judges) nor as a judge of the Supreme Court for the purposes of section 12(1) to (6) of that Act (salaries etc.);

(b) a judge of the Court of Session is not to count as a judge of that court for the purposes of section 1(l) of the Court of Session Act 1988 (maximum number of judges) or of section 9(1)(c) of the Administration of Justice Act 1973 ("the 1973 Act") (salaries etc.);

(c) a Lord Justice of Appeal or judge of the High Court in Northern Ireland is not to count as a judge of the relevant court for the purposes of section 2(1) or 3(1) of the Judicature (Northern Ireland)

Act 1978 (maximum number of judges) nor as a judge of the Court of Judicature of Northern Ireland for the purposes of section 9(1)(d) of the 1973 Act (salaries etc.);

(d) a Circuit judge is not to count as such for the purposes of section 18 of the Courts Act 1971 (salaries etc.);

(e) a sheriff is not to count as such for the purposes of section 14 of the Sheriff Courts (Scotland) Act 1907 (salaries etc.);

(f) a county court judge of Northern Ireland is not to count as such for the purposes of section 106 of the County Courts Act (Northern Ireland) 1959 (salaries etc.).

18(5) If a sheriff principal is appointed a judge of the Court, section 11(1) of the Sheriff Courts (Scotland) Act 1971 (temporary appointment of sheriff principal) applies, while he holds that appointment, as if his office is vacant.

18(6) Schedule 4 makes provision about judicial pensions in relation to the holder of a judicial office who serves as a judge of the Court.

18(7) The Lord Chancellor or the Secretary of State may by order make such transitional provision (including, in particular, provision for a temporary increase in the maximum number of judges) as he considers appropriate in relation to any holder of a judicial office who has completed his service as a judge of the Court.

18(7A) The following paragraphs apply to the making of an order under subsection (7) in relation to any holder of a judicial office listed in subsection (1)(a)–

(a) before deciding what transitional provision it is appropriate to make, the person making the order must consult the Lord Chief Justice of England and Wales;

(b) before making the order, that person must consult the Lord Chief Justice of England and Wales.

18(7B) The following paragraphs apply to the making of an order under subsection (7) in relation to any holder of a judicial office listed in subsection (1)(c)–

(a) before deciding what transitional provision it is appropriate to make, the person making the order must consult the Lord Chief Justice of Northern Ireland;

(b) before making the order, that person must consult the Lord Chief Justice of Northern Ireland.

18(7C) The Lord Chief Justice of England and Wales may nominate a judicial office holder (within the meaning of section 109(4) of the Constitutional Reform Act 2005) to exercise his functions under this section.

18(7D) The Lord Chief Justice of Northern Ireland may nominate any of the following to exercise his functions under this section–

(a) the holder of one of the offices listed in Schedule 1 to the Justice (Northern Ireland) Act 2002;

(b) a Lord Justice of Appeal (as defined in section 88 of that Act).

History – In s. 18(4)(a), the words "Senior Courts Act 1981" substituted for the words "Supreme Court Act 1981" and words "Senior Courts" substituted for the words "Supreme Court" by the Constitutional Reform Act 2005, s. 59(5) and Sch. 11, para. 1(2) and (3), with effect from 1 October 2009 (the date appointed by virtue of SI 2009/1604).

In s. 18(4)(c), the words "Court of Judicature" substituted for the words "Supreme Court" by the Constitutional Reform Act 2005, s. 59(5) and Sch. 11, para. 1(4), with effect from 1 October 2009 (the date appointed by virtue of SI 2009/1604).

S. 18(7A)–(7D) inserted by Constitutional Reform Act 2005, s. 15 and Sch. 4, para. 278, with effect from 3 April 2006 (SI 2006/1014, art. 2(a) and Sch. 1, para. 10 and 11).

Notes – S. 18 was brought into force on 2 October 2000 by the Human Rights Act 1998 (Commencement No. 2) Order 2000 (SI 2000/1851).

PARLIAMENTARY PROCEDURE

19 Statements of compatibility

19(1) A Minister of the Crown in charge of a Bill in either House of Parliament must, before Second Reading of the Bill–

(a) make a statement to the effect that in his view the provisions of the Bill are compatible with the Convention rights ("a statement of compatibility"); or

(b) make a statement to the effect that although he is unable to make a statement of compatibility the government nevertheless wishes the House to proceed with the Bill.

19(2) The statement must be in writing and be published in such manner as the Minister making it considers appropriate.

Statutory instruments – SI 1998/2882 (C. 71): appointing 24 November 1998 as the commencement day for s. 19 (statements of compatibility).

Notes – S. 19 (statements of compatibility) was brought into force on 24 November 1998 by the Human Rights Act 1998 (Commencement No. 1) Order 1998 (SI 1998/2882).

SUPPLEMENTAL

20 Orders etc. under this Act

20(1) Any power of a Minister of the Crown to make an order under this Act is exercisable by statutory instrument.

20(2) The power of the Lord Chancellor or the Secretary of State to make rules (other than rules of court) under section 2(3) or 7(9) is exercisable by statutory instrument.

20(3) Any statutory instrument made under section 14, 15 or 16(7) must be laid before Parliament.

20(4) No order may be made by the Lord Chancellor or the Secretary of State under section 1(4), 7(11) or 16(2) unless a draft of the order has been laid before, and approved by, each House of Parliament.

20(5) Any statutory instrument made under section 18(7) or Schedule 4, or to which subsection (2) applies, shall be subject to annulment in pursuance of a resolution of either House of Parliament.

20(6) The power of a Northern Ireland department to make–

(a) rules under section 2(3)(c) or 7(9)(c), or

(b) an order under section 7(11),

is exercisable by statutory rule for the purposes of the Statutory Rules (Northern Ireland) Order 1979.

20(7) Any rules made under section 2(3)(c) or 7(9)(c) shall be subject to negative resolution; and section 41(6) of the Interpretation Act (Northern Ireland) 1954 (meaning of "subject to negative resolution") shall apply as if the power to make the rules were conferred by an Act of the Northern Ireland Assembly.

20(8) No order may be made by a Northern Ireland department under section 7(11) unless a draft of the order has been laid before, and approved by, the Northern Ireland Assembly.

History – In s. 20(2) and (4), the words "the Lord Chancellor or" inserted by SI 2005/3429, art. 8 and Sch., para. 3, with effect from 12 January 2006 (SI 2005/3429, art. 1(2)).

In s. 20(2) and (4), the words "the Lord Chancellor or" repealed by SI 2003/1887, art. 9 and Sch. 2, para. 10(2), with effect from 19 August 2003.

Notes – S. 20 was brought into force on 2 October 2000 by the Human Rights Act 1998 (Commencement No. 2) Order 2000 (SI 2000/1851).

21 Interpretation, etc.

21(1) In this Act–

"amend" includes repeal and apply (with or without modifications);

"the appropriate Minister" means the Minister of the Crown having charge of the appropriate authorised government department (within the meaning of the Crown Proceedings Act 1947);

"the Commission" means the European Commission of Human Rights;

"the Convention" means the Convention for the Protection of Human Rights and Fundamental Freedoms, agreed by the Council of Europe at Rome on 4th November 1950 as it has effect for the time being in relation to the United Kingdom;

"declaration of incompatibility" means a declaration under section 4;

"Minister of the Crown" has the same meaning as in the Ministers of the Crown Act 1975;

"Northern Ireland Minister" includes the First Minister and the deputy First Minister in Northern Ireland;

"primary legislation" means any–

(a) public general Act;

(b) local and personal Act;

(c) private Act;

(d) Measure of the Church Assembly;

(e) Measure of the General Synod of the Church of England;

(f) Order in Council–

(i) made in exercise of Her Majesty's Royal Prerogative;

(ii) made under section 38(1)(a) of the Northern Ireland Constitution Act 1973 or the corresponding provision of the Northern Ireland Act 1998; or

(iii) amending an Act of a kind mentioned in paragraph (a), (b) or (c);

and includes an order or other instrument made under primary legislation (otherwise than by the Welsh Ministers, the First Minister for Wales, the Counsel General to the Welsh Assembly Government, a member of the Scottish Executive, a Northern Ireland Minister or a Northern Ireland department) to the extent to which it operates to bring one or more provisions of that legislation into force or amends any primary legislation; **"the First Protocol"** means the protocol to the Convention agreed at Paris on 20th March 1952; **"the Eleventh Protocol"** means the protocol to the Convention (restructuring the control machinery established by the Convention) agreed at Strasbourg on 11th May 1994; **"the Thirteenth Protocol"** means the protocol to the Convention (concerning the abolition of the death penalty in all circumstances) agreed at Vilnius on 3rd May 2002;**"remedial order"** means an order under section 10; **"subordinate legislation"** means any– **"transferred matters"** has the same meaning as in the Northern Ireland Act 1998; and **"tribunal"** means any tribunal in which legal proceedings may be brought.

(a) Order in Council other than one–
  (i) made in exercise of Her Majesty's Royal Prerogative;
  (ii) made under section 38(1)(a) of the Northern Ireland Constitution Act 1973 or the corresponding provision of the Northern Ireland Act 1998; or
  (iii) amending an Act of a kind mentioned in the definition of primary legislation;
(b) Act of the Scottish Parliament;
(ba) Measure of the National Assembly for Wales;
(bb) Act of the National Assembly for Wales;
(c) Act of the Parliament of Northern Ireland;
(d) Measure of the Assembly established under section 1 of the Northern Ireland Assembly Act 1973;
(e) Act of the Northern Ireland Assembly;
(f) order, rules, regulations, scheme, warrant, byelaw or other instrument made under primary legislation (except to the extent to which it operates to bring one or more provisions of that legislation into force or amends any primary legislation);
(g) order, rules, regulations, scheme, warrant, byelaw or other instrument made under legislation mentioned in paragraph (b), (c), (d) or (e) or made under an Order in Council applying only to Northern Ireland;
(h) order, rules, regulations, scheme, warrant, byelaw or other instrument made by a member of the Scottish Executive, Welsh Ministers, the First Minister for Wales, the Counsel General to the Welsh Assembly Government, a Northern Ireland Minister or a Northern Ireland department in exercise of prerogative or other executive functions of Her Majesty which are exercisable by such a person on behalf of Her Majesty;

21(2) The references in paragraphs (b) and (c) of section 2(1) to Articles are to Articles of the Convention as they had effect immediately before the coming into force of the Eleventh Protocol.

21(3) The reference in paragraph (d) of section 2(1) to Article 46 includes a reference to Articles 32 and 54 of the Convention as they had effect immediately before the coming into force of the Eleventh Protocol.

21(4) The references in section 2(1) to a report or decision of the Commission or a decision of the Committee of Ministers include references to a report or decision made as provided by paragraphs 3, 4 and 6 of Article 5 of the Eleventh Protocol (transitional provisions).

21(5) [Repealed by Armed Forces Act 2006, s. 378 and Sch. 17.]

History – In s. 21(1), in the definition of "primary legislation" the words "Welsh Ministers, the First Minister for Wales, the Counsel General to the Welsh Assembly Government" substituted by the Government of Wales Act 2006, s. 160 and Sch. 10, para. 56(2), with effect from 25 May 2007.
In s. 21(1) the definition of "the Sixth Protocol" omitted by SI 2004/1574, art. 2(2), operative from 22 June 2004.
In s. 21(1), in the definition of "subordinate legislation" para. (ba) and (bb) inserted by the Government of Wales Act 2006, s. 160 and Sch. 10, para. 56(3), with effect from 25 May 2007.
In s. 21(1), in the definition of "subordinate legislation" in para. (h) the words ", Welsh Ministers, the First Minister for Wales, the Counsel General to the Welsh Assembly Government" inserted by the Government of Wales Act 2006, s. 160 and Sch. 10, para. 56(4), with effect from 25 May 2007.
In s. 21(1) the definition of "the Thirteenth Protocol" inserted by SI 2004/1574, art. 2(2), operative from 22 June 2004.
S. 21(5) repealed by Armed Forces Act 2006, s. 378 and Sch. 17.

Notes – S. 21 was brought into force on 2 October 2000 by the Human Rights Act 1998 (Commencement No. 2) Order 2000 (SI 2000/1851).

22 Short title, commencement, application and extent

22(1) This Act may be cited as the Human Rights Act 1998.

22(2) Sections 18, 20 and 21(5) and this section come into force on the passing of this Act.

22(3) The other provisions of this Act come into force on such day as the Secretary of State may by order appoint; and different days may be appointed for different purposes.

22(4) Paragraph (b) of subsection (1) of section 7 applies to proceedings brought by or at the instigation of a public authority whenever the act in question took place; but otherwise that subsection does not apply to an act taking place before the coming into force of that section.

22(5) This Act binds the Crown.

22(6) This Act extends to Northern Ireland.

22(7) [Repealed by Armed Forces Act 2006, s. 378 and Sch. 17.]

History – S. 22(7) repealed by Armed Forces Act 2006, s. 378 and Sch. 17.

Notes – S. 22 was brought into force on 2 October 2000 by the Human Rights Act 1998 (Commencement No. 2) Order 2000 (SI 2000/1851).

SCHEDULES

SCHEDULE 1 – THE ARTICLES

Section 1(3)

Part I – The Convention

RIGHTS AND FREEDOMS

ARTICLE 2 –RIGHT TO LIFE

1 Everyone's right to life shall be protected by law. No one shall be deprived of his life intentionally save in the execution of a sentence of a court following his conviction of a crime for which this penalty is provided by law.

Notes – Sch. 1, Pt. I was brought into force on 2 October 2000 by the Human Rights Act 1998 (Commencement No. 2) Order 2000 (SI 2000/1851).

2 Deprivation of life shall not be regarded as inflicted in contravention of this Article when it results from the use of force which is no more than absolutely necessary:

(a) in defence of any person from unlawful violence;

(b) in order to effect a lawful arrest or to prevent the escape of a person lawfully detained;

(c) in action lawfully taken for the purpose of quelling a riot or insurrection.

Notes – Sch. 1, Pt. I was brought into force on 2 October 2000 by the Human Rights Act 1998 (Commencement No. 2) Order 2000 (SI 2000/1851).

ARTICLE 3

PROHIBITION OF TORTURE

No one shall be subjected to torture or to inhuman or degrading treatment or punishment.

Notes – Sch. 1, Pt. I was brought into force on 2 October 2000 by the Human Rights Act 1998 (Commencement No. 2) Order 2000 (SI 2000/1851).

ARTICLE 4

PROHIBITION OF SLAVERY AND FORCED LABOUR

1 No one shall be held in slavery or servitude.

Notes – Sch. 1, Pt. I was brought into force on 2 October 2000 by the Human Rights Act 1998 (Commencement No. 2) Order 2000 (SI 2000/1851).

2 No one shall be required to perform forced or compulsory labour.

Notes – Sch. 1, Pt. I was brought into force on 2 October 2000 by the Human Rights Act 1998 (Commencement No. 2) Order 2000 (SI 2000/1851).

3 For the purpose of this Article the term **"forced or compulsory labour"** shall not include:

(a) any work required to be done in the ordinary course of detention imposed according to the provisions of Article 5 of this Convention or during conditional release from such detention;

(b) any service of a military character or, in case of conscientious objectors in countries where they are recognised, service exacted instead of compulsory military service;

(c) any service exacted in case of an emergency or calamity threatening the life or well-being of the community;

(d) any work or service which forms part of normal civic obligations.

Notes – Sch. 1, Pt. I was brought into force on 2 October 2000 by the Human Rights Act 1998 (Commencement No. 2) Order 2000 (SI 2000/1851).

ARTICLE 5

RIGHT TO LIBERTY AND SECURITY

1 Everyone has the right to liberty and security of person. No one shall be deprived of his liberty save in the following cases and in accordance with a procedure prescribed by law:

(a) the lawful detention of a person after conviction by a competent court;

(b) the lawful arrest or detention of a person for non-compliance with the lawful order of a court or in order to secure the fulfilment of any obligation prescribed by law;

(c) the lawful arrest or detention of a person effected for the purpose of bringing him before the competent legal authority on reasonable suspicion of having committed an offence or when it is reasonably considered necessary to prevent his committing an offence or fleeing after having done so;

(d) the detention of a minor by lawful order for the purpose of educational supervision or his lawful detention for the purpose of bringing him before the competent legal authority;

(e) the lawful detention of persons for the prevention of the spreading of infectious diseases, of persons of unsound mind, alcoholics or drug addicts or vagrants;

(f) the lawful arrest or detention of a person to prevent his effecting an unauthorised entry into the country or of a person against whom action is being taken with a view to deportation or extradition.

Notes – Sch. 1, Pt. I was brought into force on 2 October 2000 by the Human Rights Act 1998 (Commencement No. 2) Order 2000 (SI 2000/1851).

2 Everyone who is arrested shall be informed promptly, in a language which he understands, of the reasons for his arrest and of any charge against him.

Notes – Sch. 1, Pt. I was brought into force on 2 October 2000 by the Human Rights Act 1998 (Commencement No. 2) Order 2000 (SI 2000/1851).

3 Everyone arrested or detained in accordance with the provisions of paragraph 1(c) of this Article shall be brought promptly before a judge or other officer authorised by law to exercise judicial power and shall be entitled to trial within a reasonable time or to release pending trial. Release may be conditioned by guarantees to appear for trial.

Notes – Sch. 1, Pt. I was brought into force on 2 October 2000 by the Human Rights Act 1998 (Commencement No. 2) Order 2000 (SI 2000/1851).

4 Everyone who is deprived of his liberty by arrest or detention shall be entitled to take proceedings by which the lawfulness of his detention shall be decided speedily by a court and his release ordered if the detention is not lawful.

Notes – Sch. 1, Pt. I was brought into force on 2 October 2000 by the Human Rights Act 1998 (Commencement No. 2) Order 2000 (SI 2000/1851).

5 Everyone who has been the victim of arrest or detention in contravention of the provisions of this Article shall have an enforceable right to compensation.

Notes – Sch. 1, Pt. I was brought into force on 2 October 2000 by the Human Rights Act 1998 (Commencement No. 2) Order 2000 (SI 2000/1851).

ARTICLE 6

RIGHT TO A FAIR TRIAL

1 In the determination of his civil rights and obligations or of any criminal charge against him, everyone is entitled to a fair and public hearing within a reasonable time by an independent and impartial tribunal established by law. Judgement shall be pronounced publicly but the press and public may be excluded from all or part of the trial in the interest of morals, public order or national security in a democratic society, where the interests of juveniles or the protection of the private life of the parties so require, or to the extent strictly necessary in the opinion of the court in special circumstances where publicity would prejudice the interests of justice.

Notes – Sch. 1, Pt. I was brought into force on 2 October 2000 by the Human Rights Act 1998 (Commencement No. 2) Order 2000 (SI 2000/1851).

2 Everyone charged with a criminal offence shall be presumed innocent until proved guilty according to law.

Notes – Sch. 1, Pt. I was brought into force on 2 October 2000 by the Human Rights Act 1998 (Commencement No. 2) Order 2000 (SI 2000/1851).

3 Everyone charged with a criminal offence has the following minimum rights:

(a) to be informed promptly, in a language which he understands and in detail, of the nature and cause of the accusation against him;

(b) to have adequate time and facilities for the preparation of his defence;

(c) to defend himself in person or through legal assistance of his own choosing or, if he has not sufficient means to pay for legal assistance, to be given it free when the interests of justice so require;

(d) to examine or have examined witnesses against him and to obtain the attendance and examination of witnesses on his behalf under the same conditions as witnesses against him;

(e) to have the free assistance of an interpreter if he cannot understand or speak the language used in court.

Notes – Sch. 1, Pt. I was brought into force on 2 October 2000 by the Human Rights Act 1998 (Commencement No. 2) Order 2000 (SI 2000/1851).

ARTICLE 7

NO PUNISHMENT WITHOUT LAW

1 No one shall be held guilty of any criminal offence on account of any act or omission which did not constitute a criminal offence under national or international law at the time when it was committed. Nor shall a heavier penalty be imposed than the one that was applicable at the time the criminal offence was committed.

Notes – Sch. 1, Pt. I was brought into force on 2 October 2000 by the Human Rights Act 1998 (Commencement No. 2) Order 2000 (SI 2000/1851).

2 This Article shall not prejudice the trial and punishment of any person for any act or omission which, at the time when it was committed, was criminal according to the general principles of law recognised by civilised nations.

Notes – Sch. 1, Pt. I was brought into force on 2 October 2000 by the Human Rights Act 1998 (Commencement No. 2) Order 2000 (SI 2000/1851).

ARTICLE 8

RIGHT TO RESPECT FOR PRIVATE AND FAMILY LIFE

1 Everyone has the right to respect for his private and family life, his home and his correspondence.

Notes – Sch. 1, Pt. I was brought into force on 2 October 2000 by the Human Rights Act 1998 (Commencement No. 2) Order 2000 (SI 2000/1851).

2 There shall be no interference by a public authority with the exercise of this right except such as is in accordance with the law and is necessary in a democratic society in the interests of national security, public safety or the economic well-being of the country, for the prevention of disorder or crime, for the protection of health or morals, or for the protection of the rights and freedoms of others.

Notes – Sch. 1, Pt. I was brought into force on 2 October 2000 by the Human Rights Act 1998 (Commencement No. 2) Order 2000 (SI 2000/1851).

ARTICLE 9

FREEDOM OF THOUGHT, CONSCIENCE AND RELIGION

1 Everyone has the right to freedom of thought, conscience and religion; this right includes freedom to change his religion or belief and freedom, either alone or in community with others and in public or private, to manifest his religion or belief, in worship, teaching, practice and observance.

Notes – Sch. 1, Pt. I was brought into force on 2 October 2000 by the Human Rights Act 1998 (Commencement No. 2) Order 2000 (SI 2000/1851).

2 Freedom to manifest one's religion or beliefs shall be subject only to such limitations as are prescribed by law and are necessary in a democratic society in the interests of public safety, for the protection of public order, health or morals, or for the protection of the rights and freedoms of others.

Notes – Sch. 1, Pt. I was brought into force on 2 October 2000 by the Human Rights Act 1998 (Commencement No. 2) Order 2000 (SI 2000/1851).

ARTICLE 10

FREEDOM OF EXPRESSION

1 Everyone has the right to freedom of expression. This right shall include freedom to hold opinions and to receive and impart information and ideas without interference by public authority and regardless of frontiers. This Article shall not prevent States from requiring the licensing of broadcasting, television or cinema enterprises.

Notes – Sch. 1, Pt. I was brought into force on 2 October 2000 by the Human Rights Act 1998 (Commencement No. 2) Order 2000 (SI 2000/1851).

2 The exercise of these freedoms, since it carries with it duties and responsibilities, may be subject to such formalities, conditions, restrictions or penalties as are prescribed by law and are necessary in a democratic society, in the interests of national security, territorial integrity or public safety, for the prevention of disorder or crime, for the protection of health or morals, for the protection of the reputation or rights of others, for preventing the disclosure of information received in confidence, or for maintaining the authority and impartiality of the judiciary.

Notes – Sch. 1, Pt. I was brought into force on 2 October 2000 by the Human Rights Act 1998 (Commencement No. 2) Order 2000 (SI 2000/1851).

ARTICLE 11

FREEDOM OF ASSEMBLY AND ASSOCIATION

1 Everyone has the right to freedom of peaceful assembly and to freedom of association with others, including the right to form and to join trade unions for the protection of his interests.

Notes – Sch. 1, Pt. I was brought into force on 2 October 2000 by the Human Rights Act 1998 (Commencement No. 2) Order 2000 (SI 2000/1851).

2 No restrictions shall be placed on the exercise of these rights other than such as are prescribed by law and are necessary in a democratic society in the interests of national security or public safety, for the prevention of disorder or crime, for the protection of health or morals or for the protection of the rights and freedoms of others. This Article shall not prevent the imposition of lawful restrictions on the exercise of these rights by members of the armed forces, of the police or of the administration of the State.

Notes – Sch. 1, Pt. I was brought into force on 2 October 2000 by the Human Rights Act 1998 (Commencement No. 2) Order 2000 (SI 2000/1851).

ARTICLE 12

RIGHT TO MARRY

Men and women of marriageable age have the right to marry and to found a family, according to the national laws governing the exercise of this right.

Notes – Sch. 1, Pt. I was brought into force on 2 October 2000 by the Human Rights Act 1998 (Commencement No. 2) Order 2000 (SI 2000/1851).

ARTICLE 14

PROHIBITION OF DISCRIMINATION

The enjoyment of the rights and freedoms set forth in this Convention shall be secured without discrimination on any ground such as sex, race, colour, language, religion, political or other opinion, national or social origin, association with a national minority, property, birth or other status.

Notes – Sch. 1, Pt. I was brought into force on 2 October 2000 by the Human Rights Act 1998 (Commencement No. 2) Order 2000 (SI 2000/1851).

ARTICLE 16

RESTRICTIONS ON POLITICAL ACTIVITY OF ALIENS

Nothing in Articles 10, 11 and 14 shall be regarded as preventing the High Contracting Parties from imposing restrictions on the political activity of aliens.

Notes – Sch. 1, Pt. I was brought into force on 2 October 2000 by the Human Rights Act 1998 (Commencement No. 2) Order 2000 (SI 2000/1851).

ARTICLE 17

PROHIBITION OF ABUSE OF RIGHTS

Nothing in this Convention may be interpreted as implying for any State, group or person any right to engage in any activity or perform any act aimed at the destruction of any of the rights and freedoms set forth herein or at their limitation to a greater extent than is provided for in the Convention

Notes – Sch. 1, Pt. I was brought into force on 2 October 2000 by the Human Rights Act 1998 (Commencement No. 2) Order 2000 (SI 2000/1851).

ARTICLE 18

LIMITATION ON USE OF RESTRICTIONS RIGHTS

The restrictions permitted under this Convention to the said rights and freedoms shall not be applied for any purpose other than those for which they have been prescribed.

Notes – Sch. 1, Pt. I was brought into force on 2 October 2000 by the Human Rights Act 1998 (Commencement No. 2) Order 2000 (SI 2000/1851).

Part II – The First Protocol

ARTICLE 1

PROTECTION OF PROPERTY

Every natural or legal person is entitled to the peaceful enjoyment of his possessions. No one shall be deprived of his possessions except in the public interest and subject to the conditions provided for by law and by the general principles of international law.

The preceding provisions shall not, however, in any way impair the right of a State to enforce such laws as it deems necessary to control the use of property in accordance with the general interest or to secure the payment of taxes or other contributions or penalties.

Notes – Sch. 1, Pt. II was brought into force on 2 October 2000 by the Human Rights Act 1998 (Commencement No. 2) Order 2000 (SI 2000/1851).

ARTICLE 2

RIGHT TO EDUCATION

No person shall be denied the right to education. In the exercise of any functions which it assumes in relation to education and to teaching, the State shall respect the right of parents to ensure such education and teaching in conformity with their own religious and philosophical convictions.

Notes – Sch. 1, Pt. II was brought into force on 2 October 2000 by the Human Rights Act 1998 (Commencement No. 2) Order 2000 (SI 2000/1851).

ARTICLE 3

RIGHT TO FREE ELECTIONS

The High Contracting Parties undertake to hold free elections at reasonable intervals by secret ballot, under conditions which will ensure the free expression of the opinion of the people in the choice of the legislature.

Notes – Sch. 1, Pt. II was brought into force on 2 October 2000 by the Human Rights Act 1998 (Commencement No. 2) Order 2000 (SI 2000/1851).

Part 3

ARTICLE 1 OF THE THIRTEENTH PROTOCOL

ABOLITION OF THE DEATH PENALTY

The death penalty shall be abolished. No one shall be condemned to such penalty or executed.

History – Part 3, art. 1 substituted by SI 2004/1574, art. 3, with effect from 22 June 2004.

Notes – Sch. 1, Pt. III was brought into force on 2 October 2000 by the Human Rights Act 1998 (Commencement No. 2) Order 2000 (SI 2000/1851).

ARTICLE 2

DEATH PENALTY IN TIME OF WAR

A State may make provision in its law for the death penalty in respect of acts committed in time of war or of imminent threat of war; such penalty shall be applied only in the instances laid down in the law and in accordance with its provisions. The State shall communicate to the Secretary General of the Council of Europe the relevant provisions of that law.

Notes – Sch. 1, Pt. III was brought into force on 2 October 2000 by the Human Rights Act 1998 (Commencement No. 2) Order 2000 (SI 2000/1851).

SCHEDULE 2 – REMEDIAL ORDERS

Section 10

ORDERS

1(1) A remedial order may–

(a) contain such incidental, supplemental, consequential or transitional provision as the person making it considers appropriate;

(b) be made so as to have effect from a date earlier than that on which it is made;

(c) make provision for the delegation of specific functions;

(d) make different provision for different cases.

1(2) The power conferred by sub-paragraph (1)(a) includes–

(a) power to amend primary legislation (including primary legislation other than that which contains the incompatible provision); and

(b) power to amend or revoke subordinate legislation (including subordinate legislation other than that which contains the incompatible provision).

1(3) A remedial order may be made so as to have the same extent as the legislation which it affects.

1(4) No person is to be guilty of an offence solely as a result of the retrospective effect of a remedial order.

Notes – Sch. 2, para. 1 was brought into force on 2 October 2000 by the Human Rights Act 1998 (Commencement No. 2) Order 2000 (SI 2000/1851).

PROCEDURE

2 No remedial order may be made unless–

(a) a draft of the order has been approved by a resolution of each House of Parliament made after the end of the period of 60 days beginning with the day on which the draft was laid; or

(b) it is declared in the order that it appears to the person making it that, because of the urgency of the matter, it is necessary to make the order without a draft being so approved.

Notes – Sch. 2, para. 2 was brought into force on 2 October 2000 by the Human Rights Act 1998 (Commencement No. 2) Order 2000 (SI 2000/1851).

ORDERS LAID IN DRAFT

3(1) No draft may be laid under paragraph 2(a) unless–

(a) the person proposing to make the order has laid before Parliament a document which contains a draft of the proposed order and the required information; and

(b) the period of 60 days, beginning with the day on which the document required by this sub-paragraph was laid, has ended.

3(2) If representations have been made during that period, the draft laid under paragraph 2(a) must be accompanied by a statement containing–

(a) a summary of the representations; and

(b) if, as a result of the representations, the proposed order has been changed, details of the changes.

Notes – Sch. 2, para. 3 was brought into force on 2 October 2000 by the Human Rights Act 1998 (Commencement No. 2) Order 2000 (SI 2000/1851).

URGENT CASES

4(1) If a remedial order ("the original order") is made without being approved in draft, the person making it must lay it before Parliament, accompanied by the required information, after it is made.

4(2) If representations have been made during the period of 60 days beginning with the day on which the original order was made, the person making it must (after the end of that period) lay before Parliament a statement containing–

(a) a summary of the representations; and

(b) if, as a result of the representations, he considers it appropriate to make changes to the original order, details of the changes.

4(3) If sub-paragraph (2)(b) applies, the person making the statement must–

(a) make a further remedial order replacing the original order; and

(b) lay the replacement order before Parliament.

4(4) If, at the end of the period of 120 days beginning with the day on which the original order was made, a resolution has not been passed by each House approving the original or replacement order, the order ceases to have effect (but without that affecting anything previously done under either order or the power to make a fresh remedial order).

Notes – Sch. 2, para. 4 was brought into force on 2 October 2000 by the Human Rights Act 1998 (Commencement No. 2) Order 2000 (SI 2000/1851).

DEFINITIONS

5 In this Schedule–

"representations" means representations about a remedial order (or proposed remedial order) made to the person making (or proposing to make) it and includes any relevant Parliamentary report or resolution; and

"required information" means–

(a) an explanation of the incompatibility which the order (or proposed order) seeks to remove, including particulars of the relevant declaration, finding or order; and

(b) a statement of the reasons for proceeding under section 10 and for making an order in those terms.

Notes – Sch. 2, para. 5 was brought into force on 2 October 2000 by the Human Rights Act 1998 (Commencement No. 2) Order 2000 (SI 2000/1851).

CALCULATING PERIODS

6 In calculating any period for the purposes of this Schedule, no account is to be taken of any time during which–

(a) Parliament is dissolved or prorogued; or

(b) both Houses are adjourned for more than four days.

Notes – Sch. 2, para. 6 was brought into force on 2 October 2000 by the Human Rights Act 1998 (Commencement No. 2) Order 2000 (SI 2000/1851).

7(1) This paragraph applies in relation to–

(a) any remedial order made, and any draft of such an order proposed to be made,–

(i) by the Scottish Ministers; or

(ii) within devolved competence (within the meaning of the Scotland Act 1998) by Her Majesty in Council;

and

(b) any document or statement to be laid in connection with such an order (or proposed order).

7(2) This Schedule has effect in relation to any such order (or proposed order), document or statement subject to the following modifications.

7(3) Any reference to Parliament, each House of Parliament or both Houses of Parliament shall be construed as a reference to the Scottish Parliament.

7(4) Paragraph 6 does not apply and instead, in calculating any period for the purposes of this Schedule, no account is to be taken of any time during which the Scottish Parliament is dissolved or is in recess for more than four days

History – Para. 7 inserted by SI 2000/2040, art. 21 with effect from 27 July 2001.

SCHEDULE 3 – DEROGATION AND RESERVATION

Sections 14 and 15

Part I – Derogation

[Repealed by SI 2005/1071, art. 2.]

History – Sch. 3, Pt. 1 repealed by SI 2005/1071, art. 2, with effect from 8 April 2005.
Former Pt. 1 inserted by SI 2001/4032, art. 2 and Schedule with effect from 20 December 2001.
Previously a former version of Pt. 1 had been repealed by SI 2001/1216, art. 4 with effect from 1 April 2001.

Part II – Reservation

RESERVATION

At the time of signing the present (First) Protocol, I declare that, in view of certain provisions of the Education Acts in the United Kingdom, the principle affirmed in the second sentence of Article 2 is accepted by the United Kingdom only so far as it is compatible with the provision of efficient instruction and training, and the avoidance of unreasonable public expenditure.

Dated 20 March 1952. Made by the United Kingdom Permanent Representative to the Council of Europe.

Notes – Sch. 3, Pt. II was brought into force on 2 October 2000 by the Human Rights Act 1998 (Commencement No. 2) Order 2000 (SI 2000/1851).

SCHEDULE 4 – JUDICIAL PENSIONS

Section 18(6)

DUTY TO MAKE ORDERS ABOUT PENSIONS

1(1) The appropriate Minister must by order make provision with respect to pensions payable to or in respect of any holder of a judicial office who serves as an ECHR judge.

1(2) A pensions order must include such provision as the Minister making it considers is necessary to secure that–

(a) an ECHR judge who was, immediately before his appointment as an ECHR judge, a member of a judicial pension scheme is entitled to remain as a member of that scheme;

(b) the terms on which he remains a member of the scheme are those which would have been applicable had he not been appointed as an ECHR judge; and

(c) entitlement to benefits payable in accordance with the scheme continues to be determined as if, while serving as an ECHR judge, his salary was that which would (but for section 18(4)) have been payable to him in respect of his continuing service as the holder of his judicial office.

Notes – Sch. 4, para. 1 was brought into force on 2 October 2000 by the Human Rights Act 1998 (Commencement No. 2) Order 2000 (SI 2000/1851).

CONTRIBUTIONS

2 A pensions order may, in particular, make provision–

(a) for any contributions which are payable by a person who remains a member of a scheme as a result of the order, and which would otherwise be payable by deduction from his salary, to be made otherwise than by deduction from his salary as an ECHR judge; and

(b) for such contributions to be collected in such manner as may be determined by the administrators of the scheme.

Notes – Sch. 4, para. 2 was brought into force on 2 October 2000 by the Human Rights Act 1998 (Commencement No. 2) Order 2000 (SI 2000/1851).

AMENDMENTS OF OTHER ENACTMENTS

3 A pensions order may amend any provision of or made under, a pensions Act in such manner and to such extent as the Minister making the order considers necessary or expedient to ensure the proper administration of any scheme to which it relates.

Notes – Sch. 4, para. 3 was brought into force on 2 October 2000 by the Human Rights Act 1998 (Commencement No. 2) Order 2000 (SI 2000/1851).

DEFINITIONS

4 In this Schedule–

"appropriate Minister" means–

(a) in relation to any judicial office whose jurisdiction is exercisable exclusively in relation to Scotland, the Secretary of State; and

(b) otherwise, the Lord Chancellor;

"ECHR judge" means the holder of a judicial office who is serving as a judge of the Court;

"judicial pension scheme" means a scheme established by and in accordance with a pensions Act;

"pensions Act" means–

(a) the County Courts Act (Northern Ireland) 1959;

(b) the Sheriff's Pensions (Scotland) Act 1961;

(c) the Judicial Pensions Act 1981; or

(d) the Judicial Pensions and Retirement Act 1993; and

(e) the Public Service Pensions Act 2013

"pensions order" means an order made under paragraph 1.

History – In para. 4, in the definition of "pensions Act", para. (e) inserted by Public Service Pensions Act 2013, s. 27 and Sch. 8, para. 26, with effect from 1 April 2014 (SI 2014/839, art. 4).

Notes – Sch. 4, para. 4 was brought into force on 2 October 2000 by the Human Rights Act 1998 (Commencement No. 2) Order 2000 (SI 2000/1851).

REGIONAL DEVELOPMENT AGENCIES ACT 1998

(1998 Chapter 45) [*19th November 1998*]

PART III – GENERAL

38 Corporation tax

38(1) The following provisions apply for the purposes of the Corporation Tax Acts.

38(2) Any trade or part of a trade transferred under a transfer scheme is to be treated as having been, at the time of its commencement and at all times since that time, a separate trade carried on by the transferee.

38(3) Where any trade, or part of a trade, is transferred under a transfer scheme, the trade carried on by the transferee after the date of the transfer is to be treated as the same trade as that which, by virtue of subsection (2), it is treated as having carried on before that date.

38(4) All property, rights and liabilities transferred under a transfer scheme are to be treated as having been, at the time when they became vested in the transferor, and at all times since that time, property, rights and liabilities of the transferee.

38(5) Anything done, in relation to property, rights and liabilities transferred under a transfer scheme, by the transferor is to be deemed to have been done by the transferee.

38(6) Where any property, rights and liabilities transferred under a transfer scheme became vested in the transferor by virtue of a transfer made by a company in which, at the time of the transfer, the transferor held an interest, that interest is to be deemed to have been held at that time by the transferee.

38(7) Where any property, rights and liabilities transferred under a transfer scheme became vested in the transferor by virtue of a qualifying transfer, or two or more successive qualifying transfers–

(a) subsection (4) has effect as if the reference to the time when the property, rights and liabilities became vested in the transferor were a reference to the time when they became vested in the original transferor (that is to say, the transferor under the qualifying transfer or, as the case may be, the first of the qualifying transfers), and

(b) if the property, rights and liabilities became vested in the transferor by virtue of a transfer made by a company in which, at the time of the transfer, the original transferor held an interest, that interest is to be deemed to have been held at that time by the transferee under the transfer scheme.

38(8) The previous provisions of this section are subject to such apportionments of unallowed tax losses and of expenditure by reference to which capital allowances may be made as may be specified in the transfer scheme concerned.

38(9) This section has effect in relation to accounting periods beginning after the final accounting period.

38(10) In this section–

"capital allowance" has the same meaning as in the Tax Acts;

"final accounting period" means the last complete accounting period of the transferor under the transfer scheme concerned;

"qualifying transfer" means a transfer made to one of the following bodies by another such body–

(a) the Development Commission,

(b) the Urban Regeneration Agency,

(c) a regional development agency;

"transfer scheme" means–

(a) an order under section 25 which includes provision for the transfer of property, rights or liabilities, and

(b) a scheme under any of sections 34 to 37 for the transfer of property, rights or liabilities;

"unallowed tax losses" means any losses, allowances or amounts which, as at the end of the final accounting period, are tax losses within the meaning given by section 400(2) of the Income and Corporation Taxes Act 1988.

SCOTLAND ACT 1998

(1998 Chapter 46)

[*19th November 1998*]

ARRANGEMENT OF SECTIONS

PART IV – THE TAX-VARYING POWER

History – Part IV omitted by SCA 2012, s. 25(2), with effect so that a tax-varying resolution may not be passed so as to relate to any tax year following 2015–16 (as the last tax year for which Pt. 4 is to have effect (SI 2015/2000, art. 2)).

73 Power to fix basic rate for Scottish taxpayers

73 [Omitted by SCA 2012, s. 25(2).]

History – S. 73 omitted by SCA 2012, s. 25(2), with effect so that a tax-varying resolution may not be passed so as to relate to any tax year following 2015–16 (as the last tax year for which Pt. 4 is to have effect (SI 2015/2000, art. 2)). Former s. 73 read as follows:

"Power to fix basic rate for Scottish taxpayers

73(1) Subject to section 74, this section applies for any year of assessment for which income tax is charged if–

(a) the Parliament has passed a resolution providing for the percentage determined to be the basic rate for that year to be increased or reduced for Scottish taxpayers in accordance with the resolution,

(b) the increase or reduction provided for is confined to an increase or reduction by a number not exceeding three which is specified in the resolution and is either a whole number or half of a whole number, and

(c) the resolution has not been cancelled by a subsequent resolution of the Parliament.

73(2) Where this section applies for any year of assessment the Income Tax Acts (excluding this Part) shall have effect in relation to the income of Scottish taxpayers as if any rate determined by the Parliament of the United Kingdom to be the basic rate for that year were increased or reduced in accordance with the resolution of the Scottish Parliament.

73(3) In subsection (2) the reference to the income of Scottish taxpayers does not include a reference to any income of Scottish taxpayers which, had it been income for the year 1998–99, would have been income to which section 1A of the Income and Corporation Taxes Act 1988 (income from savings and distributions) applied for that year.

73(4) In this section–

(a) a reference, in relation to any year of assessment, to income tax being charged for that year includes a reference to the passing of a PCTA resolution that provides for the charging of that tax for that year, and

(b) a reference, in relation to a year of assessment, to the determination by the Parliament of the United Kingdom of a rate to be the basic rate for that year includes a reference to the passing of a PCTA resolution specifying a percentage to be the basic rate for that year.

73(5) In this section **"a PCTA resolution"** means a resolution of the House of Commons containing such a declaration as is mentioned in section l(2)(b) of the Provisional Collection of Taxes Act 1968.".

74 Supplemental provision with respect to resolutions

74 [Omitted by SCA 2012, s. 25(2).]

History – S. 74 omitted by SCA 2012, s. 25(2), with effect so that a tax-varying resolution may not be passed so as to relate to any tax year following 2015–16 (as the last tax year for which Pt. 4 is to have effect (SI 2015/2000, art. 2)). Former s. 74 read as follows:

"Supplemental provision with respect to resolutions

74(1) This section applies to any resolution of the Parliament (**"a tax-varying resolution"**) which–

(a) provides, in accordance with section 73, for an increase or reduction for Scottish taxpayers of the basic rate for any year of assessment, or

(b) cancels a previous resolution of the Parliament providing for such an increase or reduction.

74(2) Subject to subsection (3), a tax-varying resolution–

(a) must be expressed so as to relate to no more than a single year of assessment beginning after, but no more than twelve months after, the passing of the resolution, but

(b) shall have effect in relation to a determination by the Parliament of the United Kingdom of the rate to be the basic rate for that year irrespective of whether that determination had been made at the time of the passing of the resolution.

74(3) Subsection (2) shall not prevent a tax-varying resolution relating to any year of assessment from being passed and having effect where–

(a) a determination by the Parliament of the United Kingdom of the rate to be the basic rate for that year is made after, or less than a month before, the beginning of that year,

(b) that determination is not confined to the passing of the enactment by which a determination of the same rate by a PCTA resolution is ratified, and

(c) the tax-varying resolution is passed within the period of one month beginning with the day of the making by the Parliament of the United Kingdom of its determination.

74(4) Where, in a case to which subsection (3) applies, a tax-varying resolution is passed after the beginning of the year of assessment to which it relates–

(a) the resolution shall have effect as from the beginning of that year, and

(b) all such payments, repayments, deductions and other adjustments shall be made as are required to restore the position to what it would have been if the resolution had been passed before the beginning of that year.

74(5) Standing orders shall ensure that only a member of the Scottish Executive may move a motion for a tax-varying resolution.

74(6) A tax-varying resolution shall not be passed so as to have effect in relation to any year of assessment before the year 2000–01.

74(7) Subsections (4) and (5) of section 73 apply for the purposes of this section as they apply for the purposes of that section.".

75 Scottish taxpayers

75 [Omitted by SCA 2012, s. 25(2).]

History – S. 75 omitted by SCA 2012, s. 25(2), with effect so that a tax-varying resolution may not be passed so as to relate to any tax year following 2015–16 (as the last tax year for which Pt. 4 is to have effect (SI 2015/2000, art. 2)). Former s. 75 read as follows:

"Scottish taxpayers

75 Sections 80D to 80F (definition of Scottish taxpayer) apply for the purposes of this Part.".
Former text of s. 75 substituted for former s. 75(1)–(6) by SCA 2012, s. 27(1), with effect from 1 July 2012.

76 Changes to income tax structure

76 [Omitted by SCA 2012, s. 25(2).]

History – S. 76 omitted by SCA 2012, s. 25(2), with effect so that a tax-varying resolution may not be passed so as to relate to any tax year following 2015–16 (as the last tax year for which Pt. 4 is to have effect (SI 2015/2000, art. 2)). Former s. 76 read as follows:

"Changes to income tax structure

76(1) This section applies where–

(a) there has been a proposal for the modification of any provision made by or under the Income Tax Acts,

(b) that proposal is one made and published by the Treasury or the Board, or (without having been so made and published) appears to the Treasury to be a proposal to which effect is likely to be given by Act of Parliament, and

(c) it appears to the Treasury that the proposed modification would have a significant effect on the practical extent for any year of assessment of the Parliament's tax-varying powers.

76(2) It shall be the duty of the Treasury, as soon as reasonably practicable after the publication of the proposal, or (as the case may be) as soon as reasonably practicable after it first appears to the Treasury that the proposal is likely to be enacted, to lay before the House of Commons–

(a) a statement of whether, in the Treasury's opinion, an amendment of the Parliament's tax-varying powers is required as a consequence of the proposal, and

(b) if in their opinion an amendment of those powers is required, the Treasury's proposals for amending those powers.

76(3) Any proposals for amending the Parliament's tax-varying powers that are laid before the House of Commons by the Treasury under this section–

(a) must be confined to income tax,

(b) must appear to the Treasury to satisfy the conditions set out in subsections (4) and (5), and

(c) must not contain any proposal for the Parliament's tax-varying powers to be exercisable in relation to the taxation of income from savings or distributions.

76(4) The first condition mentioned in subsection (3)(b) is that the proposals would secure–

(a) so far as possible, and

(b) after making due allowance for annual changes in the retail prices index,

that the practical extent of the Parliament's tax-varying powers would remain broadly the same from year to year as it would be if (apart from any resolution of the Parliament) the law relating to income tax were the same from year to year as it was in relation to the year 1997–98.

76(5) The second condition so mentioned is that the proposals would not enable the Parliament's tax-varying powers to be exercised for any year of assessment so as to have an effect on the levels of the after-tax income of Scottish taxpayers generally that would be significantly different from the effect their exercise could have had in any previous year of assessment.

76(6) References in this section to the practical extent of the Parliament's tax-varying powers are references to the amounts of income tax for any year of assessment which appear to be or (as the case may be) to have been the maximum amounts capable of being raised and foregone in that year in pursuance of a resolution of the Parliament.

76(7) In this section **"income from savings or distributions"** means income which, had it been income for the year 1998–99, would have been income to which section 1A of the Income and Corporation Taxes Act 1988 applied for that year.".

77 Accounting for additional Scottish tax

77 [Omitted by SCA 2012, s. 25(2).]

History – S. 77 omitted by SCA 2012, s. 25(2), with effect so that a tax-varying resolution may not be passed so as to relate to any tax year following 2015–16 (as the last tax year for which Pt. 4 is to have effect (SI 2015/2000, art. 2)). Former s. 77 read as follows:

"Accounting for additional Scottish tax

77(1) Where the basic rate for any year of assessment is increased for Scottish taxpayers by a resolution of the Parliament, it shall be the duty of the Board to pay amounts into the Scottish Consolidated Fund in accordance with this section.

77(2) The amounts of the payments to be made by the Board under this section, and the times at which they are to be made, shall be determined by the Board and notified to the Scottish Ministers as soon as reasonably practicable after the passing of the resolution providing for the increase to which they relate.

77(3) Any determination made by the Board under subsection (2) for any year of assessment shall be such as appears to the Board to be necessary for securing that, in the course of that year, amounts are paid into the Scottish Consolidated Fund which are equal in total to the amount estimated by the Board to represent the proportion of the income tax receipts for that year that is properly attributable to a resolution of the Parliament.

77(4) For the purposes of this section the Board shall make and maintain arrangements as to–

(a) the manner of estimating the proportion of the income tax receipts for a year of assessment that is properly attributable to a resolution of the Parliament,

(b) the circumstances and manner in which an estimate of that proportion or of those receipts may be revised before or in the course of the year of assessment to which it relates,

(c) the manner of determining the amount of each payment to be made in respect of any such estimate, and

(d) the times at which, and manner in which, those amounts are to be paid by the Board into the Scottish Consolidated Fund.

77(5) Arrangements under subsection (4) may include provision for the making of adjustments to the amounts paid by the Board where any estimate made for the purposes of this section in respect of any year of assessment (whether the current year or a previous year) turns out to have been inaccurate.

77(6) Before making or modifying any arrangements under subsection (4) or (5), the Board shall consult with the Scottish Ministers.

77(7) In this section **"income tax receipts"**, in relation to any year of assessment, means so much as is referable to income tax charged for that year of any sums which, disregarding both–

(a) subsection (8), and

(b) any regulations or direction made or given by the Treasury,

are sums that have to be paid into the Consolidated Fund under section 44 of the Commissioners for Revenue and Customs Act 2005 (payment into Consolidated Fund).

77(8) [Ceased to have effect by CRCA 2005, s. 50 and Sch. 4, para. 71(b) and repealed by s. 52 and Sch. 5.]".

In former s. 77(7), the words "section 44 of the Commissioners for Revenue and Customs Act 2005 (payment into Consolidated Fund)" substituted for "section 10 of the Exchequer and Audit Department Act 1866 (gross revenues of Board's department to be paid into that Fund after the making of specified deductions)" by CRCA 2005, s. 50 and Sch. 4, para. 71(a) with effect from 18 April 2005 (by virtue of SI 2005/1126, reg. 2(2)).

Former s. 77(8) ceased to have effect by CRCA 2005, s. 50 and Sch. 4, para. 71(b) and repealed by s. 52 and Sch. 5, with effect from 18 April 2005 (by virtue of SI 2005/1126, reg. 2(2)).

78 Effect of tax reduction for Scottish taxpayers

78 [Omitted by SCA 2012, s. 25(2).]

History – S. 78 omitted by SCA 2012, s. 25(2), with effect so that a tax-varying resolution may not be passed so as to relate to any tax year following 2015–16 (as the last tax year for which Pt. 4 is to have effect (SI 2015/2000, art. 2)). Former s. 78 read as follows:

"Effect of tax reduction for Scottish taxpayers

78(1) Where the basic rate for any year of assessment is reduced for Scottish taxpayers by a resolution of the Parliament, payments to the Board in accordance with this section shall be charged on the Scottish Consolidated Fund.

78(2) The amounts of the payments to be made out of the Scottish Consolidated Fund under this section, and the times at which they are to be made, shall be determined by the Board and notified to the Scottish Ministers as soon as reasonably practicable after the passing of the resolution providing for the reduction to which they relate.

78(3) Any determination made by the Board under subsection (2) for any year of assessment shall be such as appears to the Board to be necessary for securing that in the course of that year amounts are paid to the Board which are equal in total to the amount estimated by the Board to represent the shortfall in income tax receipts for that year that is properly attributable to a resolution of the Parliament.

78(4) For the purposes of this section the Board shall make and maintain arrangements as to–

(a) the manner of estimating the shortfall in income tax receipts for any year of assessment that is properly attributable to a resolution of the Parliament,

(b) the circumstances and manner in which an estimate of that shortfall may be revised before or in the course of the year of assessment to which it relates,

(c) the manner of determining the amount of each payment to be made in respect of any such estimate, and
(d) the times at which, and manner in which, those amounts are to be paid to the Board.

78(5) Arrangements under subsection (4) may include provision for the making of adjustments to the amounts paid to the Board where any estimate made for the purposes of this section in respect of any year of assessment (whether the current year or a previous year) turns out to have been inaccurate.

78(6) Before making or modifying any arrangements under subsection (4) or (5), the Board shall consult with the Scottish Ministers.

78(7) In this section **"income tax receipts"** has the same meaning as in section 77.

78(8) [Ceased to have effect by CRCA 2005, s. 50 and Sch. 4, para. 71(b) and repealed by s. 52 and Sch. 5.]".

Former s. 78(8) ceased to have effect by CRCA 2005, s. 50 and Sch. 4, para. 72 and repealed by CRCA 2005, s. 52 and Sch. 5, from 18 April 2005 (CRCA 2005, s. 53(1)).

79 Supplemental powers to modify enactments

79 [Omitted by SCA 2012, s. 25(2).]

History – S. 79 omitted by SCA 2012, s. 25(2), with effect so that a tax-varying resolution may not be passed so as to relate to any tax year following 2015–16 (as the last tax year for which Pt. 4 is to have effect (SI 2015/2000, art. 2)). Former s. 79 read as follows:

"Supplemental powers to modify enactments

79(1) The Treasury may by order make such modifications of any enactment as they consider necessary or expedient in consequence of–
(a) the fact that the Parliament has, or is to have, the power to pass a tax-varying resolution, or
(b) the fact (where it is the case) that the Parliament has passed such a resolution.

79(2) The Treasury may by order make provision–
(a) excluding the operation of section 73(2) in relation to any enactment, and
(b) making any such other modifications of any enactment as they consider necessary or expedient in connection with, or for the purposes of, any such exclusion.

79(3) Without prejudice to the generality of the powers conferred by the preceding provisions of this section, an order under this section may provide that, where any tax-varying resolution relating to any year of assessment is passed, that resolution does not require any change in the amounts repayable or deductible under PAYE regulations between–
(a) the beginning of that year, and
(b) such day falling after the passing of the resolution as may be specified in the order.

79(4) An order under this section may, to the extent that the Treasury consider it to be appropriate, take effect retrospectively from the beginning of the year of assessment in which it is made.

79(5) In this section **"tax-varying resolution"** has the same meaning as in section 74.".

In former s. 79(3), the words "PAYE regulations" substituted for the words "section 203 of the Income and Corporation Taxes Act 1988 (PAYE)" by ITEPA 2003, Sch. 6, para. 237 which has effect for the tax year 2003–04 and subsequent tax years.

80 Reimbursement of expenses

80 [Omitted by SCA 2012, s. 25(2).]

History – S. 80 omitted by SCA 2012, s. 25(2), with effect so that a tax-varying resolution may not be passed so as to relate to any tax year following 2015–16 (as the last tax year for which Pt. 4 is to have effect (SI 2015/2000, art. 2)). Former s. 80 read as follows:

"Reimbursement of expenses

80 The Scottish Ministers may reimburse any Minister of the Crown or government department for administrative expenses incurred by virtue of this Part at any time after the passing of this Act by the Minister or department.".

PART 4A – TAXATION

CHAPTER 1 – INTRODUCTORY

History – Ch. 1 inserted by SCA 2012, s. 23(2), with effect from 1 July 2012.

80A Overview of Part 4A

80A(1) In this Part–
(a) Chapter 2 confers on the Scottish Parliament power to set a rate of income tax to be paid by Scottish taxpayers, and
(b) The remaining Chapters specify the taxes about which the Scottish Parliament may make provision in the exercise of the power conferred by section 28(1).

80A(2) The power to make provision about a devolved tax is subject to the restrictions imposed by–
(a) subsection (3), and
(b) the other provisions of this Part.

80A(3) A devolved tax may not be imposed where to do so would be incompatible with any international obligations.

80A(4) In this Act **"devolved tax"** means a tax specified in this Part as a devolved tax.

History – In s. 80A(1), the words "The remaining Chapters" substituted for the words "Chapters 3 and 4" by SCA 2016, s. 19(1), with effect at the end of 2 months beginning with 23 March 2016.
S. 80A inserted by SCA 2012, s. 23(2), with effect from 1 July 2012.

80B Power to add new devolved taxes

80B(1) Her Majesty may by Order in Council amend this Part so as to–
(a) specify, as an additional devolved tax, a tax of any description, or

(b) make any other modifications of the provisions relating to devolved taxes which She considers necessary or expedient.

80B(2) An Order in Council under this section may also make such modifications of–

(a) any enactment or prerogative instrument (including any enactment comprised in or made under this Act), or

(b) any other instrument or document,

as Her Majesty considers necessary or expedient in connection with other provision made by the Order.

Prospective amendments – In s. 80A(1)(a), the words "or rates" substituted for the word "rate" by SCA 2016, s. 13(8), with effect in relation to the tax year to be appointed under SCA 2016, s. 13(15) and subsequent tax years.

History – S. 80B inserted by SCA 2012, s. 23(2), with effect from 1 July 2012.

CHAPTER 2 – INCOME TAX

Commencement Date – The tax year 2016–17 is appointed under SCA 2012, s. 25(5) as the first tax year for which a Scottish rate resolution made by the Scottish Parliament under s. 80C (power to set Scottish rate for Scottish taxpayers) is to have effect (SI 2015/2000, art. 3).

History – Ch. 2 inserted by SCA 2012, s. 25(3), with effect from 1 July 2012, subject to SCA 2012, s. 25(4)–(6) (the first tax year in respect of which a Scottish rate resolution under s. 80C may be made by the Scottish Parliament is the tax year 2016–17 (SI 2015/2000, art. 3)).

80C Power to set Scottish rate for Scottish taxpayers

80C(1) The Scottish Parliament may by resolution (a "Scottish rate resolution") set the Scottish rate for the purpose of calculating the rates of income tax to be paid by Scottish taxpayers.

80C(2) See section 6A of the Income Tax Act 2007 for provision about the calculation of those rates and section 11A of that Act for provision about the income charged at those rates.

80C(3) A Scottish rate resolution applies–

(a) for only one tax year, and

(b) for the whole of that year.

80C(4) A Scottish rate resolution may specify only one rate.

80C(5) The Scottish rate must be a whole number or half a whole number.

80C(6) A Scottish rate resolution–

(a) must specify the tax year for which it applies,

(b) must be made before the start of that tax year, and

(c) must not be made more than 12 months before the start of that year.

80C(7) If a Scottish rate resolution is cancelled before the start of the tax year for which it is to apply–

(a) the Income Tax Acts have effect for that year as if the resolution had never been passed, and

(b) the resolution may be replaced by another Scottish rate resolution.

80C(8) Standing orders must provide that only a member of the Scottish Government may move a motion for a Scottish rate resolution.

Prospective amendments – In s. 80C(1), the words "the Scottish basic rate, and any other rates, for the purposes of section 11A of the Income Tax Act 2007 (which provides for the income of Scottish taxpayers which is charged at those rates)" substituted for the words from "the Scottish rate" to the end by SCA 2016, s. 13(2), with effect in relation to the tax year to be appointed under SCA 2016, s. 13(15) and subsequent tax years.

S. 80C(2A)–(2C) substituted for (2) by SCA 2016, s. 13(3), with effect in relation to the tax year to be appointed under SCA 2016, s. 13(15) and subsequent tax years.

S. 80C(4) omitted by SCA 2016, s. 13(4), with effect in relation to the tax year to be appointed under SCA 2016, s. 13(15) and subsequent tax years.

In s. 80C(5), the word "A" substituted for the word "The" and the words ", or zero" inserted at the end by SCA 2016, s. 13(5), with effect in relation to the tax year to be appointed under SCA 2016, s. 13(15) and subsequent tax years.

History – S. 80C(2) substituted by FA 2014, s. 296 and Sch. 38, para. 16(2), with effect from 17 July 2014.

S. 80C inserted by SCA 2012, s. 25(3), with effect from 1 July 2012, subject to SCA 2012, s. 25(4)–(6) (the first tax year in respect of which a Scottish rate resolution under s. 80C may be made by the Scottish Parliament is the tax year 2016–17 (SI 2015/2000, art. 3)).

80D Scottish taxpayers

80D(1) For any tax year, a Scottish taxpayer is an individual (T)–

(a) who is resident in the UK for income tax purposes for that year (see Schedule 45 to the Finance Act 2013), and

(b) who, for that year, meets condition A, B or C.

80D(2) T meets condition A if T has a close connection with Scotland (see section 80E).

80D(3) T meets condition B if–

(a) T does not have a close connection with England, Wales or Northern Ireland (see section 80E), and

(b) T spends more days of that year in Scotland than in any other part of the UK (see section 80F).

80D(4) T meets condition C if, for the whole or any part of the year, T is–

(a) a member of Parliament for a constituency in Scotland,

(b) a member of the European Parliament for Scotland, or

(c) a member of the Scottish Parliament.

80D(5) In this Chapter "the UK" means the United Kingdom.

Prospective amendments – S. 80D(4A) and (4B) inserted by WA 2014, s. 11(5), with effect from a day to be appointed under s. 14.

History – In s. 80D(1) the word "For" substituted for the word "In" and in para. (a) the words "for that year (see Schedule 45 to the Finance Act 2013)" inserted by WA 2014, s. 11(3), with effect from 17 February 2015.
In s. 80D(3(a) the words "England, Wales or Northern Ireland" substituted for the words "any part of the UK other than Scotland" by WA 2014, s. 11(4), with effect from 17 February 2015.
S. 80D inserted by SCA 2012, s. 25(3), with effect from 1 July 2012, subject to SCA 2012, s. 25(4)–(6) (the first tax year in respect of which a Scottish rate resolution under s. 80C may be made by the Scottish Parliament is the tax year 2016–17 (SI 2015/2000, art. 3)).

Other material – Misc. 24/2015: HMRC guidance: Scottish rate of income tax – technical guidance on Scottish taxpayer status.

80DA Scottish taxpayers: Welsh parliamentarians

80DA [Prospectively inserted.]

Prospective amendments – S, 80DA inserted by WA 2014, s. 11(6), with effect from a day to be appointed under s. 14.

80E Close connection with Scotland or another part of the UK

80E(1) To find whether, for any year, T has a close connection with any part of the UK see–

(a) subsection (2) (where T has only one place of residence in the UK), or

(b) subsection (3) (where T has 2 or more places of residence in the UK).

80E(2) T has a close connection with a part of the UK if in that year–

(a) T has only one place of residence in the UK,

(b) that place of residence is in that part of the UK, and

(c) for at least part of the year, T lives at that place.

80E(3) T has a close connection with a part of the UK if in that year–

(a) T has 2 or more places of residence in the UK,

(b) for at least part of the year, T's main place of residence in the UK is in that part of the UK,

(c) the times in the year when T's main place of residence is in that part of the UK comprise (in aggregate) at least as much of the year as the times when T's main place of residence is in each other part of the UK (considered separately), and

(d) for at least part of the year, T lives at a place of residence in that part of the UK.

80E(4) In this section **"place"** includes a place on board a vessel or other means of transport.

Prospective amendments – In s., 80E(3)(c) the words "more of the year than" substituted for the words "at least as much of the year as" by WA 2014, s. 11(7)(a), with effect from a day to be appointed under s. 14.

History – In s., 80E(3)(c) the words "each other part of the UK (considered separately)" substituted for the words "any one other part of the UK" by WA 2014, s. 11(7)(a), with effect from 17 February 2015.
S. 80E inserted by SCA 2012, s. 25(3), with effect from 1 July 2012, subject to SCA 2012, s. 25(4)–(6) (the first tax year in respect of which a Scottish rate resolution under s. 80C may be made by the Scottish Parliament is the tax year 2016–17 (SI 2015/2000, art. 3)).

80F Days spent in Scotland or another part of the UK

80F(1) T spends more days of a year in Scotland than in any other part of the UK if (and only if)–

(a) the number of days in the year on which T is in Scotland at the end of the day

equals or exceeds

(b) the number of days in the year on which T is in any other part of the UK at the end of the day.

80F(2) T is treated as not being in the UK at the end of a day if–

(a) on that day T arrives in the UK as a passenger,

(b) T departs from the UK on the next day, and

(c) during the time between arrival and departure T does not engage in activities which are to a substantial extent unrelated to T's passage through the UK.

Prospective amendments – In s., 80F(1) the words from "if)–" to the end substituted by WA 2014, s. 11(8)(a), with effect from a day to be appointed under s. 14.

History – In s., 80F(2) the words "T is treated as not" substituted for the words "But T is not to be treated as" by WA 2014, s. 11(8)(b), with effect from a day to be appointed under s. 14.
S. 80F inserted by SCA 2012, s. 25(3), with effect from 1 July 2012, subject to SCA 2012, s. 25(4)–(6) (the first tax year in respect of which a Scottish rate resolution under s. 80C may be made by the Scottish Parliament is the tax year 2016–17 (SI 2015/2000, art. 3)).

80G Supplemental powers to modify enactments

80G(1) The Treasury may by order modify section 11A of the Income Tax Act 2007 (income charged at the Scottish basic, higher and additional rates) for the purpose of altering–

(a) the definition of the income which is charged to income tax at the rates provided for under the section, or

(b) the application of the section in relation to a particular class of income which is so charged.

80G(1A) The Treasury may by order modify any enactment not contained in Chapter 2 of Part 2 of the Income Tax Act 2007 (rates at which income tax is charged) so that it makes provision, in relation to a Scottish taxpayer, by reference to the Scottish basic rate, the Scottish higher rate or the Scottish additional rate, instead of the basic rate, the higher rate or the additional rate.

80G(1B) If the Treasury consider it necessary or expedient to do so, they may by order provide that–

(a) the Scottish rate set by the Parliament for a tax year, or

(b) the fact that the Scottish rate has not been so set for a tax year,

does not require any change in the amounts repayable or deductible under PAYE regulations between the beginning of that year and such later date as may be specified in the order.

80G(2) The Treasury may by order make such modifications of any enactment as they consider necessary or expedient in consequence of or in connection with an order under subsection (1), (1A) or (1B).

80G(3) [Omitted by FA 2014, s. 296 and Sch. 38, para. 16(6).]

80G(4) An order under this section may, to the extent that the Treasury consider it to be appropriate, take effect retrospectively from the beginning of the tax year in which the order is made.

80G(5) The power under subsection (1) does not include power to provide that any income which is–

(a) savings income, or

(b) dividend income which would otherwise be charged to income tax at a rate provided for under section 13 of the Income Tax Act 2007,

is income which is charged to income tax at a rate provided for under section 11A of that Act.

Prospective amendments – In s. 80G(1), in the words before (a), the word "Scottish" substituted for the words "the Scottish basic, higher and additional" by SCA 2016, s. 13(10)(a), with effect in relation to the tax year to be appointed under SCA 2016, s. 13(15) and subsequent tax years.
In s. 80G(1)(a), in the words "Scottish rates" substituted for the words "the rates provided for under the section" by SCA 2016, s. 13(10)(b), with effect in relation to the tax year to be appointed under SCA 2016, s. 13(15) and subsequent tax years.
S. 80G(1A)(a) and (b) and words before it substituted for the words after "enactment" by SCA 2016, s. 13(11), with effect in relation to the tax year to be appointed under SCA 2016, s. 13(15) and subsequent tax years.
S. 80G(1B)(a)–(c) substituted for (a) and (b) by SCA 2016, s. 13(12), with effect in relation to the tax year to be appointed under SCA 2016, s. 13(15) and subsequent tax years.

History – S. 80G(1), (1A) and (1B) substituted for former s. 80G(1) by FA 2014, s. 296 and Sch. 38, para. 16(4), with effect from 17 July 2014.
In s. 80G(2), the words "with an order under subsection (1), (1A) or (1B)" substituted for the former wording by FA 2014, s. 296 and Sch. 38, para. 16(5), with effect from 17 July 2014.
S. 80G(3) omitted by FA 2014, s. 296 and Sch. 38, para. 16(6), with effect from 17 July 2014.
S. 80G(5) inserted by FA 2014, s. 296 and Sch. 38, para. 16(7), with effect from 17 July 2014.
S. 80G inserted by SCA 2012, s. 25(3), with effect from 1 July 2012, subject to SCA 2012, s. 25(4)–(6) (the first tax year in respect of which a Scottish rate resolution under s. 80C may be made by the Scottish Parliament is the tax year 2016–17 (SI 2015/2000, art. 3)).

80H Reimbursement of expenses

80H The Scottish Ministers may reimburse any Minister of the Crown or government department for administrative expenses incurred by virtue of this Chapter at any time after the passing of the Scotland Act 2012 by the Minister or department.

History – S. 80H inserted by SCA 2012, s. 25(3), with effect from 1 July 2012, subject to SCA 2012, s. 25(4)–(6) (the first tax year in respect of which a Scottish rate resolution under s. 80C may be made by the Scottish Parliament is the tax year 2016–17 (SI 2015/2000, art. 3)).

80HA Report by the Comptroller and Auditor General

80HA(1) The Comptroller and Auditor General must for each financial year prepare a report on the matters set out in subsection (2).

80HA(2) Those matters are–

(a) the adequacy of any of HMRC's rules and procedures put in place, in consequence of the Scottish rate provisions, for the purpose of ensuring the proper assessment and collection of income tax charged at rates determined under those provisions,

(b) whether the rules and procedures described in paragraph (a) are being complied with,

(c) the correctness of the sums brought to account by HMRC which relate to income tax which is attributable to a Scottish rate resolution, and

(d) the accuracy and fairness of the amounts which are reimbursed to HMRC under section 80H (having been identified by it as administrative expenses incurred as a result of the charging of income tax as mentioned in paragraph (a)).

80HA(3) The "Scottish rate provisions" are–

(a) any provision made by or under this Chapter, and

(b) any provision made by or under the Income Tax Acts relating to the Scottish basic rate, the Scottish higher rate or the Scottish additional rate.

80HA(4) A report under this section may also include an assessment of the economy, efficiency and effectiveness with which HMRC has used its resources in carrying out relevant functions.

80HA(5) **"Relevant functions"** are functions of HMRC in the performance of which HMRC incurs administrative expenses which are reimbursed to HMRC under section 80H (having been identified by it as administrative expenses incurred as a result of the charging of income tax as mentioned in subsection (2)(a)).

80HA(6) HMRC must give the Comptroller and Auditor General such information as the Comptroller and Auditor General may reasonably require for the purposes of preparing a report under this section.

80HA(7) A report prepared under this section must be laid before the Scottish Parliament not later than 31 January of the financial year following that to which the report relates.

80HA(8) In this section **"HMRC"** means Her Majesty's Revenue and Customs.

Prospective amendments – In s. 80HA(3)(b), the words "a Scottish rate" substituted for the words from "the Scottish basic rate" to the end by SCA 2016, s. 13(13), with effect in relation to the tax year to be appointed under SCA 2016, s. 13(15) and subsequent tax years.

History – S. 80HA inserted by FA 2014, s. 297(1), with effect in relation to the financial year ending on 31 March 2015 and subsequent financial years.

PART V – MISCELLANEOUS AND GENERAL

SUPPLEMENTARY POWERS

104 Power to make provision consequential on legislation of, or scrutinised by, the Parliament.

104(1) Subordinate legislation may make such provision as the person making the legislation considers necessary or expedient in consequence of any provision made by or under any Act of the Scottish Parliament or made by legislation mentioned in subsection (2).

104(2) The legislation is subordinate legislation under an Act of Parliament made by–

(a) a member of the Scottish Executive,

(b) a Scottish public authority with mixed functions or no reserved functions, or

(c) any other person (not being a Minister of the Crown) if the function of making the legislation is exercisable within devolved competence.

Statutory instruments – SI 2014/3294: partly made under s. 104.

REMUNERATION OF MEMBERS OF THE PARLIAMENT AND EXECUTIVE

110 Scottish taxpayers for social security purposes

110(1) The Secretary of State may by order provide for individuals of any description specified in the order to be treated for the purposes of any of the matters that are reserved matters by virtue of Head F of Part II of Schedule 5 as if they were, or were not, Scottish taxpayers.

110(2) The Secretary of State may by order provide in relation to any year of assessment that, for those purposes, the basic rate in relation to the income of Scottish taxpayers shall be treated as being such rate as is specified in the order (instead of the rate increased or reduced for that year by virtue of any resolution of the Parliament in pursuance of section 73 passed after the beginning of the year).

110(3) An order under this section may apply in respect of any individuals whether Scotland is the part of the United Kingdom with which they have the closest connection or not.

110(4) In this section **"Scottish taxpayer"** has the same meaning as in Part IV.

Prospective amendments – In s. 110(2), the words "Scottish basic rate, Scottish higher rate or Scottish additional rate (within the meaning of the Income Tax Acts)" substituted for the words "basic rate" by FA 2014, s. 296 and Sch. 38, para. 16(8)(a), with effect from a day to be appointed under FA 2014, Sch. 38, para. 16(12).

In s. 110(2), the words "(instead of the rate increased or reduced for that year by virtue of any resolution of the Parliament in pursuance of section 73 passed after the beginning of the year)" omitted from the end by FA 2014, s. 296 and Sch. 38, para. 16(8)(b), with effect from a day to be appointed under FA 2014, Sch. 38, para. 16(12).

In s. 110(2), the words "a Scottish rate (within the meaning of the Income Tax Acts)" substituted for the words from "the Scottish basic rate" to "Scottish taxpayers" by SCA 2016, s. 15(1), with effect in relation to the tax year appointed by the Treasury under SCA 2016, s. 13(15) and subsequent tax years.

History – These provisions were brought into force with effect from 6 May 1999 by The Scotland Act 1998 (Commencement) Order 1998 (SI 1998/3178).

PART VI – SUPPLEMENTARY

SUBORDINATE LEGISLATION

112 Subordinate legislation: general.

112(1) Any power to make subordinate legislation conferred by this Act shall, if no other provision is made as to the person by whom the power is exercisable, be exercisable by Her Majesty by Order in Council or by a Minister of the Crown by order.

112(2) But the power to make subordinate legislation under section 129(1) providing–

(a) for the appropriation of sums forming part of the Scottish Consolidated Fund, or

(b) for sums received by any person to be appropriated in aid of sums appropriated as mentioned in paragraph (a),

shall be exercisable only by Her Majesty by Order in Council.

112(3) References in this Act to an open power are to a power to which subsection (1) applies (and include a power to make subordinate legislation under section 129(1) whether or not the legislation makes provision as mentioned in subsection (2)).

112(4) An Order in Council under an open power may revoke, amend or re-enact an order, as well as an Order in Council, under the power; and an order under an open power may revoke, amend or re-enact an Order in Council, as well as an order, under the power.

112(5) Any power to make subordinate legislation conferred by this Act shall, in relation to its exercise by a Minister of the Crown or a member of the Scottish Executive, be exercisable by statutory instrument.

Statutory instruments – SI 2014/3294: partly made under s. 112(1).

113 Subordinate legislation: scope of powers.

113(1) References in this section to a power are to an open power and to any other power to make subordinate legislation conferred by this Act which is exercisable by Her Majesty in Council or by a Minister of the Crown, and include a power as extended by this section.

113(2) A power may be exercised so as to make different provision for different purposes.

113(3) A power (as well as being exercisable in relation to all cases to which it extends) maybe exercised in relation to–

(a) those cases subject to specified exceptions, or

(b) any particular case or class of case.

113(4) A power includes power to make–

(a) any supplementary, incidental or consequential provision, and

(b) any transitory, transitional or saving provision,

which the person making the legislation considers necessary or expedient.

113(5) A power may be exercised by modifying–

(a) any enactment or prerogative instrument,

(b) any other instrument or document,

if the subordinate legislation (or a statutory instrument containing it) would be subject to any of the types of procedure referred to in Schedule 7.

113(6) But a power to modify enactments does not (unless otherwise stated) extend to making modifications of this Act or subordinate legislation under it.

113(7) A power may be exercised so as to make provision for the delegation of functions.

113(8) A power includes power to make provision for sums to be payable out of the Scottish Consolidated Fund or charged on the Fund.

113(9) A power includes power to make provision for the payment of sums out of money provided by Parliament or for sums to be charged on and paid out of the Consolidated Fund.

113(10) A power may not be exercised so as to create any criminal offence punishable–

(a) on summary conviction, with imprisonment for a period exceeding three months or with a fine exceeding the amount specified as level 5 on the standard scale,

(b) on conviction on indictment, with a period of imprisonment exceeding two years.

113(11) The fact that a power is conferred does not prejudice the extent of any other power.

Statutory instruments – SI 2014/3294: partly made under s. 113(2), (4) and (5).

114 Subordinate legislation: particular provisions.

114(1) A power to make subordinate legislation conferred by any of the following provisions of this Act may be exercised by modifying any enactment comprised in or made under this Act (except Schedules 4 and 5): sections 89, 104, 107, 108 and 129(1).

114(2) The reference in subsection (1) to a power to make subordinate legislation includes a power as extended by section 113.

114(3) A power to make subordinate legislation conferred by any of the following provisions of this Act may be exercised so as to make provision having retrospective effect: sections 30, 58(4), 104 and 107.

Statutory instruments – SI 2014/3294: made under s. 114(1).

FINANCE ACT 1999

(1999 Chapter 16)

[*27th July 1999*]

ARRANGEMENT OF SECTIONS

PART III – INCOME TAX, CORPORATION TAX AND CAPITAL GAINS TAX

CHARITIES

EDUCATION AND TRAINING

VARIOUS OTHER RELIEFS

SETTLEMENTS

SECURITIES AND INVESTMENTS

VENTURE CAPITAL TRUSTS

ENTERPRISE INVESTMENT SCHEME

CHARGEABLE GAINS

CAPITAL ALLOWANCES

PENSIONS AND INSURANCE, ETC.

ADVANCE PRICING AGREEMENTS AND CFCs

MANAGEMENT AND ENFORCEMENT

PART III – INCOME TAX, CORPORATION TAX AND CAPITAL GAINS TAX

INCOME TAX RATES AND CHARGE ETC.

22 Starting rate

22 [Repealed by ITA 2007, s. 1031 and Sch. 3, Pt. 1.]

History – S. 22 repealed by ITA 2007, s. 1031 and Sch. 3, Pt. 1, with effect from 6 April 2007.

Notes – S. 22 rewritten as follows:
S. 22(1): ITA 2007, s. 6(1), 10(1), (2).
S. 22(2): ITA 2007, s. 10(1), (2), 20(1).
S. 22(4): ITA 2007, s. 21(2), (3).
S. 22(6): ITA 2007, s. 17(1), (2).
S. 22(7): ITA 2007, s. 7, 17(1), (2).
S. 22(10): ITA 2007, s. 989.

23 Charge and rates for 1999–2000

23 [Repealed by ITA 2007, s. 1031 and Sch. 3, Pt. 1.]

History – S. 23 repealed by ITA 2007, s. 1031 and Sch. 3, Pt. 1, with effect from 6 April 2007.

24 Personal allowances for 1999–00 for those aged 65 or more

24 [Repealed by ITA 2007, s. 1031 and Sch. 3, Pt. 1.]

History – S. 24 repealed by ITA 2007, s. 1031 and Sch. 3, Pt. 1, with effect from 6 April 2007.

25 Operative date of indexation for PAYE

25(1) The Taxes Act 1988 shall be amended in accordance with subsections (2) and (3) below.

25(2) [Inserts ICTA 1988, s. 1(5A).]

25(3) [Omitted by FA 2009, s. 5 and Sch. 1, para. 6(j).]

25(4) This section has effect for the year 1999–00 and subsequent years of assessment.

History – S. 25(3) omitted by FA 2009, s. 5 and Sch. 1, para. 6(j), with effect for the tax year 2010–11 and subsequent tax years.

Notes – S. 25(2) rewritten as ITA 2007, s. 21(4).

RATES OF CAPITAL GAINS TAX

26 Rates of capital gains tax

26 [Omitted by FA 2008, s. 8 and Sch. 2, para. 21(d).]

History – S. 26 omitted by FA 2008, s. 8 and Sch. 2, para. 21(d), with effect for the tax year 2008–09 and subsequent tax years.

CORPORATION TAX CHARGE AND RATES

27 Charge and main rate for financial year 2000

27 [Spent: fixed corporation tax rate for 2000.]

28 Corporation tax starting rate

28 [Repealed by FA 2006, s. 178 and Sch. 26, Pt. 3(1).]

History – S. 28 repealed by FA 2006, s. 178 and Sch. 26, Pt. 3(1), with effect for the financial year 2006 and subsequent financial years, subject to provisions of FA 2006, s. 26(9)–(11). Former s. 28 inserted ICTA 1988, s. 13AA and amended ICTA 1988, s. 13A(1), 468(1A), FA 1989, Sch. 12, para. 1(a) and Sch. 18, para. 8(1).

29 Rate and fraction for corporation tax starting rate

29 [Spent: fixed corporation starting tax rate and fraction for 2000.]

INCOME TAX REDUCTIONS

30 Children's tax credit

30 [Repealed by TCA 2002, s. 60 and Sch. 6.]

History – S. 30 repealed by TCA 2002, s. 60 and Sch. 6, with effect from 6 April 2003 (by virtue of SI 2003/962, art. 2(1), (3)(c), (e) and Sch. 1).

31 Restriction of MCA to those reaching 65 before 2000–01

31 [Omitted by FA 2009, s. 5 and Sch. 1, para. 6(j).]

History – S. 31 omitted by FA 2009, s. 5 and Sch. 1, para. 6(j), with effect for the tax year 2010–11 and subsequent tax years.

32 Further provision about married couple's allowance

32 [Omitted by FA 2009, s. 5 and Sch. 1, para. 6(j).]

History – S. 32 omitted by FA 2009, s. 5 and Sch. 1, para. 6(j), with effect for the tax year 2010–11 and subsequent tax years.

33 Abolition of existing relief in respect of children

33(1) [Repeals ICTA 1988, s. 259-261A.]

33(2) This section has effect for the year 2000–01 and subsequent years of assessment.

34 Abolition of widow's bereavement allowance

34(1) [Repeals ICTA 1988, s. 262.]

34(2) Subsection (1) above has effect in relation to deaths occurring on or after 6th April 2000.

34(3) Where a woman is entitled to an income tax reduction for the year 2000-01 by virtue of paragraph (b) of section 262(1) of the Taxes Act 1988, the reference in that paragraph to the amount specified in section 257A(1) for that year shall be read as a reference to the amount specified in section 257A(5A) for that year.

35 Order of income tax reductions etc.

35 [Repealed by ITA 2007, s. 1031 and Sch. 3, Pt. 1.]

History – S. 35 repealed by ITA 2007, s. 1031 and Sch. 3, Pt. 1, with effect from 6 April 2007.

36 Maintenance payments

36(1)–(6) [Repealed by ITA 2007, s. 1031 and Sch. 3, Pt. 1.]

36(7) Sections 347A and 347B of the Taxes Act 1988 shall have effect, notwithstanding anything in subsection (3) of section 36 of the Finance Act 1988 (which provides for the application of those sections), in relation to a payment made in pursuance of an existing obligation (within the meaning of that subsection) as they have effect in relation to a payment made otherwise than in pursuance of such an obligation.

36(8) This section has effect in relation to any payment falling due on or after 6th April 2000.

History – S. 36(1)–(6) repealed by ITA 2007, s. 1031 and Sch. 3, Pt. 1, with effect from 6 April 2007.

Notes – S. 36 rewritten as follows:
S. 36(2): ITA 2007, s. 454(3).
S. 36(4): ITA 2007, s. 453(2).

RELIEF FOR INTEREST PAYMENTS

37 Limit on relief for interest

37 [Spent: fixed limit on relief for interest on certain loans for 1999–2000.]

38 Withdrawal of relief for interest on loans to buy land etc.

38(1) A payment of interest falling within subsection (3) or (4) below shall not be eligible for relief under section 353 of the Taxes Act 1988 by virtue of section 354 of that Act (interest on loans to buy land etc.).

38(2) Section 369(1) of that Act (mortgage interest payable under deduction of tax) shall not apply to any payment of interest falling within subsection (3) or (4) below which (apart from section 353(2) of that Act and subsection (1) above) would be eligible for relief under section 353 of that Act by virtue of section 354 of that Act.

38(3) A payment of interest falls within this subsection if it is–

(a) a payment made on or after 6th April 2000 (whenever falling due); or

(b) a payment made before that date, but not before 9th March 1999, of any interest that was not due until on or after 6th April 2000.

38(4) A payment of interest falls within this subsection if it is–

(a) made before 6th April 2000 but not before 9th March 1999; and

(b) made under or in accordance with any scheme made for a tax-avoidance purpose on or after 9th March 1999 (whether or not before the making of the payment).

38(5) For the purposes of subsection (4) above, a scheme is made for a tax-avoidance purpose if its main purpose, or one of its main purposes, is to secure that a payment of one or more of the following descriptions is a relievable payment, that is to say–

(a) a payment discharging an obligation to make a payment which (but for the scheme) might have been expected to be a non-relievable payment;

(b) a payment made in pursuance of any obligation which has effect, directly or indirectly, in place of an obligation under which a payment which might have been expected to be a non-relievable payment would have become due;

(c) a payment made in pursuance of an obligation which (apart from the purpose of securing that it is a relievable payment) might have been expected to take the form of an obligation–

  (i) to make a non-relievable payment, or

  (ii) to make two or more payments at least one of which would have been a non-relievable payment.

38(6) In subsection (5) above–

"non-relievable payment" means a payment falling within subsection (3) above; and

"relievable payment" means a payment which–

(a) is eligible for relief under section 353 of the Taxes Act 1988, or

(b) is a payment to which section 369(1) of that Act applies.

38(7) The references in this section to a scheme are references to any scheme, arrangements or understanding of any kind whatever, whether or not legally enforceable.

38(8) Schedule 4 to this Act (which contains amendments consequential on the preceding provisions of this section) shall have effect.

39 Withdrawal of relief for interest on new annuity loans

39(1) [Inserts ICTA 1988, s. 365(1)(aa).]

39(2) [Inserts ICTA 1988, s. 365(1AA).]

39(3) This section has effect for the year 1998–99 and subsequent years of assessment.

40 Annuity loans: residence requirements and re-mortgages

40(1) Section 365 of the Taxes Act 1988 (relief for interest on loans to buy life annuities) is amended as follows.

40(2) [Amends ICTA 1988, s.365(1)(d).]

40(3) [Inserts ICTA 1988, s. 365(1AB), (1AC) and (1AD).]

40(4) [Substitutes ICTA 1988, s. 365(1A).]

40(5) This section has effect in relation to any payment of interest (whenever falling due) made on or after the day on which this Act is passed.

41 Repayments attracting repayment supplement

41(1) Section 824 of the Taxes Act 1988 (repayment supplements for individuals) shall have effect, and be deemed always to have had effect, with the following amendments.

41(2) [Inserts ICTA 1988, s. 824(2B).]

41(3) [Inserts ICTA 1988, s. 824(3)(aa).]

41(4) This section shall be deemed to have had effect in relation to provisions corresponding to section 824 of the Taxes Act 1988 directly or indirectly re-enacted in that section as it has effect in relation to that section, subject to subsections (5) and (6) below.

41(5) For the purposes of subsection (4) above the references in the amendments of section 824 of the Taxes Act 1988 made by this section to provisions of that Act shall be taken to include references to any corresponding provision contained in the enactments directly or indirectly re-enacted in those provisions.

41(6) Subsection (4) above applies only if the payments corresponding to payments under section 375(8) of the Taxes Act 1988 were made in the year 1984–85 or a subsequent year of assessment.

EMPLOYEE BENEFITS ETC.

42 Conditional acquisition of shares

42 [Repealed by ITEPA 2003, Sch. 8, Pt. 1.]

History – Repealed by ITEPA 2003, Sch. 8, Pt. 1 which has effect for the tax year 2003–04 and subsequent tax years.

43 Meaning of conditional interests in shares

43 [Repealed by ITEPA 2003, Sch. 8, Pt. 1.]

History – Repealed by ITEPA 2003, Sch. 8, Pt. 1 which has effect for the tax year 2003–04 and subsequent tax years.

44 Exemption for mobile telephones

44 [Repealed by ITEPA 2003, Sch. 8, Pt. 1.]

History – Repealed by ITEPA 2003, Sch. 8, Pt. 1 which has effect for the tax year 2003–04 and subsequent tax years.

45 Limited exemption for computer equipment

45 [Repealed by ITEPA 2003, Sch. 8, Pt. 1.]

History – Repealed by ITEPA 2003, Sch. 8, Pt. 1 which has effect for the tax year 2003–04 and subsequent tax years.

46 PRP and agricultural pay

46 [Repealed by Statute Law (Repeals) Act 2013, s. 1 and Sch. 1, Pt. 10.]

History – S. 46 repealed by Statute Law (Repeals) Act 2013, s. 1 and Sch. 1, Pt. 10, with effect from 31 January 2013.

47 Cars available for private use

47 [Repealed by FA 2000, Sch. 40, Pt. II(3).]

History – S. 47 repealed by FA 2000, Sch. 40, Pt. II(3) with effect for the year 2002–03 and subsequent years of assessment in accordance with FA2000, s. 59.

48 Provision and support of bus services

48 [Repealed by ITEPA 2003, Sch. 8, Pt. 1.]

History – Repealed by ITEPA 2003, Sch. 8, Pt. 1 which has effect for the tax year 2003–04 and subsequent tax years.

49 Provision of motor cycle or cycle parking facilities

49 [Repealed by ITEPA 2003, Sch. 8, Pt. 1.]

History – Repealed by ITEPA 2003, Sch. 8, Pt. 1 which has effect for the tax year 2003–04 and subsequent tax years.

50 Cycles and cyclist's safety equipment

50 [Repealed by ITEPA 2003, Sch. 8, Pt. 1.]

History – Repealed by ITEPA 2003, Sch. 8, Pt. 1 which has effect for the tax year 2003–04 and subsequent tax years.

MEMBERS OF PARLIAMENTS AND ASSEMBLIES

51 EU travel expenses

51 [Repealed by ITEPA 2003, Sch. 8, Pt. 1.]

History – Repealed by ITEPA 2003, Sch. 8, Pt. 1 which has effect for the tax year 2003–04 and subsequent tax years.

52 Scottish Parliament and devolved assemblies

52 [Repealed by FA 2004, s. 326 and Sch. 42, Pt. 3.]

History – S. 52 repealed by FA 2004, s. 326 and Sch. 42, Pt. 3 with effect, subject to FA 2004, Sch. 36, from 6 April 2006.

SUB-CONTRACTORS IN THE CONSTRUCTION INDUSTRY

53 Exemption certificates

53 [Repealed by FA 2004, s. 326 and Sch. 42, Pt. 2(7).]

History – S. 53 repealed by FA 2004, s. 326 and Sch. 42, Pt. 2(7) with effect in relation to payments made under contracts relating to construction operations on or after 6 April 2007, by virtue of notice given pursuant to SI 2005/2045, reg. 1.

REVERSE PREMIUMS

54 Tax treatment of reverse premiums

54 [Omitted by CTA 2009, s. 1322 and Sch. 1, para. 456 and repealed by CTA 2009, s. 1326 and Sch. 3, Pt. 1.]

History – S. 54 omitted by CTA 2009, s. 1322 and Sch. 1, para. 456 and repealed by CTA 2009, s. 1326 and Sch. 3, Pt. 1, with effect for corporation tax purposes for accounting periods ending on or after 1 April 2009, and for income tax and capital gains tax purposes for the tax year 2009–10 and subsequent tax years.

Notes – S. 54 rewritten as follows:
S. 54(2): CTA 2009, Sch. 2, para. 24(1).
S. 54(3): CTA 2009, Sch. 2, para. 24(2).

CHARITIES

55 Gifts in kind to charities etc.

55(1) [Repealed by CTA 2009, s. 1326 and Sch. 3, Pt. 1.]

55(2) [Repeals FA 1998, s. 47.]

55(3) Subsections (1) and (2) above have effect in relation to gifts made on or after the day on which this Act is passed.

History – S. 55(1) repealed by CTA 2009, s. 1326 and Sch. 3, Pt. 1, with effect for corporation tax purposes for accounting periods ending on or after 1 April 2009, and for income tax and capital gains tax purposes for the tax year 2009–10 and subsequent tax years.

56 Gifts of money to relieve refugee poverty

56 [Repealed by FA 2011, s. 91 and Sch. 26, para. 2(2)(a).]

History – S. 56 repealed by FA 2011, s. 91 and Sch. 26, para. 2(2)(a), with effect from 19 July 2011.

57 Aggregation of money gifts for relief in poor countries

57 [Repealed by FA 2011, s. 91 and Sch. 26, para. 2(2)(a).]

History – S. 57 repealed by FA 2011, s. 91 and Sch. 26, para. 2(2)(a), with effect from 19 July 2011. .

EDUCATION AND TRAINING

58 Employees seconded to educational establishments

58 [Repealed by CTA 2009, s. 1326 and Sch. 3, Pt. 1.]

History – S. 58 repealed by CTA 2009, s. 1326 and Sch. 3, Pt. 1, with effect for corporation tax purposes for accounting periods ending on or after 1 April 2009, and for income tax and capital gains tax purposes for the tax year 2009–10 and subsequent tax years.

59 Phasing out of vocational training relief

59(1) [Substitutes FA 1991, s. 32(2)–(2B).]

59(2) That section and section 33 of that Act (provisions supplementary to section 32) shall cease to have effect.

59(3) In this section–

(a) subsection (1) has effect in relation to payments made on or after 6th April 1999; and

(b) subsection (2) shall have effect in relation to payments made on or after such date after 6th April 2000 as the Treasury may by order appoint.

Notes – The day appointed for the purposes of FA 1999, s. 59(2) and (3)(b) is 1 September 2000 (SI 2000/2004 (C. 53)).

60 Student loans: certain interest to be disregarded

60 [Repealed by ITTOIA 2005, s. 884 and Sch. 3 effective for income tax purposes for 2005–06 onwards (ITTOIA 2005, s. 883(1)).]

VARIOUS OTHER RELIEFS

61 Class 1B National Insurance contributions

61 [Repealed by CTA 2009, s. 1326 and Sch. 3, Pt. 1.]

History – S. 61 repealed by CTA 2009, s. 1326 and Sch. 3, Pt. 1, with effect for corporation tax purposes for accounting periods ending on or after 1 April 2009, and for income tax and capital gains tax purposes for the tax year 2009–10 and subsequent tax years.

62 Expenditure on film production and acquisition

62 [Amends F(No. 2)A 1997, s. 48(2)(a).]

63 Treatment of transfer fees under existing contracts

63 [Omitted by CTA 2009, s. 1322 and Sch. 1, para. 457 and repealed by CTA 2009, s. 1326 and Sch. 3, Pt. 1.]

History – S. 63 omitted by CTA 2009, s. 1322 and Sch. 1, para. 457 and repealed by CTA 2009, s. 1326 and Sch. 3, Pt. 1, with effect for corporation tax purposes for accounting periods ending on or after 1 April 2009, and for income tax and capital gains tax purposes for the tax year 2009–10 and subsequent tax years.

SETTLEMENTS

64 Income of unmarried child of settlor

64 [Repealed by ITTOIA 2005, s. 884 and Sch. 3.]

History – Repealed by ITTOIA 2005, s. 884 and Sch. 3, effective for income tax purposes for 2005–06 onwards (ITTOIA 2005, s. 883(1)).

SECURITIES AND INVESTMENTS

65 Relevant discounted securities

65(1)–(6) [Omitted by ITTOIA 2005, s. 882(1) and Sch. 1, para. 507(2); and repealed by ITTOIA 2005, s. 884 and Sch. 3.]

65(7) [Repealed by FA 2004, s. 326 and Sch. 42, Pt. 2(6).]

65(8) Subject to subsections (9) to (12) below, subsection (7) above has effect in relation to–

(a) any transfer of a security on or after 15th February 1999; or

(b) any occasion on or after that date on which a person holding a security becomes entitled to any payment on its redemption.

65(9) For the purposes of section 92 of that Act, subsection (7) above–

(a) has effect in relation to any accounting period of a company ending on or after 15th February 1999; but

(b) does not affect any amount falling to be brought into account in respect of any disposal (in whole or in part) of an asset representing a creditor relationship if the disposal was one completed before that day.

65(10) For the purposes of paragraphs 17 and 18 of Schedule 9 to that Act, subsection (7) above–

(a) has effect in relation to any accounting period of a company ending on or after 15th February 1999; but

(b) does not affect any amount falling to be brought into account in respect of a security representing a debtor relationship of a company if, on that day, the company was no longer subject to any liability under the relationship.

65(11) For the purposes of sections 117(2AA) and 251(8) of the Taxation of Chargeable Gains Act 1992, subsection (7) above has effect in relation to any disposal (in whole or in part) of an asset on or after 15th February 1999.

65(12) For the purposes of subsection (1)(c) of section 254 of that Act (which, notwithstanding its repeal by the Finance Act 1998, continues to have effect in relation to loans made before 17th March 1998), subsection (7) above has effect in relation to any claim made on or after 15th February 1999.

History – S. 65(1)–(6) omitted by ITTOIA 2005, s. 882(1) and Sch. 1, para. 507(2); and repealed by ITTOIA 2005, s. 884 and Sch. 3 effective for income tax purposes for 2005–06 onwards (ITTOIA 2005, s. 883(1)).
S. 65(7) repealed by FA 2004, s. 326 and Sch. 42, Pt. 2(6) with effect in relation to:
(a) periods of account beginning on or after 1 January 2005, and
(b) in the case of a company required to prepare accounts under the Companies Act 1985 or the Companies (Northern Ireland) Order 1986, any period of account beginning before that date for which the company is required or permitted to prepare such accounts in accordance with international accounting standards.
In s. 65(8) the words "subsection (7) above has" inserted by ITTOIA 2005, s. 882(1) and Sch. 1, para. 507(3); effective for income tax purposes for 2005–06 onwards (ITTOIA 2005, s. 883(1)).
In s. 65(9) and (10) the words: "subsection (7)", "has effect" and "does not affect" substituted for the former wordings by ITTOIA 2005, s. 882(1) and Sch. 1, para. 507(4); effective for income tax purposes for 2005–06 onwards (ITTOIA 2005, s. 883(1)).
In s. 65(11) and (12) the words "subsection (7) above has" substituted for the former wordings by ITTOIA 2005, s. 882(1) and Sch. 1, para. 507(5); effective for income tax purposes for 2005–06 onwards (ITTOIA 2005, s. 883(1)).

66 Qualifying corporate bonds: provision consequential on s. 65

66(1) This section applies where–

(a) before 15th February 1999 there occurred a transaction (**"the relevant transaction"**) to which sections 127 to 130 of the Taxation of Chargeable Gains Act 1992 applied; and

(b) the new holding (within the meaning given by section 126 of that Act) consisted of or included something (**"the new asset"**) that–

(i) did not fall to be treated as a qualifying corporate bond in relation to the relevant transaction, but

(ii) by virtue of section 65 above, does fall to be so treated in relation to a disposal on or after 15th February 1999.

66(2) Section 116 of the Taxation of Chargeable Gains Act 1992 (reorganisations etc. involving qualifying corporate bonds) shall have effect in relation to any disposal of the whole or part of the new asset on or after 15th February 1999 as if–

(a) there had been a transaction (**"the subsequent transaction"**) by which the person holding the new asset had disposed of it and immediately re-acquired it;

(b) the subsequent transaction had occurred at the time mentioned in subsection (3) below;

(c) the asset re-acquired had been a qualifying corporate bond; and

(d) the subsequent transaction had been a transaction to which section 127 of that Act would have applied but for section 116(5) of that Act.

66(3) That time is–

(a) where the relevant transaction took place before 5th April 1996, that date;

(b) where the relevant transaction took place on or after that date, immediately after the relevant transaction.

67 Deep discount and deep gain securities

67(1) [Inserts FA 1996, Sch. 15, para 19(3A).]

67(2) [Inserts FA 1996, Sch. 15, para 20(2A).]

67(3) [Substitutes FA 1996, Sch. 15, para. 19(7)(b).]

67(4) [Amends FA 1993, s. 64(5c) and s. 65(5c).]

67(5) [Inserts FA 1993, s. 65(5A).]

67(6) Subsections (1) and (2) above apply in relation to income treated as arising on or after 15th February 1999.

67(7) Subsection (3) above applies in any case where the day mentioned in paragraph 19(9) of Schedule 15 to the Finance Act 1996 falls on or after 15th February 1999.

67(8) Subsections (4) and (5) above apply for determining whether a time on or after 15th February 1999–

(a) is a time falling within section 64(5)(c) of the Finance Act 1993; or

(b) is on a day falling within section 65(5)(c) of that Act.

68 Court common investment funds

68(1) [Repealed by CTA 2010, s. 1181 and Sch. 3, Pt. 1.]

68(2) [Repeals ICTA 1988, s. 328.]

68(3) Subsections (1) and (2) above have effect in relation to–

(a) any income arising to a common investment fund on or after 6th April 1999; and

(b) any distribution made by such a fund for a distribution period beginning on or after that date.

68(4) For the purposes of the Tax Acts where any common investment fund was in existence on 5th April 1999–

(a) the distribution period of that fund which was current on that date for the purposes of section 469 of the Taxes Act 1988 shall be taken to have ended with that date; and

(b) the fund's first accounting period for the purposes of corporation tax, and its first distribution period for the purposes of the enactments relating to authorised unit trusts, shall each be taken to have begun with 6th April 1999.

68(5) In this section **"common investment fund"** means any common investment fund established under section 42 of the Administration of Justice Act 1982.

History – S. 68(1) repealed by CTA 2010, s. 1181 and Sch. 3, Pt. 1, with effect for corporation tax purposes for accounting periods ending on or after 1 April 2010, and for income tax and capital gains tax purposes for the tax year 2010–11 and subsequent tax years.

VENTURE CAPITAL TRUSTS

69 Company restructuring and convertible securities

69 [Repealed by ITA 2007, s. 1031 and Sch. 3, Pt. 1.]

History – S. 69 repealed by ITA 2007, s. 1031 and Sch. 3, Pt. 1, with effect from 6 April 2007.

Notes – S. 69 rewritten as follows:
S. 69(2): ITA 2007, s. 326(1), (2), (3), (4), (5), 327(2), (3), (4), (5), (6), (7), (8), 328(1), (2), (3), (4), (5), 329(1), (3), (4), Sch. 2, para. 87.
S. 69(3): ITA 2007, s. 285(2).
S. 69(4): ITA 2007, s. 279(1), (2), (3).
S. 69(5): ITA 2007, Sch. 2, para. 87.

70 Relief on distributions

70 [Repealed by ITTOIA 2005, s. 884 and Sch. 3.]

History – Repealed by ITTOIA 2005, s. 884 and Sch. 3, effective for income tax purposes for 2005–06 onwards and for corporation tax purposes for accounting periods ending after 5 April 2005 (ITTOIA 2005, s. 883(1)).

ENTERPRISE INVESTMENT SCHEME

71 Eligibility for EIS relief

71 [Repealed by ITA 2007, s. 1031 and Sch. 3, Pt. 2.]

History – S. 71 repealed by ITA 2007, s. 1031 and Sch. 3, Pt. 2, with effect in respect of shares issued after 5 April 2007.

72 Deferred gains: application of taper relief

72 [Omitted by FA 2008, s. 8 and Sch. 2, para. 55(b)(i).]

History – S. 72 omitted by FA 2008, s. 8 and Sch. 2, para. 55(b)(i), with effect in relation to chargeable gains accruing or treated as accruing in the tax year 2008–09 or any subsequent tax year.

73 Deferred gains: gain accruing on part disposal, etc.

73(1) Schedule 8 to this Act (which amends Schedule 5B to the Taxation of Chargeable Gains Act 1992 in relation to cases where there is a disposal of some, but not all, of the shares to which relief under that Schedule is attributable) shall have effect.

73(2) The amendments made by Schedule 8 to this Act have effect in relation to shares issued on or after 6th April 1999.

CHARGEABLE GAINS

74 Value shifting: tax-free benefits

74 Schedule 9 to this Act (which makes provision about tax-free benefits in relation to value shifting) shall have effect.

75 Allowable losses where beneficiary absolutely entitled

75(1) [Substitutes TCGA 1992, s. 71.]

75(2) This section applies in relation to any occasion on or after 16th June 1999 on which a person becomes absolutely entitled to settled property as against the trustee.

76 Concessions that defer a capital gains charge

76(1) [Inserts TCGA 1992, s. 284A, 284B.]

76(2) Sections 284A and 284B of the Taxation of Chargeable Gains Act 1992 have effect in relation to any case in which the circumstances arising as mentioned in subsection (6)(a) of section 284A are circumstances arising on or after 9th March 1999, whether the benefit mentioned in subsection (1) of that section was obtained as so mentioned before or after the passing of this Act.

CAPITAL ALLOWANCES

77 Extension of first-year allowances

77 [Repealed by CAA 2001, s. 580 and Sch. 4.]

History – S. 77 repealed by CAA 2001, s. 580 and Sch. 4, with effect for allowances and charges falling to be made for chargeable periods ending on or after 6 April 2001 for income tax purposes or 1 April 2001 for corporation tax purposes.

78 First-year allowances for investment in Northern Ireland

78 [Repealed by CAA 2001, s. 580 and Sch. 4.]

History – S. 78 repealed by CAA 2001, s. 580 and Sch. 4, with effect for allowances and charges falling to be made for chargeable periods ending on or after 6 April 2001 for income tax purposes or 1 April 2001 for corporation tax purposes

PENSIONS AND INSURANCE, ETC.

79 Sharing of pensions on divorce, etc.

79 Schedule 10 to this Act (which, for purposes connected with the sharing of pensions between ex-spouses, makes provision with respect to pensions and annuities) shall have effect.

80 Purchased life annuities

80 [Omitted by FA 2008, s. 36 and Sch. 14, para. 17(h).]

History – S. 80 omitted by FA 2008, s. 36 and Sch. 14, para. 17(h), with effect–

- so far as relating to corporation tax, for accounting periods beginning on or after 1 April 2008, and
- so far as relating to income tax, for the tax year 2008–09 and subsequent tax years.

81 Acquisitions disregarded under insurance companies concession

81(1) This section applies for the purposes of corporation tax in relation to the disposal by a company ("the relevant company") of any asset where–

(a) the asset is one acquired by the relevant company from an insurance company at a time when the relevant company and that insurance company were both members of the same group of companies;

(b) there was an occasion before the disposal (whether the occasion of the transfer of the asset to the relevant company or the occasion of an earlier transfer of the asset) in relation to which the *non-statutory arrangements* for groups of insurance companies were applied in the case of the transferring company;

(c) the application of those arrangements in relation to that occasion had the effect of preventing the cost of the asset's acquisition by the transferring company ("the previous acquisition") from being brought into account for tax purposes; and

(d) there has not, between that occasion and the making of the disposal, been any relevant event by reference to which the cost of the previous acquisition has been brought into account in computing the profits or losses of any company for tax purposes.

81(2) Subject to subsection (5) below, where the computation of the relevant company's profits or losses from any trade requires the cost of the acquisition of the asset by that company to be brought into account

Post-TCGA 1992

in the accounting period in which the disposal takes place, that cost shall be brought into account in that period as if it were an amount equal to the cost of the previous acquisition.

81(3) Subject to subsections (4) and (5) below, where–

(a) the asset disposed of represents a creditor relationship,

(b) the disposal is such that paragraph 6 of Schedule 15 to the Finance Act 1996 (adjustment for pre-commencement trading relationships) would require an amount to be brought into account in the accounting period in which the disposal takes place in any case in which there is, for that relationship, a difference such as is mentioned in sub-paragraph (1) of that paragraph, and

(c) the cost of the previous acquisition is less than the amount which for the purposes of paragraph 5(2) of that Schedule would (apart from this subsection) be the notional closing value of the relationship on 31st March 1996,

the question whether an amount falls to be brought into account in accordance with paragraph 6(2) or (3) of that Schedule, and the amount (if any) falling to be so brought into account, shall be determined as if the notional closing value of the relationship on 31st March 1996 had been equal to the cost of the previous acquisition.

81(4) In any case where the asset represents a creditor relationship in relation to which an election under paragraph 6(4) of Schedule 15 to the Finance Act 1996 has effect–

(a) [omitted by CTA 2009, s. 1322 and Sch. 1, para. 458(2)(a) and repealed by CTA 2009, s. 1326 and Sch. 2, Pt. 1;]

(b) paragraph 6(1) and (2) of that Schedule shall be treated as applying, notwithstanding paragraph 6(4) if, in the case of that relationship, the amount referred to in subsection (3)(c) above exceeds the cost of the previous acquisition; and

(c) the amount falling by virtue of paragraph (b) above to be brought into account in accordance with paragraph 6(2) of that Schedule shall be determined as if the excess referred to in paragraph 6(2)(a) were the excess mentioned in paragraph (b) above.

81(5) Where–

(a) there are two or more occasions such as are mentioned in paragraph (b) of subsection (1) above, and

(b) paragraph (d) of that subsection is satisfied in relation to each of them,

subsections (2) to (4) above shall have effect as if the references to the previous acquisition were references to the acquisition which is the previous acquisition in relation to the earliest of those occasions.

81(6) In subsection (1)(d) above **"relevant event"**, in relation to any asset, means–

(a) a disposal of the asset; or

(b) any event by reference to which the conditions of the non-statutory arrangements for groups of insurance companies has required the cost of the previous acquisition to be brought into account in computing the profits or losses of any company for tax purposes.

81(7) Section 170 of the Taxation of Chargeable Gains Act 1992 (meaning of groups etc.) shall apply for construing references in the preceding provisions of this section to a group of companies as it applies for the purposes of sections 171 to 181 of that Act.

81(8) In the preceding provisions of this section–

"creditor relationship" has the same meaning as in Part 5 of the Corporation Tax Act 2009 (see section 302(5)); and

"insurance company" means an insurance company within the meaning given by section 65 of the Finance Act 2012.

81(9) References in this section to an asset shall be construed as if section 129 of the Corporation Tax Act 2009 (cases where different assets are treated as the same) applied for the purposes of this section as it applies for the purpose of calculating the profits of a company's trade; and section 340(2) to (4) of the Corporation Tax Act 2009 (cases where different companies are treated as the same) shall apply for the purposes of this section as it applies for the purposes of Part 5 of that Act.

81(10) In this section any reference to the non-statutory arrangements for groups of insurance companies is a reference to so much of any arrangements made by the Board otherwise than by virtue of an enactment as–

(a) in relation to an accounting period beginning before 1st January 2000–

(i) provided for a single assessment of the trading profits of a group of insurance companies to be made on the principal company of the group; and

(ii) excluded trading profits on intra-group transfers of investments from the group assessment; or

(b) contains transitional provision, in connection with the withdrawal of any arrangements falling within paragraph (a) above, for allowing trading profits on intra-group transfers to be excluded from assessments of members of groups of insurance companies that relate to accounting periods beginning on or after 1st January 1999 and before 1st January 2000.

81(11) This section–

(a) shall not be construed as requiring any amount representing a gain on the disposal of the asset to be brought into account for tax purposes in so far as an amount representing that gain is or has already been brought into account, as an attributed gain, under any regulations made by virtue of Schedule 16 to the Finance Act 1993 (Forex transitional provisions); and

(b) shall be without prejudice to any power of the Board apart from this section to enforce any conditions subject to which any relief in accordance with the non-statutory arrangements for groups of insurance companies has been allowed.

81(12) This section applies in relation to disposals by the relevant company made in accounting periods beginning on or after 1st January 1999.

81(13) If the relevant company changes from–

(a) not recognising a profit or loss on an asset until it is realised, to

(b) bringing assets into account in each period of account at a fair value,

then, in calculating the amount of any adjustment required under Chapter 14 of Part 3 of the Corporation Tax Act 2009 (calculation of adjustment on change of basis), the amount to be taken into account as the cost of the asset in relation to a period of account before the change is the cost of the previous acquisition.

History – S. 81(4)(a) omitted by CTA 2009, s. 1322 and Sch. 1, para. 458(2)(a) and repealed by CTA 2009, s. 1326 and Sch. 3, Pt. 1, with effect for corporation tax purposes for accounting periods ending on or after 1 April 2009, and for income tax and capital gains tax purposes for the tax year 2009–10 and subsequent tax years.

In s. 81(4)(b), the words "paragraph 6(4)" substituted for the words "paragraph 6(4)(a)" by CTA 2009, s. 1322 and Sch. 1, para. 458(2)(b), with effect for corporation tax purposes for accounting periods ending on or after 1 April 2009, and for income tax and capital gains tax purposes for the tax year 2009–10 and subsequent tax years.

In s. 81(8), the words "meaning given by section 65 of the Finance Act 2012" substituted for the words "meaning of Chapter I of Part XII of the Taxes Act 1988" by FA 2012, s. 146 and Sch. 16, para. 93 in relation to accounting periods beginning on or after 1 January 2013 (FA 2012, s. 148) but subject to transitional provisions in FA 2012, Sch. 17. Where an accounting period would otherwise straddle 1 January 2013, it is deemed to end on 31 December 2012 (FA 2012, s. 149).

In s. 81(8), the words "Part 5 of the Corporation Tax Act 2009 (see section 302(5))" substituted for the words "Chapter II of Part IV of the Finance Act 1996" by CTA 2009, s. 1322 and Sch. 1, para. 458(3), with effect for corporation tax purposes for accounting periods ending on or after 1 April 2009, and for income tax and capital gains tax purposes for the tax year 2009–10 and subsequent tax years.

In s. 81(9), the words "section 129 of the Corporation Tax Act 2009" substituted for the words "section 473 of the Taxes Act 1988", the words "the purpose of calculating the profits of a company's trade" substituted for the words "the purposes of that Act", and the words "section 340(2) to (4) of the Corporation Tax Act 2009" and "Part 5 of that Act" substituted for, respectively, the words "paragraph 12(2) of Schedule 9 to the Finance Act 1996" and "Chapter II of Part IV of that Act of 1996" by CTA 2009, s. 1322 and Sch. 1, para. 458(4), with effect for corporation tax purposes for accounting periods ending on or after 1 April 2009, and for income tax and capital gains tax purposes for the tax year 2009–10 and subsequent tax years.

In s. 81(13), the words "Chapter 14 of Part 3 of the Corporation Tax Act 2009" substituted for the words "Schedule 22 to the Finance Act 2002" by CTA 2009, s. 1322 and Sch. 1, para. 458(5), with effect for corporation tax purposes for accounting periods ending on or after 1 April 2009, and for income tax and capital gains tax purposes for the tax year 2009–10 and subsequent tax years.

S.81(13) inserted by FA 2002, s. 67(3) in relation to a change in basis taking effect in a period of account ending on or after 1 August 2001.

82 Lloyd's: members' agent pooling arrangements

82(1) This section applies where a member has entered into a members' agent pooling arrangement ("the arrangement").

82(2) Subsections (3) to (9) below shall apply for the purpose of determining any liability of the member's to capital gains tax that may arise from transactions effected in pursuance of the arrangement.

82(3) The syndicate rights held by the member under the arrangement shall be treated as a single asset acquired by him at the time when he entered into the arrangement; but, subject to subsection (9) below, he shall not be treated as disposing of the asset (in whole or in part) except as mentioned in subsection (6) below.

82(4) The member shall be treated as having given, wholly and exclusively for the acquisition of the asset, consideration equal to any amount paid by him on entering into the arrangement

82(5) Any other amount paid by the member under the arrangement shall, on a disposal of the asset, be treated as expenditure incurred wholly and exclusively on the asset for the purpose of enhancing its value and reflected in its state or nature at the time of the disposal.

82(6) If an amount is paid to the member at any time under the arrangement, he shall be treated as disposing of the whole asset or, as the case may be, part of the asset at that time for a consideration equal to that amount.

82(7) If syndicate rights held by the member otherwise than under the arrangement become at any time rights held by him under the arrangement, he shall be treated as disposing of those rights at that time for a consideration equal to their market value at that time.

82(8) If syndicate rights held by the member under the arrangement become at any time rights held by him otherwise than under the arrangement, he shall be treated as acquiring those rights at that time for a consideration equal to their market value at that time.

82(9) Nothing in subsection (3) above shall affect the operation of section 24(1) of the Taxation of Chargeable Gains Act 1992 (disposals where assets extinguished etc.) in relation to the asset.

82(10) Subject to subsection (11) below this section applies to arrangements entered into on or after 6th April 1999 or subsisting on that date.

82(11) In the case of arrangements subsisting on 6th April 1999, this section has effect–

(a) as if the time mentioned in subsection (3) above were the earliest time ("the notional time of acquisition") at which the member acquired any of the syndicate rights held by him under the arrangement immediately before 6th April 1999;

(b) as if the consideration referred to in subsection (4) above were the consideration, in money or money's worth, given by him wholly and exclusively for the acquisition of such of those rights as he acquired at the notional time of acquisition; and

(c) in relation to times before 6th April 1999, as if the amount mentioned in subsection (5) above were the amount of any consideration, in money or money's worth, given by him wholly and exclusively for the acquisition, after the notional time of acquisition, of rights such as are mentioned in paragraph (a) above;

and the incidental costs of any acquisition falling within paragraph (b) or (c) above shall be taken to be incidental costs of the acquisition of the asset.

83 Provisions supplementary to s. 82

83(1) In section 76 above and this section, except where the context otherwise requires–

"member" means an individual who is an underwriting member of Lloyd's;

"members' agent" , in relation to a member, means a person registered as a members' agent at Lloyd's who is acting as such an agent for the member;

"members' agent pooling arrangement", in relation to a member, means an arrangement–

(i) under which a members' agent arranges for the member's participation in syndicates; and

(ii) which satisfies the conditions set out in subsection (2) below;

"syndicate" has the same meaning as in Chapter III of Part II of the Finance Act 1993; and

"syndicate rights", in relation to a member, means rights under a syndicate in which the member participates.

83(2) The conditions mentioned in paragraph (ii) of the above definition of "members' agent pooling arrangement" are that under the arrangement–

(a) the member must participate in each of the syndicates to which the arrangement relates; and

(b) the extent to which the member participates in each such syndicate is determined–

(i) by the members' agent; or

(ii) according to a formula provided for in the arrangement.

83(3) References in section 82 above to the payment of an amount are references to the payment of an amount in money or money's worth; and to the extent that an amount mentioned in subsection (4), (5) or (6) of that section is paid in money's worth, the amount of the consideration or expenditure there referred to shall be calculated by reference to the market value of the money's worth at the time of the payment mentioned in that subsection.

83(4) Section 82 above and this section have effect in relation to a Scottish partnership which is an underwriting member of Lloyd's as they have effect in relation to a member, but as if the reference in section 82(2) to any liability of the member's to capital gains tax that may arise from transactions effected in pursuance of the arrangement were a reference to any such liability of members of the partnership that may so arise.

84 Lloyd's: roll-over relief

84(1) [Amends TCGA 1992, s. 155.]

84(2) *This section applies to–*

(a) assets (or interests in them) disposed of on or after 6th April 1999;

(b) assets (or interests in them) acquired on or after that date.

ADVANCE PRICING AGREEMENTS AND CFCs

85 Advance pricing agreements etc.

85 [Omitted by TIOPA 2010, s. 374 and Sch. 8, para. 116 and repealed by TIOPA 2010, s. 378 and Sch. 10, Pt. 2.]

History – S. 85 omitted by TIOPA 2010, s. 374 and Sch. 8, para. 116 and repealed by TIOPA 2010, s. 378 and Sch. 10, Pt 2, with effect for corporation tax purposes for accounting periods ending on or after 1 April 2010, for income tax and capital gains tax purposes for the tax year 2010–11 and subsequent tax years, and for petroleum revenue tax purposes for chargeable periods beginning on or after 1 July 2010.

Notes – S. 85 rewritten in TIOPA 2010 as follows:
S. 85(1): TIOPA 2010, s. 218(1), 220(1), 223(1), (2), 230.
S. 85(2): TIOPA 2010, s. 218(2).
S. 85(3): TIOPA 2010, s. 220(2), (3), (4).
S. 85(4): TIOPA 2010, s. 220(5).
S. 85(5): TIOPA 2010, s. 223(1), (3), (4), (5), 230.
S. 85(6): TIOPA 2010, s. 157(1), 158(4), 159(1), 160(1), 219(1), (2), (3), (4).
S. 85(7): TIOPA 2010, s. 206(1), (2), (3), (4).
S. 85(8): TIOPA 2010, s. 220(1), 224(2), Sch. 9, para. 29(1).

86 Provisions supplementary to s. 85

86(1)–(8) [Omitted by TIOPA 2010, s. 374 and Sch. 8, para. 117 and repealed by TIOPA 2010, s. 378 and Sch. 10, Pt. 2.]

86(9) [Repealed by TIOPA 2010, s. 378 and Sch. 10, Pt. 2.]

86(10) [Omitted by TIOPA 2010, s. 374 and Sch. 8, para. 117 and repealed by TIOPA 2010, s. 378 and Sch. 10, Pt. 2.]

History – S. 86(1)–(8) omitted by TIOPA 2010, s. 374 and Sch. 8, para. 117 and repealed by TIOPA 2010, s. 378 and Sch. 10, Pt. 2, with effect for corporation tax purposes for accounting periods ending on or after 1 April 2010, for income tax and capital gains tax purposes for the tax year 2010–11 and subsequent tax years, and for petroleum revenue tax purposes for chargeable periods beginning on or after 1 July 2010.
S. 86(9) repealed by TIOPA 2010, s. 378 and Sch. 10, Pt. 2, with effect for corporation tax purposes for accounting periods ending on or after 1 April 2010, for income tax and capital gains tax purposes for the tax year 2010–11 and subsequent tax years, and for petroleum revenue tax purposes for chargeable periods beginning on or after 1 July 2010.
S. 86(10) omitted by TIOPA 2010, s. 374 and Sch. 8, para. 117 and repealed by TIOPA 2010, s. 378 and Sch. 10, Pt. 2 with effect for corporation tax purposes for accounting periods ending on or after 1 April 2010, for income tax and capital gains tax purposes for the tax year 2010–11 and subsequent tax years, and for petroleum revenue tax purposes for chargeable periods beginning on or after 1 July 2010.

Notes – S. 86 rewritten in TIOPA 2010 as follows:
S. 86(1): TIOPA 2010, s. 224(1).
S. 86(2): TIOPA 2010, s. 221(1), (2), (3), (4), (5), (6), 230.
S. 86(3): TIOPA 2010, s. 229(1), (2), (3), 230.
S. 86(4): TIOPA 2010, s. 228, 230.
S. 86(5): TIOPA 2010, s. 226(1), (2), (3), (4), (5), (6), 230.
S. 86(6): TIOPA 2010, s. 225(1), (2), (3), 230.
S. 86(7): TIOPA 2010, s. 224(3).
S. 86(8): TIOPA 2010, s. 227, 230.
S. 86(10): TIOPA 2010, s. 229(4).

87 Effect of section 85 agreements on non-parties

87 [Omitted by TIOPA 2010, s. 374 and Sch. 8, para. 118 and repealed by TIOPA 2010, s. 378 and Sch. 10, Pt. 2.]

History – S. 87 omitted by TIOPA 2010, s. 374 and Sch. 8, para. 118 and repealed by TIOPA 2010, s. 378 and Sch. 10, Pt. 2, with effect for corporation tax purposes for accounting periods ending on or after 1 April 2010, for income tax and capital gains tax purposes for the tax year 2010–11 and subsequent tax years, and for petroleum revenue tax purposes for chargeable periods beginning on or after 1 July 2010.

Notes – S. 87 rewritten in TIOPA 2010 as follows:
S. 87(1): TIOPA 2010, s. 222(1).
S. 87(2): TIOPA 2010, s. 222(2), (3).
S. 87(3): TIOPA 2010, s. 222(4).
S. 87(4): TIOPA 2010, s. 222(5).
S. 87(5): TIOPA 2010, s. 185(5), 222(6).

88 Controlled foreign companies

88 [Omitted by FA 2009, s. 36 and Sch. 16, para. 5(e).]

History – S. 88 omitted by FA 2009, s. 36 and Sch. 16, para. 5(e), with effect in relation to accounting periods of controlled foreign companies beginning on or after 1 July 2009, subject to rules in FA 2009, Sch. 16, para. 7 regarding accounting periods straddling that date and transitional rules in FA 2009, Sch. 16, para. 8.

MANAGEMENT AND ENFORCEMENT

89 Corporation tax: due and payable date

89(1) [Amends column 1 of the table in TMA 1970, s. 98.]

89(2) [Repealed by CTA 2010, s. 1181 and Sch. 3, Pt. 1.]

89(3) This section has effect in relation to accounting periods ending on or after 1st July 1999.

History – S. 89(2) repealed by CTA 2010, s. 1181 and Sch. 3, Pt. 1, with effect for accounting periods ending on or after 1 April 2010.

90 Release or writing off of debt: interest on tax overpaid

90(1) [Amends ICTA 1988, s. 826(4).]

90(2) This section has effect in relation to the release or writing off of the whole or part of a debt on or after 6th April 1999.

91 Advance corporation tax: consequences of abolition

91(1)–(3) [Repealed by ITA 2007, s. 1031 and Sch. 3, Pt. 1.]

91(4) [Amends FA 1998, s. 32(6).]

91(5) [Repealed by ITA 2007, s. 1031 and Sch. 3, Pt. 1.]

91(6) The amendment made by subsection (4) above shall be deemed always to have had effect.

History – S. 91(1)–(3) and (5) repealed by ITA 2007, s. 1031 and Sch. 3, Pt. 1, with effect from 6 April 2007.

92 Group relief: consequences of reduction in surrenderable amount

92(1) Part VIII of Schedule 18 to the Finance Act 1998 (claims for group relief) is amended as follows.

92(2) [Amends FA 1998, Sch. 18, para. 75.]

92(3) [Inserts FA 1998, Sch. 18, para. 75A.]

92(4) [Inserts FA 1998, Sch. 18, para. 76(3).]

92(5) [Amends TMA 1970, s. 87A(3).]

92(6) [Repeals FA 1990, s. 96.]

92(7) This section has effect in relation to accounting periods ending on or after 1st July 1999.

93 Company tax returns, etc.

93(1) The enactments mentioned in Schedule 11 to this Act have effect with the amendments specified there, which are minor amendments and amendments consequential on Schedule 18 to the Finance Act 1998 (company tax returns, assessments and claims, etc.).

93(2) The amendments made by Schedule 11 to this Act have effect in relation to accounting periods ending on or after 1st July 1999.

PART IV – OIL TAXATION

100 Sale and lease-back: ring fence profits

100 [Repealed by CTA 2010, s. 1181 and Sch. 3, Pt. 1.]

History – S. 100 repealed by CTA 2010, s. 1181 and Sch. 3, Pt. 1, with effect for corporation tax purposes for accounting periods ending on or after 1 April 2010, and for income tax and capital gains tax purposes for the tax year 2010–11 and subsequent tax years.

103 Business assets: roll-over relief

103(1) [Repeals TCGA 1992, s. 193.]

103(2) This section has effect in relation to–

(a) a disposal of a licence or an interest in a licence which occurs on or after 1st July 1999;

(b) an acquisition of a licence or an interest in a licence which occurs on or after 1st July 1999.

PART VIII – MISCELLANEOUS AND SUPPLEMENTAL

GENERAL ADMINISTRATION OF TAX

131 Economic and monetary union: taxes and duties

131 The Commissioners of Inland Revenue and the Commissioners of Customs and Excise may incur expenditure in order to secure that, if the United Kingdom were to move to the third stage of economic and monetary union, they would be able to exercise their functions relating to taxes and duties (including agricultural levies of the European Community).

132 Power to provide for use of electronic communications

132(1) Regulations may be made, in accordance with this section, for facilitating the use of electronic communications for–

(a) the delivery of information the delivery of which is authorised or required by or under any legislation relating to a taxation matter;

(b) the making of payments under any such legislation.

132(2) The power to make regulations under this section is conferred–

(a) on the Commissioners of Inland Revenue in relation to matters which are under their care and management; and

(b) on the Commissioners of Customs and Excise in relation to matters which are under their care and management.

132(3) For the purposes of this section provision for facilitating the use of electronic communications includes any of the following–

(a) provision authorising persons to use electronic communications for the delivery of information to tax authorities, or for the making of payments to tax authorities;

(b) provision requiring electronic communications to be used for the making to tax authorities of payments due from persons using such communications for the delivery of information to those authorities;

(c) provision authorising tax authorities to use electronic communications for the delivery of information to other persons or for the making of any payments;

(d) provision as to the electronic form to be taken by any information that is delivered to any tax authorities using electronic communications;

(e) provision requiring persons to prepare and keep records of information delivered to tax authorities by means of electronic communications, and of payments made to any such authorities by any such means;

(f) provision for the production of the contents of records kept in accordance with any regulations under this section;

(g) provision imposing conditions that must be complied with in connection with any use of electronic communications for the delivery of information or the making of any payment;

(h) provision, in relation to cases where use is made of electronic communications, for treating information as not having been delivered, or a payment as not having been made, unless conditions imposed by any such regulations are satisfied;

(i) provision, in relation to such cases, for determining the time when information is delivered or a payment is made;

(j) provision, in relation to such cases, for determining the person by whom information is to be taken to have been delivered or by whom a payment is to be taken to have been made;

(k) provision, in relation to cases where information is delivered by means of electronic communications, for authenticating whatever is delivered.

132(4) The power to make provision under this section for facilitating the use of electronic communications shall also include power to make such provision as the persons exercising the power think fit (including provision for the application of conclusive or other presumptions) as to the manner of proving for any purpose–

(a) whether any use of electronic communications is to be taken as having resulted in the delivery of information or the making of a payment;

(b) the time of delivery of any information for the delivery of which electronic communications have been used;

(c) the time of the making of any payment for the making of which electronic communications have been used;

(d) the person by whom information delivered by means of electronic communications was delivered;

(e) the contents of anything so delivered;

(f) the contents of any records;

(g) any other matter for which provision may be made by regulations under this section.

132(5) Regulations under this section may–

(a) allow any authorisation or requirement for which such regulations may provide to be given or imposed by means of a specific or general direction given by the Commissioners of Inland Revenue or the Commissioners of Customs and Excise;

(b) provide that the conditions of any such authorisation or requirement are to be taken to be satisfied only where such tax authorities as may be determined under the regulations are satisfied as to specified matters;

(c) allow a person to refuse to accept delivery of information in an electronic form or by means of electronic communications except in such circumstances as may be specified in or determined under the regulations;

(d) allow or require use to be made of intermediaries in connection with–

(i) the delivery of information, or the making of payments, by means of electronic communications; or

(ii) the authentication or security of anything transmitted by any such means.

132(6) Power to make provision by regulations under this section shall include power–

(a) to provide for a contravention of, or any failure to comply with, a specified provision of any such regulations to attract a penalty of a specified amount not exceeding £1,000;

(b) to provide that specified enactments relating to penalties imposed for the purposes of any taxation matter (including enactments relating to assessments, review and appeal) are to apply, with or without modifications, in relation to penalties under such regulations;

(c) to make different provision for different cases;

(d) to make such incidental, supplemental, consequential and transitional provision in connection with any provision contained in any such regulations as the persons exercising the power think fit.

132(7) The power to make regulations under this section shall be exercisable by statutory instrument subject to annulment in pursuance of a resolution of the House of Commons.

132(8) References in this section to the delivery of information include references to any of the following (however referred to)–

(a) the production or furnishing to a person of any information, account, record or document;

(b) the giving, making, issue or surrender to, or service on, any person of any notice, notification, statement, declaration, certificate or direction;

(c) the imposition on any person of any requirement or the issue to any person of any request;

(d) the making of any return, claim, election or application;

(e) the amendment or withdrawal of anything mentioned in paragraphs (a) to (d) above.

132(9) References in this section to a taxation matter are references to any of the matters which are under the care and management of the Commissioners of Inland Revenue or of the Commissioners of Customs and Excise.

132(10) In this section–

"electronic communications" includes any communications by means of an electronic communications service;

"legislation" means any enactment, Community legislation or subordinate legislation;

"payment" includes a repayment;

"records" includes records in electronic form;

"subordinate legislation" has the same meaning as in the Interpretation Act 1978;

"tax authorities" means–

(a) the Commissioners of Inland Revenue or the Commissioners of Customs and Excise,

(b) any officer of either body of Commissioners; or

(c) any other person who for the purposes of electronic communications is acting under the authority of either body of Commissioners.

History – In s. 132(10), in the definition of "electronic communications", the words "an electronic communications service" substituted for the words "a telecommunication system (within the meaning of the Telecommunications Act 1984)" by the Communications Act 2003, s. 406(1) and Sch. 17, para. 156, with effect for the purpose only of enabling the networks and services functions and the spectrum functions to be carried out by the Director General of Telecommunications and the Secretary of State respectively, during the transitional period (as provided for by the Communications Act 2003, s. 408(6)) from 25 July 2003–29 December 2003 (by virtue of SI 2003/1900, art. 2(1), 3(1), Sch. 1 and the Communications Act 2003, s. 406(6), 408, Sch. 18, para. 2); and with effect for the purpose of conferring the networks and services functions and the spectrum functions on OFCOM from 29 December 2003 (by virtue of SI 2003/3142, art. 3(2)).

Cross references – FA 2000, Sch. 38, para. 1: power to make regulations for providing incentives to use electronic communications.
Work and Families Act 2006, Sch. 1, para. 49 reads as follows:
"**49(1)** Sections 132 and 133 of the Finance Act 1999 shall have effect as if additional statutory paternity pay were a matter which is under the care and management of the Commissioners for Her Majesty's Revenue and Customs.
49(2) In this paragraph "additional statutory paternity pay" includes statutory pay under Northern Ireland legislation corresponding to the provisions of Part 12ZA of SSCBA 1992 relating to additional statutory paternity pay.".

Statutory instruments – SI 2000/2074 (regulations made under s. 132).
SI 2002/680 (regulations made under s. 132).
SI 2002/3047 (regulations made under s. 132).

SI 2003/282 (regulations made under s. 132).
SI 2003/2682 (regulations made under s. 132).
SI 2003/2718 (regulations made under s. 132).
SI 2003/3143 (regulations made under s. 132).
SI 2005/844 (regulations made under s. 132).
SI 2005/3338 (regulations made under s. 132).
SI 2006/570 (regulations made under s. 132).
SI 2007/792 (regulations made under s. 132).
SI 2012/1836 (regulations made partly under s. 132).
SI 2013/2259: partly made under s. 132.
SI 2013/2592: partly made under s. 132.

133 Use of electronic communications under other provisions

133(1) Without prejudice to section 132 above, where any power to make subordinate legislation for or in connection with the delivery of information or the making of payments is conferred in relation to any taxation matter on–

(a) the Commissioners of Inland Revenue,

(b) the Commissioners of Customs and Excise, or

(c) the Treasury,

that power shall be taken (to the extent that it would not otherwise be so taken) to include power to make any such provision in relation to the delivery of that information or the making of those payments as could be made by any person by regulations in exercise of a power conferred by that section.

133(2) Provision made in exercise of the powers conferred by section 132 above or subsection (1) above shall have effect notwithstanding so much of any enactment or subordinate legislation as (apart from the provision so made) would require–

(a) any information to be delivered, or

(b) any amount to be paid,

in a form or manner that would preclude the use of electronic communications for its delivery or payment, or the use in connection with its delivery or payment of an intermediary.

133(3) Schedule 3A to the Taxes Management Act 1970 (electronic lodgment of tax returns etc.) shall cease to have effect.

133(4) Subsection (3) above shall come into force on such day as the Treasury may by order made by statutory instrument appoint; and different days may be appointed under this subsection for different purposes.

133(5) Expressions used in this section and section 132 above have the same meanings in this section as in that section.

Cross references – Work and Families Act 2006, Sch. 1, para. 49 reads as follows:

"49(1) Sections 132 and 133 of the Finance Act 1999 shall have effect as if additional statutory paternity pay were a matter which is under the care and management of the Commissioners for Her Majesty's Revenue and Customs.

49(2) In this paragraph "additional statutory paternity pay" includes statutory pay under Northern Ireland legislation corresponding to the provisions of Part 12ZA of SSCBA 1992 relating to additional statutory paternity pay.".

Statutory instruments – SI 2000/2074 (regulations made under s. 133).
SI 2002/3047 (regulations made under s. 133).
SI 2003/282 (regulations made under s. 133).
SI 2003/2682 (regulations made under s. 133).
SI 2005/844 (regulations made under s. 133).
SI 2005/3338 (regulations made under s. 133).
SI 2006/570 made under s. 133(2).
SI 2007/792 (regulations made under s. 133(2)).
SI 2013/1844: partly made under s. 133.
SI 2013/2259: partly made under s. 133.

SUPPLEMENTAL

138 Interpretation

138 In this Act **"the Taxes Act 1988 "** means the Income and Corporation Taxes Act 1988.

139 Repeals

139(1) The enactments mentioned in Schedule 20 to this Act (which include provisions that are spent or of no practical utility) are hereby repealed to the extent specified in the third column of that Schedule.

139(2) The repeals specified in that Schedule have effect subject to the commencement provisions and savings contained or referred to in the notes set out in that Schedule.

140 Short title

140 This Act may be cited as the Finance Act 1999.

SCHEDULES

SCHEDULE 3 – NEW SCHEDULE 13B TO THE TAXES ACT 1988

Section 30

[Repealed by TCA 2002, s. 60 and Sch. 6.]

History – Repealed by TCA 2002, s. 60 and Sch. 6, with effect from 6 April 2003 (by virtue of SI 2003/962, art. 2(1), (3)(c), (e) and Sch. 1, subject to provisions of art. 3–5).

SCHEDULE 4 – WITHDRAWAL OF RELIEF FOR INTEREST ON LOANS TO BUY LAND ETC.

Section 38

AMENDMENTS OF PART IX OF THE TAXES ACT 1988

1(1) Section 353 of the Taxes Act 1988 (general provision for relief for interest payments) is amended as follows.

1(2) [Repealed by TIOPA 2010, s. 378 and Sch. 10, Pt. 13.]

1(3) [Amends ICTA 1988, s. 353(1A) and (1B)]

1(4) [Repealed by ITA 2007, s. 1031 and Sch. 3, Pt. 1.]

History – Para. 1(2) repealed by TIOPA 2010, s. 378 and Sch. 10, Pt. 13, with effect for corporation tax purposes for accounting periods ending on or after 1 April 2010, for income tax and capital gains tax purposes for the tax year 2010–11 and subsequent tax years, and for petroleum revenue tax purposes for chargeable periods beginning on or after 1 July 2010.
Para. 1(4) repealed by ITA 2007, s. 1031 and Sch. 3, Pt. 1, with effect from 6 April 2007.

2 [Repealed by Statute Law (Repeals) Act 2013, s. 1 and Sch. 1, Pt. 10.]

History – Para. 2 repealed by Statute Law (Repeals) Act 2013, s. 1 and Sch. 1, Pt. 10, with effect from 31 January 2013.

3(1) Section 367 of the Taxes Act 1988 (supplementary provisions) is amended as follows.

3(2) [Repealed by Statute Law (Repeals) Act 2013, s. 1 and Sch. 1, Pt. 10.]

3(3) [Repealed by TIOPA 2010, s. 378 and Sch. 10, Pt. 13.]

3(4) [Amends ICTA 1988, s. 367(5).]

History – Para. 3(2) repealed by Statute Law (Repeals) Act 2013, s. 1 and Sch. 1, Pt. 10, with effect from 31 January 2013.
Para. 3(3) repealed by TIOPA 2010, s. 378 and Sch. 10, Pt. 13, with effect for corporation tax purposes for accounting periods ending on or after 1 April 2010, for income tax and capital gains tax purposes for the tax year 2010–11 and subsequent tax years, and for petroleum revenue tax purposes for chargeable periods beginning on or after 1 July 2010.

4 [Substitutes ICTA 1988, s. 369(1A).]

5(1) Section 370 of the Taxes Act 1988 (meaning of "relevant loan interest") is amended as follows.

5(2)–(4) [Repealed by Statute Law (Repeals) Act 2013, s. 1 and Sch. 1, Pt. 10.]

5(5) [Amends ICTA 1988, s. 370(5).]

History – Para. 5(2)(b), (3) and (4) repealed by Statute Law (Repeals) Act 2013, s. 1 and Sch. 1, Pt. 10, with effect from 31 January 2013.

6 [Repealed by Statute Law (Repeals) Act 2013, s. 1 and Sch. 1, Pt. 10.]

History – Para. 6 repealed by Statute Law (Repeals) Act 2013, s. 1 and Sch. 1, Pt. 10, with effect from 31 January 2013.

7 [Repealed by Statute Law (Repeals) Act 2013, s. 1 and Sch. 1, Pt. 10.]

History – Para. 7 repealed by Statute Law (Repeals) Act 2013, s. 1 and Sch. 1, Pt. 10, with effect from 31 January 2013.

8 [Repealed by Statute Law (Repeals) Act 2013, s. 1 and Sch. 1, Pt. 10.]

History – Para. 8 repealed by Statute Law (Repeals) Act 2013, s. 1 and Sch. 1, Pt. 10, with effect from 31 January 2013.

9(1) [Inserts ICTA 1988, subsection (8B).]

9(2) [Repealed by Statute Law (Repeals) Act 2013, s. 1 and Sch. 1, Pt. 10.]

History – Para. 9(2) repealed by Statute Law (Repeals) Act 2013, s. 1 and Sch. 1, Pt. 10, with effect from 31 January 2013.

10 [Repealed by Statute Law (Repeals) Act 2013, s. 1 and Sch. 1, Pt. 10.]

History – Para. 10 repealed by Statute Law (Repeals) Act 2013, s. 1 and Sch. 1, Pt. 10, with effect from 31 January 2013.

11 [Repealed by Statute Law (Repeals) Act 2013, s. 1 and Sch. 1, Pt. 10.]

History – Para. 11 repealed by Statute Law (Repeals) Act 2013, s. 1 and Sch. 1, Pt. 10, with effect from 31 January 2013.

12 [Repealed by Statute Law (Repeals) Act 2013, s. 1 and Sch. 1, Pt. 10.]

History – Para. 12 repealed by Statute Law (Repeals) Act 2013, s. 1 and Sch. 1, Pt. 10, with effect from 31 January 2013.

(a) [repealed by Statute Law (Repeals) Act 2013, s. 1 and Sch. 1, Pt. 10,]

(b) amends ICTA 1988, s. 378(3).

History – Para. 13(a) repealed by Statute Law (Repeals) Act 2013, s. 1 and Sch. 1, Pt. 10, with effect from 31 January 2013.F

(a)–(b) [repealed by Statute Law (Repeals) Act 2013, s. 1 and Sch. 1, Pt. 10,]

(c) amends ICTA 1988, s. 379.

History – Para. 14(a) and (b) repealed by Statute Law (Repeals) Act 2013, s. 1 and Sch. 1, Pt. 10, with effect from 31 January 2013.

OTHER AMENDMENTS

15(1) Section 488 of the Taxes Act 1988 (tax liability of co-operative housing associations) is amended as follows.

15(2) In subsection (1)–

(a) [repealed by CTA 2010, s. 1181 and Sch. 3, Pt. 1]

(b) [repealed by Statute Law (Repeals) Act 2013, s. 1 and Sch. 1, Pt. 10.]

15(3)–(4) [Repealed by Statute Law (Repeals) Act 2013, s. 1 and Sch. 1, Pt. 10.]

15(5) [Repealed by CTA 2010, s. 1181 and Sch. 3, Pt. 1.]

15(6) [Repealed by Statute Law (Repeals) Act 2013, s. 1 and Sch. 1, Pt. 10.]

History – Para. 15(2)(a) and the word "and " immediately after it repealed by CTA 2010, s. 1181 and Sch. 3, Pt. 1, with effect for corporation tax purposes for accounting periods ending on or after 1 April 2010, and for income tax and capital gains tax purposes for the tax year 2010–11 and subsequent tax years.
Para. 15(2)(b), (3), (4) and (6) repealed by Statute Law (Repeals) Act 2013, s. 1 and Sch. 1, Pt. 10, with effect from 31 January 2013.
Para. 15(5) repealed by CTA 2010, s. 1181 and Sch. 3, Pt. 1, with effect for corporation tax purposes for accounting periods ending on or after 1 April 2010, and for income tax and capital gains tax purposes for the tax year 2010–11 and subsequent tax years.

16 [Omitted by FA 2008, s. 36 and Sch. 14, para. 17(h).]

History – Para. 16 omitted by FA 2008, s. 36 and Sch. 14, para. 17(h), with effect–

- so far as relating to corporation tax, for accounting periods beginning on or after 1 April 2008, and
- so far as relating to income tax, for the tax year 2008–09 and subsequent tax years.

17(1) Section 222 of the Taxation of Chargeable Gains Act 1992 (relief on disposal of private residence) is amended as follows.

17(2) [Repealed by Statute Law (Repeals) Act 2013, s. 1 and Sch. 1, Pt. 10.]

17(3) [Inserts TCGA 1992, s. 222(8A)–(8D).]

17(4) [Amends TCGA 1992, s. 222(9).]

History – Para. 17(2) repealed by Statute Law (Repeals) Act 2013, s. 1 and Sch. 1, Pt. 10, with effect from 31 January 2013.

COMMENCEMENT

18(1) [Repealed by Statute Law (Repeals) Act 2013, s. 1 and Sch. 1, Pt. 10.]

18(2) Paragraph 15 above has effect in relation to any claim for (or for part of) the year 2000–01 or any subsequent year of assessment.

18(3) [Omitted by FA 2008, s. 36 and Sch. 14, para. 17(h).]

18(4) Paragraph 17 above has effect for the year 2000–01 and subsequent years of assessment.

18(5) The other provisions of this Schedule have effect in relation to any payment of interest falling within subsection (3) or (4) of section 38 of this Act.

History – Para. 18(1) repealed by Statute Law (Repeals) Act 2013, s. 1 and Sch. 1, Pt. 10, with effect from 31 January 2013.
Para. 18(3) omitted by FA 2008, s. 36 and Sch. 14, para. 17(h), with effect–

- so far as relating to corporation tax, for accounting periods beginning on or after 1 April 2008, and
- so far as relating to income tax, for the tax year 2008–09 and subsequent tax years.

SCHEDULE 5 – SCOTTISH PARLIAMENT AND DEVOLVED ASSEMBLIES: EXEMPTIONS AND RELIEFS

Section 52

PAYMENTS ON DISSOLUTION, ETC., OR LOSS OF OFFICE

1 [Repealed by ITEPA 2003, Sch. 8, Pt. 1.]

History – Para. 1 repealed by ITEPA 2003, Sch. 8, Pt. 1 which has effect for the tax year 2003–04 and subsequent tax years.

PAYMENTS IN RESPECT OF OVERNIGHT EXPENSES OR EU TRAVEL

2 [Repealed by ITEPA 2003, Sch. 8, Pt. 1.]

History – Para. 2 repealed by ITEPA 2003, Sch. 8, Pt. 1 which has effect for the tax year 2003–04 and subsequent tax years.

OFFICE-HOLDERS' TRANSPORT AND SUBSISTENCE

3 [Repealed by ITEPA 2003, Sch. 8, Pt. 1.]

History – Para. 3 repealed by ITEPA 2003, Sch. 8, Pt. 1 which has effect for the tax year 2003–04 and subsequent tax years.

TRUSTEES' INCOME FROM PARLIAMENTARY PENSION FUNDS

4 [Repealed by FA 2004, s. 326 and Sch. 42, Pt. 3.]

History – Para. 4 repealed by FA 2004, s. 326 and Sch. 42, Pt. 3 with effect, subject to FA 2004, Sch. 36, from 6 April 2006.

RELEVANT STATUTORY SCHEMES

5 [Repealed by FA 2004, s. 326 and Sch. 42, Pt. 3.]

History – Para. 5 repealed by FA 2004, s. 326 and Sch. 42, Pt. 3 with effect, subject to FA 2004, Sch. 36, from 6 April 2006.

PENSIONS OF MEMBERS OF THE SCOTTISH EXECUTIVE

6(1) Sub-paragraph (2) below applies if provision under the Scotland Act 1998 is made for the salary paid to members of the Scottish Parliament who are also members of the Scottish Executive to be lower than that of other members of the Scottish Parliament.

6(2) In that case, sections 629 of the Taxes Act 1988 (under which part of the salary of the holder of certain offices is treated as remuneration as a member of the House of Commons) apply in relation to the salary of a member of the Scottish Executive who is also a member of the Scottish Parliament as they apply in relation to the salary of the holder of a qualifying office within the meaning of those sections who is also a member of the House of Commons, with such modifications as the Treasury may specify by order.

6(3) In this paragraph references to a member of the Scottish Executive include a junior Scottish Minister.

History – In para. 6(2) the words "and 654" which followed the words "sections 629" repealed by FA 2004, s. 326 and Sch. 42, Pt. 3 with effect, subject to FA 2004, Sch. 36, from 6 April 2006.

SCHEDULE 6 – TAX TREATMENT OF RECEIPTS BY WAY OF REVERSE PREMIUM

[Omitted by CTA 2009, s. 1322 and Sch. 1, para. 459 and repealed by CTA 2009, s. 1326 and Sch. 3, Pt. 1.]

History – Sch. 6 omitted by CTA 2009, s. 1322 and Sch. 1, para. 459 and repealed by CTA 2009, s. 1326 and Sch. 3, Pt. 1, with effect for corporation tax purposes for accounting periods ending on or after 1 April 2009, and for income tax and capital gains tax purposes for the tax year 2009–10 and subsequent tax years.

Notes – Sch. 6 rewritten for income tax purposes as follows:
Para. 1(1): ITTOIA 2005, s. 99(1), (2), (3), (4), 311(1), (6).
Para. 1(2): ITTOIA 2005, s. 99(1), 311(1), (6).
Para. 2(1): ITTOIA 2005, s. 101(1), 311(1), (6).
Para. 2(2): ITTOIA 2005, s. 101(2), 311(1).
Para. 2(3): ITTOIA 2005, s. 101(3), 311(1), (2).
Para. 3(1): ITTOIA 2005, s. 102(1), (3), 311(4), (5).
Para. 3(2): ITTOIA 2005, s. 102(4), 311(4), (5).
Para. 3(3): ITTOIA 2005, s. 102(5).
Para. 3(4): ITTOIA 2005, s. 102(2), 311(6).
Para. 5: ITTOIA 2005, s. 100(1), 311(6).
Para. 6: ITTOIA 2005, s. 100(2), 311(6).
Para. 7: ITTOIA 2005, s. 100(3), (4), 311(6).
Para. 8(1): ITTOIA 2005, s. 103, 311(6), 878(5).
Para. 8(2): ITTOIA 2005, s. 103, 311(6).
Sch. 6 rewritten for corporation tax purposes as follows:
Para. 1(1): CTA 2009, s. 96(1), (2), (3), (4), 250(1), (6).
Para. 1(2): CTA 2009, s. 96(1).
Para. 2(1): CTA 2009, s. 98(1).
Para. 2(2): CTA 2009, s. 98(2), 250(1).
Para. 2(3): CTA 2009, s. 98(3), 250(1), (2).
Para. 3(1): CTA 2009, s. 99(1), (3), 250(4), (5).
Para. 3(2): CTA 2009, s. 99(4), 250(4), (5).
Para. 3(3): CTA 2009, s. 99(5).
Para. 3(4): CTA 2009, s. 99(2), 250(6).
Para. 5: CTA 2009, s. 97(1), 250(6).
Para. 7: CTA 2009, s. 97(3), (4), 250(6).
Para. 8(1): CTA 2009, s. 100, 250(6), 1316(1).
Para. 8(2): CTA 2009, s. 100, 250(6).

SCHEDULE 7 – APPLICATION OF TAPER RELIEF TO EIS DEFERRED GAINS

Section 72

[Omitted by FA 2008, s. 8 and Sch. 2, para. 55(b)(ii).]

History – Sch. 7 omitted by FA 2008, s. 8 and Sch. 2, para. 55(b)(ii), with effect in relation to chargeable gains accruing or treated as accruing in the tax year 2008–09 or any subsequent tax year.

SCHEDULE 8 – EIS DEFERRED GAINS: GAINS ACCRUING ON PART DISPOSAL

Section 73

INTRODUCTORY

1 Schedule 5B to the Taxation of Chargeable Gains Act 1992 (relief in respect of re-investment under the enterprise investment scheme) is amended as follows.

PARAGRAPH 4

2(1) [Substitutes TCGA 1992, Sch. 5B, para. 4(1)(b).]

2(2) [Substitutes TCGA 1992, Sch. 5B, para. 4(5)(a).]

2(3) [Inserts TCGA 1992, Sch. 5B, para. 4(6), (7).]

PARAGRAPH 19

3(1) In paragraph 19(1) (interpretation) omit the definition of "**relevant shares**".

3(2) [Inserts TCGA 1992, Sch. 5B, para. 19(1A), (1B), (1C), (1D), and (1E).]

CONSEQUENTIAL AMENDMENTS

4 In consequence of paragraph 3 above–

(a) [amends TCGA 1992, Sch. 5B, para. 2(1), (4);]

(b) [amends TCGA 1992, Sch. 5B, para. 2(2), (3);]

(c) [amends TCGA 1992, Sch. 5B, para. 2(2)(b);]

(d) [amends TCGA 1992, Sch. 5B, para. 3(1), (5);]

(e) [amends TCGA 1992, Sch. 5B, para. 4(1), (5);]

(f) [amends TCGA 1992, Sch. 5B, para. 4(5)(b)]

(g) [amends TCGA 1992, Sch. 5B, para. 5(1);]

(h) [amends TCGA 1992, Sch. 5B, para. 6(1);]

(i) [amends TCGA 1992, Sch. 5B, para. 16(1), (2);]

(j) [amends TCGA 1992, Sch. 5B, para. 19(1).]

SCHEDULE 9 – CHARGEABLE GAINS: VALUE SHIFTING AND TAX-FREE BENEFITS

Section 74

[Repealed by FA 2011, s. 44 and Sch. 9, para. 5(b).]

History – Sch. 9 repealed by FA 2011, s. 44 and Sch. 9, para. 5(b), with effect in relation to disposals of shares and securities by companies made on or after 19 July 2011, subject to the transitional provision in FA 2011, Sch. 9, para. 6(2).

SCHEDULE 10 – SHARING OF PENSIONS ETC. ON DIVORCE OR ANNULMENT

Section 79

DEFINITION OF "PENSION BUSINESS"

1 [Repealed by FA 2004, s. 326 and Sch. 42, Pt. 3.]

History – Para. 1 repealed by FA 2004, s. 326 and Sch. 42, Pt. 3 with effect, subject to FA 2004, Sch. 36, from 6 April 2006.

APPROVAL OF RETIREMENT BENEFIT SCHEMES

2 [Repealed by FA 2004, s. 326 and Sch. 42, Pt. 3.]

History – Para. 2 repealed by FA 2004, s. 326 and Sch. 42, Pt. 3 with effect, subject to FA 2004, Sch. 36, from 6 April 2006.

DISCRETIONARY APPROVAL OF RETIREMENT BENEFIT SCHEMES

3 [Repealed by FA 2004, s. 326 and Sch. 42, Pt. 3.]

History – Para. 3 repealed by FA 2004, s. 326 and Sch. 42, Pt. 3 with effect, subject to FA 2004, Sch. 36, from 6 April 2006.

NON-APPROVED RETIREMENT BENEFIT SCHEMES

4 [Repealed by ITEPA 2003, Sch. 8, Pt. 1.]

History – Para. 4 repealed by ITEPA 2003, Sch. 8, Pt. 1 which has effect for the tax year 2003–04 and subsequent tax years.

Notes – Despite already being repealed by ITEPA 2003, para. 4 is repealed by FA 2004, s. 326 and Sch. 42, Pt. 3 with effect, subject to FA 2004, Sch. 36, from 6 April 2006.

5 [Repealed by ITEPA 2003, Sch. 8, Pt. 1.]

History – Para. 5 repealed by FA 2004, s. 326 and Sch. 42, Pt. 3 with effect, subject to FA 2004, Sch. 36, from 6 April 2006. Repealed by ITEPA 2003, Sch. 8, Pt. 1 which has effect for the tax year 2003–04 and subsequent tax years.

Notes – Despite already being repealed by ITEPA 2003, para. 5 is repealed by FA 2004, s. 326 and Sch. 42, Pt. 3 with effect, subject to FA 2004, Sch. 36, from 6 April 2006.

6 [Repealed by ITEPA 2003, Sch. 8, Pt. 1.]

History – Para. 6 repealed by ITEPA 2003, Sch. 8, Pt. 1 which has effect for the tax year 2003–04 and subsequent tax years.

Notes – Despite already being repealed by ITEPA 2003, para. 6 is repealed by FA 2004, s. 326 and Sch. 42, Pt. 3 with effect, subject to FA 2004, Sch. 36, from 6 April 2006.

CHARGE ON PENSIONS COMMUTED IN SPECIAL CIRCUMSTANCES

7 [Repealed by FA 2004, s. 326 and Sch. 42, Pt. 3.]

History – Para. 7 repealed by FA 2004, s. 326 and Sch. 42, Pt. 3 with effect, subject to FA 2004, Sch. 36, from 6 April 2006.

CHARGE ON UNAUTHORISED PAYMENTS

8 [Repealed by ITEPA 2003, Sch. 8, Pt. 1.]

History – Para. 8 repealed by ITEPA 2003, Sch. 8, Pt. 1 which has effect for the tax year 2003–04 and subsequent tax years.

Notes – Despite already being repealed by ITEPA 2003, para. 8 is repealed by FA 2004, s. 326 and Sch. 42, Pt. 3 with effect, subject to FA 2004, Sch. 36, from 6 April 2006.

DEFINITION OF "RETIREMENT BENEFITS SCHEME"

9 [Repealed by FA 2004, s. 326 and Sch. 42, Pt. 3.]

History – Para. 9 repealed by FA 2004, s. 326 and Sch. 42, Pt. 3 with effect, subject to FA 2004, Sch. 36, from 6 April 2006.

INTERPRETATION OF CHAPTER I

10 [Repealed by FA 2004, s. 326 and Sch. 42, Pt. 3.]

History – Para. 10 repealed by FA 2004, s. 326 and Sch. 42, Pt. 3 with effect, subject to FA 2004, Sch. 36, from 6 April 2006.

OVERSEAS PENSIONS

11 [Amends ICTA 1988, s. 615(6)(b).]

RULES PROHIBITING SURRENDER OR ASSIGNMENT OF ANNUITIES ETC.

12 [Repealed by FA 2004, s. 326 and Sch. 42, Pt. 3.]

History – Para. 12 repealed by FA 2004, s. 326 and Sch. 42, Pt. 3 with effect, subject to FA 2004, Sch. 36, from 6 April 2006.

ANNUITY PAYABLE ON THE DEATH OF A MEMBER

13 [Repealed by FA 2004, s. 326 and Sch. 42, Pt. 3.]

History – Para. 13 repealed by FA 2004, s. 326 and Sch. 42, Pt. 3 with effect, subject to FA 2004, Sch. 36, from 6 April 2006.

RULE IN SECTION 636A PROHIBITING ASSIGNMENT OR SURRENDER

14 [Repealed by FA 2004, s. 326 and Sch. 42, Pt. 3.]

History – Para. 14 repealed by FA 2004, s. 326 and Sch. 42, Pt. 3 with effect, subject to FA 2004, Sch. 36, from 6 April 2006.

MEANING OF "RELEVANT EARNINGS"

15 [Repealed by FA 2004, s. 326 and Sch. 42, Pt. 3.]

History – Para. 15 repealed by FA 2004, s. 326 and Sch. 42, Pt. 3 with effect, subject to FA 2004, Sch. 36, from 6 April 2006.

PURCHASED LIFE ANNUITIES

16 [Repealed by FA 2004, s. 326 and Sch. 42, Pt. 3.]

History – Para. 16 repealed by FA 2004, s. 326 and Sch. 42, Pt. 3 with effect, subject to FA 2004, Sch. 36, from 6 April 2006.

INTERPRETATION OF PART XIV

17 [Repealed by FA 2004, s. 326 and Sch. 42, Pt. 3.]

History – Para. 17 repealed by FA 2004, s. 326 and Sch. 42, Pt. 3 with effect, subject to FA 2004, Sch. 36, from 6 April 2006.

COMMENCEMENT ETC.

18 [Repealed by FA 2004, s. 326 and Sch. 42, Pt. 3.]

History – Para. 18 repealed by FA 2004, s. 326 and Sch. 42, Pt. 3 with effect, subject to FA 2004, Sch. 36, from 6 April 2006.

SCHEDULE 11 – COMPANY TAX RETURNS, ETC: MINOR AND CONSEQUENTIAL AMENDMENTS

Section 93

INCOME AND CORPORATION TAXES ACT 1988 (c.1)

1 Section 411A of the Taxes Act 1988 (group relief in substitution for loss relief) shall cease to have effect.

2 [Repealed by CTA 2009, s. 1326 and Sch. 3, Pt. 1.]

History – Para. 2 repealed by CTA 2009, s. 1326 and Sch. 3, Pt. 1, with effect for corporation tax purposes for accounting periods ending on or after 1 April 2009, and for income tax and capital gains tax purposes for the tax year 2009–10 and subsequent tax years.

FINANCE ACT 1989 (c.26)

3 [Repealed by CTA 2010, s. 1181 and Sch. 3, Pt. 1.]

History – Para. 3 repealed by CTA 2010, s. 1181 and Sch. 3, Pt. 1, with effect for corporation tax purposes for accounting periods ending on or after 1 April 2010, and for income tax and capital gains tax purposes for the tax year 2010–11 and subsequent tax years.

CAPITAL ALLOWANCES ACT 1990 (c.1)

4 [Repealed by CAA 2001, s. 580 and Sch. 4.]

5 [Repealed by CAA 2001, s. 580 and Sch. 4.]

6 [Repealed by CAA 2001, s. 580 and Sch. 4.]

7 [Repealed by CAA 2001, s. 580 and Sch. 4.]

FINANCE ACT 1994 (c.9)

8 [Repealed by CAA 2001, s. 580 and Sch. 4.]

FINANCE ACT 1998 (c.36)

9 [Omitted by SI 2009/56, art. 3(1) and Sch. 1, para. 277.]

History – Para. 4 to 8 repealed by CAA 2001, s. 580 and Sch. 4, with effect for allowances and charges falling to be made for chargeable periods ending on or after 6 April 2001 for income tax purposes or 1 April 2001 for corporation tax purposes.

Para. 9 omitted by SI 2009/56, art. 3(1) and Sch. 1, para. 277, operative from 1 April 2009, subject to transitional and saving provisions in SI 2009/56, Sch. 3.

SCHEDULE 20 – REPEALS

Section 139

Part VII – Electronic Communications

Chapter	Short title	Extent of repeal
1970 c. 9	The Taxes Management Act 1970.	Section 115A. Schedule 3A.
1988 c. 1.	The Income and Corporation Taxes Act 1988.	In section 203(10), the words from "and, in particular" onwards. Section 566(5).
1995 c. 4.	The Finance Act 1995.	Section 153. Schedule 28.
1998 c. 36.	The Finance Act 1998.	In Schedule 19, paragraph 43.

1. Subsection (4) of section 133 of this Act shall apply in relation to these repeals as it applies in relation to subsection (3) of that section.

2. Without prejudice to section 17(2) of the Interpretation Act 1978, any provision made by regulations under an enactment to which any of these repeals relates shall have effect, on and after the coming into force of the repeal and to the extent that it could have been made under section 132 or 133 of this Act, as if it were a provision made under that section of this Act.

Cross references – ITEPA 2003, s. 684: PAYE regulations.
ITEPA 2003, Sch. 7, para. 89 (Sch. 7: transitionals and savings): PAYE regulations – modification of ITEPA 2003, s. 684(2), item 5 in relation to any time before the commencement of the repeals in FA 1999, Sch. 20, Pt. 7.

TERRORISM ACT 2000

(2000 Chapter 11)

[20th July 2000]

ARRANGEMENT OF SECTIONS

PART III – TERRORIST PROPERTY

PART III – TERRORIST PROPERTY

INTERPRETATION

14 Terrorist property

14(1) In this Act **"terrorist property"** means–

(a) money or other property which is likely to be used for the purposes of terrorism (including any resources of a proscribed organisation),

(b) proceeds of the commission of acts of terrorism, and

(c) proceeds of acts carried out for the purposes of terrorism.

14(2) In subsection (1)–

(a) a reference to proceeds of an act includes a reference to any property which wholly or partly, and directly or indirectly, represents the proceeds of the act (including payments or other rewards in connection with its commission), and

(b) the reference to an organisation's resources includes a reference to any money or other property which is applied or made available, or is to be applied or made available, for use by the organisation.

Commencement Date – S. 14 brought into force on 19 February 2001 by the Terrorism Act 2000 (Commencement No. 3) Order 2001 (SI 2001/421, art. 2).

OFFENCES

18 Money laundering

18(1) A person commits an offence if he enters into or becomes concerned in an arrangement which facilitates the retention or control by or on behalf of another person of terrorist property–

(a) by concealment,

(b) by removal from the jurisdiction,

(c) by transfer to nominees, or

(d) in any other way.

18(2) It is a defence for a person charged with an offence under subsection (1) to prove that he did not know and had no reasonable cause to suspect that the arrangement related to terrorist property.

Commencement Date – S. 18 brought into force on 19 February 2001 by the Terrorism Act 2000 (Commencement No. 3) Order 2001 (SI 2001/421, art. 2).

19 Disclosure of information: duty

19(1) This section applies where a person–

(a) believes or suspects that another person has committed an offence under any of sections 15 to 18, and

(b) bases his belief or suspicion on information which comes to his attention in the course of a trade, profession, business or employment.

19(1A) But this section does not apply if the information came to the person in the course of a business in the regulated sector.

19(2) The person commits an offence if he does not disclose to a constable as soon as is reasonably practicable–

(a) his belief or suspicion, and

(b) the information on which it is based.

19(3) It is a defence for a person charged with an offence under subsection (2) to prove that he had a reasonable excuse for not making the disclosure.

19(4) Where–

(a) a person is in employment,

(b) his employer has established a procedure for the making of disclosures of the matters specified in subsection (2), and

(c) he is charged with an offence under that subsection,

it is a defence for him to prove that he disclosed the matters specified in that subsection in accordance with the procedure.

19(5) Subsection (2) does not require disclosure by a professional legal adviser of–

(a) information which he obtains in privileged circumstances, or

(b) a belief or suspicion based on information which he obtains in privileged circumstances.

19(6) For the purpose of subsection (5) information is obtained by an adviser in privileged circumstances if it comes to him, otherwise than with a view to furthering a criminal purpose–

(a) from a client or a client's representative, in connection with the provision of legal advice by the adviser to the client,

(b) from a person seeking legal advice from the adviser, or from the person's representative, or

(c) from any person, for the purpose of actual or contemplated legal proceedings.

19(7) For the purposes of subsection (1)(a) a person shall be treated as having committed an offence under one of sections 15 to 18 if–

(a) he has taken an action or been in possession of a thing, and

(b) he would have committed an offence under one of those sections if he had been in the United Kingdom at the time when he took the action or was in possession of the thing.

19(7A) The reference to a business in the regulated sector must be construed in accordance with *Schedule 3A*.

19(7B) The reference to a constable includes a reference to a National Crime Agency officer authorised for the purposes of this section by the Director General of that Agency.

19(8) A person guilty of an offence under this section shall be liable–

(a) on conviction on indictment, to imprisonment for a term not exceeding five years, to a fine or to both, or

(b) on summary conviction, to imprisonment for a term not exceeding six months, or to a fine not exceeding the statutory maximum or to both.

Commencement Date – S. 19 brought into force on 19 February 2001 by the Terrorism Act 2000 (Commencement No. 3) Order 2001 (SI 2001/421, art. 2).

History – S. 19(1A) inserted by the Anti-Terrorism, Crime and Security Act 2001, s. 3 and Sch. 2, para. 5(3), with effect from 20 December 2001 (by virtue of SI 2001/4019, art. 2).
S. 19(7A) inserted by the Anti-Terrorism, Crime and Security Act 2001, s. 3 and Sch. 2, para. 5(4), with effect from 20 December 2001, by virtue of SI 2001/4019, art. 2.
In s. 19(7B), the words "National Crime Agency officer" substituted for the words "member of the staff of the Serious Organised Crime Agency" by Crime and Courts Act 2013, s. 15(3) and Sch. 8, para. 68, with effect from 7 October 2013 (SI 2013/1682, art. 3).
In s. 19(7B) the words "member of the staff of the Serious Organised Crime Agency" substituted for the word "person" and the words "that Agency" substituted for the words "the National Criminal Intelligence Service" by SOCPA 2005, Sch. 4, para. 126, with effect from 1 April 2006 (by virtue of SI 2006/378, art. 4(1) and Schedule).
S. 19(7B) inserted by the Anti-Terrorism, Crime and Security Act 2001, s. 3 and Sch. 2, para. 5(4), with effect from 20 December 2001, by virtue of SI 2001/4019, art. 2.

Cross references – SI 2001/192, reg. 4: disapplication of s. 19 in respect of list of persons who are, in the opinion of the Secretary of State, performing or connected with the performance of regulatory, supervisory, investigative or registration functions of a public nature.

20 Disclosure of information: permission

20(1) A person may disclose to a constable–

(a) a suspicion or belief that any money or other property is terrorist property or is derived from terrorist property;

(b) any matter on which the suspicion or belief is based.

20(2) A person may make a disclosure to a constable in the circumstances mentioned in section 19(1) and (2).

20(3) Subsections (1) and (2) shall have effect notwithstanding any restriction on the disclosure of information imposed by statute or otherwise.

20(4) Where–

(a) a person is in employment, and

(b) his employer has established a procedure for the making of disclosures of the kinds mentioned in subsection (1) and section 19(2),

subsections (1) and (2) shall have effect in relation to that person as if any reference to disclosure to a constable included a reference to disclosure in accordance with the procedure.

20(5) References to a constable include references to a National Crime Agency officer authorised for the purposes of this section by the Director General of that Agency.

Commencement Date – S. 20 brought into force on 19 February 2001 by the Terrorism Act 2000 (Commencement No. 3) Order 2001 (SI 2001/421, art. 2).

History – In s. 20(5), the words "National Crime Agency officer" substituted for the words "member of the staff of the Serious Organised Crime Agency" by Crime and Courts Act 2013, s. 15(3) and Sch. 8, para. 69, with effect from 7 October 2013 (SI 2013/1682, art. 3).
In s. 20(5) the words "member of the staff of the Serious Organised Crime Agency" substituted for the word "person" and the words "that Agency" substituted for the words "the National Criminal Intelligence Service" by SOCPA 2005, Sch. 4, para. 127, with effect from 1 April 2006 (by virtue of SI 2006/378, art. 4(1) and Schedule).
S. 20(5) inserted by the Anti-Terrorism, Crime and Security Act 2001, s. 3 and Sch. 2, para. 5(5), with effect from 20 December 2001 (by virtue of SI 2001/4019, art. 2).

21 Cooperation with police

21(1) A person does not commit an offence under any of sections 15 to 18 if he is acting with the express consent of a constable.

21(2) Subject to subsections (3) and (4), a person does not commit an offence under any of sections 15 to 18 by involvement in a transaction or arrangement relating to money or other property if he discloses to a constable–

(a) his suspicion or belief that the money or other property is terrorist property, and

(b) the information on which his suspicion or belief is based.

21(3) Subsection (2) applies only where a person makes a disclosure–

(a) after he becomes concerned in the transaction concerned,

(b) on his own initiative, and

(c) as soon as is reasonably practicable.

21(4) Subsection (2) does not apply to a person if–

(a) a constable forbids him to continue his involvement in the transaction or arrangement to which the disclosure relates, and

(b) he continues his involvement.

21(5) It is a defence for a person charged with an offence under any of sections 15(2) and (3) and 16 to 18 to prove that–

(a) he intended to make a disclosure of the kind mentioned in subsections (2) and (3), and

(b) there is reasonable excuse for his failure to do so.

21(6) Where–

(a) a person is in employment, and

(b) his employer has established a procedure for the making of disclosures of the same kind as may be made to a constable under subsection (2),

this section shall have effect in relation to that person as if any reference to disclosure to a constable included a reference to disclosure in accordance with the procedure.

21(7) A reference in this section to a transaction or arrangement relating to money or other property includes a reference to use or possession.

Commencement Date – S. 21 brought into force on 19 February 2001 by the Terrorism Act 2000 (Commencement No. 3) Order 2001 (SI 2001/421, art. 2).

21ZA Arrangements with prior consent

21ZA(1) A person does not commit an offence under any of sections 15 to 18 by involvement in a transaction or an arrangement relating to money or other property if, before becoming involved, the person–

(a) discloses to an authorised officer the person's suspicion or belief that the money or other property is terrorist property and the information on which the suspicion or belief is based, and

(b) has the authorised officer's consent to becoming involved in the transaction or arrangement.

21ZA(2) A person is treated as having an authorised officer's consent if before the end of the notice period the person does not receive notice from an authorised officer that consent is refused.

21ZA(3) The notice period is the period of 7 working days starting with the first working day after the person makes the disclosure.

21ZA(4) A working day is a day other than a Saturday, a Sunday, Christmas Day, Good Friday or a day that is a bank holiday under the Banking and Financial Dealings Act 1971 (c.80) in the part of the United Kingdom in which the person is when making the disclosure.

21ZA(5) In this section **"authorised officer"** means a National Crime Agency officer authorised for the purposes of this section by the Director General of that Agency.

21ZA(6) The reference in this section to a transaction or arrangement relating to money or other property includes a reference to use or possession.

History – In s. 21ZA(5), the words "National Crime Agency officer" substituted for the words "member of the staff of the Serious Organised Crime Agency" by Crime and Courts Act 2013, s. 15(3) and Sch. 8, para. 70, with effect from 7 October 2013 (SI 2013/1682, art. 3).

S. 21ZA inserted by SI 2007/3398, reg. 2 and Sch. 1, para. 2, with effect from 26 December 2007.

21ZB Disclosure after entering into arrangements

21ZB(1) A person does not commit an offence under any of sections 15 to 18 by involvement in a transaction or an arrangement relating to money or other property if, after becoming involved, the person discloses to an authorised officer–

(a) the person's suspicion or belief that the money or other property is terrorist property, and

(b) the information on which the suspicion or belief is based.

21ZB(2) This section applies only where–

(a) there is a reasonable excuse for the person's failure to make the disclosure before becoming involved in the transaction or arrangement, and

(b) the disclosure is made on the person's own initiative and as soon as it is reasonably practicable for the person to make it.

21ZB(3) This section does not apply to a person if–

(a) an authorised officer forbids the person to continue involvement in the transaction or arrangement to which the disclosure relates, and

(b) the person continues that involvement.

21ZB(4) In this section **"authorised officer"** means a National Crime Agency officer authorised for the purposes of this section by the Director General of that Agency.

21ZB(5) The reference in this section to a transaction or arrangement relating to money or other property includes a reference to use or possession.

History – In s. 21ZB(4), the words "National Crime Agency officer" substituted for the words "member of the staff of the Serious Organised Crime Agency" by Crime and Courts Act 2013, s. 15(3) and Sch. 8, para. 71, with effect from 7 October 2013 (SI 2013/1682, art. 3).

S. 21ZB inserted by SI 2007/3398, reg. 2 and Sch. 1, para. 2, with effect from 26 December 2007.

21ZC Reasonable excuse for failure to disclose

21ZC It is a defence for a person charged with an offence under any of sections 15 to 18 to prove that–

(a) the person intended to make a disclosure of the kind mentioned in section 21ZA or 21ZB, and

(b) there is a reasonable excuse for the person's failure to do so.

History – S. 21ZC inserted by SI 2007/3398, reg. 2 and Sch. 1, para. 2, with effect from 26 December 2007.

21A Failure to disclose: regulated sector

21A(1) A person commits an offence if each of the following three conditions is satisfied.

21A(2) The first condition is that he–

(a) knows or suspects, or

(b) has reasonable grounds for knowing or suspecting,

that another person has committed or attempted to commit an offence under any of sections 15 to 18.

21A(3) The second condition is that the information or other matter–

(a) on which his knowledge or suspicion is based, or

(b) which gives reasonable grounds for such knowledge or suspicion,

came to him in the course of a business in the regulated sector.

21A(4) The third condition is that he does not disclose the information or other matter to a constable or a nominated officer as soon as is practicable after it comes to him.

21A(5) But a person does not commit an offence under this section if–

(a) he has a reasonable excuse for not disclosing the information or other matter;

(b) he is a professional legal adviser or relevant professional adviser and the information or other matter came to him in privileged circumstances; or

(c) subsection (5A) applies to him.

21A(5A) This subsection applies to a person if–

(a) the person is employed by, or is in partnership with, a professional legal adviser or relevant professional adviser to provide the adviser with assistance or support,

(b) the information or other matter comes to the person in connection with the provision of such assistance or support, and

(c) the information or other matter came to the adviser in privileged circumstances.

21A(6) In deciding whether a person committed an offence under this section the court must consider whether he followed any relevant guidance which was at the time concerned–

(a) issued by a supervisory authority or any other appropriate body,

(b) approved by the Treasury, and

(c) published in a manner it approved as appropriate in its opinion to bring the guidance to the attention of persons likely to be affected by it.

21A(7) A disclosure to a nominated officer is a disclosure which–

(a) is made to a person nominated by the alleged offender's employer to receive disclosures under this section, and

(b) is made in the course of the alleged offender's employment and in accordance with the procedure established by the employer for the purpose.

21A(8) Information or other matter comes to a professional legal adviser or relevant professional adviser in privileged circumstances if it is communicated or given to him–

(a) by (or by a representative of) a client of his in connection with the giving by the adviser of legal advice to the client,

(b) by (or by a representative of) a person seeking legal advice from the adviser, or

(c) by a person in connection with legal proceedings or contemplated legal proceedings.

21A(9) But subsection (8) does not apply to information or other matter which is communicated or given with a view to furthering a criminal purpose.

21A(10) Schedule 3A has effect for the purpose of determining what is–

(a) a business in the regulated sector;

(b) a supervisory authority.

21A(11) For the purposes of subsection (2) a person is to be taken to have committed an offence there mentioned if–

(a) he has taken an action or been in possession of a thing, and

(b) he would have committed the offence if he had been in the United Kingdom at the time when he took the action or was in possession of the thing.

21A(12) A person guilty of an offence under this section is liable–

(a) on conviction on indictment, to imprisonment for a term not exceeding five years or to a fine or to both;

(b) on summary conviction, to imprisonment for a term not exceeding six months or to a fine not exceeding the statutory maximum or to both.

21A(13) An appropriate body is any body which regulates or is representative of any trade, profession, business or employment carried on by the alleged offender.

21A(14) The reference to a constable includes a reference to a National Crime Agency officer authorised for the purposes of this section by the Director General of that Agency.

21A(15) In this section **"relevant professional adviser"** means an accountant, auditor or tax adviser who is a member of a professional body which is established for accountants, auditors or tax advisers (as the case may be) and which makes provision for–

(a) testing the competence of those seeking admission to membership of such a body as a condition for such admission; and

(b) imposing and maintaining professional and ethical standards for its members, as well as imposing sanctions for non-compliance with those standards.

History – In s. 21A(2), the words "or attempted to commit" inserted by SI 2007/3398, reg. 3(2), with effect from 26 December 2007.
In s. 21A(5), the words "or relevant professional adviser" and para. (c) inserted by SI 2007/3398, reg. 3(3), with effect from 26 December 2007.
S. 21A(5A) inserted by SI 2007/3398, reg. 3(4), with effect from 26 December 2007.
In s. 21A(8), the words "or relevant professional adviser" inserted by SI 2007/3398, reg. 3(5), with effect from 26 December 2007.
In s. 21A(14), the words "National Crime Agency officer" substituted for the words "member of the staff of the Serious Organised Crime Agency" by Crime and Courts Act 2013, s. 15(3) and Sch. 8, para. 72, with effect from 7 October 2013 (SI 2013/1682, art. 3).
In s. 21A(14) the words "member of the staff of the Serious Organised Crime Agency" substituted for the word "person" and the words "that Agency" substituted for the words "the National Criminal Intelligence Service" by SOCPA 2005, Sch. 4, para. 128, with effect from 1 April 2006 (by virtue of SI 2006/378, art. 4(1) and Schedule).
S. 21A(15) inserted by SI 2007/3398, reg. 3(6), with effect from 26 December 2007.
S. 21A inserted by the Anti-Terrorism, Crime and Security Act 2001, s. 3 and Sch. 2, para. 5(2), with effect from 20 December 2001, by virtue of SI 2001/4019, art. 2.

21B Protected disclosures

21B(1) A disclosure which satisfies the following three conditions is not to be taken to breach any restriction on the disclosure of information (however imposed).

21B(2) The first condition is that the information or other matter disclosed came to the person making the disclosure (the discloser) in the course of a business in the regulated sector.

21B(3) The second condition is that the information or other matter–

(a) causes the discloser to know or suspect, or

(b) gives him reasonable grounds for knowing or suspecting,

that another person has committed or attempted to commit an offence under any of sections 15 to 18.

21B(4) The third condition is that the disclosure is made to a constable or a nominated officer as soon as is practicable after the information or other matter comes to the discloser.

21B(5) A disclosure to a nominated officer is a disclosure which–

(a) is made to a person nominated by the discloser's employer to receive disclosures under this section, and

(b) is made in the course of the discloser's employment and in accordance with the procedure established by the employer for the purpose.

21B(6) The reference to a business in the regulated sector must be construed in accordance with Schedule 3A.

21B(7) The reference to a constable includes a reference to a National Crime Agency officer authorised for the purposes of this section by the Director General of that Agency.

History – In s. 21B(3), the words "or attempted to commit" inserted by SI 2007/3398, reg. 4, with effect from 26 December 2007.
In s. 21B(7), the words "National Crime Agency officer" substituted for the words "member of the staff of the Serious Organised Crime Agency" by Crime and Courts Act 2013, s. 15(3) and Sch. 8, para. 73, with effect from 7 October 2013 (SI 2013/1682, art. 3).

In s. 21B(7) the words "member of the staff of the Serious Organised Crime Agency" substituted for the word "person" and the words "that Agency" substituted for the words "the National Criminal Intelligence Service" by SOCPA 2005, Sch 4, para. 129, with effect from 1 April 2006 (by virtue of SI 2006/378, art. 4(1) and Schedule).
S. 21B inserted by the Anti-Terrorism, Crime and Security Act 2001, s. 3 and Sch. 2, para. 5(2), with effect from 20 December 2001, by virtue of SI 2001/4019, art. 2.

21C Disclosures to the National Crime Agency

History – In heading to s. 21C, the words "the National Crime Agency" substituted for the words "SOCA" by Crime and Courts Act 2013, s. 15(3) and Sch. 8, para. 74(2), with effect from 7 October 2013 (SI 2013/1682, art. 3).

21C(1) Where a disclosure is made under a provision of this Part to a constable, the constable must disclose it in full as soon as practicable after it has been made to a National Crime Agency officer authorised for the purposes of that provision by the Director General of that Agency.

21C(2) Where a disclosure is made under section 21 (cooperation with police) to a constable, the constable must disclose it in full as soon as practicable after it has been made to a National Crime Agency officer authorised for the purposes of this subsection by the Director General of that Agency.

History – In s. 21C(1) and (2), the words "National Crime Agency officer" substituted for the words "member of the staff of the Serious Organised Crime Agency" by Crime and Courts Act 2013, s. 15(3) and Sch. 8, para. 74(3), with effect from 7 October 2013 (SI 2013/1682, art. 3).
S. 21C inserted by SI 2007/3398, reg. 2 and Sch. 1, para. 5, with effect from 26 December 2007.

21D Tipping off: regulated sector

21D(1) A person commits an offence if–

(a) the person discloses any matter within subsection (2);

(b) the disclosure is likely to prejudice any investigation that might be conducted following the disclosure referred to in that subsection; and

(c) the information on which the disclosure is based came to the person in the course of a business in the regulated sector.

21D(2) The matters are that the person or another person has made a disclosure under a provision of this Part–

(a) to a constable,

(b) in accordance with a procedure established by that person's employer for the making of disclosures under that provision,

(c) to a nominated officer, or

(d) to a National Crime Agency officer authorised for the purposes of that provision by the Director General of that Agency,

of information that came to that person in the course of a business in the regulated sector.

21D(3) A person commits an offence if–

(a) the person discloses that an investigation into allegations that an offence under this Part has been committed is being contemplated or is being carried out;

(b) the disclosure is likely to prejudice that investigation; and

(c) the information on which the disclosure is based came to the person in the course of a business in the regulated sector.

21D(4) A person guilty of an offence under this section is liable–

(a) on summary conviction to imprisonment for a term not exceeding three months, or to a fine not exceeding level 5 on the standard scale, or to both;

(b) on conviction on indictment to imprisonment for a term not exceeding two years, or to a fine, or to both.

21D(5) This section is subject to–

(a) section 21E (disclosures within an undertaking or group etc),

(b) section 21F (other permitted disclosures between institutions etc), and

(c) section 21G (other permitted disclosures etc).

History – In s. 21D(2)(d), the words "National Crime Agency officer" substituted for the words "member of the staff of the Serious Organised Crime Agency" by Crime and Courts Act 2013, s. 15(3) and Sch. 8, para. 75, with effect from 7 October 2013 (SI 2013/1682, art. 3).
S. 21D inserted by SI 2007/3398, reg. 2 and Sch. 1, para. 5, with effect from 26 December 2007.

21E Disclosures within an undertaking or group etc

21E(1) An employee, officer or partner of an undertaking does not commit an offence under section 21D if the disclosure is to an employee, officer or partner of the same undertaking.

21E(2) A person does not commit an offence under section 21D in respect of a disclosure by a credit institution or a financial institution if–

(a) the disclosure is to a credit institution or a financial institution,

(b) the institution to whom the disclosure is made is situated in an EEA State or in a country or territory imposing equivalent money laundering requirements, and

(c) both the institution making the disclosure and the institution to whom it is made belong to the same group.

21E(3) In subsection (2) **"group"** has the same meaning as in Directive 2002/87/EC of the European Parliament and of the Council of 16th December 2002 on the supplementary supervision of credit institutions, insurance undertakings and investment firms in a financial conglomerate.

21E(4) A professional legal adviser or a relevant professional adviser does not commit an offence under section 21D if–

(a) the disclosure is to a professional legal adviser or a relevant professional adviser,

(b) both the person making the disclosure and the person to whom it is made carry on business in an EEA state or in a country or territory imposing equivalent money laundering requirements, and

(c) those persons perform their professional activities within different undertakings that share common ownership, management or control.

History – S. 21E inserted by SI 2007/3398, reg. 2 and Sch. 1, para. 5, with effect from 26 December 2007.

21F Other permitted disclosures between institutions etc

21F(1) This section applies to a disclosure–

(a) by a credit institution to another credit institution,

(b) by a financial institution to another financial institution,

(c) by a professional legal adviser to another professional legal adviser, or

(d) by a relevant professional adviser of a particular kind to another relevant professional adviser of the same kind.

21F(2) A person does not commit an offence under section 21D in respect of a disclosure to which this section applies if–

(a) the disclosure relates to–

(i) a client or former client of the institution or adviser making the disclosure and the institution or adviser to whom it is made,

(ii) a transaction involving them both, or

(iii) the provision of a service involving them both;

(b) the disclosure is for the purpose only of preventing an offence under this Part of this Act;

(c) the institution or adviser to whom the disclosure is made is situated in an EEA State or in a country or territory imposing equivalent money laundering requirements; and

(d) the institution or adviser making the disclosure and the institution or adviser to whom it is made are subject to equivalent duties of professional confidentiality and the protection of personal data (within the meaning of section 1 of the Data Protection Act 1998).

History – S. 21F inserted by SI 2007/3398, reg. 2 and Sch. 1, para. 5, with effect from 26 December 2007.

21G Other permitted disclosures etc

21G(1) A person does not commit an offence under section 21D if the disclosure is–

(a) to the authority that is the supervisory authority for that person by virtue of the Money Laundering Regulations 2007 (S.I. 2007/2157); or

(b) for the purpose of–

(i) the detection, investigation or prosecution of a criminal offence (whether in the United Kingdom or elsewhere),

(ii) an investigation under the Proceeds of Crime Act 2002, or

(iii) the enforcement of any order of a court under that Act.

21G(2) A professional legal adviser or a relevant professional adviser does not commit an offence under section 21D if the disclosure–

(a) is to the adviser's client, and

(b) is made for the purpose of dissuading the client from engaging in conduct amounting to an offence.

21G(3) A person does not commit an offence under section 21D(1) if the person does not know or suspect that the disclosure is likely to have the effect mentioned in section 21D(1)(b).

21G(4) A person does not commit an offence under section 21D(3) if the person does not know or suspect that the disclosure is likely to have the effect mentioned in section 21D(3)(b).

History – S. 21G inserted by SI 2007/3398, reg. 2 and Sch. 1, para. 5, with effect from 26 December 2007.

21H Interpretation of sections 21D to 21G

21H(1) The references in sections 21D to 21G–

(a) to a business in the regulated sector, and

(b) to a supervisory authority,

are to be construed in accordance with Schedule 3A.

21H(2) In those sections–

"credit institution" has the same meaning as in Schedule 3A;

"financial institution" means an undertaking that carries on a business in the regulated sector by virtue of any of paragraphs (b) to (i) of paragraph 1(1) of that Schedule.

21H(3) References in those sections to a disclosure by or to a credit institution or a financial institution include disclosure by or to an employee, officer or partner of the institution acting on its behalf.

21H(4) For the purposes of those sections a country or territory imposes "equivalent money laundering requirements" if it imposes requirements equivalent to those laid down in Directive 2005/60/EC of the European Parliament and of the Council of 26th October 2005 on the prevention of the use of the financial system for the purpose of money laundering and terrorist financing.

21H(5) In those sections **"relevant professional adviser"** means an accountant, auditor or tax adviser who is a member of a professional body which is established for accountants, auditors or tax advisers (as the case may be) and which makes provision for–

(a) testing the competence of those seeking admission to membership of such a body as a condition for such admission; and

(b) imposing and maintaining professional and ethical standards for its members, as well as imposing sanctions for non-compliance with those standards.

History – S. 21H inserted by SI 2007/3398, reg. 2 and Sch. 1, para. 5, with effect from 26 December 2007.

22 Penalties

22 A person guilty of an offence under any of sections 15 to 18 shall be liable–

(a) on conviction on indictment, to imprisonment for a term not exceeding 14 years, to a fine or to both, or

(b) on summary conviction, to imprisonment for a term not exceeding six months, to a fine not exceeding the statutory maximum or to both.

Commencement Date – S. 22 brought into force on 19 February 2001 by the Terrorism Act 2000 (Commencement No. 3) Order 2001 (SI 2001/421, art. 2).

23 Forfeiture

23(1) The court by or before which a person is convicted of an offence under any of sections 15 to 18 may make a forfeiture order in accordance with the provisions of this section.

23(2) Where a person is convicted of an offence under section 15(1) or (2) or 16 the court may order the forfeiture of any money or other property–

(a) which, at the time of the offence, he had in his possession or under his control, and

(b) which, at that time, he intended should be used, or had reasonable cause to suspect might be used, for the purposes of terrorism.

23(3) Where a person is convicted of an offence under section 15(3) the court may order the forfeiture of any money or other property–

(a) which, at the time of the offence, he had in his possession or under his control, and

(b) which, at that time, he knew or had reasonable cause to suspect would or might be used for the purposes of terrorism.

23(4) Where a person is convicted of an offence under section 17 the court may order the forfeiture of the money or other property–

(a) to which the arrangement in question related, and

(b) which, at the time of the offence, he knew or had reasonable cause to suspect would or might be used for the purposes of terrorism.

23(5) Where a person is convicted of an offence under section 18 the court may order the forfeiture of the money or other property to which the arrangement in question related.

23(5A) Where a person is convicted of an offence under section 17A the court may order the forfeiture of the amount paid under, or purportedly under, the insurance contract.

23(6) Where a person is convicted of an offence under any of sections 15 to 18, the court may order the forfeiture of any money or other property which wholly or partly, and directly or indirectly, is received by any person as a payment or other reward in connection with the commission of the offence.

23(7) Where a person other than the convicted person claims to be the owner of or otherwise interested in anything which can be forfeited by an order under this section, the court shall give him an opportunity to be heard before making an order.

23(8) A court in Scotland shall not make an order under this section except on the application of the prosecutor–

(a) in proceedings on indictment, when he moves for sentence, and

(b) in summary proceedings, before the court convicts the accused,

and for the purposes of any appeal or review, an order under this section made by a court in Scotland is a sentence.

23(9) Schedule 4 (which makes further provision in relation to forfeiture orders under this section) shall have effect.

Commencement Date – S. 23 brought into force for remaining purposes on 19 February 2001 by the Terrorism Act 2000 (Commencement No. 3) Order 2001 (SI 2001/421, art. 2).

S. 23(9) brought into force for certain purposes, in relation to specified paragraphs within Sch. 4, on 31 October 2000 by the Terrorism Act 2000 (Commencement No. 2) Order 2000 (SI 2000/2944, art. 2).

History – S. 23(5A) inserted by Counter-Terrorism and Security Act 2015, s. 42(2), with effect from 12 February 2015.

SCHEDULES

SCHEDULE 3A – REGULATED SECTOR AND SUPERVISORY AUTHORITIES

Part 1 – Regulated Sector

History – Pt. 1 substituted by SI 2007/3288, art. 2, with effect from 15 December 2007.

BUSINESS IN THE REGULATED SECTOR

1(1) A business is in the regulated sector to the extent that it consists of–

(a) the acceptance by a credit institution of deposits or other repayable funds from the public, or the granting by a credit institution of credits for its own account;

(b) the carrying on of one or more of the activities listed in points 2 to 12, 14 and 15 of Annex 1 to the Capital Requirements Directive by an undertaking other than–

  (i) a credit institution; or

  (ii) an undertaking whose only listed activity is trading for own account in one or more of the products listed in point 7 of Annex 1 to the Capital Requirements Directive and which does not act on behalf of a customer (that is, a third party which is not a member of the same group as the undertaking);

(c) the carrying on of activities covered by the Life Assurance Consolidation Directive by an insurance company authorised in accordance with that Directive;

(d) the provision of investment services or the performance of investment activities by a person (other than a person falling within Article 2 of the Markets in Financial Instruments Directive) whose regular occupation or business is the provision to other persons of an investment service or the performance of an investment activity on a professional basis;

(e) the marketing or other offering of units or shares by a collective investment undertaking;

(f) the activities of an insurance intermediary as defined in Article 2(5) of the Insurance Mediation Directive, other than a tied insurance intermediary as mentioned in Article 2(7) of that Directive, in respect of contracts of long-term insurance within the meaning given by article 3(1) of, and Part II of Schedule 1 to, the Financial Services and Markets Act 2000 (Regulated Activities) Order 2001;

(g) the carrying on of any of the activities mentioned in paragraphs (b) to (f) by a branch located in an EEA State of a person referred to in those paragraphs (or of an equivalent person in any other State), wherever its head office is located;

(h) the activities of the National Savings Bank;

(i) any activity carried on for the purpose of raising money authorised to be raised under the National Loans Act 1968 under the auspices of the Director of Savings;

(j) the provision of audit services by a person who is eligible for appointment as a company auditor under section 25 of the Companies Act 1989 (eligibility for appointment) or article 28 of the Companies (Northern Ireland) Order 1990;

(k) the activities of a person appointed to act as an insolvency practitioner within the meaning of section 388 of the Insolvency Act 1986 (meaning of "act as insolvency practitioner") or article 3 of the Insolvency (Northern Ireland) Order 1989;

(l) the provision to other persons of accountancy services by a firm or sole practitioner who by way of business provides such services to other persons;

(m) the provision of advice about the tax affairs of other persons by a firm or sole practitioner who by way of business provides advice about the tax affairs of other persons;

(n) the participation in financial or real property transactions concerning–

(i) the buying and selling of real property (or, in Scotland, heritable property) or business entities;

(ii) the managing of client money, securities or other assets;

(iii) the opening or management of bank, savings or securities accounts;

(iv) the organisation of contributions necessary for the creation, operation or management of companies; or

(v) the creation, operation or management of trusts, companies or similar structures,

by a firm or sole practitioner who by way of business provides legal or notarial services to other persons;

(o) the provision to other persons by way of business by a firm or sole practitioner of any of the services mentioned in sub-paragraph (4);

(p) the carrying on of estate agency work by a firm or a sole practitioner who carries on, or whose employees carry on, such work;

(q) the trading in goods (including dealing as an auctioneer) whenever a transaction involves the receipt of a payment or payments in cash of at least 15,000 euros in total, whether the transaction is executed in a single operation or in several operations which appear to be linked, by a firm or sole trader who by way of business trades in goods;

(r) operating a casino under a casino operating licence (within the meaning given by section 65(2) of the Gambling Act 2005 (nature of licence)).

1(2) For the purposes of sub-paragraph (1)(a) and (b) **"credit institution"** means–

(a) a credit institution as defined in Article 4(1)(1) of the Capital Requirements Regulation; or

(b) a branch (within the meaning of Article 4(1)(17) of that Regulation) located in an EEA state of an institution falling within paragraph (a) (or of an equivalent institution in any other State) wherever its head office is located.

1(3) For the purposes of sub-paragraph (1)(n) a person participates in a transaction by assisting in the planning or execution of the transaction or otherwise acting for or on behalf of a client in the transaction.

1(4) The services referred to in sub-paragraph (1)(o) are–

(a) forming companies or other legal persons;

(b) acting, or arranging for another person to act–

(i) as a director or secretary of a company;

(ii) as a partner of a partnership; or

(iii) in a similar position in relation to other legal persons;

(c) providing a registered office, business address, correspondence or administrative address or other related services for a company, partnership or any other legal person or arrangement;

(d) acting, or arranging for another person to act, as–

(i) a trustee of an express trust or similar legal arrangement; or

(ii) a nominee shareholder for a person other than a company whose securities are listed on a regulated market.

1(5) For the purposes of sub-paragraph (4)(d) **"regulated market"**–

(a) in relation to any EEA State, has the meaning given by point 14 of Article 4(1) of the Markets in Financial Instruments Directive; and

(b) in relation to any other State, means a regulated financial market which subjects companies whose securities are admitted to trading to disclosure obligations which are contained in international standards and are equivalent to the specified disclosure obligations.

1(6) For the purposes of sub-paragraph (5) "the specified disclosure obligations" means–

(a) disclosure requirements set out in Articles 17 and 19 of Regulation (EU) No 596/2014 of the European Parliament and of the Council of 16 April 2014 on market abuse (market abuse regulation);

(b) disclosure requirements consistent with Articles 3, 5, 7, 8, 10, 14 and 16 of Directive 2003/71/EC of the European Parliament and of the Council of 4 November 2003 on the prospectuses to be published when securities are offered to the public or admitted to trading;

(c) disclosure requirements consistent with Articles 4 to 6, 14, 16 to 19 and 30 of Directive 2004/109/EC of the European Parliament and of the Council of 15 December 2004 relating to the harmonisation of transparency requirements in relation to information about issuers whose securities are admitted to trading on a regulated market; or

(d) disclosure requirements consistent with EU legislation made under the provisions mentioned in paragraphs (a) to (c).

1(6A) For the purposes of sub-paragraph (1)(p) **"estate agency work"** is to be read in accordance with section 1 of the Estate Agents Act 1979 (estate agency work), but for those purposes references in that section to disposing of or acquiring an interest in land are (despite anything in section 2 of that Act) to be taken to include references to disposing of or acquiring an estate or interest in land outside the United Kingdom where that estate or interest is capable of being owned or held as a separate interest.

1(7) For the purposes of sub-paragraph (1)(j) and (l) to (q) **"firm"** means any entity, whether or not a legal person, that is not an individual and includes a body corporate and a partnership or other unincorporated association.

1(8) For the purposes of sub-paragraph (1)(q) **"cash"** means notes, coins or travellers' cheques in any currency.

History – In para. 1(1)(b) and (b)(ii), the words "Banking Consolidation Directive" in both places substituted by SI 2013/3115, reg. 40(2)(a), with effect from 1 January 2014.
In para. 1(1)(b), ", 14 and 15" substituted for "and 14" by SI 2011/99, reg. 79 and Sch. 4, para. 3(a)(i), with effect from 30 April 2011.
In para. 1(1)(p), the words "(within the meaning given by section 1 of the Estate Agents Act 1979 (estate agency work))" omitted by SI 2012/2299, art. 2(a), with effect from 1 October 2012.
In para. 1(2)(a), "Article 14(1)" substituted for "Article 14(1)(a)" by SI 2011/99, reg. 79 and Sch. 4, para. 3(a)(ii), with effect from 30 April 2011.
In para. 1(2)(a), the words "Article 4(1)(1) of the Capital Requirements Regulation" substituted for "Article 4(1) of the Banking Consolidation Directive" by SI 2013/3115, reg. 40(2)(b), with effect from 1 January 2014.
In para. 1(2)(b), the words "Article 4(1)(17) of that Regulation" substituted for "Article 4(3) of that Directive" by SI 2013/3115, reg. 40(2)(c), with effect from 1 January 2014.
Para. 1(6) substituted by SI 2016/680, reg. 12, with effect from 3 July 2016. Former para. 1(6) read as follows:
"**1(6)** For the purposes of sub-paragraph (5) "the specified disclosure obligations" means disclosure requirements consistent with–
(a) Article 6(1) to (4) of Directive 2003/6/EC of the European Parliament and of the Council of 28th January 2003 on insider dealing and market manipulation;
(b) Articles 3, 5, 7, 8, 10, 14 and 16 of Directive 2003/71/EC of the European Parliament and of the Council of 4th November 2003 on the prospectuses to be published when securities are offered to the public or admitted to trading;
(c) Articles 4 to 6, 14, 16 to 19 and 30 of Directive 2004/109/EC of the European Parliament and of the Council of 15th December 2004 relating to the harmonisation of transparency requirements in relation to information about issuers whose securities are admitted to trading on a regulated market; or
(d) Community legislation made under the provisions mentioned in paragraphs (a) to (c).".
Para. 1(6A) inserted by SI 2012/2299, art. 2(b), with effect from 1 October 2012.
Pt. 1 substituted by SI 2007/3288, art. 2, with effect from 15 December 2007.

EXCLUDED ACTIVITIES

2(1) A business is not in the regulated sector to the extent that it consists of–

(a) the issuing of withdrawable share capital within the limit set by section 24 of the Co–operative and Community Benefit Societies Act 2014 (maximum interest in a society's withdrawable shares), or the acceptance of deposits from the public within the limit set by section 67(2) of that Act (carrying on of banking by societies), by a society registered under that Act;

(b) the issuing of withdrawable share capital within the limit set by section 6 of the Industrial and Provident Societies Act (Northern Ireland) 1969 (maximum shareholding in society), or the acceptance of deposits from the public within the limit set by section 7(3) of that Act (carrying on of banking by societies), by a society registered under that Act;

(c) the carrying on of any activity in respect of which a person who is (or falls within a class of persons) specified in any of paragraphs 2 to 23, 25 to 38 or 40 to 49 of the Schedule to the Financial Services and Markets Act 2000 (Exemption) Order 2001 is exempt;

(d) the exercise of the functions specified in section 45 of the Financial Services Act 1986 (miscellaneous exemptions) by a person who was an exempted person for the purposes of that section immediately before its repeal;

(e) the engaging in financial activity which fulfils all of the conditions set out in paragraphs (a) to (g) of sub-paragraph (3) of this paragraph by a person whose main activity is that of a high value dealer; or

(f) the preparation of a home information pack (within the meaning of Part 5 of the Housing Act 2004 (home information packs)) or a document or information for inclusion in a home information pack.

2(2) For the purposes of sub-paragraph (1)(e) a **"high value dealer"** means a person mentioned in paragraph 1(1)(q) when carrying on the activities mentioned in that paragraph.

2(3) A business is not in the regulated sector to the extent that it consists of financial activity if–

(a) the person's total annual turnover in respect of the financial activity does not exceed £64,000;

(b) the financial activity is limited in relation to any customer to no more than one transaction exceeding 1,000 euros, whether the transaction is carried out in a single operation, or a series of operations which appear to be linked;

(c) the financial activity does not exceed 5% of the person's total annual turnover;

(d) the financial activity is ancillary to the person's main activity and directly related to that activity;

(e) the financial activity is not the transmission or remittance of money (or any representation of monetary value) by any means;

(f) the main activity of the person carrying on the financial activity is not an activity mentioned in paragraph 1(1)(a) to (p) or (r); and

(g) the financial activity is provided only to customers of the person's main activity and is not offered to the public.

2(4) A business is not in the regulated sector if it is carried on by–

(a) the Auditor General for Scotland;

(b) the Auditor General for Wales;

(c) the Bank of England;

(d) the Comptroller and Auditor General;

(e) the Comptroller and Auditor General for Northern Ireland;

(f) the Official Solicitor to the Supreme Court, when acting as trustee in his official capacity; or

(g) the Treasury Solicitor.

History – In s. 2(1)(a), the words "section 24 of the Co–operative and Community Benefit Societies Act 2014 (maximum interest in a society's withdrawable shares." substituted for the words "section 6 of the Industrial and Provident Societies Act 1965 (maximum shareholding in society)" and the words "section 67(2)" substituted for the words "section 7(3)" by the Co-operative and Community Societies Act 2014, s. 151 and Sch. 4, para. 73(2) and (3), with effect from 1 August 2014 (subject to the provisions of Sch. 5 and 6 of that Act).
Pt. 1 substituted by SI 2007/3288, art. 2, with effect from 15 December 2007.

INTERPRETATION

3(1) In this Part–

"the Capital Requirements Regulation" means Regulation (EU) No. 575/2013 of the European Parliament and of the Council

"the Insurance Mediation Directive" means directive 2002/92/EC of the European Parliament and of the Council of 9th December 2002 on insurance mediation;

"the Life Assurance Consolidation Directive" means directive 2002/83/EC of the European Parliament and of the Council of 5th November 2002 concerning life assurance; and

"the Markets in Financial Instruments Directive" means directive 2004/39/EC of the European Parliament and of the Council of 12th April 2004 on markets in financial instruments.

3(2) In this Part references to amounts in euros include references to equivalent amounts in another currency.

3(3) Terms used in this Part and in the Capital Requirements Regulation or the Markets in Financial Instruments Directive have the same meaning in this Part as in those Directives.

History – In para. 3(1), the definition of "the Banking Consolidation Directive" omitted by SI 2013/3115, reg. 40(2)(d)(i), with effect from 1 January 2014.
In para. 3(1), the definition of "the Capital Requirements Regulation" inserted by SI 2013/3115, reg. 40(2)(d)(ii), with effect from 1 January 2014.
In para. 3(1), in the definition of "the Banking Consolidation Directive", the words "as last amended by Directive 2009/111/EC" inserted by SI 2011/99, reg. 79 and Sch. 4, para. 3(a)(ii), with effect from 30 April 2011.
In para. 3(3), the words "Banking Consolidation Directive" substituted by SI 2013/3115, reg. 40(2)(e), with effect from 1 January 2014.
Pt. 1 substituted by SI 2007/3288, art. 2, with effect from 15 December 2007.

Part 2 – Supervisory Authorities

History – Pt. 2 substituted by SI 2007/3288, art. 2, with effect from 15 December 2007.

4(1) The following bodies are supervisory authorities–

(a) the Commissioners for Her Majesty's Revenue and Customs;

(b) the Department of Enterprise, Trade and Investment in Northern Ireland;

(c) the Financial Conduct Authority;

(d) the Gambling Commission;

(e) the Office of Fair Trading;

(ea) the Prudential Regulation Authority;

(f) the Secretary of State; and

(g) the professional bodies listed in sub-paragraph (2).

4(2) The professional bodies referred to in sub-paragraph (1)(g) are–

(a) the Association of Accounting Technicians;

(b) the Association of Chartered Certified Accountants;

(c) the Association of International Accountants;

(d) the Association of Taxation Technicians;

(e) the Chartered Institute of Management Accountants;

(f) the Chartered Institute of Public Finance and Accountancy;

(g) the Chartered Institute of Taxation;

(h) the Council for Licensed Conveyancers;

(i) the Faculty of Advocates;

(j) the Faculty Office of the Archbishop of Canterbury;

(k) the General Council of the Bar;

(l) the General Council of the Bar of Northern Ireland;

(m) the Insolvency Practitioners Association;

(n) the Institute of Certified Bookkeepers;

(o) the Institute of Chartered Accountants in England and Wales;

(p) the Institute of Chartered Accountants in Ireland;

(q) the Institute of Chartered Accountants of Scotland;

(r) the Institute of Financial Accountants;

(s) the International Association of Book-keepers;

(t) the Law Society;

(u) the Law Society for Northern Ireland; and

(v) the Law Society of Scotland.

History – Para. 4(1)(c) substituted by Financial Services Act 2012, s. 114(1) and Sch. 18, para. 87(2), with effect from 1 April 2013 (SI 2013/423).

Para. 4(1)(ea) inserted by Financial Services Act 2012, s. 114(1) and Sch. 18, para. 87(2), with effect from 1 April 2013 (SI 2013/423).

Pt. 2 substituted by SI 2007/3288, art. 2, with effect from 15 December 2007.

Part 3 – Power to Amend

5(1) The Treasury may by order amend Part 1 or 2 of this Schedule.

5(2) An order under sub-paragraph (1) must be made by statutory instrument subject to annulment in pursuance of a resolution of either House of Parliament.

History – Sch. 3A inserted by the Anti-Terrorism, Crime and Security Act 2001, s. 3 and Sch. 2, para. 5(6), with effect from 20 December 2001, by virtue of SI 2001/4019, art. 2.

Statutory instruments – SI 2012/2299: The Terrorism Act 2000 and Proceeds of Crime Act 2002 (Business in the Regulated Sector) (No.2) Order 2012, partly made under Sch. 3A, para. 5.

FINANCE ACT 2000

(2000 Chapter 17)

[*28th July 2000*]

ARRANGEMENT OF SECTIONS

PART III – INCOME TAX, CORPORATION TAX AND CAPITAL GAINS TAX

CHAPTER I – CHARGE AND RATES

INCOME TAX

CORPORATION TAX

CAPITAL GAINS TAX

CHAPTER II – OTHER PROVISIONS

GIVING TO CHARITY

EMPLOYEE SHARE OWNERSHIP

OTHER PROVISIONS ABOUT EMPLOYMENT

PENSION SCHEMES

PART III – INCOME TAX, CORPORATION TAX AND CAPITAL GAINS TAX

Chapter I – Charge And Rates

INCOME TAX

31 *Charge and rates for 2000–01*

31 [Repealed by ITA 2007, s. 1031 and Sch. 3, Pt. 1.]

History – S. 31 repealed by ITA 2007, s. 1031 and Sch. 3, Pt. 1, with effect from 6 April 2007.

32 Extension of starting rate to savings income of individuals

32(1) [Repealed by ITA 2007, s. 1031 and Sch. 3, Pt. 1.]

History – S. 32 repealed by ITA 2007, s. 1031 and Sch. 3, Pt. 1, with effect from 6 April 2007.

Notes – S. 32 rewritten as follows:
S. 32(2): ITA 2007, s. 13(1).
S. 32(3): ITA 2007, s. 13(1), 18(1), (2).

33 Deduction of income tax from foreign dividends

33 [Repealed by ITTOIA 2005, s. 884 and Sch. 3.]

History – S. 33 repealed by ITTOIA 2005, s. 884 and Sch. 3 effective for income tax purposes for 2005–06 onwards (ITTOIA 2005, s. 883(1)).

34 Children's tax credit

34(1) [Repealed by TCA 2002, s. 60 and Sch. 6.]

34(2) [Repealed by TCA 2002, s. 60 and Sch. 6.]

History – S. 34 repealed by TCA 2002, s. 60 and Sch. 6 with effect from 6 April 2003 by virtue of SI 2003/962, art. 2(3), Sch. 1.

CORPORATION TAX

35 Charge and main rate for financial year 2001

35 [Spent; set corporation tax rate for financial year 2001.]

36 Small companies' rate for financial year 2000

36 [Repealed by CTA 2010, s. 1181 and Sch. 3, Pt. 1.]

History – S. 36 repealed by CTA 2010, s. 1181 and Sch. 3, Pt. 1, with effect for accounting periods ending on or after 1 April 2010.

CAPITAL GAINS TAX

37 Application of starting rate to capital gains tax

37 [Omitted by FA 2008, s. 8 and Sch. 2, para. 21(e).]

History – S. 37 omitted by FA 2008, s. 8 and Sch. 2, para. 21(e), with effect for the tax year 2008–09 and subsequent tax years.

Chapter II – Other Provisions

GIVING TO CHARITY

38 Payroll deduction scheme

38 [Repealed by FA 2011, s. 91 and Sch. 26, para. 3(1).]

History – S. 38 repealed by FA 2011, s. 91 and Sch. 26, para. 3(1), with effect from 19 July 2011.

Notes – Former s. 38(5) and (7) were unnecessary and were not rewritten into the provisions of ITEPA 2003

39 Gift aid payments by individuals

39(1)–(6) [Repealed by ITA 2007, s. 1031 and Sch. 3, Pt. 1.]

39(7) [Repeals FA 1990, s. 25(12)(b), (e).]

39(8) [Omitted by FA 2009, s. 5 and Sch. 1, para. 6(k).

39(9) [Omitted by FA 2009, s. 5 and Sch. 1, para. 6(k).

39(10) This section has effect in relation to–

(a) gifts made on or after 6th April 2000 which are not covenanted payments; and

(b) covenanted payments falling to be made on or after that date;

and any regulations made under subsection (3) of section 25 of the Finance Act 1990 (as substituted by subsection (4) above) within three months of the passing of this Act may be so made as to apply to any payments in relation to which this section has effect.

History – S. 39(1)–(6) repealed by ITA 2007, s. 1031 and Sch. 3, Pt. 1, with effect from 6 April 2007.
S. 39(8) and (9) omitted by FA 2009, s. 5 and Sch. 1, para. 6(k), with effect for the tax year 2010–11 and subsequent tax years.

Notes – S. 39 rewritten as follows:
S. 39(2): ITA 2007, s. 416(1).
S. 39(3): ITA 2007, s. 416(8), 418(1), (2), 422(2), (3), (4), (5), 427(1), (2), (3), (4), 1025(2), (3), 1026.
S. 39(4): ITA 2007, s. 428(1), (2), (3).
S. 39(5): ITA 2007, s. 418(2), 419(1), (2), (3), (4), (5), (6), (7), (8).

S. 39(6): ITA 2007, s. 58(1), 414(1), (2), 423(1), (2), (4), (5), 424(1), (2), (3), (4), (5), (6), 425(2), (3), (4), (5), Sch. 1 para. 28, 536.

40 Gift aid payments by companies

40 [Repealed by CTA 2010, s. 1181 and Sch. 3, Pt. 1.]

History – S. 40 repealed by CTA 2010, s. 1181 and Sch. 3, Pt. 1, with effect for corporation tax purposes for accounting periods ending on or after 1 April 2010, and for income tax and capital gains tax purposes for the tax year 2010–11 and subsequent tax years.

41 Covenanted payments to charities

41(1) [Repealed by CTA 2010, s. 1181 and Sch. 3, Pt. 1.]

41(2) [Amends ICTA 1988, s. 347A.]

41(3) [Repealed by ITA 2007, s. 1031 and Sch. 3, Pt. 1.]

41(4) [Repealed by ITA 2007, s. 1031 and Sch. 3, Pt. 1.]

41(5) [Amends ICTA 1988, s. 505(6).]

41(6) [Repealed by ITTOIA 2005, s. 884 and Sch. 3 effective for income tax purposes for 2005–06 onwards (ITTOIA 2005, s. 883(1)).]

41(7) [Repeals FA 1989, s. 59.]

41(8) Where a deed of covenant executed by an individual before 6th April 2000 provides for the payment of specified amounts, any amount payable under the deed on or after that date shall be determined as if the individual were entitled to deduct tax from that amount at the basic rate.

41(9) This section shall have effect in relation to covenanted payments–

(a) falling to be made by individuals on or after 6th April 2000; or

(b) made by companies on or after 1st April 2000.

History – S. 41(1) repealed by CTA 2010, s. 1181 and Sch. 3, Pt. 1, with effect for corporation tax purposes for accounting periods ending on or after 1 April 2010, and for income tax and capital gains tax purposes for the tax year 2010–11 and subsequent tax years.
S. 41(3) and (4) repealed by ITA 2007, s. 1031 and Sch. 3, Pt. 1, with effect from 6 April 2007.

Notes – S. 41 rewritten as follows:
S. 41(3): ITA 2007, s. 899(5).
S. 41(4): ITA 2007, s. 899(5).

42 Millennium gift aid

42 [Repealed by FA 2011, s. 91 and Sch. 26, para. 2(2)(b).]

History – S. 42 repealed by FA 2011, s. 91 and Sch. 26, para. 2(2)(b), with effect from 19 July 2011.

43 Gifts of shares and securities to charities etc

43 [Repealed by CTA 2010, s. 1181 and Sch. 3, Pt. 1.]

History – S. 43 repealed by CTA 2010, s. 1181 and Sch. 3, Pt. 1, with effect for corporation tax purposes for accounting periods ending on or after 1 April 2010, and for income tax and capital gains tax purposes for the tax year 2010–11 and subsequent tax years.

44 Gifts to charity from certain trusts

44(1) [Omitted by ITTOIA 2005, s. 882(1) and Sch. 1, para. 512(2); and repealed by ITTOIA 2005, s. 884 and Sch. 3.]

44(2) [Omitted by ITTOIA 2005, s. 882(1) and Sch. 1, para. 512(2); and repealed by ITTOIA 2005, s. 884 and Sch. 3.]

44(3) [Omitted by ITTOIA 2005, s. 882(1) and Sch. 1, para. 512(2); and repealed by ITTOIA 2005, s. 884 and Sch. 3.]

44(4) [Effectively omitted by ITA 2007, s. 1027 and Sch. 1, para. 391.]

44(5) [Effectively omitted by ITA 2007, s. 1027 and Sch. 1, para. 391.]

44(5A) This section applies if–

(a) in a year of assessment qualifying income arises under a UK settlement,

(b) the qualifying income consists of charitable income and non-charitable income, and

(c) expenses of the trustees are to be used to reduce the charitable income for the purpose of calculating a beneficiary's liability to corporation tax.

44(5B) The amount of those expenses which can used for that purpose is limited to the amount allocated to the charitable income.

44(5C) The amount of the expenses allocated to the charitable income is determined by apportioning them rateably between the charitable income and the non-charitable income.

44(5D) In this section–

"charitable income" means income within section 628(1) or 630(1) of ITTOIA 2005,

"non-charitable income" means income which is not charitable income, and

"qualifying income" and **"UK settlement"** have the same meaning as in section 628 of ITTOIA 2005.

44(6) This section has effect in relation to qualifying income arising to a UK trust on or after 6th April 2000.

History – S. 44(1), (2) and (3) omitted by ITTOIA 2005, s. 882(1) and Sch. 1, para. 512(2); and repealed by ITTOIA 2005, s. 884 and Sch. 3 effective for income tax purposes for 2005–06 onwards (ITTOIA 2005, s. 883(1)).
S. 44(5A)–(5D) substituted for former s. 44(4) and (5) by ITA 2007, s. 1027 and Sch. 1, para. 391, with effect from 6 April 2007.
In former s. 44(4) the words "trust the trustees of which are resident in the United Kingdom (a "UK trust")" substituted for the former wording ("UK trust") and the words "section 628(1) or 630(1) of ITTOIA 2005" substituted for the former wording ("subsection (1) above") by ITTOIA 2005, s. 882(1) and Sch. 1, para. 512(3) effective for income tax purposes for 2005–06 onwards (ITTOIA 2005, s. 883(1)).
Former s. 44(5) substituted by ITTOIA 2005, s. 882(1) and Sch. 1, para. 512(4) effective for income tax purposes for 2005–06 onwards (ITTOIA 2005, s. 883(1)).

Notes – S. 44 rewritten as follows:
The rewritten income tax rules covering s. 44(1)–(3) can be principally found at ITTOIA 2005, s. 628 and s. 630.
S. 44(4): ITA 2007, Sch. 1, para. 560.
S. 44(5): ITA 2007, Sch. 1, para. 560.

45 Loans to charities

45 [Omitted by ITTOIA 2005, s. 882(1) and Sch. 1, para. 513 and repealed by ITTOIA 2005, s. 884 and Sch. 3.]

History – S. 45 omitted by ITTOIA 2005, s. 882(1) and Sch. 1, para. 513 and repealed by ITTOIA 2005, s. 884 and Sch. 3 effective for income tax purposes for 2005–06 onwards (ITTOIA 2005, s. 883(1)).

Notes – The rewritten income tax rules can be principally found at ITTOIA 2005, s. 620; 628 and 630.

46 Exemption for small trades etc.

46 [Omitted by CTA 2010, s. 1177 and Sch. 1, para. 309 and repealed by CTA 2010, s. 1181 and Sch. 3, Pt. 1.]

History – S. 46 omitted by CTA 2010, s. 1177 and Sch. 1, para. 309 and repealed by CTA 2010, s. 1181 and Sch. 3, Pt. 1 with effect for corporation tax purposes for accounting periods ending on or after 1 April 2010, and for income tax and capital gains tax purposes for the tax year 2010–11 and subsequent tax years.

Notes – S. 46 rewritten for income tax as follows:
S. 46(1): ITA 2007, s. 526(1), (2), (7), 527(1), 538(1).
S. 46(2): ITA 2007, s. 527(2).
S. 46(2A): ITA 2007, s. 527(2).
S. 46(3): ITA 2007, s. 526(4), (5), 527(4), (5), 528(1).
S. 46(4): ITA 2007, s. 528(6).
S. 46(6): ITA 2007, s. 526(3), 527(3), 528(2), (3), (4), (5).
S. 46 rewritten for corporation tax purposes as follows:
S. 46(1): CTA 2010, s. 480(1), (2), (6), (7), s. 481(1), (6).
S. 46(2): CTA 2010, s. 481(2).
S. 46(2A): CTA 2010, s. 481(2).
S. 46(3): s. 480(4), (5), s. 481(4), (5), s. 482(1).
S. 46(4): CTA 2010, s. 482(6).
S. 46(5): CTA 2010, s. 482(7).
S. 46(6): CTA 2010, s. 467, 480(3), 481(1), (3), 482(1), (2), (3), (4), (5).
S. 46(7): Spent commencement.

EMPLOYEE SHARE OWNERSHIP

47 Employee share ownership plans

47 [Repealed by ITEPA 2003, s. 724 and Sch. 8, Pt. 1.]

History – S. 47 repealed by ITEPA 2003, s. 724 and Sch. 8, Pt. 1 with effect for the year 2003-04 and subsequent tax years

Notes – S. 47 is unnecessary and has not been rewritten into the provisions of ITEPA 2003.

48 Relief for transfers to employee share ownership plans

48(1) [Inserts TCGA 1992, s. 236A.]

48(2) [Inserts TCGA 1992, Sch. 7C.]

49 Phasing out of approved profit sharing schemes

49(1) The Board shall not approve a profit sharing scheme under Schedule 9 to the Taxes Act 1988 (approval of share option schemes and profit sharing schemes) unless the application for approval is received by the Board before 6th April 2001.

49(2) For the purposes of subsection (1) an application for approval which is not accompanied by the particulars and evidence referred to in paragraph 1(2) of that Schedule is not regarded as received by the Board until the required particulars and evidence have been received by them.

49(3) [Amends ICTA 1988, s. 186(1).]

Cross references – ITEPA 2003, s. 418(3): In view of section 49, the following provisions continue in force and are not rewritten in ITEPA 2003:

- ICTA 1988, s. 186–187: APS schemes.
- ICTA 1988, Sch. 9: approval of share schemes (so far as relating to APS schemes).
- ICTA 1988, Sch. 10: further provisions about APS schemes.

50 Phasing out of relief for payments to trustees of profit sharing schemes

50 [Omitted by CTA 2009, s. 1322 and Sch. 1, para. 464 and repealed by CTA 2009, s. 1326 and Sch. 3, Pt. 1.]

History – S. 50 omitted by CTA 2009, s. 1322 and Sch. 1, para. 464 and repealed by CTA 2009, s. 1326 and Sch. 3, Pt. 1, with effect for corporation tax purposes for accounting periods ending on or after 1 April 2009, and for income tax and capital gains tax purposes for the tax year 2009–10 and subsequent tax years.

51 Approved profit sharing scheme: other awards of shares

51(1) [Inserts ICTA 1988, Sch. 9, para. 3(2)(f).]

51(2) [Inserts ICTA 1988, Sch. 9, para. 3(4)–(6).]

52 Approved profit sharing schemes: restriction on type of shares

52(1) Schedule 9 to the Taxes Act 1988 (share option schemes and profit sharing schemes) is amended in accordance with subsections (2) to (4).

52(2) [Amends ICTA 1988, Sch. 9, para. 9(1).]

52(3) [Inserts ICTA 1988, Sch. 9, para. 11A.]

52(4) In paragraph 12–

(a) [Amends ICTA 1988, Sch. 9, para. 12(1)(c).]

(b) [Inserts ICTA 1988, Sch. 9, para. 12(1A), (1B).]

52(5) Subsections (1) to (4) shall be deemed to have come into force on 21st March 2000.

52(6) Subsections (3) and (4) do not have effect in relation to shares acquired before 21st March 2000 by the trustees of a profit sharing scheme approved under Schedule 9 to the Taxes Act 1988.

53 Approved profit sharing schemes: loan arrangements

53(1) [Inserts ICTA 1988, Sch. 9, para. 2(2A), (2B).]

53(2) [Inserts ICTA 1988, Sch. 9, para. 3(2)(ca).]

53(3) This section shall be deemed to have come into force on 21st March 2000.

54 Employee share ownership trusts

54 No claim for relief under section 229(1) or (3) of the Taxation of Chargeable Gains Act 1992 (roll-over relief where disposal made to employee share ownership trust) may be made in relation to a disposal of shares, or an interest in shares, made on or after 6th April 2001.

55 Shares transferred from employee share ownership trust

55(1) Section 69 of the Finance Act 1989 (chargeable events in relation to employee share ownership trusts) is amended in accordance with subsections (2) to (5).

55(2) [Inserts FA 1989, s. 69(1)(e).]

55(3) [Inserts FA 1989, s. 69(3AA)–(3AD).]

55(4) [Amends FA 1989, s. 69(5).]

55(5) [Inserts FA 1989, s. 69(5A).]

55(6) [Inserts FA 1989, s. 70(4).]

56 Further provisions about share options

56 [Repealed by ITEPA 2003, s. 724 and Sch. 8, Pt. 1.]

History – S. 56 repealed by ITEPA 2003, s. 724 and Sch. 8, Pt. 1 with effect for the year 2003–04 and subsequent tax years.

Notes – S. 56 is unnecessary and has not been rewritten into the provisions of ITEPA 2003.

OTHER PROVISIONS ABOUT EMPLOYMENT

57 Benefits in kind: deregulatory amendments

57 [Repealed by ITEPA 2003, s. 724 and Sch. 8, Pt. 1.]

History – S. 57 repealed by ITEPA 2003, s. 724 and Sch. 8, Pt. 1 with effect for the year 2003–04 and subsequent tax years.
Notes – S. 57 is unnecessary and has not been rewritten into the provisions of ITEPA 2003.

58 Education and training

58 [Repealed by ITEPA 2003, s. 724 and Sch. 8, Pt. 1.]

History – S. 58 repealed by ITEPA 2003, s. 724 and Sch. 8, Pt. 1 with effect for the year 2003–04 and subsequent tax years.
Notes – S. 58 is unnecessary and has not been rewritten into the provisions of ITEPA 2003.

59 Cars available for private use

59 [Repealed by ITEPA 2003, s. 724 and Sch. 8, Pt. 1.]

History – S. 59 repealed by ITEPA 2003, s. 724 and Sch. 8, Pt. 1 with effect for the year 2003–04 and subsequent tax years.
Notes – S. 59 is unnecessary and has not been rewritten into the provisions of ITEPA 2003.

60 Provision of services through intermediary

60 [Repealed by ITEPA 2003, s. 724 and Sch. 8, Pt. 1.]

History – S. 60 repealed by ITEPA 2003, s. 724 and Sch. 8, Pt. 1 with effect for the year 2003–04 and subsequent tax years.
Notes – S. 60 is unnecessary and has not been rewritten into the provisions of ITEPA 2003.

PENSION SCHEMES

61 Occupational and personal pension schemes

61 [Repealed by FA 2004 s. 326, and Sch. 42, Pt. 3.]

History – S. 61 repealed by FA 2004, s. 326, and Sch. 42, Pt. 3 with effect from 6 April 2006 but subject to FA 2004, Sch. 36.

ENTERPRISE INCENTIVES

62 Enterprise management incentives

62 [Repealed by ITEPA 2003, s. 724 and Sch. 8, Pt. 1.]

History – S. 62 repealed by ITEPA 2003, s. 724 and Sch. 8, Pt. 1 with effect for the year 2003-04 and subsequent tax years.
Notes – S. 62 is unnecessary and has not been rewritten into the provisions of ITEPA 2003.

63 Corporate venturing scheme

63(1) Schedule 15 to this Act (which makes provision for the corporate venturing scheme) has effect.

63(2) Schedule 16 to this Act (which makes consequential amendments) has effect.

63(3) [Repealed by CTA 2010, s. 1181 and Sch. 3, Pt. 1.]

63(4) Subject to that, Schedules 15 and 16 apply in relation to shares issued on or after 1st April 2000 but before 1st April 2010.

History – S. 63(3) repealed by CTA 2010, s. 1181 and Sch. 3, Pt. 1, with effect for corporation tax purposes for accounting periods ending on or after 1 April 2010, and for income tax and capital gains tax purposes for the tax year 2010–11 and subsequent tax years. S. 63(3)(b) and the word "and" preceding it previously repealed by ITA 2007, s. 1031 and Sch. 3, Pt. 1, with effect from 6 April 2007.

64 Enterprise investment scheme: amendments

64 The provisions relating to the enterprise investment scheme are amended in accordance with Schedule 17 to this Act.

In that Schedule–

Part I makes amendments reducing various periods which apply in relation to the provisions which determine the reliefs under the scheme;

Part II makes amendments about qualifying companies;

Part III makes other minor amendments.

65 Venture capital trusts: amendments

65 The provisions relating to venture capital trusts are amended in accordance with Schedule 18 to this Act.

In that Schedule–

Part I makes amendments reducing various periods which apply in relation to the provisions which determine the reliefs;

History – In s. 65 the words "and Part II makes amendments about qualifying holdings" repealed by ITA 2007, s. 1031 and Sch. 3, Pt. 1, with effect from 6 April 2007.

66 Taper relief: taper for business assets

66 [Omitted by FA 2008, s. 8 and Sch. 2, para. 55(c).]

History – S. 66 omitted by FA 2008, s. 8 and Sch. 2, para. 55(c), with effect in relation to chargeable gains accruing or treated as accruing in the tax year 2008–09 or any subsequent tax year.

67 Taper relief: assets qualifying as business assets

67 [Omitted by FA 2008, s. 8 and Sch. 2, para. 55(c).]

History – S. 67 omitted by FA 2008, s. 8 and Sch. 2, para. 55(c), with effect in relation to chargeable gains accruing or treated as accruing in the tax year 2008–09 or any subsequent tax year.

Cross references – FA 2001, s. 78 and Sch. 25: amendments to the rules in TCGA 1992, Sch. A1, identifying "business assets" for the purposes of taper relief; these amendments are deemed to have effect as if they had been included with those made by FA 2000, s. 67, above.

RESEARCH AND DEVELOPMENT

68 Meaning of "research and development"

68(1) Schedule 19 to this Act (meaning of "research and development") has effect.

In that Schedule–

Part I contains a new definition of "research and development" for the purposes of the Tax Acts, and

Part II contains consequential amendments.

68(2) The amendments in Part II of that Schedule have effect–

(a) for the purposes of income tax and capital gains tax, in relation to the year 2000–01 and subsequent years of assessment, and

(b) for the purposes of corporation tax, for accounting periods ending on or after 1st April 2000.

69 Tax relief for expenditure on research and development

69(1) [Omitted by CTA 2009, s. 1322 and Sch. 1, para. 465 and repealed by CTA 2009, s. 1326 and Sch. 3, Pt. 1.]

69(2) Schedule 21 to this Act (which contains consequential amendments) has effect accordingly.

History – S. 69(1) omitted by CTA 2009, s. 1322 and Sch. 1, para. 465 and repealed by CTA 2009, s. 1326 and Sch. 3, Pt. 1, with effect for corporation tax purposes for accounting periods ending on or after 1 April 2009, and for income tax and capital gains tax purposes for the tax year 2009–10 and subsequent tax years.

CAPITAL ALLOWANCES

70 First year allowances for small or medium-sized enterprises

70 [Repealed by CAA 2001, s. 580 and Sch. 4 with effect as respects allowances and charges falling to be made for chargeable periods ending, for income tax purposes, on or after 6 April 2001, and, for corporation tax purposes, on or after 1 April 2001.]

71 First year allowances for ICT expenditure by small enterprises

71 [Repealed by CAA 2001, s. 580 and Sch. 4 with effect as respects allowances and charges falling to be made for chargeable periods ending, for income tax purposes, on or after 6 April 2001, and, for corporation tax purposes, on or after 1 April 2001.]

72 Expenditure of a small enterprise

72 [Repealed by CAA 2001, s. 580 and Sch. 4 with effect as respects allowances and charges falling to be made for chargeable periods ending, for income tax purposes, on or after 6 April 2001, and, for corporation tax purposes, on or after 1 April 2001.]

73 Repeal of notification requirements

73(1) In section 118 of the Finance Act 1994 (notification requirements)–

(a) [Amends FA 1994, s. 118(1)–(5) and (7)–(9).]

(b) [Amends FA 1994, s. 118(6).]

73(2) This section has effect for chargeable periods as respects which the period specified in subsection (3A) of that section ends on or after 1st April 2000.

74 Pool for certain leased assets and inexpensive cars

74(1) [Amended CAA 1990, s. 41(1) and (4) (both since repealed).]

74(2) Subsection (3) below applies where–

(a) immediately before the end of the relevant chargeable period, a person was treated for the purposes of sections 24, 25 and 26 of the Capital Allowances Act 1990 as having incurred expenditure on the provision of machinery or plant wholly and exclusively for the purposes of a separate trade carried on by him;

(b) the expenditure fell within subsection (1)(b) or (c) of section 41 of that Act; and

(c) qualifying expenditure in respect of the separate trade for the relevant chargeable period exceeded any disposal value brought into account in respect of that trade for that period.

74(3) The balance of the excess (after the deduction of any writing-down allowances made by reference to it) shall be treated for the purposes of sections 24, 25 and 26 of the Capital Allowances Act 1990 as capital expenditure which–

(a) was incurred by that person in the relevant chargeable period on the provision of the machinery or plant for the purposes of the trade which is the actual trade for the purposes of section 41 of that Act; and

(b) does not form part of his qualifying expenditure for that period.

74(4) In this section–

"the relevant chargeable period" means the chargeable period immediately preceding that which begins on or before and ends on or after the relevant date;

"the relevant date" means, subject to subsection (5) below, 6th April 2000 for the purposes of income tax and 1st April 2000 for the purposes of corporation tax.

74(5) A person may, by a notice given to an officer of the Board, elect that this section shall have effect in relation to any trade carried on by him as if the relevant date were 6th April 2001 or, as the case may be, 1st April 2001.

Notes – CAA 1990 repealed by CAA 2001, s. 580 and Sch. 4.

75 Machinery and plant allowances for non-residents etc.

75(1)–(3) [Repealed by CAA 2001, s. 580 and Sch. 4.]

75(4) [Repealed by SI 2006/3271, reg. 43 and Schedule, Pt. 1.]

75(5) [Repealed by CAA 2001, s. 580 and Sch. 4.]

(a) [repealed by SI 2006/3271, reg. 43 and Schedule, Pt. 1]

(b), (c) [repealed by CAA 2001, s. 580 and Sch. 4.]

History – S. 75(1)–(3) repealed by CAA 2001, s. 580 and Sch. 4 with effect as respects allowances and charges falling to be made for chargeable periods ending, for income tax purposes, on or after 6 April 2001, and, for corporation tax purposes, on or after 1 April 2001.

S. 75(4) repealed by SI 2006/3271, reg. 43 and Schedule, Pt. 1 with effect from 31 December 2006 in relation to accounting periods ending on or after that date. S. 75(4) previously inserted ICTA 1988, Sch. 19AC, para. 10B(2A).

S. 75(5) repealed by CAA 2001, s. 580 and Sch. 4 with effect as respects allowances and charges falling to be made for chargeable periods ending, for income tax purposes, on or after 6 April 2001, and, for corporation tax purposes, on or after 1 April 2001.

In s. 75(6) the words "In this section–" and para. (a) repealed by SI 2006/3271, reg. 43 and Schedule, Pt. 1 with effect from 31 December 2006 in relation to accounting periods ending on or after that date.

S. 75(6)(b) and (c) repealed by CAA 2001, s. 580 and Sch. 4 with effect as respects allowances and charges falling to be made for chargeable periods ending, for income tax purposes, on or after 6 April 2001, and, for corporation tax purposes, on or after 1 April 2001.

76 Production animals

76(1) [Repealed by CAA 2001, s. 580 and Sch. 4.]

76(2) [Amends ICTA 1988, Sch. 5, para. 9(4).]

76(3) The enactments amended by subsections (1) and (2) above shall be deemed always to have had effect with the amendments made by those subsections.

History – S. 76(1) repealed by CAA 2001, s. 580 and Sch. 4 with effect as respects allowances and charges falling to be made for chargeable periods ending, for income tax purposes, on or after 6 April 2001, and, for corporation tax purposes, on or after 1 April 2001.

77 Sale and leaseback

77 [Repealed by CAA 2001, s. 580 and Sch. 4 with effect as respects allowances and charges falling to be made for chargeable periods ending, for income tax purposes, on or after 6 April 2001, and, for corporation tax purposes, on or after 1 April 2001.]

78 Meaning of "fixture"

78 [Repealed by TIOPA 2010, s. 378 and Sch. 10, Pt. 13.]

History – S. 78 repealed by s. 378 and Sch. 10, Pt. 13, with effect for corporation tax purposes for accounting periods ending on or after 1 April 2010, for income tax and capital gains tax purposes for the tax year 2010–11 and subsequent tax years, and for petroleum revenue tax purposes for chargeable periods beginning on or after 1 July 2010.

79 Leased assets under the Affordable Warmth Programme

79 [Repealed by CAA 2001, s. 580 and Sch. 4 with effect as respects allowances and charges falling to be made for chargeable periods ending, for income tax purposes, on or after 6 April 2001, and, for corporation tax purposes, on or after 1 April 2001.]

80 Fixtures and machinery and plant on hire-purchase etc.

80 [Repealed by CAA 2001, s. 580 and Sch. 4 with effect as respects allowances and charges falling to be made for chargeable periods ending, for income tax purposes, on or after 6 April 2001, and, for corporation tax purposes, on or after 1 April 2001.]

81 Production sharing contracts

81 [Repealed by CAA 2001, s. 580 and Sch. 4 with effect as respects allowances and charges falling to be made for chargeable periods ending, for income tax purposes, on or after 6 April 2001, and, for corporation tax purposes, on or after 1 April 2001.]

TONNAGE TAX

82 Tonnage tax

82 Schedule 22 to this Act (tonnage tax) has effect.

OTHER RELIEVING PROVISIONS

83 Relief for interest on loans to buy annuities

83(1) [Amends ICTA 1988, s. 365(3).]

83(2) [Repealed by ITA 2007, s. 1031 and Sch. 3, Pt. 1.]

83(3) [Amends ICTA 1988, s. 369(1A).]

83(4) This section has effect in relation to payments of interest made on or after 6th April 2000.

History – S. 83(2) repealed by ITA 2007, s. 1031 and Sch. 3, Pt. 1, with effect from 6 April 2007.

84 Exemption of payments under New Deal 50plus

84 [Omitted by ITTOIA 2005, s. 882(1) and Sch. 1, para. 515 and repealed by ITTOIA 2005, s. 884 and Sch. 3 effective for income tax purposes for 2005–06 onwards (ITTOIA 2005, s. 883(1)).]

Notes – The rewritten income tax rules can be principally found at ITTOIA 2005, s. 781.

85 Exemption of payments under Employment Zones programme

85 [Omitted by ITTOIA 2005, s. 882(1) and Sch. 1, para. 516 and repealed by ITTOIA 2005, s. 884 and Sch. 3 effective for income tax purposes for 2005–06 onwards (ITTOIA 2005, s. 883(1)).]

Notes – The rewritten income tax rules can be principally found at ITTOIA 2005, s. 782.

86 Loan where return bears inverse relationship to results

86 [Repealed by CTA 2010, s. 1181 and Sch. 3, Pt. 1.]

History – *S. 86 repealed by CTA 2010, s. 1181 and Sch. 3, Pt. 1*, with effect for corporation tax purposes for accounting periods ending on or after 1 April 2010, and for income tax and capital gains tax purposes for the tax year 2010–11 and subsequent tax years.

87 Tax treatment of acquisition, disposal or revaluation of certain rights

87 [Omitted by ITTOIA 2005, s. 882(1) and Sch. 1, para. 517 and repealed by ITTOIA 2005, s. 884 and Sch. 3 effective for income tax purposes for 2005–06 onwards (ITTOIA 2005, s. 883(1)).]

88 Contributions to local enterprise agencies, etc.

88 [Repealed by CTA 2009, s. 1326 and Sch. 3, Pt. 1.]

History – S. 88 repealed by CTA 2009, s. 1326 and Sch. 3, Pt. 1, with effect for corporation tax purposes for accounting periods ending on or after 1 April 2009, and for income tax and capital gains tax purposes for the tax year 2009–10 and subsequent tax years.

89 Waste disposal: entitlement of successor to allowances

89 [Repealed by CTA 2009, s. 1326 and Sch. 3, Pt. 1.]

History – S. 89 repealed by CTA 2009, s. 1326 and Sch. 3, Pt. 1, with effect for corporation tax purposes for accounting periods ending on or after 1 April 2009, and for income tax and capital gains tax purposes for the tax year 2009–10 and subsequent tax years.

CAPITAL GAINS TAX: GIFTS AND TRUSTS

90 Restriction of gifts relief

90(1) [Amends TCGA 1992, s. 165(1).]

90(2) [Amends TCGA 1992, s. 260(1).]

90(3) [Amends TCGA 1992, s. 165(2)(b)(i) and Sch. 7, para. 2(2)(b)(i).]

90(4) [Amends TCGA 1992, s. 165(3)(b).]

90(5) This section has effect in relation to disposals made on or after 9th November 1999.

91 Disposal of interest in settled property: deemed disposal of underlying assets

91(1) [Inserts TCGA 1992, s. 76A.]

91(2) [Inserts TCGA 1992, Sch. 4A.]

91(3) This section applies to any disposal of an interest in settled property made, or the effective completion of which falls, on or after 21st March 2000.

Expressions used in this subsection have the same meaning as in Schedule 4A to the Taxation of Chargeable Gains Act 1992.

92 Transfers of value by trustees linked with trustee borrowing

92(1) [Inserts TCGA 1992, s. 76B.]

92(2) [Inserts TCGA 1992, Sch. 4B.]

92(3) [Inserts TCGA 1992, s. 85A.]

92(4) [Inserts TCGA 1992, Sch. 4C.]

92(5) The provisions of this section have effect in relation to any transfer of value in relation to which the material time is on or after 21st March 2000.

The expressions **"transfer of value"** and **"material time"** have the same meaning in this subsection as in Schedule 4B to the Taxation of Chargeable Gains Act 1992.

93 Restriction on set-off of trust losses

93(1) [Inserts TCGA 1992, s. 79A.]

93(2) This section applies to gains accruing on or after 21st March 2000.

94 Attribution to trustees of gains of non-resident companies

94(1) [Inserts TCGA 1992, s. 79B.]

94(2) This section applies where a chargeable gain accrues on or after 21st March 2000 to a company that is not resident in the United Kingdom.

95 Disposal of interest in non-resident settlement

95(1) Section 85 of the Taxation of Chargeable Gains Act 1992 (disposal of interest in non-resident settlements) is amended as follows.

95(2) [Amends TCGA 1992, s. 85(2).]

95(3) [Amends TCGA 1992, s. 85(5).]

95(4) [Inserts TCGA 1992, s. 85(10).]

95(5) This section applies where the material time (within the meaning of section 85(10) of the Taxation of Chargeable Gains Act 1992, inserted by subsection (4) above) falls on or after 21st March 2000.

96 Payments by trustees to non-resident companies

96(1) [Amends TCGA 1992, s. 96(5).]

96(2) This section applies to payments received on or after 21st March 2000.

GROUPS AND GROUP RELIEF

97 Group relief for non-resident companies etc.

97 Schedule 27 to this Act has effect.

In that Schedule–

Part I makes amendments of Chapter IV of Part X of the Taxes Act 1988 (group relief), and

Part II contains consequential amendments.

98 Recovery of tax payable by non-resident company

98 [Omitted by CTA 2010, s. 1177 and Sch. 1, para. 310 and repealed by CTA 2010, s. 1181 and Sch. 3, Pt. 1.]

History – S. 98 omitted by CTA 2010, s. 1177 and Sch. 1, para. 309 and repealed by CTA 2010, s. 1181 and Sch. 3, Pt. 1, with effect for corporation tax purposes for accounting periods ending on or after 1 April 2010.

99 Joint arrangements for claims

99 [Amends FA 1998, Sch. 18, para. 77(1)(a).]

100 Limit on amount of group relief in case of consortium claim

100 [Repealed by CTA 2010, s. 1181 and Sch. 3, Pt. 1.]

History – S. 100 repealed by CTA 2010, s. 1181 and Sch. 3, Pt. 1, with effect for corporation tax purposes for accounting periods ending on or after 1 April 2010, and for income tax and capital gains tax purposes for the tax year 2010–11 and subsequent tax years.

101 Notional transfers within groups of companies

101 [Omitted by FA 2009, s. 31 and Sch. 12, para. 4(a).]

History – S. 101 omitted by FA 2009, s. 31 and Sch. 12, para. 4(a), with effect in relation to chargeable gains and allowable losses accruing on or after 21 July 2009. .

102 Chargeable gains: non-resident companies and groups etc.

102 Schedule 29 to this Act has effect.

In that Schedule–

Part I makes provision with respect to the application of the Taxation of Chargeable Gains Act 1992 to companies not resident in the United Kingdom and groups of companies etc,

Part II contains minor and consequential amendments, and

Part III contains transitional provisions.

INTERNATIONAL MATTERS

103 Double taxation relief

103 Schedule 30 to this Act (double taxation relief) shall have effect.

104 Controlled foreign companies

104 Schedule 31 to this Act (which makes provision in relation to controlled foreign companies) shall have effect.

105 Corporation tax: use of currencies other than sterling

105(1) [Substitutes FA 1993, s. 92–95.]

105(2) Where any of the items referred to in section 93(2)(b) of the Finance Act 1993 (as substituted by subsection (1) above) fall to be taken into account in the first accounting period in relation to which this section has effect, the amounts of those items shall be computed and expressed in the relevant currency by reference to the London closing exchange rate for the last day of the immediately preceding accounting period.

105(3) Where any amount falls to be taken into account under Chapter 5 of Part 2 of the Capital Allowances Act as available qualifying expenditure for the first accounting period in relation to which this section has effect relate to expenditure which was incurred before the beginning of that period, the amounts of those items shall be computed and expressed in the relevant currency by reference to the London closing exchange rate for the last day of the immediately preceding accounting period.

105(4) Subject to subsection (5) below, this section has effect for accounting periods beginning on or after 1st January 2000 and ending on or after 21st March 2000.

105(5) Any company which did not, for the accounting period immediately preceding the first accounting period falling within subsection (4) above, make an election in respect of a trade or part of a trade under the Local Currency Elections Regulations 1994 may, by notice given to an officer of the Board on or before 31st August 2000, elect that this section shall not have effect in relation to it until the first accounting period beginning on or after 1st July 2000.

History – In s. 105(3), the words "any amount … available qualifying expenditure" substituted for "any of the items referred to in section 25(1) of the Capital Allowances Act 1990 which fall to be taken into account" by CAA 2001, s. 578 and Sch. 2, para. 106 with effect as respects allowances and charges falling to be made for chargeable periods ending, for income tax purposes, on or after 6 April 2001, and, for corporation tax purposes, on or after 1 April 2001.

106 Foreign exchange gains and losses: use of local currency

106 [Repealed by FA 2002, s. 141 and Sch. 40, Pt. 3(10).]

History – S. 106 repealed by FA 2002, s. 141 and Sch. 40, Pt. 3(10) with effect in relation to accounting periods beginning on or after 1 October 2002.

INSURANCE

107 General insurance reserves

107 [Omitted by FA 2007, s. 42 and Sch. 11, para. 4 and repealed by FA 2007, s. 114 and Sch. 27, Pt. 2(11).]

History – S. 107 omitted by FA 2007, s. 42 and Sch. 11, para. 4 and repealed by FA 2007, s. 114 and Sch. 27, Pt. 2(11) in accordance with the detailed commencement provisions in FA 2007, Sch. 11, para. 5(2)–(7) (which broadly provide that the repeal has effect from the date of Royal Assent (19 July 2007).

108 Overseas life assurance business

108 [Omitted by FA 2012, s. 146 and Sch. 16, para. 247(j).]

History – S. 108 omitted by FA 2012, s. 146 and Sch. 16, para. 247(j), with effect in relation to accounting periods beginning on or after 1 January 2013 (FA 2012, s. 148) but subject to transitional provisions in FA 2012, Sch. 17. Where an accounting period would otherwise straddle 1 January 2013, it is deemed to end on 31 December 2012 (FA 2012, s. 149).

109 Insurance business: apportionment rules

109 [Omitted by FA 2012, s. 146 and Sch. 16, para. 247(j).]

History – S. 109 omitted by FA 2012, s. 146 and Sch. 16, para. 247(j), with effect in relation to accounting periods beginning on or after 1 January 2013 (FA 2012, s. 148) but subject to transitional provisions in FA 2012, Sch. 17. Where an accounting period would otherwise straddle 1 January 2013, it is deemed to end on 31 December 2012 (FA 2012, s. 149).

MISCELLANEOUS

110 Rent factoring

110 [Repealed by FA 2006, s. 178 and Sch. 26, Pt. 3(12).]

History – s. 110 repealed by FA 2006, s. 178 and Sch. 26, Pt. 3(12) with effect in relation to transactions entered into on or after 6 June 2006.

111 Payments under deduction of tax

111(1) [Repeals ICTA 1988, Pt. IV, Ch. VIIA (s. 118A–118K).]

111(2)–(5) [Repealed by ITA 2007, s. 1031 and Sch. 3, Pt. 1.]

111(6) In this section–

(a) subsections (1) and (5) apply to relevant payments or receipts in relation to which the chargeable date for the purposes of Chapter VIIA of Part IV is on or after 1st April 2001;

(b) [repealed by ITA 2007, s. 1031 and Sch. 3, Pt. 1;]

(c) [repealed by ITA 2007, s. 1031 and Sch. 3, Pt. 1.]

History – S. 111(2)–(5) repealed by ITA 2007, s. 1031 and Sch. 3, Pt. 1, with effect from 6 April 2007.
S. 111(6)(b) and (c) repealed by ITA 2007, s. 1031 and Sch. 3, Pt. 1, with effect from 6 April 2007.

Notes – S. 111 rewritten as follows:
S. 111(2): ITA 2007, s. 882, 889(3), 987.
S. 111(3): ITA 2007, s. 858(2), 859(2).
S. 111(4): ITA 2007, s. 871(1), (2), (3).
S. 111(6): ITA 2007, Sch. 2, para. 156.

112 UK public revenue dividends: deduction of tax

112 [Repealed by ITA 2007, s. 1031 and Sch. 3, Pt. 1.]

History – S. 112 repealed by ITA 2007, s. 1031 and Sch. 3, Pt. 1, with effect from 6 April 2007.
Notes – S. 112 rewritten as follows:
S. 112(1): ITA 2007, s. 893(1), (2).
S. 112(2): ITA 2007, s. 892(1), (2).
S. 112(3): ITA 2007, s. 891.
S. 112(4): ITA 2007, s. 897(1), (2), (3).

113 Tax treatment of expenditure on production or acquisition of films

113 [Repealed by CAA 2001, s. 580 and Sch. 4 with effect as respects allowances and charges falling to be made for chargeable periods ending, for income tax purposes, on or after 6 April 2001, and, for corporation tax purposes, on or after 1 April 2001.]

PART VI – MISCELLANEOUS AND SUPPLEMENTARY PROVISIONS

INCENTIVES FOR ELECTRONIC COMMUNICATIONS

143 Power to provide incentives to use electronic communications

143(1) Regulations may be made in accordance with Schedule 38 to this Act for providing incentives to use electronic communications.

143(2) [Omitted by CTA 2009, s. 1322 and Sch. 1, para. 466 and repealed by CTA 2009, s. 1326 and Sch. 3, Pt. 1.]

History – S. 143(2) omitted by CTA 2009, s. 1322 and Sch. 1, para. 466 and repealed by CTA 2009, s. 1326 and Sch. 3, Pt. 1, with effect for corporation tax purposes for accounting periods ending on or after 1 April 2009, and for income tax and capital gains tax purposes for the tax year 2009–10 and subsequent tax years.
In former s. 143(2) the words "corporation tax purposes" substituted for word "purposes of the Tax Acts" by ITTOIA 2005, s. 882(1) and Sch. 1, para. 518; effective for income tax purposes for 2005–06 onwards and for corporation tax purposes for accounting periods ending after 5 April 2005 (ITTOIA 2005, s. 883(1)).
Statutory instruments – SI 2001/56: provision of incentive payments to be made if returns submitted to HMRC using electronic communications.
SI 2003/2495: income tax, incentive payments for voluntary online filing of PAYE returns.
Notes – S. 143 rewritten for corporation tax purposes as follows:
S. 143(2): CTA 2009, s. 1287.
The rewritten income tax rules can be principally found at ITTOIA 2005, s. 778.

COMPLIANCE

144 Offence of fraudulent evasion of income tax

144 [Omitted by TIOPA 2010, s. 371 and Sch. 7, para. 97 and repealed by TIOPA 2010, s. 378 and Sch. 10, Pt. 12.]

History – S. 144 omitted by TIOPA 2010, s. 371 and Sch. 7, para. 97 and repealed by TIOPA 2010, s. 378 and Sch. 10, Pt. 12, with effect for the tax year 2010–11 and subsequent tax years.
Notes – S. 144 rewritten as follows:
S. 144(1): TIOPA 2010, Sch. 7, para. 95.
S. 144(2): TIOPA 2010, Sch. 7, para. 95.
S. 144(3): TIOPA 2010, Sch. 7, para. 95.

145 Information about interest etc. paid, credited or received

145(1) [Repeals TMA 1970, s. 17(4B), (4C).]

145(2) [Amends TMA 1970, s. 17(5).]

145(3) [Inserts TMA 1970, s. 17(6)(aa).]

145(4) [Amends TMA 1970, s. 18(1).]

145(5) [Repeals TMA 1970, s. 18(3), (3AA).]

145(6) [Amends TMA 1970, s. 18(3A).]

145(7) [Amends TMA 1970, s. 18(3B).]

145(8) [Inserts TMA 1970, s. 18(3C)(aa).]

145(9) [Substitutes TMA 1970, s. 18(3D).]

145(10) [Repeals ICTA 1988, s. 482A.]

145(11) This section has effect in relation to amounts paid, credited or received on or after 6th April 2001.

146 International exchange of information: general

146 [Repealed by FA 2006, s. 178 and Sch. 26, Pt. 8(2).]

History – S. 146 repealed by FA 2006, s. 178 and Sch. 26, Pt. 8(2) with effect from 19 July 2006.

148 Use of minimum wage information

148(1) Information obtained by an officer acting for the purposes of the National Minimum Wage Act 1998 ("the 1998 Act") by virtue of section 13(1)(a) or (b) of that Act (officers) may be supplied by or with the authority of the Secretary of State to the Board for the purpose of any of its functions.

148(2) [Repealed by CRCA 2005, s. 50(6) and Sch. 4, para. 54 and s. 52(2) and Sch. 5.]

148(3) Information supplied to the Secretary of State under section 16(2) of the 1998 Act (information obtained by agricultural wages officers) may be supplied by the Secretary of State to the Board for the purpose of any of its functions.

148(4) [Substitutes National Minimum Wage Act 1998, s. 15(6).]

History – S. 148(2) repealed by CRCA 2005, s. 50(6) and Sch. 4, para. 80 and s. 52(2) and Sch. 5, with effect from 18 April 2005 (SI 2005/1126 (C. 51), art. 2(2)).

149 Orders for the delivery of documents

149(1) [Inserts TMA 1970, s. 20BA.]

149(2) After Schedule 1 to the Taxes Management Act 1970, insert the Schedule 1AA set out in Schedule 39 to this Act.

149(3) [Amends TMA 1970, s. 20BB(1)(a), (3).]

149(4) [Repealed by FA 2007, s. 114 and Sch. 27, Pt. 5(1).]

History – S. 149(4) repealed by FA 2007, s. 114 and Sch. 27, Pt. 5(1) with effect from 8 November 2007, by virtue of SI 2007/3166, art. 2(c) in accordance with s. 84(5).

150 Search warrants: miscellaneous amendments

150 [Repealed by FA 2007, s. 114 and Sch. 27, Pt. 5(1).]

History – S. 150 repealed by FA 2007, s. 114 and Sch. 27, Pt. 5(1) with effect from 8 November 2007, by virtue of SI 2007/3166, art. 2(c) in accordance with s. 84(5).

SUPPLEMENTARY PROVISIONS

155 Interpretation

155 In this Act **"the Taxes Act 1988"** means the Income and Corporation Taxes Act 1988 and **"ITTOIA 2005"** means the Income Tax (Trading and Other Income) Act 2005 and **"ITA 2007"**means the Income Tax Act 2007.

History – In s. 155 the definition of "ITA 2007" inserted by ITA 2007, s. 1027 and Sch. 1, para. 393, with effect from 6 April 2007. In s. 155 the definition for "ITTOIA 2005" (and the word "and" preceding it) inserted by ITTOIA 2005, s. 882(1) and Sch. 1, para. 519; effective for income tax purposes for 2005–06 onwards and for corporation tax purposes for accounting periods ending after 5 April 2005 (ITTOIA 2005, s. 883(1)).

156 Repeals

156(1) The enactments mentioned in Schedule 40 to this Act (which include provisions that are spent or of no practical utility) are repealed to the extent specified in the third column of that schedule.

156(2) The repeals specified in that Schedule have effect subject to the commencement provisions and savings contained or referred to in the notes set out in that Schedule.

157 Short title

157 This Act may be cited as the Finance Act 2000.

SCHEDULES

SCHEDULE 7 – CLIMATE CHANGE LEVY: CONSEQUENTIAL AMENDMENTS

Section 30

PROVISIONAL COLLECTION OF TAXES ACT 1968 (C. 2)

1 [Amends PCTA 1968, s. 1(1).]

INSOLVENCY ACT 1986 (C. 45)

3(1) [Repealed by the Enterprise Act 2002, s. 278(2), and Sch. 26.]

History – Sch. 7, para. 3 repealed by the Enterprise Act 2002, s. 278(2), and Sch. 26 with effect from 15 September 2003, by virtue of SI 2003/2093, art. 2 and Sch. 1. Art. 4 contains transitional provisions. Sch. 7, para. 3 amended IA 1986, s. 386(1) and inserted IA 1986, Sch. 6, para. 3C.

Transitional – Enterprise Act 2002 (Commencement No. 4 and Transitional Provisions and Savings) Order 2003, SI 2003/2093, art. 4, contains transitional provisions so that the former rules remain in effect where insolvency arrangements are in place prior to 15 September 2003.

INCOME AND CORPORATION TAXES ACT 1988 (C. 1)

4 [Inserts ICTA 1988, s. 827(1D).]

SCHEDULE 8 – EMPLOYEE SHARE OWNERSHIP PLANS

Section 47

[Repealed by ITEPA 2003, s. 724, and Sch. 8, Pt. 1.]

History – Sch. 8 repealed by ITEPA 2003, s. 724 and Sch. 8, Pt. 1 with effect in relation to share ownership plans approved on or after 6 April 2003.
Former wording is as follows:

"Part I – Introductory

EMPLOYEE SHARE OWNERSHIP PLANS

1(1) In this Schedule an **"employee share ownership plan"** means a plan established by a company providing–
(a) for shares ("free shares") to be appropriated to employees without payment, or
(b) for shares ("partnership shares") to be acquired on behalf of employees out of sums deducted from their salary.

1(2) A plan that provides for partnership shares may also provide for shares ("matching shares") to be appropriated without payment to employees in proportion to the partnership shares acquired by them.

1(3) Where a plan contains provision for all, or more than one, of the kinds of shares mentioned in sub-paragraphs (1) and (2), it may leave it for the company to decide when the provisions relating to each kind of share are to have effect.

1(4) In this Schedule, in relation to an employee share ownership plan **"the company"** means the company which established the plan.

GROUP PLANS

2(1) An employee share ownership plan established by a company that controls other companies (a "parent company") may extend to all or any of those other companies.
In this Schedule a plan established by a parent company which so extends is referred to as a "group plan".

2(2) In relation to a group plan a **"participating company"** means the parent company or any other company to which for the time being the plan is expressed to extend.

MEANING OF "AWARD OF SHARES", "PARTICIPANT" ETC.

3(1) For the purposes of this Schedule an award of shares is made under a plan on each occasion when in accordance with the plan–
(a) matching or free shares are appropriated to employees, or
(b) partnership shares are acquired on behalf of employees.

3(2) For the purposes of this Schedule an individual participates in an award of free, matching or partnership shares under the plan if shares ("the individual award") included in that award are–
(a) in the case of an award of free or matching shares, appropriated to him, or
(b) in the case of an award of partnership shares, acquired on his behalf,
and references to shares awarded to an individual are to free or matching shares appropriated to him, or partnership shares acquired on his behalf, under the plan.

3(3) In this Schedule **"participant"**, in relation to a plan, means an individual to whom shares have been awarded under the plan.

APPLICATION FOR APPROVAL

4(1) Where an employee share ownership plan has been established, on the application of the company the Inland Revenue shall approve the plan if they are satisfied that it meets the requirements of this Schedule.

4(2) An application for approval must contain such particulars and be supported by such evidence as the Inland Revenue may require.

APPEAL AGAINST REFUSAL OF APPROVAL

5(1) If the Inland Revenue refuse to approve the plan, the company may appeal to the Special Commissioners.

5(2) Notice of appeal must be given to the Inland Revenue within 30 days after their decision was notified to the company.

5(3) If the Special Commissioners allow the appeal they may direct the Inland Revenue to approve the plan with effect from such date (but not earlier than the application for approval) as the Commissioners may specify.

Part II – General Requirements

INTRODUCTION

6 The plan must meet the requirements of–
paragraph 7 (the purpose of plan);
paragraph 8 (all-employee nature of plan);
paragraph 9 (participation on same terms);
paragraph 10 (no preferential treatment for directors, etc.);
paragraph 11 (no further conditions);
paragraph 12 (no loan arrangements).

THE PURPOSE OF THE PLAN

7(1) The purpose of the plan must be to provide benefits to employees in the nature of shares in a company which give them a continuing stake in that company.
7(2) The plan must not contain, and the operation of the plan must not involve, features which are neither essential nor reasonably incidental to that purpose.

ALL-EMPLOYEE NATURE OF PLAN

8(1) The plan must provide that every employee who–
(a) meets the requirements mentioned in Part III (eligibility of individuals) in relation to an award of shares under the plan, and
(b) is chargeable to tax under Case I of Schedule E in respect of the employment by reference to which he satisfies the condition in paragraph 14 (the employment requirement),
is eligible to participate in the award, and invited to do so.
8(2) The plan must not contain any feature which has or would have the effect of discouraging any description of employees within sub-paragraph (1) from participating in an award of shares under the plan.
This does not apply to any provision required or authorised by this Schedule.
8(3) The plan may provide that an employee who–
(a) meets the requirements mentioned in Part III (eligibility of individuals) in relation to an award of shares under the plan, but
(b) is not chargeable to tax as mentioned in sub-paragraph (1)(b),
is eligible to participate in the award, and may be invited to do so.
8(4) For the purposes of this Schedule an individual is a **"qualifying employee"**, in relation to an award of shares, if–
(a) he is eligible to participate in the award, and
(b) either–
(i) he must be invited to participate in the award (see sub-paragraph (1)), or
(ii) under the plan he may be invited to participate in the award (see sub-paragraph (3)) and has been so invited.

PARTICIPATION ON SAME TERMS

9(1) The requirement of this paragraph is–
(a) that every employee who is invited to participate in an award must be invited to participate on the same terms, and
(b) that those who do participate must actually do so on the same terms.
9(2) The requirement of this paragraph is infringed by the awarding of free shares by reference to factors other than those mentioned in sub-paragraph (3).
9(3) The requirement of this paragraph is not infringed by the awarding of free shares by reference to an employee's–
(a) remuneration,
(b) length of service, or
(c) hours worked.
This is subject to sub-paragraph (4).
9(4) Where the awarding of free shares is by reference to more than one of the factors mentioned in sub-paragraph (3) the requirement of this paragraph is infringed unless–
(a) each factor gives rise to a separate entitlement related to the level of remuneration, length of service or (as the case may be) hours worked, and
(b) the total entitlement is the sum of those separate entitlements.
9(5) In the case of an award of free shares which provides for performance allowances, this paragraph has effect as provided in paragraph 29 (performance allowances: method one) or, as the case may be, paragraph 30 (performance allowances: method two).
For this purpose **"performance allowance"** has the meaning given in paragraph 25(1).

NO PREFERENTIAL TREATMENT FOR DIRECTORS ETC.

10(1) The first requirement of this paragraph is that no feature of the plan must have or be likely to have the effect of conferring benefits wholly or mainly–
(a) on directors, or
(b) on employees receiving higher levels of remuneration.
10(2) The second requirement of this paragraph is that in the case of a plan established by a company that is a member of a group, the identity of the company (or, if it is a group plan, the participating companies) must not be such that the plan has or is likely to have the effect of conferring benefits wholly or mainly–
(a) on employees of companies that are members of the group who receive higher levels of remuneration, or
(b) on directors of such companies.
10(3) This paragraph is subject to paragraph 9(3) (award of shares by reference to remuneration etc.).

NO FURTHER CONDITIONS

11 No conditions, other than those required or permitted by this Schedule, may be imposed on an employee's participation in an award of shares under the plan.

NO LOAN ARRANGEMENTS

12(1) The arrangements for the plan must not make any provision, or be in any way associated with any provision made, for loans to some or all of the employees of–
(a) the company, or
(b) in the case of a group plan, any participating company,
and the operation of the plan must not be in any way associated with such loans.
12(2) For the purposes of sub-paragraph (1) **"arrangements"** includes any scheme, agreement, undertaking or understanding, whether or not legally enforceable.

Part III – Eligibility of Individuals

INTRODUCTION

13(1) The plan must provide that an individual may only participate in an award of shares if–
(a) in the case of free shares, he is eligible to participate in the award at the time it is made, and
(b) in the case of partnership or matching shares–

(i) if there is no accumulation period, he is eligible to participate in the award at the time the partnership share money relating to the award is deducted, and
(ii) if there is an accumulation period, he is eligible to participate in the award at the time of the first deduction of partnership share money relating to the award.

13(2) For the purposes of sub-paragraph (1), in the case of an award of matching shares the deduction of partnership share money "relating" to the award is the deduction relating to the award of partnership shares to which the matching shares relate.

13(3) An individual is eligible to participate in an award of shares under the plan if and only if–
(a) the requirements of the plan are met as to–
(i) employment (see paragraph 14),
(ii) no material interest (see paragraph 15), and
(iii) not participating in other schemes (see paragraph 16), and
(b) in a case where the individual is not within paragraph 8(1) (employees who must be invited to participate in the award), any further eligibility requirements of the plan are met.

THE EMPLOYMENT REQUIREMENT

14(1) The plan must provide that an individual is not eligible to participate in an award of shares unless–
(a) he is an employee of the company or, in the case of a group plan, of a participating company, and
(b) where the plan provides for a qualifying period, he has at all times during that period been an employee of a qualifying company.

14(1A) Except in the case of a group plan, a qualifying company means–
(a) the company, or
(b) a company that when the individual was employed by it was an associated company–
(i) of the company, or
(ii) of another company qualifying under this paragraph.

14(1B) In the case of a group plan, a qualifying company means–
(a) a company that is a participating company at the end of the qualifying period, or
(b) a company that when the individual was employed by it was a participating company, or
(c) a company that when the individual was employed by it was an associated company of–
(i) a company qualifying under paragraph (a) or (b), or
(ii) another company qualifying under this paragraph.

14(2) If the plan provides for a qualifying period, that period must be–
(a) in the case of free shares, a period of not more than 18 months ending with the date on which the award is made,
(b) in the case of partnership or matching shares–
(i) if the plan does not provide for an accumulation period, a period of not more than 18 months ending with the deduction of partnership share money relating to the award, and
(ii) if the plan provides for an accumulation period, a period of not more than six months ending with the start of the accumulation period relating to the award.

14(3) For the purposes of sub-paragraph (2), in the case of an award of matching shares the deduction of partnership share money or accumulation period "relating" to the award is the deduction or period relating to the award of partnership shares to which the matching shares relate.

14(4) In relation to an award, the same qualifying period must apply in relation to all employees of the company or, in the case of a group plan, of the participating companies.

14(5) Subject to sub-paragraphs (2) and (4), the plan may authorise the company to specify different qualifying periods in respect of different awards of shares.

History – Para. 14(1)(b) substituted by FA 2001, s. 61, Sch. 13, para. 2(1)(a) with effect for share awards made after 11 May 2001 (FA 2001, Sch. 13, para. 2(2)).
Para. 14(1A) and (1B) inserted by FA 2001, s. 61, Sch. 13, para. 2(1)(b) with effect for share awards made after 11 May 2001 (FA 2001, Sch. 13, para. 2(2)).

THE "NO MATERIAL INTEREST" REQUIREMENT

15(1) The plan must provide that an individual is not eligible to participate in an award of shares if he has, or has within the preceding twelve months had, a material interest in–
(a) a close company whose shares may be awarded under the plan, or
(b) a company which has control of such a company or is a member of a consortium which owns such a company.

15(2) For the purposes of this paragraph an individual is regarded as having a material interest in a company if–
(a) the individual,
(b) the individual together with one or more associates of his, or
(c) any associate of the individual's, with or without any other such associates,
has a material interest in the company.

15(3) This paragraph is supplemented–
(a) as regards the meaning of "material interest", by paragraphs 17 to 19, and
(b) as regards the meaning of "associate", by paragraph 20 (read with paragraphs 21 and 22).

THE REQUIREMENT OF NON-PARTICIPATION IN OTHER RELEVANT SHARE SCHEMES

16(1) The plan must provide that an individual is not to participate in an award of free shares under the plan in a tax year if in that year–
(a) shares have been (or are at the same time to be) appropriated to him in accordance with an approved profit sharing scheme established by the company or a connected company, or
(b) he has participated (or is at the same time to participate) in another employee share ownership plan established by the company or a connected company and approved under this Schedule.

16(2) The plan must provide that an individual is not eligible to participate in an award of partnership or matching shares under the plan in any tax year if, in that year, he has participated (or at the same time participates) in an award of shares under another employee share ownership plan established by the company or a connected company and approved under this Schedule.

16(3) For the purposes of this paragraph an individual is treated as having participated in an award of free shares under an employee share ownership plan if he would have participated in that award but for his failure to obtain a performance allowance (see paragraph 25).

16(4) In this paragraph **"connected company"** means–
(a) a company which controls or is controlled by the company or which is controlled by a company which also controls the company, or
(b) a company which is a member of a consortium owning the company or which is owned in part by the company as a member of a consortium.

MEANING OF "MATERIAL INTEREST"

17(1) For the purposes of paragraph 15 (the "no material interest" requirement) a **"material interest in a company"** means–
(a) beneficial ownership of, or the ability to control, directly or through the medium of other companies or by any other indirect means, more than 25% of the ordinary share capital of the company; or

(b) where the company is a close company, possession or entitlement to acquire such rights as would, in the event of the winding up of the company or in any other circumstances, give an entitlement to receive more than 25% of the assets that would then be available for distribution among the participators.

17(2) In this paragraph–

"close company" includes a company that would be a close company but for–

(a) section 414(1)(a) of the Taxes Act 1988 (exclusion of companies not resident in the United Kingdom), or

(b) section 415 of that Act (exclusion of certain quoted companies); and

"participator" has the meaning given by section 417(1) of that Act.

17(3) This paragraph is supplemented by paragraph 18 (options etc.) and paragraph 19 (shares held by trustees of approved profit sharing scheme etc.).

MATERIAL INTEREST: OPTIONS ETC.

18(1) For the purposes of paragraph 17(1) (meaning of material interest) a right to acquire shares (however arising) is treated as a right to control them.

18(2) In any case where–

(a) the shares attributed to an individual consist of or include shares which he or another person has a right to acquire, and

(b) the circumstances are such that if that right were to be exercised the shares acquired would be shares which were previously unissued and which the company is contractually bound to issue in the event of the exercise of the right,

then in determining at any time prior to the exercise of the right whether the number of shares attributed to the individual exceeds a particular percentage of the ordinary share capital of the company, that ordinary share capital shall be taken to be increased by the number of unissued shares referred to in paragraph (b).

18(3) The references in sub-paragraph (2) to the shares attributed to an individual are to the shares which in accordance with paragraph 17(1)(a) fall to be brought into account in his case to determine whether their number exceeds a particular percentage of the company's ordinary share capital.

MATERIAL INTEREST: SHARES HELD BY TRUSTEES OF APPROVED PROFIT SHARING SCHEMES ETC.

19 In applying paragraph 17(1) (meaning of material interest) there shall be disregarded–

(a) the interest of the trustees of–

(i) any approved profit sharing scheme, or

(ii) an approved employee share ownership plan,

in any shares held by them in accordance with the scheme or plan but which have not been appropriated to or acquired on behalf of an individual; and

(b) any rights exercisable by those trustees by virtue of any such interest.

MEANING OF "ASSOCIATE"

20(1) In paragraph 15 (the "no material interest" requirement) **"associate"**, in relation to a person, means–

(a) any relative or partner of that person,

(b) the trustee or trustees of any settlement in relation to which that person, or any relative of his (living or dead), is or was a settlor, and

(c) where that person is interested in any shares or obligations of the company which are subject to any trust, or are part of the estate of a deceased person, the trustee or trustees of the settlement concerned or (as the case may be) the personal representatives of the deceased.

20(2) In sub-paragraph (1)(a) and (b) **"relative"** means husband or wife, parent or remoter forebear, child or remoter issue, or brother or sister.

20(3) In sub-paragraph (1)(b) **"settlor"** and **"settlement"** have the same meaning as in Chapter IA of Part XV of the Taxes Act 1988 (see section 660G(1) and (2)).

MEANING OF "ASSOCIATE": TRUSTEES OF EMPLOYEE BENEFIT TRUST

21(1) This paragraph applies for the purposes of paragraph 20(1)(c) (meaning of "associate": trustees of settlement) where an individual is interested as a beneficiary of an employee benefit trust in shares or obligations of a company ("the relevant company") in relation to which it falls to be determined whether that individual has an interest.

21(2) The trustees of the employee benefit trust are not regarded as associates of the individual by reason only of his being so interested if neither–

(a) the individual,

(b) the individual together with one or more associates of his, or

(c) any associate of the individual's, with or without any other such associates,

has at any time on or after 14th March 1989 been the beneficial owner of, or able (directly or through the medium of other companies or by any other indirect means) to control, more than 25% of the ordinary share capital of the company.

21(3) In this paragraph **"employee benefit trust"** has the same meaning as in paragraph 7 of Schedule 8 to the Taxes Act 1988.

21(4) Sub-paragraphs (9) to (12) of that paragraph apply for the purposes of this paragraph in relation to an individual as they apply for the purposes of that paragraph in relation to an employee.

21(5) In sub-paragraph (2)(b) and (c) **"associate"** does not include the trustees of an employee benefit trust by reason only that the individual has an interest in shares or obligations of the trust.

MEANING OF "ASSOCIATE": TRUSTEES OF DISCRETIONARY TRUST

22(1) This paragraph applies for the purposes of paragraph 20(1)(c) (meaning of "associate": trustees of settlement) where–

(a) the person in question ("the beneficiary") is one of the objects of a discretionary trust, and

(b) the property subject to the trust has at any time consisted of, or included, shares or obligations of the company ("the relevant company") in relation to which it falls to be determined whether that person has an interest.

22(2) If–

(a) the beneficiary has ceased to be eligible to benefit under the discretionary trust by reason of–

(i) an irrevocable disclaimer or release executed by him, or

(ii) the irrevocable exercise by the trustees of a power to exclude him from the objects of the trust,

(b) immediately after the beneficiary ceased to be so eligible, no associate of his was interested in the shares or obligations of the relevant company which were subject to the trust, and

(c) during the period of twelve months ending with the date when the beneficiary ceased to be so eligible neither he nor any associate of his received any benefit under the trust,

the beneficiary is not regarded by reason only of the matters mentioned in sub-paragraph (1) as having been interested in the shares or obligations of the relevant company at any time during the period of twelve months mentioned in paragraph (c).

22(3) In sub-paragraph (2) **"associate"** has the meaning given by paragraph 20, but with the omission of sub-paragraph (1)(c) of that paragraph (trusts and estates).

Part IV – Free Shares

INTRODUCTION

23 If the plan provides for free shares it must comply with the requirements of this Part of this Schedule.

MAXIMUM ANNUAL AWARD

24(1) The plan must provide that the initial market value of the free shares awarded to a participant in any tax year cannot exceed £3,000.
24(2) For this purpose the **"initial market value"** of shares means their market value on the date on which they are awarded.
24(3) For the purposes of this paragraph the market value of shares subject to restrictions or risk of forfeiture shall be determined as if there were no such restriction or risk.
For this purpose shares are **"subject to risk of forfeiture"** if the interest that may be acquired is only conditional within the meaning of section 140C of the Taxes Act 1988.

PERFORMANCE ALLOWANCES

25(1) Sub-paragraph (2) applies if the plan provides for performance allowances, that is for–
(a) whether or not free shares will be awarded to an individual, or
(b) the number or value of free shares awarded,
to be conditional on performance targets being met.
25(2) Where this paragraph applies–
(a) the requirements of–
paragraph 26 (performance allowances: general application),
paragraph 27 (performance measures and targets), and
paragraph 28 (performance allowances: information to be given to employees), and
(b) the requirements of either paragraph 29 (method one) or paragraph 30 (method two),
must be complied with.

PERFORMANCE ALLOWANCES: GENERAL APPLICATION

26 If the plan provides for performance allowances in relation to an award it must make provision for such allowances for all qualifying employees in relation to that award.

PERFORMANCE ALLOWANCES: MEASURES AND TARGETS

27(1) If the plan provides for performance allowances the following requirements must be met with respect to performance measures and performance targets.
27(2) The performance measures used must–
(a) be based on business results or other objective criteria, and
(b) be fair and objective measures of the performance of the units to which they are or may be applied.
27(3) The performance targets must be set for performance units comprising one or more employees.
27(4) For the purposes of an award of free shares under the plan an employee must not be a member of more than one performance unit.

PERFORMANCE ALLOWANCES: INFORMATION TO BE GIVEN TO EMPLOYEES

28(1) If the plan provides for performance allowances in relation to an award of shares, the plan must require the company–
(a) to notify each employee participating in the award of the performance targets and measures which, under the plan, will be used to determine the number or value of free shares awarded to him; and
(b) to notify all qualifying employees of the company or, in the case of a group plan, of any participating company, in general terms, of the performance measures to be used to determine the number or value of free shares to be awarded to each employee participating in the award.
28(2) The notices must be given as soon as reasonably practicable.
28(3) The company may exclude from the notice mentioned in sub-paragraph (1)(b) any information the disclosure of which the company reasonably considers would prejudice commercial confidentiality.

PERFORMANCE ALLOWANCES: METHOD ONE

29(1) The requirements of this paragraph are that if the plan provides for performance allowances in relation to an award of shares–
(a) at least 20% of the shares in the award must be awarded without reference to performance in accordance with the requirement of paragraph 9 (participation on same terms),
(b) the remaining shares must be awarded by reference to performance, and
(c) the highest number of shares within paragraph (b) awarded to an individual must be not more than four times the highest number of shares within paragraph (a) awarded to an individual.
29(2) In determining for the purposes of sub-paragraph (1)(a) whether the requirement of paragraph 9 (participation on same terms) is met the shares to which sub-paragraph (1)(a) above applies are treated as a separate award of free shares.
29(3) Where the plan meets the requirements of sub-paragraph (1), the requirement of paragraph 9 (participation on same terms) does not apply to any provision of the plan relating to the awarding of shares within sub-paragraph (1)(b).
29(4) If free shares of different classes are awarded, the requirements of sub-paragraph (1) apply separately in relation to each class.

PERFORMANCE ALLOWANCES: METHOD TWO

30(1) The requirements of this paragraph are that in relation to an award of free shares under the plan–
(a) some or all of the shares must be awarded by reference to performance; and
(b) the awarding of the shares to qualifying employees who are members of the same performance unit must meet the requirement of paragraph 9 (participation on same terms).
30(2) In determining for the purposes of sub-paragraph (1)(b) whether the requirement of paragraph 9 (participation on same terms) is met the free shares awarded in respect of each performance unit are treated as a separate award of free shares.
30(3) If this method is used nothing in paragraph 9 (participation on same terms) requires the awarding of shares to members of different performance units to be on the same terms.

THE HOLDING PERIOD

31(1) The plan must require the company in respect of each award of free shares to specify a period ("the holding period") during which a participant is bound by contract with the company–
(a) to permit his free shares to remain in the hands of the trustees, and
(b) not to assign, charge or otherwise dispose of his beneficial interest in the shares.
31(2) The holding period–
(a) must be a period of at least three years but not more than five years, beginning with the date on which the shares in question are awarded to the participant, and
(b) must be the same in respect of all shares in the same award.
31(3) The plan may authorise the company to specify different holding periods from time to time.
But it must prevent the company from increasing the holding period specified in respect of free shares that have been awarded under the plan.
31(4) The participant's obligations with respect to the holding period–

(a) come to an end if during the period he ceases to be in relevant employment, and
(b) are subject to–
paragraph 32 (power to authorise trustees to accept general offers etc.);
paragraph 73 (meeting PAYE obligations); and
paragraph 121(5) (termination of plan: early removal of shares with participant's consent).

HOLDING PERIOD: POWER TO AUTHORISE TRUSTEES TO ACCEPT GENERAL OFFERS ETC.

32 A participant may direct the trustees to do any of the following during the holding period–
(a) to accept an offer for any of his free shares ("the original shares") if the acceptance or agreement will result in a new holding being equated with the original shares for the purposes of capital gains tax; or
(b) to accept an offer of a qualifying corporate bond (whether alone or with other assets or cash or both) for his free shares if the offer forms part of such a general offer as is mentioned in paragraph (c); or
(c) to accept an offer of cash, with or without other assets, for his free shares if the offer forms part of a general offer which is made to holders of shares of the same class as his or of shares in the same company and which is made in the first instance on a condition such that if it is satisfied the person making the offer will have control of that company, within the meaning of section 416 of the Taxes Act 1988; or
(d) to agree to a transaction affecting his free shares or such of them as are of a particular class, if the transaction would be entered into pursuant to a compromise, arrangement or scheme applicable to or affecting–
(i) all the ordinary share capital of the company or, as the case may be, all the shares of the class in question, or
(ii) all the shares, or all the shares of the class in question, which are held by a class of shareholders identified otherwise than by reference to their employment or their participation in an approved employee share ownership plan.

Part V – Partnership Shares

INTRODUCTION

33 If the plan provides for partnership shares it must comply with the requirements of this Part of this Schedule.

PARTNERSHIP SHARE AGREEMENTS

34 The plan must provide for qualifying employees to enter into agreements with the company ("partnership share agreements") under which–
(a) the employee authorises the company to deduct part of his salary for the purchase of partnership shares, and
(b) the company undertakes to arrange for partnership shares to be awarded to the employee in accordance with the plan.

DEDUCTIONS FROM SALARY

35(1) The plan must provide for a partnership share agreement to be given effect by deductions from the employee's salary.
Amounts so deducted are referred to in this Part of this Schedule as "partnership share money".
35(2) The partnership share agreement must specify–
(a) what amounts are to be deducted, and
(b) at what intervals.
This does not prevent the employee and the company agreeing to vary those amounts or intervals.
35(3) For the purposes of sub-paragraph (2)(a) the agreement may specify a percentage of the employee's salary.
35(4) The plan must require the employer company to calculate the amounts and intervals having regard to the provisions of paragraph 36 (maximum amount of deductions from salary).
For this purpose **"the employer company"** is the company by reference to which the employee meets the requirement of paragraph 14 (the employment requirement) in relation to the plan.

MAXIMUM AMOUNT OF DEDUCTIONS

36(1) The amount of partnership share money deducted from an employee's salary must not exceed–
(a) £125 in any month, or
(b) where the salary is not paid at monthly intervals, such amount as bears to £125 the same proportion as the pay interval in question bears to one month.
36(2) The amount of partnership share money deducted from an employee's salary must not exceed 10% of the employee's salary.
This means–
(a) if the plan does not provide for an accumulation period, 10% of the salary payment from which the deduction is made;
(b) if the plan provides for an accumulation period, 10% of the total of the employee's salary payments over that period.
36(3) The plan may authorise the company to specify lower limits than those specified in sub-paragraphs (1) and (2).
Different limits may be specified in relation to different awards of shares.
36(4) Any amount deducted in excess of that allowed by sub-paragraph (1) or (2), or any lower limit in the plan, must be paid over to the employee as soon as practicable.

MINIMUM AMOUNT OF DEDUCTIONS

37(1) The plan may provide that the amount to be deducted in pursuance of a partnership share agreement in any month must not be less than a minimum amount specified in the plan.
37(2) The specified minimum amount must not be greater than £10.
37(3) Sub-paragraphs (1) and (2) apply whatever the intervals at which the employee is paid.

NOTICE OF POSSIBLE EFFECT OF DEDUCTIONS ON BENEFIT ENTITLEMENT

38(1) The plan must provide that the company may not enter into a partnership share agreement with an employee unless the agreement contains a notice under this paragraph.
38(2) A notice under this paragraph is a notice in a prescribed form containing prescribed information as to the possible effect of deductions on an employee's entitlement to social security benefits, statutory sick pay and statutory maternity pay.
38(3) In this paragraph **"prescribed"** means prescribed by regulations made by the Board.

PARTNERSHIP SHARE MONEY HELD FOR EMPLOYEE

39(1) The plan must provide that partnership share money deducted in accordance with a partnership share agreement is–
(a) paid to the trustees as soon as practicable, and
(b) held by them on behalf of the employee until such time as it is applied by them in acquiring partnership shares on the employee's behalf.
This is subject to paragraphs 40(4)(b) and 42(5)(b) and (6) (obligations to pay money to employee).
39(2) References in this Schedule to the trustees acquiring partnership shares on behalf of an employee include their appropriating to an employee shares already held by them.
39(3) The plan must provide for the trustees to keep any money required to be held by them under this paragraph in an account (interest bearing or otherwise) with–
(a) a person falling within section 840A(1)(b) of the Taxes Act 1988,
(b) a building society, or
(c) a firm falling within section 840A(1)(c) of that Act.

39(4) If the partnership share money held on behalf of an employee is held in an interest bearing account the plan must provide for the trustees to account to the employee for the interest.

History – In Para. 39(3) (partnership share money held for employees), sub-paragraphs (a) and (c) substituted, by virtue of SI 2001/3629, art. 107 which came into force on 1 December 2001.

PLAN WITH NO ACCUMULATION PERIOD

40(1) If the plan does not provide for an accumulation period, it must provide for partnership share money to be applied by the trustees in acquiring partnership shares on behalf of the employee on the acquisition date.

40(2) For this purpose **"the acquisition date"** means the date set by the trustees in relation to the award of partnership shares, being a date within 30 days after the last date on which the partnership share money to be applied in acquiring the shares was deducted.

40(3) The number of shares awarded to each employee must be determined in accordance with the market value of the shares on the acquisition date.

40(4) Any surplus partnership share money remaining after the acquisition of shares by the trustees–
(a) may with the agreement of the employee be carried forward and added to the amount of the next deduction, and
(b) in any other case must be paid over to the employee as soon as practicable.

40(5) This paragraph is subject to paragraph 43 (restriction imposed on number of shares awarded).

PLAN WITH ACCUMULATION PERIOD

41(1) The plan may provide for accumulation periods not exceeding twelve months.

41(2) Where it does so–
(a) the partnership share agreement must specify when each accumulation period begins and ends (the beginning of the first period being not later than the date on which the first deduction is made), and
(b) the accumulation period which applies in relation to each award of partnership shares must be the same for all individuals who are eligible to participate in the award.

41(3) The partnership share agreement may specify that an accumulation period comes to an end on the occurrence of a specified event. This is subject to sub-paragraph (2)(b).

41(4) Where the plan provides for accumulation periods, it may also provide that if–
(a) during an accumulation period, a transaction occurs in relation to any of the shares ("the original holding") to be acquired under a partnership share agreement which results in a new holding of shares being equated with the original holding for the purposes of capital gains tax, and
(b) the employee gives his consent for the purposes of this sub-paragraph,
the partnership share agreement shall have effect after the time of that transaction as if it were an agreement for the purchase of shares comprised in the new holding.

APPLICATION OF MONEY DEDUCTED IN ACCUMULATION PERIOD

42(1) This paragraph applies if the plan provides for one or more accumulation periods.

42(2) The plan must provide for the partnership share money deducted in each period to be applied by the trustees in acquiring partnership shares on behalf of the employee on the acquisition date.
This is subject to sub-paragraphs (6) and (7).

42(3) In sub-paragraph (2) **"the acquisition date"** means the date set by the trustees in relation to the award of partnership shares, being a date within 30 days after the end of the accumulation period which applies in relation to the award.

42(4) The number of shares awarded to each employee must be determined in accordance with the lower of–
(a) the market value of the shares at the beginning of the accumulation period, and
(b) the market value of the shares on the acquisition date.

42(5) Any surplus partnership share money remaining after the acquisition of shares by the trustees–
(a) may with the agreement of the employee be carried forward to the next accumulation period, and
(b) in any other case must be paid over to the employee as soon as practicable.

42(6) The plan must provide that where–
(a) partnership share money has been deducted in an accumulation period, and
(b) the employee ceases to be in relevant employment during that period,
the partnership share money is paid over to the individual as soon as practicable.

42(7) The partnership share agreement may provide that, where an accumulation period comes to an end on the occurrence of a specified event, the partnership share money deducted in that period must be paid over to the individual as soon as practicable instead of being applied in acquiring shares.

42(8) This paragraph is subject to paragraph 43 (restriction imposed on number of shares awarded).

RESTRICTION IMPOSED ON NUMBER OF SHARES AWARDED

43(1) The plan may authorise the company to specify the maximum number of shares ("the award maximum") to be included in an award of partnership shares. A different number may be specified in relation to different awards.

43(2) If the plan so authorises the company, it must require partnership share agreements to contain an undertaking by the company to notify the employee of any restriction on the number of shares to be included in an award.

43(3) The plan must require the notice to be given–
(a) if there is no accumulation period, before the deduction of the partnership share money relating to the award, and
(b) if there is an accumulation period, before the beginning of the accumulation period relating to the award.

43(4) The plan must provide that where the award maximum in respect of an award of partnership shares is smaller that the number of shares which would otherwise be included in the award, the number of partnership shares included in each individual award under paragraph 40(1) or 42(2) shall be reduced proportionately.

STOPPING AND RE-STARTING DEDUCTIONS

44(1) The plan must provide that an employee may at any time give notice in writing to the company to stop deductions in pursuance of a partnership share agreement.

44(2) The plan must also provide that an employee who has stopped deductions may subsequently give notice in writing to the company to re-start deductions in pursuance of the agreement, but may not make up deductions that have been missed.

44(3) If the plan makes provision for one or more accumulation periods, it may prevent an employee re-starting deductions more than once in any accumulation period.

44(4) The plan must provide that unless a later date is specified in the notice–
(a) the company must within 30 days of receiving a notice within sub-paragraph (1), ensure that no further deductions are made by it under the partnership share agreement;
(b) the company must on receiving a notice within sub-paragraph (2) re-start deductions under the partnership share agreement not later than the re-start date.

44(5) For the purposes of sub-paragraph (4)(b) **"the re-start date"** is the date of the first deduction due under the partnership share agreement more than 30 days after receipt of the notice within sub-paragraph (2).

WITHDRAWAL FROM PARTNERSHIP SHARE AGREEMENT

45(1) The plan must provide that an employee may withdraw from a partnership share agreement at any time by notice in writing to the company.

45(2) The plan must provide that, unless a later date is specified in the notice, a notice of withdrawal takes effect 30 days after it is received by the company.
45(3) The plan must provide that where an employee withdraws from a partnership share agreement, any partnership share money held on his behalf is to be paid over to him as soon as practicable.

REPAYMENT OF PARTNERSHIP SHARE MONEY ON WITHDRAWAL OF APPROVAL OR TERMINATION

46(1) The plan must provide that where–
(a) the approval of the plan is withdrawn (see paragraph 118), or
(b) a plan termination notice is issued in respect of the plan (see paragraph 120),
any partnership share money held on behalf of an employee is paid over to him.
46(2) The plan must require the payment to be made–
(a) in a case within sub-paragraph (1)(a), as soon as practicable after notice of the withdrawal is given to the company, and
(b) in a case within sub-paragraph (1)(b), as soon as practicable after the plan termination notice is notified to the trustees under paragraph 120(2).

ACCESS TO PARTNERSHIP SHARES

47(1) The plan must provide that when partnership shares have been awarded to an employee, the employee may at any time withdraw any or all of the partnership shares from the plan.
47(2) There may be a charge to tax under paragraph 86 (charge on partnership shares ceasing to be subject to plan).

MEANING OF "SALARY"

48 References in this Part of this Schedule to an employee's "salary" are to such of the emoluments of the employment by reference to which he is eligible to participate in the plan as are liable to be paid under deduction of tax pursuant to section 203 of the Taxes Act 1988 (PAYE) or which would be if that individual were within the scope of Schedule E, after deducting amounts included by virtue of Chapter II of Part V of that Act (expenses and benefits in kind) or which would have been had the individual been within the scope of Schedule E, or would be so liable apart from this Schedule.

History – In para. 48, the words "or which would be if that individual were within the scope of Schedule E" and "or which would have been had the individual been within the scope of Schedule E" inserted by FA 2001, s. 62 and Sch. 13, para. 3(1) with effect, in relation to any award of partnership shares for which the eligibility time falls, after 11 May 2001 (Sch. 13, para. 3(2)).

Cross references – FA 2001, Sch. 13, para. 3(3): meaning of the term "eligibility time".

Part VI – Matching Shares

INTRODUCTION

49 If the plan provides for matching shares it must comply with the requirements of this Part of this Schedule.

GENERAL REQUIREMENTS FOR MATCHING SHARES

50(1) The plan must provide for the matching shares–
(a) to be shares of the same class and carrying the same rights as the partnership shares to which they relate;
(b) to be awarded on the same day as the partnership shares to which they relate are awarded; and
(c) to be awarded to all employees who participate in the award on exactly the same basis.
50(2) Sub-paragraph (1) is subject to paragraph 65 (permitted restrictions: provision for forfeiture).

RATIO OF MATCHING SHARES TO PARTNERSHIP SHARES

51(1) The partnership share agreement must specify–
(a) the ratio of matching shares to partnership shares for the time being offered by the company, and
(b) the circumstances and manner in which the ratio may be changed by the company.
51(2) The ratio must not exceed 2:1 and must be applied by reference to the number of shares.
51(3) A partnership share agreement must provide for the employee to be informed by the company if the ratio offered by the company changes before partnership shares are awarded to him under the agreement.

APPLICATION OF PROVISIONS RELATING TO HOLDING PERIOD ETC.

52 The provisions of paragraphs 31 and 32 as to the holding period and related matters apply in relation to matching shares as they apply to free shares.

Part VII – Reinvestment Of Cash Dividends

REINVESTMENT

53(1) The plan may provide that where the company so directs–
(a) all cash dividends in respect of plan shares held on behalf of participants must be applied in acquiring further shares on their behalf, or
(b) all cash dividends in respect of plan shares held on behalf of participants who elect to reinvest their dividends must be applied in acquiring further shares on their behalf.
This is referred to in this Part of this Schedule as "reinvestment" and the further plan shares acquired are referred to in this Schedule as "dividend shares".
53(2) The company may revoke a direction.
53(3) Where cash dividends in respect of plan shares held on behalf of a participant are not required to be reinvested under the plan, the plan must require the dividends to be paid over to the participant as soon as practicable.
53(4) This paragraph is subject to paragraph 54 (limit on amount reinvested).

LIMIT ON AMOUNT REINVESTED

54(1) The plan must provide that the total dividend reinvestment in respect of any participant cannot exceed £1,500 in any tax year.
54(2) For this purpose **"the total dividend reinvestment"** in respect of a participant is the sum of–
(a) the amount applied by the trustees in acquiring dividend shares on behalf of the participant under the plan, and
(b) the amount applied by the trustees of other employee share ownership plans that are–
(i) established by the company or an associated company, and
(ii) approved under this Schedule,
in acquiring dividend shares on his behalf.
54(3) If the amounts received by the trustees exceed the limit in sub-paragraph (1), the plan must provide for the balance to be paid over to the participant as soon as practicable.

GENERAL REQUIREMENTS FOR DIVIDEND SHARES

55 The plan must provide that dividend shares are shares–
(a) of the same class and carrying the same rights as the shares in respect of which the dividend is paid, and
(b) which are not subject to any provision for forfeiture.

ACQUISITION OF DIVIDEND SHARES

56(1) The plan must provide that in exercising their powers in relation to the acquisition of dividend shares the trustees must treat participants fairly and equally.

56(2) The plan must provide for the trustees to apply a cash dividend in acquiring further shares on behalf of participants on the acquisition date.

This does not affect the carrying forward under paragraph 58 of any such amount as is mentioned in sub-paragraph (1) of that paragraph (amounts remaining after acquisition of shares).

56(3) For this purpose **"the acquisition date"** means the date set by the trustees in relation to the acquisition of dividend shares, being a date within 30 days after the dividend is received by them.

56(4) The number of dividend shares acquired on behalf of each participant must be determined in accordance with the market value of the shares on the acquisition date.

56(5) References in this Part of this Schedule to the trustees acquiring dividend shares on behalf of a participant include their appropriating to a participant shares already held by them.

HOLDING PERIOD FOR DIVIDEND SHARES

57 The provisions of paragraphs 31 and 32 (holding period and related matters) apply in relation to dividend shares as they apply to free shares, except that the holding period must be three years.

CERTAIN AMOUNTS NOT REINVESTED TO BE CARRIED FORWARD

58(1) Any amount that is not reinvested–

(a) because the amount of the cash dividend to which the participant is entitled is not sufficient to acquire a share, or

(b) because there is an amount remaining after acquiring one or more dividend shares on the participant's behalf,

may be retained by the trustees and carried forward to be added to the amount of the next cash dividend to be reinvested, but shall be held by them so as to be separately identifiable for the purposes of sub-paragraphs (2) and (3).

58(2) An amount retained under this paragraph shall be paid over to the participant–

(a) if or to the extent that it is not reinvested within the period of three years beginning with the date on which the dividend was paid, or

(b) if during that period the participant ceases to be in relevant employment, or

(c) if during that period a plan termination notice is issued in respect of the plan.

58(3) An amount required to be paid over to the participant under sub-paragraph (2) shall be paid over as soon as practicable.

58(4) For the purposes of this paragraph an amount carried forward under this paragraph derived from an earlier cash dividend is treated as reinvested before an amount derived from a later cash dividend.

Part VIII – Types of Share that may be Used

INTRODUCTION

59 The requirements of the following paragraphs must be met with respect to any shares that may be awarded under the plan ("eligible shares")–

paragraph 60 (must be ordinary share capital);
paragraph 61 (requirement as to listing etc.);
paragraph 62 (shares must be fully paid up and not redeemable);
paragraph 63 (only certain kinds of restriction allowed);
paragraph 67 (prohibited companies).

MUST BE ORDINARY SHARE CAPITAL

60 Eligible shares must form part of the ordinary share capital of–

(a) the company; or

(b) a company which has control of the company; or

(c) a company which either is, or has control of, a company which is a member of a consortium owning either the company or a company having control of the company.

REQUIREMENT AS TO LISTING ETC.

61 Eligible shares must be–

(a) shares of a class listed on a recognised stock exchange; or

(b) shares in a company which is not under the control of another company; or

(c) shares in a company which is under the control of a company (other than a company which is, or would if resident in the United Kingdom be, a close company) whose shares are listed on a recognised stock exchange.

SHARES MUST BE FULLY PAID UP AND NOT REDEEMABLE

62(1) Eligible shares must be–

(a) fully paid up, and

(b) not redeemable.

62(2) Shares are not regarded as fully paid up for the purposes of sub-paragraph (1)(a) if there is any undertaking to pay cash to the company at a future date.

62(3) For the purposes of sub-paragraph (1)(b) **"redeemable"** shares include shares that may become redeemable at a future date.

62(4) Sub-paragraph (1)(b) does not apply in relation to shares in a co-operative.

62(5) In sub-paragraph (4) **"co-operative"** means a registered industrial and provident society which is a co-operative society.

For this purpose–

"registered industrial and provident society" means a society registered or deemed to be registered under the Industrial and Provident Societies Act 1965 or the Industrial and Provident Societies Act (Northern Ireland) 1969; and

"co-operative society" has the same meaning as in section 1 of the 1965 Act or, as the case may be, the 1969 Act.

ONLY CERTAIN KINDS OF RESTRICTION ALLOWED

63(1) Eligible shares must not be subject to any restrictions other than–

(a) those involved in there being a holding period (see paragraphs 31, 52 and 57); or

(b) those affecting all ordinary shares in the company; or

(c) those permitted by–
paragraph 64 (voting rights),
paragraph 65 (provision for forfeiture), or
paragraph 66 (pre-emption conditions).

63(2) For this purpose there is a restriction if there is any contract, agreement, arrangement or condition–

(a) by which a person's freedom to dispose of the shares or of any interest in them or of the proceeds of their sale or to exercise any right conferred by them is restricted, or

(b) by which such a disposal or exercise may result in any disadvantage to him or to a person connected with him,

subject to sub-paragraphs (3) and (4).

63(3) Any discretion of the directors under the articles of association of the company to refuse to accept the transfer of shares shall be disregarded for the purposes of this paragraph if the directors–

(a) have undertaken to the Inland Revenue not to exercise it in such a way as to discriminate against participants, and

(b) have notified all qualifying employees of the existence of the undertaking.

63(4) There shall also be disregarded for the purposes of this paragraph so much of any contract, agreement, arrangement or condition as contains provisions similar in purpose and effect to any of the provisions of the Model Code as (for the time being) set out in the listing rules issued by the competent authority for listing in the United Kingdom under section 74(4) of the Financial Services and Markets Act 2000.

PERMITTED RESTRICTIONS: VOTING RIGHTS

64 Eligible shares may be shares carrying no voting rights or limited voting rights.

PERMITTED RESTRICTIONS: PROVISION FOR FORFEITURE

65(1) Free or matching shares may be subject to provision for forfeiture in the following circumstances.

65(2) Provision may be made for forfeiture–

(a) on the participant ceasing to be in relevant employment at any time in the forfeiture period,

(b) on the participant withdrawing the shares from the plan in that period, or

(c) in the case of matching shares, on the participant withdrawing the partnership shares in respect of which those shares were awarded from the plan within that period,

otherwise than by reason of an event within paragraph 87(2) (circumstances in which there is no charge to tax on shares ceasing to be subject to plan).

65(3) In sub-paragraph (2) **"the forfeiture period"** means the forfeiture period specified in the plan being a period of not more than three years beginning with the date on which the shares were awarded to the participant.

65(4) Forfeiture may not be linked to the performance of any person or persons.

65(5) The same provision for forfeiture must apply in relation to all free or matching shares included in the same award under the plan.

65(6) In this Schedule **"provision for forfeiture"** means any provision to the effect that a participant shall cease to be beneficially entitled to the shares on the occurrence of certain events, and references to forfeiture shall be construed accordingly.

PERMITTED RESTRICTIONS: PRE-EMPTION CONDITIONS

66(1) If the requirements of this paragraph are met, eligible shares may be subject to provision requiring shares–

(a) that were awarded to an employee under the plan, and

(b) that are held by an employee or a permitted transferee,

to be offered for sale on the employee ceasing to be in relevant employment.

66(2) For the purposes of sub-paragraph (1)(b) a **"permitted transferee"** means a person to whom, under the articles of association of the company, the employee is permitted to transfer the shares.

66(3) The requirements of this paragraph are that under the articles of association of the company–

(a) the same provision applies to all employees of the company or, in the case of a parent company, to all employees of that company or any company of which that company has control;

(b) the shares are required to be offered for sale at a specified consideration; and

(c) anyone disposing of shares of the same class (whether or not as an employee) is required to offer the shares for sale on no better terms.

PROHIBITED COMPANIES

67(1) Eligible shares must not be shares–

(a) in an employer company, or

(b) in a company that–

(i) has control of an employer company, and

(ii) is under the control of a person or persons within sub-paragraph (2)(b)(i) in relation to an employer company.

67(2) For the purposes of this paragraph a company is **"an employer company"** if–

(a) the business carried on by it consists substantially in the provision of the services of persons employed by it, and

(b) the majority of those services are provided to–

(i) a person who has, or two or more persons who together have, control of the company, or

(ii) a company associated with the company.

67(3) For the purposes of sub-paragraph (2)(b)(ii) a company shall be treated as associated with another company if both companies are under the control of the same person or persons.

67(4) For the purposes of sub-paragraphs (1) to (3)–

(a) references to a person include a partnership, and

(b) where a partner, alone or together with others, has control of a company, the partnership shall be treated as having like control of that company.

67(5) For the purposes of this paragraph the question whether a person controls a company shall be determined in accordance with section 416(2) to (6) of the Taxes Act 1988.

Part IX – The Trustees

ESTABLISHMENT OF TRUSTEES

68(1) The plan must provide for the establishment of a body of persons resident in the United Kingdom ("the trustees") who are required by the plan–

(a) in the case of free or matching shares, to acquire shares and appropriate them to employees in accordance with the plan;

(b) in the case of partnership shares, to apply partnership share money in acquiring shares on behalf of employees in accordance with the plan; and

(c) in the case of dividend shares, to apply cash dividends in acquiring shares on behalf of participants in accordance with the plan.

68(2) The functions of the trustees with respect to shares held by them must be regulated by a trust ("the plan trust")–

(a) which is constituted under the law of a part of the United Kingdom, and

(b) the terms of which are embodied in an instrument which complies with the requirements of this Part of this Schedule.

68(3) The instrument must not contain any terms which are neither essential nor reasonably incidental to complying with the requirements of this Part of this Schedule.

POWER OF TRUSTEES TO BORROW

69 The trust instrument may provide that the trustees have power to borrow–

(a) to acquire shares for the purposes of the plan, and

(b) for such other purposes as may be specified in the trust instrument.

DUTY TO GIVE NOTICE OF AWARD OF SHARES ETC.

70(1) The trust instrument must make the following provision regarding notices.

70(2) It must provide that, as soon as practicable after any free or matching shares have been awarded to an employee, the trustees shall give him notice of the award–

(a) specifying the number and description of those shares,
(b) stating their market value on the date on which they were awarded to him, and
(c) stating the holding period applicable to them.

70(3) It must provide that, as soon as practicable after any partnership shares have been awarded to an employee, the trustees shall give him notice of the award–
(a) specifying the number and description of those shares, and
(b) stating–
(i) the amount of partnership share money applied by the trustees in acquiring the shares on his behalf, and
(ii) their market value on the acquisition date (within the meaning of paragraph 40(2) or, if there is an accumulation period, paragraph 42(3)).

70(4) It must provide that, as soon as practicable after any dividend shares have been acquired on behalf of a participant, the trustees shall give him notice of the acquisition–
(a) specifying the number and description of those shares,
(b) stating their market value on the acquisition date (within the meaning of paragraph 56(3)),
(c) stating the holding period applicable to them, and
(d) informing him of any amount carried forward under paragraph 58 (certain amounts not reinvested).

70(5) It must provide that, where any foreign cash dividend is received in respect of plan shares held on behalf of a participant, the trustees shall give him notice of the amount of any foreign tax deducted from the dividend before it was paid.

GENERAL DUTIES OF TRUSTEES

71(1) The trust instrument must require the trustees–
(a) to dispose of a participant's plan shares, and
(b) to deal with any right conferred in respect of any of his plan shares to be allotted other shares, securities or rights of any description,

only pursuant to a direction given by or on behalf of the participant.

This is subject to sub-paragraph (3) and to any provision made in the plan in accordance with paragraph 73 (meeting PAYE obligations).

71(2) The plan may provide for participants to give such general directions, to such effect and in such terms, as are specified in the plan.

71(3) The trust instrument must, in the case of a participant's plan shares that are free, matching or dividend shares, prohibit the trustees from disposing of any of those shares (whether to the participant or otherwise) at any time during the holding period, unless the participant has at that time ceased to be in relevant employment.

This is subject to–

paragraph 32 (holding period: power to authorise trustees to accept general offers etc.);
paragraph 72 (power of trustees to raise funds to subscribe for rights issue);
paragraph 73 (meeting PAYE obligations);
paragraph 121(5) (termination of plan: early removal of shares with participant's consent).

71(4) The trust instrument must require the trustees to pay over to the participant as soon as practicable any money or money's worth received by them in respect of or by reference to any of his shares, other than money's worth consisting of new shares within the meaning of paragraph 115 (company reconstructions).

This is subject to–
(a) the provisions of Part VII (reinvestment of cash dividends);
(b) the trustees' obligations under paragraphs 95 and 96 (PAYE: shares ceasing to be subject to the plan and capital receipts); and
(c) the trustees' PAYE obligations.

POWER OF TRUSTEES TO RAISE FUNDS TO SUBSCRIBE FOR RIGHTS ISSUE

72(1) The trustees may dispose of some of the rights arising under a rights issue in order to be able to obtain sufficient funds to exercise other such rights.

This power is subject to paragraph 71(1) (duty to act in accordance with participant's directions).

72(2) In this paragraph references to rights arising under a rights issue are to rights conferred in respect of a participant's plan shares to be allotted, on payment, other shares or securities or rights of any description in the same company.

MEETING PAYE OBLIGATIONS

73(1) The plan must make provision to ensure that, where a PAYE obligation is imposed on the trustees as a result of any of a participant's plan shares ceasing to be subject to the plan, the trustees are able to meet that obligation–
(a) by disposing of–
(i) any of those shares, or
(ii) any of the participant's remaining plan shares (if any), or
(b) by virtue of the participant paying to the trustees a sum equal to the amount required to discharge the obligation.

73(2) In sub-paragraph (1) the reference to a PAYE obligation includes an obligation under paragraph 95 (PAYE: shares ceasing to be subject to the plan).

73(3) In sub-paragraph (1)(a) the reference to disposing of shares includes the acquisition of the shares by the trustees for the purposes of the trust.

73(4) A disposal of any of the participant's plan shares in accordance with provision made under sub-paragraph (1)(a)(ii) may give rise to a charge to tax under–

paragraph 81 (charge on free or matching shares ceasing to be subject to plan);
paragraph 86 (charge on partnership shares ceasing to be subject to plan); or
paragraph 93 (charge on dividend shares ceasing to be subject to plan).

DEEMED DISPOSAL BY TRUSTEES ON DISPOSAL OF BENEFICIAL INTEREST

74(1) If at any time the participant's beneficial interest in any of his shares is disposed of, the shares in question shall be treated for the purposes of this Schedule as having been disposed of at that time by the trustees for the like consideration as was obtained for the disposal of the beneficial interest.

74(2) For this purpose there is no disposal of the participant's beneficial interest if and at the time when–
(a) in England and Wales or Northern Ireland, that interest becomes vested in any person on the insolvency of the participant or otherwise by operation of law, or
(b) in Scotland, that interest becomes vested in a judicial factor, in a trustee of the participant's sequestrated estate or in a trustee for the benefit of the participant's creditors.

74(3) If a disposal of shares falling within this paragraph is not at arm's length, the proceeds of the disposal shall be taken for the purposes of this Schedule to be equal to the market value of the shares at the time of the disposal.

DUTIES OF TRUSTEES IN RELATION TO TAX LIABILITIES

75(1) The trust instrument must require the trustees–
(a) to maintain such records as may be necessary for the purposes of–
(i) their own PAYE obligations, or
(ii) the PAYE obligations of the employer company so far as they relate to the plan,
(b) where the participant becomes liable to income tax under Case V of Schedule D, Schedule E or Schedule F by reason of the occurrence of any event, to inform him of any facts relevant to determining that liability.

75(2) For the purposes of this paragraph–

"employer company" has the same meaning as in paragraph 95 (PAYE: shares ceasing to be subject to the plan); and

"PAYE obligations" includes obligations conferred on the trustees by paragraphs 95 and 96 (PAYE: shares ceasing to be subject to plan and capital receipts).

ACQUISITION BY TRUSTEES OF SHARES FROM EMPLOYEE SHARE OWNERSHIP TRUST

76(1) The trust instrument must provide that, where there is a qualifying transfer of shares to the trustees, those shares–

(a) must not be awarded to participants under the plan as partnership shares, and

(b) must be included in any award of free or matching shares made after the date of the transfer in priority to other shares available for inclusion in that award.

76(2) For the purposes of this paragraph there is a qualifying transfer of shares to the trustees if relevant shares–

(a) are transferred to them by the trustees of an employee share ownership trust, and

(b) the transfer is a qualifying transfer within section 69(3AA) of the Finance Act 1989 (transfer of shares in, or shares purchased from money in, an employee share ownership trust immediately before 21st March 2000).

Part X – Income Tax

INTRODUCTION

77(1) The provisions of this Part of this Schedule apply for income tax purposes in relation to an approved employee share ownership plan.

This is subject to sub-paragraph (2).

77(2) Nothing in this Part applies to an individual if, at the time of the award in question, he is not chargeable to tax under Schedule E in respect of the employment by reference to which he meets the requirement of paragraph 14 (the employment requirement) in relation to the plan.

NO CHARGE ON AWARD OF SHARES ETC.

78(1) Notwithstanding that the beneficial interest in the shares passes to the employee–

(a) on the award to him of free, matching or partnership shares under the plan, or

(b) on the acquisition on his behalf of dividend shares under the plan,

the value of that interest at the time of the award or acquisition is not treated as income of his chargeable to tax.

78(2) An employee is not chargeable to tax under Schedule E by virtue of section 162(1) of the Taxes Act 1988 (deemed loan in case of shares acquired at an under-value) in respect of the award to him of shares under the plan.

This does not affect any charge to tax under section 162(6) of that Act (stop-loss provision).

78(3) Incidental expenditure of the trustees or the employer in operating the plan is not treated as giving rise to any charge to income tax on employees.

History – Para. 78(3) inserted by FA 2001, s. 62 and Sch. 13, para. 4(1) with effect for the year 2001–02 and subsequent years of assessment (Sch. 13, para. 4(2)).

CAPITAL RECEIPTS IN RESPECT OF PARTICIPANT'S SHARES

79(1) Where–

(a) a capital receipt is received by a participant in respect of or by reference to any of his plan shares, and

(b) the plan shares in respect of or by reference to which it is received are–

(i) free, matching or partnership shares that were awarded to the participant fewer than five years before he received the capital receipt, or

(ii) dividend shares that were acquired on his behalf fewer than three years before he received that receipt,

the participant is chargeable to income tax under Schedule E for the tax year in which the capital receipt is received by him on the amount or value of the receipt.

79(2) For the purposes of this paragraph any money or money's worth is a **"capital receipt"** subject to the following provisions.

79(3) Money or money's worth is not a capital receipt for the purposes of this paragraph to the extent that–

(a) it constitutes income in the hands of the recipient for the purposes of income tax (or would do so but for this Part of this Schedule), or

(b) it consists of the proceeds of disposal of the shares, or

(c) it consists of new shares within the meaning of paragraph 115 (company reconstructions).

79(4) If, pursuant to a direction given by or on behalf of the participant for the purposes of paragraph 72(1), the trustees–

(a) dispose of some of the rights under a rights issue, and

(b) use the proceeds of that disposal to exercise other such rights,

the money or money's worth that constitutes the proceeds of that disposal is not a capital receipt for the purposes of this paragraph.

The references in this sub-paragraph to rights under a rights issue are to rights, conferred in respect of a participant's plan shares, to be allotted, on payment, other shares or securities or rights of any description in the same company.

79(5) This paragraph does not apply in relation to a capital receipt referable to the shares of a participant if it is received by the participant's personal representative after his death.

EXCLUSION OF CERTAIN CHARGES IN RELATION TO PARTICIPANT'S SHARES

80(1) There is no charge to tax on the participant under–

(a) section 140A of the Taxes Act 1988 (charge on conditional acquisition of shares), or

(b) section 78 of the Finance Act 1988 (charge on removal of restriction),

when any provision for forfeiture to which the shares are subject, in accordance with paragraph 65 (permitted restrictions: provision for forfeiture), is varied or removed.

80(2) A participant is not chargeable to tax under Schedule E by virtue of section 78 of the Finance Act 1988 (charge on removal of restriction) if the chargeable event (within the meaning of that section) is the ending of the holding period in relation to his free, matching or dividend shares.

80(3) A participant is not chargeable to tax under Schedule E by virtue of section 79 of that Act (charge on chargeable increase in value) in respect of any shares of his that are subject to the plan at the end of the period for which the chargeable increase is determined for the purposes of that section.

CHARGE ON FREE OR MATCHING SHARES CEASING TO BE SUBJECT TO PLAN

81(1) When free or matching shares cease to be subject to the plan, income tax may be chargeable depending on the period that has elapsed between–

(a) the date on which the shares were awarded to the participant, and

(b) the date on which they cease to be subject to the plan.

81(2) If the period is less than three years, the participant is chargeable to tax under Schedule E on the market value of the shares when they cease to be subject to the plan.

81(3) If the period is three years or more but less than five years, the participant is chargeable to tax under Schedule E on–

(a) the market value of the shares at the date they were awarded to him, or

(b) the market value of the shares when they cease to be subject to the plan,

whichever is less.

81(4) Where the participant is charged to tax under sub-paragraph (3)(a) the tax due shall be reduced by the amount or aggregate amount of any tax paid on any capital receipts within paragraph 79 in respect of those shares.
81(5) There is no charge to tax under this paragraph on the forfeiture of free or matching shares.
81(6) This paragraph has effect subject to–
paragraph 82 (charge to tax on disposal of beneficial interest in shares during the holding period); and
paragraph 87 (circumstances in which there is no charge to tax on shares ceasing to be subject to plan).
81(7) Except as provided by this paragraph and paragraph 82 there is no charge to tax on free or matching shares ceasing to be subject to the plan.

CHARGE ON DISPOSAL OF BENEFICIAL INTEREST DURING THE HOLDING PERIOD

82(1) Where free or matching shares cease to be subject to the plan by virtue of a participant, in breach of his obligations under paragraph 31(1)(b), assigning, charging or otherwise disposing of his beneficial interest in those shares–
(a) paragraph 81 does not apply, and
(b) the participant is chargeable to income tax under Schedule E on the market value of the shares when they cease to be subject to the plan.
82(2) [Repealed by FA 2001, s. 62 and Sch. 13, para. 5 and Sch. 33, Pt. II(2).]

History – Para. 82(2) repealed by FA 2001, s. 62 and Sch. 13, para. 5(1) and Sch. 33, Pt. II(2); such repeal deemed always to have had effect (FA 2001, s. 62 and Sch. 13, para. 5(2) and Sch. 33, Pt. II(2)).

PARTNERSHIP SHARE MONEY DEDUCTED BEFORE TAX

83(1) Partnership share money deducted from an employee's salary in accordance with a partnership share agreement is not regarded as income of the employee chargeable to tax under Schedule E.
83(2) [Repealed by FA 2004, s. 326 and Sch. 42, Pt. 3.]

History – Para. 83(2) repealed by FA 2004, s. 326 and Sch. 42, Pt. 3 with effect from 6 April 2006.

CHARGE ON PARTNERSHIP SHARE MONEY PAID OVER TO EMPLOYEE

84(1) An individual is chargeable to income tax under Schedule E on any amount paid over to him under–
paragraph 36(4) (deductions in excess of permitted maximum amount);
paragraph 40(4)(b) or 42(5)(b) (surplus partnership share money remaining after acquisition of shares);
paragraph 42(6) (partnership share money paid over on individual leaving relevant employment);
paragraph 42(7) (partnership share money paid over where accumulation period brought to an end by event specified in plan);
paragraph 45(3) (partnership share money paid over on withdrawal from partnership share agreement); or
paragraph 46 (partnership share money paid over on withdrawal of plan approval or termination of plan).
84(2) A charge to tax under sub-paragraph (1) arises at the time the amount is paid over.

CHARGE ON CANCELLATION PAYMENTS IN RESPECT OF PARTNERSHIP SHARE AGREEMENT

85 An individual is chargeable to tax under Schedule E on the amount or value of any money or money's worth received by him in respect of the cancellation of a partnership share agreement entered into by him.

CHARGE ON PARTNERSHIP SHARES CEASING TO BE SUBJECT TO PLAN

86(1) When partnership shares cease to be subject to the plan, income tax may be chargeable depending on the period that has elapsed between–
(a) the acquisition date in respect of those shares (as defined by paragraph 40(2) or, as the case may be, 42(3)), and
(b) the date on which they cease to be subject to the plan.
86(2) If the period is less than three years, the employee is chargeable to income tax under Schedule E on an amount equal to the market value of the shares when they cease to be subject to the plan.
86(3) If the period is three years or more but less than five years, the employee is chargeable to income tax under Schedule E on–
(a) the amount of partnership share money used to acquire the shares, or
(b) the market value of the shares when they cease to be subject to the plan,
whichever is less.
86(4) Where the participant is charged to tax under sub-paragraph (3)(a) the tax due shall be reduced by the amount or aggregate amount of any tax paid on any capital receipts within paragraph 79 in respect of those shares.
86(5) This paragraph has effect subject to paragraph 87 (circumstances in which there is no charge on shares ceasing to be subject to plan).
86(6) Except as provided by this paragraph, there is no charge to income tax on the employee on partnership shares ceasing to be subject to the plan.

CIRCUMSTANCES IN WHICH THERE IS NO CHARGE ON SHARES CEASING TO BE SUBJECT TO PLAN

87(1) There is no charge to tax on shares ceasing to be subject to the plan on the occurrence of any of the following events.
87(2) Those events are the participant ceasing to be in relevant employment–
(a) because of injury or disability;
(b) on being dismissed by reason of redundancy;
(c) by reason of a transfer to which the Transfer of Undertakings (Protection of Employment) Regulations 1981 apply;
(d) by reason of a change of control or other circumstances ending the associated company status of the company by which he is employed;
(e) by reason of his retirement on or after he reaches retirement age; or
(f) on his death.
87(3) In sub-paragraph (2)(b) **"redundancy"** has the same meaning as in the Employment Rights Act 1996 or the Employment Rights (Northern Ireland) Order 1996.
87(4) In sub-paragraph (2)(e) **"retirement age"** means the retirement age specified in the plan, which–
(a) must be the same for men and women, and
(b) must be not less than 50.

DIVIDENDS ETC. IN RESPECT OF UNAPPROPRIATED SHARES

88(1) This paragraph applies to income of the trustees consisting of dividends or other distributions in respect of shares held by them in relation to which the requirements of Part VIII are met.
88(2) Income to which this paragraph applies is income to which section 686 of the Taxes Act 1988 (accumulation and discretionary trusts: special rates of tax) applies only if and when–
(a) *the period applicable to the shares* under the following provisions comes to an end without the shares being awarded to a participant in accordance with the plan, or
(b) if earlier, the shares are disposed of by the trustees.
88(3) If any of the shares in the company in question are readily convertible assets at the time the shares are acquired by the trustees, the period applicable to the shares is the period of two years beginning with the date on which the shares were acquired by the trustees.
88(4) If at the time of the acquisition of the shares by the trustees none of the shares in the company in question are readily convertible assets, the period within which the shares must be awarded is–
(a) five years beginning with the date on which the shares were acquired by the trustees, or

(b) if within that period any of the shares in that company become readily convertible assets, two years beginning with the date on which they did so,

whichever ends first.

88(5) For the purposes of determining whether shares are awarded to a participant within the period applicable under the above provisions, shares acquired by the trustees at an earlier time are taken to be awarded to a participant before shares of the same class acquired by the trustees at a later time.

88(6) For the purposes of this paragraph shares which are subject to provision for forfeiture are treated as acquired by the trustees if and when the forfeiture occurs.

88(7) In this paragraph references to the shares being awarded include references to shares being acquired on behalf of a participant as dividend shares.

History – In para. 88(3) the words "If any of the shares in the company in question are readily convertible assets at the time the shares are acquired by the trustees," substituted for the words "Subject to sub-paragraph (4)," by FA 2001, s. 62 and Sch. 13, para. 6(1)(a) with effect for any shares acquired by the trustees of an employee share ownership plan after 11 May 2001 (Sch. 13, para. 6(2)).

In para. 88(4) the words "any of the shares in that company" substituted for the words "the shares in question" by FA 2001, s. 62 and Sch. 13, para. 6(1)(b) with effect for any shares acquired by the trustees of an employee share ownership plan after 11 May 2001 (Sch. 13, para. 6(2)).

Cross references – FA 2001, Sch. 13, para. 6(3): meaning of the term "the trustees of an employee share ownership plan" defined by reference to the body of persons established by FA 2000, Sch. 8, para. 68.

REINVESTMENT OF CASH DIVIDEND ON BEHALF OF PARTICIPANT

89(1) The amount applied by the trustees in acquiring dividend shares on behalf of a participant is not treated as income of the participant for any tax purposes.

89(2) The participant has no entitlement to a tax credit in respect of the amounts of dividends so applied.

89(3) Sub-paragraphs (1) and (2) do not affect–

(a) any charge under paragraph 93(1) (charge on dividend shares ceasing to be subject to plan), or

(b) any entitlement to a tax credit in respect of the amount so charged.

89(4) Section 234A(4) of the Taxes Act 1988 (information relating to distributions to be provided by nominee) shall not apply in relation to any amount applied by the trustees in acquiring dividend shares on behalf of a participant.

This is subject to paragraph 93(4).

REPAYMENT OF EXCESS CASH DIVIDEND

90 Section 234A(4) to (11) of the Taxes Act 1988 (information relating to distributions to be provided by nominee) shall apply in relation to the balance of any cash dividend paid over to the participant under paragraph 54(3) as if it were a payment to which subsection (4)(b) of that section applies.

TREATMENT OF CASH DIVIDEND RETAINED FOR REINVESTMENT

91(1) An amount retained under paragraph 58(1) (amount of cash dividend not reinvested) shall not be treated as income of the participant for any tax purposes.

91(2) The participant has no entitlement to a tax credit in respect of any such amount.

91(3) This paragraph does not affect any charge–

(a) under paragraph 92 (treatment of cash dividend retained and then later paid out), or

(b) paragraph 93 (charge on dividend shares ceasing to be subject to plan),

or any tax credit in respect of an amount so charged.

TREATMENT OF CASH DIVIDEND RETAINED AND THEN LATER PAID OUT

92(1) Where a cash dividend is paid over to a participant under paragraph 58(2) (cash dividend paid over if not reinvested), the participant is chargeable to tax on that amount–

(a) under Schedule F, or

(b) to the extent that the dividend is a foreign cash dividend, under Case V of Schedule D,

for the tax year in which the dividend is paid over to him.

92(2) For the purposes of determining the tax credit (if any) to which the participant is entitled under section 231 of the Taxes Act 1988 (tax credits for certain recipients of qualifying distributions), the reference in subsection (1) of that section to the tax credit fraction in force when the distribution is made shall be read as a reference to the fraction in force when the dividend is paid over to him.

92(3) Section 234A(4) to (11) of the Taxes Act 1988 (information relating to distributions to be provided by nominee) shall apply in relation to an amount paid under paragraph 58(2) as if–

(a) it were a payment to which subsection (4)(b) of that section applies, and

(b) the cash dividend had been paid when the payment was paid over to the participant under paragraph 58(2).

CHARGE ON DIVIDEND SHARES CEASING TO BE SUBJECT TO PLAN

93(1) If dividend shares cease to be subject to the plan before the end of the period of three years beginning with the date on which the shares were acquired on his behalf, the participant is chargeable to tax on the amount of the relevant dividend–

(a) under Schedule F, or

(b) to the extent that the amount represents a foreign cash dividend, under Case V of Schedule D,

for the tax year in which the shares cease to be subject to the plan.

For this purpose **"the relevant dividend"** is the cash dividend applied to acquire those shares on the participant's behalf.

93(2) For the purposes of determining the tax credit (if any) to which the participant is entitled under section 231 of the Taxes Act 1988 (tax credits for certain recipients of qualifying distributions), the reference in subsection (1) of that section to the tax credit fraction in force when the distribution is made shall be read as a reference to the fraction in force when the shares cease to be subject to the plan.

93(3) Where the participant is charged to tax under this paragraph the tax due shall be reduced by the amount or aggregate amount of any tax paid on any capital receipts within paragraph 79 in respect of those shares.

For this purpose **"the tax due"** means the amount of tax due after deduction of the tax credit determined under sub-paragraph (2).

93(4) Section 234A(4) to (11) of the Taxes Act 1988 (information relating to distributions to be provided by nominee) shall apply in relation to the relevant dividend as if it were a payment to which subsection (4)(b) of that section applies.

93(5) This paragraph has effect subject to paragraph 87 (circumstances in which there is no charge on shares ceasing to be subject to plan).

93(6) Except as provided by this paragraph there is no charge to tax on dividend shares ceasing to be subject to the plan.

History – In para. 93(2) the words "when the shares cease to be subject to the plan" substituted for the former wording by FA 2001, s. 62 and Sch. 13, para. 7(1); this substitution being deemed to have always had effect (Sch. 13, para. 7(2)).

PAYE: SHARES CEASING TO BE SUBJECT TO PLAN

94 Where as a result of shares ceasing to be subject to the plan a participant is chargeable to tax under this Part of this Schedule,

(a) section 203F of the Taxes Act 1988 (PAYE: readily convertible assets) shall have effect as if the participant were being provided with assessable income in the form of those shares–

(i) at the time the shares cease to be subject to the plan, and

(ii) in respect of the relevant employment in which the participant is employed at that time (or, if he is not employed in relevant employment at that time, the relevant employment in which he was last employed before that time), and

(b) subsection (3) of that section shall have effect as if the reference in that subsection to the amount of income likely to be chargeable to tax under Schedule E in respect of the provision of the asset were a reference to the amount on which tax is likely to be chargeable under this Part of this Schedule by virtue of the shares ceasing to be subject to the plan.

History – In para. 94(a) and (b) from the beginning to "that section" substituted by FA 2002, s. 39(2) with effect for 2002–03 and subsequent tax years.

PAYE: SHARES CEASING TO BE SUBJECT TO THE PLAN

95(1) Sub-paragraphs (2) to (5) apply where as a result of any shares ("the relevant shares") ceasing to be subject to the plan–
(a) a participant is chargeable to income tax under Schedule E in accordance with this Part of this Schedule, and
(b) an obligation to make a PAYE deduction arises in respect of that charge.

95(2) The trustees must pay to the employer company a sum which is sufficient to enable the employer company to discharge that obligation.
This is subject to sub-paragraphs (3) and (7).

95(3) Sub-paragraph (2) only applies where, or to the extent that, the plan does not require the participant to pay the employer company a sum that is sufficient to discharge the obligation mentioned in sub-paragraph (1)(b).

95(4) Section 203J(1) of the Taxes Act 1988 (sections 203B to 203I: accounting for tax) shall have effect as if it required the deduction of income tax to be made from any sum or sums received by the employer–
(a) from the trustees under sub-paragraph (2), or
(b) from the participant in accordance with the plan, as mentioned in sub-paragraph (3).

95(5) After making the necessary PAYE deduction from the sum or sums received as mentioned in sub-paragraph (4), the employer company shall pay any remaining amounts to the participant.

95(6) For the purposes of this paragraph **"the employer company"** means the company which employs the participant in relevant employment at the time when the shares cease to be subject to the plan (or, if the participant is not employed in relevant employment at that time, the company which last employed him in relevant employment before that time), provided that that company is one to whom the PAYE regulations (within the meaning of section 203L(3) of the Taxes Act 1988) at that time apply.

95(7) Where, as a result of any shares ceasing to be subject to the plan, a participant is chargeable to income tax under Schedule E in accordance with this Part and either–
(a) there is no company which falls within sub-paragraph (6), or
(b) the Inland Revenue are of the opinion that it is impracticable for the company which falls within that sub-paragraph to make a PAYE deduction and accordingly direct that this sub-paragraph shall apply,

then sub-paragraph (2) shall not apply and the trustees shall make a PAYE deduction in respect of an amount equal to that on which income tax is payable as if the participant were a former employee of the trustees.

95(8) In a case where sub-paragraph (7) applies, section 203C of the Taxes Act 1988 (PAYE: employee of non-UK employer) does not apply.

95(9) Where–
(a) a participant disposes of his beneficial interest in any of his plan shares to the trustees, and
(b) the trustees are deemed by virtue of paragraph 74 to have disposed of the shares in question,

this paragraph shall apply as if the consideration payable by the trustees to the participant on the disposal had been received by the trustees as the proceeds of disposal of plan shares.

95(10) For the purposes of this paragraph **"PAYE deduction"** means a deduction required by regulations under section 203 of the Taxes Act 1988.

History – In para. 95(6), the words from "a company" to "to whom" substituted by FA 2002, s. 39(3) with effect for 2002–03 and subsequent tax years.

PAYE: CAPITAL RECEIPTS

96(1) Where the trustees receive a sum of money which constitutes (or forms part of) a capital receipt in respect of which a participant is chargeable to income tax under Schedule E, in accordance with this Part of this Schedule, when it is received by him–
(a) the trustees shall pay out of that sum of money to the employer company an amount equal to that on which income tax is so payable, and
(b) the employer company shall then pay over that amount to the participant, but in so doing shall make a PAYE deduction.

This is subject to sub-paragraph (3).

96(2) For the purposes of this paragraph **"the employer company"** means the company which employs the participant in relevant employment at the time the trustees receive the sum of money referred to in sub-paragraph (1) (or, if the participant is not employed in relevant employment at that time, the company which last employed him in relevant employment before that time), provided that that company is one to whom the PAYE regulations (within the meaning of section 203L(3) of the Taxes Act 1988) at that time apply.

96(3) Where the trustees receive a sum of money to which sub-paragraph (1) applies but–
(a) there is no company which falls within sub-paragraph (2), or
(b) the Inland Revenue are of the opinion that it is impracticable for the company which falls within that sub-paragraph to make a PAYE deduction and accordingly direct that this sub-paragraph shall apply,

then, in paying over to the participant the capital receipt, the trustees shall make a PAYE deduction in respect of an amount equal to that on which income tax is payable as mentioned in sub-paragraph (1) as if the participant were a former employee of the trustees.

96(4) In a case where sub-paragraph (3) applies, section 203C of the Taxes Act 1988 (PAYE: employee of non-UK employer) does not apply.

96(5) For the purposes of this paragraph **"PAYE deduction"** means a deduction required by regulations under section 203 of the Taxes Act 1988.

History – In para. 96(2), the words from "the company" to "to whom" substituted by FA 2002, s. 39(4) with effect for 2002–03 and subsequent tax years.

Part XI – Capital Gains Tax

INTRODUCTION

97 The provisions of this Part apply for capital gains tax purposes in relation to an approved employee share ownership plan.

GAINS ACCRUING TO TRUSTEES

98(1) Any gain accruing to the trustees is not a chargeable gain if the shares–
(a) *are shares in relation to which the requirements of Part VIII are met*, and
(b) are awarded to employees, or acquired on their behalf as dividend shares, in accordance with the plan within the relevant period.

98(2) If any of the shares in the company in question are readily convertible assets at the time the shares are acquired by the trustees, the relevant period is the period of two years beginning with the date on which the shares are acquired by the trustees.

98(3) If at the time of the acquisition of the shares by the trustees none of the shares in the company in question are readily convertible assets, the relevant period is–
(a) the period of five years beginning with the date on which the shares were acquired, or

(b) if within that period any of the shares in that company become readily convertible assets, the period of two years beginning with the date on which they did so,

whichever ends first.

98(4) For the purposes of determining whether shares are awarded to employees within the relevant period, shares acquired by the trustees at an earlier time are taken to be awarded to employees before shares of the same class acquired by the trustees at a later time. This is subject to paragraph 76(1) (treatment of shares acquired from an employee share ownership trust).

History – In para. 98(2) the words "If any of the shares in the company in question are readily convertible assets at the time the shares" substituted for the former words "If the shares are readily convertible assets at the time they"; by FA 2001, s. 62 and Sch. 13 para. 8(1)(a) with effect for any shares acquired by the trustees of an employee share ownership plan after 11 May 2001 (Sch. 13, para. 8(2)).

In para. 98(3) the words "If at the time of the acquisition of the shares by the trustees none of the shares in the company in question are readily convertible assets" substituted for the former words "If at the time of their acquisition by the trustees the shares are not readily convertible assets"; by FA 2001, s. 62 and Sch. 13, para. 8(1)(b)(i) with effect for any shares acquired by the trustees of an employee share ownership plan after 11 May 2001 (Sch. 13, para. 8(2)).

In para. 98(3)(b) the words "any of the shares in that company" substituted for the former words "the shares in question"; by FA 2001, s. 62 and Sch. 13, para. 8(1)(b)(ii) with effect for any shares acquired by the trustees of an employee share ownership plan after 11 May 2001 (Sch. 13, para. 8(2)).

Cross references – FA 2001, Sch. 13, para. 8(3): meaning of the term "the trustees of an employee share ownership plan" defined by reference to the body of persons established by FA 2000, Sch. 8, para. 68.

PARTICIPANT ABSOLUTELY ENTITLED AS AGAINST TRUSTEES

99(1) A participant is treated for capital gains tax purposes as absolutely entitled as against the trustees to any shares awarded to him under the plan.

99(2) This applies notwithstanding anything in the plan or the trust instrument.

DIFFERENT CLASSES OF SHARES

100(1) For the purposes of Chapter I of Part IV of the Taxation of Chargeable Gains Act 1992 (identification of shares etc.) a participant's plan shares are treated, so long as they are subject to the plan, as of a different class from any shares (which would otherwise be treated as of the same class) that are not plan shares.

100(2) For the purposes of that Chapter, any shares transferred to the trustees of the plan trust by a qualifying transfer that have not been awarded to participants under the plan shall (notwithstanding that they would otherwise fall to be treated as of the same class) be treated as of a different class from any shares held by the trustees that were not transferred to them by a qualifying transfer.

100(3) In sub-paragraph (2) **"qualifying transfer"** has the meaning given in paragraph 76 (acquisition by trustees of shares from employee share ownership trust).

NO CHARGEABLE GAIN ON SHARES CEASING TO BE SUBJECT TO THE PLAN

101(1) Shares which cease to be subject to the plan are treated as having been disposed of and immediately reacquired by the participant at market value.

101(2) Any gain accruing on that disposal is not a chargeable gain.

TREATMENT OF FORFEITED SHARES

102(1) If any of the participant's plan shares are forfeited, they are treated as having been disposed of by the participant and acquired by the trustees at market value at the date of forfeiture.

102(2) Any gain accruing on that disposal is not a chargeable gain.

ACQUISITION BY TRUSTEES OF SHARES FROM PROFIT SHARING SCHEME

103(1) Where the trustees acquire shares from the trustees of an approved profit sharing scheme, the disposal and the acquisition by the trustees are treated as being made for such consideration as to secure that neither a gain nor a loss accrues on the disposal.

103(2) In such a case the relevant period for the purposes of paragraph 98 is determined as if the shares had been acquired by the trustees at the time they were acquired by the trustees of the other trust.

This does not affect the date on which the trustees are treated as acquiring the shares for the purposes of taper relief.

DISPOSAL OF RIGHTS UNDER RIGHTS ISSUE

104(1) Any gain accruing on the disposal of rights under paragraph 72 (power of trustees to raise funds to subscribe for rights issue) is not a chargeable gain.

104(2) Sub-paragraph (1) does not apply to a disposal of rights unless similar rights are conferred in respect of all ordinary shares in the company.

Part XII – Corporation Tax Deductions

INTRODUCTION

105 References in this Part of this Schedule to deductions are to deductions by a company in calculating for the purposes of corporation tax the profits of a trade carried on by it.

This is subject to paragraph 114 (application of provisions to expenses of management of investment companies etc.).

DEDUCTION FOR PROVIDING FREE OR MATCHING SHARES

106(1) Where, under an approved employee share ownership plan, shares are awarded to employees as free or matching shares by reason of their employment with a company, a deduction is allowed under this paragraph to that company.

106(2) Any such deduction–

(a) is of an amount equal to the market value of the shares at the time they are acquired by the trustees, and

(b) must be made for the period of account in which the shares are awarded to employees in accordance with the plan.

106(3) Except as provided by sub-paragraph (1), no deduction may be made by that company or any associated company in respect of the provision of those shares.

This is subject to paragraphs 111 (deduction for expenses of setting up the plan) and 112 (deductions for contributions to running costs of plan).

106(4) Where the shares are awarded under a group plan, the market value of the shares at the time they are acquired by the trustees shall for the purposes of this paragraph be taken to be the relevant proportion of the total market value of the shares included in the award.

For this purpose **"the relevant proportion"** means the proportion that the number of shares in the award awarded to the employees of the company concerned bears to the total number of shares in the award.

106(5) In determining the market value of any shares for the purposes of this paragraph, if shares have been acquired by the trustees on different days it shall be assumed that those acquired on an earlier day are awarded to employees under the plan before those acquired by the trustees on a later day.

106(6) If a deduction is made under this paragraph by a company, no deduction may be made by any other company under this paragraph in respect of the provision of the shares.

106(7) This paragraph has effect subject to paragraph 108 (cases in which no deduction is allowed).

DEDUCTION FOR ADDITIONAL EXPENSES IN PROVIDING PARTNERSHIP SHARES

107(1) Where under an approved employee share ownership plan–

(a) partnership shares are awarded to employees by reason of their employment with a company, and

(b) the market value of those shares at the time they are acquired by the trustees exceeds the partnership share money paid by the participants to acquire those shares,

a deduction is allowed under this paragraph to that company.

107(2) Any such deduction–

(a) is of an amount equal to the amount of the excess referred to in sub-paragraph (1)(b), and

(b) must be made for the period of account in which the shares are awarded to employees in accordance with the plan.

107(3) Except as provided by sub-paragraph (1), no deduction may be made by that company or any associated company in respect of the provision of those shares.

This is subject to paragraphs 111 (deduction for costs of setting up the plan) and 112 (deductions for contributions to running expenses of plan).

107(4) If a deduction is made under this paragraph by a company, no deduction may be made by any other company under this paragraph in respect of the provision of the shares.

107(5) This paragraph has effect subject to paragraph 108 (cases in which no deduction is allowed).

CASES IN WHICH NO DEDUCTION IS ALLOWED

108(1) No deduction is allowed under paragraph 106 or 107 in the following cases.

108(2) No deduction is allowed in respect of shares awarded to an individual who is not a Schedule E taxpayer at the date the shares are awarded to him under the plan.

A **"Schedule E taxpayer"** means an individual who–

(a) is chargeable to tax under Schedule E in respect of emoluments from the employment by reference to which he is eligible to participate in the award, or

(b) would be so chargeable if any such emoluments were remitted to the United Kingdom.

108(3) No deduction is allowed in respect of shares that are liable to depreciate substantially in value for reasons that do not apply generally to shares in the company.

108(4) No deduction is allowed if a deduction has been made–

(a) by the company, or

(b) by an associated company of the company,

in respect of the provision of the same shares for this or another trust.

This applies whatever the nature or purpose of the other trust and whatever the basis on which the deduction was made.

108(5) For the purposes of determining whether the same shares have been provided to more than one trust, if shares have been acquired by the trustees of the plan trust on different days it shall be assumed that those acquired on an earlier day are awarded under the plan before those acquired by the trustees on a later day.

NO DEDUCTION FOR EXPENSES IN PROVIDING DIVIDEND SHARES

109(1) No deduction is allowed for expenses in providing shares that are acquired on behalf of individuals under an approved employee share ownership plan as dividend shares.

109(2) This is subject to paragraph 112 (deductions for contributions to running expenses of plan).

TREATMENT OF FORFEITED SHARES

110 If any of a participant's plan shares are forfeited–

(a) the shares are treated for the purposes of this Part as acquired by the trustees–

 (i) when the forfeiture occurs, and

 (ii) for no consideration, and

(b) no deduction is allowed under paragraph 106 or 107 in respect of any subsequent award of those shares under the plan.

DEDUCTION FOR COSTS OF SETTING UP THE PLAN

111(1) A deduction is allowed under this paragraph for expenses incurred by a company in establishing an employee share ownership plan which is approved by the Inland Revenue.

111(2) No deduction may be made under this paragraph if–

(a) any employee acquires rights under the plan, or

(b) the trustees acquire any shares for the purposes of the plan,

before the Inland Revenue approve the plan.

111(3) If Inland Revenue approval of the plan is given more than nine months after the end of that period of account in which the expenses are incurred, the expenses are treated for the purposes of this paragraph as incurred in the period in which the approval is given.

111(4) No other deduction is allowed in respect of expenses for which a deduction is allowed under this paragraph.

DEDUCTIONS FOR CONTRIBUTIONS TO RUNNING EXPENSES OF PLAN

112(1) Nothing in this Part of this Schedule affects any deduction for expenses incurred by a company in contributing to the expenses of the trustees in operating an approved employee share ownership plan.

112(2) For this purpose the expenses of the trustees in operating the plan–

(a) do not include expenses in acquiring shares for the purposes of the trust, other than incidental acquisition costs, but

(b) do include the payment of interest on money borrowed by them for that purpose.

112(3) In sub-paragraph (2)(a) **"incidental acquisition costs"** means any fees, commission, stamp duty and similar incidental costs attributable to the acquisition of the shares.

WITHDRAWAL OF DEDUCTIONS ON WITHDRAWAL OF APPROVAL

113(1) If approval of an employee share ownership plan is withdrawn the Inland Revenue may by notice to a company direct that the benefit of any deductions under paragraph 106 (deduction for providing free or matching shares) or 107 (deduction for contributing to additional expenses in providing partnership shares) in relation to the plan is also withdrawn.

113(2) The effect of the direction is that the aggregate amount of the deductions is treated as a trading receipt of that company for the period of account in which the Inland Revenue give notice of the withdrawal of approval.

APPLICATION OF PROVISIONS TO EXPENSES OF MANAGEMENT OF INVESTMENT COMPANIES ETC.

114(1) The provisions of this Part apply in relation to–

(a) investment companies, and

(b) companies to which section 75 of the Taxes Act 1988 (management expenses) applies by virtue of section 76 of that Act (insurance companies),

in accordance with the following provisions.

114(2) The provisions of this Part which allow a deduction in calculating the profits of a trade apply to treat amounts as disbursed as expenses of management.

114(3) Paragraph 113(2) (effect of direction as to withdrawal of deductions) applies as if the reference to a trading receipt for the period of account in which the Inland Revenue give notice of the withdrawal of approval were a reference to profits or gains chargeable to tax under Case VI of Schedule D arising when the Inland Revenue give notice of the withdrawal.

Cross references – FA 2003, Sch. 23, para.33(3)(f): in respect of any time before ITEPA 2003 came into force, deductions available under the provisions of para. 106, 107, 112A and 112B(3) are given priority to relief under FA 2003, Sch. 23 para. 33.

Part XIII – Supplementary Provisions

COMPANY RECONSTRUCTIONS

115(1) This paragraph applies where there occurs in relation to any of the participant's plan shares ("the original holding")–
(a) a transaction which results in a new holding being equated with the original holding for the purposes of capital gains tax, or
(b) a transaction that would have that result but for the fact that what would be the new holding consists of or includes a qualifying corporate bond,
other than a transaction within sub-paragraph (2).
A transaction in relation to which this paragraph applies is referred to below as a "company reconstruction".
115(2) Where an issue of shares of any of the following descriptions (in respect of which a charge to income tax arises) is made as part of a company reconstruction, those shares shall be treated for the purposes of this paragraph as not forming part of the new holding–
(a) redeemable shares or securities issued as mentioned in section 209(2)(c) of the Taxes Act 1988;
(b) share capital issued in circumstances such that section 210(1) of that Act applies;
(c) share capital to which section 249 of that Act applies.
115(3) In this paragraph–

"corresponding shares", in relation to any new shares, means the shares in respect of which the new shares are issued or which the new shares otherwise represent;

"new shares"means shares comprised in the new holding which were issued in respect of, or otherwise represent, shares comprised in the original holding;

"original holding"has the meaning given by sub-paragraph (1).

115(4) Subject to the following provisions of this paragraph, in relation to an employee share ownership plan, references in this Schedule to a participant's plan shares shall be construed, after the time of the company reconstruction, as being or, as the case may be, as including references to any new shares.
115(5) For the purposes of this Schedule–
(a) a company reconstruction shall be treated as not involving a disposal of shares comprised in the original holding,
(b) the date on which any new shares are to be treated as having been awarded to the participant shall be that on which the corresponding shares were awarded,
(c) the conditions in Part VIII shall be treated as fulfilled with respect to any new shares if they were (or were treated as) fulfilled with respect to the corresponding shares, and
(d) the provisions of Part X (income tax) and Part XI (capital gains tax) shall apply in relation to the new shares as they would have applied to the corresponding shares.
Where the corresponding shares were dividend shares, the reference in paragraph (b) to the shares being awarded shall be read as a reference to the shares being acquired on behalf of the participant.
115(6) Sub-paragraphs (4) and (5) are subject to paragraph 116 (treatment of shares acquired under rights issue).
115(7) For the purposes of this Schedule if, as part of a company reconstruction, trustees become entitled to a capital receipt, their entitlement to the capital receipt shall be taken to arise before the new holding comes into being.
115(8) In the context of a new holding, any reference in this Schedule to shares includes securities and rights of any description which form part of the new holding for the purposes of Chapter II of Part IV of the Taxation of Chargeable Gains Act 1992.

TREATMENT OF SHARES ACQUIRED UNDER RIGHTS ISSUE

116(1) Where the trustees exercise rights under a rights issue conferred in respect of a participant's plan shares, any shares or securities or rights allotted as a result shall be treated for the purposes of this Schedule as if they were plan shares–
(a) identical to the shares in respect of which the rights were conferred, and
(b) appropriated to, or acquired on behalf of, the participant under the plan in the same way and at the same time as those shares.
This is subject to sub-paragraphs (2) to (4).
116(2) Where the funds used by the trustees to exercise rights under a rights issue are provided otherwise than by virtue of the exercise by the trustees of their powers under paragraph 72 (power of trustees to raise funds to subscribe for rights issue)–
(a) any shares, securities or rights allotted are not plan shares, and
(b) sections 127 to 130 of the Taxation of Chargeable Gains Act 1992 shall not apply in relation to them.
116(3) Sub-paragraph (1) does not apply in relation to rights arising under a rights issue unless similar rights are conferred in respect of all ordinary shares in the company.
116(4) Where sub-paragraph (1) does not apply by virtue of sub-paragraph (3)–
(a) any shares, securities or rights allotted are not plan shares, and
(b) sections 127 to 130 of the Taxation of Chargeable Gains Act 1992 shall not apply in relation to them.
116(5) In this paragraph references to rights arising under a rights issue are to be construed in accordance with paragraph 72(2).

EXEMPTIONS FROM STAMP DUTY AND STAMP DUTY RESERVE TAX

116A Where, under an approved employee share ownership plan, partnership shares or dividend shares are transferred by the trustees to an employee–
(a) no *ad valorem* stamp duty is chargeable on any instrument by which the transfer is made, and
(b) no stamp duty reserve tax is chargeable on any agreement by the trustees to make the transfer.

History – Para. 116A inserted by FA 2001, s. 95(2); effective, for instruments executed and agreements to transfer shares made after, 11 May 2001 (s. 95(3)).

POWER TO REQUIRE INFORMATION

117(1) The Inland Revenue may by notice require any person to provide them with such information as they reasonably require for the performance of their functions under this Schedule and as the person to whom the notice is addressed has or can reasonably obtain.
117(2) The power conferred by this paragraph extends, in particular, to–
(a) information to enable the Inland Revenue–
(i) to decide whether to approve an employee share ownership plan or withdraw an approval already given, or
(ii) to determine the liability to tax, including capital gains tax, of any person who has participated in a plan; and
(b) information about the administration of a plan and any proposed alteration of the terms of a plan.
117(3) The notice must require the information to be provided within a specified time, which must not be less than three months.
117(4) In section 98 of the Taxes Management Act 1970 (penalties in connection with returns, etc.), in the first column of the table, after the final entry insert–
"paragraph 117 of Schedule 8 to the Finance Act 2000".

WITHDRAWAL OF APPROVAL

118(1) If any disqualifying event occurs in relation to an approved employee share ownership plan, the Inland Revenue may by notice to the company withdraw the approval with effect from the time at which the disqualifying event occurred or such later time as the Inland Revenue may specify.
118(2) The following are disqualifying events–

(a) a contravention in relation to the operation of the plan of any of the requirements of this Schedule, the plan itself or the plan trust;
(b) any alteration being made in a key feature of the plan, or in the terms of the plan trust, without the approval of the Inland Revenue;
(c) if the plan provides for performance allowances in accordance with paragraph 30 (method two), the setting, in respect of an award of shares, of performance targets that, at the time they are set in accordance with the plan, cannot reasonably be viewed as being comparable;
(d) any alteration being made in the share capital of the company whose shares are the subject of the plan, or in the rights attaching to any shares of that company, that materially affects the value of participants' plan shares;
(e) shares of a class of which shares have been awarded to participants receiving different treatment in any respect from the other shares of that class;
(f) the trustees, the company or, in the case of a group plan, a company which is or has been a participating company failing to furnish any information which they are or it is required to furnish under paragraph 117.

118(3) For the purposes of sub-paragraph (2)(b)–
(a) an alteration is an alteration of a "key feature" of the plan if it relates to a provision that is necessary in order to meet the requirements of this Schedule; and
(b) the Inland Revenue shall not withhold their approval unless it appears to them that the plan as proposed to be altered would not now be approved on an application under paragraph 4.

118(4) For the purposes of sub-paragraph (2)(c) performance targets are comparable if they are comparable in terms of the likelihood of their being met by the performance units to which they apply.

118(5) Sub-paragraph (2)(e) applies, in particular, to different treatment in respect of–
(a) the dividend payable;
(b) repayment;
(c) the restrictions attaching to the shares; or
(d) any offer of substituted or additional shares, securities or rights of any description in respect of the shares.

This is subject to sub-paragraph (6).

118(6) Sub-paragraph (2)(e) does not apply–
(a) where the difference in treatment arises from–
(i) a key feature of the plan, or
(ii) any of the participants' shares being subject to provision for forfeiture, or
(b) on the ground only that shares which have been newly issued receive, in respect of dividends payable with respect to a period beginning before the date on which they were issued, treatment less favourable than that accorded to shares issued before that date.

118(7) The withdrawal of approval of an employee share ownership plan does not affect the operation of this Schedule in relation to shares awarded to participants in the plan before the time with effect from which approval was withdrawn.
References in this Schedule to an approved employee share ownership plan in relation to such shares are to a plan that was approved at the time the shares were awarded.

APPEAL AGAINST WITHDRAWAL OF APPROVAL

119(1) The company may appeal against a decision of the Inland Revenue–
(a) to withdraw approval of an employee share ownership plan, or
(b) to give a direction under paragraph 113 (withdrawal of corporation tax deductions on withdrawal of approval), or
(c) to refuse approval under paragraph 118(2)(b) (approval of alteration of plan or plan trust).

119(2) The appeal lies to the Special Commissioners.

119(3) Notice of appeal must be given to the Inland Revenue within 30 days after notice of their decision is given to the company.

TERMINATION OF PLAN

120(1) The plan may provide for the company to issue a plan termination notice in respect of the plan in such circumstances as are specified in the plan.

120(2) The plan must provide that, where a plan termination notice is issued, a copy of the notice is to be given, without delay, to–
(a) the Inland Revenue,
(b) the trustees, and
(c) each individual–
(i) who has plan shares, or
(ii) who has entered a partnership share agreement which was in force immediately before the notice was issued.

EFFECT OF PLAN TERMINATION NOTICE

121(1) This paragraph applies where the company has issued a plan termination notice under paragraph 120.

121(2) No further shares may be awarded to individuals under the plan.

121(3) The trustees must remove the plan shares from the plan as soon as practicable after–
(a) the end of the notice period, or
(b) if later, the first date on which the shares may be removed from the plan without giving rise to a charge to income tax under Part X of this Schedule on the participant on whose behalf they are held.

Paragraph 46 (repayment of partnership share money) and paragraph 58(2) (cash dividend paid over if not reinvested) provide for the payment to employees of money held on their behalf.

121(4) In sub-paragraph (3) **"the notice period"** means the period of three months beginning with the date on which the requirements imposed by the plan in accordance with paragraph 120(2) (copy of termination notice to Inland Revenue, participants etc.) are met in respect of the plan termination notice.

121(5) The trustees may remove the participant's shares from the plan at an earlier date with the participant's consent.

121(6) Any consent given by the participant before he receives a copy of the plan termination notice shall be disregarded for this purpose.

121(7) The trustees must as soon as practicable after the plan termination notice is issued pay to an individual any money held on his behalf.

121(8) In this paragraph references to the trustees removing the plan shares from the plan are to their–
(a) transferring the shares to the participant on behalf of whom they are held, or to another person, at his direction, or
(b) disposing of the shares and accounting (or holding themselves ready to account) for the proceeds to the participant or to another person at his direction.

121(9) Where the participant has died, the references in sub-paragraph (8) to the participant shall be read as references to his personal representatives.

MEANING OF SHARES BEING WITHDRAWN FROM OR CEASING TO BE SUBJECT TO PLAN

122(1) For the purposes of this Schedule shares are withdrawn from the plan when–
(a) they are transferred by the trustees to the participant, or another person, on the direction of the participant,
(b) the participant assigns, charges or otherwise disposes of his beneficial interest in the shares, or
(c) they are disposed of by the trustees, on the direction of the participant, in circumstances where the trustees account (or hold themselves ready to account) for the proceeds to the participant or to another person.

122(2) Where the participant has died, the references in sub-paragraph (1) to the participant shall be read as references to his personal representatives.

122(3) For the purposes of this Schedule plan shares cease to be subject to the plan when–

(a) they are withdrawn from the plan,

(b) the participant to whom the shares were awarded ceases to be in relevant employment at a time when the shares are subject to the plan, or

(c) the trustees dispose of the shares under provision made in accordance with paragraph 73 (meeting PAYE obligations).

122(4) Where an individual participates in an award of partnership shares, if he ceases to be in relevant employment at any time during the acquisition period relating to that award, he shall be treated for the purposes of sub-paragraphs (3) and (7) as ceasing to be in such employment immediately after the shares are awarded to him.

122(5) In sub-paragraph (4) **"the acquisition period"** in relation to an award means–

(a) where there was no accumulation period, the period beginning with the deduction of the partnership share money and ending with the acquisition date (within the meaning of paragraph 40(2)); and

(b) where there was an accumulation period, the period beginning with the end of that period and ending immediately before the acquisition date (within the meaning of paragraph 42(3)).

122(6) For the purposes of determining the charge to income tax (if any) arising on any of the participant's shares ceasing to be subject to the plan–

(a) shares shall be taken to cease to be subject to the plan in the order in which they were awarded to the participant under the plan,

(b) where shares are awarded to the participant on the same day, the shares shall be treated as ceasing to be subject to the plan in the order which gives rise to the lowest charge to income tax on the participant.

122(7) Where a participant ceases to be in relevant employment his plan shares shall be treated as ceasing to be subject to the plan on the date of leaving.

MEANING OF PARTICIPANT CEASING TO BE IN RELEVANT EMPLOYMENT

123(1) This paragraph explains what is meant by a participant ceasing to be in relevant employment.

123(2) Relevant employment means employment by the company or any associated company.

123(3) A participant does not cease to be in relevant employment if he remains in the employment of the company or any associated company.

EXERCISE OF FUNCTIONS CONFERRED ON "THE INLAND REVENUE"

124 References in this Schedule to "the Inland Revenue" are to any officer of the Board.

DETERMINATION OF MARKET VALUE

125(1) For the purposes of this Schedule the **"market value"** of shares has the same meaning as, for the purposes of the Taxation of Chargeable Gains Act 1992, it has by virtue of Part VIII of that Act.

This is subject to paragraph 24(3) (determination of value of shares subject to restriction or risk of forfeiture).

125(2) Where for the purposes of this Schedule the market value of shares on any date falls to be determined, the Inland Revenue and the trustees may agree that it shall be determined by reference to such date or dates, or to an average of the values on a number of dates, as may be provided in the agreement.

MEANING OF "ASSOCIATED COMPANY"

126(1) For the purposes of this Schedule one company is an **"associated company"** of another company if–

(a) one has control of the other, or

(b) both are under the control of the same person or persons.

126(2) For the purposes of this paragraph the question of whether a person controls a company shall be determined in accordance with section 416(2) to (6) of the Taxes Act 1988.

126(3) This paragraph is subject to paragraph 67(3).

JOINTLY OWNED COMPANIES

127(1) For the purposes of the provisions of this Schedule relating to group plans, each joint owner of a jointly owned company is treated as controlling–

(a) the jointly owned company, and

(b) any company controlled by that company.

This paragraph does not apply for the purposes of paragraph 61(b) (requirement that plan shares are in a company not under another company's control).

127(2) A **"jointly owned company"** means a company–

(a) of which 50% of the issued share capital is owned by one person and 50% by another, and

(b) which is not controlled by any one person.

127(3) A jointly owned company may not be a participating company in more than one group plan.

127(4) A company controlled by a jointly owned company may not–

(a) be a participating company in more than one group plan, or

(b) if the jointly owned company or any other company controlled by it is a participating company in a group plan, be a participating company in a different group plan.

History – Para. 127(4) inserted by FA 2002, s. 39(5) with effect for 2002–03 and subsequent tax years.

Notes – FA 2002, s. 39(8): nothing in para. 127(4) prevents a company from continuing to be a participating company in a group plan in which it was a participating company immediately before 24 July 2002 (date of Royal Assent to Finance Act 2002).

MEANING OF "READILY CONVERTIBLE ASSET"

128(1) For the purposes of this Schedule **"readily convertible asset"** has the same meaning as in section 203F of the Taxes Act 1988 (PAYE: tradeable assets).

This is subject to sub-paragraph (2).

128(2) In determining for the purposes of this Schedule (and that section in its application in relation to shares which cease to be subject to a plan) whether shares are readily convertible assets any market for the shares that–

(a) is created by virtue of the trustees acquiring shares for the purposes of the plan, and

(b) exists solely for the purposes of the plan,

shall be disregarded.

History – In para. 128(2), the words from "(and that section" to "subject to a plan)" inserted by FA 2002, s. 39(6) with effect for 2002–03 and subsequent tax years.

MINOR DEFINITIONS

129(1) In this Schedule–

"approved employee share ownership plan" means an employee share ownership plan approved under this Schedule;

"approved profit sharing scheme" means a profit sharing scheme approved under Schedule 9 to the Taxes Act 1988;

"articles of association", in relation to a company, includes any other written agreement between the shareholders of the company;

"company" means a body corporate;

"control", unless otherwise indicated, has the same meaning as in section 840 of the Taxes Act 1988;

"foreign cash dividend" means a cash dividend paid in respect of plan shares in a company not resident in the United Kingdom;

"group of companies" means a company and any other companies of which it has control, and

"group company" has a corresponding meaning;

"ordinary share capital" has the meaning given in section 832(1) of the Taxes Act 1988;

"participant's plan shares", in relation to an employee share ownership plan, means plan shares that have been awarded to an individual participant;

"PAYE obligations" means obligations of any person under–

(a) sections 203 to 203L of the Taxes Act 1988, or

(b) regulations under section 203 of that Act;

"plan shares", in relation to a plan, means–

(a) free, partnership or matching shares that have been awarded to participants under the plan,

(b) dividend shares that have been acquired on behalf of participants under the plan, and

(c) shares in relation to which paragraph 115(5) applies (company reconstructions: new shares),

that remain subject to the plan;

"qualifying corporate bond" has the meaning given by section 117 of the Taxation of Chargeable Gains Act 1992;

"tax year" means a year of assessment.

129(2) Section 839 of the Taxes Act 1988 (connected persons) applies for the purposes of this Schedule.

129(3) For the purposes of this Schedule references to "shares" include fractions of shares forming part of the share capital of a company registered in a foreign country the law of which recognises such fractions.

129(4) For the purposes of this Schedule a company is a member of a consortium owning another company if it is one of a number of companies–

(a) which between them beneficially own not less than three-quarters of the other company's ordinary share capital, and

(b) each of which beneficially owns not less than one-twentieth of that capital.

INDEX OF DEFINED EXPRESSIONS

130 In this Schedule the following expressions are defined or otherwise explained by the provisions indicated–

approved employee share ownership plan	paragraph 129(1) (and see paragraph 118(7))
approved profit sharing scheme	paragraph 129(1)
articles of association	paragraph 129(1)
associated company	paragraph 126 (and see paragraph 67(3))
award of shares	paragraph 3(1)
ceasing to be in relevant employment (in relation to a participant)	paragraph 123
ceasing to be subject to plan (in relation to shares)	paragraph 122
company	paragraph 129(1)
the company (in relation to an employee share ownership plan)	paragraph 1(4)
connected person	paragraph 129(2)
consortium (member of)	paragraph 129(4)
control	paragraph 129(1) (and see paragraph 127)
deduction (in Part XII)	paragraph 105
dividend shares	paragraph 53(1)
eligible shares (in Part VIII)	paragraph 59
employee share ownership plan	paragraph 1(1)
foreign cash dividend	paragraph 129(1)
forfeiture (provision for)	paragraph 65(6)
free shares	paragraph 1(1)(a)
group of companies	paragraph 129(1)
group plan	paragraph 2(1)
holding period	paragraph 31
the Inland Revenue	paragraph 124
market value (of shares)	paragraph 125
matching shares	paragraph 1(2)
ordinary share capital	paragraph 129(1)
parent company	paragraph 2(1)
participant (in relation to an employee share ownership plan)	paragraph 3(3)
participant's plan shares	paragraph 129(1) (and see paragraph 115(4))
participating company (in relation to a group plan)	paragraph 2(2)
participation in an award of shares	paragraph 3(2)
partnership share agreement	paragraph 34
partnership shares	paragraph 1(1)(b)
PAYE obligations	paragraph 129(1)

performance allowance	paragraph 25
plan shares	paragraph 129(1) (and see paragraphs 115 and 116)
the plan trust	paragraph 68(2)
qualifying corporate bond	paragraph 129(1)
qualifying employee	paragraph 8(4)
readily convertible asset	paragraph 128
reinvestment (in Part VII)	paragraph 53(1)
relevant employment	paragraph 123(2)
salary (in Part V)	paragraph 48
shares	paragraph 129(3) (and in the context of a new holding paragraph 115(8))
tax year	paragraph 129(1)
the trustees	paragraph 68(1)
withdrawal of shares from plan	paragraph 122(1)"

Cross references – ITEPA 2003, Sch. 7, para. 68–70: transitionals and savings in respect of share incentive plans approved under Sch. 8 before 6 April 2003.
ITEPA 2003, Sch. 7, para. 92: transitionals and savings in respect of corporation tax deductions under former Sch. 8, Pt. XII.
Notes – Sch. 8 has been rewritten into the provisions of ITEPA 2003, Sch. 2.

SCHEDULE 9 – NEW SCHEDULE 7C TO THE TAXATION OF CHARGEABLE GAINS ACT 1992

Section 48

1 [Inserts TCGA 1992, Sch. 7C.]

SCHEDULE 10 – BENEFITS IN KIND: DEREGULATORY AMENDMENTS

Section 57

[Repealed by ITEPA 2003, s. 724 and Sch. 8, Pt. 1.]

History – Sch. 10 repealed by ITEPA 2003, s. 724 and Sch. 8, Pt. 1 with effect for the year 2003–04 and subsequent tax years.
Notes – Sch. 10 is unnecessary and has not been rewritten into the provisions of ITEPA 2003.

SCHEDULE 11 – CARS AVAILABLE FOR PRIVATE USE

Section 59

[Repealed by ITEPA 2003, s. 724 and Sch. 8, Pt. 1.]

History – Sch. 11 repealed by ITEPA 2003, s. 724 and Sch. 8, Pt. 1 with effect for the year 2003–04 and subsequent tax years.
Notes – Sch. 11 is unnecessary and has not been rewritten into the provisions of ITEPA 2003.

SCHEDULE 12 – PROVISION OF SERVICES THROUGH AN INTERMEDIARY

Section 60

Part I – Application of this Schedule

1–6 [Repealed by ITEPA 2003, s. 724 and Sch. 8, Pt. 1.]

History – Para. 1–6 repealed by ITEPA 2003, s. 724 and Sch. 8, Pt. 1 with effect for the year 2003–04 and subsequent tax years.
Notes – Para. 1–6 rewritten as follows:
Para. 1(1)–(4): ITEPA 2003, s. 49.
Para. 1(5) is unnecessary and has not been rewritten into the provisions of ITEPA 2003.
Para. 2: ITEPA 2003, s. 7(5) and s. 50.
Para. 3: ITEPA 2003, s. 51.
Para. 4: ITEPA 2003, s. 52.
Para. 5: ITEPA 2003, s. 53.
Para. 6: ITEPA 2003, s. 48.

Part II – The deemed Schedule E payment

7–11 [Repealed by ITEPA 2003, s. 724 and Sch. 8, Pt. 1.]

History – Para. 7–11 repealed by ITEPA 2003, s. 724 and Sch. 8, Pt. 1 with effect for the year 2003–04 and subsequent tax years.
Notes – Para. 7–11 rewritten as follows:

Para. 7: ITEPA 2003, s. 54(1).
Para. 7A: ITEPA 2003, s. 54(3).
Para. 7B: ITEPA 2003, s. 54(4), (5) and (7).
Para. 8: ITEPA 2003, s. 54(2).
Para. 9: ITEPA 2003, s. 54(8).
Para. 10: ITEPA 2003, s. 55.
Para. 11: ITEPA 2003, s. 56.

Part III – Supplementary Provisions

12–16 [Repealed by ITEPA 2003, s. 724 and Sch. 8, Pt. 1.]

History – Para. 12–16 repealed by ITEPA 2003, s. 724 and Sch. 8, Pt. 1 with effect for the year 2003–04 and subsequent tax years.

Notes – Para. 12–16 rewritten as follows:
Para. 12: ITEPA 2003, s. 57.
Para. 13: ITEPA 2003, s. 58.
Para. 14: ITEPA 2003, s. 59(1), (6) and (7).
Para. 15: ITEPA 2003, s. 59(4) and (5).
Para. 16: ITEPA 2003, s. 59(4) and (5).

CALCULATION OF PROFITS OF INTERMEDIARY: DEDUCTION FOR DEEMED SCHEDULE E PAYMENT

17 [Omitted by CTA 2009, s. 1322 and Sch. 1, para. 467 and repealed by CTA 2009, s. 1326 and Sch. 3, Pt. 1.]

History – Para. 17 omitted by CTA 2009, s. 1322 and Sch. 1, para. 467 and repealed by CTA 2009, s. 1326 and Sch. 3, Pt. 1, with effect for corporation tax purposes for accounting periods ending on or after 1 April 2009, and for income tax and capital gains tax purposes for the tax year 2009–10 and subsequent tax years.

Notes – Para. 17 rewritten for corporation tax purposes as follows:
Para. 17(1): CTA 2009, s. 139(1) and (2).
Para. 17(2): CTA 2009, s. 139(3).
Para. 17(3): CTA 2009, s. 139(4).
Para. 17(4): CTA 2009, s. 139(5), s. 140(4).

CALCULATION OF PROFITS OF INTERMEDIARY: SPECIAL RULES FOR PARTNERSHIPS

18 [Omitted by CTA 2009, s. 1322 and Sch. 1, para. 467 and repealed by CTA 2009, s. 1326 and Sch. 3, Pt. 1.]

History – Para. 18 omitted by CTA 2009, s. 1322 and Sch. 1, para. 467 and repealed by CTA 2009, s. 1326 and Sch. 3, Pt. 1, with effect for corporation tax purposes for accounting periods ending on or after 1 April 2009, and for income tax and capital gains tax purposes for the tax year 2009–10 and subsequent tax years.

Notes – Para. 18 rewritten for corporation tax purposes as follows:
Para. 18(1): CTA 2009, s. 140(1).
Para. 18(2): CTA 2009, s. 140(2).
Para. 18(3): CTA 2009, s. 140(3).
The rewritten income tax rules can be principally found at s. 164.

19–24 [Repealed by ITEPA 2003, s. 724 and Sch. 8, Pt. 1.]

History – Para. 19–24 repealed by ITEPA 2003, s. 724 and Sch. 8, Pt. 1 with effect for the year 2003–04 and subsequent tax years.

Notes – Para. 19–24 rewritten as follows:
Para. 19: ITEPA 2003, s. 60 and s. 718.
Para. 20: ITEPA 2003, s. 720(1).
Para. 21: ITEPA 2003, s. 61 and s. 721(5).
Para. 22 is unnecessary and has not been rewritten into the provisions of ITEPA 2003.
Para. 23 is spent and has not been rewritten into the provisions of ITEPA 2003.
Para. 24: ITEPA 2003, s. 48.

SCHEDULE 13 – OCCUPATIONAL AND PERSONAL PENSION SCHEMES

Section 61

[Repealed by FA 2004, s. 326 and Sch. 42, Pt. 3 with effect from 6 April 2006.]

History – Sch. 13 repealed by FA 2004, s. 326 and Sch. 42, Pt. 3 with effect from 6 April 2006.

SCHEDULE 14 – ENTERPRISE MANAGEMENT INCENTIVES

Section 62

[Repealed by ITEPA 2003, s. 724 and Sch. 8, Pt. 1.]

History – Sch. 14 repealed by ITEPA 2003, s. 724 and Sch. 8, Pt. 1 with effect in relation to enterprise management incentive share options approved on or after 6 April 2003.

Cross references – ITEPA 2003, Sch. 7, para. 77–83: transitionals and savings in respect of options qualifying under Sch. 14 before 6 April 2003.
ITEPA 2003, Sch. 7, para. 67(4): transitionals and savings in respect of obligations to notify.

Notes – Sch. 14 has been rewritten into the provisions of ITEPA 2003, s. 527–541 and Sch. 5.

SCHEDULE 15 – THE CORPORATE VENTURING SCHEME

Section 63(1)

Cross references – ICTA 1988, s. 303A(9): Enterprise Investment Scheme; application of definitions in FA 2000, Sch. 15 to the restrictions on withdrawal of relief.
TCGA 1992, Sch. 5B, para. 14A(8): Enterprise Investment Scheme, Reinvestment Relief; application of definitions in FA 2000, Sch. 15 to the disregard of certain receipts when determining what value has been received.
SI 2004/712 (Research and Development (Prescribed Activities) Regulations): application of regulations in relation to shares issued on or after 6 April 2004 in relation to Sch. 15.

Official publications – HMRC booklet; IR 2000: The Corporate Venturing Scheme

Part I – Investment Relief: Introduction

MEANING OF "INVESTMENT RELIEF"

1 This Schedule makes provision for–

(a) relief against corporation tax ("investment relief") on amounts subscribed by companies for shares (see this Part and Parts II to VI of this Schedule);

(b) relief against income of companies for losses on disposals of shares to which investment relief is attributable (see Part VII of this Schedule); and

(c) the postponement of certain chargeable gains of companies where the gains are reinvested in shares to which investment relief is attributable (see Part VIII of this Schedule).

ELIGIBILITY FOR INVESTMENT RELIEF

2 A company ("the investing company") is eligible for investment relief in respect of an amount subscribed by it for an issue of shares in another company ("the issuing company") if–

(a) the shares ("the relevant shares") are issued to the investing company;

(b) the investing company is a qualifying investing company in relation to the relevant shares (see Part II of this Schedule);

(c) the issuing company is a qualifying issuing company in relation to the relevant shares (see Part III of this Schedule); and

(d) the general requirements of Part IV of this Schedule are met in respect of the relevant shares.

Other material – HMRC press release, 25 September 2000: establishment of Small Company Enterprise Centre to deal with claims regarding qualification

MEANING OF "THE QUALIFICATION PERIOD"

3(1) In this Schedule **"the qualification period"**, in relation to the relevant shares, means the period beginning with the issue of the shares and ending–

(a) immediately before the third anniversary of the issue date; or

(b) where the money raised by the issuance of the shares is employed wholly or mainly for the purposes of one or more qualifying trades that, on the issue date, were not being carried on–

  (i) by the issuing company, or

  (ii) if it is a parent company, by that company or any of its qualifying 90% subsidiaries,

immediately before the third anniversary of the trading date.

3(2) For this purpose **"the trading date"** means–

(a) the date on which the issuing company or one of its qualifying 90% subsidiaries begins to carry on the qualifying trade to which sub-paragraph (1)(b) refers, or

(b) if there is more than one such trade, the latest date on which the issuing company or one of its qualifying 90% subsidiaries begins to carry on such a trade.

History – In para. 3(1)(b)(ii) and (2)(a) and (b) the phrase "qualifying subsidiaries" substituted by the phrase "qualifying 90% subsidiaries" by FA 2004, s. 95 and Sch. 20, para. 2 with effect in relation to shares issued on or after 17 March 2004.

Cross references – Para: 102(8) when a qualifying 90% subsidiary begins to carry on a trade.

Part II – The Investing Company

INTRODUCTION

4 The investing company is a qualifying investing company in relation to the relevant shares if the requirements of this Part are met as to–

(a) no material interest (see paragraph 5);

(b) no reciprocal arrangements (see paragraph 6);

(c) no control (see paragraph 8);

(d) non-financial activities (see paragraph 10);

(e) the shares being a chargeable asset (see paragraph 13); and

(f) no tax avoidance (see paragraph 14).

THE "NO MATERIAL INTEREST" REQUIREMENT

5 The investing company must not, at any time during the qualification period relating to the shares, have a material interest in the issuing company.

THE "NO RECIPROCAL ARRANGEMENTS" REQUIREMENT

6(1) The investing company must not subscribe for the relevant shares as part of any arrangements which provide for any other person to subscribe for shares in a related company.

6(2) For this purpose–

(a) arrangements shall be disregarded to the extent that they provide for the issuing company to subscribe for shares in any of its qualifying subsidiaries, and

(b) **"a related company"** means a company in which the investing company, or any other person who is a party to the arrangements, has a material interest.

6(3) In sub-paragraph (2)(a) the reference to qualifying subsidiaries of the issuing company is not restricted to companies that were such subsidiaries at the time the arrangements were made.

MEANING OF "MATERIAL INTEREST"

7(1) For the purposes of paragraphs 5 and 6 a person has a material interest in a company if he (whether alone or together with any person connected with him) directly or indirectly possesses or is entitled to acquire more than 30% of–

(a) the ordinary share capital of the company or any subsidiary, or

(b) the voting power in the company or any subsidiary.

7(2) For the purposes of sub-paragraph (1) **"ordinary share capital"**, in relation to a company, means–

(a) all of the issued share capital (by whatever name called) of the company, other than capital comprising relevant preference shares, and

(b) all of the loan capital of the company that comprises debt which carries (directly or indirectly) any right to conversion into, or to the acquisition of, shares within paragraph (a) (or that would be within that paragraph if issued).

7(3) For the purposes of sub-paragraph (2)(b) the loan capital of a company shall be treated as including any debt incurred by the company–

(a) for any money borrowed or capital assets acquired by the company,

(b) for any right to receive income created in favour of the company, or

(c) for consideration the value of which to the company was (at the time when the debt was incurred) substantially less than the amount of the debt (including any premium on it).

This is subject to sub-paragraph (4).

7(4) For the purposes of sub-paragraph (3) a debt which–

(a) is incurred by a company or any subsidiary by overdrawing an account with a person carrying on the business of banking, and

(b) arises in the ordinary course of that business,

shall not be treated as loan capital of the company.

7(5) For the purposes of sub-paragraph (1)–

(a) a person is treated as entitled to acquire anything which he is entitled to acquire at a future date or will at a future date be entitled to acquire, and

(b) there are attributed to a person any rights or powers of any other person who is an associate of his.

7(6) For the purposes of this paragraph a company is a subsidiary of another company if it is a 51% subsidiary of that company.

THE "NO CONTROL" REQUIREMENT

8(1) The investing company must not, at any time during the qualification period relating to those shares, control the issuing company.

8(2) For this purpose the question whether the investing company controls the issuing company shall be determined in accordance with sections 450 and 451 of CTA 2010 with the following modifications.

8(3) The first modification is that, in determining whether the investing company controls the issuing company, there shall be disregarded–

(a) its or any other person's possession of, or entitlement to acquire, relevant preference shares of the issuing company; and

(b) its or any other person's possession of, or entitlement to acquire, rights as a loan creditor of the issuing company.

8(4) For the purposes of sub-paragraph (3) a person is a "loan creditor" of a company if the person is a creditor in respect of the loan capital of that company (within the meaning of paragraph 7(3))

8(5) The second modification is that in determining whether the conditions of sections 450(2) to (4) of CTA 2010 are satisfied there shall be attributed to the investing company (to the extent that it would not otherwise be the case) any rights or powers in the issuing company, or any of its subsidiaries, that are held by–

(a) any person connected with the investing company; or

(b) any person who is–

  (i) a director of the investing company, or of any company connected with that company, or

  (ii) a relative of such a director.

For this purpose **"relative"** means spouse or civil partner, parent or remoter forebear or child or remoter issue.

History – In para. 8(2), the words "sections 450 and 451 of CTA 2010" substituted for the words "section 416(2) to (6) of the Taxes Act 1988" by CTA 2010, s. 1177 and Sch. 1, para. 315(2)(a), with effect for corporation tax purposes for accounting periods ending on or after 1 April 2010, and for income tax and capital gains tax purposes for the tax year 2010–11 and subsequent tax years.
In para. 8(5), the words "sections 450(2) to (4) of CTA 2010" substituted for the words "section 416(2) of that Act" by CTA 2010, s. 1177 and Sch. 1, para. 315(2)(b), with effect for corporation tax purposes for accounting periods ending on or after 1 April 2010, and for income tax and capital gains tax purposes for the tax year 2010–11 and subsequent tax years.
In para. 8(5) the words "spouse or civil partner" substituted for the words "husband or wife" by SI 2005/3229, reg. 132, with effect from 5 December 2005.

RELEVANT PREFERENCE SHARES

9(1) In paragraphs 7 (meaning of "material interest") and 8 (the "no control" requirement) **"relevant preference shares"** means shares which–

(a) do not for the time being carry voting rights;

(b) are issued wholly for new consideration;

(c) do not carry any right either to conversion into shares or securities of any other description or to the acquisition of any additional shares or securities; and

(d) do not carry any right to dividends other than dividends which–

  (i) fall within sub-paragraph (2) or (3);

  (ii) are not to any extent dependent on the results of the company's business or any part of it or on the value of any of the company's assets; and

  (iii) together with any sum paid on a redemption, represent no more than a reasonable commercial return on the consideration for which the shares were issued.

In paragraph (b) **"new consideration"** has the meaning given by section 1115 of CTA 2010.

9(2) Dividends fall within this sub-paragraph if they are of a fixed amount or at a fixed rate per cent of the nominal value of the shares.

This includes dividends where the amount or rate may be changed to another fixed amount or fixed rate in a manner determined under the terms of issue of the shares.

9(3) Dividends fall within this sub-paragraph if they are of a rate per cent of the nominal value of the shares and the rate fluctuates in accordance with–

(a) a standard published rate of interest,

(b) a rate of tax,

(c) the retail prices index, or any similar general index of prices which is published by the government, or by an agent of the government, of the country or territory in whose currency the shares are denominated, or

(d) a published index of prices of shares quoted in the official list of a recognised stock exchange.

9(4) For the purposes of sub-paragraph (1)(d)(ii) dividends shall not be treated as being to any extent dependent on the results of the company's business (or any part of it) or on the value of any of the company's assets by reason only of the fact that the amount or rate of the dividends–

(a) reduces in the event of the results of the business (or part) improving or the value of any of the company's assets increasing, or

(b) increases in the event of the results of the business (or part) deteriorating or the value of any of the company's assets diminishing.

9(5) Dividends are not prevented from falling within sub-paragraph (2) or (3) by the fact that the shares carry no rights at all to dividends for a period or periods determined under the terms of issue of the shares.

History – In para. 9(1), the words "section 1115 of CTA 2010" substituted for the words "section 254 of the Taxes Act 1988" by CTA 2010, s. 1177 and Sch. 1, para. 315(3), with effect for corporation tax purposes for accounting periods ending on or after 1 April 2010, and for income tax and capital gains tax purposes for the tax year 2010–11 and subsequent tax years.

THE NON-FINANCIAL ACTIVITIES REQUIREMENT

10(1) Throughout the qualification period relating to the relevant shares the investing company must fall within sub-paragraph (2) or (3).

10(2) The company falls within this sub-paragraph at any time when it–

(a) is a single company, and

(b) disregarding any incidental purposes, exists wholly for the purpose of carrying on one or more non-financial trades.

10(3) The company falls within this sub-paragraph at any time when–

(a) it is a group company,

(b) the group is a non-financial trading group, and

(c) sub-paragraph (4) applies.

10(4) This sub-paragraph applies where the company–

(a) disregarding any incidental purposes, exists wholly for the purpose of carrying on one or more–

  (i) non-financial trades, or

  (ii) businesses other than trades; or

(b) is the parent company of the group.

10(5) For the purposes of determining whether the company falls within sub-paragraph (2)(b) or (4)(a), the purposes for which the company exists shall be disregarded to the extent that they consist in the carrying on of the following activities–

(a) in the case of a single company, the holding and managing of property used by the company for one or more non-financial trades carried on by it,

(b) in the case of a group company, any activities within paragraph 12(3)(a) or (b), and

(c) in any case, the holding of shares to which investment relief is attributable, unless the holding of such shares amounts to a substantial part of the company's business.

10(6) In this paragraph **"incidental purposes"** means purposes having no significant effect (other than in relation to incidental matters) on the extent of the company's activities.

MEANING OF "NON-FINANCIAL TRADE"

11(1) A trade is a **"non-financial trade"** if–

(a) it is conducted on a commercial basis and with a view to the realisation of profits, and

(b) it does not consist wholly or as to a substantial part in the carrying on of financial activities.

11(2) For this purpose **"financial activities"** includes–

(a) banking, or money-lending, carried on by a bank, building society or other person;

(b) debt-factoring, finance-leasing or hire-purchase financing;

(c) insurance;

(d) dealing in shares, securities, currency, debts or other assets of a financial nature; and

(e) dealing in commodity or financial futures or options.

MEANING OF "NON-FINANCIAL TRADING GROUP"

12(1) A group is a "non-financial trading group" unless the business of the group consists wholly or as to a substantial part in the carrying on of one or more of the following–

(a) trades other than non-financial trades;

(b) businesses which are not trades.

12(2) The business of the group means what would be the business of the group if the activities of the group companies taken together were regarded as one business.

12(3) For this purpose activities of a group company shall be disregarded to the extent that they consist in–

(a) the holding of shares in or securities of, or the making of loans to, another group company;

(b) the holding and managing of property used by a group company for the purposes of one or more non-financial trades carried on by a group company; or

(c) the holding of shares to which investment relief is attributable, unless the holding of such shares amounts to a substantial part of the company's business.

REQUIREMENT AS TO SHARES BEING A CHARGEABLE ASSET

13(1) The investing company is not a qualifying investing company in relation to the relevant shares unless the shares are a chargeable asset of the company immediately after they are issued to it.

13(2) For this purpose an asset is a chargeable asset of that company at any time if, on a disposal at that time, a gain accruing to the company would be a chargeable gain.

13(3) In this paragraph **"asset"** has the same meaning as in the 1992 Act.

REQUIREMENT AS TO NO TAX AVOIDANCE

14 The relevant shares must be subscribed for by the investing company for commercial reasons, and not as part of a scheme or arrangement the main purpose or one of the main purposes of which is the avoidance of tax.

Part III – The Issuing Company

INTRODUCTION

15 The issuing company is a qualifying issuing company in relation to the relevant shares if the requirements of this Part are met as to–

(a) unquoted status (see paragraph 16);

(b) independence (see paragraph 17);

(c) individual-owners (see paragraph 18);

(d) partnerships and joint ventures (see paragraph 19);

(e) qualifying subsidiaries (see paragraph 20);

(ea) property managing subsidiaries (see paragraph 21A);

(f) gross assets (see paragraph 22);

(fa) number of employees (see paragraph 22A); and

(g) trading activities (see paragraph 23).

History – Para. 15(ea) inserted by FA 2004, s. 95 and Sch. 20, para. 3 with effect with relation to shares issued on or after 17 March 2004.

In para. 15(f), the word "and" at the end repealed by FA 2007, s. 114 and Sch. 27, Pt. 2(16) with effect in relation to shares issued on or after Royal Assent (19 July 2007).

Para. 15(fa) inserted by FA 2007, s. 51 and Sch. 16, para. 1(2) with effect in relation to shares issued on or after Royal Assent (19 July 2007).

THE "UNQUOTED STATUS" REQUIREMENT

16(1) The unquoted status requirement is that, at the time the relevant shares are issued, none of the issuing company's shares, debentures or other securities is (and there are no arrangements in existence for any of them to be)–

(a) listed on a recognised stock exchange,

(b) listed on a designated exchange in a country outside the United Kingdom, or

(c) dealt in outside the United Kingdom by such means as may be designated.

This is subject to sub-paragraph (3).

16(2) The unquoted status requirement applies whether or not the company is resident in the United Kingdom.

16(3) The unquoted status requirement is treated as not met if at the time the relevant shares are issued–

(a) arrangements are in existence for the issuing company to become a subsidiary of another company ("the new company") by virtue of an exchange of shares, or shares and securities, in relation to which paragraph 83 (certain exchanges resulting in acquisition of share capital by new company) applies, and

(b) arrangements have been made with a view to any of the new company's shares, debentures or other securities being listed or dealt in as mentioned in paragraph (a), (b) or (c) of sub-paragraph (1).

16(4) For the purposes of sub-paragraph (1) **"designated"** means designated by an order ("a designation order") made for the purposes of subsection (1B) of section 312 of the Taxes Act 1988 or section 184(3) of ITA 2007 (definition of "unquoted company" for the purposes of EIS).

16(5) Where the issuing company meets the unquoted status requirement when the relevant shares are issued, it shall not cease to meet it by virtue of–

(a) any designation order, or

(b) any order under section 841 of the Taxes Act 1988 (designation of exchange as "recognised stock exchange"),

made after that time.

History – In para. 16(4) the words "or section 184(3) of ITA 2007" inserted by ITA 2007, s. 1027 and Sch. 1, para. 394(2), with effect from 6 April 2007.

THE INDEPENDENCE REQUIREMENT

17(1) The independence requirement is that–

(a) the issuing company is not, at any time during the qualification period relating to the relevant shares–

  (i) a 51% subsidiary of another company, or

  (ii) under the control of another company (or of another company and any other person connected with that other company), without being a 51% subsidiary of that other company, and

(b) no arrangements are in existence at any time during that period by virtue of which the company could become such a subsidiary or fall under such control (whether during that period or otherwise).

17(2) For the purposes of sub-paragraph (1)(b) arrangements with a view to such an exchange of shares, or shares and securities, as is mentioned in paragraph 83(1) (certain exchanges resulting in acquisition of share capital by new company) shall be disregarded.

17(3) In this paragraph **"control"** has the meaning given by section 1124 of CTA 2010.

History – In para. 17(3), the words "section 1124 of CTA 2010" substituted for the words "section 840 of the Taxes Act 1988" by CTA 2010, s. 1177 and Sch. 1, para. 315(4), with effect for corporation tax purposes for accounting periods ending on or after 1 April 2010, and for income tax and capital gains tax purposes for the tax year 2010–11 and subsequent tax years.

THE "INDIVIDUAL-OWNERS" REQUIREMENT

18(1) The "individual-owners" requirement is that, throughout the qualification period relating to the relevant shares, at least 20% of the ordinary share capital of the issuing company is beneficially owned by one or more independent individuals.

18(2) For the purposes of sub-paragraph (1) **"independent individual"** means an individual who is not, at any time during that period when he holds ordinary shares in the issuing company–

(a) a director or employee of–

  (i) the investing company, or

  (ii) any company connected with that company, or

(b) a relative of such a director or employee.

For this purpose **"relative"** means spouse or civil partner, parent or remoter forebear or child or remoter issue.

18(3) Where part of the ordinary share capital of the issuing company forms part of the estate of a deceased person who immediately before his death–

(a) was the beneficial owner of the shares in question, and

(b) was an independent individual for the purposes of sub-paragraph (1),

the shares in question shall, by virtue of this sub-paragraph, continue to be treated as beneficially owned by an independent individual for the purposes of sub-paragraph (1) until such time as they cease to form part of the deceased's estate.

History – In para. 18(2) the words "spouse or civil partner" substituted for the words "husband or wife" by SI 2005/3229, reg. 132, with effect from 5 December 2005.

THE PARTNERSHIPS AND JOINT VENTURES REQUIREMENT

19(1) The requirement as to partnerships and joint ventures is that neither the issuing company nor any of its qualifying subsidiaries is at any time during the qualification period relating to the relevant shares–

(a) a member of a partnership falling within sub-paragraph (2), or

(b) a party to a joint venture falling within sub-paragraph (3).

19(2) A partnership of which the issuing company, or any of its qualifying subsidiaries, is a member falls within this paragraph at any time when–

(a) the relevant trade is being carried on, or to be carried on, by the partners in partnership,

(b) the other partners include at least one other company, and

(c) the same person (or persons) are the beneficial owner (or owners) of more than 75% of the issued share capital or the ordinary share capital of both–

   (i) the issuing company, and

   (ii) at least one of the other partners.

19(3) A joint venture to which the issuing company, or any of its qualifying subsidiaries, is a party falls within this paragraph at any time when–

(a) the relevant trade is being carried on, or to be carried on, by that party in its capacity as a party to the joint venture,

(b) the other parties include at least one other company, and

(c) the same person (or persons) are the beneficial owner (or owners) of more than 75% of the issued share capital or the ordinary share capital of both–

   (i) the issuing company, and

   (ii) at least one of the other parties.

19(4) For the purposes of sub-paragraphs (2) and (3)–

(a) **"the relevant trade"** means any trade by reference to which the trading activities requirement is met in respect of the issuing company in relation to the relevant shares; and

(b) there shall be attributed to any person any issued share capital or ordinary share capital held by any other person who is an associate of his.

THE QUALIFYING SUBSIDIARIES REQUIREMENT

20(1) The issuing company is not a qualifying issuing company in relation to the relevant shares if, at any time during the qualification period relating to those shares, it has a subsidiary which is not a qualifying subsidiary.

20(2) In this paragraph **"subsidiary"** means any company which the company controls, either on its own or together with any person connected with it.

20(3) For the purpose of sub-paragraph (2), the question whether a person controls a company shall be determined in accordance with sections 450 and 451 of CTA 2010.

History – In para. 20(3), the words "sections 450 and 451 of CTA 2010" substituted for the words "section 416(2) to (6) of the Taxes Act 1988" by CTA 2010, s. 1177 and Sch. 1, para. 315(5), with effect for corporation tax purposes for accounting periods ending on or after 1 April 2010, and for income tax and capital gains tax purposes for the tax year 2010–11 and subsequent tax years.

Para. 20(2) and (3) substituted for former para. 20(2) by FA 2004, s. 95 and Sch. 20, para. 4 with effect in relation to shares issued on or after 17 March 2004.

MEANING OF "QUALIFYING SUBSIDIARY"

21(1) A company ("the subsidiary") is a qualifying subsidiary of another company ("the relevant company") if the following conditions are met.

21(2) The conditions are that–

(a)–(c) [Omitted by FA 2004 s. 95 and Sch. 20, para. 5(2)(a) and repealed by FA 2004, s. 326 and Sch. 42, Pt. 2(13).]

(ca) the subsidiary is a 51% subsidiary of the relevant company;

(d) no person other than the relevant company or another of its subsidiaries has control of the subsidiary within the meaning of section 840 of the Taxes Act 1988; and

(e) no arrangements are in existence by virtue of which either of the conditions in paragraphs (ca) and (d) would cease to be met.

21(3) The subsidiary shall not be regarded as ceasing to be a company in relation to which the conditions in sub-paragraph (2) are met by reason only of–

(a) anything done as a consequence of the subsidiary, or any other company, being in administration or receivership, or

(b) the subsidiary, or any other company, being wound up or dissolved without winding up,

if sub-paragraph (4) applies.

21(4) This paragraph applies where–

(a) in a case within sub-paragraph (3)(a)–

(i) the entry into administration or receivership, and

(ii) everything done as a consequence of the company concerned being in administration or receivership, or

(b) in a case within sub-paragraph (3)(b), the winding up or dissolution,

is for commercial reasons and is not part of a scheme or arrangement the main purpose or one of the main purposes of which is the avoidance of tax.

21(5) The subsidiary shall not be regarded, at any time when arrangements are in existence for the disposal by the relevant company or (as the case may be) by another subsidiary of that company of all its interest in the subsidiary in question, as having ceased on that account to be a qualifying subsidiary of the relevant company if the disposal is to be for commercial reasons and is not to be part of a scheme or arrangement the main purpose of which, or one of the main purposes of which, is the avoidance of tax.

History – Para. 21(2)(a)–(c) omitted by FA 2004, s. 95 and Sch. 20, para. 5(2)(a) and repealed by FA 2004, s. 326 and Sch. 42, Pt. 2(13) with effect in relation to shares issued on or after 17 March 2004.
Para. 21(2)(ca) inserted by FA 2004, s. 95 and Sch. 20, para. 5(2)(b) with effect in relation to shares issued on or after 17 March 2004.
In para. 21(2)(e), the words "either of the conditions in paragraphs (ca) and" substituted for "the conditions in paragraphs (a) to" by FA 2004, s. 95 and Sch. 20, para. 5(2)(c) with effect in relation to shares issued on or after 17 March 2004.
Para. 21(4)(a)(i) substituted by SI 2003/2096, art. 4 and Schedule, para. 34(a) with effect from 15 September 2003.
In para. 21(4)(a)(ii), the word "concerned" inserted by FA 2004, s. 95 and Sch. 20, para. 5(3) with effect in relation to shares issued on or after 17 March 2004.
In para. 21(5), the words "of the relevant company" inserted by FA 2004, s. 95 and Sch. 20, para. 5(4)(a) with effect in relation to shares issued on or after 17 March 2004.
In para. 21(5), the words "and is not to be part" substituted for "and not part" by FA 2004, s. 95 and Sch. 20, para. 5(4)(b) with effect in relation to shares issued on or after 17 March 2004.

Cross references – SI 2009/317, art. 3(2), (3): modification of para. 21(3), (4) in relation to liquidation or administration of banks.

Transitional – SI 2003/2096, art. 6, contains transitional provisions so that the former rules remain in effect where a petition for an administration order was presented prior to 15 September 2003.

THE PROPERTY MANAGING SUBSIDIARIES REQUIREMENT

21A(1) The issuing company is not a qualifying issuing company in relation to the relevant shares if, at any time during the qualification period relating to those shares, it has a property managing subsidiary which is not a qualifying 90% subsidiary of the issuing company (see paragraph 23(10) and (11)).

21A(2) **"Property managing subsidiary"** means a qualifying subsidiary of the issuing company whose business consists wholly or mainly in the holding or managing of land or any property deriving its value from land.

21A(3) In sub-paragraph (2) **"property deriving its value from land"** has the meaning given by section 833(2) of CTA 2010

History – Para. 21A(3) substituted by CTA 2010, s. 1177 and Sch. 1, para. 315(6), with effect for corporation tax purposes for accounting periods ending on or after 1 April 2010, and for income tax and capital gains tax purposes for the tax year 2010–11 and subsequent tax years.
Para. 21A inserted by FA 2004, s. 95 and Sch. 20, para. 6 with effect in relation to shares issued on or after 17 March 2004.

THE GROSS ASSETS REQUIREMENT

22(1) The gross assets requirement in the case of a single company is that the value of the company's gross assets–

(a) does not exceed £7 million immediately before the issue of the relevant shares, and

(b) does not exceed £8 million immediately afterwards.

22(2) The gross assets requirement in the case of a parent company is that the consolidated value of the group assets–

(a) does not exceed £7 million immediately before the issue of the relevant shares, and

(b) does not exceed £8 million immediately afterwards.

22(3) The consolidated value of the group assets means the aggregate value of the gross assets of the group, disregarding any that consist in rights against, or shares in or securities of, another group company.

History – In para. 22(1)(a) the words "£7 million" substituted for the words "£15 million" by FA 2006, s. 91 and Sch. 14, para. 3(1) with effect in relation to shares issued on or after 6 April 2006, subject to the transitional provision in FA 2006, Sch. 14, para. 3(3).
In para. 22(1)(b) the words "£8 million" substituted for the words "£16 million" by FA 2006, s. 91 and Sch. 14, para. 3(1) with effect in relation to shares issued on or after 6 April 2006, subject to the transitional provision in FA 2006, Sch. 14, para. 3(3).
In para. 22(2)(a) the words "£7 million" substituted for the words "£15 million" by FA 2006, s. 91 and Sch. 14, para. 3(1) with effect in relation to shares issued on or after 6 April 2006, subject to the transitional provision in FA 2006, Sch. 14, para. 3(3).
In para. 22(2)(b) the words "£8 million" substituted for the words "£16 million" by FA 2006, s. 91 and Sch. 14, para. 3(1) with effect in relation to shares issued on or after 6 April 2006, subject to the transitional provision in FA 2006, Sch. 14, para. 3(3).

Statements of practice – SP 2/00: HMRC's approach to the "gross asset" test.

THE NUMBER OF EMPLOYEES REQUIREMENT

22A(1) If the issuing company is a single company, the full-time equivalent employee number for it must be less than 50 when the relevant shares are issued.

22A(2) If the issuing company is a parent company, the sum of–

(a) the full-time equivalent employee number for it, and

(b) the full-time equivalent employee numbers for each of its qualifying subsidiaries,

must be less than 50 when the relevant shares are issued.

22A(3) The full-time equivalent employee number for a company is calculated as follows–

Step 1

Find the number of full-time employees of the company.

Step 2

Add, for each employee of the company who is not a full-time employee, such fraction as is just and reasonable. The result is the full-time equivalent employee number.

22A(4) In this paragraph references to an employee–

(a) include a director, but

(b) do not include–

 (i) an employee on maternity, paternity or shared parental leave, or

 (ii) a student on vocational training.

History – In para. 22A(4)(b)(i), the words ", paternity or shared parental" substituted for the words "or paternity" by Children and Families Act 2014, s. 126(1) and Sch. 7, para. 49, with effect from 1 December 2014 (SI 2014/1640, art. 5).
Para. 22A inserted by FA 2007, s. 51 and Sch. 16, para. 1(3) with effect in relation to shares issued on or after Royal Assent (19 July 2007).

THE TRADING ACTIVITIES REQUIREMENT

23(1) The issuing company is not a qualifying issuing company in relation to the relevant shares unless it meets the trading activities requirement throughout the qualification period relating to those shares.

23(2) The trading activities requirement in the case of a single company is that the company–

(a) disregarding any incidental purposes, exists wholly for the purpose of carrying on one or more qualifying trades, and

(b) is carrying on a qualifying trade or preparing to do so.

23(3) The trading activities requirement in the case of a parent company is that–

(a) the business of the group does not consist wholly or as to a substantial part in the carrying on of non-qualifying activities, and

(b) the issuing company or a qualifying 90% subsidiary of the issuing company–

 (i) disregarding any incidental purposes, exists wholly for the purpose of carrying on one or more qualifying trades, and

(ii) is carrying on a qualifying trade or preparing to do so.

23(4) For this purpose the business of the group means what would be the business of the group if the activities of the group companies taken together were regarded as one business.

23(5) The requirement of sub-paragraph (2) or (3) is not met at any time by reason of the issuing company or a qualifying 90% subsidiary of the issuing company preparing to carry on a qualifying trade if the company or a qualifying 90% subsidiary of the issuing company does not begin to carry on the trade within two years after the issue of the relevant shares.

23(6) For the purposes of determining whether a company falls within sub-paragraph (2)(a) or (3)(b)(i), the purposes for which it exists shall be disregarded to the extent that they consist in the carrying on of the following activities–

(a) in the case of a single company, the holding and managing of property used by the company for one or more qualifying trades carried on by it,

(b) in the case of a group company, any activities within sub-paragraph (7)(a), (b) or (d), and

(c) in any case, the holding of shares to which investment relief is attributable, unless the holding of such shares amounts to a substantial part of the company's business.

23(7) For the purposes of determining the business of a group, activities of a group company shall be disregarded to the extent that they consist in–

(a) the holding of shares in or securities of, or the making of loans to, another group company;

(b) the holding and managing of property used by a group company for the purposes of one or more qualifying trades carried on by a group company;

(c) the holding of shares to which investment relief is attributable, unless the holding of such shares amounts to a substantial part of the company's business, or

(d) incidental activities of a company which meets the trading activities requirement for a single company.

23(8) In sub-paragraph (3)(a) **"non-qualifying activities"** means–

(a) excluded activities other than–

(i) the letting of ships to which paragraph 28 applies (ships other than offshore installations or pleasure craft) in circumstances where the requirement of sub-paragraph (2) of that paragraph is met; or

(ii) the receiving of royalties or licence fees within paragraph 29 in circumstances where the requirements mentioned in sub-paragraph (2) of that paragraph are met; and

(b) activities carried on otherwise than in the course of a trade.

23(9) In this paragraph–

(a) **"incidental purposes"** means purposes having no significant effect (other than in relation to incidental matters) on the extent of the activities of the company in question;

(b) **"incidental activities"** means activities carried on in pursuance of incidental purposes.

23(10)–(11) [Omitted by FA 2007, s. 51 and Sch. 16, para. 15(2) and repealed by FA 2007, s. 114 and Sch. 27, Pt. 2(16).]

History – In para. 23(3)(b), the words "the issuing company or a qualifying 90% subsidiary of the issuing company" substituted for "at least one group company" by FA 2004, s. 95 and Sch. 20, para. 7(a) with effect in relation to shares issued on or after 17 March 2004.
In para. 23(5), the words "a qualifying 90% subsidiary of the issuing company" substituted for "a subsidiary" by FA 2004, s. 95 and Sch. 20, para. 7(b)(i) with effect in relation to shares issued on or after 17 March 2004.
In para. 23(5), the words "or a qualifying 90% subsidiary of the issuing company" substituted for "or subsidiary" by FA 2004, s. 95 and Sch. 20, para. 7(b)(ii) with effect in relation to shares issued on or after 17 March 2004.
In para. 23(6), the words "a company" substituted for "the company" by FA 2004, s. 95 and Sch. 20, para. 7(c) with effect in relation to shares issued on or after 17 March 2004.
In para. 23(8)(a)(i), the words "offshore installations" substituted for "oil rigs" by FA 2004, s. 146 and Sch. 27, para. 6(2) in relation to shares issued on or after 6 April 2004.
Para. 23(10) and (11) omitted by FA 2007, s. 51 and Sch. 16, para. 15(2) and repealed by FA 2007, s. 114 and Sch. 27, Pt. 2(16) with effect from 6 April 2007 (FA 2007, Sch. 16, para. 18).
Former para. 23(10) and (11) inserted by FA 2004, s. 95 and Sch. 20, para. 7(d) with effect in relation to shares issued on or after 17 March 2004.

Cross references – Para. 102(8) when a qualifying 90% subsidiary begins to carry on a trade.

MEANING OF "QUALIFYING 90% SUBSIDIARY"

23A(1) For the purposes of this Schedule, a company ("the subsidiary") is a qualifying 90% subsidiary of the issuing company if the following conditions are met–

(a) the issuing company possesses not less than 90% of the issued share capital of, and not less than 90% of the voting power in, the subsidiary;

(b) the issuing company would–

(i) in the event of a winding up of the subsidiary, or

(ii) in any other circumstances,

be beneficially entitled to receive not less than 90% of the assets of the subsidiary which would then be available for distribution to the shareholders of the subsidiary;

(c) the issuing company is beneficially entitled to not less than 90% of any profits of the subsidiary which are available for distribution to the shareholders of the subsidiary;

(d) no person other than the issuing company has control of the subsidiary within the meaning of section 1124 of CTA 2010;

(e) no arrangements are in existence by virtue of which any of the conditions in paragraphs (a) to (d) would cease to be met.

23A(2) Paragraph 21(3) and (4) (effect of receivership etc) apply in relation to the conditions in sub-paragraph (1) as they apply in relation to the conditions in paragraph 21(2).

23A(3) If–

(a) arrangements are in existence for the disposal by the issuing company of all its interest in the subsidiary, and

(b) the disposal is to be for commercial reasons and is not to be part of a scheme or arrangement the main purpose of which, or one of the main purposes of which, is the avoidance of tax,

the subsidiary is not to be regarded as having ceased on that account to be a qualifying 90% subsidiary of the issuing company.

23A(4) For the purposes of this Schedule, a company ("company A") which is a subsidiary of a company that is not the issuing company ("company B") is a qualifying 90% subsidiary of the issuing company if–

(a) company A would be a qualifying 90% subsidiary of company B (if company B were the issuing company), and company B is a qualifying 100% subsidiary of the issuing company; or

(b) company A is a qualifying 100% subsidiary of company B, and company B is a qualifying 90% subsidiary of the issuing company.

23A(5) For the purposes of sub-paragraph (4), no account is to be taken of any control the issuing company may have of company A.

23A(6) For those purposes, a company ("company X") is a qualifying 100% subsidiary of another company ("company Y") at any time when the conditions in sub-paragraph (1) would be met if–

(a) company X were the subsidiary;

(b) company Y were the issuing company; and

(c) in sub-paragraph (1) for "not less than 90%" in each place there were substituted "100%".

History – In para. 23A(1)(d), the words "section 1124 of CTA 2010" substituted for the words "section 840 of the Taxes Act 1988" by CTA 2010, s. 1177 and Sch. 1, para. 315(7), with effect for corporation tax purposes for accounting periods ending on or after 1 April 2010, and for income tax and capital gains tax purposes for the tax year 2010–11 and subsequent tax years.
Para. 23A inserted by FA 2007, s. 51 and Sch. 16, para. 15(3) with effect from 6 April 2007 (FA 2007, Sch 16, para. 18).

Cross references – SI 2009/317, art. 3 (2): modification of para. 23A(1) in relation to liquidation or administration of banks.

CEASING TO MEET TRADING ACTIVITIES REQUIREMENT BY REASON OF ADMINISTRATION, RECEIVERSHIP, ETC.

24(1) A company shall not be regarded as ceasing to meet the trading activities requirement by reason only of anything done as a consequence of the company, or any of its qualifying subsidiaries, being in administration or receivership.
This sub-paragraph has effect subject to sub-paragraphs (2) and (3).

24(2) Sub-paragraph (1) applies only if–

(a) the entry into administration or receivership, and

(b) everything done as a consequence of the company concerned being in administration or receivership,
is for commercial reasons and is not part of a scheme or arrangement the main purpose or one of the main purposes of which is the avoidance of tax.

24(3) A company ceases to meet the trading activities requirement if–

(a) a resolution is passed, or an order is made, for the winding up of the company or any of its qualifying subsidiaries (or, in the case of a winding up otherwise than under the Insolvency Act 1986 or the Insolvency (Northern Ireland) Order 1989, any other act is done for the like purpose), or

(b) the company, or any of its qualifying subsidiaries, is dissolved without winding up.
This is subject to sub-paragraph (4).

24(4) A company shall not be regarded as ceasing to meet the trading activities requirement if–

(a) it does so by reason only of the company or any of its qualifying subsidiaries being wound up or dissolved without winding up, and

(b) the winding up or dissolution is for commercial reasons and is not part of a scheme or arrangement the main purpose or one of the main purposes of which is the avoidance of tax.

History – In para. 24(1), the words "which is in administration or receivership" (following the words "A company") omitted by FA 2004, s. 95 and Sch. 20, para. 8(a)(i) and repealed by FA 2004, s. 326 and Sch. 42, Pt. 2(13) with effect in relation to shares issued on or after 17 March 2004.
In para. 24(1), the word "only" inserted by FA 2004, s. 95 and Sch. 20, para. 8(a)(ii).
Para. 24(2)(a) substituted by SI 2003/2096, art. 4 and Schedule, para. 34(b) with effect from 15 September 2003.
In para. 24(2)(b), the word "concerned" inserted by FA 2004, s. 95 and Sch. 20, para. 8(b) with effect in relation to shares issued on or after 17 March 2004.
In para. 24(4)(a), the words "only of the company or any of its qualifying subsidiaries" substituted for "of the company or any of its subsidiaries" by FA 2004, s. 95 and Sch. 20, para. 8(c)(i) with effect in relation to shares issued on or after 17 March 2004.
In para. 24(4)(b), the words "and is not" substituted for "and not" by FA 2004, s. 95 and Sch. 20, para. 8(c)(ii) with effect in relation to shares issued on or after 17 March 2004.

Cross references – SI 2009/317, art. 3: modification of para. 24 in relation to liquidation or administration of banks.

Transitional – SI 2003/2096, art. 6 contains transitional provisions so that the former rules remain in effect where a petition for an administration order was presented prior to 15 September 2003.

MEANING OF "QUALIFYING TRADE"

25(1) A trade is a qualifying trade if–

(a) it is carried on wholly or mainly in the United Kingdom,

(b) it is conducted on a commercial basis and with a view to the realisation of profits, and

(c) it does not consist wholly or as to a substantial part in the carrying on of excluded activities.

25(2) The carrying on of activities of research and development from which it is intended that a connected qualifying trade will be derived or benefit is treated as the carrying on of a qualifying trade.
But preparing to carry on such activities does not count as preparing to carry on a qualifying trade.

25(3) For the purposes of sub-paragraph (2) a **"connected qualifying trade"** means a qualifying trade carried on–

(a) by the company carrying on the activities of research and development, or

(b) if that company is a member of a group, by the issuing company or any of its qualifying 90% subsidiaries.

History – In para. 25(3)(b), the words "the issuing company or any of its qualifying 90% subsidiaries" substituted for "any other group company" by FA 2004, s. 95 and Sch. 20, para. 9 with effect in relation to shares issued on or after 17 March 2004.

Statements of practice – SP 3/00: HMRC's approach to the requirement for a company's trade to be carried on wholly or mainly in the UK.

EXCLUDED ACTIVITIES

26(1) The following are excluded activities–

(a) dealing in land, in commodities or futures or in shares, securities or other financial instruments;

(b) dealing in goods otherwise than in the course of an ordinary trade of wholesale or retail distribution;

(c) banking, insurance, money-lending, debt-factoring, hire-purchase financing or other financial activities;

(d) leasing (including letting ships on charter or other assets on hire) or receiving royalties or other licence fees;

(e) providing legal or accountancy services;

(f) property development;

(g) farming or market gardening;

(h) holding, managing or occupying woodlands, any other forestry activities or timber production;

(ha) shipbuilding;

(hb) producing coal;

(hc) producing steel;

(i) operating or managing hotels or comparable establishments or managing property used as a hotel or comparable establishment; and

(j) operating or managing nursing homes or residential care homes, or managing property used as a nursing home or residential care home.

26(2) Sub-paragraph (1) is supplemented by the following provisions–
paragraph 27 (wholesale and retail distribution);
paragraph 28 (leasing of ships);

paragraph 29 (receipt of royalties and licence fees);
paragraph 30 (property development);
paragraph 30A (shipbuilding);
paragraph 30B (producing coal);
paragraph 30C (producing steel);
paragraph 31 (hotels and comparable establishments);
paragraph 32 (nursing homes and residential care homes); and
paragraph 33 (provision of facilities for another business).

History – Para. 26(1)(ha) inserted by FA 2008, s. 32 and Sch. 11, para. 2(a), and is treated as having come into force on 6 April 2008, but does not have effect in relation to shares issued before that date.
Para. 26(1)(hb) inserted by FA 2008, s. 32 and Sch. 11, para. 2(a), and is treated as having come into force on 6 April 2008, but does not have effect in relation to shares issued before that date.
Para. 26(1)(hc) inserted by FA 2008, s. 32 and Sch. 11, para. 2(a), and is treated as having come into force on 6 April 2008, but does not have effect in relation to shares issued before that date.
In para. 26(2), the entries relating to para. 30A, para. 30B and para. 30C inserted by FA 2008, s. 32 and Sch. 11, para. 2(b), and is treated as having come into force on 6 April 2008, but does not have effect in relation to shares issued before that date.

Notes – Para. 26(1)(j) and (2) were to be amended by the Regulation of Care (Scotland) Act 2001 (Act of Scottish Parliament), s. 79 and Sch. 3, para. 24(3)(a) with effect from such day as the Scottish Ministers may by order made by statutory instrument appoint. However, such changes were repealed by SI 2001/2478 (S. 13), art. 2 as tax provisions fall outside the scope of the Scottish Parliament.

EXCLUDED ACTIVITIES: WHOLESALE AND RETAIL DISTRIBUTION

27(1) This paragraph supplements paragraph 26(1)(b).

27(2) A trade of wholesale distribution is one in which the goods are offered for sale and sold to persons for resale by them, or for processing and resale by them, to members of the general public for their use or consumption.

27(3) A trade of retail distribution is one in which the goods are offered for sale and sold to members of the general public for their use or consumption.

27(4) A trade is not an ordinary trade of wholesale or retail distribution if–

(a) it consists, to a substantial extent, in dealing in goods of a kind which are collected or held as an investment, or in that activity and any other excluded activity taken together, and

(b) a substantial proportion of those goods are held by the company for a period which is significantly longer than the period for which a vendor would reasonably be expected to hold them while endeavouring to dispose of them at their market value.

27(5) In determining whether a trade carried on by any person is an ordinary trade of wholesale or retail distribution, regard shall be had to the extent to which it has the following features–

(a) the goods are bought by that person in quantities larger than those in which he sells them;

(b) the goods are bought and sold by that person in different markets;

(c) that person employs staff and incurs expenses in the trade in addition to the cost of the goods and, in the case of a trade carried on by a company, to any remuneration paid to any person connected with it;

(d) there are purchases or sales from or to persons who are connected with that person;

(e) purchases are matched with forward sales or vice versa;

(f) the goods are held by that person for longer than is normal for goods of the kind in question;

(g) the trade is carried on otherwise than at a place or places commonly used for wholesale or retail trade;

(h) that person does not take physical possession of the goods.

27(6) The features specified in sub-paragraph (5)(a) to (c) are indications that the trade is such an ordinary trade.
Those in sub-paragraph (5)(d) to (h) are indications of the contrary.

EXCLUDED ACTIVITIES: LEASING OF SHIPS

28(1) This paragraph supplements paragraph 26(1)(d) so far as it relates to the leasing of ships other than offshore installations or pleasure craft.

28(2) A trade shall not be treated as not being a qualifying trade by reason only of its consisting in letting such ships on charter if the following requirements are met–

(a) every ship let on charter by the company carrying on the trade is beneficially owned by the company;

(b) every ship beneficially owned by the company is registered in the United Kingdom;

(c) the company is solely responsible for arranging the marketing of the services of its ships; and

(d) the conditions mentioned in sub-paragraph (3) are satisfied in relation to every letting of a ship on charter by the company.

28(3) The conditions are that–

(a) the letting is for a period not exceeding 12 months and no provision is made at any time (whether in the charterparty or otherwise) for extending it beyond that period otherwise than at the option of the charterer;

(b) during the period of the letting there is no provision in force (whether by virtue of being contained in the charterparty or otherwise) for the grant of a new letting to end, otherwise than at the option of the charterer, more than 12 months after that provision is made;

(c) the letting is by way of a bargain made at arm's length between the company and a person who is not connected with it;

(d) under the terms of the charter the company is responsible as principal–

(i) for taking, throughout the period of the charter, management decisions in relation to the ship, other than those of a kind generally regarded by persons engaged in trade of the kind in question as matters of husbandry; and

(ii) for defraying all expenses in connection with the ship throughout that period, or substantially all such expenses, other than those directly incidental to a particular voyage or to the employment of the ship during that period;

and

(e) no arrangements exist by virtue of which a person other than the company may be appointed to be responsible for the matters mentioned in paragraph (d) on behalf of the company.

28(4) In relation to any letting between one company and another where–

(a) one of those companies is the company carrying on the trade and the other is a qualifying subsidiary of that company, or

(b) both companies are qualifying subsidiaries of the company carrying on the trade,

sub-paragraph (3) has effect with the omission of paragraph (c).

28(5) Where any of the requirements in sub-paragraph (2) are not met in relation to any lettings, the trade shall not thereby be treated as not a qualifying trade if those lettings and any other excluded activities do not, taken together, amount to a substantial part of the trade.

28(6) In this paragraph–

"pleasure craft" means any ship of a kind primarily used for sport or recreation.

History – In para. 28(1) the words "offshore installations" substituted for "oil rigs" by FA 2004, s. 146 and Sch. 27, para. 6(3) in relation to shares issued on or after 6 April 2004.
In para. 28(6), the definition of "oil rig" omitted by FA 2004, s. 146 and Sch. 27, para. 6(3) and repealed by FA 2004, s. 326 and Sch. 42, Pt. 2(19) in relation to shares issued on or after 6 April 2004.

EXCLUDED ACTIVITIES: RECEIPT OF ROYALTIES AND LICENCE FEES

29(1) This paragraph supplements paragraph 26(1)(d) so far as it relates to the receipt of royalties and licence fees.

29(2) A trade shall not be regarded as not being a qualifying trade by reason only that at some time in the qualification period relating to the relevant shares it consists to a substantial extent in the receiving of royalties or licence fees if the royalties and licence fees (or all but for a part that is not a substantial part in terms of value) are attributable to the exploitation of relevant intangible assets.

29(3) For this purpose an intangible asset is a **"relevant intangible asset"** if the whole or greater part (in terms of value) of it has been created–

(a) by the issuing company, or

(b) by a company which was a qualifying subsidiary of the issuing company throughout a period during which it created the whole or greater part (in terms of value) of the intangible asset.

29(4) In this paragraph **"intangible asset"** means any asset which falls to be treated as an intangible asset in accordance with generally accepted accounting practice.

29(5) In the case of a relevant asset that is intellectual property, references in this paragraph to the creation of the asset by a company are to its creation in circumstances in which the right to exploit it vests in the company (whether alone or jointly with others).

29(6) In sub-paragraph (5) **"intellectual property"** means–

(a) any patent, trade mark, registered design, copyright, design right, performer's right or plant breeder's right; and

(b) any rights under the law of a country or territory outside the United Kingdom which correspond or are similar to those falling within paragraph (a).

29(7) If–

(a) the issuing company acquired all the shares ("old shares") in another company ("the old company") at a time when the only shares issued in the issuing company were subscriber shares, and

(b) the consideration for the old shares consisted wholly of the issue of shares in the issuing company, references in sub-paragraph (3) to the issuing company include the old company.

History – Para. 29(3)(a) and (b) substituted by FA 2007, s. 51 and Sch. 16, para. 9(2) with effect from 6 April 2007 (FA 2007, Sch. 16, para. 13).
In para. 29(4), the words "generally accepted accounting practice" substituted for the words "normal accounting practice" by FA 2002, s. 103(4)(f) with effect from 24 July 2002.
In para. 29(4), the second sentence containing the definition of "normal accounting practice" repealed by FA 2002, s. 141 and Sch. 40, Pt. 3(16) with effect from 24 July 2002.
Para. 29(7) inserted by FA 2007, s. 51 and Sch. 16, para. 9(3) with effect from 6 April 2007 (FA 2007, Sch. 16, para. 13).

Accounting Standard – See the selection of accounting standards in relation to ascertaining generally accepted accounting practice, in particular FRS 10.

EXCLUDED ACTIVITIES: PROPERTY DEVELOPMENT

30(1) This paragraph supplements paragraph 26(1)(f).

30(2) **"Property development"** means the development of land–

(a) by a company which has, or at any time has had, an interest in the land, and

(b) with the sole or main object of realising a gain from the disposal of an interest in the land when it is developed.

30(3) For this purpose **"interest in land"** means, subject to sub-paragraph (4)–

(a) any estate, interest or right in or over land, including any right affecting the use or disposition of land, or

(b) any right to obtain such an estate, interest or right from another which is conditional on the other's ability to grant it.

30(4) References in this paragraph to an interest in land do not include–

(a) the interest of a creditor (other than a creditor in respect of a rentcharge) whose debt is secured by way of mortgage, an agreement for a mortgage or a charge of any kind over land, or

(b) in the case of land in Scotland, the interest of a creditor in a charge or security of any kind over land.

EXCLUDED ACTIVITIES: SHIPBUILDING

30A In paragraph 26(1)(ha) **"shipbuilding"** has the same meaning as in the Framework on state aid to shipbuilding (2003/C 317/06), published in the Official Journal on 30 December 2003.

History – Para. 30A inserted by FA 2008, s. 32 and Sch. 11, para. 3, and is treated as having come into force on 6 April 2008, but does not have effect in relation to shares issued before that date.

EXCLUDED ACTIVITIES: PRODUCING COAL

30B(1) This paragraph supplements paragraph 26(1)(hb).

30B(2) **"Coal"** has the meaning given by Article 2 of Council Regulation (EC) No. 1407/2002 (state aid to coal industry).

30B(3) The production of coal includes the extraction of it.

History – Para. 30B inserted by FA 2008, s. 32 and Sch. 11, para. 3, and is treated as having come into force on 6 April 2008, but does not have effect in relation to shares issued before that date.

EXCLUDED ACTIVITIES: PRODUCING STEEL

30C In paragraph 26(1)(hc) **"steel"** means any of the steel products listed in Annex 1 to the Guidelines on national regional aid (2006/ C 54/08), published in the Official Journal on 4 March 2006.

History – Para. 30C inserted by FA 2008, s. 32 and Sch. 11, para. 3, and is treated as having come into force on 6 April 2008, but does not have effect in relation to shares issued before that date.

EXCLUDED ACTIVITIES: HOTELS AND COMPARABLE ESTABLISHMENTS

31(1) This paragraph supplements paragraph 26(1)(i).

31(2) The reference to a comparable establishment is to a guest house, hostel or other establishment the main purpose of maintaining which is the provision of facilities for overnight accommodation (with or without catering services).

31(3) The activities of a person shall not be taken to fall within paragraph 26(1)(i) unless that person has an estate or interest in, or is in occupation of, the hotel or comparable establishment in question.

EXCLUDED ACTIVITIES: NURSING HOMES AND RESIDENTIAL CARE HOMES

32(1) This paragraph supplements paragraph 26(1)(j).

32(2) **"Nursing home"** means an establishment that exists wholly or mainly for the provision of nursing care–

(a) for persons suffering from sickness, injury or infirmity, or

(b) for women who are pregnant or have given birth to children.

32(3) **"Residential care home"** means an establishment that exists wholly or mainly for the provision of residential accommodation, together with board and personal care, for persons in need of personal care by reason of–

(a) old age,

(b) mental or physical disability,

(c) past or present dependence on alcohol or drugs,

(d) any past illness, or

(e) past or present mental disorder.

32(4) The activities of a person shall not be taken to fall within paragraph 26(1)(j) unless that person has an estate or interest in, or is in occupation of, the nursing home or residential care home in question.

Notes – Para. 32 was to be amended by the Regulation of Care (Scotland) Act 2001 (Act of Scottish Parliament), s. 79 and Sch. 3, para. 24(3)(b) with effect from such day as the Scottish Ministers may by order made by statutory instrument appoint. However, the amendments were repealed by SI 2001/2478 (S. 13), art. 2 as tax provisions fall outside the scope of the Scottish Parliament.

EXCLUDED ACTIVITIES: PROVISION OF FACILITIES FOR ANOTHER BUSINESS

33(1) Providing services or facilities for a business carried on by another person is an excluded activity if–

(a) the business consists to a substantial extent of excluded activities within sub-paragraph 26(1), and

(b) a controlling interest in the business is held by a person who also has a controlling interest in the business carried on by the company providing the services or facilities.

33(2) Sub-paragraphs (3) to (5) define what is meant by a controlling interest in a business for the purposes of sub-paragraph (1)(b).

33(3) In the case of a business carried on by a company, a person has a controlling interest if–

(a) he controls the company,

(b) the company is a close company and he or an associate of his, being a director of the company, either–

  (i) is the beneficial owner of more than 30% of the ordinary share capital of the company, or

  (ii) is able, directly or through the medium of other companies or by any other indirect means, to control more than 30% of that share capital,

or

(c) not less than half of the business could, in accordance with section 942 of CTA 2010, be regarded as belonging to him for the purposes of section 941 of that Act.

33(4) In any other case, a person has a controlling interest in a business if he is entitled to not less than half of the assets used for, or of the income arising from, the business.

33(5) For the purposes of sub-paragraph (3)(a) the question whether a person controls a company shall be determined in accordance with sections 450 and 451 of CTA 2010.

33(6) For the purposes of this paragraph–

(a) there shall be attributed to any person any rights or powers of any other person who is an associate of his, and

(b) **"business"** includes any trade, profession or vocation.

History – In para. 33(3)(c), the words "section 942 of CTA 2010" substituted for the words "section 344(2) of the Taxes Act 1988" and the words "section 941" substituted for the words "section 343" by CTA 2010, s. 1177 and Sch. 1, para. 315(8), with effect for corporation tax purposes for accounting periods ending on or after 1 April 2010, and for income tax and capital gains tax purposes for the tax year 2010–11 and subsequent tax years.

In para. 33(5), the words "sections 450 and 451 of CTA 2010" substituted for the words "section 416(2) to (6) of the Taxes Act 1988" by CTA 2010, s. 1177 and Sch. 1, para. 315(9), with effect for corporation tax purposes for accounting periods ending on or after 1 April 2010, and for income tax and capital gains tax purposes for the tax year 2010–11 and subsequent tax years.

Part IV – General Requirements

INTRODUCTION

34 The investing company is not eligible for investment relief in respect of the amount subscribed by it for the relevant shares unless the requirements of this Part are met as to–

(a) the shares (see paragraph 35);

(aa) the maximum amount raised annually through risk capital schemes (see paragraph 35A);

(b) the money raised (see paragraph 36);

(c) no pre-arranged exits (see paragraph 37); and

(d) no tax avoidance (see paragraph 38).

History – Para. 34(aa) inserted by FA 2007, s. 51 and Sch. 16, para. 4(2) with effect from Royal Assent (19 July 2007).

REQUIREMENT AS TO THE SHARES

35(1) The relevant shares must satisfy sub-paragraphs (2) and (3).

35(2) Shares satisfy this sub-paragraph if they are–

(a) ordinary shares,

(b) subscribed for wholly in cash, and

(c) fully paid up at the time they are issued.

Shares are not fully paid up for the purposes of paragraph (c) if there is any undertaking to pay cash to any person at a future date in respect of the acquisition of the shares.

35(3) Shares satisfy this sub-paragraph if they do not, at any time during the qualification period relating to the relevant shares, carry–

(a) any present or future preferential right to dividends or to a company's assets on its winding up, or

(b) any present or future right to be redeemed.

History – In para. 35(2), the words "any person at a future date in respect of the acquisition of the shares" substituted for "the issuing company at a future date" by FA 2004, s. 95 and Sch. 20, para. 10 with effect in relation to shares issued on or after 17 March 2004.

Cross references – SI 2009/317, art. 3(2): modification of para. 35(3)(a) in relation to liquidation or administration of banks.

REQUIREMENT AS TO MAXIMUM AMOUNT RAISED ANNUALLY THROUGH RISK CAPITAL SCHEMES

35A(1) The total amount of relevant investments made in the issuing company in the year ending with the date the relevant shares are issued must not exceed £2 million.

35A(2) In sub-paragraph (1), the reference to relevant investments made in the issuing company includes relevant investments made in any company that is, or has at any time in the year mentioned there been, a subsidiary of the issuing company (whether or not it was such a subsidiary when the investment was made).

35A(3) A **"relevant investment"** is made in a company if–

(a) an investment (of any kind) in the company is made by a VCT, or

(b) the company issues shares (money having been subscribed for them), and (at any time) the company provides–

  (i) a compliance statement under paragraph 42, or

  (ii) a compliance statement under section 205 of ITA 2007 (enterprise investment scheme),

in respect of the shares.

35A(4) An investment within sub-paragraph (3)(b) is regarded as made when the shares are issued.

History – Para. 35A inserted by FA 2007, s. 51 and Sch. 16, para. 4(3) with effect from Royal Assent (19 July 2007) subject to the transitional rules at FA 2007, Sch. 16, para. 8.

REQUIREMENT AS TO THE MONEY RAISED

36(1) All of the money raised by the issuance of the relevant issue of shares must have been employed wholly for the purposes of a relevant trade not later than the time determined in accordance with sub-paragraph (1B).

36(1A) [Omitted by FA 2009, s. 27 and Sch. 8, para. 8(3).]

36(1B) The time referred to in sub-paragraph (1) is–

(a) the end of the period of two years beginning with the issue of the shares, or

(b) where the issuing company or a qualifying 90% subsidiary of that company had not begun to carry on the relevant trade at the time the shares were issued, the end of the period of two years beginning when the issuing company or a qualifying 90% subsidiary of that company begins to carry on the relevant trade.

36(1C) Sub-paragraph (1) is subject to sub-paragraph (5).

36(2) For the purposes of this paragraph–

"the relevant issue of shares" means the issue of shares in the issuing company which includes the relevant shares;

"relevant trade" means a trade by reference to which the issuing company meets the trading activities requirement.

36(3) In this paragraph references to employing money for the purposes of a trade (except where the carrying on of the trade is within paragraph 25(2)) include references to employing it for the purpose of preparing to carry on the trade.

36(4) In sub-paragraph (2) the reference to a trade by reference to which the trading activities requirement is met includes, where the carrying on of that trade is within paragraph 25(2), a reference to any qualifying trade–

(a) which is derived or benefits from that trade, and

(b) which is carried on–

(i) by the issuing company, or

(ii) if that company is a parent company, by that company or a qualifying 90% subsidiary of that company.

36(5) Where–

(a) any of the money raised by the issuance of the relevant issue of shares is employed for the purposes of a trade that is a relevant trade by virtue of sub-paragraph (4), and

(b) that trade was not being carried on by the issuing company, or a qualifying 90% subsidiary of that company, at the time the shares were issued,

the requirement of sub-paragraph (1) is not met unless that money is so employed before the third anniversary of the issue date.

36(6) For the purposes of this paragraph money is not treated as employed otherwise than wholly for the purposes of a trade if the only amount employed for other purposes is an amount which is not a significant amount.

History – In para. 36(1), the word "All" substituted for the words "At least 80%" by FA 2009, s. 27 and Sch. 8, para. 8(2), with effect in relation to shares issued on or after 22 April 2009.

Para. 36(1) substituted by FA 2001, s. 64 and Sch. 16, para. 5(1) with effect:

- in relation to the issue of any shares on or after 7 March 2001 (Sch. 16, para. 5(3)(a)); and
- in respect of the application of FA 2000, Sch. 15 on or after 7 March 2001; to shares issued after 31 March 2000 but before 7 March 2001 – where such shares attracted investment relief immediately before the latter date (Sch. 16, para. 5(3)(b)).

Para. 36(1A) omitted by FA 2009, s. 27 and Sch. 8, para. 8(3), with effect in relation to shares issued on or after 22 April 2009.

Former para. 36(1A) inserted by FA 2001, s. 64 and Sch. 16, para. 5(1) with effect:

- in relation to the issue of any shares on or after 7 March 2001 (Sch. 16, para. 5(3)(a)); and
- in respect of the application of FA 2000, Sch. 15 on or after 7 March 2001; to shares issued after 31 March 2000 but before 7 March 2001 – where such shares attracted investment relief immediately before the latter date (Sch. 16, para. 5(3)(b)).

In para. 36(1B), the words "two years" substituted for the words "12 months" (in both places) by FA 2009, s. 27 and Sch. 8, para. 8(4), with effect in relation to shares issued on or after 22 April 2009.

In para. 36(1B)(b), the words "issuing company or a qualifying 90% subsidiary of that company had not begun to carry on the relevant trade" substituted for "relevant trade was not being carried on" and the words "qualifying 90% subsidiary of that company" substituted for "subsidiary" by FA 2004, s. 95 and Sch. 20, para. 11 with effect in relation to shares issued on or after 17 March 2004.

Para. 36(1B) inserted by FA 2001, s. 64 and Sch. 16, para. 5(1) with effect:

- in relation to the issue of any shares on or after 7 March 2001 (Sch. 16, para. 5(3)(a)); and
- in respect of the application of FA 2000, Sch. 15 on or after 7 March 2001; to shares issued after 31 March 2000 but before 7 March 2001 – where such shares attracted investment relief immediately before the latter date (Sch. 16, para. 5(3)(b)).

In para. 36(1C), the words "Sub-paragraph (1) is" substituted for the words "Sub-paragraphs (1) and (1A) are" by FA 2009, s. 27 and Sch. 8, para. 8(5), with effect in relation to shares issued on or after 22 April 2009.

Para. 36(1C) inserted by FA 2001, s. 64 and Sch. 16, para. 5(1) with effect:

- in relation to the issue of any shares on or after 7 March 2001 (Sch. 16, para. 5(3)(a)); and
- in respect of the application of FA 2000, Sch. 15 on or after 7 March 2001; to shares issued after 31 March 2000 but before 7 March 2001 – where such shares attracted investment relief immediately before the latter date (Sch. 16, para. 5(3)(b)).

In para. 36(5), the words "does not apply and the requirement of sub-paragraph (1A)", which preceded the words "is not met", omitted by FA 2009, s. 27 and Sch. 8, para. 8(6), with effect in relation to shares issued on or after 22 April 2009.

In para. 36(5)(a) the words "any of the money raised by the issuance of the relevant issue of shares" and in end note "the requirement of sub-paragraph (1) does not apply and the requirement of sub-paragraph (1A)" substituted by FA 2001, s. 64 and Sch. 16, para. 5(2) with effect:

- in relation to the issue of any shares on or after 7 March 2001 (Sch. 16, para. 5(3)(a)); and
- in respect of the application of FA 2000, Sch. 15 on or after 7 March 2001; to shares issued after 31 March 2000 but before 7 March 2001 – where such shares attracted investment relief immediately before the latter date (Sch. 16, para. 5(3)(b)).

Cross references – Para: 102(8) when a qualifying 90% subsidiary begins to carry on a trade.

REQUIREMENT AS TO NO PRE-ARRANGED EXITS

37(1) The issuing arrangements for the relevant shares must not include–

(a) arrangements with a view to the subsequent repurchase, exchange or other disposal of those shares or of other shares in or securities of the issuing company;

(b) arrangements for or with a view to the cessation of any trade which is being or is to be or may be carried on by the issuing company or a person connected with that company;

(c) arrangements for the disposal of, or of a substantial amount (in terms of value) of, the assets of the issuing company or of a person connected with that company; or

(d) arrangements the main purpose of which, or one of the main purposes of which, is (by means of any insurance, indemnity or guarantee or otherwise) to provide partial or complete protection for persons investing in shares in the issuing company against what would otherwise be the risks attached to making the investment.

37(2) For the purposes of this paragraph **"the issuing arrangements"** means–

(a) the arrangements under which the relevant shares are issued to the investing company,

(b) any arrangements made, before the issue of the relevant shares to that company, in relation to or in connection with that issue, and

(c) if before the relevant shares were issued information on pre-arranged exits was made available to any prospective subscribers for shares in the relevant issue, any arrangements made–

(i) on or after the issue of the shares, but

(ii) before the end of the qualification period relating to them.

37(3) For the purposes of sub-paragraph (2)–

(a) **"information on pre-arranged exits"** means any information indicating the possibility of making, on or after the issue of the relevant shares but before the end of the qualification period relating to them, arrangements of the kind described in paragraph (a), (b), (c) or (d) of sub-paragraph (1), and

(b) **"the relevant issue"** means the issue of shares in the issuing company which includes the relevant shares.

37(4) The arrangements referred to in sub-paragraph (1)(a) do not include any arrangements with a view to such an exchange of shares, or shares and securities, as is mentioned in paragraph 83(1) (certain exchanges resulting in acquisition of share capital by new company).

37(5) The arrangements referred to in sub-paragraph (1)(b) and (c) do not include any arrangements applicable only on the winding up of the issuing company except in a case where–

(a) the issuing arrangements include arrangements for the issuing company to be wound up, or

(b) the issuing company is wound up otherwise than for commercial reasons.

37(6) The arrangements referred to in sub-paragraph (1)(d) do not include any arrangements which are confined to the provision–

(a) for the issuing company itself, or

(b) where the issuing company is the parent company of a group, for any group company,

of any such protection against the risks arising in the course of carrying on its business as might reasonably be expected to be provided for normal commercial reasons.

Cross references – SI 2009/317, art. 3(2): modification of para. 37(5) in relation to liquidation or administration of banks.

REQUIREMENT AS TO NO TAX AVOIDANCE

38 The relevant shares must be issued for commercial reasons, and not as part of a scheme or arrangement the main purpose or one of the main purposes of which is the avoidance of tax.

Part V – Investment Relief

FORM OF INVESTMENT RELIEF

39(1) Where–

(a) the investing company is eligible for investment relief in respect of an amount subscribed by it for an issue of shares, and

(b) it makes a claim under this Part,

the company's liability for corporation tax for the accounting period in which the shares were issued shall be reduced by the appropriate amount.

39(2) In sub-paragraph (1) **"the appropriate amount"** means whichever is the smaller of–

(a) 20% of the amount or aggregate amount–

(i) which was subscribed by the company for shares issued in that period, and

(ii) in respect of which the company is eligible for and claims investment relief, and

(b) the amount which reduces the liability to nil.

ENTITLEMENT TO CLAIM

40(1) The investing company is entitled to make a claim to investment relief in respect of the amount subscribed by it for the relevant shares if it appears to it that the requirements for the relief are for the time being met.

This is subject to sub-paragraph (2).

40(2) The investing company is not entitled to make a claim to investment relief in relation to the amount subscribed by it for the relevant shares unless–

(a) the funded trade has been carried on for four months by no person other than the issuing company or a qualifying 90% subsidiary of that company, disregarding–

(i) any time spent preparing to carry on that trade, and

(ii) any person required to be disregarded in accordance with sub-paragraph (2A) or (2B), and

(b) the investing company has received from the issuing company a compliance certificate in respect of those shares.

40(2A) At any time when the funded trade is carried on by the partners in a partnership of which the issuing company, or a qualifying 90% subsidiary of that company, is a member, there shall be disregarded for the purposes of sub-paragraph (2)(a) any other members of the partnership at that time.

40(2B) At any time when the funded trade is carried on by the parties to a joint venture to which the issuing company, or a qualifying 90% subsidiary of that company, is a party, there shall be disregarded for the purposes of sub-paragraph (2)(a) any other parties to the joint venture at that time.

40(3) For the purposes of this paragraph, **"the funded trade"** means the trade or trades by reference to which the requirement of paragraph 36 (use of money raised) is met in respect of the relevant issue of shares (as defined by sub-paragraph (2) of that paragraph).

This is subject to sub-paragraph (4).

40(4) To the extent that the funded trade would, by virtue of sub-paragraph (3), be a trade derived or benefiting from a trade within paragraph 25(2), the funded trade shall be deemed, for the purposes of this paragraph, to be the trade within that paragraph.

40(5) Where–

(a) by reason only of the issuing company or any other company being wound up or dissolved without winding up, the funded trade is carried on as mentioned in sub-paragraph (2)(a) for a period shorter than four months, and

(b) the winding up or dissolution is for commercial reasons and is not part of a scheme or arrangement the main purpose or one of the main purposes of which is the avoidance of tax,

sub-paragraph (2)(a) shall have effect as if it referred to that shorter period.

40(6) Where–

(a) by reason only of anything done as a consequence of the issuing company or any other company being in administration or receivership, the funded trade is carried on as mentioned in sub-paragraph (2)(a) for a period shorter than four months, and

(b) the entry into administration or receivership, and everything done as a consequence of the company concerned being in administration or receivership, is for commercial reasons and is not part of a scheme or arrangement the main purpose or one of the main purposes of which is the avoidance of tax,

sub-paragraph (2)(a) shall have effect as if it referred to that shorter period.

40(7) No application shall be made under section 55(3) or (4) of the Taxes Management Act 1970 (application for postponement of payment of tax pending appeal) on the ground that the investing company is eligible for investment relief unless a claim for the relief has been duly made by that company.

History – Para. 40(2)(a) substituted by FA 2004, s. 95 and Sch. 20, para. 12(a) with effect in relation to shares issued on or after 17 March 2004.

Para. 40(2A) inserted by FA 2004, s. 95 and Sch. 20, para. 12(b) with effect in relation to shares issued on or after 17 March 2004.

Para. 40(2B) inserted by FA 2004, s. 95 and Sch. 20, para. 12(b) with effect in relation to shares issued on or after 17 March 2004.

Para. 40(5)(a) substituted by FA 2004, s. 95 and Sch. 20, para. 12(c) with effect in relation to shares issued on or after 17 March 2004.
In para. 40(5)(b), all instances of the word "is" substituted for "was" by FA 2004, s. 95 and Sch. 20, para. 12(d) with effect in relation to shares issued on or after 17 March 2004.
Para. 40(6)(a) substituted by FA 2004, s. 95 and Sch. 20, para. 12(e) with effect in relation to shares issued on or after 17 March 2004.
In para. 40(6)(b), the word "concerned" inserted after the word "company" by FA 2004, s. 95 and Sch. 20, para. 12(f) with effect in relation to shares issued on or after 17 March 2004.
In para. 40(6)(b), the words "the entry into administration or receivership" substituted for the words "the making of the order within paragraph (a) or, as the case may be, (b) of paragraph 102(4) (administration orders and orders for appointment of receiver etc.)" by SI 2003/2096, art. 4 and Schedule, para. 34(c) with effect from 15 September 2003. Transitional provisions are contained in art. 6.

Cross references – SI 2009/317, art. 3(2), (3): modification of para. 40(5), (6) in relation to liquidation or administration of banks.

Transitional – SI 2003/2096, art. 6 contains transitional provisions so that the former rules remain in effect where a petition for an administration order was presented prior to 15 September 2003.

COMPLIANCE CERTIFICATES

41(1) A **"compliance certificate"** is a certificate which–

(a) is issued by the issuing company in respect of the relevant shares,

(b) states that, except so far as they fall to be met by or in relation to the investing company, the requirements for investment relief are for the time being met in relation to those shares, and

(c) is in such form as the Inland Revenue may direct.

41(2) Before issuing a compliance certificate in respect of the relevant shares, the issuing company must provide the Inland Revenue with a compliance statement in respect of the issue of shares which includes the relevant shares.

41(3) The issuing company must not issue a compliance certificate without the authority of the Inland Revenue.

41(4) Where the company or a person connected with the company has given notice to the Inland Revenue under paragraph 65 (information to be provided by issuing company etc.) the authority of the Inland Revenue must be given or renewed after the receipt of the notice.

COMPLIANCE STATEMENTS

42(1) A **"compliance statement"** is a statement, in respect of an issue of shares, to the effect that, except so far as they fall to be satisfied by or in relation to companies to which the shares included in that issue have been issued, the requirements for investment relief–

(a) are for the time being met in relation to the shares to which the statement relates, and

(b) have been so met at all times since the shares were issued.

In determining for the purposes of this sub-paragraph whether those requirements are met at any time in relation to the issue of shares, references in this Schedule to "the relevant shares" shall be read as references to the shares included in the issue.

42(2) A compliance statement must be in such form as the Inland Revenue direct and must contain–

(a) such additional information as the Inland Revenue reasonably require,

(b) a declaration that the statement is correct to the best of the issuing company's knowledge and belief, and

(c) such other declarations as the Inland Revenue reasonably require.

42(3) Without prejudice to the generality of sub-paragraph (2)(a) the information required by the Inland Revenue may include–

(a) information relating to the companies to which compliance certificates may be issued under paragraph 41 in respect of any shares included in the issue of shares to which the statement relates, and

(b) information to enable the Inland Revenue to determine whether the requirements of paragraph 35(2)(b) and (c) (shares to be subscribed for wholly in cash and fully paid up) are met in relation to shares included in that issue subscribed for by such companies.

42(4) The issuing company may not provide the Inland Revenue with a compliance statement in respect of any shares issued by it in any accounting period–

(a) before the condition in paragraph 40(2)(a) (no claim until trade carried on for four months) is satisfied; or

(b) later than two years after the end of that accounting period or, if that condition is first satisfied after the end of that accounting period, later than two years after the condition is first satisfied.

APPEAL AGAINST REFUSAL TO AUTHORISE COMPLIANCE CERTIFICATE

43 For the purposes of the provisions of the Taxes Management Act 1970 relating to appeals, the refusal of the Inland Revenue to authorise the issue of a compliance certificate shall be taken to be a decision disallowing a claim by the issuing company which is not a claim for discharge or repayment of tax.

PENALTIES FOR FRAUDULENT CERTIFICATE OR STATEMENT ETC.

44 The issuing company is liable to a penalty not exceeding £3,000 if–

(a) it issues a compliance certificate, or provides a compliance statement, which is made fraudulently or negligently, or

(b) it issues a compliance certificate in contravention of paragraph 41(3) or (4) (no certificate to be issued without Inland Revenue approval).

ATTRIBUTION OF RELIEF TO SHARES

45(1) References in this Schedule, in relation to a company, to the investment relief attributable to any shares or issue of shares shall be read as references to any reduction made in the company's liability to corporation tax that is attributed to those shares or that issue in accordance with this paragraph.
This is subject to the provisions of Part VI of this Schedule providing for the reduction or withdrawal of investment relief.

45(2) Where a company's liability to corporation tax is reduced for an accounting period under paragraph 39 (form of investment relief), then–

(a) where the reduction is obtained by reason of one issue of shares, the amount of the reduction shall be attributed to that issue, and

(b) where the reduction is obtained by reason of two or more issues of shares, the reduction–

  (i) shall be apportioned between those issues in the same proportions as the amounts subscribed by the company for each issue, and

  (ii) shall be attributed to those issues accordingly.

45(3) Where under this paragraph an amount of any reduction of corporation tax is attributed to an issue of shares ("the original issue") to a company a proportionate part of that amount shall be attributed to each share comprised in the original issue.

45(4) If corresponding bonus shares are issued to the company in respect of any shares ("the original shares") comprised in the original issue that have been continuously held by the company from the time they were issued until the issue of the bonus shares–

(a) a proportionate part of the total amount attributed to the original shares immediately before the bonus shares are issued shall be attributed to each of the shares in the holding comprising the original shares and the bonus shares, and

(b) after the issue of the bonus shares, this Schedule shall apply as if–

  (i) the original issue had included the bonus shares, and

  (ii) the bonus shares had been held by the company continuously from the time the original shares were issued until the bonus shares were issued.

45(5) In sub-paragraph (4) **"corresponding bonus shares"** means bonus shares which are in the same company, of the same class, and carry the same rights as the original shares.

45(6) If investment relief attributable to any shares falls to be withdrawn under Part VI of this Schedule the relief attributable to each of the shares shall be reduced to nil.

45(7) If investment relief attributable to any shares falls to be reduced under Part VI of this Schedule by any amount the relief attributable to each of the shares shall be reduced by a proportionate part of that amount.

Part VI – Withdrawal of Investment Relief

DISPOSAL OF SHARES

46(1) This paragraph applies where–

(a) the investing company disposes of any of the relevant shares which have been held by it continuously from the time they were issued until the disposal,

(b) the disposal takes place during the qualification period relating to the relevant shares, and

(c) investment relief is attributable to the shares.

46(2) If the disposal is not–

(a) by way of a bargain made at arm's length,

(b) by way of a distribution in the course of dissolving or winding up the issuing company,

(c) a disposal within section 24(1) of the 1992 Act (entire loss, destruction, dissipation or extinction of asset), or

(d) a deemed disposal under section 24(2) of that Act (claim that value of asset has become negligible),

the investment relief attributable to those shares must be withdrawn.

46(3) If the disposal is within paragraph (a), (b), (c) or (d) of sub-paragraph (2) the investment relief attributable to those shares must–

(a) if it is greater than an amount equal to 20% of the amount or value of the consideration (if any) which the company receives for the shares, be reduced by that amount, and

(b) in any other case, be withdrawn.

46(4) Where–

(a) the amount of the reduction ("A") in the investing company's liability to corporation tax obtained under paragraph 39 (form of investment relief) in respect of the relevant shares, is less than

(b) the amount ("B") which is equal to 20% of the amount subscribed by the investing company for those shares,

sub-paragraph (3)(a) shall have effect in relation to a disposal of any of those shares as if the amount or value referred to in that sub-paragraph were reduced by multiplying it by the fraction–

$$\frac{A}{B}$$

46(5) Where the amount of investment relief attributable to any of the relevant shares has been reduced before the investment relief was obtained, the amount of the corporation tax reduction obtained in respect of those shares shall be deemed for the purposes of sub-paragraph (4) to be the amount of the corporation tax reduction that would have been obtained had no such reduction of relief been made before the relief was obtained.

46(6) Sub-paragraph (5) does not apply to a reduction by virtue of paragraph 45(4) (attribution of investment relief where there is a corresponding issue of bonus shares).

History – In para. 46(2)(a), the words "for full consideration" (which followed the words "at arm's length") omitted by CTA 2010, s. 1177 and Sch. 1, para. 315(10) and repealed by CTA 2010, s. 1181 and Sch. 3, Pt. 1, with effect for corporation tax purposes for accounting periods ending on or after 1 April 2010, and for income tax and capital gains tax purposes for the tax year 2010–11 and subsequent tax years.

Cross references – TCGA 1992, Sch. 7AC, para. 4(2): disapplication of TCGA 1992, Sch. 7AC, para. 1 where the effect would be the reduction or withdrawal of relief under para. 46.
SI 2009/317,art. 3(2): modification of para. 46(2) in relation to liquidation or administration of banks.

VALUE RECEIVED BY INVESTING COMPANY

47(1) Sub-paragraph (2) applies where the investing company receives any value (other than insignificant value) from the issuing company during the period of restriction relating to the relevant shares.

47(2) Any investment relief attributable to the shares shall–

(a) if it exceeds the amount mentioned in sub-paragraph (3), be reduced by that amount, and

(b) in any other case, be withdrawn.

47(3) The amount referred to in sub-paragraph (2)(a) is an amount equal to 20% of the amount of the value received.

47(4) This paragraph is subject to the following paragraphs–

paragraph 51 (value received where there is more than one issue of shares);

paragraph 52 (cases where maximum investment relief not obtained); and

paragraph 54 (receipt of replacement value).

47(5) Where–

(a) value is received ("the relevant receipt") by the investing company from the issuing company at any time during the period of restriction relating to the relevant shares,

(b) the investing company has received from the issuing company one or more receipts of insignificant value at a time or times–

  (i) during that period, but

  (ii) not later than the time of the relevant receipt, and

(c) the aggregate amount of the value of the receipts within paragraph (a) and (b) is not an amount of insignificant value,

the investing company shall be treated for the purposes of this Part as if the relevant receipt had been a receipt of an amount of value equal to that aggregate amount.

For this purpose a receipt does not fall within paragraph (b) if it has been previously aggregated under this sub-paragraph.

47(6) If, at any time in the period–

(a) beginning one year before the relevant shares are issued, and

(b) expiring at the end of the issue date,

arrangements are in existence which provide for the investing company to receive, or to be entitled to receive, any value from the issuing company at any time in the period of restriction relating to those shares, no amount of value received by the investing company shall be treated as a receipt of insignificant value for the purposes of this paragraph.

47(7) For the purposes of this paragraph–

(a) references to a receipt of insignificant value (however expressed) are references to a receipt of an amount of insignificant value;

(b) **"an amount of insignificant value"** means an amount of value which–

(i) does not exceed £1,000, or

(ii) if it exceeds that amount, is insignificant in relation to the amount subscribed by the investing company for the shares.

This is subject to sub-paragraph (6).

47(8) Where by reason of the investing company's disposal of any shares any investment relief attributable to those shares is withdrawn or reduced, the investing company shall not be treated for the purposes of this paragraph as receiving value from the issuing company in respect of the disposal.

47(9) Value received shall be disregarded, for the purposes of this paragraph, to the extent to which investment relief attributable to any shares has already been reduced or withdrawn on its account.

Cross references – ICTA 1988, s. 303: restriction of Enterprise Investment Scheme relief where value received by person other than claimant; interaction with receipts of insignificant value.

TCGA 1992, Sch. 5B, para. 14(3): Enterprise Investment Scheme, Reinvestment Relief; application of para. 47 to the determination of what, if any, value has been received in respect of shares.

MEANING OF "THE PERIOD OF RESTRICTION"

48 For the purposes of this Schedule **"the period of restriction"** relating to the relevant shares means the period–

(a) beginning one year before the shares are issued, and

(b) ending at the end of the qualification period relating to the shares.

WHEN VALUE IS RECEIVED

49(1) For the purposes of paragraphs 47 (value received by investing company) and 51 (value received where there is more than one issue of shares) the investing company receives value from the issuing company at any time when the issuing company–

(a) repays, redeems or repurchases any of its share capital or securities which belong to the investing company or makes any payment to that company for giving up its right to any of the issuing company's share capital or any security on its cancellation or extinguishment;

(b) repays, in pursuance of any arrangements for or in connection with the acquisition of the relevant shares, any debt owed to the investing company other than a debt which was incurred by the issuing company–

(i) on or after the date of issue of those shares; and

(ii) otherwise than in consideration of the extinguishment of a debt incurred before that date;

(c) makes to the investing company any payment for giving up the company's right to any debt on its extinguishment;

(d) releases or waives any liability of the investing company to the issuing company or discharges, or *undertakes to discharge*, any liability of the investing company to a third person;

(e) makes a loan or advance to the investing company which has not been repaid in full before the issue of the relevant shares;

(f) provides a benefit or facility for the directors or employees of the investing company or any of their associates;

(g) disposes of an asset to the investing company for no consideration or for a consideration which is or the value of which is less than the market value of the asset;

(h) acquires an asset from the investing company for a consideration which is or the value of which is more than the market value of the asset; or

(i) makes a payment to the investing company other than a qualifying payment.

49(2) For the purposes of sub-paragraph (1)(e) there shall be treated as if it were a loan made by the issuing company to the investing company–

(a) the amount of any debt (other than an ordinary trade debt) incurred by the investing company to the issuing company, and

(b) the amount of any debt due from the investing company to a third person which has been assigned to the issuing company.

49(3) For the purposes of sub-paragraph (1)(d) the issuing company shall be treated as having released or waived a liability if the liability is not discharged within 12 months of the time when it ought to have been discharged.

49(4) For the purposes of this paragraph–

(a) references to a debt or liability do not, in relation to a person, include references to any debt or liability which would be discharged by the making by that person of a qualifying payment;

(b) references to a benefit or facility do not include references to any benefit or facility provided in circumstances such that, if a payment had been made of an amount equal to its value, that payment would be a qualifying payment; and

(c) any reference to a payment or disposal to a person includes a reference to a payment or disposal made to that person indirectly or to his order or for his benefit.

In paragraphs (a) to (c) references to "a person" include references to any person who, at any time in the period of restriction in question, is connected with that person, whether or not he is so connected at the material time.

49(5) In this paragraph–

"ordinary trade debt" means any debt for goods or services supplied in the ordinary course of a trade or business where any credit given–

(a) does not exceed six months, and

(b) is not longer than that normally given to customers of the person carrying on the trade or business; and

"qualifying payment" means–

(a) any payment by any person for any goods, services or facilities provided by the investing company (in the course of its trade or otherwise) which is reasonable in relation to the market value of those goods, services or facilities;

(b) the payment by any person of any interest which represents no more than a reasonable commercial return on money lent to that person;

(c) the payment by any company of any dividend or other distribution which does not exceed a normal return on any investment in shares in or other securities of that company;

(d) any payment for the acquisition of an asset which does not exceed its market value;

(e) the payment by any person, as rent for any property occupied by the person, of an amount not exceeding a reasonable and commercial rent for the property; and

(f) a payment in discharge of an ordinary trade debt.

THE AMOUNT OF VALUE RECEIVED

50 For the purposes of paragraph 47 the amount of the value received is–

(a) *in a case within paragraph 49(1)(a), (b) or (c)*–

(i) the amount received by the investing company, or

(ii) the market value of the shares, securities or debt in question,

whichever is greater;

(b) in a case within paragraph 49(1)(d), the amount of the liability;

(c) in a case within paragraph 49(1)(e)–

(i) the amount of the loan or advance, less

(ii) the amount of any repayment made before the issue of the relevant shares;

(d) in a case within paragraph 49(1)(f)–

(i) the cost to the issuing company of providing the benefit or facility, less

(ii) any consideration given for it by the recipient or any associate of his;

(e) in a case within paragraph 49(1)(g) or (h), the difference between the market value of the asset and the consideration (if any) received for it; and

(f) in a case within paragraph 49(1)(i), the amount of the payment.

VALUE RECEIVED WHERE THERE IS MORE THAN ONE ISSUE OF SHARES

51(1) This paragraph applies where–

(a) two or more issues of shares in the issuing company have been made to the investing company (being issues in relation to which the investing company is eligible for and claims investment relief), and

(b) the value received falls within the periods of restriction relating to two or more of those issues.

51(2) Where this paragraph applies paragraph 47 has effect in relation to the shares comprised in each of the issues referred to in sub-paragraph (1)(b) as if the amount of the value received were reduced by multiplying it by the fraction–

$$\frac{A}{B}$$

Where–

A is the amount subscribed by the investing company for the shares comprised in the issue in question to which investment relief is (or, but for paragraph 47 would be) attributable; and

B is the aggregate of that amount and the corresponding amount or amounts for the other issue or issues.

CASES WHERE MAXIMUM INVESTMENT RELIEF NOT OBTAINED

52(1) Where–

(a) the amount of the reduction ("C") in the investing company's liability to corporation tax obtained in respect of the relevant shares, is less than

(b) the amount ("D") which is equal to 20% of the amount subscribed by the investing company for those shares,

paragraph 47 has effect as if the amount of the value received were reduced by multiplying it by the fraction–

$$\frac{C}{D}$$

52(2) Where the amount of investment relief attributable to any of the relevant shares has been reduced before the investment relief was obtained, the amount of the corporation tax reduction obtained in respect of those shares shall be deemed for the purposes of sub-paragraph (1) to be the amount of the corporation tax reduction that would have been obtained had no such reduction of relief been made before the relief was obtained.

52(3) Sub-paragraph (2) does not apply to a reduction of investment relief by virtue of paragraph 45(4) (attribution of investment relief where there is a corresponding issue of bonus shares).

RECEIPTS OF VALUE BY AND FROM CONNECTED PERSONS

53 In paragraphs 47, 49 and 50 references to the investing company or the issuing company include references to any person who at any time in the period of restriction relating to the relevant shares is connected with the company concerned, whether or not he is connected at the material time.

RECEIPT OF REPLACEMENT VALUE

54(1) Where–

(a) any investment relief attributable to the relevant shares would, in the absence of this paragraph, be reduced or withdrawn under paragraph 47 by reason of a receipt of value within paragraph 49(1) ("the original value"),

(b) the original supplier receives value ("the replacement value") from the original recipient by reason of a qualifying receipt, and

(c) the amount of the replacement value is not less than the amount of the original value,

paragraph 47 shall not, by reason of the receipt of the original value, have effect to reduce or withdraw the investment relief.

54(2) For the purposes of this paragraph and paragraph 55–

"the original recipient" means the person who receives the original value; and

"the original supplier" means the person from whom that value was received.

54(2A) Where the amount of the original value is, by virtue of paragraph 51, treated as reduced for the purposes of paragraph 47, the reference in sub-paragraph (1)(c) to the amount of the original value shall be read as a reference to the amount of that value disregarding the reduction.

54(3) A receipt of the replacement value is a qualifying receipt for the purposes of sub-paragraph (1) if it arises–

(a) by reason of the original recipient doing one or more of the following–

(i) making a payment to the original supplier other than an excepted payment;

(ii) acquiring any asset from the original supplier for a consideration the amount or value of which is more than the market value of the asset;

(iii) disposing of any asset to the original supplier for no consideration or for a consideration the amount or value of which is less than the market value of the asset; or

(b) where the receipt of the original value was within paragraph 49(1)(d), by reason of an event the effect of which is to reverse the event which constituted the receipt of the original value.

54(3A) For the purposes of sub-paragraph (3)(a)(i), the following are excepted payments–

(a) any payment for any goods, services or facilities, provided (whether in the course of a trade or otherwise) by–

(i) the original supplier, or

(ii) any other person who, at any time in the period of restriction relating to the relevant shares, is an associate of, or connected with, that supplier (whether or not he is such an associate, or so connected, at the material time),

which is reasonable in relation to the market value of those goods, services or facilities;

(b) any payment of any interest which represents no more than a reasonable commercial return on money lent to–

(i) the original recipient, or

(ii) any other person who, at any time in the period of restriction relating to the relevant shares, is an associate of, or connected with, that recipient (whether or not he is such an associate, or so connected, at the material time);

(c) any payment, as rent for any property occupied by–

(i) that recipient, or

(ii) any person who, at any time in the period of restriction relating to the relevant shares, is an associate of, or connected with, that recipient (whether or not he is such an associate, or so connected, at the material time),

of an amount not exceeding a reasonable and commercial rent for the property;

(d) any payment within paragraph (c), (d) or (f) of the definition of **"qualifying payment"** in paragraph 49(5); and

(e) any payment for shares in or securities of any company in circumstances that do not fall within sub-paragraph (3)(a)(ii).

54(4) For the purposes of this paragraph, the amount of the replacement value is–

(a) in a case within paragraph (a) of sub-paragraph (3), the aggregate of–

(i) the amount of any payment within sub-paragraph (i) of that paragraph, and

(ii) the difference between the market value of any asset to which sub-paragraph (ii) or (iii) of that paragraph applies and the amount or value of the consideration (if any) received for it, and

(b) in a case within sub-paragraph (3)(b), the amount of the original value,

and paragraph 50 shall apply for the purposes of determining the amount of the original value.

History – In para. 54(1)(c) the words "the amount of" inserted by FA 2001, s. 64 and Sch. 16, para. 6(1); the inserted words being deemed to have always been in place (Sch. 16, para. 6(6)).

Para. 54(2A) inserted by FA 2001, s. 64 and Sch. 16, para. 6(2) with effect:

- in relation to any shares issued on or after 7 March 2001 (Sch. 16, para. 6(7)(a)); and
- in relation to shares issued on or after 31 March 2000 but before 7 March 2001 in respect of "value received", as defined by FA 2000, Sch. 15, para. 49 (Sch. 16, para. 6(7)(b)).

Para. 54(3)(a) and (b) substituted and para. 54(3)(c) deleted by FA 2001, s. 64 and Sch. 16, para. 6(3) with effect:

- in relation to any shares issued on or after 7 March 2001 (Sch. 16, para. 6(7)(a)); and
- in respect of shares issued on or after 31 March 2000 but before 7 March 2001 in respect of "value received", as defined by FA 2000, Sch. 15, para. 49 (Sch. 16, para. 6(7)(b)).

Para. 54(3A) inserted by FA 2001, s. 64 and Sch. 16, para. 6(4) with effect:

- in relation to any shares issued on or after 7 March 2001 (Sch. 16, para. 6(7)(a)); and
- in relation to shares issued on or after 31 March 2000 but before 7 March 2001 in respect of "value received", as defined by FA 2000, Sch. 15, para. 49 (Sch. 16, para. 6(7)(b)).

Para. 54(4) substituted by FA 2001, s. 64 and Sch. 16, para. 6(5) with effect:

- in relation to any shares issued on or after 7 March 2001 (Sch. 16, para. 6(7)(a)); and
- in respect of shares issued on or after 31 March 2000 but before 7 March 2001 in respect of "value received", as defined by FA 2000, Sch. 15, para. 49 (Sch. 16, para. 6(7)(b)).

PROVISION SUPPLEMENTARY TO PARAGRAPH 54

55(1) The receipt of the replacement value shall be disregarded for the purposes of sub-paragraph (1) of paragraph 54 to the extent to which it has previously been set (under that paragraph) against a receipt of value to prevent any reduction or withdrawal of investment relief under paragraph 47.

55(2) The receipt of the replacement value by the original supplier ("the event") shall be disregarded for the purposes of paragraph 54(1) if–

(a) the event occurs before the start of the period of restriction relating to the relevant shares,

(b) there was an unreasonable delay in the event occurring, or

(c) where an appeal has been brought by the investing company against an assessment to withdraw or reduce any investment relief attributable to the relevant shares by reason of the receipt of the original value, the event occurs more than 60 days after the amount of relief which falls to be withdrawn has been finally determined.

But nothing in paragraph 54 or this paragraph requires the replacement value to be received after the original value.

55(3) Sub-paragraph (4) applies where–

(a) the receipt of the replacement value is a qualifying receipt for the purposes of paragraph 54(1) (receipt of replacement value which prevents loss of investment relief), and

(b) the event which gives rise to the receipt is (or includes) a subscription for shares by–

 (i) the investing company, or

 (ii) any person who at any time in the period of restriction relating to the relevant shares is connected with the investing company, whether or not he is connected at the material time.

55(4) Where this sub-paragraph applies the person who subscribes for the shares shall not–

(a) be eligible for–

 (i) any investment relief, or

 (ii) any relief under Chapter III of Part VII of the Taxes Act 1988 or Part 5 of ITA 2007 (EIS income tax relief),

 in relation to those shares or any other shares in the same issue; or

(b) by virtue of his subscription for those shares or any other shares in the same issue, be treated as making a qualifying investment for the purposes of Schedule 5B to the 1992 Act (EIS: deferral relief).

55(5) In this paragraph **"the original value"** and **"the replacement value"** shall be construed in accordance with paragraph 54.

History – In para. 55(4) the words "or Part 5 of ITA 2007" inserted by ITA 2007, s. 1027 and Sch. 1, para. 394(3), with effect from 6 April 2007.

Para. 55(5) inserted by FA 2001, s. 64 and Sch. 16, para. 7(1); the inserted sub-paragraph being deemed always to have been in place (Sch. 16, para. 7(2)).

VALUE RECEIVED BY OTHER PERSONS

56(1) Where any investment relief is attributable to such of the relevant shares as are held by the investing company, sub-paragraph (2) shall apply if at any time in the period of restriction relating to the relevant shares the issuing company or any subsidiary–

(a) repays, redeems or repurchases any of its share capital which belongs to any member other than–

 (i) the investing company, or

 (ii) a person who falls within sub-paragraph (3), or

(b) makes any payment to any such member for giving up his right to any of the share capital of the company or subsidiary on its cancellation or extinguishment.

56(2) The investment relief–

(a) if it is greater than the amount mentioned in sub-paragraph (4), shall be reduced by that amount, and

(b) in any other case, must be withdrawn.

56(3) A person falls within this sub-paragraph if the repayment, redemption, repurchase or payment in question–

(a) causes any investment relief attributable to that person's shares in the issuing company to be withdrawn or reduced by virtue of–
  (i) paragraph 46 (disposal of shares), or
  (ii) paragraph 49(1)(a) (receipt of value by virtue of repayment of share capital etc.);

(b) causes any relief under Chapter III of Part VII of the Taxes Act 1988 or Part 5 of ITA 2007 (EIS income tax relief) attributable to that person's shares in the issuing company to be withdrawn or reduced by virtue of–
  (i) section 299 of the Taxes Act 1988 or section 209 of ITA 2007 (disposal of shares), or
  (ii) section 300(2)(a) of the Taxes Act 1988 or section 216(2)(a) of ITA 2007 (receipt of value by virtue of repayment of share capital etc.);

  or

(c) gives rise to a qualifying chargeable event (within the meaning of paragraph 14(4) of Schedule 5B to the 1992 Act (EIS: deferral relief)) in respect of that person,

or it would have the effect mentioned in paragraph (a), (b) or (c) were it not a receipt of insignificant value for the purposes of paragraph 47 (value received by the investing company), section 300 of the Taxes Act 1988, section 214 of ITA 2007 or paragraph 13 of Schedule 5B to the 1992 Act, as the case may be.

56(4) The amount referred to in sub-paragraph (2) is an amount equal to 20%–

(a) where sub-paragraph (1) does not apply in the case of any other company holding shares in the issuing company, of the amount received by the member, and

(b) where sub-paragraph (1) also applies in the case of one or more such other companies, of the appropriate fraction of that amount.

56(5) For the purposes of sub-paragraph (4) **"the appropriate fraction"** is–

$$\frac{A}{B}$$

Where–

A is the amount subscribed by the investing company for such of the relevant shares as are shares to which investment relief is or, but for sub-paragraph (2)(b), would be attributable, and

B is the aggregate of that amount and the amount or amounts subscribed by the other company or companies for such shares which are comprised in the same issue of shares.

56(6) Where–

(a) the amount of the reduction ("C") in the investing company's liability to corporation tax obtained under paragraph 39 (form of investment relief) in respect of the relevant shares, is less than

(b) the amount ("D") which is equal to 20% of the amount subscribed by the investing company for those shares,

sub-paragraph (4) has effect as if the amount received by the member, or (as the case may be) the appropriate fraction of that amount, were reduced by multiplying it by the fraction–

$$\frac{C}{D}$$

56(7) Where the amount of investment relief attributable to the relevant shares has been reduced before the relief was obtained, the amount of the corporation tax reduction obtained in respect of those shares shall be deemed for the purposes of sub-paragraph (6) to be the amount of the corporation tax reduction that would have been obtained had no such reduction of investment relief been made before the relief was obtained.

56(8) Sub-paragraph (7) does not apply to a reduction by virtue of paragraph 45(4) (attribution of investment relief where there is a corresponding issue of bonus shares).

History – In para. 56(3) the words "or Part 5 of ITA 2007" inserted by ITA 2007, s. 1027 and Sch. 1, para. 394(4)(a), with effect from 6 April 2007.

In para. 56(3) the words "section 299 of the Taxes Act 1988 or section 209 of ITA 2007" substituted for "section 299 of that Act" by ITA 2007, s. 1027 and Sch. 1, para. 394(4)(b), with effect from 6 April 2007.

In para. 56(3) the words "section 300(2)(a) of the Taxes Act 1988 or section 216(2)(a) of ITA 2007" substituted for "section 300(2)(a) of that Act" by ITA 2007, s. 1027 and Sch. 1, para. 394(4)(c), with effect from 6 April 2007.

In para. 56(3) the words ", section 214 of ITA 2007" inserted by ITA 2007, s. 1027 and Sch. 1, para. 394(4)(d), with effect from 6 April 2007.

The final lines of text in para. 56(3) which immediately follow subpara. (3)(c) inserted by FA 2001, s. 64 and Sch. 16, para. 8(1) with effect:

- in relation to any shares issued on or after 7 March 2001 (Sch. 16, para. 8(2)(a)); and
- in relation to shares issued on or after 31 March 2000 but before 7 March 2001 in respect of any repayment, as defined by FA 2000, Sch. 15, para. 57(2) (Sch. 16, para. 8(2)(b)).

INSIGNIFICANT REPAYMENTS DISREGARDED

57(1) Any repayment shall be disregarded for the purposes of paragraph 56(1) (repayments etc. which cause withdrawal of investment relief) if whichever is the greater of–

(a) the market value of the shares to which it relates ("the target shares") immediately before the event occurs, and

(b) the amount received by the member in question,

is insignificant in relation to the market value of the remaining issued share capital of the issuing company (or, as the case may be, subsidiary) immediately after the event occurs.

This is subject to sub-paragraph (4).

57(2) For the purposes of this paragraph **"repayment"** means a repayment, redemption, repurchase or payment mentioned in paragraph 56(1) (repayments etc. which cause withdrawal of investment relief).

57(3) For the purposes of sub-paragraph (1) it shall be assumed that the target shares are cancelled at the time the repayment is made.

57(4) Sub-paragraph (1) does not apply if, at a relevant time, arrangements are in existence that provide–

(a) for a repayment by the issuing company or any subsidiary of that company (whether or not it is such a subsidiary at the time the arrangements are made), or

(b) for anyone to be entitled to such a repayment,

at any time in the period of restriction relating to the shares.

57(5) For the purposes of sub-paragraph (4) **"a relevant time"** means any time in the period–

(a) beginning one year before the relevant shares are issued, and

(b) expiring at the end of the issue date.

History – In para. 57(1)(b), the word "issued" (in the phrase "remaining issued share capital") inserted by FA 2001, s. 64 and Sch. 16, para. 9(1) with effect:

- in relation to any shares issued on or after 7 March 2001 (Sch. 16, para. 9(3)(a)); and
- in relation to shares issued on or after 31 March 2000 but before 7 March 2001 in respect of any repayment, as defined by FA 2000, Sch. 15, para. 57(2) (Sch. 16, para. 9(3)(b)).

In para. 57(3) the word "repayment" is substituted for the former word ("payment") by FA 2001, s. 64 and Sch. 16, para. 9(2); the amendment being deemed to have always had effect (Sch. 16, para. 9(4)).

PROVISION SUPPLEMENTARY TO PARAGRAPH 56 AND 57

58(1) Any repayment shall be disregarded for the purposes of paragraph 56(1) (repayments etc. which cause withdrawal of investment relief) to the extent to which investment relief attributable to any shares has already been reduced or withdrawn on its account.

58(2) In any case where–

(a) investment relief is attributable to such of the relevant shares as are held by the investing company;

(b) the issuing company has made one or more other issues of shares each of which includes shares ("designated shares") to which investment relief is attributable, and

(c) the repayment falls–

   (i) within the period of restriction relating to the relevant shares, and

   (ii) within one or more of the equivalent periods relating to any of the designated shares,

paragraph 56(4) shall have effect in relation to each of the issues of shares as if the amount received by the member, or (as the case may be) the appropriate fraction of that amount, were reduced by multiplying it by the relevant fraction.

58(3) For the purposes of sub-paragraph (2) **"the equivalent period"**, in relation to any designated shares, means the period–

(a) beginning one year before the shares are issued, and

(b) ending at the end of the qualification period relating to the shares.

For the purposes of determining the qualification period relating to any designated shares, the references in paragraph 3 to the relevant shares shall be read as references to those designated shares.

58(4) *In sub-paragraph (2)–*

"the appropriate fraction" has the meaning given by paragraph 56(5), and

"the relevant fraction" means–

$$\frac{E}{F}$$

Where–

E is the amount subscribed by companies for shares which are included in the issue in question and to which investment relief is or, but for paragraph 56(2)(b), would be attributable; and

F is the aggregate of that amount and the corresponding amount or amounts for the other issue or issues.

58(5) Where–

(a) a company issues share capital of nominal value equal to the authorised minimum (within the meaning of the Companies Act 2006) for the purposes of complying with the requirements of section 761 of that Act (public company not to do business unless requirements as to share capital complied with), and

(b) the registrar of companies issues the company with a certificate under section 761,

paragraph 56(1) shall not apply in relation to any redemption of those shares within 12 months of the date on which they were issued.

58(6) [Omitted by SI 2008/954, art. 26, and art. 3 and Sch.]

58(7) References in paragraphs 56 and 57 and this paragraph to a subsidiary of the issuing company are references to any company which at any time in the period of restriction relating to the relevant shares is a 51% subsidiary of the issuing company whether or not it is such a subsidiary at the time of the repayment in question.

58(8) For the purposes of this paragraph **"repayment"** has the meaning given in paragraph 57(2).

History – In para. 58(5) the words "the Companies Act 2006" substituted for "the Companies Act 1985" and "section 761" substituted for "section 117" in both places by SI 2008/954, art. 26, with effect from 6 April 2008.
Para. 58(6) omitted by SI 2008/954, art. 26, and art. 3 and Schedule, with effect from 6 April 2008.

PUT OPTIONS AND CALL OPTIONS

59(1) Sub-paragraph (2) applies where–

(a) an option, the exercise of which would bind the grantor to purchase any of the relevant shares, is granted to the investing company during the qualification period relating to those shares; or

(b) an option, the exercise of which would bind the investing company to sell such shares, is granted by the investing company during that period.

59(2) Any investment relief attributable to the shares to which the option relates must be withdrawn.

59(3) The shares to which the option relates are those which, if–

(a) the option were exercised immediately after the grant, and

(b) any shares in the issuing company acquired by the investing company after the grant were disposed of immediately after being acquired,

would be treated for the purposes of this Schedule as disposed of in pursuance of the option.

59(4) Nothing in this paragraph prejudices the operation of paragraph 37 (pre-arranged exits).

WITHDRAWAL OF RELIEF

60(1) Where any investment relief has been obtained which–

(a) is subsequently found not to have been due, or

(b) falls to be withdrawn under this Part,

it shall be withdrawn by making an assessment to corporation tax for the accounting period for which the relief was obtained.

60(2) Investment relief obtained by the investing company in respect of the relevant shares may not be withdrawn on the ground–

(a) that the issuing company is not a qualifying issuing company in relation to those shares,

(b) that the requirements of Part IV of this Schedule are not met in respect of the shares,

(c) by virtue of paragraph 47 (value received by investing company), or

(d) by virtue of paragraph 56 (value received by other persons),

unless sub-paragraph (3) is satisfied.

60(3) This sub-paragraph is satisfied if–

(a) either–

(i) the issuing company has given notice under paragraph 65 (information to be provided by issuing company etc.) in relation to those shares, or

(ii) the Inland Revenue have given notice to that company stating that, by reason of the ground in question, the whole or any part of the investment relief obtained by any company or companies in respect of shares included in the relevant issue of shares was not in their opinion due,

and

(b) in the case of a withdrawal within sub-paragraph (2)(c) or (d), the Inland Revenue have given notice to the investing company stating the matters mentioned in paragraph (a)(ii) above.

60(4) In this paragraph–

(a) references to the withdrawal of investment relief include its reduction; and

(b) **"the relevant issue of shares"** means the issue of shares in the issuing company which includes the relevant shares.

History – In para. 60(1) the words "under Case VI of Schedule D" omitted by CTA 2009, s. 1322 and Sch. 1, para. 468 and repealed by CTA 2009, s. 1326 and Sch. 3, Pt. 1, with effect for corporation tax purposes for accounting periods ending on or after 1 April 2009, and for income tax and capital gains tax purposes for the tax year 2009–10 and subsequent tax years.

APPEALS AGAINST WITHDRAWAL OF RELIEF

61 For the purposes of the provisions of the Taxes Management Act 1970 relating to appeals, the giving of notice by the Inland Revenue under paragraph 60(3)(a)(ii) shall be taken to be a decision disallowing a claim by the issuing company which is not a claim for discharge or repayment of tax.

TIME LIMITS

62(1) The Inland Revenue may not–

(a) make an assessment for withdrawing or reducing the investment relief attributable to any of the relevant shares, or

(b) give a notice under paragraph 60(3)(a)(ii) or (b),

more than six years after the end of the relevant accounting period.

62(2) In sub-paragraph (1) **"the relevant accounting period"** means–

(a) the accounting period in which the time mentioned in paragraph 36(1) (time limit for employing money raised) falls, or

(b) the accounting period in which the event which causes the investment relief to be withdrawn or reduced occurs,

whichever is later.

62(3) This paragraph is subject to sub-paragraphs (2) and (3) of paragraph 46 of Schedule 18 to the Finance Act 1998 (fraud or negligence).

Those sub-paragraphs shall apply in relation to any notice under paragraph 60(3)(a)(ii) or (b) as if it were an assessment relating to the accounting period to which any assessment made by virtue of the notice would relate.

INTEREST

63(1) This paragraph applies where–

(a) investment relief is withdrawn or reduced by virtue of–

(i) a failure to meet any of the requirements of paragraphs 5 to 10 or of Part III of this Schedule (requirements to be met in relation to investing company or issuing company);

(ia) paragraph 35A (maximum amount raised annually through risk capital schemes);

(ii) paragraph 46 (disposal of shares);

(iii) paragraph 47 (value received by investing company);

(iv) paragraph 56 (value received by other persons); or

(v) paragraph 59 (put options and call options);

(b) as a result, an assessment to corporation tax is made by virtue of paragraph 60; and

(c) the relevant event occurs after the date when the tax assessed became due and payable or, if there is more than one such date, the latest of them.

63(2) Section 87A of the Taxes Management Act 1970 (interest on overdue corporation tax etc.) has effect in relation to the tax assessed as if it became due and payable on the date the relevant event occurred.

63(3) In this paragraph references to **"the relevant event"** are to the event by virtue of which the relief is withdrawn or reduced as mentioned in sub-paragraph (1)(a).

History – Para. 63(1)(a) inserted by FA 2007, s. 51 and Sch. 16, para. 4(4) with effect from Royal Assent (19 July 2007).

INFORMATION TO BE PROVIDED BY THE INVESTING COMPANY

64(1) This paragraph applies where–

(a) the investing company has obtained investment relief in respect of the relevant shares, and

(b) an event occurs by reason of which–

  (i) the company is not a qualifying investing company in relation to those shares,

  (ii) the investment relief falls to be withdrawn or reduced by virtue of paragraph 47 (receipt of value by investing company), or

  (iii) the investment relief falls to be withdrawn or reduced by virtue of paragraph 59 (put options and call options).

64(2) Where this paragraph applies the investing company must give the Inland Revenue a notice containing particulars of the event.

64(3) Where the investing company–

(a) is required under this paragraph to give notice of a receipt of value (within paragraph 49(1)), and

(b) has knowledge of any replacement value received (or expected to be received) from the original recipient by the original supplier by reason of a qualifying receipt,

the notice shall include particulars of that receipt of replacement value (or expected receipt).

In this paragraph **"replacement value"**, **"original recipient"**, **"original supplier"** and **"qualifying receipt"** shall be construed in accordance with paragraph 54.

64(4) Subject to sub-paragraph (5), any notice required to be given by the company under sub-paragraph (2) must be given–

(a) within 60 days after the event, or

(b) where the event is the receipt of value by a person connected with the company (see paragraph 53), within 60 days after the company coming to know of the event.

64(5) In a case within sub-paragraph (1)(b)(ii), where the event occurred before the issue of the relevant shares, any notice required to be given by the investing company under sub-paragraph (2) must be given–

(a) within 60 days after the issue of the shares, or

(b) where–

  (i) the event is the receipt of value by a person connected with the company (see paragraph 53), and

  (ii) the company comes to know of the event on or after the issue of the shares,

within 60 days after the company coming to know of the event.

INFORMATION TO BE PROVIDED BY THE ISSUING COMPANY ETC.

65(1) This paragraph applies where–

(a) the issuing company has provided the Inland Revenue with a compliance statement in respect of an issue of shares, and

(b) an event occurs by reason of which–

  (i) the issuing company is not a qualifying issuing company in relation to any of the shares included in that issue, or would not be such a company if investment relief had been obtained in respect of the shares in question,

  (ii) the requirements of Part IV of this Schedule are not met in respect of any of the shares included in that issue, or would not be met if investment relief had been obtained in respect of the shares in question, or

  (iii) paragraph 47 (value received by investing company) or 56 (value received by other persons) has effect to cause any investment relief attributable to any of the shares included in that issue to be withdrawn or reduced, or would have such an effect if investment relief had been obtained in respect of the shares in question.

65(2) Where this paragraph applies–

(a) the company, and

(b) any person connected with the company who has knowledge of the matters mentioned in sub-paragraph (1),

must give the Inland Revenue a notice containing particulars of the event.

65(3) Sub-paragraph (3) of paragraph 64 shall apply in relation to a person required to give notice under this paragraph of a receipt of value within paragraph 49(1) as it applies to a company required to give such a notice under paragraph 64.

65(4) Subject to sub-paragraph (6) any notice required to be given by a company under sub-paragraph (2) (a) must be given–

(a) within 60 days after the event, or

(b) where the event is–

(i) a failure by the company to meet the requirement of paragraph 18 (the "individual-owners requirement") in respect of any of those shares; or

(ii) a receipt of value within paragraph 49(1) from a person connected with the company (see paragraph 53),

within 60 days after the company coming to know of the event.

65(5) Subject to sub-paragraph (6) any notice required to be given by a person within sub-paragraph (2) (b) must be given within 60 days after the person coming to know of the event.

65(6) In a case within sub-paragraph (1)(b)(iii), any notice required to be given by a person under sub-paragraph (2) must be given within 60 days after the issue of the shares if–

(a) the event occurred, and

(b) the person came to know of it,

before those shares were issued.

POWER OF INLAND REVENUE TO OBTAIN INFORMATION

66(1) This paragraph applies where the Inland Revenue have reason to believe that a company or other person–

(a) has not given a notice which it is required to give under paragraph 64 or 65 in respect of any event, or

(b) has given or received value (within the meaning of paragraph 49(1)) which, but for the fact that the amount given or received was an amount of insignificant value, would have triggered a requirement to give such a notice.

66(2) The Inland Revenue may by notice require the person concerned to furnish them, within such time as the Inland Revenue may direct (not being less than 60 days), with such information relating to the event as the Inland Revenue may reasonably require for the purposes of this Schedule.

66(3) In sub-paragraph (1)(b) the reference to an amount of insignificant value shall be construed in accordance with paragraph 47(7)(b).

Part VII – Relief for Losses on Disposals of Shares

ELIGIBILITY FOR RELIEF AGAINST INCOME

67(1) The investing company is eligible for relief under this Part ("loss relief") if–

(a) it incurs an allowable loss on the disposal of shares to which investment relief is attributable (and not withdrawn in full as a result of the disposal), and

(b) the requirements of sub-paragraphs (2) and (3) are met.

67(2) The first requirement is that the shares must have been held continuously by the investing company from the time they were issued until the disposal.

67(3) The second requirement is that the disposal on which the loss is incurred must be a disposal of the kind described in paragraph (a), (b), (c) or (d) of paragraph 46(2).

ENTITLEMENT TO CLAIM

68(1) Where the investing company is eligible for loss relief it may make a claim requiring that the loss be set off for the purposes of corporation tax against income–

(a) of the accounting period in which the loss is incurred, and

(b) if the claim so requires, of accounting periods ending within the preceding 12 month period.

68(2) A claim under sub-paragraph (1) must be made within two years after the end of the accounting period in which the loss is incurred.

68(3) In this paragraph **"the preceding 12 month period"** means the 12 months ending immediately before the accounting period in which the loss is incurred.

FORM OF LOSS RELIEF

69(1) Where a claim is made under sub-paragraph (1) of paragraph 68, the income of any of the accounting periods mentioned in that sub-paragraph shall then be treated as reduced by the amount of the loss or by so much of it as cannot be relieved under this sub-paragraph against income of a later accounting period. This is subject to loss relief first being obtained for any earlier loss.

69(2) The amount of the reduction which may be made under this paragraph in the income of an accounting period beginning before the preceding 12 month period (within the meaning of paragraph 68(3)) shall not exceed a part of that income proportionate to the part of the accounting period falling within that period.

PRIORITY OF LOSS RELIEF

70(1) Where loss relief is claimed by the investing company it must be claimed–

(a) in priority to any relief claimed by that company under Chapter 5 of Part 4 of CTA 2010 (relief for loss on disposal of shares in certain trading companies by investment companies),

(b) [omitted by CTA 2010, s. 1177 and Sch. 1, para. 315(11)(b) and repealed by CTA 2010, s. 1181 and Sch. 3, Pt. 1]

70(2) Where loss relief is obtained for an amount of a loss no deduction shall be made in respect of that amount–

(a) by virtue of section 70 of CTA 2010 (relief for loss on disposal of shares in certain trading companies by investment companies), or

(b) for the purposes of corporation tax on chargeable gains.

History – In para. 70(1)(a), the words "Chapter 5 of Part 4 of CTA 2010" substituted for the words "section 573 of the Taxes Act 1988" by CTA 2010, s. 1177 and Sch. 1, para. 315(11)(a), with effect for corporation tax purposes for accounting periods ending on or after 1 April 2010, and for income tax and capital gains tax purposes for the tax year 2010–11 and subsequent tax years.
Para. 70(1)(b) and the word "and" immediately before it omitted by CTA 2010, s. 1177 and Sch. 1, para. 315(11)(b) and repealed by CTA 2010, s. 1181 and Sch. 3, Pt. 1, with effect for corporation tax purposes for accounting periods ending on or after 1 April 2010, and for income tax and capital gains tax purposes for the tax year 2010–11 and subsequent tax years.
In para. 70(2)(a), the words "section 70 of CTA 2010" substituted for the words "section 573(2) of the Taxes Act 1988" by CTA 2010, s. 1177 and Sch. 1, para. 315(11)(c), with effect for corporation tax purposes for accounting periods ending on or after 1 April 2010, and for income tax and capital gains tax purposes for the tax year 2010–11 and subsequent tax years.

TAX AVOIDANCE

71(1) Sub-paragraph (2) applies where shares would, in the absence of paragraph 82 (which disapplies sections 135 and 136 of the 1992 Act in respect of shares to which investment relief is attributable), be the subject of an exchange or arrangement which–

(a) is of the kind mentioned in section 135 or 136 of the 1992 Act (company reconstructions etc.), and

(b) would involve a disposal of shares, by reason of–

  (i) section 137(1) of that Act (schemes with tax avoidance purpose), or

  (ii) paragraph 96(2)(b) (company treated as disposing of shares in the case of certain schemes of reconstruction involving tax avoidance).

71(2) Where this sub-paragraph applies no loss relief may be obtained in respect of any allowable loss incurred on the disposal.

71(3) Where a claim is made under this Part in respect of a loss accruing on the disposal of shares, section 30 of the 1992 Act (value-shifting) shall have effect in relation to the disposal as if for the references in subsections (1)(b) and (5) of that section to a tax-free benefit there were substituted references to any benefit whether tax-free or not.

History – In para. 71(1)(b)(ii), the words "schemes of reconstruction" substituted for the words "reconstructions and amalgamations" by FA 2002, s. 45 and Sch. 9, para. 6(2) with effect in relation to disposals on or after 17 April 2002.

ADJUSTMENT OF CORPORATION TAX

72 The Inland Revenue shall make any adjustment of corporation tax required as a result of–

(a) loss relief being obtained in respect of an allowable loss, or

(b) loss relief not being obtained for the whole or part of a loss in respect of which a claim is made under this Part, whether by way of assessment, discharge or repayment of tax.

Part VIII – Deferral Relief

INTRODUCTION

73(1) This Part applies where–

(a) a chargeable gain ("the original gain") accrues to the investing company at any time ("the accrual time"),

(b) the gain is one accruing either–

  (i) on a disposal of shares to which investment relief was attributable immediately before the disposal, or

  (ii) by virtue of paragraph 79 on the occurrence of a chargeable event in relation to shares to which deferral relief is attributable immediately before the event,

and

(c) the investing company makes a qualifying investment.

73(2) In determining for the purposes of sub-paragraph (1)(a) whether or not a chargeable gain accrues at any time paragraph 76 (postponement of original gain) shall be disregarded.

73(3) Sub-paragraph (1)(b)(i) does not apply to a disposal of shares unless the shares were held by the investing company continuously from the time they were issued until the disposal.

MEANING OF "QUALIFYING INVESTMENT"

74(1) For the purposes of this Part the investing company makes a qualifying investment if–

(a) it subscribes for any shares to which investment relief is attributable,

(b) the shares are not issued by a prohibited company,

(c) the shares are issued to the investing company at a qualifying time, and

(d) where the shares were issued before the accrual time–

  (i) they have been held continuously by the investment company from the time they were issued until that time, and

  (ii) investment relief is attributable to the shares at that time.

74(2) For the purposes of sub-paragraph (1)–

"a prohibited company" means–

(a) the company whose shares comprised the original holding, or

(b) a company that was, at the accrual time or the time of the issue of the qualifying shares (or both), a member of the same group as that company; and

"a qualifying time" means any time in the period of four years beginning one year before the accrual time.

74(3) For the purposes of the definition of "a prohibited company" in sub-paragraph (2), **"the original holding"** means–

(a) where the original gain accrued as mentioned in sub-paragraph (i) of paragraph 73(1)(b), the shares disposed of, and

(b) where the original gain accrued as mentioned in sub-paragraph (ii) of paragraph 73(1)(b), the shares in relation to which the chargeable event occurred.

MEANING OF "THE QUALIFYING SHARES"

75(1) For the purposes of this Part **"the qualifying shares"**, in relation to a case where this Part applies, means the shares which are acquired by the investing company in making the qualifying investment. This is subject to sub-paragraphs (2) and (4).

75(2) If any corresponding bonus shares are issued to the investing company, this Part shall apply as if references to the qualifying shares were to all the shares comprising the qualifying shares and the bonus shares so issued.

75(3) In sub-paragraph (2) **"corresponding bonus shares"** means bonus shares which–

(a) are issued in respect of the qualifying shares, and

(b) are in the same company, of the same class and carry the same rights as those shares.

75(4) If in circumstances where paragraph 83 (certain exchanges resulting in acquisition of share capital by new company) applies new shares are issued in exchange for old shares, references in this Part to the qualifying shares, so far as they relate to the old shares, shall be construed as references to the new shares. For this purpose **"old shares"** and **"new shares"** have the same meaning as in that paragraph.

POSTPONEMENT OF ORIGINAL GAIN

76(1) On the making of a claim by the investing company for the purposes of this Part, so much of the investing company's unused qualifying expenditure on the qualifying shares as–

(a) is specified in the claim, and

(b) does not exceed so much of the original gain as is unmatched,

shall be set against a corresponding amount of the original gain.

76(2) Where an amount of qualifying expenditure on the qualifying shares is set under this paragraph against the whole or part of the original gain, then for the purposes of corporation tax on chargeable gains–

(a) so much of that gain as is equal to that amount shall be treated as not having accrued at the accrual time, but

(b) paragraph 79 applies for determining the gain that is to be treated as accruing on the occurrence of any chargeable event in relation to any of the qualifying shares.

76(3) For the purposes of this Part–

(a) the investing company's qualifying expenditure on the qualifying shares is the amount subscribed by it for the shares, and

(b) that expenditure is unused to the extent that it has not already been set under this paragraph against the whole or any part of a chargeable gain.

76(4) For the purposes of this paragraph the original gain is unmatched in relation to any qualifying expenditure on the qualifying shares to the extent that it has not had any other expenditure set against it under this paragraph.

MEANING OF "DEFERRAL RELIEF"

77 For the purposes of this Schedule **"deferral relief"** is attributable to any shares if–

(a) expenditure on the shares has been set under paragraph 76 against the whole or part of any gain, and

(b) there has been no chargeable event for the purposes of this Part in relation to the shares.

CHARGEABLE EVENTS

78(1) There is, for the purposes of this Part, a chargeable event in relation to any of the qualifying shares if–

(a) the investing company disposes of those shares, or

(b) any other event occurs by reason of which the investment relief attributable to those shares is reduced or withdrawn otherwise than by virtue of paragraph 46(2) or (3) (withdrawal of investment relief on disposal of shares).

78(2) For the purposes of sub-paragraph (1)(b), where the qualifying investment is made before the time at which the original gain accrues, any reduction of the investment relief attributable to the qualifying shares that is made by reason of an event that occurs before the accrual time shall be disregarded.

GAIN ACCRUING ON CHARGEABLE EVENT

79(1) This paragraph applies where a chargeable event occurs in relation to any of the qualifying shares in relation to which there has not been a previous chargeable event.

79(2) Where this paragraph applies, then for the purposes of corporation tax on chargeable gains–

(a) a chargeable gain shall be treated as accruing to the investing company at the time of the event, and

(b) the amount of the gain shall be equal to so much of the deferred gain as is attributable to the shares in relation to which the chargeable event occurs.

79(3) In order to determine, for this purpose, the amount of the deferred gain attributable to any shares, a proportionate part of the amount of the gain shall be attributed to each of the qualifying shares held immediately before the occurrence of the chargeable event in question by the investing company.

79(4) In this paragraph **"the deferred gain"** means–

(a) the amount of the original gain against which expenditure has been set under paragraph 76, less

(b) the amount of any gain treated as accruing under this paragraph previously in consequence of a chargeable event in relation to any of the qualifying shares.

79(5) For the purposes of section 10B of the 1992 Act (taxation of chargeable gains accruing to non-resident with UK branch or agency) a chargeable gain treated as accruing by virtue of this paragraph shall be treated as a chargeable gain accruing on the disposal of an asset to which subsection (3) of that section applies.

History – In para. 79(5), the words "section 10B" substituted for the words "section 10" by FA 2003, s. 155 and Sch. 27, para. 9 with effect in relation to gains accruing after 10 July 2003.

Part IX – Company Restructuring

SHARE REORGANISATIONS

80(1) Where a company ("the company") holds shares which–

(a) form part of the ordinary share capital of another company,

(b) are of the same class and held in the same capacity, and

(c) include shares falling within two or more of the categories in sub-paragraph (2),

then, where there is a reorganisation affecting those shares, to which section 116 or section 127 of the 1992 Act applies, section 116 or (as the case may be) section 127 shall apply separately to shares falling within each of those categories.

80(2) The categories referred to in sub-paragraph (1)(c) are–

(a) shares to which deferral relief is attributable;

(b) shares–

  (i) to which investment relief but not deferral relief is attributable, and

  (ii) which have been held continuously by the company since the time they were issued until the reorganisation; and

(c) shares not within paragraph (a) or (b) above.

80(3) In this paragraph **"reorganisation"** has the meaning given in section 126 of the 1992 Act.

RIGHTS ISSUES ETC.

81(1) Where–

(a) a company ("the company") holds shares ("the existing holding") which–

  (i) form part of the ordinary share capital of another company, and

  (ii) are of the same class and held in the same capacity,

(b) there is by virtue of such an allotment as is mentioned in section 126(2)(a) of the 1992 Act (an allotment of shares or debentures in respect of and in proportion to an original holding), other than an allotment of corresponding bonus shares, a reorganisation affecting the existing holding,

(c) immediately following the reorganisation, investment relief is attributable to the shares comprised in the existing holding or the shares allotted in respect of those shares, and

(d) if investment relief is attributable to the shares comprised in the existing holding at that time, those shares have been held by the company continuously from the time they were issued until the reorganisation,

sections 127 to 130 of that Act (treatment of share capital following a reorganisation) shall not apply in relation to the existing holding.

81(2) Subsection (10) of section 116 of that Act (reorganisations, conversions and reconstructions) shall not apply in any case where the old asset consists of shares held (in the same capacity) by a company–

(a) that have been held by it continuously from the time they were issued until the relevant transaction, and

(b) to which investment relief is attributable immediately before that transaction.

In this sub-paragraph **"old asset"** and **"the relevant transaction"** have the meanings given in section 116 of that Act.

81(3) For the purposes of sub-paragraph (1)–

"corresponding bonus shares" means bonus shares that–

(a) are issued in respect of shares comprised in the existing holding, and

(b) are of the same class, and carry the same rights, as those shares;

"reorganisation" has the meaning given in section 126 of that Act.

COMPANY RECONSTRUCTIONS AND AMALGAMATIONS

82(1) Where–

(a) a company ("the company") holds shares ("the existing holding") in a company ("company A"),

(b) there is a reconstruction or amalgamation affecting the existing holding,

(c) immediately before the reconstruction or amalgamation, investment relief is attributable to the shares comprised in the existing holding, and

(d) the shares comprised in the existing holding have been held by the company continuously from the time they were issued until the reconstruction or amalgamation,

sections 135 and 136 of the 1992 Act (share exchanges and company reconstructions) shall not apply in respect of the existing holding.

This is subject to paragraph 84 (no disposal on certain exchanges of shares).

82(2) Sub-paragraph (1)(a) applies only where the shares are held by the company in the same capacity.

82(3) For the purposes of sub-paragraph (1) a **"reconstruction or amalgamation"** means an issue by a company ("company B") of shares in or debentures of that company in exchange for or in respect of shares in or debentures of company A.

History – In para. 82(1), in the closing words, the words "share exchanges and company reconstructions" substituted for the words "company reconstructions and amalgamations" by FA 2002, s. 45 and Sch. 9, para. 6(3) with effect in relation to shares or debentures issued on or after 17 April 2002.

CERTAIN EXCHANGES RESULTING IN ACQUISITION OF SHARE CAPITAL BY NEW COMPANY

83(1) Paragraphs 84 and 85 apply where–

(a) arrangements are made in accordance with which a company ("the new company") acquires all the shares ("old shares") in another company ("the old company");

(b) the acquisition provided for by the arrangements falls within sub-paragraph (2); and

(c) the Inland Revenue have, before any exchange of shares takes place under the arrangements, given an approval notification.

83(2) An acquisition of shares falls within this sub-paragraph if–

(a) the consideration for the old shares consists wholly of the issue of shares ("new shares") in the new company;

(b) new shares are issued in consideration of old shares only at times when there are no issued shares in the new company other than–

 (i) subscriber shares, and

 (ii) new shares previously issued in consideration of old shares;

(c) the consideration for new shares of each description consists wholly of old shares of the corresponding description; and

(d) new shares of each description are issued to the holders of old shares of the corresponding description in respect of, and in proportion to, their holdings.

83(3) For the purposes of sub-paragraph (1)(c) an approval notification is one which, on an application by either the old company or the new company, is given to the applicant company and states that the Inland Revenue are satisfied that the exchange of shares under the arrangements–

(a) will be effected for commercial reasons, and

(b) will not form part of any such scheme or arrangements as are mentioned in section 137(1) of the 1992 Act (schemes with tax avoidance purpose).

83(4) For the purposes of this paragraph old shares and new shares are of a corresponding description if, on the assumption that they were shares in the same company, they would be of the same class and carry the same rights.

83(5) In this paragraph references to **"shares"**, except in the expression "subscriber shares", include securities.

83(6) References in paragraphs 84 to 87 to **"shares"**, **"old shares"**, **"new shares"**, **"the old company"** and **"the new company"** shall be construed in accordance with this paragraph.

NO DISPOSAL ON CERTAIN EXCHANGES OF SHARES

84(1) Where this paragraph applies (see paragraph 83), nothing in paragraph 82 has effect to disapply section 135 of the 1992 Act (exchange of shares etc. for those in another company).

Accordingly, by virtue of section 127 of that Act (as applied by section 135(3)), the exchange of shares is not treated as involving a disposal of the old shares or an acquisition of the new shares.

84(2) In its application by virtue of sub-paragraph (1), section 127 of the 1992 Act shall have effect subject to paragraph 80 (shares to which investment relief or investment and deferral relief is attributable treated as separate holdings).

Cross references – TCGA 1992, Sch. 7AC, para. 4(4): disapplication of TCGA 1992, s. 127 and FA 2000, Sch. 15, para. 85 by virtue of TCGA 1992, Sch. 7AC, para. 4(3)(a).

ATTRIBUTION OF RELIEF TO NEW SHARES

85(1) Where this paragraph applies (see paragraph 83), any investment relief or deferral relief which is attributable to any old shares shall be attributable instead to the new shares for which they are exchanged.

85(2) Where investment relief becomes so attributable to any new shares–

(a) this Schedule shall have effect as if anything which under paragraph 41, 42, 60 or 65 has been done, or is required to be done, by or in relation to the old company had been done, or were required to be done, by or in relation to the new company; and

(b) any appeal brought by the old company against–

(i) the refusal of the Inland Revenue to authorise the issue of a compliance certificate, or

(ii) a notice under paragraph 60(3)(b),

may be prosecuted by the new company as if it had been brought by that company.

Cross references – TCGA 1992, Sch. 7AC, para. 4(4): disapplication of FA 2000, Sch. 15 para. 85.

SUBSTITUTION OF NEW SHARES FOR OLD SHARES

86(1) This paragraph applies where–

(a) relief becomes attributable, by virtue of paragraph 85, to any new shares held by a company ("the company"), and

(b) the old shares for which those shares were exchanged ("the relevant old shares") were–

(i) subscribed for by and issued to the company, and

(ii) held by it continuously from the time they were issued until the exchange.

86(2) Where this paragraph applies this Schedule (except paragraph 29(7)) shall have effect as if–

(a) the matching new shares had been subscribed for by the company at the time when, and for the amount for which, the relevant old shares were subscribed for,

(b) the matching new shares had–

(i) been issued at the time when the relevant old shares were issued, and

(ii) held continuously by the company from that time until the exchange,

(c) any claim for relief under Part V (investment relief), or Part VIII (deferral relief), of this Schedule made in respect of the relevant old shares had been made in respect of the matching new shares, and

(d) the company's liability to corporation tax had been reduced under Part V of this Schedule in respect of the matching new shares for the same accounting period as that for which its liability was so reduced in respect of the relevant old shares.

86(3) For the purposes of this paragraph old shares and new shares are matching shares in relation to each other if the old shares are the shares for which those new shares are exchanged under the arrangements.

History – In para. 86(2), the words "(except paragraph 29(7))" inserted by FA 2007, s. 51 and Sch. 16, para. 10 with effect from Royal Assent (19 July 2007).

OPERATION OF REQUIREMENTS OF PARTS II AND III IN RELATION TO NEW SHARES

87(1) This paragraph applies where paragraph 86 (substitution of new shares for old shares) applies in relation to any new shares held by a company.

87(2) If, immediately before the exchange, any of the requirements of paragraphs 5, 8 and 13 (requirements to be met by a qualifying investing company in relation to the relevant shares) was (or was deemed to be) met to any extent by the company in relation to the matching old shares, the requirement shall be deemed to be met by the company to the same extent in relation to the new shares.

87(3) If, immediately before the exchange, any of the requirements of paragraphs 16 to 22 (requirements to be met by a qualifying issuing company) was (or was deemed to be) met to any extent by the old company in relation to the matching old shares, it shall be deemed to be met to the same extent by the new company in relation to the new shares.

87(4) In determining whether the requirements of paragraphs 17 (the independence requirement) and 20 (the qualifying subsidiaries requirement) are met in relation to the old company or the new company at a time in the period for giving effect to the arrangements, both–

(a) the arrangements themselves, and

(b) any exchange of new shares for old shares that has already taken place under the arrangements,

shall be disregarded.

87(5) If, immediately before the period for giving effect to the arrangements, the requirement of paragraph 23(1) (the trading activities requirement) was (or was deemed to be) met to any extent by the old company in relation to the matching old shares–

(a) it shall be deemed to be met to the same extent by the new company in relation to the new shares, and

(b) to the extent that it would not otherwise be the case, it shall also be deemed to be met by that company in relation to those shares at all times which–

  (i) fall in the period for giving effect to the arrangements, and

  (ii) do not fall after a time when (apart from the arrangements) the requirement would have ceased to have been met by the old company in relation to the matching old shares.

87(6) For the purposes of this paragraph–

(a) **"the period for giving effect to the arrangements"** means the period which–

  (i) begins when those arrangements first come into existence; and

  (ii) ends when the new company completes its acquisition under the arrangements of all the old shares; and

(b) references to matching shares shall be construed in accordance with paragraph 86(3).

RELATIONSHIP BETWEEN THIS PART AND THE 1992 ACT

88 The following provisions of the 1992 Act have effect subject to paragraphs 80, 81, 82 and 84 (which make special provision in respect of company reorganisations etc. involving shares to which investment relief is attributable)–

section 116 (reorganisations, conversions and reconstructions); and

Chapter II of Part IV (reorganisation of share capital, conversion of securities etc.).

Part X – Advance Clearance

Statements of practice – SP 1/00: Corporate Venturing Scheme; procedure for advance clearance application.
SP 2/00: HMRC's approach to the "gross asset" test.
SP 3/00: HMRC's approach to the requirement for a company's trade to be carried on wholly or mainly in the UK.

APPLICATION FOR ADVANCE CLEARANCE NOTICE

89(1) A company ("the applicant") may, before issuing any shares, make an application to the Board for an advance clearance notice in respect of that issue.

89(2) An advance clearance notice is a notice issued by the Board in respect of an issue of shares which states that, on the basis of the particulars, declarations and undertakings provided by the applicant, the Board are satisfied that, at the time the shares are issued, the requirements of Parts III and IV of this Schedule will be met (or, in the case of any requirement that cannot be met until a future date, will be met for the time being) in relation to the shares.

89(3) For the purposes of determining whether they are satisfied as mentioned in sub-paragraph (2) the Inland Revenue shall assume that the shares included in the issue of shares are "the relevant shares".

89(4) An application under this paragraph must–

(a) contain the particulars, declarations and undertakings required by the Board, and

(b) disclose all facts and circumstances material for the decision of the Board.

89(5) In this Part references to an "application" are to an application under this paragraph.

PROVISION OF FURTHER INFORMATION

90(1) On receiving an application for an advance clearance notice, the Board may by notice ("an information notice") require the applicant to provide them, within such time as the Board may direct (not being less than 30 days), with such further particulars as the Board deem necessary to enable them to decide whether or not to issue an advance clearance notice.

90(2) An information notice must be given–

(a) within 30 days after the receipt of the application, or

(b) if further particulars have already been provided in response to an earlier information notice, within 30 days after the receipt of those particulars.

90(3) If the applicant does not comply with an information notice within the period specified in the notice, the Board need not proceed further on the application.

DECISION ON APPLICATION AND REVIEW PROCEDURE

91(1) The Board must within 30 days after receiving an application or, where an information notice is given in relation to the application, within 30 days after that notice being complied with–

(a) issue an advance clearance notice in respect of the shares to which the application relates, or

(b) notify the applicant that the Board are not satisfied as mentioned in paragraph 89(2) in respect of those shares.

This is subject to sub-paragraph (3) and to paragraph 90(3) (circumstances in which Board need not proceed on application).

91(2) In a case where two or more information notices are given in relation to the application, the time limit in sub-paragraph (1) is calculated by reference to the time when the later (or last) of the notices is complied with.

91(3) If before the Board issue an advance clearance notice in respect of the issue of shares to which the application relates, or notify the applicant under sub-paragraph (1), the applicant issues the shares in question, the Board need not proceed further on the application.

91(4) If the Board–

(a) notify the applicant that they are not satisfied as mentioned in paragraph 89(2), or

(b) in a case to which sub-paragraph (3) does not apply, fail to notify their decision to the applicant in accordance with sub-paragraph (1),

the applicant may, within 30 days after the notification or failure, require the Board to transmit the application, together with any information notices given and further particulars provided under paragraph 90, to the tribunal.

91(5) Where sub-paragraph (4) applies any notification by the tribunal that it is satisfied as mentioned in paragraph 89(2) shall have effect as if it were an advance clearance notice issued by the Board in respect of the issue of shares in question.

History – In para. 91(4) the word "tribunal" substituted for the words "Special Commissioners" by SI 2009/56, art. 3(1) and Sch. 1, para. 293(2), operative from 1 April 2009, subject to transitional and saving provisions in SI 2009/56, Sch. 3.

In para. 91(5) the words "tribunal that it is" substituted for the words "Special Commissioners that they are" by SI 2009/56, art. 3(1) and Sch. 1, para. 293(2), operative from 1 April 2009, subject to transitional and saving provisions in SI 2009/56, Sch. 3.

Cross references – SI 2009/275, art. 3(f): any decision under para. 91(5) is an excluded decision for the purposes of TCEA 2007, s. 11(1) and 13(1).

EFFECT OF ADVANCE CLEARANCE NOTICE

92(1) For the purposes of this Schedule, where an advance clearance notice is issued in respect of an issue of shares before the shares are issued, the requirements of Parts III and IV of this Schedule shall be treated as met (or, in the case of any requirement that cannot be met until a future date, as met for the time being) in relation to those shares at the time they are issued.

92(2) If–

(a) any particulars provided in the application for the notice, or in response to any information notice relating to the application, do not fully and accurately disclose all facts and circumstances material for the decision of the Board or the tribunal, or

(b) the applicant or any of its subsidiaries fails to act in accordance with any declaration or undertaking which was given in, or in connection with, the application,

any resulting advance clearance notice shall be void.

92(3) Sub-paragraph (2)(b) applies in relation to a subsidiary of the applicant whether or not it was such a subsidiary at the time the declaration or undertaking in question was given.

History – In para. 92(2)(a) the word "tribunal" substituted for the words "Special Commissioners" by SI 2009/56, art. 3(1) and Sch. 1, para. 293(3), operative from 1 April 2009, subject to transitional and saving provisions in SI 2009/56, Sch. 3.

Part XI – Supplementary and General

IDENTIFICATION OF SHARES ON A DISPOSAL

93(1) In any case where–

(a) a company ("the company") disposes of part of a holding of shares ("the holding"), and

(b) the holding includes shares to which investment relief is attributable that have been held continuously by the company from the time they were issued until the disposal,

this paragraph applies for the purpose of identifying the shares disposed of.

93(2) For the purposes of this paragraph **"holding"** means any number of shares of the same class in another company held by the company in the same capacity, growing or diminishing as shares of that class are acquired or disposed of.

93(3) Where shares included in the holding have been acquired by the company on different days, then, for the purposes of corporation tax on chargeable gains and of this Schedule, any disposal by the company of any of those shares shall be treated as relating to those acquired on an earlier day rather than to those acquired on a later day.

93(4) Where shares included in the holding have been acquired by the company on the same day, then, for the purposes of corporation tax on chargeable gains and of this Schedule, if there is a disposal by the company of any of those shares, any shares–

(a) to which investment relief is attributable, and

(b) which have been held by the company continuously from the time they were issued until the time of disposal,

shall be treated as disposed of after any other shares included in the holding which were acquired by the company on that day.

93(5) Chapter I of Part IV of the 1992 Act (share pooling, etc.) shall have effect subject to this paragraph.

93(6) Sections 104, 105 and 107 of that Act (which make provision for the purposes of corporation tax on chargeable gains for the identification of shares on a disposal) shall not apply to shares to which investment relief is attributable.

93(7) In a case to which section 127 of that Act (equation of original shares and new holding) applies (including a case where that section applies by virtue of any enactment relating to chargeable gains), shares comprised in the new holding shall be treated for the purposes of sub-paragraphs (3) and (4) as acquired when the original shares were acquired.

In this sub-paragraph **"new holding"** and **"original shares"** have the same meaning as in section 127 of the 1992 Act (or, as the case may be, that section as applied by virtue of the enactment concerned).

History – In para. 93(6), the words "Sections 104, 105" substituted for the words "Sections 104 to 106" by FA 2006, s. 72(2)(e) with effect in relation to any disposal that is made on or after 5 December 2005.

In para. 93(7), the words "including a case where that section applies by virtue of any enactment relating to chargeable gains" substituted for the words "whether or not by virtue of section 135(3) of that Act" by FA 2002, s. 45 and Sch. 9, para. 6(4) with effect in relation to disposals on or after 17 April 2002.

In para. 93(7), the words "have the same meaning as in section 127 of the 1992 Act (or, as the case may be, that section as applied by virtue of the enactment concerned)" substituted for the words "shall be construed in accordance with sections 126, 127, 135 and 136 of that Act" by FA 2002, s. 45, Sch. 9, para. 6(4) in relation to disposals on or after 17 April 2002.

DETERMINATION OF LOSS WHERE INVESTMENT RELIEF IS ATTRIBUTABLE TO SHARES

94(1) This paragraph applies for the purposes of corporation tax on chargeable gains where–

(a) a company disposes of shares which were held by it continuously from the time they were issued until the disposal,

(b) investment relief is attributable to the shares (and not withdrawn in full as a result of the disposal), and

(c) apart from sub-paragraph (2), there would be a loss on the disposal.

94(2) For the purpose of determining the gain or loss on the disposal the consideration given by the company for the shares is treated as reduced by the amount of the investment relief attributable to the shares immediately after the disposal.

94(3) Any gain which accrues by virtue of sub-paragraph (2) is not a chargeable gain.

94(4) Notwithstanding the definition of "allowable loss" in section 1119 of CTA 2010 (interpretation of the Corporation Tax Acts), nothing in sub-paragraph (3) has effect in relation to any loss determined in accordance with sub-paragraph (2) to prevent it being an allowable loss.

History – In para. 94(4), the words "section 1119 of CTA 2010" substituted for the words "section 834(1) of the Taxes Act 1988" by CTA 2010, s. 1177 and Sch. 1, para. 315(12), with effect for corporation tax purposes for accounting periods ending on or after 1 April 2010, and for income tax and capital gains tax purposes for the tax year 2010–11 and subsequent tax years.

NOMINEES

95 Shares subscribed for by, issued to, acquired or held by or disposed of by a nominee for any person shall be treated for the purposes of this Schedule as subscribed for by, issued to, acquired or held by or disposed of by that person.

MEANING OF "DISPOSAL"

96(1) Subject to sub-paragraph (2), in this Schedule **"disposal"** shall be construed in accordance with the 1992 Act, and cognate expressions shall be construed accordingly.

96(2) A company shall be treated for the purposes of this Schedule, and for the purposes of corporation tax on chargeable gains, as disposing of any shares which, but for paragraph 82 (company reconstructions and amalgamations) it–

(a) would be treated as exchanging for other shares by virtue of section 136 of the 1992 Act, or

(b) would be so treated but for section 137(1) of the 1992 Act (which restricts section 136 of that Act to bona fide schemes of reconstruction.

History – In para. 96(2)(a), the words "section 136" substituted for the words "section 136(1)" substituted by FA 2002, s. 45 and Sch. 9, para. 6(5) with effect in relation to disposals on or after 17 April 2002.

In para. 96(2)(b), the words "section 136 of that Act to bona fide schemes of reconstruction" substituted for the words "sections 135 and 136 of that Act to bona fide reconstructions and amalgamations" by FA 2002, s. 45 and Sch. 9, para. 6(5) with effect in relation to disposals on or after 17 April 2002.

CONSTRUCTION OF REFERENCES TO SHARES BEING "HELD CONTINUOUSLY"

97(1) This paragraph applies where for the purposes of this Schedule it falls to be determined whether a company has held shares continuously throughout any period.

97(2) The company shall not be treated as having held shares continuously throughout a period if–

(a) it is deemed, under any provision of the 1992 Act, to have disposed of and immediately reacquired the shares at any time during the period, or

(b) it is treated as having disposed of the shares at any such time, by virtue of paragraph 96(2) (on reconstruction or amalgamation company treated as disposing of shares continuously held by it to which investment relief is attributable).

MEANING OF "ISSUE OF SHARES"

98 In this Schedule–

(a) references (however expressed) to an issue of shares in any company are to such of the shares in the company as are of the same class and issued on the same day; and

(b) references (however expressed) to an issue of shares in a company to a person are references to such of the shares in an issue of shares in that company as are issued to that person in one capacity.

MEANING OF "ASSOCIATE"

99(1) In this Schedule **"associate"**, in relation to a person, means–

(a) any relative or partner of that person,

(b) the trustee or trustees of any settlement in relation to which that person, or any relative of his (living or dead), is or was a settlor, and

(c) where that person is interested in any shares or obligations of a company which are subject to any trust, or are part of the estate of a deceased person–

(i) the trustee or trustees of the settlement concerned or, as the case may be, the personal representatives of the deceased, and

(ii) if that person is a company, any other company interested in those shares or obligations.

99(2) In sub-paragraph (1)(a) and (b) **"relative"** means spouse or civil partner, parent or remoter forebear or child or remoter issue.

99(3) In sub-paragraph (1)(b) **"settlor"** and **"settlement"** have the same meaning as in Chapter 5 of Part 5 of ITTOIA 2005 (see section 620 of that Act).

History – In para. 99(2) the words "spouse or civil partner" substituted for the words "husband or wife" by SI 2005/3229, reg. 132, with effect from 5 December 2005.

In para. 99(3) the words "Chapter 5 of Part 5 of ITTOIA 2005 (see section 620 of that Act)" substituted for the former wording by ITTOIA 2005, s. 882(1) and Sch. 1, para. 521; effective for income tax purposes for 2005–06 onwards (ITTOIA 2005, s. 883(1)).

'THE BOARD' AND 'THE INLAND REVENUE'

100 In this Schedule–

(a) **"the Board"** means the Commissioners of Inland Revenue; and

(b) references to **"the Inland Revenue"** are to any officer of the Board.

POWER TO AMEND BY TREASURY ORDER

101 The Treasury may by order amend this Schedule–

(a) to make such amendments of–

 (i) paragraphs 10 to 12 (the non-financial activities requirement), or

 (ii) paragraphs 23 to 33 (the trading activities requirement),

as they consider expedient;

(b) to substitute different sums of money for those for the time being specified in paragraph 22 (gross assets requirement).

MINOR DEFINITIONS ETC.

102(1) In this Schedule–

"allowable loss" means an allowable loss for the purposes of corporation tax on chargeable gains;

"arrangements" includes any scheme, agreement or understanding, whether or not legally enforceable;

"chargeable gain" means a chargeable gain for the purposes of corporation tax on chargeable gains;

"class", in relation to shares or securities, means a class of shares in or securities of any one company (see sub-paragraph (2));

"CTA 2010" means the Corporation Tax Act 2010;

"director" shall be construed in accordance with section 452 of CTA 2010;

"group" means a parent company and its 51% subsidiaries;

"group company", in relation to a group, means the parent company and any of its 51% subsidiaries;

"ordinary share capital", except in paragraph 7 (meaning of **"material interest"**), has the meaning given in section 1119 of CTA 2010;

"ordinary shares" means shares forming part of a company's ordinary share capital;

"parent company" means a company that–

(a) has one or more 51% subsidiaries, but

(b) is not itself a 51% subsidiary of another company;

"research and development" has the meaning given by section 1138 of CTA 2010;

"single company" means a company that is not a parent company or a 51% subsidiary of a parent company;

"the 1992 Act" means the Taxation of Chargeable Gains Act 1992.

102(2) For the purposes of this Schedule shares in or securities of a company shall not be treated as being of the same class unless they would be so treated if dealt with on the Stock Exchange.

102(3) Section 1122 of CTA 2010 (connected persons) applies for the purposes of this Schedule.

102(4) References in this Schedule to a company being in administration or receivership shall be construed as follows–

(a) references to a company being "in administration" are to the company being in administration within the meaning of Schedule B1 to the Insolvency Act 1986, or to there being in force in relation to it–

 (i) an administration order under Part III of the Insolvency (Northern Ireland) Order 1989, or

 (ii) any corresponding order under the law of a country or territory outside the United Kingdom;

(b) references to a company being "in receivership" are to there being in force in relation to it–

(i) an order for the appointment of an administrative receiver, a receiver and manager or a receiver under Chapter I or II of Part III of the Insolvency Act 1986 or Part IV of the Insolvency (Northern Ireland) Order 1989, or

(ii) any corresponding order under the law of a country or territory outside the United Kingdom.

102(5) For the purposes of this Schedule the market value at any time of any asset is the price which it might reasonably be expected to fetch on a sale at that time in the open market free from any interest or right which exists by way of security in or over it.

102(6) In this Schedule–

(a) references to investment relief obtained by a company in respect of any shares include references to investment relief obtained by it in respect of those shares at any time after it has disposed of them, and

(b) references to the withdrawal or reduction of investment relief obtained by a company in respect of any shares include references to the withdrawal or reduction of investment relief obtained in respect of those shares at any such time.

102(7) In the case of a requirement that cannot be met until a future date–

(a) references in this Schedule to a requirement being met for the time being are to nothing having occurred to prevent its being met, and

(b) references to its continuing to be met are to nothing occurring to prevent its being met.

102(8) In determining for the purposes of paragraph 3(2), 23(5) or 36(1B) when a trade is begun to be carried on by a qualifying 90% subsidiary of the issuing company there shall be disregarded any carrying on of the trade by it before it became such a subsidiary.

102(9) References in this Schedule to Part 5 of ITA 2007 or any provision of that Part are to a Part or provision that applies only in relation to shares issued after 5 April 2007.

History – In para. 102(1), the definition of "CTA 2010" inserted by CTA 2010, s. 1177 and Sch. 1, para. 315(13)(d), with effect for corporation tax purposes for accounting periods ending on or after 1 April 2010, and for income tax and capital gains tax purposes for the tax year 2010–11 and subsequent tax years.
In para. 102(1), in the definition of "director", the words "section 452 of CTA 2010" substituted for the words "section 417(5) of the Taxes Act 1988" by CTA 2010, s. 1177 and Sch. 1, para. 315(13)(a), with effect for corporation tax purposes for accounting periods ending on or after 1 April 2010, and for income tax and capital gains tax purposes for the tax year 2010–11 and subsequent tax years.
In para. 102(1), in the definition of "ordinary share capital", the words "section 1119 of CTA 2010" substituted for the words "section 832(1) of the Taxes Act 1988" by CTA 2010, s. 1177 and Sch. 1, para. 315(13)(b), with effect for corporation tax purposes for accounting periods ending on or after 1 April 2010, and for income tax and capital gains tax purposes for the tax year 2010–11 and subsequent tax years.
In para. 102(1), in the definition of "research and development", the words "section 1138 of CTA 2010" substituted for the words "section 837A of the Taxes Act 1988" by CTA 2010, s. 1177 and Sch. 1, para. 315(13)(c), with effect for corporation tax purposes for accounting periods ending on or after 1 April 2010, and for income tax and capital gains tax purposes for the tax year 2010–11 and subsequent tax years.
In para. 102(3), the words "Section 1122 of CTA 2010" substituted for the words "Section 839 of the Taxes Act 1988" by CTA 2010, s. 1177 and Sch. 1, para. 315(14), with effect for corporation tax purposes for accounting periods ending on or after 1 April 2010, and for income tax and capital gains tax purposes for the tax year 2010–11 and subsequent tax years.
Para. 102(4)(a) substituted by SI 2003/2096, art. 4 and Schedule, para. 34(d) with effect from 15 September 2003. Transitional provisions are contained in art. 6.
Para. 102(8) inserted by FA 2004, s. 95 and Sch. 20, para. 13 with effect in relation to shares issued on or after 17 March 2004.
Para. 102(9) inserted by ITA 2007, s. 1027 and Sch. 1, para. 394(5), with effect from 6 April 2007.

Cross references – SI 2009/317, art. 3(3), (4): modification of para. 102(4) in relation to liquidation or administration of banks.

Transitional – SI 2003/2096, art. 6 contains transitional provisions so that the former rules remain in effect where a petition for an administration order was presented prior to 15 September 2003.

INDEX OF DEFINED EXPRESSIONS

103 In this Schedule the following expressions are defined or otherwise explained by the provisions indicated:

in administration	paragraph 102(4)(a)
allowable loss	paragraph 102(1)
application (in Part X)	paragraph 89(5)
arrangements	paragraph 102(1)
associate	paragraph 99
the Board	paragraph 100
chargeable gain	paragraph 102(1)
class (of shares)	paragraph 102(1) and (2)
compliance certificate	paragraph 41
compliance statement	paragraph 42

connected person	paragraph 102(3)
CTA 2010	paragraph 102(1)
deferral relief	paragraph 77
director	paragraph 102(1)
disposal	paragraph 96
excluded activities	paragraph 26
group	paragraph 102(1)
group company	paragraph 102(1)
held continuously (in relation to shares)	paragraph 97
the Inland Revenue	paragraph 100
the investing company	paragraph 2
investment relief	paragraph 1
issue of shares	paragraph 98
the issuing company	paragraph 2
loss relief	paragraph 67(1)
market value	paragraph 102(5)
material interest	paragraph 7
new company (in paragraphs 83 to 87)	paragraph 83
new shares (in paragraphs 83 to 87)	paragraph 83
non-financial trade	paragraph 11
non-financial trading group	paragraph 12
old company (in paragraphs 83 to 87)	paragraph 83
old shares (in paragraphs 83 to 87)	paragraph 83
ordinary share capital	paragraphs 7 and 102(1)
ordinary shares	paragraph 102(1)
parent company	paragraph 102(1)
the period of restriction	paragraph 48
the qualification period	paragraph 3
the qualifying shares (in Part VIII)	paragraph 75
qualifying subsidiary	paragraph 21
qualifying 90% subsidiary	paragraph 23A
qualifying trade	paragraph 25
in receivership	paragraph 102(4)(b)
relevant preference shares	paragraph 9
the relevant shares	paragraph 2
relief attributable to shares	
investment relief	paragraph 45
deferral relief	paragraph 77
research and development	paragraph 102(1)
single company	paragraph 102(1)
the 1992 Act	paragraph 102(1)
trading activities requirement	paragraph 23(2) and (3)

History – In the table, the entry for "CTA 2010" inserted by CTA 2010, s. 1177 and Sch. 1, para. 315(15), with effect for corporation tax purposes for accounting periods ending on or after 1 April 2010, and for income tax and capital gains tax purposes for the tax year 2010–11 and subsequent tax years.

In the table, the entry for "qualifying 90% subsidiary" inserted by FA 2004, s. 95 and Sch. 20, para. 14 with effect in relation to shares issued on or after 17 March 2004.

In the table, in the entry for "qualifying 90% subsidiary", the reference to para. 23A substituted for the reference to para. 23(10) and (11) by FA 2007, s. 51 and Sch. 16, para. 15(4) with effect from 6 April 2007 (FA 2007, Sch. 16, para. 18)

SCHEDULE 16 – CORPORATE VENTURING SCHEME: CONSEQUENTIAL AMENDMENTS

Section 63(2)

PENALTIES IN CONNECTION WITH RETURNS ETC.

1 [Amends TMA 1970, s. 98, Table.]

ENTERPRISE INVESTMENT SCHEME

2 [Repealed by ITA 2007, s. 1031 and Sch. 3, Pt. 2.]

History – Para. 2 repealed by ITA 2007, s. 1031 and Sch. 3, Pt. 2, with effect in relation to shares issued after 5 April 2007.

LOSS RELIEF

3 [Repealed by CTA 2010, s. 1181 and Sch. 3, Pt. 1.]

History – Para. 3 repealed by CTA 2010, s. 1181 and Sch. 3, Pt. 1, with effect for corporation tax purposes for accounting periods ending on or after 1 April 2010, and for income tax and capital gains tax purposes for the tax year 2010–11 and subsequent tax years.

EIS: DEFERRAL RELIEF

4(1) The Taxation of Chargeable Gains Act 1992 is amended as follows.

4(2) In paragraph 14 of Schedule 5B (value received by persons other than claimants)–

(a) [Amends TCGA 1992, Sch. 5B, para. 14(1).]

(b) [Amends TCGA 1992, Sch. 5B, para. 14(1).]

(c) [Amends TCGA 1992, Sch. 5B, para. 14(3).]

(d) [Inserts TCGA 1992, Sch. 5B, para. 14(3)(c).]

4(3) [Inserts TCGA 1992, Sch. 5B, para. 14A.]

COMPANY TAX RETURNS, ASSESSMENTS ETC.

5(1) Schedule 18 to the Finance Act 1998 is amended as follows.

5(2) [Amends FA 1998, Sch. 18, para. 8.]

5(3) [Inserts FA 1998, Sch. 18, para. 9(4).]

SCHEDULE 17 – ENTERPRISE INVESTMENT SCHEME: AMENDMENTS

Section 64

Part I – Reduction of Applicable Periods

MEANING OF "ELIGIBLE SHARES"

1 [Repealed by ITA 2007, s. 1031 and Sch. 3, Pt. 2.]

History – Para. 1 repealed by ITA 2007, s. 1031 and Sch. 3, Pt. 2, with effect in relation to shares issued after 5 April 2007.

Notes – Para. 1 rewritten as ITA 2007, s. 173(2).

CONDITIONS RELATING TO INDIVIDUALS

2 [Repealed by FA 2001, s. 110, Sch. 33, Pt. II(2); ITA 2007, s. 1031 and Sch. 3, Pt. 2.]

History – Para. 2 repealed by ITA 2007, s. 1031 and Sch. 3, Pt. 2, with effect in relation to shares issued after 5 April 2007. Transitional and saving provisions are contained in ITA 2007, Sch. 2.

Para. 2 repealed by FA 2001, s. 110, Sch. 33, Pt. II(2) with effect (Note 6):

- in relation to any shares issued on or after 7 March 2001 (FA 2001, Sch. 15, para. 40(2)(a)); and
- in relation to application of ICTA 1988, Pt. VII, Ch. III or TCGA 1992, Sch. 5B on or after 7 March 2001; to shares issued *after 31 December 1993* but before 7 March 2001 – where such shares had attributed to them income tax relief or deferral relief immediately before the latter date (Sch. 15, para. 40(2)(b)).

Notes – Para. 2 rewritten as ITA 2007, s. 163(1).

CONDITIONS RELATING TO FURTHER INVESTMENT BY CONNECTED PERSON

3(1) [Repealed by ITA 2007, s. 1031 and Sch. 3, Pt. 2.]

3(2) [Repealed by FA 2001, s. 110, Sch. 33, Pt. II(2); ITA 2007, s. 1031 and Sch. 3, Pt. 2.]

3(3) [Repealed by ITA 2007, s. 1031 and Sch. 3, Pt. 2.]

History – Para. 3 repealed by ITA 2007, s. 1031 and Sch. 3, Pt. 2, with effect in relation to shares issued after 5 April 2007. Transitional and saving provisions are contained in ITA 2007, Sch. 2. Former para. 3 amended ICTA 1988, s. 291A(5)(c).
Para. 3(2) repealed by FA 2001, s. 110, Sch. 33, Pt. II(2) with effect (Note 6):

- in relation to any shares issued on or after 7 March 2001 (FA 2001, Sch. 15, para. 40(2)(a)); and
- in relation to application of ICTA 1988, Pt. VII, Ch. III or TCGA 1992, Sch. 5B on or after 7 March 2001; to shares issued after 31 December 1993 but before 7 March 2001 – where such shares had attributed to them income tax relief or deferral relief immediately before the latter date (Sch. 15, para. 40(2)(b)).

Notes – Para. 3(2) rewritten as ITA 2007, s. 168(1).
Para. 3(3) rewritten as ITA 2007, s. 169(4).

VALUE RECEIVED FROM COMPANY

4 [Repealed by FA 2001, s. 110, Sch. 33, Pt. II(2); ITA 2007, s. 1031 and Sch. 3, Pt. 2.]

History – Para. 4 repealed by ITA 2007, s. 1031 and Sch. 3, Pt. 2, with effect from 6 April 2007, in relation to shares issued after 5 April 2007. Transitional and saving provisions are contained in ITA 2007, Sch. 2.
Para. 4 repealed by FA 2001, s. 110, Sch. 33, Pt. II(2) with effect (Note 6):

- in relation to any shares issued on or after 7 March 2001 (FA 2001, Sch. 15, para. 40(3)(a)); and
- in relation to shares issued before 7 March 2001, in the application of ICTA 1988, Pt. VII, Ch. III or TCGA 1992, Sch. 5B on or after that date, in relation to value received and repayments made on or after 7 March 2001 (Sch. 15, para. 40(3)(b)).

Notes – Para. 4 rewritten as ITA 2007, s. 213(1), (3).

VALUE RECEIVED BY PERSONS OTHER THAN CLAIMANTS

5(1) [Repealed by ITA 2007, s. 1031 and Sch. 3, Pt. 2.]

5(2) [Repealed by FA 2001, s. 110, Sch. 33, Pt. II(2); ITA 2007, s. 1031 and Sch. 3, Pt. 2.]

5(3) [Repealed by ITA 2007, s. 1031 and Sch. 3, Pt. 2.]

5(4) [Repealed by ITA 2007, s. 1031 and Sch. 3, Pt. 2.]

5(5) [Repealed by FA 2001, s. 110, Sch. 33, Pt. II(2); ITA 2007, s. 1031 and Sch. 3, Pt. 2.]

History – Para. 5 repealed by ITA 2007, s. 1031 and Sch. 3, Pt. 2, with effect in relation to shares issued after 5 April 2007.
Para. 5(2) and para. 5(5) repealed by FA 2001, s. 110, Sch. 33, Pt. II(2) with effect (Note 6):

- in relation to any shares issued on or after 7 March 2001 (FA 2001, Sch. 15, para. 40(3)(a)); and
- in relation to shares issued before 7 March 2001, in the application of ICTA 1988, Pt. VII, Ch. III or TCGA 1992, Sch. 5B on or after that date, in relation to value received and repayments made on or after 7 March 2001 (Sch. 15, para. 40(3)(b)).

MEANING OF 'TERMINATION DATE' AND 'RELEVANT PERIOD'

6(1) [Repealed by ITA 2007, s. 1031 and Sch. 3, Pt. 2.]

6(2) [Repealed by FA 2001, s. 110, Sch. 33, Pt. II(2); ITA 2007, s. 1031 and Sch. 3, Pt. 2.]

6(3) [Repealed by ITA 2007, s. 1031 and Sch. 3, Pt. 2.]

6(4) [Repealed by ITA 2007, s. 1031 and Sch. 3, Pt. 2.]

History – Para. 6 repealed by ITA 2007, s. 1031 and Sch. 3, Pt. 2, with effect in relation to shares issued after 5 April 2007.
Para. 6(2) repealed by FA 2001, s. 110, Sch. 33, Pt. II(2) with effect (Note 6):

- in relation to any shares issued on or after 7 March 2001 (FA 2001, Sch. 15, para. 40(2)(a)); and
- in relation to application of ICTA 1988, Pt. VII, Ch. III or TCGA 1992, Sch. 5B on or after 7 March 2001; to shares issued after 31 December 1993 but before 7 March 2001 – where such shares had attributed to them income tax relief or deferral relief immediately before the latter date (Sch. 15, para. 40(2)(b)).

Notes – Para. 6(3) rewritten as ITA 2007, s. 256(1).
Para. 6(4) rewritten as ITA 2007, s. 159(2), (3).

POSTPONEMENT OF CHARGEABLE GAINS ON REINVESTMENT

7 [Repealed by FA 2001, s. 110, Sch. 33, Pt. II(2).]

History – Para. 7 repealed by FA 2001, s. 110, Sch. 33, Pt. II(2) with effect (Note 6):

- in relation to any shares issued on or after 7 March 2001 (FA 2001, Sch. 15, para. 40(2)(a)); and
- in relation to application of ICTA 1988, Pt. VII, Ch. III or TCGA 1992, Sch. 5B on or after 7 March 2001; to shares issued after 31 December 1993 but before 7 March 2001 – where such shares had attributed to them income tax relief or deferral relief immediately before the latter date (Sch. 15, para. 40(2)(b)).

COMMENCEMENT

8 The amendments in this Part of this Schedule have effect in relation to shares issued on or after 6th April 2000.

Part II – Qualifying Companies

COMPANY IN ADMINISTRATION OR RECEIVERSHIP

9 [Repealed by ITA 2007, s. 1031 and Sch. 3, Pt. 2.]

History – Para. 9 repealed by ITA 2007, s. 1031 and Sch. 3, Pt. 2, with effect in relation to shares issued after 5 April 2007.

Notes – Para. 9(1) rewritten as ITA 2007, s. 138(1), (2), 182(1), (2), Sch. 1, para. 123, Sch. 2, para. 41(3).
Para. 9(2) rewritten as ITA 2007, Sch. 1, para. 123.
Para. 9(3) rewritten as ITA 2007, s. 176(5).
Para. 9(3) rewritten as ITA 2007, s. 252(2), (3), Sch. 2, para. 57(5).

COMPANY IN LIQUIDATION

10 [Repealed by ITA 2007, s. 1031 and Sch. 3, Pt. 2.]

History – Para. 10 repealed by ITA 2007, s. 1031 and Sch. 3, Pt. 2, with effect in relation to shares issued after 5 April 2007.

Notes – Para. 10 rewritten as ITA 2007, s. 138(4), 182(4), Sch. 1, para. 123.

INDEPENDENCE OF QUALIFYING COMPANY

11 [Repealed by ITA 2007, s. 1031 and Sch. 3, Pt. 2.]

History – Para. 11 repealed by ITA 2007, s. 1031 and Sch. 3, Pt. 2, with effect in relation to shares issued after 5 April 2007.

Notes – Para. 11 rewritten as ITA 2007, s. 139(1), (2), (3), 185(1), (2), (3), 1021(2), Sch. 1, para. 124, Sch. 2, para. 42(2).

COMMENCEMENT

12(1) [Repealed by ITA 2007, s. 1031 and Sch. 3, Pt. 2.]

12(2) [Repealed by ITA 2007, s. 1031 and Sch. 3, Pt. 2.]

History – Para. 12 repealed by ITA 2007, s. 1031 and Sch. 3, Pt. 2, with effect in relation to shares issued after 5 April 2007.

Notes – Para. 12(1) rewritten as ITA 2007, Sch. 2, para. 41(3), (4), 42(2), (3), 57(5), (6).

Part III – Other Amendments

QUALIFYING TRADES

13 [Repealed by ITA 2007, s. 1031 and Sch. 3, Pt. 2.]

History – Para. 13 repealed by ITA 2007, s. 1031 and Sch. 3, Pt. 2, with effect in relation to shares issued after 5 April 2007.

Notes – Para. 13(1) rewritten as ITA 2007, s. 195(2), (3), (4), (5), (6), Sch. 2, para. 55(1).
Para. 13(2) rewritten as ITA 2007, Sch. 2, para. 55(1).

MEANING OF "ARRANGEMENTS"

14 [Repealed by ITA 2007, s. 1031 and Sch. 3, Pt. 2.]

History – Para. 14 repealed by ITA 2007, s. 1031 and Sch. 3, Pt. 2, with effect in relation to shares issued after 5 April 2007.

Notes – Para. 14(1) rewritten as ITA 2007, s. 257(1), (3).

MEANING OF "RESEARCH AND DEVELOPMENT"

15(1) [Repealed by ITA 2007, s. 1031 and Sch. 3, Pt. 2.]

15(2) [Repealed by ITA 2007, s. 1031 and Sch. 3, Pt. 2.]

15(3)

(a) [Repealed by ITA 2007, s. 1031 and Sch. 3, Pt. 2.]

(b) [Repealed by ITA 2007, s. 1031 and Sch. 3, Pt. 1.]

(c) [Repealed by ITA 2007, s. 1031 and Sch. 3, Pt. 2.]

History – Para. 15(1), (2), (3)(a) and (3)(c) repealed by ITA 2007, s. 1031 and Sch. 3, Pt. 2, with effect in relation to shares issued after 5 April 2007.
Para. 15(3)(b) repealed by ITA 2007, s. 1031 and Sch. 3, Pt. 1, with effect from 6 April 2007.

Notes – Para. 15(1) rewritten as ITA 2007, s. 137(7), 257(1), Sch. 2, para. 40(2).

SCHEDULE 18 – VENTURE CAPITAL TRUSTS: AMENDMENTS

Section 65

Part I – Reduction of Applicable Periods

RELIEF FROM INCOME TAX

1(1)–(3) [Repealed by ITA 2007, s. 1031 and Sch. 3, Pt. 1.]

1(4) [Repealed by FA 2006, s. 178 and Sch. 26, Pt. 3(16); repealed by ITA 2007, s. 1031 and Sch. 3, Pt. 1.]

History – Para. 1 repealed by ITA 2007, s. 1031 and Sch. 3, Pt. 1, with effect from 6 April 2007. Transitional and savings provisions contained in Sch. 2.
Para. 1(4) repealed by FA 2006, s. 178 and Sch. 26, Pt. 3(16) with effect in relation to shares issued on or after 6 April 2006.

Notes – Para. 1(2) rewritten as ITA 2007, s. 264(3).
Para. 1(3) rewritten as ITA 2007, s. 266(1).
Para. 1(4) rewritten as ITA 2007, s. 273(1).

DEFERRED CGT CHARGE ON REINVESTMENT

2 [Amends TCGA 1992, Sch. 5C, para. 3(2).]

COMMENCEMENT

3 The amendments made by this Part of this Schedule have effect in relation to shares issued on or after 6th April 2000.

Part II – Qualifying Holdings

INTRODUCTORY

4 [Repealed by ITA 2007, s. 1031 and Sch. 3, Pt. 1.]

History – Para. 4 repealed by ITA 2007, s. 1031 and Sch. 3, Pt. 1, with effect from 6 April 2007.

QUALIFYING TRADE: RECEIPT OF ROYALTIES OR LICENCE FEES

5 [Repealed by ITA 2007, s. 1031 and Sch. 3, Pt. 1.]

History – Para. 5 repealed by ITA 2007, s. 1031 and Sch. 3, Pt. 1, with effect from 6 April 2007.

Notes – Para. 5(1) rewritten as ITA 2007, s. 306(2), (3), (4), (5), (6), Sch. 2, para. 84.
Para. 5(2) rewritten as ITA 2007, Sch. 2, para. 84.

MEANING OF "RESEARCH AND DEVELOPMENT"

6 [Repealed by ITA 2007, s. 1031 and Sch. 3, Pt. 1.]

History – Para. 6 repealed by ITA 2007, s. 1031 and Sch. 3, Pt. 1, with effect from 6 April 2007.

Notes – Para. 6(1) rewritten as ITA 2007, s. 332, Sch. 2 para. 90(5).

COMPANY IN ADMINISTRATION OR RECEIVERSHIP

7 [Repealed by ITA 2007, s. 1031 and Sch. 3, Pt. 1.]

History – Para. 7 repealed by ITA 2007, s. 1031 and Sch. 3, Pt. 1, with effect from 6 April 2007.

Notes – Para. 7(1) rewritten as ITA 2007, s. 292(1), (2), 331(2), (3).

COMPANY REORGANISATIONS ETC. INVOLVING EXCHANGE OF SHARES

8 [Repealed by ITA 2007, s. 1031 and Sch. 3, Pt. 1.]

History – Para. 8 repealed by ITA 2007, s. 1031 and Sch. 3, Pt. 1, with effect from 6 April 2007.

Notes – Para. 8(1) rewritten as ITA 2007, s. 330(1), (2), (3), (4), (5), (6), Sch. 2, para. 88.
Para. 8(2) rewritten as ITA 2007, s. 279(4), (5).
Para. 8(4) rewritten as ITA 2007, Sch. 2, para. 88.

SCHEDULE 19 – MEANING OF "RESEARCH AND DEVELOPMENT"

Section 68

Part I – The New Definition

RESEARCH AND DEVELOPMENT

1 [Repealed by CTA 2010, s. 1181 and Sch. 3, Pt. 1.]

History – Para. 1 repealed by CTA 2010, s. 1181 and Sch. 3, Pt. 1, with effect for corporation tax purposes for accounting periods ending on or after 1 April 2010, and for income tax and capital gains tax purposes for the tax year 2010–11 and subsequent tax years.

OIL AND GAS EXPLORATION AND APPRAISAL

2 [Repealed by CTA 2010, s. 1181 and Sch. 3, Pt. 1.]

History – Para. 2 repealed by CTA 2010, s. 1181 and Sch. 3, Pt. 1, with effect for corporation tax purposes for accounting periods ending on or after 1 April 2010, and for income tax and capital gains tax purposes for the tax year 2010–11 and subsequent tax years.

Part II – Consequential Amendments

INCOME AND CORPORATION TAXES ACT 1988 (C.1)

3 The Income and Corporation Taxes Act 1988 is amended as follows.

4 [Amends ICTA 1988, s. 495(1)(b).]

5(1) [Inserts ICTA 1988, s. 82A, 82B.]

5(2) Any approval given by the Secretary of State for the purposes of section 136(b) or (c) of the Capital Allowances Act 1990 and in force immediately before the commencement of this paragraph has effect as if given under section 82B(1)(a) or (b) of the Taxes Act 1988 as inserted by sub-paragraph (1) above.

5(3) So far as is necessary for continuing its effect, any decision made by the Secretary of State under section 139(3) of the Capital Allowances Act 1990 before the commencement of this paragraph has effect as if given under section 82B(4) of the Taxes Act 1988 as inserted by sub-paragraph (1) above.

6 [Amends ICTA 1988, Sch. 18, para. (6)(b)(iii).]

CAPITAL ALLOWANCES ACT 1990 (C. 1)

7–11 [Repealed by CAA 2001, s. 580 and Sch. 4.]

History – Para. 7–11 repealed by CAA 2001, s. 580 and Sch. 4 with effect as respects allowances and charges falling to be made for chargeable periods ending, for income tax purposes, on or after 6 April 2001, and, for corporation tax purposes, on or after 1 April 2001.

TAXATION OF CHARGEABLE GAINS ACT 1992 (C. 12)

12(1) Section 195 of the Taxation of Chargeable Gains Act 1992 (allowance of certain drilling expenditure) is amended as follows.

12(2) [Amends TCGA 1992, s. 195(2), (3).]

12(3) [Amends TCGA 1992, s. 195(3).]

12(4) [Inserts TCGA 1992, s. 195(8).]

SCHEDULE 20 – TAX RELIEF FOR EXPENDITURE ON RESEARCH AND DEVELOPMENT

Section 69(1)

[Omitted by CTA 2009, s. 1322 and Sch. 1, para. 469 and repealed by CTA 2009, s. 1326 and Sch. 3, Pt. 1.]

History – Sch. 20 omitted by CTA 2009, s. 1322 and Sch. 1, para. 469 and repealed by CTA 2009, s. 1326 and Sch. 3, Pt. 1, with effect for corporation tax purposes for accounting periods ending on or after 1 April 2009, and for income tax and capital gains tax purposes for the tax year 2009–10 and subsequent tax years.

Notes – Sch. 20 rewritten for corporation tax purposes as follows:
Para. 1(1): CTA 2009, s. 1044(1), (2), (3), CTA 2009, s. 1045(1), (2), (3), CTA 2009, s. 1050(1), (2), (3).
Para. 1(2): CTA 2009, s. 1050(5).
Para. 1(3): CTA 2009, s. 1050(6).
Para. 1(3A): CTA 2009, s. 1050(7).
Para. 1(5): CTA 2009, s. 1044(9), s. 1045(9), s. 1054(5).
Para. 2(1): CTA 2009, s. 1119(1), CTA 2009, s. 1120(2)–(7).

Para. 2(2): CTA 2009, s. 1119(2).
Para. 3(1): CTA 2009, s. 1052(1), s. 1053(1).
Para. 3(3): CTA 2009, s. 1052(3), s. 1053(1) and (2).
Para. 3(4): CTA 2009, s. 1052(2), s. 1053(1).
Para. 3(5): CTA 2009, s. 1052(4), s. 1053(3).
Para. 3(6): CTA 2009, s. 1052(5), s. 1053(4).
Para. 3(7): CTA 2009, s. 1052(6), s. 1053(5).
Para. 4(1): CTA 2009, s. 1042(1).
Para. 4(2): CTA 2009, s. 1042(2).
Para. 5(1): CTA2009, s. 1123(1)–(5) and (7).
Para. 5(1ZB): CTA 2009, s. 1123(6).
Para. 5(1A): CTA 2009, s. 1123(8) and (9).
Para. 5(2): CTA 2009, s. 1124(2).
Para. 5(3): CTA 2009, s. 1124(3) and (4).
Para. 5(4): CTA 2009, s. 1124(5) and (6).
Para. 6(1): CTA 2009, s. 1125(1).
Para. 6(2): CTA 2009, s. 1125(2).
Para. 6(3): CTA 2009, s. 1126(2).
Para. 6(4): CTA 2009, s. 1126(3) and (4).
Para. 6(5): CTA 2009, s. 1126(5) and (6).
Para. 6A(1): CTA 2009, s. 1140(1).
Para. 6A(2): CTA 2009, s. 1140(2).
Para. 7: CTA 2009, s. 1139.
Para. 8(1): CTA 2009, s. 1138(1).
Para. 8(2): CTA 2009, s. 1138(2) and (3).
Para. 8(3): CTA 2009, s. 1138(4).
Para. 8A(3): CTA 2009, s. 1127(1).
Para. 8A(4): CTA 2009, s. 1132(2).
Para. 8A(5): CTA 2009, s. 1132(3) and (4).
Para. 8A(6): CTA 2009, s. 1132(5) and (6).
Para. 8B: CTA 2009, s. 1128(1)–(8).
Para. 8C(1): CTA 2009, s. 1129(1) and (2).
Para. 8C(2): CTA 2009, s. 1129(3) and (4).
Para. 8C(3): CTA 2009, s. 1129(5).
Para. 8C(4): CTA 2009, s. 1129(6).
Para. 8C(5): CTA 2009, s. 1129(7).
Para. 8D(1): CTA 2009, s. 1130(1).
Para. 8D(2): CTA 2009, s. 1130(2).
Para. 8D(3): CTA 2009, s. 1130(3).
Para. 8D(4): CTA 2009, s. 1130(4).
Para. 8D(5): CTA 2009, s. 1130(5).
Para. 8E: CTA 2009, s. 1131(1) and (2).
Para. 9(2): CTA 2009, s. 1133(1).
Para. 10(1): CTA 2009, s. 1134(1) and (2).
Para. 10(2): CTA 2009, s. 1134(3) and (4).
Para. 10(3): CTA 2009, s. 1134(5).
Para. 10(4): CTA 2009, s. 1134(6).
Para. 11(1): CTA 2009, s. 1135(1).
Para. 11(2): CTA 2009, s. 1135(2).
Para. 11(3): CTA 2009, s. 1135(3).
Para. 11(4): CTA 2009, s. 1135(4).
Para. 11(5): CTA 2009, s. 1135(5).
Para. 12: CTA 2009, s. 1136(1) and (2).
Para. 13: CTA 2009, s. 1044(1) and (4)–(8).
Para. 14(1): CTA 2009, s. 1045(1) and (4).
Para. 14(2): CTA 2009, s. 1045(5)–(7).
Para. 14(3): CTA 2009, s. 1045(8).
Para. 14(4): CTA 2009, s. 1047(1).
Para. 14(5): CTA 2009, s. 1047(2).
Para. 14(6): CTA 2009, s. 1047(3).
Para. 15(1): CTA 2009, s. 1054(1) and (2).
Para. 15(2): CTA 2009, s. 1055(1).
Para. 15(3): CTA 2009, s. 1055(2) and (3).
Para. 15(4): CTA 2009, s. 1056(2).
Para. 15(5): CTA 2009, s. 1056(3).
Para. 16(1): CTA 2009, s. 1058(1).
Para. 16(2): CTA 2009, s. 1058(2).
Para. 16(3): CTA 2009, s. 1058(3).
Para. 17(1): CTA 2009, s. 1059(1)–(5).
Para. 17(2): CTA 2009, s. 1141.
Para. 18(1): CTA 2009, s. 1054(4).
Para. 18(2): CTA 2009, s. 1060(2) and (3).
Para. 18(3): CTA 2009, s. 1060(4) and (5).
Para. 18(4): CTA 2009, s. 1060(6) and (7).
Para. 18(5): CTA 2009, s. 1054(2).
Para. 18A(1): CTA 2009, s. 1046(1), s. 1057(1).
Para. 18A(2): CTA 2009, s. 1057(2).
Para. 18A(3): CTA 2009, s. 1057(3).
Para. 18A(4): CTA 2009, s. 1046(2), s. 1057(4).
Para. 18A(5): CTA 2009, s. 1046(3), s. 1057(5).
Para. 19(1): CTA 2009, s. 1062(1) and (2).
Para. 19(2): CTA 2009, s. 1062(2) and (3).
Para. 20: CTA 2009, s. 1061.
Para. 21(1): CTA 2009, s. 1084(1) and (2).

Para. 21(2): CTA 2009, s. 1084(3).
Para. 21(3): CTA 2009, s. 1084(4).
Para. 22: CTA 2009, s. 1049(1)–(3).
Para. 23(1): CTA 2009, s. 1048(1).
Para. 23(2): CTA 2009, s. 1048(2).
Para. 23(3): CTA 2009, s. 1048(3)–(5).
Para. 23(4): CTA 2009, s. 1048(3).
Para. 25(1): CTA 2009, s. 1041, s. 1055(1).
Para. 25(2): CTA 2009, s. 1316(1).
Para. 25(3): CTA 2009, s. 1137(1) and (2).

SCHEDULE 21 – R&D TAX CREDITS: CONSEQUENTIAL AMENDMENTS

Section 69(2)

INTEREST

1(1) Section 826 of the Taxes Act 1988 (interest on tax overpaid) is amended as follows.

1(2) [Inserts ICTA 1988, s. 826(1)(d).]

1(3) [Inserts ICTA 1988, s. 826(3A).]

1(4) In subsection (8A) (recovery of overpaid interest)

(a) [Amends ICTA 1988, s. 826(8A)(a).]

(b) [Substitutes ICTA 1988, s. 826(8A)(b).]

1(5) [Inserts ICTA 1988, s. 826(8BA).]

CLAIM MUST BE MADE IN TAX RETURN

2 [Substitutes FA 1998, Sch. 18, para. 10(2).]

RECOVERY OF EXCESSIVE R&D TAX CREDIT

3 In paragraph 52 of that Schedule (recovery of excessive repayments, etc.)

(a) [Inserts FA 1998, Sch. 18, para. 52(2)(ba).]

(b) [Inserts FA 1998, Sch. 18, para. 52(5)(ab).]

(c) [Amends FA 1998, Sch. 18, para. 52(5).]

CLAIMS FOR R&D TAX CREDITS

4 [Inserts FA 1998, Sch. 18, para. 83A–83F.]

SCHEDULE 22 – TONNAGE TAX

Section 82

Cross references – ITEPA 2003, s. 357(5): business entertaining and gifts by tonnage tax companies.

Statements of practice – SP 4/00: HMRC statement covering the general operation of the tonnage tax regime for shipping companies (issued 25 August 2000).

Other material – HMRC Brief 06/13: guidance on the application of the flagging rules for tonnage tax in 2013.
HMRC Brief 37/13: guidance on qualifying ships and flagging.
HMRC Brief 1/15: tonnage tax — qualifying ships and flagging.

Part I – Introductory

TONNAGE TAX

1(1) This Schedule provides an alternative regime ("tonnage tax") for calculating the profits of a shipping company for the purposes of corporation tax.

1(2) The regime applies only if an election to that effect (a "tonnage tax election") is made (see Part II of this Schedule).

Companies that are members of a group must join in a group election.

1(3) A tonnage tax election may only be made if–

(a) the company or group is a qualifying company or group (see Part III of this Schedule), and

(b) certain requirements are met as to training (see Part IV of this Schedule) and other matters (see Part V of this Schedule).

TONNAGE TAX COMPANIES AND GROUPS

2(1) In this Schedule a **"tonnage tax company"** or **"tonnage tax group"** means a company or group in relation to which a tonnage tax election has effect.

2(2) References in this Schedule to a company entering or leaving tonnage tax are to its becoming or ceasing to be a tonnage tax company.
References to a company being subject to tonnage tax have a corresponding meaning.

PROFITS OF TONNAGE TAX COMPANY

3(1) In the case of a tonnage tax company, its tonnage tax profits are brought into charge to corporation tax in place of its relevant shipping profits (see Part VI of this Schedule).

3(2) Where profits would be relevant shipping income, any loss accruing to the company is similarly left out of account for the purposes of corporation tax.

TONNAGE TAX PROFITS: METHOD OF CALCULATION

4(1) A company's tonnage tax profits for an accounting period are calculated in accordance with this paragraph by reference to the net tonnage of the qualifying ships operated by the company.
For the purposes of the calculation the net tonnage of a ship is rounded down (if necessary) to the nearest multiple of 100 tons.

4(2) The calculation is as follows:
Step One
Determine the daily profit for each qualifying ship operated by the company by reference to the following table and the net tonnage of the ship:

For each 100 tons up to 1,000 tons	£0.60
For each 100 tons between 1,000 and 10,000 tons	£0.45
For each 100 tons between 10,000 and 25,000 tons	£0.30
For each 100 tons above 25,000 tons	£0.15

Step Two
Work out the ship's profit for the accounting period by multiplying the daily profit by–

(a) the number of days in the accounting period, or

(b) if the ship was operated by the company as a qualifying ship for only part of the period, by the number of days in that part.

Step Three
Follow Steps One and Two for each of the qualifying ships operated by the company in the accounting period.
Step Four
Add together the resulting amounts and the total is the amount of the company's tonnage tax profits for that accounting period.

TONNAGE TAX PROFITS: CALCULATION IN CASE OF JOINT OPERATION ETC.

5(1) If two or more companies fall to be regarded as operators of a ship by virtue of a joint interest in the ship, or in an agreement for the use of the ship, the tonnage tax profits of each are calculated as if each were entitled to a share of the profits proportionate to its share of that interest.

5(2) If two or more companies fall to be treated as the operator of a ship otherwise than as mentioned in sub-paragraph (1), the tonnage tax profits of each are computed as if each were the only operator.

MEASUREMENT OF TONNAGE OF SHIP

6(1) References in this Schedule to the gross or net tonnage of a ship are to that tonnage as determined–

(a) in the case of vessel of 24 metres in length or over, in accordance with the IMO International Convention on Tonnage Measurement of Ships (ITC69);

(b) in the case of a vessel under 24 metres in length, in accordance with tonnage regulations.

6(2) A ship shall not be treated as a qualifying ship for the purposes of this Schedule unless there is in force–

(a) a valid International Tonnage Certificate (1969), or

(b) a valid certificate recording its tonnage as measured in accordance with tonnage regulations.

6(3) In this paragraph **"tonnage regulations"** means regulations under section 19 of the Merchant Shipping Act 1995 or provisions of the law of a country or territory outside the United Kingdom corresponding to those regulations.

Part II – Tonnage Tax Elections

COMPANY OR GROUP ELECTION

7(1) A tonnage tax election may be made in respect of–

(a) a qualifying single company (a "company election"), or

(b) a qualifying group (a "group election").

7(2) A group election has effect in relation to all qualifying companies in the group.

METHOD OF MAKING ELECTION

8(1) A tonnage tax election is made by notice to the Inland Revenue.

8(2) The notice must contain such particulars and be supported by such evidence as the Inland Revenue may require.

PERSON BY WHOM ELECTION TO BE MADE

9(1) A company election must be made by the company concerned.

9(2) A group election must be made jointly by all the qualifying companies in the group.

WHEN ELECTION MAY BE MADE

10(1) A tonnage tax election may be made at any time before the end of the period of twelve months beginning with the day on which this Act is passed ("the initial period").
After the end of the initial period a tonnage tax election may only be made–

(a) in the circumstances specified in the following provisions of this paragraph, or

(b) as provided by an order under paragraph 11 (power to provide further opportunities for election).

10(2) An election may be made after the end of the initial period in respect of a single company that–

(a) becomes a qualifying company, and

(b) has not previously been a qualifying company at any time after the passing of this Act.

Any such election must be made before the end of the period of twelve months beginning with the day on which the company became a qualifying company.

10(3) An election may be made after the end of the initial period in respect of a group that becomes a qualifying group by virtue of a member of the group becoming a qualifying company, not previously having been a qualifying company at any time after the passing of this Act.
This does not apply if the group–

(a) was previously a qualifying group at any time after the passing of this Act, or

(b) is substantially the same as a group that was previously a qualifying group at any such time.

An election under this sub-paragraph must be made before the end of the period of twelve months beginning with the day on which the group became a qualifying group.

10(4) This paragraph does not prevent an election being made under the provisions of Part XII of this Schedule relating to mergers and demergers.

POWER TO PROVIDE FURTHER OPPORTUNITIES FOR ELECTION

11(1) The Treasury may by order provide for further periods during which tonnage tax elections may be made.

11(2) Any such order may provide for this Part of this Schedule to apply, with such consequential adaptations as appear to the Treasury to be appropriate, in relation to any such further period as it applies in relation to the initial period.

The consequential adaptations that may be made include adaptations of the references to the passing of this Act or to 1st January 2000.

Statutory instruments – SI 2005/1449: Tonnage Tax (Further Opportunity for Election) Order 2005.

WHEN ELECTION TAKES EFFECT

12(1) The general rule is that a tonnage tax election has effect from the beginning of the accounting period in which it is made.

This is subject to the following exceptions.

12(2) A tonnage tax election cannot have effect in relation to an accounting period beginning before 1st January 2000.

If the general rule would produce that effect, the election has effect instead from the beginning of the accounting period following that in which it is made.

12(3) The Inland Revenue may agree that a tonnage tax election made before the end of the initial period shall have effect from the beginning of an accounting period earlier than that in which it is made (but not one beginning before 1st January 2000).

12(4) The Inland Revenue may agree that a tonnage tax election made before the end of the initial period shall have effect from the beginning of the accounting period following that in which it is made.

In exceptional circumstances they may agree that it shall have effect from the beginning of the accounting period following that one.

12(5) In the case of a group election in respect of a group where the members have different accounting periods–

(a) sub-paragraph (1), or

(b) any agreement under sub-paragraph (3) or (4),

has effect in relation to each qualifying company by reference to that company's accounting periods.

12(6) A tonnage tax election under paragraph 10(2) or (3) (election in consequence of company becoming a qualifying company) has effect from the time at which the company in question became a qualifying company.

This is subject to paragraph 38(2)(a) and (b) (effect in certain cases of exceeding the 75% limit on chartered in tonnage).

Cross references – SI 2005/1449: adaptation of para. 12 where a tonnage tax election is made during the period from 1 July 2005 to 31 December 2006.

PERIOD FOR WHICH ELECTION IS IN FORCE

13(1) The general rule is that a tonnage tax election remains in force until it expires at the end of the period of ten years beginning–

(a) in the case of a company election, with the first day on which the election has effect in relation to the company;

(b) in the case of a group election, with the first day on which the election has effect in relation to any member of the group.

This is subject to the following exceptions.

13(2) A tonnage tax election ceases to be in force–

(a) in the case of a company election, if the company ceases to be a qualifying company;

(b) in the case of a group election, if the group ceases to be a qualifying group.

13(2A) A tonnage tax election ceases to be in force–

(a) in the case of a company election, if a withdrawal notice in respect of the company takes effect under paragraph 15A;

(b) in the case of a group election, if a withdrawal notice in respect of the group takes effect under that paragraph.

13(3) A tonnage tax election may also cease to be in force under–

(a) the provisions of Part V of this Schedule, or

(b) the provisions of Part XII of this Schedule relating to mergers and demergers.

13(4) This paragraph has effect subject to paragraph 15(4) (election superseded by renewal election).

History – Para. 13(2A) inserted by FA 2005, s. 93 and Sch. 7, para. 2, with effect from 7 April 2005.

EFFECT OF ELECTION CEASING TO BE IN FORCE

14 A tonnage tax election that ceases to be in force ceases to have effect in relation to any company.

RENEWAL ELECTION

15(1) At any time when a tonnage tax election is in force in respect of a single company or group a further tonnage tax election (a "renewal election") may be made in respect of that company or group.

15(2) This is subject to paragraph 32(5) (training requirement: no renewal election if non-compliance notice in force).

15(3) The provisions of–

paragraphs 7 to 9 (type of election, method of election and person by whom election to be made), and

paragraphs 13 and 14 (period for which election is in force and when election ceases to have effect),

apply in relation to a renewal election as they apply in relation to an original tonnage tax election.

15(4) A renewal election supersedes the existing tonnage tax election.

WITHDRAWAL NOTICES

15A(1) A withdrawal notice (see paragraph 13(2A)) may be given–

(a) in respect of a single company, or

(b) in respect of a group,

but only if the following conditions are met.

15A(2) Condition 1 is that the notice is given during the period–

(a) beginning with the day on which the Finance Act 2005 is passed, and

(b) ending with 31st March 2006.

15A(3) Condition 2 is that, for the whole of the period of three years ending with the day on which the Finance Act 2005 is passed, a tonnage tax election or a renewal election has been in force in respect of the company or group in respect of which the withdrawal notice is to be given.

15A(4) A withdrawal notice must be given to the Inland Revenue–

(a) in the case of a withdrawal notice in respect of a single company, by that company;

(b) in the case of a withdrawal notice in respect of a group, jointly by all the qualifying companies in the group.

15A(5) A withdrawal notice given in accordance with this paragraph takes effect at the end of the accounting period that precedes the first accounting period of the company to begin after 1st July 2005.

15A(6) In the case of a withdrawal notice given in respect of a group, sub-paragraph (5) has effect in relation to each qualifying company in the group by reference to that company's accounting periods.

History – Para. 15A inserted by FA 2005, s. 93 and Sch. 7, para. 3, with effect from 7 April 2005.

Cross references – FA 2005, Sch. 7, para. 19: transitional provision for qualifying activity if withdrawal notice given under para. 15A on or before 31 March 2006.

Notes – The Finance Act 2005 was passed on 7 April 2005.
The "Inland Revenue" became "Her Majesty's Revenue and Customs" from 18 April 2005 (CRCA 2005, s. 1; SI 2005/1126 (C. 51)).

POWER TO PROVIDE FURTHER OPPORTUNITIES FOR WITHDRAWAL

15B(1) The Treasury may by order provide for further periods during which withdrawal notices under paragraph 15A may be given.

15B(2) Any such order may provide for that paragraph to apply, with such consequential adaptations as appear to the Treasury to be appropriate, in relation to any such further period as it applies in relation to the period specified in sub-paragraph (2) of that paragraph.

15B(3) The consequential adaptations that may be made include adaptations of the reference in sub-paragraph (3) of that paragraph to the period of three years ending with the day on which the Finance Act 2005 is passed.

History – Para. 15B inserted by FA 2005, s. 93 and Sch. 7, para. 3, with effect from 7 April 2005.

Notes – The Finance Act 2005 was passed on 7 April 2005.

Part III – Qualifying Companies and Groups

QUALIFYING COMPANIES AND GROUPS

16(1) For the purposes of this Schedule a company is a **"qualifying company"** if–

(a) it is within the charge to corporation tax,

(b) it operates qualifying ships, and

(c) those ships are strategically and commercially managed in the United Kingdom.

16(2) A **"qualifying group"** means a group of which one or more members are qualifying companies.

EFFECT OF TEMPORARILY CEASING TO OPERATE QUALIFYING SHIPS

17(1) This paragraph applies where a company temporarily ceases to operate any qualifying ships. It does not apply where a company continues to operate a ship that temporarily ceases to be a qualifying ship.

17(2) If the company gives notice to the Inland Revenue stating–

(a) its intention to resume operating qualifying ships, and

(b) its wish to remain within tonnage tax,

the company shall be treated for the purposes of this Schedule as if it had continued to operate the qualifying ship or ships it operated immediately before the temporary cessation.

17(3) The notice must be given not later than the date which is the filing date for the company's company tax return for the accounting period in which the temporary cessation begins.

"Filing date" and **"company tax return"** here have the same meaning as in Schedule 18 to the Finance Act 1998.

17(4) This paragraph ceases to apply if and when the company–

(a) abandons its intention to resume operating qualifying ships, or

(b) again in fact operates a qualifying ship.

MEANING OF OPERATING A SHIP

18(1) A company is regarded for the purposes of this Schedule as operating any ship owned by, or chartered to, the company, subject to the following provisions.

18(2) A company is not regarded as the operator of a ship where part only of the ship has been chartered to it.

For this purpose a company is not to be taken as having part only of a ship chartered to it by reason only of the ship being chartered to it jointly with one or more other persons.

18(3) A company is not regarded as the operator of a ship that has been chartered out by it on bareboat charter terms, except as provided by the following provisions.

18(4) A company is regarded as operating a ship that has been chartered out by it on bareboat charter terms if the person to whom it is chartered is not a third party.

For this purpose a **"third party"** means–

(a) in the case of a single company, any other person;

(b) in the case of a member of a group–

 (i) any member of the group that is not a tonnage tax company (and does not become a tonnage tax company by virtue of the ship being chartered to it), or

 (ii) any person who is not a member of the group.

18(5) A company is not regarded as ceasing to operate a ship that has been chartered out by it on bareboat charter terms if–

(a) the ship is chartered out because of short-term over-capacity, and

(b) the term of the charter does not exceed three years.

18(6) A company is regarded as operating a ship that has been chartered out by it on bareboat charter terms if the ship–

(a) is registered in the United Kingdom, and

(b) is in the service of a government department by reason of a charter by demise to the Crown,

and there is in force under section 308(2) of the Merchant Shipping Act 1995 an Order in Council providing for the registration of government ships in the service of that department.

In this sub-paragraph **"government department"** includes a Northern Ireland department.

QUALIFYING SHIPS

19(1) For the purposes of this Schedule a **"qualifying ship"** means, subject to sub-paragraph (2), a seagoing ship of 100 tons or more gross tonnage used for–

(a) the carriage by sea of passengers,

(b) the carriage by sea of cargo,

(c) towage, salvage or other marine assistance carried out at sea, or

(d) transport by sea in connection with other services of a kind necessarily provided at sea.

19(2) A vessel is not a qualifying ship for the purposes of this Schedule if the main purpose for which it is used is the provision of goods or services of a kind normally provided on land.

19(3) Sub-paragraph (1) is also subject to–

(a) paragraph 20 (vessels excluded from being qualifying ships);

(b) paragraph 20A (qualifying dredgers and tugs);

(c) paragraphs 22A to 22F (flagging).

19(4) For the purposes of this paragraph a ship is a seagoing ship if it is certificated for navigation at sea by the competent authority of any country or territory.

19(5) For the purposes of sub-paragraph (1) **"sea"** does not include–

(a) a port or harbour;

(b) an estuary, a tidal or other river or an inland waterway.

History – In para. 19(1)(a), the words "by sea" inserted by FA 2005, s. 93 and Sch. 7, para. 4(2)(a), with effect from 1 July 2005 but subject to the transitional provisions at FA 2005, Sch. 7, para. 19–21.
In para. 19(1)(b), the words "by sea" inserted by FA 2005, s. 93 and Sch. 7, para. 4(2)(b), with effect from 1 July 2005 but subject to the transitional provisions at FA 2005, Sch. 7, para. 19–21.
In para. 19(1)(c), the words "carried out at sea" inserted by FA 2005, s. 93 and Sch. 7, para. 4(2)(c), with effect from 1 July 2005 but subject to the transitional provisions at FA 2005, Sch. 7, para. 19–21.
In para. 19(1)(d), the words "by sea" inserted by FA 2005, s. 93 and Sch. 7, para. 4(2)(d), with effect from 1 July 2005 but subject to the transitional provisions at FA 2005, Sch. 7, para. 19–21.
In para. 19(3), "(a)" inserted after the words "subject to" and para. (b) and (c) inserted by FA 2005, s. 93 and Sch. 7, para. 4(3), with effect from 1 July 2005 but subject to the transitional provisions at FA 2005, Sch. 7, para. 19–21.
Para. 19(5) inserted by FA 2005, s. 93 and Sch. 7, para. 4(4), with effect from 1 July 2005 but subject to the transitional provisions at FA 2005, Sch. 7, para. 19–21.

VESSELS EXCLUDED FROM BEING QUALIFYING SHIPS

20(1) The following kinds of vessel are not qualifying ships for the purposes of this Schedule–

(a) fishing vessels or factory ships;

(b) pleasure craft;

(c) harbour or river ferries;

(d) offshore installations;

(e) tankers dedicated to a particular oil field;

(f) dredgers other than qualifying dredgers.

20(2) In sub-paragraph (1)(a) **"factory ship"** means a vessel providing processing services for the fishing industry.

20(3) In sub-paragraph (1)(b) **"pleasure craft"** means a vessel of a kind whose primary use is for the purposes of sport or recreation.

20(4) In sub-paragraph (1)(c) **"harbour or river ferry"** means a vessel used for harbour, estuary or river crossings.

20(5) [Omitted by FA 2004, s. 146 and Sch. 27, para. 7(1).]

20(6) For the purposes of sub-paragraph (1)(e) whether a tanker is dedicated to a particular oil field shall be determined in accordance with section 2 of the Oil Taxation Act 1983 (dedicated mobile assets).

20(7) In this Schedule **"qualifying dredger"** means a dredger which–

(a) is self-propelled, and

(b) is constructed or adapted for the carriage of cargo;

(but see further paragraph 20A).

History – Para. 20(1)(f) substituted by FA 2005, s. 93 and Sch. 7, para. 5(2), with effect from 1 July 2005 but subject to the transitional provisions at FA 2005, Sch. 7, para. 19–21.
Para. 20(5) omitted by FA 2004, s. 146 and Sch. 27, para. 7(1) and repealed by FA 2004, s. 326 and Sch. 42, Pt. 2(19) with effect for accounting periods ending on or after 1 April 2004.
Para. 20(7) inserted by FA 2005, s. 93 and Sch. 7, para. 5(3), with effect from 1 July 2005 but subject to the transitional provisions at FA 2005, Sch. 7, para. 19–21.

QUALIFYING DREDGERS AND TUGS

20A(1) This paragraph applies where a company operates a ship in an accounting period and the ship–

(a) is a qualifying dredger or a tug, and

(b) would, apart from this paragraph, be a qualifying ship.

20A(2) The ship shall not be regarded as a qualifying ship operated by the company in that accounting period unless it is used for one or more of the activities mentioned in paragraph 19(1)(a) to (d) for more than 50% of its operational time.

20A(3) In this paragraph **"operational time"**, in relation to a ship operated by a company in an accounting period, means the time during that accounting period during which the ship is–

(a) operated by the company, and

(b) used for any activity.

20A(4) For the purposes of sub-paragraph (2) assisting a self-propelled vessel into or out of a port or harbour is not to be regarded as use for an activity mentioned in paragraph 19(1)(c).

20A(5) For the purposes of sub-paragraph (3) any waiting time spent by a tug for the purposes of a particular activity is to be treated as time during which the tug is used for that activity.

History – Para. 20A inserted by FA 2005, s. 93 and Sch. 7, para. 6, with effect from 1 July 2005 but subject to the transitional provisions at FA 2005, Sch. 7, para. 19–21.

POWER TO MODIFY EXCLUSIONS

21 The Treasury may make provision by order amending paragraph 20 so as to add any description of vessel to, or remove any description of vessel from, the kinds of vessel that are excluded from being qualifying ships for the purposes of this Schedule.

EFFECT OF CHANGE OF USE

22(1) A qualifying ship that begins to be used for non-qualifying purposes ceases to be a qualifying ship when it begins to be so used, subject to the following provisions.

22(2) If–

(a) a company operates a ship throughout an accounting period of the company, and

(b) in that period the ship is used for non-qualifying purposes on not more than 30 days,

that use shall be disregarded in determining whether the ship is a qualifying ship at any time during that period.

22(3) In the case of an accounting period shorter than a year, the figure of 30 days in sub-paragraph (2) shall be proportionately reduced.

22(4) If a company operates a ship during part only of an accounting period of the company, sub-paragraph (2) has effect as if for "30 days", or the number of days substituted by sub-paragraph (3), there were substituted the number of days that bear to the length of that part of the accounting period the same proportion that 30 days does to a year.

22(5) In this paragraph references to use for non-qualifying purposes are to–

(a) use for an activity other than any of the activities mentioned in paragraph 19(1)(a) to (d), or

(b) use as a vessel of a kind excluded by paragraph 20 from being a qualifying ship.

22(6) This paragraph does not apply for the purposes of sub-paragraphs (2) to (5) of paragraph 20A (qualifying dredgers and tugs).

History – In para. 22(1), the words "for non-qualifying purposes" substituted for the words "as a vessel of an excluded kind" by FA 2005, s. 93 and Sch. 7, para. 7(2), with effect from 7 April 2005.

In para. 22(2)(b), the words "for non-qualifying purposes" substituted for the words "as a vessel of an excluded kind" by FA 2005, s. 93 and Sch. 7, para. 7(3), with effect from 7 April 2005.

In para. 22(5), both the words "for non-qualifying purposes are to–" and new para. (a) substituted for the words "as a vessel of an excluded kind are to" by FA 2005, s. 93 and Sch. 7, para. 7(4), with effect from 7 April 2005.

Para. 22(6) inserted by FA 2005, s. 93 and Sch. 7, para. 7(5), with effect from 7 April 2005.

FLAGGING: RULE FOR SHIPS OTHER THAN DREDGERS AND TUGS

22A(1) This paragraph applies if the following conditions are satisfied in the case of a ship which–

(a) is neither a qualifying dredger nor a tug, and

(b) would, apart from this paragraph, be a qualifying ship.

22A(2) Condition 1 is that, at a time after the later of the reference date (see paragraph 22B(1)) and 30th June 2005,–

(a) in the case of a tonnage tax company which is a single company, the company begins, in a financial year which is not excepted (see paragraph 22B(2)), to operate the ship for the first time, or

(b) in the case of a tonnage tax company which is a member of a tonnage tax group, the company begins, in a financial year which is not excepted, to operate the ship for the first time, the ship not having previously been operated by any other member of the group.

22A(3) Condition 2 is that less than 60% of the company's total tonnage is Community-flagged (see paragraph 22B(3)) on average over the period–

(a) beginning with the first day of the financial year mentioned in condition 1, and

(b) ending with the day on which the company so begins to operate the ship.

22A(4) Condition 3 is that–

(a) the percentage of the company's total tonnage which is Community-flagged on average over the period mentioned in condition 2,

is less than

(b) the percentage of the company's total tonnage which was Community-flagged on the reference date.

22A(5) Condition 4 is that, on the date on which the company so begins to operate the ship, the ship is not registered in one of the Member States' registers (see paragraph 22B(7)).

22A(6) Where this paragraph applies in relation to the ship, the ship shall not, at any time on or after that date, be regarded as–

(a) a qualifying ship operated by the company, or

(b) if immediately before that date the company is a member of a tonnage tax group, a qualifying ship operated by any company that is or becomes a member of the group.

22A(7) But sub-paragraph (6) does not apply if–

(a) the ship has become registered in one of the Member States' registers by the end of the period of three months beginning with that date, or

(b) the conditions in sub-paragraph (8) are satisfied.

22A(8) Those conditions are that–

(a) a substitute ship which was not registered in one of the Member States' registers has, during the period mentioned in sub-paragraph (7)(a), become so registered, and

(b) no later than the end of that period–

(i) if the company is a single company, the company makes an election under this sub-paragraph in relation to the substitute ship, or

(ii) if the company is a member of a tonnage tax group, all the qualifying companies in the group jointly make such an election.

22A(9) In sub-paragraph (8) a **"substitute ship"** means a qualifying ship–

(a) the tonnage of which is no less than that of the ship mentioned in sub-paragraph (1), and

(b) which was first operated by the company or, if the company is a member of a tonnage tax group, by any other member of the group more than three months before that date;

and for this purpose the tonnage of a ship is to be determined on the same basis as it is under paragraph 22B(3).

22A(10) An election under sub-paragraph (8) is made by notice to the Inland Revenue.

History – Para. 22A inserted by FA 2005, s. 93 and Sch. 7, para. 8, with effect from 1 July 2005 but subject to the transitional provisions at FA 2005, Sch. 7, para. 19–21.

Cross references – SI 2005/1480: financial year 2005 designated as one in relation to which para. 22A is not to have effect. SI 2006/333: financial year 2006 designated as one in relation to which para. 22A is not to have effect.

FLAGGING: MEANING OF TERMS USED IN PARAGRAPH 22A

22B(1) In paragraph 22A **"the reference date"** means 17th January 2004 or, if later,–

(a) in the case of a single company, the date of the end of the accounting period in which the company became (or becomes) a tonnage tax company;

(b) in the case of a member of a group, the date of the end of the accounting period in which the group became (or becomes) a tonnage tax group;

but where the members of a group had (or have) different accounting periods at the time the group became (or becomes) a tonnage tax group, paragraph (b) has effect by reference to the first of those accounting periods.

22B(2) For the purposes of sub-paragraph (2) of paragraph 22A a financial year is excepted if it is designated by an order made by the Treasury as a financial year in relation to which that paragraph is not to have effect (see further paragraph 22C(1) to (3)).

22B(3) For the purposes of paragraph 22A the percentage of a company's total tonnage which is Community-flagged is–

$$\frac{CFT}{TT} \times 100$$

where–

CFT is the aggregate tonnage of such of the relevant ships as are registered in one of the Member States' registers, and

TT is the aggregate tonnage of all the relevant ships.

22B(4) For the purposes of sub-paragraph (3) the ships which are the relevant ships are–

(a) if the company is a single company, the ships operated by the company, or

(b) if the company is a member of a tonnage tax group, the ships operated by each member of the group which is a qualifying company.

22B(5) Sub-paragraphs (3) and (4) are subject to any regulations made under paragraph 22C(4).

22B(6) A ship shall not be counted more than once in determining for the purposes of sub-paragraph (3) the aggregate tonnage of relevant ships.

22B(7) In this Schedule **"Member States' registers"** has the meaning given by the Annex to Commission communication C(2004) 43 – Community guidelines on State aid to maritime transport (as from time to time amended or replaced).

History – Para. 22B inserted by FA 2005, s. 93 and Sch. 7, para. 8, with effect from 1 July 2005 but subject to the transitional provisions at FA 2005, Sch. 7, para. 19–21.

Statutory instruments – SI 2005/1480: Tonnage Tax (Exception of Financial Year 2005) Order 2005.
SI 2006/333: Tonnage Tax (Exception of Financial Year 2006) Order 2006.
SI 2007/850: made under para. 22B(2).

FLAGGING: PROVISIONS SUPPLEMENTING PARAGRAPHS 22A AND 22B

22C(1) An order under paragraph 22B(2) designating a financial year shall be made if–

(a) the Treasury are satisfied, on the basis of the information available to them, that the percentage of the tonnage tax fleet which is Community-flagged has not decreased on average over a prescribed three year period, and

(b) the order is made before the beginning of that financial year.

22C(2) The Treasury may make provision by regulations for or in connection with–

(a) specifying the meaning, for the purposes of sub-paragraph (1)(a), of the percentage of the tonnage tax fleet which is Community-flagged;

(b) specifying the way in which an average is to be calculated for those purposes;

(c) requiring any tonnage tax company or tonnage tax group to provide prescribed information for the purposes of enabling the Treasury to determine whether the condition in sub-paragraph (1)(a) is met;

(d) imposing penalties in respect of a failure to comply with a provision of the regulations made by virtue of paragraph (c) (including, in prescribed cases or circumstances, the exclusion of a company or group from tonnage tax).

22C(3) Section 828(3) of the Taxes Act 1988 shall not apply in relation to an order under paragraph 22B(2).

22C(4) The Treasury may make provision by regulations as to the way in which the percentage of a company's total tonnage which is Community-flagged is to be calculated for the purposes of paragraph 22A.

22C(5) The provision that may be made by regulations under sub-paragraph (4) includes provision for or in connection with–

(a) determining the percentage of a company's total tonnage which is Community-flagged on average over a period;

(b) specifying the basis on which the tonnage of a ship is to be determined;

(c) treating ships which would, but for the regulations, be relevant ships for the purposes of paragraph 22B(3) as not being relevant ships for those purposes;

(d) including in the calculation set out in paragraph 22B(3) only such proportion of the tonnage of a relevant ship as may be prescribed.

22C(6) Regulations under this paragraph–

(a) may make different provision for different cases or circumstances, and

(b) may contain such supplementary, incidental, consequential and transitional provisions as appear to the Treasury to be necessary or expedient.

22C(7) In this paragraph **"prescribed"** means–

(a) specified in, or

(b) determined in accordance with,

regulations under this paragraph.

History – Para. 22C inserted by FA 2005, s. 93 and Sch. 7, para. 8, with effect from 1 July 2005 but subject to the transitional provisions at FA 2005, Sch. 7, para. 19–21.

Cross references – FA 2005, Sch. 7, para. 20: in relation to the financial year 2005, FA 2000, Sch. 22 has effect with the omission of para. 22C(1).

Statutory instruments – SI 2006/333: Tonnage Tax (Exception of Financial Year 2006) Order 2006.
SI 2007/850: made under para. 22C(1).

FLAGGING: RULE ON FIRST OPERATION OF QUALIFYING DREDGER OR TUG

22D(1) This paragraph applies if–

(a) a company begins to operate a ship which–

   (i) is a qualifying dredger or a tug,

   (ii) would, apart from this paragraph, be a qualifying ship, and

   (iii) has not previously been operated by the company or, if the company is a member of a group, by any member of the group, and

(b) on the date on which the company so begins to operate the ship, the ship is not registered in one of the Member States' registers.

22D(2) The ship shall not, at any time on or after that date, be regarded as–

(a) a qualifying ship operated by the company, or

(b) if immediately before that date the company is a member of a group, a qualifying ship operated by any company that is or becomes a member of the group.

22D(3) But sub-paragraph (2) does not apply if the ship has become registered in one of the Member States' registers by the end of the period of three months beginning with that date.

History – Para. 22D inserted by FA 2005, s. 93 and Sch. 7, para. 9, with effect from 1 July 2005 but subject to the transitional provisions at FA 2005, Sch. 7, para. 19–21.

Cross references – FA 2005, Sch. 7, para. 21: where a company (whether or not a member of a group) has operated a qualifying dredger or a tug at any time before 1 July 2005, the company is treated, for the purposes of para. 22D, as not having operated the qualifying dredger or tug before that date.

FLAGGING: RULE ON SUBSEQUENT RE-FLAGGING OF QUALIFYING DREDGER OR TUG

22E(1) This paragraph applies if–

(a) a qualifying ship operated by a company ceases to be registered in any of the Member States' registers, and

(b) the ship is a qualifying dredger or a tug.

22E(2) The ship shall not, at any time on or after the date on which it ceases to be so registered, be regarded as–

(a) a qualifying ship operated by the company, or

(b) if immediately before that date the company is a member of a group, a qualifying ship operated by any company that is or becomes a member of the group.

History – Para. 22E inserted by FA 2005, s. 93 and Sch. 7, para. 9, with effect from 1 July 2005 but subject to the transitional provisions at FA 2005, Sch. 7, para. 19–21.

FLAGGING: RESTRICTIONS WHERE SHIP CEASES TO BE QUALIFYING SHIP UNDER PARAGRAPH 22E

22F(1) This paragraph applies where a qualifying ship operated by a tonnage tax company ceases to be a qualifying ship by virtue of paragraph 22E.

22F(2) No notice may be given under section 130 of the Capital Allowances Act 2001 for the postponement of all or part of a relevant allowance to which–

(a) the company, or

(b) if immediately before the date on which the ship so ceases to be a qualifying ship ("the cessation date") the company is a member of a tonnage tax group, any company that is or becomes a member of the group, becomes entitled on or after the cessation date.

22F(3) In sub-paragraph (2) **"relevant allowance"** means an allowance in respect of–

(a) qualifying expenditure on the provision of the ship, or

(b) qualifying expenditure which–

(i) is incurred on the provision of the ship, and

(ii) is allocated to a single ship pool.

22F(4) No claim may be made under section 135 of that Act for deferment of all or part of a balancing charge–

(a) to which the company or, if immediately before the cessation date the company is a member of a tonnage tax group, any company that is or becomes a member of the group becomes liable, and

(b) which arises when there is a disposal event in respect of the ship on or after the cessation date.

22F(5) Relief in respect of a relevant loss shall not be given under section 37 of the Corporation Tax Act 2010 (losses: deduction from total profits of the same, or an earlier, accounting period).

22F(6) Group relief under Part 5 of that Act shall not be available in respect of a relevant loss.

22F(7) Accordingly, relief in respect of a relevant loss shall be given only under section 45 of that Act (carry forward of trade loss).

22F(8) In sub-paragraphs (5) to (7) **"relevant loss"** means a loss which is incurred in respect of the ship on or after the cessation date in the course of a trade carried on by–

(a) the company, or

(b) if immediately before the cessation date the company is a member of a tonnage tax group, any company that is or becomes a member of the group.

History – In para. 22F(5), the words "section 37 of the Corporation Tax Act 2010 (losses: deduction from total" substituted for the words "section 393A(1) of the Taxes Act 1988 (losses: set off against" by CTA 2010, s. 1177 and Sch. 1, para. 316(2)(a), with effect for corporation tax purposes for accounting periods ending on or after 1 April 2010, and for income tax and capital gains tax purposes for the tax year 2010–11 and subsequent tax years.

In para. 22F(6), the words "Part 5" substituted for the words "Chapter 4 of Part 10" by CTA 2010, s. 1177 and Sch. 1, para. 316(2)(b), with effect for corporation tax purposes for accounting periods ending on or after 1 April 2010, and for income tax and capital gains tax purposes for the tax year 2010–11 and subsequent tax years.

In para. 22F(7), the words "section 45 of that Act (carry forward of trade loss)" substituted for the words "section 393(1) of that Act (losses other than terminal losses)" by CTA 2010, s. 1177 and Sch. 1, para. 316(2)(c), with effect for corporation tax purposes for accounting periods ending on or after 1 April 2010, and for income tax and capital gains tax purposes for the tax year 2010–11 and subsequent tax years.

Para. 22F inserted by FA 2005, s. 93 and Sch. 7, para. 10, with effect from 1 July 2005 but subject to the transitional provisions at FA 2005, Sch. 7, para. 19–21.

Part IV – The Training Requirement

INTRODUCTION

23(1) It is a condition of entering tonnage tax or making a renewal election that–

(a) in the case of a single company, the company, or

(b) in the case of a group, the group,

meets certain minimum obligations in connection with the training of seafarers.

23(2) The provisions of this Part of this Schedule have effect for securing that result.

THE MINIMUM TRAINING OBLIGATION

24(1) The Secretary of State may make provision by regulations as to the minimum obligation of a tonnage tax company as regards the training of seafarers.

24(2) The regulations may–

(a) require the company to provide training for a minimum number of seafarers calculated on such basis as may be prescribed, and

(b) impose different requirements with respect to the training of officers and ratings.

Paragraph (b) is without prejudice to the general power to make different provision for different cases (see paragraph 36(2)(a)).

24(3) The regulations may impose such requirements as to the nationality and ordinary residence of trainees as appear to the Secretary of State to be appropriate.

24(4) References in this Part of this Schedule to "the minimum training obligation" are–

(a) in relation to a single company, to the minimum obligation of that company, and

(b) in relation to a group, to the minimum obligations of the qualifying companies in the group taken as a whole.

Statutory instruments – SI 2000/2129: Training Requirement Regulations 2000.

MEANING OF "TRAINING COMMITMENT"

25(1) References in this Part of this Schedule to a "training commitment" are to a statement by a company or group setting out how it proposes to meet the minimum training obligation.

25(2) A training commitment is not effective for the purposes of this Part of the Schedule unless approved by the Secretary of State.

25(3) Sub-paragraphs (1) and (2) are subject to–

paragraph 27(4) and (5) (power of Secretary of State to set training commitment), and

paragraph 28(2) (power of Secretary of State to adjust training commitment to take account of changed circumstances).

APPROVAL OF INITIAL TRAINING COMMITMENT

26(1) A company or group proposing to make a tonnage tax election must produce, and submit to the Secretary of State for approval, an initial training commitment.

26(2) If the Secretary of State is satisfied that the proposals are adequate to meet the minimum training obligation, he shall approve the initial training commitment and issue a certificate to that effect.

26(3) A tonnage tax election is ineffective unless such a certificate of approval is in force with respect to the training commitment of the company or group in respect of which the election is made.

ANNUAL TRAINING COMMITMENT

27(1) The Secretary of State may by regulations require a tonnage tax company or tonnage tax group–

(a) to produce a training commitment at such annual or other intervals as may be prescribed in respect of such period as may be prescribed, and

(b) to submit it to the Secretary of State for approval.

27(2) If the Secretary of State is satisfied that the proposals are adequate to meet the minimum training obligation, he shall approve the training commitment and issue a certificate to that effect.

27(3) It is an offence to fail to comply with any requirement imposed by regulations under sub-paragraph (1).

27(4) The Secretary of State may make provision by regulations enabling him–

(a) to set the training commitment for a company or group if, after such period as may be prescribed, no training commitment has been submitted to and approved by him; and

(b) on the application of the company or group concerned, made after consultation with any prescribed person involved in the training of seafarers, to vary a training commitment set by him.

27(5) A training commitment set by the Secretary of State has effect as if submitted by the company or group and approved by him.

Statutory instruments – SI 2000/2129: Training Requirement Regulations 2000.

SUPPLEMENTARY PROVISIONS ABOUT TRAINING COMMITMENTS

28(1) The Secretary of State may make provision by regulations–

(a) as to the form and contents of a training commitment;

(b) requiring an application for approval of a training commitment to be in such form and contain such information as may be prescribed;

(c) authorising the Secretary of State, when considering a training commitment, to consult any prescribed person involved in the training of seafarers;

(d) as to the procedure to be followed where the Secretary of State is minded not to approve a training commitment.

28(2) The Secretary of State may make provision by regulations–

(a) enabling him, on the application of the company or group concerned, to adjust a training commitment (to any extent) to take account of changed circumstances;

(b) requiring an application for adjustment to be in such form and contain such information as may be prescribed;

(c) authorising the Secretary of State, when considering an application for adjustment, to consult any prescribed person involved in the training of seafarers;

(d) as to the procedure to be followed where the Secretary of State is minded not to make the adjustment applied for.

28(3) The Secretary of State may by regulations make such provision as he thinks appropriate as to the effect in relation to a training commitment of a merger or other transaction resulting in a change of control of one or more companies.

Statutory instruments – SI 2000/2129: Training Requirement Regulations 2000.

PAYMENTS IN LIEU OF TRAINING

29(1) The Secretary of State may make provision by regulations–

(a) allowing a company or group, in such circumstances and to such extent as may be prescribed, to propose in its training commitment to meet the minimum training obligation by making payments in lieu of training; and

(b) requiring a company or group to make payments in lieu of training–

  (i) where its training commitment provides for such payments;

  (ii) where training is not provided in accordance with its training commitment.

29(2) The regulations shall provide for payments in lieu of training–

(a) to be calculated on such basis as may be prescribed,

(b) to be made to or for the benefit of any prescribed person involved in the training of seafarers, and

(c) to be made at such intervals and in such manner as may be prescribed.

29(3) The regulations may provide that if in any case there is a failure in relation to a company or group to comply with the requirements of this Part of this Schedule with respect to–

(a) the submission of training commitments, or

(b) the making of returns or provision of information,

the Secretary of State may determine to the best of his information and belief the amount of the payments in lieu of training to be made by the company or group.

29(4) The regulations may provide that a payment in lieu of training that has become due but is unpaid–

(a) is a debt due to the Secretary of State or any prescribed person involved in the training of seafarers, and

(b) carries interest at such rate as may be prescribed.

29(5) The regulations may provide for the costs or expenses of any legal or other proceedings for recovering the debt or interest to be recoverable, and to carry interest, in the same way as the debt.

Statutory instruments – SI 2000/2129 (as amended): Training Requirement Regulations 2000.
SI 2007/2482: partly made under para. 29.

MONITORING OF COMPLIANCE WITH TRAINING COMMITMENT

30(1) The Secretary of State may make provision by regulations–

(a) requiring a return to be made to the Secretary of State or any prescribed person involved in the training of seafarers, at such intervals as may be prescribed, of such information as may be prescribed relating to–

  (i) the training provided, and

  (ii) any payments in lieu of training made,

 by a tonnage tax company or tonnage tax group;

(b) authorising the Secretary of State to direct any person to provide such information as the Secretary of State may reasonably require for the purposes of ascertaining–

  (i) what the minimum training obligation of a company or group should be,

  (ii) whether the proposals in a training commitment are adequate to meet the minimum training obligation of a company or group, or

  (iii) whether a company or group has complied with its training commitment;

(c) enabling an audit to be carried on on behalf of the Secretary of State of the accounts or other records–

  (i) of a qualifying single company, or

  (ii) of the qualifying companies in a group,

for the purpose of checking that any return or information provided to the Secretary of State is correct.

30(2) A person commits an offence if without reasonable excuse–

(a) he fails to make a return that he is required to make by regulations under sub-paragraph (1)(a),

(b) having been directed under regulations under sub-paragraph (1)(b) to provide any information, he fails to comply with the direction, or

(c) he obstructs a person carrying out an audit under regulations under sub-paragraph (1)(c).

Statutory instruments – SI 2000/2129: Training Requirement Regulations 2000.

HIGHER RATE OF PAYMENT IN CASE OF FAILURE TO MEET TRAINING COMMITMENT

31(1) The Secretary of State may by regulations provide that–

(a) if a company fails to meet its training commitment in any period, the amount of any payments in lieu of training that fall to be made by the company in a subsequent period shall be at a higher rate; and

(b) if a group fails to meet its training commitment in any period, the amount of any payments in lieu of training that fall to be made by any member of the group in a subsequent period shall be at a higher rate.

31(2) The regulations may contain provision as to–

(a) the periods by reference to which it is to be determined whether a company or group has met its training commitment;

(b) the circumstances in which a company or group is to be treated as failing to meet its training commitment;

(c) the method of calculating the higher rate of payment; and

(d) any circumstances in which the higher rate is not to be payable despite the failure of a company or group to meet its training commitment.

31(3) The regulations may make provision having the effect that the rate of payments in lieu of training is progressively increased if a company or group fails to meet its training commitment in successive periods.

Statutory instruments – SI 2000/2129: Training Requirement Regulations 2000.
SI 2007/2482: partly made under para. 31.

CERTIFICATE OF NON-COMPLIANCE

32(1) The Secretary of State may by regulations make provision authorising the Secretary of State to issue a certificate of non-compliance in the following cases.

32(2) The regulations may authorise the issue of a certificate of non-compliance in respect of a single company if–

(a) the company fails to meet its training commitment for successive periods amounting to not less than two years, or

(b) the company, or any of its officers, commits an offence under this Schedule.

32(3) The regulations may authorise the issue of a certificate of non-compliance in respect of a group if–

(a) the group fails to meet its training commitment for successive periods amounting to not less than two years, or

(b) a member of the group, or an officer of a member, commits an offence under this Schedule.

32(4) If such regulations are made they shall provide that a certificate of non-compliance must be issued unless the Secretary of State is satisfied that there are good reasons why a certificate should not be issued.

32(5) No renewal election may be made in respect of a company or group in relation to which a certificate of non-compliance is in force.

Statutory instruments – SI 2000/2129: Training Requirement Regulations 2000.

CERTIFICATES OF NON-COMPLIANCE: SUPPLEMENTARY PROVISIONS

33(1) The Secretary of State may make provision by regulations–

(a) enabling a company or group in respect of which a certificate of non-compliance has been issued to apply to the Secretary of State to cancel the certificate;

(b) requiring any such application to be in such form and contain such information as may be prescribed;

(c) *authorising or requiring* the Secretary of State, when considering such an application, to consult any prescribed person involved in the training of seafarers;

(d) as to the procedure to be followed where the Secretary of State is minded not to cancel a certificate of non-compliance.

33(2) The Secretary of State may by regulations make such provision as he thinks appropriate as to the effect on a certificate of non-compliance of a merger or demerger relating to the company or group in respect of which the certificate is in force.

Statutory instruments – SI 2000/2129: Training Requirement Regulations 2000.

DISCLOSURE OF INFORMATION

34(1) No obligation as to secrecy or other restriction on the disclosure of information imposed by statute or otherwise prevents the disclosure of information–

(a) by the Secretary of State to the Inland Revenue for the purpose of assisting the Inland Revenue to discharge their functions under the Corporation Tax Acts so far as relating to matters arising under this Schedule, or

(b) by the Inland Revenue to the Secretary of State for the purpose of assisting the Secretary of State to discharge his functions under this Part of this Schedule.

34(2) No obligation as to secrecy or other restriction on the disclosure of information imposed by statute or otherwise prevents the disclosure of information–

(a) by the Secretary of State to any prescribed person involved in the training of seafarers, or

(b) by any such person to the Secretary of State,

for the purposes of assisting the Secretary of State to discharge his functions under this Part of this Schedule.

34(3) Information obtained by such disclosure as is mentioned in sub-paragraph (1) or (2) shall not be further disclosed except for the purposes of legal proceedings arising out of the functions referred to.

Statutory instruments – SI 2000/2129: Training Requirement Regulations 2000.

OFFENCES

35(1) It is an offence for a person to provide for any of the purposes of this Part of this Schedule information that he knows or has reasonable cause to believe is false in a material particular.

35(2) A person committing any offence under this Part of this Schedule, is liable–

(a) on summary conviction, to a fine not exceeding the statutory maximum, and

(b) on conviction on indictment, to a fine.

GENERAL PROVISIONS ABOUT REGULATIONS

36(1) Regulations under this Part of this Schedule shall be made by statutory instrument which shall be subject to annulment in pursuance of a resolution of the House of Commons.

36(2) Regulations under this Part of this Schedule–

(a) may make different provision for different cases, and

(b) may contain such supplementary, incidental and transitional provisions as appear to the Secretary of State to be necessary or expedient.

36(3) In this Part of this Schedule **"prescribed"** means prescribed by regulations made by the Secretary of State.

36(4) Regulations under this Part of this Schedule may make provision as to the obligations of a company in respect of any part of the period–

(a) beginning with 1st January 2000, and

(b) ending immediately before the first regulations under this Part come into force,

during which the company is, or is treated as having been, subject to tonnage tax.

This includes power to require payments in lieu of training to be made in respect of any such part of that period.

Statutory instruments – SI 2000/2129: Training Requirement Regulations 2000.
SI 2007/2482: partly made under para. 36.

Part V – Other Requirements

THE REQUIREMENT THAT NOT MORE THAN 75% OF FLEET TONNAGE IS CHARTERED IN

37(1) It is a requirement of entering or remaining within tonnage tax–

(a) in the case of a single company, that not more than 75% of the net tonnage of the qualifying ships operated by it is chartered in;

(b) in the case of a group, that not more than 75% of the aggregate net tonnage of the qualifying ships operated by the members of the group that are qualifying companies is chartered in.

37(2) For this purpose a ship is **"chartered in"**–

(a) in relation to a single company, if it is chartered to the company otherwise than on bareboat charter terms, or

(b) in relation to a group, if it is chartered otherwise than on bareboat charter terms to a qualifying member of the group by a person who is not a qualifying member of the group.

In paragraph (b) **"qualifying member of the group"** means a qualifying company that is a member of the group.

37(3) A ship shall not be counted more than once in determining for the purposes of sub-paragraph (1)(b) the aggregate net tonnage of the qualifying ships operated by the members of a group that are qualifying companies.

37(4) In the following provisions the requirement in this paragraph is referred to as "the 75% limit"–

paragraph 38 (election not effective if limit exceeded), and

paragraphs 39 and 40 (exclusion of company or group where limit exceeded).

37(5) References to the limit being exceeded in an accounting period are to its being exceeded on average over the period in question.

THE 75% LIMIT: ELECTION NOT EFFECTIVE IF LIMIT EXCEEDED

38(1) Where a tonnage tax election is made before the end of the initial period and the 75% limit is exceeded in the first relevant accounting period, the election is treated as never having been of any effect.

38(2) Where a tonnage tax election is made after the initial period, then–

(a) if the 75% limit is exceeded in the first relevant accounting period, the election does not have effect in relation to that period;

(b) if the 75% limit is exceeded in the first and second relevant accounting periods, the election does not have effect in relation to either of those periods; and

(c) if the 75% limit is exceeded in the first, second and third relevant periods, the election is treated as never having been of effect.

38(3) For the purposes of sub-paragraphs (1) and (2) the first, second and third relevant accounting period mean–

(a) in relation to a single company, the accounting period that, if the election had been effective, would have been the first, second or third accounting period of the company after its entry into tonnage tax;

(b) in relation to a group, the accounting period that, if the election had been effective, would have been the first, second or third accounting period of a member of the group that would have been a tonnage tax company.

38(4) Sub-paragraphs (1) and (2) do not apply to a renewal election.

THE 75% LIMIT: EXCLUSION OF COMPANY IF LIMIT EXCEEDED

39(1) If the 75% limit is exceeded in two or more consecutive accounting periods of a single company subject to tonnage tax, the Inland Revenue may give notice excluding the company from tonnage tax.

39(2) The effect of the notice is that the company's tonnage tax election ceases to be in force from such date as may be specified in the notice.

The specified date must not be earlier than the beginning of the accounting period of the company that follows the second consecutive accounting period of the company in which the limit is exceeded.

THE 75% LIMIT: EXCLUSION OF GROUP IF LIMIT EXCEEDED

40(1) If the 75% limit is exceeded in relation to a tonnage tax group in two or more consecutive accounting periods of any tonnage tax company that is a member of the group ("the relevant company"), the Inland Revenue may give notice excluding the group from tonnage tax.

40(2) The effect of the notice is that the group's tonnage tax election ceases to be in force from such date as may be specified in the notice.
The specified date must not be earlier than the beginning of the accounting period of the relevant company that follows the second consecutive accounting period of that company in which the limit is exceeded.

40(3) Notice under this paragraph need only be given to the relevant company.
This is subject to any arrangements under paragraph 120 (arrangements for dealing with group matters).

THE REQUIREMENT NOT TO ENTER INTO TAX AVOIDANCE ARRANGEMENTS

41(1) It is a condition of remaining within tonnage tax that a company is not a party to any transaction or arrangement that is an abuse of the tonnage tax regime.

41(2) A transaction or arrangement is such an abuse if in consequence of its being, or having been, entered into the provisions of this Schedule fall to be applied in a way that results (or would but for this paragraph result) in–

(a) a tax advantage being obtained for–

  (i) a company other than a tonnage tax company, or

  (ii) a tonnage tax company in respect of its non-tonnage tax activities,

or

(b) the amount of the tonnage tax profits of a tonnage tax company being artificially reduced.

41(3) In this paragraph **"tax advantage"** has the meaning given by section 840ZA of the Taxes Act 1988.

41(4) A lease is not to be taken as being an abuse of the tonnage tax regime by reason of the lessor obtaining capital allowances as a result of the lease being, or having been, entered into.
In this sub-paragraph **"lease"**, and **"lessor"** in relation to a lease, have the meaning given by paragraph 89(2).

History – Para. 41(3) substituted by ITA 2007, s. 1027 and Sch. 1, para. 395, with effect from 6 April 2007.
In para. 41(4), word "finance" omitted from expression "finance lease", and the second sentence substituted, by FA 2003, s. 169 and Sch. 32, para. 2(1) and the word repealed by FA 2003, Sch. 43, Pt. 3(11) with effect in relation to any lease (within the meaning given by para. 5 of Sch. 32 to that Act) entered into on or after 19 December 2002.
In para. 41(4), reference to CAA 2001, s. 219 substituted for former reference to CAA 1990, s. 82A by CAA 2001, s. 578 and Sch. 2, para. 108(1) with effect as respects allowances and charges falling to be made for chargeable periods ending, for income tax purposes, on or after 6 April 2001, and, for corporation tax purposes, on or after 1 April 2001.

TAX AVOIDANCE: EXCLUSION FROM TONNAGE TAX

42(1) If a tonnage tax company is a party to any such transaction or arrangement as is mentioned in paragraph 41(1), the Inland Revenue may–

(a) if it is a single company, give notice excluding it from tonnage tax;

(b) if it is a member of a group, give notice excluding the group from tonnage tax.

42(2) The effect of the notice in the case of a single company is that the company's tonnage tax election ceases to be in force from the beginning of the accounting period in which the transaction or arrangement was entered into.

42(3) The effect of such a notice in the case of a group is that the group's tonnage tax election ceases to be in force from such date as may be specified in the notice.
The specified date must not be earlier than the beginning of the earliest accounting period in which any member of the group entered into the transaction or arrangement in question.

42(4) The provisions of paragraphs 138 and 139 (exit charge: chargeable gains and balancing charges) apply where a company ceases to be a tonnage tax company by virtue of this paragraph.

42(5) Notice under this sub-paragraph (1)(b) need only be given to the company mentioned in the opening words of that sub-paragraph.
This is subject to any arrangements under paragraph 120 (arrangements for dealing with group matters).

APPEALS

43(1) An appeal may be made against a notice given by the Inland Revenue under–

paragraph 39 or 40 (exclusion of company or group from tonnage tax if 75% limit exceeded), or

paragraph 42 (exclusion from tonnage tax of company or group where tax avoidance arrangement entered into).

43(2) Notice of appeal must be given to the Inland Revenue within 30 days of the date of issue of the notice appealed against.

43(3) In the case of a notice under paragraph 40 or 42(1)(b) only one appeal may be brought, but it may be brought jointly by two or more members of the group concerned.

History – In para. 43(1) the words "may be made" substituted for the words "lies to the Special Commissioners" by SI 2009/56, art. 3(1) and Sch. 1, para. 294(2), operative from 1 April 2009, subject to transitional and saving provisions in SI 2009/56, Sch. 3.

THE REQUIREMENT TO PROVE COMPLIANCE WITH SAFETY ETC STANDARDS

43A(1) The Secretary of State may make provision by regulations for or in connection with requiring qualifying companies or qualifying groups to provide evidence of compliance with prescribed standards relating to–

(a) health and safety in connection with qualifying ships which are not registered in any of the Member States' registers;

(b) environmental performance of such ships;

(c) working conditions on such ships.

43A(2) The provision that may be made by regulations under this paragraph includes provision for or in connection with–

(a) requiring returns to be made at prescribed intervals;

(b) authorising the Secretary of State to require persons to provide prescribed information in prescribed cases or circumstances;

(c) enabling audits to be carried out on behalf of the Secretary of State;

(d) authorising the Secretary of State to issue certificates of non-compliance in prescribed cases or circumstances;

(e) the effect of such a certificate (including preventing the making of a renewal election when such a certificate is in force);

(f) enabling persons to apply to the Secretary of State for the cancellation of such a certificate;

(g) requiring or enabling the Secretary of State to revoke a tonnage tax election after a prescribed period of non-compliance;

(h) the making of appeals;

(i) authorising the disclosure of information between the Secretary of State and the Inland Revenue.

43A(3) Regulations under this paragraph may create criminal offences in respect of failures to comply with requirements imposed by the regulations.

43A(4) Regulations under this paragraph shall be made by statutory instrument which shall be subject to annulment in pursuance of a resolution of the House of Commons.

43A(5) Regulations under this paragraph–

(a) may make different provision for different cases, and

(b) may contain such supplementary, incidental and transitional provisions as appear to the Secretary of State to be necessary or expedient.

43A(6) In this paragraph **"prescribed"** means prescribed by regulations under this paragraph.

History – Para. 43A inserted by FA 2005, s. 93 and Sch. 7, para. 11, with effect from 7 April 2005.

Part VI – Relevant Shipping Profits

INTRODUCTION

44(1) For the purposes of this Schedule the relevant shipping profits of a tonnage tax company are–

(a) its relevant shipping income (as defined below), and

(b) so much of its chargeable gains as is effectively excluded from the charge to tax by the provisions of Part VIII of this Schedule.

44(2) The **"relevant shipping income"** of a tonnage tax company means–

(a) its income from tonnage tax activities (see paragraphs 45 to 48), and

(b) any income that is relevant shipping income under–

paragraph 49 (distributions of overseas shipping companies), or

paragraph 50 (certain interest etc.),

but subject to paragraph 51 (general exclusion of investment income).

TONNAGE TAX ACTIVITIES

45(1) References in this Schedule to the **"tonnage tax activities"** of a tonnage tax company are to–

(a) its core qualifying activities (see paragraph 46),

(b) its qualifying secondary activities to the extent that they do not exceed the permitted level (see paragraph 47), and

(c) its qualifying incidental activities (see paragraph 48).

45(2) Sub-paragraph (1) has effect subject to paragraph 51(2) (exclusion of activities giving rise to investment income).

CORE QUALIFYING ACTIVITIES

46(1) A tonnage tax company's **"core qualifying activities"** are–

(a) its activities in operating qualifying ships, and

(b) other ship-related activities that are a necessary and integral part of the business of operating its qualifying ships.

46(2) A company's activities in operating qualifying ships means the activities mentioned in paragraph 19(1)(a) to (d) by virtue of which the ship is a qualifying ship.

QUALIFYING SECONDARY ACTIVITIES

47(1) The Inland Revenue may make provision by regulations as to–

(a) the descriptions of activity that are to be regarded as qualifying secondary activities, and

(b) the permitted level in relation to any such activity or description of activity.

47(2) The regulations may set the permitted level or provide for its determination by reference to such factors as may be specified in the regulations.

QUALIFYING INCIDENTAL ACTIVITIES

48(1) A company's incidental activities means its ship-related activities that–

(a) are incidental to its core qualifying activities, and

(b) are not qualifying secondary activities.

48(2) If the turnover in an accounting period of the company from its incidental activities (taken together) does not exceed 0.25% of the company's turnover in that period from–

(a) its core qualifying activities, and

(b) its qualifying secondary activities to the extent that they do not exceed the permitted level,

the company's incidental activities in that period are qualifying incidental activities.

RELEVANT SHIPPING INCOME: DISTRIBUTIONS OF OVERSEAS SHIPPING COMPANIES

49(1) Income of a tonnage tax company consisting in a dividend or other distribution of an overseas company is relevant shipping income if the following conditions are met.

49(2) The conditions are–

(a) that the overseas company operates qualifying ships;

(b) that more than 50% of the voting power in the overseas company is held by a company resident in a member State, or that two or more companies each of which is resident in a member State hold in aggregate more than 50% of that voting power;

(c) that the 75% limit is not exceeded in relation to the overseas company in any accounting period in respect of which the distribution is paid;

(d) that all the income of the overseas company is such that, if it were a tonnage tax company, it would be relevant shipping income;

(e) that the distribution is paid entirely out of profits arising at a time when–

  (i) the conditions in paragraphs (a) to (d) were met, and

  (ii) the tonnage tax company was subject to tonnage tax; and

(f) the profits of the overseas company out of which the distribution is paid are subject to a tax on profits (in the country of residence of the company or elsewhere, or partly in that country and partly elsewhere).

49(3) For the purposes of sub-paragraph (2)(c) the "75% limit" is the requirement set out in paragraph 37 (requirement that not more than 75% of tonnage is chartered in) as it applies to a single company.

49(4) In this paragraph an **"overseas company"** means a company that is not resident in the United Kingdom.

RELEVANT SHIPPING INCOME: CERTAIN INTEREST ETC.

50(1) Income to which this paragraph applies is relevant shipping income only to the extent that it would apart from this Schedule fall to be taken into account as trading income from a trade consisting of the company's tonnage tax activities.

50(2) This paragraph applies to–

(a) anything giving rise to a credit that would fall to be brought into account for the purposes of Part 5 of the Corporation Tax Act 2009 (loan relationships); and

(b) [repealed by FA 2002, s. 141 and Sch. 40, Pt. 3(10);]

(c) any credit falling to be brought into account in accordance with Part 7 of the Corporation Tax Act 2009 (derivative contracts).

History – In para. 50(2)(a) the words "Part 5 of the Corporation Tax Act 2009" substituted for the words "Chapter II of Part IV of the Finance Act 1996" and in para. (c) the words "in accordance with Part 7 of the Corporation Tax Act 2009 (derivative contracts)" substituted for the words "under Schedule 26 to the Finance Act 2002 (derivative contracts)" by CTA 2009, s. 1322 and Sch. 1, para. 470(2), with effect for corporation tax purposes for accounting periods ending on or after 1 April 2009, and for income tax and capital gains tax purposes for the tax year 2009–10 and subsequent tax years.

In para. 50(2), the word "and" at the end of para. 50(2)(a) inserted by FA 2002, s. 79 and Sch. 23, para. 23(2) with effect in relation to accounting periods beginning on or after 1 October 2002.

Para. 50(2)(b) repealed by FA 2002, s. 141 and Sch. 40, Pt. 3(10) with effect in relation to accounting periods beginning on or after 1 October 2002.

Para. 50(2)(c) substituted by FA 2002, s. 83 and Sch. 27, para. 23(2) with effect in relation to accounting periods ending on or after 1 October 2002.

GENERAL EXCLUSION OF INVESTMENT INCOME

51(1) Income from investments is not relevant shipping income.

51(2) To the extent that an activity gives rise to income from investments it is not regarded as part of a company's tonnage tax activities.

51(3) For the purposes of this paragraph **"income from investments"** includes anything chargeable to tax under–

(a) Part 4 of the Corporation Tax Act 2009 (property income),

(b) section 299 of that Act (loan relationships: non-trading profits),

(c) [Omitted by SI 2013/2819, reg. 35(a).]

(d) Chapter 7 of Part 10 of that Act (annual payments not otherwise charged), or

(e) regulation 15 of the Unauthorised Unit Trusts (Tax) Regulations 2013.

51(4) [Effectively omitted by CTA 2009, s. 1322 and Sch. 1, para. 470(3).]

51(5) Sub-paragraph (1) above does not affect income that is relevant shipping income under–

paragraph 49 (distributions of overseas shipping companies), or

paragraph 50 (certain interest etc.).

History – Para. 51(3)(c) (and the "or" at the end of it) omitted by SI 2013/2819, reg. 35(a), with effect from 6 April 2014.

In para. 51(3)(d), the words "Part 10 of that Act" substituted for the words "that Part", by SI 2013/2819, reg. 35(b), with effect from 6 April 2014.

Para. 51(3)(e) (and the "or" before it) inserted by SI 2013/2819, reg. 35(c), with effect from 6 April 2014.

Para. 51(3) substituted for former para. 51(3) and (4) by CTA 2009, s. 1322 and Sch. 1, para. 470(3), with effect for corporation tax purposes for accounting periods ending on or after 1 April 2009, and for income tax and capital gains tax purposes for the tax year 2009–10 and subsequent tax years.

Part VII – The Ring Fence: General Provisions

ACCOUNTING PERIOD ENDS ON ENTRY OR EXIT

52 An accounting period ends (if it would not otherwise do so) when a company enters or leaves tonnage tax.

TONNAGE TAX TRADE

53(1) The tonnage tax activities of a tonnage tax company are treated for corporation tax purposes as a separate trade (the company's "tonnage tax trade") distinct from all other activities carried on by the company.

53(2) Sub-paragraph (1) shall not be read as requiring a company to be treated–

(a) as setting up and commencing a new trade on entry into tonnage tax, or

(b) as permanently ceasing to carry on a trade on leaving tonnage tax.

PROFITS OF CONTROLLED FOREIGN COMPANIES

54(1) A tonnage tax company is not subject to any liability at step 5 in section 371BC(1) of the Taxation (International and Other Provisions) Act 2010 ("TIOPA 2010") in any accounting period in respect of profits of a CFC if in that period distributions of the CFC made to the tonnage tax company would be relevant shipping income of the latter (see paragraph 49); and, accordingly, the tonnage tax company is not to be a chargeable company for the purposes of Part 9A of TIOPA 2010 in relation to the CFC's accounting period in question.

54(2) In relation to a CFC which–

(a) is a member of a tonnage tax group, and

(b) is a tonnage tax company by virtue of the group's tonnage tax election, or would be if it were within the charge to corporation tax,

the corporation tax assumptions within the meaning of Part 9A of TIOPA 2010 are to be taken to include the following assumption.

54(3) The CFC is to be assumed to be a single company that is a tonnage tax company.

54(4) Nothing in section 371SL(1) of TIOPA 2010 affects sub-paragraphs (2) and (3) above.

54(5) In this paragraph **"CFC"** has the same meaning as in Part 9A of TIOPA 2010.

History – In para. 54(1), the words "at step 5 in section 371BC(1) of the Taxation (International and Other Provisions) Act 2010 ("TIOPA 2010")" substituted for "under section 747 of the Taxes Act 1988" by FA 2012, s. 180 and Sch. 20, para. 19(2)(a) in relation to accounting periods of controlled foreign companies beginning on or after 1 January 2013.
In para. 54(1), the word "CFC" substituted for "controlled foreign company" (in both places) by FA 2012, s. 180 and Sch. 20, para. 19(2)(b) in relation to accounting periods of controlled foreign companies beginning on or after 1 January 2013.
In para. 54(1), at the end, the words "; and, accordingly, the tonnage tax company is not to be a chargeable company for the purposes of Part 9A of TIOPA 2010 in relation to the CFC's accounting period in question." inserted by FA 2012, s. 180 and Sch. 20, para. 19(2)(c) in relation to accounting periods of controlled foreign companies beginning on or after 1 January 2013.
Para. 54(2) substituted by FA 2012, s. 180 and Sch. 20, para. 19(3) in relation to accounting periods of controlled foreign companies beginning on or after 1 January 2013.
Para. 54(3) substituted by FA 2012, s. 180 and Sch. 20, para. 19(3) in relation to accounting periods of controlled foreign companies beginning on or after 1 January 2013.
Para. 54(4) substituted by FA 2012, s. 180 and Sch. 20, para. 19(3) in relation to accounting periods of controlled foreign companies beginning on or after 1 January 2013.
Para. 54(5) substituted by FA 2012, s. 180 and Sch. 20, para. 19(3) in relation to accounting periods of controlled foreign companies beginning on or after 1 January 2013.

Notes – ICTA 1988, Sch. 24, para. 20 repealed, subject to transitional provisions, by FA 2004.

GENERAL EXCLUSION OF RELIEFS, DEDUCTIONS AND SET-OFFS

55 No relief, deduction or set-off of any description is allowed against the amount of a company's tonnage tax profits.

EXCLUSION OF LOSS RELIEF

56(1) When a company enters tonnage tax, any losses that have accrued to it before entry and are attributable–

(a) to activities that under tonnage tax become part of the company's tonnage tax trade, or

(b) to a source of income that under tonnage tax becomes relevant shipping income,

are not available for loss relief in any accounting period beginning on or after the company's entry into tonnage tax.

56(2) Any apportionment necessary to determine the losses so attributable shall be made on a just and reasonable basis.

56(3) In sub-paragraph (1) **"loss relief"** includes any means by which a loss might be used to reduce the amount in respect of which that company, or any other company, is chargeable to tax.

EXCLUSION OF RELIEF OR SET-OFF AGAINST TAX LIABILITY

57(1) Any relief or set-off against a company's tax liability for an accounting period does not apply in relation to–

(a) so much of that tax liability as is attributable to the company's tonnage tax profits, or

(b) so much of that tax liability as is attributable to tonnage profits of a CFC apportioned to the company at step 3 in section 371BC(1) of the Taxation (International and Other Provisions) Act 2010.

57(2) Relief to which this paragraph applies includes, but is not limited to, any relief or set-off under–

(a) sections 2 and 6 of the Taxation (International and Other Provisions) Act 2010 (double taxation relief by agreement with territories outside the United Kingdom),

(aa) section 18(1)(b) and (2) of that Act (unilateral relief from double taxation), or.

(b) regulations under section 32 of the Finance Act 1998 (unrelieved surplus advance corporation tax).

57(3) Sub-paragraph (1)(b) applies whether or not the company to which the profits are apportioned is subject to tonnage tax.

57(4) For the purposes of sub-paragraph (1)(b)–

(a) **"tonnage profits"** means so much of the CFC's chargeable profits for its accounting period in question as, applying the corporation tax assumptions, are calculated in accordance with paragraph 4 of this Schedule; and

(b) so much of those chargeable profits as are tonnage profits shall be treated as apportioned at step 3 in section 371BC(1) of the Taxation (International and Other Provisions) Act 2010 in the same proportions as those profits (taken generally) are apportioned.

57(4A) In sub-paragraphs (1)(b) and (4) terms defined in Part 9A of the Taxation (International and Other Provisions) Act 2010 have the same meaning as in that Part.

57(5) For the purposes of any such regulations as are mentioned in sub-paragraph (2)(b), a company's tonnage tax profits shall be left out of account in determining the company's profits charged to corporation tax.

This does not affect the computation under those regulations of shadow ACT on distributions made by a tonnage tax company, whether paid out of tonnage tax profits or other profits.

57(6) This paragraph does not affect–

(a) any reduction under Chapter 3A of Part 8 of CTA 2010 (marginal relief for companies with small ring fence profits),

(b) any set off under section 967 or 968 of the Corporation Tax Act 2010 (set off for income tax borne by deduction).

History – In para. 57(1)(b), the words "CFC apportioned to the company at step 3 in section 371BC(1) of the Taxation (International and Other Provisions) Act 2010." substituted for the words from "controlled" to the end by FA 2012, s. 180 and Sch. 20, para. 20(2) in relation to accounting periods of controlled foreign companies beginning on or after 1 January 2013.

Para. 57(2)(a) and (aa) substituted for former para. 57(2)(a) by TIOPA 2010, s. 374 and Sch. 8, para. 56(2), with effect for corporation tax purposes for accounting periods ending on or after 1 April 2010, for income tax and capital gains tax purposes for the tax year 2010–11 and subsequent tax years, and for petroleum revenue tax purposes for chargeable periods beginning on or after 1 July 2010.

Para. 57(4) and 57(4A) substituted for former para. 57(4) by FA 2012, s. 180 and Sch. 20, para. 20(3) in relation to accounting periods of controlled foreign companies beginning on or after 1 January 2013.

Para. 57(6)(a) substituted by FA 2014, s. 7 and Sch. 1, para. 7, with effect for the financial year 2015 and subsequent financial years. In former para. 57(6)(a), the words "section 19, 20 or 21 of the Corporation Tax Act 2010 (marginal relief for companies with small profits)" substituted for the words "section 13(2) of the Taxes Act 1988 (marginal small companies' relief)" by CTA 2010, s. 1177 and Sch. 1, para. 316(3)(a), with effect for corporation tax purposes for accounting periods ending on or after 1 April 2010, and for income tax and capital gains tax purposes for the tax year 2010–11 and subsequent tax years.

In para. 57(6)(b), the words "section 967 or 968 of the Corporation Tax Act 2010" substituted for the words "section 7(2) or 11(3) of the Taxes Act 1988" by CTA 2010, s. 1177 and Sch. 1, para. 316(3)(b), with effect for corporation tax purposes for accounting periods ending on or after 1 April 2010, and for income tax and capital gains tax purposes for the tax year 2010–11 and subsequent tax years.

TRANSACTIONS NOT AT ARM'S LENGTH: BETWEEN TONNAGE TAX COMPANY AND ANOTHER PERSON

58(1) In relation to provision made or imposed as between a tonnage tax company and another person by a transaction or series of transactions that–

(a) falls in relation to the tonnage tax company to be regarded as made or imposed in the course of, or with respect to, its tonnage tax trade, and

(b) does not fall in relation to the other person to be regarded as made or imposed in the course of, or with respect to, a tonnage tax trade carried on by that person,

Part 4 of the Taxation (International and Other Provisions) Act 2010 (transactions not at arm's length) has effect with the omission of sections 174 to 184, 187 to 189 and 191 to 196 (elimination of double counting etc).

58(2) Expressions used in Part 4 of the Taxation (International and Other Provisions) Act 2010 have the same meaning in this paragraph.

58(3) Nothing in this paragraph affects the computation of a company's tonnage tax profits.

History – In para. 58(1), the words "Part 4 of the Taxation (International and Other Provisions) Act 2010 (transactions not at arm's length) has effect with the omission of sections 174 to 184, 187 to 189 and 191 to 196 (elimination of double counting etc)." substituted for the words "Schedule 28AA to the Taxes Act 1988 (transactions not at arm's length) has effect with the omission of paragraphs 6 to 7A (elimination of double counting etc)." by TIOPA 2010, s. 374 and Sch. 8, para. 119(2), with effect for corporation tax purposes for accounting periods ending on or after 1 April 2010, for income tax and capital gains tax purposes for the tax year 2010–11 and subsequent tax years, and for petroleum revenue tax purposes for chargeable periods beginning on or after 1 July 2010.
In para. 58(1), the words following para. 58(1)(b) substituted by FA 2004, s. 30 and Sch. 5, para. 12 with effect in relation to chargeable periods beginning on or after 1 April 2004.
In para. 58(2), the words "Part 4 of the Taxation (International and Other Provisions) Act 2010" substituted for the words "Schedule 28AA" by TIOPA 2010, s. 374 and Sch. 8, para. 119(3), with effect for corporation tax purposes for accounting periods ending on or after 1 April 2010, for income tax and capital gains tax purposes for the tax year 2010–11 and subsequent tax years, and for petroleum revenue tax purposes for chargeable periods beginning on or after 1 July 2010.

TRANSACTIONS NOT AT ARM'S LENGTH: BETWEEN TONNAGE TAX TRADE AND OTHER ACTIVITIES OF SAME COMPANY

59(1) Part 4 of the Taxation (International and Other Provisions) Act 2010 (transactions not at arm's length) applies to provision made or imposed as between a company's tonnage tax trade and other activities carried on by it as if–

(a) that trade and those activities were carried on by two different persons,

(b) the provision were made or imposed between those persons by means of a transaction, and

(c) the two persons were both controlled by the same person at the time of the making or imposition of the provision.

59(2) As applied by sub-paragraph (1), Part 4 of the Taxation (International and Other Provisions) Act 2010 has effect with the omission of sections 174 to 184, 187 to 189 and 191 to 196 (elimination of double counting etc).

59(3) Expressions used in Part 4 of the Taxation (International and Other Provisions) Act 2010 have the same meaning in this paragraph.

59(4) Nothing in this paragraph affects the computation of a company's tonnage tax profits.

History – In para. 59(1), the words "Part 4 of the Taxation (International and Other Provisions) Act 2010" substituted for the words "Schedule 28AA of the Taxes Act 1988" by TIOPA 2010, s. 374 and Sch. 8, para. 119(4), with effect for corporation tax purposes for accounting periods ending on or after 1 April 2010, for income tax and capital gains tax purposes for the tax year 2010–11 and subsequent tax years, and for petroleum revenue tax purposes for chargeable periods beginning on or after 1 July 2010.
Para. 59(2) substituted by TIOPA 2010, s. 374 and Sch. 8, para. 119(5), with effect for corporation tax purposes for accounting periods ending on or after 1 April 2010, for income tax and capital gains tax purposes for the tax year 2010–11 and subsequent tax years, and for petroleum revenue tax purposes for chargeable periods beginning on or after 1 July 2010.
Former para. 59(2) substituted by FA 2004, s. 30 and Sch. 5, para. 13 with effect in relation to chargeable periods beginning on or after 1 April 2004.
In para. 59(3), the words "Part 4 of the Taxation (International and Other Provisions) Act 2010" substituted for the words "Schedule 28AA" by TIOPA 2010, s. 374 and Sch. 8, para. 119(6), with effect for corporation tax purposes for accounting periods ending on or after 1 April 2010, for income tax and capital gains tax purposes for the tax year 2010–11 and subsequent tax years, and for petroleum revenue tax purposes for chargeable periods beginning on or after 1 July 2010.

TRANSACTIONS NOT AT ARM'S LENGTH: DUTY TO GIVE NOTICE

60(1) Not more than 90 days after–

(a) the making of an election under this Schedule, or the occurrence of any other event, as a result of which a company enters, or is taken to have entered, tonnage tax, or

(b) the making of an election under this Schedule as a result of which a company will become a tonnage tax company at a later date,

the company shall give notice under this paragraph to any person whose tax liability may be affected by paragraph 58 (transactions not at arm's length).

60(2) The notice must state–

(a) that the company has become a tonnage tax company, or

(b) that an election has been made under this Schedule as a result of which the company will become a tonnage tax company,

and inform the person to whom it is given of the possible application of the provisions of Part 4 of the Taxation (International and Other Provisions) Act 2010 in relation to transactions between the company and that person.

History – In para. 60(2), the words "Part 4 of the Taxation (International and Other Provisions) Act 2010" substituted for the words "Schedule 28AA" by TIOPA 2010, s. 374 and Sch. 8, para. 119(7), with effect for corporation tax purposes for accounting periods ending on or after 1 April 2010, for income tax and capital gains tax purposes for the tax year 2010–11 and subsequent tax years, and for petroleum revenue tax purposes for chargeable periods beginning on or after 1 July 2010.

TREATMENT OF FINANCE COSTS: SINGLE COMPANY

61(1) This paragraph applies to a tonnage tax company which is a single company carrying on tonnage tax activities and other activities.

61(2) An adjustment shall be made if it appears, in relation to an accounting period of the company, that the company's deductible finance costs outside the ring fence exceed a fair proportion of the company's total finance costs.

61(3) The company's **"deductible finance costs outside the ring fence"** means the total of the amounts that may be brought into account in respect of finance costs in calculating for the purposes of corporation tax the company's profits other than relevant shipping profits.

61(4) A company's **"total finance costs"** means so much of the company's finance costs as could, if there were no tonnage tax election, be brought into account in calculating the company's profits for the purposes of corporation tax.

61(5) What proportion of the company's total finance costs should be deductible outside the ring fence shall be determined on a just and reasonable basis by reference to the extent to which the funding in relation to which the costs are incurred is applied in such a way that any profits arising, directly or indirectly, would be relevant shipping profits.

61(6) Where an adjustment falls to be made under this paragraph, an amount equal to the excess referred to in sub-paragraph (2) shall be brought into account as if it were a non-trading credit falling for the purposes of Part 5 of the Corporation Tax Act 2009 (loan relationships) to be brought into account in respect of a loan relationship of the company in respect of non-tonnage tax activities.

History – In para. 61(6) the words "Part 5 of the Corporation Tax Act 2009" substituted for the words "Chapter II of Part IV of the Finance Act 1996" by CTA 2009, s. 1322 and Sch. 1, para. 470(4), with effect for corporation tax purposes for accounting periods ending on or after 1 April 2009, and for income tax and capital gains tax purposes for the tax year 2009–10 and subsequent tax years.

TREATMENT OF FINANCE COSTS: GROUP COMPANY

62(1) This paragraph applies to a tonnage tax company which is a member of a tonnage tax group where the activities carried on by the members of the group include activities other than tonnage tax activities.

62(2) An adjustment shall be made if it appears, in relation to an accounting period of the company, that the group's deductible finance costs outside the ring fence exceed a fair proportion of the total finance costs of the group.

62(3) A group's **"deductible finance costs outside the ring fence"** means so much of the group's finance costs as may be brought into account in calculating for the purposes of corporation tax–

(a) in the case of a group member that is a tonnage tax company, the company's profits other than relevant shipping profits, and

(b) in the case of a group member that is not a tonnage tax company, the company's profits.

62(4) A group's **"total finance costs"** means so much of the group's finance costs as could, if there were no tonnage tax election, be brought into account in calculating for the purposes of corporation tax the profits of any member of the group.

62(5) What proportion of the group's total finance costs should be deductible outside the ring fence shall be determined on a just and reasonable basis by reference to the extent to which the funding in relation to which the costs are incurred is applied in such a way that any profits arising, directly or indirectly, would be relevant shipping profits.

62(6) Where an adjustment falls to be made under this paragraph, an amount equal to the relevant proportion of the excess referred to in sub-paragraph (2) shall be brought into account as if it were a non-trading credit falling for the purposes of "Part 5 of the Corporation Tax Act 2009" (loan relationships) to be brought into account in respect of a loan relationship of the company in respect of non-tonnage tax activities.

For this purpose **"the relevant proportion"** is the proportion that the company's tonnage tax profits bear to the tonnage tax profits of all the members of the group.

History – In para. 62(6) the words "Part 5 of the Corporation Tax Act 2009" substituted for the words "Chapter II of Part IV of the Finance Act 1996" by CTA 2009, s. 1322 and Sch. 1, para. 470(5), with effect for corporation tax purposes for accounting periods ending on or after 1 April 2009, and for income tax and capital gains tax purposes for the tax year 2009–10 and subsequent tax years.

MEANING OF "FINANCE COSTS"

63(1) For the purposes of paragraphs 61 and 62 **"finance costs"** means the costs of debt finance.

63(2) In calculating the costs of debt finance, the matters to be taken into account include–

(a) any costs giving rise to a trading or non-trading debit under Part 5 of the Corporation Tax Act 2009 (loan relationships);

(b) any credit or debit falling to be brought into account in accordance with Part 7 of the Corporation Tax Act 2009 (derivative contracts), in relation to debt finance;

(c) any exchange gain or loss within the meaning given by section 475 of the Corporation Tax Act 2009 in relation to debt finance;

(d) the finance cost–

(i) implicit in a payment under a finance lease, or

(ii) payable on debt factoring or any similar transaction;

(dd) where the tonnage tax company is the lessee under a long funding operating lease, the amount deductible (or the total amount that could, if there were no tonnage tax election, be deductible) in respect of payments under the lease in computing the profits of the lessee for the purposes of corporation tax (after first making against any such amount any reductions falling to be made by virtue of section 379 of the Corporation Tax Act 2010); and

(e) any other costs arising from what would be considered on normal accounting principles to be a financing transaction.

63(3) No adjustment shall be made under paragraph 61 or 62 if, in calculating for a period the company's, or as the case may be, the group's deductible finance costs outside the ring fence, the amount taken into account in respect of costs and losses is exceeded by the amount taken into account in respect of profits and gains.

63(4) In this paragraph **"long funding operating lease"** means a long funding operating lease for the purposes of Part 2 of the Capital Allowances Act (see section 70YI(1) of that Act).

History – In para. 63(2)(a) the words "Part 5 of the Corporation Tax Act 2009" substituted for the words "Chapter II of Part IV of the Finance Act 1996"; in para. (b) the words "in accordance with Part 7 of the Corporation Tax Act 2009 (derivative contracts)" substituted for the words "under Schedule 26 to the Finance Act 2002 (derivative contracts)"; and in para. (c) the words "section 475 of the Corporation Tax Act 2009" substituted for the words "section 103(1A) of the Finance Act 1996" by CTA 2009, s. 1322 and Sch. 1, para. 470(6), with effect for corporation tax purposes for accounting periods ending on or after 1 April 2009 and for income tax and capital gains tax purposes for the tax year 2009–10 and subsequent tax years.

Para. 63(2)(b) substituted by FA 2002, s. 83 and Sch. 27, para. 23(3) with effect in relation to accounting periods beginning on or after 1 October 2002.

In para. 63(2)(c), the words "within the meaning given by section 103(1A) of the Finance Act 1996" substituted for the words "within the meaning of Chapter II of Part II of the Finance Act 1993" by FA 2002, s. 79 and Sch. 23, para. 23(3) with effect in relation to accounting periods beginning on or after 1 October 2002.

In para. 63(2)(dd), the words "section 379 of the Corporation Tax Act 2010" substituted for the words "section 502K of the Taxes Act 1988" by CTA 2010, s. 1177 and Sch. 1, para. 316(4), with effect for corporation tax purposes for accounting periods ending on or after 1 April 2010, and for income tax and capital gains tax purposes for the tax year 2010–11 and subsequent tax years.

Para. 63(2)(dd) substituted for the word "and" at the end of para. 63(2)(d) by FA 2006, s. 81 and Sch. 9, para. 9(2) with effect in relation to payments due on or after 1 April 2006.

Para. 63(4) inserted by FA 2006, s. 81 and Sch. 9, para. 9(3) with effect in relation to payments due on or after 1 April 2006

Part VIII – Chargeable Gains and Allowable Losses on Tonnage Tax Assets

CHARGEABLE GAINS: TONNAGE TAX ASSETS

64(1) In this Part of this Schedule a **"tonnage tax asset"** means an asset that is used wholly and exclusively for the purposes of the tonnage tax activities of a tonnage tax company.

64(2) Where for one or more continuous periods of at least a year part of an asset has been used wholly and exclusively for the purposes of the tonnage tax activities of a tonnage tax company and part has not, this Part of this Schedule shall apply as if the part so used were a separate asset.

64(3) Where sub-paragraph (2) applies, any necessary apportionment of the gain or loss on the whole asset shall be made on a just and reasonable basis.

CHARGEABLE GAINS: DISPOSAL OF TONNAGE TAX ASSET

65(1) When an asset is disposed of that is or has been a tonnage tax asset–

(a) any gain or loss on the disposal is a chargeable gain or allowable loss only to the extent (if any) to which it is referable to periods during which the asset was not a tonnage tax asset, and

(b) any such chargeable gain or allowable loss on a disposal by a tonnage tax company is treated as arising otherwise than in the course of the company's tonnage tax trade.

65(2) For the purposes of sub-paragraph (1) the amount of the gain or loss on a disposal means what would be the amount of the chargeable gain or allowable loss apart from this paragraph.

65(3) The proportion of that gain or loss referable to periods during which the asset was not a tonnage tax asset is given by:

$$\frac{P - PTTA}{P}$$

where:

P is the total length of the period since the asset was created or, if later, the last third-party disposal, and

PTTA is the length of the period (or the aggregate length of the periods) since–

(a) the asset was created, or

(b) if later, the last third-party disposal,

during which the asset was a tonnage tax asset.

65(4) In sub-paragraph (3) a **"third-party disposal"** means a disposal (or deemed disposal) that is not treated as one on which neither a gain nor a loss accrues to the person making the disposal.

CHARGEABLE GAINS: LOSSES BROUGHT FORWARD

66 A tonnage tax election does not affect the deduction under section 8(1) of the Taxation of Chargeable Gains Act 1992 (corporation tax: computation of chargeable gains) of allowable losses that accrued to a company before it became a tonnage tax company.

CHARGEABLE GAINS: ROLL-OVER RELIEF FOR BUSINESS ASSETS

67(1) Sections 152 and 153 of the Taxation of Chargeable Gains Act 1992 (roll-over relief for business assets) do not apply if or to the extent that the new assets are tonnage tax assets.

67(2) Where relief under either of those sections is, or has been, claimed in respect of the disposal or deemed sale of an asset ("Asset No.1") and the acquisition of another asset ("Asset No.2") that subsequently becomes a tonnage tax asset, the claimant is not (or, as the case may be, shall cease to be) entitled under that section to–

(a) a reduction of the consideration for the disposal of Asset No.1, or, as the case may be, the deemed sale consideration and

(b) a corresponding reduction of the expenditure for the acquisition of Asset No.2,

but so much of the chargeable gain arising on the disposal or deemed sale of Asset No.1 as is equal to the amount of the reduction that would have been made is treated as not accruing until Asset No.2 is disposed of.

67(3) Any chargeable gain accruing as a result of the rules in sub-paragraph (1) or (2) is treated as arising otherwise than in the course of the company's tonnage tax trade.

History – In para. 67(2), the words "or deemed sale" in two places, and in para. 67(2)(a), the words "or, as the case may be, the deemed sale consideration" inserted by FA 2002, s. 43 and Sch. 7, para. 10 with effect in relation to a case where a company is treated by virtue of TCGA 1992, s. 179(3) as having sold and immediately reacquired an asset, where the company ceasing to be a member of the group in question happens on or after 1 April 2002; and in relation to a case where a company is so treated by virtue of TCGA 1992, s. 179(6) where the relevant time is on or after that date.

Part IX – The Ring Fence: Capital Allowances: General

INTRODUCTION

68(1) This Part of this Schedule makes provision about capital allowances where a company enters, leaves or is subject to tonnage tax.

68(2) The general scheme of this Part of this Schedule is that–

(a) entry of a company into tonnage tax does not of itself give rise to any balancing charges or balancing allowances,

(b) a company subject to tonnage tax is not entitled to capital allowances in respect of expenditure incurred for the purposes of its tonnage tax trade, whether before or after its entry into tonnage tax, and

(c) on leaving tonnage tax–

(i) a company is treated as having incurred qualifying expenditure on its tonnage tax plant and machinery assets of an amount equal to the lower of cost and market value, where it leaves tonnage tax on expiry of an election or on the taking effect of a withdrawal notice, but

(ii) otherwise, a company is put broadly in the position it would have been in if it had never been subject to tonnage tax.

68(3) A company's tonnage tax trade is not a qualifying activity for the purposes of determining the company's entitlement to capital allowances.

History – Para. 68(2)(c) substituted by FA 2005, s. 93 and Sch. 7, para. 12, with effect from 7 April 2005.

ENTRY: PLANT AND MACHINERY: ASSETS TO BE USED WHOLLY FOR TONNAGE TAX TRADE

69(1) On a company's entry into tonnage tax any unrelieved qualifying expenditure attributable to plant or machinery that is to be used wholly for the purposes of the company's tonnage tax trade is taken to a single pool (the company's **"tonnage tax pool"**).

69(2) In this paragraph **"unrelieved qualifying expenditure"** has the same meaning as in Chapter 5 of Part 2 of the Capital Allowances Act 2001.

69(3) The amount of unrelieved qualifying expenditure attributable to plant or machinery in a class pool, or the main pool, is the proportion of the whole given by:

$$\frac{AV}{PV}$$

where:

AV is the aggregate market value of the assets concerned immediately before entry into tonnage tax, and

PV is the aggregate market value at that time of all the assets in the pool.

69(4) References in this paragraph to unrelieved qualifying expenditure include qualifying expenditure to the extent to which it is unrelieved by virtue of notice having been given under section 130 of the Capital Allowances Act 2001 (notice postponing first-year or writing-down allowance).

No allowance may be claimed in respect of any such expenditure taken to the company's tonnage tax pool.

History – Para. 69(2) substituted by CAA 2001, s. 578 and Sch. 2, para. 108(2), and in para. 69(4) words "section 130 … writing-down allowance" substituted for former para. 69(4)(a) and (b) by CAA 2001, s. 578 and Sch. 2, para. 108(3) with effect as respects allowances and charges falling to be made for chargeable periods ending, for income tax purposes, on or after 6 April 2001, and, for corporation tax purposes, on or after 1 April 2001.

ENTRY: PLANT AND MACHINERY: ASSETS TO BE USED PARTLY FOR TONNAGE TAX TRADE

70(1) This paragraph applies where, on a company's entry into tonnage tax, plant and machinery is to be used partly for the purposes of the company's tonnage tax trade and partly for the purposes of a qualifying activity carried on by the company.

70(2) Sections 61(1)(e), 206(3) and 207 of the Capital Allowances Act 2001 (effect of use partly for qualifying activity and partly for other purposes) apply as follows–

(a) references to a qualifying activity shall be read as not including references to the tonnage tax trade, and

(b) references to purposes other than those of a qualifying activity shall be read as including references to the purposes of the tonnage tax trade.

History – Para. 70(2) substituted by CAA 2001, s. 578 and Sch. 2, para. 108(4) with effect as respect allowances and changes falling to be made for chargeable periods ending, for income tax purposes, on or after 6 April 2001, and for corporation tax purposes, on or after 1 April 2001.

ENTRY: SHIPS ACQUIRED AND DISPOSED OF WITHIN TWELVE MONTHS

71(1) This paragraph applies if a company–

(a) acquires a qualifying ship within the period of six months before the company enters tonnage tax, and

(b) disposes of the ship before the end of the period of twelve months beginning with the day on which the ship was acquired.

71(2) The aggregate amount of the capital allowances to which the company is entitled for the period or periods before entry into tonnage tax in respect of its expenditure on acquiring the ship is limited to the amount by which that expenditure exceeds the market value of the ship on the company's entry into tonnage tax.

ENTRY: DEFERRED BALANCING CHARGE ON DISPOSAL OF SHIP

72(1) This paragraph applies where deferment of a balancing charge has been claimed under sections 135 to 156 of the Capital Allowances Act 2001 (balancing charge on disposal of ship to be deferred and set against new expenditure incurred within six years) by a company that subsequently enters tonnage tax.

72(2) Expenditure on new shipping incurred by a company subject to tonnage tax shall not be taken into account for the purposes of those sections unless the company that incurred the balancing charge–

(a) was a qualifying company for the purposes of this Schedule at the time the balancing charge arose, or

(b) would have been such a company had this Schedule been in force at that time.

72(3) Subject to sub-paragraph (2)–

(a) the company's entry into tonnage tax does not affect the operation of those sections, and

(b) the expenditure on new shipping that is to be taken into account for the purposes of those sections shall be determined as if the company was not subject to tonnage tax.

History – In para. 72(1), reference to CAA 2001, s. 135–156 substituted for former reference to CAA 1990, s. 33A–33F, by CAA 2001, s. 578 and Sch. 2, para. 108(5) with effect as respects allowances and charges falling to be made for chargeable periods ending, for income tax purposes, on or after 6 April 2001, and, for corporation tax purposes, on or after 1 April 2001.

DURING: PLANT AND MACHINERY: NEW EXPENDITURE PARTLY FOR TONNAGE TAX PURPOSES

73(1) This paragraph applies where a company subject to tonnage tax incurs expenditure on the provision of plant or machinery partly for the purposes of its tonnage tax trade and partly for the purposes of a qualifying activity.

73(2) Sections 206(1), (2) and (4) and 207 of the Capital Allowances Act 2001 (operation of single asset pool for mixed use assets) apply as follows–

(a) references to a qualifying activity shall be read as not including references to the tonnage tax trade, and

(b) references to purposes other than those of a qualifying activity shall be read as including references to the purposes of the tonnage tax trade.

History – Para. 73(2) substituted by CAA 2001, s. 578 and Sch. 2, para. 108(6), with effect as respects allowances and charges falling to be made for chargeable periods ending, for income tax purposes, on or after 6 April 2001, and, for corporation tax purposes, on or after 1 April 2001.

Cross references – CAA 2001, Sch. 3, para. 8: changes in the law effected by CAA 2001– limited right to elect, in respect of things done, etc., before 1 or 6 April 2001, for pre-consolidation law to apply for first chargeable period ending thereafter.

DURING: PLANT AND MACHINERY: ASSET BEGINNING TO BE USED FOR TONNAGE TAX TRADE

74 A company's tonnage tax pool is not increased by reason of an asset beginning to be used for the purposes of the company's tonnage tax trade after the company's entry into tonnage tax.

DURING: PLANT AND MACHINERY: CHANGE OF USE OF TONNAGE TAX ASSET

75(1) This paragraph applies where, at a time when a company is subject to tonnage tax, plant or machinery used for the purposes of the company's tonnage tax trade begins to be used wholly or partly for purposes other than those of that trade.

75(2) If the asset was acquired before entry into tonnage tax, section 61(1)(e) of the Capital Allowances Act 2001 applies (disposal event if plant machinery begins to be used wholly or partly for purposes other than those of the qualifying activity), but reading the reference in that provision to the qualifying activity as a reference to the tonnage tax trade.

75(3) If the asset was acquired after entry into tonnage tax and begins to be used wholly or partly for the purposes of a qualifying activity carried on by the company, section 13 of the Capital Allowances Act 2001 (use for qualifying activity of plant or machinery provided for other purposes) applies as follows–

(a) references to purposes which were not those of any qualifying activity shall be read as including references to the purposes of the tonnage tax trade, and

(b) references to the qualifying activity carried on by him shall be read as not including references to the tonnage tax trade.

History – Para. 75(2), (3) substituted by CAA 2001, s. 578 and Sch. 2, para. 108(7) with effect as respects allowances and charges falling to be made for chargeable periods ending, for income tax purposes, on or after 6 April 2001, and, for corporation tax purposes, on or after 1 April 2001.:

Cross references – CAA 2001, Sch. 3, para. 8: changes in the law effected by CAA 2001– limited right to elect, in respect of things done, etc., before 1 or 6 April 2001, for pre-consolidation law to apply for first chargeable period ending thereafter.

DURING: PLANT AND MACHINERY: CHANGE OF USE OF NON-TONNAGE TAX ASSET

76(1) This paragraph applies where, at a time when a company is subject to tonnage tax, plant or machinery used for the purposes of a qualifying activity carried on by the company begins to be used wholly or partly for the purposes of the company's tonnage tax trade.

76(2) Sections 61(1)(e), 206(3) and 207 of the Capital Allowances Act 2001 (effect of use partly for qualifying activity and partly for other purposes) apply as follows–

(a) references to a qualifying activity shall be read as not including references to the tonnage tax trade, and

(b) references to purposes other than those of a qualifying activity shall be read as including references to the purposes of the tonnage tax trade.

History – Para. 76(2) substituted by CAA 2001, s. 578 and Sch. 2, para. 108(8) with effect as respects allowances and charges falling to be made for chargeable periods ending, for income tax purposes, on or after 6 April 2001, and, for corporation tax purposes, on or after 1 April 2001.

DURING: PLANT AND MACHINERY: DISPOSALS

77(1) This paragraph applies if when a company is subject to tonnage tax a disposal event occurs in relation to plant or machinery–

(a) in respect of which qualifying expenditure was incurred by the company before its entry into tonnage tax,

(b) some or all of the expenditure on which was carried to the tonnage tax pool on the company's entry into tonnage tax, and

(c) which is used by the company for the purposes of its tonnage tax trade.

77(2) A **"disposal event"** means an event as a result of which the company is required under Part 2 of the Capital Allowances Act 2001 to bring a disposal value into account.

In determining whether such an event has occurred references in that Part of that Act to a qualifying activity shall be read as including the company's tonnage tax trade.

77(3) Where this paragraph applies–

(a) the disposal value to be brought into account in respect of any plant or machinery is limited to its market value when the company entered tonnage tax, and

(b) the disposal value is set against the unrelieved qualifying expenditure in the company's tonnage tax pool.

77(4) If the amount of the disposal value is less than or equal to the amount of unrelieved qualifying expenditure in the company's tonnage tax pool, the amount of unrelieved qualifying expenditure is reduced or extinguished accordingly.

77(5) If–

(a) the amount of the disposal value exceeds the amount of unrelieved qualifying expenditure, or

(b) there is no unrelieved qualifying expenditure in the pool,

the company is liable to a balancing charge.

77(6) The amount of the balancing charge is–

(a) where sub-paragraph (5)(a) applies, the amount of the excess, or

(b) where sub-paragraph (5)(b) applies, the amount of the disposal value.

This is subject to any reduction under paragraph 78.

History – In para. 77(2), reference to CAA 2001, Pt. 2 substituted for former reference to CAA 1990, Pt. II, and words "references in that Part of that Act to a qualifying activity" substituted for "references in that Part of that Act to a trade", by CAA 2001, s. 578 and Sch. 2, para. 108(8) with effect as respects allowances and charges falling to be made for chargeable periods ending, for income tax purposes, on or after 6 April 2001, and, for corporation tax purposes, on or after 1 April 2001.

DURING: PLANT AND MACHINERY: REDUCTION OF BALANCING CHARGES

78(1) The amount of any balancing charge under this Part of this Schedule is reduced by reference to the number of whole years the company has been subject to tonnage tax at the time of the disposal event giving rise to the charge.

78(2) The following table shows the percentage reduction:

Number of years	*Percentage reduction*
1	15%
2	30%
3	45%
4	60%
5	75%
6	90%
7 or more	100%

DURING: PLANT AND MACHINERY: GIVING EFFECT TO BALANCING CHARGE

79(1) A balancing charge under this Part of this Schedule–

(a) is treated as arising in connection with a trade (other than its tonnage tax trade) carried on by the company, and

(b) is made in taxing that trade.

79(2) Subject to paragraph 80 (deferment of balancing charge in case of reinvestment), the charge must be given effect in the accounting period in which it arises.

79A(1) This paragraph applies if–

(a) a balancing charge under this Part of this Schedule arises to the company on the disposal of any plant or machinery, and

(b) the plant or machinery is taken into account in calculating income that the company is treated as receiving under section 383 or 417 of the Corporation Tax Act 2010 (sales of lessors) as a result of section 394ZA of that Act (company joining tonnage tax group).

79A(2) The balancing charge is to be reduced by the relevant part of the sales of lessors expense so far as relief has not previously been given for that expense (whether under this sub-paragraph or otherwise).

79A(3) **"The sales of lessors expense"** means–

(a) the expense which the company is treated as incurring under section 383 or 417 of the Corporation Tax Act 2010 as a result of section 394ZA of that Act, or

(b) if section 386 or 419 of that Act applies or has applied, the expense which derives from the expense within paragraph (a).

79A(4) If the sales of lessors expense is incurred at a time when the company is in tonnage tax, the "relevant part" of that expense is so much of it as, on a just and reasonable basis, is attributable to the matters set out in paragraph 56(1)(a) or (b).

79A(5) If–

(a) the sales of lessors expense is not incurred at a time when the company is in tonnage tax,

(b) that expense is taken into account in calculating a loss made by the company in a trade, and

(c) the loss is one to which paragraph 56 applies, the **"relevant part"** of the sales of lessors expense is so much of the apportioned loss as, on a just and reasonable basis, is derived from the sales of lessors expense.

79A(6) The reference here to the apportioned loss is to the loss that is attributable to the matters set out in paragraph 56(1)(a) or (b).

History – Para. 79A inserted by FA 2012, s. 24(8) with effect from 21 March 2012 where a company becomes a member of a tonnage tax group on or after that date and enters tonnage tax at the same time or 23 April 2012 where a company becomes a member of a tonnage tax group on or after that date without entering tonnage tax at the same time.

DURING: PLANT AND MACHINERY: DEFERMENT OF BALANCING CHARGE

80(1) If–

(a) a balancing charge under this Part of this Schedule arises in connection with the disposal of a qualifying ship, and

(b) within the requisite period the company incurs capital expenditure on acquiring one or more other qualifying ships, and

(c) the company claims relief under this paragraph,

only the amount (if any) by which the balancing charge exceeds that expenditure must be given effect in the accounting period in which the charge arises and the rest may be held over.

80(2) For the purposes of this paragraph–

(a) the disposal of a qualifying ship includes any event within section 61(1)(a) to (d) of the Capital Allowances Act 2001 occurring with respect to a qualifying ship, and

(b) the requisite period is the period beginning one year before, and ending two years after, the date of the disposal.

80(3) If the new qualifying ship (or any of them) is disposed of before the end of the period of seven years after the company in question entered tonnage tax–

(a) there is a balancing charge under this paragraph when the disposal occurs, and

(b) the amount of that charge is equal to the amount held over under sub-paragraph (1) by reference to the acquisition of that ship.

This is subject to any reduction under paragraph 78 and to any further deferment under this paragraph.

80(4) Sections 135 to 156 of the Capital Allowances Act 2001 (deferment of balancing charges) do not apply in relation to balancing charges arising when the company is subject to tonnage tax.

80(5) The fact that there is a balancing charge under this paragraph does not affect the operation of paragraph 77 in a case where that paragraph also applies.

History – In para. 80(2) reference to CAA 2001, s. 61(1)(a)–(d) substituted for former reference to CAA 1990, s. 24(6)(c)(i)–(iii), and in s. 80(4) references to CAA 2001, s. 135–156 substituted for former references to CAA 1990, s. 33A–33F, by CAA 2001, s. 578 and Sch. 2, para. 108(10) and (11) respectively with effect as respects allowances and charges falling to be made for chargeable periods ending, for income tax purposes, on or after 6 April 2001, and, for corporation tax purposes, on or after 1 April 2001.

DURING: PLANT AND MACHINERY: SURRENDER OF UNRELIEVED QUALIFYING EXPENDITURE

81(1) This paragraph applies where–

(a) a company subject to tonnage tax is liable to a balancing charge under this Part of this Schedule,

(b) another tonnage tax company which is a member of the same group has unrelieved qualifying expenditure in its tonnage tax pool, and

(c) the two companies have been members of the same group for not less than a year at the date of the disposal giving rise to the balancing charge.

81(2) The latter company may surrender to the former all or part of its unrelieved qualifying expenditure, and the amount of the balancing charge shall be reduced or extinguished accordingly.

81(3) The provisions of Part VIII of Schedule 18 to the Finance Act 1998 (corporation tax self-assessment: claims for group relief), except paragraph 77 (joint amended returns), apply in relation to relief under this paragraph as they apply in relation to group relief.

DURING: INDUSTRIAL BUILDINGS: MIXED USE

82 If any identifiable part of a building or structure is used for the purposes of a company's tonnage tax trade, that part is treated for the purposes of Part 3 of the Capital Allowances Act 2001 as used otherwise than as an industrial building or structure.

History – Para. 82 substituted by CAA 2001, s. 578 and Sch. 2, para. 108(12) with effect as respects allowances and charges falling to be made for chargeable periods ending, for income tax purposes, on or after 6 April 2001, and, for corporation tax purposes, on or after 1 April 2001.

DURING: INDUSTRIAL BUILDINGS: BALANCING CHARGES

83(1) This paragraph applies where, in an accounting period during which a company is subject to tonnage tax, a balancing event occurs in relation to an industrial building in respect of which qualifying expenditure was incurred by the company before its entry into tonnage tax.

83(2) A **"balancing event"** means an event by reason of which the company is required by Part 3 of the Capital Allowances Act 2001 to bring into account any proceeds.

In determining whether such an event has occurred references in that Part of that Act to a trade or undertaking shall be read as including the company's tonnage tax trade.

83(3) Where this paragraph applies–

(a) the proceeds to be brought into account in respect of the industrial building are limited to the market value of the relevant interest when the company entered tonnage tax; and

(b) the amount of any balancing charge under that Part is reduced in accordance with paragraph 78.

History – In para. 83(1), words "balancing event occurs in relation to an industrial building" substituted for "disposal event occurs in relation to an industrial building or structure" by CAA 2001, s. 578 and Sch. 2, para. 108(13) with effect as respects allowances and charges falling to be made for chargeable periods ending, for income tax purposes, on or after 6 April 2001, and, for corporation tax purposes, on or after 1 April 2001.

Para. 83(2) first sentence substituted by CAA 2001, s. 578 and Sch. 2, para. 108(14) with effect as respects allowances and charges falling to be made for chargeable periods ending, for income tax purposes, on or after 6 April 2001, and, for corporation tax purposes, on or after 1 April 2001.
Para. 83(3)(a) substituted by CAA 2001, s. 578 and Sch. 2, para. 108(15) with effect as respects allowances and charges falling to be made for chargeable periods ending, for income tax purposes, on or after 6 April 2001, and, for corporation tax purposes, on or after 1 April 2001.

DURING: INDUSTRIAL BUILDINGS: RESIDUE OF QUALIFYING EXPENDITURE

84 [Omitted by FA 2008, s. 84 and Sch. 27, para. 22.]

History – Para. 84 omitted by FA 2008, s. 84 and Sch. 27, para. 22, with effect in relation to chargeable periods (within the meaning of CAA 2001) beginning on or after 1 April 2011 (for corporation tax purposes) or 6 April 2011 (for income tax purposes).

EXIT: PLANT AND MACHINERY

85(1) If a company leaves tonnage tax–

(a) the amount of qualifying expenditure under Part 2 of the Capital Allowances Act 2001 (plant and machinery allowances), and

(b) the pools to which such expenditure is to be allocated for the purposes of that Part,

shall be determined under this paragraph.

85(1A) Sub-paragraph (1C) applies where the company leaves tonnage tax–

(a) on the expiry of a tonnage tax election, or

(b) on a tonnage tax election ceasing to be in force under paragraph 13(2A) (taking effect of withdrawal notice under paragraph 15A).

85(1B) In any other case, sub-paragraph (2) applies.

85(1C) Where this sub-paragraph applies, the amount of qualifying expenditure in respect of each asset used by the company for the purposes of its tonnage tax activities and held by the company when it leaves tonnage tax shall be taken to be–

(a) the market value of the asset at the time the company leaves tonnage tax, or

(b) if less, the amount of expenditure incurred on the provision of the asset that would have been qualifying expenditure if the company had not been subject to tonnage tax.

85(2) Where this sub-paragraph applies, for each asset used by the company for the purposes of its tonnage tax activities and held by the company when it leaves tonnage tax there shall be determined–

(a) the amount of expenditure incurred on the provision of the asset that would have been qualifying expenditure if the company had not been subject to tonnage tax, and

(b) the written down value of that amount by reference to the period since the expenditure was incurred.

85(3) The Inland Revenue shall make provision by regulations as to the basis on which the writing down is to be done.

The regulations may make different provision for different descriptions of asset.

History – In para. 85(1), words "Part 2 of the Capital Allowances Act 2001 (plant and machinery allowances)" substituted for "Part II of the Capital Allowances Act 1990 (plant and machinery)" by CAA 2001, s. 578 and Sch. 2, para. 108(18) with effect as respects allowances and charges falling to be made for chargeable periods ending, for income tax purposes, on or after 6 April 2001, and, for corporation tax purposes, on or after 1 April 2001.
Para. 85(1A) inserted by FA 2005, s. 93 and Sch. 7, para. 13(2), with effect from 7 April 2005.
Para. 85(1B) inserted by FA 2005, s. 93 and Sch. 7, para. 13(2), with effect from 7 April 2005.
Para. 85(1C) inserted by FA 2005, s. 93 and Sch. 7, para. 13(2), with effect from 7 April 2005.
In para. 85(2), the words "Where this sub-paragraph applies," inserted by FA 2005, s. 93 and Sch. 7, para. 13(3), with effect from 7 April 2005.

EXIT: INDUSTRIAL BUILDINGS

86 [Omitted by FA 2008, s. 84 and Sch. 27, para. 22.]

History – Para. 86 omitted by FA 2008, s. 84 and Sch. 27, para. 22, with effect in relation to chargeable periods (within the meaning of CAA 2001) beginning on or after 1 April 2011 (for corporation tax purposes) or 6 April 2011 (for income tax purposes).

MEANING OF "NOT ENTITLED TO CAPITAL ALLOWANCES"

87(1) Where any provision of this Part of this Schedule states that a person is not entitled to capital allowances in respect of expenditure on plant or machinery–

(a) no annual investment allowance or first-year allowance is to be be given in respect of that expenditure, and

(b) the expenditure shall be disregarded for the purposes of calculating the person's entitlement to a writing-down allowance or balancing allowance or liability to a balancing charge.

87(2) If there is no entitlement to capital allowances in respect of expenditure, there is no entitlement to capital allowances in respect of any additional VAT liability incurred in respect of it.

History – In para. 87(1)(a), the words "no annual investment allowance or first-year allowance is to be" [sic] substituted for the words "a first-year allowance shall not" by FA 2008, s. 74 and Sch. 24, para. 19(2), with effect in relation to expenditure incurred on or after 1 April 2008 (for corporation tax purposes) or 6 April 2008 (for income tax purposes), subject to the transitional provision in FA 2008, Sch. 24, para. 23(2).
Para. 87(1)(b) substituted by CAA 2001, s. 578 and Sch. 2, para. 108(20) with effect as respects allowances and charges falling to be made for chargeable periods ending, for income tax purposes, on or after 6 April 2001, and, for corporation tax purposes, on or after 1 April 2001.

INTERPRETATION

88(1) In this Part of this Schedule–

"capital allowance" means any allowance under the Capital Allowances Act 2001;

"qualifying activity" means any activity in respect of which a person may be entitled to a capital allowance;

"qualifying expenditure" means expenditure in respect of which a person may be entitled to a capital allowance.

88(2) In this Part of this Schedule any reference to pooling or to single asset pools, class pools or the main pool shall be construed in accordance with sections 53 and 54 of the Capital Allowances Act 2001.

88(4) Other expressions relating to capital allowances have the same meaning in this Part of this Schedule as in the Capital Allowances Act 2001.

History – In para. 88(1), definitions of "capital allowance" and "qualifying activity" substituted by CAA 2001, s. 578 and Sch. 2, para. 108(21), and para. 88(2) substituted for former para. 88(2) and (3) by Sch. 2, para. 108(22) with effect as respects allowances and charges falling to be made for chargeable periods ending, for income tax purposes, on or after 6 April 2001, and, for corporation tax purposes, on or after 1 April 2001.
In para. 88(4), "the Capital Allowances Act 2001" substituted for "the Capital Allowances Act 1990" by CAA 2001, s. 578 and Sch. 2, para. 108(23).

Part X – The Ring Fence: Capital Allowances: Ship Leasing

INTRODUCTION

89(1) In the case of a lease of a qualifying ship provided, directly or indirectly, to a company within tonnage tax, the provisions of Part 2 of the Capital Allowances Act 2001 have effect subject to and in accordance with the provisions of–

paragraphs 90 and 91 (defeased leasing),

paragraphs 91A to 91F (long funding leases),

paragraph 92 (sale and lease back arrangements, and

paragraphs 94 to 102 (quantitative restrictions on allowances).

This is subject to paragraph 89A (exception for ordinary charters).

89(2) In this Part of this Schedule **"lease"** means any arrangements that provide for a ship to be leased or otherwise made available by a person (**"the lessor"**) to another person (**"the lessee"**).

89(3) Other expressions used in this Part of this Schedule have the same meaning as in Part IX of this Schedule (the ring fence: capital allowances: general).

History – In para. 89(1), the words "paragraphs 91A to 91F (long funding leases)," inserted by FA 2006, s. 81 and Sch. 9, para. 10(2) with effect in accordance with the provisions of FA 2006, Sch. 8, para. 15.
In para. 89(1), reference to CAA 2001, Pt. 2 substituted for CAA 1990, Pt. II, and in para. 89(2) reference to CAA 2001, s. 219 substituted for CAA 1990, s. 82A, by CAA 2001, s. 578 and Sch. 2, para. 108(24) and (25) respectively with effect as respects allowances and charges falling to be made for chargeable periods ending, for income tax purposes, on or after 6 April 2001, and, for corporation tax purposes, on or after 1 April 2001.
In para. 89(1), word "finance" omitted from expression "finance lease", and words "this is subject to paragraph 89A (exception for ordinary charters)" added by FA 2003, s. 169 and Sch. 32, para. 1(2), (3) and the word repealed by FA 2003, Sch. 43, Pt. 3(11) with effect in relation to any lease (within the meaning given by para. 5 of Sch. 32 to that Act) entered into on or after 19 December 2002.
Para. 89(2) substituted by FA 2003, Sch. 32, para. 1(3) with effect in relation to any lease (within the meaning given by para. 5 of Sch. 32 to that Act) entered into on or after 19 December 2002.

QUANTITATIVE RESTRICTIONS NOT TO APPLY TO ORDINARY CHARTERS

89A(1) Paragraph 94 to 102, and paragraph 89(1) so far as relating to those paragraphs, do not apply in the following cases.

89A(2) The first case is where the ship is chartered out by a person who is responsible–

(a) for the operation of the ship, including the appointment of the master and those members of the crew engaged in navigation, throughout the period of the charter, and

(b) for defraying all expenses in connection with the ship throughout that period, or substantially all such expenses other than those directly incidental to a particular voyage or to the employment of the ship during that period.

For the purposes of this sub-paragraph a person is **"responsible"** if he is responsible as principal or if he appoints another person, other than the lessee or a person connected with the lessee, to be responsible in his place.

89A(3) The second case is where–

(a) the ship is chartered out by a person acting in the course of a trade that consists of, or to a significant extent includes, operating ships, and

(b) the conditions in sub-paragraph (4) are met.

89A(4) Those conditions are–

(a) that the period of the charter does not exceed seven years, and there is no provision or agreement under which it could be extended beyond seven years;

(b) that the period of the charter, together with any other periods in the same ten years during which the ship is chartered out to the lessee or a person connected with him, does not exceed seven years in total;

(c) that there are no arrangements under which the lessee or a person connected with him may acquire the ship, whether directly or indirectly, from the lessor.

In paragraph (b) **"the same ten years"** means any period of ten years that includes the period of the charter mentioned in that paragraph.

89A(5) References in this paragraph to the period of a charter are to the term specified in the lease or, if longer, the actual period during which the ship is chartered.

89A(6) Section 1122 of the Corporation Tax Act 2010 (connected persons) applies for the purposes of this paragraph.

History – In para. 89A(6), the words "Section 1122 of the Corporation Tax Act 2010" substituted for the words "Section 839 of the Taxes Act 1988" by CTA 2010, s. 1177 and Sch. 1, para. 316(5), with effect for corporation tax purposes for accounting periods ending on or after 1 April 2010, and for income tax and capital gains tax purposes for the tax year 2010–11 and subsequent tax years.
Para. 89A added by FA 2003, s. 169 and Sch. 32, para. 1(5) with effect in relation to any lease (within the meaning given by para. 5 of Sch. 32 to that Act) entered into on or after 16 April 2003, except that in sub-para. 4(b), the reference to any other periods during which the ship is chartered out does not include any period during which it is chartered out under a lease entered into before 19 December 2002.

Notes – Para. 89A does not apply in relation to any lease (within the meaning given by para. 5 of Sch. 32 to FA 2003 entered into on or after 19 December 2002 and before 16 April 2003. In such a case the following para. has effect in place of para. 89A, by virtue of FA 2003, s. 169 and Sch. 32, para. 4:

"EXCEPTION FOR ORDINARY CHARTERS

89A(1) Paragraph 89(1), and the provisions of this Part of this Schedule listed there, do not apply in the following cases.

89A(2) The first case is where the ship is chartered out by a person who is responsible–

(a) for the operation of the ship, including the appointment of the master and those members of the crew engaged in navigation, throughout the period of the charter, and

(b) for defraying all expenses in connection with the ship throughout that period, or substantially all such expenses other than those directly incidental to a particular voyage or to the employment of the ship during that period.

For the purposes of this sub-paragraph a person is **"responsible"** if he is responsible as principal or if he appoints another person, other than the lessee or a person connected with the lessee, to be responsible in his place.

89A(3) The second case is where–

(a) the ship is chartered out to another person (**"the charterer"**) because of short-term over-capacity,

(b) the person chartering out the ship does so in the course of a trade that consists of or includes operating ships, and

(c) the conditions in sub-paragraph (4) are met.

89A(4) Those conditions are–

(a) that the period of the charter does not exceed three years, and there is no provision or agreement under which it could be extended beyond three years;

(b) that the period of the charter, together with any other periods in the same five years during which the ship is chartered out to the charterer or a person connected with him, does not exceed three years in total;

(c) that neither the charterer nor any person connected with him has an option to purchase the ship.

89A(5) In sub-paragraph (4)(b)–

(a) the reference to any other periods during which the ship is chartered out does not include any period during which it is chartered out under a lease entered into before 19th December 2002;

(b) **"the same five years"** means any period of five years that includes the period of the charter mentioned in that sub- paragraph.

89A(6) References in this paragraph to the period of a charter are to the term specified in the lease or, if longer, the actual period during which the ship is chartered.

89A(7) Section 839 of the Taxes Act 1988 (connected persons) applies for the purposes of this paragraph.".

DEFEASED LEASING

90(1) *The lessor under the lease is not entitled to capital allowances in respect of expenditure on the provision of the ship if–*

(a) the lease, or

(b) any transaction or series of transaction of which the lease forms a part, makes provision the effect of which is to remove the whole, or the greater part of, any non-compliance risk which, apart from that provision, would fall directly or indirectly on the lessor.

90(2) For this purpose a **"non-compliance risk"** means a risk that a loss will be sustained by any person if payments under the lease are not made in accordance with its terms.

90(3) For the purposes of this paragraph the lessor and any persons connected with him shall be treated as the same person.

90(4) In this paragraph **"connected person"** has the meaning given by section 839 of the Taxes Act 1988.

History – In para. 90(1), word "finance" omitted from expression "finance lease" by FA 2003, s. 169 and Sch. 32, para. 1(2) and the word repealed by FA 2003, Sch. 43, Pt. 3(11) with effect in relation to any lease (within the meaning given by para. 5 of Sch. 32 to that Act) entered into on or after 19 December 2002.

DEFEASED LEASING: EXCEPTED FORMS OF SECURITY

91(1) Paragraph 90 (defeased leasing) is subject to the following exceptions.

91(2) It does not apply to the provision of security of any of the following kinds by the lessee, or a person connected with the lessee–

(a) a mortgage of the ship;

(b) security attaching–

(i) to the ship's earning, or

(ii) to the proceeds of insurance policies on the ship;

(c) security over rental rebates arising from the arm's length sale of the ship;

(d) any other form of security relating to assets, sums or rights arising from the ordinary operation of the ship or from arm's length transactions involving the ship.

In this sub-paragraph **"the ship"** means the ship that is the subject of the lease.

91(3) It does not apply to the provision of security by the lessee, or a person connected with the lessee, if the following conditions are met–

(a) no deposit of money or other property by way of security is obtained by the lessor or any third party:

(b) any payments under the security are limited to the amount of any rental payments under the lease in respect of which the lessee is in default.

91(4) It does not apply to the provision of security by a third party where no security other than security of a kind mentioned in sub-paragraph (2)(a) to (d) is held by the third party or any person connected with the third party.

91(5) It does not apply to the provision of security by a third party if the following conditions are met–

(a) no deposit of money or other property by way of security is obtained by the lessor or any third party;

(b) the security does not involve the assumption of any obligations of the lessee in return for a payment made (directly or indirectly) by the lessee or a person connected with him;

(c) the security does not give rise to any payments to the lessor unless the lessee defaults on the rental payments under the lease;

(d) any payments under the security are limited to the amount of the rental payments in default.

91(6) For the purposes of this paragraph the lessor and any persons connected with him shall be treated as the same person.

91(7) In this paragraph–

"connected person" has the meaning given by section 839 of the Taxes Act 1988; and

"third party" means a person not connected with either the lessor or lessee.

LONG FUNDING LEASES: CONDITIONS FOR ALTERNATIVE TREATMENT

91A(1) This paragraph applies if the lease would fall to be regarded as a long funding lease for the purposes of Part 2 of the Capital Allowances Act 2001, apart from this paragraph.

91A(2) The lease is to be treated for tax purposes as not being a long funding lease at any time when the lease–

(a) meets the conditions in sub-paragraph (3), or

(b) is expected to meet those conditions when the ship is first brought into use under the lease,

but this is subject to the qualification in sub-paragraph (4) and the exception in sub-paragraph (5).

91A(3) The conditions are–

(a) that the lease falls within paragraph 91B (lease to tonnage tax company or group),

(b) that the lease falls within paragraph 91C (tonnage tax company to operate and manage qualifying ship),

(c) that the lease falls within paragraph 91D (period and rate of sublease of qualifying ship).

91A(4) The condition in paragraph (c) of sub-paragraph (3) has to be met, or be expected to be met, only at times when the company within tonnage tax is leasing the ship to a company not within tonnage tax.

91A(5) The conditions in paragraphs (b) and (c) of sub-paragraph (3) do not have to be met, or be expected to be met, if the lease was finalised (within the meaning of Part 4 of Schedule 8 to the Finance Act 2006) before 1st April 2006.

91A(6) Sub-paragraph (2) is subject to paragraph 91E (anti-avoidance).

History – Para. 91A inserted by FA 2006, s. 81 and Sch. 9, para. 10(3) with effect in accordance with the provisions of FA 2006, Sch. 8, para. 15.

LEASE TO TONNAGE TAX COMPANY OR GROUP

91B(1) A lease falls within this paragraph if–

(a) it is a lease of a qualifying ship provided directly to a company within tonnage tax, or

(b) it is a lease of a qualifying ship provided indirectly to a company within tonnage tax ("T") and sub-paragraph (2) applies.

91B(2) This sub-paragraph applies where–

(a) the owner of the qualifying ship provides it directly to a company ("C") under a lease,

(b) C provides the qualifying ship directly to T under a lease, and

(c) C and T are in the same group.

History – Para. 91B inserted by FA 2006, s. 81 and Sch. 9, para. 10(3) with effect in accordance with the provisions of FA 2006, Sch. 8, para. 15.

TONNAGE TAX COMPANY TO OPERATE AND MANAGE QUALIFYING SHIP

91C(1) A lease of a qualifying ship provided, directly or indirectly, to a company within tonnage tax ("T") falls within this paragraph if T is responsible–

(a) for the operation of the ship, including the appointment of the master and those members of the crew engaged in navigation, and

(b) for defraying all expenses in connection with the ship, or substantially all such expenses other than those directly incidental to a particular voyage or to the employment of the ship during any period for which the ship is leased by T to another person.

91C(2) For the purposes of this paragraph, T is "responsible" if–

(a) he is responsible as principal, or

(b) he appoints another person ("P") to be responsible in his place and the condition in sub-paragraph (3) is met.

91C(3) The condition is that–

(a) P is not a person to whom the ship is leased by T and is not connected with such a person, or

(b) P is a company within tonnage tax.

91C(4) Any reference in this paragraph to a lease by T includes a reference to a contract of affreightment entered into by T that provides for the carriage of goods by the qualifying ship.

91C(5) Section 1122 of the Corporation Tax Act 2010 (connected persons) applies for the purposes of this paragraph.

History – In para. 91C(5), the words "Section 1122 of the Corporation Tax Act 2010" substituted for the words "Section 839 of the Taxes Act 1988" by CTA 2010, s. 1177 and Sch. 1, para. 316(6), with effect for corporation tax purposes for accounting periods ending on or after 1 April 2010, and for income tax and capital gains tax purposes for the tax year 2010–11 and subsequent tax years.
Para. 91C inserted by FA 2006, s. 81 and Sch. 9, para. 10(3) with effect in accordance with the provisions of FA 2006, Sch. 8, para. 15.

PERIOD AND RATE OF SUBLEASE OF QUALIFYING SHIP

91D(1) A lease of a qualifying ship provided, directly or indirectly, to a company within tonnage tax ("T") falls within this paragraph if each lease of the ship by T (a "sublease") to a company not within tonnage tax meets the conditions in sub-paragraph (2).

91D(2) The conditions are–

(a) that the amount payable under the sublease is the market rate, and

(b) that the period of the sublease does not exceed 7 years.

91D(3) For the purposes of this paragraph the market rate is the rate at which the qualifying ship could reasonably be expected to be leased, taking into account all the circumstances of the lease including the period of the lease, the date at which the lease commences and the size and description of the qualifying ship.

91D(4) For the purposes of this paragraph the period of a sublease is the period comprising–

(a) the term specified in the sublease, and

(b) any subsequent periods which meet the conditions in sub-paragraph (5).

91D(5) The conditions are that–

(a) there is an option to continue the sublease for that period, and

(b) the amount payable under the sublease for that period is not the market rate applicable at the start of that period.

91D(6) Where–

(a) an option to continue a sublease for a period is exercised, and

(b) the amount payable under the sublease for that period is the market rate applicable at the start of that period,

the parties to the sublease are to be treated for the purposes of this paragraph as if the sublease had terminated immediately before the commencement of the period and a new sublease had immediately been entered into.

91D(7) Where a sublease is for an indefinite period, the period of the sublease is to be taken for the purposes of this paragraph to be a period of more than 7 years, unless the condition in sub-paragraph (8) is met.

91D(8) The condition is that–

(a) the amount payable under the sublease must be reviewed at least once every 7 years, and

(b) if the amount payable under the sublease is found on such a review not to be the market rate applicable at the time of the review, it must be changed to the market rate applicable at that time.

91D(9) Where there is an option to continue a sublease for an indefinite period, the period of the sublease is to be taken for the purposes of this paragraph to be a period of more than 7 years, unless the condition in sub-paragraph (10) is met.

91D(10) The condition is that the amount payable under the sublease for any period for which the option may be exercised is the market rate applicable at the start of that period, except that–

(a) the amount for the time being payable under the sublease may subsequently be changed at any time to the market rate applicable at that time,

(b) the amount payable under the sublease must be reviewed at least once every 7 years, and

(c) if the amount payable under the sublease is found on such a review not to be the market rate applicable at the time of the review, it must be changed to the market rate applicable at that time.

91D(11) Any reference in this paragraph to a lease by T includes a reference to a contract of affreightment entered into by T that provides for the carriage of goods by the qualifying ship.

History – Para. 91D inserted by FA 2006, s. 81 and Sch. 9, para. 10(3) with effect in accordance with the provisions of FA 2006, Sch. 8, para. 15.

ANTI-AVOIDANCE

91E Paragraph 91A(2) does not have effect in the case of the lease if the main purpose, or one of the main purposes–

(a) of the leasing of the ship,

(b) of a series of transactions of which the leasing of the ship is one, or

(c) of any of the transactions in such a series,

was to obtain a writing down allowance determined without regard to any of paragraphs 90, 92 and 94 to 102 in respect of expenditure incurred by any person on the provision of the ship.

History – Para. 91E inserted by FA 2006, s. 81 and Sch. 9, para. 10(3) with effect in accordance with the provisions of FA 2006, Sch. 8, para. 15.

CONSEQUENCES OF PARAGRAPH 91A(2) CEASING TO HAVE EFFECT

91F(1) This paragraph applies if sub-paragraph (2) of paragraph 91A ceases to have effect in relation to a lease (the "existing lease") because one or more of the conditions in sub-paragraph (3) of that paragraph cease to be met.

91F(2) In any such case it is to be assumed for tax purposes that–

(a) the existing lease terminates at the time of the cessation;

(b) another lease (the "new lease") is entered into immediately after the cessation;

(c) the term of the new lease is the portion of the term of the existing lease that remains unexpired at the time of the cessation;

(d) the date on which the cessation occurs is the date of both–

(i) the inception of the new lease, and

(ii) the commencement of the term of the new lease.

91F(3) Where this paragraph applies, sub-section (4) of section 70X of the Capital Allowances Act 2001 (transfers, assignments etc by lessee) does not.

91F(4) For the purposes of this paragraph, the following expressions have the meaning given in Chapter 6A of Part 2 of the Capital Allowances Act 2001 (interpretation of provisions about long funding leases)–

"commencement", in relation to the term of a lease;

"inception", in relation to a lease;

"term", in relation to a lease;

"terminate".

History – Para. 91F inserted by FA 2006, s. 81 and Sch. 9, para. 10(3) with effect in accordance with the provisions of FA 2006, Sch. 8, para. 15.

SALE AND LEASE-BACK ARRANGEMENTS

92(1) The lessor under the lease is not entitled to capital allowances if the lease is part of sale and lease-back arrangements.

92(2) For this purpose **"sale and lease-back arrangements"** means, subject to sub-paragraphs (3) and (3A), any arrangements that take the following form:

Step One

The ship is owned by a tonnage tax company and used for the purposes of its tonnage tax trade.

Step Two

A transaction is entered into, as a result of which (apart from this paragraph) capital allowances would become available to the lessor, under which–

(a) the ship (or an interest in it) is sold, or

(b) a person enters into a contract on the performance of which he will or may become the owner of the ship (or an interest in it), or

(c) a person entitled to the benefit of any such contract assigns the benefit of it so far as it relates to the ship (or an interest in it).

Step Three

After the time of that transaction the ship is used for the purposes of a tonnage tax trade carried on–

(a) by the original company, or

(b) by another tonnage tax company that is a member of the same group,

without having been used since that time for the purposes of any other trade (except that of leasing).

92(3) This paragraph does not apply if the ship is newly-constructed and the transaction mentioned in Step Two in sub-paragraph (2) is effected not more than four months after the first occasion on which the ship is brought into use by any person for any purpose.

92(3A) This paragraph does not apply if–

(a) expenditure is incurred on enhancing the ship or on converting it to another use,

(b) the amount of that expenditure–

(i) is greater than 33% of the market value of the ship immediately after completion of the enhancement or conversion, and

(ii) is equal to or greater than the market value of the interest in the ship which is the subject of the transaction mentioned in Step Two in sub-paragraph (2), and

(c) that transaction is effected not more than four months after the first occasion following completion of the enhancement or conversion on which the ship is brought into use by any person for any purpose.

92(4) A person is regarded for the purposes of this paragraph as owning a ship if it is treated as owned by him for the purposes of Part 2 of the Capital Allowances Act 2001.

History – In para. 92(1), word "finance" omitted from expression "finance lease" by FA 2003, s. 169 and Sch. 32, para. 1(2) and the word repealed by FA 2003, Sch. 43, Pt. 3(11) with effect in relation to any lease (within the meaning given by Sch. 32, para. 5 to that Act) entered into on or after 19 December 2002.

In para. 92(2), the words "subject to sub-paragraphs (3) and (3A)" substituted for the words "subject to sub-paragraph (3)" by FA 2005, s. 93 and Sch. 7, para. 14(2), with effect from 7 April 2005.
Para. 92(3A) inserted by FA 2005, s. 93 and Sch. 7, para. 14(3), with effect from 7 April 2005.
In para. 92(4), words "owned by him for the purposes of Part 2 of the Capital Allowances Act 2001" substituted for "belonging to him for the purposes of Part II of the Capital Allowances Act 1990" by CAA 2001, s. 578 and Sch. 2, para. 108(26) with effect as respects allowances and charges falling to be made for chargeable periods ending, for income tax purposes, on or after 6 April 2001, and, for corporation tax purposes, on or after 1 April 2001.

CERTIFICATES REQUIRED TO SUPPORT CLAIM BY LESSOR

History – In heading to para. 93, word "finance" omitted from expression "finance lessor" by FA 2003, Sch. 43, Pt. 3(11) with effect in relation to any lease (within the meaning given by para. 5 of Sch. 32 to that Act) entered into on or after 19 December 2002

93(1) Any claim by the lessor under a lease for capital allowances in respect of expenditure on the provision of a qualifying ship must be accompanied by a certificate by the lessor and the lessee stating –

(a) that the ship is not leased, directly or indirectly, to a company subject to tonnage tax, or

(b) that neither paragraph 90 (defeased leasing) nor paragraph 92 (sale and lease-back arrangements) applies in relation to the lease and, if the lease is one that would (apart from paragraph 91A) fall to be regarded as a long funding lease for the purposes of Part 2 of the Capital Allowances Act 2001, that paragraph 91A(2) has effect in relation to the lease.

93(2) If any matter so certified ceases to be the case, the lessor must give notice of that fact to the Inland Revenue.

93(3) Any such notice must be given within three months after the end of the chargeable period in which the change takes place.

93(4) [Amends second column of Table in TMA 1970, s. 98.]

History – In para. 93(1)(b), the words "and, if the lease is one that would (apart from paragraph 91A) fall to be regarded as a long funding lease for the purposes of Part 2 of the Capital Allowances Act 2001, that paragraph 91A(2) has effect in relation to the lease." inserted by FA 2006, s. 81 and Sch. 9, para. 10(4) with effect in accordance with the provisions of FA 2006, Sch. 8, para. 15.
In para. 93(1), word "finance" omitted from expression "finance lease" by FA 2003, s. 169 and Sch. 32, para. 1(2) and the words "finance" and "either" repealed by FA 2003, Sch. 43, Pt. 3(11) with effect in relation to any lease (within the meaning given by para. 5 of Sch. 32 to that Act) entered into on or after 19 December 2002.
Para. 93(1) is amended in relation to any lease (within the meaning given by para. 5 of Sch. 32 to FA 2003) entered into on or after 19 December 2002 and before 16 April 2003 by virtue of FA 2003, s. 169 and Sch. 32, para. 4(3). In such a case, para. 93(1) is read as if after paragraph (a) there were inserted–
"(aa) that the lease is such that, by virtue of paragraph 89A (exception for ordinary charters), paragraph 89(1) does not apply, or".

QUANTITATIVE RESTRICTIONS ON ALLOWANCES

94(1) Where the lessor under the lease is entitled to capital allowances in respect of expenditure on the provision of the ship, the following provisions apply.

94(2) There is no entitlement to any annual investment allowance or first-year allowance.

94(3) The lessor is entitled–

(a) in respect of the first £40 million of the cost of providing the ship, to writing-down allowances at the rate determined under sub-paragraph (3A) on the reducing balance, and

(b) in respect of the next £40 million, to writing-down allowances at the rate specified in section 104D(1) of the Capital Allowances Act 2001 on the reducing balance.

94(3A) The rate mentioned in sub-paragraph (3)(a) is–

(a) if the rate of the writing down allowance to which the lessor would be entitled in respect of the expenditure apart from this paragraph is that specified in section 56(1) of the Capital Allowances Act 2001, that rate, and

(b) otherwise, the rate specified in section 104D(1) of that Act.

94(4) The expenditure shall be allocated to separate pools in accordance with sub-paragraph (4A) and dealt with under Part 2 of the Capital Allowances Act 2001 in the same way as expenditure allocated to a class pool.

94(4A) The expenditure is to be allocated to the following pools–

(a) to the extent that it is expenditure in respect of which the lessor is entitled to writing down allowance at the rate specified in section 56(1) of the Capital Allowances Act 2001, a pool to be known as "the tonnage tax (main rate) pool", and

(b) to the extent that it is expenditure in respect of which the lessor is entitled to writing down allowance at the rate specified in section 104D(1) of that Act, a pool to be known as "the tonnage tax (special rate) pool".

94(5) If the cost of providing the ship exceeds £80 million, the lessor is not entitled to capital allowances in respect of the excess.

History – In para. 94(1), word "finance" omitted from expression "finance lease" by FA 2003, s. 169 and Sch. 32, para. 1(2) and the word repealed by FA 2003, Sch. 43, Pt. 3(11) with effect in relation to any lease (within the meaning given by para. 5 of Sch. 32 to that Act) entered into on or after 19 December 2002.
In para. 94(2), the words "annual investment allowance or" inserted by FA 2008, s. 74 and Sch. 24, para. 19(3), with effect in relation to expenditure incurred on or after 1 April 2008 (for corporation tax purposes) or 6 April 2008 (for income tax purposes), subject to the transitional provision in FA 2008, Sch. 24, para. 23(2).
In para. 94(3)(a), "the rate determined under sub-paragraph (3A)" substituted for "a rate of 20% per annum" by FA 2011, s. 57(2)(a) with effect in relation to chargeable periods ending on or after 1 January 2011, but this amendment has no effect in relation to expenditure incurred before 1 January 2011. See cross-reference note below for details of the application of para. 94(3)(a) in relation to expenditure incurred before 1 January 2011. Subject to that cross-reference note, former para. 94(3)(a) read as follows:
"(a) in respect of the first £40 million of the cost of providing the ship, to writing-down allowances at a rate of 20% per annum on the reducing balance, and".
In para. 94(3)(a), "20%" substituted for "25%" by FA 2008, s. 80(6)(a), with effect in relation to chargeable periods beginning on or after the "relevant date" and beginning before, and ending on or after, the "relevant date", subject to the transitional provisions in FA 2008, s. 80(9)–(11). The "relevant date" is 1 April 2008 for corporation tax purposes and 6 April 2008 for income tax purposes.
In para. 94(3)(b), "the rate specified in section 104D(1) of the Capital Allowances Act 2001" substituted for "a rate of 10% per annum" by FA 2011, s. 57(2)(b) with effect in relation to chargeable periods ending on or after 1 January 2011, but this amendment has no effect in relation to expenditure incurred before 1 January 2011. See cross-reference note below for details of the application of para. 94(3)(b) in relation to expenditure incurred before 1 January 2011. Subject to that cross-reference note, former para. 94(3)(b) read as follows:
"(b) in respect of the next £40 million, to writing-down allowances at a rate of 10% per annum on the reducing balance.".
Para. 94(3A) inserted by FA 2011, s. 57(2)(c) with effect in relation to chargeable periods ending on or after 1 January 2011, but this amendment has no effect in relation to expenditure incurred before 1 January 2011.
In para. 94(4), the words "within each of those bands", which appeared after the words "The expenditure" omitted by FA 2011, s. 57(2)(d)(i) with effect in relation to chargeable periods ending on or after 1 January 2011, but this amendment has no effect in relation to expenditure incurred before 1 January 2011. See cross-reference note below for details of the application of para. 94(4) in relation to expenditure incurred before 1 January 2011. Subject to that cross-reference note, former para. 94(4) read as follows:
"The expenditure within each of those bands shall be allocated to separate pools and dealt with under Part 2 of the Capital Allowances Act 2001 in the same way as expenditure allocated to a class pool. These pools are referred to below as "the 20% pool" and the "10% pool"".
In para. 94(4), the words "in accordance with sub-paragraph (4A)" inserted after the words "separate pools" by FA 2011, s. 57(2)(d)(ii) with effect in relation to chargeable periods ending on or after 1 January 2011, but this amendment has no effect in relation to expenditure incurred before 1 January 2011. See cross-reference note below for details of the application of para. 94(4) in relation to expenditure incurred before 1 January 2011.
In para. 94(4), the sentence "These pools are referred to below as "the 20% pool" and "the 10% pool".", which appeared at the end of the para. 94(4), omitted by FA 2011, s. 57(2)(d)(iii), with effect in relation to chargeable periods ending on or after 1 January 2011, but this amendment has no effect in relation to expenditure incurred before 1 January 2011. See cross-reference note below for details of the application of para. 94(4) in relation to expenditure incurred before 1 January 2011.
In para. 94(4), "20%" substituted for "25%" by FA 2008, s. 80(6)(a), with effect in relation to chargeable periods beginning on or after the "relevant date" and beginning before, and ending on or after, the "relevant date", subject to the transitional provisions in FA 2008, s. 80(9)–(11). The "relevant date" is 1 April 2008 for corporation tax purposes and 6 April 2008 for income tax purposes.
In para. 94(4), reference to CAA 2001, Pt. 2 substituted for CAA 1990, Pt. II by CAA 2001, s. 578 and Sch. 2, para. 108(27) with effect as respects allowances and charges falling to be made for chargeable periods ending, for income tax purposes, on or after 6 April 2001, and, for corporation tax purposes, on or after 1 April 2001.
Para. 94(4A) inserted by FA 2011, s. 57(2)(e), with effect in relation to chargeable periods ending on or after 1 January 2011, but this amendment has no effect in relation to expenditure incurred before 1 January 2011.

Cross references – FA 2011, s. 10: in former para. 94(3)(a) and (4) as it continues to apply in respect of expenditure incurred before 1 January 2011 (see history note above), "18%" substituted for "20%".
FA 2011, s. 10: in former para. 94(3)(b) and (4) as it continues to apply in respect of expenditure incurred before 1 January 2011 (see history note above), "8%" substituted for "10%".

QUANTITATIVE RESTRICTIONS: FURTHER PROVISIONS AS TO RATE BANDS, LIMIT AND POOLING

95(1) The rate bands and limit in paragraph 94 (quantitative restrictions on allowances) apply separately in relation to each ship.

95(2) The amounts specified in that paragraph apply in relation to the whole cost of providing the ship.

95(3) If–

(a) the cost is shared by two or more persons, or

(b) a person acquires a part share in the ship,

that paragraph applies as if there were substituted in sub-paragraph (3)(a) and (b) and sub-paragraph (5) in relation to each person the proportion of the figure specified that his share of the cost bears to the whole cost.

95(4) The pools referred to in sub-paragraph (4A) of that paragraph are class pools of all expenditure of a lessor that falls to be allocated to a tonnage tax (main rate) or tonnage tax (special rate) pool in respect of ships leased by him.

History – In para. 95(4), the words "sub-paragraph (4A)" substituted for "sub-paragraph (4)" by FA 2011, s. 57(3)(a), with effect in relation to chargeable periods ending on or after 1 January 2011, but this amendment has no effect in relation to expenditure incurred before 1 January 2011. See cross-reference note below for details of the application of para. 95(4) in relation to expenditure incurred before 1 January 2011. Subject to that cross-reference note, former para. 95(4) read as follows:
"**95(4)** The pools referred to in sub-paragraph (4) of that paragraph are class pools of all expenditure of a lessor that falls to be allocated to a 20% or 10% pool in respect of ships leased by him.".
In para. 95(4), the words "tonnage tax (main rate)" substituted for "20%", and "tonnage tax (special rate)" substituted for "10%" by FA 2011, s. 57(3)(b), with effect in relation to chargeable periods ending on or after 1 January 2011, but this amendment has no effect in relation to expenditure incurred before 1 January 2011. See cross-reference note below for details of the application of para. 95(4) in relation to expenditure incurred before 1 January 2011. Subject to that cross-reference note, former para. 95(4) read as follows:
"**95(4)** The pools referred to in sub-paragraph (4) of that paragraph are class pools of all expenditure of a lessor that falls to be allocated to a 20% or 10% pool in respect of ships leased by him.".

In para. 95(4), "20%" substituted for "25%" by FA 2008, s. 80(6)(b), with effect in relation to chargeable periods beginning on or after the "relevant date" and beginning before, and ending on or after, the "relevant date", subject to the transitional provisions in FA 2008, s. 80(9)–(11). The "relevant date" is 1 April 2008 for corporation tax purposes and 6 April 2008 for income tax purposes.

Cross references – FA 2011, s. 10: in former para. 95(4) as it continues to apply in respect of expenditure incurred before 1 January 2011 (see history note above), "18%" substituted for "20%".
FA 2011, s. 10: in former para. 95(4) as it continues to apply in respect of expenditure incurred before 1 January 2011 (see history note above), "8%" substituted for "10%".

QUANTITATIVE RESTRICTIONS: MEANING OF "COST OF PROVIDING SHIP"

96(1) For the purposes of paragraph 94 (quantitative restrictions on allowances) the cost of providing the ship means the total cost of providing it in a state ready to be brought into use for the purposes for which it is normally to be used.
This includes the cost of any accessories or additional equipment, or fitting out, necessary for the operation of the ship for those purposes.

96(2) The cost of providing the ship shall be determined without regard to the provisions of the Capital Allowances Act 2001 as to–

(a) when expenditure is treated as incurred, or

(b) when expenditure may be brought into account as qualifying expenditure.

96(3) Further capital expenditure by the lessor on the ship shall be added to the original cost of providing the ship to determine–

(a) whether the lessor is entitled to capital allowances in respect of the further expenditure, and

(b) if he is, the rate of writing-down allowances to which he is entitled.

References to the cost of providing the ship shall accordingly be read as including any such further expenditure.

96(4) The amounts to be taken into account under this paragraph are limited to the amounts that would otherwise have been qualifying expenditure for the purposes of capital allowances.

History – In para. 96(2), reference to CAA 2001 substituted for CAA 1990 by CAA 2001, s. 578 and Sch. 2, para. 108(28) with effect as respects allowances and charges falling to be made for chargeable periods ending, for income tax purposes, on or after 6 April 2001, and, for corporation tax purposes, on or after 1 April 2001.

QUANTITATIVE RESTRICTIONS: TREATMENT OF DISPOSAL PROCEEDS

97(1) The following provisions apply where–

(a) there is a disposal of a ship in relation to which paragraph 94 applies to restrict the capital allowances available, and

(b) a disposal value falls to be brought into account.

The reference in paragraph (a) to a disposal of ship includes a disposal of a part of a ship, or of an interest in a ship or a part of a ship.

97(2) The disposal value is first allocated between the tonnage tax (main rate) pool and the tonnage tax (special rate) pool in the same proportions as the cost of providing the ship was allocated to those pools.

97(3) If the amount allocated to the tonnage tax (main rate) pool exceeds the amount of qualifying expenditure remaining in that pool, any excess shall be taken to the tonnage tax (special rate) pool

97(4) A balancing charge arises only if the amount taken to the tonnage tax (special rate) pool exceeds the amount of qualifying expenditure remaining in that pool.

History – In para. 97(2) and (3), "tonnage tax (main rate)" substituted for "20%" and "tonnage tax (special rate)" substituted for "10%" by FA 2011, s. 57(4)(a), with effect in relation to chargeable periods ending on or after 1 January 2011, but this amendment has no effect in relation to expenditure incurred before 1 January 2011. See cross-reference note below for details of the application of para. 97(2) and (3) in relation to expenditure incurred before 1 January 2011. Subject to that cross-reference note, former para. 97(2) and (3) read as follows:
"**97(2)** The disposal value is first allocated between the 20% pool and 10% pool in the same proportions as the cost of providing the ship was allocated to those pools.
97(3) If the amount allocated to the 20% pool exceeds the amount of qualifying expenditure remaining in that pool, any excess shall be taken to the 10% pool.".
In para. 97(2), "20%" substituted for "25%" by FA 2008, s. 80(6)(c), with effect in relation to chargeable periods beginning on or after the "relevant date" and beginning before, and ending on or after, the "relevant date", subject to the transitional provisions in FA 2008, s. 80(9)–(11). The "relevant date" is 1 April 2008 for corporation tax purposes and 6 April 2008 for income tax purposes.
In para. 97(3), "20%" substituted for "25%" by FA 2008, s. 80(6)(c), with effect in relation to chargeable periods beginning on or after the "relevant date" and beginning before, and ending on or after, the "relevant date", subject to the transitional provisions in FA 2008, s. 80(9)–(11). The "relevant date" is 1 April 2008 for corporation tax purposes and 6 April 2008 for income tax purposes.
In para. 97(4), "tonnage tax (special rate)" substituted for "10%" by FA 2011, s. 57(4)(b), with effect in relation to chargeable periods ending on or after 1 January 2011, but this amendment has no effect in relation to expenditure incurred before 1 January 2011. See cross-reference note below for details of the application of para. 97(4) in relation to expenditure incurred before 1 January 2011. Subject to that cross-reference note, former para. 97(4) read as follows:
"**97(4)** A balancing charge arises only if the amount taken to the 10% pool exceeds the amount of qualifying expenditure remaining in that pool.".

Cross references – FA 2011, s. 10: in former para. 97(2) and (3) as it continues to apply in respect of expenditure incurred before 1 January 2011 (see history note above), "18%" substituted for "20%".

FA 2011, s. 10: in former para. 97(2), (3) and (4) as it continues to apply in respect of expenditure incurred before 1 January 2011 (see history note above), "8%" substituted for "10%".

QUANTITATIVE RESTRICTIONS: CHANGE OF CIRCUMSTANCES BRINGING CASE WITHIN RESTRICTIONS

98(1) The provisions of this paragraph apply where–

(a) the lessor under a lease has been entitled to capital allowances in circumstances in which paragraph 94 (quantitative restrictions on allowances) did not apply, and

(b) a change of circumstances brings the case within paragraph 89(1) so that the restrictions in paragraph 94 do apply.

98(2) In this paragraph–

"the relevant period" means the period beginning–

(a) with the beginning of the accounting period of the lessor in which there occurs the change of circumstances in relation to which this paragraph applies, or

(b) if since the beginning of that period there has been a change of circumstances in relation to which paragraph 99 applied (change taking case out of restrictions), with the time of that change (or if there has been more than one such change, the last of them),

and ending with the time of the change of circumstances in relation to which this paragraph applies; and

"the lessor's normal pool" means the lessor's pool that contains the qualifying expenditure relating to the ship at the beginning of the relevant period.

98(3) At the beginning of the relevant period an amount ("amount A") equal to–

(a) the tax written down value of the ship as at that time, or

(b) if less, the amount of unrelieved qualifying expenditure in the lessor's normal pool at that time,

shall be brought into account as a disposal value in the lessor's normal pool.

98(4) At the same time an amount of qualifying expenditure equal to amount A shall be taken to a separate single-asset pool ("the temporary pool").

98(5) Any qualifying expenditure or other items relating to the ship that would otherwise have been brought into account in the lessor's normal pool in the relevant period shall instead be brought into account in the temporary pool.

98(6) At the end of the relevant period, the temporary pool shall be closed as if the ship had been disposed of by the lessor for an amount equal to its tax written down value at that time ("amount B"), and any resulting balancing allowance or balancing charge shall be given effect.

98(7) The lessor shall be treated as if he had incurred qualifying expenditure equal to amount B on the provision of the ship for the purposes of the lessee's tonnage tax trade immediately after the end of the relevant period.

98(8) There shall be allocated to the lessor's tonnage tax (main rate) and tonnage tax (special rate) pools the same proportions of amount B as the proportions of the actual cost of providing the ship that would have been so allocated if the case has been within paragraph 89(1) at all material times.

History – In para. 98(1)(a), the word "finance" omitted from expression "finance lease" by FA 2003, s. 169 and Sch. 32, para. 1(2) and the word repealed by FA 2003, Sch. 43, Pt. 3(11) with effect in relation to any lease (within the meaning given by para. 5 of Sch. 32 to that Act) entered into on or after 19 December 2002.

In para. 98(8), "tonnage tax (main rate)" substituted for "20%" and "tonnage tax (special rate)" substituted for "10%" by FA 2011, s. 57(5), with effect in relation to chargeable periods ending on or after 1 January 2011, but this amendment has no effect in relation to expenditure incurred before 1 January 2011. See cross-reference note below for details of the application of para. 98(8) in relation to expenditure incurred before 1 January 2011. Subject to that cross-reference note, former para. 98(8) read as follows:

"**98(8)** There shall be allocated to the lessor's 20% and 10% pools the same proportions of amount B as the proportions of the actual cost of providing the ship that would have been so allocated if the case has been within paragraph 89(1) at all material times.".

In para. 98(8), "20%" substituted for "25%" by FA 2008, s. 80(6)(d), with effect in relation to chargeable periods beginning on or after the "relevant date" and beginning before, and ending on or after, the "relevant date", subject to the transitional provisions in FA 2008, s. 80(9)–(11). The "relevant date" is 1 April 2008 for corporation tax purposes and 6 April 2008 for income tax purposes.

Cross references – FA 2011, s. 10: in former para. 98(8) as it continues to apply in respect of expenditure incurred before 1 January 2011 (see history note above), "18%" substituted for "20%".

FA 2011, s. 10: in former para. 98(8) as it continues to apply in respect of expenditure incurred before 1 January 2011 (see history note above), "8%" substituted for "10%".

QUANTITATIVE RESTRICTIONS: CHANGE OF CIRCUMSTANCES TAKING CASE OUT OF RESTRICTIONS

99(1) The provisions of this paragraph apply where–

(a) the lessor under a lease has been entitled to capital allowances in which paragraph 94 (quantitative restrictions on allowances) applied, and

(b) a change of circumstances takes the case out of paragraph 89(1) so that the restrictions in paragraph 94 no longer apply.

99(2) When the change of circumstances occurs a disposal value shall be brought into account by the lessor equal to the tax written down value of the ships as at that time.

The provisions of paragraph 97 (treatment of disposal proceeds) apply as regards the allocation of that amount to the lessor's tonnage tax (main rate) and tonnage tax (special rate) pools.

99(3) The lessor shall be treated as if he had incurred qualifying expenditure on the provision of the ship for the purposes of the lessee's non-tonnage tax trade immediately after the change of circumstances occurs.

99(4) The amount of that expenditure shall be taken to be the amount that the tax written down value of the ship would have been, at the time the change of circumstances occurs, had paragraph 94 never applied.

99(5) [Omitted by FA 2011, s. 57(6)(c).]

History – In para. 99(1)(a), the word "finance" omitted from expression "finance lease" by FA 2003, s. 169 and Sch. 32, para. 1(2) and the word repealed by FA 2003, Sch. 43, Pt. 3(11) with effect in relation to any lease (within the meaning given by para. 5 of Sch. 32 to that Act) entered into on or after 19 December 2002.

In para. 99(2), "tonnage tax (main rate)" substituted for "20%" and "tonnage tax (special rate)" substituted for "10%' by FA 2011, s. 57(6)(a), with effect in relation to chargeable periods ending on or after 1 January 2011, but this amendment has no effect in relation to expenditure incurred before 1 January 2011. See cross-reference note below for details of the application of para. 99(2) in relation to expenditure incurred before 1 January 2011. Subject to that cross-reference note, former para. 99(2) read as follows:

"**99(2)** When the change of circumstances occurs a disposal value shall be brought into account by the lessor equal to the tax written down value of the ships as at that time.

The provisions of paragraph 97 (treatment of disposal proceeds) apply as regards the allocation of that amount to the lessor's 20% and 10% pools.".

In para. 99(2), "20%" substituted for "25%" by FA 2008, s. 80(6)(e), with effect in relation to chargeable periods beginning on or after the "relevant date" and beginning before, and ending on or after, the "relevant date", subject to the transitional provisions in FA 2008, s. 80(9)–(11). The "relevant date" is 1 April 2008 for corporation tax purposes and 6 April 2008 for income tax purposes.

In para. 99(4), the words "the amount that the tax written down value of the ship would have been, at the time the change of circumstances occurs, had paragraph 94 never applied" substituted for " the whole of the expenditure on the ship that would have qualified for capital allowances if paragraph 94 had never applied, written down at the appropriate rate per annum on the reducing balance for the period beginning with the time when it was actually incurred and ending when the change of circumstances occurs. " by FA 2011, s. 57(6)(b), but this amendment has no effect in relation to expenditure incurred before 1 January 2011.

In para. 99(4), "the appropriate rate" substituted for "25%" by FA 2008, s. 80(7)(a), with effect in relation to chargeable periods beginning on or after the "relevant date" and beginning before, and ending on or after, the "relevant date". The "relevant date" is 1 April 2008 for corporation tax purposes and 6 April 2008 for income tax purposes.

Para. 99(5) omitted by FA 2011, s. 57(6)(c), with effect in relation to chargeable periods ending on or after 1 January 2011, but this amendment has no effect in relation to expenditure incurred before 1 January 2011. See cross-reference note below for details of the application of para. 99(5) in relation to expenditure incurred before 1 January 2011. Subject to that cross-reference note, former para. 99(5) read as follows:

"**99(5)** The appropriate rate is 20%; but if for any part of the period mentioned in sub-paragraph (4) the rate of writing-down allowance to which the lessor would have been entitled under section 56(1) of the Capital Allowances Act 2001 if paragraph 94 had not applied was more than 20%, for that part of the period that rate is the appropriate rate.".

Former para. 99(5) inserted by FA 2008, s. 80(7)(b), with effect in relation to chargeable periods beginning on or after the "relevant date" and beginning before, and ending on or after, the "relevant date", subject to the transitional provisions in FA 2008, s. 80(9) to (11). The "relevant date" is 1 April 2008 for corporation tax purposes and 6 April 2008 for income tax purposes.

Cross references – FA 2011, s. 10: in former para. 99(2) and (5) as it continues to apply in respect of expenditure incurred before 1 January 2011 (see history note above), "18%" substituted for "20%".

FA 2011, s. 10: in former para. 99(2) as it continues to apply in respect of expenditure incurred before 1 January 2011 (see history note above), "8%" substituted for "10%".

DETERMINATION OF TAX WRITTEN DOWN VALUE, ETC.

100(1) This paragraph supplements paragraphs 98 and 99.

100(2) the **"tax written down value"** of the ship at any time means what would be the amount of unrelieved qualifying expenditure at that time determined on the following assumptions–

(a) that the qualifying expenditure relating to the ship had been held in a single asset pool, and

(b) that there had been made to the lessor–

(i) the first-year allowance (if any) that was actually made to him,

(ii) any first-year allowance falling to be made to him that was postponed under section 130 of the Capital Allowances Act 2001, and

(iii) the maximum amount of any writing-down allowances that, on the preceding assumptions, could have been made.

100(3) The references in paragraph 98(3)(b) and sub-paragraph (2) above to the amount of "unrelieved qualifying expenditure" are to the unrelieved qualifying expenditure that would otherwise have been carried forward under Chapter 5 of Part 2 of the Capital Allowances Act 2001.

100(4) For the purpose of determining that amount at a time other than the beginning or end of an accounting period of the lessor, it shall be assumed that an accounting period of the lessor began or ended at that time.

History – In para. 100(2)(b)(ii), reference to CAA 2001, s. 130 substituted for reference to CAA 1990, s. 30(1)(a) or (c) by CAA 2001, s. 578 and Sch. 2, para. 108(29) with effect as respects allowances and charges falling to be made for chargeable periods ending, for income tax purposes, on or after 6 April 2001, and, for corporation tax purposes, on or after 1 April 2001.
In para. 100(3), words "the unrelieved qualifying expenditure" to the end substituted for "the balance that would otherwise have been carried forward under Part II of the Capital Allowances Act 1990" by CAA 2001, s. 578 and Sch. 2, para. 108(30) with effect as respects allowances and charges falling to be made for chargeable periods ending, for income tax purposes, on or after 6 April 2001, and, for corporation tax purposes, on or after 1 April 2001.

QUANTITATIVE RESTRICTIONS: POWER TO ALTER AMOUNTS BY REGULATIONS

101(1) The Inland Revenue may by regulations alter the amounts for the time being specified in sub-paragraph (3)(a) and (b) and sub-paragraph (5) of paragraph 94 (quantitative restrictions on allowances).

101(2) The regulations may contain such incidental, supplementary and transitional provisions as appear to the Inland Revenue to be appropriate.

EXCLUSION OF LEASES ENTERED INTO ON OR BEFORE 23RD DECEMBER 1999

102 The provisions of this Part do not apply in relation to a finance lease entered into on or before 23rd December 1999.

Part XI – Special Rules for Offshore Activities

INTRODUCTION

103(1) This Part of this Schedule sets out special rules that apply where a qualifying ship operated by a tonnage tax company is engaged in offshore activities.

103(2) The rules in this Part of this Schedule do not apply in an accounting period unless the total number of days in that period on which qualifying ships operated by that company are engaged in offshore activities exceeds 30.

MEANING OF "OFFSHORE ACTIVITIES"

104(1) In this Part of this Schedule **"offshore activities"** means activities in connection with the exploration or exploitation of so much of the seabed or subsoil or their natural resources as is situated in the UK sector of the continental shelf.

104(1A) But none of the following activities is to be regarded as an offshore activity–

(a) offshore supply services;

(b) towage, salvage or other marine assistance;

(c) anchor handling;

(d) carriage of liquids or gases;

(e) safety or rescue services;

(f) the carriage of cargo in connection with dredging.

104(1B) The Treasury may make provision by order amending sub-paragraph (1A) by–

(a) adding, or

(b) varying,

any description of activity.

104(2) The **"UK sector of the continental shelf"** means–

(a) any area designated by Order in Council under section 1(7) of the Continental Shelf Act 1964, and

(b) any waters within the seaward limits of the territorial sea of the United Kingdom.

History – Para. 104(1A) inserted by FA 2005, s. 93 and Sch. 7, para. 15(2), with effect from 1 July 2005 but subject to the transitional provisions at FA 2005, Sch. 7, para. 19–21.
Para. 104(1B) inserted by FA 2005, s. 93 and Sch. 7, para. 15(2), with effect from 1 July 2005 but subject to the transitional provisions at FA 2005, Sch. 7, para. 19–21.

VESSELS TO WHICH SPECIAL PROVISIONS DO NOT APPLY

105 [Omitted by FA 2005, s. 93 and Sch. 7, para. 16 and repealed by s. 104 and Sch. 11, Pt. 2(10).]

History – Para. 105 repealed by FA 2005, s. 93 and Sch. 7, para. 16 and s. 104 and Sch. 11, Pt. 2(10), with effect from 1 July 2005 but subject to the transitional provisions at FA 2005, Sch. 7, para. 19–21.

TREATMENT OF PERIODS OF INACTIVITY

106 A period between contracts when a qualifying ship is not working shall not be taken to be a period during which the ship is engaged in offshore activities unless–

(a) the period of inactivity is specifically related to a forthcoming offshore activity, and

(b) it is impractical for the vessel to undertake other work in the meantime.

PROFITS FROM OFFSHORE ACTIVITIES TO BE COMPUTED ACCORDING TO ORDINARY RULES

107(1) The profits of a tonnage tax company from a qualifying ship in respect of periods during which the ship is engaged in offshore activities (its "offshore profits") are computed and charged to tax in accordance with ordinary corporation tax principles as if they were not part of the company's relevant shipping profits.

107(2) Accordingly, the number of days in an accounting period during which a qualifying ship is so engaged shall be left out of account for the purposes of paragraph 4 (calculation of tonnage tax profits by reference to daily profit).

APPLICATION OF RING FENCE PROVISIONS

108(1) The provisions of Part VII (the ring fence: general provisions) apply in relation to a company's offshore activities as if they were not tonnage tax activities.

108(2) The provisions of this Schedule apply in relation to a company's offshore profits as they apply to profits other than relevant shipping profits.

CHARGEABLE GAINS FROM ASSETS USED FOR OFFSHORE ACTIVITIES

109 A period during which an asset is used for the purposes of offshore activities is treated for the purposes of paragraph 65 (chargeable gains on disposal of tonnage tax asset) as if it were a period during which the asset was not a tonnage tax asset.

CAPITAL ALLOWANCES: GENERAL

110(1) A tonnage tax company may claim capital allowances for capital expenditure incurred in providing plant or machinery for the purposes of its offshore activities.

110(2) In such a case Part 2 of the Capital Allowances Act 2001 applies as if–

(a) an asset used for the purposes of the company's offshore activities were provided by the company for those purposes on the first occasion after entry into tonnage tax on which it is brought into use for those purposes, and

(b) an amount of capital expenditure (the "notional qualifying expenditure") had been incurred at that time on its provision.

110(3) The amount of the notional qualifying expenditure is given by paragraph 112 (existing assets) or paragraph 113 (new assets).

110(4) Where an asset to which this paragraph applies ceases permanently to be used for the purposes of the company's offshore activities, it is treated for the purposes of Part 2 of the Capital Allowances Act 2001 as it applies by virtue of this paragraph as if it had been disposed of at market value.
This does not apply if a disposal value is required to be brought into account under section 61(1) of that Act apart from this sub-paragraph.

History – In para. 110(2), (4), references to CAA 2001, Pt. 2 substituted for references to CAA 1990, Pt. II, and in para. 110(4) reference to CAA 2001, s. 61(1) for CAA 1990, s. 24(6)(c), by CAA 2001, s. 578 and Sch. 2, para. 108(31), (32) with effect as respects allowances and charges falling to be made for chargeable periods ending, for income tax purposes, on or after 6 April 2001, and, for corporation tax purposes, on or after 1 April 2001.

CAPITAL ALLOWANCES: PROPORTIONATE REDUCTION OF ALLOWANCES

111(1) This paragraph applies where in an accounting period of the company an asset to which paragraph 110 applies is used for the purposes of the company's offshore activities on some only of the days in the period.

111(2) The amount of any writing-down allowance for that period in respect of expenditure incurred on the provision of the asset is restricted to the relevant proportion of the full allowance.

111(3) Any writing-down allowance for a subsequent accounting period of the company in respect of such expenditure shall be calculated as if an allowance had been made of an amount equal to the full allowance, whether or not that amount (or any amount) was in fact claimed.

111(4) For the purposes of this paragraph the full allowance means the allowance (if any) that would have been available apart from this paragraph.

111(5) For the purposes of this paragraph the relevant proportion of the full allowance is given by:

$$\frac{OSD}{APD}$$

where–

OSD is the number of days in the accounting period on which the asset was used for the purposes of the company's offshore activities; and

APD is the number of days in that period.

CAPITAL ALLOWANCES: NOTIONAL QUALIFYING EXPENDITURE: EXISTING ASSETS

112(1) This paragraph applies to determine the amount of notional qualifying expenditure for the purposes of paragraph 110 where the company was entitled before entry into tonnage tax to capital allowances in respect of expenditure on providing the asset.

112(2) If the asset was brought into use for the purposes of the company's offshore activities immediately on entry into tonnage tax, the notional qualifying expenditure is equal to any unrelieved qualifying expenditure attributable to the asset.

112(3) In this paragraph **"unrelieved qualifying expenditure"** means the unrelieved qualifying expenditure that would otherwise have been carried forward under Chapter 5 of Part 2 of the Capital Allowances Act 2001.

112(4) The amount of unrelieved qualifying expenditure attributable to plant or machinery in a class pool, or the main pool, is the proportion of the whole given by:

$$\frac{AV}{PV}$$

where:

AV is the market value of the asset concerned immediately before entry into tonnage tax, and

PV is the aggregate market value at that time of all the assets in the pool.

112(5) References in this paragraph to unrelieved qualifying expenditure include qualifying expenditure to the extent to which it is unrelieved by virtue of notice having been given under section 130 of the Capital Allowances Act 2001 (notice postponing first-year or writing-down allowance).

112(6) If the asset was not brought into use for the purposes of the company's offshore activities immediately on entry into tonnage tax, the notional qualifying expenditure is the amount given by sub-paragraph (2) but written down in respect of the period between the company's entry into tonnage tax and the asset being brought into use for those purposes.

112(7) The Inland Revenue shall make provision by regulations as to the basis on which the writing down mentioned in sub-paragraph (6) is to be done.
The regulations may make different provision for different descriptions of asset.

CAPITAL ALLOWANCES: NOTIONAL QUALIFYING EXPENDITURE: NEW ASSETS

113(1) This paragraph applies to determine the amount of notional qualifying expenditure for the purposes of paragraph 110 where the company was not entitled before entry into tonnage tax to capital allowances in respect of expenditure on providing the asset.

113(2) If the asset was brought into use for the purposes of the company's offshore activities immediately on being acquired by the company, the notional qualifying expenditure is equal to the amount that would fall to be brought into account as qualifying expenditure under Part 2 of the Capital Allowances Act 2001 apart from this Schedule.

113(3) If the asset was not brought into use for the purposes of the company's offshore activities immediately on being acquired by the company, the notional qualifying expenditure is the amount referred to in sub-paragraph (2) written down in respect of the period between its acquisition by the company and its being brought into use for those purposes.

113(4) The Inland Revenue shall make provision by regulations as to the basis on which the writing down mentioned in sub-paragraph (3) is to be done.
The regulations may make different provision for different descriptions of asset.

History – In para. 113(2), references to CAA 2001, Pt. 2 substituted for references to CAA 1990, Pt. II, by CAA 2001, s. 578 and Sch. 2, para. 108(35) with effect in respect of allowances and charges falling to be made for chargeable periods ending, for income tax purposes, on or after 6 April 2001 and for corporation tax purposes on or after 1 April 2001.

THE TRAINING REQUIREMENT

114(1) The fact that a qualifying ship is used for the purposes of offshore activities does not affect the training requirement but an allowance is made under this paragraph.

114(2) The amount of the allowance in an accounting period is equal to the aggregate of–

(a) the cash equivalent of the training provided that would not have had to be provided, and

(b) any payments in lieu of training made that would not have had to be made,

if the days on which the ship was engaged in offshore activities had been days on which it was not engaged in tonnage tax activities.

For the purposes of paragraph (a) the cash equivalent of training shall be calculated by reference to the current rate of payments in lieu of training.

114(3) The amount of the allowance may be deducted by the company in computing the amount of corporation tax payable for that accounting period, so far as that is attributable to offshore activities.

114(4) If in any accounting period the company is unable to deduct the full amount of–

(a) any allowance to which it is entitled under this paragraph for that period, and

(b) any amount brought forward under this sub-paragraph,

the balance may be carried forward and set against the amount of corporation tax payable in the next accounting period, so far as that is attributable to offshore activities.

114(5) No deduction may be made by a company in computing its profits from offshore activities in respect of expenditure incurred in meeting the training requirement.

INTERPRETATION

115 Expressions used in this Part of this Schedule that are defined for the purposes of Part VIII or IX of this Schedule have the same meaning in this Part.

Part XII – Groups, Mergers and Related Matters

MEANING OF 'GROUP' AND 'MEMBER OF GROUP'

116 In this Schedule a **"group"** means–

(a) all the companies controlled by an individual, or

(b) where a company that is not controlled by another person controls one or more other companies, that company and all the companies controlled by it.

References to membership of a group shall be construed accordingly.

COMPANIES TREATED AS CONTROLLED BY AN INDIVIDUAL

117(1) For the purposes of this Schedule an individual is treated as controlling any company that is controlled–

(a) by him alone, or

(b) by him together with one or more associates of his, or

(c) subject to sub-paragraph (2), by any associate of his, with or without any other such associates.

117(2) An individual shall not be treated as controlling a company by virtue of sub-paragraph (1)(c) if he does not have any significant influence over the affairs of the company in question.

MEANING OF "CONTROL"

118(1) In this Schedule **"control"**, in relation to a company, means the power of a person to secure–

(a) by means of the holding of shares or the possession of voting power in or in relation to that or any other company, or

(b) by virtue of any powers conferred by the articles of association or other document regulating that or any other company,

that the affairs of the company are conducted in accordance with his wishes.

118(2) For the purposes of this paragraph there shall be attributed to a person–

(a) any rights or powers which another person holds on his behalf or may be required to exercise at his direction or on his behalf,

(b) any rights or powers–

  (i) of a company of which he has, or he and his associates have, control, or

  (ii) of any two or more such companies, and

(c) any rights or powers of any associate of his, or of any two or more associates of his.

118(3) The references in paragraphs (b) and (c) of sub-paragraph (2) to rights or powers of a company or associate include rights or powers attributed to the company or associate under paragraph (a) of that sub-paragraph.

118(4) The references in paragraphs (b) and (c) of sub-paragraph (2) to rights or powers of an associate do not include rights or powers attributed to the associate under those paragraphs.

COMPANY NOT TO BE TREATED AS MEMBER OF MORE THAN ONE GROUP

119(1) For the purposes of this Schedule a company may not, at the same time, be a member–

(a) of a tonnage tax group and a qualifying non-tonnage tax group, or

(b) of more than one tonnage tax group.

119(2) If the rules in paragraphs 116 to 118 would produce that result in relation to a company, the following rules apply.

119(3) As between a tonnage tax group and a qualifying non-tonnage tax group, the company shall be treated as a member of the tonnage tax group and not of the non-tonnage tax group.

119(4) As between two tonnage tax groups, the company shall be treated as a member of the group whose tonnage tax election was made first and not of the other tonnage tax group.

119(5) In the case of group elections made at the same time, the company may choose which election it joins in.

It is treated for the purposes of this Schedule as a member of the group in respect of which that election is made and not of any other tonnage tax group.

ARRANGEMENTS FOR DEALING WITH GROUP MATTERS

120(1) The Inland Revenue may enter into arrangements with the qualifying companies in a group for one of those companies to deal on behalf of the group in relation to matters arising under this Schedule that may conveniently be dealt with on a group basis.

120(2) Any such arrangements–

(a) may make provision in relation to cases where companies become or cease to be members of a group;

(b) may make provision for or in connection with the termination of the arrangements; and

(c) may make such supplementary, incidental, consequential or transitional provision as is necessary or expedient for the purposes of the arrangements.

120(3) Any such arrangements do not affect–

(a) any requirement under this Schedule that an election be made jointly by all the qualifying companies in the group; or

(b) any liability under this Schedule or any other provision of the Tax Acts of a company to which the arrangements relate.

120(4) The Secretary of State may also make such arrangements in relation to matters arising under this Schedule in relation to which he has functions.

MEANING OF 'MERGER' AND 'DEMERGER'

121(1) In this Schedule–

"merger" means a transaction by which one or more companies become members of a group, and

"demerger" means a transaction by which one or more companies cease to be members of a group.

121(2) References to a merger to which a group is a party include any merger affecting a member of the group.

MERGER: BETWEEN TONNAGE TAX GROUPS OR COMPANIES

122(1) This paragraph applies where there is a merger–

(a) between two or more tonnage tax groups,

(b) between one or more tonnage tax groups and one or more tonnage tax companies, or

(c) between two or more tonnage tax companies.

122(2) In all those cases the group resulting from the merger is a tonnage tax group as if a group election had been made.

122(3) That deemed election continues in force, subject to the provisions of this Schedule–

(a) if there is a dominant party to the merger, until that party's tonnage tax election would have expired;

(b) if there is no dominant party, until whichever of the existing tonnage tax elections had the longest period left to run would have expired.

MERGER: TONNAGE TAX GROUP OR COMPANY AND QUALIFYING NON-TONNAGE TAX GROUP OR COMPANY

123(1) This paragraph applies where there is a merger between a tonnage tax group or company ("T") and a qualifying non-tonnage tax group or company ("QNT").

123(2) If T is the dominant party, the group resulting from the merger is a tonnage tax group as if a group election had been made.

That deemed election continues in force, subject to the provisions of this Schedule, until T's election would have expired.

123(3) If QNT is the dominant party, T's tonnage tax election ceases to be in force as from the date of the merger.

123(4) If there is no dominant party–

(a) the group resulting from the merger may elect that T shall be treated as the dominant party (with the result that sub-paragraph (2) applies), and

(b) if it does not do so, T's tonnage tax election ceases to be in force as from the date of the merger.

123(5) Any election under sub-paragraph (4)(a) must be made–

(a) jointly by all the qualifying companies in the group resulting from the merger,

(b) by notice to the Inland Revenue,

(c) within twelve months of the merger.

MERGER: TONNAGE TAX GROUP OR COMPANY AND NON-QUALIFYING GROUP OR COMPANY

124(1) This paragraph applies where there is a merger between a tonnage tax group or company ("T") and a non-qualifying group or company.

124(2) In that case the group resulting from the merger is a tonnage tax group by virtue of T's election.

MERGER: NON-QUALIFYING GROUP OR COMPANY AND QUALIFYING NON-TONNAGE TAX GROUP OR COMPANY

125(1) This paragraph applies where there is a merger between a non-qualifying group or company ("NQ") and a qualifying non-tonnage tax group or company.

125(2) In that case, if NQ is the dominant party the group resulting from the merger may make a tonnage tax election having effect as from the date of the merger.

125(3) Any such election must be made–

(a) jointly by all the qualifying companies in the group resulting from the merger,

(b) by notice to the Inland Revenue,

(c) within twelve months of the merger.

MEANING OF "DOMINANT PARTY" IN RELATION TO MERGER

126(1) This paragraph explains what is meant by the references in this Schedule to the "dominant party" in relation to a merger.

126(2) The **"dominant party"** is determined as follows–

(a) if the turnover generated by the relevant activities of one of the parties to the merger is more than twice that of the other, that one is the dominant party;

(b) if not, there is no dominant party.

126(3) The relevant activities of a party to a merger are–

(a) for the purposes of–

 (i) paragraph 122 (merger between tonnage tax groups or companies), or

 (ii) paragraph 123 (merger between tonnage tax group or company and qualifying non-tonnage tax group or company),

the tonnage tax activities of that party;

(b) for the purposes of paragraph 125 (merger between non-qualifying group or company and qualifying non-tonnage tax group or company), all the activities of that party.

126(4) The basis on which (and the periods by reference to which) the turnover from relevant activities is to be determined for the purposes of those paragraphs shall be such as may be agreed between the parties and the Inland Revenue.

126(5) In default of such agreement–

(a) the Inland Revenue shall decide, and

(b) an appeal may be made against their decision.

126(6) Notice of appeal must be given to the Inland Revenue within 30 days of their decision being notified to the parties.

History – In para. 126(5)(b) the words "may be made" substituted for the words "lies to the Special Commissioners" by SI 2009/56, art. 3(1) and Sch. 1, para. 294(3), operative from 1 April 2009, subject to transitional and saving provisions in SI 2009/56, Sch. 3.

DEMERGER: SINGLE COMPANY

127(1) This paragraph applies where a tonnage tax company ceases to be a member of a tonnage tax group and does not become a member of another group.

127(2) In that case–

(a) the company in question remains a tonnage tax company as if a single company election had been made, and

(b) that deemed election continues in force, subject to the provisions of this Schedule, until the group election would have expired.

127(3) If two or more members of the previous group remain, and any of them is a qualifying company, the group consisting of those companies is a tonnage tax group by virtue of the previous group election.

DEMERGER: GROUP

128(1) This paragraph applies where a tonnage tax group splits into two or more groups.

128(2) In that case each new group that contains a qualifying company that was a tonnage tax company before the demerger is a tonnage tax group as if a group election had been made.

128(3) That deemed election continues in force, subject to the provisions of this Schedule, until the group election would have expired.

DUTY TO NOTIFY INLAND REVENUE OF GROUP CHANGES

129(1) A tonnage tax company that becomes or ceases to be a member of a group, or of a particular group, must give notice to the Inland Revenue of that fact.

129(2) The notice must be given within the period of twelve months beginning with the date on which the company became or ceased to be a member of the group.

129(3) [Amends second column of Table in TMA 1970, s. 98.]

Part XIII – Application of provisions to partnerships

INTRODUCTION

130(1) The Inland Revenue may make provision by regulations as to the application of this Schedule in relation to activities carried on by a company in partnership.

130(2) Nothing in the following provisions of this Part of this Schedule shall be read as restricting the generality of this power.

CALCULATION OF PARTNERSHIP PROFITS

131 The Regulations may provide that–

(a) for the purpose of calculating the profits of a partner which is a tonnage tax company, the profits of the partnership shall be calculated as if the partnership were a tonnage tax company, and

(b) for the purposes of calculating the profits of a partner which is not a tonnage tax company, the profits of the partnership shall be calculated as if the partnership were not a tonnage tax company.

QUALIFYING PARTNERSHIPS

132(1) The regulations may provide that activities carried on by a company in partnership are not to be regarded as qualifying activities of that company unless the partnership is a qualifying partnership. **"Qualifying activities"** here means core activities, qualifying secondary activities or qualifying incidental activities.

132(2) Subject to any provision made by the regulations, a **"qualifying partnership"** means a partnership that if it were a company would meet the requirements in paragraph 16(1) (qualifying companies).

SHIPS OWNED BY OR CHARTERED TO PARTNERS

133 The regulations may provide that a ship which is not a partnership property but which–

(a) is owned by or chartered to a member (or two or more members) of a partnership, and

(b) is a ship in relation to which activities of the partnership business are carried on, shall be treated as if it were owned by or chartered to every member of the partnership and as if everything done by or to any of the partners in relation to it had been done by or to all the partners.

TRANSACTIONS NOT AT ARM'S LENGTH

134 The regulations may provide that for the purposes of paragraphs 58 and 59 (transactions not at arm's length) the partnership shall be treated–

(a) as an entity separate and distinct from the persons that are its members, and

(b) as if it were a tonnage tax company.

ADJUSTMENTS FOR CAPITAL ALLOWANCE PURPOSES

135 The regulations may provide that where a partner leaves a tonnage tax, such adjustments shall be made for capital allowance purposes, in relation to that partner and all or any of the other partners, with respect to–

(a) the amount of qualifying expenditure under Part 2 of the Capital Allowances Act 2001 (plant and machinery allowances), and

(b) the amount of the residue of qualifying expenditure under Part 3 of that Act (industrial buildings allowances),

as may be specified in the regulations.

History – In para. 135, words "Part 2 of the Capital Allowances Act 2001 (plant and machinery allowances)' substituted for "Part II of the Capital Allowances Act 1990 (plant and machinery)", and words "the residue of qualifying expenditure under Part 3 of that Act (industrial buildings allowances)" substituted for "unrelieved qualifying expenditure under Part I of that Act (industrial buildings)" by CAA 2001, s. 578 and Sch. 2, para. 108(36) with effect as respects allowances and charges falling to be made for chargeable periods ending, for income tax purposes, on or after 6 April 2001, and, for corporation tax purposes, on or after 1 April 2001.

GENERAL

136 Regulations under this Part of this Schedule–

(a) may make different provision for different cases, and

(b) may contain such supplementary, incidental and transitional provision as appears to the Inland Revenue to be appropriate.

Part XIV – Withdrawal of relief etc on company leaving tonnage tax

INTRODUCTION

137(1) This Part of this Schedule applies where a company ceases to be a tonnage tax company.

137(2) The provisions of paragraphs 138 and 139 (exit charges: chargeable gains and balancing charges) apply where a company ceases to be a tonnage tax company–

(a) on ceasing to be a qualifying company for reasons relating wholly or mainly to tax, or

(b) under paragraph 42 (exclusion from tonnage tax where tax avoidance arrangements entered into).

137(3) Paragraph 140 (ten year disqualification from re-entry into tonnage tax) applies in every case where a company ceases to be a tonnage tax company otherwise than on the expiry of a tonnage tax election.

EXIT CHARGE: CHARGEABLE GAINS

138(1) Paragraph 65(1)(a) (chargeable gain: disposal of tonnage tax assets) has effect in relation to gains (but not losses) on all relevant disposals as if the company had never been a tonnage tax company.

138(2) For this purpose a **"relevant disposal"** means a disposal–

(a) on or after the day on which the company ceases to be a tonnage tax company, or

(b) at any time during the period of six years immediately preceding that day when the company was a tonnage tax company.

138(3) Where sub-paragraph (1) operates to increase the amount of the chargeable gain on a disposal made at a time within the period mentioned in sub-paragraph (2)(b), the gain is treated to the extent of the increase–

(a) as arising immediately before the company ceased to be a tonnage tax company, and

(b) as not being relevant shipping profits of the company.

138(4) No relief, deduction or set-off of any description is allowed against the amount of that increase or the corporation tax on that amount.

EXIT CHARGE: BALANCING CHARGES

139(1) This paragraph applies if in a relevant accounting period during which the company was a tonnage tax company it was liable to a balancing charge in relation to which paragraph 78 (phasing-out of balancing charges) applied to reduce the amount of the charge.

139(2) For this purpose a **"relevant accounting period"** means an accounting period ending not more than six years before the day on which the company ceased to be a tonnage tax company.

139(3) The company is treated as having received an additional amount of profits chargeable to corporation tax equal to the aggregate of the amounts by which those balancing charges were reduced.

139(4) Those additional profits are treated–

(a) as arising immediately before the company ceased to be a tonnage tax company, and

(b) as not being relevant shipping profits of the company.

139(5) No relief, deduction or set-off of any description is allowed against those profits or against corporation tax on them.

TEN YEAR DISQUALIFICATION FROM RE-ENTRY INTO TONNAGE TAX

140(1) A company election made by a former tonnage tax company is ineffective if made before the end of the period of ten years beginning with the date on which the company ceased to be a tonnage tax company.

140(2) A group election that–

(a) is made in respect of a group whose members include a former tonnage tax company, and

(b) would result in that company becoming a tonnage tax company,

is ineffective if made before the end of the period of ten years beginning with the date on which that company ceased to be a tonnage tax company.

140(3) Sub-paragraphs (1) and (2) do not prevent a company becoming a tonnage tax company under and in accordance with the rules in Part XII of this Schedule (groups, mergers and related matters).

140(4) In this paragraph **"former tonnage tax company"** means a company that is not a tonnage tax company but has previously been a tonnage tax company.

SECOND OR SUBSEQUENT APPLICATION OF THIS PART

141 Where this Part of this Schedule applies on a second or subsequent occasion on which a company ceases to be a tonnage tax company (whether or not this Part applied on any of the previous occasions)–

(a) the references to the company ceasing to be a tonnage tax company shall be read as references to the last occasion on which it did so, and

(b) the references to the period during which the company was a tonnage tax company do not include any period before its most recent entry into tonnage tax.

Part XV – Supplementary Provisions

MEANING OF "SHIP"

142 In this Schedule **"ship"** means any vessel used in navigation, and includes a hovercraft.

MEANING OF "ON BAREBOAT CHARTER TERMS"

143 In this Schedule a charter **"on bareboat charter terms"** means a hiring of a ship for a stipulated period on terms which give the charterer possession and control of the ship, including the right to appoint the master and crew.

MEANING OF "ASSOCIATE"

144(1) In this Schedule **"associate"**, in relation to an individual, means–

(a) a relative of that individual;

(b) a partner of that individual;

(c) the trustee or trustees of any settlement in relation to which–

(i) that individual, or

(ii) any relative (whether living or dead) of that individual,

is or was a settlor;

(d) where that individual is interested in any shares or obligations of a company that are subject to a trust, the trustee or trustees of the settlement concerned;

(e) where that individual is interested in any shares or obligations of a company that are part of the estate of a deceased person, the personal representatives of the deceased.

144(2) In sub-paragraph (1)(a) and (c)(ii) **"relative"** means spouse or civil partner, parent or remoter forebear, child or remoter issue, or brother or sister.
Section 831(4) of the Taxes Act 1988 applies for the purposes of this paragraph as it applies for the purposes of that Act.

144(3) In sub-paragraph (1)(c) and (d) **"settlement"** and **"settlor"** have the same meaning as in Chapter 5 of Part 5 of ITTOIA 2005 (see section 620 of that Act).

History – In para. 144(2) the words "spouse or civil partner" substituted for the words "husband or wife" by SI 2005/3229, reg. 133, with effect from 5 December 2005.
In para. 144(3) the words "Chapter 5 of Part 5 of ITTOIA 2005 (see section 620 of that Act)" substituted for the former wording by ITTOIA 2005, s. 882(1) and Sch. 1, para. 522; effective for income tax purposes for 2005–06 onwards and for corporation tax purposes for accounting periods ending after 5 April 2005 (ITTOIA 2005, s. 883(1)).

EXERCISE OF FUNCTIONS CONFERRED ON "THE INLAND REVENUE"

145(1) Any power to make regulations conferred by this Schedule on "the Inland Revenue" is exercisable only by the Board.

145(2) Subject to that, references in this Schedule to **"the Inland Revenue"** are to any officer of the Board.

MEANING OF "COMPANY" AND RELATED EXPRESSIONS

146 In this Schedule–

"company" means a body corporate or unincorporated association, but does not include a partnership;

"controlled foreign company" has the same meaning as in Chapter IV of Part XVII of the Taxes Act 1988 (tax avoidance: controlled foreign companies);

"single company" means a company that is not a member of a group.

INDEX OF DEFINED EXPRESSIONS

147 In this Schedule the following expressions are defined or otherwise explained by the provisions indicated:

associate (of an individual)	paragraph 144
bareboat charter terms	paragraph 143
capital allowances (in Part IX)	paragraph 88(1)
certificate of non-compliance (with training requirement)	paragraph 32
company	paragraph 146
company election	paragraph 7(1)(a)
control	paragraph 118 (and see paragraph 117)
controlled foreign company	paragraph 146
core qualifying activities	paragraph 46
cost of providing the ship (in Part X)	paragraph 95
demerger	paragraph 121(1)
dominant party (in relation to a merger)	paragraph 126
entering (or leaving) tonnage tax	paragraph 2(2)
finance costs (in paragraphs 61 and 62)	paragraph 63
group	paragraph 116
group election	paragraph 7(1)(b)
initial period	paragraph 10(1) (and see paragraph 11(2))
Inland Revenue	paragraph 145
lease (and lessor and lessee) (in Part X)	paragraph 89(2)
leaving (or entering) tonnage tax	paragraph 2(2)
member of group	paragraph 116
Member States' registers	paragraph 22B(7)
merger	paragraph 121(1)
minimum training obligation	paragraph 24
offshore activities (in Part XI)	paragraph 104
offshore profits (in Part XI)	paragraph 107(1)
payments in lieu of training	paragraph 29
pooling and related expressions (in Parts IX, X and XI)	paragraph 88(2) and (3)
operating (a ship)	paragraph 18
qualifying activity and qualifying expenditure (in Parts IX, X and XI)	paragraph 88(1)
qualifying company	paragraph 16(1) (and see paragraph 17)
qualifying dredger	paragraph 20(7)
qualifying group	paragraph 16(2)
qualifying incidental activities	paragraph 48
qualifying secondary activities	paragraph 47

qualifying ship	paragraphs 19 to 22
relevant shipping income	paragraph 44(2)
relevant shipping profits	paragraph 44(1) (and see paragraph 108(2))
renewal election	paragraph 15(1)
the 75% limit (on chartered-in tonnage)	paragraph 37
ship	paragraph 142
single company	paragraph 146
subject to tonnage tax	paragraph 2(2)
tonnage	paragraph 6(1)
tonnage tax	paragraph 1(1)
tonnage tax activities	paragraph 45 (and see paragraph 108(1))
tonnage tax asset (in Parts VIII and XI)	paragraph 64
tonnage tax company	paragraph 2(1)
tonnage tax election	paragraph 1(2) (and see Part II)
tonnage tax group	paragraph 2(1)
tonnage tax pool (in Part IX)	paragraph 69
tonnage tax profits	paragraphs 3 to 5 (and see Part XI)
tonnage tax trade	paragraph 53(1)
training commitment	paragraph 25 (and see paragraphs 27(4) and (5) and 28(2)

History – In para. 147, the defined expression "Member States' registers" inserted by FA 2005, s. 93 and Sch. 7, para. 17(2), with effect from 1 July 2005 but subject to the transitional provisions at FA 2005, Sch. 7, para. 19–21.
In para. 147, the defined expression "qualifying dredger" inserted by FA 2005, s. 93 and Sch. 7, para. 17(2), with effect from 1 July 2005 but subject to the transitional provisions at FA 2005, Sch. 7, para. 19–21.

SCHEDULE 23 – TAX TREATMENT OF AMOUNTS RELATING TO ACQUISITION ETC OF CERTAIN RIGHTS

Section 87

[Omitted by ITTOIA 2005, s. 882(1) and Sch. 1, para. 523; and repealed by ITTOIA 2005, s. 884 and Sch. 3.]

History – Sch. 3 omitted by ITTOIA 2005, s. 882(1) and Sch. 1, para. 523; and repealed by ITTOIA 2005, s. 884 and Sch. 3 effective for income tax purposes for 2005–06 onwards and for corporation tax purposes for accounting periods ending after 5 April 2005 (ITTOIA 2005, s. 883(1)).

Notes – The omitted income tax material is principally rewritten at ITTOIA 2005, s. 146–148 and 614.
Sch. 23 ceased to have effect for corporation tax purposes as regards accounting periods ending on or after 1 April 2002.

SCHEDULE 24 – NEW SCHEDULE 4A TO THE TAXATION OF CHARGEABLE GAINS ACT 1992

Section 91(2)

[Inserts TCGA 1992, Sch. 4A.]

SCHEDULE 25 – NEW SCHEDULE 4B TO THE TAXATION OF CHARGEABLE GAINS ACT 1992

Section 92(2)

[Inserts TCGA 1992, Sch. 4B.]

SCHEDULE 26 – TRANSFERS OF VALUE: ATTRIBUTION OF GAINS TO BENEFICIARIES

Section 92(4)

Part I – New Schedule 4C to the Taxation of Chargeable Gains Act 1992

1 [Inserts TCGA 1992, Sch. 4C.]

Part II – Consequential Amendments

TAXATION OF CHARGEABLE GAINS ACT 1992(C.12)

2 [Inserts TCGA 1992, s. 90(5).]

3 [Amends TCGA 1992, s. 96(1), (2).]

4 [Amends TCGA 1992, s. 97(1), (3)(a), (4), (5), (7) and (8).]

5 [Inserts TCGA 1992, s. 98(3).]

TAXES ACT 1988

6 [Repealed by ITA 2007, s. 1031 and Sch. 3, Pt. 1.]

History – Para. 6 repealed by ITA 2007, s. 1031 and Sch. 3, Pt. 1, with effect from 6 April 2007.

Notes – Para. 6 rewritten as ITA 2007, s. 734(1).

SCHEDULE 27 – GROUP RELIEF IN CASE OF NON-RESIDENT COMPANIES ETC

Section 97

Part I – Amendments of Chapter IV of Part X of the Taxes Act 1988

AVAILABILITY OF RELIEF

1 [Repealed by CTA 2010, s. 1181 and Sch. 3, Pt. 1.]

History – Para. 1 repealed by CTA 2010, s. 1181 and Sch. 3, Pt. 1, with effect for accounting periods ending on or after 1 April 2010.

2 [Repealed by CTA 2010, s. 1181 and Sch. 3, Pt. 1.]

History – Para. 2 repealed by CTA 2010, s. 1181 and Sch. 3, Pt. 1, with effect for accounting periods ending on or after 1 April 2010.

LIMITS ON AMOUNT OF RELIEF

3 [Repealed by CTA 2010, s. 1181 and Sch. 3, Pt. 1.]

History – Para. 3 repealed by CTA 2010, s. 1181 and Sch. 3, Pt. 1, with effect for accounting periods ending on or after 1 April 2010. Para. 3(a) previously repealed by FA 2006, s. 178 and Sch. 26, Pt. 3(2), with effect in relation to accounting periods beginning on or after 1 April 2006, subject to the provisions of FA 2006, Sch. 1, para. 9.

4 [Repealed by CTA 2010, s. 1181 and Sch. 3, Pt. 1.]

History – Para. 4 repealed by CTA 2010, s. 1181 and Sch. 3, Pt. 1, with effect for accounting periods ending on or after 1 April 2010.

AMENDMENTS OF SCHEDULE 18 TO THE TAXES ACT 1988

5 [Repealed by CTA 2010, s. 1181 and Sch. 3, Pt. 1.]

History – Para. 5 repealed by CTA 2010, s. 1181 and Sch. 3, Pt. 1, with effect for accounting periods ending on or after 1 April 2010.

COMMENCEMENT

6 [Repealed by CTA 2010, s. 1181 and Sch. 3, Pt. 1.]

History – Para. 6 repealed by CTA 2010, s. 1181 and Sch. 3, Pt. 1, with effect for accounting periods ending on or after 1 April 2010.

Part II – Consequential Amendments

SECTION 76 OF THE TAXES ACT 1988

7 [Repealed by FA 2004, s. 326, Sch. 42, Pt. 2(3).]

History – Para. 7 repealed by FA 2004, s. 326, Sch. 42, Pt. 2(3) with effect for accounting periods beginning on or after 1 April 2004 subject to the transitional provisions in FA 2004 s. 43 and 44 and Sch. 6.

SECTION 434A OF THE TAXES ACT 1988

8 [Repealed by FA 2007, s. 114 and Sch. 27, Pt. 2(7).]

History – Para. 8 repealed by FA 2007, s. 114 and Sch. 27, Pt. 2(7) with effect (FA 2007, s. 38):

- for the purposes of corporation tax, for periods of account of insurance companies beginning on or after 1 January 2007; and
- for the purposes of income tax, for the 2007/08 tax year and subsequent tax years.

SECTION 502 OF THE TAXES ACT 1988

9 [Repealed by CTA 2010, s. 1181 and Sch. 3, Pt. 1.]

History – Para. 9 repealed by CTA 2010, s. 1181 and Sch. 3, Pt. 1, with effect for corporation tax purposes for accounting periods ending on or after 1 April 2010, and for income tax and capital gains tax purposes for the tax year 2010–11 and subsequent tax years.

SCHEDULE 24 TO THE TAXES ACT 1988

10 [Amends ICTA 1988, Sch. 24, para. 5.]

SCHEDULE 18 TO THE FINANCE ACT 1998

11 [Inserts FA 1998, Sch. 18, para. 68(3), (4).]

COMMENCEMENT

12(1) Paragraphs 7, 8, 10 and 11 have effect in relation to accounting periods ending on or after 1st April 2000.

12(2) [Repealed by CTA 2010, s. 1181 and Sch. 3, Pt. 1.]

History – Para. 12(2) repealed by CTA 2010, s. 1181 and Sch. 3, Pt. 1, with effect for corporation tax purposes for accounting periods ending on or after 1 April 2010, and for income tax and capital gains tax purposes for the tax year 2010–11 and subsequent tax years.

SCHEDULE 28 – RECOVERY OF TAX PAYABLE BY NON-RESIDENT COMPANY

[Omitted by CTA 2010, s. 1177 and Sch. 1, para. 317 and repealed by CTA 2010, s. 1181 and Sch. 3, Pt. 1.]

History – Sch. 28 omitted by CTA 2010, s. 1177 and Sch. 1, para. 317 and repealed by CTA 2010, s. 1181 and Sch. 3, Pt. 1, with effect for accounting periods ending on or after 1 April 2010. Sch. 28 is rewritten in CTA 2010 (see Note below).

Notes – Sch. 28 rewritten as follows:
Para. 1: s. 974(1), (2).
Para. 2(1): s. 976(1).
Para. 2(2): s. 975.
Para. 2(3): s. 976(2), (3).
Para. 2(4): s. 976(4).
Para. 3(1): s. 977(1).
Para. 3(2): s. 977(2).
Para. 3(3): s. 977(3).
Para. 4(1): s. 978(1).
Para. 4(2): s. 978(2).
Para. 4(3): s. 978(3), (5).
Para. 4(4): s. 978(4).
Para. 5(1): s. 979(1).
Para. 5(2): s. 977(4).
Para. 5(3): s. 979(2), (3), (4).
Para. 5(4): s. 979(5).
Para. 6(1): s. 973(3).
Para. 6(2): s. 980(1).
Para. 6(3): s. 980(2).

SCHEDULE 29 – CHARGEABLE GAINS: NON-RESIDENT COMPANIES AND GROUPS ETC

Section 102

Part I – Application of Taxation of Chargeable Gains Act 1992

MAIN AMENDMENTS

1(1) In section 170 of the Taxation of Chargeable Gains Act 1992 (groups of companies: interpretation), the following provisions shall cease to have effect

(a) [Repeals TCGA 1992, s. 170(2)(a).]

(b) [Amends TCGA 1992, s. 170(9)(b).]

1(2) The above amendments (referred to in this Schedule as "the main amendments") have effect in accordance with the following provisions of this Schedule.

TRANSFERS WITHIN A GROUP

2(1) Section 171 of the Taxation of Chargeable Gains Act 1992 (transfers within a group: general provisions) is amended as follows.

2(2) [Substitutes TCGA 1992, s. 171(1).]

2(3) [Amends TCGA 1992, s. 171(2).]

2(4) [Amends TCGA 1992, s. 171(3).]

2(5) [Inserts TCGA 1992, s. 171(6).]

2(6) The above amendments, and the main amendments so far as they apply for the purposes of section 171, have effect in relation to disposals on or after 1st April 2000.

TRANSFER OF UNITED KINGDOM BRANCH OR AGENCY

3(1) [Repeals TCGA 1992, s. 172.]

3(2) The above amendment has effect in relation to disposals on or after 1st April 2000.

DE-GROUPING CHARGE

4(1) Section 179 of the Taxation of Chargeable Gains Act 1992 (company ceasing to be member of group) is amended as follows.

4(2) [Substitutes TCGA 1992, s. 179(1).]

4(3) [Amends TCGA 1992, s. 179(2A).]

4(4) [Amends TCGA 1992, s. 179(2B)–(2D), (4), (10)(c) and (13).]

4(5) [Repeals TCGA 1992, s. 179(11), (12).]

4(6) The amendments made by sub-paragraphs (2) to (4) above, and the main amendments so far as they apply for the purposes of section 179, have effect in relation to assets acquired on or after 1st April 2000.

4(7) The amendments made by sub-paragraph (5) above have effect in relation to gains accruing on or after 1st April 2000.

RECONSTRUCTION OR AMALGAMATION INVOLVING TRANSFER OF BUSINESS

5(1) Section 139 of the Taxation of Chargeable Gains Act 1992 (reconstruction or amalgamation involving transfer of business) is amended as follows.

5(2) [Substitutes TCGA 1992, s. 139(1)(b).]

5(3) [Inserts TCGA 1992, s. 139(1A).]

5(4) The above amendments have effect in relation to disposals made on or after 1st April 2000.

DEEMED DISPOSAL ON NON-RESIDENT CEASING TO CARRY ON TRADE IN UNITED KINGDOM THROUGH BRANCH OR AGENCY

6(1) Section 25 of the Taxation of Chargeable Gains Act 1992 (non-residents: deemed disposals) is amended as follows.

6(2) [Inserts TCGA 1992, s. 25(3A).]

6(3) [Repeals TCGA 1992, s. 25(4).]

6(4) The amendment in sub-paragraph (2) above has effect in relation to cases where section 139 or, as the case may be, section 171 has effect as amended by this Schedule.

6(5) The amendment in sub-paragraph (3) above has effect in relation to cases where section 139 has effect as amended by this Schedule.

RESTRICTION ON SET-OFF OF PRE-ENTRY LOSSES

7(1) In Schedule 7A to the Taxation of Chargeable Gains Act 1992 (restriction on set-off of pre-entry losses), paragraph 1 (application and construction of Schedule) is amended as follows

7(2) [Omitted by FA 2011, s. 46 and Sch. 11, para. 10(c).]

7(3) [Omitted by FA 2011, s. 46 and Sch. 11, para. 10(c).]

7(4) [Omitted by FA 2011, s. 46 and Sch. 11, para. 10(c).]

7(5) [Omitted by FA 2011, s. 46 and Sch. 11, para. 10(c).]

7(6) The above amendments, and the main amendments so far as they apply for the purposes of Schedule 7A, have effect in relation to the amount to be included in respect of chargeable gains in a company's total profits for any accounting period ending on or after 21st March 2000.

7(7) Any question whether a company was, in relation to times before 21st March 2000, a member of a group shall be determined by reference to the position under the Taxation of Chargeable Gains Act 1992 as it stood before the main amendments.

7(8) Any question whether a company was, in relation to times before 6th April 1992, a member of a group shall be determined by reference to the position under the Capital Gains Tax Act 1979

7(9) Where–

(a) immediately before the time when the main amendments have effect in relation to a company in accordance with sub-paragraph (6), the company was not a member of a group of companies for the purposes of section 170 of the Taxation of Chargeable Gains Act 1992 (as it stood before the main amendments), and

(b) immediately after that time, the company is a member of a group of companies for the purposes of that section (as amended by the main amendments),

Schedule 7A to that Act shall not have effect in relation to any losses accruing to the company before that time or any chargeable assets (within the meaning of paragraph 1(3A) of that Schedule) held by it immediately before that time.

History – Para. 7(2) to (5) omitted by FA 2011, s. 46 and Sch. 11, para. 10(c), with effect from 19 July 2011 in relation to the deduction of any pre-entry loss within TCGA 1992, Sch. 7A, para. 1(2), subject to the provisions of FA 2011, Sch. 11, para. 11(2) and 12.

RESTRICTIONS ON SETTING LOSSES AGAINST PRE-ENTRY GAINS

8 [Repealed by FA 2006, s. 178 and Sch. 26, Pt. 3(9).]

History – Para. 8 repealed by FA 2006, s. 178 and Sch. 26, Pt. 3(9), with effect in relation to accounting periods ending on or after 5 December 2005 in accordance with FA 2006, s. 70(6) but subject to the provisions of FA 2006, s. 70(7)–(11).

RECOVERY OF UNPAID TAX

9(1) [Substitutes TCGA 1992, s. 190, 191.]

9(2) [Amends TMA 1970, s. 87A(3).]

9(3) The above amendments, and the main amendments so far as they apply for the purposes of section 190 (as substituted by sub-paragraph (1) above), have effect in relation to gains accruing on or after 1st April 2000.

9(4) Any question whether a company was a member of a group during the period of twelve months ending when such a gain accrued shall be determined in accordance with section 170 as amended by the main amendments.

REPLACEMENT OF BUSINESS ASSETS BY MEMBERS OF GROUP

10(1) Section 175 of the Taxation of Chargeable Gains Act 1992 is amended as follows.

10(2) [Amends TCGA 1992, s. 175(1).]

10(3) [Inserts TCGA 1992, s. 175(1A).]

10(4) [Inserts TCGA 1992, s. 175 (2A)(ba).]

10(5) [Inserts TCGA 1992, s. 175(2AA).]

10(6) [Substitutes TCGA 1992, s. 175(3).]

10(7) The above amendments, and the main amendments so far as they apply for the purposes of section 175, have effect in relation to cases in which–

(a) either the disposal or acquisition is on or after 1st April 2000, or

(b) both the disposal and acquisition are on or after that date.

10(8) In a case falling within paragraph (a) of sub-paragraph (7), any question whether a company was, at the time of the acquisition or disposal corresponding to the disposal or acquisition referred to in that paragraph, a member of a group shall be determined in accordance with section 170 of the Taxation of Chargeable Gains Act 1992 as amended by the main amendments.

TRANSFERS OF ASSETS WITHIN A GROUP: TRADING STOCK

11(1) [Substitutes TCGA 1992, s. 173.]

11(2) The above amendment, and the main amendments so far as they apply for the purposes of section 173 (as substituted by sub-paragraph (1) above), have effect in relation to acquisitions and disposals on or after 1st April 2000.

RESTRICTION OF LOSSES BY REFERENCE TO CAPITAL ALLOWANCES

12(1) [Inserts TCGA 1992, s. 41(8).]

12(2) The above amendment has effect in relation to cases where the disposal first referred to in section 41(8) (as inserted by sub-paragraph (1) above) is on or after 1st April 2000.

ASSETS HELD ON 6TH APRIL 1965: DISPOSAL OUTSIDE GROUP

13(1) Section 174 of the Taxation of Chargeable Gains Act 1992 is amended as follows.

13(2) [Amends TCGA 1992, s. 174(4).]

13(3) [Repeals TCGA 1992, s. 174(5).]

13(4) The above amendments, and the main amendments so far as they apply for the purposes of section 174, have effect in relation to acquisitions on or after 1st April 2000.

13(5) Any question whether a company was, in relation to times before 1st April 2000, a member of a group shall be determined in accordance with section 170 of the Taxation of Chargeable Gains Act 1992 as it stood before the main amendments.

Part II – Minor and Consequential Amendments

SECTION 97 OF THE INHERITANCE TAX ACT 1984

14 The main amendments have effect for the purposes of section 97 of the Inheritance Tax Act 1984 (transfer of asset within a group of companies) in relation to disposals on or after 1st April 2000.

SECTION 132 OF THE FINANCE ACT 1988

15(1) [Amends FA 1988, s. 132(6).]

15(2) The above amendment, and the main amendments so far as they apply for the purposes of section 132, have effect in relation to cases in which the migrating company ceases to be resident in the United Kingdom on or after 1st April 2000.

15(3) Any question whether a company was a member of a group during the period of twelve months ending when the migrating company ceased to be so resident shall be determined in accordance with section 170 of the Taxation of Chargeable Gains Act 1992 as amended by the main amendments.

SECTION 14 OF THE TAXATION OF CHARGEABLE GAINS ACT 1992

16(1) Section 14 of the Taxation of Chargeable Gains Act 1992 (non-resident groups of companies) is amended as follows.

16(2) [Substitutes TCGA 1992, s. 14(2).]

16(3) [Amends TCGA 1992, s. 14(3).]

16(4) [Amends TCGA 1992, s. 14(4)(b).]

16(5) The above amendments, and the main amendments so far as they apply for the purposes of section 14, have effect in cases in which section 41, 171, 173, 174(4), 175(1) or 179, as the case may be, have effect as amended by this Schedule.

SECTION 31A OF THE TAXATION OF CHARGEABLE GAINS ACT 1992

17 [Repealed by FA 2011, s. 44 and Sch. 9, para. 5(c).]

History – Para. 17 repealed by FA 2011, s. 44 and Sch. 9, para. 5(c) in relation to disposals of shares and securities by companies made on or after 19 July 2011, subject to the transitional provision in FA 2011, Sch. 9, para. 6(2).

SECTION 106 OF THE TAXATION OF CHARGEABLE GAINS ACT 1992

18 [Repealed by FA 2006, s. 178 and Sch. 26 Pt. 3(9).]

History – Para. 18 repealed by FA 2006, s. 178 and Sch. 26, Pt. 3(9), with effect in relation to any disposal that is made on or after 5 December 2005.

SECTION 116 OF THE TAXATION OF CHARGEABLE GAINS ACT 1992

19(1) [Amends TCGA 1992, s. 116(11).]

19(2) The above amendment has effect in accordance with paragraph 3(2).

SECTION 117A OF THE TAXATION OF CHARGEABLE GAINS ACT 1992

20 [Repealed by FA 2002, s. 141 and Sch. 40, Pt. 3(10).]

History – Para. 20 repealed by FA 2002, s. 141 and Sch. 40, Pt. 3(10) with effect in relation to accounting periods beginning on or after 1 October 2002.

SECTION 117B OF THE TAXATION OF CHARGEABLE GAINS ACT 1992

21 [Repealed by FA 2002, s. 141 and Sch. 40, Pt. 3(10).]

History – Para. 21 repealed by FA 2002, s. 141 and Sch. 40, Pt. 3(10) with effect in relation to accounting periods beginning on or after 1 October 2002.

SECTION 138A OF THE TAXATION OF CHARGEABLE GAINS ACT 1992

22 The main amendments have effect for the purposes of section 138A of the Taxation of Chargeable Gains Act 1992 (use of earn-out rights for exchange of securities) in relation to rights conferred on or after 1st April 2000.

SECTION 140 OF THE TAXATION OF CHARGEABLE GAINS ACT 1992

23(1) [Amends TCGA 1992, s. 140(6)(b).]

23(2) The above amendment has effect in relation to disposals on or after 1st April 2000.

SECTION 176 OF THE TAXATION OF CHARGEABLE GAINS ACT 1992

24(1) [Repeals TCGA 1992, s. 176(7)(c).]

24(2) The above amendment, and the main amendments so far as they apply for the purposes of section 176, have effect in relation to cases in which the depreciatory transaction (within the meaning of section 176) is on or after 1st April 2000.

SECTION 177 OF THE TAXATION OF CHARGEABLE GAINS ACT 1992

25(1) [Amends TCGA 1992, s. 177(2).]

25(2) The above amendment, and the main amendments so far as they apply for the purposes of section 177, have effect in relation to disposals on or after 1st April 2000.

SECTION 178 OF THE TAXATION OF CHARGEABLE GAINS ACT 1992

26 [Repeals TCGA 1992, s. 178.]

SECTION 180 OF THE TAXATION OF CHARGEABLE GAINS ACT 1992

27 [Repeals TCGA 1992, s. 180.]

SECTION 181 OF THE TAXATION OF CHARGEABLE GAINS ACT 1992

28(1) In section 181 of the Taxable of Chargeable Gains Act 1992 (exemption from de-grouping charge in the case of certain mergers)

(a) [Amends TCGA 1992, s. 181(1).]

(b) [Repeals TCGA 1992, s. 181(5).]

28(2) The amendment made by sub-paragraph (1)(b) above, and the main amendments so far as they apply for the purposes of section 181, have effect in relation to cases in which the company ceases to be a member of a group on or after 1st April 2000.

SECTION 192 OF THE TAXATION OF CHARGEABLE GAINS ACT 1992

29 [Amends TCGA 1992, s. 192(3).]

SECTION 211 OF THE TAXATION OF CHARGEABLE GAINS ACT 1992

30 [Repealed by FA 2007, s. 114 and Sch. 27, Pt. 2(9).]

History – Para. 30 repealed by FA 2007, s. 114 and Sch. 27, Pt. 2(9) with effect in relation to periods of account beginning on or after 1 January 2007.

SECTION 216 OF THE TAXATION OF CHARGEABLE GAINS ACT 1992

31 The main amendments have effect for the purposes of section 216 of the Taxation of Chargeable Gains Act 1992 (assets transferred from building society to company) in relation to transfers on or after 1st April 2000.

SECTION 217C OF THE TAXATION OF CHARGEABLE GAINS ACT 1992

32(1) [Substitutes TCGA 1992, s. 217C(2).]

32(2) The above amendment has effect in relation to cases in which the disposal by the incorporated society is on or after 1st April 2000.

SECTION 228 OF THE TAXATION OF CHARGEABLE GAINS ACT 1992

33 The main amendments have effect for the purposes of section 228 of the Taxation of Chargeable Gains Act 1992 (conditions for roll-over relief: supplementary) in relation to disposals on or after 1st April 2000.

SECTION 253 OF THE TAXATION OF CHARGEABLE GAINS ACT 1992

34 The main amendments have effect for the purposes of section 253 of the Taxation of Chargeable Gains Act 1992 (relief for loans to traders)–

(a) in relation to loans made on or after 1st April 2000;

(b) in relation to guarantees given on or after that date.

SECTION 276 OF THE TAXATION OF CHARGEABLE GAINS ACT 1992

35(1) [Substitutes TCGA 1992, s. 276(8).]

35(2) The above amendment has effect in cases in which section 41, 171, 173, 174(4), 179 or 181, as the case may be, have effect as amended by this Schedule.

SCHEDULE A1 TO THE TAXATION OF CHARGEABLE GAINS ACT 1992

36 The main amendments have effect for the purposes of paragraph 11 of Schedule A1 to the Taxation of Chargeable Gains Act 1992 (rules for application of taper relief) in relation to any determination whether, at any time on or after 1st April 2000, a company is a 51 per cent subsidiary of another company.

SCHEDULE 2 TO THE TAXATION OF CHARGEABLE GAINS ACT 1992

37 The main amendments have effect for the purposes of paragraph 5 of Schedule 2 to the Taxation of Chargeable Gains Act 1992 (disposals of assets held on 6th April 1965) in relation to any determination whether, at any time on or after 1st April 2000, a company is a member, or the principal company, of a group of companies.

SCHEDULE 3 TO THE TAXATION OF CHARGEABLE GAINS ACT 1992

38 The main amendments have effect for the purposes of paragraphs 8 and 9 of Schedule 3 to the Taxation of Chargeable Gains Act 1992 (disposals of assets held on 31st March 1982: supplementary provisions) in relation to any determination whether, at any time on or after 1st April 2000, a company is a member, or the principal company, of a group of companies.

SCHEDULE 7B TO THE TAXATION OF CHARGEABLE GAINS ACT 1992

39 [Repealed by SI 2006/3271, reg. 43 and Schedule, Pt. 1.]

History – Para. 39 repealed by SI 2006/3271, reg. 43 and Schedule, Pt. 1 with effect from 31 December 2006 in relation to accounting periods ending on or after that date.

SCHEDULE 7C TO THE TAXATION OF CHARGEABLE GAINS ACT 1992

40 The main amendments have effect for the purposes of Schedule 7C to the Taxation of Chargeable Gains Act 1992 (which is inserted by virtue of section 48 of this Act).

SECTION 136 OF THE FINANCE ACT 1993

41 [Repealed by FA 2002, s. 141 and Sch. 40, Pt. 3(10).]

History – Para. 41 repealed by FA 2002, s. 141 and Sch. 40, Pt. 3(10) with effect in relation to accounting periods beginning on or after 1 October 2002.

SECTION 136A OF THE FINANCE ACT 1993

42 [Repealed by FA 2002, s. 141 and Sch. 40, Pt. 3(10).]

History – Para. 42 repealed by FA 2002, s. 141 and Sch. 40, Pt. 3(10) with effect in relation to accounting periods ending on or after 1 October 2002.

SCHEDULE 17 TO THE FINANCE ACT 1993

43 [Repealed by FA 2002, s. 141 and Sch. 40, Pt. 3(10).]

History – Para. 43 repealed by FA 2002, s. 141 and Sch. 40, Pt. 3(10) with effect in relation to accounting periods ending on or after 1 October 2002.

SCHEDULE 9 TO THE FINANCE ACT 1996

44 [Repealed by CTA 2009, s. 1326 and Sch. 3, Pt. 1.]

History – Para. 44 repealed by CTA 2009, s. 1326 and Sch. 3, Pt. 1, with effect for corporation tax purposes for accounting periods ending on or after 1 April 2009, and for income tax and capital gains tax purposes for the tax year 2009–10 and subsequent tax years.

SCHEDULE 15 TO THE FINANCE ACT 1996

45(1) [Amends FA 1996, Sch. 15, para. 8(2).]

45(2) The above amendment has effect in accordance with paragraph 3(2) above.

Part III – Transitional Provisions

46(1) For the purposes of this paragraph–

(a) references to a company which was a member of an old group are references to it being, immediately before the time when the main amendments have effect in accordance with the preceding provisions of this Schedule, a member of a group for the purposes of section 170 of the Taxation of Chargeable Gains Act 1992 (as it stood before the main amendments), and

(b) references to a company which is a member of a new group are references to it being, immediately after that time, a member of a group for the purposes of that section (as amended by the main amendments).

46(2) Where the same two or more companies were members of an old group and are members of a new group, those groups shall be regarded as the same group for the purposes of the provisions amended by this Schedule in relation to which the main amendments have effect.

46(3) Sub-paragraph (2) applies irrespective of whether the new group includes companies which were not members of the old group.

46(4) Sub-paragraph (5) applies in relation to a company which–

(a) was a member of an old group, but

(b) is not a member of a new group by reason only that–

(i) the principal company of the old group is not the principal company of the new group, and

(ii) the company in question is not an effective 51 per cent subsidiary of the principal company of the new group.

46(5) For the purposes of the provisions amended by this Schedule in relation to which the main amendments have effect, section 170(3)(b) of the Taxation of Chargeable Gains Act 1992 shall not apply in relation to the company for so long as it remains an effective 51 per cent subsidiary of the company which was the principal company of the old group.

46(6) Expressions used in this paragraph and in section 170 of the Taxation of Chargeable Gains Act 1992 shall be construed for the purposes of this paragraph in accordance with that section.

DE-GROUPING CHARGE: DEFERRAL UNTIL COMPANY LEAVES NEW GROUP

47(1) This paragraph has effect for the purposes of section 179 of the Taxation of Chargeable Gains Act 1992 as that section has effect in relation to assets acquired before 1st April 2000 (**"old section 179"**).

47(2) Where–

(a) a company would (apart from this paragraph) fall to be regarded for the purposes of old section 179 as ceasing to be a member of an old group at any time, but

(b) immediately before that time, it is also a member of a new group for the purposes of new section 179,

the company shall not be regarded for the purposes of old section 179 as ceasing to be a member of the old group unless or until it also ceases to be a member of the new group for the purposes of new section 179.

47(3) Sub-paragraph (2) above does not prevent the company from being or becoming a member of another old group at any time.

47(4) Where a company ceases to be a member of a new group on any occasion, it shall not by virtue of sub-paragraph (2) above be treated for the purposes of old section 179 as if it had on that occasion ceased to be a member of the same old group more than once.

47(5) For the purposes of this paragraph–

(a) references to a company being a member of an old group are references to its being, for the purposes of old section 179, a member of a group of companies within the meaning given by old section 170;

(b) references to a company being a member of a new group are references to its being, for the purposes of new section 179, a member of a group of companies within the meaning given by new section 170; and

(c) references to a company ceasing to be a member of an old group or a new group shall be construed in accordance with paragraph (a) or (b) above, as the case may be.

47(6) Where, for the purposes of sub-paragraph (2)(b) above, a company is not a member of a new group by reason only that–

(a) the principal company of the old group is not the principal company of the new group, and

(b) the company in question is not an effective 51 per cent subsidiary of the principal company of the new group,

subsection (3)(b) of new section 170 shall not apply in relation to the company for the purposes of this paragraph for so long as it remains an effective 51 per cent subsidiary of the company which was the principal company of the old group.

47(7) In this paragraph–

(a) **"new section 179"** means section 179 of the Taxation of Chargeable Gains Act 1992 as it has effect in relation to assets acquired on or after 1st April 2000;

(b) **"new section 170"** means section 170 of that Act, as amended by the main amendments;

(c) **"old section 170"** means section 170 of the Taxation of Chargeable Gains Act 1992, as it stands before the main amendments.

47(8) Expressions used in this paragraph and in section 170 of the Taxation of Chargeable Gains Act 1992 shall be construed in accordance with that section.

History – Para. 47 is deemed to have been enacted at the same time as the other paragraphs of Sch. 29 and was inserted by FA 2001, s. 79.

SCHEDULE 30 – DOUBLE TAXATION RELIEF

Section 103

POWER TO MAKE TREATY PROVISION FOR MATCHING CREDIT FOR TAX SPARED IN FOREIGN COUNTRY

1 [Repealed by TIOPA 2010, s. 378 and Sch. 10, Pt. 1.]

History – Para. 1 repealed by TIOPA 2010, s. 378 and Sch. 10, Pt. 1, with effect for corporation tax purposes for accounting periods ending on or after 1 April 2010, for income tax and capital gains tax purposes for the tax year 2010–11 and subsequent tax years, and for petroleum revenue tax purposes for chargeable periods beginning on or after 1 July 2010.

MATCHING CREDIT FOR TAX SPARED BELOW IMMEDIATE OVERSEAS SUBSIDIARY: TREATY RELIEF

2 [Repealed by TIOPA 2010, s. 378 and Sch. 10, Pt. 1.]

History – Para. 2 repealed by TIOPA 2010, s. 378 and Sch. 10, Pt. 1, with effect for corporation tax purposes for accounting periods ending on or after 1 April 2010, for income tax and capital gains tax purposes for the tax year 2010–11 and subsequent tax years, and for petroleum revenue tax purposes for chargeable periods beginning on or after 1 July 2010.

Notes – Para. 2(2) rewritten as TIOPA 2010, s. 20(6).

MATCHING CREDIT FOR TAX SPARED BELOW IMMEDIATE OVERSEAS SUBSIDIARY: UNILATERAL RELIEF

3 [Repealed by TIOPA 2010, s. 378 and Sch. 10, Pt. 1.]

History – Para. 3 repealed by TIOPA 2010, s. 378 and Sch. 10, Pt. 1, with effect for corporation tax purposes for accounting periods ending on or after 1 April 2010, for income tax and capital gains tax purposes for the tax year 2010–11 and subsequent tax years, and for petroleum revenue tax purposes for chargeable periods beginning on or after 1 July 2010.

RELIEF FOR PERSONS RESIDENT OUTSIDE THE UK WHO HAVE BRANCHES OR AGENCIES IN THE UK

4(1)–(12) [Repealed by TIOPA 2010, s. 378 and Sch. 10, Pt. 1.]

4(13)–(14) [Repealed by Statute Law (Repeals) Act 2013, s. 1 and Sch. 1, Pt. 10.]

History – Para. 4(1)–(12) repealed by TIOPA 2010, s. 378 and Sch. 10, Pt. 1, with effect for corporation tax purposes for accounting periods ending on or after 1 April 2010, for income tax and capital gains tax purposes for the tax year 2010–11 and subsequent tax years, and for petroleum revenue tax purposes for chargeable periods beginning on or after 1 July 2010.
Para. 4(13) and (14) repealed by Statute Law (Repeals) Act 2013, s. 1 and Sch. 1, Pt. 10, with effect from 31 January 2013.
In para. 4(14) the term "chargeable periods" is substituted for the words "accounting periods" by FA 2001, s. 81, Sch. 27, para. 7(2); Para. 14 being deemed to have been originally enacted with the amendment in place (Sch. 27, para. 7(3)).

NO DOUBLE RELIEF ETC.

5 [Repealed by TIOPA 2010, s. 378 and Sch. 10, Pt. 1.]

History – Para. 5 repealed by TIOPA 2010, s. 378 and Sch. 10, Pt. 1, with effect for corporation tax purposes for accounting periods ending on or after 1 April 2010, for income tax and capital gains tax purposes for the tax year 2010–11 and subsequent tax years, and for petroleum revenue tax purposes for chargeable periods beginning on or after 1 July 2010.

Notes – Para. 5(3) rewritten as TIOPA 2010, Sch. 9, para. 13.

LIMITS ON CREDIT: MINIMISATION OF THE FOREIGN TAX

6 [Repealed by TIOPA 2010, s. 378 and Sch. 10, Pt. 1.]

History – Para. 6 repealed by TIOPA 2010, s. 378 and Sch. 10, Pt. 1, with effect for corporation tax purposes for accounting periods ending on or after 1 April 2010, for income tax and capital gains tax purposes for the tax year 2010–11 and subsequent tax years, and for petroleum revenue tax purposes for chargeable periods beginning on or after 1 July 2010.

FOREIGN TAX ON AMOUNTS UNDERLYING NON-TRADING CREDITS

7 [Repealed by TIOPA 2010, s. 378 and Sch. 10, Pt. 1.]

History – Para. 7 repealed by TIOPA 2010, s. 378 and Sch. 10, Pt. 1, with effect for corporation tax purposes for accounting periods ending on or after 1 April 2010, for income tax and capital gains tax purposes for the tax year 2010–11 and subsequent tax years, and for petroleum revenue tax purposes for chargeable periods beginning on or after 1 July 2010.

RESTRICTION OF RELIEF FOR UNDERLYING TAX

8 [Repealed by TIOPA 2010, s. 378 and Sch. 10, Pt. 1.]

History – Para. 8 repealed by TIOPA 2010, s. 378 and Sch. 10, Pt. 1, with effect for corporation tax purposes for accounting periods ending on or after 1 April 2010, for income tax and capital gains tax purposes for the tax year 2010–11 and subsequent tax years, and for petroleum revenue tax purposes for chargeable periods beginning on or after 1 July 2010.

Notes – Para. 8(5) rewritten as TIOPA 2010, s. 57(2), 65(6).

COMPUTATION OF UNDERLYING TAX: THE RELEVANT PROFITS

9 [Repealed by TIOPA 2010, s. 378 and Sch. 10, Pt. 1.]

History – Para. 9 repealed by TIOPA 2010, s. 378 and Sch. 10, Pt. 1, with effect for corporation tax purposes for accounting periods ending on or after 1 April 2010, for income tax and capital gains tax purposes for the tax year 2010–11 and subsequent tax years, and for petroleum revenue tax purposes for chargeable periods beginning on or after 1 July 2010.

Notes – Para. 9(3) rewritten as TIOPA 2010, s. 57(2).

DIVIDENDS PAID BETWEEN RELATED COMPANIES BUT NOT COVERED BY ARRANGEMENTS

10 [Repealed by Statute Law (Repeals) Act 2013, s. 1 and Sch. 1, Pt. 10.]

History – Para. 10 repealed by Statute Law (Repeals) Act 2013, s. 1 and Sch. 1, Pt. 10, with effect from 31 January 2013.

RESTRICTION OF RELIEF FOR UNDERLYING TAX: DIVIDENDS PAID BETWEEN RELATED COMPANIES

11 [Repealed by TIOPA 2010, s. 378 and Sch. 10, Pt. 1.]

History – Para. 11 repealed by TIOPA 2010, s. 378 and Sch. 10, Pt. 1, with effect for corporation tax purposes for accounting periods ending on or after 1 April 2010, for income tax and capital gains tax purposes for the tax year 2010–11 and subsequent tax years, and for petroleum revenue tax purposes for chargeable periods beginning on or after 1 July 2010.

Notes – Para. 11(3) rewritten as TIOPA 2010, s. 65(6).

DIVIDENDS PAID OUT OF TRANSFERRED PROFITS

12 [Repealed by TIOPA 2010, s. 378 and Sch. 10, Pt. 1.]

History – Para. 12 repealed by TIOPA 2010, s. 378 and Sch. 10, Pt. 1, with effect for corporation tax purposes for accounting periods ending on or after 1 April 2010, for income tax and capital gains tax purposes for the tax year 2010–11 and subsequent tax years, and for petroleum revenue tax purposes for chargeable periods beginning on or after 1 July 2010.

SEPARATE STREAMING OF DIVIDEND SO FAR AS REPRESENTING AN ADP DIVIDEND OF A CFC

13 [Omitted by FA 2009, s. 36 and Sch. 16, para. 5(f).]

History – Para. 13 omitted by FA 2009, s. 36 and Sch. 16, para. 5(f), with effect in relation to accounting periods of controlled foreign companies beginning on or after 1 July 2009, subject to rules for accounting periods straddling 1 July 2009 in FA 2009, Sch. 16, para. 7 and transitional rules in FA 2009, Sch. 16, para. 8.

UK INSURANCE COMPANIES TRADING OVERSEAS: REPEAL OF SECTION 802

14 [Repealed by Statute Law (Repeals) Act 2013, s. 1 and Sch. 1, Pt. 10.]

History – Para. 14 repealed by Statute Law (Repeals) Act 2013, s. 1 and Sch. 1, Pt. 10, with effect from 31 January 2013.

UNDERLYING TAX: FOREIGN TAXATION OF GROUP AS A SINGLE ENTITY

15 [Repealed by TIOPA 2010, s. 378 and Sch. 10, Pt. 1.]

History – Para. 15 repealed by TIOPA 2010, s. 378 and Sch. 10, Pt. 1, with effect for corporation tax purposes for accounting periods ending on or after 1 April 2010, for income tax and capital gains tax purposes for the tax year 2010–11 and subsequent tax years, and for petroleum revenue tax purposes for chargeable periods beginning on or after 1 July 2010.

Notes – Para. 15(2) rewritten as TIOPA 2010, s. 71(1).

LIFE ASSURANCE COMPANIES WITH OVERSEAS BRANCHES ETC: RESTRICTION OF CREDIT

16 [Repealed by TIOPA 2010, s. 378 and Sch. 10, Pt. 1.]

History – Para. 16 repealed by TIOPA 2010, s. 378 and Sch. 10, Pt. 1, with effect for corporation tax purposes for accounting periods ending on or after 1 April 2010, for income tax and capital gains tax purposes for the tax year 2010–11 and subsequent tax years, and for petroleum revenue tax purposes for chargeable periods beginning on or after 1 July 2010.

ALLOCATION OF FOREIGN TAX TO DIFFERENT CATEGORIES OF INSURANCE BUSINESS

17 [Repealed by TIOPA 2010, s. 378 and Sch. 10, Pt. 1.]

History – Para. 17 repealed by TIOPA 2010, s. 378 and Sch. 10, Pt. 1, with effect for corporation tax purposes for accounting periods ending on or after 1 April 2010, for income tax and capital gains tax purposes for the tax year 2010–11 and subsequent tax years, and for petroleum revenue tax purposes for chargeable periods beginning on or after 1 July 2010.

ALLOCATION OF EXPENSES ETC IN A COMPUTATION UNDER CASE I OF SCHEDULE D

18 [Repealed by Statute Law (Repeals) Act 2013, s. 1 and Sch. 1, Pt. 10.]

History – Para. 18 repealed by Statute Law (Repeals) Act 2013, s. 1 and Sch. 1, Pt. 10, with effect from 31 January 2013. Note that former para. 18(1) and (3) had previously been repealed (see notes below) and former para. 18 amended FA 1989, s. 82(1)(a).
Para. 18(1) repealed by TIOPA 2010, s. 378 and Sch. 10, Pt. 1, with effect for corporation tax purposes for accounting periods ending on or after 1 April 2010, for income tax and capital gains tax purposes for the tax year 2010–11 and subsequent tax years, and for petroleum revenue tax purposes for chargeable periods beginning on or after 1 July 2010.
Para. 18(3) repealed by FA 2003, Sch. 43, Pt. 3(12) with effect for periods of account beginning on or after 1 January 2003.

INTERPRETATION OF SECTIONS 804A TO 804E

19 [Repealed by FA 2007, s. 114 and Sch. 27, Pt. 2(10).]

History – Para. 19 repealed by FA 2007, s. 114 and Sch. 27, Pt. 2(10) with effect in relation to periods of account beginning on or after 1 January 2007.

TIME LIMITS FOR CLAIMS FOR CREDIT RELIEF

20 [Repealed by TIOPA 2010, s. 378 and Sch. 10, Pt. 1.]

History – Para. 20 repealed by TIOPA 2010, s. 378 and Sch. 10, Pt. 1, with effect for corporation tax purposes for accounting periods ending on or after 1 April 2010, for income tax and capital gains tax purposes for the tax year 2010–11 and subsequent tax years, and for petroleum revenue tax purposes for chargeable periods beginning on or after 1 July 2010.

FOREIGN DIVIDENDS: ONSHORE POOLING AND UTILISATION OF CERTAIN UNRELIEVED FOREIGN TAX

21 [Omitted by FA 2009, s. 34 and Sch. 14, para. 30(b).]

History – Para. 21 omitted by FA 2009, s. 34 and Sch. 14, para. 30(b), with effect in relation to distributions paid on or after 1 July 2009.

APPLICATION OF FOREIGN DIVIDEND PROVISIONS TO BRANCHES OR AGENCIES IN THE UK OF PERSONS RESIDENT ELSEWHERE

22 [Omitted by FA 2009, s. 34 and Sch. 14, para. 30(b).]

History – Para. 22 omitted by FA 2009, s. 34 and Sch. 14, para. 30(b), with effect in relation to distributions paid on or after 1 July 2009.

UNRELIEVED FOREIGN TAX: PROFITS OF OVERSEAS BRANCH OR AGENCY

23 [Repealed by TIOPA 2010, s. 378 and Sch. 10, Pt. 1.]

History – Para. 23 repealed by TIOPA 2010, s. 378 and Sch. 10, Pt. 1, with effect for corporation tax purposes for accounting periods ending on or after 1 April 2010, for income tax and capital gains tax purposes for the tax year 2010–11 and subsequent tax years, and for petroleum revenue tax purposes for chargeable periods beginning on or after 1 July 2010.

FOREIGN TAX ON AMOUNTS UNDERLYING NON-TRADING CREDITS

24 [Repealed by TIOPA 2010, s. 378 and Sch. 10, Pt. 1.]

History – Para. 24 repealed by TIOPA 2010, s. 378 and Sch. 10, Pt. 1, with effect for corporation tax purposes for accounting periods ending on or after 1 April 2010, for income tax and capital gains tax purposes for the tax year 2010–11 and subsequent tax years, and for petroleum revenue tax purposes for chargeable periods beginning on or after 1 July 2010.
Para. 24(3) previously repealed by FA 2002, s. 141 and Sch. 40, Pt. 3(13) with effect in relation to accounting periods beginning on or after 1 October 2002.

ROYALTIES: SPECIAL RELATIONSHIP

25 [Repealed by TIOPA 2010, s. 378 and Sch. 10, Pt. 1.]

History – Para. 25 repealed by TIOPA 2010, s. 378 and Sch. 10, Pt. 1, with effect for corporation tax purposes for accounting periods ending on or after 1 April 2010, for income tax and capital gains tax purposes for the tax year 2010–11 and subsequent tax years, and for petroleum revenue tax purposes for chargeable periods beginning on or after 1 July 2010.

POSTPONEMENT OF CAPITAL ALLOWANCES TO OBTAIN DOUBLE TAXATION RELIEF

26 [Repealed by Statute Law (Repeals) Act 2013, s. 1 and Sch. 1, Pt. 10.]

History – Para. 26 repealed by Statute Law (Repeals) Act 2013, s. 1 and Sch. 1, Pt. 10, with effect from 31 January 2013.

TIME LIMITS WHERE REDUCTION UNDER S. 811 RENDERED EXCESSIVE OR INSUFFICIENT

27 [Repealed by TIOPA 2010, s. 378 and Sch. 10, Pt. 1.]

History – Para. 27 repealed by TIOPA 2010, s. 378 and Sch. 10, Pt. 1, with effect for corporation tax purposes for accounting periods ending on or after 1 April 2010, for income tax and capital gains tax purposes for the tax year 2010–11 and subsequent tax years, and for petroleum revenue tax purposes for chargeable periods beginning on or after 1 July 2010.

MUTUAL AGREEMENT PROCEDURE

28 [Repealed by TIOPA 2010, s. 378 and Sch. 10, Pt. 1.]

History – Para. 28 repealed by TIOPA 2010, s. 378 and Sch. 10, Pt. 1, with effect for corporation tax purposes for accounting periods ending on or after 1 April 2010, for income tax and capital gains tax purposes for the tax year 2010–11 and subsequent tax years, and for petroleum revenue tax purposes for chargeable periods beginning on or after 1 July 2010.

RESTRICTION OF INTEREST ON REPAYMENT OF TAX RESULTING FROM CARRY BACK OF RELIEVABLE TAX

29(1) Amend section 826 of the Taxes Act 1988 as follows.

29(2) [Inserts ICTA 1988, s. 826(7BB) and (7BC).]

29(3) [Amends ICTA 1988, s. 826(7D).]

29(4) [Amends ICTA 1988, s. 826(7E).]

TIME LIMITS WHERE DEDUCTION UNDER S. 278 OF THE 1992 ACT RENDERED EXCESSIVE OR INSUFFICIENT

30 [Repealed by TIOPA 2010, s. 378 and Sch. 10, Pt. 1.]

History – Para. 30 repealed by TIOPA 2010, s. 378 and Sch. 10, Pt. 1, with effect for corporation tax purposes for accounting periods ending on or after 1 April 2010, for income tax and capital gains tax purposes for the tax year 2010–11 and subsequent tax years, and for petroleum revenue tax purposes for chargeable periods beginning on or after 1 July 2010.

SCHEDULE 31 – CONTROLLED FOREIGN COMPANIES

Section 104

INTRODUCTORY

1 Amend Chapter IV of Part XVII of the Taxes Act 1988 as follows.

CONDITIONS FOR COMPANY TO BE CONTROLLED FOREIGN COMPANY

2(1) Amend section 747 as follows.

2(2) [Inserts ICTA 1988, s. 747(1A).]

DESIGNER RATE TAX PROVISIONS: DEEMED LOWER LEVEL OF TAXATION

3 [Inserts ICTA 1988, s. 750A.]

"CONTROL" AND "THE TWO 40 PER CENT" TESTS

4(1) [Inserts ICTA 1988, s. 755D.]

4(2) [Amends ICTA 1988, s. 756(3).]

EXEMPT ACTIVITIES: WHOLESALE, DISTRIBUTIVE, FINANCIAL OR SERVICE BUSINESS

5(1) In Part II of Schedule 25 (exempt activities) amend paragraph 6 as follows.

5(2) [Amends ICTA 1988, Sch. 25, para. 6(2)(b).]

5(3) [Inserts ICTA 1988, Sch. 25, para. 6(2A).]

LOCAL HOLDING COMPANIES

6(1) In Part II of Schedule 25 (exempt activities) amend paragraph 6 as follows.

6(2) [Amends ICTA 1988, Sch. 25, para. 6(3).].

OTHER HOLDING COMPANIES

7(1) In Part II of Schedule 25 (exempt activities) amend paragraph 6 as follows.

7((2)–(7)) [Omitted by FA 2009, s. 36 and Sch. 16, para. 11(b).]

7(8) [Amends ICTA 1988, Sch. 25, para. 6(5).]

7(9) [Inserts ICTA 1988, Sch. 25, para. 6(5ZB).]

7(10–11) [Omitted by FA 2009, s. 36 and Sch. 16, para. 11(b).]

History – Para. 7(2)–(7), (10) and (11) omitted by FA 2009, s. 36 and Sch. 16, para. 11(b), with effect in relation to accounting periods of controlled foreign companies beginning on or after 1 July 2009 where the company is other than a "qualifying holding company" (FA 2009, Sch. 16, para. 12–15).

BUSINESSES TO WHICH REQUIREMENT AS TO DERIVATION OF RECEIPTS APPLIES

8(1) In Part II of Schedule 25 (exempt activities) amend paragraph 11 as follows.

8(2) [Amends ICTA 1988, Sch. 25, para. 11(1).]

COMMENCEMENT

9(1) Paragraph 2 has effect on and after 21st March 2000.

9(2) Paragraph 3 has effect in relation to any accounting period of a company resident outside the United Kingdom which begins on or after 6th October 1999.

9(3) Paragraph 4 has effect–

(a) for the purpose of determining whether at any time on or after 21st March 2000 a company resident outside the United Kingdom is to be regarded for the purposes of Chapter IV of Part XVII of the Taxes Act 1988 as controlled by persons resident in the United Kingdom; and

(b) for any accounting period of a company resident outside the United Kingdom which begins on or after 21st March 2000.

9(4) Paragraphs 5 to 8 have effect in relation to any accounting period of a controlled foreign company which begins on or after 21st March 2000.

9(5) In this paragraph **"accounting period"** and **"controlled foreign company"** have the same meaning as they have in Chapter IV of Part XVII of the Taxes Act 1988.

SCHEDULE 38 – REGULATIONS FOR PROVIDING INCENTIVES FOR ELECTRONIC COMMUNICATIONS

Section 143(1)

Cross references – SI 2001/56: provision of incentive payments to be made if returns submitted to HMRC using electronic communications.
SI 2003/2495: income tax, incentive payments for voluntary online filing of PAYE returns.

INTRODUCTION

1(1) Regulations may be made in accordance with this Schedule for providing incentives to use electronic communications–

(a) for the purposes mentioned in section 132(1) of the Finance Act 1999 (power to provide for use of electronic communications for delivery of information and making of payments), or

(b) for any other communications with the tax authorities or in connection with taxation matters.

1(2) The power to make regulations under this Schedule is conferred–

(a) on the Commissioners of Inland Revenue in relation to matters which are under their care and management, and

(b) on the Commissioners of Customs and Excise in relation to matters which are under their care and management.

KINDS OF INCENTIVE

2(1) The incentives shall be of such description as may be provided for in the regulations.

2(2) They may, in particular, take the form of–

(a) discounts;

(b) the allowing of additional time to comply with any obligations under tax legislation (including obligations relating to the payment of tax or other amounts); or

(c) the facility to deliver information or make payments at more convenient intervals.

CONDITIONS OF ENTITLEMENT

3(1) The regulations may make provision as to the conditions of entitlement to an incentive.

3(2) They may, in particular, make entitlement conditional–

(a) on the use of electronic communications for all communications or payments (or all communications and payments of a specified description) with, to or from the tax authority concerned, and

(b) on the use of specified means of electronic communication or payment acceptable to the tax authority concerned.

3(3) The regulations may make provision for an appeal against a decision that the conditions of entitlement are not met.

WITHDRAWAL OF ENTITLEMENT

4(1) The regulations may make provision for the withdrawal of an incentive in specified circumstances.

4(2) If they do, they may make provision–

(a) for giving notice of the withdrawal,

(b) for an appeal, and

(c) for the recovery of an amount not exceeding the value of the incentive.

4(3) The regulations may provide that specified enactments relating to assessments, reviews, appeals and recovery of tax are to apply, with such adaptations as may be specified, in relation to the withdrawal of an incentive.

History – In para. 4(3) the word "reviews," inserted by SI 2009/56, art. 3(1) and Sch. 1, para. 295(2), operative from 1 April 2009, subject to transitional and saving provisions in SI 2009/56, Sch. 3.

POWER TO AUTHORISE PROVISION BY DIRECTIONS

5 The regulations may authorise the making of any such provision as is mentioned in paragraph 3 or 4 by means of a specific or general direction given by the Commissioners of Inland Revenue or the Commissioners of Customs and Excise.

POWER TO PROVIDE FOR PENALTIES

6(1) The regulations may provide for contravention of, or failure to comply with, a specified provision of any such regulations to attract a penalty of a specified amount not exceeding £1,000.

6(2) If they do, they may provide that specified enactments relating to penalties imposed in relation to any taxation matter (including enactments relating to assessments, review and appeals) are to apply, with or without modifications, in relation to penalties under the regulations.

GENERAL SUPPLEMENTARY PROVISIONS

7(1) Power to make provision by regulations under this Schedule includes power–

(a) to make different provision for different cases; and

(b) to make such incidental, supplemental, consequential and transitional provision in connection with any provision contained in any such regulations as the persons exercising the power think fit.

7(2) The power to make regulations under this Schedule is exercisable by statutory instrument subject to annulment in pursuance of a resolution of the House of Commons.

INTERPRETATION

8(1) In this Schedule–

"discount" includes payment;

"electronic communications" includes any communications by means of a telecommunication system (within the meaning of the Telecommunications Act 1984);

"legislation" means any enactment, Community legislation or subordinate legislation;

"payment" includes a repayment;

"subordinate legislation" has the same meaning as in the Interpretation Act 1978;

"taxation matter" means any of the matters under the care and management of the Commissioners of Inland Revenue or the Commissioners of Customs and Excise;

"tax authorities" means–

(a) the Commissioners of Inland Revenue or the Commissioners of Customs and Exc se,
(b) any officer of either body of Commissioners; or
(c) any other person who for the purposes of electronic communications is acting under the authority of either body of Commissioners;

"tax legislation" means legislation relating to any taxation matter.

8(2) References in this Schedule to the delivery of information have the same meaning as in section 132 of the Finance Act 1999.

SCHEDULE 39 – NEW SCHEDULE 1AA TO THE TAXES MANAGEMENT ACT 1970

Section 149(2)

[Inserts TMA 1970, Sch. 1AA.]

FREEDOM OF INFORMATION ACT 2000

(2000 Chapter 36) [*30th November 2000*]

ARRANGEMENT OF SECTIONS

PART I – ACCESS TO INFORMATION HELD BY PUBLIC AUTHORITIES

RIGHT TO INFORMATION

REFUSAL OF REQUEST

THE INFORMATION COMMISSIONER AND THE INFORMATION TRIBUNAL

PUBLICATION SCHEMES

PART II – EXEMPT INFORMATION

PART I – ACCESS TO INFORMATION HELD BY PUBLIC AUTHORITIES

RIGHT TO INFORMATION

1 General right of access to information held by public authorities

1(1) Any person making a request for information to a public authority is entitled–

(a) to be informed in writing by the public authority whether it holds information of the description specified in the request, and

(b) if that is the case, to have that information communicated to him.

1(2) Subsection (1) has effect subject to the following provisions of this section and to the provisions of sections 2, 9, 12 and 14.

1(3) Where a public authority–

(a) reasonably requires further information in order to identify and locate the information requested, and

(b) has informed the applicant of that requirement,

the authority is not obliged to comply with subsection (1) unless it is supplied with that further information.

1(4) The information–

(a) in respect of which the applicant is to be informed under subsection (1)(a), or

(b) which is to be communicated under subsection (1)(b),

is the information in question held at the time when the request is received, except that account may be taken of any amendment or deletion made between that time and the time when the information is to be communicated under subsection (1)(b), being an amendment or deletion that would have been made regardless of the receipt of the request.

1(5) A public authority is to be taken to have complied with subsection (1)(a) in relation to any information if it has communicated the information to the applicant in accordance with subsection (1)(b).

1(6) In this Act, the duty of a public authority to comply with subsection (1)(a) is referred to as "the duty to confirm or deny".

2 Effect of the exemptions in Part II

2(1) Where any provision of Part II states that the duty to confirm or deny does not arise in relation to any information, the effect of the provision is that where either–

(a) the provision confers absolute exemption, or

(b) in all the circumstances of the case, the public interest in maintaining the exclusion of the duty to confirm or deny outweighs the public interest in disclosing whether the public authority holds the information,

section 1(1)(a) does not apply.

2(2) In respect of any information which is exempt information by virtue of any provision of Part II, section 1(1)(b) does not apply if or to the extent that–

(a) the information is exempt information by virtue of a provision conferring absolute exemption, or

(b) in all the circumstances of the case, the public interest in maintaining the exemption outweighs the public interest in disclosing the information.

2(3) For the purposes of this section, the following provisions of Part II (and no others) are to be regarded as conferring absolute exemption–

(a) section 21,

(b) section 23,

(c) section 32,

(d) section 34,

(e) section 36 so far as relating to information held by the House of Commons or the House of Lords,

(ea) in section 37, paragraphs (a) to (ab) of subsection (1), and subsection (2) so far as relating to those paragraphs,

(f) in section 40–

(i) subsection (1), and

(ii) subsection (2) so far as relating to cases where the first condition referred to in that subsection is satisfied by virtue of subsection (3)(a)(i) or (b) of that section,

(g) section 41, and

(h) section 44.

History – S. 2(3)(ea) inserted by CRGA 2011, s. 46 and Sch. 7, para. 2, with effect from 19 January 2011, but this insertion does not apply in respect of any request for information received by a public authority before that date (SI 2011/46).

3 Public authorities

3(1) In this Act **"public authority"** means–

(a) subject to section 4(4), any body which, any other person who, or the holder of any office which–

(i) is listed in Schedule 1, or

(ii) is designated by order under section 5, or

(b) a publicly-owned company as defined by section 6.

3(2) For the purposes of this Act, information is held by a public authority if–

(a) it is held by the authority, otherwise than on behalf of another person, or

(b) it is held by another person on behalf of the authority.

4 Amendment of Schedule 1

4(1) The Secretary of State or the Minister for the Cabinet Office may by order amend Schedule 1 by adding to that Schedule a reference to any body or the holder of any office which (in either case) is not for the time being listed in that Schedule but as respects which both the first and the second conditions below are satisfied.

4(2) The first condition is that the body or office–

(a) is established by virtue of Her Majesty's prerogative or by an enactment or by subordinate legislation, or

(b) is established in any other way by a Minister of the Crown in his capacity as Minister, by a government department or by the Welsh Ministers, the First Minister for Wales or the Counsel General to the Welsh Assembly Government.

4(3) The second condition is–

(a) in the case of a body, that the body is wholly or partly constituted by appointment made by the Crown, by a Minister of the Crown, by a government department or by the Welsh Ministers, the First Minister for Wales or the Counsel General to the Welsh Assembly Government, or

(b) in the case of an office, that appointments to the office are made by the Crown, by a Minister of the Crown, by a government department or by the Welsh Ministers, the First Minister for Wales or the Counsel General to the Welsh Assembly Government.

4(4) If either the first or the second condition above ceases to be satisfied as respects any body or office which is listed in Part VI or VII of Schedule 1, that body or the holder of that office shall cease to be a public authority by virtue of the entry in question.

4(5) The Secretary of State or the Minister for the Cabinet Office may by order amend Schedule 1 by removing from Part VI or VII of that Schedule an entry relating to any body or office–

(a) which has ceased to exist, or

(b) as respects which either the first or the second condition above has ceased to be satisfied.

4(6) An order under subsection (1) may relate to a specified person or office or to persons or offices falling within a specified description.

4(7) Before making an order under subsection (1), the Secretary of State or the Minister for the Cabinet Office shall–

(a) if the order adds to Part II, III, IV or VI of Schedule 1 a reference to–

(i) a body whose functions are exercisable only or mainly in or as regards Wales, or

(ii) the holder of an office whose functions are exercisable only or mainly in or as regards Wales,

consult the Welsh Ministers, and

(b) if the order relates to a body which, or the holder of any office who, if the order were made, would be a Northern Ireland public authority, consult the First Minister and deputy First Minister in Northern Ireland.

4(8) This section has effect subject to section 80.

4(9) In this section **"Minister of the Crown"** includes a Northern Ireland Minister.

History – In s. 4(1), (5) and (7), the words "Minister for the Cabinet Office" substituted for the words "Chancellor of the Duchy" by SI 2016/997, art. 13 and Sch. 2, para. 14(2)(a), with effect from 9 November 2016.

In s. 4(1), (5) and (7), the words "or the Chancellor of the Duchy" inserted by SI 2015/1897, art. 9 and Sch., para. 2(2)(a), with effect from 9 December 2015.

In s. 4(2)(b) the words "the Welsh Ministers, the First Minister for Wales or the Counsel General to the Welsh Assembly Government" substituted for the words "the National Assembly for Wales" by SI 2007/1388, art. 3 and Sch. 1, para. 78(2), with effect from 2 May 2007.

In s. 4(3)(a) and (b) the words "the Welsh Ministers, the First Minister for Wales or the Counsel General to the Welsh Assembly Government" substituted for the words "the National Assembly for Wales" by SI 2007/1388, art. 3 and Sch. 1, para. 78(3), with effect from 2 May 2007.

In s. 4(7)(a)(ii) the words "the Welsh Ministers" substituted for the words "the National Assembly for Wales' by SI 2007/1388, art. 3 and Sch. 1, para. 78(4), with effect from 2 May 2007.

5 Further power to designate public authorities

5(1) The Secretary of State or the Minister for the Cabinet Office may by order designate as a public authority for the purposes of this Act any person who is neither listed in Schedule 1 nor capable of being added to that Schedule by an order under section 4(1), but who–

(a) appears to the Secretary of State or the Chancellor of the Duchy to exercise functions of a public nature, or

(b) is providing under a contract made with a public authority any service whose provision is a function of that authority.

5(2) An order under this section may designate a specified person or office or persons or offices falling within a specified description.

5(3) Before making an order under this section, the Secretary of State or the Minister for the Cabinet Office shall consult every person to whom the order relates, or persons appearing to him to represent such persons.

5(4) This section has effect subject to section 80.

History – In s. 5(1) and (3), the words "Minister for the Cabinet Office" substituted for the words "Chancellor of the Duchy" by SI 2016/997, art. 13 and Sch. 2, para. 14(2)(b), with effect from 9 November 2016.

In s. 5(1) and (3), the words "or the Chancellor of the Duchy" inserted by SI 2015/1897, art. 9 and Sch., para. 2(2)(b), with effect from 9 December 2015.

6 Publicly-owned companies

6(1) A company is a **"publicly-owned company"** for the purposes of section 3(1)(b) if–

(a) it is wholly owned by the Crown,

(b) it is wholly owned by the wider public sector, or

(c) it is wholly owned by the Crown and the wider public sector.

6(2) For the purposes of this section–

(a) a company is wholly owned by the Crown if, and only if, every member is a person falling within sub-paragraph (i) or (ii)–

(i) a Minister of the Crown, government department or company wholly owned by the Crown, or

(ii) a person acting on behalf of a Minister of the Crown, government department or company wholly owned by the Crown,

(b) a company is wholly owned by the wider public sector if, and only if, every member is a person falling within sub-paragraph (i) or (ii)–

(i) a relevant public authority or a company wholly owned by the wider public sector, or

(ii) a person acting on behalf of a relevant public authority or of a company wholly owned by the wider public sector, and

(c) a company is wholly owned by the Crown and the wider public sector if, and only if, condition A, B or C is met.

6(2A) In subsection (2)(c)–

(a) condition A is met if–

(i) at least one member is a person falling within subsection (2)(a)(i) or (ii),

(ii) at least one member is a person falling within subsection (2)(b)(i) or (ii), and

(iii) every member is a person falling within subsection (2)(a)(i) or (ii) or (b)(i) or (ii),

(b) condition B is met if–

(i) at least one member is a person falling within subsection (2)(a)(i) or (ii) or (b)(i) or (ii),

(ii) at least one member is a company wholly owned by the Crown and the wider public sector, and

(iii) every member is a person falling within subsection (2)(a)(i) or (ii) or (b)(i) or (ii) or a company wholly owned by the Crown and the wider public sector, and

(c) condition C is met if every member is a company wholly owned by the Crown and the wider public sector.

6(3) In this section–

"company" includes any body corporate;

"Minister of the Crown" includes a Northern Ireland Minister;

"relevant public authority" means any public authority listed in Schedule 1 other than–

(a) a government department, or

(b) any authority which is listed only in relation to particular information.

History – In s. 6(1)(a), the word "or" repealed by Protection of Freedoms Act 2012, s. 115(2) and Sch. 10, Pt. 7, with effect from 1 July 2012 (SI 2012/1205).

In s. 6(1)(b), the words "the wider public sector" substituted for the words "any public authority listed in Schedule 1 other than–

(i) a government department, or

(ii) any authority which is listed only in relation to particular information"

by Protection of Freedoms Act 2012, s. 103(2), with effect from 1 September 2013 (SI 2013/1906, art. 3(b)).

S. 6(1)(c) (and the "or" before it) inserted (and the "or" after (a) omitted) by Protection of Freedoms Act 2012, s. 103(2), with effect from 1 September 2013 (SI 2013/1906, art. 3(b)).

S. 6(2) and (2A) substituted for (2) by Protection of Freedoms Act 2012, s. 103(3), with effect from 1 September 2013 (SI 2013/1906, art. 3(b)).

In s. 6(3), definition of "relevant public authority" inserted by Protection of Freedoms Act 2012, s. 103(4), with effect from 1 September 2013 (SI 2013/1906, art. 3(b)).

7 Public authorities to which Act has limited application

7(1) Where a public authority is listed in Schedule 1 only in relation to information of a specified description, nothing in Parts I to V of this Act applies to any other information held by the authority.

7(2) An order under section 4(1) may, in adding an entry to Schedule 1, list the public authority only in relation to information of a specified description.

7(3) The Secretary of State or the Minister for the Cabinet Office may by order amend Schedule 1–

(a) by limiting to information of a specified description the entry relating to any public authority, or

(b) by removing or amending any limitation to information of a specified description which is for the time being contained in any entry.

7(4) Before making an order under subsection (3), the Secretary of State or the Minister for the Cabinet Office shall–

(a) if the order relates to the National Assembly for Wales or a Welsh public authority referred to in section 83(1)(b)(ii) (subsidiary of the Assembly Commission), consult the Presiding Officer of the National Assembly for Wales,

(aa) if the order relates to the Welsh Assembly Government or a Welsh public authority other than one referred to in section 83(1)(b)(ii), consult the First Minister for Wales,

(b) if the order relates to the Northern Ireland Assembly, consult the Presiding Officer of that Assembly, and

(c) if the order relates to a Northern Ireland department or a Northern Ireland public authority, consult the First Minister and deputy First Minister in Northern Ireland.

7(5) An order under section 5(1)(a) must specify the functions of the public authority designated by the order with respect to which the designation is to have effect; and nothing in Parts I to V of this Act applies to information which is held by the authority but does not relate to the exercise of those functions.

7(6) An order under section 5(1)(b) must specify the services provided under contract with respect to which the designation is to have effect; and nothing in Parts I to V of this Act applies to information which is held by the public authority designated by the order but does not relate to the provision of those services.

7(7) Nothing in Parts I to V of this Act applies in relation to any information held by a publicly-owned company which is excluded information in relation to that company.

7(8) In subsection (7) **"excluded information"**, in relation to a publicly-owned company, means information which is of a description specified in relation to that company in an order made by the Secretary of State or the Minister for the Cabinet Office for the purposes of this subsection.

7(9) In this section **"publicly-owned company"** has the meaning given by section 6.

History – In s. 7(3), (4) and (8), the words "Minister for the Cabinet Office" substituted for the words "Chancellor of the Duchy" by SI 2016/997, art. 13 and Sch. 2, para. 14(2)(c), with effect from 9 November 2016.
In s. 7(3), (4) and (8), the words "or the Chancellor of the Duchy" inserted by SI 2015/1897, art. 9 and Sch., para. 2(2)(c), with effect from 9 December 2015.
S. 7(4)(a) and (aa) substituted for former s. 7(4)(a) by SI 2007/1388, art. 3 and Sch. 1, para. 79, with effect from 2 May 2007.

8 Request for information

8(1) In this Act any reference to a **"request for information"** is a reference to such a request which–

(a) is in writing,

(b) states the name of the applicant and an address for correspondence, and

(c) describes the information requested.

8(2) For the purposes of subsection (1)(a), a request is to be treated as made in writing where the text of the request–

(a) is transmitted by electronic means,

(b) is received in legible form, and

(c) is capable of being used for subsequent reference.

9 Fees

9(1) A public authority to whom a request for information is made may, within the period for complying with section 1(1), give the applicant a notice in writing (in this Act referred to as a "fees notice") stating that a fee of an amount specified in the notice is to be charged by the authority for complying with section 1(1).

9(2) Where a fees notice has been given to the applicant, the public authority is not obliged to comply with section 1(1) unless the fee is paid within the period of three months beginning with the day on which the fees notice is given to the applicant.

9(3) Subject to subsection (5), any fee under this section must be determined by the public authority in accordance with regulations made by the Minister for the Cabinet Office.

9(4) Regulations under subsection (3) may, in particular, provide–

(a) that no fee is to be payable in prescribed cases,

(b) that any fee is not to exceed such maximum as may be specified in, or determined in accordance with, the regulations, and

(c) that any fee is to be calculated in such manner as may be prescribed by the regulations.

9(5) Subsection (3) does not apply where provision is made by or under any enactment as to the fee that may be charged by the public authority for the disclosure of the information.

History – In s. 9(3), the words "Minister for the Cabinet Office" substituted for the words "Chancellor of the Duchy" by SI 2016/997, art. 13 and Sch. 2, para. 14(2)(d), with effect from 9 November 2016.
In s. 9(3), the words "Chancellor of the Duchy" substituted for the words "Secretary of State" by SI 2015/1897, art. 9 and Sch., para. 2(3)(a), with effect from 9 December 2015.

10 Time for compliance with request

10(1) Subject to subsections (2) and (3), a public authority must comply with section 1(1) promptly and in any event not later than the twentieth working day following the date of receipt.

10(2) Where the authority has given a fees notice to the applicant and the fee is paid in accordance with section 9(2), the working days in the period beginning with the day on which the fees notice is given to the applicant and ending with the day on which the fee is received by the authority are to be disregarded in calculating for the purposes of subsection (1) the twentieth working day following the date of receipt.

10(3) If, and to the extent that–

(a) section 1(1)(a) would not apply if the condition in section 2(1)(b) were satisfied, or

(b) section 1(1)(b) would not apply if the condition in section 2(2)(b) were satisfied,

the public authority need not comply with section 1(1)(a) or (b) until such time as is reasonable in the circumstances; but this subsection does not affect the time by which any notice under section 17(1) must be given.

10(4) The Minister for the Cabinet Office may by regulations provide that subsections (1) and (2) are to have effect as if any reference to the twentieth working day following the date of receipt were a reference to such other day, not later than the sixtieth working day following the date of receipt, as may be specified in, or determined in accordance with, the regulations.

10(5) Regulations under subsection (4) may–

(a) prescribe different days in relation to different cases, and

(b) confer a discretion on the Commissioner.

10(6) In this section–

"the date of receipt" means–

(a) the day on which the public authority receives the request for information, or

(b) if later, the day on which it receives the information referred to in section 1(3);

"working day" means any day other than a Saturday, a Sunday, Christmas Day, Good Friday or a day which is a bank holiday under the Banking and Financial Dealings Act 1971 in any part of the United Kingdom.

History – In s. 10(4), the words "Minister for the Cabinet Office" substituted for the words "Chancellor of the Duchy" by SI 2016/997, art. 13 and Sch. 2, para. 14(2)(e), with effect from 9 November 2016.
In s. 10(4), the words "Chancellor of the Duchy" substituted for the words "Secretary of State" by SI 2015/1897, art. 9 and Sch., para. 2(3)(b), with effect from 9 December 2015.

11 Means by which communication to be made

11(1) Where, on making his request for information, the applicant expresses a preference for communication by any one or more of the following means, namely–

(a) the provision to the applicant of a copy of the information in permanent form or in another form acceptable to the applicant,

(b) the provision to the applicant of a reasonable opportunity to inspect a record containing the information, and

(c) the provision to the applicant of a digest or summary of the information in permanent form or in another form acceptable to the applicant,

the public authority shall so far as reasonably practicable give effect to that preference.

11(1A) Where–

(a) an applicant makes a request for information to a public authority in respect of information that is, or forms part of, a dataset held by the public authority, and

(b) on making the request for information, the applicant expresses a preference for communication by means of the provision to the applicant of a copy of the information in electronic form,

the public authority must, so far as reasonably practical, provide the information to the applicant in an electronic form which is capable of re-use.

11(2) In determining for the purposes of this section whether it is reasonably practicable to communicate information by particular means, the public authority may have regard to all the circumstances, including the cost of doing so.

11(3) Where the public authority determines that it is not reasonably practicable to comply with any preference expressed by the applicant in making his request, the authority shall notify the applicant of the reasons for its determination.

11(4) Subject to subsections (1) and (1A), a public authority may comply with a request by communicating information by any means which are reasonable in the circumstances.

11(5) In this Act **"dataset"** means information comprising a collection of information held in electronic form where all or most of the information in the collection–

(a) has been obtained or recorded for the purpose of providing a public authority with information in connection with the provision of a service by the authority or the carrying out of any other function of the authority,

(b) is factual information which–

 (i) is not the product of analysis or interpretation other than calculation, and

 (ii) is not an official statistic (within the meaning given by section 6(1) of the Statistics and Registration Service Act 2007), and

(c) remains presented in a way that (except for the purpose of forming part of the collection) has not been organised, adapted or otherwise materially altered since it was obtained or recorded.

History – S. 11(1A) inserted by Protection of Freedoms Act 2012, s. 102(2)(a), with effect from 1 September 2013 (SI 2013/1906, art. 3(a)).

In s. 11(4), the words "subsections (1) and (1A)" substituted for the words "subsection (1)" by Protection of Freedoms Act 2012, s. 102(2)(b), with effect from 1 September 2013 (SI 2013/1906, art. 3(a)).

S. 11(5) inserted by Protection of Freedoms Act 2012, s. 102(2)(c), with effect from 1 September 2013 (SI 2013/1906, art. 3(a)).

11A Release of datasets for re-use

11A(1) This section applies where–

(a) a person makes a request for information to a public authority in respect of information that is, or forms part of, a dataset held by the authority,

(b) any of the dataset or part of a dataset so requested is a relevant copyright work,

(c) the public authority is the only owner of the relevant copyright work, and

(d) the public authority is communicating the relevant copyright work to the applicant in accordance with this Act.

11A(1A) But if the whole of the relevant copyright work is a document to which the Re-use of Public Sector Information Regulations 2015 apply, this section does not apply to the relevant copyright work.

11A(1B) If part of the relevant copyright work is a document to which those Regulations apply–

(a) this section does not apply to that part, but

(b) this section does apply to the part to which the Regulations do not apply (and references in the following provisions of this section to the relevant copyright work are to be read as references to that part).

11A(2) When communicating the relevant copyright work to the applicant, the public authority must make the relevant copyright work available for re-use by the applicant in accordance with the terms of the specified licence.

11A(3) The public authority may exercise any power that it has by virtue of regulations under section 11B to charge a fee in connection with making the relevant copyright work available for re-use in accordance with subsection (2).

11A(4) Nothing in this section or section 11B prevents a public authority which is subject to a duty under subsection (2) from exercising any power that it has by or under an enactment other than this Act to charge a fee in connection with making the relevant copyright work available for re-use.

11A(5) Where a public authority intends to charge a fee (whether in accordance with regulations under section 11B or as mentioned in subsection (4)) in connection with making a relevant copyright work available for re-use by an applicant, the authority must give the applicant a notice in writing (in this section referred to as a "re-use fee notice") stating that a fee of an amount specified in, or determined in accordance with, the notice is to be charged by the authority in connection with complying with subsection (2).

11A(6) Where a re-use fee notice has been given to the applicant, the public authority is not obliged to comply with subsection (2) while any part of the fee which is required to be paid is unpaid.

11A(7) Where a public authority intends to charge a fee as mentioned in subsection (4), the re-use fee notice may be combined with any other notice which is to be given under the power which enables the fee to be charged.

11A(8) In this section–

"copyright owner" has the meaning given by Part 1 of the Copyright, Designs and Patents Act 1988 (see section 173 of that Act);

"copyright work" has the meaning given by Part 1 of the Act of 1988 (see section 1(2) of that Act);

"database" has the meaning given by section 3A of the Act of 1988;

"database right" has the same meaning as in Part 3 of the Copyright and Rights in Databases Regulations 1997 (S.I. 1997/3032);

"owner", in relation to a relevant copyright work, means–

(a) the copyright owner, or

(b) the owner of the database right in the database;

"relevant copyright work" means–

(a) a copyright work, or

(b) a database subject to a database right,

but excludes a relevant Crown work or a relevant Parliamentary work;

"relevant Crown work" means–

(a) a copyright work in relation to which the Crown is the copyright owner, or

(b) a database in relation to which the Crown is the owner of the database right;

"relevant Parliamentary work" means–

(a) a copyright work in relation to which the House of Commons or the House of Lords is the copyright owner, or

(b) a database in relation to which the House of Commons or the House of Lords is the owner of the database right;

"the specified licence" is the licence specified by the Minister for the Cabinet Office in a code of practice issued under section 45, and the Minister for the Cabinet Office may specify different licences for different purposes.

History – S. 11A(1A) and (1B) inserted by SI 2015/1415, reg. 21(2), with effect from 18 July 2015.
In s. 11A(8), in the definition of "the specified licence", the words "Minister for the Cabinet Office" substituted for the words "Chancellor of the Duchy" by SI 2016/997, art. 13 and Sch. 2, para. 14(2)(f), with effect from 9 November 2016.
In s. 11A(8), in the definition of "the specified licence", the words "Chancellor of the Duchy" substituted for the words "Secretary of State" by SI 2015/1897, art. 9 and Sch., para. 2(3)(c), with effect from 9 December 2015.
S. 11A inserted by Protection of Freedoms Act 2012, s. 102(3), with effect from 1 September 2013 (SI 2013/1906, art. 3(a)).

11B Power to charge fees in relation to release of datasets for re-use

11B(1) The Minister for the Cabinet Office may, with the consent of the Treasury, make provision by regulations about the charging of fees by public authorities in connection with making relevant copyright works available for re-use under section 11A(2) or by virtue of section 19(2A)(c).

11B(2) Regulations under this section may, in particular–

(a) prescribe cases in which fees may, or may not, be charged,

(b) prescribe the amount of any fee payable or provide for any such amount to be determined in such manner as may be prescribed,

(c) prescribe, or otherwise provide for, times at which fees, or parts of fees, are payable,

(d) require the provision of information about the manner in which amounts of fees are determined,

(e) make different provision for different purposes.

11B(3) Regulations under this section may, in prescribing the amount of any fee payable or providing for any such amount to be determined in such manner as may be prescribed, provide for a reasonable return on investment.

11B(4) In this section **"relevant copyright work"** has the meaning given by section 11A(8).

History – In s. 11B(1), the words "Minister for the Cabinet Office" substituted for the words "Chancellor of the Duchy" by SI 2016/997, art. 13 and Sch. 2, para. 14(2)(g), with effect from 9 November 2016.
In s. 11B(1), the words "Chancellor of the Duchy" substituted for the words "Secretary of State" by SI 2015/1897, art. 9 and Sch., para. 2(3)(d), with effect from 9 December 2015.
S. 11B inserted by Protection of Freedoms Act 2012, s. 102(3), with effect from 1 August 2013 (SI 2013/1906, art. 2).

12 Exemption where cost of compliance exceeds appropriate limit

12(1) Section 1(1) does not oblige a public authority to comply with a request for information if the authority estimates that the cost of complying with the request would exceed the appropriate limit.

12(2) Subsection (1) does not exempt the public authority from its obligation to comply with paragraph (a) of section 1(1) unless the estimated cost of complying with that paragraph alone would exceed the appropriate limit.

12(3) In subsections (1) and (2) **"the appropriate limit"** means such amount as may be prescribed, and different amounts may be prescribed in relation to different cases.

12(4) The Minister for the Cabinet Office may by regulations provide that, in such circumstances as may be prescribed, where two or more requests for information are made to a public authority–

(a) by one person, or

(b) by different persons who appear to the public authority to be acting in concert or in pursuance of a campaign,

the estimated cost of complying with any of the requests is to be taken to be the estimated total cost of complying with all of them.

12(5) The Minister for the Cabinet Office may by regulations make provision for the purposes of this section as to the costs to be estimated and as to the manner in which they are to be estimated.

History – In s. 12(4) and (5), the words "Minister for the Cabinet Office" substituted for the words "Chancellor of the Duchy" by SI 2016/997, art. 13 and Sch. 2, para. 14(2)(h), with effect from 9 November 2016.

In s. 12(4) and (5), the words "Chancellor of the Duchy" substituted for the words "Secretary of State" by SI 2015/1897, art. 9 and Sch., para. 2(3)(e), with effect from 9 December 2015.

13 Fees for disclosure where cost of compliance exceeds appropriate limit

13(1) A public authority may charge for the communication of any information whose communication–

(a) is not required by section 1(1) because the cost of complying with the request for information exceeds the amount which is the appropriate limit for the purposes of section 12(1) and (2), and

(b) is not otherwise required by law,

such fee as may be determined by the public authority in accordance with regulations made by the Minister for the Cabinet Office.

13(2) Regulations under this section may, in particular, provide–

(a) that any fee is not to exceed such maximum as may be specified in, or determined in accordance with, the regulations, and

(b) that any fee is to be calculated in such manner as may be prescribed by the regulations.

13(3) Subsection (1) does not apply where provision is made by or under any enactment as to the fee that may be charged by the public authority for the disclosure of the information.

History – In s. 13(1), the words "Minister for the Cabinet Office" substituted for the words "Chancellor of the Duchy" by SI 2016/997, art. 13 and Sch. 2, para. 14(2)(i), with effect from 9 November 2016.

In s. 13(1), the words "Chancellor of the Duchy" substituted for the words "Secretary of State" by SI 2015/1897, art. 9 and Sch., para. 2(3)(f), with effect from 9 December 2015.

14 Vexatious or repeated requests

14(1) Section 1(1) does not oblige a public authority to comply with a request for information if the request is vexatious.

14(2) Where a public authority has previously complied with a request for information which was made by any person, it is not obliged to comply with a subsequent identical or substantially similar request from that person unless a reasonable interval has elapsed between compliance with the previous request and the making of the current request.

15 Special provisions relating to public records transferred to Public Record Office, etc.

15(1) Where–

(a) the appropriate records authority receives a request for information which relates to information which is, or if it existed would be, contained in a transferred public record, and

(b) either of the conditions in subsection (2) is satisfied in relation to any of that information,

that authority shall, within the period for complying with section 1(1), send a copy of the request to the responsible authority.

15(2) The conditions referred to in subsection (1)(b) are–

(a) that the duty to confirm or deny is expressed to be excluded only by a provision of Part II not specified in subsection (3) of section 2, and

(b) that the information is exempt information only by virtue of a provision of Part II not specified in that subsection.

15(3) On receiving the copy, the responsible authority shall, within such time as is reasonable in all the circumstances, inform the appropriate records authority of the determination required by virtue of subsection (3) or (4) of section 66.

15(4) In this Act **"transferred public record"** means a public record which has been transferred–

(a) to the Public Record Office,

(b) to another place of deposit appointed by the Secretary of State under the Public Records Act 1958, or

(c) to the Public Record Office of Northern Ireland.

15(5) In this Act–

"appropriate records authority", in relation to a transferred public record, means–

(a) in a case falling within subsection (4)(a), the Public Record Office,

(b) in a case falling within subsection (4)(b), the Secretary of State, and

(c) in a case falling within subsection (4)(c), the Public Record Office of Northern Ireland;

"responsible authority", in relation to a transferred public record, means–

(a) in the case of a record transferred as mentioned in subsection (4)(a) or (b) from a government department in the charge of a Minister of the Crown, the Minister of the Crown who appears to the Secretary of State to be primarily concerned,

(b) in the case of a record transferred as mentioned in subsection (4)(a) or (b) from any other person, the person who appears to the Secretary of State to be primarily concerned,

(c) in the case of a record transferred to the Public Record Office of Northern Ireland from a government department in the charge of a Minister of the Crown, the Minister of the Crown who appears to the appropriate Northern Ireland Minister to be primarily concerned,

(d) in the case of a record transferred to the Public Record Office of Northern Ireland from a Northern Ireland department, the Northern Ireland Minister who appears to the appropriate Northern Ireland Minister to be primarily concerned, or

(e) in the case of a record transferred to the Public Record Office of Northern Ireland from any other person, the person who appears to the appropriate Northern Ireland Minister to be primarily concerned.

History – In s. 15(4)(b) and (5), the words "Secretary of State" substituted for the words "Lord Chancellor" by SI 2015/1897, art. 9 and Sch., para. 2(5)(a), with effect from 9 December 2015.

16 Duty to provide advice and assistance

16(1) It shall be the duty of a public authority to provide advice and assistance, so far as it would be reasonable to expect the authority to do so, to persons who propose to make, or have made, requests for information to it.

16(2) Any public authority which, in relation to the provision of advice or assistance in any case, conforms with the code of practice under section 45 is to be taken to comply with the duty imposed by subsection (1) in relation to that case.

REFUSAL OF REQUEST

17 Refusal of request

17(1) A public authority which, in relation to any request for information, is to any extent relying on a claim that any provision of Part II relating to the duty to confirm or deny is relevant to the request or on a claim that information is exempt information must, within the time for complying with section 1(1), give the applicant a notice which–

(a) states that fact,

(b) specifies the exemption in question, and

(c) states (if that would not otherwise be apparent) why the exemption applies.

17(2) Where–

(a) in relation to any request for information, a public authority is, as respects any information, relying on a claim–

(i) that any provision of Part II which relates to the duty to confirm or deny and is not specified in section 2(3) is relevant to the request, or

(ii) that the information is exempt information only by virtue of a provision not specified in section 2(3), and

(b) at the time when the notice under subsection (1) is given to the applicant, the public authority (or, in a case falling within section 66(3) or (4), the responsible authority) has not yet reached a decision as to the application of subsection (1)(b) or (2)(b) of section 2,

the notice under subsection (1) must indicate that no decision as to the application of that provision has yet been reached and must contain an estimate of the date by which the authority expects that such a decision will have been reached.

17(3) A public authority which, in relation to any request for information, is to any extent relying on a claim that subsection (1)(b) or (2)(b) of section 2 applies must, either in the notice under subsection (1) or in a separate notice given within such time as is reasonable in the circumstances, state the reasons for claiming–

(a) that, in all the circumstances of the case, the public interest in maintaining the exclusion of the duty to confirm or deny outweighs the public interest in disclosing whether the authority holds the information, or

(b) that, in all the circumstances of the case, the public interest in maintaining the exemption outweighs the public interest in disclosing the information.

17(4) A public authority is not obliged to make a statement under subsection (1)(c) or (3) if, or to the extent that, the statement would involve the disclosure of information which would itself be exempt information.

17(5) A public authority which, in relation to any request for information, is relying on a claim that section 12 or 14 applies must, within the time for complying with section 1(1), give the applicant a notice stating that fact.

17(6) Subsection (5) does not apply where–

(a) the public authority is relying on a claim that section 14 applies,

(b) the authority has given the applicant a notice, in relation to a previous request for information, stating that it is relying on such a claim, and

(c) it would in all the circumstances be unreasonable to expect the authority to serve a further notice under subsection (5) in relation to the current request.

17(7) A notice under subsection (1), (3) or (5) must–

(a) contain particulars of any procedure provided by the public authority for dealing with complaints about the handling of requests for information or state that the authority does not provide such a procedure, and

(b) contain particulars of the right conferred by section 50.

THE INFORMATION COMMISSIONER AND THE INFORMATION TRIBUNAL

18 The Information Commissioner and the Information Tribunal

18(1) The Data Protection Commissioner shall be known instead as the Information Commissioner.

18(2) The Data Protection Tribunal shall be known instead as the Information Tribunal.

18(3) In this Act–

(a) the Information Commissioner is referred to as "the Commissioner", and

(b) the Information Tribunal is referred to as "the Tribunal".

18(4) Schedule 2 (which makes provision consequential on subsections (1) and (2) and amendments of the Data Protection Act 1998 relating to the extension by this Act of the functions of the Commissioner and the Tribunal) has effect.

18(5) [Repealed by Protection of Freedoms Act 2012, s. 115(2) and Sch. 10, Pt. 8.]

18(6) [Repealed by Protection of Freedoms Act 2012, s. 115(2) and Sch. 10, Pt. 8.]

18(7) [Repealed by Protection of Freedoms Act 2012, s. 115(2) and Sch. 10, Pt. 8.]

History – S. 18(5)–(7) repealed by Protection of Freedoms Act 2012, s. 115(2) and Sch. 10, Pt. 8, with effect from 16 March 2015 (SI 2015/587, art. 2).

PUBLICATION SCHEMES

19 Publication schemes

19(1) It shall be the duty of every public authority–

(a) to adopt and maintain a scheme which relates to the publication of information by the authority and is approved by the Commissioner (in this Act referred to as a "publication scheme"),

(b) to publish information in accordance with its publication scheme, and

(c) from time to time to review its publication scheme.

19(2) A publication scheme must–

(a) specify classes of information which the public authority publishes or intends to publish,

(b) specify the manner in which information of each class is, or is intended to be, published, and

(c) specify whether the material is, or is intended to be, available to the public free of charge or on payment.

19(2A) A publication scheme must, in particular, include a requirement for the public authority concerned–

(a) to publish–

(i) any dataset held by the authority in relation to which a person makes a request for information to the authority, and

(ii) any up-dated version held by the authority of such a dataset,

unless the authority is satisfied that it is not appropriate for the dataset to be published,

(b) where reasonably practicable, to publish any dataset the authority publishes by virtue of paragraph (a) in an electronic form which is capable of re-use,

(c) subject to subsections (2AA) and (2AB), where any information in a dataset published by virtue of paragraph (a) is a relevant copyright work in relation to which the authority is the only owner, to make the information available for re-use in accordance with the terms of the specified licence.

19(2AA) If the whole of the relevant copyright work is a document to which the Re-use of Public Sector Information Regulations 2015 apply, subsections (2A)(c) and (2B) to (2F) do not apply to the relevant copyright work.

19(2AB) If part of the relevant copyright work is a document to which those Regulations apply–

(a) subsections (2A)(c) and (2B) to (2F) do not apply to that part, but

(b) those provisions do apply to the part to which the Regulations do not apply (and references in the following provisions of this section to the relevant copyright work are to be read as references to that part).

19(2B) The public authority may exercise any power that it has by virtue of regulations under section 11B to charge a fee in connection with making the relevant copyright work available for re-use in accordance with a requirement imposed by virtue of subsection (2A)(c).

19(2C) Nothing in this section or section 11B prevents a public authority which is subject to such a requirement from exercising any power that it has by or under an enactment other than this Act to charge a fee in connection with making the relevant copyright work available for re-use.

19(2D) Where a public authority intends to charge a fee (whether in accordance with regulations under section 11B or as mentioned in subsection (2C)) in connection with making a relevant copyright work available for re-use by an applicant, the authority must give the applicant a notice in writing (in this section referred to as a "re-use fee notice") stating that a fee of an amount specified in, or determined in accordance with, the notice is to be charged by the authority in connection with complying with the requirement imposed by virtue of subsection (2A)(c).

19(2E) Where a re-use fee notice has been given to the applicant, the public authority is not obliged to comply with the requirement imposed by virtue of subsection (2A)(c) while any part of the fee which is required to be paid is unpaid.

19(2F) Where a public authority intends to charge a fee as mentioned in subsection (2C), the re-use fee notice may be combined with any other notice which is to be given under the power which enables the fee to be charged.

19(3) In adopting or reviewing a publication scheme, a public authority shall have regard to the public interest–

(a) in allowing public access to information held by the authority, and

(b) in the publication of reasons for decisions made by the authority.

19(4) A public authority shall publish its publication scheme in such manner as it thinks fit.

19(5) The Commissioner may, when approving a scheme, provide that his approval is to expire at the end of a specified period.

19(6) Where the Commissioner has approved the publication scheme of any public authority, he may at any time give notice to the public authority revoking his approval of the scheme as from the end of the period of six months beginning with the day on which the notice is given.

19(7) Where the Commissioner–

(a) refuses to approve a proposed publication scheme, or

(b) revokes his approval of a publication scheme,

he must give the public authority a statement of his reasons for doing so.

19(8) In this section–

"copyright owner" has the meaning given by Part 1 of the Copyright, Designs and Patents Act 1988 (see section 173 of that Act);

"copyright work" has the meaning given by Part 1 of the Act of 1988 (see section 1(2) of that Act);

"database" has the meaning given by section 3A of the Act of 1988;

"database right" has the same meaning as in Part 3 of the Copyright and Rights in Databases Regulations 1997 (S.I. 1997/3032);

"owner", in relation to a relevant copyright work, means–

(a) the copyright owner, or

(b) the owner of the database right in the database;

"relevant copyright work" means–

(a) a copyright work, or

(b) a database subject to a database right,

but excludes a relevant Crown work or a relevant Parliamentary work;

"relevant Crown work" means–

(a) a copyright work in relation to which the Crown is the copyright owner, or

(b) a database in relation to which the Crown is the owner of the database right;

"relevant Parliamentary work" means–

(a) a copyright work in relation to which the House of Commons or the House of Lords is the copyright owner, or

(b) a database in relation to which the House of Commons or the House of Lords is the owner of the database right;

"the specified licence" has the meaning given by section 11A(8).

History – S. 19(2A)–(2F) inserted by Protection of Freedoms Act 2012, s. 102(4), with effect from 1 September 2013 (SI 2013/1906, art. 3(a)).
In s. 19(2A)(c), the words "subject to subsections (2AA) and (2AB)" inserted by SI 2015/1415, reg. 21(3)(a), with effect from 18 July 2015.
S. 19(2AA) and (2AB) inserted by SI 2015/1415, reg. 21(3)(b), with effect from 18 July 2015.
S. 19(8) inserted by Protection of Freedoms Act 2012, s. 102(4), with effect from 1 September 2013 (SI 2013/1906, art. 3(a)).

20 Model publication schemes

20(1) The Commissioner may from time to time approve, in relation to public authorities falling within particular classes, model publication schemes prepared by him or by other persons.

20(2) Where a public authority falling within the class to which an approved model scheme relates adopts such a scheme without modification, no further approval of the Commissioner is required so long as the model scheme remains approved; and where such an authority adopts such a scheme with modifications, the approval of the Commissioner is required only in relation to the modifications.

20(3) The Commissioner may, when approving a model publication scheme, provide that his approval is to expire at the end of a specified period.

20(4) Where the Commissioner has approved a model publication scheme, he may at any time publish, in such manner as he thinks fit, a notice revoking his approval of the scheme as from the end of the period of six months beginning with the day on which the notice is published.

20(5) Where the Commissioner refuses to approve a proposed model publication scheme on the application of any person, he must give the person who applied for approval of the scheme a statement of the reasons for his refusal.

20(6) Where the Commissioner refuses to approve any modifications under subsection (2), he must give the public authority a statement of the reasons for his refusal.

20(7) Where the Commissioner revokes his approval of a model publication scheme, he must include in the notice under subsection (4) a statement of his reasons for doing so.

PART II – EXEMPT INFORMATION

21 Information accessible to applicant by other means

21(1) Information which is reasonably accessible to the applicant otherwise than under section 1 is exempt information.

21(2) For the purposes of subsection (1)–

(a) information may be reasonably accessible to the applicant even though it is accessible only on payment, and

(b) information is to be taken to be reasonably accessible to the applicant if it is information which the public authority or any other person is obliged by or under any enactment to communicate (otherwise than by making the information available for inspection) to members of the public on request, whether free of charge or on payment.

21(3) For the purposes of subsection (1), information which is held by a public authority and does not fall within subsection (2)(b) is not to be regarded as reasonably accessible to the applicant merely because the information is available from the public authority itself on request, unless the information is made available in accordance with the authority's publication scheme and any payment required is specified in, or determined in accordance with, the scheme.

22 Information intended for future publication

22(1) Information is exempt information if–

(a) the information is held by the public authority with a view to its publication, by the authority or any other person, at some future date (whether determined or not),

(b) the information was already held with a view to such publication at the time when the request for information was made, and

(c) it is reasonable in all the circumstances that the information should be withheld from disclosure until the date referred to in paragraph (a).

22(2) The duty to confirm or deny does not arise if, or to the extent that, compliance with section 1(1)(a) would involve the disclosure of any information (whether or not already recorded) which falls within subsection (1).

22A Research

22A(1) Information obtained in the course of, or derived from, a programme of research is exempt information if–

(a) the programme is continuing with a view to the publication, by a public authority or any other person, of a report of the research (whether or not including a statement of that information), and

(b) disclosure of the information under this Act before the date of publication would, or would be likely to, prejudice–

(i) the programme,

(ii) the interests of any individual participating in the programme,

(iii) the interests of the authority which holds the information, or

(iv) the interests of the authority mentioned in paragraph (a) (if it is a different authority from that which holds the information).

22A(2) The duty to confirm or deny does not arise in relation to information which is (or if it were held by the public authority would be) exempt information by virtue of subsection (1) if, or to the extent that, compliance with section 1(1)(a) would, or would be likely to, prejudice any of the matters mentioned in subsection (1)(b).

History – S. 22A inserted by Intellectual Property Act 2014, s. 20, with effect from 1 October 2014 (SI 2014/2330, art. 2).

23 Information supplied by, or relating to, bodies dealing with security matters

23(1) Information held by a public authority is exempt information if it was directly or indirectly supplied to the public authority by, or relates to, any of the bodies specified in subsection (3).

23(2) A certificate signed by a Minister of the Crown certifying that the information to which it applies was directly or indirectly supplied by, or relates to, any of the bodies specified in subsection (3) shall, subject to section 60, be conclusive evidence of that fact.

23(3) The bodies referred to in subsections (1) and (2) are–

(a) the Security Service,

(b) the Secret Intelligence Service,
(c) the Government Communications Headquarters,
(d) the special forces,
(e) the Tribunal established under section 65 of the Regulation of Investigatory Powers Act 2000,
(f) the Tribunal established under section 7 of the Interception of Communications Act 1985,
(g) the Tribunal established under section 5 of the Security Service Act 1989,
(h) the Tribunal established under section 9 of the Intelligence Services Act 1994,
(i) the Security Vetting Appeals Panel,
(j) the Security Commission,
(k) the National Criminal Intelligence Service,
(l) the Service Authority for the National Criminal Intelligence Service[,]
(m) the Serious Organised Crime Agency[,]
(n) the National Crime Agency[,]
(o) the Intelligence and Security Committee of Parliament.

23(4) In subsection (3)(c) **"the Government Communications Headquarters"** includes any unit or part of a unit of the armed forces of the Crown which is for the time being required by the Secretary of State to assist the Government Communications Headquarters in carrying out its functions.

23(5) The duty to confirm or deny does not arise if, or to the extent that, compliance with section 1(1)(a) would involve the disclosure of any information (whether or not already recorded) which was directly or indirectly supplied to the public authority by, or relates to, any of the bodies specified in subsection (3).

History – In s. 23(3)(k), the word "and" at end omitted by SOCPA 2005, Sch. 4, para. 159 and repealed by SOCPA 2005, Sch. 17, with effect from 1 April 2006 (by virtue of SI 2006/378, art. 4(1) and Schedule).
S. 23(3)(m) inserted by SOCPA 2005, Sch. 4, para. 159, with effect from 1 April 2006 (by virtue of SI 2006/378, art. 4(1) and Schedule).
S. 23(3)(n) inserted by Crime and Courts Act 2013, s. 15(3) and Sch. 8, para. 102, with effect from 27 May 2013 (SI 2013/1042).
S. 23(o) inserted by Justice and Security Act 2013, s. 19(1) and Sch. 2, para. 2, with effect from 25 June 2013 (SI 2013/1482, art. 2).

24 National security

24(1) Information which does not fall within section 23(1) is exempt information if exemption from section 1(1)(b) is required for the purpose of safeguarding national security.

24(2) The duty to confirm or deny does not arise if, or to the extent that, exemption from section 1(1)(a) is required for the purpose of safeguarding national security.

24(3) A certificate signed by a Minister of the Crown certifying that exemption from section 1(1)(b), or from section 1(1)(a) and (b), is, or at any time was, required for the purpose of safeguarding national security shall, subject to section 60, be conclusive evidence of that fact.

24(4) A certificate under subsection (3) may identify the information to which it applies by means of a general description and may be expressed to have prospective effect.

25 Certificates under ss. 23 and 24: supplementary provisions

25(1) A document purporting to be a certificate under section 23(2) or 24(3) shall be received in evidence and deemed to be such a certificate unless the contrary is proved.

25(2) A document which purports to be certified by or on behalf of a Minister of the Crown as a true copy of a certificate issued by that Minister under section 23(2) or 24(3) shall in any legal proceedings be evidence (or, in Scotland, sufficient evidence) of that certificate.

25(3) The power conferred by section 23(2) or 24(3) on a Minister of the Crown shall not be exercisable except by a Minister who is a member of the Cabinet or by the Attorney General, the Advocate General for Scotland or the Attorney General for Northern Ireland.

26 Defence

26(1) Information is exempt information if its disclosure under this Act would, or would be likely to, prejudice–
(a) the defence of the British Islands or of any colony, or
(b) the capability, effectiveness or security of any relevant forces.

26(2) In subsection (1)(b) **"relevant forces"** means–
(a) the armed forces of the Crown, and
(b) any forces co-operating with those forces,
or any part of any of those forces.

26(3) The duty to confirm or deny does not arise if, or to the extent that, compliance with section 1(1)(a) would, or would be likely to, prejudice any of the matters mentioned in subsection (1).

27 International relations

27(1) Information is exempt information if its disclosure under this Act would, or would be likely to, prejudice–

(a) relations between the United Kingdom and any other State,

(b) relations between the United Kingdom and any international organisation or international court,

(c) the interests of the United Kingdom abroad, or

(d) the promotion or protection by the United Kingdom of its interests abroad.

27(2) Information is also exempt information if it is confidential information obtained from a State other than the United Kingdom or from an international organisation or international court.

27(3) For the purposes of this section, any information obtained from a State, organisation or court is confidential at any time while the terms on which it was obtained require it to be held in confidence or while the circumstances in which it was obtained make it reasonable for the State, organisation or court to expect that it will be so held.

27(4) The duty to confirm or deny does not arise if, or to the extent that, compliance with section 1(1)(a)–

(a) would, or would be likely to, prejudice any of the matters mentioned in subsection (1), or

(b) would involve the disclosure of any information (whether or not already recorded) which is confidential information obtained from a State other than the United Kingdom or from an international organisation or international court.

27(5) In this section–

"international court" means any international court which is not an international organisation and which is established–

(a) by a resolution of an international organisation of which the United Kingdom is a member, or

(b) by an international agreement to which the United Kingdom is a party;

"international organisation" means any international organisation whose members include any two or more States, or any organ of such an organisation;

"State" includes the government of any State and any organ of its government, and references to a State other than the United Kingdom include references to any territory outside the United Kingdom.

28 Relations within the United Kingdom

28(1) Information is exempt information if its disclosure under this Act would, or would be likely to, prejudice relations between any administration in the United Kingdom and any other such administration.

28(2) In subsection (1) **"administration in the United Kingdom"** means–

(a) the government of the United Kingdom,

(b) the Scottish Administration,

(c) the Executive Committee of the Northern Ireland Assembly, or

(d) the Welsh Assembly Government.

28(3) The duty to confirm or deny does not arise if, or to the extent that, compliance with section 1(1)(a) would, or would be likely to, prejudice any of the matters mentioned in subsection (1).

History – S. 28(2)(d) substituted by SI 2007/1388, art. 3 and Sch. 1, para. 80, with effect from 2 May 2007.

29 The economy

29(1) Information is exempt information if its disclosure under this Act would, or would be likely to, prejudice–

(a) the economic interests of the United Kingdom or of any part of the United Kingdom, or

(b) the financial interests of any administration in the United Kingdom, as defined by section 28(2).

29(2) The duty to confirm or deny does not arise if, or to the extent that, compliance with section 1(1)(a) would, or would be likely to, prejudice any of the matters mentioned in subsection (1).

30 Investigations and proceedings conducted by public authorities

30(1) Information held by a public authority is exempt information if it has at any time been held by the authority for the purposes of–

(a) any investigation which the public authority has a duty to conduct with a view to it being ascertained–

(i) whether a person should be charged with an offence, or

(ii) whether a person charged with an offence is guilty of it,

(b) any investigation which is conducted by the authority and in the circumstances may lead to a decision by the authority to institute criminal proceedings which the authority has power to conduct, or

(c) any criminal proceedings which the authority has power to conduct.

30(2) Information held by a public authority is exempt information if–

(a) it was obtained or recorded by the authority for the purposes of its functions relating to–

(i) investigations falling within subsection (1)(a) or (b),

(ii) criminal proceedings which the authority has power to conduct,

(iii) investigations (other than investigations falling within subsection (1)(a) or (b)) which are conducted by the authority for any of the purposes specified in section 31(2) and either by virtue of Her Majesty's prerogative or by virtue of powers conferred by or under any enactment, or

(iv) civil proceedings which are brought by or on behalf of the authority and arise out of such investigations, and

(b) it relates to the obtaining of information from confidential sources.

30(3) The duty to confirm or deny does not arise in relation to information which is (or if it were held by the public authority would be) exempt information by virtue of subsection (1) or (2).

30(4) In relation to the institution or conduct of criminal proceedings or the power to conduct them, references in subsection (1)(b) or (c) and subsection (2)(a) to the public authority include references–

(a) to any officer of the authority,

(b) in the case of a government department other than a Northern Ireland department, to the Minister of the Crown in charge of the department, and

(c) in the case of a Northern Ireland department, to the Northern Ireland Minister in charge of the department.

30(5) In this section–

"criminal proceedings" includes–

(a) proceedings before a court-martial constituted under the Army Act 1955, the Air Force Act 1955 or the Naval Discipline Act 1957 or a disciplinary court constituted under section 52G of the Act of 1957,

(b) proceedings on dealing summarily with a charge under the Army Act 1955 or the Air Force Act 1955 or on summary trial under the Naval Discipline Act 1957,

(c) proceedings before a court established by section 83ZA of the Army Act 1955, section 83ZA of the Air Force Act 1955 or section 52FF of the Naval Discipline Act 1957 (summary appeal courts),

(d) proceedings before the Courts-Martial Appeal Court, and

(e) proceedings before a Standing Civilian Court;

"offence" includes any offence under the Army Act 1955, the Air Force Act 1955 or the Naval Discipline Act 1957.

30(6) In the application of this section to Scotland–

(a) in subsection (1)(b), for the words from "a decision" to the end there is substituted "a decision by the authority to make a report to the procurator fiscal for the purpose of enabling him to determine whether criminal proceedings should be instituted",

(b) in subsections (1)(c) and (2)(a)(ii) for "which the authority has power to conduct" there is substituted "which have been instituted in consequence of a report made by the authority to the procurator fiscal", and

(c) for any reference to a person being charged with an offence there is substituted a reference to the person being prosecuted for the offence.

31 Law enforcement

31(1) Information which is not exempt information by virtue of section 30 is exempt information if its disclosure under this Act would, or would be likely to, prejudice–

(a) the prevention or detection of crime,

(b) the apprehension or prosecution of offenders,

(c) the administration of justice,

(d) the assessment or collection of any tax or duty or of any imposition of a similar nature,

(e) the operation of the immigration controls,

(f) the maintenance of security and good order in prisons or in other institutions where persons are lawfully detained,

(g) the exercise by any public authority of its functions for any of the purposes specified in subsection (2),

(h) any civil proceedings which are brought by or on behalf of a public authority and arise out of an investigation conducted, for any of the purposes specified in subsection (2), by or on behalf of the authority by virtue of Her Majesty's prerogative or by virtue of powers conferred by or under an enactment, or

(i) any inquiry held under the Fatal Accidents and Sudden Deaths Inquiries (Scotland) Act 1976 to the extent that the inquiry arises out of an investigation conducted, for any of the purposes specified in subsection (2), by or on behalf of the authority by virtue of Her Majesty's prerogative or by virtue of powers conferred by or under an enactment.

31(2) The purposes referred to in subsection (1)(g) to (i) are–

(a) the purpose of ascertaining whether any person has failed to comply with the law,

(b) the purpose of ascertaining whether any person is responsible for any conduct which is improper,

(c) the purpose of ascertaining whether circumstances which would justify regulatory action in pursuance of any enactment exist or may arise,

(d) the purpose of ascertaining a person's fitness or competence in relation to the management of bodies corporate or in relation to any profession or other activity which he is, or seeks to become, authorised to carry on,

(e) the purpose of ascertaining the cause of an accident,

(f) the purpose of protecting charities against misconduct or mismanagement (whether by trustees or other persons) in their administration,

(g) the purpose of protecting the property of charities from loss or misapplication,

(h) the purpose of recovering the property of charities,

(i) the purpose of securing the health, safety and welfare of persons at work, and

(j) the purpose of protecting persons other than persons at work against risk to health or safety arising out of or in connection with the actions of persons at work.

31(3) The duty to confirm or deny does not arise if, or to the extent that, compliance with section 1(1)(a) would, or would be likely to, prejudice any of the matters mentioned in subsection (1).

32 Court records, etc

32(1) Information held by a public authority is exempt information if it is held only by virtue of being contained in–

(a) any document filed with, or otherwise placed in the custody of, a court for the purposes of proceedings in a particular cause or matter,

(b) any document served upon, or by, a public authority for the purposes of proceedings in a particular cause or matter, or

(c) any document created by–

(i) a court, or

(ii) a member of the administrative staff of a court,

for the purposes of proceedings in a particular cause or matter.

32(2) Information held by a public authority is exempt information if it is held only by virtue of being contained in–

(a) any document placed in the custody of a person conducting an inquiry or arbitration, for the purposes of the inquiry or arbitration, or

(b) any document created by a person conducting an inquiry or arbitration, for the purposes of the inquiry or arbitration.

32(3) The duty to confirm or deny does not arise in relation to information which is (or if it were held by the public authority would be) exempt information by virtue of this section.

32(4) In this section–

(a) **"court"** includes any tribunal or body exercising the judicial power of the State,

(b) **"proceedings in a particular cause or matter"** includes any inquest or post-mortem examination,

(c) **"inquiry"** means any inquiry or hearing held under any provision contained in, or made under, an enactment, and

(d) except in relation to Scotland, **"arbitration"** means any arbitration to which Part I of the Arbitration Act 1996 applies.

33 Audit functions

33(1) This section applies to any public authority which has functions in relation to–

(a) the audit of the accounts of other public authorities, or

(b) the examination of the economy, efficiency and effectiveness with which other public authorities use their resources in discharging their functions.

33(2) Information held by a public authority to which this section applies is exempt information if its disclosure would, or would be likely to, prejudice the exercise of any of the authority's functions in relation to any of the matters referred to in subsection (1).

33(3) The duty to confirm or deny does not arise in relation to a public authority to which this section applies if, or to the extent that, compliance with section 1(1)(a) would, or would be likely to, prejudice the exercise of any of the authority's functions in relation to any of the matters referred to in subsection (1).

34 Parliamentary privilege

34(1) Information is exempt information if exemption from section 1(1)(b) is required for the purpose of avoiding an infringement of the privileges of either House of Parliament.

34(2) The duty to confirm or deny does not apply if, or to the extent that, exemption from section 1(1)(a) is required for the purpose of avoiding an infringement of the privileges of either House of Parliament.

34(3) A certificate signed by the appropriate authority certifying that exemption from section 1(1)(b), or from section 1(1)(a) and (b), is, or at any time was, required for the purpose of avoiding an infringement of the privileges of either House of Parliament shall be conclusive evidence of that fact.

34(4) In subsection (3) **"the appropriate authority"** means–

(a) in relation to the House of Commons, the Speaker of that House, and

(b) in relation to the House of Lords, the Clerk of the Parliaments.

35 Formulation of government policy, etc.

35(1) Information held by a government department or by the Welsh Assembly Government is exempt information if it relates to–

(a) the formulation or development of government policy,

(b) Ministerial communications,

(c) the provision of advice by any of the Law Officers or any request for the provision of such advice, or

(d) the operation of any Ministerial private office.

35(2) Once a decision as to government policy has been taken, any statistical information used to provide an informed background to the taking of the decision is not to be regarded–

(a) for the purposes of subsection (1)(a), as relating to the formulation or development of government policy, or

(b) for the purposes of subsection (1)(b), as relating to Ministerial communications.

35(3) The duty to confirm or deny does not arise in relation to information which is (or if it were held by the public authority would be) exempt information by virtue of subsection (1).

35(4) In making any determination required by section 2(1)(b) or (2)(b) in relation to information which is exempt information by virtue of subsection (1)(a), regard shall be had to the particular public interest in the disclosure of factual information which has been used, or is intended to be used, to provide an informed background to decision-taking.

35(5) In this section–

"government policy" includes the policy of the Executive Committee of the Northern Ireland Assembly and the policy of the Welsh Assembly Government;

"the Law Officers" means the Attorney General, the Solicitor General, the Advocate General for Scotland, the Counsel General to the Welsh Assembly Government, the Lord Advocate, the Solicitor General for Scotland and the Attorney General for Northern Ireland;

"Ministerial communications" means any communications–

(a) between Ministers of the Crown,

(b) between Northern Ireland Ministers, including Northern Ireland junior Ministers, or

(c) between members of the Welsh Assembly Government,

and includes, in particular, proceedings of the Cabinet or of any committee of the Cabinet, proceedings of the Executive Committee of the Northern Ireland Assembly, and proceedings of the Cabinet or any committee of the Cabinet of the Welsh Assembly Government;

"Ministerial private office" means any part of a government department which provides personal administrative support to a Minister of the Crown, to a Northern Ireland Minister or a Northern Ireland junior Minister or any part of the administration of the Welsh Assembly Government providing personal administrative support to the members of the Welsh Assembly Government;

"Northern Ireland junior Minister" means a member of the Northern Ireland Assembly appointed as a junior Minister under section 19 of the Northern Ireland Act 1998.

History – In s. 35(1) the words "the Welsh Assembly Government" substituted for the words "the National Assembly for Wales" by SI 2007/1388, art. 3 and Sch. 1, para. 81(2), with effect from 2 May 2007.
In s. 35(5), in the definition of "government policy", the words "the Welsh Assembly Government" substituted for the words "the National Assembly for Wales" by SI 2007/1388, art. 3 and Sch. 1, para. 81(3), with effect from 2 May 2007.
In s. 35(5), in the definition of "the Law Officers", the words ", the Counsel General to the Welsh Assembly Government" inserted by SI 2007/1388, art. 3 and Sch. 1, para. 81(3), with effect from 2 May 2007.
In s. 35(5), in the definition of "Ministerial communications", para. (c) substituted and the words "the Cabinet or any committee of the Cabinet of the Welsh Assembly Government" substituted for the words "the executive committee of the National Assembly for Wales" by SI 2007/1388, art. 3 and Sch. 1, para. 81(3), with effect from 2 May 2007.
In s. 35(5), in the definition of "Ministerial private office", the words "any part of the administration of the Welsh Assembly Government providing personal administrative support to the members of the Welsh Assembly Government" substituted for the words "any part of the administration of the National Assembly for Wales providing personal administrative support to the Assembly First Secretary or an Assembly Secretary" by SI 2007/1388, art. 3 and Sch. 1, para. 81(3), with effect from 2 May 2007.

36 Prejudice to effective conduct of public affairs

36(1) This section applies to–

(a) information which is held by a government department or by the Welsh Assembly Government and is not exempt information by virtue of section 35, and

(b) information which is held by any other public authority.

36(2) Information to which this section applies is exempt information if, in the reasonable opinion of a qualified person, disclosure of the information under this Act–

(a) would, or would be likely to, prejudice–

(i) the maintenance of the convention of the collective responsibility of Ministers of the Crown, or

(ii) the work of the Executive Committee of the Northern Ireland Assembly, or

(iii) the work of the Cabinet of the Welsh Assembly Government.

(b) would, or would be likely to, inhibit–

(i) the free and frank provision of advice, or

(ii) the free and frank exchange of views for the purposes of deliberation, or

(c) would otherwise prejudice, or would be likely otherwise to prejudice, the effective conduct of public affairs.

36(3) The duty to confirm or deny does not arise in relation to information to which this section applies (or would apply if held by the public authority) if, or to the extent that, in the reasonable opinion of a qualified person, compliance with section 1(1)(a) would, or would be likely to, have any of the effects mentioned in subsection (2).

36(4) In relation to statistical information, subsections (2) and (3) shall have effect with the omission of the words "in the reasonable opinion of a qualified person".

36(5) In subsections (2) and (3) **"qualified person"**–

(a) in relation to information held by a government department in the charge of a Minister of the Crown, means any Minister of the Crown,

(b) in relation to information held by a Northern Ireland department, means the Northern Ireland Minister in charge of the department,

(c) in relation to information held by any other government department, means the commissioners or other person in charge of that department,

(d) in relation to information held by the House of Commons, means the Speaker of that House,

(e) in relation to information held by the House of Lords, means the Clerk of the Parliaments,

(f) in relation to information held by the Northern Ireland Assembly, means the Presiding Officer,

(g) in relation to information held by the Welsh Assembly Government, means the Welsh Ministers or the Counsel General to the Welsh Assembly Government

(h) in relation to information held by the National Assembly for Wales, means the Presiding Officer of the National Assembly for Wales,

(i) in relation to information held by any Welsh public authority (other than one referred to in section 83(1)(b)(ii) (subsidiary of the Assembly Commission), the Auditor General for Wales, the Wales Audit Office or the Public Services Ombudsman for Wales), means—

(i) the public authority, or

(ii) any officer or employee of the authority authorised by the Welsh Ministers or the Counsel General to the Welsh Assembly Government,

(j) in relation to information held by a Welsh public authority referred to in section 83(1)(b)(ii), means—

(i) the public authority, or

(ii) any officer or employee of the authority authorised by the Presiding Officer of the National Assembly for Wales,

(k) [effectively omitted by SI 2007/1388, art. 3 and Sch. 1, para. 82(4).]

(l) in relation to information held by any Welsh public authority other than the Auditor General for Wales or the Wales Audit Office, means–

(i) the public authority, or

(ii) any officer or employee of the authority authorised by the Assembly First Secretary,

(m) in relation to information held by the National Audit Office or the Comptroller and Auditor General, means the Comptroller and Auditor General,

(n) in relation to information held by the Northern Ireland Audit Office, means the Comptroller and Auditor General for Northern Ireland,

(o) in relation to information held by the Public Services Ombudsman for Wales, means the Public Services Ombudsman for Wales,

(p) in relation to information held by the Auditor General for Wales, means the Auditor General for Wales,

(q) in relation to information held by any Northern Ireland public authority other than the Northern Ireland Audit Office, means–

(i) the public authority, or

(ii) any officer or employee of the authority authorised by the First Minister and deputy First Minister in Northern Ireland acting jointly,

(r) in relation to information held by the Greater London Authority, means the Mayor of London,

(s) in relation to information held by a functional body within the meaning of the Greater London Authority Act 1999, means the chairman of that functional body, and

(t) in relation to information held by any public authority not falling within any of paragraphs (a) to (n), means–

(i) a Minister of the Crown,

(ii) the public authority, if authorised for the purposes of this section by a Minister of the Crown, or

(iii) any officer or employee of the public authority who is authorised for the purposes of this section by a Minister of the Crown.

36(6) Any authorisation for the purposes of this section–

(a) may relate to a specified person or to persons falling within a specified class,

(b) may be general or limited to particular classes of case, and

(c) may be granted subject to conditions.

36(7) A certificate signed by the qualified person referred to in subsection (5)(d) or (e) above certifying that in his reasonable opinion–

(a) disclosure of information held by either House of Parliament, or

(b) compliance with section 1(1)(a) by either House,

would, or would be likely to, have any of the effects mentioned in subsection (2) shall be conclusive evidence of that fact.

History – In s. 36(1)(a) the words "the Welsh Assembly Government" substituted for the words "the National Assembly for Wales" by SI 2007/1388, art. 3 and Sch. 1, para. 82(2), with effect from 2 May 2007.

S. 36(2)(a)(iii) substituted by SI 2007/1388, art. 3 and Sch. 1, para. 82(3), with effect from 2 May 2007.

S. 36(5)(g), (ga), (gb) and (gc) substituted for s. 36(5)(g) and (h) and s. 36(5)(ka) inserted by SI 2007/1388, art. 3 and Sch. 1, para. 82(4), with effect from 2 May 2007.

In s. 36(5)(gb), the words ", the Wales Audit Office" inserted by Public Audit (Wales) Act 2013, s. 24 and Sch. 4, para. 18(2), with effect from 1 April 2014 (by virtue of Welsh SI 2013/1466, art. 3).
In s. 36(5)(i), the words "or the Comptroller and Auditor General" inserted after the words "the National Audit Office" by the Budget Responsibility and National Audit Act 2011, s. 26 and Sch. 5, para. 22(1), with effect from 1 April 2012 (SI 2011/2576, art. 5).
In s. 36(5)(k), the words "or the Wales Audit Office" inserted by Public Audit (Wales) Act 2013, s. 24 and Sch. 4, para. 18(3), with effect from 1 April 2014 (by virtue of Welsh SI 2013/1466, art. 3).

Notes – S. 36(5) is subject to the Budget Responsibility and National Audit Act 2011, s. 26 and Sch. 5, para. 22(2), which provides that the reference there to old NAO is to be read as a reference to new NAO.

37 Communications with Her Majesty, etc. and honours

37(1) Information is exempt information if it relates to–

(a) communications with the Sovereign,

(aa) communications with the heir to, or the person who is for the time being second in line of succession to, the Throne,

(ab) communications with a person who has subsequently acceded to the Throne or become heir to, or second in line to, the Throne,

(ac) communications with other members of the Royal Family (other than communications which fall within any of paragraphs (a) to (ab) because they are made or received on behalf of a person falling within any of those paragraphs), and

(ad) communications with the Royal Household (other than communications which fall within any of paragraphs (a) to (ac) because they are made or received on behalf of a person falling within any of those paragraphs), or

(b) the conferring by the Crown of any honour or dignity.

37(2) The duty to confirm or deny does not arise in relation to information which is (or if it were held by the public authority would be) exempt information by virtue of subsection (1).

History – S. 37(1)(a)–(ad) substituted for former s. 37(1)(a) by CRGA 2011, s. 46 and Sch. 7, para. 3, with effect from 19 January 2011, but this substitution does not apply in respect of any request for information received by a public authority before that date (SI 2011/46).

38 Health and safety

38(1) Information is exempt information if its disclosure under this Act would, or would be likely to–

(a) endanger the physical or mental health of any individual, or

(b) endanger the safety of any individual.

38(2) The duty to confirm or deny does not arise if, or to the extent that, compliance with section 1(1)(a) would, or would be likely to, have either of the effects mentioned in subsection (1).

39 Environmental information

39(1) Information is exempt information if the public authority holding it–

(a) is obliged by regulations under section 74 to make the information available to the public in accordance with the regulations, or

(b) would be so obliged but for any exemption contained in the regulations.

39(2) The duty to confirm or deny does not arise in relation to information which is (or if it were held by the public authority would be) exempt information by virtue of subsection (1).

39(3) Subsection (1)(a) does not limit the generality of section 21(1).

40 Personal information

40(1) Any information to which a request for information relates is exempt information if it constitutes personal data of which the applicant is the data subject.

40(2) Any information to which a request for information relates is also exempt information if–

(a) it constitutes personal data which do not fall within subsection (1), and

(b) either the first or the second condition below is satisfied.

40(3) The first condition is–

(a) in a case where the information falls within any of paragraphs (a) to (d) of the definition of "data" in section 1(1) of the Data Protection Act 1998, that the disclosure of the information to a member of the public otherwise than under this Act would contravene–

(i) any of the data protection principles, or

(ii) section 10 of that Act (right to prevent processing likely to cause damage or distress), and

(b) in any other case, that the disclosure of the information to a member of the public otherwise than under this Act would contravene any of the data protection principles if the exemptions in section 33A(1) of the Data Protection Act 1998 (which relate to manual data held by public authorities) were disregarded.

40(4) The second condition is that by virtue of any provision of Part IV of the Data Protection Act 1998 the information is exempt from section 7(1)(c) of that Act (data subject's right of access to personal data).

40(5) The duty to confirm or deny–

(a) does not arise in relation to information which is (or if it were held by the public authority would be) exempt information by virtue of subsection (1), and

(b) does not arise in relation to other information if or to the extent that either–

(i) the giving to a member of the public of the confirmation or denial that would have to be given to comply with section 1(1)(a) would (apart from this Act) contravene any of the data protection principles or section 10 of the Data Protection Act 1998 or would do so if the exemptions in section 33A(1) of that Act were disregarded, or

(ii) by virtue of any provision of Part IV of the Data Protection Act 1998 the information is exempt from section 7(1)(a) of that Act (data subject's right to be informed whether personal data being processed).

40(6) In determining for the purposes of this section whether anything done before 24th October 2007 would contravene any of the data protection principles, the exemptions in Part III of Schedule 8 to the Data Protection Act 1998 shall be disregarded.

40(7) In this section–

"the data protection principles" means the principles set out in Part I of Schedule 1 to the Data Protection Act 1998, as read subject to Part II of that Schedule and section 27(1) of that Act;

"data subject" has the same meaning as in section 1(1) of that Act;

"personal data" has the same meaning as in section 1(1) of that Act.

41 Information provided in confidence

41(1) Information is exempt information if–

(a) it was obtained by the public authority from any other person (including another public authority), and

(b) the disclosure of the information to the public (otherwise than under this Act) by the public authority holding it would constitute a breach of confidence actionable by that or any other person.

41(2) The duty to confirm or deny does not arise if, or to the extent that, the confirmation or denial that would have to be given to comply with section 1(1)(a) would (apart from this Act) constitute an actionable breach of confidence.

42 Legal professional privilege

42(1) Information in respect of which a claim to legal professional privilege or, in Scotland, to confidentiality of communications could be maintained in legal proceedings is exempt information.

42(2) The duty to confirm or deny does not arise if, or to the extent that, compliance with section 1(1)(a) would involve the disclosure of any information (whether or not already recorded) in respect of which such a claim could be maintained in legal proceedings.

43 Commercial interests

43(1) Information is exempt information if it constitutes a trade secret.

43(2) Information is exempt information if its disclosure under this Act would, or would be likely to, prejudice the commercial interests of any person (including the public authority holding it).

43(3) The duty to confirm or deny does not arise if, or to the extent that, compliance with section 1(1)(a) would, or would be likely to, prejudice the interests mentioned in subsection (2).

44 Prohibitions on disclosure

44(1) Information is exempt information if its disclosure (otherwise than under this Act) by the public authority holding it–

(a) is prohibited by or under any enactment,

(b) is incompatible with any Community obligation, or

(c) would constitute or be punishable as a contempt of court.

44(2) The duty to confirm or deny does not arise if the confirmation or denial that would have to be given to comply with section 1(1)(a) would (apart from this Act) fall within any of paragraphs (a) to (c) of subsection (1).

PART IV – ENFORCEMENT

50 Application for decision by Commissioner

50(1) Any person (in this section referred to as "the complainant") may apply to the Commissioner for a decision whether, in any specified respect, a request for information made by the complainant to a public authority has been dealt with in accordance with the requirements of Part I.

50(2) On receiving an application under this section, the Commissioner shall make a decision unless it appears to him–

(a) that the complainant has not exhausted any complaints procedure which is provided by the public authority in conformity with the code of practice under section 45,

(b) that there has been undue delay in making the application,

(c) that the application is frivolous or vexatious, or

(d) that the application has been withdrawn or abandoned.

50(3) Where the Commissioner has received an application under this section, he shall either–

(a) notify the complainant that he has not made any decision under this section as a result of the application and of his grounds for not doing so, or

(b) serve notice of his decision (in this Act referred to as a "decision notice") on the complainant and the public authority.

50(4) Where the Commissioner decides that a public authority–

(a) has failed to communicate information, or to provide confirmation or denial, in a case where it is required to do so by section 1(1), or

(b) has failed to comply with any of the requirements of section 11 section 17,

the decision notice must specify the steps which must be taken by the authority for complying with that requirement and the period within which they must be taken.

50(5) A decision notice must contain particulars of the right of appeal conferred by section 57.

50(6) Where a decision notice requires steps to be taken by the public authority within a specified period, the time specified in the notice must not expire before the end of the period within which an appeal can be brought against the notice and, if such an appeal is brought, no step which is affected by the appeal need be taken pending the determination or withdrawal of the appeal.

50(7) This section has effect subject to section 53.

51 Information notices

51(1) If the Commissioner–

(a) has received an application under section 50, or

(b) reasonably requires any information–

(i) for the purpose of determining whether a public authority has complied or is complying with any of the requirements of Part I, or

(ii) for the purpose of determining whether the practice of a public authority in relation to the exercise of its functions under this Act conforms with that proposed in the codes of practice under sections 45 and 46,

he may serve the authority with a notice (in this Act referred to as "an information notice") requiring it, within such time as is specified in the notice, to furnish the Commissioner, in such form as may be so specified, with such information relating to the application, to compliance with Part I or to conformity with the code of practice as is so specified.

51(2) An information notice must contain–

(a) in a case falling within subsection (1)(a), a statement that the Commissioner has received an application under section 50, or

(b) in a case falling within subsection (1)(b), a statement–

(i) that the Commissioner regards the specified information as relevant for either of the purposes referred to in subsection (1)(b), and

(ii) of his reasons for regarding that information as relevant for that purpose.

51(3) An information notice must also contain particulars of the right of appeal conferred by section 57.

51(4) The time specified in an information notice must not expire before the end of the period within which an appeal can be brought against the notice and, if such an appeal is brought, the information need not be furnished pending the determination or withdrawal of the appeal.

51(5) An authority shall not be required by virtue of this section to furnish the Commissioner with any information in respect of–

(a) any communication between a professional legal adviser and his client in connection with the giving of legal advice to the client with respect to his obligations, liabilities or rights under this Act, or

(b) any communication between a professional legal adviser and his client, or between such an adviser or his client and any other person, made in connection with or in contemplation of proceedings under or arising out of this Act (including proceedings before the Tribunal) and for the purposes of such proceedings.

51(6) In subsection (5) references to the client of a professional legal adviser include references to any person representing such a client.

51(7) The Commissioner may cancel an information notice by written notice to the authority on which it was served.

51(8) In this section **"information"** includes unrecorded information.

52 Enforcement notices

52(1) If the Commissioner is satisfied that a public authority has failed to comply with any of the requirements of Part I, the Commissioner may serve the authority with a notice (in this Act referred to as "an enforcement notice") requiring the authority to take, within such time as may be specified in the notice, such steps as may be so specified for complying with those requirements.

52(2) An enforcement notice must contain–

(a) a statement of the requirement or requirements of Part I with which the Commissioner is satisfied that the public authority has failed to comply and his reasons for reaching that conclusion, and

(b) particulars of the right of appeal conferred by section 57.

52(3) An enforcement notice must not require any of the provisions of the notice to be complied with before the end of the period within which an appeal can be brought against the notice and, if such an appeal is brought, the notice need not be complied with pending the determination or withdrawal of the appeal.

52(4) The Commissioner may cancel an enforcement notice by written notice to the authority on which it was served.

52(5) This section has effect subject to section 53.

53 Exception from duty to comply with decision notice or enforcement notice

53(1) This section applies to a decision notice or enforcement notice which–

(a) is served on–

(i) a government department,

(ii) the Welsh Assembly Government, or

(iii) any public authority designated for the purposes of this section by an order made by the Minister for the Cabinet Office, and

(b) relates to a failure, in respect of one or more requests for information–

(i) to comply with section 1(1)(a) in respect of information which falls within any provision of Part II stating that the duty to confirm or deny does not arise, or

(ii) to comply with section 1(1)(b) in respect of exempt information.

53(2) A decision notice or enforcement notice to which this section applies shall cease to have effect if, not later than the twentieth working day following the effective date, the accountable person in relation to that authority gives the Commissioner a certificate signed by him stating that he has on reasonable grounds formed the opinion that, in respect of the request or requests concerned, there was no failure falling within subsection (1)(b).

53(3) Where the accountable person gives a certificate to the Commissioner under subsection (2) he shall as soon as practicable thereafter lay a copy of the certificate before–

(a) each House of Parliament,

(b) the Northern Ireland Assembly, in any case where the certificate relates to a decision notice or enforcement notice which has been served on a Northern Ireland department or any Northern Ireland public authority, or

(c) the National Assembly for Wales, in any case where the certificate relates to a decision notice or enforcement notice which has been served on–

(i) the Welsh Assembly Government,

(ii) the National Assembly for Wales, or

(iii) any Welsh public authority.

53(4) In subsection (2) **"the effective date"**, in relation to a decision notice or enforcement notice, means–

(a) the day on which the notice was given to the public authority, or

(b) where an appeal under section 57 is brought, the day on which that appeal (or any further appeal arising out of it) is determined or withdrawn.

53(5) Before making an order under subsection (1)(a)(iii), the Minister for the Cabinet Office shall–

(a) if the order relates to a Welsh public authority, consult the Welsh Ministers,

(aa) if the order relates to the National Assembly for Wales, consult the Presiding Officer of that Assembly,

(b) if the order relates to the Northern Ireland Assembly, consult the Presiding Officer of that Assembly, and

(c) if the order relates to a Northern Ireland public authority, consult the First Minister and deputy First Minister in Northern Ireland.

53(6) Where the accountable person gives a certificate to the Commissioner under subsection (2) in relation to a decision notice, the accountable person shall, on doing so or as soon as reasonably practicable after doing so, inform the person who is the complainant for the purposes of section 50 of the reasons for his opinion.

53(7) The accountable person is not obliged to provide information under subsection (6) if, or to the extent that, compliance with that subsection would involve the disclosure of exempt information.

53(8) In this section **"the accountable person"**–

(a) in relation to a Northern Ireland department or any Northern Ireland public authority, means the First Minister and deputy First Minister in Northern Ireland acting jointly,

(b) in relation the Welsh Assembly Government, the National Assembly for Wales or any Welsh public authority, means the First Minister for Wales, and

(c) in relation to any other public authority, means–

(i) a Minister of the Crown who is a member of the Cabinet, or

(ii) the Attorney General, the Advocate General for Scotland or the Attorney General for Northern Ireland.

53(9) In this section **"working day"** has the same meaning as in section 10.

History – S. 53(1)(a)(ii) substituted by SI 2007/1388, art. 3 and Sch. 1, para. 83(2), with effect from 2 May 2007.
In s. 53(1)(a)(iii), the words "Minister for the Cabinet Office" substituted for the words "Chancellor of the Duchy" by SI 2016/997, art. 13 and Sch. 2, para. 14(2)(n), with effect from 9 November 2016.
In s. 53(1)(a)(iii), the words "Chancellor of the Duchy" substituted for the words "Secretary of State" by SI 2015/1897, art. 9 and Sch., para. 2(3)(j), with effect from 9 December 2015.
S. 53(3)(c) substituted by SI 2007/1388, art. 3 and Sch. 1, para. 83(3), with effect from 2 May 2007.
In s. 53(5), the words "Minister for the Cabinet Office" substituted for the words "Chancellor of the Duchy" by SI 2016/997, art. 13 and Sch. 2, para. 14(2)(n), with effect from 9 November 2016.
In s. 53(5), the words "Chancellor of the Duchy" substituted for the words "Secretary of State" by SI 2015/1897, art. 9 and Sch., para. 2(3)(j), with effect from 9 December 2015.
In s. 53(5)(a) the words "the Welsh Ministers" substituted for the words "the National Assembly for Wales" by SI 2007/1388, art. 3 and Sch. 1, para. 83(4)(a), with effect from 2 May 2007.
S. 53(5)(aa) inserted by SI 2007/1388, art. 3 and Sch. 1, para. 83(4)(b), with effect from 2 May 2007.
S. 53(8)(b) substituted by SI 2007/1388, art. 3 and Sch. 1, para. 83(5), with effect from 2 May 2007.

54 Failure to comply with notice

54(1) If a public authority has failed to comply with–

(a) so much of a decision notice as requires steps to be taken,

(b) an information notice, or

(c) an enforcement notice,

the Commissioner may certify in writing to the court that the public authority has failed to comply with that notice.

54(2) For the purposes of this section, a public authority which, in purported compliance with an information notice–

(a) makes a statement which it knows to be false in a material respect, or

(b) recklessly makes a statement which is false in a material respect,

is to be taken to have failed to comply with the notice.

54(3) Where a failure to comply is certified under subsection (1), the court may inquire into the matter and, after hearing any witness who may be produced against or on behalf of the public authority, and after hearing any statement that may be offered in defence, deal with the authority as if it had committed a contempt of court.

54(4) In this section **"the court"** means the High Court or, in Scotland, the Court of Session.

55 Powers of entry and inspection

55 Schedule 3 (powers of entry and inspection) has effect.

56 No action against public authority

56(1) This Act does not confer any right of action in civil proceedings in respect of any failure to comply with any duty imposed by or under this Act.

56(2) Subsection (1) does not affect the powers of the Commissioner under section 54.

PART V – APPEALS

57 Appeal against notices served under Part IV

57(1) Where a decision notice has been served, the complainant or the public authority may appeal to the Tribunal against the notice.

57(2) A public authority on which an information notice or an enforcement notice has been served by the Commissioner may appeal to the Tribunal against the notice.

57(3) In relation to a decision notice or enforcement notice which relates–

(a) to information to which section 66 applies, and

(b) to a matter which by virtue of subsection (3) or (4) of that section falls to be determined by the responsible authority instead of the appropriate records authority,

subsections (1) and (2) shall have effect as if the reference to the public authority were a reference to the public authority or the responsible authority.

58 Determination of appeals

58(1) If on an appeal under section 57 the Tribunal considers–

(a) that the notice against which the appeal is brought is not in accordance with the law, or

(b) to the extent that the notice involved an exercise of discretion by the Commissioner, that he ought to have exercised his discretion differently,

the Tribunal shall allow the appeal or substitute such other notice as could have been served by the Commissioner; and in any other case the Tribunal shall dismiss the appeal.

58(2) On such an appeal, the Tribunal may review any finding of fact on which the notice in question was based.

59 Appeals from decision of Tribunal

59 Any party to an appeal to the Tribunal under section 57 may appeal from the decision of the Tribunal on a point of law to the appropriate court; and that court shall be–

(a) the High Court of Justice in England if the address of the public authority is in England or Wales,

(b) the Court of Session if that address is in Scotland, and

(c) the High Court of Justice in Northern Ireland if that address is in Northern Ireland.

60 Appeals against national security certificate

60(1) Where a certificate under section 23(2) or 24(3) has been issued–

(a) the Commissioner, or

(b) any applicant whose request for information is affected by the issue of the certificate,

may appeal to the Tribunal against the certificate.

60(2) If on an appeal under subsection (1) relating to a certificate under section 23(2), the Tribunal finds that the information referred to in the certificate was not exempt information by virtue of section 23(1), the Tribunal may allow the appeal and quash the certificate.

60(3) If on an appeal under subsection (1) relating to a certificate under section 24(3), the Tribunal finds that, applying the principles applied by the court on an application for judicial review, the Minister did not have reasonable grounds for issuing the certificate, the Tribunal may allow the appeal and quash the certificate.

60(4) Where in any proceedings under this Act it is claimed by a public authority that a certificate under section 24(3) which identifies the information to which it applies by means of a general description applies to particular information, any other party to the proceedings may appeal to the Tribunal on the ground that the certificate does not apply to the information in question and, subject to any determination under subsection (5), the certificate shall be conclusively presumed so to apply.

60(5) On any appeal under subsection (4), the Tribunal may determine that the certificate does not so apply.

61 Appeal proceedings

61(1) Schedule 4 (which contains amendments of Schedule 6 to the Data Protection Act 1998 relating to appeal proceedings) has effect.

61(2) Accordingly, the provisions of Schedule 6 to the Data Protection Act 1998 have effect (so far as applicable) in relation to appeals under this Part.

SCHEDULES

SCHEDULE 1 – PUBLIC AUTHORITIES

Part I – General

1 Any government department other than —

(a) the Competition and Markets Authority,

(b) the Office for Standards in Education, Children's Services and Ski.

History – Para. 1(a) and the dash before it inserted, and para. 1(b) created from existing wording, by Enterprise and Regulatory Reform Act 2013, s. 25 and Sch. 4, para. 25(a), with effect from 1 October 2013 (by virtue of SI 2013/2227).
In para. 1, the words "other than the Office for Standards in Education, Children's Services and Ski" inserted by Education and Inspections Act 2006, s. 157, 188(3), and Sch. 14 para. 69(2)(a), with effect from 1 April 2007.

1ZA The Competition and Markets Authority, in respect of information held otherwise than as a tribunal.

History – Para. 1ZA inserted by Enterprise and Regulatory Reform Act 2013, s. 25 and Sch. 4, para. 25(b), with effect from 1 October 2013 (by virtue of SI 2013/2227).

Part VI – Other Public Bodies And Offices: General

Notes – Included here are only the bodies relevant to the Red Book.

The Comptroller and Auditor General.

the Wales Audit Office.

History – In Pt. VI, the words "the Wales Audit Office" inserted by Public Audit (Wales) Act 2013, s. 24 and Sch. 4, para. 19, with effect from 1 April 2014 (by virtue of Welsh SI 2013/1466, art. 3).
In Pt. VI, the words "The Administrative Justice and Tribunals Council", "The Scottish Committee of the Administrative Justice and Tribunals Council" and "The Welsh Committee of the Administrative Justice and Tribunals Council" omitted by SI 2013/2042, art. 22, with effect from 19 August 2013.
In Pt. VI, the words "The Personal Accounts Delivery Authority" repealed by Statute Law (Repeals) Act 2013, s. 1 and Sch. 1, Pt. 10, with effect from 31 January 2013.
In Pt. VI, the words "The Comptroller and Auditor General" inserted at the appropriate place by the Budget Responsibility and National Audit Act 2011, s. 26 and Sch. 5, para. 23(1)(a), with effect from 1 April 2012 (SI 2011/2576, art. 5).
In Pt. VI the words "The Adjudicator for the Inland Revenue and Customs and Excise." omitted by SI 2010/939, art. 2 and Schedule, Pt. 1, with effect from 1 October 2010.
In Pt. VI the words "An Advisory Committee on General Commissioners of Income Tax" omitted by SI 2009/56, art. 3(1) and Sch. 1, para. 296(a), operative from 1 April 2009, subject to transitional and saving provisions in SI 2009/56, Sch. 3.
In Pt. VI the words "The Welsh Committee of the Administrative Justice and Tribunals Council." inserted by TCEA 2007, s. 48(1) and Sch. 8, para. 53, with effect from 1 June 2008 (SI 2007/2709, art. 6).
In Pt. VI the words "The Council on Tribunals" repealed by TCEA 2007, s. 146 and Sch. 23, Pt. 1, with effect from 1 November 2007 (SI 2007/2709, art. 3).
In Pt. VI the words "The Administrative Justice and Tribunals Council." and "The Scottish Committee of the Administrative Justice and Tribunals Council." inserted by TCEA 2007, s. 48(1) and Sch. 8, para. 53, with effect from 1 November 2007 (SI 2007/2709, art. 3).
In Pt. VI the words "The Personal Accounts Delivery Authority" inserted by PA 2007, s. 20 and Sch. 6, para. 23, with effect from 26 September 2007, s. 30(3).

Part VII – Other Public Bodies And Offices: Northern Ireland

[Omitted by SI 2009/56, art. 3(1) and Sch. 1, para. 296(b).]

History – In Pt. VII the words "An Advisory Committee on General Commissioners of Income Tax (Northern Ireland) " omitted by SI 2009/56, art. 3(1) and Sch. 1, para. 296(b), operative from 1 April 2009, subject to transitional and saving provisions in SI 2009/56, Sch. 3.

TRANSPORT ACT 2000

(2000 Chapter 38)

[*30th November 2000*]

ARRANGEMENT OF SECTIONS

PART V – MISCELLANEOUS AND SUPPLEMENTARY

SUPPLEMENTARY

SCHEDULES

PART V – MISCELLANEOUS AND SUPPLEMENTARY

SUPPLEMENTARY

275 Commencement

275(1) Subject as follows, the preceding provisions of this Act come into force in accordance with provision made by the Secretary of State by order made by statutory instrument; and different provision may be made for different purposes.

275(2) The power conferred by subsection (1) is exercisable as respects Wales by the National Assembly for Wales (and not the Secretary of State) in relation to Parts II and III (and the repeals relating to Part II).

275(3) An order making provision for the coming into force of section 151–

(a) shall provide for it to come into force on 1st April in any year, and

(b) shall be made at least three months before the day on which it is to come into force.

275(4) Section 231 (and Schedule 24), section 253 (and Schedule 28) and section 269 come into force on the day on which this Act is passed.

275(5) In section 245, subsections (1) and (3) to (5), and subsections (2) and (8) so far as relating to subsections (3) to (5), shall be treated as having come into force on 10th May 2000.

276 Transitionals and savings

276(1) The Secretary of State may by order made by statutory instrument make any transitional provisions or savings which he considers appropriate in connection with the coming into force of any provision of this Act.

276(2) The power conferred by subsection (1) is exercisable as respects Wales by the National Assembly for Wales (and not the Secretary of State) in relation to Parts II and III (and the repeals relating to Part II).

277 Power to make amendments

277(1) The Secretary of State may, in consequence of any provision of this Act or of any instrument made under it, by order made by statutory instrument make such amendments (including repeals or revocations) as appear to him to be appropriate in–

(a) any Act (whether public general or local) passed, or

(b) any subordinate legislation (within the meaning of the Interpretation Act 1978) made,

before that provision comes into force.

277(2) The power conferred by subsection (1) is exercisable as respects Wales by the National Assembly for Wales (and not the Secretary of State) in relation to Parts II and III and any instruments made under them.

277(3) No order shall be made under subsection (1) by the Secretary of State unless a draft of the order containing it has been laid before, and approved by resolution of, each House of Parliament.

278 Financial provision

278(1) There shall be paid out of money provided by Parliament–

(a) any expenditure incurred by any Minister of the Crown or government department under or by virtue of this Act (apart from any expenditure to be met from the National Loans Fund), and

(b) any increase attributable to this Act in the sums payable out of money so provided under any other enactment.

278(2) There shall be issued to the Secretary of State by the Treasury out of the National Loans Fund any sums required by him for–

(a) making loans under section 52 to a transferee, or

(b) making loans to the Strategic Rail Authority.

278(3) There shall be paid into the National Loans Fund any repayment of, or payment of interest on, loans–

(a) made under section 52 by the Secretary of State to a transferee, or

(b) made by the Secretary of State to the Strategic Rail Authority.

278(4) The assets of the National Loans Fund shall be reduced by an amount corresponding to such liability as the Secretary of State extinguishes by order under section 57.

278(5) There shall be paid into the Consolidated Fund any sums received by any Minister of the Crown or government department under or by virtue of this Act (apart from any sums required to be paid into the National Loans Fund).

279 Extent

279(1) Parts II and III, and the repeals relating to those Parts, and sections 255 and 256, 265, 267 and 268 and 270 and 271, and the repeals in Part V(2) of Schedule 31, extend only to England and Wales.

279(2) Subject as follows, Part IV, sections 257 to 260 (and Schedule 29), sections 261 to 263 (and Schedule 30) and sections 264, 266 and 269, and Part V(1) of Schedule 31, extend only to England and Wales and Scotland.

279(3) The amendments made by Parts I and IV, and the repeals and revocations relating to those Parts, have the same extent as the enactments to which they relate (except where it is otherwise provided).

279(4) Sections 247 and 250, paragraph 14 of Schedule 14 and Schedule 26 extend to England and Wales, Scotland and Northern Ireland.

280 Short title

280 This Act may be cited as the Transport Act 2000.

SCHEDULES

SCHEDULE 7 – TRANSFER SCHEMES: TAX

History – Sch. 7 brought into force on 1 February 2001 (SI 2001/57).

Interpretation

1 In this Schedule–

"the 1988 Act" means the Income and Corporation Taxes Act 1988;

"the 1990 Act" means the Capital Allowances Act 1990;

"the 1992 Act" means the Taxation of Chargeable Gains Act 1992;

"relevant transfer" means a transfer of property, rights or liabilities under a transfer scheme;

"transferee" in relation to a relevant transfer means the person to whom the property, rights or liabilities are transferred;

"transferor" in relation to a relevant transfer means the person from whom the property, rights or liabilities are transferred.

CHARGEABLE GAINS: GENERAL

2(1) For the purposes of the 1992 Act a disposal constituted by a relevant transfer is to be taken (in relation to the transferee as well as the transferor) to be for a consideration such that no gain or loss accrues to the transferor.

2(2) Sub-paragraph (1) has effect subject to the following provisions of this Schedule.

2(3) [Omitted by FA 2008, s. 8 and Sch. 2, para. 70(e)(i).]

2(4) Section 171(1) of the 1992 Act (provision in relation to disposal of assets from one member of a group of companies to another member of the group) does not apply if the disposal in question is constituted by a relevant transfer.

2(5) Expressions used in this paragraph and in the 1992 Act have the same meanings in this paragraph as in that Act.

History – Para. 2(3) omitted by FA 2008, s. 8 and Sch. 2, para. 70(e)(i), with effect in relation to disposals on or after 6 April 2008.

CHARGEABLE GAINS: SECURITIES

3(1) This paragraph applies if–

(a) assets are transferred to a company under a transfer scheme,

(b) in consequence the Secretary of State gives a direction under section 49 above, and

(c) the company issues securities in accordance with the direction.

3(2) For the purposes of the 1992 Act the person to whom the securities are issued is to be treated as acquiring them for a consideration–

(a) provided by him wholly and exclusively for the securities, and

(b) equal to the market value of the assets transferred to the company under the scheme.

3(3) This paragraph applies whether or not the person to whom the securities are issued is the person transferring the assets under the scheme.

3(4) Expressions used in this paragraph and in the 1992 Act have the same meanings in this paragraph as in that Act.

4(1) This paragraph applies if–

(a) the Secretary of State gives a direction under section 57 above requiring the CAA to release a company from liability in respect of debts,

(b) in connection with the direction the Secretary of State gives a direction or directions under section 58 above, and

(c) securities are issued in accordance with the direction or directions under section 58.

4(2) Sub-paragraph (3) applies if the direction under section 58 requires securities to be issued to one person only or the directions under that section (taken together) require securities to be issued to one person only; and sub-paragraph (4) applies in any other case.

4(3) For the purposes of the 1992 Act the person to whom the securities are issued is to be treated as acquiring them for a consideration–

(a) provided by him wholly and exclusively for the securities, and

(b) equal to the amount of the liability affected by the release required by the direction under section 57.

4(4) For the purposes of the 1992 Act a person to whom any of the securities are issued is to be treated as acquiring them for a consideration–

(a) provided by him wholly and exclusively for the securities, and

(b) equal to such part as is just and reasonable of the amount of the liability affected by the release required by the direction under section 57.

4(5) This paragraph applies whether or not the person to whom the securities are issued, or any person to whom any of the securities are issued, is a person transferring anything under the transfer scheme in connection with which the direction under section 57 is given.

4(6) Expressions used in this paragraph and in the 1992 Act have the same meanings in this paragraph as in that Act.

CHARGEABLE GAINS: VALUE SHIFTING

5 Nothing in this Chapter and nothing done under it is to be regarded as a scheme or arrangement for the purposes of section 30 of the 1992 Act (tax-free benefits).

CHARGEABLE GAINS: ROLL-OVER RELIEF

6(1) This paragraph applies if–

(a) but for section 154 of the 1992 Act (depreciating assets) a held-over gain would have been carried forward to a depreciating asset,

(b) the asset is the subject of a relevant transfer, and

(c) the Secretary of State is not the transferee under the relevant transfer.

6(2) Section 154 is to have effect as if the gain had accrued to, and the claim for it to be held over had been made by, the transferee and as if the transferor's acquisition of the depreciating asset had been the transferee's acquisition of it.

6(3) Expressions used in this paragraph and in section 154 have the same meanings in this paragraph as in that section.

CHARGEABLE GAINS: RESTRICTION OF LOSSES

7(1) If there has been a relevant transfer of an asset section 174(1) of the 1992 Act (which applies section 41 to cases where assets have been acquired without gain or loss) is to have effect as if the asset had been transferred to the transferee, and acquired by him, in relevant circumstances.

7(2) This paragraph is not to prejudice paragraph 2.

(3) Expressions used in this paragraph and in section 174(1) of the 1992 Act have the same meanings in this paragraph as in section 174(1).

CHARGEABLE GAINS: GROUPS

8(1) Sub-paragraph (2) applies if a company (the degrouped company)–

(a) acquired an asset from another company at any time when both were members of the same group of companies (the old group),

(b) ceases by virtue of a relevant transfer to be a member of the old group, and

(c) becomes by virtue of the transfer a member of another group of companies (the new group).

8(2) Section 179 of the 1992 Act (company ceasing to be member of group) is not to treat the degrouped company as having by virtue of the transfer sold and immediately reacquired the asset.

8(3) Sub-paragraph (4) applies if–

(a) sub-paragraph (2) applies to an asset, and

(b) the degrouped company ceases to be a member of the new group.

8(4) On the company so ceasing section 179 of the 1992 Act is to have effect as if the degrouped company and the company from which it acquired the asset had been members of the new group at the time of acquisition.

8(5) But sub-paragraph (4) does not apply if–

(a) at the time when the degrouped company ceases to be a member of the new group the company from which it acquired the asset also ceases to be a member of the new group,

(b) the companies are associated companies immediately before and immediately after that time, and

(c) the companies were associated companies at the time of acquisition.

8(6) Expressions used in this paragraph and in section 179 of the 1992 Act have the same meanings in this paragraph as in that section.

9(1) Sub-paragraph (3) applies if–

(a) a company (the degrouped company) ceases by virtue of a relevant transfer to be a member of a group of companies (the old group),

(b) it becomes by virtue of the transfer a member of another group of companies (the new group),

(c) it ceases to be a member of the new group, and

(d) the condition in sub-paragraph (2) is satisfied.

9(2) The condition is that–

(a) the degrouped company acquired an asset under a relevant transfer at a time falling before it ceases to be a member of the new group, and

(b) at the time of acquisition the degrouped company and the transferor were not members of the new group.

9(3) On the degrouped company ceasing to be a member of the new group section 179 of the 1992 Act is to have effect as if the degrouped company and the transferor had been members of the new group at the time of acquisition.

9(4) But sub-paragraph (3) does not apply if–

(a) at the time when the degrouped company ceases to be a member of the new group the transferor also ceases to be a member of the new group,

(b) the companies are associated companies immediately before and immediately after that time, and

(c) the companies were associated companies at the time of acquisition.

9(5) Paragraph 8(4) and sub-paragraph (3) above may apply on the same occasion; but if paragraph 8(4) applies to an asset on a given occasion sub-paragraph (3) above does not apply to that asset on that occasion.

9(6) Expressions used in this paragraph and in section 179 of the 1992 Act have the same meanings in this paragraph as in that section.

10(1) Sub-paragraph (4) applies if–

(a) a company ceases by virtue of a relevant transfer to be a member of a group of companies (the old group),

(b) it becomes by virtue of the transfer a member of another group of companies (the new group),

(c) a company falling within sub-paragraph (2) (the degrouped company) ceases to be a member of the new group, and

(d) the condition in sub-paragraph (3) is satisfied.

10(2) A company falls within this sub-paragraph if immediately before it ceases to be a member of the new group it is a subsidiary of–

(a) the company referred to in sub-paragraph (1)(a), or

(b) the principal company of the new group (if that company differs from the company referred to in sub-paragraph (1)(a)).

10(3) The condition is that–

(a) the degrouped company acquired an asset under a relevant transfer at a time falling before it ceases to be a member of the new group, and

(b) at the time of acquisition the degrouped company and the transferor were not members of the new group.

10(4) On the degrouped company ceasing to be a member of the new group section 179 of the 1992 Act is to have effect as if the degrouped company and the transferor had been members of the new group at the time of acquisition.

10(5) But sub-paragraph (4) does not apply if–

(a) at the time when the degrouped company ceases to be a member of the new group the transferor also ceases to be a member of the new group,

(b) the companies are associated companies immediately before and immediately after that time, and

(c) the companies were associated companies at the time of acquisition.

10(6) Expressions used in this paragraph and in section 179 of the 1992 Act have the same meanings in this paragraph as in that section.

CAPITAL ALLOWANCES

11(1) This paragraph applies if–

(a) property which is plant or machinery is the subject of a relevant transfer,

(b) Chapter 1 of Part 22 of the Corporation Tax Act 2010 (transfers of trade without a change of ownership) does not apply in relation to the transfer, and

(c) the transfer scheme concerned contains provision for the disposal value of the property to be taken for the purposes of the Capital Allowances Acts to be of an amount specified in or determined in accordance with the scheme.

11(2) For the purposes of the Capital Allowances Acts–

(a) the provision mentioned in sub-paragraph (1)(c) is to have effect (instead of section 26(1) or 59 of the 1990 Act) for determining an amount as the disposal value of the property or the price at which a fixture is to be treated as sold;

(b) the transferee is to be taken to have incurred expenditure of that amount on the provision of the property;

(c) in the case of a fixture, the expenditure which falls to be treated as incurred by the transferee is to be taken for the purposes of section 54 of the 1990 Act to be incurred by the giving of a consideration consisting in a capital sum of that amount.

11(3) A provision mentioned in sub-paragraph (1)(c) for the determination of an amount may include provision–

(a) for a determination to be made by the Secretary of State in a manner described in the scheme;

(b) for a determination to be made by reference to factors so described or to the opinion of a person so described;

(c) for a determination to be capable of being modified (on one or more occasions) in a manner and in circumstances so described.

11(4) The Treasury's consent is required for the making or modification of a determination under a provision mentioned in sub-paragraph (1)(c).

11(5) The transferee's consent is also required for such a modification after the relevant transfer takes effect.

11(6) If there is a determination or a modification of a determination under a provision mentioned in sub-paragraph (1)(c) all necessary adjustments–

(a) must be made by making assessments or by repayment or discharge of tax, and

(b) must be made notwithstanding any limitation on the time within which assessments may be made.

11(7) In this paragraph **"the Capital Allowances Acts"** has the same meaning as in the Tax Acts and **"fixture"** has the same meaning as in Chapter VI of Part II of the 1990 Act.

History – In para. 11(1)(b), the words "Chapter 1 of Part 22 of the Corporation Tax Act 2010 (transfers of trade without a change of ownership)" substituted for the words "section 343 of the 1988 Act (company reconstructions without a change of ownership)" by CTA 2010, s. 1177 and Sch. 1, para. 321(2), with effect for corporation tax purposes for accounting periods ending on or after 1 April 2010, and for income tax and capital gains tax purposes for the tax year 2010–11 and subsequent tax years.

TRANSFERS OF TRADING STOCK

12(1) This paragraph applies if–

(a) under a relevant transfer trading stock of the transferor is transferred to the transferee, and

(b) the stock falls, immediately after the time when the transfer takes effect, to be treated as trading stock of the transferee.

(2) Sub-paragraphs (3) and (4) have effect in computing the profits or gains of the relevant trades for the purposes of the Corporation Tax Acts; and the relevant trades are–

(a) the trade in relation to which the stock is trading stock immediately before the time when the transfer takes effect, and

(b) the trade in relation to which it is trading stock after that time.

12(3) The stock must be taken–

(a) to have been disposed of by the transferor in the course of the trade carried on by the transferor,

(b) to have been acquired by the transferee in the course of the trade carried on by the transferee, and

(c) subject to that, to have been disposed of and acquired at the time when the transfer takes effect.

12(4) The stock must be valued for the purposes of each of the relevant trades as if the disposal and acquisition had been for a consideration which in relation to the transferor would have resulted in neither a profit nor a loss being brought into account in respect of the disposal in the accounting period of the transferor which ends with, or is current at, the time when the transfer takes effect.

12(5) In this paragraph **"trading stock"** has the same meaning as in section 163 of the Corporation Tax Act 2009.

History – In para. 12(5), the words "section 163 of the Corporation Tax Act 2009" substituted for the words "section 100 of the 1988 Act" by CTA 2009, s. 1322 and Sch. 1, para. 472(2), with effect for corporation tax purposes for accounting periods ending on or after 1 April 2009, and for income tax and capital gains tax purposes for the tax year 2009–10 and subsequent tax years.

TRADING LOSSES: TRANSFER OF TRADE

13(1) This paragraph applies if a transfer scheme provides for a relevant transfer as a result of which the transferor ceases to carry on a trade and the transferee begins to carry it on.

13(2) A transferor treated as ceasing to carry on a trade for the purposes of Chapter 1 of Part 22 of the Corporation Tax Act 2010 (transfers of trade without a change of ownership) is to be so treated for the purposes of this paragraph.

13(3) A transferee treated as beginning to carry on a trade for the purposes of that Chapter is to be so treated for the purposes of this paragraph.

13(4) Sub-paragraph (5) applies if the transfer will result in the transferee being entitled to relief for an amount in respect of the trade under section 45 of the Corporation Tax Act 2010 (carry forward of trading losses) by virtue of section 944(3) of that Act.

13(5) In such a case the scheme may provide that the amount is to be treated as such amount (the replacement amount) as is specified in or determined in accordance with the scheme.

13(6) Sub-paragraph (7) applies if the trade concerned is in fact part of a trade of the transferor and the transferor is entitled to relief for an amount under section 45 of the Corporation Tax Act 2010 in respect of the part retained.

13(7) In such a case the scheme may provide that the amount is to be treated as such amount (the replacement amount) as is specified in or determined in accordance with the scheme.

13(8) A provision under sub-paragraph (5) or (7) must be such that the replacement amount is not greater than the amount it replaces; and the replacement amount may be nil.

13(9) When the scheme comes into force a provision made under sub-paragraph (5) or (7) is to have effect for the purposes of arriving at the amount of relief concerned.

History – In para. 13(2), the words "Chapter 1 of Part 22 of the Corporation Tax Act 2010 (transfers of trade without a change of ownership)" substituted for the words "section 343 of the 1988 Act (company reconstructions without a change of ownership)" by CTA 2010, s. 1177 and Sch. 1, para. 321(3)(a), with effect for corporation tax purposes for accounting periods ending on or after 1 April 2010, and for income tax and capital gains tax purposes for the tax year 2010–11 and subsequent tax years.

In para. 13(3), the words "that Chapter" substituted for the words "that section" by CTA 2010, s. 1177 and Sch. 1, para. 321(3)(b), with effect for corporation tax purposes for accounting periods ending on or after 1 April 2010, and for income tax and capital gains tax purposes for the tax year 2010–11 and subsequent tax years.

In para. 13(4), the words "under section 45 of the Corporation Tax Act 2010 (carry forward of trading losses) by virtue of section 944(3) of that Act" substituted for the words "under section 393(1) of the 1988 Act (trading losses) by virtue of section 343(3)" by CTA 2010, s. 1177 and Sch. 1, para. 321(3)(c), with effect for corporation tax purposes for accounting periods ending on or after 1 April 2010, and for income tax and capital gains tax purposes for the tax year 2010–11 and subsequent tax years.

In para. 13(6), the words "section 45 of the Corporation Tax Act 2010" substituted for "section 393(1)" by CTA 2010, s. 1177 and Sch. 1, para. 321(3)(d), with effect for corporation tax purposes for accounting periods ending on or after 1 April 2010, and for income tax and capital gains tax purposes for the tax year 2010–11 and subsequent tax years.

TRADING LOSSES: CHANGE IN OWNERSHIP

14(1) This paragraph applies if under a relevant transfer all the issued share capital of a company (the transferred company) is transferred from the CAA to–

(a) the Secretary of State, or

(b) a company whose shares are all held by the Secretary of State when the transfer takes effect.

14(2) For the purposes of Chapter 2 of Part 14 of the Corporation Tax Act 2010 (but not section 674(1) of that Act) (disallowance of trading losses on change in company's ownership) the transfer is not to be taken to result in a change in the ownership of–

(a) the transferred company, or

(b) a company which is a wholly owned subsidiary of the transferred company when the transfer takes effect.

History – In para. 14(2), the words "Chapter 2 of Part 14 of the Corporation Tax Act 2010 (but not section 674(1) of that Act)" substituted for the words "section 768 of the 1988 Act" by CTA 2010, s. 1177 and Sch. 1, para. 321(4), with effect for corporation tax purposes for accounting periods ending on or after 1 April 2010, and for income tax and capital gains tax purposes for the tax year 2010–11 and subsequent tax years.

LEASED ASSETS

15(1) This paragraph applies for the purposes of Chapter 4 of Part 19 of the Corporation Tax Act 2010 or Chapter 4 of Part 12A of the Income Tax Act 2007 (assets leased to traders and others) if the interest of the lessor or the lessee under a lease, or any other interest in an asset, is transferred to a person under a relevant transfer.

15(2) The transfer is to be treated as made without any capital sum having been obtained in respect of the interest by the transferor or the transferee; and this is so notwithstanding section 879 of the Corporation Tax Act 2010 and section 681DI of the Income Tax Act 2007.

History – In para. 15(1), the words "Chapter 4 of Part 19 of the Corporation Tax Act 2010" substituted for the words "section 781 of the 1988 Act" by CTA 2010, s. 1177 and Sch. 1, para. 321(5)(a), with effect for corporation tax purposes for accounting periods ending on or after 1 April 2010, and for income tax and capital gains tax purposes for the tax year 2010–11 and subsequent tax years.
In para. 15(1), the words "or Chapter 4 of Part 12A of the Income Tax Act 2007" inserted by TIOPA 2010, s. 374 and Sch. 8, para. 252(a), with effect for corporation tax purposes for accounting periods ending on or after 1 April 2010, for income tax and capital gains tax purposes for the tax year 2010–11 and subsequent tax years, and for petroleum revenue tax purposes for chargeable periods beginning on or after 1 July 2010.
In para. 15(2), "section 879" substituted for "section 783(4)" by CTA 2010, s. 1177 and Sch. 1, para. 321(5)(b), with effect for corporation tax purposes for accounting periods ending on or after 1 April 2010, and for income tax and capital gains tax purposes for the tax year 2010–11 and subsequent tax years.
In para. 15(2), the words "the Corporation Tax Act 2010 and section 681DI of the Income Tax Act 2007" substituted for the words "that Act" inserted by TIOPA 2010, s. 374 and Sch. 8, para. 252(b), with effect for corporation tax purposes for accounting periods ending on or after 1 April 2010, for income tax and capital gains tax purposes for the tax year 2010–11 and subsequent tax years, and for petroleum revenue tax purposes for chargeable periods beginning on or after 1 July 2010.

SECURITIES

16(1) This paragraph applies if securities are issued by a company in pursuance of a direction of the Secretary of State under section 49 or 58 above.

16(2) A share issued by the company is to be treated for the purposes of the Corporation Tax Acts as if it had been issued wholly in consideration of a subscription paid to the company of an amount equal to the nominal value of the share.

16(3) A debenture issued by the company is to be treated for the purposes of the Corporation Tax Acts as if it had been issued–

(a) wholly in consideration of a loan made to the company of an amount equal to the principal sum payable under the debenture, and

(b) wholly and exclusively for the purposes of the trade carried on by the company.

16(4) If a debenture issued by the company includes provision for the payment of a sum expressed as interest in respect of a period falling wholly or partly before the issue of the debenture, a payment made in pursuance of the provision in respect of the period is to be treated for the purposes of the Corporation Tax Acts as if the debenture had been issued at the commencement of the period and (accordingly) as interest on the principal sum payable under the debenture.

16(5) This paragraph has effect subject to paragraphs 3, 4 and 17.

17(1) This paragraph applies if–

(a) securities are issued to a company in pursuance of a direction of the Secretary of State under section 49 or 58 above, and

(b) by virtue of any such security the company has a loan relationship for the purposes of the Corporation Tax Acts.

17(2) For the purposes of Part 5 of the Corporation Tax Act 2009 (loan relationships) the company is to be taken to have acquired its rights under the security wholly in consideration of a loan made by it to the issuing company of an amount equal to the principal sum payable under the security.

17(3) Expressions used in this paragraph and in Part 5 of the Corporation Tax Act 2009 have the same meanings in this paragraph as in that Part.

History – In para. 17(2), the words "Part 5 of the Corporation Tax Act 2009" substituted for the words "Chapter II of Part IV of the Finance Act 1996" by CTA 2009, s. 1322 and Sch. 1, para. 472(3)(a), with effect for corporation tax purposes for accounting periods ending on or after 1 April 2009, and for income tax and capital gains tax purposes for the tax year 2009–10 and subsequent tax years.
In para. 17(3), the words "Part 5 of the Corporation Tax Act 2009" substituted for the words "Chapter II of Part IV of the Finance Act 1996" and the words "that Part" substituted for the words "that Chapter" by CTA 2009, s. 1322 and Sch. 1, para. 472(3)(b), with effect for corporation tax purposes for accounting periods ending on or after 1 April 2009, and for income tax and capital gains tax purposes for the tax year 2009–10 and subsequent tax years.

STAMP DUTY

18 [Neither relevant nor reproduced.]

STAMP DUTY RESERVE TAX

19 [Neither relevant nor reproduced.]

AGREEMENTS

20(1) Sub-paragraph (2) applies if the effect of–

(a) an agreement made under paragraph 9 or 11 of Schedule 6,

(b) an instrument executed under paragraph 9 of Schedule 6, or

(c) an agreement treated as made under paragraph 10 of Schedule 6,

is to modify the effect of a transfer scheme.

20(2) This Schedule, the 1988 Act, the 1990 Act and the 1992 Act are to have effect as if–

(a) the scheme had been made as modified, and

(b) anything done by or in relation to the preceding holder had (so far as relating to the property, rights or liabilities affected by the modification) been done by or in relation to the subsequent holder.

20(3) Sub-paragraph (4) applies to a disposal of an asset if the disposal–

(a) is effected in pursuance of an agreement made or treated as made under paragraph 9 or 10 of Schedule 6 or is effected by an instrument executed under paragraph 9 of that Schedule, and

(b) is the grant of a lease of land or the creation of other rights and liabilities over land.

20(4) For the purposes of the 1992 Act the disposal is to be taken (in relation to the person to whom it is made as well as the person making it) to be for a consideration such that no gain or loss accrues to the person making it.

20(5) Section 171(1) of the 1992 Act (provision in relation to disposal of assets from one member of a group of companies to another member of the group) does not apply if sub-paragraph (4) applies to the disposal in question.

20(6) References in this paragraph to an agreement or instrument include references to the agreement or instrument as varied in accordance with a direction under paragraph 19(4) of Schedule 6.

20(7) For the purposes of sub-paragraph (2) the preceding holder is the person who without the modification–

(a) became (under the transfer scheme concerned) entitled or subject to the property, rights or liabilities affected by the modification, or

(b) remained (despite the transfer scheme concerned) entitled or subject to the property, rights or liabilities affected by the modification,

as the case may be.

20(8) For the purposes of sub-paragraph (2) the subsequent holder is the person who (in consequence of the modification) becomes, or resumes being, entitled or subject to the property, rights or liabilities affected by the modification.

SCHEDULE 26 – TRANSFERS: TAX

History – Sch. 26 brought into force on 15 January 2001 (SI 2000/3376, art. 2).

PART I – INTERPRETATION

1(1) In this Schedule–

"the 1988 Act" means the Income and Corporation Taxes Act 1988,

"the 1992 Act" means the Taxation of Chargeable Gains Act 1992,

"the Capital Allowances Acts" means the Capital Allowances Act 2001 and includes, where the context admits, enactments which under the 1988 Act are to be treated as contained in the Capital Allowances Act 2001,

"fixture" has the same meaning as in Chapter 14 of Part 2 of the Capital Allowances Act,

"franchise company" means any body corporate which is, or is to be, the franchisee or the franchise operator under a franchise agreement, and

"qualifying transfer" means a transfer which is a relevant transfer for the purposes of any of Parts II to VI of this Schedule.

1(2) So far as it relates to corporation tax, this Schedule is to be construed as one with the Corporation Tax Acts.

1(3) So far as it relates to capital allowances, this Schedule is to be construed as one with the Capital Allowances Act.

History – In para. 1(1) the definition of "the 1990 Act" omitted, the definition of the Capital Allowances Acts substituted and the definition of "fixture" amended by CAA 2001, s. 578 and Sch. 2, para. 109(1), with effect for income tax purposes, as respects allowances and charges falling to be made for chargeable periods ending on or after 6 April 2001, and for corporation tax purposes, as respects allowances and charges falling to be made for chargeable periods ending on or after 1 April 2001.
Para. 1(3) amended by CAA 2001, s. 578 and Sch. 2, para. 109(2), with effect for income tax purposes, as respects allowances and charges falling to be made for chargeable periods ending on or after 6 April 2001, and for corporation tax purposes, as respects allowances and charges falling to be made for chargeable periods ending on or after 1 April 2001.

PART II – TRANSFERS TO SRA FROM FRANCHISING DIRECTOR, SECRETARY OF STATE AND REGULATOR

INTERPRETATION

2 In this Part of this Schedule–

"relevant transfer" means a transfer of property, rights or liabilities by virtue of–

(a) section 215,

(b) a scheme under paragraph 1 of Schedule 15, or

(c) a scheme under paragraph 31 of Schedule 17,

"transferee", in relation to a relevant transfer, means the Authority, and

"transferor", in relation to a relevant transfer, means the person from whom the property, rights or liabilities are transferred.

CHARGEABLE GAINS: NO GAIN NO LOSS

3 For the purposes of the 1992 Act a disposal by virtue of provision made under paragraph 34(a) of Schedule 17 is to be taken to be for a consideration such that no gain or loss accrues to the person making the disposal.

CHARGEABLE GAINS: DISPOSAL OF DEBTS

4(1) Sub-paragraph (2) applies if in the case of a relevant transfer–

(a) a debt owed to the transferor is transferred to the transferee, and

(b) the transferor would, apart from this paragraph, be the original creditor in relation to that debt for the purposes of section 251 of the 1992 Act (disposal of debts).

4(2) The 1992 Act is to have effect as if the transferee (and not the transferor) were the original creditor for those purposes.

CAPITAL ALLOWANCES FOR PLANT AND MACHINERY

5(1) This paragraph applies in relation to property if–

(a) the property is plant or machinery to which a relevant transfer relates,

(b) the property would have been treated for the purposes of the Capital Allowances Act (had the transferor incurred expenditure qualifying for allowances under Part 2 of that Act on the provision of the property) as disposed of by the transferor to the transferee on the transfer taking effect, and

(c) the relevant order or scheme contains provision for the transferee to be taken for the purposes of that Act to have incurred capital expenditure of an amount specified in or determined in accordance with the order or scheme on the provision of the property.

5(2) For the purposes of the Capital Allowances Act–

(a) the transferee is to be taken to have incurred capital expenditure of that amount on the provision of the property for the purposes for which it is used by the transferee on and after the taking effect of the transfer,

(b) the property is to be taken as belonging to the transferee in consequence of the transferee having incurred that expenditure, and

(c) in the case of a fixture, the expenditure which falls to be treated as incurred by the transferee is to be taken for the purposes of sections 181(1) and 182(1) of that Act to be incurred by the giving of a consideration consisting in a capital sum of that amount.

5(3) In sub-paragraph (1)(c) **"the relevant order or scheme"** means–

(a) in the case of a transfer by virtue of section 215, an order made by the Secretary of State by statutory instrument, or

(b) in the case of a transfer by virtue of a scheme under paragraph 1 of Schedule 15 or paragraph 31 of Schedule 17, the scheme concerned.

5(4) A provision mentioned in sub-paragraph (1)(c) for the determination of an amount may include provision–

(a) for a determination to be made by the Secretary of State in a manner described in the order or scheme,

(b) for a determination to be made by reference to factors so described or to the opinion of a person so described, and

(c) for a determination to be capable of being modified (on one or more occasions) in a manner and in circumstances so described.

5(5) The Treasury's consent is required for the making or modification of a determination under a provision mentioned in sub-paragraph (1)(c).

5(6) The transferee's consent is also required for such a modification after the relevant transfer takes effect.

5(7) If there is a determination or a modification of a determination under a provision mentioned in sub-paragraph (1)(c) all necessary adjustments–

(a) must be made by making assessments or by repayment or discharge of tax, and

(b) must be made despite any limitation on the time within which assessments may be made.

History – Para. 5(1)(c) and (2) amended by CAA 2001, s. 578 and Sch. 2, para. 109(3) (4) and (5), with effect for income tax purposes, as respects allowances and charges falling to be made for chargeable periods ending on or after 6 April 2001, and for corporation tax purposes, as respects allowances and charges falling to be made for chargeable periods ending on or after 1 April 2001.

CAPITAL ALLOWANCES FOR PLANT AND MACHINERY: CONNECTED PERSONS

6 For the purposes of Part 2 of the Capital Allowances Act references in that Part to a transaction (however described) between connected persons (see section 575 of that Act) are not to include references to a relevant transfer.

History – In para. 6, the words "(see section 575 of that Act)" substituted for the words "within the meaning of section 839 of the 1988 Act" by CTA 2010, s. 1177 and Sch. 1, para. 322(2), with effect for corporation tax purposes for accounting periods ending on or after 1 April 2010, and for income tax and capital gains tax purposes for the tax year 2010–11 and subsequent tax years.
Para. 6 amended by CAA 2001, s. 578 and Sch. 2, para. 109(6) with effect for income tax purposes, as respects allowances and charges falling to be made for chargeable periods ending on or after 6 April 2001, and for corporation tax purposes, as respects allowances and charges falling to be made for chargeable periods ending on or after 1 April 2001.

LOAN RELATIONSHIPS

7(1) Sub-paragraph (2) applies if as a result of a relevant transfer the transferee replaces, or (if the transferor had been a company) would have replaced, the transferor as a party to a loan relationship.

7(2) Part 5 of the Corporation Tax Act 2009 is to have effect in relation to the time when the relevant transfer takes effect and any later time as if–

(a) the transferee had been a party to the loan relationship at the time the transferor became, or (if the transferor had been a company) would have become, a party to the loan relationship and at all times since that time, and

(b) the loan relationship to which the transferee is a party after the time the transfer takes effect is the same loan relationship as that to which, by virtue of paragraph (a), it is treated as having been a party before that time.

7(3) For the purposes of sub-paragraph (2) the transferor (and accordingly the transferee) is to be taken to have accounted for the loan relationship in accordance with a basis of accounting corresponding to that in accordance with which the transferee accounts for the loan relationship in the accounting period in which the transfer takes effect.

7(4) Expressions used in this paragraph and in Part 5 of the Corporation Tax Act 2009 have the same meanings in this paragraph as in that Part.

History – In para. 7(2), the words "Part 5 of the Corporation Tax Act 2009" substituted for the words "Chapter II of Part IV of the Finance Act 1996" by CTA 2009, s. 1322 and Sch. 1, para. 473(2)(a), with effect for corporation tax purposes for accounting periods ending on or after 1 April 2009, and for income tax and capital gains tax purposes for the tax year 2009–10 and subsequent tax years.
In para. 7(3) the words "a basis of accounting" substituted for the words "authorised accounting method" by FA 2004 s. 52 and Sch. 10, para. 46 with effect in relation to (a) periods of account beginning on or after 1 January 2005, and (b) in the case of a company required to prepare accounts under the Companies Act 1985 or the Companies (Northern Ireland) Order 1986, any period of account beginning before that date for which the company is required or permitted to prepare such accounts in accordance with international accounting standards. Provisions in the Companies Act 1985 to be substituted by the Companies Act 2006 on dates to be appointed (expected to be between 2007 and 2008). See Accounting Standards in vol. 1C for extracts from CA 2006.
In para. 7(4), the words "Part 5 of the Corporation Tax Act 2009" substituted for the words "Chapter II of Part IV of the Finance Act 1996" and the words "that Part" substituted for the words "that Chapter" by CTA 2009, s. 1322 and Sch. 1, para. 473(2)(b), with

effect for corporation tax purposes for accounting periods ending on or after 1 April 2009, and for income tax and capital gains tax purposes for the tax year 2009–10 and subsequent tax years.

PART III – TRANSFERS FROM BR TO SRA

INTERPRETATION

8 In this Part of this Schedule–

"relevant transfer" means a transfer of property, rights or liabilities by virtue of–

(a) paragraph 11 of Schedule 18, or

(b) a scheme under paragraph 1 of Schedule 19,

"transferee", in relation to a relevant transfer, means the Authority, and

"transferor", in relation to a relevant transfer, means the Board.

CHARGEABLE GAINS: GENERAL

9 For the purposes of the 1992 Act a disposal–

(a) constituted by a relevant transfer, or

(b) by virtue of provision made under paragraph 4 of Schedule 19,

is to be taken (in relation to the person to whom the disposal is made as well as the person making the disposal) to be for a consideration such that no gain or loss accrues to the person making the disposal.

CHARGEABLE GAINS: RESTRICTION OF LOSSES

10(1) If there has been a disposal of an asset–

(a) constituted by a relevant transfer, or

(b) by virtue of provision made under paragraph 4 of Schedule 19,

subsection (8) of section 41 of the 1992 Act (which applies that section to cases where assets have been acquired without gain or loss) is to have effect as if the asset had been disposed of and acquired in circumstances mentioned in that subsection.

10(2) This paragraph is not to prejudice paragraph 9.

CHARGEABLE GAINS: GROUPS

11(1) Sub-paragraph (2) applies if a company (**"the degrouped company"**)–

(a) acquired an asset from another company at any time when both were members of the same group of companies (**"the old group"**), and

(b) ceases by virtue of a relevant transfer to be a member of the old group.

11(2) Section 179 of the 1992 Act (company ceasing to be member of group) is not to treat the degrouped company as having by virtue of the transfer sold and immediately reacquired the asset.

11(3) If sub-paragraph (2) applies to an asset, that section is to have effect on and after the first subsequent occasion on which the degrouped company ceases to be a member of a group of companies (**"the new group"**), otherwise than by virtue of a qualifying transfer, as if the degrouped company and the company from which it acquired the asset had been members of the new group at the time of acquisition.

11(4) If, disregarding any preparatory transactions, a company would be regarded for the purposes of section 179 of the 1992 Act (and, accordingly, of this paragraph) as ceasing to be a member of a group of companies by virtue of a qualifying transfer, it is to be regarded for those purposes as so doing by virtue of the qualifying transfer and not by virtue of any preparatory transactions.

11(5) In this paragraph **"preparatory transaction"** means anything done under or by virtue of this Part of this Act for the purpose of initiating, advancing or facilitating the qualifying transfer in question.

11(6) Expressions used in this paragraph and in section 179 of the 1992 Act have the same meanings in this paragraph as in that section.

CHARGEABLE GAINS: DISPOSAL OF DEBTS

12(1) Sub-paragraph (2) applies if in the case of a relevant transfer–

(a) a debt owed to the transferor is transferred to the transferee, and

(b) the transferor would, apart from this paragraph, be the original creditor in relation to that debt for the purposes of section 251 of the 1992 Act (disposal of debts).

12(2) The 1992 Act is to have effect as if the transferee (and not the transferor) were the original creditor for those purposes.

CONTINUITY IN RELATION TO CAPITAL ALLOWANCES ETC. WHERE TRADE TRANSFERRED

13(1) Sub-paragraphs (2) to (4) apply if–

(a) the transferor ceased to carry on a trade by virtue of a relevant transfer taking effect, and

(b) on the taking effect of that transfer, the transferee began to carry on the trade.

This sub-paragraph is to be read with sub-paragraph (8).

13(2) Subject to sub-paragraphs (3) and (4), in a case falling within sub-paragraph (1)–

(a) there are to be made to or on the transferee in accordance with the Capital Allowances Act all such allowances and charges as would, if the transferor had continued to carry on the trade, have fallen to be made to or on the transferor, and

(b) the amount of any such allowance or charge is to be computed as if–

(i) the transferee had been carrying on the trade since the transferor began to do so, and

(ii) everything done to or by the transferor had been done to or by the transferee (but so that the relevant transfer itself, so far as it relates to any assets in use for the purpose of the trade, shall not be treated as giving rise to any such allowance or charge).

13(3) For the purposes of the Corporation Tax Acts, only such amounts (if any) as may be specified in or determined in accordance with an order made by the Secretary of State by statutory instrument are to be allocated to the transferee in respect of expenditure by reference to which capital allowances may be made by virtue of sub-paragraph (2) in relation to anything to which the transfer relates.

13(4) Sub-paragraph (2) is to affect the amounts falling to be taken into account in relation to the transferor as expenditure by reference to which capital allowances may be made only so far as necessary to give effect to a reduction of any such amount by a sum equal to so much of that amount as is allocated to the transferee as mentioned in sub-paragraph (3).

13(5) An order under sub-paragraph (3) may include provision–

(a) for a determination to be made by the Secretary of State in a manner described in the order,

(b) for a determination to be made by reference to factors so described or to the opinion of a person so described, and

(c) for a determination to be capable of being modified (on one or more occasions) in a manner and in circumstances so described.

13(6) The Treasury's consent is required for the making or modification of a determination of any such amount as is mentioned in sub-paragraph (3).

13(7) The transferee's consent is also required for such a modification after the relevant transfer takes effect.

13(8) In determining whether sub-paragraph (1) has effect in relation to a relevant transfer in a case where–

(a) the transferor continues to carry on any trade or part of a trade after the transfer takes effect, or

(b) the transferee was carrying on any trade before the transfer takes effect,

the trade or part of a trade which is continued, or was being carried on, shall for the purposes of that sub-paragraph be treated in relation to any trade or part of a trade which is transferred by virtue of the transfer as a separate trade and shall accordingly be disregarded.

13(9) If there is a determination or a modification of a determination for any purposes of this paragraph, all necessary adjustments–

(a) must be made by making assessments or by repayment or discharge of tax, and

(b) must be made despite any limitation on the time within which assessments may be made.

History – Para. 13(1) substituted by CTA 2009, s. 1322 and Sch. 1, para. 473(3), with effect for corporation tax purposes for accounting periods ending on or after 1 April 2009, and for income tax and capital gains tax purposes for the tax year 2009–10 and subsequent tax years.

Para. 13(1) and (2)(a) amended by CAA 2001, s. 578 and Sch. 2, para. 109(7) with effect for income tax purposes, as respects allowances and charges falling to be made for chargeable periods ending on or after 6 April 2001, and for corporation tax purposes, as respects allowances and charges falling to be made for chargeable periods ending on or after 1 April 2001.

CAPITAL ALLOWANCES FOR PLANT AND MACHINERY

14(1) This paragraph applies in relation to property if–

(a) the property is plant or machinery to which a relevant transfer relates,

(b) paragraph 13 does not apply in relation to the transfer of the property to the transferee,

(c) the property would be treated for the purposes of the Capital Allowances Act as disposed of by the transferor to the transferee on the transfer taking effect, and

(d) the scheme concerned contains provision for the disposal value of the property to be taken for the purposes of that Act to be of an amount specified in or determined in accordance with the scheme.

14(2) For the purposes of the Capital Allowances Act–

(a) the provision mentioned in sub-paragraph (1)(d) is to have effect (instead of section 61(2) to (4), 72(3) to (5), 171, 196 or 423 of that Act) for determining an amount as the disposal value of the property or the price at which a fixture is to be treated as sold,

(b) the transferee is to be taken to have incurred capital expenditure of that amount on the provision of the property for the purposes for which it is used by the transferee on and after the taking effect of the transfer,

(c) the property is to be taken as belonging to the transferee in consequence of the transferee having incurred that expenditure, and

(d) in the case of a fixture, the expenditure which falls to be treated as incurred by the transferee is to be taken for the purposes of sections 181(1) and 182(1) of that Act to be incurred by the giving of a consideration consisting in a capital sum of that amount.

14(3) A provision mentioned in sub-paragraph (1)(d) for the determination of an amount may include provision–

(a) for a determination to be made by the Secretary of State in a manner described in the scheme,

(b) for a determination to be made by reference to factors so described or to the opinion of a person so described, and

(c) for a determination to be capable of being modified (on one or more occasions) in a manner and in circumstances so described.

14(4) The Treasury's consent is required for the making or modification of a determination under a provision mentioned in sub-paragraph (1)(d).

14(5) The transferee's consent is also required for such a modification after the relevant transfer takes effect.

14(6) If there is a determination or a modification of a determination under a provision mentioned in sub-paragraph (1)(d) all necessary adjustments–

(a) must be made by making assessments or by repayment or discharge of tax, and

(b) must be made despite any limitation on the time within which assessments may be made.

History – Para. 14(1) and (2) amended by CAA 2001, s. 578 and Sch. 2, para. 109(8)(9) and (10), with effect for income tax purposes, as respects allowances and charges falling to be made for chargeable periods ending on or after 6 April 2001, and for corporation tax purposes, as respects allowances and charges falling to be made for chargeable periods ending on or after 1 April 2001.

CAPITAL ALLOWANCES FOR PLANT AND MACHINERY: CONNECTED PERSONS

15 For the purposes of Part 2 of the Capital Allowances Act references in that Part to a transaction (however described) between connected persons (see section 575 of that Act) are not to include references to a relevant transfer.

History – In para. 15, the words "(see section 575 of that Act)" substituted for the words "within the meaning of section 839 of the 1988 Act" by CTA 2010, s. 1177 and Sch. 1, para. 322(3), with effect for corporation tax purposes for accounting periods ending on or after 1 April 2010, and for income tax and capital gains tax purposes for the tax year 2010–11 and subsequent tax years.

Para. 15 amended by CAA 2001, s. 578 and Sch. 2, para. 109(11) with effect for income tax purposes, as respects allowances and charges falling to be made for chargeable periods ending on or after 6 April 2001, and for corporation tax purposes, as respects allowances and charges falling to be made for chargeable periods ending on or after 1 April 2001.

LEASED ASSETS

16(1) Sub-paragraphs (2) and (3) apply for the purposes of section 781 of the 1988 Act (assets leased to traders and others) if the interest of the lessor or the lessee under a lease, or any other interest in an asset, is transferred to a person under a relevant transfer.

16(2) The transfer is to be treated as made without any capital sum having been obtained in respect of the interest by the transferor; and this is so despite section 783(4) of that Act.

16(3) If the interest is an interest under a lease, payments made by the transferor under the lease before the transfer takes effect are to be treated as if they had been made under that lease by the transferee.

16(4) Sub-paragraph (5) applies for the purposes of section 781 of the 1988 Act if a lease, or any other interest in an asset, is granted by virtue of provision made under paragraph 4 of Schedule 19.

16(5) The grant is to be treated as made without any capital sum having been obtained in respect of the lease, or interest, by the grantor; and this is so despite section 783(4) of that Act.

16(6) No charge is to arise under section 781(1) of the 1988 Act by virtue of section 783(2) of that Act in a case where the capital sum mentioned in section 781(1)(b)(i) or (ii) of that Act is or forms part of the consideration obtained (or treated by section 783(4) of that Act as obtained) by the transferor on a disposal by virtue of a relevant transfer of securities of a subsidiary of the transferor.

16(7) Expressions used in this paragraph and in sections 781 to 785 of the 1988 Act have the same meanings in this paragraph as in those sections.

LOAN RELATIONSHIPS

17(1) Sub-paragraph (2) applies if, as a result of a relevant transfer, the transferee replaces the transferor as a party to a loan relationship.

17(2) Part 5 of the Corporation Tax Act 2009 is to have effect in relation to the time when the relevant transfer takes effect and any later time as if–

(a) the transferee had been a party to the loan relationship at the time the transferor became a party to the loan relationship and at all times since that time, and

(b) the loan relationship to which the transferee is a party after the time the transfer takes effect is the same loan relationship as that to which, by virtue of paragraph (a), it is treated as having been a party before that time.

17(3) Expressions used in this paragraph and in Part 5 of the Corporation Tax Act 2009 have the same meanings in this paragraph as in that Part.

History – In para. 17(2), the words "Part 5 of the Corporation Tax Act 2009" substituted for the words "Chapter II of Part IV of the Finance Act 1996" by CTA 2009, s. 1322 and Sch. 1, para. 473(4)(a), with effect for corporation tax purposes for accounting periods ending on or after 1 April 2009, and for income tax and capital gains tax purposes for the tax year 2009–10 and subsequent tax years. In para. 17(3), the words "Part 5 of the Corporation Tax Act 2009" substituted for the words "Chapter II of Part IV of the Finance Act 1996" and the words "that Part" substituted for the words "that Chapter" by CTA 2009, s. 1322 and Sch. 1, para. 473(4)(b), with effect for corporation tax purposes for accounting periods ending on or after 1 April 2009, and for income tax and capital gains tax purposes for the tax year 2009–10 and subsequent tax years.

CHARGE TO TAX UNDER CASE I OF SCHEDULE D

18(1) This paragraph applies for the purpose of computing the profits or losses of the transferor and the transferee under Case I of Schedule D in respect of any trade or part of a trade transferred by a relevant transfer in relation to the time when the transfer takes effect and any later time.

18(2) The trade or part of a trade transferred is to be treated as having been, at the time of its commencement and at all times since that time, a separate trade carried on by the transferee.

18(3) The trade carried on by the transferee after the time the transfer takes effect is to be treated as the same trade as that which, by virtue of sub-paragraph (2), it is treated as having carried on before that time.

18(4) This paragraph is subject to paragraphs 13 and 17.

PART IV – TRANSFERS TO SECRETARY OF STATE FROM SRA AND BR

INTERPRETATION

19 In this Part of this Schedule–

"relevant transfer" means a transfer of property, rights or liabilities by virtue of–

(a) a scheme under paragraph 1 of Schedule 21 under which the property, rights or liabilities are transferred to the Secretary of State, or

(b) a scheme under paragraph 1 of Schedule 25,

"transferee", in relation to a relevant transfer, means the Secretary of State, and

"transferor", in relation to a relevant transfer, means the person from whom the property, rights or liabilities are transferred.

CHARGEABLE GAINS: GROUPS

20(1) Sub-paragraph (2) applies if a company (**"the degrouped company"**)–

(a) acquired an asset from another company at any time when both were members of the same group of companies (**"the old group"**), and

(b) ceases by virtue of a relevant transfer to be a member of the old group.

20(2) Section 179 of the 1992 Act (company ceasing to be member of group) is not to treat the degrouped company as having by virtue of the transfer sold and immediately reacquired the asset.

20(3) If, disregarding any preparatory transactions, a company would be regarded for the purposes of section 179 of the 1992 Act (and, accordingly, of this paragraph) as ceasing to be a member of a group of companies by virtue of a relevant transfer, it is to be regarded for those purposes as so doing by virtue of the relevant transfer and not by virtue of any preparatory transactions.

20(4) In this paragraph **"preparatory transaction"** means anything done under or by virtue of this Part of this Act for the purpose of initiating, advancing or facilitating the relevant transfer in question.

20(5) Expressions used in this paragraph and in section 179 of the 1992 Act have the same meanings in this paragraph as in that section.

CAPITAL ALLOWANCES: ACTUAL CONSIDERATION TO BE THE DISPOSAL VALUE

21(1) Sub-paragraphs (2) to (4) apply for the purposes of Part 3 of the Capital Allowances Act, and the other provisions of that Act which are relevant to that Part, if there is a disposal by virtue of a relevant transfer of the relevant interest in–

(a) an industrial building or structure, or

(b) a qualifying hotel or a commercial building or structure.

21(2) The disposal is to be treated as a sale of that relevant interest.

21(3) The sale moneys in respect of that sale are to be taken–

(a) if a capital sum is received by the transferor or a person connected with the transferor by way of consideration or compensation in respect of the disposal, to be an amount equal to that capital sum, or

(b) if no such capital sum is received, to be nil.

21(4) Sections 567 to 570 of that Act (sales treated as being for alternative amount) are not to have effect in relation to that sale.

21(5) Sub-paragraph (6) applies for determining, in the case of plant or machinery which is treated for the purposes of the Capital Allowances Act as disposed of by virtue of a relevant transfer, the amount which (in consequence of that disposal) is to be brought into account as the disposal value of that plant or machinery for the purposes of section 60 of that Act (meaning of "disposal value" and "disposal event").

21(6) The amount is, subject to section 62 of that Act (general limit on amount of disposal value) to be taken–

(a) if a capital sum is received by the transferor or a person connected with the transferor by way of consideration or compensation in respect of the disposal, to be an amount equal to that capital sum, or

(b) if no such capital sum is received, to be nil.

21(7) Sub-paragraph (8) applies if, in consequence of a disposal by virtue of a relevant transfer, a person is treated by section 188 of the Capital Allowances Act as ceasing to own a fixture at any time.

21(8) The amount which, in consequence of that disposal, is to be brought into account as the disposal value of the fixture for the purposes of section 60 of the Capital Allowances Act is, subject to section 62 of that Act, to be taken–

(a) if a capital sum is received by the transferor or a person connected with the transferor by way of consideration or compensation in respect of the disposal, to be an amount equal to that portion of that capital sum which falls (or, if the person to whom the disposal is made were entitled to an allowance, would fall) to be treated for the purposes of Part 2 of that Act as expenditure incurred by that person on the provision of the fixture, or

(b) if no such capital sum is received, to be nil.

21(9) Sub-paragraphs (3), (6) and (8) have effect despite any other provision of the Capital Allowances Act.

History – Para. 21 amended by CAA 2001, s. 578 and Sch. 2, para. 109(12)–(18), with effect for income tax purposes, as respects allowances and charges falling to be made for chargeable periods ending on or after 6 April 2001, and for corporation tax purposes, as respects allowances and charges falling to be made for chargeable periods ending on or after 1 April 2001.

LEASED ASSETS

22(1) Sub-paragraphs (2) and (3) apply for the purposes of section 781 of the 1988 Act (assets leased to traders and others) if the interest of the lessor or the lessee under a lease, or any other interest in an asset, is transferred to a person under a relevant transfer.

22(2) The transfer is to be treated as made without any capital sum having been obtained in respect of the interest by the transferor; and this is so despite section 783(4) of that Act.

22(3) If the interest is an interest under a lease, payments made by the transferor under the lease before the transfer takes effect are to be treated as if they had been made under that lease by the transferee.

22(4) Sub-paragraph (5) applies for the purposes of section 781 of the 1988 Act if a lease, or any other interest in an asset, is granted by the transferor by virtue of provision made under paragraph 5 of Schedule 21 or paragraph 4 of Schedule 25.

22(5) The grant is to be treated as made without any capital sum having been obtained in respect of the lease, or interest, by the transferor; and this is so despite section 783(4) of that Act.

22(6) No charge is to arise under section 781 of the 1988 Act by virtue of section 783(2) of that Act in a case where the capital sum mentioned in section 781(1)(b)(i) or (ii) of that Act is or forms part of the consideration obtained (or treated by section 783(4) of that Act as obtained) by the transferor on a disposal by virtue of a relevant transfer of securities of a subsidiary of the transferor.

22(7) Expressions used in this paragraph and in sections 781 to 785 of the 1988 Act have the same meanings in this paragraph as in those sections.

PART V – TRANSFERS FROM SRA TO FRANCHISE COMPANY

INTERPRETATION

23 In this Part of this Schedule–

"relevant transfer" means a transfer of property, rights or liabilities by virtue of a scheme under paragraph 1 of Schedule 21 under which the property, rights or liabilities are transferred to a franchise company,

"transferee", in relation to a relevant transfer, means the franchise company to whom the property, rights or liabilities are transferred, and

"transferor", in relation to a relevant transfer, means the person from whom the property, rights or liabilities are transferred.

CHARGEABLE GAINS: DISPOSALS NOT TO BE TREATED AS MADE AT MARKET VALUE

24(1) Section 17 of the 1992 Act (disposals and acquisitions treated as made at market value) is not to have effect in relation to–

(a) a disposal constituted by a relevant transfer or a disposal by virtue of provision made under paragraph 5 of Schedule 21, or

(b) the acquisition made by the person to whom the disposal is made.

24(2) But sub-paragraph (1) does not apply–

(a) if the person making the disposal is connected with the person making the acquisition, or

(b) in the case of a disposal by virtue of provision made under paragraph 5 of Schedule 21, if the disposal is made by or to a person other than the transferor or the transferee.

24(3) If sub-paragraph (1) applies to the disposal of an asset, the disposal is to be taken (in relation to the person making the acquisition as well as the person making the disposal) to be–

(a) in a case where consideration in money or money's worth is given by the person making the acquisition or on his behalf in respect of the vesting of the asset in him, for a consideration equal to the amount or value of that consideration, or

(b) in a case where no such consideration is given, for a consideration of nil.

CHARGEABLE GAINS: GROUPS

25(1) Sub-paragraph (2) applies if a company (**"the degrouped company"**)–

(a) acquired an asset from another company at any time when both were members of the same group of companies (**"the old group"**), and

(b) ceases by virtue of a relevant transfer to be a member of the old group.

25(2) Section 179 of the 1992 Act (company ceasing to be member of group) is not to treat the degrouped company as having by virtue of the transfer sold and immediately reacquired the asset.

25(3) If sub-paragraph (2) applies to an asset, that section is to have effect on and after the first subsequent occasion on which the degrouped company ceases to be a member of a group of companies (**"the new group"**), otherwise than by virtue of a qualifying transfer, as if the degrouped company and the company from which it acquired the asset had been members of the new group at the time of acquisition.

25(4) If, disregarding any preparatory transactions, a company would be regarded for the purposes of section 179 of the 1992 Act (and, accordingly, of this paragraph) as ceasing to be a member of a group of companies by virtue of a qualifying transfer, it is to be regarded for those purposes as so doing by virtue of the qualifying transfer and not by virtue of any preparatory transactions.

25(5) In this paragraph **"preparatory transaction"** means anything done under or by virtue of this Part of this Act for the purpose of initiating, advancing or facilitating the qualifying transfer in question.

25(6) Expressions used in this paragraph and in section 179 of the 1992 Act have the same meanings in this paragraph as in that section.

CHARGEABLE GAINS: DISPOSAL OF DEBTS

26(1) Sub-paragraph (2) applies if in the case of a relevant transfer–

(a) a debt owed to the transferor is transferred to the transferee, and

(b) the transferor would, apart from this paragraph, be the original creditor in relation to that debt for the purposes of section 251 of the 1992 Act (disposal of debts).

26(2) The 1992 Act is to have effect as if the transferee (and not the transferor) were the original creditor for those purposes.

CAPITAL ALLOWANCES: ACTUAL CONSIDERATION TO BE THE DISPOSAL VALUE

27(1) Sub-paragraphs (2) to (4) apply for the purposes of Part 3 of the Capital Allowances Act, and the other provisions of that Act which are relevant to that Part, if there is a disposal by virtue of a relevant transfer of the relevant interest in–

(a) an industrial building or structure, or

(b) a qualifying hotel or a commercial building or structure.

(2) The disposal is to be treated as a sale of that relevant interest.

27(3) The sale moneys in respect of that sale are to be taken–

(a) if a capital sum is received by the transferor or a person connected with the transferor by way of consideration or compensation in respect of the disposal, to be an amount equal to that capital sum, or

(b) if no such capital sum is received, to be nil.

27(4) Sections 567 to 570 of that Act (sales treated as being for alternative amount) are not to have effect in relation to that sale.

27(5) Sub-paragraph (6) applies for determining, in the case of plant and machinery which is treated for the purposes of the Capital Allowances Act as disposed of by virtue of a relevant transfer, the amount which (in consequence of that disposal) is to be brought into account as the disposal value of that plant and machinery for the purposes of section 60 of that Act (meaning of "disposal value" and "disposal event").

27(6) The amount is, subject to section 62 of that Act (general limit on amount of disposal value) to be taken–

(a) if a capital sum is received by the transferor or a person connected with the transferor by way of consideration or compensation in respect of the disposal, to be an amount equal to that capital sum, or

(b) if no such capital sum is received, to be nil.

27(7) Sub-paragraph (8) applies if, in consequence of a disposal by virtue of a relevant transfer, a person is treated by section 188 of the Capital Allowances Act as ceasing to own a fixture at any time.

27(8) The amount which, in consequence of that disposal, is to be brought into account as the disposal value of the fixture for the purposes of section 60 of the Capital Allowances Act is, subject to section 62 of that Act, to be taken–

(a) if a capital sum is received by the transferor or a person connected with the transferor by way of consideration or compensation in respect of the disposal, to be an amount equal to that portion of that capital sum which falls (or, if the person to whom the disposal is made were entitled to an allowance, would fall) to be treated for the purposes of Part 2 of that Act as expenditure incurred by that person on the provision of the fixture, or

(b) if no such capital sum is received, to be nil.

27(9) Sub-paragraphs (3), (6) and (8) have effect despite any other provision of the Capital Allowances Act.

History – Para. 27 amended by CAA 2001, s. 578 and Sch. 2, para. 109(19)–(25) with effect for income tax purposes, as respects allowances and charges falling to be made for chargeable periods ending on or after 6 April 2001, and for corporation tax purposes, as respects allowances and charges falling to be made for chargeable periods ending on or after 1 April 2001.

LEASED ASSETS

28(1) Sub-paragraphs (2) and (3) apply for the purposes of section 781 of the 1988 Act (assets leased to traders and others) if the interest of the lessor or the lessee under a lease, or any other interest in an asset, is transferred to a person under a relevant transfer.

28(2) The transfer is to be treated as made without any capital sum having been obtained in respect of the interest by the transferor; and this is so despite section 783(4) of that Act.

28(3) If the interest is an interest under a lease, payments made by the transferor under the lease before the transfer takes effect are to be treated as if they had been made under that lease by the transferee.

28(4) Sub-paragraph (5) applies for the purposes of section 781 of the 1988 Act if a lease, or any other interest in an asset, is granted by the transferor by virtue of provision made under paragraph 5 of Schedule 21.

28(5) The grant is to be treated as made without any capital sum having been obtained in respect of the lease, or interest, by the transferor; and this is so despite section 783(4) of that Act.

28(6) No charge is to arise under section 781(1) of the 1988 Act by virtue of section 783(2) of that Act in a case where the capital sum mentioned in section 781(1)(b)(i) or (ii) of that Act is or forms part of the consideration obtained (or treated by section 783(4) of that Act as obtained) by the transferor on a disposal by virtue of a relevant transfer of securities of a subsidiary of the transferor.

28(7) Expressions used in this paragraph and in sections 781 to 785 of the 1988 Act have the same meanings in this paragraph as in those sections.

LOAN RELATIONSHIPS

29(1) Sub-paragraph (2) applies if, as a result of a relevant transfer, the transferee replaces the transferor as a party to a loan relationship.

29(2) Part 5 of the Corporation Tax Act 2009 is to have effect in relation to the time when the relevant transfer takes effect and any later time as if–

(a) the transferee had been a party to the loan relationship at the time the transferor became a party to the loan relationship and at all times since that time, and

(b) the loan relationship to which the transferee is a party after the time the transfer takes effect is the same loan relationship as that to which, by virtue of paragraph (a), it is treated as having been a party before that time.

29(3) Expressions used in this paragraph and in Part 5 of the Corporation Tax Act 2009 have the same meanings in this paragraph as in that Part.

History – In para. 29(2), the words "Part 5 of the Corporation Tax Act 2009" substituted for the words "Chapter II of Part IV of the Finance Act 1996" by CTA 2009, s. 1322 and Sch. 1, para. 473(5)(a), with effect for corporation tax purposes for accounting periods ending on or after 1 April 2009, and for income tax and capital gains tax purposes for the tax year 2009–10 and subsequent tax years. In para. 29(3), the words "Part 5 of the Corporation Tax Act 2009" substituted for the words "Chapter II of Part IV of the Finance Act 1996" and the words "that Part" substituted for the words "that Chapter" by CTA 2009, s. 1322 and Sch. 1, para. 473(5)(b), with effect for corporation tax purposes for accounting periods ending on or after 1 April 2009, and for income tax and capital gains tax purposes for the tax year 2009–10 and subsequent tax years.

PART VI – TRANSFERS OF FRANCHISE ASSETS

INTERPRETATION

30 In this Part of this Schedule–

"relevant transfer" means a transfer of property, rights or liabilities by virtue of a scheme under paragraph 2 of Schedule 21 under which the property, rights or liabilities are transferred from a person which is, or has been, a franchise company,

"transferee", in relation to a relevant transfer, means the person to whom the property, rights or liabilities are transferred, and

"transferor", in relation to a relevant transfer, means the person from whom the property, rights or liabilities are transferred.

CHARGEABLE GAINS: DISPOSALS NOT TO BE TREATED AS MADE AT MARKET VALUE

31(1) Section 17 of the 1992 Act (disposals and acquisitions treated as made at market value) is not to have effect in relation to–

(a) a disposal constituted by a relevant transfer or a disposal by virtue of provision made under paragraph 5 of Schedule 21, or

(b) the acquisition made by the person to whom the disposal is made.

31(2) But sub-paragraph (1) does not apply–

(a) if the person making the disposal is connected with the person making the acquisition, or

(b) in the case of a disposal by virtue of provision made under paragraph 5 of Schedule 21, if the disposal is made by or to a person other than the transferor or the transferee.

31(3) If sub-paragraph (1) applies to the disposal of an asset, the disposal is to be taken (in relation to the person making the acquisition as well as the person making the disposal) to be–

(a) in a case where consideration in money or money's worth is given by the person making the acquisition or on his behalf in respect of the vesting of the asset in him, for a consideration equal to the amount or value of that consideration, or

(b) in a case where no such consideration is given, for a consideration of nil.

CHARGEABLE GAINS: GROUPS

32(1) Sub-paragraph (2) applies if a company (**"the degrouped company"**)–

(a) acquired an asset from another company at any time when both were members of the same group of companies (**"the old group"**), and

(b) ceases by virtue of a relevant transfer to be a member of the old group.

32(2) Section 179 of the 1992 Act (company ceasing to be member of group) is not to treat the degrouped company as having by virtue of the transfer sold and immediately reacquired the asset.

32(3) If sub-paragraph (2) applies to an asset, that section is to have effect on and after the first subsequent occasion on which the degrouped company ceases to be a member of a group of companies (**"the new group"**), otherwise than by virtue of a qualifying transfer, as if the degrouped company and the company from which it acquired the asset had been members of the new group at the time of acquisition.

32(4) If, disregarding any preparatory transactions, a company would be regarded for the purposes of section 179 of the 1992 Act (and, accordingly, of this paragraph) as ceasing to be a member of a group of companies by virtue of a qualifying transfer, it is to be regarded for those purposes as so doing by virtue of the qualifying transfer and not by virtue of any preparatory transactions.

32(5) In this paragraph **"preparatory transaction"** means anything done under or by virtue of this Part of this Act for the purpose of initiating, advancing or facilitating the qualifying transfer in question.

32(6) Expressions used in this paragraph and in section 179 of the 1992 Act have the same meanings in this paragraph as in that section.

CHARGEABLE GAINS: DISPOSAL OF DEBTS

33(1) Sub-paragraph (2) applies if in the case of a relevant transfer–

(a) a debt owed to the transferor is transferred to the transferee, and

(b) the transferor would, apart from this paragraph, be the original creditor in relation to that debt for the purposes of section 251 of the 1992 Act (disposal of debts).

33(2) The 1992 Act is to have effect as if the transferee (and not the transferor) were the original creditor for those purposes.

CAPITAL ALLOWANCES: ACTUAL CONSIDERATION TO BE THE DISPOSAL VALUE

34(1) Sub-paragraphs (2) to (5) apply for the purposes of Part 3 of the Capital Allowances Act, and the other provisions of that Act which are relevant to that Part, if there is a disposal by virtue of a relevant transfer of the relevant interest in–

(a) an industrial building or structure, or

(b) a qualifying hotel or a commercial building or structure.

34(2) The disposal is to be treated as a sale of that relevant interest.

34(3) The sale moneys in respect of that sale are to be taken–

(a) if a capital sum is received by the transferor or a person connected with the transferor by way of consideration or compensation in respect of the disposal, to be an amount equal to that capital sum, or

(b) if no such capital sum is received, to be nil.

34(4) The sale moneys in respect of that sale are to be taken, as respects the transferee only, to include in addition an amount equal to any capital sum received by a person other than the transferor or a person connected with the transferor by way of consideration or compensation in respect of the acquisition of the relevant interest by the transferee.

34(5) Sections 567 to 570 of that Act (sales treated as being for alternative amount) are not to have effect in relation to that sale.

34(6) Sub-paragraph (7) applies for determining, in the case of plant or machinery which is treated for the purposes of the Capital Allowances Act as disposed of by virtue of a relevant transfer, the amount which (in consequence of that disposal) is to be brought into account as the disposal value of that plant or machinery for the purposes of section 60 of that Act (meaning of "disposal value" and "disposal event").

34(7) The amount is, subject to section 62 of that Act (general limit on amount of disposal value) to be taken–

(a) if a capital sum is received by the transferor or a person connected with the transferor by way of consideration or compensation in respect of the disposal, to be an amount equal to that capital sum, or

(b) if no such capital sum is received, to be nil.

34(8) Sub-paragraph (9) applies if, in consequence of a disposal by virtue of a relevant transfer, a person treated by section 188 of the Capital Allowances Act as ceasing to own a fixture at any time.

34(9) The amount which, in consequence of that disposal, is to be brought into account as the disposal value of the fixture for the purposes of section 60 of the Capital Allowances Act is, subject to section 62 of that Act, to be taken–

(a) if a capital sum is received by the transferor or a person connected with the transferor by way of consideration or compensation in respect of the disposal, to be an amount equal to that portion of that capital sum which falls (or, if the person to whom the disposal is made were entitled to an allowance, would fall) to be treated for the purposes of Part 2 of that Act as expenditure incurred by that person on the provision of the fixture, or

(b) if no such capital sum is received, to be nil.

34(10) Sub-paragraphs (3), (4), (7) and (9) have effect despite any other provision of the Capital Allowances Act.

History – Para. 34 amended by CAA 2001, s. 578 and Sch. 2, para. 109(26)–(32), with effect for income tax purposes, as respects allowances and charges falling to be made for chargeable periods ending on or after 6 April 2001, and for corporation tax purposes, as respects allowances and charges falling to be made for chargeable periods ending on or after 1 April 2001.

LOAN RELATIONSHIPS

35(1) Section 444 of the Corporation Tax Act 2009 is not to have effect in a case where, as a result of a relevant transfer, the transferee replaces the transferor as a party to a loan relationship.

35(2) Expressions used in this paragraph and in Part 5 of the Corporation Tax Act 2009 have the same meanings in this paragraph as in that Part.

History – In para. 35(1) the words "Section 444 of the Corporation Tax Act 2009" substituted for the words "Paragraph 11 of Schedule 9 to the Finance Act 1996" by CTA 2009, s. 1322 and Sch. 1, para. 473(6)(a), with effect for corporation tax purposes for accounting periods ending on or after 1 April 2009, and for income tax and capital gains tax purposes for the tax year 2009–10 and subsequent tax years.
In para. 35(2), the words "Part 5 of the Corporation Tax Act 2009" substituted for the words "Chapter II of Part IV of the Finance Act 1996" and the words "that Part" substituted for the words "that Chapter" by CTA 2009, s. 1322 and Sch. 1, para. 473(6)(b), with effect for corporation tax purposes for accounting periods ending on or after 1 April 2009, and for income tax and capital gains tax purposes for the tax year 2009–10 and subsequent tax years.

PART VII – OTHER PROVISIONS CONCERNING TRANSFERS

CHARGEABLE GAINS: VALUE SHIFTING

36 Nothing in this Part of this Act and nothing done under it is to be regarded as a scheme or arrangement for the purposes of section 30 of the 1992 Act (tax-free benefits).

CHARGEABLE GAINS: CONSEQUENTIAL AMENDMENT

37 [Omitted by FA 2008, s. 8 and Sch. 2, para. 70(e)(ii).]

History – Para. 37 omitted by FA 2008, s. 8 and Sch. 2, para. 70(e)(ii), with effect in relation to disposals on or after 6 April 2008.

GROUP RELIEF

38 The existence of the powers of the Secretary of State or the Authority under this Part of this Act is not to be regarded (and nothing else in that Part is to be regarded) as–

(a) constituting arrangements falling within section 154(3) or 155(3) of the Corporation Tax Act 2010 (arrangements for transfer of company to another group or consortium), or

(b) constituting option arrangements for the purposes of section 173 of that Act.

History – In para. 38, the words "section 154(3) or 155(3) of the Corporation Tax Act 2010" substituted for the words "section 410(1) or (2) of the 1988 Act" by CTA 2010, s. 1177 and Sch. 1, para. 322(4)(a), with effect for corporation tax purposes for accounting periods ending on or after 1 April 2010, and for income tax and capital gains tax purposes for the tax year 2010–11 and subsequent tax years. In para. 38, the words "section 173 of that Act" substituted for the words "paragraph 5B of Schedule 18 to the 1988 Act" by CTA 2010, s. 1177 and Sch. 1, para. 322(4)(b), with effect for corporation tax purposes for accounting periods ending on or after 1 April 2010, and for income tax and capital gains tax purposes for the tax year 2010–11 and subsequent tax years.

MODIFICATIONS OF TRANSFER SCHEMES

39(1) Sub-paragraph (2) applies if–

(a) the effect of a scheme under paragraph 1 of Schedule 15, paragraph 31 of Schedule 17, paragraph 1 of Schedule 19 or paragraph 1 of Schedule 25 is modified by an order made by the Secretary of State, or

(b) the effect of a scheme under paragraph 1 of Schedule 21 under which the property, rights or liabilities are transferred to the Secretary of State or a franchise company is modified by an agreement made under paragraph 15 of that Schedule.

39(2) The Corporation Tax Acts (including this Schedule) are to have effect as if–

(a) the scheme had been made as modified, and

(b) anything done by or in relation to the preceding holder had (so far as relating to the property, rights or liabilities affected by the modification) been done by or in relation to the subsequent holder.

39(3) For the purposes of sub-paragraph (2) the preceding holder is the person who without the modification–

(a) became (under the scheme concerned) entitled or subject to the property, rights or liabilities affected by the modification, or

(b) remained (despite the scheme concerned) entitled or subject to the property, rights or liabilities affected by the modification,

as the case may be.

39(4) For the purposes of sub-paragraph (2) the subsequent holder is the person who (in consequence of the modification) becomes, or resumes being, entitled or subject to the property, rights or liabilities affected by the modification.

STAMP DUTY AND STAMP DUTY RESERVE TAX

40 [Neither relevant nor reproduced.]

TRUSTEES ACT 2000

(2000 Chapter 29)

[23rd November 2000]

ARRANGEMENT OF SECTIONS

PART I – THE DUTY OF CARE

PART II – INVESTMENT

PART III – ACQUISITION OF LAND

PART IV – AGENTS, NOMINEES AND CUSTODIANS

AGENTS

NOMINEES AND CUSTODIANS

REVIEW OF AND LIABILITY FOR AGENTS, NOMINEES AND CUSTODIANS ETC.

SUPPLEMENTARY

PART V – REMUNERATION

PART VI – MISCELLANEOUS AND SUPPLEMENTARY

SCHEDULES

Commencement Date – The Trustees Act 2000 entered into force on 1 February 2001, with the exception of s. 41, 42 and 43 which entered into force on 23 November 2000 (SI 2001/49, art. 2).

PART I – THE DUTY OF CARE

1 The duty of care

1(1) Whenever the duty under this subsection applies to a trustee, The duty of care. he must exercise such care and skill as is reasonable in the circumstances, having regard in particular–

(a) to any special knowledge or experience that he has or holds himself out as having, and

(b) if he acts as trustee in the course of a business or profession, to any special knowledge or experience that it is reasonable to expect of a person acting in the course of that kind of business or profession.

1(2) In this Act the duty under subsection (1) is called **"the duty of care"**.

2 Application of duty of care

2 Schedule 1 makes provision about when the duty of care applies to a trustee.

PART II – INVESTMENT

3 General power of investment

3(1) Subject to the provisions of this Part, a trustee may make any kind of investment that he could make if he were absolutely entitled to the assets of the trust.

3(2) In this Act the power under subsection (1) is called **"the general power of investment"**.

3(3) The general power of investment does not permit a trustee to make investments in land other than in loans secured on land (but see also section 8).

3(4) A person invests in a loan secured on land if he has rights under any contract under which–

(a) one person provides another with credit, and

(b) the obligation of the borrower to repay is secured on land.

3(5) **"Credit"** includes any cash loan or other financial accommodation.

3(6) **"Cash"** includes money in any form.

4 Standard investment criteria

4(1) In exercising any power of investment, whether arising under this Part or otherwise, a trustee must have regard to the standard investment criteria.

4(2) A trustee must from time to time review the investments of the trust and consider whether, having regard to the standard investment criteria, they should be varied.

4(3) The standard investment criteria, in relation to a trust, are–

(a) the suitability to the trust of investments of the same kind as any particular investment proposed to be made or retained and of that particular investment as an investment of that kind, and

(b) the need for diversification of investments of the trust, in so far as is appropriate to the circumstances of the trust.

5 Advice

5(1) Before exercising any power of investment, whether arising under this Part or otherwise, a trustee must (unless the exception applies) obtain and consider proper advice about the way in which, having regard to the standard investment criteria, the power should be exercised.

5(2) When reviewing the investments of the trust, a trustee must (unless the exception applies) obtain and consider proper advice about whether, having regard to the standard investment criteria, the investments should be varied.

5(3) The exception is that a trustee need not obtain such advice if he reasonably concludes that in all the circumstances it is unnecessary or inappropriate to do so.

5(4) Proper advice is the advice of a person who is reasonably believed by the trustee to be qualified to give it by his ability in and practical experience of financial and other matters relating to the proposed investment.

6 Restriction or exclusion of this Part etc

6(1) The general power of investment is–

(a) in addition to powers conferred on trustees otherwise than by this Act, but

(b) subject to any restriction or exclusion imposed by the trust instrument or by any enactment or any provision of subordinate legislation.

6(2) For the purposes of this Act, an enactment or a provision of subordinate legislation is not to be regarded as being, or as being part of, a trust instrument.

6(3) In this Act **"subordinate legislation"** has the same meaning as in the Interpretation Act 1978.

7 Existing trusts

7(1) This Part applies in relation to trusts whether created before or after its commencement.

7(2) No provision relating to the powers of a trustee contained in a trust instrument made before 3rd August 1961 is to be treated (for the purposes of section 6(1)(b)) as restricting or excluding the general power of investment.

7(3) A provision contained in a trust instrument made before the commencement of this Part which–

(a) has effect under section 3(2) of the Trustee Investments Act 1961 as a power to invest under that Act, or

(b) confers power to invest under that Act,

is to be treated as conferring the general power of investment on a trustee.

PART III – ACQUISITION OF LAND

8 Power to acquire freehold and leasehold land

8(1) A trustee may acquire freehold or leasehold land in the United Kingdom–

(a) as an investment,

(b) for occupation by a beneficiary, or

(c) for any other reason.

8(2) **"Freehold or leasehold land"** means–

(a) in relation to England and Wales, a legal estate in land,

(b) in relation to Scotland–

  (ii) the estate or interest of the proprietor of the dominium utile or, in the case of land not held on feudal tenure, the estate or interest of the owner, or

  (b) a tenancy, and

(c) in relation to Northern Ireland, a legal estate in land, including land held under a fee farm grant.

8(3) For the purpose of exercising his functions as a trustee, a trustee who acquires land under this section has all the powers of an absolute owner in relation to the land.

9 Restriction or exclusion of this Part etc

9 The powers conferred by this Part are–

(a) in addition to powers conferred on trustees otherwise than by this Part, but

(b) subject to any restriction or exclusion imposed by the trust instrument or by any enactment or any provision of subordinate legislation.

10 Existing trusts

10(1) This Part does not apply in relation to–

(a) a trust of property which consists of or includes land which (despite section 2 of the Trusts of Land and Appointment of Trustees Act 1996) is settled land, or

(b) a trust to which the Universities and College Estates Act 1925 applies.

10(2) Subject to subsection (1), this Part applies in relation to trusts whether created before or after its commencement.

PART IV – AGENTS, NOMINEES AND CUSTODIANS

AGENTS

11 Power to employ agents

11(1) Subject to the provisions of this Part, the trustees of a trust may authorise any person to exercise any or all of their delegable functions as their agent.

11(2) In the case of a trust other than a charitable trust, the trustees' delegable functions consist of any function other than–

(a) any function relating to whether or in what way any assets of the trust should be distributed,

(b) any power to decide whether any fees or other payment due to be made out of the trust funds should be made out of income or capital,

(c) any power to appoint a person to be a trustee of the trust, or

(d) any power conferred by any other enactment or the trust instrument which permits the trustees to delegate any of their functions or to appoint a person to act as a nominee or custodian.

11(3) In the case of a charitable trust, the trustees' delegable functions are–

(a) any function consisting of carrying out a decision that the trustees have taken;

(b) any function relating to the investment of assets subject to the trust (including, in the case of land held as an investment, managing the land and creating or disposing of an interest in the land);

(c) any function relating to the raising of funds for the trust otherwise than by means of profits of a trade which is an integral part of carrying out the trust's charitable purpose;

(d) any other function prescribed by an order made by the Secretary of State.

11(4) For the purposes of subsection (3)(c) a trade is an integral part of carrying out a trust's charitable purpose if, whether carried on in the United Kingdom or elsewhere, the profits are applied solely to the purposes of the trust and either–

(a) the trade is exercised in the course of the actual carrying out of a primary purpose of the trust, or

(b) the work in connection with the trade is mainly carried out by beneficiaries of the trust.

11(5) The power to make an order under subsection (3)(d) is exercisable by statutory instrument which shall be subject to annulment in pursuance of a resolution of either House of Parliament.

12 Persons who may act as agents

12(1) Subject to subsection (2), the persons whom the trustees may under section 11 authorise to exercise functions as their agent include one or more of their number.

12(2) The trustees may not authorise two (or more) persons to exercise the same function unless they are to exercise the function jointly.

12(3) The trustees may not under section 11 authorise a beneficiary to exercise any function as their agent (even if the beneficiary is also a trustee).

12(4) The trustees may under section 11 authorise a person to exercise functions as their agent even though he is also appointed to act as their nominee or custodian (whether under section 16, 17 or 18 or any other power).

13 Linked functions etc

13(1) Subject to subsections (2) and (5), a person who is authorised under section 11 to exercise a function is (whatever the terms of the agency) subject to any specific duties or restrictions attached to the function. For example, a person who is authorised under section 11 to exercise the general power of investment is subject to the duties under section 4 in relation to that power.

13(2) A person who is authorised under section 11 to exercise a power which is subject to a requirement to obtain advice is not subject to the requirement if he is the kind of person from whom it would have been proper for the trustees, in compliance with the requirement, to obtain advice.

13(3) Subsections (4) and (5) apply to a trust to which section 11(1) of the Trusts of Land and Appointment of Trustees Act 1996 (duties to consult beneficiaries and give effect to their wishes) applies.

13(4) The trustees may not under section 11 authorise a person to exercise any of their functions on terms that prevent them from complying with section 11(1) of the 1996 Act.

13(5) A person who is authorised under section 11 to exercise any function relating to land subject to the trust is not subject to section 11(1) of the 1996 Act.

14 Terms of agency

14(1) Subject to subsection (2) and sections 15(2) and 29 to 32, the trustees may authorise a person to exercise functions as their agent on such terms as to remuneration and other matters as they may determine.

14(2) The trustees may not authorise a person to exercise functions as their agent on any of the terms mentioned in subsection (3) unless it is reasonably necessary for them to do so.

14(3) The terms are–

(a) a term permitting the agent to appoint a substitute;

(b) a term restricting the liability of the agent or his substitute to the trustees or any beneficiary;

(c) a term permitting the agent to act in circumstances capable of giving rise to a conflict of interest.

15 Asset management: special restrictions

15(1) The trustees may not authorise a person to exercise any of their asset management functions as their agent except by an agreement which is in or evidenced in writing.

15(2) The trustees may not authorise a person to exercise any of their asset management functions as their agent unless–

(a) they have prepared a statement that gives guidance as to how the functions should be exercised ("a policy statement"), and

(b) the agreement under which the agent is to act includes a term to the effect that he will secure compliance with–

   (i) the policy statement, or

   (ii) if the policy statement is revised or replaced under section 22, the revised or replacement policy statement.

15(3) The trustees must formulate any guidance given in the policy statement with a view to ensuring that the functions will be exercised in the best interests of the trust.

15(4) The policy statement must be in or evidenced in writing.

15(5) The asset management functions of trustees are their functions relating to–

(a) the investment of assets subject to the trust,

(b) the acquisition of property which is to be subject to the trust, and

(c) managing property which is subject to the trust and disposing of, or creating or disposing of an interest in, such property.

NOMINEES AND CUSTODIANS

16 Power to appoint nominees

16(1) Subject to the provisions of this Part, the trustees of a trust may–

(a) appoint a person to act as their nominee in relation to such of the assets of the trust as they determine (other than settled land), and

(b) take such steps as are necessary to secure that those assets are vested in a person so appointed.

16(2) An appointment under this section must be in or evidenced in writing.

16(3) This section does not apply to any trust having a custodian trustee or in relation to any assets vested in the official custodian for charities.

17 Power to appoint custodians

17(1) Subject to the provisions of this Part, the trustees of a trust may appoint a person to act as a custodian in relation to such of the assets of the trust as they may determine.

17(2) For the purposes of this Act a person is a custodian in relation to assets if he undertakes the safe custody of the assets or of any documents or records concerning the assets.

17(3) An appointment under this section must be in or evidenced in writing.

17(4) This section does not apply to any trust having a custodian trustee or in relation to any assets vested in the official custodian for charities.

18 Investment in bearer securities

18(1) If trustees retain or invest in securities payable to bearer, they must appoint a person to act as a custodian of the securities.

18(2) Subsection (1) does not apply if the trust instrument or any enactment or provision of subordinate legislation contains provision which (however expressed) permits the trustees to retain or invest in securities payable to bearer without appointing a person to act as a custodian.

18(3) An appointment under this section must be in or evidenced in writing.

18(4) This section does not apply to any trust having a custodian trustee or in relation to any securities vested in the official custodian for charities.

19 Persons who may be appointed as nominees or custodians

19(1) A person may not be appointed under section 16, 17 or 18 as a nominee or custodian unless one of the relevant conditions is satisfied.

19(2) The relevant conditions are that–

(a) the person carries on a business which consists of or includes acting as a nominee or custodian;

(b) the person is a body corporate which is controlled by the trustees;

(c) the person is a body corporate recognised under section 9 of the Administration of Justice Act 1985.

19(3) The question whether a body corporate is controlled by trustees is to be determined in accordance with section 1124 of the Corporation Tax Act 2010.

19(4) The trustees of a charitable trust which is not an exempt charity must act in accordance with any guidance given by the Charity Commission concerning the selection of a person for appointment as a nominee or custodian under section 16, 17 or 18.

19(5) Subject to subsections (1) and (4), the persons whom the trustees may under section 16, 17 or 18 appoint as a nominee or custodian include–

(a) one of their number, if that one is a trust corporation, or

(b) two (or more) of their number, if they are to act as joint nominees or joint custodians.

19(6) The trustees may under section 16 appoint a person to act as their nominee even though he is also–

(a) appointed to act as their custodian (whether under section 17 or 18 or any other power), or

(b) authorised to exercise functions as their agent (whether under section 11 or any other power).

19(7) Likewise, the trustees may under section 17 or 18 appoint a person to act as their custodian even though he is also–

(a) appointed to act as their nominee (whether under section 16 or any other power), or

(b) authorised to exercise functions as their agent (whether under section 11 or any other power).

History – In s. 19(3), the words "section 1124 of the Corporation Tax Act 2010" substituted for the words "section 840 of the Income and Corporation Taxes Act 1988" by CTA 2010, s. 1177 and Sch. 1, para. 319, with effect for corporation tax purposes for accounting periods ending on or after 1 April 2010 and for income tax and capital gains tax purposes, for the tax year 2010–11 and subsequent tax years.

In s. 19(4), the words "Charity Commission" substituted for the words "Charity Commissioners" by Charities Act 2006, s. 75 and Sch. 8, para. 197, with effect from 27 February 2007 (SI 2007/309, art. 2).

20 Terms of appointment of nominees and custodians

20(1) Subject to subsection (2) and sections 29 to 32, the trustees may under section 16, 17 or 18 appoint a person to act as a nominee or custodian on such terms as to remuneration and other matters as they may determine.

20(2) The trustees may not under section 16, 17 or 18 appoint a person to act as a nominee or custodian on any of the terms mentioned in subsection (3) unless it is reasonably necessary for them to do so.

20(3) The terms are–

(a) a term permitting the nominee or custodian to appoint a substitute;

(b) a term restricting the liability of the nominee or custodian or his substitute to the trustees or to any beneficiary;

(c) a term permitting the nominee or custodian to act in circumstances capable of giving rise to a conflict of interest.

REVIEW OF AND LIABILITY FOR AGENTS, NOMINEES AND CUSTODIANS ETC.

21 Application of sections 22 and 23

21(1) Sections 22 and 23 apply in a case where trustees have, under section 11, 16, 17 or 18–

(a) authorised a person to exercise functions as their agent, or

(b) appointed a person to act as a nominee or custodian.

21(2) Subject to subsection (3), sections 22 and 23 also apply in a case where trustees have, under any power conferred on them by the trust instrument or by any enactment or any provision of subordinate legislation–

(a) authorised a person to exercise functions as their agent, or

(b) appointed a person to act as a nominee or custodian.

21(3) If the application of section 22 or 23 is inconsistent with the terms of the trust instrument or the enactment or provision of subordinate legislation, the section in question does not apply.

22 Review of agents, nominees and custodians etc

22(1) While the agent, nominee or custodian continues to act for the trust, the trustees–

(a) must keep under review the arrangements under which the agent, nominee or custodian acts and how those arrangements are being put into effect,

(b) if circumstances make it appropriate to do so, must consider whether there is a need to exercise any power of intervention that they have, and

(c) if they consider that there is a need to exercise such a power, must do so.

22(2) If the agent has been authorised to exercise asset management functions, the duty under subsection (1) includes, in particular–

(a) a duty to consider whether there is any need to revise or replace the policy statement made for the purposes of section 15,

(b) if they consider that there is a need to revise or replace the policy statement, a duty to do so, and

(c) a duty to assess whether the policy statement (as it has effect for the time being) is being complied with.

22(3) Subsections (3) and (4) of section 15 apply to the revision or replacement of a policy statement under this section as they apply to the making of a policy statement under that section.

22(4) **"Power of intervention"** includes–

(a) a power to give directions to the agent, nominee or custodian;

(b) a power to revoke the authorisation or appointment.

23 Liability for agents, nominees and custodians etc

23(1) A trustee is not liable for any act or default of the agent, nominee or custodian unless he has failed to comply with the duty of care applicable to him, under paragraph 3 of Schedule 1–

(a) when entering into the arrangements under which the person acts as agent, nominee or custodian, or

(b) when carrying out his duties under section 22.

23(2) If a trustee has agreed a term under which the agent, nominee or custodian is permitted to appoint a substitute, the trustee is not liable for any act or default of the substitute unless he has failed to comply with the duty of care applicable to him, under paragraph 3 of Schedule 1–

(a) when agreeing that term, or

(b) when carrying out his duties under section 22 in so far as they relate to the use of the substitute.

SUPPLEMENTARY

24 Effect of trustees exceeding their powers

24 A failure by the trustees to act within the limits of the powers conferred by this Part–

(a) in authorising a person to exercise a function of theirs as an agent, or

(b) in appointing a person to act as a nominee or custodian,

in appointing a person to act as a nominee or custodian,

25 Sole trustees.

25(1) Subject to subsection (2), this Part applies in relation to a trust having a sole trustee as it applies in relation to other trusts (and references in this Part to trustees–except in sections 12(1) and (3) and 19(5)–are to be read accordingly).

25(2) Section 18 does not impose a duty on a sole trustee if that trustee is a trust corporation.

26 Restriction or exclusion of this Part etc

26 The powers conferred by this Part are–

(a) in addition to powers conferred on trustees otherwise than by this Act, but

(b) subject to any restriction or exclusion imposed by the trust instrument or by any enactment or any provision of subordinate legislation.

27 Existing trusts.

27 This Part applies in relation to trusts whether created before or after its commencement.

PART V – REMUNERATION

28 Trustee's entitlement to payment under trust instrument

28(1) Except to the extent (if any) to which the trust instrument makes inconsistent provision, subsections (2) to (4) apply to a trustee if–

(a) there is a provision in the trust instrument entitling him to receive payment out of trust funds in respect of services provided by him to or on behalf of the trust, and

(b) the trustee is a trust corporation or is acting in a professional capacity.

28(2) The trustee is to be treated as entitled under the trust instrument to receive payment in respect of services even if they are services which are capable of being provided by a lay trustee.

28(3) Subsection (2) applies to a trustee of a charitable trust who is not a trust corporation only–

(a) if he is not a sole trustee, and

(b) to the extent that a majority of the other trustees have agreed that it should apply to him.

28(4) Any payments to which the trustee is entitled in respect of services are to be treated as remuneration for services (and not as a gift) for the purposes of–

(a) section 15 of the Wills Act 1837 (gifts to an attesting witness to be void), and

(b) section 34(3) of the Administration of Estates Act 1925 (order in which estate to be paid out).

28(5) For the purposes of this Part, a trustee acts in a professional capacity if he acts in the course of a profession or business which consists of or includes the provision of services in connection with–

(a) the management or administration of trusts generally or a particular kind of trust, or

(b) any particular aspect of the management or administration of trusts generally or a particular kind of trust,

and the services he provides to or on behalf of the trust fall within that description.

28(6) For the purposes of this Part, a person acts as a lay trustee if he–

(a) is not a trust corporation, and

(b) does not act in a professional capacity.

29 Remuneration of certain trustees

29(1) Subject to subsection (5), a trustee who–

(a) is a trust corporation, but

(b) is not a trustee of a charitable trust,

is entitled to receive reasonable remuneration out of the trust funds for any services that the trust corporation provides to or on behalf of the trust.

29(2) Subject to subsection (5), a trustee who–

(a) acts in a professional capacity, but

(b) is not a trust corporation, a trustee of a charitable trust or a sole trustee, is entitled to receive reasonable remuneration out of the trust funds for any services that he provides to or on behalf of the trust if each other trustee has agreed in writing that he may be remunerated for the services.

29(3) **"Reasonable remuneration"** means, in relation to the provision of services by a trustee, such remuneration as is reasonable in the circumstances for the provision of those services to or on behalf of that trust by that trustee and for the purposes of subsection (1) includes, in relation to the provision of services by a trustee who is a deposit taker and provides the services in that capacity, the deposit taker's reasonable charges for the provision of such services.

29(3A) In subsection (3), **"deposit taker"** means–

(a) a person who has permission under Part 4A of the Financial Services and Markets Act 2000 to accept deposits, or

(b) an EEA firm of the kind mentioned in paragraph 5(b) of Schedule 3 to that Act which has permission under paragraph 15 of that Schedule (as a result of qualifying for authorisation under paragraph 12(1) of that Schedule) to accept deposits.

29(3B) A reference in subsection (3A) to a person or firm with permission to accept deposits does not include a person or firm with permission to do so only for the purposes of, or in the course of, carrying on another regulated activity in accordance with that permission.

29(3C) Subsections (3A) and (3B) must be read with–

(a) section 22 of the Financial Services and Markets Act 2000,

(b) any relevant order under that section, and

(c) Schedule 2 to that Act.

29(4) A trustee is entitled to remuneration under this section even if the services in question are capable of being provided by a lay trustee.

29(5) A trustee is not entitled to remuneration under this section if any provision about his entitlement to remuneration has been made–

(a) by the trust instrument, or

(b) by any enactment or any provision of subordinate legislation.

29(6) This section applies to a trustee who has been authorised under a power conferred by Part IV or the trust instrument–

(a) to exercise functions as an agent of the trustees, or

(b) to act as a nominee or custodian,

as it applies to any other trustee.

History – In s. 29(3), the words "a deposit taker" substituted for the words "an authorised institution under the Banking Act 1987" and the words "deposit taker's" substituted for the word "institution's" by Financial Services Act 2012, s. 114(1) and Sch. 18, para. 90(2), with effect from 1 April 2013 (SI 2013/423, art. 3).

S. 29(3A) to (3C) inserted by Financial Services Act 2012, s. 114(1) and Sch. 18, para. 90(3), with effect from 1 April 2013 (SI 2013/423, art. 3).

30 Remuneration of trustees of charitable trusts

30(1) The Secretary of State may by regulations make provision for the remuneration of trustees of charitable trusts who are trust corporations or act in a professional capacity.

30(2) The power under subsection (1) includes power to make provision for the remuneration of a trustee who has been authorised under a power conferred by Part IV or any other enactment or any provision of subordinate legislation, or by the trust instrument–

(a) to exercise functions as an agent of the trustees, or

(b) to act as a nominee or custodian.

30(3) Regulations under this section may–

(a) make different provision for different cases;

(b) contain such supplemental, incidental, consequential and transitional provision as the Secretary of State considers appropriate.

30(4) The power to make regulations under this section is exercisable by statutory instrument, but no such instrument shall be made unless a draft of it has been laid before Parliament and approved by a resolution of each House of Parliament.

31 Trustees' expenses

31(1) A trustee–

(a) is entitled to be reimbursed from the trust funds, or

(b) may pay out of the trust funds,

expenses properly incurred by him when acting on behalf of the trust.

31(2) This section applies to a trustee who has been authorised under a power conferred by Part IV or any other enactment or any provision of subordinate legislation, or by the trust instrument–

(a) to exercise functions as an agent of the trustees, or

(b) to act as a nominee or custodian,

as it applies to any other trustee.

32 Remuneration and expenses of agents, nominees and custodians

32(1) This section applies if, under a power conferred by Part IV or any other enactment or any provision of subordinate legislation, or by the trust instrument, a person other than a trustee has been–

(a) authorised to exercise functions as an agent of the trustees, or

(b) appointed to act as a nominee or custodian.

32(2) The trustees may remunerate the agent, nominee or custodian out of the trust funds for services if–

(a) he is engaged on terms entitling him to be remunerated for those services, and

(b) the amount does not exceed such remuneration as is reasonable in the circumstances for the provision of those services by him to or on behalf of that trust.

32(3) The trustees may reimburse the agent, nominee or custodian out of the trust funds for any expenses properly incurred by him in exercising functions as an agent, nominee or custodian.

33 Application

33(1) Subject to subsection (2), sections 28, 29, 31 and 32 apply in relation to services provided to or on behalf of, or (as the case may be) expenses incurred on or after their commencement on behalf of, trusts whenever created.

33(2) Nothing in section 28 or 29 is to be treated as affecting the operation of–

(a) section 15 of the Wills Act 1837, or

(b) section 34(3) of the Administration of Estates Act 1925,

in relation to any death occurring before the commencement of section 28 or (as the case may be) section 29.

PART VI – MISCELLANEOUS AND SUPPLEMENTARY

34 Power to insure

34(1) For section 19 of the Trustee Act 1925 (power to insure) substitute–

"Power to insure

19(1) A trustee may–

(a) insure any property which is subject to the trust against risks of loss or damage due to any event, and

(b) pay the premiums out of the trust funds.

19(2) In the case of property held on a bare trust, the power to insure is subject to any direction given by the beneficiary or each of the beneficiaries–

(a) that any property specified in the direction is not to be insured;

(b) that any property specified in the direction is not to be insured except on such conditions as may be so specified.

19(3) Property is held on a bare trust if it is held on trust for–

(a) a beneficiary who is of full age and capacity and absolutely entitled to the property subject to the trust, or

(b) beneficiaries each of whom is of full age and capacity and who (taken together) are absolutely entitled to the property subject to the trust.

19(4) If a direction under subsection (2) of this section is given, the power to insure, so far as it is subject to the direction, ceases to be a delegable function for the purposes of section 11 of the *Trustee Act 2000* (power to employ agents).

19(5) In this section **"trust funds"** means any income or capital funds of the trust."

34(2) In section 20(1) of the Trustee Act 1925 (application of insurance money) omit "whether by fire or otherwise".

34(3) The amendments made by this section apply in relation to trusts whether created before or after its commencement.

35 Personal representatives

35(1) Subject to the following provisions of this section, this Act applies in relation to a personal representative administering an estate according to the law as it applies to a trustee carrying out a trust for beneficiaries.

35(2) For this purpose this Act is to be read with the appropriate modifications and in particular–

(a) references to the trust instrument are to be read as references to the will,

(b) references to a beneficiary or to beneficiaries, apart from the reference to a beneficiary in section 8(1)(b), are to be read as references to a person or the persons interested in the due administration of the estate, and

(c) the reference to a beneficiary in section 8(1)(b) is to be read as a reference to a person who under the will of the deceased or under the law relating to intestacy is beneficially interested in the estate.

35(3) Remuneration to which a personal representative is entitled under section 28 or 29 is to be treated as an administration expense for the purposes of–

(a) section 34(3) of the Administration of Estates Act 1925 (order in which estate to be paid out), and

(b) any provision giving reasonable administration expenses priority over the preferential debts listed in Schedule 6 to the Insolvency Act 1986.

35(4) Nothing in subsection (3) is to be treated as affecting the operation of the provisions mentioned in paragraphs (a) and (b) of that subsection in relation to any death occurring before the commencement of this section.

36 Pension schemes

36(1) In this section **"pension scheme"** means an occupational pension scheme (within the meaning of the Pension Schemes Act 1993) established under a trust and subject to the law of England and Wales.

36(2) Part I does not apply in so far as it imposes a duty of care in relation to–

(a) the functions described in paragraphs 1 and 2 of Schedule 1, or

(b) the functions described in paragraph 3 of that Schedule to the extent that they relate to trustees–

  (i) authorising a person to exercise their functions with respect to investment, or

  (ii) appointing a person to act as their nominee or custodian.

36(3) Nothing in Part II or III applies to the trustees of any pension scheme.

36(4) Part IV applies to the trustees of a pension scheme subject to the restrictions in subsections (5) to (8).

36(5) The trustees of a pension scheme may not under Part IV authorise any person to exercise any functions relating to investment as their agent.

36(6) The trustees of a pension scheme may not under Part IV authorise a person who is–

(a) an employer in relation to the scheme, or

(b) connected with or an associate of such an employer,

to exercise any of their functions as their agent.

36(7) For the purposes of subsection (6)–

(a) **"employer"**, in relation to a scheme, has the same meaning as in the Pensions Act 1995;

(b) sections 249 and 435 of the Insolvency Act 1986 apply for the purpose of determining whether a person is connected with or an associate of an employer.

36(8) Sections 16 to 20 (powers to appoint nominees and custodians) do not apply to the trustees of a pension scheme.

37 Authorised unit trusts

37(1) Parts II to IV do not apply to trustees of authorised unit trusts.

37(2) **"Authorised unit trust"** means a unit trust scheme in the case of which an order under section 78 of the Financial Services Act 1986 is in force.

38 Common investment schemes for charities etc

38(1) Parts II to IV do not apply to–

(a) trustees managing a fund under a common investment scheme made, or having effect as if made, under section 96 of the Charities Act 2011, other than such a fund the trusts of which provide that property is not to be transferred to the fund except by or on behalf of a charity the trustees of which are the trustees appointed to manage the fund, or

(b) trustees managing a fund under a common deposit scheme made, or having effect as if made, under section 100 of that Act.

History – In s. 38(1)(a), the words "section 96 of the Charities Act 2011" substituted for the words "section 24 of the Charities Act 1993" and in (b), the words "section 100" substituted for the words "section 25" by CA 2011, s. 354 and Sch. 7, para. 89, with effect at the end of the period of three months beginning with 14 December 2011.

39 Interpretation

39(1) In this Act–

"asset" includes any right or interest;

"charitable trust" means a trust under which property is held for charitable purposes and **"charitable purposes"** has the meaning given by section 11 of the Charities Act 2011;

"custodian trustee" has the same meaning as in the Public Trustee Act 1906;

"enactment" includes any provision of a Measure of the Church Assembly or of the General Synod of the Church of England;

"exempt charity" has the same meaning as in the the Charities Act 2011;

"functions" includes powers and duties;

"legal mortgage" has the same meaning as in the Law of Property Act 1925;

"personal representative" has the same meaning as in the Trustee Act 1925;

"settled land" has the same meaning as in the Settled Land Act 1925;

"trust corporation" has the same meaning as in the Trustee Act 1925;

"trust funds" means income or capital funds of the trust.

39(2) In this Act the expressions listed below are defined or otherwise explained by the provisions indicated–

asset management functions	section 15(5)
custodian	section 17(2)
the duty of care	section 1(2)
the general power of investment	section 3(2)
lay trustee	section 28(6)
power of intervention	section 22(4)
the standard investment criteria	section 4(3)
subordinate legislation	section 6(3)
trustee acting in a professional capacity	section 28(5)
trust instrument	sections 6(2) and 35(2)(a)

History – In s. 39(1), in the definition of "charitable purposes", the words "has the meaning given by section 11 of the Charities Act 2011" substituted for the words "has the same meaning as in the Charities Act 1993" by CA 2011, s. 354 and Sch. 7, para. 90(a), with effect at the end of the period of three months beginning with 14 December 2011.
In s. 39(1), in the definition of "exempt charity", the words "the Charities Act 2011" substituted for the words "the Charities Act 1993" by CA 2011, s. 354 and Sch. 7, para. 90(b), with effect at the end of the period of three months beginning with 14 December 2011.

40 Minor and consequential amendments etc

40(1) Schedule 2 (minor and consequential amendments) shall have effect.

40(2) Schedule 3 (transitional provisions and savings) shall have effect.

40(3) Schedule 4 (repeals) shall have effect.

41 Power to amend other Acts

41(1) A Minister of the Crown may by order make such amendments of any Act, including an Act extending to places outside England and Wales, as appear to him appropriate in consequence of or in connection with Part II or III.

41(2) Before exercising the power under subsection (1) in relation to a local, personal or private Act, the Minister must consult any person who appears to him to be affected by any proposed amendment.

41(3) An order under this section may–

(a) contain such transitional provisions and savings as the Minister thinks fit;

(b) make different provision for different purposes.

41(4) The power to make an order under this section is exercisable by statutory instrument which shall be subject to annulment in pursuance of a resolution of either House of Parliament.

41(5) "Minister of the Crown" has the same meaning as in the Ministers of the Crown Act 1975.

42 Commencement and extent

42(1) Section 41, this section and section 43 shall come into force on the day on which this Act is passed.

42(2) The remaining provisions of this Act shall come into force on such day as the Lord Chancellor may appoint by order made by statutory instrument; and different days may be so appointed for different purposes.

42(3) An order under subsection (2) may contain such transitional provisions and savings as the Lord Chancellor considers appropriate in connection with the order.

42(4) Subject to section 41(1) and subsection (5), this Act extends to England and Wales only.

42(5) An amendment or repeal in Part II or III of Schedule 2 or Part II of Schedule 4 has the same extent as the provision amended or repealed.

43 Short title

43 This Act may be cited as the Trustee Act 2000.

SCHEDULES

SCHEDULE 1 – APPLICATION OF DUTY OF CARE

Section 2

INVESTMENT

1 The duty of care applies to a trustee–

(a) when exercising the general power of investment or any other power of investment, however conferred;

(b) when carrying out a duty to which he is subject under section 4 or 5 (duties relating to the exercise of a power of investment or to the review of investments).

ACQUISITION OF LAND

2 The duty of care applies to a trustee–

(a) when exercising the power under section 8 to acquire land;

(b) when exercising any other power to acquire land, however conferred;

(c) when exercising any power in relation to land acquired under a power mentioned in sub-paragraph (a) or (b).

AGENTS, NOMINEES AND CUSTODIANS

3(1) The duty of care applies to a trustee–

(a) when entering into arrangements under which a person is authorised under section 11 to exercise functions as an agent;

(b) when entering into arrangements under which a person is appointed under section 16 to act as a nominee;

(c) when entering into arrangements under which a person is appointed under section 17 or 18 to act as a custodian;

(d) when entering into arrangements under which, under any other power, however conferred, a person is authorised to exercise functions as an agent or is appointed to act as a nominee or custodian;

(e) when carrying out his duties under section 22 (review of agent, nominee or custodian, etc.).

3(2) For the purposes of sub-paragraph (1), entering into arrangements under which a person is authorised to exercise functions or is appointed to act as a nominee or custodian includes, in particular–

(a) selecting the person who is to act,

(b) determining any terms on which he is to act, and

(c) if the person is being authorised to exercise asset management functions, the preparation of a policy statement under section 15.

COMPOUNDING OF LIABILITIES

4 The duty of care applies to a trustee–

(a) when exercising the power under section 15 of the Trustee Act 1925 to do any of the things referred to in that section;

(b) when exercising any corresponding power, however conferred.

INSURANCE

5 The duty of care applies to a trustee–

(a) when exercising the power under section 19 of the Trustee Act 1925 to insure property;

(b) when exercising any corresponding power, however conferred.

REVERSIONARY INTERESTS, VALUATIONS AND AUDIT

6 The duty of care applies to a trustee–

(a) when exercising the power under section 22(1) or (3) of the Trustee Act 1925 to do any of the things referred to there;

(b) when exercising any corresponding power, however conferred.

EXCLUSION OF DUTY OF CARE

7 The duty of care does not apply if or in so far as it appears from the trust instrument that the duty is not meant to apply.

CAPITAL ALLOWANCES ACT 2001

(2001 Chapter 2)

[22nd March 2001]

ARRANGEMENT OF SECTIONS

PART 1 – INTRODUCTION

CHAPTER 1 – CAPITAL ALLOWANCES: GENERAL

CHAPTER 2 – EXCLUSION OF DOUBLE RELIEF

PART 2 – PLANT AND MACHINERY ALLOWANCES

CHAPTER 1 – INTRODUCTION

CHAPTER 2 – QUALIFYING ACTIVITIES

CHAPTER 3 – QUALIFYING EXPENDITURE

BUILDINGS, STRUCTURES AND LAND

DEMOLITION COSTS

EXPENDITURE ON THERMAL INSULATION AND PERSONAL SECURITY

CHAPTER 13 – PROVISIONS AFFECTING MINING AND OIL INDUSTRIES

CHAPTER 14 – FIXTURES

CHAPTER 19 – GIVING EFFECT TO ALLOWANCES AND CHARGES

CHAPTER 20 – SUPPLEMENTARY PROVISIONS

PART 3 – INDUSTRIAL BUILDINGS ALLOWANCES

PART 3A – BUSINESS PREMISES RENOVATION ALLOWANCES

CHAPTER 1 – INTRODUCTION

CHAPTER 2 – QUALIFYING EXPENDITURE

CHAPTER 3 – QUALIFYING BUILDINGS AND QUALIFYING BUSINESS PREMISES

CHAPTER 4 – THE RELEVANT INTEREST IN THE QUALIFYING BUILDING

CHAPTER 5 – INITIAL ALLOWANCES

CHAPTER 6 – WRITING-DOWN ALLOWANCES

CHAPTER 7 – GRANTS IN RESPECT OF QUALIFYING EXPENDITURE

CHAPTER 8 – BALANCING ADJUSTMENTS

CHAPTER 9 – WRITING OFF QUALIFYING EXPENDITURE

CHAPTER 10 – ADDITIONAL VAT LIABILITIES AND REBATES

CHAPTER 11 – SUPPLEMENTARY PROVISIONS

PART 4 – AGRICULTURAL BUILDINGS ALLOWANCES

PART 4A – FLAT CONVERSION ALLOWANCES

CHAPTER 1 – INTRODUCTION

CHAPTER 2 – QUALIFYING EXPENDITURE

CHAPTER 3 – QUALIFYING BUILDINGS AND QUALIFYING FLATS

CHAPTER 4 – THE RELEVANT INTEREST IN THE FLAT

CHAPTER 5 – INITIAL ALLOWANCES

CHAPTER 6 – WRITING-DOWN ALLOWANCES

CHAPTER 7 – BALANCING ADJUSTMENTS

CHAPTER 8 – WRITING OFF QUALIFYING EXPENDITURE

CHAPTER 9 – SUPPLEMENTARY PROVISIONS

PART 5 – MINERAL EXTRACTION ALLOWANCES

CHAPTER 1 – INTRODUCTION

CHAPTER 2 – QUALIFYING EXPENDITURE ON MINERAL EXPLORATION AND ACCESS

CHAPTER 3 – QUALIFYING EXPENDITURE ON ACQUIRING A MINERAL ASSET

CHAPTER 4 – QUALIFYING EXPENDITURE: SECOND-HAND ASSETS

ASSETS REFLECTING EXPENDITURE ON MINERAL EXPLORATION AND ACCESS

QUALIFYING EXPENDITURE ON ASSETS LIMITED BY REFERENCE TO HISTORIC COSTS

CHAPTER 5 – OTHER KINDS OF QUALIFYING EXPENDITURE

CHAPTER 5A – FIRST-YEAR QUALIFYING EXPENDITURE

GENERAL

TYPES OF EXPENDITURE WHICH MAY QUALIFY FOR FIRST-YEAR ALLOWANCES

SUPPLEMENTARY

CHAPTER 6 – ALLOWANCES AND CHARGES

FIRST-YEAR ALLOWANCES

WRITING-DOWN AND BALANCING ALLOWANCES AND BALANCING CHARGES

UNRELIEVED QUALIFYING EXPENDITURE

PART 7 – KNOW-HOW ALLOWANCES

CHAPTER 1 – INTRODUCTION

CHAPTER 2 – QUALIFYING EXPENDITURE

CHAPTER 3 – ALLOWANCES AND CHARGES

PART 8 – PATENT ALLOWANCES

CHAPTER 1 – INTRODUCTION

CHAPTER 2 – QUALIFYING EXPENDITURE

CHAPTER 3 – ALLOWANCES AND CHARGES

CHAPTER 4 – GIVING EFFECT TO ALLOWANCES AND CHARGES

CHAPTER 5 – SUPPLEMENTARY PROVISIONS

PART 9 – DREDGING ALLOWANCES

QUALIFYING EXPENDITURE ON DREDGING, ETC.

CHAPTER 2 – ADDITIONAL VAT LIABILITIES AND REBATES: INTERPRETATION, ETC.

CHAPTER 3 – DISPOSALS OF OIL LICENCES: PROVISIONS RELATING TO PARTS 5 AND 6

INTRODUCTION

OIL LICENCES RELATING TO UNDEVELOPED AREAS

DISPOSAL OF OIL LICENCE WITH EXPLOITATION VALUE

MINOR DEFINITIONS

CHAPTER 4 – PARTNERSHIPS, SUCCESSIONS AND TRANSFERS

CHAPTER 5 – MISCELLANEOUS

APPORTIONMENT

PROCEDURE FOR DETERMINING CERTAIN QUESTIONS

TAX AGREEMENTS FOR INCOME TAX PURPOSES

COMPANIES NOT RESIDENT IN THE UNITED KINGDOM

SALES TREATED AS BEING FOR ALTERNATIVE AMOUNT

ANTI-AVOIDANCE

PART 1 – INTRODUCTION

Notes – M06/2006: statement form Tax Law Rewrite team summarising their goals and methods.

Chapter 1 – Capital Allowances: General

1 Capital allowances

1(1) This Act provides for allowances in respect of capital expenditure (and for charges in connection with those allowances).

1(2) The allowances for which this Act provides are those under–

(a) Part 2 (plant and machinery allowances);

(b) [Omitted by FA 2008, s. 84 and Sch. 27, para. 2(a).]

(ba) Part 3A (business premises renovation allowances)
(c) [Omitted by FA 2008, s. 84 and Sch. 27, para. 2(a).]
(ca) [Omitted by FA 2012, s. 227 and Sch. 39, para. 38(2).]
(d) Part 5 (mineral extraction allowances);
(e) Part 6 (research and development allowances);
(f) Part 7 (know-how allowances);
(g) Part 8 (patent allowances);
(h) Part 9 (dredging allowances);
(i) Part 10 (assured tenancy allowances).

1(3) This Act also provides for allowances in respect of contributions to expenditure incurred on plant or machinery for the purposes of a mineral extraction trade or on dredging (see Part 11).

1(4) But a person is not entitled to any allowance or liable to any charge under this Act in calculating the profits of a trade, profession or vocation of the person in relation to which an election under section 25A of ITTOIA 2005 (cash basis for small businesses) has effect, other than an allowance in respect of expenditure incurred on the provision of a car (or a charge in connection with such an allowance).

1(5) In subsection (4) **"car"** has the same meaning as in Part 2 (see section 268A).

History – S. 1(2)(b) and (c) omitted by FA 2008, s. 84 and Sch. 27, para. 2(a), with effect in relation to chargeable periods beginning on or after 1 April 2011 for corporation tax purposes and 6 April 2011 for income tax purposes (FA 2008, s. 84(3)).
S. 1(2)(ba) inserted by FA 2005, s. 92 and Sch. 6, para. 2 with effect in relation to expenditure incurred on or after 11 April 2007, by virtue of SI 2007/949, art. 2.
S. 1(2)(ca) omitted by FA 2012, s. 227 and Sch. 39, para. 38(2), with effect in relation to chargeable periods beginning on or after 1 April 2013 for corporation tax purposes, and 6 April 2013 for income tax purposes, subject to transitional and saving provisions in FA 2012, Sch. 39, para. 41 and 42. Former s. 1(2)(ca) read as follows:
"(ca) Part 4A (flat conversion allowances);".
Former s. 1(2)(ca) inserted by FA 2001, s. 67 and Sch. 19, Pt. 2, para. 1, in relation to expenditure incurred on or after 11 May 2001.
In s. 1(3), the words ", industrial buildings or agricultural buildings," omitted by FA 2008, s. 84 and Sch. 27, para. 2(b), with effect in relation to chargeable periods beginning on or after 1 April 2011 for corporation tax purposes and 6 April 2011 for income tax purposes (FA 2008, s. 84(3)).
S. 1(4) inserted by FA 2013, s. 17 and Sch. 4, para. 46, with effect for the tax year 2013–14 and subsequent tax years.
S. 1(5) inserted by FA 2013, s. 17 and Sch. 4, para. 46, with effect for the tax year 2013–14 and subsequent tax years.

Origin – Drafting.

Transitional – Sch. 3, Pt. 1: continuity of the law following repeal and re-enactment of provisions in this Act.
Sch. 3, Pt. 2: changes in the law effected by this Act: limited right to elect in respect of things done, etc. before 1 or 6 April 2001, for status quo ante to apply for first chargeable period ending thereafter.

HMRC Manuals – CA10040: history of capital allowances.
CA11101: types of capital allowance.

2 General means of giving effect to capital allowances

2(1) Allowances and charges are to be given effect–
(a) for income tax purposes, in calculating income for a chargeable period, and
(b) for corporation tax purposes, in calculating profits for a chargeable period.

2(2) For the meaning of **"chargeable period"**, see section 6.

2(3) Subsection (1) needs to be read with the following provisions about giving effect to allowances and charges–

sections 247 to 262A (plant and machinery allowances);
sections 360Z and 360Z1 (business premises renovation allowances);
section 432 (mineral extraction allowances);
section 450 (research and development allowances);
section 463 (know-how allowances);
sections 478 to 480 (patent allowances);
section 489 (dredging allowances);
section 529 (assured tenancy allowances).

2(4) In subsection (1)(b) **"profits"** has the same meaning as in Part 2 of CTA 2009 (see section 2(2) of that Act).

History – In s. 2(3), entry relating to section 393T omitted by FA 2012, s. 227 and Sch. 39, para. 38(3), with effect in relation to chargeable periods beginning on or after 1 April 2013 for corporation tax purposes, and 6 April 2013 for income tax purposes, subject to transitional and saving provisions in FA 2012, Sch. 39, para. 41 and 42.
In s. 2(3), the words "sections 352 to 355 (industrial buildings allowances);" and "sections 391 and 392 (agricultural buildings allowances);" omitted by FA 2008, s. 84 and Sch. 27, para. 3, with effect in relation to chargeable periods beginning on or after 1 April 2011 for corporation tax purposes and 6 April 2011 for income tax purposes (FA 2008, s. 84(3)).
In s. 2(3), the figure "262A" substituted for the figure "262" by FA 2008, s. 79 and Sch. 25, para. 2, with effect in relation to expenditure incurred on or after 1 April 2008 (FA 2008, Sch. 25, para. 9).

In s. 2(3), the words "sections 360Z and 360Z1 (business premises renovation allowances)" inserted after the entry for s. 352 to 355 by FA 2005, s. 92 and Sch. 6, para. 3, with effect in relation to expenditure incurred on or after 11 April 2007, by virtue of SI 2007/949, art. 2.
In s. 2(3), item relating to s. 393T inserted by FA 2001, s. 67 and Sch. 19, Pt. 2, para. 2, in relation to expenditure incurred on or after 11 May 2001.
In s. 2(4), the words "Part 2 of CTA 2009 (see section 2(2) of that Act)" substituted for the words "section 6 of ICTA" by CTA 2009, s. 1322 and Sch. 1, para. 475, with effect for corporation tax purposes for accounting periods ending on or after 1 April 2009, and for income tax and capital gains tax purposes for the tax year 2009–10 and subsequent tax years.

Origin – S. 2(1): CAA 1990, s. 137(1) (part), s. 140(1), (5), 144(1), (3), 161(2) ("chargeable period", part).
S. 2(2), (3): drafting.
S. 2(4): ICTA 1988, s. 834(2) (part).

HMRC Manuals – CA11110: guidance and example on how allowances are made.

3 Claims for capital allowances

3(1) No allowance is to be made under this Act, and no first-year tax credit is to be paid under Schedule A1, unless a claim for it is made.

3(2) The claim must be included in a tax return.

3(2A) Any claim for an allowance under Part 3A (business premises renovation allowances) must be separately identified as such in the return.

3(2B) Any claim for a first-year tax credit under Schedule A1 must be separately identified as such in the return.

3(3) In this Act **"tax return"** means–

(a) for income tax purposes, a return required to be made under TMA 1970, and

(b) for corporation tax purposes, a company tax return required to be made under Schedule 18 to FA 1998 (company tax returns, assessments and related matters).

3(4) Subsection (2) does not apply for income tax purposes to a claim for an allowance under–

(a) section 258 (claim for allowance in respect of special leasing of plant or machinery),

(b) [Omitted by FA 2008, s. 84 and Sch. 27, para. 4,]

(c) section 479 (claim for patent allowance in respect of non-trading expenditure),

which is instead subject to section 42 of TMA 1970 (procedure for making claims and claims not included in returns).

3(5) Subsection (2) does not apply for corporation tax purposes to a claim for an allowance under–

(a) section 260(3)(b) (claim to carry back allowance in respect of special leasing of plant or machinery), or

(b) [Omitted by FA 2008, s. 84 and Sch. 27, para. 4,]

which is instead subject to paragraphs 54 to 60 of Schedule 18 to FA 1998 (general provisions as to claims).

3(6) This section is subject to section 42(6) and (7) of TMA 1970 (special provisions relating to partnerships).

History – In s. 3(1), the words ", and no first-year tax credit is to be paid under Schedule A1," inserted by FA 2008, s. 79 and Sch. 25, para. 3(2), with effect in relation to expenditure incurred on or after 1 April 2008 (FA 2008, Sch. 25, para 9).
S. 3(2A) inserted by FA 2005, s. 92 and Sch. 6, para. 4, with effect in relation to expenditure incurred on or after 11 April 2007, by virtue of SI 2007/949, art. 2.
S. 3(2B) inserted by FA 2008, s. 70 and Sch. 25, para. 3(3), with effect in relation to expenditure incurred on or after 1 April 2008 (FA 2008, Sch. 25, para. 9).

Origin – S. 3(1): *Elliss v BP Oil Northern Ireland Refinery* [1987] BTC 38 (see Rewrite note below).
S. 3(2): CAA 1990, s. 143(3) (part), FA 1998, Sch. 18, para. 79(1) (part).
S. 3(3): CAA 1990, s. 38F(5), 51(2) ("return"), 76B(8), 140(3) (part), 147(3) (part), FA 1998, Sch. 18, para. 3(1), 79(1) (part).
S. 3(4): ICTA 1988, s. 528(2) (part), CAA 1990, s. 17(3), 141(1) (part), 141(5).
S. 3(4)(b) omitted by FA 2008, s. 84 and Sch. 27, para. 4, with effect in relation to chargeable periods beginning on or after 1 April 2011 for corporation tax purposes and 6 April 2011 for income tax purposes (FA 2008, s. 84(3)).
S. 3(5): see FA 1998, Sch. 18, para. 54–60, and Rewrite note below.
S. 3(5)(b) omitted by FA 2008, s. 84 and Sch. 27, para. 4, with effect in relation to chargeable periods beginning on or after 1 April 2011 for corporation tax purposes and 6 April 2011 for income tax purposes (FA 2008, s. 84(3)).
S. 3(6): drafting.

Cross references – FA 2006, s. 120(7): s. 3(1) shall not apply ro calculation of profits under thre real estate investment trust regime.
FA 1998, Sch. 18, para. 3(1), 79(1): a claim by a company for capital allowances must be made in the claimant company's company tax return for the accounting period for which the claim is made.

Rewrite: Technical Points – Explanatory Notes, Annex 2, Note 1: there was previously no statutory rule that capital allowances have to be claimed, but this was established in *Elliss v BP Oil Northern Ireland Refinery* [1987] BTC 38 and is incorporated in s. 3(1).
Explanatory Notes, Annex 2, Note 2: a claim under former CAA 1990, s. 17 (mining structures etc.: balancing allowances carried back to earlier chargeable periods) and s. 145(3) (carry-back of corporation tax allowances to earlier chargeable periods) can still be made under FA 1998, Sch. 18, para. 54–60 (FA 1999, Sch. 11, para. 4 and 7 notwithstanding).

Statements of practice – 5/01– corporation tax self assessment: time limits for claims to loss relief, capital allowances and group relief.

HMRC Manuals – CA11120: guidance on how claims are made.
CA11130: guidance on claims made in income tax returns.
CA11140: guidance on claims made by companies.
CT10800: guidance on claims made in corporation tax returns.

4 Capital expenditure

4(1) In this Act **"capital expenditure"** and **"capital sums"** are used in the sense given in this section.

4(2) **"Capital expenditure"** and **"capital sums"** do not include, in relation to a person incurring the expenditure or paying the sums–

(a) any expenditure or sum that may be deducted in calculating the profits or gains of a trade, profession or vocation or property business carried on by the person, or

(b) any expenditure or sum that may be allowed as a deduction under a relevant provision from the taxable earnings from an employment or office held by the person.

4(2A) In subsection (2)–

"relevant provision" means any of the following–

(a) section 262;

(b) section 232 of ITEPA 2003 (giving effect to mileage allowance relief);

(c) Chapters 2 to 6 of Part 5 of that Act (general deductions allowed from earnings); and

(d) sections 188 to 194 of FA 2004 (contributions under registered pension schemes), and

"taxable earnings" has the meaning given by section 10 of ITEPA 2003.

4(3) **"Capital expenditure"** and **"capital sums"** do not include, in relation to a recipient of the expenditure or sums–

(a) any amounts that are to be added in calculating the profits or gains of a trade, profession or vocation or property business carried on by the recipient, or

(b) any amounts that are earnings of an employment or office held by the recipient.

4(4) **"Capital expenditure"** and **"capital sums"** do not include, in relation to–

(a) a person incurring the expenditure or paying the sums, or

(b) a recipient of the expenditure or sums,

any expenditure or sum in the case of which a deduction of income tax falls or may fall to be made under Chapter 6 of Part 15 of ITA 2007 (deduction from annual payments or patent royalties) or under section 906 of that Act (certain royalties etc where usual place of abode of owner is abroad).

4(5) [Omitted by ITA 2007, s. 1027 and Sch. 1, para. 397(3), and repealed by s. 1031 and Sch. 3, Pt. 1.]

History – In s. 4(2)(b), the words "any expenditure or sum that may be allowed as a deduction under a relevant provision from the taxable earnings from an employment or office held by the person." substituted for the words "any expenditure or sum that may be deducted in calculating the emoluments of an employment or office held by the person." by ITEPA 2003, Sch. 6, para. 247(2) which has effect, for income tax purposes, for the tax year 2003–04 and subsequent tax years and, for corporation tax purposes, for accounting periods ending after 5 April 2003.

S. 4(2A)(d) substituted by FA 2004, s. 281(1) and Sch. 35, para. 48 which, by virtue of FA 2004, s. 284(1), came into force on 6 April 2006.

S. 4(2A) inserted by ITEPA 2003, Sch. 6, para. 247(3) which has effect, for income tax purposes, for the tax year 2003–04 and subsequent tax years and, for corporation tax purposes, for accounting periods ending after 5 April 2003.

In s. 4(3), the word "earnings" substituted for the word "emoluments" by ITEPA 2003, Sch. 6, para. 247(4) which has effect, for income tax purposes, for the tax year 2003–04 and subsequent tax years and, for corporation tax purposes, for accounting periods ending after 5 April 2003.

In s. 4(4), the words "Chapter 6 of Part 15 of ITA 2007 (deduction from annual payments or patent royalties) or under section 906 of that Act (certain royalties etc where usual place of abode of owner is abroad)" substituted for the words "section 348 or 349(1) of ICTA (annual payments)" by ITA 2007, s. 1027 and Sch. 1, para. 397(2), with effect from 6 April 2007.

S. 4(5) omitted by ITA 2007, s. 1027 and Sch. 1, para. 397(3), and repealed by s. 1031 and Sch. 3, Pt. 1, with effect from 6 April 2007. In former s. 4(5) the words "section 595(2) of ITTOIA 2005" and ": income and corporation tax" inserted by ITTOIA 2005, s. 882(1) and Sch. 1, para. 525(4); effective for income tax purposes for 2005–06 onwards and for corporation tax purposes for accounting periods ending after 5 April 2005 (ITTOIA 2005, s. 883(1)).

Origin – S. 4(1): CAA 1990, s. 159(1) (part).
S. 4(2), (3): CAA 1990, s. 159(1) (part), (1A) (part), 161(2A).
S. 4(4): CAA 1990, s. 159(1) (part).
S. 4(5): ICTA 1988, s. 532(4).

Cross references – ICTA 1988, s. 532 (as amended by Sch. 2, para. 49): Tax Acts have effect as though ICTA 1988, s. 524–529 and 531, 532 and 533 were contained in this Act.

Transitional – Sch. 3, para. 9: s. 4(2) and (3) apply with the omission of the words "or property business" in relation to expenditure incurred or sums paid or received before 26 November 1996.

Extra-statutory concessions – B1: expenditure on machinery or plant which has been the subject of a "renewals" deduction may qualify as capital expenditure notwithstanding s. 4(2)(a).

HMRC Manuals – CA11530: guidance on the meaning of capital expenditure.
CA11750: guidance on s. 4(1).

5 When capital expenditure is incurred

5(1) For the purposes of this Act, the general rule is that an amount of capital expenditure is to be treated as incurred as soon as there is an unconditional obligation to pay it.

5(2) The general rule applies even if the whole or a part of the expenditure is not required to be paid until a later date.

5(3) There are the following exceptions to the general rule.

5(4) If under an agreement–

(a) the capital expenditure is expenditure on the provision of an asset,

(b) an unconditional obligation to pay an amount of the expenditure comes into being as a result of the giving of a certificate or any other event,

(c) the giving of the certificate, or other event, occurs within the period of one month after the end of a chargeable period, and

(d) at or before the end of that chargeable period, the asset has become the property of, or is otherwise under the agreement attributed to, the person subject to the unconditional obligation to pay,

the expenditure is to be treated as incurred immediately before the end of that chargeable period.

5(5) If under an agreement an amount of capital expenditure is not required to be paid until a date more than 4 months after the unconditional obligation to pay has come into being, the amount is to be treated as incurred on that date.

5(6) If under an agreement–

(a) there is an unconditional obligation to pay an amount of capital expenditure on a date earlier than accords with normal commercial usage, and

(b) the sole or main benefit which might have been expected to be obtained thereby is that the amount would be treated, under the general rule, as incurred in an earlier chargeable period,

the amount is to be treated as incurred on the date on or before which it is required to be paid.

5(7) This section–

(a) is subject to any provision of this Act which has the effect that expenditure is to be treated as incurred on a date later than would result from the application of this section, and

(b) does not apply to expenditure treated as incurred as a result of a person incurring an additional VAT liability.

Origin – S. 5(1)–(3): CAA 1990, s. 159(3).
S. 5(4): CAA 1990, s. 159(4).
S. 5(5): CAA 1990, s. 159(5).
S. 5(6): CAA 1990, s. 159(6).
S. 5(7): CAA 1990, s. 159(2), (7).

Cross references – F(No. 2)A 1997, s. 48(9) (as amended by Sch. 2, para. 99): modifications of s. 5(6) in application of s. 5(1)–(5) for determining when expenditure is incurred for the purposes of production and acquisition expenditure incurred between 2 July 1997 and 2 July 2002 on certain low-budget films.

Rewrite: Technical Points – Explanatory Notes, Annex 2, Note 3: change of wording from "when the obligation to pay becomes unconditional" in CAA 1990, s. 159(3) to "as soon as there is an unconditional obligation to pay it".

HMRC Manuals – CA11700, 11800: where goods are sold subject to reservation of title ("Romalpa" contracts), the obligation to pay becomes unconditional (within CAA 2001, s. 5(1)) when the goods are delivered.

Other material – ICAEW Technical Releases 580, 602 (not reproduced): allowances for hire purchase expenditure unaffected by CAA 1990, s. 159(5) (now CAA 2001, s. 5(5)).

6 Meaning of "chargeable period"

6(1) In this Act **"chargeable period"** means–

(a) for income tax purposes, a period of account, or

(b) for corporation tax purposes, an accounting period of a company.

6(2) **"Period of account"** means–

(a) in the case of a person entitled to an allowance or liable to a charge in calculating the profits of his trade, profession or vocation, a period for which accounts are drawn up for the purposes of the trade, profession or vocation, and

(b) in the case of any other person entitled to an allowance or liable to a charge, a tax year.

6(3) Subsection (2)(a) is subject to subsections (4) to (6).

6(4) If–

(a) two periods of account overlap, or

(b) one period of account includes another,

the period common to both is to be treated as part of the first period of account only.

6(5) If there is a gap between two periods of account, the gap is to be treated as part of the first period of account.

6(6) If a period of account would (apart from this subsection) be longer than 18 months, that period must be treated as divided into separate periods of account–

(a) the first beginning with the start date of the original period, and

(b) each subsequent one beginning with an anniversary of that date,

so as to ensure that none of the periods of account is longer than 12 months.

Origin – S. 6(1): CAA 1990, s. 161(2) ("chargeable period", part).
S. 6(2): CAA 1990, s. 160(2) (part), (5), and see Rewrite note below.
S. 6(3): CAA 1990, s. 160(2) (part).
S. 6(4): CAA 1990, s. 160(3) (part), (6), and see Rewrite note below.
S. 6(5): CAA 1990, s. 160(3) (part).
S. 6(6): CAA 1990, s. 160(4).

Cross references – ICTA 1988, s. 532 (as amended by Sch. 2, para. 49): Tax Acts have effect as though ICTA 1988, s. 524–529 and 531, 532–533 were contained in this Act.

Rewrite: Technical Points – Explanatory Notes, Annex 2, Note 4: no change in law between CAA 1990, s. 160(5) and s. 6(2)(b), although former provision apparently extended only to CAA 1990, Pt. I–VI and VIII while s. 6(2)(b) extends to the whole of this Act, because:

- s. 6(2)(b) is not relevant to research and expenditure allowances, and,
- on a correct interpretation, references to "chargeable period" in ICTA 1988, s. 520–533 (know-how and patent allowances) included a period of account as defined in CAA 1990, s. 160(5).

Explanatory Notes, Annex 2, Note 5: redundancy of former words in CAA 1990, s. 160(6) "coincidence of two periods" following amendments made by FA 1994, s. 212(1), therefore they do not re-appear in s. 6(4).

HMRC Manuals – CA11510: guidance and examples on s. 6.

Chapter 1A – Trades Attracting Northern Ireland Rate of Corporation Tax

Prospective amendments – Ch. 1A inserted by CTNIA 2015, s. 2 and Sch. 1, para. 2, with effect from 26 March 2015 (Royal Assent) in respect of any power to make regulations and with effect in relation to accounting periods beginning on or after the first day of the appointed financial year for other provisions (see CTNIA 2015, s. 5). See also transitional provisions at Sch. 1, para. 19–21.

Chapter 2 – Exclusion of Double Relief

7 No double allowances

7(1) If an allowance is made under any Part of this Act to a person in respect of capital expenditure, no allowance is to be made to him under any other Part in respect of–

(a) that expenditure, or

(b) the provision of any asset to which that expenditure related.

7(2) This section does not apply in relation to Parts 7 and 8 (know-how and patent allowances).

Rewrite: Technical Points – Explanatory Notes, Annex 2, Note 6: CAA 1990, s. 147 did not refer to allowances made under ICTA 1988, Pt. XIII, Ch. I (patents and know-how) which therefore was not subject to s. 147, but "the nature of patents and know-how is such that it seems unlikely that the subject matter of patent and know-how allowances could in practice lead to claims for double relief" (see subsection (2)).

HMRC Manuals – CA31800: guidance on prevention of double allowances.

8 No double relief through pooling under Part 2 (plant and machinery allowances)

8(1) Subsection (2) applies if, under Part 2–

(a) any capital expenditure has been allocated to a pool, and

(b) an allowance or charge has been made to or on any person in respect of the pool.

8(2) The person to or on whom the allowance or charge has been made is not entitled to an allowance under any Part other than Part 2 in respect of–

(a) the expenditure allocated to the pool, or

(b) the provision of any asset to which the allocated expenditure related.

8(3) Subsection (4) applies if under any Part other than Part 2 an allowance has been made to a person in respect of any capital expenditure.

8(4) The person to whom the allowance has been made is not entitled to allocate to any pool–

(a) that expenditure, or

(b) any expenditure on the provision of any asset to which the expenditure mentioned in paragraph (a) related.

8(5) This section does not apply in relation to Parts 7 and 8 (know-how and patent allowances).

Cross references – S. 57(3): available qualifying expenditure for plant and machinery writing-down allowances does not include any expenditure excluded by s. 8(4).

Rewrite: Technical Points – Explanatory Notes, Annex 2, Note 6: CAA 1990, s. 147 did not refer to allowances made under ICTA 1988, Pt. XIII, Ch. I (patents and know-how) which therefore was not subject to s. 147, but "the nature of patents and know-how is such that it seems unlikely that the subject matter of patent and know-how allowances could in practice lead to claims for double relief" (see subs. (5)).

9 Interaction between fixtures claims and other claims

9(1) A person is not entitled to make a fixtures claim in respect of any capital expenditure relating to an asset if–

(a) any person entitled to do so has at any previous time claimed an allowance under any Part other than Part 2, and

(b) the claim was for an allowance in respect of capital expenditure relating, in whole or part, to the asset.

9(2) Subsection (1) does not prevent a person making a fixtures claim in respect of capital expenditure if–

(a) the only previous claim was under Part 3, 3A or 6 (industrial buildings and research and development allowances), and

(b) section 186(2), 186A(2) or 187(2) (limit on amount of expenditure that may be taken into account) applies to that expenditure.

9(3) If a person entitled to do so has made a fixtures claim in respect of capital expenditure relating to an asset, no one is entitled to an allowance on a later claim under any Part other than Part 2 in respect of any capital expenditure relating to the asset.

9(4) A person makes a fixtures claim in respect of expenditure if he makes a claim (in the sense given in section 202(3)) under Chapter 14 of Part 2 in respect of the expenditure as expenditure on the provision of a fixture.

History – In s. 9(2)(a) the words ", 3A" inserted by FA 2012, s. 43 and Sch. 10, para. 7(a), with effect in relation to balancing events which occur on or after 6 April 2012, for income tax purposes, and 1 April 2012, for corporation tax purposes, subject to provisions in FA 2012, Sch. 10, para. 13.
In s. 9(2)(b) the words ", 186A(2)" inserted by FA 2012, s. 43 and Sch. 10, para. 7(b), with effect in relation to balancing events which occur on or after 6 April 2012, for income tax purposes, and 1 April 2012, for corporation tax purposes, subject to provisions in FA 2012, Sch. 10, para. 13.

Cross references – S. 57(3): available qualifying expenditure for plant and machinery writing-down allowances does not include any expenditure excluded by s. 9(1).

Transitional – Sch. 3, para. 10: s. 9 does not apply in relation to expenditure incurred before 24 July 1996.

10 Interpretation

10(1) In this Chapter **"capital expenditure"** includes any contribution to capital expenditure.

10(2) For the purposes of this Chapter–

(a) expenditure relates to an asset only if it relates to its provision, and

(b) the provision of an asset includes its construction or acquisition.

PART 2 – PLANT AND MACHINERY ALLOWANCES

Cross references – S. 537, 538: contribution allowances under Pt. 2.
S. 544(1): allowances and charges in respect of the management assets of a company's life assurance business may only be given or imposed under Pt. 2.
S. 557(a): rules on partnership changes and successions (s. 557, 558) inapplicable to Pt. 2.
S. 564(2)(a): s. 563 (procedure for determining certain questions affecting two or more persons) applies in relation to any determination of the market value of property for the purposes of Pt. 2.
ICTA 1988, s. 84(2): relief for gifts by traders to educational establishments of articles qualifying under Pt. 2 as plant or machinery.
ICTA 1988, s. 116(4): arrangements for company partner to transfer relief within trading partnership, restriction of set-off to a separate trade: allowances in respect of special leasing of plant or machinery treated as an allowance given effect in calculating profits of that trade.
ICTA 1988, s. 197C(5)(b): allowances under Pt. 2 deductible in computing employee's chargeable mileage profit.
ICTA 1988, s. 359(3): eligibility for relief under ICTA 1988, s. 353 for interest paid by holder of an office or employment on a loan for capital expenditure on plant or machinery.
ICTA 1988, s. 384(6): any loss arising from expenditure incurred on the provision of plant or machinery to be disregarded in computing trading loss to be set against general income.
ICTA 1988, s. 384A: no loss relief against general income in respect of first-year allowance in respect of expenditure incurred on the provision of plant or machinery for leasing in the course of a qualifying activity carried on by an individual in partnership with a company.
ICTA 1988, s. 395: restriction of loss relief where expenditure incurred by company on provision of plant or machinery for letting, and arrangements for company reconstruction are in place during accounting period in which first-year allowance is made.
ICTA 1988, s. 487(4): a credit union is not regarded as an investment company for the purposes of Pt. 2.
ICTA 1988, s. 495: expenditure incurred between connected parties which qualifies for plant and machinery allowances and is wholly or partly met by regional development grant.
ICTA 1988, Sch. 18, para. 1(6): person providing new consideration for shares in or securities of a company, and using in his trade assets in respect of which plant and machinery allowances have been made to the company, treated as being an equity holder.
ICTA 1988, Sch. 24, para. 10: assumptions in respect of plant and machinery allowances in calculating chargeable profits, creditable tax and corresponding UK tax of foreign companies for purposes of CFC rules.
TCGA 1992, s. 37(2)(b): money or money's worth which is brought into account as the disposal value of plant or machinery under Pt. 2 is not excluded by TCGA 1992, s. 37(1) from the consideration taken into account for the purposes of tax on chargeable gains.
TCGA 1992, s. 41(7): restriction of allowable capital losses by reference to plant and machinery allowances made.
FA 1996, Sch. 8, para. 3(6)(c)(i): loan relationships – plant and machinery allowance to be given in priority to claim to carry back deficit to previous accounting periods where company is an investment company.

FA 1997, Sch. 12, para. 11(3)(a): disposal value to be brought into account if capital expenditure incurred by the lessor under a finance lease has been taken into account for the purposes of plant and machinery allowances, and a major lump sum falls to be paid in the case of the lease of the asset.
FA 2000, Sch. 12, para. 7, Step 4: deduction of plant and machinery allowances in respect of expenditure incurred by the intermediary that could have been claimed by the worker in calculating the deemed Schedule E payment under the "IR35" rules.
FA 2000, Sch. 22, para. 85(1): determination of qualifying expenditure under Pt. 2 where company leaves tonnage tax.
FA 2000, Sch. 22, para. 89(1): application of Pt. 2 in the case of a finance lease of a qualifying ship provided to a company within tonnage tax.
FA 2000, Sch. 22, para. 110(2): application of Pt. 2 when a tonnage tax company claims capital allowances for capital expenditure incurred in providing plant or machinery for the purposes of its offshore activities.
FA 2002, Sch. 29, para. 73A: intangible fixed assets: assets entirely excluded: assets in respect of which capital allowance previously made.
Atomic Energy Act 1995, Sch. 3, para. 20: transfers to Atomic Energy Authority and to and by successor companies – construction of references to connected persons.
Transport Act 2000, Sch. 26, para. 5, 6, 13–15, 21, 27, 34: treatment of inherited plant and machinery allowances under transfers to Strategic Rail Authority and/or Secretary of State, franchise companies, etc.

HMRC Manuals – CA20006: outline of plant and machinery allowances.
CA21010ff: guidance on "plant and machinery".
CA21190: lifts and escalators are machinery.
CA21200: central heating systems, hot water systems, air conditioning systems, alarm and sprinkler systems, ventilation systems, baths, wash basins and toilet suites qualify as plant.
CA29220: plant, etc. dealt with on renewals basis.

Chapter 1 – Introduction

11 General conditions as to availability of plant and machinery allowances

11(1) Allowances are available under this Part if a person carries on a qualifying activity and incurs qualifying expenditure.

11(2) **"Qualifying activity"** has the meaning given by Chapter 2.

11(3) Allowances under this Part must be calculated separately for each qualifying activity which a person carries on.

11(4) The general rule is that expenditure is qualifying expenditure if–

(a) it is capital expenditure on the provision of plant or machinery wholly or partly for the purposes of the qualifying activity carried on by the person incurring the expenditure, and

(b) the person incurring the expenditure owns the plant or machinery as a result of incurring it.

11(5) But the general rule is affected by other provisions of this Act, and in particular by Chapter 3.

Origin – S. 11(4): CAA 1990, s. 22(1) (part), s. 24(1) (part), s. 79(1) (part), (2) (part), see also Explanatory Notes, Annex 2, Note 7 (below).

Rewrite: Technical Points – Explanatory Notes, Annex 2, Note 7: "owns" in s. 11(4)(b) means the same as "belongs" in CAA 1990, s. 22(1)(b), 24(1)(b) (*Stokes (HMIT) v Costain Property Investments Ltd* [1983] BTC 2000; *Melluish (HMIT) v BMI (No. 3) Ltd* [1995] BTC 381.

HMRC interpretations – IRInt. 86: meaning of "machinery" for CGT purposes – in absence of statutory definition, given its normal meaning, including any apparatus that applies mechanical power.

Hansard – 15 February 1984, col. 203 (not reproduced): basic lighting systems not treated as machinery or plant (although installation costs may be eligible for IBAs); specialised lighting systems may qualify as plant and machinery where they perform a specific function and are not merely part of the trade's setting.

HMRC Manuals – CA11700: whether expenditure has been "incurred", etc.
CA20060: restricted meaning of "expenditure on the provision of plant", etc.
CA20070: professional fees and preliminaries only qualify as expenditure on plant or machinery if directly related to the acquisition, transport and installation of the plant.
CA22090: Revenue do not accept that all glasshouses are plant; the majority qualify for ABA as premises or setting within which a grower's trade is carried on.
CA23010: guidance on s. 11(4).
CA23050: expenditure by MPs etc. on residential accommodation not qualifying expenditure.
CA23350: abortive capital expenditure on machinery and plant may be within scope of s. 67 and therefore qualify for writing-down allowances.
CA31800: guidance on prevention of double allowances.

Other material – IR press release, 15 March 1984: cost of cable television network ducting (including installation costs) is qualifying expenditure for capital allowances on machinery or plant.
ICAEW Technical Release TR 256: Revenue practice on qualification as expenditure on machinery or plant of expenditure on "mains services" to buildings.
ICAEW Technical Release TR 500: application of ICTA 1988, s. 343(2) in determining which company obtains allowances.
ICAEW Technical Release TR 627 (not reproduced): treatment of computer software generally follows accounting treatment where this reflects commercial usage.
ICAEW Technical Release TR 713 (not reproduced): professional fees only qualify for capital allowances to the extent that the expenditure is directly related to the acquisition of plant .
Taxline 1993/40 (not reproduced): evidence that Revenue apply a more detailed formula to the allocation of professional fees for construction projects, broadly disallowing legal, surveyor and managing agent fees entirely; allowing around 30 per cent of the fees of quantity surveyors, architects and structural engineers; the fees of mechanical, electrical, service and lift engineers allowed in the same proportion as the assets to which they relate.
Revenue letter to Football League, 25 January 1991 (not reproduced): guidance on meaning of "machinery or plant" in the context of improvements to football grounds.

12 Expenditure incurred before qualifying activity carried on

12 For the purposes of this Part, expenditure incurred for the purposes of a qualifying activity by a person about to carry on the activity is to be treated as if it had been incurred by him on the first day on which he carries on the activity.

Prospective amendments – The existing provision made s. 12(1) and s. 12(2)–(6) inserted by CTNIA 2015, s. 2 and Sch. 1, para. 3, with effect from 26 March 2015 (Royal Assent) in respect of any power to make regulations and with effect in relation to accounting periods beginning on or after the first day of the appointed financial year for other provisions (see CTNIA 2015, s. 5). See also transitional provisions at Sch. 1, para. 19–21.

Origin – CAA 1990, s. 83(2).

Cross references – S. 38A(4): any effect of s. 12 on the time at which expenditure is treated as incurred is disregarded for the purposes of determining whether the expenditure is AIA qualifying expenditure.
S. 50: any effect of s. 12 on the time at which expenditure is to be treated as incurred is disregarded for the purposes of determining whether the expenditure is first-year qualifying expenditure under Pt. 2, Ch. 4.

HMRC Manuals – CA23020: guidance on s. 12.

Notes – ICTA 1988, s. 401: trading income – relief for pre-trading expenditure.

13 Use for qualifying activity of plant or machinery provided for other purposes

13(1) This section applies if a person–

(a) brings plant or machinery into use for the purposes of a qualifying activity carried on by him, and

(b) on the date when he does so, owns the plant or machinery as a result of having incurred capital expenditure (**"actual expenditure"**) on its provision for purposes other than those of that qualifying activity.

13(2) The person is to be treated–

(a) as having incurred capital expenditure (**"notional expenditure"**) on the provision of the plant or machinery for the purposes of the qualifying activity on the date on which it is brought into use for those purposes, and

(b) as owning the plant or machinery as a result as having incurred that expenditure.

13(3) Subject to subsection (4), the amount of the notional expenditure is the market value of the plant or machinery on the date when it is brought into use for the purposes of the qualifying activity.

13(4) If the market value is greater than the actual expenditure, the amount of the notional expenditure is the amount of the actual expenditure, less any amount required to be deducted under subsection (5).

13(5) The amount to be deducted is any amount that under section 218 would have been left out of account in determining the person's available qualifying expenditure if the actual expenditure had been incurred on the provision of the plant or machinery for the purposes of the qualifying activity.

13(6) The question whether the provision of the plant or machinery is to be treated as wholly or only partly for the purposes of the qualifying activity is to be determined according to whether the use referred to in subsection (1)(a) is wholly or only partly for those purposes.

13(7) This section is subject to section 161 (pre-trading expenditure on mineral exploration and access).

History – In s. 13(5) the words "or 224", which followed the words "section 28", omitted by FA 2008, s. 55 and Sch. 20, para. 6(2), with effect in the case of plant or machinery which is the subject of a sale and finance leaseback (as defined in CAA 2001, s. 221) where the date of the transaction (within the meaning of that section) is on or after 9 October 2007 (FA 2008, Sch. 20, para. 6(19)).

Origin – S. 13(1): CAA 1990, s. 81(1) (part).
S. 13(2), (3): CAA 1990, s. 81(1) (part), 1A(b) (part).
S. 13(4): CAA 1990, s. 81(2AA).
S. 13(5): CAA 1990, s. 81(2AB).
S. 13(6): CAA 1990, s. 81(2) (part).
S. 13(7): CAA 1990, s. 81(1) (part), (1A) (part).

Cross references – S. 46(2): expenditure to which s. 13 applies is not first-year qualifying expenditure under s. 40 (expenditure incurred for Northern Ireland purposes by small and medium-sized companies), 44 (expenditure incurred by small or medium-sized companies) or 45 (ICT expenditure incurred by small enterprises), subject to s. 161 (pre-trading expenditure on mineral exploration and access).
S. 84, Table, Item 1: short-life asset treatment is ruled out where expenditure is treated as incurred for the purposes of a qualifying activity under s. 13.
S. 218, s. 224: restriction on qualifying expenditure in certain sale and leasebacks etc.
ICTA 1988, Sch. 19AC, para. 10B(2A): s. 13 applies where an asset or part of an asset held by an overseas life insurance company ceases to be a non-UK asset.
ICTA 1988, Sch. 24, para. 10(1): where a company incurs capital expenditure on the provision of plant or machinery for its trade before the first accounting period in respect of which an apportionment is made under ICTA 1988, s. 747(3), or which is an ADP exempt period, that expenditure is treated as provided for purposes other than the trade, and as not having been brought into use for the purposes of the trade until the start of that accounting period, and s. 13 applies accordingly.
FA 2000, s. 75(3): application of s. 13 where asset acquired after entry into tonnage tax and begins to be used for a qualifying activity carried on by the company.
FA 2003, s. 176 and Sch. 36, para. 17(3) and 19: modified application of this section in relation to foster carers.

Transitional – Sch. 3, para. 11: s. 13(4) and (5) do not apply if the plant or machinery was brought into use before 21 March 2000.

HMRC Manuals – CA23030: guidance on s. 13.

CAA 2001

13A Use for other purposes of plant or machinery previously used for long funding leasing

13A(1) This section applies if a person who has been using plant or machinery for the purpose of leasing it under a long funding lease (see Chapter 6A)–

(a) ceases to use the plant or machinery for that purpose without ceasing to use it for the purposes of a qualifying activity carried on by him, and

(b) on the date of the cessation, owns the plant or machinery as a result of having incurred capital expenditure on its provision for the purposes of the qualifying activity.

13A(2) The person is to be treated–

(a) as having incurred capital expenditure ("notional expenditure") on the provision of the plant or machinery for the purposes of the qualifying activity on the day after the cessation,

(b) as owning the plant or machinery as a result of having incurred that expenditure, and

(c) as if the plant or machinery on and after that day were different plant or machinery from the plant or machinery before that day.

13A(3) The amount of the notional expenditure is an amount equal to the termination amount, determined in accordance with section 70YG, in the case of the long funding lease under which the plant or machinery was last leased before the cessation.

History – S. 13A inserted by FA 2006, s. 81 and Sch. 8, para. 2. The commencement and transitional provisions are complex and are set out in full in FA 2006, Sch. 8, para. 15–27.

13B Use for other purposes of plant or machinery: property businesses

13B(1) This section applies if a person who has been using plant or machinery for the purposes of a relevant qualifying activity–

(a) ceases to use the plant or machinery for that purpose without ceasing to use it for the purposes of another relevant qualifying activity ("the other activity") carried on by the person, and

(b) on the date of the cessation, owns the plant or machinery as a result of having incurred capital expenditure on its provision for the purposes of the other activity.

13B(2) The person is to be treated–

(a) as having incurred capital expenditure ("notional expenditure") on the provision of the plant or machinery for the purposes of the other activity on the day after the cessation,

(b) as owning the plant or machinery as a result of having incurred that expenditure, and

(c) as if the plant or machinery on or after that day were different plant or machinery from the plant or machinery before that day.

13B(3) Subject to subsection (4), the amount of the notional expenditure is the market value of the plant or machinery on the date of cessation.

13B(4) If the market value is greater than the actual expenditure, the amount of the notional expenditure is the amount of the actual expenditure.

13B(5) **"Relevant qualifying activity"** means–

(a) ordinary UK property business or UK furnished holiday lettings business, or

(b) ordinary overseas property business or EEA furnished holiday lettings business,

(as the case may be).

History – S. 13B inserted by FA 2011, s. 52 and Sch. 14, para. 12(2), with effect in relation to chargeable periods beginning on or after 1 April 2011 (for corporation tax purposes), and in relation to chargeable periods beginning on or after 6 April 2011 (for income tax purposes).

14 Use for qualifying activity of plant or machinery which is a gift

14(1) This section applies if a person–

(a) is the owner of plant or machinery as a result of a gift, and

(b) brings the plant or machinery into use for the purposes of a qualifying activity carried on by him.

14(2) The person is to be treated–

(a) as having incurred capital expenditure on the provision of the plant or machinery for the purposes of the qualifying activity on the date on which it is brought into use for those purposes, and

(b) as owning the plant or machinery as a result of having incurred that expenditure.

14(3) The amount of that capital expenditure is to be treated as being the market value of the plant or machinery on the date when it was brought into use for the purposes of the qualifying activity.

14(4) The question whether the provision of the plant or machinery is to be treated as wholly or only partly for the purposes of the qualifying activity is to be determined according to whether the use referred to in subsection (1)(b) is wholly or only partly for those purposes.

14(5) This section is subject to section 161 (pre-trading expenditure on mineral exploration and access).

Origin – S. 14(1): CAA 1990, s. 81(1) (part).
S. 14(2), (3): CAA 1990, s. 81(1) (part), (1A)(b) (part).
S. 14(4): CAA 1990, s. 81(2) (part).
S. 14(5): CAA 1990, s. 8192) (part), (1A) (part).

Cross references – S. 46(2): expenditure to which s. 14 applies is not first-year qualifying expenditure under s. 40 (expenditure incurred for Northern Ireland purposes by small and medium-sized companies), s. 44 (expenditure incurred by small or medium-sized companies) or 45 (ICT expenditure incurred by small enterprises), subject to s. 161 (pre-trading expenditure on mineral exploration and access).
S. 84, Table, Item 1: short-life asset treatment is ruled out where expenditure is treated as incurred for the purposes of a qualifying activity under s. 14.
S. 213(3)(a): where a person brings plant or machinery received as a gift into use for business purposes, he is treated for the purposes of Pt. 2, Ch. 17 (anti-avoidance) as having incurred capital expenditure in buying the plant or machinery from the donor.

Transitional – Sch. 3, para. 12: where plant or machinery brought into use before 27 July 1989, s. 14 does not apply unless donor required to bring into account a disposal value equal to the market value of the plant or machinery.

HMRC Manuals – CA23040: guidance on s. 14.

Chapter 2 – Qualifying Activities

15 Qualifying activities

15(1) Each of the following is a qualifying activity for the purposes of this Part–

(a) a trade,
(b) an ordinary UK property business,
(c) a UK furnished holiday lettings business,
(d) an ordinary overseas property business,
(da) an EEA furnished holiday lettings business,
(e) a profession or vocation,
(f) a concern listed in section 12(4) of ITTOIA 2005 or section 39(4) of CTA 2009 (mines, transport undertakings etc.),
(g) managing the investments of a company with investment business,
(h) special leasing of plant or machinery, and
(i) an employment or office,

but to the extent only that the profits or gains from the activity are, or (if there were any) would be, chargeable to tax.

15(2) Subsection (1) is subject to the following provisions of this Part.

15(2A) A business carried on through one or more permanent establishments outside the United Kingdom by a company in relation to which an election under section 18A of CTA 2009 has effect–

(a) is an activity separate from any other activity of the company, and
(b) is to be regarded as an activity all the profits and gains from which are not, or (if there were any) would not be, chargeable to tax.

15(2B) Subsection (2A) does not apply to the business so far as it consists of a plant or machinery lease under which the company is a lessor if any profits or losses arising from the lease are to be left out of account as mentioned in section 18C(3) of CTA 2009.

15(3) This section, in so far as it provides for–

(a) an ordinary UK property business,
(b) an ordinary overseas property business, or
(c) special leasing of plant or machinery,

to be a qualifying activity, needs to be read with section 35 (expenditure on plant or machinery for use in a dwelling-house not qualifying expenditure in certain cases).

15(4) Also, subsection (1)(i) needs to be read with sections 36 (restriction on qualifying expenditure in case of employment or office) and 80 (vehicles provided for purposes of employment or office).

Prospective amendments – S. 15(2ZA) and (2ZB) inserted by CTNIA 2015, s. 2 and Sch. 1, para. 4, with effect from 26 March 2015 (Royal Assent) in respect of any power to make regulations and with effect in relation to accounting periods beginning on or after the first day of the appointed financial year for other provisions (see CTNIA 2015, s. 5). See also transitional provisions at Sch. 1, para. 19–21.

History – In s. 15(1)(b), the word "UK" inserted after "ordinary" by FA 2011, s. 52 and Sch. 14, para. 12(3)(a), with effect in relation to chargeable periods beginning on or after 1 April 2011 (for corporation tax purposes), and in relation to chargeable periods beginning on or after 6 April 2011 (for income tax purposes).

In s. 15(1)(c), the words "UK furnished" substituted for "furnished" by FA 2011, s. 52 and Sch. 14, para. 12(3)(b), with effect in relation to chargeable periods beginning on or after 1 April 2011 (for corporation tax purposes), and in relation to chargeable periods beginning on or after 6 April 2011 (for income tax purposes).
In s. 15(1)(d), the words "ordinary overseas" substituted for "overseas" by FA 2011, s. 52 and Sch. 14, para. 12(3)(c), with effect in relation to chargeable periods beginning on or after 1 April 2011 (for corporation tax purposes), and in relation to chargeable periods beginning on or after 6 April 2011 (for income tax purposes).
S. 15(1)(da) inserted by FA 2011, s. 52 and Sch. 14, para. 12(3)(d), with effect in relation to chargeable periods beginning on or after 1 April 2011 (for corporation tax purposes), and in relation to chargeable periods beginning on or after 6 April 2011 (for income tax purposes).
In s. 15(1)(f), the words "section 39(4) of CTA 2009" substituted for the words "section 55(2) of ICTA" by CTA 2009, s. 1322 and Sch. 1, para. 476, with effect for corporation tax purposes for accounting periods ending on or after 1 April 2009, and for income tax and capital gains tax purposes for the tax year 2009–10 and subsequent tax years.
S. 15(1)(g) substituted by SI 2004/2310, Schedule, para. 52(2), with effect in relation to accounting periods beginning on or after 1 April 2004 subject to the provisions of FA 2004, s. 43 and 44.
In s. 15(1) the word "property" in paragraph (b) substituted for "Schedule A", and the words "section 12(4) of ITTOIA 2005 or" in paragraph (f) inserted, by ITTOIA 2005, s. 882(1) and Sch. 1, para. 526; in each case effective for income tax purposes for 2005–06 onwards and for corporation tax purposes for accounting periods ending after 5 April 2005 (ITTOIA 2005, s. 883(1)).
S. 15(2A) inserted by FA 2011, s. 48 and Sch. 13, para. 15, with effect from 19 July 2011.
S. 15(2B) inserted by FA 2012, s. 180 and Sch. 20, para. 9 with effect in relation to accounting periods beginning on or after 1 January 2013.
In s. 15(3) the word "property" substituted for "Schedule A" by ITTOIA 2005, s. 882(1) and Sch. 1, para. 526(2); effective for income tax purposes for 2005–06 onwards and for corporation tax purposes for accounting periods ending after 5April 2005 (ITTOIA 2005, s. 883(1)).
In s. 15(3)(a), the word "UK" inserted after "ordinary" by FA 2011, s. 52 and Sch. 14, para. 12(3)(e), with effect in relation to chargeable periods beginning on or after 1 April 2011 (for corporation tax purposes), and in relation to chargeable periods beginning on or after 6 April 2011 (for income tax purposes).
In s. 15(3)(b), the words "ordinary overseas" substituted for "overseas" by FA 2011, s. 52 and Sch. 14, para. 12(3)(f), with effect in relation to chargeable periods beginning on or after 1 April 2011 (for corporation tax purposes), and in relation to chargeable periods beginning on or after 6 April 2011 (for income tax purposes).

Origin – S. 15(1)(a): CAA 1990, s. 22(1)(a) (part), s. 24(1)(a) (part).
S. 15(1)(b): CAA 1990, s. 28A(1) (part).
S. 15(1)(c): CAA 1990, s. 29(1) (part).
S. 15(1)(d): CAA 1990, s. 28A(1) (part), s. 161(2A) (part).
S. 15(1)(e): CAA 1990, s. 27(1) (part).
S. 15(1)(f): Annex 1, Change 1.
S. 15(1)(g): CAA 1990, s. 28(1) (part), Annex 2, Note 8.
S. 15(1)(h): CAA 1990, s. 61(1) (part).
S. 15(1)(i): CAA 1990, s. 27(1) (part).
Concluding words: CAA 1990, s. 83(2A) (part).
S. 15(2): Drafting.
S. 15(3): CAA 1990, s. 28A(3) (part), s. 61(2) (part), s. 161(2A) (part).
S. 15(4): CAA 1990, s. 27(1) (part), s. 29(1) (part).

Cross references – S. 20(1): restricted meaning of "employment" (in s. 15(1)(i)) in relation to divers and diving supervisors.
S. 105(6): meaning of "qualifying activity" for purposes of overseas leasing provisions.
S. 216(2): restriction of allowances where there are sale and leaseback transactions – where seller continues to use plant and machinery for a qualifying activity – meaning of "qualifying activity".
S. 253(2): giving relief for capital allowances, in respect of investment companies.
S. 263(2): meaning of "qualifying activity" where a qualifying activity is carried on in partnership, and there is a partnership change which is not treated as a permanent discontinuance.
S. 265(1)(b): meaning of "qualifying activity" where a qualifying activity is carried on in partnership, and is treated as discontinued on a partnership change.
S. 268(8): meaning of "qualifying activity" where a beneficiary succeeds to a qualifying activity which was carried on by a deceased person, and the beneficiary elects for plant and machinery to be treated as sold to the beneficiary when the succession takes place.
ICTA 1988, s. 75: allowances to be added to a company's expenses of management in any accounting period under s. 15(1)(g).

Rewrite: Changes in Law – Explanatory Notes, Annex 1, Change 1: s. 15(1)(f) treats any concern listed in ICTA 1988, s. 55(2) (mines, quarries etc) as a qualifying activity, and s. 252 enables effect to be given to plant and machinery allowances in the case of s. 55 concerns. Previously, while ICTA 1988, s. 55(1) charged the profits of such concerns to tax under Sch. D, Case I, that does not mean that they were necessarily trades, and they could not be regarded as Sch. A businesses because of para. 2(2)(a) of Sch. A (see ICTA 1988, s. 15(1)).

Rewrite: Technical Points – Explanatory Notes, Annex 2, Note 8: redundancy of words "the business of" where they appeared in CAA 1990, s. 28(1) and (4), "management of the business of an investment company" (s. 15(1)(g) now refers to "the management of an investment company" and ICTA 1988, s. 75 to "the management of a company").

HMRC Manuals – CA20010: guidance on s. 15.

16 Ordinary UK property businesses

History – In the heading to s. 16, the word "UK" inserted after "Ordinary" by FA 2011, s. 52 and Sch. 14, para. 12(4)(a), with effect in relation to chargeable periods beginning on or after 1 April 2011 (for corporation tax purposes), and in relation to chargeable periods beginning on or after 6 April 2011 (for income tax purposes).
The heading to s. 16 substituted by ITTOIA 2005, s. 882(1) and Sch. 1, para. 527; effective for income tax purposes for 2005–06 onwards and for corporation tax purposes for accounting periods ending after 5 April 2005 (ITTOIA 2005, s. 883(1)).

In this Part **"ordinary UK property business"** means a UK property business except in so far as it is a UK furnished holiday lettings business.

History – In s. 16, the word "UK" inserted after "ordinary" by FA 2011, s. 52 and Sch. 14, para. 12(4)(b), with effect in relation to chargeable periods beginning on or after 1 April 2011 (for corporation tax purposes), and in relation to chargeable periods beginning on or after 6 April 2011 (for income tax purposes).
In s. 16, the words "UK furnished" substituted for "furnished" by FA 2011, s. 52 and Sch. 14, para. 12(4)(c), with effect in relation to chargeable periods beginning on or after 1 April 2011 (for corporation tax purposes), and in relation to chargeable periods beginning on or after 6 April 2011 (for income tax purposes).
In s. 16, the words ", or a Schedule A business,", which appeared after the words "a UK property business", omitted by CTA 2009, s. 1322 and Sch. 1, para. 477 and repealed by CTA 2009, s. 1326 and Sch. 3, Pt. 1, with effect for corporation tax purposes for

accounting periods ending on or after 1 April 2009, and for income tax and capital gains tax purposes for the tax year 2009–10 and subsequent tax years.
In s. 16 the words "ordinary property" substituted for "ordinary Schedule A" (in both the heading and the text of the section), and the words "means a UK property business, or a Schedule A business," substituted for "means a Schedule A business", by ITTOIA 2005, s. 882(1) and Sch. 1, para. 527; effective for income tax purposes for 2005–06 onwards and for corporation tax purposes for accounting periods ending after 5 April 2005 (ITTOIA 2005, s. 883(1)).

Origin – CAA 1990, s. 28A(1) (part), s. 29(1) (part).

HMRC Manuals – CA20020: guidance on s. 16.

17 UK furnished holiday lettings businesses

History – In the heading to s. 17, the words "UK furnished" substituted for "Furnished" by FA 2011, s. 52 and Sch. 14, para. 12(5)(a), with effect in relation to chargeable periods beginning on or after 1 April 2011 (for corporation tax purposes), and in relation to chargeable periods beginning on or after 6 April 2011 (for income tax purposes).

17(1) In this Part **"UK furnished holiday lettings business"** means a UK property business which consists in, or so far as it consists in, the commercial letting of furnished holiday accommodation.

17(2) All such commercial lettings of furnished holiday accommodation made by a particular person or partnership or body of persons are to be treated as one qualifying activity.

17(3) For the purposes of income tax the **"commercial letting of furnished holiday accommodation"** has the same meaning as it has for the purposes of Chapter 6 of Part 3 of ITTOIA 2005.

For the purposes of corporation tax the **"commercial letting of furnished holiday accommodation"** has the same meaning as it has for the purposes of Chapter 6 of Part 4 of CTA 2009 (see section 265).

17(4) If there is a letting of accommodation only part of which is holiday accommodation, such apportionments are to be made for the purposes of this section as are just and reasonable.

History – In s. 17(1), the words "UK furnished" substituted for "furnished" by FA 2011, s. 52 and Sch. 14, para. 12(5)(b), with effect in relation to chargeable periods beginning on or after 1 April 2011 (for corporation tax purposes), and in relation to chargeable periods beginning on or after 6 April 2011 (for income tax purposes).
In s. 17(1), the words ", or a Schedule A business,", which appeared after the words "a UK property business", omitted by CTA 2009, s. 1322 and Sch. 1, para. 478(1) and repealed by CTA 2009, s. 1326 and Sch. 3, Pt. 1, with effect for corporation tax purposes for accounting periods ending on or after 1 April 2009, and for income tax and capital gains tax purposes for the tax year 2009–10 and subsequent tax years.
In s. 17(1) the words from "a UK property business" to the end substituted by ITTOIA 2005, s. 882(1) and Sch 1, para. 528(2); effective for income tax purposes for 2005–06 onwards and for corporation tax purposes for accounting periods ending after 5 April 2005 (ITTOIA 2005, s. 883(1)).
In s. 17(2), the word "such" inserted after "All" by FA 2011, s. 52 and Sch. 14, para. 12(5)(c), with effect in relation to chargeable periods beginning on or after 1 April 2011 (for corporation tax purposes), and in relation to chargeable periods beginning on or after 6 April 2011 (for income tax purposes).
In s. 17(3), the words "has the same meaning as it has for the purposes of Chapter 6 of Part 4 of CTA 2009 (see section 265)" substituted for the words "has the meaning given by section 504 of ICTA" by CTA 2009, s. 1322 and Sch. 1, para. 478(3), with effect for corporation tax purposes for accounting periods ending on or after 1 April 2009, and for income tax and capital gains tax purposes for the tax year 2009–10 and subsequent tax years.
S. 17(3) substituted by ITTOIA 2005, s. 882(1) and Sch. 1, para. 528(3); effective for income tax purposes for 2005–06 onwards and for corporation tax purposes for accounting periods ending after 5 April 2005 (ITTOIA 2005, s. 883(1)).

Origin – S. 17(1): CAA 1990, s. 29(1) (part).
S. 17(2): ICTA 1988, s. 503(1)(b); CAA 1990, s. 29(2) (part).
S. 17(3): CAA 1990, s. 29(2) (part).
S. 17(4): CAA 1990, s. 29(3).

HMRC Manuals – CA20025: guidance on s. 17.

17A Ordinary overseas property business

17A In this Part **"ordinary overseas property business"** means an overseas property business except in so far as it is an EEA furnished holiday lettings business.

History – S. 17A inserted by FA 2011, s. 52 and Sch. 14, para. 12(6), with effect in relation to chargeable periods beginning on or after 1 April 2011 (for corporation tax purposes) and in relation to chargeable periods beginning on or after 6 April 2011 (for income tax purposes).

17B EEA furnished holiday lettings businesses

17B(1) In this Part **"EEA furnished holiday lettings business"** means an overseas property business which consists in, or so far as it consists in, the commercial letting of furnished holiday accommodation in one or more EEA states.

17B(2) All such commercial lettings of furnished holiday accommodation made by a particular person or partnership or body of persons are to be treated as one qualifying activity.

17B(3) Subsections (3) and (4) of section 17 are to apply for the purposes of this section as they apply for the purposes of that section.

History – S. 17B inserted by FA 2011, s. 52 and Sch. 14, para. 12(6), with effect in relation to chargeable periods beginning on or after 1 April 2011 (for corporation tax purposes), and in relation to chargeable periods beginning on or after 6 April 2011 (for income tax purposes).

18 Managing the investments of a company with investment business

18(1) For the purposes of this Part, managing the investments of a company with investment business consists of pursuing those purposes expenditure on which would be treated as expenses of management within section 1219 of CTA 2009.

18(2) In this Part **"company with investment business"** has the meaning given by "section 1218B of CTA 2009".

History – In s. 18(1), the words "section 1219 of CTA 2009" substituted for the words "section 75 of ICTA" by CTA 2009, s. 1322 and Sch. 1, para. 479(2), with effect for corporation tax purposes for accounting periods ending on or after 1 April 2009, and for income tax and capital gains tax purposes for the tax year 2009–10 and subsequent tax years.
In s. 18(2), "section 1218B" substituted for "section 1218" by FA 2013, s. 36 and Sch. 18, para. 21(4), with effect (for purposes other than television tax relief) from 1 April 2014 (SI 2014/1962) in relation to accounting periods beginning on or after "the relevant day" (as defined in FA 2013, Sch. 18, para. 23).
In s. 18(2), "section 1218B" substituted for "section 1218" by FA 2013, s. 36 and Sch. 18, para. 21(4), with effect for television tax relief from 19 July 2013 (SI 2013/1817) in relation to accounting periods beginning on or after "the relevant day" (as defined in FA 2013, Sch. 18, para. 23).
In s. 18(2), the words "section 1218 of CTA 2009" substituted for the words "section 130 of ICTA" by CTA 2009, s. 1322 and Sch. 1, para. 479(3), with effect for corporation tax purposes for accounting periods ending on or after 1 April 2009, and for income tax and capital gains tax purposes for the tax year 2009–10 and subsequent tax years.
S. 18 substituted by SI 2004/2310, Schedule, para. 53, with effect in relation to accounting periods beginning on or after 1 April 2004 subject to the provisions of FA 2004, s. 43 and 44.

Origin – S. 18(1): CAA 1990, s. 28(4), Annex 2, Note 8.
S. 18(2): CAA 1990, s. 28(1) (part).

Rewrite: Technical Points – Explanatory Notes, Annex 2, Note 8: redundancy of words "the business of" where they appeared in CAA 1990, s. 28(1) and (4), "management of the business of an investment company" (s. 18(1) now refers to "the management of an investment company" and ICTA 1988, s. 75 to "the management of a company").

HMRC Manuals – CA20050: guidance on s. 18.

19 Special leasing of plant or machinery

19(1) In this Part **"special leasing"**, in relation to plant or machinery, means hiring out the plant or machinery otherwise than in the course of any other qualifying activity (and references to a lessor or lessee in the context of special leasing are to be read accordingly).

19(2) A qualifying activity consisting of special leasing of plant or machinery begins when the plant or machinery is first hired out in the circumstances given in subsection (1).

19(3) A qualifying activity consisting of special leasing of plant or machinery is permanently discontinued if the lessor permanently ceases to hire out the plant or machinery otherwise than in the course of any other qualifying activity.

19(4) A person who has more than one item of plant or machinery that is the subject of special leasing has a separate qualifying activity in relation to each item.

19(5) If a company carrying on any long-term business–

(a) hires out plant or machinery which is an investment asset (as defined by section 545(2)), and

(b) does not do so in the course of a property business,

the company is to be treated for the purposes of subsection (1) as hiring out the plant or machinery otherwise than in the course of a qualifying activity.

History – In s. 19(5), "long-term business" substituted for "life assurance business" by FA 2012, s. 146 and Sch. 16, para. 95 in relation to accounting periods beginning on or after 1 January 2013 (FA 2012, s. 148) but subject to transitional provisions in FA 2012, Sch. 17. Where an accounting period would otherwise straddle 1 January 2013, it is deemed to end on 31 December 2012 (FA 2012, s. 149).

Origin – S. 19(1): CAA 1990, s. 61(1) (part), Annex 2, Note 9.
S. 19(2): CAA 1990, s. 61(1) (part).
S. 19(3): CAA 1990, s. 61(1) (part), Annex 1, Change 15.
S. 19(4): CAA 1990, s. 61(1) (part).
S. 19(5): ICTA 1988, s. 434E(1) (part), (2).

Cross references – S. 84, Table, Item 2: short-life asset treatment is ruled out where plant or machinery is the subject of special leasing as defined by s. 19.
S. 261: restrictions on carrying back excess allowances from special leasing etc. where a company carries on life assurance business.
FA 1993, s. 92: general rule that exchange profits and losses for corporation tax must be computed and expressed in sterling.

Rewrite: Changes in Law – Explanatory Notes, Annex 1, Change 15: s. 19(3), read together with s. 65(1), produces the result that there is a final chargeable period (which may give rise to a balancing allowance) if the chargeable period is one in which the taxpayer permanently ceases to hire out the plant or machinery otherwise than in the course of the qualifying activity. Under CAA 1990, s. 61(1)(b), when the lessor permanently ceased to let the machinery or plant otherwise than in the course of a trade, the machinery or plant was treated as being used wholly for purposes other than those of the deemed trade. There was no indication as to when the deemed trade was to be regarded as "permanently discontinued", so there was doubt as to whether a balancing allowance could arise. The rewrite resolves the matter in favour of the taxpayer by making it clear that a balancing allowance can arise in this final chargeable period.

Rewrite: Technical Points – Explanatory Notes, Annex 2, Note 9: unnecessary to reflect words of CAA 1990, s. 61 "whether or not it is used for the purposes of a trade carried on by the lessee" in s. 19 as those words were originally inserted in ITA 1952, s. 298 in response to a decided case (*Macsaga Investments Co Ltd v Lupton* (1967) 44 TC 659) and the legislative context has changed. Also, view of consultees adopted that it is safe to change the terminology from "let" to "hiring out".

Statements of practice – SP 3/91: finance lease rental payments where SSAP 21 (accounting for leases) is applied and where it is not applied – does not affect availability of capital allowances to the lessor.

HMRC Manuals – CA20040: guidance on s. 19.

Other material – HMRC press release, 27 October 1986: clarification of the tax treatment of leases following SSAP 21 (accounting for leases).
ICAEW Technical Release TR 588: application of the Ramsay principle to leasing.
Taxline 94/10 (not reproduced): Revenue took view, based on the pre-rewrite legislation, that a "deemed trade" did not count for the purposes of CAA 1990, s. 77 (now CAA 2001, s. 266 – election where predecessor and successor are connected persons). Given the language of the rewritten legislation, where both actual trades and deemed trades are subsumed within the concept of "qualifying activity", it is doubtful that this view is still tenable.

20 Employments and offices

20(1) In section 15(1)(i) **"employment"** does not include an employment the performance of the duties of which is treated as the carrying on of a trade under section 15 of ITTOIA 2005 (divers and diving supervisors in the North Sea etc.).

20(2) Subsection (3) applies if the earnings for any duties of an employment or office fall within section 22 or 26 of ITEPA 2003.

20(3) This Part applies in relation to–

(a) those earnings, or

(b) any other taxable earnings (as defined by section 10 of ITEPA 2003) of the employment or office,

as if the performance of the duties did not belong to that employment or office.

History – In s. 20(1), the reference to section 15 of ITTOIA 2005 substituted for the reference to "section 314 of ICTA", effective for income tax purposes for 2005–06 onwards and for corporation tax purposes for accounting periods ending after 5 April 2005 (ITTOIA 2005, s. 883(1)).
In s. 20(2), the word "earnings" substituted for the word "emoluments" by ITEPA 2003, Sch. 6, para. 248(2)(a) which has effect, for income tax purposes, for the tax year 2003–04 and subsequent tax years and, for corporation tax purposes, for accounting periods ending after 5 April 2003.
In s. 20(2), the words "fall within section 22 or 26 of ITEPA 2003" substituted for the words "do not fall within Case I or II of Schedule E" by ITEPA 2003, Sch. 6, para. 248(2)(b) which has effect, for income tax purposes, for the tax year 2003–04 and subsequent tax years and, for corporation tax purposes, for accounting periods ending after 5 April 2003.
In s. 20(3), the words "those earnings" substituted for the words "those emoluments" by ITEPA 2003, Sch. 6, para. 248(3)(a) which has effect, for income tax purposes, for the tax year 2003–04 and subsequent tax years and, for corporation tax purposes, for accounting periods ending after 5 April 2003.
In s. 20(3), the words "other taxable earnings (as defined by section 10 of ITEPA 2003)" substituted for the words "other emoluments" by ITEPA 2003, Sch. 6, para. 248(3)(b) which has effect, for income tax purposes, for the tax year 2003–04 and subsequent tax years and, for corporation tax purposes, for accounting periods ending after 5 April 2003.

Origin – S. 20(1): ICTA 1988, s. 314(1) (part), CAA 1990, s. 27(1) (part).
S. 20(2), (3): ICTA 1988, s. 198(2) (part).

HMRC Manuals – CA20015: guidance on s. 20.

Chapter 3 – Qualifying Expenditure

BUILDINGS, STRUCTURES AND LAND

21 Buildings

21(1) For the purposes of this Act, expenditure on the provision of plant or machinery does not include expenditure on the provision of a building.

21(2) The provision of a building includes its construction or acquisition.

21(3) In this section, **"building"** includes an asset which–

(a) is incorporated in the building,

(b) although not incorporated in the building (whether because the asset is moveable or for any other reason), is in the building and is of a kind normally incorporated in a building, or

(c) is in, or connected with, the building and is in list A.

LIST A
ASSETS TREATED AS BUILDINGS

1. Walls, floors, ceilings, doors, gates, shutters, windows and stairs.
2. Mains services, and systems, for water, electricity and gas.
3. Waste disposal systems.
4 Sewerage and drainage systems.
5. Shafts or other structures in which lifts, hoists, escalators and moving walkways are installed.
6. Fire safety systems.

21(4) This section is subject to section 23.

Origin – S. 21(1): CAA 1990, Sch. AA1, para. 1(1).
S. 21(2): CAA 1990, Sch. AA1, para. 5(1) (part).
S. 21(3): CAA 1990, Sch. AA1, para. 1(2).

List A: CAA 1990, Sch. AA1, para. 1, Table 1, col. (1).
S. 21(4): drafting.

Transitional – Sch. 3, para. 13: s. 21–24 do not apply in relation to expenditure incurred before 30 November 1993, or before 6 April 1996 under a contract entered into before 30 November 1993, or one entered into on or after 30 November 1993 which confirms pre-existing obligations.

Hansard – HC Debates, 10 March 1994, col. 620: statement by the Financial Secretary to the Treasury that the provisions of CAA 1990, Sch. AA1 (the precursor to s. 21–24) "will not remove entitlement to capital allowances from any taxpayer who is entitled to it under the present state of case law".

HMRC Manuals – CA21010: meaning of plant and machinery: Revenue overview.
CA22010: guidance on buildings which are not plant.
CA22000: guidance on s. 21–23.

Other material – Taxline 1995/51 (not reproduced): whether lift shafts, mechanically operated doors and gates and cold stores are plant.
Inland Revenue letter, Taxation Practitioner, Finance Act 1994 Capital Allowances provisions, August 1994 (not reproduced): CAA 1990, Sch. AA1 (the precursor to s. 21–24) aimed to strengthen the then existing plant/structure boundary and to ensure that no further erosion by judicial decisions took place. In practice, the tax treatment of specific assets was expected to be less uncertain than it had been.
In CAA 1990, Sch. AA1, para. 1(2)(b) words "moveable or otherwise" (see s. 21(3)(b) words in parentheses) are aimed at modern building techniques which, e.g., permit an entire room (such as a toilet) to be placed in a building as a complete module.

22 Structures, assets and works

22(1) For the purposes of this Act, expenditure on the provision of plant or machinery does not include expenditure on–

(a) the provision of a structure or other asset in list B, or

(b) any works involving the alteration of land.

LIST B
EXCLUDED STRUCTURES AND OTHER ASSETS

1. A tunnel, bridge, viaduct, aqueduct, embankment or cutting.
2. A way, hard standing (such as a pavement), road, railway, tramway, a park for vehicles or containers, or an airstrip or runway.
3. An inland navigation, including a canal or basin or a navigable river.
4. A dam, reservoir or barrage, including any sluices, gates, generators and other equipment associated with the dam, reservoir or barrage.
5. A dock, harbour, wharf, pier, marina or jetty or any other structure in or at which vessels may be kept, or merchandise or passengers may be shipped or unshipped.
6. A dike, sea wall, weir or drainage ditch.
7. Any structure not within items 1 to 6 other than–
   (a) a structure (but not a building) within Chapter 2 of Part 3 (meaning of "industrial building"),
   (b) a structure in use for the purposes of an undertaking for the extraction, production, processing or distribution of gas, and
   (c) a structure in use for the purposes of a trade which consists in the provision of telecommunication, television or radio services.

22(2) The provision of a structure or other asset includes its construction or acquisition.

22(3) In this section–

(a) **"structure"** means a fixed structure of any kind, other than a building (as defined by section 21(3)), and

(b) **"land"** does not include buildings or other structures, but otherwise has the meaning given in Schedule 1 to the Interpretation Act 1978.

22(4) This section is subject to section 23.

Origin – S. 22(1): CAA 1990, Sch. AA1, para. 2(1), (2).
List B: CAA 1990, Sch. AA1, para. 2, Table 2, col. (1).
S. 22(2): CAA 1990, Sch. AA1, para. 5(1) (part).
S. 22(3): CAA 1990, Sch. AA1, para. 5(1) (part), (3) (part).
S. 22(4): drafting.

Transitional – Sch. 3, para. 13: s. 21–24 do not apply in relation to expenditure incurred before 30 November 1993, or before 6 April 1996 under a contract entered into before 30 November 1993, or one entered into on or after 30 November 1993 which confirms pre-existing obligations.

Hansard – HC Debates, 10 March 1994, col. 620: statement by the Financial Secretary to the Treasury that the provisions of CAA 1990, Sch. AA1 (the precursor to s. 21–24) "will not remove entitlement to capital allowances from any taxpayer who is entitled to it under the present state of case law".

HMRC Manuals – CA22000: guidance on s. 21–23.
CA22020: guidance on buildings and structures which are not plant.

Other material – HMRC Brief 32/12: guidance relating to treatment of capital expenditure on polytunnels.
Taxline 1995/51 (not reproduced): whether lift shafts, mechanically operated doors and gates and cold stores are plant.

Inland Revenue letter, Taxation Practitioner, Finance Act 1994 Capital Allowances provisions, August 1994 (not reproduced): CAA 1990, Sch. AA1 (the precursor to s. 21–24) aimed to strengthen the then existing plant/structure boundary and to ensure that no further erosion by judicial decisions took place. In practice, the tax treatment of specific assets was expected to be less uncertain than it had been. Item 7(a)–(c) in List B is intended to let out assets which are within the definition in Pt. 3, Ch. 2. Such assets may come within other headings in List B and not be let out by List C or any of the other provisions.

23 Expenditure unaffected by sections 21 and 22

23(1) Sections 21 and 22 do not apply to any expenditure to which any of the provisions listed in subsection (2) applies.

23(2) The provisions are–

section 28 (thermal insulation of buildings);

section 33 (personal security);

section 33A (integral features);

section 71 (software and rights to software);

section 143 of ITTOIA 2005 or section 40D of F(No.2)A 1992 (election relating to tax treatment of films expenditure).

23(3) Sections 21 and 22 also do not affect the question whether expenditure on any item described in list C is, for the purposes of this Act, expenditure on the provision of plant or machinery.

23(4) But items 1 to 16 of list C do not include any asset whose principal purpose is to insulate or enclose the interior of a building or to provide an interior wall, floor or ceiling which (in each case) is intended to remain permanently in place.

LIST C

EXPENDITURE UNAFFECTED BY SECTIONS 21 AND 22

1. Machinery (including devices for providing motive power) not within any other item in this list.
2. Gas and sewerage systems provided mainly–
   (a) to meet the particular requirements of the qualifying activity, or
   (b) to serve particular plant or machinery used for the purposes of the qualifying activity.
3. [Omitted by FA 2008, s. 73(1)(b)(ii).]
4. Manufacturing or processing equipment; storage equipment (including cold rooms); display equipment; and counters, checkouts and similar equipment.
5. Cookers, washing machines, dishwashers, refrigerators and similar equipment; washbasins, sinks, baths, showers, sanitary ware and similar equipment; and furniture and furnishings.
6. Hoists.
7. Sound insulation provided mainly to meet the particular requirements of the qualifying activity.
8. Computer, telecommunication and surveillance systems (including their wiring or other links).
9. Refrigeration or cooling equipment.
10. Fire alarm systems; sprinkler and other equipment for extinguishing or containing fires.
11. Burglar alarm systems.
12. Strong rooms in bank or building society premises; safes.
13. Partition walls, where moveable and intended to be moved in the course of the qualifying activity.
14. Decorative assets provided for the enjoyment of the public in hotel, restaurant or similar trades.
15. Advertising hoardings; signs, displays and similar assets.
16. Swimming pools (including diving boards, slides and structures on which such boards or slides are mounted).
17. Any glasshouse constructed so that the required environment (namely, air, heat, light, irrigation and temperature) for the growing of plants is provided automatically by means of devices forming an integral part of its structure.
18. Cold stores.
19. Caravans provided mainly for holiday lettings.
20. Buildings provided for testing aircraft engines run within the buildings.
21. Moveable buildings intended to be moved in the course of the qualifying activity.
22. The alteration of land for the purpose only of installing plant or machinery.

LIST C
EXPENDITURE UNAFFECTED BY SECTIONS 21 AND 22

23. The provision of dry docks.

24. The provision of any jetty or similar structure provided mainly to carry plant or machinery.

25. The provision of pipelines or underground ducts or tunnels with a primary purpose of carrying utility conduits.

26. The provision of towers to support floodlights.

27. The provision of–

(a) any reservoir incorporated into a water treatment works, or

(b) any service reservoir of treated water for supply within any housing estate or other particular locality.

28. The provision of–

(a) silos provided for temporary storage, or

(b) storage tanks.

29. The provision of slurry pits or silage clamps.

30. The provision of fish tanks or fish ponds.

31. The provision of rails, sleepers and ballast for a railway or tramway.

32. The provision of structures and other assets for providing the setting for any ride at an amusement park or exhibition.

33. The provision of fixed zoo cages.

23(5) In item 19 of list C, **"caravan"** includes, in relation to a holiday caravan site, anything that is treated as a caravan for the purposes of–

(a) the Caravan Sites and Control of Development Act 1960, or

(b) the Caravans Act (Northern Ireland) 1963.

History – In s. 23(2), the entries relating to s. 30, 31 and 32 omitted by FA 2012, s. 227 and Sch. 39, para. 34(2), with effect in relation to expenditure incurred on or after 1 April 2013 for corporation tax purposes, and 6 April 2013 for income tax purposes.
In s. 23(2), in the entry for section 28, the word "industrial" omitted by FA 2008, s. 71(7), with effect in relation to expenditure incurred on or after 1 April 2008 for corporation tax purposes and 6 April 2008 for income tax purposes.
In s. 23(2), the entry "section 29 (fire safety)" omitted by FA 2008, s. 72(2), with effect in relation to expenditure incurred on or after 1 April 2008 for corporation tax purposes and 6 April 2008 for income tax purposes.
In s. 23(2), the entry "section 33A (integral features)" inserted by FA 2008, s. 73(1), with effect in relation to expenditure incurred on or after 1 April 2008 for corporation tax purposes and 6 April 2008 for income tax purposes.
In s. 23(2) the reference to section 143 of ITTOIA 2005 inserted by ITTOIA 2005, s. 882(1) and Sch. 1, para. 528(2); effective for income tax purposes for 2005–06 onwards and for corporation tax purposes for accounting periods ending after 5 April 2005 (ITTOIA 2005, s. 883(1)).
In s. 23(4), in List C, the introductory words "Electrical systems (including lighting systems) and cold water," in item 2 omitted by FA 2008, s. 73(1)(b)(i), with effect in relation to expenditure incurred on or after 1 April 2008 for corporation tax purposes and 6 April 2008 for income tax purposes.
In s. 23(4), in List C, item 3 (which formerly read "Space or water heating systems; powered systems of ventilation, air cooling or air purification; and any floor or ceiling comprised in such systems") omitted by FA 2008, s. 73(1)(b)(ii), with effect in relation to expenditure incurred on or after 1 April 2008 for corporation tax purposes and 6 April 2008 for income tax purposes.
In s. 23(4), in List C, the word "Hoists" substituted for the words "Lifts, hoists, escalators and moving walkways" in item 6 by FA 2008, s. 73(1)(b)(iii), with effect in relation to expenditure incurred on or after 1 April 2008 for corporation tax purposes and 6 April 2008 for income tax purposes.

Origin – S. 23(1), (2): CAA 1990, Sch. AA1, para. 4.
S. 23(3): CAA 1990, Sch. AA1, para. 1(3) (part), 2(3) (part), Annex 1, Change 2.
S. 23(4): CAA 1990, Sch. AA1, para. 1, Table 1, Note 1.
List C: CAA 1990, Sch. AA1, para. 1, Table 1, para. 2, Table 2, para. 5(2).
S. 23(5): ESC B50; Annex 1, Change 3.

Rewrite: Changes in Law – Explanatory Notes, Annex 1, Change 2: merger of CAA 1990, Sch. AA1, para. 1, Table 1, col. 2 and para. 2, Table 2, col. 2 into one list, List C, potentially extends the range of circumstances in which the taxpayer may obtain plant and machinery allowances. Previously, col. 2 of each Table enumerated items unaffected by the exclusions of buildings in the one case, and structures, assets and works on the other (i.e. on a literal interpretation they were mutually exclusive). However, inclusion of substance of former CAA 1990, Sch. AA1, para. 5(2) in List C, Item 17 does not necessarily restrict its effect, as there is thought to be nothing in Sch. AA1, para. 3 or 4 which might affect the question whether the type of glasshouse described might be machinery or plant.
Annex 1, Change 3: ESC B50 (which defines "caravan") is enacted in s. 23(5).

Hansard – HC Debates, 10 March 1994, col. 620: statement by the Financial Secretary to the Treasury that the provisions of CAA 1990, Sch. AA1 (the precursor to s. 21–24) "will not remove entitlement to capital allowances from any taxpayer who is entitled to it under *the present state of case law*".

HMRC Manuals – CA22000: guidance on s. 21–23.
CA22020: guidance on buildings and structures which are not plant.
CA22030: guidance on s. 23.
CA22090: glasshouses.
CA22100: HMRC treatment of caravans.

Other material – Taxline 1995/51 (not reproduced): whether lift shafts, mechanically operated doors and gates and cold stores are plant.

Inland Revenue letter, Taxation Practitioner, Finance Act 1994 Capital Allowances provisions, August 1994 (not reproduced): CAA 1990, Sch. AA1 (the precursor to s. 21–24) aimed to strengthen the then existing plant/structure boundary and to ensure that no further erosion by judicial decisions took place. In practice, the tax treatment of specific assets was expected to be less uncertain than it had been.
In relation to item 12 in list C, the Revenue did not accept that strong rooms in banks, etc., were plant in every case; an ordinary room did not become plant because better locks were fitted, bars were put on the window, and it was called a strong room.

24 Interests in land

24(1) For the purposes of this Act, expenditure on the provision of plant or machinery does not include expenditure on the acquisition of an interest in land.

24(2) In this section **"land"** does not include–

(a) buildings or other structures, or

(b) any asset which is so installed or otherwise fixed to any description of land as to become, in law, part of the land,

but otherwise has the meaning given in Schedule 1 to the Interpretation Act 1978.

24(3) Subject to subsection (2), **"interest in land"** has the meaning given by section 175 (definitions in connection with provisions about fixtures).

Origin – S. 24(1): CAA 1990, Sch. AA1, para. 3(1).
S. 24(2): CAA 1990, Sch. AA1, para. 3(2), 5(3) (part).
S. 24(3): CAA 1990, Sch. AA1, 5(3), part.

Transitional – Sch. 3, para. 13: s. 21–24 do not apply in relation to expenditure incurred before 30 November 1993, or before 6 April 1996 under a contract entered into before 30 November 1993, or one entered into on or after 30 November 1993 which confirms pre-existing obligations.

Hansard – HC Debates, 10 March 1994, col. 620: statement by the Financial Secretary to the Treasury that the provisions of CAA 1990, Sch. AA1 (the precursor to s. 21–24) "will not remove entitlement to capital allowances from any taxpayer who is entitled to it under the present state of case law".

HMRC Manuals – CA22010: guidance on buildings and structures which are not plant.
CA22040: "land includes buildings and other structures, land covered with water, and any estate, interest, easement, servitude or right in or over land".

Other material – Taxline 1995/51 (not reproduced): whether lift shafts, mechanically operated doors and gates and cold stores are plant.
Inland Revenue letter, Taxation Practitioner, Finance Act 1994 Capital Allowances provisions, August 1994 (not reproduced): CAA 1990, Sch. AA1 (the precursor to s. 21–24) aimed to strengthen the then existing plant/structure boundary and to ensure that no further erosion by judicial decisions took place. In practice, the tax treatment of specific assets was expected to be less uncertain than it had been.

25 Building alterations connected with installation of plant or machinery

25 If a person carrying on a qualifying activity incurs capital expenditure on alterations to an existing building incidental to the installation of plant or machinery for the purposes of the qualifying activity, this Part applies as if–

(a) the expenditure were expenditure on the provision of the plant or machinery, and

(b) the works representing the expenditure formed part of the plant or machinery.

Origin – CAA 1990, s. 66.

HMRC Manuals – CA21190: guidance on s. 25.
CA21230: football ground improvements.

Other material – Revenue response to ICAEW Technical Release TR 256 (1977) (not reproduced): treatment of expenditure on "mains services" as machinery or plant or as part of the cost of the building.
Revenue letter to Football League, 25 January 1991 (not reproduced): alterations to a football stand or terrace before seats can be installed are capable of falling under s. 25.

DEMOLITION COSTS

26 Demolition costs

26(1) This section applies if–

(a) plant or machinery is demolished, and

(b) the last use of the plant or machinery was for the purposes of a qualifying activity.

26(2) If the person carrying on the qualifying activity replaces the plant or machinery with other plant or machinery then, for the purposes of this Part, the net cost of the demolition to that person is treated as expenditure incurred on the provision of the other plant or machinery.

26(3) If the person carrying on the qualifying activity does not replace the plant or machinery, the net cost of the demolition to that person is allocated to the appropriate pool for the chargeable period in which the demolition takes place.

26(4) In subsection (3)–

"the appropriate pool" means the pool to which the expenditure on the demolished plant or machinery has been or would be allocated in accordance with this Part, and

CAA 2001

"the net cost of the demolition" means the amount, if any, by which the cost of the demolition exceeds any money received for the remains of the plant or machinery.

26(5) Subsection (3) is subject to section 164(4) (general decommissioning expenditure before cessation of ring fence trade: election for special allowance) and sections 165A to 165E (restrictions on allowances: anti-avoidance).

History – In s. 26(5), the words "and sections 165A to 165E (restrictions on allowances: anti-avoidance)." inserted by FA 2013, s. 93 and Sch. 32, para. 3, with effect in relation to expenditure incurred on decommissioning carried out on or after 17 July 2013.
In s. 26(5), the words "general decommissioning expenditure" substituted for the words "abandonment expenditure" by FA 2008, s. 109 and Sch. 34, para. 3, with effect in relation to expenditure incurred on or after 12 March 2008.

Origin – S. 26(1): CAA 1990, s. 62(1) (part), Annex 1, Change 4.
S. 26(2): CAA 1990, s. 62(1)(a).
S. 26(3): CAA 1990, s. 62(1)(b).
S. 26(4): CAA 1990, s. 62(2), drafting.
S. 26(5): CAA 1990, s. 62(1) (part).

Cross references – S. 164(4)(c): s. 26(3) does not apply where election made for special allowance in respect of abandonment expenditure.
S. 164(4)(b): s. 26(3) does not apply where election made under s. 164 for a special allowance to be made in respect of abandonment expenditure incurred in respect of a ring fence trade.
S. 57(2): a person's available qualifying expenditure in a pool for a chargeable period includes any amount allocated to the pool for that period under s. 26(3).

Rewrite: Changes in Law – Explanatory Notes, Annex 1, Change 4: whereas CAA 1990, s. 62(1) applied only where plant or machinery was *in use* for the purposes of the trade when demolished; s. 26 applies where the *last use* of the plant or machinery was for the purposes of the trade. So there is no risk of taxpayers being excluded from the beneficial treatment of demolition because the plant or machinery has ceased to in use at the time when the demolition occurs.

HMRC Manuals – CA22210: how 164 Revenue deal with demolition costs.

EXPENDITURE ON THERMAL INSULATION AND PERSONAL SECURITY

27 Application of Part to thermal insulation and personal security

27(1) Subsection (2) has effect in relation to expenditure if–

(a) it is expenditure to which section 28 or 33 applies, and

(b) an allowance under Part 2 or a deduction in respect of the expenditure could not, in the absence of this section, be made in calculating the income from the qualifying activity in question.

27(2) This Part (including in particular section 11(4)) applies as if–

(a) the expenditure were capital expenditure on the provision of plant or machinery for the purposes of the qualifying activity in question, and

(b) the person who incurred the expenditure owned plant or machinery as a result of incurring it.

History – In heading to s. 27, "and personal security" substituted for ", safety measures, etc", by FA 2012, s. 227 and Sch. 39, para. 34(3), with effect in relation to expenditure incurred on or after 1 April 2013 for corporation tax purposes, and 6 April 2013 for income tax purposes.
In the heading to s. 27, "and personal security" substituted for ", safety measures, etc", by FA 2012, s. 227 and Sch. 39, para. 34(3)(b), with effect in relation to expenditure incurred on or after 1 April 2013 for corporation tax purposes, and 6 April 2013 for income tax purposes.
In s. 27(1)(a) "section 28 or 33" substituted for "any of sections 28 to 33" by FA 2012, s. 227 and Sch. 39, para. 34(3)(a), with effect in relation to expenditure incurred on or after 1 April 2013 for corporation tax purposes, and 6 April 2013 for income tax purposes.

Origin – S. 7(1): CAA 1990, s. 69(1)(b), (2) (part), s. 70(1) (part), (2) (part), s. 71(1)(c), (d), s. 161(3) (part), Annex 1, Change 5, annex 2, Note 74.
S. 27(2): CAA 1990, s. 67(1) (part), s. 69(1) (part), (2) (part), s. 70(1) (part), (2) (part), s. 71(2) (part).

Cross references – S. 63(5): if expenditure is treated under s. 27(2) as having been incurred on plant or machinery, the disposal value of the plant or machinery is nil.

Rewrite: Changes in Law – Explanatory Notes, Annex 1, Change 5: s. 27(1)(b) limits the application of s. 28–33 (under which the disposal value is treated as nil) to cases where an allowance under Pt. 2 or a deduction could not otherwise be made in respect of the expenditure. This brings the former provisions CAA 1990 s. 67, 69, 70 and 71 into line by harmonising the test to "an allowance or deduction in respect of the expenditure could not, apart from this section, be made…". In respect of former s. 69 and 70 (fire safety and safety at sports grounds) the change operates in favour of the taxpayer because the former test would have excluded relief under Pt. 2 where IBAs were available. In relation to thermal insulation (former s. 67), where previously there was no test at all, introducing one is potentially adverse to the taxpayer by denying an allowance if an allowance under Pt. 2 could already be given, or the expenditure relieved as a revenue expense.

HMRC Manuals – CA22220: guidance on s. 27.

28 Thermal insulation of buildings

28(1) This section applies to expenditure if a person carrying on a qualifying activity other than an ordinary UK property business or an ordinary overseas property business has incurred it in adding *insulation against loss of heat to* a building occupied by him for the purposes of the qualifying activity.

28(2) This section also applies to expenditure if a person carrying on a qualifying activity consisting of an ordinary UK property business or an ordinary overseas property business has incurred it in adding insulation against loss of heat to a building let by him in the course of the business.

28(2A) Subsection (2) is subject to section 35 (expenditure on plant or machinery for use in dwelling-house not qualifying expenditure).

28(2B) This section does not apply to expenditure within subsection (2) if a deduction for that expenditure is allowable–

(a) under section 251 of CTA 2009, or

(b) under section 312 of ITTOIA 2005,

(deductions for expenditure on energy-saving items).

28(2C) For the purposes of subsection (2B), whether such a deduction is allowable is to be determined without regard to subsection (1)(e) of the section in question.

28(3) [Omitted by FA 2008, s. 71(5).]

History – In the heading to s. 28, the word "industrial", which preceded the word "buildings", omitted by FA 2008, s. 71(6), with effect in relation to expenditure incurred on or after 1 April 2008 for corporation tax purposes and 6 April 2008 for income tax purposes.
In s. 28(1), the word "UK" inserted after "ordinary" and the words "ordinary overseas" substituted for the word "overseas" by FA 2011, s. 52 and Sch. 14, para. 12(7), with effect in relation to chargeable periods beginning on or after 1 April 2011 (for corporation tax purposes), and in relation to chargeable periods beginning on or after 6 April 2011 (for income tax purposes).
In s. 28(1), the words "other than an ordinary property business or an overseas property business" substituted for the words "consisting of a trade", the word "a" substituted for the words "an industrial" (which preceded the word "building") and the words "the qualifying activity" substituted for the words "the trade" by FA 2008, s. 71(2), with effect in relation to expenditure incurred on or after 1 April 2008 for corporation tax purposes and 6 April 2008 for income tax purposes.
In s. 28(2), the word "UK" inserted after "ordinary" and the words "ordinary overseas" substituted for the word "overseas" by FA 2011, s. 52 and Sch. 14, para. 12(7), with effect in relation to chargeable periods beginning on or after 1 April 2011 (for corporation tax purposes), and in relation to chargeable periods beginning on or after 6 April 2011 (for income tax purposes).
In s. 28(2), the word "a" substituted for the words "an industrial" (which preceded the word "building"), with effect in relation to expenditure incurred on or after 1 April 2008 for corporation tax purposes and 6 April 2008 for income tax purposes.
In s. 28(2) the word "property" substituted for "Schedule A" by ITTOIA 2005, s. 882(1) and Sch. 1, para. 531; effective for income tax purposes for 2005–06 onwards and for corporation tax purposes for accounting periods ending after 5 April 2005 (ITTOIA 2005, s. 883(1)).
In s. 28(2), words "or an overseas property business" inserted by FA 2001, s. 69 and Sch. 21, para. 1, with effect as respects allowances and charges falling to be made for chargeable periods ending on or after:

- 6 April 2001 for income tax purposes, and
- 1 April 2001 for corporation tax purposes.

S. 28(2A) inserted by FA 2008, s. 71(4), with effect in relation to expenditure incurred on or after 1 April 2008 for corporation tax purposes and 6 April 2008 for income tax purposes.
In s. 28(2B)(a), the words "section 251 of CTA 2009" substituted for the words "section 31ZA of ICTA" by CTA 2009, s. 1322 and Sch. 1, para. 480, with effect for corporation tax purposes for accounting periods ending on or after 1 April 2009, and for income tax and capital gains tax purposes for the tax year 2009–10 and subsequent tax years.
S. 28(2B) inserted by FA 2008, s. 71(4), with effect in relation to expenditure incurred on or after 1 April 2008 for corporation tax purposes and 6 April 2008 for income tax purposes.
S. 28(2C) inserted by FA 2008, s. 71(4), with effect in relation to expenditure incurred on or after 1 April 2008 for corporation tax purposes and 6 April 2008 for income tax purposes.
S. 28(3) omitted by FA 2008, s. 71(5), with effect in relation to expenditure incurred on or after 1 April 2008 for corporation tax purposes and 6 April 2008 for income tax purposes.

Origin – S. 28(1): CAA 1990, s. 67(1).
S. 28(2): CAA 1990, s. 67(4A).
S. 28(3): CAA 1990, s. 67(4).

HMRC Manuals – CA22220: guidance on s. 28.

29 Fire safety

29 [Omitted by FA 2008, s. 72(1)]

History – S. 29 omitted by FA 2008, s. 72(1), with effect in relation to expenditure incurred on or after 1 April 2008 for corporation tax purposes and 6 April 2008 for income tax purposes.
Former s. 29(2)-(4) omitted by SI 2005/1541, art. 53 and Sch. 2, para. 49(a) and repealed by Sch. 4, with effect from 1 April 2006.

Origin – S. 29(1): CAA 1990, s. 69(1) (part), (2) (part), drafting.
S. 29(2): CAA 1990, s. 69(1) (part).
S. 29(3): CAA 1990, s. 69(2) (part).
S. 29(4): CAA 1990, s. 69(2) (part); INA 1978, s. 17(2); Annex 2, Note 10.
S. 29(5), (6): ESC B16, Annex 1, Change 6.

Rewrite: Changes in Law – Explanatory Notes, Annex 1, Change 6: ESC B16, which extended plant and machinery allowances in respect of certain expenditure on fire safety measures to Northern Ireland, is enacted in s. 29(5) and (6).

Rewrite: Technical Points – Explanatory Notes, Annex 2, Note 10: wording of s. 29(4) ("prohibition notice", "to remedy the matters specified in the notice") is updated to reflect that of Fire Precautions Act 1971, s. 10 as substituted by Fire Safety and Places of Sport Act 1987, s. 9(1). The former enactment, CAA 1990, s. 69(2)(b), reflected the wording of Fire Precautions Act 1971, s. 10 as originally enacted.

30 Safety at designated sports grounds

30 [Repealed by FA 2012, s. 227 and Sch. 39, para. 33(a).]

History – S. 30 repealed by FA 2012, s. 227 and Sch. 39, para. 33(a), with effect in relation to expenditure incurred on or after 1 April 2013 for corporation tax purposes, and 6 April 2013 for income tax purposes.

Origin – S. 30(1): CAA 1990, s. 70(1) (part), (3), (5) (part).
S. 30(2), (3): CAA 1990, s. 70(1) (part), (5) (part).

31 Safety at regulated stands at sports grounds

31 [Repealed by FA 2012, s. 227 and Sch. 39, para. 33(b).]

History – S. 31 repealed by FA 2012, s. 227 and Sch. 39, para. 33(b), with effect in relation to expenditure incurred on or after 1 April 2013 for corporation tax purposes, and 6 April 2013 for income tax purposes.

Origin – S. 31(1)–(3): CAA 1990, s. 70(1) (part), (5) (part).

32 Safety at other sports grounds

32 [Repealed by FA 2012, s. 227 and Sch. 39, para. 33(c).]

History – S. 32 repealed by FA 2012, s. 227 and Sch. 39, para. 33(c), with effect in relation to expenditure incurred on or after 1 April 2013 for corporation tax purposes, and 6 April 2013 for income tax purposes.

Origin – S. 32(1)–(2): CAA 1990, s. 70(2) (part), (5) (part).
S. 32(3): CAA 1990, s. 70(4).
S. 32(4): CAA 1990, s. 70(2) (part), (5) (part).

33 Personal security

33(1) This section applies to expenditure if–

(a) it is incurred by an individual or partnership of individuals in connection with the provision for, or for use by, the individual, or any of the individuals, of a security asset,

(b) the individual or partnership is carrying on a relevant qualifying activity, and

(c) the special threat conditions are met.

33(2) The special threat conditions are that–

(a) the asset is provided or used to meet a threat which–

(i) is a special threat to the individual's personal physical security, and

(ii) arises wholly or mainly because of the relevant qualifying activity, and

(b) the person incurring the expenditure–

(i) has the sole object of meeting that threat in incurring that expenditure, and

(ii) intends the asset to be used solely to improve personal physical security.

33(3) If–

(a) the person incurring the expenditure intends the asset to be used solely to improve personal physical security, but

(b) there is another use which is incidental to improving personal physical security,

that other use is ignored for the purposes of this section.

33(4) The fact that an asset improves the personal physical security of any member of the family or household of the individual concerned, as well as that of the individual, does not prevent this section from applying.

33(5) If–

(a) the asset is not intended to be used solely to improve personal physical security, but the expenditure incurred on it would otherwise be expenditure to which this section applies, and

(b) the person incurring the expenditure intends the asset to be used partly to improve personal physical security,

this section applies only to the proportion of the expenditure attributable to the intended use to improve personal physical security.

33(6) In this section **"security asset"** means an asset which improves personal security; and here **"asset"**–

(a) does not include–

(i) a car, ship or aircraft, or

(ii) a dwelling or grounds appurtenant to a dwelling, but

(b) subject to paragraph (a), includes equipment, a structure (such as a wall) and an asset which becomes fixed to land.

33(7) [Omitted FA 2009, s. 30 and Sch. 11, para. 13.]

33(8) In this section **"relevant qualifying activity"** means a qualifying activity consisting of–

(a) a trade,

(b) an ordinary UK property business,

(c) a UK furnished holiday lettings business,

(d) an ordinary overseas property business,

(da) an EEA furnished holiday lettings business, or

(e) a profession or vocation.

History – S. 33(7) omitted by FA 2009, s. 30 and Sch. 11, para. 13, with effect in relation to expenditure incurred on or after 1 April 2009 (for corporation tax purposes) and 6 April 2009 (for income tax purposes), subject to transitional provisions in FA 2009, Sch. 11, para. 27(2) and 30–32.
In s. 33(8)(b), the word "UK" inserted after "ordinary" by FA 2011, s. 52 and Sch. 14, para. 12(8)(a), with effect in relation to chargeable periods beginning on or after 1 April 2011 (for corporation tax purposes), and in relation to chargeable periods beginning on or after 6 April 2011 (for income tax purposes).
In s. 33(8)(b) the word "property" substituted for "Schedule A" by ITTOIA 2005, s. 882(1) and Sch. 1, para. 532; effective for income tax purposes for 2005–06 onwards and for corporation tax purposes for accounting periods ending after 5 April 2005 (ITTOIA 2005, s. 883(1)).
In s. 33(8)(c), the words "UK furnished" substituted for "furnished" by FA 2011, s. 52 and Sch. 14, para. 12(8)(b), with effect in relation to chargeable periods beginning on or after 1 April 2011 (for corporation tax purposes), and in relation to chargeable periods beginning on or after 6 April 2011 (for income tax purposes).
In s. 33(8)(d), the words "ordinary overseas" substituted for "overseas" by FA 2011, s. 52 and Sch. 14, para. 12(8)(c), with effect in relation to chargeable periods beginning on or after 1 April 2011 (for corporation tax purposes), and in relation to chargeable periods beginning on or after 6 April 2011 (for income tax purposes).
The word "or" at the end of (d) omitted and s. 33(8)(da) inserted by FA 2011, s. 52 and Sch. 14, para. 12(8)(d), with effect in relation to chargeable periods beginning on or after 1 April 2011 (for corporation tax purposes), and in relation to chargeable periods beginning on or after 6 April 2011 (for income tax purposes).

Origin – S. 33(1): CAA 1990, s. 71(1) (part), Annex 2, Note 11.
S. 33(2): CAA 1990, s. 71(3), (4), Annex 2, Note 11.
S. 33(3): CAA 1990, s. 72(2).
S. 33(4): CAA 1990, s. 72(3).
S. 33(5): CAA 1990, s. 71(5), (6).
S. 33(6): CAA 1990, s. 72(1), (4).
S. 33(7): drafting.
S. 33(8): CAA 1990, s. 28A(1) (part), s. 29(1) (part), s. 71(1) (part), s. 161(2A) (part), Annex 2, Note 11.

Rewrite: Changes in Law – Explanatory Notes, Annex 2, Note 11: explanation of how definition of "relevant qualifying activity" in s. 33(8) is derived from CAA 1990, s. 71(1)(a) as extended by CAA 1990, s. 28A, 29 and 161(2A), and exclusion of employments and offices from list.

HMRC Manuals – CA22270: examples of security assets (alarm systems, bullet resistant windows, reinforced doors and windows, and perimeter walls and fences). Excluded are cars, ships or aircraft, a dwelling (though not necessarily fixtures), or grounds appurtenant to a dwelling.
Ibid.: apportionment where asset is partly used for purposes other than personal physical security (though allowances given in full where the other use is incidental to the use for personal physical security).

CAA 2001

EXPENDITURE ON INTEGRAL FEATURES

33A Expenditure on provision or replacement of integral features

33A(1) This section applies where a person carrying on a qualifying activity incurs expenditure on the provision or replacement of an integral feature of a building or structure used by the person for the purposes of the qualifying activity.

33A(2) This Part (including in particular section 11(4)) applies as if–

(a) the expenditure were capital expenditure on the provision of plant or machinery for the purposes of the qualifying activity, and

(b) the person who incurred the expenditure owned plant or machinery as a result of incurring it.

33A(3) If the expenditure is qualifying expenditure, it may not be deducted in calculating the income from the qualifying activity.

33A(4) If the expenditure is not qualifying expenditure, whether it may be so deducted is to be determined without regard to this section.

33A(5) For the purposes of this section each of the following is an integral feature–

(a) an electrical system (including a lighting system),

(b) a cold water system,

(c) a space or water heating system, a powered system of ventilation, air cooling or air purification, and any floor or ceiling comprised in such a system,

(d) a lift, an escalator or a moving walkway,

(e) external solar shading.

33A(6) The items listed in subsection (5) do not include any asset whose principal purpose is to insulate or enclose the interior of a building or to provide an interior wall, floor or ceiling which (in each case) is intended to remain permanently in place.

33A(7) The Treasury may by order–

(a) provide that subsection (5) does not include a feature of a building or structure specifed in the order, expenditure on which would (if not within subsection (5)) be qualifying expenditure other than special rate expenditure, and

(b) add to the list in subsection (5) a feature of a building or structure expenditure on the provision of which would not (apart from the order) be expenditure on the provision of plant or machinery.

33A(8) An order under subsection (7) may make such incidental, supplemental, consequential and transitional provision as the Treasury thinks fit.

History – S. 33A inserted by FA 2008, s. 73(2), with effect in relation to expenditure incurred on or after 1 April 2008 for corporation tax purposes and 6 April 2008 for income tax purposes.

Cross references – ITTOIA 2005, s. 55A(2): disapplication of s. 33A(3) in calculating profits of a trade on the cash basis.

33B Meaning of "replacement" in section 33A

33B(1) Expenditure to which this section applies is to be treated for the purposes of section 33A as expenditure on the replacement of an integral feature.

33B(2) This section applies to expenditure incurred by a person on an integral feature if the amount of the expenditure is more than 50% of the cost of replacing the integral feature at the time the expenditure is incurred.

33B(3) Subsection (4) applies where–

(a) a person incurs expenditure ("initial expenditure") on an integral feature which is not more than 50% of the cost of replacing the integral feature at the time it is incurred, but

(b) in the period of 12 months beginning with the initial expenditure being incurred the person incurs further expenditure on the integral feature.

33B(4) If the aggregate of–

(a) the amount of the initial expenditure, and

(b) the amount (or the aggregate of the amounts) of the further expenditure,

is more than 50% of the cost of replacing the integral feature at the time the initial expenditure was incurred, this section applies to the initial expenditure and the further expenditure.

33B(5) Where section 33A applies because of subsection (4), all such assessments and adjustments of assessments are to be made as are necessary to give effect to that section.

History – S. 33B inserted by FA 2008, s. 73(2), with effect in relation to expenditure incurred on or after 1 April 2008 for corporation tax purposes and 6 April 2008 for income tax purposes.

EXCLUSION OF CERTAIN TYPES OF EXPENDITURE

34 Expenditure by MPs and others on accommodation

34(1) Expenditure is not qualifying expenditure if it is incurred by–

(a) a member of the House of Commons,

(b) a member of the Scottish Parliament,

(c) a member of the National Assembly for Wales, or

(d) a member of the Northern Ireland Assembly,

in or in connection with the provision or use of residential or overnight accommodation for the purpose given in subsection (2).

34(2) The purpose is enabling the member to perform the duties of a member of the body in or about–

(a) the place where the body sits, or

(b) the constituency or region for which the member has been returned.

Origin – S. 34(1), (2): CAA 1990, s. 74.

34A Expenditure on plant or machinery for long funding leasing not qualifying expenditure

34A Expenditure is not qualifying expenditure if it is incurred on the provision of plant or machinery for leasing under a long funding lease (see Chapter 6A).

History – S. 34A inserted by FA 2006, s. 81 and Sch. 8, para. 3. The commencement and transitional provisions are complex and are set out in full in FA 2006, Sch. 8, para. 15–27.

35 Expenditure on plant or machinery for use in dwelling-house not qualifying expenditure in certain cases

35(1) This section applies if a person is carrying on a qualifying activity consisting of–

(a) an ordinary UK property business,

(b) an ordinary overseas property business, or

(c) special leasing of plant or machinery.

35(2) The person's expenditure is not qualifying expenditure if it is incurred in providing plant or machinery for use in a dwelling-house.

35(3) If plant or machinery is provided partly for use in a dwelling-house and partly for other purposes, such apportionment of the expenditure incurred in providing that plant or machinery is to be made for the purposes of subsection (2) as is just and reasonable.

History – In s. 35(1)(a), the word "UK" inserted after "ordinary" by FA 2011, s. 52 and Sch. 14, para. 12(9)(a), with effect in relation to chargeable periods beginning on or after 1 April 2011 (for corporation tax purposes), and in relation to chargeable periods beginning on or after 6 April 2011 (for income tax purposes).
In s. 35(1)(a) the word "property" substituted for "Schedule A" by ITTOIA 2005, s. 882(1) and Sch. 1, para. 533; effective for income tax purposes for 2005–06 onwards and for corporation tax purposes for accounting periods ending after 5 April 2005 (ITTOIA 2005, s. 883(1)).
In s. 35(1)(b), the words "ordinary overseas" substituted for "overseas" by FA 2011, s. 52 and Sch. 14, para. 12(9)(b), with effect in relation to chargeable periods beginning on or after 1 April 2011 (for corporation tax purposes), and in relation to chargeable periods beginning on or after 6 April 2011 (for income tax purposes).

Origin – S. 35(1): CAA 1990, s. 28A(3) (part), s. 61(2) (part), s. 161(2A) (part).
S. 35(2): CAA 1990, s. 28A(3) (part), s. 61(2) (part).
S. 35(3): CAA 1990, s. 28A(4), Annex 2, Note 12.

Rewrite: Changes in Law – Explanatory Notes, Annex 2, Note 12: s. 35(3) reflects CAA 1990, s. 28A(4) (apportionment where expenditure on plant or machinery is incurred partly for use in a dwelling house and partly for other purposes). There is no similar apportionment rule within CAA 1990, s. 61 (special leasing), but CAA 1990, s. 79 provides an equivalent rule for reducing allowances which has the same effect.

Extra-statutory concessions – B47: furnished lettings of dwelling houses – 10 per cent of net rent deductible for wear and tear.

HMRC Manuals – CA20020: "dwelling-house" is not defined and so takes its ordinary meaning. A building, or part of a building, which is a person's home is a dwelling-house. A block of residential flats is not a dwelling-house, though the individual flats are dwelling-houses. Expenditure on an asset provided partly for use in a dwelling-house and partly for other purposes (e.g. a central heating system for the whole of a block of residential flats) is apportioned. Full allowances are given where the non-qualifying part is 25% or less of the total expenditure.
CA20040: special leasing: exclusion of assets let for use in a dwelling house.
CA23060: plant and machinery in a dwelling house – guidance and example.

Other material – HMRC Brief 45/10: revised HMRC view on the meaning of "dwelling house", based on the facilities required for day-to-day private existence.

36 Restriction on qualifying expenditure in case of employment or office

36(1) Where the qualifying activity consists of an employment or office–

(a) expenditure on the provision of a mechanically propelled road vehicle, or a cycle, is not qualifying expenditure, and

(b) other expenditure is qualifying expenditure only if the plant or machinery is necessarily provided for use in the performance of the duties of the employment or office.

36(2) In this section **"cycle"** has the meaning given by section 192(1) of the Road Traffic Act 1988.

History – S. 36 substituted by FA 2001, s. 59(1), in relation to expenditure incurred on or after 6 April 2002.

Origin – S. 36(1): drafting.
S. 36(2): CAA 1990, s. 27(2) (part).
S. 36(3): drafting.

Cross references – FA 2001, s. 59(4): cessation of capital allowances entitlement in respect of expenditure by an employee on a mechanically propelled road vehicle, or a cycle, on 6 April 2002.

HMRC Manuals – CA20015: employees are entitled to statutory authorised mileage relief in respect of qualifying business travel and so are denied capital allowances for expenditure on cars.
CA23080: no allowances for assets provided solely for the taxpayer's own convenience or other personal reasons even if the employee uses them while working.
CA23550: special rules for calculating a balancing allowance where an employee has taken part in the Fixed Car Profit scheme for some chargeable periods and claimed capital allowances for others.

37 Exclusion where sums payable in respect of depreciation

37(1) Expenditure incurred by a person in providing plant or machinery for the purposes of a qualifying activity is not qualifying expenditure if it appears–

(a) that during the period during which the plant or machinery will be used for the purposes of the qualifying activity sums are, or are to be, payable to that person directly or indirectly, and

(b) that those sums are in respect of, or take account of, the whole of the depreciation of the plant or machinery resulting from its use for those purposes.

37(2) Subsection (1) does not apply if the sums fall to be taken into account as income of the person or in calculating the profits of a qualifying activity carried on by him.

Origin – S. 37(1), (2): CAA 1990, s. 80(1) (part), Annex 2, Note 13.

Rewrite: Technical Points – Explanatory Notes, Annex 2, Note 13: in the rewrite, "depreciation … resulting from its use" preferred to the expression "wear and tear … occasioned by its use" used in CAA 1990, s. 80(1). While "depreciation" on its own seems wider than "wear and tear", including loss of value not due to any physical deterioration, its scope is limited by the expression "resulting from its use", meaning that the loss of value must be caused by "use" of the plant or machinery. Therefore it is thought that the change in wording has not brought about a real change in the effect of the provisions.

38 Production animals etc.

38 Expenditure is not qualifying expenditure if it is incurred on–

(a) animals or other creatures to which section 30 of ITTOIA 2005 or section 50 of CTA 2009 (animals kept for trade purposes) applies,

(b) animals or other creatures to which Chapter 8 of Part 2 of ITTOIA 2005 or Chapter 8 of Part 3 of CTA 2009 (herd basis rules) applies, or

(c) shares in animals or creatures such as are mentioned in paragraph (a) or (b).

History – S. 38(a), (b) and (c) substituted for former paragraphs (a) and (b) by CTA 2009, s. 1322 and Sch. 1, para. 481, with effect for corporation tax purposes for accounting periods ending on or after 1 April 2009, and for income tax and capital gains tax purposes for the tax year 2009–10 and subsequent tax years.

In former s. 38(a) the references to ITTOIA 2005 inserted by s. 882(1) and Sch. 1, para. 534 of that Act; effective for income tax purposes for 2005–06 onwards and for corporation tax purposes for accounting periods ending after 5 April 2005 (ITTOIA 2005, s. 883(1)).

Origin – CAA 1990, s. 82(2).

HMRC Manuals – CA21220: guidance on s. 38.

38ZA Vehicles for which deductions allowed at fixed rate under Part 2 of ITTOIA 2005

38ZA Expenditure is not qualifying expenditure if–

(a) it is incurred in respect of a vehicle in a period, and

(b) a deduction is made for the period in respect of the expenditure under section 94D of ITTOIA 2005 (deduction allowable at fixed rate for expenditure on vehicles).

History – S. 38ZA inserted by FA 2013, s. 18 and Sch. 5, para. 5(2), with effect for the tax year 2013–14 and subsequent tax years.

Chapter 3A – AIA Qualifying Expenditure

History – Chapter 3A inserted by FA 2008, s. 74 and Sch. 24, para. 2, with effect in relation to expenditure incurred on or after 1 April 2008 for corporation tax purposes and 6 April 2008 for income tax purposes.

38A AIA qualifying expenditure

38A(1) An annual investment allowance is not available unless the qualifying expenditure is AIA qualifying expenditure.

38A(2) Expenditure is AIA qualifying expenditure if–

(a) it is incurred by a qualifying person on or after the relevant date, and

(b) it is not excluded by any of the general exclusions in section 38B.

38A(3) **"Qualifying person"** means–

(a) an individual,

(b) a partnership of which all the members are individuals, or

(c) a company.

38A(4) In determining whether expenditure is AIA qualifying expenditure, any effect of section 12 on the time at which it is to be treated as incurred is to be disregarded.

38A(5) **"The relevant date"** means–

(a) for corporation tax purposes, 1 April 2008, and

(b) for income tax purposes, 6 April 2008.

History – S. 38A inserted by FA 2008, s. 74 and Sch. 24, para. 2, with effect in relation to expenditure incurred on or after 1 April 2008 for corporation tax purposes and 6 April 2008 for income tax purposes.

38B General exclusions applying to section 38A

38B Expenditure within any of the following general exclusions is not AIA qualifying expenditure.

General exclusion 1

The expenditure is incurred in the chargeable period in which the qualifying activity is permanently discontinued.

General exclusion 2

The expenditure is incurred on the provision of a car (as defined by section 268A).

General exclusion 3

The expenditure is incurred wholly for the purposes of a ring fence trade in respect of which tax is chargeable under section 330(1) of CTA 2010 (supplementary charge in respect of ring fence trades).

General exclusion 4

The circumstances of the incurring of the expenditure are that–

(a) the provision of the plant or machinery on which the expenditure is incurred is connected with a change in the nature or conduct of the trade or business carried on by a person other than the person incurring the expenditure, and

(b) the obtaining of an annual investment allowance is the main benefit, or one of the main benefits, which could reasonably be expected to arise from the making of the change.

General exclusion 5

Any of the following sections applies–

section 13 (use for qualifying activity of plant or machinery provided for other purposes);

section 13A (use for other purposes of plant or machinery provided for long funding leasing);

section 14 (use for qualifying activity of plant or machinery which is a gift).

This is subject to section 161 (pre-trading expenditure on mineral exploration and access).

History – In s. 38B, in general exclusion 2, "268A" substituted for "81" by FA 2009, s. 30 and Sch. 11, para. 2, with effect in relation to expenditure incurred on or after 1 April 2009 (for corporation tax purposes) and 6 April 2009 (for income tax purposes), subject to transitional provisions in FA 2009, Sch. 11, para. 27(2) and 30–32.
In s. 38B, in general exclusion 3, the words "section 330(1) of CTA 2010" substituted for "section 501A of ICTA" by CTA 2010, s. 1177 and Sch. 1, para. 324, with effect for corporation tax purposes for accounting periods ending on or after 1 April 2010, and for income tax and capital gains tax purposes for the tax year 2010–11 and subsequent tax years.
S. 38B inserted by FA 2008, s. 74 and Sch. 24, para. 2, with effect in relation to expenditure incurred on or after 1 April 2008 for corporation tax purposes and 6 April 2008 for income tax purposes.

CAA 2001

Chapter 4 – First-year Qualifying Expenditure

GENERAL

39 First-year allowances available for certain types of qualifying expenditure only

39 A first-year allowance is not available unless the qualifying expenditure is first-year qualifying expenditure under any of the following provisions–

section 45A	expenditure on energy-saving plant or machinery,
section 45D	expenditure on cars with low CO_2 emissions,
section 45DA	expenditure on zero-emission goods vehicles,
section 45E	expenditure on plant or machinery for gas refuelling station,
section 45F	expenditure on plant or machinery for use wholly in a ring fence trade,
section 45H	expenditure on environmentally beneficial plant or machinery.
section 45K	expenditure on plant and machinery for use in designated assisted areas.

History – Words "any of the following provisions" inserted by FA 2003, s. 167 and Sch. 30, para. 2.
Former entry relating to s. 40 omitted by FA 2008, s. 76(5)(a) with effect from 21 July 2008.
Former entry relating to s. 44 omitted by FA 2008, s. 75(3)(a), with effect in relation to expenditure incurred on or after 1 April 2008 for corporation tax purposes and 6 April 2008 for income tax purposes. However, where a business incurs an additional VAT liability (under the VAT Capital Goods Scheme) on or after those dates and the original expenditure was first-year qualifying expenditure by virtue of s. 44, then CAA 2001, Pt. 2, Ch. 18 will still apply to the additional VAT liability as if the entry had not been omitted (FA 2008, s. 75(6) and (7)).
Entry relating to s. 45 omitted by FA 2008, s. 76(5)(a) with effect from 21 July 2008.
Entry relating to s. 45A inserted by FA 2001, s. 65 and Sch. 17, para. 1, and word "or" that immediately preceded the words "section 45" repealed by FA 2001, s. 110 and Sch. 33, Pt. II(4), with effect as respects allowances and charges falling to be made for chargeable periods ending on or after

- 6 April 2001 for income tax purposes, and
- 1 April 2001 for corporation tax purposes.

Entry relating to s. 45D inserted by FA 2002, s. 59 and Sch. 19, para. 2, and word "or" that preceded "section 45A" repealed by FA 2002, s. 141 and Sch. 40, Pt. 3(7), with effect in relation to expenditure incurred on or after 17 April 2002.
Entry relating to s. 45DA inserted by F(No. 3)A 2010, s. 18 and Sch. 7, para. 2, with effect for chargeable periods ending on or after 1 April 2010 (corporation tax) or 6 April 2010 (income tax).
Entry relating to s. 45E inserted by FA 2002, s. 61 and Sch. 20, para. 2, with effect in relation to expenditure incurred on or after 17 April 2002.
Entry relating to s. 45F inserted by FA 2002, s. 63 and Sch. 21, para. 2, with effect in relation to expenditure incurred on or after 17 April 2002.
Entry relating to s. 45H inserted, and word "or" that followed "section 45E" repealed, by FA 2003, s.167, Sch. 30, para. 2. and Sch. 43 Pt. 3(9), with effect in relation to expenditure incurred on or after 1 April 2003.
Entry relating to s. 45K inserted by FA 2012, s. 44 and Sch. 11, para. 2, with effect for chargeable periods ending on or after 1 April 2012.

Origin – CAA 1990, s. 22(1) (part), drafting.

Cross references – S. 52: rates of first-year allowances, and conditions for claiming, etc.

S. 236: additional VAT liabilities in respect of expenditure between 1992 and 1993 or between 1997 and 1998 may generate a first-year allowance (see also Sch. 3, para. 46–51).
FA 2009, s. 24(1) (first-year capital allowances for expenditure in 2009–10): s. 39 deemed to include a reference to FA 2009, s. 24 in the list of provisions describing first-year qualifying expenditure.
HMRC Manuals – CA23110: guidance and examples.

TYPES OF EXPENDITURE WHICH MAY QUALIFY FOR FIRST-YEAR ALLOWANCES

40 Expenditure incurred for Northern Ireland purposes by small or medium-sized enterprises

40 [Omitted by FA 2008, s. 76(2).]

History – S. 40 omitted by FA 2008, s. 76(2), with effect from 21 July 2008. However, where a business incurs an additional VAT liability (under the VAT Capital Goods Scheme) on or after 21 July 2008 and the original expenditure was first-year qualifying expenditure by virtue of s. 40, then CAA 2001, Pt. 2. Ch. 18 will still apply to determine if there is an entitlement to a first-year allowance in respect of the additional VAT liability as if s. 40 had not been repealed (FA 2008, s. 76(7) and (8)). Former s. 40 read as follows:

"Expenditure incurred for Northern Ireland purposes by small or medium-sized enterprises

40(1) Expenditure is first-year qualifying expenditure if–
(a) it is incurred on or before 11th May 2002,
(b) it is incurred by a small or medium-sized enterprise,
(c) it is incurred on the provision of plant or machinery for use primarily in Northern Ireland, and
(d) it is not excluded by–
(i) section 41 (miscellaneous exclusions from this section),
(ii) section 42 (plant or machinery partly for use outside Northern Ireland), or
(iii) section 46 (general exclusions).

40(2) This section is subject to section 43 (effect of plant or machinery subsequently being primarily for use outside Northern Ireland)."

Origin – S. 40(1): CAA 1990, s. 22(3CA) (part), (3CB) (part).
S. 40(2): CAA 1990, s. 22(3CA) (part).

Notes – S. 47–49: "small or medium sized enterprise".

41 Miscellaneous exclusions from section 40 (expenditure for Northern Ireland purposes etc.)

41 [Omitted by FA 2008, s. 76(2).]

History – S. 41 omitted by FA 2008, s. 76(2), with effect from 21 July 2008. However, where a business incurs an additional VAT liability (under the VAT Capital Goods Scheme) on or after 21 July 2008 and the original expenditure was first-year qualifying expenditure by virtue of s. 41, then CAA 2001, Pt. 2. Ch. 18 will still apply to determine if there is an entitlement to a first-year allowance in respect of the additional VAT liability as if s. 41 had not been repealed (FA 2008, s. 76(7) and (8)). Former s. 41 read as follows:

"Miscellaneous exclusions from section 40 (expenditure for Northern Ireland purposes etc.)

41(1) Expenditure is not first-year qualifying expenditure under section 40 if–
(a) it is long-life asset expenditure,
(b) it is expenditure on the provision of an aircraft or hovercraft, or
(c) it is expenditure on the provision of a goods vehicle for the purposes of a trade which consists primarily of the conveyance of goods.

41(2) Expenditure is not first-year qualifying expenditure under section 40 if it is incurred on the provision of plant or machinery for use primarily in–
(a) agriculture, fishing or fish farming, or
(b) any relevant activity carried out in relation to agricultural produce, fish or any fish product for the purpose of bringing it to market,

unless it is authorised for the purposes of this section by the Department of Agriculture and Rural Development in Northern Ireland.

41(3) An authorisation given by the Department–
(a) may be given either generally or specially, and
(b) may in any case be absolute or conditional;

and, if the authorisation is given generally, it may be modified by the Department.

41(4) An authorisation is given specially if it is given so as to apply only to a specified item of expenditure or a specified person; otherwise, it is given generally.

41(5) In this section–

"agriculture" and **"agricultural produce"** have the same meaning as in section 6 of the European Communities Act 1972,

"fish" includes shellfish,

"fish farming" means the intensive rearing, on a commercial basis, of fish intended for human consumption,

"fishing" means a trade, or part of a trade, which consists of the catching or taking of fish,

"goods vehicle" has the same meaning as in the Road Traffic (Northern Ireland) Order 1995,

"hovercraft" has the same meaning as in the Hovercraft Act 1968, and

"relevant activity" means transportation, storage, preparation, processing or packaging."

Origin – *S. 41(1): CAA 1990, s. 22(3CC) (part).*
S. 41(2): CAA 1990, s. 22(3CC) (part), (3CD) (part), Departments (Northern Ireland) Order 1999 (SI 1999/283 (NI 1)), art. 3, Sch. 1
S. 41(3), (4): CAA 1990, s. 22(3CE).
S. 41(5): CAA 1990, s. 22(3CD) ("relevant activity"), (10) (part).

42 Exclusion of plant or machinery partly for use outside Northern Ireland

42 [Omitted by FA 2008, s. 76(2).]

History – S. 42 omitted by FA 2008, s. 76(2), with effect from 21 July 2008. However, where a business incurs an additional VAT liability (under the VAT Capital Goods Scheme) on or after 21 July 2008 and the original expenditure was first-year qualifying expenditure by virtue of s. 42, then CAA 2001, Pt. 2. Ch. 18 will still apply to determine if there is an entitlement to a first-year allowance in respect of the additional VAT liability as if s. 42 had not been repealed (FA 2008, s. 76(7) and (8)). Former s. 42 read as follows:

"Exclusion of plant or machinery partly for use outside Northern Ireland

42(1) Expenditure on plant or machinery is not first-year qualifying expenditure under section 40 if–
(a) at the time when it is incurred, the person incurring it intends the plant or machinery to be used partly outside Northern Ireland, and
(b) the main benefit, or one of the main benefits, which could reasonably be expected to arise from the relevant arrangements is the obtaining of a first-year allowance, or a greater first-year allowance, in respect of the part of the expenditure that is attributable to that intended use outside Northern Ireland.
42(2) For the purposes of subsection (1)–
(a) **"the relevant arrangements"** means–
(i) the transaction under which the expenditure is incurred, and
(ii) any scheme or arrangements of which that transaction forms part, and
(b) the part of the expenditure that is attributable under subsection (1)(b) is to be determined on a just and reasonable basis."

Origin – S. 42(1): CAA 1990, s. 22 (6D), (6E) ("the intended outside use").
S. 42(2): CAA 1990, s. 22 (6E) (part).

43 Effect of plant or machinery subsequently being primarily for use outside Northern Ireland

43 [Omitted by FA 2008, s. 76(2).]

History – S. 43 omitted by FA 2008, s. 76(2), with effect from 21 July 2008. However, where a business incurs an additional VAT liability (under the VAT Capital Goods Scheme) on or after 21 July 2008 and the original expenditure was first-year qualifying expenditure by virtue of s. 43, then CAA 2001, Pt. 2. Ch. 18 will still apply to determine if there is an entitlement to a first-year allowance in respect of the additional VAT liability as if s. 43 had not been repealed (FA 2008, s. 76(7) and (8)). Former s. 43 read as follows:

"Effect of plant or machinery subsequently being primarily for use outside Northern Ireland

43(1) Expenditure on the provision of plant or machinery is to be treated as never having been first-year qualifying expenditure under section 40 if, at any relevant time–
(a) the primary use to which the plant or machinery is put is a use outside Northern Ireland, or
(b) the plant or machinery is held for use otherwise than primarily in Northern Ireland.
43(2) In subsection (1) **"relevant time"** means a time which–
(a) falls within the relevant period, and
(b) is a time when the plant or machinery is owned by–
(i) the person who incurred the expenditure, or
(ii) a person who is, or at any time in that period has been, connected with that person.
43(3) **"The relevant period"** means–
(a) if the expenditure concerned exceeds £3.5 million, the period of 5 years beginning with the date of the incurring of that expenditure;
(b) in any other case, the period of 2 years beginning with that date.
43(4) All such assessments and adjustments of assessments are to be made as are necessary to give effect to subsection (1).
43(5) If a person who has made a return becomes aware that, after making it, anything in it has become incorrect because of the operation of this section, he must give notice to an officer of Revenue and Customs specifying how the return needs to be amended.
43(6) The notice must be given within 3 months beginning with the day on which the person first became aware that anything in the return had become incorrect because of the operation of this section."
In former s. 43(5), the words "an officer of Revenue and Customs" substituted for "the Inland Revenue" by CRCA 2005, s. 50(6) and Sch. 4, para. 83(1), with effect from 18 April 2005 by virtue of SI 2005/1126, art. 2(2).

Origin – S. 43(1): CAA 1990, s. 22B(1).
S. 43(2): CAA 1990, s. 22B(2).
S. 43(3): CAA 1990, s. 22B(2A).
S. 43(4): CAA 1990, s. 22B(3).
S. 43(5): (6): CAA 1990, s. 22B(4).

44 Expenditure incurred by small or medium-sized enterprises

44 [Omitted by FA 2008, s. 75(2).]

History – S. 44 omitted by FA 2008, s. 75 (2), with effect in relation to expenditure incurred on or after 1 April 2008 for corporation tax purposes and 6 April 2008 for income tax purposes. However, where a business incurs an additional VAT liability (under the VAT Capital Goods Scheme) on or after those dates and the original expenditure was first-year qualifying expenditure by virtue of s. 44, then CAA 2001, Pt. 2, Ch. 18 will still apply to determine if there is an entitlement to a first-year allowance in respect of the additional VAT liability as if s. 44 had not been repealed (FA 2008, s. 75(6) and (7)). Former s. 44 read as follows:

"Expenditure incurred by small or medium-sized enterprises

44(1) Expenditure is first-year qualifying expenditure if–
(a) it is incurred by a small or medium-sized enterprise, and
(b) it is not excluded by subsection (2) or section 46 (general exclusions).
44(2) Long-life asset expenditure is not first-year qualifying expenditure under subsection (1)."

Origin – CAA 1990 s. 22(3D) (part).

45 ICT expenditure incurred by small enterprises

45 [Omitted by FA 2008, s. 76(3).]

History – S. 45 omitted by FA 2008, s. 76(3), with effect from 21 July 2008. However, where a business incurs an additional VAT liability (under the VAT Capital Goods Scheme) on or after 21 July 2008 and the original expenditure was first-year qualifying expenditure by virtue of s. 45, then CAA 2001, Pt. 2. Ch. 18 will still apply to determine if there is an entitlement to a first-year allowance in respect of the additional VAT liability as if s. 45 had not been repealed (FA 2008, s. 76(7) and (8)). Former s. 45 read as follows:

"ICT expenditure incurred by small enterprises

45(1) Expenditure is first-year qualifying expenditure if–
(a) it is incurred on or before 31st March 2004,
(b) it is incurred by a small enterprise,
(c) it is expenditure on information and communications technology, and
(d) it is not excluded by section 46 (general exclusions) or subsection (4) below.

45(2) **"Expenditure on information and communications technology"** means expenditure on items within any of the following classes.

Class A. Computers and associated equipment

This class covers–
(a) computers,
(b) peripheral devices designed to be used by being connected to or inserted in a computer,
(c) equipment (including cabling) for use primarily to provide a data connection between–
(i) one computer and another, or
(ii) a computer and a data communications network, and
(d) dedicated electrical systems for computers.

For this purpose **"computer"** does not include computerised control or management systems or other systems that are part of a larger system whose principal function is not processing or storing information.

Class B. Other qualifying equipment

This class covers–
(a) wireless application protocol telephones,
(b) third generation mobile telephones,
(c) devices designed to be used by being connected to a television set and capable of receiving and transmitting information from and to data networks, and
(d) other devices–
(i) substantially similar to those within paragraphs (a), (b) and (c), and
(ii) capable of receiving and transmitting information from and to data networks.

This is subject to any order under subsection (3).

Class C. Software

This class covers the right to use or otherwise deal with software for the purposes of any equipment within Class A or B.

45(3) The Treasury may make provision by order–
(a) further defining the kinds of equipment within Class B, or
(b) adding further kinds of equipment to that class.

45(4) Expenditure on an item within Class C is not first-year qualifying expenditure under this section if the person incurring it does so with a view to granting to another person a right to use or otherwise deal with any of the software in question."

In former s. 45(1)(a), "31 March 2004" substituted for "31 March 2003" by FA 2003, s. 165.

In former s. 45(1)(d), words "or subsection (4) below" inserted by FA 2003, s. 166 in relation to expenditure incurred on or after 26 March 2003.

S. 45(4) inserted by FA 2003, s. 166(4) in relation to expenditure incurred on or after 26 March 2003.

Origin – S. 45(1): CAA 1990, s. 22(3E) (part).
S. 45(2): CAA 1990, s. 22(3F), (3G).
S. 45(3): CAA 1990, s. 22(3H).

Transitional – Sch. 3, para. 14: s. 45 does not apply in relation to expenditure incurred before 1 April 2000.

45A Expenditure on energy-saving plant or machinery

45A(1) Expenditure is first-year qualifying expenditure if–
(a) it is expenditure on energy-saving plant or machinery that is unused and not second-hand,
(b) it is incurred on or after 1st April 2001, and
(c) it is not excluded by section 46 (general exclusions).

45A(1A) This section is subject to section 45AA (payments under Energy Act 2008 schemes).

45A(2) Energy-saving plant or machinery means plant or machinery in relation to which the following conditions are met–
(a) when the expenditure is incurred, or
(b) when the contract for the provision of the plant or machinery is entered into.

45A(3) The conditions are that the plant or machinery–
(a) is of a description specified by Treasury order, and
(b) meets the energy-saving criteria specified by Treasury order for plant or machinery of that description.

45A(4) Any such order may make provision by reference to any technology list, or product list, issued by the Secretary of State (whether before or after the coming into force of this section).

History – S. 45A(1A) inserted by FA 2012, s. 45(2) with effect from 17 July 2012.

S. 45A inserted by FA 2001, s. 65 and Sch. 17, para. 2, with effect as respects allowances and charges falling to be made for chargeable periods ending on or after

- 6 April 2001 for income tax purposes, and
- 1 April 2001 for corporation tax purposes.

Cross references – S. 52(3): 100 per cent rate of first-year allowance on expenditure qualifying under s. 45A.
FA 2001, Sch. 17, para. 6: where expenditure is incurred on plant or machinery, or a contract entered into for its provision, before the first order under s. 45A(3) is made, the plant or machinery nevertheless qualifies as energy-saving equipment if the conditions in s. 45A(3) would have been satisfied had the order been in force at the time when the expenditure was incurred or the contract was entered into.

Statutory instruments – SI 2001/2541: partly made under s. 45A(3) and (4).

HMRC Manuals – CA23140: guidance and example on s. 45A–45C.

45AA Section 45A exclusion: feed-in tariffs and renewable heat incentives

History – In heading to s. 45AA, the words "feed-in tariffs and renewable heat incentives" substituted for the words "payments under Energy Act 2008 schemes" by FA 2013, s. 67(5), with effect from 17 July 2013.

45AA(1) Expenditure incurred on or after the relevant date on plant or machinery is to be treated as never having been first-year qualifying expenditure under section 45A if–

(a) a payment is made, or another incentive is given, under a scheme established by virtue of section 41 of the Energy Act 2008 (feed-in tariffs), or under a corresponding scheme having effect in Northern Ireland, in respect of electricity generated by the plant or machinery, or

(b) a payment is made, or another incentive is given, under a scheme established by regulations under section 100 of that Act or section 113 of the Energy Act 2011 (renewable heat incentives) in respect of heat generated, or gas or fuel produced, by the plant or machinery.

45AA(2) All such assessments and adjustments of assessments are to be made as are necessary to give effect to subsection (1).

45AA(3) If a person who has made a tax return becomes aware that, after making it, anything in it has become incorrect because of the operation of this section, the person must give notice to an officer of Revenue and Customs specifying how the return needs to be amended.

45AA(4) The notice must be given within 3 months beginning with the day on which the person first became aware that anything in the return had become incorrect because of the operation of this section.

45AA(5) Except as provided by subsections (5A) and (6), the relevant date is–

(a) for corporation tax purposes, 1 April 2012, and

(b) for income tax purposes, 6 April 2012.

45AA(5A) Except as provided by subsection (6), in the case of expenditure incurred on plant or machinery used or for use in Northern Ireland, the relevant date is–

(a) for corporation tax purposes, 1 April 2013, and

(b) for income tax purposes, 6 April 2013.

45AA(6) In the case of expenditure incurred on a combined heat and power system, the relevant date in relation to subsection (1)(b) is–

(a) for corporation tax purposes, 1 April 2014, and

(b) for income tax purposes, 6 April 2014.

History – In s. 45AA(1)(a), the words ", or under a corresponding scheme having effect in Northern Ireland," inserted by FA 2013, s. 67(2)(a), with effect from 17 July 2013.
In s. 45AA(1)(b), the words "or section 113 of the Energy Act 2011" inserted by FA 2013, s. 67(2)(b), with effect from 17 July 2013.
In s. 45AA(5), the words "subsections (5A) and (6)" substituted for the words "subsection (6)" by FA 2013, s. 67(3), with effect from 17 July 2013.
S. 45AA(5A) inserted by FA 2013, s. 67(4), with effect from 17 July 2013.
S. 45AA inserted by FA 2012, s. 45(3), with effect from 17 July 2012.

45B Certification of energy-saving plant and machinery

45B(1) The Treasury may by order provide that, in such cases as may be specified in the order, no section 45A allowance may be made unless a relevant certificate of energy efficiency is in force.

A **"section 45A allowance"** means a first-year allowance in respect of expenditure that is first-year qualifying expenditure under section 45A.

45B(2) A certificate of energy efficiency is one certifying that–

(a) particular plant or machinery, or

(b) plant or machinery constructed to a particular design,

meets the energy-saving criteria specified in relation to that description of plant or machinery by order under section 45A.

45B(3) A relevant certificate of energy efficiency means one issued–

(a) by the Secretary of State or a person authorised by the Secretary of State;

(b) in the case of plant or machinery used or for use in Scotland, by the Scottish Ministers or a person authorised by them;

(c) in the case of plant or machinery used or for use in Wales, by the National Assembly for Wales or a person authorised by it;

(d) in the case of plant or machinery used or for use in Northern Ireland, by the Department of Enterprise, Trade and Investment in Northern Ireland or a person authorised by it.

45B(4) If a certificate of energy efficiency is revoked–

(a) the certificate is to be treated for the purposes of this section as if it had never been issued, and

(b) all such assessments and adjustments of assessments are to be made as are necessary as a result of the revocation.

45B(5) If a person who has made a tax return becomes aware that, as a result of the revocation of a certificate of energy efficiency after the return was made, the return has become incorrect, he must give notice to an officer of Revenue and Customs specifying how the return needs to be amended.

45B(6) The notice must be given within 3 months beginning with the day on which the person first became aware that anything in the tax return had become incorrect because of the revocation of the certificate.

History – S. 45B inserted by FA 2001, s. 65 and Sch. 17, para. 2, with effect as respects allowances and charges falling to be made for chargeable periods ending on or after

- 6 April 2001 for income tax purposes, and
- 1 April 2001 for corporation tax purposes.

In s. 45B(5), the words "an officer of Revenue and Customs" substituted for "the Inland Revenue" by CRCA 2005, s. 50(6) and Sch. 4, para. 83(1), with effect from 18 April 2005 by virtue of SI 2005/1126, art. 2(2).

Cross references – TMA 1970, s. 98, Table: penalties for failure to comply with s. 45B(5), (6).

Statutory instruments – SI 2001/2541: partly made under s. 45B(1).

HMRC Manuals – CA23140: guidance and example on s. 45A–45C.

45C Energy-saving components of plant or machinery

45C(1) This section applies for the purpose of apportioning expenditure incurred on plant or machinery if one or more components of the plant or machinery (but not all of it) is of a description specified by Treasury order under section 45A(3).

45C(2) If–

(a) only one of the components is of such a description, and

(b) an amount is specified by the order in respect of that component,

the part of the expenditure that is section 45A expenditure must not exceed that amount.

45C(3) If–

(a) more than one of the components is of such a description, and

(b) an amount is specified by the order in respect of each of those components,

the part of the expenditure that is section 45A expenditure must not exceed the total of those amounts.

45C(4) If the expenditure is treated under this Act as incurred in instalments, the proportion of each instalment that is section 45A expenditure is the same as the proportion of the whole of the expenditure that is section 45A expenditure.

45C(5) If this section applies, the expenditure is not apportioned under section 562(3) (apportionment where property sold with other property).

45C(6) In this section **"section 45A expenditure"** means expenditure that is first-year qualifying expenditure under section 45A.

History – S. 45C inserted by FA 2001, s. 65 and Sch. 17, para. 2, with effect as respects allowances and charges falling to be made for chargeable periods ending on or after

- 6 April 2001 for income tax purposes, and
- 1 April 2001 for corporation tax purposes.

Statutory instruments – SI 2001/2541: partly made under s. 45C(2)(b) and (3)(b).

HMRC Manuals – CA23140: guidance and example on s. 45A–45C.

45D Expenditure on cars with low carbon dioxide emissions

45D(1) Expenditure is first-year qualifying expenditure if–

(a) it is incurred in the period beginning with 17th April 2002 and ending with 31st March 2021,

(b) it is expenditure on a car which is first registered on or after 17th April 2002 and which is unused and not second-hand,

(c) the car–

(i) is electrically-propelled, or

(ii) has low CO_2 emissions, and

(d) the expenditure is not excluded by section 46 (general exclusions).

45D(1A) The Treasury may by order amend subsection (1)(a) so as to extend the period specified.

45D(2) For the purposes of this section a car has low CO_2 emissions if it satisfies the conditions in subsections (3) and (4).

45D(3) The first condition is that, when the car is first registered, it is so registered on the basis of a qualifying emissions certificate.

45D(4) The second condition is that the applicable CO_2 emissions figure in relation to the car does not exceed 75 grams per kilometre driven.

45D(5) [Omitted by FA 2009, s. 30 and Sch. 11, para. 14(6).]

45D(6) [Omitted by FA 2009, s. 30 and Sch. 11, para. 14(6).]

45D(7) The Treasury may by order amend the amount from time to time specified in subsection (4).

45D(8) In this section any reference to a car is to a car within the meaning of section 268A, except that it–

(a) includes a reference to a mechanically propelled road vehicle of a type commonly used as a hackney carriage,

(b) [omitted by FA 2009, s. 30 and Sch. 11, para. 14(7)(b).]

45D(9) [Omitted by FA 2009, s. 30 and Sch. 11, para. 14(8).]

45D(10) [Omitted by FA 2009, s. 30 and Sch. 11, para. 14(8).]

45D(11) In this section–

"applicable CO_2 emissions figure" and **"qualifying emissions certificate"** have the meanings given in section 268C;

"electrically-propelled" has the meaning given in section 268B.

Prospective amendments – In s. 45D(4), "50" substituted for "75" by SI 2016/984, art. 4(b), with effect in relation to expenditure incurred on or after 1 April 2018

History – In s. 45D(1)(a), "2021" substituted for "2018" by SI 2016/984, art. 4(a), with effect from 1 November 2016.
In s. 45D(1)(a), "2018" substituted for "2015" by SI 2015/60, art. 4(a), with effect from 17 February 2015.
In s. 45D(1)(a), "2015" substituted for "2013" by FA 2013, s. 68(1)(a), with effect from 17 July 2013.
In s. 45D(1)(a), the year "2013" substituted for the year "2008" by FA 2008, s. 77(2), with effect from 21 July 2008.
S. 45D(1(c) substituted by FA 2009, s. 30 and Sch. 11, para. 14(2), with effect in relation to expenditure incurred on or after 1 April 2009 (for corporation tax purposes) and 6 April 2009 (for income tax purposes), subject to transitional provisions in FA 2009, Sch. 11, para. 27(2) and 30–32.
S. 45D(1A) inserted by FA 2014, s. 64(2) with effect from 17 July 2014.
In s. 45D(2), the words "a car has low CO_2 emissions if it" substituted for the words "a car with low CO_2 emissions is a car which" by FA 2009, s. 30 and Sch. 11, para. 14(3), with effect in relation to expenditure incurred on or after 1 April 2009 (for corporation tax purposes) and 6 April 2009 (for income tax purposes), subject to transitional provisions in FA 2009, Sch. 11, para. 27(2) and 30–32.
In s. 45D(3), the words "a qualifying emissions certificate." substituted for the former words by FA 2009, s. 30 and Sch. 11, para. 14(4), with effect in relation to expenditure incurred on or after 1 April 2009 (for corporation tax purposes) and 6 April 2009 (for income tax purposes), subject to transitional provisions in FA 2009, Sch. 11, para. 27(2) and 30–32.
In s. 45D(4), "75" substituted for "95" by SI 2015/60, art. 4(b), with effect in relation to expenditure incurred on or after 1 April 2015.
In s. 45D(4), "95" substituted for "110" by FA 2013, s. 68(1)(b), with effect in relation to expenditure incurred on or after 1 April 2013.
In s. 45D(4), the words "in relation to" substituted for the words "in the case of" by FA 2009, s. 30 and Sch. 11, para. 14(5), with effect in relation to expenditure incurred on or after 1 April 2009 (for corporation tax purposes) and 6 April 2009 (for income tax purposes), subject to transitional provisions in FA 2009, Sch. 11, para. 27(2) and 30–32.
In s. 45D(4), the figure "110" substituted for the figure "120" by FA 2008, s. 77(3), with effect in relation to expenditure incurred on or after 1 April 2008.
S. 45D(5) omitted by FA 2009, s. 30 and Sch. 11, para. 14(6), with effect in relation to expenditure incurred on or after 1 April 2009 (for corporation tax purposes) and 6 April 2009 (for income tax purposes), subject to transitional provisions in FA 2009, Sch. 11, para. 27(2) and 30–32.
S. 45D(6) omitted by FA 2009, s. 30 and Sch. 11, para. 14(6), with effect in relation to expenditure incurred on or after 1 April 2009 (for corporation tax purposes) and 6 April 2009 (for income tax purposes), subject to transitional provisions in FA 2009, Sch. 11, para. 27(2) and 30–32.
In s. 45D(8), the words "is to a car within the meaning of section 268A, except that it" inserted by FA 2009, s. 30 and Sch. 11, para. 14(7)(a), with effect in relation to expenditure incurred on or after 1 April 2009 (for corporation tax purposes) and 6 April 2009 (for income tax purposes), subject to transitional provisions in FA 2009, Sch. 11, para. 27(2) and 30–32.
S. 45D(8)(b) and the "but" before it omitted by FA 2009, s. 30 and Sch. 11, para. 14(7)(b), with effect in relation to expenditure incurred on or after 1 April 2009 (for corporation tax purposes) and 6 April 2009 (for income tax purposes), subject to transitional provisions in FA 2009, Sch. 11, para. 27(2) and 30–32.
S. 45D(9) omitted by FA 2009, s. 30 and Sch. 11, para. 14(8), with effect in relation to expenditure incurred on or after 1 April 2009 (for corporation tax purposes) and 6 April 2009 (for income tax purposes), subject to transitional provisions in FA 2009, Sch. 11, para. 27(2) and 30–32.
S. 45D(10) omitted by FA 2009, s. 30 and Sch. 11, para. 14(8), with effect in relation to expenditure incurred on or after 1 April 2009 (for corporation tax purposes) and 6 April 2009 (for income tax purposes), subject to transitional provisions in FA 2009, Sch. 11, para. 27(2) and 30–32.
S. 45D(11) inserted by FA 2009, s. 30 and Sch. 11, para. 14(9), with effect in relation to expenditure incurred on or after 1 April 2009 (for corporation tax purposes) and 6 April 2009 (for income tax purposes), subject to transitional provisions in FA 2009, Sch. 11, para. 27(2) and 30–32.
S. 45D inserted by FA 2002, s. 59 and Sch. 19, para. 3, with effect in relation to expenditure incurred on or after 17 April 2002.

Cross references – FA 2008, s. 77(6): in relation to expenditure incurred on the hiring of a car for a period of hire which begins on or before 31 March 2008 and under a contract entered into on or before 31 March 2008, ICTA 1988, s. 578A and ITTOIA 2005, s. 50 apply on or after 1 April 2008 as if the figure in CAA 2001, s. 45D(4) remained as 120 grams.

45DA Expenditure on zero-emission goods vehicles

45DA(1) Expenditure is first-year qualifying expenditure if–

(a) it is incurred in the period of 8 years beginning with the relevant date,

(b) it is incurred on the provision of a zero-emission goods vehicle,

(c) the vehicle is unused and not second-hand,

(d) the vehicle is registered, and

(e) the expenditure is not excluded by section 46 (general exclusions).

45DA(1A) The Treasury may by order amend subsection (1)(a) so as to extend the period specified.

45DA(2) For the purposes of subsection (1)(d) it does not matter whether the vehicle is first registered before or after the expenditure is incurred.

45DA(3) In this section–

"goods vehicle" means a mechanically propelled road vehicle which is of a design primarily suited for the conveyance of goods or burden of any description;

"the relevant date" means–

(a) in the case of expenditure incurred by a person within the charge to corporation tax, 1 April 2010, and

(b) in the case of expenditure incurred by a person within the charge to income tax, 6 April 2010;

"zero-emission goods vehicle" means a goods vehicle which cannot in any circumstances emit CO_2 by being driven.

45DA(4) The Treasury may by order amend this Chapter so as to provide for specified descriptions of vehicles to be treated, or not to be treated, as goods vehicles for the purposes of this section.

45DA(5) This section is subject to section 45DB.

History – In s. 45DA(1)(a), the words "8 years" substituted for the words "5 years" by FA 2015, s. 45(2), with effect from 26 March 2015.

S. 45DA(1A) inserted by FA 2014, s. 64(3) with effect from 17 July 2014.

S. 45DA inserted by F(No. 3)A 2010, s. 18 and Sch. 7, para. 3, with effect for chargeable periods ending on or after 1 April 2010 (corporation tax) or 6 April 2010 (income tax).

45DB Exclusions from allowances under section 45DA

45DB(1) Expenditure incurred by a person is not first-year qualifying expenditure under section 45DA if it is within subsection (2), (4) or (6).

45DB(2) Expenditure is within this subsection if, at the time a claim is made under section 3 for a section 45DA allowance in respect of the expenditure, the person who incurred the expenditure is, or forms part of, an undertaking within subsection (3).

45DB(3) An undertaking is within this subsection if one or both of the following conditions are met–

(a) it is reasonable to assume that the undertaking would be regarded as an undertaking in difficulty for the purposes of the General Block Exemption Regulation;

(b) the undertaking is subject to an outstanding recovery order made by virtue of Article 108(2) of the Treaty on the Functioning of the European Union (Commission Decision declaring aid illegal and incompatible with the common market).

45DB(4) Expenditure is within this subsection if it is incurred for the purposes of a qualifying activity–

(a) in the fishery or aquaculture sector, as covered by Regulation (EU) No 1379/2013 of the European Parliament and of the Council, or

(b) relating to the management of waste of undertakings.

45DB(5) In subsection (4)(b) the reference to waste of undertakings does not include waste of the person who incurred the expenditure or of any other person forming part of the same undertaking as that person.

45DB(6) Expenditure is within this subsection to the extent that it is taken into account for the purposes of a relevant grant, or relevant payment, made towards that expenditure.

45DB(7) A grant or payment is relevant if it is–

(a) a State aid, other than an allowance under this Part, or

(b) a grant or subsidy, other than a State aid, which the Treasury by order declares to be relevant for the purposes of the withholding of a section 45DA allowance.

45DB(8) If a relevant grant or relevant payment towards the expenditure is made after the making of a section 45DA allowance, the allowance is to be withdrawn.

45DB(9) All such assessments and adjustments of assessments are to be made as are necessary to give effect to subsection (8).

45DB(10) Any such assessment or adjustment is not out of time if it is made within 3 years of the end of the chargeable period in which the grant or payment was made.

45DB(11) In this section–

"General Block Exemption Regulation" means Commission Regulation (EU) No 651/2014 (General block exemption Regulation);

"management" and **"waste"** have the meaning given by Article 1 of Directive 2006/12/EC of the European Parliament and of the Council;

"section 45DA allowance" means a first year allowance in respect of expenditure that is first-year qualifying expenditure under section 45DA;

"undertaking" means–

(a) an autonomous enterprise, or

(b) an enterprise (not within paragraph (a)) and its partner enterprises (if any) and its linked enterprises (if any),

and for this purpose **"enterprise"**, **"autonomous enterprise"**, **"partner enterprises"** and **"linked enterprises"** have the meaning given by Annex 1 to the General Block Exemption Regulation.

45DB(11A) Nothing in this section limits references to "State aid" to State aid which is required to be notified to and approved by the European Commission.

45DB(12) The Treasury may by order make such provision amending this section as appears to them appropriate for the purpose of giving effect to any future amendments of or instrument replacing–

(a) the General Block Exemption Regulation,

(b) the Community Guidelines on State Aid for Rescuing and Restructuring Firms in Difficulty (2004/C 244/02),

(c) Regulation (EU) No 1379/2013 of the European Parliament and of the Council,

(d) Directive 2006/12/EC of the European Parliament and of the Council, or

(e) the Treaty on the Functioning of the European Union.

History – In s. 45DB(3)(a), the words "an undertaking in difficulty for the purposes of the General Block Exemption Regulation" substituted for the words "a firm in difficulty for the purposes of the Community Guidelines on State Aid for Rescuing and Restructuring Firms in Difficulty (2004/C 244/02)" by FA 2014, s. 65 and Sch. 13, para. 2(2), with effect in relation to expenditure incurred on or after 17 July 2014.

In s. 45DB(4)(a), the words "Regulation (EU) No 1379/2013 of the European Parliament and of the Council" substituted for the words "Council Regulation (EC) No 104/2000" by FA 2014, s. 65 and Sch. 13, para. 2(3), with effect in relation to expenditure incurred on or after 17 July 2014.

In s. 45DB(7), the word "notified" omitted (twice) by FA 2015, s. 45(4), with effect in relation to a relevant grant or relevant payment made at any time (whether before or on or after "the specified day" (6 April 2015 for income tax purposes and 1 April 2015 for corporation tax purposes) towards expenditure incurred on or after that day, and in relation to a relevant grant or relevant payment made on or after the specified day towards expenditure incurred before that day.

In s. 45DB(8), the words "to that extent" (which appeared after the word "withdrawn") omitted by FA 2015, s. 45(5), with effect in relation to a relevant grant or relevant payment made at any time (whether before or on or after "the specified day" (6 April 2015 for income tax purposes and 1 April 2015 for corporation tax purposes) towards expenditure incurred on or after that day, and in relation to a relevant grant or relevant payment made on or after the specified day towards expenditure incurred before that day.

In s. 45DB(11), in the definition of "General Block Exemption Regulation", "(EU) No 651/2014" substituted for "(EC) No 800/2008" by FA 2014, s. 65 and Sch. 13, para. 2(4), with effect in relation to expenditure incurred on or after 17 July 2014.

In s. 45DB(11), the definition of "notified State aid" omitted by FA 2015, s. 45(6), with effect in relation to a relevant grant or relevant payment made at any time (whether before or on or after "the specified day" (6 April 2015 for income tax purposes and 1 April 2015 for corporation tax purposes) towards expenditure incurred on or after that day, and in relation to a relevant grant or relevant payment made on or after the specified day towards expenditure incurred before that day.

S. 45DB(11A) inserted by FA 2015, s. 45(7), with effect in relation to a relevant grant or relevant payment made at any time (whether before or on or after "the specified day" (6 April 2015 for income tax purposes and 1 April 2015 for corporation tax purposes) towards expenditure incurred on or after that day, and in relation to a relevant grant or relevant payment made on or after the specified day towards expenditure incurred before thatday.

S. 45DB(12)(c) substituted by FA 2014, s. 65 and Sch. 13, para. 2(5), with effect in relation to expenditure incurred on or after 17 July 2014.

S. 45DB inserted by F(No. 3)A 2010, s. 18 and Sch. 7, para. 3, with effect for chargeable periods ending on or after 1 April 2010 (corporation tax) or 6 April 2010 (income tax).

45E Expenditure on plant or machinery for gas refuelling station

45E(1) Expenditure is first-year qualifying expenditure if–

(a) it is incurred in the period beginning with 17th April 2002 and ending with 31st March 2018,

(b) it is expenditure on plant or machinery for a gas refuelling station where the plant or machinery is unused and not second-hand, and

(c) it is not excluded by section 46 (general exclusions).

45E(1A) The Treasury may by order amend subsection (1)(a) so as to extend the period specified.

45E(2) For the purposes of this section expenditure on plant or machinery for a gas refuelling station is expenditure on plant or machinery installed at a gas refuelling station for use solely for or in connection with refuelling vehicles with natural gas, biogas or hydrogen fuel.

45E(3) For the purposes of subsection (2) the plant or machinery which is for use for or in connection with refuelling vehicles with natural gas, biogas or hydrogen fuel includes–

(a) any storage tank for natural gas, biogas or hydrogen fuel,

(b) any compressor, pump, control or meter used for or in connection with refuelling vehicles with natural gas, biogas or hydrogen fuel, and

(c) any equipment for dispensing natural gas, biogas or hydrogen fuel to the fuel tank of a vehicle.

45E(4) For the purposes of this section–

"biogas" means gas produced by the anaerobic conversion of organic matter and used for propelling vehicles;

"gas refuelling station" means any premises, or that part of any premises, where vehicles are refuelled with natural gas, biogas or hydrogen fuel;

"hydrogen fuel" means a fuel consisting of gaseous or cryogenic liquid hydrogen which is used for propelling vehicles; and

"vehicle" means a mechanically propelled road vehicle.

History – In s. 45E(1)(a), "2018" substituted for "2015" by SI 2015/60, art. 5, with effect from 17 February 2015.
In s. 45E(1)(a), "2015" substituted for "2013" by FA 2013, s. 69, with effect from 17 July 2013.
In s. 45E(1)(a), the year "2013" substituted for the year "2008" by FA 2008, s. 78(2), with effect from 21 July 2008.
S. 45E(1A) inserted by FA 2014, s. 64(4) with effect from 17 July 2014.
In s. 45E(2), the word "biogas" inserted by FA 2008, s. 78(3), with effect in relation to expenditure incurred on or after 1 April 2008.
In s. 45E(3), the word "biogas" inserted (in each place) by FA 2008, s. 78(3), with effect in relation to expenditure incurred on or after 1 April 2008.
In s. 45E(4), the definition of "biogas" inserted in the list of definitions by FA 2008, s. 78(4), with effect in relation to expenditure incurred on or after 1 April 2008.
In s. 45E(4), the word "biogas" inserted in the definition of "gas refuelling station" by FA 2008, s. 78(3), with effect in relation to expenditure incurred on or after 1 April 2008.
S. 45E inserted by FA 2002, s. 61 and Sch. 20, para. 3, with effect in relation to expenditure incurred on and after 17 April 2002.

45F Expenditure on plant and machinery for use wholly in a ring fence trade

45F(1) Expenditure is first-year qualifying expenditure if–

(a) it is incurred on or after 17th April 2002,

(b) it is incurred by a company,

(c) it is incurred on the provision of plant or machinery for use wholly for the purposes of a ring fence trade, and

(d) it is not excluded by section 46 (general exclusions).

45F(2) This section is subject to section 45G (plant or machinery used for less than five years in a ring fence trade).

45F(3) In this section **"ring fence trade"** means a ring fence trade in respect of which tax is chargeable under section 330(1) of CTA 2010 (supplementary charge in respect of ring fence trades).

History – In s. 45F(3), the words "section 330(1) of CTA 2010" substituted for "section 501A of the Taxes Act 1988" by CTA 2010, s. 1177 and Sch. 1, para. 325, with effect for corporation tax purposes for accounting periods ending on or after 1 April 2010, and for income tax and capital gains tax purposes for the tax year 2010–11 and subsequent tax years.
S. 45F inserted by FA 2002, s. 63 and Sch. 21, para. 3, with effect in relation to expenditure incurred on and after 17 April 2002.

45G Plant or machinery used for less than five years in a ring fence trade

45G(1) Expenditure incurred by a company on the provision of plant or machinery is to be treated as never having been first-year qualifying expenditure under section 45F if the plant or machinery–

(a) is at no time in the relevant period used in a ring fence trade carried on by the company or a company connected with it, or

(b) is at any time in the relevant period used for a purpose other than that of a ring fence trade carried on by the company or a company connected with it.

45G(2) For the purposes of this section **"the relevant period"** means whichever of the following periods, beginning with the incurring of the expenditure, first ends, namely–

(a) the period ending with the fifth anniversary of the incurring of the expenditure, or

(b) the period ending with the day preceding the first occasion on which the plant or machinery, after becoming owned by the company which incurred the expenditure, is not owned by a company which is either that company or a company connected with it.

45G(3) All such assessments and adjustments of assessments are to be made as are necessary to give effect to subsection (1).

45G(4) If a person who has made a return becomes aware that, after making it, anything in it has become incorrect because of the operation of this section, he must give notice to an officer of Revenue and Customs specifying how the return needs to be amended.

45G(5) The notice must be given within 3 months beginning with the day on which the person first became aware that anything in the return had become incorrect because of the operation of this section.

45G(6) In this section **"ring fence trade"** has the same meaning as in section 45F.

History – In s. 45G(4), the words "an officer of Revenue and Customs" substituted for "the Inland Revenue" by CRCA 2005, s. 50(6) and Sch. 4, para. 83(1), with effect from 18 April 2005 by virtue of SI 2005/1126, art. 2(2).
S. 45G inserted by FA 2002, s. 63 and Sch. 21, para. 4, with effect in relation to expenditure incurred on and after 17 April 2002.

Cross references – TMA 1970, s. 98, Table, second column: penalties for failure to give notice under s. 45G(4), (5).

45H Expenditure on environmentally beneficial plant or machinery

45H(1) Expenditure is first-year qualifying expenditure if–

(a) it is expenditure on environmentally beneficial plant or machinery that is unused and not second-hand,

(b) it is incurred on or after 1st April 2003,

(c) it is not long-life asset expenditure, and

(d) it is not excluded by section 46 (general exclusions).

45H(2) Environmentally beneficial plant or machinery means plant or machinery in relation to which the following conditions are met–

(a) when the expenditure is incurred, or

(b) when the contract for the provision of the plant or machinery is entered into.

45H(3) The conditions are that the plant or machinery–

(a) is of a description specified by Treasury order, and

(b) meets the environmental criteria specified by Treasury order for plant or machinery of that description.

45H(4) The Treasury may make such orders under subsection (3) as appear to them appropriate to promote the use of technologies, or products, designed to remedy or prevent damage to the physical environment or natural resources.

45H(5) Any such order may make provision by reference to any technology list, or product list, issued by the Secretary of State (whether before or after the coming into force of this section).

History – S. 45H inserted by FA 2003, s. 167 and Sch. 30, para. 3, in relation to expenditure incurred on or after 1 April 2003.

Cross references – FA 2003, s. 167 and Sch. 30, para. 7: where (a) expenditure on plant or machinery is incurred, or a contract for the provision of plant or machinery is entered into, before the first order is made under s. 45H(3), and (b) if that order had been made before the relevant time, the conditions in s. 45H(3) would have been met, those conditions shall be treated as if they were met at the time when the expenditure was incurred or (as the case may be) the contract was entered into.

Statutory instruments – SI 2003/2076, art. 3: partly made under s. 45(H)(3), (4).

45I Certification of environmentally beneficial plant and machinery

45I(1) The Treasury may by order provide that, in such cases as may be specified in the order, no section 45H allowance may be made unless a relevant certificate of environmental benefit is in force.

A **"section 45H allowance"** means a first-year allowance in respect of expenditure that is first-year qualifying expenditure under section 45H.

45I(2) A certificate of environmental benefit is one certifying that–

(a) particular plant or machinery, or

(b) plant or machinery constructed to a particular design,

meets the environmental criteria specified in relation to that description of plant or machinery by order under section 45H.

45I(3) A relevant certification of environmental benefit means one issued–

(a) by the Secretary of State or a person authorised by the Secretary of State;

(b) in the case of plant or machinery used or for use in Scotland, by the Scottish Ministers or a person authorised by them;

(c) in the case of plant or machinery used or for use in Wales, by the National Assembly for Wales or a person authorised by it;

(d) in the case of plant or machinery used or for use in Northern Ireland, by the Department of Enterprise, Trade and Investment in Northern Ireland or a person authorised by it.

45I(4) If a certification of environmental benefit is revoked–

(a) the certificate is treated for the purposes of this section as if it had never been issued, and

(b) all such assessments and adjustments shall be made as are necessary as a result of the revocation.

45I(5) If a person who has made a tax return becomes aware that, as a result of the revocation of a certificate of environmental benefit after the return was made, the return has become incorrect, he must give notice to an officer of Revenue and Customs specifying how the return needs to be amended.

45I(6) The notice must be given within three months beginning with the day on which the person first became aware that anything in the tax return had become incorrect because of the revocation of the certificate.

History – In s. 45I(5), the words "an officer of Revenue and Customs" substituted for "the Inland Revenue" by CRCA 2005, s. 50(6) and Sch. 4, para. 83(1), with effect from 18 April 2005 by virtue of SI 2005/1126, art. 2(2).
S. 45I inserted by FA 2003, s. 167 and Sch. 30, para. 3, in relation to expenditure incurred on or after 1 April 2003.

45J Environmentally beneficial components of plant or machinery

45J(1) This section applies for the purpose of apportioning expenditure incurred on plant or machinery where one or more of the components of the plant or machinery (but not all of it) is of a description specified by Treasury order under section 45H(3).

45J(2) If–

(a) only one of the components is of such a description, and

(b) an amount is specified by the order in respect of that component,

the part of the expenditure that is section 45H expenditure must not exceed that amount.

45J(3) If–

(a) more than one of the components is of such a description, and

(b) an amount is specified by the order in respect of each of those components,

the part of the expenditure that is section 45H expenditure must not exceed the total of those amounts.

45J(4) If the expenditure is treated under this Act as incurred in instalments, the proportion of each instalment that is section 45H expenditure is the same as the proportion of the whole expenditure that is section 45H expenditure.

45J(5) Where this section applies, the expenditure is not apportioned under section 562(3) (apportionment where property sold with other property).

45J(6) In this section **"section 45H expenditure"** means expenditure that is first-year qualifying expenditure under section 45H.

History – S. 45J inserted by FA 2003, s. 167 and Sch. 30, para. 3, in relation to expenditure incurred on or after 1 April 2003.
Statutory instruments – SI 2003/2076, art. 4: partly made under s. 45(J)(3)(b).

45K Expenditure on plant and machinery for use in designated assisted areas

45K(1) Expenditure is first-year qualifying expenditure if–

(a) it is incurred by a company on the provision of plant or machinery for use primarily in an area which at the time the expenditure is incurred is a designated assisted area,

(b) it is incurred in the period of 8 years beginning with the date on which the area is (or is treated as) designated under subsection (2)(a),

(c) Conditions A to E are met.

45K(1A) The Treasury may by order amend subsection (1)(b) so as to extend the period specified.

45K(2) **"Designated assisted area"** means an area which–

(a) is designated by an order made by the Treasury, and

(b) falls wholly within an assisted area.

45K(3) An area may be designated by an order under subsection (2)(a) only if at the time the order is made–

(a) the area falls wholly within an enterprise zone, and

(b) a memorandum of understanding, in respect of the area, relating to the availability of allowances in respect of expenditure to which this section applies has been entered into by the Treasury and the responsible authority for the area.

45K(4) An order made under subsection (2)(a) may provide that an area designated by the order is to be treated as having been so designated at times falling before the order is made.

45K(5) But where an area has previously been designated by an order under subsection (2)(a), section 14 of the Interpretation Act 1978 does not apply, by virtue of subsection (4), so as to imply a power to make an order ("the new order") treating that area (or any part of it) as if it were not so designated at times falling before the new order is made.

45K(6) Condition A is that the company is within the charge to corporation tax.

45K(7) Condition B is that the expenditure is incurred for the purposes of a qualifying activity within section 15(1)(a) or (f).

45K(8) Condition C is that the expenditure is incurred for the purposes of–

(a) a business of a kind not previously carried on by the company,

(b) expanding a business carried on by the company, or

(c) starting up an activity which relates to a fundamental change in a product or production process of, or service provided by, a business carried on by the company.

45K(8A) Condition C is met by virtue of subsection (8)(c) only if the amount of the expenditure exceeds the amount by which the relevant plant or machinery is depreciated in the period of 3 years ending immediately before the beginning of the chargeable period in which the expenditure is incurred.

45K(8B) **"Relevant plant or machinery"** means the plant or machinery being used at the end of the period of 3 years mentioned in subsection (8A) for the purposes of the product, process or service mentioned in subsection (8)(c).

45K(9) Condition D is that the plant or machinery is unused and not second hand.

45K(10) Condition E is that the expenditure is not replacement expenditure.

45K(11) **"Replacement expenditure"** means expenditure incurred on the provision of plant or machinery ("new plant or machinery") intended to perform the same or a similar function, for the purposes of the qualifying activity of the company, as other plant or machinery ("replaced plant or machinery")–

(a) on which the company has previously incurred qualifying expenditure, and

(b) which has been superseded by the new plant or machinery.

45K(12) But if and to the extent that–

(a) the expenditure is incurred on the provision of new plant or machinery that is capable of and intended to perform a significant additional function, when compared to the replaced plant or machinery, and

(b) the additional function enhances the capacity or productivity of the qualifying activity in question,

so much of the expenditure as is attributable to the additional function is not to be regarded as replacement expenditure.

45K(13) The part of the expenditure attributable to the additional function is to be determined on a just and reasonable basis.

45K(14) In this section–

"assisted area" means–

(a) an area specified as a development area under section 1 of the Industrial Development Act 1982, or

(b) Northern Ireland;

"enterprise zone" means an area recognised by the Treasury as an area in respect of which there is a special focus on economic development and identified on a map published by the Treasury for the purposes of this section;

"the responsible authority", for an area, means–

(a) if the area is in England, a local authority for all or part of the area or two or more such local authorities,

(b) if the area is in Scotland, the Scottish Ministers,

(c) if the area is in Wales, the Welsh Ministers, and

(d) if the area is in Northern Ireland, the Department of Enterprise, Trade and Investment in Northern Ireland.

45K(15) The Treasury may by order amend the definition of **"assisted area"** in subsection (14) in consequence of any changes made to the areas in the United Kingdom granted assisted area status by virtue of Article 107(3) of the Treaty on the Functioning of the European Union.

45K(16) This section is subject to–

section 45L (plant or machinery partly for use outside designated assisted areas),

section 45M (exclusions from section 45K allowances),

section 45N (effect of plant or machinery subsequently being primarily used in an area other than a designated assisted area), and

section 46 (general exclusions).

History – In s. 45K(1)(b), the words "the date on which the area is (or is treated as) designated under subsection (2)(a)" substituted for the words "1 April 2012" by FA 2016, s. 69, with effect from 15 September 2016 (Royal Assent).
In s. 45K(1)(b), the words "8 years" substituted for the words "5 years" by FA 2014, s. 64(5)(a) with effect from 17 July 2014.
S. 45K(1A) inserted by FA 2014, s. 64(5)(b) with effect from 17 July 2014.
S. 45K(8A) and (8B) inserted by FA 2014, s. 65 and Sch. 13, para. 3, with effect in relation to expenditure incurred on or after 17 July 2014.
S. 45K inserted by FA 2012, s. 44 and Sch. 11, para. 3, with effect for chargeable periods ending on or after 1 April 2012.

Statutory instruments – SI 2014/3183: made under s. 45K(2)(a), (3) and (4).
SI 2015/2047: made under s. 45K(2)(a), (3) and (4).
SI 2016/751: made under s. 45K(2)(a), (3) and (4).

45L Exclusion of plant or machinery partly for use outside designated assisted areas

45L(1) Expenditure on plant or machinery is not first-year qualifying expenditure under section 45K if–

(a) at the time when it is incurred, the company incurring it intends the plant or machinery to be used partly in a non-designated area, and

(b) the main purpose, or one of the main purposes, for which any person is a party to the relevant arrangements is the obtaining of a first-year allowance, or a greater first-year allowance, in respect of the part of the expenditure that is attributable to that intended use in a non-designated area.

45L(2) For the purposes of subsection (1)(b), the part of the expenditure that is attributable to that intended use in a non-designated area is to be determined on a just and reasonable basis.

45L(3) In this section–

"non-designated area" means an area which is not a designated assisted area within the meaning of section 45K;

"the relevant arrangements" means–

(a) the transaction under which the expenditure is incurred, and

(b) any scheme or arrangements of which that transaction forms part.

History – S. 45L inserted by FA 2012, s. 44 and Sch. 11, para. 3, with effect for chargeable periods ending on or after 1 April 2012.

45M Exclusions from allowances under section 45K

45M(1) Expenditure incurred by a person is not first-year qualifying expenditure under section 45K if it is within subsection (2), (4), (7) or (7A).

45M(2) Expenditure is within this subsection if, at the time a claim is made under section 3 for a section 45K allowance in respect of the expenditure, the person who incurred the expenditure is, or forms part of, an undertaking within subsection (3).

45M(3) An undertaking is within this subsection if one or both of the following conditions are met–

(a) it is reasonable to assume that the undertaking would be regarded as an undertaking in difficulty for the purposes of the General Block Exemption Regulation;

(b) the undertaking is subject to an outstanding recovery order made by virtue of Article 108(2) of the Treaty on the Functioning of the European Union (Commission Decision declaring aid illegal and incompatible with the common market).

45M(4) Expenditure is within this subsection if it is incurred for the purposes of a qualifying activity–

(a) in the fishery or aquaculture sector, as covered by Regulation (EU) No 1379/2013 of the European Parliament and of the Council,

(b) in the coal sector, steel sector, shipbuilding sector or synthetic fibres sector,

(ba) in the transport sector or related infrastructure,

(bb) relating to energy generation, distribution or infrastructure,

(bc) relating to the development of broadband networks,

(c) relating to the management of waste of undertakings, or

(d) relating to–

(i) the primary production of agricultural products,

(ii) on-farm activities necessary for preparing an animal or plant product for the first sale, or

(iii) the first sale of agricultural products by a primary producer to wholesalers, retailers or processors, in circumstances where that sale does not take place on separate premises reserved for that purpose.

45M(4A) Expressions used in subsection (4)(b), (ba), (bb) or (bc) and in the General Block Exemption Regulation have the same meaning as in that Regulation.

45M(5) In subsection (4)(c) the reference to waste of undertakings does not include waste of the person who incurred the expenditure or of any other person forming part of the same undertaking as that person.

45M(6) [Omitted by FA 2014, s. 65 and Sch. 13, para. 4(6).]

45M(7) Expenditure is within this subsection if a relevant grant or relevant payment is made towards–

(a) that expenditure, or

(b) any other expenditure which is incurred by any person in respect of the same designated assisted area, and on the same single investment project, as that expenditure.

45M(7A) Expenditure is within this subsection if–

(a) the area by reference to which the condition in section 45K(1)(a) is met is not an area which falls within Article 107(3)(a) of the Treaty on the Functioning of the European Union,

(b) the condition in section 45K(8)(a) is not met in relation to the expenditure, and

(c) at the time the expenditure is incurred the company is not an SME for the purposes of the General Block Exemption Regulation.

45M(8) A section 45K allowance made in respect of first-year qualifying expenditure is to be withdrawn if–

(a) after it is made, a relevant grant or relevant payment is made towards that expenditure, or

(b) within the period of 3 years beginning when that expenditure was incurred, a relevant grant or relevant payment is made towards any other expenditure which is incurred by any person in respect of the same designated assisted area, and on the same single investment project, as that expenditure.

45M(9) All such assessments and adjustments of assessments are to be made as are necessary to give effect to subsection (8).

45M(10) If a person who has made a return becomes aware that, after making it, anything in it has become incorrect because of the operation of this section, that person must give notice to an officer of Revenue and Customs specifying how the return needs to be amended.

45M(11) The notice must be given within 3 months beginning with the day on which the person first became aware that anything in the return had become incorrect because of the operation of this section.

45M(12) In this section–

"agricultural product", has the same meaning as in the General Block Exemption Regulation;

"General Block Exemption Regulation" means Commission Regulation (EU) No 651/2014 (General block exemption Regulation);

"management" and **"waste"** have the meaning given by Article 1 of Directive 2006/12/EC of the European Parliament and of the Council;

"relevant grant or relevant payment" means a grant or payment which is–

(a) a State aid, other than an allowance under this Part, or

(b) a grant or subsidy, other than a State aid, which the Treasury by order declares to be relevant for the purposes of the witholding of a section 45K allowance;

"section 45K allowance" means a first-year allowance in respect of expenditure that is first-year qualifying expenditure under section 45K;

"single investment project" has the same meaning as in the General Block Exemption Regulation;

"undertaking" means–

(a) an autonomous enterprise, or

(b) an enterprise (not within paragraph (a)) and its partner enterprises (if any) and its linked enterprises (if any),

and for this purpose **"enterprise"**, **"autonomous enterprise"**, **"partner enterprises"** and **"linked enterprises"** have the meaning given by Annex 1 to the General Block Exemption Regulation.

45M(13) Nothing in this section limits references to **"State aid"** to State aid which is required to be notified to and approved by the European Commission.

45M(14) For the purposes of this section references to expenditure incurred in respect of a designated assisted area includes expenditure incurred on the provision of things for use primarily in that area or on services to be provided primarily in that area.

45M(15) The Treasury may by order make such provision amending this section as appears to them appropriate for the purpose of giving effect to any future amendments of or instruments replacing–

(a) the General Block Exemption Regulation,

(b) the Community Guidelines on State Aid for Rescuing and Restructuring Firms in Difficulty (2004/C 244/02),

(c) Regulation (EU) No 1379/2013 of the European Parliament and of the Council,

(d) Directive 2006/12/EC of the European Parliament and of the Council, or

(e) the Treaty on the Functioning of the European Union.

History – In s. 45M(1), "(7) or (7A)" substituted for "(6) or (7)" by FA 2014, s. 65 and Sch. 13, para. 4(2), with effect in relation to expenditure incurred on or after 17 July 2014.
In s. 45M(3)(a), the words "an undertaking in difficulty for the purposes of the General Block Exemption Regulation" substituted for the words "a firm in difficulty for the purposes of the Community Guidelines on State Aid for Rescuing and Restructuring Firms in Difficulty (2004/C 244/02)" by FA 2014, s. 65 and Sch. 13, para. 4(3), with effect in relation to expenditure incurred on or after 17 July 2014.
In s. 45M(4)(a), the words "Regulation (EU) No 1379/2013 of the European Parliament and of the Council" substituted for the words "Council Regulation (EC) No 104/2000" by FA 2014, s. 65 and Sch. 13, para. 4(4)(a), with effect in relation to expenditure incurred on or after 17 July 2014.
S. 45M(4)(ba), (bb) and (bc) inserted by FA 2014, s. 65 and Sch. 13, para. 4(4)(b), with effect in relation to expenditure incurred on or after 17 July 2014.
S. 45M(4A) inserted by FA 2014, s. 65 and Sch. 13, para. 4(5), with effect in relation to expenditure incurred on or after 17 July 2014.
S. 45M(6) omitted by FA 2014, s. 65 and Sch. 13, para. 4(6), with effect in relation to expenditure incurred on or after 17 July 2014.
S. 45M(7A) inserted by FA 2014, s. 65 and Sch. 13, para. 4(7), with effect in relation to expenditure incurred on or after 17 July 2014.
In s. 45M(12), in the definition of "agricultural product", the word "has" substituted for the words "**"coal sector"**, **"steel sector"**, **"shipbuilding sector"** and **"synthetic fibres sector"** have" by FA 2014, s. 65 and Sch. 13, para. 4(8)(a), with effect in relation to expenditure incurred on or after 17 July 2014.
In s. 45M(12), in the definition of "General Block Exemption Regulation", "(EU) No 651/2014" substituted for "(EC) No 800/2008" by FA 2014, s. 65 and Sch. 13, para. 4(8)(b), with effect in relation to expenditure incurred on or after 17 July 2014.
S. 45M(15)(c) substituted by FA 2014, s. 65 and Sch. 13, para. 4(9), with effect in relation to expenditure incurred on or after 17 July 2014.
S. 45M inserted by FA 2012, s. 44 and Sch. 11, para. 3, with effect for chargeable periods ending on or after 1 April 2012.

45N Effect of plant or machinery subsequently being primarily for use outside designated assisted areas

45N(1) Expenditure on the provision of plant or machinery is to be treated as never having been first-year qualifying expenditure under section 45K if, at any relevant time–

(a) the primary use to which the plant and machinery is put is other than in an area which was a relevant area at the time the expenditure was incurred, or

(b) the plant or machinery is held for use otherwise than primarily in an area which was a relevant area at that time.

45N(2) **"Relevant time"** means a time which–

(a) falls within the relevant period, and

(b) is a time when the plant or machinery is owned by–

(i) the person who incurred the expenditure, or

(ii) a person who is, or at any time in that period has been, connected with that person.

45N(3) **"The relevant period"** means the period of 5 years beginning with–

(a) the day on which the plant or machinery in question is first brought into use for the purposes of a qualifying activity carried on by the company, or

(b) if earlier, the day on which it is first held for such use.

45N(3A) **"Relevant area"** means–

(a) in relation to expenditure which would be within subsection (7A) of section 45M if paragraph (a) of that subsection were omitted, a designated assisted area within the meaning of section 45K which falls within Article 107(3)(a) of the Treaty on the Functioning of the European Union, and

(b) in relation to any other expenditure, a designated assisted area within the meaning of section 45K.

45N(4) All such assessments and adjustments of assessments are to be made as are necessary to give effect to subsection (1).

45N(5) If a person who has made a return becomes aware that, after making it, anything in it has become incorrect because of the operation of this section, that person must give notice to an officer of Revenue and Customs specifying how the return needs to be amended.

45N(6) The notice must be given within 3 months beginning with the day on which the person first became aware that anything in the return had become incorrect because of the operation of this section.

History – In s. 45N(1)(a), the words "relevant area" substituted for the words "designated assisted area within the meaning of section 45K" by FA 2014, s. 65 and Sch. 13, para. 5(2)(a), with effect in relation to expenditure incurred on or after 17 July 2014.
In s. 45N(1)(b), the words "a relevant" substituted for the words "such a designated assisted" by FA 2014, s. 65 and Sch. 13, para. 5(2)(b), with effect in relation to expenditure incurred on or after 17 July 2014.
S. 45N(3A) inserted by FA 2014, s. 65 and Sch. 13, para. 5(3), with effect in relation to expenditure incurred on or after 17 July 2014.
S. 45N inserted by FA 2012, s. 44 and Sch. 11, para. 3, with effect for chargeable periods ending on or after 1 April 2012.

46 General exclusions

46(1) Expenditure within any of the general exclusions in subsection (2) is not first-year qualifying expenditure under any of the following provisions–

section 45A (expenditure on energy-saving plant or machinery),

section 45D (expenditure on cars with low CO_2 emissions),

section 45DA (expenditure zero-emission goods vehicles),

section 45E (expenditure on plant or machinery for gas refuelling station),

section 45F (expenditure on plant and machinery for use wholly in a ring fence trade),

section 45H (expenditure on environmentally beneficial plant and machinery).

section 45K (expenditure on plant and machinery for use in designated assisted areas).

46(2) The general exclusions are–

General exclusion 1

The expenditure is incurred in the chargeable period in which the qualifying activity is permanently discontinued.

General exclusion 2

The expenditure is incurred on the provision of a car (as defined by section 268A).

46(2) [General exclusions 3 and 4 omitted by FA 2013, s. 70(1).]

General exclusion 5

The expenditure would be long-life asset expenditure but for paragraph 20 of Schedule 3 (transitional provisions).

General exclusion 6

The expenditure is on the provision of plant or machinery for leasing (whether in the course of a trade or otherwise).

For this purpose, the letting of a ship on charter, or of any other asset on hire, is to be regarded as leasing (whether or not it would otherwise be so regarded).

General exclusion 7

The circumstances of the incurring of the expenditure are that–

(a) the provision of the plant or machinery on which the expenditure is incurred is connected with a change in the nature or conduct of a trade or business carried on by a person other than the person incurring the expenditure, and

(b) the obtaining of a first-year allowance is the main benefit, or one of the main benefits, which could reasonably be expected to arise from the making of the change.

General exclusion 8

Any of the following sections applies–

section 13 (use for qualifying activity of plant or machinery provided for other purposes);

section 13A (use for other purposes of plant or machinery provided for long funding leasing).

section 14 (use for qualifying activity of plant or machinery which is a gift).

This is subject to section 161 (pre-trading expenditure on mineral exploration and access).

46(3) Subsection (1) is subject to the following provisions of this section.

46(4) General exclusion 2 does not prevent expenditure being first-year qualifying expenditure under section 45D.

46(5) General exclusion 6 does not prevent expenditure being first-year qualifying expenditure under any of the following provisions–

section 45A, if the condition in subsection (6) is met,

section 45H, if the condition in subsection (6) is met."

46(6) The condition is that the plant or machinery is provided for leasing under an excluded lease of background plant or machinery for a building, within the meaning given by section 70R.

History – In the heading to s. 46, the words "applying to sections 40, 44 and 45" omitted by FA 2008, s. 76(5)(b)(ii), with effect from 21 July 2008.

In s. 46(1), words "any of the following provisions" inserted by FA 2003, s. 167 and Sch. 30, para. 4.

In s. 46(1), the former entry relating to s. 40 omitted by FA 2008, s. 76(5)(b)(i), with effect from 21 July 2008.

In s. 46(1), the former entry relating to s. 44 omitted by FA 2008, s. 75(3)(b), with effect in relation to expenditure incurred on or after 1 April 2008 for corporation tax purposes and 6 April 2008 for income tax purposes. However, where a business incurs an additional VAT liability (under the VAT Capital Goods Scheme) on or after those dates and the original expenditure was first-year qualifying

expenditure by virtue of s. 44, then CAA 2001, Pt. 2, Ch. 18 will still apply to the additional VAT liability as if the entry had not been omitted (FA 2008, s. 75(6) and (7)).
In s. 46(1), the former entry relating to s. 45 omitted by FA 2008, s. 76(5)(b)(i), with effect from 21 July 2008.
In s. 46(1), entry relating to s. 45A inserted by FA 2001, s. 65 and Sch. 17, para. 3, and word "or" that immediately preceded the words "section 45" repealed by FA 2001, s. 110 and Sch. 33, Pt. 2(4).
In s. 46(1), the entry relating to s. 45D added by FA 2002, s. 59 and Sch. 19, para. 4(2) with effect in relation to expenditure incurred on or after 17 April 2002.
In s. 46(1), the entry relating to s. 45DA inserted by F(No. 3)A 2010, s. 18 and Sch. 7, para. 4, with effect for chargeable periods ending on or after 1 April 2010 (corporation tax) or 6 April 2010 (income tax).
In s. 46(1) the entry relating to s. 45E added by FA 2002, s. 61 and Sch. 20, para. 4 with effect in relation to expenditure incurred on or after 17 April 2002.
In s. 46(1) the entry relating to s. 45F added by FA 2002, s. 63 and Sch. 21, para. 5 with effect in relation to expenditure incurred on or after 17 April 2002.
In s. 46(1), entry relating to s. 45H inserted, and word "or" that followed "section 45E" omitted, by FA 2003, s.167 and Sch. 30, para. 4, with effect in relation to expenditure incurred on or after 1 April 2003.
In s. 46(1), the entry relating to s. 45K inserted by FA 2012, s. 44 and Sch. 11, para. 4, with effect for chargeable periods ending on or after 1 April 2012.
In s. 46(2), general exclusion 3 and 4 (and the italicised headings preceding them) omitted by FA 2013, s. 70(1), with effect for expenditure incurred on or after 1 April 2013.
In s. 46(2), in general exclusion 2, "268A" substituted for "81" by FA 2009, s. 30 and Sch.11, para. 3, with effect in relation to expenditure incurred on or after 1 April 2009 (for corporation tax purposes) and 6 April 2009 (for income tax purposes), subject to transitional provisions in FA 2009, Sch. 11, para. 27(2) and 30–32.
In s. 46(2), the word "Any" substituted for "Either", and the entry relating to s. 13A inserted, by FA 2006, s. 81 and Sch. 8, para. 4. The commencement and transitional provisions are complex and are set out in full in FA 2006, Sch. 8, para. 15–27.
S. 46(3) and (4) inserted by FA 2002, s. 59 and Sch. 19, para. 4(3), with effect in relation to expenditure incurred on or after 17 April 2002.
In s. 46(5), entry relating to "section 45D," omitted by FA 2013, s. 68(2), with effect in relation to expenditure incurred on or after 1 April 2013.
S. 46(5) and (6) substituted for former s. 46(5) by FA 2006, s. 81 and Sch. 9, para. 11(2), with effect in relation to expenditure incurred on or after 1 April 2006.
In former s. 46(5) the reference to s. 45H inserted by FA 2003, s. 167 and Sch. 30, para. 4(2).
Former s. 46(5) inserted by FA 2002, s. 62(2), with effect in relation to expenditure incurred on or after 17 April 2002.

Origin – S. 46(1): CAA 1990, s. 22 (6B) (part), (6C) (part), s. 81(1A) (part).
S. 46(2): General exclusion 1 CAA 1990, s. 22(6B)(a). General exclusions 2–4 CAA 1990, s. 22(6B)(b). General exclusion 5 CAA 1990, s. 22(6B) (part). General exclusion 6 CAA 1990, s. 22(6B)(d), s. 50(2) (part). General exclusion 7 CAA 1990, s. 22(6C), Annex 2, Note 14. General exclusion 8 CAA 1990, s. 81(1A) (part).

Rewrite: Technical Points – Explanatory Notes, Annex 2, Note 14: by referring to a "trade or business" rather than "qualifying activity", general exclusion 7 preserves the wording of CAA 1990, s. 22(6C) from which it derives, and translates into CAA 2001 so as to make neither wider nor narrower the scope of the exclusion. It also preserves the read-across to other statutory provisions which refer to "a major change in the nature or conduct of a trade or business".

HMRC Manuals – CA23110: guidance on s. 46.

EXPENDITURE OF SMALL OR MEDIUM-SIZED ENTERPRISES

47 Expenditure of small or medium-sized enterprises: companies

47 [Omitted by FA 2008, s. 75(3)(c).]

History – S. 47 omitted by FA 2008, s. 75(3)(c), with effect in relation to expenditure incurred on or after 1 April 2008 for corporation tax purposes and 6 April 2008 for income tax purposes. However, where a business incurs an additional VAT liability (under the VAT Capital Goods Scheme) on or after those dates and the original expenditure was first-year qualifying expenditure by virtue of s. 44, then CAA 2001, Pt. 2, Ch. 18 will still apply to the additional VAT liability as if s. 47 had not been omitted (FA 2008, s. 75(6) and (7)). Former s. 47 read as follows:

"Expenditure of small or medium-sized enterprises: companies

47(1) Use this section to decide whether expenditure incurred by a company is, for the purposes of this Chapter, incurred by–
(a) a small or medium-sized enterprise, or
(b) a small enterprise.

47(2) The expenditure is incurred by a small or medium-sized enterprise if the company–
(a) qualifies (or is treated as qualifying) as small or medium-sized under the relevant companies legislation in relation to the financial year of the company in which the expenditure is incurred, and
(b) is not a member of a large group at the time when the expenditure is incurred.

47(3) The expenditure is incurred by a small enterprise if the company–
(a) qualifies (or is treated as qualifying) as small under the relevant companies legislation in relation to the financial year of the company in which the expenditure is incurred, and
(b) is not a member of a large or medium-sized group at the time when the expenditure is incurred.

47(4) In this section–
(a) **"the relevant companies legislation"** means sections 382 and 465 of the Companies Act 2006, and
(b) **"financial year"** has the same meaning as in section 390 of the Companies Act 2006.

47(5) [Omitted by SI 2008/954, art. 28(3), and art. 3 and Schedule.]

47(6) **"Company"** means–
(a) a company, or an oversea company, within the meaning of the Companies Act 1985, or
(b) a company, or a Part XXIII company, within the meaning of the Companies (Northern Ireland) Order 1986."

In former s. 47(4), the words "In this section" substituted for "Except in the case of a company formed and registered in Northern Ireland" by SI 2008/954, art. 28(2), with effect from 6 April 2008.
In former s. 47(4)(a), the words "sections 382 and 465 of the Companies Act 2006" substituted for "section 247 of the Companies Act 1985" by SI 2008/954, art. 28(2), with effect from 6 April 2008.
In former s. 47(4)(b), the words "section 390 of the Companies Act 2006" substituted for "Part VII of the 1985 Act" by SI 2008/954, art. 28(2), with effect from 6 April 2008.
S. 47(5) omitted by SI 2008/954, art. 28(3), and art. 3 and Sch., with effect from 6 April 2008.
In former s. 47(6)(a), the words "the Companies Act 1985" substituted for "the 1985 Act" by SI 2008/954, art. 28(4), with effect from 6 April 2008.

In former s. 47(6)(b), the words "the Companies (Northern Ireland) Order 1986" substituted for "the 1986 Order" by SI 2008/954, art. 28(4), with effect from 6 April 2008.

Origin – S. 47(1): CAA 1990, s. 22A(1) (part), s. 22 AA(1) (part), drafting.
S. 47(2): CAA 1990, s. 22A(1) (part), (7) (part).
S. 47(3): CAA 1990, s. 22AA(1) (part), (7) (part).
S. 47(4), (5): CAA 1990, s. 22 A(6) ("financial year"), (7) (part), s. 22AA(6) (part), (7) (part).
S. 47(6): CAA 1990, s. 22 A(6) ("company"), s. 22AA(6) (part).

48 Expenditure of small or medium-sized enterprises: businesses

48 [Omitted by FA 2008, s. 75(3)(c).]

History – S. 48 omitted by FA 2008, s. 75(3)(c), with effect in relation to expenditure incurred on or after 1 April 2008 for corporation tax purposes and 6 April 2008 for income tax purposes. However, where a business incurs an additional VAT liability (under the VAT Capital Goods Scheme) on or after those dates and the original expenditure was first-year qualifying expenditure by virtue of s. 44, then CAA 2001, Pt. 2, Ch. 18 will still apply to the additional VAT liability as if s. 48 had not been omitted (FA 2008, s. 75(6) and (7)). Former s. 48 read as follows:

"Expenditure of small or medium-sized enterprises: businesses

48(1) Use this section to decide whether expenditure incurred by a business is, for the purposes of this Chapter, incurred by–
(a) a small or medium-sized enterprise, or
(b) a small enterprise.
48(2) In this section **"business"** means–
(a) an individual,
(b) a partnership of which all the members are individuals,
(c) a registered friendly society within the meaning of Chapter II of Part XII of ICTA, or
(d) a body corporate which is not a company but is within the charge to corporation tax.
48(3) The expenditure is incurred by a small or medium-sized enterprise if–
(a) the expenditure is incurred for the purposes of a qualifying activity carried on by the business, and
(b) the business passes the hypothetical company test, in relation to that expenditure, as a small or medium-sized company.
48(4) The expenditure is incurred by a small enterprise if–
(a) the expenditure is incurred for the purposes of a qualifying activity carried on by the business, and
(b) the business passes the hypothetical company test, in relation to that expenditure, as a small company.
48(5) To apply the hypothetical company test, assume that–
(a) the qualifying activity is carried on by a company (**"the hypothetical company"**),
(b) every trade, business, profession or vocation carried on by the business is carried on by the business as part of that activity,
(c) the financial years of the hypothetical company coincide with the chargeable periods of the business, and
(d) accounts of the hypothetical company for any relevant chargeable period have been duly drawn up as if that period were a financial year of the company.
48(6) The business passes the hypothetical company test as a small or medium-sized company in relation to the expenditure in question if, on the assumptions in subsection (5), the company would qualify (or be treated as qualifying) as small or medium-sized under the relevant companies legislation in relation to the financial year in which the expenditure is assumed to be incurred.
48(7) The business passes the hypothetical company test as a small company in relation to the expenditure in question if, on the assumptions in subsection (5), the company would qualify (or be treated as qualifying) as small under the relevant companies legislation in relation to the financial year in which the expenditure is assumed to be incurred.
48(8) In this section–
(a) **"the relevant companies legislation"** means sections 382 and 465 of the Companies Act 2006, and
(b) **"financial year"** has the same meaning as in section 390 of the Companies Act 2006;
and the reference in subsection (5)(d) to accounts being duly drawn up is to their being drawn up in accordance with that Act.
48(9) [Omitted by SI 2008/954, art. 29(3), and art. 3 and Schedule.]"
In former s. 48(8), the words "In this section" substituted for "Except in the case of a business carrying on a qualifying activity wholly or mainly in Northern Ireland" by SI 2008/954, art. 29(2), with effect from 6 April 2008.
In former s. 48(8)(a), the words "sections 382 and 465 of the Companies Act 2006" substituted for "section 247 of the Companies Act 1985" by SI 2008/954, art. 29(2), with effect from 6 April 2008.
In former s. 48(8)(b), the words "section 390 of the Companies Act 2006" substituted for "Part VII of that Act" by SI 2008/954, art. 29(2), with effect from 6 April 2008.
S. 48(9) omitted by SI 2008/954, art. 29(3), and art. 3 and Sch., with effect from 6 April 2008.

Origin – S. 48(1): CAA 1990, s. 22A(2) (part), s. 22 AA(2) (part), drafting.
S. 48(2): CAA 1990, s. 22A(6) ("business"), s. 22 AA(6) (part).
S. 48(3): CAA 1990, s. 22A(2) (part).
S. 48(4): CAA 1990, s. 22AA(2) (part).
S. 48(5): CAA 1990, s. 22A(2) (part), (3) (part), s. 22 AA(2) (part), (3) (part).
S. 48(6): CAA 1990, s. 22A(2) (part).
S. 48(7): CAA 1990, s. 22AA(2) (part).
S. 48(8), (9): CAA 1990, s. 22 A(3) (part), (6) ("financial year"), (7) (part), s. 22AA(3) (part), (6) (part), (7) (part), Annex 1, Change 7.

49 Whether company is a member of a large or medium-sized group

49 [Omitted by FA 2008, s. 75(3)(c).]

History – S. 49 omitted by FA 2008, s. 75(3)(c), with effect in relation to expenditure incurred on or after 1 April 2008 for corporation tax purposes and 6 April 2008 for income tax purposes. However, where a business incurs an additional VAT liability (under the VAT Capital Goods Scheme) on or after those dates and the original expenditure was first-year qualifying expenditure by virtue of s. 44, then CAA 2001, Pt. 2, Ch. 18 will still apply to the additional VAT liability as if s. 49 had not been omitted (FA 2008, s. 75(6) and (7)). Former s. 49 read as follows:

"Whether company is a member of a large or medium-sized group

49(1) Use this section to decide whether, for the purposes of section 47, a company is–
(a) a member of a large group, or
(b) a member of a large or medium-sized group.
49(2) Subject to subsection (4), a company is a member of a large group at the time when any expenditure is incurred if–
(a) it is at that time the parent undertaking of a group which does not qualify as small or medium-sized in relation to the financial year of the parent undertaking in which that time falls, or
(b) it is at that time a subsidiary undertaking in relation to the parent undertaking of such a group.

49(3) Subject to subsection (4), a company is a member of a large or medium-sized group at the time when any expenditure is incurred if–

(a) it is at that time the parent undertaking of a group which does not qualify as small in relation to the financial year of the parent undertaking in which that time falls, or

(b) it is at that time a subsidiary undertaking in relation to the parent undertaking of such a group.

49(4) If, at the time when any expenditure is incurred by a company, any arrangements exist which are such that, had effect been given to them immediately before that time, the company or a successor of the company–

(a) would, at that time, have been a member of a large group, or

(b) would, at that time, have been a member of a large or medium-sized group,

the company incurring the expenditure is to be treated as a member of a large group or (as the case may be) a large or medium-sized group at that time.

49(5) For the purposes of subsections (2) and (3), the question whether–

(a) a group qualifies as small or medium-sized, or

(b) a group qualifies as small,

is to be decided by reference to the relevant companies legislation (but reading references in that legislation to a parent company as references to a parent undertaking).

49(6) In subsection (5) **"the relevant companies legislation"** means sections 383 and 466 of the Companies Act 2006.

49(7) For the purposes of subsection (4) a company is the successor of another if–

(a) it carries on a trade which, in whole or in part, the other company has ceased to carry on, and

(b) the circumstances are such that section 343 of ICTA (company reconstructions without a change of ownership) applies in relation to the two companies as the predecessor and the successor within the meaning of that section,

and **"arrangements"** means arrangements of any kind (whether or not in writing or legally enforceable).

49(8) In this section–

"financial year" and **"group"** have the same meaning as in Part 15 of the Companies Act 2006;

"parent undertaking" and **"subsidiary undertaking"** have the same meaning as in section 1162 of that Act."

In former s. 49(6), the words "sections 383 and 466 of the Companies Act 2006." substituted for para. (a) and (b) by SI 2008/954, art. 30(2), with effect from 6 April 2008.

Former s. 49(8) substituted by SI 2008/954, art. 30(3), with effect from 6 April 2008.

Origin – S. 49(1): drafting.
S. 49(2): CAA 1990, s. 22A(4).
S. 49(3): CAA 1990, s. 22AA(4).
S. 49(4): CAA 1990, s. 22A(5), s. 22AA(5).
S. 49(5), (6): CAA 1990, s. 22A(8), s. 22AA(8).
S. 49(7): CAA 1990, s. 22A(6) ("arrangements"), (9), s. 22AA(6) (part), (9).
S. 49(8): CAA 1990, s. 22A(6) ("financial year", "group", "parent undertaking", "subsidiary undertaking"), s. 22AA(6) (part).

SUPPLEMENTARY

50 Time when expenditure is incurred

50 In determining whether expenditure is first-year qualifying expenditure under this Chapter, any effect of section 12 on the time at which it is to be treated as incurred is to be disregarded.

Origin – CAA 1990, s. 22(3CB) (part), (3D) (part), (3E) (part).

HMRC Manuals – CA23110: guidance on s. 50.

51 Disclosure of information between UK tax authorities

51 [Omitted by FA 2008, s. 76(5)(c).]

History – S. 51 omitted by FA 2008, s. 76(5)(c), with effect from 21 July 2008.

Chapter 5 – Allowances and Charges

Cross references – FA 1993, s. 94: rules for translating amounts into a different currency.
FA 2000, s. 105(3): computation and expression in currencies other than sterling of certain amounts to be taken into account under Pt. 2 Ch. 5.
Electricity Act 1989, Sch. 11, para. 5(4): treatment of fixtures where a lease is granted in pursuance of certain transfer schemes on privatisation.
Greater London Authority Act 2000, Sch. 33, para. 4(9): transfers from London Regional Transport or its subsidiaries to Transport for London or its subsidiaries.
Greater London Authority Act 2000, Sch. 33, para. 10(10): transfers from London Regional Transport or its subsidiaries in preparation for, or in pursuance of, a private-public partnership.

ANNUAL INVESTMENT ALLOWANCE

History – S. 51A–51N inserted by FA 2008, s. 74 and Sch. 24, para. 3, with effect in relation to expenditure incurred on or after 1 April 2008 for corporation tax purposes and 6 April 2008 for income tax purposes.

51A Entitlement to annual investment allowance

Notes – For expenditure incurred during the period of two years beginning with 1 January 2013, see the cross-reference notes below.

51A(1) A person is entitled to an allowance (an "annual investment allowance") in respect of AIA *qualifying* expenditure if–

(a) the expenditure is incurred in a chargeable period to which this Act applies, and

(b) the person owns the plant and machinery at some time during that chargeable period.

51A(2) Any annual investment allowance is made for the chargeable period in which the AIA qualifying expenditure is incurred.

51A(3) If the AIA qualifying expenditure incurred in a chargeable period is less than or equal to the maximum allowance, the person is entitled to an annual investment allowance in respect of all the AIA qualifying expenditure.

51A(4) If the AIA qualifying expenditure incurred in a chargeable period is more than the maximum allowance, the person is entitled to an annual investment allowance in respect of so much of the AIA qualifying expenditure as does not exceed the maximum allowance.

51A(5) The maximum allowance is £200,000.

51A(6) But if the chargeable period is more or less than a year, the maximum allowance is proportionately increased or reduced.

51A(7) A person may claim an annual investment allowance in respect of all the AIA qualifying expenditure in respect of which the person is entitled to an allowance, or in respect of only some of it.

51A(8) The Treasury may by order substitute for the amount for the time being specified in subsection (5) such greater amount as it thinks fit.

51A(9) An order under subsection (8) may make such incidental, supplemental, consequential and transitional provision as the Treasury thinks fit.

51A(10) This section is subject to–

(a) sections 51B to 51N (restrictions on entitlement to annual investment allowance),

section 70DA(2) (transfer and long funding leaseback: no annual investment allowance for lessee),

(b) section 205 (reduction of allowance if plant or machinery provided partly for purposes other than those of qualifying activity),

(c) section 210 (reduction of allowance if it appears that a partial depreciation subsidy is or will be payable), and

(d) sections 217, 218A, 229A(2) and 241 (anti-avoidance: no allowance in certain cases),

and needs to be read with section 236 (additional VAT liabilities).

History – In s. 51A(5), "£200,000" substituted for "£25,000" by F(No. 2)A 2015, s. 8(1), with effect in relation to expenditure incurred on or after 1 January 2016, subject to transitional provisions in FA 2014, Sch. 2, para. 4 and 5.
In s. 51A(5), the word "£25,000" substituted for "£100,000" by FA 2011, s. 11(2), with effect in relation to expenditure incurred on or after 1 April 2012 (for corporation tax purposes), and 6 April 2012 (for income tax purposes), subject to transitional provisions in FA 2011, s. 11(5)–(12).
In s. 51A(5), the figure "£100,000" substituted for "£50,000" by FA 2010, s. 5(1), with effect in relation to expenditure incurred on or after 1 April 2010 (for corporation tax purposes) or 6 April 2010 (for income tax purposes), subject to transitional provisions in FA 2010, s. 5(3)–(6).
In s. 51A(8), the word "greater" substituted for the word "other" by FA 2011, s. 11(3), with effect from 19 July 2011.
In s. 51A(10), reference to s. 70DA(2) inserted (without para. designation) by FA 2009, s. 64 and Sch. 32, para. 12, with effect in relation to cases where the commencement of the term of the lease referred to in s. 70DA(1)(b) is on or after 13 November 2008.
In s. 51A(10), ", 229A(2)" inserted by FA 2009, s. 64 and Sch. 32, para. 18, with effect in relation to cases where the contract referred to in s. 229A(1)(c) is entered into on or after 13 November 2008.
S. 51A inserted by FA 2008, s. 74 and Sch. 24, para. 3, with effect in relation to expenditure incurred on or after 1 April 2008 for corporation tax purposes and 6 April 2008 for income tax purposes. However, in relation to a chargeable period that ends on or spans those April 2008 dates, the maximum allowance under s. 51A is calculated as if the period beginning with 1 April 2008 or 6 April 2008 (as the case may be) and ending with the end of the chargeable period were the chargeable period (FA 2008, Sch. 24, para. 23(2)).

Cross references – FA 2013, s. 7(1): temporary increase in annual investment allowance in relation to expenditure incurred during the period of two years beginning with 1 January 2013; s. 51A has effect as if in (5), the figure "£250,000" was substituted for "£25,000".
FA 2013, s. 7(2) and Sch. 1: annual investment allowance: periods straddling 1 January 2013 or 1 January 2015.
FA 2014, s. 10: temporary increase in annual investment allowance for periods beginning with 1 April 2014 (for corporation tax) or 6 April 2014 (for income tax) and ending with 31 December 2015: s. 51A has effect as if the maximum allowance specified in s. 51A(5) were £500,000.
FA 2014, Sch. 2, Pt. 1: transitional provisions in relation to the temporary increase in annual investment allowance provided for by FA 2014, s. 10.

51B First restriction: companies

51B(1) A company is entitled to a single annual investment allowance in respect of all the qualifying activities carried on by the company in a chargeable period.

51B(2) The company may allocate the annual investment allowance to the relevant AIA qualifying expenditure as it thinks fit.

51B(3) The relevant AIA qualifying expenditure is the AIA qualifying expenditure incurred by the company in the chargeable period mentioned in subsection (1).

51B(4) This section is subject to sections 51C, 51D and 51E.

History – S. 51B inserted by FA 2008, s. 74 and Sch. 24, para. 3, with effect in relation to expenditure incurred on or after 1 April 2008 for corporation tax purposes and 6 April 2008 for income tax purposes.

51C Second restriction: groups of companies

51C(1) This section applies in relation to–

(a) a company which, in a financial year, is a parent undertaking of one or more other companies, and

(b) those other companies.

51C(2) The companies are entitled to a single annual investment allowance between them in respect of the relevant AIA qualifying expenditure.

51C(3) The companies may allocate the annual investment allowance to the relevant AIA qualifying expenditure as they think fit.

51C(4) The relevant AIA qualifying expenditure is the AIA qualifying expenditure incurred by the companies in chargeable periods ending in the financial year mentioned in subsection (1).

51C(5) A company ("P") is a parent undertaking of another company ("C") in a financial year if P is a parent undertaking of C at the end of C's chargeable period ending in that financial year.

51C(6) In this section **"parent undertaking"** has the same meaning as in section 1162 of the Companies Act 2006.

51C(7) This section is subject to section 51D.

History – S. 51C inserted by FA 2008, s. 74 and Sch. 24, para. 3, with effect in relation to expenditure incurred on or after 1 April 2008 for corporation tax purposes and 6 April 2008 for income tax purposes.

51D Third restriction: groups of companies under common control

51D(1) Where in a financial year two or more groups of companies are–

(a) controlled by the same person (see section 51F), and

(b) related to one another (see section 51G),

this section applies in relation to the companies which are members of those groups.

51D(2) The companies are entitled to a single annual investment allowance between them in respect of the relevant AIA qualifying expenditure.

51D(3) The companies may allocate the annual investment allowance to the relevant AIA qualifying expenditure as they think fit.

51D(4) The relevant AIA qualifying expenditure is the AIA qualifying expenditure incurred by the companies in chargeable periods ending in the financial year mentioned in subsection (1).

51D(5) In this section and in sections 51F and 51G, a group of companies means–

(a) a company which, in the financial year mentioned in subsection (1), is a parent undertaking of one or more other companies, and

(b) those other companies,

(and the members of the group are the company which is the parent undertaking and those other companies).

51D(6) A company ("P") is a parent undertaking of another company ("C") in a financial year if P is a parent undertaking of C at the end of C's chargeable period ending in that financial year.

51D(7) In this section **"parent undertaking"** has the same meaning as in section 1162 of the Companies Act 2006.

History – S. 51D inserted by FA 2008, s. 74 and Sch. 24, para. 3, with effect in relation to expenditure incurred on or after 1 April 2008 for corporation tax purposes and 6 April 2008 for income tax purposes.

51E Fourth restriction: other companies under common control

51E(1) This section applies in relation to two or more companies which in a financial year are–

(a) controlled by the same person (see section 51F), and

(b) related to one another (see section 51G),

and in relation to which to neither section 51C nor section 51D applies.

51E(2) The companies are entitled to a single annual investment allowance between them in respect of the relevant AIA qualifying expenditure.

51E(3) The companies may allocate the annual investment allowance to the relevant AIA qualifying expenditure as they think fit.

51E(4) The relevant AIA qualifying expenditure is the AIA qualifying expenditure incurred by the companies in chargeable periods ending in the financial year mentioned in subsection (1).

History – S. 51E inserted by FA 2008, s. 74 and Sch. 24, para. 3, with effect in relation to expenditure incurred on or after 1 April 2008 for corporation tax purposes and 6 April 2008 for income tax purposes.

51F Companies and groups: meaning of "control"

51F(1) A company is controlled by a person in a financial year if it is controlled by that person at the end of its chargeable period ending in that financial year.

51F(2) A group of companies is controlled by a person in a financial year if the company which is the parent undertaking is controlled by that person at the end of its chargeable period ending in that financial year.

51F(3) Section 574(2) defines "control" in relation to a company which is a body corporate.

51F(4) In relation to a company ("C") which is not a body corporate, control means the power of a person ("P") to secure–

(a) by means of the holding of shares or the possession of voting power in relation to C or another body, or

(b) as a result of any powers conferred by the constitution of C or another body,

that the affairs of C are conducted in accordance with P's wishes.

51F(5) In subsection (4) **"shares"** has the meaning given by section 1161(2) of the Companies Act 2006.

History – S. 51F inserted by FA 2008, s. 74 and Sch. 24, para. 3, with effect in relation to expenditure incurred on or after 1 April 2008 for corporation tax purposes and 6 April 2008 for income tax purposes.

51G Companies and groups: meaning of "related"

51G(1) A company ("C1") is related to another company ("C2") in a financial year if one or both of–

(a) the shared premises condition, and

(b) the similar activities condition,

are met in relation to the companies in that financial year.

51G(2) Where C1 is related to C2 in a financial year, C1 is also related to any other company to which C2 is related in that financial year.

51G(3) A group of companies ("G1") is related to another group of companies ("G2") in a financial year if in that financial year a company which is a member of G1 is related to a company which is a member of G2.

51G(4) Where G1 is related to G2 in a financial year, G1 is also related to any other group of companies to which G2 is related in that financial year.

51G(5) The shared premises condition is met in relation to two companies in a financial year if, at the end of the relevant chargeable period of one or both of the companies, the companies carry on qualifying activities from the same premises.

51G(6) The similar activities condition is met in relation to two companies in a financial year if–

(a) more than 50% of the turnover of one company for the relevant chargeable period is derived from qualifying activities within a particular NACE classification, and

(b) more than 50% of the turnover of the other company for the relevant chargeable period is derived from qualifying activities within that NACE classification.

51G(7) In this section–

"NACE classification" means the first level of the common statistical classification of economic activities in the European Union established by Regulation (EC) No 1893/2006 of the European Parliament and the Council of 20 December 2006 (as that Regulation has effect from time to time), and

"relevant chargeable period", in relation to a company and a financial year, means the chargeable period of the company ending in that financial year.

History – S. 51G inserted by FA 2008, s. 74 and Sch. 24, para. 3, with effect in relation to expenditure incurred on or after 1 April 2008 for corporation tax purposes and 6 April 2008 for income tax purposes.

51H Fifth restriction: qualifying activities under common control

51H(1) This section applies in relation to two or more qualifying activities which, in a tax year–

(a) are carried on by a qualifying person other than a company,

(b) are controlled by the same person (see section 51I), and

(c) are related to one another (see section 51J).

51H(2) A qualifying activity is carried on by a qualifying person in a tax year if it is carried on by the person at the end of the chargeable period for the activity ending in the tax year.

51H(3) Where all the qualifying activities are carried on by one qualifying person, that person is entitled to a single annual investment allowance in respect of the relevant AIA qualifying expenditure.

51H(4) Where the qualifying activities are carried on by more than one qualifying person, those persons are entitled to a single annual investment allowance between them in respect of the relevant AIA qualifying expenditure.

51H(5) The person or persons carrying on the qualifying activities may allocate the annual investment allowance to the relevant AIA qualifying expenditure as the person or persons think fit.

51H(6) The relevant AIA qualifying expenditure is the AIA qualifying expenditure incurred for the purposes of the qualifying activities in the chargeable periods for those activities ending in the tax year mentioned in subsection (1).

History – S. 51H inserted by FA 2008, s. 74 and Sch. 24, para. 3, with effect in relation to expenditure incurred on or after 1 April 2008 for corporation tax purposes and 6 April 2008 for income tax purposes.

51I Qualifying activities: meaning of control

51I(1) A qualifying activity is controlled by a person in a tax year if it is controlled by the person at the end of the chargeable period for that activity which ends in that tax year.

51I(2) A qualifying activity carried on by an individual is controlled by the individual who carries it on.

51I(3) A qualifying activity carried on by a partnership is controlled by the person (if any) who controls the partnership.

51I(4) Section 574(3) defines "control" in relation to a partnership.

51I(5) Where partners who between them control one partnership also between them control another partnership, the qualifying activities carried on by the partnerships are to be treated as controlled by the same person.

History – S. 51I inserted by FA 2008, s. 74 and Sch. 24, para. 3, with effect in relation to expenditure incurred on or after 1 April 2008 for corporation tax purposes and 6 April 2008 for income tax purposes.

51J Qualifying activity: meaning of "related"

51J(1) A qualifying activity ("A1") is related to another qualifying activity ("A2") in a tax year if one or both of–

(a) the shared premises condition, and

(b) the similar activities condition,

are met in relation to the activities in the tax year.

51J(2) Where A1 is related to A2 in a tax year, A1 is also related to any other qualifying activity to which A2 is related in that tax year.

51J(3) The shared premises condition is met in relation to two qualifying activities in a tax year if, at the end of the relevant chargeable period for one or both of the activities, the activities are carried on from the same premises.

51J(4) The similar activities condition is met in relation to two qualifying activities in a tax year if, at the end of the relevant chargeable period for one or both of the activities, the activities are within the same NACE classification.

51J(5) In this section–

"NACE classification" has the same meaning as in section 51G, and

"relevant chargeable period", in relation to a qualifying activity and a tax year, means the chargeable period for that activity ending in that tax year.

History – S. 51J inserted by FA 2008, s. 74 and Sch. 24, para. 3, with effect in relation to expenditure incurred on or after 1 April 2008 for corporation tax purposes and 6 April 2008 for income tax purposes.

51JA Sixth restriction: allocation where profits chargeable at NI rate

51JA [Prospectively inserted by CTNIA 2015, s. 2 and Sch. 1, para. 5.]

Prospective amendments – S. 51JA inserted by CTNIA 2015, s. 2 and Sch. 1, para. 5, with effect from 26 March 2015 (Royal Assent) in respect of any power to make regulations and with effect in relation to accounting periods beginning on or after the first day of the appointed financial year for other provisions (see CTNIA 2015, s. 5). See also transitional provisions at Sch. 1, para. 19–21.

51K Operation of annual investment allowance where restrictions apply

51K(1) This section applies where because of section 51B, 51C, 51D, 51E or 51H a person is (or persons between them are) entitled to a single annual investment allowance in respect of relevant AIA qualifying expenditure.

51K(2) If the relevant AIA qualifying expenditure is less than or equal to the maximum allowance, the person is (or the persons between them are) entitled to an annual investment allowance in respect of all the relevant AIA qualifying expenditure.

51K(3) If the relevant AIA qualifying expenditure is more than the maximum allowance, the person is (or the persons between them are) entitled to an annual investment allowance in respect of so much of the relevant AIA qualifying expenditure as does not exceed the maximum allowance.

51K(4) The maximum allowance is the amount for the time being specified in section 51A(5); but this is subject to sections 51M and 51N (which provide that in certain cases an additional amount of annual investment allowance may be available).

51K(5) The person or persons may claim an annual investment allowance in respect of all the relevant AIA qualifying expenditure in respect of which the person is (or the persons between them are) entitled to an allowance, or in respect of only some of it.

51K(6) The amount of the annual investment allowance allocated to relevant AIA qualifying expenditure incurred in a chargeable period must not exceed the amount of the annual investment allowance to which a person would be entitled in respect of that expenditure under section 51A(5) and (6) if section 51B, 51C, 51D, 51E or 51H did not apply.

History – S. 51K inserted by FA 2008, s. 74 and Sch. 24, para. 3, with effect in relation to expenditure incurred on or after 1 April 2008 for corporation tax purposes and 6 April 2008 for income tax purposes.

Cross references – FA 2013, s. 7(2) and Sch. 1: annual investment allowance: periods straddling 1 January 2013 or 1 January 2015. FA 2014, Sch. 2, Pt. 1: transitional provisions in relation to the temporary increase in annual investment allowance provided for by FA 2014, s. 10.

51L Special provision for short chargeable periods

51L(1) This section applies where–

(a) more than one chargeable period of a company ends in a financial year, or

(b) more than one chargeable period for a qualifying activity ends in a tax year.

51L(2) Whether section 51C, 51D or 51E applies in relation to the company, or section 51H applies in relation to the qualifying activity, is to be determined in relation to each chargeable period ending in that year as if it were the only chargeable period ending in that year.

51L(3) AIA qualifying expenditure incurred in a chargeable period in relation to which the section in question does not apply is not relevant AIA qualifying expenditure for the purposes of that section.

History – S. 51L inserted by FA 2008, s. 74 and Sch. 24, para. 3, with effect in relation to expenditure incurred on or after 1 April 2008 for corporation tax purposes and 6 April 2008 for income tax purposes.

51M Special provision for long chargeable periods

51M(1) This section applies where–

(a) section 51H applies in relation to two or more qualifying activities controlled by a person ("P") in a tax year, and

(b) the relevant chargeable period for one of those qualifying activities ("A1") is longer than a year.

51M(2) An additional amount of annual investment allowance may be allocated to relevant AIA qualifying expenditure incurred for the purposes of A1.

51M(3) That additional amount is the amount, or the aggregate of the amounts, of any relevant unused allowance for each tax year (a "previous tax year")–

(a) which falls before the tax year mentioned in subsection (1)(a), and

(b) in which part of A1's relevant chargeable period falls.

51M(4) The amount of the relevant unused allowance for a previous tax year is (subject to subsections (7) and (8))–

$$MA - AM$$

but where the amount given by that formula is less than nil, the amount of the relevant unused allowance for the previous tax year is nil.

51M(5) In subsection (4)–

MA is the amount specified in section 51A(5) in relation to the previous tax year, and

AM is the amount of any annual investment allowance made under section 51A or 51K in respect of AIA qualifying expenditure incurred for the purposes of a relevant qualifying activity in the chargeable period for that activity ending in the previous tax year.

51M(6) **"Relevant qualifying activity"** means–

(a) any qualifying activity carried on by a qualifying person other than a company which was controlled by P in the previous tax year (see section 51I) and related to A1 in that tax year (see section 51J), and

(b) if A1 was controlled by P in the previous tax year (see section 51I), A1.

51M(7) Where any part of the amount calculated under subsection (4) has, on a previous application of this section, been allocated to AIA qualifying expenditure incurred for the purposes of a qualifying activity

CAA 2001

controlled by P in a tax year before that mentioned in subsection (1)(a), the amount of the relevant unused allowance is reduced accordingly.

51M(8) Where the amount of the relevant unused allowance for a previous tax year would (apart from this subsection) exceed–

$$\frac{DCPY}{DY} \times MA$$

the amount of the relevant unused allowance for that tax year is limited to the amount given by that formula.

51M(9) In subsection (8)–

DCPY is the number of days in A1's relevant chargeable period falling in the previous tax year,

DY is the number of days in that tax year, and

MA has the meaning given by subsection (5).

51M(10) Nothing in this section prevents section 51K(6) applying in relation to relevant AIA qualifying expenditure incurred for the purposes of A1.

51M(11) In this section references to a relevant chargeable period, in relation to a qualifying activity, are to the chargeable period for that activity ending in the tax year mentioned in subsection (1)(a).

History – S. 51M inserted by FA 2008, s. 74 and Sch. 24, para. 3, with effect in relation to expenditure incurred on or after 1 April 2008 for corporation tax purposes and 6 April 2008 for income tax purposes.

Cross references – FA 2013, s. 7(2) and Sch. 1: annual investment allowance: periods straddling 1 January 2013 or 1 January 2015.

51N Special provision for long chargeable periods: supplementary

51N(1) This section applies where–

(a) section 51H applies in relation to two or more qualifying activities controlled by a person ("P") in a tax year, and

(b) the relevant chargeable period for more than one of those qualifying activities is longer than a year.

51N(2) Section 51M applies in relation to each of the qualifying activities mentioned in subsection (1)(b) and the tax year mentioned in subsection (1)(a), as it applies in relation to A1 and the tax year mentioned in subsection (1)(a) of that section.

51N(3) But where two or more of the qualifying activities mentioned in subsection (1)(b) were related in a previous tax year, section 51M applies with the following modifications.

51N(4) The amount of any relevant unused allowance for that tax year is to be calculated under section 51M(4) to (7) (without regard to section 51M(8)).

51N(5) For that purpose section 51M(6) applies as if the reference to A1 were a reference to any of the qualifying activities mentioned in subsection (1)(b).

51N(6) The amount of the relevant unused allowance may be allocated between those activities, but this is subject to subsection (7).

51N(7) The amount of the relevant unused allowance allocated to any one of those activities may not exceed the amount given by the formula in section 51M(8).

History – S. 51N inserted by FA 2008, s. 74 and Sch. 24, para. 3, with effect in relation to expenditure incurred on or after 1 April 2008 for corporation tax purposes and 6 April 2008 for income tax purposes.

Cross references – FA 2013, s. 7(2) and Sch. 1: annual investment allowance: periods straddling 1 January 2013 or 1 January 2015.

FIRST-YEAR ALLOWANCES

52 First-year allowances

52(1) A person is entitled to a first-year allowance in respect of first-year qualifying expenditure if–

(a) the expenditure is incurred in a chargeable period to which this Act applies, and

(b) the person owns the plant or machinery at some time during that chargeable period.

52(2) Any first-year allowance is made for the chargeable period in which the first-year qualifying expenditure is incurred.

52(3) The amount of the allowance is a percentage of the first-year qualifying expenditure in respect of which the allowance is made, as shown in the Table–

TABLE
AMOUNT OF FIRST-YEAR ALLOWANCES

Type of first-year qualifying expenditure	*Amount*
Expenditure qualifying under section 45A (expenditure on energy-saving plant or machinery)	100%
Expenditure qualifying under section 45D (expenditure on cars with low CO_2 emissions)	100%
Expenditure qualifying under section 45DA (expenditure on zero-emission goods vehicles)	100%
Expenditure qualifying under section 45E (expenditure on plant or machinery for gas refuelling station)	100%
Expenditure qualifying under section 45F (expenditure for use wholly in a ring fence trade)	100%
Expenditure qualifying under section 45H (expenditure on environmentally beneficial plant or machinery)	100%
Expenditure qualifying under section 45K (expenditure on plant and machinery for use in designated assisted areas)	100%

52(4) A person who is entitled to a first-year allowance may claim the allowance in respect of the whole or a part of the first-year qualifying expenditure.

52(5) Subsection (1) needs to be read with section 236 (first-year allowances in respect of additional VAT liabilities) and is subject to–

section 70DA(2) (transfer and long funding leaseback: no first-year allowance for lessee),

section 205 (reduction of first-year allowance if plant or machinery provided partly for purposes other than those of qualifying activity),

section 210 (reduction of first-year allowance if it appears that a partial depreciation subsidy is or will be payable),

section 212T (cap on first-year allowances: zero-emission goods vehicles), and

sections 217, 229A(2) and 241 (anti-avoidance: no first-year allowance in certain cases).

History – In s. 52(3), in the table, the former entry relating to s. 40 omitted by FA 2008, s. 76(5)(d), with effect from 21 July 2008.
In s. 52(3), in the table, the former entry relating to s. 44 and the words following the table from "In case" to the end of the subsection, omitted by FA 2008, s. 75(3)(d), with effect in relation to expenditure incurred on or after 1 April 2008 for corporation tax purposes and 6 April 2008 for income tax purposes. However, where a business incurs an additional VAT liability (under the VAT Capital Goods Scheme) on or after those dates and the original expenditure was first-year qualifying expenditure by virtue of s. 44, then CAA 2001, Pt. 2, Ch. 18 will still apply as if the entry and those words had not been omitted (FA 2008, s. 75(6) and (7)).
In s. 52(3), in the table, the former entry relating to s. 45 omitted by FA 2008, s. 76(5)(d), with effect from 21 July 2008.
In s. 52(3), entry relating to s. 45A inserted by FA 2001, s. 65 and Sch. 17, para. 4, with effect as respects allowances and charges falling to be made for chargeable periods ending on or after:
- 6 April 2001 for income tax purposes, and
- 1 April 2001 for corporation tax purposes.

In s. 52(3), entry relating to s. 45D inserted by FA 2002, s. 59 and Sch. 19, para. 5 with effect in relation to expenditure incurred on or after 17 April 2002.
In s. 52(3), in the table, the entry relating to s. 45DA inserted by F(No. 3)A 2010, s. 18 and Sch. 7, para. 5(2), with effect for chargeable periods ending on or after 1 April 2010 (corporation tax) or 6 April 2010 (income tax).
In s. 52(3), in the table, the entry relating to s. 45E inserted by FA 2002, s. 61 and Sch. 20, para. 5 with effect in relation to expenditure incurred on or after 17 April 2002.
In s. 52(3), in the table, the entry relating to s. 45F substituted for two previous entries relating to that section by FA 2008, s. 108(1), with effect in relation to expenditure incurred on or after 12 March 2008.
In s. 52(3), in the table, the former entry relating to s. 45F inserted by FA 2002, s. 63 and Sch. 21, para. 6, with effect in relation to expenditure incurred on or after 17 April 2002.
In s. 52(3), entry relating to s. 45H inserted by FA 2003, s. 167 and Sch. 30, para. 5, with effect in relation to expenditure incurred on or after 1 April 2003.
In s. 52(3), in the table, the entry relating to s. 45K inserted by FA 2012, s. 44 and Sch. 11, para. 5(2), with effect for chargeable periods ending on or after 1 April 2012.
In s. 52(3), paragraph (c) following the table inserted by FA 2007, s. 37(3), with effect from 19 July 2007.
In s. 52(3), the wording following the table substituted by FA 2006, s. 30(3), which has effect from 19 July 2006.
In s. 52(5), the word "and" omitted from the end of the entry for s. 212T by FA 2012, s. 44 and Sch. 11, para. 5(3)(a), with effect for chargeable periods ending on or after 1 April 2012.
In s. 52(5), the entry for s. 212U inserted by FA 2012, s. 44 and Sch. 11, para. 5(3)(b), with effect for chargeable periods ending on or after 1 April 2012.
In s. 52(5), the reference to s. 212T inserted (and the "and" at the end of the entry for s. 210 omitted) by F(No. 3)A 2010, s. 18 and Sch. 7, para. 5(3), with effect for chargeable periods ending on or after 1 April 2010 (corporation tax) or 6 April 2010 (income tax).
In s. 52(5) the reference to s. 70DA(2) inserted by FA 2009, s. 64 and Sch. 32, para. 13, with effect in relation to cases where the commencement of the term of the lease referred to in s. 70DA(1)(b) is on or after 13 November 2008.
In s. 52(5), ", 229A(2)" inserted by FA 2009, s. 64 and Sch. 32, para. 19, with effect in relation to cases where the contract referred to in s. 229A(1)(c) is entered into on or after 13 November 2008.
In s. 52(5), the figure "223", which followed the words "sections 217", omitted by FA 2008, s. 55 and Sch. 20, para. 6(3), with effect in thecase of plant or machinery which is the subject of a sale and finance leaseback (as defined in CAA 2001, s. 221) where the date of the transaction (within the meaning of that section) is on or after 9 October 2007.

Origin – S. 52(1)–(3): CAA 1990, s. 22 (1) (part).
S. 52(4): CAA 1990, s. 22 (7) (part), s. 25(4) (part), s. 30(1) (part), Annex 2, Note 15.
S. 52(5): drafting.

Cross references – S. 236(3): s. 52(3), (4) apply to first-year qualifying expenditure constituted by the additional VAT liability as they apply to other first-year qualifying expenditure.
FA 2004, s. 142: first-year allowance at 50 per cent, on temporary basis, for small enterprises.
FA 2006, s. 30: first-year allowance at 50 per cent, on temporary basis, for small enterprises.
FA 2009, s. 24(1) (first-year capital allowances for expenditure in 2009–10): table in s. 52(3) deemed to include an entry for expenditure qualifying under FA 2009, s. 24 (allowance at 40 per cent).

Rewrite: Technical Points – Explanatory Notes, Annex 2, Note 15: s. 52(4) reflects the effect of CAA 1990, s. 22(7), 25(4) and 30(1)(b). S. 22(7) enabled a person claiming first-year allowances to require them to be reduced; s. 30(1)(b) made corresponding provision for first-year allowances on ships; s. 25(4) provided that part of the expenditure proportionate to the reduction in the allowance should be treated as not being expenditure in respect of which a first-year allowance is or could be made. Thus it was not prevented by CAA 1990, s. 25(1)(a)(ii) from being qualifying expenditure for writing-down allowance purposes.

Hansard – Vol. 63, col. 1077ff. (not reproduced): expenditure on which first-year allowances disclaimed or reduced goes immediately into pool of unallowed expenditure qualifying for writing-down allowances.

HMRC Manuals – CA23110: guidance on s. 52.

Notes – In s. 52(3), and in accordance with FA 2004, s. 142(1) and (2), the rate of 50 per cent for small enterprises applies to expenditure incurred by a small enterprise (within the meaning of CAA 2001, s. 44) in the period of 12 months beginning with 1 April 2004 (for corporation tax purposes) or 6 April 2004 (for income tax purposes).

PREVENTION OF DOUBLE RELIEF

52A Prevention of double relief

52A A person may not claim–

(a) an annual investment allowance and a first-year allowance in respect of the same expenditure, or

(b) first-year allowances under two or more of the provisions listed in section 39 in respect of the same expenditure.

History – S. 52A amended by FA 2012, s. 44 and Sch. 11, para. 6, with effect for chargeable periods ending on or after 1 April 2012.
S. 52A inserted by FA 2008, s. 74 and Sch. 24, para. 4, with effect in relation to expenditure incurred on or after 1 April 2008 for corporation tax purposes and 6 April 2008 for income tax purposes.

POOLING

53 Pooling of qualifying expenditure

53(1) Qualifying expenditure has to be pooled for the purpose of determining a person's entitlement to writing-down allowances and balancing allowances and liability to balancing charges.

53(2) If a person carries on more than one qualifying activity, expenditure relating to the different activities must not be allocated to the same pool.

Origin – S. 53: drafting.
HMRC Manuals – CA23210: guidance on pooling.

54 The different kinds of pools

54(1) There are single asset pools, class pools and the main pool.

54(2) A single asset pool may not contain expenditure relating to more than one asset.

54(3) The following provide for qualifying expenditure to be allocated to a single asset pool–

section 86 (short-life asset);

section 127 (ship);

section 206 (plant or machinery provided or used partly for purposes other than those of qualifying activity);

section 211 (payment of partial depreciation subsidy);

section 538 (contribution allowances: plant and machinery).

54(4) A class pool is a pool which may contain expenditure relating to more than one asset.

54(5) The following provide for qualifying expenditure to be allocated to a class pool–

section 104C (special rate expenditure);

section 107 (overseas leasing).

54(6) Qualifying expenditure may be allocated to the main pool only if it does not fall to be allocated to a *single asset pool or a class pool*.

History – In s. 54(3), "section 74 (car above the cost threshold)" omitted by FA 2009, s. 30 and Sch. 11, para. 15, with effect in relation to expenditure incurred on or after 1 April 2009 (for corporation tax purposes) and 6 April 2009 (for income tax purposes), subject to transitional provisions in FA 2009, Sch. 11, para. 27(2) and 29–32.
In s. 54(5), the words "section 104C (special rate expenditure);" substituted for the words "section 101 (long-life assets);" by FA 2008, s. 82 and Sch. 26, para. 3, with effect in relation expenditure incurred on or after 1 April 2008 for corporation tax purposes and 6 April 2008 for income tax purposes and in relation to long-life asset expenditure (within the meaning of CAA 2001, Pt. 2, Ch. 10)

incurred before those dates but allocated to a pool in a chargeable period beginning on or after those dates. This commencement provision is subject to FA 2008, s. 83 (existing long-life asset expenditure treated as special rate expenditure) and FA 2008, Sch. 26, para. 15–17 (detailed provisions relating to sales between connected persons and savings for intra-group transfers).

Origin – S. 54: drafting.

HMRC Manuals – CA23210: guidance on pooling.

WRITING-DOWN AND BALANCING ALLOWANCES AND BALANCING CHARGES

55 Determination of entitlement or liability

55(1) Whether a person is entitled to a writing-down allowance or a balancing allowance, or liable to a balancing charge, for a chargeable period is determined separately for each pool of qualifying expenditure and depends on–

(a) the available qualifying expenditure in that pool for that period ("AQE"), and

(b) the total of any disposal receipts to be brought into account in that pool for that period ("TDR").

55(2) If AQE exceeds TDR, the person is entitled to a writing-down allowance or a balancing allowance for the period.

55(3) If TDR exceeds AQE, the person is liable to a balancing charge for the period.

55(4) The entitlement under subsection (2) is to a writing-down allowance except for the final chargeable period when it is to a balancing allowance.

55(5) The final chargeable period is given by section 65.

55(6) Subsection (2) is subject to section 104F (special rate cars: discontinued activity continued by relevant company) and section 110(1) (overseas leasing: allowances prohibited in certain cases).

History – In s. 55(6), the words "section 104F (special rate cars: discontinued activity continued by relevant company) and" inserted by FA 2009, s. 30 and Sch. 11, para. 16, with effect in relation to expenditure incurred on or after 1 April 2009 (for corporation tax purposes) and 6 April 2009 (for income tax purposes), subject to transitional provisions in FA 2009, Sch. 11, para. 27(2) and 30–32.

Origin – S. 55(1), (2): CAA 1990, s. 24(2) (part).
S. 55(3): CAA 1990, s. 24(5) (part).
S. 55(4): CAA 1990, s. 24(2) (part).
S. 55(5), (6): drafting.

56 Amount of allowances and charges

56(1) The amount of the writing-down allowance to which a person is entitled for a chargeable period is 18% of the amount by which AQE exceeds TDR.

56(1A) But in relation to qualifying expenditure incurred wholly for the purposes of a ring fence trade in respect of which tax is chargeable under section 330(1) of CTA 2010 (supplementary charge in respect of ring fence trades), the amount of the writing-down allowance to which a person is entitled for a chargeable period is 25% of the amount by which AQE exceeds TDR.

56(2) Subsections (1) and (1A) are subject to–

(za) section 56A (small main pools and special rate pools),

(a) section 104D (special rate expenditure: 8% or 10%), and

(b) section 109 (overseas leasing: 10%).

56(3) If the chargeable period is more or less than a year, the amount is proportionately increased or reduced.

56(4) If the qualifying activity has been carried on for part only of the chargeable period, the amount is proportionately reduced.

56(5) A person claiming a writing-down allowance may require the allowance to be reduced to a specified amount.

56(6) The amount of the balancing charge to which a person is liable for a chargeable period is the amount by which TDR exceeds AQE.

56(7) The amount of the balancing allowance to which a person is entitled for the final chargeable period is the amount by which AQE exceeds TDR.

History – In s. 56(1), the word "18%" substituted for "20%" by FA 2011, s. 10(2), with effect in relation to chargeable periods beginning on or after 1 April 2012 (for corporation tax purposes) and 6 April 2012 (for income tax purposes), and in relation to chargeable periods straddling those dates, subject to transitional provisions in FA 2011, s. 10(9)–(12).

In s. 56(1), the percentage "20%" substituted for the percentage "25%" by FA 2008, s. 80(2), with effect in relation chargeable periods beginning on or after:

- 1 April 2008 for corporation tax purposes
- 6 April 2008 for income tax purposes,

as well as in relation to chargeable periods spanning those April 2008 dates. However, for the whole of a spanning chargeable period, s. 56(1) applies as if the reference to 20% were a reference to x%, a hybrid rate of writing-down allowance worked out on a daily basis (see FA 2008, s. 80(9)–(11) for the calculation).

In s. 56(1A), the words "section 330(1) of CTA 2010" substituted for the words "section 501A of ICTA" by CTA 2010, s. 1177 and Sch. 1, para. 326, with effect for corporation tax purposes for accounting periods ending on or after 1 April 2010, and for income tax and capital gains tax purposes for the tax year 2010–11 and subsequent tax years.
S. 56(1A) inserted by FA 2008, s. 80(3), with effect in relation chargeable periods beginning on or after:

- 1 April 2008 for corporation tax purposes
- 6 April 2008 for income tax purposes,

as well as in relation to chargeable periods ending on or spanning those April 2008 dates.
In s. 56(2)(a), the words "8% or" inserted before "10%" by FA 2011, s. 10(4)(b), with effect in relation to chargeable periods beginning on or after 1 April 2012 (for corporation tax purposes) and 6 April 2012 (for income tax purposes), and in relation to chargeable periods straddling those dates, subject to transitional provisions in FA 2011, s. 10(9)–(12).
In s. 56(2), the words "Subsections (1) and (1A) are" substituted for the words "Subsection (1) is" by FA 2008, s. 80(4), with effect in relation chargeable periods beginning on or after:

- 1 April 2008 for corporation tax purposes
- 6 April 2008 for income tax purposes,

as well as in relation to chargeable periods ending on or spanning those April 2008 dates.
S. 56(2)(za) inserted by FA 2008, s. 81(2), with effect in relation to chargeable periods beginning on or after 1 April 2008 for corporation tax purposes and 6 April 2008 for income tax purposes.
S. 56(2)(a) substituted by FA 2008, s. 82 and Sch. 26, para. 4, with effect in relation expenditure incurred on or after 1 April 2008 for corporation tax purposes and 6 April 2008 for income tax purposes and in relation to long-life asset expenditure (within the meaning of CAA 2001, Pt. 2, Ch. 10) incurred before those dates but allocated to a pool in a chargeable period beginning on or after those dates. This commencement provision is subject to FA 2008, s. 83 (existing long-life asset expenditure treated as special rate expenditure) and FA 2008, Sch. 26, para. 15–17 (detailed provisions relating to sales between connected persons and savings for intra-group transfers). Former s. 56(2)(a) read as follows:
"(a) section 102 (long-life asset expenditure: 6%), and.".

Origin – S. 56(1): CAA 1990, s. 24(2)(a) (part).
S. 56(2): drafting.
S. 56(3), (4): CAA 1990, s. 24(2)(a) (part).
S. 56(5): CAA 1990, s. 24(3), drafting.
S. 56(6): CAA 1990, s. 24(5) (part).
S. 56(7): CAA 1990, s. 24(2)(b), drafting.

HMRC Manuals – CA23220: guidance on s. 56.

56A Writing-down allowances for small pools

56A(1) This section applies in relation to the main pool and the special rate pool.

56A(2) Where the amount by which AQE exceeds TDR is less than or equal to the small pool limit, the amount of the writing-down allowance to which a person is entitled for a chargeable period is the amount by which AQE exceeds TDR.

56A(3) The small pool limit is £1,000, except that–

(a) if the chargeable period is more or less than a year, it is proportionately increased or reduced, and

(b) if the qualifying activity has been carried on for part only of the chargeable period, it is proportionately reduced.

56A(4) A person claiming a writing-down allowance under this section may require the allowance to be reduced to a specified amount.

56A(5) The Treasury may by order substitute for the amount for the time being specified in subsection (3) such other amount as it thinks fit.

56A(6) An order under subsection (5) may make such incidental, supplemental, consequential and transitional provision as the Treasury thinks fit.

History – S. 56A inserted by FA 2008, s. 81(3), with effect in relation to chargeable periods beginning on or after 1 April 2008 for corporation tax purposes and 6 April 2008 for income tax purposes.

AVAILABLE QUALIFYING EXPENDITURE

57 Available qualifying expenditure

57(1) The general rule is that a person's available qualifying expenditure in a pool for a chargeable period consists of–

(a) any qualifying expenditure allocated to the pool for that period in accordance with section 58, and

(b) any unrelieved qualifying expenditure carried forward in the pool from the previous chargeable period under section 59.

57(2) A person's available qualifying expenditure in a pool for a chargeable period also includes any amount allocated to the pool for that period under–

section 26(3) (net costs of demolition);

section 86(2) or 87(2) (allocation of expenditure in short-life asset pool);

section 111(3) (overseas leasing: standard recovery mechanism);

section 129(1), 132(2), 133(3) or 137 (provisions relating to operation of single ship pool and deferment of balancing charges in respect of ships);

section 165(3) (general decommissioning expenditure incurred after cessation of ring fence trade);

section 161C(2) (decommissioning expenditure incurred by person carrying on trade of oil extraction);

section 206(3) (plant or machinery used partly for purposes other than those of the qualifying activity);

section 211(4) (partial depreciation subsidy paid).

57(3) A person's available qualifying expenditure does not include any expenditure excluded by–

section 8(4) or 9(1) (rules against double relief);

section 70DA (transfer and long funding leaseback);

sections 165A to 165E (restrictions on allowances: anti-avoidance);

section 166(2) (transfers of interests in oil fields: anti-avoidance);

section 185(2), 186(2), 186A(2) or 187(2) (restrictions where other claims made in respect of fixture);

section 218(1), 218ZA(1) or (3), 228(2), 229A, 242(2), or 243(2) (general anti-avoidance provisions).

57(4) Subsection (1) is also subject to section 220 (allocation to chargeable periods of expenditure incurred on plant or machinery for leasing under finance lease).

History – In s. 57(2), entry relating to s. 161C(2) inserted by FA 2001, s. 68 and Sch. 20, para. 5(2).
In s. 57(2), in the entry relating to section 165(3) of CAA 2001, the words "general decommissioning expenditure" substituted for the words "abandonment expenditure" by FA 2008, s. 109 and Sch. 34, para. 4, with effect in relation to expenditure incurred on or after 12 March 2008.
In s. 57(3), reference to "sections 165A to 165E" inserted by FA 2013, s. 93 and Sch. 32, para. 4, with effect in relation to expenditure incurred on decommissioning carried out on or after 17 July 2013.
In s. 57(3) the words", 186A(2)" inserted by FA 2012, s. 43 and Sch. 10, para. 8, with effect in relation to balancing events which occur on or after 6 April 2012, for income tax purposes, and 1 April 2012, for corporation tax purposes, subject to provisions in FA 2012, Sch. 10, para. 13.
In s. 57(3) the words "218ZA(1) or (3)," inserted after the words "section 218(1)," by FA 2012, s. 42 and Sch. 9, para 2, with effect in relation to expenditure of B's that is incurred on or after 1 April 2012, for corporation tax purposes, and 6 April 2012, for income tax purposes (regardless of when the relevant transaction was entered into).
In s. 57(3), the reference to s. 70DA inserted by FA 2009, s. 64 and Sch. 32, para. 14, with effect in relation to cases where the commencement of the term of the lease referred to in s. 70DA(1)(b) is on or after 13 November 2008.
In s. 57(3), ", 229A" inserted by FA 2009, s. 64 and Sch. 33, para. 20, with effect in relation to cases where the contract referred to in s. 229A(1)(c) is entered into on or after 13 November 2008.
In s. 57(3), the reference "224(1)", which followed the words "section 218(1)", omitted by FA 2008, s. 55 and Sch. 20, para. 6(4), with effect in the case of plant or machinery which is the subject of a sale and finance leaseback (as defined in CAA 2001, s. 221) where the date of the transaction (within the meaning of that section) is on or after 9 October 2007.

Origin – S. 57(1): CAA 1990, s. 25(1) (part).
S. 57(2)–(4): drafting.

Cross references – S. 131(1)(b): postponement of allowances does not affect amount of available qualifying expenditure under s. 57–59.

HMRC Manuals – CA23230: guidance and example.

58 Initial allocation of qualifying expenditure to pools

58(1) The following rules apply to the allocation of a person's qualifying expenditure to the appropriate pool.

58(2) An amount of qualifying expenditure is not to be allocated to a pool for a chargeable period if that amount has been taken into account in determining the person's available qualifying expenditure for an earlier chargeable period.

58(3) Qualifying expenditure is not to be allocated to a pool for a chargeable period before that in which the expenditure is incurred.

58(4) Qualifying expenditure is not to be allocated to a pool for a chargeable period unless the person owns the plant or machinery at some time in that period.

58(4A) If an annual investment allowance is made to a person for a chargeable period–

(a) the AIA qualifying expenditure in respect of which the allowance is made must be allocated to the appropriate pool (or pools) in that chargeable period, and

(b) the available qualifying expenditure in a pool to which the expenditure (or some of it) is allocated is reduced by the amount of that expenditure.

58(5) If a first-year allowance is made in respect of an amount of first-year qualifying expenditure–

(a) subject to subsection (6), none of that amount is to be allocated to a pool for the chargeable period in which the expenditure is incurred, and

(b) the amount that may be allocated to a pool for any chargeable period is limited to the balance left after deducting the first-year allowance.

58(6) If–

(a) a first-year allowance is made in respect of an amount of first-year qualifying expenditure,

(b) a disposal event occurs in respect of the plant or machinery in any chargeable period, and

(c) none of the balance left after deducting the first-year allowance has been allocated to a pool for an earlier chargeable period,

the balance (or some of it) must be allocated to a pool for the chargeable period in which the disposal event occurs.

58(7) Subsection (6) applies even if the balance is nil (because of a 100% first-year allowance).

58(8) **"The appropriate pool"** means whichever pool is applicable under the provisions of this Part apart from this section.

History – S. 58(4A) inserted by FA 2008, s. 74 and Sch. 24, para. 5, with effect in relation to expenditure incurred on or after 1 April 2008 for corporation tax purposes and 6 April 2008 for income tax purposes.

Origin – S. 58: See Annex 1, Change 8.
S. 58(1): drafting.
S. 58(2), (3): CAA 1990, s. 25(1) (part).
S. 58(4): FA 1994 s. 118(6).
S. 58(5): CAA 1990, s. 25(1) (part), (3), (4) (part).
S. 58(6): CAA 1990, s. 24(6) (part), (8) (part), s. 25(5).
S. 58(7), (8): drafting.

Cross references – S. 131(1)(b): postponement of allowances does not affect amount of available qualifying expenditure under s. 57–59.
S. 205(3): where first-year allowance is reduced because asset used only partly for qualifying activity, such reduction must be disregarded in calculating, for the purposes of s. 58, the balance left after deducting a first-year allowance.
S. 210(2): where first-year allowance is reduced because a partial depreciation subsidy is payable, such reduction must be disregarded in calculating, for the purposes of s. 58, the balance left after deducting a first-year allowance.
S. 220: further provision about the allocation of qualifying expenditure in relation to finance leases.

Rewrite: Changes in Law – Explanatory Notes, Annex 2, Change 8:

- s. 58 allows a claimant to allocate expenditure to a pool in any period he chooses, while former CAA 1990, s. 25(1) probably strictly required expenditure to be allocated to a pool in the earliest possible chargeable period (i.e. the period in which incurred, or where a first-year allowance was granted, the period after that);
- nothing in s. 58 requires the taxpayer who has incurred expenditure and wishes to claim allowances to allocate the whole of the expenditure to the pool all at once, so that a taxpayer who inadvertently allocates less than the full amount of expenditure to the pool will not lose entitlement to allowances on the remainder;
- nothing in s. 58 requires the taxpayer who does not wish to claim a first-year allowance, but who wishes to claim a writing-down allowance for the period in which the first-year qualifying expenditure was incurred, to elect to do so by notice to the Revenue (former CAA 1990, s. 25(3) by contrast required such notice);
- s. 58(6) provides that the balance of expenditure after deducting a first-year allowance *must* be allocated to a pool where a disposal event occurs and none of the balance has previously been allocated to the pool. Former CAA 1990, s. 25(5) was introduced to produce this result, but depending upon the correct reading of CAA 1990, s. 25(1), may or may not have had that effect where disposal receipts were greater than any balance left in the pool after deducting the first-year allowance.

Other material – CCAB June 1972 (not reproduced): availability of writing-down allowances on liquidation of supplier of plant or machinery.

59 Unrelieved qualifying expenditure

59(1) A person has unrelieved qualifying expenditure to carry forward from a chargeable period if for that period–

(a) AQE exceeds TDR, and

(b) where section 56A(2) applies, the person does not claim a writing-down allowance of the amount by which AQE exceeds TDR.

59(2) The amount of the unrelieved qualifying expenditure is–

(a) the excess less the writing-down allowance made for the period, or

(b) if no writing-down allowance is claimed for the period, the excess.

59(3) No amount may be carried forward as unrelieved qualifying expenditure from the final chargeable period.

59(4) If a person carrying on a trade, profession or vocation enters the cash basis for a tax year, no amount may be carried forward as unrelieved qualifying expenditure from the chargeable period ending with the basis period for the previous tax year.

59(5) But subsection (4) does not apply to unrelieved qualifying expenditure incurred on the provision of a car.

59(6) Where a person has unrelieved qualifying expenditure to carry forward from a chargeable period that is not expenditure allocated to a single asset pool, the amount of unrelieved qualifying expenditure incurred on the provision of a car is to be determined on such basis as is just and reasonable in all the circumstances.

59(7) Section 240B of ITTOIA 2005 (meaning of "entering the cash basis") applies for the purposes of this section as it applies for the purposes of Chapter 17A of Part 2 of that Act.

59(8) Subsection (9) applies if–

(a) a person carrying on a trade, profession or vocation incurs expenditure in relation to a vehicle,

(b) at the end of the basis period for a tax year, the person has unrelieved qualifying expenditure incurred in relation to the vehicle to carry forward from the chargeable period ending with that basis period ("the relevant chargeable period"),

(c) in calculating the profits of a trade, profession or vocation of a person for the following tax year, a deduction is made under section 94D of ITTOIA 2005 in respect of expenditure incurred in relation to the vehicle, and

(d) the person does not enter the cash basis for that tax year.

59(9) None of the unrelieved qualifying expenditure incurred in relation to the vehicle may be carried forward as unrelieved qualifying expenditure from the relevant chargeable period.

59(10) Where a person has unrelieved qualifying expenditure to carry forward from a chargeable period that is not expenditure allocated to a single asset pool, the amount of the unrelieved qualifying expenditure incurred in relation to the vehicle is to be determined on such basis as is just and reasonable in all the circumstances.

History – In s. 59(1), "(a)" inserted after the words "that period" and para. (b) and the word ", and" preceding it inserted by FA 2008, s. 81(4), with effect in relation to chargeable periods beginning on or after 1 April 2008 for corporation tax purposes and 6 April 2008 for income tax purposes.
S. 59(4)–(7) inserted by FA 2013, s. 17 and Sch. 4, para. 47, with effect for the tax year 2013–14 and subsequent tax years.
S. 59(8)–(10) inserted by FA 2013, s. 18 and Sch. 5, para. 5(3), with effect for the tax year 2013–14 and subsequent tax years.

Origin – S. 59(1), (2): CAA 1990, s. 25(1)(b).
S. 59(3): CAA 1990, s. 24(1) (part), Annex 2, Note 16.

Cross references – S. 77(4): in calculating under s. 59 the amount of unrelieved qualifying expenditure carried forward in respect of a car in a single asset pool, a reduction of a writing-down allowance because the car is used partly for purposes other than a qualifying activity is to be disregarded.
S. 78(3): in calculating under s. 59 the amount of unrelieved qualifying expenditure carried forward in respect of a car in a single asset pool, any reduction of a writing-down allowance because a partial depreciation subsidy has been paid is to be disregarded.
S. 131(1)(b): postponement of allowances does not affect amount of available qualifying expenditure under s. 57–59.
S. 131(5): the making of a postponed writing-down allowance in a subsequent chargeable period is ignored for the purposes of s. 59.
S. 207(4): in calculating under s. 59 the amount of unrelieved qualifying expenditure carried forward in respect of plant or machinery in a single asset pool, a reduction of a writing-down allowance because the asset is used partly for purposes other than a qualifying activity is to be disregarded.
S. 212(3): in calculating under s. 59 the amount of unrelieved qualifying expenditure carried forward in respect of plant or machinery in a single asset pool, a reduction of a writing-down allowance because a partial depreciation subsidy has been paid is to be disregarded.
FA 2003, s. 176 and Sch. 36, para. 17: modified application of this section in relation to foster carers.

Rewrite: Technical Points – Explanatory Notes, Annex 2, Note 16: s. 59(3) is a more direct expression of the concept in CAA 1990 that on the permanent discontinuance of a person's actual or notional trade, any outstanding expenditure is returned to them by way of a balancing allowance.

DISPOSAL EVENTS AND DISPOSAL VALUES: GENERAL

60 Meaning of 'disposal receipt' and 'disposal event'

60(1) In this Part **"disposal receipt"** means a disposal value that a person is required to bring into account in accordance with–

(a) sections 61, 62 and 63 (disposal events, disposal values and the general limit on the amount of a disposal value),

(b) any of the provisions of this Part listed in section 66, or

(c) section 614BS of ITA 2007 or section 918 of CTA 2010 (cases where expenditure taken into account under Part 2, 5 or 8 of this Act) or any other enactment,

when read with sections 64 and 264(3) (cases in which no disposal value need be brought into account).

60(2) In this Part **"disposal event"** means any event of a kind that requires a disposal value to be brought into account under this Part (whether under section 61(1) or otherwise).

60(3) If–

(a) qualifying expenditure has been allocated to a pool, and

(b) more than one disposal event occurs in respect of the plant or machinery, a disposal value is required to be brought into account in the pool in connection with the first event only.

60(4) In subsection (3) **"disposal event"** does not include a disposal event arising under–

section 72 (computer software),

sections 140 and 143 (attribution of deferred balancing charge), or section 238(2) (additional VAT rebates).

History – In s. 60(1)(c), the words "section 614BS of ITA 2007" substituted for the words "paragraph 11 of Schedule 12 to FA 1997 (finance lease or loan: receipt of major lump sum)" by TIOPA 2010, s. 374 and Sch. 8, para. 234, with effect for income tax and capital gains tax purposes for the tax year 2010–11 and subsequent tax years.
In s. 60(1)(c), the words "section 918 of CTA 2010 (cases where expenditure taken into account under Part 2, 5 or 8 of this Act) or" inserted by CTA 2010, s. 1177 and Sch. 1, para. 327, with effect for corporation tax purposes for accounting periods ending on or after 1 April 2010.

Origin – S. 60(1), (2): drafting.
S. 60(3): CAA 1990, s. 24(6) (part), Annex 1, Change 9.
S. 60(4): drafting.

Cross references – FA 1991, s. 78(4): treatment of plant and machinery disposed of between parties to certain agreements for the sharing of transmission facilities by national broadcasting companies.

Rewrite: Changes in Law – Explanatory Notes, Annex 1, Change 9: s. 60(3) goes further than former CAA 1990, s. 24(6) in making it clear that a person is not required to bring a disposal value into account more than once in the same pool in respect of the same expenditure on plant and machinery. It is thought that the combination of CAA 1990, s. 24(6)(b) and (c) was intended to achieve the same practical result as s. 60(3).

HMRC Manuals – CA23240: guidance on s. 60(3).
CA23270: guidance on s. 60(1).

61 Disposal events and disposal values

61(1) A person who has incurred qualifying expenditure is required to bring the disposal value of the plant or machinery into account for the chargeable period in which–

(a) the person ceases to own the plant or machinery;

(b) the person loses possession of the plant or machinery in circumstances where it is reasonable to assume that the loss is permanent;

(c) the plant or machinery has been in use for mineral exploration and access and the person abandons it at the site where it was in use for that purpose;

(d) the plant or machinery ceases to exist as such (as a result of destruction, dismantling or otherwise);

(e) the plant or machinery begins to be used wholly or partly for purposes other than those of the qualifying activity;

(ee) the plant or machinery begins to be leased under a long funding lease (see Chapter 6A);

(f) the qualifying activity is permanently discontinued.

61(2) The disposal value to be brought into account depends on the disposal event, as shown in the Table–

TABLE
DISPOSAL VALUES: GENERAL

	1. Disposal event	*2. Disposal value*
1.	Sale of the plant or machinery, except in a case where item 2 applies.	The net proceeds of the sale, together with– (a) any insurance money received in respect of the plant or machinery as a result of an event affecting the price obtainable on the sale, and (b) any other compensation of any description so received, so far as it consists of capital sums.
2.	Sale of the plant or machinery where– (a) the sale is at less than market value, (b) there is no charge to tax under ITEPA 2003, and (c) the condition in subsection (4) is met by the buyer.	The market value of the plant or machinery at the time of the sale.
3.	Demolition or destruction of the plant or machinery.	The net amount received for the remains of the plant or machinery, together with– (a) any insurance money received in respect of the demolition or destruction, and (b) any other compensation of any description so received, so far as it consists of capital sums.
4.	Permanent loss of the plant or machinery otherwise than as a result of its demolition or destruction.	Any insurance money received in respect of the loss and, so far as it consists of capital sums, any other compensation of any description so received.

	1. Disposal event	*2. Disposal value*
5.	Abandonment of the plant or machinery which has been in use for mineral exploration and access at the site where it was in use for that purpose.	Any insurance money received in respect of the abandonment and, so far as it consists of capital sums, any other compensation of any description so received.
5A.	Commencement of the term of a long funding finance lease of the plant or machinery.	The greater of– (a) the market value of the plant or machinery at the commencement of the term of the lease, and (b) the qualifying lease payments.
5B.	Commencement of the term of a long funding operating lease of the plant or machinery.	An amount equal to the market value of the plant or machinery at the commencement of the term of the lease.
6.	Permanent discontinuance of the qualifying activity followed by the occurrence of an event within any of items 1 to 5B.	The disposal value for the item in question.
6A.	Disposal event to which section 62A applies.	The relevant transition value (see section 62A).
7.	Any event not falling within any of items 1 to 6A.	The market value of the plant or machinery at the time of the event.

61(3) The amounts referred to in column 2 of the Table are those received by the person required to bring the disposal value into account.

61(4) The condition referred to in item 2 of the Table is met by the buyer if–

(a) the buyer's expenditure on the acquisition of the plant or machinery cannot be qualifying expenditure under this Part or Part 6 (research and development allowances), or

(b) the buyer is a dual resident investing company which is connected with the seller.

61(5) In this section **"mineral exploration and access"** has the same meaning as in Chapter 13 (provisions affecting the mining and oil industries) and Part 5 (mineral extraction allowances).

61(5A) In item 5A of the Table **"qualifying lease payments"** means the minimum payments under the lease (including any initial payment), excluding the following–

(a) so much of any payment as, under generally accepted accounting practice, falls (or would fall) to be treated as the gross return on investment in respect of the lease,

(b) so much of any payment as represents charges for services, and

(c) so much of any payment as represents qualifying UK or foreign tax (within the meaning of section 70YE) to be paid by the lessor.

61(6) [Omitted by FA 2009, s. 64 and Sch. 32, para. 1(4).]

61(7) [Omitted by FA 2009, s. 64 and Sch. 32, para. 1(4).]

61(8) [Omitted by FA 2009, s. 64 and Sch. 32, para. 1(4).]

61(9) [Omitted by FA 2009, s. 64 and Sch. 32, para. 1(4).]

Prospective amendments – In s. 61(1), in entry 1 of the Table, the words "or 2A" inserted after the words " item 2" by CTNIA 2015, s. 2 and Sch. 1, para. 6(2), with effect from 26 March 2015 (Royal Assent) in respect of any power to make regulations and with effect in relation to accounting periods beginning on or after the first day of the appointed financial year for other provisions (see CTNIA 2015, s. 5). See also transitional provisions at Sch. 1, para. 19–21.
In s. 61(1), entry 2A of the Table inserted by CTNIA 2015, s. 2 and Sch. 1, para. 6(2), with effect from 26 March 2015 (Royal Assent) in respect of any power to make regulations and with effect in relation to accounting periods beginning on or after the first day of the appointed financial year for other provisions (see CTNIA 2015, s. 5). See also transitional provisions at Sch. 1, para. 19–21.
In s. 61(4A) and (4B) inserted by CTNIA 2015, s. 2 and Sch. 1, para. 6(3), with effect from 26 March 2015 (Royal Assent) in respect of any power to make regulations and with effect in relation to accounting periods beginning on or after the first day of the appointed financial year for other provisions (see CTNIA 2015, s. 5). See also transitional provisions at Sch. 1, para. 19–21.

History – S. 61(1)(ee) inserted by FA 2006, s. 81 and Sch. 8, para. 5(2). The commencement and transitional provisions are complex and are set out in full in FA 2006, Sch. 8, para. 15–27.
In s. 61(1), entry 6A of the Table inserted by FA 2011, s. 48 and Sch. 13, para.. 16, with effect from 19 July 2011.
In s. 61(1), in entry 7 of the Table, "6A" substituted for "6" by FA 2011, s. 48 and Sch. 13, para. 16, with effect from 19 July 2011.
In s. 61(2), entry 5A of the Table substituted by FA 2009, s. 64 and Sch. 32, para. 1(2), with effect in relation to leases whose inception is on or after 13 November 2008. In the former entry the wording in the first column was "Commencement of the term of a long funding finance lease of the plant or machinery." and the wording in the second column was "An amount equal to the market value of the plant or machinery at the commencement of the term of the lease.".
In s. 61(2), at the end of entry 5A of the Table (second column), the words "("the relevant date")" inserted by FA 2008. s. 55 and Sch. 20, para. 4(2), with effect in relation to leases granted on or after 13 December 2007.

In s. 61(2), items 5A and 5B of the Table inserted by FA 2006, s. 81 and Sch. 8, para. 5(3). The commencement and transitional provisions are set out in full in FA 2006, Sch. 8, para. 15–27.
In s. 61(2), in item 6 of the Table, the reference to "5B" substituted for "5" by FA 2006, s. 81 and Sch. 8, para. 5(4). The commencement and transitional provisions are set out in full in FA 2006, Sch. 8, para. 15–27.
In s. 61(2) in entry 2(b) of the Table, the words "ITEPA 2003" substituted for the words "Schedule E" by ITEPA 2003, Sch. 6, para. 249 which has effect, for income tax purposes, for the tax year 2003–04 and subsequent tax years and, for corporation tax purposes, for accounting periods ending after 5 April 2003.
S. 61(5A) inserted by FA 2009, s. 64 and Sch. 32, para. 1(3), with effect in relation to leases whose inception is on or after 13 November 2008.
S. 61(6) omitted by FA 2009, s. 64 and Sch. 32, para. 1(4), with effect in relation to leases whose inception is on or after 13 November 2008. Former s. 61(6) read as follows:
"**61(6)** The following provisions apply for the purposes of calculating the disposal value for item 5A of the Table.".
Former s. 61(6) inserted by FA 2008. s. 55 and Sch. 20, para. 4(3), with effect in relation to leases granted on or after 13 December 2007.
S. 61(7) omitted by FA 2009, s. 64 and Sch. 32, para. 1(4), with effect in relation to leases whose inception is on or after 13 November 2008. Former s. 61(7) read as follows:
"**61(7)** Treat any rentals under the lease made (or due) on or before the relevant date as made (and due) on the day after that date.".
Former s. 61(7) inserted by FA 2008. s. 55 and Sch. 20, para. 4(3), with effect in relation to leases granted on or after 13 December 2007.
S. 61(8) omitted by FA 2009, s. 64 and Sch. 32, para. 1(4), with effect in relation to leases whose inception is on or after 13 November 2008. Former s. 61(8) read as follows:
"**61(8)** Treat the lessor as having no liabilities of any kind at any time on the relevant date (but only if the effect of doing so would be to increase the disposal value).".
Former s. 61(8) inserted by FA 2008. s. 55 and Sch. 20, para. 4(4), with effect in relation to leases granted on or after 12 March 2008.
S. 61(9) omitted by FA 2009, s. 64 and Sch. 32, para. 1(4), with effect in relation to leases whose inception is on or after 13 November 2008. Former s. 61(9) read as follows:
"**61(9)** For the purposes of subsection (8) "liabilities" includes, where the lessor is a company, any share capital issued by the company which falls to be treated for accounting purposes as a liability.".
Former s. 61(9) inserted by FA 2008, s. 55 and Sch. 20, para. 4(4), with effect in relation to leases granted on or after 12 March 2008.

Origin – S. 61(1): CAA 1990, s. 24(6) (part).
S. 61(2): CAA 1990, s. 26(1) (part).
Table, item 1: CAA 1990, s. 26(1)(a) (part).
Table, item 2: CAA 1990, s. 26(1)(b) (part), Annex 2, Note 17.
Table, item 3: CAA 1990, s. 26(1)(c) (part).
Table, item 4: CAA 1990, s. 26(1)(d) (part).
Table, item 5: Annex 1, Change 10.
Table, item 6: CAA 1990, s. 26(1)(e) (part).
Table, item 7: CAA 1990, s. 26(1)(f) (part).
S. 61(3): CAA 1990, s. 26(1) (part).
S. 61(4): CAA 1990, s. 26(1)(b) (part).
S. 61(5): drafting.

Cross references – FA 2000, Sch. 22, para. 70(2), 75(2), 76(2): modified applications of s. 61(1)(e) for various purposes where asset used in tonnage tax trade.
RA 2005, Sch. 10. para. 2: modified application of s. 61 in the case of a transfer to a national authority.
RA 2005, Sch. 10. para. 14: disapplication of s. 61(2) to (4) in the case of certain transfers to a national authority.
SI 2012/1709, art. 3 and 4: British Waterways Board relevant transfers of trade to Canal & River Trust or Canal & River Trust Trading CIC not treated as permanent discontinuance of trade, nor new trade set up.
SI 2015/1540, reg. 7: determination of disposal value of plant and machinery in respect of transfers in accordance with transfer schemes under section 333DA of the Greater London Authority Act 1999 and under section 53A of the Housing and Regeneration Act 2008.

Rewrite: Changes in Law – Explanatory Notes, Annex 1, Change 10: on abandonment of plant or machinery used for mineral exploration and access, former CAA 1990, s. 26(1)(f) provided for the disposal value to be the price that the plant or machinery would have fetched if sold in the open market. Item 5 of the Table in s. 61 brings the treatment of plant or machinery abandoned at a site used for mineral exploration and access into line with the treatment of plant or machinery lost in circumstances where it is reasonable to assume that the loss is permanent. See also s. 402(5).

Rewrite: Technical Points – Explanatory Notes, Annex 2, Note 17: item 2 of the Table specifically provides for the market value to be ascertained "at the time of the sale". There is no such specific provision in former CAA 1990, s. 26(1)(b), but there can be no real doubt that that was how s. 26(1)(b) was meant to apply.

HMRC Manuals – CA23240: guidance on s. 61(2).
CA23250: guidance on s. 61(2)–(5).

Other material – HMRC press release, 26 July 1978 (not reproduced): item 3 of the Table in s. 61 may apply to certain car leasing schemes with variations from the traditional provisions of car leases.
ICAEW Technical Release, TR 233 (not reproduced): the "net amount received" in item 3 of the Table in s. 61 includes the cost of demolition.

62 General limit on amount of disposal value

62(1) The amount of any disposal value required to be brought into account by a person in respect of any plant or machinery is limited to the qualifying expenditure incurred by the person on its provision.

62(2) Subsection (3) applies if a person who is required to bring a disposal value into account has acquired the plant or machinery as a result of a transaction which was, or a series of transactions each of which was, between connected persons.

62(3) The amount of the disposal value is limited to the amount of the qualifying expenditure on the provision of the plant or machinery incurred by whichever party to the transaction, or to any of the transactions, incurred the greatest such expenditure.

62(4) This section is subject to section 239 (limit on disposal value where additional VAT rebate or rebates has or have been made in respect of original expenditure).

Origin – S. 62(1): CAA 1990, s. 26(2) (part).
S. 62(2): CAA 1990, s. 26(3) (part).
S. 62(3): CAA 1990, s. 26(2) (part), (3), Annex 1, Change 11.
S. 62(4): drafting.

Cross references – S. 228E: lessor's income or profits: termination of leaseback.
S. 268(6)(a): where a beneficiary succeeds to a qualifying activity under the will or intestacy of a deceased person, s. 62 applies in relation to the beneficiary to limit the disposal value by reference to expenditure incurred by the deceased.

Rewrite: Changes in Law – Explanatory Notes, Annex 1, Change 11: s. 62 limits disposal value to be brought into account by reference to qualifying expenditure incurred on provision of the plant or machinery, while former CAA 1990, s. 26(2) limited it by reference to capital expenditure. This change will generally work in favour of the taxpayer, particularly where s. 62(2) and (3) apply. But it could work against the taxpayer if the anti-avoidance provisions in Pt. 2, Ch. 17 are in point, as the benefit to the seller of a lower disposal value may result in a lower amount of qualifying expenditure for the buyer.

HMRC Manuals – CA23250: guidance on s. 62.

62A Cases in which disposal value is transition value

62A(1) Subject as follows, this section applies where an election under section 18A of CTA 2009 has effect in relation to a company and the operation of section 15(2A) brings about a disposal event consisting of plant or machinery beginning to be used for purposes other than those of a qualifying activity.

62A(2) Where this section applies to a disposal event, the disposal value is the transition value.

62A(3) The transition value is such amount as gives rise to neither a balancing allowance nor a balancing charge.

62A(4) This section does not apply if–

(a) the qualifying expenditure in respect of the plant or machinery, or of the group of assets of which it forms part at any time during a relevant accounting period, exceeds £5 million, and

(b) the company has used the plant or machinery otherwise than for the purposes of a permanent establishment in a territory outside the United Kingdom at any time during a relevant preceding accounting period.

62A(5) For the purposes of subsection (4)(a) plant or machinery used together constitutes a group of assets.

62A(6) In subsection (4) **"relevant preceding accounting period"** means the accounting period in which the election under section 18A is made or an earlier accounting period ending less than 6 years before the end of that accounting period.

History – S. 62A inserted by FA 2011, s. 48 and Sch. 13, para. 17 with effect from 19 July 2011.

63 Cases in which disposal value is nil

63(1) If a person disposes of plant or machinery by way of gift in circumstances such that there is a charge to tax under ITEPA 2003, the disposal value of the plant or machinery is nil.

63(2) If a person carrying on a relevant qualifying activity makes a gift of plant or machinery used in the course of the activity–

(a) to a charitable trust,

(aa) to a charitable company,

(ab) to a registered club within the meaning of Chapter 9 of Part 13 of CTA 2010 (community amateur sports clubs),

(b) to a body listed in section 468 of CTA 2010 (various heritage bodies and museums), or

(c) for the purposes of a designated educational establishment within the meaning of section 110 of ITTOIA 2005 or section 106 of CTA 2009 (gifts to educational establishments),

the disposal value of the plant or machinery is nil.

63(3) In subsection (2) **"relevant qualifying activity"** means a qualifying activity consisting of–

(a) a trade,

(b) an ordinary UK property business,

(c) a UK furnished holiday lettings business,

(d) an ordinary overseas property business,

(da) an EEA furnished holiday lettings business, or

(e) a profession or vocation.

63(4) Subsection (2)–

(a) needs to be read with section 109 of ITTOIA 2005 and section 108 of CTA 2009 (which provide for a charge to tax if subsection (2) applies in circumstances in which the donor or a connected person receives a benefit attributable to the gift), and

(b) is subject to section 809ZM of ITA 2007 and section 939F of CTA 2010 (removal of tax relief in respect of tainted charity donations etc).

63(5) If expenditure is treated under section 27(2) (expenditure on thermal insulation, safety measures, etc.) as having been incurred on plant or machinery, the disposal value of the plant or machinery is nil.

History – In s. 63(1), the words "ITEPA 2003" substituted for the words "Schedule E" by ITEPA 2003, Sch. 6, para. 250 which has effect, for income tax purposes, for the tax year 2003–04 and subsequent tax years and, for corporation tax purposes, for accounting periods ending after 5 April 2003.
In s. 63(2)(a), the words "within the meaning of Part 10 of ITA 2007 (see section 519 of that Act)" omitted by FA 2010, s. 30 and Sch. 6, para. 16(a), with effect for corporation tax purposes for accounting periods beginning on or after 1 April 2012 and for income tax purposes for the tax year 2012–13 and subsequent tax years (SI 2012/736, art. 12).
In s. 63(2)(aa), the words "within the meaning of Part 11 of CTA 2010 (see section 467 of that Act)" omitted by FA 2010, s. 30 and Sch. 6, para. 16(b), with effect for corporation tax purposes for accounting periods beginning on or after 1 April 2012 and for income tax purposes for the tax year 2012–13 and subsequent tax years (SI 2012/736, art. 12).
In s. 63(2)(a), the words "charitable trust within the meaning of Part 10 of ITA 2007 (see section 519 of that Act)" substituted for the words "charity within the meaning of section 506 of ICTA (charities: qualifying and non-qualifying expenditure)" by CTA 2010, s. 1177 and Sch. 1, para. 328(a), with effect for corporation tax purposes for accounting periods ending on or after 1 April 2010, and for income tax and capital gains tax purposes for the tax year 2010–11 and subsequent tax years.
S. 63(2)(aa) and (ab) inserted by CTA 2010, s. 1177 and Sch. 1, para. 328(b), with effect for corporation tax purposes for accounting periods ending on or after 1 April 2010, and for income tax and capital gains tax purposes for the tax year 2010–11 and subsequent tax years.
In s. 63(2)(b), the words "section 468 of CTA 2010" substituted for "section 507(1) of ICTA" by CTA 2010, s. 1177 and Sch. 1, para. 328(c), with effect for corporation tax purposes for accounting periods ending on or after 1 April 2010, and for income tax and capital gains tax purposes for the tax year 2010–11 and subsequent tax years.
In s. 63(2)(c), the words "section 106 of CTA 2009" substituted for the words "section 84 of ICTA" by CTA 2009, s. 1322 and Sch. 1, para. 482(2), with effect for corporation tax purposes for accounting periods ending on or after 1 April 2009, and for income tax and capital gains tax purposes for the tax year 2009–10 and subsequent tax years.
In s. 63(2)(c) the words "section 110 of ITTOIA 2005 or" inserted by ITTOIA 2005, s. 882(1) and Sch. 1, para. 535(2); effective for income tax purposes for 2005–06 onwards and for corporation tax purposes for accounting periods ending after 5 April 2005 (ITTOIA 2005, s. 883(1)).
In s. 63(3)(b), the word "UK" inserted after "ordinary" by FA 2011, s. 52 and Sch. 14, para. 12(10)(a), with effect in relation to chargeable periods beginning on or after 1 April 2011 (for corporation tax purposes), and in relation to chargeable periods beginning on or after 6 April 2011 (for income tax purposes).
In s. 63(3)(b) the word "property" substituted for "Schedule A" by ITTOIA 2005, s. 882(1) and Sch. 1, para. 535(3); effective for income tax purposes for 2005–06 onwards and for corporation tax purposes for accounting periods ending after 5 April 2005 (ITTOIA 2005, s. 883(1)).
In s. 63(3)(c), the words "UK furnished" substituted for "furnished" by FA 2011, s. 52 and Sch. 14, para. 12(10)(b), with effect in relation to chargeable periods beginning on or after 1 April 2011 (for corporation tax purposes), and in relation to chargeable periods beginning on or after 6 April 2011 (for income tax purposes).
In s. 63(3)(d), the words "ordinary overseas" substituted for "overseas" by FA 2011, s. 52 and Sch. 14, para. 12(10)(c), with effect in relation to chargeable periods beginning on or after 1 April 2011 (for corporation tax purposes), and in relation to chargeable periods beginning on or after 6 April 2011 (for income tax purposes).
S. 63(3)(da) inserted and the word "or" at the end of (d) inserted by FA 2011, s. 52 and Sch. 14, para. 12(10)(d), with effect in relation to chargeable periods beginning on or after 1 April 2011 (for corporation tax purposes), and in relation to chargeable periods beginning on or after 6 April 2011 (for income tax purposes).
In s. 63(4), the characters "– (a)" inserted by FA 2011, s. 27 and Sch. 3, para. 4(a), with effect in relation to relievable charity donations made on or after 1 April 2011.
In s. 63(4), the words ", and" and paragraph (b) inserted by FA 2011, s. 27 and Sch. 3, para. 4(b), with effect in relation to relievable charity donations made on or after 1 April 2011.
In s. 63(4), the words "section 108 of CTA 2009" substituted for the words "sections 83A(4) and 84(4) of ICTA" by CTA 2009, s. 1322 and Sch. 1, para. 482(3), with effect for corporation tax purposes for accounting periods ending on or after 1 April 2009, and for income tax and capital gains tax purposes for the tax year 2009–10 and subsequent tax years.
In s. 63(4) the words "section 109 of ITTOIA 2005 and" inserted by ITTOIA 2005, s. 882(1) and Sch. 1, para. 535(4); effective for income tax purposes for 2005–06 onwards and for corporation tax purposes for accounting periods ending after 5 April 2005 (ITTOIA 2005, s. 883(1)).

Origin – S. 63(1): CAA 1990, s. 24(6) (part), Annex 1, Change 12.
S. 63(2): ICTA 1988, s. 83A(1), (2) (part), (3)(b), s. 84(1) (part), (3)(b), Annex 1, Changes 12 and 13.
S. 63(3): ICTA 1988, s. 21A(1) (part), s. 65A(5) (part), s. 70A(5) (part), s. 83A(1) (part), s. 84(1) (part), Annex 2, Note 18.
S. 63(4): drafting.
S. 63(5): CAA 1990, s. 67(1) (part), s. 69(1) (part), s. 70(1) (part), s. 71(2) (part).

Cross references – FA 2002, Sch. 18, para. 9(3)(c): s. 63(2) has effect as if a registered community amateur sports club were a charity.

Rewrite: Changes in Law – Explanatory Notes, Annex 1, Change 12: s. 63(1) and (2) provide for a nil disposal value, while former CAA 1990, s. 24(6) (and ICTA 1988, s. 83A and 84) provide that no disposal value is required to be brought into account. This enables a person who has claimed some first-year allowances, then made a gift of the plant or machinery in the first chargeable period, to allocate the balance of their qualifying expenditure to a pool. But it could operate to the disadvantage of the recipient if the gift were a transaction within Ch. 17 as it would prevent the recipient from also claiming allowances.
Explanatory Notes, Annex 1, Change 13: s. 63 drops the two requirements of ICTA 1988, s. 84 that the person making the gift must have claimed plant and machinery allowances, and that the donor must make a claim for relief, specifying the article given and the name of the educational establishment in question.

Rewrite: Technical Points – Explanatory Notes, Annex 2, Note 18: basis for exclusion of offices and employments, special leasing and the business of an investment company from list of relevant qualifying activities in s. 63(3), and inclusion of Sch. A businesses (including furnished holiday lettings) and overseas property businesses.

HMRC Manuals – CA22220: guidance on s. 63(5).
CA23250: guidance on s. 63.

64 Case in which no disposal value need be brought into account

64(1) A person is not required to bring a disposal value into account in a pool for a chargeable period in respect of plant or machinery if none of the qualifying expenditure is or has been taken into account in *a claim in determining* the person's available qualifying expenditure in the pool for that or any previous chargeable period.

64(2) Subsection (3) applies if–

(a) a person ("C") has incurred qualifying expenditure on plant or machinery,

(b) C acquired the plant or machinery as a result of a transaction which was, or a series of transactions each of which was, between connected persons,

(c) any connected person (apart from C) who was a party to the transaction, or one of the series of transactions, is or has been required to bring a disposal value into account as a result of the transaction,

(d) a disposal event ("the relevant disposal event") occurs in respect of the plant or machinery at a time when it is owned by C, and

(e) none of C's qualifying expenditure is or has been taken into account in a claim in determining C's available qualifying expenditure for the chargeable period in which the relevant disposal event occurs or any previous chargeable period.

64(3) If this subsection applies–

(a) subsection (1) does not apply in relation to the relevant disposal event, and

(b) C's qualifying expenditure is to be treated as allocated to the appropriate pool for the chargeable period in which the relevant disposal event occurs.

64(4) In subsection (3)–

(a) **"qualifying expenditure"** means, if a first-year allowance has been made to C, the amount (including a nil amount) remaining after deducting the allowance, and

(b) **"the appropriate pool"** means whichever pool is applicable in relation to C under the provisions of this Part.

64(5) A person takes expenditure into account in a claim if he takes it into account–

(a) in a tax return;

(b) by giving notice of an amendment of a tax return;

(c) in any other claim under this Part.

Origin – S. 64(1): CAA 1990, s. 24(6) (part), Annex 1, Change 14.
S. 64(2): CAA 1990, s. 24(6) (part), s. 26(3) (part), Annex 1, Change 14.
S. 64(3): to (5): Annex 1, Change 14.

Rewrite: Changes in Law – Explanatory Notes, Annex 1, Change 14: strictly, former CAA 1990, s. 24(6) required a person to bring a disposal value into account even where they had not used the expenditure in a tax claim. However, the Revenue in practice have accepted that in general no disposal value need be brought into account where the expenditure has not been allocated to a pool, and no first-year allowances have been claimed, and s. 64(1) makes this explicit. S. 64(2)–(4) are introduced to prevent advantage being taken of this change in the law in cases where a person has not used the expenditure in a tax claim but the situation is regulated by s. 26(3) (connected persons).

HMRC Manuals – CA23260: guidance and example on s. 64.

64A Leased assets: arrangements reducing disposal value of asset

64A(1) Where–

(a) plant or machinery ("the asset") is subject to a lease,

(b) a disposal event occurs with the result that a disposal value in respect of the asset is to be brought into account under Item 1, 2 or 7 of the Table in section 61(2), and

(c) arrangements have been entered into that have the effect of reducing the disposal value of the asset in so far as it is attributable to rentals payable under the lease,

the disposal value is to be determined as if the arrangements had not been entered into.

64A(2) Subsection (1) does not apply if–

(a) the arrangements take the form of a transfer of relevant receipts within section 809AZA of ITA 2007 and the relevant amount has been treated as income under section 809AZB of that Act, or

(b) the arrangements take the form of a transfer of relevant receipts within section 752 of CTA 2010 and the relevant amount has been treated as income under section 753 of that Act.

History – S. 64A inserted by FA 2010, s. 27 and Sch. 5, para. 3(1), with effect in relation to disposal events taking place on or after 9 December 2009.

THE FINAL CHARGEABLE PERIOD

65 The final chargeable period

65(1) The final chargeable period for–

(a) the main pool, or

(b) a special rate pool,

is the chargeable period in which the qualifying activity is permanently discontinued.

65(2) The final chargeable period for a single asset pool is the first chargeable period in which any disposal event given in section 61(1) occurs.

65(3) Subsection (2) is subject to–

section 206(4) (no final chargeable period merely because plant or machinery begins to be used partly for purposes other than those of qualifying activity);

sections 86(2) and 87(2) (ending of short-life asset pool at relevant cut-off without final chargeable period);

section 132(2) (no final chargeable period for single ship pool).

65(4) The final chargeable period for a class pool under section 107 (overseas leasing) is the chargeable period at the end of which the circumstances are such that there can be no more disposal receipts in any subsequent chargeable period.

History – S. 65(1)(b) substituted by FA 2008, s. 82 and Sch. 26, para. 5, with effect in relation expenditure incurred on or after 1 April 2008 for corporation tax purposes and 6 April 2008 for income tax purposes and in relation to long-life asset expenditure (within the meaning of CAA 2001, Pt. 2, Ch. 10) incurred before those dates but allocated to a pool in a chargeable period beginning on or after those dates. This commencement provision is subject to FA 2008, s. 83 (existing long-life asset expenditure treated as special rate expenditure) and FA 2008, Sch. 26, para. 15–17 (detailed provisions relating to sales between connected persons and savings for intra-group transfers). Former s. 65(1)(b) read as follows:

"(b) a long-life asset pool,".

In s. 65(3), the word "relevant" substituted for "four-year" by FA 2011, s. 12(3), with effect from 19 July 2011.

In s. 65(3), the word "section" substituted for the words "sections 77(1) and" by FA 2009, s. 30 and Sch. 11, para. 17, with effect in relation to expenditure incurred on or after 1 April 2009 (for corporation tax purposes) and 6 April 2009 (for income tax purposes), subject to transitional provisions in FA 2009, Sch. 11, para. 27(2) and 29–32.

Origin – S. 65(1): CAA 1990, s. 24(2) (part), s. 38E(2) (part), s. 61(1), Annex 1, Change 15.

S. 65(2): CAA 1990, s. 24(6) (part), s. 31(2) (part), s. 34(2) (part), s. 37(3) (part), s. 79(4), s. 80(5) (part).

S. 65(3): drafting.

S. 65(4): CAA 1990, s. 41(4).

Cross references – S. 55: entitlement to writing-down and balancing allowance and liability to balancing charge.

Rewrite: Changes in Law – Explanatory Notes, Annex 1, Change 15: the predecessor provisions CAA 1990, s. 31(2)(b), 34(2)(b), 37(3)(b), 79(4) and 80(5)(a) use a common form of words: "without prejudice to section 24(6)(c)(i) to (iii), the [notional] trade is permanently discontinued when the [plant or machinery] begins to be used wholly or partly for purposes other than those of the actual trade". S. 65(2) reflects an interpretation of the words "without prejudice to section 24(6)(c)(i) to (iii)."

In CAA 1990, s. 31(2)(b), 34(2)(b), 37(3)(b), 79(4) and 80(5)(a) which takes them to mean that where expenditure in respect of plant or machinery is treated as incurred for the purposes of a notional trade, and an event mentioned in s. 24(6)(c)(i)–(iii) occurs, the notional trade has to be regarded as permanently discontinued. The interpretation is not free from doubt but s. 65(2) resolves it in favour of the taxpayer.

HMRC Manuals – CA23270: disposal receipt: final chargeable period.

LIST OF PROVISIONS OUTSIDE THIS CHAPTER ABOUT DISPOSAL VALUES

66 List of provisions outside this Chapter about disposal values

66 The provisions of this Part referred to in section 60(1)(b) are–

section 68	hire-purchase etc.: disposal value on cessation of notional ownership
section 70E	long funding leases: disposal events and disposal values
sections 72 and 73	grant of new software right: disposal value
sections 88 and 89	short-life assets: disposal at under-value or to connected person
section 104E	special rate expenditure: avoidance cases
section 108, section 111 and section 114	overseas leasing: disposal values in various cases
sections 132 and 143	ships: ship used for overseas leasing etc.; attribution of amount where balancing charge deferred
section 171	oil production sharing contracts: disposal values on cessation of ownership
sections 196 and 197	fixtures: disposal values on cessation of notional ownership and in avoidance cases
section 208	effect of significant reduction in use of plant or machinery for purposes of qualifying activity
section 208A	cars: disposal value in avoidance cases
section 211	effect of payment of partial depreciation subsidy
section 218ZB	disposal of plant or machinery in avoidance cases
sections 228K to 228M	Disposal of plant or machinery subject to lease where income retained
section 229	hire-purchase: disposal values in finance leasing and anti-avoidance cases
sections 238 and 239	additional VAT rebates

History – In s. 66, the entry relating to s. 70E inserted by FA 2009, s. 64 and Sch. 32, para. 6, with effect in relation to cases where the relevant event occurs on or after 13 November 2008.
In s. 66, the entry relating to s. 79 omitted by FA 2009, s. 30 and Sch. 11, para. 18(a), with effect in relation to expenditure incurred on or after 1 April 2009 (for corporation tax purposes) and 6 April 2009 (for income tax purposes), subject to transitional provisions in FA 2009, Sch. 11, para. 27(2) and 28–32.
In s. 66, the entry relating to s. 104E substituted for the entry reading "section 104 long-life assets: avoidance cases" by FA 2008, s. 82 and Sch. 26, para. 6, with effect in relation expenditure incurred on or after 1 April 2008 for corporation tax purposes and 6 April 2008 for income tax purposes and in relation to long-life asset expenditure (within the meaning of CAA 2001, Pt. 2, Ch. 10) incurred before those dates but allocated to a pool in a chargeable period beginning on or after those dates. This commencement provision is subject to FA 2008, s. 83 (existing long-life asset expenditure treated as special rate expenditure) and FA 2008, Sch. 26, para. 15–17 (detailed provisions relating to sales between connected persons and savings for intra-group transfers).
In s. 66, the entry relating to s. 208A inserted by FA 2009, s. 30 and Sch. 11, para. 18(b), with effect in relation to expenditure incurred on or after 1 April 2009 (for corporation tax purposes) and 6 April 2009 (for income tax purposes), subject to transitional provisions in FA 2009, Sch. 11, para. 27(2) and 28–32.
In s. 66, the entry relating to s. 218ZB inserted by FA 2016, s. 70(10), with effect in relation to transactions mentioned in s. 213(1)(a), (b) or (c) that take place on or after 25 November 2015.
In s. 66, the entry s. 222 omitted by FA 2008, s. 55 and Sch. 20, para. 6(5), with effect in the case of plant or machinery which is the subject of a sale and finance leaseback (as defined in CAA 2001, s. 221) where the date of the transaction (within the meaning of that section) is on or after 9 October 2007.
In s. 66, the entry relating to s. 228K to 228M inserted by FA 2006, s. 84(2), with effect in relation to any disposal made on or after 5 December 2005. But any rentals that are receivable by the lessor before 22 March 2006 are to be left out of accountin calculating the income of the lessor's leasing business for corporation tax purposes.

Origin – S. 66: drafting.

HMRC Manuals – CA23280: guidance on s. 66.

APPLICATION OF CHAPTER TO PERSON LEAVING CASH BASIS

66A Persons leaving cash basis

66A(1) This section applies if–

(a) a person carrying on a trade, profession or vocation leaves the cash basis in a chargeable period, and

(b) the person has at any time incurred expenditure which, if an election under section 25A of ITTOIA 2005 (cash basis for small businesses) had not had effect at that time, would have been qualifying expenditure.

66A(2) In this section–

(a) the **"relieved portion"** of the expenditure is the amount of that expenditure for which–

  (i) a deduction was allowed in calculating the profits of the trade, profession or vocation, or

  (ii) a deduction would have been so allowed if the expenditure had been incurred wholly and exclusively for the purposes of the trade, profession or vocation;

(b) the **"unrelieved portion"** of the expenditure is any remaining amount of the expenditure.

66A(3) For the purposes of determining any entitlement of the person to an annual investment allowance or a first-year allowance, the person is to be treated as incurring the unrelieved portion of the expenditure in the chargeable period.

66A(4) For the purposes of determining the person's available qualifying expenditure in a pool for the chargeable period (see section 58)–

(a) the whole of the expenditure must be allocated to the appropriate pool (or pools) in that chargeable period, and

(b) the available qualifying expenditure in a pool to which the expenditure (or some of it) is allocated is reduced by the relieved portion of that expenditure.

66A(5) For the purposes of determining any disposal receipts (see section 60), the expenditure incurred by the person is to be regarded as qualifying expenditure.

66A(6) For the purposes of this section a person carrying on a trade, profession or vocation leaves the cash basis in a chargeable period if–

(a) immediately before the beginning of the chargeable period an election under section 25A had effect in relation to the trade, profession or vocation, and

(b) such an election does not have effect in relation to the trade, profession or vocation for the chargeable period.

History – S. 66A inserted by FA 2013, s. 17 and Sch. 4, para. 48, with effect for the tax year 2013–14 and subsequent tax years.

EFFECT OF CHANGES IN NORTHERN IRELAND STATUS OF SME COMPANY OR SME PARTNERSHIP

66B SME company entering NI corporation tax regime

66B [Prospectively inserted by CTNIA 2015, s. 2 and Sch. 1, para. 7.]

Prospective amendments – S. 66B inserted by CTNIA 2015, s. 2 and Sch. 1, para. 7, with effect from 26 March 2015 (Royal Assent) in respect of any power to make regulations and with effect in relation to accounting periods beginning on or after the first day of the appointed financial year for other provisions (see CTNIA 2015, s. 5). See also transitional provisions at Sch. 1, para. 19–21.

66C SME partnership entering NI corporation tax regime

66C [Prospectively inserted by CTNIA 2015, s. 2 and Sch. 1, para. 7.]

Prospective amendments – S. 66C inserted by CTNIA 2015, s. 2 and Sch. 1, para. 7, with effect from 26 March 2015 (Royal Assent) in respect of any power to make regulations and with effect in relation to accounting periods beginning on or after the first day of the appointed financial year for other provisions (see CTNIA 2015, s. 5). See also transitional provisions at Sch. 1, para. 19–21.

66D SME company leaving NI corporation tax regime

66D [Prospectively inserted by CTNIA 2015, s. 2 and Sch. 1, para. 7.]

Prospective amendments – S. 66D inserted by CTNIA 2015, s. 2 and Sch. 1, para. 7, with effect from 26 March 2015 (Royal Assent) in respect of any power to make regulations and with effect in relation to accounting periods beginning on or after the first day of the appointed financial year for other provisions (see CTNIA 2015, s. 5). See also transitional provisions at Sch. 1, para. 19–21.

66E SME partnership leaving NI corporation tax regime

66E [Prospectively inserted by CTNIA 2015, s. 2 and Sch. 1, para. 7.]

Prospective amendments – S. 66E inserted by CTNIA 2015, s. 2 and Sch. 1, para. 7, with effect from 26 March 2015 (Royal Assent) in respect of any power to make regulations and with effect in relation to accounting periods beginning on or after the first day of the appointed financial year for other provisions (see CTNIA 2015, s. 5). See also transitional provisions at Sch. 1, para. 19–21.

Chapter 6 – Hire-purchase etc. and Plant or Machinery Provided by Lessee

HIRE-PURCHASE AND SIMILAR CONTRACTS

67 Plant or machinery treated as owned by person entitled to benefit of contract, etc.

67(1) This section applies if–

(a) a person carrying on a qualifying activity or corresponding overseas activity incurs capital expenditure on the provision of plant or machinery for the purposes of the qualifying activity or corresponding overseas activity, and

(b) the expenditure is incurred under a contract providing that the person shall or may become the owner of the plant or machinery on the performance of the contract.

67(2) The plant or machinery is to be treated for the purposes of this Part as owned by the person (and not by any other person) at any time when he is entitled to the benefit of the contract so far as it relates to the plant or machinery.

This subsection has effect subject to, and in accordance with, subsections (2A) to (2C).

67(2A) If the contract is one which, in accordance with generally accepted accounting practice, falls (or would fall) to be treated as a lease, subsection (2B) applies.

67(2B) Where that is the case, the plant or machinery is to be treated under subsection (2) as owned by the person at any time only if the contract falls (or would fall) to be treated by that person in accordance with generally accepted accounting practice as a finance lease.

67(2C) Where at any time the plant or machinery–

(a) is not treated under subsection (2) as owned by the person, but

(b) would be treated under that subsection as owned by the person, but for subsection (2B),

the plant or machinery is nevertheless to be treated under subsection (2) as not owned by any other person at that time.

67(3) At the time when the plant or machinery is brought into use for the purposes of the qualifying activity or corresponding overseas activity, the person is to be treated for the purposes of this Part as having incurred all capital expenditure in respect of the plant or machinery to be incurred by him under the contract after that time.

67(4) If a person–

(a) is treated under subsection (2) as owning plant or machinery,

(b) ceases to be entitled to the benefit of the contract in question so far as it relates to that plant or machinery, and

(c) does not then in fact become the owner of the plant or machinery, the person is to be treated as ceasing to own the plant or machinery at the time when he ceases to be entitled to the benefit of the contract.

67(5) [Former s. 67(5) renumbered as s. 67(7) by FA 2006, s. 81 and Sch. 9, para. 12(5).]

67(6) If–

(a) a person enters into two or more agreements, and

(b) those agreements are such that, if they together constituted a single contract, the condition in subsection (1)(b) would be met in relation to that person and that contract,

the agreements are to be treated for the purposes of this section as parts of a single contract.

In this subsection, any reference to an agreement includes a reference to an undertaking, whether or not legally enforceable.

67(7) This section is subject to section 69 (hire-purchase and fixtures) and subsection (3) is subject to section 229 (anti-avoidance).

67(8) In this section **"corresponding overseas activity"** means an activity that would be a qualifying activity if the person carrying it on were resident in the United Kingdom.

History – In s. 67(1)(a), the words "or corresponding overseas activity" inserted (twice) by FA 2006, s. 81 and Sch. 9, para. 12(2), with effect in relation to contracts that are finalised (within the meaning of FA 2006, Sch. 8, para. 15–27) on or after 1 April 2006.
In s. 67(2), the last sentence inserted by FA 2006, s. 81 and Sch. 9, para. 12(3), with effect in relation to contracts that are finalised (within the meaning of FA 2006, Sch. 8, para. 15–27) on or after 1 April 2006.
S. 67(2A) inserted by FA 2006, s. 81 and Sch. 9, para. 12(4), with effect in relation to contracts that are finalised (within the meaning of FA 2006, Sch. 8, para. 15–27) on or after 1 April 2006.
S. 67(2B) inserted by FA 2006, s. 81 and Sch. 9, para. 12(4), with effect in relation to contracts that are finalised (within the meaning of FA 2006, Sch. 8, para. 15–27) on or after 1 April 2006.
S. 67(2C) inserted by FA 2006, s. 81 and Sch. 9, para. 12(4), with effect in relation to contracts that are finalised (within the meaning of FA 2006, Sch. 8, para. 15–27) on or after 1 April 2006.
In s. 67(3), the words "or corresponding overseas activity" inserted by FA 2006, s. 81 and Sch. 9, para. 12(2), with effect in relation to contracts that are finalised (within the meaning of FA 2006, Sch. 8, para. 15–27) on or after 1 April 2006.
Former s. 67(5) renumbered as s. 67(7) by FA 2006, s. 81 and Sch. 9, para. 12(5), with effect in relation to contracts that are finalised (within the meaning of FA 2006, Sch. 8, para. 15–27) on or after 1 April 2006.
S. 67(6) inserted by FA 2006, s. 81 and Sch. 9, para. 12(6), with effect in relation to contracts that are finalised (within the meaning of FA 2006, Sch. 8, para. 15–27) on or after 1 April 2006.
S. 67(7) renumbered as such (previously s. 67(5)) by FA 2006, s. 81 and Sch. 9, para. 12(5), with effect in relation to contracts that are finalised (within the meaning of FA 2006, Sch. 8, para. 15–27) on or after 1 April 2006.
S. 67(8) inserted by FA 2006, s. 81 and Sch. 9, para. 12(7), with effect in relation to contracts that are finalised (within the meaning of FA 2006, Sch. 8, para.15–27) on or after 1 April 2006.

Origin – S. 67(1): CAA 1990, s. 60(1) (part).
S. 67(2): CAA 1990, s. 60(1)(a).
S. 67(3): CAA 1990, s. 60(1)(b).
S. 67(4): CAA 1990, s. 60(2)(a).
S. 67(5): CAA 1990, s. 60(4).

Cross references – Greater London Authority Act 1999, Sch. 33, para. 12(1)(c): entitlement to capital allowances of companies participating in a public-private agreement certified by London Regional Transport.

HMRC Manuals – CA23310: guidance on s. 67.
CA23350: abortive capital expenditure on plant and machinery may be within s. 67 and therefore qualify for capital allowances if it was incurred under a contract providing that the person "shall or may become the owner of the plant or machinery on the performance of the contract".

Other material – HMRC Brief 26/07: alternative finance arrangements – diminishing shared ownership cases – implications for capital allowances and capital gains.
HMRC press release, 27 October 1986: entitlement to capital allowances remains with the hirer under a hire purchase contract following implementation of SSAP 21: Accounting for leases and hire purchase contracts.

68 Disposal value on cessation of notional ownership

68(1) This section applies if a person–

(a) is treated under section 67(4) as ceasing to own plant or machinery, and

(b) is required to bring a disposal value into account as a result.

68(2) If the plant or machinery has been brought into use for the purposes of the qualifying activity before the person ceases to own the plant or machinery, the disposal value is the total of–

(a) any relevant capital sums, and

(b) any capital expenditure treated under section 67(3) as having been incurred when the plant or machinery was brought into use but which has not in fact been incurred.

68(3) If the plant or machinery has not been brought into use for the purposes of the qualifying activity before the person ceases to own the plant or machinery, the disposal value is the total of any relevant capital sums.

68(4) **"Relevant capital sums"** means capital sums that the person receives or is entitled to receive by way of consideration, compensation, damages or insurance money in respect of–

(a) his rights under the contract, or

(b) the plant or machinery.

68(5) This section is subject to section 229 (anti-avoidance).

Origin – S. 68(1), (2): CAA 1990, s. 60(2) (part).
S. 68(3): Annex 1, Change 16.
S. 68(4): CAA 1990, s. 60(2) (part).
S. 68(5): drafting.

Cross references – S. 60(1)(b), s. 66: general provisions about disposal values required to be brought into account ("disposal receipts").
ICTA 1988, s. 781(9): s. 781 (assets leased to traders) does not apply to turn capital sum received into income taxable under Sch. D Case VI where the capital sum is required to be brought into account under s. 68.
Greater London Authority Act 1999, Sch. 33, para. 12(1)(c): entitlement to capital allowances of companies participating in a public-private agreement certified by London Regional Transport.

Rewrite: Changes in Law – Explanatory Notes, Annex 1, Change 16: s. 68(3) provides a disposal value consisting of "relevant capital sums" where the machinery or plant being acquired under the contract has *not* been brought into use. Formerly, the disposal value where the plant or machinery had not been brought into use was its market value (CAA 1990, s. 26(1)(f)), because CAA 1990, s. 60(2) only made specific provision for the disposal value when a person ceased to be entitled to the benefit of a contract *after* bringing the plant or machinery into use.

HMRC Manuals – CA23330: examples of assignment of contract before the asset is brought into use.
CA23350: abortive capital expenditure on plant and machinery may be within s. 67 and therefore qualify for capital allowances if it was incurred under a contract providing that the person "shall or may become the owner of the plant or machinery on the performance of the contract".

Other material – HMRC press release, 27 October 1986: entitlement to capital allowances remains with the hirer under a hire purchase contract following implementation of SSAP 21: Accounting for leases and hire purchase contracts.
Taxline 1995/81 (not reproduced): lift shafts installed in existing buildings may qualify for capital allowances.

69 Hire-purchase etc. and fixtures

69(1) Section 67 does not–

(a) apply to expenditure incurred on plant or machinery which is a fixture, or

(b) prevent Chapter 14 (fixtures) applying in relation to expenditure on plant or machinery incurred under such a contract as is mentioned in section 67(1)(b).

69(2) If–

(a) a person is treated under section 67(2) as owning plant or machinery,

(b) the plant or machinery becomes a fixture, and

(c) the person is not treated under Chapter 14 as being the owner of the plant or machinery,

the person is to be treated for the purposes of this Part as ceasing to own the plant or machinery at the time when it becomes a fixture.

69(3) In this section **"fixture"** has the meaning given by section 173(1).

Origin – S. 69(1): CAA 1990, s. 60A(1).
S. 69(2): CAA 1990, s. 60A(2).
S. 69(3): CAA 1990, s. 60A(3).

Transitional – Sch. 3, para. 16: s. 69(2) does not apply if the plant or machinery became a fixture before 28 July 2000.

HMRC Manuals – CA23320: guidance one fixtures.

PLANT OR MACHINERY PROVIDED BY LESSEE

70 Plant or machinery provided by lessee

70(1) This section applies if–

(a) under the terms of a lease, a lessee is required to provide plant or machinery,

(b) the lessee incurs capital expenditure on the provision of that plant or machinery for the purposes of a qualifying activity which the lessee carries on,

(c) the plant or machinery is not so installed or otherwise fixed in or to a building or any other description of land as to become, in law, part of that building or other land, and

(d) the lessee does not own the plant or machinery.

70(2) The lessee–

(a) is to be treated as being the owner of the plant or machinery, as a result of incurring the capital expenditure, for so long as it continues to be used for the purposes of the qualifying activity, but

(b) is not required to bring a disposal value into account because the lease ends.

70(3) Subsection (4) applies if–

(a) the plant or machinery continues to be used for the purposes of the lessee's qualifying activity until the lease ends,

(b) the lessor holds the lease in the course of a qualifying activity, and

(c) on or after the ending of the lease, a disposal event occurs in respect of the plant or machinery at a time when the lessor owns the plant or machinery as a result of the requirement under the terms of the lease.

70(4) The lessor is required to bring a disposal value into account in the appropriate pool for the chargeable period in which the disposal event occurs.

70(5) **"The appropriate pool"** means the pool which would be applicable under this Part in relation to the lessor's qualifying activity if–

(a) the expenditure incurred by the lessee had been qualifying expenditure incurred by the lessor, and

(b) that qualifying expenditure were being allocated to a pool for the chargeable period in which the disposal event occurs.

70(6) In this section **"lease"** includes–

(a) an agreement for a lease if the term to be covered by the lease has begun, and

(b) any tenancy,

but does not include a mortgage (and **"lessee"** and **"lessor"** are to be read accordingly).

Origin – S. 70(1): CAA 1990, s. 61(4) (part).
S. 70(2): CAA 1990, s. 61(4) (part), Annex 1, Change 17.
S. 70(3), (4): CAA 1990, s. 24(6) (part), (8) (part), s. 61(4) (part), Annex 1, Change 17.
S. 70(5): CAA 1990, s. 61(4) (part), Annex 1, Change 17.
S. 70(6): CAA 1990, s. 61(8).

Transitional – Sch. 3, para. 17: s. 70(1)(c) and (d) do not apply if the lease was entered into before 12 July 1984, or on or after that date under an agreement made before that date.

Rewrite: Changes in Law – Explanatory Notes, Annex 1, Change 17: s. 70(4) reflects a particular interpretation of the closing words of CAA 1990, s. 61(4): "but, as from the determination of the lease, section 24(6) shall have effect as if the capital expenditure on providing the machinery or plant had been incurred by the lessor and not by the lessee". The interpretation relied upon provides that the lessee can continue to claim allowances after the determination of the lease and is not required to bring a disposal into account merely because the lease comes to an end. However, the lessor must bring a disposal value into account if a disposal event occurs in relation to the plant or machinery after the ending of the lease, but is not able to claim allowances.

HMRC Manuals – CA23340: guidance and example.

LESSEES UNDER LONG FUNDING LEASES

70A Entitlement to capital allowances

70A(1) This section applies if a person carrying on a qualifying activity incurs expenditure (whether or not of a capital nature) on the provision of plant or machinery for the purposes of the qualifying activity under a long funding lease.

70A(2) In the application of this Part in the case of that person, the plant or machinery is to be treated as owned by him at any time when he is the lessee under the long funding lease.

That is so whether or not the lease also falls to be regarded as a long funding lease in the application of this Part in the case of the lessor.

70A(3) The person is to be treated for the purposes of this Part as having incurred capital expenditure on the provision of the plant or machinery as follows.

70A(4) The capital expenditure is to be treated as incurred at the commencement of the term of the long funding lease.

70A(5) The amount of the capital expenditure varies, according to whether the long funding lease is–

(a) a long funding operating lease (subsection (6)), or

(b) a long funding finance lease (subsection (7)).

70A(6) If the long funding lease is a long funding operating lease, the amount of the capital expenditure is to be found in accordance with section 70B.

70A(7) If the long funding lease is a long funding finance lease, the amount of the capital expenditure is to be found in accordance with section 70C.

70A(8) See Chapter 6A for interpretation of this section.

History – S. 70A inserted by FA 2006, s. 81 and Sch. 8, para. 6. The commencement and transitional provisions are complex and are set out in full in FA 2006, Sch. 8, para. 15–27.

HMRC Manuals – CA23800: introductory guidance re long funding leases.

70B Long funding operating lease: amount of capital expenditure

70B(1) This section applies by virtue of section 70A(6).

70B(2) If the long funding lease is a long funding operating lease, the amount of the capital expenditure is the market value of the plant or machinery at the later of–

(a) the commencement of the term of the lease;

(b) the date on which the plant or machinery is first brought into use for the purpose of the qualifying activity.

70B(3) This section is to be construed as one with section 70A.

CAA 2001

History – S. 70B inserted by FA 2006, s. 81 and Sch. 8, para. 6. The commencement and transitional provisions are complex and are set out in full in FA 2006, Sch. 8, para. 15–27.

70C Long funding finance lease: amount of capital expenditure

70C(1) This section has effect by virtue of section 70A(7) for the purpose of determining the amount of the capital expenditure in the case of a long funding finance lease.

70C(2) If the lease is one which, under generally accepted accounting practice, falls (or would fall) to be treated as a loan, this section applies as if the lease were one which, under generally accepted accounting practice, fell to be treated as a finance lease.

70C(3) The amount of the capital expenditure is the total of–

(a) commencement PVMLP (see subsection (4)), and

(b) if subsection (6) applies, the unrelievable pre-commencement rentals ("UPR"),

but subject, in a case falling within subsection (7), to the restriction imposed by subsection (8).

70C(4) Commencement PVMLP is the amount that would fall to be recognised as the present value, at the appropriate date, of the minimum lease payments (see section 70YE) if appropriate accounts were prepared by the person.

70C(4A) But where the minimum lease payments include a relievable amount, the present value of that amount must be excluded in determining the commencement PVMLP.

70C(4B) An amount ("amount X") is a relievable amount if–

(a) an arrangement is in place under which all or part of any residual amount (as defined in section 70YE) is guaranteed by the lessee or a person connected with the lessee,

(b) amount X is within the minimum lease payments because of that arrangement (see subsection (1)(a) of that section), and

(c) it is reasonable to assume that, were amount X to be incurred under the arrangement, relief would be available as a result (beyond relief, by virtue of this section and section 70E, because amount X is within those minimum lease payments).

70C(4C) In deciding for the purposes of subsection (4B)(c) whether relief would be available as a result, no account is to be taken of–

(a) any part of the arrangement other than the part by virtue of which all or part of the residual amount is guaranteed, or

(b) any other arrangement connected with the arrangement or forming part of a set of arrangements that includes the arrangement.

70C(5) For the purposes of subsection (4)–

"appropriate accounts" are accounts prepared in accordance with generally accepted accounting practice on the date on which that value is first recognised in the books or other financial records of the person;

"the appropriate date" is the later of–

(a) the commencement of the term of the lease;

(b) the date on which the plant or machinery is first brought into use for the purpose of the qualifying activity.

70C(6) This subsection applies if–

(a) the person has paid rentals under the lease before the commencement of the term of the lease, and

(b) in the case of some or all of those rentals, relief otherwise than by virtue of this subsection–

(i) is not available, and

(ii) if the case is one where the plant or machinery was not used for the purposes of a qualifying activity in the period before the commencement of the term of the lease, would not have been available had the plant or machinery been used in that period for the purposes of a qualifying activity,

and in any such case UPR is the amount of the rentals for which relief is not, and (in a case falling within paragraph (b)(ii)) would not have been, so available.

70C(7) Subsection (8) applies if the main purpose, or one of the main purposes, of entering into–

(a) the lease,

(b) a series of transactions of which the lease is one, or

(c) any of the transactions in such a series,

is to obtain allowances under this Part in respect of an amount of capital expenditure that materially exceeds the market value of the leased asset at the commencement of the term of the lease.

70C(8) In any such case, the amount of the capital expenditure described in subsection (3) is to be restricted to an amount equal to the market value of the asset at the commencement of the term of the lease.

70C(9) In this section **"relief"** means relief by way of–

(a) an allowance under this Act,

(b) a deduction in computing profits for the purposes of income tax or corporation tax,

(c) a deduction from total profits or total income for the purposes of either of those taxes.

70C(10) This section is to be construed as one with section 70A.

History – S. 70C(4A)–(4C) inserted by FA 2011, s. 33(2), with effect in cases where the arrangement is entered into on or after 9 March 2011.

S. 70C inserted by FA 2006, s. 81 and Sch. 8, para. 6. The commencement and transitional provisions are complex and are set out in full in FA 2006, Sch. 8, para. 15–27.

HMRC Manuals – CA23810: lessees: capital expenditure.
CA23815: pre-commencement rentals; additional expenditure.

70D Long funding finance lease: additional expenditure: allowances for lessee

70D(1) This section applies where the following conditions are met–

(a) a person is the lessee of plant or machinery under a long funding finance lease,

(b) as a result of section 70A, the person falls to be regarded as having incurred qualifying expenditure on the provision of the plant or machinery, and

(c) the lessor incurs expenditure in relation to the plant or machinery,

(d) as a result of the lessor incurring the expenditure, there is in the case of the lessee an increase (the "relevant increase") in the present value of the minimum lease payments.

70D(1A) Any increase attributable to a relievable amount is to be ignored for the purposes of subsection (1)(d).

70D(1B) Subsections (4B) and (4C) of section 70C apply (with any necessary modifications) for the purposes of this section as for the purposes of that section.

70D(2) If the lease is one which, under generally accepted accounting practice, falls (or would fall) to be treated as a loan, this section applies as if the lease were one which, under generally accepted accounting practice, fell to be treated as a finance lease.

70D(3) The person is to be treated for the purposes of this Part as having incurred further capital expenditure on the provision of the plant or machinery as follows.

70D(4) The person is to be treated as having incurred the expenditure on the date of first recognition.

70D(5) The amount of the expenditure is the amount that would fall to be recognised as the amount of the relevant increase if appropriate accounts were prepared by the person.

70D(6) For that purpose, **"appropriate accounts"** are accounts prepared in accordance with generally accepted accounting practice on the date of first recognition.

70D(7) For the purposes of this section, the **"date of first recognition"** is the date on which the relevant increase is first recognised in the books or other financial records of the person.

70D(8) This section is to be construed as one with section 70A.

History – S. 70D(1A)–(1B) inserted by FA 2011, s. 33(3), with effect in cases where the arrangement is entered into on or after 9 March 2011.

S. 70D inserted by FA 2006, s. 81 and Sch. 8, para. 6. The commencement and transitional provisions are complex and are set out in full in FA 2006, Sch. 8, para. 15–27.

HMRC Manuals – CA23815: pre-commencement rentals; additional expenditure.

70DA Transfer and long funding leaseback: restrictions on lessee's allowances

70DA(1) This section applies where–

(a) a person ("S") transfers plant or machinery to another person ("B"),

(b) at any time after the date of the transfer, the plant or machinery is available to be used by S, or a person (other than B) who is connected with S ("CS"), under a plant or machinery lease, and

(c) that lease is a long funding lease.

70DA(2) No annual investment allowance or first-year allowance is to be made in respect of the expenditure of S or CS under the lease.

70DA(3) The amount, if any, by which E exceeds D is to be left out of account in determining the available qualifying expenditure of S or CS.

CAA 2001

70DA(4) E is the capital expenditure of S or CS on the provision of the plant or machinery under the long funding lease.

70DA(5) If S is required to bring a disposal value into account under this Part because of the transfer referred to in subsection (1)(a), D is that disposal value.

70DA(5A) D is nil if–

(a) S is not required to bring a disposal value into account under this Part because of the transfer referred to in subsection (1)(a), and

(b) at any time before that transfer S or a linked person became owner of the plant or machinery without incurring either capital expenditure or qualifying revenue expenditure on its provision.

70DA(6) Otherwise, D is whichever of the following is the smallest–

(a) the market value of the plant or machinery;

(b) if S incurred capital expenditure on the provision of the plant or machinery before the transfer referred to in subsection (1)(a), the amount of that expenditure;

(c) if a person connected with S incurred capital expenditure on the provision of the plant or machinery before that transfer, the amount of that expenditure.

70DA(7) Section 70Y(3) applies to references in this section to a transfer of plant or machinery by a person.

70DA(8) For the purposes of this section, a transfer involving the grant of a lease takes place on the commencement of the term of the lease.

70DA(9) **"Linked person"**, in relation to plant or machinery, means a person–

(a) who owned the plant or machinery at any time before the transfer referred to in subsection (1)(a), and

(b) who was connected with S at any time between–

(i) the time when the person became owner of the plant or machinery, and

(ii) the time of the transfer referred to in subsection (1)(a).

70DA(10) Expenditure on the provision of plant or machinery is **"qualifying revenue expenditure"** if it is expenditure of a revenue nature–

(a) that is at least equal to the amount of expenditure that would reasonably be expected to have been incurred on the provision of the plant or machinery in a transaction between persons dealing with each other at arm's length in the open market, or

(b) that is incurred by the manufacturer of the plant or machinery and is at least equal to the amount that it would have been reasonable to expect to have been the normal cost of manufacturing the plant or machinery.

History – S. 70DA(5A) inserted by FA 2015, s. 46 and Sch. 10, para. 2(2), with effect in relation to cases where the lease referred to in s. 70DA(1)(b) is entered into on or after 26 February 2015.
S. 70DA(9) and (10) inserted by FA 2015, s. 46 and Sch. 10, para. 2(3), with effect in relation to cases where the lease referred to in s. 70DA(1)(b) is entered into on or after 26 February 2015.
S. 70DA inserted by FA 2009, s. 64 and Sch. 32, para. 15, with effect in relation to cases where the commencement of the term of the lease referred to in s. 70DA(1)(b) is on or after 13 November 2008.

70E Disposal events and disposal values

70E(1) This section applies where–

(a) a person is the lessee of plant or machinery under a long funding lease,

(b) as a result of section 70A, the person falls to be regarded as having incurred qualifying expenditure on the provision of the plant or machinery, and

(c) a relevant event occurs.

70E(1A) A relevant event occurs if–

(a) the lease terminates,

(b) the plant or machinery begins to be used wholly or partly for purposes other than those of the qualifying activity, or

(c) the qualifying activity is permanently discontinued.

70E(2) In the case of that person–

(a) the relevant event is a disposal event, and

(b) the person is required to bring into account a disposal value for the chargeable period in which that disposal event occurs.

70E(2A) The amount of the disposal value is–

$$(QE - QA) + R$$

where–

QE is the person's qualifying expenditure on the provision of the plant or machinery;

QA is the qualifying amount (see subsections (2B) to (2E));

R is the sum of–

(a) any relevant rebate (see subsections (2F) and (2G)), and

(b) any other relevant lease-related payment (see subsections (2FA) and (2G)).

70E(2B) In the case of a long funding operating lease, **"the qualifying amount"** means the aggregate amount of the reductions made under section 148I of ITTOIA 2005 or section 379 of CTA 2010 for periods of account in which the person was the lessee.

70E(2C) In the case of a long funding finance lease, **"the qualifying amount"** means the aggregate of–

(a) the payments made to the lessor by the person under the lease (including any initial payment), and

(b) the payments made to the lessor by the person under a guarantee of any residual amount (as defined in section 70YE) other than any relievable payment,

subject to subsection (2D).

70E(2D) The following are excluded from the "qualifying amount" under subsection (2C)–

(a) so much of any payment as, in accordance with generally accepted accounting practice, falls (or would fall) to be shown in the person's accounts as finance charges in respect of the lease,

(b) so much of any payment as represents charges for services, and

(c) so much of any payment as represents qualifying UK or foreign tax (within the meaning of section 70YE) to be paid by the lessor.

70E(2DA) A payment ("payment X") is a relievable payment if–

(a) an arrangement is in place under which all or part of any residual amount (as defined in section 70YE) is guaranteed by the lessee or a person connected with the lessee,

(b) payment X is within the minimum lease payments because of that arrangement (see subsection (1)(a) of that section), and

(c) it is reasonable to assume that relief would be available as a result of making payment X (beyond relief, by virtue of section 70C or 70D and this section, because payment X is within those minimum lease payments).

70E(2DB) For the purposes of subsection (2DA)(c)–

(a) **"relief"** has the meaning given in section 70C, and

(b) subsection (4C) of that section applies as it applies for the purposes of subsection (4B)(c) of that section.

70E(2E) In the case of a long funding finance lease that is not a transaction at arm's length, **"the qualifying amount"** includes only so much of the amounts described in subsection (2C) as would reasonably be expected to have been paid if the lease had been such a transaction.

70E(2F) **"Relevant rebate"** means–

(a) in a case falling within subsection (1A)(a), any amount calculated by reference to the termination value that is payable for the benefit (directly or indirectly) of the person or another person connected with that person, or

(b) in a case falling within subsection (1A)(b) or (c), any such amount that would have been so payable if, when the relevant event occurred, the lease had terminated and the plant or machinery had been sold for its market value at that time.

70E(2FA) **"Relevant lease-related payment"** means any payment which–

(a) is payable at any time for the benefit (directly or indirectly) of the lessee or a person connected with the lessee,

(b) is connected with the long funding lease, or with any arrangement connected with that lease, and

(c) is not–

(i) an initial payment or any other payment made to the lessor by the lessee under the lease,

(ii) a payment made to the lessor by the lessee under a guarantee of any residual amount (as defined in section 70YE),

(iii) an initial payment or any other payment made under a relevant superior lease to the person who is the lessor under that lease by the person who is the lessee under that lease, or

(iv) a payment to the seller of the proceeds of a sale of the plant or machinery to which subsection (2FC) applies,

if, and to the extent that, the payment is not otherwise brought into account for tax purposes as income or a disposal receipt by the person for whom the benefit is payable (or would not be if that person were within the charge to tax).

70E(2FB) For the purposes of subsection (2FA)–

"payment" includes the provision of any benefit, the assumption of any liability and any other transfer of money's worth (and **"payable"** is to be construed accordingly);

"relevant superior lease" means any lease of the plant or machinery to which the long funding lease mentioned in subsection (1)(a) is inferior.

70E(2FC) This subsection applies to a sale of the plant or machinery if–

(a) a person has entered into a relevant transaction with another person in respect of the plant or machinery for the purposes of Chapter 17 of this Part (see section 213) and the sale is within section 213(1)(a),

(b) the plant or machinery is within section 216(1)(b) (sale and lease back), and

(c) the conditions in section 227(2) are met.

70E(2G) In the case of a lease that is not a transaction at arm's length, **"relevant rebate"** and **"relevant lease-related payment"** include any amount that would reasonably be expected to have fallen within subsection (2F) or, as the case may be, (2FA) if the lease had been such a transaction.

70E(2H) The amount of the disposal value brought into account under this section cannot be less than nil.

70E(3-8) [Effectively omitted by FA 2009, s. 64 and Sch. 32, para. 7(5).]

70E(9) If the relevant event gives rise to a disposal event in the case of the person apart from this section, that disposal event is to be ignored.

70E(10) This section is to be construed as one with section 70A.

History – S. 70E(1)(c) substituted by FA 2009, s. 64 and Sch. 32, para. 7(2), with effect in relation to cases where the relevant event occurs on or after 13 November 2008. The wording of former s. 70E(10(c) was: "the lease terminates.".
S. 70E(1A) inserted by FA 2009, s. 64 and Sch. 32, para. 7(3), with effect in relation to cases where the relevant event occurs on or after 13 November 2008.
In s. 70E(2)(a), the words "relevant event" substituted for the words "termination of the lease" by FA 2009, s. 64 and Sch. 32, para. 7(4), with effect in relation to cases where the relevant event occurs on or after 13 November 2008.
In s. 70E(2A), the definition of "R" substituted by FA 2012, s. 46(2), with effect in relation to cases where the relevant event occurs on or after 21 March 2012.
In s. 70E(2B), the words "section 502K of ICTA or", which appeared after "reductions made under", omitted by CTA 2010, s. 1177 and Sch. 1, para. 329 and repealed by CTA 2010, s. 1181 and Sch. 3, Pt. 1, and the words "or section 379 of CTA 2010" inserted by CTA 2010, s. 1177 and Sch. 1, para. 329, with effect for corporation tax purposes for accounting periods ending on or after 1 April 2010, and for income tax and capital gains tax purposes for the tax year 2010–11 and subsequent tax years.
In s. 70E(2C)(b), the words "other than any relievable payment" inserted after "section 70YE)" by FA 2011, s. 33(4), with effect in relation to payments made on or after 9 March 2011 (regardless of when the arrangement was entered into).
S. 70E(2DA)–(2DB) inserted by FA 2011, s. 33(5), with effect in relation to payments made on or after 9 March 2011 (regardless of when the arrangement was entered into).
S. 70E(2FA)–(2FC) inserted by FA 2012, s. 46(3), with effect in relation to cases where the relevant event occurs on or after 21 March 2012.
S. 70E(2G) substituted by FA 2012, s. 46(4), with effect in relation to cases where the relevant event occurs on or after 21 March 2012.
S. 70E(2A)–(2H) substituted for s. 70E(3) to (8) by FA 2009, s. 64 and Sch. 32, para. 7(5), with effect in relation to cases where the relevant event occurs on or after 13 November 2008.
In s. 70E(9), the words "relevant event" substituted for the words "termination of the lease" by FA 2009, s. 64 and Sch. 32, para. 7(6), with effect in relation to cases where the relevant event occurs on or after 13 November 2008.
S. 70E inserted by FA 2006, s. 81 and Sch. 8, para. 6. The commencement and transitional provisions are complex and are set out in full in FA 2006, Sch. 8, para. 15–27.

HMRC Manuals – CA23825: disposal events and disposal values.

Chapter 6A – Interpretation of Provisions About Long Funding Leases

History – Chapter 6A inserted by FA 2006, s. 81 and Sch. 8, para. 7. The commencement and transitional provisions are complex and are set out in full in FA 2006, Sch. 8, para. 15–27.

INTRODUCTORY

70F Introductory

70F This Chapter makes provision for the interpretation of this Part so far as relating to long funding leases.

History – S. 70F inserted by FA 2006, s. 81 and Sch. 8, para. 7. The commencement and transitional provisions are complex and are set out in full in FA 2006, Sch. 8, para. 15–27.

MEANING OF "LONG FUNDING LEASE" ETC

70G "Long funding lease"

70G(1) A **"long funding lease"** is a funding lease (see section 70J) which meets the following conditions–

(a) it is not a short lease (see section 70I),

(b) it is not an excluded lease of background plant or machinery for a building (see section 70R),

(c) it not excluded by section 70U (plant or machinery leased with land: low percentage value).

70G(2) Where, at the commencement of the term of a plant or machinery lease, the plant or machinery–

(a) is not being used for the purposes of a qualifying activity carried on by the person concerned, but

(b) subsequently begins to be used for the purposes of a qualifying activity carried on by that person,

the plant or machinery lease is a long funding lease if the condition in subsection (3) is met.

70G(3) The condition is that (apart from section 70H) the plant or machinery lease would have been a long funding lease at its inception had the plant or machinery been used at that time for the purposes of a qualifying activity carried on by the person concerned.

70G(4) This section is subject, in the case of the lessee, to–

(a) section 70H (requirement for tax return treating lease as long funding lease);

(b) section 70Q (leases excluded by right of lessor etc to claim capital allowances).

70G(5) See also paragraph 91A of Schedule 22 to FA 2000 (tonnage tax: certain leases to be treated as not being long funding leases).

History – In s. 70G(5), "FA" substituted for "the Finance Act" by FA 2009, s. 126(5)(a), with effect from 21 July 2009.
S. 70G inserted by FA 2006, s. 81 and Sch. 8, para. 7. The commencement and transitional provisions are complex and are set out in full in FA 2006, Sch. 8, para. 15–27.

HMRC Manuals – CA23830: definition of long funding lease.

CAA 2001

70H Lessee: requirement for tax return treating lease as long funding lease

70H(1) A lease is not a long funding lease in the case of the lessee unless he makes a tax return for the initial period on the basis that he falls to be taxed in respect of the lease in accordance with the provisions of–

(a) [omitted by CTA 2010, s. 1177 and Sch. 1, para. 330(a) and repealed by CTA 2010, s. 1181 and Sch. 3, Pt. 1,]

(b) Chapter 10A of Part 2 of ITTOIA 2005 (long funding leases: income tax), or

(c) Chapter 2 of Part 9 of CTA 2010 (long funding leases of plant or machinery).

70H(1A) Subsection (1) does not apply in respect of a lease of plant or machinery ("lease A") if, at any time in the relevant period–

(a) the lessee is the lessor of a lease of any of that plant or machinery ("lease B"), and

(b) lease B is a long funding lease.

70H(1B) In subsection (1A) **"the relevant period"** means the period–

(a) beginning with the inception of lease A, and

(b) ending with the making of the tax return for the initial period (or, if that return is amended, the making of the last amendment).

70H(1C) In a case in which paragraphs (a) and (b) of subsection (1) of section 70DA (leaseback of plant or machinery) are satisfied, subsection (1) of this section does not apply to the lease referred to in section 70DA(1)(b).

70H(2) Where, in the case of a lease, a person has made a tax return for the initial period–

(a) on the basis that he falls to be taxed in respect of the lease in accordance with those provisions, or

(b) on the basis that he does not fall to be so taxed,

he may not make a claim under the recovery provisions for relief in respect of an amount paid or liable to be paid that is excessive by reason of the tax return having been made on that basis.

70H(3) In this section–

"the recovery provisions" means–

(a) Schedule 1AB to the Taxes Management Act 1970; or

(b) paragraph 51 of Schedule 18 to FA 1998;

"the initial period" is the first accounting period or, as the case may be, tax year in which there is a difference in the amount of the profits or losses falling to be shown in the return, according to whether the lease is a long funding lease or not;

"tax return" means–

(a) a company tax return under paragraph 3 of Schedule 18 to FA 1998, or

(b) a return under section 8 of the Taxes Management Act 1970 (income tax: personal return).

History – S. 70H(1)(a) omitted by CTA 2010, s. 1177 and Sch. 1, para. 330(a), and repealed by CTA 2010, s. 1181 and Sch. 3, Pt. 1, with effect for corporation tax purposes for accounting periods ending on or after 1 April 2010, and for income tax and capital gains tax purposes for the tax year 2010–11 and subsequent tax years.
S. 70H(1)(c) (and the "or" at the end of s. 70H(1)(b)) inserted by CTA 2010, s. 1177 and Sch. 1, para. 330(b), with effect for corporation tax purposes for accounting periods ending on or after 1 April 2010, and for income tax and capital gains tax purposes for the tax year 2010–11 and subsequent tax years.
S. 70H(1A) inserted by FA 2008, s. 55 and Sch. 20, para. 8(1), with effect in relation to leases entered into on or after 13 December 2007.
S. 70H(1B) inserted by FA 2008, s. 55 and Sch. 20, para. 8(1), with effect in relation to leases entered into on or after 13 December 2007.
S. 70H(1C) inserted by FA 2009, s. 64 and Sch. 32, para. 16, with effect in relation to cases where the commencement of the term of the lease referred to in s. 70DA(1)(b) is on or after 13 November 2008.
In s. 70H(2), the words "under the recovery provisions for relief in respect of an amount paid or liable to be paid that is excessive by reason of" substituted for the words "for relief under the error or mistake provisions in respect of" by FA 2009, s. 100 and Sch. 52, para. 9(2), with effect in relation to claims made on or after 1 April 2010 (see FA 2009, s. 100).
In s. 70H(3), the words ""the recovery provisions"" substituted for the words ""the error or mistake provisions"" and the words "Schedule 1AB to" substituted for "section 33 of" by FA 2009, s. 100 and Sch. 52, para. 9(3), with effect in relation to claims made on or after 1 April 2010.
In s. 70H(3), "FA" substituted for "the Finance Act" in both places by FA 2009, s. 126(5)(a), with effect from 21 July 2009.
S. 70H inserted by FA 2006, s. 81 and Sch. 8, para. 7. The commencement and transitional provisions are complex and are set out in full in FA 2006, Sch. 8, para. 15–27.

70I "Short lease"

70I(1) Construe **"short lease"** in accordance with this section.

70I(2) A lease whose term is 5 years or less is a short lease.

70I(3) Where the term of a lease is–

(a) longer than 5 years, but

(b) not longer than 7 years,

the lease is a short lease if Conditions A, B and C are met.

70I(4) Condition A is that the lease is one which, under generally accepted accounting practice, falls (or would fall) to be treated as a finance lease.

70I(5) Condition B is that–

(a) the residual value of the plant or machinery which is implied in the terms of the lease, is not more than

(b) 5% of the market value of the plant or machinery at the commencement of the term of the lease, as estimated at the inception of the lease.

70I(6) Condition C is that under the terms of the lease–

(a) the total rentals falling due in the first reference year, if less than the total rentals falling due in the second reference year, are no more than 10% less than those rentals, and

(b) the total rentals falling due in the final year or in any reference year after the second reference year, if greater than the total rentals falling due in the second reference year, are no more than 10% greater than those rentals.

70I(7) For the purposes of Condition C–

(a) the first reference year is the period of 12 months beginning with the day next after the commencement of the term of the lease;

(b) the other reference years are successive periods of 12 months each beginning on an anniversary of that day and ending before the last day of the term of the lease;

(c) the final year is the period of 12 months ending with the last day of the term of the lease;

(d) any part of the final year, other than the last day, may accordingly also be part of a reference year.

70I(8) In determining whether Condition C is met, exclude any variation in the rentals that results from changes in a standard published base rate for interest.

70I(9) Where–

(a) a person leases an asset to another ("S") under a lease that would, apart from this subsection, be a short lease,

(b) the inception of that lease is on or after 7th April 2006,

(c) at or about the time of the inception of that lease, arrangements are entered into for the asset to be leased to one or more other persons under one or more other leases, and

(d) in the aggregate, the term of the lease to S and the terms of the leases to such of those other persons as are connected with S exceed 5 years,

the lease to S is not a short lease.

70I(9A) Where plant or machinery is the subject of a lease and finance leaseback (as defined in section 228A)–

(a) the finance lease mentioned in section 228A(2)(c), and

(b) any other finance lease forming part of the arrangements for the lease and finance leaseback (except the lease referred to in section 228A(2)(a)),

is not a short lease (if it otherwise would be).

70I(10) Where plant or machinery is the subject of a sale and finance leaseback (as defined in section 221), any finance lease of a kind mentioned in section 221(1)(c) is not a short lease (if it otherwise would be).

70I(11) But, if the conditions set out in section 227(2) are met, B and S (within the meaning of section 221) may make an election the effect of which is that–

(a) subsection (10) above does not apply,

(b) section 228(2) and (3) apply in relation to B (but this does not prevent section 225 from applying), and

(c) section 228(5) applies in relation to S.

70I(12) Subsections (4) to (6) of section 227 apply in relation to elections under this section as they apply in relation to elections under that section.

History – S. 70I(9A) inserted by FA 2008, s. 55 and Sch. 20, para. 7(1), with effect in the case of plant or machinery which is the subject of a lease and finance leaseback (as defined in CAA 2001, s. 228A) where the date of the transaction mentioned in subsection (2)(a) of that section is on or after 12 March 2008.

S. 70I(10) inserted by FA 2008, s. 55 and Sch. 20, para. 6(6), with effect in the case of plant or machinery which is the subject of a sale and finance leaseback (as defined in CAA 2001, s. 221) where the date of the transaction (within the meaning of that section) is on or after 9 October 2007. If the date of the transaction is before 12 March 2008, s. 70I(10) has effect as if the words "the finance lease" were substituted for the words "any finance lease of a kind" (FA 2008, Sch. 20, para. 6(20)).

S. 70I(11) inserted by FA 2008, s. 55 and Sch. 20, para. 6(6), with effect in the case of plant or machinery which is the subject of a sale and finance leaseback (as defined in CAA 2001, s. 221) where the date of the transaction (within the meaning of that section) is on or after 9 October 2007.

S. 70I(12) inserted by FA 2008, s. 55 and Sch. 20, para. 6(6), with effect in the case of plant or machinery which is the subject of a sale and finance leaseback (as defined in CAA 2001, s. 221) where the date of the transaction (within the meaning of that section) is on or after 9 October 2007.

S. 70I inserted by FA 2006, s. 81 and Sch. 8, para. 7. The commencement and transitional provisions are complex and are set out in full in FA 2006, Sch. 8, para. 15–27.

HMRC Manuals – CA23830: definition of short lease.

70J "Funding lease"

70J(1) A **"funding lease"** is a plant or machinery lease (see section 70K) which at its inception meets one or more of the following tests–

(a) the finance lease test (see section 70N),

(b) the lease payments test (see section 70O),

(c) the useful economic life test (see section 70P).

70J(1A) A plant or machinery lease is also a **"funding lease"** if the plant or machinery is cushion gas.

70J(2) Subsections (1) and (1A) are subject to the following provisions of this section.

70J(3) A plant or machinery lease is not a funding lease if–

(a) section 67 applies (plant or machinery treated as owned by person entitled to benefit of contract, etc), and

(b) the lease is the contract mentioned in that section.

70J(4) A plant or machinery lease is not a funding lease if–

(a) before the commencement of the term of the lease, the lessor has leased the plant or machinery under one or more other plant or machinery leases,

(b) in the aggregate, the terms of those other leases exceed 65% of the remaining useful economic life of the plant or machinery at the commencement of the term of the earliest of them, and

(c) none of those earlier leases was a funding lease.

70J(5) For the purposes of subsection (4), all persons who were lessors of the plant or machinery before 1st April 2006 are to be treated as if they were the same person as the first lessor of the plant or machinery on or after that date.

70J(6) A plant or machinery lease is not a funding lease in the case of the lessor if–

(a) before 1st April 2006, the plant or machinery had, for a period or periods totalling at least 10 years, been the subject of one or more leases, and

(b) the lessor under the plant or machinery lease was also lessor of the plant or machinery on the last day before 1st April 2006 on which the plant or machinery was the subject of a lease.

70J(7) In this section **"cushion gas"** means gas that functions or is intended to function as plant in a particular gas storage facility.

History – S. 70J(1A) inserted by FA 2010, s. 28(3), with effect in relation to leases whose inception (within the meaning given by s. 70YI(1)) is on or after 1 April 2010.

In s. 70J(2), the words "Subsections (1) and (1A) are" substituted for the words "Subsection (1) is" by FA 2010, s. 28(4), with effect in relation to leases whose inception (within the meaning given by s. 70YI(1)) is on or after 1 April 2010.

S. 70J(7) inserted by FA 2010, s. 28(5), with effect in relation to leases whose inception (within the meaning given by s. 70YI(1)) is on or after 1 April 2010.

S. 70J inserted by FA 2006, s. 81 and Sch. 8, para. 7. The commencement and transitional provisions are complex and are set out in full in FA 2006, Sch. 8, para. 15–27.

HMRC Manuals – CA23830: definition of funding lease.

MEANING OF "PLANT OR MACHINERY LEASE"

70K "Plant or machinery lease"

70K(1) A **"plant or machinery lease"** is any of the following–

(a) any agreement or arrangement to which subsection (2) applies,

(b) any other agreement or arrangement, to the extent that subsection (3) applies to it,

(c) where plant or machinery is the subject of a sale and finance leaseback, as defined in section 221, the finance lease mentioned in subsection (1)(c) of that section,

and **"lease"**, **"lessor"**, **"lessee"** and other related expressions are to be construed accordingly.

70K(2) This subsection applies to an agreement or arrangement–

(a) under which a person (the lessor) grants to another person (the lessee) the right to use plant or machinery for a period, and

(b) which, in accordance with generally accepted accounting practice, falls (or would fall) to be treated as a lease.

70K(3) This subsection applies to an agreement or arrangement to the extent that–

(a) in accordance with generally accepted accounting practice, it falls (or would fall) to be treated as a lease, and

(b) it meets the conditions in subsection (4).

70K(4) The conditions are that, for the purposes of generally accepted accounting practice,–

(a) the agreement or arrangement conveys, or falls (or would fall) to be regarded as conveying, the right to use an asset, and

(b) the asset is plant or machinery.

70K(5) In the case of an agreement or arrangement that falls (or would fall) within subsection (2) or (3) immediately after the commencement of the term of the lease, the condition in subsection (2)(b) or (3)(a) (as the case may be) is to be taken to be met as respects any time in the pre-commencement period.

70K(6) For the purposes of subsection (5), the **"pre-commencement period"** is the period that–

(a) begins with the inception of the lease, and

(b) ends with the commencement of the term of the lease.

History – S. 70K inserted by FA 2006, s. 81 and Sch. 8, para. 7. The commencement and transitional provisions are complex and are set out in full in FA 2006, Sch. 8, para. 15–27.

HMRC Manuals – CA23830: definition of plant or machinery lease.

70L Plant or machinery leased with other assets: separate derived leases

70L(1) This section applies in any case where an agreement or arrangement (the "mixed lease") at any time relates, or is to relate, or has come to relate, to both–

(a) plant or machinery of any particular description (the "relevant plant or machinery"), and

(b) other assets (whether or not also plant or machinery).

70L(2) A mixed lease is an **"eligible mixed lease"** if–

(a) under generally accepted accounting practice, it falls (or would fall) to be treated as a lease, or

(b) the relevant plant or machinery is the subject of a sale and finance leaseback, as defined in section 221, and the mixed lease is or includes the finance lease mentioned in subsection (1)(c) of that section.

70L(3) In the case of an agreement or arrangement that falls (or would fall) within paragraph (a) of subsection (2) immediately after the commencement of the term of the lease, the condition in that paragraph is to be taken to be met as respects any time in the pre-commencement period.

70L(4) For the purposes of subsection (3), the **"pre-commencement period"** is the period that–

(a) begins with the inception of the lease, and

(b) ends with the commencement of the term of the lease.

70L(5) Where this section applies–

(a) the eligible mixed lease, so far as relating to the relevant plant or machinery, and

(b) the eligible mixed lease, so far as relating to other assets,

shall be treated for the purposes of this Part (other than this section) as if they were separate agreements or arrangements.

70L(6) Any such notional separate agreement or arrangement is referred to in this Part as a "derived lease".

70L(7) Section 70M makes further provision with respect to derived leases of plant or machinery.

History – S. 70L inserted by FA 2006, s. 81 and Sch. 8, para. 7. The commencement and transitional provisions are complex and are set out in full in FA 2006, Sch. 8, para. 15–27.

HMRC Manuals – CA23835: definition of derived lease.

70M Derived leases of plant or machinery: term and rentals

70M(1) This section has effect in any case where, as a result of applying section 70L, there is a derived lease of the relevant plant or machinery.

70M(2) This section makes provision with respect to–

(a) determining whether the derived lease is a plant or machinery lease (see subsection (3)),

(b) the term of the derived lease (see subsection (4)),

(c) the rentals to be regarded as payable under the derived lease (see subsections (5) to (7)).

70M(3) Any question whether the derived lease–

(a) is a plant or machinery lease, or

(b) if it is such a lease, whether it is also a long funding lease,

is to be determined in accordance with the provisions of this Part.

70M(4) The term of the derived lease–

(a) is limited to the remaining useful economic life of the relevant plant or machinery at the commencement of the term of the derived lease, but

(b) subject to that, is to be determined in accordance with section 70YF (the "term" of a lease).

70M(5) The rentals that are to be regarded as payable under the derived lease shall be such rentals (the "deemed rentals") as are just and reasonable in all the circumstances of the case.

70M(6) It shall be assumed that rentals under the derived lease are payable in equal instalments throughout the term of the lease, unless it is reasonable to draw a different conclusion from all the circumstances of the case.

70M(7) In determining the amount of any deemed rentals, regard shall be had to–

(a) all the provisions of the eligible mixed lease,

(b) the nature of the relevant plant or machinery,

(c) the value of the relevant plant or machinery at the commencement of the term of the derived lease,

(d) the amount which, at the commencement of the term of the derived lease, is expected to be the market value of the relevant plant or machinery at the end of the term of the derived lease,

(e) the remaining useful economic life of the relevant plant or machinery at the commencement of the term of the derived lease;

(f) the term of the derived lease.

70M(8) Expressions used in section 70L have the same meaning in this section.

History – S. 70M inserted by FA 2006, s. 81 and Sch. 8, para. 7. The commencement and transitional provisions are complex and are set out in full in FA 2006, Sch. 8, para. 15–27.

HMRC Manuals – CA23835: definition of derived lease.

THE TESTS FOR BEING A FUNDING LEASE

70N The finance lease test

70N(1) A lease meets the finance lease test in the case of any person if the lease is one which, under generally accepted accounting practice, falls (or would fall) to be treated as a finance lease or a loan in the accounts–

(a) of that person, or

(b) where that person is the lessor, of any person connected with him.

70N(2) In this section **"accounts"**, in relation to a company, includes any accounts which–

(a) relate to two or more companies of which that company is one, and

(b) are drawn up in accordance with generally accepted accounting practice.

70N(3) Where for any period–

(a) a person is not within the charge to income tax or corporation tax by reason of not being resident in the United Kingdom, and

(b) accounts are not prepared in accordance with international accounting standards or UK generally accepted accounting practice,

any question relating to generally accepted accounting practice is to be determined for the purposes of this section by reference to generally accepted accounting practice with respect to accounts prepared in accordance with international accounting standards.

History – S. 70N inserted by FA 2006, s. 81 and Sch. 8, para. 7. The commencement and transitional provisions are complex and are set out in full in FA 2006, Sch. 8, para. 15–27.

70O The lease payments test

70O(1) A lease meets the lease payments test if–

(a) the present value of the minimum lease payments (see section 70YE),

is equal to

(b) 80% or more of the fair value of the leased plant or machinery.

70O(2) The present value of the minimum lease payments is to be calculated by using the interest rate implicit in the lease.

70O(3) In this section **"fair value"** means–

(a) the market value of the leased plant or machinery,

less

(b) any grants receivable towards the purchase or use of that plant or machinery.

70O(4) For the purposes of this section–

(a) the interest rate implicit in the lease is the interest rate that would apply in accordance with normal commercial criteria, including, in particular, generally accepted accounting practice (where applicable), but

(b) if the interest rate implicit in the lease cannot be determined in accordance with paragraph (a), it is the temporal discount rate for the purposes of section 70 of FA 2005 (companies: film relief: valuation of "rights to guaranteed income" and "disposed rights").

History – In s. 70O(4)(b), "FA" substituted for "the Finance Act" by FA 2009, s. 126(5(a), with effect from 21 July 2009.
S. 70O inserted by FA 2006, s. 81 and Sch. 8, para. 7. The commencement and transitional provisions are complex and are set out in full in FA 2006, Sch. 8, para. 15–27.

70P The useful economic life test

70P A lease meets the useful economic life test if the term of the lease is more than 65% of the remaining useful economic life of the leased plant or machinery.

History – S. 70P inserted by FA 2006, s. 81 and Sch. 8, para. 7. The commencement and transitional provisions are complex and are set out in full in FA 2006, Sch. 8, para. 15–27.

LEASES EXCLUDED BY RIGHT OF LESSOR ETC TO CLAIM CAPITAL ALLOWANCES

70Q Leases excluded by right of lessor etc to claim capital allowances

70Q(1) A lease is not a long funding lease in the case of the lessee if it is excluded by virtue of subsection (2) (but see also subsection (5)).

70Q(2) A lease is excluded if the lessor, or any superior lessor (see subsections (7) to (9))–

(a) is entitled, at the commencement of the term of the lease, to claim a relevant allowance (see subsection (6)),

(b) would have been so entitled at that time, but for section 70V (tax avoidance involving international leasing),

(c) has at any earlier time been entitled to claim such an allowance, but has not been required to bring a disposal value into account in accordance with section 61(1)(ee), or

(d) would fall within any one or more of paragraphs (a) to (c), if he had been within the charge to income tax or corporation tax at the inception of the lease and any earlier times.

70Q(3) Where for any period the lessor, or any superior lessor, is a person–

(a) who is not within the charge to income tax or corporation tax by reason of not being resident in the United Kingdom, and

(b) who does not prepare accounts in accordance with international accounting standards or UK generally accepted accounting practice,

subsection (4) applies.

70Q(4) In determining whether the condition in subsection (2)(d) is met, any question relating to generally accepted accounting practice in relation to that person and that period is to be determined by reference to generally accepted accounting practice with respect to accounts prepared in accordance with international accounting standards.

70Q(5) A lease is not excluded by virtue of subsection (2) if–

(a) the inception of the lease is before 28th June 2006, and

(b) by virtue only of section 70J(6), the lease is not a funding lease in the case of the lessor.

70Q(6) A **"relevant allowance"** is an allowance under this Act in respect of the leased plant or machinery.

70Q(7) There is a "superior lessor" only if the leased plant or machinery is the subject of a chain of superior leases.

70Q(8) Leased plant or machinery is the subject of a chain of superior leases if–

(a) the lessor has his interest in relation to the plant or machinery under or by virtue of a lease from a third person (P), or

(b) the circumstances are as in paragraph (a), but P has his interest in relation to the plant or machinery under or by virtue of a lease from a fourth person (Q), or

(c) the circumstances are as in paragraph (b), but Q has his interest in relation to the plant or machinery under or by virtue of a lease from a fifth person (R),

and so on, where there is more than a fifth person involved.

70Q(9) Where any leased plant or machinery is the subject of a chain of superior leases, the superior lessors are the persons described in subsection (8) as P, Q, R, and so on.

70Q(10) Subsections (6) to (9) have effect for the interpretation of this section.

History – S. 70Q inserted by FA 2006, s. 81 and Sch. 8, para. 7. The commencement and transitional provisions are complex and are set out in full in FA 2006, Sch. 8, para. 15–27.

HMRC Manuals – CA23820: chains of leases.

EXCLUDED LEASES OF BACKGROUND PLANT OR MACHINERY FOR A BUILDING

70R Excluded leases of background plant or machinery for a building

70R(1) Construe references to an excluded lease of background plant or machinery for a building in accordance with this section.

70R(2) This section applies where–

(a) plant or machinery is affixed to, or otherwise installed in or on, any land which consists of or includes a building,

(b) the plant or machinery is background plant or machinery for the building (see subsections (4) and (5)),

(c) the plant or machinery is leased with the land under a mixed lease, and

(d) none of the disqualifications set out in section 70S applies.

70R(3) In any such case, the derived lease of the plant or machinery is an excluded lease of background plant or machinery for a building.

70R(4) The background plant or machinery for a building is any plant or machinery–

(a) which is of such a description that plant or machinery of that description might reasonably be expected to be installed in, or in or on the sites of, a variety of buildings of different descriptions, and

(b) whose sole or main purpose is to contribute to the functionality of the building or its site as an environment within which activities can be carried on.

70R(5) Subsection (4) has effect subject to the provisions of any order under section 70T.

History – S. 70R inserted by FA 2006, s. 81 and Sch. 8, para. 7. The commencement and transitional provisions are complex and are set out in full in FA 2006, Sch. 8, para. 15–27.

HMRC Manuals – CA23835: definition of excluded lease (background plant and machinery).

70S The disqualifications

70S(1) This section sets out the disqualifications mentioned in subsection (2)(d) of section 70R and is to be construed as one with that section.

70S(2) Disqualification A is that the amounts payable–

(a) under the mixed lease, or

(b) under any other arrangement,

vary, or may be varied, by reference to the value from time to time to the lessor of allowances under this Act in respect of expenditure incurred by him in the provision of the background plant or machinery for the building.

70S(3) Disqualification B is that the main purpose, or one of the main purposes, of entering into–

(a) the mixed lease,

(b) a series of transactions of which the mixed lease is one, or

(c) any of the transactions in such a series,

is to secure that allowances under this Act are available to the lessor in respect of expenditure incurred in the provision of background plant or machinery for a building.

History – S. 70S inserted by FA 2006, s. 81 and Sch. 8, para. 7. The commencement and transitional provisions are complex and are set out in full in FA 2006, Sch. 8, para. 15–27.

70T Orders relating to background plant or machinery for a building

70T(1) This section supplements section 70R and is to be construed as one with it.

70T(2) The Treasury may by order prescribe–

(a) descriptions of plant or machinery to be used as examples of the kinds of plant or machinery that may be regarded as falling within the definition of background plant or machinery for a building in determining whether any particular plant or machinery does or does not fall within that definition;

(b) descriptions of plant or machinery to be deemed to be background plant or machinery for a building;

(c) descriptions of plant or machinery to be deemed not to be background plant or machinery for a building.

70T(3) An order under this section–

(a) may make different provision for different cases (including different descriptions of building),

(b) may contain incidental, consequential, supplemental, or transitional provision or savings.

70T(4) The first order made under this section may include provisions having effect in relation to times before the making of the order (but not times earlier than 1st April 2006).

History – S. 70T inserted by FA 2006, s. 81 and Sch. 8, para. 7. The commencement and transitional provisions are complex and are set out in full in FA 2006, Sch. 8, para. 15–27.

Statutory instruments – SI 2007/303: made under s. 70T.

EXCLUSION FOR CERTAIN PLANT OR MACHINERY LEASED WITH LAND

70U Plant or machinery leased with land: low percentage value

70U(1) This section applies where–

(a) any plant or machinery (the "relevant plant or machinery") is affixed to, or otherwise installed, in or on any land,

(b) the plant or machinery is not background plant or machinery for any building situated in or on the land,

(c) the plant or machinery is leased with the land under a mixed lease, and

(d) none of the relevant disqualifications applies.

70U(2) For the purposes of this section the **"relevant disqualifications"** are the disqualifications set out in section 70S, but for this purpose–

(a) take the reference in subsection (1) of that section to subsection (2)(d) of section 70R as a reference to this subsection (and, accordingly, construe the second reference to that section as a reference to this section), and

(b) take references in section 70S to background plant or machinery for a building as references to relevant plant or machinery.

70U(3) Where this section applies, the derived lease of the relevant plant or machinery is excluded by this section if the condition in subsection (4) is met at the commencement of the term of that lease.

70U(4) The condition is that AMV does not exceed both–

(a) 10% of BMV; and

(b) 5% of LMV.

70U(5) For that purpose–

AMV is the aggregate of–

(a) the market value of the relevant plant or machinery, and

(b) the market value of any other plant or machinery that falls within subsection (1) in the case of the leased land;

BMV is the aggregate market value of all the background plant or machinery leased with the land;

LMV is the market value of the land (including buildings and fixtures).

70U(6) For this purpose the market value of any land at any time is to be determined on the assumption of a sale by an absolute owner of the land free from all leases and other encumbrances.

History – S. 70U inserted by FA 2006, s. 81 and Sch. 8, para. 7. The commencement and transitional provisions are complex and are set out in full in FA 2006, Sch. 8, para. 15–27.

HMRC Manuals – CA23835: plant or machinery leased with land: low percentage value.

AVOIDANCE

70V Tax avoidance involving international leasing

70V(1) This section applies where matters are so arranged that there are plant or machinery leases such that–

(a) under a lease by a non-resident, an asset is provided directly or indirectly to a resident,

(b) the direct provision of the asset to the resident is by a lease which, in the case of the resident, is a long funding lease or a lease to which section 67 (hire purchase etc) applies,

(c) the asset is used by the resident for the purpose of leasing it under a lease (the "relevant lease") that would not (apart from this section) be a long funding lease in the case of the resident, and

(d) under the relevant lease, the asset is provided directly or indirectly (but by a lease) to a non-resident.

70V(2) Subsection (3) applies if the sole or main purpose of arranging matters in that way is to obtain a tax advantage by securing that allowances under this Part are available to a resident by virtue of–

(a) section 67 (hire purchase), or

(b) section 70A (long funding leases).

70V(3) In any such case, the relevant lease is deemed to be a long funding lease in the case of the resident who is the lessor under it.

70V(4) The reference in this section to a person obtaining a tax advantage (see section 577(4)) also includes a reference to a person obtaining a tax advantage within the meaning of section 1139 of CTA 2010.

70V(5) In this section–

"non-resident" means a person who–

(a) is not resident in the United Kingdom, and

(b) does not use the plant or machinery exclusively for earning profits chargeable to tax;

"resident" means a person who–

(a) is resident in the United Kingdom, or

(b) uses the plant or machinery exclusively for earning profits chargeable to tax.

History – In s. 70V(4), the words "section 1139 of CTA 2010" substituted for "section 840ZA of ICTA" by CTA 2010, s. 1177 and Sch. 1, para. 331, with effect for corporation tax purposes for accounting periods ending on or after 1 April 2010, and for income tax and capital gains tax purposes for the tax year 2010–11 and subsequent tax years.

In s. 70V(4), the words "section 840ZA of ICTA" substituted for "Chapter 1 of Part 17 of ICTA (see section 709 of that Act)" by ITA 2007, s. 1027 and Sch. 1, para. 398, with effect from 6 April 2007.

S. 70V inserted by FA 2006, s. 81 and Sch. 8, para. 7. The commencement and transitional provisions are complex and are set out in full in FA 2006, Sch. 8, para. 15–27.

HMRC Manuals – CA23845: avoidance involving international leasing: where an overseas lessor leases to an overseas lessee via a UK resident and the UK resident claims capital allowances HMRC will initially assume that the main purpose, or one of the main purposes, of the arrangements is to let the UK resident claim capital allowances.

TRANSFERS, ASSIGNMENTS, NOVATIONS, LEASEBACK, VARIATIONS ETC

70W Transfers, assignments etc by lessor

70W(1) This section applies in any case where the following conditions are met–

(a) a person (the "old lessor") is lessor of plant or machinery under a plant or machinery lease (the "old lease"),

(b) during the term of the lease, the old lessor transfers the plant or machinery to another person (the "new lessor"),

(c) the transfer is not the grant of a plant or machinery lease by the old lessor,

(d) immediately after the transfer, the new lessor is the lessor of the plant or machinery under a lease ("the new lease") (whether or not the same lease as the old lease).

70W(2) If it is not otherwise the case,–

(a) the old lessor is to be treated as if the old lease terminated immediately before the transfer, and

(b) the new lessor is to be treated as if the new lease had been entered into immediately after the transfer.

70W(3) The new lessor is also to be treated as if the date of the transfer were the date of both–

(a) the inception of the new lease, and

(b) the commencement of the term of the new lease,

if it is not otherwise the case.

70W(4) If, immediately before the transfer, the old lease was (or was treated by virtue of this subsection as being) in the case of the old lessor a lease of either of the following descriptions–

(a) a long funding lease, or

(b) a lease which is not a long funding lease,

the new lease is to be treated in the case of the new lessor as being a lease of the same description, if the conditions in subsection (5) are met.

70W(5) The conditions are that–

(a) the term of the new lease is the unexpired portion of the term of the old lease, and

(b) the amounts receivable under the new lease are the same as would have been receivable under the old lease, assuming it to have continued in effect.

70W(6) If–

(a) it is not otherwise the case, and

(b) the conditions in subsection (5) are met,

the lessee is to be treated as if the old lease and the new lease were the same continuing lease.

70W(7) Any reference in this section to a transfer of plant or machinery by a person includes a reference to–

(a) any kind of disposal of, or of the person's interest in, the plant or machinery,

(b) any arrangements under which the person's interest in the plant or machinery is terminated and another person becomes lessor of the plant or machinery,

(c) in a case where the plant or machinery is a fixture and the person is treated under section 176 as the owner, any cessation of ownership under section 188, 190, 191, 192 or 192A).

History – S. 70W inserted by FA 2006, s. 81 and Sch. 8, para. 7. The commencement and transitional provisions are complex and are set out in full in FA 2006, Sch. 8, para. 15–27.

HMRC Manuals – CA23840: transfers or assignments by the lessor.

70X Transfers, assignments etc by lessee

70X(1) This section applies in any case where the following conditions are met–

(a) a person (the "old lessee") is lessee of plant or machinery under a plant or machinery lease (the "old lease"),

(b) during the term of the lease, the old lessee transfers the plant or machinery to another person (the "new lessee"),

(c) the transfer is not the grant of a plant or machinery lease by the old lessee,

(d) immediately after the transfer, the new lessee is the lessee of the plant or machinery under a lease ("the new lease") (whether or not the same lease as the old lease).

70X(2) If it is not otherwise the case,–

(a) the old lessee is to be treated as if the old lease terminated immediately before the transfer, and

(b) the new lessee is to be treated as if the new lease had been entered into immediately after the transfer.

70X(3) The new lessee is also to be treated as if the date of the transfer were the date of both–

(a) the inception of the new lease, and

(b) the commencement of the term of the new lease,

if it is not otherwise the case.

70X(4) If, immediately before the transfer, the old lease was (or was treated by virtue of this subsection as being) in the case of the old lessee a lease of one of the following descriptions–

(a) a long funding lease, or

(b) a lease which is not a long funding lease,

the new lease is to be treated in the case of the new lessee as being a lease of the same description, if the conditions in subsection (5) are met.

70X(5) The conditions are that–

(a) the term of the new lease is the unexpired portion of the term of the old lease, and

(b) the amounts payable under the new lease are the same as would have been payable under the old lease, assuming it to have continued in effect.

70X(6) If–

(a) it is not otherwise the case, and

(b) the conditions in subsection (5) are met,

the lessor is to be treated as if the old lease and the new lease were the same continuing lease.

70X(7) Any reference in this section to a transfer of plant or machinery by a person includes a reference to–

(a) any kind of disposal of, or of the person's interest in, the plant or machinery,

(b) any arrangements under which the person's interest in the plant or machinery is terminated and another person becomes lessee of the plant or machinery,

(c) in a case where the plant or machinery is a fixture and the person is treated under section 176 as the owner, any cessation of ownership under section 188, 190, 191, 192 or 192A).

History – S. 70X inserted by FA 2006, s. 81 and Sch. 8, para. 7. The commencement and transitional provisions are complex and are set out in full in FA 2006, Sch. 8, para. 15–27.

HMRC Manuals – CA23840: transfers or assignments by the lessee.

70Y Sale and leaseback, lease and leaseback etc: lessors

70Y(1) Where–

(a) a person (B) transfers plant or machinery to another person (A),

(b) the plant or machinery is directly or indirectly leased back to B,

(c) immediately before the commencement of the term of the lease back to B, B is the lessor of the plant or machinery to another person under a lease which is, in B's case, a long funding lease,

the lease back to B is, in the case of both A and B, a long funding lease.

70Y(2) If, in any such case, the plant or machinery is leased back from A to B indirectly, any leases by means of which the indirect lease back from A to B is effected are also long funding leases in the case of each of the parties to them.

70Y(3) Any reference in this section to a transfer of plant or machinery by a person includes a reference to–

(a) any kind of disposal of, or of the person's interest in, the plant or machinery (including the grant of a lease),

(b) any arrangements under which the person's interest in the plant or machinery is terminated and another person becomes entitled to, or to an interest in, the plant or machinery,

(c) in a case where the plant or machinery is a fixture and the person is treated under section 176 as the owner, any cessation of ownership under section 188, 190, 191, 192 or 192A.

History – S. 70Y inserted by FA 2006, s. 81 and Sch. 8, para. 7. The commencement and transitional provisions are complex and are set out in full in FA 2006, Sch. 8, para. 15–27.

HMRC Manuals – CA23840: sales and leasebacks; leases and leasebacks: if the asset is leased back indirectly any of the leases involved in the leaseback are long funding leases.

70YA Change in accountancy classification of long funding lease

70YA(1) This section applies in any case where–

(a) a person is lessor or lessee under a long funding lease, and

(b) at any time after the inception of the lease, the accountancy classification of the lease as a finance lease or an operating lease changes in the relevant accounts.

70YA(2) The person is to be treated as if–

(a) the lease had terminated immediately before the time of the change,

(b) another lease (the "new lease") had been entered into immediately after the time of the change, and

(c) the new lease were a long funding lease in the case of the lessor.

70YA(3) The person is also to be treated as if the date on which the change occurs were the date of both–

(a) the inception of the new lease, and

(b) the commencement of the term of the new lease.

70YA(4) The cases where the accountancy classification of a long funding lease as a finance lease or an operating lease changes at any time (the "relevant time") in the relevant accounts are those set out in subsections (5) and (6).

70YA(5) Case 1 is where–

(a) immediately before the relevant time, the lease is one that falls (or would fall) to be treated in the relevant accounts in accordance with generally accepted accounting practice as a finance lease for accounting purposes, and

(b) at the relevant time the lease becomes one that falls (or would fall) to be treated in the relevant accounts in accordance with generally accepted accounting practice as not being a finance lease for accounting purposes.

70YA(6) Case 2 is where–

(a) immediately before the relevant time, the lease is one that falls (or would fall) to be treated in the relevant accounts in accordance with generally accepted accounting practice as not being a finance lease for accounting purposes, and

(b) at the relevant time the lease becomes one that falls (or would fall) to be treated in the relevant accounts in accordance with generally accepted accounting practice as a finance lease for accounting purposes.

70YA(7) The Treasury may by regulations make provision for or in connection with restricting the application or operation of this section.

70YA(8) In this section, any reference to a finance lease includes a reference to a loan.

70YA(9) In the application of this section in relation to any person, the **"relevant accounts"** are the accounts–

(a) of that person, or

(b) where that person is the lessor, of any person connected with that person,

but only to the extent that the treatment of the lease in those accounts as a finance lease or otherwise falls (or would fall) to be determined by reference to that person as the lessor or lessee under the lease.

70YA(10) Subsections (2) and (3) of section 70N (finance lease test: group accounts, and generally accepted accounting practice for persons outside the charge to tax) also apply for the purposes of this section.

History – S. 70YA inserted by FA 2006, s. 81 and Sch. 8, para. 7. The commencement and transitional provisions are complex and are set out in full in FA 2006, Sch. 8, para. 15–27.

HMRC Manuals – CA23845: change in accountancy classification.

70YB Long funding operating lease: extension of term of lease

70YB(1) This section applies in any case where–

(a) a person is lessor or lessee under a long funding operating lease (the "existing lease"),

(b) an event occurs which has the effect of extending the term of the lease (whether by variation of the provisions of the lease, the grant or exercise of an option or in any other way), and

(c) the event is not one by reason of which, within the meaning of section 70YA, the accountancy classification of the lease as an operating lease changes in the relevant accounts.

70YB(2) For this purpose an event has the effect of extending the term of the lease if it meets any of the following conditions–

(a) it has the effect of making a further period a non-cancellable period;

(b) it is the grant of an option to the lessee to continue to lease the plant or machinery for a further period, where it is reasonably certain at the time the option is granted that the lessee will exercise it;

(c) it is the exercise by the lessee of an option to continue to lease the plant or machinery for a further period;

(d) it does not fall within the preceding paragraphs, but it has the effect that the lessee will continue, or is reasonably certain to continue, to lease the plant or machinery for a further period.

For this purpose **"further period"** means a period falling wholly or partly after the end of the pre-existing term.

70YB(3) The person is to be treated as if–

(a) the existing lease terminated at the end of the day before the effective date,

(b) another lease (the "new lease") were entered into on the effective date, and

(c) the term of the new lease were the unexpired portion of the term of the existing lease, as extended.

70YB(4) The person is also to be treated as if the effective date were the date of both–

(a) the inception of the new lease, and

(b) the commencement of the term of the new lease.

70YB(5) The new lease is to be taken to be a long funding operating lease.

70YB(6) For the purposes of this section the **"effective date"** is the earlier of–

(a) the day after the end of the pre-existing term of the existing lease;

(b) if the rentals payable are varied as a result of or otherwise in connection with the event, the date on which the variation takes effect.

70YB(7) In this section–

"non-cancellable period" has the same meaning as in section 70YF (the "term" of a lease);

"pre-existing term", in relation to a lease, means the term of the lease apart from the extension in question.

History – S. 70YB inserted by FA 2006, s. 81 and Sch. 8, para. 7. The commencement and transitional provisions are complex and are set out in full in FA 2006, Sch. 8, para. 15–27.

HMRC Manuals – CA23845: extension of term of long funding operating lease: ways in which the term of the lease may be extended.

70YC Extension of term of lease that is not a long funding lease

70YC(1) This section applies where–

(a) a person is lessor under a plant or machinery lease (the "existing lease") that is not a long funding lease, and

(b) an event occurs which has the effect of extending the term of the lease (whether by variation of the provisions of the lease, the grant or exercise of an option or in any other way).

70YC(2) Subsection (2) of section 70YB (events having the effect of extending the term of a lease) also has effect for the purposes of this section.

70YC(3) Make the following assumptions–

(a) the existing lease terminates immediately before the effective date,

(b) another lease (the "new lease") is entered into on the effective date,

(c) the term of the new lease is the portion of the term of the existing lease, as extended, that remains unexpired as at the effective date;

(d) the effective date is the date of both–

(i) the inception of the new lease, and

(ii) the commencement of the term of the new lease.

70YC(4) If, on those assumptions, the new lease would be a long funding lease, the person is to be treated on those assumptions.

70YC(5) If subsection (4) does not apply, then, for the purposes of any subsequent application of this section or section 70YD in the case of the existing lease, the term of the existing lease is to be taken to be the term as extended (or further extended).

70YC(6) For the purposes of this section the **"effective date"** is the earlier of–

(a) the day after the end of the pre-existing term of the existing lease;

(b) if the rentals payable are varied as a result of or otherwise in connection with the event, the date on which the variation takes effect.

70YC(7) In this section **"pre-existing term"**, in relation to a lease, means the term of the lease apart from the extension in question.

History – S. 70YC inserted by FA 2006, s. 81 and Sch. 8, para. 7. The commencement and transitional provisions are complex and are set out in full in FA 2006, Sch. 8, para. 15–27.

HMRC Manuals – CA23845: extension of term of lease that is not a long funding lease.

70YD Increase in proportion of residual amount guaranteed: review of status

70YD(1) This section applies where–

(a) a person is lessor under a lease (the "existing lease") that is not a long funding lease,

(b) the person enters into an arrangement which meets, or arrangements which (taken together) meet, the conditions in subsection (2).

70YD(2) The conditions are that–

(a) as a result of the arrangement or arrangements, there is an increase, after the inception of the lease, in the proportion of the residual amount that is guaranteed as mentioned in section 70YE(1)(b), and

(b) had the arrangement or arrangements been entered into before the inception of the lease, the lease would have been a long funding lease.

70YD(3) The person is to be treated as if–

(a) the existing lease had terminated immediately before the time of the relevant transaction,

(b) another lease (the "new lease") had been entered into immediately after the time of the relevant transaction,

(c) the term of the new lease were the portion of the term of the existing lease that remains unexpired as at the date of the relevant transaction;

(d) the date of the relevant transaction were the date of both–

 (i) the inception of the new lease, and

 (ii) the commencement of the term of the new lease.

70YD(4) For the purposes of this section, the **"relevant transaction"** is the arrangement or, where two or more arrangements have been entered into, the latest of them.

70YD(5) The Treasury may by regulations make provision for or in connection with restricting the application or operation of this section.

History – S. 70YD inserted by FA 2006, s. 81 and Sch. 8, para. 7. The commencement and transitional provisions are complex and are set out in full in FA 2006, Sch. 8, para. 15–27.

HMRC Manuals – CA23845: increase in proportion of residual amount guaranteed: example.

INTERPRETATION

70YE "Minimum lease payments"

70YE(1) In the case of any lease, the minimum lease payments are the minimum payments under the lease over the term of the lease (including any initial payment) together with–

(a) in the case of the lessee, so much of any residual amount as is guaranteed by him or a person connected with him, or

(b) in the case of the lessor, so much of any residual amount as is guaranteed by the lessee or a person who is not connected with the lessor.

70YE(2) In determining the minimum payments, exclude so much of any payment as represents–

(a) charges for services, or

(b) qualifying UK or foreign tax to be paid by the lessor.

70YE(3) In this section–

"qualifying UK or foreign tax" means any tax or duty chargeable under the law of any part of the United Kingdom, or under the law of any foreign country, other than–

 (a) income tax,

 (b) corporation tax,

 (c) any tax chargeable under the law of a foreign country which is similar to income tax or corporation tax,

and here **"foreign country"** means any territory outside the United Kingdom;

"residual amount" means so much of the fair value of the plant or machinery subject to the lease as cannot reasonably be expected to be recovered by the lessor from the payments under the lease.

70YE(4) *In the definition* of "residual amount" in subsection (3), **"fair value"** means–

(a) the market value of the leased plant or machinery,

less

(b) any grants receivable towards the purchase or use of that plant or machinery.

History – S. 70YE inserted by FA 2006, s. 81 and Sch. 8, para. 7. The commencement and transitional provisions are complex and are set out in full in FA 2006, Sch. 8, para. 15–27.

HMRC Manuals – CA23850: minimum lease payments: meaning and example.

70YF The "term" of a lease

70YF(1) The term of a lease is the period comprising–

(a) so much of the post-commencement period as is a non-cancellable period, and

(b) any subsequent periods which meet the conditions in subsection (2).

70YF(2) The conditions are that–

(a) the lessee has an option to continue to lease the asset for the period (whether with or without further payment), and

(b) it is reasonably certain, at the inception of the lease, that the lessee will exercise that option.

70YF(3) The **"post-commencement period"** is so much of the period of the lease as begins with the commencement of the term of the lease.

70YF(4) A **"non-cancellable period"** is any period during which the lessee may terminate the lease only–

(a) upon the occurrence of some remote contingency, or

(b) upon payment by the lessee of such an additional amount that, at the inception of the lease, continuation of the lease is reasonably certain.

70YF(5) If, at the commencement of the term of the lease,–

(a) the market value of the asset exceeds £1 million, and

(b) the estimated market value of the asset 5 years after the commencement of the term of the lease is more than half of the market value of the asset at the commencement of the term of the lease,

subsection (6) applies.

70YF(6) If, in any such case, the term of the lease (apart from this subsection) would be 5 years or less, but–

(a) the lessee has one or more options to continue to lease the asset,

(b) on the assumption that it is reasonably certain, at the inception of the lease, that the lessee will exercise those options, the term of the lease would exceed 7 years, and

(c) on failing to exercise any one of those options, the lessee may be required to make a payment to the lessor,

it is to be assumed for the purposes of this section that any option to continue to lease the asset will be exercised, unless it is reasonably certain, at the inception of the lease, that the option will not be exercised.

70YF(7) Subsection (6) does not apply if, leaving out of account any options that would, by virtue of that subsection, result in the term of the lease exceeding 7 years, Conditions A, B and C in section 70I (meaning of "short lease") are met.

70YF(8) See also section 70YC(5) (extension, for certain purposes, of term of lease that is not a long funding lease).

History – S. 70YF inserted by FA 2006, s. 81 and Sch. 8, para. 7. The commencement and transitional provisions are complex and are set out in full in FA 2006, Sch. 8, para. 15–27.

HMRC Manuals – CA23850: term of lease: explanation of rules.

70YG "Termination amount"

70YG(1) This section applies where plant or machinery is or has been, or is to be, leased under a long funding lease.

70YG(2) Construe **"termination amount"**, in the case of a long funding lease, in accordance with the following provisions of this section.

70YG(3) If–

(a) the lease terminates as a result of a plant or machinery disposal event, or

(b) a plant or machinery disposal event occurs as a result of, or otherwise in connection with, the termination of the lease,

the termination amount is the disposal value that would have fallen to be brought into account by the lessor by reason of the plant or machinery disposal event on the assumptions in subsection (4).

70YG(4) Those assumptions are–

(a) that section 34A (which prevents the lessor's expenditure for long funding leasing from being qualifying expenditure) did not apply in the case of the lessor, and

(b) that the lessor had claimed all the capital allowances that would in consequence have been available to him.

CAA 2001

70YG(5) If–

(a) subsection (3) does not apply, and

(b) the lease is a long funding finance lease,

the termination amount is the value at which, immediately after the termination of the lease, the plant or machinery is recognised in the books or other financial records of the lessor.

70YG(6) If–

(a) subsection (3) does not apply, and

(b) the lease is a long funding operating lease,

the termination amount is the market value of the plant or machinery immediately after the termination of the lease.

70YG(7) For the purposes of this section a **"plant or machinery disposal event"** is an event that would have been a disposal event in relation to the plant or machinery in the case of the lessor on the assumptions in subsection (4).

History – S. 70YG inserted by FA 2006, s. 81 and Sch. 8, para. 7. The commencement and transitional provisions are complex and are set out in full in FA 2006, Sch. 8, para. 15–27.

HMRC Manuals – CA23850: termination amount: explanation of rules.

70YH Termination value

70YH(1) This section applies where plant or machinery is or has been, or is to be, leased under a long funding lease.

70YH(2) Construe **"termination value"** in accordance with the following provisions of this section.

70YH(3) The general rule is that the termination value of any plant or machinery is the value of the plant or machinery at or about the time when the lease terminates.

70YH(4) Any reference to calculation by reference to the termination value includes a reference to calculation by reference to any one or more of–

(a) the proceeds of sale, if the plant or machinery is sold after the lease comes to an end,

(b) any insurance proceeds, compensation or similar sums in respect of the plant or machinery,

(c) an estimate of the market value of the plant or machinery.

70YH(5) Any reference to calculation by reference to the termination value also includes a reference to–

(a) determination in a way which, or by reference to factors or criteria which, might reasonably be expected to produce a broadly similar result to calculation by reference to the termination value, or

(b) any other form of calculation indirectly by reference to the termination value.

History – S. 70YH inserted by FA 2006, s. 81 and Sch. 8, para. 7. The commencement and transitional provisions are complex and are set out in full in FA 2006, Sch. 8, para. 15–27.

HMRC Manuals – CA23850: termination value: explanation of rules.

70YI General definitions

70YI(1) Construe these expressions as follows–

"absolute owner", in the application of this Chapter in relation to Scotland, means the owner;

"arrangement" includes any transaction or series of transactions;

"background plant or machinery for a building" is to be construed in accordance with sections 70R to 70T;

"building" includes a reference to–

(a) a structure,

(b) part of a building or structure;

"commencement", in relation to the term of a lease, means the date on and after which the lessee is entitled to exercise his right to use the complete leased asset under the lease; for this purpose an asset is to be regarded as complete if its construction is substantially complete;

"derived lease" is to be construed in accordance with section 70L;

"the finance lease test" means the finance lease test in section 70N;

"fixture"–

(a) means any plant or machinery that is so installed or otherwise fixed in or to a building or other description of land as to become, in law, part of that building or other land, and

(b) includes any boiler or water-filled radiator installed in a building as part of a space or water heating system;

"funding lease" has the meaning given by section 70J;

"inception", in relation to a plant or machinery lease, means the earliest date on which the following conditions are met–

(a) there is a contract in writing for the lease between the lessor and the lessee,

(b) either–

(i) the contract is unconditional, or

(ii) if it is conditional, the conditions have been met,

(c) no terms remain to be agreed;

"initial payment", in the case of a plant or machinery lease, means a payment by the lessee–

(a) at or before the time when the lease is entered into, and

(b) in respect of the plant or machinery which is the subject of the lease;

"lease" includes any agreement or arrangement which is or includes a plant or machinery lease (and **"lessor"**, **"lessee"** and other related expressions are to be construed accordingly);

"lease", in relation to land, includes–

(a) an underlease, sublease or any tenancy,

(b) in England and Wales or Northern Ireland, an agreement for a lease, underlease, sublease, or tenancy,

(c) in Scotland, an agreement (including missives of let not constituting a lease) under which a lease, sublease, tenancy is to be executed,

(d) in the case of land situated outside the United Kingdom, any interest corresponding to a lease as so defined,

and **"lessor"**, **"lessee"** and other related expressions are to be construed accordingly;

"lease", in relation to plant or machinery, includes a sublease (and **"lessor"**, **"lessee"** and other related expressions are to be construed accordingly);

"lessee", in relation to a lease, includes any person entitled to the lessee's interest under the lease;

"lessor", in relation to a lease, includes any person entitled to the lessor's interest under the lease;

"long funding lease" has the meaning given by section 70G;

"long funding finance lease" means a long funding lease that meets the finance lease test by virtue of section 70N(1)(a);

"long funding operating lease" means a long funding lease which is not a long funding finance lease;

"market value", in relation to plant or machinery, is to be construed in accordance with subsection (2);

"minimum lease payments" has the meaning given by section 70YE;

"mixed lease" is to be construed in accordance with section 70L;

"plant or machinery lease" has the meaning given by section 70K (and see also sections 70L and 70M);

"remaining useful economic life", in the case of any leased plant or machinery, is the period–

(a) beginning with the commencement of the term of the lease, and

(b) ending when the asset is no longer used, and no longer likely to be used, by any person for any purpose as a fixed asset of a business;

"short lease" is to be construed in accordance with section 70I;

"the term", in relation to a lease, is to be construed in accordance with section 70YF (but see also section 70YC(5) (extension, for certain purposes, of term of lease that is not a long funding lease));

"termination", in relation to a lease,–

(a) means the coming to an end of the lease, whether by effluxion of time or in any other way, and

(b) includes in particular the bringing to an end of the lease by any person or by operation of law,

and related expressions are to be construed accordingly;

"termination amount" is to be construed in accordance with section 70YG;

"termination value" is to be construed in accordance with section 70YH.

70YI(2) The market value of any plant or machinery at any time is to be determined on the assumption of a disposal by an absolute owner free from all leases and other encumbrances.

70YI(3) In relation to a lease, any reference to plant or machinery includes a reference to fixtures.

70YI(4) [Omitted by ITA 2007, s. 1027 and Sch. 1, para. 399, and repealed by s. 1031 and Sch. 3, Pt. 1.]

70YI(5) Any necessary apportionments under or by virtue of this Chapter are to be made on a just and reasonable basis.

History – S. 70YI(4) omitted by ITA 2007, s. 1027 and Sch. 1, para. 399 and repealed by s. 1031 and Sch. 3, Pt. 1, with effect from 6 April 2007.
S. 70YI inserted by FA 2006, s. 81 and Sch. 8, para. 7. The commencement and transitional provisions are complex and are set out in full in FA 2006, Sch. 8, para. 15–27.

70YJ Power to vary the meaning of certain expressions

70YJ(1) The Treasury may by regulations make provision amending this Chapter so as to vary–

(a) the meaning of "plant or machinery lease", or

(b) the finance lease test.

70YJ(2) A statutory instrument containing regulations under this section is not to be made unless a draft of the instrument has been laid before, and approved by a resolution of, the House of Commons.

History – S. 70YJ inserted by FA 2006, s. 81 and Sch. 8, para. 7. The commencement and transitional provisions are complex and are set out in full in FA 2006, Sch. 8, para. 15–27.

Chapter 7 – Computer Software

71 Software and rights to software

71(1) For the purposes of this Part computer software is treated as plant (whether or not it would constitute plant apart from this section).

71(2) If a person carrying on a qualifying activity incurs capital expenditure in acquiring, for the purposes of the qualifying activity, a right to use or otherwise deal with computer software, this Part applies as if–

(a) the right and the software to which it relates were plant,

(b) the plant were provided for the purposes of the qualifying activity, and

(c) so long as the person is entitled to the right, the person owned the plant as a result of incurring the capital expenditure.

Origin – S. 71(1): CAA 1990, s. 67A(2).
S. 71(2): CAA 1990, s. 67A(1).

Cross references – S. 23(2): s. 21 and 22 (expenditure on provision of plant or machinery does not include expenditure on provision of a building or structure or work involving the alteration of land) do not apply to any expenditure to which s. 71 applies.

Transitional – Sch. 3, para. 18: s. 71 does not apply to expenditure incurred before 10 March 1992.

HMRC Manuals – CA22280 and CA23410: guidance on the meaning of computer software, etc; no physical asset is necessary for expenditure to qualify.
BIM35801: Capital/revenue treatment of expenditure on computer software.

72 Disposal values

72(1) This section applies if a person–

(a) has incurred qualifying expenditure on the provision of plant consisting of computer software or the right to use or otherwise deal with computer software, and

(b) grants to another a right to use or otherwise deal with the whole or part of the computer software in circumstances in which the consideration for the grant–

(i) consists of a capital sum, or

(ii) would consist of a capital sum if the consideration were in money.

72(2) The person is required to bring a disposal value into account unless–

(a) while the person owned the computer software or the right to use or otherwise deal with the computer software, and

(b) before the grant of the right referred to in subsection (1)(b),

there has been a disposal event falling within section 61(1)(e) (use for purposes other than those of the qualifying activity) or 61(1)(f) (permanent discontinuance of the qualifying activity).

72(3) The disposal value to be brought into account under this section depends on the circumstances of the grant of the right, as shown in the Table–

TABLE
DISPOSAL VALUES: GRANT OF SOFTWARE RIGHT

	1. Circumstances of grant	*2. Disposal value*
1.	The grant is for a consideration not consisting entirely of money.	The market value of the right granted at the time of the grant.
2.	The grant is made where– (a) it is for no consideration or at less than market value, (b) there is no charge to tax under ITEPA 2003, and (c) the condition in subsection (5) is met by the grantee.	The market value of the right granted at the time of the grant.
3.	The grant is made in circumstances other than those given in item 1 or 2.	The net consideration in money received in respect of the grant, together with– (a) any insurance money received in respect of the computer software as a result of an event affecting the consideration obtainable on the grant, and (b) any other compensation of any description so received, so far as it consists of capital sums.

72(4) The amounts referred to in column 2 of the Table are those received by the person required to bring the disposal value into account.

72(5) The condition referred to in item 2 of the Table is met by the grantee if–

(a) the grantee's expenditure on the acquisition of the plant cannot be qualifying expenditure under this Part or Part 6 (research and development allowances), or

(b) the grantee is a dual resident investing company which is connected with the grantor.

History – In entry 2(b) of the Table in s. 72(3), the words "ITEPA 2003" substituted for the words "Schedule E" by ITEPA 2003, Sch. 6, para. 251 which has effect, for income tax purposes, for the tax year 2003–04 and subsequent tax years and, for corporation tax purposes, for accounting periods ending after 5 April 2003.

Origin – S. 72(1), (2): CAA 1990, s. 24(6A).
S. 72(3): CAA 1990, s. 26(1) (part).
Table, item 1: CAA 1990, s. 26(1)(ea).
Table, item 2: CAA 1990, s. 26(1)(eb) (part).
Table, item 3: CAA 1990, s. 26(1)(ec) (part).
S. 72(4): CAA 1990, s. 26(1)(ec) (part).
S. 72(5): CAA 1990, s. 26(1)(eb) (part).

Cross references – S. 60(1)(b), 66: general provisions about disposal values required to be brought into account ("disposal receipts").
FA 2002, Sch. 29, para. 83(3)(d): gains and losses of a company from intangible fixed assets: election to exclude from code of capital expenditure by company on computer software – credit brought into account under Sch. 29 to extent that receipts do not fall to be taken into account in computing disposal values under s. 72.
RA 2005, Sch. 10, para. 14: disapplication of s. 72(3) to (5) in the case of certain transfers to a national authority.

HMRC Manuals – CA23420: guidance.

73 Limit on disposal values

73(1) This section applies if a person is required to bring into account a disposal value in respect of–

(a) computer software, or

(b) the right to use or otherwise deal with computer software.

73(2) For the purpose only of–

(a) determining whether the limit on the disposal value under section 62 is exceeded, and

(b) reducing the amount of that disposal value so that the limit is not exceeded,

the disposal value is to be taken to be increased by the amount given in subsection (3).

73(3) The amount is the total of any disposal values which, in respect of that person and that plant, fall or have fallen to be brought into account under section 72.

Origin – S. 73(1)–(3): CAA 1990, s. 26(2) (part), (2AA).

Cross references – S. 60(1)(b), 66: general provisions about disposal values required to be brought into account ("disposal receipts").
S. 268(7): where a beneficiary succeeds to a qualifying activity on under the will or intestacy of a deceased person, s. 73 applies as if the previous disposal values to be taken into account in determining whether the limit under s. 62 is exceeded were those of the deceased.

HMRC Manuals – CA23430: guidance and example.

Chapter 8 – Cars, etc.

CARS ABOVE THE COST THRESHOLD

74 Single asset pool

74 [Omitted by FA 2009, s. 30 and Sch. 11, para. 4.]

History – S. 74 omitted by FA 2009, s. 30 and Sch. 11, para. 4, with effect in relation to expenditure incurred on or after 1 April 2009 (for corporation tax purposes) and 6 April 2009 (for income tax purposes), subject to transitional provisions in FA 2009, Sch. 11, para. 27(2) and 29–32. Former s. 74 read as follows:

"Single asset pool

74(1) Qualifying expenditure incurred on the provision of a car to which this section applies, if allocated to a pool, must be allocated to a single asset pool.
74(2) This section applies to a car if–
(a) the car is not a qualifying hire car (as defined by section 82),
(b) the capital expenditure incurred on its provision for the purposes of the qualifying activity exceeds £12,000, and
(c) the qualifying expenditure incurred on the provision of the car is not first-year qualifying expenditure under section 45D (expenditure on cars with low CO_2 emissions)
74(3) In this Chapter **"car"** has the meaning given by section 81 (extended meaning of "car").
74(4) The Treasury may by order increase or further increase the sums of money specified in subsection (2) and in sections 75 and 76.".
Former s. 74(2)(c) and preceding word "and" inserted by FA 2002, s. 59 and Sch. 19, para. 6, with effect in relation to expenditure incurred on or after 17 April 2002.
In former s. 74(2), the word "and" preceding s. 74(2)(b) repealed by FA 2002, s. 141 and Sch. 40, Pt. 3(7), with effect in relation to expenditure incurred on or after 17 April 2002.

Origin – S. 74(1), (2): CAA 1990, s. 34(1), (2) (part), s. 35(1) (part).
S. 74(3): CAA 1990, s. 36(1) (part).
S. 74(4): CAA 1990, s. 36(5) (part).

Transitional – Sch. 3, para. 19: in relation to expenditure incurred or treated as incurred before 11 March 1992, or incurred under a contract entered into before that date, s. 74(2) applies with the substitution of "£8,000" for "£12,000". (See also ITTOIA 2005, s. 883 and Sch. 2, para. 16 for the equivalent transitional rules for car hire expenditure.)

75 General limit on amount of writing-down allowance

75 [Omitted by FA 2009, s. 30 and Sch. 11, para. 4.]

History – S. 75 omitted by FA 2009, s. 30 and Sch. 11, para. 4, with effect in relation to expenditure incurred on or after 1 April 2009 (for corporation tax purposes) and 6 April 2009 (for income tax purposes), subject to transitional provisions in FA 2009, Sch. 11, para. 27(2) and 29–32. Former s. 75 read as follows:

"General limit on amount of writing-down allowance

75(1) The amount of the writing-down allowance to be made to a person for a chargeable period in respect of qualifying expenditure incurred on the provision of a car to which section 74 applies must not exceed £3,000.
75(2) The limit under subsection (1) is proportionately increased or reduced if the chargeable period is more or less than a year.
75(3) The amount of the writing-down allowance may be further limited under–
section 76 (expenditure met by another person),
section 77 (effect of use partly for other purposes), or
section 78 (effect of partial depreciation subsidy).".

Origin – S. 75(1), (2): CAA 1990, s. 34(3) (part).
S. 75(3) drafting.

Transitional – Sch. 3, para. 19: in relation to expenditure incurred or treated as incurred before 11 March 1992, or incurred under a contract entered into before that date, s. 75(1) applies with the substitution of "£2,000" for "£3,000".

76 Limit where part of expenditure met by another person

76 [Omitted by FA 2009, s. 30 and Sch. 11, para. 4.]

History – S. 76 omitted by FA 2009, s. 30 and Sch. 11, para. 4, with effect in relation to expenditure incurred on or after 1 April 2009 (for corporation tax purposes) and 6 April 2009 (for income tax purposes), subject to transitional provisions in FA 2009, Sch. 11, para. 27(2) and 29–32. Former s. 76 read as follows:

"Limit where part of expenditure met by another person

76(1) Subsection (2) applies if, as a result of section 532 (general rule excluding contributions), only part of the capital expenditure incurred on the provision of a car to which section 74 applies is treated as incurred by a person.
76(2) The amount of the writing-down allowance to be made to that person for a chargeable period in respect of the qualifying expenditure on the car must not exceed–

$$£3{,}000 \times \frac{E - X}{E}$$

where–
E is the amount of capital expenditure incurred on the provision of the car, and
X is the amount of the expenditure excluded by section 532.
76(3) Subsection (4) applies if–
(a) capital expenditure exceeding £12,000 is incurred on the provision of a car to which section 74 applies, and
(b) a person (**"the contributor"**) is entitled to writing-down allowances as a result of section 538 (contribution allowances for plant and machinery).

76(4) The amount of the writing-down allowance to be made to the contributor for a chargeable period in respect of his contribution to the expenditure on the car must not exceed–

$$£3,000 \times \frac{C}{E}$$

where–
E is the amount of capital expenditure incurred on the provision of the car, and
C is the amount of the contribution.
76(5) The limit under subsection (2) or (4) is proportionately increased or reduced if the chargeable period is more or less than a year.".

Origin – S. 76(1), (2): CAA 1990, s. 34(3) (part).
S. 76(3), (4): CAA 1990, s. 35(1) (part), Annex 2, Note 19.
S. 76(5): CAA 1990, s. 34(3) (part), s. 35(1) (part).

Transitional – Sch. 3, para. 19: in relation to expenditure incurred or treated as incurred before 11 March 1992, or incurred under a contract entered into before that date, s. 76(2) and (4) apply with the substitution of "£2,000" for "£3,000", and s. 76(3) applies with the substitution of "£8,000" for "£12,000".

Rewrite: Technical Points – Explanatory Notes, Annex 2, Note 19: unlike former CAA 1990, s. 35(1), s. 76(3) and (4) do not create a separate pool for contributions to a car costing more than £12,000. There is no longer any need for a special pool because s. 538(3) now makes it clear (unlike CAA 1990, s. 155(6)) that a contributor's pool is a "single asset pool" not a "class pool".

77 Car used partly for purposes other than those of qualifying activity

77 [Omitted by FA 2009, s. 30 and Sch. 11, para. 4.]

History – S. 77 omitted by FA 2009, s. 30 and Sch. 11, para. 4, with effect in relation to expenditure incurred on or after 1 April 2009 (for corporation tax purposes) and 6 April 2009 (for income tax purposes), subject to transitional provisions in FA 2009, Sch. 11, para. 27(2) and 29–32. Former s. 77 read as follows:

"Car used partly for purposes other than those of qualifying activity

77(1) In the case of a single asset pool under section 74 there is no final chargeable period or disposal event merely because the car begins to be used partly for purposes other than those of the qualifying activity.
77(2) For any chargeable period in which the car is used partly for purposes other than those of the qualifying activity–
(a) any writing-down allowance or balancing allowance to which the person is entitled, or
(b) any balancing charge to which the person is liable,
must be reduced to an amount which is just and reasonable having regard to the relevant circumstances.
77(3) The relevant circumstances include, in particular, the extent to which the car is used in that chargeable period for purposes other than those of the qualifying activity.
77(4) In calculating under section 59 the amount of unrelieved qualifying expenditure carried forward, a reduction of a writing-down allowance under this section is to be disregarded.
77(5) If this section applies, Chapter 15 (plant or machinery provided or used partly for purposes other than those of the qualifying activity) does not apply.".

Origin – S. 77(1): CAA 1990, s. 34(5) (part), Annex 2, Note 20.
S. 77(2), (3): CAA 1990, s. 34(5) (part).
S. 77(4): Annex 2, Note 21.
S. 77(5): CAA 1990, s. 34(5) (part).

Rewrite: Technical Points – Explanatory Notes, Annex 2, Note 20: s. 77(1) provides that in the case of a single asset pool for a car above the cost threshold, there is no final chargeable period merely because the car begins to be used for purposes other than those of the qualifying activity. By contrast, CAA 1990, s. 34(2)(b) provided that the separate trade was permanently discontinued when the car began to be used wholly *or partly* for purpose other than those of the actual trade. But because s. 34(5) provided for allowances to continue to be made for the chargeable period when the change of use occurred and subsequent chargeable periods, the only possible inference is that the words "or partly" in s. 34(2)(b) were included by mistake.
Explanatory Notes, Annex 2, Note 21: s. 77(4) provides explicitly that in calculating unrelieved qualifying expenditure to be carried forward, any reduction in the writing-down allowance is to be disregarded. Although in terms the interaction between former CAA 1990, s. 34(5) and CAA 1990, s. 25(1)(b) would seem to suggest otherwise, the real effect is no different since if more expenditure was carried forward, the just and reasonable reduction would have been proportionately greater.

78 Effect of partial depreciation subsidy

78 [Omitted by FA 2009, s. 30 and Sch. 11, para. 4.]

History – S. 78 omitted by FA 2009, s. 30 and Sch. 11, para. 4, with effect in relation to expenditure incurred on or after 1 April 2009 (for corporation tax purposes) and 6 April 2009 (for income tax purposes), subject to transitional provisions in FA 2009, Sch. 11, para. 27(2) and 29–32. Former s. 78 read as follows:

"Effect of partial depreciation subsidy

78(1) This section applies if–
(a) a car to which section 74 applies is in use for the purposes of the qualifying activity,
(b) there is paid to the person carrying on that activity a sum in respect of, or which takes account of, part of the depreciation of the car resulting from that use, and
(c) the sum does not fall to be taken into account as income of that person or in calculating the profits of any qualifying activity carried on by him.
78(2) The amount of–
(a) any writing-down allowance or balancing allowance to which the person is entitled, or
(b) any balancing charge to which the person is liable,
must be reduced to an amount which is just and reasonable having regard to the relevant circumstances.
78(3) In calculating under section 59 the amount of unrelieved qualifying expenditure carried forward, a reduction of a writing-down allowance under subsection (2) is to be disregarded.
78(4) This section has effect for the chargeable period in which any such sum as is mentioned in subsection (1)(b) is first paid and for any subsequent chargeable period.
78(5) If this section applies, Chapter 16 (partial depreciation subsidies) does not apply.".

Origin – S. 78(1), (2): CAA 1990, s. 34(5) (part).
S. 78(3): Annex 2, Note 21.
S. 78(4), (5): CAA 1990, s. 34(5).

Rewrite: Technical Points – Explanatory Notes, Annex 2, Note 21: s. 78(3) provides explicitly that in calculating unrelieved qualifying expenditure to be carried forward, any reduction in the writing-down allowance is to be disregarded. Although in terms the interaction between former CAA 1990, s. 34(5) and CAA 1990, s. 25(1)(b) would seem to suggest otherwise, the real effect is no different since if more expenditure was carried forward, the just and reasonable reduction would have been proportionately greater.

79 Cases where Chapter 17 (anti-avoidance) applies

79 [Omitted by FA 2009, s. 30 and Sch. 11, para. 4.]

History – S. 79 omitted by FA 2009, s. 30 and Sch. 11, para. 4, with effect in relation to expenditure incurred on or after 1 April 2009 (for corporation tax purposes) and 6 April 2009 (for income tax purposes), subject to transitional provisions in FA 2009, Sch. 11, para. 27(2) and 28–32. Former s. 79 read as follows:

"Cases where Chapter 17 (anti-avoidance) applies

79(1) This section applies if–
(a) a disposal value is required to be brought into account under section 61, and
(b) the disposal event is that the person concerned ceases to own a car to which section 74 applies because of–
(i) a sale, or
(ii) the performance of a contract,
which is a relevant transaction for the purposes of Chapter 17 (anti-avoidance).
79(2) The disposal value to be brought into account is–
(a) the market value of the car at the time of the event referred to in subsection (1), or
(b) if less, the capital expenditure incurred, or treated as incurred, on the provision of the car by the person disposing of it.
79(3) The person acquiring the car is to be treated as having incurred capital expenditure on its provision of an amount equal to the disposal value required to be brought into account under subsection (2).".

Origin – S. 79(1) to (3): CAA 1990, s. 34(4).

VEHICLES PROVIDED FOR PURPOSES OF EMPLOYMENT OR OFFICE

80 Vehicles provided for purposes of employment or office

80 [Repealed by FA 2001, s. 59(2), 110 and Sch. 33, Pt. 2(1).]

History – S. 80 repealed by FA 2001, s. 59(2), 110 and Sch. 33, Pt. 2(1), in relation to expenditure incurred on or after 6 April 2002.
Origin – S. 80(1): CAA 1990, s. 27(2B) (part), (2C).
S. 80(2): CAA 1990, s. 27(2A), (2B) (part), Annex 1, Change 18.
S. 80(3): CAA 1990, s. 27(2D), (2E).
S. 80(4): CAA 1990, s. 27(2B) (part).

Rewrite: Changes in Law – Explanatory Notes, Annex 1, Change 18: s. 80(2) differs from former CAA 1990, s. 27(2B) because it extends the availability of capital allowances so as to come into line with the availability of deductions for travelling expenses under ICTA 1988, s. 198, following amendment by FA 1998, s. 61. Under CAA 1990, s. 27(2A) and (2B), allowances were available if the car was "provided" for use in the performance of the duties of employment (rather than "necessarily provided" in CAA 1990, s. 27(2)). The 1998 amendments to ICTA 1988, s. 198 extended the scope of allowable deductions so that they were no longer limited to travelling in the performance of duties. The restriction of entitlement to balancing allowance in s. 80(3) reflects the fact that in practice many employees will receive recognition of the capital depreciation on a car under the FPCS scheme rather than under the statutory scheme.

INTERPRETATION

81 Extended meaning of "car"

81 [Omitted by FA 2009, s. 30 and Sch. 11, para. 5.]

History – S. 81 omitted by FA 2009, s. 30 and Sch. 11, para. 5, with effect in relation to expenditure incurred on or after 1 April 2009 (for corporation tax purposes) and 6 April 2009 (for income tax purposes), subject to transitional provisions in FA 2009, Sch. 11, para. 27(2) and 30–32. Former s. 81 read as follows:

"Extended meaning of "car"

81 In this Part **"car"** means a mechanically propelled road vehicle other than one–
(a) of a construction primarily suited for the conveyance of goods or burden of any description, or
(b) of a type not commonly used as a private vehicle and unsuitable for such use.
References to a car accordingly include a motor cycle.".

Origin – CAA 1990, s. 36(1) (part), drafting.

82 Qualifying hire cars

82 [Omitted by FA 2009, s. 30 and Sch. 11, para. 5.]

History – S. 82 omitted by FA 2009, s. 30 and Sch. 11, para. 5, with effect in relation to expenditure incurred on or after 1 April 2009 (for corporation tax purposes) and 6 April 2009 (for income tax purposes), subject to transitional provisions in FA 2009, Sch. 11, para. 27(2) and 30–32. Former s. 82 read as follows:

"Qualifying hire cars

82(1) For the purposes of this Part a car is a qualifying hire car if–
(a) it is provided wholly or mainly for hire to, or the carriage of, members of the public in the ordinary course of a trade, and
(b) the case is within subsection (2), (3) or (4).
82(2) The first case is where the following conditions are met–
(a) the number of consecutive days for which the car is on hire to, or used for the carriage of, the same person will normally be less than 30, and
(b) the total number of days for which it is on hire to, or used for the carriage of, the same person in any period of 12 months will normally be less than 90.
82(3) The second case is where the car is provided for hire to a person who will himself use it–
(a) wholly or mainly for hire to, or for the carriage of, members of the public in the ordinary course of a trade, and

(b) in a way that meets the conditions in subsection (2).

82(4) The third case is where the car is provided wholly or mainly for the use of a person in receipt of–

(a) a disability living allowance under–

(i) the Social Security Contributions and Benefits Act 1992, or

(ii) the Social Security Contributions and Benefits (Northern Ireland) Act 1992, because of entitlement to the mobility component,

(b) a mobility supplement under a scheme made under the Personal Injuries (Emergency Provisions) Act 1939,

(c) a mobility supplement under an Order in Council made under section 12 of the Social Security (Miscellaneous Provisions) Act 1977, or

(d) any payment appearing to the Treasury to be of a similar kind and specified by them by order.

82(5) For the purposes of subsection (2) persons who are connected with each other are to be treated as the same person.".

Origin – S. 82(1): CAA 1990, s. 36(1)(c).
S. 82(2): CAA 1990, s. 36(2)(a).
S. 82(3): CAA 1990, s. 36(2)(b).
S. 82(4): CAA 1990, s. 22 (6), s. 36(4).
S. 82(5): CAA 1990, s. 36(3).

Chapter 9 – Short-life Assets

83 Meaning of "short-life asset"

83 Plant or machinery in respect of which qualifying expenditure has been incurred is a short-life asset if–

(a) its treatment as a short-life asset is not ruled out by section 84, and

(b) the person incurring the expenditure elects for the plant or machinery to be treated as a short-life asset.

Origin – CAA 1990, s. 37(1) (part).

Cross references – TMA 1970, s. 42(6) and (7)(c): claims made by partnerships.

HMRC Manuals – CA23620: guidance on assets within s. 83.

84 Cases in which short-life asset treatment is ruled out

84 Treatment of plant or machinery as a short-life asset is ruled out in any of the cases listed in column 1 of the Table, unless an exception listed in column 2 applies.

TABLE
SHORT-LIFE ASSET TREATMENT

	1. Short-life asset treatment ruled out	*2. Exception (if any)*
1.	The expenditure is treated as incurred for the purposes of a qualifying activity under– (a) section 13 (use for qualifying activity of plant or machinery provided for other purposes), or (aa) section 13A (use for other purposes of plant or machinery provided for long funding leasing), or (b) section 14 (use for qualifying activity of plant or machinery which is a gift).	
2.	The plant or machinery is the subject of special leasing (as defined by section 19).	
3.	The plant or machinery is a car (as defined by section 268A).	The car is a hire car for a disabled person (as defined by section 268D).
4.	The expenditure is special rate expenditure (see Chapter 10A).	The expenditure is incurred on the provision of a car which is a hire car for a disabled person (as defined by section 268D).
5.	The plant or machinery is provided for leasing.	The plant or machinery is a car which is a hire car for a disabled person (as defined by section 268D). The plant or machinery will be used within the designated period (as defined by section 106) for a qualifying purpose (as defined by sections 122 to 125).

	1. Short-life asset treatment ruled out	*2. Exception (if any)*
6.	Section 109 provides only a 10% writing-down allowance in respect of expenditure on the plant or machinery.	
7.	The plant or machinery is leased to two or more persons jointly in circumstances such that section 116 applies.	
8.	The plant or machinery is a ship.	
9.	The expenditure was incurred partly for the purposes of a qualifying activity and partly for other purposes (see Chapter 15).	
10.	The expenditure is required to be allocated to a single asset pool under section 211 (partial depreciation subsidy).	

History – In s. 84, in item 3, "268A" substituted for "81" by FA 2009, s. 30 and Sch. 11, para. 6, with effect in relation to expenditure incurred on or after 1 April 2009 (for corporation tax purposes) and 6 April 2009 (for income tax purposes), subject to transitional provisions in FA 2009, Sch. 11, para. 27(2) and 30–32.
In s. 84, in item 3, the words "The car is a hire car for a disabled person (as defined by section 268D)." substituted for the words "The car is within section 82(4) (cars hired out to persons receiving disability allowances etc.)." by FA 2009, s. 30 and Sch. 11, para. 19(2), with effect in relation to expenditure incurred on or after 1 April 2009 (for corporation tax purposes) and 6 April 2009 (for income tax purposes), subject to transitional provisions in FA 2009, Sch. 11, para. 27(2) and 30–32.
In s. 84, in item 4, the words "The expenditure is incurred on the provision of a car which is a hire car for a disabled person (as defined by section 268D)" inserted by FA 2009, s. 30 and Sch. 11, para. 19(3), with effect in relation to expenditure incurred on or after 1 April 2009 (for corporation tax purposes) and 6 April 2009 (for income tax purposes), subject to transitional provisions in FA 2009, Sch. 11, para. 27(2) and 30–32.
In s. 84, item 4 in column 1 substituted for the former item 4 (which read "The expenditure is long-life asset expenditure (see Chapter 10)") by FA 2008, s. 82 and Sch. 26, para. 7, with effect in relation expenditure incurred on or after 1 April 2008 for corporation tax purposes and 6 April 2008 for income tax purposes and in relation to long-life asset expenditure (within the meaning of CAA 2001, Pt. 2, Ch. 10) incurred before those dates but allocated to a pool in a chargeable period beginning on or after those dates. This commencement provision is subject to FA 2008, s. 83 (existing long-life asset expenditure treated as special rate expenditure) and FA 2008, Sch. 26, para. 15–17 (detailed provisions relating to sales between connected persons and savings for intra-group transfers).
In s. 84, in item 5, the words "a hire car for a disabled person (as defined by section 268D)" substituted for the words "within section 82(4) (cars hired out to persons receivingdisability allowances etc)" by FA 2009, s. 30 and Sch. 11, para. 19(4), with effect in relation to expenditure incurred on or after 1 April 2009 (for corporation tax purposes) and 6 April 2009 (for income tax purposes), subject to transitional provisions in FA 2009, Sch. 11, para. 27(2) and 30–32.
In s. 84 in para. 1 of the Table, subpara. (aa) inserted by FA 2006, s. 81 and Sch. 8, para. 8. The commencement and transitional provisions are complex and are set out in full in FA 2006, Sch. 8, Pt. 4.

Origin – Table, item 1: CAA 1990, s. 38(f).
Table, item 2: CAA 1990, s. 38(c).
Table, item 3: CAA 1990, s. 38(b).
Table, item 4: CAA 1990, s. 37(1)(ba).
Table, item 5: CAA 1990, s. 38(h).
Table, item 6: CAA 1990, s. 38(l).
Table, item 7: CAA 1990, s. 38(j).
Table, item 8: CAA 1990, s. 38(a).
Table, item 9: CAA 1990, s. 38(d).
Table, item 10: CAA 1990, s. 38(e).

HMRC Manuals – CA23620: guidance on assets excluded from short-life asset treatment.

85 Election for short-life asset treatment: procedure

85(1) An election under section 83 must specify–

(a) the plant or machinery which is the subject of the election,

(b) the qualifying expenditure incurred in respect of it, and

(c) the date on which the expenditure was incurred.

85(2) An election under section 83 must be made by notice given to an officer of Revenue and Customs–

(a) for income tax purposes, on or before the normal time limit for amending a tax return for the tax year in which the relevant chargeable period ends;

(b) for corporation tax purposes, no later than 2 years after the end of the relevant chargeable period.

85(3) **"The relevant chargeable period"** means–

(a) the chargeable period in which the qualifying expenditure was incurred, or

(b) *if the qualifying* expenditure was incurred in different chargeable periods, the first chargeable period in which any of the qualifying expenditure was incurred.

85(4) An election under section 83 is irrevocable.

85(5) All such assessments and adjustments of assessments are to be made as are necessary to give effect to the election.

History – In s. 85(2), the words "an officer of Revenue and Customs" substituted for "the Inland Revenue" by CRCA 2005, s. 50(6) and Sch. 4, para. 83(1), with effect from 18 April 2005 by virtue of SI 2005/1126, art. 2(2).

Origin – S. 85(1): CAA 1990, s. 37(1)(c), (2) (part).
S. 85(2): CAA 1990, s. 37(2) (part), (2A) (part).
S. 85(3): CAA 1990, s. 37(2A) (part).
S. 85(4): CAA 1990, s. 37(2) (part).
S. 85(5): CAA 1990, s. 37(4) (part).

Statements of practice – 1/86: guidance on some practical aspects of short-life asset elections, including identification of assets, form of computation for large numbers of assets where individual identification impracticable, and submission of elections and computations.

HMRC Manuals – CA23640: guidance and examples.

86 Short-life asset pool

86(1) Qualifying expenditure in respect of a short-life asset, if allocated to a pool, must be allocated to a single asset pool (a **"short-life asset pool"**).

86(2) If the final chargeable period for the short-life asset pool has not occurred before the relevant cut-off–

(a) the pool ends at the relevant cut-off without a final chargeable period,

(b) the available qualifying expenditure in the pool is allocated to the appropriate pool for the first chargeable period ending after the relevant cut-off, and

(c) the asset ceases to be a short-life asset.

86(3) In this Chapter **"the relevant cut-off"** means–

(a) if any of the qualifying expenditure incurred on the provision of the short-life asset was incurred before the designated day, the fourth anniversary of the end of the relevant chargeable period, and

(b) in any other case, the eighth anniversary of the end of the relevant chargeable period.

86(3A) In subsection (3)–

"the designated day" means–

(a) for corporation tax purposes, 1 April 2011, and

(b) for income tax purposes, 6 April 2011;

"the relevant chargeable period" means–

(a) the chargeable period in which the qualifying expenditure was incurred on the provision of the short-life asset, or

(b) if the qualifying expenditure was incurred in different chargeable periods, the first chargeable period in which any of the qualifying expenditure was incurred.

86(4) For the purposes of subsection (2), the final chargeable period occurs before the relevant cut-off only if it ends on or before it.

86(5) In subsection (2)(b) **"appropriate pool"** means–

(a) in the case of expenditure incurred on the provision of a car that is not a main rate car (as defined by section 104AA), the special rate pool, and

(b) in any other case, the main pool.

History – In s. 86(2), the words "relevant" substituted for "four-year" (in each place) by FA 2011, s. 12(2)(a), with effect from 19 July 2011.
In s. 86(2)(b), the words "appropriate pool" substituted for the words "main pool" by FA 2009, s. 30 and Sch. 11, para. 20(2), with effect in relation to expenditure incurred on or after 1 April 2009 (for corporation tax purposes) and 6 April 2009 (for income tax purposes), subject to transitional provisions in FA 2009, Sch. 11, para. 27(2) and 30–32.
S. 86(3) and (3A) substituted for former s. 86(3) by FA 2011, s. 12(2)(b), with effect from 19 July 2011.
In s. 86(4), the word "relevant" substituted for "four-year" by FA 2011, s. 12(2)(c), with effect from 19 July 2011.
S. 86(5) inserted by FA 2009, s. 30 and Sch. 11, para. 20(3), with effect in relation to expenditure incurred on or after 1 April 2009 (for corporation tax purposes) and 6 April 2009 (for income tax purposes), subject to transitional provisions in FA 2009, Sch. 11, para. 27(2) and 30–32.

Origin – S. 86(1): CAA 1990, s. 37(3) (part).
S. 86(2)–(4): CAA 1990, s. 37(5) (part).

HMRC Manuals – CA23640: guidance and examples.

87 Short-life assets provided for leasing

87(1) This section applies if–

(a) plant or machinery is a short-life asset on the basis that it has been provided for leasing but will be used within the designated period for a qualifying purpose (see item 5 of the Table in section 84),

(b) in a chargeable period ending on or before the relevant cut-off, the short-life asset begins to be used otherwise than for a qualifying purpose, and

(c) the time when it begins to be so used falls within the first 8 years of the designated period.

87(2) If this section applies–

CAA 2001

(a) the short-life asset pool ends without a final chargeable period,

(b) the available qualifying expenditure in the pool is allocated to the main pool for the chargeable period in which the asset begins to be used otherwise than for a qualifying purpose, and

(c) the asset ceases to be a short-life asset.

History – In s. 87(1)(b), the word "relevant" substituted for "four-year" by FA 2011, s. 12(4)(a), with effect from 19 July 2011.
In s. 87(1)(c), the words "8 years" substituted for "4 years" by FA 2011, s. 12(4)(b), with effect from 19 July 2011.

Origin – S. 87(1): CAA 1990, s. 37(6) (part), s. 40(4) (part).
S. 87(2): CAA 1990, s. 37(6) (part).

HMRC Manuals – CA23650: guidance.

88 Sales at under-value

88 If–

(a) a short-life asset is disposed of at less than market value,

(b) the disposal is not one in respect of which an election is made under section 89(6), and

(c) there is no charge to tax under ITEPA 2003,

the disposal value to be brought into account for the purposes of Chapter 5 is the market value of the asset.

History – In s. 88(c), the words "ITEPA 2003" substituted for the words "Schedule E" by ITEPA 2003, Sch. 6, para. 252 which has effect, for income tax purposes, for the tax year 2003–04 and subsequent tax years and, for corporation tax purposes, for accounting periods ending after 5 April 2003.

Origin – CAA 1990, s. 26(1)(b), s. 37(10).

Cross references – S. 60(1)(b), s. 66: general provisions about disposal values required to be brought into account ("disposal receipts").
RA 2005, Sch. 10. para. 2, 14 and 22: disregard of s. 88 in the case of a transfer to a national authority.

HMRC Manuals – CA23660: guidance.

89 Disposal to connected person

89(1) This section applies if, at any time before the relevant cut-off, a person (**"the transferor"**) disposes of a short-life asset to a connected person.

89(2) Subject to subsection (6)–

(a) the transferor is to be treated as having sold the short-life asset to the connected person for an amount equal to the available qualifying expenditure in the short-life asset pool for the chargeable period in which the disposal occurs, and

(b) the connected person is to be treated as having incurred qualifying expenditure of the same amount in buying the short-life asset.

89(3) Subject to subsection (6)–

(a) sections 217 and 218 (restrictions on first-year and other allowances in the case of certain transactions between connected persons, to obtain a tax advantage etc.), and

(b) section 225 (further restrictions in the case of sale and finance leaseback),

do not apply to the disposal.

89(4) Immediately after the disposal of the short-life asset, the connected person is to be taken to have made an election under section 83 (so that the plant or machinery is a short-life asset in his hands).

89(5) In relation to the connected person, **"the relevant cut-off"** means the date that would have been the relevant cut-off in relation to the transferor.

89(6) Subsections (2) and (3) apply in relation to a disposal only if–

(a) the transferor, and

(b) the connected person,

elect that they should apply.

89(7) An election under subsection (6) must be made by notice given to an officer of Revenue and Customs no later than 2 years after the end of the chargeable period in which the disposal occurred.

History – In s. 89(1), the word "relevant" substituted for "four-year" by FA 2011, s. 12(5), with effect from 19 July 2011.
In s. 89(3)(b), the word "section" substituted for "sections 222 to" by FA 2008, s. 55 and Sch. 20, para. 6(7), with effect in the case of plant or machinery which is the subject of a sale and finance leaseback (as defined in CAA 2001, s. 221) where the date of the transaction (within the meaning of that section) is on or after 9 October 2007.
In s. 89(5), the word "relevant" substituted for "four-year" (in each place) by FA 2011, s. 12(5), with effect from 19 July 2011.
In s. 89(7), the words "an officer of Revenue and Customs" substituted for "the Inland Revenue" by CRCA 2005, s. 50(6) and Sch. 4, para. 83(1), *with effect from 18 April 2005* by virtue of SI 2005/1126, art. 2(2).

Origin – S. 89(1)–(5): CAA 1990, s. 37(8).
S. 89(6), (7): CAA 1990, s. 37(9).

Cross references – S. 60(1)(b), s. 66: general provisions about disposal values required to be brought into account ("disposal receipts").

HMRC Manuals – CA23660: guidance.

Chapter 10 – Long-life Assets

Cross references – S. 84, Table, item 4: long-life asset expenditure is excluded from short-life asset treatment.

Transitional – Sch. 3, para. 20: expenditure incurred before 26 November 1996 or expenditure incurred before 1 January 2001 on contracts entered into before 26 November 1996 is excluded from long-life asset treatment. Also, treatment of plant and machinery allowances on long-life assets passed to a purchaser on or after 26 November 1996.

HMRC Manuals – CA23710: outline of long-life asset rules.
CA23780: industry wide agreements about which assets are or are not long-life.
CA 23781: agreement between HMRC and the British Air Transport Association on application of the long-life asset legislation to jet aircraft.
CA23782: aircraft not within agreement.
CA23785: greenhouses.
CA 23790: application of long-life asset legislation to modern printing equipment.

Other material – Tax Bulletin Article TB08/97-1: HMRC guidance on "how we interpret and plan to operate the rules for capital allowances on long-life assets".

LONG-LIFE ASSET EXPENDITURE

90 Long-life asset expenditure

90 **"Long-life asset expenditure"** means qualifying expenditure–

(a) incurred on the provision of a long-life asset for the purposes of a qualifying activity, and

(b) not excluded from being long-life asset expenditure by any of sections 93 to 100.

Origin – CAA 1990, s. 38A(1).

91 Meaning of "long-life asset"

91(1) For the purposes of this Chapter **"long-life asset"** means plant or machinery which–

(a) if new, can reasonably be expected to have a useful economic life of at least 25 years, and

(b) if not new, could reasonably have been expected when new to have a useful economic life of at least 25 years.

91(2) **"New"** means unused and not second-hand.

91(3) The useful economic life of plant or machinery is the period–

(a) beginning when it is first brought into use by any person for any purpose, and

(b) ending when it is no longer used or likely to be used by anyone for any purpose as a fixed asset of a business.

Origin – S. 91(1): CAA 1990, s. 38A(2).
S. 91(2): CAA 1990, s. 83(1) ("new").
S. 91(3): CAA 1990, s. 38A(3).

HMRC Manuals – CA23720: meaning of long-life asset.

Other material – Tax Bulletin Article TB08/97-1: capital allowances and long-life assets.

92 Application of Chapter to part of expenditure

92 [Omitted by FA 2008, s. 82 and Sch. 26, para. 8.]

History – S. 92 omitted by FA 2008, s. 82 and Sch. 26, para. 8, with effect in relation expenditure incurred on or after 1 April 2008 for corporation tax purposes and 6 April 2008 for income tax purposes and in relation to long-life asset expenditure (within the meaning of CAA 2001, Pt. 2, Ch. 10) incurred before those dates but allocated to a pool in a chargeable period beginning on or after those dates. This commencement provision is subject to FA 2008, s. 83 (existing long-life asset expenditure treated as special rate expenditure) and FA 2008, Sch. 26, para. 15–17 (detailed provisions relating to sales between connected persons and savings for intra-group transfers). Former s. 92 read as follows:

"*Application of Chapter to part of expenditure*

92(1) If, under any of the following provisions of this Chapter, this Chapter applies to part only of the capital expenditure on plant and machinery–

(a) the part to which this Chapter applies, and

(b) the part to which it does not,

are to be treated for the purposes of this Act as expenditure on separate items of plant or machinery.

92(2) For the purposes of subsection (1), all such apportionments are to be made as are just and reasonable."

Origin – S. 92(1): CAA 1990, s. 38A(4).
S. 92(2): CAA 1990, s. 38A(5).

Other material – Tax Bulletin Article TB08/97-1: capital allowances and long-life assets.

EXPENDITURE EXCLUDED FROM BEING LONG-LIFE ASSET EXPENDITURE

93 Fixtures etc.

93(1) Expenditure is not long-life asset expenditure if it is incurred on the provision of plant or machinery which is a fixture in, or is provided for use in, any building used wholly or mainly–

(a) as a dwelling-house, hotel, office, retail shop or showroom, or

(b) for purposes ancillary to the use referred to in paragraph (a).

93(2) In this section–

"fixture" has the meaning given by section 173(1);

"retail shop" includes any premises of a similar character where a retail trade or business, including repair work, is carried on.

Origin – S. 93(1): CAA 1990, s. 38B(1).
S. 93(2): CAA 1990, s. 38B(5) ("fixture", "retail shop").

HMRC Manuals – CA23730: guidance on exclusions.

94 Ships

94(1) Expenditure is not long-life asset expenditure if–

(a) it is incurred before 1st January 2011 on the provision of a ship of a sea-going kind, and

(b) each of the conditions in subsection (2) is met.

94(2) The conditions are that–

(a) the ship is not an offshore installation,

(b) [omitted by FA 2004, s. 146 and Sch. 27, para. 8 and repealed by FA 2004, s. 326 and Sch. 42, Pt. 2(19),]

(c) the primary use to which ships of the same kind are put by their owners (or, if their use is made available to others, those others) is a use otherwise than for sport or recreation.

94(3) [Omitted by FA 2004, s. 146 and Sch. 27, para. 8 and repealed by FA 2004, s. 326 and Sch. 42, Pt. 2(19).]

History – S. 94(2)(b) omitted by FA 2004, s. 146 and Sch. 27, para. 8 and repealed by FA 2004, s. 326 and Sch. 42, Pt. 2(19) which have effect, by virtue of FA 2004, Sch. 27, para. 11(1), as respects allowances and charges falling to be made for chargeable periods (as defined by CAA 2001, s. 6) ending on or after either 6 April 2004 (for income tax purposes) or 1 April 2004 (for corporation tax purposes).
S. 94(3) omitted by FA 2004, s. 146 and Sch. 27, para. 8 and repealed by FA 2004, s. 326 and Sch. 42, Pt. 2(19) which have effect, by virtue of FA 2004, Sch. 27, para. 11(1), as respects allowances and charges falling to be made for chargeable periods (as defined by CAA 2001, s. 6) ending on or after either 6 April 2004 (for income tax purposes) or 1 April 2004 (for corporation tax purposes).

Origin – S. 94(1) to (3): CAA 1990, s. 38B(3).

Cross references – S. 46(2): expenditure of the kind described in s. 94 is generally excluded from being expenditure qualifying for first-year allowances for small or medium-sized enterprises.

95 Railway assets

95(1) Expenditure is not long-life asset expenditure if it is incurred before 1st January 2011 on the provision of a railway asset used by any person wholly and exclusively for the purposes of a railway business.

95(2) **"Railway asset"** means–

(a) a locomotive, tram or other vehicle, or a carriage, wagon or other rolling stock designed or adapted for use on a railway;

(b) anything which is, or is to be, comprised in any railway station, railway track or light maintenance depot or any apparatus which is, or is to be, installed in association with such a station, track or depot.

95(3) **"Railway business"** means a business so far as carried on to provide a service to the public for carrying goods or passengers by means of a railway in the United Kingdom or the Channel Tunnel.

95(4) For the purposes of subsection (1), a railway asset of a kind described in subsection (2)(a) is not to be treated as used otherwise than wholly and exclusively for the purposes of a railway business merely because it is used to carry goods or passengers–

(a) from places inside the United Kingdom to places outside the United Kingdom, or

(b) from places outside the United Kingdom to places inside the United Kingdom.

95(5) In subsections (2) and (3), **"railway"** has the same meaning as in section 81(2) of the 1993 Act (**"railway"** includes tramways and other modes of guided transport).

95(6) In this section–

"the 1993 Act" means the Railways Act 1993;

"goods" has the same meaning as in Part I of the 1993 Act;

"railway station" and **"railway track"** include–

(a) anything included in the definitions of "station" and "track" in section 83 of the 1993 Act, and

(b) anything else that would be included if in section 83 "railway" had the meaning given in section 81(2) of the 1993 Act;

"light maintenance depot" means–

(a) any light maintenance depot within the meaning of Part I of the 1993 Act, and

(b) any land or other property which is the equivalent of such a depot in relation to anything which is a railway only when "railway" has the meaning given by section 81(2) of the 1993 Act.

Origin – S. 95(1): CAA 1990, s. 38B(4).
S. 95(2): CAA 1990, s. 38B(5) ("railway asset").
S. 95(3): CAA 1990, s. 38B(5) ("railway business").
S. 95(4): CAA 1990, s. 38B(6).
S. 95(5): CAA 1990, s. 38B(5) ("railway").
S. 95(6): CAA 1990, s. 38B(5) ("goods", "light maintenance depot", "railway station", and "railway track").

Cross references – S. 46(2): expenditure of the kind described in s. 95 is generally excluded from being expenditure qualifying for first-year allowances for small or medium-sized enterprises.
Railways Act 1993: the relevant provisions of the Railways Act 1993 read as follows:
"**81(2)** Where it is stated for the purposes of any provision of this Part that railway has its wider meaning, "railway" shall be taken, for the purposes of that provision, to mean:
(a) a railway
(b) a tramway; or
(c) a transport system which uses another mode of guided transport but which is not a trolley vehicle system, and cognate expressions shall be construed accordingly.

81(3) In paragraphs (a) to (c) of subsection (2) above "guided transport", "railway", "tramway" and "trolley vehicle system" have the meaning given by section 67(1) of the Transport and Works Act 1992.".
The Transport and Works Act 1992, s. 67(1) gives the following further definitions:
""**guided transport system**" means transport by vehicles guided by means external to the vehicles (whether or not the vehicles are also capable of being operated in some other way)
"**railway**" means a system of transport employing parallel rails which–
(a) provide support and guidance for vehicles carried on flanged wheels
(b) form a track which either is of a gauge of at least 350 millimetres or crosses a carriageway (whether or not on the same level).
"**tramway**" means a system of transport used wholly or mainly for the carriage of passengers and employing parallel rails which–
(a) provide support and guidance for vehicles carried on flanged wheels, and
(b) are laid wholly or mainly along a street or in any other place to which the public has access (including a place to which the public only has access on making a payment).
"**trolley vehicle system**" means a system of transport by vehicles constructed or adapted for use on roads without rails under electric power transmitted to them by overhead wires (whether or not there is in addition a source of power on board the vehicles).".
Other definitions given by s. 95(6) by reference to the Railways Act 1993 are as follows:
""**goods**" includes mail, parcels, animals, plants and any other creature, substance or thing capable of being transported, but does not include passengers;
"**light maintenance depot**" means any land or other property which is normally used for or in connection with the provision of light maintenance services, whether or not it is also used for other purposes;
"**station**" means any land or other property which consists of premises used as, or for the purposes of, or otherwise in connection with, a railway passenger station or railway passenger terminal (including any approaches, forecourt, cycle store or car park), whether or not the land or other property is, or the premises are, also used for other purposes;
"**track**" means any land or other property comprising the permanent way of any railway, taken together with the ballast, sleepers and metals laid thereon, whether or not the land or other property is also used for other purposes; and any reference to track includes a reference to–
(a) any level crossings, bridges, viaducts, tunnels, culverts, retaining walls, or other structures used or to be used for the support of, or otherwise in connection with, track; and
(b) any walls, fences or other structures bounding the railway or bounding an adjacent or adjoining property;".

96 Cars

96 Expenditure is not long-life asset expenditure if it is incurred on the provision of a car or motor cycle (as defined by section 268A).

History – In s. 96, the words "car or motor cycle (as defined by section 268A)" substituted for the words "car (as defined by section 81)" by FA 2009, s. 30 and Sch. 11, para. 21, with effect in relation to expenditure incurred on or after 1 April 2009 (for corporation tax purposes) and 6 April 2009 (for income tax purposes), subject to transitional provisions in FA 2009, Sch. 11, para. 27(2) and 30–32.

Origin – CAA 1990, s. 38B(2).

97 Expenditure within the relevant monetary limit: general

97 Expenditure is not long-life asset expenditure if it is–

(a) expenditure to which the monetary limits apply, and

(b) incurred in a chargeable period for which the relevant monetary limit is not exceeded.

Origin – S. 97: CAA 1990, s. 38C(1) (part), s. 38D(1) (part).

HMRC Manuals – CA23740: guidance on monetary limits.

98 Expenditure to which the monetary limits apply

98(1) The monetary limits apply to expenditure incurred by an individual for a chargeable period if–

(a) the expenditure was incurred by him for the purposes of a qualifying activity carried on by him,

(b) the whole of his time is substantially devoted in that period to the carrying on of that qualifying activity, and

(c) the expenditure is not within subsection (4).

98(2) The monetary limits apply to expenditure incurred by a partnership for a chargeable period if–

(a) all of the members of the partnership are individuals,

(b) the expenditure was incurred by the partnership for the purposes of a qualifying activity carried on by it,

(c) at all times throughout that period at least half the partners for the time being devote the whole or a substantial part of their time to the carrying on of that qualifying activity, and

(d) the expenditure is not within subsection (4).

98(3) The monetary limits apply for the purposes of corporation tax to any expenditure incurred by a company for a chargeable period other than expenditure within subsection (4).

98(4) Expenditure is within this subsection if it is–

(a) incurred on the provision of a share in plant or machinery,

(b) treated as a result of section 538 (contribution allowances: plant and machinery) as incurred on the provision of plant or machinery, or

(c) incurred on the provision of plant or machinery for leasing (whether or not the leasing is in the course of a trade).

Origin – S. 98(1): CAA 1990, s. 38C(1) (part), (2) (part), (3), Annex 1, Change 19.
S. 98(2): CAA 1990, s. 38C(1) (part), (2) (part), (4).
S. 98(3): CAA 1990, s. 38D(1) (part), (2) (part).
S. 98(4): CAA 1990, s. 38C(5) (part), s. 38D(7) (part).

Rewrite: Changes in Law – Explanatory Notes, Annex 1, Change 19: "qualifying activity" in s. 98(1) and (2) is wider than "trade or profession" in former CAA 1990, s. 38C(3)(a) and (4)(a) because "qualifying activity" brings in employees, office holders, those carrying on vocations and s. 55 concerns, whereas "trade or profession" does not. However, "trade or profession" does already include the management of an investment company, carrying on a property business and special leasing of plant or machinery.

HMRC Manuals – CA23740: guidance on monetary limits.

99 The monetary limit

99(1) The monetary limit in the case of a chargeable period of 12 months is £100,000.

99(2) If, in the case of an individual or partnership, the chargeable period is longer or shorter than 12 months, the monetary limit is the amount given by a proportional increase or reduction of £100,000.

99(3) If, in the case of a company, the chargeable period is shorter than 12 months, the monetary limit is the amount given by a proportional reduction of £100,000.

99(4) In the case of a company ("C"), if, in a chargeable period, one or more companies are related 51% group companies of C, the monetary limit for that period is–

$$\frac{L}{N + 1}$$

where–

L is the monetary limit applicable under subsection (1) or (3), and

N is the number of related 51% group companies.

99(5) [Omitted by FA 2014, s. 7 and Sch. 1, para. 8(b).]

History – In s. 99(4), the words "In the case of a company ("C"), if, in a chargeable period, one or more companies are related 51% group companies of C" substituted for the words "If, in a chargeable period, a company has one or more associated companies" by FA 2014, s. 7 and Sch. 1, para. 8(a)(i), with effect in relation to accounting periods beginning on or after 1 April 2015.
In s. 99(4), the words "number of related 51% group" substituted for the words "number of associated" by FA 2014, s. 7 and Sch. 1, para. 8(a)(ii), with effect in relation to accounting periods beginning on or after 1 April 2015.
S. 99(5) omitted by FA 2014, s. 7 and Sch. 1, para. 8(b), with effect in relation to accounting periods beginning on or after 1 April 2015.
Former s. 99(5) read as follows:
"**99(5)** Sections 25 to 30 of CTA 2010 (interpretation of references to associated companies) apply for the purposes of subsection (4)."
Former s. 99(5) substituted by CTA 2010, s. 1177 and Sch. 1, para. 332, with effect for corporation tax purposes for accounting periods ending on or after 1 April 2010, and for income tax and capital gains tax purposes for the tax year 2010–11 and subsequent tax years.

Origin – S. 99(1): CAA 1990, s. 38C(6), s. 38D(3).
S. 99(2): CAA 1990, s. 38C(7).
S. 99(3): CAA 1990, s. 38D(4).
S. 99(4): CAA 1990, s. 38D(5).
Former s. 99(5): CAA 1990, s. 38D(6).

Cross references – FA 1993, s. 93A(6)(b): application of s. 99(1), (2) and (3) in calculating profits or losses where company uses currency other than sterling.

HMRC Manuals – CA23740: guidance on monetary limits.

100 Exceeding the monetary limit

100(1) The monetary limit for a chargeable period is exceeded if the total expenditure in that period that meets the conditions in subsection (2) exceeds that limit.

100(2) The conditions are that the expenditure–

(a) is long-life asset expenditure, or would be long-life asset expenditure in the absence of section 97 (expenditure within monetary limit), and

(b) is expenditure to which the monetary limits apply.

100(3) Subsection (4) applies if, in the case of any contract for the provision of plant or machinery, the capital expenditure which is (or is to be) incurred under the contract is (or may fall to be) treated for the purposes of this Act as incurred in different chargeable periods.

100(4) All of the expenditure falling to be incurred under the contract on the provision of the plant or machinery is to be treated for the purposes of this section as incurred in the first chargeable period in which any of the expenditure is incurred.

Origin – S. 100(1), (2): CAA 1990, s. 38C(1) (part), (2) (part), s. 38D(1) (part), (2) (part).
S. 100(3), (4): CAA 1990, s. 38C(8), s. 38D(7) (part).

HMRC Manuals – CA23740: guidance on monetary limits.

RULES APPLYING TO LONG-LIFE ASSET EXPENDITURE

101 Allocation of long-life asset expenditure to pool

101 Chapter 10A (special rate expenditure and the special rate pool) provides for long-life asset expenditure to be allocated to the special rate pool.

History – S. 101 substituted by FA 2008, s. 82 and Sch. 26, para. 9, with effect in relation expenditure incurred on or after 1 April 2008 for corporation tax purposes and 6 April 2008 for income tax purposes and in relation to long-life asset expenditure (within the meaning of CAA 2001, Pt. 2, Ch. 10) incurred before those dates but allocated to a pool in a chargeable period beginning on or after those dates. This commencement provision is subject to FA 2008, s. 83 (existing long-life asset expenditure treated as special rate expenditure) and FA 2008, Sch. 26, para. 15–17 (detailed provisions relating to sales between connected persons and savings for intra-group transfers). Former s. 101 read as follows:

"*Long-life asset pool*

101(1) Long-life asset expenditure to which this section applies, if allocated to a pool, must be allocated to a class pool (**"the long-life asset pool"**).

101(2) This section applies to long-life asset expenditure if–
(a) it is incurred on the provision of long-life assets wholly and exclusively for the purposes of a qualifying activity, and
(b) it is not expenditure which is required to be allocated to a single asset pool."

Origin – S. 101(1): CAA 1990, s. 38E(2) (part), (5).
S. 101(2): CAA 1990, s. 38E(1) (part), (6), Annex 2, Note 22.

Rewrite: Technical Points – Explanatory Notes, Annex 2, Note 22: assets which are leased abroad are placed in a separate pool and are subject to a reduced rate of writing down allowance. Moreover, the reduced rate of allowance applies to assets which, besides being leased abroad, are also assets which are leased *other than* in the course of a trade or other qualifying activity (now known as "special leasing" in accordance with s. 15(1), (3) and 19). The previous legislation effectively excluded special leasing assets from the overseas leasing pool because a separate deemed trade was established (CAA 1990, s. 61(1)). Accordingly the reduced rate for overseas leasing had to be re-applied independently to any expenditure on special leasing assets outside the overseas leasing pool (CAA 1990, s. 42(2)(e)). The rewritten legislation is considered to achieve the same result but by a more straightforward approach. Instead, all expenditure on assets leased abroad in the course of a qualifying activity, including special leasing, comes within the overseas leasing pool. The reduced rate of allowance in s. 109 is applied to the pool, automatically including any special leased assets within the pool.

102 Writing-down allowance in respect of long-life asset expenditure

102 Chapter 10A (special rate expenditure and the special rate pool) provides for the writing-down allowance to which a person is entitled in respect of long-life asset expenditure.

History – S. 102 substituted by FA 2008, s. 82 and Sch. 26, para. 10, with effect in relation expenditure incurred on or after 1 April 2008 for corporation tax purposes and 6 April 2008 for income tax purposes and in relation to long-life asset expenditure (within the meaning of CAA 2001, Pt. 2, Ch. 10) incurred before those dates but allocated to a pool in a chargeable period beginning on or after those dates. This commencement provision is subject to FA 2008, s. 83 (existing long-life asset expenditure treated as special rate expenditure) and FA 2008, Sch. 26, para. 15–17 (detailed provisions relating to sales between connected persons and savings for intra-group transfers). Former s. 102 read as follows:

"*Writing-down allowances at 6%*

102(1) The amount of the writing-down allowance to which a person is entitled for a chargeable period in respect of expenditure which is long-life asset expenditure is 6% of the amount by which AQE exceeds TDR (see Chapter 5).

102(2) Subsection (1) applies even if the long-life asset expenditure is in a single asset pool.

102(3) In the case of expenditure which is within section 107(2)(a) and (b) (overseas leasing which is not protected leasing), this section is subject to sections 110, 114 and 115 (allowances prohibited in certain cases etc.).

102(4) Subsections (3) and (4) of section 56 (proportionate increases or reductions in amount in certain cases) apply for the purposes of subsection (1) of this section as they apply for the purposes of subsection (1) of that section."

Origin – S. 102(1): CAA 1990, s. 38F(1).
S. 102(2): CAA 1990, s. 38F(2), Annex 2, Notes 22, 23.
S. 102(3): CAA 1990, s. 38F(6).
S. 102(4): CAA 1990, s. 24(2)(a)(ii), s. 38F(1).

Rewrite: Technical Points – Explanatory Notes, Annex 2, Note 22: the 6 per cent reduced rate of allowance applies to assets which, besides being long-life assets, are also assets which are leased *other than* in the course of a trade or other qualifying activity ("special leasing"). The previous legislation effectively excluded special leasing assets from the long-life asset pool because a separate deemed trade was established (CAA 1990, s. 61(1)). Accordingly the reduced rate for long-life assets had to be re-applied independently to any expenditure on special leasing assets outside the long-life assets pool (CAA 1990, s. 38F(1)(b)). The rewritten legislation is considered to achieve the same result but by a more straightforward approach. Instead, all expenditure on long-life assets in the course of a qualifying activity, including special leasing, comes within the long-life assets pool. The reduced 6 per cent rate of allowance is applied to the pool, automatically including any special leased assets within the pool.
Explanatory Notes, Annex 2, Note 23: s. 102(2) provides that the 6 per cent rate of writing-down allowances applies to long-life assets expenditure even if the expenditure is in a single asset pool. By contrast, CAA 1990, s. 38F(2) did not mention the provisions relating to contributions. But the better view is that the notional separate trade for contributions provided for by CAA 1990, s. 155(6) can be

the trade for the purposes of s. 38E(1) and (2), so as to create a pool for long-life asset expenditure. This is reinforced by the fact that CAA 1990, s. 38E(6) did not mention s. 155(6), the implication being that s. 155(6) could generate a s. 38E pool.

ANTI-AVOIDANCE PROVISIONS

103 Later claims

103(1) Subsection (2) applies if–

(a) a person entitled to do so has made a Part 2 claim in respect of expenditure incurred on the provision of plant or machinery, and

(b) the expenditure fell to be treated as long-life asset expenditure for the purposes of the claim.

103(2) If–

(a) at any time after making the Part 2 claim, that claimant or another person makes a Part 2 claim in respect of any qualifying expenditure incurred at any time (including a time before the incurring of the expenditure to which the earlier claim relates) on the provision of the same plant or machinery, and

(b) the expenditure to which the later claim relates–

(i) would not (but for this subsection) be treated for the purposes of the later claim as long-life asset expenditure, and

(ii) is not prevented from being long-life asset expenditure by any of sections 93 to 96,

this Part has effect in relation to the later claim as if the expenditure to which it relates were long-life asset expenditure.

103(3) A person makes a Part 2 claim in respect of any expenditure if he–

(a) makes a tax return in which the expenditure is taken into account in determining his available qualifying expenditure for the purposes of this Part;

(b) gives notice of an amendment of a tax return which provides for the expenditure to be so taken into account;

(c) makes a claim in any other way for the expenditure to be so taken into account.

Origin – S. 103(1), (2): CAA 1990, s. 38F(3).
S. 103(3): CAA 1990, s. 38F(4).

HMRC Manuals – CA23750: guidance and example on s. 103.

104 Disposal value of long-life assets

104 [Omitted by FA 2008, s. 82 and Sch. 26, para. 11.]

History – S. 104 omitted by FA 2008, s. 82 and Sch. 26, para. 11, with effect in relation expenditure incurred on or after 1 April 2008 for corporation tax purposes and 6 April 2008 for income tax purposes and in relation to long-life asset expenditure (within the meaning of CAA 2001, Pt. 2, Ch. 10) incurred before those dates but allocated to a pool in a chargeable period beginning on or after those dates. This commencement provision is subject to FA 2008, s. 83 (existing long-life asset expenditure treated as special rate expenditure) and FA 2008, Sch. 26, para. 15–17 (detailed provisions relating to sales between connected persons and savings for intra-group transfers). Former s. 104 read as follows:

"*Disposal value of long-life assets*

104(1) This section applies if–

(a) section 102 (writing-down allowances at 6%) has had effect in relation to any long-life asset expenditure incurred by a person (**"the taxpayer"**),

(b) any disposal event occurs in relation to the long-life asset,

(c) the disposal value to be brought into account by the taxpayer would (but for this section) be less than the notional written-down value of the long-life asset, and

(d) the disposal event is part of, or occurs as a result of, a scheme or arrangement the main purpose or one of the main purposes of which is the obtaining by the taxpayer of a tax advantage under this Part.

104(2) The disposal value that the taxpayer must bring into account is the notional written-down value of the long-life asset.

104(3) The notional written-down value is–

$$QE - A$$

where–

QE is the taxpayer's expenditure on the plant or machinery that is qualifying expenditure, and

A is the total of all allowances which could have been made to the taxpayer in respect of that expenditure if–

(a) that expenditure had been the only expenditure that had ever been taken into account in determining his available qualifying expenditure,

(b) that expenditure had not been prevented by the application of a monetary limit from being long-life asset expenditure, and

(c) all allowances had been made in full."

Origin – S. 104(1), (2): CAA 1990, s. 38G(1).
S. 104(3): CAA 1990, s. 38G(2), (3), Annex 2, Note 24.

Chapter 10A – Special Rate Expenditure

History – Chapter 10A inserted by FA 2008, s. 82 and Sch. 26, para. 2, with effect in relation expenditure incurred on or after 1 April 2008 for corporation tax purposes and 6 April 2008 for income tax purposes and in relation to long-life asset expenditure (within the meaning of CAA 2001, Pt. 2, Ch. 10) incurred before those dates but allocated to a pool in a chargeable period beginning on or after those dates. This commencement provision is subject to FA 2008, s. 83 (existing long-life asset expenditure treated as special rate expenditure) and FA 2008, Sch. 26, para. 15–17 (detailed provisions relating to sales between connected persons and savings for intra-group transfers).

SPECIAL RATE EXPENDITURE

104A Special rate expenditure

104A(1) **"Special rate expenditure"** means–

(a) expenditure incurred on or after the first relevant date to which section 28 (thermal insulation) applies,

(b) expenditure incurred on or after that date to which section 33A (integral features) applies,

(c) long-life asset expenditure (within the meaning of Chapter 10) incurred on or after that date,

(d) long-life asset expenditure (within the meaning of that Chapter) incurred before that date but allocated to a pool in a chargeable period beginning on or after that date,

(e) expenditure incurred on or after the second relevant date on the provision of a car that is not a main rate car,

(f) expenditure incurred on or after 1 April 2010 on the provision of cushion gas (within the meaning given by section 70J(7)), and

(g) expenditure incurred on or after the third relevant date on the provision of solar panels.

104A(2) The first relevant date is–

(a) for corporation tax purposes, 1 April 2008, and

(b) for income tax purposes, 6 April 2008.

104A(3) The second relevant date is–

(a) for corporation tax purposes, 1 April 2009, and

(b) for income tax purposes, 6 April 2009.

104A(3A) The third relevant date is–

(a) for corporation tax purposes, 1 April 2012, and

(b) for income tax purposes, 6 April 2012.

104A(4) In this section–

"car" has the meaning given in section 268A;

"main rate car" has the meaning given in section 104AA.

History – In s. 104A(1)(a), the word "first" inserted by FA 2009, s. 30 and Sch. 11, para. 7(2)(a), with effect in relation to expenditure incurred on or after 1 April 2009 (for corporation tax purposes) and 6 April 2009 (for income tax purposes), subject to transitional provisions in FA 2009, Sch. 11, para. 27(2) and 30–32.

In s. 104A(1)(c), the word "and" omitted by FA 2009, s. 30 and Sch. 11, para. 7(2)(b), with effect in relation to expenditure incurred on or after 1 April 2009 (for corporation tax purposes) and 6 April 2009 (for income tax purposes), subject to transitional provisions in FA 2009, Sch. 11, para. 27(2) and 30–32.

S. 104A(1)(e) and the word "and" before it inserted by FA 2009, s. 30 and Sch. 11, para. 7(2)(c), with effect in relation to expenditure incurred on or after 1 April 2009 (for corporation tax purposes) and 6 April 2009 (for income tax purposes), subject to transitional provisions in FA 2009, Sch. 11, para. 27(2) and 30–32.

S. 104A(1)(f) inserted (and the "and" at the end of s. 104A(1)(d) omitted and the "and" at the end of s. 104A(1)(e) inserted) by FA 2010, s. 28(6), with effect in relation to expenditure incurred on or after 1 April 2010.

S. 104A(1)(g) inserted (and the "and" at the end of s. 104A(1)(e) omitted and the "and" at the end of s 104A(1)(f) inserted) by FA 2012, s. 45(4)(a), with effect from 17 July 2012.

In s. 104A(2), the word "first" inserted by FA 2009, s. 30 and Sch. 11, para. 7(3), with effect in relation to expenditure incurred on or after 1 April 2009 (for corporation tax purposes) and 6 April 2009 (for income tax purposes), subject to transitional provisions in FA 2009, Sch. 11, para. 27(2) and 30–32.

S. 104A(3) inserted by FA 2009, s. 30 and Sch. 11, para. 7(4), with effect in relation to expenditure incurred on or after 1 April 2009 (for corporation tax purposes) and 6 April 2009 (for income tax purposes), subject to transitional provisions in FA 2009, Sch. 11, para. 27(2) and 30–32.

S. 104A(3A) inserted by FA 2012, s. 45(4)(b), with effect from 17 July 2012.

S. 104A(4) inserted by FA 2009, s. 30 and Sch. 11, para.7(4), with effect in relation to expenditure incurred on or after 1 April 2009 (for corporation tax purposes) and 6 April 2009 (for income tax purposes), subject to transitional provisions in FA 2009, Sch. 11, para. 27(2) and 30–32.

S. 104A inserted by FA 2008, s. 82 and Sch. 26, para. 2, with effect in relation expenditure incurred on or after 1 April 2008 for corporation tax purposes and 6 April 2008 for income tax purposes and in relation to long-life asset expenditure (within the meaning of CAA 2001, Pt. 2, Ch. 10) incurred before those dates but allocated to a pool in a chargeable period beginning on or after those dates. This commencement provision is subject to FA 2008, s. 83 (existing long-life asset expenditure treated as special rate expenditure) and FA 2008, Sch. 26, para. 15–17 (detailed provisions relating to sales between connected persons and savings for intra-group transfers).

104AA Meaning of "main rate car"

104AA(1) **"Main rate car"** means–

(a) a car that is first registered before 1 March 2001,

(b) a car that has low CO_2 emissions, or

(c) a car that is electrically-propelled.

104AA(2) For the purposes of this section a car has low CO_2 emissions if it meets conditions A and B.

104AA(3) Condition A is that, when the car is first registered, it is so registered on the basis of a qualifying emissions certificate.

104AA(4) Condition B is that the applicable CO_2 emissions figure in relation to the car does not exceed 130 grams per kilometre driven.

104AA(5) The Treasury may by order amend the amount from time to time specified in subsection (4).

104AA(6) An order under subsection (5) may contain transitional provision and savings.

104AA(7) In this section–

"applicable CO_2 emissions figure" and **"qualifying emissions certificate"** have the meanings given in section 268C;

"car" has the meaning given in section 268A;

"electrically-propelled" has the meaning given in section 268B.

Prospective amendments – In s. 104AA(4), "110" substituted for "130" by SI 2016/984, art. 5, with effect in relation to expenditure incurred on or after 1 April 2018.

History – In s. 104AA(4), "130" substituted for "160", by FA 2013, s. 68(3), with effect in relation to expenditure incurred on or after 6 April 2013 in the case of income tax and 1 April 2013 in the case of corporation tax, subject to savings in FA 2013, s. 68(7) in relation to the application of ITTOIA 2005, s. 49(1A) and CTA 2009, s. 57(1A) in relation to expenditure incurred on the hiring of a car for a period of hire beginning before 1 or 6 April 2013 (as applicable) under a contract entered into before that date.
S. 104AA inserted by FA 2009, s. 30 and Sch. 11, para. 8, with effect in relation to expenditure incurred on or after 1 April 2009 (for corporation tax purposes) and 6 April 2009 (for income tax purposes), subject to transitional provisions in FA 2009, Sch. 11, para. 27(2) and 30–32.

104B Application of Chapter to part of expenditure

104B(1) If part only of the capital expenditure on plant and machinery is special rate expenditure–

(a) the part which is such expenditure, and

(b) the part which is not,

are to be treated for the purposes of this Act as expenditure on separate items of plant or machinery.

104B(2) For the purposes of subsection (1), all such apportionments are to be made as are just and reasonable.

History – S. 104B inserted by FA 2008, s. 82 and Sch. 26, para. 2, with effect in relation expenditure incurred on or after 1 April 2008 for corporation tax purposes and 6 April 2008 for income tax purposes and in relation to long-life asset expenditure (within the meaning of CAA 2001, Pt. 2, Ch. 10) incurred before those dates but allocated to a pool in a chargeable period beginning on or after those dates. This commencement provision is subject to FA 2008, s. 83 (existing long-life asset expenditure treated as special rate expenditure) and FA 2008, Sch. 26, para. 15–17 (detailed provisions relating to sales between connected persons and savings for intra-group transfers).

RULES APPLYING TO SPECIAL RATE EXPENDITURE

104C Special rate pool

104C(1) Special rate expenditure to which this section applies, if allocated to a pool, must be allocated to a class pool ("the special rate pool").

104C(2) This section applies to special rate expenditure if–

(a) it is incurred wholly and exclusively for the purposes of a qualifying activity, and

(b) it is not expenditure which is required to be allocated to a single asset pool.

History – S. 104C inserted by FA 2008, s. 82 and Sch. 26, para. 2, with effect in relation expenditure incurred on or after 1 April 2008 for corporation tax purposes and 6 April 2008 for income tax purposes and in relation to long-life asset expenditure (within the meaning of CAA 2001, Pt. 2, Ch. 10) incurred before those dates but allocated to a pool in a chargeable period beginning on or after those dates. This commencement provision is subject to FA 2008, s. 83 (existing long-life asset expenditure treated as special rate expenditure) and FA 2008, Sch. 26, para. 15–17 (detailed provisions relating to sales between connected persons and savings for intra-group transfers).

104D Writing-down allowances at 8% or 10%

104D(1) The amount of the writing-down allowance to which a person is entitled for a chargeable period in respect of expenditure which is special rate expenditure is 8% of the amount by which AQE exceeds TDR (see Chapter 5).

104D(1A) But, in relation to special rate expenditure incurred wholly for the purposes of a ring fence trade in respect of which tax is chargeable under section 330(1) of CTA 2010 (supplementary charge in respect of ring fence trades), the amount of the writing-down allowance to which a person is entitled for a chargeable period is 10% of the amount by which AQE exceeds TDR.

104D(2) Subsection (1) applies even if the special rate expenditure is in a single asset pool.

104D(3) In the case of expenditure in the special rate pool, this section is subject to section 56A (writing-down allowance for small pools).

104D(4) Subsections (3) and (4) of section 56 (proportionate increases or reductions in amount in certain cases) apply for the purposes of subsection (1) of this section as they apply for the purposes of subsection (1) of that section.

History – In the heading for section 104D, the words "8% or" inserted after "at" by FA 2011, s. 10(4)(a), with effect in relation to chargeable periods beginning on or after 1 April 2012 (for corporation tax purposes) and 6 April 2012 (for income tax purposes), and in relation to chargeable periods straddling those dates, subject to transitional provisions in FA 2011, s. 10(9)–(12).
In s. 104D(1), the word "8%" substituted for "10%" by FA 2011, s. 10(3)(a), with effect in relation to chargeable periods beginning on or after 1 April 2012 (for corporation tax purposes) and 6 April 2012 (for income tax purposes), and in relation to chargeable periods straddling those dates, subject to transitional provisions in FA 2011, s. 10(9)–(12).
S. 104D(1A) inserted by FA 2011, s. 10(3)(b), with effect in relation to chargeable periods beginning on or after 1 April 2012 (for corporation tax purposes) and 6 April 2012 (for income tax purposes) and in relation to chargeable periods straddling those dates, subject to transitional provisions in FA 2011, s. 10(9)–(12).
S. 104D inserted by FA 2008, s. 82 and Sch. 26, para. 2, with effect in relation expenditure incurred on or after 1 April 2008 for corporation tax purposes and 6 April 2008 for income tax purposes and in relation to long-life asset expenditure (within the meaning of CAA 2001, Pt. 2, Ch. 10) incurred before those dates but allocated to a pool in a chargeable period beginning on or after those dates. This commencement provision is subject to FA 2008, s. 83 (existing long-life asset expenditure treated as special rate expenditure) and FA 2008, Sch. 26, para. 15–17 (detailed provisions relating to sales between connected persons and savings for intra-group transfers).

104E Disposal value of special rate assets

104E(1) This section applies if–

(a) section 104D (writing-down allowances at 8% or 10%) has had effect in relation to any special rate expenditure incurred by a person ("the taxpayer"),

(b) any disposal event occurs in relation to the item on which the expenditure was incurred,

(c) the disposal value to be brought into account by the taxpayer would (but for this section) be less than the notional written-down value of the item, and

(d) the disposal event is part of, or occurs as a result of, a scheme or arrangement the main purpose or one of the main purposes of which is the obtaining by the taxpayer of a tax advantage under this Part.

104E(2) The disposal value that the taxpayer must bring into account is the notional written-down value of the item.

104E(3) The notional written-down value is–

$$QE - A$$

where–

QE is the taxpayer's expenditure on the item that is qualifying expenditure, and

A is the total of all allowances which could have been made to the taxpayer in respect of that expenditure if–

(a) that expenditure had been the only expenditure that had ever been taken into account in determining the taxpayer's available qualifying expenditure,

(b) where the item is a long-life asset, that expenditure had not been prevented by the application of a monetary limit from being long-life asset expenditure, and

(c) all allowances had been made in full.

History – In s. 104E(1)(a), the words "8% or" inserted before "10%" by FA 2011, s. 10(4)(b), with effect in relation to chargeable periods beginning on or after 1 April 2012 for corporation tax purposes and 6 April 2012 for income tax purposes and in relation to chargeable periods straddling those dates.
S. 104E inserted by FA 2008, s. 82 and Sch. 26, para. 2, with effect in relation expenditure incurred on or after 1 April 2008 for corporation tax purposes and 6 April 2008 for income tax purposes and in relation to long-life asset expenditure (within the meaning of CAA 2001, Pt. 2, Ch. 10) incurred before those dates but allocated to a pool in a chargeable period beginning on or after those dates. This commencement provision is subject to FA 2008, s. 83 (existing long-life asset expenditure treated as special rate expenditure) and FA 2008, Sch. 26, para. 15–17 (detailed provisions relating to sales between connected persons and savings for intra-group transfers).

104F Special rate cars: discontinued activity continued by relevant company

104F(1) This section applies if–

(a) a company ("the taxpayer") has incurred special rate expenditure within section 104A(1)(e) (expenditure on a car other than a main rate car) to which section 104C applies (allocation to special rate pool),

(b) the qualifying activity carried on by the taxpayer is permanently discontinued, and

(c) conditions A, B and C are met.

104F(2) Condition A is that the qualifying activity carried on by the taxpayer consisted of or included (other than incidentally) making cars available to other persons.

104F(3) Condition B is that, at any time in the 6 months after the taxpayer's qualifying activity is permanently discontinued, the qualifying activity of a group relief company consists of or includes (other than incidentally) making cars available to other persons.

104F(4) Condition C is that the balancing allowance ("SBA") to which the taxpayer would be entitled (but for this section) in respect of the special rate pool is greater than–

$$BC - OBA$$

where–

BC is the total of the balancing charges (if any) to which the taxpayer is liable for the final chargeable period in respect of any pool, and

OBA is the total of the balancing allowances to which the taxpayer is entitled for that period in respect of any pool other than the special rate pool.

For the purposes of this section, if BC – OBA is a negative amount, it is to be treated as if it were nil.

104F(5) The balancing allowance to which the taxpayer is entitled in respect of the special rate pool is reduced to an amount equal to BC – OBA.

104F(6) The relevant company is to be treated as having incurred qualifying expenditure within section 104A(1)(e) ("notional expenditure"), whether or not the relevant company owns cars previously owned by the taxpayer.

104F(7) The amount of the notional expenditure is an amount equal to the amount by which SBA exceeds BC – OBA.

104F(8) The relevant company is to be treated as having incurred the notional expenditure on the day after the end of the taxpayer's final chargeable period.

104F(9) If part of the chargeable period in which the relevant company is treated as incurring expenditure under this section ("the acquisition period") overlaps with the taxpayer's penultimate chargeable period–

(a) the part of the expenditure which is proportional to that part of the acquisition period is not to be taken into account in determining the relevant company's available qualifying expenditure for the acquisition period, but

(b) this does not prevent that part of the expenditure being taken into account in determining the relevant company's available qualifying expenditure for any subsequent chargeable period.

104F(10) In this section–

"car" has the meaning given in section 268A;

"company" means any body corporate;

"group relief company" means–

(a) a company to which group relief under Part 5 of CTA 2010 would be available (on the making of a claim) in respect of balancing allowances surrendered by the taxpayer in the taxpayer's final chargeable period, and

(b) a company to which such relief would be available (on the making of a claim) in respect of balancing allowances surrendered by a company within paragraph (a);

"main rate car" has the meaning given in section 104AA;

"penultimate chargeable period" means the chargeable period preceding the final chargeable period;

"the relevant company" means the group relief company mentioned in subsection (3) or, if there is more than one, the one–

(a) nominated by the taxpayer not more than 6 months after the end of the taxpayer's final chargeable period, or

(b) in the absence of such a nomination, nominated by Her Majesty's Revenue and Customs.

History – In s. 104F(10), in para. (a) of the definition of "group relief company", the words "Part 5 of CTA 2010" substituted for "Chapter 4 of Part 10 of ICTA" by CTA 2010, s. 1177 and Sch. 1, para. 333, with effect for corporation tax purposes for accounting periods ending on or after 1 April 2010, and for income tax and capital gains tax purposes for the tax year 2010–11 and subsequent tax years.

S. 104F inserted by FA 2009, s. 30 and Sch. 11, para. 9, with effect in relation to expenditure incurred on or after 1 April 2009 (for corporation tax purposes) and 6 April 2009 (for income tax purposes), subject to transitional provisions in FA 2009, Sch. 11, para. 27(2) and 30–32.

104G Disposal events in respect of cushion gas

104G(1) This section applies if expenditure incurred by a person on the provision of cushion gas used in a particular gas storage facility includes both new expenditure and old expenditure.

104G(2) Any disposal event which concerns any of that cushion gas is to be treated for the purposes of this Part as relating to cushion gas which is the subject of the new expenditure before cushion gas which is the subject of the old expenditure.

104G(3) The result of subsection (2) (including any further application of that subsection) is that a disposal event may be treated as relating–

(a) only to cushion gas which is the subject of the new expenditure,

(b) both to–

 (i) cushion gas which is the subject of the new expenditure, and

 (ii) cushion gas which is the subject of the old expenditure, or

(c) only to cushion gas which is the subject of the old expenditure.

104G(4) If a disposal event is treated, as a result of subsection (2), as relating both to–

(a) cushion gas which is the subject of the new expenditure, and

(b) cushion gas which is the subject of the old expenditure,

it is to be treated for the purposes of this Part as two separate disposal events, the first relating to cushion gas within paragraph (a) and the second relating to cushion gas within paragraph (b).

104G(5) In this section–

"cushion gas" has the meaning given by section 70J(7),

"new expenditure" means expenditure incurred on or after 1 April 2010, and

"old expenditure" means expenditure incurred before that date.

History – S. 104G inserted by FA 2010, s. 28(7), with effect in relation to disposal events on or after 1 April 2010.

CAA 2001

Chapter 11 – Overseas Leasing

BASIC TERMS

105 "Leasing", "overseas leasing" etc.

105(1) In this Chapter–

(a) **"leasing"** includes letting a ship or aircraft on charter or letting any other asset on hire, and

(b) references to a lease include a sub-lease (and references to a lessor or lessee are to be read accordingly).

105(2) Plant or machinery is used for overseas leasing if it is used for the purpose of being leased to a person who–

(a) is not resident in the United Kingdom, and

(b) does not use the plant or machinery exclusively for earning profits chargeable to tax.

105(2A) In determining whether plant or machinery is used for overseas leasing, no account shall be taken of any lease finalised, within the meaning of Part 4 of Schedule 8 to FA 2006, on or after 1st April 2006.

105(3) In this Chapter **"profits chargeable to tax"**–

(a) includes profits chargeable under section 1313(2) of CTA 2009 (profits from exploration and exploitation of the seabed etc.), but

(b) excludes profits arising to a person who, under double taxation arrangements, is afforded or is entitled to claim any relief from the tax chargeable on those profits.

105(4) **"Double taxation arrangements"** means arrangements which have effect under section 2(1) of the Taxation (International and Other Provisions) Act 2010 (double taxation relief by agreement with territories outside the United Kingdom).

105(5) **"Protected leasing"** of plant or machinery means–

(a) short-term leasing of the plant or machinery (as defined in section 121), or

(b) if the plant or machinery is a ship, aircraft or transport container, the use of the ship, aircraft or transport container for a qualifying purpose under section 123 or 124 (letting on charter to UK resident etc.).

105(6) In this Chapter **"qualifying activity"** includes (subject to any provision to the contrary) any activity listed in section 15(1) even if any profits or gains from it are not chargeable to tax.

History – In s. 105(2A), "FA" substituted for "the Finance Act" by FA 2009, s. 126(5)(a), with effect from 21 July 2009.
S. 105(2A) inserted by FA 2006, s. 81 and Sch. 9, para. 13(2), with effect from 19 July 2006.
In s. 105(3)(a), the words "section 1313(2) of CTA 2009" substituted for the words "section 830(4) of ICTA" by CTA 2009, s. 1322 and Sch. 1, para. 483, with effect for corporation tax purposes for accounting periods ending on or after 1 April 2009, and for income tax and capital gains tax purposes for the tax year 2009–10 and subsequent tax years.
In s. 105(4), the words "which have effect under section 2(1) of the Taxation (International and Other Provisions) Act 2010 (double taxation relief by agreement with territories outside the United Kingdom)" substituted for "specified in an Order in Council making any such provisions as are referred to in section 788 of ICTA" by TIOPA 2010, s. 374 and Sch. 8, para. 58, with effect for corporation tax purposes for accounting periods ending on or after 1 April 2010, for income tax and capital gains tax purposes for the tax year 2010–11 and subsequent tax years, and for petroleum revenue tax purposes for chargeable periods beginning on or after 1 July 2010.
Origin – S. 105(1): CAA 1990, s. 50(1), (2).
S. 105(2): CAA 1990, s. 42(1) (part).
S. 105(3): CAA 1990, s. 42(1) (part), 50(3A) (part).
S. 105(4): CAA 1990, s. 42(1) (part), 50(3A) (part).
S. 105(5): CAA 1990, s. 50(3) ("permitted leasing").
S. 105(6): CAA 1990, s. 83(2A) (part).
Cross references – S. 15: qualifying activities.
S. 19: special leasing of plant or machinery let otherwise than in the course of a trade.
S. 37: sums payable in respect of depreciation.
S. 46(2) *General exclusion 6*: unavailability of first-year allowances under s. 40 (expenditure incurred for Northern Ireland purposes by small or medium-sized enterprises), 44 (expenditure incurred by small or medium-sized enterprises) and 45 (ICT expenditure incurred by small enterprises) where expenditure is on the provision of machinery or plant for leasing, whether in the course of a trade or otherwise, including letting of a ship on charter or any other asset on hire.
S. 84 (table): short-life asset treatment ruled out where s. 109 provides ten per cent writing-down allowance on plant or machinery provided for leasing.
S. 102(3): pooling rules for long-life assets – expenditure which is within section 107(2)(a) and (b) (overseas leasing which is not protected leasing) subject to s. 110, 114 and 115 (allowances prohibited in certain cases etc.).
S. 128(1)(a): single ship pool not to include expenditure if the ship is provided for leasing unless the ship is not used for overseas leasing at any time in the designated period, or if it is, is used only for protected leasing.
S. 209: partial depreciation subsidy.
Sch. 3, para. 47(5), (6): first-year allowances for regional projects, expenditure incurred 1 November 1992 to 31 October 1993, Pt. 2, Ch. 11 applying – preclusion by reference to leased assets not used for a qualifying purpose in the designated period.
ICTA 1988, s. 830(4): charge on certain exploration or exploitation activities.
Transitional – Sch. 3, para. 21: s. 105(2) applies with the substitution for paragraph (b) of the following wording:
"does not use the plant or machinery for the purposes of a qualifying activity carried on there or for earning profits chargeable to tax by virtue of section 830(4) of ICTA,"
in relation to the use of plant or machinery for leasing under a lease entered into before 16 March 1993.
Rewrite: Technical Points – Explanatory Notes, Annex 2, Note 25: in s. 105(1)(a), the addition of the word "aircraft" to the legislation derived from CAA 1990, s. 50(2) is intended to correct an omission by oversight from the original wording. Letting an aircraft has always been a qualifying purpose (see s. 123(2) and the origin note thereto) and therefore CAA 1990, s. 50(2) should have included a reference to aircraft as well.
Explanatory Notes, Annex 2, Note 26: the rewritten statute in s. 105(3) contains two alterations to the original legislative wording:

- taken as a single statement, the introduction plus s. 105(3)(a) uses a different form of words to define "profits chargeable to tax" from the legislation in CAA 1990, s. 42(1)(b), and
- s. 105(3)(b) omits the word "or gains" (after the word "profits") which appeared in CAA 1990, s. 50(3A),

from both of which previous provisions s. 105(3) in total derives (see Origin note above). Neither of these changes is intended to alter the law; rather, they reflect current interpretation of statutory phrasing at the time the rewritten statute was drafted.
HMRC interpretations – IRInt. 194: where there is a chain of lessees, s. 42 applied to any lessee in the chain. But see now revised guidance issued by the Revenue on 3 February 2005: "where there is a chain of leases, each of the leases, not just the end lease, must be examined to determine whether the leasing under it is protected leasing. If the leasing under any of the leases is not protected leasing, the overseas leasing legislation applies.". Transitional arrangements are applied for leases entered into before 3 February 2005.
HMRC Manuals – CA24010: outline, definitions and examples.
CA24100: guidance, etc. on "protected leasing".

106 The designated period

106(1) Subject to subsection (2), the designated period, in relation to expenditure incurred by a person on the provision of plant or machinery, is the period of 10 years beginning with the date on which he first brought the plant or machinery into use.

106(2) If the person who incurred the expenditure ceases to own the plant or machinery before the end of the 10 year period, the designated period ends on the date when he ceases to own it.

106(3) For the purposes of subsection (2), a person is to be treated as continuing to own plant or machinery so long as it is owned by a person who–

(a) is connected with him, or

(b) acquired it from him as a result of one or more disposals on the occasion of which, or each of which there was a change in the persons carrying on the qualifying activity in relation to which Condition A or Condition B was met.

106(3A) Condition A is that–

(a) at least one person who carried on the qualifying activity immediately before or immediately after the change was within the charge to income tax in respect of that activity, and

(b) at least one person who carried on the qualifying activity before the change continued to carry it on after the change.

106(3B) Condition B is that–

(a) the qualifying activity was carried on in partnership both immediately before and immediately after the change,

(b) a company that was within the charge to corporation tax in respect of the activity carried it on immediately before or immediately after the change, and

(c) at least one company which carried the activity on before the change continued to carry it on after the change.

106(4) [Omitted by ITTOIA 2005, s. 882(1) and Sch. 1, para. 536(3), and repealed by ITTOIA 2005, s. 884 and Sch. 3.]

History – In s. 106(3)(b), the words "each of which there was a change in the persons carrying on the qualifying activity in relation to which Condition A or Condition B was met." substituted for the former words by CTA 2009, s. 1322 and Sch. 1, para. 484(2), with effect for corporation tax purposes for accounting periods ending on or after 1 April 2009, and for income tax and capital gains tax purposes for the tax year 2009–10 and subsequent tax years.
The wording in s. 106(3)(b) formerly amended by ITTOIA 2005, s. 882(1) and Sch. 1, para. 536(2); effective for income tax purposes for 2005–06 onwards and for corporation tax purposes for accounting periods ending after 5 April 2005 (ITTOIA 2005, s. 883(1)).
S. 106(3A) inserted by CTA 2009, s. 1322 and Sch. 1, para. 484(3), with effect for corporation tax purposes for accounting periods ending on or after 1 April 2009, and for income tax and capital gains tax purposes for the tax year 2009–10 and subsequent tax years.
S. 106(3B) inserted by CTA 2009, s. 1322 and Sch. 1, para. 484(3), with effect for corporation tax purposes for accounting periods ending on or after 1 April 2009, and for income tax and capital gains tax purposes for the tax year 2009–10 and subsequent tax years.
S. 106(4) omitted by ITTOIA 2005, s. 882(1) and Sch. 1, para. 536(3), and repealed by ITTOIA 2005, s. 884 and Sch. 3; effective for income tax purposes for 2005–06 onwards and for corporation tax purposes for accounting periods ending after 5 April 2005 (ITTOIA 2005, s. 883(1)).

Origin – S. 106(1), (2): CAA 1990 s. 40(4) (part), 50(3) ("the requisite period").
S. 106(3), (4): CAA 1990 s. 40(5).

Cross references – S. 84 (table): exception to rule that machinery or plant provided for leasing cannot be a short-life asset where used for a qualifying purpose (per s. 122–125) within the designated period as defined by s. 106.
S. 87: short-life assets provided for leasing within the designated period.
ICTA 1988, s. 113(2), 114(1): change in persons carrying on a trade etc. not a discontinuance where election involving continuing partner etc. or there is a company partner.
ICTA 1988, s. 839: meaning of "connected persons".

HMRC Manuals – CA24050: guidance and example on the "designated period".

CAA 2001

CERTAIN EXPENDITURE TO BE POOLED

107 The overseas leasing pool

107(1) Qualifying expenditure to which this section applies, if allocated to a pool, must be allocated to a class pool (**"the overseas leasing pool"**).

107(2) This section applies to qualifying expenditure if–

(a) it is incurred on the provision of plant or machinery for leasing,

(b) the plant or machinery is at any time in the designated period used for overseas leasing which is not protected leasing, and

(c) the expenditure is not–

(i) long-life asset expenditure, or

(ii) expenditure that is required to be allocated to a single asset pool.

Origin – S. 107(1): CAA 1990, s. 41(2) (part).
S. 107(2): CAA 1990, s. 41(1), (6).

Cross references – S. 35: expenditure on plant and machinery for use in dwelling house not qualifying expenditure.
S. 37: sums payable in respect of depreciation.
S. 54(5): summary of pools – allocation to class pool under s. 107.
S. 65(4): final chargeable period for a class pool under s. 107 is that at the end of which no more disposal receipts can arise in subsequent periods.
S. 102(3): pooling rules for long-life assets – expenditure which is within section 107(2)(a) and (b) subject to s. 110, 114 and 115 (allowances prohibited in certain cases etc.).
S. 128(1)(a): single ship pool not to include expenditure if the ship is provided for leasing unless the ship is not used for overseas leasing at any time in the designated period, or if it is, is used only for protected leasing.
S. 149(1)(c): expenditure on the provision of a ship with respect to which s. 107 applies is treated as never having been expenditure on new shipping.
Sch. 3, para. 47(5), (6): first-year allowances for regional projects, expenditure incurred 1 November 1992 to 31 October 1993, Pt. 2, Ch. 11 applying – preclusion by reference to leased assets not used for a qualifying purpose in the designated period.

Rewrite: Technical Points – Explanatory Notes, Annex 2, Note 22: assets which are leased abroad are placed in a separate pool and are subject to a reduced rate of writing down allowance. Moreover, the reduced rate of allowance applies to assets which, besides being leased abroad, are also assets which are leased *other than* in the course of a trade or other qualifying activity (now known as "special leasing" in accordance with s. 15(1), (3) and 19). The previous legislation effectively excluded special leasing assets from the overseas leasing pool because a separate deemed trade was established (CAA 1990, s. 61(1)). Accordingly the reduced rate for overseas leasing had to be re-applied independently to any expenditure on special leasing assets outside the overseas leasing pool (CAA 1990, s. 42(2)(e)). The rewritten legislation is considered to achieve the same result but by a more straightforward approach. Instead, all expenditure on assets leased abroad in the course of a qualifying activity, including special leasing, comes within the overseas leasing pool. The reduced rate of allowance in s. 109 is applied to the pool, automatically including any special leased assets within the pool.

HMRC Manuals – CA24200: guidance and example on s. 107–109.

108 Effect of disposal to connected person on overseas leasing pool

108(1) This section applies if–

(a) a person who has incurred qualifying expenditure which has been allocated to an overseas leasing pool disposes of the plant or machinery to a connected person,

(b) the disposal does not occur on the occasion of a change in the persons carrying on the qualifying activity–

  (i) which falls within Chapter 1 of Part 22 of CTA 2010 (transfers of trade without a change of ownership), or

  (ii) in relation to which Condition A or Condition B is met, and

(c) a disposal value is required to be brought into account on that occasion under this Part.

108(1A) Condition A is that–

(a) at least one person who carried on the qualifying activity immediately before or immediately after the change was within the charge to income tax in respect of that activity, and

(b) at least one person who carried on the qualifying activity before the change continued to carry it on after the change.

108(1B) Condition B is that–

(a) the qualifying activity was carried on in partnership both immediately before and immediately after the change,

(b) a company that was within the charge to corporation tax in respect of the activity carried it on immediately before or immediately after the change, and

(c) at least one company which carried the activity on before the change continued to carry it on after the change.

108(2) The disposal value to be brought into account is–

(a) the market value of the plant or machinery at the time of the disposal, or

(b) if less, the qualifying expenditure incurred by the person disposing of the plant or machinery.

108(3) The person acquiring the plant or machinery is to be treated for the purposes of this Part as having incurred expenditure on its provision of an amount equal to the disposal value given by subsection (2).

108(4) [Omitted by ITTOIA 2005, s. 882(1) and Sch. 1, para. 537(3), and repealed by ITTOIA 2005, s. 884 and Sch. 3.]

History – In s. 108(1)(b), the words from "does not occur on the occasion of a change in the persons carrying on the qualifying activity– " to "Condition B is met" in s. 108(1)(b)(ii) substituted for the former words by CTA 2009, s. 1322 and Sch. 1, para. 485(2), with effect for corporation tax purposes for accounting periods ending on or after 1 April 2009, and for income tax and capital gains tax purposes for the tax year 2009–10 and subsequent tax years.
In s. 108(1)(b)(i), the words "Chapter 1 of Part 22 of CTA 2010" substituted for "section 343(1) of ICTA (company reconstructions without change of ownership)" by CTA 2010, s. 1177 and Sch. 1, para. 334, with effect for corporation tax purposes for accounting periods ending on or after 1 April 2010, and for income tax and capital gains tax purposes for the tax year 2010–11 and subsequent tax years.
S. 108(1)(b) substituted by ITTOIA 2005, s. 882(1) and Sch. 1, para. 537(2); effective for income tax purposes for 2005–06 onwards and for corporation tax purposes for accounting periods ending after 5 April 2005 (ITTOIA 2005, s. 883(1)).
S. 108(1A) inserted by CTA 2009, s. 1322 and Sch. 1, para. 485(3), with effect for corporation tax purposes for accounting periods ending on or after 1 April 2009, and for income tax and capital gains tax purposes for the tax year 2009–10 and subsequent tax years.
S. 108(1B) inserted by CTA 2009, s. 1322 and Sch. 1, para. 485(3), with effect for corporation tax purposes for accounting periods ending on or after 1 April 2009, and for income tax and capital gains tax purposes for the tax year 2009–10 and subsequent tax years.
S. 108(4) omitted by ITTOIA 2005, s. 882(1) and Sch. 1, para. 537(3), and repealed by ITTOIA 2005, s. 884 and Sch. 3; effective for income tax purposes for 2005–06 onwards and for corporation tax purposes for accounting periods ending after 5 April 2005 (ITTOIA 2005, s. 883(1)).

Origin – S. 108: CAA 1990 s.41(5).

Cross references – S. 60(1)(b): meaning of "disposal receipt" includes a value that a person is required to bring into account for purposes of any of the provisions listed in s. 66 (see note below).
S. 66: list of provisions about disposal values includes s. 108.
S. 266, 267: election where predecessor and successor to trade are connected persons.
ICTA 1988, s. 113(2), 114(1): change in persons carrying on a trade etc. not a discontinuance where there is a continuing partner etc. or a company partner.
ICTA 1988, s. 343(2): transfer of trade between companies where no significant change in ownership.

HMRC Manuals – CA24200: guidance and example on s. 107–109.

ALLOWANCES REDUCED OR, IN CERTAIN CASES, PROHIBITED

109 Writing-down allowances at 10%

109(1) The amount of the writing-down allowance to which a person is entitled for a chargeable period in respect of expenditure to which this section applies is 10% of the amount by which AQE exceeds TDR (see Chapter 5).

109(2) This section applies to expenditure incurred on the provision of plant or machinery for leasing if–

(a) the plant or machinery is at any time in the designated period used for overseas leasing which is not protected leasing, and

(b) the expenditure is not long-life asset expenditure.

109(3) Subsection (2) applies to expenditure even if the expenditure is in a single asset pool.

109(4) Subsections (3) and (4) of section 56 (proportionate increases or reductions in amount in certain cases) apply for the purposes of subsection (1) of this section as they apply for the purposes of subsection (1) of that section.

Origin – S. 109(1): CAA 1990 s. 42(2) (part).
S. 109(2): CAA 1990 s. 42(1) (part), (2) (part).
S. 109(3): CAA 1990 s. 42(2) (part).
S. 109(4): CAA 1990 s. 24(2)(a)(ii), 42(2) (part).

Cross references – S. 56(2): amount of general writing down allowances subject to s. 109 allowance for overseas leasing.
S. 84 (table): short-life asset treatment ruled out where s. 109 provides ten per cent writing-down allowance.
S. 102(3): pooling rules for long-life assets – expenditure which is within s. 107(2)(a) and (b) subject to s. 110, 114 and 115 (allowances prohibited in certain cases etc.).

Rewrite: Changes in Law – Explanatory Notes, Annex 1, Change 20: the reduced rate applicable to overseas leasing did not previously apply specifically to assets which were kept in a pool of their own (by virtue of CAA 1990, s. 79) because they were used partly for purposes other than a qualifying activity. Under the rewritten provision, such assets will be subject to the reduced rate by dint of s. 109(3). There is a right of election for the previous position to apply to a period which straddles 6 April (income tax) or 1 April (corporation tax) 2001 (Sch. 3, para. 8).

Rewrite: Technical Points – Explanatory Notes, Annex 2, Note 22: assets which are leased abroad are placed in a separate pool and are subject to a reduced rate of writing down allowance. Moreover, the reduced rate of allowance applies to assets which, besides being leased abroad, are also assets which are leased *other than* in the course of a trade or other qualifying activity (now known as "special leasing" in accordance with s. 15(1), (3) and 19). The previous legislation effectively excluded special leasing assets from the overseas leasing pool because a separate deemed trade was established (CAA 1990, s. 61(1)). Accordingly the reduced rate for overseas leasing had to be re-applied independently to any expenditure on special leasing assets outside the overseas leasing pool (CAA 1990, s. 42(2)(e)). The rewritten legislation is considered to achieve the same result but by a more straightforward approach Instead, all expenditure on assets leased abroad in the course of a qualifying activity, including special leasing, comes within the overseas leasing pool (s. 107(2)). The reduced rate of allowance is applied to the pool, automatically including any special leased assets within the pool. Explanatory Notes, Annex 2, Note 23: s. 109(3) provides for the reduced rate applicable to assets leased abroad to apply to expenditure in a single asset pool as well as to expenditure pooled in a s. 107 overseas leasing pool. The note considers whether the wording of s. 109(3) constitutes a change to the original legislation in CAA 1990 s. 42 (from which s. 109 is, in part, derived: see Origin note above) in the light of the debate whether the statute relating to contributions to expenditure (previously in CAA 1990, s. 155(6)) created a single asset pool or a pool which could constitute the trade for an offshore leasing pool. The note concludes that the debate is irrelevant here. The wording of CAA 1990, s. 41(6) (now subsumed into s. 107(2) and which lists exclusions from a CAA 1990, s. 42 overseas leasing pool) did not exclude contributions within CAA 1990, s. 155(6) from the pool of assets leased overseas. Thus they were subject to the reduced rate and the law has not changed (unlike that for assets used partly for non-qualifying purposes: see change in law note above). See also the Rewrite note which accompanies s. 538 for comment on the issue of single asset pools for contributions to expenditure.

HMRC Manuals – CA24200: guidance and example on s. 107–109.

Other material – HMRC Brief 40/07: Overseas leasing – sections 109 and 110 Capital Allowances Act 2001 – leases entered into before 1 April 2006.

110 Cases where allowances are prohibited

110(1) A person is not entitled to any writing-down or balancing allowances in respect of qualifying expenditure which is within subsection (2).

110(2) Expenditure is within this subsection if–

(a) it is incurred on the provision of plant or machinery for leasing,

(b) the plant or machinery is at any time in the designated period used for overseas leasing which is not protected leasing,

(c) the plant or machinery is used otherwise than for a qualifying purpose (see sections 122 to 125), and

(d) the lease is within any of the items in the list below.

LIST
LEASES IN RELATION TO WHICH ALLOWANCES ARE PROHIBITED

1. The lease is expressed to be for a period of more than 13 years.
2. The lease, or a separate agreement, provides for–
   (a) extending or renewing the lease, or
   (b) the grant of a new lease, making it possible for the plant or machinery to be leased for a period of more than 13 years.
3. There is a period of more than one year between the dates on which any two consecutive payments become due under the lease.
4. Any payments are due under the lease or a collateral agreement other than periodical payments.
5. If payments due under the lease or a collateral agreement are expressed as monthly amounts due over a period, any payment due for that period is not the same as any of the others.

CAA 2001

But, for this purpose, ignore variations made under the terms of the lease which are attributable to changes in–

(a) the rate of corporation tax or income tax,

(b) the rate of capital allowances,

(c) any rate of interest where the changes are linked to changes in the rate of interest applicable to inter-bank loans, or

(d) the premiums charged for insurance of any description by a person who is not connected with the lessor or the lessee.

6. The lessor or a person connected with the lessor will, or may in certain circumstances, become entitled at any time to receive from the lessee or any other person a payment, other than a payment of insurance money, which is–

(a) of an amount determined before the expiry of the lease, and

(b) referable to a value of the plant or machinery at or after the expiry of the lease.

For this purpose, it does not matter whether the payment relates to a disposal of the plant or machinery.

110(3) In items 4 and 5 of the list **"collateral agreement"** means an agreement which might reasonably be construed as being collateral to the lease.

Origin – S. 110: CAA 1990 s. 42(3).

Cross references – S. 55(6): entitlement to general writing down allowances subject to s. 110(1) prohibition of allowances for certain overseas leasing.

S. 102(3): pooling rules for long-life assets – expenditure which is within s. 107(2)(a) and (b) (overseas leasing which is not protected leasing) subject to s. 110, 114 and 115 (allowances prohibited in certain cases etc.).

HMRC Manuals – CA24300: guidance and example on s. 110.

Other material – HMRC Brief 40/07: Overseas leasing – sections 109 and 110 Capital Allowances Act 2001 – leases entered into before 1 April 2006.

RECOVERY OF EXCESS ALLOWANCES

111 Excess allowances: standard recovery mechanism

111(1) If–

(a) expenditure incurred by a person in providing plant or machinery has qualified for a first-year allowance or a normal writing-down allowance, and

(b) at any time in the designated period, the plant or machinery is used for overseas leasing which is not protected leasing,

the following provisions of this section have effect in relation to the person who is the owner of the plant or machinery when it is first so used.

111(2) For the chargeable period in which the plant or machinery is first used as described in subsection (1)(b), the owner is–

(a) liable to a balancing charge of an amount given by subsection (4), and

(b) required to bring into account a disposal value of an amount given by that subsection.

111(3) For the chargeable period following that in which the plant or machinery is first used as described in subsection (1)(b), an amount given by subsection (4) is to be allocated to whatever pool is appropriate for plant or machinery which is of that description and is provided for leasing and used for overseas leasing.

111(4) The amounts are–

The balancing charge

The amount, if any, by which F + N exceeds T, where–

F is the amount of any first-year allowance made in respect of the qualifying expenditure referred to in subsection (1)(a) ("E"),

N is the total of any normal writing-down allowances made in respect of E for the relevant chargeable periods, and

T is the total of the allowances that could have been made for the relevant chargeable periods if no first-year allowance or normal writing-down allowances had been or could have been made.

The disposal value

The amount, if any, by which E exceeds (F + N), where *E*, *F* and *N* have the meaning given in relation to the amount of the balancing charge.

The amount to be allocated to the pool

The aggregate of the balancing charge and the disposal value.

111(5) For the purpose of calculating N, the normal writing-down allowances that were made in respect of expenditure on an item of plant or machinery are to be determined as if that item were the only item of plant or machinery in relation to which Chapter 5 had effect.

111(6) "The relevant chargeable periods" means the chargeable period in which the qualifying expenditure was incurred and any subsequent chargeable period up to and including the one in which the plant or machinery was first used as described in subsection (1)(b).

Origin – S. 111(1): CAA 1990 s. 46(1) (part), (8) (part).
S. 111(2): CAA 1990 s. 46(1) (part), (2) (part), (3) (part).
S. 111(3): CAA 1990 s. 46(1) (part).
S. 111(4): CAA 1990 s. 46(1) (part), (2) (part), (3) (part), (8) (part).
S. 111(5): CAA 1990 s. 46(4).
S. 111(6): CAA 1990 s. 46(2) (part).

Cross references – S. 57(2): "available qualifying expenditure" in a pool for a chargeable period includes any amount allocated to the pool under s. 111(3).
S. 60(1)(b): meaning of "disposal receipt" includes a value that a person is required to bring into account for purposes of any of the provisions listed in s. 66 (see note below).
S. 66: list of provisions about disposal values includes s. 111.

HMRC Manuals – CA24210: guidance and examples on s. 111–113.

112 Excess allowances: connected persons

112(1) Section 111 applies with the modifications in subsections (2) to (4) in a case in which–

(a) the owner acquired the plant or machinery as a result of a transaction between connected persons (or a series of transactions each of which was between connected persons),

(b) the transaction was not effected (or, if more than one, none of the transactions was effected) on the occasion of a change in the persons carrying on the qualifying activity–

  (i) which falls within Chapter 1 of Part 22 of CTA 2010 (transfers of trade without change of ownership), or

  (ii) in relation to which Condition A or Condition B is met, and

(c) any of the connected persons is a person to whom–

  (i) a first-year allowance or a normal writing-down allowance has been made in respect of expenditure on the provision of the plant or machinery, or

  (ii) a balancing allowance has been made in respect of such expenditure without a first-year allowance or normal writing-down allowance having been claimed.

112(1A) Condition A is that–

(a) at least one person who carried on the qualifying activity immediately before or immediately after the change was within the charge to income tax in respect of that activity, and

(b) at least one person who carried on the qualifying activity before the change continued to carry it on after the change.

112(1B) Condition B is that–

(a) the qualifying activity was carried on in partnership both immediately before and immediately after the change,

(b) a company that was within the charge to corporation tax in respect of the activity carried it on immediately before or immediately after the change, and

(c) at least one company which carried the activity on before the change continued to carry it on after the change.

112(2) For the purposes of section 111(2) and (3)–

E is the amount of the expenditure in respect of which an allowance within subsection (1)(c) has been made,

F is the amount of any first-year allowance within subsection (1)(c), and

N is the amount of any normal writing-down allowance or balancing allowance within subsection (1)(c).

112(3) For the purposes of section 111(2) and (3), any consideration paid or received on a disposal of the plant or machinery between the connected persons is to be disregarded.

112(4) If a balancing allowance or a balancing charge has been made in respect of any of the transactions, the amount representing F + N is to be adjusted in a just and reasonable manner.

112(5) [Omitted by ITTOIA 2005, s. 882(1) and Sch. 1, para. 538(3), and repealed by ITTOIA 2005, s. 884 and Sch. 3.]

History – S. 112(1)(b) substituted for former s. 112(1)(b) by CTA 2009, s. 1322 and Sch. 1, para. 486(2), with effect for corporation tax purposes for accounting periods ending on or after 1 April 2009, and for income tax and capital gains tax purposes for the tax year 2009–10 and subsequent tax years.
Former s. 112(1)(b) substituted by ITTOIA 2005, s. 882(1) and Sch. 1, para. 538(2); effective for income tax purposes for 2005–06 onwards and for corporation tax purposes for accounting periods ending after 5 April 2005 (ITTOIA 2005, s. 883(1)).
In s. 112(1)(b)(i), the words "Chapter 1 of Part 22 of CTA 2010 (transfers of trade" substituted for "section 343(1) of ICTA (company reconstructions" by CTA 2010, s. 1177 and Sch. 1, para. 335, with effect for corporation tax purposes for accounting periods ending on or after 1 April 2010, and for income tax and capital gains tax purposes for the tax year 2010–11 and subsequent tax years.
S. 112(1A) inserted by CTA 2009, s. 1322 and Sch. 1, para. 486(3), with effect for corporation tax purposes for accounting periods ending on or after 1 April 2009, and for income tax and capital gains tax purposes for the tax year 2009–10 and subsequent tax years.
S. 112(1B) inserted by CTA 2009, s. 1322 and Sch. 1, para. 486(3), with effect for corporation tax purposes for accounting periods ending on or after 1 April 2009, and for income tax and capital gains tax purposes for the tax year 2009–10 and subsequent tax years.
S. 112(5) omitted by ITTOIA 2005, s. 882(1) and Sch. 1, para. 538(3), and repealed by ITTOIA 2005, s. 884 and Sch. 3; effective for income tax purposes for 2005–06 onwards and for corporation tax purposes for accounting periods ending after 5 April 2005 (ITTOIA 2005, s. 883(1)).

Origin – S. 112(1): CAA 1990 s. 46(5) (part), (6), (8) (part).
S. 112(2): CAA 1990 s. 46(5) (part), (8) (part).
S. 112(3) to (5): CAA 1990 s. 46(5) (part).

Cross references – ICTA 1988, s. 113(2), 114(1): change in persons carrying on a trade etc. not a discontinuance where there is a continuing partner etc. or a company partner.
ICTA 1988, s. 343(2): transfer of trade between companies where no significant change in ownership.

HMRC Manuals – CA24210: guidance and examples on s. 111–113.

113 Excess allowances: special provision for ships

113(1) If the plant or machinery referred to in section 111 is a ship–

(a) no allowance is to be made in respect of the ship under section 131(3) (postponed allowances) for the first chargeable period of overseas use or any subsequent chargeable period,

(b) nothing in section 132(2) (disposal events and single ship pool) restricts the operation of section 111, and

(c) the amount of any first-year or writing-down allowance in respect of the ship which has been postponed under section 130 and not made is to be allocated to a long-life asset pool or an overseas leasing pool for the chargeable period following the first chargeable period of overseas use.

113(2) **"The first chargeable period of overseas use"** means the chargeable period in which the plant or machinery is first used for overseas leasing which is not protected leasing.

Origin – S. 113(1): CAA 1990, s. 46(7) (part), (8) (part).
S. 113(2): CAA 1990, s. 46(8) (part).

Cross references – S. 123: qualifying purposes – ships let on charter.
S. 127–158: special basis for writing-down allowances on certain ships permitting postponement and subsequent claim and requiring individual pooling, with transfer to general pool where disposal value falls to be brought into account.

HMRC Manuals – CA24210: guidance and examples on s. 111–113.

RECOVERY OF ALLOWANCES GIVEN IN CASES WHERE PROHIBITION APPLIES

114 Prohibited allowances: standard recovery mechanism

114(1) If–

(a) a first-year allowance, a writing-down allowance or a balancing allowance has been made in respect of expenditure incurred in providing plant or machinery, and

(b) at any time in the designated period, an event occurs such that the expenditure is brought within section 110(2) (cases where allowances are prohibited),

the following provisions have effect in relation to the person owning the plant or machinery immediately before that event.

114(2) For the chargeable period in which the event occurs, the owner is–

(a) liable to a balancing charge of an amount equal to A – R, and

(b) required to bring into account a disposal value of an amount equal to E – (A – R).

114(3) For the purposes of subsection (2)–

A is the amount of any allowances within subsection (1)(a),

R is any amount previously recovered under section 111 or 112 (recovery of excess allowances), and

E is the amount of the expenditure referred to in subsection (1)(a).

114(4) For the purpose of calculating A, the amount of the allowances made in respect of expenditure on an item of plant or machinery is to be determined as if that item were the only item of plant or machinery in relation to which Chapter 5 had effect.

Origin – S. 114(1): CAA 1990, s. 42(4) (part), (9) (part).
S. 114(2): CAA 1990, s. 42(4) (part).
S. 114(3): CAA 1990, s. 42(4), (part), (9) (part).
S. 114(4): CAA 1990, s. 42(5).

Cross references – S. 60(1)(b): meaning of "disposal receipt" includes a value that a person is required to bring into account for purposes of any of the provisions listed in s. 66 (see note below).
S. 66: list of provisions about disposal values includes s. 114.
S. 102(3): pooling rules for long-life assets – expenditure which is within s. 107(2)(a) and (b) (overseas leasing which is not protected leasing) subject to s. 110, 114 and 115 (allowances prohibited in certain cases etc.).

Rewrite: Technical Points – Explanatory Notes, Annex 2, Note 27: where allowances have been given on leased assets and the machinery or plant is subsequently used in the designated period for prohibited leasing under s. 110, a clawback is made of those allowances. In order not only to recover allowances already given, but also to ensure that no further allowances are granted on the prohibited expenditure, the person is liable to a balancing charge to the extent of the erroneous unrecovered allowances and they are also required to bring a disposal value into account equal to the prohibited expenditure less the balancing charge (s. 114(2)(b)). Although not in the previous statute (CAA 1990, s. 42(4)), the second requirement is simply to remove the balance of unrelieved prohibited expenditure from the pool and is not a change in the legislation (because no allowances would be due on that amount in any event). The change is "cosmetic".

HMRC Manuals – CA24350: guidance on recovery mechanism, etc.

115 Prohibited allowances: connected persons

115(1) Section 114 applies with the modifications in subsection (2) in a case in which–

(a) an amount falls to be treated as a balancing charge under that section,

(b) the person on whom the balancing charge is to be imposed acquired the plant or machinery in question as a result of a transaction between connected persons (or a series of transactions each of which was between connected persons),

(c) the transaction was not effected (or, if more than one, none of the transactions was effected) on the occasion of a change in the persons carrying on the qualifying activity–

(i) which falls within Chapter 1 of Part 22 of CTA 2010 (transfers of trade without change of ownership), or

(ii) in relation to which Condition A or Condition B is met, and

(d) a first-year allowance, a writing-down allowance or a balancing allowance in respect of expenditure on the provision of that plant or machinery has been made to any of those persons.

115(1A) Condition A is that–

(a) at least one person who carried on the qualifying activity immediately before or immediately after the change was within the charge to income tax in respect of that activity, and

(b) at least one person who carried on the qualifying activity before the change continued to carry it on after the change.

115(1B) Condition B is that–

(a) the qualifying activity was carried on in partnership both immediately before and immediately after the change,

(b) a company that was within the charge to corporation tax in respect of the activity carried it on immediately before or immediately after the change, and

(c) at least one company which carried the activity on before the change continued to carry it on after the change.

115(2) For the purpose of calculating the balancing charge–

(a) *A* is the amount of any allowances within subsection (1)(d),

(b) any consideration paid or received on a disposal of the plant or machinery between the connected persons is to be disregarded, and

(c) if a balancing allowance or a balancing charge has been made in respect of any of the transactions, *A* is to be adjusted in a just and reasonable manner.

115(3) [Omitted by ITTOIA 2005, s. 882(1) and Sch. 1, para. 539(2), and repealed by ITTOIA 2005, s. 884 and Sch. 3.]

History – S. 115(1)(c) substituted for former s. 115(1)(c) by CTA 2009, s. 1322 and Sch. 1, para. 487(2), with effect for corporation tax purposes for accounting periods ending on or after 1 April 2009, and for income tax and capital gains tax purposes for the tax year 2009–10 and subsequent tax years.
Former s. 115(1)(c) substituted by ITTOIA 2005, s. 882(1) and Sch. 1, para. 539(2); effective for income tax purposes for 2005–06 onwards and for corporation tax purposes for accounting periods ending after 5 April 2005 (ITTOIA 2005, s. 883(1)).
In s. 115(1)(c)(i), the words "Chapter 1 of Part 22 of CTA 2010 (transfers of trade" substituted for "section 343(1) of ICTA (company reconstructions" by CTA 2010, s. 1177 and Sch. 1, para. 336, with effect for corporation tax purposes for accounting periods ending on or after 1 April 2010, and for income tax and capital gains tax purposes for the tax year 2010–11 and subsequent tax years.

CAA 2001

S. 115(1A) inserted by CTA 2009, s. 1322 and Sch. 1, para. 487(3), with effect for corporation tax purposes for accounting periods ending on or after 1 April 2009, and for income tax and capital gains tax purposes for the tax year 2009–10 and subsequent tax years.
S. 115(1B) inserted by CTA 2009, s. 1322 and Sch. 1, para. 487(3), with effect for corporation tax purposes for accounting periods ending on or after 1 April 2009, and for income tax and capital gains tax purposes for the tax year 2009–10 and subsequent tax years.
S. 115(3) omitted by ITTOIA 2005, s. 882(1) and Sch. 1, para. 539(3), and repealed by ITTOIA 2005, s. 884 and Sch. 3; effective for income tax purposes for 2005–06 onwards and for corporation tax purposes for accounting periods ending after 5 April 2005 (ITTOIA 2005, s. 883(1)).

Origin – S. 115(1): CAA 1990, s. 42(6) (part).
S. 115(2): CAA 1990, s. 42(7).
S. 115(3): CAA 1990, s. 42(6) (part).

Cross references – S. 102(3): pooling rules for long-life assets – expenditure which is within s. 107(2)(a) and (b) (overseas leasing which is not protected leasing) subject to a. 110, 114 and 115 (allowances prohibited in certain cases etc.).

HMRC Manuals – CA24350: guidance on recovery mechanism, etc.

APPLICATION OF CHAPTER IN RELATION TO JOINT LESSEES

116 Mitigation of regime

116(1) This section applies if–

(a) plant or machinery is leased to two or more persons jointly,

(b) at least one of them is a person who–

(i) is not resident in the United Kingdom, and

(ii) does not use the plant or machinery exclusively for earning profits chargeable to tax, and

(c) the leasing is not protected leasing.

116(2) Subsection (3) applies if, at any time when the plant or machinery is leased as described in subsection (1), the lessees use the plant or machinery for the purposes of a qualifying activity or activities but not for leasing.

116(3) The expenditure on the provision of the plant or machinery is to be treated as not subject to sections 107, 109 and 110 if, and to the extent to which, it appears that the profits of the qualifying activity or activities will be chargeable to tax throughout–

(a) the designated period, or

(b) if shorter, the period of the lease.

116(4) Subsection (5) applies if, under subsection (3), part of the expenditure is treated as not subject to section 107, 109 or 110.

116(5) Whether or not the plant or machinery continues to be leased as described in subsection (1), Chapters 5 (allowances and charges) and 10 (long-life assets) and this Chapter have effect as if–

(a) the part of the expenditure that is not subject to section 107, 109 or 110 were expenditure on the provision of a separate item of plant or machinery, and

(b) the rest were expenditure which has been incurred on the provision of another item of plant or machinery (and which is subject to those sections).

116(6) All such apportionments are to be made as are necessary as a result of subsection (5).

Origin – S. 116(1): CAA 1990, s. 43(1) (part).
S. 116(2), (3): CAA 1990, s. 43(2).
S. 116(4)–(6): CAA 1990, s. 43(3).

Cross references – S. 84 (table): short-life asset treatment ruled out where plant or machinery leased jointly such that s. 116 applies.

Rewrite: Technical Points – Explanatory Notes, Annex 2, Note 28: s. 116 does not include the provisions previously contained in CAA 1990, s. 43(5). It was felt that these provisions were incapable of application because they concerned first-year allowances which were not available on leased assets. For this reason, they have not been reproduced in the rewritten legislation.

HMRC Manuals – CA24400: guidance and examples on joint lessees legislation.

117 Recovery of allowances in case of joint lessees

117(1) If–

(a) expenditure is incurred on the provision of plant or machinery which is leased as described in section 116(1),

(b) the whole or a part of the expenditure has qualified for a normal writing-down allowance under section 116(3),

(c) at any time in the designated period while the plant or machinery is so leased, no lessee uses the plant or machinery for the purposes of a qualifying activity or activities the profits of which are chargeable to tax, and

(d) section 114 (recovery of prohibited allowances) does not apply at that time and has not applied at any earlier time, sections 111 and 112 (recovery of excess allowances) apply as if the plant or machinery or (as the case may be) the separate item of plant or machinery referred to in section 116(5)(a) had at that time begun to be used for overseas leasing which is not protected leasing.

117(2) If–

(a) the whole or a part of any expenditure has qualified for–

(i) a normal writing-down allowance otherwise than as a result of section 116(3), or

(ii) a first-year allowance,

(b) subsequently, but during the designated period, the plant or machinery is leased as described in section 116(1),

(c) at any time in the designated period while the plant or machinery is so leased, no lessee uses the plant or machinery for the purposes of a qualifying activity or activities the profits of which are chargeable to tax, and

(d) section 114 (recovery of prohibited allowances) does not apply at that time and has not applied at any earlier time,

sections 111 and 112 (recovery of excess allowances) apply as if the plant or machinery (and not any separate item of plant or machinery referred to in section 116(5)(a)) had at that time begun to be used for overseas leasing which is not protected leasing.

117(3) Subsections (4) and (5) apply if–

(a) expenditure is incurred on the provision of plant or machinery which is leased as described in section 116(1),

(b) the whole or a part of the expenditure has qualified for a normal writing-down allowance under section 116(3),

(c) at the end of the designated period, the plant or machinery is leased as described in section 116(1) but subsection (1) has not had effect, and

(d) it appears that the extent to which the plant or machinery has been used for the purposes of a qualifying activity or activities the profits of which are chargeable to tax is less than the extent of such use taken into account in determining the amount of the expenditure which qualified for a normal writing-down allowance.

117(4) Sections 111 and 112 (recovery of excess allowances) apply as if–

(a) a part of the expenditure corresponding to the reduction in the extent of use referred to in subsection (3)(d) were expenditure on the provision of a separate item of plant or machinery, and

(b) the separate item of plant or machinery had been used, on the last day of the designated period, for overseas leasing which is not protected leasing.

117(5) Any disposal value subsequently brought into account under this Part in respect of the plant or machinery must be apportioned by reference to the extent of its use (determined at the end of the designated period) for the purposes of a qualifying activity or activities the profits of which are chargeable to tax.

117(6) If an apportionment is made under subsection (5), section 116(6) does not apply.

Origin – S. 117(1): CAA 1990, s. 44(1), (2).
S. 117(2): CAA 1990, s. 44(3), (5) (part).
S. 117(3)–(6): CAA 1990, s. 44(4).

Transitional – Sch. 3, para. 22: if expenditure has been incurred on the provision of plant or machinery which is leased (as described in s. 116(1)) and the expenditure has qualified for a first-year allowance (FYA: wholly or in part) under CAA 1990, s. 43(4) (joint lessees: new expenditure) or Sch. 3, paragraph 47(7)(b) (expenditure incurred between 1 November 1992 and 31 October 1993), then s. 117(1) and (3)–(5) apply as if the references in s. 117(1)(b) and 117(3)(b) respectively to expenditure qualifying for a normal writing down allowance under s. 116(3) include a reference to expenditure qualifying for the FYA.

Rewrite: Technical Points – Explanatory Notes, Annex 2, Note 29: the note explains the reasons for the introduction of the words "the plant or machinery or (as the case may be)" into the rewritten legislation at the end of s. 177(1). These words clarify the original statute in CAA 1990, s. 44(2) which only referred to the "separate item of machinery or plant" provisions applying in specific circumstances and is now considered to have been inconsistent with CAA 1990, s. 43 and the rest of s. 44.

HMRC Manuals – CA24400: guidance and examples on joint lessees legislation.

DUTIES TO SUPPLY INFORMATION

118 Certificate relating to protected leasing

118(1) If–

(a) expenditure is incurred on the provision of plant or machinery, and

(b) before the expenditure has qualified for a normal writing-down allowance, the plant or machinery is used for overseas leasing which is protected leasing,

a claim for a writing-down allowance which takes account of that expenditure must be accompanied by a certificate.

118(2) The certificate must specify–

(a) the description of protected leasing,

(b) the person to whom the plant or machinery has been leased, and

(c) if the certificate is given by reference to a chargeable period, all the items of plant or machinery (if more than one) relevant to that period.

118(3) Subsection (1) applies, for the purposes of claims to first-year allowances, as if the references to a normal writing-down allowance and to a writing-down allowance included a first-year allowance.

118(4) But nothing in subsection (3) prevents subsection (1) from continuing to apply if the use for protected leasing occurs after the expenditure has qualified for one allowance and before it qualifies for another.

Origin – S. 118(1): CAA 1990, s. 48(1) (part).
S. 118(2): CAA 1990, s. 48(1) (part), (4) (part).
S. 118(3), (4): CAA 1990, s. 48(7) (part).

Cross references – TMA 1970, s. 98 (as amended by Sch. 2, para. 4): penalties in respect of s. 118.

HMRC Manuals – CA24100: guidance, etc. on protected leasing.
CA24500: guidance on s. 118 certificate.

119 Notice of change of use of plant or machinery

119(1) If–

(a) any expenditure on plant or machinery has qualified for a first-year allowance or a normal writing-down allowance, and

(b) the plant or machinery is subsequently used at any time in the designated period for overseas leasing which is not protected leasing,

the person who then owns the plant or machinery must give notice of the fact to an officer of Revenue and Customs.

119(2) The notice must specify–

(a) the person who is not resident in the United Kingdom to whom the plant or machinery has been leased, and

(b) if the notice is given by reference to a chargeable period, all the items of plant or machinery (if more than one) relevant to that period.

119(3) The notice must be given–

(a) no later than 3 months after the end of the chargeable period in which the plant or machinery is first used for overseas leasing which is not protected leasing, or

(b) if at the end of the 3 months the person required to give the notice does not know and cannot reasonably be expected to know that the plant or machinery is being so used, within 30 days of coming to know of it.

History – In s. 119(1), the words "an officer of Revenue and Customs" substituted for "the Inland Revenue" by CRCA 2005, s. 50(6) and Sch. 4, para. 83(1), with effect from 18 April 2005 by virtue of SI 2005/1126, art. 2(2).

Origin – S. 119(1): CAA 1990, s. 48(2) (part), (7) (part).
S. 119(2): CAA 1990, s. 48(4) (part).
S. 119(3): CAA 1990, s. 48(3) (part), (6) (part).

Cross references – TMA 1970, s. 98 (as amended by Sch. 2, para. 4): penalties in respect of s. 119.

HMRC Manuals – CA24500: guidance on s. 119 notice.

120 Notice and joint lessees

120(1) If expenditure is incurred on the provision of plant or machinery which is leased as described in section 116(1) (joint lessees: mitigation of regime), the lessor must give notice to an officer of Revenue and Customs.

120(2) A notice under subsection (1) must specify–

(a) the names and addresses of the persons to whom the asset is jointly leased,

(b) the part of the expenditure properly attributable to each of them, and

(c) which of them (so far as the lessor knows) is resident in the United Kingdom.

120(3) If circumstances occur such that section 117(1) or (2) (recovery of allowances) applies, the person who is then the lessor must give notice of the fact to an officer of Revenue and Customs.

120(4) A notice under subsection (3) must specify–

(a) any of the joint lessees who is not resident in the United Kingdom to whom the plant or machinery has been leased, and

(b) if it is given by reference to a chargeable period, all the items of plant or machinery (if more than one) relevant to that period.

120(5) A notice under this section must be given–

(a) no later than 3 months after the end of the chargeable period in which the plant or machinery is first leased as described in section 116(1) or (as the case may be) in which the circumstances referred to in subsection (3) occur, or

(b) if at the end of the 3 months the person required to give the notice does not know and cannot reasonably be expected to know that the plant or machinery is being so used, within 30 days of coming to know of it.

History – In s. 120(1), the words "an officer of Revenue and Customs" substituted for "the Inland Revenue" by CRCA 2005, s. 50(6) and Sch. 4, para. 83(1), with effect from 18 April 2005 by virtue of SI 2005/1126, art. 2(2).
In s. 120(3), the words "an officer of Revenue and Customs" substituted for "the Inland Revenue" by CRCA 2005, s. 50(6) and Sch. 4, para. 83(1) with effect from 18 April 2005 by virtue of SI 2005/1126, art. 2(2).

Origin – S. 120(1), (2): CAA 1990, s. 48(5).
S. 120(3): CAA 1990, s. 44(2) (part), 48(2) (part), (3) (part).
S. 120(4): Interpretation Act 1978, s. 20(2), CAA 1990, s. 44(2) (part), (3) (part), 48(2) (part), (4) (part).
S. 120(5): Interpretation Act 1978 s. 20(2), CAA 1990, s. 44(2) (part), (3) (part), 48(2) (part), (3) (part), (5) (part), (6) (part).

Cross references – TMA 1970, s. 98 (as amended by Sch. 2, para. 4): penalties in respect of s. 120.

HMRC Manuals – CA 24110: HMRC guidance on meaning of "qualifying purpose".

Other material – ICAEW Technical Releases TR 390, 394 (not reproduced): equipment out of use through repair, changes in leases or otherwise is not regarded as being used for a purpose other than a qualifying purpose.

QUALIFYING PURPOSES

Other material – ICAEW Technical Releases TR 390, 394 (not reproduced): equipment out of use through repair, changes in leases or otherwise is not regarded as being used for a purpose other than a qualifying purpose.

121 Meaning of "short-term leasing"

121(1) Leasing of plant or machinery is short-term leasing if–

(a) the number of consecutive days for which it is leased to the same person will normally be less than 30, and

(b) the total number of days for which it is leased to that person in any period of 12 months will normally be less than 90.

121(2) Leasing of plant or machinery is also short-term leasing if–

(a) the number of consecutive days for which the plant or machinery is leased to the same person will not normally exceed 365, and

(b) the total length of the periods for which it is leased in any consecutive period of 4 years within the designated period to lessees in circumstances not falling within section 125(4) (other qualifying purposes: non-leasing use) will not exceed 2 years.

121(3) If any plant or machinery is leased as a number of items which–

(a) form part of a group of items of the same or a similar description, and

(b) are not separately identifiable,

all items in the group may be treated as used for short-term leasing if substantially the whole of the items in the group are so used.

121(4) For the purposes of subsections (1) and (2) persons who are connected with each other are to be treated as the same person.

Origin – S. 121(1): CAA 1990, s. 40(1) (part).
S. 121(2): CAA 1990, s. 40(1) (part), (2).
S. 121(3), (4): CAA 1990, s. 40(3).

Cross references – S. 84 (table): exception to rule that machinery or plant provided for leasing cannot be a short-life asset where used for a qualifying purpose (per s. 122–125) within the designated period.
S. 87: if a short-life asset provided for leasing ceases to be used for a qualifying purposes in the requisite period, tax written-down value is transferred to the general pool.

HMRC Manuals – CA24100: guidance, etc. on "short-term leasing".

122 Short-term leasing by buyer, lessee, etc.

122(1) Plant or machinery is used for a qualifying purpose at any time when any of the persons listed in subsection (2) uses it for short-term leasing (as defined by section 121).

122(2) The persons are–

(a) the person ("X") who incurred expenditure on the provision of the plant or machinery;

(b) a person who is connected with X;

(c) a person who acquired the plant or machinery from X as a result of a disposal on the occasion of which, or two or more disposals on the occasion of each of which there was a change in the persons carrying on the qualifying activity in relation to which Condition A or B was met;

(d) a person to whom the plant or machinery is leased and who is resident in the United Kingdom;

(e) a person to whom the plant or machinery is leased, who is carrying on a qualifying activity in the United Kingdom and who uses the plant or machinery for the short-term leasing in the course of that activity.

122(2A) Condition A is that–

(a) at least one person who carried on the qualifying activity immediately before or immediately after the change was within the charge to income tax in respect of that activity, and

(b) at least one person who carried on the qualifying activity before the change continued to carry it on after the change.

122(2B) Condition B is that–

(a) the qualifying activity was carried on in partnership both immediately before and immediately after the change,

(b) a company that was within the charge to corporation tax in respect of the activity carried it on immediately before or immediately after the change, and

(c) at least one company which carried the activity on before the change continued to carry it on after the change.

122(3) [Omitted by ITTOIA 2005, s. 882(1) and Sch. 1, para. 540(3), and repealed by ITTOIA 2005, s. 884 and Sch. 3.]

History – In s. 122(2)(c), the words "on the occasion of each of which there was a change in the persons carrying on the qualifying activity in relation to which Condition A or B was met" substituted for the former words by CTA 2009, s. 1322 and Sch. 1, para. 488(2), with effect for corporation tax purposes for accounting periods ending on or after 1 April 2009, and for income tax and capital gains tax purposes for the tax year 2009–10 and subsequent tax years.
Former s. 122(2)(c) substituted by ITTOIA 2005, s. 882(1) and Sch. 1, para. 540(2); effective for income tax purposes for 2005–06 onwards and for corporation tax purposes for accounting periods ending after 5 April 2005 (ITTOIA 2005, s. 883(1)).
S. 122(2A) inserted by CTA 2009, s. 1322 and Sch. 1, para. 488(3), with effect for corporation tax purposes for accounting periods ending on or after 1 April 2009, and for income tax and capital gains tax purposes for the tax year 2009–10 and subsequent tax years.
S. 122(2B) inserted by CTA 2009, s. 1322 and Sch. 1, para. 488(3), with effect for corporation tax purposes for accounting periods ending on or after 1 April 2009, and for income tax and capital gains tax purposes for the tax year 2009–10 and subsequent tax years.
S. 122(3) omitted by ITTOIA 2005, s. 882(1) and Sch. 1, para. 540(3), and repealed by ITTOIA 2005, s. 884 and Sch. 3; effective for income tax purposes for 2005–06 onwards and for corporation tax purposes for accounting periods ending after 5 April 2005 (ITTOIA 2005, s. 883(1)).

Origin – S. 122(1): CAA 1990, s. 39(1) (part), (3) (part), (4) (part).
S. 122(2): CAA 1990, s. 39(1) (part), (3) (part), (4) (part), (10) (part), 40(5) (part).
S. 122(3): CAA 1990, s. 40(5) (part).

Cross references – S. 84 (table): exception to rule that machinery or plant provided for leasing cannot be a short-life asset where used for a qualifying purpose (per s. 122) within the designated period.
S. 87: if a short-life asset provided for leasing ceases to be used for a qualifying purposes in the requisite period, tax written-down value is transferred to the general pool.
Sch. 3, para. 47(5), (6): first-year allowances for regional projects, expenditure incurred 1 November 1992 to 31 October 1993, Pt. 2, Ch. 11 applying – preclusion by reference to leased assets not used for a qualifying purpose in the designated period.
ICTA 1988, s. 113(2), 114(1): change in persons carrying on a trade etc. not a discontinuance where election involving continuing partner etc. or there is a company partner.

HMRC Manuals – CA24110: guidance on s. 122.

123 Ships and aircraft

123(1) A ship is used for a qualifying purpose at any time when it is let on charter in the course of a trade which consists of or includes operating ships by a person who is–

(a) resident in the United Kingdom or carries on the trade there, and

(b) responsible for navigating and managing the ship throughout the period of the charter and for defraying–

(i) all expenses in connection with the ship throughout that period, or

(ii) substantially all such expenses other than those directly incidental to a particular voyage or to the employment of the ship during that period.

123(2) Subsection (1) applies, with the necessary modifications, in relation to aircraft as it applies in relation to ships.

123(3) For the purposes of subsection (1)(b) a person is responsible for something if he–

(a) is responsible as principal, or

(b) appoints another person to be responsible in his place.

123(4) *Subsections (1) and (2)* do not apply if the main object, or one of the main objects–

(a) of the letting of the ship or aircraft on charter,

(b) of a series of transactions of which the letting of the ship or aircraft on charter was one, or

(c) of any of the transactions in such a series,

was to obtain a writing-down allowance determined without regard to section 109 (writing-down allowances at 10%) in respect of expenditure incurred by any person on the provision of the ship or aircraft.

Origin – S. 123(1): CAA 1990, s. 39(6) (part).
S. 123(2): CAA 1990, s. 39(7).
S. 123(3): CAA 1990, s. 39(6) (part).
S. 123(4): CAA 1990, s. 39(8).

Cross references – S. 84 (table): exception to rule that machinery or plant provided for leasing cannot be a short-life asset where used for a qualifying purpose (per s. 123) within the designated period.

Transitional – Sch. 3, para. 23: s. 123(1), (2) do not apply if the main object (or one of the main objects) of the letting of the ship or aircraft on charter, or of a series of transactions including the letting, or of any of the transactions in such a series, was to obtain a first-year allowance in respect of expenditure which was first-year qualifying expenditure under Sch. 3, para 47 (expenditure incurred between 1 November 1992 and 31 October 1993) and was incurred by any person on the provision of the ship or aircraft.

HMRC Manuals – CA24120: guidance on s. 123.

124 Transport containers

124(1) A transport container is used for a qualifying purpose at any time when it is leased in the course of a trade which is carried on by a person who–

(a) is resident in the United Kingdom, or

(b) carries on the trade there,

and either of the conditions given below is met.

124(2) The first condition is that–

(a) the person's trade consists of or includes the operation of ships or aircraft, and

(b) the container is at other times used by that person in connection with the operation of the ships or aircraft.

124(3) The second condition is that the container is leased under a succession of leases to different persons who are not, or most of whom are not, connected with each other.

Origin – S. 124: CAA 1990, s. 39(9).

Cross references – S. 84 (table): exception to rule that machinery or plant provided for leasing cannot be a short-life asset where used for a qualifying purpose (per s. 124) within the designated period.

HMRC Manuals – CA24130: guidance on s. 124.

125 Other qualifying purposes

125(1) Plant or machinery is used for a qualifying purpose at any time when subsection (2) or (4) applies.

125(2) This subsection applies if any of the persons listed in subsection (3) uses the plant or machinery for the purpose of a qualifying activity without leasing it.

125(3) The persons are–

(a) the person ("X") who incurred expenditure on the provision of the plant or machinery;

(b) a person who is connected with X;

(c) a person who acquired the plant or machinery from X as a result of a disposal on the occasion of each of which there was a change in the persons carrying on the qualifying activity in relation to which Condition A or B was met.

125(3A) Condition A is that–

(a) at least one person who carried on the qualifying activity immediately before or immediately after the change was within the charge to income tax in respect of that activity, and

(b) at least one person who carried on the qualifying activity before the change continued to carry it on after the change.

125(3B) Condition B is that–

(a) the qualifying activity was carried on in partnership both immediately before and immediately after the change,

(b) a company which was within the charge to corporation tax in respect of the activity carried it on immediately before or immediately after the change, and

(c) at least one company which carried the activity on before the change continued to carry it on after the change.

125(4) This subsection applies if–

(a) a lessee uses the plant or machinery for the purposes of a qualifying activity without leasing it, and

(b) if he had incurred expenditure on the provision of the plant or machinery at that time, the expenditure would have fallen to be included, in whole or in part, in his available qualifying expenditure for a chargeable period.

125(5) [Omitted by ITTOIA 2005, s. 882(1) and Sch. 1, para. 541(3), and repealed by ITTOIA 2005, s. 884 and Sch. 3.]

History – In s. 125(3)(c), the words "on the occasion of each of which there was a change in the persons carrying on the qualifying activity in relation to which Condition A or B was met." substituted for the former words by CTA 2009, s. 1322 and Sch. 1, para. 489(2), with effect for corporation tax purposes for accounting periods ending on or after 1 April 2009, and for income tax and capital gains tax purposes for the tax year 2009–10 and subsequent tax years.

S. 125(3)(c) substituted by ITTOIA 2005, s. 882(1) and Sch. 1, para. 541(2); effective for income tax purposes for 2005–06 onwards and for corporation tax purposes for accounting periods ending after 5 April 2005 (ITTOIA 2005, s. 883(1)).

S. 125(3A) inserted by CTA 2009, s. 1322 and Sch. 1, para. 489(3), with effect for corporation tax purposes for accounting periods ending on or after 1 April 2009, and for income tax and capital gains tax purposes for the tax year 2009–10 and subsequent tax years.

S. 125(3B) inserted by CTA 2009, s. 1322 and Sch. 1, para. 489(3), with effect for corporation tax purposes for accounting periods ending on or after 1 April 2009, and for income tax and capital gains tax purposes for the tax year 2009–10 and subsequent tax years.

S. 125(5) omitted by ITTOIA 2005, s. 882(1) and Sch. 1, para. 541(3), and repealed by ITTOIA 2005, s. 884 and Sch. 3; effective for income tax purposes for 2005–06 onwards and for corporation tax purposes for accounting periods ending after 5 April 2005 (ITTOIA 2005, s. 883(1)).

Origin – S. 125(1): CAA 1990, s. 39(1) (part).
S. 125(2): CAA 1990, s. 39(5) (part).
S. 125(3): CAA 1990, s. 39(5) (part), (10) (part), 40(5) (part).
S. 125(4): CAA 1990, s. 39(2) (part).
S. 125(5): CAA 1990, s. 40(5) (part).

Cross references – S. 84 (table): exception to rule that machinery or plant provided for leasing cannot be a short-life asset where used for a qualifying purpose (per s. 125) within the designated period.
Sch. 3, para. 47(5), (6): first-year allowances for regional projects, expenditure incurred 1 November 1992 to 31 October 1993, Pt. 2, Ch. 11 applying – preclusion by reference to leased assets not used for a qualifying purpose in the designated period.

HMRC Manuals – CA24110: guidance on s. 125.

MINOR DEFINITIONS

126 Minor definitions

126(1) In this Chapter **"normal writing-down allowance"** means a writing-down allowance of an amount determined without regard to sections 102 and 109 (reduced rates).

126(2) In this Chapter any reference, in relation to any person, to expenditure having qualified for a normal writing-down allowance is to–

(a) the expenditure, or part of it, having fallen to be included in that person's available qualifying expenditure for any chargeable period, and

(b) that available qualifying expenditure being expenditure which is not subject to section 102 or 109.

126(3) Any reference in this Chapter to a person's expenditure having qualified for a first-year allowance is to such an allowance having fallen to be made in respect of the whole or any part of the expenditure.

Origin – S. 126(1): CAA 1990, s. 50(3) ("normal writing-down allowances").
S. 126(2): CAA 1990, s. 50(4).
S. 126(3): CAA 1990, s. 50(4A).

HMRC Manuals – CA24010: a "normal writing-down allowance" is one at an annual rate of 25%.

Chapter 12 – Ships

POOLING AND POSTPONEMENT OF ALLOWANCES

127 Single ship pool

127(1) Qualifying expenditure incurred on the provision of a ship for the purposes of a qualifying activity, if allocated to a pool, must be allocated to a single asset pool (a **"single ship pool"**).

127(2) Subsection (1) is subject to the exceptions given in section 128 and any election under section 129 to use the appropriate non-ship pool.

127(3) In this Chapter **"the appropriate non-ship pool"**, in relation to a ship, means the pool to which the expenditure incurred on the provision of the ship would be allocated, or would have been allocated, apart from this Chapter.

Origin – S. 127(1), (2): CAA 1990, s. 31(1) (part), (2) (part).
S. 127(3): see Rewrite note below.

Cross references – S. 15–20: qualifying activities.
S. 54(3): different kinds of pools – provisions that provide for single asset pools include s. 127.
S. 84 (table): exception to rule that machinery or plant provided for leasing cannot be a short-life asset where used for a qualifying purpose (including a ship let on charter per s. 123) within the designated period.
S. 101(2)(b): expenditure allocated to a single asset pool cannot be allocated to the class pool for long-life asset expenditure.
S. 102(2): 6 per cent rate of writing-down allowance on expenditure on long-life assets still applies to expenditure allocated to a single asset pool.

Rewrite: Technical Points – Explanatory Notes, Annex 2, Note 30: the note explains that the effect of the introduction in the rewritten statute of pooling for expenditure on a ship, including the definition of a non-ship (or normal) pool in s. 127(3) (which is a direct consequence of the introduction of pooling and does not derive from any previous provision), is regarded as being the same as the previous position where expenditure was deemed to be for the purposes of a separate notional trade.

HMRC Manuals – CA25150: guidance and example on s. 127–129.

128 Expenditure which is not to be allocated to single ship pool

128(1) The expenditure is not to be allocated to a single ship pool if the ship is provided for leasing unless–

(a) the ship is not used for overseas leasing at any time in the designated period, or if it is, is used only for protected leasing, and

(b) it appears that the ship will be used for a qualifying purpose in the designated period and will not be used for any other purpose at any time in that period.

128(2) The expenditure is not to be allocated to a single ship pool if the qualifying activity for the purposes of which the ship is provided is special leasing of plant or machinery.

128(3) In subsection (1) **"leasing"**, **"overseas leasing"**, **"protected leasing"**, **"qualifying purpose"** and **"designated period"** have the same meaning as in Chapter 11 (overseas leasing).

Origin – S. 128(1), (2): CAA 1990, s. 31(1) (part).
S. 128(3): CAA 1990, s. 31(11) (part).

Cross references – S. 84 (table): exception to rule that machinery or plant provided for leasing cannot be a short-life asset where used for a qualifying purpose (including a ship let on charter per s. 123) within the designated period.
S. 107: overseas leasing pool.

HMRC Manuals – CA25150: guidance and example on s. 127–129.

129 Election to use the appropriate non-ship pool

129(1) A person who has incurred qualifying expenditure on the provision of a ship may, by an election made for a chargeable period, allocate to the appropriate non-ship pool–

(a) all or a part of any qualifying expenditure that would otherwise be allocated to a single ship pool, or

(b) all or a part of the available qualifying expenditure in a single ship pool.

129(2) An election under this section must be made by notice given to an officer of Revenue and Customs–

(a) for income tax purposes, on or before the normal time limit for amending a tax return for the tax year in which the relevant chargeable period ends;

(b) for corporation tax purposes, no later than 2 years after the end of the relevant chargeable period.

129(3) **"The relevant chargeable period"** means the chargeable period for which the election is made.

History – In s. 129(2), the words "an officer of Revenue and Customs" substituted for "the Inland Revenue" by CRCA 2005, s. 50(6) and Sch. 4, para. 83(1), with effect from 18 April 2005 by virtue of SI 2005/1126, art. 2(2).

Origin – S. 129(1): CAA 1990, s. 33(1) (part), (3) (part), (4) (part), (5) (part).
S. 129(2), (3): CAA 1990, s. 33(5A) (part).

Cross references – S. 57(2): "available qualifying expenditure" in a pool for a chargeable period includes any amount allocated to the pool under s. 129(1).
TMA 1970, s. 42(6), (7)(c) (as amended by Sch. 2, para. 1): claims made by partnerships.

Rewrite: Changes in Law – Explanatory Notes, Annex 1, Change 21: s. 129 replaces the previous entitlement (in CAA 1990, s. 33(1)) to give *notice* not to apply the separate notional trade rules for ships with a right of election to allocate expenditure to the non-ship (i.e. normal) pool instead. This is a change in the context of the introduction of pooling for ships (see s. 127 Rewrite note) but is also a small change in the law which means a claim must be made in an open return and thus allows for an error or mistake claim to be made if appropriate. The time limit for making a claim is not affected. Although this change is intended to be beneficial, there is a right of election for the previous position to apply to a period which straddles 6 April (income tax) or 1 April (corporation tax) 2001 (Sch. 3, para. 8).

Rewrite: Technical Points – Explanatory Notes, Annex 2, Notes 31 to 33: these three notes explain the omission of parts of the previous statute in CAA 1990, s. 33, from the rewritten legislation in the light of the introduction of pooling and the change to an election to disapply pooling referred to in the note above. They may be summarised:

> s. 33(3)(a) is omitted because, once allowances have been given, a notice to disapply the separate notional trade rule triggers a deemed a discontinuance of the notional trade and introduction of a disposal value, but with no balancing charge or allowance. As the expenditure for the purposes of the actual trade is the same as the balance for the notional trade **ignoring** s. 33, the bringing in of a disposal value is of no consequence (Note 31);
>
> the notice under s. 33(1) had effect "from the beginning of a chargeable period", whereas the election under s. 129 applies "for a chargeable period". The introduction of pooling, coupled with the change in wording in s. 132 (see Rewrite note under that section), means it is no longer necessary to spell out that an election applies from the beginning of a chargeable period as the effect will be the same as that under the separate notional trade rules (note 32); and
>
> a notice under s. 33(1) could not be made for "the chargeable period relating to the permanent discontinuance of that [notional] trade" whereas an election to use a non-ship pool under the rewritten provision has no such restriction. However, the omission of CAA 1990, s. 33(3)(a) (see above), coupled with the changes in s. 132 (see Rewrite note under that section), mean that there will be no balance of expenditure for which an election can be made in any event. The overall effect on discontinuance is therefore unchanged (note 33).

In addition, the main Explanatory Notes (Note 499) explain the omission from s. 129 of the previous provision in CAA 1990, s. 33(2) (which is purely a feature of the superseded notional trade régime and therefore obviated by pooling).

HMRC Manuals – CA25150: guidance and example on s. 127–129.

130 Notice postponing first-year or writing-down allowance

130(1) A person who is entitled to a first-year allowance for a chargeable period in respect of qualifying expenditure on the provision of a ship may, by notice, postpone all or part of the allowance.

130(2) A person who is entitled to a writing-down allowance for a chargeable period in respect of qualifying expenditure allocated to a single ship pool may, by notice, postpone all or part of the allowance.

130(3) A notice under this section must specify the amount postponed.

130(4) A notice under this section must be given to an officer of Revenue and Customs–

(a) for income tax purposes, on or before the normal time limit for amending a tax return for the tax year in which the relevant chargeable period ends;

(b) for corporation tax purposes, no later than 2 years after the end of the relevant chargeable period.

130(5) **"The relevant chargeable period"** means the chargeable period for which the person is entitled to the allowance.

130(6) If a person entitled to a first-year allowance in respect of qualifying expenditure on the provision of a ship claims the allowance in respect of part of the expenditure, subsection (1) applies to the allowance claimed.

130(7) If a person entitled to a writing-down allowance in respect of qualifying expenditure allocated to a single ship pool requires the allowance to be reduced to a specified amount, subsection (2) applies to the allowance as so reduced.

History – In s. 130(4), the words "an officer of Revenue and Customs" substituted for "the Inland Revenue" by CRCA 2005, s. 50(6) and Sch. 4, para. 83(1), with effect from 18 April 2005 by virtue of SI 2005/1126, art. 2(2).

Origin – S. 130(1): CAA 1990, s. 30(1) (part).
S. 130(2): CAA 1990, s. 31(1) (part), (3) (part).
S. 130(3): CAA 1990, s. 30(1) (part), 31(3) (part).
S. 130(4), (5): CAA 1990, s. 30(1) (part), (1A) (part), 31(3) (part), (3A) (part).
S. 130(6): CAA 1990, s. 30(5).
S. 130(7): CAA 1990, s. 31(6).

Cross references – S. 113(1)(c), (2): overseas leasing, recovery of excess allowances where asset is a ship – allowances postponed under s. 130 to be allocated to a long-life asset or overseas leasing pool for the chargeable period following the chargeable period in which the ship is first used for overseas leasing which is not protected leasing.
FA 2000, Sch. 22, para. 22F: no notice to be given under s. 130 if a ship ceases to be a qualifying ship by virtue of FA 2000, Sch. 22, para. 22E (re-flagging); qualifying ship operated by tonnage tax company ceasing to be qualifying ship.
FA 2000, Sch. 22, para. 69(4) (as amended by Sch. 2, para. 108(3)): entry into tonnage tax – unrelieved qualifying expenditure includes qualifying expenditure unrelieved by virtue of notice under s. 130.
FA 2000, Sch. 22, para. 100(2)(b)(ii)) (as amended by Sch. 2, para. 108(29)): tonnage tax – determination of tax written down value of a ship assumes that there had been made to the lessor any first year allowances which had been postponed by virtue of a notice under s. 130.
FA 2000, Sch. 22, para. 112(5)) (as amended by Sch. 2, para. 108(34)): tonnage tax elections – qualifying expenditure for capital allowances claim; unrelieved qualifying expenditure includes qualifying expenditure unrelieved by virtue of notice under s. 130.

HMRC Manuals – CA25200: guidance and example on s. 130 and 131.

131 Effect of postponement

131(1) If a person gives notice in respect of a chargeable period under section 130–

(a) the allowance is withheld or withdrawn to the extent that it is postponed, but

(b) sections 57 to 59 (calculation of available qualifying expenditure) apply as if the allowance had been made to the person without any postponement.

131(2) On making a claim, the person is entitled to have all or part of a postponed first-year allowance made to him as a first-year allowance for one or more subsequent chargeable periods in which he is carrying on the qualifying activity.

131(3) On making a claim, the person is entitled to have all or part of a postponed writing-down allowance made to him as a writing-down allowance for one or more subsequent chargeable periods in which he is carrying on the qualifying activity.

131(4) The total amount of any first-year allowances made under subsection (2) or writing-down allowances made under subsection (3) must not exceed the amount of the postponed allowance in question.

131(5) A writing-down allowance made under subsection (3) is ignored for the purposes of section 59 (unrelieved qualifying expenditure).

131(6) The fact that a postponed writing-down allowance is claimed for a chargeable period does not affect entitlement to, or the amount of, any other writing-down allowance to which the person is otherwise entitled for that chargeable period.

131(7) A postponed allowance is not, merely because of the postponement, included in the reference in section 101(3) of CTA 2010 (group relief: meaning of "capital allowance excess") to an allowance or amount brought forward from an earlier period.

History – In s. 131(7), the words "section 101(3) of CTA 2010 (group relief: meaning of "capital allowance excess")" substituted for "section 403ZB(2) of ICTA (group relief)" and "brought" substituted for "carried" by CTA 2010, s. 1177 and Sch. 1, para. 337, with effect for corporation tax purposes for accounting periods ending on or after 1 April 2010, and for income tax and capital gains tax purposes for the tax year 2010–11 and subsequent tax years.

Origin – S. 131(1): CAA 1990, s. 30(2) (part), 31(4) (part).
S. 131(2): CAA 1990, s. 30(2) (part).
S. 131(3): CAA 1990, s. 31(4) (part).
S. 131(4): CAA 1990, s. 30(2) (part), 31(4) (part).
S. 131(5): Drafting.
S. 131(6): CAA 1990, s. 31(5).
S. 131(7): CAA 1990, s. 30(4), 31(10).

Cross references – S. 113(1)(a), (2): overseas leasing, recovery of excess allowances where asset is a ship – no allowance to be made under s. 131(3) for the chargeable period following the chargeable period in which the ship is first used for overseas leasing which is not protected leasing or for any subsequent chargeable period.
TMA 1970, s. 42(6), (7)(c) (as amended by Sch. 2, para. 1): claims made by partnerships.

Rewrite: Technical Points – Explanatory Notes, Annex 2, Note 34: under s. 130, a first-year allowance (FYA) or writing down allowance (WDA) may be postponed in whole or in part. When a FYA is postponed, expenditure equal to the full amount of the FYA is not available for pooling, but the remaining expenditure is still available for WDAs. In rewriting the statute derived from CAA 1990, s. 30(2), s. 131(1)(b) avoids the approach of the previous provision (which "disregards" expenditure equal to the amount of the FYA) in favour of calculating the pool of expenditure which qualifies for WDAs ignoring any postponement; i.e. as if full FYAs had been claimed and given. This is intended to clarify:

- that, notwithstanding postponement, for the purposes of calculating the pool maximum FYAs are still treated as having been given on the expenditure; and
- the situation where there is only a partial postponement, which could have been interpreted as requiring expenditure equal to the FYAs actually claimed to be disregarded, as well as the total FYAs,

and is not a change of law. It removes any need for CAA 1990, s. 30(5) and 31(6) (interpretation of relief for postponed allowances where there has been a partial postponement of FYAs and WDAs respectively) to be rewritten into the new legislation.

HMRC Manuals – CA25200: guidance and example on s. 130 and 131.

132 Disposal events and single ship pool

132(1) A person is required to bring a disposal value into account in a single ship pool if the ship–

(a) is provided for leasing, and

(b) begins to be used otherwise than for a qualifying purpose within the first 4 years of the designated period.

132(2) If any disposal event (including one under subsection (1)) occurs in relation to a single ship pool–

(a) the available qualifying expenditure in the single ship pool is allocated, for the chargeable period in which the event occurs, to the appropriate non-ship pool,

(b) the disposal value must be brought into account as a disposal value for that chargeable period in the appropriate non-ship pool, and

(c) the single ship pool ends without a final chargeable period and without any liability to a balancing charge arising.

132(3) Subsections (1) and (2) apply even if, as a result of an election under section 129, some of the qualifying expenditure on the provision of the ship has been allocated to the appropriate non-ship pool.

132(4) In subsection (1) **"leasing"**, **"qualifying purpose"** and **"designated period"** have the same meaning as in Chapter 11 (overseas leasing).

Origin – S. 132(1): CAA 1990, s. 31(2) (part), 40(4) (part).
S. 132(2): CAA 1990, s. 24(6) (part), (8) (part), 31(7) (part).
S. 132(3): CAA 1990, s. 31(7) (part), 33(5) (part), drafting.
S. 132(4): CAA 1990, s. 31(11) (part).

Cross references – S. 57(2): "available qualifying expenditure" in a pool for a chargeable period includes any amount allocated to the pool under s. 132(2).
S. 60(1)(b): meaning of "disposal receipt" includes a value that a person is required to bring into account for purposes of any of the provisions listed in s. 66 (see note further below re s. 66).
S. 65(3): definition of "final chargeable period" for a single asset pool is subject to there being no such period under s. 132(2)(c).
S. 66: list of provisions about disposal values includes s. 132.
S. 113(1)(b): overseas leasing, recovery of excess allowances where asset is a ship – nothing in s. 132(2) restricts the operation of s. 111.

Rewrite: Technical Points – Explanatory Notes, Annex 2, Note 35: following the introduction of pooling in place of the previous notional trade régime, the opportunity was taken to adopt a change in approach to the treatment of disposals. S. 132(2) continues the previous rule (in CAA 1990, s. 31(7)) that there is no cessation and no balancing charge arises when there is a disposal out of a single ship pool. However, in allocating any balance of qualifying expenditure to the s. 127(3) non-ship pool, the remaining unallowed expenditure in the single ship pool is first transferred to the non-ship pool and then the disposal value of the ship is brought into the non-ship pool (which now includes the unallowed expenditure on that ship). This is in contrast to the previous approach whereby, having already said that no balancing charge or allowance would arise, the disposal value was first brought into the calculation of a deemed balancing charge (or allowance) on the notional trade and that balancing charge (or allowance) was then deducted from (or added to) the normal pool. The overall effect is the same but, having repeated that no balancing charge arises on the disposal, the rewritten legislation avoids the potentially confusing need to calculate a deemed allowance or charge first.

HMRC Manuals – CA25250: guidance and example on s. 132.

133 Ship not used

133(1) This section applies if–

(a) a person has incurred qualifying expenditure on the provision of a ship for the purposes of a qualifying activity, and

CAA 2001

(b) the ship ceases to be owned by the person without having been brought into use for the purposes of the qualifying activity.

133(2) Any writing-down allowances that have previously been made in respect of qualifying expenditure in the single ship pool (or which have been postponed) must be withdrawn.

133(3) The amount of any writing-down allowances withdrawn under subsection (2) is allocated, for the chargeable period in which the person ceases to own the ship, to the appropriate non-ship pool.

133(4) Any adjustments required by this section are in addition to any adjustments required under section 132 (disposal events and single ship pool).

Origin – S. 133(1): CAA 1990, s. 31(1) (part), 32(1) (part).
S. 133(2) to (4): CAA 1990, s. 32(1) (part).

Cross references – S. 57(2): "available qualifying expenditure" in a pool for a chargeable period includes any amount allocated to the pool under s. 133(3).
S. 58(6): where no allocation made for a previous period, balance of qualifying expenditure after first-year allowance must be allocated to a pool for a period in which a disposal is made (even where first-year allowance made in same period).
FA 2000, Sch. 22, para. 72(1): entry into tonnage tax – conditions in which expenditure on new shipping will be taken into account where claim for deferment of balancing charge made under s. 135–156.
FA 2000, Sch. 22, para. 80(4): disapplication of s. 135–156 when company subject to tonnage tax.

HMRC Manuals – CA25275: guidance on s. 133.

DEFERMENT OF BALANCING CHARGES

Cross references – FA 2000, Sch. 22, para. 72(1): entry into tonnage tax – conditions in which expenditure on new shipping will be taken into account where claim for deferment of balancing charge made under s. 135–156.
FA 2000, Sch. 22, para. 80(4): disapplication of s. 135–156 when company subject to tonnage tax.

134 Deferment of balancing charges: introduction

134(1) Sections 135 to 156 enable a balancing charge that arises when there is a disposal event in respect of a ship to be deferred and attributed to qualifying expenditure on another ship.

134(2) In this Chapter **"the deferment rules"** means sections 135 to 156.

Origin – S. 134: Drafting.

135 Claim for deferment

135(1) A person (**"the shipowner"**) who is liable to a balancing charge for a chargeable period may claim deferment of all or part of the charge if–

(a) in the chargeable period there is a disposal event (**"the relevant disposal event"**) in respect of a ship (**"the old ship"**),

(b) the old ship–

(i) was provided for the purposes of a qualifying activity carried on by the shipowner, and

(ii) was owned by the shipowner at some time in the chargeable period, and

(c) the conditions in section 136 are met.

135(2) The amount which may be deferred is subject to the limit in section 138.

135(3) For income tax purposes, a claim for deferment must be made on or before the normal time limit for amending a tax return for the tax year in which the relevant chargeable period ends.

135(4) **"The relevant chargeable period"** means the chargeable period for which the shipowner is liable to the balancing charge.

135(5) For corporation tax purposes, Part IX of Schedule 18 to FA 1998 applies in relation to the making of a claim for deferment as it applies in relation to the making of a claim for an allowance.

Origin – S. 135(1): CAA 1990, s. 33A(1) (part), (2) (part).
S. 135(2): CAA 1990, s. 33A(2) (part).
S. 135(3), (4): CAA 1990, s. 33F(2) (part).
S. 135(5): CAA 1990, s. 33F(1).

Cross references – TMA 1970, s. 42(6), (7)(c) (as amended by Sch. 2, para. 1): claims made by partnerships.
FA 2000, Sch. 22, para. 22F: qualifying ship operated by tonnage tax company ceasing to be qualifying ship.
FA 2000, Sch. 22, para. 72(1): entry into tonnage tax – conditions in which expenditure on new shipping will be taken into account where claim for deferment of balancing charge made under s. 135–156.
FA 2000, Sch. 22, para. 80(4): disapplication of s. 135–156 when company subject to tonnage tax.

HMRC Manuals – CA25400: guidance on s. 135–137.

136 Further conditions for deferment

136 The conditions referred to in section 135(1)(c) are that–

(a) the relevant disposal event is of a kind mentioned in section 61(1)(a) to (d) (cessation of ownership, loss, abandonment, destruction etc. of ship),

(b) the old ship was a qualifying ship immediately before the relevant disposal event,

(c) the shipowner has not incurred a loss in respect of the qualifying activity for the chargeable period for which he is liable to the balancing charge, and

(d) no amount in respect of the old ship has been allocated to–

(i) the overseas leasing pool,

(ii) a single asset pool under section 206 (plant or machinery provided or used partly for purposes other than those of the qualifying activity),

(iii) a single asset pool under section 211 (payment of partial depreciation subsidy), or

(iv) a pool for a qualifying activity consisting of special leasing.

Origin – S. 136: CAA 1990, s. 33A(1) (part), (7) (part).

Cross references – FA 2000, Sch. 22, para. 80(4): disapplication of s. 135–156 when company subject to tonnage tax.

HMRC Manuals – CA25400: guidance on s. 135–137.

137 Effect of deferment

137 A claim for deferment is given effect by allocating the amount deferred, for the chargeable period in respect of which the claim is made, to the appropriate non-ship pool.

Origin – S. 137: CAA 1990, s. 33A(2) (part).

Cross references – S. 57(2): "available qualifying expenditure" in a pool for a chargeable period includes any amount allocated to the pool under s. 137.
FA 2000, Sch. 22, para. 80(4): disapplication of s. 135–156 when company subject to tonnage tax.

HMRC Manuals – CA25400: guidance on s. 135–137.

138 Limit on amount deferred

138(1) The amount deferred must not exceed the smallest of the following amounts–

(a) the amount of any balancing charge which, if the claim for deferment had not been made, would have been made for the chargeable period for which deferment is claimed in the appropriate non-ship pool;

(b) the amount given by section 139 (amount taken into account in respect of the old ship);

(c) the amount which is, or is expected to be, the amount of expenditure on new shipping incurred–

(i) by the shipowner or, if the shipowner is a company, by another company which is a member of the same group at the time when the expenditure is incurred, and

(ii) within the period of 6 years beginning with the relevant disposal event;

(d) the amount of the shipowner's profits or income from the qualifying activity for the chargeable period for which deferment is claimed.

138(2) In determining profits or income for the purposes of subsection (1)(d)–

(a) any other amounts deferred under section 135 are to be taken into account, and

(b) any amounts brought forward under section 83 of ITA 2007 or section 45 of CTA 2010 (losses) are to be disregarded.

History – In s. 138(2)(b), the words "section 45 of CTA 2010" substituted for "section 393 of ICTA" by CTA 2010, s. 1177 and Sch. 1, para. 338, with effect for corporation tax purposes for accounting periods ending on or after 1 April 2010, and for income tax and capital gains tax purposes for the tax year 2010–11 and subsequent tax years.
In s. 138(2)(b) the words "section 83 of ITA 2007 or section" substituted for the words "section 385 or" by ITA 2007, s. 1027 and Sch. 1, para. 400, with effect from 6 April 2007.

Origin – S. 138(1): CAA 1990, s. 33A(2) (part), (3) (part), (6).
S. 138(2): CAA 1990, s. 33A(3) (part).

Cross references – FA 2000, Sch. 22, para. 80(4): disapplication of s. 135–156 when company subject to tonnage tax.

Rewrite: Changes in Law – Explanatory Notes, Annex 1, Change 22: the amount of a balancing charge that can be deferred under s. 135 cannot exceed the smallest of four certain other amounts. The first of these is the amount of any balancing charge which, in the absence of a claim to defer, would otherwise have arisen in *the non-ship pool* to which the expenditure would have been allocated if the ship rules did not apply (s. 138(1)(a)). This is a tighter limitation than that which applied previously and which was by reference to any balancing charge on the actual trade (CAA 1990, s. 33A(3)(c)). In practice, this could extend to include balancing charges on other separate notional trades, subject to specific exclusions (in CAA 1990, s. 33A(6)). Because those exclusions were meant to be comprehensive, they stipulated each statutory balancing charge. However, in time the list of exclusions apparently became deficient, thus creating an ability to increase the deferral to an amount greater than that originally intended by including balancing charges on, for example, short or long-life assets. These had been introduced subsequently, but the need to add them to the list of exclusions had been overlooked. By making the restriction specific, the rewritten statute becomes sufficiently unequivocal and restores the position to what was intended. It also obviates the need to update the exclusions. There is a right of election for the previous position to apply to a period which straddles 6 April (income tax) or 1 April (corporation tax) 2001 (Sch. 3, para. 8).

HMRC Manuals – CA25450: guidance and example on s. 138.

139 Amount taken into account in respect of old ship

139(1) The amount taken into account in respect of the old ship for the purposes of section 138(1)(b) is–

(a) amount A, if no election has been made under section 129 (election to use appropriate non-ship pool) in respect of any of the qualifying expenditure incurred on the provision of the ship, or

(b) amount B, in any other case.

CAA 2001

139(2) Amount A is the amount which falls to be brought into account as a disposal value in the appropriate non-ship pool under section 132(2)(b) as a result of the relevant disposal event, less the available qualifying expenditure allocated to the appropriate non-ship pool under section 132(2)(a).

139(3) Amount B is–

$$DV - (QE - WDA - FYA)$$

where–

DV is the amount of the disposal value required to be brought into account in respect of the old ship,

QE is all the qualifying expenditure incurred in respect of the old ship,

WDA is the maximum amount of any writing-down allowances which (on the assumptions in subsection (4)) could have been made in respect of that qualifying expenditure for chargeable periods up to (but not including) the one in respect of which the claim for deferment is made, and

FYA is the total of any first-year allowances actually made or postponed in respect of the old ship.

139(4) The assumptions are that–

(a) all the qualifying expenditure in respect of the old ship is (and has always been) allocated to the appropriate non-ship pool, and

(b) no other qualifying expenditure has been allocated to that pool.

139(5) If an election is made under section 129 (election to use appropriate non-ship pool) after the determination under this section of the amount taken into account in respect of the old ship, the amount is, and is treated as always having been, amount B and not amount A.

Origin – S. 139(1): CAA 1990, s. 33B(1) (part), (2) (part).
S. 139(2): CAA 1990, s. 33B(1) (part).
S. 139(3): CAA 1990, s. 33B(2) (part), (3) (part).
S. 139(4): CAA 1990, s. 33B(3) (part).
S. 139(5): CAA 1990, s. 33B(4).

Cross references – FA 2000, Sch. 22, para. 80(4): disapplication of s. 135–156 when company subject to tonnage tax.

HMRC Manuals – CA25475: guidance and example on s. 139.

ATTRIBUTION OF DEFERRED AMOUNTS

140 Notice attributing deferred amounts to new expenditure

140(1) The shipowner may, by notice to an officer of Revenue and Customs, attribute all or part of an amount deferred under section 135 to expenditure on new shipping.

140(2) An amount attributed under this section is attributed to an equal amount of the expenditure on new shipping.

140(3) Subsection (1) is subject to subsections (4) and (5) and section 141 (deferred amounts attributed to earlier expenditure first).

140(4) Subsection (1) applies only if the expenditure on new shipping is incurred–

(a) by the shipowner or, if the shipowner is a company, by another company which is a member of the same group at the time when the expenditure is incurred, and

(b) within the period of 6 years beginning with the relevant disposal event.

140(5) An amount may be attributed to expenditure on new shipping only to the extent that amounts have not already been attributed to it under this section.

140(6) A notice given in respect of expenditure incurred by another company does not have effect unless the other company joins the shipowner in giving it.

History – In s. 140(1), the words "an officer of Revenue and Customs" substituted for "the Inland Revenue" by CRCA 2005, s. 50(6) and Sch. 4, para. 83(1), with effect from 18 April 2005 by virtue of SI 2005/1126, art. 2(2).

Origin – S. 140(1)–(3): CAA 1990, s. 33A(5) (part).
S. 140(4): CAA 1990, s. 33A(5) (part), (8).
S. 140(5): CAA 1990, s. 33A(5) (part).
S. 140(6): CAA 1990, s. 33A(5A).

Cross references – S. 60(4): general meaning of "disposal event" does not include a disposal event under s. 140.
FA 2000, Sch. 22, para. 80(4): disapplication of s. 135–156 when company subject to tonnage tax.

HMRC Manuals – CA25500: guidance and example on s. 140–142.

141 Deferred amounts attributed to earlier expenditure first

141(1) No part of an amount deferred under section 135 is to be attributed to the whole or a part of any expenditure on new shipping (**"the current expenditure"**) if there is other expenditure (**"the earlier expenditure"**) which–

(a) was incurred before the current expenditure but at the same time as or after the relevant disposal event,

(b) was incurred by the shipowner or, if the shipowner is a company, by another company which was a member of the same group at the time the earlier expenditure was incurred, and

(c) is expenditure on new shipping, or would be treated as such but for an election under section 129 (election to use appropriate non-ship pool),

unless the condition in subsection (2) is met in relation to the earlier expenditure.

141(2) The condition is that–

(a) amounts have been attributed to all the earlier expenditure under section 140, and

(b) the attributions have been made in the case of the amount deferred and any other amounts deferred under section 135 as a result of disposal events occurring at the same time as or before the relevant disposal event.

Origin – S. 141(1): CAA 1990, s. 33D(6) (part).
S. 141(2): CAA 1990, s. 33D(6) (part).

Cross references – FA 2000, Sch. 22, para. 80(4): disapplication of s. 135–156 when company subject to tonnage tax.

Rewrite: Changes in Law – Explanatory Notes, Annex 1, Change 23: s. 141 (2)(b) widens the circumstances in which deferred balancing charges can be attributed to new expenditure (known as "roll-over relief for balancing charges") where two ships are disposed of simultaneously. Under the previous statute (CAA 1990, s. 33D(6)), a deferred charge must be attributed to the earliest unattributed possible expenditure on new shipping incurred in the six-year period (now in s. 138(1)(c)(ii)). Specifically, a deferred charge cannot be attributed to later expenditure where there is earlier expenditure, unless the earlier expenditure has been attributed to that charge already (i.e. the expenditure is less than the deferred charge) or else it has been attributed to a deferred charge which arose on an earlier disposal. The relaxation allows an attribution to be made to the earlier expenditure of another deferred charge which arose *at the same time* as the first deferred charge for which attribution is sought, as well as one which arose earlier. This gives greater flexibility in attribution than was previously the case. Although this change is intended to be beneficial, there is a right of election for the previous position to apply to a period which straddles 6 April (income tax) or 1 April (corporation tax) 2001 (Sch. 3, para. 8).

HMRC Manuals – CA25500: guidance and example on s. 140–142.

142 Variation of attribution

142(1) The shipowner may, by notice, vary an attribution under section 140 (notice attributing deferred amounts to new expenditure).

142(2) The notice must be given to an officer of Revenue and Customs on or before the time limit for the shipowner to make a claim for deferment in respect of the relevant chargeable period.

142(3) For the time limit for making a claim for deferment, see section 135(3) to (5).

142(4) For the purposes of subsection (2), it is to be assumed that–

(a) the shipowner is liable to a balancing charge for the relevant chargeable period, and

(b) a claim for deferment of that balancing charge can be made for the relevant chargeable period.

142(5) **"The relevant chargeable period"** means the earliest chargeable period in which expenditure to which the variation relates is incurred.

142(6) If the person to whose expenditure the notice relates is not the shipowner, a notice under subsection (1) does not have effect unless the person joins the shipowner in giving it.

History – In s. 142(2), the words "an officer of Revenue and Customs" substituted for "the Inland Revenue" by CRCA 2005, s. 50(6) and Sch. 4, para. 83(1), with effect from 18 April 2005 by virtue of SI 2005/1126, art. 2(2).

Origin – S. 142(1)–(5): CAA 1990, s. 33F(4) (part).
S. 142(6): CAA 1990, s. 33F(4A).

Cross references – FA 2000, Sch. 22, para. 80(4): disapplication of s. 135–156 when company subject to tonnage tax.

HMRC Manuals – CA25500: guidance and example on s. 140–142.

143 Effect of attribution

143(1) This section applies if a notice is given under section 140 attributing an amount to expenditure on new shipping.

143(2) The amount must be brought into account as a disposal value–

(a) for the chargeable period in which the expenditure is incurred, and

(b) in the single ship pool to which the expenditure is allocated.

Origin – S. 143: CAA 1990, s. 33C(1), (2).

Cross references – S. 60(1)(b): meaning of "disposal receipt" includes a value that a person is required to bring into account for purposes of any of the provisions listed in s. 66 (see note further below).
S. 60(4): general meaning of "disposal event" does not include a disposal event under s. 143.
S. 66: list of provisions about disposal values includes s. 143.
FA 2000, Sch. 22, para. 80(4): disapplication of s. 135–156 when company subject to tonnage tax.

144 Amounts which cease to be attributable

144(1) This section applies if–

(a) an amount has been deferred under section 135, and

(b) circumstances arise in which any part of the amount ceases (otherwise than by being attributed) to be attributable.

144(2) The shipowner is assumed not to have been entitled to defer so much of the amount as ceases to be attributable.

144(3) For the purposes of this section an amount is attributable if it may be attributed to expenditure on new shipping in accordance with section 140.

Origin – S. 144: CAA 1990, s. 33A(4).

Cross references – FA 2000, Sch. 22, para. 80(4): disapplication of s. 135–156 when company subject to tonnage tax.

145 Requirement to notify where no entitlement to defer amounts

145(1) This section applies if–

(a) an amount has been deferred under section 135, and

(b) circumstances arise that require the shipowner to be treated as if he was not entitled to defer all or part of the amount.

145(2) The shipowner must give notice of the fact to an officer of Revenue and Customs, specifying the circumstances.

145(3) The notice must be given no later than 3 months after the end of the chargeable period in which the circumstances first arise.

145(4) An assessment to tax chargeable as a result of the circumstances may be made at any time in the period which–

(a) begins when those circumstances arise, and

(b) ends 12 months after the shipowner gives notice of them to an officer of Revenue and Customs.

145(5) Subsection (4) applies in spite of any limitation on the time for making assessments.

History – In s. 145(2), the words "an officer of Revenue and Customs" substituted for "the Inland Revenue" by CRCA 2005, s. 50(6) and Sch. 4, para. 83(1), with effect from 18 April 2005 by virtue of SI 2005/1126, art. 2(2).
In s. 145(4), the words "an officer of Revenue and Customs" substituted for "the Inland Revenue" by CRCA 2005, s. 50(6) and Sch. 4, para. 83(1) with effect from 18 April 2005 by virtue of SI 2005/1126, art. 2(2).

Origin – S. 145(1)–(3): CAA 1990, s. 33F(5).
S. 145(4), (5): CAA 1990, s. 33F(6) (part).

Cross references – TMA 1970, s. 98 (as amended by Sch. 2, para. 4): penalties in respect of s. 145(2), (3).
FA 2000, Sch. 22, para. 80(4): disapplication of s. 135–156 when company subject to tonnage tax.

EXPENDITURE ON NEW SHIPPING

146 Basic meaning of expenditure on new shipping

146(1) For the purposes of the deferment rules, expenditure on the provision of a ship is expenditure on new shipping if the conditions in subsection (3) are met.

146(2) Subsection (1) is subject to sections 147 to 150.

146(3) The conditions are that–

(a) the expenditure is qualifying expenditure incurred by a person wholly and exclusively for the purposes of a qualifying activity carried on by him,

(b) when the expenditure is incurred, it appears that the ship will–

(i) be brought into use for the purposes of the qualifying activity as a qualifying ship, and

(ii) continue to be a qualifying ship for at least 3 years after that, and

(c) the expenditure is allocated to a single ship pool.

Origin – S. 146: CAA 1990, s. 33D(1).

Cross references – FA 2000, Sch. 22, para. 80(4): disapplication of s. 135–156 when company subject to tonnage tax.

HMRC Manuals – CA25600: guidance on s. 146–150.

147 Exclusions: ship previously owned

147(1) Expenditure on the provision of a ship is not expenditure on new shipping if the person who incurred the expenditure–

(a) has already owned the ship in the period of 6 years ending with the time when he first owns it as a result of incurring the expenditure, or

(b) was connected at a material time with a person who owned the ship at any time during that period.

147(2) For this purpose a material time is–

(a) the time when the expenditure was incurred, or

(b) any earlier time in the 6 year period beginning with the relevant disposal event.

Origin – S. 147(1): CAA 1990, s. 33D(4) (part).
S. 147(2): CAA 1990, s. 33D(5).

Cross references – FA 2000, Sch. 22, para. 80(4): disapplication of s. 135–156 when company subject to tonnage tax.

HMRC Manuals – CA25600: guidance on s. 146–150.

148 Exclusions: object to secure deferment

148 Expenditure on the provision of a ship is not expenditure on new shipping if the object, or one of the main objects, of–

(a) the transaction by which the ship was provided for the purposes of a qualifying activity carried on by the person who incurred the expenditure,

(b) any series of transactions of which that transaction was one, or

(c) any transaction in such a series,

was to secure the deferment of a balancing charge under section 135.

Origin – S. 148: CAA 1990, s. 33D(4) (part).

Cross references – FA 2000, Sch. 22, para. 80(4): disapplication of s. 135–156 when company subject to tonnage tax.

HMRC Manuals – CA25600: guidance on s. 146–150.

149 Exclusions: later events

149(1) Expenditure on the provision of a ship is not, and is treated as never having been, expenditure on new shipping if–

(a) at a time during the period mentioned in subsection (2), the ship is not a qualifying ship,

(b) the expenditure is allocated to a pool as a result of an election under section 129 (election to use appropriate non-ship pool), or

(c) section 107 applies in relation to the expenditure (overseas leasing).

149(2) The period referred to in subsection (1)(a) is–

(a) the period of 3 years beginning with the time when the ship is first brought into use for the purposes of a qualifying activity carried on–

  (i) by the person ("A") who incurred the expenditure, or

  (ii) if earlier, by a person connected with A, or

(b) if shorter, the period beginning with that time and ending when neither A nor a person connected with A owns the ship.

Origin – S. 149(1): CAA 1990, s. 33D(2) (part), (3).
S. 149(2): CAA 1990, s. 33D(2) (part).

Cross references – FA 2000, Sch. 22, para. 80(4): disapplication of s. 135–156 when company subject to tonnage tax.

HMRC Manuals – CA25600: guidance on s. 146–150.

150 Exclusions where expenditure not incurred by shipowner

150(1) Expenditure on the provision of a ship is not, and is treated as never having been, expenditure on new shipping if–

(a) it is incurred by a company which is a member of the same group as the shipowner at the time when the expenditure is incurred, and

(b) subsection (2) or (4) applies.

150(2) This subsection applies (subject to subsection (3)) if–

(a) the ship ceases to be owned by the company before it has been brought into use for the purposes of a qualifying activity carried on by the company, or

(b) a disposal event occurs in respect of the ship within 3 years of its first being brought into use for the purposes of a qualifying activity carried on by the company.

150(3) But subsection (2) does not apply if the event which would otherwise result in that subsection applying is, or is the result of, the total loss of the ship or irreparable damage to it.

150(4) This subsection applies if–

(a) after the expenditure is incurred, there is a time when the company and the shipowner are not members of the same group, and

(b) if the ship is brought into use for the purposes of a qualifying activity carried on by the company, that time is within 3 years of the ship first being so brought into use.

150(5) A time falling after the total loss of the ship or irreparable damage to it is to be disregarded for the purposes of subsection (4).

150(6) In this section **"irreparable damage"**, in relation to a ship, means damage that puts it in a condition in which it is impossible, or not commercially worthwhile, to undertake the repairs required for restoring it to its previous use.

Origin – S. 150(1): CAA 1990, s. 33A(8) (part), 33D(2A) (part).
S. 150(2): CAA 1990, s. 33D(2A) (part).
S. 150(3): CAA 1990, s. 33D(2B) (part).
S. 150(4): CAA 1990, s. 33D(2A) (part).
S. 150(5), (6): CAA 1990, s. 33D(2B) (part).

Cross references – FA 2000, Sch. 22, para. 80(4): disapplication of s. 135–156 when company subject to tonnage tax.

HMRC Manuals – CA25600: guidance on s. 146–150.

QUALIFYING SHIPS

151 Basic meaning of qualifying ship

151(1) For the purposes of the deferment rules, a ship is a qualifying ship if it is–

(a) of a sea-going kind, and

(b) registered as a ship with a gross tonnage of 100 tons or more in a register of shipping established and maintained under the law of any country or territory.

151(2) This is subject to sections 152 to 154.

Origin – S. 151: CAA 1990, s. 33E(1).

Cross references – FA 2000, Sch. 22, para. 80(4): disapplication of s. 135–156 when company subject to tonnage tax.

HMRC Manuals – CA25350: guidance and examples on s. 151–154.

152 Ships under 100 tons

152(1) This section applies if the relevant disposal event is, or results from–

(a) the total loss of the old ship, or

(b) damage to the old ship that puts it in a condition in which it is impossible, or not commercially worthwhile, to undertake the repairs required for restoring it to its previous use.

152(2) A registered ship may be a qualifying ship for the purposes of–

(a) section 136(b) (further conditions for deferment), or

(b) sections 146(3)(b) and 149(1)(a) (expenditure on new shipping),

even if it is not registered as a ship with a gross tonnage of 100 tons or more.

152(3) In subsection (2) **"registered ship"** means a ship registered in a register of shipping established and maintained under the law of any country or territory.

Origin – S. 152: CAA 1990, s. 33E(2).

Cross references – FA 2000, Sch. 22, para. 80(4): disapplication of s. 135–156 when company subject to tonnage tax.

HMRC Manuals – CA25350: guidance and examples on s. 151–154.

153 Ships which are not qualifying ships

153(1) A ship is not a qualifying ship if the primary use to which ships of the same kind as that ship are put–

(a) by the persons who own them, or

(b) by others to whom they are made available,

is use for sport or recreation.

153(2) A ship is not a qualifying ship at any time when it is an offshore installation.

153(3) [Omitted by FA 2004, s. 146 and Sch. 27, para. 9(3) and repealed by FA 2004, s. 326 and Sch. 42, Pt. 2(19).]

History – S. 153(2) substituted by FA 2004, s. 146 and Sch. 27, para. 9(2) which have effect, by virtue of FA 2004, Sch. 27, para. 11(1), as respects allowances and charges falling to be made for chargeable periods (as defined by CAA 2001, s. 6) ending on or after either 6 April 2004 (for income tax purposes) or 1 April 2004 (for corporation tax purposes).
S. 153(3) omitted by FA 2004, s. 146 and Sch. 27, para. 9(3), and repealed by FA 2004, s. 326 and Sch. 42, Pt. 2(19), which have effect, by virtue of FA 2004, Sch. 27, para. 11(1), as respects allowances and charges falling to be made for chargeable periods (as defined by CAA 2001, s. 6) ending on or after either 6 April 2004 (for income tax purposes) or 1 April 2004 (for corporation tax purposes).

Origin – S. 153(1): CAA 1990, s. 33E(3).
S. 153(2), (3): CAA 1990, s. 33E(4).

Cross references – FA 2000, Sch. 22, para. 80(4): disapplication of s. 135–156 when company subject to tonnage tax.

HMRC Manuals – CA25350: guidance and examples on s. 151–154.

154 Further registration requirement

154(1) If–

(a) a person ("A") has incurred expenditure on the provision of a ship, and

(b) there is a time in the qualifying period, but more than 3 months after the beginning of that period, when the ship is not registered in a relevant register,

the ship is not a qualifying ship after that time.

154(2) The qualifying period is–

(a) the period of 3 years beginning with the time when the ship is first brought into use for the purposes of a qualifying activity carried on–

(i) by A, or

(ii) if earlier, by a person connected with A, or

(b) if shorter, the period beginning with that time and ending when neither A nor a person connected with A owns the ship.

154(3) In determining the qualifying period for the old ship, a qualifying activity carried on at any time by a person ("B") is taken to be carried on at that time by a person connected with A if–

(a) it is subsequently carried on by A or a person connected with A, and

(b) the only changes in the persons carrying it on between the time that B does so and the time that A or a person connected with A does so are changes–

(i) which do not involve all of the persons carrying it on before the changes permanently ceasing to carry it on, or

(ii) in respect of which the qualifying activity is treated as continuing under section 948 of CTA 2010.

154(4) In this section **"relevant register"** means a register of shipping established and maintained–

(a) under the laws of any part of the British Islands, or

(b) under the laws of any country or territory which, at a time in the qualifying period for the ship, is an EEA State or a colony.

154(5) **"EEA State"** means a State which is a contracting party to the Agreement on the European Economic Area signed at Oporto on 2nd May 1992 as adjusted by the Protocol signed at Brussels on 17th March 1993 (except that for the period before the Agreement came into force in relation to Liechtenstein it does not include the State of Liechtenstein).

History – The wording of s. 154(3)(b) substituted by ITTOIA 2005, s. 882(1) and Sch. 1, para. 542; effective for income tax purposes for 2005–06 onwards and for corporation tax purposes for accounting periods ending after 5 April 2005 (ITTOIA 2005, s. 883(1)).
In s. 154(3)(b)(ii), the words "section 948 of CTA 2010" substituted for "section 343(2) of ICTA" by CTA 2010, s. 1177 and Sch. 1, para. 339, with effect for corporation tax purposes for accounting periods ending on or after 1 April 2010, and for income tax and capital gains tax purposes for the tax year 2010–11 and subsequent tax years.

Origin – S. 154(1): CAA 1990, s. 33E(5) (part), (9) (part).
S. 154(2): CAA 1990, s. 33E(6), (9) (part).
S. 154(3): CAA 1990, s. 33E(8) (part), (9) (part).
S. 154(4), (5): CAA 1990, s. 33E(7).

Cross references – ICTA 1988, s. 113(2): partnership changes not treated as a discontinuance of the old trade and the commencement of the new trade.
ICTA 1988, s. 343: company reconstructions without a change of ownership.
FA 2000, Sch. 22, para. 80(4): disapplication of s. 135–156 when company subject to tonnage tax.

Transitional – Sch. 3, para. 24: s. 154 does not apply in the case of a ship that was brought into use before 20 July 1994 for the purposes of a qualifying activity carried on by the person incurring the expenditure on the provision of the ship or a person connected with him.

HMRC Manuals – CA25350: guidance and examples on s. 151–154; "relevant register" further explained.

DEFERMENT OF BALANCING CHARGES: SUPPLEMENTARY PROVISIONS

155 Change in the persons carrying on the qualifying activity

155(1) This section applies if–

(a) a person is carrying on the qualifying activity previously carried on by the shipowner, and

(b) the only changes in the persons carrying on the qualifying activity since the shipowner carried it on are changes–

(i) which do not involve all of the persons carrying it on before the changes permanently ceasing to carry it on, or

(ii) in respect of which the qualifying activity is treated as continuing under section 948 of CTA 2010.

155(2) For the purposes of the deferment rules–

(a) expenditure incurred by a person mentioned in subsection (1)(a) for the purposes of the qualifying activity is to be treated as incurred by the shipowner, and

(b) in relation to the giving of any notice, a reference to the shipowner is to be read as a reference to the person carrying on the qualifying activity when the notice is given or is required to be given.

History – In s. 155(1)(b)(ii), the words "section 948 of CTA 2010" substituted for "section 343(2) of ICTA" by CTA 2010, s. 1177 and Sch. 1, para. 340, with effect for corporation tax purposes for accounting periods ending on or after 1 April 2010, and for income tax and capital gains tax purposes for the tax year 2010–11 and subsequent tax years.
S. 155(1)(b) substituted by ITTOIA 2005, s. 882(1) and Sch. 1, para. 543; effective for income tax purposes for 2005–06 onwards and for corporation tax purposes for accounting periods ending after 5 April 2005 (ITTOIA 2005, s. 883(1)).

Origin – S. 155(1): CAA 1990, s. 33D(7) (part), 33F(7) (part).
S. 155(2): CAA 1990, s. 33D(7) (part), 33F(7) (part).

Cross references – ICTA 1988, s. 113(2): partnership changes not treated as a discontinuance of the old trade and the commencement of the new trade.
ICTA 1988, s. 343(2): company reconstructions without a change of ownership.
FA 2000, Sch. 22, para. 80(4): disapplication of s. 135–156 when company subject to tonnage tax.

Rewrite: Changes in Law – Explanatory Notes, Annex 1, Change 24: s. 155(2)(b) extends slightly the application of the deferment rules where there is a change in the person carrying on the activity from the shipowner and the trade is not treated as having been discontinued. Previously only a notice under CAA 1990, s. 33F itself could be made where there have been changes in the persons carrying on the trade (either a notice to vary attribution of expenditure or a notice that there was no entitlement to deferment – CAA 1990, s. 33F(4) and (5)). Under the rewritten legislation, a notice to attribute a deferred charge to new expenditure (under s. 140: previously CAA 1990, s. 33A(5)) may also be made by the successor to the qualifying activity. Although this change is intended to be beneficial, there is a right of election for the previous position to apply to a period which straddles 6 April (income tax) or 1 April (corporation tax) 2001 (Sch. 3, para. 8).

Rewrite: Technical Points – Explanatory Notes, Annex 2, Note 36: conversely, s. 155(2)(a) only applies for the deferment rules, whereas its predecessor (CAA 1990, s. 33D(7)) applied for the whole of the statute applicable to allowances for ships (CAA 1990, Pt. II, Ch. II). In practice, notwithstanding this restriction to the scope of s. 155(2)(a), expenditure incurred by a successor continues to be treated for the purposes of deferment as incurred by the shipowner and the treatment of successors throughout the rewritten legislation applicable to ships remains consistent with that which preceded it (with one minor exception, where the provision is not felt to be capable of a construction with any adverse consequences for a successor).

HMRC Manuals – CA25650: guidance and examples on s. 155–158.

156 Connected persons

156(1) For the purposes of the deferment rules a person ("B") is connected with another person ("A") at any time if, at that time–

(a) B is connected (in the sense given in section 575) with A,

(b) B is carrying on a qualifying activity previously carried on by A and the condition in subsection (2) is met, or

(c) B is connected (in the sense given in section 575) with a person who is carrying on a qualifying activity previously carried on by A and the condition in subsection (2) is met.

156(2) The condition is that the only changes in the persons carrying on the qualifying activity since A carried it on are changes–

(a) which do not involve all of the persons carrying it on before the changes permanently ceasing to carry it on, or

(b) in respect of which the qualifying activity is treated as continuing under section 948 of CTA 2010.

156(3) If expenditure is incurred by a person who is not the shipowner, the persons connected with him at any time include any person connected with the shipowner at that time as a result of subsection (1).

History – In s. 156(1)(a) the words "section 575" substituted for the words "section 839 of ICTA" by ITA 2007, s. 1027 and Sch. 1, para. 401, with effect from 6 April 2007.
In s. 156(1)(c) the words "section 575" substituted for the words "section 839 of ICTA" by ITA 2007, s. 1027 and Sch. 1, para. 401, with effect from 6 April 2007.
S. 156(2) substituted by ITTOIA 2005, s. 882(1) and Sch. 1, para. 544; effective for income tax purposes for 2005–06 onwards and for corporation tax purposes for accounting periods ending after 5 April 2005 (ITTOIA 2005, s. 883(1)).
In s. 156(2)(b), the words "section 948 of CTA 2010" substituted for "section 343(2) of ICTA" by CTA 2010, s. 1177 and Sch. 1, para. 341, with effect for corporation tax purposes for accounting periods ending on or after 1 April 2010, and for income tax and capital gains tax purposes for the tax year 2010–11 and subsequent tax years.

Origin – S. 156: CAA 1990, s. 33D(8), 33E(8) (part).

Cross references – S. 575(2): general meaning of "connected persons" subject to provisions of s. 156.
FA 2000, Sch. 22, para. 80(4): disapplication of s. 135–156 when company subject to tonnage tax.

HMRC Manuals – CA25650: guidance and examples on s. 155–158.

FURTHER PROVISIONS

157 Adjustment of assessments etc.

157(1) All such assessments and adjustments of assessments are to be made as are necessary to give effect to this Chapter.

157(2) Subsection (1) does not apply for the purposes of section 145 (see instead section 145(4) and (5)).

Origin – S. 157(1): CAA 1990, s. 30(3), 31(9), 33F(6) (part).
S. 157(2): CAA 1990, s. 33F(6) (part).

HMRC Manuals – CA25650: guidance and examples on s. 155–158.

158 Members of same group

158 For the purposes of this Chapter two companies are members of the same group at any time if they would be treated as members of the same group of companies at that time for the purposes of Part 5 of CTA 2010 (group relief).

History – In s. 158, the words "Part 5 of CTA 2010" substituted for "Chapter IV of Part X of ICTA" by CTA 2010, s. 1177 and Sch. 1, para. 342, with effect for corporation tax purposes for accounting periods ending on or after 1 April 2010, and for income tax and capital gains tax purposes for the tax year 2010–11 and subsequent tax years.

Origin – S. 158: CAA 1990, s. 33A(8) (part), 33D(2A) (part).

HMRC Manuals – CA25650: guidance on membership of same group.

Chapter 13 – Provisions Affecting Mining and Oil Industries

EXPENDITURE CONNECTED WITH MINERAL EXTRACTION TRADES

HMRC Manuals – Guidance on chapter 13 is to be found in the Oil Taxation manuals.

159 Meaning of "mineral extraction trade" etc.

159 In this Chapter–

"mineral extraction trade", and

"mineral exploration and access",

have the same meaning as in Part 5 (mineral extraction allowances).

Origin – S. 159: CAA 1990, s. 83(1) ("mineral exploration and access" and "trade of mineral extraction").

160 Expenditure treated as incurred for purposes of mineral extraction trade

160(1) For the purposes of this Part, expenditure incurred by a person–

(a) on the provision of plant or machinery for mineral exploration and access, and

(b) in connection with a mineral extraction trade carried on by him,

is to be treated as incurred for the purposes of that trade.

160(2) Subsection (1) does not apply to expenditure if–

(a) when it is incurred, the person is carrying on the trade but the trade is not at that time a mineral extraction trade, or

(b) when it is incurred, the person has not begun to carry on the trade and, when the person begins to carry on the trade, the trade is not a mineral extraction trade.

160(3) Section 577(2) (references to commencement etc of a trade) does not apply to subsection (2).

History – S. 160(1) created from existing text of s. 160 by FA 2014, s. 67(4)(a), with effect in relation to claims made on or after 1 April 2014 (for corporation tax purposes) or 6 April 2014 (for income tax purposes), and in relation to those claims this amendment is treated as always having had effect.
S. 160(2) and (3) inserted by FA 2014, s. 67(4)(b), with effect in relation to claims made on or after 1 April 2014 (for corporation tax purposes) or 6 April 2014 (for income tax purposes), and in relation to those claims this amendment is treated as always having had effect.

Origin – S. 160: CAA 1990, s. 83(6).

161 Pre-trading expenditure on mineral exploration and access

161(1) This section applies if a person–

(a) incurs pre-trading expenditure on the provision of plant or machinery for the purposes of mineral exploration and access, and

(b) owns the plant or machinery on the first day of trading.

But this is subject to subsection (5).

161(2) The person is to be treated for the purposes of this Part as if he had–

(a) sold the plant or machinery immediately before the first day of trading, and

(b) on that first day incurred capital expenditure on the provision of the plant or machinery for the purposes of the trade.

161(3) The amount of the capital expenditure that the person is to be treated as having incurred is an amount equal to–

(a) the pre-trading expenditure, or

(b) if there has been an actual sale and re-acquisition before the first day of trading, the amount last incurred on the provision of the plant or machinery.

161(4) In this section–

(a) **"pre-trading expenditure"** means capital expenditure incurred–before the day on which a person begins to carry on a trade that is a mineral extraction trade, but only if there is no prior time when the person carried on that trade and the trade was not a mineral extraction trade,

(b) **"the first day of trading"**, in relation to a person's pre-trading expenditure, means the day on which that person begins to carry on the mineral extraction trade.

161(4A) Section 577(2) (references to commencement etc of a trade) does not apply to subsection (4)(a).

161(5) This section does not apply if the plant or machinery on which the pre-trading expenditure was incurred is sold, demolished, destroyed or abandoned before the first day of trading (but see section 402 (mineral extraction allowances: pre-trading expenditure on plant or machinery)).

History – S. 161(4)(a) substituted by FA 2014, s. 67(5), with effect in relation to claims made on or after 1 April 2014 (for corporation tax purposes) or 6 April 2014 (for income tax purposes), and in relation to those claims this amendment is treated as always having had effect.
S. 161(4A) inserted by FA 2014, s. 67(6), with effect in relation to claims made on or after 1 April 2014 (for corporation tax purposes) or 6 April 2014 (for income tax purposes), and in relation to those claims this amendment is treated as always having had effect.

Origin – S. 161(1)–(3): CAA 1990, s. 63(1) (part).
S. 161(4): CAA 1990, s. 63(1) (part).
S. 161(5): CAA 1990, s. 63(1) (part).

Cross references – S. 13(7): provision dealing with use for qualifying activity of plant or machinery provided for other purposes is subject to (allowance under) s. 161.
S. 14(5): provision dealing with use for qualifying activity of plant or machinery which is a gift is subject to (allowance under) s. 161.
S. 46(2): general exclusions from first year allowances provisions for Northern Ireland, for small or medium-sized enterprises and for ICT expenditure incurred by small enterprises all subject to (allowance under) s. 161.
S. 402(1): mineral extraction allowances for expenditure on mineral exploration and access in respect of machinery or plant sold, demolished, destroyed or abandoned before commencement of trade (see also notes below).

Transitional – Sch. 3, para. 25: s. 161 does not apply if the person incurred the pre-trading expenditure before 1 April 1986 and before the first day of trading, the mineral exploration and access at the source in question had ceased.

Rewrite: Changes in Law – Explanatory Notes, Annex 1, Change 25: s. 161(4)(a) alters the previous statute (in CAA 1990, s. 63(1)) by introducing the word "capital" in the rewritten definition of "pre-trading expenditure". This change is felt to be consistent with the fact that s. 161 is only required for cases where allowances for expenditure connected with research and development are not available, as well as the existence of a Sch. D, Case I allowance for pre-trading revenue expenditure incurred up to seven years before commencement of trading (ICTA 1988, s. 401). The combination of these means that the restriction of s. 161 to capital expenditure effectively only prevents allowance of one sort or another being given for revenue expenditure incurred outside the seven year period. In the context of legislation the intention of which is to give allowances for capital expenditure, this does not seem anomalous. There is a right of election for the previous position to apply to a period which straddles 6 April (income tax) or 1 April (corporation tax) 2001 (Sch. 3, para. 8).

Notes – S. 399(1): except as provided for by s. 402, asset previously treated as machinery and plant not generally eligible for mineral extraction allowances.

EXPENDITURE CONNECTED WITH REUSE ETC. OF OFFSHORE OIL INFRASTRUCTURE

161A Meaning of "offshore infrastructure"

161A(1) In sections 161C and 161D **"offshore infrastructure"** means–

(a) an offshore installation within the meaning given by section 44 of the Petroleum Act 1998 or a part of such an installation, or

(b) something that would be, or would be a part of, an offshore installation within that meaning if in subsection (3) of that section **"relevant waters"** meant waters in a foreign sector of the continental shelf and other foreign tidal waters, or

(c) a pipeline within the meaning of section 26 of that Act, or a part of such a pipeline, that is in, under or over waters in–

  (i) the territorial sea adjacent to the United Kingdom, or

  (ii) an area designated under section 1(7) of the Continental Shelf Act 1964, or

(d) a pipeline within the meaning of section 26 of the Petroleum Act 1998, or a part of such a pipeline, that is in, under or over waters in a foreign sector of the continental shelf.

161A(2) In subsection (1)(b) and (d)–

"foreign sector of the continental shelf" means an area within which rights are exercisable with respect to the sea bed and subsoil and their natural resources by a country or territory outside the United Kingdom;

"foreign tidal waters" means tidal waters in an area within which rights are exercisable with respect to the bed and subsoil of the body of water in question and their natural resources by a country or territory outside the United Kingdom.

History – S. 161A inserted by FA 2001, s. 68 and Sch. 20, para. 5(1), with effect (FA 2001, Sch. 20, para. 9) in relation to expenditure that is incurred

- on or after 7 August 2000, and
- in a chargeable period ending on or after 6 April 2001 for income tax purposes, or 1 April 2001 for corporation tax purposes (a "relevant chargeable period").

It also applies in relation to expenditure incurred before 7 August 2000 if the expenditure is incurred in a relevant chargeable period, and it is decommissioning expenditure (within s. 161C and 161D):

- on UK infrastructure, and is incurred in connection with an abandonment programme approved on or after 7 August 2000; or
- not on UK infrastructure, and is incurred in connection with a decommissioning activity (within s. 161B(1)(a)–(c)) that takes place on or after 7 August 2000.

161B Meaning of "decommissioning expenditure"

161B(1) In sections 161C and 161D **"decommissioning expenditure"** means expenditure in connection with–

(a) preserving plant or machinery pending its reuse or demolition,

(b) preparing plant or machinery for reuse, or

(c) arranging for the reuse of plant or machinery.

161B(2) It is immaterial for the purposes of subsection (1)(a) whether the plant or machinery is reused, is demolished or is partly reused and partly demolished.

161B(3) It is immaterial for the purposes of subsection (1)(b) and (c) whether the plant or machinery is in fact reused.

History – S. 161B inserted by FA 2001, s. 68 and Sch. 20, para. 5(1), with effect (FA 2001, Sch. 20, para. 9) in relation to expenditure that is incurred

- on or after 7 August 2000, and
- in a chargeable period ending on or after 6 April 2001 for income tax purposes, or 1 April 2001 for corporation tax purposes (a "relevant chargeable period").

It also applies in relation to expenditure incurred before 7 August 2000 if the expenditure is incurred in a relevant chargeable period, and it is decommissioning expenditure (within s. 161C and 161D):

- on UK infrastructure, and is incurred in connection with an abandonment programme approved on or after 7 August 2000; or
- not on UK infrastructure, and is incurred in connection with a decommissioning activity (within s. 161B(1)(a)–(c)) that takes place on or after 7 August 2000.

161C Expenditure related to reuse etc. qualifies for writing-down allowances

161C(1) This section applies where–

(a) a person carrying on a trade of oil extraction incurs decommissioning expenditure, and

(b) the plant or machinery concerned–

(i) has been brought into use for the purposes of the trade, and

(ii) is, or was when last in use for those purposes, offshore infrastructure.

161C(2) The decommissioning expenditure is allocated to the appropriate pool for the chargeable period in which it is incurred.

161C(3) Subsection (2) is subject to sections 161D, 164(4) and 165A to 165E.

161C(4) In subsection (2) **"the appropriate pool"** means the pool to which the expenditure on the plant or machinery concerned has been or would be allocated in accordance with this Part.

History – In s. 161C(3), the words ", 164(4) and 165A to 165E" substituted for the words "and 164(4)" by FA 2013, s. 93 and Sch. 32, para. 5, with effect in relation to expenditure incurred on decommissioning carried out on or after 17 July 2013.

S. 161C inserted by FA 2001, s. 68 and Sch. 20, para. 5(1), with effect (FA 2001, Sch. 20, para. 9) in relation to expenditure that is incurred

- on or after 7 August 2000, and
- in a chargeable period ending on or after 6 April 2001 for income tax purposes, or 1 April 2001 for corporation tax purposes (a "relevant chargeable period").

It also applies in relation to expenditure incurred before 7 August 2000 if the expenditure is incurred in a relevant chargeable period, and it is decommissioning expenditure (within s. 161C and 161D):

- on UK infrastructure, and is incurred in connection with an abandonment programme approved on or after 7 August 2000; or
- not on UK infrastructure, and is incurred in connection with a decommissioning activity (within s. 161B(1)(a)–(c)) that takes place on or after 7 August 2000.

Cross references – S. 57(2): decommissioning expenditure under s. 161C(2) qualifies for pooling.

161D Exceptions to section 161C(2)

161D(1) Subsection (2) of section 161C does not apply to decommissioning expenditure on UK infrastructure unless it is incurred in connection with measures taken, wholly or substantially, in order to comply with–

(a) an abandonment programme within the meaning given by section 29 of the Petroleum Act 1998, or

(b) any condition to which the approval of such a programme is subject.

161D(2) Subsection (2) of section 161C does not apply to expenditure in respect of which an allowance or deduction could be made apart from that subsection in taxing, or computing, the person's income for any tax purpose.

161D(3) For the purposes of subsection (1), decommissioning expenditure is "on UK infrastructure" if the plant or machinery concerned–

(a) is offshore infrastructure within section 161A(1)(a) or (c), or

(b) is not offshore infrastructure but was offshore infrastructure within section 161A(1)(a) or (c) when last in use for the purposes of the trade.

History – S. 161D inserted by FA 2001, s. 68 and Sch. 20, para. 5(1), with effect (FA 2001, Sch. 20, para. 9) in relation to expenditure that is incurred

- on or after 7 August 2000, and
- in a chargeable period ending on or after 6 April 2001 for income tax purposes, or 1 April 2001 for corporation tax purposes (a "relevant chargeable period").

It also applies in relation to expenditure incurred before 7 August 2000 if the expenditure is incurred in a relevant chargeable period, and it is decommissioning expenditure (within s. 161C and 161D):

- on UK infrastructure, and is incurred in connection with an abandonment programme approved on or after 7 August 2000; or
- not on UK infrastructure, and is incurred in connection with a decommissioning activity (within s. 161B(1)(a)–(c)) that takes place on or after 7 August 2000.

PROVISIONS RELATING TO RING FENCE TRADES

162 Ring fence trade a separate qualifying activity

162(1) If a person carries on a ring fence trade, it is a separate qualifying activity for the purposes of this Part.

162(2) In this Chapter **"ring fence trade"** means activities which–

(a) fall within the definition of **"oil-related activities"** in section 16(2) of ITTOIA 2005 or section 274 of CTA 2010, and

(b) constitute a separate trade (whether as a result of section 16(1) of ITTOIA 2005 or section 279 of CTA 2010 or otherwise).

History – The wording of s. 162(2) amended by ITTOIA 2005, s. 882(1) and Sch. 1, para. 545; effective for income tax purposes for 2005–06 onwards and for corporation tax purposes for accounting periods ending after 5 April 2005 (ITTOIA 2005, s. 883(1)).
In s. 162(2)(a), the words "or section 274 of CTA 2010" substituted for the words "or within any of paragraphs (a) to (c) of section 492(1) of ICTA (oil extraction activities, the acquisition, enjoyment or exploitation of oil rights, etc.)" by CTA 2010, s. 1177 and Sch. 1, para. 343(a), with effect for corporation tax purposes for accounting periods ending on or after 1 April 2010.
In s. 162(2)(b), the words "section 279 of CTA 2010" substituted for "section 492(1) of ICTA" by CTA 2010, s. 1177 and Sch. 1, para. 343(b), with effect for corporation tax purposes for accounting periods ending on or after 1 April 2010.

Origin – S. 162(1): ICTA s. 492(1), drafting.
S. 162(2): CAA 1990, s. 62A(2), 62B(5).

Cross references – ICTA 1988, s. 393A(12) (as amended by Sch. 2, para. 32(4)): applies s. 162 meaning of "ring fence trade ".

163 Meaning of "general decommissioning expenditure"

163(1) Expenditure is "general decommissioning expenditure" for the purposes of sections 164 and 165 if

(a) the conditions in subsections (3), (3A) and (4) are met, or

(b) the conditions in subsections (3B) and (4) are met.

163(2) But that is subject to subsections (4ZA) to (4ZC).

163(3) The expenditure must have been incurred on decommissioning plant or machinery–

(a) which has been brought into use wholly or partly for the purposes of a ring fence trade, and

(b) which–

(i) is, or forms part of, an offshore installation or a submarine pipeline, or

(ii) when last in use for the purposes of a ring fence trade, was, or formed part of, such an installation or pipeline.

163(3A) The expenditure must have been incurred wholly or substantially in complying with–

(a) an approved abandonment programme,

(b) a condition to which the approval of an abandonment programme is subject, or

(c) a condition imposed by the Secretary of State, or an agreement made with the Secretary of State–
 (i) before the approval of an abandonment programme, and
 (ii) in relation to the decommissioning of the plant or machinery.

163(3B) The expenditure must have been incurred on decommissioning plant or machinery–
(a) which has been brought into use wholly or partly for the purposes of a ring fence trade, and
(b) which–
 (i) is, or forms part of, a relevant onshore installation, or
 (ii) when last in use for the purposes of a ring fence trade, was, or formed part of, such an installation.

163(3C) In subsection (3B) **"relevant onshore installation"** means any building or structure which–
(a) falls within any of sub-paragraphs (ii) to (iv) of section 3(4)(c) of OTA 1975,
(b) is not an offshore installation, and
(c) is or has been used for purposes connected with the winning of oil from an oil field any part of which lies within–
 (i) the boundaries of the territorial sea of the United Kingdom, or
 (ii) an area designated under section 1(7) of the Continental Shelf Act 1964.

163(4) The plant or machinery must not be replaced.

163(4ZA) An amount of general decommissioning expenditure determined in accordance with subsection (1) is to be reduced under subsection (4ZB) if it appears that the decommissioned plant and machinery–
(a) was not brought into use wholly for qualifying purposes, or
(b) has, at any time since it was brought into use, not been used wholly for qualifying purposes.

163(4ZB) The amount determined in accordance with subsection (1) is to be reduced to an amount which is just and reasonable having regard to the relevant circumstances.

163(4ZC) The relevant circumstances include, in particular, the extent to which the decommissioned plant and machinery has not been used for qualifying purposes.

163(4A) In this section **"decommissioning"**, in relation to any plant or machinery, means–
(a) demolishing the plant or machinery,
(b) preserving the plant or machinery pending its reuse or demolition,
(c) preparing the plant or machinery for reuse, or
(d) arranging for the reuse of the plant or machinery.

163(4B) In determining whether expenditure is incurred on preserving plant or machinery pending its reuse or demolition, it is immaterial whether the plant or machinery is reused, is demolished or is partly reused and partly demolished.

163(4C) In determining whether expenditure is incurred on preparing plant or machinery for reuse, or on arranging for the reuse of plant or machinery, it is immaterial whether the plant or machinery is in fact reused.

163(4D) In this section a reference to use for qualifying purposes is a reference to–
(a) use for the purposes of any ring fence trade of any person, or
(b) other use in–
 (i) the United Kingdom,
 (ii) the territorial sea of the United Kingdom, or
 (iii) an area designated under section 1(7) of the Continental Shelf Act 1964,

 except use wholly or partly in connection with an oil field (within the meaning given by section 12(2) of the Oil Taxation Act 1975).

163(5) In this section–
(a) **"oil"** and **"oil field"** have the same meaning as in Part I of OTA 1975, and
(b) **"abandonment programme"**,**"approval"** and **"approved"** (in relation to an abandonment programme),**"offshore installation"** and **"submarine pipeline"** have the same meaning as in Part IV of the Petroleum Act 1998.

History – The heading "Meaning of "general decommissioning expenditure"" substituted for the heading "Meaning of 'abandonment expenditure"" by FA 2008, s. 109(2), with effect in relation to expenditure incurred on or after 12 March 2008.
In s. 163(1), words after "if" became (a) and therein the words "subsections (3), (3A) and (4)" substituted for "subsections (3) to (4)" by FA 2013, s. 90(2), with effect in relation to expenditure incurred on decommissioning carried out on or after 17 July 2013.
S. 163(1)(b) inserted by FA 2013, s. 90(2)(c), with effect in relation to expenditure incurred on decommissioning carried out on or after 17 July 2013.

In s. 163(1), "(3) to (4)" substituted for "(3) and (4)" by FA 2009, s. 84 and Sch. 38, para. 2(2), with effect in relation to expenditure incurred on or after 22 April 2009.
S. 163(1) substituted by FA 2008, s. 109(3), with effect in relation to expenditure incurred on or after 12 March 2008.
S. 163(2) substituted by FA 2008, s. 109(3), with effect in relation to expenditure incurred on or after 12 March 2008.
In s. 163(3)(a), the words "wholly or partly" inserted by FA 2009, s. 87 and Sch. 41, para. 5(2), with effect in relation to expenditure incurred on or after 22 April 2009.
S. 163(3) substituted by FA 2008, s. 109(3), with effect in relation to expenditure incurred on or after 12 March 2008.
S. 163(3A) inserted by FA 2009, s. 84 and Sch. 38, para. 2(3), with effect in relation to expenditure incurred on or after 22 April 2009.
S. 163(3B) inserted by FA 2013, s. 90(3), with effect in relation to expenditure incurred on decommissioning carried out on or after 17 July 2013.
S. 163(3C) inserted by FA 2013, s. 90(3), with effect in relation to expenditure incurred on decommissioning carried out on or after 17 July 2013.
S. 163(4ZA)(a) and (b) substituted by FA 2009, s. 87 and Sch. 41, para. 5(3), with effect in relation to expenditure incurred on or after 22 April 2009.
S. 163(4ZA) inserted by FA 2008, s. 109(4), with effect in relation to expenditure incurred on or after 12 March 2008.
S. 163(4ZB) inserted by FA 2008, s. 109(4), with effect in relation to expenditure incurred on or after 12 March 2008.
In s. 163(4ZC), the words "qualifying purposes" substituted for the words "the purposes of the ring fence trade" by FA 2009, s. 87 and Sch. 41, para. 5(4), with effect in relation to expenditure incurred on or after 22 April 2009.
S. 163(4ZC) inserted by FA 2008, s. 109(4), with effect in relation to expenditure incurred on or after 12 March 2008.
S. 163(4D) inserted by FA 2009, s. 87 and Sch. 41, para. 5(5), with effect in relation to expenditure incurred on or after 22 April 2009.
In s. 163(5)(a), the words ""oil" and "oil field" have" substituted for the words ""oil field" has" by FA 2013, s. 90(4), with effect in relation to expenditure incurred on decommissioning carried out on or after 17 July 2013.
In s. 163(5)(b), the words ""abandonment programme", "approval" and "approved" (in relation to an abandonment programme)," inserted by FA 2009, s. 84 and Sch. 38, para. 2(4), with effect in relation to expenditure incurred on or after 22 April 2009.
In s. 163(5)(b), the words "abandonment programme" omitted by FA 2008, s. 109(5), with effect in relation to expenditure incurred on or after 12 March 2008.
S. 163 amended by FA 2001, s. 68 and Sch. 20, para. 6, by:

- substituting "decommissioning" for "demolition" in s. 163(2)(b) and s. 163(3);
- in s. 163(2)(b)(ii), inserting words "or which, when last in use" to the end;
- inserting s. 163(4A)–(4C).

These amendments have effect (FA 2001, Sch. 20, para. 9) in relation to expenditure that is incurred:

- on or after 7 August 2000, and
- in a chargeable period ending on or after 6 April 2001 for income tax purposes, or 1 April 2001 for corporation tax purposes (a "relevant chargeable period").

They also apply to expenditure incurred before 7 August 2000 if the expenditure

- is incurred in a relevant chargeable period, and
- is incurred in connection with an abandonment programme approved on or after 7 August 2000.

Origin – S. 163(1), (2): CAA 1990, s. 62A(1) (part).
S. 163(3): CAA 1990, s. 62A(3) (part).
S. 163(4): CAA 1990, s. 62(1)(b) (part), 62A(1) (part).
S. 163(5): CAA 1990, s. 62A(1) (part), (3) (part).
Other material – Law Society note of meeting with Revenue on Finance Bill 1990 (not reproduced): term "demolition" in former s. 62A(1), (3) sufficiently wide in meaning to ensure that relief would normally be granted for expenditure incurred in removing or dismantling offshore installations and pipelines on abandonment.

164 General decommissioning expenditure incurred before cessation of ring fence trade

164(1) A person ("R") carrying on a ring fence trade may elect to have a special allowance made to R for a chargeable period (the "relevant chargeable period") if conditions A and B are met.

164(1A) Condition A is that one or more of these paragraphs applies–

(a) R incurs general decommissioning expenditure in the relevant chargeable period in respect of decommissioning carried out in that period;

(b) R incurs general decommissioning expenditure in the relevant chargeable period in respect of decommissioning carried out in a previous chargeable period;

(c) R incurred general decommissioning expenditure in a previous chargeable period in respect of decommissioning that has not been carried out until the relevant chargeable period.

164(1B) Condition B is that the plant or machinery concerned has been brought into use for the purposes of the ring fence trade.

164(2) The election–

(a) must be made by notice to an officer of Revenue and Customs no later than 2 years after the end of the relevant chargeable period, and

(b) is irrevocable.

164(1C) If the plant or machinery concerned is incidentally-acquired redundant plant or machinery (see subsection (1D)), it is to be regarded for the purposes of this section as having been brought into use for the purposes of the ring fence trade.

164(1D) Plant or machinery is **"incidentally-acquired redundant plant or machinery"** if–

(a) it has not been brought into use for the purposes of the ring fence trade,

(b) it forms part of a relevant installation (see subsection (1E)) which has been brought into use for the purposes of the ring fence trade,

(c) at the time R acquired an interest in the relevant installation, the plant or machinery was not being used for any purposes, and

(d) the acquisition of the interest in the plant or machinery was merely incidental to the acquisition of the interest in the relevant installation.

164(1E) For the purposes of subsection (1D)–

"relevant installation" means–

(a) an offshore installation,

(b) a submarine pipeline, or

(c) a relevant onshore installation;

"offshore installation" and **"submarine pipeline"** have the same meaning as in Part 4 of the Petroleum Act 1998;

"relevant onshore installation" has the meaning given by section 163(3C).

164(3) The election must specify–

(a) the general decommissioning expenditure to which it relates,

(aa) the chargeable period in which the expenditure was incurred,

(ab) the decommissioning to which the expenditure relates,

(ac) the chargeable period in which the decommissioning was carried out, and

(b) where the plant or machinery concerned has been or is to be demolished, any amounts received for its remains.

164(4) If a person makes an election under this section–

(a) he is entitled to a special allowance for the relevant chargeable period, and

(b) neither of sections 26(3) and 161C(2) (net cost of demolition where plant or machinery not replaced, or cost of preparing for reuse, added to existing pool) applies.

164(5) The amount of the special allowance for the relevant chargeable period is equal to the amount of the general decommissioning expenditure to which the election relates.

164(5A) But subsection (5) is subject to subsections (5B) and (6) and sections 165A to 165E.

164(5B) If an amount of general decommissioning expenditure to which the election relates is disproportionate to the relevant decommissioning carried out in the specified decommissioning period then, for the purposes of this section, the election is to be taken to specify only the allowable expenditure.

164(5C) The application of subsection (5B) to an amount of general decommissioning expenditure does not prevent a person from making an election under this section for a subsequent chargeable period specifying the non-allowable expenditure.

164(5D) In subsections (5B) and (5C)–

"allowable expenditure", in relation to general decommissioning expenditure, means the amount of the expenditure that is proportionate to the relevant decommissioning carried out in the specified decommissioning period;

"non-allowable expenditure", in relation to general decommissioning expenditure, means so much of that expenditure as is not allowable expenditure;

"relevant decommissioning", in relation to general decommissioning expenditure, means the decommissioning to which the expenditure relates;

"specified decommissioning period", in relation to relevant decommissioning, means the chargeable period specified in the election as the period in which the decommissioning was carried out;

"specified expenditure period", in relation to general decommissioning expenditure, means the chargeable period specified in the election as the period in which the expenditure was incurred.

164(6) If plant or machinery is demolished, the total of any special allowances in respect of expenditure on decommissioning the plant or machinery is reduced by any amount received for the remains of the plant or machinery.

Here **"decommissioning"** has the meaning given by section 163(4A).

164(7) Effect is given to subsection (6) by setting the amount (until wholly utilised)–

first, against any special allowance for the chargeable period in which the amount is received (as previously reduced in giving effect to subsection (6));

second, against special allowances for earlier chargeable periods (as so reduced and taking later such periods before earlier ones); and third, against special allowances for later chargeable periods (as so reduced and taking earlier such periods before later ones).

History – In the heading to s. 164, the words "general decommissioning expenditure" substituted for the words "abandonment expenditure" by FA 2008, s. 109 and Sch. 34, para. 5(2), with effect in relation to expenditure incurred on or after 12 March 2008.

S. 164(1), (1A) and (1B) substituted for former s. 164(1) by FA 2009, s. 84 and Sch. 38, para. 3(2), with effect in relation to expenditure incurred on or after 22 April 2009.

In former s. 164(1), the words "general decommissioning expenditure" substituted for the words "abandonment expenditure" by FA 2008, s. 109 and Sch. 34, para. 5(3), with effect in relation to expenditure incurred on or after 12 March 2008.

In former s. 164(1), words "and the plant or machinery concerned has been brought into use for the purposes of that trade," inserted by FA 2001, s. 68 and Sch. 20, para. 7(2), and deemed always to have had effect.

S. 164(1C) inserted by FA 2013, s. 91(1), with effect in relation to expenditure incurred on decommissioning carried out on or after 17 July 2013.

S. 164(1D) inserted by FA 2013, s. 91(1), with effect in relation to expenditure incurred on decommissioning carried out on or after 17 July 2013.

S. 164(1E) inserted by FA 2013, s. 91(1), with effect in relation to expenditure incurred on decommissioning carried out on or after 17 July 2013.

In s. 164(2)(a), the words "the relevant chargeable period, and" substituted for the words "the chargeable period in which the general decommissioning expenditure is incurred, and" by FA 2009, s. 84 and Sch. 38, para. 3(3), with effect in relation to expenditure incurred on or after 22 April 2009.

In s. 164(2)(a), the words "general decommissioning expenditure" substituted for the words "abandonment expenditure" by FA 2008, s. 109 and Sch. 34, para. 5(3), with effect in relation to expenditure incurred on or after 12 March 2008.

In s. 164(2)(a), the words "an officer of Revenue and Customs" substituted for "the Inland Revenue" by CRCA 2005, s. 50(6) and Sch. 4, para. 83(1), with effect from 18 April 2005 by virtue of SI 2005/1126, art. 2(2).

In s. 164(3)(a), the word "and" at the end omitted by FA 2009, s. 84 and Sch. 38, para. 3(4)(a), with effect in relation to expenditure incurred on or after 22 April 2009.

In s. 164(3)(a), the words "general decommissioning expenditure" substituted for the words "abandonment expenditure" by FA 2008, s. 109 and Sch. 34, para. 5(3), with effect in relation to expenditure incurred on or after 12 March 2008.

S. 164(3)(aa), (ab) and (ac) inserted by FA 2009, s. 84 and Sch. 38, para. 3(4)(b), with effect in relation to expenditure incurred on or after 22 April 2009.

S. 164(3)(b) substituted by FA 2001, s. 68 and Sch. 20, para. 7(3)–(6) with effect in relation to:

- expenditure incurred:
  - on or after 7 August 2000, and
  - in a chargeable period ending on or after 6 April 2001 for income tax purposes, or 1 April 2001 for corporation tax purposes (a "relevant chargeable period"); and
- expenditure incurred before 7 August 2000 if the expenditure:
  - is incurred in a relevant chargeable period, and
  - is incurred in connection with an abandonment programme approved on or after 7 August 2000.

In s. 164(4)(a), the words "the relevant chargeable period, and" substituted for the words "the chargeable period in which the general decommissioning expenditure is incurred, and" by FA 2009, s. 84 and Sch. 38, para. 3(5), with effect in relation to expenditure incurred on or after 22 April 2009.

In s. 164(4)(a), the words "general decommissioning expenditure" substituted for the words "abandonment expenditure" by FA 2008, s. 109 and Sch. 34, para. 5(3), with effect in relation to expenditure incurred on or after 12 March 2008.

In s. 164(4)(a), the words ", of an amount equal to the net abandonment cost," which occurred after "special allowance" omitted by FA 2001, s. 68 and Sch. 20, para. 7(3)–(6) with effect in relation to:

- expenditure incurred:
  - on or after 7 August 2000, and
  - in a chargeable period ending on or after 6 April 2001 for income tax purposes, or 1 April 2001 for corporation tax purposes (a "relevant chargeable period"); and
- expenditure incurred before 7 August 2000 if the expenditure:
  - is incurred in a relevant chargeable period, and
  - is incurred in connection with an abandonment programme approved on or after 7 August 2000.

S. 164(4)(b) substituted by FA 2001, s. 68 and Sch. 20, para. 7(3)–(6) with effect in relation to

- expenditure incurred:
  - on or after 7 August 2000, and
  - in a chargeable period ending on or after 6 April 2001 for income tax purposes, or 1 April 2001 for corporation tax purposes (a "relevant chargeable period"); and
- expenditure incurred before 7 August 2000 if the expenditure:
  - is incurred in a relevant chargeable period, and
  - is incurred in connection with an abandonment programme approved on or after 7 August 2000.

Words omitted from s. 164(4)(a) also repealed by FA 2001, s. 110 and Sch. 33, Pt. II(5).

These amendments have effect (FA 2001, Sch. 20, para. 9) in relation to expenditure that is incurred:

- on or after 7 August 2000, and
- in a chargeable period ending on or after 6 April 2001 for income tax purposes, or 1 April 2001 for corporation tax purposes (a "relevant chargeable period").

In s. 164(5), the words "the relevant chargeable period is equal to the amount of the general decommissioning expenditure to which the election relates." substituted for the words "a chargeable period is equal to so much of the general decommissioning expenditure to which the election relates as is incurred in that period." by FA 2009, s. 84 and Sch. 38, para. 3(6), with effect in relation to expenditure incurred on or after 22 April 2009.

In s. 164(5), the words "general decommissioning expenditure" substituted for the words "abandonment expenditure" by FA 2008, s. 109 and Sch. 34, para. 3, with effect in relation to expenditure incurred on or after 12 March 2008.

S. 164(5)–(7) substituted for former s. 164(5) by FA 2001, s. 68 and Sch. 20, para. 7(3)–(6) with effect in relation to:

- expenditure incurred:
  - on or after 7 August 2000, and
  - in a chargeable period ending on or after 6 April 2001 for income tax purposes, or 1 April 2001 for corporation tax purposes (a "relevant chargeable period"); and
- expenditure incurred before 7 August 2000 if the expenditure:
  - is incurred in a relevant chargeable period, and
  - is incurred in connection with an abandonment programme approved on or after 7 August 2000.

In s. 164(5A), the words "and sections 165A to 165E." inserted by FA 2013, s. 93 and Sch. 32, para. 6, with effect in relation to expenditure incurred on decommissioning carried out on or after 17 July 2013.

S. 164(5A), (5B), (5C) and (5D) inserted by FA 2009, s. 84 and Sch. 38, para. 3(7), with effect in relation to expenditure incurred on or after 22 April 2009.

Origin – S. 164(1): CAA 1990, s. 62A(4) (part).

S. 164(2), (3): CAA 1990, s. 62A(5) (part).
S. 164(4), (5): CAA 1990, s. 62A(4) (part).

Cross references – S. 26(5): allocation of net demolition costs of plant and machinery to appropriate pool for allowances generally subject to effect of election for special allowance under s. 164(4).
ICTA 1988, s. 393A(2C)(b) (as amended by Sch. 2, para. 32(1)): carry-back of certain losses incurred by a company in its ring fence trade in an accounting period for which an allowance is made under s. 164.

Transitional – Sch. 3, para. 26: s. 164 does not apply if the chargeable period in which the abandonment expenditure was incurred ended before 1 July 1991.

165 General decommissioning expenditure after ceasing ring fence trade

165(1) This section applies if–

(a) a person (**"the former trader"**) has ceased to carry on a ring fence trade,

(b) the decommissioning condition is met in relation to a notional accounting period, and

(c) the general decommissioning expenditure is not otherwise deductible in calculating the income of the former trader for any tax purpose.

165(1A) The decommissioning condition is met in relation to a notional accounting period (the "relevant period") if one or more of these paragraphs applies–

(a) the former trader incurs general decommissioning expenditure in the relevant period in respect of decommissioning carried out in that period,

(b) the former trader incurs general decommissioning expenditure in the relevant period in respect of decommissioning carried out in–

(i) a previous notional accounting period, or

(ii) a chargeable period falling before the first notional accounting period, and

(c) the former trader incurred general decommissioning expenditure in–

(i) a previous notional accounting period, or

(ii) a chargeable period falling before the first notional accounting period,

in respect of decommissioning that has not been carried out until the relevant period.

165(1B) **"Notional accounting period"** means each of the following periods–

(a) the period that–

(i) begins with the day following the last day on which the former trader carried on the ring fence trade, and

(ii) ends with the day on which the first termination event subsequently occurs, and

(b) each period that–

(i) begins with the day following the last day of a period determined under paragraph (a) or this paragraph, and

(ii) ends with the day on which the first termination event subsequently occurs;

but there are to be no notional accounting periods after the end of the post-cessation period.

165(1C) **"Termination event"**, in relation to a notional accounting period, means each of the following–

(a) the end of the period of 12 months beginning with the first day of the notional accounting period,

(b) the occurrence of an accounting date of the former trader or, if there is a period for which the former trader does not make up accounts, the end of that period (but see subsections (6A) and (6B)), and

(c) the end of the post-cessation period.

165(2) **"The post-cessation period"** means the period that–

(a) begins with the day following the last day on which the former trader carried on the ring fence trade, and

(b) ends with the day on which condition A and condition B are both met (or, if they are met on different days, the later of those days).

165(2A) Condition A is met if each approved abandonment programme that relates wholly or partly to relevant plant and machinery has ceased to have effect.

165(2B) Condition B is met if the Secretary of State is satisfied that no other abandonment programmes that relate wholly or partly to relevant plant and machinery will be approved.

165(2C) For the purposes of condition A, an approved abandonment programme ceases to have effect if and when–

(a) the programme has been carried out to the satisfaction of the Secretary of State, or

(b) approval of the programme has been withdrawn.

165(3) If this section applies in relation to a notional accounting period–

(a) an amount equal to the relevant decommissioning cost for that period, or the aggregate of all the relevant decommissioning costs for that period, is allocated to the appropriate pool for the chargeable period in which the former trader ceased to carry on the ring fence trade, and

(b) where any of the general decommissioning expenditure was incurred on the demolition of plant or machinery, any amount received within the post-cessation period for the remains of the plant or machinery does not constitute income of the former trader for any tax purpose.

165(3A) Subsection (3) is subject to sections 165A to 165E.

165(4) In subsection (3)–

"the appropriate pool" means the pool to which the expenditure on the demolished plant or machinery has been allocated, and

"relevant decommissioning cost", for a notional accounting period, means the amount by which general decommissioning expenditure falling within paragraph (a), (b) or (c) of subsection (1A) in relation to that period exceeds any amounts received before or during that period for the remains of any plant or machinery on whose demolition any of the general decommissioning expenditure was incurred.

165(4A) General decommissioning expenditure is to be disregarded for the purposes of this section if the expenditure is incurred in decommissioning plant and machinery at a time–

(a) after an abandonment programme relating wholly or partly to the plant and machinery has had its approval withdrawn, and

(b) when no other abandonment programme relating wholly or partly to the plant and machinery is approved.

165(4B) If an amount of general decommissioning expenditure is disproportionate to the relevant decommissioning carried out in the decommissioning period then, for the purposes of this section, only the allowable expenditure is to be taken to have been incurred in the expenditure period.

165(4C) The application of subsection (4B) to an amount of general decommissioning expenditure does not prevent the non-allowable expenditure from being taken into account under this section in relation to a subsequent notional accounting period.

165(4D) In subsections (4B) and (4C)–

"allowable expenditure", in relation to general decommissioning expenditure, means the amount of the expenditure that is proportionate to the relevant decommissioning carried out in the decommissioning period;

"decommissioning period", in relation to relevant decommissioning, means the notional accounting period or chargeable period in which the decommissioning was carried out;

"expenditure period", in relation to general decommissioning expenditure, means the notional accounting period or chargeable period in which the expenditure was incurred;

"non-allowable expenditure", in relation to general decommissioning expenditure, means so much of that expenditure as is not allowable expenditure;

"relevant decommissioning", in relation to general decommissioning expenditure, means the decommissioning to which the expenditure relates.

165(5) All such adjustments, by discharge or repayment of tax or otherwise, are to be made as are necessary to give effect to this section.

165(6) For the purposes of this section, it does not matter if approval of an abandonment programme that relates to relevant plant and machinery (including approval of the first such programme) is given before or after the start of the post-cessation period.

165(6A) If the former trader–

(a) carries on more than one trade,

(b) makes up accounts of any of them to different dates, and

(c) does not make up general accounts for the whole of the company's activities,

subsection (1C)(b) applies with reference to the accounting date of such one of the trades as the former trader may determine.

165(6B) If the Commissioners for Her Majesty's Revenue and Customs are of the opinion, on reasonable grounds, that a date determined by the former trader for the purposes of subsection (6A) is inappropriate, the Commissioners may by notice direct that the accounting date of such other of the trades referred to in that subsection as appears to the Commissioners to be appropriate is to be used instead.

165(7) In this section–

"abandonment programme" means an abandonment programme under Part 4 of the Petroleum Act 1998;

"approved", in relation to an abandonment programme, means approved or revised under Part 4 of the Petroleum Act 1998 (and **"approval"** is to be construed accordingly);

"relevant plant and machinery" means plant and machinery–

(a) which has been brought into use for the purposes of the ring fence trade that has ceased, and

(b) which, when last in use for the purposes of that ring fence trade, was, or formed part of, an offshore installation or submarine pipeline;

and for this purpose **"offshore installation"** and **"submarine pipeline"** have the same meaning as in Part 4 of the Petroleum Act 1998;

"withdrawn", in relation to approval of an abandonment programme, means withdrawn under Part 4 of the Petroleum Act 1998.

History – In the heading to s. 165, the words "General decommissioning expenditure" substituted for the words "Abandonment expenditure" by FA 2008, s. 109 and Sch. 34, para. 6(2), with effect in relation to expenditure incurred on or after 12 March 2008.
In the heading to s. 165, the word "after" substituted for the words "within 3 years of" by FA 2008, s. 110(2), with effect in relation to ring fence trades that cease to be carried on after 12 March 2008.
S. 165(1)(b) substituted by FA 2009, s. 84 and Sch. 38, para. 4(2), with effect in relation to expenditure incurred on or after 22 April 2009.
In s. 165(1)(b) and (c), the words "general decommissioning expenditure" substituted for the words "abandonment expenditure" by FA 2008, s. 109 and Sch. 34, para. 6(3), with effect in relation to expenditure incurred on or after 12 March 2008.
In s. 165(1)(b), words "on the demolition of plant or machinery", which occurred after "abandonment expenditure", repealed by FA 2001, s. 68 and Sch. 20, para. 8(2), s. 110 and Sch. 33, Pt. 2(5), and deemed always to have had effect.
S. 165(1A), (1B) and (1C) inserted by FA 2009, s. 84 and Sch. 38, para. 4(3), with effect in relation to expenditure incurred on or after 22 April 2009.
S. 165(2), (2A), (2B) and (2C) substituted for former s. 165(2) by FA 2008, s. 110(3), with effect in relation to ring fence trades that cease to be carried on after 12 March 2008.
In s. 165(3), the words "in relation to a notional accounting period" inserted by FA 2009, s. 84 and Sch. 38, para. 4(4)(a), with effect in relation to expenditure incurred on or after 22 April 2009.
In s. 165(3)(a), the words "for that period, or the aggregate of all the relevant decommissioning costs for that period " inserted by FA 2009, s. 84 and Sch. 38, para. 4(4)(b), with effect in relation to expenditure incurred on or after 22 April 2009.
In s. 165(3)(a), the words "relevant decommissioning cost" substituted for the words "relevant abandonment cost" by FA 2008, s. 109 and Sch. 34, para. 6(4), with effect in relation to expenditure incurred on or after 12 March 2008.
In s. 165(3)(b), the words "general decommissioning expenditure" substituted for the words "abandonment expenditure" by FA 2008, s. 109 and Sch. 34, para. 6(4), with effect in relation to expenditure incurred on or after 12 March 2008.
In s. 165(3)(b), words "where any of the abandonment expenditure was incurred on the demolition of plant or machinery," inserted by FA 2001, s. 68 and Sch. 20, para. 8(3), and in s. 165(4), in the definition of "the relevant abandonment cost", words "any plant or machinery on whose demolition any of the abandonment expenditure was incurred" substituted by FA 2001, s. 68 and Sch. 20, para. 8(4). These amendments have effect (FA 2001, Sch. 20, para. 9) in relation to expenditure that is incurred:

- on or after 7 August 2000, and
- in a chargeable period ending on or after 6 April 2001 for income tax purposes, or 1 April 2001 for corporation tax purposes (a "relevant chargeable period").

They also apply to expenditure incurred before 7 August 2000 if the expenditure

- is incurred in a relevant chargeable period, and
- is incurred in connection with an abandonment programme approved on or after 7 August 2000.

S. 165(3A) inserted by FA 2013, s. 93 and Sch. 32, para. 7, with effect in relation to expenditure incurred on decommissioning carried out on or after 17 July 2013.
In s. 165(4), the definition of "relevant decommissioning cost" substituted by FA 2009, s. 84 and Sch. 38, para. 4(5), with effect in relation to expenditure incurred on or after 22 April 2009.
In s. 165(4) the words "relevant decommissioning cost" substituted for the words "relevant abandonment cost" and the words "general decommissioning expenditure" substituted (in each place) for the words "abandonment expenditure" by FA 2008, s. 109 and Sch. 34, para. 6(5), with effect in relation to expenditure incurred on or after 12 March 2008.
In s. 165(4A), the words "general decommissioning expenditure" substituted for the words "abandonment expenditure" by FA 2090, s. 87 and Sch. 41, para. 6, with effect in relation to ring fence trades that cease to be carried on or after 12 March 2008. It is assumed that initial capitalisation was intended and this is reflected the CCH text.
S. 165(4A) inserted by FA 2008, s. 110(4), with effect in relation to ring fence trades that cease to be carried on after 12 March 2008.
S. 165(4B), (4C) and (4D) inserted by FA 2009, s. 84 and Sch. 38, para. 4(6), with effect in relation to expenditure incurred on or after 22 April 2009.
S. 165(6) inserted by FA 2008, s. 110(5), with effect in relation to ring fence trades that cease to be carried on after 12 March 2008.
S. 165(6A) and (6B) inserted by FA 2009, s. 84 and Sch. 38, para. 4(7), with effect in relation to expenditure incurred on or after 22 April 2009.
S. 165(7) inserted by FA 2008, s. 110(5), with effect in relation to ring fence trades that cease to be carried on after 12 March 2008.

Origin – S. 165(1), (2): CAA 1990, s. 62B(1).
S. 165(3): CAA 1990, s. 62B(2) (part), (3).
S. 165(4): CAA 1990, s. 62B(2) (part).
S. 165(5): CAA 1990, s. 62B(4).

Cross references – S. 57(2): "available qualifying expenditure" in a pool for a chargeable period includes any amount allocated to the pool under s. 165(3).
ICTA 1988, s. 393A(11)(a) (as amended by Sch. 2, para. 32(3)(a)): where by virtue of s. 165 the qualifying expenditure of the company for the chargeable period related to the cessation of its ring fence trade is treated as increased, a claim for carry-back may be made within five years following the accounting period of the loss related to the expenditure.

Transitional – Sch. 3, para. 27: s. 165 does not apply if the abandonment expenditure was incurred before 1 July 1991.

RESTRICTIONS ON ALLOWANCES: ANTI-AVOIDANCE

165A Decommissioning services supplied by connected person

165A(1) Allowances under this Part are restricted under section 165B(1) if–

(a) a person ("R") who is carrying on, or has ceased to carry on, a ring fence trade enters into an arrangement,

(b) under the arrangement, a person ("S") who is connected with R provides a service to R, and

(c) all or part of the consideration for the service is decommissioning expenditure.

165A(2) Subsection (1)(b) may be satisfied whether the service is provided to R directly or indirectly; and in particular it does not matter–

(a) whether R and S are parties to the same contract, or

(b) whether payments are made by R directly to S.

165A(3) Subsections (4) to (9) apply for the purposes of this section and sections 165B to 165E.

165A(4) References to providing a service include–

(a) letting a ship on charter or any other asset on hire, and

(b) providing goods which are to be used up in the course of providing a service.

165A(5) **"Decommissioning expenditure"** means expenditure in connection with decommissioning.

165A(6) **"Decommissioning"** means–

(a) demolishing plant or machinery,

(b) preserving plant or machinery pending its reuse or demolition,

(c) preparing plant or machinery for reuse, or

(d) arranging for the reuse of plant or machinery.

165A(7) It is immaterial for the purposes of subsection (6)(b) whether the plant or machinery is reused, is demolished or is partly reused and partly demolished.

165A(8) It is immaterial for the purposes of subsection (6)(c) and (d) whether the plant or machinery is in fact reused.

165A(9) References to R's expenditure under the arrangement are to so much of the consideration for the service as is decommissioning expenditure incurred by R.

History – S. 165A inserted by FA 2013, s. 93 and Sch. 32, para. 2, with effect in relation to expenditure incurred on decommissioning carried out on or after 17 July 2013.

165B Restriction on allowance available

165B(1) The amount, if any, by which R's expenditure under the arrangement exceeds D is to be left out of account in determining R's available qualifying expenditure.

165B(2) D is the cost to S of providing the service or, if R's expenditure under the arrangement relates to only part of the service, that part.

165B(3) Subsection (2) is subject to sections 165C and 165D, which provide for D to be calculated differently in certain circumstances.

165B(4) But if, under any arrangement, a particular service or part of a service is provided by more than one person who is connected with R (so that without this subsection there would be more than one amount for D in relation to that service or part), D is the lowest of those amounts.

History – S. 165B inserted by FA 2013, s. 93 and Sch. 32, para. 2, with effect in relation to expenditure incurred on decommissioning carried out on or after 17 July 2013.

165C Allowance in respect of certain services related to decommissioning

165C(1) This section applies to so much of R's expenditure under the arrangement as relates to the supply by S of a service if–

(a) the service is a planning or project management service, and

(b) the cost plus method is an appropriate method of applying the arm's length principle to the provision of it.

165C(2) D is the sum of–

(a) the cost to S of providing the service or, if R's expenditure under the arrangement relates to only part of the service, that part, and

(b) the appropriate percentage of that amount.

165C(3) The appropriate percentage is the smaller of–

(a) the appropriate mark up determined in accordance with the cost plus method, and

(b) 10%.

165C(4) Any expression which is used in this section and in the transfer pricing guidelines has the meaning given in those guidelines.

"The transfer pricing guidelines" has the meaning given by section 164(4) of TIOPA 2010.

History – S. 165C inserted by FA 2013, s. 93 and Sch. 32, para. 2, with effect in relation to expenditure incurred on decommissioning carried out on or after 17 July 2013.

165D Allowance where decommissioning undertaken for other participators in oil field

165D(1) This section applies where–

(a) S decommissions the plant or machinery,

(b) there are, in addition to R, one or more other participators in the relevant field, and

(c) the expenditure incurred in respect of the decommissioning is apportioned between the participators (including R) in accordance with their shares in the oil won from the relevant field or their shares in the equity of that field.

165D(2) D is the part of the expenditure referred to in subsection (1)(c) which is incurred by R.

165D(3) Where–

(a) plant or machinery is or has been used in connection with the winning of oil from more than one relevant field, and

(b) the expenditure incurred in respect of the decommissioning is apportioned between those fields in accordance with the contribution from each field to the total of the oil won using that plant or machinery,

subsections (1) and (2) apply to each such field as if subsection (1)(c) referred to the expenditure apportioned to that field.

165D(4) But subsections (2) and (3) do not apply (and section 165B(2) applies instead) if–

(a) the amount of consideration, or the method of determining the amount of consideration, to be received by S under the arrangement or arrangements, or

(b) the apportionment of the liability for that consideration (whether between the participators as mentioned in subsection (1)(c) or between the fields as mentioned in subsection (3)(b)),

has been agreed as, or as part of, an avoidance scheme.

165D(5) A scheme is an **"avoidance scheme"** if the main purpose, or one of the main purposes, of a party in entering into the scheme is to enable a person to obtain a tax advantage under this Part that would not otherwise be obtained.

165D(6) The reference in subsection (5) to obtaining a tax advantage that would not otherwise be obtained includes obtaining an allowance that is in any way more favourable to a person than the one that would otherwise be obtained.

165D(7) In this section–

"licensee", **"oil"** and **"oil field"** have the same meaning as in Part 1 of OTA 1975,

"other participator" means a person, not connected with R, who is a licensee in respect of any licensed area wholly or partly included in the oil field in question, and

"relevant field" means an oil field–

(a) in which plant or machinery is located, or

(b) in connection with which the plant or machinery is being or has been used for the purposes of a ring fence trade.

History – S. 165D inserted by FA 2013, s. 93 and Sch. 32, para. 2, with effect in relation to expenditure incurred on decommissioning carried out on or after 17 July 2013.

165E Transaction to obtain tax advantage

165E(1) Allowances under this Part are restricted under subsection (5) if–

(a) a person ("R") who is carrying on, or has ceased to carry on, a ring fence trade enters into a transaction with another person ("S"),

(b) S receives from R consideration for services provided in pursuance of the transaction,

(c) all or part of that consideration is decommissioning expenditure, and

(d) the transaction either has an avoidance purpose, or is part of, or occurs as a result of, a scheme or arrangement that has an avoidance purpose.

165E(2) Subsection (1)(d) may be satisfied–

(a) whether the scheme or arrangement was made before or after the transaction was entered into, and

(b) whether or not the scheme or arrangement is legally enforceable.

165E(3) A transaction, scheme or arrangement has an **"avoidance purpose"** if the main purpose, or one of the main purposes, of a party in–

(a) entering into the transaction, scheme or arrangement, or

(b) agreeing an amount of consideration, or a method of determining an amount of consideration, to be paid in pursuance of the transaction, scheme or arrangement,

is to enable a person to obtain a tax advantage under this Part that would not otherwise be obtained.

165E(4) The reference in subsection (3) to obtaining a tax advantage that would not otherwise be obtained includes obtaining an allowance that is in any way more favourable to a person than the one that would otherwise be obtained.

165E(5) All or part of R's expenditure under the transaction is to be left out of account in determining R's available qualifying expenditure.

165E(6) The amount of expenditure to be left out of account is–

(a) such amount as would or would in effect cancel out the tax advantage mentioned in subsection (3) (whether that advantage is obtained by R or another person and whether it relates to the transaction or something else), or

(b) if the amount found under paragraph (a) exceeds the whole of R's expenditure under the transaction, the whole of that expenditure.

History – S. 165E inserted by FA 2013, s. 93 and Sch. 32, para. 2, with effect in relation to expenditure incurred on decommissioning carried out on or after 17 July 2013.

TRANSFERS OF INTERESTS IN OIL FIELDS: ANTI-AVOIDANCE

166 Transfers of interests in oil fields: anti-avoidance

166(1) This section applies if–

(a) there is, for the purposes of Schedule 17 to FA 1980, a transfer by a participator in an oil field of the whole or part of his interest in the field, and

(b) as part of the transfer, the old participator disposes of, and the new participator acquires–

(i) plant or machinery used, or expected to be used, in connection with the field, or

(ii) a share in such plant or machinery.

166(2) The amount, if any, by which the new participator's expenditure exceeds the old participator's disposal value is to be left out of account in determining the new participator's available qualifying expenditure.

166(3) In subsection (2)–

(a) **"the new participator's expenditure"** means the expenditure incurred by the new participator on the acquisition of the plant or machinery, and

(b) **"the old participator's disposal value"** means the disposal value to be brought into account by the old participator as a result of the disposal of the plant or machinery to the new participator.

166(4) In this section–

(a) **"oil field"** and **"participator"** have the same meaning as in Part I of OTA 1975,

(b) **"the old participator"** means the participator whose interest in the oil field is wholly or partly transferred, and

(c) **"the new participator"** means the person to whom the interest in the oil field is transferred.

166(5) Nothing in this section affects the operation of Chapter 17 (anti-avoidance).

Origin – S. 166(1): CAA 1990, s. 64(1).
S. 166(2), (3): CAA 1990, s. 64(2).
S. 166(4): CAA 1990, s. 64(3).
S. 166(5): CAA 1990, s. 64(4).

Cross references – S. 57(3): "available qualifying expenditure" (in a pool for a chargeable period) does not include any expenditure excluded by s. 166(2).
FA 1980, Sch. 17: transfer where the whole or part of a participator's share in the oil to be won and saved becomes that of another person who is or becomes a participator excluding certain associated companies and re-determinations under unitisation agreements.

OIL PRODUCTION SHARING CONTRACTS

167 Oil production sharing contracts

167(1) Sections 168 to 170 apply if–

(a) a person (**"the contractor"**) is entitled to an interest in a contract made with, or with the authorised representative of, the government of a country or territory in which oil is or may be produced, and

(b) the contract provides (among other things) for any plant or machinery of a description specified in the contract which–

(i) is provided by the contractor, and

(ii) has an oil-related use under the contract,

to be transferred (immediately or later) to the government or representative.

167(2) For the purposes of this section and sections 168 to 170, plant or machinery has an oil-related use if it is used–

(a) to explore for, win access to or extract oil,

(b) for the initial storage or treatment of oil, or

(c) for other purposes ancillary to the extraction of oil.

167(3) In this section and sections 168 to 170 **"oil"** has the meaning given by section 556(3).

Origin – S. 167(1): CAA 1990, s. 64A(1)(a), (b), (3) (part), (5) (part).
S. 167(2): CAA 1990, s. 64A(11).
S. 167(3): CAA 1990, s. 64A(12).

Transitional – Sch. 3, para. 28: s. 167 does not apply if the expenditure was incurred before 21 March 2000 or the expenditure is treated as incurred by virtue of s. 13 and the conditions mentioned in 13(1) were fulfilled before that date.

CAA 2001

168 Expenditure on plant or machinery incurred by contractor

168(1) This section applies if–

(a) the contractor incurs capital expenditure on the provision of plant or machinery of a description specified in the contract,

(b) the plant or machinery is to have an oil-related use under the contract, for the purposes of a trade of oil extraction carried on by the contractor,

(c) the amount of the expenditure is commensurate with the value of the contractor's interest under the contract, and

(d) the plant or machinery is transferred to the government or representative in accordance with the contract.

168(2) Despite the transfer, the plant or machinery is to be treated for the purposes of this Part as owned by the contractor (and not by any other person) until–

(a) it ceases to be owned by the government or representative, or

(b) it ceases to be used, or held for use, by any person under the contract.

This is subject to section 170(2).

Origin – S. 168(1): CAA 1990, s. 64A(1)(c), (d), (e), 83(2A) (part).
S. 168(2): CAA 1990, s. 64A(2).

Transitional – Sch. 3, para. 28: s. 168 does not apply if the expenditure was incurred before 21 March 2000 or the expenditure is treated as incurred by virtue of s. 13 and the conditions mentioned in 13(1) were fulfilled before that date.

169 Expenditure on plant or machinery incurred by participator

169(1) This section applies if–

(a) a person (**"the participator"**) acquires an interest in the contract from–

(i) the contractor, or

(ii) another person who has acquired it (directly or indirectly) from the contractor,

(b) the participator incurs capital expenditure on the provision of plant or machinery,

(c) the plant or machinery is to have an oil-related use under the contract, for the purposes of a trade of oil extraction carried on by the participator,

(d) the amount of the expenditure is commensurate with the value of the participator's interest under the contract, and

(e) the plant or machinery is transferred to the government or representative in accordance with the contract.

169(2) Despite the transfer, the plant or machinery is to be treated for the purposes of this Part as owned by the participator (and not by any other person) until–

(a) it ceases to be owned by the government or representative, or

(b) it ceases to be used, or held for use, by any person under the contract.

This is subject to section 170(2).

Origin – S. 169(1): CAA 1990, s. 64A(3), 83(2A) (part).
S. 169(2): CAA 1990, s. 64A(4).

Transitional – Sch. 3, para. 28: s. 169 does not apply if the expenditure was incurred before 21 March 2000 or the expenditure is treated as incurred by virtue of s. 13 and the conditions mentioned in 13(1) were fulfilled before that date.

170 Participator's expenditure attributable to plant or machinery

170(1) This section applies if–

(a) a person (**"the relevant participator"**) acquires an interest in the contract from–

(i) the contractor, or

(ii) another person who has acquired it (directly or indirectly) from the contractor, and

(b) some of the expenditure incurred by the relevant participator to acquire the interest in the contract is attributable to plant or machinery which–

(i) is treated by section 168 as owned by the contractor, or

(ii) is treated by section 169 or subsection (2) as owned by another person (**"the other participator"**).

170(2) The plant or machinery is to be treated for the purposes of this Part as owned by the relevant participator (and not by any other person) until–

(a) it ceases to be owned by the government or representative, or

(b) it ceases to be used, or held for use, by any person under the contract.

This is subject to a later application of this subsection.

170(3) The person who, until subsection (2) applies, is treated as owning the plant or machinery is to be treated for the purposes of this Part as if he had disposed of it for a consideration equal to the relevant participator's expenditure attributable to it.

170(4) The relevant participator is to be treated for the purposes of this Part as if–

(a) he had incurred capital expenditure of an amount given by subsection (5), and

(b) he owned the plant or machinery (in accordance with subsection (2)) as a result of having incurred that expenditure.

170(5) The amount of that expenditure is–

(a) the amount of the relevant participator's expenditure attributable to the plant or machinery, or

(b) if less, the disposal value to be brought into account by the contractor or the other participator as a result of subsection (3).

170(6) The expenditure attributable to plant or machinery for the purposes of this section is to be determined having regard to what is just and reasonable in the circumstances.

Origin – S. 170(1): CAA 1990, s. 64A(5).
S. 170(2): CAA 1990, s. 64A(6).
S. 170(3): CAA 1990, s. 64A(7).
S. 170(4): CAA 1990, s. 64A(8) (part).
S. 170(5): CAA 1990, s. 64A(8) (part), (9).
S. 170(6): CAA 1990, s. 64A(10).

Transitional – Sch. 3, para. 28: s. 170 does not apply if the expenditure was incurred before 21 March 2000 or the expenditure is treated as incurred by virtue of s. 13 and the conditions mentioned in 13(1) were fulfilled before that date.

171 Disposal values on cessation of ownership

171(1) This section applies if a person treated as owning plant or machinery under section 168(2), 169(2) or 170(2) ceases to be treated as owning it solely as a result of one of those provisions.

171(2) If the person receives capital compensation, the disposal value to be brought into account is the amount of the compensation.

171(3) If the person does not receive capital compensation, the disposal value to be brought into account is nil.

Origin – S. 171(1): CAA 1990, s. 26(1)(ef), (eg).
S. 171(2): CAA 1990, s. 26(1)(ef).
S. 171(3): CAA 1990, s. 26(1)(eg).

Cross references – S. 9: a person is not entitled to make a fixtures claim under Pt. 2, Ch. 14 if any person has previously claimed an allowance under any part other than Pt. 2.
S. 60(1)(b): meaning of "disposal receipt" includes a value that a person is required to bring into account for purposes of any of the provisions listed in s. 66 (see note below).
S. 66: list of provisions about disposal values includes s. 171.

S. 166(2): where transfer of interest in oilfield includes transfer of machinery or plant, new participator's expenditure eligible for allowances limited to old participator's disposal value.
FA 1994, Sch. 24, para. 21(3)(a) (as amended by Sch. 2, para. 91(7)(c)), Coal Industry Act 1994, Sch. 4, para. 20(3)(a) (as amended by Sch. 2, para. 93(6)(c)) and Transport Act 2000, Sch. 26, para. 14(2)(a) (as amended by Sch. 2, para. 109(10)(b)): under a scheme of restructuring in connection with privatisation of the railways or coal industry, where a trade is treated as permanently discontinued and a new trade set up and where the relevant scheme contains provision for the disposal value of property to be deemed for the purposes of capital allowances in accordance with the scheme, s. 171 is disapplied and the scheme provision shall have effect for determining disposal value of property instead (the transferee being deemed to have incurred expenditure of that amount on the provision of that property).
Electricity Act 1989, Sch. 11, para. 5(4), (5) (as amended by Sch. 2, para. 71): treatment of fixtures where a lease is granted in pursuance of certain transfer schemes on privatisation.
FA 1994, Sch. 24, para. 21(3)(c) (as amended by Sch. 2, para. 91(7)(d)), Coal Industry Act 1994, Sch. 4 (as amended by Sch. 2, para. 93) and Transport Act 2000, Sch. 26, para. 14(2)(d) (as amended by Sch. 2, para. 109(10)(c)): treatment of fixtures under a scheme of restructuring in connection with privatisation of the railways or coal industry.
Greater London Authority Act 1999, Sch. 33, para. 11 (as amended by Sch. 2, para. 105(7), (8)): application of Pt. 2, Ch. 14 in defining terms for leases of land in connection with public private partnerships certified by London Regional Transport.
RA 2005, Sch. 10. para. 14: disapplication of s.171 in the case of certain transfers to a national authority.

Transitional – Sch. 3, para. 28: s. 171 does not apply if the expenditure was incurred before 21 March 2000 or the expenditure is treated as incurred by virtue of s. 13 and the conditions mentioned in 13(1) were fulfilled before that date.

Chapter 14 – Fixtures

INTRODUCTION

Cross references – S. 9: a person is not entitled to make a fixtures claim under Pt. 2, Ch. 14 if any person has previously claimed an allowance under any part other than Pt. 2.
Electricity Act 1989, Sch. 11, para. 5(4), (5) (as amended by Sch. 2, para. 71): treatment of fixtures where a lease is granted in pursuance of certain transfer schemes on privatisation.
FA 1994, Sch. 24, para. 21(3)(c) (as amended by Sch. 2, para. 91(7)(d)), Coal Industry Act 1994, Sch. 4 (as amended by Sch. 2, para. 93) and Transport Act 2000, Sch. 26, para. 14(2)(d) (as amended by Sch. 2, para. 109(10)(c)): treatment of fixtures under a scheme of restructuring in connection with privatisation of the railways or coal industry.
Greater London Authority Act 1999, Sch. 33, para. 11 (as amended by Sch. 2, para. 105(7), (8)): application of Pt. 2, Ch. 14 in defining terms for leases of land in connection with public private partnerships certified by London Regional Transport.

172 Scope of Chapter etc.

172(1) This Chapter applies to determine entitlement to allowances under this Part in respect of expenditure on plant or machinery that is, or becomes, a fixture.

172(2) For the purposes of this Part, ownership of plant or machinery that is, or becomes, a fixture is determined under this Chapter.

172(2A) Subsections (1) and (2) are subject to section 172A.

172(3) The provisions of this Chapter that treat a person as being the owner of a fixture (see sections 176 to 184 and 193 to 195B) are subject to the provisions of this Chapter which treat a person as ceasing to be the owner of a fixture (see sections 188 to 192A).

172(4) References in this Chapter to a person being treated–

(a) as the owner of plant or machinery, or

(b) as ceasing to be the owner of plant or machinery,

are to be read as references to the person being so treated for the purposes of this Part.

172(5) This Chapter does not affect any entitlement a person has to an allowance as a result of section 538 (contribution allowances for plant and machinery).

History – S. 172(2A) inserted by FA 2006, s. 81 and Sch. 8, para. 9(1). The commencement and transitional provisions are complex and are set out in full in FA 2006, Sch. 8, para. 15–27.
In s. 172(3), references to s. 195B and s. 192A substituted by FA 2001, s. 66 and Sch. 18, para. 1, with effect in relation to chargeable expenditure incurred on or after 1 April 2001, with effect as respects allowances and charges falling to be made for chargeable periods ending on or after

- 6 April 2001 for income tax purposes, and
- 1 April 2001 for corporation tax purposes.

Origin – S. 172(1), (2) CAA 1990, s. 51(1) (part).
S. 172(3): CAA 1990, s. 52(1) (part), 53(1) (part), 54(1) (part), 55(1) (part), 56 (part), drafting.
S. 172(4): CAA 1990, s. 52(1) (part), (2) (part), 53(1) (part), (3) (part), 54(1) (part), 55(1) (part), 56 (part), 56A(2)(c) (part), 56B(1)(a) (part), 56C(1)(d) (part), 57(2) (part), (5) (part), (6) (part), (7) (part), 58(1) (part), (2), (part), (3) (part), (4) (part).
S. 172(5): CAA 1990, s. 51(8).

Rewrite: Changes in Law – Explanatory Notes, Annex 1, Change 26: s. 172(2) omits the restriction in the previous wording in CAA 1990, s. 51(1) that,
"at any time when, by virtue of this Chapter, any machinery or plant is treated as belonging to any person, no other person shall be entitled to such an allowance in respect of it.".
This wording was given close scrutiny in the judgment in the case of *Melluish (HMIT) v BMI (No 3) Ltd* [1995] BTC 381 (where the House of Lords dismissed the Revenue's claim that, because a local authority lessee was exempt from tax, the asset would not have been treated as "belonging to" the lessee). The original intention of these words was simply to prevent double allowances being given at the same time for the same expenditure. The change removes an interpretation, hinted at in the *Melluish* judgment that, on a literal reading, no person would be entitled to an allowance where there is more than one owner of a fixture. Although this change is intended to be beneficial, there is a right of election for the previous position to apply to a period which straddles 6 April (income tax) or 1 April (corporation tax) 2001 (Sch. 3, para. 8).

HMRC Manuals – CA26050: guidance and example on fixtures legislation.

172A Long funding leases etc: cases where this Chapter does not apply

172A(1) This section applies where plant or machinery that is or becomes a fixture is the subject of a long funding lease (see Chapter 6A).

172A(2) This section also applies if, in any such case,–

(a) the lessee under the long funding lease is or becomes the lessor of some or all of the plant or machinery under a further lease, and

(b) the further lease is not itself a long funding lease within subsection (1).

172A(3) This Chapter does not apply to determine the entitlement of the lessor or the lessee (under either lease) to allowances under this Part in respect of expenditure on the plant or machinery.

172A(4) This Chapter does not apply to determine whether the lessor or the lessee (under either lease) is to be treated as the owner of the plant or machinery.

History – S. 172A inserted by FA 2006, s. 81 and Sch. 8, para. 9(2). The commencement and transitional provisions are complex and are set out in full in FA 2006, Sch. 8, para. 15–27.

173 Meaning of "fixture" and "relevant land"

173(1) In this Chapter **"fixture"**–

(a) means plant or machinery that is so installed or otherwise fixed in or to a building or other description of land as to become, in law, part of that building or other land, and

(b) includes any boiler or water-filled radiator installed in a building as part of a space or water heating system.

173(2) In this Chapter **"relevant land"**, in relation to a fixture means–

(a) the building or other description of land of which the fixture becomes part, or

(b) in the case of a boiler or water-filled radiator which is a fixture as a result of subsection (1)(b), the building in which it is installed as part of a space or water heating system.

Origin – S. 173(1): CAA 1990, s. 51(2) ("fixture"), (2A) (part).
S. 173(2): CAA 1990, s. 51(2) ("relevant land"), (2A) (part).

HMRC Manuals – CA26025: meaning of "fixture" amplified.
CA26100: meaning of "relevant land" amplified.

174 Meaning of "equipment lease" and "lease"

174(1) In this Chapter **"equipment lease"** means–

(a) an agreement entered into in the circumstances given in subsection (2), or

(b) a lease entered into under or as a result of such an agreement.

174(2) The circumstances are that–

(a) a person incurs capital expenditure on the provision of plant or machinery for leasing,

(b) an agreement is entered into for the lease, directly or indirectly from that person, of the plant or machinery to another person,

(c) the plant or machinery becomes a fixture, and

(d) the agreement is not an agreement for the plant or machinery to be leased as part of the relevant land.

174(3) In this Chapter–

"equipment lessor" means the person from whom (directly or indirectly) the equipment lease provides for the plant or machinery to be leased, and

"equipment lessee" means the person to whom the equipment lease provides for the plant or machinery to be leased.

174(4) Except in the context of leasing plant or machinery, any reference in this Chapter to a lease is to–

(a) any leasehold estate in or, in Scotland, lease of, the land (whether in the nature of a head-lease, sub-lease or under-lease), or

(b) any agreement to acquire such an estate or, in Scotland, lease;

and, in relation to such an agreement, **"grant"** is to be read accordingly.

Origin – S. 174(1): CAA 1990, s. 51(2) ("equipment lease"), 53(4).
S. 174(2: CAA 1990, s. 53(1) (part).
S. 174(3) CAA 1990, s. 51(2) ("equipment lessor" and "equipment lessee"), 53(1) (part).
S. 174(4): CAA 1990, s. 51(2) ("lease"), (3) (part).

HMRC Manuals – CA26100: guidance on meaning of "lease".
CA26200: guidance on s. 174.

175 Meaning of "interest in land", etc.

175(1) In this Chapter **"interest in land"** means–

(a) the fee simple estate in the land or an agreement to acquire such an estate,

(b) in relation to Scotland, the interest of the owner or an agreement to acquire such an interest,

(c) a lease,

(d) an easement or servitude or an agreement to acquire an easement or servitude, and

(e) a licence to occupy land.

175(2) If an interest in land is–

(a) conveyed or assigned by way of security, and

(b) subject to a right of redemption,

the person with the right of redemption is treated for the purposes of this Chapter as having that interest, and not the creditor.

Origin – S. 175(1): CAA 1990, s. 51(2) ("interest in land"), (3) (part).
S. 175(2): CAA 1990, s. 51(4).

Cross references – Greater London Authority Act 1999, Sch. 33, para. 11(4) (as amended by Sch. 2, para. 105(8)(c)): application of s. 175(1) in defining terms for leases of land in connection with public private partnerships certified by London Regional Transport.

Transitional – Sch. 3, para. 29: if s. 175 commences before the Abolition of Feudal Tenure etc. (Scotland) Act 2000 Sch. 12, para. 51 comes into force, then the following should be substituted for s. 175(1)(b) until the appointed day for that act to come into force (under s. 71 of that Act)–
"in Scotland, the estate or interest of the proprietor of the *dominium utile* (or, in the case of property other than feudal property, of the owner) and any agreement to acquire such an estate or interest,".

HMRC Manuals – CA26100: meaning of "interest in land" amplified; Revenue view is that a licence to occupy is not such an interest unless it is an exclusive licence.

175A Meaning of "energy services agreement"

175A(1) In this Chapter **"energy services agreement"** means an agreement entered into by an energy services provider (**"the energy services provider"**) and another person (**"the client"**) that makes provision, with a view to saving energy or using energy more efficiently, for–

(a) the design of plant or machinery, or one or more systems incorporating plant or machinery,

(b) obtaining and installing the plant or machinery,

(c) the operation of the plant or machinery,

(d) the maintenance of the plant or machinery, and

(e) the amount of any payments in respect of the operation of the plant or machinery to be linked (wholly or in part) to energy savings or increases in energy efficiency resulting from the provision or operation of the plant or machinery.

175A(2) In this Chapter **"energy services provider"** means a person carrying on a qualifying activity consisting wholly or mainly in the provision of energy management services.

History – S. 175A inserted by FA 2001, s. 66 and Sch. 18, para. 2, with effect in relation to expenditure incurred on or after 1 April 2001, with effect as respects allowances and charges falling to be made for chargeable periods ending, for income tax purposes, on or after 6 April 2001, and, for corporation tax purposes, on or after 1 April 2001.

HMRC Manuals – CA23150: guidance on s. 175A.

PERSONS WHO ARE TREATED AS OWNERS OF FIXTURES

176 Person with interest in relevant land having fixture for purposes of qualifying activity

176(1) If–

(a) a person incurs capital expenditure on the provision of plant or machinery for the purposes of a qualifying activity carried on by him,

(b) the plant or machinery becomes a fixture, and

(c) that person has an interest in the relevant land at the time the plant or machinery becomes a fixture,

that person is to be treated, on and after that time, as the owner of the fixture as a result of incurring the expenditure.

176(2) If there are two or more persons with different interests in the relevant land who would be treated as the owner of the same fixture as a result of subsection (1), one interest only is taken into account under that subsection.

176(3) The interest to be taken into account is given by the following rules–

CAA 2001

Rule 1

If one of the interests is an easement or servitude or any agreement to acquire an easement or servitude, that interest is the interest to be taken into account.

Rule 2

If Rule 1 does not apply, but one of the interests is a licence to occupy land, that interest is the interest to be taken into account.

Rule 3

In any other case–

(a) except in Scotland, the interest to be taken into account is the interest which is not in reversion (at law or in equity and whether directly or indirectly) on any other interest in the relevant land which is held by any of the persons referred to in subsection (2), and

(b) in Scotland, the interest to be taken into account is the interest of whichever of the persons referred to in subsection (2) has, or last had, the right of use of the relevant land.

176(4) Subsection (1) is subject to sections 177(4) and 180A.

History – In s. 176(4), reference to s. 180A added by FA 2001, s. 66 and Sch. 18, para. 3, with effect in relation to expenditure incurred on or after 1 April 2001, with effect as respects allowances and charges falling to be made for chargeable periods ending, for income tax purposes, on or after 6 April 2001, and, for corporation tax purposes, on or after 1 April 2001.

Origin – S. 176(1): CAA 1990, s. 52(1) (part).
S. 176(2), (3): CAA 1990, s. 52(2) (part).
S. 176(4): CAA 1990, s. 52(1) (part).

Cross references – S. 172(3): the provisions of s. 176 are subject to the provisions of s. 188–192 (which treat a person as ceasing to be the owner of a fixture).
Greater London Authority Act 1999, Sch. 33, para. 12(1)(b) (as amended by Sch. 2, para. 105(9)(b)): nothing in s. 176(2) or (3) shall, by reason only of any provision made under a public private partnership agreement certified by London Regional Transport, affect the entitlement of any company participating in an agreement to capital allowances in respect of capital expenditure incurred by it.

HMRC Manuals – CA26150: guidance and examples on s. 176.

177 Equipment lessors

177(1) If–

(a) the conditions in–

(i) section 178 (equipment lessee has qualifying activity etc.),

(ii) section 179 (equipment lessor has right to sever fixture that is not part of building), or

(iii) section 180 (equipment lease is part of affordable warmth programme),

are met in relation to an equipment lease,

(b) the equipment lessor and the equipment lessee are not connected persons, and

(c) they elect that this section should apply,

the equipment lessor is to be treated, on and after the relevant time, as the owner of the fixture as a result of incurring the capital expenditure on the provision of the plant or machinery that is the subject of the equipment lease.

177(2) The relevant time for the purposes of subsection (1) is (unless subsection (3) applies) the time when the equipment lessor incurs the expenditure.

177(3) If–

(a) the conditions in section 178 are met in relation to an equipment lease (but the conditions in sections 179 and 180 are not), and

(b) the equipment lessor incurs the capital expenditure before the equipment lessee begins to carry on the qualifying activity,

the relevant time is the time when the equipment lessee begins to carry on the qualifying activity.

177(4) If an election is made under this section, the equipment lessee is not to be treated under section 176 as the owner of the fixture.

177(5) An election under this section must be made by notice to an officer of Revenue and Customs–

(a) for income tax purposes, on or before the normal time limit for amending a tax return for the tax year in which the relevant chargeable period ends;

(b) for corporation tax purposes, no later than 2 years after the end of the relevant chargeable period.

177(6) **"The relevant chargeable period"** means the chargeable period in which the capital expenditure was incurred.

History – In s. 177(5), the words "an officer of Revenue and Customs" substituted for "the Inland Revenue" by CRCA 2005, s. 50(6) and Sch. 4, para. 83(1), with effect from 18 April 2005 by virtue of SI 2005/1126, art. 2(2).

Origin – S. 177(1): CAA 1990, s. 53(1) (part), (1B) (part), (1D) (part), (2) (part).
S. 177(2): CAA 1990, s. 53(1) (part)), (1B) (part), (1D) (part).

S. 177(3): CAA 1990, s. 53(1A).
S. 177(4): CAA 1990, s. 53(3) (part).
S. 177(5): CAA 1990, s. 53(2) (part), (2A) (part).
S. 177(6): CAA 1990, s. 53(2A) (part).

Cross references – S. 172(3): the provisions of s. 177 are subject to the provisions of s. 188–192 (which treat a person as ceasing to be the owner of a fixture).
TMA 1970, s. 42(6), (7)(c) (as amended by Sch. 2, para. 1): claims made by partnerships.

Transitional – Sch. 3, para. 30: s. 177(1)(a)(i) does not apply if the agreement for the lease of the plant or machinery was entered into before 19 March 1997.

Rewrite: Technical Points – Explanatory Notes, Annex 2, Note 37: allowances are available to an equipment lessor on fixtures leased for the purposes of a trade to be carried on by the lessee, and the fixture is treated as belonging to the lessor from the date when the lessee starts to trade. The wording of s. 177(3) which restricts this treatment to situations where the lessee leases the asset for the purposes of a "qualifying activity" under s. 178 (and not to other circumstances under s. 179 and 180 where the lessee may have a trade but is not *required* to have one in order for allowances to be given to the lessor) is based on an interpretation of the previous wording of CAA 1990, s. 53(1A).

Statements of practice – 3/91: finance lease rental payments.

HMRC Manuals – CA26200: guidance on s. 177.

178 Equipment lessee has qualifying activity etc.

178 The conditions referred to in section 177(1)(a)(i) are that–

(a) the equipment lease is for the lease of the plant or machinery for the purposes of a qualifying activity which is, or is to be, carried on by the equipment lessee,

(b) if the equipment lessee had incurred the capital expenditure incurred by the equipment lessor on the provision of the plant or machinery that is the subject of the equipment lease, he would, as a result of section 176, have been entitled to an allowance in respect of it, and

(c) the equipment lease is not for the lease of the plant or machinery for use in a dwelling-house.

Origin – S. 178: CAA 1990, s. 53(1) (part).

Cross references – S. 172(3): the provisions of s. 178 are subject to the provisions of s. 188–192 (which treat a person as ceasing to be the owner of a fixture).

Transitional – Sch. 3, para. 31: if:

- the agreement for the lease of the plant or machinery was entered into before 19 March 1997, the words "which is or is to be" in s. 178(a) are to be omitted and the word "and" added at the end of that paragraph; and
- if the expenditure in s. 178(b) was incurred before 24 July 1996, then the following should be substituted for para. (b)–

"if the equipment lessee had incurred the capital expenditure incurred by the equipment lessor on the provision of the plant or machinery, he would, by virtue of section 176, be treated as the owner of the fixture as a result of incurring the expenditure."
and s. 178(c) should be omitted.

HMRC Manuals – CA26200: guidance on s. 178.

179 Equipment lessor has right to sever fixture that is not part of building

179(1) The conditions referred to in section 177(1)(a)(ii) are that–

(a) the plant or machinery becomes a fixture by being fixed to land that is neither a building nor part of a building,

(b) the equipment lessee has an interest in the land when taking possession of the plant or machinery under the equipment lease,

(c) under the terms of the equipment lease, the equipment lessor is entitled to sever the plant or machinery, at the end of the period for which it is leased, from the land to which it is fixed at that time,

(d) under the terms of the equipment lease, the equipment lessor will own the plant or machinery on its severance in accordance with the equipment lease,

(e) the nature of the plant or machinery and the way in which it is fixed to land are such that its use on one set of premises does not, to any material extent, prevent it from being used, once severed, for the same purposes on a different set of premises,

(f) the equipment lease is one which under generally accepted accounting practice falls (or would fall) to be treated in the accounts of the equipment lessor as an operating lease, and

(g) the equipment lease is not for the lease of the plant or machinery for use in a dwelling-house.

179(2) [Repealed by FA 2002, s. 141 and Sch. 40, Pt. 3(16).]

History – In s. 179(1)(f), words "generally accepted accounting practice" substituted for "normal accountancy practice" by FA 2002, s. 103(4)(g) with effect from 24 July 2002.
S. 179(2) (which qualified former reference to normal accountancy practice in s. 179(1)(f) as that applicable to a company incorporated in the UK) repealed by FA 2002, s. 141 and Sch. 40, Pt. 3(16).

Origin – S. 179(1): CAA 1990, s. 53(1B), (1C) (part).
S. 179(2): CAA 1990, s. 53(1C) (part).

Cross references – S. 172(3): the provisions of s. 179 are subject to the provisions of s. 188–192 (which treat a person as ceasing to be the owner of a fixture).
ICTA 1988, s. 836A: definition of "generally accepted accounting practice" in s. 179(1)(f).

Transitional – Sch. 3, para. 32: if:

- the agreement for the lease of the plant or machinery was entered into before 19 March 1997, s. 179(1) does not apply and
- if the expenditure of the equipment lessor was incurred before 24 July 1996, s. 179(1) applies with the omission of para. (g) (and the moving of the word "and" to the end of para. (e).

HMRC Manuals – CA26200: guidance on s. 179.

180 Equipment lease is part of affordable warmth programme

180(1) The conditions referred to in section 177(1)(a)(iii) are that–

(a) the plant or machinery which is the subject of the equipment lease consists of a boiler, heat exchanger, radiator or heating control that is installed in a building as part of a space or water heating system,

(b) the expenditure of the equipment lessor is incurred before 1st January 2008, and

(c) the equipment lease is approved for the purposes of this section as entered into as part of the affordable warmth programme.

180(2) The approval mentioned in subsection (1)(c) may be given, with the consent of the Treasury–

(a) by the Secretary of State;

(b) in the case of buildings in Scotland, by the Scottish Ministers;

(c) in the case of buildings in Wales, by the National Assembly for Wales;

(d) in the case of buildings in Northern Ireland, by the Department for Social Development in Northern Ireland.

180(3) If an approval is withdrawn, it is to be treated for the purposes of subsection (1)(c) as never having had effect.

Origin – S. 180(1): CAA 1990, s. 53(1D), (1E).
S. 180(2): CAA 1990, s. 53(1F).
S. 180(3): CAA 1990, s. 53(1G) (part).

Cross references – S. 172(3): the provisions of s. 180 are subject to the provisions of s. 188–192 (which treat a person as ceasing to be the owner of a fixture).

Transitional – Sch. 3, para. 33: s. 180 does not apply if the expenditure of the equipment lessor was incurred before 28 July 2000.

HMRC Manuals – CA26200: guidance on s. 180.

180A Energy services providers

180A(1) If–

(a) an energy services agreement is entered into,

(b) the energy services provider incurs capital expenditure under the agreement on the provision of plant or machinery,

(c) the plant or machinery becomes a fixture,

(d) at the time the plant or machinery becomes a fixture–

 (i) the client has an interest in the relevant land, and

 (ii) the energy services provider does not,

(e) the plant or machinery–

 (i) is not provided for leasing, and

 (ii) is not provided for use in a dwelling-house,

(f) the operation of the plant or machinery is carried out wholly or substantially by the energy services provider or a person connected with him,

(g) the energy services provider and the client are not connected persons, and

(h) they elect that this section should apply,

the energy services provider is to be treated, on and after the time at which he incurs the expenditure, as the owner of the fixture as a result of incurring the expenditure.

180A(2) But if the client would not have been entitled to a section 176 allowance in respect of the expenditure if he had incurred it, subsection (1) does not apply unless the plant or machinery belongs to a class of plant or machinery specified by Treasury order.

180A(3) In subsection (2) a **"section 176 allowance"** means an allowance to which a person is entitled as a result of section 176.

180A(4) If an election is made under this section, the client is not to be treated under section 176 as the owner of the fixture.

180A(5) An election under this section must be made by notice to an officer of Revenue and Customs–

(a) for income tax purposes, on or before the normal time limit for amending a tax return for the tax year in which the relevant chargeable period ends;

(b) for corporation tax purposes, no later than 2 years after the end of the relevant chargeable period.

180A(6) The **"relevant chargeable period"** means the chargeable period in which the capital expenditure was incurred.

History – In s. 180A(5), the words "an officer of Revenue and Customs" substituted for "the Inland Revenue" by CRCA 2005, s. 50(6) and Sch. 4, para. 83(1), with effect from 18 April 2005 by virtue of SI 2005/1126, art. 2(2).
S. 180A inserted by FA 2001, s. 66 and Sch. 18, para. 4, with effect in relation to expenditure incurred on or after 1 April 2001, with effect as respects allowances and charges falling to be made for chargeable periods ending, for income tax purposes, on or after 6 April 2001, and, for corporation tax purposes, on or after 1 April 2001.

Statutory instruments – SI 2001/2541: partly made under s. 180A(2).

HMRC Manuals – CA23150: guidance on s. 180A.

181 Purchaser of land giving consideration for fixture

181(1) If–

(a) after any plant or machinery has become a fixture, a person (**"the purchaser"**) acquires an interest in the relevant land,

(b) that interest was in existence before the purchaser's acquisition of it, and

(c) the consideration which the purchaser gives for the interest is or includes a capital sum that, in whole or in part, falls to be treated for the purposes of this Part as expenditure on the provision of the fixture,

the purchaser is to be treated, on and after the time of the acquisition, as the owner of the fixture as a result of incurring that expenditure.

181(2) Subsection (1) does not apply, and is to be treated as never having applied, if, immediately after the time of the acquisition, a person has a prior right in relation to the fixture.

181(3) For the purposes of subsection (2), a person has a prior right in relation to the fixture if he–

(a) is treated as the owner of the fixture immediately before the time referred to in subsection (2) as a result of incurring expenditure on the provision of the fixture,

(b) is not so treated as a result of section 538 (contribution allowances for plant and machinery),

(c) is entitled to an allowance in respect of that expenditure, and

(d) makes or has made a claim in respect of that expenditure.

181(4) Subsection (1) is subject to sections 182 and 182A.

History – S. 181(2) substituted by FA 2001, s. 69 and Sch. 21, para. 2(1), (2), with effect as respects allowances and charges falling to be made for chargeable periods ending, for income tax purposes, on or after 6 April 2001, and, for corporation tax purposes, on or after 1 April 2001.
In s. 181(3) the words "subsection (2), a person" and "subsection (2)", substituted by FA 2001, s. 69 and Sch. 21, para. 2(1), (2), with effect as respects allowances and charges falling to be made for chargeable periods ending, for income tax purposes, on or after 6 April 2001, and, for corporation tax purposes, on or after 1 April 2001.
In s. 181(4), reference to s. 182A added by FA 2001, s. 66 and Sch. 18, para. 5, with effect in relation to expenditure incurred on or after 1 April 2001, with effect as respects allowances and charges falling to be made for chargeable periods ending, for income tax purposes, on or after 6 April 2001, and, for corporation tax purposes, on or after 1 April 2001.

Origin – S. 181(1): CAA 1990, s. 54(1) (part).
S. 181(2): CAA 1990, s. 56A(1) (part), (2) (part).
S. 181(3): CAA 1990, s. 56A(2) (part), (3) (part).
S. 181(4): CAA 1990, s. 54(2) (part), drafting.

Cross references – S. 172(3): the provisions of s. 181 are subject to the provisions of s. 188–192 (which treat a person as ceasing to be the owner of a fixture).
Electricity Act 1989, Sch. 11, para. 5(4), (5) (as amended by Sch. 2, para. 71): treatment of fixtures where a lease is granted in pursuance of certain transfer schemes on privatisation.
FA 1994, Sch. 24, para. 21(3)(c) (as amended by Sch. 2, para. 91(7)(d)), Coal Industry Act 1994, Sch. 4, para. 20(3)(c) (as amended by Sch. 2, para. 93(6)(d)) and Transport Act 2000, Sch. 26, para. 14(2)(d) (as amended by Sch. 2, para. 109(10)(c)): under a scheme of restructuring in connection with privatisation of the railways or coal industry, where a trade is treated as permanently discontinued and a new trade set up and where the relevant scheme contains provision for the disposal value of property to be deemed for the purposes of capital allowances in accordance with the scheme, s. 196 is disapplied and expenditure which falls to be treated as incurred by the transferee under the scheme on a fixture is deemed for the purposes of s. 181(1) to be incurred for consideration of an amount specified in accordance with the scheme.
Transport Act 2000, Sch. 26, para. 5(2) (as amended by Sch. 2, para. 109(5)): expenditure which falls to be treated as incurred by the transferee for the purposes of s. 181(1) to be a capital sum of an amount specified in the transfer scheme under the act where there is plant or machinery which would have been treated as disposed of by the transferor to the transferee.

Transitional – Sch. 3, para. 34: if the purchaser acquired the interest in the relevant land before 24 July 1996, the word "and" at the end of s. 181(1)(b) is omitted and the following inserted after para. (b):
"(bb) at the time of the purchaser's acquisition of the interest, either no person has previously become entitled to an allowance in respect of any capital expenditure incurred on the provision of the fixture or, if any person has become so entitled, that person has been or is required to bring the disposal value of the fixture into account under Chapter 5, and".

HMRC Manuals – CA26250: guidance on s. 181.

182 Purchaser of land discharging obligations of equipment lessee

182(1) If–

(a) after any plant or machinery has become a fixture, a person (**"the purchaser"**) acquires an interest in the relevant land,

(b) that interest was in existence before the purchaser's acquisition of it,

(c) before that acquisition, the plant or machinery was let under an equipment lease, and

(d) in connection with that acquisition, the purchaser pays a capital sum to discharge the obligations of the equipment lessee under the equipment lease,

the purchaser is to be treated, on and after the time of the acquisition, as the owner of the fixture as a result of incurring expenditure, consisting of that capital sum, on the provision of the fixture.

182(2) Subsection (1) does not apply, and is to be treated as never having applied, if, immediately after the time of the acquisition, a person has a prior right in relation to the fixture.

182(3) Section 181(3) (test for whether person has a prior right) applies for the purposes of subsection (2).

History – S. 182(2) and (3) substituted by FA 2001, s. 69 and Sch. 21, para. 2(3), with effect as respects allowances and charges falling to be made for chargeable periods ending, for income tax purposes, on or after 6 April 2001, and, for corporation tax purposes, on or after 1 April 2001.

Origin – S. 182(1): CAA 1990, s. 54(1) (part), (2).
S. 182(2): CAA 1990, s. 56A(1) (part), (2) (part).
S. 182(3): CAA 1990, s. 56A(2) (part), (3) (part), drafting.

Cross references – S. 172(3): the provisions of s. 182 are subject to the provisions of s. 188–192 (which treat a person as ceasing to be the owner of a fixture).
FA 1994, Sch. 24, para. 21(3)(c) (as amended by Sch. 2, para. 91(7)(d)), Coal Industry Act 1994, Sch. 4, para. 20(3)(c) (as amended by Sch. 2, para. 93(6)(d)) and Transport Act 2000, Sch. 26, para. 14(2)(d) (as amended by Sch. 2, para. 109(10)(c)): under a scheme of restructuring in connection with privatisation of the railways or coal industry, where a trade is treated as permanently discontinued and a new trade set up and where the relevant scheme contains provision for the disposal value of property to be deemed for the purposes of capital allowances in accordance with the scheme, s. 196 is disapplied and expenditure which falls to be treated as incurred by the transferee under the scheme on a fixture is deemed for the purposes of s. 182(1) to be incurred for consideration of an amount specified in accordance with the scheme.
Transport Act 2000, Sch. 26, para. 5(2) (as amended by Sch. 2, para. 109(5)): expenditure which falls to be treated as incurred by the transferee for the purposes of s. 182(1) to be a capital sum of an amount specified in the transfer scheme under the act where there is plant or machinery which would have been treated as disposed of by the transferor to the transferee.

Transitional – Sch. 3, para. 35: if the purchaser acquired the interest in the relevant land before 24 July 1996, the word "and" at the end of s. 182(1)(c) is omitted and the following inserted after para. (c):

"(cc) at the time of the purchaser's acquisition of the interest, either no person has previously become entitled to an allowance in respect of any capital expenditure incurred on the provision of the fixture or, if any person has become so entitled, that person has been or is required to bring the disposal value of the fixture into account under Chapter 5, and".

HMRC Manuals – CA26300: guidance and example on s. 182.

182A Purchaser of land discharging obligations of client under energy services agreement

182A(1) If–

(a) after any plant or machinery has become a fixture, a person (**"the purchaser"**) acquires an interest in the relevant land,

(b) that interest was in existence before the purchaser's acquisition of it,

(c) before that acquisition, the plant or machinery was provided under an energy services agreement, and

(d) in connection with that acquisition, the purchaser pays a capital sum to discharge the obligations of the client under the energy services agreement,

the purchaser is to be treated, on and after the time of the acquisition, as the owner of the fixture as a result of incurring expenditure, consisting of that capital sum, on the provision of the fixture.

182A(2) Subsection (1) does not apply, and is to be treated as never having applied, if, immediately after the time of the acquisition, a person has a prior right in relation to the fixture.

182A(3) Section 181(3) (test for whether person has a prior right) applies for the purposes of subsection (2).

History – S. 182A inserted by FA 2001, s. 66 and Sch. 18, para. 6, with effect in relation to expenditure incurred on or after 1 April 2001, with effect as respects allowances and charges falling to be made for chargeable periods ending, for income tax purposes, on or after 6 April 2001, and, for corporation tax purposes, on or after 1 April 2001.

HMRC Manuals – CA23150: guidance on s. 182A.

183 Incoming lessee where lessor entitled to allowances

183(1) If–

(a) after any plant or machinery has become a fixture, a person (**"the lessor"**) who has an interest in the relevant land grants a lease,

(b) the lessor is entitled to an allowance in respect of the fixture for the chargeable period in which the lease is granted or would be if he were within the charge to tax,

(c) the consideration which the lessee gives for the lease is or includes a capital sum that, in whole or in part, falls to be treated for the purposes of this Part as expenditure on the provision of the fixture,

(d) the lessor and the lessee are not connected persons, and

(e) the lessor and the lessee make an election under this section,

the lessee is to be treated, on and after the time when the lease is granted, as the owner of the fixture as a result of incurring that expenditure.

183(2) An election under this section must be made by notice to an officer of Revenue and Customs within 2 years after the date on which the lease takes effect.

History – In s. 183(2), the words "an officer of Revenue and Customs" substituted for "the Inland Revenue" by CRCA 2005, s. 50(6) and Sch. 4, para. 83(1), with effect from 18 April 2005 by virtue of SI 2005/1126, art. 2(2).

Origin – S. 183(1): CAA 1990, s. 55(1) (part), (2), (4).
S. 183(2): CAA 1990, s. 55(3).

Cross references – S. 172(3): the provisions of s. 183 are subject to the provisions of s. 188–192 (which treat a person as ceasing to be the owner of a fixture).
TMA 1970, s. 42(6), (7)(c) (as amended by Sch. 2, para. 1): claims made by partnerships.
Electricity Act 1989, Sch. 11, para. 5(4), (5) (as amended by Sch. 2, para. 71): treatment of fixtures where a lease is granted in pursuance of certain transfer schemes on privatisation.
F(No. 2)A 1992, Sch. 17, para. 6(4) (as amended by Sch. 2, para. 87(2), (4)): Northern Ireland Electricity privatisation – restriction of losses by reference to capital allowances.
Broadcasting Act 1996, Sch. 7, para. 15(2) (as amended by Sch. 2, para. 97(7)): treatment of leased fixtures where there is a transfer pursuant to a privatisation scheme involving the undertaking of the BBC.

Transitional – Sch. 3, para. 36: if the person who had the interest in the relevant land granted the lease before 24 July 1996, the following is inserted after s. 183(2):
"**183(3)** No election may be made under this section if it appears that the sole or main benefit that may be expected to accrue to the lessor from the grant of the lease and the making of an election is the obtaining of an allowance or deduction or a greater allowance or deduction or the avoidance or reduction of a charge under this Part.".

HMRC Manuals – CA26350: guidance and examples on s. 183.

184 Incoming lessee where lessor not entitled to allowances

184(1) If–

(a) after any plant or machinery has become a fixture, a person (**"the lessor"**) who has an interest in the relevant land grants a lease,

(b) the lessor is not within section 183(1)(b),

(c) before the lease is granted, the fixture has not been used for the purposes of a qualifying activity carried on by the lessor or any person connected with the lessor, and

(d) the consideration which the lessee gives for the lease is or includes a capital sum that, in whole or in part, falls to be treated for the purposes of this Part as expenditure on the provision of the fixture,

the lessee is to be treated, on and after the time when the lease is granted, as the owner of the fixture as a result of incurring that expenditure.

184(2) Subsection (1) does not apply, and is to be treated as never having applied, if, immediately after the time when the lease is granted, a person has a prior right in relation to the fixture.

184(3) Section 181(3) (test for whether person has a prior right) applies for the purposes of subsection (2).

History – S. 184(2) and (3) substituted by FA 2001, s. 69 and Sch. 21, para. 2(4), with effect as respects allowances and charges falling to be made for chargeable periods ending, for income tax purposes, on or after 6 April 2001, and, for corporation tax purposes, on or after 1 April 2001.

Origin – S. 184(1): CAA 1990, s. 56 (part).
S. 184(2): CAA 1990, s. 56A(1) (part), (2) (part).
S. 184(3): CAA 1990, s. 56A(2) (part), (3) (part), drafting.

Cross references – S. 172(3): the provisions of s. 184 are subject to the provisions of s. 188–192 (which treat a person as ceasing to be the owner of a fixture).
Broadcasting Act 1996, Sch. 7, para. 15(3) (as amended by Sch. 2, para. 97(8)): treatment of leased fixtures where there is a transfer pursuant to a privatisation scheme involving the undertaking of the BBC.

Transitional – Sch. 3, para. 37: if the person who had the interest in the relevant land granted the lease before 24 July 1996, the word "and" at the end of paragraph s. 184(1)(c) is omitted and the following inserted after para. (c):

"(cc) at the time of the grant of the lease, no person has previously become entitled to an allowance in respect of any capital expenditure incurred on the provision of the fixture, and".

HMRC Manuals – CA26350: guidance on s. 184.

RESTRICTIONS ON AMOUNT OF QUALIFYING EXPENDITURE

185 Fixture on which a plant and machinery allowance has been claimed

185(1) This section applies if–

(a) a person (**"the current owner"**) is treated as the owner of a fixture as a result of incurring capital expenditure (**"new expenditure"**) on its provision,

(b) the plant or machinery is treated as having been owned at a relevant earlier time by any person (**"the past owner"**) as a result of incurring other expenditure,

(c) the plant or machinery is within paragraph (b) otherwise than as a result of section 538 (contribution allowances for plant and machinery), and

(d) the past owner is or has been required to bring the disposal value of the plant or machinery into account (as a result of having made a claim in respect of that other expenditure).

185(2) If the new expenditure exceeds the maximum allowable amount, the excess–

(a) is to be left out of account in determining the current owner's qualifying expenditure, or

(b) if the new expenditure has already been taken into account for this purpose, is to be treated as expenditure that should never have been taken into account.

185(3) The maximum allowable amount is–

$$D + I$$

where–

D is the disposal value of the plant or machinery which the past owner has been or is required to bring into account, and

I is any of the new expenditure that is treated under section 25 (building alterations in connection with installation) as expenditure on the provision of the plant or machinery.

185(4) If more than one disposal event has occurred requiring the past owner to bring the disposal value of the plant or machinery into account, the maximum allowable amount is calculated by reference only to the most recent of those events.

185(5) For the purposes of this section, the current owner and the past owner may be the same person.

185(6) In subsection (1)(b) **"relevant earlier time"** means (subject to subsection (7)) any time before the earliest time when the current owner is treated as owning the plant or machinery as a result of incurring the new expenditure.

185(7) If, before the earliest time when the current owner is treated as owning the plant or machinery as a result of incurring the new expenditure–

(a) any person has ceased to own the plant or machinery as a result of a sale,

(b) the sale was not a sale of the plant or machinery as a fixture, and

(c) the buyer and seller were not connected persons at the time of the sale,

the relevant earlier time does not include any time before the seller ceased to own the plant or machinery.

Origin – S. 185(1): CAA 1990, s. 56B(1) (part), (2) (part).
S. 185(2): CAA 1990, s. 56B(1) (part).
S. 185(3): CAA 1990, s. 56B(4).
S. 185(4): CAA 1990, s. 56B(5).
S. 185(5): CAA 1990, s. 56B(3).
S. 185(6): CAA 1990, s. 56B(6) (part).
S. 185(7): CAA 1990, s. 56B(6) (part), (7).

Cross references – S. 57(3): "available qualifying expenditure" (in a pool for a chargeable period) does not include any expenditure excluded by s. 185(2).
Electricity Act 1989, Sch. 11, para. 5(4), (5) (as amended by Sch. 2, para. 71): treatment of fixtures where a lease is granted in pursuance of certain transfer schemes on privatisation.

Transitional – Sch. 3, para. 38: if the disposal event which required the disposal value to be brought into account as mentioned in s. 185(1)(d) occurred before 24 July 1996, s. 185 does not apply.

HMRC Manuals – CA26400: guidance on s. 185.

186 Fixture on which an industrial buildings allowance has been made

186(1) This section applies if–

(a) a person (**"the past owner"**) has at any time claimed an allowance to which he was entitled under Part 3 (industrial buildings allowances) in respect of expenditure which was or included expenditure on the provision of plant or machinery,

(b) the past owner has transferred the interest which was the relevant interest for the purposes of Part 3, and

(c) the current owner of the plant or machinery makes a claim in respect of expenditure (**"new expenditure"**) incurred–

(i) on the provision of the plant or machinery, and

(ii) at a time when it is a fixture in the building.

186(2) If the new expenditure exceeds the maximum allowable amount, the excess is to be left out of account in determining the current owner's qualifying expenditure.

186(3) If the total consideration for the transfer by the past owner exceeds R, the maximum allowable amount is–

$$\frac{F}{T} \times R$$

where–

F is the part of the consideration for the transfer by the past owner that is attributable to the fixture,

T is the total consideration for that transfer, and

R is the residue of qualifying expenditure which would have been attributable to the relevant interest immediately after that transfer, calculated on the assumption that the transfer was a sale of the relevant interest, had the time immediately after the transfer fallen immediately before the repeal of Part 3 by section 81 of FA 2008.

186(3A) Where subsection (3) does not apply, the maximum allowable amount is the part of the consideration for the transfer by the past owner that is attributable to the fixture.

186(4) For the purposes of this section the current owner of the plant or machinery is–

(a) the person to whom the past owner transferred the relevant interest, or

(b) any person who is subsequently treated as the owner of the plant or machinery.

186(5) In this section **"building"** and **"residue of qualifying expenditure"** have the same meaning as for the purposes of Part 3 immediately before its repeal by section 81 of FA 2008.

History – In s. 186(1)(a) and (b), the word "was" substituted for the word "is" by FA 2008, s. 84 and Sch. 27, para. 5(2), with effect in relation to a transfer by the past owner in chargeable periods beginning on or after 1 April 2011 for corporation tax purposes and 6 April 2011 for income tax purposes (FA 2008, Sch. 27, para. 30(2)).

In s. 186(3), at the beginning, the words "If the total consideration for the transfer by the past owner exceeds R." inserted by FA 2008, s. 84 and Sch. 27, para. 5(3)(a), with effect in relation to a transfer by the past owner in chargeable periods beginning on or after 1 April 2011 for corporation tax purposes and 6 April 2011 for income tax purposes (FA 2008, Sch. 27, para. 30(2)).

In s. 186(3), in the definition of "R", the words "which would have been" inserted after "expenditure" and the words ", had the time immediately after the transfer fallen immediately before the repeal of Part 3 by section 81 of FA 2008" inserted at the end by FA 2008, s. 84 and Sch. 27, para. 5(3)(b), with effect in relation to a transfer by the past owner in chargeable periods beginning on or after 1 April 2011 for corporation tax purposes and 6 April 2011 for income tax purposes (FA 2008, Sch. 27, para. 30(2)).

S. 186(3A) inserted by FA 2008, s. 84 and Sch. 27, para. 5(4), with effect in relation to a transfer by the past owner in chargeable periods beginning on or after 1 April 2011 for corporation tax purposes and 6 April 2011 for income tax purposes (FA 2008, Sch. 27, para. 30(2)).

In s. 186(5), the words "for the purposes of Part 3 immediately before its repeal by section 81 of FA 2008." substituted for the words "in Part 3." by FA 2008, s. 84 and Sch. 27, para. 5(5), with effect in relation to a transfer by the past owner in chargeable periods beginning on or after 1 April 2011 for corporation tax purposes and 6 April 2011 for income tax purposes (FA 2008, Sch. 27, para. 30(2)).

Origin – S. 186(1), (2): CAA 1990, s. 56C(1) (part).

S. 186(3): CAA 1990, s. 56C(2), (3).

S. 186(4): CAA 1990, s. 56C(1) (part).

S. 186(5): CAA 1990, s. 56C(4).

Cross references – S. 9(2): relaxation of prohibition on double allowances where industrial buildings allowance previously claimed and s. 186(2) applies to that expenditure.

S. 57(3): "available qualifying expenditure" (in a pool for a chargeable period) does not include any expenditure excluded by s. 186(2).

Transitional – Sch. 3, para. 39: if the time mentioned in s. 186(1)(c)(ii) is before 24 July 1996, s. 186 does not apply.

HMRC Manuals – CA26450: guidance on s. 186.

186A Fixtures on which a business premises renovation allowance has been made

186A(1) This section applies if–

(a) a person ("the past owner") has at any time claimed an allowance to which that person was entitled under Part 3A (business premises renovation allowances) in respect of qualifying expenditure under that Part incurred in respect of a qualifying building ("Part 3A expenditure"),

(b) there has been a balancing event within section 360N(1) as a result of which an asset representing the whole or part of the Part 3A expenditure ("the Part 3A asset") ceased to be owned by the past owner,

(c) the Part 3A asset was or included plant or machinery, and

(d) the current owner makes a claim under this Part in respect of expenditure ("new expenditure") incurred–

(i) on the provision of the plant or machinery, and

(ii) at a time when it is a fixture.

186A(2) If the new expenditure exceeds the maximum allowable amount, the excess is to be left out of account in determining the current owner's qualifying expenditure.

186A(3) If the proceeds from the balancing event mentioned in subsection (1)(b) exceed R, the maximum allowance amount is–

$$\frac{F}{T} \times R$$

where–

F is so much of the proceeds from the balancing event as are attributable to the fixture,

T is the total amount of the proceeds from the balancing event, and

R is the qualifying expenditure incurred by the past owner on the Part 3A asset less the net Part 3A allowances in respect of that asset.

186A(4) Where subsection (3) does not apply, the maximum allowable amount is so much of the proceeds from the balancing event as are attributable to the fixture.

186A(5) For the purposes of subsection (3) the **"net Part 3A allowances"** in respect of the Part 3A asset means–

(a) the total of any allowances made under Part 3A in respect of the past owner's qualifying expenditure, less

(b) the total of any balancing charges made under that Part in respect of that expenditure.

186A(6) For the purposes of this section, the current owner of the plant or machinery is–

(a) the person who acquired the Part 3A asset from the past owner, or

(b) any person who is subsequently treated as the owner of the plant or machinery.

History – S. 186A inserted by FA 2012, s. 43 and Sch. 10, para. 6, with effect in relation to balancing events which occur on or after 6 April 2012, for income tax purposes, and 1 April 2012, for corporation tax purposes, subject to provisions in FA 2012, Sch. 10, para. 13.

187 Fixture on which a research and development allowance has been made

187(1) This section applies if–

(a) a person has at any time claimed an allowance to which he is entitled under Part 6 (research and development allowances) in respect of qualifying expenditure under that Part (**"Part 6 expenditure"**),

(b) an asset representing the whole or part of the Part 6 expenditure (**"the Part 6 asset"**) has ceased to be owned by that person **"the past owner"**),

(c) the Part 6 asset was or included plant or machinery, and

(d) the current owner makes a claim under this Part in respect of expenditure (**"new expenditure"**) incurred–

(i) on the provision of the plant or machinery, and

(ii) at a time when it is a fixture.

187(2) If the new expenditure exceeds the maximum allowable amount, the excess is to be left out of account in determining the current owner's qualifying expenditure.

187(3) The maximum allowable amount is–

$$\frac{F}{T} \times A$$

where–

F is the part of the consideration for the disposal of the Part 6 asset by the past owner that is attributable to the fixture,

T is the total consideration for that disposal, and

A is an amount equal to whichever is the smaller of–

(a) the disposal value of the Part 6 asset when the past owner ceased to own it, and

(b) so much of the Part 6 expenditure as related to the provision of the Part 6 asset.

187(4) For the purposes of this section the current owner of the plant or machinery is–

(a) the person who acquired the Part 6 asset from the past owner, or

(b) any person who is subsequently treated as the owner of the plant or machinery.

Origin – S. 187(1), (2): CAA 1990, s. 56D(1) (part).
S. 187(3): CAA 1990, s. 56D(2), (3).
S. 187(4): CAA 1990, s. 56D(1) (part).

Cross references – S. 9(2): relaxation of prohibition on double allowances where research and development allowance previously claimed and s. 187(2) applies to that expenditure.
S. 57(3): "available qualifying expenditure" (in a pool for a chargeable period) does not include any expenditure excluded by s. 187(2).

Transitional – Sch. 3, para. 40: if the time mentioned in s. 187(1)(d)(ii) is before 24 July 1996, s. 187 does not apply.

HMRC Manuals – CA26450: guidance on s. 187.

187A Effect of changes in ownership of a fixture

187A(1) This section applies if–

(a) a person ("the current owner") is treated as the owner of a fixture as a result of incurring capital expenditure ("new expenditure") on its provision for the purposes of a qualifying activity carried on by the current owner,

(b) the plant or machinery is treated as having been owned at a relevant earlier time by a person as a result of incurring other capital expenditure ("historic expenditure") on its provision for the purposes of a qualifying activity carried on by that person,

(c) the plant or machinery is within paragraph (b) otherwise than as a result of section 538 (contribution allowances for plant and machinery), and

(d) a person mentioned in paragraph (b) was entitled to claim an allowance under this Part in respect of the historic expenditure.

187A(2) In this section–

"the past owner" means–

(a) the person mentioned in paragraph (d) of subsection (1), or

(b) if there is more than one amount of historic expenditure in respect of which a person was entitled to claim as mentioned in that paragraph, the person by whom expenditure was incurred most recently;

"relevant earlier time" has the meaning given by section 187B(4) and (5).

187A(3) In determining the current owner's qualifying expenditure, the new expenditure is to be treated as nil if–

(a) the pooling requirement is not satisfied,

(b) the fixed value requirement applies but is not satisfied, or

(c) the disposal value statement requirement applies but is not satisfied,

in relation to the past owner.

187A(4) The pooling requirement is that–

(a) the historic expenditure has been allocated to a pool in a chargeable period beginning on or before the day on which the past owner ceases to be treated as the owner of the fixture, or

(b) a first-year allowance has been claimed in respect of that expenditure (or any part of it).

187A(5) The fixed value requirement applies if the past owner is or has been required (as a result of having made a claim in respect of the historic expenditure) to bring the disposal value of the plant or machinery into account in accordance with item 1, 5 or 9 of the Table in section 196.

187A(6) The fixed value requirement is that either–

(a) a relevant apportionment of the apportionable sum has been made, or

(b) the current owner has obtained the statements mentioned in subsection (8), or copies of them, (directly or indirectly) from the persons who made them and the case is one where the purchaser from the past owner or, as the case may be, lessee was not entitled to claim an allowance under this Part in respect of capital expenditure incurred on the fixture.

187A(7) For the purposes of subsection (6)(a) a relevant apportionment of the apportionable sum is made if–

(a) the tribunal determines the part of the apportionable sum that constitutes the disposal value, on an application made by one of the affected parties before the end of the relevant 2 year period, or

(b) an election is made, in respect of the apportionable sum, by the affected parties jointly–

(i) before the end of the relevant 2 year period, or

(ii) if an application is made as mentioned in paragraph (a) and not determined or withdrawn by the end of that period, before that application is determined or withdrawn.

187A(8) The statements referred to in subsection (6)(b) are–

CAA 2001

(a) a written statement made by the purchaser from the past owner or, as the case may be, lessee, that the requirement of subsection (6)(a) has not been met and is no longer capable of being met, and

(b) a written statement made by the past owner of the amount of the disposal value that the past owner has in fact brought into account.

187A(9) In subsections (6) to (8)–

(a) in a case falling within item 1 or 9 of the Table in section 196–

"affected parties" means the past owner and the purchaser from the past owner;

"apportionable sum" means the sale price;

"election" means an election under section 198;

"relevant 2 year period" means the period of 2 years beginning with the date when the purchaser from the past owner acquires the qualifying interest;

(b) in a case falling within item 5 of that Table–

"affected parties" means the past owner and the lessee;

"apportionable sum" means the capital sum given by the lessee for the lease;

"election" means an election under section 199;

"relevant 2 year period" means the period of 2 years beginning with the date when the lessee is granted the lease.

187A(10) The disposal value statement requirement applies if the past owner is or has been required (as a result of having made a claim in respect of the historic expenditure) to bring the disposal value of the plant or machinery into account in accordance with item 2 or 3 of the Table in section 196 or in accordance with item 7 of the Table in section 61.

187A(11) The disposal value statement requirement is–

(a) that the past owner has, no later than 2 years after the date when the past owner ceased to own the plant or machinery, made a written statement of the amount of the disposal value that the past owner is or has been required to bring into account, and

(b) the current owner has obtained that statement or a copy of it (directly or indirectly) from the past owner.

History – S. 187A inserted by FA 2012, s. 43 and Sch. 10, para. 2 with effect in relation to new expenditure incurred on or after 6 April 2012, for income tax purposes, and 1 April 2012, for corporation tax purposes, subject to the provisions in FA 2012, Sch. 10, para. 13.

187B Section 187A: supplementary provision

187B(1) It is for the current owner to show–

(a) whether the fixed value requirement applies and, if so, is satisfied, and

(b) whether the disposal value statement requirement applies and, if so, is satisfied,

and, for this purpose, to provide an officer of Revenue and Customs, on request, with a copy of any tribunal decision, election or statement by reason of which a requirement mentioned in paragraph (a) or (b) is satisfied.

187B(2) Where–

(a) the fixed value requirement applies and is met by reason of section 187A(6)(b) being satisfied, or

(b) the disposal value requirement applies,

subsections (2) and (4) of section 200 apply in relation to the making of a statement within section 187A(8)(b) or (11)(a) and an amount specified in such a statement, as they apply in relation to an election and an amount specified in an election.

187B(3) For the purposes of section 187A, the current owner and the past owner may be the same person.

187B(4) In that section **"relevant earlier time"** means (subject to subsection (5)) any time which falls before the earliest time when the current owner is treated as owning the plant or machinery as a result of incurring the new expenditure.

187B(5) If, before the earliest time when the current owner is treated as owning the plant or machinery as a result of incurring the new expenditure–

(a) any person has ceased to own the plant or machinery as a result of a sale,

(b) the sale was not a sale of the plant or machinery as a fixture, and

(c) the buyer and seller were not connected persons at the time of the sale,

the relevant earlier time does not include any time before the seller ceased to own the plant or machinery.

187B(6) Nothing in section 187A(3) affects the disposal value (if any) which falls to be brought into account by the past owner (as a result of having made a claim in respect of the historic expenditure).

187B(7) Expressions used in this section have the same meaning as in section 187A.

History – S. 187B inserted by FA 2012, s. 43 and Sch. 10, para. 2 with effect in relation to new expenditure incurred on or after 6 April 2012, for income tax purposes, and 1 April 2012, for corporation tax purposes, subject to the provisions in FA 2012, Sch. 10, para. 13.

CESSATION OF OWNERSHIP OF FIXTURES

188 Cessation of ownership when person ceases to have qualifying interest

188(1) This section applies if a person is treated as the owner of a fixture under–

(a) section 176 (person with interest in land having fixture for purposes of qualifying activity),

(b) section 181 (purchaser of land giving consideration for fixture),

(c) section 182 (purchaser of land discharging obligations of equipment lessee),

(ca) section 182A (purchaser of land discharging obligations of client under energy services agreement),

(d) section 183 (incoming lessee where lessor entitled to allowances), or

(e) section 184 (incoming lessee where lessor not entitled to allowances).

188(2) If the person ceases at any time to have the qualifying interest, he is to be treated as ceasing to be the owner of the fixture at that time.

188(3) In this Chapter **"the qualifying interest"** means–

(a) if section 176, 181, 182 or 182A applies, the interest in the relevant land referred to in that section, and

(b) if section 183 or 184 applies, the lease referred to in that section.

188(4) This section is subject to section 189.

History – S. 188(1)(ca) inserted, and in s. 188(3)(a) reference to s. 182A added, by FA 2001, s. 66 and Sch. 18, para. 7(2), (3), with effect in relation to expenditure incurred on or after 1 April 2001, with effect as respects allowances and charges falling to be made for chargeable periods ending, for income tax purposes, on or after 6 April 2001, and, for corporation tax purposes, on or after 1 April 2001.

Origin – S. 188(1), (2): CAA 1990, s. 57(2) (part).
S. 188(3): CAA 1990, s. 57(3) (part).
S. 188(4): CAA 1990, s. 57(2) (part).

Cross references – Transport Act 2000, Sch. 26, para. 21(7), 27(7) and 34(8) (as amended by Sch. 2, para. 109(16), (23) and (30) respectively): amount which is to be brought into account as the disposal value of a fixture where a fixture is treated by s. 188 as ceasing to belong to a person at any time as a consequence of a disposal by virtue of a relevant transfer under the act.

HMRC Manuals – CA26500: guidance on s. 188.

189 Identifying the qualifying interest in special cases

189(1) If–

(a) a person's qualifying interest is an agreement to acquire an interest in land, and

(b) that interest is subsequently transferred or granted to that person,

the interest transferred or granted is to be treated as the qualifying interest.

189(2) If a person's qualifying interest ceases to exist as a result of its being merged in another interest acquired by that person, that other interest is to be treated as the qualifying interest.

189(3) If–

(a) the qualifying interest is a lease, and

(b) on its termination, a new lease of the relevant land (with or without other land) is granted to the lessee,

the new lease is to be treated as the qualifying interest.

189(4) If–

(a) the qualifying interest is a licence, and

(b) on its termination, a new licence to occupy the relevant land (with or without other land) is granted to the licensee,

the new licence is to be treated as the qualifying interest.

189(5) If–

(a) the qualifying interest is a lease, and

(b) with the consent of the lessor, the lessee remains in possession of the relevant land after the termination of the lease without a new lease being granted to him,

the qualifying interest is to be treated as continuing so long as the lessee remains in possession of the relevant land.

Origin – S. 189(1): CAA 1990, s. 57(3) (part).
S. 189(2)–(5): CAA 1990, s. 57(4).

HMRC Manuals – CA26500: guidance and examples on s. 189.

190 Cessation of ownership of lessor where section 183 applies

190(1) This section applies if a lessee is treated under section 183 (incoming lessee where lessor entitled to allowances) as the owner of a fixture.

190(2) The lessor is to be treated as ceasing to be the owner of the fixture when the lessee begins to be treated as the owner.

Origin – S. 190: CAA 1990, s. 57(5).
HMRC Manuals – CA26550: guidance on s. 190.

191 Cessation of ownership on severance of fixture

191 If–

(a) a person is treated as the owner of the fixture as a result of any provision of this Chapter,

(b) the fixture is permanently severed from the relevant land (so that it ceases to be a fixture), and

(c) once it is severed, it is not in fact owned by that person,

that person is to be treated as ceasing to be the owner of the fixture when it is severed.

Origin – S. 191: CAA 1990, s. 57(7) (part).
HMRC Manuals – CA26550: guidance and example on s. 191.

192 Cessation of ownership of equipment lessor

192(1) This section applies if an equipment lessor is treated under section 177 as the owner of a fixture.

192(2) If–

(a) the equipment lessor at any time assigns his rights under the equipment lease, or

(b) the financial obligations of the equipment lessee under an equipment lease are at any time discharged (on the payment of a capital sum or otherwise),

the equipment lessor is to be treated as ceasing to be the owner of the fixture at that time (or, as the case may be, at the earliest of those times).

192(3) The reference in subsection (2)(b) to the equipment lessee is, in a case where the financial obligations of the equipment lessee have become vested in another person (by assignment, operation of law or otherwise), a reference to the person in whom the obligations are vested when the capital sum is paid.

Origin – S. 192(1), (2): CAA 1990, s. 58(1) (part).
S. 192(3): CAA 1990, s. 58(5).
HMRC Manuals – CA26550: guidance on s. 192.

192A Cessation of ownership of energy services provider

192A(1) This section applies if an energy services provider is treated under section 180A as the owner of a fixture.

192A(2) If–

(a) the energy services provider at any time assigns his rights under the energy services agreement, or

(b) the financial obligations of the client in respect of the fixture under an energy services agreement are at any time discharged (on the payment of a capital sum or otherwise),

the energy services provider is to be treated as ceasing to be the owner of the fixture at that time (or, as the case may be, the earliest of those times).

192A(3) The reference in subsection (2)(b) to the client is, in a case where the financial obligations of the client have become vested in another person (by assignment, operation of law or otherwise), a reference to the person in whom the obligations are vested when the capital sum is paid.

History – S. 192A inserted by FA 2001, s. 66 and Sch. 18, para. 8, with effect in relation to expenditure incurred on or after 1 April 2001, with effect as respects allowances and charges falling to be made for chargeable periods ending, for income tax purposes, on or after 6 April 2001, and, for corporation tax purposes, on or after 1 April 2001.
HMRC Manuals – CA23150: guidance on s. 192A.

ACQUISITION OF OWNERSHIP OF FIXTURE WHEN ANOTHER CEASES TO OWN IT

193 *Acquisition* of ownership by lessor or licensor on termination of lease or licence

193 If, on the termination of a lease or licence, the outgoing lessee or licensee is treated under section 188 as ceasing to be the owner of a fixture, the lessor or licensor is to be treated, on and after the termination of the lease or licence, as the owner of the fixture.

Origin – S. 193: CAA 1990, s. 57(6) (part).

Cross references – S. 172(3): the provisions of s. 193 are subject to the provisions of s. 188–192 (which treat a person as ceasing to be the owner of a fixture).

HMRC Manuals – CA26600: guidance and examples on s. 193–195.

194 Acquisition of ownership by assignee of equipment lessor

194(1) If section 192(2)(a) applies (cessation of ownership of equipment lessor as a result of assignment), the assignee is to be treated, on and after the assignment–

(a) as having incurred expenditure, consisting of the consideration given by him for the assignment, on the provision of the fixture, and

(b) as being the owner of the fixture.

194(2) For the purposes of section 192 (and subsection (1) and section 195) the assignee is to be treated as being an equipment lessor who owns the fixture under section 177.

Origin – S. 194(1): CAA 1990, s. 58(2) (part).
S. 194(2): CAA 1990, s. 58(3) (part).

Cross references – S. 172(3): the provisions of s. 194 are subject to the provisions of s. 188–192 (which treat a person as ceasing to be the owner of a fixture).

HMRC Manuals – CA26600: guidance and examples on s. 193–195.

195 Acquisition of ownership by equipment lessee

195(1) If section 192(2)(b) applies (discharge of obligations of equipment lessee) because the equipment lessee has paid a capital sum, the equipment lessee is to be treated–

(a) as having incurred expenditure, consisting of the capital sum, on the provision of the fixture, and

(b) as being, on and after the time of payment, the owner of the fixture.

195(2) Section 192(3) (assignee of equipment lessee) applies in relation to subsection (1).

Origin – S. 195(1): CAA 1990, s. 58(4) (part).
S. 195(2): CAA 1990, s. 58(5) (part).

Cross references – S. 172(3): the provisions of s. 195 are subject to the provisions of s. 188–192 (which treat a person as ceasing to be the owner of a fixture).

HMRC Manuals – CA26600: guidance and examples on s. 193–195.

195A Acquisition of ownership by assignee of energy services provider

195A(1) If section 192A(2)(a) applies (cessation of ownership of energy services provider as a result of assignment), the assignee is to be treated, on and after the assignment–

(a) as having incurred expenditure, consisting of the consideration given by him for the assignment, on the provision of the fixture, and

(b) as being the owner of the fixture.

195A(2) For the purposes of section 192A (and subsection (1) and section 195B) the assignee is to be treated as being an energy services provider who owns the fixture under section 180A.

History – S. 195A inserted by FA 2001, s. 66 and Sch. 18, para. 9, with effect in relation to expenditure incurred on or after 1 April 2001, with effect as respects allowances and charges falling to be made for chargeable periods ending, for income tax purposes, on or after 6 April 2001, and, for corporation tax purposes, on or after 1 April 2001.

HMRC Manuals – CA23150: guidance on s. 195A.

195B Acquisition of ownership by client

195B(1) If section 192A(2)(b) applies (discharge of obligations of client) because the client has paid a capital sum, the client is to be treated–

(a) as having incurred expenditure, consisting of the capital sum, on the provision of the fixture, and

(b) as being, on and after the time of payment, the owner of the fixture.

195B(2) Section 192A(3) (assignee of client) applies in relation to subsection (1).

History – S. 195B inserted by FA 2001, s. 66 and Sch. 18, para. 9, with effect in relation to expenditure incurred on or after 1 April 2001, with effect as respects allowances and charges falling to be made for chargeable periods ending, for income tax purposes, on or after 6 April 2001, and, for corporation tax purposes, on or after 1 April 2001.

DISPOSAL VALUES

196 Disposal values in relation to fixtures: general

196(1) The disposal value to be brought into account in relation to a fixture depends on the nature of the disposal event, as shown in the Table–

TABLE
DISPOSAL VALUES: FIXTURES

	1. Disposal event	*2. Disposal value*
1.	Cessation of ownership of the fixture under section 188 because of a sale of the qualifying interest except where item 2 applies.	The part of the sale price that– (a) falls to be treated for the purposes of this Part as expenditure incurred by the purchaser on the provision of the fixture, or (b) would fall to be so treated if the purchaser were entitled to an allowance.
2.	Cessation of ownership of the fixture under section 188 because of a sale of the qualifying interest where– (a) the sale is at less than market value, and (b) the condition in subsection (2) is met by the purchaser.	The part of the price that would be treated for the purposes of this Part as expenditure by the purchaser on the provision of the fixture if– (a) the qualifying interest were sold at market value, (b) that sale took place immediately before the event which causes the former owner to be treated as ceasing to be owner of the fixture, and (c) that event were disregarded in determining that market value.
3.	Cessation of ownership of the fixture under section 188 where– (a) neither item 1 nor 2 applies, but (b) the qualifying interest continues in existence after that time or would so continue but for its become merged in another interest.	The disposal value given for item 2.
4.	Cessation of ownership of the fixture under section 188 because of the expiry of the qualifying interest.	If the person receives a capital sum, by way of compensation or otherwise, by reference to the fixture, the amount of the capital sum. In any other case, nil.
5.	Cessation of ownership of the fixture under section 190 because the lessee has become the owner under section 183.	The part of the capital sum given by the lessee for the lease referred to in section 183 that falls to be treated for the purposes of this Part as the lessee's expenditure on the provision of the fixture.
6.	Cessation of ownership of the fixture under section 191 (severance).	The market value of the fixture at the time of the severance.
7.	Cessation of ownership of the fixture because section 192(2)(a) (assignment of rights) applies.	The consideration given by the assignee for the assignment.
8.	Cessation of ownership of the fixture because section 192(2)(b) (discharge of equipment lessee's obligations) applies on the payment of a capital sum.	The capital sum paid to discharge the financial obligations of the equipment lessee.
8A.	Cessation of ownership of the fixture because section 192A(2)(a) (assignment of rights) applies	The consideration given by the assignee for the assignment.
8B.	Cessation of ownership of the fixture because section 192A(2)(b) (discharge of client's obligations) applies on the payment of a capital sum.	The capital sum paid to discharge the financial obligations of the client.
9.	Permanent discontinuance of the qualifying activity followed by the sale of the qualifying interest.	The part of the sale price that– (a) falls to be treated as expenditure incurred by the purchaser on the provision of the fixture, or (b) would fall to be so treated if the purchaser were entitled to an allowance.

	1. Disposal event	2. Disposal value
10.	Permanent discontinuance of the qualifying activity followed by the demolition or destruction of the fixture.	The net amount received for the remains of the fixture, together with– (a) any insurance money received in respect of the demolition or destruction, or (b) any other compensation of any description so received, so far as it consists of capital sums.
11.	Permanent discontinuance of the qualifying activity followed by the permanent loss of the fixture otherwise than as a result of its demolition or destruction.	Any insurance money received in respect of the loss and, so far as it consists of capital sums, any other compensation of any description so received.
12.	The fixture begins to be used wholly or partly for purposes other than those of the qualifying activity.	The part of the price that would fall to be treated for the purposes of this Part as expenditure incurred by the purchaser on the provision of the fixture if the qualifying interest were sold at market value.

196(2) The condition referred to in item 2 of the Table is met by the purchaser if–

(a) the purchaser's expenditure on the provision of the fixture cannot be qualifying expenditure under this Part or Part 6 (research and development allowances), or

(b) the purchaser is a dual resident investing company which is connected with the former owner.

196(3) Items 1 and 5 of the Table are subject to sections 198 and 199 (election to fix apportionment on sale of qualifying interest or grant of lease).

196(4) Section 192(3) (assignee of equipment lessee) applies in relation to item 8 of the Table.

196(4A) Section 192A(3) (assignee of client) applies in relation to item 8B of the Table.

196(5) Nothing in sections 188 to 192A or this section prevents a disposal value having to be brought into account under Chapter 5 because of a disposal event not dealt with in these sections.

196(6) This section is subject to section 197.

History – In the Table in s. 196(1), items 8A and 8B inserted by FA 2001, s. 66 and Sch. 18, para. 10(2), s. 196(4A) inserted by FA 2001, s. 66 and Sch. 18, para. 10(3), and in s. 196(5) reference to s. 192A substituted by FA 2001, s. 66 and Sch. 18, para. 10(4), with effect in relation to expenditure incurred on or after 1 April 2001, with effect as respects allowances and charges falling to be made for chargeable periods ending, for income tax purposes, on or after 6 April 2001, and, for corporation tax purposes on or after 1 April 2001.

Origin – S. 196(1)
Table, item 1: CAA 1990, s. 59(1) (part), (2).
Table, item 2: CAA 1990, s. 59(1) (part), (6).
Table, item 3: CAA 1990, s. 59(1) (part), (4), (5) (part).
Table, item 4: CAA 1990, s. 59(7).
Table, item 5: CAA 1990, s. 59(1) (part), (3).
Table, item 6: CAA 1990, s. 26(1)(f) (part).
Table, item 7: CAA 1990, s. 58(2) (part).
Table, item 8: CAA 1990, s. 58(4) (part).
Table, items 9 to 11: CAA 1990, s. 59(8).
Table, item 12: CAA 1990, s. 59(9).
S. 196(2): CAA 1990, s. 59(6) (part).
S. 196(3): CAA 1990, s. 59(1) (part).
S. 196(4): CAA 1990, s. 58(5) (part).
S. 196(5): CAA 1990, s. 57(1).
S. 196(6): CAA 1990, s. 59(1) (part).

Cross references – S. 60(1)(b): meaning of "disposal receipt" includes a value that a person is required to bring into account for purposes of any of the provisions listed in s. 66 (see note below).
S. 66: list of provisions about disposal values includes s. 196.
TCGA 1992, s. 27: hire-purchase etc. treated for chargeable gains purposes as a disposal.
FA 1994, Sch. 24, para. 21(3)(a) (as amended by Sch. 2, para. 91(7)(c)), Coal Industry Act 1994, Sch. 4, para. 20(3)(a) (as amended by Sch. 2, para. 93(6)(c)) and Transport Act 2000, Sch. 26, para. 14(2)(a) (as amended by Sch. 2, para. 109(10)(b)): under a scheme of restructuring in connection with privatisation of the railways or coal industry, where a trade is treated as permanently discontinued and a new trade set up and where the relevant scheme contains provision for the disposal value of property to be deemed for the purposes of capital allowances in accordance with the scheme, s. 196 is disapplied and the scheme provision shall have effect for determining disposal value of property instead (the transferee being deemed to have incurred expenditure of that amount on the provision of that property).
RA 2005, Sch. 10. para. 3 and 23: modified application of s. 196 in the case of a transfer to a national authority.
RA 2005, Sch. 10. para. 14: disapplication of s.196 in the case of certain transfers to a national authority.
SI 2015/1540, reg. 8: determination of disposal value of fixtures in respect of transfers in accordance with transfer schemes under section 333DA of the Greater London Authority Act 1999 and under section 53A of the Housing and Regeneration Act 2008.

Transitional – Sch. 3, para. 41: if a person is treated as ceasing to own a fixture before 24 July 1996, the following subsections are substituted for s. 196(6) in relation to that fixture:

"**196(6)** If–
(a) a person (**"the former owner"**) is treated by virtue of section 188, 190 or 191 as ceasing to own a fixture,
(b) another person incurs expenditure on the provision of the fixture, and
(c) the former owner brings a disposal value into account under Chapter 5,

there is to be disregarded for the purposes of this Part so much (if any) of that expenditure as exceeds that disposal value.

196(7) In relation to expenditure incurred before 27th July 1989, subsection 6 has effect with the substitution for the words following "the fixture" in paragraph (b) of the words "there is to be disregarded for the purposes of this Part so much (if any) of that expenditure as exceeds the disposal value which the former owner is required to bring into account under Chapter 5"".

HMRC Manuals – CA26700: guidance on disposal values.

197 Disposal values in avoidance cases

197(1) This section applies if–

(a) a person (**"the taxpayer"**) is treated under this Chapter as the owner of any plant or machinery as a result of incurring any expenditure,

(b) any disposal event occurs in relation to the plant or machinery,

(c) the disposal value to be brought into account by the taxpayer would (but for this section) be less than the notional written-down value of the plant or machinery, and

(d) the disposal event is part of, or occurs as a result of, a scheme or arrangement the main purpose or one of the main purposes of which is the obtaining by the taxpayer of a tax advantage under this Part.

197(2) The disposal value that the taxpayer must bring into account is the notional written-down value of the plant or machinery.

197(3) The notional written-down value is–

$$QE - A$$

where–

QE is the taxpayer's expenditure on the plant or machinery that is qualifying expenditure,

A is the total of all allowances which could have been made to the taxpayer in respect of that expenditure if–

(a) that expenditure had been the only expenditure that had ever been taken into account in determining his available qualifying expenditure, and

(b) all allowances had been made in full.

Origin – S. 197(1), (2): CAA 1990, s. 59A(1).
S. 197(3): CAA 1990, s. 59A(2), (3).

Cross references – S. 60(1)(b): meaning of "disposal receipt" includes a value that a person is required to bring into account for purposes of any of the provisions listed in s. 66 (see note below).
S. 66: list of provisions about disposal values includes s. 197.

Rewrite: Technical Points – Explanatory Notes, Annex 2, Note 24: s. 197(3) substitutes most of the text in the former wording of CAA 1990, s. 59A(2), (3) with a formula instead. Because it is based upon the same assumptions, the effect is the same; i.e. that the disposal value is equal to the qualifying expenditure less allowances which could have been made, looking at the expenditure in isolation.

HMRC Manuals – CA26750: guidance and example on s. 197.

ELECTION TO FIX APPORTIONMENT

198 Election to apportion sale price on sale of qualifying interest

198(1) This section applies if the disposal value of a fixture is required to be brought into account in accordance with item 1 or 9 of the Table in section 196 (sale of qualifying interest at not less than market value, etc.).

198(2) The seller and the purchaser may jointly, by an election, fix the amount that is to be treated–

(a) for the purposes of item 1 or (as the case may be) 9 of the Table, and

(b) for the other purposes of this Part,

as the part of the sale price that is expenditure incurred by the purchaser on the provision of the fixture.

198(3) The amount fixed by the election must not exceed–

(a) the amount of the capital expenditure which was treated as incurred by the seller on the provision of the fixture or of the plant or machinery which became the fixture, or

(b) the actual sale price.

198(4) If an election fixes the amount to be treated as the part of the sale price–

(a) the remaining amount (if any) of the sale price is to be treated for the purposes of this Act as expenditure attributable to the acquisition of the property which is not the fixture but is acquired for that amount, and

(b) if there is no remaining amount, the expenditure so attributable is to be treated for the purposes of this Act as nil.

198(5) This section is subject to–

(a) sections 186, 186A and 187 (fixtures on which industrial buildings allowance, business premises renovation allowance or research and development allowance has been made),

(b) section 197 (disposal values in avoidance cases), and

(c) sections 200 and 201 (further provisions about elections).

History – In s. 198(1) the words "or 9" inserted by FA 2012, s. 43 and Sch. 10, para. 3(a) with effect in relation to new expenditure incurred on or after 6 April 2012, for income tax purposes, and 1 April 2012, for corporation tax purposes, subject to the provisions in FA 2012, Sch. 10, para. 13.
In s. 198(2)(a) the words "or (as the case may be) 9" inserted by FA 2012, s. 43 and Sch. 10, para. 3(b) with effect in relation to new expenditure incurred on or after 6 April 2012, for income tax purposes, and 1 April 2012, for corporation tax purposes, subject to the provisions in FA 2012, Sch. 10, para. 13.
S. 198(5)(a) substituted by FA 2012, s. 43 and Sch. 10, para. 9, with effect in relation to balancing events which occur on or after 6 April 2012, for income tax purposes, and 1 April 2012, for corporation tax purposes, subject to provisions in FA 2012, Sch. 10, para. 13.

Origin – S. 198(1): CAA 1990, s. 59B(1) (part).
S. 198(2): CAA 1990, s. 59B(2) (part).
S. 198(3): CAA 1990, s. 59B(3) (part).
S. 198(4): CAA 1990, s. 59B(4) (part).
S. 198(5): CAA 1990, s. 59B(2) (part), drafting.

HMRC Manuals – CA26800: guidance on s. 198 elections.
CA26850: elections accepted by reference to groups of assets provided this does not distort the tax computation, but no such joint election accepted for fixtures in different properties.

199 Election to apportion capital sum given by lessee on grant of lease

199(1) This section applies if the disposal value of a fixture is required to be brought into account in accordance with item 5 of the Table in section 196 (on acquisition of ownership by incoming lessee under section 183).

199(2) The persons who are the lessor and the lessee for the purposes of section 183 may jointly, by an election, fix the amount that is to be treated–

(a) for the purposes of item 5 of the Table, and

(b) for the other purposes of this Part,

as the part of the capital sum that is expenditure incurred by the lessee on the provision of the fixture.

199(3) The amount fixed by the election must not exceed–

(a) the amount of the capital expenditure which was treated as incurred by the lessor on the provision of the fixture or of the plant or machinery which became the fixture, or

(b) the actual capital sum.

199(4) If an election fixes the amount to be treated as the part of the capital sum–

(a) the remaining amount (if any) of the capital sum is to be treated for the purposes of this Act as expenditure attributable to the acquisition of the property which is not the fixture but is acquired for that amount, and

(b) if there is no remaining amount, the expenditure so attributable is to be treated for the purposes of this Act as nil.

199(5) This section is subject to–

(a) sections 186, 186A and 187 (fixtures on which industrial buildings allowance, business premises renovation allowance or research and development allowance has been made),

(b) section 197 (disposal values in avoidance cases), and

(c) sections 200 and 201 (further provisions about elections).

History – S. 199(5)(a) substituted by FA 2012, s. 43 and Sch. 10, para. 10, with effect in relation to balancing events which occur on or after 6 April 2012, for income tax purposes, and 1 April 2012, for corporation tax purposes, subject to provisions in FA 2012, Sch. 10, para. 13.

Origin – S. 199(1): CAA 1990, s. 59B(1) (part).
S. 199(2): CAA 1990, s. 59B(2) (part).
S. 199(3): CAA 1990, s. 59B(3) (part).
S. 199(4): CAA 1990, s. 59B(4) (part).
S. 199(5): CAA 1990, s. 59B(2) (part), drafting.

HMRC Manuals – CA26800: guidance on s. 199 elections.
CA26850: elections accepted by reference to groups of assets provided this does not distort the tax computation, but no such joint election accepted for fixtures in different properties.

200 Elections under sections 198 and 199: supplementary

200(1) In this section and section 201, references to an election are to an election under section 198 or 199.

200(2) An apportionment made by an election has effect in place of any apportionment that would otherwise be made under sections 562, 563 and 564(1) (apportionment and procedure for determining apportionment).

200(3) An election is irrevocable.

200(4) If, as a result of circumstances arising after the making of an election, the maximum amount which could be fixed by the election is reduced to an amount which is less than the amount specified in the election, the election is to be treated, for the purposes of this Act, as having specified the amount to which the maximum is reduced.

Origin – S. 200(1): Drafting.
S. 200(2): CAA 1990, s. 59B(5).
S. 200(3): CAA 1990, s. 59C(6).
S. 200(4): CAA 1990, s. 59C(3) (part).

HMRC Manuals – CA26800 and CA26850: guidance on s. 198 and 199 elections.

201 Elections under sections 198 and 199: procedure

201(1) An election must be made by notice to an officer of Revenue and Customs no later than 2 years after the date when–

(a) the purchaser acquires the qualifying interest, in the case of an election under section 198, or

(b) the lessee is granted the lease, in the case of an election under section 199.

But this is subject to subsection (1A).

201(1A) Where–

(a) the requirement of subsection (6) of section 187A (effect of changes in ownership of fixture: fixed value requirement) applies, or may in future apply by reason of a person being required to bring the disposal value of plant and machinery into account in accordance with item 1, 5 or 9 of the Table in section 196,

(b) an application is made to the tribunal for the purposes of section 187A(7)(a), and

(c) that application is not determined before the end of the period mentioned in subsection (1) of this section,

subsection (1) does not apply and an election within section 187A(7)(b) may be made by notice to an officer of Revenue and Customs at any time before the tribunal determines the application or the application is withdrawn.

201(2) The amount fixed by an election must be quantified at the time when the election is made.

201(3) The notice must state–

(a) the amount fixed by the election,

(b) the name of each of the persons making the election,

(c) information sufficient to identify the plant or machinery,

(d) information sufficient to identify the relevant land,

(e) particulars of–

  (i) the interest acquired by the purchaser, in the case of an election under section 198, or

  (ii) the lease granted to the lessee, in the case of an election under section 199, and

(f) in relation to each of the persons making the election–

  (i) that person's Unique Taxpayer Reference, or

  (ii) that the person does not have a Unique Taxpayer Reference.

201(4) If a person–

(a) has joined in making an election, and

(b) subsequently makes a tax return for a period which is the first period for which he is making a tax return in which the election has an effect for tax purposes in his case,

a copy of the notice containing the election must accompany the return.

201(5) The following provisions do not apply to the election–

(a) section 42 of, and Schedule 1A to TMA 1970 (claims and elections for income tax purposes);

(b) paragraphs 54 to 60 of Schedule 18 to FA 1998 (claims and elections for corporation tax purposes).

201(6) References in this section to a tax return, in the case of an election for the purposes of a trade, profession or business carried on by persons in partnership, are to be read, in relation to those persons, as references to a return under section 12AA of TMA 1970 (partnership returns).

History – *In s. 201(1) the words* "But this is subject to subsection (1A)." inserted by FA 2012, s. 43 and Sch. 10, para. 4(2) with effect in relation to new expenditure incurred on or after 6 April 2012, for income tax purposes, and 1 April 2012, for corporation tax purposes, subject to the provisions in FA 2012, Sch. 10, para. 13.
In s. 201(1), the words "an officer of Revenue and Customs" substituted for "the Inland Revenue" by CRCA 2005, s. 50(6) and Sch. 4, para. 83(1), with effect from 18 April 2005 by virtue of SI 2005/1126, art. 2(2).
S. 201(1A) inserted by FA 2012, s. 43 and Sch. 10, para. 4(3) with effect in relation to new expenditure incurred on or after 6 April 2012, for income tax purposes, and 1 April 2012, for corporation tax purposes, subject to the provisions in FA 2012, Sch. 10, para. 13.

S. 201(3)(f) substituted by FA 2012, s. 43 and Sch. 10, para. 4(4) with effect in relation to new expenditure incurred on or after 6 April 2012, for income tax purposes, and 1 April 2012, for corporation tax purposes, subject to the provisions in FA 2012, Sch. 10, para. 13.

Origin – S. 201(1): CAA 1990, s. 59C(1), (4).
S. 201(2): CAA 1990, s. 59C(3) (part).
S. 201(3): CAA 1990, s. 59C(2).
S. 201(4): CAA 1990, s. 51(2) ("return"), s. 59C(5), (9) ("relevant period").
S. 201(5): CAA 1990, s. 59C(7).
S. 201(6): CAA 1990, s. 59C(10).

HMRC Manuals – CA26850: guidance on s. 201.

FURTHER PROVISIONS

202 Interpretation

202(1) Any reference in this Chapter to a person being entitled to an allowance in respect of expenditure on the provision of a fixture includes the person having a pool to which expenditure on the provision of the fixture has been allocated.

But this is subject to subsection (2).

202(2) If–

(a) expenditure on the provision of the fixture has been allocated to a pool, and

(b) the person is required under section 61(1) to bring the disposal value of the fixture into account in the pool,

the person is not entitled to an allowance in respect of the expenditure allocated to that pool for any chargeable period after that in which the disposal event occurs.

202(3) For the purposes of this Chapter, a person makes a claim in respect of expenditure if he–

(a) makes a claim for an allowance in respect of that expenditure,

(b) makes a tax return in which that expenditure is taken into account in determining his available qualifying expenditure for the purposes of this Part, or

(c) gives notice of an amendment of a tax return which provides for that expenditure to be so taken into account.

Origin – S. 202(1), (2): CAA 1990, s. 51(5) (part).
S. 202(3): CAA 1990, s. 51(2) ("return"), (5A), s. 147(2D).

203 Amendment of returns etc.

203(1) If a person who has made a tax return (**"the taxpayer"**) becomes aware that, after making it, anything in it has become incorrect for any of the reasons given in subsection (2), the taxpayer must give notice to an officer of Revenue and Customs specifying how the return needs to be amended.

203(2) The reasons are that–

(a) an approval given for the purposes of section 180 (affordable warmth programme) has been withdrawn;

(b) section 181(2), 182(2), 182A(2) or 184(2) (another person has a prior right) applies in the taxpayer's case;

(c) section 185 (restriction on qualifying expenditure where another person has claimed an allowance) applies in the taxpayer's case;

(d) an election is made under section 198 or 199 (election to fix apportionment);

(e) section 200(4) (reduction in amount which can be fixed by an election) applies in the taxpayer's case.

203(3) The notice must be given within 3 months beginning with the day on which the taxpayer first became aware that anything contained in the tax return had become incorrect for any of the reasons given in subsection (2).

203(4) All such assessments and adjustments of assessments are to be made as are necessary to give effect to this Chapter.

History – In s. 203(1), the words "an officer of Revenue and Customs" substituted for "the Inland Revenue" by CRCA 2005, s. 50(6) and Sch. 4, para. 83(1), with effect from 18 April 2005 by virtue of SI 2005/1126, art. 2(2).
In s. 203(2)(b), reference to s. 182A(2) inserted by FA 2001, s. 66 and Sch. 18, para. 11, with effect in relation to expenditure incurred on or after 1 April 2001, with effect as respects allowances and charges falling to be made for chargeable periods ending, for income tax purposes, on or after 6 April 2001, and, for corporation tax purposes, on or after 1 April 2001.

Origin – S. 203(1): CAA 1990, s. 51(2) ("return"), (6A) (part), 53(1H) (part).
S. 203(2): CAA 1990, s. 51(6A) (part), 53(1H) (part).
S. 203(3): CAA 1990, s. 51(2) ("return"), (6A) (part), 53(1H) (part).
S. 203(4): CAA 1990, s. 51(6), 53(1G).

Cross references – TMA 1970, s. 98 (as amended by Sch. 2, para. 4): penalties in respect of s. 203.

204 Appeals etc.

204(1) Subsections (2) and (3) apply if–

(a) any question arises as to whether any plant or machinery has become, in law, part of a building or other land, and

(b) that question is material to the tax liability (for whatever period) of two or more persons.

204(2) The question is to be determined, for the purposes of the tax of all the persons concerned, by the tribunal.

204(3) An application for the tribunal to determine the question is to be subject to the relevant provisions of Part 5 of the Taxes Management Act 1970 (see, in particular, section 48(2)(b) of that Act), and each of the persons concerned is entitled to be a party to the proceedings on the application.

204(4) Subsections (5) and (6) apply if any question relating to an election under section 198 or 199 (apportionments) arises for determination by the tribunal for the purposes of any proceedings before it.

204(5) The tribunal must determine the question separately from any other questions in those proceedings.

204(6) Each of the persons who has joined in the election is entitled to be a party to the proceedings of the tribunal concerned with the determination of the question; and the tribunal's determination has effect as if made in an appeal to which each of those persons was a party.

History – In s. 204(2), the word "tribunal" substituted for the words "Special Commissioners" by SI 2009/56, art. 3(1) and Sch. 1, para. 298(2), operative from 1 April 2009, subject to transitional and saving provisions in SI 2009/56, Sch. 3.
S. 204(3) substituted by SI 2009/56, art. 3(1) and Sch. 1, para. 298(3), operative from 1 April 2009, subject to transitional and saving provisions in SI 2009/56, Sch. 3.
In s. 204(4), the words "the tribunal" substituted for the words "any body of Commissioners" and the word "it" substituted for the word "them" by SI 2009/56, art. 3(1) and Sch. 1, para. 298(4), operative from 1 April 2009, subject to transitional and saving provisions in SI 2009/56, Sch. 3.
In s. 204(5), the word "tribunal" substituted for the word "Commissioners" by SI 2009/56, art. 3(1) and Sch. 1, para. 298(5), operative from 1 April 2009, subject to transitional and saving provisions in SI 2009/56, Sch. 3.
S. 204(6) substituted by SI 2009/56, art. 3(1) and Sch. 1, para. 298(6), operative from 1 April 2009, subject to transitional and saving provisions in SI 2009/56, Sch. 3.

Origin – S. 204(1)–(3): CAA 1990, s. 51(7).
S. 204(4)–(6): CAA 1990, s. 59C(8).

Chapter 15 – Asset Provided or Used Only Partly for Qualifying Activity

Cross references – TCGA 1992, s. 41: restriction of losses by reference to capital allowances, etc.

205 Reduction of annual investment allowance and first-year allowances

205(1) If it appears that a person carrying on a qualifying activity has incurred expenditure on the provision of plant or machinery–

(a) partly for the purposes of the qualifying activity, and

(b) partly for other purposes,

any annual investment allowance or first-year allowance to which he is entitled in respect of the expenditure must be reduced to an amount which is just and reasonable having regard to the relevant circumstances.

205(2) The relevant circumstances include, in particular, the extent to which it appears that the plant or machinery is likely to be used for purposes other than those of the qualifying activity in question.

205(3) In calculating for the purposes of section 58 the balance left after deducting a first-year allowance, a reduction under subsection (1) is to be disregarded.

History – In the heading to s. 205, the words "annual investment allowance and" inserted by FA 2008, s. 74 and Sch. 24, para. 6(3), with effect in relation to expenditure incurred on or after 1 April 2008 for corporation tax purposes and 6 April 2008 for income tax purposes.
In s. 205(1), the words "annual investment allowance or" inserted by FA 2008, s. 74 and Sch. 24, para. 6(2), with effect in relation to expenditure incurred on or after 1 April 2008 for corporation tax purposes and 6 April 2008 for income tax purposes.

Origin – S. 205(1),(2): CAA 1990, s. 79(1).
S. 205(3): see Rewrite note below.

Rewrite: Technical Points – Explanatory Notes, Annex 2, Note 38: the point made in s. 205(3) and s. 210(2) used to be addressed explicitly in FA 1971, Sch. 8, para. 5(4)(d) and 6(5)(d) before the paragraphs were amended by FA 1985, Sch. 14, para. 6 and 7.

206 Single asset pool etc.

206(1) *Qualifying expenditure* to which this subsection applies, if allocated to a pool, must be allocated to a single asset pool.

206(2) Subsection (1) applies to qualifying expenditure incurred by a person carrying on a qualifying activity–

(a) partly for the purposes of the qualifying activity, and

(b) partly for other purposes.

206(3) If a person is required to bring a disposal value into account in a pool for a chargeable period because the plant or machinery begins to be used partly for purposes other than those of the qualifying activity, an amount equal to that disposal value is allocated (as expenditure on the plant or machinery) to a single asset pool for that chargeable period.

206(4) In the case of a single asset pool under subsection (1), there is no final chargeable period or disposal event merely because the plant or machinery begins to be used partly for purposes other than those of the qualifying activity.

Origin – S. 206(1), (2): CAA 1990, s. 79(2) (part).
S. 206(3): CAA 1990, s. 79(3).
S. 206(4): CAA 1990, s. 79(4).

Cross references – FA 2000, Sch. 22, para. 70: entry: plant and machinery: assets to be used partly for tonnage tax trade.
FA 2000, Sch. 22, para. 73: during: plant and machinery: new expenditure partly for tonnage tax purposes.
FA 2000, Sch. 22, para. 76: during: plant and machinery: change of use of non-tonnage tax asset.

207 Reduction of allowances and charges on expenditure in single asset pool

207(1) This section applies if a person's expenditure is in a single asset pool under section 206(1) or (3).

207(2) The amount of–

(a) any writing-down allowance or balancing allowance to which the person is entitled, or

(b) any balancing charge to which the person is liable,

must be reduced to an amount which is just and reasonable having regard to the relevant circumstances.

207(3) The relevant circumstances include, in particular, the extent to which it appears that the plant or machinery was used in the chargeable period in question for purposes other than those of the person's qualifying activity.

207(4) In calculating under section 59 the amount of unrelieved qualifying expenditure carried forward, a reduction of a writing-down allowance under subsection (2) is to be disregarded.

207(5) If a person entitled to a writing-down allowance for a chargeable period–

(a) does not claim the allowance, or

(b) claims less than the full amount of the allowance,

the unrelieved qualifying expenditure carried forward from the period is to be treated as not reduced or (as the case may be) only proportionately reduced.

Origin – S. 207(1): CAA 1990, s. 79(2) (part).
S. 207(2) and (3): CAA 1990, s. 79(5).
S. 207(4): see Rewrite note below.
S. 207(5): CAA 1990, s. 79(6).

Cross references – FA 2000, Sch. 22, para. 70: entry: plant and machinery: assets to be used partly for tonnage tax trade.
FA 2000, Sch. 22, para. 73: during: plant and machinery: new expenditure partly for tonnage tax purposes.
FA 2000, Sch. 22, para. 76: during: plant and machinery: change of use of non-tonnage tax asset.

Rewrite: Technical Points – Explanatory Notes, Annex 2, Note 38: the point dealt with in s. 207(4) and 212(3) arises because CAA 1990, s. 79(6) and 80(6) provide that, for the purpose of determining allowances and charges for subsequent chargeable periods, the allowance is to be treated as not claimed or as proportionately reduced; this is the same as saying that the unrelieved qualifying expenditure carried forward need not be reduced.

208 Effect of significant reduction in use for purposes of qualifying activity

208(1) This section applies if–

(a) expenditure is allocated to a single asset pool under this Chapter,

(b) there is such a change of circumstances as would make it appropriate for any reduction falling to be made under section 207–

(i) for the chargeable period in which the change takes place (**"the relevant chargeable period"**), or

(ii) for any subsequent chargeable period,

to represent a larger proportion of the amount reduced than would have been appropriate apart from the change,

(c) no disposal value in respect of the plant or machinery would, apart from this section, fall to be brought into account for the relevant chargeable period, and

(d) the market value of the plant or machinery at the end of the relevant chargeable period exceeds the available qualifying expenditure in that pool for that period by more than £1 million.

208(2) If this section applies–

(a) a disposal value is required to be brought into account in the single asset pool for the relevant chargeable period, and

(b) section 206 applies as if, at the beginning of the following chargeable period, expenditure had been incurred on the provision of the plant or machinery of an amount equal to the disposal value brought into account as a result of paragraph (a).

Origin – S. 208(1): CAA 1990, s. 79A(1).
S. 208(2): CAA 1990, s. 79A(2), (3).

Cross references – FA 1993, s. 93A(6)(b): application of s. 208(1) in calculating profits or losses where company uses a currency other than sterling.

Transitional – Sch. 3, para. 42: s. 208 does not apply if the change of circumstances, referred to in s. 208(1)(b), occurs before 21 March 2000.

HMRC Manuals – CA27300: guidance and example on scope s. 208.

208A Cars: disposal value in avoidance cases

208A(1) This section applies if–

(a) a disposal value is required to be brought into account under section 61,

(b) the disposal event is that the person ceases to own a section 206 car because of a sale or the performance of a contract, and

(c) allowances under this Part in respect of the person's expenditure under that transaction are restricted under section 217 or 218 (anti-avoidance).

208A(2) A car is a section 206 car if expenditure on the provision of the car is required to be allocated to a single asset pool under that section.

208A(3) The disposal value to be brought into account is–

(a) the market value of the car at the time of the disposal event, or

(b) if less, the capital expenditure incurred, or treated as incurred, on the provision of the car by the person disposing of it.

208A(4) The person acquiring the car is to be treated as having incurred capital expenditure on its provision of an amount equal to the disposal value required to be brought into account under subsection (3).

208A(5) In this section **"car"** has the meaning given in section 268A.

History – S. 208A inserted by FA 2009, s. 30 and Sch. 11, para. 10, with effect in relation to expenditure incurred on or after 1 April 2009 (for corporation tax purposes) and 6 April 2009 (for income tax purposes), subject to transitional provisions in FA 2009, Sch. 11, para. 27(2), 28(2) and 30–32.

Chapter 16 – Partial Depreciation Subsidies

Cross references – TCGA 1992, s. 41: restriction of losses by reference to capital allowances, etc.

209 Meaning of "partial depreciation subsidy"

209 In this Chapter **"partial depreciation subsidy"** means a sum which–

(a) is payable directly or indirectly to a person who has incurred qualifying expenditure for the purposes of a qualifying activity,

(b) is in respect of, or takes account of, part of the depreciation of the plant or machinery resulting from its use for the purposes of that activity, and

(c) does not fall to be taken into account as income of that person or in calculating the profits of any qualifying activity carried on by him.

Origin – S. 209: CAA 1990, s. 80(1) (part), (2) (part), (3) (part) and see Rewrite note below.

Rewrite: Changes in Law – Explanatory Notes, Annex 2, Note 13: The phrase "wear and tear", as used in CAA 1990, s. 80, is substituted by the word "depreciation" in conjunction with the word "use"; the substitution is not intended to result in a change of law.

HMRC Manuals – CA27500: guidance on partial depreciation subsidies.

210 Reduction of annual investment allowance and first-year allowances

210(1) If–

(a) a person has incurred qualifying expenditure for the purposes of a qualifying activity carried on by him, and

(b) it appears that a partial depreciation subsidy is, or will be, payable to him in the period during which the plant or machinery will be used for the purposes of that qualifying activity,

the amount of any annual investment allowance or first-year allowance in respect of that expenditure must be reduced to an amount which is just and reasonable having regard to the relevant circumstances.

210(2) In calculating for the purposes of section 58 the balance left after deducting a first-year allowance, a reduction under subsection (1) is to be disregarded.

History – In the heading to s. 210, the words "annual investment allowance and" inserted by FA 2008, s. 74 and Sch. 24, para. 7(3), with effect in relation to expenditure incurred on or after 1 April 2008 for corporation tax purposes and 6 April 2008 for income tax purposes.
In s. 210(1), the words "annual investment allowance or" inserted by FA 2008, s. 74 and Sch. 24, para. 7(2), with effect in relation to expenditure incurred on or after 1 April 2008 for corporation tax purposes and 6 April 2008 for income tax purposes.

Origin – S. 210(1): CAA 1990, s. 80(2) (part).
S. 210(2): see Rewrite note below.

Rewrite: Technical Points – Explanatory Notes, Annex 2, Note 38: the point made in s. 205(3) and s. 210(2) used to be addressed explicitly in FA 1971, Sch. 8, para. 5(4)(d) and 6(5)(d) before the paragraphs were amended by FA 1985, Sch. 14, para. 5 and 7.

HMRC Manuals – CA27500: guidance on partial depreciation subsidies.

211 Single asset pool etc.

211(1) Qualifying expenditure to which this subsection applies, if allocated to a pool, must be allocated to a single asset pool.

211(2) Subsection (1) applies to qualifying expenditure if a partial depreciation subsidy relating to the plant or machinery has been paid to the person who incurred the expenditure.

211(3) Subsection (4) applies if–

(a) qualifying expenditure has been allocated to a pool, and

(b) a partial depreciation subsidy relating to the plant or machinery is paid to that person.

211(4) For the chargeable period in which the partial depreciation subsidy is paid–

(a) the person is required to bring a disposal value into account in the pool referred to in subsection (3), and

(b) an amount equal to the disposal value is allocated (as expenditure on the plant or machinery) to a single asset pool.

211(5) If qualifying expenditure in respect of any plant or machinery is in a single asset pool under this section, there is no further allocation of that qualifying expenditure because a further partial depreciation subsidy is paid in respect of that plant or machinery.

Origin – S. 211(1): CAA 1990, s. 80(5) (part).
S. 211(2): CAA 1990, s. 80(3) (part).
S. 211(3): CAA 1990, s. 80(4).
S. 211(4): CAA 1990, s. 80(5).
S. 211(5): CAA 1990, s. 80(7).

HMRC Manuals – CA27500: guidance on partial depreciation subsidies.

212 Reduction of allowances and charges on expenditure in single asset pool

212(1) This section applies if expenditure is in a single asset pool under section 211(1) or (4).

212(2) The amount of–

(a) any writing-down allowance or balancing allowance to which the person is entitled, or

(b) any balancing charge to which the person is liable,

must be reduced to an amount which is just and reasonable having regard to the relevant circumstances.

212(3) In calculating under section 59 the amount of unrelieved qualifying expenditure carried forward, a reduction of a writing-down allowance under subsection (2) is to be disregarded.

212(4) If a person entitled to a writing-down allowance for a chargeable period–

(a) does not claim the allowance, or

(b) claims less than the full amount of the allowance,

the unrelieved qualifying expenditure carried forward from the period is to be treated as not reduced or (as the case may be) only proportionately reduced.

Origin – S. 212(1): CAA 1990, s. 80(5) (part).
S. 212(2): CAA 1990, s. 80(5)(b).
S. 212(3): see Rewrite note below.
S. 212(4): CAA 1990, s. 80(6).

Rewrite: Technical Points – Explanatory Notes, Annex 2, Note 38: the point dealt with in s. 207(4) and 212(3) arises because CAA 1990, s. 79(6) and 80(6) provide that, for the purpose of determining allowances and charges for subsequent chargeable periods, the allowance is to be treated as not claimed or as proportionately reduced; this is the same as saying that the unrelieved qualifying expenditure carried forward need not be reduced.

HMRC Manuals – CA27500: guidance on partial depreciation subsidies.

Chapter 16ZA – Asset Provided or Used only Partly for NI Rate Activity

Prospective amendments – Ch. 16ZA inserted by CTNIA 2015, s. 2 and Sch. 1, para. 8, with effect from 26 March 2015 (Royal Assent) in respect of any power to make regulations and with effect in relation to accounting periods beginning on or after the first day of the appointed financial year for other provisions (see CTNIA 2015, s. 5). See also transitional provisions at Sch. 1, para. 19–21.

Chapter 16A – Restrictions on Allowance Buying

History – Heading to Ch. 16A substituted by FA 2013, s. 71 and Sch. 26, para. 4, with effect in relation to a qualifying change if the relevant day (within the meaning of CAA 2001, Pt. 2, Ch. 16A) is on or after 20 March 2013, subject to savings in FA 2013, Sch. 26, para. 13(2). The heading formerly read "Avoidance Involving Allowance Buying".
Ch. 16A inserted by FA 2010, s. 26 and Sch. 4, para. 2, with effect where the relevant day is on or after 21 July 2009, subject to earlier modified commencement as provided by FA 2010, Sch. 4, para. 6.

INTRODUCTION

212A Scope of Chapter

212A This Chapter provides for restrictions on the ways in which effect may be given to an allowance in certain circumstances where there has been a qualifying change in relation to a company ("C").

History – S. 212A inserted by FA 2010, s. 26 and Sch. 4, para. 2, with effect where the relevant day is on or after 21 July 2009, subject to earlier modified commencement as provided by FA 2010, Sch. 4, para. 6.

212B Where Chapter applies

212B(1) This Chapter applies where–

(a) C carries on a qualifying activity ("the relevant activity") (whether or not in partnership with another person or other persons),

(b) there is a qualifying change in relation to C on any day ("the relevant day"),

(c) C, or (where the relevant activity is carried on in partnership) the partnership ("P"), has a relevant excess of allowances in relation to the relevant activity, and

(d) the qualifying change meets one of the limiting conditions.

212B(2) Sections 212C to 212I specify when there is a qualifying change in relation to C on the relevant day.

212B(3) Sections 212J to 212L specify when C or P has a relevant excess of allowances in relation to the relevant activity.

212B(4) Sections 212LA and 212M set out the limiting conditions and specify when those conditions are met.

212B(5) Sections 212N to 212S make provision about what happens when this Chapter applies.

History – In s. 212B(1)(a), the words "a qualifying activity ("the relevant activity")" substituted for the words "a trade ("the relevant trade")" by FA 2013, s. 71 and Sch. 26, para. 5(2)(a), with effect in relation to a qualifying change if the relevant day (within the meaning of CAA 2001, Pt. 2, Ch. 16A) is on or after 20 March 2013, subject to savings in FA 2013, Sch. 26, para. 13(2).
In s. 212B(1)(c), the word "activity" substituted for the word "trade" (in both places) by FA 2013, s. 71 and Sch. 26, para. 5(2)(b), with effect in relation to a qualifying change if the relevant day (within the meaning of CAA 2001, Pt. 2, Ch. 16A) is on or after 20 March 2013, subject to savings in FA 2013, Sch. 26, para. 13(2).
S. 212B(1)(d) substituted by FA 2013, s. 71 and Sch. 26, para. 2(2), with effect in relation to a qualifying change if the relevant day (within the meaning of CAA 2001, Pt. 2, Ch. 16A) is on or after 20 March 2013, subject to savings in FA 2013, Sch. 26, para. 13(2). Former s. 212B(1)(d) read as follows:
"(d) the qualifying change has an unallowable purpose."
In s. 212B(3), the word "activity" substituted for the word "trade" by FA 2013, s. 71 and Sch. 26, para. 5(3), with effect in relation to a qualifying change if the relevant day (within the meaning of CAA 2001, Pt. 2, Ch. 16A) is on or after 20 March 2013, subject to savings in FA 2013, Sch. 26, para. 13(2).
S. 212B(4) substituted by FA 2013, s. 71 and Sch. 26, para. 2(3), with effect in relation to a qualifying change if the relevant day (within the meaning of CAA 2001, Pt. 2, Ch. 16A) is on or after 20 March 2013, subject to savings in FA 2013, Sch. 26, para. 13(2). Former s. 212B(4) read as follows:
"**212B(4)** Section 212M specifies when the qualifying change has an unallowable purpose.".
S. 212B inserted by FA 2010, s. 26 and Sch. 4, para. 2, with effect where the relevant day is on or after 21 July 2009, subject to earlier modified commencement as provided by FA 2010, Sch. 4, para. 6.

QUALIFYING CHANGE

212C When there is qualifying change in relation to C

212C(1) There is a qualifying change in relation to C on the relevant day if one or more of conditions A to D is met.

212C(2) Condition A is that–

(a) the principal company or companies of C at the beginning of the relevant day is not, or are not, the same as at the end of that day, or

(b) there is no principal company of C at the beginning of the relevant day but there is one, or are more than one, at the end of the relevant day.

212C(3) Condition B is that–

(a) any principal company of C is a consortium principal company ("CPC"), and

(b) CPC's ownership proportion at the end of the relevant day is more than at the beginning of the relevant day.

212C(4) Condition C is that the relevant activity is a trade (within the meaning of this Part) and on the relevant day–

(a) C ceases to carry on the whole or part of the relevant activity, and

(b) it begins to be carried on in partnership by two or more companies,

in circumstances in which Chapter 1 of Part 22 of CTA 2010 (transfers of trade without change of ownership) applies in relation to the transfer of the relevant activity.

212C(5) Condition D is that–

(a) the relevant activity is, at the beginning of the relevant day, carried on by C in partnership, and

(b) C's relevant percentage share in the relevant activity at the end of the relevant day is less than at the beginning of the relevant day (or is nil).

History – In s. 212C(4), the words "the relevant activity is a trade (within the meaning of this Part) and" inserted and the word "activity" substituted for the word "trade" (in both places) by FA 2013, s. 71 and Sch. 26, para. 6(2), with effect in relation to a qualifying change if the relevant day (within the meaning of CAA 2001, Pt. 2, Ch. 16A) is on or after 20 March 2013, subject to savings in FA 2013, Sch. 26, para. 13(2).
In s. 212C(5), the word "activity" substituted for the word "trade" by FA 2013, s. 71 and Sch. 26, para. 6(3) with effect in relation to a qualifying change if the relevant day (within the meaning of CAA 2001, Pt. 2, Ch. 16A) is on or after 20 March 2013, subject to savings in FA 2013, Sch. 26, para. 13(2).
S. 212C inserted by FA 2010, s. 26 and Sch. 4, para. 2, with effect where the relevant day is on or after 21 July 2009, subject to earlier modified commencement as provided by FA 2010, Sch. 4, para. 6.

212D Guide to sections explaining section 212C

212D(1) Section 212E explains–

(a) what are principal companies of C, and

(b) which are consortium principal companies of C,

for the purposes of section 212C(2) and (3).

212D(2) Section 212F explains–

(a) when a company is owned by a consortium, and

(b) who are the members of the consortium,

for the purposes of section 212E.

212D(3) Section 212G explains the meaning of **"qualifying 75% subsidiary"** for the purposes of sections 212E and 212F.

212D(4) Section 212H explains the meaning of **"ownership proportion"** in section 212C(3).

212D(5) Section 212I explains the meaning of **"relevant percentage share"** in section 212C(5).

History – S. 212D inserted by FA 2010, s. 26 and Sch. 4, para. 2, with effect where the relevant day is on or after 21 July 2009, subject to earlier modified commencement as provided by FA 2010, Sch. 4, para. 6.

212E Principal companies

212E(1) A company ("U") is a principal company of C if–

(a) C is a qualifying 75% subsidiary of U, and

(b) U is not a qualifying 75% subsidiary of another company.

212E(2) A company ("V") is a principal company of C if–

(a) C is a qualifying 75% subsidiary of U,

(b) U is a qualifying 75% subsidiary of V, and

(c) V is not a qualifying 75% subsidiary of another company.

212E(3) If V is a qualifying 75% subsidiary of another company ("W"), W is a principal company of C unless W is a qualifying 75% subsidiary of another company, and so on.

212E(4) A company ("X") is a principal company of C if–

(a) C is owned by a consortium of which X is a member, or

(b) C is a qualifying 75% subsidiary of a company owned by a consortium of which X is a member,

and X is not a qualifying 75% subsidiary of another company.

212E(5) A company ("Y") is a principal company of C if–

(a) C is owned by a consortium of which X is a member, or

(b) C is a qualifying 75% subsidiary of a company owned by a consortium of which X is a member,

and X is a qualifying 75% subsidiary of Y but Y is not a qualifying 75% subsidiary of another company.

212E(6) If Y is a qualifying 75% subsidiary of another company ("Z"), Z is a principal company of C unless Z is a qualifying 75% subsidiary of another company, and so on.

212E(7) A company that is a principal company of C by virtue of any of subsections (4) to (6) is a consortium principal company of C.

History – S. 212E inserted by FA 2010, s. 26 and Sch. 4, para. 2, with effect where the relevant day is on or after 21 July 2009, subject to earlier modified commencement as provided by FA 2010, Sch. 4, para. 6.

212F When company is owned by consortium and consortium members

212F(1) This section defines what a company being owned by, or a member of, a consortium means for the purposes of section 212E.

212F(2) A company is owned by a consortium if–

(a) it is not a qualifying 75% subsidiary of another company,

(b) at least 75% of its ordinary share capital is beneficially owned between them by other companies, and

(c) none of those other companies owns less than 5% of that capital.

212F(3) Those other companies are the members of the consortium.

History – S. 212F inserted by FA 2010, s. 26 and Sch. 4, para. 2, with effect where the relevant day is on or after 21 July 2009, subject to earlier modified commencement as provided by FA 2010, Sch. 4, para. 6.

212G Qualifying 75% subsidiaries

212G(1) For the purposes of sections 212E and 212F a company ("the subsidiary company") is a qualifying 75% subsidiary of another company ("the parent company") if condition 1 or 2 is met and condition 3 is met.

212G(2) Condition 1 is that–

(a) the subsidiary company has ordinary share capital, and

(b) the subsidiary company is a 75% subsidiary of the parent company (see section 1154(3) of CTA 2010).

212G(3) Condition 2 is that–

(a) the subsidiary company does not have ordinary share capital, and

(b) the parent company has control of the subsidiary company.

212G(4) Condition 3 is that the parent company–

(a) is beneficially entitled to at least 75% of any profits available for distribution to equity holders of the subsidiary company, and

(b) would be beneficially entitled to at least 75% of any assets of the subsidiary company available for distribution to its equity holders on a winding-up.

212G(5) Chapter 6 of Part 5 of CTA 2010 (equity holders and profits or assets available for distribution) applies for the purposes of subsection (4) as that Chapter applies for the purposes of section 151(4)(a) and (b) of that Act (meaning of "75% subsidiary").

212G(6) But in a case where the subsidiary company does not have ordinary share capital, Chapter 6 of Part 5 of that Act applies for those purposes as if the members of that company were equity holders of that company for the purposes of that Chapter.

History – S. 212G inserted by FA 2010, s. 26 and Sch. 4, para. 2, with effect where the relevant day is on or after 21 July 2009, subject to earlier modified commencement as provided by FA 2010, Sch. 4, para. 6.

212H Ownership proportion

212H(1) For the purposes of section 212C(3) CPC's **"ownership proportion"** is the lowest of–

(a) the percentage of the ordinary share capital of C that is beneficially owned by CPC,

(b) the percentage to which CPC is beneficially entitled of any profits available for distribution to equity holders of C, and

(c) the percentage to which CPC would be beneficially entitled of any assets of C available for distribution to its equity holders on a winding-up.

212H(2) Chapter 6 of Part 5 of CTA 2010 applies for the purposes of subsection (1) as that Chapter applies for the purposes of section 143(3)(b) and (c) (condition 1: surrendering company owned by consortium) and section 144(3)(b) and (c) (condition 1: claimant company owned by consortium) of that Act.

212H(3) But in a case where the subsidiary company does not have ordinary share capital, Chapter 6 of Part 5 of that Act applies for those purposes as if the members of that company were equity holders of that company for the purposes of that Chapter.

History – S. 212H inserted by FA 2010, s. 26 and Sch. 4, para. 2, with effect where the relevant day is on or after 21 July 2009, subject to earlier modified commencement as provided by FA 2010, Sch. 4, para. 6.

212I Relevant percentage share

212I(1) For the purposes of section 212C(5) C's **"relevant percentage share"** is C's percentage share in the profits or losses of the activity.

212I(2) For this purpose C's percentage share in the profits or losses of an activity at any time is determined on a just and reasonable basis.

212I(3) In making that determination regard must be had, in particular, to any matter that would be taken into account in determining under section 1262 of CTA 2009 (but without regard to sections 1263 and 1264 of that Act) the company's share at that time in the profits or losses of the activity.

History – In s. 212I(1), the word "activity" substituted for the word "trade" by FA 2013, s. 71 and Sch. 26 para. 7(2), with effect in relation to a qualifying change if the relevant day (within the meaning of CAA 2001, Pt. 2, Ch. 16A) is on or after 20 March 2013, subject to savings in FA 2013, Sch. 26, para. 13(2).

In s. 212(2), the words "an activity" substituted for the words "a trade" by FA 2013, s. 71 and Sch. 26, para. 7(3) with effect in relation to a qualifying change if the relevant day (within the meaning of CAA 2001, Pt. 2, Ch. 16A) is on or after 20 March 2013, subject to savings in FA 2013, Sch. 26, para. 13(2).

In s. 212I(3), the word "activity" substituted for the word "trade" by FA 2013, s. 71 and Sch. 26, para. 7(2), with effect in relation to a qualifying change if the relevant day (within the meaning of CAA 2001, Pt. 2, Ch. 16A) is on or after 20 March 2013, subject to savings in FA 2013, Sch. 26, para. 13(2).

S. 212I inserted by FA 2010, s. 26 and Sch. 4, para. 2, with effect where the relevant day is on or after 21 July 2009, subject to earlier modified commencement as provided by FA 2010, Sch. 4, para. 6.

RELEVANT EXCESS OF ALLOWANCES

212J Relevant excess of allowances

212J(1) C or P has a relevant excess of allowances in relation to the relevant activity if–

RTWDV > BSV

212J(2) Section 212K defines RTWDV and section 212L defines BSV.

212J(3) References in this Chapter to plant and machinery do not include excluded plant and machinery.

212J(4) Plant and machinery is **"excluded plant and machinery"** if–

(a) expenditure incurred on the provision of it is not, as a result of section 34A, qualifying expenditure for the purposes of this Part, or

(b) it is, as a result of section 67, treated for the purposes of this Part as owned otherwise than by C or P.

History – In s. 212J(1), the word "activity" substituted for the word "trade" by FA 2013, s. 71 and Sch. 26, para. 8, with effect in relation to a qualifying change if the relevant day (within the meaning of CAA 2001, Pt. 2, Ch. 16A) is on or after 20 March 2013, subject to savings in FA 2013, Sch. 26, para. 13(2).

S. 212J inserted by FA 2010, s. 26 and Sch. 4, para. 2, with effect where the relevant day is on or after 21 July 2009, subject to earlier modified commencement as provided by FA 2010, Sch. 4, para. 6.

212K Relevant tax written-down value

212K(1) RTWDV is the relevant tax written-down value and is to be found by adding together amounts 1 and 2.

212K(2) Amount 1 is the total amount of any unrelieved qualifying expenditure in respect of plant and machinery contained in–

(a) single asset pools,

(b) class pools, or

(c) the main pool,

which is available to be carried forward (in accordance with section 59) from the old period and used in calculating the profits of the relevant activity.

212K(3) Amount 2 is the total of any qualifying expenditure incurred on the provision of a ship for the purposes of the relevant activity which, at the end of the old period, is unrelieved by virtue of notice having been given under section 130.

212K(4) For the purposes of this Part the amount of unrelieved qualifying expenditure contained in any pool which is available to be carried forward (in accordance with section 59) from the old period and used in calculating the profits of the relevant activity is to be calculated on the assumptions–

(a) that any qualifying expenditure that could have been (but was not) allocated to the pool before the end of the old period had been so allocated at the end of the old period,

(b) that any qualifying expenditure prevented from being allocated to the pool by section 58(5) had been so allocated at the end of the old period, and

(c) that any transaction taking place on the relevant day that has the effect of reducing the amount of unrelieved qualifying expenditure in the pool had not taken place.

212K(5) Where condition C in section 212C is met–

(a) references in subsection (2) to any unrelieved qualifying expenditure in respect of plant and machinery contained in a pool which is available to be carried forward (in accordance with section 59) from the old period and used in calculating the profits of the relevant activity, and

(b) the reference in subsection (3) to any qualifying expenditure incurred on the provision of a ship for the purposes of the relevant activity which, at the end of the old period, is unrelieved by virtue of notice having been given under section 130,

are to what it would have been but for the qualifying change.

212K(6) In this section **"the old period"** means the period which is the old period for the purposes of section 212O (or would be if this Chapter applied): see section 212N(3).

212K(7) The plant and machinery in respect of which there is unrelieved qualifying expenditure such as is mentioned in subsection (2), or qualifying expenditure such as is mentioned in subsection (3), is referred to in the following provisions as "the relevant plant and machinery".

History – In s. 212K(2)–(5), the word "activity" substituted for the word "trade" by FA 2013, s. 71 and Sch. 26, para. 9, with effect in relation to a qualifying change if the relevant day (within the meaning of CAA 2001, Pt. 2, Ch. 16A) is on or after 20 March 2013, subject to savings in FA 2013, Sch. 26, para. 13(2).

S. 212K inserted by FA 2010, s. 26 and Sch. 4, para. 2, with effect where the relevant day is on or after 21 July 2009, subject to earlier modified commencement as provided by FA 2010, Sch. 4, para. 6.

212L Balance sheet value

212L(1) BSV is the balance sheet value of the relevant plant and machinery and is to be found by adding together the amounts (if any) which would be shown in respect of it in the appropriate balance sheet of C or P.

212L(2) For this purpose the amounts shown in the appropriate balance sheet in respect of the relevant plant or machinery are–

(a) the amounts shown in that balance sheet as the net book value (or carrying amount) in respect of it, and

(b) the amounts shown in that balance sheet as the net investment in respect of finance leases of it.

212L(3) If–

(a) any of the relevant plant or machinery is a fixture in any land, and

(b) the amount which falls (or would fall) to be shown in the appropriate balance sheet as the net book value (or carrying amount) of the land would include an amount in respect of the fixture,

the amount of the net book value (or carrying amount) in respect of the fixture is determined on a just and reasonable basis.

212L(4) If–

(a) any of the relevant plant or machinery is subject to a finance lease, and

(b) any land or asset which is not plant or machinery is subject to that lease,

the amount of the net investment in respect of the finance lease of that plant or machinery is determined on a just and reasonable basis.

212L(5) In this section any reference to any amount shown in the appropriate balance sheet of C or P is the amount which, assuming that a balance sheet of C or P were drawn up in accordance with subsection (6), would fall to be shown in that balance sheet.

212L(6) A balance sheet is drawn up in accordance with this subsection if it is drawn up in accordance with generally accepted accounting practice so as to reflect the position as at the beginning of the relevant day but adjusted to reflect the disposal of any of the relevant plant or machinery which is disposed of on the relevant day.

212L(7) In this section–

"finance lease" means a lease which, in accordance with generally accepted accounting practice, falls (or would fall) to be treated as a finance lease or loan in accounts of C or P;

"fixture"–

(a) means any plant or machinery that is so installed or otherwise fixed in or to a building or other description of land as to become, in law, part of that building or other land, and

(b) includes any boiler or water-filled radiator installed in a building as part of a space or water heating system.

History – S. 212L inserted by FA 2010, s. 26 and Sch. 4, para. 2, with effect where the relevant day is on or after 21 July 2009, subject to earlier modified commencement as provided by FA 2010, Sch. 4, para. 6.

LIMITING CONDITIONS

212LA Limiting conditions

212LA(1) The qualifying change meets one of the limiting conditions if condition A, B, C or D is met.

212LA(2) Condition A is that the amount of the relevant excess of allowances is £50 million or more.

212LA(3) Condition B is that the amount of the relevant excess of allowances–

(a) is £2 million or more but less than £50 million, and

(b) is not insignificant as a proportion of the total amount or value of the benefits derived by any relevant person by virtue of the qualifying change or change arrangements.

212LA(4) **"Relevant person"** means a person who, at the end of the relevant day, is–

(a) a principal company of C,

(b) a person carrying on the relevant activity in partnership, or

(c) a person who is connected to a person within paragraph (a) or (b) (within the meaning of section 1122 of CTA 2010).

212LA(5) Condition C is that–

(a) the amount of the relevant excess of allowances is less than £2 million, and

(b) the qualifying change has an unallowable purpose.

See section 212M for the meaning of "unallowable purpose".

212LA(6) Condition D is that the main purpose, or one of the main purposes, of any arrangements is to procure that condition A or B or paragraph (a) of condition C is not met.

212LA(7) In this section–

the amount of the relevant excess of allowances is the difference between RTWDV and BSV (see sections 212K and 212L);

"change arrangements" and **"arrangements"** have the same meaning as in section 212M.

History – S. 212LA inserted by FA 2013, s. 71 and Sch. 26, para. 3, with effect in relation to a qualifying change if the relevant day (within the meaning of CAA 2001, Pt. 2, Ch. 16A) is on or after 20 March 2013, subject to savings in FA 2013, Sch. 26, para. 13(2).

UNALLOWABLE PURPOSE

212M Unallowable purpose

212M(1) The qualifying change has an unallowable purpose if the main purpose, or one of the main purposes, of change arrangements is to obtain a relevant tax advantage (for any person).

212M(2) **"Change arrangements"** means any arrangements made to bring about, or otherwise connected with, the qualifying change; and **"arrangements"** includes any agreement, understanding, scheme, transaction or series of transactions (whether or not legally enforceable).

212M(3) **"Obtain a relevant tax advantage"** means become entitled to a reduction in profits, or an increase in losses, for the purposes of corporation tax in consequence of a claim to allowances in respect of qualifying expenditure in respect of the relevant plant and machinery or qualifying expenditure within section 212K(3).

History – S. 212M inserted by FA 2010, s. 26 and Sch. 4, para. 2, with effect where the relevant day is on or after 21 July 2009, subject to earlier modified commencement as provided by FA 2010, Sch. 4, para. 6.

WHAT HAPPENS WHEN CHAPTER APPLIES

212N Old and new accounting periods

212N(1) The accounting period of C which is current on the relevant day ends with that day and a new accounting period of C begins with the following day (but subject to subsection (2)).

212N(2) In a case in which condition A, B or D in section 212C is met and the relevant activity was, at the beginning of the relevant day, carried on by C in partnership with another company or other companies subsection (1) does not apply but–

(a) the period which, for the purposes of Part 17 of CTA 2009, is the accounting period of the partnership current on the relevant day ends with that day, and

(b) there begins with the following day a new accounting period–

(i) of the partnership, or

(ii) where condition D is met and C's relevant percentage share in the relevant activity is nil after the qualifying change, of the company or partnership by which the relevant activity is carried on after the relevant change.

212N(3) For the purposes of section 212O **"the old period"** means the accounting period of C or the partnership in which C carries on the relevant activity which ends with the relevant day.

212N(4) For the purposes of section 212P **"the new period"** means the accounting period–

(a) of C or that partnership, or

(b) where condition D is met and C's relevant percentage share in the relevant activity is nil after the qualifying change, of the company or partnership by which the relevant activity is carried on after the relevant change,

which begins with the following day.

History – In s. 212N(2), (3) and (4), the word "activity" substituted for the word "trade" by FA 2013, s. 71 and Sch. 26, para. 10, with effect in relation to a qualifying change if the relevant day (within the meaning of CAA 2001, Pt. 2, Ch. 16A) is on or after 20 March 2013, subject to savings in FA 2013, Sch. 26, para. 13(2).
S. 212N inserted by FA 2010, s. 26 and Sch. 4, para. 2, with effect where the relevant day is on or after 21 July 2009, subject to earlier modified commencement as provided by FA 2010, Sch. 4, para. 6.

212O When there is excess of allowances in pool: amount of excess

212O(1) Section 212P has effect where C or P has an excess of allowances in any single asset pool, any class pool or the main pool at the end of the old period; and a pool in the case of which there is an excess of allowances is referred to in this section and section 212P as a "relevant pool".

212O(2) For the purposes of this section C or P has an excess of allowances in a pool if–

$$PA > BSVP$$

212O(3) In this section and section 212Q–

PA, in relation to a pool, is the amount specified in section 212K(2) in relation to the pool, and

BSVP, in relation to a pool, is so much of BSV as, on a just and reasonable apportionment, it is appropriate to attribute to the pool.

212O(4) For the purposes of section 212P the amount of the excess of allowances in relation to any relevant pool ("the relevant pool in question") is the difference between PA and BSVP.

212O(5) But if, in relation to any other pool–

$$BSVP > PA$$

what would otherwise be the amount of the excess of allowances in relation to the relevant pool in question for the purposes of section 212P is reduced by so much of the difference between BSVP and PA as is not taken into account under this subsection in relation to another relevant pool or under section 212Q(8).

History – S. 212O inserted by FA 2010, s. 26 and Sch. 4, para. 2, with effect where the relevant day is on or after 21 July 2009, subject to earlier modified commencement as provided by FA 2010, Sch. 4, para. 6.

212P Effect of excess of allowances on pools

212P(1) The unrelieved qualifying expenditure in each relevant pool is to be taken to be reduced at the beginning of the new period by the amount of the excess of allowances in relation to the pool.

212P(2) The amount of the excess of allowances is to be treated from the beginning of the new period as if it were qualifying expenditure in a new pool of the same description as the relevant pool (and so subject to the same provisions of this Part, other than this Chapter).

212P(3) Where, following the qualifying change, a person ceases to carry on a qualifying activity (or part of a qualifying activity) and C begins to carry on (whether or not in partnership) that activity (or that part of an activity) as part of its trade or business, for the purposes of claiming any allowance in respect of qualifying expenditure in the new pool the carrying on of that activity (or that part) by C is to be regarded as the carrying on of a separate trade or business.

212P(4) A loss attributable to an allowance claimed in respect of qualifying expenditure in the new pool may not be set off under section 37, 62 or 66 of CTA 2010 (loss relief against total profits of same or other accounting period) or section 259 or 260(3) of this Act (special leasing) otherwise than against the profits of a qualifying activity carried on by C, or any company that is a member of P, at the beginning of the relevant day.

212P(5) And the amount of such a loss which may be so set off by any person is not to exceed the amount of the loss which would have been available for such set off by the person but for the qualifying change.

212P(6) A loss attributable to an allowance claimed in respect of qualifying expenditure in the new pool may not be set off by way of group relief in accordance with Part 5 of CTA 2010 (surrender of losses by way of group relief) by a company ("the claimant company") unless it would have been available for such set off but for the qualifying change.

212P(7) And the amount of such a loss which is available for such set off by the claimant company is not to exceed the amount of the loss which would have been available for such set off by the claimant company but for the qualifying change.

212P(8) Where any activity not carried on by C, or a company that is a member of P, at the beginning of the relevant day would otherwise be regarded for the purposes of corporation tax as forming part of a qualifying activity carried on by C or the member of P at that time it is not to be so regarded for the purposes of subsection (4).

212P(9) In a case in which condition C in section 212C is met, the references in subsections (1) and (2) to the beginning of the new period are to the time of the qualifying change (and section 948 of CTA 2010 has effect subject to this section).

History – In s. 212P(3), the words "a qualifying activity (or part of a qualifying activity)" substituted for the words "a trade (or part of a trade)", the words "that activity (or that part of an activity)" substituted for the words "the activities of that trade (or part of a trade)", the words "or business" inserted (in both places) and the words "that activity (or that part)" substituted for the words "those activities" by FA 2013, s. 71 and Sch. 26, para. 11(2), with effect in relation to a qualifying change if the relevant day (within the meaning of CAA 2001, Pt. 2, Ch. 16A) is on or after 20 March 2013, subject to savings in FA 2013, Sch. 26, para. 13(2).

In s. 212P(4), the words ", 62 or 66" and the words "or section 259 or 260(3) of this Act (special leasing)" inserted, the word "trade" omitted and the word "other" substituted for the word "earlier" by FA 2013, s. 71 and Sch. 26, para. 11(3), with effect in relation to a qualifying change if the relevant day (within the meaning of CAA 2001, Pt. 2, Ch. 16A) is on or after 20 March 2013, subject to savings in FA 2013, Sch. 26, para. 13(2).

S. 212P inserted by FA 2010, s. 26 and Sch. 4, para. 2, with effect where the relevant day is on or after 21 July 2009, subject to earlier modified commencement as provided by FA 2010, Sch. 4, para. 6.

212Q When there are postponed capital allowances

212Q(1) This section has effect where C or P has relevant postponed capital allowances.

212Q(2) C or P has relevant postponed capital allowances if amount 2 in section 212K(3) is an amount other than nil.

212Q(3) Where, following the qualifying change, a person ceases to carry on a qualifying activity (or part of a qualifying activity) and C begins to carry on (whether or not in partnership) that activity (or that part of an activity) as part of its trade or business, for the purposes of claiming any allowance in respect of qualifying expenditure such as is mentioned in section 212K(3) the carrying on of that activity (or that part) by C is to be regarded as the carrying on of a separate trade or business.

212Q(4) A loss attributable to an allowance claimed in respect of qualifying expenditure such as is mentioned in section 212K(3) may not be set off under section 37, 62 or 66 of CTA 2010 or section 259 or 260(3) of this Act otherwise than against the profits of a qualifying activity carried on by C, or any company that is a member of P, at the beginning of the relevant day.

212Q(5) And the amount of such a loss which may be so set off by any person is not to exceed the amount of the loss which would have been available for such set off by the person but for the qualifying change.

212Q(6) A loss attributable to an allowance claimed in respect of qualifying expenditure such as is mentioned in section 212K(3) may not be set off by way of group relief in accordance with Part 5 of CTA 2010 by a company ("the claimant company") unless it would have been available for such set off but for the qualifying change.

212Q(7) And the amount of such a loss which is available for such set off by the claimant company is not to exceed the amount of the loss which would have been available for such set off by the claimant company but for the qualifying change.

212Q(8) If, in relation to any pool–

$$BSVP > PA$$

what would otherwise be the amount of qualifying expenditure such as is mentioned in section 212K(3) is to be treated for the purposes of this section as reduced by so much of the difference between BSVP and PA in relation to the pool as is not taken into account under section 212O(5) in relation to a relevant pool.

212Q(9) Where any activity not carried on by C, or a company that is a member of P, at the beginning of the relevant day would otherwise be regarded for the purposes of corporation tax as forming part of a qualifying activity carried on by C or the member of P at that time it is not to be so regarded for the purposes of subsection (4).

History – In s. 212Q(3), the words "a qualifying activity (or part of a qualifying activity)" substituted for the words "a trade (or part of a trade)", the words "that activity (or that part of an activity)" substituted for the words "the activities of that trade (or part of a trade)", the words "or business" inserted (in both places) and the words "that activity (or that part)" substituted for the words "those activities" by FA 2013, s. 71 and Sch. 26, para. 12(2), with effect in relation to a qualifying change if the relevant day (within the meaning of CAA 2001, Pt. 2, Ch. 16A) is on or after 20 March 2013, subject to savings in FA 2013, Sch. 26, para. 13(2).
In s. 212Q(4), the words ", 62 or 66" and the words "or section 259 or 260(3) of this Act" inserted by FA 2013, s. 71 and Sch. 26, para. 12(3), with effect in relation to a qualifying change if the relevant day (within the meaning of CAA 2001, Pt. 2, Ch. 16A) is on or after 20 March 2013, subject to savings in FA 2013, Sch. 26, para. 13(2).
S. 212Q inserted by FA 2010, s. 26 and Sch. 4, para. 2, with effect where the relevant day is on or after 21 July 2009 (see FA 2010, Sch. 4, para. 6).

212R Apportionment of proceeds of disposal of relevant plant and machinery

212R Any amount required to be brought into account in connection with a disposal event in respect of any relevant plant and machinery is to be apportioned between the new pool and the relevant pool concerned on a just and reasonable basis.

History – S. 212R inserted by FA 2010, s. 26 and Sch. 4, para. 2, with effect where the relevant day is on or after 21 July 2009, subject to earlier modified commencement as provided by FA 2010, Sch. 4, para. 6.

212S Transactions on relevant day

212S(1) This section applies if any plant and machinery is transferred on the relevant day and (apart from subsection (4)(c) of section 212K) the transfer would have the effect of reducing RTWDV (as determined in accordance with that section).

212S(2) No person other than C or P is entitled to claim an allowance in respect of the plant or machinery after the transfer.

History – S. 212S inserted by FA 2010, s. 26 and Sch. 4, para. 2, with effect where the relevant day is on or after 21 July 2009 (see FA 2010, Sch. 4, para. 6).

Chapter 16B – Cap on First-Year Allowances

History – In the heading of Ch. 16B, the words ": zero-emission goods vehicles" omitted by FA 2012, s. 44 and Sch. 11, para. 7(2), with effect for chargeable periods ending on or after 1 April 2012.
Ch. 16B inserted by F(No. 3)A 2010, s. 18 and Sch. 7, para. 6, with effect for chargeable periods ending on or after 1 April 2010 (corporation tax) or 6 April 2010 (income tax).

212T Cap on first-year allowances: zero-emission goods vehicles

212T(1) A section 45DA allowance is not available in respect of expenditure ("the current expenditure") incurred by a person ("the investor")–

(a) if section 45DA allowances have previously been made in respect of undertaking expenditure of 85 million euros, or

(b) (where paragraph (a) does not apply) if, and to the extent that, the aggregate of–
   (i) the undertaking expenditure in respect of which section 45DA allowances have previously been made, and
   (ii) the current expenditure,

exceeds 85 million euros.

212T(2) **"Undertaking expenditure"** means–

(a) expenditure incurred by the investor,

(b) if the investor is a partnership, expenditure incurred (at any time) by a person who is a partner enterprise forming part of the investor at the time the current expenditure is incurred, and

(c) if the investor and one or more other persons together form, or have at any time formed, an undertaking, expenditure which is–
   (i) incurred by that undertaking, or
   (ii) incurred by any of those other persons at a relevant time.

212T(3) Expenditure is incurred by a person at a **"relevant time"** if it is incurred–

(a) at a time when the investor and the person are part of the same undertaking, or

(b) at a time before the investor and the person became part of the same undertaking (or, if they became part of the same undertaking on more than one occasion, before the last time).

212T(4) For the purposes of subsection (1), expenditure incurred in a currency other than the euro is to be converted into its equivalent in euros using the spot rate of exchange for the day on which the expenditure is incurred.

212T(5) The Treasury may by regulations increase the amount specified in subsection (1)(a) and (b).

212T(6) In this section–

"section 45DA allowance" means a first-year allowance in respect of expenditure that is first-year qualifying expenditure under section 45DA;

"undertaking" means–

(a) an autonomous enterprise, or

(b) an enterprise (not within paragraph (a)) and its partner enterprises (if any) and its linked enterprises (if any),

and **"enterprise"**, **"autonomous enterprise"**, **"partner enterprise"** and **"linked enterprise"** have the meaning given by Annex 1 to the Commission Regulation (EU) No 651/2014 (General block exemption Regulation).

History – In s. 212T(6), in the definition of "undertaking", "(EU) No 651/2014" substituted for "(EC) No 800/2008" by FA 2014, s. 65 and Sch. 13, para. 6, with effect in relation to expenditure incurred on or after 17 July 2014.
S. 212T inserted by F(No. 3)A 2010, s. 18 and Sch. 7, para. 6, with effect for chargeable periods ending on or after 1 April 2010 (corporation tax) or 6 April 2010 (income tax).

212U Cap on first-year allowances: expenditure on plant and machinery for use in designated assisted areas

212U(1) A section 45K allowance is not available in respect of expenditure ("the current expenditure") incurred by a person ("the investor") in respect of a particular designated assisted area–

(a) if section 45K allowances have previously been made to any person in respect of P&M expenditure of 125 million euros incurred in respect of that area and on the same single investment project as the current expenditure, or

(b) (where paragraph (a) does not apply) if, and to the extent that, the aggregate of–

(i) the P&M expenditure incurred by any person in respect of that area, and on the same single investment project as the current expenditure, in respect of which section 45K allowances have previously been made, and

(ii) the current expenditure,

exceeds 125 million euros.

212U(2) For the purposes of subsection (1), any reference to P&M expenditure incurred in respect of a designated assisted area is a reference to expenditure incurred on the provision of plant or machinery for use primarily in that area.

212U(3) For the purposes of subsection (1), expenditure incurred in a currency other than the euro is to be converted into its equivalent in euros using the spot rate of exchange for the day on which the expenditure is incurred.

212U(4) The Treasury may by regulations increase the amount specified in subsection (1)(a) and (b).

212U(5) In this section–

"designated assisted area" has the meaning given by section 45K;

"section 45K allowance" means a first-year allowance in respect of expenditure that is first-year qualifying expenditure under section 45K;

"single investment project" has the same meaning as in Commission Regulation (EU) No 651/2014 (General block exemption Regulation).

History – In s. 212U(5), in the definition of "single investment project", "(EU) No 651/ 2014" substituted for "(EC) No 800/2008" by FA 2014, s. 65 and Sch. 13, para. 7, with effect in relation to expenditure incurred on or after 17 July 2014.
S. 212U inserted by FA 2012, s. 44 and Sch. 11, para. 7(1), with effect for chargeable periods ending on or after 1 April 2012.

Chapter 17 – Other Anti-avoidance

History – Heading to Pt. 2, Ch. 17 substituted by FA 2010, s. 26 and Sch. 4, para. 3, with effect where the relevant day is on or after 21 July 2009.

RELEVANT TRANSACTIONS

213 Relevant transactions: sale, hire-purchase (etc.) and assignment

213(1) For the purposes of this Chapter, a person ("B") and another person ("S") enter into a relevant transaction if–

(a) S sells plant or machinery to B,

(b) B enters into a contract with S providing that B shall or may become the owner of plant or machinery on the performance of the contract, or

(c) S assigns to B the benefit of a contract providing that S shall or may become the owner of plant or machinery on the performance of the contract.

213(2) For the purposes of this Chapter, references to B's expenditure under a relevant transaction are references–

(a) in the case of a sale within subsection (1)(a), to B's capital expenditure on the provision of the plant or machinery by purchase,

(b) in the case of a contract within subsection (1)(b), to B's capital expenditure under the contract so far as it relates to the plant or machinery, or

(c) in the case of an assignment within subsection (1)(c), to B's capital expenditure under the contract so far as it relates to the plant or machinery or is by way of consideration for the assignment.

213(3) If–

(a) B is treated under section 14 (use for qualifying activity of plant or machinery which is a gift) as having incurred capital expenditure on the provision of plant or machinery, and

(b) the donor of the plant or machinery was S,

B is to be treated for the purposes of this Chapter as having incurred capital expenditure on the provision of the plant or machinery by purchasing it from S.

213(4) For the purposes of this Chapter, references to the disposal value of the plant or machinery under a relevant transaction are references to the disposal value that is to be brought into account by S as a result of the sale, contract or assignment in question.

History – In s. 213(1), the words "and another person ("S") enter into a relevant transaction" substituted for the words "into a relevant transaction with another ("S")" by FA 2016, s. 70(3), with effect in relation to transactions mentioned in s. 213(1)(a), (b) or (c) that take place on or after 25 November 2015.

S. 213(4) inserted by FA 2016, s. 70(4), with effect in relation to transactions mentioned in s. 213(1)(a), (b) or (c) that take place on or after 25 November 2015.

Origin – S. 213(1), (2): CAA 1990, s. 75(1) (part), (2) (part), (3) (part), drafting.

S. 213(3): CAA 1990, s. 81(3).

Transitional – Sch. 3, para. 43: s. 213(3) does not apply if the plant or machinery was brought into use before 27 July 1989.

HMRC Manuals – CA28200: guidance and example on s. 213.

Other material – Tax Bulletin Article TB06/98-1: background on the changes to the regime introduced in Finance (No. 2) Act 1997.

RESTRICTIONS ON ALLOWANCES

214 Connected persons

214 Allowances under this Part are restricted under sections 217 and 218 (or, as the case may be, 218ZA(3)) if–

(a) B enters into a relevant transaction with S, and

(b) B and S are connected with each other.

History – In s. 214, the words "(or, as the case may be, 218ZA(3))" inserted after "218" by FA 2012, s. 42 and Sch. 9, para. 3, with effect in relation to expenditure of B's that is incurred on or after 1 April 2012, for corporation tax purposes, and 6 April 2012, for income tax purposes (regardless of when the relevant transaction was entered into).

Origin – S. 214: CAA 1990, s. 75(1) (part), (2) (part), (3) (part).

HMRC Manuals – CA28300: guidance and example on restrictions on allowances.

215 Transactions to obtain tax advantages

215(1) Allowances under this Part are restricted, and balancing charges are imposed or increased, under the applicable sections if B and S enter into a relevant transaction that either–

(a) has an avoidance purpose, or

(b) is part of, or occurs as a result of, a scheme or arrangement that has an avoidance purpose.

215(2) Subsection (1)(b) may be satisfied–

(a) whether the scheme or arrangement was made before or after the relevant transaction was entered into, and

(b) whether or not the scheme or arrangement is legally enforceable.

215(3) A transaction, scheme or arrangement has an **"avoidance purpose"** if the main purpose, or one of the main purposes, of a party in entering into the transaction, scheme or arrangement is to enable a person to obtain a tax advantage under this Part that would not otherwise be obtained.

215(4) The reference in subsection (3) to obtaining a tax advantage that would not otherwise be obtained includes–

(a) obtaining an allowance that is in any way more favourable to a person than the one that would otherwise be obtained, and

(b) avoiding liability for the whole or part of a balancing charge to which a person would otherwise be liable.

215(4A) If the tax advantage relates to the disposal value of the plant or machinery under the relevant transaction (whether by obtaining a more favourable allowance or by avoiding the whole or part of a balancing charge) then–

(a) the applicable section is section 218ZB, and

(b) the tax advantage is to be disregarded for the purposes of subsection (6) and (8)(b).

215(5) If the tax advantage is of a kind described in subsection (7), **"the applicable sections"** are sections 217 and 218ZA(5).

215(6) Otherwise, **"the applicable sections"** are sections 217 and 218ZA(1) or, as the case may be, 218ZA(3).

215(7) The kinds of tax advantage are–

(a) that an allowance to which B is entitled for a chargeable period is calculated using a percentage rate that is higher than the one that would otherwise be used, or

(b) that B is entitled to an allowance in respect of an amount of capital expenditure sooner than B would otherwise be entitled to it.

215(8) If a transaction, scheme or arrangement involves–

(a) a tax advantage of a kind described in subsection (7), and

(b) a tax advantage not of such a kind,

subsections (5) and (6) have effect separately in relation to each tax advantage.

History – In s. 215(1), the words", and balancing charges are imposed or increased," inserted and the words "B and S enter into a relevant transaction" substituted for the words "B enters into a relevant transaction with S" by FA 2016, s. 70(6), with effect in relation to transactions mentioned in s. 213(1)(a), (b) or (c) that take place on or after 25 November 2015.

In s. 215(4), para. (a) created from existing text and para. (b) (and the ", and" preceding it) inserted by FA 2016, s. 70(7), with effect in relation to transactions mentioned in s. 213(1)(a), (b) or (c) that take place on or after 25 November 2015.

S. 215(4A) inserted by FA 2016, s. 70(8), with effect in relation to transactions mentioned in s. 213(1)(a), (b) or (c) that take place on or after 25 November 2015.

S. 215 substituted by FA 2012, s. 42 and Sch. 9, para. 1, with effect in relation to expenditure of B's that is incurred on or after 1 April 2012, for corporation tax purposes, and 6 April 2012, for income tax purposes (regardless of when the relevant transaction was entered into).

HMRC Manuals – CA28300: guidance and example on restrictions on allowances.

216 Sale and leaseback, etc.

216(1) Allowances under this Part are restricted under sections 217 and 218 (or, as the case may be, 218ZA(3)) if–

(a) B enters into a relevant transaction with S, and

(b) the plant or machinery–

(i) continues to be used for the purposes of a qualifying activity carried on by S or by a person (other than B) who is connected with S, or

(ii) is used after the date of the transaction for the purposes of a qualifying activity carried on by S or by a person (other than B) who is connected with S, without having been used since that date for the purposes of any other qualifying activity except that of leasing the plant or machinery.

216(2) In this section–

"the date of the transaction" means the date of the sale, the making of the contract or the assignment referred to in section 213(1)(a) to (c), and

"qualifying activity" includes any activity listed in section 15(1) even if any profits or gains from it are not chargeable to tax.

History – In s. 216(1), the words "(or, as the case may be, 218ZA(3))" inserted after "218" by FA 2012, s. 42 and Sch. 9, para. 4, with effect in relation to expenditure of B's that is incurred on or after 1 April 2012, for corporation tax purposes, and 6 April 2012, for income tax purposes (regardless of when the relevant transaction was entered into).

In s. 216(1)(b)(i), the words "or by a person (other than B) who is connected with S" inserted by FA 2009, s. 64 and Sch. 32, para. 23, with effect where the date of the transaction referred to in s. 216(1)(a) is on or after 22 April 2009, and for the purposes of s. 227 (which applies s. 216(1)(b), where the date of the transaction referred to in s. 227(1)(a) is on or after 22 April 2009.

Origin – S. 216(1): CAA 1990, s. 75(1) (part), (2) (part), (3) (part), s. 76(1).

S. 216(2): CAA 1990, s. 83(2A) (part), drafting.

HMRC Manuals – CA28300: guidance and example on restrictions on allowances.

217 No annual investment allowance or first-year allowance for B's expenditure

217(1) If this section applies as a result of section 214, 215 or 216, no annual investment allowance or first-year allowance is to be made in respect of B's expenditure under the relevant transaction.

217(2) Any annual investment allowance or first-year allowance which is prohibited by subsection (1), but which has already been made, is to be withdrawn.

217(3) This section does not apply if plant or machinery is the subject of a sale and finance leaseback (as defined in section 221).

History – In the heading to s. 217, the words "annual investment allowance or" inserted by FA 2008, s. 74 and Sch. 24, para. 8(4), with effect in relation to expenditure incurred on or after 1 April 2008 for corporation tax purposes and 6 April 2008 for income tax purposes.

In s. 217(1), the words "no annual investment allowance or first-year allowance is" substituted for the words "a first-year allowance is not" by FA 2008, s. 74 and Sch. 24, para. 8(2), with effect in relation to expenditure incurred on or after 1 April 2008 for corporation tax purposes and 6 April 2008 for income tax purposes.

In s. 217(2), the words "annual investment allowance or" inserted by FA 2008, s. 74 and Sch. 24, para. 8(3), with effect in relation to expenditure incurred on or after 1 April 2008 for corporation tax purposes and 6 April 2008 for income tax purposes.

S. 217(3) substituted by FA 2008, s. 55 and Sch. 20, para. 6(8), with effect in the case of plant or machinery which is the subject of a sale and finance leaseback (as defined in CAA 2001, s. 221) where the date of the transaction (within the meaning of that section) is on or after 9 October 2007.

Origin – S. 217(1)–(3): CAA 1990, s. 75(1) part, (2) (part), (3) (part).

HMRC Manuals – CA28300: guidance and example on restrictions on allowances.

218 Restriction on B's qualifying expenditure: section 214 or 216

218(1) If this section applies as a result of section 214 or 216, the amount, if any, by which B's expenditure under the relevant transaction exceeds D is to be left out of account in determining B's available qualifying expenditure.

D is defined in subsections (2), (2A) and (3).

218(2) If S is required to bring a disposal value into account under this Part because of the relevant transaction, D is that disposal value.

218(2A) D is nil if–

(a) S is not required to bring a disposal value into account under this Part because of the relevant transaction, and

(b) at any time before that transaction S or a linked person became owner of the plant or machinery without incurring either capital expenditure or qualifying revenue expenditure on its provision.

218(3) Otherwise, D is whichever of the following is the smallest–

(a) the market value of the plant or machinery;

(b) if S incurred capital expenditure on the provision of the plant or machinery, the amount of that expenditure;

(c) if a person connected with S incurred capital expenditure on the provision of the plant or machinery, the amount of that expenditure.

218(3A) **"Linked person"**, in relation to plant or machinery, means a person–

(a) who owned the plant or machinery at any time before the relevant transaction, and

(b) who was connected with S at any time between–

   (i) the time when the person became owner of the plant or machinery, and

   (ii) the time of the relevant transaction.

218(3B) Expenditure on the provision of plant or machinery is **"qualifying revenue expenditure"** if it is expenditure of a revenue nature–

(a) that is at least equal to the amount of expenditure that would reasonably be expected to have been incurred on the provision of the plant or machinery in a transaction between persons dealing with each other at arm's length in the open market, or

(b) that is incurred by the manufacturer of the plant or machinery and is at least equal to the amount that it would have been reasonable to expect to have been the normal cost of manufacturing the plant or machinery.

218(4) This section does not apply if plant or machinery is the subject of a sale and finance leaseback (as defined in section 221), but see section 225.

218(5) This section is subject to section 218ZA(3).

History – In the heading of s. 218, ": section 214 or 216" inserted by FA 2012, s. 42 and Sch. 9, para. 5(4), with effect in relation to expenditure of B's that is incurred on or after 1 April 2012, for corporation tax purposes, and 6 April 2012, for income tax purposes (regardless of when the relevant transaction was entered into).

In s. 218(1), the words "(2), (2A) and" substituted for the words "(2) and" by FA 2015, s. 46 and Sch. 10, para. 3(2), with effect in relation to expenditure of B's that is incurred on or after 26 February 2015.
In s. 218(1), "section 214 or 216" substituted for "section 214, 215 or 216" by FA 2012, s. 42 and Sch. 9, para. 5(2), with effect in relation to expenditure of B's that is incurred on or after 1 April 2012, for corporation tax purposes, and 6 April 2012, for income tax purposes (regardless of when the relevant transaction was entered into).
S. 218(2A) inserted by FA 2015, s. 46 and Sch. 10, para. 3(3), with effect in relation to expenditure of B's that is incurred on or after 26 February 2015.
In s. 218(3), the word "Otherwise," substituted for the words "If S is not required to bring a disposal value into account under this Part because of the relevant transaction," by FA 2015, s. 46 and Sch. 10, para. 3(4), with effect in relation to expenditure of B's that is incurred on or after 26 February 2015.
S. 218(3A) and (3B) inserted by FA 2015, s. 46 and Sch. 10, para. 3(5), with effect in relation to expenditure of B's that is incurred on or after 26 February 2015.
S. 218(4) substituted by FA 2008, s. 55 and Sch. 20, para. 6(9), with effect in the case of plant or machinery which is the subject of a sale and finance leaseback (as defined in CAA 2001, s. 221) where the date of the transaction (within the meaning of that section) is on or after 9 October 2007.
S. 218(5) inserted by FA 2012, s. 42 and Sch. 9, para. 5(3), with effect in relation to expenditure of B's that is incurred on or after 1 April 2012, for corporation tax purposes, and 6 April 2012, for income tax purposes (regardless of when the relevant transaction was entered into).
Origin – S. 218(1), (2): CAA 1990, s. 75(1) (part), (2) (part), (3) (part).
S. 218(3): CAA 1990, s. 76(2) (part), (4) (part).
S. 218(4): CAA 1990, s. 75(1) (part), (2) (part), (3) (part), s. 76(7).
HMRC Manuals – CA28300: guidance and example on restrictions on allowances.

218ZA Restrictions on writing-down allowances: section 215

218ZA(1) If this subsection applies as a result of section 215, all or part of B's expenditure under the relevant transaction is to be left out of account in determining B's available qualifying expenditure.

218ZA(2) The amount of expenditure to be left out of account is–

(a) such amount as would or would in effect cancel out the tax advantage mentioned in section 215 (whether that advantage is obtained by B or another person and whether it relates to the relevant transaction or something else), or

(b) if the amount found under paragraph (a) exceeds the whole of B's expenditure under the relevant transaction, the whole of that expenditure.

218ZA(3) But if subsection (1) applies as a result of section 215 and–

(a) section 218 also applies as a result of section 214 or 216, or

(b) section 228 also applies by virtue of an election under section 70I(11) or 227,

the amount of expenditure to be left out of account is the greater of X and Y.

218ZA(4) For the purposes of subsection (3)–

"X" is the amount found under subsection (2), and

"Y" is the amount by which B's expenditure under the relevant transaction exceeds D (as defined in section 218 or, as the case may be, section 228).

218ZA(5) If this subsection applies as a result of section 215–

(a) the allowance mentioned in subsection (7)(a) of that section is to be calculated using the rate that would be used without the tax advantage, or (as the case may be)

(b) the entitlement mentioned in subsection (7)(b) of that section is to be available as and when it would be available without the tax advantage.

218ZA(6) Subsection (5) applies whether or not section 218 also applies as a result of section 214 or 216, or section 228 also applies by virtue of an election under section 70I(11) or 227.

History – S. 218ZA inserted by FA 2012, s. 42 and Sch. 9, para. 6, with effect in relation to expenditure of B's that is incurred on or after 1 April 2012, for corporation tax purposes, and 6 April 2012, for income tax purposes (regardless of when the relevant transaction was entered into).

218ZB Disposal values: section 215

218ZB(1) If–

(a) this section applies as a result of section 215,

(b) a payment is payable to any person under the transaction, scheme or arrangement mentioned in that section,

(c) some or all of the payment would not (apart from this section) be taken into account in determining the disposal value of the plant or machinery under the relevant transaction, and

(d) as a result of the matters mentioned in paragraphs (b) and (c) S would otherwise obtain a tax advantage as mentioned in section 215(3) and (4),

the disposal value of the plant or machinery under the relevant transaction is to be adjusted in a just and reasonable manner so as to include an amount representing so much of the payment as would or would in effect cancel out the tax advantage.

CAA 2001

218ZB(2) In subsection (1) **"payment"** includes the provision of any benefit, the assumption of any liability and any other transfer of money or money's worth, and **"payable"** is to be construed accordingly.

History – S. 218ZB inserted by FA 2016, s. 70(9), with effect in relation to transactions mentioned in s. 213(1)(a), (b) or (c) that take place on or after 25 November 2015.

218A Further restriction on annual investment allowance

218A(1) This section applies where an arrangement is entered into wholly or mainly for a disqualifying purpose.

218A(2) Arrangements are entered into for a disqualifying purpose if their main purpose, or one of their main purposes, is to enable a person to obtain an annual investment allowance to which the person would not otherwise be entitled.

218A(3) The annual investment allowance mentioned in subsection (2) is not to be made.

218A(4) Any annual investment allowance which is prohibited by subsection (3), but which has already been made, is to be withdrawn.

History – S. 218A inserted by FA 2008, s. 74 and Sch. 24, para. 9, with effect in relation to expenditure incurred on or after 1 April 2008 for corporation tax purposes and 6 April 2008 for income tax purposes.

FINANCE LEASES AND CERTAIN OPERATING LEASES

History – In the above cross-heading, the words "and certain operating leases" added by FA 2006, s. 81 and Sch. 9, para. 15(5), with effect in relation to expenditure incurred on or after 1 April 2006.

219 Meaning of "finance lease"

219(1) In this Chapter **"finance lease"** means any arrangements–

(a) which provide for plant or machinery to be leased or otherwise made available by a person (**"the lessor"**) to another person (**"the lessee"**), and

(b) which, under generally accepted accounting practice–

(i) fall (or would fall) to be treated, in the accounts of the lessor or a person connected with the lessor, as a finance lease or a loan, or

(ii) are comprised in arrangements which fall (or would fall) to be so treated.

219(2) [Repealed by FA 2002, s. 141 and Sch. 40, Pt. 3(16).]

219(3) In this section **"accounts"**, in relation to a company, includes any accounts which–

(a) relate to two or more companies of which that company is one, and

(b) are drawn up in accordance with generally accepted accounting practice.

History – In s. 219(1), the words "and which are not a long funding lease in the case of the lessor", which were positioned immediately after the end of para. (b)(ii), omitted by FA 2008, s. 55 and Sch. 20, para. 6(10), with effect in the case of plant or machinery which is the subject of a sale and finance leaseback (as defined in CAA 2001, s. 221) where the date of the transaction (within the meaning of that section) is on or after 9 October 2007.

In s. 219(1)(b), after subpara. (ii), the words "and which are not a long funding lease in the case of the lessor" inserted by FA 2006, s. 81 and Sch. 9, para. 14. The commencement and transitional provisions are complex and are set out in full in FA 2006, Sch. 8, para. 15–27.

In s. 219(1), words "generally accepted accounting practice" substituted for "normal accountancy practice" by FA 2002, s. 103(4)(g) with effect from 24 July 2002.

S. 219(2) (which qualified former reference to normal accountancy practice in s. 179(1)(f) as that applicable to a company incorporated in the UK) repealed by FA 2002, s. 141 and Sch. 40, Pt. 3(16) with effect from 24 July 2002.

S. 219(3)(b) substituted by FA 2005, s. 80(1) and Sch. 4, para. 33 with effect for accounting periods beginning on or after 1 January 2005 (FA 2005, s. 80(4)).

Origin – S. 219(1), (2): CAA 1990, s. 82A(1), (2) (part), and see Rewrite note below. S. 219(3): CAA 1990, s. 82A(2) (part).

Cross references – FA 2000, Sch. 22, para. 89: the ring fence: capital allowances: ship leasing: introduction.

ICTA 1988, s. 836A: definition of "generally accepted accounting practice" in s. 219(1).

Rewrite: Technical Points – Explanatory Notes, Annex 2, Note 39: CAA 1990, s. 82A(1)(b) could in theory be read as to apply only where the lessor and connected persons are UK companies. But this would mean that, where non-UK companies are involved, one would only need to look at CAA 1990, s. 82A(1)(a) and so any arrangements for leasing plant or machinery could constitute a finance lease. Therefore, to ensure that the definition of finance lease is in accordance with normal accountancy practice that apply to UK companies. S. 219(2) treats non-UK companies as UK companies for this purpose.

HMRC Manuals – CA28400: guidance on finance leases legislation.

Other material – Tax Bulletin Article TB06/98-1: background on the changes to the regime introduced in Finance (No. 2) Act 1997.

220 Allocation of expenditure to a chargeable period

220(A1) Subsection (1) applies to a company for a chargeable period if–

(a) at the end of the CTA period of account which is the basis period for the chargeable period, the company is a member of a group, and

(b) the last day of that CTA period of account is not also the last day of a CTA period of account of the principal company of the group.

220(1) Subject to subsection (2), if the company incurs at any time in the chargeable period capital expenditure on the provision of plant or machinery for leasing under a finance lease or under a qualifying operating lease (see subsection (4))–

(a) the part of the expenditure which is proportional to the part of that chargeable period falling before that time is not to be taken into account in determining that company's available qualifying expenditure for that period, but

(b) this does not prevent that part of the expenditure being taken into account in determining that company's available qualifying expenditure for any subsequent chargeable period.

220(2) Subsection (1)(a) does not apply to a chargeable period if a disposal event occurs in that period in respect of the plant or machinery.

220(3) The following provisions have effect for the interpretation of this section.

220(4) A **"qualifying operating lease"** is a plant or machinery lease that meets the following conditions–

(a) it is not a finance lease,

(b) it is a funding lease,

(c) its term is longer than 4 years but not longer than 5 years.

220(5) A CTA period of account is the basis period for a chargeable period if the chargeable period coincides with, or falls within, the CTA period of account.

220(6) A **"CTA period of account"** is a period of account as defined in section 1119 of CTA 2010.

220(7) The provisions of section 170(3) to (6) of TCGA 1992 apply to determine for the purposes of this section–

(a) whether a company is member of a group, and

(b) which company is the principal company of the group.

220(8) But, in applying those provisions for the purposes of this section, a company ("the subsidiary company") that does not have ordinary share capital is to be treated as being a qualifying 75% subsidiary of another company ("the parent company") if the parent company–

(a) has control of the subsidiary company, and

(b) is beneficially entitled to the appropriate proportion of profits and assets.

220(9) The parent company is beneficially entitled to the appropriate proportion of profits and assets if (and only if) it–

(a) is beneficially entitled to at least 75% of any profits available for distribution to equity holders of the subsidiary company, and

(b) would be beneficially entitled to at least 75% of any assets of the subsidiary company available for distribution to its equity holders on a winding-up.

220(10) The provisions of Chapter 6 of Part 5 of CTA 2010 (equity holders and profits or assets etc) also apply for the purposes of this section.

220(11) In this section, the following expressions have the same meaning as in Chapter 6A of Part 2 (interpretation of provisions about long funding leases)–

"funding lease",

"plant or machinery lease",

"term", in relation to a lease.

History – S. 220(A1) inserted by FA 2006, s. 81 and Sch. 9, para. 15(1), with effect in relation to expenditure incurred on or after 1 April 2006.

In s. 220(A1)(a), "CTA" substituted for "ICTA" by CTA 2010, s. 1177 and Sch. 1, para. 344(2)(a), with effect for corporation tax purposes for accounting periods ending on or after 1 April 2010, and for income tax and capital gains tax purposes for the tax year 2010–11 and subsequent tax years.

In s. 220(A1)(b), "CTA" substituted for "ICTA" and "a CTA" substituted for "an ICTA" by CTA 2010, s. 1177 and Sch. 1, para. 344(2)(b), with effect for corporation tax purposes for accounting periods ending on or after 1 April 2010, and for income tax and capital gains tax purposes for the tax year 2010–11 and subsequent tax years.

In s. 220(1), the words "the company" substituted for "a person", the words "the chargeable period" substituted for "a chargeable period", and the words "or under a qualifying operating lease (see subsection (4))" inserted, all by FA 2006, s. 81 and Sch. 9, para. 15(3), with effect in relation to expenditure incurred on or after 1 April 2006.

In s. 220(1)(a) and (b), the word "company's" substituted for "person's" by FA 2006, s. 81 and Sch. 9, para. 15(3), with effect in relation to expenditure incurred on or after 1 April 2006.

S. 220(3) inserted by FA 2006, s. 81 and Sch. 9, para. 15(4), with effect in relation to expenditure incurred on or after 1 April 2006.

S. 220(4) inserted by FA 2006, s. 81 and Sch. 9, para. 15(4), with effect in relation to expenditure incurred on or after 1 April 2006.

In s. 220(5), "A CTA" substituted for "An ICTA" and "CTA" substituted for"ICTA" by CTA 2010, s. 1177 and Sch. 1, para. 344(3), with effect for corporation tax purposes for accounting periods ending on or after 1 April 2010, and for income tax and capital gains tax purposes for the tax year 2010–11 and subsequent tax years.

S. 220(5) inserted by FA 2006, s. 81 and Sch. 9, para. 15(4), with effect in relation to expenditure incurred on or after 1 April 2006.

In s. 220(6), "A CTA" substituted for "An ICTA" and "section 1119 of CTA 2010" substituted for "section 832(1) of ICTA" by CTA 2010, s. 1177 and Sch. 1, para. 344(4), with effect for corporation tax purposes for accounting periods ending on or after 1 April 2010, and for income tax and capital gains tax purposes for the tax year 2010–11 and subsequent tax years.

S. 220(6) inserted by FA 2006, s. 81 and Sch. 9, para. 15(4), with effect in relation to expenditure incurred on or after 1 April 2006.

S. 220(7) inserted by FA 2006, s. 81 and Sch. 9, para. 15(4), with effect in relation to expenditure incurred on or after 1 April 2006.
In s. 220(8)(a), the words "within the meaning of section 840 of ICTA" omitted by ITA 2007, s. 1027 and Sch.1, para. 402 and repealed by s. 1031 and Sch. 3, Pt. 1, with effect from 6 April 2007.
S. 220(8) inserted by FA 2006, s. 81 and Sch. 9, para. 15(4), with effect in relation to expenditure incurred on or after 1 April 2006.
S. 220(9) inserted by FA 2006, s. 81 and Sch. 9, para. 15(4), with effect in relation to expenditure incurred on or after 1 April 2006.
In s. 220(10), the words "Chapter 6 of Part 5 of CTA 2010" substituted for "Schedule 18 to ICTA" by CTA 2010, s. 1177 and Sch. 1, para. 344(5), with effect for corporation tax purposes for accounting periods ending on or after 1 April 2010, and for income tax and capital gains tax purposes for the tax year 2010–11 and subsequent tax years.
S. 220(10) inserted by FA 2006, s. 81 and Sch. 9, para. 15(4), with effect in relation to expenditure incurred on or after 1 April 2006.
S. 220(11) inserted by FA 2006, s. 81 and Sch. 9, para. 15(4), with effect in relation to expenditure incurred on or after 1 April 2006.

Origin – S. 220(1): CAA 1990, s. 25(5A), (5C).
S. 220(2): CAA 1990, s. 24(6) (part), (8) (part), s. 25(5B).

Transitional – Sch. 3, para. 44: s. 220 does not apply in relation to expenditure incurred before 2 July 1997, or in the 12 months beginning with that date in pursuance of a contract entered into before that date.

HMRC Manuals – CA28450: guidance and examples on s. 220.

Other material – Tax Bulletin Article TB06/98-1: background on the changes to the regime introduced in Finance (No. 2) Act 1997.

SALE AND FINANCE LEASEBACKS

221 Meaning of "sale and finance leaseback"

221(1) For the purposes of this section and section 225, plant or machinery is the subject of a sale and finance leaseback if–

(a) B enters into a relevant transaction with S,

(b) after the date of the transaction, the plant or machinery–

(i) continues to be used for the purposes of an activity carried on by S or by a person (other than B) who is connected with S,

(ii) is used for the purposes of a qualifying activity carried on by S or by a person (other than B) who is connected with S, without having been used since that date for the purposes of any other qualifying activity except that of leasing the plant or machinery, or

(iii) is used for the purposes of a non-qualifying activity carried on by S or by a person (other than B) who is connected with S, without having been used since that date for the purposes of a qualifying activity except that of leasing the plant or machinery, and

(c) it is directly or indirectly as a consequence of having been leased under a finance lease that the plant or machinery is available to be so used after that date.

221(2) In this section–

"the date of the transaction" means the date of the sale, the making of the contract or the assignment referred to in section 213(1)(a) to (c),

"non-qualifying activity" means any activity which is not a qualifying activity, and

"qualifying activity" includes any activity listed in section 15(1) even if any profits or gains from it are not chargeable to tax.

History – In s. 221(1)(b)(i), the words "an activity carried on by S or by a person (other than B) who is connected with S," substituted for the words "a qualifying activity carried on by S" by FA 2009, s. 64 and Sch. 32, para. 24, with effect where the date of the transaction referred to in s. 221(1)(a) is on or after 22 April 2009, and for the purposes of s. 228A (which applies section 221(1)(b)), where the date of the transaction referred to in s. 228A(2)(a) is on or after 22 April 2009.
In s. 221(1), the words "section 225" substituted for the words "sections 222 to 228" by FA 2008, s. 55 and Sch. 20, para. 6(11), with effect in the case of plant or machinery which is the subject of a sale and finance leaseback (as defined in CAA 2001, s. 221) where the date of the transaction (within the meaning of that section) is on or after 9 October 2007.
In s. 221(1)(b)(iii), words "S or by a person (other than B) who is connected with S" substituted by FA 2001, s. 69 and Sch. 21, para. 3, with effect as respects allowances and charges falling to be made for chargeable periods ending, for income tax purposes, on or after 6 April 2001, and, for corporation tax purposes, on or after 1 April 2001.

Origin – S. 221(1): CAA 1990, s. 75(1)(b), (2)(b), (3)(b), s. 76(1) (part), s. 76A(1) (part), (2)(a), (2)(b).
S. 221(2): CAA 1990, s. 76A(2)(b), (12) ("non-trading activities"), s. 83(2A) (part), drafting.

Cross references – S. 228A: finance leaseback: parties' income and profits.
S. 228F: lease and finance leaseback.

Transitional – Sch. 3, para. 45: s. 221 does not apply in relation to expenditure incurred before 2 July 1998 if the relevant transaction is (a) a purchase under a contract entered into before 2 July 1997, (b) itself a contract entered into before 2 July 1997, (c) an assignment made before 2 July 1997, or (d) an assignment made in pursuance of a contract entered into before 2 July 1997.

HMRC Manuals – CA28500: guidance and examples on s. 221.

222 Disposal value restricted

222 [Omitted by FA 2008, s. 55 and Sch. 20, para. 6(12)(a).]

History – S. 222 omitted by FA 2008, s. 55 and Sch. 20, para. 6(12)(a), with effect in the case of plant or machinery which is the subject of a sale and finance leaseback (as defined in CAA 2001, s. 221) where the date of the transaction (within the meaning of that section) is on or after 9 October 2007.

Origin – S. 222(1), (2): CAA 1990, s. 76(2) (part), s. 76A(2) (part), (5) (part), (9)(a).
S. 222(3): CAA 1990, s. 76A(9) (part), (10), and see Rewrite note below.
S. 222(4): CAA 1990, s. 76A(6), (7)(b) (part).

Cross references – S. 228A: finance leaseback: parties' income and profits.
S. 228H: supplementary provision to provisions of s. 228A–228G: restricted disposal value is disposal value under s. 222.

Transitional – Sch. 3, para. 45: s. 222 does not apply in relation to expenditure incurred before 2 July 1998 if the relevant transaction is (a) a purchase under a contract entered into before 2 July 1997, (b) itself a contract entered into before 2 July 1997, (c) an assignment made before 2 July 1997, or (d) an assignment made in pursuance of a contract entered into before 2 July 1997.

Rewrite: Technical Points – Explanatory Notes, Annex 2, Note 24: the definition of the notional written-down value remains the same except the approach taken in s. 222 is by way of the formula QE – A whereas the approach taken in CAA 1990, s. 76A(9) is to find a disposal value which would not give rise to a balancing charge or balancing allowance.

HMRC Manuals – CA28550: guidance and example on s. 222–224.

223 No first-year allowance for B's expenditure

223 [S. 223 omitted by FA 2008, s. 55 and Sch. 20, para. 6(12)(b).]

History – S. 223 omitted by FA 2008, s. 55 and Sch. 20, para. 6(12)(b), with effect in the case of plant or machinery which is the subject of a sale and finance leaseback (as defined in CAA 2001, s. 221) where the date of the transaction (within the meaning of that section) is on or after 9 October 2007.

Origin – S. 223(1), (2): CAA 1990, s. 75(1) (part), (2) (part), (3) (part), s. 76(1) (part), s. 76A(1) (part).

HMRC Manuals – CA28550: guidance and example on s. 222–224.

224 Restriction on B's qualifying expenditure

224 [S. 224 omitted by FA 2008, s. 55 and Sch. 20, para. 6(12)(c).]

History – S. 224 omitted by FA 2008, s. 55 and Sch. 20, para. 6(12)(c), with effect in the case of plant or machinery which is the subject of a sale and finance leaseback (as defined in CAA 2001, s. 221) where the date of the transaction (within the meaning of that section) is on or after 9 October 2007.

Origin – S. 224(1)–(3): CAA 1990, s. 75(1) (part), (2) (part), (3) (part), s. 76(2) (part), s. 76A(2) (part), (5) (part).
S. 224(4): CAA 1990, s. 76A(9), (10), drafting.
S. 224(5): CAA 1990, s. 76A(6) (part), (7) (part).

Transitional – Sch. 3, para. 45: s. 224 does not apply in relation to expenditure incurred before 2 July 1998 if the relevant transaction is (a) a purchase under a contract entered into before 2 July 1997, (b) itself a contract entered into before 2 July 1997, (c) an assignment made before 2 July 1997, or (d) an assignment made in pursuance of a contract entered into before 2 July 1997.

HMRC Manuals – CA28550: guidance and example on s. 222–224.

225 B's qualifying expenditure if lessor not bearing non-compliance risk

225(1) This section applies if plant or machinery is the subject of a sale and finance leaseback, and the finance lease, or any transaction or series of transactions of which it forms a part, makes provision which–

(a) removes from the lessor the whole, or the greater part, of any risk, which would otherwise fall directly or indirectly on the lessor, of any person sustaining a loss if payments under the lease are not made in accordance with its terms, and

(b) does so otherwise than by means of guarantees from persons connected with the lessee.

225(2) In such a case the following are not qualifying expenditure for the purposes of this Part–

(a) B's expenditure under the relevant transaction;

(b) if the lessor is a different person from B, the expenditure incurred by the lessor on the provision of the plant or machinery.

225(3) For the purposes of determining whether this section applies, the lessor and the persons connected with the lessor are treated as the same person.

Origin – S. 225(1): CAA 1990, s. 76A(6) (part), (12) ("non-compliance risk").
S. 225(2): CAA 1990, s. 76A(7) (part), (8) (part).
S. 225(3): CAA 1990, s. 76A(6) (part).

Transitional – Sch. 3, para. 45: s. 225 does not apply in relation to expenditure incurred before 2 July 1998 if the relevant transaction is (a) a purchase under a contract entered into before 2 July 1997, (b) itself a contract entered into before 2 July 1997, (c) an assignment made before 2 July 1997, or (d) an assignment made in pursuance of a contract entered into before 2 July 1997.

HMRC Manuals – CA28600: guidance on s. 225.

226 Qualifying expenditure limited in subsequent transactions

226 [S. 226 omitted by FA 2008, s. 55 and Sch. 20, para. 6(12)(d).]

History – S. 226 omitted by FA 2008, s. 55 and Sch. 20, para. 6(12)(d), with effect in the case of plant or machinery which is the subject of a sale and finance leaseback (as defined in CAA 2001, s. 221) where the date of the transaction (within the meaning of that section) is on or after 9 October 2007.

Origin – S. 226(1), (2): CAA 1990, s. 76A(3), (4) (part), (7) (part).

Transitional – Sch. 3, para. 45: s. 226 does not apply in relation to expenditure incurred before 2 July 1998 if the relevant transaction is (a) a purchase under a contract entered into before 2 July 1997, (b) itself a contract entered into before 2 July 1997, (c) an assignment made before 2 July 1997, or (d) an assignment made in pursuance of a contract entered into before 2 July 1997.

SALE AND LEASEBACK: ELECTION FOR SPECIAL TREATMENT

History – The heading "SALE AND LEASEBACK: ELECTION FOR SPECIAL TREATMENT" substituted for the former heading "SALE AND LEASEBACK OR SALE AND FINANCE LEASEBACK: ELECTION FOR SPECIAL TREATMENT" by FA 2008, s. 55

and Sch. 20, para. 6(13), with effect in the case of plant or machinery which is the subject of a sale and finance leaseback (as defined in CAA 2001, s. 221) where the date of the transaction (within the meaning of that section) is on or after 9 October 2007.

227 Circumstances in which election may be made

227(1) Section 228 applies if–

(a) B enters into a relevant transaction with S,

(b) the plant or machinery–

(i) is within section 216(1)(b) (sale and leaseback),

(ii) [omitted by FA 2008, s. 55 and Sch. 20, para. 6(13)(a)],

(c) the conditions set out in subsection (2) are met, and

(d) B and S elect that section 228 should apply.

227(2) The conditions are–

(a) that S incurred capital expenditure on the provision of the plant or machinery,

(b) that the plant or machinery was unused and not second-hand at or after the time when it was acquired by S,

(c) that the plant or machinery was acquired by S otherwise than as a result of a transaction to which section 217 or 218 applies,

(d) that the relevant transaction is effected not more than 4 months after the first occasion on which the plant or machinery is brought into use by any person for any purpose, and

(e) that S has not–

(i) made a claim for an allowance under this Act in respect of expenditure incurred on the provision of the plant or machinery,

(ii) made a tax return in which such expenditure is taken into account in determining his available qualifying expenditure for the purposes of this Part, or

(iii) given notice of any such amendment of a tax return as provides for such expenditure to be so taken into account.

227(3) In subsection (2)(b) and (c), the references to the plant or machinery being acquired by S are, in a case where the relevant transaction between S and B falls within section 213(1)(c) (assignment), references to the making of the contract the benefit of which S assigns to B.

227(4) An election under this section–

(a) must be made by notice to an officer of Revenue and Customs no later than 2 years after the date of the transaction, and

(b) is irrevocable.

227(5) Nothing in–

(a) section 42 of, or Schedule 1A to, TMA 1970 (claims and elections for income tax purposes), or

(b) paragraphs 54 to 60 of Schedule 18 to FA 1998 (claims and elections for corporation tax purposes),

applies to such an election.

227(6) In subsection (4) **"the date of the transaction"** means the date of the sale, the making of the contract or the assignment referred to in section 213(1)(a) to (c).

History – S. 227(1)(b)(ii) (which read "is the subject of a sale and finance leaseback (see section 221") and the word "or" which preceded it omitted by FA 2008, s. 55 and Sch. 20, para. 6(13)(a), with effect in the case of plant or machinery which is the subject of a sale and finance leaseback (as defined in CAA 2001, s. 221) where the date of the transaction (within the meaning of that section) is on or after 9 October 2007.

In s. 227(2)(c), the words "217 or 218" substituted for the words "217, 218, 223 or 224" by FA 2008, s. 55 and Sch. 20, para. 6(13)(b), with effect in the case of plant or machinery which is the subject of a sale and finance leaseback (as defined in CAA 2001, s. 221) where the date of the transaction (within the meaning of that section) is on or after 9 October 2007.

In s. 227(4), the words "an officer of Revenue and Customs" substituted for "the Inland Revenue" by CRCA 2005, s. 50(6) and Sch. 4, para. 83(1), with effect from 18 April 2005 by virtue of SI 2005/1126, art. 2(2).

Origin – S. 227(1): CAA 1990, s. 76B(1).

S. 227(2): CAA 1990, s. 76B(2), (6), (7) (part), s. 83(1) ("new").

S. 227(3): CAA 1990, s. 76B(7) (part).

S. 227(4): CAA 1990, s. 76B(4), (5) (part).

S. 227(5): CAA 1990, s. 76B(5) (part).

S. 227(6): CAA 1990, s. 76B(6) (part), (7) (part).

HMRC Manuals – CA28650: guidance on s. 227 and 228.

228 Effect of election: relaxation of restriction on B's qualifying expenditure, etc.

228(1) The effect of an election under section 227 in relation to B is that subsections (2) and (3) apply instead of section 218 (restriction on B's qualifying expenditure).

228(2) The amount, if any, by which B's expenditure under the relevant transaction exceeds D is to be left out of account in determining B's available qualifying expenditure.

228(3) D is whichever of the following is the smaller–

(a) if S incurred capital expenditure on the provision of the plant or machinery, the amount of that expenditure;

(b) if a person connected with S incurred capital expenditure on the provision of the plant or machinery, the amount of that expenditure.

228(4) [Omitted by FA 2008, s. 55 and Sch. 20, para. 6(14(b).]

228(5) The effect of an election under section 227 in relation to S is–

(a) that no allowance is to be made to S under this Act in respect of the capital expenditure on the provision of the plant or machinery, and

(b) that the whole of that expenditure must be left out of account in determining the amount for any period of S's available qualifying expenditure for the purposes of this Part.

History – In s. 228(1), the words "or 224", which followed the words "section 218", omitted by FA 2008, s. 55 and Sch. 20, para. 6(14)(a), with effect in the case of plant or machinery which is the subject of a sale and finance leaseback (as defined in CAA 2001, s. 221) where the date of the transaction (within the meaning of that section) is on or after 9 October 2007.

S. 228(4) omitted by FA 2008, s. 55 and Sch. 20, para. 6(14)(b), with effect in the case of plant or machinery which is the subject of a sale and finance leaseback (as defined in CAA 2001, s. 221) where the date of the transaction (within the meaning of that section) is on or after 9 October 2007.

Origin – S. 228(1)–(4): CAA 1990, s. 76B(3)(c), (d).

S. 228(5): CAA 1990, s. 76B(3)(a) (part), (b) (part).

HMRC Manuals – CA28650: guidance on s. 227 and 228.

FINANCE LEASEBACK: PARTIES' INCOME AND PROFITS

228A Application of sections 228B and 228C

228A(1) Sections 228B and 228C apply where plant or machinery is the subject of a lease and finance leaseback.

228A(2) Plant or machinery is the subject of a lease and finance leaseback if–

(a) a person ("S") leases the plant or machinery to another ("B"),

(b) after the date of that transaction, the use of the plant or machinery falls within sub-paragraph (i), (ii) or (iii) of section 221(1)(b), and

(c) it is directly as a consequence of having been leased under a finance lease that the plant or machinery is available to be so used after that date.

228A(3) For the purposes of subsection (2), S leases the plant or machinery to B only if–

(a) S grants B rights over the plant or machinery,

(b) consideration is given for that grant, and

(c) S is not required to bring all of that consideration into account under this Part.

History – S. 228A substituted by FA 2008, s. 55 and Sch. 20, para. 12(2), with effect in relation to plant and machinery lease and finance leaseback transactions entered into on or after 9 October 2007 (FA 2008, Sch. 20, para. 12(12)).

In former s. 228A(2), the words "Sections 228B and 228C" substituted for the words "Sections 228B to 228D" by FA 2007, s. 30 and Sch. 5, para. 17(2), with effect from 6 December 2006, subject to the rules in Sch. 5, para. 17(5)–(9).

Former S. 228A inserted by FA 2004, s. 134(1) which applies to income tax and corporation tax chargeable in relation to periods that end on or after 17 March 2004 and which has effect on 22 July 2004.

Cross references – S. 228H: s. 228A–28G: supplementary.

FA 2004, Sch. 23: finance leasebacks: transitional provision.

Notes – FA 2004, s. 134(2) states that, in CAA 2001, s. 228A–228J, a reference to a provision in CAA 2001 includes a reference to an equivalent provision of CAA 1990 (with any necessary modification).

228B S's income or profits etc: deductions

228B(1) For the purpose of income tax or corporation tax, in calculating S's income or profits for a period of account the amount deducted in respect of amounts payable under the leaseback may not exceed the permitted maximum.

228B(2) The permitted maximum is the amount of the finance charges shown in the accounts.

228B(3) In relation to a period of account during which the leaseback terminates, the permitted maximum shall also include an amount calculated in accordance with subsection (4).

228B(4) The calculation is–

$$\text{Current Book Value} \times \frac{\text{Original Consideration}}{\text{Original Book Value}}$$

where–

"Current Book Value" means the net book value of the leased plant or machinery immediately before the termination,

"Original Consideration" means the consideration payable to S for granting B rights over the plant or machinery, and

"Original Book Value" means the net book value of the leased plant or machinery at the beginning of the leaseback.

228B(5) If the use mentioned in section 228A(2)(b) includes use by a person (other than B) who is connected with S, this section applies in relation to that person as it applies in relation to S.

History – The heading of s. 228B changed to "S's income or profits: deductions" from "Lessee's income or profits: deductions" by FA 2008, s. 55 and Sch. 20, para. 12(3)(d), with effect in relation to plant and machinery lease and finance leaseback transactions entered into on or after 9 October 2007 (FA 2008, Sch. 20, para. 12(12)).
In the heading of s. 228B, the word "etc" inserted after the word "profits" by FA 2008, s. 55 and Sch. 20, para. 13(3), with effect in relation to plant and machinery lease and finance leaseback transactions entered into on or after 12 March 2008 (FA 2008, Sch. 20, para. 13(4)).
In s. 228B(1), the word "S's" substituted for the word "the lessee's " by FA 2008, s. 55 and Sch. 22, para. 12(3)(a), with effect in relation to plant and machinery lease and finance leaseback transactions entered into on or after 9 October 2007 (FA 2008, Sch. 20, para. 12(12)).
In s. 228B(2), the words "the amount of the finance charges shown in the accounts." substituted for the words "the total of (a) finance charges shown in the accounts, and (b) depreciation, taking the value of the plant or machinery at the beginning of the leaseback to be the restricted disposal value." by FA 2008, s. 55 and Sch. 20, para. 12(3)(b), with effect in relation to plant and machinery lease and finance leaseback transactions entered into on or after 9 October 2007 (FA 2008, Sch. 20, para. 12(12)).
In s. 228B(4), the words "granting B rights over the plant or machinery" substituted for the words "entering into the relevant transaction" by FA 2008, s. 55 and Sch. 20, para. 12(3)(c), with effect in relation to plant and machinery lease and finance leaseback transactions entered into on or after 9 October 2007 (FA 2008, Sch. 20, para. 12(12)).
S. 228B(5) inserted by FA 2008, s. 55 and Sch. 20, para. 13(2), with effect in relation to plant and machinery lease and finance leaseback transactions entered into on or after 12 March 2008 (FA 2008, Sch. 20, para. 13(4)).
S. 228B inserted by FA 2004, s. 134(1) which applies to income tax and corporation tax chargeable in relation to periods that end on or after 17 March 2004 and which has effect on 22 July 2004. However, application of s. 228B is subject to transitional provisions of FA 2004, Sch. 23, para. 1, 2 and 3.

Cross references – S. 228H: s. 228A to 228G: supplementary.
FA 2004, Sch. 23, para. 1, 2 and 3: finance leasebacks: transitional provision.

Notes – FA 2004, s. 134(2) states that, in CAA 2001, s. 228A–228J, a reference to a provision in CAA 2001 includes a reference to an equivalent provision of CAA 1990 (with any necessary modification).
FA 2004, Sch. 23, para. 1(1) states that CAA 2001, s. 228B–228E (as inserted by FA 2004, s. 134) are subject to FA 2004, Sch. 23, para. 2–9 in their application in relation to existing leasebacks.

228C S's income or profits: termination of leaseback

228C(1) Subsection (2) applies where the leaseback terminates.

228C(2) For the purpose of the calculation of income tax or corporation tax, the income or profits of S from the relevant qualifying activity for the period in which the termination occurs shall be increased by an amount calculated in accordance with subsection (3).

228C(3) The calculation is–

$$\text{Original Consideration} \times \frac{\text{Current Book Value}}{\text{Original Book Value}}$$

where–

"Original Consideration" means the consideration payable to S for granting B rights over the plant or machinery,

"Current Book Value" means the net book value of the leased plant or machinery immediately before the termination, and

"Original Book Value" means the net book value of the leased plant or machinery at the beginning of the leaseback.

228C(4) In this section **"relevant qualifying activity"** means the qualifying activity for the purposes of which the leased plant or machinery was used immediately before the termination.

228C(5) Section 228B has no effect on the treatment for the purposes of income tax or corporation tax of amounts received by way of refund on the termination of a leaseback of amounts payable under it.

228C(6) In subsection (5), **"amounts received by way of refund"** includes any amount that would be so received in respect of S's interest under the leaseback if any amounts due to B (or, where appropriate, an assignee of B) under the leaseback were disregarded.

History – The heading of s. 228C changed to "S's income or profits: termination of leaseback" from "Lessee's income or profits: termination of leaseback" by FA 2008, s. 55 and Sch. 20, para. 12(4)(d), with effect in relation to plant and machinery lease and finance leaseback transactions entered into on or after 9 October 2007 (FA 2008, Sch. 20, para. 12(12)).
In s. 228C(2), the word "S" substituted for the word "the lessee" by FA 2008, s. 55 and Sch. 20, para. 12(4)(a), with effect in relation to plant and machinery lease and finance leaseback transactions entered into on or after 9 October 2007 (FA 2008, Sch. 20, para. 12(12)).
In s. 228C(3), the word "Original" substituted for the word "Net " in the formula and the definition of "Original Consideration" substituted for that of "Net Consideration" (which read as follows: ""Net Consideration" means the consideration payable to S for entering into the relevant transaction, minus the restricted disposal value") by FA 2008, s. 55 and Sch. 20, para. 12(4)(b), with effect

in relation to plant and machinery lease and finance leaseback transactions entered into on or after 9 October 2007 (FA 2008, Sch. 20, para. 12(12)).
In s. 228C(6), the word "S's" substituted for "the lessee's" and the words "B (or, where appropriate, an assignee of B)" substituted for the words "the lessor" by FA 2008, s. 55 and Sch. 20, para. 12(4)(c), with effect in relation to plant and machinery lease and finance leaseback transactions entered into on or after 9 October 2007 (FA 2008, Sch. 20, para. 12(12)).
S. 228C inserted by FA 2004, s. 134(1) which applies to income tax and corporation tax chargeable in relation to periods that end on or after 17 March 2004 and which has effect on 22 July 2004. However, application of s. 228C is subject to transitional provisions of FA 2004, Sch. 23, para. 1, 4, 5 and 6.

Cross references – S. 228H: s. 228A–228G: supplementary.
FA 2004, Sch. 23, para. 1, 4, 5, 6 and 10: finance leasebacks: transitional provision.

Notes – FA 2004, s. 134(2) states that, in CAA 2001, s. 228A–228J, a reference to a provision in CAA 2001 includes a reference to an equivalent provision of CAA 1990 (with any necessary modification).
FA 2004, Sch. 23, para. 1(1) states that CAA 2001, s. 228B–228E (as inserted by FA 2004, s. 134) are subject to FA 2004, Sch. 23, para. 2–9 in their application in relation to existing leasebacks.

228D Lessor's income or profits

228D [Omitted by FA 2008, s. 55 and Sch. 20, para. 12(5)(a).]

History – S. 228D omitted by FA 2008, s. 55 and Sch. 20, para. 12(5)(a), with effect in relation to plant and machinery lease and finance leaseback transactions entered into on or after 9 October 2007 (FA 2008, Sch. 20, para. 12(12)).

228E Lessor's income or profits: termination of leaseback

228E [Omitted by FA 2008, s. 55 and Sch. 20, para. 12(5)(b).]

History – S. 228E omitted by FA 2008, s. 55 and Sch. 20, para. 12(5)(b), with effect in relation to plant and machinery lease and finance leaseback transactions entered into on or after 9 October 2007 (FA 2008, Sch. 20, para. 12(12)).

228F Lease and finance leaseback

228F [Omitted by FA 2008, s. 55 and Sch. 20, para. 12(5)(c).]

History – S. 228F omitted by FA 2008, s. 55 and Sch. 20, para. 12(5)(c), with effect in relation to plant and machinery lease and finance leaseback transactions entered into on or after 9 October 2007 (FA 2008, Sch. 20, para. 12(12)).

228G Leaseback not accounted for as finance lease in S's accounts

228G(1) Sections 228B and 228C are subject to this section in their application in relation to a leaseback that is not accounted for as a finance lease in the accounts of S.

228G(2) Subsection (3) applies where the leaseback is accounted for as a finance lease in the accounts of a person connected with S; and in that subsection **"relevant calculation"** means the calculation of–

(a) the permitted maximum for the purposes of section 228B, or

(b) the amount by which the income or profits of S are to be increased in accordance with section 228C.

228G(3) Where an amount that falls to be used for the purposes of a relevant calculation–

(a) cannot be ascertained by reference to S's accounts because the leaseback is not accounted for as a finance lease in those accounts, but

(b) can be ascertained by reference to the connected person's accounts for one or more periods,

that amount as ascertained by reference to the connected person's accounts shall be used for the purposes of the relevant calculation.

228G(4) Subsections (5) and (6) apply in a case where the leaseback is not accounted for as a finance lease in the accounts of a person connected with S.

228G(5) Sections 228B and 228C do not apply in relation to the leaseback.

228G(6) If the term of the leaseback begins on or after 18 May 2004 then, for the purposes of income tax or corporation tax, the income or profits of S from the relevant qualifying activity for the period of account during which the term of the leaseback begins shall be increased by the consideration payable to S for granting B rights over the plant or machinery.

228G(7) For the purposes of this section the leaseback is accounted for as a finance lease in a person's accounts if–

(a) the leaseback falls, under generally accepted accounting practice, to be treated in that person's accounts as a finance lease or loan, or

(b) in a case where the leaseback is comprised in other arrangements, those arrangements fall, under generally accepted accounting practice, to be so treated.

History – The heading of s. 228G changed to "Leaseback not accounted for as finance lease in S's accounts" from "Leaseback not accounted for as finance lease in accounts of lessee" by FA 2008, s. 55 and Sch. 20, para. 12(6)(f), with effect in relation to plant and machinery lease and finance leaseback transactions entered into on or after 9 October 2007 (FA 2008, Sch. 20, para. 12(12)).
In s. 228G(1), the word "S" substituted for the word "the lessee" by FA 2008, s. 55 and Sch. 20, para. 12(6)(a), with effect in relation to plant and machinery lease and finance leaseback transactions entered into on or after 9 October 2007 (FA 2008, Sch. 20, para. 12(12)).
In s. 228G(2), the word "S" substituted for the word "the lessee" (in both places) by FA 2008, s. 55 and Sch. 20, para. 12(6)(b), with effect in relation to plant and machinery lease and finance leaseback transactions entered into on or after 9 October 2007 (FA 2008, Sch. 20, para. 12(12)).

In s. 228G(3), the word "S's" substituted for the word "the lessee's" by FA 2008, s. 55 and Sch. 20, para. 12(6)(c), with effect in relation to plant and machinery lease and finance leaseback transactions entered into on or after 9 October 2007 (FA 2008, Sch. 20, para. 12(12)).
In s. 228G(4), the word "S" substituted for the word "the lessee" by FA 2008, s. 55 and Sch. 20, para. 12(6)(d), with effect in relation to plant and machinery lease and finance leaseback transactions entered into on or after 9 October 2007 (FA 2008, Sch. 20, para. 12(12)).
In s. 228G(6), the words "increased by the consideration payable to S for granting B rights over the plant or machinery" substituted for the words "increased by the net consideration for the purposes of section 228C(3) (in the case of a sale and finance leaseback), or the consideration referred to in section 228F(6)(b)(in the case of a lease and finance leaseback)" by FA 2008, s. 55 and Sch. 20, para. 12(6)(e), with effect in relation to plant and machinery lease and finance leaseback transactions entered into on or after 9 October 2007 (FA 2008, Sch. 20, para. 12(12)).
S. 228G inserted by FA 2004, s. 134 which applies to income tax and corporation tax chargeable in relation to periods that end on or after 17 March 2004 and which has effect on 22 July 2004.

Cross references – S. 228H: s. 228A–228G: supplementary.

Notes – FA 2004, s. 134(2) states that, in CAA 2001, s. 228A–228J, a reference to a provision in CAA 2001 includes a reference to an equivalent provision of CAA 1990 (with any necessary modification).

228H Sections 228A to 228G: supplementary

228H(1) In sections 228A to 228G–

"consideration" does not include rentals;

the **"net book value"** of leased plant or machinery means the book value of the plant or machinery having regard to any relevant entry in S's accounts, but–

(a) also having regard to depreciation up to the time in question, and

(b) disregarding any revaluation gains or losses and any impairments;

"S" does not include an assignee of S;

"termination" in relation to a leaseback includes–

(a) the assignment of S's interest,

(b) the making of any arrangements (apart from an assignment of S's interest) under which a person other than S becomes liable to make some or all payments under the leaseback, and

(c) a variation as a result of which the leaseback ceases to be a finance lease.

228H(1A) For the purposes of sections 228A to 228G, references to consideration given (or payable to S) for the grant to B of rights over the plant or machinery do not include–

(a) rentals payable under that grant, or

(b) any relevant capital payment (within the meaning of section 890 of CTA 2010 or section 809ZA of ITA 2007) to which either of those sections applies.

228H(1B) In relation to a case where some but not all of the consideration mentioned in subsection (1A) falls within paragraph (b) of that subsection, sections 228B to 228G or section 228J have effect subject to such modifications as are just and reasonable.

228H(2) In a case where accounts drawn up are not correct accounts, or no accounts are drawn up–

(a) the provisions of sections 228A to 228G apply as if correct accounts had been drawn up, and

(b) amounts referred to in any of those sections as shown in accounts are those that would have been shown in correct accounts.

228H(3) In a case where accounts are drawn up in reliance upon amounts derived from an earlier period of account for which correct accounts were not drawn up, or no accounts were drawn up, amounts referred to in sections 228A to 228G as shown in the accounts for the later period are those that would have been shown if correct accounts had been drawn up for the earlier period.

228H(4) In subsections (2) and (3) **"correct accounts"** means accounts drawn up in accordance with generally accepted accounting practice.

History – In s. 228H(1), the following amendments made by FA 2008, s. 55 and Sch. 20, para. 12(8), with effect in relation to plant and machinery lease and finance leaseback transactions entered into on or after 9 October 2007 (FA 2008, Sch. 20, para. 12(12)):

- definition of "consideration" inserted;
- definition of "lessee" (which read "lessee does not include a person who is lessee by way of an assignment") omitted;
- in the definition of "net book value", the word "S's" substituted for the word "the lessee's";
- definition of "restricted disposal value" (which read "restricted disposal value means the disposal value under section 222") omitted;
- definition of "S" inserted; and
- in the definition of "termination", the words "(except in section 228E)", which followed the words "a leaseback includes", omitted and the word "S's" and "S" substituted for the words "the lessee's" (in both places) and "S" respectively.

In s. 228H(1A), the words "section 890 of CTA 2010" substituted for "section 785B of ICTA" by CTA 2010, s. 1177 and Sch. 1, para. 345, with effect for corporation tax purposes for accounting periods ending on or after 1 April 2010, and for income tax and capital gains tax purposes for the tax year 2010–11 and subsequent tax years.
S. 228H(1A) inserted by FA 2008, s. 55 and Sch. 20, para. 12(9), with effect in relation to plant and machinery lease and finance leaseback transactions entered into on or after 9 October 2007 (FA 2008, Sch. 20, para. 12(12)).
S. 228H(1B) inserted by FA 2008, s. 55 and Sch. 20, para. 12(9), with effect in relation to plant and machinery lease and finance leaseback transactions entered into on or after 9 October 2007 (FA 2008, Sch. 20, para. 12(12)).
S. 228H inserted by FA 2004, s. 134(1) which applies to income tax and corporation tax chargeable in relation to periods that end on or after 17 March 2004 and which has effect on 22 July 2004.

Cross references – FA 2004, Sch. 23, para. 1 and 10: finance leasebacks: transitional provision.

Notes – FA 2004, s. 134(2) states that, in CAA 2001, s. 228A–228J, a reference to a provision in CAA 2001 includes a reference to an equivalent provision of CAA 1990 (with any necessary modification).

228J Plant or machinery subject to further operating lease

228J(1) This section applies where–

(a) plant or machinery is the subject of–

(i) a sale and finance leaseback, or

(ii) a lease and finance leaseback, and

(b) some or all of the plant or machinery becomes, while the subject of the leaseback, also the subject of a lease in relation to which the following conditions are met–

(i) the term of the lease begins on or after 18 May 2004;

(ii) S, or a person connected with S, is the lessee under the lease;

(iii) the lease is not accounted for as a finance lease in the accounts of the lessee.

228J(2) For the purpose of income tax or corporation tax, in calculating the lessee's income or profits for a period of account the amount deducted in respect of amounts payable under the operating lease shall not exceed the relevant amount.

228J(3) Subsections (4) and (5) apply in relation to the calculation of the lessor's income or profits for a period of account for the purpose of income tax or corporation tax.

228J(4) Where–

(a) an amount receivable in respect of the lessor's interest under the operating lease falls to be taken into account in that calculation, and

(b) that amount is reduced by an amount due to the lessee under the operating lease,

that reduction shall be disregarded when taking the amount receivable into account.

228J(5) The amounts receivable in respect of the lessor's interest under the operating lease that fall to be taken into account in that calculation may be disregarded to the extent that they exceed the relevant amount (whether or not subsection (4) applies).

228J(6) Where only some of the plant or machinery is the subject of the operating lease, subsections (2) to (5) shall apply subject to such apportionments as may be just and reasonable.

228J(7) For the purposes of this section a lease is accounted for as a finance lease in a person's accounts if–

(a) the lease falls, under generally accepted accounting practice, to be treated in that person's accounts as a finance lease or loan, or

(b) in a case where the lease is comprised in other arrangements, those arrangements fall, under generally accepted accounting practice, to be so treated.

228J(8) In this section–

"lease and finance leaseback" has the meaning given in section 228A;

"lessee" means the lessee under the operating lease;

"lessor" means the lessor under the operating lease;

"operating lease" means the lease referred to in subsection (1)(b);

"relevant amount" means an amount equal to the permitted maximum under section 228B as it applies in relation to the leaseback.

History – In s. 228J(8), in the definition of "lease and finance leaseback", the words "section 228A" substituted for the words "section 228F" by FA 2008, s. 55 and Sch. 20, para. 12(10), with effect in relation to plant and machinery lease and finance leaseback transactions entered into on or after 9 October 2007 (FA 2008, Sch. 20, para. 12(12)).

S. 228J inserted by FA 2004, s. 134(1) which applies to income tax and corporation tax chargeable in relation to periods that end on or after 17 March 2004 and which has effect on 22 July 2004.

Cross references – FA 2004, Sch. 23: finance leasebacks: transitional provision.

Notes – FA 2004, s. 134(2) states that, in CAA 2001, s. 228A–228J, a reference to a provision in CAA 2001 includes a reference to an equivalent provision of CAA 1990 (with any necessary modification).

DISPOSAL OF PLANT OR MACHINERY SUBJECT TO LEASE WHERE INCOME RETAINED

228K Disposal of plant or machinery subject to lease where income retained

228K(1) This section applies for corporation tax purposes if–

(a) on any day ("the relevant day") a person ("the lessor") carries on a business of leasing plant or machinery (the "leasing business"),

(b) on the relevant day the lessor sells or otherwise disposes of any relevant plant or machinery subject to a lease to another person,

(c) the lessor remains entitled immediately after the disposal to some or all of the rentals under the lease in respect of the plant or machinery which are payable on or after the relevant day, and

(d) the lessor is required to bring a disposal value of the plant or machinery into account under this Part.

228K(2) The disposal value to be brought into account is determined as follows.

228K(3) If the amount or value of the consideration for the disposal exceeds the limit that would otherwise be imposed on the amount of the disposal value by section 62 (general limit) or 239 (limit on disposal value where additional VAT rebate)–

(a) that limit is not to apply, and

(b) the whole of the amount or value of the consideration for the disposal is to be the disposal value to be brought into account.

228K(4) In any other case, the disposal value to be brought into account is the sum of–

(a) the amount or value of the consideration for the disposal, and

(b) the value of the rentals under the lease in respect of the plant or machinery (see subsections (7) and (8)) which are payable on or after the relevant day and to which the lessor remains entitled immediately after the disposal,

but subject to the limit imposed on the amount of the disposal value by section 62 or 239.

228K(5) If–

(a) any of the rentals under the lease are receivable by the lessor on or after the relevant day, and

(b) the value of any of those rentals is represented in the amount of the disposal value under subsection (4)(b),

the amount of those rentals that is equal to their value as so represented is left out of account in calculating the income of the lessor's leasing business for corporation tax purposes.

228K(6) If, in determining under subsection (5) the amount of any rental to be so left out of account, it is necessary to apportion the amount of the rental, the apportionment is to be made on a just and reasonable basis.

228K(7) For the purposes of this section, the value of any rentals under the lease in respect of the plant or machinery is taken to be the amount of the net present value of the rentals (see section 228L).

228K(8) If any land or other asset which is not plant or machinery is subject to the lease, the value of any rentals under the lease in respect of the plant or machinery is taken to be so much of the amount of the net present value of the rentals as, on a just and reasonable basis, relates to the plant or machinery.

228K(9) This section is supplemented by–

(a) section 228L (which provides rules for determining the net present value of the rentals), and

(b) section 228M (which defines other expressions used in this section).

History – S. 228K inserted by FA 2006, s. 84(3), with effect in relation to any disposal made on or after 5 December 2005. But any rentals that are receivable by the lessor before 22 March 2006 are to be left out of account in calculating the income of the lessor's leasing business for corporation tax purposes (FA 2006, s. 84(5), (6)).

228L Determining the net present value of the rentals for purposes of s. 228K

228L(1) For the purposes of section 228K, the amount of the net present value of the rentals is calculated as follows–

Step 1

Find the amount ("RI") of each rental payment–

(a) which is payable at any time during the term of the lease, and

(b) which is payable on or after the relevant day.

Step 2

For each rental payment find the day ("the payment day") on which it becomes payable.

Step 3

For each rental payment find the number of days in the period ("P") which–

(a) begins with the relevant day, and

(b) ends with the payment day.

Step 4

Calculate the net present value of each payment ("NPVRI") by applying the following formula–

$$\frac{RI}{(1+T)^i}$$

where–

T is the temporal discount rate, and

^{i} is the number of days in P divided by 365.

Step 5

Add together each amount of NPVRI determined under step 4.

228L(2) For the purposes of this section the **"term"** of a lease has the meaning given in Chapter 6A of this Part.

228L(3) For the purposes of this section the "temporal discount rate" is 3.5% or such other rate as may be specified by regulations made by the Treasury.

228L(4) The regulations may make such provision as is mentioned in subsection (3)(b) to (f) of section 178 of FA 1989 (power of Treasury to set rates of interest).

228L(5) Subsection (5) of that section (power of Commissioners to specify rate by order in certain circumstances) applies in relation to regulations under this section as it applies in relation to regulations under that section.

History – S. 228L inserted by FA 2006, s. 84(3), with effect in relation to any disposal made on or after 5 December 2005. But any rentals that are receivable by the lessor before 22 March 2006 are to be left out of account in calculating the income of the lessor's leasing business for corporation tax purposes (FA 2006, s. 84(5), (6)).

228M Other definitions for the purposes of s. 228K

228M(1) This section applies for the purposes of section 228K.

228M(2) **"Business of leasing plant or machinery"**–

(a) has the same meaning as in Chapter 3 of Part 9 of CTA 2010 (if the business is carried on otherwise than in partnership), or

(b) has the same meaning as in Chapter 4 of that Part (if the business is carried on in partnership).

228M(3) **"Lease"** includes–

(a) an underlease, sublease, tenancy or licence, and

(b) an agreement for any of those things.

228M(4) **"Relevant plant or machinery"**, in relation to a business of leasing plant or machinery, means plant or machinery on whose provision expenditure is incurred wholly or partly for the purposes of the business.

History – In s. 228M(2)(a), the words "Chapter 3 of Part 9 of CTA 2010" substituted for "Part 2 of Schedule 10 to FA 2006 (sale etc of lessor companies etc)" by CTA 2010, s. 1177 and Sch. 1, para. 346(a), with effect for corporation tax purposes for accounting periods ending on or after 1 April 2010, and for income tax and capital gains tax purposes for the tax year 2010–11 and subsequent tax years. In s. 228M(2)(b), the words "Chapter 4 of that Part" substituted for "Part 3 of that Schedule" by CTA 2010, s. 1177 and Sch. 1, para. 346(b), with effect for corporation tax purposes for accounting periods ending on or after 1 April 2010, and for income tax and capital gains tax purposes for the tax year 2010–11 and subsequent tax years.
S. 228M inserted by FA 2006, s. 84(3), with effect in relation to any disposal made on or after 5 December 2005. But any rentals that are receivable by the lessor before 22 March 2006 are to be left out of account in calculating the income of the lessor's leasing business for corporation tax purposes (FA 2006, s. 84(5), (6)).

RESTRICTION OF QUALIFYING EXPENDITURE IN CASE OF CERTAIN LEASED ASSETS

History – Heading and s. 228MA–228MC inserted by FA 2010, s. 27 and Sch. 5, para. 1(1), with effect in relation to capital expenditure incurred on or after 9 December 2009.

228MA Restriction of qualifying expenditure

228MA(1) This section applies where capital expenditure is incurred on the provision of plant or machinery ("the asset") and at the time the expenditure is incurred–

(a) the asset is leased or arrangements exist under which it is to be leased, and

(b) arrangements have been entered into in relation to payments under the lease that have the effect of reducing the value of the asset to the lessor ("V").

228MA(2) For the purposes of capital allowances the lessor's qualifying expenditure on the asset is restricted to V.

228MA(3) The value of the asset to the lessor is given by–

$$V = VI + VR$$

where –

VI is the present value of the lessor's income from the asset, and

VR is the present value of the residual value of the asset reduced by the amount of any rental rebate.

228MA(4) For this purpose–

(a) the lessor's income from the asset is the total of all the amounts that–

(i) have been received by the lessor, or it is reasonable to expect the lessor will receive, in connection with the lease, and

(ii) have been brought into account by the lessor, or it is reasonable to expect the lessor will bring into account, as income in computing profits chargeable to tax, and

(b) the residual value of the asset is what it is reasonable to expect will be the market value of the lessor's interest in the asset immediately after the termination of the lease.

228MA(5) In determining the lessor's income from the asset, exclude–

(a) disposal receipts brought, or to be brought, into account under Part 2, and

(b) so much of any amount as represents charges for services or qualifying UK or foreign tax (within the meaning of section 70YE) to be paid by the lessor.

228MA(6) Where capital expenditure has previously been incurred by the lessor on the provision of the asset, the reference in subsection (2) to the lessor's qualifying expenditure on the asset is to be read as a reference to the total amount of the lessor's qualifying expenditure on the asset.

228MA(7) The following provisions supplement this section–

(a) section 228MB provides for the calculation of "present value", and

(b) section 228MC defines what is meant by a rental rebate.

228MA(8) In this section and sections 228MB and 228MC **"lease"** includes any arrangements which provide for plant or machinery to be leased or otherwise made available by a person ("the lessor") to another person ("the lessee").

History – S. 228MA inserted by FA 2010, s. 27 and Sch. 5, para. 1(1), with effect in relation to capital expenditure incurred on or after 9 December 2009.

228MB Calculation of present value

228MB(1) For the purposes of section 228MA the **"present value"** of an amount is to be calculated by using the interest rate implicit in the lease.

228MB(2) The general rule is that the interest rate implicit in the lease is the interest rate that would apply in accordance with normal commercial criteria, including, in particular, generally accepted accounting practice (where applicable).

228MB(3) If the interest rate implicit in the lease cannot be determined in accordance with subsection (2), it is taken to be 1% above LIBOR.

228MB(4) For this purpose–

(a) **LIBOR** means the London interbank offered rate on the relevant day for deposits for a term of 12 months in the relevant currency,

(b) **the relevant day** is the day on which the lease was entered into (or if that was not a business day, the first business day after that day), and

(c) **the relevant currency** is the currency in which rentals under the lease are payable.

History – S. 228MB inserted by FA 2010, s. 27 and Sch. 5, para. 1(1), with effect in relation to capital expenditure incurred on or after 9 December 2009.

228MC Rental rebate

228MC(1) For the purposes of section 228MA **"rental rebate"** means any sum payable to the lessee that is calculated by reference to the termination value of the asset.

228MC(2) The general rule is that the termination value of an asset is the value of the asset at or about the time when the lease terminates.

228MC(3) Calculation by reference to the termination value includes calculation by reference to any one or more of–

(a) the proceeds of sale, if the asset is sold,

(b) any insurance proceeds, compensation or similar sums in respect of the asset, and

(c) an estimate of the market value of the asset.

228MC(4) Calculation by reference to the termination value also includes–

(a) determination in a way which, or by reference to factors or criteria which, might reasonably be expected to produce a broadly similar result to calculation by reference to the termination value, or

(b) any other form of calculation indirectly by reference to the termination value.

History – S. 228MC inserted by FA 2010, s. 27 and Sch. 5, para. 1(1), with effect in relation to capital expenditure incurred on or after 9 December 2009.

MISCELLANEOUS AND SUPPLEMENTARY

229 Hire-purchase etc.

229(1) This section applies if–

(a) a person carrying on a qualifying activity incurs capital expenditure on the provision of plant or machinery for the purposes of the qualifying activity, and

(b) the expenditure is incurred under a contract providing that the person shall or may become the owner of the plant or machinery on the performance of the contract.

229(2) If–

(a) the person assigns the benefit of the contract to another before the plant or machinery is brought into use, and

(b) the circumstances are such that allowances to the assignee fall to be restricted under this Chapter,

section 68(3) (disposal value where person ceases to be entitled to benefit of contract before plant or machinery brought into use) does not apply.

229(3) If the expenditure is incurred on the provision of plant or machinery for leasing under a finance lease–

(a) section 67(3) (expenditure due to be incurred under contract treated as incurred when plant or machinery brought into use), and

(b) section 68 (disposal values where person ceases to be entitled to benefit of contract),

do not apply.

229(4) Subsection (5) applies if–

(a) a person is treated under section 67(4) as ceasing to own plant or machinery, and

(b) as a result of subsection (2) or (3), section 68(3) or (as the case may be) section 68 does not apply.

229(5) If this subsection applies–

(a) the disposal value is the total of–

(i) any relevant capital sums, and

(ii) any capital expenditure that the person would have incurred if he had wholly performed the contract, but

(b) the person is to be treated, for the purpose only of bringing the disposal value into account, as having incurred the capital expenditure mentioned in paragraph (a)(ii) in the relevant chargeable period.

229(6) **"Relevant capital sums"** means capital sums that the person receives or is entitled to receive by way of consideration, compensation, damages or insurance money in respect of–

(a) his rights under the contract, or

(b) the plant or machinery.

229(7) The relevant chargeable period, for the purposes of subsection (5)(b), is the chargeable period in which the person is treated under section 67(4) as ceasing to own the plant or machinery.

Origin – S. 229(1): Drafting.

CAA 2001

S. 229(2): CAA 1990, s. 25(6), and see Rewrite note below.
S. 229(3): CAA 1990, s. 60(2A).
S. 229(4)–(7): CAA 1990, s. 25(6), and see Rewrite note below.

Rewrite: Changes in Law – Explanatory Notes, Annex 1, Change 27: In anti-avoidance cases, the assignee's qualifying expenditure may, depending on the circumstances, be limited to the disposal value brought into account by the assignor. S. 229 is designed to protect the assignee in an anti-avoidance context from an unduly depressed disposal value, by having the disposal value include the capital expenditure that will be incurred under the contract if it is wholly performed. Accordingly, s. 229 leaves the assignor in the same position that he/she would be in if s. 68 applied to him/her. For cases where a finance lease is not involved, s. 229 applies in any case where a person, who has not brought plant or machinery into use, assigns the benefit of a contract. Whereas if the law had not been changed then s. 229 would have applied only if the person has assigned the benefit of the contract in the chargeable period in which a first-year allowance is claimed. For cases where a finance lease is involved, s. 226 applies in any case where the finance lessor, or would be finance lessor, assigns the benefit of the contract. Whereas if the law had not been changed then s. 229 would have applied only where the assignment takes place in the chargeable period in which the expenditure is incurred.

Official publications – M06/72: CCAB press release, June 1972: availability of writing-down allowances on liquidation of supplier of plant or machinery.

HMRC Manuals – CA28700: guidance and examples on s. 229.

229A Transfer followed by hire-purchase etc: restrictions on hirer's allowances

229A(1) This section applies where–

(a) a person ("S") transfers plant or machinery to another person ("B"),

(b) at any time after the date of the transfer, the plant or machinery is available to be used by S, or a person (other than B) who is connected with S ("CS"),

(c) it is available to be so used under a contract which provides that S or CS is to or may become the owner of the plant or machinery on the performance of the contract, and

(d) S or CS incurs capital expenditure on the provision of the plant or machinery under that contract.

229A(2) No annual investment allowance or first-year allowance is to be made in respect of the expenditure of S or CS under the contract.

229A(3) The amount, if any, by which E exceeds D is to be left out of account in determining the available qualifying expenditure of S or CS.

229A(4) E is the capital expenditure of S or CS on the provision of the plant or machinery under the contract referred to in subsection (1)(c).

229A(5) If S is required to bring a disposal value into account under this Part because of the transfer referred to in subsection (1)(a), D is that disposal value.

229A(5A) D is nil if–

(a) S is not required to bring a disposal value into account under this Part because of the transfer referred to in subsection (1)(a), and

(b) at any time before that transfer S or a linked person became owner of the plant or machinery without incurring either capital expenditure or qualifying revenue expenditure on its provision.

229A(6) Otherwise, D is whichever of the following is the smallest–

(a) the market value of the plant or machinery;

(b) if S incurred capital expenditure on the provision of the plant or machinery before the transfer referred to in subsection (1)(a), the amount of that expenditure;

(c) if a person connected with S incurred capital expenditure on the provision of the plant or machinery before that transfer, the amount of that expenditure.

229A(7) Sections 214 and 215 do not apply in relation to the contract referred to in subsection (1)(c).

229A(8) Section 70Y(3) applies to references in this section to a transfer of plant or machinery by a person.

229A(9) For the purposes of this section, a transfer involving the grant of a lease takes place on the commencement of the term of the lease.

229A(10) **"Linked person"**, in relation to plant or machinery, means a person–

(a) who owned the plant or machinery at any time before the transfer referred to in subsection (1)(a), and

(b) who was connected with S at any time between–

(i) the time when the person became owner of the plant or machinery, and

(ii) the time of the transfer referred to in subsection (1)(a).

229A(11) Expenditure on the provision of plant or machinery is **"qualifying revenue expenditure"** if it is expenditure of a revenue nature–

(a) that is at least equal to the amount of expenditure that would reasonably be expected to have been incurred on the provision of the plant or machinery in a transaction between persons dealing with each other at arm's length in the open market, or

(b) that is incurred by the manufacturer of the plant or machinery and is at least equal to the amount that it would have been reasonable to expect to have been the normal cost of manufacturing the plant or machinery.

History – S. 229A(5A) inserted by FA 2015. s. 46 and Sch. 10, para. 4(2), with effect in relation to cases where the contract referred to in s. 229A(1)(c) is entered into on or after 26 February 2015.
S. 229A(10) and (11) inserted by FA 2015. s. 46 and Sch. 10, para. 4(3), with effect in relation to cases where the contract referred to in s. 229A(1)(c) is entered into on or after 26 February 2015.
S. 229A inserted by FA 2009, s. 64 and Sch. 32, para. 21, with effect in relation to cases where the contract referred to in s. 229A(1)(c) is entered into on or after 13 November 2008.

230 Exception for manufacturers and suppliers

230(1) The restrictions in sections 217 and 218 do not apply in relation to any plant or machinery if–

(a) the relevant transaction is within section 213(1)(a) or (b),

(b) the case does not fall within section 215, and

(c) the conditions in subsection (3) are met.

230(2) [Omitted by FA 2012, s. 42 and Sch. 9, para. 7(3).]

230(3) The conditions are that–

(a) the plant or machinery has never been used before the sale or the making of the contract,

(b) S's business, or part of S's business, is the manufacture or supply of plant or machinery of that class, and

(c) the sale is effected or the contract made in the ordinary course of that business.

History – S. 230(1) substituted by FA 2012, s. 42 and Sch. 9, para. 7(2), with effect in relation to expenditure of B's that is incurred on or after 1 April 2012, for corporation tax purposes, and 6 April 2012, for income tax purposes (regardless of when the relevant transaction was entered into).
In former s. 230(1) "restriction in section 218 does" substituted for "restrictions in sections 217 and 218 do" by FA 2012, s. 41(1) with effect in relation to expenditure of B's that is incurred on or after 12 August 2011 (regardless of when the relevant transaction was entered into), but subject to transitional provisions in FA 2012, s. 41(3)–(5).
S. 230(2) omitted by FA 2012, s. 42 and Sch. 9, para. 7(3), with effect in relation to expenditure of B's that is incurred on or after 1 April 2012, for corporation tax purposes, and 6 April 2012, for income tax purposes (regardless of when the relevant transaction was entered into).

Origin – S. 230(1)–(3): CAA 1990, s. 76(5).

HMRC Manuals – CA28300: guidance on restrictions on allowances.

231 Adjustments of assessments etc.

231 All such assessments and adjustments of assessments are to be made as are necessary to give effect to this Chapter.

History – In s. 230(2), the word "section" preceding the figure "225" substituted for the words "sections 222 to" by FA 2008, s. 55 and Sch. 20, para. 6(15), with effect in the case of plant or machinery which is the subject of a sale and finance leaseback (as defined in CAA 2001, s. 221) where the date of the transaction (within the meaning of that section) is on or after 9 October 2007.

Origin – S. 231: CAA 1990, s. 76(5) (part).

232 Meaning of connected person

232(1) For the purposes of this Chapter one person is to be treated as connected with another if–

(a) they would be treated as connected under section 575, or

(b) they are to be treated as connected under subsection (2).

232(2) If–

(a) a public authority has at any time acquired plant or machinery from another public authority otherwise than by purchase, and

(b) it is directly or indirectly as a consequence of having been leased under a finance lease that the plant or machinery is available for any use to which it is put,

the authority from whom the plant or machinery was acquired is to be treated, in relation to that plant or machinery, as connected with the acquiring authority and with every person connected with the acquiring authority.

232(3) In subsection (2), **"public authority"** includes the Crown or any government or local authority.

232(4) Subsection (2) does not apply in relation to section 219 (meaning of **"finance lease"**).

History – In s. 232(1)(a) the words "section 575" substituted for the words "section 839 of ICTA" by ITA 2007, s. 1027 and Sch. 1, para. 403, with effect from 6 April 2007.

Origin – S. 232(1): CAA 1990, s. 75(4), s. 76(6)(b), s. 76A(11) (part).
S. 232(2): CAA 1990, s. 76A(11), s. 82A(2) (part).
S. 232(3): CAA 1990, s. 76A(12) ("public authority").

S. 232(4): CAA 1990, s. 76A(11), drafting.
HMRC Manuals – CA28800: guidance on s. 232.

233 Additional VAT liabilities and rebates

233 This Chapter needs to be read with sections 241 to 245 (provision for cases where a person involved in a relevant transaction or a sale and finance leaseback incurs an additional VAT liability or receives an additional VAT rebate).
Origin – S. 233: Drafting.

Chapter 18 – Additional VAT Liabilities and Rebates

INTRODUCTION

234 Introduction

234 For the purposes of this Chapter–
(a) **"additional VAT liability"** and **"additional VAT rebate"** have the meaning given by section 547,
(b) the time when–
(i) a person incurs an additional VAT liability, or
(ii) an additional VAT rebate is made to a person,
is given by section 548, and
(c) the chargeable period in which an additional VAT liability or an additional VAT rebate accrues is given by section 549.
Origin – S. 234: Drafting.
HMRC Manuals – CA29230: guidance and example on additional VAT liabilities, etc.

ADDITIONAL VAT LIABILITY

235 Additional VAT liability treated as qualifying expenditure

235(1) This section applies if a person–
(a) has incurred qualifying expenditure (**"the original expenditure"**), and
(b) incurs an additional VAT liability in respect of the original expenditure at a time when the plant or machinery is provided for the purposes of the qualifying activity.
235(2) The additional VAT liability is to be treated as qualifying expenditure–
(a) which is incurred on the same plant or machinery as the original expenditure, and
(b) which may be taken into account in determining the person's available qualifying expenditure for the chargeable period in which the additional VAT liability accrues.
Origin – S. 235(1): CAA 1990, s. 24(1A).
S. 235(2): CAA 1990, s. 24(1A), s. 159A(3) (part).
European material – Directive 2006/112: directive on the common system of value added tax.
HMRC Manuals – CA29230: guidance on additional VAT liabilities.

236 Additional VAT liability generates first-year allowance or annual investment allowance

236(1) Subsection (2) applies if–
(a) the original expenditure was first-year qualifying expenditure, and
(b) the additional VAT liability is incurred at a time when the plant or machinery is provided for the purposes of the qualifying activity.
236(2) The additional VAT liability is to be regarded for the purposes of this Part as first-year qualifying expenditure which–
(a) is incurred on the same plant or machinery and is the same type of first-year qualifying expenditure as the original expenditure, and
(b) entitles the person incurring the liability to a first-year allowance for the chargeable period in which the liability accrues.
236(3) Subsections (3) and (4) of section 52 apply to first-year qualifying expenditure constituted by the additional VAT liability as they apply to other first-year qualifying expenditure.
236(3A) Subsection (3B) applies if–
(a) the original expenditure was AIA qualifying expenditure, and

(b) the additional VAT liability is incurred at a time when the plant or machinery is provided for the purposes of the qualifying activity.

236(3B) The additional VAT liability is to be regarded for the purposes of this Part as AIA qualifying expenditure incurred on the same plant or machinery as the original expenditure in the chargeable period in which the liability accrues.

236(3C) Section 51A(7) applies to AIA qualifying expenditure constituted by the additional VAT liability as it applies to other AIA qualifying expenditure.

236(4) This section is subject to sections 237 and 241.

History – In the heading to s. 236, the words "or annual investment allowance" inserted by FA 2008, s. 74 and Sch. 24, para. 10(3), with effect in relation to expenditure incurred on or after 1 April 2008 for corporation tax purposes and 6 April 2008 for income tax purposes.
S. 236(3A) inserted by FA 2008, s. 74 and Sch. 24, para. 10(2), with effect in relation to expenditure incurred on or after 1 April 2008 for corporation tax purposes and 6 April 2008 for income tax purposes.
S. 236(3B) inserted by FA 2008, s. 74 and Sch. 24, para. 10(2), with effect in relation to expenditure incurred on or after 1 April 2008 for corporation tax purposes and 6 April 2008 for income tax purposes.
S. 236(3C) inserted by FA 2008, s. 74 and Sch. 24, para. 10(2), with effect in relation to expenditure incurred on or after 1 April 2008 for corporation tax purposes and 6 April 2008 for income tax purposes.

Origin – S. 236(1): CAA 1990, s. 22(1A).
S. 236(2): CAA 1990, s. 22(1B), s. 159A(3) (part).
S. 236(3): CAA 1990, s. 22(1B).
S. 236(4): Drafting.

Cross references – Sch. 3, para. 46–50: additional VAT liabilities and rebates.

HMRC Manuals – CA29230: guidance on additional VAT liabilities.

237 Exceptions to section 236

237(1) An additional VAT liability is not AIA qualifying expenditure or first-year qualifying expenditure if at the time when the liability is incurred the plant or machinery is used for overseas leasing which is not protected leasing.

237(2) [Omitted by FA 2008, s. 76(5)(e).]

History – In s. 237(1), the words "AIA qualifying expenditure or" inserted by FA 2008, s. 74 and Sch. 24, para. 11, with effect in relation to expenditure incurred on or after 1 April 2008 for corporation tax purposes and 6 April 2008 for income tax purposes.
S. 237(2) omitted by FA 2008, s. 76(5)(e), with effect from 21 July 2008.

Origin – S. 237(1): CAA 1990, s. 22(6A) (part), (6B) (part), s. 46(1) (part), and see Rewrite note below.
S. 237(2): CAA 1990, s. 22(3CA) (part), s. 22B(1) (part), and see Rewrite note below.

Cross references – S. 40–43: expenditure incurred for Northern Ireland purposes by small or medium-sized enterprises.
S. 47, s. 48: expenditure of small or medium-sized enterprises in respect of companies and other businesses.
S. 105: meanings of basic terms with regards to overseas leasing.
S. 241: other circumstances, which relate to anti-avoidance, in which first-year allowances are unavailable.
ICTA 1988, s. 395: restriction of relief for terminal loss of company where arrangements exist for succession to leasing contract for plant or machinery by reference to which predecessor is eligible for first-year allowance.
FA 1998, s. 83(7) and SI 1999/2119: no claims for allowances under CAA 1990, s. 22(3CA) may be made before 27 July 1999 (the appointed day); time limit for making such a claim.
Value Added Tax Regulations 1995 (SI 1995/2518), reg. 112–116: adjustments to the deduction of input tax on capital items.

Rewrite: Changes in Law – Explanatory Notes, Annex 1, Change 28: With regards to CAA 2001, s. 237(1): CAA 1990, s. 22(1B) deems the additional VAT liability to be expenditure incurred on the provision of the plant or machinery for the purposes of the trade. But it is unclear whether s. 22(6B)(d) prevents a first-year allowance being made where the plant or machinery is leased when the additional VAT liability is incurred. The lack of clarity arises because CAA 1990, s. 22(1B) does not ascribe any actual purpose to the incurring of the imaginary expenditure. Therefore, to clarify the position, s. 237(1) prevents a first-year allowance being made when the plant or machinery is used for overseas leasing which is not protected leasing – protected leasing is defined in CAA 2001, s. 105(5). With regards to CAA 2001, s. 237(2): The wording of CAA 1990, s. 22(3CA) appears to establish that a shift of primary use from Northern Ireland to another place does not affect a person's entitlement to a first-year allowance in respect of the additional VAT liability. But, under CAA 1990, s. 22B(1) a first-year allowance, given by CAA 1990, s. 22(3CA) on the original expenditure incurred, is withdrawn where the primary use shifts to a place outside of Northern Ireland at any relevant time – relevant time is defined in CAA 1990, s. 22B(2). CAA 1990, s. 237(2) prevents a first-year allowance being made in respect of the additional VAT liability in the first place, rather than allowing it to be made and then clawing it back. With regards to change of circumstances: CAA 1990, s. 22(6B)(a) appears to prevent a first-year allowance being made in respect of an additional VAT liability incurred in the chargeable period in which the trade is permanently discontinued. But, because CAA 2001, s. 237 is silent on this point, the Revenue state that s. 237 enables first-year allowances to be made in respect of an additional VAT liability incurred in the chargeable period in which the trade is permanently discontinued.

HMRC Manuals – CA29230: guidance on additional VAT liabilities.

ADDITIONAL VAT REBATE

238 Additional VAT rebate generates disposal value

238(1) This section applies if–

(a) a person has incurred qualifying expenditure (**"the original expenditure"**),

(b) an additional VAT rebate is made to the person in respect of the original expenditure, and

(c) the person owns the plant or machinery on which the original expenditure was incurred at any time in the chargeable period in which the rebate is made.

238(2) If (apart from this section) there would not be a disposal value to be brought into account in respect of the plant or machinery for the chargeable period in which the rebate accrues, the amount of the rebate must be brought into account as a disposal value for that chargeable period.

238(3) If (apart from this section) there would be a disposal value to be brought into account in respect of the plant or machinery for the chargeable period in which the rebate accrues, the amount of the rebate must be brought into account as an addition to that disposal value.

Origin – S. 238(1): CAA 1990, s. 24(7) (part).
S. 238(2), (3): CAA 1990, s. 24(7) (part), s. 26(1)(ee), s. 159A(3) (part).

Cross references – S. 239: limit or cap on disposal value where additional VAT rebate accrues.

HMRC Manuals – CA29230: guidance and example on additional VAT rebates.

239 Limit on disposal value where additional VAT rebate

239(1) Subsection (2) applies if–

(a) a person is required to bring a disposal value into account in respect of any plant or machinery, and

(b) any additional VAT rebate or rebates has or have been made to him in respect of the original expenditure.

239(2) The amount of the disposal value is limited to the amount of the original expenditure reduced by the total of any additional VAT rebates accruing in previous chargeable periods in respect of that expenditure.

But this is subject to subsections (3) to (6).

239(3) Subsection (4) applies if the disposal value is required to be brought into account by section 238(2) (disposal value for additional VAT rebate on its own).

239(4) The amount of the disposal value to be brought into account is limited to the amount of the original expenditure reduced by the amount of any disposal values brought into account in respect of the plant or machinery as a result of any earlier event.

239(5) If–

(a) the person required to bring the disposal value into account has acquired the plant or machinery as a result of a transaction which was, or a series of transactions each of which was, between connected persons, and

(b) an additional VAT rebate has been made to any party to the transaction, or to any of the transactions,

the amount of the disposal value is limited to the greatest relevant expenditure of any of the parties.

239(6) The relevant expenditure of a party is that party's qualifying expenditure on the provision of the plant or machinery, less any additional VAT rebate made to that party.

Origin – S. 239(1): Drafting.
S. 239(2): CAA 1990, s. 26(2) (part).
S. 239(3), (4): CAA 1990, s. 26(2A), and see Rewrite note below.
S. 239(5): CAA 1990, s. 26(2) (part), (3) (part), (4) (part).
S. 239(6): CAA 1990, s. 26(2) (part).

Rewrite: Changes in Law – Explanatory Notes, Annex 1, Change 29: The words at the end of CAA 1990, s. 26(2A) state that previous additional VAT rebates should not be taken into account when operating the cap on disposal values. The consequence of this is that, in some situations where a VAT rebate accrues after the plant or machinery concerned has been disposed, a disposal value may be brought into the capital allowances computation which exceeds the total qualifying expenditure incurred. This anomaly has been removed by omitting the last words, mentioned at the start of this explanatory note, and by making small adjustments in the wording. This is the approach taken in CAA 2001, s. 239(3) and (4).

HMRC Manuals – CA29230: guidance and example on additional VAT rebates.

SHORT-LIFE ASSETS: BALANCING ALLOWANCE

240 Additional VAT liability

240(1) This section applies if a person–

(a) was entitled to a balancing allowance for the final chargeable period for a short-life asset pool for a qualifying activity,

(b) has incurred, after the end of that period, an additional VAT liability in respect of the original expenditure on the provision of the short-life asset, and

(c) has not brought the liability into account in determining the amount of the balancing allowance.

240(2) The person is entitled to a further balancing allowance, of an amount equal to the additional VAT liability, for the chargeable period of the qualifying activity in which the additional VAT liability accrues.

Origin – S. 240(1): CAA 1990, s. 37(4A) (part).
S. 240(2): CAA 1990, s. 37(4A) (part), s. 159A(3) (part).

Cross references – S. 83–89: short-life assets.

HMRC Manuals – CA29230: guidance on additional VAT liabilities.

ANTI-AVOIDANCE

241 No annual investment allowance or first-year allowance in respect of additional VAT liability

241(1) This section applies if–

(a) one person ("B") enters into a transaction with another person ("S") which is a relevant transaction for the purposes of Chapter 17 (anti-avoidance), and

(b) an annual investment allowance or a first-year allowance in respect of B's expenditure under the relevant transaction is prohibited by section 217(1).

241(2) No annual investment allowance or first-year allowance is to be made in respect of any additional VAT liability incurred by B in respect of his expenditure under the relevant transaction.

241(3) Any annual investment allowance or first-year allowance which is prohibited by subsection (2), but which has already been made, is to be withdrawn.

History – In the heading to s. 241, the words "annual investment allowance or" inserted by FA 2008, s. 74 and Sch. 24, para. 12(5), with effect in relation to expenditure incurred on or after 1 April 2008 for corporation tax purposes and 6 April 2008 for income tax purposes.
In s. 241(1)(b), the words "an annual investment allowance or" inserted by FA 2008, s. 74 and Sch. 24, para. 12(2), with effect in relation to expenditure incurred on or after 1 April 2008 for corporation tax purposes and 6 April 2008 for income tax purposes.
In s. 241(1)(b), the words "or 223(1)", which followed the words "section 217(1)", omitted by FA 2008, s. 55 and Sch. 20, para. 6(16), with effect in the case of plant or machinery which is the subject of a sale and finance leaseback (as defined in CAA 2001, s. 221) where the date of the transaction (within the meaning of that section) is on or after 9 October 2007.
In s. 241(2), the words "No annual investment allowance or first-year allowance is" substituted for the words "A first-year allowance is not" by FA 2008, s. 74 and Sch. 24, para. 12(3), with effect in relation to expenditure incurred on or after 1 April 2008 for corporation tax purposes and 6 April 2008 for income tax purposes.
In s. 241(3), the words "annual investment allowance or" inserted by FA 2008, s. 74 and Sch. 24, para. 12(4), with effect in relation to expenditure incurred on or after 1 April 2008 for corporation tax purposes and 6 April 2008 for income tax purposes.

Origin – S. 241(1)–(3): CAA 1990, s. 75(1) (part), (2) (part), (3) (part), s. 76(1) (part), s. 76A(1) (part).

Cross references – S. 213: relevant transactions: sale, hire-purchase (etc.) and assignment.

HMRC Manuals – CA29240: guidance on s. 241–246.

242 Restriction on B's qualifying expenditure: general

242(1) This section applies instead of section 218 (restriction on B's qualifying expenditure in case other than sale and finance leaseback) if–

(a) apart from this subsection, section 218 would apply, and

(b) an additional VAT liability has been incurred by, or an additional rebate has been made to, any of the persons mentioned in that section.

242(2) The amount, if any, by which E exceeds D is to be left out of account in determining B's available qualifying expenditure.

E and D are defined in subsections (3) to (6).

242(3) Except where subsection (6) applies, E is the sum of–

(a) B's expenditure under the relevant transaction, and

(b) any additional VAT liability incurred by B in respect of that expenditure.

242(4) If S is required to bring a disposal value into account under this Part because of the relevant transaction, D is that disposal value.

242(4A) D is nil if–

(a) S is not required to bring a disposal value into account under this Part because of the relevant transaction, and

(b) at any time before that transaction S or a linked person became owner of the plant or machinery without incurring either capital expenditure or qualifying revenue expenditure on its provision.

242(5) Otherwise, D is whichever of the following is the smallest–

(a) the market value of the plant or machinery;

(b) if S incurred capital expenditure on the provision of the plant or machinery, the amount of that expenditure–

  (i) increased by the amount of any additional VAT liability incurred by S in respect of that expenditure, and

  (ii) reduced by the amount of any additional VAT rebate made to S in respect of that expenditure;

(c) if a person connected with S incurred capital expenditure on the provision of the plant or machinery, the amount of that expenditure–

  (i) increased by the amount of any additional VAT liability incurred by that person in respect of that expenditure, and

(ii) reduced by the amount of any additional VAT rebate made to that person in respect of that expenditure.

242(6) If–

(a) [omitted by FA 2015, s. 46 and Sch. 10, para. 5(4)(a),]

(b) subsection (5) applies and the smallest amount under that subsection is the market value of the plant or machinery, and

(c) that value is determined inclusive of value added tax,

E is the amount of B's expenditure under the relevant transaction.

242(7) "Linked person", in relation to plant or machinery, means a person–

(a) who owned the plant or machinery at any time before the relevant transaction, and

(b) who was connected with S at any time between–

(i) the time when the person became owner of the plant or machinery, and

(ii) the time of the relevant transaction.

242(8) Expenditure on the provision of plant or machinery is **"qualifying revenue expenditure"** if it is expenditure of a revenue nature–

(a) that is at least equal to the amount of expenditure that would reasonably be expected to have been incurred on the provision of the plant or machinery in a transaction between persons dealing with each other at arm's length in the open market, or

(b) that is incurred by the manufacturer of the plant or machinery and is at least equal to the amount that it would have been reasonable to expect to have been the normal cost of manufacturing the plant or machinery.

History – S. 242(4A) inserted by FA 2015, s. 46 and Sch. 10, para. 5(2), with effect in relation to expenditure of B's that is incurred on or after 26 February 2015.

In s. 242(5), the word "Otherwise," substituted for the words "If S is not required to bring a disposal value into account under this Part because of the relevant transaction," by FA 2015, s. 46 and Sch. 10, para. 5(3), with effect in relation to expenditure of B's that is incurred on or after 26 February 2015.

S. 242(6)(a) omitted by FA 2015, s. 46 and Sch. 10, para. 5(4)(a), with effect in relation to expenditure of B's that is incurred on or after 26 February 2015.

In s. 242(6)(b), the words "subsection (5) applies and the smallest amount under that subsection" substituted for the words "the smallest amount under subsection (5)" by FA 2015, s. 46 and Sch. 10, para. 5(4)(b), with effect in relation to expenditure of B's that is incurred on or after 26 February 2015.

S. 242(7) and (8) inserted by FA 2015, s. 46 and Sch. 10, para. 5(5), with effect in relation to expenditure of B's that is incurred on or after 26 February 2015.

Origin – S. 242(1)–(4): CAA 1990, s. 75(1) (part), (2) (part), (3) (part).
S. 242(5): CAA 1990, 76(2), (2B), (4) (part).
S. 242(6): CAA 1990, s. 76(2A), (4) (part).

HMRC Manuals – CA29240: guidance on s. 241–246.

243 Restriction on B's qualifying expenditure: sale and finance leaseback

243 [Omitted by FA 2008, s. 55 and Sch. 20, para. 6(17).]

History – S. 243 omitted by FA 2008, s. 55 and Sch. 20, para. 6(17), with effect in the case of plant or machinery which is the subject of a sale and finance leaseback (as defined in CAA 2001, s. 221) where the date of the transaction (within the meaning of that section) is on or after 9 October 2007.

Origin – S. 243(1)–(5): CAA 1990, s. 75(1) (part), (2) (part), (3) (part), s. 76A(2) (part), (5) (part).
S. 243(6): CAA 1990, s. 76A(9), (10), drafting.
S. 243(7): CAA 1990, s. 76(2A), (4) (part).

Transitional – Sch. 3, para. 51: section 243(7) does not apply to expenditure incurred before 2 July 1998 if the relevant transaction is–

(a) a purchase under a contract entered into before 2 July 1997,

(b) itself a contract entered into before that date, or

(c) an assignment made before that date, or in pursuance of a contract entered into before that date.

244 B's qualifying expenditure if lessor not bearing non-compliance risk

244 An additional VAT liability is not qualifying expenditure for the purposes of this Part if–

(a) section 225 (restriction on B's qualifying expenditure if lessor not bearing compliance risk) applies, and

(b) the additional VAT liability is incurred–

(i) by B, in respect of the expenditure referred to in section 225(2)(a), or

(ii) by the lessor, in respect of the expenditure referred to in section 225(2)(b).

Origin – S. 244: CAA 1990, s. 76A(6) (part), (7) (part), (8) (part).

Transitional – Sch. 3, para. 51: section 243(7) does not apply to expenditure incurred before 2 July 1998 if the relevant transaction is–

(a) a purchase under a contract entered into before 2 July 1997,

(b) itself a contract entered into before that date, or

(c) an assignment made before that date, or in pursuance of a contract entered into before that date.

HMRC Manuals – CA29240: guidance on s. 241–246.

245 Effect of election under section 227 on additional VAT liability

245(1) This section applies if–

(a) an election is made under section 227 (sale and leaseback or sale and finance leaseback: election for special treatment), and

(b) an additional VAT liability is incurred by S in respect of the capital expenditure incurred on the provision of the plant or machinery to which the election relates.

245(2) The effect of the election is–

(a) that no allowance is to be made to S under this Act in respect of the additional VAT liability, and

(b) that the additional VAT liability must be left out of account in determining S's available qualifying expenditure for any period.

Origin – S. 245(1), (2): CAA 1990, s. 76B(3)(a) (part), (b) (part).

HMRC Manuals – CA29240: guidance on s. 241–246.

246 Miscellaneous

246(1) All such assessments and adjustments of assessments are to be made as are necessary to give effect to sections 241 to 245.

246(2) Section 232 (meaning of connected person) applies for the purposes of sections 242 and 243.

Origin – S. 246(1): CAA 1990, s. 75(5) (part).
S. 246(2): CAA 1990, s. 76A(11).

HMRC Manuals – CA29240: guidance on s. 241–246.

Chapter 19 – Giving Effect to Allowances and Charges

TRADES

247 Trades

247(1) If the qualifying activity of a person who is entitled or liable to an allowance or charge for a chargeable period is a trade, the allowance or charge is to be given effect in calculating the profits of that person's trade, by treating–

(a) the allowance as an expense of the trade, and

(b) the charge as a receipt of the trade.

247(2) See Chapter 16A for provision restricting in certain circumstances the ways in which effect may be given to an allowance by virtue of subsection (1)(a).

Prospective amendments – S. 247(1A) inserted by CTNIA 2015, s. 2 and Sch. 1, para. 9, with effect from 26 March 2015 (Royal Assent) in respect of any power to make regulations and with effect in relation to accounting periods beginning on or after the first day of the appointed financial year for other provisions (see CTNIA 2015, s. 5). See also transitional provisions at Sch. 1, para. 19–21.

History – S. 247(1) created from existing text of s. 247, and s. 247(2) inserted, by FA 2010. s. 26 and Sch. 4, para. 4, with effect where the relevant day (for the purposes of Ch. 16A) is on or after 21 July 2009.

Origin – S. 247: CAA 1990, 73(1), s. 140(2) (part), s. 144(2) (part), s. 161(2) ("chargeable period"), (5) (part).

PROPERTY BUSINESSES

248 Ordinary UK property businesses

History – In the heading to s. 248, the word "UK" inserted after "Ordinary" by FA 2011, s. 52 and Sch. 14, para. 12(11)(a), with effect in relation to chargeable periods beginning on or after 1 April 2011 (for corporation tax purposes), and in relation to chargeable periods beginning on or after 6 April 2011 (for income tax purposes).
The heading to s. 248 amended (previously "Ordinary Schedule A businesses"), by ITTOIA 2005, effective for income tax purposes for 2005–06 onwards and for corporation tax purposes for accounting periods ending after 5 April 2005.

If the qualifying activity of a person who is entitled or liable to an allowance or charge for a chargeable period is an ordinary UK property business, the allowance or charge is to be given effect in calculating the profits of that business, by treating–

(a) the allowance as an expense of that business, and

(b) the charge as a receipt of that business.

History – In s. 248, the word "UK" inserted after "ordinary" by FA 2011, s. 52 and Sch. 14, para. 12(11)(b), with effect in relation to chargeable periods beginning on or after 1 April 2011 (for corporation tax purposes), and in relation to chargeable periods beginning on or after 6 April 2011 (for income tax purposes).
In s. 248 the word "property" substituted for " Schedule A" (in both the heading and the text of the section) by ITTOIA 2005, s. 882(1) and Sch. 1, para. 546; effective for income tax purposes for 2005–06 onwards and for corporation tax purposes for accounting periods ending after 5 April 2005 (ITTOIA 2005, s. 883(1)).

Origin – S. 248: CAA 1990, s. 28A(1) (part).

Cross references – S. 16: ordinary Schedule A businesses.

249 UK furnished holiday lettings businesses

History – In the heading to s. 249, the words "UK furnished" substituted for "Furnished" by FA 2011, s. 52 and Sch. 14, para. 12(12)(a), with effect in relation to chargeable periods beginning on or after 1 April 2011 (for corporation tax purposes), and in relation to chargeable periods beginning on or after 6 April 2011 (for income tax purposes).

249(1) If the qualifying activity of a person who is entitled or liable to an allowance or charge for a chargeable period is a UK furnished holiday lettings business, the allowance or charge is to be given effect in calculating the profits of that business, by treating–

(a) the allowance as an expense of that business, and

(b) the charge as a receipt of that business.

249(2) Section 65 of CTA 2010 (letting of furnished holiday accommodation treated as trade for purposes of loss relief rules, etc.) applies to profits calculated in accordance with subsection (1).

History – In s. 249(1), the words "UK furnished" substituted for "furnished" by FA 2011, s. 52 and Sch. 14, para. 12(12)(b), with effect in relation to chargeable periods beginning on or after 1 April 2011 (for corporation tax purposes), and in relation to chargeable periods beginning on or after 6 April 2011 (for income tax purposes).

In s. 249(2), the words "Section 65 of CTA 2010" substituted for "Section 503 of ICTA" by CTA 2010, s. 1177 and Sch. 1, para. 347, with effect for corporation tax purposes for accounting periods ending on or after 1 April 2010, and for income tax and capital gains tax purposes for the tax year 2010–11 and subsequent tax years.

Origin – S. 249(1): CAA 1990, s. 29(1) (part).
S. 249(2): CAA 1990, s. 29(2) (part).

Cross references – ICTA 1988, s. 504: meaning of "commercial letting of furnished holiday accommodation".
CAA 2001, s. 17: meaning of "furnished holiday lettings business".

250 Ordinary overseas property businesses

History – In the heading to s. 250, the words "Ordinary overseas" substituted for "Overseas" by FA 2011, s. 52 and Sch. 14, para. 12(13)(a), with effect in relation to chargeable periods beginning on or after 1 April 2011 (for corporation tax purposes), and in relation to chargeable periods beginning on or after 6 April 2011 (for income tax purposes).

If the qualifying activity of a person who is entitled or liable to an allowance or charge for a chargeable period is an ordinary overseas property business, the allowance or charge is to be given effect in calculating the profits of that business, by treating–

(a) the allowance as an expense of that business, and

(b) the charge as a receipt of that business.

History – In s. 250, the words "ordinary overseas" substituted for "overseas" by FA 2011, s. 52 and Sch. 14, para. 12(13)(b), with effect in relation to chargeable periods beginning on or after 1 April 2011 (for corporation tax purposes), and in relation to chargeable periods beginning on or after 6 April 2011 (for income tax purposes).

Origin – S. 250: CAA 1990, s. 28A(1) (part), s. 161(2A).

Cross references – S. 15: qualifying activities.
S. 35: expenditure on plant or machinery for use in dwelling house not qualifying expenditure in certain cases.
ICTA 1988, s. 65A(4): Schedule D Case V income from land outside UK: income tax: meaning of "overseas property business".
ICTA 1988, s. 70A(4): Schedule D Case V income from land outside UK: corporation tax: meaning of "overseas property business".

HMRC Manuals – CA20030: guidance on overseas property businesses.

250A EEA furnished holiday lettings businesses

250A(1) If the qualifying activity of a person who is entitled or liable to an allowance or charge for a chargeable period is an EEA furnished holiday lettings business, the allowance or charge is to be given effect in calculating the profits of that business by treating–

(a) the allowance as an expense of that business, and

(b) the charge as a receipt of that business.

250A(2) Section 67A of CTA 2010 (letting of EEA furnished holiday accommodation treated as trade for purposes of loss relief rules, etc) applies to profits calculated in accordance with subsection (1).

History – S. 250A inserted by FA 2011, s. 52 and Sch. 14, para. 12(14), with effect in relation to chargeable periods beginning on or after 1 April 2011 (for corporation tax purposes), and in relation to chargeable periods beginning on or after 6 April 2011 (for income tax purposes).

ACTIVITIES ANALOGOUS TO TRADES

251 Professions and vocations

251 If the qualifying activity of a person who is entitled or liable to an allowance or charge for a chargeable period is carrying on a profession or vocation, the allowance or charge is to be given effect in calculating the profits or gains of that person's profession or vocation, by treating–

(a) the allowance as an expense of the profession or vocation, and

(b) the charge as a receipt of the profession or vocation.

Origin – CAA 1990, s. 27(1) (part), s. 140(4).

252 Mines, transport undertakings etc.

252 If the qualifying activity of a person who is entitled or liable to an allowance or charge for a chargeable period is a concern listed in section 12(4) of ITTOIA 2005 or section 39(4) of CTA 2009 (mines, transport undertakings etc.) the allowance or charge is to be given effect in calculating the profits of the concern under Chapter 2 of Part 2 of ITTOIA 2005 or, as the case may be, under Case I of Schedule D, by treating–

(a) the allowance as an expense of the concern, and

(b) the charge as a receipt of the concern.

History – In s. 252, the words "section 39(4) of CTA 2009" substituted for the words "section 55(2) of ICTA" by CTA 2009, s. 1322 and Sch. 1, para. 490, with effect for corporation tax purposes for accounting periods ending on or after 1 April 2009, and for income tax and capital gains tax purposes for the tax year 2009–10 and subsequent tax years.
In s. 252, the references to ITTOIA 2005 inserted by ITTOIA 2005, s. 882(1) and Sch. 1, para. 547; effective for income tax purposes for 2005–06 onwards and for corporation tax purposes for accounting periods ending after 5 April 2005 (ITTOIA 2005, s. 883(1)).

Origin – see Rewrite note below

Cross references – S. 15(1)(f).
ICTA 1988, s. 15(1), para. 2(2)(a): Sch. A not to apply to any profits or gains charged to tax under Sch. D by virtue of ICTA 1988, s. 55.

Rewrite: Changes in Law – Explanatory Notes, Annex 1, Change 1: ICTA 1988, s. 55(1) charges the profits of the concerns in s. 55(2) ibid. (i.e., s. 55 concerns) to tax under Schedule D Case I. The implication is that not all s. 55 concerns are trades. The change in law is introduced by CAA 2001, s. 15(1)(f). Under CAA 2001, s. 15(1)(f), any s. 55 concern is a qualifying activity. CAA 2001, s. 252 provides for giving effect to plant and machinery allowances in the case of s. 55 concerns. Hence, CAA 2001, s. 252 is a consequence of s. 15(1)(f)d.

COMPANIES WITH INVESTMENT BUSINESS

History – This heading substituted by SI 2004/2310, Schedule, para. 54(3), with effect in relation to accounting periods beginning on or after 1 April 2004 subject to the provisions of FA 2004, s. 43 and 44. The heading was previously "Investment companies".

253 Companies with investment business

History – The heading to s. 253 substituted by SI 2004/2310, Schedule, para. 54(3), with effect in relation to accounting periods beginning on or after 1 April 2004 subject to the provisions of FA 2004, s. 43 and 44. The heading was previously "Investment companies".

253(1) This section applies if the qualifying activity of a person entitled to an allowance or liable to a charge for a chargeable period is managing the investment business.

253(2) The allowance is, as far as possible, to be given effect by deducting the amount of the allowance from any income for the period of the business; and section 1233 of CTA 2009 (addition of allowances to company's expenses of management) applies only in so far as it cannot be given effect in this way.

253(3) The charge is to be given effect by treating the amount of the charge as income of the business.

253(4) Except as provided by subsections (2) and (3), the Corporation Tax Acts apply in relation to the allowance or charge as if they were required to be given effect in calculating the profits of that person's trade for the purposes of Part 3 of CTA 2009.

253(5) Corresponding allowances or charges in the case of the same plant or machinery are not to be made under this Part both under this section and in another way.

253(6) Expenditure to which this section applies is not to be taken into account otherwise than under this Part or as provided by section 1233 of CTA 2009.

253(7) This section is subject to sections 682(3) and 699(3) of CTA 2010.

History – In s. 253(1) the words "managing the investment business" substituted for the words "the management of an investment company" by SI 2004/2310, Schedule, para. 54(2), with effect in relation to accounting periods beginning on or after 1 April 2004 subject to the provisions of FA 2004, s. 43 and 44.
In s. 253(2), the words "section 1233 of CTA 2009" substituted for the words "section 75(4) of ICTA" by CTA 2009, s. 1322 and Sch. 1, para. 491(2), with effect for corporation tax purposes for accounting periods ending on or after 1 April 2009, and for income tax and capital gains tax purposes for the tax year 2009–10 and subsequent tax years.
In s. 253(4), the words "Part 3 of CTA 2009" substituted for the words "Case I of Schedule D" by CTA 2009, s. 1322 and Sch. 1, para. 491(3), with effect for corporation tax purposes for accounting periods ending on or after 1 April 2009, and for income tax and capital gains tax purposes for the tax year 2009–10 and subsequent tax years.
In s. 253(6), the words "section 1233 of CTA 2009" substituted for the words "section 75(4) of ICTA" by CTA 2009, s. 1322 and Sch. 1, para. 491(4), with effect for corporation tax purposes for accounting periods ending on or after 1 April 2009, and for income tax and capital gains tax purposes for the tax year 2009–10 and subsequent tax years.
In s. 253(7), the words "sections 682(3) and 699(3) of CTA 2010" substituted for "sections 768B(8) and 768C(11) of ICTA" by CTA 2010, s. 1177 and Sch. 1, para. 348, with effect for corporation tax purposes for accounting periods ending on or after 1 April 2010, and for income tax and capital gains tax purposes for the tax year 2010–11 and subsequent tax years.

Origin – S. 253(1): CAA 1990, s. 28(1) (part).
S. 253(2): CAA 1990, s. 28(2) (part).
S. 253(3): CAA 1990, s. 28(2) (part).
S. 253(4): CAA 1990, s. 28(3).
S. 253(5): CAA 1990, s. 28(5).
S. 253(6): CAA 1990, s. 28(6).
S. 253(7): Drafting.

Cross references – S. 15(1)(g): qualifying activities: the management of an investment company.
S. 18: management of investment companies.
ICTA 1988, s. 73: manner of making allowances and charges.
ICTA 1988, s. 75: expenses of management: investment companies.
ICTA 1988, s. 130: meaning of investment company.

ICTA 1988, s. 487(4): a credit union is not an investment company for the purposes of these provisions (although the reference to the predecessor of this section, ICTA 1970, s. 306, has not been amended to reflect the later consolidation).
ICTA 1988, s. 768B(8): change in ownership of an investment company: deduction generally.
ICTA 1988, Sch. 28A, para. 6(d): change in ownership of investment company: deductions.
FA 1993, s. 92: the basic rule: sterling to be used.

LONG–TERM BUSINESS

History – In the heading before s. 254 "long-term" substituted for "life assurance" by FA 2012, s. 146 and Sch. 16, para. 96 in relation to accounting periods beginning on or after 1 January 2013 (FA 2012, s. 148) but subject to transitional provisions in FA 2012, Sch. 17. Where an accounting period would otherwise straddle 1 January 2013, it is deemed to end on 31 December 2012 (FA 2012, s. 149).

HMRC Manuals – Guidance on life assurance business is to be found in the Life Assurance manual.

254 Introductory

254(1) Sections 255 and 256 apply if a company which is carrying on any long-term business is entitled or liable to any allowances or charges for a chargeable period in respect of plant or machinery consisting of a management asset.

254(2) In this Chapter **"management asset"** has the same meaning as in Chapter 1 of Part 12 (life assurance business).

History – In s. 254(1) "long-term business" substituted for "life assurance business" by FA 2012, s. 146 and Sch. 16, para. 97 in relation to accounting periods beginning on or after 1 January 2013 (FA 2012, s. 148) but subject to transitional provisions in FA 2012, Sch. 17. Where an accounting period would otherwise straddle 1 January 2013, it is deemed to end on 31 December 2012 (FA 2012, s. 149).

Origin – S. 254(1): ICTA 1988, s. 434D(1) (part).
S. 254(2): Drafting.

255 Apportionment of allowances and charges

255(1) This section applies if the long-term business of the company consists of–

(a) basic life assurance and general annuity business, and

(b) non-BLAGAB long-term business.

255(2) In that case–

(a) any allowance to which the company is entitled for a chargeable period in respect of a management asset, and

(b) any charge to which it is liable for a chargeable period in respect of a management asset,

must be apportioned between the businesses in accordance with Chapter 7 of Part 2 of FA 2012.

History – S. 255 substituted by FA 2012, s. 146 and Sch. 16, para. 98 in relation to accounting periods beginning on or after 1 January 2013 (FA 2012, s. 148) but subject to transitional provisions in FA 2012, Sch. 17. Where an accounting period would otherwise straddle 1 January 2013, it is deemed to end on 31 December 2012 (FA 2012, s. 149).
Former s. 255(1)–(1B) substituted for former s. 255(1) and (1A) by FA 2007, s. 38 and Sch. 7, para. 69(2), with effect for periods of account of insurance companies beginning on or after 1 January 2007, subject to the transitional provisions in FA 2007, Sch. 7, Pt. 2.
In former s. 255(1), in the definition of B, the words "(but taking that mean to be nil if it would otherwise be below nil)" inserted, and the words "This is subject to sub-paragraph (1A)." inserted by SI 2007/1031, art. 15(2), with effect from 17 April 2007, in relation to accounting periods ending on or after 31 December 2006, whenever beginning.
Former s. 255(1A) inserted by SI 2007/1031, art. 15(3), with effect from 17 April 2007, in relation to accounting periods ending on or after 31 December 2006, whenever beginning.
S. 255(2) omitted by FA 2007, s. 38 and Sch. 7, para. 69(3) and repealed by FA 2007, s. 114 and Sch. 27, Pt. 2(7), with effect for periods of account of insurance companies beginning on or after 1 January 2007, subject to the transitional provisions in FA 2007, Sch. 7, Pt. 2.
In former s. 255(3)(a), the words "section 436A of ICTA (gross roll-up business)" substituted for the words "section 441 of ICTA in respect of its overseas life assurance business" by FA 2007, s. 38 and Sch. 7, para. 69(4)(a), with effect for periods of account of insurance companies beginning on or after 1 January 2007, subject to the transitional provisions in FA 2007, Sch. 7, Pt. 2.
In former s. 255(3)(b), the words "held for the purposes of a permanent establishment outside the United Kingdom at or through which the company carries on gross roll-up business" substituted for the words "provided outside the United Kingdom for use for the management of that business" by FA 2007, s. 38 and Sch. 7, para. 69(4)(b), with effect for periods of account of insurance companies beginning on or after 1 January 2007, subject to the transitional provisions in FA 2007, Sch. 7, Pt. 2.

Origin – S. 255(1): ICTA 1988, s. 434D(4).
S. 255(2): ICTA 1988, Sch. 19AC, para. 9C.
S. 255(3): ICTA 1988, s. 434D(3).

Cross references – SI 2012/3008, reg. 4: modification of s. 255(1), with effect in relation to accounting periods beginning on or after 1 January 2013, in specified circumstances where the Corporation Tax Acts apply to the life assurance business and other long-term business carried on by a friendly society; where any part of the business of an insurance company is exempt from corporation tax as a result of a transfer of business from a friendly society, or as a result of a conversion by a friendly society to a company under Friendly Societies Act 1992, s. 91.
SI 2004/2200, reg. 10: modification of s. 255(2) for the purposes of taxation of overseas life insurance companies.
SI 2006/3271, reg. 36: modification of s. 255 for the purposes of taxation of overseas life insurance companies with effect from 31 December 2006 in relation to accounting periods ending on or after that date.
SI 2007/2145, reg. 15: modification of s. 255(1) where any part of the business of a company is business which is exempt from corporation tax under ICTA 1988, s. 460(11) or (12), s. 461(4) or (4A) or s. 461B(5) or (6A).

256 Different giving effect rules for BLAGAB

256(1) Subsection (2) applies if a company–

(a) carries on basic life assurance and general annuity business, and

(b) is charged to tax in accordance with the I – E rules in respect of that business.

256(2) If this subsection applies–

(a) any allowances (or parts of allowances) to which the company is entitled in respect of the basic life assurance and general annuity business are to be given effect by treating them for the purposes of section 76 of FA 2012 as deemed BLAGAB management expenses for the chargeable period in question, and

(b) any charges (or parts of charges) to which the company is liable in respect of that business are to be given effect by treating the company as receiving for the chargeable period in question an amount which is equal to the amount of the charges (or parts of charges) and to which the charge to corporation tax on income applies.

256(3) [Omitted by FA 2012, s. 146 and Sch. 16, para. 99(4).]

256(4) [Omitted by FA 2012, s. 146 and Sch. 16, para. 99(4).]

History – In the heading to s. 256, "BLAGAB" substituted for "different categories of business" by FA 2012, s. 146 and Sch. 16, para. 99(5) in relation to accounting periods beginning on or after 1 January 2013 (FA 2012, s. 148) but subject to transitional provisions in FA 2012, Sch. 17. Where an accounting period would otherwise straddle 1 January 2013, it is deemed to end on 31 December 2012 (FA 2012, s. 149).

In s. 256(1)(b) "in accordance with the I – E rules" substituted for "under the I minus E basis", and "that business" substituted for "its life assurance business", by FA 2012, s. 146 and Sch. 16, para. 99(2) in relation to accounting periods beginning on or after 1 January 2013 (FA 2012, s. 148) but subject to transitional provisions in FA 2012, Sch. 17. Where an accounting period would otherwise straddle 1 January 2013, it is deemed to end on 31 December 2012 (FA 2012, s. 149).

S. 256(1)(b) substituted by FA 2007, s. 39 and Sch. 8, para. 23, with effect for periods of account of insurance companies beginning on or after 1 January 2007, subject to the transitional provisions in FA 2007, Sch. 8, Pt. 2.

In s. 256(2)(a) "for the purposes of section 76 of FA 2012 as deemed BLAGAB management expenses for the chargeable period in question" substituted for the words "as expenses payable which fall to [be] brought into account at Step 3 in section 76(7) of ICTA", by FA 2012, s. 146 and Sch. 16, para. 99(3) in relation to accounting periods beginning on or after 1 January 2013 (FA 2012, s. 148) but subject to transitional provisions in FA 2012, Sch. 17. Where an accounting period would otherwise straddle 1 January 2013, it is deemed to end on 31 December 2012 (FA 2012, s. 149).

In s. 256(2)(a) the words "expenses payable which fall to brought into account at Step 3 in section 76(7)" (the word "be" appears to have been omitted) substituted for the words "additional expenses of management within section 76" by SI 2004/2310, Schedule, para. 55(2), with effect in relation to accounting periods beginning on or after 1 April 2004 subject to the provisions of FA 2004, s. 43 and 44.

In s. 256(2)(b), the words "company as receiving for the chargeable period in question an amountwhich is equal to the amount of the charges (or parts of charges) and to which the charge to corporation tax on income applies" substituted for the words "amount of the charges (or parts of charges) as income under Case VI of Schedule D for the chargeable period in question" by CTA 2009, s. 1322 and Sch. 1, para. 492(2), with effect for corporation tax purposes for accounting periods ending on or after 1 April 2009, and for income tax and capital gains tax purposes for the tax year 2009–10 and subsequent tax years.

In s. 256(3) and (4) omitted by FA 2012, s. 146 and Sch. 16, para. 99(4) in relation to accounting periods beginning on or after 1 January 2013 (FA 2012, s. 148) but subject to transitional provisions in FA 2012, Sch. 17. Where an accounting period would otherwise straddle 1 January 2013, it is deemed to end on 31 December 2012 (FA 2012, s. 149).

In former s. 256(3), the words "section 436A of ICTA (gross roll-up business)" substituted for paragraphs (a) to (c) by FA 2007, s. 38 and Sch. 7, para. 70(2), with effect for periods of account of insurance companies beginning on or after 1 January 2007, subject to the transitional provisions in FA 2007, Sch. 7, Pt. 2.

In former s. 256(4), for the words "chargeable under section 436A of ICTA" substituted for the words "under Case VI of Schedule D" by CTA 2009, s. 1322 and Sch. 1, para. 492(3), with effect for corporation tax purposes for accounting periods ending on or after 1 April 2009, and for income tax and capital gains tax purposes for the tax year 2009–10 and subsequent tax years.

In former s. 256(4), the word "profits" substituted for the word "profit" and, in both paragraphs (a) and (b), the words "gross roll-up business" substituted for the words "any particular category of business" and the words "its gross roll-up business" substituted for the words "that category of business" by FA 2007, s. 38 and Sch. 7, para. 70(3), with effect for periods of account of insurance companies beginning on or after 1 January 2007, subject to the transitional provisions in FA 2007, Sch. 7, Pt. 2.

Origin – S. 256(1), (2): ICTA 1988, s. 434D(6) (part).
Former s. 256(3), (4): ICTA 1988, s. 434D(3) (part), (5) (part).

Cross references – ICTA 1988, s. 76: deduction of expenses of insurance companies.
SI 1998/1871, reg. 12: modification of ICTA 1988, s. 434D(5) so far as concerns individual savings account business of insurance companies.
SI 2005/2014, reg. 44: modification of s. 256 so as to make it applicable to friendly societies carrying on life insurance business (which is not entirely tax exempt).

257 Supplementary

257(1) Allowances and charges to which sections 255 and 256 apply are not to be given effect otherwise than in accordance with those sections.

257(2) Subsection (1) does not prevent any allowance which is to be given effect under those sections from being taken into account in any calculation for the purposes of–

(a) section 93(5) of FA 2012 (minimum profits test), or

(b) section 103 of FA 2012 (rules for determining policyholders' share of I – E profit).

257(3) [Omitted by FA 2007, s. 41 and Sch. 10, para. 14(8)(a) and repealed by FA 2007, s. 114 and Sch. 27, Pt. 2(10).]

History – S. 257(2)(a) and (b) substituted by FA 2012, s. 146 and Sch. 16, para. 100 in relation to accounting periods beginning on or after 1 January 2013 (FA 2012, s. 148) but subject to transitional provisions in FA 2012, Sch. 17. Where an accounting period would otherwise straddle 1 January 2013, it is deemed to end on 31 December 2012 (FA 2012, s. 149).
In former s. 257(2)(a), "FA" substituted for "the Finance Act" by FA 2009, s. 126(5)(a), with effect from 21 July 2009.
In former s. 257(2)(a), the words "life assurance trade" substituted for the words "Case I" by CTA 2009, s. 1322 and Sch. 1, para. 493, with effect for corporation tax purposes for accounting periods ending on or after 1 April 2009, and for income tax and capital gains tax purposes for the tax year 2009–10 and subsequent tax years.
Former s. 257(2)(a) and (b) substituted by FA 2007, s. 39 and Sch. 8, para. 24, with effect for periods of account of insurance companies beginning on or after 1 January 2007, subject to the transitional provisions in FA 2007, Sch. 8, Pt. 2.
S. 257(2)(b) substituted SI 2004/2310, Schedule, para. 56(2), with effect in relation to accounting periods beginning on or after 1 April 2004 subject to the provisions of FA 2004, s. 43 and 44.
S. 257(3) omitted by FA 2007, s. 41 and Sch. 10, para. 14(8)(a) and repealed by FA 2007, s. 114 and Sch. 27, Pt. 2(10), with effect in relation to periods of account beginning on or after 1 January 2007.

Origin – S. 257(1), (2): ICTA 1988, s. 434D(8) (part).
S. 257(3): Drafting.
Cross references – FA 1989, s. 82ff: life assurance.

FRIENDLY SOCIETIES

257A Apportionment of allowances and charges

257A [Has effect for certain purposes by virtue of modification to CAA 2001 made by SI 2008/1942.]

Cross references – SI 2008/1942: modifies CAA 2001 by inserting s. 257A where a friendly society carries on business other than life or endowment business in certain circumstances.

SPECIAL LEASING OF PLANT OR MACHINERY

258 Special leasing: income tax

258(1) This section applies for income tax purposes if the qualifying activity of a person entitled or liable to an allowance or charge for a chargeable period (**"the current tax year"**) is special leasing of plant or machinery.

258(2) Subject to subsection (3), the allowance is to be given effect by deducting it from the person's income for the current tax year from any qualifying activity the person has of special leasing of plant or machinery.

258(3) If the plant or machinery leased under the special leasing was not used for the whole or any part of the current tax year for the purposes of a qualifying activity carried on by the lessee–

(a) the allowance, or

(b) a proportionate part of it,

is to be given effect by deducting the allowance, or the part of the allowance, from the person's income for the current tax year from that special leasing only.

258(3A) The allowance or (as the case may be) the proportionate part of the allowance is given effect at Step 2 of the calculation in section 23 of ITA 2007.

258(4) Any charge is to be given effect by treating the charge as income to be assessed to income tax.

258(5) If the amount to be deducted from a description of income specified in subsection (2) or (3) exceeds the person's income of that description for the current tax year, the excess must be deducted from the person's income of the same description for the next tax year, and so on for subsequent tax years.

258(6) For the purposes of this section, income from special leasing of plant or machinery includes any charge treated as income under subsection (4).

258(7) In this section, references to deducting an allowance (or a part of an allowance) from income include setting it off against income.

History – In s. 258(4), the words "assessed to income tax" substituted for "taxed under Case VI of Schedule D" by ITTOIA 2005, s. 882(1) and Sch. 1, para. 548; effective for income tax purposes for 2005–06 onwards and for corporation tax purposes for accounting periods ending after 5 April 2005 (ITTOIA 2005, s. 883(1)).

Origin – S. 258: see Rewrite note below.
S. 258(1): CAA 1990, s. 141(1) (part).
S. 258(2): CAA 1990, s. 73(2) (part), s. 141(2) (part).
S. 258(3): CAA 1990, s. 27(1) (part), s. 28(1) (part), s. 28A(1) (part), s. 29(1) (part), s. 73(3) (part), s. 141(2) (part), s. 161(2A) (part).
S. 258(3A) inserted by ITA 2007, s. 1027 and Sch. 1, para. 404, with effect from 6 April 2007.
S. 258(4): CAA 1990, s. 73(2) (part).
S. 258(5): CAA 1990, s. 141(2) (part).
S. 258(6): CAA 1990, s. 83(1) ("income").
S. 258(7): CAA 1990, s. 141(2) (part).

Cross references – S. 3(4): claims for capital allowances.
S. 19: meaning of special leasing of plant or machinery.
TMA 1970, s. 42: procedure for making claims not included in tax returns.
TMA 1970, Sch. 1A, para. 4: giving effect to claims.
ICTA 1988, s. 434D: capital allowances: management assets.

Rewrite: Technical Points – Explanatory Notes, Annex 2, Note 40: Two technical points are made. (1) The extended meaning of "income" in s. 258(6), enabling balancing charges to be included as income, originates from CAA 1990, s. 83(1) which is particular to CAA 1990, Pt. II and not from CAA 1990, s. 161(2) which relates to the whole of the CAA 1990. The extended meaning given in CAA 1990, s. 161(2) is unnecessary as it has effect only in CAA 1990, Pt. II. Accordingly, the extended meaning of "income" in CAA 1990, s. 161(2) has not been incorporated elsewhere in CAA 2001. (2) It is unnecessary to incorporate the words "and tax shall be discharged or repaid accordingly", which are at the end of CAA 1990, s. 141(2)(b), into s. 258. TMA 1970, Sch. 1A, para. 4(1) provides already for a claim made otherwise than by being included in a return to be given effect by discharge or repayment of tax. This paragraph is relevant to s. 258 because s. 3(4)(a) provides that the requirement to include the claim for capital allowances in a tax return does not apply in the case of s. 258.

HMRC Manuals – CA29450: guidance on special leasing.

259 Special leasing: corporation tax (general)

259(1) This section applies for corporation tax purposes if the qualifying activity of a company entitled or liable to an allowance or charge for a chargeable period (**"the current accounting period"**) is special leasing of plant or machinery.

259(2) Subject to subsection (3), the allowance is to be given effect by deducting it from the company's income for the current accounting period from any qualifying activity it has of special leasing of plant or machinery.

259(3) If the plant or machinery leased under the special leasing was not used for the whole or any part of the current accounting period for the purposes of a qualifying activity carried on by the lessee–

(a) the allowance, or

(b) a proportionate part of it,

is to be given effect by deducting the allowance, or the part of the allowance, from the company's income for the current accounting period from that special leasing only.

259(4) Any charge is to be given effect by treating the charge as income from special leasing of plant or machinery.

Origin – S. 259(1): CAA 1990, s. 145(1) (part).
S. 259(2): CAA 1990, s. 73(2) (part), s. 145(1) (part).
S. 259(3): CAA 1990, s. 27(1) (part), s. 28(1) (part), s. 28A(1) (part), s. 29(1) (part), s. 73(3) (part), s. 145(1) (part), s. 161(2A) (part).
S. 259(4): CAA 1990, s. 73(2) (part).

Cross references – S. 19: meaning of special leasing of plant or machinery.
ICTA 1988, s. 118(1), (2): restriction of relief for partner companies.
ICTA 1988, s. 434D: capital allowances: management assets.

HMRC Manuals – CA29450: guidance and example on special leasing.

260 Special leasing: corporation tax (excess allowance)

260(1) This section applies if the amount to be deducted from a description of income specified in section 259(2) or (3) exceeds the company's income of that description for the current accounting period.

260(2) Subject to subsections (3) to (6), the excess must (if the company remains within the charge to tax) be deducted from the company's income of the same description for the next accounting period (and so on for subsequent accounting periods).

260(3) The company may, on making a claim, require the excess to be deducted from any profits–

(a) of the current accounting period, and

(b) if the company was then within the charge to tax, of any previous accounting period ending within the carry-back period.

260(4) The carry-back period is a period which–

(a) is of the same length as the current accounting period, and

(b) ends at the start of the current accounting period.

260(5) If the preceding accounting period began before the start of the carry-back period, the total amount of deductions that may be made from the profits of the preceding accounting period under–

(a) subsection (3), and

(b) any corresponding provision of the Corporation Tax Acts relating to losses,

must not exceed a part of those profits proportionate to the part of the period falling within the carry-back period.

260(6) A claim under subsection (3) must be made no later than 2 years after the end of the current accounting period.

260(7) If the deduction of the allowance (or of part of it) was subject to the restriction in section 259(3)–

(a) subsections (3) to (6), and

(b) sections 99 and 113 of CTA 2010 (group relief),

do not apply in relation to the allowance (or part of it).

CAA 2001

260(8) In this section **"profits"** has the same meaning as in Part 2 of CTA 2009 (see section 2(2) of that Act).

History – In s. 260(7)(b), the words "sections 99 and 113 of CTA 2010" substituted for "section 403 of ICTA" by CTA 2010, s. 1177 and Sch. 1, para. 349, with effect for corporation tax purposes for accounting periods ending on or after 1 April 2010.
In s. 260(8), the words "Part 2 of CTA 2009 (see section 2(2) of that Act)" substituted for the words "section 6 of ICTA (charge to corporation tax etc)" by CTA 2009, s. 1322 and Sch. 1, para. 494, with effect for corporation tax purposes for accounting periods ending on or after 1 April 2009, and for income tax and capital gains tax purposes for the tax year 2009–10 and subsequent tax years.

Origin – S. 260(1): CAA 1990, s. 145(2) (part), drafting.
S. 260(2): CAA 1990, s. 145(2) (part).
S. 260(3): CAA 1990, s. 145(3) (part).
S. 260(4), (5): CAA 1990, s. 145(4) (part).
S. 260(6): CAA 1990, s. 145(5).
S. 260(7): CAA 1990, s. 61(5).
S. 260(8): CAA 1990, s. 834(2) (part).

Cross references – ICTA 1988, s. 400: write-off of government investment.
ICTA 1988, s. 403ZB: amounts eligible for group relief: excess capital allowances.
ICTA 1988, s. 407: relationship between group relief and other relief.

HMRC Manuals – CA29450: guidance and example on special leasing.

261 Special leasing: long-term business

261 In the case of a company which is carrying on any long-term business–

(a) subsections (3) to (6) of section 260, and

(b) sections 99 and 113 of CTA 2010 (group relief),

do not apply in relation to an allowance to which the company is entitled under section 19 (special leasing of plant or machinery).

History – In the heading to s. 261 "long-term business" substituted for "life assurance business" by FA 2012, s. 146 and Sch. 16, para. 101(3) in relation to accounting periods beginning on or after 1 January 2013 (FA 2012, s. 148) but subject to transitional provisions in FA 2012, Sch. 17. Where an accounting period would otherwise straddle 1 January 2013, it is deemed to end on 31 December 2012 (FA 2012, s. 149).
In s. 261 "long-term business" substituted for "life assurance business" by FA 2012, s. 146 and Sch. 16, para. 101(2) in relation to accounting periods beginning on or after 1 January 2013 (FA 2012, s. 148) but subject to transitional provisions in FA 2012, Sch. 17. Where an accounting period would otherwise straddle 1 January 2013, it is deemed to end on 31 December 2012 (FA 2012, s. 149).
In s. 261, the words "sections 99 and 113 of CTA 2010" substituted for "section 403 of ICTA" by CTA 2010, s. 1177 and Sch. 1, para. 350, with effect for corporation tax purposes for accounting periods ending on or after 1 April 2010.

Origin – ICTA 1988, s. 434E(6).

Cross references – ICTA 1988, s. 431(2): life assurance business includes annuity business.

HMRC Manuals – CA29450: guidance and example on special leasing.

261A Special leasing: leasing partnerships

261A(1) This section applies for corporation tax purposes if–

(a) a company carries on a business in partnership with other persons in a chargeable period of the partnership,

(b) the business ("the leasing business") is, on any day in that period, a business of leasing plant or machinery,

(c) the company is entitled to an allowance under section 19 (special leasing of plant or machinery) for any chargeable period comprised (wholly or partly) in the chargeable period of the partnership, and

(d) the interest of the company in the leasing business during the chargeable period of the partnership is not determined on an allowable basis.

261A(2) Subsections (3) to (6) of section 260 do not apply in relation to the allowance.

261A(3) For the purposes of this section–

(a) **"business of leasing plant or machinery"** has the same meaning as in Chapter 4 of Part 9 of CTA 2010 (sales of lessors: leasing business carried on by a company in partnership), and

(b) section 887 of CTA 2010 applies for determining whether the interest of the company in the leasing business during the chargeable period of the partnership is determined on an allowable basis.

History – S. 261A inserted by FA 2006, s. 83(3), with effect in relation to any business carried on by a company in partnership in any accounting period of the partnership ending on or after 5 December 2005. But, in relation to any accounting period of the partnership beginning before 5 December 2005 (and ending on or after that date) the amendment has effect only if the company starts to carry on the business in partnership on or after that date, or a relevant change in the interest of the company in the business occurs on or after that date. Such a relevant change occurs at any time if:

(a) immediately before that time its interest in the business during any accounting period of the partnership is determined on an allowable basis (within the meaning given by section 785ZA of ICTA), and

(b) *immediately* after that time its interest in the business during that period is not so determined.

In s. 261A(3)(a), the words "Chapter 4 of Part 9 of CTA 2010 (sales of lessors: leasing business carried on by a company in partnership)" substituted for "Part 3 of Schedule 10 to FA 2006 (sale etc of lessor companies etc)" by CTA 2010, s. 1177 and Sch. 1, para. 351(a), with effect for corporation tax purposes for accounting periods ending on or after 1 April 2010, and for income tax and capital gains tax purposes for the tax year 2010–11 and subsequent tax years.
In s. 261A(3)(b), the words "section 887 of CTA 2010" substituted for "section 785ZA of ICTA" by CTA 2010, s. 1177 and Sch. 1, para. 351(b), with effect for corporation tax purposes for accounting periods ending on or after 1 April 2010, and for income tax and capital gains tax purposes for the tax year 2010–11 and subsequent tax years.

EMPLOYMENTS AND OFFICES

262 Employments and offices

262 If the qualifying activity of a person who is entitled or liable to an allowance or charge for a chargeable period is an employment or office, the allowance or charge is to be given effect, by treating–

(a) the allowance as a deduction from the taxable earnings from the employment or office, and

(b) the charge as earnings of the employment or office.

History – In s. 262(a), the words "a deduction from the taxable earnings from" substituted for the words "an amount to be deducted from the emoluments of" by ITEPA 2003, Sch. 6, para. 253(a) which has effect, for income tax purposes, for the tax year 2003–04 and subsequent tax years and, for corporation tax purposes, for accounting periods ending after 5 April 2003.
In s. 262(b), the word "earnings" substituted for the words "an emolument" by ITEPA 2003, Sch. 6, para. 253(b) which has effect, for income tax purposes, for the tax year 2003–04 and subsequent tax years and, for corporation tax purposes, for accounting periods ending after 5 April 2003.

Origin – CAA 1990, s. 27(1) (part), s. 140(4), and see Rewrite note below.

Cross references – S. 20: employments and offices.
ITEPA 2003, s. 7: meaning of "employment income", "general earnings" and "specific employment income"
ITEPA 2003, s. 23: calculation of "chargeable overseas earnings".
ITEPA 2003, s. 54: calculation of deemed employment payment.
ITEPA 2003, s. 218: calculation of earnings rate for a tax year.
ITEPA 2003, s. 315: limited exemption for expenses connected with certain living accommodation.
ITEPA 2003, s. 327: deductions from earnings: general.
ITEPA 2003, s. 381: taking account of other deductions.
FA 2004, s. 188–195: contributions to registered pension schemes.

Rewrite: Technical Points – Explanatory Notes, Annex 2, Note 41: A mechanical approach to rewriting parts of CAA 1990, s. 140 would appear to require an allowance to be treated as an expense of the employment and a charge to be treated as a receipt of the employment. However, the Revenue believe that the actual wording used in s. 262 fits better with the language of Sch. E and that the change in language does not result in a change in legal effect. The Revenue give two illustrations. With respect to losses (see ICTA 1988, s. 380(1)), the Inland Revenue believe that the actual wording in s. 262 clarifies the point that capital allowances can generate a loss. In the Revenue's view, expenses falling within ICTA 1988, s. 198 (s. 198 expenses) cannot generate a loss. If a mechanical approach to rewriting ICTA 1988, s. 140 had been followed then this might have led to the belief that capital allowances were s. 198 expenses and therefore the capital allowances would be unable to generate a loss. With respect to determining whether emoluments are at the rate of £8,500 a year or more for the purposes of benefits of kind (see ICTA 1988, Pt. V, Ch. II), the Revenue believe that the words "the allowance or charge is to be given effect, by treating–" in s. 262 are limiting words. By applying the reasoning adopted by the Court of Appeal in *Elliss v BP Oil Northern Ireland Refinery Ltd* [1987] BTC 38 the implication is that a charge is not treated as an emolument for all the purposes of the Tax Acts, but only for the limited purpose of giving effect to the charge.

FIRST-YEAR TAX CREDITS

262A First-year tax credits

262A Schedule A1 contains provision about the payment of first-year tax credits to companies in connection with certain first-year qualifying expenditure.

History – S. 262A inserted by FA 2008, s. 79 and Sch. 25, para. 4, with effect in relation to expenditure incurred on or after 1 April 2008.

Chapter 20 – Supplementary Provisions

Cross references – Pt. 12, Ch. 4: partnerships, successions and transfers.

PARTNERSHIPS AND SUCCESSIONS

263 Qualifying activities carried on in partnership

263(1) This section applies if–

(a) a qualifying activity has been set up and is at any time carried on in partnership

(b) there has been a change in the persons engaged in carrying on the qualifying activity, and

(c) if the qualifying activity is a trade or property business, the condition in subsection (1A) or (1B) (whichever is appropriate) is met.

263(1A) For income tax purposes, the condition is that a person carrying on the trade or property business immediately before the change continues to carry it on after the change.

263(1B) For corporation tax purposes, the condition is that a company carrying on the trade or property business in partnership immediately before the change continues to carry it on in partnership after the change.

263(2) In this section–

"the present partners" means the person or persons for the time being carrying on the qualifying activity,

"the partners at the time of the event" means the person or persons carrying on the qualifying activity at the time of the event in question,

"predecessors"–

(a) in relation to the present partners, means their predecessors in carrying on the qualifying activity, and

(b) in relation to the partners at the time of the event, means their predecessors in carrying on the qualifying activity, and

"qualifying activity"–

(a) does not include an employment or office, but

(b) includes any other activity listed in section 15(1) even if any profits or gains from it are not chargeable to tax.

263(3) Any annual investment allowance, first-year allowance or writing-down allowance under this Part is to be made to the present partners.

263(4) The amount of any allowance arising under subsection (3) is to be calculated as if–

(a) the present partners had at all times been carrying on the qualifying activity, and

(b) everything done to or by their predecessors in carrying on the qualifying activity had been done to or by the present partners.

263(5) If any event occurs which gives rise or may give rise to a balancing allowance or a balancing charge under this Part, the allowance or charge is to be made to or on the partners at the time of the event.

263(6) The amount of any allowance or charge arising under subsection (5) is to be calculated as if–

(a) the partners at the time of the event had at all times been carrying on the qualifying activity, and

(b) everything done to or by their predecessors in carrying on the qualifying activity had been done to or by the partners at the time of the event.

History – S. 263(1)(c) substituted by CTA 2009, s. 1322 and Sch. 1, para. 495(2), with effect for corporation tax purposes for accounting periods ending on or after 1 April 2009, and for income tax and capital gains tax purposes for the tax year 2009–10 and subsequent tax years.
Former s. 263(1)(c) substituted by ITTOIA 2005, s. 882(1) and Sch. 1, para. 549(2); effective for income tax purposes for 2005–06 onwards and for corporation tax purposes for accounting periods ending after 5 April 2005 (ITTOIA 2005, s. 883(1)).
Former s. 263(1)(c) substituted by FA 2001, s. 69 and Sch. 21, para. 4(1), with effect as respects allowances and charges falling to be made for chargeable periods ending, for income tax purposes, on or after 6 April 2001, and, for corporation tax purposes, on or after 1 April 2001 (but see further History note above).
S. 263(1A) and (1B) substituted for former s. 263(1A) by CTA 2009, s. 1322 and Sch. 1, para. 495(3), with effect for corporation tax purposes for accounting periods ending on or after 1 April 2009, and for income tax and capital gains tax purposes for the tax year 2009–10 and subsequent tax years.
Former s. 263(1A) inserted by ITTOIA 2005, s. 882(1) and Sch. 1, para. 549(3); effective for income tax purposes for 2005–06 onwards and for corporation tax purposes for accounting periods ending after 5 April 2005 (ITTOIA 2005, s. 883(1)).
In s. 263(3), the words "annual investment allowance," inserted by FA 2008, s. 74 and Sch. 24, para. 13, with effect in relation to expenditure incurred on or after 1 April 2008 for corporation tax purposes and 6 April 2008 for income tax purposes.

Origin – S. 263(1): CAA 1990, s. 78(3) (part), (4) (part), drafting.
S. 263(2): CAA 1990, s. 78(3) (part), (4) (part), (5) (part), s. 83(2A) (part).
S. 263(3), (4): CAA 1990, s. 78(3) (part).
S. 263(5), (6): CAA 1990, s. 78(4) (part).

Cross references – S. 266: election where predecessor and successor are connected persons.

HMRC Manuals – CA29010: guidance on s. 263.

264 Partnership using property of a partner

264(1) Subsection (2) applies if–

(a) a qualifying activity is carried on in partnership,

(b) plant or machinery is used for the purposes of the qualifying activity, and

(c) the plant or machinery is owned by one or more of the partners but is not partnership property.

264(2) The same allowances, deductions and charges are to be made under this Part in respect of the plant or machinery as would fall to be made if–

(a) the plant or machinery had at all material times been owned by all the partners and been partnership property, and

(b) everything done by or to any of the partners in relation to that plant or machinery had been done by or to all the partners.

264(3) The disposal value of plant or machinery is not required to be brought into account if–

(a) the plant or machinery is used for the purposes of a qualifying activity carried on in partnership,

(b) a sale or gift of the plant or machinery is made by one or more of the partners to one or more of the partners, and

(c) the plant or machinery continues to be used after the sale or gift for the purposes of the qualifying activity.

264(4) The references in this section to use for the purposes of a qualifying activity do not include use–

(a) as a result of a letting by the partner or partners in question to the partnership, or

(b) in consideration of the making to the partner or partners in question of any payment which may be deducted in calculating the profits of the qualifying activity.

Origin – S. 264(1), (2): CAA 1990, s. 65(1).
S. 264(3): CAA 1990, s. 65(2).
S. 264(4): CAA 1990, s. 65(3).

Cross references – ICTA 1988, s. 359: loan to buy plant or machinery.

HMRC Manuals – CA29020: guidance and example on s. 264.

265 Successions: general

265(1) This section applies if–

(a) a person (**"the successor"**) succeeds to a qualifying activity which until that time was carried on by another person (**"the predecessor"**), and

(b) if the qualifying activity is a trade or property business, the condition in subsection (1A) or (1B) (whichever is appropriate) is met.

265(1A) For income tax purposes, the condition is that no person carrying on the trade or property business immediately before the succession continues to carry it on after the succession.

265(1B) For corporation tax purposes, the condition is that no company carrying on the trade or property business in partnership immediately before the succession continues to carry it on in partnership after the succession.

265(2) Relevant property is to be treated for the purposes of this Part as if–

(a) it had been sold to the successor when the succession takes place, and

(b) the net proceeds of the sale were the market value of the property.

265(3) **"Relevant property"** means any property which–

(a) immediately before the succession, was owned by the predecessor and was either in use or provided and available for use for the purposes of the discontinued qualifying activity, and

(b) immediately after the succession, and without being sold, is either in use or provided and available for use for the purposes of the new qualifying activity.

265(4) No entitlement to an annual investment allowance or a first-year allowance arises under this section.

265(5) In this section **"qualifying activity"**–

(a) does not include an employment or office, but

(b) includes any other activity listed in section 15(1) even if any profits or gains from it are not chargeable to tax.

History – S. 265(1)(b) substituted by CTA 2009, s. 1322 and Sch. 1, para. 496(2), with effect for corporation tax purposes for accounting periods ending on or after 1 April 2009, and for income tax and capital gains tax purposes for the tax year 2009–10 and subsequent tax years.
Former s. 265(1)(b) substituted by ITTOIA 2005, s. 882(1) and Sch. 1, para. 550(2); effective for income tax purposes for 2005–06 onwards and for corporation tax purposes for accounting periods ending after 5 April 2005 (ITTOIA 2005, s. 883(1)).
S. 265(1A) and (1B) substituted for former s. 265(1A) by CTA 2009, s. 1322 and Sch. 1, para. 496(3), with effect for corporation tax purposes for accounting periods ending on or after 1 April 2009, and for income tax and capital gains tax purposes for the tax year 2009–10 and subsequent tax years.
Former s. 265(1A) inserted by ITTOIA 2005, s. 882(1) and Sch. 1, para. 550(3); effective for income tax purposes for 2005–06 onwards and for corporation tax purposes for accounting periods ending after 5 April 2005 (ITTOIA 2005, s. 883(1)).
In s. 265(4), the words "an annual investment allowance or" inserted by FA 2008, s. 74 and Sch. 24, para. 14, with effect in relation to expenditure incurred on or after 1 April 2008 for corporation tax purposes and 6 April 2008 for income tax purposes.

Origin – S. 265(1), (2): CAA 1990, s. 78(1) (part).
S. 265(3): CAA 1990, s. 78(1) (part), and see Rewrite note below.
S. 265(4): CAA 1990, s. 78(1) (part).
S. 265(5): CAA 1990, s. 78(5) (part), s. 83(2A) (part).

Cross references – S. 266(7): an election under s. 266 prevents s. 265 applying.
SI 2013/2242, art. 4: continuity of treatment in relation to any allowances or charges which relate to part of BRB (Residuary) Limited's property business transferred to London & Continental Railways Limited by a relevant transfer.

Rewrite: Changes in Law – Explanatory Notes, Annex 1, Change 30: CAA 1990, s. 78(1) requires that the property was in use, or provided and available for use, for the purposes of the discontinued trade immediately before the succession occurs. CAA 1990, s. 78 (1) does not require the predecessor to have owned the property immediately before the succession. Hence, on a literal reading of CAA 1990, s. 78(1), the successor might have been able to claim capital allowances on his/her deemed acquisition even where the predecessor has not owned the property. The change in law is made in s. 265(3), which requires the predecessor to have owned the property immediately before the succession.

HMRC Manuals – CA29030: guidance and example on s. 265.
CA29060: effect of succession by surviving spouse.

266 Election where predecessor and successor are connected persons

266(1) This section applies if a person (**"the successor"**) succeeds to a qualifying activity which was until that time carried on by another person (**"the predecessor"**) and–

CAA 2001

(a) the two persons are connected with each other,

(b) each of them is within the charge to tax on the profits of the qualifying activity, and

(c) the successor is not a dual resident investing company.

266(2) If this section applies, the predecessor and the successor may jointly elect for the provisions of section 267 to have effect.

266(3) The election may be made whether or not any plant or machinery has actually been sold or transferred.

266(4) The election must be made by notice to an officer of Revenue and Customs within 2 years after the date on which the succession takes effect.

266(5) For the purposes of this section, the predecessor and the successor are connected with each other if any of the following conditions is met–

(a) they would be treated as connected persons under section 575;

(b) one of them is a partnership and the other has the right to a share in that partnership;

(c) one of them is a body corporate and the other has control over that body;

(d) both of them are partnerships and another person has the right to a share in both of them;

(e) both of them are bodies corporate, or one of them is a partnership and the other is a body corporate, and (in either case) another person has control over both of them.

266(6) In subsection (5) any reference to a right to a share in a partnership is to be read as a reference to a right to a share of the assets or income of the partnership.

266(7) Sections 104E, 108 and 265 (disposal value in connection with special rate expenditure, effect of disposal to connected person on overseas leasing pool and general provisions about successions) do not apply if an election is made under this section (but see section 267A).

266(8) This section does not apply if section 561 applies (transfer of UK trade to a company in another member State).

History – In s. 266(4), the words "an officer of Revenue and Customs" substituted for "the Inland Revenue" by CRCA 2005, s. 50(6) and Sch. 4, para. 83(1), with effect from 18 April 2005 by virtue of SI 2005/1126, art. 2(2).
In s. 266(5)(a) the words "section 575" substituted for "section 839 of ICTA" by ITA 2007, s. 1027 and Sch. 1, para. 405, with effect from 6 April 2007.
In s. 266(7), the figure "104E" substituted for the figure "104" and the words "in connection with special rate expenditure" substituted for the words "of long-life assets" by FA 2008, s. 82 and Sch. 26, para. 12, with effect in relation expenditure incurred on or after 1 April 2008 for corporation tax purposes and 6 April 2008 for income tax purposes and in relation to long-life asset expenditure (within the meaning of CAA 2001, Pt. 2, Ch. 10) incurred before those dates but allocated to a pool in a chargeable period beginning on or after those dates. This commencement provision is subject to FA 2008, s. 83 (existing long-life asset expenditure treated as special rate expenditure) and FA 2008, Sch. 26, para. 15–17 (detailed provisions relating to sales between connected persons and savings for intra-group transfers).
In s. 266(7), at the end, the words "(but see section 267A)" inserted by FA 2006, s. 85(2), with effect in relation to any succession occurring on or after 5 December 2005.

Origin – S. 266(1): CAA 1990, s. 77(3) (part), and see Rewrite note (note 42) below.
S. 266(2): CAA 1990, s. 77(3) (part), and see Rewrite note (note 43) below.
S. 266(3): CAA 1990, s. 77(4)(a) (part).
S. 266(4): CAA 1990, s. 77(3) (part).
S. 266(5): CAA 1990, s. 77(5).
S. 266(6): CAA 1990, s. 77(6) (part).
S. 266(7): CAA 1990, s. 77(8).
S. 266(8): CAA 1990, s. 152B(10) (part).

Cross references – S. 574: meaning of control.
ICTA 1988, s. 832(3): meaning of tax.
FA 1994, Sch. 24, para. 20(8): CAA 1990, s. 77 does not apply in certain circumstances connected with the privatisation of the railways in the UK.
SI 1995/352, reg. 15, Schedules: extended time limit under CAA 1990, s. 77(3) for Lloyd' underwriters for 1994–95 only.
Broadcasting Act 1996, Sch. 7, para. 14: transfers of property etc. between BBC and successor organisations.
Greater London Authority Act 1999, Sch. 33, para. 4(8)(b): transfers from London Regional Transport or its subsidiaries to Transport for London or its subsidiaries.
Greater London Authority Act 1999, Sch. 33, para. 10(9): transfers from London Regional Transport or its subsidiaries in preparation for, or in pursuance of, a private-public partnership.

Transitional – S. 266(7) does not apply if the succession occurred before 27 July 1989.

Rewrite: Technical Points – Explanatory Notes, Annex 2, Note 42: CAA 1990, s. 77(3)(b) requires that the predecessor and the successor are subject to tax in the United Kingdom on the profits of the trade. S. 266(1)(b) does not include the words "in the United Kingdom" and relies on ICTA 1988, s. 832(3) which defines the word "tax" as either income tax or corporation tax where neither is specified. Therefore, with income tax and corporation tax being UK taxes, if a person is within the charge to tax then he/she has to be regarded as being within the charge to tax in the United Kingdom.
Explanatory Notes, Annex 2, Note 43: CAA 1990, s. 77(3) provides that the predecessor and successor may make an election by giving notice to the inspector. S. 266(2) states that the election is made jointly by the predecessor and successor. The Revenue believe that CAA 1990, s. 77(3) implies a joint election and so s. 266(2) merely makes this explicit.

HMRC Manuals – CA29040: guidance on s. 266 and 267.

Other material – ICAEW Technical Release TR 713: treatment of transfer of building by group property investment company for purposes of CAA 1990, s. 77.
Revenue guidance dated 17 August 2004 re interaction of this section with ICTA 1988, s. 785A (rent factoring of leases of plant or machinery): "A transfer of a trade within the meaning of s. 343 ICTA 1988 will not give rise to a charge under section 785A. Similarly

a transfer of an asset between connected parties as part of a succession to a qualifying activity within section 266 will not give rise to a charge under section 785A.".

267 Effect of election

267(1) If an election is made under section 266, the following provisions have effect.

267(2) For the purposes of making allowances and charges under this Part, relevant plant or machinery is treated as sold by the predecessor to the successor–

(a) when the succession takes place, and

(b) at a price which gives rise to neither a balancing allowance nor a balancing charge.

267(3) **"Relevant plant or machinery"** means any plant or machinery which–

(a) immediately before the succession, was owned by the predecessor, and was either in use or provided and available for use for the purposes of the qualifying activity, and

(b) immediately after the succession, is owned by the successor, and is either in use or provided and available for use for the purposes of the qualifying activity.

267(4) Allowances and charges are to be made under this Part to or on the successor as if everything done to or by the predecessor had been done to or by the successor.

267(5) All such assessments and adjustments of assessments are to be made as are necessary to give effect to the election.

267(6) This section is subject to section 267A.

History – S. 267(6) inserted by FA 2006, s. 85(3), with effect in relation to any succession occurring on or after 5 December 2005.

Origin – S. 267(1): CAA 1990, s. 77(4) (part).
S. 267(2), (3): CAA 1990, s. 77(4)(a) (part), and see Rewrite note below.
S. 267(4): CAA 1990, s. 77(4)(b).
S. 267(5): CAA 1990, s. 77(7).

Cross references – S. 266(7): s. 104, s. 108 and s. 265 do not apply if an election is made under s. 266.
S. 266(8): s. 266 and s. 267 do not apply if s. 561 applies.
FA 1994, Sch. 24, para. 20(8): CAA 1990, s. 77 does not apply in certain circumstances connected with the privatisation of the railways in the UK.
SI 1995/352, reg. 15, Schedules: extended time limit under CAA 1990, s. 77(3) for Lloyd's underwriters for 1994–95 only.
Broadcasting Act 1996, Sch. 7, para. 14: transfers of property etc. between BBC and successor organisations.
Greater London Authority Act 1999, Sch. 33, para. 4(8)(b): transfers from London Regional Transport or its subsidiaries to Transport for London or its subsidiaries.
Greater London Authority Act 1999, Sch. 33, para. 10(9): transfers from London Regional Transport or its subsidiaries in preparation for, or in pursuance of, a private-public partnership.

Rewrite: Changes in Law – Explanatory Notes, Annex 1, Change 31: With respect to s. 267(2), CAA 1990, s. 77(4)(a) does not state explicitly when the deemed sale of the plant and machinery occurs. To avoid contention, s. 267(2)(a) stipulates that the deemed sale occurs at the time of the succession. In the Revenue's view, it is difficult to find anything in CAA 1990, s. 77 to suggest that the deemed sale occurs at a different time. This is because CAA 1990, s. 77(4)(a)(i) and (ii) are couched in terms of the time of the succession. If a different time were possible then a different deemed selling price might be possible as well. With respect to s. 267(3), under CAA 1990, s. 77(4)(a), the plant and machinery, which is subject to the deemed sale, had to be in use for the purposes of the trade concerned. S. 267(3) extends the relevant plant and machinery to that which is provided and available for use for the purposes of the qualifying activity concerned.

HMRC Manuals – CA29040: guidance on s. 266 and 267.

Other material – ICAEW Technical Release TR 713: treatment of transfer of building by group property investment company for purposes of CAA 1990, s. 77.
Revenue guidance dated 17 August 2004 re interaction of this section with ICTA 1988, s. 785A (rent factoring of leases of plant or machinery): "A transfer of a trade within the meaning of s. 343 ICTA 1988 will not give rise to a charge under section 785A. Similarly a transfer of an asset between connected parties as part of a succession to a qualifying activity within section 266 will not give rise to a charge under section 785A.".

267A Restriction on effect of election

267A(1) This section applies for corporation tax purposes if–

(a) on any day ("the relevant day") a person ("the predecessor") carries on a business of leasing plant or machinery,

(b) on the relevant day another person ("the successor") succeeds to the business, and

(c) the predecessor and the successor make an election under section 266.

267A(2) Neither–

(a) section 266(7), nor

(b) the provisions of section 267,

have effect in relation to any plant or machinery which, in determining whether the business is a business of leasing plant or machinery on the relevant day, falls within section 387(7) of CTA 2010 (if the business is carried on otherwise than in partnership) or within section 410(6) of that Act (if the business is carried on in partnership).

267A(3) In this section **"business of leasing plant or machinery"**–

(a) has the same meaning as in Chapter 3 of Part 9 of CTA 2010 (if the business is carried on otherwise than in partnership), or

(b) has the same meaning as in Chapter 4 of that Part (if the business is carried on in partnership).

History – In s. 267A(2), the words "falls within section 387(7) of CTA 2010 (if the business is carried on otherwise than in partnership) or within section 410(6) of that Act (if the business is carried on in partnership)" substituted for "is qualifying leased plant or machinery" by FA 2011, s. 32 and Sch. 6, para. 23, with effect in relation to transfers or successions taking place on or after 23 March 2011.

In s. 267A(3)(a), the words "Chapter 3 of Part 9 of CTA 2010" substituted for "Part 2 of Schedule 10 to FA 2006 (sale etc of lessor companies etc)" by CTA 2010, s. 1177 and Sch. 1, para. 352(a), with effect for corporation tax purposes for accounting periods ending on or after 1 April 2010.

In s. 267A(3)(b), the words "Chapter 4 of that Part" substituted for "Part 3 of that Schedule" by CTA 2010, s. 1177 and Sch. 1, para. 352(b), with effect for corporation tax purposes for accounting periods ending on or after 1 April 2010.

S. 267A inserted by FA 2006, s. 85(4), with effect in relation to any succession occurring on or after 5 December 2005.

268 Successions by beneficiaries

268(1) This section applies if–

(a) a person succeeds to a qualifying activity as a beneficiary under the will or on the intestacy of a deceased person who carried on the qualifying activity,

(b) all of the persons carrying on the qualifying activity before the succession permanently cease to carry it on, and

(c) the beneficiary elects by notice to an officer of Revenue and Customs for this section to apply.

268(2) In relation to the succession and any previous succession occurring on or after the death of the deceased, relevant plant or machinery is treated as if it had been sold to the beneficiary when the succession takes place.

268(3) The net proceeds of the sale are treated as being the lesser of–

(a) the market value of the plant or machinery, and

(b) the unrelieved qualifying expenditure which would have been taken into account in calculating the amount of a balancing allowance for the appropriate chargeable period if the disposal value of the plant or machinery had been nil.

"Appropriate chargeable period" means the chargeable period in which the deceased person's qualifying activity was permanently discontinued.

268(4) **"Relevant plant or machinery"** means plant or machinery which–

(a) was previously owned by the deceased,

(b) passes to the beneficiary with the qualifying activity, and

(c) is either used or provided and available for use by the beneficiary for the purposes of the qualifying activity.

268(5) Subsections (6) and (7) apply if the beneficiary is required to bring a disposal value into account in respect of relevant plant or machinery.

268(6) The provisions limiting the amount of the disposal value of property, that is–

(a) section 62 (limit on disposal value: general), and

(b) section 239 (limit on disposal value where additional VAT rebate),

apply in relation to the beneficiary to limit the disposal value by reference to expenditure incurred by the deceased or additional VAT rebates made to the deceased.

268(7) Section 73 (limit on disposal value: software and rights to software) applies as if the previous disposal values to be taken into account in determining whether the limit under those provisions is exceeded were those of the deceased.

268(8) In this section **"qualifying activity"**–

(a) does not include an employment or office, but

(b) includes any other activity listed in section 15(1) even if any profits or gains from it are not chargeable to tax.

History – In s. 268(1), the words "an officer of Revenue and Customs" substituted for "the Inland Revenue" by CRCA 2005, s. 50(6) and Sch. 4, para. 83(1), with effect from 18 April 2005 by virtue of SI 2005/1126, art. 2(2).

S. 268(1)(b) substituted by ITTOIA 2005, s. 882(1) and Sch. 1, para. 551; effective for income tax purposes for 2005–06 onwards and for corporation tax purposes for accounting periods ending after 5 April 2005 (ITTOIA 2005, s. 883(1)).

Origin – S. 268(1): CAA 1990, s. 78(1) (part), (2) (part).
S. 268(2)–(4): CAA 1990, s. 78(2) (part).
S. 268(5)–(7): CAA 1990, s. 78(2A) (part).
S. 268(8): CAA 1990, s. 78(5) (part), s. 83(2A) (part).

Cross references – TCGA 1992, s. 41: capital loss restricted by reference to capital allowances of transferor as well as disponer where acquisition within s. 78(2).

Transitional – S. 268(6) and (7) do not apply if the election under s. 268(1)(c) was made before 6 April 1990.

HMRC Manuals – CA29050: guidance and example on s. 268.

CARS ETC

268A Meaning of 'car' and 'motor cycle'

268A(1) In this Part **"car"** means a mechanically propelled road vehicle other than–

(a) a motor cycle,

(b) a vehicle of a construction primarily suited for the conveyance of goods or burden of any description, or

(c) a vehicle of a type not commonly used as a private vehicle and unsuitable for such use.

268A(2) In this Part **"motor cycle"** has the meaning given by section 185(1) of the Road Traffic Act 1988.

History – S. 268A and the heading before it inserted by FA 2009, s. 30 and Sch. 11, para. 11, with effect in relation to expenditure incurred on or after 1 April 2009 (for corporation tax purposes) and 6 April 2009 (for income tax purposes), subject to transitional provisions in FA 2009, Sch. 11, para. 27(2) and 30–32.

268B Electrically-propelled vehicles

268B For the purposes of this Part a vehicle is electrically-propelled only if–

(a) it is propelled solely by electrical power, and

(b) that power is derived from–

(i) a source external to the vehicle, or

(ii) an electrical storage battery which is not connected to any source of power when the vehicle is in motion.

History – S. 268B inserted by FA 2009, s. 30 and Sch. 11, para. 11, with effect in relation to expenditure incurred on or after 1 April 2009 (for corporation tax purposes) and 6 April 2009 (for income tax purposes), subject to transitional provisions in FA 2009, Sch. 11, para. 27(2) and 30–32.

268C Terms relating to emissions

268C(1) In this Part **"qualifying emissions certificate"**, in relation to a vehicle, means an EC certificate of conformity, or a UK approval certificate, that specifies–

(a) in the case of a vehicle other than a bi-fuel vehicle, a CO_2 emissions figure in terms of grams per kilometre driven, or

(b) in the case of a bi-fuel vehicle, separate CO_2 emissions figures in terms of grams per kilometre driven for different fuels.

268C(2) For the purposes of this Part, in relation to a vehicle other than a bi-fuel vehicle, the applicable CO_2 emissions figure is–

(a) where the qualifying emissions certificate specifies only one CO_2 emissions figure, that figure, and

(b) where the certificate specifies more than one CO_2 emissions figure, the figure specified as the CO_2 emissions (combined) figure.

268C(3) For the purposes of this Part, in relation to a bi-fuel vehicle, the applicable CO_2 emissions figure is–

(a) where the qualifying emissions certificate specifies more than one CO_2 emissions figure in relation to each fuel, the lowest CO_2 emissions (combined) figure specified, and

(b) in any other case, the lowest CO_2 figure specified by the certificate.

268C(4) In this section–

"bi-fuel", in relation to a vehicle, means capable of being propelled by–

(a) petrol and road fuel gas, or

(b) diesel and road fuel gas;

"diesel" means any diesel fuel within the definition in Article 2 of Directive 98/70/EC of the European Parliament and of the Council;

"EC certificate of conformity" means a certificate of conformity issued by a manufacturer under any provision of the law of a member State implementing Article 6 of Council Directive 70/156/EEC, as amended;

"petrol" has the meaning given by Article 2 of Directive 98/70/ EC of the European Parliament and of the Council;

"road fuel gas" has the same meaning as in section 171(1) of ITEPA 2003;

"UK approval certificate" means a certificate issued under–

(a) section 58(1) or (4) of the Road Traffic Act 1988, or

(b) Article 31A(4) or (5) of the Road Traffic (Northern Ireland) Order 1981 (S.I. 1981/154 (N.I. 1)).

History – S. 268C inserted by FA 2009, s. 30 and Sch. 11, para. 11, with effect in relation to expenditure incurred on or after 1 April 2009 (for corporation tax purposes) and 6 April 2009 (for income tax purposes), subject to transitional provisions in FA 2009, Sch. 11, para. 27(2) and 30–32.

268D Hire cars for disabled persons

268D(1) For the purposes of this Part a car is a hire car for a disabled person if it is provided wholly or mainly for hire to, or the carriage of, disabled persons in the ordinary course of a trade.

268D(2) **"Disabled person"** means a person in receipt of–

(a) a disability living allowance under–

  (i) the Social Security Contributions and Benefits Act 1992, or

  (ii) the Social Security Contributions and Benefits (Northern Ireland) Act 1992,

  because of entitlement to the mobility component,

(aa) personal independence payment under the Welfare Reform Act 2012, or the corresponding provision having effect in Northern Ireland, because of entitlement to the mobility component,

(ab) armed forces independence payment under a scheme established under section 1 of the Armed Forces (Pensions and Compensation) Act 2004,

(b) a mobility supplement under a scheme made under the Personal Injuries (Emergency Provisions) Act 1939,

(c) a mobility supplement under an Order in Council made under section 12 of the Social Security (Miscellaneous Provisions) Act 1977, or

(d) a payment that appears to the Treasury to be similar to those mentioned in paragraphs (a) to (c) and that is specified by order made by the Treasury.

Prospective amendments – S. 268D(2)(a)(i) repealed by WRA 2012, s. 147 and Sch. 14, Pt. 9, with effect from a date to be set by order of the Secretary of State.

History – S. 268D(2)(aa) and (ab) inserted by FA 2013, s. 72(1), with effect in relation to expenditure incurred on or after 1 April 2013. S. 268D inserted by FA 2009, s. 30 and Sch. 11, para. 22, with effect in relation to expenditure incurred on or after 1 April 2009 (for corporation tax purposes) and 6 April 2009 (for income tax purposes), subject to transitional provisions in FA 2009, Sch. 11, para. 27(2) and 30–32.

268E Meaning of "assigns"

268E(1) For the purposes of this Part–

(a) a person ("A") is taken to assign the benefit of a contract, or rights under a contract, to another person ("B") whenever B becomes entitled, and A ceases to be entitled, to the benefit or rights (whether by assignment, novation, variation or replacement of the contract, by operation of law or otherwise), and

(b) references to an assignment are to be read accordingly.

268E(2) Any reference in this Part to the benefit of a contract or to rights under a contract includes a reference to part of the benefit of a contract or to part of the rights under a contract.

History – S. 268E inserted by FA 2012, s. 42 and Sch. 9, para. 8 with effect in relation to expenditure that is incurred on or after 1 April 2012, for corporation tax purposes, and 6 April 2012, for income tax purposes.

MISCELLANEOUS

269 Use of plant or machinery for business entertainment

269(1) If–

(a) a person carrying on a qualifying activity, or

(b) an employee of that person,

provides business entertainment in connection with that activity, the use of plant or machinery for providing the entertainment is to be treated as use for purposes other than those of that activity.

269(2) For the purposes of this section–

(a) **"entertainment"** includes hospitality of any kind, and

(b) the use of an asset for providing entertainment includes the use of an asset for providing anything incidental to the entertainment.

269(3) **"Business entertainment"** does not include anything provided by a person for employees unless its provision for them is incidental to its provision for others.

269(4) **"Business entertainment"** does not include the use of plant or machinery for the provision of anything by a person if–

(a) it is a function of that person's qualifying activity to provide it, and
(b) it is provided by that person in the ordinary course of that qualifying activity–
  (i) for payment, or
  (ii) free of charge with the object of advertising to the public generally.

269(5) For the purposes of this section–
(a) directors of a company, or
(b) persons engaged in the management of a company,

are to be regarded as employed by the company.

Origin – S. 269(1): ICTA 1988, s. 577(1)(c), (5) (part), (7)(b), (c) (part).
S. 269(2): ICTA 1988, s. 577(5) (part), (7)(a) (part).
S. 269(3): ICTA 1988, s. 577(5) (part), (7)(c) (part).
S. 269(4): ICTA 1988, s. 577(10) (part).
S. 269(5): ICTA 1988, s. 577(7)(c) (part).

270 Shares in plant or machinery

270(1) This Part applies in relation to a share in plant or machinery as it applies (under section 571) in relation to a part of plant or machinery.

270(2) For the purposes of this Part, a share in plant or machinery is treated as used for the purposes of a qualifying activity so long as, and only so long as, the plant or machinery is used for the purposes of the qualifying activity.

Origin – S. 270(1), (2): CAA 1990, s. 83(4).

Cross references – S. 166: transfers of interests in oil fields: anti-avoidance.
S. 435: mineral extraction allowances: shares in assets.

HMRC Manuals – CA20080: guidance on s. 270.
CA29210: guidance and example on s. 270.

PART 3 – INDUSTRIAL BUILDINGS ALLOWANCES

[Pt. 3 omitted by FA 2008, s. 84(2).]

History – Pt. 3 of CAA 2001 does not apply in relation to expenditure incurred on or after 1 April 2011 for corporation tax purposes and 6 April 2011 for income tax purposes (FA 2008, s. 84(1)). Part 3 is accordingly omitted by FA 2008, s. 84(2) with effect in relation to chargeable periods beginning on or after those April 2011 dates (FA 2008, s. 84(3) and (4)). Savings provisions in FA 2008, Sch. 27, Pt. 2 apply in certain circumstances. Former Pt. 3 read as follows:

"PART 3 – INDUSTRIAL BUILDINGS ALLOWANCES

Cross references – S. 9(2)(a): the rule that allowances can not be claimed under two parts for the same fixture is relaxed if the first claim was under this part.
S. 537(1), s. 539, s. 542: conditions under which contributions can qualify for an allowance.
S. 564(1): apportionments that effect two or more people are to be heard by Commissioners in one hearing.
S. 567(1), s. 569(3)(a), (5): sales may be treated as being at an alternative amount.
S. 573(1): a transfer of a relevant interest may be treated as a sale.
ICTA 1988, s. 495 (as amended by Sch. 2, para. 42): definition of regional development grant.
ICTA 1988, Sch. 21, para. 6 (as amended by Sch. 2, para. 65): tax relief in connection with schemes for rationalising industry and other redundancy schemes.
FA 1994, Sch. 24, para. 22(2) (as amended by Sch. 2, para. 91(8)(b)): treatment of disposals under the Railways Act 1993.
The Broadcasting Act 1996, Sch. 7, para. 13 (as amended by Sch. 2, para. 97(4), (5)): transfer of assets relating to the BBC transmission network.
The Great London Authority Act 1999, Sch. 33, para. 4(9) (as amended by Sch. 2, para. 105): qualifying transfers do not give rise to allowances.
FA 2000 Sch. 22, para. 82, 83, 86, 135 (as amended by Sch. 2, para. 108(12), (14), (19), (36)): definitions relevant to tonnage tax.
The Transport Act 2000, Sch. 26, para. 21, 27, 34 (as amended by Sch. 2, para. 109(12), (19), (26)): matters concerning transfers.
FA 2008, s. 85: phasing out of allowances before abolition.
FA 2008, s. 86: transitional provision relating to qualifying enterprise zone expenditure.

Transitional – Sch. 3, para. 79: where provisions concerning expenditure on preparatory work on land where the building was used before 6 April 1956 applied, Pt. 3 (excluding Ch. 5) applies to the part of the expenditure separate from the remainder.

Chapter 1 – Introduction

Industrial buildings allowances

271(1) Allowances are available under this Part if–
(a) expenditure has been incurred on the construction of a building or structure,
(b) the building or structure is (or, in the case of an initial allowance, is to be)–
  (i) in use for the purposes of a qualifying trade,
  (ii) a qualifying hotel,
  (iii) a qualifying sports pavilion, or
  (iv) in relation to qualifying enterprise zone expenditure, a commercial building or structure, and
(c) the expenditure incurred on the construction of the building or structure, or other expenditure, is qualifying expenditure.

271(2) In the rest of this Part–
(a) **"building"** is short for "building or structure", and
(b) **"industrial building"** means, subject to Chapter 2 (which defines terms used in subsection (1)(b) etc.), a building or structure which is within subsection (1)(b).

271(3) Allowances under this Part are made to the person who for the time being has the relevant interest in the building (see Chapter 3) in relation to the qualifying expenditure (see Chapter 4).

Origin – S. 271(1): CAA 1990, s. 1(1) (part), (2), s. 3(1) (part), s. 6(1) (part), s. 7(1) (part), s. 14 (part), s. 18(1) (part).
S. 271(2): drafting.
S. 271(3): CAA 1990, s. 1(1) (part), s. 3(1) (part), s. 10(1) (part), (3) (part), s. 10A(2) (part), (9) (part), s. 10B(2) (part), (8) (part).

Notes – CAA 1968, Pt. I, Ch. I: industrial buildings etc. including initial allowances; the appointed day was 6 April 1946 or 6 April 1956.

Expenditure on the construction of a building

272(1) For the purposes of this Part, expenditure on the construction of a building does not include expenditure on the acquisition of land or rights in or over land.
272(2) This Part has effect in relation to capital expenditure incurred by a person on repairs to a part of a building as if it were capital expenditure on the construction of that part of the building for the first time.
272(3) For the purposes of subsection (2), expenditure incurred for the purposes of a trade on repairs to a building is to be treated as capital expenditure if it is not expenditure that would be allowed to be deducted in calculating the profits of the trade for tax purposes.

Origin – S. 272(1): CAA 1990, s. 21(1).
S. 272(2), (3): CAA 1990, s. 12.

Preparation of sites for plant or machinery

273(1) Subsection (2) applies if–
(a) capital expenditure is or has been incurred in preparing, cutting, tunnelling or levelling land for the purposes of preparing the land as a site for the installation of plant or machinery, and
(b) no allowance could (apart from this section) be made in respect of that expenditure under this Part or Part 2 (plant and machinery allowances).

273(2) This Part has effect in relation to the expenditure as if–
(a) the purpose of incurring the expenditure were to prepare the land as a site for the construction of a building, and
(b) the installed plant or machinery were a building.

Origin – S. 273(1): CAA 1990, s. 13 (part).
S. 273(2): CAA 1990, s. 13 (part), Annex 2, Note 44.

Rewrite: Technical Points – Explanatory Notes, Annex 2, Note 44: subs. 2(a) has been added to make it clear that IBAs are due for the costs of installing certain types of plant or machinery.

Chapter 2 – Industrial Buildings

BUILDINGS IN USE FOR THE PURPOSES OF A QUALIFYING TRADE

Transitional – Sch. 3, para. 79: where provisions concerning expenditure on preparatory work on land where the building was used before 6 April 1956 applied, Pt. 3 (excluding Ch. 5) applies to the part of the expenditure separate from the remainder.

Trades and undertakings which are "qualifying trades"

274(1) **"Qualifying trade"** means–
(a) a trade of a kind described in Table A, or
(b) an undertaking of a kind described in Table B, if the undertaking is carried on by way of trade.

TABLE A
TRADES WHICH ARE "QUALIFYING TRADES"

1.	*Manufacturing*	A trade consisting of manufacturing goods or materials.
2.	*Processing*	A trade consisting of subjecting goods or materials to a process. This includes (subject to section 276(3)) maintaining or repairing goods or materials.
3.	*Storage*	A trade consisting of storing goods or materials– (a) which are to be used in the manufacture of other goods or materials, (b) which are to be subjected, in the course of a trade, to a process, (c) which, having been manufactured or produced or subjected, in the course of a trade, to a process, have not yet been delivered to any purchaser, or (d) on their arrival in the United Kingdom from a place outside the United Kingdom.
4.	*Agricultural contracting*	A trade consisting of– (a) ploughing or cultivating land occupied by another, (b) carrying out any other agricultural operation on land occupied by another, or (c) threshing another's crops. For this purpose "crops" includes vegetable produce.
5.	*Working foreign plantations*	A trade consisting of working land outside the United Kingdom used for– (a) growing and harvesting crops, (b) husbandry, or (c) forestry. For this purpose "crops" includes vegetable produce and "harvesting crops" includes the collection of vegetable produce (however effected).
6.	*Fishing*	A trade consisting of catching or taking fish or shellfish.

TABLE A
TRADES WHICH ARE "QUALIFYING TRADES"

7.	*Mineral extraction*	A trade consisting of working a source of mineral deposits. **"Mineral deposits"** includes any natural deposits capable of being lifted or extracted from the earth, and for this purpose geothermal energy is to be treated as a natural deposit. **"Source of mineral deposits"** includes a mine, an oil well and a source of geothermal energy.

TABLE B
UNDERTAKINGS WHICH ARE "QUALIFYING TRADES" IF CARRIED ON BY WAY OF TRADE

1.	*Electricity*	An undertaking for the generation, transformation, conversion, transmission or distribution of electrical energy.
2.	*Water*	An undertaking for the supply of water for public consumption.
3.	*Hydraulic power*	An undertaking for the supply of hydraulic power.
4.	*Sewerage*	An undertaking for the provision of sewerage services within the meaning of the Water Industry Act 1991.
5.	*Transport*	A transport undertaking.
6.	*Highway undertakings*	A highway undertaking, that is, so much of any undertaking relating to the design, building, financing and operation of roads as is carried on– (a) for the purposes of, or (b) in connection with, the exploitation of highway concessions.
7.	*Tunnels*	A tunnel undertaking.
8.	*Bridges*	A bridge undertaking.
9.	*Inland navigation*	An inland navigation undertaking.
10.	*Docks*	A dock undertaking. A dock includes– (a) any harbour, and (b) any wharf, pier, jetty or other works in or at which vessels can ship or unship merchandise or passengers, other than a pier or jetty primarily used for recreation.

274(2) Item 6 of Table B needs to be read with Chapter 9 (application of this Part to highway undertakings).

Origin – S. 274(1): CAA 1990, s. 18(1) (part), s. 18(9) ("undertaking"), Annex 2, Note 45.
Table A, item 1: CAA 1990, s. 18(1)(e) (part).
Table A, item 2: CAA 1990, s. 18(1)(e) (part), (3) (part).
Table A, item 3: CAA 1990, s. 18(1)(f).
Table A, item 4: CAA 1990, s. 18(1)(h), (9) ("crops").
Table A, item 5: CAA 1990, s. 18(1)(g) (part), (9) ("crops", "harvesting", "foreign plantation"), (10) (part).
Table A, item 6: CAA 1990, s. 18(1)(j).
Table A, item 7: CAA 1990, s. 18(1)(g) (part), s. 161(2) ("mineral deposits"), Annex 2, Note 46.
Table B, item 1: CAA 1990, s. 18(1)(b) (part), (9) ("electricity undertaking").
Table B, item 2: CAA 1990, s. 18(1)(b) (part), (9) ("water undertaking").
Table B, item 3: CAA 1990, s. 18(1)(b) (part), (9) ("hydraulic power undertaking").
Table B, item 4: CAA 1990, s. 18(1)(b) (part), (9) ("sewerage undertaking").
Table B, item 5: CAA 1990, s. 18(1)(b) (part).
Table B, item 6: CAA 1990, s. 18(1)(da), s. 21(5AA) ("highway undertaking").
Table B, item 7: CAA 1990, s. 18(1)(c).
Table B, item 8: CAA 1990, s. 18(1)(d).
Table B, item 9: CAA 1990, s. 18(1)(b) (part).
Table B, item 10: CAA 1990, s. 18(1)(b) (part), (9) ("dock").
S. 274(2): drafting.

Transitional – Sch. 3, para. 56: Table B, item 8 does not apply if the expenditure was treated as incurred before 6 April 1957

Rewrite: Technical Points – Explanatory Notes, Annex 2, Note 45: the phrase in CAA 1990, s. 18(1)(a) "a trade carried on in a mill, factory or other similar premises" has been omitted as it is redundant and adds nothing to Table A item 2 (*Vibroplant v Holland* (1981) 54 TC 658).
Explanatory Notes, Annex 2, Note 46: the phrase "whether in the form of hot dry rocks or otherwise" has been omitted from the definition of mineral deposits as it is redundant following the addition of "geothermal energy" to the definition in 1985.
Explanatory Notes, Annex 2, Note 78: former CAA 1990, s. 18(11) is not reproduced in Table B, item 7 as the need for it (being a point of Parliamentary procedure when FA 1952, s. 25 was amended at Report stage) has long since passed.

Building used for welfare of workers

275 A building is in use for the purposes of a qualifying trade if it is–
(a) provided by the person carrying on the qualifying trade for the welfare of workers employed in that qualifying trade, and
(b) in use for the welfare of such workers.

Origin – CAA 1990, s. 18(1) (part).

Parts of trades and undertakings

276(1) Sections 274 and 275 apply in relation to part of a trade or undertaking as they apply in relation to a trade or undertaking. But this is subject to subsections (2) and (3).
276(2) If–
(a) a building is in use for the purpose of a trade or undertaking, and
(b) part only of the trade or undertaking is a qualifying trade,
the building is in use for the purposes of the qualifying trade only if it is in use for the purposes of that part of the trade or undertaking.
276(3) Maintaining or repairing goods or materials is not a qualifying trade if–
(a) the goods or materials are employed in a trade or undertaking,

(b) the maintenance or repair is carried out by the person employing the goods or materials, and
(c) the trade or undertaking is not itself a qualifying trade.

Origin – S. 276(1), (2): CAA 1990, s. 18(2).
S. 276(3): CAA 1990, s. 18(3) (part).

Exclusion of dwelling-houses, retail shops, showrooms, hotels and offices etc.

277(1) A building is not in use for the purposes of a qualifying trade if it is in use as, or as part of, or for any purpose ancillary to the purposes of–
(a) a dwelling-house;
(b) a retail shop, or premises of a similar character where a retail trade or business (including repair work) is carried on;
(c) a showroom;
(d) a hotel;
(e) an office.

277(2) Subsection (3) is about buildings constructed for occupation by, or for the welfare of persons employed–
(a) on, or in connection with, working land outside the United Kingdom which is used as described in item 5 of Table A in section 274 (foreign plantations), or
(b) at, or in connection with, working a source of mineral deposits as defined in item 7 of Table A (mineral extraction).

277(3) Subsection (1) does not apply to a building which this subsection is about if the building–
(a) is likely to be of little or no value to the person carrying on the trade when the land or source is no longer worked, or
(b) will cease to be owned by that person on the ending of a foreign concession under which the land or source is worked.

277(4) **"Foreign concession"** means a right or privilege granted by the government of, or any municipality or other authority in, a territory outside the United Kingdom.

277(5) Subsection (1) is subject to section 283 (non-industrial part of building disregarded).

Origin – S. 277(1): CAA 1990, s. 18(4) (part), (9) ("retail shop").
S. 277(2): CAA 1990, s. 18(5) (part), (9) ("foreign plantation"), (10) (part).
S. 277(3): CAA 1990, s. 18(5) (part).
S. 277(4): CAA 1990, s. 161(2) ("foreign concession").
S. 277(5): CAA 1990, s. 18(4) (part).

Building used by more than one licensee

278 A building used by more than one licensee of the same person is not in use for the purposes of a qualifying trade unless each licensee uses it, or the part to which the licence relates, for the purposes of a qualifying trade.

Origin – CAA 1990, s. 18(6) (part), Annex 1, Change 32.

Transitional – Sch. 3, para. 57; provision does not apply if licence was granted before 10 March 1982.

Rewrite: Changes in Law – Explanatory notes, Annex 1, Change 32: the provisions of CAA 1990, s. 86 are extended to allow a building to qualify for IBAs where it is occupied by licenses who carry on different undertakings (as opposed to trades), if the undertakings are "qualifying trades" as defined in s. 274, Table B.

QUALIFYING HOTELS AND SPORTS PAVILIONS

Qualifying hotels

279(1) A hotel is a qualifying hotel if the following conditions are met–
(a) the accommodation in the hotel is in a building of a permanent nature,
(b) the hotel is open for at least 4 months during April to October, and
(c) when the hotel is open during April to October–
(i) it has 10 or more letting bedrooms,
(ii) the sleeping accommodation it offers consists wholly or mainly of letting bedrooms, and
(iii) the services provided for guests normally include the provision of breakfast and an evening meal, the making of beds and the cleaning of rooms.

279(2) Whether a hotel meets the conditions in subsection (1)(b) and (c) at any time in a chargeable period is to be determined by reference to the period given under subsections (3) to (5) (**"the reference period"**).

279(3) If the hotel was in use for the purposes of a trade carried on by–
(a) the person claiming the allowance, or
(b) a lessee occupying the hotel under a lease to which the relevant interest is reversionary,
throughout the 12 month period ending with the last day of the chargeable period, the reference period is that 12 month period.

279(4) If the hotel was first used for the purposes of a trade carried on as described in subsection (3) after the beginning of the 12 month period referred to there, the reference period is the 12 month period beginning with the date on which it was first so used.

279(5) If a hotel does not qualify under subsection (3) because it had fewer than 10 letting bedrooms until too late a date, the reference period is the 12 month period beginning with the date when it had 10 or more letting bedrooms.

279(6) A hotel is not to be treated as meeting the conditions in subsection (1)(b) and (c) at any time in a chargeable period after it has ceased altogether to be used.

279(7) A building (whether or not on the same site as any other part of the hotel) which is–
(a) provided by the person carrying on the trade for the welfare of workers employed in the hotel, and
(b) in use for the welfare of such workers,
is to be treated for the purposes of this section as part of the hotel.

279(8) If a qualifying hotel is carried on by an individual (alone or in partnership), accommodation which, when the hotel is open during April to October, is normally used as a dwelling by–
(a) that individual, or
(b) a member of his family or household,
is to be treated for the purposes of this section as not being part of the hotel.

279(9) In this section–

"building" does not include a structure, and

"letting bedroom" means a private bedroom available for letting to the public generally and not normally in the same occupation for more than one month.

Origin – *S. 279(1): CAA 1990, s. 19(1) (part), (2) ("the season").*
S. 279(2) to (4): CAA 1990, s. 19(3) (part).
S. 279(5): CAA 1990, s. 19(4).
S. 279(6): CAA 1990, s. 19(3) (part).
S. 279(7): CAA 1990, s. 19(5) (part).
S. 279(8): CAA 1990, s. 19(5) (part), (2) ("the season").
S. 279(9): CAA 1990, s. 19(1) (part), (2) (part).

Transitional – Sch. 3, para. 58: section does not apply if the expenditure was incurred before 12 April 1978.

Qualifying sports pavilions

280 A building is a qualifying sports pavilion if it is–
(a) occupied by a person carrying on a trade, and
(b) used as a sports pavilion for the welfare of all or any of the workers employed in that trade.

Origin – CAA 1990, s. 14.

COMMERCIAL BUILDINGS (ENTERPRISE ZONES)

Commercial buildings (enterprise zones)

281 For the purposes of this Part as it applies in relation to qualifying enterprise zone expenditure, **"commercial building"** means a building which is used–
(a) for the purposes of a trade, profession or vocation, or
(b) as an office or offices (whether or not for the purposes of a trade, profession or vocation),
and which is not in use as, or as part of, a dwelling-house.

Origin – CAA 1990, s. 6(1) (part), s. 21(5).

Cross references – S. 271(1(b)(iv): industrial building allowances
S. 298–301: enterprise zone expenditure.

SUPPLEMENTARY PROVISIONS

Buildings outside the United Kingdom

282 A building outside the United Kingdom which is in use for the purposes of a trade is not an industrial building at any time when the profits of the trade are not assessable in accordance with the rules that apply in calculating trade profits for income tax purposes or corporation tax purposes.

History – In s. 282, the words "or corporation tax purposes" substituted for the words "or that apply to Case I of Schedule D for corporation tax purposes" by CTA 2009, s. 1322 and Sch. 1, para. 497, with effect for corporation tax purposes for accounting periods ending on or after 1 April 2009, and for income tax and capital gains tax purposes for the tax year 2009–10 and subsequent tax years. S. 282 amended by ITTOIA 2005, s. 882(1) and Sch. 1, para. 552; effective for income tax purposes for 2005–06 onwards and for corporation tax purposes for accounting periods ending after 5 April 2005 (ITTOIA 2005, s. 883(1)).

Origin – CAA 1990, s. 18(13), (14) (part).

Rewrite: Technical Points – Explanatory notes; this provision applies to all building including commercial building, but as commercial buildings are by definition located within enterprise zones in the UK, the provision can not apply to them.

Non-industrial part of building disregarded

283(1) This section applies if, apart from this section, but taking into account section 571 (parts of buildings etc.)–
(a) part of a building would be an industrial building, and
(b) part (**"the non-industrial part"**) would not.

283(2) If the qualifying expenditure relating to the non-industrial part is no more than 25% of the qualifying expenditure relating to the whole of the building, the whole of the building is an industrial building.

Origin – S. 283(1), (2): CAA 1990, s. 18(7), (14) (part).

Transitional – Sch. 3, para. 59: s. 283(2) figure 10% substituted for 25% for expenditure incurred before 16 March 1983.

Roads on industrial estates etc.

284(1) A road on an industrial estate is an industrial building if the estate consists wholly or mainly of buildings that are treated under this Part as industrial buildings.

284(2) For the purposes of this Part as it applies in relation to qualifying enterprise zone expenditure, **"industrial estate"** includes an area (such as a business park) which consists wholly or mainly of commercial buildings.

Origin – S. 284(1): CAA 1990, s. 18(8), Annex 1, Change 33.
S. 284(2) Annex 1, Change 33.

Rewrite: Changes in Law – Explanatory notes, Annex 1, Change 33: IBAs are extended to roads on industrial estates where the buildings qualify for IBAs as commercial buildings or due to other qualities which allow it to qualify under this part, such as being a qualifying hotel.

Cessation of use and temporary disuse of building

285 For the purposes of this Part–
(a) a building is not to be regarded as ceasing altogether to be used merely because it falls temporarily out of use, and
(b) if a building is an industrial building immediately before a period of temporary disuse, it is to be treated as being an industrial building during the period of temporary disuse.

Origin – CAA 1990, s. 6(1) (part), s. 7(1) (part), s. 15(1).

Chapter 3 – The Relevant Interest in the Building

Transitional – Sch. 3, para. 79: where provisions concerning expenditure on preparatory work on land where the building was used before 6 April 1956 applied, Pt. 3 (excluding Ch. 5) applies to the part of the expenditure separate from the remainder.

General rule as to what is the relevant interest

286(1) The relevant interest in relation to any qualifying expenditure is the interest in the building to which the person who incurred the expenditure on the construction of the building was entitled when the expenditure was incurred.

286(2) Subsection (1) is subject to the following provisions of this Chapter and to sections 342 (highway undertakings) and 359 (provisions applying on termination of lease).

286(3) If–
(a) the person who incurred the expenditure on the construction of the building was entitled to more than one interest in the building when the expenditure was incurred, and
(b) one of those interests was reversionary on all the others,
the reversionary interest is the relevant interest.

Origin – S. 286(1), (2): CAA 1990, s. 20(1).
S. 286(3): CAA 1990, s. 20(2).

Interest acquired on completion of construction

287 For the purposes of determining the relevant interest, a person who–
(a) incurs expenditure on the construction of a building, and
(b) is entitled to an interest in the building on or as a result of the completion of the construction,
is treated as having had that interest when the expenditure was incurred.

Origin – CAA 1990, s. 21(2), Annex 1, Change 34.

Rewrite: Changes in Law – Explanatory notes, Annex 1, Change 34: former CAA 1990, s. 21(2) was applied even if there was a short delay between completion of the building and the granting of an interest (e.g. a lease). This provision codifies that informal concession to allow IBAs to be claimed by the person who is entitled to an interest in the building as a result of its completion (i.e. the delay is not relevant).

Effect of creation of subordinate interest

288(1) An interest does not cease to be the relevant interest merely because of the creation of a lease or other interest to which that interest is subject.
288(2) This is subject to any election under section 290.

Origin – S. 288(1): CAA 1990, s. 20(3) (part).
S. 288(2): CAA 1990, s. 11(5).

Merger of leasehold interest

289 If the relevant interest is a leasehold interest which is extinguished on–
(a) being surrendered, or
(b) the person entitled to the interest acquiring the interest which is reversionary on it,
the interest into which the leasehold interest merges becomes the relevant interest when the leasehold interest is extinguished.

Origin – CAA 1990, s. 20(3) (part).

Election to treat grant of lease exceeding 50 years as sale

290(1) Subsection (2) applies if–
(a) expenditure has been incurred on the construction of a building,
(b) a lease of the building is granted out of the interest which is the relevant interest in relation to the expenditure,
(c) the duration of the lease exceeds 50 years, and
(d) the lessor and the lessee elect for subsection (2) to apply.
290(2) This Part applies as if–
(a) the grant of the lease were a sale of the relevant interest by the lessor to the lessee at the time when the lease takes effect,
(b) any capital sum paid by the lessee in consideration for the grant of the lease were the purchase price on the sale, and
(c) the interest out of which the lease was granted had at that time ceased to be, and the interest granted by the lease had at that time become, the relevant interest.
290(3) The election has effect in relation to all the expenditure–
(a) in relation to which the interest out of which the lease is granted is the relevant interest, and
(b) which relates to the building (or buildings) that is (or are) the subject of the lease.

Origin – S. 290(1): CAA 1990, s. 11(1) (part), (4)(i) long lease.
S. 290(2): CAA 1990, s. 11(1) (part).
S. 290(3): CAA 1990, s. 11(2).

Supplementary provisions with respect to elections

291(1) No election may be made under section 290 by a lessor and lessee who are connected persons unless–
(a) the lessor is a body discharging statutory functions, and
(b) the lessee is a company of which it has control.
291(2) No election may be made under section 290 if it appears that the sole or main benefit which may be expected to accrue to the lessor from the grant of the lease and the making of an election is obtaining a balancing allowance.
291(3) Whether the duration of a lease exceeds 50 years is to be determined–
(a) in accordance with sections 243 and 244 of CTA 2009, and
(b) without regard to section 359(3) (new lease granted as a result of the exercise of an option treated as continuation of old lease).
291(4) An election under section 290 must be made by notice to an officer of Revenue and Customs within 2 years after the date on which the lease takes effect.
291(5) All such adjustments, by discharge or repayment of tax or otherwise, are to be made as are necessary to give effect to the election.

History – In s. 291(3)(a), the words "sections 243 and 244 of CTA 2009," substituted for the words "section 38(1) to (4) and (6) of ICTA," by CTA 2009, s. 1322 and Sch. 1, para. 498, with effect for corporation tax purposes for accounting periods ending on or after 1 April 2009, and for income tax and capital gains tax purposes for the tax year 2009–10 and subsequent tax years. This amendment does not have effect for leases granted before 1 April 2009 (CTA 2009, Sch. 2, para. 47).
In s. 291(4), the words "an officer of Revenue and Customs" substituted for "the Inland Revenue" by CRCA 2005, s. 50(6) and Sch. 4, para. 83(1), with effect from 18 April 2005 by virtue of SI 2005/1126, art. 2(2).

Origin – S. 291(1), (2): CAA 1990, s. 11(6).
S. 291(3): CAA 1990, s. 11(4) (part).
S. 291(4), (5): CAA 1990, s. 11(3).

Chapter 4 – Qualifying Expenditure

Transitional – Sch. 3, para. 79: where provisions concerning expenditure on preparatory work on land where the building was used before 6 April 1956 applied, Pt. 3 (excluding Ch. 5) applies to the part of the expenditure separate from the remainder.

INTRODUCTION

Meaning of "qualifying expenditure"

292 In this Part **"qualifying expenditure"** means expenditure which is qualifying expenditure under–

section 294	capital expenditure on construction of a building
section 295	purchase of unused building where developer not involved
section 296	purchase of building which has been sold unused by developer
section 301	qualifying expenditure on sale within 2 years of first use where all of expenditure is qualifying enterprise zone expenditure
section 303	qualifying expenditure on sale within 2 years of first use where part of expenditure is qualifying enterprise zone expenditure.

Origin – S. 292: drafting.

Meaning of references to carrying on a trade as a developer

293 For the purposes of this Chapter–
(a) a developer is a person who carries on a trade which consists in whole or in part in the construction of buildings with a view to their sale, and
(b) an interest in a building is sold by the developer in the course of the development trade if the developer sells it in the course of the trade or (as the case may be) that part of the trade that consists in the construction of buildings with a view to their sale.

Origin – CAA 1990, s. 10(3) (part), (4) (part), s. 10A(9) (part).

QUALIFYING EXPENDITURE

Capital expenditure on construction of a building

294 If–
(a) capital expenditure is incurred on the construction of a building, and
(b) the relevant interest in the building has not been sold or, if it has been sold, it has been sold only after the first use of the building,

the capital expenditure is qualifying expenditure.

Origin – CAA 1990, s. 1(1) (part), s. 3(1) (part), s. 6(1) (part), s. 10(1)(a) (part), s. 10A(1) (part), (2)(a) (part).

Transitional – Sch. 3, para. 75–77: an initial allowances may be due in respect of additional VAT liabilities arising if the original capital expenditure was incurred in the year ended 31 October 1993.

Purchase of unused building where developer not involved

295(1) This section applies if–
(a) expenditure is incurred on the construction of a building,
(b) the relevant interest in the building is sold before the building is first used,
(c) a capital sum is paid by the purchaser for the relevant interest, and
(d) section 296 (purchase of building which has been sold unused by developer) does not apply.

295(2) The lesser of–
(a) the capital sum paid by the purchaser for the relevant interest, and
(b) the expenditure incurred on the construction of the building,

is qualifying expenditure.

295(3) The qualifying expenditure is to be treated as incurred by the purchaser when the capital sum became payable.

295(4) If the relevant interest is sold more than once before the building is first used, subsection (2) has effect only in relation to the last of those sales.

Origin – S. 295(1): CAA 1990, s. 10(1) (part), (3) (part), s. 10A(1) (part), (9) (part).
S. 295(2), (3): CAA 1990, s. 10(1) (part), s. 10A(2) (part).
S. 295(4): CAA 1990, s. 10(2), s. 10A(8).

Transitional – Sch. 3, para. 75–77: an initial allowances may be due in respect of additional VAT liabilities arising if the original capital expenditure was incurred in the year ended 31 October 1993.

Purchase of building which has been sold unused by developer

296(1) This section applies if–
(a) expenditure is incurred by a developer on the construction of a building, and
(b) the relevant interest in the building is sold by the developer in the course of the development trade before the building is first used.

296(2) If–
(a) the sale of the relevant interest by the developer was the only sale of that interest before the building is used, and
(b) a capital sum is paid by the purchaser for the relevant interest,

the capital sum is qualifying expenditure.

296(3) If–
(a) the sale by the developer was not the only sale before the building is used, and
(b) a capital sum is paid by the purchaser for the relevant interest on the last sale,

the lesser of that capital sum and the price paid for the relevant interest on its sale by the developer is qualifying expenditure.

296(4) The qualifying expenditure is to be treated as incurred by the purchaser when the capital sum referred to in subsection (2)(b) or (3)(b) became payable.

Origin – S. 296(1): CAA 1990, s. 10(3) (part), s. 10A(9) (part).
S. 296(2), (3): CAA 1990, s. 10(1) (part), (3) (part), s. 10A(2) (part), (9) (part).
S. 296(4): CAA 1990, s. 10(1) (part), s. 10A(2) (part).

Transitional – Sch. 3, para. 75–77: an initial allowances may be due in respect of additional VAT liabilities arising if the original capital expenditure was incurred in the year ended 31 October 1993.

Purchase of used building from developer

297(1) This section applies if–
(a) expenditure is incurred by a developer on the construction of a building, and

(b) the relevant interest is sold by the developer in the course of the development trade after the building has been used.

297(2) This Part has effect in relation to the person to whom the relevant interest is sold as if–

(a) the expenditure on the construction of the building had been qualifying expenditure,

(b) all appropriate writing-down allowances had been made to the developer, and

(c) any appropriate balancing adjustment had been made on the occasion of the sale.

297(3) This section is subject to sections 301 and 303 (purchase of building in enterprise zone within 2 years of first use).

Origin – S. 297(1): CAA 1990, s. 10(4) (part).
S. 297(2): CAA 1990, s. 10(5).
S. 297(3): CAA 1990, s. 10(4) (part).

Transitional – Sch. 3, para. 60: section does not apply if purchase price in (1)(b) payable before 27 July 1989.

QUALIFYING ENTERPRISE ZONE EXPENDITURE

Cross references – FA 2008, s. 86: transitional provision relating to qualifying enterprise zone expenditure.

The time limit for qualifying enterprise zone expenditure

298(1) For the purposes of sections 299 to 304, the time limit for expenditure on the construction of a building on a site in an enterprise zone is–

(a) 10 years after the site was first included in the zone, or

(b) if the expenditure is incurred under a contract entered into within those 10 years, 20 years after the site was first included in the zone.

298(2) In those sections **"EZ building"** is short for "building on a site in an enterprise zone".

298(3) In this Part **"enterprise zone"** means an area designated as such by an order–

(a) made by the Secretary of State, the Scottish Ministers or the National Assembly for Wales, under powers conferred by Schedule 32 to the Local Government, Planning and Land Act 1980, or

(b) in Northern Ireland, made by the Department of the Environment under Article 7 of the Enterprise Zones (Northern Ireland) Order 1981.

History – In s. 298(3), words ", the Scottish Ministers or the National Assembly for Wales," inserted by FA 2001, s. 69 and Sch. 21, para. 5, with effect as respects allowances and charges falling to be made for chargeable periods ending, for income tax purposes, on or after 6 April 2001, and, for corporation tax purposes, on or after 1 April 2001.

Origin – S. 298(1): CAA 1990, s. 1(1) (part), (11), s. 6(1) (part), (4A), s. 10A(1) (part), (7) (part), (10), s. 10B(1) (part), (9) (part), (10), s. 17A.
S. 298(2): drafting.
S. 298(3): CAA 1990, s. 21(4).

Statutory instruments – Enterprise zones have been designated by statutory instruments as detailed below:
SI 1981/309: Belfast (21 October 1981)
SI 1981/757: Lower Swansea Valley (11 June 1981)
SI 1981/764: Corby (22 June 1981)
SI 1981/852: Dudley (not Round Oak) (10 July 1981)
SI 1981/950: Wakefield (Langthwaite Grange) (31 July 1981)
SI 1981/975: Clydebank (3 August 1981)
SI 1981/1024: Salford (12 August 1981)
SI 1981/1025: Trafford Park (12 August 1981)
SI 1981/1069: Glasgow (18 August 1981)
SI 1981/1070: Gateshead (25 August 1981)
SI 1981/1071: Newcastle (25 August 1981)
SI 1981/1072: Speke (25 August 1981)
SI 1981/1378: Hartlepool (23 October 1981)
SI 1982/462: Isle of Dogs (26 April 1982)
SI 1983/226: Londonderry (13 September 1983)
SI 1983/896: Delyn and Flint (21 July 1983)
SI 1983/907: Wellingborough (26 July 1983)
SI 1983/1007: Rotherham (16 August 1983)
SI 1983/1304: Scunthorpe (excluding Glanford) (23 September 1983)
SI 1983/1305: Wakefield (extended to Dale Lane and Kinsley) (23 September 1983)
SI 1983/1331: Workington (Allerdale) (4 October 1983)
SI 1983/1359: Invergordon (7 October 1983)
SI 1983/1452: North-West Kent (Gillingham and Gravesend) (31 October 1983)
SI 1983/1473: Middlesborough (Britannia) (8 November 1983)
SI 1983/1639: North-East Lancashire (Burnley, Hyndburn, Pendle and Rossendale) (7 December 1983)
SI 1983/1816: Arbroath (9 January 1984)
SI 1983/1817: Dundee (9 January 1984)
SI 1983/1852: Telford (13 January 1984)
SI 1984/347: Glanford (Flixborough) (13 April 1984)
SI 1984/443, 444: Milford Haven Waterway (24 April 1984)
SI 1984/1403: Dudley (extended to Round Oak) (3 October 1984)
SI 1985/137: Lower Swansea Valley (extended) (6 March 1985)
SI 1986/1557: North-West Kent (extended to Chatham and Rochester-upon-Medway) (10 October 1986)
SI 1989/145: Inverclyde (3 March 1989)
SI 1990/794: Sunderland (Castletown and Doxford Park) (27 April 1990)
SI 1990/795: Sunderland (Hylton Riverside and Southwick) (27 April 1990)
SI 1993/23: Lanarkshire (Hamilton) (1 February 1993)
SI 1993/24: Lanarkshire (Motherwell) (1 February 1993)
SI 1993/25: Lanarkshire (Monklands) (1 February 1993)
SI 1995/2624: Dearne Valley (3 November 1995)
SI 1995/2625: East Midlands (North East Derbyshire) (3 November 1995)
SI 1995/2738: East Midlands (Bassetlaw) (16 November 1995)
SI 1995/2758: East Midlands (Ashfield) (21 November 1995)
SI 1995/2812: East Durham (29 November 1995)
SI 1996/106: North Tyneside (19 February 1996)
SI 1996/1981: North Tyneside (26 August 1996)
SI 1996/2435: North Tyneside and South Tyneside (21 October 1996).

Application of section 294

299 If–
(a) capital expenditure is incurred on the construction of an EZ building, and
(b) the expenditure is incurred within the time limit,
the qualifying expenditure given by section 294 is qualifying enterprise zone expenditure.

Origin – CAA 1990, s. 1(1) (part), s. 6(1) (part).

Application of sections 295 and 296

300 If–
(a) expenditure is incurred on the construction of an EZ building, and
(b) all the expenditure is incurred within the time limit,
any qualifying expenditure given by sections 295 and 296 in relation to that expenditure is qualifying enterprise zone expenditure.

Origin – CAA 1990, s. 10A(1) (part), (2) (part), (8) (part), (9) (part).

Transitional – Sch. 3, para. 61: provision does not apply for purchases before 16 December 1991, if conditions apply.

Purchase of building within 2 years of first use

301(1) This section applies if–
(a) expenditure is incurred on the construction of an EZ building,
(b) all the expenditure is incurred within the time limit,
(c) the relevant interest in the building is sold–
(i) after the building has been used, but
(ii) within the period of 2 years beginning with the date on which the building was first used, and
(d) that sale (**"the relevant sale"**) is the first sale in that period after the building has been used.

301(2) If this section applies–
(a) any balancing adjustment which falls to be made on the occasion of the relevant sale is to be made, and
(b) the residue of qualifying expenditure immediately after the relevant sale is to be disregarded for the purposes of this Part.

301(3) If a capital sum is paid by the purchaser for the relevant interest on the relevant sale–
(a) the purchaser is to be treated as having incurred qualifying expenditure that is qualifying enterprise zone expenditure of an amount given in subsection (4), (6) or (7), and
(b) in relation to that qualifying enterprise zone expenditure, this Part applies as if the building had not been used before the date of the relevant sale.

301(4) Unless subsection (6) or (7) applies, the amount of the qualifying enterprise zone expenditure is the lesser of–
(a) the capital sum paid by the purchaser for the relevant interest on the relevant sale, and
(b) the expenditure incurred on the construction of the building.

301(5) Subsections (6) and (7) apply if–
(a) the expenditure incurred on the construction of the EZ building was incurred by a developer, and
(b) the relevant interest in the building has been sold by the developer in the course of the development trade.

301(6) If the sale by the developer is the relevant sale, the amount of the qualifying enterprise zone expenditure is the capital sum paid by the purchaser for the relevant interest on that sale.

301(7) If the sale by the developer is not the relevant sale, the amount of the qualifying enterprise zone expenditure is the lesser of–
(a) the capital sum paid by the purchaser for the relevant interest on the relevant sale, and
(b) the price paid for the relevant interest on its sale by the developer.

301(8) The qualifying expenditure is to be treated as incurred when the capital sum on the relevant sale became payable.

Origin – S. 301(1): CAA 1990, s. 10B(1) (part).
S. 301(2): CAA 1990, s. 10B(2) (part).
S. 301(3): CAA 1990, s. 1(1) (part), s. 3(1) (part), s. 6(1) (part), s. 10B(2) (part).
S. 301(4): CAA 1990, s. 10B(4) (part), (5) ("A").
S. 301(5)–(7): CAA 1990, s. 10B(8) (part).
S. 301(8): CAA 1990, s. 10B(2)(c) (part).

Transitional – Sch. 3, para. 63: section does not apply to buildings first used before 16 December 1991 if conditions are met.

PART OF EXPENDITURE WITHIN TIME LIMIT FOR QUALIFYING ENTERPRISE ZONE EXPENDITURE

Qualifying enterprise zone expenditure where section 295 or 296 applies

302(1) This section applies if–
(a) expenditure is incurred on the construction of an EZ building,
(b) only a part of the expenditure is incurred within the time limit, and
(c) the circumstances are as described in–
(i) section 295(1) (purchase of unused building where developer not involved), or
(ii) section 296(1) (purchase of building which has been sold unused by developer).

302(2) Only a part of the qualifying expenditure given by section 295(2) or 296(2) or (3) (as the case may be) is qualifying enterprise zone expenditure.

302(3) The part of the qualifying expenditure that is qualifying enterprise zone expenditure is–

$$QE \times \frac{E}{T}$$

where–
QE is the qualifying expenditure,
E is the part of the expenditure on the construction of the EZ building that is incurred within the time limit, and
T is the total expenditure on the construction of the building.

Origin – S. 302(1): CAA 1990, s. 10A(1) (part), (9) (part).
S. 302(2): CAA 1990, s. 10A(3) (part), (6).
S. 302(3): CAA 1990, s. 10A(4) (part), (5).

Transitional – Sch. 3, para. 61: provision does not apply for purchases before 16 December 1991, if conditions apply.

Purchase of building within 2 years of first use

303(1) This section applies if–
(a) expenditure is incurred on the construction of an EZ building,
(b) only a part of the expenditure is incurred within the time limit,
(c) the relevant interest in the building is sold–

(i) after the building has been used, but
(ii) within the period of 2 years beginning with the date on which the building was first used, and
(d) that sale (**"the relevant sale"**) is the first sale in that period after the building has been used.

303(2) If this section applies–
(a) any balancing adjustment which falls to be made on the occasion of the relevant sale is to be made, and
(b) the residue of qualifying expenditure immediately after the relevant sale is to be disregarded for the purposes of this Part.

303(3) If a capital sum is paid by the purchaser for the relevant interest on the relevant sale–
(a) the purchaser is to be treated as having incurred qualifying expenditure–
(i) part of which is qualifying enterprise zone expenditure ("Z"), and
(ii) part of which is not ("N"), and
(b) in relation to that qualifying expenditure, this Part applies as if the building had not been used before the date of the relevant sale.

303(4) Unless section 304 (cases where developer involved) applies–

$$Z = L \times \frac{E}{T}$$

and

$$N = L - Z$$

where–
L is the lesser of–
(a) the capital sum paid for the relevant interest on the relevant sale, and
(b) the expenditure incurred on the construction of the building,
E is the part of the expenditure on the construction of the EZ building that is incurred within the time limit, and
T is the total expenditure on the construction of the building.

303(5) Any qualifying expenditure arising under this section or section 304 is to be treated as incurred when the capital sum on the relevant sale became payable.

Origin – S. 303(1): CAA 1990, s. 10B(1) (part).
S. 303(2): CAA 1990, s. 10B(2) (part).
S. 303(3): CAA 1990, s. 1(1) (part), s. 3(1) (part), s. 6(1) (part), s. 10B(2) (part), (3).
S. 303(4): CAA 1990, s. 10B(4) (part), (5) (part), (6), (7), (8) (part).
S. 303(5): CAA 1990, s. 10B(2) (part).

Transitional – Sch. 3, para. 63: section does not apply to buildings first used before 16 December 1991 if conditions are met.

Application of section 303 where developer involved

304(1) This section applies if section 303 applies but–
(a) the expenditure on the construction of the building was incurred by a developer, and
(b) the relevant interest in the building has been sold by the developer in the course of the development trade;
and in this section Z, N, E and T have the same meaning as in section 303.

304(2) If the sale by the developer is the relevant sale–

$$Z = C \times \frac{E}{T}$$

and

$$N = L - L \times \frac{E}{T}$$

where–
C is the capital sum paid for the relevant interest by the purchaser, and
L is the lesser of–
(a) the capital sum paid for the relevant interest on the relevant sale, and
(b) the expenditure incurred on the construction of the building.

304(3) If the sale by the developer is not the relevant sale–

$$Z = D \times \frac{E}{T}$$

and

$$N = D - Z$$

where D is the lesser of–
(a) the price paid for the relevant interest on its sale by the developer, and
(b) the capital sum paid for the relevant interest on the relevant sale.

Origin – S. 304(1) to (3): CAA 1990, s. 10B(8).

Transitional – Sch. 3, para. 63: section does not apply to buildings first used before 16 December 1991 if conditions are met.

Chapter 5 – Initial Allowances

Transitional – Sch. 3, para. 79: where provisions concerning expenditure on preparatory work on land where the building was used before 6 April 1956 applied, Pt. 3 (excluding Ch. 5) applies to the part of the expenditure separate from the remainder.

Initial allowances for qualifying enterprise zone expenditure

305(1) A person who has incurred qualifying enterprise zone expenditure is entitled to an initial allowance in respect of the expenditure if the building on which the expenditure is incurred is to be an industrial building–
(a) occupied by that person or a qualifying lessee, or
(b) used by a qualifying licensee.

305(2) In this section–

"qualifying lessee" means a lessee under a lease to which the relevant interest is reversionary, and

"qualifying licensee" means a licensee of–

(a) the person incurring the qualifying expenditure, or
(b) a lessee of the person incurring the qualifying expenditure.

Origin – S. 305(1): CAA 1990, s. 1(1) (part), (4) (part), Annex 1, Change 35.
S. 305(2): CAA 1990, s. 1(3), (4) (part).

Transitional – Sch. 3, para. 47(6): expenditure incurred between 1 November 1992 and 31 October 1993.
Sch. 3, para. 64(1)(b): does not apply if licence was granted before 10 January 1992.

Rewrite: Changes in Law – Explanatory Notes, Annex 1, Change 35, clarification that initial IBAs are available to all commercial buildings in an EZ whether or not they are occupied for the purposes of a trade. This restores the original aim of the provision as introduced by FA 1980.

Amount of initial allowance and period for which allowance made

306(1) The amount of the initial allowance is 100% of the qualifying enterprise zone expenditure.
306(2) A person claiming an initial allowance under this section may require the allowance to be reduced to a specified amount.
306(3) The initial allowance is made for the chargeable period in which the qualifying expenditure is incurred.
306(4) For the purposes of subsection (3), expenditure incurred for the purposes of a trade, profession or vocation by a person about to carry it on is to be treated as if it had been incurred on the first day on which the person carries on the trade, profession or vocation.

Origin – S. 306(1): CAA 1990, s. 1(1) (part).
S. 306(2): CAA 1990, s. 1(5) (part).
S. 306(3): CAA 1990, s. 1(1) (part).
S. 306(4): CAA 1990, s. 1(10), Annex 1, Change 36.

Transitional – Sch. 3, para. 47(6): expenditure incurred between 1 November 1992 and 31 October 1993.

Rewrite: Changes in Law – Explanatory Notes, Annex 1, Change 36: s. 306(4) applies to trades, professions and vocations whereas, former CAA 1990, s. 1(10) referred only to a trade.

Building not industrial building when first used etc.

307(1) No initial allowance is to be made under section 305 if, when the building is first used, it is not an industrial building.
307(2) An initial allowance which has been made in respect of a building which is to be an industrial building is to be withdrawn if, when the building is first used, it is not an industrial building.
307(3) An initial allowance which has been made in respect of a building which has not been used is to be withdrawn if the person to whom the allowance was made sells the relevant interest before the building is first used.
307(4) All such assessments and adjustments of assessments are to be made as are necessary to give effect to this section.

Origin – S. 307(1), (2): CAA 1990, s. 1(6) (part).
S. 307(3): CAA 1990, s. 10(1)(a), s. 10A(2)(a).
S. 307(4): CAA 1990, s. 1(6) (part).

Transitional – Sch. 3, para. 47(6): treatment for expenditure incurred between 1 November 1992 and 31 October 1993.

Rewrite: Changes in Law – Explanatory Notes, Annex 1 Change 37: former CAA 1990 only allowed for withdrawal of allowances by assessment under (2), now assessments may be made under this Act for withdrawal of allowances under (2) and (3).

Grants affecting entitlement to initial allowances

308(1) No initial allowance is to be made in respect of expenditure to the extent that it is taken into account for the purposes of a relevant grant or relevant payment made towards that expenditure.
308(2) A grant or payment is relevant if it is–
(a) a grant made under section 32, 34 or 56(1) of the Transport Act 1968,
(b) a payment made under section 56(2) of the Transport Act 1968, or
(c) a grant made under section 101 of the Greater London Authority Act 1999,
which is declared by the Treasury by order to be relevant for the purposes of the withholding of initial allowances
308(3) If a relevant grant or relevant payment towards the expenditure is made after the making of an initial allowance, the allowance is to be withdrawn to that extent.
308(4) If the amount of the grant or payment is repaid by the grantee to the grantor, in whole or in part, the grant or payment is treated, to that extent, as never having been made.
308(5) All such assessments and adjustments of assessments are to be made as are necessary to give effect to subsection (3) or (4).
308(6) Any such assessment or adjustment is not out of time if it is made within 3 years of the end of the chargeable period in which the grant, payment or repayment was made.

Origin – S. 308(1), (2): CAA 1990, s. 1(7).
S. 308(3), (4): CAA 1990, s. 1(8).
S. 308(5), (6): CAA 1990, s. 1(9).

Transitional – Sch. 3, para. 47(6): expenditure incurred between 1/11/1992 and 31/10/1993. Sch. 3, Para. 65: the grant in (2)(c) applies equally to grants under the London Regional Transport Act 1984, s. 12 or Transport (London) Act 1969, s. 3.

Chapter 6 – Writing-down Allowances

Transitional – Sch. 3, para. 79: where provisions concerning expenditure on preparatory work on land where the building was used before 6 April 1956 applied, Pt. 3 (excluding Ch. 5) applies to the part of the expenditure separate from the remainder.

Entitlement to writing-down allowance

309(1) A person is entitled to a writing-down allowance for a chargeable period if–
(a) qualifying expenditure has been incurred on a building,
(b) at the end of that chargeable period, the person is entitled to the relevant interest in the building in relation to that expenditure, and
(c) at the end of that chargeable period, the building is an industrial building.
309(2) A person claiming a writing-down allowance may require the allowance to be reduced to a specified amount.

Origin – S. 309(1): CAA 1990, s. 3(1) (part).
S. 309(2) Annex 1, Change 38.

Rewrite: Changes in Law – Explanatory Notes, Annex 1, change 38: brings the law into line with the current practice of allowing the taxpayer to claim any amount of the WDA from zero to the full allowance permitted.

Basic rule for calculating amount of allowance

310(1) The basic rule is that the writing-down allowance for a chargeable period is–

(a) in the case of qualifying enterprise zone expenditure, 25% of the expenditure, and

(b) in the case of other qualifying expenditure, 4% of the expenditure.

310(2) The allowance is proportionately increased or reduced if the chargeable period is more or less than a year.

310(3) This basic rule does not apply if section 311 applies.

Origin – S. 310(1): CAA 1990, s. 3(2) (part), s. 6(2).
S. 310(2): CAA 1990, s. 3(2) (part).
S. 310(3): drafting.

Transitional – Sch. 3, para. 66: the WDA in s. 310(1)(b) is 2 per cent for expenditure incurred before 6 November 1962.

Calculation of allowance after sale of relevant interest

311(1) If a relevant event occurs, the writing-down allowance for any chargeable period ending after the event is–

$$RQE \times \frac{A}{B}$$

where–

RQE is the amount of the residue of qualifying expenditure immediately after the event,

A is the length of the chargeable period, and

B is the length of the period from the date of the event to the end of the period of 25 years beginning with the day on which the building was first used.

311(2) On any later relevant event, the writing-down allowance is further adjusted in accordance with this section.

311(3) **"Relevant event"** means–

(a) a sale of the relevant interest in the building which is a balancing event to which section 314 applies, or

(b) an event which is a relevant event for the purposes of this section under section 347 or 349 (additional VAT liabilities and rebates).

Origin – S. 311(1)–(3): CAA 1990, s. 3(2B) (part), (2C) (part), (3) (part).

Transitional – Sch. 3, para. 67: in the definition of "B" in (1) the length of the period is 50 years for expenditure incurred before 6 November 1962.

Allowance limited to residue of qualifying expenditure

312(1) The amount of the writing-down allowance for a chargeable period is limited to the residue of qualifying expenditure.

312(2) For this purpose the residue is ascertained immediately before writing off the writing-down allowance at the end of the chargeable period.

Origin – S. 311(1)–(3): CAA 1990, s. 3(2B) (part), (2C) (part), (3) (part).

Meaning of "the residue of qualifying expenditure"

313 The residue of qualifying expenditure is the qualifying expenditure that has not yet been written off in accordance with Chapter 8.

Origin – CAA 1990, s. 8(1) (part).

Calculation of allowance after sale of relevant interest: anti-avoidance

313A(1) This section applies where–

(a) there is a sale of the relevant interest in the building which is a balancing event to which section 314 applies,

(b) the buyer and seller have different chargeable periods,

(c) the control test (within the meaning of section 567) is met, and

(d) the purpose, or one of the main purposes, of the sale is the obtaining of a tax advantage by the buyer under this Part.

313A(2) The writing-down allowance to which the buyer is entitled for the chargeable period in which the sale takes place is–

$$\frac{DI}{CP} \times WDA$$

where–

DI is the number of days in the chargeable period for which the buyer is entitled to the relevant interest,

CP is the number of days in the chargeable period, and

WDA is the writing-down allowance to which the buyer would be entitled apart from this section.

History – S. 313A inserted by FA 2008, s. 87(1), with effect in relation to the sale of a relevant interest on or after 12 March 2008, except for such a sale in pursuance of a relevant pre-commencement contract ("sale" having the same meaning as for the purposes of CAA 2001, Pt. 3). The term "relevant pre-commencement contract" is defined in FA 2008, s. 87(3).

Chapter 7 – Balancing Adjustments

Cross references – FA 2007, s. 36: Industrial and agricultural buildings allowances.
FA 1994, Sch. 25, para. 5(3), (as amended by Sch. 2, para. 92): leasehold interestest in industrial structures held by Northern Ireland Airports Limited.

Transitional – Sch. 3, para. 79: where provisions concerning expenditure on preparatory work on land where the building was used before 6 April 1956 applied, Pt. 3 (excluding Ch. 5) applies to the part of the expenditure separate from the remainder.

GENERAL

When balancing adjustments are made

314(1) A balancing adjustment is made if–

(a) qualifying expenditure has been incurred on a building, and

(b) a balancing event occurs while the building is an industrial building or after it has ceased to be an industrial building.

314(2) A balancing adjustment is either a balancing allowance or a balancing charge and is made for the chargeable period in which the balancing event occurs.

314(3) A balancing allowance or balancing charge is made to or on the person entitled to the relevant interest in the building immediately before the balancing event.

314(4) No balancing adjustment is made if the balancing event occurs more than 25 years after the building was first used.

314(5) If more than one balancing event within section 315(1) occurs during a period when the building is not an industrial building, a balancing adjustment is made only on the first of them.

Origin – S. 314(1)–(3): CAA 1990, s. 4(1).
S. 314(4), (5): CAA 1990, s. 4(2) (part).

Transitional – Sch. 3, para. 68: in (4) the period of 50 years applies for expenditure incurred before 6 November 1962.

Main balancing events

315(1) The following are balancing events for the purposes of this Part–
(a) the relevant interest in the building is sold;
(b) if the relevant interest is a lease, the lease ends otherwise than on the person entitled to it acquiring the interest reversionary on it;
(c) the building is demolished or destroyed;
(d) the building ceases altogether to be used (without being demolished or destroyed);
(e) if the relevant interest depends on the duration of a foreign concession, the concession ends.

315(2) **"Foreign concession"** means a right or privilege granted by the government of, or any municipality or other authority in, a territory outside the United Kingdom.

315(3) Other balancing events are provided for by–
section 328 (realisation of capital value where site of building is in enterprise zone);
section 343 (ending of highway concession);
section 350 (additional VAT rebates and balancing adjustments);
and a balancing event under this section may also occur as a result of section 317 (hotel not qualifying hotel for 2 years).

Origin – S. 315(1): CAA 1990, s. 4(1) (part).
S. 315(2): CAA 1990, s. 161(2) ("foreign concession").
S. 315(3): drafting.

Proceeds from main balancing events

316(1) References in this Part to the proceeds from a balancing event within section 315(1) are to the amounts received or receivable in connection with the event, as shown in the Table–

TABLE
BALANCING EVENTS AND PROCEEDS

	1. Balancing event	*2. Proceeds from event*
1.	The sale of the relevant interest.	The net proceeds of the sale.
2.	The demolition or destruction of the building.	The net amount received for the remains of the building, together with– (a) any insurance money received in respect of the demolition or destruction, and (b) any other compensation of any description so received, so far as it consists of capital sums.
3.	The building ceases altogether to be used.	Any compensation of any description received in respect of the event, so far as it consists of capital sums.
4.	A foreign concession ends.	Any compensation payable in respect of the relevant interest.

316(2) The amounts referred to in column 2 of the Table are those received or receivable by the person whose entitlement to a balancing allowance or liability to a balancing charge is in question.

Origin – S. 316(1), (2): CAA 1990, s. 156 (part).

Balancing event where hotel not qualifying hotel for 2 years

317(1) This section applies if–
(a) a building ceases to be a qualifying hotel otherwise than on the occurrence of a balancing event which is within section 315(1), and
(b) after the building ceases to be a qualifying hotel, a period of 2 years elapses–
(i) in which it is not a qualifying hotel, and
(ii) without the occurrence of a balancing event.

317(2) This Part has effect as if–
(a) the relevant interest in the building had been sold at the end of the 2 year period, and
(b) the net proceeds of the sale were equal to the market value of that interest.

317(3) Subsection (2) does not affect section 285 (building treated as industrial building during period of temporary disuse).

317(4) But a building is not to be treated under section 285(b) as continuing to be a qualifying hotel for more than 2 years after the end of the chargeable period in which it falls temporarily out of use.

317(5) This section does not apply to qualifying enterprise zone expenditure.

Origin – S. 317(1), (2): CAA 1990, s. 7(1) (part).
S. 317(3), (4): CAA 1990, s. 7(2).
S. 317(5): CAA 1990, s. 6(3).

CALCULATION OF BALANCING ADJUSTMENTS

Building an industrial building etc. throughout

318(1) This section provides for balancing adjustments where the building was–
(a) an industrial building, or
(b) used for research and development,
for the whole of the relevant period of ownership.

318(2) A balancing allowance is made if–
(a) there are no proceeds from the balancing event, or
(b) the proceeds from the balancing event are less than the residue of qualifying expenditure immediately before the event.

318(3) The amount of the balancing allowance is the amount of–
(a) the residue (if there are no proceeds);

(b) the difference (if the proceeds are less than the residue).
318(4) A balancing charge is made if the proceeds from the balancing event are more than the residue, if any, of qualifying expenditure immediately before the event.
318(5) The amount of the balancing charge is the amount of–
(a) the difference, or
(b) the proceeds (if the residue is nil).

Origin – S. 318(1): CAA 1990, s. 4(5) (part).
S. 318(2), (3): CAA 1990, s. 4(3).
S. 318(4), (5): CAA 1990, s. 4(4).

Building not an industrial building etc. throughout

319(1) This section provides for balancing adjustments where the building was not–
(a) an industrial building, or
(b) used for research and development,
for a part of the relevant period of ownership.
319(2) A balancing allowance is made if–
(a) there are no proceeds from the balancing event or the proceeds are less than the starting expenditure, and
(b) the net allowances made are less than the adjusted net cost of the building.
319(3) The amount of the balancing allowance is the amount of the difference between the adjusted net cost of the building and the net allowances made.
319(4) A balancing charge is made if the proceeds from the balancing event are equal to or more than the starting expenditure.
319(5) The amount of the balancing charge is an amount equal to the net allowances made.
319(6) A balancing charge is also made if–
(a) there are no proceeds from the balancing event or the proceeds are less than the starting expenditure, and
(b) the net allowances made are more than the adjusted net cost of the building.
319(7) The amount of the balancing charge is the amount of the difference between the net allowances made and the adjusted net cost of the building.

Origin – S. 319(1): CAA 1990, s. 4(5) (part).
S. 319(2), (3): CAA 1990, s. 4(7) (part).
S. 319(4), (5): CAA 1990, s. 4(6).
S. 319(6), (7): CAA 1990, s. 4(7) (part).

Overall limit on balancing charge

320 The amount of a balancing charge made on a person must not exceed the amount of the net allowances made.
Origin – CAA 1990, s. 4(10) (part).

MEANING OF "THE RELEVANT PERIOD OF OWNERSHIP" ETC.

The relevant period of ownership

321 The relevant period of ownership is the period beginning–
(a) with the day on which the building was first used for any purpose, or
(b) if the relevant interest has been sold after that day, with the day following that on which the sale (or the last such sale) occurred,
and ending with the day on which the balancing event occurs.

Origin – CAA 1990, s. 4(9) ("the relevant period").

Starting expenditure

322(1) This section gives the starting expenditure for the purposes of this Chapter.
322(2) If the person to or on whom the balancing allowance or balancing charge falls to be made is the person who incurred the qualifying expenditure, that expenditure is the starting expenditure.
322(3) Otherwise, the starting expenditure is the residue of qualifying expenditure at the beginning of the relevant period of ownership.
322(4) If section 340 (treatment of demolition costs) applies, the starting expenditure is increased by an amount equal to the net cost of the demolition.

Origin – S. 322(1)–(4): CAA 1990, s. 4(9) ("the capital expenditure", part).

Adjusted net cost

323 The amount of the adjusted net cost is–

$$(S - P) \times \frac{I}{R}$$

where–
S is the starting expenditure,
P is the amount of any proceeds from the balancing event,
I is the number of days in the relevant period of ownership on which the building was an industrial building or used for research and development, and
R is the number of days in the whole of the relevant period of ownership.

Origin – CAA 1990, s. 4(9) ("the adjusted net cost").

Net allowances

324 For the purposes of this Chapter, the amount of the net allowances made, in relation to any qualifying expenditure, is–

$$(I + WDA + RDA) - B$$

where–
I is the amount of any initial allowances made to the person in relation to that qualifying expenditure,
WDA is the amount of any writing-down allowances made to the person for chargeable periods ending on or before the date of the balancing event giving rise to the balancing adjustment,
RDA is the amount of any allowances under Part 6 (research and development allowances) made to the person for such chargeable periods, and
B is the amount of any balancing charges made on the person for such chargeable periods.

Origin – CAA 1990, s. 4(10) (part).

Transitional – Sch. 3, para. 69: s. 324 also applies to a mills, factories or exceptional depreciation allowance.
Sch. 3, para. 70: impact of independent taxation on allowances given.

BALANCING ALLOWANCES RESTRICTED WHERE SALE SUBJECT TO SUBORDINATE INTEREST

Balancing allowances restricted where sale subject to subordinate interest

325(1) This section applies if–
(a) the relevant interest in a building is sold subject to a subordinate interest,
(b) the person entitled to the relevant interest immediately before the sale (**"the former owner"**) would, apart from this section, be entitled to a balancing allowance under this Chapter as a result of the sale, and
(c) condition A or B is met.
325(2) Condition A is that–
(a) the former owner,
(b) the person who acquires the relevant interest, and
(c) the person to whom the subordinate interest was granted,
or any two of them, are connected persons.
325(3) Condition B is that it appears that the sole or main benefit which might have been expected to accrue to the parties or any of them from the sale or the grant, or transactions including the sale or grant, was the obtaining of an allowance under this Part.
325(4) For the purpose of deciding what balancing adjustment is to be made in a case to which this section applies, the net proceeds to the former owner of the sale are to be increased–
(a) by an amount equal to any premium receivable by him for the grant of the subordinate interest, and
(b) if no rent, or no commercial rent, is payable in respect of the subordinate interest, by the amount by which the proceeds would have been greater if a commercial rent had been payable and the relevant interest had been sold in the open market.
325(5) But the net proceeds of the sale are not to be treated as being greater than the amount which secures that no balancing allowance is made.
325(6) If the terms on which a subordinate interest is granted are varied before the sale of the relevant interest–
(a) any capital consideration for the variation is to be treated for the purposes of this section as a premium for the grant of the interest, and
(b) the question whether any, and if so what, rent is payable in respect of the interest is to be determined by reference to the terms in force immediately before the sale.
325(7) If this section applies in relation to a sale to deny or reduce a balancing allowance, the residue of qualifying expenditure immediately after the sale is nevertheless calculated as if the balancing allowance had been made or not reduced.

Origin – S. 325(1)–(3): CAA 1990, s. 5(1).
S. 325(4), (5): CAA 1990, s. 5(2).
S. 325(6): CAA 1990, s. 5(5).
S. 325(7): CAA 1990, s. 5(3).

CAA 2001

Interpretation of section 325

326(1) In section 325–

"commercial rent" means such rent as may reasonably be expected to have been required in respect of the subordinate interest (having regard to any premium payable for the grant of the interest) if the transaction had been at arm's length;

"premium" includes any capital consideration, except so much of any sum as corresponds to–
(a) an amount brought into account as a receipt in calculating the profits of a property business under sections 217 to 221 of CTA 2009 that is calculated by reference to the sum, or
(b) an amount brought into account as a receipt in calculating the profits of a UK property business under sections 277 to 281 of ITTOIA 2005 that is calculated by reference to the sum;

"subordinate interest" means an interest in or right over the building, whether granted by the former owner or anyone else.
326(2) In section 325 and this section–

"capital consideration" means consideration which consists of a capital sum or would be a capital sum if it had consisted of a money payment, and

"rent" includes any consideration which is not capital consideration.

History – In s. 326(1), para. (a) in the definition of "premium" substituted by CTA 2009, s. 1322 and Sch. 1, para. 499, with effect for corporation tax purposes for accounting periods ending on or after 1 April 2009, and for income tax and capital gains tax purposes for the tax year 2009–10 and subsequent tax years.
S. 326(1) amended by ITTOIA 2005, s. 882(1) and Sch. 1, para. 553; effective for income tax purposes for 2005–06 onwards and for corporation tax purposes for accounting periods ending after 5 April 2005 (ITTOIA 2005, s. 883(1)).

Origin – S. 326(1), (2): CAA 1990, s. 5(4).

QUALIFYING ENTERPRISE ZONE EXPENDITURE: EFFECT OF REALISING CAPITAL VALUE

Capital value provisions: application of provisions

327 Sections 328 to 331 apply only if expenditure on the construction of a building has been incurred–
(a) at a time–
(i) when the site of the building was wholly or mainly in an enterprise zone, and
(ii) which was not more than 10 years after the site was first included in the zone, or
(b) under a contract entered into at such a time.

Origin – FA 1994, s. 120(7) (part), (8) (part).

Balancing adjustment on realisation of capital value

328(1) There is a balancing event if, while the building is an industrial building or after it has ceased to be one, any capital value is realised.
328(2) No balancing allowance is to be made because of a balancing event under this section.
328(3) The amount of capital value realised is to be treated as the proceeds from the balancing event.
328(4) If a balancing event under this section occurs–
(a) section 319 (balancing adjustment where building not an industrial building etc. throughout) has effect as if, immediately after the balancing event, the starting expenditure were reduced by the amount of capital value realised, and
(b) if the net proceeds of a sale of the relevant interest fall to be increased under section 325(4) (balancing allowances restricted where sale subject to subordinate interest), those proceeds as so increased are reduced by the amount of any capital value realised before the sale.

328(5) Capital value is realised if an amount of capital value is paid which is attributable to an interest in land (**"the subordinate interest"**) to which the relevant interest in the building is or will be subject.
328(6) The capital value is realised on the making of the payment.
328(7) The amount of capital value realised is the amount of capital value that is attributable to the subordinate interest under section 329.
Origin – S. 328(1): CAA 1990, s. 4(1) (part).
S. 328(2), (3): CAA 1990, s. 4(9A) (part).
S. 328(4): CAA 1990, s. 4(9A) (part), s. 5(2A).
S. 328(5)–(7): CAA 1990, s. 4A(1) (part).
Transitional – Sch. 3, para. 71: section does not apply if the capital expenditure was incurred under a contract entered into before 13 January 1994, and was not a conditional contract which become unconditional on or after 26 February 1994.

Capital value that is attributable to subordinate interest

329(1) Capital value is attributable to the subordinate interest if it is paid–
(a) in consideration of the grant of the subordinate interest,
(b) instead of any rent payable by the person entitled to the subordinate interest,
(c) in consideration of the assignment of such rent, or
(d) in consideration of–
(i) the surrender of the subordinate interest, or
(ii) the variation or waiver of any of the terms on which it was granted.
329(2) If–
(a) no premium is given in consideration of the grant of the subordinate interest or any premium so given is less than the commercial premium, and
(b) no commercial rent is payable in respect of the subordinate interest,
capital value is attributable under subsection (1)(a) as if the commercial premium had been paid on and in consideration of the grant of the subordinate interest.
329(3) If any value given instead of any rent payable by the person entitled to the subordinate interest is less than the commercial amount, capital value is attributable under subsection (1)(b) as if the commercial amount had been paid.
329(4) If–
(a) any rent payable in respect of the subordinate interest is assigned, but
(b) no value is given in consideration of the assignment or any value so given is less than the commercial amount,
capital value is attributable under subsection (1)(c) as if the commercial amount had been given on and in consideration of the assignment.
329(5) If–
(a) the subordinate interest is surrendered, or any of the terms on which the subordinate interest was granted are varied or waived, but
(b) no value is given in consideration of the surrender, variation or waiver or any value so given is less than the commercial amount,
capital value is attributable under subsection (1)(d) as if the commercial amount had been given on and in consideration of the surrender, variation or waiver.
329(6) Capital value is not attributable to the subordinate interest if it is paid in consideration of the grant of a lease to which an election under section 290 (treating grant of lease exceeding 50 years as sale) applies.
Origin – S. 329(1): CAA 1990, s. 4A(2).
S. 329(2): CAA 1990, s. 4A(4) (part).
S. 329(3): CAA 1990, s. 4A(6) (part).
S. 329(4), (5): CAA 1990, s. 4A(5).
S. 329(6): CAA 1990, s. 4A(8).
Transitional – Sch. 3, para. 71: section does not apply if the capital expenditure was incurred under a contract entered into before 13 January 1994, and was not a conditional contract which become unconditional on or after 26 February 1994.

Exception for payments more than 7 years after agreement

330(1) Capital value is not realised for the purposes of section 328 if the payment is made more than 7 years after–
(a) the agreement under which the qualifying expenditure was incurred was entered into, or
(b) if that agreement was conditional, the time when the agreement became unconditional.
330(2) If an agreement is made to pay in respect of any event an amount of capital value which would be attributable to the subordinate interest, and–
(a) the agreement is made, or if conditional becomes unconditional, before the end of the period of 7 years referred to in subsection (1), and
(b) the event occurs, or any payment in consideration of the event is made, after the end of that period,
the event or payment is treated for the purposes of subsection (1) as occurring or made before the end of the 7 years.
330(3) Subsection (1) does not apply if arrangements–
(a) under which the person entitled to the relevant interest acquired it, or
(b) which were made in connection with its acquisition,
include provision which requires, or makes substantially more likely, any of the events set out in subsection (4).
330(4) The events are–
(a) the subsequent sale of the relevant interest;
(b) the subsequent grant of an interest in land out of the relevant interest;
(c) any other event on which capital value attributable to the subordinate interest would be paid or treated as paid.
Origin – S. 330(1): CAA 1990, s. 4A(1) (part), (12).
S. 330(2): CAA 1990, s. 4A(11).
S. 330(3), (4): CAA 1990, s. 4A(7).
Transitional – Sch. 3, para. 71: section does not apply if the capital expenditure was incurred under a contract entered into before 13 January 1994, and was not a conditional contract which become unconditional on or after 26 February 1994.

Capital value provisions: interpretation

Notes – ITTOIA 2005 amends s. 331, effective for income tax purposes for 2005–06 onwards and for corporation tax purposes for accounting periods ending after 5 April 2005: see the History notes for details.
331(1) **"Capital value"** means any capital sum–
(a) including what would have been a capital sum if it had been a money payment (and references to payment are to be read accordingly), but
(b) excluding so much of any sum as corresponds to–

(i) an amount brought into account as a receipt in calculating the profits of a property business under sections 217 to 221 of CTA 2009 that is calculated by reference to the sum, or
(ii) an amount brought into account as a receipt in calculating the profits of a UK property business under sections 277 to 281 of ITTOIA 2005 that is calculated by reference to the sum.

331(2) **"Interest in land"** means–
(a) a leasehold estate in the land, whether in the nature of a head lease, sub-lease or under-lease;
(b) an easement or servitude;
(c) a licence to occupy land.

331(3) References to granting an interest in land include agreeing to grant any such interest.

331(4) In section 329–

"commercial amount" means the amount that would have been given if the transaction had been at arm's length,

"commercial premium" means the premium that would have been given if the transaction had been at arm's length, and

"commercial rent" means such rent as may reasonably be expected to have been required in respect of the subordinate interest (having regard to any premium paid in consideration of the grant of the interest) if the transaction had been at arm's length.

331(5) In the application of section 329 to Scotland, references to assignment are to be read as references to assignation.

History – S. 331(1)(b)(i) substituted by CTA 2009, s. 1322 and Sch. 1, para. 500, with effect for corporation tax purposes for accounting periods ending on or after 1 April 2009, and for income tax and capital gains tax purposes for the tax year 2009–10 and subsequent tax years.

S. 331(1)(b) amended by ITTOIA 2005, s. 882(1) and Sch. 1, para. 554; effective for income tax purposes for 2005–06 onwards and for corporation tax purposes for accounting periods ending after 5 April 2005 (ITTOIA 2005, s. 883(1)).

Origin – S. 331(1): CAA 1990, s. 4A(3).
S. 331(2), (3): CAA 1990, s. 4A(9).
S. 331(4): CAA 1990, s. 4A(4) (part), (5) (part), (6) (part), (10).
S. 331(5): CAA 1990, s. 4A(13) (part).

Transitional – Sch. 3, para. 71: section does not apply if the capital expenditure was incurred under a contract entered into before 13 January 1994, and was not a conditional contract which become unconditional on or after 26 February 1994.

Chapter 8 – Writing Off Qualifying Expenditure

Transitional – Sch. 3, para. 79: where provisions concerning expenditure on preparatory work on land where the building was used before 6 April 1956 applied, Pt. 3 (excluding Ch. 5) applies to the part of the expenditure separate from the remainder.

Introduction

332 For the purposes of this Part qualifying expenditure is written off to the extent and at the times specified in this Chapter.

Origin – CAA 1990, s. 8(1) (part), Annex 1, Change 39.

Writing off initial allowances

333 If an initial allowance is made in respect of the qualifying expenditure, the amount of the allowance is written off at the time when the building is first used.

Origin – CAA 1990, s. 8(2) (part).

Writing off writing-down allowances

334(1) If a writing-down allowance is made in respect of the qualifying expenditure, the amount of the allowance is written off at the end of the chargeable period for which the allowance is made.

334(2) If a balancing event occurs at the end of the chargeable period referred to in subsection (1), the amount written off under that subsection is to be taken into account in calculating the residue of qualifying expenditure immediately before the event to determine what balancing adjustment (if any) is to be made.

Origin – S. 334(1): CAA 1990, s. 8(3).
S. 334(2): CAA 1990, s. 8(4).

Writing off research and development allowances

335(1) If an allowance under Part 6 (research and development allowances) is made in respect of the qualifying expenditure, the amount of the allowance is written off at the end of the chargeable period for which the allowance is made.

335(2) If a balancing event occurs at the end of the chargeable period referred to in subsection (1), the amount written off under that subsection is to be taken into account in calculating the residue of qualifying expenditure immediately before that event to determine what balancing adjustment (if any) is to be made.

Origin – S. 335(1): CAA 1990, s. 8(5) (part), Annex 1, Change 39.
S. 335(2): CAA 1990, s. 8(6) (part).

Rewrite: Changes in Law – Explanatory Notes, Annex 1, Change 39: the net allowance given (including balancing events) under Pt. 6 is written off, rather than as previously the gross allowance.

Writing off expenditure when building not an industrial building

336(1) This section applies if for any period or periods between–
(a) the time when the building was first used for any purpose, and
(b) the time when the residue of qualifying expenditure falls to be ascertained,
the building was not an industrial building.

336(2) An amount equal to the notional writing-down allowances for the period or periods is written off at the time when the residue falls to be ascertained.

336(3) The notional writing-down allowances are the allowances that would have been made for the period or periods in question (if the building had remained an industrial building), at such rate or rates as would have been appropriate having regard to any relevant sale.

336(4) In subsection (3) **"relevant sale"** means a sale of the relevant interest as a result of which a balancing adjustment falls to be made under section 314.

Origin – S. 336(1)–(4): CAA 1990, s. 8(7).

Transitional – Sch. 3, para. 72(a): a building is not treated as an industrial building for this section under s. 274, table A, items 5(b) and (c) for period before 6 April 1953.

CAA 2001

Sch. 3, para. 72(b): a building is not treated as an industrial building for this section under s. 274, table A, item 7 for period before 6 April 1952.

Writing off or increase of expenditure where balancing adjustment made

337(1) This section applies if the relevant interest in the building is sold.
337(2) If a balancing allowance is made, the amount by which the residue of qualifying expenditure before the sale exceeds the net proceeds of the sale is written off at the time of the sale.
337(3) If a balancing charge is made, the amount of the residue of qualifying expenditure is increased at the time of the sale by the amount of the charge.
337(4) But if the balancing charge is made under section 319(6) (difference between net allowances made and adjusted net cost), the residue of qualifying expenditure immediately after the sale is limited to the net proceeds of the sale.

Origin – S. 337(1): CAA 1990, s. 8(9) (part), (10) (part), (11) (part).
S. 337(2): CAA 1990, s. 8(9) (part).
S. 337(3): CAA 1990, s. 8(10) (part).
S. 337(4): CAA 1990, s. 8(11) (part).

Writing off capital value which has been realised

338 If a balancing event within section 328 occurs (realisation of capital value), an amount equal to any capital value realised is written off at the time of the event.

Origin – CAA 1990, s. 8(12B).

Crown or other person not within the charge to tax entitled to the relevant interest

339(1) This section applies if at any time–
(a) the Crown, or
(b) a person who is not within the charge to tax,
("A") is entitled to the relevant interest in a building.
339(2) Sections 333 to 338 (writing off qualifying expenditure) have effect as if all writing-down allowances and balancing adjustments had been made as could have been made if–
(a) a person ("B") who–
(i) is not the Crown,
(ii) is within the charge to tax, and
(iii) is not a company,
had been entitled to the relevant interest, and
(b) the other assumptions in subsection (3) had been made.
339(3) The assumptions are that–
(a) while A was entitled to the relevant interest, all things which were done in relation to the building–
(i) by or to A, or
(ii) by or to a person using the building under the authority of A,
were done by or to B for the purposes of, and in the course of, a trade carried on by B,
(b) any sale of the relevant interest in the building by or on behalf of A was made in connection with the termination of the trade carried on by B, and
(c) B's periods of account for that trade had, in the case of each tax year, ended immediately before the beginning of the next tax year.

Origin – S. 339(1), (2): CAA 1990, s. 8(13) (part), (14) (part), Annex 2, Note 42.
S. 339(3): CAA 1990, s. 8(13) (part), (14) (part).

Transitional – Sch. 3, para. 73: this section does not apply if the interest was sold before 29 July 1988.

Rewrite: Changes in Law – Explanatory Notes, Annex 2, Note 42: words "within the charge to tax" refer to UK tax as defined in ICTA 1928, s. 832(2) and thus the words "in the United Kingdom" are unnecessary and have been omitted.

Treatment of demolition costs

340(1) This section applies if–
(a) a building is demolished, and
(b) the person to or on whom any balancing allowance or balancing charge is or might be made is the person incurring the cost of the demolition.
340(2) The net cost of the demolition is added to the residue of qualifying expenditure immediately before the demolition.
340(3) **"The net cost of the demolition"** means the amount, if any, by which the cost of the demolition exceeds any money received for the remains of the property.
340(4) If this section applies, neither the cost of the demolition nor the net cost of the demolition is treated for the purposes of any Part of this Act other than Part 10 (assured tenancy allowances) as expenditure on any other property replacing the property demolished.

Origin – S. 340(1)–(4): CAA 1990, s. 8(12).

Chapter 9 – Highway Undertakings

Transitional – Sch. 3, para. 79: where provisions concerning expenditure on preparatory work on land where the building was used before 6 April 1956 applied, Pt. 3 (excluding Ch. 5) applies to the part of the expenditure separate from the remainder.

Carrying on of highway undertakings

341(1) For the purposes of this Part the carrying on of a highway undertaking is to be treated as the carrying on of an undertaking by way of trade; and accordingly references in this Part (except sections 274 and 276) to a trade include a highway undertaking.
341(2) For the purposes of this Part a person carrying on a highway undertaking is to be treated as occupying, for the purposes of the undertaking, any road in relation to which it is carried on.
341(3) In this Chapter **"highway undertaking"** has the meaning given in item 6 of Table B in section 274.
341(4) In that item and this Chapter **"highway concession"**, in relation to a road, means–
(a) a right to receive sums from the relevant authority because the road is or will be used by the general public, or
(b) if the road is a toll road, the right to charge tolls in respect of the road.
341(5) In subsection (4) **"the relevant authority"** means–
(a) the Secretary of State,
(b) the Scottish Ministers,

(c) the National Assembly for Wales, or
(d) the Department for Regional Development in Northern Ireland.

History – In s. 341(4), words "the relevant authority" substituted, and s. 341(5) added, by FA 2001, s. 69 and Sch. 21, para. 6, with effect as respects allowances and charges falling to be made for chargeable periods ending, for income tax purposes, on or after 6 April 2001, and, for corporation tax purposes, on or after 1 April 2001.

Origin – S. 341(1): CAA 1990, s. 21(5A).
S. 341(2): CAA 1990, s. 21(5B).
S. 341(3): drafting.
S. 341(4): CAA 1990, s. 21(5AA) ("highway concession").

Transitional – Sch. 3, para. 74: s. 341(4)(a) does not apply in relation to expenditure incurred before 6 April 1995.

The relevant interest

342(1) For the purposes of Chapter 3 (the relevant interest in the building) as it applies to expenditure incurred on the construction of a road, a highway concession is not to be treated as an interest in the road.
342(2) But if the person who incurred the expenditure on the construction of the road–
(a) was not entitled to an interest in the road when he incurred the expenditure, but
(b) was at that time entitled to a highway concession in respect of the road,
the highway concession is to be treated as the relevant interest in relation to that expenditure.
342(3) Any question as to what is the relevant interest is to be determined on the assumption that, if section 344 (renewed or new concession treated as extension of earlier concession) applies, the renewed or new concession is a continuation of the earlier concession.

Origin – S. 342(1): CAA 1990, s. 20(5).
S. 342(2): CAA 1990, s. 20(6).
S. 342(3): CAA 1990, s. 4(2AB) (part).

Balancing adjustment on ending of concession

343(1) If–
(a) the relevant interest is a highway concession, and
(b) the concession is brought to or comes to an end without being treated as extended under section 344,
the ending of the concession is a balancing event.
343(2) The proceeds from such a balancing event are–
(a) any insurance money received by the person entitled to the highway concession in respect of any qualifying expenditure, and
(b) other compensation so received so far as it consists of capital sums.

CAA 2001

Origin – S. 343(1): CAA 1990, s. 4(1) (part), (2AA) (part).
S. 343(2): CAA 1990, s. 156 (part).

Transitional – Sch. 3, para. 74: section 343 does not apply in relation to expenditure incurred before 6 April 1995.

Cases where highway concession is to be treated as extended

344(1) A highway concession in respect of a road is to be treated as extended if–
(a) the person entitled to the concession takes up a renewed concession in respect of the whole or a part of the road, or
(b) that person or a person connected with him takes up a new concession in respect of–
(i) the whole or a part of the road, or
(ii) a road that includes the whole or a part of the road.
344(2) But the concession is to be treated as extended only–
(a) to the extent that the concession which has in fact ended, and the renewed or new concession, relate to the same road, and
(b) for the period of the renewed or new concession.
344(3) A person takes up a renewed or new concession if he is afforded, whether or not under legally enforceable arrangements, an opportunity to be granted the renewed or new concession and takes advantage of the opportunity.
344(4) For the purposes of subsection (3) it does not matter whether the renewed or new concession is on the same terms as the previous concession or on modified terms.
344(5) If–
(a) a highway concession is treated as extended under this section, and
(b) the period of the extension is different in relation to different parts of the road in relation to which the concession has been granted,
such apportionments are to be made for the purposes of section 343 as are just and reasonable.

Origin – S. 344(1)–(4): CAA 1990, s. 4(2AB) (part).
S. 344(5): CAA 1990, s. 4(2AA) (part).

Transitional – Sch. 3, para. 74: s. 344 does not apply in relation to expenditure incurred before 6 April 1995.

Chapter 10 – Additional VAT Liabilities and Rebates

Transitional – Sch. 3, para. 79: where provisions concerning expenditure on preparatory work on land where the building was used before 6 April 1956 applied, Pt. 3 (excluding Ch. 5) applies to the part of the expenditure separate from the remainder.

INTRODUCTION

Introduction

345 For the purposes of this Chapter–
(a) **"additional VAT liability"** and **"additional VAT rebate"** have the meaning given by section 547,
(b) the time when–
(i) a person incurs an additional VAT liability, or
(ii) an additional VAT rebate is made to a person,
is given by section 548, and
(c) the chargeable period in which, and the time when, an additional VAT liability or an additional VAT rebate accrues are given by section 549.

Origin – S. 345: drafting.

Transitional – Sch. 3, para. 74: s. 344 does not apply in relation to expenditure incurred before 6 April 1995.

ADDITIONAL VAT LIABILITIES

Additional VAT liabilities and initial allowances

346(1) This section applies if–
(a) a person was entitled to an initial allowance in respect of qualifying enterprise zone expenditure,
(b) the person entitled to the relevant interest in relation to that expenditure incurs an additional VAT liability in respect of that expenditure,
(c) the additional VAT liability is incurred at a time when the building is, or is to be, an industrial building–
(i) occupied by the person entitled to the relevant interest or a qualifying lessee, or
(ii) used by a qualifying licensee, and
(d) the additional VAT liability is incurred not more than 10 years after the site of the building was first included in the enterprise zone.

346(2) If this section applies, the person entitled to the relevant interest is entitled to an initial allowance on the amount of the additional VAT liability.
346(3) The amount of the initial allowance is 100% of the amount of the additional VAT liability.
346(4) A person claiming an initial allowance under this section may require the allowance to be reduced to a specified amount.
346(5) The allowance is made for the chargeable period in which the additional VAT liability accrues.
346(6) The persons mentioned in subsection (1)(a) and (b) need not be the same.

Origin – S. 346(1)–(3): CAA 1990, s. 1(1A) (part).
S. 346(4): CAA 1990, s. 1(5) (part).
S. 346(5): CAA 1990, s. 1(1A) (part), s. 159A(3) (part).
S. 346(6): drafting.

Transitional – Sch. 3, para. 75–77: initial allowances may be due in respect of additional VAT liabilities arising if the original capital expenditure was incurred in the year ended 31 October 1993.

Additional VAT liabilities and writing-down allowances

347(1) This section applies if the person entitled to the relevant interest in relation to qualifying expenditure incurs an additional VAT liability in respect of that expenditure.
347(2) If this section applies–
(a) the additional VAT liability is treated as qualifying expenditure, and
(b) the amount of the residue of qualifying expenditure is accordingly increased at the time when the liability accrues by the amount of the liability.

347(3) The incurring of the additional VAT liability is a relevant event for the purposes of section 311 (calculation of writing-down allowances) that is to be treated as occurring at the time when the liability accrues.

Origin – S. 347(1): CAA 1990, s. 3(2A) (part).
S. 347(2): CAA 1990, s. 3(2A) (part), s. 159A(3) (part).
S. 347(3): CAA 1990, s. 3(2B) (part), s. 159A(3) (part).

Additional VAT liabilities and writing off initial allowances

348 If an initial allowance is made in respect of an additional VAT liability incurred after the building is first used, the amount of the allowance is written off at the time when the liability accrues.

Origin – CAA 1990, s. 8(2) (part), s. 159A(3) (part).

Transitional – Sch. 3, para. 75–77: intial allowances may be due in respect of additional VAT liabilities arising if the original capital expenditure was incurred in the year ended 31 October 1993.

ADDITIONAL VAT REBATES

Additional VAT rebates and writing-down allowances

349(1) This section applies if–
(a) an additional VAT rebate is made in respect of qualifying expenditure to the person entitled to the relevant interest in relation to that qualifying expenditure, and
(b) immediately before the rebate accrues, the residue of that qualifying expenditure is equal to, or greater than, the amount of the rebate.

349(2) The making of the additional VAT rebate is a relevant event for the purposes of section 311 (calculation of writing-down allowances) that is to be treated as occurring at the time when the rebate accrues.

Origin – S. 349(1): CAA 1990, s. 3(2C) (part).
S. 349(2): CAA 1990, s. 3(2C) (part), s. 159A(3) (part).

Additional VAT rebates and balancing adjustments

350(1) If an additional VAT rebate is made in respect of qualifying expenditure to the person entitled to the relevant interest in relation to that qualifying expenditure–
(a) the making of the rebate is a balancing event for the purposes of this Part, but
(b) the making of balancing adjustments as a result of the event is subject to subsections (2) and (3).

350(2) No balancing allowance is not to be made as a result of the event.
350(3) A balancing charge is not to be made as a result of the event unless–
(a) the amount of the additional VAT rebate is more than the amount of the residue of qualifying expenditure immediately before the time when the rebate accrues, or
(b) there is no such residue.

350(4) The amount of the balancing charge is–
(a) the amount of the difference, or
(b) the amount of the rebate (if there is no residue).

350(5) If a balancing charge is made under this section, the starting expenditure is reduced by the amount of that charge in a case where section 322(2) applies (person subject to balancing adjustment is the person who incurred the qualifying expenditure).

Origin – S. 350(1): CAA 1990, s. 4(1) (part).
S. 350(2): CAA 1990, s. 4(2A) (part).
S. 350(3): CAA 1990, s. 4(2A) (part), s. 159A(3) (part).
S. 350(4): CAA 1990, s. 4(2A) (part).
S. 350(5): CAA 1990, s. 4(9) ("the capital expenditure", part).

Additional VAT rebates and writing off qualifying expenditure

351 If an additional VAT rebate is made in respect of qualifying expenditure, an amount equal to the rebate is written off at the time when the rebate accrues.

Origin – CAA 1990, s. 8(12A), s. 159A(3) (part).

Chapter 11 – Giving Effect to Allowances and Charges

Transitional – Sch. 3, para. 79: where provisions concerning expenditure on preparatory work on land where the building was used before 6 April 1956 applied, Pt. 3 (excluding Ch. 5) applies to the part of the expenditure separate from the remainder.

Trades

352(1) An allowance or charge to which a person is entitled or liable under this Part is to be given effect in calculating the profits of that person's trade, by treating–
(a) the allowance as an expense of the trade, and
(b) the charge as a receipt of the trade.
352(2) In the case of a person who–
(a) is entitled to an allowance or liable to a charge in respect of a commercial building, and
(b) occupies the building in the course of a profession or vocation,
the references in subsection (1) to a trade are to be read as references to the profession or vocation.
352(3) Subsection (1) is subject to the following provisions of this Chapter.

Origin – S. 352(1): CAA 1990, s. 9(1) (part), s. 140(2) (part), s. 144(2) (part), s. 161(5) (part).
S. 352(2) Annex 1, Change 36.
S. 352(3) drafting.

Transitional – ICTA 1988, s. 388 (pre-self assessment): capital allowances included in relief for certain terminal losses.
FA 1994, Sch. 20, para. 9(2): former CAA 1990, s. 140 has effect as if the allowances (to traders, etc. who set up before 6 April 1994) for the first period of account ending after 5 April 1997 include allowances brought forward from earlier years to the extent that they were not used in 1996–97. Thus any unused, brought-forward allowances are treated as current-year allowances of 1997–98.

Rewrite: Changes in Law – Explanatory Notes, Annex 1, Change 36: s. 352(2) applies to trades, professions and vocations whereas, former CAA 1990, s. 9(1) referred only to a trade.

Lessors and licensors

353(1) This section applies if–
(a) a person is entitled or liable to an allowance or charge for a chargeable period (**"the relevant period"**), but
(b) his interest in the building in question is or was subject to a lease or a licence at the relevant time.
353(2) If the person's interest in the building is an asset of a UK property business carried on by him at any time in the relevant period, the allowance or charge is to be given effect in calculating the profits of that business for the relevant period, by treating–
(a) the allowance as an expense of that business, and
(b) the charge as a receipt of that business.
353(3) If the person's interest in the building is an asset of an overseas property business carried on by him at any time in the relevant period, the allowance or charge is to be given effect in calculating the profits of the overseas property business for the relevant period, by treating–
(a) the allowance as an expense of that business, and
(b) the charge as a receipt of that business.
353(3A) If the person is within the charge to income tax in respect of the allowance or charge and his interest in the building is not an asset of any property business carried on by him at any time in the relevant period, the allowance or charge is to be given effect by treating him as if he had been carrying on a UK property business in that period and as if–
(a) the allowance were an expense of that business, and
(b) the charge were a receipt of that business.
353(4) If the person is a company within the charge to corporation tax in respect of the allowance or charge and its interest in the building is not an asset of any property business carried on by it at any time in the relevant period, the allowance or charge is to be given effect by treating the company as if it had been carrying on a UK property business in that period and as if–
(a) the allowance were an expense of that business, and
(b) the charge were a receipt of that business.
353(5) In subsection (1) **"the relevant time"** means–
(a) in relation to an initial allowance, the time when the expenditure was incurred or any subsequent time before the building is used for any purpose;
(b) in relation to a writing-down allowance, the end of the relevant period;
(c) in relation to a balancing allowance or balancing charge, the time immediately before the event giving rise to the allowance or charge.

History – In s. 353(2), the words ", or a Schedule A business,", which appeared after the words "UK property business", omitted by CTA 2009, s. 1322 and Sch. 1, para. 501(2) and repealed by CTA 2009, s. 1326 and Sch. 3, Pt. 1, with effect for corporation tax purposes for accounting periods ending on or after 1 April 2009, and for income tax and capital gains tax purposes for the tax year 2009–10 and subsequent tax years.
In s. 353(2) the words "a UK property business, or a Schedule A business," substituted for "a Schedule A business" by ITTOIA 2005, s. 882(1) and Sch. 1, para. 555(2); effective for income tax purposes for 2005–06 onwards and for corporation tax purposes for accounting periods ending after 5 April 2005 (ITTOIA 2005, s. 883(1)).
S. 353(3A) inserted by ITTOIA 2005, s. 882(1) and Sch. 1, para. 555(3); effective for income tax purposes for 2005–06 onwards and for corporation tax purposes for accounting periods ending after 5 April 2005 (ITTOIA 2005, s. 883(1)).
In s. 353(4), the words "UK property business" substituted for the words "Schedule A business" by CTA 2009, s. 1322 and Sch. 1, para. 501(3), with effect for corporation tax purposes for accounting periods ending on or after 1 April 2009, and for income tax and capital gains tax purposes for the tax year 2009–10 and subsequent tax years.
S. 353(4) amended (in various places) by ITTOIA 2005, s. 882(1) and Sch. 1, para. 555(4); effective for income tax purposes for 2005–06 onwards and for corporation tax purposes for accounting periods ending after 5 April 2005 (ITTOIA 2005, s. 883(1)).

Origin – S. 353(1): CAA 1990, s. 9(2) (part), (4).
S. 353(2): CAA 1990, s. 9(1) (part), (2) (part), Annex 2, Note 47.
S. 353(3): CAA 1990, s. 9(1) (part), (2) (part), s. 161(2A) (part), Annex 2, Note 47.
S. 353(4): CAA 1990, s. 9(1) (part), (2) (part), Annex 2, Note 47.
S. 353(5): CAA 1990, s. 9(3).

Rewrite: Changes in Law – Explanatory Notes, Annex 2, Note 47: the allowance is given effect in connection with the business of which the lease is an asset, whether this is a Sch. A business or overseas property business. This clarifies the combined effect of former CAA 1990, s. 9 and 161(2A).

Buildings temporarily out of use

354(1) This section applies if a person is entitled to an allowance or liable to a charge for a chargeable period during which the building is treated as an industrial building under section 285 (building still industrial building despite temporary disuse).
354(2) If, when the building was last in use as an industrial building–
(a) it was in use for the purposes of a trade which has since been permanently discontinued, or
(b) the relevant interest in the building was subject to a lease or a licence which has since come to an end,
section 353(4) applies to the person as if the relevant interest were subject to a lease or licence at the relevant time.
354(3) If–
(a) the person is liable to a balancing charge, and
(b) when the building was last in use as an industrial building, it was in use as an industrial building for the purposes of a trade which was carried on by the person but which has since been permanently discontinued,
the same deductions may be made from the amount of the balancing charge as may be made under section 254 of ITTOIA 2005 or section 196 of CTA 2009 (deductions allowed in case of post-cessation receipts) from an amount chargeable to tax under Chapter 18 of Part 2 of ITTOIA 2005 or, as the case may be, under Chapter 15 of Part 3 of CTA 2009.
354(4) Subsection (3) does not affect the making of any deduction allowed under any other provision of the Tax Acts.
354(5) For the purposes of this section the permanent discontinuance of a trade does not include an event treated as a permanent discontinuance under section 577(2A) of this Act or section 18 of ITTOIA 2005 (effect of company ceasing to trade etc).
354(6) In this section **"trade"**, in relation to a commercial building, includes a profession or vocation.

History – In s. 354(3), the words "section 196 of CTA 2009" substituted for the words "section 105 of ICTA" and the words "Chapter 15 of Part 3 of CTA 2009" substituted for the words "section 103 or 104(1) of ICTA" by CTA 2009, s. 1322 and Sch. 1, para. 502(2), with effect for corporation tax purposes for accounting periods ending on or after 1 April 2009, and for income tax and capital gains tax purposes for the tax year 2009–10 and subsequent tax years.
S. 354(3) amended by ITTOIA 2005, s. 882(1) and Sch. 1, para. 556(2); effective for income tax purposes for 2005–06 onwards and for corporation tax purposes for accounting periods ending after 5 April 2005 (ITTOIA 2005, s. 883(1)).
In s. 354(5), the words "section 577(2A) of this Act or section 18 of ITTOIA 2005" substituted for the words "section 18 of ITTOIA 2005 or section 337(1) of ICTA" by CTA 2009, s. 1322 and Sch. 1, para. 502(3), with effect for corporation tax purposes for accounting periods ending on or after 1 April 2009, and for income tax and capital gains tax purposes for the tax year 2009–10 and subsequent tax years.
S. 354(5) amended by ITTOIA 2005, s. 882(1) and Sch. 1, para. 556(3); effective for income tax purposes for 2005–06 onwards and for corporation tax purposes for accounting periods ending after 5 April 2005 (ITTOIA 2005, s. 883(1)).

Origin – S. 354(1): CAA 1990, s. 15ZA(1) (part), (2) (part), (5) (part).
S. 354(2): CAA 1990, s. 15ZA(2) (part), (5) (part).
S. 354(3), (4): CAA 1990, s. 15ZA(3).
S. 354(5): CAA 1990, s. 15ZA(4).
S. 354(6): Annex 1, Change 36.

Rewrite: Changes in Law – Explanatory Notes, Annex 1, Change 36: s. 354(6) applies to trades, professions and vocations whereas, former CAA 1990, s. 15ZA(2) referred only to a trade.

Buildings for miners etc.: carry-back of balancing allowances

355(1) This section applies if–
(a) a trade consists of or includes the working of a source of mineral deposits (within the meaning of item 7 of Table A in section 274),
(b) a balancing allowance falls to be made under this Part for the last chargeable period in which the trade is carried on,
(c) the event giving rise to the allowance is–
 (i) the source of mineral deposits ceasing to be worked, or
 (ii) the coming to an end of a foreign concession,
(d) the allowance is made for expenditure on a building which was constructed for occupation by, or for the welfare of, persons employed at or in connection with the working of the source of mineral deposits, and
(e) full effect cannot be given to the allowance because there are insufficient profits for that chargeable period.
355(2) If this section applies, the person entitled to the allowance may claim that the balance of the allowance is to be given for the last preceding chargeable period, and so on for other preceding chargeable periods.
355(2A) For income tax purposes the allowance is given effect at Step 2 of the calculation in section 23 of ITA 2007.
355(3) But allowances are not to be given under subsection (2) for chargeable periods amounting in total to more than 5 years; but a proportionately reduced allowance may be given for a chargeable period of which part is required to make up the 5 years.
355(4) In counting the 5 years, include any period for which an allowance might be made but cannot be given effect because there are insufficient profits.
355(5) If this section applies to a company, no allowance may be given under this section so as to create or increase a loss in any accounting period.
355(6) If this section applies to a company and a claim is made both under this section and under section 37 of CTA 2010 (relief for company trading losses)–
(a) effect is to be given to the claim under that section before this section is applied, and
(b) for the purposes of giving effect to the claim under that section, the allowance for which the claim under this section is made is to be disregarded.

History – S. 355(2A) inserted by ITA 2007, s. 1027 and Sch. 1, para. 406, with effect from 6 April 2007.
In s. 355(6), the words "section 37 of CTA 2010" substituted for "section 393A(1) of ICTA" by CTA 2010, s. 1177 and Sch. 1, para. 353, with effect for corporation tax purposes for accounting periods ending on or after 1 April 2010.

Origin – S. 355(1)–(4): CAA 1990, s. 17(1).
S. 355(5), (6): CAA 1990, s. 17(2).

Chapter 12 – Supplementary Provisions

Transitional – Sch. 3, para. 79: where provisions concerning expenditure on preparatory work on land where the building was used before 6 April 1956 applied, Pt. 3 (excluding Ch. 5) applies to the part of the expenditure separate from the remainder.

Apportionment of sums partly referable to non-qualifying assets

356(1) If the sum paid for the sale of the relevant interest in a building is attributable–

(a) partly to assets representing expenditure for which an allowance can be made under this Part, and
(b) partly to assets representing other expenditure,

only so much of the sum as on a just and reasonable apportionment is attributable to the assets referred to in paragraph (a) is to be taken into account for the purposes of this Part.

356(2) Subsection (1) applies to other proceeds from a balancing event in respect of a building as it applies to a sum given for the sale of the relevant interest in the building.

356(3) Subsection (1) does not affect any other provision of this Act requiring an apportionment of the proceeds of a balancing event.

Origin – S. 356(1)–(3): CAA 1990, s. 21(3), Annex 1, Change 40.

Rewrite: Changes in Law – Explanatory Notes, Annex 1, change 40: "and reasonable" included to make the wording consistent with other provisions of this Act.

Arrangements having an artificial effect on pricing

357(1) If–
(a) the relevant interest in a building is sold,
(b) related arrangements have been entered into, at or before the time when the sale price is fixed, which had the effect at that time of enhancing the value of the relevant interest, and
(c) the arrangements contain a provision which has an artificial effect on pricing (see subsection (4)),

the sum paid on the sale of the relevant interest is to be treated for the purposes of arriving at qualifying expenditure as reduced to what it would have been if the arrangements had not contained the provision having that artificial effect.

357(2) If–
(a) qualifying expenditure is equal to a price paid on a sale of the relevant interest in a building,
(b) related arrangements have been entered into, at or before the time when the sale price is fixed, which had the effect at that time of enhancing the value of the relevant interest, and
(c) the arrangements contain a provision which has an artificial effect on pricing,

the proceeds from any balancing event subsequently occurring in relation to the building are to be treated for the purposes of this Part as reduced to what they would have been if the arrangements had not contained the provision having that artificial effect.

357(3) **"Related arrangements"** means arrangements between two or more persons which relate–
(a) to an interest in or right over the building, or
(b) to other arrangements made with respect to such an interest or right;

and for this purpose it is immaterial whether the interest or right in question is granted by the person entitled to the relevant interest or another person.

357(4) Arrangements contain a provision having an artificial effect on pricing to the extent that they go beyond what could reasonably have been regarded as required in comparable commercial transactions by the market conditions prevailing when the arrangements were entered into.

357(5) **"Comparable commercial transactions"** means transactions–
(a) involving interests in or rights over buildings of the same kind as (or of a similar kind to) the building to which the arrangements relate, and
(b) made by persons dealing with each other at arm's length in the open market.

Origin – S. 357(1), (2): CAA 1990, s. 10D(1) (part), (2) (part), (3) (part), (5) (part).
S. 357(3): CAA 1990, s. 10D(3) (part).
S. 357(4), (5): CAA 1990, s. 10D(4).

Transitional – Sch. 3, para. 78: s. 357 does not apply if the sale price became payable before 29 November 1994 or was fixed by contract entered into before that date and became payable before 6 April 1995.

Requisitioned land

358(1) This section applies in relation to any period (**"period of requisition"**) for which compensation–
(a) is payable, or
(b) but for any agreement would be payable,

under section 2(1)(a) of the Compensation (Defence) Act 1939.

358(2) This Part has effect in relation to the period of requisition as if the Crown had been in possession of the land for that period under a lease.

358(3) If a person carrying on a trade is authorised by the Crown to occupy the land (or part of it) during the whole or a part of the period of requisition, this Part has effect as if the Crown had granted a sub-lease of the land (or that part of it) to the occupier.

358(4) If subsection (2) or (3) applies, references in this Part to–
(a) the surrender of a leasehold interest,
(b) a leasehold interest being extinguished on the person entitled to it acquiring the interest which is reversionary on it, or
(c) the merger of a leasehold interest,

apply (with the necessary modifications) in relation to the lease under subsection (2) or the sub-lease under subsection (3).

358(5) If the person who (subject to the rights of the Crown) is entitled to possession of the land pays any sum to–
(a) the Crown, or
(b) if subsection (3) applies, the occupier,

in respect of a building constructed on the land during the period of requisition, the sum is to be treated for the purposes of this Part as paid in consideration of the surrender of the lease or sub-lease (as the case may be).

Origin – S. 358(1): CAA 1990, s. 16(1) (part), (3).
S. 358(2): CAA 1990, s. 16(1) (part).
S. 358(3): CAA 1990, s. 16(2) (part).
S. 358(4), (5): CAA 1990, s. 16(1) (part), (2) (part).

Provisions applying on termination of lease

359(1) This section applies for the purposes of this Part if a lease is terminated.

359(2) If, with the consent of the lessor, the lessee of a building remains in possession of the building after the termination without a new lease being granted to him the lease is treated as continuing so long as the lessee remains in possession.

359(3) If on the termination a new lease is granted to the lessee as a result of the exercise of an option available to him under the terms of the first lease, the second lease is treated as a continuation of the first.

359(4) If on the termination the lessor pays a sum to the lessee in respect of a building comprised in the lease, the lease is treated as if it had come to an end by surrender in consideration of the payment.

359(5) If on the termination–
(a) another lease is granted to a different lessee, and
(b) in connection with the transaction that lessee pays a sum to the person who was the lessee under the first lease,

the two leases are to be treated as if they were the same lease which had been assigned by the lessee under the first lease to the lessee under the second lease in consideration of the payment.

Origin – S. 359(1): CAA 1990, s. 16(4) (part), (5) (part), (6) (part), (7) (part).
S. 359(2): CAA 1990, s. 16(4) (part).
S. 359(3): CAA 1990, s. 16(5) (part).
S. 359(4): CAA 1990, s. 16(6) (part).
S. 359(5): CAA 1990, s. 16(7) (part).

Meaning of "lease" etc.

360(1) In this Part **"lease"** includes–
(a) an agreement for a lease if the term to be covered by the lease has begun, and
(b) any tenancy,
but does not include a mortgage (and **"lessee"**, **"lessor"** and **"leasehold interest"** are to be read accordingly).
360(2) In the application of this Part to Scotland–
(a) **"leasehold interest"** (or **"leasehold estate"**) means the interest of a tenant in property subject to a lease, and
(b) any reference to an interest which is reversionary on a leasehold interest or on a lease is to be read as a reference to the interest of the landlord in the property subject to the leasehold interest or lease.

Origin – S. 360(1): CAA 1990, s. 161(2) ("lease").
S. 360(2): CAA 1990, s. 4A(13) (part), s. 162 (part).

PART 3A – BUSINESS PREMISES RENOVATION ALLOWANCES

History – Pt. 3A inserted by FA 2005, s. 92 and Sch. 6, para. 1 in relation to expenditure incurred on or after 11 April 2007, by virtue of SI 2007/949, art. 2.

Chapter 1 – Introduction

360A Business premises renovation allowances

360A(1) Allowances are available under this Part if a person incurs qualifying expenditure in respect of a qualifying building.
360A(2) Allowances under this Part are made to the person who–
(a) incurred the expenditure, and
(b) has the relevant interest in the qualifying building.

History – Pt. 3A inserted by FA 2005, s. 92 and Sch. 6, para. 1 in relation to expenditure incurred on or after 11 April 2007, by virtue of SI 2007/949, art. 2.

Chapter 2 – Qualifying Expenditure

360B Meaning of "qualifying expenditure"

360B(1) In this Part **"qualifying expenditure"** means capital expenditure incurred before the expiry date–
(a) in respect of which Conditions A and B are met, and
(b) which is not excluded by subsection (3), (3B) or (3D).
360B(2) In subsection (1) **"the expiry date"** means–
(a) the fifth anniversary of the day appointed under section 92 of FA 2005, or
(b) such later date as the Treasury may prescribe by regulations.
360B(2A) Condition A is that the expenditure is incurred on–
(a) the conversion of a qualifying building into qualifying business premises,
(b) the renovation of a qualifying building if it is or will be qualifying business premises, or
(c) repairs to a qualifying building or, where the building is part of a building, to the building of which the qualifying building forms part, to the extent that the repairs are incidental to expenditure within paragraph (a) or (b).
360B(2B) Condition B is that the expenditure is incurred on–
(a) building works,
(b) architectural or design services,
(c) surveying or engineering services,
(d) planning applications, or
(e) statutory fees or statutory permissions.

360B(2C) But Condition B is treated as met in respect of expenditure incurred on matters not mentioned in that Condition to the extent that that expenditure (in total) does not exceed 5% of the qualifying expenditure incurred on the matters mentioned in subsection (2B)(a) to (c).

360B(3) Expenditure is excluded if it is incurred on or in connection with–

(a) the acquisition of land or rights in or over land,

(b) the extension of a qualifying building (except to the extent required for the purpose of providing a means of getting to or from qualifying business premises),

(c) the development of land adjoining or adjacent to a qualifying building, or

(d) the provision of plant and machinery, other than plant or machinery which is or becomes a fixture (as defined by section 173(1)) and falls within subsection (3A).

360B(3A) The fixtures which fall within this subsection are–

(a) integral features within the meaning of section 33A (taking account of section 33A(6) and any provision for the time being made under section 33A(7)) or part of such a feature;

(b) automatic control systems for opening and closing doors, windows and vents;

(c) window cleaning installations;

(d) fitted cupboards and blinds;

(e) protective installations such as lightning protection, sprinkler and other equipment for containing or fighting fires, fire alarm systems and fire escapes;

(f) building management systems;

(g) cabling in connection with telephone, audio-visual data installations and computer networking facilities, which are incidental to the occupation of the building;

(h) sanitary appliances, and bathroom fittings which are hand driers, counters, partitions, mirrors or shower facilities;

(i) kitchen and catering facilities for producing and storing food and drink for the occupants of the building;

(j) signs;

(k) public address systems;

(l) intruder alarm systems.

360B(3B) Expenditure is excluded if, and to the extent that, it exceeds the market value amount for the works, services or other matters to which it relates.

360B(3C) **"The market value amount"** means the amount of expenditure which it would have been normal and reasonable to incur on the works, services or other matters–

(a) in the market conditions prevailing when the expenditure was incurred, and

(b) assuming the transaction as a result of which the expenditure was incurred was between persons dealing with each other at arm's length in the open market.

360B(3D) Expenditure is excluded if the qualifying building was used at any time during the period of 12 months ending with the day on which the expenditure is incurred.

360B(4) For the purposes of this section, expenditure incurred on repairs to a building is to be treated as capital expenditure if it is not expenditure that would be allowed to be deducted in calculating the profits of a property business, or of a trade, profession or vocation, for tax purposes.

360B(5) The Treasury may by regulations –

(a) amend this section so as to add a description of fixture to the list in subsection (3A), or vary or remove a description of fixture in that list;

(b) make further provision as to expenditure which is, or is not, qualifying expenditure.

History – S. 360B(1) substituted by FA 2014, s. 66(2), with effect for expenditure incurred on or after 1 April 2014 (for corporation tax purposes) or 6 April 2014 (for income tax purposes).

In s. 360B(2)(a), "FA" substituted for "the Finance Act" by FA 2009, s. 126(5)(a), with effect from 21 July 2009.

S. 360B(2A), (2B) and (2C) inserted by FA 2014, s. 66(3), with effect for expenditure incurred on or after 1 April 2014 (for corporation tax purposes) or 6 April 2014 (for income tax purposes).

In s. 360B(3), the word "excluded" substituted for the words "not qualifying expenditure" by FA 2014, s. 66(4)(a), with effect for expenditure incurred on or after 1 April 2014 (for corporation tax purposes) or 6 April 2014 (for income tax purposes).

In s. 360B(3)(d), the words "(as defined by section 173(1)) and falls within subsection (3A)" substituted for the words "as defined by section 173(1)" by FA 2014, s. 66(4)(b), with effect for expenditure incurred on or after 1 April 2014 (for corporation tax purposes) or 6 April 2014 (for income tax purposes).

S. 360B(3A), (3B), (3C) and (3D) inserted by FA 2014, s. 66(5), with effect for expenditure incurred on or after 1 April 2014 (for corporation tax purposes) or 6 April 2014 (for income tax purposes).

In s. 360B(5), para. (b) created from existing text, and para. (a) (and the dash before it) inserted, by FA 2014, s. 66(6), with effect for expenditure incurred on or after 1 April 2014 (for corporation tax purposes) or 6 April 2014 (for income tax purposes).

Pt. 3A inserted by FA 2005, s. 92 and Sch. 6, para. 1 in relation to expenditure incurred on or after 11 April 2007, by virtue of SI 2007/949, art. 2.

360BA Expenditure not treated as qualifying expenditure if delay in carrying out works etc

360BA(1) This section applies where–

(a) (ignoring this section) qualifying expenditure is incurred on works, services or other matters in a chargeable period, and

(b) those works, services or other matters are not completed or provided before the end of the period of 36 months beginning with the date the expenditure was incurred.

360BA(2) To the extent that it relates to so much of those works, services or other matters as are not completed or provided before the end of that period, the expenditure is to be treated for the purposes of this Part as never having been incurred (unless and until subsection (6) applies).

360BA(3) All such assessments and adjustments of assessments are to be made as are necessary to give effect to subsection (2).

360BA(4) If a person who has made a tax return becomes aware that, after making it, anything in it has become incorrect because of the operation of this section, the person must give notice to an officer of Revenue and Customs specifying how the return needs to be amended.

360BA(5) The notice must be given within 3 months beginning with the day on which the person first became aware that anything in the return had become incorrect because of the operation of this section.

360BA(6) If, at any time after the end of the period mentioned in subsection (1)(b), those works, services or other matters are completed or provided, the expenditure to which subsection (2) applies is to be treated for the purposes of this Part as incurred at that time.

History – S. 360BA inserted by FA 2014, s. 66(7), with effect for expenditure incurred on or after 1 April 2014 (for corporation tax purposes) or 6 April 2014 (for income tax purposes).

Chapter 3 – Qualifying Buildings and Qualifying Business Premises

360C Meaning of "qualifying building"

360C(1) In this Part **"qualifying building"**, in relation to any conversion or renovation work, means any building or structure, or part of a building or structure, which–

(a) is situated in an area which, on the date on which the conversion or renovation work began, was a disadvantaged area,

(b) was unused throughout the period of one year ending immediately before that date,

(c) on that date, had last been used–
  (i) for the purposes of a trade, profession or vocation, or
  (ii) as an office or offices (whether or not for the purposes of a trade, profession or vocation),

(d) on that date, had not last been used as, or as part of, a dwelling, and

(e) in the case of part of a building or structure, on that date had not last been occupied and used in common with any other part of the building or structure other than a part–
  (i) as respects which the condition in paragraph (b) is met, or
  (ii) which had last been used as a dwelling.

360C(2) In this section **"disadvantaged area"** means–

(a) an area designated as a disadvantaged area for the purposes of this section by regulations made by the Treasury,

(b) [omitted by FA 2012, s. 227 and Sch. 39, para. 8(2)(a).]

360C(3) Regulations under subsection (2)(a) may–

(a) designate specified areas as disadvantaged areas, or

(b) provide for areas of a description specified in the regulations to be designated as disadvantaged areas.

360C(4) If regulations under subsection (2)(a) so provide, the designation of an area as a disadvantaged area shall have effect for such period as may be specified in or determined in accordance with the regulations.

360C(5) Regulations under subsection (2)(a) may–

(a) make different provision for different cases, and

(b) contain such incidental, supplementary, consequential or transitional provision as appears to the Treasury to be necessary or expedient.

360C(6) Where a building or structure (or part of a building or structure) which would otherwise be a qualifying building is on the date mentioned in subsection (1)(a) situated partly in a disadvantaged area and partly outside it, only so much of the expenditure incurred in accordance with section 360B as, on a just and reasonable apportionment, is attributable to the part of the building or structure located in the disadvantaged area is to be treated as qualifying expenditure.

360C(7) The Treasury may by regulations make further provision as to the circumstances in which a building or structure or part of a building or structure is, or is not, a qualifying building.

History – S. 360C(2)(b) (and the "or" before it) omitted by FA 2012, s. 227 and Sch. 39, para. 8(2)(a), with effect in relation to transactions for which the effective date is on or after 6 April 2013, subject to the transitional provisions in FA 2012, Sch. 39, para. 12. Former s. 360C(2)(b) read as follows:

"(a) if no regulations are made under paragraph (a), an area for the time being designated as a disadvantaged area for the purposes of Schedule 6 to FA 2003 (stamp duty land tax: disadvantaged areas relief).".

In s. 360C(2)(b), "FA" substituted for "the Finance Act" by FA2009, s. 126(5)(a), with effect from 21 July 2009.

Pt. 3A inserted by FA 2005, s. 92 and Sch. 6, para. 1 in relation to expenditure incurred on or after 11 April 2007, by virtue of SI 2007/949, art. 2.

Statutory instruments – SI 2007/945 partly made under s. 360C(2)(a) and (3).

360D Meaning of "qualifying business premises"

360D(1) In this Part **"qualifying business premises"** means any premises in respect of which the following requirements are met–

(a) the premises must be a qualifying building,

(b) the premises must be used, or available and suitable for letting for use,–

 (i) for the purposes of a trade, profession or vocation, or

 (ii) as an office or offices (whether or not for the purposes of a trade, profession or vocation),

(c) the premises must not be used, or available for use as, or as part of, a dwelling.

360D(2) In this section **"premises"** means any building or structure or part of a building or structure.

360D(3) For the purposes of this Part, if premises are qualifying business premises immediately before a period when they are temporarily unsuitable for use for the purposes mentioned in subsection (1)(b), they are to be treated as being qualifying business premises during that period.

360D(4) The Treasury may by regulations make further provision as to the circumstances in which premises are, or are not, qualifying business premises.

History – Pt. 3A inserted by FA 2005, s. 92 and Sch. 6, para. 1 in relation to expenditure incurred on or after 11 April 2007, by virtue of SI 2007/949, art. 2.

Statutory instruments – SI 2007/945 partly made under s. 360D(4).

Chapter 4 – The Relevant Interest in the Qualifying Building

360E General rule as to what is the relevant interest

360E(1) The relevant interest in a qualifying building in relation to any qualifying expenditure is the interest in the qualifying building to which the person who incurred the qualifying expenditure was entitled when it was incurred.

360E(2) Subsection (1) is subject to the following provisions of this Chapter and to section 360Z3 (provisions applying on termination of lease).

360E(3) If–

(a) the person who incurred the qualifying expenditure was entitled to more than one interest in the qualifying building when the expenditure was incurred, and

(b) one of those interests was reversionary on all the others, the reversionary interest is the relevant interest in the qualifying building.

360E(4) An interest does not cease to be the relevant interest merely because of the creation of a lease or other interest to which that interest is subject.

360E(5) If–

(a) the relevant interest is a leasehold interest, and

(b) that interest is extinguished on the person entitled to it acquiring the interest which is reversionary on it,

the interest into which the leasehold interest merges becomes the relevant interest when the leasehold interest is extinguished.

History – Pt. 3A inserted by FA 2005, s. 92 and Sch. 6, para. 1 in relation to expenditure incurred on or after 11 April 2007, by virtue of SI 2007/949, art. 2.

360F Interest acquired on completion of conversion

360F For the purposes of determining the relevant interest in a qualifying building, a person who–

(a) incurs expenditure on the conversion of a qualifying building into qualifying business premises, and

(b) is entitled to an interest in the qualifying building on or as a result of the completion of the conversion,

is treated as having had that interest when the expenditure was incurred.

History – Pt. 3A inserted by FA 2005, s. 92 and Sch. 6, para. 1 in relation to expenditure incurred on or after 11 April 2007, by virtue of SI 2007/949, art. 2.

Chapter 5 – Initial Allowances

360G Initial allowances

360G(1) A person who has incurred qualifying expenditure in respect of any qualifying building is entitled to an initial allowance in respect of the expenditure.

360G(2) The amount of the initial allowance is 100% of the qualifying expenditure.

360G(3) A person claiming an initial allowance under this section may require the allowance to be reduced to a specified amount.

360G(4) The initial allowance is made for the chargeable period in which the qualifying expenditure is incurred.

History – Pt. 3A inserted by FA 2005, s. 92 and Sch. 6, para. 1 in relation to expenditure incurred on or after 11 April 2007, by virtue of SI 2007/949, art. 2.

360H Premises not qualifying business premises or relevant interest sold before premises first used or let

360H(1) No initial allowance is to be made under section 360G if, at the relevant time, the qualifying building does not constitute qualifying business premises.

360H(2) An initial allowance which has been made in respect of a qualifying building which is to be qualifying business premises is to be withdrawn if–

(a) the qualifying building does not constitute qualifying business premises at the relevant time, or

(b) the person to whom the allowance was made has sold the relevant interest in the qualifying building before the relevant time.

360H(3) All such assessments and adjustments of assessments are to be made as are necessary to give effect to this section.

360H(4) In this section **"the relevant time"** means the time when the premises are first used by the person with the relevant interest or, if they are not so used, the time when they are first suitable for letting for either of the purposes mentioned in section 360D(1)(b).

History – Pt. 3A inserted by FA 2005, s. 92 and Sch. 6, para. 1 in relation to expenditure incurred on or after 11 April 2007, by virtue of SI 2007/949, art. 2.

Chapter 6 – Writing-down Allowances

360I Entitlement to writing-down allowances

360I(1) A person is entitled to a writing-down allowance for a chargeable period if he has incurred qualifying expenditure in respect of a qualifying building and, at the end of the chargeable period–

(a) the person is entitled to the relevant interest in the qualifying building,

(b) the person has not granted a long lease of the qualifying building out of the relevant interest in consideration of the payment of a capital sum, and

(c) the qualifying building constitutes qualifying business premises.

360I(2) In subsection (1)(b) **"long lease"** means a lease the duration of which exceeds 50 years.

360I(3) Whether the duration of a lease exceeds 50 years is to be determined–

(a) in accordance with section 303 of ITTOIA 2005, and

(b) without regard to section 360Z3(3) of this Act (new lease granted as a result of the exercise of an option treated as continuation of old lease).

360I(4) A person claiming a writing-down allowance may require the allowance to be reduced to a specified amount.

History – Pt. 3A inserted by FA 2005, s. 92 and Sch. 6, para. 1 in relation to expenditure incurred on or after 11 April 2007, by virtue of SI 2007/949, art. 2.

360J Amount of allowance

360J(1) The writing-down allowance for a chargeable period is 25% of the qualifying expenditure.

360J(2) The allowance is proportionately increased or reduced if the chargeable period is more or less than a year.

360J(3) The amount of the writing-down allowance for a chargeable period is limited to the residue of qualifying expenditure.

360J(4) For this purpose the residue is ascertained immediately before writing off the writing-down allowance at the end of the chargeable period.

History – Pt. 3A inserted by FA 2005, s. 92 and Sch. 6, para. 1 in relation to expenditure incurred on or after 11 April 2007, by virtue of SI 2007/949, art. 2.

360K Meaning of "the residue of qualifying expenditure"

360K The residue of qualifying expenditure is the qualifying expenditure that has not yet been written off in accordance with Chapter 9.

History – Pt. 3A inserted by FA 2005, s. 92 and Sch. 6, para. 1 in relation to expenditure incurred on or after 11 April 2007, by virtue of SI 2007/949, art. 2.

Chapter 7 – Grants in Respect of Qualifying Expenditure

360L Grants affecting entitlement to allowances

360L(1) No initial allowance or writing-down allowance under this Part is to be made in respect of qualifying expenditure in respect of a qualifying building if a relevant grant or relevant payment is made towards–

(a) that expenditure, or

(b) any other expenditure which is incurred by any person in respect of the same building, and on the same single investment project as that expenditure.

360L(2) An initial allowance or writing-down allowance made in respect of qualifying expenditure is to be withdrawn if–

(a) after it is made, a relevant grant or relevant payment is made towards that expenditure, or

(b) within the period of 3 years beginning when that expenditure was incurred, a relevant grant or relevant payment is made towards any other expenditure which is incurred by any person in respect of the same building, and on the same single investment project, as that expenditure.

360L(3) All such assessments and adjustments of assessments are to be made as are necessary to give effect to subsection (2).

360L(4) If a person who has made a return becomes aware that, after making it, anything in it has become incorrect because of the operation of this section, that person must give notice to an officer of Revenue and Customs specifying how the return needs to be amended.

360L(5) The notice must be given within 3 months beginning with the day on which the person first became aware that anything in the return had become incorrect because of the operation of this section.

360L(6) In this section–

"General Block Exemption Regulation" means Commission Regulation (EU) No 651/2014 (General block exemption Regulation);

"relevant grant or relevant payment" means a grant or payment which is–

(a) a State aid, other than an allowance under this Part, or

(b) a grant or subsidy, other than a State aid, which the Treasury by order declares to be relevant for the purposes of the withholding of allowances under this Part;

"single investment project" has the same meaning as in the General Block Exemption Regulation.

360L(7) Nothing in this section limits references to **"State aid"** to State aid which is required to be notified to and approved by the European Commission.

360L(8) The Treasury may by order amend this section to make provision consequential upon the General Block Exemption Regulation being replaced by another instrument.

History – S. 360L substituted by FA 2014, s. 66(8), with effect for expenditure incurred on or after 1 April 2014 (for corporation tax purposes) or 6 April 2014 (for income tax purposes), subject to the transitional provisions in FA 2014, s. 66(11) and (13). Former s. 360L read as follows:

"Grants affecting entitlement to allowances

360L(1) No initial allowance or writing-down allowance under this Part is to be made in respect of expenditure to the extent that it is taken into account for the purposes of a relevant grant or relevant payment made towards that expenditure.

360L(2) A grant or payment is relevant if it is–

(a) a notified State aid other than an allowance under this Part, or

(b) a grant or subsidy, other than a notified State aid, which the Treasury by order declares to be relevant for the purposes of the withholding of initial allowances or writing-down allowances.

360L(3) For the purposes of subsection (2), **"notified State aid"** means a State aid notified to and approved by the European Commission.

360L(4) If a relevant grant or relevant payment towards the expenditure is made after the making of an initial allowance or a writing-down allowance, the allowance is to be withdrawn to that extent.

360L(5) If the amount of the relevant grant or relevant payment is repaid by the grantee to the grantor, in whole or in part, the grant or payment is treated, to that extent, as never having been made.

360L(6) All such assessments and adjustments of assessments are to be made as are necessary to give effect to subsection (4) or (5).

360L(7) Any such assessment or adjustment is not out of time if it is made within 3 years of the end of the chargeable period in which the grant, payment or adjustment was made.

History – Pt. 3A inserted by FA 2005, s. 92 and Sch. 6, para. 1 in relation to expenditure incurred on or after 11 April 2007, by virtue of SI 2007/949, art. 2.".

Chapter 8 – Balancing Adjustments

360M When balancing adjustments are made

360M(1) A balancing adjustment is made if–

(a) qualifying expenditure has been incurred in respect of a qualifying building, and

(b) a balancing event occurs.

360M(2) A balancing adjustment is either a balancing allowance or a balancing charge and is made for the chargeable period in which the balancing event occurs.

360M(3) A balancing allowance or balancing charge is made to or on the person who incurred the qualifying expenditure.

360M(4) No balancing adjustment is made if the balancing event occurs more than 5 years after the time when the premises were first used, or suitable for letting, for either of the purposes mentioned in section 360D(1)(b).

360M(5) If more than one balancing event within section 360N occurs, a balancing adjustment is made only on the first of them.

History – In s. 360M(4), "5" substituted for "7" by FA 2014, s. 66(9), with effect for expenditure incurred on or after 1 April 2014 (for corporation tax purposes) or 6 April 2014 (for income tax purposes).
Pt. 3A inserted by FA 2005, s. 92 and Sch. 6, para. 1 in relation to expenditure incurred on or after 11 April 2007, by virtue of SI 2007/949, art. 2.

360N Balancing events

360N(1) The following are balancing events for the purposes of this Part–

(a) the relevant interest in the qualifying building is sold;

(b) a long lease of the qualifying building is granted out of the relevant interest in consideration of the payment of a capital sum;

(c) if the relevant interest is a lease, the lease ends otherwise than on the person entitled to it acquiring the interest reversionary on it;

(d) the person who incurred the qualifying expenditure dies;

(e) the qualifying building is demolished or destroyed;

(f) the qualifying building ceases to be qualifying business premises (without being demolished or destroyed).

360N(2) Section 360I(2) and (3) (meaning of **"long lease"**) applies for the purposes of subsection (1)(b).

History – Pt. 3A inserted by FA 2005, s. 92 and Sch. 6, para. 1 in relation to expenditure incurred on or after 11 April 2007, by virtue of SI 2007/949, art. 2.

360O Proceeds from balancing events

360O(1) References in this Part to the proceeds from a balancing event are to the amounts received or receivable in connection with the event, as shown in the Table–

TABLE: BALANCING EVENTS AND PROCEEDS

1 Balancing Event	2 Proceeds from event
1 The sale of the relevant interest.	The net proceeds of the sale.
2 The grant of a long lease out of the relevant interest.	If the capital sum paid in consideration of the grant is less than the commercial premium, the commercial premium. In any other case, the capital sum paid in consideration of the grant.
3 The coming to an end of a lease, where a person entitled to the lease and a person entitled to any superior interest are connected persons.	The market value of the relevant interest in the qualifying building at the time of the event.
4 The death of the person who incurred the qualifying expenditure.	The residue of qualifying expenditure immediately before the death.
5 The demolition or destruction of the qualifying building.	The net amount received for the remains of the qualifying building, together with– (a) any insurance money received in respect of the demolition or destruction, and (b) any other compensation of any description so received, so far as it consists of capital sums.
6 The qualifying building ceases to be qualifying business premises.	The market value of the relevant interest in the qualifying building at the time of the event.

360O(2) The amounts referred to in column 2 of the Table are those received or receivable by the person who incurred the qualifying expenditure.

360O(3) In Item 2 of the Table **"the commercial premium"** means the premium that would have been given if the transaction had been at arm's length.

History – Pt. 3A inserted by FA 2005, s. 92 and Sch. 6, para. 1 in relation to expenditure incurred on or after 11 April 2007, by virtue of SI 2007/949, art. 2.

360P Calculation of balancing adjustments

360P(1) A balancing allowance is made if–

(a) there are no proceeds from the balancing event, or

(b) the proceeds from the balancing event are less than the residue of qualifying expenditure immediately before the event.

360P(2) The amount of the balancing allowance is the amount of–

(a) the residue (if there are no proceeds);

(b) the difference (if the proceeds are less than the residue).

360P(3) A balancing charge is made if the proceeds from the balancing event are more than the residue, if any, of qualifying expenditure immediately before the event.

360P(4) The amount of the balancing charge is the amount of–

(a) the difference, or

(b) the proceeds (if the residue is nil).

360P(5) The amount of a balancing charge made on a person must not exceed the total amount of–

(a) any initial allowances made to the person in respect of the expenditure, and

(b) any writing-down allowances made to the person in respect of the expenditure for chargeable periods ending on or before the date of the balancing event giving rise to the balancing adjustment.

History – Pt. 3A inserted by FA 2005, s. 92 and Sch. 6, para. 1 in relation to expenditure incurred on or after 11 April 2007, by virtue of SI 2007/949, art. 2.

Chapter 9 – Writing off Qualifying Expenditure

360Q Introduction

360Q For the purposes of this Part qualifying expenditure is written off to the extent and at the times specified in this Chapter.

History – Pt. 3A inserted by FA 2005, s. 92 and Sch. 6, para. 1 in relation to expenditure incurred on or after 11 April 2007, by virtue of SI 2007/949, art. 2.

360R Writing off initial allowances and writing-down allowances

360R(1) If an initial allowance is made in respect of the qualifying expenditure, the amount of the allowance is written off at the time when the qualifying business premises are first used, or suitable for letting for use, for either of the purposes mentioned in section 360D(1)(b).

360R(2) If a writing-down allowance is made in respect of the qualifying expenditure, the amount of the allowance is written off at the end of the chargeable period for which the allowance is made.

360R(3) If a balancing event occurs at the end of the chargeable period referred to in subsection (2), the amount written off under that subsection is to be taken into account in calculating the residue of qualifying expenditure immediately before the event to determine what balancing adjustment (if any) is to be made.

History – Pt. 3A inserted by FA 2005, s. 92 and Sch. 6, para. 1 in relation to expenditure incurred on or after 11 April 2007, by virtue of SI 2007/949, art. 2.

360S Treatment of demolition costs

360S(1) This section applies if–

(a) a qualifying building is demolished, and

(b) the person who incurred the qualifying expenditure incurs the cost of the demolition.

360S(2) The net cost of the demolition is added to the residue of qualifying expenditure immediately before the demolition.

360S(3) **"The net cost of the demolition"** means the amount, if any, by which the cost of the demolition exceeds any money received for the remains of the qualifying building.

360S(4) If this section applies, neither the cost of the demolition nor the net cost of the demolition is treated for the purposes of any Part of this Act as expenditure on any other property replacing the qualifying building demolished.

History – Pt. 3A inserted by FA 2005, s. 92 and Sch. 6, para. 1 in relation to expenditure incurred on or after 11 April 2007, by virtue of SI 2007/949, art. 2.

Chapter 10 – Additional VAT Liabilities and Rebates

360T Introduction

360T For the purposes of this Chapter–

(a) **"additional VAT liability"** and **"additional VAT rebate"** have the meanings given by section 547,

(b) the time when–

(i) a person incurs an additional VAT liability, or

(ii) an additional VAT rebate is made to a person,

is given by section 548, and

(c) the chargeable period in which, and the time when, an additional VAT liability or an additional VAT rebate accrues are given by section 549.

History – Pt. 3A inserted by FA 2005, s. 92 and Sch. 6, para. 1 in relation to expenditure incurred on or after 11 April 2007, by virtue of SI 2007/949, art. 2.

360U Additional VAT liabilities and initial allowances

360U(1) This section applies if–

(a) a person was entitled to an initial allowance under this Part in respect of qualifying expenditure on a qualifying building,

(b) that person incurs an additional VAT liability in respect of that expenditure, and

(c) the additional VAT liability is incurred at a time when the qualifying building is, or is about to be, qualifying business premises.

360U(2) If this section applies, the person entitled to the relevant interest is entitled to an initial allowance on the amount of the additional VAT liability.

360U(3) The amount of the initial allowance is 100% of the amount of the additional VAT liability.

360U(4) A person claiming an initial allowance under this section may require the allowance to be reduced to a specified amount.

360U(5) The allowance is made for the chargeable period in which the additional VAT liability accrues.

History – Pt. 3A inserted by FA 2005, s. 92 and Sch. 6, para. 1 in relation to expenditure incurred on or after 11 April 2007, by virtue of SI 2007/949, art. 2.

360V Additional VAT liabilities and writing-down allowances

360V(1) This section applies if the person entitled to the relevant interest in relation to qualifying expenditure incurs an additional VAT liability in respect of that expenditure.

360V(2) If this section applies–

(a) the additional VAT liability is treated as qualifying expenditure, and

(b) the amount of the residue of qualifying expenditure is accordingly increased at the time when the liability accrues by the amount of the liability.

History – Pt. 3A inserted by FA 2005, s. 92 and Sch. 6, para. 1 in relation to expenditure incurred on or after 11 April 2007, by virtue of SI 2007/949, art. 2.

360W Additional VAT liabilities and writing off initial allowances

360W If an initial allowance is made in respect of an additional VAT liability incurred after the qualifying business premises are first used or suitable for letting for business use, the amount of the allowance is written off at the time when the liability accrues.

History – Pt. 3A inserted by FA 2005, s. 92 and Sch. 6, para. 1 in relation to expenditure incurred on or after 11 April 2007, by virtue of SI 2007/949, art. 2.

360X Additional VAT rebates and balancing adjustments

360X(1) If an additional VAT rebate is made in respect of qualifying expenditure to the person entitled to the relevant interest in relation to that qualifying expenditure–

(a) the making of the rebate is a balancing event for the purposes of this Part, but

(b) the making of balancing adjustments as a result of the event is subject to subsections (2) and (3).

360X(2) No balancing allowance is to be made as a result of the event.

360X(3) A balancing charge is not to be made as a result of the event unless–

(a) the amount of the additional VAT rebate is more than the amount of the residue of qualifying expenditure immediately before the time when the rebate accrues, or

(b) there is no such residue.

360X(4) The amount of the balancing charge is–

(a) the amount of the difference, or

(b) the amount of the rebate (if there is no residue).

History – Pt. 3A inserted by FA 2005, s. 92 and Sch. 6, para. 1 in relation to expenditure incurred on or after 11 April 2007, by virtue of SI 2007/949, art. 2.

360Y Additional VAT rebates and writing off qualifying expenditure

360Y If an additional VAT rebate is made in respect of qualifying expenditure, an amount equal to the rebate is written off at the time when the rebate accrues.

History – Pt. 3A inserted by FA 2005, s. 92 and Sch. 6, para. 1 in relation to expenditure incurred on or after 11 April 2007, by virtue of SI 2007/949, art. 2.

Chapter 11 – Supplementary Provisions

360Z Giving effect to allowances and charges: trades

360Z(1) An allowance or charge to which a person is entitled or liable under this Part is to be given effect in calculating the profits of that person's trade, by treating–

(a) the allowance as an expense of the trade, and

(b) the charge as a receipt of the trade.

360Z(2) In the case of a person who–

(a) is entitled to an allowance or liable to a charge in respect of a qualifying building, and

(b) occupies that building in the course of a profession or vocation,

the references in subsection (1) to a trade are to be read as references to the profession or vocation.

360Z(3) Subsection (1) is subject to the following provisions of this Chapter.

Prospective amendments – In s. 360Z(3) the words below substituted for the words "subject to the following provisions of this Chapter" by CTNIA 2015, s. 2 and Sch. 1, para. 11(2), with effect from 26 March 2015 (Royal Assent) in respect of any power to make regulations and with effect in relation to accounting periods beginning on or after the first day of the appointed financial year for other provisions (see CTNIA 2015, s. 5). See also transitional provisions at Sch. 1, para. 19–21. The wording is:

"subject to–

(a) section 6E (giving effect to allowances and charges: NI rate activity cases), and

(b) the following provisions of this Chapter."

CAA 2001

In s. 360Z(4)–(6) inserted by CTNIA 2015, s. 2 and Sch. 1, para. 11(3), with effect from 26 March 2015 (Royal Assent) in respect of any power to make regulations and with effect in relation to accounting periods beginning on or after the first day of the appointed financial year for other provisions (see CTNIA 2015, s. 5). See also transitional provisions at Sch. 1, para. 19–21.

History – Pt. 3A inserted by FA 2005, s. 92 and Sch. 6, para. 1 in relation to expenditure incurred on or after 11 April 2007, by virtue of SI 2007/949, art. 2.

360Z1 Giving effect to allowances and charges: lessors and licensees

360Z1(1) This section applies if–

(a) a person is entitled or liable to an allowance or charge under this Part for a chargeable period ("the relevant period"), but

(b) his interest in the building in question is or was subject to a lease or a licence at any time in that period.

360Z1(2) If the person's interest in the building is an asset of a property business carried on by him at any time in the relevant period, the allowance or charge is to be given effect in calculating the profits of that business for the relevant period by treating–

(a) the allowance as an expense of that business, and

(b) the charge as a receipt of that business.

360Z1(3) If the person's interest in the building is not an asset of a property business carried on by him at any time in the relevant period, the allowance or charge is to be given effect by treating him as if he had been carrying on a property business in that period and as if–

(a) the allowance were an expense of that business, and

(b) the charge were a receipt of that business.

History – Pt. 3A inserted by FA 2005, s. 92 and Sch. 6, para. 1 in relation to expenditure incurred on or after 11 April 2007, by virtue of SI 2007/949, art. 2.

360Z2 Apportionment of sums partly referable to non-qualifying assets

360Z2(1) If the sum paid for the sale of the relevant interest in a qualifying building is attributable–

(a) partly to assets representing expenditure for which an allowance can be made under this Part, and

(b) partly to assets representing other expenditure,

only so much of the sum as on a just and reasonable apportionment is attributable to the assets referred to in paragraph (a) is to be taken into account for the purposes of this Part.

360Z2(2) Subsection (1) applies to other proceeds from a balancing event in respect of a qualifying building as it applies to a sum given for the sale of the relevant interest in the qualifying building.

360Z2(3) Subsection (1) does not affect any other provision of this Act requiring an apportionment of the proceeds of a balancing event.

History – Pt. 3A inserted by FA 2005, s. 92 and Sch. 6, para. 1 in relation to expenditure incurred on or after 11 April 2007, by virtue of SI 2007/949, art. 2.

360Z3 Provisions applying on termination of lease

360Z3(1) This section applies for the purposes of this Part if a lease is terminated.

360Z3(2) If, with the consent of the lessor, the lessee of the qualifying building remains in possession of the qualifying building after the termination without a new lease being granted to him, the lease is treated as continuing so long as the lessee remains in possession.

360Z3(3) If on the termination a new lease is granted to a lessee as a result of the exercise of an option available to him under the terms of the first lease, the second lease is treated as a continuation of the first.

360Z3(4) If on the termination the lessor pays a sum to the lessee in respect of business premises comprised in the lease, the lease is treated as if it had come to an end by surrender in consideration of the payment.

360Z3(5) If on the termination–

(a) another lease is granted to a different lessee, and

(b) in connection with the transaction that lessee pays a sum to the person who was the lessee under the first lease,

the two leases are to be treated as if they were the same lease which had been assigned by the lessee under the first lease to the lessee under the second lease in consideration of the payment.

History – Pt. 3A inserted by FA 2005, s. 92 and Sch. 6, para. 1 in relation to expenditure incurred on or after 11 April 2007, by virtue of SI 2007/949, art. 2.

360Z4 Meaning of "lease" etc.

360Z4(1) In this Part **"lease"** includes–

(a) an agreement for a lease if the term to be covered by the lease has begun, and

(b) any tenancy,

but does not include a mortgage (and "lessee", "lessor" and "leasehold interest" are to be read accordingly).

360Z4(2) In the application of this Part to Scotland–

(a) **"leasehold interest"** or **"leasehold estate"** means the interest of a tenant in property subject to a lease, and

(b) any reference to an interest which is reversionary on a leasehold interest or on a lease is to be read as a reference to the interest of the landlord in the property subject to the leasehold interest or lease.

History – Pt. 3A inserted by FA 2005, s. 92 and Sch. 6, para. 1 in relation to expenditure incurred on or after 11 April 2007, by virtue of SI 2007/949, art. 2.

PART 4 – AGRICULTURAL BUILDINGS ALLOWANCES

[Pt. 4 omitted by FA 2008, s. 84(1).]

History – Pt. 4 of CAA 2001 does not apply in relation to expenditure incurred on or after 1 April 2011 for corporation tax purposes and 6 April 2011 for income tax purposes (FA 2008, s. 84(1)). Part 4 is accordingly omitted by FA 2008, s. 84(2), with effect in relation to chargeable periods beginning on or after those April 2011 dates (FA 2008, s. 84(3) and (4)).

CAA 2001

PART 4A – FLAT CONVERSION ALLOWANCES

History – Pt. 4A repealed by FA 2012, s. 227 and Sch. 39, para. 37, with effect in relation to chargeable periods beginning on or after 1 April 2013 for corporation tax purposes, and 6 April 2013 for income tax purposes, subject to transitional and saving provisions in FA 2012, Sch. 39, para. 41 and 42.

Pt. 4A inserted by FA 2001, s. 67 and Sch. 19, Pt. I, with effect in relation to expenditure incurred on or after 11 May 2001.

Chapter 1 – Introduction

393A Flat conversion allowances

393A [Repealed by FA 2012, s. 227 and Sch. 39, para. 37.]

History – S. 393A repealed by FA 2012, s. 227 and Sch. 39, para. 37, with effect in relation to chargeable periods beginning on or after 1 April 2013 for corporation tax purposes, and 6 April 2013 for income tax purposes, subject to transitional and saving provisions in FA 2012, Sch. 39, para. 41 and 42. Former s. 393A read as follows:

"Chapter 1 – Introduction

Flat conversion allowances

393A(1) Allowances are available under this Part if a person incurs qualifying expenditure in respect of a flat.

393A(2) Allowances under this Part are made to the person who–

(a) incurred the expenditure, and

(b) has the relevant interest in the flat.

393A(3) In this Part **"flat"** means a dwelling which–

(a) is a separate set of premises (whether or not on the same floor),

(b) forms part of a building, and

(c) is divided horizontally from another part of the building.

393A(4) In this Part **"dwelling"** means a building or part of a building occupied or intended to be occupied as a separate dwelling.".

Former s. 393A inserted by FA 2001, s. 67 and Sch. 19, Pt. I, with effect in relation to expenditure incurred on or after 11 May 2001.

Chapter 2 – Qualifying Expenditure

393B Meaning of "qualifying expenditure"

393B [Repealed by FA 2012, s. 227 and Sch. 39, para. 37.]

History – S. 393B repealed by FA 2012, s. 227 and Sch. 39, para. 37, with effect in relation to chargeable periods beginning on or after 1 April 2013 for corporation tax purposes, and 6 April 2013 for income tax purposes, subject to transitional and saving provisions in FA 2012, Sch. 39, para. 41 and 42. Former s. 393B read as follows:

"Meaning of "qualifying expenditure"

393B(1) In this Part **"qualifying expenditure"** means capital expenditure incurred on, or in connection with–

(a) the conversion of part of a qualifying building into a qualifying flat,

(b) the renovation of a flat in a qualifying building if the flat is, or will be, a qualifying flat, or

(c) repairs to a qualifying building, to the extent that the repairs are incidental to expenditure within paragraph (a) or (b).

393B(2) Expenditure within subsection (1)(a) or (b) is not qualifying expenditure unless the part of the building, or the flat, in respect of which the expenditure is incurred–

(a) was unused, or

(b) was used only for storage,

throughout the period of one year ending immediately before the date on which the conversion or renovation work began.

393B(3) Expenditure is not qualifying expenditure if it is incurred on or in connection with–

(a) the acquisition of land or rights in or over land,

(b) the extension of a qualifying building (except to the extent required for the purpose of providing a means of getting to or from a qualifying flat),

(c) the development of land adjoining or adjacent to a qualifying building, or

(d) the provision of furnishings or chattels.

393B(4) For the purposes of this section, expenditure incurred on repairs to a building is to be treated as capital expenditure if it is not expenditure that would be allowed to be deducted in calculating the profits of a UK property business for tax purposes.

393B(5) Treasury regulations may make further provision as to expenditure which is, or is not, qualifying expenditure.".

In former s. 393B(4), the words " or Schedule A business", which appeared after the words "UK property business", omitted by CTA 2009, s. 1322 and Sch. 1, para. 505 and repealed by CTA 2009, s. 1326 and Sch. 3, Pt. 1, with effect for corporation tax purposes for accounting periods ending on or after 1 April 2009, and for income tax and capital gains tax purposes for the tax year 2009–10 and subsequent tax years.

In former s. 393B(4) the words "UK property business or" inserted by ITTOIA 2005, s. 882(1) and Sch. 1, para. 559; effective for income tax purposes for 2005–06 onwards and for corporation tax purposes for accounting periods ending after 5 April 2005 (ITTOIA 2005, s. 883(1)).

Former s. 393B inserted by FA 2001, s. 67 and Sch. 19, Pt. I, with effect in relation to expenditure incurred on or after 11 May 2001.

Chapter 3 – Qualifying Buildings and Qualifying Flats

393C Meaning of "qualifying building"

393C [Repealed by FA 2012, s. 227 and Sch. 39, para. 37.]

History – S. 393C repealed by FA 2012, s. 227 and Sch. 39, para. 37, with effect in relation to chargeable periods beginning on or after 1 April 2013 for corporation tax purposes, and 6 April 2013 for income tax purposes, subject to transitional and saving provisions in FA 2012, Sch. 39, para. 41 and 42. Former s. 393C read as follows:

"Meaning of "qualifying building"

393C(1) In this Part **"qualifying building"** means a building in respect of which the following requirements are met–

(a) all or most of the ground floor of the building must be authorised for business use,

(b) it must appear that, when the building was constructed, the storeys above the ground floor were for use primarily as one or more dwellings,

(c) the building must not have more than 4 storeys above the ground floor, and

(d) the construction of the building must have been completed before 1st January 1980.

393C(2) In subsection (1)(a) **"authorised for business use"** means–

(a) in the case of a building in England or Wales, authorised for use within class A1, A2, A3, B1 or D1(a) specified in the Schedule to the Town and Country Planning (Use Classes) Order 1987,

(b) in the case of a building in Scotland–

(i) authorised for use within class 1, 2, 3 or 4 specified in the Schedule to the Town and Country Planning (Use Classes) (Scotland) Order 1997,

(ii) authorised for a use specified in Article 3(5)(j) of that Order, or

(iii) authorised for use for the provision of medical or health services other than from premises attached to the residence of the consultant or practitioner;

(c) in the case of a building in Northern Ireland–

(i) authorised for use within class 1, 2, 3, 4 or 15(a) specified in the Schedule to the Planning (Use Classes) Order (Northern Ireland) 1989, or

(ii) authorised for a use specified in Article 3(5)(b), (c) or (h) of that Order.

393C(3) The attic storey does not count for the purposes of subsection (1)(c) unless it is or has been in use as a dwelling or part of a dwelling.

393C(4) The requirement in subsection (1)(d) is met even if the building has been extended on or after 1st January 1980, provided any extension was completed on or before 31st December 2000.

393C(5) Treasury regulations may make further provision as to the circumstances in which a building is, or is not, a qualifying building.".

Former s. 393C inserted by FA 2001, s. 67 and Sch. 19, Pt. I, with effect in relation to expenditure incurred on or after 11 May 2001.

393D Meaning of "qualifying flat"

393D [Repealed by FA 2012, s. 227 and Sch. 39, para. 37.]

History – S. 393D repealed by FA 2012, s. 227 and Sch. 39, para. 37, with effect in relation to chargeable periods beginning on or after 1 April 2013 for corporation tax purposes, and 6 April 2013 for income tax purposes, subject to transitional and saving provisions in FA 2012, Sch. 39, para. 41 and 42. Former s. 393D read as follows:

"Meaning of "qualifying flat"

393D(1) In this Part **"qualifying flat"** means a flat in respect of which the following requirements are met–

(a) the flat must be in a qualifying building,

(b) the flat must be suitable for letting as a dwelling,

(c) the flat must be held for the purpose of short-term letting,

(d) it must be possible to gain access to the flat without using the part of the ground floor of the building that is authorised for business use (as defined in section 393C(2)),

(e) the flat must not have more than 4 rooms,

(f) the flat must not be a high value flat,

(g) the flat must not be (or have been) created or renovated as part of a scheme involving the creation or renovation of one or more high value flats, and

(h) the flat must not be let to a person connected with the person who incurred the expenditure on its conversion or renovation.

393D(2) In subsection (1)(c) **"short-term letting"** means letting as a dwelling on a lease for a term (or, in Scotland, period) of not more than 5 years.

393D(3) For the purposes of subsection (1)(e), the following are ignored in determining the number of rooms in a flat–

(a) any kitchen or bathroom, and

(b) any closet, cloakroom or hallway not exceeding 5 square metres in area.

393D(4) For the purposes of this Part, if a flat is a qualifying flat immediately before a period when it is temporarily unsuitable for letting as a dwelling, it is to be treated as being a qualifying flat during that period.

393D(5) Treasury regulations may make further provision as to the circumstances in which a flat is, or is not, a qualifying flat.".
Former s. 393D inserted by FA 2001, s. 67 and Sch. 19, Pt. I, with effect in relation to expenditure incurred on or after 11 May 2001.

393E High value flats

393E [Repealed by FA 2012, s. 227 and Sch. 39, para. 37.]

History – S. 393E repealed by FA 2012, s. 227 and Sch. 39, para. 37, with effect in relation to chargeable periods beginning on or after 1 April 2013 for corporation tax purposes, and 6 April 2013 for income tax purposes, subject to transitional and saving provisions in FA 2012, Sch. 39, para. 41 and 42. Former s. 393E read as follows:

"High value flats

393E(1) For the purposes of section 393D(1) a flat is a high value flat if the notional rent exceeds the relevant limit set out in the Table in subsection (5).
393E(2) The **"notional rent"** means the rent that could reasonably be expected for the flat on the relevant date, on the assumption that, on that date–
(a) the conversion or renovation has been completed,
(b) the flat is let furnished,
(c) the lease does not require the tenant to pay a premium or make any other payments to the landlord or a person connected with the landlord,
(d) the tenant is not connected with the person incurring the expenditure on the conversion or renovation of the flat, and
(e) in the case of a flat in England or Wales or Scotland, the flat is let on a shorthold tenancy.
393E(3) The **"relevant date"** means the date on which expenditure on–
(a) the conversion of part of the building into the flat, or
(b) (as the case may be) the renovation of the flat,
is first incurred.
393E(4) **"Shorthold tenancy"** means–
(a) in the case of a flat in England or Wales, an assured shorthold tenancy;
(b) in the case of a flat in Scotland, a short assured tenancy.
393E(5) The limit for the notional rent is as shown in the Table–

TABLE
NOTIONAL RENT LIMITS

Number of rooms in flat	*Flats in Greater London*	*Flats elsewhere*
1. 1 or 2 rooms	£350 per week	£150 per week
2. 3 rooms	£425 per week	£225 per week
3. 4 rooms	£480 per week	£300 per week

393E(6) Treasury regulations may make provision amending the notional rent limits in the Table in subsection (5).
393E(7) Section 393D(3) (determination of number of rooms in flat) applies for the purposes of this section.".
Former s. 393E inserted by FA 2001, s. 67 and Sch. 19, Pt. I, with effect in relation to expenditure incurred on or after 11 May 2001.

Chapter 4 – The Relevant Interest in the Flat

393F General rule as to what is the relevant interest

393F [Repealed by FA 2012, s. 227 and Sch. 39, para. 37.]

History – S. 393F repealed by FA 2012, s. 227 and Sch. 39, para. 37, with effect in relation to chargeable periods beginning on or after 1 April 2013 for corporation tax purposes, and 6 April 2013 for income tax purposes, subject to transitional and saving provisions in FA 2012, Sch. 39, para. 41 and 42. Former s. 393F read as follows:

"General rule as to what is the relevant interest

393F(1) The relevant interest in a flat in relation to any qualifying expenditure is the interest in the flat to which the person who incurred the expenditure was entitled when it was incurred.
393F(2) Subsection (1) is subject to the following provisions of this Chapter and to section 393V (provisions applying on termination of lease).
393F(3) If–
(a) the person who incurred the qualifying expenditure was entitled to more than one interest in the flat when the expenditure was incurred, and
(b) one of those interests was reversionary on all the others,
the reversionary interest is the relevant interest in the flat.
393F(4) An interest does not cease to be the relevant interest merely because of the creation of a lease or other interest to which that interest is subject.
393F(5) If–
(a) the relevant interest is a leasehold interest, and
(b) that interest is extinguished on the person entitled to it acquiring the interest which is reversionary on it,
the interest into which the leasehold interest merges becomes the relevant interest when the leasehold interest is extinguished.".
Former s. 393F inserted by FA 2001, s. 67 and Sch. 19, Pt. I, with effect in relation to expenditure incurred on or after 11 May 2001.

393G Interest acquired on completion of conversion

393G [Repealed by FA 2012, s. 227 and Sch. 39, para. 37.]

History – S. 393G repealed by FA 2012, s. 227 and Sch. 39, para. 37, with effect in relation to chargeable periods beginning on or after 1 April 2013 for corporation tax purposes, and 6 April 2013 for income tax purposes, subject to transitional and saving provisions in FA 2012, Sch. 39, para. 41 and 42. Former s. 393G read as follows:
"393G For the purposes of determining the relevant interest in a flat, a person who–

(a) incurs expenditure on the conversion of part of a building into the flat, and
(b) is entitled to an interest in the flat on or as a result of the completion of the conversion,
is treated as having had that interest when the expenditure was incurred."
Former s. 393G inserted by FA 2001, s. 67 and Sch. 19, Pt. I, with effect in relation to expenditure incurred on or after 11 May 2001.

Chapter 5 – Initial Allowances

393H Initial allowances

393H [Repealed by FA 2012, s. 227 and Sch. 39, para. 37.]

History – S. 393H repealed by FA 2012, s. 227 and Sch. 39, para. 37, with effect in relation to chargeable periods beginning on or after 1 April 2013 for corporation tax purposes, and 6 April 2013 for income tax purposes, subject to transitional and saving provisions in FA 2012, Sch. 39, para. 41 and 42. Former s. 393H read as follows:

"393H(1) A person who has incurred qualifying expenditure in respect of a flat is entitled to an initial allowance in respect of the expenditure.
393H(2) The amount of the initital allowance is 100% of the qualifying expenditure.
393H(3) A person claiming an initial allowance under this section may require the allowance to be reduced to a specified amount.
393H(4) The initial allowance is made for the chargeable period in which the qualifying expenditure is incurred.".
Former s. 393H inserted by FA 2001, s. 67 and Sch. 19, Pt. I, with effect in relation to expenditure incurred on or after 11 May 2001.

393I Flat not qualifying flat or relevant interest sold before flat first let

393I [Repealed by FA 2012, s. 227 and Sch. 39, para. 37.]

History – S. 393I repealed by FA 2012, s. 227 and Sch. 39, para. 37, with effect in relation to chargeable periods beginning on or after 1 April 2013 for corporation tax purposes, and 6 April 2013 for income tax purposes, subject to transitional and saving provisions in FA 2012, Sch. 39, para. 41 and 42. Former s. 393I read as follows:

"Flat not qualifying flat or relevant interest sold before flat first let

393I(1) No initial allowance is to be made under section 393H if, at the relevant time, the flat is not a qualifying flat.
393I(2) An initial allowance which has been made in respect of a flat which is to be a qualifying flat is to be withdrawn if–
(a) the flat is not a qualifying flat at the relevant time, or
(b) the person to whom the allowance was made has sold the relevant interest in the flat before the relevant time.
393I(3) All such assessments and adjustments of assessments are to be made as are necessary to give effect to this section.
393I(4) In this section **"the relevant time"** means the time when the flat is first suitable for letting as a dwelling.".
Former s. 393I inserted by FA 2001, s. 67 and Sch. 19, Pt. I, with effect in relation to expenditure incurred on or after 11 May 2001.

Chapter 6 – Writing-Down Allowances

393J Entitlement to writing-down allowances

393J [Repealed by FA 2012, s. 227 and Sch. 39, para. 37.]

History – S. 393J repealed by FA 2012, s. 227 and Sch. 39, para. 37, with effect in relation to chargeable periods beginning on or after 1 April 2013 for corporation tax purposes, and 6 April 2013 for income tax purposes, subject to transitional and saving provisions in FA 2012, Sch. 39, para. 41 and 42. Former s. 393J read as follows:

"Entitlement to writing-down allowances

393J(1) A person is entitled to a writing-down allowance for a chargeable period if he has incurred qualifying expenditure in respect of a flat and, at the end of the chargeable period–
(a) the person is entitled to the relevant interest in the flat,
(b) the person has not granted a long lease of the flat out of the relevant interest in consideration of the payment of a capital sum, and
(c) the flat is a qualifying flat.
393J(2) In subsection (1)(b) **"long lease"** means a lease the duration of which exceeds 50 years.
393J(3) Whether the duration of a lease exceeds 50 years is to be determined–
(a) in accordance with sections 243 and 244 of CTA 2009, and
(b) without regard to section 393V(3) (new lease granted as a result of the exercise of an option treated as continuation of old lease).
393J(4) A person claiming a writing-down allowance may require the allowance to be reduced to a specified amount.".
In former s. 393J(3)(a), the words "sections 243 and 244 of CTA 2009," substituted for the words "section 38(1) to (4) and (6) of ICTA," by CTA 2009, s. 1322 and Sch. 1, para. 506, with effect for corporation tax purposes for accounting periods ending on or after 1 April 2009, and for income tax and capital gains tax purposes for the tax year 2009–10 and subsequent tax years. This amendment does not have effect for leases granted before 1 April 2009 (CTA 2009, Sch. 2, para. 47).
Former s. 393J inserted by FA 2001, s. 67 and Sch. 19, Pt. I, with effect in relation to expenditure incurred on or after 11 May 2001.

393K Amount of allowance

393K [Repealed by FA 2012, s. 227 and Sch. 39, para. 37.]

History – S. 393K repealed by FA 2012, s. 227 and Sch. 39, para. 37, with effect in relation to chargeable periods beginning on or after 1 April 2013 for corporation tax purposes, and 6 April 2013 for income tax purposes, subject to transitional and saving provisions in FA 2012, Sch. 39, para. 41 and 42. Former s. 393K read as follows:

"Amount of allowance

393K(1) The writing-down allowance for a chargeable period is 25% of the qualifying expenditure.
393K(2) The allowance is proportionately increased or reduced if the chargeable period is more or less than a year.
393K(3) The amount of the writing-down allowance for a chargeable period is limited to the residue of qualifying expenditure.
393K(4) For this purpose the residue is ascertained immediately before writing off the writing-down allowance at the end of the chargeable period.".
Former s. 393K inserted by FA 2001, s. 67 and Sch. 19, Pt. I, with effect in relation to expenditure incurred on or after 11 May 2001.

393L Meaning of "the residue of qualifying expenditure"

393L [Repealed by FA 2012, s. 227 and Sch. 39, para. 37.]

History – S. 393L repealed by FA 2012, s. 227 and Sch. 39, para. 37, with effect in relation to chargeable periods beginning on or after 1 April 2013 for corporation tax purposes, and 6 April 2013 for income tax purposes, subject to transitional and saving provisions in FA 2012, Sch. 39, para. 41 and 42. Former s. 393L read as follows:

"Meaning of "the residue of qualifying expenditure"

393L The residue of qualifying expenditure is the qualifying expenditure that has not yet been written off in accordance with Chapter 8.".

Former s. 393L inserted by FA 2001, s. 67 and Sch. 19, Pt. I, with effect in relation to expenditure incurred on or after 11 May 2001.

Chapter 7 – Balancing Adjustments

393M When balancing adjustments are made

393M [Repealed by FA 2012, s. 227 and Sch. 39, para. 37.]

History – S. 393M repealed by FA 2012, s. 227 and Sch. 39, para. 37, with effect in relation to chargeable periods beginning on or after 1 April 2013 for corporation tax purposes, and 6 April 2013 for income tax purposes, subject to transitional and saving provisions in FA 2012, Sch. 39, para. 41 and 42. Former s. 393M read as follows:

"When balancing adjustments are made

393M(1) A balancing adjustment is made if–
(a) qualifying expenditure has been incurred in respect of a flat, and
(b) a balancing event occurs.

393M(2) A balancing adjustment is either a balancing allowance or a balancing charge and is made for the chargeable period in which the balancing event occurs.

393M(3) A balancing allowance or balancing charge is made to or on the person who incurred the qualifying expenditure.

393M(4) No balancing adjustment is made if the balancing event occurs more than 7 years after the time when the flat was first suitable for letting as a dwelling.

393M(5) If more than one balancing event occurs, a balancing adjustment is made only on the first of them.".

Former s. 393M inserted by FA 2001, s. 67 and Sch. 19, Pt. I, with effect in relation to expenditure incurred on or after 11 May 2001.

CAA 2001

393N Balancing events

393N [Repealed by FA 2012, s. 227 and Sch. 39, para. 37.]

History – S. 393N repealed by FA 2012, s. 227 and Sch. 39, para. 37, with effect in relation to chargeable periods beginning on or after 1 April 2013 for corporation tax purposes, and 6 April 2013 for income tax purposes, subject to transitional and saving provisions in FA 2012, Sch. 39, para. 41 and 42. Former s. 393N read as follows:

"Balancing events

393N(1) The following are balancing events for the purposes of this Part–
(a) the relevant interest in the flat is sold;
(b) a long lease of the flat is granted out of the relevant interest in consideration of the payment of a capital sum;
(c) if the relevant interest is a lease, the lease ends otherwise than on the person entitled to it acquiring the interest reversionary on it;
(d) the person who incurred the qualifying expenditure dies;
(e) the flat is demolished or destroyed;
(f) the flat ceases to be a qualifying flat (without being demolished or destroyed).

393N(2) Section 393J(2) and (3) (meaning of **"long lease"**) apply for the purposes of subsection (1)(b).".

Former s. 393N inserted by FA 2001, s. 67 and Sch. 19, Pt. I, with effect in relation to expenditure incurred on or after 11 May 2001.

393O Proceeds from balancing events

393O [Repealed by FA 2012, s. 227 and Sch. 39, para. 37.]

History – S. 393O repealed by FA 2012, s. 227 and Sch. 39, para. 37, with effect in relation to chargeable periods beginning on or after 1 April 2013 for corporation tax purposes, and 6 April 2013 for income tax purposes, subject to transitional and saving provisions in FA 2012, Sch. 39, para. 41 and 42. Former s. 393O read as follows:

"Proceeds from balancing events

393O(1) References in this Part to the proceeds from a balancing event are to the amounts received or receivable in connection with the event, as shown in the Table–

TABLE
BALANCING EVENTS AND PROCEEDS

	1. Balancing event	*2. Proceeds from event*
1.	The sale of the relevant interest.	The net proceeds of the sale.
2.	The grant of a long lease out of the relevant interest.	If the capital sum paid in consideration of the grant is less than the commercial premium, the commercial premium. In any other case, the capital sum paid in consideration of the grant.
3.	The coming to an end of a lease, where a person entitled to the lease and a person entitled to any superior interest are connected persons.	The market value of the relevant interest in the flat at the time of the event.

	1. *Balancing event*	2. *Proceeds from event*
4.	The death of the person who incurred the qualifying expenditure.	The residue of qualifying expenditure immediately before the death.
5.	The demolition or destruction of the flat.	The net amount received for the remains of the flat, together with– (a) any insurance money received in respect of the demolition or destruction, and (b) any other compensation of any description so received, so far as it consists of capital sums.
6.	The flat ceases to be a qualifying flat.	The market value of the relevant interest in the flat at the time of the event.

393O(2) The amounts referred to in column 2 of the Table are those received or receivable by the person who incurred the qualifying expenditure.
393O(3) In Item 2 of the Table **"the commercial premium"** means the premium that would have been given if the transaction had been at arm's length.".
Former s. 393O inserted by FA 2001, s. 67 and Sch. 19, Pt. I, with effect in relation to expenditure incurred on or after 11 May 2001.

393P Calculation of balancing adjustments

393P [Repealed by FA 2012, s. 227 and Sch. 39, para. 37.]

History – S. 393P repealed by FA 2012, s. 227 and Sch. 39, para. 37, with effect in relation to chargeable periods beginning on or after 1 April 2013 for corporation tax purposes, and 6 April 2013 for income tax purposes, subject to transitional and saving provisions in FA 2012, Sch. 39, para. 41 and 42. Former s. 393P read as follows:

"Calculation of balancing adjustments

393P(1) A balancing allowance is made if–
(a) there are no proceeds from the balancing event, or
(b) the proceeds from the balancing event are less than the residue of qualifying expenditure immediately before the event.
393P(2) The amount of the balancing allowance is the amount of–
(a) the residue (if there are no proceeds);
(b) the difference (if the proceeds are less than the residue).
393P(3) A balancing charge is made if the proceeds from the balancing event are more than the residue, if any, of qualifying expenditure immediately before the event.
393P(4) The amount of the balancing charge is the amount of–
(a) the difference, or
(b) the proceeds (if the residue is nil).
393P(5) The amount of a balancing charge made on a person must not exceed the total amount of–
(a) any initial allowances made to the person in respect of the expenditure, and
(b) any writing-down allowances made to the person in respect of the expenditure for chargeable periods ending on or before the date of the balancing event giving rise to the balancing adjustment.".
Former s. 393P inserted by FA 2001, s. 67 and Sch. 19, Pt. I, with effect in relation to expenditure incurred on or after 11 May 2001.

Chapter 8 – Writing Off Qualifying Expenditure

393Q Introduction

393Q [Repealed by FA 2012, s. 227 and Sch. 39, para. 37.]

History – S. 393Q repealed by FA 2012, s. 227 and Sch. 39, para. 37, with effect in relation to chargeable periods beginning on or after 1 April 2013 for corporation tax purposes, and 6 April 2013 for income tax purposes, subject to transitional and saving provisions in FA 2012, Sch. 39, para. 41 and 42. Former s. 393Q read as follows:

"Introduction

393Q For the purposes of this Part qualifying expenditure is written off to the extent and at the times specified in this Chapter.".
Former s. 393Q inserted by FA 2001, s. 67 and Sch. 19, Pt. I, with effect in relation to expenditure incurred on or after 11 May 2001.

393R Writing off initial allowances and writing-down allowances

393R [Repealed by FA 2012, s. 227 and Sch. 39, para. 37.]

History – S. 393R repealed by FA 2012, s. 227 and Sch. 39, para. 37, with effect in relation to chargeable periods beginning on or after 1 April 2013 for corporation tax purposes, and 6 April 2013 for income tax purposes, subject to transitional and saving provisions in FA 2012, Sch. 39, para. 41 and 42. Former s. 393R read as follows:

"Writing off initial allowances and writing-down allowances

393R(1) If an initial allowance is made in respect of the qualifying expenditure, the amount of the allowance is written off at the time when the flat is first suitable for letting as a dwelling.
393R(2) If a writing-down allowance is made in respect of the qualifying expenditure, the amount of the allowance is written off at the end of the chargeable period for which the allowance is made.
393R(3) If a balancing event occurs at the end of the chargeable period referred to in subsection (2), the amount written off under that subsection is to be taken into account in calculating the residue of qualifying expenditure immediately before the event to determine what balancing adjustment (if any) is to be made.".
Former s. 393R inserted by FA 2001, s. 67 and Sch. 19, Pt. I, with effect in relation to expenditure incurred on or after 11 May 2001.

393S Treatment of demolition costs

393S [Repealed by FA 2012, s. 227 and Sch. 39, para. 37.]

History – S. 393S repealed by FA 2012, s. 227 and Sch. 39, para. 37, with effect in relation to chargeable periods beginning on or after 1 April 2013 for corporation tax purposes, and 6 April 2013 for income tax purposes, subject to transitional and saving provisions in FA 2012, Sch. 39, para. 41 and 42. Former s. 393S read as follows:

"Treatment of demolition costs

393S(1) This section applies if–

(a) a qualifying flat is demolished, and

(b) the person who incurred the qualifying expenditure incurs the cost of the demolition.

393S(2) The net cost of the demolition is added to the residue of qualifying expenditure immediately before the demolition.

393S(3) **"The net cost of the demolition"** means the amount, if any, by which the cost of the demolition exceeds any money received for the remains of the flat.

393S(4) If this section applies, neither the cost of the demolition nor the net cost of the demolition is treated for the purposes of any Part of this Act as expenditure on any other property replacing the flat demolished.".

Former s. 393S inserted by FA 2001, s. 67 and Sch. 19, Pt. I, with effect in relation to expenditure incurred on or after 11 May 2001.

Chapter 9 – Supplementary Provisions

393T Giving effect to allowances and charges

393T [Repealed by FA 2012, s. 227 and Sch. 39, para. 37.]

History – S. 393T repealed by FA 2012, s. 227 and Sch. 39, para. 37, with effect in relation to chargeable periods beginning on or after 1 April 2013 for corporation tax purposes, and 6 April 2013 for income tax purposes, subject to transitional and saving provisions in FA 2012, Sch. 39, para. 41 and 42.

Former s. 393T(3) omitted by CTA 2009, s. 1322 and Sch. 1, para. 507(4) and repealed by CTA 2009, s. 1326 and Sch. 3, Pt. 1, with effect for corporation tax purposes for accounting periods ending on or after 1 April 2009, and for income tax and capital gains tax purposes for the tax year 2009–10 and subsequent tax years.

Former s. 393T inserted by FA 2001, s. 67 and Sch. 19, Pt. I, with effect in relation to expenditure incurred on or after 11 May 2001.

CAA 2001

393U Apportionment of sums partly referable to non-qualifying assets

393U [Repealed by FA 2012, s. 227 and Sch. 39, para. 37.]

History – S. 393U repealed by FA 2012, s. 227 and Sch. 39, para. 37, with effect in relation to chargeable periods beginning on or after 1 April 2013 for corporation tax purposes, and 6 April 2013 for income tax purposes, subject to transitional and saving provisions in FA 2012, Sch. 39, para. 41 and 42. Former s. 393U read as follows:

"Apportionment of sums partly referable to non-qualifying assets

393U(1) If the sum paid for the sale of the relevant interest in a flat is attributable–

(a) partly to assets representing expenditure for which an allowance can be made under this Part, and

(b) partly to assets representing other expenditure,

only so much of the sum as on a just and reasonable apportionment is attributable to the assets referred to in paragraph (a) is to be taken into account for the purposes of this Part.

393U(2) Subsection (1) applies to other proceeds from a balancing event in respect of a flat as it applies to a sum given for the sale of the relevant interest in the flat.

393U(3) Subsection (1) does not affect any other provision of this Act requiring an apportionment of the proceeds of a balancing event.".

Former s. 393U inserted by FA 2001, s. 67 and Sch. 19, Pt. I, with effect in relation to expenditure incurred on or after 11 May 2001.

393V Provisions applying on termination of lease

393V [Repealed by FA 2012, s. 227 and Sch. 39, para. 37.]

History – S. 393V repealed by FA 2012, s. 227 and Sch. 39, para. 37, with effect in relation to chargeable periods beginning on or after 1 April 2013 for corporation tax purposes, and 6 April 2013 for income tax purposes, subject to transitional and saving provisions in FA 2012, Sch. 39, para. 41 and 42. Former s. 393V read as follows:

"Provisions applying on termination of lease

393V(1) This section applies for the purposes of this Part if a lease is terminated.

393V(2) If, with the consent of the lessor, the lessee of a flat remains in possession of the flat after the termination without a new lease being granted to him the lease is treated as continuing so long as the lessee remains in possession.

393V(3) If on the termination a new lease is granted to the lessee as a result of the exercise of an option available to him under the terms of the first lease, the second lease is treated as a continuation of the first.

393V(4) If on the termination the lessor pays a sum to the lessee in respect of a flat comprised in the lease, the lease is treated as if it had come to an end by surrender in consideration of the payment.

393V(5) If on the termination–

(a) another lease is granted to a different lessee, and

(b) in connection with the transaction that lessee pays a sum to the person who was the lessee under the first lease,

the two leases are to be treated as if they were the same lease which had been assigned by the lessee under the first lease to the lessee under the second lease in consideration of the payment.".

Former s. 393V inserted by FA 2001, s. 67 and Sch. 19, Pt. I, with effect in relation to expenditure incurred on or after 11 May 2001.

393W Meaning of "lease" etc.

393W [Repealed by FA 2012, s. 227 and Sch. 39, para. 37.]

History – S. 393W repealed by FA 2012, s. 227 and Sch. 39, para. 37, with effect in relation to chargeable periods beginning on or after 1 April 2013 for corporation tax purposes, and 6 April 2013 for income tax purposes, subject to transitional and saving provisions in FA 2012, Sch. 39, para. 41 and 42. Former s. 393W read as follows:

"Meaning of "lease" etc.

393W(1) In this Part **"lease"** includes–

(a) an agreement for a lease if the term to be covered by the lease has begun, and

(b) any tenancy,

but does not include a mortgage (and "lessee", "lessor" and "leasehold interest" are to be read accordingly).

393W(2) In the application of this Part to Scotland–

(a) **"leasehold interest"** (or **"leasehold estate"**) means the interest of a tenant in property subject to a lease, and

(b) any reference to an interest which is reversionary on a leasehold interest or on a lease is to be read as a reference to the interest of the landlord in the property subject to the leasehold interest or lease.".

Former s. 393W inserted by FA 2001, s. 67 and Sch. 19, Pt. I, with effect in relation to expenditure incurred on or after 11 May 2001.

PART 5 – MINERAL EXTRACTION ALLOWANCES

Cross references – FA 1997, Sch. 12, para. 11(3): receipt of a "major lump sum" under certain leasing arrangements gives rise to a balancing adjustment where an allowance has been granted or a charge made under the rules relating to Mineral Extraction Allowances.
S. 532–537, 541 and 542: allowances for amounts contributed towards capital expenditure.
S. 553: certain forms of consideration given for the disposal of some types of oil production licence to be treated as nil for the purposes of Pt. 5.
S. 562: apportionment of sale or purchase moneys.
S. 564: procedures for determining the market value of assets and the apportionment of that value between two or more persons.
S. 567–570: circumstances where sales treated as if made at market value and elections available.
ICTA 1988, s. 87: disapplication of the relief, for Sch. A premiums paid, in computing trading profits where mineral extraction allowances claimed in respect of the expenditure.
ICTA 1988, s. 389(2): rules assigning priority to claims to carry back relief for terminal losses under ICTA 1988, s. 388 and final period balancing allowances under s. 355.
FA 1997, Sch. 12, para. 11: provisions relating to certain finance lease or loan arrangements where sums are received as a return on investment and the conditions which require a disposal value to be brought into account.

Chapter 1 – Introduction

394 Mineral extraction allowances

394(1) Allowances are available under this Part if a person carries on a mineral extraction trade and incurs qualifying expenditure.

394(2) In this Part **"mineral extraction trade"** means a trade which consists of, or includes, the working of a source of mineral deposits but to the extent only that the profits or gains from that trade are, or (if there were any) would be, chargeable to tax.

394(3) In this Part **"mineral deposits"** includes any natural deposits capable of being lifted or extracted from the earth, and for this purpose geothermal energy is to be treated as a natural deposit.

394(4) Any reference in this Part to mineral deposits is to mineral deposits of a wasting nature.

394(5) In this Part **"source of mineral deposits"** includes a mine, an oil well and a source of geothermal energy.

Prospective amendments – S. 394(2A) inserted by CTNIA 2015, s. 2 and Sch. 1, para. 12, with effect from 26 March 2015 (Royal Assent) in respect of any power to make regulations and with effect in relation to accounting periods beginning on or after the first day of the appointed financial year for other provisions (see CTNIA 2015, s. 5). See also transitional provisions at Sch. 1, para. 19–21.

History – In s. 394(2), the words "but to the extent only that the profits or gains from that trade are, or (if there were any) would be, chargeable to tax" inserted by FA 2014, s. 67(2), with effect in relation to claims made on or after 1 April 2014 (for corporation tax purposes) or 6 April 2014 (for income tax purposes), and in relation to those claims this amendment is treated as always having had effect.

Origin – S. 394(1): CAA 1990, s. 98(1) (part), s. 105(1) (part), s. 109(1) (part).
S. 394(2): CAA 1990, s. 121(1) ("trade of mineral extraction").
S. 394(3): CAA 1990, s. 161(2) ("mineral deposits"), Annex 2, Note 46.
S. 394(4): CAA 1990, s. 121(2) (part).
S. 394(5): CAA 1990, s. 121(1) ("source of mineral deposits").

Cross references – ICTA 1988, s. 91C: denial of revenue deduction on intangible costs of drilling second and subsequent production oil wells in any area.
TCGA 1992, s. 41: exclusion from base cost etc. in computation of gain for amounts allowable as regards tax on income etc. does not include expenditure for which "capital allowance" made, although a loss may be restricted.
TCGA 1992, Sch. 3, para. 7(8): election for 31 March 1982 market value to apply, may not be made for assets connected with a trade of working mineral deposits.

Rewrite: Technical Points – Explanatory Notes, Annex 2, Note 46: in s. 394(3) the identification of "geothermal energy" as a "natural deposit" does not include the extended illustration of the term given at CAA 1990, s. 161(2) ("whether in the form of aquifers, hot dry rocks or otherwise"). It is considered that the extended definition was unhelpful and no legal change is effected by its removal.

HMRC Manuals – CA11700: whether expenditure has been "incurred", etc.
CA13100ff.: sales treated as being at market value, etc.
CA31800: guidance on prevention of double allowances.
CA50120ff.: scope of mineral extraction allowances.
CA50410: how mineral extraction allowances are given.

Other material – ICAEW Technical Release TR 631 (not reproduced): Revenue stated that since it was not strictly possible to exploit a mineral asset until planning permission was granted, relief would not be due before that point.

395 Qualifying expenditure

395(1) In this Part **"qualifying expenditure"** means–

(a) expenditure on mineral exploration and access which is qualifying expenditure under Chapter 2,

(b) expenditure on acquiring a mineral asset which is qualifying expenditure under Chapter 3,

(c) expenditure which is treated as qualifying expenditure on mineral exploration and access under section 407(5) or 408(2), and

(d) expenditure which is qualifying expenditure under Chapter 5 (expenditure on works likely to become valueless and restoration expenditure).

But this is subject to subsections (2) and (3).

395(2) Expenditure is not qualifying expenditure if it is excluded from being qualifying expenditure by section 399.

395(3) Chapters 4 and 5 contain provisions limiting in certain cases the amount of expenditure which is qualifying expenditure.

History – In s. 395(1)(d), the words "post-trading" omitted by FA 2013, s. 92(2), with effect in relation to expenditure incurred on restoration carried out on or after 17 July 2013.
In s. 395(3), the words "Chapters 4 and 5 contain" substituted for the words "Chapter 4 contains" by FA 2013, s. 93 and Sch. 32, para. 10, with effect in relation to expenditure incurred on restoration carried out on or after 17 July 2013.

Origin – S. 395(1): CAA 1990, s. 105(1) (part), Annex 2, Note 50.
S. 395(2): CAA 1990, s. 105(1) (part).
S. 395(3): CAA 1990, s. 105(3) (part).

Cross references – ICTA 1988, s. 87: disapplication of the relief, for Sch. A premiums paid, in computing trading profits where mineral extraction allowances claimed in respect of the expenditure.

Rewrite: Technical Points – Explanatory Notes, Annex 2, Note 50: s. 395(1)(c) in defining "qualifying expenditure" makes it explicit that the acquisition of certain mineral assets and oil licences from other persons is treated as incurred on exploration and access; previously it could only be inferred from the legislation.

HMRC Manuals – CA50210ff.: guidance on qualifying expenditure.
CA50300: guidance on planning permission costs.

Other material – ICAEW Technical Release TR 631 (not reproduced): Revenue stated that since it was not strictly possible to exploit a mineral asset until planning permission was granted, relief would not be due before that point.

CAA 2001

396 Meaning of "mineral exploration and access"

396(1) In this Part **"mineral exploration and access"** means–

(a) searching for or discovering and testing the mineral deposits of a source, or

(b) winning access to such deposits.

396(2) Expenditure on seeking planning permission necessary to enable–

(a) mineral exploration and access to be undertaken at any place, or

(b) any mineral deposits to be worked,

is treated as expenditure on mineral exploration and access and not as expenditure on acquiring a mineral asset.

396(3) **"Seeking planning permission"** includes pursuing an appeal against a refusal to grant planning permission.

History – In s. 396(2), the words "and not as expenditure on acquiring a mineral asset" substituted for the words "if planning permission is not granted" by FA 2014, s. 68(2), with effect in relation to expenditure incurred on or after 17 July 2014.

Origin – S. 396(1): CAA 1990, s. 121(1) ("mineral exploration and access").
S. 396(2), (3): CAA 1990, s. 105(6).

Cross references – ICTA 1988, s. 91C: denial of revenue deduction on intangible costs of drilling second and subsequent production oil wells in any area; incorporation of definition of "mineral exploration and access".

HMRC Manuals – CA50230: guidance on s. 396.
CA50300: guidance on planning permission costs.

397 Meaning of "mineral asset"

397 In this Part **"mineral asset"** means–

(a) any mineral deposits or land comprising mineral deposits, or

(b) any interest in or right over such deposits or land.

Origin – CAA 1990, s. 121(1) ("mineral asset").

HMRC Manuals – CA50330: guidance on s. 397.

398 Relationship between main types of qualifying expenditure

398 Subject to section 396(2) and Chapter 4, expenditure on–

(a) the acquisition of, or of rights over, the site of a source of mineral deposits, or

(b) the acquisition of, or of rights over, mineral deposits,

is to be treated as expenditure on acquiring a mineral asset and not as expenditure on mineral exploration and access.

History – In s. 398, the words "section 396(2) and" inserted by FA 2014, s. 68(3) with effect in relation to expenditure incurred on or after 17 July 2014.

Origin – CAA 1990, s. 105(7).

399 Expenditure excluded from being qualifying expenditure

399(1) Expenditure on the provision of plant or machinery is not qualifying expenditure except as provided by section 402 (pre-trading expenditure on plant or machinery).

399(1A) Expenditure incurred by a person for the purposes of a mineral extraction trade is not qualifying expenditure if–

(a) when the expenditure is incurred, the person is carrying on the trade but the trade is not at that time a mineral extraction trade, or

(b) the person has not begun to carry on the trade when the expenditure is incurred and, when the person begins to carry on the trade, the trade is not a mineral extraction trade.

399(1B) Section 577(2) (references to commencement etc of a trade) does not apply to subsection (1A).

399(2) Expenditure on works constructed wholly or mainly for subjecting the raw product of a source to any process is not qualifying expenditure, unless the process is designed for preparing the raw product for use as such.

399(3) Expenditure on buildings or structures provided for occupation by, or for the welfare of, workers is not qualifying expenditure except as provided by section 415.

399(4) Expenditure on a building is not qualifying expenditure if the whole of the building was constructed for use as an office.

399(5) Subsection (6) applies if part of a building or structure has been constructed for use as an office.

399(6) The expenditure on the office part is not qualifying expenditure if it was more than 10% of the capital expenditure incurred on the construction of the whole.

History – S. 399(1A) and (1B) inserted by FA 2014, s. 67(3), with effect in relation to claims made on or after 1 April 2014 (for corporation tax purposes) or 6 April 2014 (for income tax purposes), and in relation to those claims this amendment is treated as always having had effect.

Origin – S. 399(1): CAA 1990, s. 105(4).
S. 399(2) to (6): CAA 1990, s. 105(5) (part).

HMRC Manuals – CA50320: guidance on s. 399.

Chapter 2 – Qualifying Expenditure on Mineral Exploration and Access

400 Qualifying expenditure on mineral exploration and access

400(1) Expenditure on mineral exploration and access is qualifying expenditure if–

(a) it is capital expenditure, and

(b) it is incurred for the purposes of a mineral extraction trade.

400(2) Expenditure on mineral exploration and access incurred by a person in connection with a mineral extraction trade which that person carries on then or subsequently is to be treated as incurred for the purposes of that trade.

400(3) But pre-trading expenditure on mineral exploration and access is qualifying expenditure only to the extent provided by–

section 401 (pre-trading exploration expenditure), or

section 402 (pre-trading expenditure on plant or machinery).

400(4) Any pre-trading expenditure that is qualifying expenditure under either of those sections is to be treated as incurred on the first day of trading.

400(5) In this Chapter–

(a) **"pre-trading expenditure"** means capital expenditure incurred before the day on which a person begins to carry on a mineral extraction trade, and

(b) **"the first day of trading"**, in relation to a person's pre-trading expenditure, means the day on which that person begins to carry on the mineral extraction trade.

Origin – S. 400(1): CAA 1990, s. 98(1) (part), s. 105(1) (part), Annex 1, Change 47.
S. 400(2): CAA 1990, s. 102.
S. 400(3): CAA 1990, s. 105(2).
S. 400(4): CAA 1990, s. 106(2) (part), s. 107(3) (part), s. 120(2), Annex 2, Note 51.
S. 400(5): drafting.

Cross references – S. 434: expenditure incurred by person about to commence trade (which is not pre-trading expenditure) to be treated as incurred on first day of trading.
S. 416C: rule in s. 400(4) disregarded in determining whether expenditure incurred for purposes of a ring-fence trade qualifies for first-year allowances under Ch. 5A.

Transitional – Sch. 3, para. 91: where during the transitional period an oil licence is disposed of and part of its value is attributable to exploration expenditure incurred by the transferor an election may be made specifying the amount to be so attributable.

Rewrite: Changes in Law – Explanatory Notes, Annex 1, Change 47: CAA 1990, s. 98(1) appeared to require a continuing trade in order for any expenditure to be "qualifying". In practice this apparent requirement was not interpreted as applying in the case of restoration expenditure incurred after a trade ceased (CAA 1990, s. 109). The change requires expenditure to be "incurred for the purposes of a mineral extraction trade" without any reference to it being carried on at the time the expenditure is incurred. See Sch. 3, para. 8 for the election to apply the original law to this matter where a chargeable period straddles 1 April 2001 (for corporation tax) or 6 April 2001 (for income tax).

Rewrite: Technical Points – Explanatory Notes, Annex 2, Note 51: in s. 400(4) the reference to expenditure being treated as incurred on the first day of trading eliminates duplication of the deeming provision that was present in the previous legislation.

HMRC Manuals – CA50230, CA50270: guidance on s. 400.

401 Pre-trading exploration expenditure

401(1) This section applies if–

(a) a person incurs pre-trading expenditure on mineral exploration and access at a source, and

(b) the expenditure is not incurred on the provision of plant or machinery.

401(2) The amount of the expenditure (**"pre-trading exploration expenditure"**) that is qualifying expenditure depends on whether mineral exploration and access is continuing at the source on the first day of trading.

401(3) If it is, so much of the pre-trading exploration expenditure as exceeds any relevant receipts is qualifying expenditure.

401(4) If it is not, only so much of the pre-trading exploration expenditure as–

(a) was incurred within 6 years ending on the first day of trading, and

(b) exceeds any relevant receipts,

is qualifying expenditure.

401(5) **"Relevant receipts"** means capital sums received–

(a) by the person incurring the pre-trading exploration expenditure referred to in subsection (3) or (4), and

(b) before the first day of trading,

so far as they are reasonably attributable to that expenditure.

Origin – S. 401(1): CAA 1990, s. 107(1).
S. 401(2): CAA 1990, s. 107(2) (part), (3) (part), (5).
S. 401(3): CAA 1990, s. 107(2) (part).
S. 401(4): CAA 1990, s. 107(3) (part).
S. 401(5): CAA 1990, s. 107(4).

Cross references – S. 426: entitlement to balancing allowance where trade commences during chargeable period in which expenditure incurred.
S. 562: expenditure deemed to include expenditure on the acquisition of, or rights in or over, mineral deposits, or the acquisition of land or mineral assets and the apportionment of sale or purchase moneys.

Transitional – Sch. 3, para. 88: transitional provisions relating to expenditure incurred before 1 April 1986 (i.e. under the old scheme of Mines and Oil Wells Allowance – MOWA). The provision ensures that excessive allowances; for expenditure incurred under the old rules and relieved under MOWA; can be recovered under Pt. 5.

HMRC Manuals – CA50240ff.: guidance on s. 401.

402 Pre-trading expenditure on plant or machinery

402(1) This section applies if–

(a) a person incurs pre-trading expenditure on the provision of plant or machinery for mineral exploration and access,

(b) the plant or machinery was used in connection with mineral exploration and access at a source, and

(c) before the first day of trading, the plant or machinery is sold, demolished, destroyed or abandoned.

402(2) The amount of the expenditure (**"pre-trading expenditure on plant or machinery"**) that is qualifying expenditure depends on whether mineral exploration and access is continuing at the source on the first day of trading.

402(3) If it is, so much of the pre-trading expenditure on plant or machinery as exceeds any relevant receipts is qualifying expenditure.

402(4) If it is not, only so much of the pre-trading expenditure on plant or machinery as–

(a) was incurred within 6 years ending on the first day of trading, and

(b) exceeds any relevant receipts,

is qualifying expenditure.

402(5) **"Relevant receipts"** means–

(a) if the plant or machinery is sold, the net proceeds to the person of the sale;

(b) if the plant or machinery is demolished or destroyed, the net amount received by the person for the remains of the plant or machinery, together with–

CAA 2001

(i) any insurance money received by him in respect of the demolition or destruction, and

(ii) any other compensation of any description so received, so far as it consists of capital sums;

(c) if the plant or machinery is abandoned–

(i) any insurance money received by the person in respect of the abandonment, and

(ii) any other compensation of any description so received, so far as it consists of capital sums.

Origin – S. 402(1): CAA 1990, s. 106(1) (part), (4) (part).
S. 402(2): CAA 1990, s. 106(4) (part).
S. 402(3): CAA 1990, s. 106(2) (part), (3) (part).
S. 402(4): CAA 1990, s. 106(3) (part), (4) (part).
S. 402(5): CAA 1990, s. 106(3) (part), s. 156 (part), Annex 1, Change 10.

Cross references – S. 161: relief for plant and machinery which is still owned when a trade of mineral extraction commences.
S. 426: entitlement to balancing allowance where trade commences during chargeable period in which expenditure incurred.
S. 562: expenditure deemed to include expenditure on the acquisition of, or rights in or over, mineral deposits, or the acquisition of land or mineral assets and the apportionment of sale or purchase moneys.

Transitional – Sch. 3, para. 88: transitional provisions relating to expenditure incurred before 1 April 1986 (i.e. under the old scheme of Mines and Oil Wells Allowance – MOWA). The provision ensures that excessive allowances for expenditure incurred under the old rules; and relieved under MOWA; can be recovered under Pt. 5.

Rewrite: Changes in Law – Explanatory Notes, Annex 1, Change 10: The original provisions determining the disposal value to be included did not explicitly deal with the abandonment of plant etc. (thus the value to be used would be the market value). S. 402(5)(c) includes specific provisions dealing with abandonment and requires any insurance and/or capital compensation receipts to be treated as the disposal value. See Sch. 3, para. 8 for the election to apply the original law to this matter where a chargeable period straddles 1 April 2001 (for corporation tax) or 6 April 2001 (for income tax).

HMRC Manuals – CA50240: guidance on s. 402.

Chapter 3 – Qualifying Expenditure on Acquiring a Mineral Asset

403 Qualifying expenditure on acquiring a mineral asset

403(1) Expenditure on acquiring a mineral asset is qualifying expenditure if–

(a) it is capital expenditure, and

(b) it is incurred for the purposes of a mineral extraction trade.

403(2) Subsection (1) is subject to–

section 404 (exclusion of undeveloped market value of land), and

section 406 (reduction where premium relief previously allowed).

403(2A) For the purposes of this section the reference to expenditure on acquiring a mineral asset does not include expenditure incurred on the restoration of a relevant site (within the meaning of section 416 or 416ZA).

403(3) In this Chapter **"the buyer"**, in relation to the acquisition of a mineral asset, means the person acquiring it.

History – S. 403(2A) inserted by FA 2013, s. 92(3), with effect in relation to expenditure incurred on restoration carried out on or after 17 July 2013.

Origin – S. 403(1): CAA 1990, s. 98(1) (part), s. 105(1) (part), Annex 1, Change 47.
S. 403(2): CAA 1990, s. 105(3) (part).
S. 403(3): drafting.

Cross references – S. 395: meaning of; and limitations to; the term "qualifying expenditure".
ICTA 1988, s. 87: disapplication of the relief, for Sch. A premiums paid, in computing trading profits where mineral extraction allowances claimed in respect of the expenditure.

Rewrite: Changes in Law – Explanatory Notes, Annex 1, Change 47: CAA 1990, s. 98(1) appeared to require a continuing trade in order for any expenditure to be "qualifying". In practice this apparent requirement was not interpreted as applying in the case of restoration expenditure incurred after a trade ceased (CAA 1990, s. 109). The change requires expenditure to be "incurred for the purposes of a mineral extraction trade" without any reference to it being carried on at the time the expenditure is incurred. See Sch. 3, para. 8 for the election to apply the original law to this matter where a chargeable period straddles 1 April 2001 (for corporation tax) or 6 April 2001 (for income tax).

404 Exclusion of undeveloped market value of land

404(1) If the mineral asset is an interest in land, so much of the buyer's expenditure on acquiring the asset as is equal to the undeveloped market value of the interest is not qualifying expenditure.

404(2) **"The undeveloped market value of the interest"** means the amount that, at the time of the acquisition, the interest might reasonably be expected to fetch on a sale in the open market on the assumptions in subsection (3).

404(3) The assumptions are that–

(a) there is no source of mineral deposits on or in the land, and

(b) it will only ever be lawful to carry out existing permitted development.

404(4) Development is existing permitted development if at the time of the acquisition–

(a) it has been, or had begun to be, lawfully carried out, or

(b) it could be lawfully carried out under planning permission granted by a general development order.

404(5) In applying subsection (4) in relation to land outside the United Kingdom–

(a) whether, at the time of the acquisition, development has been, or had begun to be, lawfully carried out is to be determined according to the law of the territory in which the land is situated, and

(b) whether, at that time, development could be lawfully carried out under planning permission granted by a general development order is to be determined as if the land were in England.

404(6) References in this section to the time of acquisition are not affected by section 434 (expenditure incurred before trade carried on).

404(7) This section does not apply to the buyer's expenditure if an election under section 569 (election to treat sale as being for alternative amount) is made in relation to the acquisition.

Origin – S. 404(1): CAA 1990, s. 110(1) (part).
S. 404(2)–(4): CAA 1990, s. 110(2) (part).
S. 404(5): CAA 1990, s. 110(3) (part), Annex 1, Change 48.
S. 404(6): CAA 1990, s. 110(6) (part).
S. 404(7): drafting.

Cross references – S. 412(5): intra-group transfers of mineral assets; original acquisition by any group company determines allowances etc.
S. 436: meaning of "development"; "development order"; "general development order"; and "planning permission".

Transitional – Sch. 3, para. 88: transitional provisions relating to expenditure incurred before 1 April 1986 (i e. under the old scheme of Mines and Oil Wells Allowance – MOWA). The provision ensures that excessive allowances for expenditure incurred under the old rules; and relieved under MOWA; can be recovered under Pt. 5.

Rewrite: Changes in Law – Explanatory Notes, Annex 1, Change 48: following the setting up of the Welsh Assembly it is possible for differing general development orders to be produced for England and Wales. To avoid difficulties the deemed requirement in s. 404(5)(b); which requires a hypothetical general development order to be assumed for overseas land; is now formulated by reference only to general development orders in England (and not England *and* Wales as previously). See Sch. 3, para. 8 for the election to apply the original law to this matter where a chargeable period straddles 1 April 2001 (for corporation tax) or 6 April 2001 (for income tax).

HMRC Manuals – CA50330ff.: guidance on s. 404.

CAA 2001

405 Qualifying expenditure where buildings or structures cease to be used

405(1) This section applies if–

(a) section 404 (exclusion of undeveloped market value of land) applies to limit the buyer's qualifying expenditure on acquiring the mineral asset,

(b) the undeveloped market value of the interest in land includes the value of any buildings or structures on the land, and

(c) at the time of the acquisition, or at any later time, the buildings or structures permanently cease to be used for any purpose.

405(2) The buyer is to be treated–

(a) as having incurred qualifying expenditure, on acquiring a mineral asset, of an amount equal to the unrelieved value of the buildings or structures, and

(b) as having incurred it when the buildings or structures permanently cease to be used for any purpose.

405(3) The unrelieved value of the buildings or structures is–

$$V - (A - B)$$

where–

V is the value of the buildings or structures at the date of the acquisition (disregarding any value properly attributable to the land on which they stand),

A is the amount of any allowances made to the buyer under the provisions of this Act other than Part 10 (assured tenancy allowances) in respect of–

(a) the buildings or structures, or

(b) assets in the buildings or structures, and

B is the amount of any balancing charges made on the buyer under those provisions in respect of those buildings or structures or assets in them.

405(4) References in this section to the time of acquisition are not affected by section 434 (time when expenditure incurred).

Origin – S. 405(1), (2): CAA 1990, s. 110(4).
S. 405(3): CAA 1990, s. 110(5).
S. 405(4): CAA 1990, s. 110(6) (part).

Cross references – S. 412(5): intra-group transfers of mineral assets; original acquisition by any group company determines allowances etc.

Transitional – Sch. 3, para. 84: where buildings etc. cease to be used prior to 27 July 1089 "A" does not include any Agricultural Buildings Allowances.

406 Reduction where premium relief previously allowed

406(1) This section applies if–

(a) the mineral asset is or includes an interest in land, and

(b) for chargeable periods previous to the chargeable period for which the buyer first becomes entitled to an allowance under this Part in respect of the expenditure on acquiring the mineral asset, deductions are made under sections 60 to 67 of ITTOIA 2005 or under sections 62 to 67 of CTA 2009 (deductions in calculating trading profits where premiums etc. taxable).

406(2) The amount of the expenditure on the acquisition of the mineral asset that is qualifying expenditure is reduced by–

$$D \times \frac{E}{T}$$

where–

D is the total of the deductions made under sections 60 to 67 of ITTOIA 2005 or under sections 62 to 67 of CTA 2009 in the earlier chargeable periods mentioned in subsection (1)(b),

E is the amount of the capital expenditure on the acquisition of the interest in land that would have been qualifying expenditure if the buyer had been entitled to allowances under this Part in those earlier periods, and

T is the total amount of the capital expenditure on the acquisition of the interest in land.

History – In s. 406(1)(b), the words "sections 62 to 67 of CTA 2009" substituted for the words "sections 87 and 87A of ICTA" by CTA 2009, s. 1322 and Sch. 1, para. 508(2), with effect for corporation tax purposes for accounting periods ending on or after 1 April 2009, and for income tax and capital gains tax purposes for the tax year 2009–10 and subsequent tax years.
S. 406(1) amended by ITTOIA 2005, s. 882(1) and Sch. 1, para. 561(2); effective for income tax purposes for 2005–06 onwards and for corporation tax purposes for accounting periods ending after 5 April 2005 (ITTOIA 2005, s. 883(1)).
In s. 406(2), the words "sections 62 to 67 of CTA 2009" substituted for the words "sections 87 and 87A of ICTA" by CTA 2009, s. 1322 and Sch. 1, para. 508(3), with effect for corporation tax purposes for accounting periods ending on or after 1 April 2009, and for income tax and capital gains tax purposes for the tax year 2009–10 and subsequent tax years.
S. 406(2) amended by ITTOIA 2005, s. 882(1) and Sch. 1, para. 561(3); effective for income tax purposes for 2005–06 onwards and for corporation tax purposes for accounting periods ending after 5 April 2005 (ITTOIA 2005, s. 883(1)).
Origin – S. 406(1), (2): CAA 1990, s. 111.

Chapter 4 – Qualifying Expenditure: Second-hand Assets

ASSETS REFLECTING EXPENDITURE ON MINERAL EXPLORATION AND ACCESS

407 Acquisition of mineral asset owned by previous trader

407(1) This section applies if–

(a) a person carrying on a mineral extraction trade (**"the buyer"**) incurs capital expenditure on acquiring a mineral asset (**"asset X"**) for the purposes of that trade, and

(b) the conditions in subsection (3) are met.

407(2) In this section **"the buyer's expenditure"** means the expenditure referred to in subsection (1)(a), less any amount which, under section 404 (exclusion of undeveloped market value of land), is not qualifying expenditure on the acquisition of the mineral asset.

407(3) The conditions are that–

(a) expenditure was previously incurred on acquiring asset X or bringing it into existence by–

(i) the person from whom the buyer acquired asset X, or

(ii) an earlier owner of asset X,

in connection with a mineral extraction trade carried on by the person incurring that expenditure,

(b) part of the value of asset X is properly attributable to expenditure (**"E1"**) on mineral exploration and access by the previous trader, and

(c) it is just and reasonable to attribute part of the buyer's expenditure (**"E2"**) to that part of the value of asset X.

407(4) In arriving at E1, any expenditure that is or has been deducted in calculating, for tax purposes, the profits of a trade carried on by the previous trader must be excluded.

407(5) If this section applies–

(a) so much of the buyer's expenditure as is equal to the lesser of E1 and E2 is to be treated as qualifying expenditure on mineral exploration and access, and

(b) the buyer's expenditure on acquiring the mineral asset is reduced by the same amount.

407(6) **"The previous trader"** means–

(a) the person incurring the expenditure mentioned in subsection (3)(a), or

(b) if there has been more than one such person, the last before the buyer acquired asset X.

407(7) In this section references to asset X include–

(a) two or more assets which together make up asset X, and

(b) one asset from which, or two or more assets from the combination of which, asset X is derived.

Origin – S. 407: Annex 2, Note 52.
S. 407(1): CAA 1990, s. 113(1) (part), Annex 1, Change 47.
S. 407(2): CAA 1990, s. 114(1) (part), s. 115(3) (part).
S. 407(3): CAA 1990, s. 113(3) (part), s. 115(1) (part), (2) (part).
S. 407(4): CAA 1990, s. 115(2A).
S. 407(5): CAA 1990, s. 115(2) (part).
S. 407(6): CAA 1990, s. 113(4) (part), s. 115(3) (part).
S. 407(7): CAA 1990, s. 113(5) (part), s. 115(3) (part).

Cross references – S. 413: disapplication of s. 412 (restrictions on intra-group transfers) for the purposes of s. 407(5).
S. 562(5): apportionment of amounts on sale or purchase of mineral assets.

Transitional – Sch. 3, para. 85: s. 407(4) does not apply to claims made before 26 Novemeber 1996.
Sch. 3, para. 87: s. 407 does not apply if "X" is a UK situated mineral asset and the payments for capital expenditure are required under the buyer's contract if entered into prior to 16 July 1985. Where s. 407 does apply references to an earlier owner do not include a person who has not owned the asset at any time after 31 March 1986.

Rewrite: Changes in Law – Explanatory Notes, Annex 1, Change 47: CAA 1990, s. 98(1) appeared to require a continuing trade in order for any expenditure to be "qualifying". In practice this apparent requirement was not interpreted as applying in the case of restoration expenditure incurred after a trade ceased (CAA 1990, s. 109). The change requires expenditure to be "incurred for the purposes of a mineral extraction trade" without any reference to it being carried on at the time the expenditure is incurred. See Sch. 3, para. 8 for the election to apply the original law to this matter where a chargeable period straddles 1 April 2001 (for corporation tax) or 6 April 2001 (for income tax).

Rewrite: Technical Points – Explanatory Notes, Annex 2, Note 52: part of s. 407 is based on CAA 1990, s. 115(2); however s. 115(2)(b) is not reflected in the new section as it is considered to be redundant; serving no useful purpose.

HMRC Manuals – CA50470: guidance on s. 407.

408 Acquisition of oil licence from non-trader

408(1) This section applies if–

(a) a person carrying on a mineral extraction trade (**"the buyer"**) incurs capital expenditure on acquiring an interest in an oil licence for the purposes of that trade,

(b) the person from whom the interest was acquired (**"the seller"**) disposed of the interest without having carried on a mineral extraction trade,

(c) part of the value of the interest is attributable to expenditure (**"E1"**) on mineral exploration and access by the seller, and

(d) it is just and reasonable to attribute part of the buyer's expenditure (**"E2"**) to that part of the value of the interest.

408(2) If this section applies–

(a) so much of the buyer's expenditure as is equal to the lesser of E1 and E2 is to be treated as qualifying expenditure on mineral exploration and access, and

(b) the buyer's expenditure on acquiring the interest in the oil licence is reduced by an amount equal to E2.

408(3) In this section **"oil licence"** and **"interest in an oil licence"** have the same meaning as in Chapter 3 of Part 12.

Origin – S. 408(1): CAA 1990, s. 118(1) (part), (2), s. 138A(1) (part), (2) (part), (3) (part), Annex 1, Change 47.
S. 408(2): CAA 1990, s. 118(2) (part), s. 138A(1) (part), (2) (part).
S. 408(3): CAA 1990, s. 118(2) (part), s. 138A(4) ("interest", "oil licence").

Cross references – S. 413: disapplication of s. 412 (restrictions on intra-group transfers) for the purposes of s. 408(2).
S. 552–556: supplementary rules relating to disposals of oil licences in certain undeveloped areas.
S. 562(5): apportionment of amounts on sale or purchase of mineral assets or licences.
TCGA 1992, s. 194: Capital gains rules for disposals of oil licences.

Transitional – Sch. 3, para. 86: s. 408 does not apply to acquisitions occurring before 13 September 1985.
Sch. 3, para. 91: where during the transitional period an oil licence is disposed of and part of its value is attributable to exploration expenditure incurred by the transferor an election may be made specifying the amount to be so attributable.

Rewrite: Changes in Law – Explanatory Notes, Annex 1, Change 47: CAA 1990, s. 98(1) appeared to require a continuing trade in order for any expenditure to be "qualifying". In practice this apparent requirement was not interpreted as applying in the case of restoration expenditure incurred after a trade ceased (CAA 1990, s. 109). The change requires expenditure to be "incurred for the purposes of a mineral extraction trade" without any reference to it being carried on at the time the expenditure is incurred. See Sch. 3, para. 8 for the election to apply the original law to this matter where a chargeable period straddles 1 April 2001 (for corporation tax) or 6 April 2001 (for income tax).

409 Acquisition of other assets from non-traders

409(1) This section applies if–

(a) a person carrying on a mineral extraction trade (**"the buyer"**) incurs capital expenditure on acquiring any assets for the purposes of that trade,

(b) the person from whom the assets were acquired (**"the seller"**) disposed of the assets without having carried on a mineral extraction trade,

(c) the assets represent expenditure on mineral exploration and access incurred by the seller, and

(d) section 408 (acquisition of oil licence from non-trader) does not apply in relation to the acquisition.

409(2) If this section applies, the buyer's expenditure is qualifying expenditure only to the extent that it does not exceed the amount of the seller's expenditure on mineral exploration and access that is represented by the assets.

409(3) The references in this section to assets representing expenditure on mineral exploration and access include any results obtained from any search, exploration or inquiry on which the expenditure was incurred.

Origin – S. 409(1), (2): CAA 1990, s. 118(1) (part), Annex 1, Change 47.
S. 409(3): CAA 1990, s. 121(3).

Rewrite: Changes in Law – Explanatory Notes, Annex 1, Change 47: CAA 1990, s. 98(1) appeared to require a continuing trade in order for any expenditure to be "qualifying". In practice this apparent requirement was not interpreted as applying in the case of restoration expenditure incurred after a trade ceased (CAA 1990, s. 109). The change requires expenditure to be "incurred for the purposes of a mineral extraction trade" without any reference to it being carried on at the time the expenditure is incurred. See Sch. 3, para. 8 for the election to apply the original law to this matter where a chargeable period straddles 1 April 2001 (for corporation tax) or 6 April 2001 (for income tax).

QUALIFYING EXPENDITURE ON ASSETS LIMITED BY REFERENCE TO HISTORIC COSTS

410 UK oil licence: limit is original licence payment

410(1) This section applies if a person carrying on a mineral extraction trade (**"the buyer"**) incurs capital expenditure on acquiring a mineral asset which is a UK oil licence, or an interest in such a licence, for the purposes of that trade.

410(2) If this section applies, the buyer's expenditure is qualifying expenditure only to the extent that it does not exceed–

(a) the original licence payment, or

(b) if the mineral asset is an interest in a UK oil licence, such part of the original licence payment as it is just and reasonable to attribute to the interest.

410(3) In this section **"the original licence payment"** means the amount paid to the relevant authority for the purpose of obtaining the licence by the person to whom the licence was granted.

410(4) This section does not affect any expenditure that is treated as qualifying expenditure on mineral exploration and access under–

section 407(5) (acquisition of mineral asset owned by previous trader), or

section 408(2) (acquisition of oil licence from non-trader).

410(5) In this section **"UK oil licence"** and **"the relevant authority"** have the same meaning as in Chapter 3 of Part 12.

Origin – S. 410(1): CAA 1990, s. 116(1) (part).
S. 410(2): CAA 1990, s. 116(1) (part), (2) (part).
S. 410(3): CAA 1990, s. 116(2) (part), (3) (part).
S. 410(4), (5): drafting.

Cross references – S. 562(5): apportionment of amounts on sale or purchase of mineral assets or licences.

Transitional – Sch. 3, para. 87: s. 410 does not apply if "X" is a UK situated mineral asset and the payments for capital expenditure are required under the buyer's contract if entered into prior to 16 July 1985.

411 Assets generally: limit is residue of previous trader's qualifying expenditure

411(1) This section applies if–

(a) a person carrying on a mineral extraction trade (**"the buyer"**) incurs capital expenditure on acquiring an asset (**"asset X"**) for the purposes of that trade, and

(b) expenditure was previously incurred on acquiring asset X or bringing it into existence by–

(i) the person from whom the buyer acquired asset X, or

(ii) an earlier owner of asset X,

in connection with a mineral extraction trade carried on by the person incurring that expenditure.

411(2) In this section **"the buyer's expenditure"** means the expenditure referred to in subsection (1)(a) less any amount which, under section 404 (exclusion of undeveloped market value of land), is not qualifying expenditure on the acquisition of the mineral asset.

411(3) If this section applies, the buyer's expenditure is qualifying expenditure only to the extent that it does not exceed the residue of the previous trader's qualifying expenditure.

411(4) The residue of the previous trader's qualifying expenditure is–

$$QE - (A - B)$$

where–

QE is so much of the expenditure incurred by the previous trader on the acquisition or bringing into existence of asset X as constitutes qualifying expenditure for the purposes of this Part,

A is the total of any allowances made under this Part in respect of the previous trader's qualifying expenditure, and

B is the total of any balancing charges made under this Part in respect of the previous trader's qualifying expenditure.

411(5) **"The previous trader"** means–

(a) the person incurring the expenditure mentioned in subsection (1)(b), or

(b) if there has been more than one such person, the last before the buyer acquired asset X.

411(6) In this section references to asset X include–

(a) two or more assets which together make up asset X, and

(b) one asset from which, or two or more assets from the combination of which, asset X is derived.

411(7) For the purposes of subsection (4), if the previous trader incurred expenditure on the acquisition or bringing into existence of one or more assets from which asset X is derived, QE is so much of that expenditure as–

(a) was qualifying expenditure for the purposes of this Part, and

(b) is just and reasonable to attribute to asset X;

and a similar apportionment is to be made to arrive at A and B.

411(8) This section does not affect any expenditure that is treated as qualifying expenditure on mineral exploration and access under–

section 407(5) (acquisition of mineral asset owned by previous trader), or

section 408(2) (acquisition of oil licence from non-trader).

Origin – S. 411(1): CAA 1990, s. 113(1) (part), (3) (part).
S. 411(2): CAA 1990, s. 114(1).
S. 411(3): CAA 1990, s. 114(2), (3).
S. 411(4): CAA 1990, s. 114(4), (6) (part).
S. 411(5): CAA 1990, s. 113(4) (part), s. 114(6) (part).
S. 411(6): CAA 1990, s. 113(5) (part), s. 114(6) (part).
S. 411(7): CAA 1990, s. 113(6) (part), s. 114(5).
S. 411(8): drafting.

Cross references – S. 562(5): apportionment of amounts on sale or purchase of mineral assets or licences.

Transitional – Sch. 3, para. 87: s. 411 does not apply if "X" is a UK situated mineral asset and the payments for capital expenditure are required under the buyer's contract if entered into prior to 16 July 1985. Where s. 411 does apply references to an earlier owner do not include a person who has not owned the asset at any time after 31 March 1986.

412 Transfers of mineral assets within group: limit is initial group expenditure

412(1) Subject to section 413, this section applies if–

(a) a company (**"the buyer"**) incurs capital expenditure on acquiring a mineral asset (**"asset X"**) from another company (**"the seller"**), and

(b) the seller is a group company in relation to the buyer at the time of the acquisition.

412(2) The buyer's expenditure on acquiring asset X is to be left out of account for the purposes of this Part to the extent that it exceeds–

(a) the capital expenditure incurred by the seller on acquiring asset X, or

(b) if asset X is an interest or right granted by the seller in a mineral asset acquired by the seller (**"asset Y"**), so much of the capital expenditure incurred by the seller on asset Y as on a just and reasonable apportionment is referable to asset X.

412(3) If there is a sequence of acquisitions within subsection (1), apply subsection (2) in the same sequence (starting with the first acquisition in the sequence).

412(4) Subsections (5) to (7) apply if–

(a) the buyer is carrying on a mineral extraction trade, and

(b) the asset is an interest in land.

412(5) Section 404 (exclusion of undeveloped market value of land) applies to the buyer as if the time of the buyer's acquisition of the interest in land were–

(a) the time of the seller's acquisition of the interest, or

(b) if there is a sequence of acquisitions within subsection (1), the time when the interest was acquired by the company which is the seller in the first acquisition in the sequence.

412(6) Subject to subsection (7), section 405 (qualifying expenditure where buildings or structures cease to be used) applies to the buyer as if the time of the buyer's acquisition of the interest in land were the time of the seller's acquisition of the interest.

412(7) If there is a sequence of acquisitions within subsection (1), section 405 applies as if–

(a) the time of the acquisition were the time when the interest was acquired by the company which is the seller in the first acquisition in the sequence, but

(b) the allowances and balancing charges to be taken into account in calculating (under section 405(3)) the unrelieved value of the buildings or structures included any allowances or charges made to or on any seller in the sequence.

Origin – S. 412(1): CAA 1990, s. 117(1) (part).
S. 412(2): CAA 1990, s. 117(3), (4), Annex 1, Change 40.
S. 412(3): drafting.
S. 412(4)–(6): CAA 1990, s. 117(5) (part).
S. 412(7): CAA 1990, s. 117(5) (part), (6).

Cross references – S. 413: disapplication of s. 412 for the purposes of s. 407(5), 408(2), 410, 569.
S. 562(5): apportionment of amounts on sale or purchase of mineral assets or licences.
S. 567–570: circumstances where sales treated as if made at market value and elections available.

Rewrite: Changes in Law – Explanatory Notes, Annex 1, Change 40: a minor change is effected to make the nature of the apportionment requirement in s. 384(1) consistent with other provisions in that it must be "just and reasonable"; as opposed to simply "just" as in CAA 1990, s. 133(7). See Sch. 3, para. 8 for the election to apply the original law to this matter where a chargeable period straddles 1 April 2001 (for corporation tax) or 6 April 2001 (for income tax).

413 Transfers of mineral assets within group: supplementary

413(1) For the purposes of section 412, a company is a group company in relation to another company if–

(a) it controls, or is controlled by, the other company, or

(b) both companies are under the control of another person.

413(2) Section 412 does not apply if–

(a) section 410 (UK oil licences: limit is original licence payment) applies to the acquisition, or

(b) the acquisition is a sale in respect of which an election is made under section 569 (election to treat sale as being for an alternative amount).

413(3) Section 412 applies regardless of section 568 (sales between connected persons etc., or to obtain tax advantage, treated as at market value).

413(4) Section 412 does not affect any expenditure that is treated as qualifying expenditure on mineral exploration and access under–

section 407(5) (acquisition of mineral asset owned by previous trader), or

section 408(2) (acquisition of oil licence from non-trader).

Origin – S. 413(1): CAA 1990, s. 117(1) (part).
S. 413(2), (3): CAA 1990, s. 117(2).
S. 413(4): drafting.

Cross references – S. 562(5): apportionment of amounts on sale or purchase of mineral assets or licences.
S. 567–570: circumstances where sales treated as if made at market value and elections available.

Chapter 5 – Other Kinds of Qualifying Expenditure

414 Expenditure on works likely to become valueless

414(1) Expenditure is qualifying expenditure if–

(a) it is capital expenditure on constructing works in connection with the working of a source of mineral deposits,

(b) it is incurred for the purposes of a mineral extraction trade, and

(c) the works–

(i) are likely to be of little or no value, when the source is no longer worked, to the last person working the source, or

(ii) if the source is worked under a foreign concession, are likely to become valueless, when the concession ends, to the last person working the source under the concession.

414(2) For the purposes of subsection (1), expenditure on constructing works does not include expenditure on acquiring the site of the works or any right in or over the site.

414(3) In subsection (1)(c) **"foreign concession"** means a right or privilege granted by the government of, or any municipality or other authority in, a territory outside the United Kingdom.

Origin – S. 414(1): CAA 1990, s. 98(1), s. 105(1) (part), Annex 1, Change 47.
S. 414(2): CAA 1990, s. 105(5) (part).
S. 414(3): CAA 1990, s. 161(2) ("foreign concession").

Cross references – S. 395: other types of "qualifying expenditure" for mineral extraction allowances.

Rewrite: Changes in Law – Explanatory Notes, Annex 1, Change 47: CAA 1990, s. 98(1) appeared to require a continuing trade in order for any expenditure to be "qualifying". In practice this apparent requirement was not interpreted as applying in the case of restoration expenditure incurred after a trade ceased (CAA 1990, s. 109). The change requires expenditure to be "incurred for the purposes of a mineral extraction trade" without any reference to it being carried on at the time the expenditure is incurred. See Sch. 3, para. 8 for the election to apply the original law to this matter where a chargeable period straddles 1 April 2001 (for corporation tax) or 6 April 2001 (for income tax).

HMRC Manuals – CA50230: guidance on s. 414.

415 Contribution to buildings or works for benefit of employees abroad

415(1) Subject to subsection (3), expenditure is qualifying expenditure if–

(a) it is incurred by a person carrying on a mineral extraction trade outside the United Kingdom and for the purposes of that trade,

(b) it is a contribution consisting of a capital sum to the cost of buildings or works to which this section applies, and

(c) the buildings or works are likely to be of little or no value, when the source is no longer worked, to the last person working the source.

415(2) The buildings or works to which this section applies are–

(a) buildings to be occupied by persons employed at or in connection with the working of a source outside the United Kingdom;

(b) works for the supply of water, gas or electricity wholly or mainly to buildings occupied or to be occupied by persons so employed;

(c) works to be used to provide other services or facilities wholly or mainly for the welfare of persons so employed or their dependants.

415(3) Expenditure is not qualifying expenditure if the person making the contribution–

(a) acquires an asset as a result of the expenditure, or

(b) is entitled to an allowance for the expenditure under any other provision of the Tax Acts.

Origin – S. 415(1) Interpretation Act 1978 (c. 30) s. 6(c), CAA 1990, s. 108(1) (part), (2), Annex 1, Change 47.
S. 415(2): CAA 1990, s. 108(1) (part).
S. 415(3) Interpretation Act 1978 (c. 30) s. 6(c), CAA 1990, s. 108(3).

Cross references – S. 399: certain expenditure not within s. 415 cannot be "qualifying expenditure".
S. 429: entitlement to balancing allowance where buildings etc. cease to be used for the purposes of a mineral extraction trade and s. 415 has applied.

Rewrite: Changes in Law – Explanatory Notes, Annex 1, Change 47: CAA 1990, s. 98(1) appeared to require a continuing trade in order for any expenditure to be "qualifying". In practice this apparent requirement was not interpreted as applying after a trade ceased (CAA 1990, s. 108). The change requires expenditure to be "incurred for the purposes of a mineral extraction trade" without any reference to it being carried on at the time the expenditure is incurred. See Sch. 3, para. 8 for the election to apply the original law to this matter where a chargeable period straddles 1 April 2001 (for corporation tax) or 6 April 2001 (for income tax).

HMRC Manuals – CA50290: guidance on s. 415.

416 Non-ring fence trades: expenditure on restoration within 3 years of ceasing to trade

History – Heading to s. 416 substituted by FA 2013, s. 92(4)(d), with effect in relation to expenditure incurred on restoration carried out on or after 17 July 2013.

416(1) If–

(a) a person who has ceased to carry on a relevant mineral extraction trade incurs expenditure on the restoration of a relevant site, and

(b) the expenditure is incurred within 3 years from the last day of trading and meets the further conditions in subsection (3),

the net cost of the restoration is qualifying expenditure.

416(2) The qualifying expenditure is treated as incurred on the last day of trading.

416(3) The further conditions are that the expenditure–

(a) has not been deducted in calculating for tax purposes the profits of any trade carried on by that person, and

(b) would have been–

(i) deductible in calculating the profits of the trade, or

(ii) capable of being qualifying expenditure under this Chapter,

if the expenditure had been incurred while the trade was being carried on.

416(4) If any expenditure incurred by a person is qualifying expenditure under this section–

(a) the whole of the expenditure on the restoration (not just the net cost) is not deductible in calculating the person's income for any tax purposes, and

(b) none of the amounts subtracted to produce the net cost is to be treated as the person's income for any tax purposes.

416(5) **"Restoration"** includes–

(a) landscaping,

(b) in relation to land in the United Kingdom, the carrying out of any works required as a condition of granting planning permission for development consisting of the winning and working of minerals, and

(c) in relation to land outside the United Kingdom, the carrying out of any works required by any equivalent condition imposed under the law of the territory in which the land is situated.

But it does not include decommissioning any plant or machinery (within the meaning of section 163).

416(6) A **"relevant site"** means–

(a) the site of a source to the working of which the relevant mineral extraction trade related, or

(b) land used in connection with working such a source.

416(7) **"The net cost of the restoration"** means the expenditure incurred on the restoration less any amounts–

(a) received within 3 years from the last day of trading, and

(b) attributable to the restoration of the relevant site (for instance, amounts for spoil or other assets removed from the site or for tipping rights).

416(7A) **"Relevant mineral extraction trade"** means a mineral extraction trade that is not a ring fence trade within the meaning of Part 8 of CTA 2010 (see section 277 of that Act).

416(8) All such adjustments are to be made, by way of discharge or repayment of tax or otherwise, as are necessary to give effect to this section.

History – In s. 416(1)(a), the word "relevant" inserted by FA 2013, s. 92(4)(a), with effect in relation to expenditure incurred on restoration carried out on or after 17 July 2013.

In s. 416(5), the words "But it does not include decommissioning any plant or machinery (within the meaning of section 163)." inserted by FA 2013, s. 92(4)(b), with effect in relation to expenditure incurred on restoration carried out on or after 17 July 2013.

In s. 416(6)(a), the word "relevant" inserted by FA 2013, s. 92(4)(a), with effect in relation to expenditure incurred on restoration carried out on or after 17 July 2013.

S. 416(7A) inserted by FA 2013, s. 92(4)(c), with effect in relation to expenditure incurred on restoration carried out on or after 17 July 2013.

Origin – S. 416(1)–(3): CAA 1990, s. 109(1) (part).

S. 416(4): CAA 1990, s. 109(5).

S. 416(5): CAA 1990, s. 109(3).

S. 416(6): CAA 1990, s. 109(1) (part), (2).

S. 416(7): CAA 1990, s. 109(4).

S. 416(8): CAA 1990, s. 109(6).

Cross references – S. 562: apportionment of purchase and sale for the purposes of allowances.

ICTA 1988, s. 393A(11)(b): where by virtue of s. 416 expenditure is treated as qualifying expenditure incurred by the company on the last day of trading, time limit for a claim for three-year carry-back of the loss related to the expenditure is extended to five years following accounting period of the loss.

HMRC Manuals – CA50280: guidance on s. 416.

Other material – ICAEW Technical Release TR 631 (not reproduced): site restoration period of three years applicable only where single or last mineral asset being worked, not where a continuing trade.

416ZA Ring fence trades: expenditure on site restoration

416ZA(1) If–

(a) a person who is carrying on, or has ceased to carry on, a ring fence trade incurs expenditure on the restoration of a relevant site,

(b) that part of the restoration work to which the expenditure relates has been carried out, and

(c) the expenditure has not been deducted in calculating for tax purposes the profits of any trade carried on by the person, the net cost of the restoration is qualifying expenditure for the relevant period in which that part of the work to which the expenditure relates was carried out.

416ZA(2) **"Relevant period"** means–

(a) in the case of restoration work carried out while the person is carrying on the trade, a chargeable period, and

(b) in the case of restoration work carried out after the person has ceased to carry on the trade, a notional accounting period.

For the meaning of **"notional accounting period"**, see section 416ZB.

416ZA(3) The qualifying expenditure for a notional accounting period is treated as incurred on the last day of trading.

416ZA(4) If the amount of expenditure incurred on any part of the restoration work carried out in a relevant period is disproportionate to that part of the restoration work, only so much of the net cost of the restoration as is proportionate to that part of the restoration work (the "allowable expenditure for the period") is to be treated as qualifying expenditure for that period.

416ZA(5) But subsection (4) does not prevent that part of the expenditure that is not allowable expenditure for the period from being treated as qualifying expenditure for a subsequent relevant period.

416ZA(6) If any expenditure incurred by a person is qualifying expenditure under this section–

(a) the whole of the expenditure on the restoration (not just the net cost) is not deductible in calculating the person's income for any tax purposes, and

(b) none of the amounts subtracted to produce the net cost is to be treated as the person's income for any tax purposes.

416ZA(7) **"Restoration"** includes–

(a) landscaping,

(b) in relation to land in the United Kingdom, the carrying out of any works required as a condition of granting planning permission for development relating to the winning of oil from an oil field,

(c) in relation to land in the UK marine area, the carrying out of any works required in order to comply with–

  (i) an approved abandonment programme,

  (ii) a condition to which the approval of an abandonment programme is subject, or

  (iii) a requirement imposed by the Secretary of State, or an agreement made with the Secretary of State, in relation to a relevant site, and

(d) in relation to land in a foreign sector of the continental shelf, the carrying out of any works required in order to comply with anything corresponding to a matter within paragraph (c)(i), (ii) or (iii) under the law of a territory outside the United Kingdom.

But it does not include decommissioning any plant or machinery (within the meaning of section 163).

416ZA(8) A **"relevant site"** means–

(a) the site of a source to the working of which the ring fence trade relates (or related), or

(b) land used in connection with working such a source.

416ZA(9) **"The net cost of the restoration"** means the expenditure incurred on the restoration less any amounts that–

(a) are received, or are to be received, by the person, and

(b) are attributable to the restoration of the relevant site.

416ZA(10) All such adjustments are to be made, by way of discharge or repayment of tax or otherwise, as are necessary to give effect to this section.

416ZA(11) In this section–

"abandonment programme", **"approval"** and **"approved"** (in relation to an abandonment programme) have the same meaning as in Part 4 of the Petroleum Act 1998,

"foreign sector of the continental shelf" means an area within which rights are exercisable with respect to the sea bed and subsoil and their natural resources by a territory outside the United Kingdom,

"oil" and **"oil field"** have the same meaning as in Part 1 of OTA 1975,

"ring fence trade" has the same meaning as in Part 8 of CTA 2010 (see section 277 of that Act), and

"UK marine area" has the meaning given by section 42 of the Marine and Coastal Access Act 2009.

History – S. 416ZA inserted by FA 2013, s. 92(5), with effect in relation to expenditure incurred on restoration carried out on or after 17 July 2013.

416ZB "Notional accounting period"

416ZB(1) For the purposes of section 416ZA **"notional accounting period"**, in relation to a person ("the former trader") who has ceased to carry on a ring fence trade, means each of the following periods–

(a) the period that–

(i) begins with the day following the last day on which the former trader carried on the ring fence trade, and

(ii) ends with the day on which the first termination event subsequently occurs, and

(b) each period that–

(i) begins with the day following the last day of a period determined under paragraph (a) or this paragraph, and

(ii) ends with the day on which the first termination event subsequently occurs.

416ZB(2) But there are to be no notional accounting periods after the end of the post-cessation period (see subsection (4)).

416ZB(3) **"Termination event"**, in relation to a notional accounting period, means each of the following–

(a) the end of the period of 12 months beginning with the first day of the notional accounting period,

(b) the occurrence of an accounting date of the former trader or, if there is a period for which the former trader does not make up accounts, the end of that period (but see subsections (6) and (7)), and

(c) the end of the post-cessation period.

416ZB(4) **"The post-cessation period"** means the period that–

(a) begins with the day following the last day on which the former trader carried on the ring fence trade, and

(b) ends with the day on which the appropriate authority is satisfied that the restoration of the relevant site has been completed.

416ZB(5) In subsection (4) **"the appropriate authority"** means–

(a) in the case of restoration falling within section 416ZA(7)(c), the Secretary of State, and

(b) in any other case, such person or body as the Commissioners for Her Majesty's Revenue and Customs may specify.

416ZB(6) If the former trader–

(a) carries on more than one trade,

(b) makes up accounts of any of them to different dates, and

(c) does not make up general accounts for the whole of the former trader's activities,

subsection (3)(b) applies with reference to the accounting date of such one of the trades as the former trader may determine.

416ZB(7) If the Commissioners for Her Majesty's Revenue and Customs are of the opinion, on reasonable grounds, that a date determined by the former trader for the purposes of subsection (6) is inappropriate, the Commissioners may by notice direct that the accounting date of such other of the trades referred to in that subsection as appears to the Commissioners to be appropriate is to be used instead.

416ZB(8) Expressions used in this section and in section 416ZA have the same meaning in this section as they do in that section.

History – S. 416ZB inserted by FA 2013, s. 92(5), with effect in relation to expenditure incurred on restoration carried out on or after 17 July 2013.

416ZC Site restoration services supplied by connected person

416ZC(1) Where–

(a) a person ("R") who is carrying on, or has ceased to carry on, a ring fence trade enters into an arrangement,

(b) under the arrangement, a person ("S") who is connected with R provides a service to R in connection with work on the restoration of a relevant site, and

(c) (in the absence of this section) all or part of the consideration for the service would be qualifying expenditure of R under section 416ZA,

the amount of the expenditure which is qualifying expenditure is restricted under section 416ZD(1).

416ZC(2) Subsection (1)(b) may be satisfied whether the service is provided to R directly or indirectly; and in particular it does not matter–

(a) whether R and S are parties to the same contract, or

(b) whether payments are made by R directly to S.

416ZC(3) Subsections (4) and (5) apply for the purposes of this section and sections 416ZD and 416ZE.

416ZC(4) **"Relevant site"** has the meaning given by section 416ZA(8).

416ZC(5) References to providing a service include–

(a) letting a ship on charter or any other asset on hire, and

(b) providing goods which are to be used up in the course of providing a service.

History – S. 416ZC inserted by FA 2013, s. 93 and Sch. 32, para. 9, with effect in relation to expenditure incurred on restoration carried out on or after 17 July 2013.

416ZD Restriction on allowance available

416ZD(1) In determining how much of the consideration for the service is qualifying expenditure, there is to be left out of account the amount (if any) by which that consideration exceeds D.

416ZD(2) D is the cost to S of providing the service or, if the qualifying expenditure relates to only part of the service, that part.

416ZD(3) Subsection (2) is subject to–

(a) subsection (4), and

(b) section 416ZE,

which provide for D to be calculated differently in certain circumstances.

416ZD(4) The following provisions apply in relation to an amount restricted under subsection (1) as they apply in relation to an amount restricted under section 165B(1)–

(a) section 165C;

(b) section 165E, subject to the modifications in subsection (5).

416ZD(5) The modifications are that–

(a) the references to Part 2 are to be read as references to this Part,

(b) in subsection (1)(c), the reference to decommissioning expenditure is to be read as a reference to qualifying expenditure under section 416ZA, and

(c) in subsection (5), the reference to R's available qualifying expenditure is to be read as a reference to R's qualifying expenditure on the restoration of the site.

416ZD(6) But if, under the arrangement, a particular service or part of a service is provided by more than one person who is connected with R (so that without this subsection there would be more than one amount for D in relation to that service or part), D is the lowest of those amounts.

History – S. 416ZD inserted by FA 2013, s. 93 and Sch. 32, para. 9, with effect in relation to expenditure incurred on restoration carried out on or after 17 July 2013.

416ZE Allowance where site restoration undertaken for other participators in oil field

416ZE(1) This section applies where–

(a) S carries out the restoration of a relevant site,

(b) there are, in addition to R, one or more other participators in the relevant field, and

(c) the expenditure incurred in carrying out the restoration is apportioned between the participators (including R) in accordance with their shares in the oil won from the relevant field or their shares in the equity of that field.

416ZE(2) D is the part of the expenditure referred to in subsection (1)(c) which is incurred by R.

416ZE(3) Where–

(a) a relevant site has been used in connection with the winning of oil from more than one relevant field, and

(b) the expenditure incurred in respect of the restoration is apportioned between those fields in accordance with the contribution from each field to the total of the oil won using that site,

subsections (1) and (2) apply to each such field as if subsection (1)(c) referred to the expenditure apportioned to that field.

416ZE(4) But subsections (2) and (3) do not apply (and section 416ZD(2) applies instead) if–

(a) the amount of consideration, or the method of determining the amount of consideration, to be received by S under the arrangement or arrangements, or

(b) the apportionment of the liability for that consideration (whether between the participators as mentioned in subsection (1)(c) or between the fields as mentioned in subsection (3)(b)),

has been agreed as, or as part of, an avoidance scheme.

416ZE(5) A scheme is an **"avoidance scheme"** if the main purpose, or one of the main purposes, of a party in entering into the scheme is to enable a person to obtain a tax advantage under this Part that would not otherwise be obtained.

416ZE(6) The reference in subsection (5) to obtaining a tax advantage that would not otherwise be obtained includes obtaining an allowance that is in any way more favourable to a person than the one that would otherwise be obtained.

416ZE(7) In relation to the restoration of a relevant site, **"relevant field"** means any of the following–

(a) the oil field in which the site is located;

(b) if the site is the site of a source to the working of which a ring fence trade relates (or related), an oil field from which oil is or has been won by means of working the source;

(c) if the site is land used in connection with working such a source, an oil field from which oil is or has been won by means of working the source.

416ZE(8) In this section–

"licensee", **"oil"** and **"oil field"** have the same meaning as in Part 1 of OTA 1975, and

"other participator" means a person, not connected with R, who is a licensee in respect of any licensed area wholly or partly included in the oil field in question.

History – S. 416ZE inserted by FA 2013, s. 93 and Sch. 32, para. 9, with effect in relation to expenditure incurred on restoration carried out on or after 17 July 2013.

Chapter 5A – First-Year Qualifying Expenditure

History – Ch. 5A inserted by FA 2002, s. 63 and Sch. 21, para. 9, with effect in relation to expenditure incurred on or after 17 April 2002.

GENERAL

416A First-year allowances available for certain types of qualifying expenditure

416A A first-year allowance is not available unless the qualifying expenditure is first-year qualifying expenditure under section 416B (expenditure incurred wholly for purposes of a ring fence trade).

History – S. 416A inserted by FA 2002, s. 63 and Sch. 21, para. 9, with effect in relation to expenditure incurred on or after 17 April 2002.

TYPES OF EXPENDITURE WHICH MAY QUALIFY FOR FIRST-YEAR ALLOWANCES

416B Expenditure incurred by company for purposes of a ring fence trade

416B(1) Expenditure is first-year qualifying expenditure if–

(a) it is incurred on or after 17th April 2002,

(b) it is incurred by a company,

(c) it is incurred wholly for the purposes of a ring fence trade, and

(d) it is not excluded by–

(i) subsection (2) (acquisition of mineral asset), or

(ii) subsection (3) (acquisition of asset representing expenditure of connected company).

416B(2) Expenditure is not first-year qualifying expenditure under this section if it is expenditure on acquiring a mineral asset (within the meaning of section 403).

416B(3) Expenditure is not first-year qualifying expenditure under this section if it is expenditure incurred by a company on the acquisition of an asset representing expenditure incurred by a company connected with that company.

416B(4) To the extent that references in this section to an asset representing expenditure incurred by a company include a reference to an asset representing expenditure on mineral exploration and access, they also include a reference to any results obtained from any search, exploration or inquiry on which any such expenditure was incurred.

416B(5) In this section **"ring fence trade"** means a ring fence trade in respect of which tax is chargeable under section 330(1) of CTA 2010 (supplementary charge in respect of ring fence trades).

History – In s. 416B(2), the words "(within the meaning of section 403)" inserted by FA 2013, s. 92(6), with effect in relation to expenditure incurred on restoration carried out on or after 17 July 2013.
In s. 416B(5), the words "section 330(1) of CTA 2010" substituted for "section 501A of the Taxes Act 1988" by CTA 2010, s. 1177 and Sch. 1, para. 355, with effect for corporation tax purposes for accounting periods ending on or after 1 April 2010.
S. 416B inserted by FA 2002, s. 63 and Sch. 21, para. 9, with effect in relation to expenditure incurred on or after 17 April 2002.

SUPPLEMENTARY

416C Time when expenditure is incurred

416C(1) In determining whether expenditure is first-year qualifying expenditure under this Chapter, any effect of the provisions specified in subsection (2) on the time at which the expenditure is to be treated as incurred is to be disregarded.

416C(2) The provisions are–

(a) section 400(4) (which treats certain pre-trading expenditure as incurred on the first day of trading), and

(b) section 434 (which treats certain other expenditure incurred for the purposes of a trade about to be carried on as incurred on that day).

History – S. 416C inserted by FA 2002, s. 63 and Sch. 21, para. 9, with effect in relation to expenditure incurred on or after 17 April 2002.

Chapter 6 – Allowances and Charges

FIRST-YEAR ALLOWANCES

416D First-year allowances

416D(1) A person is entitled to a first-year allowance in respect of first-year qualifying expenditure if the expenditure is incurred in a chargeable period to which this Act applies.

416D(2) Any first-year allowance is made for the chargeable period in which the first-year qualifying expenditure is incurred.

416D(3) The amount of the allowance is a percentage of the first-year qualifying expenditure in respect of which the allowance is made, as shown in the Table–

TABLE : AMOUNT OF FIRST-YEAR ALLOWANCES

Type of first-year qualifying expenditure	*Amount*
Expenditure qualifying under section 416B (expenditure incurred wholly for the purposes of a ring fence trade)	100%"

416D(4) A person who is entitled to a first-year allowance may claim the allowance in respect of the whole or a part of the first-year qualifying expenditure.

416D(5) This section is subject to section 416E (artificially inflated claims for first-year allowances).

History – S. 416D inserted by FA 2002, s. 63 and Sch. 21, para. 10, with effect in relation to expenditure incurred on or after 17 April 2002.

416E Artificially inflated claims for first-year allowances

416E(1) To the extent that a transaction is attributable to arrangements entered into wholly or mainly for a disqualifying purpose, it shall be disregarded in determining for a chargeable period the amount of any first-year allowance to which a person is entitled.

416E(2) For the purposes of this section, arrangements are entered into wholly or mainly for a "disqualifying purpose" if their main object, or one of their main objects, is to enable a person to obtain–

(a) a first-year allowance to which he would not otherwise be entitled, or

(b) a first-year allowance of a greater amount than that to which he would otherwise be entitled.

416E(3) In this section **"arrangements"** includes any scheme, agreement or understanding, whether or not legally enforceable.

History – S. 416E inserted by FA 2002, s. 63 and Sch. 21, para. 11, with effect in relation to expenditure incurred on or after 17 April 2002.

WRITING-DOWN AND BALANCING ALLOWANCES AND BALANCING CHARGES

417 Determination of entitlement or liability

417(1) Whether a person who has incurred qualifying expenditure is entitled to a writing-down allowance or a balancing allowance, or liable to a balancing charge, for a chargeable period depends on–

(a) how much of the expenditure is unrelieved qualifying expenditure for that period (**"UQE"**), and

(b) the total of any disposal receipts to be brought into account for that period (**"TDR"**) by reference to the expenditure.

417(2) If UQE exceeds TDR, the person is entitled to a writing-down allowance or a balancing allowance for the period.

417(3) If TDR exceeds UQE, the person is liable to a balancing charge for the period.

417(4) The entitlement under subsection (2) is to a writing-down allowance except in cases for which sections 426 to 431 provide for the entitlement to be to a balancing allowance.

Origin – S. 417(1): CAA 1990, s. 98(2), (3), s. 100(1).
S. 417(2): CAA 1990, s. 98(2), (3).
S. 417(3): CAA 1990, s. 100(1).
S. 417(4): drafting.

Cross references – S. 6: meaning of "chargeable period".
S. 395: meaning of "qualifying expenditure" generally.
S. 420: meaning of "disposal receipt".
TCGA 1992, s. 37(1), (2): exclusion from disposal consideration in computation of gain of amounts charged to tax as income etc. does not include amounts taken into account in the making of a balancing charge.
TCGA 1992, s. 41: exclusion from base cost etc. in computation of gain of amounts allowable as regards tax on income etc. does not include expenditure for which "capital allowance" made though a loss may be restricted.

HMRC Manuals – CA50420: guidance on disposal receipts.

418 Amount of allowances and charges

418(1) The amount of the writing-down allowance to which a person is entitled for any chargeable period in respect of qualifying expenditure is–

(a) in the case of qualifying expenditure on the acquisition of a mineral asset, 10% of the amount by which UQE exceeds TDR;

(b) in the case of other qualifying expenditure, 25% of the amount by which UQE exceeds TDR.

418(2) If the chargeable period is more or less than a year, the amount of the writing-down allowance is proportionately increased or reduced.

418(3) If the mineral extraction trade has been carried on for part only of the chargeable period, the amount of the writing-down allowance is proportionately reduced.

418(4) The amount of the balancing charge to which a person is liable for a chargeable period in respect of qualifying expenditure is–

(a) the amount by which TDR exceeds UQE, or

(b) if less, the allowances for earlier chargeable periods in respect of the expenditure less the total of any balancing charges for those periods in respect of the expenditure.

Where a person is liable to a balancing charge in respect of first-year qualifying expenditure for the chargeable period in which he incurred the expenditure, any first-year allowance made in respect of the expenditure shall be treated for the purposes of paragraph (b) as if it were an allowance for an earlier chargeable period.

418(5) The amount of the balancing allowance to which a person is entitled for a chargeable period in respect of qualifying expenditure is the amount by which UQE exceeds TDR.

418(6) A person claiming a writing-down allowance or a balancing allowance may require the allowance to be reduced to a specified amount.

History – In s. 418(4), after (b), words inserted as a second sentence by FA 2002, s. 63 and Sch. 21, para. 12, with effect in relation to expenditure incurred on or after 17 April 2002.

Origin – S. 418(1): CAA 1990, s. 98(5).
S. 418(2), (3): CAA 1990, s. 98(6).
S. 418(4): CAA 1990, s. 100(2), (3).
S. 418(5): CAA 1990, s. 98(4).
S. 418(6) Annex 1, Change 38.

Cross references – S. 6: meaning of "chargeable period".
S. 395: meaning of "qualifying expenditure" generally.
S. 570A: avoidance affecting proceeds of balancing event.
TCGA 1992, s. 37(1), (2): exclusion from disposal consideration in computation of gain of amounts charged to tax as income etc. does not include amounts taken into account in the making of a balancing charge.

TCGA 1992, s. 41: exclusion from base cost etc. in computation of gain of amounts allowable as regards tax on income etc. does not include expenditure for which "capital allowance" made though a loss may be restricted.

Transitional – Sch. 3, para. 88: transitional provisions relating to expenditure incurred before 1 April 1986 (i.e. under the old scheme of Mines and Oil Wells Allowance – MOWA). The provision ensures that excessive allowances for expenditure incurred under the old rules; and relieved under MOWA; can be recovered under Pt. 5.

Rewrite: Changes in Law – Explanatory Notes, Annex 1, Change 38: a person claiming a writing down allowance may require the amount of the allowance to be reduced to a specified amount under s. 418(6); previously there was no specific provision enabling a reduced allowance to be given, although in practice this was usually permitted. See Sch. 3, para. 8 for the election to apply the original law to this matter where a chargeable period straddles 1 April 2001 (for corporation tax) or 6 April 2001 (for income tax).

UNRELIEVED QUALIFYING EXPENDITURE

419 Unrelieved qualifying expenditure

419(1) A person's unrelieved qualifying expenditure for the chargeable period in which the qualifying expenditure is incurred is

(a) the whole of it, unless the expenditure is first-year qualifying expenditure, or

(b) if the expenditure is first-year qualifying expenditure, none of it,

but paragraph (b) is subject to subsections (3) to (5).

419(2) A person's unrelieved qualifying expenditure for a chargeable period after that in which the qualifying expenditure is incurred is the amount, if any, by which it exceeds the aggregate of–

(a) the allowances made in respect of the expenditure for earlier chargeable periods, and

(b) the total of any disposal receipts for earlier chargeable periods.

419(3) If, in the case of expenditure which is first-year qualifying expenditure, a disposal receipt falls to be brought into account for the chargeable period in which the expenditure is incurred (**"the initial period"**), subsection (4) below applies.

419(4) Where this subsection applies, the unrelieved balance of the expenditure shall be taken to be unrelieved qualifying expenditure for the initial period, but only for the purpose specified in subsection (5).

419(5) The purpose is that of determining in accordance with sections 417 and 418–

(a) any question whether the person who incurred the expenditure–

(i) is entitled to a balancing allowance for the initial period, or

(ii) is liable to a balancing charge for that period, and

(b) if so, the amount of that balancing allowance or balancing charge.

419(6) In this section **"the unrelieved balance of the expenditure"** means so much of the first-year qualifying expenditure in question as remains after deducting the amount of any first-year allowance given in respect of the whole or any part of that expenditure.

History – S. 419(1)(a), (b) and endpiece substituted for the words "the whole of it" by FA 2002, s .63 and Sch. 21, para. 13, with effect in relation to expenditure incurred on or after 17 April 2002.

S. 419(3)–(6) inserted by FA 2002, s. 63 and Sch. 21, para. 12, with effect in relation to expenditure incurred on or after 17 April 2002.

Origin – S. 419(1), (2): CAA 1990, s. 98(2), (3).

S. 419(3): drafting.

Cross references – S. 6: meaning of "chargeable period".

S. 395: meaning of "qualifying expenditure" generally.

S. 570A: avoidance affecting proceeds of balancing event. Unrelieved qualifying expenditure calculated as if balancing allowance made.

DISPOSAL VALUES

420 Meaning of "disposal receipt"

420 In sections 417 to 419 **"disposal receipt"** means a disposal value that a person is required to bring into account in accordance with–

(a) sections 421 to 425, or

(b) section 614BS of ITA 2007 or section 918 of CTA 2010 (cases where expenditure taken into account under Part 2, 5 or 8 of this Act) or any other enactment.

History – In s. 420(b), the words "section 614BS of ITA 2007" substituted for the words "paragraph 11 of Schedule 12 to FA 1997 (finance lease or loan: receipt of major lump sum)" by TIOPA 2010, s. 374 and Sch. 8, para. 235, with effect for income tax and capital gains tax purposes for the tax year 2010–11 and subsequent tax years.

In s. 420(b), the words "section 918 of CTA 2010 (cases where expenditure taken into account under Part 2, 5 or 8 of this Act) or" inserted by CTA 2010, s. 1177 and Sch. 1, para. 356, with effect for corporation tax purposes for accounting periods ending on or after 1 April 2010.

Origin – S. 420: drafting.

421 Disposal of, or ceasing to use, asset

421(1) This section applies if–

(a) a person has incurred qualifying expenditure on providing assets (including the construction of works), and

(b) any of those assets–

(i) is disposed of, or

(ii) permanently ceases to be used by him for the purposes of a mineral extraction trade (whether because of the discontinuance of the trade or for any other reason).

421(2) The person is required to bring the disposal value of the asset into account for the chargeable period in which the disposal or cessation occurs.

Origin – S. 421(1), (2): CAA 1990, s. 99(1) (part).

Cross references – S. 6: meaning of "chargeable period".
S. 395: meaning of "qualifying expenditure" generally.
S. 404: exclusions from "qualifying expenditure".
S. 410–413: limits to "qualifying expenditure".
Coal Industry Act 1994, Sch. 4, para. 20: taxation provisions relating to disposal receipts.

422 Use of asset otherwise than for permitted development etc.

422(1) This section applies if–

(a) a person has acquired a mineral asset,

(b) at any time after the acquisition, the asset begins to be used (by him or another person) in a way which constitutes development, and

(c) the development is not–

(i) existing permitted development, or

(ii) development for the purposes of a mineral extraction trade carried on by the person.

422(2) The person is required to bring the disposal value of the mineral asset into account for the chargeable period in which the use begins.

422(3) Development is existing permitted development if at the time of the acquisition–

(a) it has been, or had begun to be, lawfully carried out, or

(b) it could be lawfully carried out under planning permission granted by a general development order.

422(4) In applying subsection (3) in relation to land outside the United Kingdom–

(a) whether, at the time of the acquisition, development has been, or had begun to be, lawfully carried out is to be determined according to the law of the territory in which the land is situated, and

(b) whether, at that time, development could be lawfully carried out under planning permission granted by a general development order is to be determined as if the land were in England.

Origin – S. 422(1), (2): CAA 1990, s. 99(1) (part), (2) (part).
S. 422(3): CAA 1990, s. 99(2) (part).
S. 422(4): CAA 1990, s. 99(2) (part), s. 110(3) (part), Annex 1, Change 48.

Cross references – S. 6: meaning of "chargeable period".
S. 395: meaning of "qualifying expenditure" generally.
S. 404: exclusions from "qualifying expenditure".
S. 410–413: limits to "qualifying expenditure".
S. 436: meaning of "development"; "development order"; "general development order"; and "planning permission".
Coal Industry Act 1994, Sch. 4, para. 20: taxation provisions relating to disposal receipts.

Rewrite: Changes in Law – Explanatory Notes, Annex 1, Change 48: following the setting up of the Welsh Assembly it is possible for differing general development orders to be produced for England and Wales. To avoid difficulties the deemed requirement in s. 422(4)(b); which requires a hypothetical general development order to be assumed for overseas land; is now formulated by reference only to general development orders in England (and not England *and* Wales as previously). See Sch. 3, para. 8 for the election to apply the original law to this matter where a chargeable period straddles 1 April 2001 (for corporation tax) or 6 April 2001 (for income tax).

HMRC Manuals – CA50430: guidance on "existing permitted development".

423 Sections 421 and 422: amount of disposal value to be brought into account

423(1) The disposal value to be brought into account under section 421 or 422 depends on the event requiring it to be brought into account, as shown in the Table–

TABLE
DISPOSAL VALUE FOR SECTIONS 421 AND 422

	1. Event	*2. Disposal value*
1.	Sale of the asset, except in a case where item 2 applies.	The net proceeds of the sale, together with– (a) any insurance money received in respect of the asset as a result of an event affecting the price obtainable on the sale, and (b) any other compensation of any description so received, so far as it consists of capital sums.
2.	Sale of the asset where– (a) the sale is at less than market value, (b) there is no charge to tax under ITEPA 2003, and (c) the condition in subsection (3) is met by the buyer.	The market value of the asset at the time of the sale.
3.	Demolition or destruction of the asset.	The net amount received for the remains of the asset, together with– (a) any insurance money received in respect of the demolition or destruction, and (b) any other compensation of any description so received, so far as it consists of capital sums.
4.	Permanent loss of the asset otherwise than as a result of its demolition or destruction.	Any insurance money received in respect of the loss and, so far as it consists of capital sums, any other compensation of any description so received.
5.	Permanent discontinuance of the trade followed by the occurrence of an event within any of items 1 to 4.	The disposal value for the item in question.
6.	Any event not falling within any of items 1 to 5.	The market value of the asset at the time of the event.

423(2) The amounts referred to in column 2 of the Table are those received by the person required to bring the disposal value into account.

423(3) The condition referred to in item 2 of the Table is met by the buyer if–

(a) the buyer's expenditure on the acquisition of the asset cannot be qualifying expenditure under Part 2 or 6 (plant and machinery and research and development allowances), or

(b) the buyer is a dual resident investing company which is connected with the seller.

History – In entry 2(b) of the Table in s. 423(1), the words "ITEPA 2003" substituted for the words "Schedule E" by ITEPA 2003, Sch. 6, para. 254 which has effect, for income tax purposes, for the tax year 2003–04 and subsequent tax years and, for corporation tax purposes, for accounting periods ending after 5 April 2003.

Origin – S. 423(1): CAA 1990, s. 26(1) (part), s. 99(3) (part).
Table, item 1: CAA 1990, s. 26(1)(a) (part).
Table, item 2: CAA 1990, s. 26(1)(b) (part), Annex 2, Note 17.
Table, item 3: CAA 1990, s. 26(1)(c) (part).
Table, item 4: CAA 1990, s. 26(1)(d) (part).
Table, item 5: CAA 1990, s. 26(1)(e) (part).
Table, item 6: CAA 1990, s. 26(1)(f) (part).
S. 423(2): CAA 1990, s. 26(1) (part), s. 99(3) (part).
S. 423(3): CAA 1990, s. 26(1)(b) (part), s. 99(3) (part).

Cross references – S. 563, 564: rules for which body of Appeal Commissioners should determine the apportionment of amounts in the case of a dispute.
S. 567, 568 and 570: sales treated to made at market value.
FA 1994, Sch. 24, para. 21(3): provisions relating to the Railways Act 1993.
Coal Industry Act 1994, Sch. 4, para. 20: taxation provisions relating to disposal receipts.
Transport Act 2000, Sch. 26, para. 14(2): transfers of assets.
RA 2005, Sch. 10. para. 14: disapplication of s. 423 in the case of certain transfers to a national authority.

Transitional – Sch. 3, para. 91: where during the transitional period an oil licence is disposed of and part of its value is attributable to exploration expenditure incurred by the transferor an election may be made specifying the amount to be so attributable.

Rewrite: Technical Points – Explanatory Notes, Annex 2, Note 17: s. 423(1), Table, Item 2 is based on s. 26(1)(b) which does not make it clear that the market value to be used is that at the time of the actual sale. To clarify this point and to make Item 2 consistent with Item 6 (based on s. 26(1)(f)) an explicit reference to the date is included at Item 2.

Notes – ICAEW Technical Release TR 233 (not reproduced): the "net amount received" in s. 423(1), Table, Item 3 (old s. 26(1)(c)) includes the cost of demolition.
CCAB June 1971 (not reproduced): Where assets are not likely to be sold for a long time after the end of trading, inspectors finalise on the basis of market value at the time of permanent cessation; s. 423, Table, Item 5 (old s. 26(1)(e)).

424 Disposal value restricted in case of interest in land

424(1) If the asset in relation to which a disposal value is required to be brought into account under section 421 or 422 is an interest in land, the disposal value is restricted by excluding the undeveloped market value of the interest.

424(2) **"The undeveloped market value of the interest"** means the amount that, at the time of the disposal, the interest might reasonably be expected to fetch on a sale in the open market on the assumptions in subsection (3).

424(3) The assumptions are that–

(a) there is no source of mineral deposits on or in the land, and

(b) it will only ever be lawful to carry out existing permitted development.

424(4) Development is existing permitted development if at the time of the disposal–

(a) it has been, or had begun to be, lawfully carried out, or

(b) it could be lawfully carried out under planning permission granted by a general development order.

424(5) In applying subsection (4) in relation to land outside the United Kingdom–

(a) whether, at the time of the disposal, development has been, or had begun to be, lawfully carried out is to be determined according to the law of the territory in which the land is situated, and

(b) whether, at that time, development could be lawfully carried out under planning permission granted by a general development order is to be determined as if the land were in England.

Origin – S. 424(1): CAA 1990, s. 99(3) (part), s. 112(1) (part).
S. 424(2): CAA 1990, s. 110(2) (part), s. 112(1) (part), (2) (part).
S. 424(3), (4): CAA 1990, s. 110(2) (part), s. 112(2) (part).
S. 424(5): CAA 1990, s. 110(3) (part), s. 112(2) (part), Annex 1, Change 48.

Cross references – S. 436: meaning of "development"; "development order"; "general development order"; and "planning permission".
S. 562: apportionment of sale or purchase moneys.
S. 564: procedures for determining the market value of assets and the apportionment of that value between two or more persons.
Coal Industry Act 1994, Sch. 4, para. 20: taxation provisions relating to disposal receipts.

Transitional – Sch. 3, para. 88(3): s. 424 disapplied where FA 1986, Sch. 14, para. 6(4) applied to the old expenditure. A transitional provision relating to expenditure incurred before 1 April 1986 (i.e. under the old scheme of Mines and Oil Wells Allowance – MOWA). The provisions ensure that excessive allowances for expenditure incurred under the old rules; and relieved under MOWA; can be recovered under Pt. 5.

Rewrite: Changes in Law – Explanatory Notes, Annex 1, Change 48: following the setting up of the Welsh Assembly it is possible for differing general development orders to be produced for England and Wales. To avoid difficulties the deemed requirement in s. 422(4)(b); which requires a hypothetical general development order to be assumed for overseas land; is now formulated by reference only to general development orders in England (and not England *and* Wales as previously). See Sch. 3, para. 8 for the election to apply the original law to this matter where a chargeable period straddles 1 April 2001 (for corporation tax) or 6 April 2001 (for income tax).

425 Receipt of capital sum

425(1) This section applies if a person–

(a) has incurred qualifying expenditure, and

(b) receives a capital sum which, in whole or in part, it is reasonable to attribute to that expenditure.

425(2) The person is required to bring into account as a disposal value for the chargeable period in which the capital sum is received so much of the capital sum as is reasonably attributable to the qualifying expenditure.

425(3) This section does not apply if the capital sum falls to be brought into account under section 421 or 422.

Origin – S. 425(1)–(3): CAA 1990, s. 99(4).

Cross references – S. 6: meaning of "chargeable period".
S. 395: meaning of "qualifying expenditure" generally.
S. 562: apportionment of sale or purchase moneys.
S. 564: procedures for determining the market value of assets and the apportionment of that value between two or more persons.

CASES IN WHICH A PERSON IS ENTITLED TO A BALANCING ALLOWANCE

426 Pre-trading expenditure

426 A person's entitlement to an allowance for a chargeable period is to a balancing allowance if–

(a) the expenditure is qualifying expenditure under–

(i) section 401(4) (pre-trading exploration expenditure where exploration etc. has ceased before first day of trading), or

(ii) section 402 (pre-trading expenditure on plant or machinery), and

(b) the first day of trading occurs in that chargeable period.

Origin – CAA 1990, s. 101(5).

Cross references – S. 6: meaning of "chargeable period".
S. 395: meaning of "qualifying expenditure" generally.
S. 562: apportionment of sale or purchase moneys.

HMRC Manuals – CA50240ff.: guidance on s. 426.

427 Giving up exploration, search or inquiry

427 A person's entitlement to an allowance for a chargeable period is to a balancing allowance if–

(a) the qualifying expenditure is expenditure on mineral exploration and access,

(b) he gives up the exploration, search or inquiry to which the expenditure related in that chargeable period, and

(c) he does not then or later carry on a mineral extraction trade which consists of or includes the working of mineral deposits to which the expenditure related.

Origin – CAA 1990, s. 101(6).

Cross references – S. 6: meaning of "chargeable period".
S. 395: meaning of "qualifying expenditure" generally.
S. 562: apportionment of sale or purchase moneys.

428 Ceasing to work mineral deposits

428(1) A person's entitlement to an allowance for a chargeable period is to a balancing allowance if–

(a) in that chargeable period he permanently ceases to work particular mineral deposits, and

(b) the qualifying expenditure is expenditure incurred–

(i) on mineral exploration and access relating solely to those deposits, or

(ii) on acquiring a mineral asset consisting of those deposits or part of them.

428(2) If the person carrying on the mineral extraction trade is entitled to two or more mineral assets which at any time were–

(a) comprised in a single mineral asset, or

(b) otherwise derived from a single mineral asset,

subsection (1) does not apply until such time as the person permanently ceases to work the deposits comprised in all the mineral assets concerned taken together.

428(3) For the purposes of subsection (2), if a mineral asset relates to, but does not actually consist of, mineral deposits, the deposits to which the asset relates are to be treated as comprised in the asset.

Origin – S. 428(1): CAA 1990, s. 101(2).
S. 428(2), (3): CAA 1990, s. 101(3).

Cross references – S. 6: meaning of "chargeable period".
S. 395: meaning of "qualifying expenditure" generally.
S. 562: apportionment of sale or purchase moneys.

429 Buildings etc. for benefit of employees abroad ceasing to be used

429 A person's entitlement to an allowance for a chargeable period is to a balancing allowance if–

(a) the expenditure is qualifying expenditure under section 415 (contributions to buildings or works for benefit of employees abroad), and

(b) in that chargeable period the buildings or works permanently cease to be used for the purposes of or in connection with the mineral extraction trade.

Origin – CAA 1990, s. 101(7).

Cross references – S. 6: meaning of "chargeable period".
S. 395: meaning of "qualifying expenditure" generally.
S. 562: apportionment of sale or purchase moneys.

430 Disposal of asset, etc.

430(1) A person's entitlement to an allowance for a chargeable period is to a balancing allowance if–

(a) the qualifying expenditure was incurred on the provision of any assets, and

(b) in that chargeable period any of those assets–

(i) is disposed of, or

(ii) otherwise permanently ceases to be used by him for the purposes of the mineral extraction trade.

430(2) A person's entitlement to an allowance for a chargeable period is to a balancing allowance if any of the following events occurs in that chargeable period in relation to assets representing the qualifying expenditure–

(a) the person loses possession of the assets in circumstances where it is reasonable to assume that the loss is permanent;

(b) the assets cease to exist as such (as a result of destruction, dismantling or otherwise);

(c) the assets begin to be used wholly or partly for purposes other than those of the mineral extraction trade carried on by the person.

Origin – S. 430(1): CAA 1990, s. 99(1) (part), s. 101(4).
S. 430(2): CAA 1990, s. 101(8).

Cross references – S. 6: meaning of "chargeable period".
S. 395: meaning of "qualifying expenditure" generally.
S. 562: apportionment of sale or purchase moneys.

431 Discontinuance of trade

431 A person's entitlement to an allowance for a chargeable period is to a balancing allowance if in that chargeable period the mineral extraction trade is permanently discontinued.

Origin – CAA 1990, s. 101(1).

Cross references – S. 6: meaning of "chargeable period".
S. 395: meaning of "qualifying expenditure" generally.
S. 562: apportionment of sale or purchase moneys.

431A Foreign permanent establishment exemption

431A(1) Subsection (2) applies if–

(a) an election under section 18A of CTA 2009 has effect in relation to a company, and

(b) the company carries on any trade which consists of, or includes, the working of a source of mineral deposits.

431A(2) That trade so far as carried on through one or more permanent establishments outside the United Kingdom is treated for the purposes of this Part as a trade–

(a) separate from any other trade of the company, and

(b) all the profits and gains from which are not, or (if there were any) would not be, chargeable to tax.

History – S. 431A inserted by FA 2014, s. 67(7), with effect in relation to elections under CTA 2009, s. 18A which start to have effect on or after 1 April 2014.

431B Disposal value: no allowance/no charge cases

431B(1) If–

(a) an election under section 18A of CTA 2009 has effect in relation to a company, and

(b) the operation of sections 431A and 421(1)(b)(ii) and (2) requires the company to bring the disposal value of an asset into account,

the disposal value is such an amount as gives rise to neither a balancing allowance nor a balancing charge.

431B(2) Subsection (1) does not apply if–

(a) the company's qualifying expenditure in respect of the asset exceeds £5 million,

(b) the company has claimed any capital allowance in respect of any of that expenditure, and

(c) the company has, at any time in a relevant accounting period, used the asset otherwise than for the purposes of a permanent establishment outside the United Kingdom.

431B(3) In subsection (2)(c) **"relevant accounting period"** means an accounting period ending before, but ending not more than 6 years before, **"the relevant day"** as defined by section 18F of CTA 2009.

History – S. 431B inserted by FA 2014, s. 67(7), with effect in relation to elections under CTA 2009, s. 18A which start to have effect on or after 1 April 2014.

431C Notional allowances

431C(1) Subsection (2) applies if–

(a) an election under section 18A of CTA 2009 has effect in relation to a company, and

(b) but for section 18A of CTA 2009 and section 431A(2)(b), an allowance under this Part ("the notional allowance") could be claimed under section 3(1) in respect of assets provided for the purposes of a permanent establishment outside the United Kingdom through which business is or has been carried on by the company.

431C(2) The notional allowance (and any charge in connection with it which would have arisen if the allowance had been claimed) is to be made automatically and reflected in any calculation, for any relevant accounting period of the company, of the profits or losses attributable to business carried on by the company through such a permanent establishment.

431C(3) Subsection (4) applies if, at the time an election under section 18A of CTA 2009 takes effect in relation to a company, the company is, by reason of sections 431A and 421(1)(b)(ii) and (2), required to bring into account the disposal value of any asset provided for the purposes of a foreign permanent establishment through which business is or has been carried on by the company.

431C(4) For the purposes of subsections (1) and (2), the company is treated as having incurred at that time, for the purposes of the trade mentioned in section 431A(2), qualifying expenditure of an amount equal to that disposal value.

431C(5) In subsection (2) **"relevant accounting period"** in relation to a company by which an election under section 18A of CTA 2009 is made, means an accounting period of the company to which the election applies (as to which see section 18F of that Act).

History – S. 431C inserted by FA 2014, s. 67(7), with effect in relation to elections under CTA 2009, s. 18A which start to have effect on or after 1 April 2014.

Chapter 7 – Supplementary Provisions

432 Giving effect to allowances and charges

432 An allowance or charge to which a person is entitled or liable under this Part is to be given effect in calculating the profits of that person's mineral extraction trade, by treating–

(a) the allowance as an expense of the trade, and

(b) the charge as a receipt of the trade.

Prospective amendments – The existing provision made s. 432(1) and s. 432(2) inserted by CTNIA 2015, s. 2 and Sch. 1, para. 13, with effect from 26 March 2015 (Royal Assent) in respect of any power to make regulations and with effect in relation to accounting periods beginning on or after the first day of the appointed financial year for other provisions (see CTNIA 2015, s. 5). See also transitional provisions at Sch. 1, para. 19–21.

Origin – CAA 1990, s. 104, s. 140(2) (part), s. 144(2) (part), s. 161(5) (part).

Cross references – S. 2: general means of giving effect to capital allowances.
S. 6: meaning of "chargeable period".
S. 394: meaning of "mineral extraction trade" and related terms.
ICTA 1988, s. 411(10): references to the making of an allowance includes reference to one which would be made but for group relief etc.

433 Treatment of demolition costs

433(1) The net cost to a person of demolishing an asset which represents qualifying expenditure is added to that qualifying expenditure in determining the amount of any balancing allowance or balancing charge for the chargeable period in which the demolition occurs.

433(2) **"The net cost of the demolition"** means the amount, if any, by which the cost of the demolition exceeds any money received for the remains of the asset.

433(3) If this section applies, the net cost of the demolition is not treated as expenditure incurred on any other asset which replaces the demolished asset.

Origin – S. 433(1): CAA 1990, s. 103(1).
S. 433(2): CAA 1990, s. 103(3).
S. 433(3): CAA 1990, s. 103(2).

Cross references – S. 562: apportionment of sale or purchase moneys.

Other material – ICAEW Technical Release TR 233 (not reproduced): the "net amount received" in s. 423(1), Table, Item 3 includes the cost of demolition.

434 Time when expenditure incurred

434(1) For the purposes of this Part, expenditure incurred for the purposes of a mineral extraction trade by a person about to carry it on is treated as incurred by that person on the first day on which that person does carry it on.

434(2) Subsection (1) does not apply to pre-trading expenditure on mineral exploration and access (for which specific provision is made by section 400(4)).

Origin – S. 434(1): CAA 1990, s. 120(1).
S. 434(2) drafting, Annex 2, Note 51.

Cross references – S. 404(6): disapplication of s. 434 in relation to the acquisition of the undeveloped market value of land.
S. 405(4): disapplication of s. 434 where buildings or structures cease to be used.
S. 416C: rule in s. 400(4) disregarded in determining whether expenditure incurred for purposes of a ring-fence trade qualifies for first-year allowances under Ch. 5A.

Rewrite: Technical Points – Explanatory Notes, Annex 2, Note 51: in s. 434 the reference to expenditure being treated as incurred on the first day of trading eliminates duplication of the deeming provision that was present in the previous legislation.

435 Shares in assets

435(1) This Part applies in relation to a share in an asset as it applies (under section 571) in relation to a part of an asset.

435(2) For the purposes of those provisions, a share in an asset is treated as used for the purposes of a trade so long as, and only so long as, the asset is used for the purposes of the trade.

Origin – S. 434(1): CAA 1990, s. 120(1).
S. 434(2): drafting, Annex 2, Note 51.
Cross references – S. 562: apportionment of sale or purchase moneys.
S. 564: procedures for determining the market value of assets and the apportionment of that value between two or more persons.

436 Meaning of "development" etc.

436(1) In this Part–

"development"

"development order",

"general development order", and

"planning permission",

have the meaning given by the relevant planning enactment.

436(2) **"The relevant planning enactment"** means–

(a) in relation to land in England or Wales, section 336(1) of the Town and Country Planning Act 1990;

(b) in relation to land in Scotland, section 277(1) of the Town and Country Planning (Scotland) Act 1997;

(c) in relation to land in Northern Ireland, Article 2(2) of the Planning (Northern Ireland) Order 1991.

Origin – S. 436(1): CAA 1990, s. 121(1) ("development", "development order", "planning permission").
S. 436(2): CAA 1990, s. 121(1) ("relevant planning enactment").

PART 6 – RESEARCH AND DEVELOPMENT ALLOWANCES

Cross references – S. 6: meaning of "chargeable period".
S. 9(2): entitlement to claim allowances for fixtures, where a prior claim under Pt. 6 made.
S. 324: calculation of net allowances given for the purposes of balancing adjustments for IBAs to include any research and development allowances given.
S. 335: research and development allowances to be treated as given at the end of a chargeable period.
S. 553: certain forms of consideration given for the disposal of some types of oil production licence to be treated as nil for the purposes of Pt. 6.
S. 555: part of consideration for an oil licence treated as if it were for a notional asset represented by the qualifying expenditure for research and development allowances.
S. 557: disapplication of general rules for partnership changes and successions for research and development allowance purposes.
S. 562: apportionment of sale or purchase moneys.
S. 564: procedures for determining the market value of assets and the apportionment of that value between two or more persons.
S. 567–570: circumstances where sales treated as if made at market value and elections available.
S. 572(4): disapplication of general rules for ascertaining the time of sale of property.
Sch. 3, para. 90: equivalence of the term "research and development" to the term "scientific research" for trades set up during 1999–2000.
ICTA 1988, s. 82A: relief for revenue expenditure on research and development.
ICTA 1988, s. 411(10): references to the making of an allowance does not include any reference to one which would be made but for group relief etc.
ICTA 1988, Sch. 19B, para. 1, 6, 9 and 17: petroleum extraction activities: exploration expenditure supplement.
TCGA 1992, s. 37(2): moneys forming the disposal value of assets that are part of a research and development allowances claim are not excluded from the consideration for a disposal in the computation of a capital gain.
TCGA 1992, s. 195: allowance in computing capital gains for certain drilling expenditure.
Atomic Energy Authority Act 1995, Sch. 3, para. 17: transfer of allowances to a successor company.
FA 2000, s. 69, Sch. 20: extended tax reliefs for small and medium sized companies' revenue expenditure on research and development (where the definition of research and development does not include oil and gas exploration).

Chapter 1 – Introduction

437 Research and development allowances

437(1) Allowances are available under this Part if a person incurs qualifying expenditure on research and development.

437(2) In this Part **"research and development"**–

(a) means activities that fall to be treated as research and development in accordance with generally accepted accounting practice, and

(b) includes oil and gas exploration and appraisal.

437(3) But–

(a) activities that, as a result of regulations made under section 1006 of ITA 2007, are "research and development" for the purposes of that section are also "research and development" for the purposes of this Part, and

(b) activities that, as a result of any such regulations, are not "research and development" for the purposes of that section are also not "research and development" for the purposes of this Part.

History – S. 437(2) and (3) substituted for previous s. 437(2) by ITA 2007, s. 1027 and Sch. 1, para. 407, with effect from 6 April 2007. In former s. 437(2)(a), the words "generally accepted accounting practice" substituted for "normal accounting practice" by FA 2002, s. 103(4)(g) with effect from 24 July 2002.

Origin – S. 437(1) drafting.
S. 437(2): CAA 1990, s. 139(1) (part).

Cross references – ICTA 1988 s. 836A: definition of "generally accepted accounting practice" in s. 437(2)(a).
ICTA 1988, Sch. 19B, para. 6: petroleum extraction activities: exploration expenditure supplement: qualifying E & A expenditure.

HMRC Manuals – CA11700: whether expenditure has been "incurred", etc.
CA13100, CA32000: sales treated as being at market value, etc.
CA31800: guidance on prevention of double allowances.
CA60100: outline of R&D allowances.
CA60200, CA61000: guidance on meaning of "R&D".

438 Expenditure on research and development

438(1) Expenditure on research and development includes all expenditure incurred for–

(a) carrying out research and development, or

(b) providing facilities for carrying out research and development.

438(2) But it does not include expenditure incurred in the acquisition of–

(a) rights in research and development, or

(b) rights arising out of research and development.

438(3) Nor does it include expenditure on the provision of a dwelling.

438(4) But if–

(a) part of a building consists of a dwelling and the rest of the building is used for research and development, and

(b) no more than 25% of the capital expenditure referable to the construction or acquisition of the whole building is referable to the construction or acquisition of the dwelling,

the whole of the building is to be treated as used for research and development.

438(5) For the purposes of subsection (4)(b), the expenditure referable to the construction or acquisition of the building is to be apportioned in a just and reasonable manner.

438(6) Any additional VAT liability or rebate (as to which see Chapter 4) is to be disregarded in applying subsection (4)(b).

Origin – S. 438(1), (2): CAA 1990, s. 139(1) (part).
S. 438(3)–(6): CAA 1990, s. 137(3), Annex 1, Change 40, Annex 2, Note 53.

Cross references – FA 1988, s. 63: allowance of certain drilling expenditure etc. in determining chargeable gains.

Rewrite: Changes in Law – Explanatory Notes, Annex 1, Change 40: a minor change is effected to make the nature of the apportionment requirement in s. 438(5) consistent with other provisions in that it must be "just and reasonable"; as opposed to simply "just" as in CAA 1990, s. 137(3). See Sch. 3, para. 8 for the election to apply the original law to this matter where a chargeable period straddles 1 April 2001 (for corporation tax) or 6 April 2001 (for income tax).

Rewrite: Technical Points – Explanatory Notes, Annex 2, Note 53: s. 438(4) clarifies an ambiguity in the former wording of CAA 1990, s. 137(3) so that where no more than 25 per cent of the costs are referable to a dwelling and the rest of the building is used for research and development, the whole building can be treated as qualifying.

HMRC Manuals – CA60300: guidance and examples on s. 438.

Notes – Joint statement by the Revenue and the UK Oil Industry Taxation Committee, 7 February 1967 (not reproduced): treatment of expenditure on exploration for oil and natural gas.

Chapter 2 – Qualifying Expenditure

439 Qualifying expenditure

439(1) In this Part **"qualifying expenditure"** means capital expenditure incurred by a person on research and development directly undertaken by him or on his behalf if–

(a) he is carrying on a trade when the expenditure is incurred and the research and development relates to that trade, or

(b) after incurring the expenditure he sets up and commences a trade connected with the research and development.

439(2) The same expenditure may not be taken into account as qualifying expenditure in relation to more than one trade.

439(3) The trade by reference to which expenditure is qualifying expenditure is referred to in this Part as **"the relevant trade"** in relation to that expenditure.

439(4) If capital expenditure is partly within subsection (1) and partly not, the expenditure is to be apportioned in a just and reasonable manner.

439(5) References in this Chapter to research and development related to a trade include–

(a) research and development which may lead to or facilitate an extension of that trade, and

(b) research and development of a medical nature which has a special relation to the welfare of workers employed in that trade.

Origin – S. 439(1): CAA 1990, s. 137(1) (part).
S. 439(2): CAA 1990, s. 139(2).
S. 439(3) drafting.
S. 439(4): CAA 1990, s. 137(4) (part), Annex 1, Change 40.
S. 439(5): CAA 1990, s. 139(1) (part).

Cross references – FA 1988, s. 63: allowance of certain drilling expenditure etc. in determining chargeable gains.

Transitional – Sch. 3, para. 89: s. 439(4) does not apply to expenditure incurred before 27 July 1989.

Rewrite: Changes in Law – Explanatory Notes, Annex 1, Change 40: a minor change is effected to make the nature of the apportionment requirement in s. 439(4) consistent with other provisions in that it must be "just and reasonable"; as opposed to simply "just" as in CAA 1990, s. 137(4). See Sch. 3, para. 8 for the election to apply the original law to this matter where a chargeable period straddles 1 April 2001 (for corporation tax) or 6 April 2001 (for income tax).

HMRC Manuals – CA60400: guidance and example on s. 439.

Notes – Joint statement by the Revenue and the UK Oil Industry Taxation Committee, 7 February 1967 (not reproduced): treatment of expenditure on exploration for oil and natural gas.

439A Qualifying expenditure incurred for purposes of NI rate activity

439A [Prospectively inserted by CTNIA 2015, s. 2 and Sch. 1, para. 14.]

Prospective amendments – S. 439A inserted by CTNIA 2015, s. 2 and Sch. 1, para. 14, with effect from 26 March 2015 (Royal Assent) in respect of any power to make regulations and with effect in relation to accounting periods beginning on or after the first day of the appointed financial year for other provisions (see CTNIA 2015, s. 5). See also transitional provisions at Sch. 1, para. 19–21.

440 Excluded expenditure: land

440(1) Expenditure on the acquisition of land, or rights in or over land, is not qualifying expenditure.

440(2) But that does not prevent such expenditure from being qualifying expenditure so far as it is referable to the acquisition of–

(a) a building or structure already constructed on the land,

(b) rights in or over such a building or structure, or

(c) plant or machinery which forms part of such a building or structure.

440(3) For the purposes of subsection (2), the expenditure is to be apportioned in a just and reasonable manner.

Origin – CAA 1990, s. 137(2), Annex 1, Change 40, Annex 2, Note 54.

Rewrite: Changes in Law – Explanatory Notes, Annex 1, Change 40: a minor change is effected to make the nature of the apportionment requirement in s. 440(3) consistent with other provisions in that it must be "just and reasonable"; as opposed to simply "just" as in CAA 1990, s. 137(2). See Sch. 3, para. 8 for the election to apply the original law to this matter where a chargeable period straddles 1 April 2001 (for corporation tax) or 6 April 2001 (for income tax).

Rewrite: Technical Points – Explanatory Notes, Annex 2, Note 54: different wording to that in CAA 1990, s. 137(2) is used to ensure that the acquisition of land (without any building or structure on it) cannot qualify for allowances; however the overall effects of the provisions are considered to be the same.

HMRC Manuals – CA12300, CA60400: guidance on s. 440.

Chapter 3 – Allowances and Charges

441 Allowances

441(1) A person who incurs qualifying expenditure is entitled to an allowance in respect of that expenditure for the relevant chargeable period equal to–

(a) the amount of the qualifying expenditure, or

(b) if a disposal value is required to be brought into account for that period in respect of that expenditure, the amount (if any) by which that expenditure exceeds the disposal value.

441(2) The relevant chargeable period is–

(a) the chargeable period in which the expenditure is incurred, or

(b) if the expenditure was incurred before the chargeable period in which the relevant trade is set up and commenced, that chargeable period.

441(3) A person claiming an allowance under this section may require the allowance to be reduced to a specified amount.

Origin – S. 441(1): CAA 1990, s. 137(1) (part), s. 138(1) (part), (2) (part), (3A) (part), (5) (part), Annex 1, Change 39, Annex 2, Note 55.
S. 441(2): CAA 1990, s. 137(5) (part), Annex 2, Note 56.
S. 441(3) Annex 1, Change 38.

Cross references – S. 6: meaning of "chargeable period".
S. 335: research and development allowances to be treated as given at the end of a chargeable period when considering the effect of balancing events for IBA purposes.
S. 447(3): additional VAT liability can be treated as additional expenditure; rules for allocating it to a chargeable period.
S. 450: the method of giving effect to allowances and charges.
ICTA 1988, Sch. 18, para. (1): identification of person beneficially entitled to share capital of company for corporation Tax Group Relief purposes.
ICTA 1988, Sch. 19B, para. 6: petroleum extraction activities: exploration expenditure supplement: qualifying E & A expenditure.
ICTA 1988, Sch. 19B, para. 9 and 14: petroleum extraction activities: exploration expenditure supplement: supplement in respect of a pre-commencement accounting period.
TCGA 1992, s. 195: allowance of certain drilling expenditure for CGT purposes, if the person incurring it is entitled to an allowance under s. 441 (Ch. 3).
Coal Industry Act 1994, Sch. 4, para. 20: taxation provisions relating to balancing events.

Transitional – Sch. 3, para. 91(2), (8): where during the transitional period an oil licence is disposed of and part of its value is attributable to exploration expenditure incurred by the transferor an election may be made specifying the amount to be so attributable.

Rewrite: Changes in Law – Explanatory Notes, Annex 1, Change 38: a person claiming a writing down allowance may require the amount of the allowance to be reduced to a specified amount under s. 441(3); previously there was no specific provision enabling a reduced allowance to be given, although in practice this was usually permitted. See Sch. 3, para. 8 for the election to apply the original law to this matter where a chargeable period straddles 1 April 2001 (for corporation tax) or 6 April 2001 (for income tax).
Explanatory Notes, Annex 1, Change 39: when computing the amount of expenditure that qualifies for IBAs under Pt. 3 account is taken of any Research and Development allowances given; the change to entitlement to net allowances (as opposed to allowance less balancing charge under CAA 1990, s. 137(1)) means that a lesser reduction in IBAs may be required under the rewritten rules. See Sch. 3, para. 8 for the election to apply the original law to this matter where a chargeable period straddles 1 April 2001 (for corporation tax) or 6 April 2001 (for income tax).

Rewrite: Technical Points – Explanatory Notes, Annex 2, Note 55: the use of the term "entitled to an allowance" does not alter the law even though the previous legislation (CAA 1990, s. 137(1)) used the term "a deduction ... shall be allowed in taxing the trade"; because s. 450(a) links the entitlement to an allowance to an expense of the trade.
Explanatory Notes, Annex 2, Note 56: To avoid possible conflict in the interpretation of CAA 1990, s. 137(5) it is made clear in s. 441(2) that where expenditure is incurred in any chargeable period prior to the one in which the trade starts is to be treated as producing an allowance in the chargeable period in which the trade is started. It is considered that this is a clarification of the previous rules.

HMRC Manuals – CA60500: guidance on s. 441.

442 Balancing charges

442(1) This section applies if–

(a) an allowance is made to a person for a chargeable period in respect of qualifying expenditure, and

(b) the person is required to bring a disposal value into account for a later chargeable period in respect of that expenditure.

442(2) The person is liable to a balancing charge for the later chargeable period in respect of the qualifying expenditure.

442(3) The amount of the balancing charge is–

(a) the amount (if any) by which the disposal value to be brought into account for the period exceeds any unclaimed allowance, or

(b) if less, the allowance made in respect of the qualifying expenditure.

442(4) **"Unclaimed allowance"** means any part of the allowance to which the person was entitled in respect of the qualifying expenditure but which has not been claimed.

442(5) This section is to be read with section 449 (effect on balancing charges of additional VAT rebates in earlier chargeable periods).

Origin – S. 442(1): CAA 1990, s. 138(1) (part), (2) (part), (3A) (part), Annex 1, Change 39.
S. 442(2), (3): CAA 1990, s. 138(2) (part), (3A) (part), Annex 1, Change 49, Annex 2, Note 55.
S. 442(4): CAA 1990, s. 138(2) (part), Annex 1, Change 49.
S. 442(5): drafting.

Cross references – S. 6: meaning of "chargeable period".
S. 448, 449: effect of additional VAT liabilities on disposal values and balancing charges.
S. 450: the method of giving effect to allowances and charges.

Rewrite: Changes in Law – Explanatory Notes, Annex 1, Change 39: when computing the amount of expenditure that qualifies for IBAs under Part 3 account is taken of any Research and Development allowances given; the change to entitlement to net allowances (as opposed to allowance less balancing charge under CAA 1990, s. 137(1)) means that a lesser reduction in IBAs may be required under the rewritten rules. See Sch. 3, para. 8 for the election to apply the original law to this matter where a chargeable period straddles 1 April 2001 (for corporation tax) or 6 April 2001 (for income tax).
Explanatory Notes, Annex 1, Change 49: under the new legislation it is possible to claim only part of the allowance to which there may be an entitlement (see s. 441(3)); the changes in s. 442(3), (4) ensure that a balancing charge cannot arise where the disposal value is less than or equal to the unclaimed allowances (achieved with the words "exceeds any unclaimed allowance"). See Sch. 3,

para. 8 for the election to apply the original law to this matter where a chargeable period straddles 1 April 2001 (for corporation tax) or 6 April 2001 (for income tax).

Rewrite: Technical Points – Explanatory Notes, Annex 2, Note 55: the use of the term "liable to a balancing charge" does not alter the law even though the previous legislation (CAA 1990, s. 138(2)) used the term "a trading receipt of the trade accruing"; because s. 450(a) links the liability to a balancing charge to an receipt of the trade.

HMRC Manuals – CA60500: guidance and example on s. 442.

443 Disposal values and disposal events

443(1) A person is required to bring a disposal value into account in respect of qualifying expenditure incurred by him if–

(a) he ceases to own an asset representing the expenditure, or

(b) an asset representing the expenditure is demolished or destroyed at a time when he owns the asset.

443(2) Subsection (1) is to be read with section 555 (disposal of oil licence with exploitation value).

443(3) But a person is not required to bring a disposal value into account under subsection (1) if the disposal event gives rise to a balancing charge under Part 2 (plant and machinery allowances).

443(4) The disposal value to be brought into account under subsection (1) depends on the disposal event, as shown in the Table–

TABLE
DISPOSAL VALUES

	1. Disposal event	*2. Disposal value*
1.	Sale of the asset at not less than market value.	The net proceeds of the sale.
2.	Demolition or destruction of the asset.	The net amount received for the remains of the asset, together with– (a) any insurance money received in respect of the demolition or destruction, and (b) any other compensation of any description so received, so far as it consists of capital sums.
3.	Any event not falling within item 1 or 2.	The market value of the asset at the time of the event.

443(5) Subsection (4) is subject to–

section 445 (costs of demolition),

section 553 (nil value in case of disposal of oil licence relating to undeveloped area), and

section 555 (disposal of oil licence with exploitation value).

443(6) A person is also required to bring a disposal value into account by section 448 (additional VAT rebate generates disposal value).

443(7) In this Chapter **"disposal event"** means an event of a kind that requires a disposal value to be brought into account under subsection (1).

History – In s. 443(3), the words "or 3", which followed the words "Part 2", and "and industrial building allowances", which followed the words "machinery allowances", omitted by FA 2008, s. 84 and Sch. 27, para. 6, with effect in relation to chargeable periods beginning on or after 1 April 2011 for corporation tax purposes and 6 April 2011 for income tax purposes (FA 2008, Sch. 27, para. 30(1)).

Origin – S. 443(1): CAA 1990, s. 138(1) (part), (5) (part).
S. 443(2): drafting.
S. 443(3): CAA 1990, s. 138(6).
S. 443(4): CAA 1990, s. 138(4) (part).
Table, item 1 CAA 1990, s. 138(4) (part), Annex 1, Change 50.
Table, item 2 CAA 1990, s. 138(4) (part), (5) (part), Annex 1, Change 50.
Table, item 3 CAA 1990, s. 138(4) (part).
S. 443(5): CAA 1990, s. 138(7A), drafting.
S. 443(6): drafting.
S. 443(7): CAA 1990, s. 138(1) (part).

Cross references – S. 335(1): expenditure on industrial building etc. written-off by reference to allowances under s. 441–443 at the time the asset ceases to be used by the person in question for scientific research connected with the trade.
S. 448, 449: *effect of additional VAT liabilities on disposal values and balancing charges.*
S. 553: disposals of oil licences relating to undeveloped areas.
TCGA 1992, s. 195: allowance of certain drilling expenditure for CGT purposes, if the person incurring it is subject to a disposal value under s. 443 (Ch. 3).

Rewrite: Changes in Law – Explanatory Notes, Annex 1, Change 50: two minor changes in the determination of disposal values ensure that the rules for Research and Development Allowances are consistent with the equivalent rules in other Parts (e.g. s. 383, 423 and

515). The first change limits disposal value to the *net* proceeds/amount, in the Table, Items 1 and 2. The second limits the disposal value for demolition or destruction to *capital sums* of compensation etc. thus excluding revenue compensation.

HMRC Manuals – CA60600: guidance on s. 443 and 444.

Notes – ICAEW Technical Release TR 233 (not reproduced): the "net amount received" in s. 423(1), Table, Item 3 (old s. 26(1)(c)) includes the cost of demolition – presumably a similar interpretation applies for RDA.

444 Disposal events: chargeable period for which disposal value is to be brought into account

444(1) The chargeable period for which a disposal value is to be brought into account under section 443(1) in respect of qualifying expenditure is given by this section.

444(2) Subsection (3) applies if the disposal event occurs in or after the chargeable period for which the allowance in respect of the expenditure is made.

444(3) The disposal value is to be brought into account for–

(a) the chargeable period in which the event occurs, or

(b) if the event occurs after the chargeable period in which the relevant trade is permanently discontinued, that chargeable period.

444(4) If the disposal event occurs before the chargeable period for which the allowance in respect of the expenditure is made, the disposal value is to be brought into account for that chargeable period.

Origin – S. 444: Annex 2, Note 57.
S. 444(1) drafting.
S. 444(2), (3): CAA 1990, s. 138(2) (part), Annex 1, Change 51.
S. 444(4): Annex 1, Change 51.

Cross references – S. 6: meaning of "chargeable period".

Rewrite: Changes in Law – Explanatory Notes, Annex 1, Change 51: the former rules (CAA 1990, s. 138(1),(2)) allocating the chargeable period in which a disposal value was to be brought into account failed to deal with the (unusual) situation of an asset ceasing to belong to a trader *prior* to the chargeable period for which any allowances could be made. S. 444(3)(a) and (4) address this particular issue, allocating a chargeable period to this sort of event. See Sch. 3, para. 8 for the election to apply the original law to this matter where a chargeable period straddles 1 April 2001 (for corporation tax) or 6 April 2001 (for income tax).

Rewrite: Technical Points – Explanatory Notes, Annex 2, Note 57: in the former legislation balancing charges are treated as arising at the specific time that an asset ceases to belong to a trader, under the rewritten rules (s. 444(1)) any disposal values are allocated to a "chargeable period" rather than a particular date. This is not considered to represent a change in the law.

HMRC Manuals – CA60600: guidance on s. 443 and 444.

445 Costs of demolition

445(1) This section applies if–

(a) an asset representing qualifying expenditure incurred by a person is demolished at a time when the person owns the asset, and

(b) the person incurred costs of demolition.

445(2) The disposal value which the person is required to bring into account in respect of the qualifying expenditure is to be reduced by the cost to the person of the demolition.

445(3) If the amount of the disposal value is reduced to nil (or less than nil) under subsection (2), the person is not required to bring a disposal value into account.

445(4) If–

(a) the cost to the person of the demolition exceeds the disposal value, and

(b) before its demolition the asset had not begun to be used for purposes other than research and development related to the relevant trade,

the person is to be treated as incurring qualifying expenditure equal to the excess.

445(5) That qualifying expenditure is to be treated as incurred–

(a) when the demolition occurs, or

(b) if that is on or after the date on which the relevant trade is permanently discontinued, immediately before the discontinuance.

445(6) If this section applies, the cost to the person of the demolition is not to be treated for the purposes of this Act as expenditure on any property that replaces the demolished asset.

Origin – S. 445(1): CAA 1990, s. 138(5) (part), Annex 1, Change 52.
S. 445(2): CAA 1990, s. 138(5) (part).
S. 445(3): drafting.
S. 445(4), (5): CAA 1990, s. 138(5) (part).
S. 445(6): CAA 1990, s. 139(5).

Rewrite: Changes in Law – Explanatory Notes, Annex 1, Change 52: CAA 1990, s. 138(5)(a) could be taken to restrict an allowance for the costs of demolition to cases where the trade is still actively carried on ("the person carrying on the trade shall"); in the rewritten version of this rule (s. 445(1)) it is made clear that an allowance is available even where the trade has ceased. See Sch. 3, para. 8 for the election to apply the original law to this matter where a chargeable period straddles 1 April 2001 (for corporation tax) or 6 April 2001 (for income tax).

HMRC Manuals – CA60700: guidance on s. 445.

Chapter 4 – Additional VAT Liabilities and Rebates

446 Introduction

446 For the purposes of this Chapter–

(a) **"additional VAT liability"** and **"additional VAT rebate"** have the meaning given by section 547,

(b) the time when–

(i) a person incurs an additional VAT liability, or

(ii) an additional VAT rebate is made to a person,

is given by section 548, and

(c) the chargeable period in which, and the time when, an additional VAT liability or an additional VAT rebate accrues are given by section 549.

Origin – S. 446: drafting.

Cross references – S. 546–551: further rules relating to additional VAT liabilities and rebates.

HMRC Manuals – CA60750: guidance on s. 446–449.

447 Additional VAT liability treated as additional expenditure etc.

447(1) If a person–

(a) has incurred qualifying expenditure (**"the original expenditure"**), and

(b) incurs an additional VAT liability in respect of that expenditure,

the liability is to be treated as capital expenditure incurred on the same research and development as the original expenditure.

447(2) But subsection (1) does not apply if by the time the liability is incurred–

(a) the person who incurred the original expenditure has ceased to own the asset representing that expenditure, or

(b) that asset has been demolished or destroyed.

447(3) Any allowance arising as a result of this section is available for–

(a) the chargeable period in which the liability accrues, or

(b) if the liability accrued before the chargeable period in which the relevant trade is set up and commenced, that chargeable period,

rather than for the relevant chargeable period specified in section 441(2).

Origin – S. 447(1): CAA 1990, s. 137(1A) (part).
S. 447(2): CAA 1990, s. 137(1A) (part), s. 138(1) (part).
S. 447(3): CAA 1990, s. 137(5) (part), s. 159A(3) (part), drafting,
Annex 2, Note 56.

Cross references – S. 6: meaning of "chargeable period".
S. 443: disposal values and disposal events.

Rewrite: Technical Points – Explanatory Notes, Annex 2, Note 56: to avoid possible conflict in the interpretation of CAA 1990, s. 137(5) it is made clear in s. 447(3) that where expenditure is incurred in any chargeable period prior to the one in which the trade starts is to be treated as producing an allowance in the chargeable period in which the trade is started. It is considered that this is a clarification of the previous rules.

HMRC Manuals – CA60750: guidance on s. 446–449.

448 Additional VAT rebate generates disposal value

448(1) This section applies if–

(a) a person has incurred qualifying expenditure, and

(b) an additional VAT rebate is made to the person in respect of that expenditure.

448(2) But this section does not apply if by the time the rebate is made–

(a) the person has ceased to own the asset representing that expenditure, or

(b) that asset has been demolished or destroyed.

448(3) And this section does not apply if the rebate falls to be brought into account for the purpose of making allowances and charges under Part 2 (plant and machinery allowances).

448(4) The person must bring the amount of the rebate into account–

(a) as a disposal value in respect of the qualifying expenditure for the appropriate chargeable period, or

(b) if the person would have to bring a disposal value into account under section 443(1) in respect of that expenditure for that chargeable period, as an addition to that disposal value.

448(5) **"Appropriate chargeable period"** means–

(a) the chargeable period in which the rebate accrues, or

(b) if the rebate accrued before the chargeable period in which the relevant trade is set up and commenced, that chargeable period.

History – In s. 448(3), the words "or 3" and "and industrial buildings allowances" omitted by FA 2008, s. 84 and Sch. 27, para. 7, with effect in relation to chargeable periods beginning on or after 1 April 2011 for corporation tax purposes and 6 April 2011 for income tax purposes (FA 2008, Sch. 27, para. 30(1)).

Origin – S. 448(1): CAA 1990, s. 138(3A) (part).
S. 448(2): CAA 1990, s. 138(1) (part), (3A) (part).
S. 448(3): CAA 1990, s. 138(3A) (part).
S. 448(4), (5): CAA 1990, s. 138(3A) (part), s. 159A(3) (part), Annex 1, Change 53, Annex 2, Note 58.

Cross references – S. 6: meaning of "chargeable period".

Rewrite: Changes in Law – Explanatory Notes, Annex 1, Change 53: the former rules (CAA 1990, s. 138(3A)) failed to deal with the (unusual) situation of an asset ceasing to belong to a trader *prior* to the chargeable period for which any allowances could be made. S. 448(5)(b) addresses this particular issue, allocating a chargeable period to this sort of event. This change ensures that s. 448 is consistent with s. 444. See Sch. 3, para. 8 for the election to apply the original law to this matter where a chargeable period straddles 1 April 2001 (for corporation tax) or 6 April 2001 (for income tax).

Rewrite: Technical Points – Explanatory Notes, Annex 2, Note 58: CAA 1990, s. 138(3A) specifically identifies the chargeable period to which rebates received after discontinuance should be allocated. S. 448 makes no specific reference to discontinuance but this not considered to result in any change in the law because the former reference to discontinuance is considered to have been unnecessary.

HMRC Manuals – CA60750: guidance on s. 446–449.

449 Effect on balancing charges of additional VAT rebates in earlier chargeable periods

449(1) Section 442 (balancing charges) has effect subject to this section if–

(a) an allowance is made to a person for a chargeable period (**"the original period"**) in respect of qualifying expenditure,

(b) the person is required to bring a disposal value into account for a later chargeable period in respect of that expenditure, and

(c) the person has been required by section 448(4)(a) to bring one or more disposal values (**"VAT disposal values"**) into account in respect of that expenditure for one or more chargeable periods after the original period but before the later chargeable period.

449(2) In relation to the later chargeable period, subsection (3)(a) of section 442 applies as if the unclaimed allowance were reduced by–

$$DV - BC$$

where–

DV is the total amount of the VAT disposal values, and

BC is the total amount of any balancing charges to which the person is liable under that section as a result of bringing into account the VAT disposal values.

449(3) In relation to the later chargeable period, subsection (3)(b) of section 442 applies as if the allowance made in respect of the qualifying expenditure were reduced by BC.

Origin – S. 449(1): CAA 1990, s. 138(1) (part), (2) (part), (2A) (part), (3A) (part).
S. 449(2): CAA 1990, s. 138(2A) (part), Annex 1, Change 49.
S. 449(3): CAA 1990, s. 138(2A) (part).

Rewrite: Changes in Law – Explanatory Notes, Annex 1, Change 49: under the new legislation it is possible to claim only part of the allowance to which there may be an entitlement (see s. 441(3)); s. 449 (which amends the operation of s. 442 where there are additional VAT rebates) ensures that where a disposal value is effectively reduced by an unclaimed allowance (under s. 442), that unclaimed allowance cannot be so utilised again. See Sch. 3, para. 8 for the election to apply the original law to this matter where a chargeable period straddles 1 April 2001 (for corporation tax) or 6 April 2001 (for income tax).

HMRC Manuals – CA60750: guidance on s. 446–449.

Chapter 5 – Supplementary Provisions

450 Giving effect to allowances and charges

450 An allowance or charge to which a person is entitled or liable under this Part for a chargeable period is to be given effect in calculating the profits of the relevant trade, by treating–

(a) the allowance as an expense of the trade, and

(b) the charge as a receipt of the trade.

Prospective amendments – The existing provision made s. 450(1) and s. 450(2) inserted by CTNIA 2015, s. 2 and Sch. 1, para. 15, with effect from 26 March 2015 (Royal Assent) in respect of any power to make regulations and with effect in relation to accounting periods beginning on or after the first day of the appointed financial year for other provisions (see CTNIA 2015, s. 5). See also transitional provisions at Sch. 1, para. 19–21.

Origin – CAA 1990, s. 137(1) (part), s. 138(2) (part), (3A) (part), (5) (part), s. 140(2) (part), (5) (part), s. 144(2) (part), (3) (part), s. 161(5) (part), Annex 2, Note 55.

Cross references – S. 6: meaning of "chargeable period".
S. 441, 442: entitlement to allowances and liability to charges.

451 Sales: time of cessation of ownership

451 Any reference in this Part to the time when a person ceases to own an asset is to be read, in the case of a sale, as a reference to whichever is the earlier of–

(a) the time of completion, and

(b) the time when possession is given.

Origin – CAA 1990, s. 139(4).

PART 7 – KNOW-HOW ALLOWANCES

Cross references – S. 7(2): the rules preventing double allowances for the same expenditure do not apply to this part.
S. 8(5): the rule preventing double relief through pooling does not apply to this part.
S. 564(1): apportionments that effect two or more people are to be heard by the Commissioners in one hearing.
The Atomic Energy Authority Act 1995, Sch. 3, para. 20 (as amended by Sch. 2, para. 94(11)): the taxation provisions of that Act.

Rewrite: Technical Points – Explanatory Notes, Annex 2, Note 6: it is unlikely that expenditure which qualifies for know-how allowances could also qualify for any other allowances.

Chapter 1 – Introduction

452 Know-how allowances

452(1) Allowances are available under this Part if a person incurs qualifying expenditure on the acquisition of know-how.

452(2) In this Part **"know-how"** means any industrial information or techniques likely to assist in–

(a) manufacturing or processing goods or materials,

(b) working a source of mineral deposits (including searching for, discovering or testing mineral deposits or obtaining access to them), or

(c) carrying out any agricultural, forestry or fishing operations.

452(3) In subsection (2)(b)–

(a) **"mineral deposits"** includes any natural deposits capable of being lifted or extracted from the earth and for this purpose geothermal energy is to be treated as a natural deposit, and

(b) **"source of mineral deposits"** includes a mine, an oil well and a source of geothermal energy.

Origin – S. 452(1) drafting.
S. 452(2): ICTA 1988, s. 533(7) (part).
S. 452(3): ICTA 1988, s. 532(1) (part), s. 533(7) (part), CAA 1990, s. 161(2) ("mineral deposits"), Annex 2, Note 46.

Cross references – S. 274, Table A, items 4, 6 and 7: definitions of trades.
The Atomic Energy Act 1995, Sch. 3, para. 19(3), (as amended by Sch. 2, para. 94(10)): taxation provisions of that Act.

Rewrite: Technical Points – Explanatory Notes, Annex 2, Note 46: in s. 452(3)(a) the phrase "whether in the form of hot dry rocks or otherwise" has been omitted from the definition of mineral deposits as it is redundant following the addition of "geothermal energy" to the definition in 1986.

HMRC Manuals – CA11700: whether expenditure has been "incurred", etc.
CA70010: guidance on meaning of "know-how".
CA70020: outline of know-how allowances.
CA70030: commercial know-how and franchise agreements.
CA70040: know-how acquired by holding company.
CA73000: guidance on payments to acquire know-how.
CA74000: guidance on costs of diving courses.

453 Know-how as property

453(1) Know-how is to be treated as property for the purposes of this Act.

453(2) References in this Act to the purchase or sale of property include the acquisition or disposal of know-how.

Origin – ICTA 1988, s. 532(5) (part).

Chapter 2 – Qualifying Expenditure

454 Qualifying expenditure

454(1) In this Part **"qualifying expenditure"** means, subject to section 455, capital expenditure incurred on the acquisition of know-how by a person if–

(a) the person is carrying on a trade at the time of the acquisition and the know-how is acquired for use in that trade,

(b) the person acquires the know-how and subsequently sets up and commences a trade in which it is used,

(c) the person acquires the know-how together with the trade or part of a trade in which it was used and the parties to the acquisition make an election under section 194 of ITTOIA 2005 or under section 178 of CTA 2009 (consideration for know-how on disposal of trade to be treated as payment for goodwill unless parties otherwise elect), or

(d) the person acquires the know-how together with the trade or part of a trade in which it was used and the trade in question was, before the acquisition, carried on wholly outside the United Kingdom.

454(2) The same expenditure may not be taken into account as qualifying expenditure in relation to more than one trade.

454(3) Qualifying expenditure incurred before the setting up and commencement of the relevant trade is to be treated for the purposes of this Part as incurred when the trade is set up and commenced.

454(4) **"Relevant trade"** means the trade by reference to which expenditure is qualifying expenditure.

History – In s. 454(1)(c), the words "section 178 of CTA 2009" substituted for the words "section 531(3)(a) of ICTA" by CTA 2009, s. 1322 and Sch. 1, para. 509, with effect for corporation tax purposes for accounting periods ending on or after 1 April 2009, and for income tax and capital gains tax purposes for the tax year 2009–10 and subsequent tax years.
S. 454(1)(c) amended by ITTOIA 2005, s. 882(1) and Sch. 1, para. 562; effective for income tax purposes for 2005–06 onwards and for corporation tax purposes for accounting periods ending after 5 April 2005 (ITTOIA 2005, s. 883(1)).

Origin – S. 453(1): ICTA 1988, s. 530(1) (part), (4) (part), s. 531(2) (part), (3) (part).
S. 453(2): ICTA 1988, s. 530(1) (part), Annex 2, Note 59.
S. 453(3), (4): ICTA 1988, s. 530(7) (part).

Cross references – ICTA 1988, s. 531(3)(a): consideration for know-how to be treated as goodwill.
The Atomic Energy Act 1995, Sch. 3, para. 19(1), (as amended by Sch. 2, para. 94(8)): taxation provisions of that Act.

Rewrite: Technical Points – Explanatory Notes, Annex 2, Note 59: s. 454(2) clarifies that expenditure on know-how can not be taken into account for a claim for allowances in more than one trade.

HMRC Manuals – CA71000: guidance on s. 454.
CA74000: course expenditure by divers that qualifies as know-how.

455 Excluded expenditure

455(1) Expenditure on the acquisition of know-how is not qualifying expenditure to the extent that it is otherwise deducted for tax purposes.

455(2) Expenditure on the acquisition of know-how is not qualifying expenditure if–

(a) the buyer is a body of persons over whom the seller has control,

(b) the seller is a body of persons over whom the buyer has control, or

(c) the buyer and the seller are both bodies of persons and another person has control over both of them.

455(3) In subsection (2) **"body of persons"** includes a partnership.

455(4) Expenditure on the acquisition of know-how is not qualifying expenditure if it is treated as a payment for goodwill under section 194(3) of ITTOIA 2005 or under section 178(3) of CTA 2009 (consideration for know-how on disposal of trade to be treated as payment for goodwill, unless parties otherwise elect etc.).

History – In s. 455(4), the words "section 178(3) of CTA 2009" substituted for the words "section 531(2) of ICTA" by CTA 2009, s. 1322 and Sch. 1, para. 510, with effect for corporation tax purposes for accounting periods ending on or after 1 April 2009, and for income tax and capital gains tax purposes for the tax year 2009–10 and subsequent tax years.
S. 455(4) amended by ITTOIA 2005, s. 882(1) and Sch. 1, para. 563; effective for income tax purposes for 2005–06 onwards and for corporation tax purposes for accounting periods ending after 5 April 2005 (ITTOIA 2005, s. 883(1)).

Origin – S. 455(1): ICTA 1988, s. 530(1) (part).
S. 455(2), (3): ICTA 1988, s. 531(7) (part).
S. 455(4): ICTA 1988, s. 531(2) (part).

Cross references – TMA 1970, s. 42(6), (7): procedure for claims by partnerships under self-assessment.
ICTA 1988, s. 531(2): consideration for know-how to be treated as goodwill unless parties elect otherwise.
The Atomic Energy Act 1995, Sch. 3, para. 19(2), (as amended by Sch. 2, para. 94(9)): taxation provisions of that Act.

HMRC Manuals – CA70030: payments for commercial know-how or franchise agreements.

Chapter 3 – Allowances and Charges

456 Pooling of expenditure

456(1) Qualifying expenditure has to be pooled for the purpose of determining a person's entitlement to writing-down allowances and balancing allowances and liability to balancing charges.

456(2) There is a separate pool for each trade in respect of which the person has qualifying expenditure.

Origin – ICTA 1988, s. 530(2) (part), (3) (part), (4) (part), (5) (part), drafting.

Cross references – S. 454: qualifying expenditure
HMRC Manuals – CA71100: guidance on s. 456.

457 Determination of entitlement or liability

457(1) Whether a person is entitled to a writing-down allowance or a balancing allowance, or liable to a balancing charge, for a chargeable period is determined separately for each pool of qualifying expenditure and depends on–

(a) the available qualifying expenditure in that pool for that period (**"AQE"**), and

(b) the total of any disposal values to be brought into account in that pool for that period (**"TDV"**).

457(2) If AQE exceeds TDV, the person is entitled to a writing-down allowance or a balancing allowance for the period.

457(3) If TDV exceeds AQE, the person is liable to a balancing charge for the period.

457(4) The entitlement under subsection (2) is to a writing-down allowance except for the final chargeable period when it is to a balancing allowance.

457(5) The final chargeable period is the chargeable period in which the trade is permanently discontinued.

Origin – S. 457(1): ICTA 1988, s. 530(2) (part), (3) (part).
S. 457(2): ICTA 1988, s. 530(2) (part).
S. 457(3): ICTA 1988, s. 530(3) (part).
S. 457(4), (5): ICTA 1988, s. 530(2) (part).

Cross references – S. 6: meaning of chargeable period.

Extra-statutory concessions – B8: payments made by a non-resident for the use of UK intellectual property are normally treated as foreign source income for double taxation relief purposes.

HMRC Manuals – CA71200: guidance on s. 457.

458 Amount of allowances and charges

458(1) The amount of the writing-down allowance to which a person is entitled for a chargeable period is 25% of the amount by which AQE exceeds TDV.

458(2) If the chargeable period is more or less than a year, the amount is proportionately increased or reduced.

458(3) If the trade has been carried on for part only of the chargeable period, the amount is proportionately reduced.

458(4) A person claiming a writing-down allowance may require the allowance to be reduced to a specified amount.

458(5) The amount of the balancing charge to which a person is liable for a chargeable period is the amount by which TDV exceeds AQE.

458(6) The amount of the balancing allowance to which a person is entitled for the final chargeable period is the amount by which AQE exceeds TDV.

Origin – S. 457(1): ICTA 1988, s. 530(2) (part), (3) (part).
S. 457(2): ICTA 1988, s. 530(2) (part).
S. 457(3): ICTA 1988, s. 530(3) (part).
S. 457(4), (5): ICTA 1988, s. 530(2) (part).

Cross references – S. 6: meaning of chargeable period.

Rewrite: Changes in Law – Explanatory Notes, Annex 1, Change 38: brings the law into line with the current practice of allowing the taxpayer to claim any amount of the WDA from zero to the full allowance permitted.

HMRC Manuals – CA71200: guidance on s. 458.

459 Available qualifying expenditure

459 A person's available qualifying expenditure in a pool for a chargeable period consists of–

(a) any qualifying expenditure allocated to the pool for that period in accordance with section 460, and

(b) any unrelieved qualifying expenditure carried forward in the pool from the previous chargeable period under section 461.

Origin – ICTA 1988, s. 530(4) (part).

Cross references – S. 6: meaning of chargeable period.
S. 454: qualifying expenditure

HMRC Manuals – CA71100: guidance on s. 459.

460 Allocation of qualifying expenditure to pools

460(1) The following rules apply to the allocation of a person's qualifying expenditure to a pool.

460(2) An amount of qualifying expenditure is not to be allocated to the pool for a chargeable period if that amount has been taken into account in determining the person's available qualifying expenditure for an earlier chargeable period.

460(3) Qualifying expenditure is not to be allocated to the pool for a chargeable period before that in which the expenditure is incurred.

Origin – S. 460(1): drafting.
S. 460(2), (3): ICTA 1988, s. 530(4) (part), Annex 1, Change 54.

Cross references – S. 6: meaning of chargeable period.
S. 454: qualifying expenditure.

Rewrite: Changes in Law – Explanatory Notes, Annex 1, Change 54: the taxpayer can allocate all or some of the qualifying expenditure to the pool in the period it was incurred or a later period. This is a relaxation of the law that previously required the taxpayer to allocate all of the qualifying expenditure to the pool in the period it was incurred.

HMRC Manuals – CA71100: guidance on s. 460.

461 Unrelieved qualifying expenditure

461(1) A person has unrelieved qualifying expenditure to carry forward from a chargeable period if for that period AQE exceeds TDV.

461(2) The amount of the unrelieved qualifying expenditure is–

(a) the excess less the writing-down allowance made for the period, or

(b) if no writing-down allowance is claimed for the period, the excess.

461(3) No amount may be carried forward as unrelieved qualifying expenditure from the final chargeable period.

Origin – S. 461(1), (2): ICTA 1988, s. 530(4) (part).
S. 461(3): ICTA 1988, s. 530(1) (part), (2) (part), drafting, Annex 2, Note 60.

Cross references – S. 6: meaning of chargeable period.
S. 454: qualifying expenditure.

Rewrite: Technical Points – Explanatory Notes, Annex 2, Note 60: s. 461(3) makes it explicit that no amount in the pool can be carried forward once the trade has ceased. This achieves the same result as ICTA 1988, s. 530(1) by a different route.

462 Disposal values

462(1) A person is required to bring a disposal value into account for the chargeable period in which he sells know-how on which he has incurred qualifying expenditure.

462(2) The disposal value to be brought into account is the net proceeds of the sale, so far as they consist of capital sums.

462(3) But no disposal value need be brought into account if the consideration received for the sale is treated as a payment for goodwill under section 194(2) of ITTOIA 2005 or under section 178(2) of CTA 2009 (consideration for know-how on disposal of trade to be treated as payment for goodwill, unless parties otherwise elect).

History – In s. 462(3), the words "section 178(2) of CTA 2009" substituted for the words "section 531(2) of ICTA" by CTA 2009, s. 1322 and Sch. 1, para. 511, with effect for corporation tax purposes for accounting periods ending on or after 1 April 2009, and for income tax and capital gains tax purposes for the tax year 2009–10 and subsequent tax years.
S. 462(3) amended by ITTOIA 2005, s. 882(1) and Sch. 1, para. 564; effective for income tax purposes for 2005–06 onwards and for corporation tax purposes for accounting periods ending after 5 April 2005 (ITTOIA 2005, s. 883(1)).

Origin – S. 462(1): ICTA 1988, s. 530(5) (part).
S. 462(2): ICTA 1988, s. 530(5) (part), Annex 1, Change 55.
S. 462(3): ICTA 1988, s. 531(2) (part).

Cross references – S. 6: meaning of the chargeable period
ICTA 1988, s. 531: disposal of know-how.

Rewrite: Changes in Law – Explanatory Notes, Annex 1, Change 55: only capital sums received on the sale of know-how need be brought into the pool as a disposal value. This benefits the taxpayer as sale proceeds often give rise to a trading receipt for tax purposes, see *Jeffrey v Rolls-Royce Ltd* (1962) 40 TC 443.

HMRC Manuals – CA71300: guidance on s. 462.

463 Giving effect to allowances and charges

463 An allowance or charge to which a person is entitled or liable under this Part for a chargeable period is to be given effect in calculating the profits of the trade, by treating–

(a) the allowance as an expense of the trade, and

(b) the charge as a receipt of the trade.

Origin – ICTA 1988, s. 532(1) (part), CAA 1990, s. 140(2) (part), s. 144(2) (part), s. 161(5) (part), Annex 2, Note 61.

Cross references – S. 2(3): general means for giving effect to capital allowances.
S. 6: meaning of chargeable period.

Rewrite: Changes in Law – Explanatory Notes, Annex 2, Note 61: this section corrects an apparent drafting omission in CAA 1990, making it clear that allowances should be given as an expense of the trade.

PART 8 – PATENT ALLOWANCES

Cross references – S. 7(2): the rules preventing double allowances for the same expenditure do not apply to this part.
S. 8(5): the rule preventing double relief through pooling does not apply to this part.
S. 564(1): apportionments that effect two or more people are to be heard by Commissioners in one hearing.

The Atomic Energy Authority Act 1995, Sch. 3, para. 20 (as amended by Sch. 2, para. 94(11)): the taxation provisions of that Act.
FA 1997, Sch. 12, para. 11(3)(c), (as amended by Sch. 2, para. 98(1)): capital allowance provisions concerning finance leasing and loans.

Rewrite: Technical Points – Explanatory Notes, Annex 2, Note 6: it is unlikely that expenditure which qualifies for patent allowances could also qualify for any other allowances.

Chapter 1 – Introduction

464 Patent allowances

464(1) Allowances are available under this Part if a person incurs qualifying expenditure on the purchase of patent rights.

464(2) In this Part **"patent rights"** means the right to do or authorise the doing of anything which would, but for that right, be an infringement of a patent.

Origin – S. 464(1): drafting.
S. 464(2): ICTA 1988, s. 533(1) ("patent rights").

Cross references – The Atomic Energy Act 1995, Sch. 3, para. 18(2) (as amended by Sch. 2, para. 94(7)): taxation provisions of that Act.
Patents Act 1949, s. 46–49; Patents Act 1977, s. 55–59: circumstances in which the government may exploit patented inventions.

HMRC Manuals – CA11700: whether expenditure has been "incurred", etc.
CA75010: guidance and example on meaning of "patent".
CA75020: guidance on meaning of "patent rights" etc.

465 Future patent rights

465(1) References in this Part to expenditure incurred on the purchase of patent rights include expenditure incurred on obtaining a right to acquire future patent rights.

465(2) If a person–

(a) incurs expenditure on obtaining a right to acquire future patent rights, and

(b) subsequently acquires those rights,

the expenditure is to be treated as having been expenditure on the purchase of those rights.

465(3) **"A right to acquire future patent rights"** means a right to acquire in the future patent rights relating to an invention in respect of which the patent has not yet been granted.

465(4) References in this Part to the proceeds of a sale of patent rights include a sum received from a person which is treated under this section as expenditure incurred by him on the purchase of patent rights.

Origin – S. 465(1)–(3): ICTA 1988, s. 533(5) (part).
S. 465(4): ICTA 1988, s. 533(6) (part).

HMRC Manuals – CA75020: rights in a patent which has not yet been granted.

466 Grant of licences

466(1) The acquisition of a licence in respect of a patent is to be treated as the purchase of patent rights.

466(2) The grant of a licence in respect of a patent is to be treated as a sale of part of patent rights.

466(3) But the grant by a person entitled to patent rights of an exclusive licence is to be treated as a sale of the whole of those rights.

466(4) **"Exclusive licence"** means a licence to exercise those rights to the exclusion of the grantor and all other persons for the period remaining until the rights come to an end.

Origin – S. 466(1), (2): ICTA 1988, s. 533(2) (part).
S. 466(3), (4): ICTA 1988, s. 533(3) (part).

Cross references – S. 468: qualifying trade expenditure.
S. 476: disposal value of patent rights.

HMRC Manuals – CA75030: guidance on s. 466.

Chapter 2 – Qualifying Expenditure

467 Qualifying expenditure

467 Expenditure is qualifying expenditure only if it is–

(a) qualifying trade expenditure, or

(b) qualifying non-trade expenditure.

Origin – S. 467: drafting.

Cross references – S. 575: meaning of connected persons.

Transitional – Sch. 3, para. 92–102: writing down allowances for patent expenditure incurred before 1 April 1986.

HMRC Manuals – CA75100: guidance on s. 467–469.

468 Qualifying trade expenditure

468(1) **"Qualifying trade expenditure"** means capital expenditure incurred by a person on the purchase of patent rights for the purposes of a trade within the charge to tax carried on by the person.

468(2) The same expenditure may not be taken into account as qualifying trade expenditure in relation to more than one trade.

468(3) Expenditure incurred for the purposes of a trade by a person about to carry on the trade is to be treated as if it had been incurred by him on the first day on which he carries on the trade.

468(4) But subsection (3) does not apply if the person has before that day sold all the rights on the purchase of which the expenditure was incurred.

Origin – S. 468(1): ICTA 1988, s. 520(1) (part), (2) (part), s. 528(1) (part), s. 532(1) (part), CAA 1990, s 161(3) (part), Annex 2, Note 74.
S. 468(2): ICTA 1988, s. 520(1) (part), Annex 2, Note 59.
S. 468(3), (4): ICTA 1988, s. 520(3).

Cross references – S. 2(3): general means of giving effect to capital allowances.
S. 6: meaning of chargeable period.

Rewrite: Technical Points – Explanatory Notes, Annex 2, Note 61: this section corrects an apparent drafting omission in CAA 1990, making it clear that allowances for patents acquired as trading expenditure should be given as an expense of the trade.

HMRC Manuals – CA75100: guidance on s. 467–469.

469 Qualifying non-trade expenditure

469 **"Qualifying non-trade expenditure"** means capital expenditure incurred by a person on the purchase of patent rights if–

(a) any income receivable by the person in respect of the rights would be liable to tax, and

(b) the expenditure is not qualifying trade expenditure.

Origin – ICTA 1988, s. 520(1) (part), (2) (part).

Cross references – FA 1997, Sch. 12, para. 11(3): capital allowances on leased assets.

Transitional – Sch. 3, para. 92–102: provisions for expenditure incurred before 1 April 1986.

HMRC Manuals – CA75100: guidance on s. 467–469.

Chapter 3 – Allowances and Charges

470 Pooling of expenditure

470(1) Qualifying expenditure has to be pooled for the purpose of determining a person's entitlement to writing-down allowances and balancing allowances and liability to balancing charges.

470(2) There is a separate pool–

(a) for each trade in respect of which the person has qualifying trade expenditure, and

(b) for all of the person's qualifying non-trade expenditure.

Origin – ICTA 1988, s. 520(4) (part), (6) (part), s. 521(1) (part), (2) (part), drafting.

Cross references – S. 468: qualifying trade expenditure.

Transitional – Sch. 3, para. 92–102: provisions for expenditure incurred before 1 April 1986.

HMRC Manuals – CA75110: guidance and examples on s. 470–477.

471 Determination of entitlement or liability

471(1) Whether a person is entitled to a writing-down allowance or a balancing allowance, or liable to a balancing charge, for a chargeable period is determined separately for each pool of qualifying expenditure and depends on–

(a) the available qualifying expenditure in that pool for that period ("AQE"), and

(b) the total of any disposal receipts to be brought into account in that pool for that period ("TDR").

471(2) If AQE exceeds TDR, the person is entitled to a writing-down allowance or a balancing allowance for the period.

471(3) If TDR exceeds AQE, the person is liable to a balancing charge for the period.

471(4) The entitlement under subsection (2) is to a writing-down allowance except for the final chargeable period when it is to a balancing allowance.

471(5) The final chargeable period for a pool to which qualifying trade expenditure has been allocated is the chargeable period in which the trade is permanently discontinued.

471(6) The final chargeable period for a pool to which qualifying non-trade expenditure has been allocated is the chargeable period in which the last of the patent rights on which the person has incurred qualifying non-trade expenditure–

(a) comes to an end without any of those rights being revived, or

(b) is wholly disposed of.

Origin – S. 471(1): ICTA 1988, s. 520(4) (part), (6) (part).
S. 471(2): ICTA 1988, s. 520(4) (part).
S. 471(3): ICTA 1988, s. 520(6) (part).
S. 471(4), (5): ICTA 1988, s. 520(4) (part).
S. 471(6): ICTA 1988, s. 520(4) (part), (5) (part), Annex 1, Change 56.

Cross references – S. 6: meaning of chargeable period.

Transitional – Sch. 3, para. 92–102: provisions for expenditure incurred before 1 April 1986.

Rewrite: Changes in Law – Explanatory Notes, Annex 1, Change 56: s. 471(6) allows the taxpayer to receive a balancing allowance in the chargeable period in which the last of the patent rights in the pool comes to an end. Previously ICTA 1988, s. 520(4)(c) only entitled the taxpayer to a balancing allowance when the last of the patent rights was sold rather than expired.

HMRC Manuals – CA75110: guidance and examples on s. 470–477.

472 Amount of allowances and charges

472(1) The amount of the writing-down allowance to which a person is entitled for a chargeable period is 25% of the amount by which AQE exceeds TDR.

472(2) If the chargeable period is more or less than a year, the amount is proportionately increased or reduced.

472(3) If in the case of qualifying trade expenditure the trade has been carried on for part only of the chargeable period, the amount is proportionately reduced.

472(4) A person claiming a writing-down allowance may require the allowance to be reduced to a specified amount.

472(5) The amount of the balancing charge to which a person is liable for a chargeable period is the amount by which TDR exceeds AQE.

472(6) The amount of the balancing allowance to which a person is entitled for the final chargeable period is the amount by which AQE exceeds TDR.

Origin – S. 472(1)–(3): ICTA 1988, s. 520(4) (part).
S. 472(4) Annex 1, Change 38.
S. 472(5): ICTA 1988, s. 520(6) (part).
S. 472(6): ICTA 1988, s. 520(4) (part).

Cross references – ICTA 1988, s. 533(1): interpretation of patents and know-how provisions.
FA 1997, Sch. 12, para. 11(3): capital allowances on leased assets.

Rewrite: Changes in Law – Explanatory Notes, Annex 1, Change 38: s. 472(4) brings the law into line with the current practice of allowing the taxpayer to claim any amount of the WDA from zero to the full allowance permitted.

HMRC Manuals – CA75110: guidance and examples on s. 470–477.
CA75120: guidance on s. 472.

473 Available qualifying expenditure

473 A person's available qualifying expenditure in a pool for a chargeable period consists of–

(a) any qualifying expenditure allocated to the pool for that period in accordance with section 474, and

(b) any unrelieved qualifying expenditure carried forward in the pool from the previous chargeable period under section 475.

Origin – ICTA 1988, s. 521(1) (part).

Cross references – S. 6: meaning of chargeable period.
S. 467: qualifying expenditure.

HMRC Manuals – CA75110: guidance and examples on s. 470–477.

474 Allocation of qualifying expenditure to pools

474(1) The following rules apply to the allocation of a person's qualifying expenditure to a pool.

474(2) An amount of qualifying expenditure is not to be allocated to the pool for a chargeable period if that amount has been taken into account in determining the person's available qualifying expenditure for an earlier chargeable period.

474(3) Qualifying expenditure is not to be allocated to the pool for a chargeable period before that in which the expenditure is incurred.

474(4) Qualifying expenditure incurred on patent rights is not to be allocated to the pool for a chargeable period if in any earlier period those rights–

(a) have come to an end without any of them having been revived, or

(b) have been wholly disposed of.

Origin – S. 474(1): drafting.
S. 474(2) to (4): ICTA 1988, s. 520(2) (part), s. 521(1) (part), s. 528(1) (part), Annex 1, Change 54.

Cross references – S. 6: meaning of chargeable period.
S. 467: qualifying expenditure.

FA 1997, Sch. 12, para. 11(3): capital allowances on leased assets.

Rewrite: Changes in Law – Explanatory Notes, Annex 1, Change 54: the taxpayer can allocate all or some of the qualifying expenditure to the pool in the period it was incurred or a later period. This is a relaxation of the law that previously required the taxpayer to allocate all of the qualifying expenditure to the pool in the period it was incurred.

HMRC Manuals – CA75110: guidance and examples on s. 470–477.

475 Unrelieved qualifying expenditure

475(1) A person has unrelieved qualifying expenditure to carry forward from a chargeable period if for that period AQE exceeds TDR.

475(2) The amount of the unrelieved qualifying expenditure is–

(a) the excess less the writing-down allowance made for the period, or

(b) if no writing-down allowance is claimed for the period, the excess.

475(3) No amount may be carried forward as unrelieved qualifying expenditure from the final chargeable period.

Origin – S. 475(1), (2): ICTA 1988, s. 521(1) (part).
S. 475(3): ICTA 1988, s. 520(1) (part), (2) (part), (4) (part), (5) (part), s. 528(1) (part), drafting, Annex 2, Note 60.

Cross references – S. 6: meaning of chargeable period.
S. 468: qualifying trade expenditure.

Rewrite: Technical Points – Explanatory Notes, Annex 2, Note 60: s. 475(3) makes it explicit that no amount in the pool can be carried forward once the trade has ceased.

HMRC Manuals – CA75110: guidance and examples on s. 470–477.

476 Disposal value of patent rights

476(1) In this Chapter **"disposal receipt"** means a disposal value that a person is required to bring into account in accordance with–

(a) this section, or

(b) section 614BS of ITA 2007 or section 918 of CTA 2010 (cases where expenditure taken into account under Part 2, 5 or 8 of this Act) or any other enactment.

476(2) A person is required to bring a disposal value into account for the chargeable period in which he sells the whole or a part of any patent rights on which he has incurred qualifying expenditure.

476(3) Subject to section 477, the disposal value to be brought into account is the net proceeds of the sale, so far as they consist of capital sums.

History – In s. 476(1)(b), the words "section 614BS of ITA 2007" substituted for the words "paragraph 11 of Schedule 12 to FA 1997 (finance lease or loan: receipt of major lump sum)" by TIOPA 2010, s. 374 and Sch. 8, para. 235, with effect for income tax and capital gains tax purposes for the tax year 2010–11 and subsequent tax years.
In s. 476(1)(b), the words "section 918 of CTA 2010 (cases where expenditure taken into account under Part 2, 5 or 8 of this Act) or" inserted by CTA 2010, s. 1177 and Sch. 1, para. 357, with effect for corporation tax purposes for accounting periods ending on or after 1 April 2010.

Origin – S. 476(1): drafting.
S. 476(2): ICTA 1988, s. 521(2) (part).
S. 476(3): ICTA 1988, s. 521(2) (part), Annex 1, Change 55.

Cross references – FA 1997, Sch. 12, para. 11: finance lease or loan: receipt of major lump sum.

Transitional – Sch. 3, para. 92, 97: writing down allowances for patent expenditure incurred before 1 April 1986.

Rewrite: Changes in Law – Explanatory Notes, Annex 1, Change 55: only capital sums received on the sale of patent rights need be brought into the pool as a disposal value. This benefits the taxpayer as sale proceeds often give rise to a trading receipt for tax purposes, see *Jeffrey v Rolls-Royce Ltd* (1962) 40 TC 443.

HMRC Manuals – CA75110: guidance and examples on s. 470–477.
CA75120: guidance and example on s. 476.

477 Limit on amount of disposal value

477(1) The amount of any disposal value, or the total amount of any disposal values, required to be brought into account by a person–

(a) on the sale of the whole of any patent rights, or

(b) on one or more sales of part of any patent rights,

is limited to the capital expenditure incurred by the person on purchasing the rights.

477(2) But subsection (3) applies if the person acquired the rights as a result of–

(a) a transaction which was between connected persons, or

(b) a series of transactions each of which was between connected persons.

477(3) That amount, or total amount, is limited to the capital expenditure on purchasing the rights incurred by whichever party to the transaction, or to any of the transactions, incurred the greatest such expenditure.

Origin – S. 477(1): ICTA 1988, s. 521(3).
S. 477(2), (3): ICTA 1988, s. 521(4) (part).

Cross references – S. 575: meaning of connected persons.

Transitional – Sch. 3, para. 92–102: writing down allowances for patent expenditure incurred before 1 April 1986.
HMRC Manuals – CA75110: guidance and examples on s. 470–477.
CA75120: guidance and example on s. 477.

Chapter 4 – Giving Effect to Allowances and Charges

478 Persons having qualifying trade expenditure

478 An allowance or charge to which a person is entitled or liable under this Part for a chargeable period in respect of qualifying trade expenditure is to be given effect in calculating the profits of the trade, by treating–

(a) the allowance as an expense of the trade, and

(b) the charge as a receipt of the trade.

Origin – ICTA 1988, s. 528(1) (part), s. 532(1) (part), CAA 1990, s. 140(2) (part), s. 144(2) (part), s. 161(5) (part), Annex 2, Note 61.
Cross references – S. 2(3): general means of giving effect to capital allowances.
S. 6: meaning of chargeable period.
Rewrite: Changes in Law – Explanatory Notes, Annex 2, Note 61: this section corrects an apparent drafting omission in CAA 1990, making it clear that allowances for patents acquired as trading expenditure should be given as an expense of the trade.
HMRC Manuals – CA75130: guidance on s. 478–480.

479 Persons having qualifying non-trade expenditure: income tax

479(1) This section applies for income tax purposes if a person is entitled or liable under this Part to an allowance or charge for a chargeable period (**"the current tax year"**) in respect of qualifying non-trade expenditure.

479(2) An allowance is to be given effect by deducting it from or setting it off against the person's income from patents for the current tax year.

479(2A) The allowance is given effect at Step 2 of the calculation in section 23 of ITA 2007.

479(3) If the amount to be deducted from or set off against the person's income from patents for that tax year exceeds the amount of that income, the excess must be deducted from or set off against the person's income from patents for the next tax year, and so on for subsequent tax years.

479(4) A charge is to be given effect by treating the charge as income to be assessed to income tax.

History – S. 479(2A) inserted by ITA 2007, s. 1027 and Sch. 1, para. 408, with effect from 6 April 2007.
In s. 479(4), the words "assessed to income tax" substituted for "taxed under Case VI of Schedule D" by ITTOIA 2005, s. 882(1) and Sch. 1, para. 565; effective for income tax purposes for 2005–06 onwards and for corporation tax purposes for accounting periods ending after 5 April 2005 (ITTOIA 2005, s. 883(1)).
Origin – S. 479: Annex 2, Notes 62, 63.
S. 479(1): ICTA 1988, s. 528(2) (part), (4) (part).
S. 479(2), (3): ICTA 1988, s. 528(2) (part).
S. 479(4): ICTA 1988, s. 528(4) (part).
Cross references – S. 2(3): general means of giving effect to capital allowances.
S. 6: meaning of chargeable period.
S. 469: qualifying non-trade expenditure.
S. 483: meaning of "income from patents".
ICTA 1988, s. 835(8)(c), (as amended by Sch. 2, para. 62): definition of total income.
ICTA 1988, s. 528(3A), (as amended by Sch. 2, para. 46): the manner of making allowances and charges for patents.
Transitional – Sch. 3, para. 101(4): giving effect to allowances and charges for expenditure incurred before 1 April 1986.
Rewrite: Changes in Law – Explanatory Notes, Annex 2, Note 62: words in ICTA 1988, s. 532(1) referring to allowances given "by way of discharge or repayment of tax and to be available or available primarily against a specified class of income", are not reproduced in this Act as it is clear that they are not intended to apply to non-trade patent allowances.
Explanatory Notes, Annex 2, Note 63: the phrases from ICTA 1988 s. 528(2): "and tax shall be discharged or repaid accordingly" and "relief shall be given under this subsection on the making of a claim" are not reproduced in this Act as they are redundant.
HMRC Manuals – CA75130: guidance on s. 478–480.

480 Persons having qualifying non-trade expenditure: corporation tax

480(1) This section applies for corporation tax purposes if a company is entitled or liable under this Part to an allowance or charge for a chargeable period (**"the current accounting period"**) in respect of qualifying non-trade expenditure.

480(2) An allowance is to be given effect by deducting it from the company's income from patents for the current accounting period.

480(3) If the amount to be deducted from the company's income from patents for that period exceeds the amount of that income, the excess must (if the company remains within the charge to tax) be deducted from its income from patents for the next accounting period, and so on for subsequent accounting periods.

480(4) A charge is to be given effect by treating the charge as income of the company from patents.

Origin – S. 480: Annex 2, Note 62.
S. 480(1): ICTA 1988, s. 528(3) (part), (4) (part).

S. 480(2), (3): ICTA 1988, s. 528(3) (part).
S. 480(4): ICTA 1988, s. 528(4) (part).

Cross references – S. 2(3): general means of giving effect to capital allowances.
S. 6: meaning of chargeable period.
S. 469: qualifying non-trade expenditure.
S. 483: meaning of "income from patents".
ICTA 1988, s. 528(3A), (as amended by Sch. 2, para. 46): the manner of making allowances and charges for patents.

Transitional – Sch. 3, para. 101(4): giving effect to allowances and charges for expenditure incurred before 1 April 1986.

Rewrite: Technical Points – Explanatory Notes, Annex 2, Note 62: words in ICTA 1988, s. 532(1) referring to allowances given "by way of discharge or repayment of tax and to be available or available primarily against a specified class of income", are not reproduced in this Act as it is clear that they are not intended to apply to non-trade patent allowances.

HMRC Manuals – CA75130: guidance on s. 478–480.

Chapter 5 – Supplementary Provisions

481 Anti-avoidance: limit on qualifying expenditure

481(1) In the two cases given below, the amount (if any) by which the capital expenditure incurred by a person (**"the buyer"**) on the purchase of patent rights exceeds the relevant limit is to be left out of account in determining the buyer's qualifying expenditure.

481(2) The first case is where the buyer and the seller are connected with each other.

481(3) The second case is where it appears that the sole or main benefit which (but for this section) might have been expected to accrue to the parties from–

(a) the sale, or

(b) transactions of which the sale is one,

was obtaining an allowance under this Part.

481(4) If the seller is required to bring a disposal value into account under this Part because of the sale, the relevant limit is that disposal value.

481(5) If subsection (4) does not apply but the seller–

(a) receives a capital sum on the sale, and

(b) is chargeable to tax in respect of that sum in accordance with section 587 of ITTOIA 2005 or section 912 of CTA 2009,

the relevant limit is that sum.

481(6) If neither subsection (4) nor subsection (5) applies, the relevant limit is whichever of the following is the smallest–

(a) the market value of the rights;

(b) if the seller incurred capital expenditure on acquiring the rights, the amount of that expenditure;

(c) if a person connected with the seller incurred capital expenditure on acquiring the rights, the amount of that expenditure.

History – In s. 481(5)(b), the words "section 912 of CTA 2009" substituted for the words "section 524 of ICTA" by CTA 2009, s. 1322 and Sch. 1, para. 512, with effect for corporation tax purposes for accounting periods ending on or after 1 April 2009, and for income tax and capital gains tax purposes for the tax year 2009–10 and subsequent tax years.
S. 481(5)(b) amended by ITTOIA 2005, s. 882(1) and Sch. 1, para. 566; effective for income tax purposes for 2005–06 onwards and for corporation tax purposes for accounting periods ending after 5 April 2005 (ITTOIA 2005, s. 883(1)).

Origin – S. 481(1)–(3): ICTA 1988, s. 521(5).
S. 481(4)–(6): ICTA 1988, s. 521(6) (part).

Cross references – S. 4: meaning of capital sum and capital expenditure.
S. 467: qualifying expenditure.
S. 577(1): meaning of market value.
S. 575: connected persons.
ICTA 1988, s. 524: taxation of receipts from sale of patent rights.

Transitional – Sch. 3, para. 102: this section does not apply to expenditure incurred before 1 April 1986 and s. 481(5) and (6) do not apply to expenditure incurred before 27 July 1989.

HMRC Manuals – CA75100: guidance on s. 481.

482 Sums paid for Crown use etc. treated as paid under licence

482(1) This section applies if an invention which is the subject of a patent is used by or for the services of–

(a) the Crown under sections 55 to 59 of the Patents Act 1977, or

(b) the government of a country outside the United Kingdom under corresponding provisions of the law of that country.

482(2) The use is to be treated as having taken place under a licence.

482(3) Sums paid in respect of the use are to be treated as having been paid under a licence.

CAA 2001

Origin – ICTA 1988, s. 533(4) (part).

Cross references – Patents Act 1949, s. 46–49; Patents Act 1977, s. 55–59: circumstances in which the government may exploit patented inventions.

HMRC Manuals – CA75030: guidance on s. 482.

483 Meaning of "income from patents"

483 For the purposes of this Part a person's **"income from patents"** means–

(a) royalties or other sums paid in respect of the use of a patent,

(b) balancing charges to which the person is liable under this Part, and

(c) amounts on which tax is payable under section 587, 593 or 594 of ITTOIA 2005 or under section 912 or 918 of CTA 2009 (taxation of receipts from sale of patent rights).

History – In s. 483(c), the words "section 912 or 918 of CTA 2009" substituted for the words "section 524 or 525 of ICTA" by CTA 2009, s. 1322 and Sch. 1, para. 513, with effect for corporation tax purposes for accounting periods ending on or after 1 April 2009, and for income tax and capital gains tax purposes for the tax year 2009–10 and subsequent tax years.
S. 483(c) amended by ITTOIA 2005, s. 882(1) and Sch. 1, para. 567; effective for income tax purposes for 2005–06 onwards and for corporation tax purposes for accounting periods ending after 5 April 2005 (ITTOIA 2005, s. 883(1)).

Origin – ICTA 1988, s. 533(1) ("income from patents").

Cross references – ICTA 1988, s. 524: taxation of receipts from sale of patent rights.
ICTA 1988, s. 525: charge on winding up of partnership.

HMRC Manuals – CA 75010: meaning of "patent".

PART 9 – DREDGING ALLOWANCES

Cross references – S. 532(3): general rule for excluding contributions does not apply for this part.
S. 533(1): exclusion of contributions to dredging.
S. 543: contributions allowances as they apply to this part.
S. 564(1): procedure to determine questions arising form this part.

QUALIFYING EXPENDITURE ON DREDGING, ETC.

484 Dredging allowances

484(1) Allowances are available under this Part if a person carries on a qualifying trade and qualifying expenditure has been incurred on dredging.

484(2) In this Part **"qualifying trade"** means a trade or undertaking the whole or part of which–

(a) consists of the maintenance or improvement of the navigation of a harbour, estuary or waterway, or

(b) is of a kind listed in Table A or B in section 274 (meaning of qualifying trade for purposes of industrial buildings allowances).

484(3) **"Dredging"** does not include anything done otherwise than in the interests of navigation.

484(4) Subject to subsection (3), **"dredging"** includes–

(a) the removal of anything forming part of, or projecting from the bed of, the sea or any inland water–

  (i) by whatever means it is removed, and

  (ii) even if, at the time of removal, it is wholly or partly above water, and

(b) the widening of an inland waterway.

Prospective amendments – S. 484(2A) inserted by CTNIA 2015, s. 2 and Sch. 1, para. 16, with effect from 26 March 2015 (Royal Assent) in respect of any power to make regulations and with effect in relation to accounting periods beginning on or after the first day of the appointed financial year for other provisions (see CTNIA 2015, s. 5). See also transitional provisions at Sch. 1, para. 19–21.

Origin – S. 484(1): drafting.
S. 484(2): CAA 1990, s. 135(1) (part).
S. 484(3), (4): CAA 1990, s. 135(3).

Cross references – S. 274: meaning of qualifying trade.

HMRC Manuals – CA11700: whether expenditure has been "incurred", etc.
CA31800: guidance on prevention of double allowances.
CA80100: outline of dredging allowances.
CA80200: guidance on meaning of "dredging".
CA80300: guidance on meaning of "qualifying trades".
CA80400: guidance on dredging of marinas.

485 Qualifying expenditure

485(1) Expenditure on dredging is qualifying expenditure if–

(a) it is capital expenditure,

(b) it is incurred for the purposes of a qualifying trade by the person carrying on the trade, and

(c) if the person does not carry on a qualifying trade within section 484(2)(a), the dredging is for the benefit of vessels coming to, leaving or using a dock or other premises occupied by the person for the purposes of the qualifying trade.

485(2) If capital expenditure is incurred–

(a) partly for the purposes of a qualifying trade, and

(b) partly for other purposes,

the qualifying expenditure is the part of the capital expenditure that, on a just and reasonable apportionment, is referable to the purposes of the qualifying trade.

485(3) If part only of a trade or undertaking is within section 484(2), subsection (2) of this section applies as if–

(a) the part which is within section 484(2), and

(b) the part which is not,

were separate trades.

Origin – S. 485(1): CAA 1990, s. 134(1) (part).
S. 485(2): CAA 1990, s. 134(6), Annex 1, Change 40.
S. 485(3): CAA 1990, s. 135(1) (part).

Cross references – S. 4: meaning of capital expenditure.
S. 274: meaning of qualifying trade.

Rewrite: Changes in Law – Explanatory Notes, Annex 1, Change 40: words "and reasonable" included to make the wording consistent with other provisions of this Act.

HMRC Manuals – CA80500: guidance on s. 485.

486 Pre-trading expenditure of qualifying trades, etc.

486(1) If a person incurs capital expenditure with a view to carrying on a trade or a part of a trade, this Part applies as if the expenditure were incurred by the person on the first day on which the trade or part of the trade is carried on.

486(2) If a person incurs capital expenditure–

(a) in connection with a dock or other premises, and

(b) with a view to occupying the dock or premises for the purposes of a qualifying trade which is not a qualifying trade within section 484(2)(a),

this Part applies as if the expenditure were incurred by the person when he first occupies the dock or premises for the purposes of the qualifying trade.

Origin – S. 486(1): CAA 1990, s. 134(7) (part), s. 135(2) (part), Annex 1, Change 57.
S. 486(2): CAA 1990, s. 134(7) (part), s. 135(2).

Rewrite: Changes in Law – Explanatory Notes, Annex 1, Change 57: former CAA 1990 s. 135(2)(b) permitted the allowance to be claimed in a trade qualifying for IBAs without the requirement to occupy the waterway. This section requires occupation of the waterway for both types of trade which qualify for the allowance.

HMRC Manuals – CA80600: guidance on s. 486.

WRITING-DOWN AND BALANCING ALLOWANCES

487 Writing-down allowances

487(1) A person is entitled to a writing-down allowance for a chargeable period if–

(a) qualifying expenditure has been incurred on dredging,

(b) at any time during the chargeable period, the person is carrying on the qualifying trade for the purposes of which the qualifying expenditure was incurred, and

(c) that time falls within the writing-down period.

487(2) The writing-down period, in relation to qualifying expenditure incurred by a person, is 25 years beginning with the first day of the chargeable period of that person in which the qualifying expenditure was incurred.

487(3) The amount of the writing-down allowance is 4% of the qualifying expenditure.

487(4) The allowance is proportionately increased or reduced if the chargeable period is more or less than a year.

487(5) The total amount of any writing-down allowances made in respect of any qualifying expenditure, whether to the same or different persons, must not exceed the amount of the expenditure.

487(6) A person claiming a writing-down allowance may require the allowance to be reduced to a specified amount.

487(7) A person is not entitled to a writing-down allowance for the chargeable period in which a balancing allowance is made to him in respect of the qualifying expenditure.

Origin – S. 487(1), (2): CAA 1990, s. 134(1) (part).
S. 487(3): CAA 1990, s. 134(1) (part), s. 146(1) (part), (2) (part).
S. 487(4): CAA 1990, s. 146(1) (part), (2) (part).
S. 487(5): CAA 1990, s. 146(1) (part), (3) (part).
S. 487(6) Annex 1, Change 38.
S. 487(7) Annex 2, Note 64.

Cross references – S. 6: meaning of chargeable period.

Transitional – Sch. 3, para. 103: in s. 487(2) and (3) the period of 50 years and the rate of 2 per cent apply respectively in the case of expenditure incurred before 6 November 1962.
Sch. 3, para. 105: length of writing-down period where allowances were made under FA 1965, Sch. 14, para. 27(2) for 1964–65, or 1985–66, or for accounting periods of a company falling wholly or partly with either of those years.

Rewrite: Changes in Law – Explanatory Notes, Annex 1, Change 38: s. 487(6) brings the law into line with the current practice of allowing the taxpayer to claim any amount of the WDA from zero to the full allowance permitted.

Rewrite: Technical Points – Explanatory Notes, Annex 2, Note 64: s. 487(7) prevents a WDA in the same period as a BA, former CAA 1990, s. 134(2) permitted this but the total allowances given is the same.

HMRC Manuals – CA80700: disapplication of normal contributions, etc. rules.
CA81100: guidance and example on s. 487(2).
CA81300: guidance and example on s. 487(3), (4).
CA81400: guidance on s. 487(6).
CA81500: guidance on s. 487(5).

488 Balancing allowances

488(1) A person is entitled to a balancing allowance for a chargeable period if–

(a) qualifying expenditure has been incurred on dredging,

(b) in that chargeable period, the qualifying trade for the purposes of which the expenditure was incurred has been–

  (i) permanently discontinued, or

  (ii) sold,

(c) the person is the last person carrying on the qualifying trade before its discontinuance or sale, and

(d) the amount of the expenditure exceeds the amount of the allowances previously made in respect of it, whether to the same or different persons.

488(2) The amount of the balancing allowance is the amount of the difference.

488(3) For the purposes of subsection (1)–

(a) the permanent discontinuance of a trade does not include an event treated as a permanent discontinuance under section 577(2A) of this Act or section 18 of ITTOIA 2005 (effect of company ceasing to trade etc.), and

(b) a sale does not include a sale which is within subsection (4) or (5).

488(4) A sale is within this subsection if any of the following conditions is met–

(a) the buyer is a body of persons over whom the seller has control;

(b) the seller is a body of persons over whom the buyer has control;

(c) both the seller and the buyer are bodies of persons and another person has control over both of them;

(d) the seller and the buyer are connected persons.

In this subsection **"body of persons"** includes a partnership.

488(5) A sale is within this subsection if it appears that the sole or main benefit which might be expected to accrue to the parties, or any of them, from–

(a) the sale, or

(b) transactions of which the sale is one,

is the obtaining of a tax advantage under any of the provisions of this Act apart from Part 2 (plant and machinery allowances).

History – In s. 488(3)(a), the words "section 577(2A) of this Act or section 18 of ITTOIA 2005" substituted for the words "section 18 of ITTOIA or section 337(1) of ICTA" by CTA 2009, s. 1322 and Sch. 1, para. 514, with effect for corporation tax purposes for accounting periods ending on or after 1 April 2009, and for income tax and capital gains tax purposes for the tax year 2009–10 and subsequent tax years.
S. 488(3)(a) amended by ITTOIA 2005, s. 882(1) and Sch. 1, para. 568; effective for income tax purposes for 2005–06 onwards and for corporation tax purposes for accounting periods ending after 5 April 2005 (ITTOIA 2005, s. 883(1)).

Origin – S. 488: Annex 2, Note 64.
S. 488(1): CAA 1990, s. 134(2) (part), s. 134(4) (part).
S. 488(2): CAA 1990, s. 134(2) (part).
S. 488(3)–(5): CAA 1990, s. 134(4) (part).

Cross references – S. 6: meaning of chargeable period.
Pt. 2: plant and machinery allowances.
ICTA 1988, s. 113: change in persons carrying on a trade.
ICTA 1988, s. 337(1): effect of company ceasing to trade.

Transitional – Sch. 3, para. 104: meaning of reference in s. 488(1) to allowances previously made in respect of the expenditure.

Rewrite: Technical Points – Explanatory Notes, Annex 2, Note 64: s. 487(7) prevents a WDA in the same period as a BA, former CAA 1990, s. 134(2) permitted this but the total allowances given is the same.

HMRC Manuals – CA81600: guidance on s. 488.

GIVING EFFECT TO ALLOWANCES

489 Giving effect to allowances

489 An allowance to which a person is entitled under this Part is to be given effect in calculating the profits of that person's trade, by treating the allowance as an expense of the trade.

Prospective amendments – The existing provision made s. 489(1) and s. 489(2) inserted by CTNIA 2015, s. 2 and Sch. 1, para. 17, with effect from 26 March 2015 (Royal Assent) in respect of any power to make regulations and with effect in relation to accounting periods beginning on or after the first day of the appointed financial year for other provisions (see CTNIA 2015, s. 5). See also transitional provisions at Sch. 1, para. 19–21.

Origin – CAA 1990, s. 134(5), s. 140(2) (part), s. 144(2) (part), s. 161(5) (part).

Cross references – S. 2(3): general means of giving effect to capital allowances.

PART 10 – ASSURED TENANCY ALLOWANCES

Cross references – S. 557(c): s. 558 and 559 do not apply for this Part.
S. 564(1): procedure to determine questions arising from this Part.
S. 567(1): s. 568–570 apply for this Part.
S. 569(3)(a), (5): determination of the alternative amount.
S. 573(1): "transfers treated as sales" applies for this Part.
ICTA 1988, s. 411(10)(b), (as amended by Sch. 2, para. 38): exclusion of double allowances
TCGA 1992, s. 37(2)(a), (as amended by Sch. 2, para. 77): consideration chargeable to tax on income.

CAA 2001

Chapter 1 – Introduction

490 Assured tenancy allowances

490(1) Allowances are available under this Part if qualifying expenditure has been incurred on a building which consists of or includes a qualifying dwelling-house.

490(2) A dwelling house is not a qualifying dwelling-house unless–

(a) it is let on a tenancy which is for the time being an assured tenancy, or

(b) it has been let on an assured tenancy and the conditions in subsection (4) are met.

490(3) **"Assured tenancy"** means–

(a) an assured tenancy within the meaning of section 56 of the Housing Act 1980, or

(b) an assured tenancy (but not an assured shorthold tenancy) for the purposes of the Housing Act 1988.

490(4) The conditions referred to in subsection (2)(b) are that–

(a) the dwelling-house is for the time being subject to a regulated tenancy or a housing association tenancy, and

(b) the landlord under the tenancy is an approved body or was an approved body but has ceased to be such for any reason.

490(5) In subsection (4) **"regulated tenancy"** and **"housing association tenancy"** have the same meaning as in the Rent Act 1977.

490(6) Further requirements that have to be met for a dwelling-house to be a qualifying dwelling-house are given in sections 504 and 505; and subsection (2) is subject to section section 506(2)(b) (temporary disuse of dwelling-house ignored).

Origin – S. 490(1): CAA 1990, s. 84(1) (part).
S. 490(2): CAA 1990, s. 86(1), (2) (part).
S. 490(3): CAA 1990, s. 97(1) ("assured tenancy").
S. 490(4): CAA 1990, s. 86(2) (part).
S. 490(5): CAA 1990, s. 86(4).
S. 490(6): drafting.

Cross references – S. 504: requirements for landlord to qualify.
S. 505: exclusions from definition of qualifying dwelling house.
S. 506: temporary disuse of dwelling house.
Rent Act 1977, s. 18(1): definition of regulated tenancy.
Rent Act 1977, s. 86(1): definition of housing association tenancy.
Housing Act 1980, s. 56: definition of assured tenancy rather than a housing association tenancy.
Housing Act 1988, s. 1(1): definition of assured tenancy, and not a short hold tenancy.

HMRC Manuals – CA11540: transfers treated as sales.
CA11700: whether expenditure has been "incurred", etc.
CA13100ff.: sales treated as being at market value, etc.
CA31800: guidance on prevention of double allowances.
CA85200: background, etc. to assured tenancy allowances.
CA85400: guidance on meaning of "qualifying dwelling-house".

491 Allowances available in relation to old expenditure only

491(1) Allowances under this Part are not available unless–

(a) the qualifying expenditure was incurred after 9th March 1982 and before 1st April 1992, and

(b) if the tenancy is an assured tenancy for the purposes of the Housing Act 1988, expenditure has been incurred which is within subsection (2) or (3).

491(2) Expenditure is within this subsection if it was incurred by–

(a) a company which was an approved body on 15th March 1988, or

(b) a person who sold the relevant interest in the building, before any of the dwelling-houses comprised in it were used, to a company which was an approved body on 15th March 1988,

and either it was incurred before 15th March 1988 or it consists of the payment of sums under a contract entered into before that date.

491(3) Expenditure is within this subsection if it was incurred by a company which–

(a) was an approved body on 15th March 1988, and

(b) bought or contracted to buy the relevant interest in the building before that date.

Origin – S. 491(1): CAA 1990, s. 84(1) (part), (2) (part), s. 96(3).
S. 491(2), (3): CAA 1990, s. 84(2) (part), (3).

Cross references – Housing Act 1988, s. 1(1): definition of assured tenancy.

HMRC Manuals – CA85300: guidance on s. 491.

492 Meaning of "approved body"

492 In this Part **"approved body"** has the meaning given in section 56(4) of the Housing Act 1980.

Origin – CAA 1990, s. 97(1) ("approved body").

Cross references – Housing Act 1980, s. 56(4): definition of approved body.

HMRC Manuals – CA85350: guidance on s. 492.

493 Expenditure on the construction of a building

493(1) For the purposes of this Part, expenditure on the construction of a building does not include expenditure on the acquisition of land or rights in or over land.

493(2) This Part has effect in relation to capital expenditure incurred by a person on repairs to a part of a building as if it were capital expenditure on the construction of that part of the building for the first time.

Origin – S. 493(1): CAA 1990, s. 97(2).
S. 493(2): CAA 1990, s. 93(1).

HMRC Manuals – CA85200: background, etc. to assured tenancy allowances.
Capital Allowances, CA85250: guidance on s. 493.

Chapter 2 – The Relevant Interest

INTRODUCTION

494 Introduction

494 This Chapter identifies, in a case where a person has incurred expenditure on the construction of a building which is to be or include a qualifying dwelling-house–

(a) the relevant interest in the building, and

(b) the relevant interest in a dwelling-house comprised in the building.

Origin – S. 494: drafting.

THE RELEVANT INTEREST IN THE BUILDING

495 General rule as to what is the relevant interest in the building

495(1) The relevant interest in the building is the interest in the building to which the person who incurred the expenditure on the construction of the building was entitled when the expenditure was incurred.

495(2) Subsection (1) is subject to the following provisions of this Chapter.

495(3) If–

(a) the person who incurred the expenditure on the construction of the building was entitled to more than one interest in the building when the expenditure was incurred, and

(b) one of those interests was reversionary on all the others,

the reversionary interest is the relevant interest.

Origin – S. 495(1), (2): CAA 1990, s. 95(1) (part).
S. 495(3): CAA 1990, s. 95(2).
HMRC Manuals – CA85500: guidance on s. 495.

496 Interest acquired on completion of construction

496 For the purpose of determining the relevant interest, a person who–

(a) incurs expenditure on the construction of a building, and

(b) is entitled to an interest in the building on or as a result of the completion of the construction,

is treated as having had that interest when the expenditure was incurred.

Origin – CAA 1990, s. 97(3), Annex 1, Change 34.

Rewrite: Changes in Law – Explanatory Notes, Annex 1, Change 34: former CAA 1990, s. 97(3) was applied even if there was a short delay between completion of the building and the granting of an interest (e.g. a lease). This provision codifies that informal concession to allow Assured Tenancy Allowances to be claimed by the person who is entitled to an interest in the building as a result of its completion (i.e. the delay is not relevant).

497 Effect of creation of subordinate interest

497 An interest does not cease to be the relevant interest merely because of the creation of a lease or other interest to which that interest is subject.

Origin – CAA 1990, s. 95(3) (part).

498 Merger of leasehold interest

498 If the relevant interest is a leasehold interest which is extinguished on–

(a) being surrendered, or

(b) the person entitled to it acquiring the interest which is reversionary on it,

the interest into which the leasehold interest merges becomes the relevant interest when the leasehold interest is extinguished.

Origin – CAA 1990, s. 95(3) (part).

499 Provisions applying on termination of lease

499(1) This section applies if the relevant interest in relation to expenditure on the construction of a building is a lease.

499(2) If, with the consent of the lessor, the lessee of a building remains in possession after the termination of the lease without a new lease being granted to him, the lease is treated as continuing as long as the lessee remains in possession.

499(3) If on the termination of the lease a new lease is granted to the lessee as a result of the exercise of an option available to him under the terms of the first lease, the second lease is treated as a continuation of the first.

499(4) If on the termination of the lease the lessor pays a sum to the lessee in respect of a building comprised in the lease, the lease is treated as if it had come to an end by surrender in consideration of the payment.

499(5) If on the termination of the lease–

(a) a new lease is granted to a different lessee, and

(b) in connection with the transaction that lessee makes a payment to the former lessee,

the two leases are treated as if they were the same lease which had been assigned by the former lessee to the new lessee in consideration of the payment.

Origin – S. 499(1): CAA 1990, s. 94(1), drafting.
S. 499(2): CAA 1990, s. 94(2).
S. 499(3): CAA 1990, s. 94(3).
S. 499(4): CAA 1990, s. 94(4).
S. 499(5): CAA 1990, s. 94(5).

Cross references – S. 514(a): balancing events.
S. 572(1)(b): sale of property and time of sale.

THE RELEVANT INTEREST IN THE DWELLING-HOUSE

500 The relevant interest in the dwelling-house

500 The relevant interest in a dwelling-house comprised in a building is the relevant interest in the building, to the extent that it subsists in the dwelling-house.

Origin – CAA 1990, s. 95(1) (part).
HMRC Manuals – CA85500: guidance on s. 500.

Chapter 3 – Qualifying Expenditure

501 Capital expenditure on construction

501 If–

(a) capital expenditure has been incurred on the construction of a building which was to be or include a qualifying dwelling-house, and

(b) the relevant interest in the building has not been sold or, if it has been sold, it has been sold only after the first use of the building,

the capital expenditure is qualifying expenditure.

Origin – CAA 1990, s. 85(1) (part), (2) (part), s. 87(1) (part).
Cross references – S. 4: meaning of capital expenditure.
HMRC Manuals – CA85250: guidance on s. 501.

502 Purchase of unused dwelling-house where developer not involved

502(1) This section applies if–

(a) expenditure has been incurred on the construction of a building which was to be or include a qualifying dwelling-house,

(b) the relevant interest was sold before the first use of any dwelling-house comprised in the building,

(c) a capital sum was paid by the purchaser for the relevant interest, and

(d) section 503 (purchase of dwelling-house sold unused by developer) does not apply.

502(2) The lesser of–

(a) the capital sum paid by the purchaser for the relevant interest, and

(b) the expenditure incurred on the construction of the building,

is qualifying expenditure.

502(3) The qualifying expenditure is to be treated as having been incurred when the capital sum became payable.

502(4) If the relevant interest was sold more than once before the first use of any dwelling-house comprised in the building, subsection (2) has effect only in relation to the last of those sales.

Origin – S. 502(1)–(3): CAA 1990, s. 91(1) (part), Annex 2, Note 65.
S. 502(4): CAA 1990, s. 91(2) (part).
Rewrite: Technical Points – Explanatory Notes, Annex 2, Note 65: correction of drafting error in former CAA 1990, s. 91(1), so s. 511 (attributable expenditure) will apply to expenditure defined by this section.
HMRC Manuals – CA85250: guidance on s. 502.

503 Purchase of dwelling-house sold unused by developer

503(1) This section applies if–

(a) expenditure has been incurred by a developer on the construction of a building which was to be or include a qualifying dwelling-house, and

(b) the relevant interest was sold by the developer in the course of the development trade before the first use of any dwelling-house comprised in the building.

503(2) If–

(a) the sale of the relevant interest by the developer was the only sale of that interest before the first use of any dwelling-house comprised in the building, and

(b) a capital sum was paid by the purchaser for the relevant interest,

the capital sum is qualifying expenditure.

503(3) If–

(a) the sale by the developer was not the only sale before the first use of any dwelling-house comprised in the building, and

(b) a capital sum was paid by the purchaser for the relevant interest on the last sale,

the lesser of that capital sum and the price paid for the relevant interest on its sale by the developer is qualifying expenditure.

503(4) The qualifying expenditure is treated as having been incurred when the capital sum referred to in subsection (2)(b) or (3)(b) became payable.

503(5) For the purposes of this section–

(a) a developer is a person who carries on a trade which consists in whole or in part in the construction of buildings with a view to their sale, and

(b) an interest in a building is sold by the developer in the course of the development trade if the developer sells it in the course of the trade or (as the case may be) that part of the trade that consists in the construction of buildings with a view to their sale.

Origin – S. 503(1)–(4): CAA 1990, s. 91(1) (part), (3) (part), Annex 2, Note 65.
S. 503(5): CAA 1990, s. 91(3) (part).

Rewrite: Technical Points – Explanatory Notes, Annex 2, Note 65: correction of drafting error in former CAA 1990, s. 91(1), so s. 511 (attributable expenditure) will apply to expenditure defined by this section.

HMRC Manuals – CA85250: guidance on s. 503.

Chapter 4 – Qualifying Dwelling-houses

504 Requirements relating to the landlord

504(1) A dwelling-house is a qualifying dwelling-house only if the landlord is–

(a) a company, and

(b) the person who–

(i) incurred the qualifying expenditure on the building in which the dwelling-house is comprised, or

(ii) is for the time being entitled to the relevant interest in the dwelling-house.

504(2) The requirement that the landlord must be a company does not apply in relation to expenditure incurred–

(a) before 5th May 1983, or

(b) on or after that date pursuant to a contract entered into before that date,

unless a person other than a company became entitled to the relevant interest on or after that date.

Origin – S. 504(1): CAA 1990, s. 86(3) (part).
S. 504(2): CAA 1990, s. 86(5).

Cross references – S. 490(6): requirements for assured tenancy allowances.

HMRC Manuals – CA85400: guidance on qualifying dwelling-houses.

505 Qualifying dwelling-houses: exclusions

505(1) A dwelling-house is not a qualifying dwelling-house if any of the exclusions given below apply.

Exclusion 1

The landlord under the tenancy is–

(a) a housing association which is approved for the purposes of Chapter 7 of Part 13 of CTA 2010, or

(b) a self-build society within the meaning of the Housing Associations Act 1985.

Exclusion 2

The landlord and the tenant are connected persons.

Exclusion 3

The tenant is a director of a company which is or is connected with the landlord.

Exclusion 4

The landlord is a close company and the tenant is, for the purposes of Part XI of ICTA–

(a) a participator in that company, or

(b) an associate of such a participator.

Exclusion 5

The tenancy is entered into as part of a mutual arrangement for avoidance.

505(2) In exclusion 5, a **"mutual arrangement for avoidance"** means an arrangement–

(a) between the landlords (or owners) of different dwelling-houses, and

(b) under which one landlord takes a person as a tenant in circumstances in which, if that person was the tenant of a dwelling-house let by the other landlord, that dwelling-house would not be a qualifying dwelling-house because of exclusion 2, 3 or 4.

History – In s. 505(1), in paragraph (a) of exclusion 1, the words "Chapter 7 of Part 13 of CTA 2010" substituted for "section 488 of ICTA" by CTA 2010, s. 1177 and Sch. 1, para. 358, with effect for corporation tax purposes for accounting periods ending on or after 1 April 2010, and for income tax and capital gains tax purposes for the tax year 2010–11 and subsequent tax years.

Origin – S. 505(1), (2): CAA 1990, s. 86(3) (part).

Cross references – S. 490(6): requirements for assured tenancy allowances.
ICTA 1988, s. 488: co-operative housing associations.

HMRC Manuals – CA85400: guidance on qualifying dwelling-houses.

506 Dwelling-house ceasing to be qualifying dwelling-house

506(1) If a dwelling-house ceases to be a qualifying dwelling-house otherwise than on a sale of the relevant interest in the dwelling-house, this Part has effect as if–

(a) the relevant interest in the dwelling-house had been sold at that time, and

(b) the net proceeds of the sale were equal to the market value of that interest at that time.

506(2) For the purposes of this Part–

(a) a dwelling-house is not to be regarded as ceasing altogether to be used merely because it falls temporarily out of use, and

(b) if, immediately before any period of temporary disuse, a dwelling-house is a qualifying dwelling-house, it is to be regarded as continuing to be a qualifying dwelling-house during the period of temporary disuse.

Origin – S. 506(1): CAA 1990, s. 89(1).
S. 506(2): CAA 1990, s. 89(2).

Cross references – S. 490(6): requirements for assured tenancy allowances.

HMRC Manuals – CA85400: guidance on qualifying dwelling-houses.

Chapter 5 – Writing-down Allowances

ENTITLEMENT TO AND CALCULATION OF WRITING-DOWN ALLOWANCES

507 Entitlement to writing-down allowance

507(1) A person is entitled to a writing-down allowance for a chargeable period if–

(a) qualifying expenditure has been incurred on a building,

(b) that person is or has been an approved body,

(c) at the end of that chargeable period the person is entitled to the relevant interest in the building, and

(d) at the end of that chargeable period, the building is or includes a qualifying dwelling-house or two or more qualifying dwelling-houses.

507(2) A person claiming a writing-down allowance may require the allowance to be reduced to a specified amount.

Origin – S. 507(1): CAA 1990, s. 85(1) (part).
S. 507(2) Annex 1, Change 38.

Rewrite: Changes in Law – Explanatory Notes, Annex 1, Change 38: s. 507(2) brings the law into line with the current practice of allowing the taxpayer to claim any amount of the WDA from zero to the full allowance permitted.

HMRC Manuals – CA86000: guidance on s. 507–510.

508 Basic rule for calculating amount of allowance

508(1) The basic rule is that the writing-down allowance for a chargeable period is 4% of the qualifying expenditure attributable to the dwelling-house or (as the case may be) each dwelling-house falling within section 507(1)(d).

508(2) The allowance is proportionately increased or reduced if the chargeable period is more or less than a year.

508(3) The basic rule does not apply if section 509 applies.

Origin – S. 508(1), (2): CAA 1990, s. 85(2) (part).
S. 508(3) drafting.

HMRC Manuals – CA86000: guidance on s. 507–510.

509 Calculation of allowance after sale of relevant interest

509(1) This section applies if–

(a) the relevant interest in a qualifying dwelling-house is sold, and

(b) a balancing adjustment falls to be made under section 513 as a result of the sale.

509(2) If this section applies, the writing-down allowance for any chargeable period ending after the sale is–

$$RQE \times \frac{A}{B}$$

where–

RQE is the amount of the residue of qualifying expenditure attributable to the dwelling-house immediately after the sale,

A is the length of the chargeable period, and

B is the length of the period from the date of the sale to the end of the period of 25 years beginning with the day on which the dwelling-house was first used.

509(3) On any later such sale, the writing-down allowance is further adjusted in accordance with this section.

Origin – S. 509(1)–(3): CAA 1990, s. 85(3), Annex 2, Note 66.

Rewrite: Technical Points – Explanatory Notes, Annex 2, Note 66: correction of drafting error in former CAA 1990, s. 85(3) which referred to the date the building was first used rather then when the dwelling house was first used.

HMRC Manuals – CA86000: guidance on s. 507–510.

510 Allowance limited to residue of qualifying expenditure attributable to dwelling-house

510(1) The amount of the writing-down allowance for a chargeable period in respect of a dwelling-house is limited to the residue of qualifying expenditure attributable to it.

510(2) For this purpose the residue is ascertained immediately before writing off the writing-down allowance at the end of the chargeable period.

Origin – S. 510(1), (2): CAA 1990, s. 85(4).

HMRC Manuals – CA86000: guidance on s. 507–510.

INTERPRETATION

511 Qualifying expenditure attributable to dwelling-house

511(1) If the building concerned consists of a single qualifying dwelling-house, then, subject to the relevant limit, the whole of the qualifying expenditure is attributable to the dwelling-house.

511(2) If the qualifying dwelling-house forms part of a building, the qualifying expenditure attributable to the dwelling-house is, subject to the relevant limit, the total of–

(a) the part of the qualifying expenditure properly attributable to that dwelling-house, and

(b) if there are common parts of the building, such part of the qualifying expenditure on those common parts–

(i) as it is just and reasonable to attribute to that dwelling-house, and

(ii) as does not exceed 10% of the part referred to in paragraph (a).

511(3) In this section **"the relevant limit"** means–

(a) £60,000, if the dwelling-house is in Greater London, and

(b) £40,000, if the dwelling-house is elsewhere.

511(4) In subsection (2) **"common parts"**, in relation to a building, means common parts of the building which–

(a) are not intended to be in separate occupation (whether for domestic, commercial or other purposes), but

(b) are intended to be of benefit to some or all of the qualifying dwelling-houses included in the building.

511(5) For the purposes of subsection (2), the qualifying expenditure on any common parts of a building is so much of the expenditure on the construction of the building as it is just and reasonable to attribute to those parts.

Origin – S. 511(1)–(3): CAA 1990, s. 96(1).
S. 511(4), (5): CAA 1990, s. 96(2).

Cross references – ICTA 1988, Sch. 24, para. 11A(4), (as amended by Sch. 2, para. 66(3)(b)): assumptions for calculating chargeable profits, creditable tax and corresponding UK tax of foreign companies. It is assumed that any sterling sum mentioned in s. 511 is the equivalent, expressed in the relevant foreign currency, of the amount expressed in sterling.

HMRC Manuals – CA85450: guidance on s. 511.

512 Residue of qualifying expenditure attributable to dwelling-house

512(1) The residue of qualifying expenditure attributable to a dwelling-house is the qualifying expenditure attributable to that dwelling-house that has not yet been written off in accordance with Chapter 7.

512(2) Subsection (1) is subject to section 528 (treatment of demolition costs).

Origin – S. 512(1): CAA 1990, s. 90(1) (part), drafting.
S. 512(2): drafting.

Cross references – S. 528: treatment of demolition costs.
S. 570A: avoidance affecting proceeds of balancing event. Residue calculated as if balancing allowance made.

Chapter 6 – Balancing Adjustments

GENERAL

513 When balancing adjustments are made

513(1) A balancing adjustment is made if–

(a) qualifying expenditure has been incurred on a building, and

(b) a balancing event occurs in relation to a dwelling-house comprised in the building while it is a qualifying dwelling-house.

513(2) A balancing adjustment is either a balancing allowance or a balancing charge and is made for the chargeable period in which the balancing event occurs.

513(3) A balancing allowance or balancing charge is made to or on the person entitled to the relevant interest in the dwelling-house immediately before the balancing event.

513(4) No balancing adjustment is made if the balancing event occurs more than 25 years after the dwelling-house was first used.

Origin – S. 512(1): CAA 1990, s. 90(1) (part), drafting.
S. 512(2): drafting.

Cross references – S. 570A: avoidance affecting proceeds of balancing event.

HMRC Manuals – CA86500: guidance on s. 513–515.

514 Balancing events

514 The following are balancing events in relation to a qualifying dwelling-house–

(a) the relevant interest in the dwelling-house is sold;

(b) if the relevant interest in the dwelling-house is a lease, the lease ends otherwise than on the person entitled to it acquiring the interest reversionary on it;

(c) the dwelling-house is demolished or destroyed;

(d) the dwelling-house ceases altogether to be used (without being demolished or destroyed).

Origin – CAA 1990, s. 87(1) (part).

Cross references – S. 495: general rule as to what is the relevant interest in the building.
S. 506: dwelling house ceasing to be qualifying dwelling house.
S. 573: except in the case of the transfer of a UK trade to a company resident in another member State, a transfer of the relevant interest that is not a sale is treated as a sale of the relevant interest. The sale will be at market value, subject to an election under CAA 2001, s. 569 to treat the sale as being for an alternative amount.

HMRC Manuals – CA86500: guidance on s. 513–515.

515 Proceeds from balancing events

515(1) References in this Part to the proceeds from a balancing event are to the amounts received or receivable in connection with the event, as shown in the Table–

TABLE
BALANCING EVENTS AND PROCEEDS

1. Balancing event	*2. Proceeds from event*
1. The sale of the relevant interest.	The net proceeds of the sale.
2. The demolition or destruction of the dwelling-house.	The net amount received for the remains of the dwelling-house, together with– (a) any insurance money received in respect of the demolition or destruction, and (b) any other compensation of any description so received, so far as it consists of capital sums.
3. The dwelling-house ceases altogether to be used.	Any compensation of any description received in respect of the event, so far it consists of capital sums.

515(2) The amounts referred to in column 2 of the Table are those received or receivable by the person whose entitlement to a balancing allowance or liability to a balancing charge is in question.

Origin – S. 515(1), (2): CAA 1990, s. 156 (part).

Cross references – SI 1996/1585, reg. 10(2)(h): responsibility of trustee of pension funds pooling scheme to negotiate with inspector the amount of any sale, insurance, salvage or compensation moneys within s. 156 which are relevant to any balancing event.

HMRC Manuals – CA86500: guidance on s. 513–515.

CALCULATION OF BALANCING ADJUSTMENTS

516 Dwelling-house a qualifying dwelling-house throughout

516(1) This section provides for balancing adjustments in cases where the dwelling-house was a qualifying dwelling-house for the whole of the relevant period of ownership.

516(2) A balancing allowance is made if–

(a) there are no proceeds from the balancing event, or

(b) the proceeds from the balancing event are less than the residue of qualifying expenditure attributable to the dwelling-house immediately before the event.

516(3) The amount of the balancing allowance is the amount of–

(a) the residue (if there are no proceeds);

(b) the difference (if the proceeds are less than the residue).

516(4) A balancing charge is made if the proceeds from the balancing event are more than the residue of qualifying expenditure attributable to the dwelling-house immediately before the event.

516(5) The amount of the balancing charge is the amount of the difference.

Origin – S. 516(1): CAA 1990, s. 88(1) (part), drafting.
S. 516(2), (3): CAA 1990, s. 87(3).
S. 516(4), (5): CAA 1990, s. 87(4).

Cross references – S. 567: sales treated as being for an alternative amount.
S. 570A: avoidance affecting proceeds of balancing event.

HMRC Manuals – CA87000: guidance, etc. on s. 516–523.

517 Dwelling-house not a qualifying dwelling-house throughout

517(1) This section provides for balancing adjustments where the building was not a qualifying dwelling-house for a part of the relevant period of ownership.

517(2) A balancing allowance is made if–

(a) the proceeds from the balancing event are less than the starting expenditure attributable to the dwelling-house, and

(b) the total amount of the relevant allowances in respect of that expenditure is less than the adjusted net cost of the dwelling-house.

517(3) The amount of the balancing allowance is the amount of the difference between the adjusted net cost of the dwelling-house and the total amount of the relevant allowances.

517(4) A balancing charge is made if the proceeds from the balancing event are equal to or more than the starting expenditure attributable to the dwelling-house.

517(5) The amount of the balancing charge is equal to the total amount of the relevant allowances.

517(6) A balancing charge is also made if–

(a) the proceeds from the balancing event are less than the starting expenditure attributable to the dwelling-house, and

(b) the total amount of the relevant allowances in respect of that expenditure is more than the adjusted net cost in relation to the dwelling-house.

517(7) The amount of the balancing charge is the amount of the difference between the total amount of those allowances and the adjusted net cost.

517(8) **"The relevant allowances"** means–

(a) any initial allowance under paragraph 1 of Schedule 12 to FA 1982, and

(b) any writing-down allowance made for a chargeable period ending on or before the date of the balancing event in question.

Origin – S. 517(1): CAA 1990, s. 88(1) (part).
S. 517(2), (3): CAA 1990, s. 88(3) (part).
S. 517(4), (5): CAA 1990, s. 88(2).
S. 517(6), (7): CAA 1990, s. 88(3) (part).
S. 517(8): CAA 1990, s. 88(5) ("the allowances given").

Cross references – S. 521(1): starting expenditure.
S. 527(4): writing off or increase of expenditure where BA made.
S. 569(5): election to treat sale as being for alternative amount.
S. 570A: avoidance affecting proceeds of balancing event.
FA 1982, Sch. 12, para. 1: initial allowance.

HMRC Manuals – CA87000: guidance, etc. on s. 516–523.

518 Overall limit on balancing charge

518(1) The amount of a balancing charge made on a person in respect of any qualifying expenditure attributable to a dwelling-house must not exceed the total amount of the relevant allowances made to that person.

518(2) **"The relevant allowances"** has the meaning given by section 517(8).

Origin – CAA 1990, s. 87(6).

HMRC Manuals – CA87000: guidance, etc. on s. 516–523.

519 Recovery of old initial allowances made on incorrect assumptions

519(1) This section applies if–

(a) an initial allowance has been made under paragraph 1 of Schedule 12 to FA 1982 in respect of expenditure relating to a dwelling-house, and

(b) when the dwelling-house comes to be used, it is not a qualifying dwelling-house.

519(2) All such assessments and adjustments of assessments are to be made as are necessary to secure that, despite the repeal of Schedule 12 to FA 1982, effect is given to the prohibition in paragraph 1(3) of that Schedule (on the making of initial allowances in respect of dwelling-houses which are not qualifying dwelling-houses).

Origin – S. 519(1): CAA 1990, s. 87(7) (part), (8).
S. 519(2): CAA 1990, s. 87(7) (part).

Cross references – FA 1982, Sch. 12, para. 1: intial allowance.
TCGA 1992, s. 37(1), (2): exclusion from disposal consideration in computation of gain for amounts charged to tax as income etc. does not include amounts taken into account in the making of a balancing charge except under this Part.

HMRC Manuals – CA87000: guidance, etc. on s. 516–523.

MEANING OF "THE RELEVANT PERIOD OF OWNERSHIP" ETC.

520 The relevant period of ownership

520 The relevant period of ownership is the period beginning–

(a) with the day on which the dwelling-house was first used for any purpose, or

(b) if the relevant interest in the dwelling-house has been sold after that day, with the day following that on which the sale (or the last such sale) occurred,

and ending with the day on which the balancing event occurs.

Origin – CAA 1990, s. 88(5) ("the relevant period").

Cross references – S. 500: the relevant interest in the dwelling-house.

HMRC Manuals – CA87000: guidance, etc. on s. 516–523.

521 Starting expenditure

521(1) This section gives the starting expenditure attributable to a dwelling-house for the purposes of section 517.

521(2) If the person to or on whom the balancing allowance or balancing charge falls to be made is the person who incurred the qualifying expenditure attributable to the dwelling-house, that expenditure is the starting expenditure.

521(3) Otherwise, the starting expenditure is the residue of qualifying expenditure attributable to the dwelling-house at the beginning of the relevant period of ownership.

521(4) If section 528 (treatment of demolition costs) applies, the starting expenditure is increased by an amount equal to the net cost of the demolition.

Origin – S. 521(1) to (4): CAA 1990, s. 88(5) ("the capital expenditure").

Cross references – S. 528: treatment of demolition costs.

HMRC Manuals – CA87000: guidance, etc. on s. 516–523.

522 Adjusted net cost

522 The amount of the adjusted net cost in relation to a dwelling-house is–

$$(S - P) \times \frac{I}{R}$$

where–

S is the starting expenditure attributable to the dwelling-house,

P is the amount of any proceeds from the balancing event,

I is the number of days in the relevant period of ownership on which the dwelling-house was a qualifying dwelling-house, and

R is the number of days in the whole of the relevant period of ownership.

Origin – CAA 1990, s. 88(5) ("adjusted net cost").

Cross references – S. 567: sales treated as being for an alternative amount.

HMRC Manuals – CA87000: guidance, etc. on s. 516–523.

Chapter 7 – Writing Off Qualifying Expenditure Attributable to Dwelling-house

523 Introduction

523 For the purposes of this Part qualifying expenditure attributable to a dwelling-house is written off to the extent and at the times specified in this Chapter.

Origin – CAA 1990, s. 90(1) (part).

HMRC Manuals – CA87000: guidance, etc. on s. 516–523.
CA87500: guidance on s. 523–528.

524 Writing off initial allowances

524 If an initial allowance was made under paragraph 1 of Schedule 12 to FA 1982 in respect of a qualifying dwelling-house, the amount of the allowance is written off at the time of the first use of the dwelling-house.

Origin – CAA 1990, s. 90(2).

Cross references – FA 1982, Sch. 12, para. 1: initial allowances.

HMRC Manuals – CA87500: guidance on s. 523–528.

525 Writing off writing-down allowances

525(1) If a writing-down allowance is made in respect of qualifying expenditure attributable to a dwelling-house, the amount of the allowance is written off at the end of the chargeable period for which the allowance is made.

525(2) If a balancing event occurs at the end of a chargeable period, the amount written off under subsection (1) is to be taken into account in calculating the residue of qualifying expenditure immediately before the event to determine what balancing adjustment (if any) is to be made.

Origin – S. 525(1): CAA 1990, s. 90(3).
S. 525(2): CAA 1990, s. 90(4).

Cross references – Pt. 10, Ch. 3: qualifying expenditure.

HMRC Manuals – CA87500: guidance on s. 523–528.

526 Writing off expenditure for periods when building not used as qualifying dwelling-house

526(1) This section applies if for any period or periods between–

(a) the time when the whole or a part of the building was first used for any purpose, and

(b) the time when the residue of qualifying expenditure attributable to a dwelling-house falls to be ascertained,

the building or part has not been a qualifying dwelling-house.

526(2) An amount equal to the notional writing-down allowances for the period or periods is written off at the time when the residue falls to be ascertained.

526(3) The notional writing-down allowances are the allowances that would have been made for the period or periods in question (if the building or part had remained a qualifying dwelling-house), at such rate or rates as would have been appropriate, having regard to any relevant sale.

526(4) In subsection (3) **"relevant sale"** means a sale of the relevant interest as a result of which a balancing adjustment falls to be made under section 513.

Origin – S. 526(1)–(4): CAA 1990, s. 90(5).

Cross references – S. 513: when balancing adjustments are made.

HMRC Manuals – CA87500: guidance on s. 523–528.

527 Writing off or increase of expenditure where balancing adjustment made

527(1) This section applies if the relevant interest in the dwelling-house is sold.

527(2) If a balancing allowance is made, the amount by which the residue of qualifying expenditure attributable to the dwelling-house before the balancing event exceeds the net proceeds from the event is written off at the time of the event.

527(3) If a balancing charge is made, the amount of the residue of qualifying expenditure attributable to the dwelling-house is increased at the time of the balancing event by the amount of the charge.

527(4) But if the balancing charge is made under section 517(6) (difference between relevant allowances and adjusted net cost), the residue of qualifying expenditure attributable to the dwelling-house immediately after the balancing event is limited to the net proceeds from the event.

Origin – S. 527(1), (2): CAA 1990, s. 90(6).
S. 527(3): CAA 1990, s. 90(7).
S. 527(4): CAA 1990, s. 90(8).

Cross references – S. 517(6): balance charge when dwelling house not qualifying throughout.

HMRC Manuals – CA87500: guidance on s. 523–528.

528 Treatment of demolition costs

528(1) This section applies if–

(a) a dwelling-house is demolished, and

(b) the person to or on whom any balancing allowance or balancing charge is or might be made is the person incurring the cost of the demolition.

528(2) The net cost of the demolition is added to the residue of qualifying expenditure attributable to the qualifying dwelling-house immediately before the demolition.

528(3) **"The net cost of the demolition"** means the amount, if any, by which the cost of the demolition exceeds any money received for the remains of the property.

528(4) If this section applies, the net cost of the demolition is not treated for the purposes of this Part as expenditure on any other property replacing the property demolished.

Origin – S. 528(1)–(4): CAA 1990, s. 90(9).

Cross references – S. 512(2): residue of qualifying expenditure attributable to dwelling house.
S. 521(4): starting expenditure.

HMRC Manuals – CA87500: guidance on s. 523–528.

Chapter 8 – Supplementary Provisions

529 Giving effect to allowances and charges

529(1) If a person who is entitled or liable to an allowance or charge for a chargeable period was carrying on a UK property business at any time in that period, the allowance or charge is to be given effect in calculating the profits of that business, by treating–

(a) the allowance as an expense of that business, and

(b) the charge as a receipt of that business.

529(1A) If the person entitled or liable to an allowance or charge for a chargeable period was not carrying on a UK property business at any time in that period, the allowance or charge is to be given effect by treating the person as having carried on such a business in that period and as if–

(a) the allowance were an expense of that business, and

(b) the charge were a receipt of that business.

529(2) [Omitted by CTA 2009, s. 1322 and Sch. 1, para. 515(4) and repealed by CTA 2009, s. 1326 and Sch. 3, Pt. 1.]

History – In s. 529(1), the words ", or a Schedule A business,", which appeared after the words "UK property business", omitted by CTA 2009, s. 1322 and Sch. 1, para. 515(2) and repealed by CTA 2009, s. 1326 and Sch. 3, Pt. 1, with effect for corporation tax purposes for accounting periods ending on or after 1 April 2009, and for income tax and capital gains tax purposes for the tax year 2009–10 and subsequent tax years.

In s. 529(1) the words "a UK property business, or a Schedule A business," substituted for "a Schedule A business" by ITTOIA 2005, s. 882(1) and Sch. 1, para. 569(2); effective for income tax purposes for 2005–06 onwards and for corporation tax purposes for accounting periods ending after 5 April 2005 (ITTOIA 2005, s. 883(1)).

In s. 529(1A), the words "is within the charge to income tax in respect of the allowance or charge and he", which appeared after the words "a chargeable period", omitted and the words "treating the person as having carried on" substituted for the words "treating him as if he had been carrying on" by CTA 2009, s. 1322 and Sch. 1, para. 515(3) and repealed by CTA 2009, s. 1326 and Sch. 3, Pt. 1, with effect for corporation tax purposes for accounting periods ending on or after 1 April 2009, and for income tax and capital gains tax purposes for the tax year 2009–10 and subsequent tax years.

S. 529(1A) inserted by ITTOIA 2005, s. 882(1) and Sch. 1, para. 569(3); effective for income tax purposes for 2005–06 onwards and for corporation tax purposes for accounting periods ending after 5 April 2005 (ITTOIA 2005, s. 883(1)).

S. 529(2) omitted by CTA 2009, s. 1322 and Sch. 1, para. 515(4) and repealed by CTA 2009, s. 1326 and Sch. 3, Pt. 1, with effect for corporation tax purposes for accounting periods ending on or after 1 April 2009, and for income tax and capital gains tax purposes for the tax year 2009–10 and subsequent tax years.

Former s. 529(2) amended (in various places) by ITTOIA 2005, s. 882(1) and Sch. 1, para. 569(4); effective for income tax purposes for 2005–06 onwards and for corporation tax purposes for accounting periods ending after 5 April 2005 (ITTOIA 2005, s. 883(1)).

Origin – S. 529(1), (2): CAA 1990, s. 92(2), s. 140(2) (part), s. 144(2) (part), drafting, Annex 2, Note 67.

Cross references – S. 2(3): general means of giving effect to capital allowances.

Rewrite: Technical Points – Explanatory Notes, Annex 2, Note 67: wording of former CAA 1990, s. 92(1) is omitted as it is not needed, as those who can claim these allowances will be carrying on a Sch. A business.

HMRC Manuals – CA88000: guidance on s. 529.

530 Apportionment of sums partly referable to non-qualifying assets

530(1) If the sum paid for the sale of the relevant interest in a building is attributable–

(a) partly to assets representing expenditure for which an allowance can be made under this Part, and

(b) partly to assets representing other expenditure,

only so much of the sum paid as on a just and reasonable apportionment is attributable to the assets referred to in paragraph (a) is to be taken into account for the purposes of this Part.

530(2) Subsection (1) applies to other proceeds from a balancing event in respect of a building as it applies to a sum given for the sale of the relevant interest in the building.

530(3) Subsection (1) does not affect any other provision of this Part requiring an apportionment of the proceeds of a balancing event.

Origin – S. 530(1): CAA 1990, s. 97(4) (part), Annex 1, Change 40.
S. 530(2), (3): CAA 1990, s. 97(4) (part).

Cross references – S. 495: general rule as to what is the relevant interest in the building.

Rewrite: Changes in Law – Explanatory Notes, Annex 1, Change 40: words "and reasonable" included to make the wording consistent with other provisions of this Act.

531 Meaning of "dwelling-house", "lease" etc.

531(1) In this Part **"dwelling-house"** has the same meaning as in the Rent Act 1977.

531(2) In this Part **"lease"** includes–

(a) an agreement for a lease if the term to be covered by the lease has begun, and

(b) any tenancy,

but does not include a mortgage (and "lessee", "lessor" and "leasehold interest" are to be read accordingly).

531(3) In the application of this Part to Scotland–

(a) **"leasehold interest"** means the interest of a tenant in property subject to a lease, and

(b) any reference to an interest which is reversionary on a leasehold interest or on a lease is to be read as a reference to the interest of the landlord in the property subject to the leasehold interest or lease.

Origin – S. 531(1): CAA 1990, s. 97(1) ("dwelling-house").
S. 531(2): CAA 1990, s. 161(2) ("lease").
S. 531(3): CAA 1990, s. 162 (part).

HMRC Manuals – CA11520: guidance on s. 531.

PART 11 – CONTRIBUTIONS

Chapter 1 – Exclusion of Expenditure Met by Contributions

RULES EXCLUDING CONTRIBUTIONS

532 The general rule excluding contributions

532(1) For the purposes of this Act, the general rule is that a person ("R") is to be regarded as not having incurred expenditure to the extent that it has been, or is to be, met (directly or indirectly) by–

(a) a public body, or

(b) a person other than R.

532(2) In this Chapter **"public body"** means the Crown or any government or public or local authority (whether in the United Kingdom or elsewhere).

532(3) The general rule does not apply for the purposes of Part 9 (dredging allowances).

532(4) The general rule is subject to the exceptions in sections 534 to 536.

Origin – S. 532(1): ICTA 1988, s. 532(1) (part), CAA 1990, s. 153(1) (part).
S. 532(2): CAA 1990, s. 134(8) (part), s. 153(1) (part).
S. 532(3): CAA 1990, s. 153(4) (part), drafting.
S. 532(4): drafting.

Cross references – S. 76(1): restriction on writing-down allowances on a car above the cost threshold where, as a result of s. 532, only part of the capital expenditure incurred on its provision is treated as incurred by the claimant.
ICTA 1988, s. 91(9): application to allowances in respect of cemeteries.

ICTA 1988, s. 400(6): expenditure not treated as met by the Crown by reason only of the writing-off of a government investment.
FA 1990, s. 126(4): s. 532 not to apply to contributions to football ground safety improvements etc. resulting from reduction in pool betting duty (under FA 1990, s. 4) (see also under other material below).
FA 1991, s. 65(8): s. 532 does not apply to treat the incurring of reimbursement expenditure, by an oil field participator to a co-participator in respect of oil field abandonment expenditure, as a subsidy etc.
FA 1996, s. 151: Treasury order may be made to exclude benefits payable by a Government pilot scheme from provisions of s. 532.
FA 1999, Sch. 6, para. 5: that Schedule (tax treatment of receipts by way of reverse premium) does not apply to a payment or benefit if or to the extent that it is taken into account under s. 532 to reduce the recipient's expenditure qualifying for capital allowances.

Extra-statutory concessions – ESC B49: where expenditure met out of the grant would otherwise fall to be disregarded in giving capital allowances, any amount of the grant repaid will be treated as expenditure on which capital allowances will be given.

HMRC Manuals – CA14100: guidance on s. 532.

Other material – Revenue letter to Football League, 25 January 1991 (not reproduced): grants from the Football Trust towards a club's capital expenditure not to reduce capital allowance entitlement where paid out of moneys from "spot-the-ball" competitions (see also cross reference to FA 1990, s. 126(4) above).

533 Exclusion of contributions to dredging

533(1) For the purposes of Part 9, a person ("D") who has incurred expenditure is to be regarded as not having incurred it for the purposes of a trade carried on or to be carried on by D to the extent that it has been, or is to be, met (directly or indirectly) by–

(a) a public body, or

(b) capital sums contributed by another person for purposes other than those of D's trade.

533(2) Subsection (1) is not subject to the exceptions in sections 534 to 536.

Origin – S. 533(1): CAA 1990, s. 134(8) (part).
S. 533(2): drafting.

HMRC Manuals – CA14100: guidance on s. 533.

EXCEPTIONS TO THE GENERAL RULE EXCLUDING CONTRIBUTIONS

534 Northern Ireland regional development grants

534(1) A person is to be regarded as having incurred expenditure (despite section 532(1)) to the extent that it is met (directly or indirectly) by a grant–

(a) made under Northern Ireland legislation, and

(b) declared by the Treasury by order to correspond to a grant under Part II of the Industrial Development Act 1982.

534(2) Subject to subsection (3), the grant is to be treated as not falling within subsection (1) if, by virtue of paragraph 8 of Schedule 3 to OTA 1975, expenditure which has been or is to be met by the grant is not to be regarded for any of the purposes of Part I of OTA 1975 as having been incurred by any person.

534(3) If only a proportion of the expenditure which has been or is to be met by the grant is expenditure which, if it were not so met, would be allowable under section 3 or 4 of OTA 1975, only a corresponding proportion of the grant is to be treated as not falling within subsection (1).

Origin – S. 534(1): ICTA 1988, s. 532(1) (part), CAA 1990, s. 153(1) (part).
S. 534(2): FA 1982 s. 137(2).
S. 534(3): FA 1982 s. 137(3).

Cross references – ICTA 1988, s. 495: regional development grants – income and corporation tax treatment.

Transitional – Sch. 3, para. 106(1): application of s. 534(1) to grants made under Industrial Development Act 1982, Pt. II on an application made before 1 April 1988, or under Industry Act 1972, Pt. I or a corresponding Northern Ireland grant.
Sch. 3, para. 106(2): s. 534(2) does not apply if expenditure incurred, or grant paid, before 10 March 1982.

HMRC Manuals – CA14200: guidance on s. 534.

535 Insurance or compensation money

535 A person is to be regarded as having incurred expenditure (despite section 532(1)) to the extent that it is met (directly or indirectly) by–

(a) insurance money, or

(b) other compensation money,

payable in respect of an asset which has been destroyed, demolished or put out of use.

Origin – ICTA 1988, s. 532(1) (part), CAA 1990, s. 153(2) (part), Annex 1, Change 58.

Rewrite: Changes in Law – Explanatory Notes, Annex 1, Change 58: in CAA 1990, part of s. 153(4) provided that the exception for insurance or compensation money did not apply to Pt. VII of that Act (research and development allowances). That part of s. 153(4) is not rewritten, so that expenditure is not now denied R&D allowances because it was met by insurance, etc.

HMRC Manuals – CA14200: guidance on s. 535.

536 Contributions not made by public bodies and not eligible for tax relief

536(1) A person ("R") is to be regarded as having incurred expenditure (despite section 532(1)) to the extent that the requirements in subsections (2) and (3) are satisfied in relation to the expenditure.

536(2) The first requirement is that the person meeting R's expenditure ("C") is not a public body.

536(3) The second requirement is that–

(a) no allowance can be made under Chapter 2 in respect of C's expenditure, and

(b) the expenditure is not allowed to be deducted in calculating the profits of a trade or relevant activity carried on by C.

536(4) When determining for the purposes of subsection (3)(a) whether an allowance can be made under Chapter 2, assume that C is within the charge to tax.

536(5) In subsection (3)(b) **"relevant activity"** means–

(a) for the purposes of Part 2–

  (i) an ordinary UK property business;

  (ii) a UK furnished holiday lettings business;

  (iii) an ordinary overseas property business;

  (iiia) an EEA furnished holiday lettings business;

  (iv) a profession or vocation;

  (v) any concern listed in section 12(4) of ITTOIA 2005 or section 39(5) of CTA 2009 (mines, transport undertakings etc.);

  (vi) the management of an investment company;

(b) for other purposes, a profession or vocation.

History – In s. 536(5)(a)(i), the word "UK" inserted after "ordinary" by FA 2011, s. 52 and Sch. 14, para. 12(15)(a), with effect in relation to chargeable periods beginning on or after 1 April 2011 (for corporation tax purposes), and in relation to chargeable periods beginning on or after 6 April 2011 (for income tax purposes).
In s. 536(5)(a)(ii), the words "UK furnished" substituted for "furnished" by FA 2011, s. 52 and Sch. 14, para. 12(15)(b), with effect in relation to chargeable periods beginning on or after 1 April 2011 (for corporation tax purposes), and in relation to chargeable periods beginning on or after 6 April 2011 (for income tax purposes).
In s. 536(5)(a)(iii), the words "ordinary overseas" substituted for "overseas" by FA 2011, s. 52 and Sch. 14, para. 12(15)(c), with effect in relation to chargeable periods beginning on or after 1 April 2011 (for corporation tax purposes), and in relation to chargeable periods beginning on or after 6 April 2011 (for income tax purposes).
S. 536(5)(a)(iiia) inserted by FA 2011, s. 52 and Sch. 14, para. 12(15)(d), with effect in relation to chargeable periods beginning on or after 1 April 2011 (for corporation tax purposes) and in relation to chargeable periods beginning on or after 6 April 2011 (for income tax purposes).
In s. 536(5)(a)(v), the words "section 39(5) of CTA 2009" substituted for the words "section 55(2) of ICTA" by CTA 2009, s. 1322 and Sch. 1, para. 516, with effect for corporation tax purposes for accounting periods ending on or after 1 April 2009, and for income tax and capital gains tax purposes for the tax year 2009–10 and subsequent tax years.
S. 536(5)(a) amended by ITTOIA 2005, s. 882(1) and Sch. 1, para. 570; effective for income tax purposes for 2005–06 onwards and for corporation tax purposes for accounting periods ending after 5 April 2005 (ITTOIA 2005, s. 883(1)).

Origin – S. 536: Annex 1, Change 58.
S. 536(1)–(3): ICTA 1988, s. 532(1) (part), CAA 1990, s. 153(2) (part).
S. 536(4): ICTA 1988, s. 532(1) (part), CAA 1990, s. 153(3).
S. 536(5): ICTA 1988, s. 532(1) (part), CAA 1990, s. 153(2) (part), Annex 1, Change 59.

Cross references – FA 2013, s. 73(5): amendments to s. 538 made by FA 2013, s. 73 are to be treated as always having had effect for purposes of s. 536(3)(a) for expenditure and claims at s. 73(4).
ICTA 1988, s. 400(6): expenditure not treated as met by the Crown by reason only of the writing-off of a government investment.

Transitional – Sch. 3, para. 107: in relation to contributions made before 27 July 1989, s. 536 applies with the omission of subsection (3)(b).
Sch. 3, para. 108: in s. 536(5), as it applies for the purposes of s. 537(2), para. (a)(iv) and (b) do not apply in relation to contributions made before 27 July 1989.

Rewrite: Changes in Law – Explanatory Notes, Annex 1, Change 58: in CAA 1990, part of s. 153(4) provided that the exception for contributions by persons other than public bodies, etc. did not apply to Pt. VII of that Act (research and development allowances). That part of s. 153(4) is not rewritten, so that expenditure is not now denied R&D allowances because it was met by such persons.
Explanatory Notes, Annex 1, Change 59: definition of "relevant activity" in s. 536(5) extends the meaning of "trade" for the purposes of provisions relating to both recipients of contributions and contributors in connection with Pt. 2. This clearly represents a change in the law as respects a concern listed in ICTA 1988, s. 55(2), and almost certainly a change in relation to the management of an investment company. It may also be a change in relation to a property business. The rewritten definition also specifically includes trades and professions for purposes other than those of Pt. 2 (plant and machinery allowances). Compare and contrast CAA 1990, s. 153(2)(b) read with s. 154(1) and (5).

HMRC Manuals – CA14200: guidance on s. 536.

Chapter 2 – Contribution Allowances

CONTRIBUTION ALLOWANCES UNDER PARTS 2, 3, 4 AND 5

History – In the cross-heading, the words "Parts 2, 3, 4 and 5" substituted for "Parts 2 to 4 and 5" by FA 2005, s. 92 and Sch. 6, para. 5, with effect in relation to expenditure incurred on or after 11 April 2007, by virtue of SI 2007/949, art. 2.
Previously in the cross-heading, "Parts 2 to 4 and 5" substituted for "Parts 2 to 5" by FA 2001, s. 67 and Sch. 19, Pt. 2, para. 3, with effect in relation to expenditure incurred on or after 11 May 2001.

537 Conditions for contribution allowances under Parts 2 and 5

537(1) This section gives general conditions for making contribution allowances under Parts 2 and 5.

537(2) The general conditions are that–

(a) a person ("C") has contributed a capital sum to expenditure on the provision of an asset,

(b) the expenditure would (ignoring section 532(1))–

(i) have been regarded as wholly incurred by another person ("R"), and

(ii) if R is not a public body, have entitled R to allowances under Part 2 or 5 or to allocate the expenditure to a pool under Part 2, and

(c) C and R are not connected persons.

537(3) In this section **"public body"** means the Crown or any public or local authority in the United Kingdom.

537(4) In this Chapter **"relevant activity"** has the meaning given by section 536(5).

History – In the heading to s. 537, the words ", 3, 4" omitted by FA 2008, s. 84 and Sch. 27, para. 8(c), with effect in relation to chargeable periods beginning on or after 1 April 2011 for corporation tax purposes and 6 April 2011 for income tax purposes (FA 2008, Sch. 27, para. 30(1)).
In s. 537(1), the words ", 3, 4" omitted by FA 2008, s. 84 and Sch. 27, para. 8(a), with effect in relation to chargeable periods beginning on or after 1 April 2011 for corporation tax purposes and 6 April 2011 for income tax purposes (FA 2008, Sch. 27, para. 30(1)).
In s. 537(1) and in the section heading to s. 537, the words "Parts 2, 3, 4 and 5" substituted for "Parts 2 to 4 and 5" by FA 2005, s. 92 and Sch. 6, para. 5 with effect in relation to expenditure incurred on or after 11 April 2007, by virtue of SI 2007/949, art. 2.
Previously in s. 537(1) and in the section heading, "Parts 2 to 4 and 5" substituted for "Parts 2 to 5" by FA 2001, s. 67 and Sch. 19, Pt. 2, para. 3, with effect in relation to expenditure incurred on or after 11 May 2001.
In s. 537(2)(b)(ii), the words ", 3, 4" omitted by FA 2008, s. 84 and Sch. 27, para. 8(b), with effect in relation to chargeable periods beginning on or after 1 April 2011 for corporation tax purposes and 6 April 2011 for income tax purposes (FA 2008, Sch. 27, para. 30(1)).

Origin – S. 537(1): CAA 1990, s. 154(1) (part), (2) (part).
S. 537(2): CAA 1990, s. 154(1) (part), (2) (part), (3) (part), (4) (part).
S. 537(3): CAA 1990, s. 154(4) (part).
S. 537(4): CAA 1990, s. 154(5), Annex 1, Change 59.

Cross references – FA 1997, Sch. 12, para. 11(13): clawback of allowances given under s. 537 where certain leasing arrangements involve payment of a "major lump sum".

Rewrite: Changes in Law – Explanatory Notes, Annex 1, Change 59: definition of "relevant activity" in s. 537(4) extends the meaning of "trade" for the purposes of provisions relating to both recipients of contributions and contributors in connection with Pt. 2. This clearly represents a change in the law as respects a concern listed in ICTA 1988, s. 55(2), and almost certainly a change in relation to the management of an investment company. It may also be a change in relation to a property business. The rewritten definition also specifically includes trades and professions for purposes other than those of Pt. 2 (plant and machinery allowances). Compare and contrast CAA 1990, s. 153(2)(b) read with s. 154(1) and (5).

Extra-statutory concessions – B16: relief where lessor incurs expenditure on fire safety.

HMRC Manuals – CA14400: guidance on s. 537.

538 Plant and machinery

538(1) This section is about contribution allowances under Part 2 and applies if–

(a) the general conditions for contribution allowances are met,

(aa) C's contribution is to expenditure on the provision of plant or machinery, and

(b) C's contribution is made for the purposes of a trade or relevant activity carried on, or to be carried on, by C.

538(2) C is to be treated for the purposes of allowances under Part 2 as if–

(a) the contribution were expenditure incurred by C on the provision, for the purposes of C's trade or relevant activity, of the plant or machinery,

(b) C owned the plant or machinery as a result of incurring that expenditure at any time when R owns it or is treated under Part 2 as owning it, and

(c) the plant or machinery were at all material times plant or machinery in use for the purposes of C's trade or relevant activity.

538(3) Expenditure treated as incurred under subsection (2)(a), if allocated to any pool, must be allocated to a single asset pool.

538(4) Subsections (5) and (6) apply for the purposes of contribution allowances under Part 2 if the whole or a part of the trade or relevant activity for the purposes of which C's contribution was made is transferred.

538(5) If the whole of the trade or relevant activity is transferred, writing-down allowances for chargeable periods ending after the date of the transfer are to be made to the transferee instead of to the transferor.

538(6) If a part of the trade or relevant activity is transferred, writing-down allowances for chargeable periods ending after the date of the transfer are to be made to the transferee instead of to the transferor to the extent that they are properly referable to the part transferred.

History – S. 538(1)(aa) inserted (and the "and" after (a) omitted) by FA 2013, s. 73(2), with effect in relation to expenditure pooled, and to claims made, on or after 29 May 2013 ("the commencement date"), subject to transitional provisions in FA 2013, 73(5)–(11).
In s. 538(2)(a), the words "plant or machinery" substituted for the words "asset provided by means of C's contribution" by FA 2013, s. 73(3)(a), with effect in relation to expenditure pooled, and to claims made, on or after 29 May 2013 ("the commencement date"), subject to transitional provisions in FA 2013, 73(5)–(11).
In s. 538(2)(b), the words "plant or machinery" substituted for the word "asset" by FA 2013, s. 73(3)(b), with effect in relation to expenditure pooled, and to claims made, on or after 29 May 2013 ("the commencement date"), subject to transitional provisions in FA 2013, 73(5)–(11).
In s. 538(2)(c), the words "plant or machinery" substituted for the word "asset" and the words "plant or machinery" inserted (after "times") by FA 2013, s. 73(3)(c), with effect in relation to expenditure pooled, and to claims made, on or after 29 May 2013 ("the commencement date"), subject to transitional provisions in FA 2013, 73(5)–(11).

Origin – S. 538(1): CAA 1990, s. 154(1) (part), (2) (part), Annex 2, Note 68.
S. 538(2): CAA 1990, s. 154(1) (part), (2) (part), s. 155(2) (part).
S. 538(3): CAA 1990, s. 155(6), Annex 1, Change 60.
S. 538(4)–(6): CAA 1990, s. 155(3) (part).

Cross references – S. 76(3)(b), (4): restriction of writing-down allowance on cars above the cost threshold where a contributor is entitled to writing-down allowances as a result of s. 538.
S. 172(5): Pt. 2, Ch. 14 (plant and machinery allowances on fixtures) does not affect any entitlement a person has to an allowance as a result of s. 538.
FA 1997, Sch. 12, para. 11(13): clawback of allowances given under s. 538 where certain leasing arrangements involve payment of a "major lump sum".

Transitional – Sch. 3, para. 109: s. 538(2)(b)(ii) applies in relation to contributions made before 6 April 1990 with the omission of "or to allocate the expenditure to a pool under Part 2".

Rewrite: Changes in Law – Explanatory Notes, Annex 1, change 60: it is uncertain whether CAA 1990, s. 155(6), the precursor to s. 538(3), had the effect of creating a single asset pool, or a class pool. The uncertainty hangs on whether the words in s 155(6) "contributes a capital sum to expenditure on the provision of an asset" include the plural ("capital sums . . . assets") in accordance with Interpretation Act 1978, s. 6(c), or whether there is a contrary intention. If the former, then a class pool is created, if the latter, a single asset pool. But if there were a class pool, the intention behind an amendment made to s. 155(6) by FA 1989, Sch. 13, para. 5 – to ensure that entitlement to allowances could not be transferred when the contributor's trade was transferred – would not be achieved. Therefore, by creating a single asset pool, s. 538(3) is intended to achieve the original intention underlying the 1989 amendment.

Rewrite: Technical Points – Explanatory Notes, Annex 2, note 19: because of the effect of change 60 above, it is no longer necessary for there to be a separate pool for contributions to cars above the cost threshold, as was provided for by CAA 1990, s. 35. See now CAA 2001, s. 76(3), (4).
Explanatory Notes, Annex 2, note 23: there is compelling evidence in favour of the view that CAA 1990, s. 38F(2) and 42(2) (6 per cent and 10 per cent rates of writing-down allowance for long-life asset and overseas leasing expenditure) applied to the separate trades created by CAA 1990, s. 154(2) and 155(6), the precursors to s. 538. Therefore the single asset pool for contributions on plant and machinery leads to writing-down allowances at 25 per cent, 10 per cent or 6 per cent as appropriate.
Explanatory Notes, Annex 2, note 68: change 59 in Annex 1 (see notes to s. 536 and 537 above) has extended contributions allowances to contributions made for the purposes of property businesses. Therefore, where a landlord makes a contribution for the purposes of a tenant's trade, there is no need for s. 538(1) to make specific reference to such expenditure.

Extra-statutory concessions – B16: relief where lessor incurs expenditure on fire safety.

HMRC Manuals – CA14500: guidance and example.

539 Industrial buildings

539 [Omitted by FA 2008, s. 84 and Sch. 27, para. 9.]

History – S. 539 omitted by FA 2008, s. 84 and Sch. 27, para. 9, with effect in relation to chargeable periods beginning on or after 1 April 2011 for corporation tax purposes and 6 April 2011 for income tax purposes (FA 2008, Sch. 27, para. 30(1)).

Origin – S. 539(1): CAA 1990, s. 154(1) (part).
S. 539(2): CAA 1990, s. 154(1) (part), s. 155(2).
S. 539(3)–(5): CAA 1990, s. 155(4) (part).
S. 539(6): CAA 1990, s. 155(5).

HMRC Manuals – CA14600: guidance on s. 539.

540 Agricultural buildings

540 [Omitted by FA 2008, s. 84 and Sch. 27, para. 10.]

History – S. 540 omitted by FA 2008, s. 84 and Sch. 27, para. 10, with effect in relation to chargeable periods beginning on or after 1 April 2011 for corporation tax purposes and 6 April 2011 for income tax purposes (FA 2008, Sch. 27, para. 30(1)).

Origin – S. 540(1): CAA 1990, s. 154(1) (part).
S. 540(2): CAA 1990, s. 154(1) (part), s. 155(2) (part).
S. 540(3), (4): CAA 1990, s. 155(4) (part).
S. 540(5): CAA 1990, s. 155(4) (part), (8).

Transitional – Sch. 3, para. 110: contributions made before 27 July 1989 – s. 368, 375 and 379 apply with the necessary modifications, instead than s. 540 (this preserves the effect of CAA 1990, s. 155(7)).

HMRC Manuals – CA14700: guidance on s. 540.

541 Mineral extraction

541(1) This section is about contribution allowances under Part 5 and applies if–

(a) the general conditions for contribution allowances are met, and

(b) C's contribution is made for the purposes of a trade carried on, or to be carried on, by C.

541(2) C is to be treated for the purposes of allowances under Part 5 as if–

(a) the contribution were expenditure incurred by C on the provision, for the purposes of C's trade, of an asset similar to that provided by means of C's contribution, and

(b) the asset were at all material times in use for the purposes of C's trade.

Origin – S. 541(1): CAA 1990, s. 154(1) (part), Annex 2, Note 68.
S. 541(2): CAA 1990, s. 154(1) (part), s. 155(2) (part).

Rewrite: Technical Points – Explanatory Notes, Annex 2, note 68: change 59 in Annex 1 (see notes to s. 536 and 537 above) has extended contributions allowances to contributions made for the purposes of property businesses. Therefore, where a landlord makes a contribution for the purposes of a tenant's trade, there is no need for s. 541(1) to make specific reference to such expenditure.

HMRC Manuals – CA14800: guidance on s. 541.

EFFECT OF TRANSFERS OF C'S TRADE ON CONTRIBUTION ALLOWANCES UNDER PARTS 3, 4 AND 5

542 Transfer of C's trade

542(1) Subsections (2) and (3) apply for the purposes of contribution allowances under Part 5 if–

(a) C's contribution was made for the purposes of C's trade, and

(b) the whole or a part of the trade is subsequently transferred.

542(2) If the whole of the trade is transferred, writing-down allowances for chargeable periods ending after the date of the transfer are to be made to the transferee instead of to the transferor.

542(3) If a part of the trade is transferred, writing-down allowances for chargeable periods ending after the date of the transfer are to be made to the transferee instead of to the transferor to the extent that they are properly referable to the part transferred.

History – In s. 542, the words "or relevant activity" (in four places and in the sub-heading) repealed by Statute Law (Repeals) Act 2013, s. 1 and Sch. 1, Pt. 10, with effect from 31 January 2013.
In s. 542(1), the words "Part 5" substituted for the words "Parts 3, 4 and 5" by FA 2008, s. 84 and Sch 27, para. 11, with effect in relation to chargeable periods beginning on or after 1 April 2011 for corporation tax purposes and 6 April 2011 for income tax purposes (FA 2008, Sch. 27, para. 30(1)).
In s. 542(1), "Parts 3, 4 and 5" substituted for "Parts 3 to 5" by FA 2001, s. 67 and Sch. 19, Pt. 2, para. 4, with effect in relation to expenditure incurred on or after 11 May 2001.

Origin – S. 542(1)–(3): CAA 1990, s. 155(3) (part).

HMRC Manuals – CA14600ff.: guidance on s. 542.

CONTRIBUTION ALLOWANCES UNDER PART 9

543 Contribution allowances under Part 9

543 A person who contributes a capital sum to expenditure incurred by another person on dredging is to be regarded for the purposes of Part 9 as incurring capital expenditure on that dredging.

Origin – CAA 1990, s. 134(8) (part).

PART 12 – SUPPLEMENTARY PROVISIONS

Chapter 1 – Long-term Business

History – In the heading to Pt. 12, Ch. 1 "Long-term" substituted for "Life assurance" by FA 2012, s. 146 and Sch. 16, para. 102 in relation to accounting periods beginning on or after 1 January 2013 (FA 2012, s. 148) but subject to transitional provisions in FA 2012, Sch. 17. Where an accounting period would otherwise straddle 1 January 2013, it is deemed to end on 31 December 2012 (FA 2012, s. 149).

544 Management assets

544(1) No allowances are to be given or charges imposed in respect of management assets of any long-term business carried on by a company except under Part 2 (plant and machinery allowances).

544(2) An asset is a management asset of any long-term business carried on by a company if it is provided for use, or used, for the management of that business of that company.

544(3) [Omitted by FA 2012, s. 146 and Sch. 16, para. 103(3).]

544(4) [Effectively repealed by SI 2004/2310, Schedule, para. 57(2).]

544(5) [Omitted by FA 2007, s. 41 and Sch. 10, para. 14(8)(b) and repealed by FA 2007, s. 114 and Sch. 27, Pt. 2(10).]

History – In s. 544(1) and (2) "long-term business" substituted for "life assurance business" by FA 2012, s. 146 and Sch. 16, para. 103(2) in relation to accounting periods beginning on or after 1 January 2013 (FA 2012, s. 148) but subject to transitional provisions in FA 2012, Sch. 17. Where an accounting period would otherwise straddle 1 January 2013, it is deemed to end on 31 December 2012 (FA 2012, s. 149).

S. 544(3) omitted by FA 2012, s. 146 and Sch. 16, para. 103(3) in relation to accounting periods beginning on or after 1 January 2013 (FA 2012, s. 148) but subject to transitional provisions in FA 2012, Sch. 17. Where an accounting period would otherwise straddle 1 January 2013, it is deemed to end on 31 December 2012 (FA 2012, s. 149).
Former s. 544(3) substituted for s. 544(3) and (4) by SI 2004/2310, Schedule, para. 57(2), with effect in relation to accounting periods beginning on or after 1 April 2004 subject to the provisions of FA 2004, s. 43 and 44.
S. 544(5) omitted by FA 2007, s. 41 and Sch. 10, para. 14(8)(b) and repealed by FA 2007, s. 114 and Sch. 27, Pt. 2(10), with effect in relation to periods of account beginning on or after 1 January 2007.

Origin – S. 544(1): ICTA 1988, s. 434D(2).
S. 544(2): ICTA 1988, s. 434D(1) (part).
Former s. 544(3): ICTA 1988, s. 434D(7).
Former s. 544(4): Annex 2, Note 69.
Former s. 544(5): drafting.

Rewrite: Technical Points – Explanatory Notes, Annex 2, note 69: s. 544(4) provides for ICTA 1988, s. 76(1)(d) to be disregarded in applying definition of "expenses of management" in s. 76, although ICTA 1988, s. 434D(7), on which it is based, contains no such explicit provision. However, if s. 76(1)(d) were not disregarded in applying s. 434D(7), the special rules in s. 434D(3)–(5) for giving effect to plant and machinery allowances in the case of the categories of life assurance business mentioned in s. 76(1)(d) would be completely pointless. Therefore, s. 544(4) reflects the view that it cannot have been the intention that ICTA 1988, s. 76(1)(d) was meant to be taken into account in applying ICTA 1988, s. 434D(7).

545 Investment assets

545(1) This section applies if a company which is carrying on any long-term business holds an asset for purposes other than the management of that business.

545(2) **"Investment asset"** means an asset that is within subsection (1).

545(3) No allowance in respect of an investment asset is to be taken into account in calculating for corporation tax purposes the profits of any non-BLAGAB long-term business carried on by the company.

History – In s. 545(1) "long-term business" substituted for "life assurance business" by FA 2012, s. 146 and Sch. 16, para. 104(2) in relation to accounting periods beginning on or after 1 January 2013 (FA 2012, s. 148) but subject to transitional provisions in FA 2012, Sch. 17. Where an accounting period would otherwise straddle 1 January 2013, it is deemed to end on 31 December 2012 (FA 2012, s. 149).
S. 545(3) to (5) substituted by FA 2012, s. 146 and Sch. 16, para. 104(3) in relation to accounting periods beginning on or after 1 January 2013 (FA 2012, s. 148) but subject to transitional provisions in FA 2012, Sch. 17. Where an accounting period would otherwise straddle 1 January 2013, it is deemed to end on 31 December 2012 (FA 2012, s. 149).
In s. 545(3), the words "section 432A" substituted for the words "sections 432ZA to 432E, or section 438B," by FA s. 38 and Sch. 7, para. 71(2), with effect for periods of account of insurance companies beginning on or after 1 January 2007, subject to the transitional provisions in FA 2007, Sch. 7, Pt. 2.
S. 545(3) substituted by FA 2001, s. 76 and Sch. 25, para. 7, with deemed effect from 6 April 2001.
In former s. 545(4), the words "section 35 of CTA 2009 (charge on trade profits)" substituted for the words "Case I of Schedule D" by CTA 2009, s. 1322 and Sch. 1, para. 517, with effect for corporation tax purposes for accounting periods ending on or after 1 April 2009, and for income tax and capital gains tax purposes for the tax year 2009–10 and subsequent tax years.
In former s. 545(5), the words "under section 436A of ICTA (gross roll-up business), no allowance" substituted for the following words:
"under–
(a) section 436 of ICTA (pension business and ISA business),
(b) section 439B of ICTA (life reinsurance business), or
(c) section 441 of ICTA (overseas life assurance business),
no allowance"
and the words "gross roll-up business" at the end substituted for the words "the category of life assurance business in question" by FA 2007, s. 38 and Sch. 7, para. 71(3), with effect for periods of account of insurance companies beginning on or after 1 January 2007, subject to the transitional provisions in FA 2007, Sch. 7, Pt. 2.

Origin – S. 545(1), (2): ICTA 1988, s. 434E(1) (part), Annex 1, Change 61.
S. 545(3): ICTA 1988, s. 434E(4).
Former s. 545(4), (5): ICTA 1988, s. 434E(5).

Rewrite: Technical Points – Explanatory Notes, Annex 1, Change 61: s. 545(1) and (2) do not reproduce the effect of ICTA 1988, s. 434E(1)(b), which excluded from the definition of "investment asset" one that was "let in the course of a business the profits or gains of which are chargeable to tax under Schedule A or the income of which is chargeable to tax under Case V". In most cases, the effect of leaving out s. 434E(1)(b) will be to remove a provision that does not achieve anything, because of the way in which various statutory provisions (such as FA 1989, s. 83) remove the charge to tax under Sch. A or Case V in relation to the cases dealt with in s. 434E(5)(a) and (b). But the omission of s. 434E(1)(b) could conceivably change the law in a way that is adverse to the taxpayer where ICTA 1988, s. 432AA and 432B–432F effectively create various separate land exploitation businesses where assets are held for the purposes of different funds. In relation to companies dealt with under ICTA 1988, s. 436, 439B or 441, the effect of FA 1989, s. 83 as read with ICTA 1988, s. 432AA–432F is that sometimes all the profits from the land exploitation business in question will be turned into Case I receipts, and sometimes part will be turned into Case I receipts, and part not. In the former case the company will have no assets let in the course of a Schedule A or overseas property business, and the omission of s. 434E(1)(b) will make no difference. In the latter case the position is less clear and it is possible that the omission of s. 434E(1)(b) has changed the law.

Chapter 2 – Additional VAT Liabilities and Rebates: Interpretation, Etc.

546 Introduction

546 This Chapter has effect for the interpretation of, and for otherwise supplementing–
(a) Chapter 18 of Part 2 (plant and machinery allowances: additional VAT liabilities and rebates),
(b) [Omitted by FA 2008, s. 84 and Sch. 27, para. 12.]
(ba) Chapter 10 of Part 3A (business premises renovation allowances: additional VAT liabilities and rebates), and

(c) Chapter 4 of Part 6 (research and development allowances: additional VAT liabilities and rebates).

History – S. 546(b) omitted by FA 2008, s. 84 and Sch. 27, para. 12, with effect in relation to chargeable periods beginning on or after 1 April 2011 for corporation tax purposes and 6 April 2011 for income tax purposes (FA 2008, Sch. 27, para. 30(1)).
S. 546(ba) inserted before the "and" at the end of s. 546(b) by FA 2005, s. 92 and Sch. 6, para. 6 with effect in relation to expenditure incurred on or after 11 April 2007, by virtue of SI 2007/949, art. 2.
Origin – S. 546: drafting.
HMRC Manuals – CA11900: guidance on s. 546–551.

547 'Additional VAT liability' and 'additional VAT rebate'

547(1) "Additional VAT liability" means an amount which a person becomes liable to pay by way of adjustment under the VAT capital items legislation in respect of input tax.

547(2) "Additional VAT rebate" means an amount which a person becomes entitled to deduct by way of adjustment under the VAT capital items legislation in respect of input tax.

Origin – S. 547(1): CAA 1990, s. 159A(6) ("additional VAT liability").
S. 547(2): CAA 1990, s. 159A(6) ("additional VAT rebate").
HMRC Manuals – CA11900: guidance on s. 546–551.

548 Time when additional VAT liability or rebate is incurred or made

548(1) The time when a person incurs an additional VAT liability or an additional VAT rebate is made to a person is the last day of the period–

(a) which is one of the periods making up the VAT period of adjustment applicable to the asset in question under the VAT capital items legislation, and

(b) in which the increase or decrease in use giving rise to the liability or rebate occurs.

548(2) "VAT period of adjustment" means a period specified under the VAT capital items legislation by reference to which adjustments are made in respect of input tax.

Origin – S. 548(1): CAA 1990, s. 159A(1) (part), (2) (part).
S. 548(2): CAA 1990, s. 159A(1) (part), (2) (part), (6) ("VAT capital items legislation" (part), "VAT period of adjustment").
HMRC Manuals – CA11900: guidance on s. 546–551.

549 Chargeable period in which, and time when, additional VAT liability or rebate accrues

549(1) The chargeable period in which, and the time when, an additional VAT liability or additional VAT rebate accrues is set out in the Table.

TABLE
ACCRUAL OF VAT LIABILITIES AND REBATES

Circumstances	*Chargeable period*	*Time of accrual*
The liability or rebate is accounted for in a VAT return.	The chargeable period which includes the last day of the period to which the VAT return relates.	The last day of the period to which the VAT return relates.
The Commissioners of Customs and Excise assess the liability or rebate as due before a VAT return is made.	The chargeable period which includes the day on which the assessment is made.	The day on which the assessment is made.
The relevant activity is permanently discontinued before the liability or rebate is accounted for in a VAT return or assessed by the Commissioners.	The chargeable period in which the relevant activity is permanently discontinued.	The last day of the chargeable period in which the relevant activity is permanently discontinued.

549(2) In the Table–

(a) **"VAT return"** means a return made to the Commissioners of Customs and Excise for the purposes of value added tax, and

(b) **"the relevant activity"** means the trade or, in relation to Part 2, the qualifying activity to which the additional VAT liability or additional VAT rebate relates.

Origin – S. 549(1): CAA 1990, s. 159A(3) (part), (4) (part), Annex 2, Notes 58, 70.
S. 549(2): CAA 1990, s. 159A(4) (part), (7) (part).
Rewrite: Technical Points – Explanatory Notes, Annex 2, Note 70: Item 1 of the Table in s. 549(1) reflects an interpretation of CAA 1990, s. 159A(4)(a) which would indicate the last day of the period to which the VAT return relates (i.e. as though para. (a) had said "on" instead of "in the chargeable period which includes").
HMRC Manuals – CA11900: guidance on s. 546–551.

550 Apportionment of additional VAT liabilities and rebates

550(1) This section applies if–

(a) any provision of this Act requires an allowance or charge to which a person is entitled or liable in respect of any qualifying expenditure to be determined by reference to–

(i) a proportion only of that expenditure, or

(ii) a proportion only of what that allowance or charge would have been apart from that provision, and

(b) the person incurs an additional VAT liability or an additional VAT rebate is made to the person in respect of that expenditure.

550(2) The additional VAT liability or rebate is subject to the same apportionment as the original expenditure, allowance or charge.

Origin – S. 550(1), (2): CAA 1990, s. 159A(5).

HMRC Manuals – CA11900: guidance on s. 546–551.

551 Supplementary

551(1) In this Chapter, **"the VAT capital items legislation"** means any Act or instrument (whenever passed or made) providing for the proportion of input tax on an asset of a specified description which may be deducted by a person from his output tax to be adjusted from time to time as a result of–

(a) an increase, or

(b) a decrease,

in the extent to which the asset is used by him for making taxable supplies (or taxable supplies of a specified class or description) during a specified period.

551(2) In this Chapter **"the VAT capital items legislation"** also includes any other Act or instrument (whenever passed or made) which provides for Article 20(2) to (4) of the Sixth VAT Directive to be given effect.

551(3) **"The Sixth VAT Directive"** means the Sixth Directive of the Council of the European Communities on Value Added Tax, dated 17th May 1977.

551(4) In this Chapter **"input tax"**, **"output tax"** and **"taxable supply"** have the same meaning as in VATA 1994.

Origin – S. 551(1)–(3): CAA 1990, s. 159A(6) ("VAT capital items legislation" (part)).
S. 551(4): CAA 1990, s. 159A(6) ("VAT capital items legislation" (part)), (7) (part).

HMRC Manuals – CA11900: guidance on s. 546–551.

Chapter 3 – Disposals of Oil Licences: Provisions Relating to Parts 5 and 6

INTRODUCTION

552 Meaning of 'oil licence' and 'interest in an oil licence'

552(1) In this Chapter **"oil licence"** means a UK oil licence or a foreign oil concession.

552(2) In this Chapter **"UK oil licence"** means a licence under–

(a) Part I of the Petroleum Act 1998 ("the 1998 Act"), or

(b) the Petroleum (Production) Act (Northern Ireland) 1964 ("the 1964 Act"),

authorising the winning of oil.

552(3) In this Chapter **"foreign oil concession"** means any right which–

(a) is a right to search for or win oil that exists in its natural condition in a place to which neither the 1998 Act nor the 1964 Act applies, and

(b) is conferred or exercisable (whether or not under a licence) in relation to a particular area.

552(4) In this Chapter **"interest in an oil licence"** includes, if there is an agreement which–

(a) relates to oil from the whole or a part of the licensed area, and

(b) was made before the extraction of the oil to which it relates,

any entitlement under the agreement to, or to a share of, that oil or the proceeds of its sale.

Origin – S. 552(1): CAA 1990, s. 138A(4) ("oil licence"), drafting.
S. 552(2): Oil Taxation Act 1975 s. 12(1) ("licence"), CAA 1990, s. 116(2) (part), s. 118A(4) (part), s. 138A(4) ("UK licence"), TCGA 1992, s. 196(5) ("UK licence").

S. 552(3): CAA 1990, s. 118A(4) (part), s. 138A(4) ("foreign oil concession", "overseas petroleum"), TCGA 1992, s. 196(5) ("foreign oil concession", "overseas petroleum").
S. 552(4): CAA 1990, s. 118A(4) (part), s. 138A(4) ("interest"), TCGA1992, s. 196(5) ("interest").

Cross references – S. 555: disposal of oil licence with exploitation value.
ICTA 1988, Sch. 19B, para. 11: petroleum extraction activities: exploration expenditure supplement: treatment of disposal value on disposal of oil licence with exploitation value: meaning of oil licence as in CAA 2001, s. 555 but with reference to CAA 2001, s. 552(1).

OIL LICENCES RELATING TO UNDEVELOPED AREAS

553 Consideration to be treated as nil

553(1) This section applies if–

(a) there is a material disposal of an oil licence which, at the time of the disposal, relates to an undeveloped area, and

(b) any of the consideration for the disposal consists of–

(i) another oil licence, or an interest in another oil licence, which at that time relates to an undeveloped area, or

(ii) an obligation to undertake exploration work or appraisal work in an area which is or forms part of the licensed area in relation to the licence disposed of.

553(2) The value of the consideration within subsection (1)(b) is to be treated as nil for the purposes of–

(a) Part 5 (mineral extraction allowances),

(b) Part 6 (research and development allowances), and

(c) section 555 (disposal of oil licence with exploitation value).

553(3) A **"material disposal"** of an oil licence means any disposal (including a part disposal and a disposal of an interest in an oil licence) other than a disposal in relation to which section 568 or 569 (sales treated as being for alternative amount) has effect.

553(4) If–

(a) the material disposal is part of a larger transaction under which one party makes to another material disposals of two or more licences, and

(b) at the time of disposal, each of those licences relates to an undeveloped area,

the licensed area for the purposes of subsection (1)(b) is the totality of the licensed areas in relation to those licences.

553(5) In relation to a material disposal of a licence under which the buyer acquires an interest in the licence only so far as it relates to part of the licensed area, any reference in this section and section 554 to the licensed area is to be read as a reference only to that part of the licensed area to which the buyer's acquisition relates.

553(6) In subsection (1)(b)–

"exploration work", in relation to an area, means work carried out for the purpose of searching for oil anywhere in that area, and

"appraisal work", in relation to an area, means work carried out for the purpose of ascertaining–

(a) the extent or characteristics of any oil-bearing area the whole or part of which lies in that area, or

(b) what the reserves of oil of any such oil-bearing area are.

Origin – S. 553(1), (2): CAA 1990, s. 118A(1) (part).
S. 553(3): CAA 1990, s. 118A(2), (4) (part), TCGA 1992, s. 196(5A) (part), Annex 2, Note 71.
S. 553(4): CAA 1990, s. 118A(3).
S. 553(5): CAA 1990, s. 118A(4) (part), TCGA 1992, s. 196(4) (part).
S. 553(6): CAA 1990, s. 118A(4) (part), TCGA 1992, s. 196(6).

Rewrite: Technical Points – Explanatory Notes, Annex 2, Note 71: s. 553(3), in defining a "material disposal", does not import the definition in TCGA 1992, s. 194(1) as that would appear to be the intention behind FA 1988, s. 62(2)(a). That provision expressed the exclusion of disposals made otherwise than by way of bargains at arm's length to be "so far as concerns the 1979 Act", and s. 553(3) proceeds on the basis that CAA 1990, s. 118A(4) did not inadvertently change the law. Also, s. 553(3) refers to "section 562 or 563" because the CAA 1990, s. 118A(2) incorrectly translated FA 1988, s. 62(2)(b) by referring to "a disposal in relation to which sections 157 and 158 have effect", where the use of the word "and" was clearly a mistake.

554 Circumstances in which oil licence relates to undeveloped area

554(1) A UK oil licence relates to an undeveloped area if–

(a) no consent for development has been granted to the licensee for any part of the licensed area by the relevant authority, and

(b) no programme of development has been served on the licensee or approved for any part of the licensed area by the relevant authority.

554(2) A foreign oil concession relates to an undeveloped area if–

(a) no development has actually taken place in any part of the licensed area, and

(b) no condition for the carrying out of development anywhere in that area has been satisfied–

(i) by the grant of any consent by the authorities of a country or territory exercising jurisdiction in relation to the area, or

(ii) by the approval or service on the licensee, by any such authorities, of any programme of development.

554(3) Subsections (4) and (5) of section 36 of FA 1983 (meaning of development) apply for the purposes of subsections (1) and (2).

554(4) In subsection (1) **"licensee"** means–

(a) the person entitled to the benefit of the licence or, if two or more persons are entitled to the benefit, each of those persons, and

(b) a person who has rights under an agreement which is–

(i) approved by the Commissioners for Her Majesty's Revenue and Customs, and

(ii) certified by the relevant authority to confer on that person rights which are the same as, or similar to, those conferred by a licence.

554(5) In subsection (2) **"licensee"** means the person with the concession or any person having an interest in it.

History – In s. 554(4)(b)(i), the reference to "the Commissioners for Her Majesty's Revenue and Customs" substituted for "the Board of Inland Revenue" by CRCA 2005, s. 50(6) and Sch. 4, para. 83(2) with effect from 18 April 2005 by virtue of SI 2005/1126, art. 2(2).

Origin – S. 554(1): CAA 1990, s. 118A(4) (part), TCGA 1992, s. 196(1) (part).
S. 554(2): CAA 1990, s. 118A(4) (part), TCGA 1992, s. 196(1A) (part).
S. 554(3): CAA 1990, s. 118A(4) (part), TCGA 1992, s. 196(3) (part).
S. 554(4): Oil Taxation Act 1975 s. 12(1) ("licensee",), CAA 1990, s. 118A(4) (part), TCGA 1992, s. 196(5) ("licensee" (part)).
S. 554(5): CAA 1990, s. 118A(4) (part), TCGA 1992, s. 196(5) ("licensee" (part)).

CAA 2001

DISPOSAL OF OIL LICENCE WITH EXPLOITATION VALUE

555 Disposal of oil licence with exploitation value

555(1) This section applies if–

(a) a person (**"the seller"**) disposes of an interest in an oil licence to another (**"the buyer"**), and

(b) part of the value of the interest is attributable to allowable exploration expenditure incurred by the seller.

555(2) For the purposes of Part 6 (research and development allowances) the disposal is to be treated as a disposal by which the seller ceases to own an asset representing the allowable exploration expenditure to which that part of the value of the interest is attributable.

555(3) Part 6 applies as if the disposal value to be brought into account were equal to so much of the buyer's expenditure on acquiring the interest as it is just and reasonable to attribute to that part of the value of the interest.

555(4) In this section **"allowable exploration expenditure"** means expenditure which–

(a) is incurred on mineral exploration and access within the meaning of Part 5 (mineral extraction allowances), and

(b) is qualifying expenditure for the purposes of Part 6.

Origin – S. 555(1), (2): CAA 1990, s. 138A(1) (part).
S. 555(3): CAA 1990, s. 138A(2) (part).
S. 555(4): CAA 1990, s. 138A(3), (4) ("mineral exploration and access").

Cross references – ICTA 1988, Sch. 19B, para. 1 and 11: petroleum extraction activities: exploration expenditure supplement.

MINOR DEFINITIONS

556 Minor definitions

556(1) In this Chapter **"licensed area"** means (subject to section 553(4) and (5))–

(a) in relation to a UK oil licence, the area to which the licence applies, and

(b) in relation to a foreign oil concession, the area in relation to which the right to search for or win oil is conferred or exercisable under the concession.

556(2) In this Chapter **"the relevant authority"**, in relation to a UK oil licence means–

(a) in the case of a licence under Part I of the 1998 Act, the Oil and Gas Authority, and

(b) in the case of a licence under the 1964 Act, the Department of Enterprise, Trade and Investment in Northern Ireland.

556(3) In this Chapter **"oil"**–

(a) in relation to a UK oil licence, means any substance won or capable of being won under the authority of a licence granted under Part I of the 1998 Act or the 1964 Act, other than methane gas won in the course of operations for making and keeping mines safe, and

(b) in relation to a foreign oil concession, means any petroleum (as defined by section 1 of the 1998 Act).

Origin – S. 556(1): CAA 1990, s. 118A(4) (part), TCGA 1992, s. 196(5) ("licensed area" (part)).
In s. 556(2)(a), the words "Oil and Gas Authority" substituted for the words "Secretary of State" by SI 2016/898, reg. 14, with effect from 1 October 2016 (as the 21st day after being made on 10 September 2016).
S. 556(2) Oil Taxation 1975 s. 12(1) ("licensee" (part)), CAA 1990, s. 118A(4) (part), TCGA 1992, s. 196(1) (part), Departments (Northern Ireland) Order 1999, S.I.1999/283 (N.I.1) Art. 3, Sch. 1.
S. 556(3) Oil Taxation Act 1975 s. 1(1), CAA 1990, s. 64A(12), s. 118A(4) (part), s. 138A(4) ("oil", "petroleum"), TCGA 1992, s. 196(5) ("oil").

Chapter 4 – Partnerships, Successions and Transfers

557 Application of sections 558 and 559

557 Sections 558 (effect of partnership changes) and 559 (effect of successions) apply for the purposes of this Act other than–

(a) Part 2 (plant and machinery allowances),

(b) Part 6 (research and development allowances), and

(c) Part 10 (assured tenancy allowances).

Origin – CAA 1990, s. 152(1) (part), (3) (part).

Cross references – S. 263, 265: partnerships and successions for plant and machinery allowances.
ICTA 1988, s. 343(2): treatment of capital allowances in company reconstructions without change of ownership.

558 Effect of partnership changes

558(1) This section applies if–

(a) a relevant activity has been set up and is at any time carried on in partnership,

(b) there has been a change in the persons engaged in carrying on the relevant activity, and

(c) the condition in subsection (1A) or (1B) (whichever is appropriate) is met.

558(1A) For income tax purposes, the condition is that a person carrying on the relevant activity immediately before the change continues to carry it on after the change.

558(1B) For corporation tax purposes, the condition is that a company carrying on the relevant activity in partnership immediately before the change continues to carry it on in partnership after the change.

558(2) In this section–

"the present partners" means the person or persons for the time being carrying on the relevant activity, and

"predecessors", in relation to the present partners, means their predecessors in carrying on the relevant activity.

558(3) Any allowance or charge is to be made to or on the present partners.

558(4) The amount of any allowance or charge arising under subsection (3) is to be calculated as if–

(a) the present partners had at all times been carrying on the relevant activity, and

(b) everything done to or by their predecessors in carrying on the relevant activity had been done to or by the present partners.

558(5) In this section **"relevant activity"** means a trade, property business, profession or vocation.

History – S. 558(1)(c) substituted by CTA 2009, s. 1322 and Sch. 1, para. 518(2), with effect for corporation tax purposes for accounting periods ending on or after 1 April 2009, and for income tax and capital gains tax purposes for the tax year 2009–10 and subsequent tax years.
Former s. 558(1)(c) amended by ITTOIA 2005, s. 882(1) and Sch. 1, para. 571; effective for income tax purposes for 2005–06 onwards and for corporation tax purposes for accounting periods ending after 5 April 2005 (ITTOIA 2005, s. 883(1)).
Former s. 558(1)(c) substituted by FA 2001, s. 69 and Sch. 21, para. 4(2), with effect as respects allowances and charges falling to be made for chargeable periods ending, for income tax purposes, on or after 6 April 2001, and, for corporation tax purposes, on or after 1 April 2001.
S. 558(1A) inserted by CTA 2009, s. 1322 and Sch. 1, para. 518(3), with effect for corporation tax purposes for accounting periods ending on or after 1 April 2009, and for income tax and capital gains tax purposes for the tax year 2009–10 and subsequent tax years.
S. 558(1B) inserted by CTA 2009, s. 1322 and Sch. 1, para. 518(3), with effect for corporation tax purposes for accounting periods ending on or after 1 April 2009, and for income tax and capital gains tax purposes for the tax year 2009–10 and subsequent tax years.

Origin – S. 558(1)–(4): CAA 1990, s. 152(3) (part).
S. 558(5) Annex 1, Change 62.

Rewrite: Changes in Law – Explanatory Notes, Annex 1, Change 62: s. 558(5) applies the provisions for the effect of partnership changes to a "property business" as well as trades, professions or vocations. The previous provisions (in CAA 1990, s. 152) applied to Sch. A businesses (ICTA 1988, s. 21B, via CAA 1990, s 161(9) and ICTA 1988, s. 113 and 337), but it is not entirely clear whether they applied in a similar fashion to an overseas property business (although it is, at the least, arguable that they did). In practice, they were generally applied to such a business. Under the rewritten legislation this lack of clarity is removed to reflect the previous practical approach for an overseas property business as well as the indubitable statutory approach to other activities. Where this change has an adverse effect, there is a right of election for the previous position to apply to a period which straddles 6 April (income tax) or 1 April (corporation tax) 2001 (Sch. 3, para. 8).

HMRC Manuals – CA15200: guidance and example on s. 558.
CA15300: guidance on death of sole trader.

559 Effect of successions

559(1) This section applies if–

(a) a person (**"the successor"**) succeeds to a relevant activity which until that time was carried on by another person (**"the predecessor"**), and

(b) the condition in subsection (1A) or (1B) (whichever is appropriate) is met.

559(1A) For income tax purposes, the condition is that no person carrying on the relevant activity immediately before the succession continues to carry it on after the succession.

559(1B) For corporation tax purposes, the condition is that no company carrying on the relevant activity in partnership immediately before the succession continues to carry it on in partnership after the succession.

559(2) The property in question is to be treated as if–

(a) it had been sold to the successor when the succession takes place, and

(b) the net proceeds of the sale were the market value of the property.

559(3) The property in question is any property which–

(a) immediately before the succession, was in use for the purposes of the discontinued relevant activity, and

(b) immediately after the succession, and without being sold, is in use for the purposes of the new relevant activity.

559(4) No entitlement to an initial allowance arises under this section.

559(5) In this section **"relevant activity"** means a trade, property business, profession or vocation.

History – S. 559(1)(b) substituted by CTA 2009, s. 1322 and Sch. 1, para. 519(2), with effect for corporation tax purposes for accounting periods ending on or after 1 April 2009, and for income tax and capital gains tax purposes for the tax year 2009–10 and subsequent tax years.
Former s. 559(1)(b) amended by ITTOIA 2005, s. 882(1) and Sch. 1, para. 572(2); effective for income tax purposes for 2005–06 onwards and for corporation tax purposes for accounting periods ending after 5 April 2005 (ITTOIA 2005, s. 883(1)).
S. 559(1A) and (1B) substituted for former s. 559(1A) by CTA 2009, s. 1322 and Sch. 1, para. 519(3), with effect for corporation tax purposes for accounting periods ending on or after 1 April 2009, and for income tax and capital gains tax purposes for the tax year 2009–10 and subsequent tax years.
Former s. 559(1A) inserted by ITTOIA 2005, s. 882(1) and Sch. 1, para. 572(3); effective for income tax purposes for 2005–06 onwards and for corporation tax purposes for accounting periods ending after 5 April 2005 (ITTOIA 2005, s. 883(1)).

Origin – S. 559(1)–(3): CAA 1990, s. 152(1) (part).
S. 559(4): CAA 1990, s. 152(2).
S. 559(5): CAA 1990, s. 152(1) (part), Annex 1, Change 62.

Cross references – S. 265: successions for plant and machinery allowances.
S. 564(2)(c): application of s. 563 in determination of market value for purposes of s. 559.
ICTA 1988, s. 525(3): receipts from sale of patent rights taxed on persons jointly carrying on a trade cease to be charged after trade discontinued.
Broadcasting Act 1996, s. 135 and Sch. 7, para. 12–17: transfers of property etc. between BBC and successor organisations.
SI 2013/2242, art. 4: continuity of treatment in relation to any allowances or charges which relate to part of BRB (Residuary) Limited's property business transferred to London & Continental Railways Limited by a relevant transfer.

Rewrite: Changes in Law – Explanatory Notes, Annex 1, Change 62: s. 559(5) applies the provisions for the effect of successions to a "property business" as well as trades, professions or vocations. The previous provisions (in CAA 1990, s. 152) applied to Sch. A businesses (ICTA 1988, s. 21B, via CAA 1990, s 161(9) and ICTA 1988, s. 113 and 337), but it is not entirely clear whether they applied in a similar fashion to an overseas property business (although it is, at the least, arguable that they did). In practice, they were generally applied to such a business. Under the rewritten legislation this lack of clarity is removed to reflect the previous practical approach for an overseas property business as well as the indubitable statutory approach to other activities. Where this change has an adverse effect, there is a right of election for the previous position to apply to a period which straddles 6 April (income tax) or 1 April (corporation tax) 2001 (Sch. 3, para. 8).

HMRC Manuals – CA15100: guidance on s. 559.

560 Transfer of insurance company business

560(1) This section applies if–

(a) assets are transferred as part of, or in connection with, the transfer of the whole or part of the business of an insurance company to another company,

(b) the transfer is–

  (i) in accordance with an insurance business transfer scheme to transfer business which consists of the effecting or carrying out of contracts of long-term insurance, or

  (ii) a qualifying overseas transfer.

560(2) But this section does not apply in relation to any asset transferred to a non-resident company unless the asset will fall to be treated, immediately after the transfer, as an asset which is held for the purposes of the whole or a part of so much of any business carried on by the non-resident company as is carried on through a permanent establishment in the United Kingdom.

560(3) This section also does not apply if section 561 applies (transfer of a UK trade to a company in another member State).

560(4) If this section applies–

(a) any allowances and charges that would have been made to or on the transferor are to be made instead to or on the transferee, and

(b) the amount of any such allowance or charge is to be calculated as if everything done to or by the transferor had been done to or by the transferee,

but no sale or transfer of assets made to the transferee by the transferor is to be treated as giving rise to any such allowance or charge.

560(5) In this section–

(a) [omitted by FA 2007, s. 41 and Sch. 10, para. 14(8)(c) and repealed by FA 2007, s. 114 and Sch. 27, Pt. 2(10),]

(b) [omitted by FA 2007, s. 40 and Sch. 9, para. 1(2)(f) and repealed by FA 2007, s. 114 and Sch. 27, Pt. 2(9),]

(c) [omitted by FA 2007, s. 41 and Sch. 10, para. 14(8)(c) and repealed by FA 2007, s. 114 and Sch. 27, Pt. 2(10),]

(d) **"non-resident company"** means a company resident outside the United Kingdom.

(e) **"qualifying overseas transfer"** means so much of a transfer of the whole or any part of the business of an overseas life insurance company carried on through a permanent establishment in the United Kingdom as takes place in accordance with an authorisation granted outside the United Kingdom for the purposes of Article 14 of the Council Directive of 5 November 2002 concerning life assurance (2002/83/EC).

History – In s. 560(1)(b)(i), the words "a scheme sanctioned by a court under Part I of Schedule 2C to the Insurance Companies Act 1982 (transfers of long term business), or" substituted by the words "an insurance business transfer scheme to transfer business which consists of the effecting or carrying out of contracts of long-term insurance, or", by virtue of SI 2001/3629, art. 108(2) which has effect in relation to any transfer under a scheme falling within section 105 of the Financial Services and Markets Act 2000, including an excluded scheme falling within Case 2, 3 or 4 of subsection (3) of that section.

In s. 560(1)(b)(ii) the words "within the meaning of paragraph 4A of Schedule 19AC to ICTA (overseas life insurance companies)" (which appeared after the word "transfer") omitted by FA 2012, s. 146 and Sch. 16, para. 105(2) in relation to accounting periods beginning on or after 1 January 2013 (FA 2012, s. 148) but subject to transitional provisions in FA 2012, Sch. 17. Where an accounting period would otherwise straddle 1 January 2013, it is deemed to end on 31 December 2012 (FA 2012, s. 149).

In s. 560(2), the words "permanent establishment" substituted for "branch or agency" by FA 2003, s. 153(1)(d) in relation to accounting periods beginning on or after 1 January 2003.

S. 560(5)(a) omitted by FA 2007, s. 41 and Sch. 10, para. 14(8)(c) and repealed by FA 2007, s. 114 and Sch. 27, Pt. 2(10), with effect in relation to periods of account beginning on or after 1 January 2007.

S. 560(5)(b) omitted by FA 2007, s. 40 and Sch. 9, para. 1(2)(f) and repealed by FA 2007, s. 114 and Sch. 27, Pt. 2(9) with effect in relation to periods of account beginning on or after 1 January 2007.

S. 560(5)(c) omitted by FA 2007, s. 41 and Sch. 10, para. 14(8)(c) and repealed by FA 2007, s. 114 and Sch. 27, Pt. 2(10), with effect in relation to periods of account beginning on or after 1 January 2007.

In s. 560(5), the word "and" at the end of paragraph (a) omitted, by virtue of SI 2001/3629, art. 108(3)(a) which has effect in relation to any transfer under a scheme falling within s. 105 of the Financial Services and Markets Act 2000, including an excluded scheme falling within Case 2, 3 or 4 of subsection (3) of that section.

In s. 560(5), sub-paragraph (b) substituted, and also sub-paragraphs (c) and (d) inserted, by virtue of SI 2001/3629, art. 108(3)(b) which has effect in relation to any transfer under a scheme falling within s. 105 of the Financial Services and Markets Act 2000, including an excluded scheme falling within Case 2, 3 or 4 of subsection (3) of that section.

In s. 560(5)(e) inserted by FA 2012, s. 146 andSch. 16, para. 105(3) in relation to accounting periods beginning on or after 1 January 2013 (FA 2012, s. 148) but subject to transitional provisions in FA 2012, Sch. 17. Where an accounting period would otherwise straddle 1 January 2013, it is deemed to end on 31 December 2012 (FA 2012, s. 149).

Origin – S. 560(1): CAA 1990, s. 152A(1).
S. 560(2): CAA 1990, s. 152A(1A) (part).
S. 560(3): CAA 1990, s. 152B(10) (part).
S. 560(4): CAA 1990, s. 152A(2).
S. 560(5): CAA 1990, s. 152A(1B) (part), drafting.

Cross references – ICTA 1988, s. 75: expenses of management: investment companies.
ICTA 1988, s. 76: expenses of management: insurance companies.
ICTA 1988, s. 431: "insurance company" defined for the purposes of ICTA 1988, Pt. XII, Ch. I as a company to which the Insurance Companies Act 1982, Pt. II applies or a UK branch or agency of an EC company.
ICTA 1988, s. 444A: treatment of expenses of corporation tax when long term business is transferred between insurance companies.
ICTA 1988, Sch. 19AC, para. 4A: "qualifying overseas transfer" is so much of any transfer of the whole or any part of the business of an overseas life insurance company carried on through a branch or agency in the UK as takes place in accordance with any authorisation granted outside the UK for the purposes of art. 11 of the third long term insurance directive.
ICTA 1988, *Pt. XII, Ch. I: insurance companies, underwriters and capital redemption business.*
SI 1997/473, reg. 53D: modification of s. 560 as it applies to specified transactions involving friendly societies.

Transitional – Sch. 3, para. 111: s. 560 applies with the substitution for subs. (1) of the following:

"**560(1)** This section applies if assets are transferred as part of, or in connection with, a transfer of the whole or part of the long term business of an insurance company to another company in accordance with a scheme sanctioned by a court under section 49 of the Insurance Companies Act 1982."
and with the omission of subsection (2), in relation to transfers sanctioned or authorised before 1 July 1994.

HMRC Manuals – CA15500: guidance on s. 560.

560A Transfers of trade without a change of ownership

560A(1) This Act has effect subject to Chapter 1 of Part 22 of CTA 2010 (unless section 561 or 561A below applies in relation to the transfer in question).

560A(2) See, in particular, section 948 of that Act.

History – S. 560A inserted by CTA 2010, s. 1177 and Sch. 1, para. 359, with effect for corporation tax purposes for accounting periods ending on or after 1 April 2010.

561 Transfer or division of UK business

561(1) This section applies if and in so far as–

(a) a qualifying company resident in one member State ("the transferor") transfers the whole or part of a business carried on by it in the United Kingdom to one or more qualifying companies resident in one or more other member States ("the transferee" or "the transferees"),

(b) section 140A of TCGA 1992 (transfer of assets treated as no-gain no-loss disposal) applies in relation to the transfer, and

(c) immediately after the transfer the transferee (or one or more of the transferees)–

  (i) is resident in the United Kingdom, or

  (ii) carries on in the United Kingdom through a permanent establishment a business which consists of, or includes, the business or part of the business transferred.

561(2) If this section applies–

(a) the transfer itself does not give rise to any allowances or charges under this Act, and

(b) in relation to assets included in the transfer, anything done to or by the transferor before the transfer is to be treated after the transfer as having been done to or by the transferee (or each transferee).

561(3) If, for the purposes of subsection (2)(b), expenditure falls to be apportioned between assets included in the transfer and other assets, the apportionment is to be made in a just and reasonable manner.

561(4) In this section **"qualifying company"** means a body incorporated under the law of a member State.

561(5) If this section applies, section 948 of CTA 2010 (modified application of CAA 2001 in relation to trade transfers without a change of ownership) does not apply.

History – Heading amended to read "Transfer or division of UK business" by virtue of SI 2007/3186, reg. 3(1) and Sch. 1, para. 25(4), with effect in relation to transfers which take place on or after 1 January 2007, and in relation to cross-border mergers taking place on or after that date, but in the case of mergers relating to the formation of an SE or SCE, in relation to those taking place on or after 18 August 2006 (see SI 2008/1579, reg. 4(1)).
S. 561(1) substituted by SI 2007/3186, reg. 3(1) and Sch. 1, para. 25(2), with effect in relation to transfers which take place on or after 1 January 2007, and in relation to cross-border mergers taking place on or after that date, but in the case of mergers relating to the formation of an SE or SCE, in relation to those taking place on or after 18 August 2006 (see SI 2008/1579, reg. 4(1)).
In s. 561(1)(c)(i), the words "permanent establishment" substituted for "branch or agency" by FA 2003, s.153(1)(d) in relation to accounting periods beginning on or after 1 January 2003.
In s. 561(2)(b) "the transferor" substituted for "company A" and "the transferee (or each transferee)" substituted for "company B" by SI 2007/3186, reg. 3(1) and Sch. 1, para. 25(3), with effect in relation to transfers which take place on or after 1 January 2007, and in relation to cross-border mergers taking place on or after that date, but in the case of mergers relating to the formation of an SE or SCE, in relation to those taking place on or after 18 August 2006 (see SI 2008/1579, reg. 4(1)).
In s. 561(5), the words "section 948 of CTA 2010 (modified application of CAA 2001 in relation to trade transfers without a change of ownership) does not apply" substituted for "section 343(2) of ICTA does not apply (effect of company reconstruction without change of ownership)" by CTA 2010, s. 1177 and Sch. 1, para. 360, with effect for corporation tax purposes for accounting periods ending on or after 1 April 2010.

Origin – S. 561(1): CAA 1990, s. 152B(1) to (3), TCGA 1992, s. 140A(1) (part).
S. 561(2): CAA 1990, s. 152B(4) to (6).
S. 561(3): CAA 1990, s. 152B(7).
S. 561(4): TCGA 1992, s. 140A(7).
S. 561(5): CAA 1990, s. 152B(10) (part).

Cross references – S. 77: successions to trades – connected persons.
S. 266(8): election for successions to trades between connected persons does not apply where s. 561 applies.
S. 564(4): applies the procedure for determining questions in 563 to the tax of company A and company B and to any question of apportionment of expenditure under 561(3).
S. 567(5): s. 568–570 (provisions for sales being treated as being for an alternative amount) do not apply where s. 561 applies.
S. 573(4): provision which treats transfers as sales does not apply where s. 561 applies.
ICTA 1988, s. 343(2): capital allowance consequences of company reconstruction without change of ownership.
TCGA 1992, s. 140A: chargeable gains treatment of transfer by a qualifying company resident in one member state of the whole or part of a trade carried on in the UK to a qualifying company resident in another member state.

European material – Directive 90/434, art. 4.

HMRC Manuals – CA15560: guidance on s. 561.

561A Transfer of asset by reason of cross-border merger

561A(1) This section applies to the transfer of a qualifying asset as part of the process of a merger to which section 140E of TCGA 1992 (mergers: assets within UK tax charge) applies (or would apply but for section 140E(2)(c)).

561A(2) Where this section applies to a transfer–

(a) the transfer does not give rise to any allowance or charge under this Act,

(b) anything done to or by the transferor in relation to assets transferred is to be treated after the transfer as having been done to or by the transferee (with any necessary apportionment of expenditure being made in a reasonable manner), and

(c) section 948 of CTA 2010 (modified application of CAA 2001 in relation to trade transfers without a change of ownership) does not apply.

561A(3) For the purposes of subsection (1) an asset is a "qualifying asset" if–

(a) it is transferred to the transferee as part of the process of the merger, and

(b) subsections (4) and (5) are satisfied in respect of it.

561A(4) This subsection is satisfied in respect of an asset if–

(a) the transferor is resident in the United Kingdom at the time of the transfer, or

(b) the asset is an asset of a permanent establishment in the United Kingdom of the transferor.

561A(5) This subsection is satisfied in respect of an asset if–

(a) the transferee is resident in the United Kingdom at the time of the transfer, or

(b) the asset is an asset of a permanent establishment of the transferee in the United Kingdom immediately following the transfer.

History – S. 561A(2)(c) substituted by CTA 2010, s. 1177 and Sch. 1, para. 361, with effect for corporation tax purposes for accounting periods ending on or after 1 April 2010.
S. 561A substituted by SI 2007/3186, reg. 3(2) and Sch. 2, para. 14, in relation to mergers relating to the formation of an SE or SCE which take place on or after 18 August 2006, and in relation to all other mergers which take place on or after 1 January 2007.

Chapter 5 – Miscellaneous

APPORTIONMENT

562 Apportionment where property sold together

562(1) Any reference in this Act to the sale of property includes the sale of that property together with any other property.

562(2) For the purposes of subsection (1), all property sold as a result of one bargain is to be treated as sold together even though–

(a) separate prices are, or purport to be, agreed for separate items of that property, or

(b) there are, or purport to be, separate sales of separate items of that property.

562(3) If an item of property is sold together with other property, then, for the purposes of this Act–

(a) the net proceeds of the sale of that item are to be treated as being so much of the net proceeds of sale of all the property as, on a just and reasonable apportionment, is attributable to that item, and

(b) the expenditure incurred on the provision or purchase of that item is to be treated as being so much of the consideration given for all the property as, on a just and reasonable apportionment, is attributable to that item.

562(4) This section applies, with the necessary modifications, to other proceeds (consisting of insurance money or other compensation) as it applies in relation to the net proceeds of a sale.

562(5) This section applies in relation to Part 5 as if expenditure on the provision or purchase of an item of property included expenditure on the acquisition of–

(a) a mineral asset (as defined by section 397), or

(b) land outside the United Kingdom.

Origin – S. 562(1): CAA 1990, s. 150(1) (part).
S. 562(2): CAA 1990, s. 150(2).
S. 562(3): CAA 1990, s. 150(1) (part), Annex 1, Change 40.
S. 562(4): CAA 1990, s. 150(3).
S. 562(5): CAA 1990, s. 150(5), Annex 2, Note 72.

Cross references – S. 45C(5): s. 562(3) does not apply where s. 45C applies for the purpose of apportioning expenditure incurred on plant or machinery with energy-saving components.
S. 200(2): precedence of apportionment made by election under s. 198 or 199 over s. 562 apportionment.
S. 370(4): apportionment of capital sum paid for relevant interest in an agricultural building under s. 370(3)(b) does not affect apportionment under s. 562.

S. 384(3): apportionment of proceeds of a balancing event under s. 384(1) does not affect apportionment under s. 562.

Rewrite: Changes in Law – Explanatory Notes, Annex 1, Change 40: A minor change is effected to make the nature of apportionment requirement in s. 562(3) consistent with other provisions in that it must be "just and reasonable"; as opposed to simply "just" as in the previous provision (CAA 1990, s. 150(1)). See Sch. 3, para. 8 for the election to apply the original law to this matter where a chargeable period straddles 1 April 2001 (for corporation tax) or 6 April 2001 (for income tax).

Rewrite: Technical Points – Explanatory Notes, Annex 2, Note 72: S. 562(5) omits to include the definition in former CAA 1990, s. 150(5)(a) which is redundant. That definition is now covered by the broader scope of the general definition of "mineral asset" in s. 12(1) and is no longer required separately.

HMRC Manuals – CA12100ff.: guidance on s. 562(1)–(3).

Other material – HMRC Practice Note: apportioning the price paid for a business transferred as a going concern.

PROCEDURE FOR DETERMINING CERTAIN QUESTIONS

563 Procedure for determining certain questions affecting one or more persons

563(1) This section applies in relation to the determination of a question if–

(a) at the time when the question falls to be determined, it appears that the determination is material to the liability to tax (for whatever period) of one or more persons, and

(b) section 564 provides for this section to apply.

563(2) [Omitted by SI 2009/56, art. 3(1) and Sch. 1, para. 299(2).]

563(3) [Omitted by SI 2009/56, art. 3(1) and Sch. 1, para. 299(2).]

563(4) [Omitted by SI 2009/56, art. 3(1) and Sch. 1, para. 299(2).]

563(5) [Omitted by SI 2009/56, art. 3(1) and Sch. 1, para. 299(2).]

563(6) An application for the tribunal to determine the question is to be subject to the relevant provisions of Part 5 of the Taxes Management Act 1970 (see, in particular, section 48(2)(b) of that Act), and each of the persons concerned is entitled to be a party to the proceedings on the application.

History – In s. 563(1)(a) and the heading to s. 563, "one" substituted for "two" by FA 2012, s. 43 and Sch. 10, para. 5 with effect in relation to new expenditure incurred on or after 6 April 2012, for income tax purposes, and 1 April 2012, for corporation tax purposes, subject to the provisions in FA 2012, Sch. 10, para. 13.

S. 563(2) omitted by SI 2009/56, art. 3(1) and Sch. 1, para. 299(2), operative from 1 April 2009, subject to transitional and saving provisions in SI 2009/56, Sch. 3.

S. 563(3) omitted by SI 2009/56, art. 3(1) and Sch. 1, para. 299(2), operative from 1 April 2009, subject to transitional and saving provisions in SI 2009/56, Sch. 3.

S. 563(4) omitted by SI 2009/56, art. 3(1) and Sch. 1, para. 299(2), operative from 1 April 2009, subject to transitional and saving provisions in SI 2009/56, Sch. 3.

In former s. 563(4)(b), the reference to "the Commissioners for Her Majesty's Revenue and Customs" substituted for "the Board of Inland Revenue" by CRCA 2005, s. 50(6) and Sch. 4, para. 83(2), with effect from 18 April 2005 by virtue of SI 2005/1126, art. 2(2).

S. 563(5) omitted by SI 2009/56, art. 3(1) and Sch. 1, para. 299(2), operative from 1 April 2009, subject to transitional and saving provisions in SI 2009/56, Sch. 3.

S. 563(6) substituted by SI 2009/56, art. 3(1) and Sch. 1, para. 299(3), operative from 1 April 2009, subject to transitional and saving provisions in SI 2009/56, Sch. 3.

Origin – S. 563(1): ICTA 1988, s. 532(1) (part), CAA 1990, s. 151(1) (part).

S. 563(2)–(6): CAA 1990, s. 151(1) (part).

Cross references – S. 200(2): precedence of apportionment made by election under s. 198 or 199 over s. 563 apportionment determination procedure.

S. 370(4): apportionment of capital sum paid for relevant interest in an agricultural building under s. 370(3)(b) does not affect apportionment determination procedure under s. 563.

S. 384(3): apportionment of proceeds of a balancing event under s. 384(1) does not affect apportionment determination procedure under s. 563.

S. 564: applications of the procedure in 563.

TMA 1970, s. 57(3)(b): regulations about appeals in respect of chargeable gains etc. may contain incidental provisions corresponding to s. 563.

TMA 1970, s. 58(3)(b): application of proceedings before Court of Appeal in Northern Ireland in certain cases including s. 563.

TMA 1970, Sch. 3: priority of s. 563 procedure over rules for assigning proceedings to commissioners.

HMRC Manuals – CA12500: guidance on s. 563.

564 Questions to which procedure in section 563 applies

564(1) Section 563 applies in relation to the determination for the purposes of any of Parts 3A to 11 or this Part of any question about the way in which a sum is to be apportioned.

564(2) Section 563 applies in relation to any determination of the market value of property for the purposes of–

(a) any provision of Part 2 (plant and machinery allowances),

(b) section 423 (mineral extraction allowances: amount of disposal value to be brought into account),

(c) section 559 (effect of successions),

(d) section 568 or 569 (sales treated as being for alternative amount), or

(e) section 573 (transfers treated as sales).

564(3) [Omitted by FA 2008, s. 84 and Sch. 27, para. 13(b).]

564(4) If section 561 (transfer of a UK trade to a company in another member State) applies, section 563 applies–

(a) for the purposes of the tax of both company A and company B referred to in that section, and

(b) in relation to the determination of any question of apportionment of expenditure under section 561(3).

History – In s. 564(1), the figure "3A" substituted for the figure "3" by FA 2008, s. 84 and Sch. 27, para. 13(a), with effect in relation to chargeable periods beginning on or after 1 April 2011 for corporation tax purposes and 6 April 2011 for income tax purposes (FA 2008, Sch. 27, para. 30(1)).
S. 564(3) omitted by FA 2008, s. 84 and Sch. 27, para. 13(b), with effect in relation to chargeable periods beginning on or after 1 April 2011 for corporation tax purposes and 6 April 2011 for income tax purposes (FA 2008, Sch. 27, para. 30(1)).

Origin – S. 564(1): CAA 1990, s. 151(1) (part).
S. 564(2): CAA 1990, s. 151(2).
S. 564(3): CAA 1990, s. 151(1A).
S. 564(4): CAA 1990, s. 152B(8), (9), Annex 1, Change 63.

Cross references – S. 200(2): precedence of apportionment made by election under s. 198 or 199 over apportionment procedure under s. 564(1).
S. 370(4): apportionment of capital sum paid for relevant interest in an agricultural building under s. 370(3)(b) does not affect apportionment procedure under s. 564(1).
S. 384(3): apportionment of proceeds of a balancing event under s. 384(1) does not affect apportionment procedure under s. 564(1).

Rewrite: Changes in Law – Explanatory Notes, Annex 1, Change 63: s. 564(4)(b) applies the procedure for determining questions in 563 to 561(3) (transfer of a UK trade to a company in another member state – apportionment of expenditure between assets transferred and other assets). The change allows any consequential references in other acts to the procedure in 563 to be tracked through to its application by s. 564(4) as well (which was not the case when the predecessor provision to s. 561(3) (CAA 1990, s. 152B) had its own, separate but similar, determination provisions). Such reference is made in TMA 1970, s. 58(3) and Sch. 3, para. 10. In the event this change has an adverse effect, there is a right of election for the previous position to apply to a period which straddles 6 April (income tax) or 1 April (corporation tax) 2001 (Sch. 3, para. 8).

HMRC Manuals – CA12500: guidance on s. 564.

TAX AGREEMENTS FOR INCOME TAX PURPOSES

565 Tax agreements for income tax purposes

565(1) This section applies if–

(a) a person is entitled to an allowance for income tax purposes,

(b) that person enters into a tax agreement with an officer of Revenue and Customs for the tax year in which the allowance would be given effect, and

(c) no assessment giving effect to the allowance is made for that tax year.

565(2) In this section **"tax agreement"** means an agreement in writing as to the extent to which the allowance in question is to be given effect for the tax year in question.

565(3) If this section applies, the allowance is to be treated as if it had been given effect under an assessment–

(a) for the tax year for which the tax agreement is made, and

(b) to the extent set out in the tax agreement.

565(4) A tax agreement may relate to any method by which allowances are given effect under this Act.

History – In s. 565(1), the words "an officer of Revenue and Customs" substituted for "the Inland Revenue" by CRCA 2005, s. 50(6) and Sch. 4, para. 83(1), with effect from 18 April 2005 by virtue of SI 2005/1126, art. 2(2).

Origin – S. 565(1), (2): CAA 1990, s. 143(1) (part).
S. 565(3): CAA 1990, s. 143(2).
S. 565(4): CAA 1990, s. 143(1) (part).

HMRC Manuals – CA11150: guidance on s. 565.

COMPANIES NOT RESIDENT IN THE UNITED KINGDOM

566 Companies not resident in the United Kingdom

566(1) This section applies if a company not resident in the United Kingdom is–

(a) within the charge to corporation tax in respect of one source of income, and

(b) within the charge to income tax in respect of another source.

566(2) Allowances related to any source of income are to be given effect against income chargeable to the same tax as is chargeable on income from that source.

Origin – S. 566(1), (2): CAA 1990, s. 149(1).

SALES TREATED AS BEING FOR ALTERNATIVE AMOUNT

567 Sales treated as being for alternative amount: introductory

567(1) Sections 568 to 570 apply for the purposes of Parts 3A, 5, 6 and 10.

567(2) For the purposes of sections 568 to 570, the control test is met if–

(a) the buyer is a body of persons over whom the seller has control,

(b) the seller is a body of persons over whom the buyer has control,

(c) both the seller and the buyer are bodies of persons and another person has control over both of them, or

(d) the seller and the buyer are connected persons.

567(3) In subsection (2) **"body of persons"** includes a partnership.

567(4) For the purposes of sections 568 to 570, the tax advantage test is met if it appears that the sole or main benefit which might be expected to accrue from–

(a) the sale, or

(b) transactions of which the sale is one,

is the obtaining of a tax advantage by all or any of the parties under any provision of this Act except Part 2.

567(5) Sections 568 to 570 do not apply if section 561 applies (transfer of a UK trade to a company in another member State).

History – In s. 567(1), "4A," omitted by FA 2012, s. 227 and Sch. 39, para. 38(4), with effect in relation to chargeable periods beginning on or after 1 April 2013 for corporation tax purposes, and 6 April 2013 for income tax purposes, subject to transitional and saving provisions in FA 2012, Sch. 39, para. 41 and 42.
In s. 567(1), "3," and "4," omitted by FA 2008, s. 84 and Sch. 27, para. 14, with effect in relation to chargeable periods beginning on or after 1 April 2011 for corporation tax purposes and 6 April 2011 for income tax purposes (FA 2008, Sch. 27, para. 30(1)).
In s. 567(1) "3A," inserted after "3," by FA 2005, s. 92 and Sch. 6, para. 7, with effect in relation to expenditure incurred on or after 11 April 2007, by virtue of SI 2007/949, art. 2.
In s. 567(1), reference to Pt. 4A inserted by FA 2001, s. 67 and Sch. 19, Pt. 2, para. 5, with effect in relation to expenditure incurred on or after 11 May 2001.

Origin – S. 567: Annex 2, Note 73.
S. 567(1): ICTA 1988, s. 532(1) (part), (2) (part), (5) (part), CAA 1990, s. 157(1) (part), (4) (part), (5).
S. 567(2): CAA 1990, s. 157(1) (part).
S. 567(3): CAA 1990, s. 157(2).
S. 567(4): CAA 1990, s. 157(1) (part).
S. 567(5): CAA 1990, s. 152B(10) (part).

Cross references – F(No. 2)A 1992, s. 77 and Sch. 17, para. 5(4): Northern Ireland Electricity privatisation – arrangements in favour of other successor companies.
FA 1994, Sch. 24, para. 21(2) and 22(2): disapplication of s. 567–570 in certain circumstances connected with railways privatisation.
Coal Industry Act 1994, Sch. 4, para. 20(2) (as amended by Sch. 2, para. 93(5)(d)) and Transport Act 2000, Sch. 26, para. 21(4), 27(4) and 34(5) (as amended by Sch. 2, para. 109(13), (20) and (27) respectively): disapplication of s. 567–570 to scheme of restructuring in connection with privatisation of the coal industry or railways.
RA 2005, Sch. 10. para. 4 and 24: disapplication of s. 567 to 570 in the case of a transfer to a national authority.

Rewrite: Technical Points – Explanatory Notes, Annex 2, Note 73: s. 567–570 do not include anywhere the wording in former CAA 1990, s. 157(3) which confirmed that former s. 157 and 158 applied notwithstanding the fact that one of the parties to a sale was non-resident. This had been helpful when this legislation was originally enacted and an election was prevented where one of the parties was not resident. However, since then the wording relating to elections had been superseded (by Finance Act 1993) with wording which ignored residence status, so it had become self-evident that the amended statute was applicable regardless of the residence status of either of the parties. The law is not changed by omission of the unnecessary wording.

HMRC Manuals – CA13100: guidance on s. 567.

568 Sales treated as being at market value

568(1) A sale of property that is not at market value is treated as being at market value if–

(a) the control test is met, or

(b) the tax advantage test is met.

568(2) This section is subject to any election under section 569.

Origin – S. 568: Annex 2, Note 73.
S. 568(1): CAA 1990, s. 157(1) (part), (4) (part).
S. 568(2): CAA 1990, s. 157(4) (part).

Cross references – S. 382(3): s. 568 disregarded in determining sole or main benefit expected to accrue from the acquisition of an agricultural building where election for balancing event possible.
S. 413(3): priority of s. 412 (special provisions for transfers of mineral assets within a group) over s. 568.
S. 553(3): material disposal of oil licence does not include disposal within s. 568, 569.
S. 564(2)(d): application of s. 563 in determination of market value for purposes of s. 568.
S. 573: transfers treated as sales.
F(No. 2)A 1992, s. 77 and Sch. 17, para. 5(4): Northern Ireland Electricity privatisation – arrangements in favour of other successor companies.
FA 1994, Sch. 24, para. 21(2) and 22(2): disapplication of s. 567–570 in certain circumstances connected with railways privatisation.
Coal Industry Act 1994, Sch. 4, para. 20(2), (7) (as amended by Sch. 2, para. 93(5)(d), (10)) and Transport Act 2000, Sch. 26, para. 21(4), 27(4) and 34(5) (as amended by Sch. 2, para. 109(13), (20) and (27) respectively): disapplication of s. 567–570 to scheme of restructuring in connection with privatisation of the coal industry or railways.
RA 2005, Sch. 10. para. 4 and 24: disapplication of s. 567 to 570 in the case of a transfer to a national authority.

Rewrite: Technical Points – Explanatory Notes, Annex 2, Note 73: see Rewrite note under s. 567.

HMRC Manuals – CA13100: guidance and examples on s. 568.

569 Election to treat sale as being for alternative amount

569(1) The parties to a sale of property that is not for the alternative amount may elect for the sale to be treated as being for the alternative amount if–

(a) the control test is met or section 573 applies (transfers treated as sales), and

(b) the tax advantage test is not met.

569(2) Subsection (1) is subject to section 570.

569(3) The alternative amount is the lower of market value and–

(a) if the sale is relevant for the purposes of Part 10, the residue of the qualifying expenditure immediately before the sale;

(b) if the sale is relevant for the purposes of Part 5, the unrelieved qualifying expenditure immediately before the sale;

(c) if the sale is relevant for the purposes of Part 6–

(i) in a case where an allowance under Part 6 is given for the expenditure represented by the asset sold, nil;

(ii) in any other case, the qualifying expenditure represented by the asset sold.

569(4) In subsection (3) **"residue of qualifying expenditure"**, **"unrelieved qualifying expenditure"** and **"qualifying expenditure"** have the same meaning as in the Part for the purposes of which the sale is relevant.

569(5) If the sale–

(a) is relevant for the purposes of Part 10, and

(b) is treated as being for the residue of the qualifying expenditure immediately before the sale,

no balancing adjustment is to be made as a result of the sale under section 517 (building not a qualifying dwelling-house throughout).

569(6) If, after the date of the sale, an event occurs as a result of which a balancing charge would have fallen to be made on the seller if–

(a) he had continued to own the property, and

(b) he had done all such things, and been allowed all such allowances, as were done by or allowed to the buyer,

the balancing charge is to be made on the buyer.

569(7) All such assessments and adjustments of assessments are to be made as are necessary to give effect to the election.

569(8) For the purposes of this section and section 570, a sale is relevant for the purposes of a Part if it is of property of a kind that is relevant for deciding whether an allowance or charge is made under that Part.

History – In s. 569(3)(a), the words "3 or" omitted by FA 2008, s. 84 and Sch. 27, para. 15(a), with effect in relation to chargeable periods beginning on or after 1 April 2011 for corporation tax purposes and 6 April 2011 for income tax purposes (FA 2008, Sch. 27, para. 30(1)).

In s. 569(5), the words "3 or" and "319 (building not an industrial building, etc throughout) or" omitted by FA 2008, s. 84 and Sch. 27, para. 15, with effect in relation to chargeable periods beginning on or after 1 April 2011 for corporation tax purposes and 6 April 2011 for income tax purposes (FA 2008, Sch. 27, para. 30(1)).

Origin – S. 569: Annex 2, Note 73.
S. 569(1), (2): CAA 1990, s. 158(1) (part).
S. 569(3): CAA 1990, s. 158(1) (part), (2) (part).
S. 569(4): CAA 1990, s. 158(2) (part).
S. 569(5): CAA 1990, s. 4(8), s. 88(4).
S. 569(6): CAA 1990, s. 158(1) (part).
S. 569(7): CAA 1990, s. 158(4).
S. 569(8): drafting.

Cross references – S. 404(7) (mineral extraction allowances): exclusion of expenditure equal to undeveloped market value does not apply to buyer's expenditure where election under s. 569 made.
S. 413(2)(b): s. 412 (special provisions for transfers of mineral assets within a group) does not apply where election under s. 569 made.
S. 553(3): material disposal of oil licence does not include disposal within s. 568, 569.
S. 564(2)(d): application of s. 563 in determination of market value for purposes of s. 569.
S. 573(3): transfers treated as sales take place at market value subject to election under s. 569.
TMA 1970, s. 42(6), (7)(c) (as amended by Sch. 2, para. 1): claims made by partnerships.
F(No. 2)A 1992, s. 77 and Sch. 17, para. 5(4): Northern Ireland Electricity privatisation – arrangements in favour of other successor companies.
TCGA 1992, s. 41(3): capital loss restricted by reference to capital allowances of transferor as well as disponor where acquisition subject to election under s. 569.
FA 1994, Sch. 24, para. 21(2) and 22(2): disapplication of s. 567–570 in certain circumstances connected with railways privatisation.
Coal Industry Act 1994, Sch. 4, para. 20(2) (as amended by Sch. 2, para. 93(5)(d)) and Transport Act 2000, Sch. 26, para. 21(4), 27(4) and 34(5) (as amended by Sch. 2, para. 109(13), (20) and (27) respectively): disapplication of s. 567–570 to scheme of restructuring in connection with privatisation of the coal industry or railways.
RA 2005, Sch. 10. para. 4 and 24: disapplication of s. 567 to 570 in the case of a transfer to a national authority.

Transitional – Sch. 3, para. 112: s. 569(3) applies with the substitution for para. (a) of the following:

"(a) any of the parties is not resident in the United Kingdom at the time of the transfer and the circumstances are not at that time such that a relevant allowance or charge falls or might fall to be made to or on that party as a result of the transfer;".

to a transfer –

(a) before 16th March 1993;

(b) in pursuance of a contract entered into before that date; and

(c) in pursuance of a contract entered into for the purpose of securing that obligations under a contract entered into before that date are complied with.

Rewrite: Technical Points – Explanatory Notes, Annex 2, Note 73: see Rewrite note under s. 567.

HMRC Manuals – CA13200: guidance and examples on s. 569.

570 Elections: supplementary

570(1) Section 569(1) does not apply to a sale that is relevant for the purposes of Part 3A.

570(2) No election under section 569 may be made if–

(a) the circumstances of the sale or the parties to it mean that a relevant allowance or charge will not be capable of falling to be made, or

(b) the buyer is a dual resident investing company.

570(3) In subsection (2)(a) **"relevant allowance or charge"** means an allowance or charge under Part 5, 6, 9 or 10 which (ignoring the circumstances mentioned in subsection (2)(a)) would or might fall to be made, as a result of the sale, to or on any of the parties to it.

570(4) If the sale is relevant for the purposes of Part 10, no election under section 569 may be made unless, at the time of the sale or any earlier time, both the seller and the buyer are or have been approved bodies (as defined in section 492).

570(5) An election under section 569 must be made by notice to an officer of Revenue and Customs not later than 2 years after the sale.

CAA 2001

History – In s. 570(1), "or 4A" omitted by FA 2012, s. 227 and Sch. 39, para. 38(5), with effect in relation to chargeable periods beginning on or after 1 April 2013 for corporation tax purposes, and 6 April 2013 for income tax purposes, subject to transitional and saving provisions in FA 2012, Sch. 39, para. 41 and 42.

In s. 570(1), ", 4" omitted by FA 2008, s. 84 and Sch. 27, para. 16(a), with effect in relation to chargeable periods beginning on or after 1 April 2011 for corporation tax purposes and 6 April 2011 for income tax purposes (FA 2008, Sch. 27, para. 30(1)).

In s. 570(1) "3A," inserted after "Part" by FA 2005, s. 92 and Sch. 6, para. 8, with effect in relation to expenditure incurred on or after 11 April 2007, by virtue of SI 2007/949, art. 2.

In s. 570(1), reference to Pt. 4A inserted by FA 2001, s. 67 and Sch. 19, Pt. 2, para. 6, with effect in relation to expenditure incurred on or after 11 May 2001.

In s. 570(3), "3," omitted by FA 2008, s. 84 and Sch. 27, para. 16(b), with effect in relation to chargeable periods beginning on or after 1 April 2011 for corporation tax purposes and 6 April 2011 for income tax purposes (FA 2008, Sch. 27, para. 30(1)).

In s. 570(5), the words "an officer of Revenue and Customs" substituted for "the Inland Revenue" by CRCA 2005, s 50(6) and Sch. 4, para. 83(1), with effect from 18 April 2005 by virtue of SI 2005/1126, art. 2(2).

Origin – S. 570: Annex 2, Note 73.

S. 570(1): CAA 1990, s. 158(5).

S. 570(2) to (4): CAA 1990, s. 158(3).

S. 570(5): CAA 1990, s. 158(1) (part).

Cross references – F(No. 2)A 1992, s. 77 and Sch. 17, para. 5(4): Northern Ireland Electricity privatisation – arrangements in favour of other successor companies.

FA 1994, Sch. 24, para. 21(2) and 22(2): disapplication of s. 567–570 in certain circumstances connected with railways privatisation.

Coal Industry Act 1994, Sch. 4, para. 20(2) (as amended by Sch. 2, para. 93(5)(d)) and Transport Act 2000, Sch. 26, para. 21(4), 27(4) and 34(5) (as amended by Sch. 2, para. 109(13), (20) and (27) respectively): disapplication of s. 567–570 to scheme of restructuring in connection with privatisation of the coal industry or railways.

RA 2005, Sch. 10. para. 4 and 24: disapplication of s. 567 to 570 in the case of a transfer to a national authority.

Rewrite: Technical Points – Explanatory Notes, Annex 2, Note 73: see Rewrite note under s. 567.

HMRC Manuals – CA13200: guidance on s. 570.

ANTI-AVOIDANCE

570A Avoidance affecting proceeds of balancing event

570A(1) This section applies where an event occurs in relation to an asset (a **"balancing event"**) as a result of which a balancing allowance would (but for this section) fall to be made to a person (**"the taxpayer"**) under Part 3A, 5 or 10.

570A(2) The taxpayer is not entitled to any balancing allowance if, as a result of a tax avoidance scheme, the amount to be brought into account as the proceeds from the event is less than it would otherwise have been.

570A(3) In subsection (2) a **"tax avoidance scheme"** means a scheme or arrangement the main purpose, or one of the main purposes, of which is the obtaining of a tax advantage by the taxpayer.

570A(4) Where this section applies to deny a balancing allowance, the residue of qualifying expenditure immediately after the balancing event is nevertheless calculated as if the balancing allowance had been made.

570A(5) In this section as it applies for the purposes of Part 5 (mineral extraction allowances)–

(a) the references to the proceeds from the balancing event that are to be brought into account shall be read as references to the disposal value to be brought into account, and

(b) the reference to the residue of qualifying expenditure shall be read as a reference to the unrelieved qualifying expenditure.

History – In s. 570A(1), "4A," omitted by FA 2012, s. 227 and Sch. 39, para. 38(6), with effect in relation to chargeable periods beginning on or after 1 April 2013 for corporation tax purposes, and 6 April 2013 for income tax purposes, subject to transitional and saving provisions in FA 2012, Sch. 39, para. 41 and 42.
In s. 570A(1), the numbers "3," and "4," omitted by FA 2008, s. 84 and Sch. 27, para. 17, with effect in relation to chargeable periods beginning on or after 1 April 2011 for corporation tax purposes and 6 April 2011 for income tax purposes (FA 2008, Sch. 27, para. 30(1)).
In s. 570A(1) "3A," inserted after "3," by FA 2005, s. 92 and Sch. 6, para. 9, with effect in relation to expenditure incurred on or after 11 April 2007, by virtue of SI 2007/949, art. 2.
S. 570A inserted by FA 2003, s. 164 in relation to any "balancing event" (within the meaning of this section 570A) occurring on or after 27 November 2002, except where the event occurs in pursuance of a contract entered into before that date, and does not occur in consequence of the exercise on or after that date of an option, right of pre-emption or similar right.

Chapter 6 – Final Provisions

ORDERS AND REGULATIONS

History – The heading "Orders and regulations" inserted by ITA 2007, s. 1027 and Sch. 1, para. 409, with effect from 6 April 2007.

570B Orders and regulations made by Treasury or Commissioners

570B(1) Any orders or regulations made by the Treasury or the Commissioners for Her Majesty's Revenue and Customs under this Act must be made by statutory instrument.

570B(2) Any orders or regulations made by the Treasury or the Commissioners under this Act are subject to annulment in pursuance of a resolution of the House of Commons.

570B(3) Subsection (2) does not apply to any regulations made under section 70YJ or any order made under section 82(4)(d).

History – S. 570B inserted by ITA 2007, s. 1027 and Sch. 1, para. 409, with effect from 6 April 2007.

GENERAL INTERPRETATION

571 Application of Act to parts of assets

571(1) In this Act references to an asset of any kind (including a building or structure, plant or machinery or works) include a part of an asset.

571(2) But subsection (1) does not apply if the context otherwise requires.

Origin – S. 571(1): CAA 1990, s. 97(1) ("building"), s. 161(7) (part).
S. 571(2): CAA 1990, s. 161(1).

Cross references – S. 283(1): disregard of certain levels of expenditure on non-industrial parts of buildings to take account of s. 571.
S. 435(1): application of mineral extraction allowances to a share of any asset as in relation to a part under s. 571.

HMRC Manuals – CA20080, CA31550: guidance on s. 571.
CA32650: application to parts of buildings.

572 References to sale of property and time of sale

572(1) In this Act references to the sale of property include–

(a) the exchange of property, and

(b) the surrender for valuable consideration of a leasehold interest (or, in Scotland, the interest of the tenant in property subject to a lease).

572(2) For the purposes of subsection (1), any provision of this Act referring to a sale has effect with the necessary modifications, including, in particular, those in subsection (3).

572(3) The modifications are that–

(a) references to the net proceeds of sale and to the price include the consideration for the exchange or surrender, and

(b) references to capital sums included in the net proceeds of sale or paid on a sale include so much of the consideration for the exchange or surrender as would have been a capital sum if it had been a money payment.

572(4) Any reference in this Act (except in Part 6) to the time of any sale is to be read as a reference to whichever is the earlier of–

(a) the time of completion, and

(b) the time when possession is given.

Origin – S. 572(1): CAA 1990, s. 150(4) (part), s. 162 (part).

S. 572(2), (3): CAA 1990, s. 150(4) (part).
S. 572(4): CAA 1990, s. 161(8).
HMRC Manuals – CA11530, CA11540, CA12300: guidance, etc. on s. 572.

573 Transfers treated as sales

573(1) This section applies for the purposes of Part 3A, and 10 and other provisions of this Act relevant to those Parts if–

(a) there is a transfer of the interest which is the relevant interest for the purposes of the Part in question, and

(b) the transfer is not a sale.

573(2) The transfer is treated as a sale of the relevant interest.

573(3) The sale is treated as being at market value, subject to any election under section 569 (election to treat sale as being for alternative amount).

573(4) This section does not apply if section 561 applies (transfer of a UK trade to a company resident in another member State).

History – In s. 573(1), ", 4A" omitted by FA 2012, s. 227 and Sch. 39, para. 38(7), with effect in relation to chargeable periods beginning on or after 1 April 2013 for corporation tax purposes, and 6 April 2013 for income tax purposes, subject to transitional and saving provisions in FA 2012, Sch. 39, para. 41 and 42.
In s. 573(1), the numbers "3," and "4," omitted by FA 2008, s. 84 and Sch. 27, para. 18, with effect in relation to chargeable periods beginning on or after 1 April 2011 for corporation tax purposes and 6 April 2011 for income tax purposes (FA 2008, Sch. 27, para. 30(1)).
In s. 573(1) "3A," inserted after "3," by FA 2005, s. 92 and Sch. 6, para. 10, with effect in relation to expenditure incurred on or after 11 April 2007, by virtue of SI 2007/949, art. 2.
In s. 573(1), reference to Part 4A inserted by FA 2001, s. 67 and Sch. 19, Pt. 2, para. 7, with effect in relation to expenditure incurred on or after 11 May 2001.

Origin – S. 573(1), (2): CAA 1990, s. 21(6) (part), s. 87(5) (part), s. 133(8) (part).
S. 573(3): CAA 1990, s. 21(6) (part), (7), s. 87(5) (part), s. 133(8) (part), (9), s. 157(4) (part).
S. 573(4): CAA 1990, s. 152B(10) (part).

Cross references – S. 382(3): s. 573 disregarded in determining sole or main benefit expected to accrue from the acquisition of an agricultural building where election for balancing event possible.
S. 564(2)(e): application of s. 563 in determination of market value for purposes of s. 573.
S. 569(1)(a) (election to treat sale as being for alternative amount): election may be made where s. 573 applies and tax advantage test not met.
FA 1994, Sch. 24, para. 21(2)(a) (as amended by Sch. 2, para. 91(6)(a)): privatisation of railways – for the purpose of s. 573 as it applies for industrial buildings allowances, the deemed sale price is the price determined in accordance with the relevant scheme.
Coal Industry Act 1994, Sch. 4, para. 20(2) (as amended by Sch. 2, para. 93(5)(a)): privatisation of coal industry – for the purpose of s. 573 as it applies for industrial buildings allowances, the deemed sale price is the price determined in accordance with the relevant scheme.
RA 2005, Sch. 10. para. 15: disapplication of s. 573 in the case of certain transfers to a national authority.

HMRC Manuals – CA11540: guidance on s. 573.

574 Meaning of "control"

574(1) In this Act **"control"** is used in the sense given in this section (but, for the purposes of section 575, this definition applies only where expressly indicated).

574(2) In relation to a body corporate ("company A"), **"control"** means the power of a person ("P") to secure–

(a) by means of the holding of shares or the possession of voting power in relation to that or any other body corporate, or

(b) as a result of any powers conferred by the articles of association or other document regulating that or any other body corporate,

that the affairs of company A are conducted in accordance with P's wishes.

574(3) In relation to a partnership, **"control"** means the right to a share of more than half of the assets, or of more than one half of the income, of the partnership.

History – In s. 574(1), the words "but, for the purposes of section 575, this definition applies only where expressly indicated" inserted by ITA 2007, s. 1027 and Sch. 1, para. 410, with effect from 6 April 2007.

Origin – CAA 1990, s. 77(6) (part), s. 161(2) ("control").

HMRC Manuals – CA11650: guidance and examples on s. 574.

575 Meaning of "connected" persons

575(1) For the purposes of this Act whether a person is connected with another is determined in accordance with this section unless otherwise indicated.

575(2) An individual ("A") is connected with another individual ("B") if–

(a) A is B's spouse or civil partner,

(b) A is a relative of B,

(c) A is the spouse or civil partner of a relative of B,

(d) A is a relative of B's spouse or civil partner, or

(e) A is the spouse or civil partner of a relative of B's spouse or civil partner.

575(3) A person, in the capacity as trustee of a settlement, is connected with–

(a) any individual who is a settlor in relation to the settlement,

(b) any person connected with such an individual,

(c) any close company whose participators include the trustees of the settlement,

(d) any non-UK resident company which, if it were UK resident, would be a close company whose participators include the trustees of the settlement,

(e) any body corporate controlled (within the meaning of section 574) by a company within paragraph (c) or (d),

(f) if the settlement is the principal settlement in relation to one or more sub-fund settlements, a person in the capacity as trustee of such a sub-fund settlement, and

(g) if the settlement is a sub-fund settlement in relation to a principal settlement, a person in the capacity as trustee of any other sub-fund settlements in relation to the principal settlement.

575(4) A person who is a partner in a partnership is connected with–

(a) any partner in the partnership,

(b) the spouse or civil partner of any individual who is a partner in the partnership, and

(c) a relative of any individual who is a partner in the partnership.

But this subsection does not apply in relation to acquisitions or disposals of assets of the partnership pursuant to genuine commercial arrangements.

575(5) A company is connected with another company if–

(a) the same person has control of both companies,

(b) a person ("A") has control of one company and persons connected with A have control of the other company,

(c) A has control of one company and A together with persons connected with A have control of the other company, or

(d) a group of two or more persons has control of both companies and the groups either consist of the same persons or could be so regarded if (in one or more cases) a member of either group were replaced by a person with whom the member is connected.

575(6) A company is connected with another person ("A") if–

(a) A has control of the company, or

(b) A together with persons connected with A have control of the company.

575(7) In relation to a company, any two or more persons acting together to secure or exercise control of the company are connected with–

(a) one another, and

(b) any person acting on the directions of any of them to secure or exercise control of the company.

History – S. 575 (and s. 575A – see note re that section below) substituted for previous s. 575 by ITA 2007, s. 1027 and Sch. 1, para. 411, with effect from 6 April 2007.

Origin – Former s. 575(1): ICTA 1988, s. 521(4) (part), (7), CAA 1990, s. 4(2AB) (part), s. 5(1)(c) (part), s. 11(6)(a) (part), s. 22(6A)(b)(iii) (part), s. 22 B(2)(b) (part), s. 26(1)(b) (part), (eb)(i) (part), (3) (part), s. 36(3) (part), s. 37(8) (part), s. 50(6), s. 53(2) (part), s. 55(4) (a) (part), s. 56(d) (part), s. 56B(7)(b) (part), s. 86(3) (part), s. 130(1)(c)(i) (part), s. 138B(12), s. 154(3) (part), s. 157(1)(a) (part). Former s. 575(2): drafting.

575A Section 575: supplementary

575A(1) In section 575 and this section–

"company" includes any body corporate or unincorporated association, but does not include a partnership (and see also subsection (2)),

"control" is to be read in accordance with sections 450 and 451 of CTA 2010 (except where otherwise indicated),

"principal settlement" has the meaning given by paragraph 1 of Schedule 4ZA to TCGA 1992,

"relative" means brother, sister, ancestor or lineal descendant,

"settlement" has the same meaning as in Chapter 5 of Part 5 of ITTOIA 2005 (see section 620 of that Act), and

"sub-fund settlement" has the meaning given by paragraph 1 of Schedule 4ZA to TCGA 1992.

575A(2) For the purposes of section 575–

(a) a unit trust scheme is treated as if it were a company, and

(b) the rights of the unit holders are treated as if they were shares in the company.

575A(3) For the purposes of section 575 **"trustee"**, in the case of a settlement in relation to which there would be no trustees apart from this subsection, means any person–

(a) in whom the property comprised in the settlement is for the time being vested, or

(b) in whom the management of that property is for the time being vested.

Section 466(4) of ITA 2007 does not apply for the purposes of this subsection.

575A(4) If any provision of section 575 provides that a person ("A") is connected with another person ("B"), it also follows that B is connected with A.

History – In s. 575A(1), in the definition of "control", the words "sections 450 and 451 of CTA 2010" substituted for "section 416 of ICTA" by CTA 2010, s. 1177 and Sch. 1, para. 362, with effect for corporation tax purposes for accounting periods ending on or after 1 April 2010, and for income tax and capital gains tax purposes for the tax year 2010–11 and subsequent tax years.
S. 575A effectively inserted by ITA 2007, s. 1027 and Sch. 1, para. 411, with effect from 6 April 2007.

576 Meaning of "the Inland Revenue" etc.

576 [Ceased to have effect by CRCA 2005, s. 50 and Sch. 4, para. 85 and repealed by CRCA 2005, s. 52 and Sch. 5.]

History – S. 576 ceased to have effect by virtue of CRCA 2005, s. 50(6) and Sch. 4, para. 85 and repealed by CRCA 2005, s. 52 and Sch. 5 with effect from 18 April 2005 by virtue of SI 2005/1126, art. 2.

577 Other definitions

577(1) In this Act–

"dual resident investing company" has the same meaning as in section 949 of CTA 2010 (dual resident investing companies);

"market value", in relation to any asset, means the price the asset would fetch in the open market;

"the normal time limit for amending a tax return", in relation to a tax year, means the first anniversary of the 31st January following the tax year;

"notice" means a notice in writing;

"property business" means a UK property business or an overseas property business;

"tax return" has the meaning given by section 3(3);

577(2) Any reference to the setting up, commencement or permanent discontinuance of–

(a) a trade,

(b) a property business,

(c) a profession, or

(d) a vocation,

includes, except where the contrary is expressly provided, the occurring of an event which, under any provision of the Income Tax Acts or Corporation Tax Acts, is to be treated as equivalent to the setting up, commencement or permanent discontinuance of a trade, property business, profession or vocation.

577(2A) A person's ceasing to carry on a trade, property business, profession or vocation is treated for the purposes of this Act as the permanent discontinuance of the trade, property business, profession or vocation, whether or not it is in fact discontinued.

577(2B) For income tax purposes, a change in the persons carrying on a trade, property business, profession or vocation is not treated as the permanent discontinuance of the trade, property business, profession or vocation if a person carrying it on immediately before the change continues to carry it on after the change.

577(2C) For corporation tax purposes, a change in the persons carrying on a trade or property business is not treated as the permanent discontinuance of the trade or property business if a company carrying it on in partnership immediately before the change continues to carry it on in partnership after the change.

577(3) Any reference in this Act to an allowance made includes an allowance which would be made but for an insufficiency of profits, or other income, against which to make it.

577(4) For the purposes of this Act a person obtains a tax advantage if he–

(a) obtains an allowance or a greater allowance, or

(b) avoids a charge or secures the reduction of a charge.

577(5) In Schedule 1–

(a) Part 1 gives the meaning of abbreviated references in this Act to Acts about tax, and

(b) Part 2 lists where expressions used in this Act are defined or otherwise explained.

History – In s. 577(1), the words "section 949 of CTA 2010 (dual resident investing companies);" substituted for "section 404 of ICTA (limitation of group relief in relation to certain dual resident companies);" in the definition of "dual resident investing company" by CTA 2010, s. 1177 and Sch. 1, para. 363, with effect for corporation tax purposes for accounting periods ending on or after 1 April 2010, and for income tax and capital gains tax purposes for the tax year 2010–11 and subsequent tax years.
In s. 577(1), in the definition of "property business", the words ", a Schedule A business" omitted by CTA 2009, s. 1322 and Sch. 1, para. 520(2) and repealed by CTA 2009, s. 1326 and Sch. 3, Pt. 1, with effect for corporation tax purposes for accounting periods ending on or after 1 April 2009, and for income tax and capital gains tax purposes for the tax year 2009–10 and subsequent tax years.
In s. 577(1), the definition of "property business" amended by ITTOIA 2005, s. 882(1) and Sch. 1, para. 573; effective for income tax purposes for 2005–06 onwards and for corporation tax purposes for accounting periods ending after 5 April 2005 (ITTOIA 2005, s. 883(1)).
In s. 577(1), the definition of "tax year" omitted by ITA 2007, s. 1027 and Sch. 1, para. 412 and repealed by s. 1031 and Sch. 3, Pt. 1, with effect from 6 April 2007.
In s. 577(1), the definition of "the tax year 2001–02" omitted by ITA 2007, s. 1027 and Sch. 1, para. 412 and repealed by s. 1031 and Sch. 3, Pt. 1, with effect from 6 April 2007.
S. 577(2A) inserted by CTA 2009, s. 1322 and Sch. 1, para. 520(3), with effect for corporation tax purposes for accounting periods ending on or after 1 April 2009, and for income tax and capital gains tax purposes for the tax year 2009–10 and subsequent tax years.
S. 577(2B) inserted by CTA 2009, s. 1322 and Sch. 1, para. 520(3), with effect for corporation tax purposes for accounting periods ending on or after 1 April 2009, and for income tax and capital gains tax purposes for the tax year 2009–10 and subsequent tax years.
S. 577(2C) inserted by CTA 2009, s. 1322 and Sch. 1, para. 520(3), with effect for corporation tax purposes for accounting periods ending on or after 1 April 2009, and for income tax and capital gains tax purposes for the tax year 2009–10 and subsequent tax years.

Origin – S. 577: Annex 2, Note 74.
S. 577(1): "dual resident investing company".
CAA 1990, s. 161(2) ("dual resident investing company").

Rewrite: Changes in Law – Explanatory Notes, Annex 1, Change 62: s. 577(2)(b) provides a definition of the setting up, commencement or discontinuance of a "property business" as well as trades, professions or vocations. Although the previous provisions in CAA 1990, s. 161 applied the 1990 act generally to an overseas property business (CAA 1990, s 161(2A)), it is not entirely clear whether these specific interpretative provisions (formerly in CAA 1990, s. 161(9)) applied to an overseas property business in a similar fashion as they were applied to Sch. A businesses (by ICTA 1988, s. 21B, via s. 113 and 337), although it is arguable that they indeed did. In practice, they were usually applied to an overseas property business. Under the rewritten legislation this lack of clarity is removed to reflect the previous practical approach for an overseas property business as well as the statutory approach to other activities. Where this change has an adverse effect, there is a right of election for the previous position to apply to a period which straddles 6 April (income tax) or 1 April (corporation tax) 2001 (Sch. 3, para. 8).

Rewrite: Technical Points – Explanatory Notes, Annex 2, Note 74: CAA 1990, s. 161(3) (which applied the 1990 Act to income of trades, professions or vocations taxable under Sch. D, Case IV or V as well as to Case I and II) is not reproduced in the "other definitions" statute in s. 577 because it is, largely, a relic of the position before the introduction of self assessment. Suitable wording has been introduced into those remaining provisions, derived from legislation in CAA 1990 where specific reference was made to Sch. D, Case I or II, in order to ensure that they apply to trading, etc generally however taxable.

HMRC Manuals – CA11550ff.: guidance on s. 577.

Notes – S. 577(1) rewritten as ITA 2007, s. 989.

AMENDMENTS, REPEALS, CITATION ETC.

578 Consequential amendments

578 Schedule 2 contains consequential amendments.

579 Commencement and transitional provisions and savings

579(1) This Act has effect–

(a) for income tax purposes, as respects allowances and charges falling to be made for chargeable periods ending on or after 6th April 2001, and

(b) for corporation tax purposes, as respects allowances and charges falling to be made for chargeable periods ending on or after 1st April 2001.

579(2) References in this Act to a chargeable period to which this Act applies are to the chargeable periods given in subsection (1).

579(3) Subsection (1) is subject to Schedule 3, which contains transitional provisions and savings.

580 Repeals

580 Schedule 4 contains repeals.

581 Citation

581 This Act may be cited as the Capital Allowances Act 2001.

SCHEDULES

SCHEDULE A1 – FIRST-YEAR TAX CREDITS

Section 262A

History – Sch. A1 inserted by FA 2008, s. 79 and Sch. 25, para. 5, with effect in relation to expenditure incurred on or after 1 April 2008.

Part 1 – Entitlement to First-Year Tax Credits

ENTITLEMENT TO FIRST-YEAR TAX CREDITS

1(1) A company may claim a first-year tax credit for a chargeable period in which it has a surrenderable loss, unless it is an excluded company in relation to that chargeable period.

1(2) A company has a surrenderable loss in a chargeable period if in that chargeable period–

(a) a first-year allowance is made to the company in respect of relevant first-year expenditure (see paragraph 3) incurred for the purposes of a qualifying activity the profits of which are chargeable to corporation tax, and

(b) the company incurs a loss in carrying on that qualifying activity (see paragraphs 4 to 9).

1(3) The amount of the surrenderable loss is equal to–

(a) so much of the loss incurred in carrying on the qualifying activity as is unrelieved (see paragraphs 10 to 16), or

(b) if less, the amount of the first-year allowance made in respect of the relevant first-year expenditure in the chargeable period in question.

1(4) A company is an excluded company in relation to a chargeable period if at any time during that period it is entitled to make–

(a) a claim under section 642 or 643 of CTA 2010 (reliefs for cooperative housing associations),

(b) a claim under section 651 or 652 of CTA 2010 (reliefs for self-build societies), or

(c) a relevant claim under Part 11 of CTA 2010 (charitable companies etc).

1(5) For the purposes of sub-paragraph (4)(c) a claim under Part 11 of CTA 2010 is a relevant claim unless–

(a) it is a claim for exemption under–

(i) section 475 or 476 (reliefs for certain heritage bodies etc),

(ii) section 480 (exemption for profits of small-scale trades), or

(iii) section 481 (exemption from charges under provisions to which section 1173 of CTA 2010 applies), or

(b) the company is entitled to make it only by virtue of section 490 (application of exemptions to certain heritage bodies etc).

History – In para. 1(4), the words "entitled to make– " and the following paras. (a), (b) and (c) substituted for the former words by CTA 2010, s. 1177 and Sch. 1, para. 364(2)(a), with effect for corporation tax purposes for accounting periods ending on or after 1 April 2010, and for income tax and capital gains tax purposes for the tax year 2010–11 and subsequent tax years.
Para. 1(5) inserted by CTA 2010, s. 1177 and Sch. 1, para. 364(2)(b), with effect for corporation tax purposes for accounting periods ending on or after 1 April 2010, and for income tax and capital gains tax purposes for the tax year 2010–11 and subsequent tax years.

AMOUNT OF FIRST-YEAR TAX CREDIT

2(1) The amount of the first-year tax credit to which a company is entitled for a chargeable period in which it has a surrenderable loss is an amount equal to–

(a) 19% of the amount of the surrenderable loss for the chargeable period, or

(b) if the amount mentioned in paragraph (a) exceeds the upper limit, the upper limit.

2(2) The upper limit is the greater of–

(a) the total amount of the company's PAYE and NICs liabilities for payment periods ending in the chargeable period (see paragraph 17), and

(b) £250,000.

2(3) A company which is entitled to an amount of first-year tax credit may claim the whole amount or part only of the amount.

2(4) The Treasury may by order substitute for the percentage for the time being specified in sub-paragraph (1)(a) such other percentage as it thinks fit.

2(5) An order under sub-paragraph (4) may make such incidental, supplemental, consequential and transitional provision as the Treasury thinks fit.

Prospective amendments – Para. 2(3A) inserted by CTNIA 2015, s. 2 and Sch. 1, para. 10, with effect from 26 March 2015 (Royal Assent) in respect of any power to make regulations and with effect in relation to accounting periods beginning on or after the first day of the appointed financial year for other provisions (see CTNIA 2015, s. 5). See also transitional provisions at Sch. 1, para. 19–21.

MEANING OF "RELEVANT FIRST-YEAR EXPENDITURE"

3(1) In this Schedule **"relevant first-year expenditure"** means expenditure which–

(a) is first-year qualifying expenditure by virtue of section 45A (energy-saving plant or machinery) or section 45H (environmentally beneficial plant or machinery), and

(b) is incurred in the period beginning with 1 April 2008 and ending with 31 March 2018,

but does not include expenditure which is treated as first-year qualifying expenditure within paragraph (a) by virtue of section 236 (additional VAT liability treated as expenditure).

3(2) In determining whether expenditure is relevant first-year expenditure, any effect of section 12 on the time at which it is to be treated as incurred is to be disregarded.

3(3) The Treasury may by order substitute, for the date for the time being specified in sub-paragraph (1)(b) as the date with which the period ends, such later date as it thinks fit.

3(4) An order under sub-paragraph (3) may make such incidental, supplemental, consequential and transitional provision as the Treasury thinks fit.

History – In para. 3(1)(b), the date "31 March 2018" substituted for the date "31 March 2013" by SI 2013/464, art. 2, with effect from 28 March 2013.

INCURRING A LOSS IN CARRYING ON A QUALIFYING ACTIVITY

4 Paragraphs 5 to 9 apply for the interpretation of paragraph 1(2)(b).

5(1) This paragraph applies where the qualifying activity is an ordinary UK property business or an ordinary overseas property business and paragraph 7 does not apply.

5(2) References in this Schedule to a loss incurred in carrying on the qualifying activity are to a loss incurred in carrying on that part of the business (if any) to which sections 62 and 63 of CTA 2010 (UK property business losses) apply (see section 64 of that Act).

History – In para. 5(1), the words "an ordinary UK property business or an ordinary overseas property business" substituted for "a UK property business other than a furnished holiday lettings business" by FA 2011, s. 52 and Sch. 14, para. 12(16)(a), with effect in relation to chargeable periods beginning on or after 1 April 2011 (for corporation tax purposes), and in relation to chargeable periods beginning on or after 6 April 2011 (for income tax purposes).
In para. 5(1), the words "UK property business" substituted for the words "Schedule A business" by CTA 2009, s. 1322 and Sch. 1, para. 521(2)(a), with effect for corporation tax purposes for accounting periods ending on or after 1 April 2009, and for income tax and capital gains tax purposes for the tax year 2009–10 and subsequent tax years.
In para. 5(2), the words "sections 62 and 63 of CTA 2010 (UK property business losses) apply (see section 64 of that Act)" substituted for "section 392A of ICTA (UK property business losses) applies" by CTA 2010, s. 1177 and Sch. 1, para. 364(3), with effect for corporation tax purposes for accounting periods ending on or after 1 April 2010, and for income tax and capital gains tax purposes for the tax year 2010–11 and subsequent tax years.
In para. 5(2), the words "(UK property business losses)" substituted for the words "(Schedule A losses)" by CTA 2009, s. 1322 and Sch. 1, para. 521(2)(b), with effect for corporation tax purposes for accounting periods ending on or after 1 April 2009, and for income tax and capital gains tax purposes for the tax year 2009–10 and subsequent tax years.

6(1) This paragraph applies where the qualifying activity is an overseas property business and paragraph 7 does not apply.

6(2) References in this Schedule to a loss incurred in carrying on the qualifying activity are to a loss incurred in carrying on that part of the business (if any) to which section 66 of CTA 2010 (losses from overseas property business) applies (see section 67 of that Act).

History – In para. 6(2) the words "section 66 of CTA 2010" substituted for "section 392B of ICTA" and the words "(see section 67 of that Act)" inserted by CTA 2010, s. 1177 and Sch. 1, para. 364(4), with effect for corporation tax purposes for accounting periods ending on or after 1 April 2010, and for income tax and capital gains tax purposes for the tax year 2010–11 and subsequent tax years.

7(1) This paragraph applies where–

(a) the qualifying activity is a UK property business or an overseas property business, and

(b) the company is an insurance company.

7(2) References in this Schedule to a loss incurred in carrying on the qualifying activity are to a loss which, as a result of section 87(3) of FA 2012, is treated for the purposes of section 76 of that Act as a deemed BLAGAB management expense for an accounting period.

7(3) Where the insurance company is treated under section 86 of that Act as carrying on more than one UK property business or overseas property business, references in this Schedule to a loss incurred in carrying on the qualifying activity are to be construed in accordance with section 87(4) of that Act (aggregation of losses).

History – In para. 7(1)(a), the words "UK property business" substituted for the words "Schedule A business" by CTA 2009, s. 1322 and Sch. 1, para. 521(3)(a), with effect for corporation tax purposes for accounting periods ending on or after 1 April 2009, and for income tax and capital gains tax purposes for the tax year 2009–10 and subsequent tax years.
In para. 7(2), the words "which, as a result of section 87(3) of FA 2012, is treated for the purposes of section 76 of that Act as a deemed BLAGAB management expense for an accounting period" substituted for the words "which is treated under section 432AB(3) of ICTA, for the purposes of section 76 of that Act, as expenses payable which fall to be brought into account at Step 3 of subsection (7) of that section." by FA 2012, s. 146 and Sch. 16, para. 106(2)(a) in relation to accounting periods beginning on or after 1 January 2013 (FA 2012, s. 148) but subject to transitional provisions in FA 2012, Sch. 17. Where an accounting period would otherwise straddle 1 January 2013, it is deemed to end on 31 December 2012 (FA 2012, s. 149).
In para. 7(3), "section 86" substituted for "section 432AA", and "section 87(4)" substituted for "section 432AB(4)" by FA 2012, s. 146 and Sch. 16, para. 106(2)(b) in relation to accounting periods beginning on or after 1 January 2013 (FA 2012, s. 148) but subject to transitional provisions in FA 2012, Sch. 17. Where an accounting period would otherwise straddle 1 January 2013, it is deemed to end on 31 December 2012 (FA 2012, s. 149).
In para. 7(3), the words "UK property business" substituted for the words "Schedule A business" by CTA 2009, s. 1322 and Sch. 1, para. 521(3)(b), with effect for corporation tax purposes for accounting periods ending on or after 1 April 2009, and for income tax and capital gains tax purposes for the tax year 2009–10 and subsequent tax years.

8(1) This paragraph applies where the qualifying activity is managing the investments of a company with investment business.

8(2) The company incurs a loss in carrying on that activity in a chargeable period if in that chargeable period–

(a) the sum of the amounts mentioned in section 1223(2) of CTA 2009, exceeds

(b) the amount of the profits from which those expenses and charges are deductible,

and the amount of the loss is the amount of the excess.

History – Para. 8(2)(a) substituted by CTA 2009, s. 1322 and Sch. 1, para. 521(4), with effect for corporation tax purposes for accounting periods ending on or after 1 April 2009, and for income tax and capital gains tax purposes for the tax year 2009–10 and subsequent tax years.

9(1) This paragraph applies where the qualifying activity is basic life assurance and general annuity business and the profits of that business are charged to tax in accordance with the I – E rules.

9(2) The company incurs a loss in a chargeable period if in that chargeable period an amount falls to be carried forward to a succeeding chargeable period under section 73 of FA 2012 (carrying forward unrelieved expenses).

9(3) The amount of the loss is the amount which falls to be so carried forward.

History – In para. 9(1), the words "basic life assurance and general annuity business" substituted for the words "life assurance business", and "in accordance with the I – E rules" substituted for "under the I minus E basis", by FA 2012, s. 146 and Sch. 16, para. 106(3)(a) in relation to accounting periods beginning on or after 1 January 2013 (FA 2012, s. 148) but subject to transitional provisions in FA 2012, Sch. 17. Where an accounting period would otherwise straddle 1 January 2013, it is deemed to end on 31 December 2012 (FA 2012, s. 149).
In para. 9(2), "section 73 of FA 2012" substituted for "section 76(12) of ICTA" by FA 2012, s. 146 and Sch. 16, para. 106(3)(b) in relation to accounting periods beginning on or after 1 January 2013 (FA 2012, s. 148) but subject to transitional provisions in FA 2012, Sch. 17. Where an accounting period would otherwise straddle 1 January 2013, it is deemed to end on 31 December 2012 (FA 2012, s. 149).

UNRELIEVED LOSS

10 Paragraphs 11 to 16 apply for the interpretation of paragraph 1(3)(a).

11(1) This paragraph applies where the qualifying activity is a trade, a UK furnished holiday lettings business or an EEA furnished holiday lettings business and paragraph 14 or 16 does not apply.

11(2) The amount of the loss that is unrelieved is the amount of the loss, reduced by the amount of–

(a) any relief that was or could have been obtained by the company making a claim under section 37(3)(a) of CTA 2010 to deduct the loss from total profits of the same chargeable period,

(b) any other relief obtained by the company making a claim under section 37(3)(b) or 42 of that Act (losses deducted from profits of an earlier chargeable period),

(c) any loss that was or could have been surrendered under Part 5 of that Act (surrender of relief to group or consortium members),

(d) any loss surrendered under a relevant tax credit provision, and

(e) any amount set off against the loss under Chapter 7 of Part 4 of that Act (write-off of government investment).

11(3) For this purpose no account is to be taken of any losses–

(a) brought forward from an earlier chargeable period under section 45 of CTA 2010,

(b) carried back from a later chargeable period under section 37(3)(b) or 42 of that Act, or

(c) incurred on a leasing contract (within the meaning of section 53 of that Act) in circumstances to which that section applies.

11(4) In sub-paragraph (2)(d) **"relevant tax credit provision"** means–

(a) Chapter 2 or 7 of Part 13 of CTA 2009 (tax credits for expenditure on research and development or vaccine research etc),

(b) Chapter 3 of Part 14 of that Act (tax credits for remediation of contaminated land),
(c) Chapter 3 of Part 15 of that Act (film tax credits),
(d) Chapter 3 of Part 15A of that Act (television tax credits),
(e) Chapter 3 of Part 15B of that Act (video game tax credits),
(f) section 1217K of that Act (theatre tax credits), and
(g) Chapter 3 of Part 15D of that Act (orchestra tax credits).

History – In para. 11(1), the words ", a UK furnished holiday lettings business or an EEA furnished holiday lettings business" substituted for "or a furnished holiday lettings business" by FA 2011, s. 52 and Sch. 14, para. 12(16)(b), with effect in relation to chargeable periods beginning on or after 1 April 2011 (for corporation tax purposes), and in relation to chargeable periods beginning on or after 6 April 2011 (for income tax purposes).
In para. 11(2)(a), the words "section 37(3)(a) of CTA 2010 to deduct the loss from total profits" substituted for "section 393A(1)(a) of ICTA to set the loss against profits of whatever description" by CTA 2010, s. 1177 and Sch. 1, para. 364(5)(a), with effect for corporation tax purposes for accounting periods ending on or after 1 April 2010, and for income tax and capital gains tax purposes for the tax year 2010–11 and subsequent tax years.
In para. 11(2)(b), the words "section 37(3)(b) or 42 of that Act (losses deducted from" substituted for "section 393A(1)(b) or 393B(3) of that Act (losses set against" by CTA 2010, s. 1177 and Sch. 1, para. 364(5)(b), with effect for corporation tax purposes for accounting periods ending on or after 1 April 2010, and for income tax and capital gains tax purposes for the tax year 2010–11 and subsequent tax years.
In para. 11(2)(c), the words "Part 5" substituted for "section 403(1)" by CTA 2010, s. 1177 and Sch. 1, para. 364(5)(c), with effect for corporation tax purposes for accounting periods ending on or after 1 April 2010, and for income tax and capital gains tax purposes for the tax year 2010–11 and subsequent tax years.
In para. 11(2)(e), the words "Chapter 7 of Part 4" substituted for "section 400" by CTA 2010, s. 1177 and Sch. 1, para. 364(5)(d), with effect for corporation tax purposes for accounting periods ending on or after 1 April 2010, and for income tax and capital gains tax purposes for the tax year 2010–11 and subsequent tax years.
In para. 11(3)(a), the words "section 45 of CTA 2010" substituted for "section 393(1) of ICTA" by CTA 2010, s. 1177 and Sch. 1, para. 364(5)(e), with effect for corporation tax purposes for accounting periods ending on or after 1 April 2010, and for income tax and capital gains tax purposes for the tax year 2010–11 and subsequent tax years.
In para. 11(3)(b), the words "section 37(3)(b) or 42" substituted for "section 393A(1)(b) or 393B(3)" by CTA 2010, s. 1177 and Sch. 1, para. 364(5)(f), with effect for corporation tax purposes for accounting periods ending on or after 1 April 2010, and for income tax and capital gains tax purposes for the tax year 2010–11 and subsequent tax years.
In para. 11(3)(c), the words "section 53" substituted for "section 395" by CTA 2010, s. 1177 and Sch. 1, para. 364(5)(g), with effect for corporation tax purposes for accounting periodsending on or after 1 April 2010, and for income tax and capital gains tax purposes for the tax year 2010–11 and subsequent tax years.
Para. 11(4)(a)–(c) substituted for former para. (a)–(d) by CTA 2009, s. 1322 and Sch. 1, para. 521(5), with effect for corporation tax purposes for accounting periods ending on or after 1 April 2009, and for income tax and capital gains tax purposes for the tax year 2009–10 and subsequent tax years.
Para. 11(4)(d) inserted (and the "and" after (b) omitted) by FA 2013, s. 36 and Sch. 18, para. 6, with effect from 19 July 2013 (SI 2013/1817) in relation to accounting periods beginning on or after "the relevant day" (as defined in FA 2013, Sch. 18, para. 23).
Para. 11(4)(e) inserted by FA 2013, s. 36 and Sch. 18, para. 6, with effect from 1 April 2014 (SI 2014/1962) in relation to accounting periods beginning on or after "the relevant day" (as defined in FA 2013, Sch. 18, para. 23).
Para. 11(4)(f) inserted (and the "and" at the end of para. 11(4)(d) omitted, and an ", and" inserted at the end of para. 11(4)(e)) by FA 2014, s. 36 and Sch. 4, para. 7, with effect from 22 August 2014, in relation to accounting periods beginning on or after 1 September 2014, subject to the transitional provisions in FA 2014, Sch. 4, para. 17.
Para. 11(4)(g) (and the word ", and" preceding it) inserted (and the word "and" at the end of para. (e) omitted) by FA 2016, s. 54 and Sch. 8, para. 7, with effect in relation to accounting periods beginning on or after 1 April 2016 (subject to the provisions of Sch. 8, para. 17(2) and (3)).

12(1) This paragraph applies where the qualifying activity is an ordinary UK property business or an ordinary overseas property business and paragraph 14 does not apply.

12(2) The amount of the loss that is unrelieved is the amount of the loss, reduced by the amount of–
(a) any relief that was or could have been obtained by the company making a claim under section 62(1) to (3) of CTA 2010 to deduct the loss from total profits of the same chargeable period,
(b) any loss that was or could have been surrendered under Part 5 of that Act (surrender of relief to group or consortium members),
(c) any loss surrendered under Chapter 3 of Part 14 of CTA 2009 (tax credits for remediation of contaminated land), and
(d) any amount set off against the loss under Chapter 7 of Part 4 of CTA 2010 (write-off of government investment).

12(3) For this purpose, no account is to be taken of any losses brought forward from an earlier chargeable period under section 62(5) of CTA 2010.

History – In para. 12(1), the words "an ordinary UK property business or an ordinary overseas property business" substituted for "a UK property business other than a furnished holiday lettings business" by FA 2011, s. 52 and Sch. 14, para. 12(16)(c), with effect in relation to chargeable periods beginning on or after 1 April 2011 (for corporation tax purposes), and in relation to chargeable periods beginning on or after 6 April 2011 (for income tax purposes).
In para. 12(1), the words "UK property business" substituted for the words "Schedule A business" by CTA 2009, s. 1322 and Sch. 1, para. 521(6)(a), with effect for corporation tax purposes for accounting periods ending on or after 1 April 2009, and for income tax and capital gains tax purposes for the tax year 2009–10 and subsequent tax years.
In para. 12(2)(a), the words "section 62(1) to (3) of CTA 2010 to deduct the loss from total profits" substituted for "section 392A(1) of ICTA to set the loss against profits of whatever description" by CTA 2010, s. 1177 and Sch. 1, para. 364(6)(a), with effect for corporation tax purposes for accounting periods ending on or after 1 April 2010, and for income tax and capital gains tax purposes for the tax year 2010–11 and subsequent tax years.
In para. 12(2)(b), the words "Part 5" substituted for "section 403(1)" by CTA 2010, s. 1177 and Sch. 1, para. 364(6)(b), with effect for corporation tax purposes for accounting periods ending on or after 1 April 2010, and for income tax and capital gains tax purposes for the tax year 2010–11 and subsequent tax years.

In para. 12(2)(c), the words "Chapter 3 of Part 14 of CTA 2009" substituted for the words "Part 3 of Schedule 22 to FA 2001" by CTA 2009, s. 1322 and Sch. 1, para. 521(6)(b), with effect for corporation tax purposes for accounting periods ending on or after 1 April 2009, and for income tax and capital gains tax purposes for the tax year 2009–10 and subsequent tax years.
In para. 12(2)(d), the words "Chapter 7 of Part 4 of CTA 2010" substituted for "section 400 of ICTA" by CTA 2010, s. 1177 and Sch. 1, para. 364(6)(c), with effect for corporation tax purposes for accounting periods ending on or after 1 April 2010, and for income tax and capital gains tax purposes for the tax year 2010–11 and subsequent tax years.
In para. 12(3), the words "section 62(5) of CTA 2010" substituted for "section 392A(2) of ICTA" by CTA 2010, s. 1177 and Sch. 1, para. 364(6)(d), with effect for corporation tax purposes for accounting periods ending on or after 1 April 2010, and for income tax and capital gains tax purposes for the tax year 2010–11 and subsequent tax years.

13(1) This paragraph applies where the qualifying activity is an overseas property business and paragraph 14 does not apply.

13(2) The amount of the loss that is unrelieved is the amount of the loss, reduced by any amount set off against the loss under Chapter 7 of Part 4 of CTA 2010 (write-off of government investment).

13(3) For this purpose, no account is to be taken of any losses brought forward from an earlier chargeable period under section 66 of CTA 2010.

History – In para. 13(2), the words "Chapter 7 of Part 4 of CTA 2010" substituted for "section 400 of ICTA" by CTA 2010, s. 1177 and Sch. 1, para. 364(7)(a), with effect for corporation tax purposes for accounting periods ending on or after 1 April 2010, and for income tax and capital gains tax purposes for the tax year 2010–11 and subsequent tax years.
In para. 13(3), the words "section 66 of CTA 2010" substituted for "section 392B(1) of ICTA" by CTA 2010, s. 1177 and Sch. 1, para. 364(7)(b), with effect for corporation tax purposes for accounting periods ending on or after 1 April 2010, and for income tax and capital gains tax purposes for the tax year 2010–11 and subsequent tax years.

14(1) This paragraph applies where–

(a) the qualifying activity is a UK property business or an overseas property business, and

(b) the company is an insurance company.

14(2) If no amount falls to be carried forward to a succeeding chargeable period under section 73 of FA 2012 (carrying forward unrelieved expenses), no amount of the loss is unrelieved.

14(3) If an amount falls to be carried forward to a succeeding chargeable period under section 73 of that Act, the amount of the loss that is unrelieved is equal to the lesser of–

(a) the amount of the loss (see paragraph 7), reduced by any amount within sub-paragraph (4), and

(b) the total amount which so falls to be carried forward.

14(4) The amounts mentioned in sub-paragraph (3)(a) are–

(a) the amount of any loss surrendered under Chapter 3 of Part 14 of CTA 2009 (tax credits for remediation of contaminated land), and

(b) any amount set off against the loss under Chapter 7 of Part 4 of CTA 2010 (write-off of government investment).

14(5) Sub-paragraph (6) applies for determining whether there is an amount which falls to be carried forward under section 73 of FA 2012.

14(6) Disregard any amounts brought forward from an earlier chargeable period which fall to be taken into account in calculating for the purposes of section 73 of FA 2012 the amount of adjusted BLAGAB management expenses of the company for the period in question as a result of–

(a) the previous application of section 73 or 93 of FA 2012, or

(b) the carry forward to the period in question of an amount under section 391(3) of CTA 2009 (loan relationship deficit carried forward).

History – In para. 14(1)(a), the words "UK property business" substituted for the words "Schedule A business" by CTA 2009, s. 1322 and Sch. 1, para. 521(7)(a), with effect for corporation tax purposes for accounting periods ending on or after 1 April 2009, and for income tax and capital gains tax purposes for the tax year 2009–10 and subsequent tax years.
In para. 14(2), "section 73 of FA 2012" substituted for "section 76(12) of ICTA", by FA 2012, s. 146 and Sch. 16, para. 106(4)(a) in relation to accounting periods beginning on or after 1 January 2013 (FA 2012, s. 148) but subject to transitional provisions in FA 2012, Sch. 17. Where an accounting period would otherwise straddle 1 January 2013, it is deemed to end on 31 December 2012 (FA 2012, s. 149).
In para. 14(3), "section 73" substituted for "section 76(12)", by FA 2012, s. 146 and Sch. 16, para. 106(4)(b) in relation to accounting periods beginning on or after 1 January 2013 (FA 2012, s. 148) but subject to transitional provisions in FA 2012, Sch. 17. Where an accounting period would otherwise straddle 1 January 2013, it is deemed to end on 31 December 2012 (FA 2012, s. 149).
In para. 14(4)(a), the words "Chapter 3 of Part 14 of CTA 2009" substituted for the words "Part 3 of Schedule 22 to FA 2001" by CTA 2009, s. 1322 and Sch. 1, para. 521(7)(b), with effect for corporation tax purposes for accounting periods ending on or after 1 April 2009, and for income tax and capital gains tax purposes for the tax year 2009–10 and subsequent tax years.
In para. 14(4)(b), the words "set off against the loss under Chapter 7 of Part 4 of CTA 2010" substituted for "set of against the loss under section 400 of ICTA" by CTA 2010, s. 1177 and Sch. 1, para. 364(8), with effect for corporation tax purposes for accounting periods ending on or after 1 April 2010, and for income tax and capital gains tax purposes for the tax year 2010–11 and subsequent tax years.
In para. 14(5), "section 73 of FA 2012" substituted for "section 76(12) of ICTA", by FA 2012, s. 146 and Sch. 16, para. 106(4)(c) in relation to accounting periods beginning on or after 1 January 2013 (FA 2012, s. 148) but subject to transitional provisions in FA 2012, Sch. 17. Where an accounting period would otherwise straddle 1 January 2013, it is deemed to end on 31 December 2012 (FA 2012, s. 149).
Para. 14(6) substituted by FA2012, s. 146 and Sch. 16, para. 106(4)(d) in relation to accounting periods beginning on or after 1 January 2013 (FA 2012, s. 148) but subject to transitional provisions in FA 2012, Sch. 17. Where an accounting period would otherwise straddle 1 January 2013, it is deemed to end on 31 December 2012 (FA 2012, s. 149).

In para. 14(6)(b), the words "section 391(3)(b) of CTA 2009" substituted for the words "paragraph 4(4) of Schedule 11 to FA 1996" by CTA 2009, s. 1322 and Sch. 1, para. 521(7)(c), with effect for corporation tax purposes for accounting periods ending on or after 1 April 2009, and for income tax and capital gains tax purposes for the tax year 2009–10 and subsequent tax years.

15(1) This paragraph applies where the qualifying activity is managing the investments of a company with investment business.

15(2) The amount of the loss that is unrelieved is the amount of the loss (see paragraph 8), reduced by the amount of–

(a) any loss that was or could have been surrendered under Part 5 of CTA 2010 (surrender of relief to group or consortium members), and

(b) any amount set off against the loss under Chapter 7 of Part 4 of that Act (write-off of government investment).

15(3) For this purpose, no account is to be taken of any amount brought forward from an earlier chargeable period under section 1223 of CTA 2009.

History – In para. 15(2)(a), the words "Part 5 of CTA 2010" substituted for "section 403(1) of ICTA" by CTA 2010, s. 1177 and Sch. 1, para. 364(9)(a), with effect for corporation tax purposes for accounting periods ending on or after 1 April 2010, and for income tax and capital gains tax purposes for the tax year 2010–11 and subsequent tax years.
In para. 15(2)(b), the words "Chapter 7 of Part 4" substituted for "section 400" by CTA 2010, s. 1177 and Sch. 1, para. 364(9)(b), with effect for corporation tax purposes for accounting periods ending on or after 1 April 2010, and for income tax and capital gains tax purposes for the tax year 2010–11 and subsequent tax years.
In para. 15(3), the words "section 1223 of CTA 2009" substituted for the words "section 75(9) of that Act" by CTA 2009, s. 1322 and Sch. 1, para. 521(8), with effect for corporation tax purposes for accounting periods ending on or after 1 April 2009, and for income tax and capital gains tax purposes for the tax year 2009–10 and subsequent tax years.

16(1) This paragraph applies where the qualifying activity is basic life assurance and general annuity business and the profits of that business are charged to tax in accordance with the I – E rules.

16(2) The amount of the unrelieved loss is the amount of the loss (see paragraph 9), reduced by–

(a) any loss surrendered under Chapter 4 of Part 14 of CTA 2009 (tax credits for remediation of contaminated land), and

(b) any amount set off against the loss under Chapter 7 of Part 4 of CTA 2010 (write-off of government investment).

16(3) For this purpose, no account is to be taken of any amounts brought forward from an earlier chargeable period which fall to be taken into account in calculating for the purposes of section 73 of FA 2012 the amount of adjusted BLAGAB management expenses of the company for the period in question as a result of–

(a) the previous application of section 73 or 93 of FA 2012, or

(b) the carry forward to the period in question of an amount under section 391(3) of CTA 2009 (loan relationship deficit carried forward).

History – In para. 16(1), the words "basic life assurance and general annuity business" substituted for the words "life assurance business", and "in accordance with the I – E rules" substituted for "under the I minus E basis", by FA 2012, s. 146 and Sch. 16, para. 106(5)(a) in relation to accounting periods beginning on or after 1 January 2013 (FA 2012, s. 148) but subject to transitional provisions in FA 2012, Sch. 17. Where an accounting period would otherwise straddle 1 January 2013, it is deemed to end on 31 December 2012 (FA 2012, s. 149).
In para. 16(2)(a), the words "Chapter 4 of Part 14 of CTA 2009" substituted for the words "Part 4 of Schedule 22 to FA 2001" by CTA 2009, s. 1322 and Sch. 1, para. 521(9)(a), with effect for corporation tax purposes for accounting periods ending on or after 1 April 2009, and for income tax and capital gains tax purposes for the tax year 2009–10 and subsequent tax years.
In para. 16(2)(b), the words "Chapter 7 of Part 4 of CTA 2010" substituted for "section 400 of ICTA" by CTA 2010, s. 1177 and Sch. 1, para. 364(10), with effect for corporation tax purposes for accounting periods ending on or after 1 April 2010, and for income tax and capital gains tax purposes for the tax year 2010–11 and subsequent tax years.
Para. 16(3) substituted by FA 2012, s. 146 and Sch. 16, para. 106(5)(b) in relation to accounting periods beginning on or after 1 January 2013 (FA 2012, s. 148) but subject to transitional provisions in FA 2012, Sch. 17. Where an accounting period would otherwise straddle 1 January 2013, it is deemed to end on 31 December 2012 (FA 2012, s. 149).
In para. 16(3)(b), the words "section 391(3)(b) of CTA 2009" substituted for the words "paragraph 4(4) of Schedule 11 to FA 1996" by CTA 2009, s. 1322 and Sch. 1, para. 521(9)(b), with effect for corporation tax purposes for accounting periods ending on or after 1 April 2009, and for income tax and capital gains tax purposes for the tax year 2009–10 and subsequent tax years.

TOTAL AMOUNT OF COMPANY'S PAYE AND NICS LIABILITIES

17(1) For the purposes of paragraph 2(2)(a) the total amount of the company's PAYE and NICs liabilities for a payment period is the total of–

(a) the amount of income tax for which the company is required to account to HMRC for that period under the PAYE regulations, disregarding any deduction the company is authorised to make in respect of child tax credit or working tax credit, and

(b) the Class 1 national insurance contributions for which the company is required to account to HMRC for that period, disregarding any deduction the company is authorised to make in respect of payments of statutory sick pay, statutory maternity pay, child tax credit or working tax credit.

17(2) A **"payment period"** means a period which ends on the 5th day of a month and for which the company is liable to account for income tax and national insurance contributions to HMRC.

Prospective amendments – In para. 17(1)(a), the words from "disregarding any" to "working tax credit" repealed by WRA 2012, s. 147 and Sch. 14, Pt. 1, with effect from a date to be set by order of the Secretary of State.
In para. 17(1)(b), after the words "sick pay,", the word "or" inserted by WRA 2012, s. 33 and Sch. 3, para. 14, with effect from a date to be set by order of the Secretary of State.
In para. 17(1)(b), the words "child tax credit or working tax credit" repealed by WRA 2012, s. 147 and Sch. 14, Pt. 1, with effect from a date to be set by order of the Secretary of State.

Part 2 – Giving Effect to First-Year Tax Credits

PAYMENT IN RESPECT OF FIRST-YEAR TAX CREDIT

18(1) Where a company is entitled to a first-year tax credit for a chargeable period and makes a claim for payment of the credit, HMRC must pay to the company the amount of the credit.

18(2) An amount payable in respect of–

(a) a first-year tax credit, or

(b) interest on a first-year tax credit under section 826 of ICTA,

may be applied in discharging any liability of the company's to pay corporation tax.

18(3) To the extent that it is so applied, HMRC's obligation under sub-paragraph (1) is discharged.

18(4) Where HMRC enquires into the company's company tax return for the chargeable period, no payment in respect of a first-year tax credit for that chargeable period need be made before HMRC's enquiries are completed (see paragraph 32 of Schedule 18 to FA 1998).

18(5) In those circumstances HMRC may make a payment on a provisional basis of such amount as it thinks fit.

18(6) No payment need be made in respect of a first-year tax credit for a chargeable period before the company has paid to HMRC any amount that it is required to pay for payment periods (within the meaning of paragraph 17(2)) ending in that chargeable period–

(a) under the PAYE regulations, or

(b) in respect of Class 1 national insurance contributions.

CAA 2001

RESTRICTION ON LOSSES CARRIED FORWARD

19(1) For the purposes of the relieving provisions (see paragraph 20), the company's loss from the qualifying activity for a chargeable period in which it claims a first-year tax credit is treated as reduced by the amount of the loss surrendered.

19(2) For the purposes of this Schedule, the amount of the loss surrendered is–

(a) where the amount of first-year tax credit mentioned in paragraph 2(1)(a) is claimed, the whole of the surrenderable loss for that period, and

(b) where less than that amount is claimed, a corresponding proportion of the surrenderable loss for that period.

20 The relieving provisions are–

(a) where the qualifying activity is a trade, a UK furnished holiday lettings business or an EEA furnished holiday lettings business and paragraph 21 or 22 does not apply, section 45 of CTA 2010 (relief of trading losses against future profits),

(b) where the qualifying activity is managing the investments of a company with investment business, section 1223 of CTA 2009 (carrying expenses forward),

(c) where the qualifying activity is an ordinary UK property business or an ordinary overseas property business and paragraph 21 does not apply, section 62(5) of CTA 2010 (relief of UK property business losses against future profits), and

(d) where the qualifying activity is an overseas property business and paragraph 21 does not apply, section 66 of CTA 2010 (relief of overseas property losses against future profits).

History – In para. 20(a), the words ", a UK furnished holiday lettings business or an EEA furnished holiday lettings business" substituted for "or a furnished holiday lettings business" by FA 2011, s. 52 and Sch. 14, para. 12(16)(d)(i), with effect in relation to chargeable periods beginning on or after 1 April 2011 (for corporation tax purposes), and in relation to chargeable periods beginning on or after 6 April 2011 (for income tax purposes).
In para. 20(a), the words "section 45 of CTA 2010" substituted for "section 393 of ICTA" by CTA 2010, s. 1177 and Sch. 1, para. 364(11)(a), with effect for corporation tax purposes for accounting periods ending on or after 1 April 2010, and for income tax and capital gains tax purposes for the tax year 2010–11 and subsequent tax years.
In para. 20(b), the words "section 1223 of CTA 2009 (carrying expenses forward)" substituted for the words "section 75(9) of that Act (relief of expenses and charges against future profits)" by CTA 2009, s. 1322 and Sch. 1, para. 521(10)(a), with effect for corporation tax purposes for accounting periods ending on or after 1 April 2009, and for income tax and capital gains tax purposes for the tax year 2009–10 and subsequent tax years.
In para. 20(c), the words "an ordinary UK property business or an ordinary overseas property business" substituted for "a UK property business (other than a furnished holiday lettings business)" by FA 2011, s. 52 and Sch. 14, para. 12(16)(d)(ii), with effect in relation to

chargeable periods beginning on or after 1 April 2011 (for corporation tax purposes), and in relation to chargeable periods beginning on or after 6 April 2011 (for income tax purposes).
In para. 20(c), the words "section 62(5) of CTA 2010" substituted for "section 392A(2) of ICTA" by CTA 2010, s. 1177 and Sch. 1, para. 364(11)(b), with effect for corporation tax purposes for accounting periods ending on or after 1 April 2010, and for income tax and capital gains tax purposes for the tax year 2010–11 and subsequent tax years.
In para. 20(c), the words "UK property business" substituted for the words "Schedule A business", the words "UK property business losses" substituted for the words "Schedule A losses" and the word "ICTA" substituted for the words "that Act" by CTA 2009, s. 1322 and Sch. 1, para. 521(1)(b), with effect for corporation tax purposes for accounting periods ending on or after 1 April 2009, and for income tax and capital gains tax purposes for the tax year 2009–10 and subsequent tax years.
In para. 20(d), the words "section 66 of CTA 2010" substituted for "section 392B of ICTA" by CTA 2010, s. 1177 and Sch. 1, para. 364(10), with effect for corporation tax purposes for accounting periods ending on or after 1 April 2010, and for income tax and capital gains tax purposes for the tax year 2010–11 andsubsequent tax years.
In para. 20(d), the word "ICTA" substituted for the words "that Act" by CTA 2009, s. 1322 and Sch. 1, para. 521(1)(c), with effect for corporation tax purposes for accounting periods ending on or after 1 April 2009, and for income tax and capital gains tax purposes for the tax year 2009–10 and subsequent tax years.

21(1) This paragraph applies if the qualifying activity is an ordinary UK property business or an ordinary overseas property business, and in a chargeable period–

(a) the company's loss in carrying on that activity is a loss which, as a result of section 87(3) of FA 2012, is treated for the purposes of section 76 of that Act as a deemed BLAGAB management expense for the chargeable period,

(b) an amount falls to be carried forward to a succeeding chargeable period under section 73 of FA 2012 (carrying forward unrelieved expenses on income), and

(c) the company claims a first-year tax credit for the chargeable period.

21(2) The total amount which falls to be carried forward to a succeeding chargeable period under section 73 of FA 2012 is treated as reduced by the amount of the loss surrendered.

History – In para. 21(1), the words "an ordinary UK" substituted for "a UK" by FA 2011, s. 52 and Sch. 14, para. 12(16)(e)(i), with effect in relation to chargeable periods beginning on or after 1 April 2011 (for corporation tax purposes), and in relation to chargeable periods beginning on or after 6 April 2011 (for income tax purposes).
In para. 21(1), the words "ordinary overseas" substituted for "overseas" by FA 2011, s. 52 and Sch. 14, para. 12(16)(e)(ii), with effect in relation to chargeable periods beginning on or after 1 April 2011 (for corporation tax purposes), and in relation to chargeable periods beginning on or after 6 April 2011 (for income tax purposes).
In para. 21(1), the words "UK property business" substituted for the words "Schedule A business" by CTA 2009, s. 1322 and Sch. 1, para. 521(11), with effect for corporation tax purposes for accounting periods ending on or after 1 April 2009, and for income tax and capital gains tax purposes for the tax year 2009–10 and subsequent tax years.
In para. 21(1)(a), the words "which, as a result of section 87(3) of FA 2012, is treated for the purposes of section 76 of that Act as a deemed BLAGAB management expense for the chargeable period" substituted for the words "treated under section 432AB(3) of ICTA, for the purposes of section 76 of that Act, as expenses payable which fall to be brought into account at Step 3 in subsection (7) of that section" by FA 2012, s. 146 and Sch. 16, para. 106(6)(a) in relation to accounting periods beginning on or after 1 January 2013 (FA 2012, s. 148) but subject to transitional provisions in FA 2012, Sch. 17. Where an accounting period would otherwise straddle 1 January 2013, it is deemed to end on 31 December 2012 (FA 2012, s. 149).
In para. 21(1)(b), the words "section 73 of FA 2012" substituted for the words "section 76(12) of that Act" by FA 2012, s. 146 and Sch. 16, para. 106(6)(b) in relation to accounting periods beginning on or after 1 January 2013 (FA 2012, s. 148) but subject to transitional provisions in FA 2012, Sch. 17. Where an accounting period would otherwise straddle 1 January 2013, it is deemed to end on 31 December 2012 (FA 2012, s. 149).
In para. 21(2), the words "section 73 of FA 2012" substituted for the words "section 76(12) of ICTA" by FA 2012, s. 146 and Sch. 16, para. 106(6)(c) in relation to accounting periods beginning on or after 1 January 2013 (FA 2012, s. 148) but subject to transitional provisions in FA 2012, Sch. 17. Where an accounting period would otherwise straddle 1 January 2013, it is deemed to end on 31 December 2012 (FA 2012, s. 149).

22(1) This paragraph applies where the qualifying activity is basic life assurance and general annuity business and the profits of that business are charged to tax in accordance with the I – E rules.

22(2) For the purposes of those rules, the total amount which may–

(a) be carried forward under section 73 of FA 2012 from a chargeable period in which the company claims a first-year tax credit, and

(b) be brought into account for the next chargeable period in accordance with step 5 in section 76 of FA 2012,

is treated as reduced by the amount of the loss surrendered.

History – In para. 22(1), the words "basic life assurance and general annuity business" substituted for the words "life assurance business", and "in accordance with the I – E rules" substituted for "under the I minus E basis", by FA 2012, s. 146 and Sch. 16, para. 106(7)(a) in relation to accounting periods beginning on or after 1 January 2013 (FA 2012, s. 148) but subject to transitional provisions in FA 2012, Sch. 17. Where an accounting period would otherwise straddle 1 January 2013, it is deemed to end on 31 December 2012 (FA 2012, s. 149).
Para. 22(2) substituted by FA 2012, s. 146 and Sch. 16, para. 106(7)(b) in relation to accounting periods beginning on or after 1 January 2013 (FA 2012, s. 148) but subject to transitional provisions in FA 2012, Sch. 17. Where an accounting period would otherwise straddle 1 January 2013, it is deemed to end on 31 December 2012 (FA 2012, s. 149).

PAYMENT IN RESPECT OF FIRST-YEAR TAX CREDIT NOT INCOME

23 A payment in respect of a first-year tax credit is not income of the company for any tax purposes.

Part 3 – Clawback of First-Year Tax Credit

CIRCUMSTANCES IN WHICH FIRST-YEAR TAX CREDIT CLAWED BACK

24(1) This paragraph applies where–

(a) a company to which a first-year tax credit is paid for a chargeable period disposes of an item of tax-relieved plant or machinery before the end of the clawback period in relation to that item, and

(b) after the disposal the amount (or the aggregate of the amounts) of the original expenditure on the retained tax-relieved plant and machinery is less than the amount of loss surrendered under this Schedule in the chargeable period for which the first-year tax credit was paid.

24(2) The appropriate part ("the restored loss") of the loss surrendered under this Schedule in that chargeable period is to be treated as if it were not a surrenderable loss in that chargeable period.

24(3) The amount of the restored loss is to be calculated in accordance with paragraph 26.

24(4) The amount of first-year tax credit paid to the company in respect of the restored loss is to be treated as if it ought never to have been paid.

24(5) The amount of first-year tax credit paid to the company in respect of the restored loss is the relevant percentage of the restored loss.

24(6) **"Relevant percentage"** means the percentage specified in paragraph 2(1)(a) for the chargeable period for which the first-year tax credit is paid.

24(7) This Part of this Schedule applies to an amount of first-year tax credit which is payable for a chargeable period but not yet paid, as it applies to an amount of first-year tax credit which is paid.

INTERPRETATION

25(1) This paragraph applies for the interpretation of this Part of this Schedule.

25(2) References to a first-year tax credit being paid include the case where an amount payable in respect of first-year tax credit is applied in discharging any liability of the company's to pay corporation tax.

25(3) An item of plant or machinery is tax-relieved if any expenditure on the item was relevant first-year expenditure in respect of which a first-year allowance was made for the chargeable period for which the first-year tax credit was paid.

25(4) The original expenditure on the item is the amount of the relevant first-year expenditure on the item.

25(5) A company disposes of an item of tax-relieved plant or machinery if–

(a) an event listed in section 61(1) occurs in relation to the item, or

(b) there is a change in the ownership of the item in relation to which a continuity of business provision applies.

25(6) The disposal value of the item is the disposal value required to be brought into account by the company in respect of the item.

25(7) But where–

(a) the company disposes of the item to a person connected with the company for less than its market value, or

(b) there is a change in the ownership of the item in relation to which a continuity of business provision applies,

the disposal value of the item is its market value (whether or not the company is required to bring that value into account).

25(8) A **"continuity of business provision"** is an enactment under which anything done to or by the company which ceases to be the owner of the item is treated, for the purpose of making allowances and charges under this Act, as having been done to or by the person who becomes the owner of the item.

25(9) The retained tax-relieved plant and machinery is the tax-relieved plant and machinery which the company has not disposed of.

25(10) The clawback period, in relation to an item of tax-relieved plant and machinery–

(a) begins when the relevant first-year expenditure on the item is incurred, and

(b) ends 4 years after the end of the chargeable period for which the tax credit was paid.

AMOUNT OF RESTORED LOSS

26(1) The amount of the restored loss is–

$$(LS - OERPM) - (OE - DV) - ARL$$

but where the amount given by that formula is less than nil, the amount of the restored loss is nil.

26(2) In sub-paragraph (1)–

LS is the amount of loss surrendered under this Schedule in the chargeable period for which the first-year tax credit was paid,

OERPM is the amount (or the aggregate of the amounts) of the original expenditure on the retained tax-relieved plant and machinery after the item is disposed of,

OE is the aggregate of the amount of the original expenditure on the item disposed of, and the amounts of the original expenditure on any items of tax-relieved plant and machinery which the company has previously disposed of,

DV is the aggregate of the disposal value of the item disposed of, and the disposal values of any items of tax-relieved plant and machinery which the company has previously disposed of, and

ARL is the amount of the restored loss (or the aggregate of the amounts of the restored loss) on any previous application of this paragraph.

CLAWBACK OF FIRST-YEAR TAX CREDITS: ADMINISTRATIVE PROVISION

27(1) Where paragraph 24 applies, all such assessments and adjustments of assessments are to be made as are necessary.

27(2) If a company which has made a tax return becomes aware that, as a result of that paragraph applying after the return was made, the return has become incorrect, it must give notice to HMRC specifying how the return needs to be amended.

27(3) The notice must be given within 3 months beginning with the day on which the company became aware that anything in the tax return had become incorrect because of paragraph 24.

Part 4 – Supplementary

ARTIFICIALLY INFLATED CLAIMS

28(1) To the extent that a transaction is attributable to arrangements entered into wholly or mainly for a disqualifying purpose, it shall be disregarded in determining for a chargeable period the amount of any first-year tax credit to which a company is entitled under this Schedule.

28(2) Arrangements are entered into wholly or mainly for a disqualifying purpose if their main object, or one of their main objects, is to enable a company to obtain a first-year tax credit–

(a) to which it would not otherwise be entitled, or

(b) of a greater amount than that to which it would otherwise be entitled.

28(3) **"Arrangements"** includes any scheme, agreement or understanding, whether or not legally enforceable.

INTERPRETATION

29 In this Schedule–

"HMRC" means the Commissioners for Her Majesty's Revenue and Customs;

"national insurance contributions" means contributions under Part 1 of the Social Security Contributions and Benefits Act 1992 or Part 1 of the Social Security Contributions and Benefits (Northern Ireland) Act 1992.

SCHEDULE 1 – ABBREVIATIONS AND DEFINED EXPRESSIONS

Section 577

Part 1 – Abbreviations

FA followed by a year	The Finance Act of that year
F(No.2)A followed by a year	The Finance (No.2) Act of that year
CAA 1968	The Capital Allowances Act 1968 (c. 3)
TMA 1970	The Taxes Management Act 1970 (c. 1)
OTA 1975	The Oil Taxation Act 1975 (c. 22)
ICTA	The Income and Corporation Taxes Act 1988 (c. 1)
CAA 1990	The Capital Allowances Act 1990 (c. 1)
TCGA 1992	The Taxation of Chargeable Gains Act 1992 (c. 12)
VATA 1994	The Value Added Tax Act 1994 (c. 23)
ITEPA 2003	The Income Tax (Earnings and Pensions) Act 2003
ITTOIA 2005	The Income Tax (Trading and Other Income) Act 2005
ITA 2007	The Income Tax Act 2007
CTA 2009	The Corporation Tax Act 2009
CTA 2010	The Corporation Tax Act 2010

History – In Pt. 1, the entry for "CTA 2010" inserted by CTA 2010, s. 1177 and Sch. 1, para. 365(2), with effect for corporation tax purposes for accounting periods ending on or after 1 April 2010, and for income tax and capital gains tax purposes for the tax year 2010–11 and subsequent tax years.

In Pt. 1, the entries for "FA followed by a year" and "F(No. 2)A followed by a year" inserted by FA 2009, s. 126(3), with effect from 21 July 2009 (Royal Assent).

In Pt. 1, all entries relating to a Finance Act or a Finance (No. 2) Act omitted by FA 2009, s. 126(4), with effect from 21 July 2009 (Royal Assent).

In Pt. 1, the words "CTA 2009" and "The Corporation Tax Act 2009" inserted by CTA 2009, s. 1322 and Sch. 1, para. 522(2), with effect for corporation tax purposes for accounting periods ending on or after 1 April 2009, and for income tax and capital gains tax purposes for the tax year 2009–10 and subsequent tax years.

In Pt. 1, the entries for "FA 2000", "FA 2001" and "FA 2002" inserted by FA 2008, s. 79 and Sch. 25, para. 6, with effect in relation to expenditure incurred on or after 1 April 2008.

In Pt. 1, the words "ITA 2007" and "The Income Tax Act 2007" inserted by ITA 2007, s. 1027 and Sch. 1, para. 413(2), with effect from 6 April 2007.

In Pt. 1, the words "FA 2006" and "The Finance Act 2006 (c. 25)" inserted by FA 2006, s. 84(4), with effect in relation to any disposal made on or after 5 December 2005.

In Pt. 1, the words "ITTOIA 2005" and "The Income Tax (Trading and Other Income) Act 2005" inserted by ITTOIA 2005, s. 882(1) and Sch. 1, para. 574(2); effective for income tax purposes for 2005–06 onwards and for corporation tax purposes for accounting periods ending after 5 April 2005 (ITTOIA 2005, s. 883(1)).

In Pt. 1, the words "FA 2004" and "The Finance Act 2004 (c. 12)" inserted by FA 2004, s. 281 and Sch. 35, para. 49 which, by virtue of FA 2004, s. 284(1), came into force on 6 April 2006.

In Pt. 1, the words "ITEPA 2003" and "The Income Tax (Earnings and Pensions) Act 2003" inserted by ITEPA 2003, Sch. 6, para. 255 which has effect, for income tax purposes, for the tax year 2003–04 and subsequent tax years and, for corporation tax purposes, for accounting periods ending after 5 April 2003.

Part 2 – Defined Expressions

accounting period	Chapter 2 of Part 2 of CTA 2009
additional VAT liability	section 547(1)
additional VAT rebate	section 547(2)
adjusted net cost (in Chapter 6 of Part 10)	section 522
AIA qualifying expenditure	section 38A
applicable CO_2 emissions figure (in Part 2)	section 268C
approved body (in Part 10)	section 492
assured tenancy	section 490(3)
available qualifying expenditure (in Part 2)	section 57

available qualifying expenditure (in Part 7)	section 459
available qualifying expenditure (in Part 8)	section 473
balancing adjustment (in Part 3A)	section 360M
balancing adjustment (in Part 10)	section 513
balancing event (in Part 3A)	section 360N
balancing event (in Part 10)	section 514
basic life assurance and general annuity business	sections 57 and 67(5) of FA 2012 (as applied by section 141(2) of that Act)
body of persons	section 989 of ITA 2007 and section 1119 of CTA 2010
capital expenditure	section 4 and (in Chapter 2 of Part 1) section 10(1)
capital sum	section 4
car (in Part 2)	section 268A
the charge to corporation tax on income	section 2(3) of CTA 2009 (as applied by section 1119 of CTA 2010)
chargeable period	section 6
connected persons (general meaning)	section 575
connected persons (special extended meaning for certain purposes)	sections 156, 232, 246(2) and 266(5)
control	section 574
the Corporation Tax Acts	section 831(1) of ICTA
development and development order (in Part 5)	section 436
disposal event (in Part 2)	section 60(2)
disposal event (in Chapter 3 of Part 6)	section 443(7)
disposal receipt (in Part 2)	section 60
disposal receipt (in Part 5)	section 420
disposal receipt (in Chapter 3 of Part 8)	section 476(1)
dredging	section 484(3), (4)
dual resident investing company	section 577(1) and section 949 of CTA 2010
dwelling-house	section 531(1)
EEA furnished holiday lettings business	section 17B
electrically-propelled (in Part 2)	section 268B
expenditure on the construction of a building (in Part 10)	section 493
final chargeable period (in Part 2)	section 65
final chargeable period (in Part 7)	section 457(5)
final chargeable period (in Part 8)	section 471(5) and (6)
first-year qualifying expenditure	Chapter 4 of Part 2
fixture (in Part 2)	section 173(1)
general development order (in Part 5)	section 436
hire car for a disabled person (in Part 2)	section 268D
I – E rules	section 70(1) and (2) of FA 2012 (as applied by section 141(2) of that Act)
income from patents (in Part 8)	section 483 and paragraph 101(5) of Schedule 3
insurance company	section 65 of FA 2012 (as applied by section 141(2) of that Act)

interest in an oil licence (in Chapter 3 of Part 12)	section 552(4)
investment company	section 130 of ICTA
investment asset (in relation to life assurance business)	section 545(2)
know-how (in Part 7)	section 452(2)
lease and related expressions (in Part 3A)	section 360Z4
lease and related expressions (in Part 10)	section 531
long-life asset (in Chapter 10 of Part 2)	section 91
long-life asset expenditure (in Part 2)	section 90
long-term business	section 63(1) of FA 2012 (as applied by section 141(2) of that Act)
market value	section 577(1)
mineral asset (in Part 5)	section 397
mineral exploration and access (in Part 5)	section 396
mineral extraction trade (in Part 5)	section 394(2)
mineral deposits (in Part 5)	section 394(3)
motor cycle (in Part 2)	section 268A
non-BLAGAB long-term business	sections 66 and 67 of FA 2012 (as applied by section 141(2) of that Act)
normal time limit for amending a tax return	section 577(1)
notice	section 577(1)
offshore installation (except in Chapter 13 of Part 2)	sections 1001 and 1002 of ITA 2007 and section 1132 of CTA 2010
oil (in Chapter 3 of Part 12)	section 556(3)
oil licence (in Chapter 3 of Part 12)	section 552(1)
ordinary UK property business	section 16
ordinary overseas property business	section 17A
overseas property business	Chapter 2 of Part 3 of ITTOIA 2005 (as applied by section 989 of ITA 2007) and Chapter 2 of Part 4 of CTA 2009 (as applied by section 1119 of CTA 2010)
partial depreciation subsidy	section 209
patent rights (in Part 8)	section 464(2)
planning permission (in Part 5)	section 436
proceeds from a balancing event (in Part 3A)	section 360O
proceeds from a balancing event (in Part 10)	section 515
property business	section 577(1)
public body (in Chapter 1 of Part 11)	section 532(2)
qualifying activity (in Part 2)	Chapter 2 of part 2
qualifying building (in Part 3A)	section 360C
qualifying business premises (in Part 3A)	section 360D
qualifying dwelling-house (in Part 10)	section 490(2) and Chapter 4 of Part 10
qualifying emissions certificate (in Part 2)	section 268C
qualifying expenditure (in Part 3A)	section 360B
qualifying expenditure attributable to a dwelling-house (in Part 10)	section 511

qualifying hire car (in Part 2)	section 82
qualifying non-trade expenditure (in Part 8)	section 469
qualifying trade expenditure (in Part 8)	section 468
qualifying trade (in Part 9)	section 484(2)
related 51% group company	section 279F of CTA 2010 (as applied by 1119 of that Act)
relevant cut-off (in Chapter 9 of Part 2)	section 86(3)
relevant interest (in Part 3A)	Chapter 4 of Part 3A
relevant interest (in Part 10)	Chapter 2 of Part 10
relevant trade (in Part 6)	section 439(3)
research and development	437(2) and (3)
residue of qualifying expenditure attributable to a dwelling-house (in Part 10)	section 512
residue of qualifying interest (in Part 3A)	section 360K
ring fence trade (in Chapter 13 of Part 2)	section 162(2)
sale	section 572(1) to (3)
sale, time of	section 572(4)
sale, transfers under Parts 3A and 10 treated as	section 573
sale, treated as occurring on successions, for purposes of Parts other than Parts 2, 6 and 10	section 559
short-life asset (in Part 2)	section 83
source of mineral deposits (in Part 5)	section 394(5)
special leasing (in Part 2)	section 19
special rate expenditure (in Part 2)	section 104A
tax	section 1119 of CTA 2010
the Tax Acts	Schedule 1 to the Interpretation Act 1978 and section 831 of ICTA
tax advantage	section 577(4)
tax return	section 3(3)
tax year	section 4(2) of ITA 2007 (as applied by section 989 of that Act)
UK furnished holiday lettings business	section 17
UK oil licence	section 552(2)
UK property business	Chapter 2 of Part 3 of ITTOIA 2005 (as applied by section 989 of ITA 2007) and Chapter 2 of Part 4 of CTA 2009 (as applied by section 1119 of CTA 2010)
United Kingdom	section 1013 of ITA 2007 and section 1170 of CTA 2010
unrelieved qualifying expenditure (in Part 2)	section 59
unrelieved qualifying expenditure (in Part 5)	section 419
unrelieved qualifying expenditure (in Part 7)	section 461
unrelieved qualifying expenditure (in Part 8)	section 475
within the charge to tax	section 1009 of ITA 2007 and section 1167 of CTA 2010
writing-down period (in Part 9)	section 487(2)

Prospective amendments – In Sch. 1, Pt. 2 definitions of "the corporate partner calculation (in relation to a trade carried on by a Northern Ireland firm)", "NI rate activity", "NIRE company", "Northern Ireland Chapter 6 firm", "Northern Ireland Chapter 7 firm", "Northern Ireland firm" and "Northern Ireland SME company" inserted by CTNIA 2015, s. 2 and Sch. 1, para. 18, with effect from 26 March 2015 (Royal Assent) in respect of any power to make regulations and with effect in relation to accounting periods beginning on or after the first day of the appointed financial year for other provisions (see CTNIA 2015, s. 5). See also transitional provisions at Sch. 1, para. 19–21.

History – In Sch. 1, Pt. 2:

Entry for "related 51% group company" inserted by FA 2014, s. 7 and Sch. 1, para. 9, with effect in relation to accounting periods beginning on or after 1 April 2015.

The following entries omitted by FA 2012, s. 227 and Sch. 39, para. 38(8), with effect in relation to chargeable periods beginning on or after 1 April 2013 for corporation tax purposes, and 6 April 2013 for income tax purposes, subject to transitional and saving provisions in FA 2012, Sch. 39, para. 41 and 42:

- "balancing adjustment (in Part 4A)",
- "balancing event (in Part 4A)",
- "dwelling (in Part 4A)",
- "flat (in Part 4A)",
- "lease and related expressions (in Part 4A)",
- "proceeds from a balancing event (in Part 4A)",
- "qualifying building (in Part 4A)",
- "qualifying flat (in Part 4A)",
- "relevant interest (in Part 4A)", and
- "residue of qualifying expenditure (in Part 4A)".

Entry for "life assurance business" omitted by FA 2012, s. 146 and Sch. 16, para. 107(2), in relation to accounting periods beginning on or after 1 January 2013 (FA 2012, s. 148) but subject to transitional provisions in FA 2012, Sch. 17. Where an accounting period would otherwise straddle 1 January 2013, it is deemed to end on 31 December 2012 (FA 2012, s. 149).

The following entries inserted by FA 2012, s. 146 and Sch. 16, para. 107(3), in relation to accounting periods beginning on or after 1 January 2013 (FA 2012, s. 148) but subject to transitional provisions in FA 2012, Sch. 17. Where an accounting period would otherwise straddle 1 January 2013, it is deemed to end on 31 December 2012 (FA 2012, s. 149):

- basic life assurance and general annuity business
- I – E rules
- insurance company
- long-term business
- non-BLAGAB long-term business

The following entries inserted by FA 2011, s. 52 and Sch. 14, para. 12(17)(b) with effect in relation to chargeable periods beginning on or after 1 April 2011 (for corporation tax purposes) and in relation to chargeable periods beginning on or after 6 April 2011 (for income tax purposes):

- EEA furnished holiday lettings business
- ordinary UK property business
- ordinary overseas property business
- UK furnished holiday lettings business

In the entry for "accounting period", the words "Chapter 2 of Part 2 of CTA 2009" substituted for the words "section 12 of ICTA" by CTA 2009, s. 1322 and Sch. 1, para. 522(3)(a), with effect for corporation tax purposes for accounting periods ending on or after 1 April 2009, and for income tax and capital gains tax purposes for the tax year 2009–10 and subsequent tax years.

The entry for "AIA qualifying expenditure" inserted by FA 2008, s. 74 and Sch. 24, para. 15, with effect in relation to expenditure incurred on or after 1 April 2008 for corporation tax purposes and 6 April 2008 for income tax purposes.

The entry for "applicable CO_2 emissions figure (in Part 2)" inserted by FA 2009, s. 30 and Sch. 11, para. 23(3), with effect in relation to expenditure incurred on or after 1 April 2009 (for corporation tax purposes) and 6 April 2009 (for income tax purposes), subject to transitional provisions in FA 2009, Sch. 11, para. 27(2) and 30–32.

The entries relating to Pt. 3A inserted in the appropriate places by FA 2005, s. 92 and Sch. 6, para. 11(2), with effect in relation to expenditure incurred on or after 11 April 2007, by virtue of SI 2007/949, art. 2.

In the entry for "sale, transfers under Parts 3, 4, 4A and 10 treated as", ", 3A" inserted by FA 2005, s. 92 and Sch. 6, para. 11(3), with effect in relation to expenditure incurred on or after 11 April 2007, by virtue of SI 2007/949, art. 2.

The entry for "balancing adjustment (in Pt. 4A)" inserted by FA 2001, s. 67 and Sch. 19, Pt. 2, para. 8(2), with effect in relation to expenditure incurred on or after 11 May 2001.

The entry for "balancing event (in Pt. 4A)" inserted by FA 2001, s. 67 and Sch. 19, Pt. 2, para. 8(2), with effect in relation to expenditure incurred on or after 11 May 2001.

The entry for "the Board of Inland Revenue" ceased to have effect by virtue of CRCA 2005, s. 50(6) and Sch. 4, para. 86 and repealed by CRCA 2005, s. 52 and Sch. 5, with effect from 18 April 2005 by virtue of SI 2005/1126, art. 2(2).

In the entry for "body of persons", the words "section 1119 of CTA 2010" substituted for "section 832(1) of ICTA" by CTA 2010, s. 1177 and Sch. 1, para. 365(3)(a), with effect for corporation tax purposes for accounting periods ending on or after 1 April 2010.

In the entry for "body of persons", the words "section 989 of ITA 2007 and" inserted by ITA 2007, s. 1027 and Sch. 1, para. 413(3)(a), with effect from 6 April 2007.

In the entry for "car", "section 268A" substituted for "section 81" by FA 2009, s. 30 and Sch. 11, para. 23(2), with effect in relation to expenditure incurred on or after 1 April 2009 (for corporation tax purposes) and 6 April2009 (for income tax purposes), subject to transitional provisions in FA 2009, Sch. 11, para. 27(2) and 30–32.

In the entry for "the charge to corporation tax on income", the words "section 1119 of CTA 2010" substituted for "section 834(1) of ICTA" by CTA 2010, s. 1177 and Sch. 1, para. 365(3)(b), with effect for corporation tax purposes for accounting periods ending on or after 1 April 2010.

The entry for "the charge to corporation tax on income" inserted by CTA 2009, s. 1322 and Sch. 1, para. 522(3)(b), with effect for corporation tax purposes for accounting periods ending on or after 1 April 2009, and for income tax and capital gains tax purposes for the tax year 2009–10 and subsequent tax years.

In the entry for "connected persons (general meaning)", the words "section 575" substituted for "section 575(1)" by ITA 2007, s. 1027 and Sch. 1, para. 413(3)(b), with effect from 6 April 2007.

In the entry for "dual resident investing company", the words "section 949 of CTA 2010" substituted for "section 404 of ICTA" by CTA 2010, s. 1177 and Sch. 1, para. 365(3)(c), with effect for corporation tax purposes for accounting periods ending on or after 1 April 2010.

The entry for "dwelling (in Pt. 4A)" inserted by FA 2001, s. 67 and Sch. 19, Pt. 2, para. 8(2), with effect in relation to expenditure incurred on or after 11 May 2001.

The entry for "electrically-propelled (in Part 2)" inserted by FA 2009, s. 30 and Sch. 11, para. 23(3), with effect in relation to expenditure incurred on or after 1 April 2009 (for corporation tax purposes) and 6 April 2009 (for income tax purposes), subject to transitional provisions in FA 2009, Sch. 11, para. 27(2) and 30–32.

The entry for "four-year cut-off" omitted by FA 2011, s, 12(6)(b), with effect from 19 July 2011.

The entry for "flat (in Pt. 4A)" inserted by FA 2001, s. 67 and Sch. 19, Pt. 2, para. 8(2), with effect in relation to expenditure incurred on or after 11 May 2001.

The entry for "furnished holiday lettings business" omitted by FA 2011, s. 52 and Sch. 14, para.. 12(17)(a), with effect in relation to chargeable periods beginning on or after 1 April 2011 (for corporation tax purposes), and in relation to chargeable periods beginning on or after 6 April 2011 (for income tax purposes).
The entry for "hire car for a disabled person (in Part 2)" inserted by FA 2009, s. 30 and Sch. 11, para. 23(3), with effect in relation to expenditure incurred on or after 1 April 2009 (for corporation tax purposes) and 6 April 2009 (for income tax purposes), subjectto transitional provisions in FA 2009, Sch. 11, para. 27(2) and 30–32.
The entry for "the Inland Revenue" ceased to have effect by virtue of CRCA 2005, s. 50(6) and Sch. 4, para. 86 and repealed by CRCA 2005, s. 52 and Sch. 5, with effect from 18 April 2005 by virtue of SI 2005/1126, art. 2(2).
The entry for "lease and related expressions (in Pt. 4A)" inserted by FA 2001, s. 67 and Sch. 19, Pt. 2, para. 8(2), with effect in relation to expenditure incurred on or after 11 May 2001.
In the entry for "long-life asset expenditure", the words "in Chapter 10 of Part 2" amended to "in Part 2" by FA 2003, Sch. 43, Pt. 3(9) in relation to expenditure incurred on or after 1 April 2003.
The entry for "motor cycle (in Part 2)" inserted by FA 2009, s. 30 and Sch. 11, para. 23(3), with effect in relation to expenditure incurred on or after 1 April 2009 (for corporation tax purposes) and 6 April 2009 (for income tax purposes), subject to transitional provisions in FA 2009, Sch. 11, para. 27(2) and 30–32.
In the entry for "offshore installation", the words "section 1132 of CTA 2010" substituted for "section 837C of ICTA" by CTA 2010, s. 1177 and Sch. 1, para. 365(3)(d), with effect for corporation tax purposes for accounting periods ending on or after 1 April 2010.
In the entry for "offshore installation", the words "sections 1001 and 1002 of ITA 2007 and" inserted by ITA 2007, s. 1027 and Sch. 1, para. 413(3)(c), with effect from 6 April 2007.
In the definition of "offshore installation", the words "offshore installation (except in Chapter 13 of Part 2)" and "section 837C of ICTA" inserted by FA 2004, s. 146 and Sch. 27, para. 10 which have effect, by virtue of FA 2004, Sch. 27, para. 11(1), as respects allowances and charges falling to be made for chargeable periods ending on or after either 6 April 2004 (for income tax purposes) or 1 April 2004 (for corporation tax purposes).
The entry for "ordinary property business" omitted by FA 2011, s. 52 and Sch. 14, para.. 12(17)(a), with effect in relation to chargeable periods beginning on or after 1 April 2011 (for corporation tax purposes), and in relation to chargeable periods beginning on or after 6 April 2011 (for income tax purposes).
The entry for "ordinary property business" substituted for "ordinary Schedule A business" by virtue of ITTOIA 2005, s. 882(1) and Sch. 1, para. 574(3); effective for income tax purposes for 2005–06 onwards and for corporation tax purposes for accounting periods ending after 5 April 2005 (ITTOIA 2005, s. 883(1)).
In the entry for "overseas property business", the words "section 1119 of CTA 2010" substituted for "section 834B of ICTA" by CTA 2010, s. 1177 and Sch. 1, para. 365(3)(e), with effect for corporation tax purposes for accounting periods ending on or after 1 April 2010.
In the entry for "overseas property business", the words "Chapter 2 of Part 3 of ITTOIA 2005 (as applied by section 989 of ITA 2007) and Chapter 2 of Part 4 of CTA 2009 (as applied by section 834B of ICTA)" substituted for the words "sections 70A(4) and 832(1) of ICTA and Chapter 2 of Part 3 of ITTOIA 2005 (as applied by section 989 of ITA 2007)" by CTA 2009, s. 1322 and Sch. 1, para. 522(3)(c), with effect for corporation tax purposes for accounting periods ending on or after 1 April 2009, and for income tax and capital gains tax purposes for the tax year 2009–10 and subsequent tax years.
In the entry for "overseas property business", the words "(as applied by section 989 of ITA 2007)" inserted by ITA 2007, s. 1027 and Sch. 1, para. 413(3)(d), with effect from 6 April 2007.
The entry for "overseas property business" expanded by virtue of ITTOIA 2005, s. 882(1) and Sch. 1, para. 574(3); effective for income tax purposes for 2005–06 onwards and for corporation tax purposes for accounting periods ending after 5 April 2005 (ITTOIA 2005, s. 883(1)).
The entry for "proceeds from a balancing event (in Pt. 4A)" inserted by FA 2001, s. 67 and Sch. 19, Pt. 2, para. 8(2), with effect in relation to expenditure incurred on or after 11 May 2001.
The entry for "qualifying building (in Pt. 4A)" inserted by FA 2001, s. 67 and Sch. 19, Pt. 2, para. 8(2), with effect in relation to expenditure incurred on or after 11 May 2001.
The entry for "qualifying emissions certificate (in Part 2)" inserted by FA 2009, s. 30 and Sch. 11, para. 23(3), with effect in relation to expenditure incurred on or after 1 April 2009 (for corporation tax purposes) and 6 April 2009 (for income tax purposes), subject to transitional provisions in FA 2009, Sch. 11, para. 27(2) and 30–32.
The entry for "qualifying flat (in Pt. 4A)" inserted by FA 2001, s. 67 and Sch. 19, Pt. 2, para. 8(2), with effect in relation to expenditure incurred on or after 11 May 2001.
The entry for "relevant cut-off" inserted by FA 2011, s, 12(6)(a), with effect from 19 July 2011.
The entry for "relevant interest (in Pt. 4A)" inserted by FA 2001, s. 67 and Sch. 19, Pt. 2, para. 8(2), with effect in relation to expenditureincurred on or after 11 May 2001.
The entry for "research and development", the words "437(2) and (3)" substituted for "437(2) and section 837A of ICTA" by ITA 2007, s. 1027 and Sch. 1, para. 413(3)(e), with effect from 6 April 2007.
The entry for "residue of qualifying expenditure (in Pt. 4A)" inserted by FA 2001, s. 67 and Sch. 19, Pt. 2, para. 8(2), with effect in relation to expenditure incurred on or after 11 May 2001.
In the entry for sale, transfers under Parts 3, 4, 4A and 10 treated as, reference to Part 4A inserted by FA 2001, s. 67 and Sch. 19, Pt. 2, para. 8(3).
In Sch. 1, Pt. 2, ", 4A" omitted from the entry for "sale, transfers under Parts 3A, 4A and 10 treated as", by FA 2012, s. 227 and Sch. 39, para. 38(9), with effect in relation to chargeable periods beginning on or after 1 April 2013 for corporation tax purposes, and 6 April 2013 for income tax purposes, subject to transitional and saving provisions in FA 2012, Sch. 39, para. 41 and 42.
In Sch. 1, Pt. 2 in the entry relating to "sale, transfers under Parts 3, 3A, 4, 4A and 10 treated as", "3," and "4," omitted by FA 2008, s. 84 and Sch. 27, para. 19(3), with effect in relation to chargeable periods beginning on or after 1 April 2011 for corporation tax purposes and 6 April 2011 for income tax purposes (FA 2008, Sch. 27, para. 30(1)).
The entry for "Schedule A business" omitted by CTA 2009, s. 1322 and Sch. 1, para. 522(3)(d) and repealed by CTA 2009, s. 1326 and Sch. 3, Pt. 1, with effect for corporation tax purposes for accounting periods ending on or after 1 April 2009, and for income tax and capital gains tax purposes for the tax year 2009–10 and subsequent tax years. The second column of that former entry read "section 989 of ITA 2007 and section 832(1) of ICTA".
In the former entry for "Schedule A business", the words "section 989 of ITA 2007 and" inserted by ITA 2007, s. 1027 and Sch. 1, para. 413(3)(f), with effect from 6 April 2007.
The entry for "special rate expenditure (in Part 2)" inserted by FA 2008, s. 82 and Sch. 26, para. 13, with effect in relation expenditure incurred on or after 1 April 2008 for corporation tax purposes and 6 April 2008 for income tax purposes and in relation to long-life asset expenditure (within the meaning of CAA 2001, Pt. 2, Ch. 10) incurred before those dates but allocated to a pool in a chargeable period beginning on or after those dates. This commencement provision is subject to FA 2008, s. 83 (existing long-life asset expenditure treated as special rate expenditure) and FA 2008, Sch. 26, para. 15–17 (detailedprovisions relating to sales between connected persons and savings for intra-group transfers).
In the entry for "Tax", the words "section 1119 of CTA 2010" substituted for "section 832(3) of ICTA" by CTA 2010, s. 1177 and Sch. 1, para. 365(3)(f), with effect for corporation tax purposes for accounting periods ending on or after 1 April 2010.
In the entry for "tax year", the words "section 4(2) of ITA 2007 (as applied by section 989 of that Act)" substituted for "section 577(1)" by ITA 2007, s. 1027 and Sch. 1, para. 413(3)(g), with effect from 6 April 2007.
In the entry for "UK property business", the words "section 1119 of CTA 2010" substituted for "section 834B of ICTA" by CTA 2010, s. 1177 and Sch. 1, para. 365(3)(g), with effect for corporation tax purposes for accounting periods ending on or after 1 April 2010.

In the entry for "UK property business", the words "and Chapter 2 of Part 4 of CTA 2009 (as applied by section 834B of ICTA)" inserted by CTA 2009, s. 1322 and Sch. 1, para. 522(3)(e), with effect for corporation tax purposes for accounting periods ending on or after 1 April 2009, and for income tax and capital gains tax purposes for the tax year 2009–10 and subsequent tax years.
In the entry for "UK property business", the words "section 832(1) of ICTA and" omitted, and the words "(as applied by section 989 of ITA 2007)" inserted, by ITA 2007, s. 1027 and Sch. 1, para. 413(3)(h); and the words "section 832(1) of ICTA and" also repealed by ITA 2007, s. 1031 and Sch. 3, Pt. 1; all with effect from 6 April 2007.
In the entry for "UK property business" inserted by ITTOIA 2005, s. 882(1) and Sch. 1, para. 574(3); effective for income tax purposes for 2005–06 onwards and for corporation tax purposes for accounting periods ending after 5 April 2005 (ITTOIA 2005, s. 883(1)).
In the entry for "United Kingdom", the words "section 1170 of CTA 2010" substituted for "section 830(1) of ICTA" by CTA 2010, s. 1177 and Sch. 1, para. 365(3)(h), with effect for corporation tax purposes for accounting periods ending on or after 1 April 2010.
In the entry for "United Kingdom", the words "section 1013 of ITA 2007 and section 830(1) of ICTA" substituted for "section 830 of ICTA and section 41 of ITEPA 2003" by ITA 2007, s. 1027 and Sch. 1, para. 413(3)(i), with effect from 6 April 2007.
In the entry relating to "United Kingdom", the words "and section 41 of ITEPA 2003" inserted by ITEPA 2003, Sch. 6, para. 256 with effect, for income tax purposes, for the tax year 2003–04 and subsequent tax years and, for corporation tax purposes, for accounting periods ending after 5 April 2003.
In the entry for "within the charge to tax", the words "section 1167 of CTA 2010" substitutedfor "section 832(1) of ICTA" by CTA 2010, s. 1177 and Sch. 1, para. 365(3)(i), with effect for corporation tax purposes for accounting periods ending on or after 1 April 2010.
In the entry for "within the charge to tax", the words "section 1009 of ITA 2007 and" inserted by ITA 2007, s. 1027 and Sch. 1, para. 413(3)(j), with effect from 6 April 2007.

SCHEDULE 2 – CONSEQUENTIAL AMENDMENTS

Section 578

THE TAXES MANAGEMENT ACT 1970 (C. 9)

Section 42 (procedure for making claims etc.)

1 [Amends TMA 1970, s. 42(7).]

Section 57 (regulations about appeals)

2 [Substitutes TMA 1970, s. 57(3)(b).]

Section 58 (proceedings in tax cases in Northern Ireland)

3 [Amends TMA 1970, s. 58(3)(b).]

Section 98 (special returns, etc.)

4(1) [Amends TMA 1970, s. 98, Table (Column 1).]

4(2) [Amends TMA 1970, s. 98, Table (Column 2).]

Schedule 3 (rules for assigning proceedings to General Commissioners)

5 [Repealed by CTA 2009, s. 1326 and Sch. 3, Pt. 1 and omitted by SI 2009/56, art 3(1) and Sch. 1, para. 300.]

History – Para. 5 repealed by CTA 2009, s. 1326 and Sch. 3, Pt. 1, with effect for corporation tax purposes for accounting periods ending on or after 1 April 2009, and for income tax and capital gains tax purposes for the tax year 2009–10 and subsequent tax years and also omitted by SI 2009/56, art. 3(1) and Sch. 1, para. 300, operative from 1 April 2009, subject to transitional and saving provisions in SI 2009/56, Sch. 3. Former para. 5 amended TMA 1970, Sch. 3, para. 10.

THE FINANCE ACT 1982 (C. 39)

Section 137 (expenditure met by regional development plans to be disregarded for certain purposes)

6 [Omits FA 1982, s. 137(2), (3), (6) and (7).]

THE LONDON REGIONAL TRANSPORT ACT 1984 (C. 32)

Schedule 5 (transitional provisions and savings)

7 [Amends London Regional Transport Act 1984, Sch. 5, para. 5.]

THE FILMS ACT 1985 (C. 21)

Section 6 (certification of films as British films)

8 [Amends Films Act 1985, s. 6(1).].

Schedule 1 (certification of films as British films)

9(1) [Amends Films Act 1985, Sch. 1, para. 2(1).].

9(2) [Amends Films Act 1985, Sch. 1, para. 3(1).].

THE TRUSTEE SAVINGS BANKS ACT 1985(C. 58)

Schedule 2 (taxation)

10 [Amends Trustee Savings Bank Act 1985, Sch. 2, para. 1.]

THE INCOME AND CORPORATION TAXES ACT 1988 (C. 1)

Section 43C (transfer of rent: exceptions, etc.)

11 [Repealed by FA 2006, s. 178 and Sch. 26, Pt. 3(12).]

History – Para. 11 repealed by FA 2006, s. 178 and Sch. 26, Pt. 3(12), with effect in relation to transactions entered into on or after 6 June 2006.

Section 43E (interposed lease: exceptions, etc.)

12 [Repealed by FA 2006, s. 178 and Sch. 26, Pt. 3(12).]

History – Para. 12 repealed by FA 2006, s. 178 and Sch. 26, Pt. 3(12), with effect in relation to transactions entered into on or after 6 June 2006.

Section 65A (Case V income from land outside UK: income tax)

13 [Amends ICTA 1988, s. 65A(7).]

Section 70A (Case V income from land outside UK: corporation tax)

14 [Repealed by CTA 2009, s. 1326 and Sch. 3, Pt. 1.]

History – Para. 14 repealed by CTA 2009, s. 1326 and Sch. 3, Pt. 1, with effect for corporation tax purposes for accounting periods ending on or after 1 April 2009, and for income tax and capital gains tax purposes for the tax year 2009–10 and subsequent tax years.

Section 75 (expenses of management: investment companies)

15 [Repealed by FA 2004, s. 326 and Sch. 42, Pt. 2(3).]

History – Para. 15 repealed by FA 2004, s. 326 and Sch. 42, Pt. 2(3) which have effect, by virtue of, and in accordance with, FA 2004, s. 42, for accounting periods beginning on or after 1 April 2004 but subject to the transitional provisions in FA 2004, s. 43 and 44 and Sch. 6.

Section 83A (gifts in kind to charities, etc.)

16 [Repealed by CTA 2009, s. 1326 and Sch. 3, Pt. 1; amended ICTA 1988, s. 83A.]

History – Para. 16 repealed by CTA 2009, s. 1326 and Sch. 3, Pt. 1, with effect for corporation tax purposes for accounting periods ending on or after 1 April 2009, and for income tax and capital gains tax purposes for the tax year 2009–10 and subsequent tax years.

Section 84 (gifts to educational establishments)

17 [Repealed by CTA 2009, s. 1326 and Sch. 3, Pt. 1.]

History – Para. 17 repealed by CTA 2009, s. 1326 and Sch. 3, Pt. 1, with effect for corporation tax purposes for accounting periods ending on or after 1 April 2009, and for income tax and capital gains tax purposes for the tax year 2009–10 and subsequent tax years.

Section 87 (taxable premiums etc.)

18 [Repealed by CTA 2009, s. 1326 and Sch. 3, Pt. 1.]

History – Para. 18 repealed by CTA 2009, s. 1326 and Sch. 3, Pt. 1, with effect for corporation tax purposes for accounting periods ending on or after 1 April 2009, and for income tax and capital gains tax purposes for the tax year 2009–10 and subsequent tax years.

Section 91 (cemeteries)

19 [Repealed by CTA 2009, s. 1326 and Sch. 3, Pt. 1.]

History – Para. 19 repealed by CTA 2009, s. 1326 and Sch. 3, Pt. 1, with effect for corporation tax purposes for accounting periods ending on or after 1 April 2009, and for income tax and capital gains tax purposes for the tax year 2009–10 and subsequent tax years.

Section 91C (mineral exploration and access)

20 [Repealed by CTA 2009, s. 1326 and Sch. 3, Pt. 1.]

History – Para. 20 repealed by CTA 2009, s. 1326 and Sch. 3, Pt. 1, with effect for corporation tax purposes for accounting periods ending on or after 1 April 2009, and for income tax and capital gains tax purposes for the tax year 2009–10 and subsequent tax years.

Section 116 (arrangements for transferring relief)

21 [Repealed by CTA 2010, s. 1181 and Sch. 3, Pt. 1.]

History – Para. 21 repealed by CTA 2010, s. 1181 and Sch. 3, Pt. 1, with effect for corporation tax purposes for accounting periods ending on or after 1 April 2010, and for income tax and capital gains tax purposes for the tax year 2010–11 and subsequent tax years.

Section 117 (restriction on relief: individuals)

22 [Repealed by ITA 2007, s. 1031 and Sch. 3, Pt. 1.]

History – Para. 22 repealed by ITA 2007, s. 1031 and Sch. 3, Pt. 1, with effect from 6 April 2007.

Rewrite: Technical Points – Explanatory Notes, Annex 2, Note 75: former para. 22 repealed provisions that no longer had any effect following the Rewrite, essentially because there were no longer any allowances that could be given to traders by way of discharge or repayment of tax.

Notes – Para. 22(3) rewritten as ITA 2007, Sch. 2, para. 27(1).

Section 118 (restriction on relief: companies)

23 [Repealed by CTA 2010, s. 1181 and Sch. 3, Pt. 1.]

History – Para. 23 repealed by CTA 2010, s. 1181 and Sch. 3, Pt. 1, with effect for corporation tax purposes for accounting periods ending on or after 1 April 2010, and for income tax and capital gains tax purposes for the tax year 2010–11 and subsequent tax years.

Section 197C (definition of mileage profit)

24 [Repealed by ITEPA 2003, Sch. 8, Pt. 1.]

History – Para. 24 repealed by ITEPA 2003, Sch. 8, Pt. 1 which has effect for the tax year 2003–04 and subsequent tax years.

Section 198 (relief for necessary expenses)

25 [Repealed by ITEPA 2003, Sch. 8, Pt. 1.]

History – Para. 25 repealed by ITEPA 2003, Sch. 8, Pt. 1 which has effect for the tax year 2003–04 and subsequent tax years.

Section 343 (company reconstructions without a change of ownership)

26 [Repealed by CTA 2010, s. 1181 and Sch. 3, Pt. 1.]

History – Para. 26 repealed by CTA 2010, s. 1181 and Sch. 3, Pt. 1, with effect for corporation tax purposes for accounting periods ending on or after 1 April 2010, and for income tax and capital gains tax purposes for the tax year 2010–11 and subsequent tax years.

Section 359 (loan to buy machinery or plant)

27 [Repealed by ITA 2007, s. 1031 and Sch. 3, Pt. 1.]

History – Para. 27 repealed by ITA 2007, s. 1031 and Sch. 3, Pt. 1, with effect from 6 April 2007.

Notes – Para. 27 rewritten as ITA 2007, Sch. 2, para. 388(1), (2), 390(1), (2).

Section 379A (Schedule A losses)

28 [Repealed by ITA 2007, s. 1031 and Sch. 3, Pt. 1.]

History – Para. 28 repealed by ITA 2007, s. 1031 and Sch. 3, Pt. 1, with effect from 6 April 2007.

Notes – Para. 28 rewritten as ITA 2007, Sch. 2, para. 123(2).

Section 384 (restrictions on right of set-off)

29 [Repealed by ITA 2007, s. 1031 and Sch. 3, Pt. 1.]

29(2) [Amends ICTA 1988, s. 384(1).]

History – Para. 29(1) repealed by ITA 2007, s. 1031 and Sch. 3, Pt. 1, with effect from 6 April 2007.
In para. 29(2), a former reference to inserting ICTA 1988, s. 384(11) repealed by ITA 2007, s. 1031 and Sch. 3, Pt. 1, with effect from 6 April 2007.

Notes – Para. 29 rewritten as ITA 2007, s. 75(2), 79(2).

New section 384A (restriction of set-off of plant and machinery allowances)

30 [Repealed by ITA 2007, s. 1031 and Sch. 3, Pt. 1.]

History – Para. 30 repealed by ITA 2007, s. 1031 and Sch. 3, Pt. 1, with effect from 6 April 2007.

Notes – Para. 30 rewritten as ITA 2007, s. 76, 77(1), (2), (3), 78(1), (2), (3), (4), (5), (6), 79(1), (2).

Section 389 (supplementary provisions relating to carry-back of terminal losses)

31 [Repealed by ITA 2007, s. 1031 and Sch. 3, Pt. 1.]

History – Para. 31 repealed by ITA 2007, s. 1031 and Sch. 3, Pt. 1, with effect from 6 April 2007.

Notes – Para. 31 rewritten as ITA 2007, s. 93(1), (2), (3), (4).

Section 393A (losses: set off against profits of the same, or an earlier, accounting period)

32 [Repealed by CTA 2010, s. 1181 and Sch. 3, Pt. 1.]

History – Para. 32 repealed by CTA 2010, s. 1181 and Sch. 3, Pt. 1, with effect for corporation tax purposes for accounting periods ending on or after 1 April 2010, and for income tax and capital gains tax purposes for the tax year 2010–11 and subsequent tax years.

Section 395 (leasing contracts and company reconstructions)

33 [Repealed by CTA 2010, s. 1181 and Sch. 3, Pt. 1.]

History – Para. 33 repealed by CTA 2010, s. 1181 and Sch. 3, Pt. 1, with effect for corporation tax purposes for accounting periods ending on or after 1 April 2010, and for income tax and capital gains tax purposes for the tax year 2010–11 and subsequent tax years.

Section 397 (restriction of relief in case of farming and market gardening)

34 [Repealed by CTA 2010, s. 1181 and Sch. 3, Pt. 1.]

History – Para. 34 repealed by CTA 2010, s. 1181 and Sch. 3, Pt. 1, with effect for corporation tax purposes for accounting periods ending on or after 1 April 2010, and for income tax and capital gains tax purposes for the tax year 2010–11 and subsequent tax years.

Section 400 (write-off of government investment)

35 [Repealed by CTA 2010, s. 1181 and Sch. 3, Pt. 1.]

History – Para. 35 repealed by CTA 2010, s. 1181 and Sch. 3, Pt. 1, with effect for corporation tax purposes for accounting periods ending on or after 1 April 2010, and for income tax and capital gains tax purposes for the tax year 2010–11 and subsequent tax years.

Section 403ZB (amounts eligible for group relief: excess capital allowances)

36 [Repealed by CTA 2010, s. 1181 and Sch. 3, Pt. 1.]

History – Para. 36 repealed by CTA 2010, s. 1181 and Sch. 3, Pt. 1, with effect for corporation tax purposes for accounting periods ending on or after 1 April 2010, and for income tax and capital gains tax purposes for the tax year 2010–11 and subsequent tax years.

Section 407 (relationship between group relief and other relief)

37 [Repealed by CTA 2010, s. 1181 and Sch. 3, Pt. 1.]

History – Para. 37 repealed by CTA 2010, s. 1181 and Sch. 3, Pt. 1, with effect for corporation tax purposes for accounting periods ending on or after 1 April 2010, and for income tax and capital gains tax purposes for the tax year 2010–11 and subsequent tax years.

Section 411 (exclusion of double allowance)

38 [Repealed by CTA 2010, s. 1181 and Sch. 3, Pt. 1.]

History – Para. 38 repealed by CTA 2010, s. 1181 and Sch. 3, Pt. 1, with effect for corporation tax purposes for accounting periods ending on or after 1 April 2010, and for income tax and capital gains tax purposes for the tax year 2010–11 and subsequent tax years.

Sections 434D and 434E (capital allowances: management assets; investment assets)

39 [Omits ICTA 1988, s. 434D and 434E.]

Notes – ICTA 1988, s. 434A and 434E are rewritten as CAA 2001, s. 255 to 257, and 544 and 545.

Section 487 (credit unions)

40 [Repealed by CTA 2009, s. 1326 and Sch. 3, Pt. 1.]

History – Para. 40 repealed by CTA 2009, s. 1326 and Sch. 3, Pt. 1, with effect for corporation tax purposes for accounting periods ending on or after 1 April 2009, and for income tax and capital gains tax purposes for the tax year 2009–10 and subsequent tax years.

Section 492 (treatment of oil extraction activities etc. for tax purposes)

41 [Repealed by CTA 2010, s. 1181 and Sch. 3, Pt. 1.]

History – Para. 41 repealed by CTA 2010, s. 1181 and Sch. 3, Pt. 1, with effect for corporation tax purposes for accounting periods ending on or after 1 April 2010, and for income tax and capital gains tax purposes for the tax year 2010–11 and subsequent tax years.

Section 495 (regional development grants)

42 [Repealed by CTA 2010, s. 1181 and Sch. 3, Pt. 2; also repealed by TIOPA 2010, s. 378 and Sch. 10, Pt. 6.]

History – Para. 42 repealed by CTA 2010, s. 1181 and Sch. 3, Pt. 2, for corporation tax purposes only, with effect for accounting periods ending on or after 1 April 2010. Para. 42 also repealed by TIOPA 2010, s. 378 and Sch. 10, Pt. 6, with effect for corporation tax purposes for accounting periods ending on or after 1 April 2010, for income tax and capital gains tax purposes for the tax year 2010–11 and subsequent tax years, and for petroleum revenue tax purposes for chargeable periods beginning on or after 1 July 2010.

Section 518 (harbour reorganisation schemes)

43 [Repealed by CTA 2010, s. 1181 and Sch. 3, Pt. 1.]

History – Para. 43 repealed by CTA 2010, s. 1181 and Sch. 3, Pt. 1, with effect for corporation tax purposes for accounting periods ending on or after 1 April 2010, and for income tax and capital gains tax purposes for the tax year 2010–11 and subsequent tax years.

Sections 520 to 523 (patents)

44 [Omits ICTA 1988, s. 520 to 523.]

Notes – ICTA 1988, s. 520 to 523 are rewritten by CAA 2001, Pt. 8 (patent allowances).

Section 525 (capital sums: death, winding up or partnership change)

45 [Repealed by CTA 2009, s. 1326 and Sch. 3, Pt. 1.]

History – Para. 45 repealed by CTA 2009, s. 1326 and Sch. 3, Pt. 1, with effect for corporation tax purposes for accounting periods ending on or after 1 April 2009, and for income tax and capital gains tax purposes for the tax year 2009–10 and subsequent tax years.

Section 528 (patents: manner of making allowances and charges)

46 [Repealed by CTA 2009, s. 1326 and Sch. 3, Pt. 1.]

History – Para. 46 repealed by CTA 2009, s. 1326 and Sch. 3, Pt. 1, with effect for corporation tax purposes for accounting periods ending on or after 1 April 2009, and for income tax and capital gains tax purposes for the tax year 2009–10 and subsequent tax years.

Section 530 (disposal of know-how)

47 [Omits ICTA 1988, s. 530.]

Notes – ICTA 1988, s. 530 is rewritten by CAA 2001, Pt. 7 (know-how allowances).

Section 531 (disposal of know-how: supplementary provisions)

48 [Repealed by CTA 2009, s. 1326 and Sch. 3, Pt. 1.]

History – Para. 48 repealed by CTA 2009, s. 1326 and Sch. 3, Pt. 1, with effect for corporation tax purposes for accounting periods ending on or after 1 April 2009, and for income tax and capital gains tax purposes for the tax year 2009–10 and subsequent tax years.

Section 532 (application of 1990 Act)

49 [Repealed by CTA 2009, s. 1326 and Sch. 3, Pt. 1.]

History – Para. 49 repealed by CTA 2009, s. 1326 and Sch. 3, Pt. 1, with effect for corporation tax purposes for accounting periods ending on or after 1 April 2009, and for income tax and capital gains tax purposes for the tax year 2009–10 and subsequent tax years.

Section 533 (interpretation of sections 520 to 532)

50 [Repealed by CTA 2009, s. 1326 and Sch. 3, Pt. 1.]

History – Para. 50 repealed by CTA 2009, s. 1326 and Sch. 3, Pt. 1, with effect for corporation tax purposes for accounting periods ending on or after 1 April 2009, and for income tax and capital gains tax purposes for the tax year 2009–10 and subsequent tax years.

Section 577 (business entertaining expenses)

51 [Repealed by CTA 2009, s. 1326 and Sch. 3, Pt. 1.]

History – Para. 51 repealed by CTA 2009, s. 1326 and Sch. 3, Pt. 1, with effect for corporation tax purposes for accounting periods ending on or after 1 April 2009, and for income tax and capital gains tax purposes for the tax year 2009–10 and subsequent tax years.

New sections 578A and 578B (expenditure on car hire)

52 [Repealed by CTA 2009, s. 1326 and Sch. 3, Pt. 1.]

History – Para. 52 repealed by CTA 2009, s. 1326 and Sch. 3, Pt. 1, with effect for corporation tax purposes for accounting periods ending on or after 1 April 2009, and for income tax and capital gains tax purposes for the tax year 2009–10 and subsequent tax years.

Section 623 (retirement annuities: relevant earnings)

53 [Repealed by FA 2004, s. 326 and Sch. 42, Pt. 3.]

History – Para. 53 repealed by FA 2004, s. 326 and Sch. 42, Pt. 3 with effect from 6 April 2006 but subject to FA 2004, Sch. 36. Para. 53 amended ICTA 1988, s. 623(5).

Section 646 (meaning of "net relevant earnings")

54 [Repealed by FA 2004, s. 326 and Sch. 42, Pt. 3.]

History – Para. 54 repealed by FA 2004, s. 326 and Sch. 42, Pt. 3 with effect from 6 April 2006 but subject to FA 2004, Sch. 36. Para. 54 amended ICTA 1988, s. 646(3).

Section 768 (change in ownership of company: disallowance of trading losses)

55 [Repealed by CTA 2010, s. 1181 and Sch. 3, Pt. 1.]

History – Para. 55 repealed by CTA 2010, s. 1181 and Sch. 3, Pt. 1, with effect for corporation tax purposes for accounting periods ending on or after 1 April 2010, and for income tax and capital gains tax purposes for the tax year 2010–11 and subsequent tax years.

Section 768B (change in ownership of investment company: deductions generally)

56 [Repealed by CTA 2010, s. 1181 and Sch. 3, Pt. 1.]

History – Para. 56 repealed by CTA 2010, s. 1181 and Sch. 3, Pt. 1, with effect for corporation tax purposes for accounting periods ending on or after 1 April 2010, and for income tax and capital gains tax purposes for the tax year 2010–11 and subsequent tax years.

Section 781 (assets leased to traders and others)

57 [Repealed by CTA 2010, s. 1181 and Sch. 3, Pt. 2; also repealed by TIOPA 2010, s. 378 and Sch. 10, Pt. 9.]

History – Para. 57 repealed by CTA 2010, s. 1181 and Sch. 3, Pt. 2, for corporation tax purposes only, with effect for accounting periods ending on or after 1 April 2010. Para. 57 also repealed by TIOPA 2010, s. 378 and Sch. 10, Pt. 9, with effect for corporation tax purposes for accounting periods ending on or after 1 April 2010, for income tax and capital gains tax purposes for the tax year 2010–11 and subsequent tax years, and for petroleum revenue tax purposes for chargeable periods beginning on or after 1 July 2010.

Section 828 (orders and regulations made by the Treasury or the Board)

58 [Repealed by ITA 2007, s. 1031 and Sch. 3, Pt. 1.]

History – Para. 58 repealed by ITA 2007, s. 1031 and Sch. 3, Pt. 1, with effect from 6 April 2007.

Notes – Para. 58 rewritten as ITA 2007, Sch. 1, para. 409.

Section 831 (interpretation of Act)

59 Section 831(3) continues to have effect with the addition of the definition of **"the 1990 Act"** (an amendment originally made by paragraph 8(35) of Schedule 1 to the Capital Allowances Act 1990).

Section 832 (interpretation of the Tax Acts)

60 [Repealed by CTA 2010, s. 1181 and Sch. 3, Pt. 1.]

History – Para. 60 repealed by CTA 2010, s. 1181 and Sch. 3, Pt. 1, with effect for corporation tax purposes for accounting periods ending on or after 1 April 2010, and for income tax and capital gains tax purposes for the tax year 2010–11 and subsequent tax years.

Section 834 (interpretation of the Corporation Tax Acts)

61 [Amends ICTA 1988, s. 834(2).]

Section 835 ("total income" in the Income Tax Acts)

62 [Repealed by ITA 2007, s. 1031 and Sch. 3, Pt. 1.]

History – Para. 62 repealed by ITA 2007, s. 1031 and Sch. 3, Pt. 1, with effect from 6 April 2007.

Schedule 18 (group relief)

63 [Repealed by CTA 2010, s. 1181 and Sch. 3, Pt. 1.]

History – Para. 63 repealed by CTA 2010, s. 1181 and Sch. 3, Pt. 1, with effect for corporation tax purposes for accounting periods ending on or after 1 April 2010, and for income tax and capital gains tax purposes for the tax year 2010–11 and subsequent tax years.

Schedule 19AC (modification of Act in relation to overseas life insurance companies)

64(1) [Omits ICTA 1988, Sch. 19AC, para. 9C.]

64(2) [Repealed by SI 2006/3271, reg. 43 and Sch., Pt. 1.]

History – Sch. 2, para. 64(2) repealed by SI 2006/3271, reg. 43 and Sch., Pt. 1 with effect from 31 December 2006 in relation to accounting periods ending on or after that date.

Schedule 21 (tax relief in connection with schemes for rationalising industry and other redundancy schemes)

65 [Amends ICTA 1988, Sch. 21, para. 6(1)(a).]

Schedule 24 (assumptions for calculating chargeable profits, creditable tax and corresponding United Kingdom tax of foreign companies)

66(1) [Amends ICTA 1988, Sch. 24, para. 10(1).]

66(2) [Amends ICTA 1988, Sch. 24, para. 10(2).]

66(3) [Repealed by FA 2005, s. 104 and Sch. 11, Pt. 2(6).]

History – Para. 66(3) repealed by FA 2005, s. 104 and Sch. 11, Pt. 2(6), with effect for periods of account beginning on or after 16 March 2005.

Schedule 28A (change in ownership of investment company: deductions)

67 [Repealed by CTA 2010, s. 1181 and Sch. 3, Pt. 1.]

History – Para. 67 repealed by CTA 2010, s. 1181 and Sch. 3, Pt. 1, with effect for corporation tax purposes for accounting periods ending on or after 1 April 2010, and for income tax and capital gains tax purposes for the tax year 2010–11 and subsequent tax years.

Schedule 28AA (provision not at arm's length)

68 [Repealed by TIOPA 2010, s. 378 and Sch. 10, Pt. 2.]

History – Para. 68 repealed by TIOPA 2010, s. 378 and Sch. 10, Pt. 2, with effect for corporation tax purposes for accounting periods ending on or after 1 April 2010, for income tax and capital gains tax purposes for the tax year 2010–11 and subsequent tax years, and for petroleum revenue tax purposes for chargeable periods beginning on or after 1 July 2010.

THE FINANCE ACT 1988 (C. 39)

Schedule 12 (building societies: change of status)

69 [Amends FA 1988, Sch. 12, para. 3(1).]

THE FINANCE ACT 1989 (C. 26)

Section 86 (spreading of relief for acquisition expenses)

70 [Repealed by FA 2004, s. 326 and Sch. 42, Pt. 2(3).]

History – Para. 70 repealed by FA 2004, s. 326 and Sch. 42, Pt. 2(3) which have effect, by virtue of, and in accordance with, FA 2004, s. 42, for accounting periods beginning on or after 1 April 2004 but subject to the transitional provisions in FA 2004, s. 43 and 44 and Sch. 6. Para. 70 amended FA 1989, s. 86(5A).

THE ELECTRICITY ACT 1989 (C. 29)

Schedule 11 (taxation provisions)

71 [Amends Electricity Act 1989, Sch. 11.]

THE FINANCE ACT 1990 (C. 29)

Section 126 (pools payments for football ground improvements)

72 [Repealed by FA 2012, s. 227 and Sch. 39, para. 19(2).]

History – Para. 72 repealed by FA 2012, s. 227 and Sch. 39, para. 19(2), with effect in relation to payments made on or after 1 April 2013 for corporation tax purposes, and in relation to payments made on or after 6 April 2013 for income tax purposes.

THE FINANCE ACT 1991 (C. 31)

Section 65 (reimbursement by defaulter in respect of certain abandonment expenditure)

73 [Repealed by CTA 2010, s. 1181 and Sch. 3, Pt. 2; also repealed by TIOPA 2010, s. 378 and Sch. 10, Pt. 6.]

History – Para. 73 repealed by CTA 2010, s. 1181 and Sch. 3, Pt. 2, for corporation tax purposes only, with effect for accounting periods ending on or after 1 April 2010. Para. 73 also repealed by TIOPA 2010, s. 378 and Sch. 10, Pt. 6, with effect for corporation tax purposes for accounting periods ending on or after 1 April 2010, for income tax and capital gains tax purposes for the tax year 2010–11 and subsequent tax years, and for petroleum revenue tax purposes for chargeable periods beginning on or after 1 July 2010.

Section 78 (sharing of transmission facilities)

74(1) [Amends FA 1991, s. 78(4).]

74(2) [Amends FA 1991, s. 78(5).]

THE SOCIAL SECURITY CONTRIBUTIONS AND BENEFITS ACT 1992 (C. 4)

Schedule 2 (levy of Class 4 contributions with income tax)

75(1) [Omits SSCBA 1992, Sch. 2, para. 1(b).]

75(2) [Partially repeals SSCBA 1992, Sch. 2, para. 2.]

Rewrite: Technical Points – Explanatory Notes, Annex 2, Note 75: para. 75 repeals provisions that no longer have any effect following the Rewrite, essentially because there are no longer any allowances that can be given to traders by way of discharge or repayment of tax.

THE SOCIAL SECURITY CONTRIBUTIONS AND BENEFITS (NORTHERN IRELAND) ACT 1992 (C. 7)

Schedule 2 (levy of Class 4 contributions with income tax)

76(1) [Omits SSCB(NI)A 1992, Sch. 2, para. 1(b).]

76(2) [Partially repeals SSCB(NI)A 1992, Sch. 2, para. 2.]

Rewrite: Technical Points – Explanatory Notes, Annex 2, Note 75: para. 76 repeals provisions that no longer have any effect following the Rewrite, essentially because there are no longer any allowances that can be given to traders by way of discharge or repayment of tax.

THE TAXATION OF CHARGEABLE GAINS ACT 1992 (C. 12)

Section 37 (consideration chargeable to tax on income)

77 [Substitutes TCGA 1992, s. 37(2)(a), (b) and (c) for former (a) and (b).]

Section 41 (restriction of losses by reference to capital allowances etc.)

78(1) [Substitutes TCGA 1992, s. 41(3)(a) and (b).]

78(2) [Substitutes TCGA 1992, s. 41(4)(a).]

78(3) [Amends TCGA 1992, s. 41(7).]

Section 195 (allowance of certain drilling expenditure)

79(1) [Substitutes TCGA 1992, s. 195(2)(b) and (c).]

79(2) [Amends TCGA 1992, s. 195(3).]

79(3) [Amends TCGA 1992, s. 195(4) and substitutes para. (a) and (b).]

79(4) [Omits TCGA 1992, s. 195(5).]

79(5) [Amends TCGA 1992, s. 195(6) and omits para. (b).]

79(6) [Amends TCGA 1992, s. 195(8).]

Section 288 (interpretation)

80 [Amends TCGA 1992, s. 288(1).]

Schedule 3 (assets held on 31st March 1982)

81 [Amends TCGA 1992, Sch. 3, para. 7(8).]

THE FINANCE (NO. 2) ACT 1992 (C. 48)

New sections 40A to 40D (films)

82 [Inserts F(No. 2)A 1992, s. 40A–40D.]

Section 41 (relief for preliminary expenditure)

83 [Amends F(No. 2)A 1992, s. 41(1)(c).]

Section 42 (relief for production or acquisition expenditure)

84(1) [Amends F(No. 2)A 1992, s. 42(1)(b).]

84(2) [Amends F(No. 2)A 1992, s. 42(4)(c).]

84(3) [Amends F(No. 2)A 1992, s. 42(7).]

Section 43 (interpretation of sections 41 and 42)

85 [Amends F(No. 2)A 1992, s. 43(1).]

Schedule 10 (furnished accommodation)

86 [Repealed by ITTOIA 2005, s. 884 and Sch. 3.]

History – Para. 86 repealed by ITTOIA 2005, s. 884 and Sch. 3; effective for income tax purposes for 2005–06 onwards and for corporation tax purposes for accounting periods ending after 5 April 2005 (ITTOIA 2005, s. 883(1)).

Schedule 17 (Northern Ireland electricity)

87(1) [Amends F(No. 2)A 1992, Sch. 17, para. 5(4).]

87(2) [Amends F(No. 2)A 1992, Sch. 17, para. 5(5).]

87(3) [Amends F(No. 2)A 1992, Sch. 17, para. 6(1).]

87(4) [Amends F(No. 2)A 1992, Sch. 17, para. 6(4).]

THE FINANCE ACT 1993 (C. 34)

Section 92 (the basic rule: sterling to be used)

88 [Repealed by FA 2004, s. 326 and Sch. 42, Pt. 2(6), but see History note below.]

History – Para. 88 repealed by FA 2004, s. 326 and Sch. 42, Pt. 2(6) which have effect, by virtue of FA 2004, s. 52(3), in relation to (a) periods of account beginning on or after 1 January 2005, and (b) in the case of a company required to prepare accounts under CA 1985 (superseded by CA 2006) or the Companies (Northern Ireland) Order 1986, any period of account beginning before that date for which the company is required or permitted to prepare such accounts in accordance with international accounting standards.

Section 93 (use of currency other than sterling)

89 [Repealed by FA 2004, s. 326 and Sch. 42, Pt. 2(6), but see History note below.]

History – Para. 89 repealed by FA 2004, s. 326 and Sch. 42, Pt. 2(6) which have effect, by virtue of FA 2004, s. 52(3), in relation to (a) periods of account beginning on or after 1 January 2005, and (b) in the case of a company required to prepare accounts under CA 1985 (superseded by CA 2006) or the Companies (Northern Ireland) Order 1986, any period of account beginning before that date for which the company is required or permitted to prepare such accounts in accordance with international accounting standards.

THE AGRICULTURE ACT 1993 (C. 37)

Schedule 2 (provisions relating to carrying out approved schemes or reorganisation)

90 [Amends Agriculture Act 1993, Sch. 2, para. 19.]

THE FINANCE ACT 1994 (C. 9)

Schedule 24 (provisions relating to the Railways Act 1993)

91(1) [Amends FA 1994, Sch. 24, para. 1(1).]

91(2) [Amends FA 1994, Sch. 24, para. (1)(4)(c).]

91(3) [Amends FA 1994, Sch. 24, para. 20(1) and (2)(a).]

91(4) [Amends FA 1994, Sch. 24, para. 20(8).]

91(5) [Amends FA 1994, Sch. 24, para. 21(1).]

91(6) [Amends FA 1994, Sch. 24, para. 21(2).]

91(7) [Amends FA 1994, Sch. 24, para. 21(3).]

91(8) [Amends FA 1994, Sch. 24, para. 22(2).]

91(9) [Amends FA 1994, Sch. 24, para. 22(3).]

91(10) [Amends FA 1994, Sch. 24, para. 22(4).]

Schedule 25 (Northern Ireland Airports Limited)

92(1) [Amends FA 1994, Sch. 25, para. 5(2).]

92(2) [Amends FA 1994, Sch. 25, para. 5(3).]

THE COAL INDUSTRY ACT 1994 (C. 21)

Schedule 4 (taxation provisions)

93 [Amends Coal Industry Act 1994, Sch. 4.]

THE ATOMIC ENERGY AUTHORITY ACT 1995 (C. 37)

Schedule 3 (taxation provisions)

94 [Amends Atomic Energy Authority Act 1995, Sch. 3.]

THE FINANCE ACT 1996 (C. 8)

Section 151 (benefits under pilot schemes)

95 [Amends FA 1996, s. 151(2).]

Schedule 8 (loan relationships)

96 [Repealed by CTA 2009, s. 1326 and Sch. 3, Pt. 1.]

History – Para. 96 repealed by CTA 2009, s. 1326 and Sch. 3, Pt. 1, with effect for corporation tax purposes for accounting periods ending on or after 1 April 2009, and for income tax and capital gains tax purposes for the tax year 2009–10 and subsequent tax years.

THE BROADCASTING ACT 1996 (C. 55)

Schedule 7 (transfer schemes relating to BBC transmission network: taxation provisions)

97 [Amends Broadcasting Act 1996, Sch. 7.]

THE FINANCE ACT 1997 (C. 16)

Schedule 12 (leasing arrangements: finance leases and loans)

98 [Repealed by CTA 2010, s. 1181 and Sch. 3, Pt. 2; also repealed by TIOPA 2010, s. 378 and Sch. 10, Pt. 8.]

History – Para. 98 repealed by CTA 2010, s. 1181 and Sch. 3, Pt. 2, for corporation tax purposes only, with effect for accounting periods ending on or after 1 April 2010. Para. 98 also repealed by TIOPA 2010, s. 378 and Sch. 10, Pt. 8, with effect for corporation tax purposes for accounting periods ending on or after 1 April 2010, for income tax and capital gains tax purposes for the tax year 2010–11 and subsequent tax years, and for petroleum revenue tax purposes for chargeable periods beginning on or after 1 July 2010.

THE FINANCE (NO. 2) ACT 1997 (C. 58)

Section 48 (films: relief for production or acquisition expenditure)

99(1) [Amends F(No. 2)A 1997, s. 48(1).]

99(2) [Substitutes F(No. 2)A 1997, s. 48(9).]

THE FINANCE ACT 1998 (C. 36)

Section 117 (company tax returns, assessments and related matters)

100(1) [Amends FA 1998, s. 117(1)(b).]

100(2) [Substitutes FA 1998, s. 117(1), former para. (d).]

Section 118 (claims for income tax purposes)

101 [Repealed by TIOPA 2010, s. 378 and Sch. 10, Pt. 12.]

History – Para. 101 repealed by TIOPA 2010, s. 378 and Sch. 10, Pt. 12, with effect for corporation tax purposes for accounting periods ending on or after 1 April 2010, for income tax and capital gains tax purposes for the tax year 2010–11 and subsequent tax years, and for petroleum revenue tax purposes for chargeable periods beginning on or after 1 July 2010.

Schedule 6 (adjustment on change of accounting basis)

102 [Amends FA 1998, Sch. 6, para. 4(4).]

Schedule 18 (company tax returns, assessments and related matters)

103(1) [Substitutes FA 1998, Sch. 18, para. 78.]

103(2) [Substitutes FA 1998, Sch. 18, para. 79(1).]

THE FINANCE ACT 1999 (C. 16)

Schedule 6 (tax treatment of receipts by way of reverse premium)

104 [Repealed by CTA 2009, s. 1326 and Sch. 3, Pt. 1.]

History – Para. 104 repealed by CTA 2009, s. 1326 and Sch. 3, Pt. 1, with effect for corporation tax purposes for accounting periods ending on or after 1 April 2009, and for income tax and capital gains tax purposes for the tax year 2009–10 and subsequent tax years.

THE GREATER LONDON AUTHORITY ACT 1999 (C. 29)

Schedule 33 (taxation)

105 [Amends Greater London Authority Act 1999, Sch. 33.]

THE FINANCE ACT 2000 (C. 17)

Section 105 (corporation tax: use of currencies other than sterling)

106 [Amends FA 2000, s. 105(3).]

Schedule 12 (provision of services through an intermediary)

107 [Repealed by ITEPA 2003, Sch. 8, Pt. 1.]

History – Para. 107 repealed by ITEPA 2003, Sch. 8, Pt. 1 which has effect for the tax year 2003–04 and subsequent tax years.

Schedule 22 (tonnage tax)

108(1) [Amends FA 2000, Sch. 22, para. 41(4).]

108(2) [Substitutes FA 2000, Sch. 22, para. 69(2).]

108(3) [Substitutes FA 2000, Sch. 22, para. 69(4)(a) and (b).]

108(4) [Substitutes FA 2000, Sch. 22, para. 70(2).]

108(5) [Amends FA 2000, Sch. 22, para. 72(1).]

108(6) [Substitutes FA 2000, Sch. 22, para. 73(2).]

108(7) [Substitutes FA 2000, Sch. 22, para. 75(2) and (3).]

108(8) [Substitutes FA 2000, Sch. 22, para. 76(2).]

108(9) [Amends FA 2000, Sch. 22, para. 77(2).]

108(10) [Amends FA 2000, Sch. 22, para. 80(2).]

108(11) [Amends FA 2000, Sch. 22, para. 80(4).]

108(12) [Substitutes FA 2000, Sch. 22, para. 82.]

108(13) [Amends FA 2000, Sch. 22, para. 83(1).]

108(14) [Substitutes FA 2000, Sch. 22, para. 83(2), first sentence.]

108(15) [Substitutes FA 2000, Sch. 22, para. 83(3)(a).]

108(16) [Amends FA 2000, Sch. 22, para. 84(1).]
108(17) [Amends FA 2000, Sch. 22, para. 84(2).]
108(18) [Amends FA 2000, Sch. 22, para. 85(1).]
108(19) [Amends FA 2000, Sch. 22, para. 86(1).]
108(20) [Substitutes FA 2000, Sch. 22, para. 87(1)(b).]
108(21) [Amends FA 2000, Sch. 22, para. 88(1).]
108(22) [Substitutes FA 2000, Sch. 22, para. 88(2) and (3).]
108(23) [Amends FA 2000, Sch. 22, para. 88(4).]
108(24) [Amends FA 2000, Sch. 22, para. 89(1).]
108(25) [Amends FA 2000, Sch. 22, para. 89(2).]
108(26) [Amends FA 2000, Sch. 22, para. 92(4).]
108(27) [Amends FA 2000, Sch. 22, para. 94(4).]
108(28) [Amends FA 2000, Sch. 22, para. 96(2).]
108(29) [Amends FA 2000, Sch. 22, para. 100(2)(b)(ii).]
108(30) [Amends FA 2000, Sch. 22, para. 100(3).]
108(31) [Amends FA 2000, Sch. 22, para. 110(2).]
108(32) [Amends FA 2000, Sch. 22, para. 110(4).]
108(33) [Amends FA 2000, Sch. 22, para. 112(3).]
108(34) [Amends FA 2000, Sch. 22, para. 112(5).]
108(35) [Amends FA 2000, Sch. 22, para. 113(2).]
108(36) [Amends FA 2000, Sch. 22, para. 135.]

THE TRANSPORT ACT 2000 (C. 38)

Schedule 26 (transfers: tax)

109 [Amends Transport Act 2000, Sch. 26.]

SCHEDULE 3 – TRANSITIONALS AND SAVINGS

Section 579

Part 1 – Continuity of the Law

Notes – The "continuity" clause in CAA 1990 was contained in s. 163 of that Act.

1 The repeal of provisions and their enactment in a rewritten form in this Act does not affect the continuity of the law.

2 Paragraph 1–

(a) does not apply to any change in the law effected by this Act, and

(b) is subject to paragraph 8.

3 Any subordinate legislation or other thing which–

(a) has been made or done, or has effect as if made or done, under or for the purposes of a repealed provision, and

(b) is in force or effective immediately before the commencement of the corresponding rewritten provision,

has effect after that commencement as if made or done under or for the purposes of the rewritten provision.

4 Any reference (express or implied) in any enactment, instrument or document to–

(a) a rewritten provision, or

(b) things done or falling to be done under or for the purposes of a rewritten provision,

is to be read as including, in relation to times, circumstances or purposes in relation to which any corresponding repealed provision had effect, a reference to the repealed provision or (as the case may be) things done or falling to be done under or for the purposes of the repealed provision.

Cross references – ITTOIA 2005, s. 883 and Sch. 2, para. 5(3) and 14(2): interaction of this paragraph with ITTOIA transitional provisions.

5 Any reference (express or implied) in any enactment, instrument or document to–

(a) a repealed provision, or

(b) things done or falling to be done under or for the purposes of a repealed provision, is to be read as including, in relation to times, circumstances or purposes in relation to which any corresponding rewritten provision has effect, a reference to the rewritten provision or (as the case may be) things done or falling to be done under or for the purposes of the rewritten provision.

6 Paragraphs 1 to 5 have effect instead of section 17(2) of the Interpretation Act 1978 (but are without prejudice to any other provision of that Act).

7 Paragraphs 4 and 5 apply only in so far as the context permits.

Part 2 – Changes in the Law

8(1) This paragraph applies where, in the case of any person–

(a) a thing is done or an event occurs before the relevant date, and

(b) by reason of a change in the law effected by this Act, the tax consequences of that thing or event for a relevant chargeable period are different from what they would otherwise have been.

8(2) If that person so elects, this Act has effect in relation to that period with such modifications as may be necessary to secure that those consequences are the same as they would have been without the change in the law.

8(3) If this paragraph applies in the case of two or more persons in relation to the same thing or event, an election made under sub-paragraph (2) by any one of those persons is of no effect unless a corresponding election is made by the other or each of the others.

8(4) An election under sub-paragraph (2) must be made by notice given to an officer of Revenue and Customs–

(a) for income tax purposes, within the normal time limit for amending a tax return for the tax year in which the chargeable period ends;

(b) for corporation tax purposes, no later than 2 years after the end of the chargeable period.

8(5) In this paragraph–

"relevant chargeable period" means–

(a) in relation to a change effected by section 536(5)(a) or 537(4), the earliest chargeable period for which the tax consequences of the thing or event are different from what they would otherwise have been;

(b) in relation to any other change, a chargeable period which begins before and ends on or after the relevant date;

"the relevant date" means 6th April 2001 for income tax purposes and 1st April 2001 for corporation tax purposes.

History – In para. 8(4), the words "an officer of Revenue and Customs" substituted for "the Inland Revenue" by CRCA 2005, s. 50(6) and Sch. 4, para. 83(1), with effect from 18 April 2005 by virtue of SI 2005/1126, art. 2(2).

Part 3 – General

CAPITAL EXPENDITURE

9 Subsections (2) and (3) of section 4 apply with the omission of the words "or property business" in relation to expenditure incurred or sums paid or received before 26th November 1996.

EXCLUSION OF DOUBLE RELIEF

10 Section 9 does not apply in relation to expenditure incurred before 24th July 1996.

Part 4 – Plant and Machinery Allowances

INTRODUCTION

Use for qualifying activity of plant or machinery provided for other purposes

11 Subsections (4) and (5) of section 13 do not apply if the plant or machinery was brought into use before 21st March 2000.

Use for qualifying activity of plant or machinery which is a gift

12 Section 14 applies with the insertion after subsection (1) of–

"**14(1A)** This section does not apply unless the donor was required by section 24(6) of CAA 1990 to bring into account for the purposes there mentioned a disposal value equal to the price which the plant or machinery would have fetched if sold in the open market at the time of the gift.", if the plant or machinery was brought into use before 27th July 1989.

QUALIFYING EXPENDITURE

Buildings, structures and land

13 Sections 21 to 24 do not apply in relation to expenditure–

(a) incurred before 30th November 1993;

(b) incurred before 6th April 1996 in pursuance of a contract entered into before 30th November 1993; or

(c) incurred before 6th April 1996 in pursuance of a contract entered into on or after 30th November 1993 for the purpose of securing that obligations under a contract entered into before 30th November 1993 are complied with.

FIRST-YEAR QUALIFYING EXPENDITURE

ICT expenditure incurred by small companies

14 [Omitted by FA 2008, s. 76(5)(f).]

History – Para. 14 omitted by FA 2008, s. 76(5)(f), with effect from 21 July 2008.

HIRE-PURCHASE AND SIMILAR CONTRACTS

Plant or machinery acquired under hire purchase etc.

15 Section 67(2) applies with the omission of the words in brackets if the contract under which the expenditure was incurred was entered into before 27th July 1989.

Plant or machinery on hire purchase etc.: fixtures

16 Section 69(2) does not apply if the plant or machinery became a fixture before 28th July 2000.

Plant or machinery provided by lessee

17 In section 70(1), paragraphs (c) and (d) do not apply if the lease was entered into before 12th July 1984, or on or after that date under an agreement made before that date.

COMPUTER SOFTWARE

Software and rights to software

18 Section 71 does not apply to expenditure incurred before 10th March 1992.

19 [Omitted by FA 2009, s. 30 and Sch. 11, para. 24.]

History – Para. 19 (and the headings before it) omitted by FA 2009, s. 30 and Sch. 11, para. 24, with effect in relation to expenditure incurred on or after 1 April 2009 (for corporation tax purposes) and 6 April 2009 (for income tax purposes), subject to transitional provisions in FA 2009, Sch. 11, para. 27(2) and 30–32. Former para. 19 (and the headings before it) read as follows:

"CARS, ETC.

Cars above the cost threshold

19 In relation to expenditure incurred or treated as incurred before 11th March 1992, or incurred under a contract entered into before that date–

(a) sections 74(2) and 76(3) apply with the substitution of "£8,000" for "£12,000"; and

(b) sections 75(1) and 76(2) and (4) apply with the substitution of "£2,000" for "£3,000"."

LONG-LIFE ASSETS

Long-life asset expenditure

20(1) Chapter 10 of Part 2 does not apply to any expenditure incurred–

(a) before 26th November 1996, or

(b) before 1st January 2001 in pursuance of a contract entered into before 26th November 1996.

20(2) Chapter 10 of Part 2 does not apply to expenditure incurred by any person (**"the purchaser"**) on the acquisition of a long-life asset from another (**"the seller"**) if–

(a) the seller has made a Part 2 claim in respect of expenditure incurred on the provision of the asset (**"the seller's expenditure"**),

(b) the claim is one which the seller was entitled to make,

(c) the seller's expenditure did not fall to be treated as long-life asset expenditure for the purposes of the claim, and

(d) the seller's expenditure would have been so treated if one or more of the assumptions specified in sub-paragraph (3) were made.

20(3) The assumptions are that–

(a) expenditure falling within sub-paragraph (1) is not prevented by that sub-paragraph from being long-life asset expenditure,

(b) the seller's expenditure was not prevented by sub-paragraph (2) from being long-life asset expenditure, and

(c) Chapter 10 of Part 2 or any provision corresponding to it applied for chargeable periods ending before 26th November 1996.

20(4) The reference in sub-paragraph (1) to expenditure incurred in pursuance of a contract entered into before 26th November 1996 does not, in the case of a contract varied at any time on or after that date, include a reference to any expenditure incurred under the contract that exceeds the expenditure that would have been incurred if the contract had not been varied.

20(5) Expressions used in this paragraph and in Chapter 10 of Part 2 have the same meaning in this paragraph as in that Chapter; and in particular references in this paragraph to a "Part 2 claim" are to be read in accordance with section 103(3).

OVERSEAS LEASING

Meaning of "overseas leasing"

21 Section 105(2) applies with the substitution for paragraph (b) of–

"(b) does not use the plant or machinery for the purposes of a qualifying activity carried on there or for earning profits chargeable to tax by virtue of section 830(4) of ICTA, ",

in relation to the use of plant or machinery for leasing under a lease entered into before 16th March 1993.

Recovery of first-year allowances in case of joint lessees

22(1) Sub-paragraphs (2) and (3) apply if–

(a) expenditure has been incurred on the provision of plant or machinery which is leased as described in section 116(1),

(b) the whole or a part of the expenditure has qualified for a first-year allowance under–

(i) section 43(4) of CAA 1990, or

(ii) paragraph 47(7).

22(2) Section 117(1) applies as if the reference in paragraph (b) to expenditure qualifying for a normal writing-down allowance under section 116(3) included a reference to expenditure qualifying for the first-year allowance.

22(3) Subsections (3) to (5) of section 117 apply as if the reference in section 117(3)(b) to expenditure qualifying for a normal writing-down allowance under section 116(3) included a reference to expenditure qualifying for the first-year allowance.

Letting ships or aircraft to obtain old first-year allowance not a qualifying purpose

23 Subsections (1) and (2) of section 123 do not apply if the main object, or one of the main objects–

(a) of the letting of the ship or aircraft on charter,

(b) of a series of transactions of which the letting of the ship or aircraft on charter was one, or

(c) of any of the transactions in such a series,

was to obtain a first-year allowance in respect of expenditure which was first-year qualifying expenditure under paragraph 47 and was incurred by any person on the provision of the ship or aircraft.

SHIPS: DEFERMENTS ETC.

Further registration requirement

24 Section 154 does not apply in the case of a ship that was brought into use before 20th July 1994 for the purposes of a qualifying activity carried on by the person incurring the expenditure on the provision of the ship or a person connected with him.

MINING AND OIL INDUSTRIES

Pre-trading expenditure on mineral exploration and access

25 Section 161 does not apply if–

(a) the person incurred the pre-trading expenditure before 1st April 1986; and

(b) before the first day of trading, the mineral exploration and access at the source in question had ceased.

Abandonment expenditure incurred before cessation of ring fence trade

26 Section 164 does not apply if the chargeable period in which the abandonment expenditure was incurred ended before 1st July 1991.

Abandonment expenditure incurred after cessation of ring fence trade

27 Section 165 does not apply if the abandonment expenditure was incurred before 1st July 1991.

Oil production sharing contracts

28 Sections 167 to 171 do not apply if–

(a) the expenditure was incurred before 21st March 2000; or

(b) the expenditure is treated as incurred by virtue of section 13 and the conditions mentioned in subsection (1) of that section were fulfilled before that date.

FIXTURES

Meaning of "interest in land" for purposes of Chapter 14 of Part 2 (fixtures)

29(1) Sub-paragraph (2) applies if paragraph 51 of Schedule 12 to the Abolition of Feudal Tenure etc. (Scotland) Act 2000 has not come into force before the commencement of section 175.

29(2) Section 175(1) has effect until the appointed day as if for paragraph (b) there were substituted–

"(b) in Scotland, the estate or interest of the proprietor of the *dominium utile* (or, in the case of property other than feudal property, of the owner) and any agreement to acquire such an estate or interest,".

29(3) In sub-paragraph (2) **"the appointed day"** means such day as may be appointed by the Scottish Ministers under section 71 of the Abolition of Feudal Tenure etc. (Scotland) Act 2000 for the coming into force of the Act.

Equipment lessors

30 Section 177(1)(a)(i) does not apply if the agreement for the lease of the plant or machinery was entered into before 19th March 1997.

Equipment lessee has qualifying activity etc.

31 Section 178 applies–

(a) if the agreement for the lease of the plant or machinery was entered into before 19th March 1997, with the omission of the words "which is or is to be" in paragraph (a) and the addition of the word "and" at the end of that paragraph; and

(b) if that expenditure was incurred before 24th July 1996, with the omission of paragraph (c) and the substitution for paragraph (b) of–

"(b) if the equipment lessee had incurred the capital expenditure incurred by the equipment lessor on the provision of the plant or machinery, he would, by virtue of section 176, be treated as the owner of the fixture as a result of incurring the expenditure".

Equipment lessor has right to sever fixture that is not part of building

32 Section 179(1) does not apply if the agreement for the lease of the plant or machinery was entered into before 19th March 1997 and applies with–

(a) the addition at the end of paragraph (e) of the word "and", and

(b) the omission of paragraph (g) and the word "and" immediately before it,

if the expenditure of the equipment lessor was incurred before 24th July 1996.

Equipment lease is part of affordable warmth programme

33 Section 180 does not apply if the expenditure of the equipment lessor was incurred before 28th July 2000.

Purchaser of land giving consideration for fixture

34 Section 181 applies with–

(a) the omission of the word "and" at the end of paragraph (b) of subsection (1); and

(b) the insertion after that paragraph of–

"(bb) at the time of the purchaser's acquisition of the interest, either no person has previously become entitled to an allowance in respect of any capital expenditure incurred on the provision of the fixture or, if any person has become so entitled, that person has been or is required to bring the disposal value of the fixture into account under Chapter 5, and",

if the purchaser acquired the interest in the relevant land before 24th July 1996.

Purchaser of land discharging obligations of equipment lessee

35 Section 182 applies with–

(a) the omission of the word “and” at the end of paragraph (c) of subsection (1); and

(b) the insertion after that paragraph of–

“(cc) at the time of the purchaser’s acquisition of the interest, either no person has previously become entitled to an allowance in respect of any capital expenditure incurred on the provision of the fixture or, if any person has become so entitled, that person has been or is required to bring the disposal value of the fixture into account under Chapter 5, and”,

if the purchaser acquired the interest in the relevant land before 24th July 1996.

Incoming lessee where lessor entitled to allowances

36 Section 183 applies with the insertion after subsection (2) of–

“**183(3)** No election may be made under this section if it appears that the sole or main benefit that may be expected to accrue to the lessor from the grant of the lease and the making of an election is the obtaining of an allowance or deduction or a greater allowance or deduction or the avoidance or reduction of a charge under this Part.”,

if the person who had the interest in the relevant land granted the lease before 24th July 1996.

Incoming lessee where lessor not entitled to allowances

37 Section 184 applies with–

(a) the omission of the word “and” at the end of paragraph (c) of subsection (1); and

(b) the insertion after that paragraph of–

“(cc) at the time of the grant of the lease, no person has previously become entitled to an allowance in respect of any capital expenditure incurred on the provision of the fixture, and”,

if the person who had the interest in the relevant land granted the lease before 24th July 1996.

Fixture on which a plant and machinery allowance has been claimed

38 Section 185 does not apply if the disposal event which required the disposal value to be brought into account as mentioned in subsection (1)(d) occurred before 24th July 1996.

Fixture on which industrial buildings allowance has been made

39 Section 186 does not apply if the time mentioned in subsection (1)(c)(ii) is before 24th July 1996.

Fixture on which research and development allowance has been made

40 Section 187 does not apply if the time mentioned in subsection (1)(d)(ii) is before 24th July 1996.

Disposal value in relation to fixtures: general

41 In relation to a fixture which a person is treated as ceasing to own before 24th July 1996, section 196 applies with the substitution for subsection (6) of–

“**196(6)** If–

(a) a person (**“the former owner”**) is treated by virtue of section 188, 190 or 191 as ceasing to own a fixture,

(b) another person incurs expenditure on the provision of the fixture, and

(c) the former owner brings a disposal value into account under Chapter 5,

there is to be disregarded for the purposes of this Part so much (if any) of that expenditure as exceeds that disposal value.

196(7) In relation to expenditure incurred before 27th July 1989, subsection 6 has effect with the substitution for the words following “the fixture” in paragraph (b) of the words “there is to be disregarded for the purposes of this Part so much (if any) of that expenditure as exceeds the disposal value which the former owner is required to bring into account under Chapter 5””.

ASSETS PROVIDED OR USED ONLY PARTLY FOR QUALIFYING ACTIVITY

Effect of significant reduction in use for purposes of qualifying activity

42 Section 208 does not apply if the change of circumstances referred to in subsection (1)(b) of that section occurs before 21st March 2000.

ANTI-AVOIDANCE

Relevant transactions: sale, hire-purchase (etc.) and assignment

43 Section 213(3) does not apply if the plant or machinery was brought into use before 27th July 1989.

Hire purchase etc. and finance leases

44 Sections 220 and 229 do not apply in relation to expenditure incurred before 2nd July 1997, or in the 12 months beginning with that date in pursuance of a contract entered into before that date.

Sale and finance leasebacks

45 Sections 221, 222 and 224 to 226 do not apply in relation to expenditure incurred before 2nd July 1998 if the relevant transaction–

(a) is a purchase under a contract entered into before 2nd July 1997;

(b) is itself a contract entered into before that date; or

(c) is an assignment made before that date, or in pursuance of a contract entered into before that date.

ADDITIONAL VAT LIABILITIES AND REBATES

Expenditure which is first-year qualifying expenditure: general

46 [Omitted by FA 2008, s. 76(4).]

History – Para. 46 omitted by FA 2008, s. 76(4), with effect from 21 July 2008. However, where a business incurs an additional VAT liability (under the VAT Capital Goods Scheme) on or after 21 July 2008 and the original expenditure was first-year qualifying expenditure by virtue of para. 46, then CAA 2001, Pt. 2. Ch. 18 will still apply to determine if there is an entitlement to a first-year allowance in respect of the additional VAT liability as if para. 46 had not been repealed (FA 2008, s. 76(7) and (8)). Former para. 46 read as follows:

"**46(1)** For the purposes of section 236(1)(a) (entitlement to first-year allowance in respect of additional VAT liability where original expenditure was first-year qualifying expenditure), first-year qualifying expenditure includes expenditure which is first-year qualifying expenditure under paragraph 47 or 48.

46(2) A first-year allowance under this paragraph is made for the chargeable period in which the additional VAT liability accrues.

46(3) The amount of such an allowance is a percentage of the additional VAT liability in respect of which the allowance is made, as shown in the Table–

TABLE
AMOUNT OF FIRST-YEAR ALLOWANCES
(PRE-COMMENCEMENT ORIGINAL EXPENDITURE)

Type of original first-year qualifying expenditure	*Amount*
Expenditure qualifying under paragraph 47 (expenditure incurred 1992–93).	40%
Expenditure qualifying under paragraph 48 (expenditure incurred 1997–98 by small or medium-sized enterprises) which is not long-life asset expenditure.	50%
Expenditure qualifying under paragraph 48 (expenditure incurred 1997–98 by small or medium-sized enterprises) which is long-life asset expenditure.	12%"

Expenditure incurred 1992–93

47 [Omitted by FA 2008, s. 76(4).]

History – Para. 47 omitted by FA 2008, s. 76(4), with effect from 21 July 2008. However, where a business incurs an additional VAT liability (under the VAT Capital Goods Scheme) on or after 21 July 2008 and the original expenditure was first-year qualifying expenditure by virtue of para. 47, then CAA 2001, Pt. 2. Ch. 18 will still apply to determine if there is an entitlement to a first-year allowance in respect of the additional VAT liability as if para. 47 had not been repealed (FA 2008, s. 76(7) and (8)). Former para. 47 read as follows:

"**47(1)** Expenditure is first-year qualifying expenditure under this paragraph if–

(a) it was incurred in the period beginning with 1st November 1992 and ending with 31st October 1993, and

(b) it is not excluded by sub-paragraphs (3) to (8).

47(2) In determining whether expenditure is first-year qualifying expenditure under this paragraph, any effect of section 12 on the time at which it is to be treated as incurred is to be disregarded.

47(3) Expenditure is not first-year qualifying expenditure under this paragraph if it was incurred–

(a) in the chargeable period in which there was a permanent discontinuance of the qualifying activity, or

(b) on the provision of a car other than a qualifying hire car (as defined by section 82).

47(4) Expenditure on the provision of plant or machinery for leasing is not first-year qualifying expenditure under this paragraph if it appears that the expenditure is of the kind described in section 109(2) or 110(2) (expenditure on plant or machinery which is used for overseas leasing etc.).

47(5) Expenditure on the provision of plant or machinery for leasing is not first-year qualifying expenditure under this paragraph if–

(a) the expenditure was incurred on or after 14th April 1993,

(b) the person to whom the plant or machinery is to be or is leased, or a person who is connected with that person, used the plant or machinery for any purpose at any time before its provision for leasing, and

(c) the expenditure does not fall within any of the categories of expenditure on plant or machinery for leasing given in sub-paragraph (6).

47(6) The categories referred to in sub-paragraph (5)(c) are as follows.

Category 1. Expenditure on leasing qualifying by reference to Chapter 11 of Part 2 (overseas leasing)

It appears that the plant or machinery–

(a) will be used for a qualifying purpose (as defined by sections 122 to 125) in the designated period (as defined by section 106), and

(b) will not be used for any other purpose at any time in that period.

Category 2. Enterprise zones

The circumstances of the incurring of the expenditure are that–

(a) the expenditure is incurred on the provision of plant or machinery which is to be an integral part of a building or structure, and

(b) expenditure incurred at that time on the construction of the building or structure would be qualifying enterprise zone expenditure to which Chapter 5 of Part 3 (initial allowances for qualifying enterprise zone expenditure) would apply.

Category 3. Fixtures
The circumstances of the incurring of the expenditure are that–
(a) expenditure is incurred on the provision of plant or machinery which is fixed to land or a building,
(b) the person who incurs it is the lessor of the land or building, and
(c) a transfer of the person's interest in the land or building would operate to transfer that person's interest in the plant or machinery.

Category 4. Cars hired out to the disabled etc.
The expenditure is incurred on the provision of a car which is within section 82(4) (cars hired out to persons receiving disability allowances etc.).

47(7) Sub-paragraph (4) does not prevent expenditure being first-year qualifying expenditure, if it appears that–
(a) the plant or machinery will be leased as described in section 116(1), and
(b) the circumstances are such that section 116(3) will require the whole or any part of the expenditure to be treated as not subject to section 107, 109 or 110.

47(8) Any first-year allowance under sub-paragraph (7) (when read with section 236) is to be made on the same basis and subject to the same apportionments (if any) as would be applicable in the case of a writing-down allowance under section 116(5)."

Expenditure by small or medium-sized enterprises, 1997–98

48 [Omitted by FA 2008, s. 76(4).]

History – Para. 48 omitted by FA 2008, s. 76(4), with effect from 21 July 2008. However, where a business incurs an additional VAT liability (under the VAT Capital Goods Scheme) on or after 21 July 2008 and the original expenditure was first-year qualifying expenditure by virtue of para. 48, then CAA 2001, Pt. 2. Ch. 18 will still apply to determine if there is an entitlement to a first-year allowance in respect of the additional VAT liability as if para. 48 had not been repealed (FA 2008, s. 76(7) and (8)). Former para. 48 read as follows:

"**48(1)** Expenditure is first-year qualifying expenditure under this paragraph if–
(a) it was incurred in the period beginning with 2nd July 1997 and ending with 1st July 1998;
(b) it was incurred by a small or medium-sized enterprise; and
(c) it is not excluded by sub-paragraph (3).

48(2) In determining whether expenditure is first-year qualifying expenditure under this paragraph, any effect of section 12 on the time at which it is to be treated as incurred is to be disregarded.

48(3) Expenditure is not first-year qualifying expenditure under this paragraph if it is within any of the general exclusions given in section 46(2).

48(4) In this paragraph, **"small or medium-sized enterprise"** is to be read in accordance with sections 47 to 49, read with paragraph 50."

Whether a company is a member of large or medium-sized group

49 [Omitted by FA 2008, s. 76(4).]

History – Para. 49 omitted by FA 2008, s. 76(4), with effect from 21 July 2008. However, where a business incurs an additional VAT liability (under the VAT Capital Goods Scheme) on or after 21 July 2008 and the original expenditure was first-year qualifying expenditure by virtue of para. 49, then CAA 2001, Pt. 2. Ch. 18 will still apply to determine if there is an entitlement to a first-year allowance in respect of the additional VAT liability as if para. 49 had not been repealed (FA 2008, s. 76(7) and (8)). Former para. 49 read as follows:

"**49(1)** This paragraph applies in relation to any expenditure incurred before 12th May 1998, and for the purpose of determining–
(a) whether expenditure incurred under a contract entered into before that date is first-year qualifying expenditure under section 44, or
(b) whether expenditure is first-year qualifying expenditure under paragraph 46 or 48.

49(2) Section 49 applies with the substitution in subsection (2) of "parent company" for "parent undertaking" and the omission of the words in brackets in subsection (5).

49(3) In section 49 as it so applies **"parent company"**–
(a) except in the case of a company formed and registered in Northern Ireland, has the same meaning as in Part VII of the Companies Act 1985;
(b) in the case of such a company, has the same meaning as in Part VIII of the Companies (Northern Ireland) Order 1986."

Expenditure which is not first-year qualifying expenditure

50 [Omitted by FA 2008, s. 76(4).]

History – Para. 50 omitted by FA 2008, s. 76(4), with effect from 21 July 2008. However, where a business incurs an additional VAT liability (under the VAT Capital Goods Scheme) on or after 21 July 2008 and the original expenditure was first-year qualifying expenditure by virtue of para. 50, then CAA 2001, Pt. 2. Ch. 18 will still apply to determine if there is an entitlement to a first-year allowance in respect of the additional VAT liability as if para. 50 had not been repealed (FA 2008, s. 76(7) and (8)). Former para. 50 read as follows:

"**50** For the purposes of section 236(1)(a)–
(a) section 40 (expenditure for Northern Ireland purposes by small or medium-sized enterprises) does not apply if the expenditure was incurred before 12th May 1998;
(b) section 44 (expenditure by small or medium-sized enterprises) does not apply if the expenditure was incurred before 2nd July 1998;
(c) section 45 (ICT expenditure by small enterprises) does not apply if the expenditure was incurred before 1st April 2000."

Anti-avoidance

51 [Omitted by FA 2008, s. 76(4).]

History – Para. 51 omitted by FA 2008, s. 76(4), with effect from 21 July 2008. However, where a business incurs an additional VAT liability (under the VAT Capital Goods Scheme) on or after 21 July 2008 and the original expenditure was first-year qualifying expenditure by virtue of para. 51, then CAA 2001, Pt. 2. Ch. 18 will still apply to determine if there is an entitlement to a first-year allowance in respect of the additional VAT liability as if para. 51 had not been repealed (FA 2008, s. 76(7) and (8)). Former para. 51 read as follows:

"**51** Sections 243(7) and 244 do not apply in relation to expenditure incurred before 2nd July 1998 if the relevant transaction–
(a) is a purchase under a contract entered into before 2nd July 1997;
(b) is itself a contract entered into before that date; or
(c) is an assignment made before that date, or in pursuance of a contract entered into before that date."

SUPPLEMENTARY PROVISIONS

Successions by beneficiaries

52 Section 266(7) does not apply if the succession occurred before 27th July 1989.

53 Subsections (6) and (7) of section 268 do not apply if the election under that section was made before 6th April 1990.

GENERAL

Vehicles provided by employees in 1990–91

54(1) This paragraph applies if–

(a) at the beginning of the tax year 1990–91 machinery consisting of a mechanically propelled road vehicle was provided by a person for use in the performance of the duties of an office or employment held by him, and

(b) the machinery was also provided by him at the end of the tax year 1989–90 for use in the performance of the duties of that office or employment but without that provision being necessary.

54(2) Part 2 of this Act has effect as if the person had incurred capital expenditure on the provision of the machinery for the purposes of the office or employment in the tax year 1990–91–

(a) the amount of that expenditure being taken as the price which the machinery would have fetched if sold in the open market on 6th April 1990, and

(b) the person being treated as owning the machinery as a result of his having incurred that expenditure.

Certain expenditure incurred before 6th April 1976

55 Part 2 of this Act does not apply to capital expenditure–

(a) which was not eligible expenditure within the meaning of section 39 of FA 1976 (which brought expenditure previously not within Chapter I of Part III of FA 1971 within that Chapter but with certain exceptions), and

(b) which was incurred in a chargeable period ending before 6th April 1976.

Part 5 – Industrial Buildings Allowances

INDUSTRIAL BUILDINGS

Bridge undertakings

56 [Omitted by FA 2008, s. 84 and Sch. 27, para. 20(a) and 30.]

History – Para. 56 omitted by FA 2008, s. 84 and Sch. 27, para. 20(a), with effect in relation to chargeable periods beginning on or after 1 April 2011 for corporation tax purposes and 6 April 2011 for income tax purposes (FA 2008, Sch. 27, para. 30(1)).

Building used by more than one licensee

57 [Omitted by FA 2008, s. 84 and Sch. 27, para. 20(a) and 30.]

History – Para. 57 omitted by FA 2008, s. 84 and Sch. 27, para. 20(a), with effect in relation to chargeable periods beginning on or after 1 April 2011 for corporation tax purposes and 6 April 2011 for income tax purposes (FA 2008, Sch. 27, para. 30(1)).

Qualifying hotels

58 [Omitted by FA 2008, s. 84 and Sch. 27, para. 20(a) and 30.]

History – Para. 58 omitted by FA 2008, s. 84 and Sch. 27, para. 20(a), with effect in relation to chargeable periods beginning on or after 1 April 2011 for corporation tax purposes and 6 April 2011 for income tax purposes (FA 2008, Sch. 27, para. 30(1)).

Non-industrial part of building disregarded

59 [Omitted by FA 2008, s. 84 and Sch. 27, para. 20(a) and 30.]

History – Para. 59 omitted by FA 2008, s. 84 and Sch. 27, para. 20(a), with effect in relation to chargeable periods beginning on or after 1 April 2011 for corporation tax purposes and 6 April 2011 for income tax purposes (Sch. 27, para. 30(1)).

QUALIFYING EXPENDITURE

Purchase of used building from developer

60 [Omitted by FA 2008, s. 84 and Sch. 27, para. 20(a) and 30.]

History – Para. 60 omitted by FA 2008, s. 84 and Sch. 27, para. 20(a), with effect in relation to chargeable periods beginning on or after 1 April 2011 for corporation tax purposes and 6 April 2011 for income tax purposes (FA 2008, Sch. 27, para. 30(1)).

Qualifying enterprise zone expenditure

61 [Omitted by FA 2008, s. 84 and Sch. 27, para. 20(a) and 30.]

History – Para. 61 omitted by FA 2008, s. 84 and Sch. 27, para. 20(a), with effect in relation to chargeable periods beginning on or after 1 April 2011 for corporation tax purposes and 6 April 2011 for income tax purposes (FA 2008, Sch. 27, para. 30(1)).

62 [Omitted by FA 2008, s. 84 and Sch. 27, para. 20(a) and 30.]

History – Para. 62 omitted by FA 2008, s. 84 and Sch. 27, para. 20(a), with effect in relation to chargeable periods beginning on or after 1 April 2011 for corporation tax purposes and 6 April 2011 for income tax purposes (FA 2008, Sch. 27, para. 30(1)).

63 [Omitted by FA 2008, s. 84 and Sch. 27, para. 20(a) and 30.]

History – Para. 63 omitted by FA 2008, s. 84 and Sch. 27, para. 20(a), with effect in relation to chargeable periods beginning on or after 1 April 2011 for corporation tax purposes and 6 April 2011 for income tax purposes (FA 2008, Sch. 27, para. 30(1)).

INITIAL ALLOWANCES

Building occupied by qualifying licensee

64 [Omitted by FA 2008, s. 84 and Sch. 27, para. 20(a) and 30.]

History – Para. 64 omitted by FA 2008, s. 84 and Sch. 27, para. 20(a), with effect in relation to chargeable periods beginning on or after 1 April 2011 for corporation tax purposes and 6 April 2011 for income tax purposes (FA 2008, Sch. 27, para. 30(1)).

Grants affecting entitlement to initial allowances

65 [Omitted by FA 2008, s. 84 and Sch. 27, para. 20(a) and 30.]

History – Para. 65 omitted by FA 2008, s. 84 and Sch. 27, para. 20(a), with effect in relation to chargeable periods beginning on or after 1 April 2011 for corporation tax purposes and 6 April 2011 for income tax purposes (FA 2008, Sch. 27, para. 30(1)).

WRITING-DOWN ALLOWANCES

Basic rule for calculating amount of allowance

66 [Omitted by FA 2008, s. 84 and Sch. 27, para. 20(a) and 30.]

History – Para. 66 omitted by FA 2008, s. 84 and Sch. 27, para. 20(a), with effect in relation to chargeable periods beginning on or after 1 April 2011 for corporation tax purposes and 6 April 2011 for income tax purposes (FA 2008, Sch. 27, para. 30(1)).

Calculation of amount after relevant event

67 [Omitted by FA 2008, s. 84 and Sch. 27, para. 20(a) and 30.]

History – Para. 67 omitted by FA 2008, s. 84 and Sch. 27, para. 20(a), with effect in relation to chargeable periods beginning on or after 1 April 2011 for corporation tax purposes and 6 April 2011 for income tax purposes (FA 2008, Sch. 27, para. 30(1)).

BALANCING ADJUSTMENTS

When balancing adjustments are made

68 [Omitted by FA 2008, s. 84 and Sch. 27, para. 20(a) and 30.]

History – Para. 68 omitted by FA 2008, s. 84 and Sch. 27, para. 20(a), with effect in relation to chargeable periods beginning on or after 1 April 2011 for corporation tax purposes and 6 April 2011 for income tax purposes (FA 2008, FA 2008 Sch. 27, para. 30(1)).

Net allowance given

69 [Omitted by FA 2008, s. 84 and Sch. 27, para. 20(a) and 30.]

History – Para. 69 omitted by FA 2008, s. 84 and Sch. 27, para. 20(a), with effect in relation to chargeable periods beginning on or after 1 April 2011 for corporation tax purposes and 6 April 2011 for income tax purposes (FA 2008, Sch. 27, para. 30(1)).

70 [Omitted by FA 2008, s. 84 and Sch. 27, para. 20(a) and 30.]

History – Para. 70 omitted by FA 2008, s. 84 and Sch. 27, para. 20(a), with effect in relation to chargeable periods beginning on or after 1 April 2011 for corporation tax purposes and 6 April 2011 for income tax purposes (FA 2008, Sch. 27, para. 30(1)).

Balancing adjustment on realisation of capital value

71 [Omitted by FA 2008, s. 84 and Sch. 27, para. 20(a) and 30.]

History – Para. 71 omitted by FA 2008, s. 84 and Sch. 27, para. 20(a), with effect in relation to chargeable periods beginning on or after 1 April 2011 for corporation tax purposes and 6 April 2011 for income tax purposes (FA 2008, Sch. 27, para. 30(1)).

WRITING OFF QUALIFYING EXPENDITURE

Writing off qualifying expenditure when building not an industrial building

72 [Omitted by FA 2008, s. 84 and Sch. 27, para. 20(a) and 30.]

History – Para. 72 omitted by FA 2008, s. 84 and Sch. 27, para. 20(a), with effect in relation to chargeable periods beginning on or after 1 April 2011 for corporation tax purposes and 6 April 2011 for income tax purposes (FA 2008, Sch. 27, para. 30(1)).

Crown or other person not within the charge to tax entitled to the relevant interest

73 [Omitted by FA 2008, s. 84 and Sch. 27, para. 20(a) and 30.]

History – Para. 73 omitted by FA 2008, s. 84 and Sch. 27, para. 20(a), with effect in relation to chargeable periods beginning on or after 1 April 2011 for corporation tax purposes and 6 April 2011 for income tax purposes (FA 2008, Sch. 27, para. 30(1)).

HIGHWAY UNDERTAKINGS

Special provisions relating to highway concessions

74 [Omitted by FA 2008, s. 84 and Sch. 27, para. 20(a) and 30.]

History – Para. 74 omitted by FA 2008, s. 84 and Sch. 27, para. 20(a), with effect in relation to chargeable periods beginning on or after 1 April 2011 for corporation tax purposes and 6 April 2011 for income tax purposes (FA 2008, Sch. 27, para. 30(1)).

ADDITIONAL VAT LIABILITIES AND REBATES

Additional VAT liabilities and initial allowances: 1992–93 cases

75 [Omitted by FA 2008, s. 84 and Sch. 27, para. 20(a) and 30.]

History – Para. 75 omitted by FA 2008, s. 84 and Sch. 27, para. 20(a), with effect in relation to chargeable periods beginning on or after 1 April 2011 for corporation tax purposes and 6 April 2011 for income tax purposes (FA 2008, Sch. 27, para. 30(1)).

Additional VAT liabilities and initial allowances: further case

76 [Omitted by FA 2008, s. 84 and Sch. 27, para. 20(a) and 30.]

History – Para. 76 omitted by FA 2008, s. 84 and Sch. 27, para. 20(a), with effect in relation to chargeable periods beginning on or after 1 April 2011 for corporation tax purposes and 6 April 2011 for income tax purposes (FA 2008, Sch. 27, para. 30(1)).

1992–93 qualifying expenditure

77 [Omitted by FA 2008, s. 84 and Sch. 27, para. 20(a) and 30.]

History – Para. 77 omitted by FA 2008, s. 84 and Sch. 27, para. 20(a), with effect in relation to chargeable periods beginning on or after 1 April 2011 for corporation tax purposes and 6 April 2011 for income tax purposes (FA 2008, Sch. 27, para. 30(1)).

SUPPLEMENTARY PROVISIONS

Arrangements having an artificial effect on pricing

78 [Omitted by FA 2008, s. 84 and Sch. 27, para. 20(a) and 30.]

History – Para. 78 omitted by FA 2008, s. 84 and Sch. 27, para. 20(a), with effect in relation to chargeable periods beginning on or after 1 April 2011 for corporation tax purposes and 6 April 2011 for income tax purposes (FA 2008, Sch. 27, para. 30(1)).

GENERAL

Expenditure on preparatory work on land where building used before 6th April 1956

79 [Omitted by FA 2008, s. 84 and Sch. 27, para. 20(a) and 30.]

History – Para. 79 omitted by FA 2008, s. 84 and Sch. 27, para. 20(a), with effect in relation to chargeable periods beginning on or after 1 April 2011 for corporation tax purposes and 6 April 2011 for income tax purposes (FA 2008, Sch. 27, para. 30(1)).

Part 6 – Agricultural Buildings Allowances

Overall limit on balancing charge

80 [Omitted by FA 2008, s. 84 and Sch. 27, para. 20(a) and 30.]

History – Para. 80 omitted by FA 2008, s. 84 and Sch. 27, para. 20(a), with effect in relation to chargeable periods beginning on or after 1 April 2011 for corporation tax purposes and 6 April 2011 for income tax purposes (FA 2008, Sch. 27, para. 30(1)).

Meaning of "freehold interest in land" for purposes of Part 4

81 [Omitted by FA 2008, s. 84 and Sch. 27, para. 20(a) and 30.]

History – Para. 81 omitted by FA 2008, s. 84 and Sch. 27, para. 20(a), with effect in relation to chargeable periods beginning on or after 1 April 2011 for corporation tax purposes and 6 April 2011 for income tax purposes (FA 2008, Sch. 27, para. 30(1)).

Exclusion of expenditure incurred before 1st April 1986

82 [Omitted by FA 2008, s. 84 and Sch. 27, para. 20(a) and 30.]

History – Para. 82 omitted by FA 2008, s. 84 and Sch. 27, para. 20(a), with effect in relation to chargeable periods beginning on or after 1 April 2011 for corporation tax purposes and 6 April 2011 for income tax purposes (FA 2008, Sch. 27, para. 30(1)).

The writing-down period

83 [Omitted by FA 2008, s. 84 and Sch. 27, para. 20(a) and 30.]

History – Para. 83 omitted by FA 2008, s. 84 and Sch. 27, para. 20(a), with effect in relation to chargeable periods beginning on or after 1 April 2011 for corporation tax purposes and 6 April 2011 for income tax purposes (FA 2008, Sch. 27, para. 30(1)).

Part 7 – Mineral Extraction Allowances

QUALIFYING EXPENDITURE ON ACQUIRING A MINERAL ASSET

Qualifying expenditure where buildings or structures cease to be used

84 In section 405(3) "A" does not include, in cases where the buildings or structures have permanently ceased to be used for any purpose before 27th July 1989, the amount of any agricultural buildings allowances.

QUALIFYING EXPENDITURE: SECOND-HAND ASSETS

Claims before 26th November 1996 in respect of acquisition of mineral asset owned by previous trader

85 Section 407(4) does not apply in relation to claims made before 26th November 1996.

Acquisition of oil licence from non-trader before 13th September 1995

86 Section 408 does not apply to acquisitions occurring before 13th September 1995.

Restrictions on qualifying expenditure in case of UK oil licence and certain other assets inapplicable for expenditure pre-16th July 1985

87(1) The sections listed in sub-paragraph (2) do not apply if–

(a) asset X is a mineral asset situated in the United Kingdom, and

(b) the capital expenditure incurred by the buyer consists of the payment of sums under a contract entered into by him before 16th July 1985.

87(2) The sections are–

(a) section 407 (acquisition of mineral asset owned by previous trader),

(b) section 410 (UK oil licence: qualifying expenditure limited by reference to original licence payment), and

(c) section 411 (assets generally: qualifying expenditure limited by reference to previous trader's unrelieved qualifying expenditure).

87(3) Sections 407 and 411 apply, in relation to a case where asset X is a mineral asset situated in the United Kingdom, as if the references to an earlier owner of the asset did not include a person who has not owned the asset at any time after 31st March 1986.

87(4) In the case of a mineral asset which consists of or includes an interest in or right over mineral deposits or land, the asset is not to be regarded for the purposes of this paragraph as situated in the United Kingdom unless the deposits or land are or is so situated.

87(5) Expressions used in this paragraph and Chapter 4 of Part 5 have the same meaning in this paragraph as they have in that Chapter.

Expenditure incurred pre-1st April 1986

88(1) Part 5 of this Act does not apply in relation to expenditure incurred before 1st April 1986 (**"old expenditure"**) except as provided by the following provisions of this paragraph.

88(2) Sections 401 and 402 apply to old expenditure if–

(a) that expenditure was incurred on mineral exploration and access,

(b) immediately before 1st April 1986, no allowance had been made under Chapter III of Part I of CAA 1968 in respect of it, and

(c) after that day and before mineral exploration and access ceases at the source in question, the person by whom the expenditure was incurred began or begins to carry on a trade of mineral extraction.

In this sub-paragraph **"source"** has the same meaning as it had in Schedule 14 to FA 1986.

88(3) For the purposes of Part 5–

(a) expenditure which by virtue of any provision of section 119 of CAA 1990 (read with any provision of Schedule 14 to FA 1986) was treated immediately before the coming into force of this Act as expenditure incurred on 1st April 1986 for any purpose or purposes is to continue to be so treated;

(b) any allowances treated as having been made under Schedule 13 to FA 1986 is to continue to be so treated;

(c) any amount treated as qualifying expenditure for the purposes of that Schedule is to continue to be so treated; and

(d) in relation to any expenditure to which paragraph 6(4)(a) of Schedule 14 to FA 1986 applied, section 424 does not apply (so that no deduction is to be made from the amount of any disposal receipt by reference to the undeveloped market value of the land in question).

88(4) In the case of expenditure incurred in the acquisition of a mineral asset, nothing in sub-paragraph (3)(c) affects the time as at which under section 404 the undeveloped market value of an interest is to be determined.

88(5) In a case where–

(a) by virtue of any provision of this paragraph, the whole or any part of the outstanding balance (within the meaning of paragraph 1 of Schedule 14 to FA 1986) of an item of old expenditure is treated for the purposes of Part 5 as qualifying expenditure, and

(b) a balancing charge falls to be made under Chapter 6 of that Part in respect of the expenditure, then, in determining the amount on which that charge falls to be made, subsection (4) of section 418 has effect (subject to sub-paragraph (6)) as if paragraph (b) of that subsection included a reference to allowances made in respect of the item under Chapter III of Part I of CAA 1968.

88(6) Where the qualifying expenditure in respect of which a balancing charge falls to be made represents part only of the outstanding balance of an item of old expenditure, the reference in sub-paragraph (5) to allowances made in respect of that item is to be construed as a reference to such part of those allowances as it is just and reasonable to apportion to that part of the balance (having regard to any apportionment made under paragraph 3(2) of Schedule 14 to FA 1986).

Part 8 – Research and Development Allowances

Expenditure incurred partly on research and development

89 Section 439(4) does not apply to expenditure incurred before 27th July 1989.

References to research and development in relation to new trades

90(1) Where–

(a) a trade is set up and commenced in the year of assessment 1999–00, and

(b) its first period of account ends after 6th April 2001,

Part 6 of this Act has effect in relation to that year as if references to research and development were references to scientific research.

90(2) In this paragraph **"scientific research"** means any activities in the fields of natural or applied science for the extension of knowledge.

Disposal of oil licences

91(1) Sub-paragraphs (2) and (3) apply where–

(a) a person (**"the transferor"**) disposes of any interest in an oil licence to another (**"the transferee"**) during the transitional period,

(b) part of the value of the interest is attributable to allowable exploration expenditure incurred by the transferor, and

(c) an election is made in accordance with this paragraph specifying an amount as the amount to be treated as so attributable.

91(2) Chapter 3 of Part 6 has effect in relation to the disposal as if–

(a) the disposal were a disposal by which an asset representing the allowable exploration expenditure ceases to belong to the transferor, and

(b) the disposal value of that asset were an amount equal to the amount specified in the election.

91(3) For the purposes of Part 5 of this Act, the amount of any expenditure incurred–

(a) by the transferee in acquiring the interest from the transferor, or

(b) by any person subsequently acquiring the interest (or an interest deriving from the interest),

which is taken to be attributable to expenditure incurred, before the disposal to the transferee, on mineral exploration and access is the lesser of the amount specified in the election and the amount which, apart from this sub-paragraph, would be taken to be so attributable.

91(4) An election–

(a) must be made by notice to the Commissioners for Her Majesty's Revenue and Customs given by the transferor, and

(b) subject to sub-paragraph (5), does not have effect unless a copy of it is served on the transferee and the transferee consents to it.

91(5) If the tribunal is satisfied–

(a) that the disposal was made under or in pursuance of an agreement entered into by the transferor and the transferee on the mutual understanding that a quantified (or quantifiable) part of the value of the interest disposed of was attributable to allowable exploration expenditure, and

(b) that the part quantified in accordance with that understanding and the amount specified in the election are the same,

the tribunal may dispense with the need for the transferee to consent to the election.

91(6) An application for the tribunal to determine the question is to be subject to the relevant provisions of Part 5 of the Taxes Management Act 1970 (see, in particular, section 48(2)(b) of that Act), and each of the persons concerned is entitled to be a party to the proceedings on the application.

91(7) Subject to sub-paragraph (8), an election may specify any amount, including a nil amount, as the amount to be treated as mentioned in sub-paragraph (1)(c).

91(8) Where–

(a) a return has been made for a chargeable period of the transferor, and

(b) the return includes, at the time when it is made, an amount which, disregarding the provisions of this paragraph, would be treated under Chapter 3 of Part 6 as a trading receipt accruing in that period,

the election must not specify an amount less than the amount included in the return unless the Commissioners for Her Majesty's Revenue and Customs agrees the lesser amount in question.

91(9) An election made in accordance with this paragraph–

(a) is irrevocable, and

(b) may not be varied after it is made.

91(10) For the purposes of this paragraph a disposal is a disposal made during the transitional period if it is one made–

(a) before 13th September 1995, or

(b) on or after that date in pursuance of any obligation to make the disposal which, immediately before that date, was an unconditional obligation.

91(11) For the purposes of sub-paragraph (10), the fact that a third party who is not connected with the transferor or the transferee may, by exercising any right or withholding any permission, prevent the fulfilment of an obligation does not prevent the obligation from being treated as unconditional.

91(12) In sub-paragraph (11) the reference to a third party is a reference to any person, body, government or public authority, whether within or outside the United Kingdom.

91(13) In this paragraph–

"allowable exploration expenditure" has the same meaning as in section 555;

"mineral exploration and access" has the same meaning as in Part 5.

91(14) All such assessments and adjustments of assessments are to be made as are necessary to give effect to this paragraph.

History – In para. 91(4) and (8), the references to "the Commissioners for Her Majesty's Revenue and Customs" substituted for "the Board of Inland Revenue" by CRCA 2005, s. 50(6) and Sch. 4, para. 83(2), with effect from 18 April 2005 by virtue of SI 2005/1126, art. 2(2).

In para. 91(5), the words "the tribunal is" substituted for the words "the Special Commissioners are" and the words "the tribunal" substituted for the word "they" by SI 2009/56, art. 3(1) and Sch. 1, para. 301(2), operative from 1 April 2009, subject to transitional and saving provisions in SI 2009/56, Sch. 3.

Para. 91(6) substituted by SI 2009/56, art. 3(1) and Sch. 1, para. 301(3), operative from 1 April 2009, subject to transitional and saving provisions in SI 2009/56, Sch. 3.

Part 9 – Patent Allowances

EXPENDITURE INCURRED BEFORE 1ST APRIL 1986

Scope of paragraphs 93 to 101

92(1) Paragraphs 93 to 101 apply to capital expenditure incurred by a person before 1st April 1986 on the purchase of patent rights.

92(2) Chapters 2 to 4 of Part 8 do not apply to such expenditure, except for certain provisions which are specifically applied by paragraph 101.

Qualifying expenditure and unrelieved qualifying expenditure

93(1) In this paragraph and paragraphs 94 to 101, **"qualifying expenditure"** means capital expenditure incurred before 1st April 1986 on the purchase of patent rights.

93(2) The result of Steps 1 to 3 is the unrelieved qualifying expenditure for a chargeable period.

Step 1

Take an item of qualifying expenditure.

Step 2

Subtract any writing-down allowances made in respect of that expenditure for earlier chargeable periods.

Step 3

If the person who incurred the expenditure sold any part of the patent rights before the beginning of the chargeable period, subtract the net proceeds of sale (so far as they consist of capital sums).

Entitlement to writing-down allowances

94(1) A writing-down allowance is made for a chargeable period in respect of an item of qualifying expenditure if–

(a) the chargeable period falls wholly or partly within the writing-down period for that expenditure (as determined in accordance with paragraph 95),

(b) paragraph 97 does not prohibit writing-down allowances for that period, and

(c) either–

(i) the trade use condition is met for that period, or

(ii) any income receivable by that person in respect of the patent rights in that period would be liable to tax.

94(2) The trade use condition is that–

(a) the person is carrying on in the chargeable period a trade which is within the charge to tax, and

(b) at any time in the chargeable period the patent rights, or other rights out of which they were granted, were, or were to be, used for the purposes of the trade.

94(3) The total writing-down allowances made in respect of an item of qualifying expenditure (whether to the same or to different persons) must not exceed the amount of that expenditure.

The writing-down period

95(1) The writing-down period for an item of qualifying expenditure–

(a) begins at the beginning of the chargeable period in respect of which the expenditure is incurred, and

(b) is of a length determined in accordance with the Table, which shows the basic rule, and the rules which apply instead of the basic rule in the cases described in items 2 and 3.

TABLE
LENGTH OF WRITING-DOWN PERIODS FOR QUALIFYING EXPENDITURE

Rule		*Length of writing-down period*
1.	Basic rule.	17 years.
2.	Patent rights are purchased for a specified period.	Whichever is shorter – (a) 17 years; (b) the number of years comprised within the specified period.
3.	Patent rights begin one complete year or more after the commencement of the patent, and item 2 does not apply.	17 years, less the number of complete years which, when the rights began, have elapsed since the commencement of the patent; or if 17 complete years have so elapsed, one year.

95(2) For the purpose of determining the writing-down period, expenditure incurred for the purposes of a trade by a person about to carry on the trade is treated as if incurred on the first day on which that person carries on that trade, unless that person has by then sold all the rights on which the expenditure was incurred.

95(3) **"The commencement of the patent"**, means, in relation to a patent, the date as from which the patent rights become effective.

Calculation of writing-down allowances

96(1) The basic rule for calculating a writing-down allowance for an item of qualifying expenditure is–

$$E \times \frac{C}{W}$$

where–

E is the amount of the qualifying expenditure;

C is the length of the part of the chargeable period falling within the writing-down period;

W is the length of the writing-down period.

96(2) The basic rule is subject to the rules about–

(a) cessation of writing-down allowances (paragraph 97), and

(b) reduced writing-down allowances (paragraph 98).

End of writing-down allowances

97(1) No writing-down allowance is to be made to a person for a chargeable period in respect of qualifying expenditure incurred on the purchase of patent rights if any of the following occur in that period–

(a) the patent rights come to an end without being subsequently revived,

(b) the person sells all of those rights, or so much of them as that person still owned at the beginning of the chargeable period, or

(c) the person sells part of those rights, and the net proceeds of sale for that period (so far as they consist of capital sums) are not less than the amount of the unrelieved qualifying expenditure for that period.

97(2) If a writing-down allowance in respect of qualifying expenditure is prohibited by sub-paragraph (1) for a chargeable period, no writing-down allowance is to be made in respect of that expenditure for any subsequent chargeable period.

Reduced writing-down allowance

98(1) If a person sells part of any patent rights in a chargeable period, and for that period U is greater than N, the writing-down allowance for that period is–

$$\frac{U - N}{Y}$$

where–

U is the unrelieved qualifying expenditure for the chargeable period,

N is the net proceeds of any sales of the patent rights which take place in the chargeable period (so far as those proceeds consist of capital sums), and

Y is the number of complete years of the writing-down period remaining at the beginning of the chargeable period.

98(2) If an amount is calculated under sub-paragraph (1) for a chargeable period, that amount is also the amount of the writing-down allowance for subsequent chargeable periods until another sale in a period for which U is greater than N causes a fresh calculation to be made under sub-paragraph (1).

98(3) If a chargeable period is more or less than a year, an allowance calculated under sub-paragraph (1) or (2) is proportionately increased or reduced.

Balancing allowance on sale or expiry of patent rights

99(1) A person is entitled to a balancing allowance for a chargeable period in respect of qualifying expenditure if there is unrelieved qualifying expenditure for that period and any of the following occur in that period–

(a) the patent rights come to an end without subsequently being revived, or

(b) the person sells all of those rights, or so much of them as that person still owned at the beginning of the period.

This is subject to sub-paragraph (2).

99(2) The person is not entitled to a balancing allowance unless–

(a) a writing-down allowance has been given in respect of the expenditure, or

(b) a writing-down allowance could, but for the rights coming to an end or being sold, have been given in respect of the expenditure.

99(3) The amount of the balancing allowance is–

(a) in the case of a sale, equal to the unrelieved qualifying expenditure for the chargeable period, less the net proceeds of sales taking place in the chargeable period (so far as they consist of capital sums), and

(b) in any other case, equal to the unrelieved qualifying expenditure for the chargeable period.

Balancing charges

100(1) A balancing charge is made on a person for a chargeable period in respect of qualifying expenditure if in that period–

(a) the person sells some or all of the patent rights, and

(b) the net proceeds of sale (so far as they consist of capital sums) from the sales in that period exceed any unrelieved qualifying expenditure for that period.

The charge is calculated in accordance with sub-paragraphs (2) to (5).

100(2) If there is no unrelieved qualifying expenditure, the amount of the balancing charge is equal to the net proceeds of sale (so far as they consist of capital sums).

This is subject to sub-paragraphs (4) and (5).

100(3) If there is some unrelieved qualifying expenditure, the amount of the balancing charge is equal to the amount by which the net proceeds of sale (so far as they consist of capital sums) exceed the unrelieved qualifying expenditure.

This is subject to sub-paragraphs (4) and (5).

100(4) The total amount of the first balancing charge must not exceed the total writing-down allowances actually given in respect of the expenditure.

100(5) The total amount on which a second or further balancing charge is made must not exceed the total writing-down allowances actually made in respect of the expenditure, less the amount of any earlier charge.

Giving effect to allowances and charges

101(1) Sub-paragraph (2) applies if–

(a) a person is entitled to a writing-down allowance or a balancing allowance or liable to a balancing charge in respect of qualifying expenditure, and

(b) the trade use condition is met.

101(2) The allowance or charge is to be given effect in calculating the profits of that person's trade, by treating–

(a) the allowance as an expense of the trade, and

(b) the charge as a receipt of the trade.

101(3) Sub-paragraph (4) applies if–

(a) a person is entitled to a writing-down allowance or a balancing allowance or liable to a balancing charge in respect of qualifying expenditure, and

(b) the trade use condition is not met.

101(4) Sections 479 and 480 apply in relation to giving effect to the allowance or charge referred to in sub-paragraph (3) as they apply in relation to giving effect to an allowance or charge under Chapter 3 of Part 8 in respect of qualifying non-trade expenditure.

101(5) For the purposes of Part 8 a person's **"income from patents"** includes balancing charges to which the person is liable in respect of qualifying expenditure.

SUPPLEMENTARY PROVISIONS

Limit on qualifying expenditure

102 Section 481 does not apply to expenditure incurred before 1st April 1986, and subsections (5) and (6) of that section do not apply to expenditure incurred before 27th July 1989.

Part 10 – Dredging allowances

Writing-down allowances

103(1) Section 487(2) applies with the substitution of "50 years" for "25 years" in the case of expenditure incurred before 6th November 1962.

103(2) Section 487(3) applies with the substitution of "2%" for "4%" in the case of expenditure incurred before 6th November 1962.

Balancing allowances

104 The reference in section 488(1)(d) to allowances previously made in respect of the expenditure–

(a) includes any initial allowance made in respect of it under section 17 of FA 1956 or section 67 of CAA 1968, and

(b) except in relation to initial allowances, is to be construed as if section 17 of FA 1956 had always had effect (instead of having effect only for chargeable periods after the year 1955–56).

The writing-down period

105(1) This paragraph applies where it is provided under Part 9 that writing-down allowances are to be made in respect of any expenditure during a writing-down period of any specified length.

105(2) If allowances were made under paragraph 27(2) of Schedule 14 to FA 1965–

(a) for income tax purposes, for either of the tax years 1964–65 and 1965–66, and

(b) for accounting periods of a company falling wholly or partly within either of those years,

the periods for which allowances were made are added together in calculating the writing-down period, even though (according to the calendar) the same time is counted twice.

History – In para. 105(2), "FA" substituted for "the Finance Act" by FA 2009, s. 126(5)(a), with effect from 21 July 2009.

Part 11 – Contributions

Regional development grants

106(1) Section 534(1) applies as if a grant falling within that subsection included–

(a) a grant made under Part II of the Industrial Development Act 1982 on an application made before 1st April 1988;

(b) a grant made under Part I of the Industry Act 1972, or a grant made under Northern Ireland legislation and declared by the Treasury to correspond to a grant under that Part.

106(2) Section 534(2) does not apply if the expenditure was incurred, or the grant was paid, before 10th March 1982.

Contributions not made by public bodies and not eligible for tax relief

107 Section 536 applies with the omission of subsection (3)(b) in relation to contributions made before 27th July 1989.

Conditions for allowances

108 In section 536(5), as it applies for the purposes of section 537(2), paragraphs (a)(iv) and (b) do not apply in relation to contributions made before 27th July 1989.

109 Section 538(2)(b)(ii) applies in relation to contributions made before 6th April 1990 with the omission of "or to allocate the expenditure to a pool under Part 2".

Agricultural buildings

110 [Omitted by FA 2008, s. 84 and Sch. 27, para. 20(b) and 30(1).]

History – Para. 110 omitted by FA 2008, s. 84 and Sch. 27, para. 20(b), with effect in relation to chargeable periods beginning on or after 1 April 2011 for corporation tax purposes and 6 April 2011 for income tax purposes (FA 2008, Sch. 27, para. 30(1)).

Part 12 – Supplemental

Transfer of insurance company business

111 Section 560 applies with–

(a) the substitution for subsection (1) of–

"**560(1)** This section applies if assets are transferred as part of, or in connection with, a transfer of the whole or part of the long term business of an insurance company to another company in accordance with a scheme sanctioned by a court under section 49 of the Insurance Companies Act 1982."; and

(b) the omission of subsection (2),

in relation to transfers sanctioned or authorised before 1st July 1994.

Election regarding sale consideration

112(1) In relation to a transfer to which this paragraph applies, section 569(3) applies with the substitution for paragraph (a) of–

"(a) any of the parties is not resident in the United Kingdom at the time of the transfer and the circumstances are not at that time such that a relevant allowance or charge falls or might fall to be made to or on that party as a result of the transfer;".

112(2) This paragraph applies to–

(a) a transfer before 16th March 1993;

(b) a transfer in pursuance of a contract entered into before that date; and

(c) a transfer in pursuance of a contract entered into for the purpose of securing that obligations under a contract entered into before that date are complied with.

Part 13 – Other Enactments

113(1) Subsections (2) and (3) of section 578A of ICTA (expenditure on car hire) apply with the substitution of "£8,000" for "£12,000" in relation to expenditure incurred under a contract entered into before 11th March 1992.

113(2) Subsection (4) of that section does not apply in relation to rebates made or transactions occurring before 29th April 1996.

114 [Repealed by ITTOIA 2005, s. 884 and Sch. 3.]

History – Para. 114 repealed by ITTOIA 2005, s. 884 and Sch. 3; effective for income tax purposes for 2005–06 onwards and for corporation tax purposes for accounting periods ending after 5 April 2005 (ITTOIA 2005, s. 883(1)).

115 The repeals made by CAA 1990 do not have effect in relation to capital expenditure–

(a) which was not eligible expenditure within the meaning of section 39 of FA 1976 (which brought expenditure previously not within Chapter I of Part III of FA 1971 within that Chapter but with certain exceptions), and

(b) which was incurred in a chargeable period ending before 6th April 1976.

116(1) Sections 40A to 40D of F(No.2)A 1992 (films) apply with the necessary modifications in relation to–

(a) expenditure on the production of a film–

 (i) completed before 21st March 2000, or

 (ii) completed on or after that date, if the first day of principal photography is before that date, unless the person incurring the expenditure elects that those modifications should not apply;

(b) expenditure on the acquisition of a film, tape or disc incurred before 6th April 2000.

116(2) The necessary modifications are–

(a) the substitution for section 40A(1) of–

 "**40A(1)** Expenditure which–

 (a) is incurred on the production or acquisition of a film, tape or disc, and

 (b) would, apart from this subsection, constitute capital expenditure on the provision of plant or machinery for the purposes of Part 2 of the Capital Allowances Act,

 is to be regarded for the purposes of the Tax Acts as expenditure of a revenue nature unless an election under section 40D below has effect with respect to it.";

(b) in section 40A(2), the substitution of "the production or acquisition of a film, tape or disc" for "the original master version of a film" and of "of the film, tape or disc" for "of the original master version";

(c) in section 40A(3), the substitution of "a film, tape or disc" for "the original master version of a film" and of "the film, tape or disc" for "the original master version" (in both places);

(d) the insertion after section 40A(4) of–

 "**40A(5)** In this section and sections 40B to 40D below–

 (a) any reference to a film is a reference to an original master negative of the film and its soundtrack, if any;

 (b) any reference to a tape is a reference to an original master film tape or original master audio tape; and

 (c) any reference to a disc is a reference to an original master film disc or original master audio disc;

 and any reference to the acquisition of a film, tape or disc includes a a reference to the acquisition of any description of rights in a film, tape or disc.";

(e) in section 40B(1), the substitution of "films, tapes or discs" for "original master versions of films" and of "a film, tape or disc" for "the original master version of a film";

(f) in section 40B(4), the substitution of "film, tape or disc" for "original master version of the film" and of "film, tape or disc" for "original master version";

(g) in section 40B(5), the substitution of "film, tape or disc" for "original master version of the film";

(h) in section 40C(1), the substitution of "film, tape or disc" for "original master version of the film";

(i) in section 40C(2), the substitution of "film, tape or disc" for "original master version of the film";

(j) in section 40D(2), the substitution of "films, tapes or discs" for "original master versions of films", of "a film, tape or disc" for "the original master version of a film" and of "film, tape or disc" for "original master version" (in both places);

(k) in section 40D(3), the substitution of "film, tape or disc" for "original master version";

(l) in section 40D(4), the substitution of "film, tape or disc" for "original master version of the film" (in both places);

(m) in section 40D(6), the substitution of "a film, tape or disc" for "the original master version of a film" and of "of the film, tape or disc" for "of the original master version"; and

(n) *in section 40D(7), the substitution* of "a film, tape or disc" for "the original master version of a film".

116(3) An election under sub-paragraph (1)(a) is irrevocable.

116(4) For the purposes of sub-paragraph (1)(a) a film is completed at the time when it is first in a form in which it can reasonably be regarded as ready for copies of it to be made and distributed for presentation to the general public.

116(5) In sub-paragraph (1)(b)–

(a) **"film"** means an original master negative of the film and its soundtrack, if any;

(b) **"tape"** means an original master film tape or original master audio tape; and

(c) **"disc"** means an original master film disc or original master audio disc;

and the acquisition of a film, tape or disc includes the acquisition of any description of rights in a film, tape or disc.

History – In para. 116(2)(b), the words "original master" substituted for "master" in both places by FA 2005, s. 59 and Sch. 3, para. 27(2) with effect from 2 December 2004 (FA 2005, Sch. 3, para. 31(3)).
In para. 116(2)(c), the words "a film", "the original master" and "original master" substituted for "film", the first "master" and the second "master" respectively by FA 2005, s. 59 and Sch. 3, para. 27(3) with effect from 2 December 2004 (FA 2005, Sch. 3, para. 31(3)).
In para. 116(2)(d), the words "insertion after section 40A(4)" substituted for "substitution for section 40A(5)" by FA 2005, s. 59 and Sch. 3, para. 27(4) with effect from 2 December 2004 (FA 2005, Sch. 3, para. 31(3)).
In para. 116(2)(e), the words "original master", "a film" and "the original master" substituted for the first "master", "film" and the second "master" respectively by FA 2005, s. 59 and Sch. 3, para. 27(5) with effect from 2 December 2004 (FA 2005, Sch. 3, para. 31(3)).
In para. 116(2)(f)–(i), the words "original master" substituted for "master" in each place by FA 2005, s. 59 and Sch. 3, para. 27(6) with effect from 2 December 2004 (FA 2005, Sch. 3, para. 31(3)).
In para. 116(2)(j), the words "for "original master versions of films", of "a film, tape or disc" for "the original master version of a film" and of "film, tape or disc" for "original master version" (in both places);" substituted for "for "master versions of films", of "film, tape or disc" for "master version of a film" and of "the film, tape or disc" for "the master version" (in both places);" by FA 2005, s. 59 and Sch. 3, para. 27(7) with effect from 2 December 2004 (FA 2005, Sch. 3, para. 31(3)).
In para. 116(2)(k)–(m), the words "original master" substituted for "master" in each place by FA 2005, s. 59 and Sch. 3, para. 27(8) with effect from 2 December 2004 (FA 2005, Sch. 3, para. 31(3)).
In para. 116(2)(n), the words "a film" and"the original master" substituted for "film" and "master" respectively by FA 2005, s. 59 and Sch. 3, para. 27(9) with effect from 2 December 2004 (FA 2005, Sch. 3, para. 31(3)).

Cross references – FI 1985, Sch. 1, para. 1: meaning of film.
F(No. 2)A 1992, s. 43: meaning of original master version.

117 Section 40D of F(No. 2)A 1992 (election relating to tax treatment of films expenditure) applies with the omission of–

(a) paragraph (a) of subsection (1); and

(b) subsections (3) to (7),

if the film, tape or disc of the film was completed before 10th March 1992.